Calendrical Tabulations, 1900–2200

The momentous task of assembling such a comprehensive and accurate collection of calendars could only have been achieved by the authors of the definitive work on calendar algorithms, *Calendrical Calculations*. Using the algorithms from that book, Professors Reingold and Dershowitz have achieved the near-impossible task of simultaneously displaying the date on fifteen different calendars over a three-hundred-year period. Represented here are the Gregorian, ISO, Hebrew, Chinese, Coptic, Ethiopic, Persian, Hindu lunar, Hindu solar, and Islamic calendars; another five are easily obtained from the tables with minimal arithmetic (JD, R.D., Julian, arithmetical Persian, and arithmetical Islamic). The tables also include phases of the moon, dates of solstices and equinoxes, and religious and other special holidays for all the calendars shown.

This set of beautifully produced tables will be of use for centuries by anyone with an interest in calendars and the societies that produce them. It should also prove an invaluable reference tool for astronomers and genealogists.

Edward M. Reingold was born in Chicago, Illinois, in 1945. He has an undergraduate degree in mathematics from the Illinois Institute of Technology and a doctorate in computer science from Cornell University. Reingold was a faculty member in the Department of Computer Science at the University of Illinois at Urbana-Champaign from 1970–2000; he retired as a Professor Emeritus of Computer Science in December 2000 and is now chair of the Department of Computer Science at the Illinois Institute of Technology. His research interests are in theoretical computer science—especially the design and analysis of algorithms and data structures. A Fellow of the Association for Computing Machinery since 1995, Reingold has authored or coauthored more than 50 research papers and 9 books; his papers on backtrack search, generation of combinations, weight-balanced binary trees, and drawing of trees and graphs are considered classics. He has won awards for his undergraduate and graduate teaching. Reingold is intensely interested in calendars and their computer implementation; in addition to *Calendrical Calculations*, he is the author and maintainer of the calendar/diary part of GNU Emacs.

Beyond his expertise in calendars, Nachum Dershowitz is a leading figure in software verification in general and termination of programs in particular; he is an international authority on equational inference and term rewriting. Other areas in which he has made major contributions include program semantics and combinatorial enumeration. Dershowitz has authored or coauthored more than 100 research papers and several books and has held visiting positions at prominent institutions around the globe. He has won numerous awards for his research and teaching. He was born in 1951, and his graduate degrees in applied mathematics are from the Weizmann Institute in Israel. He is currently a professor of computer science at Tel Aviv University.

Calendrical Tabulations 1900–2200

Edward M. Reingold
University of Illinois at Urbana-Champaign
and
Illinois Institute of Technology

Nachum Dershowitz
Tel Aviv University

CAMBRIDGE
UNIVERSITY PRESS

University Printing House, Cambridge CB2 8BS, United Kingdom

One Liberty Plaza, 20th Floor, New York, NY 10006, USA

477 Williamstown Road, Port Melbourne, VIC 3207, Australia

314-321, 3rd Floor, Plot 3, Splendor Forum, Jasola District Centre, New Delhi - 110025, India

79 Anson Road, #06-04/06, Singapore 079906

Cambridge University Press is part of the University of Cambridge.

It furthers the University's mission by disseminating knowledge in the pursuit of education, learning and research at the highest international levels of excellence.

www.cambridge.org
Information on this title: www.cambridge.org/9780521782531

First published 2002

A catalogue record for this publication is available from the British Library

Library of Congress Cataloging in Publication data
Reingold, Edward M., 1945–
Calendrical tabulations, 1900–2200 / Edward M. Reingold, Nachum Dershowitz.
p. cm.
Includes bibliographical references.
ISBN 0-521-78253-8
1. Calendar –Mathematics. 2. Calendar – Conversion tables. 3. Computer algorithms.
4. Chronology, Historical. I. Dershowitz, Nachum. II. Title.
CE12 .R46 2002
529′.3 – dc21 2001035654

ISBN 978-0-521-78253-1 Hardback

To our beloved wives

Ruth Nothmann Reingold
Schulamith Chava Halevy

ראה חיים עם אשה אשר אהבת כל ימי חיי הבלך קהלת ט,ט

Contents

Preface

> The reader... may complain that he could recite the calendar for himself and so save his pocket whatever sum the publisher may think proper to charge for this book.
>
> —Virginia Woolf: *Orlando* (1928)

We give tables for easy conversion of fifteen different calendars. Ten calendars are given explicitly (Gregorian, ISO, Hebrew, Chinese, Coptic, Ethiopic, astronomical Persian, Hindu lunar, Hindu solar, and astronomical Islamic); another five are easily obtained from the tables with minimal arithmetic (JD, R.D., Julian, arithmetical Persian, and arithmetical Islamic). Detailed explanations of the structure and determination of these and many other calendars can be found in [10].

Why produce yet another book of tables given the large number available? And why produce it in book form at all in the computer age? For the latter question, we point out that all available computer programs cover only one or two calendars, have limited ranges, are of dubious accuracy, are difficult for a non-expert to use, or work only on a small subset of computers. Also, books are less ephemeral.

As to the former question, why bother with a new book of tables, all published books of tables have significant flaws: Among general tables, by far the best is Schram [14], which is extensive, but hard to find (a search of the OCLC WorldCat database found fewer than 50 copies, of which a dozen were in non-lending institutions), awkward to use, only goes to 2000, and is in German. The most ubiquitous is Parise [8], so filled with errors as to be useless.

For conversions to and from specific exotic calendars, there are some excellent tables, but usually with a caveat:

- For the Chinese calendar, [9] is hard to find, is in Chinese, and only goes to 2050. [17] and [18] are hard to find and go to only 1951. [20] is in Chinese and only goes to 2050. [7] is very rare and only goes to 1921.

- For the Hebrew calendar, [16] is excellent and goes to 2100. [11] goes only to 2050 and is awkward to use. The index volume of [12] contains readable tables for 1920–2020. [2] is extensive, rare, and in Hebrew; it also contains somewhat awkward tables for the Julian, Gregorian, Islamic, and French Revolutionary calendars over various ranges. The self-published [13] contains extensive tables for the Hebrew calendar, equinoxes, and lunar conjunctions for 1826–2240; it is extremely rare and primarily in Yiddish with some Hebrew, though with enough English to make it usable without knowledge of Yiddish or Hebrew.
- For the Islamic calendar, [19] is hard to find (a search of the OCLC WorldCat database found fewer than 40 copies, of which half a dozen were in non-lending institutions), in German, and only goes to 2077. [6] is awkward to use.
- For the Coptic/Ethiopic calendar, [5] goes only to 1930, is hard to find (a search of the OCLC WorldCat database found fewer than 40 copies, of which ten were in non-lending institutions), and is in French.
- For the Persian calendar, [3] follows (one of) the arithmetical calendars that is still under debate and is somewhat awkward to use. As noted above, [19] is hard to find.
- For the Hindu calendars, [15] goes only until 2000. [4] is limited to 1879–2000.

Using the Tables

Following this preface is an extended description of the usage of the tables. The description contains sufficient explanatory material to make conversion among the calendars easy, even for readers without a detailed familiarity with the calendars' idiosyncrasies. The reader is strongly cautioned to read the description carefully and to pay close attention to the warnings; for the reader's convenience, the warnings are reprinted at the end of the tables.

Production of the Tables

These tables were produced by Common Lisp driver code that executed the algorithms in [10] (available on a compact disk accompanying that book) to produce LaTeX output, which was in turn used to produce the tables in this book. Because the LaTeX was produced algorithmically, idiosyncratic cases were not handled in an ad hoc way, as would be done in a conventionally typeset book. This has led to minor typographical inadequacies (most notably, instances of overprinting); we preferred to live with these difficulties and eliminate the possibility of corrupting the tables by human editing. There are no typographical errors in the more than one million numbers in these tables!

Though intended as single-use, the driver code had to be run many times as the content and typography of the tables evolved. The final run, which produced the tables in this book, was made over January 7–9, 2002 and required 51.5 hours on a dual-processor Sun Blade® 1000 workstation; that is, the average year's table took about 10.26 minutes. Of that, over two-thirds was for the Hindu lunar calendar.[1] Detailed statistics of the times required to compute the various calendars are given in Table 1.

[1] Only the Hindu lunar and Chinese calendars had any significant variation in the computation times: Of the 301 years, only six Hindu lunar calendars had unusually long computation times (due usually to the rare

Table 1: Statistics for the computation time (in minutes) of the 301 years of calendars; σ is the standard deviation. The total time for all 301 calendars was somewhat over two full days (3088 minutes = 51.5 hours).

	Average			Shortest		Longest	
Calendar	**Time**	σ	**%**	**Time**	**Year**	**Time**	**Year**
Gregorian (verso)	0.51	0.02	4.96	0.47	1999	0.60	2111
ISO Week	0.00	0.00	0.01	0.00	1999	0.02	2189
Julian Day (JD)	0.00	0.00	0.01	0.00	1999	0.02	1972
Hebrew	0.02	0.01	0.22	0.02	2002	0.03	2100
Chinese	0.68	0.26	6.62	0.42	2003	1.23	1976
Coptic/Ethiopic	0.01	0.01	0.13	0.00	2011	0.12	1972
Persian	0.18	0.02	1.77	0.15	2091	0.23	2101
Hindu Lunar	6.94	2.64	67.69	4.98	2011	22.80	2048
Hindu Solar	1.08	0.05	10.56	0.98	1998	1.28	1999
Islamic	0.81	0.04	7.92	0.73	1998	0.95	2136
Gregorian (recto)	0.01	0.01	0.12	0.00	2003	0.02	1974
Year	10.26	2.66	100.00	7.92	2011	26.00	2048

These should be taken with a grain of salt because they are based on file modification times and the workstation was not always otherwise idle during the computation of the tables; moreover, values near zero should be regarded as noise.

Our method of production makes these tables unique in two ways. First, they are the only published calendar tables for which the *precise* details of the underlying calendrical algorithms are public [10]. Second, and much more important, these tables are uniquely accurate—more accurate than any existing tables of any scope. However, the nature of calendars is such that no tables can be completely accurate: Some calendars are based on observation, not calculation, and climatic conditions can unpredictably alter theoretical calculations of visibility. Some calendars are a matter of dispute or regional variation. Some calendars depend on astronomical calculations whose accuracy depends on the underlying model, and these models have and will continue to vary as our understanding of such phenomena improves. Definitions of holidays can change. Finally, we admit that there is an infinitesimal chance that our algorithms in [10] could be flawed.

The Web Page

To facilitate electronic communication with our readers, we have established a home page for [10] and this book on the World Wide Web:

`http://www.calendarists.com`

occurrence of an expunged month in a leap year): 1983 (22.3 minutes), 2048 (22.8 minutes), 2067 (19.7 minutes), 2086 (20.0 minutes), 2124 (20.1 minutes), and 2189 (21.7 minutes); the remaining years all took between 5.0 and 13.3 minutes with an average of 6.7 minutes and a standard deviation of 1.7. Times for the Chinese calendar were bimodal, with the 111 leap years taking an average of 1.0 minutes each and the 190 common years taking an average of 0.5 minutes each, with standard deviations of 0.06 and 0.03, respectively.

Acknowledgments

We thank William Adams for his lunar font, Ruth N. Reingold for gathering the statistics on runtimes, Schulamith Halevy for help in cross checking dates, and Jeffrey L. Copeland, Robert H. van Gent, Mitchell A. Harris, Denis B. Roegel, and G. Sivakumar for their helpful comments.

We thank our editor Alan Harvey for putting up with us.

January 21, 2002
Chicago, Illinois — E.M.R.
Tel Aviv, Israel — N.D.

Reading the Tables

Each pair of facing pages shows the weeks of a Gregorian year: The leftmost major column of the verso (left) page and the rightmost major column of the recto (right) page show the year as a sequence of weeks, beginning with the week containing January 1 and ending with the week containing December 31. The remaining major column divisions of the verso page give the ISO week number for the week beginning on the corresponding Monday, the Julian day number (JD) for that Sunday at noon, and the corresponding weeks on the Hebrew, Chinese, Coptic, and Ethiopic calendars:

1900

	GREGORIAN 1900							Lunar Phases	ISO WEEK	JULIAN DAY		HEBREW 5660‡/5661							Molad		CHINESE Jǐ-Hài/Gēng-Zǐ‡							Solar Term		COPTIC 1616/1617 ETHIOPIC 1892/1893							
	Sun	Mon	Tue	Wed	Thu	Fri	Sat		(Mon)	(Sun noon)		Sun	Mon	Tue	Wed	Thu	Fri	Sat			Sun	Mon	Tue	Wed	Thu	Fri	Sat			Sun	Mon	Tue	Wed	Thu	Fri	Sat	
JANUARY 1900	31	●[a]	2	3	4	5	6	13:52	1	2415020	SHEVAT 5660	29	1	2	3	4	5	6	Mon 10h24m0p	MONTH 12 Jǐ-Hài	29	1	2	3	4	5	6	Xiǎo hán	KOIAK 1616	22	23	24	25	26	27	28	TĀKHŚĀŚ 1892
	7	◐	9	10	11	12	13	5:40	2	2415027		7	8	9	10	11	12	13			7	8	9	10	11	12	13			29[c]	30	1	2	3	4	5	
	14	○	16	17	18	19	20	19:07	3	2415034		14	15	16	17	18	19	20			14	15	16	17	18	19	**20**	Dà hán	ṬŌBE 1616	6[d]	7	8	9	10	11[e]	12	ṬER 1892
	21	22	◑	24	25	26	27	23:5[illegible]	4	2415041		21	22	23	24	25	26	27			21	22	23	24	25	26	27			13	14	15	16	17	18	19	
	28	29	30	●	1	2	3	1:22	5	2415048		28	29	30	1	2	3	4	Tue 23h8m1p		28	29	30	1[a]	2	3	4			20	21	22	23	24	25	26	
FEBRUARY 1900	4	5	◐	7	8	9	10	16:23	6	2415055	ADAR I 5660	5	6	7	8	9	10	11		MONTH 1 Gēng-Zǐ	5	6	7	8	9	10	11	Lì chūn		27	28	29	30	1	2	3	
	11	12	13	○	15	16	17	13:50	7	2415062		12	13	14	15	16	17	18			12	13	14	15[b]	16	17	18		MESHIR 1616	4	5	6	7	8	9	10	YAKĀTIT 1892
	18	19	20	21	◑	23	24	16:44	8	2415069		19	20	21	22	23	24	25			19	**20**	21*	22	23	24	25	Yǔ shuǐ		11	12	13	14	15	16	17	
	25	26	27	28	●	2	3	11:25	9	2415076		26	27	28	29	30	1	2	Thu 11h52m2p		26	27	28	29	1	2	3			18	19	20	21	22	23	24	
MARCH 1900	4	5	6	7	◐	9	10	5:34	10	2415083	ADAR II 5660	3	4	5	6	7	8	9		MONTH 2 Gēng-Zǐ	4	5	6	7	8	9	10	Jīng zhé		25	26	27	28	29	30	1	
	11	12	13	14	15	○	17	8:1	11	2415090		10	11	12	13	14[f]	15	16			11	12	13	14	15	16	17		EP	2	3	4	5	6	7	8	M

Footnotes at the bottom of the major columns give holidays and other special dates:

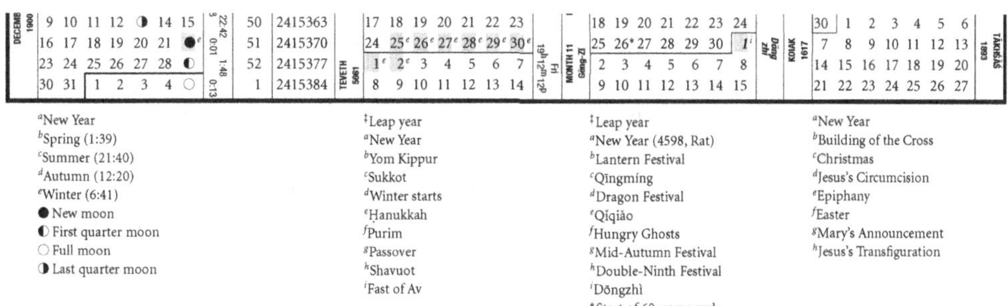

	Sun	Mon	Tue	Wed	Thu	Fri	Sat	Lunar Phases	ISO WEEK	JULIAN DAY		Sun	Mon	Tue	Wed	Thu	Fri	Sat	Molad		Sun	Mon	Tue	Wed	Thu	Fri	Sat	Solar Term		Sun	Mon	Tue	Wed	Thu	Fri	Sat	
DECEMB 1900	9	10	11	12	◑	14	15	22:42	50	2415363		17	18	19	20	21	22	23		–	18	19	20	21	22	23	24		KOIAK 1617	30	1	2	3	4	5	6	TĀKHŚĀŚ 1893
	16	17	18	19	20	21	●[e]	0:01	51	2415370		24	25[e]	26[e]	27[e]	28[e]	29[e]	30[e]		MONTH 11 Gēng-Zǐ	25	26*	27	28	29	30	***1***[i]	Dōng zhì		7	8	9	10	11	12	13	
	23	24	25	26	27	28	◐	1:48	52	2415377	TEVETH 5661	1[e]	2[e]	3	4	5	6	7	Fri 19h12m12p		2	3	4	5	6	7	8			14	15	16	17	18	19	20	
	30	31	1	2	3	4	○	0:13	1	2415384		8	9	10	11	12	13	14			9	10	11	12	13	14	15			21	22	23	24	25	26	27	

[a]New Year
[b]Spring (1:39)
[c]Summer (21:40)
[d]Autumn (12:20)
[e]Winter (6:41)
● New moon
◐ First quarter moon
○ Full moon
◑ Last quarter moon

‡Leap year
[a]New Year
[b]Yom Kippur
[c]Sukkot
[d]Winter starts
[e]Ḥanukkah
[f]Purim
[g]Passover
[h]Shavuot
[i]Fast of Av

‡Leap year
[a]New Year (4598, Rat)
[b]Lantern Festival
[c]Qīngmíng
[d]Dragon Festival
[e]Qǐqiǎo
[f]Hungry Ghosts
[g]Mid-Autumn Festival
[h]Double-Ninth Festival
[i]Dōngzhì
*Start of 60-name cycle

[a]New Year
[b]Building of the Cross
[c]Christmas
[d]Jesus's Circumcision
[e]Epiphany
[f]Easter
[g]Mary's Announcement
[h]Jesus's Transfiguration

The remaining major column divisions of the recto page give the corresponding weeks on the Persian, Hindu, and Islamic calendars:

1900

PERSIAN (ASTRONOMICAL) 1278/1279								HINDU LUNAR 1956/1957								HINDU SOLAR 1821/1822								ISLAMIC (ASTRONOMICAL) 1317/1318‡								Julian‡ (Sun)	GREGORIAN 1900							
	Sun	Mon	Tue	Wed	Thu	Fri	Sat		Sun	Mon	Tue	Wed	Thu	Fri	Sat		Sun	Mon	Tue	Wed	Thu	Fri	Sat		Sun	Mon	Tue	Wed	Thu	Fri	Sat		Sun	Mon	Tue	Wed	Thu	Fri	Sat	
	10	11	12	13	14	15	16		29	30	1	2	3	4	**5**	PAUSHA 1821	18	19	20	21	22	23	24		28	29	30	*1*[e]	2	3	4	Dec 19	*31*	1	2	3	4	5	6[a]	
DEY 1278	17	18	19	20	21	22	23		7	8	9	10	11	12	13		25	26	27	28	29	1[b]	2		5	6	7	8	9	10	11		7	8	9	10	11	12	13[b]	
	24	25	26	27	28	29	30	PAUSHA 1956	14	15	16	17	18	19	20	MĀGHA 1821	3	4	5	6	7	8	9	RAMAḌĀN 1317	12	13	14	15	16	17	18	Jan 2	*14*	15	16	17	18	19	20	JANUARY 1900
	1	2	3	4	5	6	7		*20*	21	22	23	24	25	26		10	11	12	13	14	15	16		19	20	21	22	23	24	25		21	22	23	24	25	26	27	
	8	9	10	11	12	13	14		27	28	**29**	1	2	3	4		17	18	19	20	21	22	23		26	27	28	29	*1*[f]	2	3	Jan 16	*28*	29	30	31	1	2	3	
BAHMAN 1278	15	16	17	18	19	20	21		5	6	7	8	9	10	11		24	25	26	27	28	29	30		4	5	6	7	8	9	10		4	5	6	7	8	9	10	
	22	23	24	25	26	27	28	MĀGHA 1956	12	13	14	15	16	17	18		1	2	3	4	5	6	7	SHAWWĀL 1317	11	12	13	14	15	16	17	Jan 30	*11*	12	13	14	15	16	17	FEBRUARY 1900
	29	30	*1*	2	3	4	5		19	20	21	22	23	24	25		8	9	10	11	12	13	14		18	19	20	21	22	23	24		18	19	20	21	22	23	24	
	6	7	8	9	10	11	12		26	27	28[h]	29	30	1	2	PHĀLGUNA 1821	15	16	17	18	19	20	21		25	26	27	28	29	30	*1*	Feb 13	*25*	26	27	28[c]	1	2	3	
ESFAND 1278	13	14	15	16	17	18	19		3	**4**	6	7	8	9	10		22	23	24	25	26	27	28		2	3	4	5	6	7	8		4	5	6	7	8	9	10	
	20	21	22	23	24	25	26	PHĀLGUNA 1956	11	12	*12*	13	14	15[i]	16		29	30	1	2	3	4	5	DHU AL-QA'DA 1317	9	10	11	12	13	14	15	Feb 27	*11*[d]	12	13	14	15	16	17	MARCH 1900
	27	28	29	*1*[a]	2	3	4		17	18	19	20	21	22	23	RA	6	7	8	9	10	11	12		16	17	18	19	20	21	22		18	19	20	21	22	23	24	

Again, footnotes at the bottom of the major columns give holidays and other special dates:

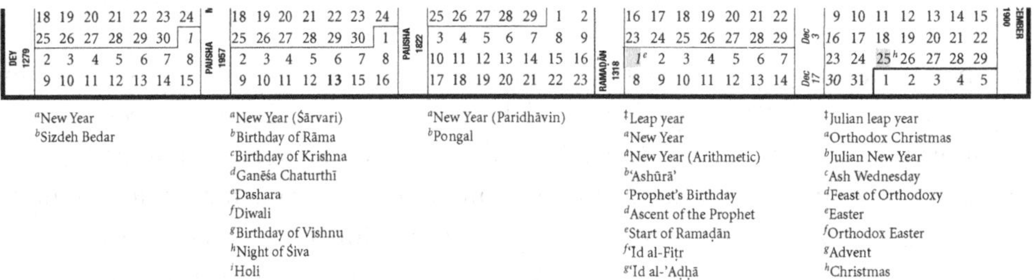

	18	19	20	21	22	23	24		18	19	20	21	22	23	24		25	26	27	28	29	1	2		16	17	18	19	20	21	22		9	10	11	12	13	14	15	DECEMBER 1900
DEY 1279	25	26	27	28	29	30	*1*	PAUSHA 1957	25	26	27	28	29	30	1	PAUSHA 1822	3	4	5	6	7	8	9		23	24	25	26	27	28	29	Dec 3	*16*	17	18	19	20	21	22	
	2	3	4	5	6	7	8		2	3	4	5	6	7	8		10	11	12	13	14	15	16	RAMAḌĀN 1318	*1*[e]	2	3	4	5	6	7		23	24	25[h]	26	27	28	29	
	9	10	11	12	13	14	15		9	10	11	12	**13**	15	16		17	18	19	20	21	22	23		8	9	10	11	12	13	14	Dec 17	*30*	31	1	2	3	4	5	

[a]New Year
[b]Sizdeh Bedar

[a]New Year (Śārvari)
[b]Birthday of Rāma
[c]Birthday of Krishna
[d]Ganēśa Chaturthī
[e]Dashara
[f]Diwali
[g]Birthday of Vishnu
[h]Night of Śiva
[i]Holi

[a]New Year (Paridhāvin)
[b]Pongal

‡Leap year
[a]New Year
[a]New Year (Arithmetic)
[b]'Ashūrā'
[c]Prophet's Birthday
[d]Ascent of the Prophet
[e]Start of Ramaḍān
[f]'Id al-Fiṭr
[g]'Id al-'Aḍḥā

‡Julian leap year
[a]Orthodox Christmas
[b]Julian New Year
[c]Ash Wednesday
[d]Feast of Orthodoxy
[e]Easter
[f]Orthodox Easter
[g]Advent
[h]Christmas

The weeks are shown in parallel, so that conversion of a date from one calendar to another requires only looking left or right on the same line to the corresponding day of the week in the other calendar's column (the reader is aided in this by the inclusion with the book of a matching column-ruled bookmark). Month boundaries are shown by a thin line; year boundaries are shown by a thicker line. Additional information for some of the calendars is given in adjacent columns; the details are explained below.

WARNING

- *Changes in font (roman or italic, lightface or bold) are important in the tables. The sections below explain the significance for each calendar.*

The Gregorian and Julian Calendars

A week on the Gregorian calendar (the most widely used calendar in the world) is shown twice, in the major columns on the extreme left and the extreme right of a pair of facing pages. The Gregorian calendar on the extreme left has the month names and year numbers in a minor column at the left; the Gregorian calendar on the extreme right has month names and year numbers in a minor column at the right. The month names and lengths are:

(1)	January	31 days	(7) July	31 days
(2)	February	28 {29} days	(8) August	31 days
(3)	March	31 days	(9) September	30 days
(4)	April	30 days	(10) October	31 days
(5)	May	31 days	(11) November	30 days
(6)	June	30 days	(12) December	31 days

In leap years, indicated by ‡ after the year number, February has 29 days, as indicated in curly brackets.

The leftmost Gregorian calendar,

GREGORIAN 1900	Sun	Mon	Tue	Wed	Thu	Fri	Sat	Lunar Phases
JANUARY 1900	31	●[a]	2	3	4	5	6	13:52
	7	◐	9	10	11	12	13	5:40
	14	○	16	17	18	19	20	19:07
	21	22	◑	24	25	26	27	23:53
	28	29	30	●	1	2	3	1:22
FEBRUARY 1900	4	5	◐	7	8	9	10	16:23
	11	12	13	○	15	16	17	13:50
	18	19	20	21	◑	23	24	16:44
	25	26	27	28	●	2	3	11:25
MARCH 1900	4	5	6	7	◐	9	10	5:34
	11	12	13	14	15	○	17	8:1

includes matters of astronomical interest:

Event	Key	When
New Year	*a*	January 1
Vernal (spring) equinox	*b*	March 19–21
Summer solstice	*c*	June 20–22
Autumnal equinox	*d*	September 21–24
Winter solstice	*e*	December 20–23
New Moon	●	About every four weeks
First Quarter	◐	About every four weeks
Full Moon	○	About every four weeks
Last Quarter	◑	About every four weeks

Dates of solstices and equinoxes are shaded and keyed to footnotes giving the exact time (to within a few minutes)—times given are in Universal Time (U.T.), formerly called Greenwich Mean Time (G.M.T.); see Figure 1 for a map relating U.T. to various time zones. The phases of the moon are given by the standard symbols in place of the date—new moons by ●, full moons by ○, first quarter moons by ◐, and last quarter moons by ◑. The exact times of the phases (to within a few minutes) are given in the column just to the right of Saturday, aligned with the week of occurrence; times are given in Universal Time. When, rarely, two phases occur during the same week, the two times are given and correspond, left to right, to the phases shown in that week.

WARNING

❖ ***Times for lunar phases, equinoxes, and solstices are given in Universal Time. The times are close approximations, but may be in error by a few minutes.***

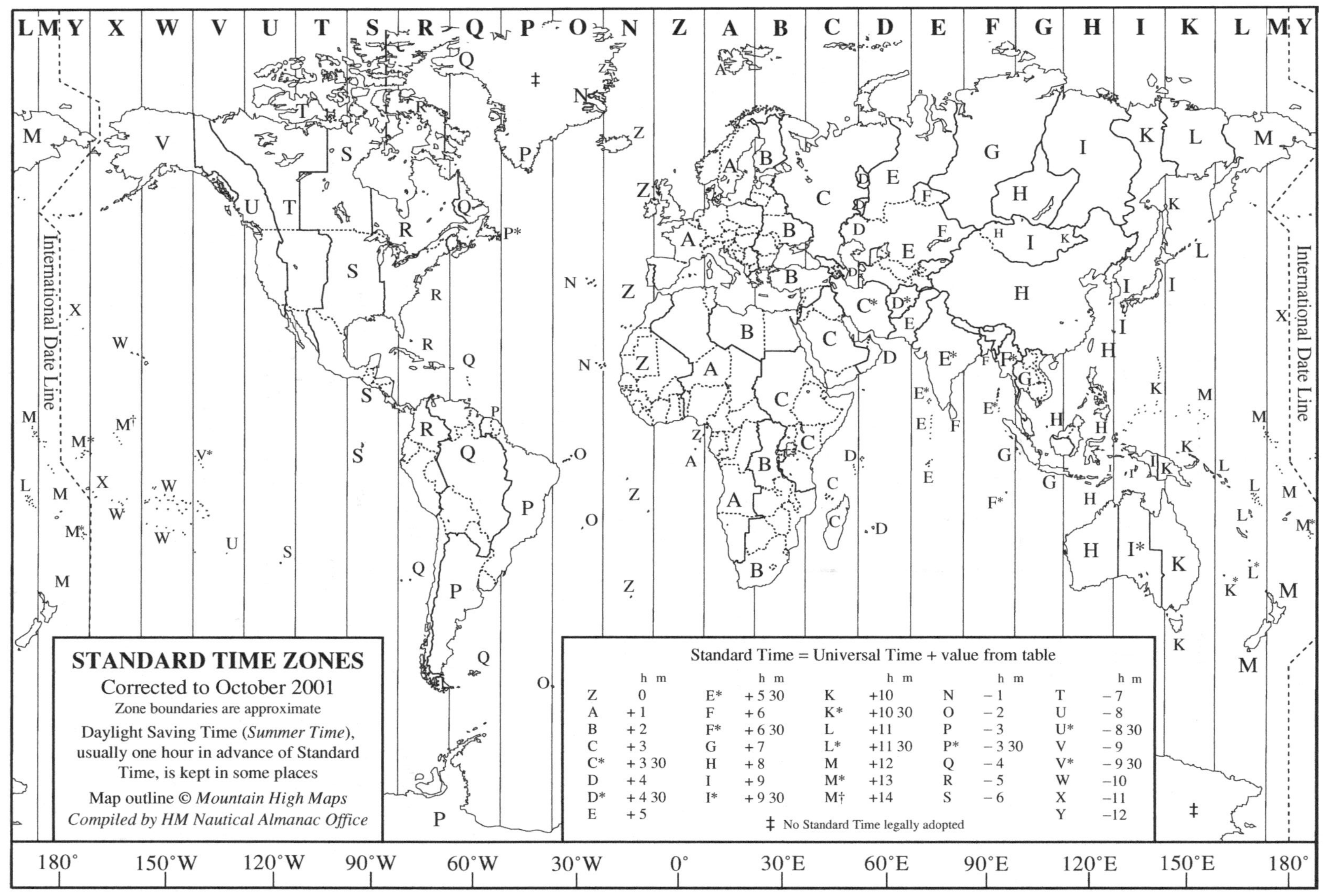

Figure 1: Standard time zones of the world as of 2001. Data supplied by H. M. Nautical Almanac Office; copyright Council for the Central Laboratory of the Research Councils. Used with permission.

The Gregorian calendar on the extreme right,

	Julian‡ (Sun)	GREGORIAN 1900							
Sat		Sun	Mon	Tue	Wed	Thu	Fri	Sat	
4	*Dec 19*	*31*	1	2	3	4	5	6[a]	
11		7	8	9	10	11	12	13[b]	JANUARY 1900
18	*Jan 2*	*14*	15	16	17	18	19	20	
25		21	22	23	24	25	26	27	
3	*Jan 16*	*28*	29	30	31	1	2	3	
10		4	5	6	7	8	9	10	FEBRUARY 1900
17	*Jan 30*	*11*	12	13	14	15	16	17	
24		18	19	20	21	22	23	24	
1	*Feb 13*	*25*	26	27	28[c]	1	2	3	
8		4	5	6	7	8	9	10	MARCH 1900
15	*Feb 27*	*11*[d]	12	13	14	15	16	17	
22		18	19	20	21	22	23	24	

indicates matters of Christian interest: dates of Christmas (both Western and Orthodox), Ash Wednesday, the Feast of Orthodoxy, Easter (both Western and Orthodox), and Advent are shaded and keyed to footnotes:

Event	Key	When
Orthodox Christmas	*a*	December 25 (Julian)
Julian New Year	*b*	January 1 (Julian)
Ash Wednesday	*c*	46 days before Easter
Feast of Orthodoxy	*d*	42 days before Orthodox Easter
Easter	*e*	March 22–April 25
Orthodox Easter	*f*	March 22–April 25 (Julian)
Advent	*g*	Sunday near November 30
Christmas	*h*	December 25

Julian New Year is also shaded and keyed to a footnote, with Julian leap years indicated by ‡ after the word "Julian" in the column heading. A minor column to the left of Sunday gives in italics the corresponding Julian (old style) calendar date for alternate Sundays, which are also shown in italics. This makes conversion of the Gregorian calendar to and from the Julian calendar possible with only minimal arithmetic. Aside from Eastern Europe and Turkey, most countries adopted the Gregorian calendar prior to 1900; an extensive list of dates of adoption of the Gregorian calendar in place of the Julian calendar can be found in [1, pages 414–416].

The ISO Week

The ISO week number (used in parts of Europe) for the seven-day week beginning on the Monday of the week shown, is given as the second major column on the verso page:

ISO WEEK
(Mon)
1
2
3
4
5
6
7
8
9

The Julian Day

The Julian day number (JD), as of noon on Sunday of the week shown, is given as the third major column on the verso page:

JULIAN DAY (Sun noon)
2415020
2415027
2415034
2415041
2415048
2415055
2415062
2415069
2415076
2415083

This value is easily used to compute, with minimal arithmetic, the JD of any date, the ordinal number of a day in the year, the number of days between two dates, or the number of days remaining in the year on any of the calendars. Similarly, it is easy to compute the modified Julian day number (MJD), which at midnight between Sunday and Monday is JD − 2400000, or the fixed date (R.D. of [10], with epoch January 1, 1 on the proleptic Gregorian calendar), which at midnight between Sunday and Monday is JD − 1721424.

WARNING

❖ ***Julian day numbers count days from noon to noon, but modified Julian day numbers and fixed day numbers count days from midnight to midnight.***

The Hebrew Calendar

The Hebrew (Jewish) calendar is given as the fourth major column on the verso page, with the month names and year numbers in a minor column on its left:

HEBREW 5660‡/5661								Molad
	Sun	Mon	Tue	Wed	Thu	Fri	Sat	
	29	1	2	3	4	5	6	Mon $10^h24^m0^p$
SHEVAT 5660	7	8	9	10	11	12	13	
	14	15	16	17	18	19	20	
	21	22	23	24	25	26	27	
	28	29	30	1	2	3	4	Tue $23^h8^m1^p$
	5	6	7	8	9	10	11	
ADAR I 5660	12	13	14	15	16	17	18	
	19	20	21	22	23	24	25	
	26	27	28	29	30	1	2	Thu $11^h52^m2^p$
ADAR II 5660	3	4	5	6	7	8	9	
	10	11	12	13	14[f]	15	16	

Common years have twelve months; leap years, indicated by ‡ after the year number, have thirteen months. The month names and lengths are:

(1)	Nisan	30 days	(7)	Tishri	30 days
(2)	Iyyar	29 days	(8)	Ḥeshvan	29 or 30 days
(3)	Sivan	30 days	(9)	Kislev	29 or 30 days
(4)	Tammuz	29 days	(10)	Teveth	29 days
(5)	Av	30 days	(11)	Shevat	30 days
(6)	Elul	29 days	{(12)	*Adar I*	30 days}
			(12) {(13)}	Adar {II}	29 days

The name of the leap month (*Adar I*) is given in italics when it occurs.

This calendar indicates matters of Jewish interest. Starting dates of major holidays, some minor holidays, and other significant days are shaded and keyed to footnotes, as follows:

Event	Key	When
New Year (Rosh ha-Shanah)	*a*	Tishri 1 and 2
Yom Kippur (Day of Atonement)	*b*	Tishri 10
Sukkot (Tabernacles), first day	*c*	Tishri 15
'Winter' starts (Sh'ela)	*d*	Athôr 26 (Coptic)
Ḥanukkah	*e*	Kislev 25 to Teveth 2 or 3
Purim	*f*	Adar {II} 14
Passover, first day	*g*	Nisan 15
Shavuot (Pentecost), first day	*h*	Sivan 6
Fast of Av (Tishah be-Av)	*i*	Av 9 or 10
Solar cycle begins (Birkath ha-Ḥama)	*	Paremotep 30 (Coptic), every 28 years

Two of these events, the beginning of winter and the solar cycle, are correlated with the Coptic calendar (see below).

A minor column to the right of Saturday gives the time of the mean new moon, called the *molad.* This is given with the traditional Hebrew time unit "parts" ($3\frac{1}{3}$ seconds per part).[2]

WARNING

❖ ***On the Hebrew calendar each day begins the prior evening at local sunset.***

The Chinese Calendar

The Chinese calendar is given as the fifth major column on the verso page, with the month numbers and year names in a minor column on its left:

[2] The function given for the calculation of the molad was flawed in the first printing of [10]; a corrected version, used in subsequent printings of [10], was used in preparing these tables.

	CHINESE Jǐ-Hài/Gēng-Zǐ‡							Solar Term
	Sun	Mon	Tue	Wed	Thu	Fri	Sat	
MONTH 12 Jǐ-Hài	29	1	2	3	4	5	6	*Xiǎo hán*
	7	8	9	10	11	12	13	
	14	15	16	17	18	19	***20***	***Dà hán***
	21	22	23	24	25	26	27	
	28	29	30	1[a]	2	3	4	
MONTH 1 Gēng-Zǐ	5	6	7	8	9	10	11	*Lì chūn*
	12	13	14	15[b]	16	17	18	
	19	***20***	21*	22	23	24	25	***Yǔ shuǐ***
	26	27	28	29	1	2	3	
MONTH 2 Gēng-Zǐ	4	5	6	7	8	9	10	*Jīng zhé*
	11	12	13	14	15	16	17	

Common years have twelve months; leap years, indicated by ‡ after the year name (see below), have thirteen months. Months are numbered, not named, and month lengths vary in accordance with the actual lunar cycle.

Dates of the festivals are shaded and keyed to footnotes:

Event	Key	When
Chinese New Year	*a*	Day 1 of Month 1
Lantern Festival	*b*	Day 15 of Month 1
Qīngmíng	*c*	April 4–6
Dragon Festival	*d*	Day 5 of Month 5
Qǐqiǎo (Chinese Valentine's Day)	*e*	Day 7 of Month 7
Hungry Ghosts	*f*	Day 15 of Month 7
Mid-Autumn Festival	*g*	Day 15 of Month 8
Double-Ninth Festival	*h*	Day 9 of Month 9
Dōngzhì (Winter solstice)	*i*	December 21–23
Start of 60-name cycle	*	Every 60 days

A minor column to the right of Saturday gives the 24 solar terms or *jiéqì*: The twelve major solar terms called *zhōngqì* are in bold italics and the twelve minor solar terms known by the general term *jiéqì* are given in lightface italics. The dates of occurrence are likewise shown in either bold or lightface italics. The solar terms correspond to 15° segments of solar longitude, with the twelve major terms at 0°, 30°, 60°, . . . , 300°, and 330° of solar longitude and the twelve minor terms at 15°, 45°, . . . , 315°, and 345°.

The Chinese calendar uses a cycle of sixty names. The name is formed by combining a celestial stem, *tiān gān*, with a terrestrial branch, *dì zhī*. The celestial stems,

(1) Jiǎ	(6) Jǐ
(2) Yǐ	(7) Gēng
(3) Bǐng	(8) Xīn
(4) Dīng	(9) Rén
(5) Wù	(10) Guǐ

are untranslatable, though they are sometimes associated with the five elements (tree, fire, earth, metal, and water), each in its male and female form. The terrestrial branches,

(1) Zǐ	(Rat)	(7) Wǔ	(Horse)
(2) Chǒu	(Ox)	(8) Wèi	(Sheep)
(3) Yín	(Tiger)	(9) Shēn	(Monkey)
(4) Mǎo	(Hare)	(10) Yǒu	(Fowl)
(5) Chén	(Dragon)	(11) Xū	(Dog)
(6) Sì	(Snake)	(12) Hài	(Pig)

are also untranslatable; the English names—traditional animal totems—given for the twelve branches corresponding to the years of the Chinese "Zodiac" are not translations from the Chinese. Names are assigned sequentially, running through the decimal and duodenary lists simultaneously: The first name is *jiǎ-zǐ*, the second is *yǐ-chǒu*, the third is *bǐng-yín*, and so on. Since the least common multiple of 10 and 12 is 60, the cycle of names repeats after the sixtieth name, *guǐ-hài*. The *n*th name of the sexagesimal cycle of names is as follows:

(1) Jiǎ-zǐ	(21) Jiǎ-shēn	(41) Jiǎ-chén
(2) Yǐ-chǒu	(22) Yǐ-yǒu	(42) Yǐ-sì
(3) Bǐng-yín	(23) Bǐng-xū	(43) Bǐng-wǔ
(4) Dīng-mǎo	(24) Dīng-hài	(44) Dīng-wèi
(5) Wù-chén	(25) Wù-zǐ	(45) Wù-shēn
(6) Jǐ-sì	(26) Jǐ-chǒu	(46) Jǐ-yǒu
(7) Gēng-wǔ	(27) Gēng-yín	(47) Gēng-xū
(8) Xīn-wèi	(28) Xīn-mǎo	(48) Xīn-hài
(9) Rén-shēn	(29) Rén-chén	(49) Rén-zǐ
(10) Guǐ-yǒu	(30) Guǐ-sì	(50) Guǐ-chǒu
(11) Jiǎ-xū	(31) Jiǎ-wǔ	(51) Jiǎ-yín
(12) Yǐ-hài	(32) Yǐ-wèi	(52) Yǐ-mǎo
(13) Bǐng-zǐ	(33) Bǐng-shēn	(53) Bǐng-chén
(14) Dīng-chǒu	(34) Dīng-yǒu	(54) Dīng-sì
(15) Wù-yín	(35) Wù-xū	(55) Wù-wǔ
(16) Jǐ-mǎo	(36) Jǐ-hài	(56) Jǐ-wèi
(17) Gēng-chén	(37) Gēng-zǐ	(57) Gēng-shēn
(18) Xīn-sì	(38) Xīn-chǒu	(58) Xīn-yǒu
(19) Rén-wǔ	(39) Rén-yín	(59) Rén-xū
(20) Guǐ-wèi	(40) Guǐ-mǎo	(60) Guǐ-hài

This sexagesimal cycle is used to name years, days, and (in earlier times) months. The starting day of each cycle is indicated by an asterisk. Since leap months (shown in the tables in italics) were unnamed, the cycle of month names repeats after five years; the starting month of each cycle, always an eleventh month, is indicated by an asterisk.

The Chinese calendar does not traditionally count years; rather, years are generally given as regnal years and by sexagesimal name. The popular press, however, usually gives a year number. This year number is given in the footnote marking the new year, along with the animal totem for the year.

WARNINGS

- *Historically, on the Chinese calendar for the Gregorian year 1906, Month 4 began on April 24, not April 23 as shown; it thus had 29 days instead of the 30 days shown. The disagreement occurs because our calculations of times of solar and lunar events are more accurate than the seventeenth-century methods used by the Chinese until 1913.*
- *The year number we give for Chinese New Year is the popular version of the Huángdi era.*

The Coptic and Ethiopic Calendars

The rightmost major column on the verso page gives the Coptic and Ethiopic calendars:

	COPTIC 1616/1617			ETHIOPIC 1892/1893				
	Sun	Mon	Tue	Wed	Thu	Fri	Sat	
KOIAK 1616	22	23	24	25	26	27	28	TĀKHŚĀŚ 1892
	29[c]	30	1	2	3	4	5	
TÔBE 1616	6[d]	7	8	9	10	11[e]	12	ṬER 1892
	13	14	15	16	17	18	19	
	20	21	22	23	24	25	26	
	27	28	29	30	1	2	3	
MESHIR 1616	4	5	6	7	8	9	10	YAKĀTIT 1892
	11	12	13	14	15	16	17	
	18	19	20	21	22	23	24	
	25	26	27	28	29	30	1	
TEP	2	3	4	5	6	7	8	M

These calendars are identical except for the names of the months and year numbers. Coptic month names and year numbers are given in a minor column on the left; Ethiopic month names and year numbers are given in a minor column on the right. The month names and lengths are:

	Coptic Name		*Ethiopic Name*	
(1)	Thoout	(1)	Maskaram	30 days
(2)	Paope	(2)	Teqemt	30 days
(3)	Athôr	(3)	Ḫedār	30 days
(4)	Koiak	(4)	Tākhśāś	30 days
(5)	Tôbe	(5)	Ṭer	30 days
(6)	Meshir	(6)	Yakātit	30 days
(7)	Paremotep	(7)	Magābit	30 days
(8)	Parmoute	(8)	Miyāzyā	30 days
(9)	Pashons	(9)	Genbot	30 days
(10)	Paône	(10)	Sanē	30 days
(11)	Epêp	(11)	Ḥamlē	30 days
(12)	Mesorê	(12)	Naḥasē	30 days
(13)	Epagomenê	(13)	Pāguemēn	5 {6} days

Leap years have 366 days and are indicated by ‡ after the year number.

The dates of New Year, Coptic/Ethiopic Christmas, Orthodox Easter, and several Coptic holidays are shaded and keyed to footnotes:

Event	Key	When
New Year	*a*	Thoout 1
Building of the Cross	*b*	Thoout 17
Christmas	*c*	Koiak 29
Jesus's Circumcision	*d*	Tôbe 6
Coptic Epiphany	*e*	Tôbe 11
Easter	*f*	Orthodox Easter
Mary's Announcement	*g*	Parmoute 29
Jesus's Transfiguration	*h*	Mesorê 13

The Persian Calendar

The leftmost major column on the recto page gives the astronomical Persian calendar:

PERSIAN (ASTRONOMICAL) 1278/1279	Sun	Mon	Tue	Wed	Thu	Fri	Sat
DEY 1278	10	11	12	13	14	15	16
	17	18	19	20	21	22	23
	24	25	26	27	28	29	30
BAHMAN 1278	*1*	2	3	4	5	6	7
	8	9	10	11	12	13	14
	15	16	17	18	19	20	21
	22	23	24	25	26	27	28
ESFAND 1278	29	30	*1*	2	3	4	5
	6	7	8	9	10	11	12
	13	14	15	16	17	18	19
	20	21	22	23	24	25	26
	27	28	29	*1*[a]	2	3	4

When the equinox occurs very close to noon in Tehran (specifically, when the solar longitude θ at noon satisfies $0 \leq |\theta| \leq 2'$), this is indicated, and the note for the neighboring day gives the solar longitude at noon of the day marked as the new year (Naw Ruz). When the arithmetic calculation of Birashk [3] differs from the astronomically indicated date, the arithmetic start of the year is also noted. The first day of the month on the arithmetic calendar is always shown in italics, so the date on the arithmetic calendar can be determined by counting forward from there; the first days of the astronomical and arithmetic months coincide with very few exceptions (2025-26, 2058-59, 2153-54, 2186-87, and 2190-91) in these tables.

The month names and lengths are:

(1) Farvardīn	31 days	(7) Mehr	30 days
(2) Ordībehesht	31 days	(8) Abān	30 days
(3) Xordād	31 days	(9) Āzar	30 days
(4) Tīr	31 days	(10) Dey	30 days
(5) Mordād	31 days	(11) Bahman	30 days
(6) Shahrīvar	31 days	(12) Esfand	29 {30} days

Leap years have 366 days and are indicated by ‡ after the year number. Leap years on the astronomical calendar are shown, *not* leap years on the arithmetic calendar.

The dates of the Persian holidays Naw Ruz (New Year) and Sizdeh Bedar are keyed to footnotes:

Event	Key	When
New Year (Naw Ruz)	a	Farvardīn 1
Near New Year	*	Day before or after Naw Ruz
New Year (Arithmetic)	â	Farvardīn 1
Sizdeh Bedar	b	Farvardīn 14

WARNINGS

- ***Our Persian calendar is astronomical and the decision to use it or one of the proposed arithmetic forms is uncertain.***
- ***When the equinox occurs very close to noon, our Persian calendar may be off by a day.***

The Hindu Calendars

The second and third major columns on the recto page give the Hindu lunar and solar calendars:

HINDU LUNAR 1956/1957								HINDU SOLAR 1821/1822							
	Sun	Mon	Tue	Wed	Thu	Fri	Sat		Sun	Mon	Tue	Wed	Thu	Fri	Sat
	29	30	1	2	3	4	**5**	PAUSHA 1821	18	19	20	21	22	23	24
PAUSHA 1956	7	8	9	10	11	12	13		25	26	27	28	29	1[b]	2
	14	15	16	17	18	19	20	MĀGHA 1821	3	4	5	6	7	8	9
	20	21	22	23	24	25	26		10	11	12	13	14	15	16
	27	28	**29**	1	2	3	4		17	18	19	20	21	22	23
MĀGHA 1956	5	6	7	8	9	10	11		24	25	26	27	28	29	30
	12	13	14	15	16	17	18		1	2	3	4	5	6	7
	19	20	21	22	23	24	25	PHĀLGUNA 1821	8	9	10	11	12	13	14
	26	27	28[h]	29	30	1	2		15	16	17	18	19	20	21
PHĀLGUNA 1956	3	**4**	6	7	8	9	10		22	23	24	25	26	27	28
	11	12	*12*	13	14	15[i]	16		29	30	1	2	3	4	5
	17	18	19	20	21	22	23	TRA 21	6	7	8	9	10	11	12

The month names are:

(1)	Chaitra	(7)	Āśvina
(2)	Vaiśākha	(8)	Kārttika
(3)	Jyaishṭha	(9)	Mārgaśīra
(4)	Āshāḍha	(10)	Pausha
(5)	Śrāvaṇa	(11)	Māgha
(6)	Bhādrapada	(12)	Phālguna

Intercalated days are given in italics. Because there are extracalated (omitted) days, dates in the calendar may not be consecutive; in such cases, the (civil) day that wholly contains the omitted "lunar" day is given in boldface. Similarly, when a month is skipped on the lunar calendar, the previous month name is in lightface italics.

Lunar years are given according to the elapsed Vikrama era; leap years, indicated by ‡ after the year number, have thirteen months. Solar years are given according to the elapsed Śaka era; leap years, which have 366 days, are indicated by ‡ after the year number. Various different eras have been used in India. The year number of the major eras can be calculated using the following table of offsets from the Śaka:

Era	Current Year	Elapsed Year
Vikrama	+136	+135
Kali Yuga	+3180	+3179
Śaka	+1	0
Bengal		−515
Kollam	+901	
Nepalese		+955

Significant dates are shaded and keyed to footnotes. For the lunar calendar:

Event	Key	When
New Year (Chandramana Ugadi)	*a*	Chaitra 1
Birthday of Rāma	*b*	Chaitra 9
Birthday of Krishna (Janmāshṭamī)	*c*	Śrāvaṇa 23
Ganēśa Chaturthī	*d*	Bhādrapada 3 or 4
Dashara (Nava Rathri), last 3 days	*e*	Āśvina 8–10
Diwali, last day	*f*	Kārttika 1
Birthday of Vishnu (Ekadashi)	*g*	Mārgaśīra 11
Night of Śiva	*h*	Māgha 28 or 29
Holi	*i*	Phālguna 15

and for the solar calendar:

Event	Key	When
New Year (Sowramana Ugadi)	*a*	Vaiśākha 1
Pongal (Makara Saṃkrāti), main day	*b*	Māgha 1

The name of the Hindu years in the sixty-name *samvatsara* cycle is given in two versions: the common southern version is given with the lunar calendar, and a northern scheme (which skips a name in 1943, 2028, 2114, and 2199) is used with the solar calendar. The year names are:

(1) Vijaya
(2) Jaya
(3) Manmatha
(4) Durmukha
(5) Hemalamba
(6) Vilamba
(7) Vikārin
(8) Śārvari
(9) Plava
(10) Śubhakṛit
(11) Śobhana
(12) Krodhin
(13) Viśvāvasu
(14) Parābhava
(15) Plavaṅga
(16) Kīlaka
(17) Saumya
(18) Sādhāraṇa
(19) Virodhakṛit
(20) Paridhāvin
(21) Praṃādin
(22) Ānanda
(23) Rākshasa
(24) Anala
(25) Piṅgala
(26) Kālayukta
(27) Siddhārthin
(28) Rāudra
(29) Durmati
(30) Dundubhi

(31) Rudhirodgārin	(41) Śrīmukha	(51) Subhānu
(32) Raktāksha	(42) Bhāva	(52) Tāraṇa
(33) Krodhana	(43) Yuvan	(53) Pārthiva
(34) Kshaya	(44) Dhātṛi	(54) Vyaya
(35) Prabhava	(45) Īśvara	(55) Sarvajit
(36) Vibhava	(46) Bahudhānya	(56) Sarvadhārin
(37) Śukla	(47) Pramāthin	(57) Virodhin
(38) Pramoda	(48) Vikrama	(58) Vikṛita
(39) Prajāpati	(49) Vṛisha	(59) Khara
(40) Aṅgiras	(50) Chitrabhānu	(60) Nandana

WARNINGS

- *There are numerous variants of the Hindu calendar, human calendar calculators use approximations, and dates are determined regionally. Some calendar makers prefer modern astronomical methods.*
- *For the Hindu lunar calendar, we follow the rules of the Sūrya-Siddhānta, as amended by Gaṇesa Daivajna, except that the actual time of sunrise in Ujjain is used.*
- *Hindu lunar months are shown from new moon to new moon; in many regional variants full moon to full moon would be used. The day numbers of the second ("dark") half of each lunar month typically start over from 1; we use 16–30, instead.*
- *Our Hindu solar calendar follows the Orissa rule and actual sunrise in Calcutta, which can differ by a day or two from the rules used elsewhere.*
- *The sequence of Hindu months, and their names, differ regionally. Ours begins the solar year with Vaiśākha, the name of the second month of the lunar year.*
- *On the Hindu calendars each day begins at local sunrise.*
- *There is very wide variance in the precise date of celebration of the various Hindu holidays, and in the length of the celebration.*

The Islamic Calendar

The fourth major column on the recto page gives the astronomical Islamic (Moslem) calendar:[3]

[3] In the first printing of [10], the definition and usage of the crescent visibility function were inconsistent. A corrected version, used in subsequent printings of [10], was used in preparing these tables, and Los Angeles was substituted for the viewing location.

		ISLAMIC (ASTRONOMICAL) 1317/1318‡						
at		Sun	Mon	Tue	Wed	Thu	Fri	Sat
4		28	29	30	*1*[e]	2	3	4
2	RAMAḌĀN 1317	5	6	7	8	9	10	11
9		12	13	14	15	16	17	18
5		19	20	21	22	23	24	25
3		26	27	28	29	1[f]	*2*	3
0	SHAWWĀL 1317	4	5	6	7	8	9	10
7		11	12	13	14	15	16	17
4		18	19	20	21	22	23	24
1		25	26	27	28	29	30	*1*
3	DHU AL-QA'DA 1317	2	3	4	5	6	7	8
5		9	10	11	12	13	14	15
2		16	17	18	19	20	21	22

The months are:

(1)	Muḥarram	30 days	(7)	Rajab	30 days
(2)	Ṣafar	29 days	(8)	Sha'bān	29 days
(3)	Rabī' I (Rabī' al-Awwal)	30 days	(9)	Ramaḍān	30 days
(4)	Rabī' II (Rabī' al-Āḥir)	29 days	(10)	Shawwāl	29 days
(5)	Jumada I (Jumādā al-Ūlā)	30 days	(11)	Dhu al-Qa'da	30 days
(6)	Jumādā II (Jumādā al-Āḥira)	29 days	(12)	Dhu al-Ḥijja	29 {30} days

Month lengths on the astronomical calendar vary according to the actual lunar cycle; the lengths given above are for the *arithmetic* calendar only. The first day of the month on the arithmetic calendar is always shown in italics, so the date on the arithmetic calendar can be determined by counting forward from there; the first days of the astronomical and arithmetic months are always within one or two days of each other.

Leap years, which have 355 days, are indicated by ‡ after the year number. Leap years on the astronomical calendar are shown, *not* leap years on the arithmetic calendar. An Islamic year y is a leap year on the arithmetic calendar if $(14 + 11y) \bmod 30 < 11$.

Dates of significance in the Islamic year are shaded and keyed to footnotes. The dates so indicated are approximate because the actual dates of occurrence depend on human observations, not calculations.

Event	Key	When
New Year	*a*	Muḥarram 1
New Year (Arithmetic)	*â*	Muḥarram 1
'Ashūrā'	*b*	Muḥarram 10
Prophet's Birthday (Mawlid an-Nabī)	*c*	Rabī' I 12
Ascent of the Prophet	*d*	Rajab 27
Start of Ramaḍān	*e*	Ramaḍān 1
'Īd al-Fiṭr	*f*	Shawwāl 1
'Īd al-'Aḍḥā	*g*	Dhu al-Ḥijja 10

WARNINGS

- ***Our Islamic calendar is an approximation based on astronomical determination of when the new crescent moon is likely to be visible in Los Angeles, California; however, the actual date depends on human observation of the crescent moon. Thus, month beginnings and endings can be in error by a day or so, and vary from country to country. Holiday dates are therefore also only approximate and vary from country to country.***

- *On the Islamic calendar each day begins the prior evening at local sunset.*
- *The italicized dates of the arithmetic Islamic calendar indicated in the tables are based on a fixed thirty-year cycle in which years 2, 5, 7, 10, 13, 16, 18, 21, 24, 26, and 29 are leap years.*

References

[1] *Explanatory Supplement to the Astronomical Ephemeris and the American Ephemeris and Nautical Almanac*, Her Majesty's Stationery Office, London, 1961.

[2] A. A. Akavia (A. L. Jacobowitz), *Luaḥ l'Sheshet Alafim Shanah: Luaḥ l'Hashva'ah l'Mininim ha'Shonim mi'Bri'at ha'Olam 'ad Sof ha'Elef ha'Shishi* (*Calendar for 6000 Years: Comparative Calendar of All Chronological Tables from the Creation until the End of the Sixth Millennium*), prepared by N. Fried, edited by D. Zakai, Mossad Harav Kook, Jerusalem, 5736 (1975–1976).

[3] A. Birashk, *A Comparative Calendar of the Iranian, Muslim Lunar, and Christian Eras for Three Thousand Years*, Mazda Publishers (in association with Bibliotheca Persica), Costa Mesa, CA, 1993.

[4] Bureau of Economics & Statistics, *Diglott Calendar*, volumes I and II, 4th ed., Government of Andhra Pradesh, Hyderabad, India, 1961.

[5] M. Chaîne, *La chronologie des temps Chrétiens de l'Égypte et de l'Éthiopie*, Paul Geuthner, Paris, 1925.

[6] G. S. P. Freeman-Grenville, *The Islamic and Christian Calendars*, Garnet Publishing, Reading, England, 1995.

[7] H. Fritsche, *On Chronology and the Construction of the Calendar with Special Regard to the Chinese Computation of Time Compared with the European*, R. Laverentz, St. Petersburg, 1886.

[8] F. Parise, ed., *The Book of Calendars*, Facts on File, New York, 1982.

[9] Purple Mountain Observatory, *Xīn biān wàn nián lì* (*The Newly Compiled Perpetual Chinese Calendar*) *1840–2050*, Kē xué pǔ jí chū bǎn shè (Popular Science Press), Beijing, 1984. Third and subsequent printings correct the structure of the year 2033.

[10] E. M. Reingold and N. Dershowitz, *Calendrical Calculations: The Millennium Edition*, Cambridge University Press, Cambridge, 2001.

[11] F. Reiss, *The Standard Guide to the Jewish and Civil Calendars*, Behrman House, West Orange, NJ, 1995.

[12] C. Roth, ed., *Encyclopædia Judaica*, Macmillan, New York, 1971.

[13] S. J. Scheinman, *'Amudai Shai'ish: Luaḥ 'al Arb'a Me'ot v'Arb'a 'Esrei Shanah* [*Agmudai Shaish* (*Marble Pillars*)*: A Calendar for a Period of 414 Years, from 1826 to 2240*], New York, 1900.

[14] R. G. Schram, *Kalendariographische und chronologische Tafeln*, J. C. Hinrichs'sche Buchhandlung, Leipzig, 1908.

[15] R. Sewell and S. B. Dîkshit, *The Indian Calendar, with Tables for the Conversion of Hindu and Muhammadan into A.D. Dates, and Vice Versa, with Tables of Eclipses Visible in India by R. Schram*, Motilal Banarsidass Publishers, Delhi, 1995. Originally published in 1896.

[16] A. Spier, *The Comprehensive Hebrew Calendar*, 3rd ed., Feldheim Publishers, New York, 1986.

[17] W. C. Welch, *Chinese-American Calendar for the 102 Chinese Years Commencing January 24, 1849 and Ending February 5, 1951*, U.S. Department of Labor, Bureau of Immigration, United States Government Printing Office, Washington, DC, 1928.

[18] W. C. Welch, *Chinese-American Calendar for the 40th through the 89th Year of the Chinese Republic, February 6, 1951 to January 23, 2001*, U.S. Department of Justice, Immigration and Naturalization Service, United States Government Printing Office, Washington, DC, 1957.

[19] F. Wüstenfeld and E. Mahler, *Wüstenfeld-Mahler'sche Vergleichungs-Tabellen zur muslimischen und iranischen Zeitrechung mit Tafeln zur Umrechnung orient-christlicher Ären*, 3rd ed. Revised by J. Mayr and B. Spuler, Deutsche Morgenländische Gesellschaft, Wiesbaden, 1961.

[20] H. C. Xú, *Xīn biān Zhōng-guó sān qiān nián lì rì jiǎn suǒ biǎo* (*The Newly Compiled Chinese 3000-Year Calendar Indexing Table*), Rén mín jiào yù chū bǎn shè (People's Education Press), Beijing, 1992.

Calendars, 1900–2200

1900

Gregorian 1900 / ISO Week / Julian Day

Month	Sun	Mon	Tue	Wed	Thu	Fri	Sat	Lunar Phases	ISO Week (Mon)	Julian Day (Sun noon)
JANUARY 1900	31	●[a]	2	3	4	5	6	13:52	1	2415020
	7	◐	9	10	11	12	13	5:40	2	2415027
	14	○	16	17	18	19	20	19:07	3	2415034
	21	22	◑	24	25	26	27	23:53	4	2415041
	28	29	30	●	1	2	3	1:22	5	2415048
FEBRUARY 1900	4	5	◐	7	8	9	10	16:23	6	2415055
	11	12	13	○	15	16	17	13:50	7	2415062
	18	19	20	21	◑	23	24	16:44	8	2415069
	25	26	27	28	●	2	3	11:25	9	2415076
MARCH 1900	4	5	6	7	◐	9	10	5:34	10	2415083
	11	12	13	14	15	○	17	8:12	11	2415090
	18	19	20	21[b]	22	23	◑	5:37	12	2415097
	25	26	27	28	29	●	31	20:30	13	2415104
APRIL 1900	1	2	3	4	5	◐	7	20:55	14	2415111
	8	9	10	11	12	13	14		15	2415118
	○	16	17	18	19	20	21	1:02	16	2415125
	◑	23	24	25	26	27	28	14:33	17	2415132
	●	30	1	2	3	4	5	5:23	18	2415139
MAY 1900	◐	7	8	9	10	11	12	13:39	19	2415146
	13	○	15	16	17	18	19	15:37	20	2415153
	20	◑	22	23	24	25	26	20:31	21	2415160
	27	●	29	30	31	1	2	14:50	22	2415167
JUNE 1900	3	4	◐	6	7	8	9	6:59	23	2415174
	10	11	12	○	14	15	16	3:39	24	2415181
	17	18	19	◑	21[c]	22	23	0:57	25	2415188
	24	25	26	●	28	29	30	1:27	26	2415195
JULY 1900	1	2	3	4	◐	6	7	0:14	27	2415202
	8	9	10	11	○	13	14	13:22	28	2415209
	15	16	17	18	◑	20	21	5:31	29	2415216
	22	23	24	25	●	27	28	13:43	30	2415223
	29	30	31	1	2	◐	4	16:46	31	2415230
AUGUST 1900	5	6	7	8	9	○	11	21:30	32	2415237
	12	13	14	15	16	◑	18	11:46	33	2415244
	19	20	21	22	23	24	●	3:53	34	2415251
	26	27	28	29	30	31	1		35	2415258
SEPTEMBER 1900	◐	3	4	5	6	7	8	7:56	36	2415265
	○	10	11	12	13	14	◑	5:06 20:57	37	2415272
	16	17	18	19	20	21	22		38	2415279
	●[d]	24	25	26	27	28	29	19:57	39	2415286
	30	◐	2	3	4	5	6	21:10	40	2415293
OCTOBER 1900	7	○	9	10	11	12	13	13:18	41	2415300
	14	◑	16	17	18	19	20	9:51	42	2415307
	21	22	●	24	25	26	27	13:27	43	2415314
	28	29	30	◐	1	2	3	8:17	44	2415321
NOVEMBER 1900	4	5	○	7	8	9	10	23:00	45	2415328
	11	12	13	◑	15	16	17	2:37	46	2415335
	18	19	20	21	●	23	24	7:17	47	2415342
	25	26	27	28	◐	30	1	17:35	48	2415349
DECEMBER 1900	2	3	4	5	○	7	8	10:38	49	2415356
	9	10	11	12	◑	14	15	22:42	50	2415363
	16	17	18	19	20	21	●[e]	0:01	51	2415370
	23	24	25	26	27	28	◐	1:48	52	2415377
	30	31	1	2	3	4	○	0:13	1	2415384

Hebrew 5660‡/5661

ISO Week	Month	Sun	Mon	Tue	Wed	Thu	Fri	Sat	Molad
1	SHEVAT 5660	29	1	2	3	4	5	6	Mon 10h24m0p
2		7	8	9	10	11	12	13	
3		14	15	16	17	18	19	20	
4		21	22	23	24	25	26	27	
5	ADAR I 5660	28	29	30	1	2	3	4	Tue 23h8m1p
6		5	6	7	8	9	10	11	
7		12	13	14	15	16	17	18	
8		19	20	21	22	23	24	25	
9	ADAR II 5660	26	27	28	29	30	1	2	Thu 11h52m2p
10		3	4	5	6	7	8	9	
11		10	11	12	13	14[f]	15	16	
12		17	18	19	20	21	22	23	
13	NISAN 5660	24	25	26	27	28	29	1	Sat 0h36m3p
14		2	3	4	5	6	7	8	
15		9	10	11	12	13	14	15[g]	
16		16	17	18	19	20	21	22	
17		23	24	25	26	27	28	29	
18	IYAR 5660	30	1	2	3	4	5	6	Sun 13h20m4p
19		7	8	9	10	11	12	13	
20		14	15	16	17	18	19	20	
21		21	22	23	24	25	26	27	
22	SIVAN 5660	28	29	1	2	3	4	5	Tue 2h4m5p
23		6[h]	7	8	9	10	11	12	
24		13	14	15	16	17	18	19	
25		20	21	22	23	24	25	26	
26	TAMMUZ 5660	27	28	29	30	1	2	3	Wed 14h48m6p
27		4	5	6	7	8	9	10	
28		11	12	13	14	15	16	17	
29		18	19	20	21	22	23	24	
30	AV 5660	25	26	27	28	29	1	2	Fri 3h32m7p
31		3	4	5	6	7	8	9	
32		10[i]	11	12	13	14	15	16	
33		17	18	19	20	21	22	23	
34		24	25	26	27	28	29	30	
35	ELUL 5660	1	2	3	4	5	6	7	Sat 16h16m8p
36		8	9	10	11	12	13	14	
37		15	16	17	18	19	20	21	
38		22	23	24	25	26	27	28	
39	TISHRI 5661	29	1[a]	2[a]	3	4	5	6	Mon 5h0m9p
40		7	8	9	10[b]	11	12	13	
41		14	15[c]	16	17	18	19	20	
42		21	22	23	24	25	26	27	
43	HESHVAN 5661	28	29	30	1	2	3	4	Tue 17h44m10p
44		5	6	7	8	9	10	11	
45		12	13	14	15	16	17	18	
46		19	20	21	22	23	24	25	
47	KISLEV 5661	26	27	28	29	30	1	2	Thu 6h28m11p
48		3	4	5	6	7	8	9	
49		10	11	12	13[d]	14	15	16	
50		17	18	19	20	21	22	23	
51		24	25[e]	26[e]	27[e]	28[e]	29[e]	30[e]	
52	TEVETH 5661	1[e]	2[e]	3	4	5	6	7	Fri 19h12m12p
1		8	9	10	11	12	13	14	

Chinese Jǐ-Hài/Gēng-Zǐ‡

ISO Week	Month	Sun	Mon	Tue	Wed	Thu	Fri	Sat	Solar Term
1	MONTH 12 Jǐ-Hài	29	1	2	3	4	5	*6*	Xiǎo hán
2		7	8	9	10	11	12	13	
3		14	15	16	17	18	19	**20**	Dà hán
4		21	22	23	24	25	26	27	
5	MONTH 1 Gēng-Zǐ	28	29	30	1[a]	2	3	4	
6		5	6	7	8	9	10	11	Lì chūn
7		12	13	14	15[b]	16	17	18	
8		19	**20**	21*	22	23	24	25	Yǔ shuǐ
9	MONTH 2 Gēng-Zǐ	26	27	28	29	1	2	3	
10		4	5	6	7	8	9	10	Jīng zhé
11		11	12	13	14	15	16	17	
12		18	19	20	**21**	22	23	24	Chūn fēn
13	MONTH 3 Gēng-Zǐ	25	26	27	28	29	30	1	
14		2	3	4	5	6[c]	7	8	Qīng míng
15		9	10	11	12	13	14	15	
16		16	17	18	19	20	**21**	22*	Gǔ yǔ
17		23	24	25	26	27	28	29	
18	MONTH 4 Gēng-Zǐ	1	2	3	4	5	6	7	
19		*8*	9	10	11	12	13	14	Lì xià
20		15	16	17	18	19	20	21	
21		22	**23**	24	25	26	27	28	Xiǎo mǎn
22	MONTH 5 Gēng-Zǐ	29	1	2	3	4	5[d]	6	
23		7	8	9	*10*	11	12	13	Máng zhòng
24		14	15	16	17	18	19	20	
25		21	22	23	24*	25	**26**	27	Xià zhì
26	MONTH 6 Gēng-Zǐ	28	29	30	1	2	3	4	
27		5	6	7	8	9	10	*11*	Xiǎo shǔ
28		12	13	14	15	16	17	18	
29		19	20	21	22	23	24	25	
30	MONTH 7 Gēng-Zǐ	26	**27**	28	29	1	2	3	Dà shǔ
31		4	5	6	7[e]	8	9	10	
32		11	12	13	*14*	15[f]	16	17	Lì qiū
33		18	19	20	21	22	23	24	
34	MONTH 8 Gēng-Zǐ	25*	26	27	28	**29**	30	1	Chǔ shǔ
35		2	3	4	5	6	7	8	
36		9	10	11	12	13	14	*15*[g]	Bái lù
37		16	17	18	19	20	21	22	
38		23	24	25	26	27	28	29	
39	LEAP MONTH 8 Gēng-Zǐ	**30**	1	2	3	4	5	6	Qiū fēn
40		7	8	9	10	11	12	13	
41		14	15	*16*	17	18	19	20	Hán lù
42		21	22	23	24	25*	26	27	
43	MONTH 9 Gēng-Zǐ	28	29	1	**2**	3	4	5	Shuāng jiàng
44		6	7	8	9[h]	10	11	12	
45		13	14	15	16	*17*	18	19	Lì dōng
46		20	21	22	23	24	25	26	
47	MONTH 10 Gēng-Zǐ	27	28	29	30	1	**2**	3	Xiǎo xuě
48		4	5	6	7	8	9	10	
49		11	12	13	14	15	*16*	17	Dà xuě
50		18	19	20	21	22	23	24	
51	MONTH 11 Gēng-Zǐ	25	26*	27	28	29	30	1[i]	Dōng zhì
52		2	3	4	5	6	7	8	
1		9	10	11	12	13	14	15	

Coptic 1616/1617 — Ethiopic 1892/1893

ISO Week	Coptic Month	Sun	Mon	Tue	Wed	Thu	Fri	Sat	Ethiopic Month
1	KOIAK 1616	22	23	24	25	26	27	28	TĀḪŚĀŚ 1892
2	TŌBE 1616	29[c]	30	1	2	3	4	5	ṬER 1892
3		6[d]	7	8	9	10	11[e]	12	
4		13	14	15	16	17	18	19	
5		20	21	22	23	24	25	26	
6	MESHIR 1616	27	28	29	30	1	2	3	YAKĀTIT 1892
7		4	5	6	7	8	9	10	
8		11	12	13	14	15	16	17	
9		18	19	20	21	22	23	24	
10	PAREMOTEP 1616	25	26	27	28	29	30	1	MAGĀBIT 1892
11		2	3	4	5	6	7	8	
12		9	10	11	12	13	14	15	
13		16	17	18	19	20	21	22	
14		23	24	25	26	27	28	29	
15	PARMOUTE 1616	30	1	2	3	4	5	6	MIYĀZYĀ 1892
16		7	8	9	10	11	12	13	
17		14[f]	15	16	17	18	19	20	
18		21	22	23	24	25	26	27	
19	PASHONS 1616	28	29[g]	30	1	2	3	4	GENBOT 1892
20		5	6	7	8	9	10	11	
21		12	13	14	15	16	17	18	
22		19	20	21	22	23	24	25	
23	PAŌNE 1616	26	27	28	29	30	1	2	SANĒ 1892
24		3	4	5	6	7	8	9	
25		10	11	12	13	14	15	16	
26		17	18	19	20	21	22	23	
27		24	25	26	27	28	29	30	
28	EPĒP 1616	1	2	3	4	5	6	7	ḤAMLĒ 1892
29		8	9	10	11	12	13	14	
30		15	16	17	18	19	20	21	
31		22	23	24	25	26	27	28	
32	MESORĒ 1616	29	30	1	2	3	4	5	NAḤASĒ 1892
33		6	7	8	9	10	11	12	
34		13[h]	14	15	16	17	18	19	
35		20	21	22	23	24	25	26	
36	EPAG. 1616	27	28	29	30	1	2	3	PĀG. 1892
37	THOOUT 1617	4	5	1[a]	2	3	4	5	MASKARAM 1893
38		6	7	8	9	10	11	12	
39		13	14	15	16	17[b]	18	19	
40		20	21	22	23	24	25	26	
41	PAOPE 1617	27	28	29	30	1	2	3	ṬEQEMT 1893
42		4	5	6	7	8	9	10	
43		11	12	13	14	15	16	17	
44		18	19	20	21	22	23	24	
45	ATHŌR 1617	25	26	27	28	29	30	1	ḪEDĀR 1893
46		2	3	4	5	6	7	8	
47		9	10	11	12	13	14	15	
48		16	17	18	19	20	21	22	
49		23	24	25	26	27	28	29	
50	KOIAK 1617	30	1	2	3	4	5	6	TĀḪŚĀŚ 1893
51		7	8	9	10	11	12	13	
52		14	15	16	17	18	19	20	
1		21	22	23	24	25	26	27	

Gregorian notes:
[a]New Year
[b]Spring (1:39)
[c]Summer (21:40)
[d]Autumn (12:20)
[e]Winter (6:41)
● New moon
◐ First quarter moon
○ Full moon
◑ Last quarter moon

Hebrew notes:
‡Leap year
[a]New Year
[b]Yom Kippur
[c]Sukkot
[d]Winter starts
[e]Ḥanukkah
[f]Purim
[g]Passover
[h]Shavuot
[i]Fast of Av

Chinese notes:
‡Leap year
[a]New Year (4598, Rat)
[b]Lantern Festival
[c]Qīngmíng
[d]Dragon Festival
[e]Qǐqiǎo
[f]Hungry Ghosts
[g]Mid-Autumn Festival
[h]Double-Ninth Festival
[i]Dōngzhì
*Start of 60-name cycle

Coptic/Ethiopic notes:
[a]New Year
[b]Building of the Cross
[c]Christmas
[d]Jesus's Circumcision
[e]Epiphany
[f]Easter
[g]Mary's Announcement
[h]Jesus's Transfiguration

PERSIAN (ASTRONOMICAL) 1278/1279

Month	Sun	Mon	Tue	Wed	Thu	Fri	Sat
DEY 1278	10	11	12	13	14	15	16
	17	18	19	20	21	22	23
	24	25	26	27	28	29	30
BAHMAN 1278	1	2	3	4	5	6	7
	8	9	10	11	12	13	14
	15	16	17	18	19	20	21
	22	23	24	25	26	27	28
ESFAND 1278	29	30	1	2	3	4	5
	6	7	8	9	10	11	12
	13	14	15	16	17	18	19
	20	21	22	23	24	25	26
FARVARDĪN 1279	27	28	29	1[a]	2	3	4
	5	6	7	8	9	10	11
	12	13[b]	14	15	16	17	18
	19	20	21	22	23	24	25
ORDĪBEHEŠT 1279	26	27	28	29	30	31	1
	2	3	4	5	6	7	8
	9	10	11	12	13	14	15
	16	17	18	19	20	21	22
	23	24	25	26	27	28	29
XORDĀD 1279	30	31	1	2	3	4	5
	6	7	8	9	10	11	12
	13	14	15	16	17	18	19
	20	21	22	23	24	25	26
TĪR 1279	27	28	29	30	31	1	2
	3	4	5	6	7	8	9
	10	11	12	13	14	15	16
	17	18	19	20	21	22	23
	24	25	26	27	28	29	30
MORDĀD 1279	31	1	2	3	4	5	6
	7	8	9	10	11	12	13
	14	15	16	17	18	19	20
	21	22	23	24	25	26	27
SHAHRĪVAR 1279	28	29	30	31	1	2	3
	4	5	6	7	8	9	10
	11	12	13	14	15	16	17
	18	19	20	21	22	23	24
	25	26	27	28	29	30	31
MEHR 1279	1	2	3	4	5	6	7
	8	9	10	11	12	13	14
	15	16	17	18	19	20	21
	22	23	24	25	26	27	28
ĀBĀN 1279	29	30	1	2	3	4	5
	6	7	8	9	10	11	12
	13	14	15	16	17	18	19
	20	21	22	23	24	25	26
ĀZAR 1279	27	28	29	30	1	2	3
	4	5	6	7	8	9	10
	11	12	13	14	15	16	17
	18	19	20	21	22	23	24
DEY 1279	25	26	27	28	29	30	1
	2	3	4	5	6	7	8
	9	10	11	12	13	14	15

[a]New Year
[b]Sizdeh Bedar

HINDU LUNAR 1956/1957

Month	Sun	Mon	Tue	Wed	Thu	Fri	Sat
PAUSHA 1956	29	30	1	2	3	4	5
	7	8	9	10	11	12	13
	14	15	16	17	18	19	20
	20	21	22	23	24	25	26
MĀGHA 1956	27	28	29	1	2	3	4
	5	6	7	8	9	10	11
	12	13	14	15	16	17	18
	19	20	21	22	23	24	25
PHĀLGUNA 1956	26	27	28[h]	29	30	1	2
	3	4	6	7	8	9	10
	11	12	12	13	14	15[i]	16
	17	18	19	20	21	22	23
CHAITRA 1957	24	25	26	27	28	30	1[a]
	2	3	4	5	6	7	8
	9[b]	10	11	12	13	14	15
	15	16	17	18	19	20	21
	23	24	25	26	27	28	29
VAIŚĀKHA 1957	30	1	2	3	4	5	6
	7	8	9	10	11	12	13
	14	15	16	17	18	19	20
	21	22	23	24	25	27	28
JYAISHTHA 1957	29	30	1	2	3	4	5
	6	7	8	9	10	11	11
	12	13	14	15	16	17	19
	20	21	22	23	24	25	26
ĀSHĀḌHA 1957	27	28	29	30	1	2	3
	4	5	6	7	8	9	10
	11	12	13	14	15	16	17
	18	19	20	22	23	24	25
ŚRĀVAṆA 1957	26	27	28	29	30	1	2
	3	4	5	6	7	8	8
	9	10	11	12	13	15	16
	17	18	19	20	21	22	23[c]
	24	25	27	28	29	29	30
BHĀDRAPADA 1957	1	2	3	4[d]	5	6	7
	8	9	10	11	12	13	14
	15	16	18	19	20	21	22
	23	24	25	26	27	28	29
ĀŚVINA 1957	30	1	2	3	4	4	5
	6	7	8[e]	9[e]	11	12	13
	14	15	16	17	18	19	20
	21	22	23	24	25	26	27
KĀRTTIKA 1957	28	29	30	1[f]	2	3	4
	5	6	7	8	9	10	11
	12	13	14	16	17	18	19
	20	21	22	23	24	25	26
MĀRGAŚIRA 1957	27	27	28	29	30	1	2
	3	4	5	6	7	8	10
	11[g]	12	13	14	15	16	17
	18	19	20	21	22	23	24
PAUSHA 1957	25	26	27	28	29	30	1
	2	3	4	5	6	7	8
	9	10	11	12	13	15	16

[a]New Year (Śārvari)
[b]Birthday of Rāma
[c]Birthday of Krishna
[d]Ganēśa Chaturthī
[e]Dashara
[f]Diwali
[g]Birthday of Vishnu
[h]Night of Śiva
[i]Holi

HINDU SOLAR 1821/1822

Month	Sun	Mon	Tue	Wed	Thu	Fri	Sat
PAUSHA 1821	18	19	20	21	22	23	24
MĀGHA 1821	25	26	27	28	29	1[b]	2
	3	4	5	6	7	8	9
	10	11	12	13	14	15	16
	17	18	19	20	21	22	23
	24	25	26	27	28	29	30
PHĀLGUNA 1821	1	2	3	4	5	6	7
	8	9	10	11	12	13	14
	15	16	17	18	19	20	21
	22	23	24	25	26	27	28
CHAITRA 1821	29	30	1	2	3	4	5
	6	7	8	9	10	11	12
	13	14	15	16	17	18	19
	20	21	22	23	24	25	26
VAIŚĀKHA 1822	27	28	29	30	1[a]	2	3
	4	5	6	7	8	9	10
	11	12	13	14	15	16	17
	18	19	20	21	22	23	24
	25	26	27	28	29	30	31
JYAIṢHṬHA 1822	1	2	3	4	5	6	7
	8	9	10	11	12	13	14
	15	16	17	18	19	20	21
	22	23	24	25	26	27	28
ĀSHĀḌHA 1822	29	30	31	1	2	3	4
	5	6	7	8	9	10	11
	12	13	14	15	16	17	18
	19	20	21	22	23	24	25
	26	27	28	29	30	31	32
ŚRĀVAṆA 1822	1	2	3	4	5	6	7
	8	9	10	11	12	13	14
	15	16	17	18	19	20	21
	22	23	24	25	26	27	28
BHĀDRAPADA 1822	29	30	31	32	1	2	3
	4	5	6	7	8	9	10
	11	12	13	14	15	16	17
	18	19	20	21	22	23	24
	25	26	27	28	29	30	31
ĀŚVINA 1822	1	2	3	4	5	6	7
	8	9	10	11	12	13	14
	15	16	17	18	19	20	21
	22	23	24	25	26	27	28
KĀRTTIKA 1822	29	30	1	2	3	4	5
	6	7	8	9	10	11	12
	13	14	15	16	17	18	19
	20	21	22	23	24	25	26
MĀRGAŚIRA 1822	27	28	29	30	1	2	3
	4	5	6	7	8	9	10
	11	12	13	14	15	16	17
	18	19	20	21	22	23	24
PAUSHA 1822	25	26	27	28	29	1	2
	3	4	5	6	7	8	9
	10	11	12	13	14	15	16
	17	18	19	20	21	22	23

[a]New Year (Paridhāvin)
[b]Pongal

ISLAMIC (ASTRONOMICAL) 1317/1318‡

Month	Sun	Mon	Tue	Wed	Thu	Fri	Sat
RAMAḌĀN 1317	28	29	30	1[e]	2	3	4
	5	6	7	8	9	10	11
	12	13	14	15	16	17	18
	19	20	21	22	23	24	25
SHAWWĀL 1317	26	27	28	29	1[f]	2	3
	4	5	6	7	8	9	10
	11	12	13	14	15	16	17
	18	19	20	21	22	23	24
DHU AL-QA'DA 1317	25	26	27	28	29	30	1
	2	3	4	5	6	7	8
	9	10	11	12	13	14	15
	16	17	18	19	20	21	22
	23	24	25	26	27	28	29
DHU AL-ḤIJJA 1317	1	2	3	4	5	6	7
	8	9	10[g]	11	12	13	14
	15	16	17	18	19	20	21
	22	23	24	25	26	27	28
MUḤARRAM 1318	29	1[a]	2[d]	3	4	5	6
	7	8	9	10[b]	11	12	13
	14	15	16	17	18	19	20
	21	22	23	24	25	26	27
ṢAFAR 1318	28	29	30	1	2	3	4
	5	6	7	8	9	10	11
	12	13	14	15	16	17	18
	19	20	21	22	23	24	25
RABĪ' I 1318	26	27	28	29	30	1	2
	3	4	5	6	7	8	9
	10	11	12[c]	13	14	15	16
	17	18	19	20	21	22	23
	24	25	26	27	28	29	30
RABĪ' II 1318	1	2	3	4	5	6	7
	8	9	10	11	12	13	14
	15	16	17	18	19	20	21
	22	23	24	25	26	27	28
JUMĀDĀ I 1318	29	30	1	2	3	4	5
	6	7	8	9	10	11	12
	13	14	15	16	17	18	19
	20	21	22	23	24	25	26
JUMĀDĀ II 1318	27	28	29	1	2	3	4
	5	6	7	8	9	10	11
	12	13	14	15	16	17	18
	19	20	21	22	23	24	25
RAJAB 1318	26	27	28	29	1	2	3
	4	5	6	7	8	9	10
	11	12	13	14	15	16	17
	18	19	20	21	22	23	24
SHA'BĀN 1318	25	26	27[d]	28	29	30	1
	2	3	4	5	6	7	8
	9	10	11	12	13	14	15
	16	17	18	19	20	21	22
	23	24	25	26	27	28	29
RAMAḌĀN 1318	1[e]	2	3	4	5	6	7
	8	9	10	11	12	13	14

‡Leap year
[a]New Year
[d]New Year (Arithmetic)
[b]'Ashūrā'
[c]Prophet's Birthday
[d]Ascent of the Prophet
[e]Start of Ramaḍān
[f]'Īd al-Fiṭr
[g]'Īd al-'Aḍḥā

GREGORIAN 1900

Julian‡ (Sun)	Month	Sun	Mon	Tue	Wed	Thu	Fri	Sat
Dec 19	JANUARY 1900	31	1	2	3	4	5	6[a]
		7	8	9	10	11	12	13[b]
Jan 2		14	15	16	17	18	19	20
		21	22	23	24	25	26	27
Jan 16	FEBRUARY 1900	28	29	30	31	1	2	3
		4	5	6	7	8	9	10
Jan 30		11	12	13	14	15	16	17
		18	19	20	21	22	23	24
Feb 13	MARCH 1900	25	26	27	28[c]	1	2	3
		4	5	6	7	8	9	10
Feb 27		11[d]	12	13	14	15	16	17
		18	19	20	21	22	23	24
Mar 12		25	26	27	28	29	30	31
	APRIL 1900	1	2	3	4	5	6	7
Mar 26		8	9	10	11	12	13	14
		15[e]	16	17	18	19	20	21
Apr 9		22[f]	23	24	25	26	27	28
	MAY 1900	29	30	1	2	3	4	5
Apr 23		6	7	8	9	10	11	12
		13	14	15	16	17	18	19
May 7		20	21	22	23	24	25	26
	JUNE 1900	27	28	29	30	31	1	2
May 21		3	4	5	6	7	8	9
		10	11	12	13	14	15	16
Jun 4		17	18	19	20	21	22	23
		24	25	26	27	28	29	30
Jun 18	JULY 1900	1	2	3	4	5	6	7
		8	9	10	11	12	13	14
Jul 2		15	16	17	18	19	20	21
		22	23	24	25	26	27	28
Jul 16	AUGUST 1900	29	30	31	1	2	3	4
		5	6	7	8	9	10	11
Jul 30		12	13	14	15	16	17	18
		19	20	21	22	23	24	25
Aug 13	SEPTEMBER 1900	26	27	28	29	30	31	1
		2	3	4	5	6	7	8
Aug 27		9	10	11	12	13	14	15
		16	17	18	19	20	21	22
Sep 10		23	24	25	26	27	28	29
	OCTOBER 1900	30	1	2	3	4	5	6
Sep 24		7	8	9	10	11	12	13
		14	15	16	17	18	19	20
Oct 8		21	22	23	24	25	26	27
	NOVEMBER 1900	28	29	30	31	1	2	3
Oct 22		4	5	6	7	8	9	10
		11	12	13	14	15	16	17
Nov 5		18	19	20	21	22	23	24
	DECEMBER 1900	25	26	27	28	29	30	1
Nov 19		2[g]	3	4	5	6	7	8
		9	10	11	12	13	14	15
Dec 3		16	17	18	19	20	21	22
		23	24	25[h]	26	27	28	29
Dec 17		30	31	1	2	3	4	5

‡Julian leap year
[a]Orthodox Christmas
[b]Julian New Year
[c]Ash Wednesday
[d]Feast of Orthodoxy
[e]Easter
[f]Orthodox Easter
[g]Advent
[h]Christmas

1901

Gregorian 1901 month	Gregorian 1901 (Sun Mon Tue Wed Thu Fri Sat)	Lunar Phases	ISO WEEK (Mon)	JULIAN DAY (Sun noon)	Hebrew month	HEBREW 5661/5662‡ (Sun Mon Tue Wed Thu Fri Sat)	Molad	Chinese month	CHINESE Gēng-Zǐ‡/Xīn-Chǒu (Sun Mon Tue Wed Thu Fri Sat)	Solar Term	Coptic month	COPTIC 1617/1618 – ETHIOPIC 1893/1894 (Sun Mon Tue Wed Thu Fri Sat)	Ethiopic month
JANUARY 1901	30 31 1[a] 2 3 4 ○	0:13	1	2415384		8 9 10 11 12 13 14		MONTH 11 Gēng-Zǐ	9 10 11 12 13 14 15		KOAK 1617	21 22 23 24 25 26 27	TĀKHŚĀŚ 1893
	6 7 8 9 10 11 ◑	20:38	2	2415391	TEVETH 5661	15 16 17 18 19 20 21			16 17 18 19 20 21 22	Xiǎo hán		28 29[c] 30 | 1 2 3 4	
	13 14 15 16 17 18 19		3	2415398		22 23 24 25 26 27 28			23 24 25 26 27 28 29		TŌBE 1617	5 6[d] 7 8 9 10 11[e]	ṬER 1893
	● 21 22 23 24 25 26	14:36	4	2415405		29 | 1 2 3 4 5 6	Sun 7h56m13p		1 2 3 4 5 6 7	Dà hán		12 13 14 15 16 17 18	
	◐ 28 29 30 31 | 1 2	9:52	5	2415412	SHEVAT 5661	7 8 9 10 11 12 13		MONTH 12 Gēng-Zǐ	8 9 10 11 12 13 14			19 20 21 22 23 24 25	
FEBRUARY 1901	○ 4 5 6 7 8 9	15:30	6	2415419		14 15 16 17 18 19 20			15 16 17 18 19 20 21	Lì chūn		26 27 28 29 30 | 1 2	
	10 ◑ 12 13 14 15 16	18:12	7	2415426		21 22 23 24 25 26 27			22 23 24 25 26 27* 28		MESHIR 1617	3 4 5 6 7 8 9	YAKĀTIT 1893
	17 18 ● 20 21 22 23	2:45	8	2415433		28 29 30 | 1 2 3 4	Mon 20h40m14p		29 30 | 1[a] 2 3 4 5	Yǔ shuǐ		10 11 12 13 14 15 16	
	24 ◐ 26 27 28 | 1 2	18:38	9	2415440	ADAR 5661	5 6 7 8 9 10 11		MONTH 1 Xīn-Chǒu	6 7 8 9 10 11 12			17 18 19 20 21 22 23	
MARCH 1901	3 4 ○ 6 7 8 9	8:04	10	2415447		12 13 14[f] 15 16 17 18			13 14 15[b] 16 17 18 19	Jīng zhé		24 25 26 27 28 29 30	
	10 11 12 ◑ 14 15 16	13:06	11	2415454		19 20 21 22 23 24 25			20 21 22 23 24 25 26		PAREMOTEP 1617	1 2 3 4 5 6 7	MAGĀBIT 1893
	17 18 19 ● 21[b] 22 23	12:53	12	2415461		26 27 28 29 | 1 2 3	Wed 9h24m1p		27 28 29 | 1 2 3 4	Chūn fēn		8 9 10 11 12 13 14	
	24 25 26 ◐ 28 29 30	4:39	13	2415468	NISAN 5661	4 5 6 7 8 9 10		MONTH 2 Xīn-Chǒu	5 6 7 8 9 10 11			15 16 17 18 19 20 21	
	31 | 1 2 3 ○ 5 6	1:20	14	2415475		11 12 13 14 15[g] 16 17			12 13 14 15 16 17[c] 18	Qīng míng		22 23 24 25 26 27 28	
APRIL 1901	7 8 9 10 11 ◑ 13	3:57	15	2415482		18 19 20 21 22 23 24			19 20 21 22 23 24 25			29 30 | 1 2 3 4 5	MIYĀZYĀ 1893
	14 15 16 17 ● 19 20	21:37	16	2415489		25 26 27 28 29 30 | 1	Thu 22h8m16p		26 27 28* 29 30 | 1 2	Gǔ yǔ	PARMOUTE 1617	6[f] 7 8 9 10 11 12	
	21 22 23 24 ◐ 26 27	16:15	17	2415496	IYYAR 5661	2 3 4 5 6 7 8		MONTH 3 Xīn-Chǒu	3 4 5 6 7 8 9			13 14 15 16 17 18 19	
	28 29 30 | 1 2 ○ 4	18:19	18	2415503		9 10 11 12 13 14 15			10 11 12 13 14 15 16			20 21 22 23 24 25 26	
MAY 1901	5 6 7 8 9 10 ◑	14:38	19	2415510		16 17 18 19 20 21 22			17 18 19 20 21 22 23	Lì xià		27 28 29[g] 30 | 1 2 3	GENBOT 1893
	12 13 14 15 16 17 ●	5:38	20	2415517		23 24 25 26 27 28 29	Sat 10h52m17p		24 25 26 27 28 29 | 1		PASHONS 1617	4 5 6 7 8 9 10	
	19 20 21 22 23 24 ◐	5:40	21	2415524	SIVAN 5661	1 2 3 4 5 6[h] 7		MONTH 4 Xīn-Chǒu	2 3 4 5 6 7 8	Xiǎo mǎn		11 12 13 14 15 16 17	
	26 27 28 29 30 31 | 1		22	2415531		8 9 10 11 12 13 14			9 10 11 12 13 14 15			18 19 20 21 22 23 24	
JUNE 1901	○ 3 4 5 6 7 8	9:53	23	2415538		15 16 17 18 19 20 21			16 17 18 19 20 21 22	Máng zhòng		25 26 27 28 29 30 | 1	SANĒ 1893
	◑ 10 11 12 13 14 15	22:00	24	2415545		22 23 24 25 26 27 28			23 24 25 26 27 28 29*			2 3 4 5 6 7 8	
	● 17 18 19 20 21 22[c]	13:33	25	2415552		29 30 | 1 2 3 4 5	Sun 23h37m0p		1 2 3 4 5[d] 6 7	Xià zhì	PAŌNE 1617	9 10 11 12 13 14 15	
	◐ 24 25 26 27 28 29	20:59	26	2415559	TAMMUZ 5661	6 7 8 9 10 11 12		MONTH 5 Xīn-Chǒu	8 9 10 11 12 13 14			16 17 18 19 20 21 22	
	30 | ○ 2 3 4 5 6	23:18	27	2415566		13 14 15 16 17 18 19			15 16 17 18 19 20 21			23 24 25 26 27 28 29	
JULY 1901	7 8 ◑ 10 11 12 13	3:20	28	2415573		20 21 22 23 24 25 26			22 23 24 25 26 27 28	Xiǎo shǔ		30 | 1 2 3 4 5 6	ḤAMLĒ 1893
	14 ● 16 17 18 19 20	22:10	29	2415580		27 28 29 | 1 2 3 4	Tue 12h21m1p		29 30 | 1 2 3 4 5		EPĒP 1617	7 8 9 10 11 12 13	
	21 22 ◐ 24 25 26 27	13:58	30	2415587	AV 5661	5 6 7 8 9[i] 10 11		MONTH 6 Xīn-Chǒu	6 7 8 9 10 11 12	Dà shǔ		14 15 16 17 18 19 20	
	28 29 30 ○ | 1 2 3	10:34	31	2415594		12 13 14 15 16 17 18			13 14 15 16 17 18 19			21 22 23 24 25 26 27	
AUGUST 1901	4 5 6 ◑ 8 9 10	8:02	32	2415601		19 20 21 22 23 24 25			20 21 22 23 24 25 26	Lì qiū		28 29 30 | 1 2 3 4	NAḤASĒ 1893
	11 12 13 ● 15 16 17	8:27	33	2415608		26 27 28 29 30 | 1 2	Thu 1h5m2p		27 28 29 | 1* 2 3 4		MESORĒ 1617	5 6 7 8 9 10 11	
	18 19 20 21 ◐ 23 24	7:52	34	2415615	ELUL 5661	3 4 5 6 7 8 9		MONTH 7 Xīn-Chǒu	5 6 7[e] 8 9 10 11	Chǔ shǔ		12 13[h] 14 15 16 17 18	
	25 26 27 28 ○ 30 31	20:21	35	2415622		10 11 12 13 14 15 16			12 13 14 15[f] 16 17 18			19 20 21 22 23 24 25	
SEPTEMBER 1901	1 2 3 4 ◑ 6 7	13:27	36	2415629		17 18 19 20 21 22 23			19 20 21 22 23 24 25		EPAG. 1617	26 27 28 29 30 | 1 2	PĀG. 1893
	8 9 10 11 ● 13 14	21:19	37	2415636		24 25 26 27 28 29 | 1[a]	Fri 13h49m3p		26 27 28 29 30 | 1 2	Bái lù		3 4 5 | 1[a] 2 3 4	MASKARAM 1894
	15 16 17 18 19 20 ◐	1:33	38	2415643	TISHRI 5662	2[a] 3 4 5 6 7 8		MONTH 8 Xīn-Chǒu	3 4 5 6 7 8 9		THOOUT 1618	5 6 7 8 9 10 11	
	22 23[d] 24 25 26 27 ○	5:36	39	2415650		9 10[b] 11 12 13 14 15[c]			10 11 12 13 14 15[g] 16	Qiū fēn		12 13 14 15 16 17[b] 18	
	29 30 | 1 2 3 ◑ 5	20:52	40	2415657		16 17 18 19 20 21 22			17 18 19 20 21 22 23			19 20 21 22 23 24 25	
OCTOBER 1901	6 7 8 9 10 11 ●	13:11	41	2415664		23 24 25 26 27 28 29			24 25 26 27 28 29 | 1	Hán lù		26 27 28 29 30 | 1 2	ṬEQEMT 1894
	13 14 15 16 17 18 19		42	2415671		30 | 1 2 3 4 5 6	Sun 2h33m4p	MONTH 9 Xīn-Chǒu	2* 3 4 5 6 7 8		PAOPE 1618	3 4 5 6 7 8 9	
	◐ 21 22 23 24 25 26	17:58	43	2415678	HESHVAN 5662	7 8 9 10 11 12 13			9[h] 10 11 12 13 14 15	Shuāng jiàng		10 11 12 13 14 15 16	
	○ 28 29 30 31 | 1 2	15:06	44	2415685		14 15 16 17 18 19 20			16 17 18 19 20 21 22			17 18 19 20 21 22 23	
NOVEMBER 1901	◑ 4 5 6 7 8 9	7:24	45	2415692		21 22 23 24 25 26 27			23 24 25 26 27 28 29	Lì dōng		24 25 26 27 28 29 30	ḪEDĀR 1894
	10 ● 12 13 14 15 16	7:34	46	2415699		28 29 | 1 2 3 4 5	Mon 15h17m5p		30 | 1 2 3 4 5 6		ATHŌR 1618	1 2 3 4 5 6 7	
	17 18 ◐ 20 21 22 23	8:23	47	2415706	KISLEV 5662	6 7 8 9 10 11 12		MONTH 10 Xīn-Chǒu	7 8 9 10 11 12 13	Xiǎo xuě		8 9 10 11 12 13 14	
	24 25 ○ 27 28 29 30	1:18	48	2415713		13 14 15 16 17 18 19			14 15 16 17 18 19 20			15 16 17 18 19 20 21	
DECEMBER 1901	1 ◑ 3 4 5 6 7	21:50	49	2415720		20 21 22 23 24[d] 25[e] 26[e]			21 22 23 24 25 26 27			22 23 24 25 26 27 28	
	8 9 10 ● 12 13 14	2:53	50	2415727		27[e] 28[e] 29[e] | 1[e] 2[e] 3[e] 4	Wed 4h1m6p		28 29 30 | 1 2* 3 4	Dà xuě		29 30 | 1 2 3 4 5	TĀKHŚĀŚ 1894
	15 16 17 ◐ 19 20 21	20:35	51	2415734	TEVETH 5662	5 6 7 8 9 10 11		MONTH 11 Xīn-Chǒu	5 6 7 8 9 10 11		KOIAK 1618	6 7 8 9 10 11 12	
	22[e] 23 24 ○ 26 27 28	12:16	52	2415741		12 13 14 15 16 17 18			12[i] 13 14 15 16 17 18	Dōng zhì		13 14 15 16 17 18 19	
	29 30 31 | ◑ 2 3 4	16:08	1	2415748		19 20 21 22 23 24 25			19 20 21 22 23 24 25			20 21 22 23 24 25 26	

Gregorian notes:
[a]New Year
[b]Spring (7:23)
[c]Summer (3:28)
[d]Autumn (18:09)
[e]Winter (12:36)
● New moon
◐ First quarter moon
○ Full moon
◑ Last quarter moon

Hebrew notes:
‡Leap year
[a]New Year
[b]Yom Kippur
[c]Sukkot
[d]Winter starts
[e]Ḥanukkah
[f]Purim
[g]Passover
[h]Shavuot
[i]Fast of Av

Chinese notes:
‡Leap year
[a]New Year (4599, Ox)
[b]Lantern Festival
[c]Qīngmíng
[d]Dragon Festival
[e]Qīqiǎo
[f]Hungry Ghosts
[g]Mid-Autumn Festival
[h]Double-Ninth Festival
[i]Dōngzhì
*Start of 60-name cycle

Coptic/Ethiopic notes:
[a]New Year
[b]Building of the Cross
[c]Christmas
[d]Jesus's Circumcision
[e]Epiphany
[f]Easter
[g]Mary's Announcement
[h]Jesus's Transfiguration

1901

PERSIAN (ASTRONOMICAL) 1279/1280‡

Month	Sun	Mon	Tue	Wed	Thu	Fri	Sat
DEY 1279	9	10	11	12	13	14	15
	16	17	18	19	20	21	22
	23	24	25	26	27	28	29
BAHMAN 1279	30	1	2	3	4	5	6
	7	8	9	10	11	12	13
	14	15	16	17	18	19	20
	21	22	23	24	25	26	27
ESFAND 1279	28	29	30	1	2	3	4
	5	6	7	8	9	10	11
	12	13	14	15	16	17	18
	19	20	21	22	23	24	25
FARVARDĪN 1280	26	27	28	29	1[a]	2	3
	4	5	6	7	8	9	10
	11	12	13[b]	14	15	16	17
	18	19	20	21	22	23	24
	25	26	27	28	29	30	31
ORDĪBEHEŠT 1280	1	2	3	4	5	6	7
	8	9	10	11	12	13	14
	15	16	17	18	19	20	21
	22	23	24	25	26	27	28
XORDĀD 1280	29	30	31	1	2	3	4
	5	6	7	8	9	10	11
	12	13	14	15	16	17	18
	19	20	21	22	23	24	25
TĪR 1280	26	27	28	29	30	31	1
	2	3	4	5	6	7	8
	9	10	11	12	13	14	15
	16	17	18	19	20	21	22
	23	24	25	26	27	28	29
MORDĀD 1280	30	31	1	2	3	4	5
	6	7	8	9	10	11	12
	13	14	15	16	17	18	19
	20	21	22	23	24	25	26
SHAHRĪVAR 1280	27	28	29	30	31	1	2
	3	4	5	6	7	8	9
	10	11	12	13	14	15	16
	17	18	19	20	21	22	23
	24	25	26	27	28	29	30
MEHR 1280	31	1	2	3	4	5	6
	7	8	9	10	11	12	13
	14	15	16	17	18	19	20
	21	22	23	24	25	26	27
ĀBĀN 1280	28	29	30	1	2	3	4
	5	6	7	8	9	10	11
	12	13	14	15	16	17	18
	19	20	21	22	23	24	25
ĀZAR 1280	26	27	28	29	30	1	2
	3	4	5	6	7	8	9
	10	11	12	13	14	15	16
	17	18	19	20	21	22	23
	24	25	26	27	28	29	30
DEY 1280	1	2	3	4	5	6	7
	8	9	10	11	12	13	14

‡Leap year
[a]New Year
[b]Sizdeh Bedar

HINDU LUNAR 1957/1958‡

Month	Sun	Mon	Tue	Wed	Thu	Fri	Sat
PAUSHA 1957	9	10	11	12	13	15	16
	17	18	19	20	20	21	22
	23	24	25	26	27	28	29
MĀGHA 1957	30	1	2	3	4	5	6
	8	9	10	11	12	13	14
	15	16	17	18	19	20	21
	22	22	23	24	25	26	27
PHĀLGUNA 1957	28[h]	29	30	2	3	4	5
	6	7	8	9	10	11	12
	13	14	15[i]	16	17	18	19
	20	21	22	23	24	25	26
CHAITRA 1958	27	28	29	30	1[a]	2	3
	4	5	7	8	9[b]	10	11
	12	13	14	15	16	16	17
	18	19	20	21	22	23	24
VAIŚĀKHA 1958	25	26	27	28	30	1	2
	3	4	5	6	7	8	9
	10	11	12	13	14	15	16
	17	18	19	20	21	22	23
	24	25	26	27	28	29	30
JYAISHṬHA 1958	1	2	4	5	6	7	8
	9	10	11	11	12	13	14
	15	16	17	18	19	20	21
	22	23	24	25	27	28	29
LEAP ĀSHĀḌHA 1958	30	1	2	3	4	5	6
	7	8	9	10	11	12	13
	14	15	16	17	18	19	20
	21	22	23	24	25	26	27
ĀSHĀḌHA 1958	28	30	1	2	3	4	5
	6	7	8	8	9	10	11
	12	13	14	15	16	17	18
	19	20	22	23	24	25	26
ŚRĀVAṆA 1958	27	28	29	30	1	2	3
	4	5	6	7	8	9	10
	11	12	13	14	15	16	17
	18	19	20	21	22	23[c]	24
BHĀDRAPADA 1958	26	27	28	29	30	1	2
	3	4[d]	4	5	6	7	8
	9	10	11	12	13	14	15
	16	17	19	20	21	22	23
	24	25	26	27	28	29	30
ĀŚVINA 1958	1	2	3	4	5	6	7
	8[e]	9[e]	10[e]	11	12	13	14
	15	16	17	18	19	20	21
	23	24	25	26	27	28	28
KĀRTTIKA 1958	29	30	1[f]	2	3	4	5
	6	7	8	9	10	11	12
	13	14	15	17	18	19	20
	21	22	23	24	25	26	27
MĀRGAŚĪRA 1958	28	29	30	30	1	2	3
	4	5	6	7	8	10	11[g]
	12	13	14	15	16	17	18
	19	20	21	22	23	24	25

‡Leap year
[a]New Year (Plava)
[b]Birthday of Rāma
[c]Birthday of Krishna
[d]Ganēśa Chaturthī
[e]Dashara
[f]Diwali
[g]Birthday of Vishnu
[h]Night of Śiva
[i]Holi

HINDU SOLAR 1822/1823‡

Month	Sun	Mon	Tue	Wed	Thu	Fri	Sat
PAUSHA 1822	17	18	19	20	21	22	23
	24	25	26	27	28	29	30
MĀGHA 1822	1[b]	2	3	4	5	6	7
	8	9	10	11	12	13	14
	15	16	17	18	19	20	21
	22	23	24	25	26	27	28
PHĀLGUNA 1822	29	1	2	3	4	5	6
	7	8	9	10	11	12	13
	14	15	16	17	18	19	20
	21	22	23	24	25	26	27
CHAITRA 1822	28	29	30	1	2	3	4
	5	6	7	8	9	10	11
	12	13	14	15	16	17	18
	19	20	21	22	23	24	25
VAIŚĀKHA 1823	26	27	28	29	30	1[a]	2
	3	4	5	6	7	8	9
	10	11	12	13	14	15	16
	17	18	19	20	21	22	23
	24	25	26	27	28	29	30
JYAISHṬHA 1823	31	1	2	3	4	5	6
	7	8	9	10	11	12	13
	14	15	16	17	18	19	20
	21	22	23	24	25	26	27
ĀSHĀḌHA 1823	28	29	30	31	32	1	2
	3	4	5	6	7	8	9
	10	11	12	13	14	15	16
	17	18	19	20	21	22	23
	24	25	26	27	28	29	30
ŚRĀVAṆA 1823	31	1	2	3	4	5	6
	7	8	9	10	11	12	13
	14	15	16	17	18	19	20
	21	22	23	24	25	26	27
BHĀDRAPADA 1823	28	29	30	31	32	1	2
	3	4	5	6	7	8	9
	10	11	12	13	14	15	16
	17	18	19	20	21	22	23
	24	25	26	27	28	29	30
ĀŚVINA 1823	31	1	2	3	4	5	6
	7	8	9	10	11	12	13
	14	15	16	17	18	19	20
	21	22	23	24	25	26	27
KĀRTTIKA 1823	28	29	30	1	2	3	4
	5	6	7	8	9	10	11
	12	13	14	15	16	17	18
	19	20	21	22	23	24	25
MĀRGAŚĪRA 1823	26	27	28	29	30	1	2
	3	4	5	6	7	8	9
	10	11	12	13	14	15	16
	17	18	19	20	21	22	23
	24	25	26	27	28	29	30
PAUSHA 1823	1	2	3	4	5	6	7
	8	9	10	11	12	13	14
	15	16	17	18	19	20	21

‡Leap year
[a]New Year (Pramādin)
[b]Pongal

ISLAMIC (ASTRONOMICAL) 1318‡/1319‡

Month	Sun	Mon	Tue	Wed	Thu	Fri	Sat
RAMAḌĀN 1318	8	9	10	11	12	13	14
	15	16	17	18	19	20	21
	22	23	24	25	26	27	28
SHAWWĀL 1318	29	30	1[f]	2	3	4	5
	6	7	8	9	10	11	12
	13	14	15	16	17	18	19
	20	21	22	23	24	25	26
DHU AL-QA'DA 1318	27	28	29	1	2	3	4
	5	6	7	8	9	10	11
	12	13	14	15	16	17	18
	19	20	21	22	23	24	25
DHU AL-ḤIJJA 1318	26	27	28	29	30	1	2
	3	4	5	6	7	8	9
	10[g]	11	12	13	14	15	16
	17	18	19	20	21	22	23
MUḤARRAM 1319	24	25	26	27	28	29	1[a]
	2	3	4	5	6	7	8
	9	10[b]	11	12	13	14	15
	16	17	18	19	20	21	22
	23	24	25	26	27	28	29
ṢAFAR 1319	1	2	3	4	5	6	7
	8	9	10	11	12	13	14
	15	16	17	18	19	20	21
	22	23	24	25	26	27	28
RABĪʿ I 1319	29	30	1	2	3	4	5
	6	7	8	9	10	11	12[c]
	13	14	15	16	17	18	19
	20	21	22	23	24	25	26
RABĪʿ II 1319	27	28	29	30	1	2	3
	4	5	6	7	8	9	10
	11	12	13	14	15	16	17
	18	19	20	21	22	23	24
JUMĀDĀ I 1319	25	26	27	28	29	30	1
	2	3	4	5	6	7	8
	9	10	11	12	13	14	15
	16	17	18	19	20	21	22
	23	24	25	26	27	28	29
JUMĀDĀ II 1319	1	2	3	4	5	6	7
	8	9	10	11	12	13	14
	15	16	17	18	19	20	21
	22	23	24	25	26	27	28
RAJAB 1319	29	1	2	3	4	5	6
	7	8	9	10	11	12	13
	14	15	16	17	18	19	20
	21	22	23	24	25	26	27[d]
SHAʿBĀN 1319	28	29	30	1	2	3	4
	5	6	7	8	9	10	11
	12	13	14	15	16	17	18
	19	20	21	22	23	24	25
RAMAḌĀN 1319	26	27	28	29	1[e]	2	3
	4	5	6	7	8	9	10
	11	12	13	14	15	16	17
	18	19	20	21	22	23	24

‡Leap year
[a]New Year
[b]ʿAshūrā'
[c]Prophet's Birthday
[d]Ascent of the Prophet
[e]Start of Ramaḍān
[f]ʿId al-Fiṭr
[g]ʿId al-'Aḍḥā

GREGORIAN 1901

Julian (Sun)	Month	Sun	Mon	Tue	Wed	Thu	Fri	Sat
Dec 17	JANUARY 1901	30	31	1	2	3	4	5
		6	7[a]	8	9	10	11	12
Dec 31		13	14[b]	15	16	17	18	19
		20	21	22	23	24	25	26
Jan 14	FEBRUARY 1901	27	28	29	30	31	1	2
		3	4	5	6	7	8	9
Jan 28		10	11	12	13	14	15	16
		17	18	19	20[c]	21	22	23
Feb 11	MARCH 1901	24	25	26	27	28	1	2
		3[d]	4	5	6	7	8	9
Feb 25		10	11	12	13	14	15	16
		17	18	19	20	21	22	23
Mar 11		24	25	26	27	28	29	30
	APRIL 1901	31	1	2	3	4	5	6
Mar 25		7[e]	8	9	10	11	12	13
		14[f]	15	16	17	18	19	20
Apr 8		21	22	23	24	25	26	27
	MAY 1901	28	29	30	1	2	3	4
Apr 22		5	6	7	8	9	10	11
		12	13	14	15	16	17	18
May 6		19	20	21	22	23	24	25
	JUNE 1901	26	27	28	29	30	31	1
May 20		2	3	4	5	6	7	8
		9	10	11	12	13	14	15
Jun 3		16	17	18	19	20	21	22
		23	24	25	26	27	28	29
Jun 17	JULY 1901	30	1	2	3	4	5	6
		7	8	9	10	11	12	13
Jul 1		14	15	16	17	18	19	20
		21	22	23	24	25	26	27
Jul 15	AUGUST 1901	28	29	30	31	1	2	3
		4	5	6	7	8	9	10
Jul 29		11	12	13	14	15	16	17
		18	19	20	21	22	23	24
Aug 12		25	26	27	28	29	30	31
	SEPTEMBER 1901	1	2	3	4	5	6	7
Aug 26		8	9	10	11	12	13	14
		15	16	17	18	19	20	21
Sep 9		22	23	24	25	26	27	28
	OCTOBER 1901	29	30	1	2	3	4	5
Sep 23		6	7	8	9	10	11	12
		13	14	15	16	17	18	19
Oct 7		20	21	22	23	24	25	26
	NOVEMBER 1901	27	28	29	30	31	1	2
Oct 21		3	4	5	6	7	8	9
		10	11	12	13	14	15	16
Nov 4		17	18	19	20	21	22	23
		24	25	26	27	28	29	30
Nov 18	DECEMBER 1901	1[g]	2	3	4	5	6	7
		8	9	10	11	12	13	14
Dec 2		15	16	17	18	19	20	21
		22	23	24	25[h]	26	27	28
Dec 16		29	30	31	1	2	3	4

[a]Orthodox Christmas
[b]Julian New Year
[c]Ash Wednesday
[d]Feast of Orthodoxy
[e]Easter
[f]Orthodox Easter
[g]Advent
[h]Christmas

1902

GREGORIAN 1902	Sun	Mon	Tue	Wed	Thu	Fri	Sat	Lunar Phases	ISO WEEK (Mon)	JULIAN DAY (Sun noon)
	29	30	31	◑[a]	2	3	4	16:08	1	2415748
JANUARY 1902	5	6	7	8	●	10	11	21:14	2	2415755
	12	13	14	15	16	◐	18	6:38	3	2415762
	19	20	21	22	23	○	25	0:06	4	2415769
	26	27	28	29	30	◑	1	13:08	5	2415776
FEBRUARY 1902	2	3	4	5	6	7	●	13:21	6	2415783
	9	10	11	12	13	14	◐	14:56	7	2415790
	16	17	18	19	20	21	○	13:03	8	2415797
	23	24	25	26	27	28	1		9	2415804
MARCH 1902	◑	3	4	5	6	7	8	10:39	10	2415811
	9	●	11	12	13	14	15	2:50	11	2415818
	◐	17	18	19	20	21[b]	22	22:13	12	2415825
	23	○	25	26	27	28	29	3:21	13	2415832
	30	31	◑	2	3	4	5	6:24	14	2415839
APRIL 1902	6	7	●	9	10	11	12	13:50	15	2415846
	13	14	◐	16	17	18	19	5:25	16	2415853
	20	21	○	23	24	25	26	18:49	17	2415860
	27	28	29	◑	1	2	3	22:58	18	2415867
MAY 1902	4	5	6	●	8	9	10	22:45	19	2415874
	11	12	13	◐	15	16	17	13:40	20	2415881
	18	19	20	21	○	23	24	10:46	21	2415888
	25	26	27	28	29	◑	31	12:00	22	2415895
JUNE 1902	1	2	3	4	5	●	7	6:11	23	2415902
	8	9	10	11	◐	13	14	23:54	24	2415909
	15	16	17	18	19	20	○	2:17	25	2415916
	22[c]	23	24	25	26	27	◑	21:52	26	2415923
	29	30	1	2	3	4	●	12:59	27	2415930
JULY 1902	6	7	8	9	10	11	◐	12:47	28	2415937
	13	14	15	16	17	18	19		29	2415944
	○	21	22	23	24	25	26	16:45	30	2415951
	27	◑	29	30	31	1	2	5:15	31	2415958
AUGUST 1902	●	4	5	6	7	8	9	20:17	32	2415965
	10	◐	12	13	14	15	16	4:24	33	2415972
	17	18	○	20	21	22	23	6:03	34	2415979
	24	25	◑	27	28	29	30	11:04	35	2415986
	31	1	●	3	4	5	6	5:19	36	2415993
SEPTEMBER 1902	7	8	◐	10	11	12	13	22:15	37	2416000
	14	15	16	○	18	19	20	18:23	38	2416007
	21	22	23[d]	◑	25	26	27	16:32	39	2416014
	28	29	30	●	2	3	4	17:09	40	2416021
OCTOBER 1902	5	6	7	8	◐	10	11	17:21	41	2416028
	12	13	14	15	16	○	18	6:01	42	2416035
	19	20	21	22	◑	24	25	22:58	43	2416042
	26	27	28	29	30	●	1	8:14	44	2416049
NOVEMBER 1902	2	3	4	5	6	7	◐	12:30	45	2416056
	9	10	11	12	13	14	○	17:06	46	2416063
	16	17	18	19	20	21	◑	7:47	47	2416070
	23	24	25	26	27	28	29		48	2416077
	●	1	2	3	4	5	6	2:05	49	2416084
DECEMBER 1902	7	◐	9	10	11	12	13	6:27	50	2416091
	14	○	16	17	18	19	20	3:47	51	2416098
	◑	22[e]	23	24	25	26	27	20:00	52	2416105
	28	●	30	31	1	2	3	21:25	1	2416112

ISO WEEK	HEBREW 5662‡/5663	Sun	Mon	Tue	Wed	Thu	Fri	Sat	Molad
1	TEVETH 5662	19	20	21	22	23	24	25	
2		26	27	28	29	1	2	3	Thu 16h45m7p
3	SHEVAT 5662	4	5	6	7	8	9	10	
4		11	12	13	14	15	16	17	
5		18	19	20	21	22	23	24	
6		25	26	27	28	29	30	1	Sat 5h29m8p
7	ADAR I 5662	2	3	4	5	6	7	8	
8		9	10	11	12	13	14	15	
9		16	17	18	19	20	21	22	
10		23	24	25	26	27	28	29	
11		30	1	2	3	4	5	6	Sun 18h13m9p
12	ADAR II 5662	7	8	9	10	11	12	13	
13		14[f]	15	16	17	18	19	20	
14		21	22	23	24	25	26	27	
15		28	29	1	2	3	4	5	Tue 6h57m10p
16	NISAN 5662	6	7	8	9	10	11	12	
17		13	14	15[g]	16	17	18	19	
18		20	21	22	23	24	25	26	
19		27	28	29	30	1	2	3	Wed 19h41m11p
20	IYAR 5662	4	5	6	7	8	9	10	
21		11	12	13	14	15	16	17	
22		18	19	20	21	22	23	24	
23		25	26	27	28	29	1	2	Fri 8h25m12p
24	SIVAN 5662	3	4	5	6[h]	7	8	9	
25		10	11	12	13	14	15	16	
26		17	18	19	20	21	22	23	
27		24	25	26	27	28	29	30	
28		1	2	3	4	5	6	7	Sat 21h9m13p
29	TAMMUZ 5662	8	9	10	11	12	13	14	
30		15	16	17	18	19	20	21	
31		22	23	24	25	26	27	28	
32		29	1	2	3	4	5	6	Mon 9h53m14p
33	AV 5662	7	8	9[i]	10	11	12	13	
34		14	15	16	17	18	19	20	
35		21	22	23	24	25	26	27	
36		28	29	30	1	2	3	4	Tue 22h37m15p
37	ELUL 5662	5	6	7	8	9	10	11	
38		12	13	14	15	16	17	18	
39		19	20	21	22	23	24	25	
40		26	27	28	29	1[a]	2[a]	3	Thu 11h21m16p
41	TISHRI 5663	4	5	6	7	8	9	10[b]	
42		11	12	13	14	15[c]	16	17	
43		18	19	20	21	22	23	24	
44		25	26	27	28	29	30	1	Sat 0h5m17p
45	ḤESHVAN 5663	2	3	4	5	6	7	8	
46		9	10	11	12	13	14	15	
47		16	17	18	19	20	21	22	
48		23	24	25	26	27	28	29	
49		30	1	2	3	4	5[d]	6	Sun 12h50m0p
50	KISLEV 5663	7	8	9	10	11	12	13	
51		14	15	16	17	18	19	20	
52		21	22	23	24	25[e]	26[e]	27[e]	
1		28[e]	29[e]	30[e]	1[e]	2[e]	3	4	Tue 1h34m1p

ISO WEEK	CHINESE Xīn-Chǒu/Rén-Yín	Sun	Mon	Tue	Wed	Thu	Fri	Sat	Solar Term
1	MONTH 11 Xīn-Chǒu	19	20	21	22	23	24	25	
2		26	27	28	29	30	1	2	Xiǎo hán
3	MONTH 12 Xīn-Chǒu	3	4	5	6	7	8	9	
4		10	11	12	13	14	15	16	Dà hán
5		17	18	19	20	21	22	23	
6		24	25	26	27	28	29	1[a]	Lì chūn
7	MONTH 1 Rén-Yín	2	3*	4	5	6	7	8	
8		9	10	11	12	13	14	15[b]	Yǔ shuǐ
9		16	17	18	19	20	21	22	
10		23	24	25	26	27	28	29	Jīng zhé
11		30	1	2	3	4	5	6	
12	MONTH 2 Rén-Yín	7	8	9	10	11	12	13	Chūn fēn
13		14	15	16	17	18	19	20	
14		21	22	23	24	25	26	27	
15		28[c]	29	1	2	3	4*	5	Qīng míng
16	MONTH 3 Rén-Yín	6	7	8	9	10	11	12	
17		13	14	15	16	17	18	19	Gǔ yǔ
18		20	21	22	23	24	25	26	
19		27	28	29	30	1	2	3	Lì xià
20	MONTH 4 Rén-Yín	4	5	6	7	8	9	10	
21		11	12	13	14	15	16	17	Xiǎo mǎn
22		18	19	20	21	22	23	24	
23		25	26	27	28	29	1	2	Máng zhòng
24	MONTH 5 Rén-Yín	3	4	5[d]*	6	7	8	9	
25		10	11	12	13	14	15	16	
26		17	18	19	20	21	22	23	Xià zhì
27		24	25	26	27	28	29	1	
28	MONTH 6 Rén-Yín	2	3	4	5	6	7	8	Xiǎo shǔ
29		9	10	11	12	13	14	15	
30		16	17	18	19	20	21	22	Dà shǔ
31		23	24	25	26	27	28	29	
32		30	1	2	3	4	5	6*	Lì qiū
33	MONTH 7 Rén-Yín	7[e]	8	9	10	11	12	13	
34		14	15[f]	16	17	18	19	20	
35		21	22	23	24	25	26	27	Chǔ shǔ
36		28	29	1	2	3	4	5	
37	MONTH 8 Rén-Yín	6	7	8	9	10	11	12	Bái lù
38		13	14	15[g]	16	17	18	19	
39		20	21	22	23	24	25	26	Qiū fēn
40		27	28	29	30	1	2	3	
41	MONTH 9 Rén-Yín	4	5	6	7*	8	9[h]	10	Hán lù
42		11	12	13	14	15	16	17	
43		18	19	20	21	22	23	24	Shuāng jiàng
44		25	26	27	28	29	1	2	
45	MONTH 10 Rén-Yín	3	4	5	6	7	8	9	Lì dōng
46		10	11	12	13	14	15	16	
47		17	18	19	20	21	22	23	
48		24	25	26	27	28	29	30	Xiǎo xuě
49		1	2	3	4	5	6	7	
50	MONTH 11 Rén-Yín	8*	9	10	11	12	13	14	Dà xuě
51		15	16	17	18	19	20	21	
52		22	23	24[i]	25	26	27	28	Dōng zhì
1		29	30	1	2	3	4	5	

ISO WEEK	COPTIC 1618/1619‡	Sun	Mon	Tue	Wed	Thu	Fri	Sat	ETHIOPIC 1894/1895‡
1	KOIAK 1618	20	21	22	23	24	25	26	TĀKHŚĀŚ 1894
2		27	28	29[c]	30	1	2	3	
3	TÔBE 1618	4	5	6[d]	7	8	9	10	ṬER 1894
4		11[e]	12	13	14	15	16	17	
5		18	19	20	21	22	23	24	
6		25	26	27	28	29	30	1	
7	MESHIR 1618	2	3	4	5	6	7	8	YAKĀTIT 1894
8		9	10	11	12	13	14	15	
9		16	17	18	19	20	21	22	
10		23	24	25	26	27	28	29	
11		30	1	2	3	4	5	6	
12	PAREMOTEP 1618	7	8	9	10	11	12	13	MAGĀBIT 1894
13		14	15	16	17	18	19	20	
14		21	22	23	24	25	26	27	
15		28	29	30	1	2	3	4	
16	PARMOUTE 1618	5	6	7	8	9	10	11	MIYĀZYĀ 1894
17		12	13	14	15	16	17	18	
18		19[f]	20	21	22	23	24	25	
19		26	27	28	29[g]	30	1	2	
20	PASHONS 1618	3	4	5	6	7	8	9	GENBOT 1894
21		10	11	12	13	14	15	16	
22		17	18	19	20	21	22	23	
23		24	25	26	27	28	29	30	
24	PAÔNE 1618	1	2	3	4	5	6	7	SANĒ 1894
25		8	9	10	11	12	13	14	
26		15	16	17	18	19	20	21	
27		22	23	24	25	26	27	28	
28		29	30	1	2	3	4	5	
29	EPÊP 1618	6	7	8	9	10	11	12	ḤAMLĒ 1894
30		13	14	15	16	17	18	19	
31		20	21	22	23	24	25	26	
32		27	28	29	30	1	2	3	
33	MESORÊ 1618	4	5	6	7	8	9	10	NAḤASĒ 1894
34		11	12	13[h]	14	15	16	17	
35		18	19	20	21	22	23	24	
36		25	26	27	28	29	30	1	
37	EPAG. 1618	2	3	4	5	1[a]	2	3	PĀG. 1894
38	THOOUT 1619	4	5	6	7	8	9	10	MASKARAM 1895
39		11	12	13	14	15	16	17[b]	
40		18	19	20	21	22	23	24	
41		25	26	27	28	29	30	1	
42	PAOPE 1619	2	3	4	5	6	7	8	ṬEQEMT 1895
43		9	10	11	12	13	14	15	
44		16	17	18	19	20	21	22	
45		23	24	25	26	27	28	29	
46		30	1	2	3	4	5	6	
47	ATHÔR 1619	7	8	9	10	11	12	13	ḪEDĀR 1895
48		14	15	16	17	18	19	20	
49		21	22	23	24	25	26	27	
50		28	29	30	1	2	3	4	
51	KOIAK 1619	5	6	7	8	9	10	11	TĀKHŚĀŚ 1895
52		12	13	14	15	16	17	18	
1		19	20	21	22	23	24	25	

Gregorian:
[a] New Year
[b] Spring (13:17)
[c] Summer (9:15)
[d] Autumn (23:55)
[e] Winter (18:35)
● New moon
◐ First quarter moon
○ Full moon
◑ Last quarter moon

Hebrew:
‡ Leap year
[a] New Year
[b] Yom Kippur
[c] Sukkot
[d] Winter starts
[e] Ḥanukkah
[f] Purim
[g] Passover
[h] Shavuot
[i] Fast of Av

Chinese:
[a] New Year (4600, Tiger)
[b] Lantern Festival
[c] Qīngmíng
[d] Dragon Festival
[e] Qīqiǎo
[f] Hungry Ghosts
[g] Mid-Autumn Festival
[h] Double-Ninth Festival
[i] Dōngzhì
* Start of 60-name cycle

Coptic/Ethiopic:
‡ Leap year
[a] New Year
[b] Building of the Cross
[c] Christmas
[d] Jesus's Circumcision
[e] Epiphany
[f] Easter
[g] Mary's Announcement
[h] Jesus's Transfiguration

PERSIAN (ASTRONOMICAL) 1280‡/1281

Month	Sun	Mon	Tue	Wed	Thu	Fri	Sat
	8	9	10	11	12	13	14
DEY 1280	15	16	17	18	19	20	21
	22	23	24	25	26	27	28
	29	30	1	2	3	4	5
BAHMAN 1280	6	7	8	9	10	11	12
	13	14	15	16	17	18	19
	20	21	22	23	24	25	26
	27	28	29	30	1	2	3
ESFAND 1280	4	5	6	7	8	9	10
	11	12	13	14	15	16	17
	18	19	20	21	22	23	24
	25	26	27	28	29	30	1[a]
	2	3	4	5	6	7	8
FARVARDĪN 1281	9	10	11	12	13[b]	14	15
	16	17	18	19	20	21	22
	23	24	25	26	27	28	29
	30	31	1	2	3	4	5
ORDĪBEHEŠT 1281	6	7	8	9	10	11	12
	13	14	15	16	17	18	19
	20	21	22	23	24	25	26
	27	28	29	30	31	1	2
	3	4	5	6	7	8	9
XORDĀD 1281	10	11	12	13	14	15	16
	17	18	19	20	21	22	23
	24	25	26	27	28	29	30
	31	1	2	3	4	5	6
	7	8	9	10	11	12	13
TĪR 1281	14	15	16	17	18	19	20
	21	22	23	24	25	26	27
	28	29	30	31	1	2	3
	4	5	6	7	8	9	10
MORDĀD 1281	11	12	13	14	15	16	17
	18	19	20	21	22	23	24
	25	26	27	28	29	30	31
	1	2	3	4	5	6	7
	8	9	10	11	12	13	14
SHAHRĪVAR 1281	15	16	17	18	19	20	21
	22	23	24	25	26	27	28
	29	30	31	1	2	3	4
	5	6	7	8	9	10	11
MEHR 1281	12	13	14	15	16	17	18
	19	20	21	22	23	24	25
	26	27	28	29	30	1	2
	3	4	5	6	7	8	9
ĀBĀN 1281	10	11	12	13	14	15	16
	17	18	19	20	21	22	23
	24	25	26	27	28	29	30
	1	2	3	4	5	6	7
	8	9	10	11	12	13	14
ĀZAR 1281	15	16	17	18	19	20	21
	22	23	24	25	26	27	28
	29	30	1	2	3	4	5
DEY 1281	6	7	8	9	10	11	12

‡Leap year
[a]New Year
[b]Sizdeh Bedar

HINDU LUNAR 1958‡/1959

Month	Sun	Mon	Tue	Wed	Thu	Fri	Sat
MĀRGAŚĪRA 1958	19	20	21	22	23	24	25
	26	27	28	29	30	1	2
PAUSHA 1958	3	4	5	6	7	8	9
	10	11	12	**13**	15	16	17
	18	19	20	21	22	23	*23*
	24	25	26	27	28	29	30
	1	2	3	4	5	6	**7**
MĀGHA 1958	9	10	11	12	13	14	15
	16	17	18	19	20	21	22
	23	24	25	*25*	26	27	28[h]
	29	30	**1**	3	4	5	6
	7	8	9	10	11	12	13
PHĀLGUNA 1958	14	15[i]	16	17	18	19	20
	21	22	23	24	25	26	27
	28	29	30	1[a]	2	3	4
CHAITRA 1959	**5**	7	8	9[b]	10	11	12
	13	14	15	16	17	18	19
	19	20	21	22	23	24	25
	26	27	28	**29**	1	2	3
VAIŚĀKHA 1959	4	5	6	7	8	9	10
	11	12	13	14	15	16	17
	18	19	20	21	22	23	24
	25	26	27	28	29	30	1
JYAISHTHA 1959	**2**	4	5	6	7	8	9
	10	11	12	13	14	15	*15*
	16	17	18	19	20	21	22
	23	24	**25**	27	28	29	30
	1	2	3	4	5	6	7
ĀSHĀḌHA 1959	8	9	10	11	12	13	14
	15	16	17	18	19	20	21
	22	23	24	25	26	27	**28**
	30	1	2	3	4	5	6
	7	8	9	10	11	12	*12*
ŚRĀVAṆA 1959	13	14	15	16	17	18	19
	20	22	23[c]	24	25	26	27
	28	29	30	1	2	3[d]	4
	5	6	7	8	9	10	11
BHĀDRAPADA 1959	12	13	14	15	16	17	18
	19	20	21	22	23	**24**	26
	27	28	29	30	1	2	3
	4	5	6	7	*7*	8[e]	9[e]
ĀŚVINA 1959	10[e]	11	12	13	14	15	16
	17	19	20	21	22	23	24
	25	26	27	28	29	30	1[f]
	2	3	4	5	6	7	8
KĀRTTIKA 1959	9	10	11	12	13	14	15
	16	17	18	19	20	21	**22**
	24	25	26	27	28	29	30
	1	*1*	2	3	4	5	6
MĀRGAŚĪRA 1959	7	8	9	10	11[g]	12	13
	14	15	**16**	18	19	20	21
	22	23	24	25	26	27	28
	29	30	1	2	3	*3*	4

‡Leap year
[a]New Year (Śubhakṛit)
[b]Birthday of Rāma
[c]Birthday of Krishna
[d]Ganēśa Chaturthī
[e]Dashara
[f]Diwali
[g]Birthday of Vishnu
[h]Night of Śiva
[i]Holi

HINDU SOLAR 1823‡/1824

Month	Sun	Mon	Tue	Wed	Thu	Fri	Sat
	15	16	17	18	19	20	21
PAUSHA 1823	22	23	24	25	26	27	28
	29	1[b]	2	3	4	5	6
MĀGHA 1823	7	8	9	10	11	12	13
	14	15	16	17	18	19	20
	21	22	23	24	25	26	27
	28	29	1	2	3	4	5
PHĀLGUNA 1823	6	7	8	9	10	11	12
	13	14	15	16	17	18	19
	20	21	22	23	24	25	26
	27	28	29	30	1	2	3
CHAITRA 1823	4	5	6	7	8	9	10
	11	12	13	14	15	16	17
	18	19	20	21	22	23	24
	25	26	27	28	29	30	31
	1[a]	2	3	4	5	6	7
VAIŚĀKHA 1824	8	9	10	11	12	13	14
	15	16	17	18	19	20	21
	22	23	24	25	26	27	28
	29	30	31	1	2	3	4
JYAISHTHA 1824	5	6	7	8	9	10	11
	12	13	14	15	16	17	18
	19	20	21	22	23	24	25
	26	27	28	29	30	31	1
	2	3	4	5	6	7	8
ĀSHĀḌHA 1824	9	10	11	12	13	14	15
	16	17	18	19	20	21	22
	23	24	25	26	27	28	29
	30	31	32	1	2	3	4
ŚRĀVAṆA 1824	5	6	7	8	9	10	11
	12	13	14	15	16	17	18
	19	20	21	22	23	24	25
	26	27	28	29	30	31	1
	2	3	4	5	6	7	8
BHĀDRAPADA 1824	9	10	11	12	13	14	15
	16	17	18	19	20	21	22
	23	24	25	26	27	28	29
	30	31	1	2	3	4	5
	6	7	8	9	10	11	12
ĀŚVINA 1824	13	14	15	16	17	18	19
	20	21	22	23	24	25	26
	27	28	29	30	31	1	2
	3	4	5	6	7	8	9
KĀRTTIKA 1824	10	11	12	13	14	15	16
	17	18	19	20	21	22	23
	24	25	26	27	28	29	1
	2	3	4	5	6	7	8
MĀRGAŚĪRA 1824	9	10	11	12	13	14	15
	16	17	18	19	20	21	22
	23	24	25	26	27	28	29
PAUSHA 1824	30	1	2	3	4	5	6
	7	8	9	10	11	12	13
	14	15	16	17	18	19	20

‡Leap year
[a]New Year (Ānanda)
[b]Pongal

ISLAMIC (ASTRONOMICAL) 1319‡/1320

Month	Sun	Mon	Tue	Wed	Thu	Fri	Sat
RAMAḌĀN 1319	18	19	20	21	22	23	24
	25	26	27	28	29	30	1[f]
	2	3	4	5	6	7	8
SHAWWĀL 1319	9	10	11	12	13	14	15
	16	17	18	19	20	21	22
	23	24	25	26	27	28	29
	30	1	2	3	4	5	6
DHU AL-QA'DA 1319	7	8	9	10	11	12	13
	14	15	16	17	18	19	20
	21	22	23	24	25	26	27
	28	29	1	2	3	4	5
DHU AL-ḤIJJA 1319	6	7	8	9	10[g]	11	12
	13	14	15	16	17	18	19
	20	21	22	23	24	25	26
	27	28	29	30	1[a]	2	3
MUḤARRAM 1320	4	5	6	7	8	9	10[b]
	11	12	13	14	15	16	17
	18	19	20	21	22	23	24
	25	26	27	28	29	1	2
ṢAFAR 1320	3	4	5	6	7	8	9
	10	11	12	13	14	15	16
	17	18	19	20	21	22	23
	24	25	26	27	28	29	30
	1	2	3	4	5	6	7
RABĪ' I 1320	8	9	10	11	12[c]	13	14
	15	16	17	18	19	20	21
	22	23	24	25	26	27	28
	29	1	2	3	4	5	6
RABĪ' II 1320	7	8	9	10	11	12	13
	14	15	16	17	18	19	20
	21	22	23	24	25	26	27
	28	29	30	1	2	3	4
JUMĀDĀ I 1320	5	6	7	8	9	10	11
	12	13	14	15	16	17	18
	19	20	21	22	23	24	25
	26	27	28	29	1	2	3
JUMĀDĀ II 1320	4	5	6	7	8	9	10
	11	12	13	14	15	16	17
	18	19	20	21	22	23	24
	25	26	27	28	29	1	2
RAJAB 1320	3	4	5	6	7	8	9
	10	11	12	13	14	15	16
	17	18	19	20	21	22	23
	24	25	26	27[d]	28	29	30
	1	2	3	4	5	6	7
SHA'BĀN 1320	8	9	10	11	12	13	14
	15	16	17	18	19	20	21
	22	23	24	25	26	27	28
	29	1[e]	2	3	4	5	6
RAMAḌĀN 1320	7	8	9	10	11	12	13
	14	15	16	17	18	19	20
	21	22	23	24	25	26	27
	28	29	30	1[f]	2	3	4

‡Leap year
[a]New Year
[b]'Ashūrā'
[c]Prophet's Birthday
[d]Ascent of the Prophet
[e]Start of Ramaḍān
[f]'Īd al-Fiṭr
[g]'Īd al-'Aḍḥā

GREGORIAN 1902

Julian (Sun)	Sun	Mon	Tue	Wed	Thu	Fri	Sat	Month
Dec 16	29	30	31	1	2	3	4	
	5	6	7[a]	8	9	10	11	JANUARY 1902
Dec 30	12	13	14[b]	15	16	17	18	
	19	20	21	22	23	24	25	
Jan 13	26	27	28	29	30	31	1	
	2	3	4	5	6	7	8	FEBRUARY 1902
Jan 27	9	10	11	12[c]	13	14	15	
	16	17	18	19	20	21	22	
Feb 10	23	24	25	26	27	28	1	
	2	3	4	5	6	7	8	
Feb 24	9	10	11	12	13	14	15	MARCH 1902
	16[d]	17	18	19	20	21	22	
Mar 10	23	24	25	26	27	28	29	
	30[e]	31	1	2	3	4	5	
Mar 24	6	7	8	9	10	11	12	APRIL 1902
	13	14	15	16	17	18	19	
Apr 7	20	21	22	23	24	25	26	
	27[f]	28	29	30	1	2	3	
Apr 21	4	5	6	7	8	9	10	
	11	12	13	14	15	16	17	MAY 1902
May 5	18	19	20	21	22	23	24	
	25	26	27	28	29	30	31	
May 19	1	2	3	4	5	6	7	
	8	9	10	11	12	13	14	JUNE 1902
Jun 2	15	16	17	18	19	20	21	
	22	23	24	25	26	27	28	
Jun 16	29	30	1	2	3	4	5	
	6	7	8	9	10	11	12	JULY 1902
Jun 30	13	14	15	16	17	18	19	
	20	21	22	23	24	25	26	
Jul 14	27	28	29	30	31	1	2	
	3	4	5	6	7	8	9	
Jul 28	10	11	12	13	14	15	16	AUGUST 1902
	17	18	19	20	21	22	23	
Aug 11	24	25	26	27	28	29	30	
	31	1	2	3	4	5	6	
Aug 25	7	8	9	10	11	12	13	SEPTEMBER 1902
	14	15	16	17	18	19	20	
Sep 8	21	22	23	24	25	26	27	
	28	29	30	1	2	3	4	
Sep 22	5	6	7	8	9	10	11	OCTOBER 1902
	12	13	14	15	16	17	18	
Oct 6	19	20	21	22	23	24	25	
	26	27	28	29	30	31	1	
Oct 20	2	3	4	5	6	7	8	NOVEMBER 1902
	9	10	11	12	13	14	15	
Nov 3	16	17	18	19	20	21	22	
	23	24	25	26	27	28	29	
Nov 17	30[g]	1	2	3	4	5	6	
	7	8	9	10	11	12	13	DECEMBER 1902
Dec 1	14	15	16	17	18	19	20	
	21	22	23	24	25[h]	26	27	
Dec 15	28	29	30	31	1	2	3	

[a]Orthodox Christmas
[b]Julian New Year
[c]Ash Wednesday
[d]Feast of Orthodoxy
[e]Easter
[f]Orthodox Easter
[g]Advent
[h]Christmas

1903

Gregorian 1903	Sun Mon Tue Wed Thu Fri Sat	Lunar Phases	ISO WEEK (Mon)	JULIAN DAY (Sun noon)	Hebrew 5663/5664	Sun Mon Tue Wed Thu Fri Sat	Molad	Chinese Rén-Yín/Guǐ-Mǎo‡	Sun Mon Tue Wed Thu Fri Sat	Solar Term	Coptic 1619‡/1620	Sun Mon Tue Wed Thu Fri Sat	Ethiopic 1895‡/1896
JANUARY 1903	28 ● 30 31 1[a] 2 3	21:25	1	2416112	TEVETH 5663	28[e] 29[e] 30[e] 1[e] 2[e] 3 4	Tue 1h34m1p	MONTH 12 Rén-Yín	29 30 1 2 3 4 5		KOIAK 1619	19 20 21 22 23 24 25	TĀKHŚĀŚ 1895
	4 5 ◐ 7 8 9 10	21:57	2	2416119		5 6 7 8 9 10 11			6 7 8 9 10 11 12	Xiǎo hán		26 27 28 29[c] 30 1 2	
	11 12 ○ 14 15 16 17	14:17	3	2416126		12 13 14 15 16 17 18			13 14 15 16 17 18 19		TÔBE 1619	3 4 5 6[d] 7 8 9	ṬER 1895
	18 19 ◑ 21 22 23 24	11:49	4	2416133		19 20 21 22 23 24 25			20 21 22 23 24 25 26	Dà hán		10 11[e] 12 13 14 15 16	
	25 26 27 ● 29 30 31	16:38	5	2416140	SHEVAT 5663	26 27 28 29 1 2 3	Wed 14h18m2p	MONTH 1 Guǐ-Mǎo	27 28 29 30 1[a] 2 3			17 18 19 20 21 22 23	
FEBRUARY 1903	1 2 3 4 ◐ 6 7	10:12	6	2416147		4 5 6 7 8 9 10			4 5 6 7 8* 9 10	Lì chūn		24 25 26 27 28 29 30	
	8 9 10 11 ○ 13 14	0:58	7	2416154		11 12 13 14 15 16 17			11 12 13 14 15[b] 16 17		MESHIR 1619	1 2 3 4 5 6 7	YAKĀTIT 1895
	15 16 17 18 ◑ 20 21	6:23	8	2416161		18 19 20 21 22 23 24			18 19 20 21 22 23 24	Yǔ shuǐ		8 9 10 11 12 13 14	
	22 23 24 25 26 ● 28	10:19	9	2416168	ADAR 5663	25 26 27 28 29 30 1	Fri 3h2m3p	MONTH 2 Guǐ-Mǎo	25 26 27 28 29 1 2			15 16 17 18 19 20 21	
MARCH 1903	1 2 3 4 5 ◐ 7	19:14	10	2416175		2 3 4 5 6 7 8			3 4 5 6 7 8 9	Jīng zhé		22 23 24 25 26 27 28	
	8 9 10 11 12 ○ 14	12:13	11	2416182		9 10 11 12 13 14[f] 15			10 11 12 13 14 15 16		PAREMOTEP 1619	29 30 1 2 3 4 5	MAGĀBIT 1895
	15 16 17 18 19 20 ◑[b]	2:08	12	2416189		16 17 18 19 20 21 22			17 18 19 20 21 22 23	Chūn fēn		6 7 8 9 10 11 12	
	22 23 24 25 26 27 28		13	2416196		23 24 25 26 27 28 29			24 25 26 27 28 29 30			13 14 15 16 17 18 19	
	● 30 31 1 2 3 4	1:26	14	2416203	NISAN 5663	1 2 3 4 5 6 7	Sat 15h46m4p	MONTH 3 Guǐ-Mǎo	1 2 3 4 5 6 7			20 21 22 23 24 25 26	
APRIL 1903	◐ 6 7 8 9 10 11	1:51	15	2416210		8 9 10 11 12 13 14			8 9[c]* 10 11 12 13 14	Qīng míng	PARMOUTE 1619	27 28 29 30 1 2 3	MIYĀZYĀ 1895
	○ 13 14 15 16 17 18	0:18	16	2416217		15[g] 16 17 18 19 20 21			15 16 17 18 19 20 21			4 5 6 7 8 9 10	
	◑ 20 21 22 23 24 25	21:30	17	2416224		22 23 24 25 26 27 28			22 23 24 25 26 27 28	Gǔ yǔ		11[f] 12 13 14 15 16 17	
	26 ● 28 29 30 1 2	13:31	18	2416231	IYYAR 5663	29 30 1 2 3 4 5	Mon 4h30m5p	MONTH 4 Guǐ-Mǎo	29 1 2 3 4 5 6			18 19 20 21 22 23 24	
MAY 1903	3 ◐ 5 6 7 8 9	7:26	19	2416238		6 7 8 9 10 11 12			7 8 9 10 11 12 13	Lì xià	PASHONS 1619	25 26 27 28 29[g] 30 1	GENBOT 1895
	10 ○ 12 13 14 15 16	13:18	20	2416245		13 14 15 16 17 18 19			14 15 16 17 18 19 20			2 3 4 5 6 7 8	
	17 18 ◑ 20 21 22 23	15:18	21	2416252		20 21 22 23 24 25 26			21 22 23 24 25 26 27	Xiǎo mǎn		9 10 11 12 13 14 15	
	24 25 ● 27 28 29 30	22:50	22	2416259	SIVAN 5663	27 28 29 1 2 3 4	Tue 17h14m6p	MONTH 5 Guǐ-Mǎo	28 29 30 1 2 3 4			16 17 18 19 20 21 22	
	31 1 ◐ 3 4 5 6	13:24	23	2416266		5 6[h] 7 8 9 10 11			5[d] 6 7 8 9 10* 11			23 24 25 26 27 28 29	
JUNE 1903	7 8 9 ○ 11 12 13	3:08	24	2416273		12 13 14 15 16 17 18			12 13 14 15 16 17 18	Máng zhòng	PAÔNE 1619	30 1 2 3 4 5 6	SANĒ 1895
	14 15 16 17 ◑ 19 20	6:44	25	2416280		19 20 21 22 23 24 25			19 20 21 22 23 24 25			7 8 9 10 11 12 13	
	21 22[c] 23 24 ● 26 27	6:11	26	2416287	TAMMUZ 5663	26 27 28 29 30 1 2	Thu 5h58m7p	LEAP MONTH 5 Guǐ-Mǎo	26 27 28 29 1 2 3	Xià zhì		14 15 16 17 18 19 20	
	28 29 30 ◐ 2 3 4	21:02	27	2416294		3 4 5 6 7 8 9			4 5 6 7 8 9 10			21 22 23 24 25 26 27	
JULY 1903	5 6 7 8 ○ 10 11	17:43	28	2416301		10 11 12 13 14 15 16			11 12 13 14 15 16 17	Xiǎo shǔ	EPÊP 1619	28 29 30 1 2 3 4	ḤAMLĒ 1895
	12 13 14 15 16 ◑ 18	19:24	29	2416308		17 18 19 20 21 22 23			18 19 20 21 22 23 24			5 6 7 8 9 10 11	
	19 20 21 22 23 ● 25	12:46	30	2416315	AV 5663	24 25 26 27 28 29 1	Fri 18h42m8p	MONTH 6 Guǐ-Mǎo	25 26 27 28 29 1 2	Dà shǔ		12 13 14 15 16 17 18	
	26 27 28 29 30 ◐ 1	7:15	31	2416322		2 3 4 5 6 7 8			3 4 5 6 7 8 9			19 20 21 22 23 24 25	
AUGUST 1903	2 3 4 5 6 7 ○	8:54	32	2416329		9[i] 10 11 12 13 14 15			10 11 12* 13 14 15 16		MESORÊ 1619	26 27 28 29 30 1 2	NAḤASĒ 1895
	9 10 11 12 13 14 15		33	2416336		16 17 18 19 20 21 22			17 18 19 20 21 22 23	Lì qiū		3 4 5 6 7 8 9	
	◑ 17 18 19 20 21 ●	5:23 20:34	34	2416343		23 24 25 26 27 28 29			24 25 26 27 28 29 30			10 11 12 13[h] 14 15 16	
	23 24 25 26 27 28 ◐	19:51	35	2416350	ELUL 5663	30 1 2 3 4 5 6	Sun 7h26m9p	MONTH 7 Guǐ-Mǎo	1 2 3 4 5 6 7[e]	Chǔ shǔ		17 18 19 20 21 22 23	
	30 31 1 2 3 4 5		36	2416357		7 8 9 10 11 12 13			8 9 10 11 12 13 14			24 25 26 27 28 29 30	
SEPTEMBER 1903	6 ○ 8 9 10 11 12	0:20	37	2416364		14 15 16 17 18 19 20			15[f] 16 17 18 19 20 21	Bái lù	EPAG. 1619	1 2 3 4 5 6 1[a]	PĀG. 1895
	13 ◑ 15 16 17 18 19	13:14	38	2416371		21 22 23 24 25 26 27			22 23 24 25 26 27 28		THOOUT 1620	2 3 4 5 6 7 8	MASKARAM 1896
	20 ● 22 23 24[d] 25 26	4:30	39	2416378	TISHRI 5664	28 29 1[a] 2[a] 3 4 5	Mon 20h10m10p	MONTH 8 Guǐ-Mǎo	29 1 2 3 4 5 6	Qiū fēn		9 10 11 12 13 14 15	
	27 ◐ 29 30 1 2 3	13:08	40	2416385		6 7 8 9 10[b] 11 12			7 8 9 10 11 12 13*			16 17[b] 18 19 20 21 22	
OCTOBER 1903	4 5 ○ 7 8 9 10	15:24	41	2416392		13 14 15[c] 16 17 18 19			14 15[g] 16 17 18 19 20	Hán lù		23 24 25 26 27 28 29	
	11 12 ◑ 14 15 16 17	19:57	42	2416399		20 21 22 23 24 25 26			21 22 23 24 25 26 27		PAOPE 1620	30 1 2 3 4 5 6	TEQEMT 1896
	18 19 ● 21 22 23 24	15:30	43	2416406	ḤESHVAN 5664	27 28 29 30 1 2 3	Wed 8h54m11p	MONTH 9 Guǐ-Mǎo	28 29 1 2 3 4 5	Shuāng jiàng		7 8 9 10 11 12 13	
	25 26 27 ◐ 29 30 31	8:33	44	2416413		4 5 6 7 8 9 10			6 7 8 9[h] 10 11 12			14 15 16 17 18 19 20	
NOVEMBER 1903	1 2 3 4 ○ 6 7	5:27	45	2416420		11 12 13 14 15 16 17			13 14 15 16 17 18 19			21 22 23 24 25 26 27	
	8 9 10 11 ◑ 13 14	2:46	46	2416427		18 19 20 21 22 23 24			20 21 22 23 24 25 26	Lì dōng	ATHÔR 1620	28 29 30 1 2 3 4	ḪEDĀR 1896
	15 16 17 18 ● 20 21	5:10	47	2416434	KISLEV 5664	25 26 27 28 29 1 2	Thu 21h38m12p	MONTH 10 Guǐ-Mǎo	27 28 29 30 1 2 3			5 6 7 8 9 10 11	
	22 23 24 25 26 ◐ 28	5:37	48	2416441		3 4 5 6 7 8 9			4 5 6 7 8 9 10	Xiǎo xuě		12 13 14 15 16 17 18	
	29 30 1 2 3 ○ 5	18:13	49	2416448		10 11 12 13 14 15 16			11 12 13 14* 15 16 17			19 20 21 22 23 24 25	
DECEMBER 1903	6 7 8 9 10 ◑ 12	10:53	50	2416455		17[d] 18 19 20 21 22 23			18 19 20 21 22 23 24	Dà xuě	KOIAK 1620	26 27 28 29 30 1 2	TĀKHŚĀŚ 1896
	13 14 15 16 17 ● 19	21:26	51	2416462		24 25[e] 26[e] 27[e] 28[e] 29[e] 30[e]		MONTH 11* Guǐ-Mǎo	25 26 27 28 29 30 1			3 4 5 6 7 8 9	
	20 21 22 23[e] 24 25 26		52	2416469	TEVETH 5664	1[e] 2[e] 3 4 5 6 7	Sat 10h22m13p		2 3 4 5[i] 6 7 8	Dōng zhì		10 11 12 13 14 15 16	
	◐ 28 29 30 31 1 2	2:22	53	2416476		8 9 10 11 12 13 14			9 10 11 12 13 14 15			17 18 19 20 21 22 23	

[a]New Year
[b]Spring (19:15)
[c]Summer (15:05)
[d]Autumn (5:44)
[e]Winter (0:20)
● New moon
◐ First quarter moon
○ Full moon
◑ Last quarter moon

[a]New Year
[b]Yom Kippur
[c]Sukkot
[d]Winter starts
[e]Ḥanukkah
[f]Purim
[g]Passover
[h]Shavuot
[i]Fast of Av

‡Leap year
[a]New Year (4601, Hare)
[b]Lantern Festival
[c]Qīngmíng
[d]Dragon Festival
[e]Qīqiǎo
[f]Hungry Ghosts
[g]Mid-Autumn Festival
[h]Double-Ninth Festival
[i]Dōngzhì
*Start of 60-name cycle

‡Leap year
[a]New Year
[b]Building of the Cross
[c]Christmas
[d]Jesus's Circumcision
[e]Epiphany
[f]Easter
[g]Mary's Announcement
[h]Jesus's Transfiguration

PERSIAN (ASTRONOMICAL) 1281/1282

Month	Sun	Mon	Tue	Wed	Thu	Fri	Sat
	6	7	8	9	10	11	12
DEY 1281	13	14	15	16	17	18	19
	20	21	22	23	24	25	26
BAHMAN 1281	27	28	29	30	*1*	2	3
	4	5	6	7	8	9	10
	11	12	13	14	15	16	17
	18	19	20	21	22	23	24
ESFAND 1281	25	26	27	28	29	30	*1*
	2	3	4	5	6	7	8
	9	10	11	12	13	14	15
	16	17	18	19	20	21	22
	23	24	25	26	27	28	29
FARVARDĪN 1282	*1*[a]	2	3	4	5	6	7
	8	9	10	11	12	13[b]	14
	15	16	17	18	19	20	21
	22	23	24	25	26	27	28
ORDĪBEHEŠT 1282	29	30	31	*1*	2	3	4
	5	6	7	8	9	10	11
	12	13	14	15	16	17	18
	19	20	21	22	23	24	25
XORDĀD 1282	26	27	28	29	30	31	*1*
	2	3	4	5	6	7	8
	9	10	11	12	13	14	15
	16	17	18	19	20	21	22
	23	24	25	26	27	28	29
TĪR 1282	30	31	*1*	2	3	4	5
	6	7	8	9	10	11	12
	13	14	15	16	17	18	19
	20	21	22	23	24	25	26
MORDĀD 1282	27	28	29	30	31	*1*	2
	3	4	5	6	7	8	9
	10	11	12	13	14	15	16
	17	18	19	20	21	22	23
	24	25	26	27	28	29	30
SHAHRĪVAR 1282	31	*1*	2	3	4	5	6
	7	8	9	10	11	12	13
	14	15	16	17	18	19	20
	21	22	23	24	25	26	27
MEHR 1282	28	29	30	31	*1*	2	3
	4	5	6	7	8	9	10
	11	12	13	14	15	16	17
	18	19	20	21	22	23	24
ĀBĀN 1282	25	26	27	28	29	30	*1*
	2	3	4	5	6	7	8
	9	10	11	12	13	14	15
	16	17	18	19	20	21	22
	23	24	25	26	27	28	29
ĀZAR 1282	30	*1*	2	3	4	5	6
	7	8	9	10	11	12	13
	14	15	16	17	18	19	20
	21	22	23	24	25	26	27
DEY 1282	28	29	30	*1*	2	3	4
	5	6	7	8	9	10	11

HINDU LUNAR 1959/1960

Month	Sun	Mon	Tue	Wed	Thu	Fri	Sat
PAUSHA 1959	29	30	1	2	3	3	4
	5	6	7	8	**9**	11	12
	13	14	15	16	17	18	19
	20	21	22	23	24	25	26
MĀGHA 1959	27	28	29	30	1	2	3
	4	5	6	7	8	9	10
	11	12	13	**14**	16	17	18
	19	20	21	22	23	24	25
PHĀLGUNA 1959	26	*26*	27	28[h]	29	30	1
	2	3	4	5	6	7	**8**
	10	11	12	13	14	15[i]	16
	17	18	19	20	21	22	23
	24	25	26	27	28	29	*29*
CHAITRA 1960	30	1[a]	3	4	5	6	7
	8	9[b]	10	11	12	13	**14**
	16	17	18	19	*19*	20	21
	22	23	24	25	26	27	28
VAIŚĀKHA 1960	29	30	1	2	3	4	5
	6	8	9	10	11	12	13
	14	15	16	17	18	19	20
	21	22	23	*23*	24	25	26
JYAISHTHA 1960	27	28	**29**	1	2	3	4
	5	6	7	8	9	10	11
	12	13	14	15	16	17	18
	19	20	21	22	23	24	25
ĀSHĀDHA 1960	26	27	28	29	30	1	**2**
	4	5	6	7	8	9	10
	11	12	13	14	15	16	17
	18	19	20	*20*	21	22	23
ŚRĀVANA 1960	**24**	26	27	28	29	30	1
	2	3	4	5	**6**	8	9
	10	11	*11*	12	13	14	15
	16	17	18	19	20	21	22
	23[c]	24	25	26	27	**28**	30
BHĀDRAPADA 1960	1	2	3	4[d]	5	6	7
	8	9	10	11	12	13	14
	15	16	*16*	17	18	19	**20**
	22	23	24	25	26	27	28
ĀŚVINA 1960	29	30	1	**2**	4	5	6
	7	*7*	8[e]	9[e]	10[e]	11	12
	13	14	15	16	17	18	19
	20	21	22	23	**24**	26	27
KĀRTTIKA 1960	28	29	30	1[f]	2	3	4
	5	6	7	8	9	10	*10*
	11	12	13	14	15	16	17
	18	20	21	22	23	24	25
MĀRGAŚĪRA 1960	26	27	28	29	30	1	2
	3	4	5	6	7	8	9
	10	11[g]	12	13	14	15	16
	17	18	19	20	21	22	**23**
PAUSHA 1960	25	26	27	28	29	30	1
	2	3	4	*4*	5	6	7
	8	9	10	11	12	13	14

HINDU SOLAR 1824/1825

Month	Sun	Mon	Tue	Wed	Thu	Fri	Sat
	14	15	16	17	18	19	20
PAUSHA 1824	21	22	23	24	25	26	27
MĀGHA 1824	28	29	1[b]	2	3	4	5
	6	7	8	9	10	11	12
	13	14	15	16	17	18	19
	20	21	22	23	24	25	26
PHĀLGUNA 1824	27	28	29	30	1	2	3
	4	5	6	7	8	9	10
	11	12	13	14	15	16	17
	18	19	20	21	22	23	24
CHAITRA 1824	25	26	27	28	29	30	1
	2	3	4	5	6	7	8
	9	10	11	12	13	14	15
	16	17	18	19	20	21	22
	23	24	25	26	27	28	29
VAIŚĀKHA 1825	30	1[a]	2	3	4	5	6
	7	8	9	10	11	12	13
	14	15	16	17	18	19	20
	21	22	23	24	25	26	27
JYAISHTHA 1825	28	29	30	31	1	2	3
	4	5	6	7	8	9	10
	11	12	13	14	15	16	17
	18	19	20	21	22	23	24
	25	26	27	28	29	30	31
ĀSHĀDHA 1825	1	2	3	4	5	6	7
	8	9	10	11	12	13	14
	15	16	17	18	19	20	21
	22	23	24	25	26	27	28
ŚRĀVANA 1825	29	30	31	32	1	2	3
	4	5	6	7	8	9	10
	11	12	13	14	15	16	17
	18	19	20	21	22	23	24
	25	26	27	28	29	30	31
BHĀDRAPADA 1825	1	2	3	4	5	6	7
	8	9	10	11	12	13	14
	15	16	17	18	19	20	21
	22	23	24	25	26	27	28
ĀŚVINA 1825	29	30	31	1	2	3	4
	5	6	7	8	9	10	11
	12	13	14	15	16	17	18
	19	20	21	22	23	24	25
KĀRTTIKA 1825	26	27	28	29	30	31	1
	2	3	4	5	6	7	8
	9	10	11	12	13	14	15
	16	17	18	19	20	21	22
	23	24	25	26	27	28	29
MĀRGAŚĪRA 1825	30	1	2	3	4	5	6
	7	8	9	10	11	12	13
	14	15	16	17	18	19	20
	21	22	23	24	25	26	27
PAUSHA 1825	28	29	1	2	3	4	5
	6	7	8	9	10	11	12
	13	14	15	16	17	18	19

ISLAMIC (ASTRONOMICAL) 1320/1321‡

Month	Sun	Mon	Tue	Wed	Thu	Fri	Sat
	28	29	30	1	*2*	3	4
SHAWWĀL 1320	5	6	7	8	9	10	11
	12	13	14	15	16	17	18
	19	20	21	22	23	24	25
DHU AL-QA'DA 1320	26	27	28	29	30	*1*	2
	3	4	5	6	7	8	9
	10	11	12	13	14	15	16
	17	18	19	20	21	22	23
	24	25	26	27	28	29	30
DHU AL-HIJJA 1320	*1*	2	3	4	5	6	7
	8	9	10[g]	11	12	13	14
	15	16	17	18	19	20	21
	22	23	24	25	26	27	28
MUHARRAM 1321	29	*1*[a]	2	3	4	5	6
	7	8	9	10[b]	11	12	13
	14	15	16	17	18	19	20
	21	22	23	24	25	26	27
SAFAR 1321	28	29	30	*1*	2	3	4
	5	6	7	8	9	10	11
	12	13	14	15	16	17	18
	19	20	21	22	23	24	25
RABĪ' I 1321	26	27	28	29	*1*	2	3
	4	5	6	7	8	9	10
	11	12[c]	13	14	15	16	17
	18	19	20	21	22	23	24
RABĪ' II 1321	25	26	27	28	29	30	*1*
	2	3	4	5	6	7	8
	9	10	11	12	13	14	15
	16	17	18	19	20	21	22
	23	24	25	26	27	28	29
JUMĀDĀ I 1321	*1*	2	3	4	5	6	7
	8	9	10	11	12	13	14
	15	16	17	18	19	20	21
	22	23	24	25	26	27	28
JUMĀDĀ II 1321	29	30	*1*	2	3	4	5
	6	7	8	9	10	11	12
	13	14	15	16	17	18	19
	20	21	22	23	24	25	26
RAJAB 1321	27	28	29	*1*	2	3	4
	5	6	7	8	9	10	11
	12	13	14	15	16	17	18
	19	20	21	22	23	24	25
SHA'BĀN 1321	26	27[d]	28	29	1	2	3
	4	5	6	7	8	9	10
	11	12	13	14	15	16	17
	18	19	20	21	22	23	24
RAMAḌĀN 1321	25	26	27	28	29	1[e]	2
	3	4	5	6	7	8	9
	10	11	12	13	14	15	16
	17	18	19	20	21	22	23
	24	25	26	27	28	29	30
SHAWWĀL 1321	1[f]	2	3	4	5	6	7
	8	9	10	11	12	13	14

GREGORIAN 1903

Julian (Sun)	Sun	Mon	Tue	Wed	Thu	Fri	Sat	Month
Dec 15	*28*	29	30	31	1	2	3	JANUARY 1903
	4	5	6	7[a]	8	9	10	
Dec 29	*11*	12	13	14[b]	15	16	17	
	18	19	20	21	22	23	24	
Jan 12	*25*	26	27	28	29	30	31	
	1	2	3	4	5	6	7	FEBRUARY 1903
Jan 26	*8*	9	10	11	12	13	14	
	15	16	17	18	19	20	21	
Feb 9	*22*	23	24	25[c]	26	27	28	
	1	2	3	4	5	6	7	MARCH 1903
Feb 23	*8*[d]	9	10	11	12	13	14	
	15	16	17	18	19	20	21	
Mar 9	*22*	23	24	25	26	27	28	
	29	30	31	1	2	3	4	APRIL 1903
Mar 23	*5*	6	7	8	9	10	11	
	12[e]	13	14	15	16	17	18	
Apr 6	*19*[f]	20	21	22	23	24	25	
	26	27	28	29	30	1	2	MAY 1903
Apr 20	*3*	4	5	6	7	8	9	
	10	11	12	13	14	15	16	
May 4	*17*	18	19	20	21	22	23	
	24	25	26	27	28	29	30	
May 18	*31*	1	2	3	4	5	6	JUNE 1903
	7	8	9	10	11	12	13	
Jun 1	*14*	15	16	17	18	19	20	
	21	22	23	24	25	26	27	
Jun 15	*28*	29	30	1	2	3	4	JULY 1903
	5	6	7	8	9	10	11	
Jun 29	*12*	13	14	15	16	17	18	
	19	20	21	22	23	24	25	
Jul 13	*26*	27	28	29	30	31	1	AUGUST 1903
	2	3	4	5	6	7	8	
Jul 27	*9*	10	11	12	13	14	15	
	16	17	18	19	20	21	22	
Aug 10	*23*	24	25	26	27	28	29	
	30	31	1	2	3	4	5	SEPTEMBER 1903
Aug 24	*6*	7	8	9	10	11	12	
	13	14	15	16	17	18	19	
Sep 7	*20*	21	22	23	24	25	26	
	27	28	29	30	1	2	3	OCTOBER 1903
Sep 21	*4*	5	6	7	8	9	10	
	11	12	13	14	15	16	17	
Oct 5	*18*	19	20	21	22	23	24	
	25	26	27	28	29	30	31	
Oct 19	*1*	2	3	4	5	6	7	NOVEMBER 1903
	8	9	10	11	12	13	14	
Nov 2	*15*	16	17	18	19	20	21	
	22	23	24	25	26	27	28	
Nov 16	*29*[g]	30	1	2	3	4	5	DECEMBER 1903
	6	7	8	9	10	11	12	
Nov 30	*13*	14	15	16	17	18	19	
	20	21	22	23	24	25[h]	26	
Dec 14	*27*	28	29	30	31	1	2	

Persian: [a]New Year; [b]Sizdeh Bedar

Hindu Lunar: [a]New Year (Śobhana); [b]Birthday of Rāma; [c]Birthday of Krishna; [d]Ganēśa Chaturthī; [e]Dashara; [f]Diwali; [g]Birthday of Vishnu; [h]Night of Śiva; [i]Holi

Hindu Solar: [a]New Year (Rākshasa); [b]Pongal

Islamic: ‡Leap year; [a]New Year; [b]'Ashūrā'; [c]Prophet's Birthday; [d]Ascent of the Prophet; [e]Start of Ramaḍān; [f]'Id al-Fiṭr; [g]'Id al-'Aḍḥā

Gregorian: [a]Orthodox Christmas; [b]Julian New Year; [c]Ash Wednesday; [d]Feast of Orthodoxy; [e]Easter; [f]Orthodox Easter; [g]Advent; [h]Christmas

1904

GREGORIAN 1904‡								Lunar Phases	ISO WEEK	JULIAN DAY	HEBREW 5664/5665‡								Molad	CHINESE Guǐ-Mǎo‡/Jiǎ-Chén								Solar Term	COPTIC 1620/1621								ETHIOPIC 1896/1897
	Sun	Mon	Tue	Wed	Thu	Fri	Sat		(Mon)	(Sun noon)		Sun	Mon	Tue	Wed	Thu	Fri	Sat			Sun	Mon	Tue	Wed	Thu	Fri	Sat			Sun	Mon	Tue	Wed	Thu	Fri	Sat	
JANUARY 1904	◐	29	30	31	1[a]	2	28	2:22	53	2416476	TEVETH 5664	8	9	10	11	12	13	14		MONTH 11* Guǐ-Mǎo	9	10	11	12	13	14	15		KOIAK 1620	17	18	19	20	21	22	23	TĀKHŚĀŚ 1896
	○	4	5	6	7	8	◑	5:47 21:10	1	2416483		15	16	17	18	19	20	21			16	17	18	19	20	21	22	Xiǎo hán		24	25	26	27	28	29[c]	30	
	10	11	12	13	14	15	16		2	2416490		22	23	24	25	26	27	28			23	24	25	26	27	28	29		TÔBE 1620	1	2	3	4	5	6[d]	7	ṬER 1896
	●	18	19	20	21	22	23	15:47	3	2416497	SHEVAT 5664	29	1	2	3	4	5	6	Sun 23h 6m 14p	MONTH 12 Guǐ-Mǎo	1	2	3	4	5	6	7	Dà hán		8	9	10	11[e]	12	13	14	
	24	◐	26	27	28	29	30	20:41	4	2416504		7	8	9	10	11	12	13			8	9	10	11	12	13	14			15	16	17	18	19	20	21	
FEBRUARY 1904	31	○	2	3	4	5	6	16:33	5	2416511		14	15	16	17	18	19	20			15*	16	17	18	19	20	21	Lì chūn		22	23	24	25	26	27	28	
	7	◑	9	10	11	12	13	9:56	6	2416518		21	22	23	24	25	26	27			22	23	24	25	26	27	28		MESHIR 1620	29	30	1	2	3	4	5	YAKĀTIT 1896
	14	15	●	17	18	19	20	11:05	7	2416525	ADAR 5664	28	29	30	1	2	3	4	Tue 11h 50m 15p	MONTH 1 Jiǎ-Chén	29	30	1[a]	2	3	4	5	Yǔ shuǐ		6	7	8	9	10	11	12	
	21	22	23	◐	25	26	27	11:08	8	2416532		5	6	7	8	9	10	11			6	7	8	9	10	11	12			13	14	15	16	17	18	19	
	28	29	1	○	3	4	5	2:48	9	2416539		12	13	14[f]	15	16	17	18			13	14	15[b]	16	17	18	19			20	21	22	23	24	25	26	
MARCH 1904	6	7	8	◑	10	11	12	1:01	10	2416546		19	20	21	22	23	24	25			20	21	22	23	24	25	26	Jīng zhé	PAREMOTEP 1620	27	28	29	30	1	2	3	MAGĀBIT 1896
	13	14	15	16	●	18	19	5:39	11	2416553	NISAN 5664	26	27	28	29	1	2	3	Thu 0h 34m 16p	MONTH 2 Jiǎ-Chén	27	28	29	30	1	2	3			4	5	6	7	8	9	10	
	20	21[b]	22	23	◐	25	26	21:36	12	2416560		4	5	6	7	8	9	10			4	5	6	7	8	9	10	Chūn fēn		11	12	13	14	15	16	17	
	27	28	29	30	○	1	2	12:44	13	2416567		11	12	13	14	15[g]	16	17			11	12	13	14	15*	16	17			18	19	20	21	22	23	24	
APRIL 1904	3	4	5	6	◑	8	9	17:53	14	2416574		18	19	20	21	22	23	24			18	19	20[c]	21	22	23	24	Qīng míng	PARMOUTE 1620	25	26	27	28	29	30	1	MIYĀZYĀ 1896
	10	11	12	13	14	●	16	21:53	15	2416581	IYYAR 5664	25	26	27	28	29	30	1	Fri 13h 18m 17p	MONTH 3 Jiǎ-Chén	25	26	27	28	29	30	1			2[f]	3	4	5	6	7	8	
	17	18	19	20	21	22	◐	4:54	16	2416588		2	3	4	5	6	7	8			2	3	4	5	6	7	8	Gǔ yǔ		9	10	11	12	13	14	15	
	24	25	26	27	28	○	30	22:36	17	2416595		9	10	11	12	13	14	15			9	10	11	12	13	14	15			16	17	18	19	20	21	22	
MAY 1904	1	2	3	4	5	6	◑	11:50	18	2416602		16	17	18	19	20	21	22			16	17	18	19	20	21	22	Lì xià		23	24	25	26	27	28	29[g]	
	8	9	10	11	12	13	14		19	2416609		23	24	25	26	27	28	29			23	24	25	26	27	28	29		PASHONS 1620	30	1	2	3	4	5	6	GENBOT 1896
	●	16	17	18	19	20	21	10:58	20	2416616	SIVAN 5664	1	2	3	4	5	6[h]	7	Sun 2h 3m 0p	MONTH 4 Jiǎ-Chén	1	2	3	4	5	6	7	Xiǎo mǎn		7	8	9	10	11	12	13	
	◐	23	24	25	26	27	28	10:18	21	2416623		8	9	10	11	12	13	14			8	9	10	11	12	13	14			14	15	16	17	18	19	20	
	○	30	31	1	2	3	4	8:54	22	2416630		15	16	17	18	19	20	21			15	16*	17	18	19	20	21			21	22	23	24	25	26	27	
JUNE 1904	5	◑	7	8	9	10	11	5:53	23	2416637		22	23	24	25	26	27	28			22	23	24	25	26	27	28	Máng zhòng	PAÔNE 1620	28	29	30	1	2	3	4	SANĒ 1896
	12	●	14	15	16	17	18	21:10	24	2416644	TAMMUZ 5664	29	30	1	2	3	4	5	Mon 14h 47m 1p	MONTH 5 Jiǎ-Chén	29	30	1	2	3	4	5[d]			5	6	7	8	9	10	11	
	19	◐	21[c]	22	23	24	25	15:10	25	2416651		6	7	8	9	10	11	12			6	7	8	9	10	11	12	Xià zhì		12	13	14	15	16	17	18	
	26	○	28	29	30	1	2	20:23	26	2416658		13	14	15	16	17	18	19			13	14	15	16	17	18	19			19	20	21	22	23	24	25	
JULY 1904	3	4	◑	6	7	8	9	22:54	27	2416665		20	21	22	23	24	25	26			20	21	22	23	24	25	26	Xiǎo shǔ	EPÊP 1620	26	27	28	29	30	1	2	ḤAMLĒ 1896
	10	11	12	●	14	15	16	5:27	28	2416672	AV 5664	27	28	29	1	2	3	4	Wed 3h 31m 2p	MONTH 6 Jiǎ-Chén	27	28	29	1	2	3	4			3	4	5	6	7	8	9	
	17	18	◐	20	21	22	23	20:48	29	2416679		5	6	7	8	9[i]	10	11			5	6	7	8	9	10	11	Dà shǔ		10	11	12	13	14	15	16	
	24	25	26	○	28	29	30	9:42	30	2416686		12	13	14	15	16	17	18			12	13	14	15	16	17*	18			17	18	19	20	21	22	23	
AUGUST 1904	31	1	2	3	◑	5	6	14:03	31	2416693		19	20	21	22	23	24	25			19	20	21	22	23	24	25			24	25	26	27	28	29	30	
	7	8	9	10	●	12	13	12:58	32	2416700	ELUL 5664	26	27	28	29	30	1	2	Thu 16h 15m 3p	MONTH 7 Jiǎ-Chén	26	27	28	29	1	2	3	Lì qiū	MESORÊ 1620	1	2	3	4	5	6	7	NAHASĒ 1896
	14	15	16	17	◐	19	20	4:27	33	2416707		3	4	5	6	7	8	9			4	5	6	7[e]	8	9	10			8	9	10	11	12	13[h]	14	
	21	22	23	24	25	○	27	1:02	34	2416714		10	11	12	13	14	15	16			11	12	13	14	15[f]	16	17	Chǔ shǔ		15	16	17	18	19	20	21	
	28	29	30	31	1	2	◑	2:58	35	2416721		17	18	19	20	21	22	23			18	19	20	21	22	23	24			22	23	24	25	26	27	28	
SEPTEMBER 1904	4	5	6	7	8	●	10	20:43	36	2416728	TISHRI 5665	24	25	26	27	28	29	1[a]	Sat 4h 59m 4p	MONTH 8 Jiǎ-Chén	25	26	27	28	29	30	1	Bái lù	EPAG. 1620	29	30	1	2	3	4	5	PĀG. 1896
	11	12	13	14	15	◐	17	15:13	37	2416735		2[a]	3	4	5	6	7	8			2	3	4	5	6	7	8		THOOUT 1621	1[a]	2	3	4	5	6	7	MASKARAM 1897
	18	19	20	21	22	23[d]	○	17:50	38	2416742		9	10[b]	11	12	13	14	15[c]			9	10	11	12	13	14	15[g]	Qiū fēn		8	9	10	11	12	13	14	
	25	26	27	28	29	30	1		39	2416749		16	17	18	19	20	21	22			16	17	18*	19	20	21	22			15	16	17[b]	18	19	20	21	
OCTOBER 1904	◑	3	4	5	6	7	8	13:52	40	2416756		23	24	25	26	27	28	29			23	24	25	26	27	28	29			22	23	24	25	26	27	28	
	●	10	11	12	13	14	15	5:25	41	2416763	ḤESHVAN 5665	30	1	2	3	4	5	6	Sun 17h 43m 5p	MONTH 9 Jiǎ-Chén	1	2	3	4	5	6	7	Hán lù	PAOPE 1621	29	30	1	2	3	4	5	ṬEQEMT 1897
	◐	17	18	19	20	21	22	5:54	42	2416770		7	8	9	10	11	12	13			8	9[h]	10	11	12	13	14			6	7	8	9	10	11	12	
	23	○	25	26	27	28	29	10:56	43	2416777		14	15	16	17	18	19	20			15	16	17	18	19	20	21	Shuāng jiàng		13	14	15	16	17	18	19	
	30	◑	1	2	3	4	5	23:13	44	2416784		21	22	23	24	25	26	27			22	23	24	25	26	27	28			20	21	22	23	24	25	26	
NOVEMBER 1904	6	●	8	9	10	11	12	15:37	45	2416791	KISLEV 5665	28	29	30	1	2	3	4	Tue 6h 27m 6p	MONTH 10 Jiǎ-Chén	29	1	2	3	4	5	6	Lì dōng	ATHÔR 1621	27	28	29	30	1	2	3	ḪEDĀR 1897
	13	14	◐	16	17	18	19	0:35	46	2416798		5	6	7	8	9	10	11			7	8	9	10	11	12	13			4	5	6	7	8	9	10	
	20	21	22	○	24	25	26	3:12	47	2416805		12	13	14	15	16	17	18			14	15	16	17	18	19	20*	Xiǎo xuě		11	12	13	14	15	16	17	
	27	28	29	◑	1	2	3	7:38	48	2416812		19	20	21	22	23	24	25[e]			21	22	23	24	25	26	27			18	19	20	21	22	23	24	
DECEMBER 1904	4	5	6	●	8	9	10	3:46	49	2416819	TEVETH 5665	26[e]	27[d,e]	28[e]	29[e]	30[e]	1[e]	2[e]	Wed 19h 11m 7p	MONTH 11 Jiǎ-Chén	28	29	30	1	2	3	4	Dà xuě	KOIAK 1621	25	26	27	28	29	30	1	TĀKHŚĀŚ 1897
	11	12	13	◐	15	16	17	22:07	50	2416826		3	4	5	6	7	8	9			5	6	7	8	9	10	11			2	3	4	5	6	7	8	
	18	19	20	21	○[e]	23	24	18:01	51	2416833		10	11	12	13	14	15	16			12	13	14	15	16[i]	17	18	Dōng zhì		9	10	11	12	13	14	15	
	25	26	27	28	◑	30	31	15:46	52	2416840		17	18	19	20	21	22	23			19	20	21	22	23	24	25			16	17	18	19	20	21	22	

‡Leap year
[a]New Year
[b]Spring (0:58)
[c]Summer (20:51)
[d]Autumn (11:40)
[e]Winter (6:14)
● New moon
◐ First quarter moon
○ Full moon
◑ Last quarter moon

‡Leap year
[a]New Year
[b]Yom Kippur
[c]Sukkot
[d]Winter starts
[e]Ḥanukkah
[f]Purim
[g]Passover
[h]Shavuot
[i]Fast of Av

‡Leap year
[a]New Year (4602, Dragon)
[b]Lantern Festival
[c]Qīngmíng
[d]Dragon Festival
[e]Qīqiǎo
[f]Hungry Ghosts
[g]Mid-Autumn Festival
[h]Double-Ninth Festival
[i]Dōngzhì
*Start of 60-name cycle

[a]New Year
[b]Building of the Cross
[c]Christmas
[d]Jesus's Circumcision
[e]Epiphany
[f]Easter
[g]Mary's Announcement
[h]Jesus's Transfiguration

PERSIAN (ASTRONOMICAL) 1282/1283

Month	Sun	Mon	Tue	Wed	Thu	Fri	Sat
	5	6	7	8	9	10	11
DEY 1282	12	13	14	15	16	17	18
	19	20	21	22	23	24	25
	26	27	28	29	30	*1*	2
	3	4	5	6	7	8	9
BAHMAN 1282	10	11	12	13	14	15	16
	17	18	19	20	21	22	23
	24	25	26	27	28	29	30
	1	2	3	4	5	6	7
ESFAND 1282	8	9	10	11	12	13	14
	15	16	17	18	19	20	21
	22	23	24	25	26	27	28
	29	*1*[a]	2	3	4	5	6
FARVARDĪN 1283	7	8	9	10	11	12	13[b]
	14	15	16	17	18	19	20
	21	22	23	24	25	26	27
	28	29	30	31	*1*	2	3
ORDĪBEHEŠT 1283	4	5	6	7	8	9	10
	11	12	13	14	15	16	17
	18	19	20	21	22	23	24
	25	26	27	28	29	30	31
	1	2	3	4	5	6	7
XORDĀD 1283	8	9	10	11	12	13	14
	15	16	17	18	19	20	21
	22	23	24	25	26	27	28
	29	30	31	*1*	2	3	4
TĪR 1283	5	6	7	8	9	10	11
	12	13	14	15	16	17	18
	19	20	21	22	23	24	25
	26	27	28	29	30	31	*1*
	2	3	4	5	6	7	8
MORDĀD 1283	9	10	11	12	13	14	15
	16	17	18	19	20	21	22
	23	24	25	26	27	28	29
	30	31	*1*	2	3	4	5
SHAHRĪVAR 1283	6	7	8	9	10	11	12
	13	14	15	16	17	18	19
	20	21	22	23	24	25	26
	27	28	29	30	31	*1*	2
	3	4	5	6	7	8	9
MEHR 1283	10	11	12	13	14	15	16
	17	18	19	20	21	22	23
	24	25	26	27	28	29	30
	1	2	3	4	5	6	7
ĀBĀN 1283	8	9	10	11	12	13	14
	15	16	17	18	19	20	21
	22	23	24	25	26	27	28
	29	30	*1*	2	3	4	5
ĀZAR 1283	6	7	8	9	10	11	12
	13	14	15	16	17	18	19
	20	21	22	23	24	25	26
DEY 1283	27	28	29	30	*1*	2	3
	4	5	6	7	8	9	10

[a]New Year
[b]Sizdeh Bedar

HINDU LUNAR 1960/1961‡

Month	Sun	Mon	Tue	Wed	Thu	Fri	Sat
	8	9	10	11	12	13	14
PAUSHA 1960	15	16	**17**	19	20	21	22
	23	24	25	26	27	28	29
	30	1	2	3	4	5	6
MĀGHA 1960	*6*	7	8	9	**10**	12	13
	14	15	16	17	18	19	20
	21	22	23	24	25	26	27
	28[h]	29	30	1	2	3	4
PHĀLGUNA 1960	5	6	7	8	9	10	11
	12	13	14	**15**[i]	17	18	19
	20	21	22	23	24	25	26
	27	28	*28*	29	30	1[a]	2
CHAITRA 1961	3	4	5	6	7	8[b]	**9**
	11	12	13	14	15	16	17
	18	19	20	21	22	23	24
	25	26	27	28	29	30	1
VAIŚĀKHA 1961	2	3	4	5	6	7	8
	9	10	11	12	**13**	15	16
	17	18	19	20	21	22	23
	23	24	25	26	27	28	29
	30	1	2	3	4	5	**6**
LEAP JYAISHTHA 1961	8	9	10	11	12	13	14
	15	16	17	18	19	20	21
	22	23	24	25	26	27	28
	29	30	1	2	3	4	5
JYAISHTHA 1961	6	7	8	**9**	11	12	13
	14	15	16	17	18	19	*19*
	20	21	22	23	24	25	26
	27	28	29	30	1	**2**	4
ĀSHĀḌHA 1961	5	6	7	8	9	10	11
	12	13	14	15	16	17	18
	19	20	21	22	23	24	25
	26	27	28	29	30	1	2
ŚRĀVAṆA 1961	3	4	**5**	7	8	9	10
	11	12	13	14	15	16	*16*
	17	18	19	20	21	22	23[c]
	24	25	26	27	**28**	30	1
BHĀDRAPADA 1961	2	3	4[d]	5	6	7	8
	9	10	11	12	13	14	15
	16	17	18	19	20	21	22
	23	24	25	26	27	28	29
	30	1	**2**	4	5	6	7
ĀŚVINA 1961	8[e]	9[e]	10[e]	11	*11*	12	13
	14	15	16	17	18	19	20
	21	22	23	24	**25**	27	28
	29	30	1[f]	2	3	4	5
KĀRTTIKA 1961	6	7	8	9	10	11	12
	13	14	*14*	15	16	17	**18**
	20	21	22	23	24	25	26
	27	28	29	30	1	2	3
MĀRGAŚĪRA 1961	4	5	6	7	8	9	10
	11[g]	12	13	14	15	16	17
	18	19	20	21	22	**23**	25

‡Leap year
[a]New Year (Krodhin)
[b]Birthday of Rāma
[c]Birthday of Krishna
[d]Ganēśa Chaturthī
[e]Dashara
[f]Diwali
[g]Birthday of Vishnu
[h]Night of Śiva
[i]Holi

HINDU SOLAR 1825/1826

Month	Sun	Mon	Tue	Wed	Thu	Fri	Sat
	13	14	15	16	17	18	19
PAUSHA 1825	20	21	22	23	24	25	26
	27	28	29	1[b]	2	3	4
	5	6	7	8	9	10	11
MĀGHA 1825	12	13	14	15	16	17	18
	19	20	21	22	23	24	25
	26	27	28	29	30	1	2
	3	4	5	6	7	8	9
PHĀLGUNA 1825	10	11	12	13	14	15	16
	17	18	19	20	21	22	23
	24	25	26	27	28	29	30
	1	2	3	4	5	6	7
	8	9	10	11	12	13	14
CHAITRA 1825	15	16	17	18	19	20	21
	22	23	24	25	26	27	28
	29	30	1[a]	2	3	4	5
	6	7	8	9	10	11	12
VAIŚĀKHA 1826	13	14	15	16	17	18	19
	20	21	22	23	24	25	26
	27	28	29	30	31	1	2
	3	4	5	6	7	8	9
JYAISHTHA 1826	10	11	12	13	14	15	16
	17	18	19	20	21	22	23
	24	25	26	27	28	29	30
	31	32	1	2	3	4	5
	6	7	8	9	10	11	12
ĀSHĀḌHA 1826	13	14	15	16	17	18	19
	20	21	22	23	24	25	26
	27	28	29	30	31	1	2
	3	4	5	6	7	8	9
ŚRĀVAṆA 1826	10	11	12	13	14	15	16
	17	18	19	20	21	22	23
	24	25	26	27	28	29	30
	31	32	1	2	3	4	5
	6	7	8	9	10	11	12
BHĀDRAPADA 1826	13	14	15	16	17	18	19
	20	21	22	23	24	25	26
	27	28	29	30	31	1	2
	3	4	5	6	7	8	9
ĀŚVINA 1826	10	11	12	13	14	15	16
	17	18	19	20	21	22	23
	24	25	26	27	28	29	30
	1	2	3	4	5	6	7
	8	9	10	11	12	13	14
KĀRTTIKA 1826	15	16	17	18	19	20	21
	22	23	24	25	26	27	28
	29	30	1	2	3	4	5
MĀRGAŚĪRA 1826	6	7	8	9	10	11	12
	13	14	15	16	17	18	19
	20	21	22	23	24	25	26
	27	28	29	1	2	3	4
PAUSHA 1826	5	6	7	8	9	10	11
	12	13	14	15	16	17	18

[a]New Year (Anala)
[b]Pongal

ISLAMIC (ASTRONOMICAL) 1321‡/1322

Month	Sun	Mon	Tue	Wed	Thu	Fri	Sat
	8	9	10	11	12	13	14
SHAWWĀL 1321	15	16	17	18	19	20	21
	22	23	24	25	26	27	28
	29	30	*1*	2	3	4	5
	6	7	8	9	10	11	12
DHU AL-QA'DA 1321	13	14	15	16	17	18	19
	20	21	22	23	24	25	26
	27	28	29	30	*1*	2	3
	4	5	6	7	8	9	10[g]
DHU AL-ḤIJJA 1321	11	12	13	14	15	16	17
	18	19	20	21	22	23	24
	25	26	27	28	29	30[d]	1[a]
	2	3	4	5	6	7	8
MUḤARRAM 1322	9	10[b]	11	12	13	14	15
	16	17	18	19	20	21	22
	23	24	25	26	27	28	29
	1	2	3	4	5	6	7
ṢAFAR 1322	8	9	10	11	12	13	14
	15	16	17	18	19	20	21
	22	23	24	25	26	27	28
	29	30	1	2	3	4	5
	6	7	8	9	10	11	12[c]
RABĪ' I 1322	13	14	15	16	17	18	19
	20	21	22	23	24	25	26
	27	28	29	*1*	2	3	4
	5	6	7	8	9	10	11
RABĪ' II 1322	12	13	14	15	16	17	18
	19	20	21	22	23	24	25
	26	27	28	29	*30*	1	2
	3	4	5	6	7	8	9
JUMĀDĀ I 1322	10	11	12	13	14	15	16
	17	18	19	20	21	22	23
	24	25	26	27	28	29	*1*
	2	3	4	5	6	7	8
JUMĀDĀ II 1322	9	10	11	12	13	14	15
	16	17	18	19	20	21	22
	23	24	25	26	27	28	29
	1	2	3	4	5	6	7
	8	9	10	11	12	13	14
RAJAB 1322	15	16	17	18	19	20	21
	22	23	24	25	26	27[d]	28
	29	1	2	3	4	5	6
	7	8	9	10	11	12	13
SHA'BĀN 1322	14	15	16	17	18	19	20
	21	22	23	24	25	26	27
	28	29	30	*1*[e]	2	3	4
	5	6	7	8	9	10	11
RAMAḌĀN 1322	12	13	14	15	16	17	18
	19	20	21	22	23	24	25
	26	27	28	29	1[f]	2	3
SHAWWĀL 1322	4	5	6	7	8	9	10
	11	12	13	14	15	16	17
	18	19	20	21	22	23	24

‡Leap year
[a]New Year
[d]New Year (Arithmetic)
[b]'Ashūrā'
[c]Prophet's Birthday
[d]Ascent of the Prophet
[e]Start of Ramaḍān
[f]'Id al-Fiṭr
[g]'Id al-'Aḍḥā

GREGORIAN 1904‡

Julian† (Sun)	Sun	Mon	Tue	Wed	Thu	Fri	Sat	Month
Dec 14	*27*	28	29	30	31	1	2	
	3	4	5	6	7[a]	8	9	JANUARY 1904
Dec 28	*10*	11	12	13	14[b]	15	16	
	17	18	19	20	21	22	23	
Jan 11	*24*	25	26	27	28	29	30	
	31	1	2	3	4	5	6	
Jan 25	*7*	8	9	10	11	12	13	FEBRUARY 1904
	14	15	16	17[c]	18	19	20	
Feb 8	*21*	22	23	24	25	26	27	
	28[d]	29	1	2	3	4	5	
Feb 22	*6*	7	8	9	10	11	12	MARCH 1904
	13	14	15	16	17	18	19	
Mar 7	*20*	21	22	23	24	25	26	
	27	28	29	30	31	1	2	
Mar 21	*3*[e]	4	5	6	7	8	9	APRIL 1904
	10[f]	11	12	13	14	15	16	
Apr 4	*17*	18	19	20	21	22	23	
	24	25	26	27	28	29	30	
Apr 18	*1*	2	3	4	5	6	7	
	8	9	10	11	12	13	14	MAY 1904
May 2	*15*	16	17	18	19	20	21	
	22	23	24	25	26	27	28	
May 16	*29*	30	31	1	2	3	4	
	5	6	7	8	9	10	11	JUNE 1904
May 30	*12*	13	14	15	16	17	18	
	19	20	21	22	23	24	25	
Jun 13	*26*	27	28	29	30	1	2	
	3	4	5	6	7	8	9	JULY 1904
Jun 27	*10*	11	12	13	14	15	16	
	17	18	19	20	21	22	23	
Jul 11	*24*	25	26	27	28	29	30	
	31	1	2	3	4	5	6	
Jul 25	*7*	8	9	10	11	12	13	AUGUST 1904
	14	15	16	17	18	19	20	
Aug 8	*21*	22	23	24	25	26	27	
	28	29	30	31	1	2	3	
Aug 22	*4*	5	6	7	8	9	10	SEPTEMBER 1904
	11	12	13	14	15	16	17	
Sep 5	*18*	19	20	21	22	23	24	
	25	26	27	28	29	30	1	
Sep 19	*2*	3	4	5	6	7	8	OCTOBER 1904
	9	10	11	12	13	14	15	
Oct 3	*16*	17	18	19	20	21	22	
	23	24	25	26	27	28	29	
Oct 17	*30*	31	1	2	3	4	5	
	6	7	8	9	10	11	12	NOVEMBER 1904
Oct 31	*13*	14	15	16	17	18	19	
	20	21	22	23	24	25	26	
Nov 14	27[g]	28	29	30	1	2	3	
	4	5	6	7	8	9	10	DECEMBER 1904
Nov 28	*11*	12	13	14	15	16	17	
	18	19	20	21	22	23	24	
Dec 12	25[h]	26	27	28	29	30	31	

‡Leap year
[a]Orthodox Christmas
[b]Julian New Year
[c]Ash Wednesday
[d]Feast of Orthodoxy
[e]Easter
[f]Orthodox Easter
[g]Advent
[h]Christmas

1905

Gregorian 1905 / ISO week / Julian day

Month	Sun	Mon	Tue	Wed	Thu	Fri	Sat	Lunar Phases	ISO Week (Mon)	Julian Day (Sun noon)
January 1905	1[a]	2	3	4	●	6	7	18:17	1	2416847
	8	9	10	11	12	◐	14	20:11	2	2416854
	15	16	17	18	19	20	○	7:14	3	2416861
	22	23	24	25	26	27	◑	0:20	4	2416868
February 1905	29	30	31	1	2	3	●	11:06	5	2416875
	5	6	7	8	9	10	11		6	2416882
	◐	13	14	15	16	17	18	16:20	7	2416889
	○	20	21	22	23	24	25	18:52	8	2416896
March 1905	◑	27	28	1	2	3	4	10:04	9	2416903
	5	●	7	8	9	10	11	5:19	10	2416910
	12	13	◐	15	16	17	18	8:59	11	2416917
	19	20	○[b]	22	23	24	25	4:55	12	2416924
April 1905	26	◑	28	29	30	31	1	21:35	13	2416931
	2	3	●	5	6	7	8	23:23	14	2416938
	9	10	11	◐	13	14	15	21:41	15	2416945
	16	17	18	○	20	21	22	13:38	16	2416952
	23	24	25	◑	27	28	29	11:14	17	2416959
May 1905	30	1	2	3	●	5	6	15:50	18	2416966
	7	8	9	10	11	◐	13	6:46	19	2416973
	14	15	16	17	○	19	20	21:36	20	2416980
	21	22	23	24	25	◑	27	2:50	21	2416987
June 1905	28	29	30	31	1	2	●	5:56	22	2416994
	4	5	6	7	8	9	◐	13:04	23	2417001
	11	12	13	14	15	16	○	5:51	24	2417008
	18	19	20	21	22[c]	23	◑	19:46	25	2417015
July 1905	25	26	27	28	29	30	1		26	2417022
	●	3	4	5	6	7	8	17:50	27	2417029
	◐	10	11	12	13	14	15	17:46	28	2417036
	○	17	18	19	20	21	22	15:32	29	2417043
	23	◑	25	26	27	28	29	13:08	30	2417050
August 1905	30	31	●	2	3	4	5	4:02	31	2417057
	6	◐	8	9	10	11	12	22:16	32	2417064
	13	14	○	16	17	18	19	3:31	33	2417071
	20	21	22	◑	24	25	26	6:10	34	2417078
September 1905	27	28	29	●	31	1	2	13:13	35	2417085
	3	4	5	◐	7	8	9	4:09	36	2417092
	10	11	12	○	14	15	16	18:10	37	2417099
	17	18	19	20	◑	22	23[d]	22:13	38	2417106
	24	25	26	27	●	29	30	21:59	39	2417113
October 1905	1	2	3	4	◐	6	7	12:54	40	2417120
	8	9	10	11	12	○	14	11:02	41	2417127
	15	16	17	18	19	20	◑	12:50	42	2417134
	22	23	24	25	26	27	●	6:58	43	2417141
November 1905	29	30	31	1	2	3	◐	1:39	44	2417148
	5	6	7	8	9	10	11		45	2417155
	○	13	14	15	16	17	18	5:11	46	2417162
	19	◑	21	22	23	24	25	1:34	47	2417169
December 1905	●	27	28	29	30	1	2	16:47	48	2417176
	◐	4	5	6	7	8	9	18:37	49	2417183
	10	○	12	13	14	15	16	23:25	50	2417190
	17	18	◑	20	21	22[e]	23	12:09	51	2417197
	24	25	●	27	28	29	30	4:04	52	2417204
	31	1	◐	3	4	5	6	14:52	1	2417211

Hebrew 5665‡/5666

ISO Week	Month	Sun	Mon	Tue	Wed	Thu	Fri	Sat	Molad
1	Shevat 5665	24	25	26	27	28	29	1	Fri 7h55m8p
2		2	3	4	5	6	7	8	
3		9	10	11	12	13	14	15	
4		16	17	18	19	20	21	22	
5		23	24	25	26	27	28	29	Sat 20h39m9p
6	Adar I 5665	30	1	2	3	4	5	6	
7		7	8	9	10	11	12	13	
8		14	15	16	17	18	19	20	
9		21	22	23	24	25	26	27	Mon 9h23m10p
10	Adar II 5665	28	29	30	1	2	3	4	
11		5	6	7	8	9	10	11	
12		12	13	14[f]	15	16	17	18	
13		19	20	21	22	23	24	25	Tue 22h7m11p
14	Nisan 5665	26	27	28	29	1	2	3	
15		4	5	6	7	8	9	10	
16		11	12	13	14	15[g]	16	17	
17		18	19	20	21	22	23	24	Thu 10h51m12p
18	Iyar 5665	25	26	27	28	29	30	1	
19		2	3	4	5	6	7	8	
20		9	10	11	12	13	14	15	
21		16	17	18	19	20	21	22	
22		23	24	25	26	27	28	29	Fri 23h35m13p
23	Sivan 5665	1	2	3	4	5	6[h]	7	
24		8	9	10	11	12	13	14	
25		15	16	17	18	19	20	21	
26		22	23	24	25	26	27	28	Sun 12h19m14p
27	Tammuz 5665	29	30	1	2	3	4	5	
28		6	7	8	9	10	11	12	
29		13	14	15	16	17	18	19	
30		20	21	22	23	24	25	26	Tue 1h3m15p
31	Av 5665	27	28	29	1	2	3	4	
32		5	6	7	8	9[i]	10	11	
33		12	13	14	15	16	17	18	
34		19	20	21	22	23	24	25	Wed 13h47m16p
35	Elul 5665	26	27	28	29	30	1	2	
36		3	4	5	6	7	8	9	
37		10	11	12	13	14	15	16	
38		17	18	19	20	21	22	23	Fri 2h31m17p
39	Tishri 5666	24	25	26	27	28	29	1[a]	
40		2[a]	3	4	5	6	7	8	
41		9	10[b]	11	12	13	14	15[c]	
42		16	17	18	19	20	21	22	
43		23	24	25	26	27	28	29	Sat 15h16m0p
44	Heshvan 5666	30	1	2	3	4	5	6	
45		7	8	9	10	11	12	13	
46		14	15	16	17	18	19	20	
47		21	22	23	24	25	26	27	Mon 4h0m1p
48	Kislev 5666	28	29	30	1	2	3	4	
49		5	6	7[d]	8	9	10	11	
50		12	13	14	15	16	17	18	
51		19	20	21	22	23	24	25[e]	Tue 16h44m2p
52	Teveth 5666	26[e]	27[e]	28[e]	29[e]	30[e]	1[e]	2[e]	
1		3	4	5	6	7	8	9	

Chinese Jiă-Chén/Yĭ-Sì

ISO Week	Month	Sun	Mon	Tue	Wed	Thu	Fri	Sat	Solar Term
1	Month 12 Jiă-Chén	26	27	28	29	30	1	2	Xiăo hán
2		3	4	5	6	7	8	9	
3		10	11	12	13	14	15	16	Dà hán
4		17	18	19	20*	21	22	23	
5	Month 1 Yĭ-Sì	24	25	26	27	28	29	1[a]	Lì chūn
6		2	3	4	5	6	7	8	
7		9	10	11	12	13	14	15[b]	
8		16	17	18	19	20	21	22	Yŭ shuĭ
9		23	24	25	26	27	28	29	
10	Month 2 Yĭ-Sì	30	1	2	3	4	5	6	Jīng zhé
11		7	8	9	10	11	12	13	
12		14	15	16	17	18	19	20	Chūn fēn
13		21*	22	23	24	25	26	27	
14	Month 3 Yĭ-Sì	28	29	30	1[c]	2	3	4	Qīng míng
15		5	6	7	8	9	10	11	
16		12	13	14	15	16	17	18	Gŭ yŭ
17		19	20	21	22	23	24	25	
18	Month 4 Yĭ-Sì	26	27	28	29	1	2	3	Lì xià
19		4	5	6	7	8	9	10	
20		11	12	13	14	15	16	17	
21		18	19	20	21	22*	23	24	Xiăo măn
22	Month 5 Yĭ-Sì	25	26	27	28	29	30	1	
23		2	3	4	5[d]	6	7	8	Máng zhòng
24		9	10	11	12	13	14	15	
25		16	17	18	19	20	21	22	Xià zhì
26		23	24	25	26	27	28	29	
27	Month 6 Yĭ-Sì	30	1	2	3	4	5	6	Xiăo shŭ
28		7	8	9	10	11	12	13	
29		14	15	16	17	18	19	20	
30		21	22*	23	24	25	26	27	Dà shŭ
31	Month 7 Yĭ-Sì	28	29	1	2	3	4	5	
32		6	7[e]	8	9	10	11	12	Lì qiū
33		13	14	15[f]	16	17	18	19	
34		20	21	22	23	24	25	26	Chŭ shŭ
35	Month 8 Yĭ-Sì	27	28	29	1	2	3	4	
36		5	6	7	8	9	10	11	Bái lù
37		12	13	14	15[g]	16	17	18	
38		19	20	21	22	23	24*	25	
39	Month 9 Yĭ-Sì	26	27	28	29	30	1	2	Qiū fēn
40		3	4	5	6	7	8	9[h]	
41		10	11	12	13	14	15	16	Hán lù
42		17	18	19	20	21	22	23	
43	Month 10 Yĭ-Sì	24	25	26	27	28	29	1	Shuāng jiàng
44		2	3	4	5	6	7	8	
45		9	10	11	12	13	14	15	Lì dōng
46		16	17	18	19	20	21	22	
47		23	24	25*	26	27	28	29	Xiăo xuě
48	Month 11 Yĭ-Sì	30	1	2	3	4	5	6	
49		7	8	9	10	11	12	13	Dà xuě
50		14	15	16	17	18	19	20	
51		21	22	23	24	25	26[i]	27	Dōng zhì
52	Month 12 Yĭ-Sì	28	29	1	2	3	4	5	
1		6	7	8	9	10	11	12	Xiăo hán

Coptic 1621/1622 – Ethiopic 1897/1898

ISO Week	Coptic Month	Sun	Mon	Tue	Wed	Thu	Fri	Sat	Ethiopic Month
1	Koiak 1621	23	24	25	26	27	28	29[c]	Tāḫśāś 1897
2	Tōbe 1621	30	1	2	3	4	5	6[d]	Ṭer 1897
3		7	8	9	10	11[e]	12	13	
4		14	15	16	17	18	19	20	
5		21	22	23	24	25	26	27	
6	Meshir 1621	28	29	30	1	2	3	4	Yakātit 1897
7		5	6	7	8	9	10	11	
8		12	13	14	15	16	17	18	
9		19	20	21	22	23	24	25	
10	Paremotep 1621	26	27	28	29	30	1	2	Magābit 1897
11		3	4	5	6	7	8	9	
12		10	11	12	13	14	15	16	
13		17	18	19	20	21	22	23	
14		24	25	26	27	28	29	30	
15	Parmoute 1621	1	2	3	4	5	6	7	Miyāzyā 1897
16		8	9	10	11	12	13	14	
17		15	16	17	18	19	20	21	
18		22[f]	23	24	25	26	27	28	
19	Pashons 1621	29[g]	30	1	2	3	4	5	Genbot 1897
20		6	7	8	9	10	11	12	
21		13	14	15	16	17	18	19	
22		20	21	22	23	24	25	26	
23	Paōne 1621	27	28	29	30	1	2	3	Sanē 1897
24		4	5	6	7	8	9	10	
25		11	12	13	14	15	16	17	
26		18	19	20	21	22	23	24	
27	Epēp 1621	25	26	27	28	29	30	1	Ḥamlē 1897
28		2	3	4	5	6	7	8	
29		9	10	11	12	13	14	15	
30		16	17	18	19	20	21	22	
31		23	24	25	26	27	28	29	
32	Mesorē 1621	30	1	2	3	4	5	6	Naḥasē 1897
33		7	8	9	10	11	12	13[h]	
34		14	15	16	17	18	19	20	
35		21	22	23	24	25	26	27	
36	Epag. 1621	28	29	30	1	2	3	4	Pāg. 1897
37	Thoout 1622	5	1[a]	2	3	4	5	6	Maskaram 1898
38		7	8	9	10	11	12	13	
39		14	15	16	17[b]	18	19	20	
40		21	22	23	24	25	26	27	
41	Paope 1622	28	29	30	1	2	3	4	Ṭeqemt 1898
42		5	6	7	8	9	10	11	
43		12	13	14	15	16	17	18	
44		19	20	21	22	23	24	25	
45	Athōr 1622	26	27	28	29	30	1	2	Ḫedār 1898
46		3	4	5	6	7	8	9	
47		10	11	12	13	14	15	16	
48		17	18	19	20	21	22	23	
49		24	25	26	27	28	29	30	
50	Koiak 1622	1	2	3	4	5	6	7	Tāḫśāś 1898
51		8	9	10	11	12	13	14	
52		15	16	17	18	19	20	21	
1		22	23	24	25	26	27	28	

Gregorian notes:
[a]New Year
[b]Spring (6:57)
[c]Summer (2:52)
[d]Autumn (17:30)
[e]Winter (12:03)
● New moon
◐ First quarter moon
○ Full moon
◑ Last quarter moon

Hebrew notes:
‡Leap year
[a]New Year
[b]Yom Kippur
[c]Sukkot
[d]Winter starts
[e]Ḥanukkah
[f]Purim
[g]Passover
[h]Shavuot
[i]Fast of Av

Chinese notes:
[a]New Year (4603, Snake)
[b]Lantern Festival
[c]Qīngmíng
[d]Dragon Festival
[e]Qīqiăo
[f]Hungry Ghosts
[g]Mid-Autumn Festival
[h]Double-Ninth Festival
[i]Dōngzhì
*Start of 60-name cycle

Coptic/Ethiopic notes:
[a]New Year
[b]Building of the Cross
[c]Christmas
[d]Jesus's Circumcision
[e]Epiphany
[f]Easter
[g]Mary's Announcement
[h]Jesus's Transfiguration

1905

PERSIAN (ASTRONOMICAL) 1283/1284‡

Month	Sun	Mon	Tue	Wed	Thu	Fri	Sat
	11	12	13	14	15	16	17
DEY 1283	18	19	20	21	22	23	24
	25	26	27	28	29	30	1
	2	3	4	5	6	7	8
BAHMAN 1283	9	10	11	12	13	14	15
	16	17	18	19	20	21	22
	23	24	25	26	27	28	29
	30	1	2	3	4	5	6
	7	8	9	10	11	12	13
ESFAND 1283	14	15	16	17	18	19	20
	21	22	23	24	25	26	27
	28	29	1[a]	2	3	4	5
	6	7	8	9	10	11	12
FARVARDĪN 1284	13[b]	14	15	16	17	18	19
	20	21	22	23	24	25	26
	27	28	29	30	31	1	2
	3	4	5	6	7	8	9
ORDĪBEHEŠT 1284	10	11	12	13	14	15	16
	17	18	19	20	21	22	23
	24	25	26	27	28	29	30
	31	1	2	3	4	5	6
XORDĀD 1284	7	8	9	10	11	12	13
	14	15	16	17	18	19	20
	21	22	23	24	25	26	27
	28	29	30	31	1	2	3
	4	5	6	7	8	9	10
TĪR 1284	11	12	13	14	15	16	17
	18	19	20	21	22	23	24
	25	26	27	28	29	30	31
	1	2	3	4	5	6	7
MORDĀD 1284	8	9	10	11	12	13	14
	15	16	17	18	19	20	21
	22	23	24	25	26	27	28
	29	30	31	1	2	3	4
	5	6	7	8	9	10	11
SHAHRĪVAR 1284	12	13	14	15	16	17	18
	19	20	21	22	23	24	25
	26	27	28	29	30	31	1
	2	3	4	5	6	7	8
MEHR 1284	9	10	11	12	13	14	15
	16	17	18	19	20	21	22
	23	24	25	26	27	28	29
	30	1	2	3	4	5	6
	7	8	9	10	11	12	13
ABĀN 1284	14	15	16	17	18	19	20
	21	22	23	24	25	26	27
	28	29	30	1	2	3	4
	5	6	7	8	9	10	11
ĀZAR 1284	12	13	14	15	16	17	18
	19	20	21	22	23	24	25
	26	27	28	29	30	1	2
DEY 1284	3	4	5	6	7	8	9
	10	11	12	13	14	15	16

HINDU LUNAR 1961‡/1962

Month	Sun	Mon	Tue	Wed	Thu	Fri	Sat
	26	27	28	29	30	1	2
PAUSHA 1961	3	4	5	6	6	7	8
	9	10	11	12	13	14	15
	16	17	**18**	20	21	22	23
	24	25	26	27	28	29	30
	1	2	3	4	5	6	7
MĀGHA 1961	8	9	10	11	12	13	14
	15	16	17	18	19	20	21
	22	**23**	25	26	27	28	28[h]
	29	30	1	2	3	4	5
	6	7	8	9	10	11	12
PHĀLGUNA 1961	13	14	15[i]	**16**	18	19	20
	21	22	23	24	25	26	27
	28	29	30	1[a]	2	2	3
	4	5	6	7	8[b]	9	**10**
CHAITRA 1962	12	13	14	15	16	17	18
	19	20	21	22	23	24	25
	26	27	28	29	30	1	2
	3	4	5	6	7	8	9
VAIŚĀKHA 1962	10	11	12	**13**	15	16	17
	18	19	20	21	22	23	24
	25	26	27	27	28	29	30
	1	2	3	4	5	**6**	8
	9	10	11	12	13	14	15
JYAISHṬHA 1962	16	17	18	19	20	21	22
	23	24	25	26	27	28	29
	30	1	2	3	4	5	6
	7	8	**9**	11	12	13	14
ĀSHĀḌHA 1962	15	16	17	18	19	20	21
	22	23	24	24	25	26	27
	28	29	30	1	**2**	4	5
	6	7	8	9	10	11	12
ŚRĀVAṆA 1962	13	14	15	16	17	18	19
	20	21	22	23[c]	24	25	26
	27	28	29	30	1	2	3
	4[d]	**5**	7	8	9	10	11
BHĀDRAPADA 1962	12	13	14	15	16	17	18
	19	20	20	21	22	23	24
	25	26	27	**28**	30	1	2
	3	4	5	6	7	8[e]	9[e]
ĀŚVINA 1962	10[e]	11	12	13	14	15	16
	17	18	19	20	21	22	23
	24	25	26	27	28	29	30
	1[f]	**2**	4	5	6	7	8
	9	10	11	12	13	14	14
KĀRTTIKA 1962	15	16	17	18	19	20	21
	22	23	24	25	**26**	28	29
	30	1	2	3	4	5	6
	7	8	9	10	11[g]	12	13
MĀRGAŚĪRA 1962	14	15	16	17	18	19	20
	21	22	23	24	25	26	27
	28	29	30	1	**2**	4	5
PAUSHA 1962	6	6	7	8	9	10	11

HINDU SOLAR 1826/1827‡

Month	Sun	Mon	Tue	Wed	Thu	Fri	Sat
PAUSHA 1826	19	20	21	22	23	24	25
	26	27	28	29	30	1[b]	2
MĀGHA 1826	3	4	5	6	7	8	9
	10	11	12	13	14	15	16
	17	18	19	20	21	22	23
	24	25	26	27	28	29	1
	2	3	4	5	6	7	8
PHĀLGUNA 1826	9	10	11	12	13	14	15
	16	17	18	19	20	21	22
	23	24	25	26	27	28	29
	30	1	2	3	4	5	6
	7	8	9	10	11	12	13
CHAITRA 1826	14	15	16	17	18	19	20
	21	22	23	24	25	26	27
	28	29	30	1[a]	2	3	4
	5	6	7	8	9	10	11
VAIŚĀKHA 1827	12	13	14	15	16	17	18
	19	20	21	22	23	24	25
	26	27	28	29	30	31	1
	2	3	4	5	6	7	8
JYAISHṬHA 1827	9	10	11	12	13	14	15
	16	17	18	19	20	21	22
	23	24	25	26	27	28	29
	30	31	32	1	2	3	4
	5	6	7	8	9	10	11
ĀSHĀḌHA 1827	12	13	14	15	16	17	18
	19	20	21	22	23	24	25
	26	27	28	29	30	31	1
	2	3	4	5	6	7	8
ŚRĀVAṆA 1827	9	10	11	12	13	14	15
	16	17	18	19	20	21	22
	23	24	25	26	27	28	29
	30	31	32	1	2	3	4
BHĀDRAPADA 1827	5	6	7	8	9	10	11
	12	13	14	15	16	17	18
	19	20	21	22	23	24	25
	26	27	28	29	30	31	1
ĀŚVINA 1827	2	3	4	5	6	7	8
	9	10	11	12	13	14	15
	16	17	18	19	20	21	22
	23	24	25	26	27	28	29
	30	1	2	3	4	5	6
KĀRTTIKA 1827	7	8	9	10	11	12	13
	14	15	16	17	18	19	20
	21	22	23	24	25	26	27
	28	29	30	1	2	3	4
	5	6	7	8	9	10	11
MĀRGAŚĪRA 1827	12	13	14	15	16	17	18
	19	20	21	22	23	24	25
	26	27	28	29	30	1	2
	3	4	5	6	7	8	9
PAUSHA 1827	10	11	12	13	14	15	16
	17	18	19	20	21	22	23

ISLAMIC (ASTRONOMICAL) 1322/1323

Month	Sun	Mon	Tue	Wed	Thu	Fri	Sat
	25	26	27	28	29	30	1
	2	3	4	5	6	7	8
DHU AL-QA'DA 1322	9	10	11	12	13	14	15
	16	17	18	19	20	21	22
	23	24	25	26	27	28	29
	30	1	2	3	4	5	6
DHU AL-ḤIJJA 1322	7	8	9	10[g]	11	12	13
	14	15	16	17	18	19	20
	21	22	23	24	25	26	27
	28	29	30	1[a]	2	3	4
	5	6	7	8	9	10[b]	11
MUḤARRAM 1323	12	13	14	15	16	17	18
	19	20	21	22	23	24	25
	26	27	28	29	1	2	3
	4	5	6	7	8	9	10
ṢAFAR 1323	11	12	13	14	15	16	17
	18	19	20	21	22	23	24
	25	26	27	28	29	30	1
	2	3	4	5	6	7	8
RABĪ' I 1323	9	10	11	12[c]	13	14	15
	16	17	18	19	20	21	22
	23	24	25	26	27	28	29
	30	1	2	3	4	5	6
	7	8	9	10	11	12	13
RABĪ' II 1323	14	15	16	17	18	19	20
	21	22	23	24	25	26	27
	28	29	1	2	3	4	5
	6	7	8	9	10	11	12
JUMĀDĀ I 1323	13	14	15	16	17	18	19
	20	21	22	23	24	25	26
	27	28	29	30	1	2	3
	4	5	6	7	8	9	10
JUMĀDĀ II 1323	11	12	13	14	15	16	17
	18	19	20	21	22	23	24
	25	26	27	28	29	1	2
	3	4	5	6	7	8	9
RAJAB 1323	10	11	12	13	14	15	16
	17	18	19	20	21	22	23
	24	25	26	27[d]	28	29	1
	2	3	4	5	6	7	8
SHA'BĀN 1323	9	10	11	12	13	14	15
	16	17	18	19	20	21	22
	23	24	25	26	27	28	29
	1[e]	2	3	4	5	6	7
	8	9	10	11	12	13	14
RAMAḌĀN 1323	15	16	17	18	19	20	21
	22	23	24	25	26	27	28
	29	30	1[f]	2	3	4	5
	6	7	8	9	10	11	12
SHAWWĀL 1323	13	14	15	16	17	18	19
	20	21	22	23	24	25	26
	27	28	29	1	2	3	4
DHU AL-QA'DA 1323	5	6	7	8	9	10	11

GREGORIAN 1905

Julian (Sun)	Sun	Mon	Tue	Wed	Thu	Fri	Sat	Month
Dec 19	1	2	3	4	5	6	7[a]	
	8	9	10	11	12	13	14[b]	
Jan 2	15	16	17	18	19	20	21	JANUARY 1905
	22	23	24	25	26	27	28	
Jan 16	29	30	31	1	2	3	4	
	5	6	7	8	9	10	11	
Jan 30	12	13	14	15	16	17	18	FEBRUARY 1905
	19	20	21	22	23	24	25	
Feb 13	26	27	28	1	2	3	4	
	5	6	7	8[c]	9	10	11	
Feb 27	12	13	14	15	16	17	18	MARCH 1905
	19[d]	20	21	22	23	24	25	
Mar 13	26	27	28	29	30	31	1	
	2	3	4	5	6	7	8	
Mar 27	9	10	11	12	13	14	15	APRIL 1905
	16	17	18	19	20	21	22	
Apr 10	23[e]	24	25	26	27	28	29	
	30[f]	1	2	3	4	5	6	
Apr 24	7	8	9	10	11	12	13	
	14	15	16	17	18	19	20	MAY 1905
May 8	21	22	23	24	25	26	27	
	28	29	30	31	1	2	3	
May 22	4	5	6	7	8	9	10	JUNE 1905
	11	12	13	14	15	16	17	
Jun 5	18	19	20	21	22	23	24	
	25	26	27	28	29	30	1	
Jun 19	2	3	4	5	6	7	8	
	9	10	11	12	13	14	15	JULY 1905
Jul 3	16	17	18	19	20	21	22	
	23	24	25	26	27	28	29	
Jul 17	30	31	1	2	3	4	5	
	6	7	8	9	10	11	12	
Jul 31	13	14	15	16	17	18	19	AUGUST 1905
	20	21	22	23	24	25	26	
Aug 14	27	28	29	30	31	1	2	
	3	4	5	6	7	8	9	
Aug 28	10	11	12	13	14	15	16	SEPTEMBER 1905
	17	18	19	20	21	22	23	
Sep 11	24	25	26	27	28	29	30	
	1	2	3	4	5	6	7	
Sep 25	8	9	10	11	12	13	14	OCTOBER 1905
	15	16	17	18	19	20	21	
Oct 9	22	23	24	25	26	27	28	
	29	30	31	1	2	3	4	
Oct 23	5	6	7	8	9	10	11	
	12	13	14	15	16	17	18	NOVEMBER 1905
Nov 6	19	20	21	22	23	24	25	
	26	27	28	29	30	1	2	
Nov 20	3[g]	4	5	6	7	8	9	
	10	11	12	13	14	15	16	DECEMBER 1905
Dec 4	17	18	19	20	21	22	23	
	24	25[h]	26	27	28	29	30	
Dec 18	31	1	2	3	4	5	6	

Persian: ‡Leap year; [a]New Year; [b]Sizdeh Bedar

Hindu Lunar: ‡Leap year; [a]New Year (Viśvāvasu); [b]Birthday of Rāma; [c]Birthday of Krishna; [d]Ganēśa Chaturthī; [e]Dashara; [f]Diwali; [g]Birthday of Vishnu; [h]Night of Śiva; [i]Holi

Hindu Solar: ‡Leap year; [a]New Year (Piṅgala); [b]Pongal

Islamic: [a]New Year; [b]'Ashūrā'; [c]Prophet's Birthday; [d]Ascent of the Prophet; [e]Start of Ramaḍān; [f]'Id al-Fiṭr; [g]'Id al-'Aḍḥā

Gregorian: [a]Orthodox Christmas; [b]Julian New Year; [c]Ash Wednesday; [d]Feast of Orthodoxy; [e]Easter; [f]Orthodox Easter; [g]Advent; [h]Christmas

1906

Gregorian 1906

ISO Week (Mon)	Julian Day (Sun noon)	Month	Sun	Mon	Tue	Wed	Thu	Fri	Sat	Lunar Phases
1	2417211	January 1906	31	1[a]	◐	3	4	5	6	14:52
2	2417218		7	8	9	○	11	12	13	16:36
3	2417225		14	15	16	◑	18	19	20	20:49
4	2417232		21	22	23	●	25	26	27	17:09
5	2417239	February 1906	28	29	30	31	◐	2	3	12:31
6	2417246		4	5	6	7	8	○	10	7:46
7	2417253		11	12	13	14	15	◑	17	4:23
8	2417260		18	19	20	21	22	●	24	7:57
9	2417267	March 1906	25	26	27	28	1	2	◐	9:28
10	2417274		4	5	6	7	8	9	○	20:17
11	2417281		11	12	13	14	15	16	◑	11:58
12	2417288		18	19	20	21[b]	22	23	●	23:52
13	2417295		25	26	27	28	29	30	31	
14	2417302	April 1906	1	◐	3	4	5	6	7	4:02
15	2417309		8	○	10	11	12	13	14	6:12
16	2417316		◑	16	17	18	19	20	21	20:37
17	2417323		22	●	24	25	26	27	28	16:07
18	2417330	May 1906	29	30	◐	2	3	4	5	19:07
19	2417337		6	7	○	9	10	11	12	14:09
20	2417344		13	14	◑	16	17	18	19	7:03
21	2417351		20	21	22	●	24	25	26	8:01
22	2417358	June 1906	27	28	29	30	◐	1	2	6:24
23	2417365		3	4	5	○	7	8	9	21:12
24	2417372		10	11	12	◑	14	15	16	19:34
25	2417379		17	18	19	20	●	22[c]	23	23:05
26	2417386		24	25	26	27	28	◐	30	14:19
27	2417393	July 1906	1	2	3	4	5	○	7	4:27
28	2417400		8	9	10	11	12	◑	14	10:13
29	2417407		15	16	17	18	19	20	●	12:59
30	2417414		22	23	24	25	26	27	◐	19:56
31	2417421	August 1906	29	30	31	1	2	3	○	13:00
32	2417428		5	6	7	8	9	10	11	
33	2417435		◑	13	14	15	16	17	18	2:47
34	2417442		19	●	21	22	23	24	25	1:27
35	2417449	September 1906	26	◐	28	29	30	31	1	0:42
36	2417456		○	3	4	5	6	7	8	23:36
37	2417463		9	◑	11	12	13	14	15	20:54
38	2417470		16	17	●	19	20	21	22	12:33
39	2417477		23[d]	24	◐	26	27	28	29	6:11
40	2417484	October 1906	30	1	○	3	4	5	6	12:48
41	2417491		7	8	9	◑	11	12	13	15:39
42	2417498		14	15	16	●	18	19	20	22:43
43	2417505		21	22	23	◐	25	26	27	13:50
44	2417512	November 1906	28	29	30	31	○	2	3	4:46
45	2417519		4	5	6	7	8	◑	10	9:45
46	2417526		11	12	13	14	15	●	17	8:37
47	2417533		18	19	20	21	22	◐	24	0:39
48	2417540	December 1906	25	26	27	28	29	○	1	23:07
49	2417547		2	3	4	5	6	7	8	
50	2417554		◑	10	11	12	13	14	●	1:45 18:54
51	2417561		16	17	18	19	20	21	◐[e]	15:04
52	2417568		23	24	25	26	27	28	29	
1	2417575		○	31	1	2	3	4	5	18:44

Hebrew 5666/5667

ISO Week	Month	Sun	Mon	Tue	Wed	Thu	Fri	Sat	Molad
1	Teveth 5666	3	4	5	6	7	8	9	
2		10	11	12	13	14	15	16	
3		17	18	19	20	21	22	23	
4	Shevat 5666	24	25	26	27	28	29	1	Thu 5h28m3p
5		2	3	4	5	6	7	8	
6		9	10	11	12	13	14	15	
7		16	17	18	19	20	21	22	
8		23	24	25	26	27	28	29	
9	Adar 5666	30	1	2	3	4	5	6	Fri 18h12m4p
10		7	8	9	10	11	12	13	
11		14[f]	15	16	17	18	19	20	
12		21	22	23	24	25	26	27	
13	Nisan 5666	28	29	1	2	3	4	5	Sun 6h56m5p
14		6	7	8	9	10	11	12	
15		13	14	15[g]	16	17	18	19	
16		20	21	22	23	24	25	26	
17	Iyyar 5666	27	28	29	30	1	2	3	Mon 19h40m6p
18		4	5	6	7	8	9	10	
19		11	12	13	14	15	16	17	
20		18	19	20	21	22	23	24	
21	Sivan 5666	25	26	27	28	29	1	2	Wed 8h24m7p
22		3	4	5	6[h]	7	8	9	
23		10	11	12	13	14	15	16	
24		17	18	19	20	21	22	23	
25		24	25	26	27	28	29	30	
26	Tammuz 5666	1	2	3	4	5	6	7	Thu 21h8m8p
27		8	9	10	11	12	13	14	
28		15	16	17	18	19	20	21	
29		22	23	24	25	26	27	28	
30	Av 5666	29	1	2	3	4	5	6	Sat 9h52m9p
31		7	8	9[i]	10	11	12	13	
32		14	15	16	17	18	19	20	
33		21	22	23	24	25	26	27	
34	Elul 5666	28	29	30	1	2	3	4	Sun 22h36m10p
35		5	6	7	8	9	10	11	
36		12	13	14	15	16	17	18	
37		19	20	21	22	23	24	25	
38	Tishri 5667	26	27	28	29	1[a]	2[a]	3	Tue 11h20m11p
39		4	5	6	7	8	9	10[b]	
40		11	12	13	14	15[c]	16	17	
41		18	19	20	21	22	23	24	
42	Heshvan 5667	25	26	27	28	29	30	1	Thu 0h4m12p
43		2	3	4	5	6	7	8	
44		9	10	11	12	13	14	15	
45		16	17	18	19	20	21	22	
46		23	24	25	26	27	28	29	
47	Kislev 5667	1	2	3	4	5	6	7	Fri 12h48m13p
48		8	9	10	11	12	13	14	
49		15	16	17	18[d]	19	20	21	
50		22	23	24	25[e]	26[e]	27[e]	28[e]	
51	Teveth 5667	29[e]	30[e]	1[e]	2[e]	3	4	5	Sun 1h32m14p
52		6	7	8	9	10	11	12	
1		13	14	15	16	17	18	19	

Chinese Yǐ-Sì/Bǐng-Wǔ‡

ISO Week	Month	Sun	Mon	Tue	Wed	Thu	Fri	Sat	Solar Term
1	Month 12 Yǐ-Sì	6	7	8	9	10	11	12	Xiǎo hán
2		13	14	15	16	17	18	19	
3		20	21	22	23	24	25	26*	
4	Month 1 Bǐng-Wǔ	27	28	29	30	1[a]	2	3	Dà hán
5		4	5	6	7	8	9	10	
6		11	12	13	14	15[b]	16	17	Lì chūn
7		18	19	20	21	22	23	24	
8	Month 2 Bǐng-Wǔ	25	26	27	28	29	1	2	Yǔ shuǐ
9		3	4	5	6	7	8	9	
10		10	11	12	13	14	15	16	Jīng zhé
11		17	18	19	20	21	22	23	
12		24	25	26	27*	28	29	30	Chūn fēn
13	Month 3 Bǐng-Wǔ	1	2	3	4	5	6	7	
14		8	9	10	11	12	13[c]	14	Qīng míng
15		15	16	17	18	19	20	21	
16		22	23	24	25	26	27	28	Gǔ yǔ
17	Month 4 Bǐng-Wǔ	29	1†	2†	3†	4†	5†	6†	
18		7†	8†	9†	10†	11†	12†	13†	
19		14†	15†	16†	17†	18†	19†	20†	Lì xià
20		21†	22†	23†	24†	25†	26†	27†	
21	Leap Month 4 Bǐng-Wǔ	28†*	29†	30†	1	2	3	4	Xiǎo mǎn
22		5	6	7	8	9	10	11	
23		12	13	14	15	16	17	18	Máng zhòng
24		19	20	21	22	23	24	25	
25	Month 5 Bǐng-Wǔ	26	27	28	29	30	1	2	Xià zhì
26		3	4	5[d]	6	7	8	9	
27		10	11	12	13	14	15	16	
28		17	18	19	20	21	22	23	Xiǎo shǔ
29	Month 6 Bǐng-Wǔ	24	25	26	27	28*	29	1	
30		2	3	4	5	6	7	8	Dà shǔ
31		9	10	11	12	13	14	15	
32		16	17	18	19	20	21	22	Lì qiū
33		23	24	25	26	27	28	29	
34	Month 7 Bǐng-Wǔ	30	1	2	3	4	5	6	Chǔ shǔ
35		7[e]	8	9	10	11	12	13	
36		14	15[f]	16	17	18	19	20	Bái lù
37		21	22	23	24	25	26	27	
38	Month 8 Bǐng-Wǔ	28	29*	1	2	3	4	5	
39		6	7	8	9	10	11	12	Qiū fēn
40		13	14	15[g]	16	17	18	19	
41		20	21	22	23	24	25	26	Hán lù
42	Month 9 Bǐng-Wǔ	27	28	29	30	1	2	3	
43		4	5	6	7	8	9[h]	10	Shuāng jiàng
44		11	12	13	14	15	16	17	
45		18	19	20	21	22	23	24	Lì dōng
46	Month 10 Bǐng-Wǔ	25	26	27	28	29	1*	2	
47		3	4	5	6	7	8	9	Xiǎo xuě
48		10	11	12	13	14	15	16	
49		17	18	19	20	21	22	23	Dà xuě
50		24	25	26	27	28	29	30	
51	Month 11 Bǐng-Wǔ	1	2	3	4	5	6	7	
52		8[i]	9	10	11	12	13	14	Dōng zhì
1		15	16	17	18	19	20	21	

Coptic 1622/1623‡ — Ethiopic 1898/1899‡

ISO Week	Coptic Month	Sun	Mon	Tue	Wed	Thu	Fri	Sat	Ethiopic Month
1	Koiak 1622	22	23	24	25	26	27	28	Tākhśāś 1898
2	Tôbe 1622	29[c]	30	1	2	3	4	5	Ṭer 1898
3		6[d]	7	8	9	10	11[e]	12	
4		13	14	15	16	17	18	19	
5		20	21	22	23	24	25	26	
6	Meshir 1622	27	28	29	30	1	2	3	Yakātit 1898
7		4	5	6	7	8	9	10	
8		11	12	13	14	15	16	17	
9		18	19	20	21	22	23	24	
10	Paremotep 1622	25	26	27	28	29	30	1	Magābit 1898
11		2	3	4	5	6	7	8	
12		9	10	11	12	13	14	15	
13		16	17	18	19	20	21	22	
14		23	24	25	26	27	28	29	
15	Parmoute 1622	30	1	2	3	4	5	6	Miyāzyā 1898
16		7[f]	8	9	10	11	12	13	
17		14	15	16	17	18	19	20	
18		21	22	23	24	25	26	27	
19	Pashons 1622	28	29[g]	30	1	2	3	4	Genbot 1898
20		5	6	7	8	9	10	11	
21		12	13	14	15	16	17	18	
22		19	20	21	22	23	24	25	
23	Paône 1622	26	27	28	29	30	1	2	Sanē 1898
24		3	4	5	6	7	8	9	
25		10	11	12	13	14	15	16	
26		17	18	19	20	21	22	23	
27		24	25	26	27	28	29	30	
28	Epêp 1622	1	2	3	4	5	6	7	Ḥamlē 1898
29		8	9	10	11	12	13	14	
30		15	16	17	18	19	20	21	
31		22	23	24	25	26	27	28	
32	Mesorê 1622	29	30	1	2	3	4	5	Naḥasē 1898
33		6	7	8	9	10	11	12	
34		13[h]	14	15	16	17	18	19	
35		20	21	22	23	24	25	26	
36	Epag. 1622	27	28	29	30	1	2	3	Pāg. 1898
37	Thoout 1623	4	5	1[a]	2	3	4	5	Maskaram 1899
38		6	7	8	9	10	11	12	
39		13	14	15	16	17[b]	18	19	
40		20	21	22	23	24	25	26	
41	Paope 1623	27	28	29	30	1	2	3	Ṭeqemt 1899
42		4	5	6	7	8	9	10	
43		11	12	13	14	15	16	17	
44		18	19	20	21	22	23	24	
45	Athôr 1623	25	26	27	28	29	30	1	Hedār 1899
46		2	3	4	5	6	7	8	
47		9	10	11	12	13	14	15	
48		16	17	18	19	20	21	22	
49		23	24	25	26	27	28	29	
50	Koiak 1623	30	1	2	3	4	5	6	Tākhśāś 1899
51		7	8	9	10	11	12	13	
52		14	15	16	17	18	19	20	
1		21	22	23	24	25	26	27	

[a]New Year
[b]Spring (12:52)
[c]Summer (8:41)
[d]Autumn (23:15)
[e]Winter (17:53)
● New moon
◐ First quarter moon
○ Full moon
◑ Last quarter moon

[a]New Year
[b]Yom Kippur
[c]Sukkot
[d]Winter starts
[e]Ḥanukkah
[f]Purim
[g]Passover
[h]Shavuot
[i]Fast of Av

‡Leap year
[a]New Year (4604, Horse)
[b]Lantern Festival
[c]Qīngmíng
†See warnings!
[d]Dragon Festival
[e]Qīqiǎo
[f]Hungry Ghosts
[g]Mid-Autumn Festival
[h]Double-Ninth Festival
[i]Dōngzhì
*Start of 60-name cycle

‡Leap year
[a]New Year
[b]Building of the Cross
[c]Christmas
[d]Jesus's Circumcision
[e]Epiphany
[f]Easter
[g]Mary's Announcement
[h]Jesus's Transfiguration

PERSIAN (ASTRONOMICAL) 1284‡/1285

Month	Sun	Mon	Tue	Wed	Thu	Fri	Sat
DEY 1284	10	11	12	13	14	15	16
	17	18	19	20	21	22	23
	24	25	26	27	28	29	30
BAHMAN 1284	1	2	3	4	5	6	7
	8	9	10	11	12	13	14
	15	16	17	18	19	20	21
	22	23	24	25	26	27	28
	29	30	1	2	3	4	5
ESFAND 1284	6	7	8	9	10	11	12
	13	14	15	16	17	18	19
	20	21	22	23	24	25	26
	27	28	29	30	1[a]	2	3
FARVARDĪN 1285	4	5	6	7	8	9	10
	11	12	13[b]	14	15	16	17
	18	19	20	21	22	23	24
	25	26	27	28	29	30	31
ORDĪBEHEŠT 1285	1	2	3	4	5	6	7
	8	9	10	11	12	13	14
	15	16	17	18	19	20	21
	22	23	24	25	26	27	28
	29	30	31	1	2	3	4
XORDĀD 1285	5	6	7	8	9	10	11
	12	13	14	15	16	17	18
	19	20	21	22	23	24	25
	26	27	28	29	30	31	1
TĪR 1285	2	3	4	5	6	7	8
	9	10	11	12	13	14	15
	16	17	18	19	20	21	22
	23	24	25	26	27	28	29
	30	31	1	2	3	4	5
MORDĀD 1285	6	7	8	9	10	11	12
	13	14	15	16	17	18	19
	20	21	22	23	24	25	26
	27	28	29	30	31	1	2
SHAHRĪVAR 1285	3	4	5	6	7	8	9
	10	11	12	13	14	15	16
	17	18	19	20	21	22	23
	24	25	26	27	28	29	30
	31	1	2	3	4	5	6
MEHR 1285	7	8	9	10	11	12	13
	14	15	16	17	18	19	20
	21	22	23	24	25	26	27
	28	29	30	1	2	3	4
ĀBĀN 1285	5	6	7	8	9	10	11
	12	13	14	15	16	17	18
	19	20	21	22	23	24	25
	26	27	28	29	30	1	2
ĀZAR 1285	3	4	5	6	7	8	9
	10	11	12	13	14	15	16
	17	18	19	20	21	22	23
	24	25	26	27	28	29	30
DEY 1285	1	2	3	4	5	6	7
	8	9	10	11	12	13	14

HINDU LUNAR 1962/1963

Month	Sun	Mon	Tue	Wed	Thu	Fri	Sat
PAUSHA 1962	6	6	7	8	9	10	11
	12	13	14	15	16	17	18
	19	20	21	22	23	24	**25**
	27	28	29	30	1	2	3
MĀGHA 1962	4	5	6	7	8	9	9
	10	11	12	13	14	15	16
	17	18	**19**	21	22	23	24
	25	26	27	28[h]	29	30	1
PHĀLGUNA 1962	2	3	4	5	6	7	8
	9	10	11	12	13	14	15[i]
	16	17	18	19	20	21	22
	23	**24**	26	27	28	29	30
CHAITRA 1963	1[a]	2	2	3	4	5	6
	7	8	9[b]	10	11	12	13
	14	15	16	**17**	19	20	21
	22	23	24	25	26	27	28
	29	30	1	2	3	4	5
VAIŚĀKHA 1963	6	6	7	8	**9**	11	12
	13	14	15	16	17	18	19
	20	21	**22**	24	25	26	26
	27	28	29	30	1	2	3
JYAISHTHA 1963	4	5	6	7	8	9	10
	11	12	**13**	15	16	17	18
	19	20	21	22	23	24	25
	26	27	28	29	30	1	2
ĀSHĀDHA 1963	2	3	4	**5**	7	8	9
	10	11	12	13	14	15	16
	17	19	20	21	22	23	23
	24	25	26	27	28	29	30
	1	2	3	4	5	6	7
ŚRĀVAṆA 1963	8	**9**	11	12	13	14	15
	16	17	18	19	20	21	22
	23[c]	24	25	26	27	28	29
	29	**30**	2	3	4[d]	5	6
BHĀDRAPADA 1963	7	8	9	10	11	12	**13**
	15	16	17	18	19	20	20
	21	22	23	24	25	26	27
	28	29	30	1	2	3	4
ĀŚVINA 1963	**5**	7	8[e]	9[e]	10[e]	11	12
	13	14	15	16	17	18	19
	20	21	22	23	24	24	25
	26	27	**28**	30	1[f]	2	3
KĀRTTIKA 1963	4	5	6	7	8	9	10
	11	12	13	14	15	16	17
	18	19	20	21	22	23	24
	25	26	27	28	29	30	1
MĀRGAŚĪRA 1963	2	**3**	5	6	7	8	9
	10	11[g]	12	13	14	15	16
	17	17	18	19	20	21	22
	23	24	25	26	**27**	29	30
PAUSHA 1963	1	2	3	4	5	6	7
	8	9	10	11	12	13	14
	15	16	17	18	19	20	21

HINDU SOLAR 1827‡/1828

Month	Sun	Mon	Tue	Wed	Thu	Fri	Sat
PAUSHA 1827	17	18	19	20	21	22	23
	24	25	26	27	28	29	1[b]
MĀGHA 1827	2	3	4	5	6	7	8
	9	10	11	12	13	14	15
	16	17	18	19	20	21	22
	23	24	25	26	27	28	29
PHĀLGUNA 1827	1	2	3	4	5	6	7
	8	9	10	11	12	13	14
	15	16	17	18	19	20	21
	22	23	24	25	26	27	28
	29	30	1	2	3	4	5
CHAITRA 1827	6	7	8	9	10	11	12
	13	14	15	16	17	18	19
	20	21	22	23	24	25	26
	27	28	29	30	31	1[a]	2
VAIŚĀKHA 1828	3	4	5	6	7	8	9
	10	11	12	13	14	15	16
	17	18	19	20	21	22	23
	24	25	26	27	28	29	30
	31	1	2	3	4	5	6
JYAISHTHA 1828	7	8	9	10	11	12	13
	14	15	16	17	18	19	20
	21	22	23	24	25	26	27
	28	29	30	31	1	2	3
ĀSHĀDHA 1828	4	5	6	7	8	9	10
	11	12	13	14	15	16	17
	18	19	20	21	22	23	24
	25	26	27	28	29	30	31
	32	1	2	3	4	5	6
ŚRĀVAṆA 1828	7	8	9	10	11	12	13
	14	15	16	17	18	19	20
	21	22	23	24	25	26	27
	28	29	30	31	1	2	3
BHĀDRAPADA 1828	4	5	6	7	8	9	10
	11	12	13	14	15	16	17
	18	19	20	21	22	23	24
	25	26	27	28	29	30	31
ĀŚVINA 1828	1	2	3	4	5	6	7
	8	9	10	11	12	13	14
	15	16	17	18	19	20	21
	22	23	24	25	26	27	28
	29	30	31	1	2	3	4
KĀRTTIKA 1828	5	6	7	8	9	10	11
	12	13	14	15	16	17	18
	19	20	21	22	23	24	25
	26	27	28	29	1	2	3
MĀRGAŚĪRA 1828	4	5	6	7	8	9	10
	11	12	13	14	15	16	17
	18	19	20	21	22	23	24
	25	26	27	28	29	30	1
PAUSHA 1828	2	3	4	5	6	7	8
	9	10	11	12	13	14	15
	16	17	18	19	20	21	22

ISLAMIC (ASTRONOMICAL) 1323/1324

Month	Sun	Mon	Tue	Wed	Thu	Fri	Sat
DHU AL-QA'DA 1323	5	6	7	8	9	10	11
	12	13	14	15	16	17	18
	19	20	21	22	23	24	25
	26	27	28	29	30	1	2
DHU AL-ḤIJJA 1323	3	4	5	6	7	8	9
	10[g]	11	12	13	14	15	16
	17	18	19	20	21	22	23
	24	25	26	27	28	29	30
MUḤARRAM 1324	1[a]	2	3	4	5	6	7
	8	9	10[b]	11	12	13	14
	15	16	17	18	19	20	21
	22	23	24	25	26	27	28
	29	1	2	3	4	5	6
ṢAFAR 1324	7	8	9	10	11	12	13
	14	15	16	17	18	19	20
	21	22	23	24	25	26	27
	28	29	30	1	2	3	4
RABĪ' I 1324	5	6	7	8	9	10	11
	12[c]	13	14	15	16	17	18
	19	20	21	22	23	24	25
	26	27	28	29	30	1	2
RABĪ' II 1324	3	4	5	6	7	8	9
	10	11	12	13	14	15	16
	17	18	19	20	21	22	23
	24	25	26	27	28	29	30
JUMĀDĀ I 1324	1	2	3	4	5	6	7
	8	9	10	11	12	13	14
	15	16	17	18	19	20	21
	22	23	24	25	26	27	28
	29	1	2	3	4	5	6
JUMĀDĀ II 1324	7	8	9	10	11	12	13
	14	15	16	17	18	19	20
	21	22	23	24	25	26	27
	28	29	1	2	3	4	5
RAJAB 1324	6	7	8	9	10	11	12
	13	14	15	16	17	18	19
	20	21	22	23	24	25	26
	27[d]	28	29	30	1	2	3
SHA'BĀN 1324	4	5	6	7	8	9	10
	11	12	13	14	15	16	17
	18	19	20	21	22	23	24
	25	26	27	28	29	1[e]	2
RAMAḌĀN 1324	3	4	5	6	7	8	9
	10	11	12	13	14	15	16
	17	18	19	20	21	22	23
	24	25	26	27	28	29	1[f]
SHAWWĀL 1324	2	3	4	5	6	7	8
	9	10	11	12	13	14	15
	16	17	18	19	20	21	22
	23	24	25	26	27	28	29
	30	1	2	3	4	5	6
DHU AL-QA'DA 1324	7	8	9	10	11	12	13
	14	15	16	17	18	19	20

GREGORIAN 1906

Julian (Sun)	Sun	Mon	Tue	Wed	Thu	Fri	Sat	Month
Dec 18	31	1	2	3	4	5	6	JANUARY 1906
	7[a]	8	9	10	11	12	13	
Jan 1	14[b]	15	16	17	18	19	20	
	21	22	23	24	25	26	27	
Jan 15	28	29	30	31	1	2	3	FEBRUARY 1906
	4	5	6	7	8	9	10	
Jan 29	11	12	13	14	15	16	17	
	18	19	20	21	22	23	24	
Feb 12	25	26	27	28[c]	1	2	3	MARCH 1906
	4[d]	5	6	7	8	9	10	
Feb 26	11	12	13	14	15	16	17	
	18	19	20	21	22	23	24	
Mar 12	25	26	27	28	29	30	31	
	1	2	3	4	5	6	7	APRIL 1906
Mar 26	8	9	10	11	12	13	14	
	15[e]	16	17	18	19	20	21	
Apr 9	22	23	24	25	26	27	28	
	29	30	1	2	3	4	5	MAY 1906
Apr 23	6	7	8	9	10	11	12	
	13	14	15	16	17	18	19	
May 7	20	21	22	23	24	25	26	
	27	28	29	30	31	1	2	JUNE 1906
May 21	3	4	5	6	7	8	9	
	10	11	12	13	14	15	16	
Jun 4	17	18	19	20	21	22	23	
	24	25	26	27	28	29	30	
Jun 18	1	2	3	4	5	6	7	JULY 1906
	8	9	10	11	12	13	14	
Jul 2	15	16	17	18	19	20	21	
	22	23	24	25	26	27	28	
Jul 16	29	30	31	1	2	3	4	AUGUST 1906
	5	6	7	8	9	10	11	
Jul 30	12	13	14	15	16	17	18	
	19	20	21	22	23	24	25	
Aug 13	26	27	28	29	30	31	1	SEPTEMBER 1906
	2	3	4	5	6	7	8	
Aug 27	9	10	11	12	13	14	15	
	16	17	18	19	20	21	22	
Sep 10	23	24	25	26	27	28	29	
	30	1	2	3	4	5	6	OCTOBER 1906
Sep 24	7	8	9	10	11	12	13	
	14	15	16	17	18	19	20	
Oct 8	21	22	23	24	25	26	27	
	28	29	30	31	1	2	3	NOVEMBER 1906
Oct 22	4	5	6	7	8	9	10	
	11	12	13	14	15	16	17	
Nov 5	18	19	20	21	22	23	24	
	25	26	27	28	29	30	1	DECEMBER 1906
Nov 19	2[g]	3	4	5	6	7	8	
	9	10	11	12	13	14	15	
Dec 3	16	17	18	19	20	21	22	
	23	24	25[h]	26	27	28	29	
Dec 17	30	31	1	2	3	4	5	

Persian:
‡Leap year
[a]New Year
[b]Sizdeh Bedar

Hindu Lunar:
[a]New Year (Parābhava)
[b]Birthday of Rāma
[c]Birthday of Krishna
[d]Ganēśa Chaturthī
[e]Dashara
[f]Diwali
[g]Birthday of Vishnu
[h]Night of Śiva
[i]Holi

Hindu Solar:
‡Leap year
[a]New Year (Kālayukta)
[b]Pongal

Islamic:
[a]New Year
[b]'Ashūrā'
[c]Prophet's Birthday
[d]Ascent of the Prophet
[e]Start of Ramaḍān
[f]'Id al-Fiṭr
[g]'Id al-'Aḍḥā

Gregorian:
[a]Orthodox Christmas
[b]Julian New Year
[c]Ash Wednesday
[d]Feast of Orthodoxy
[e]Easter (also Orthodox)
[g]Advent
[h]Christmas

1907

	GREGORIAN 1907							Lunar Phases	ISO WEEK	JULIAN DAY		HEBREW 5667/5668‡							Molad		CHINESE Bǐng-Wǔ‡/Dīng-Wèi							Solar Term		COPTIC 1623‡/1624							ETHIOPIC 1899‡/1900
	Sun	Mon	Tue	Wed	Thu	Fri	Sat		(Mon)	(Sun noon)		Sun	Mon	Tue	Wed	Thu	Fri	Sat			Sun	Mon	Tue	Wed	Thu	Fri	Sat			Sun	Mon	Tue	Wed	Thu	Fri	Sat	
JANUARY 1907	○ 31	1[a]	2	3	4	5	18:44	1	2417575	TEVETH 5667	13	14	15	16	17	18	19		MONTH 11 Bǐng-Wǔ	15	16	17	18	19	20	21		KOIAK 1623	21	22	23	24	25	26	27	TĀKHŚĀŚ 1899
	6	◑	8	9	10	11	12	14:47	2	2417582		20	21	22	23	24	25	26			22	23	24	25	26	27	28	Xiǎo hán	TŌBE 1623	28	29[c]	30	1	2	3	4	ṬER 1899
	13	●	15	16	17	18	19	5:57	3	2417589	SHEVAT 5667	27	28	29	1	2	3	4	Mon $14^{h}16^{m}15^{p}$	MONTH 12 Bǐng-Wǔ	29	1	2*	3	4	5	6			5	6[d]	7	8	9	10	11[e]	
	20	◐	22	23	24	25	26	8:42	4	2417596		5	6	7	8	9	10	11			7	**8**	9	10	11	12	13	Dà hán		12	13	14	15	16	17	18	
FEBRUARY 1907	27	28	○	30	31	1	2	13:45	5	2417603		12	13	14	15	16	17	18			14	15	16	17	18	19	20			19	20	21	22	23	24	25	
	3	4	5	◑	7	8	9	0:52	6	2417610		19	20	21	22	23	24	25			21	22	23	24	25	26	27	Lì chūn	MESHIR 1623	26	27	28	29	30	1	2	YAKĀTIT 1899
	10	11	●	13	14	15	16	17:43	7	2417617	ADAR 5667	26	27	28	29	30	1	2	Wed $3^{h}0^{m}16^{p}$	MONTH 1 Dīng-Wèi	28	29	30	1[a]	2	3	4			3	4	5	6	7	8	9	
	17	18	19	◐	21	22	23	4:35	8	2417624		3	4	5	6	7	8	9			5	6	7	**8**	9	10	11	Yǔ shuǐ		10	11	12	13	14	15	16	
MARCH 1907	24	25	26	27	○	1	2	6:23	9	2417631		10	11	12	13	14[f]	15	16			12	13	14	15[b]	16	17	18			17	18	19	20	21	22	23	
	3	4	5	6	◑	8	9	8:42	10	2417638		17	18	19	20	21	22	23			19	20	21	22	23	24	25	Jīng zhé		24	25	26	27	28	29	30	
	10	11	12	13	●	15	16	6:05	11	2417645	NISAN 5667	24	25	26	27	28	29	1	Thu $15^{h}44^{m}17^{p}$	MONTH 2 Dīng-Wèi	26	27	28	29	1	2	3*		PAREMOTEP 1623	1	2	3	4	5	6	7	MAGĀBIT 1899
	17	18	19	20	21[b]	◐	23	1:10	12	2417652		2	3	4	5	6	7	8			4	5	6	7	8	**9**	10	Chūn fēn		8	9	10	11	12	13	14	
	24	25	26	27	28	○	30	19:44	13	2417659		9	10	11	12	13	14	15[g]			11	12	13	14	15	16	17			15	16	17	18	19	20	21	
APRIL 1907	31	1	2	3	4	◑	6	15:20	14	2417666		16	17	18	19	20	21	22			18	19	20	21	22	23	24[c]	Qīng míng		22	23	24	25	26	27	28	
	7	8	9	10	11	●	13	19:06	15	2417673		23	24	25	26	27	28	29		MONTH 3 Dīng-Wèi	25	26	27	28	29	30	1		PARMOUTE 1623	29	30	1	2	3	4	5	MIYĀZYĀ 1899
	14	15	16	17	18	19	◐	20:38	16	2417680	IYYAR 5667	30	1	2	3	4	5	6	Sat $4^{h}29^{m}0^{p}$		2	3	4	5	6	7	8			6	7	8	9	10	11	12	
	21	22	23	24	25	26	27		17	2417687		7	8	9	10	11	12	13			**9**	10	11	12	13	14	15	Gǔ yǔ		13	14	15	16	17	18	19	
MAY 1907	○	29	30	1	2	3	◑	6:04 21:53	18	2417694		14	15	16	17	18	19	20			16	17	18	19	20	21	22			20	21	22	23	24	25	26	
	5	6	7	8	9	10	11		19	2417701		21	22	23	24	25	26	27			23	24	25	26	27	28	29	Lì xià	PASHONS 1623	27[f]	28	29[g]	30	1	2	3	GENBOT 1899
	●	13	14	15	16	17	18	8:59	20	2417708	SIVAN 5667	28	29	1	2	3	4	5	Sun $17^{h}13^{m}1^{p}$	MONTH 4 Dīng-Wèi	1	2	3	4*	5	6	7			4	5	6	7	8	9	10	
	19	◐	21	22	23	24	25	13:27	21	2417715		6[h]	7	8	9	10	11	12			8	9	10	**11**	12	13	14	Xiǎo mǎn		11	12	13	14	15	16	17	
JUNE 1907	26	○	28	29	30	31	1	14:18	22	2417722		13	14	15	16	17	18	19			15	16	17	18	19	20	21			18	19	20	21	22	23	24	
	2	◑	4	5	6	7	8	5:19	23	2417729		20	21	22	23	24	25	26			22	23	24	25	26	27	28	Máng zhòng	PAŌNE 1623	25	26	27	28	29	30	1	SANĒ 1899
	9	●	11	12	13	14	15	23:50	24	2417736	TAMMUZ 5667	27	28	29	30	1	2	3	Tue $5^{h}57^{m}2^{p}$	MONTH 5 Dīng-Wèi	29	30	1	2	3	4	5[d]			2	3	4	5	6	7	8	
	16	17	18	◐	20	21	22[c]	2:55	25	2417743		4	5	6	7	8	9	10			6	7	8	9	10	11	**12**	Xià zhì		9	10	11	12	13	14	15	
	23	24	○	26	27	28	29	21:27	26	2417750		11	12	13	14	15	16	17			13	14	15	16	17	18	19			16	17	18	19	20	21	22	
JULY 1907	30	1	◑	3	4	5	6	14:34	27	2417757		18	19	20	21	22	23	24			20	21	22	23	24	25	26			23	24	25	26	27	28	29	
	7	8	9	●	11	12	13	15:17	28	2417764	AV 5667	25	26	27	28	29	1	2	Wed $18^{h}41^{m}3^{p}$	MONTH 6 Dīng-Wèi	27	28	29	1	2	3	4	Xiǎo shǔ	EPĒP 1623	30	1	2	3	4	5	6	ḤAMLĒ 1899
	14	15	16	17	◐	19	20	13:12	29	2417771		3	4	5	6	7	8	9			5*	6	7	8	9	10	11			7	8	9	10	11	12	13	
	21	22	23	24	○	26	27	4:29	30	2417778		10[i]	11	12	13	14	15	16			12	13	14	**15**	16	17	18	Dà shǔ		14	15	16	17	18	19	20	
AUGUST 1907	28	29	30	31	◑	2	3	2:25	31	2417785		17	18	19	20	21	22	23			19	20	21	22	23	24	25			21	22	23	24	25	26	27	
	4	5	6	7	8	●	10	6:36	32	2417792		24	25	26	27	28	29	30		MONTH 7 Dīng-Wèi	26	27	28	29	30	1	2	Lì qiū	MESORĒ 1623	28	29	30	1	2	3	4	NAḤASĒ 1899
	11	12	13	14	15	◐	17	21:05	33	2417799	ELUL 5667	1	2	3	4	5	6	7	Fri $7^{h}25^{m}4^{p}$		3	4	5	6	7[e]	8	9			5	6	7	8	9	10	11	
	18	19	20	21	22	○	24	12:15	34	2417806		8	9	10	11	12	13	14			10	11	12	13	14	15[f]	**16**	Chǔ shǔ		12	13[h]	14	15	16	17	18	
	25	26	27	28	29	◑	31	17:28	35	2417813		15	16	17	18	19	20	21			17	18	19	20	21	22	23			19	20	21	22	23	24	25	
SEPTEMBER 1907	1	2	3	4	5	6	●	21:04	36	2417820		22	23	24	25	26	27	28			24	25	26	27	28	29	30		EPAG. 1623	26	27	28	29	30	1	2	PĀG. 1899
	8	9	10	11	12	13	14		37	2417827	TISHRI 5668	29	1[a]	2[a]	3	4	5	6	Sat $20^{h}9^{m}5^{p}$	MONTH 8 Dīng-Wèi	1	2	3	4	5*	6	7	Bái lù	THOOUT 1624	3	4	5	6	1[a]	2	3	MASKARAM 1900
	◐	16	17	18	19	20	○	3:40 21:34	38	2417834		7	8	9	10[b]	11	12	13			8	9	10	11	12	13	14			4	5	6	7	8	9	10	
	22	23	24[d]	25	26	27	28		39	2417841		14	15[c]	16	17	18	19	20			15[g]	16	**17**	18	19	20	21	Qiū fēn		11	12	13	14	15	16	17[b]	
OCTOBER 1907	◑	30	1	2	3	4	5	11:37	40	2417848		21	22	23	24	25	26	27			22	23	24	25	26	27	28			18	19	20	21	22	23	24	
	6	●	8	9	10	11	12	10:20	41	2417855	HESHVAN 5668	28	29	30	1	2	3	4	Mon $8^{h}53^{m}6^{p}$	MONTH 9 Dīng-Wèi	29	1	2	3	4	5	6	Hán lù	PAOPE 1624	25	26	27	28	29	30	1	ṬEQEMT 1900
	13	◐	15	16	17	18	19	10:02	42	2417862		5	6	7	8	9	10	11			7	8	9[h]	10	11	12	13			2	3	4	5	6	7	8	
	20	○	22	23	24	25	26	9:17	43	2417869		12	13	14	15	16	17	18			14	15	16	17	**18**	19	20	Shuāng jiàng		9	10	11	12	13	14	15	
NOVEMBER 1907	27	28	◑	30	31	1	2	7:51	44	2417876		19	20	21	22	23	24	25			21	22	23	24	25	26	27			16	17	18	19	20	21	22	
	3	4	●	6	7	8	9	22:39	45	2417883	KISLEV 5668	26	27	28	29	1	2	3	Tue $21^{h}37^{m}7^{p}$	MONTH 10 Dīng-Wèi	28	29	30	1	2	3	4	Lì dōng		23	24	25	26	27	28	29	
	10	11	◐	13	14	15	16	17:14	46	2417890		4	5	6	7	8	9	10			5	6*	7	8	9	10	11		ATHŌR 1624	30	1	2	3	4	5	6	ḪEDĀR 1900
	17	18	19	○	21	22	23	0:04	47	2417897		11	12	13	14	15	16	17			12	13	14	15	16	17	**18**	Xiǎo xuě		7	8	9	10	11	12	13	
	24	25	26	27	◑	29	30	4:21	48	2417904		18	19	20	21	22	23	24			19	20	21	22	23	24	25			14	15	16	17	18	19	20	
DECEMBER 1907	1	2	3	4	●	6	7	10:22	49	2417911	TEVETH 5668	25[e]	26[e]	27[e]	28[e]	29[e]	1[d,e]	2[e]	Thu $10^{h}21^{m}8^{p}$	MONTH 11 Dīng-Wèi	26	27	28	29	1	2	3			21	22	23	24	25	26	27	
	8	9	10	11	◐	13	14	2:16	50	2417918		3[e]	4	5	6	7	8	9			4	5	6	7	8	9	10	Dà xuě	KOIAK 1624	28	29	30	1	2	3	4	TĀKHŚĀŚ 1900
	15	16	17	18	○	20	21	17:55	51	2417925		10	11	12	13	14	15	16			11	12	13	14	15	16	17			5	6	7	8	9	10	11	
	22[e]	23	24	25	26	◑	28	23:10	52	2417932		17	18	19	20	21	22	23			18	**19**[i]	20	21	22	23	24	Dōng zhì		12	13	14	15	16	17	18	
	29	30	31	1	2	●	4	21:43	1	2417939	SHEVAT 5668	24	25	26	27	28	29	1	Fri $23^{h}5^{m}9^{p}$		25	26	27	28	29	30	1			19	20	21	22	23	24	25	

[a]New Year
[b]Spring (18:33)
[c]Summer (14:23)
[d]Autumn (5:09)
[e]Winter (23:51)
● New moon
◐ First quarter moon
○ Full moon
◑ Last quarter moon

‡Leap year
[a]New Year
[b]Yom Kippur
[c]Sukkot
[d]Winter starts
[e]Ḥanukkah
[f]Purim
[g]Passover
[h]Shavuot
[i]Fast of Av

‡Leap year
[a]New Year (4605, Sheep)
[b]Lantern Festival
[c]Qīngmíng
[d]Dragon Festival
[e]Qīqiǎo
[f]Hungry Ghosts
[g]Mid-Autumn Festival
[h]Double-Ninth Festival
[i]Dōngzhì
*Start of 60-name cycle

‡Leap year
[a]New Year
[b]Building of the Cross
[c]Christmas
[d]Jesus's Circumcision
[e]Epiphany
[f]Easter
[g]Mary's Announcement
[h]Jesus's Transfiguration

PERSIAN (ASTRONOMICAL) 1285/1286

Month	Sun	Mon	Tue	Wed	Thu	Fri	Sat
	8	9	10	11	12	13	14
DEY 1285	15	16	17	18	19	20	21
	22	23	24	25	26	27	28
	29	30	1	2	3	4	5
BAHMAN 1285	6	7	8	9	10	11	12
	13	14	15	16	17	18	19
	20	21	22	23	24	25	26
	27	28	29	30	1	2	3
ESFAND 1285	4	5	6	7	8	9	10
	11	12	13	14	15	16	17
	18	19	20	21	22	23	24
	25	26	27	28	29	1[a]	2
	3	4	5	6	7	8	9
FARVARDĪN 1286	10	11	12	13[b]	14	15	16
	17	18	19	20	21	22	23
	24	25	26	27	28	29	30
	31	1	2	3	4	5	6
ORDĪBEHEŠT 1286	7	8	9	10	11	12	13
	14	15	16	17	18	19	20
	21	22	23	24	25	26	27
	28	29	30	31	1	2	3
XORDĀD 1286	4	5	6	7	8	9	10
	11	12	13	14	15	16	17
	18	19	20	21	22	23	24
	25	26	27	28	29	30	31
	1	2	3	4	5	6	7
TĪR 1286	8	9	10	11	12	13	14
	15	16	17	18	19	20	21
	22	23	24	25	26	27	28
	29	30	31	1	2	3	4
MORDĀD 1286	5	6	7	8	9	10	11
	12	13	14	15	16	17	18
	19	20	21	22	23	24	25
	26	27	28	29	30	31	1
SHAHRĪVAR 1286	2	3	4	5	6	7	8
	9	10	11	12	13	14	15
	16	17	18	19	20	21	22
	23	24	25	26	27	28	29
	30	31	1	2	3	4	5
MEHR 1286	6	7	8	9	10	11	12
	13	14	15	16	17	18	19
	20	21	22	23	24	25	26
	27	28	29	30	1	2	3
ĀBĀN 1286	4	5	6	7	8	9	10
	11	12	13	14	15	16	17
	18	19	20	21	22	23	24
	25	26	27	28	29	30	1
ĀZAR 1286	2	3	4	5	6	7	8
	9	10	11	12	13	14	15
	16	17	18	19	20	21	22
	23	24	25	26	27	28	29
	30	1	2	3	4	5	6
DEY 1286	7	8	9	10	11	12	13

[a]New Year
[b]Sizdeh Bedar

HINDU LUNAR 1963/1964‡

Month	Sun	Mon	Tue	Wed	Thu	Fri	Sat
	15	16	17	18	19	20	21
PAUSHA 1963	22	23	24	25	26	27	28
	29	30	1	2	4	5	6
	7	8	9	9	10	11	12
MĀGHA 1963	13	14	15	16	17	18	19
	20	21	22	23	24	25	26
	28	29[h]	30	1	2	3	4
	5	6	7	8	9	10	11
PHĀLGUNA 1963	12	12	13	14	15[i]	16	17
	18	19	20	22	23	24	25
	26	27	28	29	30	1[a]	2
	3	4	5	6	7	8	9
LEAP CHAITRA 1964	10	11	12	13	14	15	16
	17	18	19	20	21	22	23
	24	26	27	28	29	30	1
	2	3	4	5	5	6	7
CHAITRA 1964	8[b]	9	10	11	12	13	14
	15	16	17	19	20	21	22
	23	24	25	26	27	28	29
	30	1	2	3	4	5	6
VAIŚĀKHA 1964	7	8	9	10	11	12	13
	14	15	16	17	18	19	20
	21	23	24	25	26	27	28
	29	30	1	1	2	3	4
JYAISHTHA 1964	5	6	7	8	9	10	11
	12	13	14	16	17	18	19
	20	21	22	23	24	25	26
	27	28	29	30	1	2	3
ĀSHĀDHA 1964	4	5	6	7	8	9	10
	11	12	13	14	15	16	18
	19	20	21	22	23	24	25
	26	27	28	28	29	30	1
ŚRĀVAṆA 1964	2	3	4	5	6	7	8
	9	11	12	13	14	15	16
	17	18	19	20	21	22	23[c]
	24	25	26	27	28	29	30
	1	2	3	4[d]	5	6	7
BHĀDRAPADA 1964	8	9	10	11	12	14	15
	16	17	18	19	20	21	22
	23	24	24	25	26	27	28
	29	30	1	2	3	4	5
ĀŚVINA 1964	6	8[e]	9[e]	10[e]	11	12	13
	14	15	16	17	18	19	20
	21	22	23	24	25	26	27
	28	29	30	1[f]	2	3	4
KĀRTTIKA 1964	5	6	7	8	9	10	12
	13	14	15	16	17	17	18
	19	20	21	22	23	24	25
	26	27	28	29	30	1	2
MĀRGAŚIRA 1964	3	4	6	7	8	9	10
	11[g]	12	13	14	15	16	17
	18	19	20	20	21	22	23
	24	25	26	27	28	30	1

‡Leap year
[a]New Year (Plavaṅga)
[b]Birthday of Rāma
[c]Birthday of Krishna
[d]Gaṇēśa Chaturthī
[e]Dashara
[f]Diwali
[g]Birthday of Vishnu
[h]Night of Śiva
[i]Holi

HINDU SOLAR 1828/1829

Month	Sun	Mon	Tue	Wed	Thu	Fri	Sat
	16	17	18	19	20	21	22
PAUSHA 1828	23	24	25	26	27	28	29
	1[b]	2	3	4	5	6	7
	8	9	10	11	12	13	14
MĀGHA 1828	15	16	17	18	19	20	21
	22	23	24	25	26	27	28
	29	30	1	2	3	4	5
	6	7	8	9	10	11	12
PHĀLGUNA 1828	13	14	15	16	17	18	19
	20	21	22	23	24	25	26
	27	28	29	30	1	2	3
	4	5	6	7	8	9	10
CHAITRA 1828	11	12	13	14	15	16	17
	18	19	20	21	22	23	24
	25	26	27	28	29	30	1[a]
	2	3	4	5	6	7	8
VAIŚĀKHA 1829	9	10	11	12	13	14	15
	16	17	18	19	20	21	22
	23	24	25	26	27	28	29
	30	31	1	2	3	4	5
JYAISHTHA 1829	6	7	8	9	10	11	12
	13	14	15	16	17	18	19
	20	21	22	23	24	25	26
	27	28	29	30	31	1	2
	3	4	5	6	7	8	9
ĀSHĀDHA 1829	10	11	12	13	14	15	16
	17	18	19	20	21	22	23
	24	25	26	27	28	29	30
	31	32	1	2	3	4	5
ŚRĀVAṆA 1829	6	7	8	9	10	11	12
	13	14	15	16	17	18	19
	20	21	22	23	24	25	26
	27	28	29	30	31	1	2
	3	4	5	6	7	8	9
BHĀDRAPADA 1829	10	11	12	13	14	15	16
	17	18	19	20	21	22	23
	24	25	26	27	28	29	30
	31	1	2	3	4	5	6
ĀŚVINA 1829	7	8	9	10	11	12	13
	14	15	16	17	18	19	20
	21	22	23	24	25	26	27
	28	29	30	31	1	2	3
	4	5	6	7	8	9	10
KĀRTTIKA 1829	11	12	13	14	15	16	17
	18	19	20	21	22	23	24
	25	26	27	28	29	30	1
	2	3	4	5	6	7	8
MĀRGAŚIRA 1829	9	10	11	12	13	14	15
	16	17	18	19	20	21	22
	23	24	25	26	27	28	29
	1	2	3	4	5	6	7
PAUSHA 1829	8	9	10	11	12	13	14
	15	16	17	18	19	20	21

[a]New Year (Siddhārthin)
[b]Pongal

ISLAMIC (ASTRONOMICAL) 1324/1325

Month	Sun	Mon	Tue	Wed	Thu	Fri	Sat
	14	15	16	17	18	19	20
DHU AL-QA'DA 1324	21	22	23	24	25	26	27
	28	29	1	2	3	4	5
DHU AL-ḤIJJA 1324	6	7	8	9	10[g]	11	12
	13	14	15	16	17	18	19
	20	21	22	23	24	25	26
	27	28	29	30	1[a]	2	3
MUḤARRAM 1325	4	5	6	7	8	9	10[b]
	11	12	13	14	15	16	17
	18	19	20	21	22	23	24
	25	26	27	28	29	1	2
	3	4	5	6	7	8	9
ṢAFAR 1325	10	11	12	13	14	15	16
	17	18	19	20	21	22	23
	24	25	26	27	28	29	30
	1	2	3	4	5	6	7
RABĪ' I 1325	8	9	10	11	12[c]	13	14
	15	16	17	18	19	20	21
	22	23	24	25	26	27	28
	29	30	1	2	3	4	5
RABĪ' II 1325	6	7	8	9	10	11	12
	13	14	15	16	17	18	19
	20	21	22	23	24	25	26
	27	28	29	1	2	3	4
JUMĀDĀ I 1325	5	6	7	8	9	10	11
	12	13	14	15	16	17	18
	19	20	21	22	23	24	25
	26	27	28	29	30	1	2
JUMĀDĀ II 1325	3	4	5	6	7	8	9
	10	11	12	13	14	15	16
	17	18	19	20	21	22	23
	24	25	26	27	28	29	30
	1	2	3	4	5	6	7
RAJAB 1325	8	9	10	11	12	13	14
	15	16	17	18	19	20	21
	22	23	24	25	26	27[d]	28
	29	1	2	3	4	5	6
SHA'BĀN 1325	7	8	9	10	11	12	13
	14	15	16	17	18	19	20
	21	22	23	24	25	26	27
	28	29	30	1[e]	2	3	4
RAMAḌĀN 1325	5	6	7	8	9	10	11
	12	13	14	15	16	17	18
	19	20	21	22	23	24	25
	26	27	28	29	1[f]	2	3
SHAWWĀL 1325	4	5	6	7	8	9	10
	11	12	13	14	15	16	17
	18	19	20	21	22	23	24
	25	26	27	28	29	30	1
DHU AL-QA'DA 1325	2	3	4	5	6	7	8
	9	10	11	12	13	14	15
	16	17	18	19	20	21	22
	23	24	25	26	27	28	29

[a]New Year
[b]'Ashūrā'
[c]Prophet's Birthday
[d]Ascent of the Prophet
[e]Start of Ramaḍān
[f]'Id al-Fiṭr
[g]'Id al-'Aḍḥā

GREGORIAN 1907

Julian (Sun)	Sun	Mon	Tue	Wed	Thu	Fri	Sat	Month
Dec 17	30	31	1	2	3	4	5	
	6	7[a]	8	9	10	11	12	JANUARY 1907
Dec 31	13	14[b]	15	16	17	18	19	
	20	21	22	23	24	25	26	
Jan 14	27	28	29	30	31	1	2	
	3	4	5	6	7	8	9	FEBRUARY 1907
Jan 28	10	11	12	13[c]	14	15	16	
	17	18	19	20	21	22	23	
Feb 11	24	25	26	27	28	1	2	
	3	4	5	6	7	8	9	
Feb 25	10	11	12	13	14	15	16	MARCH 1907
	17	18	19	20	21	22	23	
Mar 11	24[d]	25	26	27	28	29	30	
	31[e]	1	2	3	4	5	6	
Mar 25	7	8	9	10	11	12	13	
	14	15	16	17	18	19	20	APRIL 1907
Apr 8	21	22	23	24	25	26	27	
	28	29	30	1	2	3	4	
Apr 22	5[f]	6	7	8	9	10	11	
	12	13	14	15	16	17	18	MAY 1907
May 6	19	20	21	22	23	24	25	
	26	27	28	29	30	31	1	
May 20	2	3	4	5	6	7	8	
	9	10	11	12	13	14	15	JUNE 1907
Jun 3	16	17	18	19	20	21	22	
	23	24	25	26	27	28	29	
Jun 17	30	1	2	3	4	5	6	
	7	8	9	10	11	12	13	
Jul 1	14	15	16	17	18	19	20	JULY 1907
	21	22	23	24	25	26	27	
Jul 15	28	29	30	31	1	2	3	
	4	5	6	7	8	9	10	
Jul 29	11	12	13	14	15	16	17	AUGUST 1907
	18	19	20	21	22	23	24	
Aug 12	25	26	27	28	29	30	31	
	1	2	3	4	5	6	7	
Aug 26	8	9	10	11	12	13	14	SEPTEMBER 1907
	15	16	17	18	19	20	21	
Sep 9	22	23	24	25	26	27	28	
	29	30	1	2	3	4	5	
Sep 23	6	7	8	9	10	11	12	OCTOBER 1907
	13	14	15	16	17	18	19	
Oct 7	20	21	22	23	24	25	26	
	27	28	29	30	31	1	2	
Oct 21	3	4	5	6	7	8	9	NOVEMBER 1907
	10	11	12	13	14	15	16	
Nov 4	17	18	19	20	21	22	23	
	24	25	26	27	28	29	30	
Nov 18	1[g]	2	3	4	5	6	7	
	8	9	10	11	12	13	14	DECEMBER 1907
Dec 2	15	16	17	18	19	20	21	
	22	23	24	25[h]	26	27	28	
Dec 16	29	30	31	1	2	3	4	

[a]Orthodox Christmas
[b]Julian New Year
[c]Ash Wednesday
[d]Feast of Orthodoxy
[e]Easter
[f]Orthodox Easter
[g]Advent
[h]Christmas

1908

GREGORIAN 1908‡

Month	Sun	Mon	Tue	Wed	Thu	Fri	Sat	Lunar Phases	ISO WEEK (Mon)	JULIAN DAY (Sun noon)
JANUARY 1908	29	30	31	1[a]	2	●	4	21:43	1	2417939
	5	6	7	8	9	◐	11	13:53	2	2417946
	12	13	14	15	16	17	○	13:37	3	2417953
	19	20	21	22	23	24	25		4	2417960
	◑	27	28	29	30	31	1	15:01	5	2417967
FEBRUARY 1908	●	3	4	5	6	7	8	8:36	6	2417974
	◐	10	11	12	13	14	15	4:27	7	2417981
	16	○	18	19	20	21	22	9:05	8	2417988
	23	24	◑	26	27	28	29	3:24	9	2417995
MARCH 1908	1	●	3	4	5	6	7	18:57	10	2418002
	8	◐	10	11	12	13	14	21:42	11	2418009
	15	16	17	○	19	20	21[b]	2:28	12	2418016
	22	23	24	◑	26	27	28	12:31	13	2418023
	29	30	31	●	2	3	4	5:02	14	2418030
APRIL 1908	5	6	7	◐	9	10	11	16:31	15	2418037
	12	13	14	15	○	17	18	16:55	16	2418044
	19	20	21	22	◑	24	25	19:07	17	2418051
	26	27	28	29	●	1	2	15:33	18	2418058
MAY 1908	3	4	5	6	7	◐	9	11:23	19	2418065
	10	11	12	13	14	15	○	4:32	20	2418072
	17	18	19	20	21	22	◑	0:17	21	2418079
	24	25	26	27	28	29	●	3:14	22	2418086
	31	1	2	3	4	5	6		23	2418093
JUNE 1908	◐	8	9	10	11	12	13	4:56	24	2418100
	○	15	16	17	18	19	20	13:55	25	2418107
	◑[c]	22	23	24	25	26	27	5:26	26	2418114
	●	29	30	1	2	3	4	16:31	27	2418121
JULY 1908	5	◐	7	8	9	10	11	20:25	28	2418128
	12	○	14	15	16	17	18	21:48	29	2418135
	19	◑	21	22	23	24	25	12:01	30	2418142
	26	27	●	29	30	31	1	7:17	31	2418149
AUGUST 1908	2	3	4	◐	6	7	8	9:40	32	2418156
	9	10	11	○	13	14	15	4:59	33	2418163
	16	17	◑	19	20	21	22	21:25	34	2418170
	23	24	25	●	27	28	29	22:59	35	2418177
	30	31	1	2	◐	4	5	20:50	36	2418184
SEPTEMBER 1908	6	7	8	9	○	11	12	12:23	37	2418191
	13	14	15	16	◑	18	19	10:33	38	2418198
	20	21	22	23[d]	24	●	26	14:59	39	2418205
	27	28	29	30	1	2	◐	6:13	40	2418212
OCTOBER 1908	4	5	6	7	8	○	10	21:03	41	2418219
	11	12	13	14	15	16	◑	3:35	42	2418226
	18	19	20	21	22	23	24		43	2418233
	●	26	27	28	29	30	31	6:46	44	2418240
NOVEMBER 1908	◐	2	3	4	5	6	7	14:16	45	2418247
	○	9	10	11	12	13	14	7:58	46	2418254
	◑	16	17	18	19	20	21	23:41	47	2418261
	22	●	24	25	26	27	28	21:53	48	2418268
	29	◐	1	2	3	4	5	21:44	49	2418275
DECEMBER 1908	6	○	8	9	10	11	12	21:44	50	2418282
	13	14	◑	16	17	18	19	21:12	51	2418289
	20	21	22[e]	●	24	25	26	11:50	52	2418296
	27	28	29	◐	31	1	2	5:40	53	2418303

HEBREW 5668‡/5669

ISO WEEK	Month	Sun	Mon	Tue	Wed	Thu	Fri	Sat	Molad
1		24	25	26	27	28	29	1	Fri $23^h5^m9^p$
2	SHEVAT 5668	2	3	4	5	6	7	8	
3		9	10	11	12	13	14	15	
4		16	17	18	19	20	21	22	
5		23	24	25	26	27	28	29	
6		30	1	2	3	4	5	6	Sun $11^h49^m10^p$
7	ADAR I 5668	7	8	9	10	11	12	13	
8		14	15	16	17	18	19	20	
9		21	22	23	24	25	26	27	
10		28	29	30	1	2	3	4	Tue $0^h33^m11^p$
11	ADAR II 5668	5	6	7	8	9	10	11	
12		12	13	14[f]	15	16	17	18	
13		19	20	21	22	23	24	25	
14		26	27	28	29	1	2	3	Wed $13^h17^m12^p$
15	NISAN 5668	4	5	6	7	8	9	10	
16		11	12	13	14	15[g]	16	17	
17		18	19	20	21	22	23	24	
18		25	26	27	28	29	30	1	Fri $2^h1^m13^p$
19	IYAR 5668	2	3	4	5	6	7	8	
20		9	10	11	12	13	14	15	
21		16	17	18	19	20	21	22	
22		23	24	25	26	27	28	29	Sat $14^h45^m14^p$
23		1	2	3	4	5	6[h]	7	
24	SIVAN 5668	8	9	10	11	12	13	14	
25		15	16	17	18	19	20	21	
26		22	23	24	25	26	27	28	
27		29	30	1	2	3	4	5	Mon $3^h29^m15^p$
28	TAMMUZ 5668	6	7	8	9	10	11	12	
29		13	14	15	16	17	18	19	
30		20	21	22	23	24	25	26	
31		27	28	29	1	2	3	4	Tue $16^h13^m16^p$
32	AV 5668	5	6	7	8	9[i]	10	11	
33		12	13	14	15	16	17	18	
34		19	20	21	22	23	24	25	
35		26	27	28	29	30	1	2	Thu $4^h57^m17^p$
36	ELUL 5668	3	4	5	6	7	8	9	
37		10	11	12	13	14	15	16	
38		17	18	19	20	21	22	23	
39		24	25	26	27	28	29	1[a]	Fri $17^h42^m0^p$
40	TISHRI 5669	2[a]	3	4	5	6	7	8	
41		9	10[b]	11	12	13	14	15[c]	
42		16	17	18	19	20	21	22	
43		23	24	25	26	27	28	29	
44		30	1	2	3	4	5	6	Sun $6^h26^m1^p$
45	HESHVAN 5669	7	8	9	10	11	12	13	
46		14	15	16	17	18	19	20	
47		21	22	23	24	25	26	27	
48		28	29	30	1	2	3	4	Mon $19^h10^m2^p$
49	KISLEV 5669	5	6	7	8	9	10	11[d]	
50		12	13	14	15	16	17	18	
51		19	20	21	22	23	24	25[e]	
52		26[e]	27[e]	28[e]	29[e]	30[e]	1[e]	2[e]	Wed $7^h54^m3^p$
53	TEVETH 5669	3	4	5	6	7	8	9	

CHINESE Dīng-Wèi/Wù-Shēn

ISO WEEK	Month	Sun	Mon	Tue	Wed	Thu	Fri	Sat	Solar Term
1		25	26	27	28	29	30	1	
2	MONTH 12 Dīng-Wèi	2	3	*4*	5	6	7*	8	Xiǎo hán
3		9	10	11	12	13	14	15	
4		16	17	**18**	19	20	21	22	Dà hán
5		23	24	25	26	27	28	29	
6		1[a]	2	3	*4*	5	6	7	Lì chūn
7	MONTH 1 Wù-Shēn	8	9	10	11	12	13	14	
8		15[b]	16	17	18	**19**	20	21	Yǔ shuǐ
9		22	23	24	25	26	27	28	
10		29	30	1	2	3	*4*	5	Jīng zhé
11	MONTH 2 Wù-Shēn	6	7	8*	9	10	11	12	
12		13	14	15	16	17	18	**19**	Chūn fēn
13		20	21	22	23	24	25	26	
14		27	28	29	1	2	3	4	
15	MONTH 3 Wù-Shēn	5[c]	6	7	8	9	10	11	Qīng míng
16		12	13	14	15	16	17	18	
17		19	**20**	21	22	23	24	25	Gǔ yǔ
18		26	27	28	29	1	2	3	
19	MONTH 4 Wù-Shēn	4	5	6	7	8	9	10*	Lì xià
20		11	12	13	14	15	16	17	
21		18	19	20	21	**22**	23	24	Xiǎo mǎn
22		25	26	27	28	29	30	1	
23		2	3	4	5[d]	6	7	*8*	Máng zhòng
24	MONTH 5 Wù-Shēn	9	10	11	12	13	14	15	
25		16	17	18	19	20	21	22	
26		23	**24**	25	26	27	28	29	Xià zhì
27		30	1	2	3	4	5	6	
28	MONTH 6 Wù-Shēn	7	8	9	10*	11	12	13	Xiǎo shǔ
29		14	15	16	17	18	19	20	
30		21	22	23	24	**25**	26	27	Dà shǔ
31		28	29	1	2	3	4	5	
32	MONTH 7 Wù-Shēn	6	7[e]	8	9	10	11	*12*	Lì qiū
33		13	14	15[f]	16	17	18	19	
34		20	21	22	23	24	25	26	
35		**27**	28	29	30	1	2	3	Chǔ shǔ
36	MONTH 8 Wù-Shēn	4	5	6	7	8	9	10	
37		11*	12	*13*	14	15[g]	16	17	Bái lù
38		18	19	20	21	22	23	24	
39		25	26	27	**28**	29	1	2	Qiū fēn
40	MONTH 9 Wù-Shēn	3	4	5	6	7	8	9[h]	
41		10	11	12	13	14	*15*	16	Hán lù
42		17	18	19	20	21	22	23	
43		24	25	26	27	28	29	**30**	Shuāng jiàng
44		1	2	3	4	5	6	7	
45	MONTH 10 Wù-Shēn	8	9	10	11	12*	13	14	
46		*15*	16	17	18	19	20	21	Lì dōng
47		22	23	24	25	26	27	28	
48		29	**30**	1	2	3	4	5	Xiǎo xuě
49	MONTH 11* Wù-Shēn	6	7	8	9	10	11	12	
50		13	*14*	15	16	17	18	19	Dà xuě
51		20	21	22	23	24	25	26	
52	MONTH 12 Wù-Shēn	27	28	29[i]	1	2	3	4	Dōng zhì
53		5	6	7	8	9	10	11	

COPTIC 1624/1625 — ETHIOPIC 1900/1901

ISO WEEK	Coptic	Sun	Mon	Tue	Wed	Thu	Fri	Sat	Ethiopic
1	KOIAK 1624	19	20	21	22	23	24	25	TĀKHŚĀŚ 1900
2		26	27	28	29[c]	30	1	2	
3	TŌBE 1624	3	4	5	6[d]	7	8	9	TER 1900
4		10	11[e]	12	13	14	15	16	
5		17	18	19	20	21	22	23	
6		24	25	26	27	28	29	30	
7	MESHIR 1624	1	2	3	4	5	6	7	YAKĀTIT 1900
8		8	9	10	11	12	13	14	
9		15	16	17	18	19	20	21	
10		22	23	24	25	26	27	28	
11	PAREMOTEP 1624	29	30	1	2	3	4	5	MAGĀBIT 1900
12		6	7	8	9	10	11	12	
13		13	14	15	16	17	18	19	
14		20	21	22	23	24	25	26	
15	PARMOUTE 1624	27	28	29	30	1	2	3	MIYĀZYĀ 1900
16		4	5	6	7	8	9	10	
17		11	12	13	14	15	16	17	
18		18[f]	19	20	21	22	23	24	
19		25	26	27	28	29[g]	30	1	
20	PASHONS 1624	2	3	4	5	6	7	8	GENBOT 1900
21		9	10	11	12	13	14	15	
22		16	17	18	19	20	21	22	
23		23	24	25	26	27	28	29	
24		30	1	2	3	4	5	6	
25	PAŌNE 1624	7	8	9	10	11	12	13	SANĒ 1900
26		14	15	16	17	18	19	20	
27		21	22	23	24	25	26	27	
28		28	29	30	1	2	3	4	
29	EPĒP 1624	5	6	7	8	9	10	11	HAMLĒ 1900
30		12	13	14	15	16	17	18	
31		19	20	21	22	23	24	25	
32		26	27	28	29	30	1	2	
33	MESORĒ 1624	3	4	5	6	7	8	9	NAHASĒ 1900
34		10	11	12	13[h]	14	15	16	
35		17	18	19	20	21	22	23	
36		24	25	26	27	28	29	30	
37	EPAG. 1624 / THOOUT 1625	1	2	3	4	5	1[a]	2	PĀG. 1900 / MASKARAM 1901
38		3	4	5	6	7	8	9	
39		10	11	12	13	14	15	16	
40		17[b]	18	19	20	21	22	23	
41		24	25	26	27	28	29	30	
42	PAOPE 1625	1	2	3	4	5	6	7	TEQEMT 1901
43		8	9	10	11	12	13	14	
44		15	16	17	18	19	20	21	
45		22	23	24	25	26	27	28	
46	ATHŌR 1625	29	30	1	2	3	4	5	HEDĀR 1901
47		6	7	8	9	10	11	12	
48		13	14	15	16	17	18	19	
49		20	21	22	23	24	25	26	
50	KOIAK 1625	27	28	29	30	1	2	3	TĀKHŚĀŚ 1901
51		4	5	6	7	8	9	10	
52		11	12	13	14	15	16	17	
53		18	19	20	21	22	23	24	

‡Leap year
[a]New Year
[b]Spring (0:27)
[c]Summer (20:19)
[d]Autumn (10:58)
[e]Winter (5:33)
● New moon
◐ First quarter moon
○ Full moon
◑ Last quarter moon

‡Leap year
[a]New Year
[b]Yom Kippur
[c]Sukkot
[d]Winter starts
[e]Ḥanukkah
[f]Purim
[g]Passover
[h]Shavuot
[i]Fast of Av

[a]New Year (4606, Monkey)
[b]Lantern Festival
[c]Qīngmíng
[d]Dragon Festival
[e]Qīqiǎo
[f]Hungry Ghosts
[g]Mid-Autumn Festival
[h]Double-Ninth Festival
[i]Dōngzhì
*Start of 60-name cycle

[a]New Year
[b]Building of the Cross
[c]Christmas
[d]Jesus's Circumcision
[e]Epiphany
[f]Easter
[g]Mary's Announcement
[h]Jesus's Transfiguration

1908

PERSIAN (ASTRONOMICAL) 1286/1287

Month	Sun	Mon	Tue	Wed	Thu	Fri	Sat
DEY 1286	7	8	9	10	11	12	13
	14	15	16	17	18	19	20
	21	22	23	24	25	26	27
BAHMAN 1286	28	29	30	1	2	3	4
	5	6	7	8	9	10	11
	12	13	14	15	16	17	18
	19	20	21	22	23	24	25
ESFAND 1286	26	27	28	29	30	1	2
	3	4	5	6	7	8	9
	10	11	12	13	14	15	16
	17	18	19	20	21	22	23
FARVARDIN 1287	24	25	26	27	28	29	1[a]
	2	3	4	5	6	7	8
	9	10	11	12	13[b]	14	15
	16	17	18	19	20	21	22
	23	24	25	26	27	28	29
ORDIBEHEŠT 1287	30	31	1	2	3	4	5
	6	7	8	9	10	11	12
	13	14	15	16	17	18	19
	20	21	22	23	24	25	26
XORDĀD 1287	27	28	29	30	31	1	2
	3	4	5	6	7	8	9
	10	11	12	13	14	15	16
	17	18	19	20	21	22	23
	24	25	26	27	28	29	30
TĪR 1287	31	1	2	3	4	5	6
	7	8	9	10	11	12	13
	14	15	16	17	18	19	20
	21	22	23	24	25	26	27
MORDĀD 1287	28	29	30	31	1	2	3
	4	5	6	7	8	9	10
	11	12	13	14	15	16	17
	18	19	20	21	22	23	24
	25	26	27	28	29	30	31
SHAHRĪVAR 1287	1	2	3	4	5	6	7
	8	9	10	11	12	13	14
	15	16	17	18	19	20	21
	22	23	24	25	26	27	28
MEHR 1287	29	30	31	1	2	3	4
	5	6	7	8	9	10	11
	12	13	14	15	16	17	18
	19	20	21	22	23	24	25
ĀBĀN 1287	26	27	28	29	30	1	2
	3	4	5	6	7	8	9
	10	11	12	13	14	15	16
	17	18	19	20	21	22	23
	24	25	26	27	28	29	30
ĀZAR 1287	1	2	3	4	5	6	7
	8	9	10	11	12	13	14
	15	16	17	18	19	20	21
	22	23	24	25	26	27	28
DEY 1287	29	30	1	2	3	4	5
	6	7	8	9	10	11	12

HINDU LUNAR 1964‡/1965

Month	Sun	Mon	Tue	Wed	Thu	Fri	Sat
PAUSHA 1964	24	25	26	27	**28**	30	1
	2	3	4	5	6	7	8
	9	10	11	12	13	14	15
	16	17	18	19	20	21	22
	23	24	25	26	27	28	29
MĀGHA 1964	30	1	2	**3**	5	6	7
	8	9	10	11	12	12	13
	14	15	16	17	18	19	20
	21	22	23	24	25	26	**27**
PHĀLGUNA 1964	29[h]	30	1	2	3	4	5
	6	7	8	9	10	11	12
	13	14	15	15[i]	16	17	18
	19	**20**	22	23	24	25	26
CHAITRA 1965	27	28	29	30	1[a]	2	3
	4	5	6	7	8[b]	9	10
	11	12	13	14	15	16	17
	18	19	20	21	22	23	**24**
VAIŚĀKHA 1965	26	27	28	29	30	1	2
	3	4	5	6	7	8	9
	9	10	11	12	13	14	15
	16	17	**18**	20	21	22	23
	24	25	26	27	28	29	30
JYAISHTHA 1965	1	2	3	4	5	6	7
	8	9	10	11	12	13	14
	15	16	17	18	19	20	**21**
	23	24	25	26	27	28	29
ĀSHĀDHA 1965	30	1	2	3	4	5	5
	6	7	8	9	10	11	12
	13	15	16	17	18	19	20
	21	22	23	24	25	26	27
ŚRĀVANA 1965	28	29	30	1	2	3	4
	5	6	7	8	9	10	11
	12	13	14	15	**16**	18	19
	20	21	22	23[c]	24	25	26
BHĀDRAPADA 1965	27	28	29	30	1	2	2
	3[d]	4	5	6	7	8	**9**
	11	12	13	14	15	16	17
	18	19	20	21	22	23	24
ĀŚVINA 1965	25	26	27	28	29	30	1
	2	3	4	5	6	7	8[e]
	9[e]	10[e]	11	12	**13**	15	16
	17	18	19	20	21	22	23
	24	25	26	27	27	28	29
KĀRTTIKA 1965	30	1[f]	2	3	4	5	**6**
	8	9	10	11	12	13	14
	15	16	17	18	19	20	21
	22	23	24	25	26	27	28
MĀRGAŚĪRA 1965	29	30	1	2	3	4	5
	6	7	8	9	10	**11**[g]	13
	14	15	16	17	18	19	20
	20	21	22	23	24	25	26
PAUSHA 1965	27	28	29	30	1	2	3
	4	**5**	7	8	9	10	11

HINDU SOLAR 1829/1830

Month	Sun	Mon	Tue	Wed	Thu	Fri	Sat
PAUSHA 1829	15	16	17	18	19	20	21
	22	23	24	25	26	27	28
MĀGHA 1829	29	30	1[b]	2	3	4	5
	6	7	8	9	10	11	12
	13	14	15	16	17	18	19
	20	21	22	23	24	25	26
PHĀLGUNA 1829	27	28	29	1	2	3	4
	5	6	7	8	9	10	11
	12	13	14	15	16	17	18
	19	20	21	22	23	24	25
CHAITRA 1829	26	27	28	29	30	1	2
	3	4	5	6	7	8	9
	10	11	12	13	14	15	16
	17	18	19	20	21	22	23
	24	25	26	27	28	29	30
VAIŚĀKHA 1830	1[a]	2	3	4	5	6	7
	8	9	10	11	12	13	14
	15	16	17	18	19	20	21
	22	23	24	25	26	27	28
JYAISHTHA 1830	29	30	31	1	2	3	4
	5	6	7	8	9	10	11
	12	13	14	15	16	17	18
	19	20	21	22	23	24	25
	26	27	28	29	30	31	32
ĀSHĀDHA 1830	1	2	3	4	5	6	7
	8	9	10	11	12	13	14
	15	16	17	18	19	20	21
	22	23	24	25	26	27	28
ŚRĀVANA 1830	29	30	31	1	2	3	4
	5	6	7	8	9	10	11
	12	13	14	15	16	17	18
	19	20	21	22	23	24	25
	26	27	28	29	30	31	32
BHĀDRAPADA 1830	1	2	3	4	5	6	7
	8	9	10	11	12	13	14
	15	16	17	18	19	20	21
	22	23	24	25	26	27	28
ĀŚVINA 1830	29	30	31	1	2	3	4
	5	6	7	8	9	10	11
	12	13	14	15	16	17	18
	19	20	21	22	23	24	25
KĀRTTIKA 1830	26	27	28	29	30	1	2
	3	4	5	6	7	8	9
	10	11	12	13	14	15	16
	17	18	19	20	21	22	23
	24	25	26	27	28	29	30
MĀRGAŚĪRA 1830	1	2	3	4	5	6	7
	8	9	10	11	12	13	14
	15	16	17	18	19	20	21
	22	23	24	25	26	27	28
PAUSHA 1830	29	1	2	3	4	5	6
	7	8	9	10	11	12	13
	14	15	16	17	18	19	20

ISLAMIC (ASTRONOMICAL) 1325/1326‡

Month	Sun	Mon	Tue	Wed	Thu	Fri	Sat
DHU AL-HIJJA 1325	23	24	25	26	27	28	29
	1	2	3	4	5	6	7
	8	9	10[g]	11	12	13	14
	15	16	17	18	19	20	21
	22	23	24	25	26	27	28
MUHARRAM 1326	29	1[a]	2[d]	3	4	5	6
	7	8	9	10[b]	11	12	13
	14	15	16	17	18	19	20
	21	22	23	24	25	26	27
SAFAR 1326	28	29	30	1	2	3	4
	5	6	7	8	9	10	11
	12	13	14	15	16	17	18
	19	20	21	22	23	24	25
RABĪ' I 1326	26	27	28	29	1	2	3
	4	5	6	7	8	9	10
	11	12[c]	13	14	15	16	17
	18	19	20	21	22	23	24
RABĪ' II 1326	25	26	27	28	29	30	1
	2	3	4	5	6	7	8
	9	10	11	12	13	14	15
	16	17	18	19	20	21	22
	23	24	25	26	27	28	29
JUMĀDĀ I 1326	1	2	3	4	5	6	7
	8	9	10	11	12	13	14
	15	16	17	18	19	20	21
	22	23	24	25	26	27	28
JUMĀDĀ II 1326	29	30	1	2	3	4	5
	6	7	8	9	10	11	12
	13	14	15	16	17	18	19
	20	21	22	23	24	25	26
RAJAB 1326	27	28	29	30	1	2	3
	4	5	6	7	8	9	10
	11	12	13	14	15	16	17
	18	19	20	21	22	23	24
SHA'BĀN 1326	25	26	27[d]	28	29	1	2
	3	4	5	6	7	8	9
	10	11	12	13	14	15	16
	17	18	19	20	21	22	23
	24	25	26	27	28	29	30
RAMAḌĀN 1326	1[e]	2	3	4	5	6	7
	8	9	10	11	12	13	14
	15	16	17	18	19	20	21
	22	23	24	25	26	27	28
SHAWWĀL 1326	29	30	1[f]	2	3	4	5
	6	7	8	9	10	11	12
	13	14	15	16	17	18	19
	20	21	22	23	24	25	26
DHU AL-QA'DA 1326	27	28	29	1	2	3	4
	5	6	7	8	9	10	11
	12	13	14	15	16	17	18
	19	20	21	22	23	24	25
DHU AL-HIJJA 1326	26	27	28	29	30	1	2
	3	4	5	6	7	8	9

GREGORIAN 1908‡

Julian† (Sun)	Sun	Mon	Tue	Wed	Thu	Fri	Sat	Month
Dec 16	29	30	31	1	2	3	4	JANUARY 1908
	5	6	7[a]	8	9	10	11	
Dec 30	12	13	14[b]	15	16	17	18	
	19	20	21	22	23	24	25	
Jan 13	26	27	28	29	30	31	1	
	2	3	4	5	6	7	8	FEBRUARY 1908
Jan 27	9	10	11	12	13	14	15	
	16	17	18	19	20	21	22	
Feb 10	23	24	25	26	27	28	29	
	1	2	3	4[c]	5	6	7	MARCH 1908
Feb 24	8	9	10	11	12	13	14	
	15[d]	16	17	18	19	20	21	
Mar 9	22	23	24	25	26	27	28	
	29	30	31	1	2	3	4	APRIL 1908
Mar 23	5	6	7	8	9	10	11	
	12	13	14	15	16	17	18	
Apr 6	19[e]	20	21	22	23	24	25	
	26[f]	27	28	29	30	1	2	MAY 1908
Apr 20	3	4	5	6	7	8	9	
	10	11	12	13	14	15	16	
May 4	17	18	19	20	21	22	23	
	24	25	26	27	28	29	30	
May 18	31	1	2	3	4	5	6	JUNE 1908
	7	8	9	10	11	12	13	
Jun 1	14	15	16	17	18	19	20	
	21	22	23	24	25	26	27	
Jun 15	28	29	30	1	2	3	4	JULY 1908
	5	6	7	8	9	10	11	
Jun 29	12	13	14	15	16	17	18	
	19	20	21	22	23	24	25	
Jul 13	26	27	28	29	30	31	1	
	2	3	4	5	6	7	8	AUGUST 1908
Jul 27	9	10	11	12	13	14	15	
	16	17	18	19	20	21	22	
Aug 10	23	24	25	26	27	28	29	
	30	31	1	2	3	4	5	SEPTEMBER 1908
Aug 24	6	7	8	9	10	11	12	
	13	14	15	16	17	18	19	
Sep 7	20	21	22	23	24	25	26	
	27	28	29	30	1	2	3	OCTOBER 1908
Sep 21	4	5	6	7	8	9	10	
	11	12	13	14	15	16	17	
Oct 5	18	19	20	21	22	23	24	
	25	26	27	28	29	30	31	
Oct 19	1	2	3	4	5	6	7	NOVEMBER 1908
	8	9	10	11	12	13	14	
Nov 2	15	16	17	18	19	20	21	
	22	23	24	25	26	27	28	
Nov 16	29[g]	30	1	2	3	4	5	DECEMBER 1908
	6	7	8	9	10	11	12	
Nov 30	13	14	15	16	17	18	19	
	20	21	22	23	24	25[h]	26	
Dec 14	27	28	29	30	31	1	2	

Persian: [a]New Year; [b]Sizdeh Bedar

Hindu Lunar: ‡Leap year; [a]New Year (Kīlaka); [b]Birthday of Rāma; [c]Birthday of Krishna; [d]Ganēśa Chaturthī; [e]Dashara; [f]Diwali; [g]Birthday of Vishnu; [h]Night of Śiva; [i]Holi

Hindu Solar: [a]New Year (Rāudra); [b]Pongal

Islamic: ‡Leap year; [a]New Year; [d]New Year (Arithmetic); [b]'Ashūrā'; [c]Prophet's Birthday; [d]Ascent of the Prophet; [e]Start of Ramaḍān; [f]'Id al-Fiṭr; [g]'Id al-'Aḍḥā

Gregorian: ‡Leap year; [a]Orthodox Christmas; [b]Julian New Year; [c]Ash Wednesday; [d]Feast of Orthodoxy; [e]Easter; [f]Orthodox Easter; [g]Advent; [h]Christmas

1909

Gregorian 1909	Sun	Mon	Tue	Wed	Thu	Fri	Sat	Lunar Phases	ISO Week (Mon)	Julian Day (Sun noon)	Hebrew 5669/5670‡	Sun	Mon	Tue	Wed	Thu	Fri	Sat	Molad	Chinese Wù-Shēn/Jǐ-Yǒu‡	Sun	Mon	Tue	Wed	Thu	Fri	Sat	Solar Term	Coptic 1625/1626	Sun	Mon	Tue	Wed	Thu	Fri	Sat	Ethiopic 1901/1902
January 1909	27	28	29	◐	31	1[a]	2	5:40	53	2418303	Teveth 5669	3	4	5	6	7	8	9		Month 12 Wù-Shēn	5	6	7	8	9	10	11		Koiak 1625	18	19	20	21	22	23	24	Tākhśāś 1901
	3	4	5	○	7	8	9	14:12	1	2418310		10	11	12	13	14	15	16			12	13*	14	15	16	17	18	Xiǎo hán	Tôbe 1625	25	26	27	28	29[c]	30	1	Ṭer 1901
	10	11	12	13	◑	15	16	18:11	2	2418317		17	18	19	20	21	22	23			19	20	21	22	23	24	25			2	3	4	5	6[d]	7	8	
	17	18	19	20	21	●	23	0:12	3	2418324	Shevat 5669	24	25	26	27	28	29	1	Thu $20^h38^m4^p$	Month 1 Jǐ-Yǒu	26	27	28	29	30	1[a]	2	Dà hán		9	10	11[e]	12	13	14	15	
	24	25	26	27	◐	29	30	15:07	4	2418331		2	3	4	5	6	7	8			3	4	5	6	7	8	9			16	17	18	19	20	21	22	
February 1909	31	1	2	3	4	○	6	8:24	5	2418338		9	10	11	12	13	14	15			10	11	12	13	14	15[b]	16	Lì chūn		23	24	25	26	27	28	29	
	7	8	9	10	11	12	◑	12:47	6	2418345		16	17	18	19	20	21	22			17	18	19	20	21	22	23		Meshir 1625	30	1	2	3	4	5	6	Yakātit 1901
	14	15	16	17	18	19	●	10:52	7	2418352		23	24	25	26	27	28	29		Month 2 Jǐ-Yǒu	24	25	26	27	28	29	1	Yǔ shuǐ		7	8	9	10	11	12	13	
	21	22	23	24	25	26	◐	2:49	8	2418359	Adar 5669	30	1	2	3	4	5	6	Sat $9^h22^m5^p$		2	3	4	5	6	7	8			14	15	16	17	18	19	20	
March 1909	28	1	2	3	4	5	6		9	2418366		7	8	9	10	11	12	13			9	10	11	12	13	14*	15	Jīng zhé		21	22	23	24	25	26	27	
	○	8	9	10	11	12	13	2:55	10	2418373		14[f]	15	16	17	18	19	20			16	17	18	19	20	21	22		Paremotep 1625	28	29	30	1	2	3	4	Magābit 1901
	14	◑	16	17	18	19	20	3:41	11	2418380		21	22	23	24	25	26	27			23	24	25	26	27	28	29			5	6	7	8	9	10	11	
	●[b]	22	23	24	25	26	27	20:11	12	2418387	Nisan 5669	28	29	1	2	3	4	5	Sun $22^h6^m6^p$	Leap Month 2 Jǐ-Yǒu	30	1	2	3	4	5	6	Chūn fēn		12	13	14	15	16	17	18	
April 1909	◐	29	30	31	1	2	3	16:49	13	2418394		6	7	8	9	10	11	12			7	8	9	10	11	12	13			19	20	21	22	23	24	25	
	4	○	6	7	8	9	10	20:28	14	2418401		13	14	15[g]	16	17	18	19			14	15[c]	16	17	18	19	20	Qīng míng	Parmoute 1625	26	27	28	29	30	1	2	Miyāzyā 1901
	11	12	◑	14	15	16	17	14:30	15	2418408		20	21	22	23	24	25	26			21	22	23	24	25	26	27			3[f]	4	5	6	7	8	9	
	18	19	●	21	22	23	24	4:51	16	2418415	Iyyar 5669	27	28	29	30	1	2	3	Tue $10^h50^m7^p$	Month 3 Jǐ-Yǒu	28	29	1	2	3	4	5	Gǔ yǔ		10	11	12	13	14	15	16	
May 1909	25	26	◐	28	29	30	1	8:36	17	2418422		4	5	6	7	8	9	10			6	7	8	9	10	11	12			17	18	19	20	21	22	23	
	2	3	4	○	6	7	8	12:08	18	2418429		11	12	13	14	15	16	17			13	14	15*	16	17	18	19	Lì xià		24	25	26	27	28	29[g]	30	
	9	10	11	◑	13	14	15	21:45	19	2418436		18	19	20	21	22	23	24			20	21	22	23	24	25	26		Pashons 1625	1	2	3	4	5	6	7	Genbot 1901
	16	17	18	●	20	21	22	13:42	20	2418443	Sivan 5669	25	26	27	28	29	1	2	Wed $23^h34^m8^p$	Month 4 Jǐ-Yǒu	27	28	29	1	2	3	4	Xiǎo mǎn		8	9	10	11	12	13	14	
	23	24	25	26	◐	28	29	1:27	21	2418450		3	4	5	6[h]	7	8	9			5	6	7	8	9	10	11			15	16	17	18	19	20	21	
June 1909	30	31	1	2	3	○	5	1:25	22	2418457		10	11	12	13	14	15	16			12	13	14	15	16	17	18			22	23	24	25	26	27	28	
	6	7	8	9	10	◑	12	2:43	23	2418464		17	18	19	20	21	22	23			19	20	21	22	23	24	25	Máng zhòng	Paōne 1625	29	30	1	2	3	4	5	Sanē 1901
	13	14	15	16	●	18	19	23:28	24	2418471		24	25	26	27	28	29	30		Month 5 Jǐ-Yǒu	26	27	28	29	30	1	2			6	7	8	9	10	11	12	
	20	21	22[c]	23	24	◐	26	18:43	25	2418478	Tammuz 5669	1	2	3	4	5	6	7	Fri $12^h18^m9^p$		3	4	5[d]	6	7	8	9	Xià zhì		13	14	15	16	17	18	19	
July 1909	27	28	29	30	1	2	○	12:17	26	2418485		8	9	10	11	12	13	14			10	11	12	13	14	15	16*			20	21	22	23	24	25	26	
	4	5	6	7	8	9	◑	6:58	27	2418492		15	16	17	18	19	20	21			17	18	19	20	21	22	23	Xiǎo shǔ	Epêp 1625	27	28	29	30	1	2	3	Ḥamlē 1901
	11	12	13	14	15	16	●	10:45	28	2418499		22	23	24	25	26	27	28		Month 6 Jǐ-Yǒu	24	25	26	27	28	29	1			4	5	6	7	8	9	10	
	18	19	20	21	22	23	24		29	2418506	Av 5669	29	1	2	3	4	5	6	Sun $1^h2^m10^p$		2	3	4	5	6	7	8	Dà shǔ		11	12	13	14	15	16	17	
	◐	26	27	28	29	30	31	11:45	30	2418513		7	8	9[i]	10	11	12	13			9	10	11	12	13	14	15			18	19	20	21	22	23	24	
August 1909	○	2	3	4	5	6	7	21:14	31	2418520		14	15	16	17	18	19	20			16	17	18	19	20	21	22		Mesorē 1625	25	26	27	28	29	30	1	Naḥasē 1901
	◑	9	10	11	12	13	14	12:10	32	2418527		21	22	23	24	25	26	27			23	24	25	26	27	28	29	Lì qiū		2	3	4	5	6	7	8	
	●	16	17	18	19	20	21	23:55	33	2418534	Elul 5669	28	29	30	1	2	3	4	Mon $13^h46^m11^p$	Month 7 Jǐ-Yǒu	30	1	2	3	4	5	6			9	10	11	12	13[h]	14	15	
	22	23	◐	25	26	27	28	3:55	34	2418541		5	6	7	8	9	10	11			7[e]	8	9	10	11	12	13	Chǔ shǔ		16	17	18	19	20	21	22	
September 1909	29	30	○	1	2	3	4	5:08	35	2418548		12	13	14	15	16	17	18			14	15[f]	16	17*	18	19	20			23	24	25	26	27	28	29	
	5	◑	7	8	9	10	11	19:44	36	2418555		19	20	21	22	23	24	25			21	22	23	24	25	26	27	Bái lù	Epag. 1625 / Thoout 1626	30	1	2	3	4	5	1[a]	Pāg. 1901 / Maskaram 1902
	12	13	●	15	16	17	18	15:08	37	2418562	Tishri 5670	26	27	28	29	1[a]	2[a]	3	Wed $2^h30^m12^p$	Month 8 Jǐ-Yǒu	28	29	1	2	3	4	5			2	3	4	5	6	7	8	
	19	20	21	◐	23[d]	24	25	18:31	38	2418569		4	5	6	7	8	9	10[b]			6	7	8	9	10	11	12	Qiū fēn		9	10	11	12	13	14	15	
October 1909	26	27	28	○	30	1	2	13:06	39	2418576		11	12	13	14	15[c]	16	17			13	14	15[g]	16	17	18	19			16	17[b]	18	19	20	21	22	
	3	4	5	◑	7	8	9	6:44	40	2418583		18	19	20	21	22	23	24			20	21	22	23	24	25	26	Hán lù		23	24	25	26	27	28	29	
	10	11	12	13	●	15	16	8:13	41	2418590	Ḥeshvan 5670	25	26	27	28	29	30	1	Thu $15^h14^m13^p$	Month 9 Jǐ-Yǒu	27	28	29	30	1	2	3		Paope 1626	30	1	2	3	4	5	6	Ṭeqemt 1902
	17	18	19	20	21	◐	23	7:03	42	2418597		2	3	4	5	6	7	8			4	5	6	7	8	9[h]	10			7	8	9	10	11	12	13	
	24	25	26	27	○	29	30	22:07	43	2418604		9	10	11	12	13	14	15			11	12	13	14	15	16	17	Shuāng jiàng		14	15	16	17	18	19	20	
November 1909	31	1	2	3	◑	5	6	21:38	44	2418611		16	17	18	19	20	21	22			18*	19	20	21	22	23	24			21	22	23	24	25	26	27	
	7	8	9	10	11	12	●	2:18	45	2418618		23	24	25	26	27	28	29		Month 10 Jǐ-Yǒu	25	26	27	28	29	30	1	Lì dōng	Athōr 1626	28	29	30	1	2	3	4	Ḫedār 1902
	14	15	16	17	18	19	◐	17:29	46	2418625	Kislev 5670	1	2	3	4	5	6	7	Sat $3^h58^m14^p$		2	3	4	5	6	7	8			5	6	7	8	9	10	11	
	21	22	23	24	25	26	○	8:52	47	2418632		8	9	10	11	12	13	14			9	10	11	12	13	14	15	Xiǎo xuě		12	13	14	15	16	17	18	
December 1909	28	29	30	1	2	3	◑	16:12	48	2418639		15	16	17	18	19	20	21			16	17	18	19	20	21	22			19	20	21	22	23	24	25	
	5	6	7	8	9	10	11		49	2418646		22[d]	23	24	25[e]	26[e]	27[e]	28[e]			23	24	25	26	27	28	29	Dà xuě	Koiak 1626	26	27	28	29	30	1	2	Tākhśāś 1902
	●	13	14	15	16	17	18	19:59	50	2418653	Teveth 5670	29[e]	1[e]	2[e]	3[e]	4	5	6	Sun $16^h42^m15^p$	Month 11 Jǐ-Yǒu	30	1	2	3	4	5	6			3	4	5	6	7	8	9	
	19	◐	21	22[e]	23	24	25	2:17	51	2418660		7	8	9	10	11	12	13			7	8	9	10[i]	11	12	13	Dōng zhì		10	11	12	13	14	15	16	
	○	27	28	29	30	31	1	21:30	52	2418667		14	15	16	17	18	19	20			14	15	16	17	18*	19	20			17	18	19	20	21	22	23	

[a]New Year
[b]Spring (6:13)
[c]Summer (2:06)
[d]Autumn (16:45)
[e]Winter (11:20)
● New moon
◐ First quarter moon
○ Full moon
◑ Last quarter moon

‡Leap year
[a]New Year
[b]Yom Kippur
[c]Sukkot
[d]Winter starts
[e]Ḥanukkah
[f]Purim
[g]Passover
[h]Shavuot
[i]Fast of Av

‡Leap year
[a]New Year (4607, Fowl)
[b]Lantern Festival
[c]Qīngmíng
[d]Dragon Festival
[e]Qīqiǎo
[f]Hungry Ghosts
[g]Mid-Autumn Festival
[h]Double-Ninth Festival
[i]Dōngzhì
*Start of 60-name cycle

[a]New Year
[b]Building of the Cross
[c]Christmas
[d]Jesus's Circumcision
[e]Epiphany
[f]Easter
[g]Mary's Announcement
[h]Jesus's Transfiguration

1909

PERSIAN (ASTRONOMICAL) 1287/1288‡

Month	Sun	Mon	Tue	Wed	Thu	Fri	Sat
DEY 1287	6	7	8	9	10	11	12
	13	14	15	16	17	18	19
	20	21	22	23	24	25	26
	27	28	29	30	1	2	3
BAHMAN 1287	4	5	6	7	8	9	10
	11	12	13	14	15	16	17
	18	19	20	21	22	23	24
	25	26	27	28	29	30	1
ESFAND 1287	2	3	4	5	6	7	8
	9	10	11	12	13	14	15
	16	17	18	19	20	21	22
	23	24	25	26	27	28	29
FARVARDĪN 1288	1[a]	2	3	4	5	6	7
	8	9	10	11	12	13[b]	14
	15	16	17	18	19	20	21
	22	23	24	25	26	27	28
	29	30	31	1	2	3	4
ORDĪBEHEŠT 1288	5	6	7	8	9	10	11
	12	13	14	15	16	17	18
	19	20	21	22	23	24	25
	26	27	28	29	30	31	1
XORDĀD 1288	2	3	4	5	6	7	8
	9	10	11	12	13	14	15
	16	17	18	19	20	21	22
	23	24	25	26	27	28	29
	30	31	1	2	3	4	5
TĪR 1288	6	7	8	9	10	11	12
	13	14	15	16	17	18	19
	20	21	22	23	24	25	26
	27	28	29	30	31	1	2
MORDĀD 1288	3	4	5	6	7	8	9
	10	11	12	13	14	15	16
	17	18	19	20	21	22	23
	24	25	26	27	28	29	30
	31	1	2	3	4	5	6
SHAHRĪVAR 1288	7	8	9	10	11	12	13
	14	15	16	17	18	19	20
	21	22	23	24	25	26	27
	28	29	30	31	1	2	3
MEHR 1288	4	5	6	7	8	9	10
	11	12	13	14	15	16	17
	18	19	20	21	22	23	24
	25	26	27	28	29	30	1
ĀBĀN 1288	2	3	4	5	6	7	8
	9	10	11	12	13	14	15
	16	17	18	19	20	21	22
	23	24	25	26	27	28	29
	30	1	2	3	4	5	6
ĀZAR 1288	7	8	9	10	11	12	13
	14	15	16	17	18	19	20
	21	22	23	24	25	26	27
	28	29	30	1	2	3	4
DEY 1288	5	6	7	8	9	10	11

HINDU LUNAR 1965/1966‡

Month	Sun	Mon	Tue	Wed	Thu	Fri	Sat
PAUSHA 1965	4	5	7	8	9	10	11
	12	13	14	15	16	17	18
	19	20	21	22	22	23	24
	25	26	27	28	29	1	2
MĀGHA 1965	3	4	5	6	7	8	9
	10	11	12	13	14	15	16
	17	18	19	20	21	22	23
	24	25	26	27	28[h]	29	30
PHĀLGUNA 1965	1	2	3	4	6	7	8
	9	10	11	12	13	14	15
	15[i]	16	17	18	19	20	21
	22	23	24	25	26	27	28
CHAITRA 1966	30	1[a]	2	3	4	5	6
	7	8	9[b]	10	11	12	13
	14	15	16	17	18	19	20
	21	22	23	24	25	26	27
	28	29	30	1	2	4	5
VAIŚĀKHA 1966	6	7	8	9	9	10	11
	12	13	14	15	16	17	18
	19	20	21	22	23	24	25
	27	28	29	30	1	2	3
JYAISHTHA 1966	4	5	6	7	8	9	10
	11	12	13	14	14	15	16
	17	19	20	21	22	23	24
	25	26	27	28	29	1	2
ĀSHĀDHA 1966	3	4	5	5	6	7	8
	9	10	11	12	13	14	15
	16	17	18	19	20	21	23
	24	25	26	27	28	29	30
LEAP ŚRĀVAṆA 1966	1	2	3	4	5	6	7
	8	9	10	11	12	13	14
	15	16	17	18	19	20	21
	22	23	24	26	27	28	29
	30	1	2	2	3	4	5
ŚRĀVAṆA 1966	6	7	8	9	10	11	12
	13	14	15	16	18	19	20
	21	22	23[c]	24	25	26	27
	28	29	30	1	2	3	4[d]
BHĀDRAPADA 1966	5	6	7	8	9	10	11
	12	13	14	15	16	17	18
	19	20	21	23	24	25	26
	27	27	28	29	30	1	2
ĀŚVINA 1966	3	4	5	6	7	8[e]	9[e]
	10[e]	11	12	13	15	16	17
	18	19	20	21	22	23	24
	25	26	27	28	29	30	30
KĀRTTIKA 1966	1[f]	2	3	4	5	6	7
	9	10	11	12	13	14	15
	16	17	18	19	20	21	22
	23	24	25	26	27	28	29
	30	1	2	3	4	5	6
MĀRGAŚIRA 1966	7	8	9	10	11[g]	12	14
	15	16	17	18	19	20	21

HINDU SOLAR 1830/1831‡

Month	Sun	Mon	Tue	Wed	Thu	Fri	Sat
PAUSHA 1830	14	15	16	17	18	19	20
	21	22	23	24	25	26	27
	28	29	30	1[b]	2	3	4
MĀGHA 1830	5	6	7	8	9	10	11
	12	13	14	15	16	17	18
	19	20	21	22	23	24	25
	26	27	28	29	1	2	3
PHĀLGUNA 1830	4	5	6	7	8	9	10
	11	12	13	14	15	16	17
	18	19	20	21	22	23	24
	25	26	27	28	29	30	1
CHAITRA 1830	2	3	4	5	6	7	8
	9	10	11	12	13	14	15
	16	17	18	19	20	21	22
	23	24	25	26	27	28	29
	30	1[a]	2	3	4	5	6
VAIŚĀKHA 1831	7	8	9	10	11	12	13
	14	15	16	17	18	19	20
	21	22	23	24	25	26	27
	28	29	30	31	1	2	3
JYAISHTHA 1831	4	5	6	7	8	9	10
	11	12	13	14	15	16	17
	18	19	20	21	22	23	24
	25	26	27	28	29	30	31
	32	1	2	3	4	5	6
ĀSHĀDHA 1831	7	8	9	10	11	12	13
	14	15	16	17	18	19	20
	21	22	23	24	25	26	27
	28	29	30	31	1	2	3
ŚRĀVAṆA 1831	4	5	6	7	8	9	10
	11	12	13	14	15	16	17
	18	19	20	21	22	23	24
	25	26	27	28	29	30	31
	32	1	2	3	4	5	6
BHĀDRAPADA 1831	7	8	9	10	11	12	13
	14	15	16	17	18	19	20
	21	22	23	24	25	26	27
	28	29	30	31	1	2	3
ĀŚVINA 1831	4	5	6	7	8	9	10
	11	12	13	14	15	16	17
	18	19	20	21	22	23	24
	25	26	27	28	29	30	1
KĀRTTIKA 1831	2	3	4	5	6	7	8
	9	10	11	12	13	14	15
	16	17	18	19	20	21	22
	23	24	25	26	27	28	29
	30	1	2	3	4	5	6
MĀRGAŚIRA 1831	7	8	9	10	11	12	13
	14	15	16	17	18	19	20
	21	22	23	24	25	26	27
	28	29	30	1	2	3	4
PAUSHA 1831	5	6	7	8	9	10	11
	12	13	14	15	16	17	18

ISLAMIC (ASTRONOMICAL) 1326‡/1327‡

Month	Sun	Mon	Tue	Wed	Thu	Fri	Sat
DHU AL-HIJJA 1326	3	4	5	6	7	8	9
	10[g]	11	12	13	14	15	16
	17	18	19	20	21	22	23
	24	25	26	27	28	29	1[a]
MUHARRAM 1327	2	3	4	5	6	7	8
	9	10[b]	11	12	13	14	15
	16	17	18	19	20	21	22
	23	24	25	26	27	28	29
	30	1	2	3	4	5	6
SAFAR 1327	7	8	9	10	11	12	13
	14	15	16	17	18	19	20
	21	22	23	24	25	26	27
	28	29	1	2	3	4	5
RABĪ' I 1327	6	7	8	9	10	11	12[c]
	13	14	15	16	17	18	19
	20	21	22	23	24	25	26
	27	28	29	1	2	3	4
RABĪ' II 1327	5	6	7	8	9	10	11
	12	13	14	15	16	17	18
	19	20	21	22	23	24	25
	26	27	28	29	30	1	2
JUMĀDĀ I 1327	3	4	5	6	7	8	9
	10	11	12	13	14	15	16
	17	18	19	20	21	22	23
	24	25	26	27	28	29	1
JUMĀDĀ II 1327	2	3	4	5	6	7	8
	9	10	11	12	13	14	15
	16	17	18	19	20	21	22
	23	24	25	26	27	28	29
	30	1	2	3	4	5	6
RAJAB 1327	7	8	9	10	11	12	13
	14	15	16	17	18	19	20
	21	22	23	24	25	26	27[d]
	28	29	1	2	3	4	5
SHA'BĀN 1327	6	7	8	9	10	11	12
	13	14	15	16	17	18	19
	20	21	22	23	24	25	26
	27	28	29	30	1[e]	2	3
RAMAḌĀN 1327	4	5	6	7	8	9	10
	11	12	13	14	15	16	17
	18	19	20	21	22	23	24
	25	26	27	28	29	30	1[f]
SHAWWĀL 1327	2	3	4	5	6	7	8
	9	10	11	12	13	14	15
	16	17	18	19	20	21	22
	23	24	25	26	27	28	29
	30	1	2	3	4	5	6
DHU AL-QA'DA 1327	7	8	9	10	11	12	13
	14	15	16	17	18	19	20
	21	22	23	24	25	26	27
	28	29	1	2	3	4	5
DHU AL-HIJJA 1327	6	7	8	9	10[g]	11	12
	13	14	15	16	17	18	19

GREGORIAN 1909

Julian (Sun)	Sun	Mon	Tue	Wed	Thu	Fri	Sat	Month
Dec 14	27	28	29	30	31	1	2	
	3	4	5	6	7[a]	8	9	JANUARY 1909
Dec 28	10	11	12	13	14[b]	15	16	
	17	18	19	20	21	22	23	
Jan 11	24	25	26	27	28	29	30	
	31	1	2	3	4	5	6	FEBRUARY 1909
Jan 25	7	8	9	10	11	12	13	
	14	15	16	17	18	19	20	
Feb 8	21	22	23	24[c]	25	26	27	
	28[d]	1	2	3	4	5	6	MARCH 1909
Feb 22	7	8	9	10	11	12	13	
	14	15	16	17	18	19	20	
Mar 8	21	22	23	24	25	26	27	
	28	29	30	31	1	2	3	APRIL 1909
Mar 22	4	5	6	7	8	9	10	
	11[e]	12	13	14	15	16	17	
Apr 5	18	19	20	21	22	23	24	
	25	26	27	28	29	30	1	MAY 1909
Apr 19	2	3	4	5	6	7	8	
	9	10	11	12	13	14	15	
May 3	16	17	18	19	20	21	22	
	23	24	25	26	27	28	29	
May 17	30	31	1	2	3	4	5	JUNE 1909
	6	7	8	9	10	11	12	
May 31	13	14	15	16	17	18	19	
	20	21	22	23	24	25	26	
Jun 14	27	28	29	30	1	2	3	JULY 1909
	4	5	6	7	8	9	10	
Jun 28	11	12	13	14	15	16	17	
	18	19	20	21	22	23	24	
Jul 12	25	26	27	28	29	30	31	
	1	2	3	4	5	6	7	AUGUST 1909
Jul 26	8	9	10	11	12	13	14	
	15	16	17	18	19	20	21	
Aug 9	22	23	24	25	26	27	28	
	29	30	31	1	2	3	4	SEPTEMBER 1909
Aug 23	5	6	7	8	9	10	11	
	12	13	14	15	16	17	18	
Sep 6	19	20	21	22	23	24	25	
	26	27	28	29	30	1	2	OCTOBER 1909
Sep 20	3	4	5	6	7	8	9	
	10	11	12	13	14	15	16	
Oct 4	17	18	19	20	21	22	23	
	24	25	26	27	28	29	30	
Oct 18	31	1	2	3	4	5	6	NOVEMBER 1909
	7	8	9	10	11	12	13	
Nov 1	14	15	16	17	18	19	20	
	21	22	23	24	25	26	27	
Nov 15	28[g]	29	30	1	2	3	4	DECEMBER 1909
	5	6	7	8	9	10	11	
Nov 29	12	13	14	15	16	17	18	
	19	20	21	22	23	24	25[h]	
Dec 13	26	27	28	29	30	31	1	

Persian: ‡Leap year; [a]New Year; [b]Sizdeh Bedar

Hindu Lunar: ‡Leap year; [a]New Year (Saumya); [b]Birthday of Rāma; [c]Birthday of Krishna; [d]Ganēśa Chaturthī; [e]Dashara; [f]Diwali; [g]Birthday of Vishnu; [h]Night of Śiva; [i]Holi

Hindu Solar: ‡Leap year; [a]New Year (Durmati); [b]Pongal

Islamic: ‡Leap year; [a]New Year; [b]'Ashūrā'; [c]Prophet's Birthday; [d]Ascent of the Prophet; [e]Start of Ramaḍān; [f]'Īd al-Fiṭr; [g]'Īd al-'Aḍḥā

Gregorian: [a]Orthodox Christmas; [b]Julian New Year; [c]Ash Wednesday; [d]Feast of Orthodoxy; [e]Easter (also Orthodox); [g]Advent; [h]Christmas

1910

Gregorian 1910

Month	Sun	Mon	Tue	Wed	Thu	Fri	Sat	Lunar Phases	ISO Week (Mon)	Julian Day (Sun noon)
	○	27	28	29	30	31	1[a]	21:30	52	2418667
JANUARY 1910	2	◑	4	5	6	7	8	13:27	1	2418674
	9	10	●	12	13	14	15	11:51	2	2418681
	16	17	◐	19	20	21	22	10:20	3	2418688
	23	24	○	26	27	28	29	11:50	4	2418695
	30	31	1	◑	3	4	5	11:27	5	2418702
FEBRUARY 1910	6	7	8	9	●	11	12	1:13	6	2418709
	13	14	15	◐	17	18	19	18:32	7	2418716
	20	21	22	23	○	25	26	3:36	8	2418723
	27	28	1	2	3	◑	5	7:52	9	2418730
MARCH 1910	6	7	8	9	10	●	12	12:12	10	2418737
	13	14	15	16	17	◐	19	3:37	11	2418744
	20	21[b]	22	23	24	○	26	20:21	12	2418751
	27	28	29	30	31	1	2		13	2418758
APRIL 1910	◑	4	5	6	7	8	●	0:47 21:25	14	2418765
	10	11	12	13	14	15	◐	14:04	15	2418772
	17	18	19	20	21	22	23		16	2418779
	○	25	26	27	28	29	30	13:22	17	2418786
MAY 1910	1	◑	3	4	5	6	7	13:29	18	2418793
	8	●	10	11	12	13	14	5:33	19	2418800
	15	◐	17	18	19	20	21	2:13	20	2418807
	22	23	○	25	26	27	28	5:39	21	2418814
	29	30	◑	1	2	3	4	22:24	22	2418821
JUNE 1910	5	6	●	8	9	10	11	13:16	23	2418828
	12	13	◐	15	16	17	18	16:19	24	2418835
	19	20	21	○[c]	23	24	25	20:12	25	2418842
	26	27	28	29	◑	1	2	4:39	26	2418849
JULY 1910	3	4	5	●	7	8	9	21:20	27	2418856
	10	11	12	13	◐	15	16	8:24	28	2418863
	17	18	19	20	21	○	23	8:37	29	2418870
	24	25	26	27	28	◑	30	9:34	30	2418877
	31	1	2	3	4	●	6	6:37	31	2418884
AUGUST 1910	7	8	9	10	11	12	◐	2:01	32	2418891
	14	15	16	17	18	19	○	19:14	33	2418898
	21	22	23	24	25	26	◑	14:33	34	2418905
	28	29	30	31	1	2	●	18:06	35	2418912
SEPTEMBER 1910	4	5	6	7	8	9	10		36	2418919
	◐	12	13	14	15	16	17	20:10	37	2418926
	18	○	20	21	22	23[d]	24	4:52	38	2418933
	◑	26	27	28	29	30	1	20:54	39	2418940
OCTOBER 1910	2	●	4	5	6	7	8	8:32	40	2418947
	9	10	◐	12	13	14	15	13:40	41	2418954
	16	17	○	19	20	21	22	14:24	42	2418961
	23	24	◑	26	27	28	29	5:48	43	2418968
	30	31	1	●	3	4	5	1:56	44	2418975
NOVEMBER 1910	6	7	8	9	◐	11	12	5:29	45	2418982
	13	14	15	16	○	18	19	0:25	46	2418989
	20	21	22	◑	24	25	26	18:13	47	2418996
	27	28	29	30	●	2	3	21:10	48	2419003
DECEMBER 1910	4	5	6	7	8	◐	10	19:05	49	2419010
	11	12	13	14	15	○	17	11:05	50	2419017
	18	19	20	21	22[e]	◑	24	10:35	51	2419024
	25	26	27	28	29	30	●	16:21	52	2419031

Hebrew 5670‡/5671

ISO Week	Month	Sun	Mon	Tue	Wed	Thu	Fri	Sat	Molad
52	TEVETH 5670	14	15	16	17	18	19	20	
1		21	22	23	24	25	26	27	
2		28	29	1	2	3	4	5	Tue 5h26m16p
3	SHEVAT 5670	6	7	8	9	10	11	12	
4		13	14	15	16	17	18	19	
5		20	21	22	23	24	25	26	
6		27	28	29	30	1	2	3	Wed 18h10m17p
7	ADAR I 5670	4	5	6	7	8	9	10	
8		11	12	13	14	15	16	17	
9		18	19	20	21	22	23	24	
10		25	26	27	28	29	30	1	Fri 6h55m0p
11	ADAR II 5670	2	3	4	5	6	7	8	
12		9	10	11	12	13	14[f]	15	
13		16	17	18	19	20	21	22	
14		23	24	25	26	27	28	29	Sat 19h39m1p
15	NISAN 5670	1	2	3	4	5	6	7	
16		8	9	10	11	12	13	14	
17		15[g]	16	17	18	19	20	21	
18		22	23	24	25	26	27	28	Mon 8h23m2p
19	IYAR 5670	29	30	1	2	3	4	5	
20		6	7	8	9	10	11	12	
21		13	14	15	16	17	18	19	
22		20	21	22	23	24	25	26	Tue 21h7m3p
23		27	28	29	1	2	3	4	
24	SIVAN 5670	5	6[h]	7	8	9	10	11	
25		12	13	14	15	16	17	18	
26		19	20	21	22	23	24	25	Thu 9h51m4p
27		26	27	28	29	30	1	2	
28	TAMMUZ 5670	3	4	5	6	7	8	9	
29		10	11	12	13	14	15	16	
30		17	18	19	20	21	22	23	Fri 22h35m5p
31		24	25	26	27	28	29	1	
32	AV 5670	2	3	4	5	6	7	8	
33		9[i]	10	11	12	13	14	15	
34		16	17	18	19	20	21	22	
35		23	24	25	26	27	28	29	Sun 11h19m6p
36		30	1	2	3	4	5	6	
37	ELUL 5670	7	8	9	10	11	12	13	
38		14	15	16	17	18	19	20	
39		21	22	23	24	25	26	27	Tue 0h3m7p
40		28	29	1[a]	2[a]	3	4	5	
41	TISHRI 5671	6	7	8	9	10[b]	11	12	
42		13	14	15[c]	16	17	18	19	
43		20	21	22	23	24	25	26	Wed 12h47m8p
44		27	28	29	30	1	2	3	
45	HESHVAN 5671	4	5	6	7	8	9	10	
46		11	12	13	14	15	16	17	
47		18	19	20	21	22	23	24	Fri 1h31m9p
48		25	26	27	28	29	1	2	
49	KISLEV 5671	3	4[d]	5	6	7	8	9	
50		10	11	12	13	14	15	16	
51		17	18	19	20	21	22	23	
52		24	25[e]	26[e]	27[e]	28[e]	29[e]	30[e]	

Chinese Jĭ-Yŏu‡/Gēng-Xū

ISO Week	Month	Sun	Mon	Tue	Wed	Thu	Fri	Sat	Solar Term
52	MONTH 11 Jĭ-Yŏu	14	15	16	17	18	19	20	
1		21	22	23	24	25	26	27	Xiăo hán
2		28	29	1	2	3	4	5	
3	MONTH 12 Jĭ-Yŏu	6	7	8	9	10	**11**	12	Dà hán
4		13	14	15	16	17	18	19	
5		20	21	22	23	24	25	26	Lì chūn
6		27	28	29	30	1[a]	2	3	
7	MONTH 1 Gēng-Xū	4	5	6	7	8	9	**10**	Yŭ shuĭ
8		11	12	13	14	15[b]	16	17	
9		18	19*	20	21	22	23	24	
10		25	26	27	28	29	1	2	Jīng zhé
11	MONTH 2 Gēng-Xū	3	4	5	6	7	8	9	
12		10	**11**	12	13	14	15	16	Chūn fēn
13		17	18	19	20	21	22	23	
14		24	25	26	27[c]	28	29	30	Qīng míng
15	MONTH 3 Gēng-Xū	1	2	3	4	5	6	7	
16		8	9	10	11	**12**	13	14	Gŭ yŭ
17		15	16	17	18	19	20*	21	
18		22	23	24	25	26	27	28	Lì xià
19		29	1	2	3	4	5	6	
20	MONTH 4 Gēng-Xū	7	8	9	10	11	12	13	
21		**14**	15	16	17	18	19	20	Xiăo măn
22		21	22	23	24	25	26	27	
23		28	29	1	2	3	4	5[d]	Máng zhòng
24	MONTH 5 Gēng-Xū	6	7	8	9	10	11	12	
25		13	14	15	**16**	17	18	19	Xià zhì
26		20	21	22*	23	24	25	26	
27		27	28	29	30	1	2	3	Xiăo shŭ
28	MONTH 6 Gēng-Xū	4	5	6	7	8	9	10	
29		11	12	13	14	15	16	17	
30		**18**	19	20	21	22	23	24	Dà shŭ
31		25	26	27	28	29	1	2	
32	MONTH 7 Gēng-Xū	3	4	5	6	7[e]	8	9	Lì qiū
33		10	11	12	13	14	15[f]	16	
34		17	18	19	**20**	21	22	23*	Chŭ shŭ
35		24	25	26	27	28	29	30	
36	MONTH 8 Gēng-Xū	1	2	3	4	5	6	7	Bái lù
37		8	9	10	11	12	13	14	
38		15[g]	16	17	18	19	20	**21**	Qiū fēn
39		22	23	24	25	26	27	28	
40		29	1	2	3	4	5	6	
41	MONTH 9 Gēng-Xū	7	8	9[h]	10	11	12	13	Hán lù
42		14	15	16	17	18	19	20	
43		21	**22**	23	24*	25	26	27	Shuāng jiàng
44		28	29	30	1	2	3	4	
45	MONTH 10 Gēng-Xū	5	6	7	8	9	10	11	Lì dōng
46		12	13	14	15	16	17	18	
47		19	20	21	**22**	23	24	25	Xiăo xuě
48		26	27	28	29	30	1	2	
49	MONTH 11 Gēng-Xū	3	4	5	6	7	8	9	Dà xuě
50		10	11	12	13	14	15	16	
51		17	18	19	20	21	22[i]	23	Dōng zhì
52		24*	25	26	27	28	29	30	

Coptic 1626/1627‡ — Ethiopic 1902/1903‡

ISO Week	Coptic Month	Sun	Mon	Tue	Wed	Thu	Fri	Sat	Ethiopic Month
52	KOIAK 1626	17	18	19	20	21	22	23	TĀKHŚĀŚ 1902
1		24	25	26	27	28	29[c]	30	
2	TÔBE 1626	1	2	3	4	5	6[d]	7	ṬER 1902
3		8	9	10	11[e]	12	13	14	
4		15	16	17	18	19	20	21	
5		22	23	24	25	26	27	28	
6		29	30	1	2	3	4	5	
7	MESHIR 1626	6	7	8	9	10	11	12	YAKĀTIT 1902
8		13	14	15	16	17	18	19	
9		20	21	22	23	24	25	26	
10		27	28	29	30	1	2	3	
11	PAREMOTEP 1626	4	5	6	7	8	9	10	MAGĀBIT 1902
12		11	12	13	14	15	16	17	
13		18	19	20	21	22	23	24	
14		25	26	27	28	29	30	1	
15	PARMOUTE 1626	2	3	4	5	6	7	8	MIYĀZYĀ 1902
16		9	10	11	12	13	14	15	
17		16	17	18	19	20	21	22	
18		23[f]	24	25	26	27	28	29[g]	
19		30	1	2	3	4	5	6	
20	PASHONS 1626	7	8	9	10	11	12	13	GENBOT 1902
21		14	15	16	17	18	19	20	
22		21	22	23	24	25	26	27	
23		28	29	30	1	2	3	4	
24	PAÔNE 1626	5	6	7	8	9	10	11	SANĒ 1902
25		12	13	14	15	16	17	18	
26		19	20	21	22	23	24	25	
27		26	27	28	29	30	1	2	
28	EPÊP 1626	3	4	5	6	7	8	9	ḤAMLĒ 1902
29		10	11	12	13	14	15	16	
30		17	18	19	20	21	22	23	
31		24	25	26	27	28	29	30	
32	MESORĒ 1626	1	2	3	4	5	6	7	NAHASĒ 1902
33		8	9	10	11	12	13[h]	14	
34		15	16	17	18	19	20	21	
35		22	23	24	25	26	27	28	
36	EPAG. 1626	29	30	1	2	3	4	5	PĀG. 1902
37	THOOUT 1627	1[a]	2	3	4	5	6	7	MASKARAM 1903
38		8	9	10	11	12	13	14	
39		15	16	17[b]	18	19	20	21	
40		22	23	24	25	26	27	28	
41		29	30	1	2	3	4	5	
42	PAOPE 1627	6	7	8	9	10	11	12	TEQEMT 1903
43		13	14	15	16	17	18	19	
44		20	21	22	23	24	25	26	
45		27	28	29	30	1	2	3	
46	ATHÔR 1627	4	5	6	7	8	9	10	ḪEDĀR 1903
47		11	12	13	14	15	16	17	
48		18	19	20	21	22	23	24	
49		25	26	27	28	29	30	1	
50	KOIAK 1627	2	3	4	5	6	7	8	TĀKHŚĀŚ 1903
51		9	10	11	12	13	14	15	
52		16	17	18	19	20	21	22	

[a]New Year
[b]Spring (12:03)
[c]Summer (7:49)
[d]Autumn (22:31)
[e]Winter (17:12)
● New moon
◐ First quarter moon
○ Full moon
◑ Last quarter moon

‡Leap year
[a]New Year
[b]Yom Kippur
[c]Sukkot
[d]Winter starts
[e]Ḥanukkah
[f]Purim
[g]Passover
[h]Shavuot
[i]Fast of Av

‡Leap year
[a]New Year (4608, Dog)
[b]Lantern Festival
[c]Qīngmíng
[d]Dragon Festival
[e]Qīqiăo
[f]Hungry Ghosts
[g]Mid-Autumn Festival
[h]Double-Ninth Festival
[i]Dōngzhì
*Start of 60-name cycle

‡Leap year
[a]New Year
[b]Building of the Cross
[c]Christmas
[d]Jesus's Circumcision
[e]Epiphany
[f]Easter
[g]Mary's Announcement
[h]Jesus's Transfiguration

PERSIAN (ASTRONOMICAL) 1288‡/1289

Month	Sun	Mon	Tue	Wed	Thu	Fri	Sat
DEY 1288	5	6	7	8	9	10	11
	12	13	14	15	16	17	18
	19	20	21	22	23	24	25
BAHMAN 1288	26	27	28	29	30	1	2
	3	4	5	6	7	8	9
	10	11	12	13	14	15	16
	17	18	19	20	21	22	23
	24	25	26	27	28	29	30
ESFAND 1288	1	2	3	4	5	6	7
	8	9	10	11	12	13	14
	15	16	17	18	19	20	21
	22	23	24	25	26	27	28
FARVARDĪN 1289	29	30	1[a]	2	3	4	5
	6	7	8	9	10	11	12
	13[b]	14	15	16	17	18	19
	20	21	22	23	24	25	26
ORDĪBEHEŠT 1289	27	28	29	30	31	1	2
	3	4	5	6	7	8	9
	10	11	12	13	14	15	16
	17	18	19	20	21	22	23
	24	25	26	27	28	29	30
XORDĀD 1289	31	1	2	3	4	5	6
	7	8	9	10	11	12	13
	14	15	16	17	18	19	20
	21	22	23	24	25	26	27
TĪR 1289	28	29	30	31	1	2	3
	4	5	6	7	8	9	10
	11	12	13	14	15	16	17
	18	19	20	21	22	23	24
	25	26	27	28	29	30	31
MORDĀD 1289	1	2	3	4	5	6	7
	8	9	10	11	12	13	14
	15	16	17	18	19	20	21
	22	23	24	25	26	27	28
SHAHRĪVAR 1289	29	30	31	1	2	3	4
	5	6	7	8	9	10	11
	12	13	14	15	16	17	18
	19	20	21	22	23	24	25
MEHR 1289	26	27	28	29	30	31	1
	2	3	4	5	6	7	8
	9	10	11	12	13	14	15
	16	17	18	19	20	21	22
	23	24	25	26	27	28	29
ĀBĀN 1289	30	1	2	3	4	5	6
	7	8	9	10	11	12	13
	14	15	16	17	18	19	20
	21	22	23	24	25	26	27
ĀZAR 1289	28	29	30	1	2	3	4
	5	6	7	8	9	10	11
	12	13	14	15	16	17	18
	19	20	21	22	23	24	25
DEY 1289	26	27	28	29	30	1	2
	3	4	5	6	7	8	9

HINDU LUNAR 1966‡/1967

Month	Sun	Mon	Tue	Wed	Thu	Fri	Sat
MĀRGAŚĪRA 1966	15	16	17	18	19	20	21
	22	23	*23*	24	25	26	27
PAUSHA 1966	28	29	30	1	2	3	4
	5	**6**	8	9	10	11	12
	13	14	15	16	17	18	19
	20	21	22	23	24	25	*25*
MĀGHA 1966	26	27	28	**29**	1	2	3
	4	5	6	7	8	9	10
	11	12	13	14	15	16	17
	18	19	20	21	22	23	24
PHĀLGUNA 1966	25	26	27	**28**[h]	29	30	1
	2	3	4	**5**	7	8	9
	10	11	12	13	14	15[i]	16
	17	18	*18*	19	20	21	22
	23	24	25	26	27	**28**	30
CHAITRA 1967	1[a]	2	3	4	5	6	7
	8[b]	9	10	11	12	13	14
	15	16	17	18	19	20	21
	22	23	24	25	26	27	28
VAIŚĀKHA 1967	29	30	1	**2**	4	5	6
	7	8	9	10	11	12	13
	13	14	15	16	17	18	19
	20	21	22	23	24	**25**	27
JYAISHTHA 1967	28	29	30	1	2	3	4
	5	6	7	8	9	10	11
	12	13	14	15	16	17	18
	19	20	21	22	23	24	25
ĀSHĀDHA 1967	26	27	**28**	30	1	2	3
	4	5	6	7	8	9	10
	10	11	12	13	14	15	16
	17	18	19	20	**21**	23	24
ŚRĀVANA 1967	25	26	27	28	29	30	1
	2	3	4	5	6	7	8
	9	10	11	12	13	14	15
	16	17	18	19	20	21	22
	23[c]	**24**	26	27	28	29	30
BHĀDRAPADA 1967	1	2	3	4[d]	5	6	*6*
	7	8	9	10	11	12	13
	14	15	16	**17**	19	20	21
	22	23	24	25	26	27	28
ĀŚVINA 1967	29	30	1	2	3	4	5
	6	7	8[e]	9[e]	10[e]	11	12
	13	14	15	16	17	18	19
	20	**21**	23	24	25	26	27
KĀRTTIKA 1967	28	29	30	1	*1*[f]	2	3
	4	5	6	7	8	9	10
	11	12	13	**14**	16	17	18
	19	20	21	22	23	24	25
MĀRGAŚĪRA 1967	26	27	28	29	30	1	2
	3	*3*	4	5	6	**7**	9
	10	*11*[g]	12	13	14	15	16
	17	18	19	20	21	22	23
	24	25	26	27	28	29	30

HINDU SOLAR 1831‡/1832

Month	Sun	Mon	Tue	Wed	Thu	Fri	Sat
PAUSHA 1831	12	13	14	15	16	17	18
	19	20	21	22	23	24	25
MĀGHA 1831	26	27	28	29	1[b]	2	3
	4	5	6	7	8	9	10
	11	12	13	14	15	16	17
	18	19	20	21	22	23	24
PHĀLGUNA 1831	25	26	27	28	29	1	2
	3	4	5	6	7	8	9
	10	11	12	13	14	15	16
	17	18	19	20	21	22	23
	24	25	26	27	28	29	30
CHAITRA 1831	1	2	3	4	5	6	7
	8	9	10	11	12	13	14
	15	16	17	18	19	20	21
	22	23	24	25	26	27	28
VAIŚĀKHA 1832	29	30	31	1[a]	2	3	4
	5	6	7	8	9	10	11
	12	13	14	15	16	17	18
	19	20	21	22	23	24	25
JYAISHTHA 1832	26	27	28	29	30	31	1
	2	3	4	5	6	7	8
	9	10	11	12	13	14	15
	16	17	18	19	20	21	22
	23	24	25	26	27	28	29
ĀSHĀDHA 1832	30	31	1	2	3	4	5
	6	7	8	9	10	11	12
	13	14	15	16	17	18	19
	20	21	22	23	24	25	26
ŚRĀVANA 1832	27	28	29	30	31	32	1
	2	3	4	5	6	7	8
	9	10	11	12	13	14	15
	16	17	18	19	20	21	22
	23	24	25	26	27	28	29
BHĀDRAPADA 1832	30	31	1	2	3	4	5
	6	7	8	9	10	11	12
	13	14	15	16	17	18	19
	20	21	22	23	24	25	26
ĀŚVINA 1832	27	28	29	30	31	1	2
	3	4	5	6	7	8	9
	10	11	12	13	14	15	16
	17	18	19	20	21	22	23
	24	25	26	27	28	29	30
KĀRTTIKA 1832	31	1	2	3	4	5	6
	7	8	9	10	11	12	13
	14	15	16	17	18	19	20
	21	22	23	24	25	26	27
MĀRGAŚĪRA 1832	28	29	30	1	2	3	4
	5	6	7	8	9	10	11
	12	13	14	15	16	17	18
	19	20	21	22	23	24	25
PAUSHA 1832	26	27	28	29	1	2	3
	4	5	6	7	8	9	10
	11	12	13	14	15	16	17

ISLAMIC (ASTRONOMICAL) 1327‡/1328

Month	Sun	Mon	Tue	Wed	Thu	Fri	Sat
DHU AL-HIJJA 1327	13	14	15	16	17	18	19
	20	21	22	23	24	25	26
MUHARRAM 1328	27	28	29	30	1[a]	2	3
	4	5	6	7	8	9	10[b]
	11	12	13	14	15	16	17
	18	19	20	21	22	23	24
SAFAR 1328	25	26	27	28	29	1	2
	3	4	5	6	7	8	9
	10	11	12	13	14	15	16
	17	18	19	20	21	22	23
	24	25	26	27	28	29	30
RABĪ' I 1328	1	2	3	4	5	6	7
	8	9	10	11	12[c]	13	14
	15	16	17	18	19	20	21
	22	23	24	25	26	27	28
RABĪ' II 1328	29	1	2	3	4	5	6
	7	8	9	10	11	12	13
	14	15	16	17	18	19	20
	21	22	23	24	25	26	27
JUMĀDĀ I 1328	28	29	1	2	3	4	5
	6	7	8	9	10	11	12
	13	14	15	16	17	18	19
	20	21	22	23	24	25	26
JUMĀDĀ II 1328	27	28	29	30	1	2	3
	4	5	6	7	8	9	10
	11	12	13	14	15	16	17
	18	19	20	21	22	23	24
RAJAB 1328	25	26	27	28	29	1	2
	3	4	5	6	7	8	9
	10	11	12	13	14	15	16
	17	18	19	20	21	22	23
SHA'BĀN 1328	24	25	26	27[d]	28	29	1
	2	3	4	5	6	7	8
	9	10	11	12	13	14	15
	16	17	18	19	20	21	22
	23	24	25	26	27	28	29
RAMAḌĀN 1328	30	1[e]	2	3	4	5	6
	7	8	9	10	11	12	13
	14	15	16	17	18	19	20
	21	22	23	24	25	26	27
SHAWWĀL 1328	28	29	30	1[f]	2	3	4
	5	6	7	8	9	10	11
	12	13	14	15	16	17	18
	19	20	21	22	23	24	25
DHU AL-QA'DA 1328	26	27	28	29	30	1	2
	3	4	5	6	7	8	9
	10	11	12	13	14	15	16
	17	18	19	20	21	22	23
	24	25	26	27	28	29	30
DHU AL-HIJJA 1328	1	2	3	4	5	6	7
	8	9	10[g]	11	12	13	14
	15	16	17	18	19	20	21
	22	23	24	25	26	27	28

GREGORIAN 1910

Julian (Sun)	Sun	Mon	Tue	Wed	Thu	Fri	Sat	Month
Dec 13	26	27	28	29	30	31	1	JANUARY 1910
	2	3	4	5	6	7[a]	8	
Dec 27	9	10	11	12	13	14[b]	15	
	16	17	18	19	20	21	22	
Jan 10	23	24	25	26	27	28	29	
	30	31	1	2	3	4	5	FEBRUARY 1910
Jan 24	6	7	8	9[c]	10	11	12	
	13	14	15	16	17	18	19	
Feb 7	20	21	22	23	24	25	26	
	27	28	1	2	3	4	5	MARCH 1910
Feb 21	6	7	8	9	10	11	12	
	13	14	15	16	17	18	19	
Mar 7	20[d]	21	22	23	24	25	26	
	27[e]	28	29	30	31	1	2	APRIL 1910
Mar 21	3	4	5	6	7	8	9	
	10	11	12	13	14	15	16	
Apr 4	17	18	19	20	21	22	23	
	24	25	26	27	28	29	30	
Apr 18	1[f]	2	3	4	5	6	7	MAY 1910
	8	9	10	11	12	13	14	
May 2	15	16	17	18	19	20	21	
	22	23	24	25	26	27	28	
May 16	29	30	31	1	2	3	4	JUNE 1910
	5	6	7	8	9	10	11	
May 30	12	13	14	15	16	17	18	
	19	20	21	22	23	24	25	
Jun 13	26	27	28	29	30	1	2	JULY 1910
	3	4	5	6	7	8	9	
Jun 27	10	11	12	13	14	15	16	
	17	18	19	20	21	22	23	
Jul 11	24	25	26	27	28	29	30	
	31	1	2	3	4	5	6	AUGUST 1910
Jul 25	7	8	9	10	11	12	13	
	14	15	16	17	18	19	20	
Aug 8	21	22	23	24	25	26	27	
	28	29	30	31	1	2	3	SEPTEMBER 1910
Aug 22	4	5	6	7	8	9	10	
	11	12	13	14	15	16	17	
Sep 5	18	19	20	21	22	23	24	
	25	26	27	28	29	30	1	OCTOBER 1910
Sep 19	2	3	4	5	6	7	8	
	9	10	11	12	13	14	15	
Oct 3	16	17	18	19	20	21	22	
	23	24	25	26	27	28	29	
Oct 17	30	31	1	2	3	4	5	NOVEMBER 1910
	6	7	8	9	10	11	12	
Oct 31	13	14	15	16	17	18	19	
	20	21	22	23	24	25	26	
Nov 14	27[g]	28	29	30	1	2	3	DECEMBER 1910
	4	5	6	7	8	9	10	
Nov 28	11	12	13	14	15	16	17	
	18	19	20	21	22	23	24	
Dec 12	25[h]	26	27	28	29	30	31	

Persian:
‡Leap year
[a]New Year
[b]Sizdeh Bedar

Hindu Lunar:
‡Leap year
[a]New Year (Sādhāraṇa)
[b]Birthday of Rāma
[c]Birthday of Krishna
[d]Ganēśa Chaturthī
[e]Dashara
[f]Diwali
[g]Birthday of Vishnu
[h]Night of Śiva
[i]Holi

Hindu Solar:
‡Leap year
[a]New Year (Dundubhi)
[b]Pongal

Islamic:
‡Leap year
[a]New Year
[b]'Ashūrā'
[c]Prophet's Birthday
[d]Ascent of the Prophet
[e]Start of Ramaḍān
[f]'Īd al-Fiṭr
[g]'Īd al-'Aḍḥā

Gregorian:
[a]Orthodox Christmas
[b]Julian New Year
[c]Ash Wednesday
[d]Feast of Orthodoxy
[e]Easter
[f]Orthodox Easter
[g]Advent
[h]Christmas

1911

	GREGORIAN 1911							Lunar Phases	ISO WEEK	JULIAN DAY		HEBREW 5671/5672							Molad		CHINESE Gēng-Xū/Xīn-Hài‡							Solar Term		COPTIC 1627‡/1628 ETHIOPIC 1903‡/1904							
	Sun	Mon	Tue	Wed	Thu	Fri	Sat		(Mon)	(Sun noon)		Sun	Mon	Tue	Wed	Thu	Fri	Sat			Sun	Mon	Tue	Wed	Thu	Fri	Sat			Sun	Mon	Tue	Wed	Thu	Fri	Sat	
JANUARY 1911	1[a]	2	3	4	5	6	7		1	2419038	TEVETH 5671	1[e]	2[e]	3	4	5	6	7	Sat 14h15m10p	MONTH 12 Gēng-Xū	1	2	3	4	5	6	7	Xiǎo hán	KOIAK 1627	23	24	25	26	27	28	29[c]	TĀKHŚĀŚ 1903
	◐	9	10	11	12	13	○	6:20 22:26	2	2419045		8	9	10	11	12	13	14			8	9	10	11	12	13	14		TŌBE 1627	30	1	2	3	4	5	6[d]	ṬER 1903
	15	16	17	18	19	20	21		3	2419052		15	16	17	18	19	20	21			15	16	17	18	19	20	21	Dà hán		7	8	9	10	11[e]	12	13	
	◑	23	24	25	26	27	28	6:21	4	2419059		22	23	24	25	26	27	28			22	23	24	25	26	27	28			14	15	16	17	18	19	20	
FEBRUARY 1911	29	●	31	1	2	3	4	9:44	5	2419066	SHEVAT 5671	29	1	2	3	4	5	6	Mon 2h59m11p	MONTH 1 Xīn-Hài	29	1[a]	2	3	4	5	6			21	22	23	24	25	26	27	
	5	◐	7	8	9	10	11	15:27	6	2419073		7	8	9	10	11	12	13			7	8	9	10	11	12	13	Lì chūn	MESHIR 1627	28	29	30	1	2	3	4	YAKĀTIT 1903
	12	○	14	15	16	17	18	10:37	7	2419080		14	15	16	17	18	19	20			14	15[b]	16	17	18	19	20			5	6	7	8	9	10	11	
	19	20	◑	22	23	24	25	3:44	8	2419087		21	22	23	24	25	26	27			21	22	23	24	25*	26	27	Yǔ shuǐ		12	13	14	15	16	17	18	
MARCH 1911	26	27	28	●	2	3	4	0:31	9	2419094	ADAR 5671	28	29	30	1	2	3	4	Tue 15h43m12p	MONTH 2 Xīn-Hài	28	29	30	1	2	3	4			19	20	21	22	23	24	25	
	5	6	◐	8	9	10	11	23:01	10	2419101		5	6	7	8	9	10	11			5	6	7	8	9	10	11	Jīng zhé	PAREMOTEP 1627	26	27	28	29	30	1	2	MAGĀBIT 1903
	12	13	○	15	16	17	18	23:58	11	2419108		12	13	14[f]	15	16	17	18			12	13	14	15	16	17	18			3	4	5	6	7	8	9	
	19	20	21[b]	22	◑	24	25	0:26	12	2419115		19	20	21	22	23	24	25			19	20	21	22	23	24	25	Chūn fēn		10	11	12	13	14	15	16	
APRIL 1911	26	27	28	29	●	31	1	12:38	13	2419122	NISAN 5671	26	27	28	29	1	2	3	Thu 4h27m13p	MONTH 3 Xīn-Hài	26	27	28	29	1	2	3			17	18	19	20	21	22	23	
	2	3	4	5	◐	7	8	5:55	14	2419129		4	5	6	7	8	9	10			4	5	6	7	8[c]	9	10	Qīng míng		24	25	26	27	28	29	30	
	9	10	11	12	○	14	15	14:36	15	2419136		11	12	13	14	15[g]	16	17			11	12	13	14	15	16	17		PARMOUTE 1627	1	2	3	4	5	6	7	MIYĀZYĀ 1903
	16	17	18	19	20	◑	22	18:35	16	2419143		18	19	20	21	22	23	24			18	19	20	21	22	23	24	Gǔ yǔ		8	9	10	11	12	13	14	
	23	24	25	26	27	●	29	22:25	17	2419150	IYYAR 5671	25	26	27	28	29	30	1	Fri 17h11m14p	MONTH 4 Xīn-Hài	25	26*	27	28	29	30	1			15[f]	16	17	18	19	20	21	
MAY 1911	30	1	2	3	4	◐	6	13:13	18	2419157		2	3	4	5	6	7	8			2	3	4	5	6	7	8	Lì xià		22	23	24	25	26	27	28	
	7	8	9	10	11	12	○	6:09	19	2419164		9	10	11	12	13	14	15			9	10	11	12	13	14	15		PASHONS 1627	29[g]	30	1	2	3	4	5	GENBOT 1903
	14	15	16	17	18	19	20		20	2419171		16	17	18	19	20	21	22			16	17	18	19	20	21	22			6	7	8	9	10	11	12	
	◑	22	23	24	25	26	27	9:22	21	2419178		23	24	25	26	27	28	29			23	24	25	26	27	28	29	Xiǎo mǎn		13	14	15	16	17	18	19	
JUNE 1911	●	29	30	31	1	2	◐	6:24 22:04	22	2419185	SIVAN 5671	1	2	3	4	5	6[h]	7	Sun 5h55m15p	MONTH 5 Xīn-Hài	1	2	3	4	5[d]	6	7			20	21	22	23	24	25	26	
	4	5	6	7	8	9	10		23	2419192		8	9	10	11	12	13	14			8	9	10	11	12	13	14	Máng zhòng	PAŌNE 1627	27	28	29	30	1	2	3	SANĒ 1903
	○	12	13	14	15	16	17	21:50	24	2419199		15	16	17	18	19	20	21			15	16	17	18	19	20	21			4	5	6	7	8	9	10	
	18	◑	20	21	22[c]	23	24	20:50	25	2419206		22	23	24	25	26	27	28			22	23	24	25	26	27*	28	Xià zhì		11	12	13	14	15	16	17	
JULY 1911	25	●	27	28	29	30	1	13:19	26	2419213	TAMMUZ 5671	29	30	1	2	3	4	5	Mon 18h39m16p	MONTH 6 Xīn-Hài	29	1	2	3	4	5	6			18	19	20	21	22	23	24	
	2	◐	4	5	6	7	8	9:20	27	2419220		6	7	8	9	10	11	12			7	8	9	10	11	12	13	Xiǎo shǔ	EPĒP 1627	25	26	27	28	29	30	1	ḤAMLĒ 1903
	9	10	○	12	13	14	15	12:53	28	2419227		13	14	15	16	17	18	19			14	15	16	17	18	19	20			2	3	4	5	6	7	8	
	16	17	18	◑	20	21	22	5:31	29	2419234		20	21	22	23	24	25	26			21	22	23	24	25	26	27			9	10	11	12	13	14	15	
	23	24	●	26	27	28	29	20:12	30	2419241	AV 5671	27	28	29	1	2	3	4	Wed 7h23m17p	LEAP MONTH 6 Xīn-Hài	28	29	30	1	2	3	4	Dà shǔ		16	17	18	19	20	21	22	
AUGUST 1911	30	31	◐	2	3	4	5	23:29	31	2419248		5	6	7	8	9[i]	10	11			5	6	7	8	9	10	11			23	24	25	26	27	28	29	
	6	7	8	9	○	11	12	2:54	32	2419255		12	13	14	15	16	17	18			12	13	14	15	16	17	18	Lì qiū	MESORĒ 1627	30	1	2	3	4	5	6	NAḤASĒ 1903
	13	14	15	16	◑	18	19	12:11	33	2419262		19	20	21	22	23	24	25			19	20	21	22	23	24	25			7	8	9	10	11	12	13[h]	
	20	21	22	23	●	25	26	4:14	34	2419269	ELUL 5671	26	27	28	29	30	1	2	Thu 20h8m0p	MONTH 7 Xīn-Hài	26	27	28*	29	1	2	3	Chǔ shǔ		14	15	16	17	18	19	20	
SEPTEMBER 1911	27	28	29	30	◐	1	2	16:20	35	2419276		3	4	5	6	7	8	9			4	5	6	7[e]	8	9	10			21	22	23	24	25	26	27	
	3	4	5	6	7	○	9	15:56	36	2419283		10	11	12	13	14	15	16			11	12	13	14	15[f]	16	17	Bái lù	EPAG. 1627	28	29	30	1	2	3	4	PĀG. 1903
	10	11	12	13	14	◑	16	17:51	37	2419290		17	18	19	20	21	22	23			18	19	20	21	22	23	24		THOOUT 1628	5	6	1[a]	2	3	4	5	MASKARAM 1904
	17	18	19	20	21	●	23	14:37	38	2419297	TISHRI 5672	24	25	26	27	28	29	1[a]	Sat 8h52m1p	MONTH 8 Xīn-Hài	25	26	27	28	29	1	2			6	7	8	9	10	11	12	
	24[d]	25	26	27	28	29	◐	11:07	39	2419304		2[a]	3	4	5	6	7	8			3	4	5	6	7	8	9	Qiū fēn		13	14	15	16	17[b]	18	19	
OCTOBER 1911	1	2	3	4	5	6	7		40	2419311		9	10[b]	11	12	13	14	15[c]			10	11	12	13	14	15[g]	16			20	21	22	23	24	25	26	
	○	9	10	11	12	13	◑	4:11 23:46	41	2419318		16	17	18	19	20	21	22			17	18	19	20	21	22	23	Hán lù	PAOPE 1628	27	28	29	30	1	2	3	ṬEQEMT 1904
	15	16	17	18	19	20	21		42	2419325		23	24	25	26	27	28	29			24	25	26	27	28	29	30*			4	5	6	7	8	9	10	
	●	23	24	25	26	27	28	4:09	43	2419332	ḤESHVAN 5672	30	1	2	3	4	5	6	Sun 21h36m2p	MONTH 9 Xīn-Hài	1	2	3	4	5	6	7	Shuāng jiàng		11	12	13	14	15	16	17	
NOVEMBER 1911	29	◐	31	1	2	3	4	6:41	44	2419339		7	8	9	10	11	12	13			8	9[h]	10	11	12	13	14			18	19	20	21	22	23	24	
	5	○	7	8	9	10	11	15:48	45	2419346		14	15	16	17	18	19	20			15	16	17	18	19	20	21	Lì dōng	ATHŌR 1628	25	26	27	28	29	30	1	ḪEDĀR 1904
	12	◑	14	15	16	17	18	7:19	46	2419353		21	22	23	24	25	26	27			22	23	24	25	26	27	28			2	3	4	5	6	7	8	
	19	●	21	22	23	24	25	20:49	47	2419360	KISLEV 5672	28	29	30	1	2	3	4	Tue 10h20m3p	MONTH 10 Xīn-Hài	29	30	1	2	3	4	5	Xiǎo xuě		9	10	11	12	13	14	15	
DECEMBER 1911	26	27	28	◐	30	1	2	1:42	48	2419367		5	6	7	8	9	10	11			6	7	8	9	10	11	12			16	17	18	19	20	21	22	
	3	4	5	○	7	8	9	2:52	49	2419374		12	13	14	15[d]	16	17	18			13	14	15	16	17	18	19	Dà xuě		23	24	25	26	27	28	29	
	10	11	◑	13	14	15	16	17:45	50	2419381		19	20	21	22	23	24	25[e]			20	21	22	23	24	25	26		KOIAK 1628	30	1	2	3	4	5	6	TĀKHŚĀŚ 1904
	17	18	19	●	21	22[e]	23	15:40	51	2419388	TEVETH 5672	26[e]	27[e]	28[e]	29[e]	30[e]	1[e]	2[e]	Wed 23h4m4p	MONTH 11 Xīn-Hài	27	28	29	1*	2	3	4[i]	Dōng zhì		7	8	9	10	11	12	13	
	24	25	26	27	◐	29	30	18:47	52	2419395		3	4	5	6	7	8	9			5	6	7	8	9	10	11			14	15	16	17	18	19	20	
	31	1	2	3	○	5	6	13:29	1	2419402		10	11	12	13	14	15	16			12	13	14	15	16	17	18	Xiǎo hán		21	22	23	24	25	26	27	

[a]New Year
[b]Spring (17:54)
[c]Summer (13:35)
[d]Autumn (4:17)
[e]Winter (22:53)
● New moon
◐ First quarter moon
○ Full moon
◑ Last quarter moon

[a]New Year
[b]Yom Kippur
[c]Sukkot
[d]Winter starts
[e]Ḥanukkah
[f]Purim
[g]Passover
[h]Shavuot
[i]Fast of Av

‡Leap year
[a]New Year (4609, Pig)
[b]Lantern Festival
[c]Qīngmíng
[d]Dragon Festival
[e]Qīqiǎo
[f]Hungry Ghosts
[g]Mid-Autumn Festival
[h]Double-Ninth Festival
[i]Dōngzhì
*Start of 60-name cycle

‡Leap year
[a]New Year
[b]Building of the Cross
[c]Christmas
[d]Jesus's Circumcision
[e]Epiphany
[f]Easter
[g]Mary's Announcement
[h]Jesus's Transfiguration

PERSIAN (ASTRONOMICAL) 1289/1290

Month	Sun	Mon	Tue	Wed	Thu	Fri	Sat
DEY 1289	10	11	12	13	14	15	16
	17	18	19	20	21	22	23
	24	25	26	27	28	29	30
BAHMAN 1289	1	2	3	4	5	6	7
	8	9	10	11	12	13	14
	15	16	17	18	19	20	21
	22	23	24	25	26	27	28
ESFAND 1289	29	30	1	2	3	4	5
	6	7	8	9	10	11	12
	13	14	15	16	17	18	19
	20	21	22	23	24	25	26
FARVARDĪN 1290	27	28	29	1[a]	2	3	4
	5	6	7	8	9	10	11
	12	13[b]	14	15	16	17	18
	19	20	21	22	23	24	25
ORDĪBEHEŠT 1290	26	27	28	29	30	31	1
	2	3	4	5	6	7	8
	9	10	11	12	13	14	15
	16	17	18	19	20	21	22
	23	24	25	26	27	28	29
XORDĀD 1290	30	31	1	2	3	4	5
	6	7	8	9	10	11	12
	13	14	15	16	17	18	19
	20	21	22	23	24	25	26
TĪR 1290	27	28	29	30	31	1	2
	3	4	5	6	7	8	9
	10	11	12	13	14	15	16
	17	18	19	20	21	22	23
	24	25	26	27	28	29	30
MORDĀD 1290	31	1	2	3	4	5	6
	7	8	9	10	11	12	13
	14	15	16	17	18	19	20
	21	22	23	24	25	26	27
SHAHRĪVAR 1290	28	29	30	31	1	2	3
	4	5	6	7	8	9	10
	11	12	13	14	15	16	17
	18	19	20	21	22	23	24
	25	26	27	28	29	30	31
MEHR 1290	1	2	3	4	5	6	7
	8	9	10	11	12	13	14
	15	16	17	18	19	20	21
	22	23	24	25	26	27	28
ABĀN 1290	29	30	1	2	3	4	5
	6	7	8	9	10	11	12
	13	14	15	16	17	18	19
	20	21	22	23	24	25	26
ĀZAR 1290	27	28	29	30	1	2	3
	4	5	6	7	8	9	10
	11	12	13	14	15	16	17
	18	19	20	21	22	23	24
DEY 1290	25	26	27	28	29	30	1
	2	3	4	5	6	7	8
	9	10	11	12	13	14	15

HINDU LUNAR 1967/1968

Month	Sun	Mon	Tue	Wed	Thu	Fri	Sat
PAUSHA 1967	1	2	3	4	5	6	7
	8	9	10	11	12	**13**	15
	16	17	18	19	20	21	22
	23	24	25	26	26	27	28
MĀGHA 1967	29	30	1	2	3	4	5
	6	**7**	9	10	11	12	13
	14	15	16	17	18	19	20
	21	22	23	24	25	26	27
PHĀLGUNA 1967	28	29[h]	30	1	2	3	4
	5	6	7	8	9	10	11
	12	14	15[i]	16	17	18	18
	19	20	21	22	23	24	25
CHAITRA 1968	26	27	28	29	30	1[a]	2
	3	4	**5**	7	8	9[b]	10
	11	12	13	14	15	16	17
	18	19	20	21	22	22	23
VAIŚĀKHA 1968	24	25	26	27	28	**29**	1
	2	3	4	5	6	7	8
	9	10	11	12	13	14	15
	16	17	18	19	20	21	22
	23	24	25	26	27	28	29
JYAISHṬHA 1968	30	1	**2**	4	5	6	7
	8	9	10	11	12	13	14
	15	16	17	17	18	19	20
	21	22	23	24	**25**	27	28
ĀSHĀḌHA 1968	29	30	1	2	3	4	5
	6	7	8	9	10	11	12
	13	14	15	16	17	18	19
	20	21	22	23	24	25	26
ŚRĀVAṆA 1968	27	**28**	30	1	2	3	4
	5	6	7	8	9	10	11
	12	13	14	14	15	16	17
	18	19	**20**	22	23[c]	24	25
BHĀDRAPADA 1968	26	27	28	29	30	1	2
	3[d]	4	5	6	7	8	9
	10	11	12	13	14	15	16
	17	18	19	20	21	22	23
ĀŚVINA 1968	**24**	26	27	28	29	30	1
	2	3	4	5	6	7	8[e]
	9[e]	10[e]	10[e]	11	12	13	14
	15	16	**17**	19	20	21	22
	23	24	25	26	27	28	29
KĀRTTIKA 1968	30	1[f]	2	3	4	5	6
	7	8	9	10	11	12	13
	14	15	16	17	18	19	20
	21	23	24	25	26	27	28
MĀRGAŚIRA 1968	29	30	1	2	3	4	4
	5	6	7	8	9	10	11[g]
	12	13	14	**15**	17	18	19
	20	21	22	23	24	25	26
PAUSHA 1968	27	28	29	30	1	2	3
	4	5	6	7	8	9	10
	11	12	13	14	15	16	17

HINDU SOLAR 1832/1833

Month	Sun	Mon	Tue	Wed	Thu	Fri	Sat
PAUSHA 1832	18	19	20	21	22	23	24
MĀGHA 1832	25	26	27	28	29	1[b]	2
	3	4	5	6	7	8	9
	10	11	12	13	14	15	16
	17	18	19	20	21	22	23
	24	25	26	27	28	29	30
PHĀLGUNA 1832	1	2	3	4	5	6	7
	8	9	10	11	12	13	14
	15	16	17	18	19	20	21
	22	23	24	25	26	27	28
CHAITRA 1832	29	30	1	2	3	4	5
	6	7	8	9	10	11	12
	13	14	15	16	17	18	19
	20	21	22	23	24	25	26
VAIŚĀKHA 1833	27	28	29	30	1[a]	2	3
	4	5	6	7	8	9	10
	11	12	13	14	15	16	17
	18	19	20	21	22	23	24
	25	26	27	28	29	30	31
JYAISHṬHA 1833	1	2	3	4	5	6	7
	8	9	10	11	12	13	14
	15	16	17	18	19	20	21
	22	23	24	25	26	27	28
ĀSHĀḌHA 1833	29	30	31	1	2	3	4
	5	6	7	8	9	10	11
	12	13	14	15	16	17	18
	19	20	21	22	23	24	25
	26	27	28	29	30	31	32
ŚRĀVAṆA 1833	1	2	3	4	5	6	7
	8	9	10	11	12	13	14
	15	16	17	18	19	20	21
	22	23	24	25	26	27	28
BHĀDRAPADA 1833	29	30	31	1	2	3	4
	5	6	7	8	9	10	11
	12	13	14	15	16	17	18
	19	20	21	22	23	24	25
ĀŚVINA 1833	26	27	28	29	30	31	1
	2	3	4	5	6	7	8
	9	10	11	12	13	14	15
	16	17	18	19	20	21	22
	23	24	25	26	27	28	29
KĀRTTIKA 1833	30	31	1	2	3	4	5
	6	7	8	9	10	11	12
	13	14	15	16	17	18	19
	20	21	22	23	24	25	26
MĀRGAŚIRA 1833	27	28	29	30	1	2	3
	4	5	6	7	8	9	10
	11	12	13	14	15	16	17
	18	19	20	21	22	23	24
PAUSHA 1833	25	26	27	28	29	1	2
	3	4	5	6	7	8	9
	10	11	12	13	14	15	16
	17	18	19	20	21	22	23

ISLAMIC (ASTRONOMICAL) 1328/1329/1330‡

Month	Sun	Mon	Tue	Wed	Thu	Fri	Sat
MUḤARRAM 1329	29	1[a]	2	3	4	5	6
	7	8	9	10[b]	11	12	13
	14	15	16	17	18	19	20
	21	22	23	24	25	26	27
ṢAFAR 1329	28	29	30	1	2	3	4
	5	6	7	8	9	10	11
	12	13	14	15	16	17	18
	19	20	21	22	23	24	25
RABĪ' I 1329	26	27	28	29	1	2	3
	4	5	6	7	8	9	10
	11	12[c]	13	14	15	16	17
	18	19	20	21	22	23	24
RABĪ' II 1329	25	26	27	28	29	30	1
	2	3	4	5	6	7	8
	9	10	11	12	13	14	15
	16	17	18	19	20	21	22
	23	24	25	26	27	28	29
JUMĀDĀ I 1329	1	2	3	4	5	6	7
	8	9	10	11	12	13	14
	15	16	17	18	19	20	21
	22	23	24	25	26	27	28
JUMĀDĀ II 1329	29	1	2	3	4	5	6
	7	8	9	10	11	12	13
	14	15	16	17	18	19	20
	21	22	23	24	25	26	27
RAJAB 1329	28	29	30	1	2	3	4
	5	6	7	8	9	10	11
	12	13	14	15	16	17	18
	19	20	21	22	23	24	25
SHA'BĀN 1329	26	27[d]	28	29	1	2	3
	4	5	6	7	8	9	10
	11	12	13	14	15	16	17
	18	19	20	21	22	23	24
RAMAḌĀN 1329	25	26	27	28	29	1[e]	2
	3	4	5	6	7	8	9
	10	11	12	13	14	15	16
	17	18	19	20	21	22	23
	24	25	26	27	28	29	30
SHAWWĀL 1329	1[f]	2	3	4	5	6	7
	8	9	10	11	12	13	14
	15	16	17	18	19	20	21
	22	23	24	25	26	27	28
DHU AL-QA'DA 1329	29	30	1	2	3	4	5
	6	7	8	9	10	11	12
	13	14	15	16	17	18	19
	20	21	22	23	24	25	26
DHU AL-ḤIJJA 1329	27	28	29	30	1	2	3
	4	5	6	7	8	9	10[g]
	11	12	13	14	15	16	17
	18	19	20	21	22	23	24
MUḤARRAM 1330	25	26	27	28	29	1[a]	2
	3	4	5	6	7	8	9
	10[b]	11	12	13	14	15	16

GREGORIAN 1911

Julian (Sun)	Month	Sun	Mon	Tue	Wed	Thu	Fri	Sat
Dec 19	JANUARY 1911	1	2	3	4	5	6	7[a]
		8	9	10	11	12	13	14[b]
Jan 2		15	16	17	18	19	20	21
		22	23	24	25	26	27	28
Jan 16	FEBRUARY 1911	29	30	31	1	2	3	4
		5	6	7	8	9	10	11
Jan 30		12	13	14	15	16	17	18
		19	20	21	22	23	24	25
Feb 13	MARCH 1911	26	27	28	1[c]	2	3	4
		5	6	7	8	9	10	11
Feb 27		12[d]	13	14	15	16	17	18
		19	20	21	22	23	24	25
Mar 13	APRIL 1911	26	27	28	29	30	31	1
		2	3	4	5	6	7	8
Mar 27		9	10	11	12	13	14	15
		16[e]	17	18	19	20	21	22
Apr 10		23[f]	24	25	26	27	28	29
	MAY 1911	30	1	2	3	4	5	6
Apr 24		7	8	9	10	11	12	13
		14	15	16	17	18	19	20
May 8		21	22	23	24	25	26	27
	JUNE 1911	28	29	30	31	1	2	3
May 22		4	5	6	7	8	9	10
		11	12	13	14	15	16	17
Jun 5		18	19	20	21	22	23	24
	JULY 1911	25	26	27	28	29	30	1
Jun 19		2	3	4	5	6	7	8
		9	10	11	12	13	14	15
Jul 3		16	17	18	19	20	21	22
		23	24	25	26	27	28	29
Jul 17	AUGUST 1911	30	31	1	2	3	4	5
		6	7	8	9	10	11	12
Jul 31		13	14	15	16	17	18	19
		20	21	22	23	24	25	26
Aug 14	SEPTEMBER 1911	27	28	29	30	31	1	2
		3	4	5	6	7	8	9
Aug 28		10	11	12	13	14	15	16
		17	18	19	20	21	22	23
Sep 11		24	25	26	27	28	29	30
	OCTOBER 1911	1	2	3	4	5	6	7
Sep 25		8	9	10	11	12	13	14
		15	16	17	18	19	20	21
Oct 9		22	23	24	25	26	27	28
	NOVEMBER 1911	29	30	31	1	2	3	4
Oct 23		5	6	7	8	9	10	11
		12	13	14	15	16	17	18
Nov 6		19	20	21	22	23	24	25
	DECEMBER 1911	26	27	28	29	30	1	2
Nov 20		3[g]	4	5	6	7	8	9
		10	11	12	13	14	15	16
Dec 4		17	18	19	20	21	22	23
		24	25[h]	26	27	28	29	30
Dec 18		31	1	2	3	4	5	6

Persian:
[a] New Year
[b] Sizdeh Bedar

Hindu Lunar:
[a] New Year (Virodhakṛit)
[b] Birthday of Rāma
[c] Birthday of Krishna
[d] Ganēśa Chaturthī
[e] Dashara
[f] Diwali
[g] Birthday of Vishnu
[h] Night of Śiva
[i] Holi

Hindu Solar:
[a] New Year (Rudhirodgārin)
[b] Pongal

Islamic:
‡ Leap year
[a] New Year
[b] 'Ashūrā'
[c] Prophet's Birthday
[d] Ascent of the Prophet
[e] Start of Ramaḍān
[f] 'Id al-Fiṭr
[g] 'Id al-'Aḍḥā

Gregorian:
[a] Orthodox Christmas
[b] Julian New Year
[c] Ash Wednesday
[d] Feast of Orthodoxy
[e] Easter
[f] Orthodox Easter
[g] Advent
[h] Christmas

1912

	GREGORIAN 1912‡							Lunar Phases	ISO WEEK	JULIAN DAY		HEBREW 5672/5673‡							Molad		CHINESE Xīn-Hài‡/Rén-Zǐ							Solar Term		COPTIC 1628/1629 ETHIOPIC 1904/1905							
	Sun	Mon	Tue	Wed	Thu	Fri	Sat		(Mon)	(Sun noon)		Sun	Mon	Tue	Wed	Thu	Fri	Sat			Sun	Mon	Tue	Wed	Thu	Fri	Sat			Sun	Mon	Tue	Wed	Thu	Fri	Sat	
JANUARY 1912	31	1[a]	2	3	○	5	6	13:29	1	2419402	TEVETH 5672	10	11	12	13	14	15	16		MONTH 11 Xīn-Hài	12	13	14	15	16	17	18	Xiǎo hán	KOIAK 1628	21	22	23	24	25	26	27	TĀKHŚĀŚ 1904
	7	8	9	10	◑	12	13	7:43	2	2419409		17	18	19	20	21	22	23	Fri 11h48m5p		19	20	21	22	23	24	25			28	29[c]	30	1	2	3	4	ṬER 1904
	14	15	16	17	18	●	20	11:09	3	2419416		24	25	26	27	28	29	1			26	27	28	29	30	1	2		TŌBE 1628	5	6[d]	7	8	9	10	11[e]	
	21	22	23	24	25	26	◐	8:51	4	2419423	SHEVAT 5672	2	3	4	5	6	7	8		MONTH 12 Xīn-Hài	3	4	5	6	7	8	9	Dà hán		12	13	14	15	16	17	18	
	28	29	30	31	1	○	3	23:58	5	2419430		9	10	11	12	13	14	15			10	11	12	13	14	15	16			19	20	21	22	23	24	25	
FEBRUARY 1912	4	5	6	7	8	9	◑	0:50	6	2419437		16	17	18	19	20	21	22			17	18	19	20	21	22	23			26	27	28	29	30	1	2	
	11	12	13	14	15	16	17		7	2419444		23	24	25	26	27	28	29			24	25	26	27	28	29	30	Lì chūn	MESHIR 1628	3	4	5	6	7	8	9	YAKĀTIT 1904
	●	19	20	21	22	23	24	5:44	8	2419451	ADAR 5672	30	1	2	3	4	5	6	Sun 0h32m6p	MONTH 1 Rén-Zǐ	1[a]*	2	3	4	5	6	7	Yǔ shuǐ		10	11	12	13	14	15	16	
	◐	26	27	28	29	1	2	19:26	9	2419458		7	8	9	10	11	12	13			8	9	10	11	12	13	14			17	18	19	20	21	22	23	
MARCH 1912	○	4	5	6	7	8	9	10:42	10	2419465		14[f]	15	16	17	18	19	20			15[b]	16	17	18	19	20	21	Jīng zhé		24	25	26	27	28	29	30	
	◑	11	12	13	14	15	16	19:55	11	2419472		21	22	23	24	25	26	27			22	23	24	25	26	27	28		PAREMOTEP 1628	1	2	3	4	5	6	7	MAGĀBIT 1904
	17	●	19	20[b]	21	22	23	22:08	12	2419479	NISAN 5672	28	29	1	2	3	4	5	Mon 13h16m7p	MONTH 2 Rén-Zǐ	29	30	1	2	3	4	5	Chūn fēn		8	9	10	11	12	13	14	
	24	25	◐	27	28	29	30	3:01	13	2419486		6	7	8	9	10	11	12			6	7	8	9	10	11	12			15	16	17	18	19	20	21	
	31	○	2	3	4	5	6	22:04	14	2419493		13	14	15[g]	16	17	18	19			13	14	15	16	17	18[c]	19	Qīng míng		22	23	24	25	26	27	28	
APRIL 1912	7	8	◑	10	11	12	13	15:23	15	2419500		20	21	22	23	24	25	26			20	21	22	23	24	25	26		PARMOUTE 1628	29[f]	30	1	2	3	4	5	MIYĀZYĀ 1904
	14	15	16	●	18	19	20	11:40	16	2419507	IYYAR 5672	27	28	29	30	1	2	3	Wed 2h0m8p	MONTH 3 Rén-Zǐ	27	28	29	1	2*	3	4	Gǔ yǔ		6	7	8	9	10	11	12	
	21	22	23	◐	25	26	27	8:47	17	2419514		4	5	6	7	8	9	10			5	6	7	8	9	10	11			13	14	15	16	17	18	19	
	28	29	30	○	2	3	4	10:19	18	2419521		11	12	13	14	15	16	17			12	13	14	15	16	17	18			20	21	22	23	24	25	26	
MAY 1912	5	6	7	8	◑	10	11	9:56	19	2419528		18	19	20	21	22	23	24			19	20	21	22	23	24	25	Lì xià		27	28	29[g]	30	1	2	3	
	12	13	14	15	●	17	18	22:13	20	2419535	SIVAN 5672	25	26	27	28	29	1	2	Thu 14h44m9p	MONTH 4 Rén-Zǐ	26	27	28	29	30	1	2		PASHONS 1628	4	5	6	7	8	9	10	GENBOT 1904
	19	20	21	22	◐	24	25	14:11	21	2419542		3	4	5	6[h]	7	8	9			3	4	5	6	7	8	9	Xiǎo mǎn		11	12	13	14	15	16	17	
	26	27	28	29	○	31	1	23:29	22	2419549		10	11	12	13	14	15	16			10	11	12	13	14	15	16			18	19	20	21	22	23	24	
JUNE 1912	2	3	4	5	6	7	◑	2:35	23	2419556		17	18	19	20	21	22	23			17	18	19	20	21	22	23	Máng zhòng		25	26	27	28	29	30	1	
	9	10	11	12	13	14	●	6:23	24	2419563		24	25	26	27	28	29	30	Sat 3h28m10p		24	25	26	27	28	29	1		PAŌNE 1628	2	3	4	5	6	7	8	SANĒ 1904
	16	17	18	19	20	◐[c]	22	20:38	25	2419570	TAMMUZ 5672	1	2	3	4	5	6	7		MONTH 5 Rén-Zǐ	2	3*	4	5[d]	6	7	8	Xià zhì		9	10	11	12	13	14	15	
	23	24	25	26	27	28	○	13:34	26	2419577		8	9	10	11	12	13	14			9	10	11	12	13	14	15			16	17	18	19	20	21	22	
	30	1	2	3	4	5	6		27	2419584		15	16	17	18	19	20	21			16	17	18	19	20	21	22			23	24	25	26	27	28	29	
JULY 1912	◑	8	9	10	11	12	13	16:47	28	2419591		22	23	24	25	26	27	28			23	24	25	26	27	28	29	Xiǎo shǔ	EPĒP 1628	30	1	2	3	4	5	6	ḤAMLĒ 1904
	●	15	16	17	18	19	20	13:13	29	2419598	AV 5672	29	1	2	3	4	5	6	Sun 16h12m11p	MONTH 6 Rén-Zǐ	1	2	3	4	5	6	7			7	8	9	10	11	12	13	
	◐	22	23	24	25	26	27	5:18	30	2419605		7	8	9[i]	10	11	12	13			8	9	10	11	12	13	14	Dà shǔ		14	15	16	17	18	19	20	
	28	○	30	31	1	2	3	4:28	31	2419612		14	15	16	17	18	19	20			15	16	17	18	19	20	21			21	22	23	24	25	26	27	
AUGUST 1912	4	5	◑	7	8	9	10	4:17	32	2419619		21	22	23	24	25	26	27			22	23	24	25	26	27	28			28	29	30	1	2	3	4	
	11	●	13	14	15	16	17	19:57	33	2419626	ELUL 5672	28	29	30	1	2	3	4	Tue 4h56m12p	MONTH 7 Rén-Zǐ	29	30	1	2	3	4*	5	Lì qiū	MESORĒ 1628	5	6	7	8	9	10	11	NAḤASĒ 1904
	18	◐	20	21	22	23	24	16:56	34	2419633		5	6	7	8	9	10	11			6	7[e]	8	9	10	11	12	Chǔ shǔ		12	13[h]	14	15	16	17	18	
	25	26	○	28	29	30	31	19:58	35	2419640		12	13	14	15	16	17	18			13	14	15[f]	16	17	18	19			19	20	21	22	23	24	25	
SEPTEMBER 1912	1	2	3	◑	5	6	7	13:23	36	2419647		19	20	21	22	23	24	25			20	21	22	23	24	25	26		EPAG. 1628	26	27	28	29	30	1	2	PĀG. 1904
	8	9	10	●	12	13	14	3:48	37	2419654	TISHRI 5673	26	27	28	29	1[a]	2[a]	3	Wed 17h40m13p	MONTH 8 Rén-Zǐ	27	28	29	1	2	3	4	Bái lù	THOOUT 1629	3	4	5	1[a]	2	3	4	MASKARAM 1905
	15	16	17	◐	19	20	21	7:54	38	2419661		4	5	6	7	8	9	10[b]			5	6	7	8	9	10	11			5	6	7	8	9	10	11	
	22	23[d]	24	25	○	27	28	11:34	39	2419668		11	12	13	14	15[c]	16	17			12	13	14	15[g]	16	17	18	Qiū fēn		12	13	14	15	16	17[b]	18	
	29	30	1	2	◑	4	5	20:48	40	2419675		18	19	20	21	22	23	24			19	20	21	22	23	24	25			19	20	21	22	23	24	25	
OCTOBER 1912	6	7	8	9	●	11	12	13:40	41	2419682	HESHVAN 5673	25	26	27	28	29	30	1	Fri 6h24m14p	MONTH 9 Rén-Zǐ	26	27	28	29	1	2	3	Hán lù	PAOPE 1629	26	27	28	29	30	1	2	ṬEQEMT 1905
	13	14	15	16	17	◐	19	2:06	42	2419689		2	3	4	5	6	7	8			4	5	6*	7	8	9[h]	10			3	4	5	6	7	8	9	
	20	21	22	23	24	25	○	2:30	43	2419696		9	10	11	12	13	14	15			11	12	13	14	15	16	17	Shuāng jiàng		10	11	12	13	14	15	16	
	27	28	29	30	31	1	◑	3:38	44	2419703		16	17	18	19	20	21	22			18	19	20	21	22	23	24			17	18	19	20	21	22	23	
NOVEMBER 1912	3	4	5	6	7	8	●	2:05	45	2419710		23	24	25	26	27	28	29			25	26	27	28	29	30	1	Lì dōng		24	25	26	27	28	29	30	
	10	11	12	13	14	15	◐	22:43	46	2419717	KISLEV 5673	30	1	2	3	4	5	6	Sat 19h8m15p	MONTH 10 Rén-Zǐ	2	3	4	5	6	7	8		ATHŌR 1629	1	2	3	4	5	6	7	HEDĀR 1905
	17	18	19	20	21	22	23		47	2419724		7	8	9	10	11	12	13			9	10	11	12	13	14	15	Xiǎo xuě		8	9	10	11	12	13	14	
	○	25	26	27	28	29	30	16:12	48	2419731		14	15	16	17	18	19	20			16	17	18	19	20	21	22			15	16	17	18	19	20	21	
DECEMBER 1912	◑	2	3	4	5	6	7	11:05	49	2419738		21	22	23	24	25[d][e]	26[e]	27[e]			23	24	25	26	27	28	29	Dà xuě		22	23	24	25	26	27	28	
	●	9	10	11	12	13	14	17:07	50	2419745	TEVETH 5673	28[e]	29[e]	30[e]	1[e]	2[e]	3	4	Mon 7h52m16p	MONTH 11 Rén-Zǐ	30	1	2	3	4	5	6*		KOIAK 1629	29	30	1	2	3	4	5	TĀKHŚĀŚ 1905
	15	◐	17	18	19	20	21	20:06	51	2419752		5	6	7	8	9	10	11			7	8	9	10	11	12	13			6	7	8	9	10	11	12	
	22[e]	23	○	25	26	27	28	4:30	52	2419759		12	13	14	15	16	17	18			14[i]	15	16	17	18	19	20	Dōng zhì		13	14	15	16	17	18	19	
	29	◑	31	1	2	3	4	20:12	1	2419766		19	20	21	22	23	24	25			21	22	23	24	25	26	27			20	21	22	23	24	25	26	

‡Leap year
[a]New Year
[b]Spring (23:29)
[c]Summer (19:17)
[d]Autumn (10:08)
[e]Winter (4:45)
● New moon
◐ First quarter moon
○ Full moon
◑ Last quarter moon

‡Leap year
[a]New Year
[b]Yom Kippur
[c]Sukkot
[d]Winter starts
[e]Ḥanukkah
[f]Purim
[g]Passover
[h]Shavuot
[i]Fast of Av

‡Leap year
[a]New Year (4610, Rat)
[b]Lantern Festival
[c]Qīngmíng
[d]Dragon Festival
[e]Qīqiǎo
[f]Hungry Ghosts
[g]Mid-Autumn Festival
[h]Double-Ninth Festival
[i]Dōngzhì
*Start of 60-name cycle

[a]New Year
[b]Building of the Cross
[c]Christmas
[d]Jesus's Circumcision
[e]Epiphany
[f]Easter
[g]Mary's Announcement
[h]Jesus's Transfiguration

PERSIAN (ASTRONOMICAL) 1290/1291

Month	Sun	Mon	Tue	Wed	Thu	Fri	Sat
DEY 1290	9	10	11	12	13	14	15
	16	17	18	19	20	21	22
	23	24	25	26	27	28	29
BAHMAN 1290	30	1	2	3	4	5	6
	7	8	9	10	11	12	13
	14	15	16	17	18	19	20
	21	22	23	24	25	26	27
ESFAND 1290	28	29	30	1	2	3	4
	5	6	7	8	9	10	11
	12	13	14	15	16	17	18
	19	20	21	22	23	24	25
FARVARDĪN 1291	26	27	28	29	1[a]	2	3
	4	5	6	7	8	9	10
	11	12	13[b]	14	15	16	17
	18	19	20	21	22	23	24
	25	26	27	28	29	30	31
ORDĪBEHEŠT 1291	1	2	3	4	5	6	7
	8	9	10	11	12	13	14
	15	16	17	18	19	20	21
	22	23	24	25	26	27	28
XORDĀD 1291	29	30	31	1	2	3	4
	5	6	7	8	9	10	11
	12	13	14	15	16	17	18
	19	20	21	22	23	24	25
TĪR 1291	26	27	28	29	30	31	1
	2	3	4	5	6	7	8
	9	10	11	12	13	14	15
	16	17	18	19	20	21	22
	23	24	25	26	27	28	29
MORDĀD 1291	30	31	1	2	3	4	5
	6	7	8	9	10	11	12
	13	14	15	16	17	18	19
	20	21	22	23	24	25	26
SHAHRĪVAR 1291	27	28	29	30	31	1	2
	3	4	5	6	7	8	9
	10	11	12	13	14	15	16
	17	18	19	20	21	22	23
	24	25	26	27	28	29	30
MEHR 1291	31	1	2	3	4	5	6
	7	8	9	10	11	12	13
	14	15	16	17	18	19	20
	21	22	23	24	25	26	27
ABĀN 1291	28	29	30	1	2	3	4
	5	6	7	8	9	10	11
	12	13	14	15	16	17	18
	19	20	21	22	23	24	25
ĀZAR 1291	26	27	28	29	30	1	2
	3	4	5	6	7	8	9
	10	11	12	13	14	15	16
	17	18	19	20	21	22	23
	24	25	26	27	28	29	30
DEY 1291	1	2	3	4	5	6	7
	8	9	10	11	12	13	14

[a]New Year
[b]Sizdeh Bedar

HINDU LUNAR 1968/1969‡

Month	Sun	Mon	Tue	Wed	Thu	Fri	Sat
PAUSHA 1968	11	12	13	14	15	16	17
	18	19	20	**21**	23	24	25
MĀGHA 1968	26	26	27	28	29	30	1
	2	3	4	5	6	7	8
	9	10	11	12	13	**14**	16
	17	18	19	20	21	22	23
	24	25	26	27	28	28[h]	29
PHĀLGUNA 1968	30	1	2	3	4	5	6
	7	**8**	10	11	12	13	14
	15[i]	16	17	18	19	20	21
	22	23	24	25	26	27	28
CHAITRA 1969	29	30	1[a]	2	3	4	5
	6	7	8	9[b]	10	11	12
	13	15	16	17	18	19	20
	21	22	22	23	24	25	26
VAIŚĀKHA 1969	27	28	29	30	1	2	3
	4	5	**6**	8	9	10	11
	12	13	14	15	16	17	18
	19	20	21	22	23	24	25
JYAISHṬHA 1969	26	27	27	29	30	1	2
	3	4	5	6	7	8	9
	10	12	13	14	15	16	17
	17	18	19	20	21	22	23
	24	25	26	27	28	29	30
LEAP ĀSHĀḌHA 1969	1	**2**	4	5	6	7	8
	9	10	11	12	13	14	15
	16	17	18	19	20	21	22
	23	24	25	26	27	28	29
ĀSHĀḌHA 1969	30	1	2	3	4	**5**	7
	8	9	10	11	12	13	14
	14	15	16	17	18	19	20
	21	22	23	24	25	26	27
ŚRĀVAṆA 1969	**28**	30	1	2	3	4	5
	6	7	8	9	10	11	12
	13	14	15	16	17	18	19
	20	21	22	23[c]	24	25	26
BHĀDRAPADA 1969	27	28	29	30	**1**	3	4[d]
	5	6	7	8	9	10	10
	11	12	13	14	15	16	17
	18	19	20	21	22	23	**24**
ĀŚVINA 1969	26	27	28	29	30	1	2
	3	4	5	6	7	8[e]	9[e]
	10[e]	11	12	13	14	14	15
	16	**17**	19	20	21	22	23
	24	25	26	27	28	29	30[f]
KĀRTTIKA 1969	2	3	3	4	5	6	7
	8	9	10	11	12	13	14
	15	16	17	18	19	20	21
	22	24	25	26	27	28	29
MĀRGAŚIRA 1969	30	1	2	3	4	5	6
	6	7	8	9	10	11[g]	12
	13	14	15	**16**	18	19	20
	21	22	23	24	25	26	27

‡Leap year
[a]New Year (Paridhāvin)
[b]Birthday of Rāma
[c]Birthday of Krishna
[d]Ganēśa Chaturthī
[e]Dashara
[f]Diwali
[g]Birthday of Vishnu
[h]Night of Śiva
[i]Holi

HINDU SOLAR 1833/1834

Month	Sun	Mon	Tue	Wed	Thu	Fri	Sat
PAUSHA 1833	17	18	19	20	21	22	23
	24	25	26	27	28	29	30
MĀGHA 1833	1[b]	2	3	4	5	6	7
	8	9	10	11	12	13	14
	15	16	17	18	19	20	21
	22	23	24	25	26	27	28
PHĀLGUNA 1833	29	1	2	3	4	5	6
	7	8	9	10	11	12	13
	14	15	16	17	18	19	20
	21	22	23	24	25	26	27
CHAITRA 1833	28	29	30	1	2	3	4
	5	6	7	8	9	10	11
	12	13	14	15	16	17	18
	19	20	21	22	23	24	25
VAIŚĀKHA 1834	26	27	28	29	30	1[a]	2
	3	4	5	6	7	8	9
	10	11	12	13	14	15	16
	17	18	19	20	21	22	23
	24	25	26	27	28	29	30
JYAISHṬHA 1834	31	1	2	3	4	5	6
	7	8	9	10	11	12	13
	14	15	16	17	18	19	20
	21	22	23	24	25	26	27
ĀSHĀḌHA 1834	28	29	30	31	32	1	2
	3	4	5	6	7	8	9
	10	11	12	13	14	15	16
	17	18	19	20	21	22	23
	24	25	26	27	28	29	30
ŚRĀVAṆA 1834	31	1	2	3	4	5	6
	7	8	9	10	11	12	13
	14	15	16	17	18	19	20
	21	22	23	24	25	26	27
BHĀDRAPADA 1834	28	29	30	31	32	1	2
	3	4	5	6	7	8	9
	10	11	12	13	14	15	16
	17	18	19	20	21	22	23
	24	25	26	27	28	29	30
ĀŚVINA 1834	31	1	2	3	4	5	6
	7	8	9	10	11	12	13
	14	15	16	17	18	19	20
	21	22	23	24	25	26	27
KĀRTTIKA 1834	28	29	30	1	2	3	4
	5	6	7	8	9	10	11
	12	13	14	15	16	17	18
	19	20	21	22	23	24	25
MĀRGAŚĪRA 1834	26	27	28	29	30	1	2
	3	4	5	6	7	8	9
	10	11	12	13	14	15	16
	17	18	19	20	21	22	23
PAUSHA 1834	24	25	26	27	28	29	1
	2	3	4	5	6	7	8
	9	10	11	12	13	14	15
	16	17	18	19	20	21	22

[a]New Year (Raktāksha)
[b]Pongal

ISLAMIC (ASTRONOMICAL) 1330‡/1331

Month	Sun	Mon	Tue	Wed	Thu	Fri	Sat
MUHARRAM 1330	10	11	12	13	14	15	16
	17	18	19	20	21	22	23
	24	25	26	27	28	29	30
ṢAFAR 1330	1	2	3	4	5	6	7
	8	9	10	11	12	13	14
	15	16	17	18	19	20	21
	22	23	24	25	26	27	28
RABĪ' I 1330	29	30	1	2	3	4	5
	6	7	8	9	10	11	12[c]
	13	14	15	16	17	18	19
	20	21	22	23	24	25	26
RABĪ' II 1330	27	28	29	1	2	3	4
	5	6	7	8	9	10	11
	12	13	14	15	16	17	18
	19	20	21	22	23	24	25
JUMĀDĀ I 1330	26	27	28	29	30	1	2
	3	4	5	6	7	8	9
	10	11	12	13	14	15	16
	17	18	19	20	21	22	23
JUMĀDĀ II 1330	24	25	26	27	28	29	1
	2	3	4	5	6	7	8
	9	10	11	12	13	14	15
	16	17	18	19	20	21	22
	23	24	25	26	27	28	29
RAJAB 1330	1	2	3	4	5	6	7
	8	9	10	11	12	13	14
	15	16	17	18	19	20	21
	22	23	24	25	26	27[d]	28
SHA'BĀN 1330	29	30	1	2	3	4	5
	6	7	8	9	10	11	12
	13	14	15	16	17	18	19
	20	21	22	23	24	25	26
RAMAḌĀN 1330	27	28	29	1[e]	2	3	4
	5	6	7	8	9	10	11
	12	13	14	15	16	17	18
	19	20	21	22	23	24	25
SHAWWĀL 1330	26	27	28	29	30	1[f]	2
	3	4	5	6	7	8	9
	10	11	12	13	14	15	16
	17	18	19	20	21	22	23
DHU AL-QA'DA 1330	24	25	26	27	28	29	1
	2	3	4	5	6	7	8
	9	10	11	12	13	14	15
	16	17	18	19	20	21	22
	23	24	25	26	27	28	29
DHU AL-HIJJA 1330	30	1	2	3	4	5	6
	7	8	9	10[g]	11	12	13
	14	15	16	17	18	19	20
	21	22	23	24	25	26	27
MUHARRAM 1331	28	29	30	1[a]	2	3	4
	5	6	7	8	9	10[b]	11
	12	13	14	15	16	17	18
	19	20	21	22	23	24	25

‡Leap year
[a]New Year
[b]'Ashūrā'
[c]Prophet's Birthday
[d]Ascent of the Prophet
[e]Start of Ramaḍān
[f]'Id al-Fiṭr
[g]'Id al-'Aḍḥā

GREGORIAN 1912‡

Julian‡ (Sun)	Sun	Mon	Tue	Wed	Thu	Fri	Sat	Month
Dec 18	31	1	2	3	4	5	6	JANUARY 1912
	7[a]	8	9	10	11	12	13	
Jan 1	14[b]	15	16	17	18	19	20	
	21	22	23	24	25	26	27	
Jan 15	28	29	30	31	1	2	3	FEBRUARY 1912
	4	5	6	7	8	9	10	
Jan 29	11	12	13	14	15	16	17	
	18	19	20	21[c]	22	23	24	
Feb 12	25[d]	26	27	28	29	1	2	MARCH 1912
	3	4	5	6	7	8	9	
Feb 26	10	11	12	13	14	15	16	
	17	18	19	20	21	22	23	
Mar 11	24	25	26	27	28	29	30	
	31	1	2	3	4	5	6	APRIL 1912
Mar 25	7[e]	8	9	10	11	12	13	
	14	15	16	17	18	19	20	
Apr 8	21	22	23	24	25	26	27	
	28	29	30	1	2	3	4	MAY 1912
Apr 22	5	6	7	8	9	10	11	
	12	13	14	15	16	17	18	
May 6	19	20	21	22	23	24	25	
	26	27	28	29	30	31	1	JUNE 1912
May 20	2	3	4	5	6	7	8	
	9	10	11	12	13	14	15	
Jun 3	16	17	18	19	20	21	22	
	23	24	25	26	27	28	29	
Jun 17	30	1	2	3	4	5	6	JULY 1912
	7	8	9	10	11	12	13	
Jul 1	14	15	16	17	18	19	20	
	21	22	23	24	25	26	27	
Jul 15	28	29	30	31	1	2	3	AUGUST 1912
	4	5	6	7	8	9	10	
Jul 29	11	12	13	14	15	16	17	
	18	19	20	21	22	23	24	
Aug 12	25	26	27	28	29	30	31	
	1	2	3	4	5	6	7	SEPTEMBER 1912
Aug 26	8	9	10	11	12	13	14	
	15	16	17	18	19	20	21	
Sep 9	22	23	24	25	26	27	28	
	29	30	1	2	3	4	5	OCTOBER 1912
Sep 23	6	7	8	9	10	11	12	
	13	14	15	16	17	18	19	
Oct 7	20	21	22	23	24	25	26	
	27	28	29	30	31	1	2	NOVEMBER 1912
Oct 21	3	4	5	6	7	8	9	
	10	11	12	13	14	15	16	
Nov 4	17	18	19	20	21	22	23	
	24	25	26	27	28	29	30	
Nov 18	1[g]	2	3	4	5	6	7	DECEMBER 1912
	8	9	10	11	12	13	14	
Dec 2	15	16	17	18	19	20	21	
	22	23	24	25[h]	26	27	28	
Dec 16	29	30	31	1	2	3	4	

‡Leap year
[a]Orthodox Christmas
[b]Julian New Year
[c]Ash Wednesday
[d]Feast of Orthodoxy
[e]Easter (also Orthodox)
[g]Advent
[h]Christmas

1913

Gregorian 1913	Sun	Mon	Tue	Wed	Thu	Fri	Sat	Lunar Phases	ISO Week (Mon)	Julian Day (Sun noon)
JANUARY 1913	29	◑	31	1[a]	2	3	4	20:12	1	2419766
	5	6	●	8	9	10	11	10:28	2	2419773
	12	13	14	◐	16	17	18	16:01	3	2419780
	19	20	21	○	23	24	25	15:40	4	2419787
	26	27	28	◑	30	31	1	7:34	5	2419794
FEBRUARY 1913	2	3	4	5	●	7	8	5:21	6	2419801
	9	10	11	12	13	◐	15	8:34	7	2419808
	16	17	18	19	20	○	22	2:03	8	2419815
	23	24	25	26	◑	28	1	21:15	9	2419822
MARCH 1913	2	3	4	5	6	7	●	0:22	10	2419829
	9	10	11	12	13	14	◐	20:58	11	2419836
	16	17	18	19	20	21[b]	○	11:56	12	2419843
	23	24	25	26	27	28	◑	12:57	13	2419850
	30	31	1	2	3	4	5		14	2419857
APRIL 1913	●	7	8	9	10	11	12	17:48	15	2419864
	13	◐	15	16	17	18	19	5:39	16	2419871
	○	21	22	23	24	25	26	21:32	17	2419878
	27	◑	29	30	1	2	3	6:09	18	2419885
MAY 1913	4	5	●	7	8	9	10	8:24	19	2419892
	11	12	◐	14	15	16	17	11:44	20	2419899
	18	19	○	21	22	23	24	7:18	21	2419906
	25	26	27	◑	29	30	31	0:03	22	2419913
JUNE 1913	1	2	3	●	5	6	7	19:57	23	2419920
	8	9	10	◐	12	13	14	16:37	24	2419927
	15	16	17	○	19	20	21	17:53	25	2419934
	22[c]	23	24	25	◑	27	28	17:40	26	2419941
	29	30	1	2	3	●	5	5:06	27	2419948
JULY 1913	6	7	8	9	◐	11	12	21:37	28	2419955
	13	14	15	16	17	○	19	6:06	29	2419962
	20	21	22	23	24	25	◑	9:58	30	2419969
	27	28	29	30	31	1	●	12:58	31	2419976
AUGUST 1913	3	4	5	6	7	8	◐	4:03	32	2419983
	10	11	12	13	14	15	○	20:26	33	2419990
	17	18	19	20	21	22	23		34	2419997
	24	◑	26	27	28	29	30	0:17	35	2420004
SEPTEMBER 1913	●	1	2	3	4	5	6	20:38	36	2420011
	◐	8	9	10	11	12	13	13:05	37	2420018
	14	○	16	17	18	19	20	12:45	38	2420025
	21	22	◑[d]	24	25	26	27	12:30	39	2420032
	28	29	●	1	2	3	4	4:56	40	2420039
OCTOBER 1913	5	6	◐	8	9	10	11	1:46	41	2420046
	12	13	14	○	16	17	18	6:06	42	2420053
	19	20	21	◑	23	24	25	22:53	43	2420060
	26	27	28	●	30	31	1	14:29	44	2420067
NOVEMBER 1913	2	3	4	◐	6	7	8	18:34	45	2420074
	9	10	11	12	○	14	15	23:11	46	2420081
	16	17	18	19	20	◑	22	7:56	47	2420088
	23	24	25	26	27	●	29	1:41	48	2420095
DECEMBER 1913	30	1	2	3	4	◐	6	14:58	49	2420102
	7	8	9	10	11	12	○	15:00	50	2420109
	14	15	16	17	18	19	◑	16:15	51	2420116
	21	22[e]	23	24	25	26	●	14:58	52	2420123
	28	29	30	31	1	2	3		1	2420130

Julian Day	Hebrew 5673‡/5674	Sun	Mon	Tue	Wed	Thu	Fri	Sat	Molad
2419766	TEVETH 5673	19	20	21	22	23	24	25	
2419773		26	27	28	29	1	2	3	Tue 20h36m17p
2419780	SHEVAT 5673	4	5	6	7	8	9	10	
2419787		11	12	13	14	15	16	17	
2419794		18	19	20	21	22	23	24	
2419801		25	26	27	28	29	30	1	Thu 9h21m0p
2419808	ADAR I 5673	2	3	4	5	6	7	8	
2419815		9	10	11	12	13	14	15	
2419822		16	17	18	19	20	21	22	
2419829		23	24	25	26	27	28	29	
2419836	ADAR II 5673	30	1	2	3	4	5	6	Fri 22h5m1p
2419843		7	8	9	10	11	12	13	
2419850		14[f]	15	16	17	18	19	20	
2419857		21	22	23	24	25	26	27	
2419864	NISAN 5673	28	29	1	2	3	4	5	Sun 10h49m2p
2419871		6	7	8	9	10	11	12	
2419878		13	14	15[g]	16	17	18	19	
2419885		20	21	22	23	24	25	26	
2419892	IYAR 5673	27	28	29	30	1	2	3	Mon 23h33m3p
2419899		4	5	6	7	8	9	10	
2419906		11	12	13	14	15	16	17	
2419913		18	19	20	21	22	23	24	
2419920	SIVAN 5673	25	26	27	28	29	1	2	Wed 12h17m4p
2419927		3	4	5	6[h]	7	8	9	
2419934		10	11	12	13	14	15	16	
2419941		17	18	19	20	21	22	23	
2419948		24	25	26	27	28	29	30	
2419955	TAMMUZ 5673	1	2	3	4	5	6	7	Fri 1h1m5p
2419962		8	9	10	11	12	13	14	
2419969		15	16	17	18	19	20	21	
2419976		22	23	24	25	26	27	28	
2419983	AV 5673	29	1	2	3	4	5	6	Sat 13h45m6p
2419990		7	8	9[i]	10	11	12	13	
2419997		14	15	16	17	18	19	20	
2420004		21	22	23	24	25	26	27	
2420011	ELUL 5673	28	29	30	1	2	3	4	Mon 2h29m7p
2420018		5	6	7	8	9	10	11	
2420025		12	13	14	15	16	17	18	
2420032		19	20	21	22	23	24	25	
2420039	TISHRI 5674	26	27	28	29	1[a]	2[a]	3	Tue 15h13m8p
2420046		4	5	6	7	8	9	10[b]	
2420053		11	12	13	14	15[c]	16	17	
2420060		18	19	20	21	22	23	24	
2420067		25	26	27	28	29	30	1	Thu 3h57m9p
2420074	ḤESHVAN 5674	2	3	4	5	6	7	8	
2420081		9	10	11	12	13	14	15	
2420088		16	17	18	19	20	21	22	
2420095		23	24	25	26	27	28	29	
2420102	KISLEV 5674	1	2	3	4	5	6[d]	7	Fri 16h41m10p
2420109		8	9	10	11	12	13	14	
2420116		15	16	17	18	19	20	21	
2420123		22	23	24	25[e]	26[e]	27[e]	28[e]	Sun 5h25m11p
2420130		29[e]	30[e]	1[e]	2[e]	3	4	5	

Julian Day	Chinese Rén-Zǐ/Guǐ-Chǒu	Sun	Mon	Tue	Wed	Thu	Fri	Sat	Solar Term
2419766	MONTH 11 Rén-Zǐ	21	22	23	24	25	26	27	
2419773		28	29	1	2	3	4	5	Xiǎo hán
2419780	MONTH 12 Rén-Zǐ	6	7	8	9	10	11	12	
2419787		13	***14***	15	16	17	18	19	Dà hán
2419794		20	21	22	23	24	25	26	
2419801		27	28	29	30	1[a]	2	3	Lì chūn
2419808	MONTH 1 Guǐ-Chǒu	4	5	6	7*	8	9	10	
2419815		11	12	13	***14***	15[b]	16	17	Yǔ shuǐ
2419822		18	19	20	21	22	23	24	
2419829		25	26	27	28	29	30	1	Jīng zhé
2419836	MONTH 2 Guǐ-Chǒu	2	3	4	5	6	7	8	
2419843		9	10	11	12	13	***14***	15	Chūn fēn
2419850		16	17	18	19	20	21	22	
2419857		23	24	25	26	27	28	29[c]	Qīng míng
2419864		30	1	2	3	4	5	6	
2419871	MONTH 3 Guǐ-Chǒu	7*	8	9	10	11	12	13	
2419878		14	***15***	16	17	18	19	20	Gǔ yǔ
2419885		21	22	23	24	25	26	27	
2419892		28	29	*1*	2	3	4	5	Lì xià
2419899	MONTH 4 Guǐ-Chǒu	6	7	8	9	10	11	12	
2419906		13	14	15	16	***17***	18	19	Xiǎo mǎn
2419913		20	21	22	23	24	25	26	
2419920		27	28	29	30	1	2	3	Máng zhòng
2419927	MONTH 5 Guǐ-Chǒu	4	5[d]	6	7	8*	9	10	
2419934		11	12	13	14	15	16	17	
2419941		***18***	19	20	21	22	23	24	Xià zhì
2419948		25	26	27	28	29	1	2	
2419955	MONTH 6 Guǐ-Chǒu	3	4	5	6	7	8	9	Xiǎo shǔ
2419962		10	11	12	13	14	15	16	
2419969		17	18	19	***20***	21	22	23	Dà shǔ
2419976		24	25	26	27	28	29	1	
2419983	MONTH 7 Guǐ-Chǒu	2	3	4	5	6	7[e]	8	Lì qiū
2419990		9	10*	11	12	13	14	15[f]	
2419997		16	17	18	19	20	21	22	
2420004		***23***	24	25	26	27	28	29	Chǔ shǔ
2420011		30	1	2	3	4	5	6	
2420018	MONTH 8 Guǐ-Chǒu	7	*8*	9	10	11	12	13	Bái lù
2420025		14	15[g]	16	17	18	19	20	
2420032		21	22	***23***	24	25	26	27	Qiū fēn
2420039		28	29	1	2	3	4	5	
2420046	MONTH 9 Guǐ-Chǒu	6	7	8	9[h]	*10*	11*	12	Hán lù
2420053		13	14	15	16	17	18	19	
2420060		20	21	22	23	24	***25***	26	Shuāng jiàng
2420067		27	28	29	1	2	3	4	
2420074	MONTH 10 Guǐ-Chǒu	5	6	7	8	9	10	*11*	Lì dōng
2420081		12	13	14	15	16	17	18	
2420088		19	20	21	22	23	24	25	
2420095		***26***	27	28	29	30	1	2	Xiǎo xuě
2420102	MONTH 11* Guǐ-Chǒu	3	4	5	6	7	8	9	
2420109		10	*11*	12*	13	14	15	16	Dà xuě
2420116		17	18	19	20	21	22	23	
2420123	MONTH 12 Guǐ-Chǒu	24	***25***[i]	26	27	28	29	1	Dōng zhì
2420130		2	3	4	5	6	7	8	

Julian Day	Coptic 1629/1630	Sun	Mon	Tue	Wed	Thu	Fri	Sat	Ethiopic 1905/1906
2419766	KOIAK 1629	20	21	22	23	24	25	26	TĀKHŚĀŚ 1905
2419773		27	28	29[c]	30	1	2	3	
2419780	ṬŌBE 1629	4	5	6[d]	7	8	9	10	ṬER 1905
2419787		11[e]	12	13	14	15	16	17	
2419794		18	19	20	21	22	23	24	
2419801		25	26	27	28	29	30	1	
2419808	MESHIR 1629	2	3	4	5	6	7	8	YAKĀTIT 1905
2419815		9	10	11	12	13	14	15	
2419822		16	17	18	19	20	21	22	
2419829		23	24	25	26	27	28	29	
2419836	PAREMOTEP 1629	30	1	2	3	4	5	6	MAGĀBIT 1905
2419843		7	8	9	10	11	12	13	
2419850		14	15	16	17	18	19	20	
2419857		21	22	23	24	25	26	27	
2419864	PARMOUTE 1629	28	29	30	1	2	3	4	MIYĀZYĀ 1905
2419871		5	6	7	8	9	10	11	
2419878		12	13	14	15	16	17	18	
2419885		19[f]	20	21	22	23	24	25	
2419892		26	27	28	29[g]	30	1	2	
2419899	PASHONS 1629	3	4	5	6	7	8	9	GENBOT 1905
2419906		10	11	12	13	14	15	16	
2419913		17	18	19	20	21	22	23	
2419920		24	25	26	27	28	29	30	
2419927	PAŌNE 1629	1	2	3	4	5	6	7	SANĒ 1905
2419934		8	9	10	11	12	13	14	
2419941		15	16	17	18	19	20	21	
2419948		22	23	24	25	26	27	28	
2419955	EPĒP 1629	29	30	1	2	3	4	5	ḤAMLĒ 1905
2419962		6	7	8	9	10	11	12	
2419969		13	14	15	16	17	18	19	
2419976		20	21	22	23	24	25	26	
2419983	MESORĒ 1629	27	28	29	30	1	2	3	NAḤASĒ 1905
2419990		4	5	6	7	8	9	10	
2419997		11	12	13[h]	14	15	16	17	
2420004		18	19	20	21	22	23	24	
2420011		25	26	27	28	29	30	1	
2420018	EPAG. 1629 / THOOUT 1630	2	3	4	5	1[a]	2	3	PĀG. 1905 / MASKARAM 1906
2420025		4	5	6	7	8	9	10	
2420032		11	12	13	14	15	16	17[b]	
2420039		18	19	20	21	22	23	24	
2420046		25	26	27	28	29	30	1	
2420053	PAOPE 1630	2	3	4	5	6	7	8	ṬEQEMT 1906
2420060		9	10	11	12	13	14	15	
2420067		16	17	18	19	20	21	22	
2420074		23	24	25	26	27	28	29	
2420081	ATHŌR 1630	30	1	2	3	4	5	6	ḪEDĀR 1906
2420088		7	8	9	10	11	12	13	
2420095		14	15	16	17	18	19	20	
2420102		21	22	23	24	25	26	27	
2420109	KOIAK 1630	28	29	30	1	2	3	4	TĀKHŚĀŚ 1906
2420116		5	6	7	8	9	10	11	
2420123		12	13	14	15	16	17	18	
2420130		19	20	21	22	23	24	25	

Gregorian:
[a]New Year
[b]Spring (5:18)
[c]Summer (1:10)
[d]Autumn (15:52)
[e]Winter (10:35)
● New moon
◐ First quarter moon
○ Full moon
◑ Last quarter moon

Hebrew:
‡Leap year
[a]New Year
[b]Yom Kippur
[c]Sukkot
[d]Winter starts
[e]Ḥanukkah
[f]Purim
[g]Passover
[h]Shavuot
[i]Fast of Av

Chinese:
[a]New Year (4611, Ox)
[b]Lantern Festival
[c]Qīngmíng
[d]Dragon Festival
[e]Qīqiǎo
[f]Hungry Ghosts
[g]Mid-Autumn Festival
[h]Double-Ninth Festival
[i]Dōngzhì
*Start of 60-name cycle

Coptic/Ethiopic:
[a]New Year
[b]Building of the Cross
[c]Christmas
[d]Jesus's Circumcision
[e]Epiphany
[f]Easter
[g]Mary's Announcement
[h]Jesus's Transfiguration

PERSIAN (ASTRONOMICAL) 1291/1292‡

Month	Sun	Mon	Tue	Wed	Thu	Fri	Sat
DEY 1291	8	9	10	11	12	13	14
	15	16	17	18	19	20	21
	22	23	24	25	26	27	28
	29	30	1	2	3	4	5
BAHMAN 1291	6	7	8	9	10	11	12
	13	14	15	16	17	18	19
	20	21	22	23	24	25	26
	27	28	29	30	1	2	3
ESFAND 1291	4	5	6	7	8	9	10
	11	12	13	14	15	16	17
	18	19	20	21	22	23	24
	25	26	27	28	29	1[a]	2
FARVARDIN 1292	3	4	5	6	7	8	9
	10	11	12	13[b]	14	15	16
	17	18	19	20	21	22	23
	24	25	26	27	28	29	30
	31	1	2	3	4	5	6
ORDIBEHEŠT 1292	7	8	9	10	11	12	13
	14	15	16	17	18	19	20
	21	22	23	24	25	26	27
	28	29	30	31	1	2	3
XORDĀD 1292	4	5	6	7	8	9	10
	11	12	13	14	15	16	17
	18	19	20	21	22	23	24
	25	26	27	28	29	30	31
TĪR 1292	1	2	3	4	5	6	7
	8	9	10	11	12	13	14
	15	16	17	18	19	20	21
	22	23	24	25	26	27	28
	29	30	31	1	2	3	4
MORDĀD 1292	5	6	7	8	9	10	11
	12	13	14	15	16	17	18
	19	20	21	22	23	24	25
	26	27	28	29	30	31	1
SHAHRĪVAR 1292	2	3	4	5	6	7	8
	9	10	11	12	13	14	15
	16	17	18	19	20	21	22
	23	24	25	26	27	28	29
	30	31	1	2	3	4	5
MEHR 1292	6	7	8	9	10	11	12
	13	14	15	16	17	18	19
	20	21	22	23	24	25	26
	27	28	29	30	1	2	3
ĀBĀN 1292	4	5	6	7	8	9	10
	11	12	13	14	15	16	17
	18	19	20	21	22	23	24
	25	26	27	28	29	30	1
ĀZAR 1292	2	3	4	5	6	7	8
	9	10	11	12	13	14	15
	16	17	18	19	20	21	22
	23	24	25	26	27	28	29
DEY 1292	30	1	2	3	4	5	6
	7	8	9	10	11	12	13

HINDU LUNAR 1969‡/1970

Month	Sun	Mon	Tue	Wed	Thu	Fri	Sat
MĀRGAŚĪRA 1969	21	22	23	24	25	26	27
	28	29	30	1	2	3	4
PAUSHA 1969	5	6	7	8	9	10	11
	12	13	14	15	16	17	18
	19	20	**21**	23	24	25	26
	27	28	29	29	30	1	2
MĀGHA 1969	3	4	5	6	7	8	9
	10	11	12	13	14	**15**	17
	18	19	20	21	22	23	24
	25	26	27	28	29[h]	30	1
PHĀLGUNA 1969	1	2	3	4	5	6	7
	8	**9**	11	12	13	14	15[i]
	16	17	18	19	20	21	22
	23	24	25	26	27	28	29
	30	1[a]	2	3	4	5	6
CHAITRA 1970	7	8	9[b]	10	11	12	**13**
	15	16	17	18	19	20	21
	22	23	24	25	25	26	27
	28	29	30	1	2	3	4
VAIŚĀKHA 1970	5	**6**	8	9	10	11	12
	13	14	15	16	17	18	19
	20	21	22	23	24	25	26
	27	28	29	30	1	2	3
JYAISHTHA 1970	4	5	6	7	8	**9**	11
	12	13	14	15	16	17	18
	19	20	21	22	22	23	24
	25	26	27	28	29	30	1
ĀSHĀḌHA 1970	**2**	4	5	6	7	8	9
	10	11	12	13	14	15	16
	17	18	19	20	21	22	23
	24	25	26	27	28	29	30
	1	2	3	4	**5**	7	8
ŚRĀVAṆA 1970	9	10	11	12	13	14	15
	16	17	18	18	19	20	21
	22	23[c]	24	25	26	27	**28**
	30	1	2	3	4[d]	5	6
BHĀDRAPADA 1970	7	8	9	10	11	12	13
	14	15	16	17	18	19	20
	21	22	23	24	25	26	27
	28	29	30	**1**	3	4	5
ĀŚVINA 1970	6	7	8[e]	9[e]	10[e]	11	12
	13	14	14	15	16	17	18
	19	20	21	22	23	24	**25**
	27	28	29	30	1[f]	2	3
KĀRTTIKA 1970	4	5	6	7	8	9	10
	11	12	13	14	15	16	17
	18	19	20	21	22	23	24
	25	26	27	28	29	**30**	2
MĀRGAŚĪRA 1970	3	4	5	6	7	7	8
	9	10	11[g]	12	13	14	15
	16	17	18	19	20	21	22
	23	25	26	27	28	29	30
	1	2	3	4	5	6	7

HINDU SOLAR 1834/1835‡

Month	Sun	Mon	Tue	Wed	Thu	Fri	Sat
PAUSHA 1834	16	17	18	19	20	21	22
	23	24	25	26	27	28	29
	30	1[b]	2	3	4	5	6
MĀGHA 1834	7	8	9	10	11	12	13
	14	15	16	17	18	19	20
	21	22	23	24	25	26	27
	28	29	1	2	3	4	5
PHĀLGUNA 1834	6	7	8	9	10	11	12
	13	14	15	16	17	18	19
	20	21	22	23	24	25	26
	27	28	29	30	1	2	3
CHAITRA 1834	4	5	6	7	8	9	10
	11	12	13	14	15	16	17
	18	19	20	21	22	23	24
	25	26	27	28	29	30	1[a]
VAIŚĀKHA 1835	2	3	4	5	6	7	8
	9	10	11	12	13	14	15
	16	17	18	19	20	21	22
	23	24	25	26	27	28	29
	30	31	1	2	3	4	5
JYAISHTHA 1835	6	7	8	9	10	11	12
	13	14	15	16	17	18	19
	20	21	22	23	24	25	26
	27	28	29	30	31	32	1
ĀSHĀḌHA 1835	2	3	4	5	6	7	8
	9	10	11	12	13	14	15
	16	17	18	19	20	21	22
	23	24	25	26	27	28	29
	30	31	1	2	3	4	5
ŚRĀVAṆA 1835	6	7	8	9	10	11	12
	13	14	15	16	17	18	19
	20	21	22	23	24	25	26
	27	28	29	30	31	32	1
BHĀDRAPADA 1835	2	3	4	5	6	7	8
	9	10	11	12	13	14	15
	16	17	18	19	20	21	22
	23	24	25	26	27	28	29
	30	31	1	2	3	4	5
ĀŚVINA 1835	6	7	8	9	10	11	12
	13	14	15	16	17	18	19
	20	21	22	23	24	25	26
	27	28	29	30	1	2	3
KĀRTTIKA 1835	4	5	6	7	8	9	10
	11	12	13	14	15	16	17
	18	19	20	21	22	23	24
	25	26	27	28	29	30	1
MĀRGAŚĪRA 1835	2	3	4	5	6	7	8
	9	10	11	12	13	14	15
	16	17	18	19	20	21	22
	23	24	25	26	27	28	29
PAUSHA 1835	30	1	2	3	4	5	6
	7	8	9	10	11	12	13
	14	15	16	17	18	19	20

ISLAMIC (ASTRONOMICAL) 1331/1332

Month	Sun	Mon	Tue	Wed	Thu	Fri	Sat
MUHARRAM 1331	19	20	21	22	23	24	25
	26	27	28	29	1	2	3
SAFAR 1331	4	5	6	7	8	9	10
	11	12	13	14	15	16	17
	18	19	20	21	22	23	24
	25	26	27	28	29	30	1
RABĪ' I 1331	2	3	4	5	6	7	8
	9	10	11	12[c]	13	14	15
	16	17	18	19	20	21	22
	23	24	25	26	27	28	29
	1	2	3	4	5	6	7
RABĪ' II 1331	8	9	10	11	12	13	14
	15	16	17	18	19	20	21
	22	23	24	25	26	27	28
	29	30	1	2	3	4	5
JUMĀDĀ I 1331	6	7	8	9	10	11	12
	13	14	15	16	17	18	19
	20	21	22	23	24	25	26
	27	28	29	30	1	2	3
JUMĀDĀ II 1331	4	5	6	7	8	9	10
	11	12	13	14	15	16	17
	18	19	20	21	22	23	24
	25	26	27	28	29	1	2
RAJAB 1331	3	4	5	6	7	8	9
	10	11	12	13	14	15	16
	17	18	19	20	21	22	23
	24	25	26	27[d]	28	29	1
SHA'BĀN 1331	2	3	4	5	6	7	8
	9	10	11	12	13	14	15
	16	17	18	19	20	21	22
	23	24	25	26	27	28	29
	30	1[e]	2	3	4	5	6
RAMAḌĀN 1331	7	8	9	10	11	12	13
	14	15	16	17	18	19	20
	21	22	23	24	25	26	27
	28	29	1[f]	2	3	4	5
SHAWWĀL 1331	6	7	8	9	10	11	12
	13	14	15	16	17	18	19
	20	21	22	23	24	25	26
	27	28	29	30	1	2	3
DHU AL-QA'DA 1331	4	5	6	7	8	9	10
	11	12	13	14	15	16	17
	18	19	20	21	22	23	24
	25	26	27	28	29	30	1
DHU AL-HIJJA 1331	2	3	4	5	6	7	8
	9	10[g]	11	12	13	14	15
	16	17	18	19	20	21	22
	23	24	25	26	27	28	29
MUHARRAM 1332	1[a]	2	3	4	5	6	7
	8	9	10[b]	11	12	13	14
	15	16	17	18	19	20	21
	22	23	24	25	26	27	28
	29	1	2	3	4	5	6

GREGORIAN 1913

Julian (Sun)	Sun	Mon	Tue	Wed	Thu	Fri	Sat	Month
Dec 16	29	30	31	1	2	3	4	
	5	6	7[a]	8	9	10	11	JANUARY 1913
Dec 30	12	13	14[b]	15	16	17	18	
	19	20	21	22	23	24	25	
Jan 13	26	27	28	29	30	31	1	
	2	3	4	5[c]	6	7	8	FEBRUARY 1913
Jan 27	9	10	11	12	13	14	15	
	16	17	18	19	20	21	22	
Feb 10	23	24	25	26	27	28	1	
	2	3	4	5	6	7	8	MARCH 1913
Feb 24	9	10	11	12	13	14	15	
	16[d]	17	18	19	20	21	22	
Mar 10	23[e]	24	25	26	27	28	29	
	30	31	1	2	3	4	5	
Mar 24	6	7	8	9	10	11	12	APRIL 1913
	13	14	15	16	17	18	19	
Apr 7	20	21	22	23	24	25	26	
	27[f]	28	29	30	1	2	3	
Apr 21	4	5	6	7	8	9	10	MAY 1913
	11	12	13	14	15	16	17	
May 5	18	19	20	21	22	23	24	
	25	26	27	28	29	30	31	
May 19	1	2	3	4	5	6	7	
	8	9	10	11	12	13	14	JUNE 1913
Jun 2	15	16	17	18	19	20	21	
	22	23	24	25	26	27	28	
Jun 16	29	30	1	2	3	4	5	
	6	7	8	9	10	11	12	JULY 1913
Jun 30	13	14	15	16	17	18	19	
	20	21	22	23	24	25	26	
Jul 14	27	28	29	30	31	1	2	
	3	4	5	6	7	8	9	AUGUST 1913
Jul 28	10	11	12	13	14	15	16	
	17	18	19	20	21	22	23	
Aug 11	24	25	26	27	28	29	30	
	31	1	2	3	4	5	6	
Aug 25	7	8	9	10	11	12	13	SEPTEMBER 1913
	14	15	16	17	18	19	20	
Sep 8	21	22	23	24	25	26	27	
	28	29	30	1	2	3	4	
Sep 22	5	6	7	8	9	10	11	OCTOBER 1913
	12	13	14	15	16	17	18	
Oct 6	19	20	21	22	23	24	25	
	26	27	28	29	30	31	1	
Oct 20	2	3	4	5	6	7	8	NOVEMBER 1913
	9	10	11	12	13	14	15	
Nov 3	16	17	18	19	20	21	22	
	23	24	25	26	27	28	29	
Nov 17	30[g]	1	2	3	4	5	6	
	7	8	9	10	11	12	13	DECEMBER 1913
Dec 1	14	15	16	17	18	19	20	
	21	22	23	24	25[h]	26	27	
Dec 15	28	29	30	31	1	2	3	

Persian: ‡Leap year; [a]New Year; [b]Sizdeh Bedar

Hindu Lunar: ‡Leap year; [a]New Year (Pramādin); [b]Birthday of Rāma; [c]Birthday of Krishna; [d]Ganēśa Chaturthī; [e]Dashara; [f]Diwali; [g]Birthday of Vishnu; [h]Night of Śiva; [i]Holi

Hindu Solar: ‡Leap year; [a]New Year (Krodhana); [b]Pongal

Islamic: [a]New Year; [b]'Ashūrā'; [c]Prophet's Birthday; [d]Ascent of the Prophet; [e]Start of Ramaḍān; [f]'Īd al-Fiṭr; [g]'Īd al-'Aḍḥā

Gregorian: [a]Orthodox Christmas; [b]Julian New Year; [c]Ash Wednesday; [d]Feast of Orthodoxy; [e]Easter; [f]Orthodox Easter; [g]Advent; [h]Christmas

1914

GREGORIAN 1914	Sun	Mon	Tue	Wed	Thu	Fri	Sat	Lunar Phases	ISO WEEK (Mon)	JULIAN DAY (Sun noon)	HEBREW 5674/5675	Sun	Mon	Tue	Wed	Thu	Fri	Sat	Molad	CHINESE Guǐ-Chǒu/Jiǎ-Yín‡	Sun	Mon	Tue	Wed	Thu	Fri	Sat	Solar Term	COPTIC 1630/1631‡	Sun	Mon	Tue	Wed	Thu	Fri	Sat	ETHIOPIC 1906/1907‡
	28	29	30	31	1[a]	2	3		1	2420130		29[e]	30[e]	1[e]	2[e]	3	4	5	Sun 5h25m11p		2	3	4	5	6	7	8			19	20	21	22	23	24	25	TĀKHŚĀŚ 1906
JANUARY 1914	◐	5	6	7	8	9	10	13:09	2	2420137	TEVETH 5674	6	7	8	9	10	11	12		MONTH 12 Guǐ-Chǒu	9	10	*11*	12	13	14	15	Xiǎo hán	KOIAK 1630	26	27	28	29[c]	30	1	2	
	11	○	13	14	15	16	17	5:09	3	2420144		13	14	15	16	17	18	19			16	17	18	19	20	21	22			3	4	5	6[d]	7	8	9	
	18	◑	20	21	22	23	24	0:30	4	2420151		20	21	22	23	24	25	26			23	24	25	**26**	27	28	29	Dà hán	TŌBE 1630	10	11[e]	12	13	14	15	16	TER 1906
	25	●	27	28	29	30	31	6:34	5	2420158		27	28	29	1	2	3	4	Mon 18h9m12p		30	1[a]	2	3	4	5	6			17	18	19	20	21	22	23	
FEBRUARY 1914	1	2	◐	4	5	6	7	10:32	6	2420165	SHEVAT 5674	5	6	7	8	9	10	11		MONTH 1 Jiǎ-Yín	7	8	9	*10*	11	12	13*	Lì chūn		24	25	26	27	28	29	30	
	8	9	○	11	12	13	14	17:34	7	2420172		12	13	14	15	16	17	18			14	15[b]	16	17	18	19	20			1	2	3	4	5	6	7	
	15	16	◑	18	19	20	21	9:23	8	2420179		19	20	21	22	23	24	25			21	22	23	24	**25**	26	27	Yǔ shuǐ	MESHIR 1630	8	9	10	11	12	13	14	
	22	23	24	●	26	27	28	0:02	9	2420186		26	27	28	29	30	1	2	Wed 6h53m13p		28	29	30	1	2	3	4			15	16	17	18	19	20	21	YAKĀTIT 1906
MARCH 1914	1	2	3	4	◐	6	7	5:03	10	2420193	ADAR 5674	3	4	5	6	7	8	9		MONTH 2 Jiǎ-Yín	5	6	7	8	9	*10*	11	Jīng zhé		22	23	24	25	26	27	28	
	8	9	10	11	○	13	14	4:18	11	2420200		10	11	12	13	14[f]	15	16			12	13	14	15	16	17	18			29	30	1	2	3	4	5	
	15	16	17	◑	19	20	21[b]	19:39	12	2420207		17	18	19	20	21	22	23			19	20	21	22	23	24	**25**	Chūn fēn	PAREMOTEP 1630	6	7	8	9	10	11	12	MAGĀBIT 1906
	22	23	24	25	●	27	28	18:09	13	2420214		24	25	26	27	28	29	1	Thu 19h37m14p		26	27	28	29	30	1	2			13	14	15	16	17	18	19	
	29	30	31	1	2	◐	4	19:41	14	2420221		2	3	4	5	6	7	8		MONTH 3 Jiǎ-Yín	3	4	5	6	7	8	9			20	21	22	23	24	25	26	
APRIL 1914	5	6	7	8	9	○	11	13:28	15	2420228	NISAN 5674	9	10	11	12	13	14	15[g]			*10*[c]	11	12	13*	14	15	16	Qīng míng		27	28	29	30	1	2	3	
	12	13	14	15	16	◑	18	7:52	16	2420235		16	17	18	19	20	21	22			17	18	19	20	21	22	23		PARMOUTE 1630	4	5	6	7	8	9	10	MIYĀZYĀ 1906
	19	20	21	22	23	24	●	11:21	17	2420242		23	24	25	26	27	28	29			24	25	**26**	27	28	29	1	Gǔ yǔ		11[f]	12	13	14	15	16	17	
	26	27	28	29	30	1	2		18	2420249		30	1	2	3	4	5	6	Sat 8h21m15p	MONTH 4 Jiǎ-Yín	2	3	4	5	6	7	8			18	19	20	21	22	23	24	
MAY 1914	◐	4	5	6	7	8	○	21:30 6:29	19	2420256	IYYAR 5674	7	8	9	10	11	12	13			9	10	11	*12*	13	14	15	Lì xià		25	26	27	28	29[g]	30	1	
	10	11	12	13	14	15	◑	22:12	20	2420263		14	15	16	17	18	19	20			16	17	18	19	20	21	22			2	3	4	5	6	7	8	
	17	18	19	20	21	22	23		21	2420270		21	22	23	24	25	26	27			23	24	25	26	27	**28**	29	Xiǎo mǎn	PASHONS 1630	9	10	11	12	13	14	15	GENBOT 1906
	24	●	26	27	28	29	30	2:34	22	2420277		28	29	1	2	3	4	5	Sun 21h5m16p		30	1	2	3	4	5[d]	6			16	17	18	19	20	21	22	
	31	◐	2	3	4	5	6	14:03	23	2420284	SIVAN 5674	6[h]	7	8	9	10	11	12		MONTH 5 Jiǎ-Yín	7	8	9	10	11	12	*13*	Máng zhòng		23	24	25	26	27	28	29	
JUNE 1914	7	○	9	10	11	12	13	5:13	24	2420291		13	14	15	16	17	18	19			14*	15	16	17	18	19	20			30	1	2	3	4	5	6	
	14	◑	16	17	18	19	20	14:20	25	2420298		20	21	22	23	24	25	26			21	22	23	24	25	26	27			7	8	9	10	11	12	13	
	21	22[c]	●	24	25	26	27	15:33	26	2420305		27	28	29	30	1	2	3	Tue 9h49m17p		28	**29**	1	2	3	4	5	Xià zhì	PAŌNE 1630	14	15	16	17	18	19	20	SANĒ 1906
	28	29	◐	1	2	3	4	19:24	27	2420312	TAMMUZ 5674	4	5	6	7	8	9	10		LEAP MONTH 5 Jiǎ-Yín	6	7	8	9	10	11	12			21	22	23	24	25	26	27	
JULY 1914	5	6	○	8	9	10	11	14:00	28	2420319		11	12	13	14	15	16	17			13	14	15	*16*	17	18	19	Xiǎo shǔ		28	29	30	1	2	3	4	
	12	13	14	◑	16	17	18	7:31	29	2420326		18	19	20	21	22	23	24			20	21	22	23	24	25	26			5	6	7	8	9	10	11	
	19	20	21	22	●	24	25	2:38	30	2420333		25	26	27	28	29	1	2	Wed 22h34m0p		27	28	29	30	1	**2**	3	Dà shǔ	EPĒP 1630	12	13	14	15	16	17	18	HAMLĒ 1906
	26	27	28	◐	30	31	1	23:51	31	2420340	AV 5674	3	4	5	6	7	8	9		MONTH 6 Jiǎ-Yín	4	5	6	7	8	9	10			19	20	21	22	23	24	25	
AUGUST 1914	2	3	4	5	○	7	8	0:40	32	2420347		10[i]	11	12	13	14	15	16			11	12	13	14	15*	16	*17*	Lì qiū		26	27	28	29	30	1	2	
	9	10	11	12	13	◑	15	0:56	33	2420354		17	18	19	20	21	22	23			18	19	20	21	22	23	24			3	4	5	6	7	8	9	
	16	17	18	19	20	●	22	12:26	34	2420361		24	25	26	27	28	29	30			25	26	27	28	29	1	2		MESORĒ 1630	10	11	12	13[h]	14	15	16	NAHASĒ 1906
	23	24	25	26	27	◐	29	4:52	35	2420368		1	2	3	4	5	6	7	Fri 11h18m1p	MONTH 7 Jiǎ-Yín	3	**4**	5	6	7[e]	8	9	Chǔ shǔ		17	18	19	20	21	22	23	
	30	31	1	2	3	○	5	14:01	36	2420375	ELUL 5674	8	9	10	11	12	13	14			10	11	12	13	14	15[f]	16			24	25	26	27	28	29	30	
SEPTEMBER 1914	6	7	8	9	10	11	◑	17:48	37	2420382		15	16	17	18	19	20	21			17	18	*19*	20	21	22	23	Bái lù	EPAG. 1630	1	2	3	4	5	1[a]	2	PĀG. 1906
	13	14	15	16	17	18	●	21:33	38	2420389		22	23	24	25	26	27	28			24	25	26	27	28	29	30			3	4	5	6	7	8	9	MASKARAM 1907
	20	21	22	23[d]	24	25	◐	12:03	39	2420396		29	1[a]	2[a]	3	4	5	6	Sun 0h2m2p		1	2	3	4	**5**	6	7	Qiū fēn	THOOUT 1631	10	11	12	13	14	15	16	
	27	28	29	30	1	2	3		40	2420403	TISHRI 5675	7	8	9	10[b]	11	12	13		MONTH 8 Jiǎ-Yín	8	9	10	11	12	13	14			17[b]	18	19	20	21	22	23	
OCTOBER 1914	○	5	6	7	8	9	10	5:58	41	2420410		14	15[c]	16	17	18	19	20			15[g]	16*	17	18	19	*20*	21	Hán lù		24	25	26	27	28	29	30	
	11	◑	13	14	15	16	17	9:33	42	2420417		21	22	23	24	25	26	27			22	23	24	25	26	27	28			1	2	3	4	5	6	7	
	18	●	20	21	22	23	24	6:33	43	2420424		28	29	30	1	2	3	4	Mon 12h46m3p		29	1	2	3	4	5	**6**	Shuāng jiàng	PAOPE 1631	8	9	10	11	12	13	14	TEQEMT 1907
	◐	26	27	28	29	30	31	22:44	44	2420431	HESHVAN 5675	5	6	7	8	9	10	11		MONTH 9 Jiǎ-Yín	7	8	9[h]	10	11	12	13			15	16	17	18	19	20	21	
NOVEMBER 1914	1	○	3	4	5	6	7	23:48	45	2420438		12	13	14	15	16	17	18			14	15	16	17	18	19	20			22	23	24	25	26	27	28	
	8	9	◑	11	12	13	14	23:36	46	2420445		19	20	21	22	23	24	25			*21*	22	23	24	25	26	27	Lì dōng		29	30	1	2	3	4	5	
	15	16	●	18	19	20	21	16:02	47	2420452		26	27	28	29	1	2	3	Wed 1h30m4p		28	29	1	2	3	4	5			6	7	8	9	10	11	12	
	22	23	◐	25	26	27	28	13:38	48	2420459	KISLEV 5675	4	5	6	7	8	9	10		MONTH 10 Jiǎ-Yín	6	*7*	8	9	10	11	12	Xiǎo xuě	ATHŌR 1631	13	14	15	16	17	18	19	HEDĀR 1907
	29	30	1	○	3	4	5	18:20	49	2420466		11	12	13	14	15	16	17[d]			13	14	15	16	17	18*	19			20	21	22	23	24	25	26	
DECEMBER 1914	6	7	8	9	◑	11	12	11:31	50	2420473		18	19	20	21	22	23	24			20	21	*22*	23	24	25	26	Dà xuě		27	28	29	30	1	2	3	
	13	14	15	16	●	18	19	2:35	51	2420480		25[e]	26[e]	27[e]	28[e]	29[e]	1[e]	2[e]	Thu 14h14m5p	MONTH 11 Jiǎ-Yín	27	28	29	30	1	2	3		KOIAK 1631	4	5	6	7	8	9	10	TĀKHŚĀŚ 1907
	20	21	22[e]	23	◐	25	26	8:24	52	2420487	TEVETH 5675	3[e]	4	5	6	7	8	9			4	5	6	7[i]	8	9	10	Dōng zhì		11	12	13	14	15	16	17	
	27	28	29	30	31	○	2	12:20	53	2420494		10	11	12	13	14	15	16			11	12	13	14	15	16	17			18	19	20	21	22	23	24	

Gregorian:
[a]New Year
[b]Spring (11:11)
[c]Summer (6:55)
[d]Autumn (21:34)
[e]Winter (16:22)
● New moon
◐ First quarter moon
○ Full moon
◑ Last quarter moon

Hebrew:
[a]New Year
[b]Yom Kippur
[c]Sukkot
[d]Winter starts
[e]Ḥanukkah
[f]Purim
[g]Passover
[h]Shavuot
[i]Fast of Av

Chinese:
‡Leap year
[a]New Year (4612, Tiger)
[b]Lantern Festival
[c]Qīngmíng
[d]Dragon Festival
[e]Qīqiǎo
[f]Hungry Ghosts
[g]Mid-Autumn Festival
[h]Double-Ninth Festival
[i]Dōngzhì
*Start of 60-name cycle

Coptic/Ethiopic:
‡Leap year
[a]New Year
[b]Building of the Cross
[c]Christmas
[d]Jesus's Circumcision
[e]Epiphany
[f]Easter
[g]Mary's Announcement
[h]Jesus's Transfiguration

1914

PERSIAN (ASTRONOMICAL) 1292‡/1293

Month	Sun	Mon	Tue	Wed	Thu	Fri	Sat
	7	8	9	10	11	12	13
DEY 1292	14	15	16	17	18	19	20
	21	22	23	24	25	26	27
	28	29	30	1	2	3	4
BAHMAN 1292	5	6	7	8	9	10	11
	12	13	14	15	16	17	18
	19	20	21	22	23	24	25
	26	27	28	29	30	1	2
ESFAND 1292	3	4	5	6	7	8	9
	10	11	12	13	14	15	16
	17	18	19	20	21	22	23
	24	25	26	27	28	29	30
	1[a]	2	3	4	5	6	7
FARVARDĪN 1293	8	9	10	11	12	13[b]	14
	15	16	17	18	19	20	21
	22	23	24	25	26	27	28
	29	30	31	1	2	3	4
ORDĪBEHEŠT 1293	5	6	7	8	9	10	11
	12	13	14	15	16	17	18
	19	20	21	22	23	24	25
	26	27	28	29	30	31	1
	2	3	4	5	6	7	8
XORDĀD 1293	9	10	11	12	13	14	15
	16	17	18	19	20	21	22
	23	24	25	26	27	28	29
	30	31	1	2	3	4	5
TĪR 1293	6	7	8	9	10	11	12
	13	14	15	16	17	18	19
	20	21	22	23	24	25	26
	27	28	29	30	31	1	2
MORDĀD 1293	3	4	5	6	7	8	9
	10	11	12	13	14	15	16
	17	18	19	20	21	22	23
	24	25	26	27	28	29	30
	31	1	2	3	4	5	6
SHAHRĪVAR 1293	7	8	9	10	11	12	13
	14	15	16	17	18	19	20
	21	22	23	24	25	26	27
	28	29	30	31	1	2	3
MEHR 1293	4	5	6	7	8	9	10
	11	12	13	14	15	16	17
	18	19	20	21	22	23	24
	25	26	27	28	29	30	1
ĀBĀN 1293	2	3	4	5	6	7	8
	9	10	11	12	13	14	15
	16	17	18	19	20	21	22
	23	24	25	26	27	28	29
	30	1	2	3	4	5	6
ĀZAR 1293	7	8	9	10	11	12	13
	14	15	16	17	18	19	20
	21	22	23	24	25	26	27
DEY 1293	28	29	30	1	2	3	4
	5	6	7	8	9	10	11

HINDU LUNAR 1970/1971

Month	Sun	Mon	Tue	Wed	Thu	Fri	Sat
	1	2	3	4	5	6	7
PAUSHA 1970	8	9	9	10	11	12	13
	14	15	16	**17**	19	20	21
	22	23	24	25	26	27	28
	29	30	1	2	3	4	5
MĀGHA 1970	6	7	8	9	10	11	12
	13	14	15	16	17	18	19
	20	21	**22**	24	25	26	27
	28	29[h]	30	1	2	2	3
PHĀLGUNA 1970	4	5	6	7	8	9	10
	11	12	13	14	15[i]	**16**	18
	19	20	21	22	23	24	25
	26	27	28	29	30	1[a]	2
CHAITRA 1971	3	4	5	5	6	7	8[b]
	9	11	12	13	14	15	16
	17	18	19	20	21	22	23
	24	25	26	27	28	29	30
	1	2	3	4	5	6	7
VAIŚĀKHA 1971	8	9	10	11	12	**13**	15
	16	17	18	19	20	21	22
	23	24	25	26	27	28	29
	29	30	1	2	3	4	5
JYAISHTHA 1971	**6**	8	9	10	11	12	13
	14	15	16	17	18	19	20
	21	22	23	24	25	26	27
	28	29	30	1	2	3	4
ĀSHĀDHA 1971	5	6	7	8	**9**	11	12
	13	14	15	16	17	18	19
	20	21	22	23	24	25	26
	26	27	28	29	30	**1**	3
ŚRĀVANA 1971	4	5	6	7	8	9	10
	11	12	13	**14**	16	17	17
	18	19	20	21	22	23[c]	24
	25	26	27	28	29	30	1
BHĀDRAPADA 1971	2	3	4[d]	**5**	7	8	9
	10	11	12	13	14	15	16
	17	18	19	20	21	22	22
	23	24	25	26	27	**28**	30
	1	2	3	4	5	6	7
ĀŚVINA 1971	8[e]	9[e]	10[e]	11	12	13	14
	15	16	17	18	19	20	21
	22	23	24	25	26	27	28
	29	30	1[f]	**2**	4	5	6
KĀRTTIKA 1971	7	8	9	10	11	12	13
	14	15	16	17	17	18	19
	20	21	22	23	24	25	**26**
	28	29	30	1	2	3	4
MĀRGAŚĪRA 1971	5	6	7	8	9	10	11[g]
	12	13	14	15	16	17	18
	19	20	21	22	23	24	25
	26	27	28	29	**30**	2	3
PAUSHA 1971	4	5	6	7	8	9	10
	10	11	12	13	14	15	16

HINDU SOLAR 1835‡/1836

Month	Sun	Mon	Tue	Wed	Thu	Fri	Sat
PAUSHA 1835	14	15	16	17	18	19	20
	21	22	23	24	25	26	27
	28	29	1[b]	2	3	4	5
	6	7	8	9	10	11	12
MĀGHA 1835	13	14	15	16	17	18	19
	20	21	22	23	24	25	26
	27	28	29	30	1	2	3
	4	5	6	7	8	9	10
PHĀLGUNA 1835	11	12	13	14	15	16	17
	18	19	20	21	22	23	24
	25	26	27	28	29	1	2
	3	4	5	6	7	8	9
CHAITRA 1835	10	11	12	13	14	15	16
	17	18	19	20	21	22	23
	24	25	26	27	28	29	30
	31	1[a]	2	3	4	5	6
VAIŚĀKHA 1836	7	8	9	10	11	12	13
	14	15	16	17	18	19	20
	21	22	23	24	25	26	27
	28	29	30	31	1	2	3
JYAISHTHA 1836	4	5	6	7	8	9	10
	11	12	13	14	15	16	17
	18	19	20	21	22	23	24
	25	26	27	28	29	30	31
	1	2	3	4	5	6	7
ĀSHĀDHA 1836	8	9	10	11	12	13	14
	15	16	17	18	19	20	21
	22	23	24	25	26	27	28
	29	30	31	32	1	2	3
ŚRĀVANA 1836	4	5	6	7	8	9	10
	11	12	13	14	15	16	17
	18	19	20	21	22	23	24
	25	26	27	28	29	30	31
	1	2	3	4	5	6	7
BHĀDRAPADA 1836	8	9	10	11	12	13	14
	15	16	17	18	19	20	21
	22	23	24	25	26	27	28
	29	30	31	1	2	3	4
ĀŚVINA 1836	5	6	7	8	9	10	11
	12	13	14	15	16	17	18
	19	20	21	22	23	24	25
	26	27	28	29	30	31	1
	2	3	4	5	6	7	8
KĀRTTIKA 1836	9	10	11	12	13	14	15
	16	17	18	19	20	21	22
	23	24	25	26	27	28	29
	30	1	2	3	4	5	6
MĀRGAŚĪRA 1836	7	8	9	10	11	12	13
	14	15	16	17	18	19	20
	21	22	23	24	25	26	27
	28	29	1	2	3	4	5
PAUSHA 1836	6	7	8	9	10	11	12
	13	14	15	16	17	18	19

ISLAMIC (ASTRONOMICAL) 1332/1333‡

Month	Sun	Mon	Tue	Wed	Thu	Fri	Sat
	29	1	2	3	4	5	6
ṢAFAR 1332	7	8	9	10	11	12	13
	14	15	16	17	18	19	20
	21	22	23	24	25	26	27
	28	29	30	1	2	3	4
RABĪ' I 1332	5	6	7	8	9	10	11
	12[c]	13	14	15	16	17	18
	19	20	21	22	23	24	25
	26	27	28	29	1	2	3
RABĪ' II 1332	4	5	6	7	8	9	10
	11	12	13	14	15	16	17
	18	19	20	21	22	23	24
	25	26	27	28	29	30	1
JUMĀDĀ I 1332	2	3	4	5	6	7	8
	9	10	11	12	13	14	15
	16	17	18	19	20	21	22
	23	24	25	26	27	28	29
	30	1	2	3	4	5	6
JUMĀDĀ II 1332	7	8	9	10	11	12	13
	14	15	16	17	18	19	20
	21	22	23	24	25	26	27
	28	29	1	2	3	4	5
RAJAB 1332	6	7	8	9	10	11	12
	13	14	15	16	17	18	19
	20	21	22	23	24	25	26
	27[d]	28	29	30	1	2	3
SHA'BĀN 1332	4	5	6	7	8	9	10
	11	12	13	14	15	16	17
	18	19	20	21	22	23	24
	25	26	27	28	29	1[e]	2
RAMAḌĀN 1332	3	4	5	6	7	8	9
	10	11	12	13	14	15	16
	17	18	19	20	21	22	23
	24	25	26	27	28	29	30
	1[f]	2	3	4	5	6	7
SHAWWĀL 1332	8	9	10	11	12	13	14
	15	16	17	18	19	20	21
	22	23	24	25	26	27	28
	29	30	1	2	3	4	5
DHU AL-QA'DA 1332	6	7	8	9	10	11	12
	13	14	15	16	17	18	19
	20	21	22	23	24	25	26
	27	28	29	1	2	3	4
DHU AL-ḤIJJA 1332	5	6	7	8	9	10[g]	11
	12	13	14	15	16	17	18
	19	20	21	22	23	24	25
	26	27	28	29	1[a]	2	3
MUHARRAM 1333	4	5	6	7	8	9	10[b]
	11	12	13	14	15	16	17
	18	19	20	21	22	23	24
	25	26	27	28	29	30	1
ṢAFAR 1333	2	3	4	5	6	7	8
	9	10	11	12	13	14	15

GREGORIAN 1914

Julian (Sun)	Sun	Mon	Tue	Wed	Thu	Fri	Sat	Month
Dec 15	28	29	30	31	1	2	3	
	4	5	6	7[a]	8	9	10	JANUARY 1914
Dec 29	11	12	13	14[b]	15	16	17	
	18	19	20	21	22	23	24	
Jan 12	25	26	27	28	29	30	31	
	1	2	3	4	5	6	7	
Jan 26	8	9	10	11	12	13	14	FEBRUARY 1914
	15	16	17	18	19	20	21	
Feb 9	22	23	24	25[c]	26	27	28	
	1	2	3	4	5	6	7	
Feb 23	8[d]	9	10	11	12	13	14	MARCH 1914
	15	16	17	18	19	20	21	
Mar 9	22	23	24	25	26	27	28	
	29	30	31	1	2	3	4	
Mar 23	5	6	7	8	9	10	11	APRIL 1914
	12[e]	13	14	15	16	17	18	
Apr 6	19[f]	20	21	22	23	24	25	
	26	27	28	29	30	1	2	
Apr 20	3	4	5	6	7	8	9	MAY 1914
	10	11	12	13	14	15	16	
May 4	17	18	19	20	21	22	23	
	24	25	26	27	28	29	30	
May 18	31	1	2	3	4	5	6	
	7	8	9	10	11	12	13	JUNE 1914
Jun 1	14	15	16	17	18	19	20	
	21	22	23	24	25	26	27	
Jun 15	28	29	30	1	2	3	4	
	5	6	7	8	9	10	11	JULY 1914
Jun 29	12	13	14	15	16	17	18	
	19	20	21	22	23	24	25	
Jul 13	26	27	28	29	30	31	1	
	2	3	4	5	6	7	8	
Jul 27	9	10	11	12	13	14	15	AUGUST 1914
	16	17	18	19	20	21	22	
Aug 10	23	24	25	26	27	28	29	
	30	31	1	2	3	4	5	
Aug 24	6	7	8	9	10	11	12	SEPTEMBER 1914
	13	14	15	16	17	18	19	
Sep 7	20	21	22	23	24	25	26	
	27	28	29	30	1	2	3	
Sep 21	4	5	6	7	8	9	10	OCTOBER 1914
	11	12	13	14	15	16	17	
Oct 5	18	19	20	21	22	23	24	
	25	26	27	28	29	30	31	
Oct 19	1	2	3	4	5	6	7	
	8	9	10	11	12	13	14	NOVEMBER 1914
Nov 2	15	16	17	18	19	20	21	
	22	23	24	25	26	27	28	
Nov 16	29[g]	30	1	2	3	4	5	
	6	7	8	9	10	11	12	DECEMBER 1914
Nov 30	13	14	15	16	17	18	19	
	20	21	22	23	24	25[h]	26	
Dec 14	27	28	29	30	31	1	2	

Persian: ‡Leap year; [a]New Year; [b]Sizdeh Bedar

Hindu Lunar: [a]New Year (Ānanda); [b]Birthday of Rāma; [c]Birthday of Krishna; [d]Ganēśa Chaturthī; [e]Dashara; [f]Diwali; [g]Birthday of Vishnu; [h]Night of Śiva; [i]Holi

Hindu Solar: ‡Leap year; [a]New Year (Kshaya); [b]Pongal

Islamic: ‡Leap year; [a]New Year; [b]'Ashūrā'; [c]Prophet's Birthday; [d]Ascent of the Prophet; [e]Start of Ramaḍān; [f]'Id al-Fiṭr; [g]'Id al-'Aḍḥā

Gregorian: [a]Orthodox Christmas; [b]Julian New Year; [c]Ash Wednesday; [d]Feast of Orthodoxy; [e]Easter; [f]Orthodox Easter; [g]Advent; [h]Christmas

1915

GREGORIAN 1915	Sun	Mon	Tue	Wed	Thu	Fri	Sat	Lunar Phases	ISO WEEK (Mon)	JULIAN DAY (Sun noon)	HEBREW 5675/5676‡	Sun	Mon	Tue	Wed	Thu	Fri	Sat	Molad	CHINESE Jiă-Yín‡/Yĭ-Măo	Sun	Mon	Tue	Wed	Thu	Fri	Sat	Solar Term	COPTIC 1631‡/1632	Sun	Mon	Tue	Wed	Thu	Fri	Sat	ETHIOPIC 1907‡/1908
	27	28	29	30	31	○[a]	2	12:20	53	2420494		10	11	12	13	14	15	16		MONTH 11 Jiă-Yín	11	12	13	14	15	16	17		KOIAK 1631	18	19	20	21	22	23	24	TĀKHŚĀŚ 1907
	3	4	5	6	7	◑	9	21:12	1	2420501	TEVETH 5675	17	18	19	20	21	22	23			18	19	20	21	22	23	24	Xiăo hán		25	26	27	28	29[c]	30	1	
JANUARY 1915	10	11	12	13	14	●	16	14:42	2	2420508		24	25	26	27	28	29	1	Sat 2h58m6p		25	26	27	28	29	1	2			2	3	4	5	6[d]	7	8	
	17	18	19	20	21	22	◐	5:32	3	2420515		2	3	4	5	6	7	8		MONTH 12 Jiă-Yín	3	4	5	6	7	8	9	Dà hán	TŌBE 1631	9	10	11[e]	12	13	14	15	ṬER 1907
	24	25	26	27	28	29	30		4	2420522	SHEVAT 5675	9	10	11	12	13	14	15			10	11	12	13	14	15	16			16	17	18	19	20	21	22	
	○	1	2	3	4	5	6	4:41	5	2420529		16	17	18	19	20	21	22			17	18	19*	20	21	22	23	Lì chūn		23	24	25	26	27	28	29	
	◑	8	9	10	11	12	13	5:11	6	2420536		23	24	25	26	27	28	29			24	25	26	27	28	29	30			30	1	2	3	4	5	6	
FEBRUARY 1915	●	15	16	17	18	19	20	4:31	7	2420543		30	1	2	3	4	5	6	Sun 15h42m7p		1[a]	2	3	4	5	6	7	Yŭ shuĭ		7	8	9	10	11	12	13	
	21	◐	23	24	25	26	27	2:58	8	2420550	ADAR 5675	7	8	9	10	11	12	13		MONTH 1 Yĭ-Măo	8	9	10	11	12	13	14		MESHIR 1631	14	15	16	17	18	19	20	YAKĀTIT 1907
	28	○	2	3	4	5	6	18:32	9	2420557		14[f]	15	16	17	18	19	20			15[b]	16	17	18	19	20	21	Jīng zhé		21	22	23	24	25	26	27	
	7	◑	9	10	11	12	13	12:27	10	2420564		21	22	23	24	25	26	27			22	23	24	25	26	27	28			28	29	30	1	2	3	4	
MARCH 1915	14	●	16	17	18	19	20	19:42	11	2420571		28	29	1	2	3	4	5	Tue 4h26m8p		29	30	1	2	3	4	5			5	6	7	8	9	10	11	
	21[b]	22	◐	24	25	26	27	22:48	12	2420578		6	7	8	9	10	11	12		MONTH 2 Yĭ-Măo	6	7	8	9	10	11	12	Chūn fēn	PAREMOTEP 1631	12	13	14	15	16	17	18	MAGĀBIT 1907
	28	29	30	○	1	2	3	5:37	13	2420585	NISAN 5675	13	14	15[g]	16	17	18	19			13	14	15	16	17	18	19*			19	20	21	22	23	24	25	
	4	5	◑	7	8	9	10	20:12	14	2420592		20	21	22	23	24	25	26			20	21	22[c]	23	24	25	26	Qīng míng		26[f]	27	28	29	30	1	2	
APRIL 1915	11	12	13	●	15	16	17	11:35	15	2420599		27	28	29	30	1	2	3	Wed 17h10m9p		27	28	29	1	2	3	4			3	4	5	6	7	8	9	
	18	19	20	21	◐	23	24	15:38	16	2420606	IYYAR 5675	4	5	6	7	8	9	10		MONTH 3 Yĭ-Măo	5	6	7	8	9	10	11	Gŭ yŭ	PARMOUTE 1631	10	11	12	13	14	15	16	MIYĀZYĀ 1907
	25	26	27	28	○	30	1	14:19	17	2420613		11	12	13	14	15	16	17			12	13	14	15	16	17	18			17	18	19	20	21	22	23	
	2	3	4	5	◑	7	8	5:22	18	2420620		18	19	20	21	22	23	24			19	20	21	22	23	24	25	Lì xià		24	25	26	27	28	29[g]	30	
MAY 1915	9	10	11	12	13	●	15	3:31	19	2420627		25	26	27	28	29	1	2	Fri 5h54m10p		26	27	28	29	30	1	2			1	2	3	4	5	6	7	
	16	17	18	19	20	21	◐	4:49	20	2420634	SIVAN 5675	3	4	5	6[h]	7	8	9		MONTH 4 Yĭ-Măo	3	4	5	6	7	8	9	Xiăo măn	PASHONS 1631	8	9	10	11	12	13	14	GENBOT 1907
	23	24	25	26	27	○	29	21:32	21	2420641		10	11	12	13	14	15	16			10	11	12	13	14	15	16			15	16	17	18	19	20	21	
	30	31	1	2	3	◑	5	16:32	22	2420648		17	18	19	20	21	22	23			17	18	19	20*	21	22	23			22	23	24	25	26	27	28	
	6	7	8	9	10	11	●	18:57	23	2420655		24	25	26	27	28	29	30	Sat 18h38m11p		24	25	26	27	28	29	30	Máng zhòng		29	30	1	2	3	4	5	
JUNE 1915	13	14	15	16	17	18	19		24	2420662		1	2	3	4	5	6	7			1	2	3	4	5[d]	6	7			6	7	8	9	10	11	12	
	◐	21	22[c]	23	24	25	26	14:24	25	2420669	TAMMUZ 5675	8	9	10	11	12	13	14		MONTH 5 Yĭ-Măo	8	9	10	11	12	13	14	Xià zhì	PAŌNE 1631	13	14	15	16	17	18	19	SANĒ 1907
	○	28	29	30	1	2	3	4:27	26	2420676		15	16	17	18	19	20	21			15	16	17	18	19	20	21			20	21	22	23	24	25	26	
	◑	5	6	7	8	9	10	5:54	27	2420683		22	23	24	25	26	27	28	Mon 7h22m12p		22	23	24	25	26	27	28	Xiăo shŭ		27	28	29	30	1	2	3	
JULY 1915	11	●	13	14	15	16	17	9:30	28	2420690		29	1	2	3	4	5	6			29	1	2	3	4	5	6			4	5	6	7	8	9	10	
	18	◐	20	21	22	23	24	21:08	29	2420697	AV 5675	7	8	9[i]	10	11	12	13		MONTH 6 Yĭ-Măo	7	8	9	10	11	12	13	Dà shŭ	EPĒP 1631	11	12	13	14	15	16	17	ḤAMLĒ 1907
	25	○	27	28	29	30	31	12:11	30	2420704		14	15	16	17	18	19	20			14	15	16	17	18	19	20			18	19	20	21	22	23	24	
	1	◑	3	4	5	6	7	21:27	31	2420711		21	22	23	24	25	26	27	Tue 20h6m13p		21*	22	23	24	25	26	27			25	26	27	28	29	30	1	
AUGUST 1915	8	9	●	11	12	13	14	22:52	32	2420718		28	29	30	1	2	3	4			28	29	30	1	2	3	4	Lì qiū		2	3	4	5	6	7	8	
	15	16	17	◐	19	20	21	2:17	33	2420725	ELUL 5675	5	6	7	8	9	10	11		MONTH 7 Yĭ-Măo	5	6	7[e]	8	9	10	11		MESORĒ 1631	9	10	11	12	13[h]	14	15	NAḤASĒ 1907
	22	23	○	25	26	27	28	21:40	34	2420732		12	13	14	15	16	17	18			12	13	14	15[f]	16	17	18	Chŭ shŭ		16	17	18	19	20	21	22	
	29	30	31	◑	2	3	4	14:56	35	2420739		19	20	21	22	23	24	25			19	20	21	22	23	24	25			23	24	25	26	27	28	29	
SEPTEMBER 1915	5	6	7	8	●	10	11	10:52	36	2420746		26	27	28	29	1[a]	2[a]	3	Thu 8h50m14p		26	27	28	29	1	2	3	Bái lù	EPAG. 1631	30	1	2	3	4	5	6	PĀG. 1907
	12	13	14	15	◐	17	18	7:21	37	2420753	TISHRI 5676	4	5	6	7	8	9	10[b]		MONTH 8 Yĭ-Măo	4	5	6	7	8	9	10			1[a]	2	3	4	5	6	7	
	19	20	21	22	○	24[d]	25	9:35	38	2420760		11	12	13	14	15[c]	16	17			11	12	13	14	15[g]	16	17	Qiū fēn	THOOUT 1632	8	9	10	11	12	13	14	MASKARAM 1908
	26	27	28	29	30	◑	2	9:44	39	2420767		18	19	20	21	22	23	24			18	19	20	21	22*	23	24			15	16	17[b]	18	19	20	21	
	3	4	5	6	7	●	9	21:42	40	2420774		25	26	27	28	29	30	1	Fri 21h34m15p		25	26	27	28	29	30	1	Hán lù		22	23	24	25	26	27	28	
OCTOBER 1915	10	11	12	13	14	◐	16	13:51	41	2420781		2	3	4	5	6	7	8		MONTH 9 Yĭ-Măo	2	3	4	5	6	7	8			29	30	1	2	3	4	5	
	17	18	19	20	21	22	○	0:15	42	2420788	HESHVAN 5676	9	10	11	12	13	14	15			9[h]	10	11	12	13	14	15	Shuāng jiàng	PAOPE 1632	6	7	8	9	10	11	12	ṬEQEMT 1908
	24	25	26	27	28	29	30		43	2420795		16	17	18	19	20	21	22			16	17	18	19	20	21	22			13	14	15	16	17	18	19	
	◑	1	2	3	4	5	6	4:39	44	2420802		23	24	25	26	27	28	29			23	24	25	26	27	28	29			20	21	22	23	24	25	26	
NOVEMBER 1915	●	8	9	10	11	12	◐	7:52 23:03	45	2420809		30	1	2	3	4	5	6	Sun 10h18m16p		1	2	3	4	5	6	7	Lì dōng		27	28	29	30	1	2	3	
	14	15	16	17	18	19	20		46	2420816	KISLEV 5676	7	8	9	10	11	12	13		MONTH 10 Yĭ-Măo	8	9	10	11	12	13	14		ATHŌR 1632	4	5	6	7	8	9	10	
	○	22	23	24	25	26	27	17:36	47	2420823		14	15	16	17	18	19	20			15	16	17	18	19	20	21	Xiăo xuě		11	12	13	14	15	16	17	ḪEDĀR 1908
	28	◑	30	1	2	3	4	22:10	48	2420830		21	22	23	24	25[e]	26[e]	27[e]	Mon 23h2m17p		22	23*	24	25	26	27	28			18	19	20	21	22	23	24	
	5	●	7	8	9	10	11	18:04	49	2420837		28[e]	29[d][e]	30[e]	1[e]	2[e]	3	4			29	30	1	2	3	4	5	Dà xuě		25	26	27	28	29	30	1	
DECEMBER 1915	12	◐	14	15	16	17	18	11:38	50	2420844	TEVETH 5676	5	6	7	8	9	10	11		MONTH 11 Yĭ-Măo	6	7	8	9	10	11	12		KOIAK 1632	2	3	4	5	6	7	8	TĀKHŚĀŚ 1908
	19	20	○	22[e]	23	24	25	12:52	51	2420851		12	13	14	15	16	17	18			13	14	15	16	17[i]	18	19	Dōng zhì		9	10	11	12	13	14	15	
	26	27	28	◑	30	31	1	12:59	52	2420858		19	20	21	22	23	24	25			20	21	22	23	24	25	26			16	17	18	19	20	21	22	

[a]New Year
[b]Spring (16:51)
[c]Summer (12:29)
[d]Autumn (3:24)
[e]Winter (22:15)
● New moon
◐ First quarter moon
○ Full moon
◑ Last quarter moon

‡Leap year
[a]New Year
[b]Yom Kippur
[c]Sukkot
[d]Winter starts
[e]Ḥanukkah
[f]Purim
[g]Passover
[h]Shavuot
[i]Fast of Av

‡Leap year
[a]New Year (4613, Hare)
[b]Lantern Festival
[c]Qīngmíng
[d]Dragon Festival
[e]Qīqiăo
[f]Hungry Ghosts
[g]Mid-Autumn Festival
[h]Double-Ninth Festival
[i]Dōngzhì
*Start of 60-name cycle

‡Leap year
[a]New Year
[b]Building of the Cross
[c]Christmas
[d]Jesus's Circumcision
[e]Epiphany
[f]Easter
[g]Mary's Announcement
[h]Jesus's Transfiguration

PERSIAN (ASTRONOMICAL) 1293/1294

Month	Sun	Mon	Tue	Wed	Thu	Fri	Sat
	5	6	7	8	9	10	11
DEY 1293	12	13	14	15	16	17	18
	19	20	21	22	23	24	25
	26	27	28	29	30	1	2
BAHMAN 1293	3	4	5	6	7	8	9
	10	11	12	13	14	15	16
	17	18	19	20	21	22	23
	24	25	26	27	28	29	30
ESFAND 1293	1	2	3	4	5	6	7
	8	9	10	11	12	13	14
	15	16	17	18	19	20	21
	22	23	24	25	26	27	28
	29	1[a]	2	3	4	5	6
FARVARDĪN 1294	7	8	9	10	11	12	13[b]
	14	15	16	17	18	19	20
	21	22	23	24	25	26	27
	28	29	30	31	1	2	3
ORDĪBEHEŠT 1294	4	5	6	7	8	9	10
	11	12	13	14	15	16	17
	18	19	20	21	22	23	24
	25	26	27	28	29	30	31
XORDĀD 1294	1	2	3	4	5	6	7
	8	9	10	11	12	13	14
	15	16	17	18	19	20	21
	22	23	24	25	26	27	28
	29	30	31	1	2	3	4
TĪR 1294	5	6	7	8	9	10	11
	12	13	14	15	16	17	18
	19	20	21	22	23	24	25
	26	27	28	29	30	31	1
MORDĀD 1294	2	3	4	5	6	7	8
	9	10	11	12	13	14	15
	16	17	18	19	20	21	22
	23	24	25	26	27	28	29
	30	31	1	2	3	4	5
SHAHRĪVAR 1294	6	7	8	9	10	11	12
	13	14	15	16	17	18	19
	20	21	22	23	24	25	26
	27	28	29	30	31	1	2
MEHR 1294	3	4	5	6	7	8	9
	10	11	12	13	14	15	16
	17	18	19	20	21	22	23
	24	25	26	27	28	29	30
ĀBĀN 1294	1	2	3	4	5	6	7
	8	9	10	11	12	13	14
	15	16	17	18	19	20	21
	22	23	24	25	26	27	28
	29	30	1	2	3	4	5
ĀZAR 1294	6	7	8	9	10	11	12
	13	14	15	16	17	18	19
	20	21	22	23	24	25	26
	27	28	29	30	1	2	3
DEY 1294	4	5	6	7	8	9	10

[a]New Year
[b]Sizdeh Bedar

HINDU LUNAR 1971/1972‡

Month	Sun	Mon	Tue	Wed	Thu	Fri	Sat
PAUSHA 1971	*10*	11	12	13	14	15	16
	17	18	19	20	21	22	23
	24	26	27	28	29	30	1
MĀGHA 1971	2	3	4	5	6	7	8
	9	10	11	12	*12*	13	14
	15	16	17	**18**	20	21	22
	23	24	25	26	27	28[h]	29
PHĀLGUNA 1971	30	1	2	3	4	5	6
	7	8	9	10	11	12	13
	14	15[i]	16	17	18	19	20
	21	22	**23**	25	26	27	28
	29	30	1[a]	2	3	4	5
CHAITRA 1972	5	6	7	8	9[b]	10	11
	12	13	14	15	16	**17**	19
	20	21	22	23	24	25	26
LEAP VAIŚĀKHA 1972	27	28	29	30	1	2	3
	4	5	6	7	8	9	10
	11	12	13	14	15	16	17
	18	19	20	**21**	23	24	25
	26	27	28	29	*29*	30	1
VAIŚĀKHA 1972	2	3	4	5	6	7	8
	9	10	11	12	13	**14**	16
	17	18	19	20	21	22	23
	24	25	26	27	28	29	30
JYAISHTHA 1972	1	2	3	4	5	6	7
	8	9	10	11	12	13	14
	15	16	**17**	19	20	21	22
	23	24	25	26	*26*	27	28
ĀSHĀDHA 1972	29	30	1	2	3	4	5
	6	7	8	**9**	11	12	13
	14	15	16	17	18	19	20
	21	22	23	24	25	26	27
ŚRĀVAṆA 1972	28	29	30	1	2	3	4
	5	6	7	8	9	10	11
	12	14	15	16	17	18	19
	20	21	22	*22*	23[c]	24	25
BHĀDRAPADA 1972	26	27	28	29	30	1	2
	3	4[d]	**5**	7	8	9	10
	11	12	13	14	15	16	17
	18	19	20	21	22	23	24
ĀŚVINA 1972	25	26	27	28	29	30	1
	2	3	4	5	6	7	8[e]
	9[e]	11	12	13	14	15	16
	17	*17*	18	19	20	21	22
	23	24	25	26	27	28	29
KĀRTTIKA 1972	30	1[f]	2	**3**	5	6	7
	8	9	10	11	12	13	14
	15	16	17	18	19	20	*20*
	21	22	23	24	25	**26**	28
MĀRGAŚĪRA 1972	29	30	1	2	3	4	5
	6	7	8	9	10	11[g]	12
	13	14	15	16	17	18	19
	20	21	22	23	24	25	26

‡Leap year
[a]New Year (Rākshasa)
[b]Birthday of Rāma
[c]Birthday of Krishna
[d]Ganēśa Chaturthī
[e]Dashara
[f]Diwali
[g]Birthday of Vishnu
[h]Night of Śiva
[i]Holi

HINDU SOLAR 1836/1837

Month	Sun	Mon	Tue	Wed	Thu	Fri	Sat
	13	14	15	16	17	18	19
PAUSHA 1836	20	21	22	23	24	25	26
	27	28	29	1[b]	2	3	4
MĀGHA 1836	5	6	7	8	9	10	11
	12	13	14	15	16	17	18
	19	20	21	22	23	24	25
	26	27	28	29	30	1	2
PHĀLGUNA 1836	3	4	5	6	7	8	9
	10	11	12	13	14	15	16
	17	18	19	20	21	22	23
	24	25	26	27	28	29	30
	1	2	3	4	5	6	7
CHAITRA 1836	8	9	10	11	12	13	14
	15	16	17	18	19	20	21
	22	23	24	25	26	27	28
	29	30	1[a]	2	3	4	5
VAIŚĀKHA 1837	6	7	8	9	10	11	12
	13	14	15	16	17	18	19
	20	21	22	23	24	25	26
	27	28	29	30	31	1	2
JYAISHTHA 1837	3	4	5	6	7	8	9
	10	11	12	13	14	15	16
	17	18	19	20	21	22	23
	24	25	26	27	28	29	30
	31	1	2	3	4	5	6
ĀSHĀDHA 1837	7	8	9	10	11	12	13
	14	15	16	17	18	19	20
	21	22	23	24	25	26	27
	28	29	30	31	32	1	2
ŚRĀVAṆA 1837	3	4	5	6	7	8	9
	10	11	12	13	14	15	16
	17	18	19	20	21	22	23
	24	25	26	27	28	29	30
	31	1	2	3	4	5	6
BHĀDRAPADA 1837	7	8	9	10	11	12	13
	14	15	16	17	18	19	20
	21	22	23	24	25	26	27
	28	29	30	31	1	2	3
ĀŚVINA 1837	4	5	6	7	8	9	10
	11	12	13	14	15	16	17
	18	19	20	21	22	23	24
	25	26	27	28	29	30	31
	1	2	3	4	5	6	7
KĀRTTIKA 1837	8	9	10	11	12	13	14
	15	16	17	18	19	20	21
	22	23	24	25	26	27	28
	29	30	1	2	3	4	5
MĀRGAŚĪRA 1837	6	7	8	9	10	11	12
	13	14	15	16	17	18	19
	20	21	22	23	24	25	26
	27	28	29	1	2	3	4
PAUSHA 1837	5	6	7	8	9	10	11
	12	13	14	15	16	17	18

[a]New Year (Prabhava)
[b]Pongal

ISLAMIC (ASTRONOMICAL) 1333‡/1334‡

Month	Sun	Mon	Tue	Wed	Thu	Fri	Sat
	9	10	11	12	13	14	15
ṢAFAR 1333	16	17	18	19	20	21	22
	23	24	25	26	27	28	29
	1	2	3	4	5	6	7
RABĪʿ I 1333	8	9	10	11	12[c]	13	14
	15	16	17	18	19	20	21
	22	23	24	25	26	27	28
	29	1	2	3	4	5	6
RABĪʿ II 1333	7	8	9	10	11	12	13
	14	15	16	17	18	19	20
	21	22	23	24	25	26	27
	28	29	30	1	2	3	4
JUMĀDĀ I 1333	5	6	7	8	9	10	11
	12	13	14	15	16	17	18
	19	20	21	22	23	24	25
	26	27	28	29	30	1	2
JUMĀDĀ II 1333	3	4	5	6	7	8	9
	10	11	12	13	14	15	16
	17	18	19	20	21	22	23
	24	25	26	27	28	29	1
RAJAB 1333	2	3	4	5	6	7	8
	9	10	11	12	13	14	15
	16	17	18	19	20	21	22
	23	24	25	26	27[d]	28	29
SHAʿBĀN 1333	30	1	2	3	4	5	6
	7	8	9	10	11	12	13
	14	15	16	17	18	19	20
	21	22	23	24	25	26	27
RAMAḌĀN 1333	28	29	30	1[e]	2	3	4
	5	6	7	8	9	10	11
	12	13	14	15	16	17	18
	19	20	21	22	23	24	25
	26	27	28	29	30	1[f]	2
SHAWWĀL 1333	3	4	5	6	7	8	9
	10	11	12	13	14	15	16
	17	18	19	20	21	22	23
	24	25	26	27	28	29	30
DHU AL-QAʿDA 1333	1	2	3	4	5	6	7
	8	9	10	11	12	13	14
	15	16	17	18	19	20	21
	22	23	24	25	26	27	28
DHU AL-ḤIJJA 1333	29	1	2	3	4	5	6
	7	8	9	10[g]	11	12	13
	14	15	16	17	18	19	20
	21	22	23	24	25	26	27
MUḤARRAM 1334	28	29	1[a]	2	3	4	5
	6	7	8	9	10[b]	11	12
	13	14	15	16	17	18	19
	20	21	22	23	24	25	26
	27	28	29	1	2	3	4
ṢAFAR 1334	5	6	7	8	9	10	11
	12	13	14	15	16	17	18
	19	20	21	22	23	24	25

‡Leap year
[a]New Year
[b]ʿAshūrā'
[c]Prophet's Birthday
[d]Ascent of the Prophet
[e]Start of Ramaḍān
[f]ʿId al-Fiṭr
[g]ʿId al-'Aḍḥā

GREGORIAN 1915

Julian (Sun)	Sun	Mon	Tue	Wed	Thu	Fri	Sat	Month
Dec 14	27	28	29	30	31	1	2	
	3	4	5	6	7[a]	8	9	JANUARY 1915
Dec 28	10	11	12	13	14[b]	15	16	
	17	18	19	20	21	22	23	
Jan 11	24	25	26	27	28	29	30	
	31	1	2	3	4	5	6	
Jan 25	7	8	9	10	11	12	13	FEBRUARY 1915
	14	15	16	17[c]	18	19	20	
Feb 8	21[d]	22	23	24	25	26	27	
	28	1	2	3	4	5	6	
Feb 22	7	8	9	10	11	12	13	MARCH 1915
	14	15	16	17	18	19	20	
Mar 8	21	22	23	24	25	26	27	
	28	29	30	31	1	2	3	
Mar 22	4[e]	5	6	7	8	9	10	APRIL 1915
	11	12	13	14	15	16	17	
Apr 5	18	19	20	21	22	23	24	
	25	26	27	28	29	30	1	
Apr 19	2	3	4	5	6	7	8	MAY 1915
	9	10	11	12	13	14	15	
May 3	16	17	18	19	20	21	22	
	23	24	25	26	27	28	29	
May 17	30	31	1	2	3	4	5	
	6	7	8	9	10	11	12	JUNE 1915
May 31	13	14	15	16	17	18	19	
	20	21	22	23	24	25	26	
Jun 14	27	28	29	30	1	2	3	
	4	5	6	7	8	9	10	JULY 1915
Jun 28	11	12	13	14	15	16	17	
	18	19	20	21	22	23	24	
Jul 12	25	26	27	28	29	30	31	
	1	2	3	4	5	6	7	
Jul 26	8	9	10	11	12	13	14	AUGUST 1915
	15	16	17	18	19	20	21	
Aug 9	22	23	24	25	26	27	28	
	29	30	31	1	2	3	4	
Aug 23	5	6	7	8	9	10	11	SEPTEMBER 1915
	12	13	14	15	16	17	18	
Sep 6	19	20	21	22	23	24	25	
	26	27	28	29	30	1	2	
Sep 20	3	4	5	6	7	8	9	
	10	11	12	13	14	15	16	OCTOBER 1915
Oct 4	17	18	19	20	21	22	23	
	24	25	26	27	28	29	30	
Oct 18	31	1	2	3	4	5	6	
	7	8	9	10	11	12	13	NOVEMBER 1915
Nov 1	14	15	16	17	18	19	20	
	21	22	23	24	25	26	27	
Nov 15	28[g]	29	30	1	2	3	4	
	5	6	7	8	9	10	11	DECEMBER 1915
Nov 29	12	13	14	15	16	17	18	
	19	20	21	22	23	24	25[h]	
Dec 13	26	27	28	29	30	31	1	

[a]Orthodox Christmas
[b]Julian New Year
[c]Ash Wednesday
[d]Feast of Orthodoxy
[e]Easter (also Orthodox)
[g]Advent
[h]Christmas

1916

GREGORIAN 1916‡	Sun Mon Tue Wed Thu Fri Sat	Lunar Phases	ISO WEEK (Mon)	JULIAN DAY (Sun noon)	HEBREW 5676‡/5677	Sun Mon Tue Wed Thu Fri Sat	Molad	CHINESE Yǐ-Mǎo/Bǐng-Chén	Sun Mon Tue Wed Thu Fri Sat	Solar Term	COPTIC 1632/1633	Sun Mon Tue Wed Thu Fri Sat	ETHIOPIC 1908/1909
	26 27 28 ◑ 30 31 1[a]	12:59	52	2420858	TEVETH 5676	19 20 21 22 23 24 25		MONTH 11 Yǐ-Mǎo	20 21 22 23 24 25 26			16 17 18 19 20 21 22	
	2 3 4 ● 6 7 8	4:45	1	2420865		26 27 28 29 1 2 3	Wed 11h47m0p		27 28 29 1 2 3 4	Xiǎo hán	KOIAK 1632	23 24 25 26 27 28 29[c]	TĀKHŠĀŠ 1908
JANUARY 1916	9 10 11 ◐ 13 14 15	3:37	2	2420872		4 5 6 7 8 9 10		MONTH 12 Yǐ-Mǎo	5 6 7 8 9 10 11			30 1 2 3 4 5 6[d]	
	16 17 18 19 ○ 21 22	8:29	3	2420879	SHEVAT 5676	11 12 13 14 15 16 17			12 13 14 15 16 **17** 18	Dà hán		7 8 9 10 11[e] 12 13	
	23 24 25 26 27 ◑ 29	0:35	4	2420886		18 19 20 21 22 23 24			19 20 21 22 23 24* 25		TŌBE 1632	14 15 16 17 18 19 20	ṬER 1908
	30 31 1 2 ● 4 5	16:05	5	2420893		25 26 27 28 29 30 1	Fri 0h31m1p		26 27 28 29 1[a] 2 3	Lì chūn		21 22 23 24 25 26 27	
FEBRUARY 1916	6 7 8 9 ◐ 11 12	22:20	6	2420900		2 3 4 5 6 7 8			4 5 6 7 8 9 10			28 29 30 1 2 3 4	
	13 14 15 16 17 18 ○	2:28	7	2420907	ADAR I 5676	9 10 11 12 13 14 15		MONTH 1 Bǐng-Chén	11 12 13 14 15[b] 16 17			5 6 7 8 9 10 11	
	20 21 22 23 24 25 ◑	9:23	8	2420914		16 17 18 19 20 21 22			**18** 19 20 21 22 23 24	Yǔ shuǐ	MESHIR 1632	12 13 14 15 16 17 18	YAKĀTIT 1908
	27 28 29 1 2 3 ●	3:57	9	2420921		23 24 25 26 27 28 29			25 26 27 28 29 30 1			19 20 21 22 23 24 25	
	5 6 7 8 9 10 ◐	18:33	10	2420928		30 1 2 3 4 5 6	Sat 13h15m2p		2 3 4 5 6 7 8	Jīng zhé		26 27 28 29 30 1 2	
MARCH 1916	12 13 14 15 16 17 18		11	2420935		7 8 9 10 11 12 13		MONTH 2 Bǐng-Chén	9 10 11 12 13 14 15			3 4 5 6 7 8 9	
	○ 20[b] 21 22 23 24 25	17:26	12	2420942	ADAR II 5676	14[f] 15 16 17 18 19 20			16 17 **18** 19 20 21 22	Chūn fēn	PAREMOTEP 1632	10 11 12 13 14 15 16	MAGĀBIT 1908
	◑ 27 28 29 30 31 1	16:22	13	2420949		21 22 23 24 25 26 27			23 24 25* 26 27 28 29			17 18 19 20 21 22 23	
	● 3 4 5 6 7 8	16:21	14	2420956		28 29 1 2 3 4 5	Mon 1h59m3p		30 1 2 3[c] 4 5 6	Qīng míng		24 25 26 27 28 29 30	
APRIL 1916	9 ◐ 11 12 13 14 15	14:35	15	2420963		6 7 8 9 10 11 12			7 8 9 10 11 12 13			1 2 3 4 5 6 7	
	16 17 ○ 19 20 21 22	5:07	16	2420970	NISAN 5676	13 14 15[g] 16 17 18 19		MONTH 3 Bǐng-Chén	14 15 16 17 **18** 19 20	Gǔ yǔ		8 9 10 11 12 13 14	
	23 ◑ 25 26 27 28 29	22:38	17	2420977		20 21 22 23 24 25 26			21 22 23 24 25 26 27		PARMOUTE 1632	15[f] 16 17 18 19 20 21	MIYĀZYĀ 1908
	30 1 ● 3 4 5 6	5:28	18	2420984		27 28 29 30 1 2 3	Tue 14h43m4p		28 29 1 2 3 4 5	Lì xià		22 23 24 25 26 27 28	
	7 8 9 ◐ 11 12 13	8:47	19	2420991		4 5 6 7 8 9 10			6 7 8 9 10 11 12			29[g] 30 1 2 3 4 5	
MAY 1916	14 15 16 ○ 18 19 20	14:11	20	2420998	IYAR 5676	11 12 13 14 15 16 17		MONTH 4 Bǐng-Chén	13 14 15 16 17 18 19			6 7 8 9 10 11 12	
	21 22 23 ◑ 25 26 27	5:16	21	2421005		18 19 20 21 22 23 24			**20** 21 22 23 24 25 26*	Xiǎo mǎn	PASHONS 1632	13 14 15 16 17 18 19	GENBOT 1908
	28 29 30 ● 1 2 3	19:37	22	2421012		25 26 27 28 29 1 2	Thu 3h27m5p		27 28 29 30 1 2 3			20 21 22 23 24 25 26	
	4 5 6 7 ◐ 9 10	23:59	23	2421019		3 4 5 6[h] 7 8 9			4 5[d] 6 7 8 9 10	Máng zhòng		27 28 29 30 1 2 3	
JUNE 1916	11 12 13 14 ○ 16 17	21:41	24	2421026	SIVAN 5676	10 11 12 13 14 15 16		MONTH 5 Bǐng-Chén	11 12 13 14 15 16 17			4 5 6 7 8 9 10	
	18 19 20 21[c] ◑ 23 24	13:16	25	2421033		17 18 19 20 21 22 23			18 19 20 21 **22** 23 24	Xià zhì	PAŌNE 1632	11 12 13 14 15 16 17	SANĒ 1908
	25 26 27 28 29 ● 1	10:43	26	2421040		24 25 26 27 28 29 30			25 26 27 28 29 1 2			18 19 20 21 22 23 24	
	2 3 4 5 6 7 ◐	11:55	27	2421047		1 2 3 4 5 6 7	Fri 16h11m6p		3 4 5 6 7 *8* 9	Xiǎo shǔ		25 26 27 28 29 30 1	
JULY 1916	9 10 11 12 13 14 ○	4:40	28	2421054		8 9 10 11 12 13 14		MONTH 6 Bǐng-Chén	10 11 12 13 14 15 16			2 3 4 5 6 7 8	
	16 17 18 19 20 ◑ 22	23:32	29	2421061	TAMMUZ 5676	15 16 17 18 19 20 21			17 18 19 20 21 22 23		EPĒP 1632	9 10 11 12 13 14 15	ḤAMLĒ 1908
	23 24 25 26 27 28 29		30	2421068		22 23 24 25 26 27 28			**24** 25 26 27* 28 29 30	Dà shǔ		16 17 18 19 20 21 22	
	● 31 1 2 3 4 5	2:15	31	2421075		29 1 2 3 4 5 6	Sun 4h55m7p		1 2 3 4 5 6 7[e]			23 24 25 26 27 28 29	
	◐ 7 8 9 10 11 12	21:05	32	2421082		7 8 9[i] 10 11 12 13			8 9 *10* 11 12 13 14	Lì qiū		30 1 2 3 4 5 6	
AUGUST 1916	○ 14 15 16 17 18 19	12:00	33	2421089	AV 5676	14 15 16 17 18 19 20		MONTH 7 Bǐng-Chén	15[f] 16 17 18 19 20 21			7 8 9 10 11 12 13[h]	
	◑ 21 22 23 24 25 26	12:52	34	2421096		21 22 23 24 25 26 27			22 23 24 **25** 26 27 28	Chǔ shǔ	MESORĒ 1632	14 15 16 17 18 19 20	NAHASĒ 1908
	27 ● 29 30 31 1 2	17:24	35	2421103		28 29 30 1 2 3 4	Mon 17h39m8p		29 30 1 2 3 4 5			21 22 23 24 25 26 27	
	3 4 ◐ 6 7 8 9	4:26	36	2421110		5 6 7 8 9 10 11			6 7 8 9 10 *11* 12	Bái lù		28 29 30 1 2 3 4	
SEPTEMBER 1916	10 ○ 12 13 14 15 16	20:30	37	2421117	ELUL 5676	12 13 14 15 16 17 18		MONTH 8 Bǐng-Chén	13 14 15[g] 16 17 18 19		EPAG. 1632	5 1[a] 2 3 4 5 6	PĀG. 1908
	17 18 ◑ 20 21 22 23[d]	5:35	38	2421124		19 20 21 22 23 24 25			20 21 22 23 24 25 **26**	Qiū fēn		7 8 9 10 11 12 13	
	24 25 26 ● 28 29 30	7:34	39	2421131		26 27 28 29 1[a] 2[a] 3	Wed 6h23m9p		27* 28 29 1 2 3 4		THOOUT 1633	14 15 16 17[b] 18 19 20	MASKARAM 1909
	1 2 3 ◐ 5 6 7	11:00	40	2421138		4 5 6 7 8 9 10[b]			5 6 7 8 9[h] 10 11	Hán lù		21 22 23 24 25 26 27	
OCTOBER 1916	8 9 10 ○ 12 13 14	7:01	41	2421145	TISHRI 5677	11 12 13 14 15[c] 16 17		MONTH 9 Bǐng-Chén	*12* 13 14 15 16 17 18			28 29 30 1 2 3 4	
	15 16 17 18 ◑ 20 21	1:08	42	2421152		18 19 20 21 22 23 24			19 20 21 22 23 24 25		PAOPE 1633	5 6 7 8 9 10 11	ṬEQEMT 1909
	22 23 24 25 ● 27 28	20:37	43	2421159		25 26 27 28 29 30 1	Thu 19h7m10p		26 27 **28** 29 30 1 2	Shuāng jiàng		12 13 14 15 16 17 18	
	29 30 31 1 ◐ 3 4	17:50	44	2421166		2 3 4 5 6 7 8			3 4 5 6 7 8 9			19 20 21 22 23 24 25	
NOVEMBER 1916	5 6 7 8 ○ 10 11	20:18	45	2421173	HESHVAN 5677	9 10 11 12 13 14 15		MONTH 10 Bǐng-Chén	10 11 12 *13* 14 15 16	Lì dōng		26 27 28 29 30 1 2	
	12 13 14 15 16 ◑ 18	22:00	46	2421180		16 17 18 19 20 21 22			17 18 19 20 21 22 23			3 4 5 6 7 8 9	
	19 20 21 22 23 24 ●	8:50	47	2421187		23 24 25 26 27 28 29			24 25 26 **27** 28* 29 1	Xiǎo xuě	ATHŌR 1633	10 11 12 13 14 15 16	ḪEDĀR 1909
	26 27 28 29 30 1 ◐	1:55	48	2421194		1 2 3 4 5 6 7	Sat 7h51m11p		2 3 4 5 6 7 8			17 18 19 20 21 22 23	
	3 4 5 6 7 8 ○	12:43	49	2421201	KISLEV 5677	8 9 10[d] 11 12 13 14		MONTH 11 Bǐng-Chén	9 10 11 12 *13* 14 15	Dà xuě		24 25 26 27 28 29 30	
DECEMBER 1916	10 11 12 13 14 15 16		50	2421208		15 16 17 18 19 20 21			16 17 18 19 20 21 22			1 2 3 4 5 6 7	
	◑ 18 19 20 21 22[e] 23	18:06	51	2421215		22 23 24 25[e] 26[e] 27[e] 28[e]			23 24 25 26 27 **28**[i] 29	Dōng zhì	KOIAK 1633	8 9 10 11 12 13 14	TĀKHŠĀŠ 1909
	● 25 26 27 28 29 30	20:31	52	2421222	TEVETH 5677	29[e] 30[e] 1[e] 2[e] 3 4 5	Sun 20h35m12p	MONTH 12 Bǐng-Chén	30 1 2 3 4 5 6			15 16 17 18 19 20 21	
	◐ 1 2 3 4 5 6	12:07	1	2421229		6 7 8 9 10 11 12			7 8 9 10 11 12 *13*	Xiǎo hán		22 23 24 25 26 27 28	

‡Leap year
[a]New Year
[b]Spring (22:47)
[c]Summer (18:24)
[d]Autumn (9:15)
[e]Winter (3:58)
● New moon
◐ First quarter moon
○ Full moon
◑ Last quarter moon

‡Leap year
[a]New Year
[b]Yom Kippur
[c]Sukkot
[d]Winter starts
[e]Ḥanukkah
[f]Purim
[g]Passover
[h]Shavuot
[i]Fast of Av

[a]New Year (4614, Dragon)
[b]Lantern Festival
[c]Qīngmíng
[d]Dragon Festival
[e]Qīqiǎo
[f]Hungry Ghosts
[g]Mid-Autumn Festival
[h]Double-Ninth Festival
[i]Dōngzhì
*Start of 60-name cycle

[a]New Year
[b]Building of the Cross
[c]Christmas
[d]Jesus's Circumcision
[e]Epiphany
[f]Easter
[g]Mary's Announcement
[h]Jesus's Transfiguration

PERSIAN (ASTRONOMICAL) 1294/1295

Month	Sun	Mon	Tue	Wed	Thu	Fri	Sat
DEY 1294	4	5	6	7	8	9	10
	11	12	13	14	15	16	17
	18	19	20	21	22	23	24
	25	26	27	28	29	30	1
BAHMAN 1294	2	3	4	5	6	7	8
	9	10	11	12	13	14	15
	16	17	18	19	20	21	22
	23	24	25	26	27	28	29
	30	1	2	3	4	5	6
ESFAND 1294	7	8	9	10	11	12	13
	14	15	16	17	18	19	20
	21	22	23	24	25	26	27
	28	29	1[a]	2	3	4	5
FARVARDĪN 1295	6	7	8	9	10	11	12
	13[b]	14	15	16	17	18	19
	20	21	22	23	24	25	26
	27	28	29	30	31	1	2
ORDĪBEHEŠT 1295	3	4	5	6	7	8	9
	10	11	12	13	14	15	16
	17	18	19	20	21	22	23
	24	25	26	27	28	29	30
	31	1	2	3	4	5	6
XORDĀD 1295	7	8	9	10	11	12	13
	14	15	16	17	18	19	20
	21	22	23	24	25	26	27
	28	29	30	31	1	2	3
TĪR 1295	4	5	6	7	8	9	10
	11	12	13	14	15	16	17
	18	19	20	21	22	23	24
	25	26	27	28	29	30	31
MORDĀD 1295	1	2	3	4	5	6	7
	8	9	10	11	12	13	14
	15	16	17	18	19	20	21
	22	23	24	25	26	27	28
	29	30	31	1	2	3	4
SHAHRĪVAR 1295	5	6	7	8	9	10	11
	12	13	14	15	16	17	18
	19	20	21	22	23	24	25
	26	27	28	29	30	31	1
MEHR 1295	2	3	4	5	6	7	8
	9	10	11	12	13	14	15
	16	17	18	19	20	21	22
	23	24	25	26	27	28	29
	30	1	2	3	4	5	6
ĀBĀN 1295	7	8	9	10	11	12	13
	14	15	16	17	18	19	20
	21	22	23	24	25	26	27
	28	29	30	1	2	3	4
ĀZAR 1295	5	6	7	8	9	10	11
	12	13	14	15	16	17	18
	19	20	21	22	23	24	25
	26	27	28	29	30	1	2
DEY 1295	3	4	5	6	7	8	9
	10	11	12	13	14	15	16

HINDU LUNAR 1972‡/1973

Month	Sun	Mon	Tue	Wed	Thu	Fri	Sat
PAUSHA MĀRGAŚIRA 1972	20	21	22	23	24	25	26
	27	28	29	30	1	3	4
PAUSHA 1972	5	6	7	8	9	10	11
	12	12	13	14	15	16	17
	18	19	20	21	22	23	24
	25	27	28	29	30	1	2
MĀGHA 1972	3	4	5	6	7	8	9
	10	11	12	13	14	15	15
	16	17	18	**19**	21	22	23
	24	25	26	27	28[h]	29	30
PHĀLGUNA 1972	1	2	3	4	5	6	7
	8	9	10	11	12	13	14
	15[i]	16	17	18	19	20	21
	22	23	**24**	26	27	28	29
CHAITRA 1973	30	1[a]	2	3	4	5	6
	7	8	8[b]	9	10	11	12
	13	14	15	16	**17**	19	20
	21	22	23	24	25	26	27
VAIŚĀKHA 1973	28	29	30	1	2	3	4
	5	6	7	8	9	10	11
	12	13	14	15	16	17	18
	19	20	**21**	23	24	25	26
JYAISHṬHA 1973	27	28	29	30	1	2	3
	3	4	5	6	7	8	9
	10	11	12	13	**14**	16	17
	18	19	20	21	22	23	24
ĀSHĀḌHA 1973	25	26	27	28	29	30	1
	2	3	4	5	6	7	8
	9	10	11	12	13	14	15
	16	18	19	20	21	22	23
	24	25	26	27	28	29	30
ŚRĀVAṆA 1973	30	1	2	3	4	5	6
	7	8	**9**	11	12	13	14
	15	16	17	18	19	20	21
	22	23[c]	24	25	26	27	28
BHĀDRAPADA 1973	29	30	1	2	3	4[d]	5
	6	7	8	9	10	11	**12**
	14	15	16	17	18	19	20
	21	22	23	24	25	26	26
ĀŚVINA 1973	27	28	29	30	1	2	3
	4	5	**6**	8[e]	9[e]	10[e]	11
	12	13	14	15	16	17	18
	19	20	21	22	23	24	25
KĀRTTIKA 1973	26	27	28	29	30	1[f]	2
	3	4	5	6	7	8	9
	10	12	13	14	15	16	17
	18	19	20	20	21	22	23
	24	25	26	27	28	29	30
MĀRGAŚIRA 1973	1	2	3	**4**	6	7	8
	9	10	11[g]	12	13	14	15
	16	17	18	19	20	21	22
	23	23	24	25	26	**27**	29
PAUSHA 1973	30	1	2	3	4	5	6
	7	8	9	10	11	12	13

HINDU SOLAR 1837/1838‡

Month	Sun	Mon	Tue	Wed	Thu	Fri	Sat
PAUSHA 1837	12	13	14	15	16	17	18
	19	20	21	22	23	24	25
	26	27	28	29	30	1[b]	2
MĀGHA 1837	3	4	5	6	7	8	9
	10	11	12	13	14	15	16
	17	18	19	20	21	22	23
	24	25	26	27	28	29	1
PHĀLGUNA 1837	2	3	4	5	6	7	8
	9	10	11	12	13	14	15
	16	17	18	19	20	21	22
	23	24	25	26	27	28	29
	30	1	2	3	4	5	6
CHAITRA 1837	7	8	9	10	11	12	13
	14	15	16	17	18	19	20
	21	22	23	24	25	26	27
	28	29	30	1[a]	2	3	4
VAIŚĀKHA 1838	5	6	7	8	9	10	11
	12	13	14	15	16	17	18
	19	20	21	22	23	24	25
	26	27	28	29	30	31	1
JYAISHṬHA 1838	2	3	4	5	6	7	8
	9	10	11	12	13	14	15
	16	17	18	19	20	21	22
	23	24	25	26	27	28	29
	30	31	32	1	2	3	4
ĀSHĀḌHA 1838	5	6	7	8	9	10	11
	12	13	14	15	16	17	18
	19	20	21	22	23	24	25
	26	27	28	29	30	31	1
ŚRĀVAṆA 1838	2	3	4	5	6	7	8
	9	10	11	12	13	14	15
	16	17	18	19	20	21	22
	23	24	25	26	27	28	29
	30	31	32	1	2	3	4
BHĀDRAPADA 1838	5	6	7	8	9	10	11
	12	13	14	15	16	17	18
	19	20	21	22	23	24	25
	26	27	28	29	30	31	1
ĀŚVINA 1838	2	3	4	5	6	7	8
	9	10	11	12	13	14	15
	16	17	18	19	20	21	22
	23	24	25	26	27	28	29
	30	1	2	3	4	5	6
KĀRTTIKA 1838	7	8	9	10	11	12	13
	14	15	16	17	18	19	20
	21	22	23	24	25	26	27
	28	29	30	1	2	3	4
MĀRGAŚIRA 1838	5	6	7	8	9	10	11
	12	13	14	15	16	17	18
	19	20	21	22	23	24	25
	26	27	28	29	30	1	2
PAUSHA 1838	3	4	5	6	7	8	9
	10	11	12	13	14	15	16
	17	18	19	20	21	22	23

ISLAMIC (ASTRONOMICAL) 1334‡/1335

Month	Sun	Mon	Tue	Wed	Thu	Fri	Sat
ṢAFAR 1334	19	20	21	22	23	24	25
	26	27	28	29	1	2	3
RABĪʿ I 1334	4	5	6	7	8	9	10
	11	12[c]	13	14	15	16	17
	18	19	20	21	22	23	24
	25	26	27	28	29	30	1
RABĪʿ II 1334	2	3	4	5	6	7	8
	9	10	11	12	13	14	15
	16	17	18	19	20	21	22
	23	24	25	26	27	28	29
JUMĀDĀ I 1334	1	2	3	4	5	6	7
	8	9	10	11	12	13	14
	15	16	17	18	19	20	21
	22	23	24	25	26	27	28
JUMĀDĀ II 1334	29	30	1	2	3	4	5
	6	7	8	9	10	11	12
	13	14	15	16	17	18	19
	20	21	22	23	24	25	26
RAJAB 1334	27	28	29	1	2	3	4
	5	6	7	8	9	10	11
	12	13	14	15	16	17	18
	19	20	21	22	23	24	25
SHAʿBĀN 1334	26	27[d]	28	29	30	1	2
	3	4	5	6	7	8	9
	10	11	12	13	14	15	16
	17	18	19	20	21	22	23
	24	25	26	27	28	29	30
RAMAḌĀN 1334	1[e]	2	3	4	5	6	7
	8	9	10	11	12	13	14
	15	16	17	18	19	20	21
	22	23	24	25	26	27	28
SHAWWĀL 1334	29	30	1[f]	2	3	4	5
	6	7	8	9	10	11	12
	13	14	15	16	17	18	19
	20	21	22	23	24	25	26
DHU AL-QAʿDA 1334	27	28	29	30	1	2	3
	4	5	6	7	8	9	10
	11	12	13	14	15	16	17
	18	19	20	21	22	23	24
	25	26	27	28	29	30	1
DHU AL-ḤIJJA 1334	2	3	4	5	6	7	8
	9	10[g]	11	12	13	14	15
	16	17	18	19	20	21	22
	23	24	25	26	27	28	29[a]
MUḤARRAM 1335	1[a]	2	3	4	5	6	7
	8	9	10[b]	11	12	13	14
	15	16	17	18	19	20	21
	22	23	24	25	26	27	28
ṢAFAR 1335	29	1	2	3	4	5	6
	7	8	9	10	11	12	13
	14	15	16	17	18	19	20
	21	22	23	24	25	26	27
RABĪʿ I 1335	28	29	1	2	3	4	5
	6	7	8	9	10	11	12

GREGORIAN 1916‡

Julian‡ (Sun)	Sun	Mon	Tue	Wed	Thu	Fri	Sat	Month
Dec 13	26	27	28	29	30	31	1	JANUARY 1916
	2	3	4	5	6	7[a]	8	
Dec 27	9	10	11	12	13	14[b]	15	
	16	17	18	19	20	21	22	
Jan 10	23	24	25	26	27	28	29	
	30	31	1	2	3	4	5	FEBRUARY 1916
Jan 24	6	7	8	9	10	11	12	
	13	14	15	16	17	18	19	
Feb 7	20	21	22	23	24	25	26	
	27	28	29	1	2	3	4	MARCH 1916
Feb 21	5	6	7	8[c]	9	10	11	
	12[d]	13	14	15	16	17	18	
Mar 6	19	20	21	22	23	24	25	
	26	27	28	29	30	31	1	APRIL 1916
Mar 20	2	3	4	5	6	7	8	
	9	10	11	12	13	14	15	
Apr 3	16	17	18	19	20	21	22	
	23[e]	24	25	26	27	28	29	
Apr 17	30	1	2	3	4	5	6	MAY 1916
	7	8	9	10	11	12	13	
May 1	14	15	16	17	18	19	20	
	21	22	23	24	25	26	27	
May 15	28	29	30	31	1	2	3	JUNE 1916
	4	5	6	7	8	9	10	
May 29	11	12	13	14	15	16	17	
	18	19	20	21	22	23	24	
Jun 12	25	26	27	28	29	30	1	JULY 1916
	2	3	4	5	6	7	8	
Jun 26	9	10	11	12	13	14	15	
	16	17	18	19	20	21	22	
Jul 10	23	24	25	26	27	28	29	
	30	31	1	2	3	4	5	AUGUST 1916
Jul 24	6	7	8	9	10	11	12	
	13	14	15	16	17	18	19	
Aug 7	20	21	22	23	24	25	26	
	27	28	29	30	31	1	2	SEPTEMBER 1916
Aug 21	3	4	5	6	7	8	9	
	10	11	12	13	14	15	16	
Sep 4	17	18	19	20	21	22	23	
	24	25	26	27	28	29	30	
Sep 18	1	2	3	4	5	6	7	OCTOBER 1916
	8	9	10	11	12	13	14	
Oct 2	15	16	17	18	19	20	21	
	22	23	24	25	26	27	28	
Oct 16	29	30	31	1	2	3	4	NOVEMBER 1916
	5	6	7	8	9	10	11	
Oct 30	12	13	14	15	16	17	18	
	19	20	21	22	23	24	25	
Nov 13	26	27	28	29	30	1	2	DECEMBER 1916
	3[g]	4	5	6	7	8	9	
Nov 27	10	11	12	13	14	15	16	
	17	18	19	20	21	22	23	
Dec 11	24	25[h]	26	27	28	29	30	
	31	1	2	3	4	5	6	

Persian: [a]New Year; [b]Sizdeh Bedar

Hindu Lunar: ‡Leap year; [a]New Year (Anala); [b]Birthday of Rāma; [c]Birthday of Krishna; [d]Ganēśa Chaturthī; [e]Dashara; [f]Diwali; [g]Birthday of Vishnu; [h]Night of Śiva; [i]Holi

Hindu Solar: ‡Leap year; [a]New Year (Vibhava); [b]Pongal

Islamic: ‡Leap year; [a]New Year; [a]New Year (Arithmetic); [b]ʿAshūrāʾ; [c]Prophet's Birthday; [d]Ascent of the Prophet; [e]Start of Ramaḍān; [f]ʿId al-Fiṭr; [g]ʿId al-ʾAḍḥā

Gregorian: ‡Leap year; [a]Orthodox Christmas; [b]Julian New Year; [c]Ash Wednesday; [d]Feast of Orthodoxy; [e]Easter (also Orthodox); [g]Advent; [h]Christmas

1917

GREGORIAN 1917	Sun	Mon	Tue	Wed	Thu	Fri	Sat	Lunar Phases	ISO WEEK (Mon)	JULIAN DAY (Sun noon)	HEBREW 5677/5678	Sun	Mon	Tue	Wed	Thu	Fri	Sat	Molad	CHINESE Bǐng-Chén/Dīng-Sì‡	Sun	Mon	Tue	Wed	Thu	Fri	Sat	Solar Term	COPTIC 1633/1634	Sun	Mon	Tue	Wed	Thu	Fri	Sat	ETHIOPIC 1909/1910
JANUARY 1917	◐	1[a]	2	3	4	5	6	12:07	1	2421229	TEVETH 5677	6	7	8	9	10	11	12		MONTH 12 Bǐng-Chén	7	8	9	10	11	12	13	Xiǎo hán	KOIAK 1633	22	23	24	25	26	27	28	TĀKHŠĀŠ 1909
	7	○	9	10	11	12	13	7:42	2	2421236		13	14	15	16	17	18	19			14	15	16	17	18	19	20		TŌBE 1633	29[c]	30	1	2	3	4	5	TER 1909
	14	15	◑	17	18	19	20	11:42	3	2421243		20	21	22	23	24	25	26	Tue $9^h19^m13^p$		21	22	23	24	25	26	27	Dà hán		6[d]	7	8	9	10	11[e]	12	
	21	22	●	24	25	26	27	7:40	4	2421250	SHEVAT 5677	27	28	29	1	2	3	4		MONTH 1 Dīng-Sì	28	29*	1[a]	2	3	4	5			13	14	15	16	17	18	19	
FEBRUARY 1917	28	29	◐	31	1	2	3	1:01	5	2421257		5	6	7	8	9	10	11			6	7	8	9	10	11	12			20	21	22	23	24	25	26	
	4	5	6	○	8	9	10	3:28	6	2421264		12	13	14	15	16	17	18			13	14	15[b]	16	17	18	19	Lì chūn	MESHIR 1633	27	28	29	30	1	2	3	YAKĀTIT 1909
	11	12	13	14	◑	16	17	1:53	7	2421271		19	20	21	22	23	24	25			20	21	22	23	24	25	26			4	5	6	7	8	9	10	
	18	19	20	●	22	23	24	18:08	8	2421278	ADAR 5677	26	27	28	29	30	1	2	Wed $22^h3^m14^p$	MONTH 2 Dīng-Sì	27	28	29	30	1	2	3	Yǔ shuǐ		11	12	13	14	15	16	17	
MARCH 1917	25	26	27	◐	1	2	3	16:43	9	2421285		3	4	5	6	7	8	9			4	5	6	7	8	9	10			18	19	20	21	22	23	24	
	4	5	6	7	○	9	10	21:58	10	2421292		10	11	12	13	14[f]	15	16			11	12	13	14	15	16	17	Jīng zhé	PAREMOTEP 1633	25	26	27	28	29	30	1	MAGĀBIT 1909
	11	12	13	14	15	◑	17	12:33	11	2421299		17	18	19	20	21	22	23			18	19	20	21	22	23	24			2	3	4	5	6	7	8	
	18	19	20	21[b]	22	●	24	4:05	12	2421306	NISAN 5677	24	25	26	27	28	29	1	Fri $10^h47^m15^p$	LEAP MONTH 2 Dīng-Sì	25	26	27	28	29	1*	2	Chūn fēn		9	10	11	12	13	14	15	
	25	26	27	28	29	◐	31	10:36	13	2421313		2	3	4	5	6	7	8			3	4	5	6	7	8	9			16	17	18	19	20	21	22	
APRIL 1917	1	2	3	4	5	6	○	13:48	14	2421320		9	10	11	12	13	14	15[g]			10	11	12	13	14[c]	15	16	Qīng míng		23	24	25	26	27	28	29	
	8	9	10	11	12	13	◑	20:12	15	2421327		16	17	18	19	20	21	22			17	18	19	20	21	22	23		PARMOUTE 1633	30	1	2	3	4	5	6	MIYĀZYĀ 1909
	15	16	17	18	19	20	●	14:01	16	2421334		23	24	25	26	27	28	29		MONTH 3 Dīng-Sì	24	25	26	27	28	29	1	Gǔ yǔ		7[f]	8	9	10	11	12	13	
	22	23	24	25	26	27	28		17	2421341	IYYAR 5677	30	1	2	3	4	5	6	Sat $23^h31^m16^p$		2	3	4	5	6	7	8			14	15	16	17	18	19	20	
MAY 1917	◐	30	1	2	3	4	5	5:21	18	2421348		7	8	9	10	11	12	13			9	10	11	12	13	14	15			21	22	23	24	25	26	27	
	6	○	8	9	10	11	12	2:43	19	2421355		14	15	16	17	18	19	20			16	17	18	19	20	21	22	Lì xià	PASHONS 1633	28	29[g]	30	1	2	3	4	GENBOT 1909
	13	◑	15	16	17	18	19	1:48	20	2421362		21	22	23	24	25	26	27			23	24	25	26	27	28	29			5	6	7	8	9	10	11	
	20	●	22	23	24	25	26	0:46	21	2421369	SIVAN 5677	28	29	1	2	3	4	5	Mon $12^h15^m17^p$	MONTH 4 Dīng-Sì	30	1	2*	3	4	5	6	Xiǎo mǎn		12	13	14	15	16	17	18	
JUNE 1917	27	◐	29	30	31	1	2	23:33	22	2421376		6[h]	7	8	9	10	11	12			7	8	9	10	11	12	13			19	20	21	22	23	24	25	
	3	4	○	6	7	8	9	13:06	23	2421383		13	14	15	16	17	18	19			14	15	16	17	18	19	20	Máng zhòng	PAŌNE 1633	26	27	28	29	30	1	2	SANĒ 1909
	10	11	◑	13	14	15	16	6:33	24	2421390		20	21	22	23	24	25	26			21	22	23	24	25	26	27			3	4	5	6	7	8	9	
	17	18	●	20	21	22[c]	23	13:02	25	2421397	TAMMUZ 5677	27	28	29	30	1	2	3	Wed $1^h0^m0^p$	MONTH 5 Dīng-Sì	28	29	1	2	3	4	5[d]	Xià zhì		10	11	12	13	14	15	16	
	24	25	26	◐	28	29	30	16:08	26	2421404		4	5	6	7	8	9	10			6	7	8	9	10	11	12			17	18	19	20	21	22	23	
JULY 1917	1	2	3	○	5	6	7	21:40	27	2421411		11	12	13	14	15	16	17			13	14	15	16	17	18	19			24	25	26	27	28	29	30	
	8	9	10	◑	12	13	14	12:12	28	2421418		18	19	20	21	22	23	24			20	21	22	23	24	25	26	Xiǎo shǔ	EPĒP 1633	1	2	3	4	5	6	7	HAMLĒ 1909
	15	16	17	18	●	20	21	3:00	29	2421425	AV 5677	25	26	27	28	29	1	2	Thu $13^h44^m1^p$	MONTH 6 Dīng-Sì	27	28	29	30	1	2	3*			8	9	10	11	12	13	14	
	22	23	24	25	26	◐	28	6:40	30	2421432		3	4	5	6	7	8	9			4	5	6	7	8	9	10	Dà shǔ		15	16	17	18	19	20	21	
AUGUST 1917	29	30	31	1	2	○	4	5:11	31	2421439		10[i]	11	12	13	14	15	16			11	12	13	14	15	16	17			22	23	24	25	26	27	28	
	5	6	7	8	◑	10	11	19:56	32	2421446		17	18	19	20	21	22	23			18	19	20	21	22	23	24	Lì qiū	MESORĒ 1633	29	30	1	2	3	4	5	NAHASĒ 1909
	12	13	14	15	16	●	18	18:21	33	2421453		24	25	26	27	28	29	30		MONTH 7 Dīng-Sì	25	26	27	28	29	30	1			6	7	8	9	10	11	12	
	19	20	21	22	23	24	◐	19:08	34	2421460	ELUL 5677	1	2	3	4	5	6	7	Sat $2^h28^m2^p$		2	3	4	5	6	7[e]	8	Chǔ shǔ		13[h]	14	15	16	17	18	19	
SEPTEMBER 1917	26	27	28	29	30	31	○	12:28	35	2421467		8	9	10	11	12	13	14			9	10	11	12	13	14	15[f]			20	21	22	23	24	25	26	
	2	3	4	5	6	7	◑	7:05	36	2421474		15	16	17	18	19	20	21			16	17	18	19	20	21	22	Bái lù	EPAG. 1633	27	28	29	30	1	2	3	PĀG. 1909
	9	10	11	12	13	14	15		37	2421481		22	23	24	25	26	27	28			23	24	25	26	27	28	29		THOOUT 1634	4	5	1[a]	2	3	4	5	MASKARAM 1910
	●	17	18	19	20	21	22	10:27	38	2421488	TISHRI 5678	29	1[a]	2[a]	3	4	5	6	Sun $15^h12^m3^p$	MONTH 8 Dīng-Sì	1	2	3	4*	5	6	7			6	7	8	9	10	11	12	
	23[d]	◐	25	26	27	28	29	5:41	39	2421495		7	8	9	10[b]	11	12	13			8	9	10	11	12	13	14	Qiū fēn		13	14	15	16	17[b]	18	19	
OCTOBER 1917	○	1	2	3	4	5	6	20:31	40	2421502		14	15[c]	16	17	18	19	20			15[g]	16	17	18	19	20	21			20	21	22	23	24	25	26	
	◑	8	9	10	11	12	13	22:14	41	2421509		21	22	23	24	25	26	27			22	23	24	25	26	27	28	Hán lù	PAOPE 1634	27	28	29	30	1	2	3	TEQEMT 1910
	14	15	●	17	18	19	20	2:41	42	2421516	HESHVAN 5678	28	29	30	1	2	3	4	Tue $3^h56^m4^p$	MONTH 9 Dīng-Sì	29	30	1	2	3	4	5			4	5	6	7	8	9	10	
	21	22	◐	24	25	26	27	14:37	43	2421523		5	6	7	8	9	10	11			6	7	8	9[h]	10	11	12	Shuāng jiàng		11	12	13	14	15	16	17	
NOVEMBER 1917	28	29	○	31	1	2	3	6:19	44	2421530		12	13	14	15	16	17	18			13	14	15	16	17	18	19			18	19	20	21	22	23	24	
	4	5	◑	7	8	9	10	17:03	45	2421537		19	20	21	22	23	24	25			20	21	22	23	24	25	26	Lì dōng	ATHŌR 1634	25	26	27	28	29	30	1	HEDĀR 1910
	11	12	13	●	15	16	17	18:28	46	2421544	KISLEV 5678	26	27	28	29	30	1	2	Wed $16^h40^m5^p$	MONTH 10 Dīng-Sì	27	28	29	30	1	2	3			2	3	4	5	6	7	8	
	18	19	20	◐	22	23	24	22:28	47	2421551		3	4	5	6	7	8	9			4*	5	6	7	8	9	10	Xiǎo xuě		9	10	11	12	13	14	15	
DECEMBER 1917	25	26	27	○	29	30	1	18:41	48	2421558		10	11	12	13	14	15	16			11	12	13	14	15	16	17			16	17	18	19	20	21	22	
	2	3	4	5	◑	7	8	14:13	49	2421565		17	18	19	20[d]	21	22	23			18	19	20	21	22	23	24	Dà xuě		23	24	25	26	27	28	29	
	9	10	11	12	13	●	15	9:17	50	2421572		24	25[e]	26[e]	27[e]	28[e]	29[e]	30[e]		MONTH 11 Dīng-Sì	25	26	27	28	29	1	2		KOIAK 1634	30	1	2	3	4	5	6	TĀKHŠĀŠ 1910
	16	17	18	19	20	◐	22[e]	6:07	51	2421579	TEVETH 5678	1[e]	2[e]	3	4	5	6	7	Fri $5^h24^m6^p$		3	4	5	6	7	8	9[i]	Dōng zhì		7	8	9	10	11	12	13	
	23	24	25	26	27	○	29	9:51	52	2421586		8	9	10	11	12	13	14			10	11	12	13	14	15	16			14	15	16	17	18	19	20	
	30	31	1	2	3	4	◑	11:49	1	2421593		15	16	17	18	19	20	21			17	18	19	20	21	22	23			21	22	23	24	25	26	27	

[a]New Year
[b]Spring (4:37)
[c]Summer (0:14)
[d]Autumn (15:00)
[e]Winter (9:45)
● New moon
◐ First quarter moon
○ Full moon
◑ Last quarter moon

[a]New Year
[b]Yom Kippur
[c]Sukkot
[d]Winter starts
[e]Ḥanukkah
[f]Purim
[g]Passover
[h]Shavuot
[i]Fast of Av

‡Leap year
[a]New Year (4615, Snake)
[b]Lantern Festival
[c]Qīngmíng
[d]Dragon Festival
[e]Qīqiǎo
[f]Hungry Ghosts
[g]Mid-Autumn Festival
[h]Double-Ninth Festival
[i]Dōngzhì
*Start of 60-name cycle

[a]New Year
[b]Building of the Cross
[c]Christmas
[d]Jesus's Circumcision
[e]Epiphany
[f]Easter
[g]Mary's Announcement
[h]Jesus's Transfiguration

PERSIAN (ASTRONOMICAL) 1295/1296‡

Month	Sun	Mon	Tue	Wed	Thu	Fri	Sat
DEY 1295	10	11	12	13	14	15	16
	17	18	19	20	21	22	23
	24	25	26	27	28	29	30
BAHMAN 1295	1	2	3	4	5	6	7
	8	9	10	11	12	13	14
	15	16	17	18	19	20	21
	22	23	24	25	26	27	28
	29	30	1	2	3	4	5
ESFAND 1295	6	7	8	9	10	11	12
	13	14	15	16	17	18	19
	20	21	22	23	24	25	26
	27	28	29	1[a]	2	3	4
FARVARDĪN 1296	5	6	7	8	9	10	11
	12	13[b]	14	15	16	17	18
	19	20	21	22	23	24	25
	26	27	28	29	30	31	1
ORDĪBEHEŠT 1296	2	3	4	5	6	7	8
	9	10	11	12	13	14	15
	16	17	18	19	20	21	22
	23	24	25	26	27	28	29
	30	31	1	2	3	4	5
XORDĀD 1296	6	7	8	9	10	11	12
	13	14	15	16	17	18	19
	20	21	22	23	24	25	26
	27	28	29	30	31	1	2
TĪR 1296	3	4	5	6	7	8	9
	10	11	12	13	14	15	16
	17	18	19	20	21	22	23
	24	25	26	27	28	29	30
	31	1	2	3	4	5	6
MORDĀD 1296	7	8	9	10	11	12	13
	14	15	16	17	18	19	20
	21	22	23	24	25	26	27
	28	29	30	31	1	2	3
SHAHRĪVAR 1296	4	5	6	7	8	9	10
	11	12	13	14	15	16	17
	18	19	20	21	22	23	24
	25	26	27	28	29	30	31
MEHR 1296	1	2	3	4	5	6	7
	8	9	10	11	12	13	14
	15	16	17	18	19	20	21
	22	23	24	25	26	27	28
	29	30	1	2	3	4	5
ĀBĀN 1296	6	7	8	9	10	11	12
	13	14	15	16	17	18	19
	20	21	22	23	24	25	26
	27	28	29	30	1	2	3
ĀZAR 1296	4	5	6	7	8	9	10
	11	12	13	14	15	16	17
	18	19	20	21	22	23	24
	25	26	27	28	29	30	1
DEY 1296	2	3	4	5	6	7	8
	9	10	11	12	13	14	15

HINDU LUNAR 1973/1974‡

Month	Sun	Mon	Tue	Wed	Thu	Fri	Sat
PAUSHA 1973	7	8	9	10	11	12	13
	14	15	16	17	18	19	20
	21	22	23	24	25	26	27
	28	29	30	1	**2**	4	5
MĀGHA 1973	6	7	8	9	10	11	12
	13	14	15	15	16	17	18
	19	20	21	22	23	24	25
	26	28	29[h]	30	1	2	3
PHĀLGUNA 1973	4	5	6	7	8	9	10
	11	12	13	14	15[i]	16	17
	18	19	20	21	22	23	24
	25	26	27	28	29	30	1[a]
CHAITRA 1974	3	4	5	6	7	8	8[b]
	9	10	11	12	13	14	15
	16	17	18	19	20	21	22
	23	**24**	26	27	28	29	30
VAIŚĀKHA 1974	1	2	3	4	5	6	7
	8	9	10	11	12	12	13
	14	15	16	**17**	19	20	21
	22	23	24	25	26	27	28
	29	30	1	2	3	4	5
JYAISHTHA 1974	6	7	8	9	10	11	12
	13	14	15	16	17	18	19
	20	**21**	23	24	25	26	27
	28	29	30	1	2	3	4
ĀSHĀDHA 1974	5	6	7	8	8	9	10
	11	12	**13**	15	16	17	18
	19	20	21	22	23	24	**25**
	27	28	29	29	30	1	2
ŚRĀVANA 1974	3	4	5	6	7	8	9
	10	11	12	13	14	15	**16**
	18	19	20	21	22	23[c]	24
	25	26	27	28	29	30	1
LEAP BHĀDRAPADA 1974	2	3	4	5	5	6	7
	8	10	11	12	13	14	15
	16	17	18	19	**20**	22	23
	24	25	26	26	27	28	29
	30	1	2	3	4[d]	5	6
BHĀDRAPADA 1974	7	8	9	10	11	12	**13**
	15	16	17	18	19	20	21
	22	23	24	25	26	27	28
	29	30	30	1	2	3	4
ĀŚVINA 1974	5	**6**	8[e]	9[e]	10[e]	11	12
	13	14	15	16	17	18	19
	20	21	22	23	24	25	26
	27	28	29	30	1[f]	2	3
KĀRTTIKA 1974	4	5	6	7	8	9	**10**
	12	13	14	15	16	17	18
	19	20	21	22	23	23	24
	25	26	27	28	29	30	1
MĀRGAŚĪRA 1974	2	3	**4**	6	7	8	9
	10	**11**[g]	12	13	14	15	16
	17	18	19	20	21	22	23

HINDU SOLAR 1838‡/1839

Month	Sun	Mon	Tue	Wed	Thu	Fri	Sat
PAUSHA 1838	17	18	19	20	21	22	23
	24	25	26	27	28	29	1[b]
MĀGHA 1838	2	3	4	5	6	7	8
	9	10	11	12	13	14	15
	16	17	18	19	20	21	22
	23	24	25	26	27	28	29
	1	2	3	4	5	6	7
PHĀLGUNA 1838	8	9	10	11	12	13	14
	15	16	17	18	19	20	21
	22	23	24	25	26	27	28
	29	30	1	2	3	4	5
CHAITRA 1838	6	7	8	9	10	11	12
	13	14	15	16	17	18	19
	20	21	22	23	24	25	26
	27	28	29	30	31	1[a]	2
VAIŚĀKHA 1839	3	4	5	6	7	8	9
	10	11	12	13	14	15	16
	17	18	19	20	21	22	23
	24	25	26	27	28	29	30
	1	2	3	4	5	6	7
JYAISHTHA 1839	8	9	10	11	12	13	14
	15	16	17	18	19	20	21
	22	23	24	25	26	27	28
	29	30	31	32	1	2	3
ĀSHĀDHA 1839	4	5	6	7	8	9	10
	11	12	13	14	15	16	17
	18	19	20	21	22	23	24
	25	26	27	28	29	30	31
	32	1	2	3	4	5	6
ŚRĀVANA 1839	7	8	9	10	11	12	13
	14	15	16	17	18	19	20
	21	22	23	24	25	26	27
	28	29	30	31	1	2	3
BHĀDRAPADA 1839	4	5	6	7	8	9	10
	11	12	13	14	15	16	17
	18	19	20	21	22	23	24
	25	26	27	28	29	30	31
	1	2	3	4	5	6	7
ĀŚVINA 1839	8	9	10	11	12	13	14
	15	16	17	18	19	20	21
	22	23	24	25	26	27	28
	29	30	1	2	3	4	5
KĀRTTIKA 1839	6	7	8	9	10	11	12
	13	14	15	16	17	18	19
	20	21	22	23	24	25	26
	27	28	29	30	1	2	3
MĀRGAŚĪRA 1839	4	5	6	7	8	9	10
	11	12	13	14	15	16	17
	18	19	20	21	22	23	24
	25	26	27	28	29	30	1
PAUSHA 1839	2	3	4	5	6	7	8
	9	10	11	12	13	14	15
	16	17	18	19	20	21	22

ISLAMIC (ASTRONOMICAL) 1335/1336

Month	Sun	Mon	Tue	Wed	Thu	Fri	Sat
RABĪ' I 1335	6	7	8	9	10	11	12[c]
	13	14	15	16	17	18	19
	20	21	22	23	24	25	26
	27	28	29	1	2	3	4
RABĪ' II 1335	5	6	7	8	9	10	11
	12	13	14	15	16	17	18
	19	20	21	22	23	24	25
	26	27	28	29	30	1	2
JUMĀDĀ I 1335	3	4	5	6	7	8	9
	10	11	12	13	14	15	16
	17	18	19	20	21	22	23
	24	25	26	27	28	29	1
JUMĀDĀ II 1335	2	3	4	5	6	7	8
	9	10	11	12	13	14	15
	16	17	18	19	20	21	22
	23	24	25	26	27	28	29
	30	1	2	3	4	5	6
RAJAB 1335	7	8	9	10	11	12	13
	14	15	16	17	18	19	20
	21	22	23	24	25	26	27[d]
	28	29	1	2	3	4	5
SHA'BĀN 1335	6	7	8	9	10	11	12
	13	14	15	16	17	18	19
	20	21	22	23	24	25	26
	27	28	29	30	1[e]	2	3
RAMADĀN 1335	4	5	6	7	8	9	10
	11	12	13	14	15	16	17
	18	19	20	21	22	23	24
	25	26	27	28	29	30	1[f]
SHAWWĀL 1335	2	3	4	5	6	7	8
	9	10	11	12	13	14	15
	16	17	18	19	20	21	22
	23	24	25	26	27	28	29
	30	1	2	3	4	5	6
DHU AL-QA'DA 1335	7	8	9	10	11	12	13
	14	15	16	17	18	19	20
	21	22	23	24	25	26	27
	28	29	30	1	2	3	4
DHU AL-HIJJA 1335	5	6	7	8	9	10[g]	11
	12	13	14	15	16	17	18
	19	20	21	22	23	24	25
	26	27	28	29[d]	1[a]	2	3
MUHARRAM 1336	4	5	6	7	8	9	10[b]
	11	12	13	14	15	16	17
	18	19	20	21	22	23	24
	25	26	27	28	29	30	1
SAFAR 1336	2	3	4	5	6	7	8
	9	10	11	12	13	14	15
	16	17	18	19	20	21	22
	23	24	25	26	27	28	29
RABĪ' I 1336	1	2	3	4	5	6	7
	8	9	10	11	12[c]	13	14
	15	16	17	18	19	20	21

GREGORIAN 1917

Julian (Sun)	Sun	Mon	Tue	Wed	Thu	Fri	Sat	Month
Dec 18	31	1	2	3	4	5	6	
	7[a]	8	9	10	11	12	13	JANUARY 1917
Jan 1	14[b]	15	16	17	18	19	20	
	21	22	23	24	25	26	27	
Jan 15	28	29	30	31	1	2	3	
	4	5	6	7	8	9	10	FEBRUARY 1917
Jan 29	11	12	13	14	15	16	17	
	18	19	20	21[c]	22	23	24	
Feb 12	25	26	27	28	1	2	3	
	4[d]	5	6	7	8	9	10	MARCH 1917
Feb 26	11	12	13	14	15	16	17	
	18	19	20	21	22	23	24	
Mar 12	25	26	27	28	29	30	31	
	1	2	3	4	5	6	7	APRIL 1917
Mar 26	8[e]	9	10	11	12	13	14	
	15[f]	16	17	18	19	20	21	
Apr 9	22	23	24	25	26	27	28	
	29	30	1	2	3	4	5	MAY 1917
Apr 23	6	7	8	9	10	11	12	
	13	14	15	16	17	18	19	
May 7	20	21	22	23	24	25	26	
	27	28	29	30	31	1	2	JUNE 1917
May 21	3	4	5	6	7	8	9	
	10	11	12	13	14	15	16	
Jun 4	17	18	19	20	21	22	23	
	24	25	26	27	28	29	30	
Jun 18	1	2	3	4	5	6	7	JULY 1917
	8	9	10	11	12	13	14	
Jul 2	15	16	17	18	19	20	21	
	22	23	24	25	26	27	28	
Jul 16	29	30	31	1	2	3	4	AUGUST 1917
	5	6	7	8	9	10	11	
Jul 30	12	13	14	15	16	17	18	
	19	20	21	22	23	24	25	
Aug 13	26	27	28	29	30	31	1	SEPTEMBER 1917
	2	3	4	5	6	7	8	
Aug 27	9	10	11	12	13	14	15	
	16	17	18	19	20	21	22	
Sep 10	23	24	25	26	27	28	29	
	30	1	2	3	4	5	6	OCTOBER 1917
Sep 24	7	8	9	10	11	12	13	
	14	15	16	17	18	19	20	
Oct 8	21	22	23	24	25	26	27	
	28	29	30	31	1	2	3	NOVEMBER 1917
Oct 22	4	5	6	7	8	9	10	
	11	12	13	14	15	16	17	
Nov 5	18	19	20	21	22	23	24	
	25	26	27	28	29	30	1	DECEMBER 1917
Nov 19	2[g]	3	4	5	6	7	8	
	9	10	11	12	13	14	15	
Dec 3	16	17	18	19	20	21	22	
	23	24	25[h]	26	27	28	29	
Dec 17	30	31	1	2	3	4	5	

Persian: ‡Leap year; [a]New Year; [b]Sizdeh Bedar

Hindu lunar: ‡Leap year; [a]New Year (Piṅgala); [b]Birthday of Rāma; [c]Birthday of Krishna; [d]Ganēśa Chaturthī; [e]Dashara; [f]Diwali; [g]Birthday of Vishnu; [h]Night of Śiva; [i]Holi

Hindu solar: ‡Leap year; [a]New Year (Śukla); [b]Pongal

Islamic: [a]New Year; [d]New Year (Arithmetic); [b]'Ashūrā'; [c]Prophet's Birthday; [d]Ascent of the Prophet; [e]Start of Ramaḍān; [f]'Id al-Fiṭr; [g]'Id al-'Aḍḥā

Gregorian: [a]Orthodox Christmas; [b]Julian New Year; [c]Ash Wednesday; [d]Feast of Orthodoxy; [e]Easter; [f]Orthodox Easter; [g]Advent; [h]Christmas

1918

GREGORIAN 1918	Sun	Mon	Tue	Wed	Thu	Fri	Sat	Lunar Phases	ISO WEEK (Mon)	JULIAN DAY (Sun noon)	HEBREW 5678/5679‡	Sun	Mon	Tue	Wed	Thu	Fri	Sat	Molad	CHINESE Dīng-Sì‡/Wù-Wǔ	Sun	Mon	Tue	Wed	Thu	Fri	Sat	Solar Term	COPTIC 1634/1635‡	Sun	Mon	Tue	Wed	Thu	Fri	Sat	ETHIOPIC 1910/1911‡
JANUARY 1918	30	31	1[a]	2	3	4	◑	11:49	1	2421593	TEVETH 5678	15	16	17	18	19	20	21		MONTH 11 Dīng-Sì	17	18	19	20	21	22	23		KOIAK 1634	21	22	23	24	25	26	27	TĀKHŚĀŚ 1910
	6	7	8	9	10	11	●	22:35	2	2421600		22	23	24	25	26	27	28			*24*	25	26	27	28	29	30	Xiǎo hán		28	29[c]	30	1	2	3	4	
	13	14	15	16	17	18	◐	14:38	3	2421607		29	1	2	3	4	5	6	Sat 18h8m7p	MONTH 12 Dīng-Sì	1	2	3	4	5*	6	7		TÔBE 1634	5	6[d]	7	8	9	10	11[e]	ṬER 1910
	20	21	22	23	24	25	26		4	2421614	SHEVAT 5678	7	8	9	10	11	12	13			8	***9***	10	11	12	13	14	Dà hán		12	13	14	15	16	17	18	
	○	28	29	30	31	1	2	3:14	5	2421621		14	15	16	17	18	19	20			15	16	17	18	19	20	21			19	20	21	22	23	24	25	
FEBRUARY 1918	3	◑	5	6	7	8	9	7:52	6	2421628		21	22	23	24	25	26	27			22	*23*	24	25	26	27	28	Lì chūn		26	27	28	29	30	1	2	
	10	●	12	13	14	15	16	10:04	7	2421635		28	29	30	1	2	3	4	Mon 6h52m8p	MONTH 1 Wù-Wǔ	29	1[a]	2	3	4	5	6		MESHIR 1634	3	4	5	6	7	8	9	YAKĀTIT 1910
	17	◐	19	20	21	22	23	0:56	8	2421642	ADAR 5678	5	6	7	8	9	10	11			7	8	***9***	10	11	12	13	Yǔ shuǐ		10	11	12	13	14	15	16	
	24	○	26	27	28	1	2	21:34	9	2421649		12	13	14[f]	15	16	17	18			14	15[b]	16	17	18	19	20			17	18	19	20	21	22	23	
MARCH 1918	3	4	5	◑	7	8	9	0:43	10	2421656		19	20	21	22	23	24	25			21	22	23	*24*	25	26	27	Jīng zhé		24	25	26	27	28	29	30	
	10	11	●	13	14	15	16	19:52	11	2421663		26	27	28	29	1	2	3	Tue 19h36m9p		28	29	30	1	2	3	4		PAREMOTEP 1634	1	2	3	4	5	6	7	MAGĀBIT 1910
	17	18	◐	20	21[b]	22	23	13:30	12	2421670	NISAN 5678	4	5	6	7	8	9	10		MONTH 2 Wù-Wǔ	5	6*	7	8	***9***	10	11	Chūn fēn		8	9	10	11	12	13	14	
	24	25	26	○	28	29	30	15:33	13	2421677		11	12	13	14	15[g]	16	17			12	13	14	15	16	17	18			15	16	17	18	19	20	21	
	31	1	2	3	◑	5	6	13:33	14	2421684		18	19	20	21	22	23	24			19	20	21	22	23	24[c]	25	Qīng míng		22	23	24	25	26	27	28	
APRIL 1918	7	8	9	10	●	12	13	4:34	15	2421691		25	26	27	28	29	30	1	Thu 8h20m10p		26	27	28	29	1	2	3			29	30	1	2	3	4	5	
	14	15	16	17	◐	19	20	4:07	16	2421698	IYYAR 5678	2	3	4	5	6	7	8		MONTH 3 Wù-Wǔ	4	5	6	7	8	9	10		PARMOUTE 1634	6	7	8	9	10	11	12	MIYĀZYĀ 1910
	21	22	23	24	25	○	27	8:05	17	2421705		9	10	11	12	13	14	15			***11***	12	13	14	15	16	17	Gǔ yǔ		13	14	15	16	17	18	19	
	28	29	30	1	2	◑	4	22:26	18	2421712		16	17	18	19	20	21	22			18	19	20	21	22	23	24			20	21	22	23	24	25	26	
MAY 1918	5	6	7	8	9	●	11	13:00	19	2421719		23	24	25	26	27	28	29			25	*26*	27	28	29	1	2	Lì xià		27[f]	28	29[g]	30	1	2	3	
	12	13	14	15	16	◐	18	20:14	20	2421726	SIVAN 5678	1	2	3	4	5	6[h]	7	Fri 21h4m11p	MONTH 4 Wù-Wǔ	3	4	5	6	7	8*	9		PASHONS 1634	4	5	6	7	8	9	10	GENBOT 1910
	19	20	21	22	23	24	○	22:32	21	2421733		8	9	10	11	12	13	14			10	11	12	***13***	14	15	16	Xiǎo mǎn		11	12	13	14	15	16	17	
	26	27	28	29	30	31	1		22	2421740		15	16	17	18	19	20	21			17	18	19	20	21	22	23			18	19	20	21	22	23	24	
JUNE 1918	◑	3	4	5	6	7	●	4:20 22:02	23	2421747		22	23	24	25	26	27	28			24	25	26	27	*28*	29	30	Máng zhòng		25	26	27	28	29	30	1	
	9	10	11	12	13	14	15		24	2421754		29	30	1	2	3	4	5	Sun 9h48m12p		1	2	3	4	5[d]	6	7		PAÔNE 1634	2	3	4	5	6	7	8	SANÉ 1910
	◐	17	18	19	20	21	22[c]	13:11	25	2421761	TAMMUZ 5678	6	7	8	9	10	11	12		MONTH 5 Wù-Wǔ	8	9	10	11	12	13	***14***	Xià zhì		9	10	11	12	13	14	15	
	23	○	25	26	27	28	29	10:38	26	2421768		13	14	15	16	17	18	19			15	16	17	18	19	20	21			16	17	18	19	20	21	22	
	30	◑	2	3	4	5	6	8:43	27	2421775		20	21	22	23	24	25	26			22	23	24	25	26	27	28			23	24	25	26	27	28	29	
JULY 1918	7	●	9	10	11	12	13	8:22	28	2421782		27	28	29	1	2	3	4	Mon 22h32m13p		29	*1*	2	3	4	5	6	Xiǎo shǔ		30	1	2	3	4	5	6	
	14	15	◐	17	18	19	20	6:24	29	2421789	AV 5678	5	6	7	8	9[i]	10	11		MONTH 6 Wù-Wǔ	7	8	9*	10	11	12	13		EPÊP 1634	7	8	9	10	11	12	13	ḤAMLĒ 1910
	21	22	○	24	25	26	27	20:34	30	2421796		12	13	14	15	16	17	18			14	15	16	***17***	18	19	20	Dà shǔ		14	15	16	17	18	19	20	
	28	29	◑	31	1	2	3	13:14	31	2421803		19	20	21	22	23	24	25			21	22	23	24	25	26	27			21	22	23	24	25	26	27	
AUGUST 1918	4	5	●	7	8	9	10	20:29	32	2421810		26	27	28	29	30	1	2	Wed 11h16m14p		28	29	30	1	*2*	3	4	Lì qiū		28	29	30	1	2	3	4	
	11	12	13	◐	15	16	17	23:16	33	2421817	ELUL 5678	3	4	5	6	7	8	9		MONTH 7 Wù-Wǔ	5	6	7[e]	8	9	10	11		MESORÊ 1634	5	6	7	8	9	10	11	NAḤASĒ 1910
	18	19	20	21	○	23	24	5:02	34	2421824		10	11	12	13	14	15	16			12	13	14	15[f]	16	17	***18***	Chǔ shǔ		12	13[h]	14	15	16	17	18	
	25	26	27	◑	29	30	31	19:27	35	2421831		17	18	19	20	21	22	23			19	20	21	22	23	24	25			19	20	21	22	23	24	25	
SEPTEMBER 1918	1	2	3	4	●	6	7	10:43	36	2421838		24	25	26	27	28	29	1[a]	Fri 0h0m15p		26	27	28	29	1	2	3		EPAG. 1634	26	27	28	29	30	1	2	PĀG. 1910
	8	9	10	11	12	◐	14	15:02	37	2421845	TISHRI 5679	2[a]	3	4	5	6	7	8		MONTH 8 Wù-Wǔ	*4*	5	6	7	8	9	10*	Bái lù	THOOUT 1635	3	4	5	1[a]	2	3	4	MASKARAM 1911
	15	16	17	18	19	○	21	13:01	38	2421852		9	10[b]	11	12	13	14	15[c]			11	12	13	14	15[g]	16	17			5	6	7	8	9	10	11	
	22	23[d]	24	25	26	◑	28	4:38	39	2421859		16	17	18	19	20	21	22			18	19	***20***	21	22	23	24	Qiū fēn		12	13	14	15	16	17[b]	18	
	29	30	1	2	3	4	●	3:05	40	2421866		23	24	25	26	27	28	29			25	26	27	28	29	30	1			19	20	21	22	23	24	25	
OCTOBER 1918	6	7	8	9	10	11	12		41	2421873	HESHVAN 5679	30	1	2	3	4	5	6	Sat 12h44m16p	MONTH 9 Wù-Wǔ	2	3	4	5	6	7	8	Hán lù	PAOPE 1635	26	27	28	29	30	1	2	TEQEMT 1911
	◐	14	15	16	17	18	○	4:59 21:35	42	2421880		7	8	9	10	11	12	13			9[h]	10	11	12	13	14	15			3	4	5	6	7	8	9	
	20	21	22	23	24	25	◑	17:35	43	2421887		14	15	16	17	18	19	20			16	17	18	19	***20***	21	22	Shuāng jiàng		10	11	12	13	14	15	16	
	27	28	29	30	31	1	2		44	2421894		21	22	23	24	25	26	27			23	24	25	26	27	28	29			17	18	19	20	21	22	23	
NOVEMBER 1918	●	4	5	6	7	8	9	21:01	45	2421901	KISLEV 5679	28	29	1	2	3	4	5	Mon 1h28m17p		30	1	2	3	4	5	6	Lì dōng		24	25	26	27	28	29	30	
	10	◐	12	13	14	15	16	16:46	46	2421908		6	7	8	9	10	11	12		MONTH 10 Wù-Wǔ	7	8	9	10*	11	12	13		ATHÔR 1635	1	2	3	4	5	6	7	ḤEDĀR 1911
	17	○	19	20	21	22	23	7:33	47	2421915		13	14	15	16	17	18	19			14	15	16	17	18	19	***20***	Xiǎo xuě		8	9	10	11	12	13	14	
	24	◑	26	27	28	29	30	10:25	48	2421922		20	21	22	23	24	25[e]	26[e]			21	22	23	24	25	26	27			15	16	17	18	19	20	21	
DECEMBER 1918	1	2	●	4	5	6	7	15:19	49	2421929		27[e]	28[e]	29[e]	1[e]	2[d,e]	3[e]	4	Tue 14h13m0p		28	29	1	2	3	4	5			22	23	24	25	26	27	28	
	8	9	10	◐	12	13	14	2:31	50	2421936	TEVETH 5679	5	6	7	8	9	10	11		MONTH 11* Wù-Wǔ	6	7	8	9	10	11	12	Dà xuě	KOIAK 1635	29	30	1	2	3	4	5	TĀKHŚĀŚ 1911
	15	16	○	18	19	20	21	19:17	51	2421943		12	13	14	15	16	17	18			13	14	15	16	17	18	19			6	7	8	9	10	11	12	
	22[e]	23	24	◑	26	27	28	6:30	52	2421950		19	20	21	22	23	24	25			***20***[i]	21	22	23	24	25	26	Dōng zhì		13	14	15	16	17	18	19	
	29	30	31	1	●	3	4	8:24	1	2421957		26	27	28	29	1	2	3	Thu 2h57m1p		27	28	29	30	1	2	3			20	21	22	23	24	25	26	

[a]New Year
[b]Spring (10:25)
[c]Summer (5:59)
[d]Autumn (20:45)
[e]Winter (15:41)
● New moon
◐ First quarter moon
○ Full moon
◑ Last quarter moon

‡Leap year
[a]New Year
[b]Yom Kippur
[c]Sukkot
[d]Winter starts
[e]Ḥanukkah
[f]Purim
[g]Passover
[h]Shavuot
[i]Fast of Av

‡Leap year
[a]New Year (4616, Horse)
[b]Lantern Festival
[c]Qīngmíng
[d]Dragon Festival
[e]Qīqiǎo
[f]Hungry Ghosts
[g]Mid-Autumn Festival
[h]Double-Ninth Festival
[i]Dōngzhì
*Start of 60-name cycle

‡Leap year
[a]New Year
[b]Building of the Cross
[c]Christmas
[d]Jesus's Circumcision
[e]Epiphany
[f]Easter
[g]Mary's Announcement
[h]Jesus's Transfiguration

1918

PERSIAN (ASTRONOMICAL) 1296‡/1297

Month	Sun	Mon	Tue	Wed	Thu	Fri	Sat
DEY 1296	9	10	11	12	13	14	15
	16	17	18	19	20	21	22
	23	24	25	26	27	28	29
BAHMAN 1296	30	1	2	3	4	5	6
	7	8	9	10	11	12	13
	14	15	16	17	18	19	20
	21	22	23	24	25	26	27
ESFAND 1296	28	29	30	1	2	3	4
	5	6	7	8	9	10	11
	12	13	14	15	16	17	18
	19	20	21	22	23	24	25
FARVARDĪN 1297	26	27	28	29	30	1[a]	2
	3	4	5	6	7	8	9
	10	11	12	13[b]	14	15	16
	17	18	19	20	21	22	23
	24	25	26	27	28	29	30
ORDĪBEHEŠT 1297	31	1	2	3	4	5	6
	7	8	9	10	11	12	13
	14	15	16	17	18	19	20
	21	22	23	24	25	26	27
XORDĀD 1297	28	29	30	31	1	2	3
	4	5	6	7	8	9	10
	11	12	13	14	15	16	17
	18	19	20	21	22	23	24
	25	26	27	28	29	30	31
TĪR 1297	1	2	3	4	5	6	7
	8	9	10	11	12	13	14
	15	16	17	18	19	20	21
	22	23	24	25	26	27	28
MORDĀD 1297	29	30	31	1	2	3	4
	5	6	7	8	9	10	11
	12	13	14	15	16	17	18
	19	20	21	22	23	24	25
SHAHRĪVAR 1297	26	27	28	29	30	31	1
	2	3	4	5	6	7	8
	9	10	11	12	13	14	15
	16	17	18	19	20	21	22
	23	24	25	26	27	28	29
MEHR 1297	30	31	1	2	3	4	5
	6	7	8	9	10	11	12
	13	14	15	16	17	18	19
	20	21	22	23	24	25	26
ĀBĀN 1297	27	28	29	30	1	2	3
	4	5	6	7	8	9	10
	11	12	13	14	15	16	17
	18	19	20	21	22	23	24
ĀZAR 1297	25	26	27	28	29	30	1
	2	3	4	5	6	7	8
	9	10	11	12	13	14	15
	16	17	18	19	20	21	22
	23	24	25	26	27	28	29
DEY 1297	30	1	2	3	4	5	6
	7	8	9	10	11	12	13

‡Leap year
[a]New Year
[b]Sizdeh Bedar

HINDU LUNAR 1974‡/1975

Month	Sun	Mon	Tue	Wed	Thu	Fri	Sat
MĀRGAŚĪRA 1974	17	18	19	20	21	22	23
	24	25	26	27	28	29	30
PAUSHA 1974	1	2	3	4	5	6	7
	8	9	**10**	12	13	14	15
	15	16	17	18	19	20	21
	22	23	24	25	26	27	28
MĀGHA 1974	29	30	1	2	**3**	5	6
	7	8	9	10	11	12	13
	14	15	16	17	18	*18*	19
	20	21	22	23	24	25	26
PHĀLGUNA 1974	**27**	29[h]	30	1	2	3	4
	5	6	7	8	9	10	11
	12	13	14	15[i]	16	17	18
	19	20	21	22	23	24	25
CHAITRA 1975	26	27	28	29	30	1[a]	**2**
	4	5	6	7	8	9[b]	10
	11	12	*12*	13	14	15	16
	17	18	19	20	21	22	23
VAIŚĀKHA 1975	24	**25**	27	28	29	30	1
	2	3	4	5	6	7	8
	9	10	11	12	13	14	15
	16	17	18	19	20	21	22
	23	24	25	26	27	**28**	30
JYAISHTHA 1975	1	2	3	4	5	6	7
	8	*8*	9	10	11	12	13
	14	15	16	17	18	19	20
	21	23	24	25	26	27	28
ĀSHĀDHA 1975	29	30	1	2	3	4	5
	6	7	8	9	10	11	12
	13	14	15	16	17	18	19
	20	21	22	23	**24**	26	27
ŚRĀVAṆA 1975	28	29	30	1	2	3	4
	4	5	6	7	8	9	10
	11	12	13	14	15	**16**	18
	19	20	21	22	23[c]	24	25
BHĀDRAPADA 1975	26	27	28	29	30	1	2
	3	4[d]	5	6	7	8	9
	10	11	12	13	14	15	16
	17	18	19	**20**	22	23	24
	25	26	27	28	29	30	*30*
ĀŚVINA 1975	1	2	3	4	5	6	7
	8[e]	9[e]	10[e]	11	12	**13**	15
	16	17	18	19	20	21	22
	23	24	25	26	27	28	29
KĀRTTIKA 1975	30	1[f]	2	3	4	*4*	5
	6	8	9	10	11	12	13
	14	15	16	17	18	**19**	21
	22	23	*23*	24	25	26	27
MĀRGAŚĪRA 1975	28	29	30	1	2	3	4
	5	6	7	8	9	10	**11**[g]
	13	14	15	16	17	18	19
	20	21	22	23	24	25	26
	26	27	28	29	30	1	2

‡Leap year
[a]New Year (Kālayukta)
[b]Birthday of Rāma
[c]Birthday of Krishna
[d]Ganēśa Chaturthī
[e]Dashara
[f]Diwali
[g]Birthday of Vishnu
[h]Night of Śiva
[i]Holi

HINDU SOLAR 1839/1840

Month	Sun	Mon	Tue	Wed	Thu	Fri	Sat
PAUSHA 1839	16	17	18	19	20	21	22
	23	24	25	26	27	28	29
MĀGHA 1839	1[b]	2	3	4	5	6	7
	8	9	10	11	12	13	14
	15	16	17	18	19	20	21
	22	23	24	25	26	27	28
PHĀLGUNA 1839	29	30	1	2	3	4	5
	6	7	8	9	10	11	12
	13	14	15	16	17	18	19
	20	21	22	23	24	25	26
CHAITRA 1839	27	28	29	1	2	3	4
	5	6	7	8	9	10	11
	12	13	14	15	16	17	18
	19	20	21	22	23	24	25
VAIŚĀKHA 1840	26	27	28	29	30	31	1[a]
	2	3	4	5	6	7	8
	9	10	11	12	13	14	15
	16	17	18	19	20	21	22
	23	24	25	26	27	28	29
JYAISHTHA 1840	30	31	1	2	3	4	5
	6	7	8	9	10	11	12
	13	14	15	16	17	18	19
	20	21	22	23	24	25	26
ĀSHĀDHA 1840	27	28	29	30	31	1	2
	3	4	5	6	7	8	9
	10	11	12	13	14	15	16
	17	18	19	20	21	22	23
	24	25	26	27	28	29	30
ŚRĀVAṆA 1840	31	32	1	2	3	4	5
	6	7	8	9	10	11	12
	13	14	15	16	17	18	19
	20	21	22	23	24	25	26
BHĀDRAPADA 1840	27	28	29	30	31	1	2
	3	4	5	6	7	8	9
	10	11	12	13	14	15	16
	17	18	19	20	21	22	23
	24	25	26	27	28	29	30
ĀŚVINA 1840	31	1	2	3	4	5	6
	7	8	9	10	11	12	13
	14	15	16	17	18	19	20
	21	22	23	24	25	26	27
KĀRTTIKA 1840	28	29	30	31	1	2	3
	4	5	6	7	8	9	10
	11	12	13	14	15	16	17
	18	19	20	21	22	23	24
MĀRGAŚĪRA 1840	25	26	27	28	29	30	1
	2	3	4	5	6	7	8
	9	10	11	12	13	14	15
	16	17	18	19	20	21	22
	23	24	25	26	27	28	29
PAUSHA 1840	1	2	3	4	5	6	7
	8	9	10	11	12	13	14
	15	16	17	18	19	20	21

[a]New Year (Pramoda)
[b]Pongal

ISLAMIC (ASTRONOMICAL) 1336/1337

Month	Sun	Mon	Tue	Wed	Thu	Fri	Sat
RABĪ' I 1336	15	16	17	18	19	20	21
	22	23	24	25	26	27	28
RABĪ' II 1336	29	*1*	2	3	4	5	6
	7	8	9	10	11	12	13
	14	15	16	17	18	19	20
	21	22	23	24	25	26	27
JUMĀDĀ I 1336	28	29	*30*	1	2	3	4
	5	6	7	8	9	10	11
	12	13	14	15	16	17	18
	19	20	21	22	23	24	25
JUMĀDĀ II 1336	26	27	28	29	*1*	2	3
	4	5	6	7	8	9	10
	11	12	13	14	15	16	17
	18	19	20	21	22	23	24
RAJAB 1336	25	26	27	28	29	*1*	2
	3	4	5	6	7	8	9
	10	11	12	13	14	15	16
	17	18	19	20	21	22	23
	24	25	26	27[d]	28	29	30
SHA'BĀN 1336	*1*	2	3	4	5	6	7
	8	9	10	11	12	13	14
	15	16	17	18	19	20	21
	22	23	24	25	26	27	28
RAMAḌĀN 1336	29	1[e]	2	3	4	5	6
	7	8	9	10	11	12	13
	14	15	16	17	18	19	20
	21	22	23	24	25	26	27
SHAWWĀL 1336	28	29	30	1[f]	2	3	4
	5	6	7	8	9	10	11
	12	13	14	15	16	17	18
	19	20	21	22	23	24	25
DHU AL-QA'DA 1336	26	27	28	29	*30*	1	2
	3	4	5	6	7	8	9
	10	11	12	13	14	15	16
	17	18	19	20	21	22	23
	24	25	26	27	28	29	*30*
DHU AL-ḤIJJA 1336	1	2	3	4	5	6	7
	8	9	10[g]	11	12	13	14
	15	16	17	18	19	20	21
	22	23	24	25	26	27	28
MUHARRAM 1337	29	1[a]	2	3	4	5	6
	7	8	9	10[b]	11	12	13
	14	15	16	17	18	19	20
	21	22	23	24	25	26	27
ṢAFAR 1337	28	29	30	*1*	2	3	4
	5	6	7	8	9	10	11
	12	13	14	15	16	17	18
	19	20	21	22	23	24	25
RABĪ' I 1337	26	27	28	29	*1*	2	3
	4	5	6	7	8	9	10
	11	12[c]	13	14	15	16	17
	18	19	20	21	22	23	24
	25	26	27	28	29	30	*1*

[a]New Year
[b]'Ashūrā'
[c]Prophet's Birthday
[d]Ascent of the Prophet
[e]Start of Ramaḍān
[f]'Id al-Fiṭr
[g]'Id al-'Aḍḥā

GREGORIAN 1918

Julian (Sun)	Month	Sun	Mon	Tue	Wed	Thu	Fri	Sat
Dec 17	JANUARY 1918	*30*	31	1	2	3	4	5
		6	7[a]	8	9	10	11	12
Dec 31		*13*	14[b]	15	16	17	18	19
		20	21	22	23	24	25	26
Jan 14	FEBRUARY 1918	*27*	28	29	30	31	1	2
		3	4	5	6	7	8	9
Jan 28		*10*	11	12	13[c]	14	15	16
		17	18	19	20	21	22	23
Feb 11	MARCH 1918	*24*	25	26	27	28	1	2
		3	4	5	6	7	8	9
Feb 25		*10*	11	12	13	14	15	16
		17	18	19	20	21	22	23
Mar 11		*24*[d]	25	26	27	28	29	30
	APRIL 1918	31[e]	1	2	3	4	5	6
Mar 25		*7*	8	9	10	11	12	13
		14	15	16	17	18	19	20
Apr 8		*21*	22	23	24	25	26	27
	MAY 1918	28	29	30	1	2	3	4
Apr 22		*5*[f]	6	7	8	9	10	11
		12	13	14	15	16	17	18
May 6		*19*	20	21	22	23	24	25
	JUNE 1918	26	27	28	29	30	31	1
May 20		*2*	3	4	5	6	7	8
		9	10	11	12	13	14	15
Jun 3		*16*	17	18	19	20	21	22
		23	24	25	26	27	28	29
Jun 17	JULY 1918	*30*	1	2	3	4	5	6
		7	8	9	10	11	12	13
Jul 1		*14*	15	16	17	18	19	20
		21	22	23	24	25	26	27
Jul 15	AUGUST 1918	*28*	29	30	31	1	2	3
		4	5	6	7	8	9	10
Jul 29		*11*	12	13	14	15	16	17
		18	19	20	21	22	23	24
Aug 12		*25*	26	27	28	29	30	31
	SEPTEMBER 1918	1	2	3	4	5	6	7
Aug 26		*8*	9	10	11	12	13	14
		15	16	17	18	19	20	21
Sep 9		*22*	23	24	25	26	27	28
	OCTOBER 1918	29	30	1	2	3	4	5
Sep 23		*6*	7	8	9	10	11	12
		13	14	15	16	17	18	19
Oct 7		*20*	21	22	23	24	25	26
	NOVEMBER 1918	27	28	29	30	31	1	2
Oct 21		*3*	4	5	6	7	8	9
		10	11	12	13	14	15	16
Nov 4		*17*	18	19	20	21	22	23
		24	25	26	27	28	29	30
Nov 18	DECEMBER 1918	*1*[g]	2	3	4	5	6	7
		8	9	10	11	12	13	14
Dec 2		*15*	16	17	18	19	20	21
		22	23	24	25[h]	26	27	28
Dec 16		*29*	30	31	1	2	3	4

[a]Orthodox Christmas
[b]Julian New Year
[c]Ash Wednesday
[d]Feast of Orthodoxy
[e]Easter
[f]Orthodox Easter
[g]Advent
[h]Christmas

1919

Gregorian 1919

Month	Sun	Mon	Tue	Wed	Thu	Fri	Sat	Lunar Phases	ISO Week (Mon)	Julian Day (Sun noon)
JANUARY 1919	29	30	31	1[a]	●	3	4	8:24	1	2421957
	5	6	7	8	◐	10	11	10:55	2	2421964
	12	13	14	15	○	17	18	8:44	3	2421971
	19	20	21	22	23	◑	25	4:22	4	2421978
FEBRUARY 1919	26	27	28	29	30	●	1	23:07	5	2421985
	2	3	4	5	6	◐	8	18:52	6	2421992
	9	10	11	12	13	○	15	23:38	7	2421999
	16	17	18	19	20	21	22		8	2422006
MARCH 1919	◑	24	25	26	27	28	1	1:47	9	2422013
	●	3	4	5	6	7	8	11:11	10	2422020
	◐	10	11	12	13	14	15	3:14	11	2422027
	○	17	18	19	20	21[b]	22	15:41	12	2422034
	23	◑	25	26	27	28	29	20:34	13	2422041
APRIL 1919	30	●	1	2	3	4	5	21:05	14	2422048
	6	◐	8	9	10	11	12	12:38	15	2422055
	13	14	○	16	17	18	19	8:25	16	2422062
	20	21	22	◑	24	25	26	11:21	17	2422069
MAY 1919	27	28	29	●	1	2	3	5:30	18	2422076
	4	5	◐	7	8	9	10	23:33	19	2422083
	11	12	13	14	○	16	17	1:01	20	2422090
	18	19	20	21	◑	23	24	22:04	21	2422097
	25	26	27	28	●	30	31	13:12	22	2422104
JUNE 1919	1	2	3	4	◐	6	7	12:22	23	2422111
	8	9	10	11	12	○	14	16:28	24	2422118
	15	16	17	18	19	20	◑	5:33	25	2422125
	22[c]	23	24	25	26	●	28	20:52	26	2422132
JULY 1919	29	30	1	2	3	4	◐	3:17	27	2422139
	6	7	8	9	10	11	12		28	2422146
	○	14	15	16	17	18	19	6:02	29	2422153
	◑	21	22	23	24	25	26	11:03	30	2422160
AUGUST 1919	●	28	29	30	31	1	2	5:21	31	2422167
	◐	4	5	6	7	8	9	20:11	32	2422174
	10	○	12	13	14	15	16	17:39	33	2422181
	17	◑	19	20	21	22	23	15:56	34	2422188
	24	●	26	27	28	29	30	15:37	35	2422195
SEPTEMBER 1919	31	1	◐	3	4	5	6	14:21	36	2422202
	7	8	9	○	11	12	13	3:54	37	2422209
	14	15	◑	17	18	19	20	21:32	38	2422216
	21	22	23	●[d]	25	26	27	4:34	39	2422223
OCTOBER 1919	28	29	30	1	◐	3	4	8:37	40	2422230
	5	6	7	8	○	10	11	13:38	41	2422237
	12	13	14	15	◑	17	18	5:05	42	2422244
	19	20	21	22	●	24	25	20:39	43	2422251
NOVEMBER 1919	26	27	28	29	30	31	◐	1:43	44	2422258
	2	3	4	5	6	○	8	23:35	45	2422265
	9	10	11	12	13	◑	15	15:40	46	2422272
	16	17	18	19	20	21	●	15:19	47	2422279
	23	24	25	26	27	28	29		48	2422286
DECEMBER 1919	◐	1	2	3	4	5	6	16:47	49	2422293
	○	8	9	10	11	12	13	10:03	50	2422300
	◑	15	16	17	18	19	20	6:02	51	2422307
	21	●[e]	23	24	25	26	27	10:55	52	2422314
	28	29	◐	31	1	2	3	5:24	1	2422321

Hebrew 5679‡/5680

ISO Week	Month	Sun	Mon	Tue	Wed	Thu	Fri	Sat	Molad
1	SHEVAT 5679	26	27	28	29	1	2	3	Thu $2^h57^m1^p$
2		4	5	6	7	8	9	10	
3		11	12	13	14	15	16	17	
4		18	19	20	21	22	23	24	
5	ADAR I 5679	25	26	27	28	29	30	1	Fri $15^h41^m2^p$
6		2	3	4	5	6	7	8	
7		9	10	11	12	13	14	15	
8		16	17	18	19	20	21	22	
9		23	24	25	26	27	28	29	
10	ADAR II 5679	30	1	2	3	4	5	6	Sun $4^h25^m3^p$
11		7	8	9	10	11	12	13	
12		14[f]	15	16	17	18	19	20	
13		21	22	23	24	25	26	27	
14	NISAN 5679	28	29	1	2	3	4	5	Mon $17^h9^m4^p$
15		6	7	8	9	10	11	12	
16		13	14	15[g]	16	17	18	19	
17		20	21	22	23	24	25	26	
18	IYAR 5679	27	28	29	30	1	2	3	Wed $5^h53^m5^p$
19		4	5	6	7	8	9	10	
20		11	12	13	14	15	16	17	
21		18	19	20	21	22	23	24	
22	SIVAN 5679	25	26	27	28	29	1	2	Thu $18^h37^m6^p$
23		3	4	5	6[h]	7	8	9	
24		10	11	12	13	14	15	16	
25		17	18	19	20	21	22	23	
26		24	25	26	27	28	29	30	
27	TAMMUZ 5679	1	2	3	4	5	6	7	Sat $7^h21^m7^p$
28		8	9	10	11	12	13	14	
29		15	16	17	18	19	20	21	
30		22	23	24	25	26	27	28	
31	AV 5679	29	1	2	3	4	5	6	Sun $20^h5^m8^p$
32		7	8	9[i]	10	11	12	13	
33		14	15	16	17	18	19	20	
34		21	22	23	24	25	26	27	
35	ELUL 5679	28	29	30	1	2	3	4	Tue $8^h49^m9^p$
36		5	6	7	8	9	10	11	
37		12	13	14	15	16	17	18	
38		19	20	21	22	23	24	25	
39	TISHRI 5680	26	27	28	29	1[a]	2[a]	3	Wed $21^h33^m10^p$
40		4	5	6	7	8	9	10[b]	
41		11	12	13	14	15[c]	16	17	
42		18	19	20	21	22	23	24	
43	HEṢHVAN 5680	25	26	27	28	29	30	1	Fri $10^h17^m11^p$
44		2	3	4	5	6	7	8	
45		9	10	11	12	13	14	15	
46		16	17	18	19	20	21	22	
47		23	24	25	26	27	28	29	
48	KISLEV 5680	1	2	3	4	5	6	7	Sat $23^h1^m12^p$
49		8	9	10	11	12	13	14[d]	
50		15	16	17	18	19	20	21	
51		22	23	24	25[e]	26[e]	27[e]	28[e]	
52	TEVETH 5680	29[e]	30[e]	1[e]	2[e]	3	4	5	Mon $11^h45^m13^p$
1		6	7	8	9	10	11	12	

Chinese Wù-Wǔ/Jǐ-Wèi‡

ISO Week	Month	Sun	Mon	Tue	Wed	Thu	Fri	Sat	Solar Term
1	MONTH 12 Wù-Wǔ	27	28	29	30	1	2	3	
2		4	*5*	6	7	8	9	10	*Xiǎo hán*
3		11*	12	13	14	15	16	17	
4		18	19	**20**	21	22	23	24	**Dà hán**
5	MONTH 1 Jǐ-Wèi	25	26	27	28	29	30	1[a]	
6		2	3	4	*5*	6	7	8	*Lì chūn*
7		9	10	11	12	13	14	15[b]	
8		16	17	18	19	**20**	21	22	**Yǔ shuǐ**
9		23	24	25	26	27	28	29	
10	MONTH 2 Jǐ-Wèi	1	2	3	4	*5*	6	7	*Jīng zhé*
11		8	9	10	11	12*	13	14	
12		15	16	17	18	19	20	**21**	**Chūn fēn**
13		22	23	24	25	26	27	28	
14	MONTH 3 Jǐ-Wèi	29	30	1	2	3	4	5	
15		*6*[c]	7	8	9	10	11	12	*Qīng míng*
16		13	14	15	16	17	18	19	
17		20	**21**	22	23	24	25	26	**Gǔ yǔ**
18	MONTH 4 Jǐ-Wèi	27	28	29	1	2	3	4	
19		5	6	*7*	8	9	10	11	*Lì xià*
20		12	13*	14	15	16	17	18	
21		19	20	21	22	**23**	24	25	**Xiǎo mǎn**
22	MONTH 5 Jǐ-Wèi	26	27	28	29	1	2	3	
23		4	5[d]	6	7	8	9	*10*	*Máng zhòng*
24		11	12	13	14	15	16	17	
25		18	19	20	21	22	23	24	
26	MONTH 6 Jǐ-Wèi	**25**	26	27	28	29	30	1	**Xià zhì**
27		2	3	4	5	6	7	8	
28		9	10	*11*	12	13	14*	15	*Xiǎo shǔ*
29		16	17	18	19	20	21	22	
30		23	24	25	26	**27**	28	29	**Dà shǔ**
31	MONTH 7 Jǐ-Wèi	1	2	3	4	5	6	7[e]	
32		8	9	10	11	12	*13*	14	*Lì qiū*
33		15[f]	16	17	18	19	20	21	
34		22	23	24	25	26	27	28	
35	LEAP MONTH 7 Jǐ-Wèi	**29**	1	2	3	4	5	6	**Chǔ shǔ**
36		7	8	9	10	11	12	13	
37		14	15	*16**	17	18	19	20	*Bái lù*
38		21	22	23	24	25	26	27	
39	MONTH 8 Jǐ-Wèi	28	29	30	**1**	2	3	4	**Qiū fēn**
40		5	6	7	8	9	10	11	
41		12	13	14	15[g]	*16*	17	18	*Hán lù*
42		19	20	21	22	23	24	25	
43	MONTH 9 Jǐ-Wèi	26	27	28	29	30	**1**	2	**Shuāng jiàng**
44		3	4	5	6	7	8	9[h]	
45		10	11	12	13	14	15	*16**	*Lì dōng*
46		17	18	19	20	21	22	23	
47	MONTH 10 Jǐ-Wèi	24	25	26	27	28	29	1	
48		**2**	3	4	5	6	7	8	**Xiǎo xuě**
49		9	10	11	12	13	14	15	
50		16	*17*	18	19	20	21	22	*Dà xuě*
51		23	24	25	26	27	28	29	
52	MONTH 11 Jǐ-Wèi	30	1	**2**[i]	3	4	5	6	**Dōng zhì**
1		7	8	9	10	11	12	13	

Coptic 1635‡/1636 — Ethiopic 1911‡/1912

ISO Week	Coptic Month	Sun	Mon	Tue	Wed	Thu	Fri	Sat	Ethiopic Month
1	KOIAK 1635	20	21	22	23	24	25	26	TĀKHŚĀŚ 1911
2	TŌBE 1635	27	28	29[c]	30	1	2	3	ṬER 1911
3		4	5	6[d]	7	8	9	10	
4		11[e]	12	13	14	15	16	17	
5		18	19	20	21	22	23	24	
6	MESHIR 1635	25	26	27	28	29	30	1	YAKĀTIT 1911
7		2	3	4	5	6	7	8	
8		9	10	11	12	13	14	15	
9		16	17	18	19	20	21	22	
10		23	24	25	26	27	28	29	
11	PAREMOTEP 1635	30	1	2	3	4	5	6	MAGĀBIT 1911
12		7	8	9	10	11	12	13	
13		14	15	16	17	18	19	20	
14		21	22	23	24	25	26	27	
15	PARMOUTE 1635	28	29	30	1	2	3	4	MIYĀZYĀ 1911
16		5	6	7	8	9	10	11	
17		12[f]	13	14	15	16	17	18	
18		19	20	21	22	23	24	25	
19	PASHONS 1635	26	27	28	29[g]	30	1	2	GENBOT 1911
20		3	4	5	6	7	8	9	
21		10	11	12	13	14	15	16	
22		17	18	19	20	21	22	23	
23		24	25	26	27	28	29	30	
24	PAŌNE 1635	1	2	3	4	5	6	7	SANĒ 1911
25		8	9	10	11	12	13	14	
26		15	16	17	18	19	20	21	
27		22	23	24	25	26	27	28	
28	EPĒP 1635	29	30	1	2	3	4	5	ḤAMLĒ 1911
29		6	7	8	9	10	11	12	
30		13	14	15	16	17	18	19	
31		20	21	22	23	24	25	26	
32	MESORĒ 1635	27	28	29	30	1	2	3	NAḤASĒ 1911
33		4	5	6	7	8	9	10	
34		11	12	13[h]	14	15	16	17	
35		18	19	20	21	22	23	24	
36	EPAG. 1635	25	26	27	28	29	30	1	PĀG. 1911
37	THOOUT 1636	2	3	4	5	6	1[a]	2	MASKARAM 1912
38		3	4	5	6	7	8	9	
39		10	11	12	13	14	15	16	
40		17[b]	18	19	20	21	22	23	
41		24	25	26	27	28	29	30	
42	PAOPE 1636	1	2	3	4	5	6	7	ṬEQEMT 1912
43		8	9	10	11	12	13	14	
44		15	16	17	18	19	20	21	
45		22	23	24	25	26	27	28	
46	ATHŌR 1636	29	30	1	2	3	4	5	ḪEDĀR 1912
47		6	7	8	9	10	11	12	
48		13	14	15	16	17	18	19	
49		20	21	22	23	24	25	26	
50	KOIAK 1636	27	28	29	30	1	2	3	TĀKHŚĀŚ 1912
51		4	5	6	7	8	9	10	
52		11	12	13	14	15	16	17	
1		18	19	20	21	22	23	24	

Gregorian notes:

[a]New Year
[b]Spring (16:19)
[c]Summer (11:54)
[d]Autumn (2:35)
[e]Winter (21:27)
● New moon
◐ First quarter moon
○ Full moon
◑ Last quarter moon

Hebrew notes:

‡Leap year
[a]New Year
[b]Yom Kippur
[c]Sukkot
[d]Winter starts
[e]Ḥanukkah
[f]Purim
[g]Passover
[h]Shavuot
[i]Fast of Av

Chinese notes:

‡Leap year
[a]New Year (4617, Sheep)
[b]Lantern Festival
[c]Qīngmíng
[d]Dragon Festival
[e]Qīqiǎo
[f]Hungry Ghosts
[g]Mid-Autumn Festival
[h]Double-Ninth Festival
[i]Dōngzhì
*Start of 60-name cycle

Coptic/Ethiopic notes:

‡Leap year
[a]New Year
[b]Building of the Cross
[c]Christmas
[d]Jesus's Circumcision
[e]Epiphany
[f]Easter
[g]Mary's Announcement
[h]Jesus's Transfiguration

1919

PERSIAN (ASTRONOMICAL) 1297/1298	Sun	Mon	Tue	Wed	Thu	Fri	Sat
DEY 1297	7	8	9	10	11	12	13
	14	15	16	17	18	19	20
	21	22	23	24	25	26	27
	28	29	30	1	2	3	4
BAHMAN 1297	5	6	7	8	9	10	11
	12	13	14	15	16	17	18
	19	20	21	22	23	24	25
	26	27	28	29	30	1	2
ESFAND 1297	3	4	5	6	7	8	9
	10	11	12	13	14	15	16
	17	18	19	20	21	22	23
	24	25	26	27	28	29	1[a]
FARVARDĪN 1298	2	3	4	5	6	7	8
	9	10	11	12	13[b]	14	15
	16	17	18	19	20	21	22
	23	24	25	26	27	28	29
	30	31	1	2	3	4	5
ORDĪBEHEŠT 1298	6	7	8	9	10	11	12
	13	14	15	16	17	18	19
	20	21	22	23	24	25	26
	27	28	29	30	31	1	2
XORDĀD 1298	3	4	5	6	7	8	9
	10	11	12	13	14	15	16
	17	18	19	20	21	22	23
	24	25	26	27	28	29	30
	31	1	2	3	4	5	6
TĪR 1298	7	8	9	10	11	12	13
	14	15	16	17	18	19	20
	21	22	23	24	25	26	27
	28	29	30	31	1	2	3
MORDĀD 1298	4	5	6	7	8	9	10
	11	12	13	14	15	16	17
	18	19	20	21	22	23	24
	25	26	27	28	29	30	31
SHAHRĪVAR 1298	1	2	3	4	5	6	7
	8	9	10	11	12	13	14
	15	16	17	18	19	20	21
	22	23	24	25	26	27	28
	29	30	31	1	2	3	4
MEHR 1298	5	6	7	8	9	10	11
	12	13	14	15	16	17	18
	19	20	21	22	23	24	25
	26	27	28	29	30	1	2
ABĀN 1298	3	4	5	6	7	8	9
	10	11	12	13	14	15	16
	17	18	19	20	21	22	23
	24	25	26	27	28	29	30
ĀZAR 1298	1	2	3	4	5	6	7
	8	9	10	11	12	13	14
	15	16	17	18	19	20	21
	22	23	24	25	26	27	28
DEY 1298	29	30	1	2	3	4	5
	6	7	8	9	10	11	12

HINDU LUNAR 1975/1976	Sun	Mon	Tue	Wed	Thu	Fri	Sat
PAUSHA 1975	26	27	28	29	30	1	2
	3	4	5	**6**	8	9	10
	11	12	13	14	15	16	17
	18	19	20	21	22	23	24
	25	26	27	28	29	30	1
MĀGHA 1975	2	3	4	5	6	7	8
	9	10	**11**	13	14	15	16
	17	18	18	19	20	21	22
	23	24	25	26	27	28[h]	29
	30	1	2	3	**4**	6	7
PHĀLGUNA 1975	8	9	10	11	12	13	14
	15[i]	16	17	18	19	20	21
	21	22	23	24	25	26	27
	28	30	1[a]	2	3	4	5
CHAITRA 1976	6	7	8[b]	9	10	11	12
	13	14	15	16	17	18	19
	20	21	22	23	24	25	26
	27	28	29	30	1	**2**	4
VAIŚĀKHA 1976	5	6	7	8	9	10	11
	12	13	14	15	15	16	17
	18	19	20	21	22	23	24
	25	27	28	29	30	1	2
JYAISHTHA 1976	3	4	5	6	7	8	9
	10	11	12	13	14	15	16
	17	18	19	20	21	22	23
	24	25	26	27	**28**	30	1
ĀSHĀDHA 1976	2	3	4	5	6	7	8
	9	10	11	12	12	13	14
	15	16	17	18	19	20	**21**
	23	24	25	26	27	28	29
ŚRĀVANA 1976	30	1	2	3	4	5	6
	7	8	9	10	11	12	13
	14	15	16	17	18	19	20
	21	22	23[c]	**24**	26	27	28
BHĀDRAPADA 1976	29	30	1	2	3	4[d]	5
	6	7	8	8	9	10	11
	12	13	14	15	16	**17**	19
	20	21	22	23	24	25	26
ĀŚVINA 1976	27	28	29	30	1	2	3
	4	5	6	7	8[e]	9[e]	10[e]
	11	12	13	14	15	16	17
	18	19	**20**	22	23	24	25
	26	27	28	29	30	1[f]	2
KĀRTTIKA 1976	3	3	4	5	6	7	8
	9	10	11	12	13	**14**	16
	17	18	19	20	21	22	23
	24	25	26	27	28	29	30
MĀRGAŚIRA 1976	1	2	3	4	5	6	7
	8	9	10	11[g]	12	13	14
	15	16	17	18	**19**	21	22
	23	24	25	26	26	27	28
PAUSHA 1976	29	30	1	2	3	4	5
	6	7	8	9	10	11	**12**

HINDU SOLAR 1840/1841	Sun	Mon	Tue	Wed	Thu	Fri	Sat
PAUSHA 1840	15	16	17	18	19	20	21
	22	23	24	25	26	27	28
	29	1[b]	2	3	4	5	6
MĀGHA 1840	7	8	9	10	11	12	13
	14	15	16	17	18	19	20
	21	22	23	24	25	26	27
	28	29	30	1	2	3	4
PHĀLGUNA 1840	5	6	7	8	9	10	11
	12	13	14	15	16	17	18
	19	20	21	22	23	24	25
	26	27	28	29	30	1	2
CHAITRA 1840	3	4	5	6	7	8	9
	10	11	12	13	14	15	16
	17	18	19	20	21	22	23
	24	25	26	27	28	29	30
VAIŚĀKHA 1841	1[a]	2	3	4	5	6	7
	8	9	10	11	12	13	14
	15	16	17	18	19	20	21
	22	23	24	25	26	27	28
	29	30	31	1	2	3	4
JYAISHTHA 1841	5	6	7	8	9	10	11
	12	13	14	15	16	17	18
	19	20	21	22	23	24	25
	26	27	28	29	30	31	1
ĀSHĀDHA 1841	2	3	4	5	6	7	8
	9	10	11	12	13	14	15
	16	17	18	19	20	21	22
	23	24	25	26	27	28	29
	30	31	32	1	2	3	4
ŚRĀVANA 1841	5	6	7	8	9	10	11
	12	13	14	15	16	17	18
	19	20	21	22	23	24	25
	26	27	28	29	30	31	32
BHĀDRAPADA 1841	1	2	3	4	5	6	7
	8	9	10	11	12	13	14
	15	16	17	18	19	20	21
	22	23	24	25	26	27	28
	29	30	31	1	2	3	4
ĀŚVINA 1841	5	6	7	8	9	10	11
	12	13	14	15	16	17	18
	19	20	21	22	23	24	25
	26	27	28	29	30	1	2
KĀRTTIKA 1841	3	4	5	6	7	8	9
	10	11	12	13	14	15	16
	17	18	19	20	21	22	23
	24	25	26	27	28	29	30
MĀRGAŚIRA 1841	1	2	3	4	5	6	7
	8	9	10	11	12	13	14
	15	16	17	18	19	20	21
	22	23	24	25	26	27	28
PAUSHA 1841	29	1	2	3	4	5	6
	7	8	9	10	11	12	13
	14	15	16	17	18	19	20

ISLAMIC (ASTRONOMICAL) 1337/1338	Sun	Mon	Tue	Wed	Thu	Fri	Sat
RABĪʿ II 1337	25	26	27	28	29	30	1
	2	3	4	5	6	7	8
	9	10	11	12	13	14	15
	16	17	18	19	20	21	22
	23	24	25	26	27	28	29
JUMĀDĀ I 1337	1	2	3	4	5	6	7
	8	9	10	11	12	13	14
	15	16	17	18	19	20	21
	22	23	24	25	26	27	28
JUMĀDĀ II 1337	29	30	1	2	3	4	5
	6	7	8	9	10	11	12
	13	14	15	16	17	18	19
	20	21	22	23	24	25	26
RAJAB 1337	27	28	29	1	2	3	4
	5	6	7	8	9	10	11
	12	13	14	15	16	17	18
	19	20	21	22	23	24	25
SHAʿBĀN 1337	26	27[d]	28	29	1	2	3
	4	5	6	7	8	9	10
	11	12	13	14	15	16	17
	18	19	20	21	22	23	24
RAMAḌĀN 1337	25	26	27	28	29	30	1[e]
	2	3	4	5	6	7	8
	9	10	11	12	13	14	15
	16	17	18	19	20	21	22
	23	24	25	26	27	28	29
SHAWWĀL 1337	1[f]	2	3	4	5	6	7
	8	9	10	11	12	13	14
	15	16	17	18	19	20	21
	22	23	24	25	26	27	28
DHU AL-QAʿDA 1337	29	30	1	2	3	4	5
	6	7	8	9	10	11	12
	13	14	15	16	17	18	19
	20	21	22	23	24	25	26
DHU AL-ḤIJJA 1337	27	28	29	30	1	2	3
	4	5	6	7	8	9	10[g]
	11	12	13	14	15	16	17
	18	19	20	21	22	23	24
MUḤARRAM 1338	25	26	27	28	29	1[a]	2
	3	4	5	6	7	8	9
	10[b]	11	12	13	14	15	16
	17	18	19	20	21	22	23
	24	25	26	27	28	29	30
ṢAFAR 1338	1	2	3	4	5	6	7
	8	9	10	11	12	13	14
	15	16	17	18	19	20	21
	22	23	24	25	26	27	28
RABĪʿ I 1338	29	1	2	3	4	5	6
	7	8	9	10	11	12[c]	13
	14	15	16	17	18	19	20
	21	22	23	24	25	26	27
RABĪʿ II 1338	28	29	30	1	2	3	4
	5	6	7	8	9	10	11

Julian (Sun)	GREGORIAN 1919	Sun	Mon	Tue	Wed	Thu	Fri	Sat
Dec 16		29	30	31	1	2	3	4
	JANUARY 1919	5	6	7[a]	8	9	10	11
Dec 30		12	13	14[b]	15	16	17	18
		19	20	21	22	23	24	25
Jan 13		26	27	28	29	30	31	1
	FEBRUARY 1919	2	3	4	5	6	7	8
Jan 27		9	10	11	12	13	14	15
		16	17	18	19	20	21	22
Feb 10		23	24	25	26	27	28	1
	MARCH 1919	2	3	4	5[c]	6	7	8
Feb 24		9[d]	10	11	12	13	14	15
		16	17	18	19	20	21	22
Mar 10		23	24	25	26	27	28	29
		30	31	1	2	3	4	5
Mar 24	APRIL 1919	6	7	8	9	10	11	12
		13	14	15	16	17	18	19
Apr 7		20[e]	21	22	23	24	25	26
		27	28	29	30	1	2	3
Apr 21	MAY 1919	4	5	6	7	8	9	10
		11	12	13	14	15	16	17
May 5		18	19	20	21	22	23	24
		25	26	27	28	29	30	31
May 19	JUNE 1919	1	2	3	4	5	6	7
		8	9	10	11	12	13	14
Jun 2		15	16	17	18	19	20	21
		22	23	24	25	26	27	28
Jun 16		29	30	1	2	3	4	5
	JULY 1919	6	7	8	9	10	11	12
Jun 30		13	14	15	16	17	18	19
		20	21	22	23	24	25	26
Jul 14		27	28	29	30	31	1	2
	AUGUST 1919	3	4	5	6	7	8	9
Jul 28		10	11	12	13	14	15	16
		17	18	19	20	21	22	23
Aug 11		24	25	26	27	28	29	30
		31	1	2	3	4	5	6
Aug 25	SEPTEMBER 1919	7	8	9	10	11	12	13
		14	15	16	17	18	19	20
Sep 8		21	22	23	24	25	26	27
		28	29	30	1	2	3	4
Sep 22	OCTOBER 1919	5	6	7	8	9	10	11
		12	13	14	15	16	17	18
Oct 6		19	20	21	22	23	24	25
		26	27	28	29	30	31	1
Oct 20	NOVEMBER 1919	2	3	4	5	6	7	8
		9	10	11	12	13	14	15
Nov 3		16	17	18	19	20	21	22
		23	24	25	26	27	28	29
Nov 17		30[g]	1	2	3	4	5	6
	DECEMBER 1919	7	8	9	10	11	12	13
Dec 1		14	15	16	17	18	19	20
		21	22	23	24	25[h]	26	27
Dec 15		28	29	30	31	1	2	3

Persian: [a]New Year; [b]Sizdeh Bedar

Hindu lunar: [a]New Year (Siddhārthin); [b]Birthday of Rāma; [c]Birthday of Krishna; [d]Ganēśa Chaturthī; [e]Dashara; [f]Diwali; [g]Birthday of Vishnu; [h]Night of Śiva; [i]Holi

Hindu solar: [a]New Year (Prajāpati); [b]Pongal

Islamic: [a]New Year; [b]ʿAshūrāʾ; [c]Prophet's Birthday; [d]Ascent of the Prophet; [e]Start of Ramaḍān; [f]ʿĪd al-Fiṭr; [g]ʿĪd al-ʾAḍḥā

Gregorian: [a]Orthodox Christmas; [b]Julian New Year; [c]Ash Wednesday; [d]Feast of Orthodoxy; [e]Easter (also Orthodox); [g]Advent; [h]Christmas

1920

Gregorian 1920‡	Sun	Mon	Tue	Wed	Thu	Fri	Sat	Lunar Phases	ISO WEEK (Mon)	JULIAN DAY (Sun noon)	Hebrew 5680/5681‡	Sun	Mon	Tue	Wed	Thu	Fri	Sat	Molad
JANUARY 1920	28	29	◐	31	1[a]	2	3	5:24	1	2422321	TEVETH 5680	6	7	8	9	10	11	12	
	4	○	6	7	8	9	10	21:04	2	2422328		13	14	15	16	17	18	19	
	11	12	◑	14	15	16	17	0:08	3	2422335		20	21	22	23	24	25	26	
	18	19	20	●	22	23	24	5:26	4	2422342	SHEVAT 5680	27	28	29	1	2	3	4	Wed 0h29m14p
	25	26	27	◐	29	30	31	15:37	5	2422349		5	6	7	8	9	10	11	
FEBRUARY 1920	1	2	3	○	5	6	7	8:42	6	2422356		12	13	14	15	16	17	18	
	8	9	10	◑	12	13	14	20:49	7	2422363		19	20	21	22	23	24	25	
	15	16	17	18	●	20	21	21:34	8	2422370	ADAR 5680	26	27	28	29	30	1	2	Thu 13h13m15p
	22	23	24	25	◐	27	28	23:49	9	2422377		3	4	5	6	7	8	9	
MARCH 1920	29	1	2	3	○	5	6	21:12	10	2422384		10	11	12	13	14[f]	15	16	
	7	8	9	10	11	◑	13	17:57	11	2422391		17	18	19	20	21	22	23	
	14	15	16	17	18	19	●[b]	10:55	12	2422398	NISAN 5680	24	25	26	27	28	29	1	Sat 1h57m16p
	21	22	23	24	25	26	◐	6:45	13	2422405		2	3	4	5	6	7	8	
APRIL 1920	28	29	30	31	1	2	○	10:54	14	2422412		9	10	11	12	13	14	15[g]	
	4	5	6	7	8	9	10		15	2422419		16	17	18	19	20	21	22	
	◑	12	13	14	15	16	17	13:24	16	2422426		23	24	25	26	27	28	29	
	●	19	20	21	22	23	24	21:43	17	2422433	IYYAR 5680	30	1	2	3	4	5	6	Sun 14h41m17p
MAY 1920	◐	26	27	28	29	30	1	13:27	18	2422440		7	8	9	10	11	12	13	
	2	○	4	5	6	7	8	1:47	19	2422447		14	15	16	17	18	19	20	
	9	10	◑	12	13	14	15	5:51	20	2422454		21	22	23	24	25	26	27	
	16	17	●	19	20	21	22	6:25	21	2422461	SIVAN 5680	28	29	1	2	3	4	5	Tue 3h26m0p
	23	◐	25	26	27	28	29	21:07	22	2422468		6[h]	7	8	9	10	11	12	
JUNE 1920	30	31	○	2	3	4	5	17:18	23	2422475		13	14	15	16	17	18	19	
	6	7	8	◑	10	11	12	18:58	24	2422482		20	21	22	23	24	25	26	
	13	14	15	●	17	18	19	13:41	25	2422489	TAMMUZ 5680	27	28	29	30	1	2	3	Wed 16h10m1p
	20	21[c]	22	◐	24	25	26	6:49	26	2422496		4	5	6	7	8	9	10	
JULY 1920	27	28	29	30	○	2	3	8:40	27	2422503		11	12	13	14	15	16	17	
	4	5	6	7	8	◑	10	5:05	28	2422510		18	19	20	21	22	23	24	
	11	12	13	14	●	16	17	20:25	29	2422517	AV 5680	25	26	27	28	29	1	2	Fri 4h54m2p
	18	19	20	21	◐	23	24	19:20	30	2422524		3	4	5	6	7	8	9	
	25	26	27	28	29	○	31	23:19	31	2422531		10[i]	11	12	13	14	15	16	
AUGUST 1920	1	2	3	4	5	6	◑	12:50	32	2422538		17	18	19	20	21	22	23	
	8	9	10	11	12	13	●	3:44	33	2422545		24	25	26	27	28	29	30	
	15	16	17	18	19	20	◐	10:51	34	2422552	ELUL 5680	1	2	3	4	5	6	7	Sat 17h38m3p
	22	23	24	25	26	27	28		35	2422559		8	9	10	11	12	13	14	
SEPTEMBER 1920	○	30	31	1	2	3	4	13:03	36	2422566		15	16	17	18	19	20	21	
	◑	6	7	8	9	10	11	19:05	37	2422573		22	23	24	25	26	27	28	
	●	13	14	15	16	17	18	12:51	38	2422580	TISHRI 5681	29	1[a]	2[a]	3	4	5	6	Mon 6h22m4p
	19	◐	21	22	23[d]	24	25	4:55	39	2422587		7	8	9	10[b]	11	12	13	
OCTOBER 1920	26	27	○	29	30	1	2	1:56	40	2422594		14	15[c]	16	17	18	19	20	
	3	4	◑	6	7	8	9	0:53	41	2422601		21	22	23	24	25	26	27	
	10	11	●	13	14	15	16	0:50	42	2422608	HESHVAN 5681	28	29	30	1	2	3	4	Tue 19h6m5p
	17	18	19	◐	21	22	23	0:28	43	2422615		5	6	7	8	9	10	11	
	24	25	26	○	28	29	30	14:09	44	2422622		12	13	14	15	16	17	18	
NOVEMBER 1920	31	1	2	◑	4	5	6	7:35	45	2422629		19	20	21	22	23	24	25	
	7	8	9	●	11	12	13	16:05	46	2422636	KISLEV 5681	26	27	28	29	30	1	2	Thu 7h50m6p
	14	15	16	17	◐	19	20	20:12	47	2422643		3	4	5	6	7	8	9	
	21	22	23	24	25	○	27	1:42	48	2422650		10	11	12	13	14	15	16	
DECEMBER 1920	28	29	30	1	◑	3	4	16:29	49	2422657		17	18	19	20	21	22	23	
	5	6	7	8	9	●	11	10:04	50	2422664		24[d]	25[e]	26[e]	27[e]	28[e]	29[e]	30[e]	
	12	13	14	15	16	17	◐	14:40	51	2422671	TEVETH 5681	1[e]	2[e]	3	4	5	6	7	Fri 20h34m7p
	19	20	21	22[e]	23	24	○	12:38	52	2422678		8	9	10	11	12	13	14	
	26	27	28	29	30	31	◑	4:34	53	2422685		15	16	17	18	19	20	21	

ISO WEEK	Chinese Jǐ-Wèi‡/Gēng-Shēn	Sun	Mon	Tue	Wed	Thu	Fri	Sat	Solar Term	Coptic 1636/1637	Sun	Mon	Tue	Wed	Thu	Fri	Sat	Ethiopic 1912/1913
1	MONTH 11 Jǐ-Wèi	7	8	9	10	11	12	13		KOIAK 1636	18	19	20	21	22	23	24	TĀKHŚĀŚ 1912
2		14	15	16	17*	18	19	20	Xiǎo hán	TŌBE 1636	25	26	27	28	29[c]	30	1	ṬER 1912
3		21	22	23	24	25	26	27			2	3	4	5	6[d]	7	8	
4	MONTH 12 Jǐ-Wèi	28	29	30	1	2	3	4	Dà hán		9	10	11[e]	12	13	14	15	
5		5	6	7	8	9	10	11			16	17	18	19	20	21	22	
6		12	13	14	15	16	17	18	Lì chūn		23	24	25	26	27	28	29	
7		19	20	21	22	23	24	25		MESHIR 1636	30	1	2	3	4	5	6	YAKĀTIT 1912
8	MONTH 1 Gēng-Shēn	26	27	28	29	30	1[a]	2	Yǔ shuǐ		7	8	9	10	11	12	13	
9		3	4	5	6	7	8	9			14	15	16	17	18	19	20	
10		10	11	12	13	14	15[b]	16	Jīng zhé		21	22	23	24	25	26	27	
11		17*	18	19	20	21	22	23		PAREMOTEP 1636	28	29	30	1	2	3	4	MAGĀBIT 1912
12	MONTH 2 Gēng-Shēn	24	25	26	27	28	29	1			5	6	7	8	9	10	11	
13		2	3	4	5	6	7	8	Chūn fēn		12	13	14	15	16	17	18	
14		9	10	11	12	13	14	15			19	20	21	22	23	24	25	
15		16	17[c]	18	19	20	21	22	Qīng míng	PARMOUTE 1636	26	27	28	29	30	1	2	MIYĀZYĀ 1912
16		23	24	25	26	27	28	29			3[f]	4	5	6	7	8	9	
17	MONTH 3 Gēng-Shēn	30	1	2	3	4	5	6	Gǔ yǔ		10	11	12	13	14	15	16	
18		7	8	9	10	11	12	13			17	18	19	20	21	22	23	
19		14	15	16	17	18*	19	20	Lì xià		24	25	26	27	28	29[g]	30	
20		21	22	23	24	25	26	27		PASHONS 1636	1	2	3	4	5	6	7	GENBOT 1912
21	MONTH 4 Gēng-Shēn	28	29	1	2	3	4	5	Xiǎo mǎn		8	9	10	11	12	13	14	
22		6	7	8	9	10	11	12			15	16	17	18	19	20	21	
23		13	14	15	16	17	18	19			22	23	24	25	26	27	28	
24		20	21	22	23	24	25	26	Máng zhòng	PAŌNE 1636	29	30	1	2	3	4	5	SANĒ 1912
25	MONTH 5 Gēng-Shēn	27	28	29	1	2	3	4			6	7	8	9	10	11	12	
26		5[d]	6	7	8	9	10	11	Xià zhì		13	14	15	16	17	18	19	
27		12	13	14	15	16	17	18			20	21	22	23	24	25	26	
28		19	20*	21	22	23	24	25	Xiǎo shǔ	EPĒP 1636	27	28	29	30	1	2	3	HAMLĒ 1912
29	MONTH 6 Gēng-Shēn	26	27	28	29	30	1	2			4	5	6	7	8	9	10	
30		3	4	5	6	7	8	9	Dà shǔ		11	12	13	14	15	16	17	
31		10	11	12	13	14	15	16			18	19	20	21	22	23	24	
32		17	18	19	20	21	22	23		MESORĒ 1636	25	26	27	28	29	30	1	NAHASĒ 1912
33	MONTH 7 Gēng-Shēn	24	25	26	27	28	29	1	Lì qiū		2	3	4	5	6	7	8	
34		2	3	4	5	6	7[e]	8			9	10	11	12	13[h]	14	15	
35		9	10	11	12	13	14	15[f]	Chǔ shǔ		16	17	18	19	20	21	22	
36		16	17	18	19	20	21*	22			23	24	25	26	27	28	29	
37		23	24	25	26	27	28	29	Bái lù	EPAG. 1636; THOOUT 1637	30	1	2	3	4	5	1[a]	PĀG. 1912; MASKARAM 1913
38	MONTH 8 Gēng-Shēn	1	2	3	4	5	6	7			2	3	4	5	6	7	8	
39		8	9	10	11	12	13	14	Qiū fēn		9	10	11	12	13	14	15	
40		15[g]	16	17	18	19	20	21			16	17[b]	18	19	20	21	22	
41		22	23	24	25	26	27	28	Hán lù		23	24	25	26	27	28	29	
42	MONTH 9 Gēng-Shēn	29	30	1	2	3	4	5		PAOPE 1637	30	1	2	3	4	5	6	ṬEQEMT 1913
43		6	7	8	9[h]	10	11	12			7	8	9	10	11	12	13	
44		13	14	15	16	17	18	19	Shuāng jiàng		14	15	16	17	18	19	20	
45		20	21	22*	23	24	25	26			21	22	23	24	25	26	27	
46	MONTH 10 Gēng-Shēn	27	28	29	1	2	3	4	Lì dōng	ATHŌR 1637	28	29	30	1	2	3	4	HEDĀR 1913
47		5	6	7	8	9	10	11			5	6	7	8	9	10	11	
48		12	13	14	15	16	17	18	Xiǎo xuě		12	13	14	15	16	17	18	
49		19	20	21	22	23	24	25			19	20	21	22	23	24	25	
50	MONTH 11 Gēng-Shēn	26	27	28	29	30	1	2	Dà xuě	KOIAK 1637	26	27	28	29	30	1	2	TĀKHŚĀŚ 1913
51		3	4	5	6	7	8	9			3	4	5	6	7	8	9	
52		10	11	12	13[i]	14	15	16	Dōng zhì		10	11	12	13	14	15	16	
53		17	18	19	20	21	22	23			17	18	19	20	21	22	23	

Gregorian:
‡Leap year
[a]New Year
[b]Spring (21:59)
[c]Summer (17:40)
[d]Autumn (8:28)
[e]Winter (3:17)
● New moon
◐ First quarter moon
○ Full moon
◑ Last quarter moon

Hebrew:
‡Leap year
[a]New Year
[b]Yom Kippur
[c]Sukkot
[d]Winter starts
[e]Ḥanukkah
[f]Purim
[g]Passover
[h]Shavuot
[i]Fast of Av

Chinese:
‡Leap year
[a]New Year (4618, Monkey)
[b]Lantern Festival
[c]Qīngmíng
[d]Dragon Festival
[e]Qīqiǎo
[f]Hungry Ghosts
[g]Mid-Autumn Festival
[h]Double-Ninth Festival
[i]Dōngzhì
*Start of 60-name cycle

Coptic/Ethiopic:
[a]New Year
[b]Building of the Cross
[c]Christmas
[d]Jesus's Circumcision
[e]Epiphany
[f]Easter
[g]Mary's Announcement
[h]Jesus's Transfiguration

1920

PERSIAN (ASTRONOMICAL) 1298/1299

Month	Sun	Mon	Tue	Wed	Thu	Fri	Sat
DEY 1298	6	7	8	9	10	11	12
	13	14	15	16	17	18	19
	20	21	22	23	24	25	26
	27	28	29	30	1	2	3
BAHMAN 1298	4	5	6	7	8	9	10
	11	12	13	14	15	16	17
	18	19	20	21	22	23	24
	25	26	27	28	29	30	1
ESFAND 1298	2	3	4	5	6	7	8
	9	10	11	12	13	14	15
	16	17	18	19	20	21	22
	23	24	25	26	27	28	29
FARVARDĪN 1299	1[a]	2	3	4	5	6	7
	8	9	10	11	12	13[b]	14
	15	16	17	18	19	20	21
	22	23	24	25	26	27	28
	29	30	31	1	2	3	4
ORDĪBEHEŠT 1299	5	6	7	8	9	10	11
	12	13	14	15	16	17	18
	19	20	21	22	23	24	25
	26	27	28	29	30	31	1
XORDĀD 1299	2	3	4	5	6	7	8
	9	10	11	12	13	14	15
	16	17	18	19	20	21	22
	23	24	25	26	27	28	29
	30	31	1	2	3	4	5
TĪR 1299	6	7	8	9	10	11	12
	13	14	15	16	17	18	19
	20	21	22	23	24	25	26
	27	28	29	30	31	1	2
MORDĀD 1299	3	4	5	6	7	8	9
	10	11	12	13	14	15	16
	17	18	19	20	21	22	23
	24	25	26	27	28	29	30
	31	1	2	3	4	5	6
SHAHRĪVAR 1299	7	8	9	10	11	12	13
	14	15	16	17	18	19	20
	21	22	23	24	25	26	27
	28	29	30	31	1	2	3
MEHR 1299	4	5	6	7	8	9	10
	11	12	13	14	15	16	17
	18	19	20	21	22	23	24
	25	26	27	28	29	30	1
ĀBĀN 1299	2	3	4	5	6	7	8
	9	10	11	12	13	14	15
	16	17	18	19	20	21	22
	23	24	25	26	27	28	29
	30	1	2	3	4	5	6
ĀZAR 1299	7	8	9	10	11	12	13
	14	15	16	17	18	19	20
	21	22	23	24	25	26	27
	28	29	30	1	2	3	4
DEY 1299	5	6	7	8	9	10	11

[a]New Year
[b]Sizdeh Bedar

HINDU LUNAR 1976/1977‡

Month	Sun	Mon	Tue	Wed	Thu	Fri	Sat
PAUSHA 1976	6	7	8	9	10	11	12
	14	15	16	17	18	19	20
	21	22	23	24	25	26	27
	28	28	29	30	1	2	3
MĀGHA 1976	4	5	6	7	9	10	11
	12	13	14	15	16	17	18
	19	20	21	22	23	24	25
	26	27	28	29[h]	30	1	2
PHĀLGUNA 1976	3	4	5	6	7	8	9
	10	11	13	14	15[i]	16	17
	18	19	20	21	21	22	23
	24	25	26	27	28	29	30
CHAITRA 1977	1[a]	2	3	4	5	7	8
	9[b]	10	11	12	13	14	15
	16	17	18	19	20	21	22
	23	24	25	25	26	27	28
	30	1	2	3	4	5	6
VAIŚĀKHA 1977	7	8	9	10	12	13	14
	15	15	16	17	18	19	20
	21	22	23	24	25	26	27
	28	29	30	1	2	4	5
JYAISHTHA 1977	6	7	8	9	10	11	12
	13	14	15	16	17	18	19
	20	20	21	22	23	24	26
	27	28	29	30	1	2	3
ĀSHĀḌHA 1977	4	5	6	8	9	10	11
	11	12	13	14	15	16	17
	18	19	20	21	22	23	24
	25	26	27	28	30	1	2
LEAP ŚRĀVAṆA 1977	3	4	5	6	7	8	9
	10	11	12	13	14	15	16
	17	17	18	19	21	22	23
	24	25	26	27	28	29	30
ŚRĀVAṆA 1977	1	3	4	5	6	7	8
	8	9	10	11	12	13	14
	15	16	17	18	19	20	21
	22	23[c]	24	26	27	28	29
	30	1	2	3	4[d]	5	6
BHĀDRAPADA 1977	7	8	9	10	11	12	13
	13	14	15	16	18	19	20
	21	22	23	24	25	26	27
	28	29	1	2	3	3	4
ĀŚVINA 1977	5	6	7	8[e]	9[e]	10[e]	11
	12	13	14	15	16	17	18
	19	20	21	23	24	25	26
	27	28	29	30	1[f]	2	3
KĀRTTIKA 1977	4	5	6	6	7	8	9
	10	11	12	13	14	15	17
	18	19	20	21	22	23	24
	25	26	27	28	29	30	1
MĀRGAŚĪRA 1977	2	3	4	5	6	7	8
	9	10	11[g]	12	13	14	15
	16	17	18	19	20	22	23

‡Leap year
[a]New Year (Rāudra)
[b]Birthday of Rāma
[c]Birthday of Krishna
[d]Ganēśa Chaturthī
[e]Dashara
[f]Diwali
[g]Birthday of Vishnu
[h]Night of Śiva
[i]Holi

HINDU SOLAR 1841/1842‡

Month	Sun	Mon	Tue	Wed	Thu	Fri	Sat
PAUSHA 1841	14	15	16	17	18	19	20
	21	22	23	24	25	26	27
	28	29	30	1[b]	2	3	4
MĀGHA 1841	5	6	7	8	9	10	11
	12	13	14	15	16	17	18
	19	20	21	22	23	24	25
	26	27	28	29	1	2	3
PHĀLGUNA 1841	4	5	6	7	8	9	10
	11	12	13	14	15	16	17
	18	19	20	21	22	23	24
	25	26	27	28	29	30	1
CHAITRA 1841	2	3	4	5	6	7	8
	9	10	11	12	13	14	15
	16	17	18	19	20	21	22
	23	24	25	26	27	28	29
	30	1[a]	2	3	4	5	6
VAIŚĀKHA 1842	7	8	9	10	11	12	13
	14	15	16	17	18	19	20
	21	22	23	24	25	26	27
	28	29	30	31	1	2	3
JYAISHTHA 1842	4	5	6	7	8	9	10
	11	12	13	14	15	16	17
	18	19	20	21	22	23	24
	25	26	27	28	29	30	31
	32	1	2	3	4	5	6
ĀSHĀḌHA 1842	7	8	9	10	11	12	13
	14	15	16	17	18	19	20
	21	22	23	24	25	26	27
	28	29	30	31	1	2	3
ŚRĀVAṆA 1842	4	5	6	7	8	9	10
	11	12	13	14	15	16	17
	18	19	20	21	22	23	24
	25	26	27	28	29	30	31
	32	1	2	3	4	5	6
BHĀDRAPADA 1842	7	8	9	10	11	12	13
	14	15	16	17	18	19	20
	21	22	23	24	25	26	27
	28	29	30	31	1	2	3
ĀŚVINA 1842	4	5	6	7	8	9	10
	11	12	13	14	15	16	17
	18	19	20	21	22	23	24
	25	26	27	28	29	30	1
KĀRTTIKA 1842	2	3	4	5	6	7	8
	9	10	11	12	13	14	15
	16	17	18	19	20	21	22
	23	24	25	26	27	28	29
	30	1	2	3	4	5	6
MĀRGAŚĪRA 1842	7	8	9	10	11	12	13
	14	15	16	17	18	19	20
	21	22	23	24	25	26	27
	28	29	30	1	2	3	4
PAUSHA 1842	5	6	7	8	9	10	11
	12	13	14	15	16	17	18

‡Leap year
[a]New Year (Aṅgiras)
[b]Pongal

ISLAMIC (ASTRONOMICAL) 1338/1339‡

Month	Sun	Mon	Tue	Wed	Thu	Fri	Sat
	5	6	7	8	9	10	11
RABĪ' II 1338	12	13	14	15	16	17	18
	19	20	21	22	23	24	25
	26	27	28	29	1	2	3
JUMĀDĀ I 1338	4	5	6	7	8	9	10
	11	12	13	14	15	16	17
	18	19	20	21	22	23	24
	25	26	27	28	29	30	1
JUMĀDĀ II 1338	2	3	4	5	6	7	8
	9	10	11	12	13	14	15
	16	17	18	19	20	21	22
	23	24	25	26	27	28	29
	30	1	2	3	4	5	6
RAJAB 1338	7	8	9	10	11	12	13
	14	15	16	17	18	19	20
	21	22	23	24	25	26	27[d]
	28	29	1	2	3	4	5
SHA'BĀN 1338	6	7	8	9	10	11	12
	13	14	15	16	17	18	19
	20	21	22	23	24	25	26
	27	28	29	1[e]	2	3	4
RAMAḌĀN 1338	5	6	7	8	9	10	11
	12	13	14	15	16	17	18
	19	20	21	22	23	24	25
	26	27	28	29	30	1[f]	2
SHAWWĀL 1338	3	4	5	6	7	8	9
	10	11	12	13	14	15	16
	17	18	19	20	21	22	23
	24	25	26	27	28	29	30
DHU AL-QA'DA 1338	1	2	3	4	5	6	7
	8	9	10	11	12	13	14
	15	16	17	18	19	20	21
	22	23	24	25	26	27	28
	29	1	2	3	4	5	6
DHU AL-ḤIJJA 1338	7	8	9	10[g]	11	12	13
	14	15	16	17	18	19	20
	21	22	23	24	25	26	27
	28	29	1[a]	2[A]	3	4	5
MUḤARRAM 1339	6	7	8	9	10[b]	11	12
	13	14	15	16	17	18	19
	20	21	22	23	24	25	26
	27	28	29	30	1	2	3
ṢAFAR 1339	4	5	6	7	8	9	10
	11	12	13	14	15	16	17
	18	19	20	21	22	23	24
	25	26	27	28	29	1	2
RABĪ' I 1339	3	4	5	6	7	8	9
	10	11	12[c]	13	14	15	16
	17	18	19	20	21	22	23
	24	25	26	27	28	29	30
RABĪ' II 1339	1	2	3	4	5	6	7
	8	9	10	11	12	13	14
	15	16	17	18	19	20	21

‡Leap year
[a]New Year
[A]New Year (Arithmetic)
[b]'Ashūrā'
[c]Prophet's Birthday
[d]Ascent of the Prophet
[e]Start of Ramaḍān
[f]'Id al-Fiṭr
[g]'Id al-'Aḍḥā

GREGORIAN 1920‡

Julian‡ (Sun)	Month	Sun	Mon	Tue	Wed	Thu	Fri	Sat
Dec 15		28	29	30	31	1	2	3
	JANUARY 1920	4	5	6	7[a]	8	9	10
Dec 29		11	12	13	14[b]	15	16	17
		18	19	20	21	22	23	24
Jan 12		25	26	27	28	29	30	31
	FEBRUARY 1920	1	2	3	4	5	6	7
Jan 26		8	9	10	11	12	13	14
		15	16	17	18[c]	19	20	21
Feb 9		22	23	24	25	26	27	28
	MARCH 1920	29[d]	1	2	3	4	5	6
Feb 23		7	8	9	10	11	12	13
		14	15	16	17	18	19	20
Mar 8		21	22	23	24	25	26	27
		28	29	30	31	1	2	3
Mar 22	APRIL 1920	4[e]	5	6	7	8	9	10
		11[f]	12	13	14	15	16	17
Apr 5		18	19	20	21	22	23	24
		25	26	27	28	29	30	1
Apr 19	MAY 1920	2	3	4	5	6	7	8
		9	10	11	12	13	14	15
May 3		16	17	18	19	20	21	22
		23	24	25	26	27	28	29
May 17		30	31	1	2	3	4	5
	JUNE 1920	6	7	8	9	10	11	12
May 31		13	14	15	16	17	18	19
		20	21	22	23	24	25	26
Jun 14		27	28	29	30	1	2	3
	JULY 1920	4	5	6	7	8	9	10
Jun 28		11	12	13	14	15	16	17
		18	19	20	21	22	23	24
Jul 12		25	26	27	28	29	30	31
	AUGUST 1920	1	2	3	4	5	6	7
Jul 26		8	9	10	11	12	13	14
		15	16	17	18	19	20	21
Aug 9		22	23	24	25	26	27	28
		29	30	31	1	2	3	4
Aug 23	SEPTEMBER 1920	5	6	7	8	9	10	11
		12	13	14	15	16	17	18
Sep 6		19	20	21	22	23	24	25
		26	27	28	29	30	1	2
Sep 20	OCTOBER 1920	3	4	5	6	7	8	9
		10	11	12	13	14	15	16
Oct 4		17	18	19	20	21	22	23
		24	25	26	27	28	29	30
Oct 18		31	1	2	3	4	5	6
	NOVEMBER 1920	7	8	9	10	11	12	13
Nov 1		14	15	16	17	18	19	20
		21	22	23	24	25	26	27
Nov 15		28[g]	29	30	1	2	3	4
	DECEMBER 1920	5	6	7	8	9	10	11
Nov 29		12	13	14	15	16	17	18
		19	20	21	22	23	24	25[h]
Dec 13		26	27	28	29	30	31	1

‡Leap year
[a]Orthodox Christmas
[b]Julian New Year
[c]Ash Wednesday
[d]Feast of Orthodoxy
[e]Easter
[f]Orthodox Easter
[g]Advent
[h]Christmas

1921

GREGORIAN 1921	Sun	Mon	Tue	Wed	Thu	Fri	Sat	Lunar Phases	ISO WEEK (Mon)	JULIAN DAY (Sun noon)	HEBREW 5681‡/5682	Sun	Mon	Tue	Wed	Thu	Fri	Sat	Molad
JANUARY 1921	26	27	28	29	30	31	◑[a]	4:34	53	2422685	TEVETH 5681	15	16	17	18	19	20	21	
	2	3	4	5	6	7	8		1	2422692		22	23	24	25	26	27	28	
	●	10	11	12	13	14	15	5:27	2	2422699	SHEVAT 5681	29	1	2	3	4	5	6	Sun $9^h18^m8^p$
	16	◐	18	19	20	21	22	6:30	3	2422706		7	8	9	10	11	12	13	
	○	24	25	26	27	28	29	23:07	4	2422713		14	15	16	17	18	19	20	
FEBRUARY 1921	◑	31	1	2	3	4	5	20:02	5	2422720		21	22	23	24	25	26	27	
	6	7	●	9	10	11	12	0:36	6	2422727	ADAR I 5681	28	29	30	1	2	3	4	Mon $22^h2^m9^p$
	13	14	◐	16	17	18	19	18:53	7	2422734		5	6	7	8	9	10	11	
	20	21	○	23	24	25	26	9:32	8	2422741		12	13	14	15	16	17	18	
MARCH 1921	27	28	◑	2	3	4	5	14:03	9	2422748		19	20	21	22	23	24	25	
	6	7	8	●	10	11	12	18:09	10	2422755	ADAR II 5681	26	27	28	29	30	1	2	Wed $10^h46^m10^p$
	13	14	15	16	◐	18	19	3:49	11	2422762		3	4	5	6	7	8	9	
	20	21[b]	22	○	24	25	26	20:19	12	2422769		10	11	12	13	14[f]	15	16	
APRIL 1921	27	28	29	30	◑	1	2	9:13	13	2422776		17	18	19	20	21	22	23	
	3	4	5	6	7	●	9	9:05	14	2422783	NISAN 5681	24	25	26	27	28	29	1	Thu $23^h30^m11^p$
	10	11	12	13	14	◐	16	10:11	15	2422790		2	3	4	5	6	7	8	
	17	18	19	20	21	○	23	7:49	16	2422797		9	10	11	12	13	14	15[g]	
	24	25	26	27	28	29	◑	4:08	17	2422804		16	17	18	19	20	21	22	
MAY 1921	1	2	3	4	5	6	●	21:01	18	2422811		23	24	25	26	27	28	29	
	8	9	10	11	12	13	◐	15:24	19	2422818	IYAR 5681	30	1	2	3	4	5	6	Sat $12^h14^m12^p$
	15	16	17	18	19	20	○	20:15	20	2422825		7	8	9	10	11	12	13	
	22	23	24	25	26	27	28		21	2422832		14	15	16	17	18	19	20	
JUNE 1921	◑	30	31	1	2	3	4	21:44	22	2422839		21	22	23	24	25	26	27	
	5	●	7	8	9	10	11	6:[illegible]4	23	2422846	SIVAN 5681	28	29	1	2	3	4	5	Mon $0^h58^m13^p$
	◐	13	14	15	16	17	18	20:59	24	2422853		6[h]	7	8	9	10	11	12	
	19	○	21[c]	22	23	24	25	9:41	25	2422860		13	14	15	16	17	18	19	
JULY 1921	26	27	◑	29	30	1	2	13:17	26	2422867		20	21	22	23	24	25	26	
	3	4	●	6	7	8	9	13:36	27	2422874	TAMMUZ 5681	27	28	29	30	1	2	3	Tue $13^h42^m14^p$
	10	11	◐	13	14	15	16	4:15	28	2422881		4	5	6	7	8	9	10	
	17	18	19	○	21	22	23	0:07	29	2422888		11	12	13	14	15	16	17	
	24	25	26	27	◑	29	30	2:20	30	2422895		18	19	20	21	22	23	24	
AUGUST 1921	31	1	2	●	4	5	6	20:17	31	2422902	AV 5681	25	26	27	28	29	1	2	Thu $2^h26^m15^p$
	7	8	9	◐	11	12	13	14:13	32	2422909		3	4	5	6	7	8	9	
	14	15	16	17	○	19	20	15:28	33	2422916		10[i]	11	12	13	14	15	16	
	21	22	23	24	25	◑	27	12:51	34	2422923		17	18	19	20	21	22	23	
SEPTEMBER 1921	28	29	30	31	1	●	3	3:33	35	2422930		24	25	26	27	28	29	30	
	4	5	6	7	8	◐	10	3:29	36	2422937	ELUL 5681	1	2	3	4	5	6	7	Fri $15^h10^m16^p$
	11	12	13	14	15	16	○	7:20	37	2422944		8	9	10	11	12	13	14	
	18	19	20	21	22	23[d]	◑	21:17	38	2422951		15	16	17	18	19	20	21	
	25	26	27	28	29	30	●	12:26	39	2422958		22	23	24	25	26	27	28	
OCTOBER 1921	2	3	4	5	6	7	◐	20:11	40	2422965	TISHRI 5682	29	1[a]	2[a]	3	4	5	6	Sun $3^h54^m17^p$
	9	10	11	12	13	14	15		41	2422972		7	8	9	10[b]	11	12	13	
	○	17	18	19	20	21	22	22:59	42	2422979		14	15[c]	16	17	18	19	20	
	23	◑	25	26	27	28	29	4:31	43	2422986		21	22	23	24	25	26	27	
NOVEMBER 1921	●	31	1	2	3	4	5	23:38	44	2422993	HESHVAN 5682	28	29	30	1	2	3	4	Mon $16^h39^m0^p$
	6	◐	8	9	10	11	12	15:53	45	2423000		5	6	7	8	9	10	11	
	13	14	○	16	17	18	19	13:39	46	2423007		12	13	14	15	16	17	18	
	20	21	◑	23	24	25	26	11:41	47	2423014		19	20	21	22	23	24	25	
DECEMBER 1921	27	28	●	30	1	2	3	13:25	48	2423021	KISLEV 5682	26	27	28	29	30	1	2	Wed $5^h23^m1^p$
	4	5	6	◐	8	9	10	13:19	49	2423028		3	4[d]	5	6	7	8	9	
	11	12	13	14	○	16	17	2:50	50	2423035		10	11	12	13	14	15	16	
	18	19	20	◑	22[e]	23	24	19:54	51	2423042		17	18	19	20	21	22	23	
	25	26	27	28	●	30	31	5:39	52	2423049		24	25[e]	26[e]	27[e]	28[e]	29[e]	30[e]	

ISO WEEK	CHINESE Gēng-Shēn/Xīn-Yǒu	Sun	Mon	Tue	Wed	Thu	Fri	Sat	Solar Term	COPTIC 1637/1638	Sun	Mon	Tue	Wed	Thu	Fri	Sat	ETHIOPIC 1913/1914
53	MONTH 11 Gēng-Shēn	17	18	19	20	21	22	23*		KOIAK 1637	17	18	19	20	21	22	23	TĀKHŚĀŚ 1913
1		24	25	26	27	*28*	29	30	Xiǎo hán		24	25	26	27	28	29[c]	30	
2	MONTH 12 Gēng-Shēn	1	2	3	4	5	6	7		TÔBE 1637	1	2	3	4	5	6[d]	7	ṬER 1913
3		8	9	10	11	**12**	13	14	**Dà hán**		8	9	10	11[e]	12	13	14	
4		15	16	17	18	19	20	21			15	16	17	18	19	20	21	
5		22	23	24	25	26	*27*	28	Lì chūn		22	23	24	25	26	27	28	
6	MONTH 1 Xīn-Yǒu	29	30	1[a]	2	3	4	5		MESHIR 1637	29	30	1	2	3	4	5	YAKĀTIT 1913
7		6	7	8	9	10	11	**12**	**Yǔ shuǐ**		6	7	8	9	10	11	12	
8		13	14	15[b]	16	17	18	19			13	14	15	16	17	18	19	
9		20	21	22	23*	24	25	26			20	21	22	23	24	25	26	
10	MONTH 2 Xīn-Yǒu	*27*	28	29	30	1	2	3	Jīng zhé	PAREMOTEP 1637	27	28	29	30	1	2	3	MAGĀBIT 1913
11		4	5	6	7	8	9	10			4	5	6	7	8	9	10	
12		11	**12**	13	14	15	16	17	**Chūn fēn**		11	12	13	14	15	16	17	
13		18	19	20	21	22	23	24			18	19	20	21	22	23	24	
14	MONTH 3 Xīn-Yǒu	25	26	*27*[c]	28	29	1	2	Qīng míng	PARMOUTE 1637	25	26	27	28	29	30	1	MIYĀZYĀ 1913
15		3	4	5	6	7	8	9			2	3	4	5	6	7	8	
16		10	11	12	**13**	14	15	16	**Gǔ yǔ**		9	10	11	12	13	14	15	
17		17	18	19	20	21	22	23			16	17	18	19	20	21	22	
18		24*	25	26	27	28	*29*	30	Lì xià		23[f]	24	25	26	27	28	29[g]	
19	MONTH 4 Xīn-Yǒu	1	2	3	4	5	6	7		PASHONS 1637	30	1	2	3	4	5	6	GENBOT 1913
20		8	9	10	11	12	13	**14**	**Xiǎo mǎn**		7	8	9	10	11	12	13	
21		15	16	17	18	19	20	21			14	15	16	17	18	19	20	
22		22	23	24	25	26	27	28			21	22	23	24	25	26	27	
23	MONTH 5 Xīn-Yǒu	29	*1*	2	3	4	5[d]	6	Máng zhòng	PAÔNE 1637	28	29	30	1	2	3	4	SANĒ 1913
24		7	8	9	10	11	12	13			5	6	7	8	9	10	11	
25		14	15	16	**17**	18	19	20	**Xià zhì**		12	13	14	15	16	17	18	
26		21	22	23	24	25*	26	27			19	20	21	22	23	24	25	
27	MONTH 6 Xīn-Yǒu	28	29	1	2	3	*4*	5	Xiǎo shǔ	EPÊP 1637	26	27	28	29	30	1	2	ḤAMLĒ 1913
28		6	7	8	9	10	11	12			3	4	5	6	7	8	9	
29		13	14	15	16	17	18	**19**	**Dà shǔ**		10	11	12	13	14	15	16	
30		20	21	22	23	24	25	26			17	18	19	20	21	22	23	
31	MONTH 7 Xīn-Yǒu	27	28	29	30	1	2	3			24	25	26	27	28	29	30	
32		4	*5*	6	7[e]	8	9	10	Lì qiū	MESORÊ 1637	1	2	3	4	5	6	7	NAḤASĒ 1913
33		11	12	13	14	15[f]	16	17			8	9	10	11	12	13[h]	14	
34		18	19	20	**21**	22	23	24	**Chǔ shǔ**		15	16	17	18	19	20	21	
35	MONTH 8 Xīn-Yǒu	25	26*	27	28	29	1	2			22	23	24	25	26	27	28	
36		3	4	5	6	*7*	8	9	Bái lù	EPAG. 1637	29	30	1	2	3	4	5	PĀG. 1913
37		10	11	12	13	14	15[g]	16		THOOUT 1638	1[a]	2	3	4	5	6	7	MASKARAM 1914
38		17	18	19	20	21	**22**	23	**Qiū fēn**		8	9	10	11	12	13	14	
39	MONTH 9 Xīn-Yǒu	24	25	26	27	28	29	1			15	16	17[b]	18	19	20	21	
40		2	3	4	5	6	7	8			22	23	24	25	26	27	28	
41		*9*[h]	10	11	12	13	14	15	Hán lù	PAOPE 1638	29	30	1	2	3	4	5	TEQEMT 1914
42		16	17	18	19	20	21	22			6	7	8	9	10	11	12	
43		23	**24**	25	26	27	28*	29	**Shuāng jiàng**		13	14	15	16	17	18	19	
44	MONTH 10 Xīn-Yǒu	30	1	2	3	4	5	6			20	21	22	23	24	25	26	
45		7	8	9	10	11	12	13	Lì dōng	ATHÔR 1638	27	28	29	30	1	2	3	ḪEDĀR 1914
46		14	15	16	17	18	19	20			4	5	6	7	8	9	10	
47		21	22	23	**24**	25	26	27	**Xiǎo xuě**		11	12	13	14	15	16	17	
48	MONTH 11 Xīn-Yǒu	28	29	1	2	3	4	5			18	19	20	21	22	23	24	
49		6	7	8	*9*	10	11	12	Dà xuě	KOIAK 1638	25	26	27	28	29	30	1	TĀKHŚĀŚ 1914
50		13	14	15	16	17	18	19			2	3	4	5	6	7	8	
51		20	21	22	23	**24**[i]	25	26	**Dōng zhì**		9	10	11	12	13	14	15	
52		27	28	29*	30	1	2	3			16	17	18	19	20	21	22	

Gregorian:

[a]New Year
[b]Spring (3:51)
[c]Summer (23:36)
[d]Autumn (14:20)
[e]Winter (9:07)
● New moon
◐ First quarter moon
○ Full moon
◑ Last quarter moon

Hebrew:

‡Leap year
[a]New Year
[b]Yom Kippur
[c]Sukkot
[d]Winter starts
[e]Ḥanukkah
[f]Purim
[g]Passover
[h]Shavuot
[i]Fast of Av

Chinese:

[a]New Year (4619, Fowl)
[b]Lantern Festival
[c]Qīngmíng
[d]Dragon Festival
[e]Qǐqiǎo
[f]Hungry Ghosts
[g]Mid-Autumn Festival
[h]Double-Ninth Festival
[i]Dōngzhì
*Start of 60-name cycle

Coptic/Ethiopic:

[a]New Year
[b]Building of the Cross
[c]Christmas
[d]Jesus's Circumcision
[e]Epiphany
[f]Easter
[g]Mary's Announcement
[h]Jesus's Transfiguration

PERSIAN (ASTRONOMICAL) 1299/1300‡

Month	Sun	Mon	Tue	Wed	Thu	Fri	Sat
DEY 1299	5	6	7	8	9	10	11
	12	13	14	15	16	17	18
	19	20	21	22	23	24	25
	26	27	28	29	30	1	2
BAHMAN 1299	3	4	5	6	7	8	9
	10	11	12	13	14	15	16
	17	18	19	20	21	22	23
	24	25	26	27	28	29	30
ESFAND 1299	1	2	3	4	5	6	7
	8	9	10	11	12	13	14
	15	16	17	18	19	20	21
	22	23	24	25	26	27	28
	29	1[a]	2	3	4	5	6
FARVARDĪN 1300	7	8	9	10	11	12	13[b]
	14	15	16	17	18	19	20
	21	22	23	24	25	26	27
	28	29	30	31	1	2	3
ORDĪBEHEŠT 1300	4	5	6	7	8	9	10
	11	12	13	14	15	16	17
	18	19	20	21	22	23	24
	25	26	27	28	29	30	31
	1	2	3	4	5	6	7
XORDĀD 1300	8	9	10	11	12	13	14
	15	16	17	18	19	20	21
	22	23	24	25	26	27	28
	29	30	31	1	2	3	4
TĪR 1300	5	6	7	8	9	10	11
	12	13	14	15	16	17	18
	19	20	21	22	23	24	25
	26	27	28	29	30	31	1
	2	3	4	5	6	7	8
MORDĀD 1300	9	10	11	12	13	14	15
	16	17	18	19	20	21	22
	23	24	25	26	27	28	29
	30	31	1	2	3	4	5
	6	7	8	9	10	11	12
SHAHRĪVAR 1300	13	14	15	16	17	18	19
	20	21	22	23	24	25	26
	27	28	29	30	31	1	2
	3	4	5	6	7	8	9
MEHR 1300	10	11	12	13	14	15	16
	17	18	19	20	21	22	23
	24	25	26	27	28	29	30
	1	2	3	4	5	6	7
ĀBĀN 1300	8	9	10	11	12	13	14
	15	16	17	18	19	20	21
	22	23	24	25	26	27	28
	29	30	1	2	3	4	5
ĀZAR 1300	6	7	8	9	10	11	12
	13	14	15	16	17	18	19
	20	21	22	23	24	25	26
	27	28	29	30	1	2	3
DEY 1300	4	5	6	7	8	9	10

HINDU LUNAR 1977‡/1978

Month	Sun	Mon	Tue	Wed	Thu	Fri	Sat
MĀRGAŚĪRA 1977	16	17	18	19	**20**	22	23
	24	25	26	27	28	29	29
	30	1	2	3	4	5	6
PAUSHA 1977	7	8	9	10	11	12	13
	14	16	17	18	19	20	21
	22	23	24	25	26	27	28
	29	30	1	1	2	3	4
MĀGHA 1977	5	6	**7**	9	10	11	12
	13	14	15	16	17	18	19
	20	21	22	23	24	25	26
	27	28[h]	29	30	1	2	3
PHĀLGUNA 1977	4	5	6	7	8	9	10
	11	**12**	14	15[i]	16	17	18
	19	20	21	22	23	24	24
	25	26	27	28	29	30	1[a]
CHAITRA 1978	2	3	4	5	**6**	8	9[b]
	10	11	12	13	14	15	16
	17	18	19	20	21	22	23
	24	25	26	27	28	29	30
	1	2	3	4	5	6	7
VAIŚĀKHA 1978	8	**9**	11	12	13	14	15
	16	17	18	19	20	20	21
	22	23	24	25	26	27	28
	29	30	1	**2**	4	5	6
JYAISHTHA 1978	7	8	9	10	11	12	13
	14	15	16	17	18	19	20
	21	22	23	24	25	26	27
	28	29	30	1	2	3	4
ĀSHĀDHA 1978	**5**	7	8	9	10	11	12
	13	14	15	16	16	17	18
	19	20	21	22	23	24	25
	26	27	**28**	30	1	2	3
ŚRĀVAṆA 1978	4	5	6	7	8	9	10
	11	12	13	14	15	16	17
	18	19	20	21	22	23[c]	24
	25	26	27	28	29	30	**1**
BHĀDRAPADA 1978	3	4[d]	5	6	7	8	9
	10	11	12	12	13	14	15
	16	17	18	19	20	21	22
	23	**24**	26	27	28	29	30
	1	2	3	4	5	6	7
ĀŚVINA 1978	8[e]	9[e]	10[e]	11	12	13	14
	15	16	17	18	19	20	21
	22	23	24	25	26	27	**28**
	30	1[f]	2	3	4	5	6
KĀRTTIKA 1978	7	7	8	9	10	11	12
	13	14	15	16	17	18	19
	20	21	**22**	24	25	26	27
	28	29	30	1	2	3	4
MĀRGAŚĪRA 1978	5	6	7	8	9	9	10
	11[g]	12	13	14	**15**	17	18
	19	20	21	22	23	24	25
	26	27	28	29	30	1	2

HINDU SOLAR 1842‡/1843

Month	Sun	Mon	Tue	Wed	Thu	Fri	Sat
PAUSHA 1842	12	13	14	15	16	17	18
	19	20	21	22	23	24	25
	26	27	28	29	1[b]	2	3
MĀGHA 1842	4	5	6	7	8	9	10
	11	12	13	14	15	16	17
	18	19	20	21	22	23	24
	25	26	27	28	29	1	2
PHĀLGUNA 1842	3	4	5	6	7	8	9
	10	11	12	13	14	15	16
	17	18	19	20	21	22	23
	24	25	26	27	28	29	30
	1	2	3	4	5	6	7
CHAITRA 1842	8	9	10	11	12	13	14
	15	16	17	18	19	20	21
	22	23	24	25	26	27	28
	29	30	31	1[a]	2	3	4
VAIŚĀKHA 1843	5	6	7	8	9	10	11
	12	13	14	15	16	17	18
	19	20	21	22	23	24	25
	26	27	28	29	30	1	2
JYAISHTHA 1843	3	4	5	6	7	8	9
	10	11	12	13	14	15	16
	17	18	19	20	21	22	23
	24	25	26	27	28	29	30
	31	32	1	2	3	4	5
ĀSHĀDHA 1843	6	7	8	9	10	11	12
	13	14	15	16	17	18	19
	20	21	22	23	24	25	26
	27	28	29	30	31	32	1
ŚRĀVAṆA 1843	2	3	4	5	6	7	8
	9	10	11	12	13	14	15
	16	17	18	19	20	21	22
	23	24	25	26	27	28	29
	30	31	1	2	3	4	5
BHĀDRAPADA 1843	6	7	8	9	10	11	12
	13	14	15	16	17	18	19
	20	21	22	23	24	25	26
	27	28	29	30	31	1	2
ĀŚVINA 1843	3	4	5	6	7	8	9
	10	11	12	13	14	15	16
	17	18	19	20	21	22	23
	24	25	26	27	28	29	30
	1	2	3	4	5	6	7
KĀRTTIKA 1843	8	9	10	11	12	13	14
	15	16	17	18	19	20	21
	22	23	24	25	26	27	28
	29	30	1	2	3	4	5
MĀRGAŚĪRA 1843	6	7	8	9	10	11	12
	13	14	15	16	17	18	19
	20	21	22	23	24	25	26
	27	28	29	30	1	2	3
PAUSHA 1843	4	5	6	7	8	9	10
	11	12	13	14	15	16	17

ISLAMIC (ASTRONOMICAL) 1339‡/1340

Month	Sun	Mon	Tue	Wed	Thu	Fri	Sat
RABĪ' II 1339	15	16	17	18	19	20	21
	22	23	24	25	26	27	28
	29	30	1	2	3	4	5
JUMĀDĀ I 1339	6	7	8	9	10	11	12
	13	14	15	16	17	18	19
	20	21	22	23	24	25	26
	27	28	29	1	2	3	4
JUMĀDĀ II 1339	5	6	7	8	9	10	11
	12	13	14	15	16	17	18
	19	20	21	22	23	24	25
	26	27	28	29	30	1	2
RAJAB 1339	3	4	5	6	7	8	9
	10	11	12	13	14	15	16
	17	18	19	20	21	22	23
	24	25	26	27[d]	28	29	30
	1	2	3	4	5	6	7
SHA'BĀN 1339	8	9	10	11	12	13	14
	15	16	17	18	19	20	21
	22	23	24	25	26	27	28
	29	1[e]	2	3	4	5	6
RAMAḌĀN 1339	7	8	9	10	11	12	13
	14	15	16	17	18	19	20
	21	22	23	24	25	26	27
	28	29	30	1[f]	2	3	4
SHAWWĀL 1339	5	6	7	8	9	10	11
	12	13	14	15	16	17	18
	19	20	21	22	23	24	25
	26	27	28	29	1	2	3
DHU AL-QA'DA 1339	4	5	6	7	8	9	10
	11	12	13	14	15	16	17
	18	19	20	21	22	23	24
	25	26	27	28	29	30	1
DHU AL-ḤIJJA 1339	2	3	4	5	6	7	8
	9	10[g]	11	12	13	14	15
	16	17	18	19	20	21	22
	23	24	25	26	27	28	29
	1[a]	2	3	4	5	6	7
MUḤARRAM 1340	8	9	10[b]	11	12	13	14
	15	16	17	18	19	20	21
	22	23	24	25	26	27	28
	29	1	2	3	4	5	6
ṢAFAR 1340	7	8	9	10	11	12	13
	14	15	16	17	18	19	20
	21	22	23	24	25	26	27
	28	29	1	2	3	4	5
RABĪ' I 1340	6	7	8	9	10	11	12[c]
	13	14	15	16	17	18	19
	20	21	22	23	24	25	26
	27	28	29	30	1	2	3
RABĪ' II 1340	4	5	6	7	8	9	10
	11	12	13	14	15	16	17
	18	19	20	21	22	23	24
	25	26	27	28	29	30	1

GREGORIAN 1921

Julian (Sun)	Sun	Mon	Tue	Wed	Thu	Fri	Sat	Month
Dec 13	26	27	28	29	30	31	1	
	2	3	4	5	6	7[a]	8	JANUARY 1921
Dec 27	9	10	11	12	13	14[b]	15	
	16	17	18	19	20	21	22	
Jan 10	23	24	25	26	27	28	29	
	30	31	1	2	3	4	5	
Jan 24	6	7	8	9[c]	10	11	12	FEBRUARY 1921
	13	14	15	16	17	18	19	
Feb 7	20	21	22	23	24	25	26	
	27	28	1	2	3	4	5	
Feb 21	6	7	8	9	10	11	12	MARCH 1921
	13	14	15	16	17	18	19	
Mar 7	20[d]	21	22	23	24	25	26	
	27[e]	28	29	30	31	1	2	
Mar 21	3	4	5	6	7	8	9	APRIL 1921
	10	11	12	13	14	15	16	
Apr 4	17	18	19	20	21	22	23	
	24	25	26	27	28	29	30	
Apr 18	1[f]	2	3	4	5	6	7	
	8	9	10	11	12	13	14	MAY 1921
May 2	15	16	17	18	19	20	21	
	22	23	24	25	26	27	28	
May 16	29	30	31	1	2	3	4	
	5	6	7	8	9	10	11	JUNE 1921
May 30	12	13	14	15	16	17	18	
	19	20	21	22	23	24	25	
Jun 13	26	27	28	29	30	1	2	
	3	4	5	6	7	8	9	
Jun 27	10	11	12	13	14	15	16	JULY 1921
	17	18	19	20	21	22	23	
Jul 11	24	25	26	27	28	29	30	
	31	1	2	3	4	5	6	
Jul 25	7	8	9	10	11	12	13	AUGUST 1921
	14	15	16	17	18	19	20	
Aug 8	21	22	23	24	25	26	27	
	28	29	30	31	1	2	3	
Aug 22	4	5	6	7	8	9	10	SEPTEMBER 1921
	11	12	13	14	15	16	17	
Sep 5	18	19	20	21	22	23	24	
	25	26	27	28	29	30	1	
Sep 19	2	3	4	5	6	7	8	
	9	10	11	12	13	14	15	OCTOBER 1921
Oct 3	16	17	18	19	20	21	22	
	23	24	25	26	27	28	29	
Oct 17	30	31	1	2	3	4	5	
	6	7	8	9	10	11	12	NOVEMBER 1921
Oct 31	13	14	15	16	17	18	19	
	20	21	22	23	24	25	26	
Nov 14	27[g]	28	29	30	1	2	3	
	4	5	6	7	8	9	10	DECEMBER 1921
Nov 28	11	12	13	14	15	16	17	
	18	19	20	21	22	23	24	
Dec 12	25[h]	26	27	28	29	30	31	

Persian: ‡Leap year; [a]New Year; [b]Sizdeh Bedar

Hindu lunar: ‡Leap year; [a]New Year (Durmati); [b]Birthday of Rāma; [c]Birthday of Krishna; [d]Ganēśa Chaturthī; [e]Dashara; [f]Diwali; [g]Birthday of Vishnu; [h]Night of Śiva; [i]Holi

Hindu solar: ‡Leap year; [a]New Year (Śrīmukha); [b]Pongal

Islamic: ‡Leap year; [a]New Year; [b]'Ashūrā'; [c]Prophet's Birthday; [d]Ascent of the Prophet; [e]Start of Ramaḍān; [f]'Īd al-Fiṭr; [g]'Īd al-'Aḍḥā

Gregorian: [a]Orthodox Christmas; [b]Julian New Year; [c]Ash Wednesday; [d]Feast of Orthodoxy; [e]Easter; [f]Orthodox Easter; [g]Advent; [h]Christmas

1922

GREGORIAN 1922								Lunar Phases	ISO WEEK	JULIAN DAY	HEBREW 5682/5683								Molad	CHINESE Xīn-Yǒu/Rén-Xū‡								Solar Term	COPTIC 1638/1639‡								ETHIOPIC 1914/1915‡
	Sun	Mon	Tue	Wed	Thu	Fri	Sat		(Mon)	(Sun noon)		Sun	Mon	Tue	Wed	Thu	Fri	Sat			Sun	Mon	Tue	Wed	Thu	Fri	Sat			Sun	Mon	Tue	Wed	Thu	Fri	Sat	
JANUARY 1922	1[a]	2	3	4	5	◐	7	10:23	1	2423056	TEVETH 5682	1[e]	2[e]	3	4	5	6	7	Thu 18h7m2p	MONTH 12 Xīn-Yǒu	4	5	6	7	8	9	10	Xiǎo hán	KOIAK 1638	23	24	25	26	27	28	29[c]	TĀKHŚĀŚ 1914
	8	9	10	11	12	○	14	14:36	2	2423063		8	9	10	11	12	13	14			11	12	13	14	15	16	17		TŌBE 1638	30	1	2	3	4	5	6[d]	ṬER 1914
	15	16	17	18	19	◑	21	6:00	3	2423070		15	16	17	18	19	20	21			18	19	20	21	22	23	**24**	Dà hán		7	8	9	10	11[e]	12	13	
	22	23	24	25	26	●	28	23:48	4	2423077		22	23	24	25	26	27	28			25	26	27	28	29	30	1[a]			14	15	16	17	18	19	20	
FEBRUARY 1922	29	30	31	1	2	3	4		5	2423084	SHEVAT 5682	29	1	2	3	4	5	6	Sat 6h51m3p	MONTH 1 Rén-Xū	2	3	4	5	6	7	8	Lì chūn		21	22	23	24	25	26	27	
	◐	6	7	8	9	10	11	4:52	6	2423091		7	8	9	10	11	12	13			9	10	11	12	13	14	15[b]		MESHIR 1638	28	29	30	1	2	3	4	YAKĀTIT 1914
	○	13	14	15	16	17	◑	1:17 18:18	7	2423098		14	15	16	17	18	19	20			16	17	18	19	20	21	22	Yǔ shuǐ		5	6	7	8	9	10	11	
	19	20	21	22	23	24	25		8	2423105		21	22	23	24	25	26	27			**23**	24	25	26	27	28	29*			12	13	14	15	16	17	18	
MARCH 1922	●	27	28	1	2	3	4	18:47	9	2423112	ADAR 5682	28	29	30	1	2	3	4	Sun 19h35m4p	MONTH 2 Rén-Xū	30	1	2	3	4	5	6			19	20	21	22	23	24	25	
	5	◐	7	8	9	10	11	19:21	10	2423119		5	6	7	8	9	10	11			7	8	9	10	11	12	13	Jīng zhé	PAREMOTEP 1638	26	27	28	29	30	1	2	MAGĀBIT 1914
	12	○	14	15	16	17	18	11:14	11	2423126		12	13	14[f]	15	16	17	18			14	15	16	17	18	19	20			3	4	5	6	7	8	9	
	19	◑	21[b]	22	23	24	25	8:43	12	2423133		19	20	21	22	23	24	25			21	22	**23**	24	25	26	27	Chūn fēn		10	11	12	13	14	15	16	
APRIL 1922	26	27	●	29	30	31	1	13:03	13	2423140	NISAN 5682	26	27	28	29	1	2	3	Tue 8h19m5p	MONTH 3 Rén-Xū	28	29	1	2	3	4	5			17	18	19	20	21	22	23	
	2	3	4	◐	6	7	8	5:45	14	2423147		4	5	6	7	8	9	10			6	7	8	9[c]	10	11	12	Qīng míng		24	25	26	27	28	29	30	
	9	10	○	12	13	14	15	20:43	15	2423154		11	12	13	14	15[g]	16	17			13	14	15	16	17	18	19		PARMOUTE 1638	1	2	3	4	5	6	7	MIYĀZYĀ 1914
	16	17	18	◑	20	21	22	0:53	16	2423161		18	19	20	21	22	23	24			20	21	22	23	24	**25**	26	Gǔ yǔ		8[f]	9	10	11	12	13	14	
	23	24	25	26	●	28	29	5:03	17	2423168	IYYAR 5682	25	26	27	28	29	30	1	Wed 21h3m6p	MONTH 4 Rén-Xū	27	28	29	30*	1	2	3			15	16	17	18	19	20	21	
MAY 1922	30	1	2	3	◐	5	6	12:55	18	2423175		2	3	4	5	6	7	8			4	5	6	7	8	9	*10*	Lì xià		22	23	24	25	26	27	28	
	7	8	9	10	○	12	13	6:06	19	2423182		9	10	11	12	13	14	15			11	12	13	14	15	16	17		PASHONS 1638	29[g]	30	1	2	3	4	5	GENBOT 1914
	14	15	16	17	◑	19	20	18:17	20	2423189		16	17	18	19	20	21	22			18	19	20	21	22	23	24			6	7	8	9	10	11	12	
	21	22	23	24	25	●	27	18:04	21	2423196		23	24	25	26	27	28	29		MONTH 5 Rén-Xū	25	**26**	27	28	29	30	1	Xiǎo mǎn		13	14	15	16	17	18	19	
JUNE 1922	28	29	30	31	1	◐	3	18:10	22	2423203	SIVAN 5682	1	2	3	4	5	6[h]	7	Fri 9h47m7p		2	3	4	5[d]	6	7	8			20	21	22	23	24	25	26	
	4	5	6	7	8	○	10	15:58	23	2423210		8	9	10	11	12	13	14			9	10	*11*	12	13	14	15	Máng zhòng	PAŌNE 1638	27	28	29	30	1	2	3	SANĒ 1514
	11	12	13	14	15	16	◑	12:03	24	2423217		15	16	17	18	19	20	21			16	17	18	19	20	21	22			4	5	6	7	8	9	10	
	18	19	20	21	22[c]	23	24		25	2423224		22	23	24	25	26	27	28			23	24	25	26	**27**	28	29	Xià zhì		11	12	13	14	15	16	17	
JULY 1922	●	26	27	28	29	30	◐	4:19 22:52	26	2423231	TAMMUZ 5682	29	30	1	2	3	4	5	Sat 22h31m8p	LEAP MONTH 5 Rén-Xū	1*	2	3	4	5	6	7			18	19	20	21	22	23	24	
	2	3	4	5	6	7	8		27	2423238		6	7	8	9	10	11	12			8	9	10	11	12	13	*14*	Xiǎo shǔ	EPĒP 1638	25	26	27	28	29	30	1	ḤAMLĒ 1914
	○	10	11	12	13	14	15	3:07	28	2423245		13	14	15	16	17	18	19			15	16	17	18	19	20	21			2	3	4	5	6	7	8	
	16	◑	18	19	20	21	22	5:11	29	2423252		20	21	22	23	24	25	26			22	23	24	25	26	27	28			9	10	11	12	13	14	15	
	23	●	25	26	27	28	29	12:47	30	2423259	AV 5682	27	28	29	1	2	3	4	Mon 11h15m9p	MONTH 6 Rén-Xū	29	*1*	2	3	4	5	6	Dà shǔ		16	17	18	19	20	21	22	
AUGUST 1922	30	◐	1	2	3	4	5	4:21	31	2423266		5	6	7	8	9[i]	10	11			7	8	9	10	11	12	13			23	24	25	26	27	28	29	
	6	○	8	9	10	11	12	16:19	32	2423273		12	13	14	15	16	17	18			14	15	*16*	17	18	19	20	Lì qiū	MESORĒ 1638	30	1	2	3	4	5	6	NAHASĒ 1914
	13	14	◑	16	17	18	19	20:45	33	2423280		19	20	21	22	23	24	25			21	22	23	24	25	26	27			7	8	9	10	11	12	13[h]	
	20	21	●	23	24	25	26	20:34	34	2423287	ELUL 5682	26	27	28	29	30	1	2	Tue 23h59m10p	MONTH 7 Rén-Xū	28	29	30	1	2*	3	4	Chǔ shǔ		14	15	16	17	18	19	20	
SEPTEMBER 1922	27	28	◐	30	31	1	2	11:55	35	2423294		3	4	5	6	7	8	9			5	6	7[e]	8	9	10	11			21	22	23	24	25	26	27	
	3	4	5	○	7	8	9	7:47	36	2423301		10	11	12	13	14	15	16			12	13	14	15[f]	16	*17*	18	Bái lù	EPAG. 1638	28	29	30	1	2	3	4	PĀG. 1914
	10	11	12	13	◑	15	16	10:20	37	2423308		17	18	19	20	21	22	23			19	20	21	22	23	24	25		THOOUT 1639	5	1[a]	2	3	4	5	6	MASKARAM 1915
	17	18	19	20	●	22	23[d]	4:38	38	2423315	TISHRI 5683	24	25	26	27	28	29	1[a]	Thu 12h43m11p	MONTH 8 Rén-Xū	26	27	28	29	1	2	3			7	8	9	10	11	12	13	
	24	25	26	◐	28	29	30	22:40	39	2423322		2[a]	3	4	5	6	7	8			**4**	5	6	7	8	9	10	Qiū fēn		14	15	16	17[b]	18	19	20	
OCTOBER 1922	1	2	3	4	5	○	7	0:58	40	2423329		9	10[b]	11	12	13	14	15[c]			11	12	13	14	15[g]	16	17			21	22	23	24	25	26	27	
	8	9	10	11	12	◑	14	21:55	41	2423336		16	17	18	19	20	21	22			18	*19*	20	21	22	23	24	Hán lù	PAOPE 1639	28	29	30	1	2	3	4	ṬEQEMT 1915
	15	16	17	18	19	●	21	13:40	42	2423343		23	24	25	26	27	28	29		MONTH 9 Rén-Xū	25	26	27	28	29	1	2			5	6	7	8	9	10	11	
	22	23	24	25	26	◐	28	13:26	43	2423350	HESHVAN 5683	30	1	2	3	4	5	6	Sat 1h27m12p		3	4*	**5**	6	7	8	9[h]	Shuāng jiàng		12	13	14	15	16	17	18	
NOVEMBER 1922	29	30	31	1	2	3	○	18:36	44	2423357		7	8	9	10	11	12	13			10	11	12	13	14	15	16			19	20	21	22	23	24	25	
	5	6	7	8	9	10	11		45	2423364		14	15	16	17	18	19	20			17	18	19	*20*	21	22	23	Lì dōng	ATHŌR 1639	26	27	28	29	30	1	2	HEDĀR 1915
	◑	13	14	15	16	17	18	7:52	46	2423371		21	22	23	24	25	26	27			24	25	26	27	28	29	30			3	4	5	6	7	8	9	
	●	20	21	22	23	24	25	0:06	47	2423378	KISLEV 5683	28	29	1	2	3	4	5	Sun 14h11m13p	MONTH 10 Rén-Xū	1	2	3	4	**5**	6	7	Xiǎo xuě		10	11	12	13	14	15	16	
DECEMBER 1922	◐	27	28	29	30	1	2	8:15	48	2423385		6	7	8	9	10	11	12			8	9	10	11	12	13	14			17	18	19	20	21	22	23	
	3	○	5	6	7	8	9	11:23	49	2423392		13	14	15[d]	16	17	18	19			15	16	17	18	19	*20*	21	Dà xuě		24	25	26	27	28	29	30	
	10	◑	12	13	14	15	16	16:40	50	2423399		20	21	22	23	24	25[e]	26[e]			22	23	24	25	26	27	28		KOIAK 1639	1	2	3	4	5	6	7	TĀKHŚĀŚ 1915
	17	●	19	20	21	22[e]	23	12:20	51	2423406	TEVETH 5683	27[e]	28[e]	29[e]	1[e]	2[e]	3[e]	4	Tue 2h55m14p	MONTH 11 Rén-Xū	29	1	2	3	4	5[i]*	6	Dōng zhì		8	9	10	11	12	13	14	
	24	25	◐	27	28	29	30	5:53	52	2423413		5	6	7	8	9	10	11			7	8	9	10	11	12	13			15	16	17	18	19	20	21	
	31	1	2	○	4	5	6	2:33	1	2423420		12	13	14	15	16	17	18			14	15	16	17	18	19	*20*	Xiǎo hán		22	23	24	25	26	27	28	

[a]New Year
[b]Spring (9:48)
[c]Summer (5:27)
[d]Autumn (20:10)
[e]Winter (14:57)
● New moon
◐ First quarter moon
○ Full moon
◑ Last quarter moon

[a]New Year
[b]Yom Kippur
[c]Sukkot
[d]Winter starts
[e]Ḥanukkah
[f]Purim
[g]Passover
[h]Shavuot
[i]Fast of Av

‡Leap year
[a]New Year (4620, Dog)
[b]Lantern Festival
[c]Qīngmíng
[d]Dragon Festival
[e]Qīqiǎo
[f]Hungry Ghosts
[g]Mid-Autumn Festival
[h]Double-Ninth Festival
[i]Dōngzhì
*Start of 60-name cycle

‡Leap year
[a]New Year
[b]Building of the Cross
[c]Christmas
[d]Jesus's Circumcision
[e]Epiphany
[f]Easter
[g]Mary's Announcement
[h]Jesus's Transfiguration

PERSIAN (ASTRONOMICAL) 1300‡/1301

Month	Sun	Mon	Tue	Wed	Thu	Fri	Sat
	11	12	13	14	15	16	17
DEY 1300	18	19	20	21	22	23	24
	25	26	27	28	29	30	1
	2	3	4	5	6	7	8
BAHMAN 1300	9	10	11	12	13	14	15
	16	17	18	19	20	21	22
	23	24	25	26	27	28	29
	30	1	2	3	4	5	6
ESFAND 1300	7	8	9	10	11	12	13
	14	15	16	17	18	19	20
	21	22	23	24	25	26	27
	28	29	30	1[a]	2	3	4
FARVARDĪN 1301	5	6	7	8	9	10	11
	12	13[b]	14	15	16	17	18
	19	20	21	22	23	24	25
	26	27	28	29	30	31	1
ORDĪBEHEŠT 1301	2	3	4	5	6	7	8
	9	10	11	12	13	14	15
	16	17	18	19	20	21	22
	23	24	25	26	27	28	29
	30	31	1	2	3	4	5
XORDĀD 1301	6	7	8	9	10	11	12
	13	14	15	16	17	18	19
	20	21	22	23	24	25	26
	27	28	29	30	31	1	2
	3	4	5	6	7	8	9
TĪR 1301	10	11	12	13	14	15	16
	17	18	19	20	21	22	23
	24	25	26	27	28	29	30
	31	1	2	3	4	5	6
MORDĀD 1301	7	8	9	10	11	12	13
	14	15	16	17	18	19	20
	21	22	23	24	25	26	27
	28	29	30	31	1	2	3
SHAHRĪVAR 1301	4	5	6	7	8	9	10
	11	12	13	14	15	16	17
	18	19	20	21	22	23	24
	25	26	27	28	29	30	31
MEHR 1301	1	2	3	4	5	6	7
	8	9	10	11	12	13	14
	15	16	17	18	19	20	21
	22	23	24	25	26	27	28
	29	30	1	2	3	4	5
ĀBĀN 1301	6	7	8	9	10	11	12
	13	14	15	16	17	18	19
	20	21	22	23	24	25	26
	27	28	29	30	1	2	3
ĀZAR 1301	4	5	6	7	8	9	10
	11	12	13	14	15	16	17
	18	19	20	21	22	23	24
	25	26	27	28	29	30	1
DEY 1301	2	3	4	5	6	7	8
	9	10	11	12	13	14	15

‡Leap year
[a]New Year
[b]Sizdeh Bedar

HINDU LUNAR 1978/1979

Month	Sun	Mon	Tue	Wed	Thu	Fri	Sat
	3	4	5	6	7	8	9
PAUSHA 1978	10	11	12	13	14	15	16
	17	18	19	**20**	22	23	24
	25	26	27	28	29	30	1
	2	2	3	4	5	6	7
MĀGHA 1978	8	9	10	11	12	13	14
	15	17	18	19	20	21	22
	23	24	25	26	27	28[h]	29
	30	1	2	3	4	4	5
PHĀLGUNA 1978	6	7	**8**	10	11	12	13
	14	15[i]	16	17	18	19	20
	21	22	23	24	25	26	27
	28	29	30	1[a]	2	3	4
	5	6	7	8	9[b]	10	11
CHAITRA 1979	12	**13**	15	16	17	18	19
	20	21	22	23	24	25	26
	27	28	*28*	29	30	1	2
VAIŚĀKHA 1979	3	4	5	**6**	8	9	10
	11	12	13	14	15	16	17
	18	19	20	21	22	23	24
	25	26	27	28	29	30	1
	2	3	4	5	6	7	8
JYAISHTHA 1979	**9**	11	12	13	14	15	16
	17	18	19	20	21	22	23
	24	*24*	25	26	27	28	29
	30	1	**2**	4	5	6	7
ĀSHĀḌHA 1979	8	9	10	11	12	13	14
	15	16	17	18	19	20	21
	22	23	24	25	26	27	28
	29	30	1	2	3	4	**5**
ŚRĀVAṆA 1979	7	8	9	10	11	12	13
	14	15	16	17	18	19	20
	21	*21*	22	23[c]	24	25	26
	27	**28**	30	1	2	3	4[d]
	5	6	7	8	9	10	11
BHĀDRAPADA 1979	12	13	14	15	16	17	18
	19	20	21	22	23	24	25
	26	27	28	29	30	**1**	3
	4	5	6	7	8[e]	9[e]	10[e]
ĀŚVINA 1979	11	12	13	14	15	16	*16*
	17	18	19	20	21	22	23
	24	**25**	27	28	29	30	1[f]
	2	3	4	5	6	7	8
KĀRTTIKA 1979	9	10	11	12	13	14	15
	16	17	18	19	20	21	22
	23	24	25	26	27	28	**29**
	1	2	3	4	5	6	7
MĀRGAŚIRA 1979	8	9	10	*10*	11[g]	12	13
	14	15	16	17	18	19	20
	21	22	**23**	25	26	27	28
	29	30	1	2	3	4	5
PAUSHA 1979	6	7	8	9	10	11	12
	12	13	14	15	**16**	18	19

[a]New Year (Dundubhi)
[b]Birthday of Rāma
[c]Birthday of Krishna
[d]Ganēśa Chaturthī
[e]Dashara
[f]Diwali
[g]Birthday of Vishnu
[h]Night of Śiva
[i]Holi

HINDU SOLAR 1843/1844

Month	Sun	Mon	Tue	Wed	Thu	Fri	Sat
	18	19	20	21	22	23	24
PAUSHA 1843	25	26	27	28	29	1[b]	2
	3	4	5	6	7	8	9
MĀGHA 1843	10	11	12	13	14	15	16
	17	18	19	20	21	22	23
	24	25	26	27	28	29	30
	1	2	3	4	5	6	7
	8	9	10	11	12	13	14
PHĀLGUNA 1843	15	16	17	18	19	20	21
	22	23	24	25	26	27	28
	29	1	2	3	4	5	6
	7	8	9	10	11	12	13
CHAITRA 1843	14	15	16	17	18	19	20
	21	22	23	24	25	26	27
	28	29	30	31	1[a]	2	3
	4	5	6	7	8	9	10
VAIŚĀKHA 1844	11	12	13	14	15	16	17
	18	19	20	21	22	23	24
	25	26	27	28	29	30	31
	1	2	3	4	5	6	7
	8	9	10	11	12	13	14
JYAISHTHA 1844	15	16	17	18	19	20	21
	22	23	24	25	26	27	28
	29	30	31	1	2	3	4
ĀSHĀḌHA 1844	5	6	7	8	9	10	11
	12	13	14	15	16	17	18
	19	20	21	22	23	24	25
	26	27	28	29	30	31	32
	1	2	3	4	5	6	7
	8	9	10	11	12	13	14
ŚRĀVAṆA 1844	15	16	17	18	19	20	21
	22	23	24	25	26	27	28
	29	30	31	1	2	3	4
	5	6	7	8	9	10	11
BHĀDRAPADA 1844	12	13	14	15	16	17	18
	19	20	21	22	23	24	25
	26	27	28	29	30	31	1
	2	3	4	5	6	7	8
ĀŚVINA 1844	9	10	11	12	13	14	15
	16	17	18	19	20	21	22
	23	24	25	26	27	28	29
	30	31	1	2	3	4	5
	6	7	8	9	10	11	12
KĀRTTIKA 1844	13	14	15	16	17	18	19
	20	21	22	23	24	25	26
	27	28	29	30	1	2	3
	4	5	6	7	8	9	10
MĀRGAŚIRA 1844	11	12	13	14	15	16	17
	18	19	20	21	22	23	24
	25	26	27	28	29	1	2
PAUSHA 1844	3	4	5	6	7	8	9
	10	11	12	13	14	15	16
	17	18	19	20	21	22	23

[a]New Year (Bhāva)
[b]Pongal

ISLAMIC (ASTRONOMICAL) 1340/1341‡

Month	Sun	Mon	Tue	Wed	Thu	Fri	Sat
	2	3	4	5	6	7	8
JUMADA I 1340	9	10	11	12	13	14	15
	16	17	18	19	20	21	22
	23	24	25	26	27	28	29
	1	2	3	4	5	6	7
	8	9	10	11	12	13	14
JUMADA II 1340	15	16	17	18	19	20	21
	22	23	24	25	26	27	28
	29	30	1	2	3	4	5
	6	7	8	9	10	11	12
RAJAB 1340	13	14	15	16	17	18	19
	20	21	22	23	24	25	26
	27[d]	28	29	30	1	2	3
SHA'BAN 1340	4	5	6	7	8	9	10
	11	12	13	14	15	16	17
	18	19	20	21	22	23	24
	25	26	27	28	29	1[e]	2
RAMADAN 1340	3	4	5	6	7	8	9
	10	11	12	13	14	15	16
	17	18	19	20	21	22	23
	24	25	26	27	28	29	30
	1[f]	2	3	4	5	6	7
SHAWWAL 1340	8	9	10	11	12	13	14
	15	16	17	18	19	20	21
	22	23	24	25	26	27	28
	29	30	1	2	3	4	5
DHU AL-QA'DA 1340	6	7	8	9	10	11	12
	13	14	15	16	17	18	19
	20	21	22	23	24	25	26
	27	28	29	1	2	3	4
DHU AL-HIJJA 1340	5	6	7	8	9	10[g]	11
	12	13	14	15	16	17	18
	19	20	21	22	23	24	25
	26	27	28	29	1[a]	2	3
MUHARRAM 1341	4	5	6	7	8	9	10[b]
	11	12	13	14	15	16	17
	18	19	20	21	22	23	24
	25	26	27	28	29	30	1
	2	3	4	5	6	7	8
SAFAR 1341	9	10	11	12	13	14	15
	16	17	18	19	20	21	22
	23	24	25	26	27	28	29
	1	2	3	4	5	6	7
RABI' I 1341	8	9	10	11	12[c]	13	14
	15	16	17	18	19	20	21
	22	23	24	25	26	27	28
	29	1	2	3	4	5	6
	7	8	9	10	11	12	13
RABI' II 1341	14	15	16	17	18	19	20
	21	22	23	24	25	26	27
	28	29	30	1	2	3	4
JUMADA I 1341	5	6	7	8	9	10	11
	12	13	14	15	16	17	18

‡Leap year
[a]New Year
[b]'Ashūrā'
[c]Prophet's Birthday
[d]Ascent of the Prophet
[e]Start of Ramaḍān
[f]'Id al-Fiṭr
[g]'Id al-'Aḍḥā

GREGORIAN 1922

Julian (Sun)	Sun	Mon	Tue	Wed	Thu	Fri	Sat	Month
Dec 19	1	2	3	4	5	6	7[a]	
	8	9	10	11	12	13	14[b]	JANUARY 1922
Jan 2	15	16	17	18	19	20	21	
	22	23	24	25	26	27	28	
Jan 16	29	30	31	1	2	3	4	
	5	6	7	8	9	10	11	FEBRUARY 1922
Jan 30	12	13	14	15	16	17	18	
	19	20	21	22	23	24	25	
Feb 13	26	27	28	1[c]	2	3	4	
	5[d]	6	7	8	9	10	11	MARCH 1922
Feb 27	12	13	14	15	16	17	18	
	19	20	21	22	23	24	25	
Mar 13	26	27	28	29	30	31	1	
	2	3	4	5	6	7	8	
Mar 27	9	10	11	12	13	14	15	APRIL 1922
	16[e]	17	18	19	20	21	22	
Apr 10	23	24	25	26	27	28	29	
	30	1	2	3	4	5	6	
Apr 24	7	8	9	10	11	12	13	MAY 1922
	14	15	16	17	18	19	20	
May 8	21	22	23	24	25	26	27	
	28	29	30	31	1	2	3	
May 22	4	5	6	7	8	9	10	JUNE 1922
	11	12	13	14	15	16	17	
Jun 5	18	19	20	21	22	23	24	
	25	26	27	28	29	30	1	
Jun 19	2	3	4	5	6	7	8	
	9	10	11	12	13	14	15	JULY 1922
Jul 3	16	17	18	19	20	21	22	
	23	24	25	26	27	28	29	
Jul 17	30	31	1	2	3	4	5	
	6	7	8	9	10	11	12	AUGUST 1922
Jul 31	13	14	15	16	17	18	19	
	20	21	22	23	24	25	26	
Aug 14	27	28	29	30	31	1	2	
	3	4	5	6	7	8	9	SEPTEMBER 1922
Aug 28	10	11	12	13	14	15	16	
	17	18	19	20	21	22	23	
Sep 11	24	25	26	27	28	29	30	
	1	2	3	4	5	6	7	OCTOBER 1922
Sep 25	8	9	10	11	12	13	14	
	15	16	17	18	19	20	21	
Oct 9	22	23	24	25	26	27	28	
	29	30	31	1	2	3	4	
Oct 23	5	6	7	8	9	10	11	NOVEMBER 1922
	12	13	14	15	16	17	18	
Nov 6	19	20	21	22	23	24	25	
	26	27	28	29	30	1	2	
Nov 20	3[g]	4	5	6	7	8	9	DECEMBER 1922
	10	11	12	13	14	15	16	
Dec 4	17	18	19	20	21	22	23	
	24	25[h]	26	27	28	29	30	
Dec 18	31	1	2	3	4	5	6	

[a]Orthodox Christmas
[b]Julian New Year
[c]Ash Wednesday
[d]Feast of Orthodoxy
[e]Easter (also Orthodox)
[g]Advent
[h]Christmas

1923

Gregorian 1923, Lunar Phases, ISO Week, Julian Day

Month	Sun	Mon	Tue	Wed	Thu	Fri	Sat	Lunar Phases	ISO WEEK (Mon)	JULIAN DAY (Sun noon)
	31	1[a]	2	○	4	5	6	2:33	1	2423420
	7	8	9	◑	11	12	13	0:54	2	2423427
JANUARY 1923	14	15	16	●	18	19	20	2:41	3	2423434
	21	22	23	24	◐	26	27	3:59	4	2423441
	28	29	30	31	○	2	3	15:53	5	2423448
	4	5	6	7	◑	9	10	9:16	6	2423455
FEBRUARY 1923	11	12	13	14	●	16	17	19:07	7	2423462
	18	19	20	21	22	23	◐	0:06	8	2423469
	25	26	27	28	1	2	○	3:23	9	2423476
	4	5	6	7	8	◑	10	18:31	10	2423483
MARCH 1923	11	12	13	14	15	16	●	12:51	11	2423490
	18	19	20	21[b]	22	23	24		12	2423497
	◐	26	27	28	29	30	31	16:41	13	2423504
	○	2	3	4	5	6	7	13:09	14	2423511
APRIL 1923	◑	9	10	11	12	13	14	5:22	15	2423518
	15	●	17	18	19	20	21	6:28	16	2423525
	22	23	◐	25	26	27	28	5:20	17	2423532
	29	○	1	2	3	4	5	21:30	18	2423539
	6	◑	8	9	10	11	12	18:18	19	2423546
MAY 1923	13	14	●	16	17	18	19	22:38	20	2423553
	20	21	22	◐	24	25	26	14:25	21	2423560
	27	28	29	○	31	1	2	5:07	22	2423567
	3	4	5	◑	7	8	9	9:19	23	2423574
JUNE 1923	10	11	12	13	●	15	16	12:42	24	2423581
	17	18	19	20	◐	22[c]	23	20:46	25	2423588
	24	25	26	27	○	29	30	13:04	26	2423595
	1	2	3	4	5	◑	7	1:56	27	2423602
	8	9	10	11	12	13	●	0:45	28	2423609
JULY 1923	15	16	17	18	19	20	◐	1:32	29	2423616
	22	23	24	25	26	○	28	22:33	30	2423623
	29	30	31	1	2	3	◑	19:22	31	2423630
	5	6	7	8	9	10	11		32	2423637
AUGUST 1923	●	13	14	15	16	17	18	11:16	33	2423644
	◐	20	21	22	23	24	25	6:07	34	2423651
	○	27	28	29	30	31	1	10:29	35	2423658
	2	◑	4	5	6	7	8	12:47	36	2423665
SEPTEMBER 1923	9	●	11	12	13	14	15	20:52	37	2423672
	16	◐	18	19	20	21	22	12:04	38	2423679
	23	24[d]	○	26	27	28	29	1:16	39	2423686
	30	1	2	◑	4	5	6	5:29	40	2423693
	7	8	9	●	11	12	13	6:06	41	2423700
OCTOBER 1923	14	15	◐	17	18	19	20	20:53	42	2423707
	21	22	23	○	25	26	27	18:26	43	2423714
	28	29	30	31	◑	2	3	20:49	44	2423721
	4	5	6	7	●	9	10	15:27	45	2423728
NOVEMBER 1923	11	12	13	14	◐	16	17	9:41	46	2423735
	18	19	20	21	22	○	24	12:58	47	2423742
	25	26	27	28	29	30	◑	10:09	48	2423749
	2	3	4	5	6	7	●	1:30	49	2423756
DECEMBER 1923	9	10	11	12	13	14	◐	2:38	50	2423763
	16	17	18	19	20	21	22[e]		51	2423770
	○	24	25	26	27	28	29	7:33	52	2423777
	◑	31	1	2	3	4	5	21:07	1	2423784

Hebrew 5683/5684‡

ISO Week	Month	Sun	Mon	Tue	Wed	Thu	Fri	Sat	Molad
1		12	13	14	15	16	17	18	
2	TEVETH 5683	19	20	21	22	23	24	25	
3		26	27	28	29	1	2	3	Wed 15h39m15p
4		4	5	6	7	8	9	10	
5	SHEVAT 5683	11	12	13	14	15	16	17	
6		18	19	20	21	22	23	24	
7		25	26	27	28	29	30	1	Fri 4h23m16p
8		2	3	4	5	6	7	8	
9	ADAR 5683	9	10	11	12	13	14[f]	15	
10		16	17	18	19	20	21	22	
11		23	24	25	26	27	28	29	
12		1	2	3	4	5	6	7	Sat 17h7m17p
13		8	9	10	11	12	13	14	
14	NISAN 5683	15[g]	16	17	18	19	20	21	
15		22	23	24	25	26	27	28	
16		29	30	1	2	3	4	5	Mon 5h52m0p
17		6	7	8	9	10	11	12	
18	IYYAR 5683	13	14	15	16	17	18	19	
19		20	21	22	23	24	25	26	
20		27	28	29	1	2	3	4	Tue 18h36m1p
21		5	6[h]	7	8	9	10	11	
22	SIVAN 5683	12	13	14	15	16	17	18	
23		19	20	21	22	23	24	25	
24		26	27	28	29	30	1	2	Thu 7h20m2p
25		3	4	5	6	7	8	9	
26	TAMMUZ 5683	10	11	12	13	14	15	16	
27		17	18	19	20	21	22	23	
28		24	25	26	27	28	29	1	Fri 20h4m3p
29		2	3	4	5	6	7	8	
30	AV 5683	9[i]	10	11	12	13	14	15	
31		16	17	18	19	20	21	22	
32		23	24	25	26	27	28	29	
33		30	1	2	3	4	5	6	Sun 8h48m4p
34		7	8	9	10	11	12	13	
35	ELUL 5683	14	15	16	17	18	19	20	
36		21	22	23	24	25	26	27	
37		28	29	1[a]	2[a]	3	4	5	Mon 21h32m5p
38		6	7	8	9	10[b]	11	12	
39	TISHRI 5684	13	14	15[c]	16	17	18	19	
40		20	21	22	23	24	25	26	
41		27	28	29	30	1	2	3	Wed 10h16m6p
42		4	5	6	7	8	9	10	
43	HESHVAN 5684	11	12	13	14	15	16	17	
44		18	19	20	21	22	23	24	
45		25	26	27	28	29	1	2	Thu 23h0m7p
46		3	4	5	6	7	8	9	
47	KISLEV 5684	10	11	12	13	14	15	16	
48		17	18	19	20	21	22	23	
49		24	25[e]	26[e]	27[e]	28[d][e]	29[e]	30[e]	
50		1[e]	2[e]	3	4	5	6	7	Sat 11h44m8p
51	TEVETH 5684	8	9	10	11	12	13	14	
52		15	16	17	18	19	20	21	
1		22	23	24	25	26	27	28	

Chinese Rén-Xū‡/Guǐ-Hài

ISO Week	Month	Sun	Mon	Tue	Wed	Thu	Fri	Sat	Solar Term
1		14	15	16	17	18	19	20	Xiǎo hán
2	MONTH 11 Rén-Xū	21	22	23	24	25	26	27	
3		28	29	30	1	2	3	4	
4		5	6	7	8	9	10	11	Dà hán
5	MONTH 12 Rén-Xū	12	13	14	15	16	17	18	
6		19	20	21	22	23	24	25	Lì chūn
7		26	27	28	29	30	1[a]	2	
8		3	4	5*	6	7	8	9	Yǔ shuǐ
9	MONTH 1 Guǐ-Hài	10	11	12	13	14	15[b]	16	
10		17	18	19	20	21	22	23	Jīng zhé
11		24	25	26	27	28	29	1	
12		2	3	4	5	6	7	8	Chūn fēn
13	MONTH 2 Guǐ-Hài	9	10	11	12	13	14	15	
14		16	17	18	19	20	21[c]	22	Qīng míng
15		23	24	25	26	27	28	29	
16		30	1	2	3	4	5	6*	Gǔ yǔ
17	MONTH 3 Guǐ-Hài	7	8	9	10	11	12	13	
18		14	15	16	17	18	19	20	
19		21	22	23	24	25	26	27	Lì xià
20		28	29	30	1	2	3	4	
21		5	6	7	8	9	10	11	Xiǎo mǎn
22	MONTH 4 Guǐ-Hài	12	13	14	15	16	17	18	
23		19	20	21	22	23	24	25	Máng zhòng
24		26	27	28	29	1	2	3	
25		4	5[d]	6	7*	8	9	10	Xià zhì
26	MONTH 5 Guǐ-Hài	11	12	13	14	15	16	17	
27		18	19	20	21	22	23	24	
28		25	26	27	28	29	30	1	Xiǎo shǔ
29		2	3	4	5	6	7	8	
30	MONTH 6 Guǐ-Hài	9	10	11	12	13	14	15	Dà shǔ
31		16	17	18	19	20	21	22	
32		23	24	25	26	27	28	29	Lì qiū
33		1	2	3	4	5	6	7[e]	
34		8*	9	10	11	12	13	14	Chǔ shǔ
35	MONTH 7 Guǐ-Hài	15[f]	16	17	18	19	20	21	
36		22	23	24	25	26	27	28	
37		29	30	1	2	3	4	5	Bái lù
38		6	7	8	9	10	11	12	
39	MONTH 8 Guǐ-Hài	13	14	15[g]	16	17	18	19	Qiū fēn
40		20	21	22	23	24	25	26	
41		27	28	29	1	2	3	4	Hán lù
42		5	6	7	8	9[h]*	10	11	
43	MONTH 9 Guǐ-Hài	12	13	14	15	16	17	18	Shuāng jiàng
44		19	20	21	22	23	24	25	
45		26	27	28	29	1	2	3	Lì dōng
46		4	5	6	7	8	9	10	
47	MONTH 10 Guǐ-Hài	11	12	13	14	15	16	17	Xiǎo xuě
48		18	19	20	21	22	23	24	
49		25	26	27	28	29	30	1	Dà xuě
50		2	3	4	5	6	7	8	
51	MONTH 11* Guǐ-Hài	9	10*	11	12	13	14	15	
52		16[i]	17	18	19	20	21	22	Dōng zhì
1		23	24	25	26	27	28	29	

Coptic 1639‡/1640, Ethiopic 1915‡/1916

ISO Week	Coptic Month	Sun	Mon	Tue	Wed	Thu	Fri	Sat	Ethiopic Month
1		22	23	24	25	26	27	28	TĀKHŚĀŚ 1915
2	KOIAK 1639	29[c]	30	1	2	3	4	5	
3		6[d]	7	8	9	10	11[e]	12	
4	TŌBE 1639	13	14	15	16	17	18	19	ṬER 1915
5		20	21	22	23	24	25	26	
6		27	28	29	30	1	2	3	
7		4	5	6	7	8	9	10	
8	MESHIR 1639	11	12	13	14	15	16	17	YAKĀTIT 1915
9		18	19	20	21	22	23	24	
10		25	26	27	28	29	30	1	
11		2	3	4	5	6	7	8	
12	PAREMOTEP 1639	9	10	11	12	13	14	15	MAGĀBIT 1915
13		16	17	18	19	20	21	22	
14		23	24	25	26	27	28	29	
15		30[f]	1	2	3	4	5	6	
16		7	8	9	10	11	12	13	
17	PARMOUTE 1639	14	15	16	17	18	19	20	MIYĀZYĀ 1915
18		21	22	23	24	25	26	27	
19		28	29[g]	30	1	2	3	4	
20		5	6	7	8	9	10	11	
21	PASHONS 1639	12	13	14	15	16	17	18	GENBOT 1915
22		19	20	21	22	23	24	25	
23		26	27	28	29	30	1	2	
24		3	4	5	6	7	8	9	
25	PAŌNE 1639	10	11	12	13	14	15	16	SANĒ 1915
26		17	18	19	20	21	22	23	
27		24	25	26	27	28	29	30	
28		1	2	3	4	5	6	7	
29		8	9	10	11	12	13	14	
30	EPĒP 1639	15	16	17	18	19	20	21	HAMLĒ 1915
31		22	23	24	25	26	27	28	
32		29	30	1	2	3	4	5	
33		6	7	8	9	10	11	12	
34	MESORĒ 1639	13[h]	14	15	16	17	18	19	NAHASĒ 1915
35		20	21	22	23	24	25	26	
36		27	28	29	30	1	2	3	
37	EPAG. 1639	4	5	6	1[a]	2	3	4	PĀG. 1915
38		5	6	7	8	9	10	11	
39	THOOUT 1640	12	13	14	15	16	17[b]	18	MASKARAM 1916
40		19	20	21	22	23	24	25	
41		26	27	28	29	30	1	2	
42		3	4	5	6	7	8	9	
43	PAOPE 1640	10	11	12	13	14	15	16	ṬEQEMT 1916
44		17	18	19	20	21	22	23	
45		24	25	26	27	28	29	30	
46		1	2	3	4	5	6	7	
47	ATHŌR 1640	8	9	10	11	12	13	14	HEDĀR 1916
48		15	16	17	18	19	20	21	
49		22	23	24	25	26	27	28	
50		29	30	1	2	3	4	5	
51	KOIAK 1640	6	7	8	9	10	11	12	TĀKHŚĀŚ 1916
52		13	14	15	16	17	18	19	
1		20	21	22	23	24	25	26	

[a]New Year
[b]Spring (15:28)
[c]Summer (11:03)
[d]Autumn (2:03)
[e]Winter (20:53)
● New moon
◐ First quarter moon
○ Full moon
◑ Last quarter moon

‡Leap year
[a]New Year
[b]Yom Kippur
[c]Sukkot
[d]Winter starts
[e]Ḥanukkah
[f]Purim
[g]Passover
[h]Shavuot
[i]Fast of Av

‡Leap year
[a]New Year (4621, Pig)
[b]Lantern Festival
[c]Qīngmíng
[d]Dragon Festival
[e]Qīqiǎo
[f]Hungry Ghosts
[g]Mid-Autumn Festival
[h]Double-Ninth Festival
[i]Dōngzhì
*Start of 60-name cycle

‡Leap year
[a]New Year
[b]Building of the Cross
[c]Christmas
[d]Jesus's Circumcision
[e]Epiphany
[f]Easter
[g]Mary's Announcement
[h]Jesus's Transfiguration

PERSIAN (ASTRONOMICAL) 1301/1302

Month	Sun	Mon	Tue	Wed	Thu	Fri	Sat
DEY 1301	9	10	11	12	13	14	15
	16	17	18	19	20	21	22
	23	24	25	26	27	28	29
	30	1	2	3	4	5	6
BAHMAN 1301	7	8	9	10	11	12	13
	14	15	16	17	18	19	20
	21	22	23	24	25	26	27
	28	29	30	1	2	3	4
ESFAND 1301	5	6	7	8	9	10	11
	12	13	14	15	16	17	18
	19	20	21	22	23	24	25
	26	27	28	29	1[a]	2	3
FARVARDĪN 1302	4	5	6	7	8	9	10
	11	12	13[b]	14	15	16	17
	18	19	20	21	22	23	24
	25	26	27	28	29	30	31
ORDĪBEHEŠT 1302	1	2	3	4	5	6	7
	8	9	10	11	12	13	14
	15	16	17	18	19	20	21
	22	23	24	25	26	27	28
	29	30	31	1	2	3	4
XORDĀD 1302	5	6	7	8	9	10	11
	12	13	14	15	16	17	18
	19	20	21	22	23	24	25
	26	27	28	29	30	31	1
TĪR 1302	2	3	4	5	6	7	8
	9	10	11	12	13	14	15
	16	17	18	19	20	21	22
	23	24	25	26	27	28	29
	30	31	1	2	3	4	5
MORDĀD 1302	6	7	8	9	10	11	12
	13	14	15	16	17	18	19
	20	21	22	23	24	25	26
	27	28	29	30	31	1	2
SHAHRĪVAR 1302	3	4	5	6	7	8	9
	10	11	12	13	14	15	16
	17	18	19	20	21	22	23
	24	25	26	27	28	29	30
	31	1	2	3	4	5	6
MEHR 1302	7	8	9	10	11	12	13
	14	15	16	17	18	19	20
	21	22	23	24	25	26	27
	28	29	30	1	2	3	4
ĀBĀN 1302	5	6	7	8	9	10	11
	12	13	14	15	16	17	18
	19	20	21	22	23	24	25
	26	27	28	29	30	1	2
ĀZAR 1302	3	4	5	6	7	8	9
	10	11	12	13	14	15	16
	17	18	19	20	21	22	23
	24	25	26	27	28	29	30
DEY 1302	1	2	3	4	5	6	7
	8	9	10	11	12	13	14

[a]New Year
[b]Sizdeh Bedar

HINDU LUNAR 1979/1980‡

Month	Sun	Mon	Tue	Wed	Thu	Fri	Sat
PAUSHA 1979	12	13	14	15	16	18	19
	20	21	22	23	24	25	26
	27	28	29	30	1	2	3
MĀGHA 1979	4	5	6	7	8	9	10
	11	12	13	14	15	16	17
	18	19	20	21	22	24	25
	26	27	28[h]	29	30	1	2
PHĀLGUNA 1979	3	4	5	5	6	7	8
	9	10	11	12	13	14	15[i]
	16	18	19	20	21	22	23
	24	25	26	27	28	29	30
CHAITRA 1980	1[a]	2	3	4	5	6	7
	8	9[b]	10	11	12	13	14
	15	16	17	18	19	20	22
	23	24	25	26	27	28	28
	29	30	1	2	3	4	5
VAIŚĀKHA 1980	6	7	8	9	10	11	12
	13	15	16	17	18	19	20
	21	22	23	24	25	26	27
	28	29	30	1	2	2	3
LEAP JYAISHṬHA 1980	4	5	7	8	9	10	11
	12	13	14	15	16	17	19
	20	21	22	23	23	24	25
	26	27	28	29	30	1	2
JYAISHṬHA 1980	3	4	5	6	7	8	9
	11	12	13	14	15	16	17
	18	19	20	21	22	23	24
	25	26	27	28	29	30	30
ĀSHĀḌHA 1980	2	3	4	5	6	7	8
	9	10	11	12	13	15	16
	17	18	19	20	20	21	22
	23	24	25	26	27	28	29
	30	1	2	3	4	5	7
ŚRĀVAṆA 1980	8	9	10	11	12	13	14
	15	16	17	18	19	20	21
	22	23[c]	24	25	26	27	28
	29	30	1	2	3	4[d]	5
BHĀDRAPADA 1980	6	7	8	9	11	12	13
	14	15	16	16	17	18	19
	20	21	22	23	24	25	26
	27	28	29	30	1	2	4
ĀŚVINA 1980	5	6	7	8[e]	9[e]	10[e]	11
	12	13	14	15	16	17	18
	19	20	20	21	22	23	24
	25	27	28	29	30	1[f]	2
KĀRTTIKA 1980	3	4	5	6	7	8	9
	10	11	12	13	14	15	16
	17	18	19	20	21	22	23
	24	25	26	27	28	29	30
MĀRGAŚIRA 1980	2	3	4	5	6	7	8
	9	10	11[g]	12	13	13	14
	15	16	17	18	19	20	21
	22	23	24	26	27	28	29

‡Leap year
[a]New Year (Rudhirodgārin)
[b]Birthday of Rāma
[c]Birthday of Krishna
[d]Ganēśa Chaturthī
[e]Dashara
[f]Diwali
[g]Birthday of Vishnu
[h]Night of Śiva
[i]Holi

HINDU SOLAR 1844/1845

Month	Sun	Mon	Tue	Wed	Thu	Fri	Sat
PAUSHA 1844	17	18	19	20	21	22	23
	24	25	26	27	28	29	1[b]
MĀGHA 1844	2	3	4	5	6	7	8
	9	10	11	12	13	14	15
	16	17	18	19	20	21	22
	23	24	25	26	27	28	29
	30	1	2	3	4	5	6
PHĀLGUNA 1844	7	8	9	10	11	12	13
	14	15	16	17	18	19	20
	21	22	23	24	25	26	27
	28	29	30	1	2	3	4
CHAITRA 1844	5	6	7	8	9	10	11
	12	13	14	15	16	17	18
	19	20	21	22	23	24	25
	26	27	28	29	30	1[a]	2
VAIŚĀKHA 1845	3	4	5	6	7	8	9
	10	11	12	13	14	15	16
	17	18	19	20	21	22	23
	24	25	26	27	28	29	30
	31	1	2	3	4	5	6
JYAISHṬHA 1845	7	8	9	10	11	12	13
	14	15	16	17	18	19	20
	21	22	23	24	25	26	27
	28	29	30	31	1	2	3
ĀSHĀḌHA 1845	4	5	6	7	8	9	10
	11	12	13	14	15	16	17
	18	19	20	21	22	23	24
	25	26	27	28	29	30	31
	32	1	2	3	4	5	6
ŚRĀVAṆA 1845	7	8	9	10	11	12	13
	14	15	16	17	18	19	20
	21	22	23	24	25	26	27
	28	29	30	31	32	1	2
BHĀDRAPADA 1845	3	4	5	6	7	8	9
	10	11	12	13	14	15	16
	17	18	19	20	21	22	23
	24	25	26	27	28	29	30
	31	1	2	3	4	5	6
ĀŚVINA 1845	7	8	9	10	11	12	13
	14	15	16	17	18	19	20
	21	22	23	24	25	26	27
	28	29	30	1	2	3	4
KĀRTTIKA 1845	5	6	7	8	9	10	11
	12	13	14	15	16	17	18
	19	20	21	22	23	24	25
	26	27	28	29	30	1	2
MĀRGAŚIRA 1845	3	4	5	6	7	8	9
	10	11	12	13	14	15	16
	17	18	19	20	21	22	23
	24	25	26	27	28	29	1
PAUSHA 1845	2	3	4	5	6	7	8
	9	10	11	12	13	14	15
	16	17	18	19	20	21	22

[a]New Year (Yuvan)
[b]Pongal

ISLAMIC (ASTRONOMICAL) 1341‡/1342

Month	Sun	Mon	Tue	Wed	Thu	Fri	Sat
JUMĀDĀ I 1341	12	13	14	15	16	17	18
	19	20	21	22	23	24	25
	26	27	28	29	1	2	3
JUMĀDĀ II 1341	4	5	6	7	8	9	10
	11	12	13	14	15	16	17
	18	19	20	21	22	23	24
	25	26	27	28	29	30	1
RAJAB 1341	2	3	4	5	6	7	8
	9	10	11	12	13	14	15
	16	17	18	19	20	21	22
	23	24	25	26	27[d]	28	29
	30	1	2	3	4	5	6
SHA'BĀN 1341	7	8	9	10	11	12	13
	14	15	16	17	18	19	20
	21	22	23	24	25	26	27
	28	29	30	1[e]	2	3	4
RAMAḌĀN 1341	5	6	7	8	9	10	11
	12	13	14	15	16	17	18
	19	20	21	22	23	24	25
	26	27	28	29	1[f]	2	3
SHAWWĀL 1341	4	5	6	7	8	9	10
	11	12	13	14	15	16	17
	18	19	20	21	22	23	24
	25	26	27	28	29	30	1
DHU AL-QA'DA 1341	2	3	4	5	6	7	8
	9	10	11	12	13	14	15
	16	17	18	19	20	21	22
	23	24	25	26	27	28	29
	30	1	2	3	4	5	6
DHU AL-ḤIJJA 1341	7	8	9	10[g]	11	12	13
	14	15	16	17	18	19	20
	21	22	23	24	25	26	27
	28	29	1[a]	2	3	4	5
MUḤARRAM 1342	6	7	8	9	10[b]	11	12
	13	14	15	16	17	18	19
	20	21	22	23	24	25	26
	27	28	29	1	2	3	4
ṢAFAR 1342	5	6	7	8	9	10	11
	12	13	14	15	16	17	18
	19	20	21	22	23	24	25
	26	27	28	29	1	2	3
RABĪ' I 1342	4	5	6	7	8	9	10
	11	12[c]	13	14	15	16	17
	18	19	20	21	22	23	24
	25	26	27	28	29	30	1
RABĪ' II 1342	2	3	4	5	6	7	8
	9	10	11	12	13	14	15
	16	17	18	19	20	21	22
	23	24	25	26	27	28	29
JUMĀDĀ I 1342	1	2	3	4	5	6	7
	8	9	10	11	12	13	14
	15	16	17	18	19	20	21
	22	23	24	25	26	27	28

‡Leap year
[a]New Year
[b]'Ashūrā'
[c]Prophet's Birthday
[d]Ascent of the Prophet
[e]Start of Ramaḍān
[f]'Id al-Fiṭr
[g]'Id al-'Aḍḥā

GREGORIAN 1923

Julian (Sun)	Sun	Mon	Tue	Wed	Thu	Fri	Sat	Month
Dec 18	31	1	2	3	4	5	6	
	7[a]	8	9	10	11	12	13	JANUARY 1923
Jan 1	14[b]	15	16	17	18	19	20	
	21	22	23	24	25	26	27	
Jan 15	28	29	30	31	1	2	3	
	4	5	6	7	8	9	10	FEBRUARY 1923
Jan 29	11	12	13	14[c]	15	16	17	
	18	19	20	21	22	23	24	
Feb 12	25[d]	26	27	28	1	2	3	
	4	5	6	7	8	9	10	MARCH 1923
Feb 26	11	12	13	14	15	16	17	
	18	19	20	21	22	23	24	
Mar 12	25	26	27	28	29	30	31	
	1[e]	2	3	4	5	6	7	APRIL 1923
Mar 26	8[f]	9	10	11	12	13	14	
	15	16	17	18	19	20	21	
Apr 9	22	23	24	25	26	27	28	
	29	30	1	2	3	4	5	
Apr 23	6	7	8	9	10	11	12	MAY 1923
	13	14	15	16	17	18	19	
May 7	20	21	22	23	24	25	26	
	27	28	29	30	31	1	2	
May 21	3	4	5	6	7	8	9	JUNE 1923
	10	11	12	13	14	15	16	
Jun 4	17	18	19	20	21	22	23	
	24	25	26	27	28	29	30	
Jun 18	1	2	3	4	5	6	7	
	8	9	10	11	12	13	14	JULY 1923
Jul 2	15	16	17	18	19	20	21	
	22	23	24	25	26	27	28	
Jul 16	29	30	31	1	2	3	4	
	5	6	7	8	9	10	11	AUGUST 1923
Jul 30	12	13	14	15	16	17	18	
	19	20	21	22	23	24	25	
Aug 13	26	27	28	29	30	31	1	
	2	3	4	5	6	7	8	SEPTEMBER 1923
Aug 27	9	10	11	12	13	14	15	
	16	17	18	19	20	21	22	
Sep 10	23	24	25	26	27	28	29	
	30	1	2	3	4	5	6	
Sep 24	7	8	9	10	11	12	13	OCTOBER 1923
	14	15	16	17	18	19	20	
Oct 8	21	22	23	24	25	26	27	
	28	29	30	31	1	2	3	
Oct 22	4	5	6	7	8	9	10	NOVEMBER 1923
	11	12	13	14	15	16	17	
Nov 5	18	19	20	21	22	23	24	
	25	26	27	28	29	30	1	
Nov 19	2[g]	3	4	5	6	7	8	
	9	10	11	12	13	14	15	DECEMBER 1923
Dec 3	16	17	18	19	20	21	22	
	23	24	25[h]	26	27	28	29	
Dec 17	30	31	1	2	3	4	5	

[a]Orthodox Christmas
[b]Julian New Year
[c]Ash Wednesday
[d]Feast of Orthodoxy
[e]Easter
[f]Orthodox Easter
[g]Advent
[h]Christmas

1924

GREGORIAN 1924‡

Month	Sun	Mon	Tue	Wed	Thu	Fri	Sat	Lunar Phases	ISO WEEK (Mon)	JULIAN DAY (Sun noon)
January 1924	◑	31	1[a]	2	3	4	5	21:07	1	2423784
	●	7	8	9	10	11	12	12:48	2	2423791
	◐	14	15	16	17	18	19	22:44	3	2423798
	20	21	○	23	24	25	26	0:57	4	2423805
	27	28	◑	30	31	1	2	5:53	5	2423812
February 1924	3	4	●	6	7	8	9	1:38	6	2423819
	10	11	◐	13	14	15	16	20:09	7	2423826
	17	18	19	○	21	22	23	16:07	8	2423833
	24	25	26	◑	28	29	1	13:15	9	2423840
March 1924	2	3	4	●	6	7	8	15:58	10	2423847
	9	10	11	12	◐	14	15	16:50	11	2423854
	16	17	18	19	20[b]	○	22	4:30	12	2423861
	23	24	25	26	◑	28	29	20:24	13	2423868
	30	31	1	2	3	●	5	7:17	14	2423875
April 1924	6	7	8	9	10	11	◐	11:12	15	2423882
	13	14	15	16	17	18	○	14:10	16	2423889
	20	21	22	23	24	25	◑	4:28	17	2423896
	27	28	29	30	1	2	●	23:00	18	2423903
May 1924	4	5	6	7	8	9	10		19	2423910
	11	◐	13	14	15	16	17	2:13	20	2423917
	○	19	20	21	22	23	24	21:52	21	2423924
	◑	26	27	28	29	30	31	14:16	22	2423931
June 1924	1	●	3	4	5	6	7	14:34	23	2423938
	8	9	◐	11	12	13	14	13:37	24	2423945
	15	16	○	18	19	20	21[c]	4:41	25	2423952
	22	23	◑	25	26	27	28	2:16	26	2423959
	29	30	1	●	3	4	5	5:35	27	2423966
July 1924	6	7	8	◐	10	11	12	21:46	28	2423973
	13	14	15	○	17	18	19	11:49	29	2423980
	20	21	22	◑	24	25	26	16:35	30	2423987
	27	28	29	30	●	1	2	19:42	31	2423994
August 1924	3	4	5	6	7	◐	9	3:41	32	2424001
	10	11	12	13	○	15	16	20:19	33	2424008
	17	18	19	20	21	◑	23	9:10	34	2424015
	24	25	26	27	28	29	●	8:37	35	2424022
	31	1	2	3	4	5	◐	8:45	36	2424029
September 1924	7	8	9	10	11	12	○	7:00	37	2424036
	14	15	16	17	18	19	20		38	2424043
	◑	22	23[d]	24	25	26	27	3:35	39	2424050
	●	29	30	1	2	3	4	20:16	40	2424057
October 1924	◐	6	7	8	9	10	11	14:30	41	2424064
	○	13	14	15	16	17	18	20:21	42	2424071
	19	◑	21	22	23	24	25	22:54	43	2424078
	26	27	●	29	30	31	1	6:57	44	2424085
November 1924	2	◐	4	5	6	7	8	22:18	45	2424092
	9	10	○	12	13	14	15	12:31	46	2424099
	16	17	18	◑	20	21	22	17:38	47	2424106
	23	24	25	●	27	28	29	17:16	48	2424113
	30	1	2	◐	4	5	6	9:10	49	2424120
December 1924	7	8	9	10	○	12	13	7:03	50	2424127
	14	15	16	17	18	◑	20	10:11	51	2424134
	21	22[e]	23	24	25	●	27	3:46	52	2424141
	28	29	30	31	◐	2	3	23:25	1	2424148

HEBREW 5684‡/5685

ISO Week	Month	Sun	Mon	Tue	Wed	Thu	Fri	Sat	Molad
1	Teveth 5684	22	23	24	25	26	27	28	
2		29	1	2	3	4	5	6	Mon 0h28m9p
3	Shevat 5684	7	8	9	10	11	12	13	
4		14	15	16	17	18	19	20	
5		21	22	23	24	25	26	27	
6		28	29	30	1	2	3	4	Tue 13h12m10p
7	Adar I 5684	5	6	7	8	9	10	11	
8		12	13	14	15	16	17	18	
9		19	20	21	22	23	24	25	
10		26	27	28	29	30	1	2	Thu 1h56m11p
11	Adar II 5684	3	4	5	6	7	8	9	
12		10	11	12	13	14[f]	15	16	
13		17	18	19	20	21	22	23	
14		24	25	26	27	28	29	1	Fri 14h40m12p
15	Nisan 5684	2	3	4	5	6	7	8	
16		9	10	11	12	13	14	15[g]	
17		16	17	18	19	20	21	22	
18		23	24	25	26	27	28	29	
19		30	1	2	3	4	5	6	Sun 3h24m13p
20	Iyar 5684	7	8	9	10	11	12	13	
21		14	15	16	17	18	19	20	
22		21	22	23	24	25	26	27	
23		28	29	1	2	3	4	5	Mon 16h8m14p
24	Sivan 5684	6[h]	7	8	9	10	11	12	
25		13	14	15	16	17	18	19	
26		20	21	22	23	24	25	26	
27		27	28	29	30	1	2	3	Wed 4h52m15p
28	Tammuz 5684	4	5	6	7	8	9	10	
29		11	12	13	14	15	16	17	
30		18	19	20	21	22	23	24	
31		25	26	27	28	29	1	2	Thu 17h36m16p
32	Av 5684	3	4	5	6	7	8	9	
33		10[i]	11	12	13	14	15	16	
34		17	18	19	20	21	22	23	
35		24	25	26	27	28	29	30	
36		1	2	3	4	5	6	7	Sat 6h20m17p
37	Elul 5684	8	9	10	11	12	13	14	
38		15	16	17	18	19	20	21	
39		22	23	24	25	26	27	28	
40		29	1[a]	2[a]	3	4	5	6	Sun 19h5m0p
41	Tishri 5685	7	8	9	10[b]	11	12	13	
42		14	15[c]	16	17	18	19	20	
43		21	22	23	24	25	26	27	
44		28	29	30	1	2	3	4	Tue 7h49m1p
45	Heshvan 5685	5	6	7	8	9	10	11	
46		12	13	14	15	16	17	18	
47		19	20	21	22	23	24	25	
48		26	27	28	29	30	1	2	Wed 20h33m2p
49	Kislev 5685	3	4	5	6	7	8[d]	9	
50		10	11	12	13	14	15	16	
51		17	18	19	20	21	22	23	
52		24	25[e]	26[e]	27[e]	28[e]	29[e]	30[e]	Fri 9h17m3p
1		1[e]	2[e]	3	4	5	6	7	

CHINESE Guǐ-Hài/Jiǎ-Zǐ

ISO Week	Month	Sun	Mon	Tue	Wed	Thu	Fri	Sat	Solar Term
1	Month 12 Guǐ-Hài	23	24	25	26	27	28	29	
2		*1*	2	3	4	5	6	7	Xiǎo hán
3		8	9	10	11	12	13	14	
4		15	***16***	17	18	19	20	21	Dà hán
5		22	23	24	25	26	27	28	
6	Month 1 Jiǎ-Zǐ	29	30	*1*[a]	2	3	4	5	Lì chūn
7		6	7	8	9	10	11*	12	
8		13	14	15[b]	***16***	17	18	19	Yǔ shuǐ
9		20	21	22	23	24	25	26	
10		27	28	29	1	*2*	3	4	Jīng zhé
11	Month 2 Jiǎ-Zǐ	5	6	7	8	9	10	11	
12		12	13	14	15	16	***17***	18	Chūn fēn
13		19	20	21	22	23	24	25	
14		26	27	28	29	30	1	*2*[c]	Qīng míng
15	Month 3 Jiǎ-Zǐ	3	4	5	6	7	8	9	
16		10	11	12*	13	14	15	16	
17		***17***	18	19	20	21	22	23	Gǔ yǔ
18		24	25	26	27	28	29	30	
19	Month 4 Jiǎ-Zǐ	1	2	3	4	5	6	7	Lì xià
20		8	9	10	11	12	13	14	
21		15	16	17	***18***	19	20	21	Xiǎo mǎn
22		22	23	24	25	26	27	28	
23	Month 5 Jiǎ-Zǐ	29	1	2	3	4	5[d]	6	Máng zhòng
24		7	8	9	10	11	12	13*	
25		14	15	16	17	18	19	20	
26		***21***	22	23	24	25	26	27	Xià zhì
27	Month 6 Jiǎ-Zǐ	28	29	30	1	2	3	4	
28		5	6	7	8	9	10	11	Xiǎo shǔ
29		12	13	14	15	16	17	18	
30		19	20	21	***22***	23	24	25	Dà shǔ
31	Month 7 Jiǎ-Zǐ	26	27	28	29	30	1	2	
32		3	4	5	6	7[e]	*8*	9	Lì qiū
33		10	11	12	13*	14	15[f]	16	
34		17	18	19	20	21	22	***23***	Chǔ shǔ
35		24	25	26	27	28	29	1	
36	Month 8 Jiǎ-Zǐ	2	3	4	5	6	7	8	
37		9	*10*	11	12	13	14	15[g]	Bái lù
38		16	17	18	19	20	21	22	
39		23	24	***25***	26	27	28	29	Qiū fēn
40	Month 9 Jiǎ-Zǐ	30	1	2	3	4	5	6	
41		7	8	9[h]	*10*	11	12	13	Hán lù
42		14*	15	16	17	18	19	20	
43		21	22	23	24	25	***26***	27	Shuāng jiàng
44	Month 10 Jiǎ-Zǐ	28	29	1	2	3	4	5	
45		6	7	8	9	10	11	*12*	Lì dōng
46		13	14	15	16	17	18	19	
47		20	21	22	23	24	25	***26***	Xiǎo xuě
48		27	28	29	30	1	2	3	
49	Month 11 Jiǎ-Zǐ	4	5	6	7	8	9	10	
50		*11*	12	13	14	15*	16	17	Dà xuě
51		18	19	20	21	22	23	24	
52		25	***26***[i]	27	28	29	1	2	Dōng zhì
1	Month 12 Jiǎ-Zǐ	3	4	5	6	7	8	9	

COPTIC 1640/1641 — ETHIOPIC 1916/1917

ISO Week	Coptic Month	Sun	Mon	Tue	Wed	Thu	Fri	Sat	Ethiopic Month
1	Koiak 1640	20	21	22	23	24	25	26	Tākhśāś 1916
2		27	28	29[c]	30	1	2	3	
3	Tōbe 1640	4	5	6[d]	7	8	9	10	Ṭer 1916
4		11[e]	12	13	14	15	16	17	
5		18	19	20	21	22	23	24	
6		25	26	27	28	29	30	1	
7	Meshir 1640	2	3	4	5	6	7	8	Yakātit 1916
8		9	10	11	12	13	14	15	
9		16	17	18	19	20	21	22	
10		23	24	25	26	27	28	29	
11	Paremotep 1640	30	1	2	3	4	5	6	Magābit 1916
12		7	8	9	10	11	12	13	
13		14	15	16	17	18	19	20	
14		21	22	23	24	25	26	27	
15	Parmoute 1640	28	29	30	1	2	3	4	Miyāzyā 1916
16		5	6	7	8	9	10	11	
17		12	13	14	15	16	17	18	
18		19[f]	20	21	22	23	24	25	
19	Pashons 1640	26	27	28	29[g]	30	1	2	Genbot 1916
20		3	4	5	6	7	8	9	
21		10	11	12	13	14	15	16	
22		17	18	19	20	21	22	23	
23	Paōne 1640	24	25	26	27	28	29	30	Sanē 1916
24		1	2	3	4	5	6	7	
25		8	9	10	11	12	13	14	
26		15	16	17	18	19	20	21	
27		22	23	24	25	26	27	28	
28	Epēp 1640	29	30	1	2	3	4	5	Ḥamlē 1916
29		6	7	8	9	10	11	12	
30		13	14	15	16	17	18	19	
31		20	21	22	23	24	25	26	
32	Mesorē 1640	27	28	29	30	1	2	3	Naḥasē 1916
33		4	5	6	7	8	9	10	
34		11	12	13[h]	14	15	16	17	
35		18	19	20	21	22	23	24	
36	Epag. 1640	25	26	27	28	29	30	1	Ṗāg. 1916
37	Thoout 1641	2	3	4	5	1[a]	2	3	Maskaram 1917
38		4	5	6	7	8	9	10	
39		11	12	13	14	15	16	17[b]	
40		18	19	20	21	22	23	24	
41	Paope 1641	25	26	27	28	29	30	1	Ṭeqemt 1917
42		2	3	4	5	6	7	8	
43		9	10	11	12	13	14	15	
44		16	17	18	19	20	21	22	
45	Athōr 1641	23	24	25	26	27	28	29	Ḫedār 1917
46		30	1	2	3	4	5	6	
47		7	8	9	10	11	12	13	
48		14	15	16	17	18	19	20	
49		21	22	23	24	25	26	27	
50	Koiak 1641	28	29	30	1	2	3	4	Tākhśāś 1917
51		5	6	7	8	9	10	11	
52		12	13	14	15	16	17	18	
1		19	20	21	22	23	24	25	

‡Leap year
[a]New Year
[b]Spring (21:20)
[c]Summer (16:59)
[d]Autumn (7:58)
[e]Winter (2:45)
● New moon
◐ First quarter moon
○ Full moon
◑ Last quarter moon

‡Leap year
[a]New Year
[b]Yom Kippur
[c]Sukkot
[d]Winter starts
[e]Ḥanukkah
[f]Purim
[g]Passover
[h]Shavuot
[i]Fast of Av

[a]New Year (4622, Rat)
[b]Lantern Festival
[c]Qīngmíng
[d]Dragon Festival
[e]Qīqiǎo
[f]Hungry Ghosts
[g]Mid-Autumn Festival
[h]Double-Ninth Festival
[i]Dōngzhì
*Start of 60-name cycle

[a]New Year
[b]Building of the Cross
[c]Christmas
[d]Jesus's Circumcision
[e]Epiphany
[f]Easter
[g]Mary's Announcement
[h]Jesus's Transfiguration

1924

PERSIAN (ASTRONOMICAL) 1302/1303

Month	Sun	Mon	Tue	Wed	Thu	Fri	Sat
DEY 1302	8	9	10	11	12	13	14
	15	16	17	18	19	20	21
	22	23	24	25	26	27	28
BAHMAN 1302	29	30	1	2	3	4	5
	6	7	8	9	10	11	12
	13	14	15	16	17	18	19
	20	21	22	23	24	25	26
ESFAND 1302	27	28	29	30	1	2	3
	4	5	6	7	8	9	10
	11	12	13	14	15	16	17
	18	19	20	21	22	23	24
FARVARDĪN 1303	25	26	27	28	29	1[a]	2
	3	4	5	6	7	8	9
	10	11	12	13[b]	14	15	16
	17	18	19	20	21	22	23
	24	25	26	27	28	29	30
ORDĪBEHEŠT 1303	31	1	2	3	4	5	6
	7	8	9	10	11	12	13
	14	15	16	17	18	19	20
	21	22	23	24	25	26	27
XORDĀD 1303	28	29	30	31	1	2	3
	4	5	6	7	8	9	10
	11	12	13	14	15	16	17
	18	19	20	21	22	23	24
	25	26	27	28	29	30	31
TĪR 1303	1	2	3	4	5	6	7
	8	9	10	11	12	13	14
	15	16	17	18	19	20	21
	22	23	24	25	26	27	28
MORDĀD 1303	29	30	31	1	2	3	4
	5	6	7	8	9	10	11
	12	13	14	15	16	17	18
	19	20	21	22	23	24	25
SHAHRĪVAR 1303	26	27	28	29	30	31	1
	2	3	4	5	6	7	8
	9	10	11	12	13	14	15
	16	17	18	19	20	21	22
	23	24	25	26	27	28	29
MEHR 1303	30	31	1	2	3	4	5
	6	7	8	9	10	11	12
	13	14	15	16	17	18	19
	20	21	22	23	24	25	26
ĀBĀN 1303	27	28	29	30	1	2	3
	4	5	6	7	8	9	10
	11	12	13	14	15	16	17
	18	19	20	21	22	23	24
ĀZAR 1303	25	26	27	28	29	30	1
	2	3	4	5	6	7	8
	9	10	11	12	13	14	15
	16	17	18	19	20	21	22
	23	24	25	26	27	28	29
DEY 1303	30	1	2	3	4	5	6
	7	8	9	10	11	12	13

HINDU LUNAR 1980‡/1981

Month	Sun	Mon	Tue	Wed	Thu	Fri	Sat
MĀRGAŚIRA 1980	22	23	24	26	27	28	29
PAUSHA 1980	30	1	2	3	4	5	6
	7	8	9	10	11	12	13
	14	15	16	17	18	19	20
	21	22	23	24	25	26	27
MĀGHA 1980	28	29	30	2	3	4	4
	5	6	7	8	9	10	11
	12	13	14	15	16	17	18
	19	20	21	22	23	25	26
PHĀLGUNA 1980	27	28[h]	29	30	1	2	3
	4	5	6	7	7	8	9
	10	11	12	13	14	15[i]	16
	18	19	20	21	22	23	24
CHAITRA 1981	25	26	27	28	29	30	1[a]
	2	3	4	5	6	7	8
	9[b]	10	11	12	13	14	15
	16	17	18	19	20	22	23
	24	25	26	27	28	29	30
VAIŚĀKHA 1981	1	2	2	3	4	5	6
	7	8	9	10	11	12	13
	14	16	17	18	19	20	21
	22	23	24	25	26	27	28
JYAISHTHA 1981	29	30	1	2	3	4	5
	6	7	8	9	10	11	12
	13	14	15	16	17	19	20
	21	22	23	24	25	26	27
ĀSHĀḌHA 1981	28	28	29	30	1	2	3
	4	5	6	7	8	9	11
	12	13	14	15	16	17	18
	19	20	21	22	23	24	25
ŚRĀVAṆA 1981	26	27	28	29	30	1	2
	3	4	5	6	7	8	9
	10	11	12	14	15	16	17
	18	19	20	21	22	23[c]	24
	25	25	26	27	28	29	30
BHĀDRAPADA 1981	1	2	3	4[d]	5	7	8
	9	10	11	12	13	14	15
	16	17	18	19	20	21	22
	23	24	25	26	27	28	29
ĀŚVINA 1981	30	1	2	3	4	5	6
	7	8[e]	9[e]	11	12	13	14
	15	16	17	18	19	20	20
	21	22	23	24	25	26	27
KĀRTTIKA 1981	28	29	30	1[f]	2	4	5
	6	7	8	9	10	11	12
	13	14	15	16	17	18	19
	20	21	22	23	24	24	26
MĀRGAŚIRA 1981	27	28	29	30	1	2	3
	4	5	6	7	8	10	11[g]
	12	13	13	14	15	16	17
	18	19	20	21	22	23	24
PAUSHA 1981	25	26	27	28	29	30	1
	3	4	5	6	7	8	9

HINDU SOLAR 1845/1846‡

Month	Sun	Mon	Tue	Wed	Thu	Fri	Sat
PAUSHA 1845	16	17	18	19	20	21	22
	23	24	25	26	27	28	29
MĀGHA 1845	30	1[b]	2	3	4	5	6
	7	8	9	10	11	12	13
	14	15	16	17	18	19	20
	21	22	23	24	25	26	27
PHĀLGUNA 1845	28	29	1	2	3	4	5
	6	7	8	9	10	11	12
	13	14	15	16	17	18	19
	20	21	22	23	24	25	26
CHAITRA 1845	27	28	29	30	1	2	3
	4	5	6	7	8	9	10
	11	12	13	14	15	16	17
	18	19	20	21	22	23	24
VAIŚĀKHA 1846	25	26	27	28	29	30	1[a]
	2	3	4	5	6	7	8
	9	10	11	12	13	14	15
	16	17	18	19	20	21	22
	23	24	25	26	27	28	29
JYAISHTHA 1846	30	31	1	2	3	4	5
	6	7	8	9	10	11	12
	13	14	15	16	17	18	19
	20	21	22	23	24	25	26
ĀSHĀḌHA 1846	27	28	29	30	31	32	1
	2	3	4	5	6	7	8
	9	10	11	12	13	14	15
	16	17	18	19	20	21	22
	23	24	25	26	27	28	29
ŚRĀVAṆA 1846	30	31	1	2	3	4	5
	6	7	8	9	10	11	12
	13	14	15	16	17	18	19
	20	21	22	23	24	25	26
BHĀDRAPADA 1846	27	28	29	30	31	32	1
	2	3	4	5	6	7	8
	9	10	11	12	13	14	15
	16	17	18	19	20	21	22
	23	24	25	26	27	28	29
ĀŚVINA 1846	30	31	1	2	3	4	5
	6	7	8	9	10	11	12
	13	14	15	16	17	18	19
	20	21	22	23	24	25	26
KĀRTTIKA 1846	27	28	29	30	1	2	3
	4	5	6	7	8	9	10
	11	12	13	14	15	16	17
	18	19	20	21	22	23	24
MĀRGAŚIRA 1846	25	26	27	28	29	30	1
	2	3	4	5	6	7	8
	9	10	11	12	13	14	15
	16	17	18	19	20	21	22
	23	24	25	26	27	28	29
PAUSHA 1846	30	1	2	3	4	5	6
	7	8	9	10	11	12	13
	14	15	16	17	18	19	20

ISLAMIC (ASTRONOMICAL) 1342/1343

Month	Sun	Mon	Tue	Wed	Thu	Fri	Sat
JUMĀDĀ I 1342	22	23	24	25	26	27	28
JUMĀDĀ II 1342	29	30	1	2	3	4	5
	6	7	8	9	10	11	12
	13	14	15	16	17	18	19
	20	21	22	23	24	25	26
RAJAB 1342	27	28	29	1	2	3	4
	5	6	7	8	9	10	11
	12	13	14	15	16	17	18
	19	20	21	22	23	24	25
SHA'BĀN 1342	26	27[d]	28	29	30	1	2
	3	4	5	6	7	8	9
	10	11	12	13	14	15	16
	17	18	19	20	21	22	23
	24	25	26	27	28	29	30
RAMAḌĀN 1342	1[e]	2	3	4	5	6	7
	8	9	10	11	12	13	14
	15	16	17	18	19	20	21
	22	23	24	25	26	27	28
SHAWWĀL 1342	29	1[f]	2	3	4	5	6
	7	8	9	10	11	12	13
	14	15	16	17	18	19	20
	21	22	23	24	25	26	27
DHU AL-QA'DA 1342	28	29	30	1	2	3	4
	5	6	7	8	9	10	11
	12	13	14	15	16	17	18
	19	20	21	22	23	24	25
DHU AL-ḤIJJA 1342	26	27	28	29	30	1	2
	3	4	5	6	7	8	9
	10[g]	11	12	13	14	15	16
	17	18	19	20	21	22	23
MUḤARRAM 1343	24	25	26	27	28	29	1[a]
	2	3	4	5	6	7	8
	9	10[b]	11	12	13	14	15
	16	17	18	19	20	21	22
	23	24	25	26	27	28	29
ṢAFAR 1343	30	1	2	3	4	5	6
	7	8	9	10	11	12	13
	14	15	16	17	18	19	20
	21	22	23	24	25	26	27
RABĪ' I 1343	28	29	1	2	3	4	5
	6	7	8	9	10	11	12[c]
	13	14	15	16	17	18	19
	20	21	22	23	24	25	26
RABĪ' II 1343	27	28	29	1	2	3	4
	5	6	7	8	9	10	11
	12	13	14	15	16	17	18
	19	20	21	22	23	24	25
JUMĀDĀ I 1343	26	27	28	29	30	1	2
	3	4	5	6	7	8	9
	10	11	12	13	14	15	16
	17	18	19	20	21	22	23
JUMĀDĀ II 1343	24	25	26	27	28	29	1
	2	3	4	5	6	7	8

GREGORIAN 1924‡

Julian‡ (Sun)	Sun	Mon	Tue	Wed	Thu	Fri	Sat	Month
Dec 17	30	31	1	2	3	4	5	JANUARY 1924
	6	7[a]	8	9	10	11	12	
Dec 31	13	14[b]	15	16	17	18	19	
	20	21	22	23	24	25	26	
Jan 14	27	28	29	30	31	1	2	FEBRUARY 1924
	3	4	5	6	7	8	9	
Jan 28	10	11	12	13	14	15	16	
	17	18	19	20	21	22	23	
Feb 11	24	25	26	27	28	29	1	MARCH 1924
	2	3	4	5[c]	6	7	8	
Feb 25	9	10	11	12	13	14	15	
	16[d]	17	18	19	20	21	22	
Mar 10	23	24	25	26	27	28	29	
	30	31	1	2	3	4	5	APRIL 1924
Mar 24	6	7	8	9	10	11	12	
	13	14	15	16	17	18	19	
Apr 7	20[e]	21	22	23	24	25	26	
	27[f]	28	29	30	1	2	3	MAY 1924
Apr 21	4	5	6	7	8	9	10	
	11	12	13	14	15	16	17	
May 5	18	19	20	21	22	23	24	
	25	26	27	28	29	30	31	
May 19	1	2	3	4	5	6	7	JUNE 1924
	8	9	10	11	12	13	14	
Jun 2	15	16	17	18	19	20	21	
	22	23	24	25	26	27	28	
Jun 16	29	30	1	2	3	4	5	JULY 1924
	6	7	8	9	10	11	12	
Jun 30	13	14	15	16	17	18	19	
	20	21	22	23	24	25	26	
Jul 14	27	28	29	30	31	1	2	AUGUST 1924
	3	4	5	6	7	8	9	
Jul 28	10	11	12	13	14	15	16	
	17	18	19	20	21	22	23	
Aug 11	24	25	26	27	28	29	30	
	31	1	2	3	4	5	6	SEPTEMBER 1924
Aug 25	7	8	9	10	11	12	13	
	14	15	16	17	18	19	20	
Sep 8	21	22	23	24	25	26	27	
	28	29	30	1	2	3	4	OCTOBER 1924
Sep 22	5	6	7	8	9	10	11	
	12	13	14	15	16	17	18	
Oct 6	19	20	21	22	23	24	25	
	26	27	28	29	30	31	1	NOVEMBER 1924
Oct 20	2	3	4	5	6	7	8	
	9	10	11	12	13	14	15	
Nov 3	16	17	18	19	20	21	22	
	23	24	25	26	27	28	29	
Nov 17	30[g]	1	2	3	4	5	6	DECEMBER 1924
	7	8	9	10	11	12	13	
Dec 1	14	15	16	17	18	19	20	
	21	22	23	24	25[h]	26	27	
Dec 15	28	29	30	31	1	2	3	

Persian: [a]New Year; [b]Sizdeh Bedar

Hindu Lunar: ‡Leap year; [a]New Year (Raktāksha); [b]Birthday of Rāma; [c]Birthday of Krishna; [d]Ganēśa Chaturthī; [e]Dashara; [f]Diwali; [g]Birthday of Vishnu; [h]Night of Śiva; [i]Holi

Hindu Solar: ‡Leap year; [a]New Year (Dhātṛi); [b]Pongal

Islamic: [a]New Year; [b]'Āshūrā'; [c]Prophet's Birthday; [d]Ascent of the Prophet; [e]Start of Ramaḍān; [f]'Id al-Fiṭr; [g]'Id al-'Aḍḥā

Gregorian: ‡Leap year; [a]Orthodox Christmas; [b]Julian New Year; [c]Ash Wednesday; [d]Feast of Orthodoxy; [e]Easter; [f]Orthodox Easter; [g]Advent; [h]Christmas

1925

Month	Sun	Mon	Tue	Wed	Thu	Fri	Sat	Lunar Phases	ISO WEEK (Mon)	JULIAN DAY (Sun noon)
JANUARY 1925	28	29	30	31	◐[a]	2	3	23:25	1	2424148
	4	5	6	7	8	9	○	2:47	2	2424155
	11	12	13	14	15	16	◑	23:33	3	2424162
	18	19	20	21	22	23	●	14:45	4	2424169
	25	26	27	28	29	30	◐	16:43	5	2424176
FEBRUARY 1925	1	2	3	4	5	6	7		6	2424183
	○	9	10	11	12	13	14	21:49	7	2424190
	15	◑	17	18	19	20	21	9:41	8	2424197
	22	●	24	25	26	27	28	2:12	9	2424204
MARCH 1925	1	◐	3	4	5	6	7	12:06	10	2424211
	8	9	○	11	12	13	14	14:21	11	2424218
	15	16	◑	18	19	20	21[b]	17:21	12	2424225
	22	23	●	25	26	27	28	14:03	13	2424232
	29	30	31	◐	2	3	4	8:12	14	2424239
APRIL 1925	5	6	7	8	○	10	11	3:33	15	2424246
	12	13	14	◑	16	17	18	23:40	16	2424253
	19	20	21	22	●	24	25	2:28	17	2424260
	26	27	28	29	30	◐	2	3:20	18	2424267
MAY 1925	3	4	5	6	7	○	9	13:42	19	2424274
	10	11	12	13	14	◑	16	5:46	20	2424281
	17	18	19	20	21	●	23	15:48	21	2424288
	24	25	26	27	28	29	◐	20:04	22	2424295
	31	1	2	3	4	5	○	21:48	23	2424302
JUNE 1925	7	8	9	10	11	12	◑	12:44	24	2424309
	14	15	16	17	18	19	20		25	2424316
	●[c]	22	23	24	25	26	27	6:17	26	2424323
	28	◐	30	1	2	3	4	9:43	27	2424330
JULY 1925	5	○	7	8	9	10	11	4:54	28	2424337
	◑	13	14	15	16	17	18	21:34	29	2424344
	19	●	21	22	23	24	25	21:40	30	2424351
	26	27	◐	29	30	31	1	20:23	31	2424358
AUGUST 1925	2	3	○	5	6	7	8	11:59	32	2424365
	9	10	◑	12	13	14	15	9:10	33	2424372
	16	17	18	●	20	21	22	13:15	34	2424379
	23	24	25	26	◐	28	29	4:46	35	2424386
	30	31	1	○	3	4	5	19:53	36	2424393
SEPTEMBER 1925	6	7	8	9	◑	11	12	0:11	37	2424400
	13	14	15	16	17	●	19	4:12	38	2424407
	20	21	22	23[d]	24	◐	26	11:51	39	2424414
	27	28	29	30	1	○	3	5:23	40	2424421
OCTOBER 1925	4	5	6	7	8	◑	10	18:34	41	2424428
	11	12	13	14	15	16	●	18:06	42	2424435
	18	19	20	21	22	23	◐	18:38	43	2424442
	25	26	27	28	29	30	○	17:17	44	2424449
NOVEMBER 1925	1	2	3	4	5	6	7		45	2424456
	◑	9	10	11	12	13	14	15:13	46	2424463
	15	●	17	18	19	20	21	6:58	47	2424470
	22	◐	24	25	26	27	28	2:06	48	2424477
	29	○	1	2	3	4	5	8:11	49	2424484
DECEMBER 1925	6	7	◑	9	10	11	12	12:11	50	2424491
	13	14	●	16	17	18	19	19:05	51	2424498
	20	21	◐[e]	23	24	25	26	11:08	52	2424505
	27	28	29	○	31	1	2	2:01	53	2424512

ISO WEEK	HEBREW 5685/5686	Sun	Mon	Tue	Wed	Thu	Fri	Sat	Molad
1	TEVETH 5685	1[e]	2[e]	3	4	5	6	7	Fri 9h17m3p
2		8	9	10	11	12	13	14	
3		15	16	17	18	19	20	21	
4		22	23	24	25	26	27	28	
5	SHEVAT 5685	29	1	2	3	4	5	6	Sat 22h1m4p
6		7	8	9	10	11	12	13	
7		14	15	16	17	18	19	20	
8		21	22	23	24	25	26	27	
9	ADAR 5685	28	29	30	1	2	3	4	Mon 10h45m5p
10		5	6	7	8	9	10	11	
11		12	13	14[f]	15	16	17	18	
12		19	20	21	22	23	24	25	
13	NISAN 5685	26	27	28	29	1	2	3	Tue 23h29m6p
14		4	5	6	7	8	9	10	
15		11	12	13	14*	15[g]	16	17	
16		18	19	20	21	22	23	24	
17	IYYAR 5685	25	26	27	28	29	30	1	Thu 12h13m7p
18		2	3	4	5	6	7	8	
19		9	10	11	12	13	14	15	
20		16	17	18	19	20	21	22	
21		23	24	25	26	27	28	29	
22	SIVAN 5685	1	2	3	4	5	6[h]	7	Sat 0h57m8p
23		8	9	10	11	12	13	14	
24		15	16	17	18	19	20	21	
25		22	23	24	25	26	27	28	
26	TAMMUZ 5685	29	30	1	2	3	4	5	Sun 13h41m9p
27		6	7	8	9	10	11	12	
28		13	14	15	16	17	18	19	
29		20	21	22	23	24	25	26	
30	AV 5685	27	28	29	1	2	3	4	Tue 2h25m10p
31		5	6	7	8	9[i]	10	11	
32		12	13	14	15	16	17	18	
33		19	20	21	22	23	24	25	
34	ELUL 5685	26	27	28	29	30	1	2	Wed 15h9m11p
35		3	4	5	6	7	8	9	
36		10	11	12	13	14	15	16	
37		17	18	19	20	21	22	23	
38	TISHRI 5686	24	25	26	27	28	29	1[a]	Fri 3h53m12p
39		2[a]	3	4	5	6	7	8	
40		9	10[b]	11	12	13	14	15[c]	
41		16	17	18	19	20	21	22	
42		23	24	25	26	27	28	29	
43	HESHVAN 5686	30	1	2	3	4	5	6	Sat 16h37m13p
44		7	8	9	10	11	12	13	
45		14	15	16	17	18	19	20	
46		21	22	23	24	25	26	27	
47	KISLEV 5686	28	29	30	1	2	3	4	Mon 5h21m14p
48		5	6	7	8	9	10	11	
49		12	13	14	15	16	17	18[d]	
50		19	20	21	22	23	24	25[e]	
51	TEVETH 5686	26[e]	27[e]	28[e]	29[e]	30[e]	1[e]	2[e]	Tue 18h5m15p
52		3	4	5	6	7	8	9	
53		10	11	12	13	14	15	16	

ISO WEEK	CHINESE Jiǎ-Zǐ/Yǐ-Chǒu‡	Sun	Mon	Tue	Wed	Thu	Fri	Sat	Solar Term
1	MONTH 12 Jiǎ-Zǐ	3	4	5	6	7	8	9	
2		10	11	12	13	14	15	16	Xiǎo hán
3		17	18	19	20	21	22	23	
4		24	25	**26**	27	28	29	1[a]	Dà hán
5	MONTH 1 Yǐ-Chǒu	2	3	4	5	6	7	8	
6		9	10	11	12	13	14	15[b]	Lì chūn
7		16	17*	18	19	20	21	22	
8		23	24	25	26	**27**	28	29	Yǔ shuǐ
9	MONTH 2 Yǐ-Chǒu	30	1	2	3	4	5	6	
10		7	8	9	10	11	12	13	Jīng zhé
11		14	15	16	17	18	19	20	
12		21	22	23	24	25	26	**27**	Chūn fēn
13	MONTH 3 Yǐ-Chǒu	28	29	1	2	3	4	5	
14		6	7	8	9	10	11	12	
15		13[c]	14	15	16	17	18*	19	Qīng míng
16		20	21	22	23	24	25	26	
17	MONTH 4 Yǐ-Chǒu	27	**28**	29	30	1	2	3	Gǔ yǔ
18		4	5	6	7	8	9	10	
19		11	12	13	14	15	16	17	Lì xià
20		18	19	20	21	22	23	24	
21	LEAP MONTH 4 Yǐ-Chǒu	25	26	27	28	**29**	1	2	Xiǎo mǎn
22		3	4	5	6	7	8	9	
23		10	11	12	13	14	15	16	Máng zhòng
24		17	18	19*	20	21	22	23	
25		24	25	26	27	28	29	30	
26	MONTH 5 Yǐ-Chǒu	1	**2**	3	4	5[d]	6	7	Xià zhì
27		8	9	10	11	12	13	14	
28		15	16	17	18	19	20	21	Xiǎo shǔ
29		22	23	24	25	26	27	28	
30	MONTH 6 Yǐ-Chǒu	29	30	1	2	**3**	4	5	Dà shǔ
31		6	7	8	9	10	11	12	
32		13	14	15	16	17	18	19*	Lì qiū
33		20	21	22	23	24	25	26	
34	MONTH 7 Yǐ-Chǒu	27	28	29	1	2	3	4	
35		5	**6**	7[e]	8	9	10	11	Chǔ shǔ
36		12	13	14	15[f]	16	17	18	
37		19	20	21	22	23	24	25	Bái lù
38	MONTH 8 Yǐ-Chǒu	26	27	28	29	30	1	2	
39		3	4	5	**6**	7	8	9	Qiū fēn
40		10	11	12	13	14	15[g]	16	
41		17	18	19	20*	21	22	23	Hán lù
42		24	25	26	27	28	29	30	
43	MONTH 9 Yǐ-Chǒu	1	2	3	4	5	6	**7**	Shuāng jiàng
44		8	9[h]	10	11	12	13	14	
45		15	16	17	18	19	20	21	
46		22	23	24	25	26	27	28	Lì dōng
47	MONTH 10 Yǐ-Chǒu	29	1	2	3	4	5	6	
48		7	**8**	9	10	11	12	13	Xiǎo xuě
49		14	15	16	17	18	19	20	
50		21*	22	23	24	25	26	27	Dà xuě
51	MONTH 11 Yǐ-Chǒu	28	29	30	1	2	3	4	
52		5	6	7[i]	8	9	10	11	Dōng zhì
53		12	13	14	15	16	17	18	

ISO WEEK	COPTIC 1641/1642	Sun	Mon	Tue	Wed	Thu	Fri	Sat	ETHIOPIC 1917/1918
1	KOIAK 1641	19	20	21	22	23	24	25	TĀKHŚĀŚ 1917
2	TŌBE 1641	26	27	28	29[c]	30	1	2	TER 1917
3		3	4	5	6[d]	7	8	9	
4		10	11[e]	12	13	14	15	16	
5		17	18	19	20	21	22	23	
6		24	25	26	27	28	29	30	
7	MESHIR 1641	1	2	3	4	5	6	7	YAKĀTIT 1917
8		8	9	10	11	12	13	14	
9		15	16	17	18	19	20	21	
10		22	23	24	25	26	27	28	
11	PAREMOTEP 1641	29	30	1	2	3	4	5	MAGĀBIT 1917
12		6	7	8	9	10	11	12	
13		13	14	15	16	17	18	19	
14		20	21	22	23	24	25	26	
15	PARMOUTE 1641	27	28	29	30	1	2	3	MIYĀZYĀ 1917
16		4	5	6	7	8	9	10	
17		11[f]	12	13	14	15	16	17	
18		18	19	20	21	22	23	24	
19	PASHONS 1641	25	26	27	28	29[g]	30	1	GENBOT 1917
20		2	3	4	5	6	7	8	
21		9	10	11	12	13	14	15	
22		16	17	18	19	20	21	22	
23		23	24	25	26	27	28	29	
24	PAŌNE 1641	30	1	2	3	4	5	6	SANĒ 1917
25		7	8	9	10	11	12	13	
26		14	15	16	17	18	19	20	
27		21	22	23	24	25	26	27	
28	EPĒP 1641	28	29	30	1	2	3	4	HAMLĒ 1917
29		5	6	7	8	9	10	11	
30		12	13	14	15	16	17	18	
31		19	20	21	22	23	24	25	
32	MESORĒ 1641	26	27	28	29	30	1	2	NAHASĒ 1917
33		3	4	5	6	7	8	9	
34		10	11	12	13[h]	14	15	16	
35		17	18	19	20	21	22	23	
36		24	25	26	27	28	29	30	
37	EPAG. 1641 / THOOUT 1642	1	2	3	4	5	1[a]	2	PĀG. 1917 / MASKARAM 1918
38		3	4	5	6	7	8	9	
39		10	11	12	13	14	15	16	
40		17[b]	18	19	20	21	22	23	
41		24	25	26	27	28	29	30	
42	PAOPE 1642	1	2	3	4	5	6	7	TEQEMT 1918
43		8	9	10	11	12	13	14	
44		15	16	17	18	19	20	21	
45		22	23	24	25	26	27	28	
46	ATHŌR 1642	29	30	1	2	3	4	5	HEDĀR 1918
47		6	7	8	9	10	11	12	
48		13	14	15	16	17	18	19	
49		20	21	22	23	24	25	26	
50	KOIAK 1642	27	28	29	30	1	2	3	TĀKHŚĀŚ 1918
51		4	5	6	7	8	9	10	
52		11	12	13	14	15	16	17	
53		18	19	20	21	22	23	24	

[a] New Year
[b] Spring (3:12)
[c] Summer (22:50)
[d] Autumn (13:43)
[e] Winter (8:36)
● New moon
◐ First quarter moon
○ Full moon
◑ Last quarter moon

[a] New Year
[b] Yom Kippur
[c] Sukkot
[d] Winter starts
[e] Ḥanukkah
[f] Purim
[g] Passover
[h] Shavuot
[i] Fast of Av
* New solar cycle

‡ Leap year
[a] New Year (4623, Ox)
[b] Lantern Festival
[c] Qīngmíng
[d] Dragon Festival
[e] Qīqiǎo
[f] Hungry Ghosts
[g] Mid-Autumn Festival
[h] Double-Ninth Festival
[i] Dōngzhì
* Start of 60-name cycle

[a] New Year
[b] Building of the Cross
[c] Christmas
[d] Jesus's Circumcision
[e] Epiphany
[f] Easter
[g] Mary's Announcement
[h] Jesus's Transfiguration

1925

PERSIAN (ASTRONOMICAL) 1303/1304‡

Month	Sun	Mon	Tue	Wed	Thu	Fri	Sat
DEY 1303	7	8	9	10	11	12	13
	14	15	16	17	18	19	20
	21	22	23	24	25	26	27
	28	29	30	1	2	3	4
BAHMAN 1303	5	6	7	8	9	10	11
	12	13	14	15	16	17	18
	19	20	21	22	23	24	25
	26	27	28	29	30	1	2
ESFAND 1303	3	4	5	6	7	8	9
	10	11	12	13	14	15	16
	17	18	19	20	21	22	23
	24	25	26	27	28	29	1[a]
FARVARDĪN 1304	2	3	4	5	6	7	8
	9	10	11	12	13[b]	14	15
	16	17	18	19	20	21	22
	23	24	25	26	27	28	29
	30	31	1	2	3	4	5
ORDĪBEHEŠT 1304	6	7	8	9	10	11	12
	13	14	15	16	17	18	19
	20	21	22	23	24	25	26
	27	28	29	30	31	1	2
XORDĀD 1304	3	4	5	6	7	8	9
	10	11	12	13	14	15	16
	17	18	19	20	21	22	23
	24	25	26	27	28	29	30
	31	1	2	3	4	5	6
TĪR 1304	7	8	9	10	11	12	13
	14	15	16	17	18	19	20
	21	22	23	24	25	26	27
	28	29	30	31	1	2	3
MORDĀD 1304	4	5	6	7	8	9	10
	11	12	13	14	15	16	17
	18	19	20	21	22	23	24
	25	26	27	28	29	30	31
SHAHRĪVAR 1304	1	2	3	4	5	6	7
	8	9	10	11	12	13	14
	15	16	17	18	19	20	21
	22	23	24	25	26	27	28
	29	30	31	1	2	3	4
MEHR 1304	5	6	7	8	9	10	11
	12	13	14	15	16	17	18
	19	20	21	22	23	24	25
	26	27	28	29	30	1	2
ABĀN 1304	3	4	5	6	7	8	9
	10	11	12	13	14	15	16
	17	18	19	20	21	22	23
	24	25	26	27	28	29	30
ĀZAR 1304	1	2	3	4	5	6	7
	8	9	10	11	12	13	14
	15	16	17	18	19	20	21
	22	23	24	25	26	27	28
DEY 1304	29	30	1	2	3	4	5
	6	7	8	9	10	11	12

‡Leap year
[a]New Year
[b]Sizdeh Bedar

HINDU LUNAR 1981/1982

Month	Sun	Mon	Tue	Wed	Thu	Fri	Sat
PAUSHA 1981	3	4	5	6	7	8	9
	10	11	12	13	14	15	15
	16	17	18	19	20	21	22
	23	24	**25**	27	28	29	30
MĀGHA 1981	1	2	3	4	5	6	7
	8	9	10	11	12	13	14
	15	16	17	18	19	20	21
	22	23	24	25	26	27	28[h]
	29	**30**	2	3	4	5	6
PHĀLGUNA 1981	7	8	8	9	10	11	12
	13	14	15[i]	16	17	18	19
	20	21	22	**23**	25	26	27
	28	29	30	1[a]	2	3	4
CHAITRA 1982	5	6	7	8	9[b]	10	11
	11	12	13	14	15	16	**17**
	19	20	21	22	23	24	25
	26	27	28	29	30	1	2
VAIŚĀKHA 1982	3	4	5	6	7	8	9
	10	11	12	13	14	15	16
	17	18	19	20	**21**	23	24
	25	26	27	28	29	30	1
JYAISHTHA 1982	2	3	4	5	6	6	7
	8	9	10	11	12	13	**14**
	16	17	18	19	20	21	22
	23	24	25	26	27	28	29
	30	1	2	3	4	5	6
ĀSHĀDHA 1982	7	8	9	10	11	12	13
	14	15	16	**17**	19	20	21
	22	23	24	25	26	27	28
	29	30	1	2	3	3	4
ŚRĀVANA 1982	5	6	7	8	**9**	11	12
	13	14	15	16	17	18	19
	20	21	22	23[c]	24	25	26
	27	28	29	30	1	2	3
BHĀDRAPADA 1982	4[d]	5	6	7	8	9	10
	11	**12**	14	15	16	17	18
	19	20	21	22	23	24	25
	26	27	28	29	29	30	1
ĀŚVINA 1982	2	3	4	**5**	7	8[e]	9[e]
	10[e]	11	12	13	14	15	16
	17	18	19	20	21	22	23
	24	25	26	27	28	29	30
KĀRTTIKA 1982	1[f]	2	3	4	5	6	7
	8	**9**	11	12	13	14	15
	16	17	18	19	20	21	22
	23	23	24	25	26	27	28
	29	30	1	2	**3**	5	6
MĀRGAŚĪRA 1982	7	8	9	10	11[g]	12	13
	14	15	16	17	18	19	20
	21	22	23	24	25	26	27
	28	29	30	1	2	3	4
PAUSHA 1982	5	6	7	**8**	10	11	12
	13	14	15	16	16	17	18

[a]New Year (Krodhana)
[b]Birthday of Rāma
[c]Birthday of Krishna
[d]Ganēśa Chaturthī
[e]Dashara
[f]Diwali
[g]Birthday of Vishnu
[h]Night of Śiva
[i]Holi

HINDU SOLAR 1846‡/1847

Month	Sun	Mon	Tue	Wed	Thu	Fri	Sat
PAUSHA 1846	14	15	16	17	18	19	20
	21	22	23	24	25	26	27
	28	29	1[b]	2	3	4	5
MĀGHA 1846	6	7	8	9	10	11	12
	13	14	15	16	17	18	19
	20	21	22	23	24	25	26
	27	28	29	1	2	3	4
PHĀLGUNA 1846	5	6	7	8	9	10	11
	12	13	14	15	16	17	18
	19	20	21	22	23	24	25
	26	27	28	29	30	1	2
CHAITRA 1846	3	4	5	6	7	8	9
	10	11	12	13	14	15	16
	17	18	19	20	21	22	23
	24	25	26	27	28	29	30
	31	1[a]	2	3	4	5	6
VAIŚĀKHA 1847	7	8	9	10	11	12	13
	14	15	16	17	18	19	20
	21	22	23	24	25	26	27
	28	29	30	31	1	2	3
JYAISHTHA 1847	4	5	6	7	8	9	10
	11	12	13	14	15	16	17
	18	19	20	21	22	23	24
	25	26	27	28	29	30	31
ĀSHĀDHA 1847	1	2	3	4	5	6	7
	8	9	10	11	12	13	14
	15	16	17	18	19	20	21
	22	23	24	25	26	27	28
	29	30	31	32	1	2	3
ŚRĀVANA 1847	4	5	6	7	8	9	10
	11	12	13	14	15	16	17
	18	19	20	21	22	23	24
	25	26	27	28	29	30	31
BHĀDRAPADA 1847	1	2	3	4	5	6	7
	8	9	10	11	12	13	14
	15	16	17	18	19	20	21
	22	23	24	25	26	27	28
	29	30	31	1	2	3	4
ĀŚVINA 1847	5	6	7	8	9	10	11
	12	13	14	15	16	17	18
	19	20	21	22	23	24	25
	26	27	28	29	30	31	1
KĀRTTIKA 1847	2	3	4	5	6	7	8
	9	10	11	12	13	14	15
	16	17	18	19	20	21	22
	23	24	25	26	27	28	29
MĀRGAŚĪRA 1847	1	2	3	4	5	6	7
	8	9	10	11	12	13	14
	15	16	17	18	19	20	21
	22	23	24	25	26	27	28
	29	30	1	2	3	4	5
PAUSHA 1847	6	7	8	9	10	11	12
	13	14	15	16	17	18	19

‡Leap year
[a]New Year (Iśvara)
[b]Pongal

ISLAMIC (ASTRONOMICAL) 1343/1344

Month	Sun	Mon	Tue	Wed	Thu	Fri	Sat
	2	3	4	5	6	7	8
JUMĀDĀ II 1343	9	10	11	12	13	14	15
	16	17	18	19	20	21	22
	23	24	25	26	27	28	29
	30	1	2	3	4	5	6
RAJAB 1343	7	8	9	10	11	12	13
	14	15	16	17	18	19	20
	21	22	23	24	25	26	27[d]
	28	29	1	2	3	4	5
SHA'BĀN 1343	6	7	8	9	10	11	12
	13	14	15	16	17	18	19
	20	21	22	23	24	25	26
	27	28	29	30	1[e]	2	3
RAMADĀN 1343	4	5	6	7	8	9	10
	11	12	13	14	15	16	17
	18	19	20	21	22	23	24
	25	26	27	28	29	1[f]	2
SHAWWĀL 1343	3	4	5	6	7	8	9
	10	11	12	13	14	15	16
	17	18	19	20	21	22	23
	24	25	26	27	28	29	30
DHU AL-QA'DA 1343	1	2	3	4	5	6	7
	8	9	10	11	12	13	14
	15	16	17	18	19	20	21
	22	23	24	25	26	27	28
	29	30	1	2	3	4	5
DHU AL-HIJJA 1343	6	7	8	9	10[g]	11	12
	13	14	15	16	17	18	19
	20	21	22	23	24	25	26
	27	28	29	1[a]	2	3	4
MUHARRAM 1344	5	6	7	8	9	10[b]	11
	12	13	14	15	16	17	18
	19	20	21	22	23	24	25
	26	27	28	29	30	1	2
SAFAR 1344	3	4	5	6	7	8	9
	10	11	12	13	14	15	16
	17	18	19	20	21	22	23
	24	25	26	27	28	29	1
RABĪ' I 1344	2	3	4	5	6	7	8
	9	10	11	12[c]	13	14	15
	16	17	18	19	20	21	22
	23	24	25	26	27	28	29
	30	1	2	3	4	5	6
RABĪ' II 1344	7	8	9	10	11	12	13
	14	15	16	17	18	19	20
	21	22	23	24	25	26	27
	28	29	1	2	3	4	5
JUMĀDĀ I 1344	6	7	8	9	10	11	12
	13	14	15	16	17	18	19
	20	21	22	23	24	25	26
	27	28	29	30	1	2	3
JUMĀDĀ II 1344	4	5	6	7	8	9	10
	11	12	13	14	15	16	17

[a]New Year
[b]'Ashūrā'
[c]Prophet's Birthday
[d]Ascent of the Prophet
[e]Start of Ramaḍān
[f]'Id al-Fiṭr
[g]'Id al-'Aḍḥā

GREGORIAN 1925

Julian (Sun)	Sun	Mon	Tue	Wed	Thu	Fri	Sat	Month
Dec 15	28	29	30	31	1	2	3	
	4	5	6	7[a]	8	9	10	JANUARY 1925
Dec 29	11	12	13	14[b]	15	16	17	
	18	19	20	21	22	23	24	
Jan 12	25	26	27	28	29	30	31	
	1	2	3	4	5	6	7	
Jan 26	8	9	10	11	12	13	14	FEBRUARY 1925
	15	16	17	18	19	20	21	
Feb 9	22	23	24	25[c]	26	27	28	
	1	2	3	4	5	6	7	
Feb 23	8[d]	9	10	11	12	13	14	MARCH 1925
	15	16	17	18	19	20	21	
Mar 9	22	23	24	25	26	27	28	
	29	30	31	1	2	3	4	
Mar 23	5	6	7	8	9	10	11	APRIL 1925
	12[e]	13	14	15	16	17	18	
Apr 6	19[f]	20	21	22	23	24	25	
	26	27	28	29	30	1	2	
Apr 20	3	4	5	6	7	8	9	
	10	11	12	13	14	15	16	MAY 1925
May 4	17	18	19	20	21	22	23	
	24	25	26	27	28	29	30	
May 18	31	1	2	3	4	5	6	
	7	8	9	10	11	12	13	
Jun 1	14	15	16	17	18	19	20	JUNE 1925
	21	22	23	24	25	26	27	
Jun 15	28	29	30	1	2	3	4	
	5	6	7	8	9	10	11	
Jun 29	12	13	14	15	16	17	18	JULY 1925
	19	20	21	22	23	24	25	
Jul 13	26	27	28	29	30	31	1	
	2	3	4	5	6	7	8	
Jul 27	9	10	11	12	13	14	15	AUGUST 1925
	16	17	18	19	20	21	22	
Aug 10	23	24	25	26	27	28	29	
	30	31	1	2	3	4	5	
Aug 24	6	7	8	9	10	11	12	SEPTEMBER 1925
	13	14	15	16	17	18	19	
Sep 7	20	21	22	23	24	25	26	
	27	28	29	30	1	2	3	
Sep 21	4	5	6	7	8	9	10	
	11	12	13	14	15	16	17	OCTOBER 1925
Oct 5	18	19	20	21	22	23	24	
	25	26	27	28	29	30	31	
Oct 19	1	2	3	4	5	6	7	
	8	9	10	11	12	13	14	NOVEMBER 1925
Nov 2	15	16	17	18	19	20	21	
	22	23	24	25	26	27	28	
Nov 16	29[g]	30	1	2	3	4	5	
	6	7	8	9	10	11	12	DECEMBER 1925
Nov 30	13	14	15	16	17	18	19	
	20	21	22	23	24	25[h]	26	
Dec 14	27	28	29	30	31	1	2	

[a]Orthodox Christmas
[b]Julian New Year
[c]Ash Wednesday
[d]Feast of Orthodoxy
[e]Easter
[f]Orthodox Easter
[g]Advent
[h]Christmas

1926

Gregorian 1926	Sun	Mon	Tue	Wed	Thu	Fri	Sat	Lunar Phases	ISO WEEK (Mon)	JULIAN DAY (Sun noon)	Hebrew 5686/5687‡	Sun	Mon	Tue	Wed	Thu	Fri	Sat	Molad	Chinese Yǐ-Chǒu‡/Bǐng-Yín	Sun	Mon	Tue	Wed	Thu	Fri	Sat	Solar Term	Coptic 1642/1643‡	Sun	Mon	Tue	Wed	Thu	Fri	Sat	Ethiopic 1918/1919‡
	27	28	29	○	31	1[a]	2	2:01	53	2424512		10	11	12	13	14	15	16			12	13	14	15	16	17	18			18	19	20	21	22	23	24	TĀKHŚĀŚ 1918
JANUARY 1926	3	4	5	6	◑	8	9	7:22	1	2424519	TEVETH 5686	17	18	19	20	21	22	23		MONTH 11 Yǐ-Chǒu	19	20	21	22	23	24	25	Xiǎo hán	KOIAK 1642	25	26	27	28	29[c]	30	1	
	10	11	12	13	●	15	16	6:35	2	2424526		24	25	26	27	28	29	1	Thu 6h49m16p		26	27	28	29	1	2	3			2	3	4	5	6[d]	7	8	
	17	18	19	◐	21	22	23	22:31	3	2424533		2	3	4	5	6	7	8		MONTH 12 Yǐ-Chǒu	4	5	6	7	8	9	10	Dà hán	TŌBE 1642	9	10	11[e]	12	13	14	15	ṬER 1918
	24	25	26	27	○	29	30	21:35	4	2424540	SHEVAT 5686	9	10	11	12	13	14	15			11	12	13	14	15	16	17			16	17	18	19	20	21	22	
	31	1	2	3	4	◑	6	23:25	5	2424547		16	17	18	19	20	21	22			18	19	20	21	22*	23	24	Lì chūn		23	24	25	26	27	28	29	
FEBRUARY 1926	7	8	9	10	11	●	13	17:20	6	2424554		23	24	25	26	27	28	29			25	26	27	28	29	30	1[a]			30	1	2	3	4	5	6	
	14	15	16	17	18	◐	20	12:36	7	2424561		30	1	2	3	4	5	6	Fri 19h33m17p	MONTH 1 Bǐng-Yín	2	3	4	5	6	7	8	Yǔ shuǐ	MESHIR 1642	7	8	9	10	11	12	13	YAKĀTIT 1918
	21	22	23	24	25	26	○	16:51	8	2424568	ADAR 5686	7	8	9	10	11	12	13			9	10	11	12	13	14	15[b]			14	15	16	17	18	19	20	
	28	1	2	3	4	5	6		9	2424575		14[f]	15	16	17	18	19	20			16	17	18	19	20	21	22	Jīng zhé		21	22	23	24	25	26	27	
MARCH 1926	◑	8	9	10	11	12	13	11:49	10	2424582		21	22	23	24	25	26	27			23	24	25	26	27	28	29			28	29	30	1	2	3	4	
	●	15	16	17	18	19	20	3:20	11	2424589		28	29	1	2	3	4	5	Sun 8h18m0p		1	2	3	4	5	6	7		PAREMOTEP 1642	5	6	7	8	9	10	11	MAGĀBIT 1918
	◐[b]	22	23	24	25	26	27	5:12	12	2424596	NISAN 5686	6	7	8	9	10	11	12		MONTH 2 Bǐng-Yín	8	9	10	11	12	13	14	Chūn fēn		12	13	14	15	16	17	18	
	28	○	30	31	1	2	3	10:00	13	2424603		13	14	15[g]	16	17	18	19			15	16	17	18	19	20	21			19	20	21	22	23	24	25	
APRIL 1926	4	◑	6	7	8	9	10	20:50	14	2424610		20	21	22	23	24	25	26			22	23[c]*	24	25	26	27	28	Qīng míng		26	27	28	29	30	1	2	
	11	●	13	14	15	16	17	12:56	15	2424617		27	28	29	30	1	2	3	Mon 21h2m1p		29	1	2	3	4	5	6		PARMOUTE 1642	3	4	5	6	7	8	9	MIYĀZYĀ 1918
	18	◐	20	21	22	23	24	23:23	16	2424624	IYYAR 5686	4	5	6	7	8	9	10		MONTH 3 Bǐng-Yín	7	8	9	10	11	12	13	Gǔ yǔ		10	11	12	13	14	15	16	
	25	26	27	○	29	30	1	0:16	17	2424631		11	12	13	14	15	16	17			14	15	16	17	18	19	20			17	18	19	20	21	22	23	
MAY 1926	2	3	4	◑	6	7	8	3:13	18	2424638		18	19	20	21	22	23	24			21	22	23	24	25	26	27	Lì xià		24[f]	25	26	27	28	29[g]	30	
	9	10	●	12	13	14	15	22:55	19	2424645		25	26	27	28	29	1	2	Wed 9h46m2p		28	29	30	1	2	3	4		PASHONS 1642	1	2	3	4	5	6	7	
	16	17	18	◐	20	21	22	17:48	20	2424652	SIVAN 5686	3	4	5	6[h]	7	8	9		MONTH 4 Bǐng-Yín	5	6	7	8	9	10	11	Xiǎo mǎn		8	9	10	11	12	13	14	GENBOT 1918
	23	24	25	26	○	28	29	11:49	21	2424659		10	11	12	13	14	15	16			12	13	14	15	16	17	18			15	16	17	18	19	20	21	
	30	31	1	2	◑	4	5	8:09	22	2424666		17	18	19	20	21	22	23			19	20	21	22	23	24*	25			22	23	24	25	26	27	28	
JUNE 1926	6	7	8	9	●	11	12	10:08	23	2424673		24	25	26	27	28	29	30			26	27	28	29	1	2	3	Máng zhòng		29	30	1	2	3	4	5	
	13	14	15	16	17	◐	19	11:13	24	2424680		1	2	3	4	5	6	7	Thu 22h30m3p	MONTH 5 Bǐng-Yín	4	5[d]	6	7	8	9	10		PAŌNE 1642	6	7	8	9	10	11	12	SANĒ 1918
	20	21	22[c]	23	24	○	26	21:13	25	2424687	TAMMUZ 5686	8	9	10	11	12	13	14			11	12	13	14	15	16	17	Xià zhì		13	14	15	16	17	18	19	
	27	28	29	30	1	◑	3	13:02	26	2424694		15	16	17	18	19	20	21			18	19	20	21	22	23	24			20	21	22	23	24	25	26	
JULY 1926	4	5	6	7	8	●	10	23:06	27	2424701		22	23	24	25	26	27	28			25	26	27	28	29	30	1	Xiǎo shǔ		27	28	29	30	1	2	3	
	11	12	13	14	15	16	17		28	2424708		29	1	2	3	4	5	6	Sat 11h14m4p	MONTH 6 Bǐng-Yín	2	3	4	5	6	7	8		EPĒP 1642	4	5	6	7	8	9	10	HAMLĒ 1918
	◐	19	20	21	22	23	24	2:55	29	2424715	AV 5686	7	8	9[i]	10	11	12	13			9	10	11	12	13	14	15	Dà shǔ		11	12	13	14	15	16	17	
	○	26	27	28	29	30	◑	5:13 19:24	30	2424722		14	15	16	17	18	19	20			16	17	18	19	20	21	22			18	19	20	21	22	23	24	
AUGUST 1926	1	2	3	4	5	6	7		31	2424729		21	22	23	24	25	26	27			23	24	25*	26	27	28	29			25	26	27	28	29	30	1	
	●	9	10	11	12	13	14	13:49	32	2424736		28	29	30	1	2	3	4	Sun 23h58m5p		1	2	3	4	5	6	7[e]	Lì qiū		2	3	4	5	6	7	8	
	15	◐	17	18	19	20	21	16:39	33	2424743	ELUL 5686	5	6	7	8	9	10	11		MONTH 7 Bǐng-Yín	8	9	10	11	12	13	14		MESORĒ 1642	9	10	11	12	13[h]	14	15	NAHASĒ 1918
	22	○	24	25	26	27	28	12:38	34	2424750		12	13	14	15	16	17	18			15[f]	16	17	18	19	20	21	Chǔ shǔ		16	17	18	19	20	21	22	
	29	◑	31	1	2	3	4	4:40	35	2424757		19	20	21	22	23	24	25			22	23	24	25	26	27	28			23	24	25	26	27	28	29	
SEPTEMBER 1926	5	6	●	8	9	10	11	5:45	36	2424764		26	27	28	29	1[a]	2[a]	3	Tue 12h42m6p		29	30	1	2	3	4	5	Bái lù	EPAG. 1642	30	1	2	3	4	5	1[a]	PĀG. 1918
	12	13	14	◐	16	17	18	4:26	37	2424771	TISHRI 5687	4	5	6	7	8	9	10[b]		MONTH 8 Bǐng-Yín	6	7	8	9	10	11	12		THOOUT 1643	2	3	4	5	6	7	8	MASKARAM 1919
	19	20	○	22	23[d]	24	25	20:19	38	2424778		11	12	13	14	15[c]	16	17			13	14	15[g]	16	17	18	19	Qiū fēn		9	10	11	12	13	14	15	
	26	27	◑	29	30	1	2	17:48	39	2424785		18	19	20	21	22	23	24			20	21	22	23	24	25	26*			16	17[b]	18	19	20	21	22	
OCTOBER 1926	3	4	5	●	7	8	9	22:13	40	2424792		25	26	27	28	29	30	1	Thu 1h26m7p		27	28	29	30	1	2	3	Hán lù		23	24	25	26	27	28	29	
	10	11	12	13	◐	15	16	14:28	41	2424799	HESHVAN 5687	2	3	4	5	6	7	8		MONTH 9 Bǐng-Yín	4	5	6	7	8	9[h]	10			30	1	2	3	4	5	6	
	17	18	19	20	○	22	23	5:15	42	2424806		9	10	11	12	13	14	15			11	12	13	14	15	16	17		PAOPE 1643	7	8	9	10	11	12	13	TEQEMT 1919
	24	25	26	27	◑	29	30	10:57	43	2424813		16	17	18	19	20	21	22			18	19	20	21	22	23	24	Shuāng jiàng		14	15	16	17	18	19	20	
	31	1	2	3	4	●	6	14:34	44	2424820		23	24	25	26	27	28	29			25	26	27	28	29	1	2			21	22	23	24	25	26	27	
NOVEMBER 1926	7	8	9	10	11	◐	13	23:01	45	2424827		1	2	3	4	5	6	7	Fri 14h10m8p	MONTH 10 Bǐng-Yín	3	4	5	6	7	8	9	Lì dōng		28	29	30	1	2	3	4	
	14	15	16	17	18	○	20	16:21	46	2424834	KISLEV 5687	8	9	10	11	12	13	14			10	11	12	13	14	15	16		ATHŌR 1643	5	6	7	8	9	10	11	HEDĀR 1919
	21	22	23	24	25	26	◑	7:15	47	2424841		15	16	17	18	19	20	21			17	18	19	20	21	22	23	Xiǎo xuě		12	13	14	15	16	17	18	
	28	29	30	1	2	3	4		48	2424848		22	23	24	25[e]	26[e]	27[e]	28[e]			24	25	26	27*	28	29	30			19	20	21	22	23	24	25	
DECEMBER 1926	●	6	7	8	9	10	11	6:11	49	2424855		29[d][e]	1[e]	2[e]	3[e]	4	5	6	Sun 2h54m9p		1	2	3	4	5	6	7	Dà xuě		26	27	28	29	30	1	2	
	◐	13	14	15	16	17	18	6:47	50	2424862	TEVETH 5687	7	8	9	10	11	12	13		MONTH 11 Bǐng-Yín	8	9	10	11	12	13	14		KOIAK 1643	3	4	5	6	7	8	9	TĀKHŚĀŚ 1919
	○	20	21	22[e]	23	24	25	6:09	51	2424869		14	15	16	17	18	19	20			15	16	17	18[i]	19	20	21	Dōng zhì		10	11	12	13	14	15	16	
	26	◑	28	29	30	31	1	4:59	52	2424876		21	22	23	24	25	26	27			22	23	24	25	26	27	28			17	18	19	20	21	22	23	

Gregorian notes:
[a]New Year
[b]Spring (9:01)
[c]Summer (4:30)
[d]Autumn (19:26)
[e]Winter (14:33)
● New moon
◐ First quarter moon
○ Full moon
◑ Last quarter moon

Hebrew notes:
‡Leap year
[a]New Year
[b]Yom Kippur
[c]Sukkot
[d]Winter starts
[e]Ḥanukkah
[f]Purim
[g]Passover
[h]Shavuot
[i]Fast of Av

Chinese notes:
‡Leap year
[a]New Year (4624, Tiger)
[b]Lantern Festival
[c]Qīngmíng
[d]Dragon Festival
[e]Qīqiǎo
[f]Hungry Ghosts
[g]Mid-Autumn Festival
[h]Double-Ninth Festival
[i]Dōngzhì
*Start of 60-name cycle

Coptic/Ethiopic notes:
‡Leap year
[a]New Year
[b]Building of the Cross
[c]Christmas
[d]Jesus's Circumcision
[e]Epiphany
[f]Easter
[g]Mary's Announcement
[h]Jesus's Transfiguration

Persian (Astronomical) 1304†/1305	Sun	Mon	Tue	Wed	Thu	Fri	Sat	Hindu Lunar 1982/1983‡	Sun	Mon	Tue	Wed	Thu	Fri	Sat	Hindu Solar 1847/1848	Sun	Mon	Tue	Wed	Thu	Fri	Sat	Islamic (Astronomical) 1344/1345	Sun	Mon	Tue	Wed	Thu	Fri	Sat	Julian (Sun)	Sun	Mon	Tue	Wed	Thu	Fri	Sat	Gregorian 1926
	6	7	8	9	10	11	12		13	14	15	16	*16*	17	18		13	14	15	16	17	18	19		11	12	13	14	15	16	17	Dec 14	27	28	29	30	31	1	2	
DEY 1304	13	14	15	16	17	18	19	PAUSHA 1982	19	20	21	22	23	24	25	PAUSHA 1847	20	21	22	23	24	25	26	JUMĀDĀ II 1344	18	19	20	21	22	23	24		3	4	5	6	7[a]	8	9	
	20	21	22	23	24	25	26		26	27	28	29	30	1	**2**		27	28	29	1[b]	2	3	4		25	26	27	28	29	*1*	2	Dec 28	*10*	11	12	13	14[b]	15	16	JANUARY 1926
	27	28	29	30	*1*	2	3		4	5	6	7	8	9	10		5	6	7	8	9	10	11		3	4	5	6	7	8	9		17	18	19	20	21	22	23	
	4	5	6	7	8	9	10	MĀGHA 1982	11	12	13	14	15	16	17	MĀGHA 1847	12	13	14	15	16	17	18	RAJAB 1344	10	11	12	13	14	15	16	Jan 11	*24*	25	26	27	28	29	30	
BAHMAN 1304	11	12	13	14	15	16	17		18	*18*	19	20	21	22	23		19	20	21	22	23	24	25		17	18	19	20	21	22	23		31	1	2	3	4	5	6	
	18	19	20	21	22	23	24		24	25	**26**	28	29[h]	30	1		26	27	28	29	30	1	2		24	25	26	27[d]	28	29	30	Jan 25	*7*	8	9	10	11	12	13	
	25	26	27	28	29	30	*1*		2	3	4	5	6	7	8		3	4	5	6	7	8	9		*1*	2	3	4	5	6	7		14	15	16	17[c]	18	19	20	FEBRUARY 1926
	2	3	4	5	6	7	8	PHĀLGUNA 1982	9	10	11	12	13	14	15[i]	PHĀLGUNA 1847	10	11	12	13	14	15	16	SHA'BĀN 1344	8	9	10	11	12	13	14	Feb 8	*21*	22	23	24	25	26	27	
ESFAND 1304	9	10	11	12	13	14	15		16	17	18	19	20	21	22		17	18	19	20	21	22	23		15	16	17	18	19	20	21		28	1	2	3	4	5	6	
	16	17	18	19	20	21	22		23	24	25	26	27	28	29		24	25	26	27	28	29	1		22	23	24	25	26	27	28	Feb 22	*7*	8	9	10	11	12	13	
	23	24	25	26	27	28	29		30	1[a]	3	4	5	6	7		2	3	4	5	6	7	8		29	1[e]	2	3	4	5	6		14	15	16	17	18	19	20	MARCH 1926
	30*	*1*[a]	2	3	4	5	6		8	9	10	11	*11*	12	13	CHAITRA 1847	9	10	11	12	13	14	15	RAMAḌĀN 1344	7	8	9	10	11	12	13	Mar 8	*21*[d]	22	23	24	25	26	27	
	7	8	9	10	11	12	13[b]	LEAP CHAITRA 1983	14	15	16	17	18	19	20		16	17	18	19	20	21	22		14	15	16	17	18	19	20		28	29	30	31	1	2	3	
FARVARDĪN 1305	14	15	16	17	18	19	20		21	22	23	**24**	26	27	28		23	24	25	26	27	28	29		21	22	23	24	25	26	27	Mar 22	*4*[e]	5	6	7	8	9	10	
	21	22	23	24	25	26	27		29	30	1	2	3	4	5		30	31	1[a]	2	3	4	5		28	29	30	*1*[f]	2	3	4		11	12	13	14	15	16	17	APRIL 1926
	28	29	30	31	*1*	2	3		6	7	8	9[b]	10	11	12		6	7	8	9	10	11	12		5	6	7	8	9	10	11	Apr 5	*18*	19	20	21	22	23	24	
	4	5	6	7	8	9	10	CHAITRA 1983	13	14	15	16	17	18	19	VAIŚĀKHA 1848	13	14	15	16	17	18	19	SHAWWĀL 1344	12	13	14	15	16	17	18		25	26	27	28	29	30	1	
ORDĪBEHEŠT 1305	11	12	13	14	15	16	17		20	21	22	23	24	25	26		20	21	22	23	24	25	26		19	20	21	22	23	24	25	Apr 19	*2*[f]	3	4	5	6	7	8	
	18	19	20	21	22	23	24		27	**28**	30	1	2	3	4		27	28	29	30	31	1	2		26	27	28	29	*1*	2	3		9	10	11	12	13	14	15	MAY 1926
	25	26	27	28	29	30	31		5	6	*6*	7	8	9	10		3	4	5	6	7	8	9		4	5	6	7	8	9	10	May 3	*16*	17	18	19	20	21	22	
	1	2	3	4	5	6	7	VAIŚĀKHA 1983	11	12	13	14	15	16	17	JYAISHṬHA 1848	10	11	12	13	14	15	16	DHU AL-QA'DA 1344	11	12	13	14	15	16	17		23	24	25	26	27	28	29	
	8	9	10	11	12	13	14		18	19	20	**21**	23	24	25		17	18	19	20	21	22	23		18	19	20	21	22	23	24	May 17	*30*	31	1	2	3	4	5	
XORDĀD 1305	15	16	17	18	19	20	21		26	27	28	29	30	1	2		24	25	26	27	28	29	30		25	26	27	28	29	30	*1*		6	7	8	9	10	11	12	
	22	23	24	25	26	27	28		3	4	5	6	7	8	9		31	1	2	3	4	5	6		2	3	4	5	6	7	8	May 31	*13*	14	15	16	17	18	19	JUNE 1926
	29	30	31	*1*	2	3	4	JYAISHṬHA 1983	10	11	12	13	14	15	16	ĀSHĀḌHA 1848	7	8	9	10	11	12	13	DHU AL-ḤIJJA 1344	9	10[g]	11	12	13	14	15		20	21	22	23	24	25	26	
	5	6	7	8	9	10	11		17	18	19	20	21	22	23		14	15	16	17	18	19	20		16	17	18	19	20	21	22	Jun 14	*27*	28	29	30	1	2	3	
TĪR 1305	12	13	14	15	16	17	18		**24**	26	27	28	29	30	1		21	22	23	24	25	26	27		23	24	25	26	27	28	29		4	5	6	7	8	9	10	
	19	20	21	22	23	24	25		2	*2*	3	4	5	6	7		28	29	30	31	32	1	2		1[a]	2[â]	3	4	5	6	7	Jun 28	*11*	12	13	14	15	16	17	JULY 1926
	26	27	28	29	30	31	*1*	ĀSHĀḌHA 1983	8	9	10	11	12	13	14		3	4	5	6	7	8	9	MUḤARRAM 1345	8	9	10[b]	11	12	13	14		18	19	20	21	22	23	24	
	2	3	4	5	6	7	8		15	16	**17**	19	20	21	22	ŚRĀVAṆA 1848	10	11	12	13	14	15	16		15	16	17	18	19	20	21	Jul 12	*25*	26	27	28	29	30	31	
MORDĀD 1305	9	10	11	12	13	14	15		23	24	25	26	27	28	29		17	18	19	20	21	22	23		22	23	24	25	26	27	28		1	2	3	4	5	6	7	
	16	17	18	19	20	21	22		30	1	2	3	4	5	6		24	25	26	27	28	29	30		29	30	1	2	3	4	5	Jul 26	*8*	9	10	11	12	13	14	
	23	24	25	26	27	28	29		7	8	9	10	11	12	13		31	1	2	3	4	5	6		6	7	8	9	10	11	12		15	16	17	18	19	20	21	AUGUST 1926
	30	31	*1*	2	3	4	5	ŚRĀVAṆA 1983	14	15	16	17	18	19	**20**		7	8	9	10	11	12	13	ṢAFAR 1345	13	14	15	16	17	18	19	Aug 9	*22*	23	24	25	26	27	28	
	6	7	8	9	10	11	12		22	23[c]	24	25	26	27	28	BHĀDRAPADA 1848	14	15	16	17	18	19	20		20	21	22	23	24	25	26		29	30	31	1	2	3	4	
SHAHRĪVAR 1305	13	14	15	16	17	18	19		29	*29*	30	1	2	3	4[d]		21	22	23	24	25	26	27		27	28	29	30	*1*	2	3	Aug 23	*5*	6	7	8	9	10	11	
	20	21	22	23	24	25	26		5	6	7	8	9	10	11		28	29	30	31	1	2	3		4	5	6	7	8	9	10		12	13	14	15	16	17	18	SEPTEMBER 1926
	27	28	29	30	31	*1*	2	BHĀDRAPADA 1983	12	**13**	15	16	17	18	19		4	5	6	7	8	9	10	RABĪ' I 1345	11	12[c]	13	14	15	16	17	Sep 6	*19*	20	21	22	23	24	25	
	3	4	5	6	7	8	9		20	21	22	23	24	25	26	ĀŚVINA 1848	11	12	13	14	15	16	17		18	19	20	21	22	23	24		26	27	28	29	30	1	2	
MEHR 1305	10	11	12	13	14	15	16		27	28	29	30	1	2	3		18	19	20	21	22	23	24		25	26	27	28	29	*1*	2	Sep 20	*3*	4	5	6	7	8	9	
	17	18	19	20	21	22	23		4	*4*	6	7	8[e]	9[e]	10[e]		25	26	27	28	29	30	31		3	4	5	6	7	8	9		10	11	12	13	14	15	16	OCTOBER 1926
	24	25	26	27	28	29	30	ĀŚVINA 1983	11	12	13	14	15	16	**17**		1	2	3	4	5	6	7	RABĪ' II 1345	10	11	12	13	14	15	16	Oct 4	*17*	18	19	20	21	22	23	
	1	2	3	4	5	6	7		19	20	21	22	23	*23*	24	KĀRTTIKA 1848	8	9	10	11	12	13	14		17	18	19	20	21	22	23		24	25	26	27	28	29	30	
ĀBĀN 1305	8	9	10	11	12	13	14		25	26	27	28	29	30	1[f]		15	16	17	18	19	20	21		24	25	26	27	28	29	30	Oct 18	*31*	1	2	3	4	5	6	
	15	16	17	18	19	20	21		2	3	4	5	6	7	8		22	23	24	25	26	27	28		*1*	2	3	4	5	6	7		7	8	9	10	11	12	13	
	22	23	24	25	26	27	28	KĀRTTIKA 1983	9	**10**	12	13	14	15	16		29	30	1	2	3	4	5	JUMĀDĀ I 1345	8	9	10	11	12	13	14	Nov 1	*14*	15	16	17	18	19	20	NOVEMBER 1926
	29	30	*1*	2	3	4	5		17	18	19	20	21	22	23	MĀRGAŚIRA 1848	6	7	8	9	10	11	12		15	16	17	18	19	20	21		21	22	23	24	25	26	27	
	6	7	8	9	10	11	12		24	25	26	*26*	27	28	29		13	14	15	16	17	18	19		22	23	24	25	26	27	28	Nov 15	*28*[g]	29	30	1	2	3	4	
ĀZAR 1305	13	14	15	16	17	18	19		30	1	2	3	**4**	6	7		20	21	22	23	24	25	26		29	30	*1*	2	3	4	5		5	6	7	8	9	10	11	
	20	21	22	23	24	25	26	MĀRGAŚIRA 1983	8	9	10	11[g]	12	13	14		27	28	29	1	2	3	4	JUMĀDĀ II 1345	6	7	8	9	10	11	12	Nov 29	*12*	13	14	15	16	17	18	DECEMBER 1926
	27	28	29	30	*1*	2	3		15	16	17	18	19	20	21	PAUSHA 1848	5	6	7	8	9	10	11		13	14	15	16	17	18	19		19	20	21	22	23	24	25[h]	
DEY 1305	4	5	6	7	8	9	10		22	23	24	25	26	27	28		12	13	14	15	16	17	18		20	21	22	23	24	25	26	Dec 13	*26*	27	28	29	30	31	1	

†Leap year
[a]New Year (or prior day)
*Near New Year: −0′47″
[b]Sizdeh Bedar

‡Leap year
[a]New Year (Kshaya)
[b]Birthday of Rāma
[c]Birthday of Krishna
[d]Ganēśa Chaturthī
[e]Dashara
[f]Diwali
[g]Birthday of Vishnu
[h]Night of Śiva
[i]Holi

[a]New Year (Bahudhānya)
[b]Pongal

[a]New Year
[â]New Year (Arithmetic)
[b]'Ashūrā'
[c]Prophet's Birthday
[d]Ascent of the Prophet
[e]Start of Ramaḍān
[f]'Īd al-Fiṭr
[g]'Īd al-'Aḍḥā

[a]Orthodox Christmas
[b]Julian New Year
[c]Ash Wednesday
[d]Feast of Orthodoxy
[e]Easter
[f]Orthodox Easter
[g]Advent
[h]Christmas

1927

Gregorian month	GREGORIAN 1927 (Sun Mon Tue Wed Thu Fri Sat)	Lunar Phases	ISO WEEK (Mon)	JULIAN DAY (Sun noon)	Hebrew month	HEBREW 5687‡/5688 (Sun Mon Tue Wed Thu Fri Sat)	Molad	Chinese month	CHINESE Bĭng-Yín/Dīng-Mǎo (Sun Mon Tue Wed Thu Fri Sat)	Solar Term	Coptic month	COPTIC 1643‡/1644 – ETHIOPIC 1919‡/1920 (Sun Mon Tue Wed Thu Fri Sat)	Ethiopic month
JANUARY 1927	26 ◑ 28 29 30 31 1[a]	4:59	52	2424876	TEVETH 5687	21 22 23 24 25 26 27		MONTH 11 Bĭng-Yín	22 23 24 25 26 27 28		KOIAK 1643	17 18 19 20 21 22 23	TĀKHŚĀŚ 1919
	2 ● 4 5 6 7 8	20:28	1	2424883	SHEVAT 5687	28 29 1 2 3 4 5	Mon 15h38m10p	MONTH 12 Bĭng-Yín	29 30 1 2 *3* 4 5	Xiǎo hán		24 25 26 27 28 29[c] 30	
	9 ◐ 11 12 13 14 15	14:43	2	2424890		6 7 8 9 10 11 12			6 7 8 9 10 11 12		TÔBE 1643	1 2 3 4 5 6[d] 7	ṬER 1919
	16 ○ 18 19 20 21 22	22:27	3	2424897		13 14 15 16 17 18 19			13 14 15 16 17 **18** 19	Dà hán		8 9 10 11[e] 12 13 14	
	23 24 25 ◑ 27 28 29	2:05	4	2424904		20 21 22 23 24 25 26			20 21 22 23 24 25 26			15 16 17 18 19 20 21	
FEBRUARY 1927	30 31 1 ● 3 4 5	8:54	5	2424911	ADAR I 5687	27 28 29 30 1 2 3	Wed 4h22m11p	MONTH 1 Dīng-Mǎo	27* 28 29 1[a] 2 3 *4*	Lì chūn		22 23 24 25 26 27 28	
	6 7 ◐ 9 10 11 12	23:54	6	2424918		4 5 6 7 8 9 10			5 6 7 8 9 10 11		MESHIR 1643	29 30 1 2 3 4 5	YAKĀTIT 1919
	13 14 15 ○ 17 18 19	16:18	7	2424925		11 12 13 14 15 16 17			12 13 14 15[b] 16 17 **18**	Yǔ shuǐ		6 7 8 9 10 11 12	
	20 21 22 23 ◑ 25 26	20:42	8	2424932		18 19 20 21 22 23 24			19 20 21 22 23 24 25			13 14 15 16 17 18 19	
MARCH 1927	27 28 1 2 ● 4 5	19:25	9	2424939	ADAR II 5687	25 26 27 28 29 30 1	Thu 17h6m12p	MONTH 2 Dīng-Mǎo	26 27 28 29 30 1 2			20 21 22 23 24 25 26	
	6 7 8 9 ◐ 11 12	11:03	10	2424946		2 3 4 5 6 7 8			*3* 4 5 6 7 8 9	Jīng zhé	PAREMOTEP 1643	27 28 29 30 1 2 3	MAGĀBIT 1919
	13 14 15 16 17 ○ 19	10:24	11	2424953		9 10 11 12 13 14[f] 15			10 11 12 13 14 15 16			4 5 6 7 8 9 10	
	20 21[b] 22 23 24 25 ◑	11:35	12	2424960		16 17 18 19 20 21 22			17 **18** 19 20 21 22 23	Chūn fēn		11 12 13 14 15 16 17	
APRIL 1927	27 28 29 30 31 1 ●	4:24	13	2424967		23 24 25 26 27 28 29	Sat 5h50m13p	MONTH 3 Dīng-Mǎo	24 25 26 27 28* 29 1			18 19 20 21 22 23 24	
	3 4 5 6 7 8 ◐	0:21	14	2424974	NISAN 5687	1 2 3 4 5 6 7			2 3 4 *5*[c] 6 7 8	Qīng míng	PARMOUTE 1643	25 26 27 28 29 30 1	MIYĀZYĀ 1919
	10 11 12 13 14 15 16		15	2424981		8 9 10 11 12 13 14			9 10 11 12 13 14 15			2 3 4 5 6 7 8	
	○ 18 19 20 21 22 23	3:35	16	2424988		15[g] 16 17 18 19 20 21			16 17 18 19 **20** 21 22	Gǔ yǔ		9 10 11 12 13 14 15	
	◑ 25 26 27 28 29 30	22:21	17	2424995		22 23 24 25 26 27 28			23 24 25 26 27 28 29			16[f] 17 18 19 20 21 22	
MAY 1927	● 2 3 4 5 6 7	12:40	18	2425002	IYAR 5687	29 30 1 2 3 4 5	Sun 18h34m14p	MONTH 4 Dīng-Mǎo	1 2 3 4 5 6 7	Lì xià		23 24 25 26 27 28 29[g]	
	◐ 9 10 11 12 13 14	15:27	19	2425009		6 7 8 9 10 11 12			8 9 10 11 12 13 14		PASHONS 1643	30 1 2 3 4 5 6	GENBOT 1919
	15 ○ 17 18 19 20 21	19:03	20	2425016		13 14 15 16 17 18 19			15 16 17 18 19 20 21			7 8 9 10 11 12 13	
	22 23 ◑ 25 26 27 28	5:34	21	2425023		20 21 22 23 24 25 26			**22** 23 24 25 26 27 28	Xiǎo mǎn		14 15 16 17 18 19 20	
JUNE 1927	29 ● 31 1 2 3 4	21:06	22	2425030	SIVAN 5687	27 28 29 1 2 3 4	Tue 7h18m15p	MONTH 5 Dīng-Mǎo	29 30* 1 2 3 4 5[d]			21 22 23 24 25 26 27	
	5 6 ◐ 8 9 10 11	7:48	23	2425037		5 6[h] 7 8 9 10 11			6 7 *8* 9 10 11 12	Máng zhòng	PAÔNE 1643	28 29 30 1 2 3 4	SANĒ 1919
	12 13 14 ○ 16 17 18	8:19	24	2425044		12 13 14 15 16 17 18			13 14 15 16 17 18 19			5 6 7 8 9 10 11	
	19 20 21 ◑[c] 23 24 25	10:29	25	2425051		19 20 21 22 23 24 25			20 21 22 **23** 24 25 26	Xià zhì		12 13 14 15 16 17 18	
JULY 1927	26 27 28 ● 30 1 2	6:32	26	2425058	TAMMUZ 5687	26 27 28 29 30 1 2	Wed 20h2m16p	MONTH 6 Dīng-Mǎo	27 28 29 1 2 3 4			19 20 21 22 23 24 25	
	3 4 5 6 ◐ 8 9	0:52	27	2425065		3 4 5 6 7 8 9			5 6 7 8 9 *10* 11	Xiǎo shǔ	EPÊP 1643	26 27 28 29 30 1 2	ḤAMLĒ 1919
	10 11 12 13 ○ 15 16	19:22	28	2425072		10 11 12 13 14 15 16			12 13 14 15 16 17 18			3 4 5 6 7 8 9	
	17 18 19 20 ◑ 22 23	14:43	29	2425079		17 18 19 20 21 22 23			19 20 21 22 23 24 25			10 11 12 13 14 15 16	
	24 25 26 27 ● 29 30	17:36	30	2425086	AV 5687	24 25 26 27 28 29 1	Fri 8h46m17p	MONTH 7 Dīng-Mǎo	**26** 27 28 29 30 1* 2	Dà shǔ		17 18 19 20 21 22 23	
AUGUST 1927	31 1 2 3 4 ◐ 6	18:05	31	2425093		2 3 4 5 6 7 8			3 4 5 6 7[e] 8 9			24 25 26 27 28 29 30	
	7 8 9 10 11 12 ○	4:37	32	2425100		9[i] 10 11 12 13 14 15			10 *11* 12 13 14 15[f] 16	Lì qiū	MESORĒ 1643	1 2 3 4 5 6 7	NAḤASĒ 1919
	14 15 16 17 18 ◑ 20	19:54	33	2425107		16 17 18 19 20 21 22			17 18 19 20 21 22 23			8 9 10 11 12 13[h] 14	
	21 22 23 24 25 26 ●	6:45	34	2425114		23 24 25 26 27 28 29		MONTH 8 Dīng-Mǎo	24 25 26 **27** 28 29 1	Chǔ shǔ		15 16 17 18 19 20 21	
SEPTEMBER 1927	28 29 30 31 1 2 3		35	2425121	ELUL 5687	30 1 2 3 4 5 6	Sat 21h31m0p		2 3 4 5 6 7 8			22 23 24 25 26 27 28	
	◐ 5 6 7 8 9 10	10:44	36	2425128		7 8 9 10 11 12 13			9 10 11 12 *13* 14 15[g]	Bái lù	EPAG. 1643	29 30 1 2 3 4 5	PĀG. 1919
	○ 12 13 14 15 16 17	12:54	37	2425135		14 15 16 17 18 19 20			16 17 18 19 20 21 22		THOOUT 1644	6 1[a] 2 3 4 5 6	MASKARAM 1920
	◑ 19 20 21 22 23 24[d]	3:29	38	2425142		21 22 23 24 25 26 27			23 24 25 26 27 28 **29**	Qiū fēn		7 8 9 10 11 12 13	
OCTOBER 1927	● 26 27 28 29 30 1	22:11	39	2425149	TISHRI 5688	28 29 1[a] 2[a] 3 4 5	Mon 10h15m1p	MONTH 9 Dīng-Mǎo	30 1 2* 3 4 5 6			14 15 16 17[b] 18 19 20	
	2 3 ◐ 5 6 7 8	2:01	40	2425156		6 7 8 9 10[b] 11 12			7 8 9[h] 10 11 12 13			21 22 23 24 25 26 27	
	9 ○ 11 12 13 14 15	21:15	41	2425163		13 14 15[c] 16 17 18 19			*14* 15 16 17 18 19 20	Hán lù	PAOPE 1644	28 29 30 1 2 3 4	ṬEQEMT 1920
	16 ◑ 18 19 20 21 22	14:32	42	2425170		20 21 22 23 24 25 26			21 22 23 24 25 26 27			5 6 7 8 9 10 11	
	23 24 ● 26 27 28 29	15:37	43	2425177	HESHVAN 5688	27 28 29 30 1 2 3	Tue 22h59m2p	MONTH 10 Dīng-Mǎo	28 **29** 1 2 3 4 5	Shuāng jiàng		12 13 14 15 16 17 18	
NOVEMBER 1927	30 31 1 ◐ 3 4 5	15:16	44	2425184		4 5 6 7 8 9 10			6 7 8 9 10 11 12			19 20 21 22 23 24 25	
	6 7 8 ○ 10 11 12	6:36	45	2425191		11 12 13 14 15 16 17			13 14 *15* 16 17 18 19	Lì dōng	ATHÔR 1644	26 27 28 29 30 1 2	ḪEDĀR 1920
	13 14 15 ◑ 17 18 19	5:28	46	2425198		18 19 20 21 22 23 24			20 21 22 23 24 25 26			3 4 5 6 7 8 9	
	20 21 22 23 ● 25 26	10:09	47	2425205	KISLEV 5688	25 26 27 28 29 1 2	Thu 11h43m3p	MONTH 11 Dīng-Mǎo	27 28 29 **30** 1 2 3*	Xiǎo xuě		10 11 12 13 14 15 16	
DECEMBER 1927	27 28 29 30 1 ◐ 3	2:15	48	2425212		3 4 5 6 7 8 9			4 5 6 7 8 9 10			17 18 19 20 21 22 23	
	4 5 6 7 ○ 9 10	17:32	49	2425219		10 11 12[d] 13 14 15 16			11 12 13 14 *15* 16 17	Dà xuě		24 25 26 27 28 29 30	
	11 12 13 14 15 ◑ 17	0:03	50	2425226		17 18 19 20 21 22 23			18 19 20 21 22 23 24		KOIAK 1644	1 2 3 4 5 6 7	TĀKHŚĀŚ 1920
	18 19 20 21 22[e] 23 ●	4:13	51	2425233		24 25[e] 26[e] 27[e] 28[e] 29[e] 30[e]	Sat 0h27m4p	MONTH 12 Dīng-Mǎo	25 26 27 28 29 **30**[i] 1	Dōng zhì		8 9 10 11 12 13 14	
	25 26 27 28 29 30 ◐	11:22	52	2425240		1[e] 2[e] 3 4 5 6 7			2 3 4 5 6 7 8			15 16 17 18 19 20 21	

[a]New Year
[b]Spring (14:59)
[c]Summer (10:22)
[d]Autumn (1:17)
[e]Winter (20:18)
● New moon
◐ First quarter moon
○ Full moon
◑ Last quarter moon

‡Leap year
[a]New Year
[b]Yom Kippur
[c]Sukkot
[d]Winter starts
[e]Ḥanukkah
[f]Purim
[g]Passover
[h]Shavuot
[i]Fast of Av

[a]New Year (4625, Hare)
[b]Lantern Festival
[c]Qīngmíng
[d]Dragon Festival
[e]Qīqiǎo
[f]Hungry Ghosts
[g]Mid-Autumn Festival
[h]Double-Ninth Festival
[i]Dōngzhì
*Start of 60-name cycle

‡Leap year
[a]New Year
[b]Building of the Cross
[c]Christmas
[d]Jesus's Circumcision
[e]Epiphany
[f]Easter
[g]Mary's Announcement
[h]Jesus's Transfiguration

1927

PERSIAN (ASTRONOMICAL) 1305/1306

Month	Sun	Mon	Tue	Wed	Thu	Fri	Sat
	4	5	6	7	8	9	10
DEY 1305	11	12	13	14	15	16	17
	18	19	20	21	22	23	24
	25	26	27	28	29	30	*1*
	2	3	4	5	6	7	8
BAHMAN 1305	9	10	11	12	13	14	15
	16	17	18	19	20	21	22
	23	24	25	26	27	28	29
	30	*1*	2	3	4	5	6
ESFAND 1305	7	8	9	10	11	12	13
	14	15	16	17	18	19	20
	21	22	23	24	25	26	27
	28	29	*1*[a]	2	3	4	5
FARVARDĪN 1306	6	7	8	9	10	11	12
	13[b]	14	15	16	17	18	19
	20	21	22	23	24	25	26
	27	28	29	30	31	*1*	2
	3	4	5	6	7	8	9
ORDĪBEHEŠT 1306	10	11	12	13	14	15	16
	17	18	19	20	21	22	23
	24	25	26	27	28	29	30
	31	*1*	2	3	4	5	6
	7	8	9	10	11	12	13
XORDĀD 1306	14	15	16	17	18	19	20
	21	22	23	24	25	26	27
	28	29	30	31	*1*	2	3
	4	5	6	7	8	9	10
TĪR 1306	11	12	13	14	15	16	17
	18	19	20	21	22	23	24
	25	26	27	28	29	30	31
	1	2	3	4	5	6	7
	8	9	10	11	12	13	14
MORDĀD 1306	15	16	17	18	19	20	21
	22	23	24	25	26	27	28
	29	30	31	*1*	2	3	4
	5	6	7	8	9	10	11
SHAHRĪVAR 1306	12	13	14	15	16	17	18
	19	20	21	22	23	24	25
	26	27	28	29	30	31	*1*
	2	3	4	5	6	7	8
MEHR 1306	9	10	11	12	13	14	15
	16	17	18	19	20	21	22
	23	24	25	26	27	28	29
	30	*1*	2	3	4	5	6
	7	8	9	10	11	12	13
ĀBĀN 1306	14	15	16	17	18	19	20
	21	22	23	24	25	26	27
	28	29	30	*1*	2	3	4
	5	6	7	8	9	10	11
ĀZAR 1306	12	13	14	15	16	17	18
	19	20	21	22	23	24	25
	26	27	28	29	30	*1*	2
DEY 1306	3	4	5	6	7	8	9

HINDU LUNAR 1983‡/1984

Month	Sun	Mon	Tue	Wed	Thu	Fri	Sat
MĀRGAŚĪRA 1983	22	23	24	25	26	27	28
	29	30	1	2	3	4	5
PAUSHA 1983	6	7	8	**9**	11	12	13
	14	15	16	17	18	19	*19*
	20	21	22	23	24	25	26
	27	28	29	30	1	2	**3**
MĀGHA 1983	5	6	7	8	9	10	11
	12	13	14	15	16	17	18
	19	20	21	*21*	22	23	24
	25	26	**27**	29[h]	30	1	2
PHĀLGUNA 1983	3	4	5	6	7	8	9
	10	11	12	13	14	15[i]	16
	17	18	19	20	21	22	23
	24	25	26	27	28	29	30
	1[a]	3	4	5	6	7	8
CHAITRA 1984	9[b]	10	11	12	13	14	*14*
	15	16	17	18	19	20	21
	22	23	24	**25**	27	28	29
	30	1	2	3	4	5	6
VAIŚĀKHA 1984	7	8	9	10	11	12	13
	14	15	16	17	18	19	20
	21	22	23	24	25	26	27
	28	30	1	2	3	4	5
JYAISHṬHA 1984	6	7	8	9	10	*10*	11
	12	13	14	15	16	17	18
	19	20	**21**	23	24	25	26
	27	28	29	30	1	2	3
ĀSHĀḌHA 1984	4	5	6	7	8	9	10
	11	12	13	14	15	16	17
	18	19	20	21	22	23	**24**
	26	27	28	29	30	1	2
ŚRĀVAṆA 1984	3	4	5	6	7	*7*	8
	9	10	11	12	13	14	15
	16	18	19	20	21	22	23[c]
	24	25	26	27	28	29	30
	1	2	3	4[d]	5	6	7
BHĀDRAPADA 1984	8	9	10	11	12	13	14
	15	16	17	18	19	**20**	22
	23	24	25	26	27	28	29
	30	1	2	*2*	3	4	5
ĀŚVINA 1964	6	7	8[e]	9[e]	10[e]	11	12
	13	15	16	17	18	19	20
	21	22	23	24	25	26	27
	28	29	30	1[f]	2	3	4
KĀRTTIKA 1984	5	6	7	8	9	10	11
	12	13	14	15	16	**17**	19
	20	21	22	23	24	25	26
	26	27	28	29	30	1	2
MĀRGAŚĪRA 1984	3	4	5	6	7	8	9
	10	**11**[g]	13	14	15	16	17
	18	19	20	21	22	23	24
	25	26	27	28	29	*29*	30
	1	2	3	4	**5**	7	8

HINDU SOLAR 1848/1849

Month	Sun	Mon	Tue	Wed	Thu	Fri	Sat
	12	13	14	15	16	17	18
PAUSHA 1848	19	20	21	22	23	24	25
	26	27	28	29	1[b]	2	3
	4	5	6	7	8	9	10
MĀGHA 1848	11	12	13	14	15	16	17
	18	19	20	21	22	23	24
	25	26	27	28	29	30	1
	2	3	4	5	6	7	8
PHĀLGUNA 1848	9	10	11	12	13	14	15
	16	17	18	19	20	21	22
	23	24	25	26	27	28	29
	30	1	2	3	4	5	6
	7	8	9	10	11	12	13
CHAITRA 1848	14	15	16	17	18	19	20
	21	22	23	24	25	26	27
	28	29	30	1[a]	2	3	4
	5	6	7	8	9	10	11
VAIŚĀKHA 1849	12	13	14	15	16	17	18
	19	20	21	22	23	24	25
	26	27	28	29	30	31	1
	2	3	4	5	6	7	8
JYAISHṬHA 1849	9	10	11	12	13	14	15
	16	17	18	19	20	21	22
	23	24	25	26	27	28	29
	30	31	1	2	3	4	5
	6	7	8	9	10	11	12
ĀSHĀḌHA 1849	13	14	15	16	17	18	19
	20	21	22	23	24	25	26
	27	28	29	30	31	32	1
	2	3	4	5	6	7	8
ŚRĀVAṆA 1849	9	10	11	12	13	14	15
	16	17	18	19	20	21	22
	23	24	25	26	27	28	29
	30	31	32	1	2	3	4
	5	6	7	8	9	10	11
BHĀDRAPADA 1849	12	13	14	15	16	17	18
	19	20	21	22	23	24	25
	26	27	28	29	30	31	1
	2	3	4	5	6	7	8
ĀŚVINA 1849	9	10	11	12	13	14	15
	16	17	18	19	20	21	22
	23	24	25	26	27	28	29
	30	1	2	3	4	5	6
	7	8	9	10	11	12	13
KĀRTTIKA 1849	14	15	16	17	18	19	20
	21	22	23	24	25	26	27
	28	29	30	1	2	3	4
	5	6	7	8	9	10	11
MĀRGAŚĪRA 1849	12	13	14	15	16	17	18
	19	20	21	22	23	24	25
	26	27	28	29	1	2	3
PAUSHA 1849	4	5	6	7	8	9	10
	11	12	13	14	15	16	17

ISLAMIC (ASTRONOMICAL) 1345/1346‡

Month	Sun	Mon	Tue	Wed	Thu	Fri	Sat
JUMĀDĀ II 1345	20	21	22	23	24	25	26
	27	28	29	*1*	2	3	4
RAJAB 1345	5	6	7	8	9	10	11
	12	13	14	15	16	17	18
	19	20	21	22	23	24	25
	26	27[d]	28	29	30	*1*	2
SHA'BĀN 1345	3	4	5	6	7	8	9
	10	11	12	13	14	15	16
	17	18	19	20	21	22	23
	24	25	26	27	28	29	*1*[e]
RAMAḌĀN 1345	2	3	4	5	6	7	8
	9	10	11	12	13	14	15
	16	17	18	19	20	21	22
	23	24	25	26	27	28	29
	1[f]	*2*	3	4	5	6	7
SHAWWĀL 1345	8	9	10	11	12	13	14
	15	16	17	18	19	20	21
	22	23	24	25	26	27	28
	29	30	*1*	2	3	4	5
DHU AL-QA'DA 1345	6	7	8	9	10	11	12
	13	14	15	16	17	18	19
	20	21	22	23	24	25	26
	27	28	29	1	*2*	3	4
DHU AL-ḤIJJA 1345	5	6	7	8	9	10[g]	11
	12	13	14	15	16	17	18
	19	20	21	22	23	24	25
	26	27	28	29	1[a]	*2*[â]	3
MUḤARRAM 1346	4	5	6	7	8	9	10[b]
	11	12	13	14	15	16	17
	18	19	20	21	22	23	24
	25	26	27	28	29	30	1
ṢAFAR 1346	*2*	3	4	5	6	7	8
	9	10	11	12	13	14	15
	16	17	18	19	20	21	22
	23	24	25	26	27	28	29
	1	*2*	3	4	5	6	7
RABĪ' I 1346	8	9	10	11	12[c]	13	14
	15	16	17	18	19	20	21
	22	23	24	25	26	27	28
	29	30	1	*2*	3	4	5
RABĪ' I 1346	6	7	8	9	10	11	12
	13	14	15	16	17	18	19
	20	21	22	23	24	25	26
	27	28	29	30	*1*	2	3
JUMĀDĀ I 1346	4	5	6	7	8	9	10
	11	12	13	14	15	16	17
	18	19	20	21	22	23	24
	25	26	27	28	29	30	*1*
JUMĀDĀ II 1346	2	3	4	5	6	7	8
	9	10	11	12	13	14	15
	16	17	18	19	20	21	22
	23	24	25	26	27	28	29
	30	1	2	3	4	5	6

GREGORIAN 1927

Julian (Sun)	Sun	Mon	Tue	Wed	Thu	Fri	Sat	Month
Dec 13	*26*	27	28	29	30	31	1	
	2	3	4	5	6	7[a]	8	
Dec 27	*9*	10	11	12	13	14[b]	15	JANUARY 1927
	16	17	18	19	20	21	22	
Jan 10	*23*	24	25	26	27	28	29	
	30	31	1	2	3	4	5	
Jan 24	*6*	7	8	9	10	11	12	FEBRUARY 1927
	13	14	15	16	17	18	19	
Feb 7	*20*	21	22	23	24	25	26	
	27	28	1	2[c]	3	4	5	
Feb 21	*6*	7	8	9	10	11	12	MARCH 1927
	13[d]	14	15	16	17	18	19	
Mar 7	*20*	21	22	23	24	25	26	
	27	28	29	30	31	1	2	
Mar 21	*3*	4	5	6	7	8	9	APRIL 1927
	10	11	12	13	14	15	16	
Apr 4	*17*[e]	18	19	20	21	22	23	
	24[f]	25	26	27	28	29	30	
Apr 18	*1*	2	3	4	5	6	7	
	8	9	10	11	12	13	14	MAY 1927
May 2	*15*	16	17	18	19	20	21	
	22	23	24	25	26	27	28	
May 16	*29*	30	31	1	2	3	4	
	5	6	7	8	9	10	11	JUNE 1927
May 30	*12*	13	14	15	16	17	18	
	19	20	21	22	23	24	25	
Jun 13	*26*	27	28	29	30	1	2	
	3	4	5	6	7	8	9	JULY 1927
Jun 27	*10*	11	12	13	14	15	16	
	17	18	19	20	21	22	23	
Jul 11	*24*	25	26	27	28	29	30	
	31	1	2	3	4	5	6	
Jul 25	*7*	8	9	10	11	12	13	AUGUST 1927
	14	15	16	17	18	19	20	
Aug 8	*21*	22	23	24	25	26	27	
	28	29	30	31	1	2	3	
Aug 22	*4*	5	6	7	8	9	10	SEPTEMBER 1927
	11	12	13	14	15	16	17	
Sep 5	*18*	19	20	21	22	23	24	
	25	26	27	28	29	30	1	
Sep 19	*2*	3	4	5	6	7	8	
	9	10	11	12	13	14	15	OCTOBER 1927
Oct 3	*16*	17	18	19	20	21	22	
	23	24	25	26	27	28	29	
Oct 17	*30*	31	1	2	3	4	5	
	6	7	8	9	10	11	12	NOVEMBER 1927
Oct 31	*13*	14	15	16	17	18	19	
	20	21	22	23	24	25	26	
Nov 14	*27*[g]	28	29	30	1	2	3	
	4	5	6	7	8	9	10	DECEMBER 1927
Nov 28	*11*	12	13	14	15	16	17	
	18	19	20	21	22	23	24	
Dec 12	*25*[h]	26	27	28	29	30	31	

[a]New Year
[b]Sizdeh Bedar

‡Leap year
[a]New Year (Prabhava)
[b]Birthday of Rāma
[c]Birthday of Krishna
[d]Ganēśa Chaturthī
[e]Dashara
[f]Diwali
[g]Birthday of Vishnu
[h]Night of Śiva
[i]Holi

[a]New Year (Pramāthin)
[b]Pongal

‡Leap year
[a]New Year
[â]New Year (Arithmetic)
[b]'Ashūrā'
[c]Prophet's Birthday
[d]Ascent of the Prophet
[e]Start of Ramaḍān
[f]'Id al-Fiṭr
[g]'Id al-'Aḍḥā

[a]Orthodox Christmas
[b]Julian New Year
[c]Ash Wednesday
[d]Feast of Orthodoxy
[e]Easter
[f]Orthodox Easter
[g]Advent
[h]Christmas

1928

Gregorian 1928‡	Sun Mon Tue Wed Thu Fri Sat	Lunar Phases	ISO Week (Mon)	Julian Day (Sun noon)	Hebrew 5688/5689‡	Sun Mon Tue Wed Thu Fri Sat	Molad	Chinese Dīng-Mǎo/Wù-Chén‡	Sun Mon Tue Wed Thu Fri Sat	Solar Term	Coptic 1644/1645	Sun Mon Tue Wed Thu Fri Sat	Ethiopic 1920/1921
JANUARY 1928	1[a] 2 3 4 5 6 ○	6:08	1	2425247		8 9 10 11 12 13 14		MONTH 12 Dīng-Mǎo	9 10 11 12 13 14 15	Xiǎo hán	KOIAK 1644	22 23 24 25 26 27 28	TĀKHŚĀŚ 1920
	8 9 10 11 12 13 ◑	21:14	2	2425254	TEVETH 5688	15 16 17 18 19 20 21			16 17 18 19 20 21 22			29[c] 30 1 2 3 4 5	ṬER 1920
	15 16 17 18 19 20 21		3	2425261		22 23 24 25 26 27 28			23 24 25 26 27 28 29	Dà hán	TŌBE 1644	6[d] 7 8 9 10 11[e] 12	
	● 23 24 25 26 27 28	20:19	4	2425268		29 1 2 3 4 5 6	Sun 13h11m5p	MONTH 1 Wù-Chén	30 1[a] 2 3* 4 5 6			13 14 15 16 17 18 19	
	◐ 30 31 1 2 3 4	19:25	5	2425275	SHEVAT 5688	7 8 9 10 11 12 13			7 8 9 10 11 12 13			20 21 22 23 24 25 26	
FEBRUARY 1928	○ 6 7 8 9 10 11	20:11	6	2425282		14 15 16 17 18 19 20			14 15[b] 16 17 18 19 20	Lì chūn		27 28 29 30 1 2 3	
	12 ◑ 14 15 16 17 18	19:05	7	2425289		21 22 23 24 25 26 27			21 22 23 24 25 26 27		MESHIR 1644	4 5 6 7 8 9 10	YAKĀTIT 1920
	19 20 ● 22 23 24 25	9:41	8	2425296		28 29 30 1 2 3 4	Tue 1h55m6p		28 29 1 2 3 4 5	Yǔ shuǐ		11 12 13 14 15 16 17	
	26 27 ◐ 29 1 2 3	3:21	9	2425303	ADAR 5688	5 6 7 8 9 10 11		MONTH 2 Wù-Chén	6 7 8 9 10 11 12			18 19 20 21 22 23 24	
MARCH 1928	4 5 ○ 7 8 9 10	11:27	10	2425310		12 13 14[f] 15 16 17 18			13 14 15 16 17 18 19	Jīng zhé		25 26 27 28 29 30 1	
	11 12 13 ◑ 15 16 17	15:20	11	2425317		19 20 21 22 23 24 25			20 21 22 23 24 25 26		PAREMOTEP 1644	2 3 4 5 6 7 8	MAGĀBIT 1920
	18 19 20[b] ● 22 23 24	20:29	12	2425324		26 27 28 29 1 2 3	Wed 14h39m7p		27 28 29 30 1 2 3	Chūn fēn		9 10 11 12 13 14 15	
	25 26 27 ◐ 29 30 31	11:54	13	2425331	NISAN 5688	4 5 6 7 8 9 10		LEAP MONTH 2 Wù-Chén	4* 5 6 7 8 9 10			16 17 18 19 20 21 22	
APRIL 1928	1 2 3 4 ○ 6 7	3:38	14	2425338		11 12 13 14 15[g] 16 17			11 12 13 14 15[c] 16 17	Qīng míng		23 24 25 26 27 28 29	
	8 9 10 11 12 ◑ 14	8:09	15	2425345		18 19 20 21 22 23 24			18 19 20 21 22 23 24			30 1 2 3 4 5 6	
	15 16 17 18 19 ● 21	5:25	16	2425352		25 26 27 28 29 30 1	Fri 3h23m8p		25 26 27 28 29 1 2	Gǔ yǔ	PARMOUTE 1644	7[f] 8 9 10 11 12 13	MIYĀZYĀ 1920
	22 23 24 25 ◐ 27 28	21:42	17	2425359	IYYAR 5688	2 3 4 5 6 7 8		MONTH 3 Wù-Chén	3 4 5 6 7 8 9			14 15 16 17 18 19 20	
	29 30 1 2 3 ○ 5	20:12	18	2425366		9 10 11 12 13 14 15			10 11 12 13 14 15 16			21 22 23 24 25 26 27	
MAY 1928	6 7 8 9 10 11 ◑	20:50	19	2425373		16 17 18 19 20 21 22			17 18 19 20 21 22 23	Lì xià		28 29[g] 30 1 2 3 4	
	13 14 15 16 17 18 ●	13:14	20	2425380		23 24 25 26 27 28 29			24 25 26 27 28 29 1		PASHONS 1644	5 6 7 8 9 10 11	GENBOT 1920
	20 21 22 23 24 25 ◐	9:11	21	2425387	SIVAN 5688	1 2 3 4 5 6[h] 7	Sat 16h7m9p	MONTH 4 Wù-Chén	2 3 4 5 6* 7 8	Xiǎo mǎn		12 13 14 15 16 17 18	
	27 28 29 30 31 1 2		22	2425394		8 9 10 11 12 13 14			9 10 11 12 13 14 15			19 20 21 22 23 24 25	
JUNE 1928	○ 4 5 6 7 8 9	12:13	23	2425401		15 16 17 18 19 20 21			16 17 18 19 20 21 22	Máng zhòng		26 27 28 29 30 1 2	
	10 ◑ 12 13 14 15 16	5:51	24	2425408		22 23 24 25 26 27 28			23 24 25 26 27 28 29		PAŌNE 1644	3 4 5 6 7 8 9	SANĒ 1920
	● 18 19 20 21[c] 22 23	20:42	25	2425415		29 30 1 2 3 4 5	Mon 4h51m10p		30 1 2 3 4 5[d] 6	Xià zhì		10 11 12 13 14 15 16	
	◐ 25 26 27 28 29 30	22:47	26	2425422	TAMMUZ 5688	6 7 8 9 10 11 12		MONTH 5 Wù-Chén	7 8 9 10 11 12 13			17 18 19 20 21 22 23	
JULY 1928	1 2 ○ 4 5 6 7	2:48	27	2425429		13 14 15 16 17 18 19			14 15 16 17 18 19 20	Xiǎo shǔ		24 25 26 27 28 29 30	
	8 9 ◑ 11 12 13 14	12:16	28	2425436		20 21 22 23 24 25 26			21 22 23 24 25 26 27		EPĒP 1644	1 2 3 4 5 6 7	ḤAMLĒ 1920
	15 16 ● 18 19 20 21	4:35	29	2425443		27 28 29 1 2 3 4	Tue 17h35m11p		28 29 1 2 3 4 5			8 9 10 11 12 13 14	
	22 23 ◐ 25 26 27 28	14:38	30	2425450	AV 5688	5 6 7 8 9[i] 10 11		MONTH 6 Wù-Chén	6 7* 8 9 10 11 12	Dà shǔ		15 16 17 18 19 20 21	
	29 30 31 ○ 2 3 4	15:30	31	2425457		12 13 14 15 16 17 18			13 14 15 16 17 18 19			22 23 24 25 26 27 28	
AUGUST 1928	5 6 7 ◑ 9 10 11	17:24	32	2425464		19 20 21 22 23 24 25			20 21 22 23 24 25 26	Lì qiū		29 30 1 2 3 4 5	
	12 13 14 ● 16 17 18	13:48	33	2425471		26 27 28 29 30 1 2	Thu 6h19m12p		27 28 29 1 2 3 4		MESORĒ 1644	6 7 8 9 10 11 12	NAḤASĒ 1920
	19 20 21 22 ◐ 24 25	8:21	34	2425478	ELUL 5688	3 4 5 6 7 8 9		MONTH 7 Wù-Chén	5 6 7[e] 8 9 10 11	Chǔ shǔ		13[h] 14 15 16 17 18 19	
	26 27 28 29 30 ○ 1	2:34	35	2425485		10 11 12 13 14 15 16			12 13 14 15[f] 16 17 18			20 21 22 23 24 25 26	
SEPTEMBER 1928	2 3 4 5 ◑ 7 8	22:35	36	2425492		17 18 19 20 21 22 23			19 20 21 22 23 24 25	Bái lù	EPAG. 1644	27 28 29 30 1 2 3	PĀG. 1920
	9 10 11 12 13 ● 15	1:20	37	2425499		24 25 26 27 28 29 1[a]	Fri 19h3m13p		26 27 28 29 30 1 2			4 5 1[a] 2 3 4 5	MASKARAM 1921
	16 17 18 19 20 21 ◐	2:57	38	2425506	TISHRI 5689	2[a] 3 4 5 6 7 8		MONTH 8 Wù-Chén	3 4 5 6 7 8* 9		THOOUT 1645	6 7 8 9 10 11 12	
	23[d] 24 25 26 27 28 ○	12:43	39	2425513		9 10[b] 11 12 13 14 15[c]			10 11 12 13 14 15[g] 16	Qiū fēn		13 14 15 16 17[b] 18 19	
	30 1 2 3 4 5 ◑	5:06	40	2425520		16 17 18 19 20 21 22			17 18 19 20 21 22 23			20 21 22 23 24 25 26	
OCTOBER 1928	7 8 9 10 11 12 ●	15:56	41	2425527		23 24 25 26 27 28 29			24 25 26 27 28 29 1	Hán lù		27 28 29 30 1 2 3	
	14 15 16 17 18 19 20		42	2425534		30 1 2 3 4 5 6	Sun 7h47m14p	MONTH 9 Wù-Chén	2 3 4 5 6 7 8		PAOPE 1645	4 5 6 7 8 9 10	ṬEQEMT 1921
	◐ 22 23 24 25 26 27	21:06	43	2425541	HESHVAN 5689	7 8 9 10 11 12 13			9[h] 10 11 12 13 14 15	Shuāng jiàng		11 12 13 14 15 16 17	
	○ 29 30 31 1 2 3	22:43	44	2425548		14 15 16 17 18 19 20			16 17 18 19 20 21 22			18 19 20 21 22 23 24	
NOVEMBER 1928	◑ 5 6 7 8 9 10	14:06	45	2425555		21 22 23 24 25 26 27			23 24 25 26 27 28 29	Lì dōng		25 26 27 28 29 30 1	
	11 ● 13 14 15 16 17	9:35	46	2425562		28 29 30 1 2 3 4	Mon 20h31m15p		30 1 2 3 4 5 6		ATHŌR 1645	2 3 4 5 6 7 8	ḪEDĀR 1921
	18 19 ◐ 21 22 23 24	13:36	47	2425569	KISLEV 5689	5 6 7 8 9 10 11		MONTH 10 Wù-Chén	7 8 9* 10 11 12 13	Xiǎo xuě		9 10 11 12 13 14 15	
	25 26 ○ 28 29 30 1	9:06	48	2425576		12 13 14 15 16 17 18			14 15 16 17 18 19 20			16 17 18 19 20 21 22	
DECEMBER 1928	2 3 ◑ 5 6 7 8	2:31	49	2425583		19 20 21 22[d] 23 24 25[e]			21 22 23 24 25 26 27	Dà xuě		23 24 25 26 27 28 29	
	9 10 11 ● 13 14 15	5:06	50	2425590		26[e] 27[e] 28[e] 29[e] 30[e] 1[e] 2[e]	Wed 9h15m16p		28 29 30 1 2 3 4		KOIAK 1645	30 1 2 3 4 5 6	TĀKHŚĀŚ 1921
	16 17 18 19 ◐ 21 22[e]	3:43	51	2425597	TEVETH 5689	3 4 5 6 7 8 9		MONTH 11* Wù-Chén	5 6 7 8 9 10 11[i]	Dōng zhì		7 8 9 10 11 12 13	
	23 24 25 ○ 27 28 29	19:55	52	2425604		10 11 12 13 14 15 16			12 13 14 15 16 17 18			14 15 16 17 18 19 20	
	30 31 1 ◑ 3 4 5	18:44	1	2425611		17 18 19 20 21 22 23			19 20 21 22 23 24 25			21 22 23 24 25 26 27	

‡Leap year
[a]New Year
[b]Spring (20:44)
[c]Summer (16:06)
[d]Autumn (7:05)
[e]Winter (2:03)
● New moon
◐ First quarter moon
○ Full moon
◑ Last quarter moon

‡Leap year
[a]New Year
[b]Yom Kippur
[c]Sukkot
[d]Winter starts
[e]Ḥanukkah
[f]Purim
[g]Passover
[h]Shavuot
[i]Fast of Av

‡Leap year
[a]New Year (4626, Dragon)
[b]Lantern Festival
[c]Qīngmíng
[d]Dragon Festival
[e]Qīqiǎo
[f]Hungry Ghosts
[g]Mid-Autumn Festival
[h]Double-Ninth Festival
[i]Dōngzhì
*Start of 60-name cycle

[a]New Year
[b]Building of the Cross
[c]Christmas
[d]Jesus's Circumcision
[e]Epiphany
[f]Easter
[g]Mary's Announcement
[h]Jesus's Transfiguration

PERSIAN (ASTRONOMICAL) 1306/1307

Month	Sun	Mon	Tue	Wed	Thu	Fri	Sat
DEY 1306	10	11	12	13	14	15	16
	17	18	19	20	21	22	23
	24	25	26	27	28	29	30
BAHMAN 1306	1	2	3	4	5	6	7
	8	9	10	11	12	13	14
	15	16	17	18	19	20	21
	22	23	24	25	26	27	28
	29	30	1	2	3	4	5
ESFAND 1306	6	7	8	9	10	11	12
	13	14	15	16	17	18	19
	20	21	22	23	24	25	26
	27	28	29	1[a]	2	3	4
FARVARDĪN 1307	5	6	7	8	9	10	11
	12	13[b]	14	15	16	17	18
	19	20	21	22	23	24	25
	26	27	28	29	30	31	1
ORDĪBEHEŠT 1307	2	3	4	5	6	7	8
	9	10	11	12	13	14	15
	16	17	18	19	20	21	22
	23	24	25	26	27	28	29
	30	31	1	2	3	4	5
XORDĀD 1307	6	7	8	9	10	11	12
	13	14	15	16	17	18	19
	20	21	22	23	24	25	26
	27	28	29	30	31	1	2
TĪR 1307	3	4	5	6	7	8	9
	10	11	12	13	14	15	16
	17	18	19	20	21	22	23
	24	25	26	27	28	29	30
	31	1	2	3	4	5	6
MORDĀD 1307	7	8	9	10	11	12	13
	14	15	16	17	18	19	20
	21	22	23	24	25	26	27
	28	29	30	31	1	2	3
SHAHRĪVAR 1307	4	5	6	7	8	9	10
	11	12	13	14	15	16	17
	18	19	20	21	22	23	24
	25	26	27	28	29	30	31
MEHR 1307	1	2	3	4	5	6	7
	8	9	10	11	12	13	14
	15	16	17	18	19	20	21
	22	23	24	25	26	27	28
	29	30	1	2	3	4	5
ĀBĀN 1307	6	7	8	9	10	11	12
	13	14	15	16	17	18	19
	20	21	22	23	24	25	26
	27	28	29	30	1	2	3
ĀZAR 1307	4	5	6	7	8	9	10
	11	12	13	14	15	16	17
	18	19	20	21	22	23	24
	25	26	27	28	29	30	1
DEY 1307	2	3	4	5	6	7	8
	9	10	11	12	13	14	15

HINDU LUNAR 1984/1985‡

Month	Sun	Mon	Tue	Wed	Thu	Fri	Sat
PAUSHA 1984	9	10	11	12	13	14	15
	16	17	18	19	20	21	22
	23	24	25	26	27	28	29
	30	1	2	3	4	5	6
MĀGHA 1984	7	8	9	**10**	12	13	14
	15	16	17	18	19	20	21
	21	22	23	24	25	26	27
	28[h]	29	30	1	2	3	**4**
PHĀLGUNA 1984	6	7	8	9	10	11	12
	13	14	15[i]	16	17	18	19
	20	21	22	23	24	*24*	25
	26	**27**	29	30	1[a]	2	3
CHAITRA 1985	4	5	6	7	8[b]	9	**10**
	12	13	14	*14*	15	16	17
	18	19	20	21	22	23	24
	25	26	27	28	29	30	1
VAIŚĀKHA 1985	**2**	4	5	6	7	8	9
	10	11	12	13	14	15	16
	17	18	*18*	19	20	21	22
	23	24	**25**	27	28	29	30
	1	2	3	4	5	6	7
JYAISHṬHA 1985	8	9	10	11	12	13	14
	15	16	17	18	19	20	21
	22	23	24	25	26	27	**28**
	30	1	2	3	4	5	6
ĀSHĀḌHA 1985	7	8	9	10	11	12	13
	14	*14*	15	16	17	18	19
	20	22	23	24	25	26	27
	28	29	30	1	2	3	4
LEAP ŚRĀVAṆA 1985	5	6	7	8	9	10	11
	12	13	14	15	16	17	18
	19	20	21	22	23	**24**	26
	27	28	29	30	1	2	3
ŚRĀVAṆA 1985	4	5	6	7	8	9	10
	11	*11*	12	13	14	15	**16**
	18	19	20	21	22	23[c]	24
	25	26	27	28	**29**	1	*1*
BHĀDRAPADA 1985	2	3[d]	4	5	6	7	8
	9	10	11	12	13	14	15
	16	17	18	19	**20**	22	23
	24	25	26	27	28	29	30
	1	2	3	4	5	6	*6*
ĀŚVINA 1985	7	8[e]	9[e]	10[e]	11	12	13
	14	16	17	18	19	20	21
	22	23	24	25	26	27	28
	29	30	1[f]	2	3	4	5
KĀRTTIKA 1985	6	7	8	9	10	11	12
	13	14	15	16	17	**18**	20
	21	22	23	24	25	26	27
	28	29	*29*	30	1	2	3
MĀRGAŚĪRA 1985	4	5	6	7	8	9	10
	11[g]	**12**	14	15	16	17	18
	19	20	21	22	23	24	25

HINDU SOLAR 1849/1850‡

Month	Sun	Mon	Tue	Wed	Thu	Fri	Sat
PAUSHA 1849	18	19	20	21	22	23	24
	25	26	27	28	29	30	1[b]
MĀGHA 1849	2	3	4	5	6	7	8
	9	10	11	12	13	14	15
	16	17	18	19	20	21	22
	23	24	25	26	27	28	29
	1	2	3	4	5	6	7
PHĀLGUNA 1849	8	9	10	11	12	13	14
	15	16	17	18	19	20	21
	22	23	24	25	26	27	28
	29	30	1	2	3	4	5
CHAITRA 1849	6	7	8	9	10	11	12
	13	14	15	16	17	18	19
	20	21	22	23	24	25	26
	27	28	29	30	1[a]	2	3
VAIŚĀKHA 1850	4	5	6	7	8	9	10
	11	12	13	14	15	16	17
	18	19	20	21	22	23	24
	25	26	27	28	29	30	31
	1	2	3	4	5	6	7
JYAISHṬHA 1850	8	9	10	11	12	13	14
	15	16	17	18	19	20	21
	22	23	24	25	26	27	28
	29	30	31	32	1	2	3
ĀSHĀḌHA 1850	4	5	6	7	8	9	10
	11	12	13	14	15	16	17
	18	19	20	21	22	23	24
	25	26	27	28	29	30	31
	1	2	3	4	5	6	7
ŚRĀVAṆA 1850	8	9	10	11	12	13	14
	15	16	17	18	19	20	21
	22	23	24	25	26	27	28
	29	30	31	32	1	2	3
BHĀDRAPADA 1850	4	5	6	7	8	9	10
	11	12	13	14	15	16	17
	18	19	20	21	22	23	24
	25	26	27	28	29	30	31
	1	2	3	4	5	6	7
ĀŚVINA 1850	8	9	10	11	12	13	14
	15	16	17	18	19	20	21
	22	23	24	25	26	27	28
	29	30	1	2	3	4	5
KĀRTTIKA 1850	6	7	8	9	10	11	12
	13	14	15	16	17	18	19
	20	21	22	23	24	25	26
	27	28	29	30	1	2	3
MĀRGAŚĪRA 1850	4	5	6	7	8	9	10
	11	12	13	14	15	16	17
	18	19	20	21	22	23	24
	25	26	27	28	29	30	1
PAUSHA 1850	2	3	4	5	6	7	8
	9	10	11	12	13	14	15
	16	17	18	19	20	21	22

ISLAMIC (ASTRONOMICAL) 1346‡/1347‡

Month	Sun	Mon	Tue	Wed	Thu	Fri	Sat
RAJAB 1346	7	8	9	10	11	12	13
	14	15	16	17	18	19	20
	21	22	23	24	25	26	27[d]
	28	29	1	2	3	4	5
SHA'BĀN 1346	6	7	8	9	10	11	12
	13	14	15	16	17	18	19
	20	21	22	23	24	25	26
	27	28	29	30	1[e]	2	3
RAMAḌĀN 1346	4	5	6	7	8	9	10
	11	12	13	14	15	16	17
	18	19	20	21	22	23	24
	25	26	27	28	29	1[f]	2
SHAWWĀL 1346	3	4	5	6	7	8	9
	10	11	12	13	14	15	16
	17	18	19	20	21	22	23
	24	25	26	27	28	29	1
DHU AL-QA'DA 1346	2	3	4	5	6	7	8
	9	10	11	12	13	14	15
	16	17	18	19	20	21	22
	23	24	25	26	27	28	29
	30	1	2	3	4	5	6
DHU AL-ḤIJJA 1346	7	8	9	10[g]	11	12	13
	14	15	16	17	18	19	20
	21	22	23	24	25	26	27
	28	29	1[a]	2[A]	3	4	5
MUḤARRAM 1347	6	7	8	9	10[b]	11	12
	13	14	15	16	17	18	19
	20	21	22	23	24	25	26
	27	28	29	1	2	3	4
ṢAFAR 1347	5	6	7	8	9	10	11
	12	13	14	15	16	17	18
	19	20	21	22	23	24	25
	26	27	28	29	30	1	2
RABĪ' I 1347	3	4	5	6	7	8	9
	10	11	12[c]	13	14	15	16
	17	18	19	20	21	22	23
	24	25	26	27	28	29	1
RABĪ' II 1347	2	3	4	5	6	7	8
	9	10	11	12	13	14	15
	16	17	18	19	20	21	22
	23	24	25	26	27	28	29
	30	1	2	3	4	5	6
JUMĀDĀ I 1347	7	8	9	10	11	12	13
	14	15	16	17	18	19	20
	21	22	23	24	25	26	27
	28	29	30	1	2	3	4
JUMĀDĀ II 1347	5	6	7	8	9	10	11
	12	13	14	15	16	17	18
	19	20	21	22	23	24	25
	26	27	28	29	30	1	2
RAJAB 1347	3	4	5	6	7	8	9
	10	11	12	13	14	15	16
	17	18	19	20	21	22	23

GREGORIAN 1928‡

Julian† (Sun)	Sun	Mon	Tue	Wed	Thu	Fri	Sat	Month
Dec 19	1	2	3	4	5	6	7[a]	JANUARY 1928
	8	9	10	11	12	13	14[b]	
Jan 2	15	16	17	18	19	20	21	
	22	23	24	25	26	27	28	
Jan 16	29	30	31	1	2	3	4	
	5	6	7	8	9	10	11	FEBRUARY 1928
Jan 30	12	13	14	15	16	17	18	
	19	20	21	22[c]	23	24	25	
Feb 13	26	27	28	29	1	2	3	
	4[d]	5	6	7	8	9	10	MARCH 1928
Feb 27	11	12	13	14	15	16	17	
	18	19	20	21	22	23	24	
Mar 12	25	26	27	28	29	30	31	
	1	2	3	4	5	6	7	
Mar 26	8[e]	9	10	11	12	13	14	APRIL 1928
	15[f]	16	17	18	19	20	21	
Apr 9	22	23	24	25	26	27	28	
	29	30	1	2	3	4	5	
Apr 23	6	7	8	9	10	11	12	MAY 1928
	13	14	15	16	17	18	19	
May 7	20	21	22	23	24	25	26	
	27	28	29	30	31	1	2	
May 21	3	4	5	6	7	8	9	JUNE 1928
	10	11	12	13	14	15	16	
Jun 4	17	18	19	20	21	22	23	
	24	25	26	27	28	29	30	
Jun 18	1	2	3	4	5	6	7	
	8	9	10	11	12	13	14	JULY 1928
Jul 2	15	16	17	18	19	20	21	
	22	23	24	25	26	27	28	
Jul 16	29	30	31	1	2	3	4	
	5	6	7	8	9	10	11	AUGUST 1928
Jul 30	12	13	14	15	16	17	18	
	19	20	21	22	23	24	25	
Aug 13	26	27	28	29	30	31	1	
	2	3	4	5	6	7	8	SEPTEMBER 1928
Aug 27	9	10	11	12	13	14	15	
	16	17	18	19	20	21	22	
Sep 10	23	24	25	26	27	28	29	
	30	1	2	3	4	5	6	
Sep 24	7	8	9	10	11	12	13	OCTOBER 1928
	14	15	16	17	18	19	20	
Oct 8	21	22	23	24	25	26	27	
	28	29	30	31	1	2	3	
Oct 22	4	5	6	7	8	9	10	NOVEMBER 1928
	11	12	13	14	15	16	17	
Nov 5	18	19	20	21	22	23	24	
	25	26	27	28	29	30	1	
Nov 19	2[g]	3	4	5	6	7	8	DECEMBER 1928
	9	10	11	12	13	14	15	
Dec 3	16	17	18	19	20	21	22	
	23	24	25[h]	26	27	28	29	
Dec 17	30	31	1	2	3	4	5	

Persian:
[a] New Year
[b] Sizdeh Bedar

Hindu Lunar:
‡ Leap year
[a] New Year (Vibhava)
[b] Birthday of Rāma
[c] Birthday of Krishna
[d] Ganēśa Chaturthī
[e] Dashara
[f] Diwali
[g] Birthday of Vishnu
[h] Night of Śiva
[i] Holi

Hindu Solar:
‡ Leap year
[a] New Year (Vikrama)
[b] Pongal

Islamic:
‡ Leap year
[a] New Year
[A] New Year (Arithmetic)
[b] 'Ashūrā'
[c] Prophet's Birthday
[d] Ascent of the Prophet
[e] Start of Ramaḍān
[f] 'Id al-Fiṭr
[g] 'Id al-'Aḍḥā

Gregorian:
‡ Leap year
[a] Orthodox Christmas
[b] Julian New Year
[c] Ash Wednesday
[d] Feast of Orthodoxy
[e] Easter
[f] Orthodox Easter
[g] Advent
[h] Christmas

1929

Month	Gregorian 1929 Sun	Mon	Tue	Wed	Thu	Fri	Sat	Lunar Phases	ISO WEEK (Mon)	JULIAN DAY (Sun noon)	Hebrew month	HEBREW 5689‡/5690 Sun	Mon	Tue	Wed	Thu	Fri	Sat	Molad	Chinese month	CHINESE Wù-Chén‡/Jĭ-Sì Sun	Mon	Tue	Wed	Thu	Fri	Sat	Solar Term	Coptic month	COPTIC 1645/1646 / ETHIOPIC 1921/1922 Sun	Mon	Tue	Wed	Thu	Fri	Sat	Ethiopic month
JANUARY 1929	30	31	1[a]	◑	3	4	5	18:44	1	2425611	TEVETH 5689	17	18	19	20	21	22	23		MONTH 11* Wù-Chén	19	20	21	22	23	24	25		KOIAK 1645	21	22	23	24	25	26	27	TĀKHŚĀŚ 1921
	6	7	8	9	10	●	12	0:28	2	2425618	SHEVAT 5689	24	25	26	27	28	29	1	Thu 21h59m17p	MONTH 12 Wù-Chén	*26*	27	28	29	30	1	2	Xiǎo hán	TŌBE 1645	28	29[c]	30	1	2	3	4	ṬER 1921
	13	14	15	16	17	◐	19	15:15	3	2425625		2	3	4	5	6	7	8			3	4	5	6	7	8	9*			5	6[d]	7	8	9	10	11[e]	
	20	21	22	23	24	○	26	7:09	4	2425632		9	10	11	12	13	14	15			**10**	11	12	13	14	15	16	Dà hán		12	13	14	15	16	17	18	
FEBRUARY 1929	27	28	29	30	31	◑	2	14:10	5	2425639		16	17	18	19	20	21	22			17	18	19	20	21	22	23			19	20	21	22	23	24	25	
	3	4	5	6	7	8	●	17:55	6	2425646		23	24	25	26	27	28	29			24	*25*	26	27	28	29	30	Lì chūn	MESHIR 1645	26	27	28	29	30	1	2	YAKĀTIT 1921
	10	11	12	13	14	15	16		7	2425653	ADAR I 5689	30	1	2	3	4	5	6	Sat 10h44m0p	MONTH 1 Jĭ-Sì	1[a]	2	3	4	5	6	7			3	4	5	6	7	8	9	
	◐	18	19	20	21	22	○	0:22 18:59	8	2425660		7	8	9	10	11	12	13			8	9	**10**	11	12	13	14	Yǔ shuǐ		10	11	12	13	14	15	16	
	24	25	26	27	28	1	2		9	2425667		14	15	16	17	18	19	20			15[b]	16	17	18	19	20	21			17	18	19	20	21	22	23	
MARCH 1929	◑	4	5	6	7	8	9	11:09	10	2425674		21	22	23	24	25	26	27			22	23	24	*25*	26	27	28	Jīng zhé		24	25	26	27	28	29	30	
	10	●	12	13	14	15	16	8:37	11	2425681	ADAR II 5689	28	29	30	1	2	3	4	Sun 23h28m1p	MONTH 2 Jĭ-Sì	29	1	2	3	4	5	6		PAREMOTEP 1645	1	2	3	4	5	6	7	MAGĀBIT 1921
	17	◐	19	20	21[b]	22	23	7:41	12	2425688		5	6	7	8	9	10	11			7	8	9	10*	**11**	12	13	Chūn fēn		8	9	10	11	12	13	14	
	24	○	26	27	28	29	30	7:46	13	2425695		12	13	14[f]	15	16	17	18			14	15	16	17	18	19	20			15	16	17	18	19	20	21	
APRIL 1929	31	1	◑	3	4	5	6	7:29	14	2425702		19	20	21	22	23	24	25			21	22	23	24	25	*26*[c]	27	Qīng míng		22	23	24	25	26	27	28	
	7	8	●	10	11	12	13	20:33	15	2425709	NISAN 5689	26	27	28	29	1	2	3	Tue 12h12m2p	MONTH 3 Jĭ-Sì	28	29	30	1	2	3	4		PARMOUTE 1645	29	30	1	2	3	4	5	MIYĀZYĀ 1921
	14	15	◐	17	18	19	20	14:09	16	2425716		4	5	6	7	8	9	10			5	6	7	8	9	10	**11**	Gǔ yǔ		6	7	8	9	10	11	12	
	21	22	○	24	25	26	27	21:47	17	2425723		11	12	13	14	15[g]	16	17			12	13	14	15	16	17	18			13	14	15	16	17	18	19	
MAY 1929	28	29	30	1	◑	3	4	1:25	18	2425730		18	19	20	21	22	23	24			19	20	21	22	23	24	25			20	21	22	23	24	25	26	
	5	6	7	8	●	10	11	6:07	19	2425737	IYAR 5689	25	26	27	28	29	30	1	Thu 0h56m3p	MONTH 4 Jĭ-Sì	26	*27*	28	29	1	2	3	Lì xià	PASHONS 1645	27[f]	28	29[g]	30	1	2	3	GENBOT 1921
	12	13	14	◐	16	17	18	20:56	20	2425744		2	3	4	5	6	7	8			4	5	6	7	8	9	10			4	5	6	7	8	9	10	
	19	20	21	22	○	24	25	12:50	21	2425751		9	10	11	12	13	14	15			11*	12	**13**	14	15	16	17	Xiǎo mǎn		11	12	13	14	15	16	17	
JUNE 1929	26	27	28	29	30	◑	1	16:13	22	2425758		16	17	18	19	20	21	22			18	19	20	21	22	23	24			18	19	20	21	22	23	24	
	2	3	4	5	6	●	8	13:57	23	2425765		23	24	25	26	27	28	29		MONTH 5 Jĭ-Sì	25	26	27	28	29	1	2	Máng zhòng	PAŌNE 1645	25	26	27	28	29	30	1	SANĒ 1921
	9	10	11	12	13	◐	15	5:14	24	2425772	SIVAN 5689	1	2	3	4	5	6[h]	7	Fri 13h40m4p		3	4	5[d]	6	7	8	9			2	3	4	5	6	7	8	
	16	17	18	19	20	21[c]	○	4:15	25	2425779		8	9	10	11	12	13	14			10	11	12	13	14	15	**16**	Xià zhì		9	10	11	12	13	14	15	
	23	24	25	26	27	28	29		26	2425786		15	16	17	18	19	20	21			17	18	19	20	21	22	23			16	17	18	19	20	21	22	
JULY 1929	◑	1	2	3	4	5	●	3:53 20:47	27	2425793		22	23	24	25	26	27	28			24	25	26	27	28	29	30			23	24	25	26	27	28	29	
	7	8	9	10	11	12	◐	16:05	28	2425800	TAMMUZ 5689	29	30	1	2	3	4	5	Sun 2h24m5p	MONTH 6 Jĭ-Sì	*1*	2	3	4	5	6	7	Xiǎo shǔ	EPĒP 1645	30	1	2	3	4	5	6	ḤAMLĒ 1921
	14	15	16	17	18	19	20		29	2425807		6	7	8	9	10	11	12			8	9	10	11	12*	13	14			7	8	9	10	11	12	13	
	○	22	23	24	25	26	27	19:20	30	2425814		13	14	15	16	17	18	19			15	16	**17**	18	19	20	21	Dà shǔ		14	15	16	17	18	19	20	
AUGUST 1929	28	◑	30	31	1	2	3	12:56	31	2425821		20	21	22	23	24	25	26			22	23	24	25	26	27	28			21	22	23	24	25	26	27	
	4	●	6	7	8	9	10	3:40	32	2425828	AV 5689	27	28	29	1	2	3	4	Mon 15h8m6p	MONTH 7 Jĭ-Sì	29	1	2	3	*4*	5	6	Lì qiū	MESORĒ 1645	28	29	30	1	2	3	4	NAHASĒ 1921
	11	◐	13	14	15	16	17	6:01	33	2425835		5	6	7	8	9[i]	10	11			7[e]	8	9	10	11	12	13			5	6	7	8	9	10	11	
	18	19	○	21	22	23	24	9:42	34	2425842		12	13	14	15	16	17	18			14	15[f]	16	17	18	**19**	20	Chǔ shǔ		12	13[h]	14	15	16	17	18	
	25	26	◑	28	29	30	31	20:02	35	2425849		19	20	21	22	23	24	25			21	22	23	24	25	26	27			19	20	21	22	23	24	25	
SEPTEMBER 1929	1	2	●	4	5	6	7	11:47	36	2425856	ELUL 5689	26	27	28	29	30	1	2	Wed 3h52m7p	MONTH 8 Jĭ-Sì	28	29	1	2	3	4	5		EPAG. 1645	26	27	28	29	30	1	2	PĀG. 1921
	8	9	◐	11	12	13	14	22:57	37	2425863		3	4	5	6	7	8	9			6	7	8	9	10	11	12	Bái lù	THOOUT 1646	3	4	5	1[a]	2	3	4	MASKARAM 1922
	15	16	17	○	19	20	21	23:16	38	2425870		10	11	12	13	14	15	16			13	14*	15[g]	16	17	18	19			5	6	7	8	9	10	11	
	22	23[d]	24	25	◑	27	28	2:07	39	2425877		17	18	19	20	21	22	23			20	**21**	22	23	24	25	26	Qiū fēn		12	13	14	15	16	17[b]	18	
OCTOBER 1929	29	30	1	●	3	4	5	22:19	40	2425884	TISHRI 5690	24	25	26	27	28	29	1[a]	Thu 16h36m8p	MONTH 9 Jĭ-Sì	27	28	29	30	1	2	3			19	20	21	22	23	24	25	
	6	7	8	9	◐	11	12	18:05	41	2425891		2[a]	3	4	5	6	7	8			4	5	6	*7*	8	9[h]	10	Hán lù	PAOPE 1646	26	27	28	29	30	1	2	TEQEMT 1922
	13	14	15	16	17	○	19	12:06	42	2425898		9	10[b]	11	12	13	14	15[c]			11	12	13	14	15	16	17			3	4	5	6	7	8	9	
	20	21	22	23	24	◑	26	8:21	43	2425905		16	17	18	19	20	21	22			18	19	20	21	**22**	23	24	Shuāng jiàng		10	11	12	13	14	15	16	
NOVEMBER 1929	27	28	29	30	31	●	2	12:01	44	2425912		23	24	25	26	27	28	29		MONTH 10 Jĭ-Sì	25	26	27	28	29	1	2			17	18	19	20	21	22	23	
	3	4	5	6	7	8	◐	14:10	45	2425919	HESHVAN 5690	30	1	2	3	4	5	6	Sat 5h20m9p		3	4	5	6	7	*8*	9	Lì dōng		24	25	26	27	28	29	30	
	10	11	12	13	14	15	16		46	2425926		7	8	9	10	11	12	13			10	11	12	13	14	15*	16		ATHŌR 1646	1	2	3	4	5	6	7	ḪEDĀR 1922
	○	18	19	20	21	22	◑	0:14 16:04	47	2425933		14	15	16	17	18	19	20			17	18	19	20	21	22	**23**	Xiǎo xuě		8	9	10	11	12	13	14	
	24	25	26	27	28	29	30		48	2425940		21	22	23	24	25	26	27			24	25	26	27	28	29	30			15	16	17	18	19	20	21	
DECEMBER 1929	●	2	3	4	5	6	7	4:48	49	2425947	KISLEV 5690	28	29	1	2	3[d]	4	5	Sun 18h4m10p	MONTH 11 Jĭ-Sì	1	2	3	4	5	6	*7*	Dà xuě		22	23	24	25	26	27	28	
	8	◐	10	11	12	13	14	9:42	50	2425954		6	7	8	9	10	11	12			8	9	10	11	12	13	14		KOIAK 1646	29	30	1	2	3	4	5	TĀKHŚĀŚ 1922
	15	○	17	18	19	20	21	11:38	51	2425961		13	14	15	16	17	18	19			15	16	17	18	19	20	21			6	7	8	9	10	11	12	
	22[e]	◑	24	25	26	27	28	2:27	52	2425968		20	21	22	23	24	25[e]	26[e]			**22**[i]	23	24	25	26	27	28	Dōng zhì		13	14	15	16	17	18	19	
	29	●	31	1	2	3	4	23:42	1	2425975		27[e]	28[e]	29[e]	1[e]	2[e]	3[e]	4	Tue 6h48m11p		29	30	1	2	3	4	5			20	21	22	23	24	25	26	

[a]New Year
[b]Spring (2:35)
[c]Summer (22:01)
[d]Autumn (12:52)
[e]Winter (7:53)
● New moon
◐ First quarter moon
○ Full moon
◑ Last quarter moon

‡Leap year
[a]New Year
[b]Yom Kippur
[c]Sukkot
[d]Winter starts
[e]Ḥanukkah
[f]Purim
[g]Passover
[h]Shavuot
[i]Fast of Av

‡Leap year
[a]New Year (4627, Snake)
[b]Lantern Festival
[c]Qīngmíng
[d]Dragon Festival
[e]Qīqiǎo
[f]Hungry Ghosts
[g]Mid-Autumn Festival
[h]Double-Ninth Festival
[i]Dōngzhì
*Start of 60-name cycle

[a]New Year
[b]Building of the Cross
[c]Christmas
[d]Jesus's Circumcision
[e]Epiphany
[f]Easter
[g]Mary's Announcement
[h]Jesus's Transfiguration

PERSIAN (ASTRONOMICAL) 1307/1308

Month	Sun	Mon	Tue	Wed	Thu	Fri	Sat
DEY 1307	9	10	11	12	13	14	15
	16	17	18	19	20	21	22
	23	24	25	26	27	28	29
BAHMAN 1307	30	1	2	3	4	5	6
	7	8	9	10	11	12	13
	14	15	16	17	18	19	20
	21	22	23	24	25	26	27
ESFAND 1307	28	29	30	1	2	3	4
	5	6	7	8	9	10	11
	12	13	14	15	16	17	18
	19	20	21	22	23	24	25
FARVARDĪN 1308	26	27	28	29	1[a]	2	3
	4	5	6	7	8	9	10
	11	12	13[b]	14	15	16	17
	18	19	20	21	22	23	24
	25	26	27	28	29	30	31
ORDĪBEHEŠT 1308	1	2	3	4	5	6	7
	8	9	10	11	12	13	14
	15	16	17	18	19	20	21
	22	23	24	25	26	27	28
XORDĀD 1308	29	30	31	1	2	3	4
	5	6	7	8	9	10	11
	12	13	14	15	16	17	18
	19	20	21	22	23	24	25
TĪR 1308	26	27	28	29	30	31	1
	2	3	4	5	6	7	8
	9	10	11	12	13	14	15
	16	17	18	19	20	21	22
	23	24	25	26	27	28	29
MORDĀD 1308	30	31	1	2	3	4	5
	6	7	8	9	10	11	12
	13	14	15	16	17	18	19
	20	21	22	23	24	25	26
SHAHRĪVAR 1308	27	28	29	30	31	1	2
	3	4	5	6	7	8	9
	10	11	12	13	14	15	16
	17	18	19	20	21	22	23
	24	25	26	27	28	29	30
MEHR 1308	31	1	2	3	4	5	6
	7	8	9	10	11	12	13
	14	15	16	17	18	19	20
	21	22	23	24	25	26	27
ABĀN 1308	28	29	30	1	2	3	4
	5	6	7	8	9	10	11
	12	13	14	15	16	17	18
	19	20	21	22	23	24	25
ĀZAR 1308	26	27	28	29	30	1	2
	3	4	5	6	7	8	9
	10	11	12	13	14	15	16
	17	18	19	20	21	22	23
	24	25	26	27	28	29	30
DEY 1308	1	2	3	4	5	6	7
	8	9	10	11	12	13	14

[a]New Year
[b]Sizdeh Bedar

HINDU LUNAR 1985‡/1986

Month	Sun	Mon	Tue	Wed	Thu	Fri	Sat
MĀRGAŚĪRA 1985	19	20	21	22	23	24	25
PAUSHA 1985	26	27	28	29	30	1	2
	2	3	4	**5**	7	8	9
	10	11	12	13	14	15	16
	17	18	19	20	21	22	23
	24	25	26	27	28	29	30
MĀGHA 1985	1	2	3	4	5	6	7
	8	9	10	**11**	13	14	15
	16	17	18	19	20	21	22
	23	24	*24*	25	26	27	28[h]
PHĀLGUNA 1985	29	30	1	2	3	4	**5**
	7	8	9	10	11	12	13
	14	15[i]	16	17	18	19	20
	21	22	23	24	25	26	27
CHAITRA 1986	28	29	30	1[a]	2	3	4
	5	6	7	8[b]	**9**	11	12
	13	14	15	16	17	18	*18*
	19	20	21	22	23	24	25
VAIŚĀKHA 1986	26	27	28	29	30	1	**2**
	4	5	6	7	8	9	10
	11	12	13	14	15	16	17
	18	19	20	21	22	23	24
JYAISHṬHA 1986	25	26	27	28	29	30	1
	2	3	4	5	**6**	8	9
	10	11	12	13	14	*14*	15
	16	17	18	19	20	21	22
	23	24	25	26	27	**28**	30
ĀSHĀḌHA 1986	1	2	3	4	5	6	7
	8	9	10	11	12	13	14
	15	16	17	18	19	20	21
	22	23	24	25	26	27	28
ŚRĀVAṆA 1986	29	30	**1**	3	4	5	6
	7	8	9	10	11	*11*	12
	13	14	15	16	17	18	19
	20	21	22	23[c]	**24**	26	27
BHĀDRAPADA 1986	28	29	30	1	2	3	4[d]
	5	6	7	8	9	10	11
	12	13	14	15	16	17	18
	19	20	21	22	23	24	25
ĀŚVINA 1986	26	27	**28**	30	1	2	3
	4	5	6	*6*	7	8[e]	9[e]
	10[e]	11	12	13	14	15	16
	17	18	19	20	**21**	23	24
KĀRTTIKA 1986	25	26	27	28	29	30	1[f]
	2	3	4	5	6	7	8
	9	*9*	10	11	12	13	**14**
	16	17	18	19	20	21	22
	23	24	25	26	27	28	29
MĀRGAŚĪRA 1986	30	1	2	3	4	5	6
	7	8	9	10	11[g]	12	13
	14	15	16	17	18	**19**	21
	22	23	24	25	26	27	28
	29	30	1	2	*2*	3	4

‡Leap year
[a]New Year (Śukla)
[b]Birthday of Rāma
[c]Birthday of Krishna
[d]Ganēśa Chaturthī
[e]Dashara
[f]Diwali
[g]Birthday of Vishnu
[h]Night of Śiva
[i]Holi

HINDU SOLAR 1850‡/1851

Month	Sun	Mon	Tue	Wed	Thu	Fri	Sat
PAUSHA 1850	16	17	18	19	20	21	22
	23	24	25	26	27	28	29
MĀGHA 1850	1[b]	2	3	4	5	6	7
	8	9	10	11	12	13	14
	15	16	17	18	19	20	21
	22	23	24	25	26	27	28
PHĀLGUNA 1850	29	1	2	3	4	5	6
	7	8	9	10	11	12	13
	14	15	16	17	18	19	20
	21	22	23	24	25	26	27
CHAITRA 1850	28	29	30	1	2	3	4
	5	6	7	8	9	10	11
	12	13	14	15	16	17	18
	19	20	21	22	23	24	25
VAIŚĀKHA 1851	26	27	28	29	30	31	1[a]
	2	3	4	5	6	7	8
	9	10	11	12	13	14	15
	16	17	18	19	20	21	22
	23	24	25	26	27	28	29
JYAISHṬHA 1851	30	31	1	2	3	4	5
	6	7	8	9	10	11	12
	13	14	15	16	17	18	19
	20	21	22	23	24	25	26
ĀSHĀḌHA 1851	27	28	29	30	31	1	2
	3	4	5	6	7	8	9
	10	11	12	13	14	15	16
	17	18	19	20	21	22	23
	24	25	26	27	28	29	30
ŚRĀVAṆA 1851	31	32	1	2	3	4	5
	6	7	8	9	10	11	12
	13	14	15	16	17	18	19
	20	21	22	23	24	25	26
BHĀDRAPADA 1851	27	28	29	30	31	1	2
	3	4	5	6	7	8	9
	10	11	12	13	14	15	16
	17	18	19	20	21	22	23
	24	25	26	27	28	29	30
ĀŚVINA 1851	31	1	2	3	4	5	6
	7	8	9	10	11	12	13
	14	15	16	17	18	19	20
	21	22	23	24	25	26	27
KĀRTTIKA 1851	28	29	30	31	1	2	3
	4	5	6	7	8	9	10
	11	12	13	14	15	16	17
	18	19	20	21	22	23	24
MĀRGAŚĪRA 1851	25	26	27	28	29	1	2
	3	4	5	6	7	8	9
	10	11	12	13	14	15	16
	17	18	19	20	21	22	23
	24	25	26	27	28	29	30
PAUSHA 1851	1	2	3	4	5	6	7
	8	9	10	11	12	13	14
	15	16	17	18	19	20	21

‡Leap year
[a]New Year (Vṛisha)
[b]Pongal

ISLAMIC (ASTRONOMICAL) 1347‡/1348

Month	Sun	Mon	Tue	Wed	Thu	Fri	Sat
RAJAB 1347	17	18	19	20	21	22	23
	24	25	26	27[d]	28	29	30
SHA'BĀN 1347	1	2	3	4	5	6	7
	8	9	10	11	12	13	14
	15	16	17	18	19	20	21
	22	23	24	25	26	27	28
RAMAḌĀN 1347	29	1[e]	2	3	4	5	6
	7	8	9	10	11	12	13
	14	15	16	17	18	19	20
	21	22	23	24	25	26	27
SHAWWĀL 1347	28	29	30	1[f]	2	3	4
	5	6	7	8	9	10	11
	12	13	14	15	16	17	18
	19	20	21	22	23	24	25
DHU AL-QA'DA 1347	26	27	28	29	1	2	3
	4	5	6	7	8	9	10
	11	12	13	14	15	16	17
	18	19	20	21	22	23	24
DHU AL-ḤIJJA 1347	25	26	27	28	29	1	2
	3	4	5	6	7	8	9
	10[g]	11	12	13	14	15	16
	17	18	19	20	21	22	23
	24	25	26	27	28	29	30
MUḤARRAM 1348	1[a]	2	3	4	5	6	7
	8	9	10[b]	11	12	13	14
	15	16	17	18	19	20	21
	22	23	24	25	26	27	28
ṢAFAR 1348	29	1	2	3	4	5	6
	7	8	9	10	11	12	13
	14	15	16	17	18	19	20
	21	22	23	24	25	26	27
RABĪ' I 1348	28	29	1	2	3	4	5
	6	7	8	9	10	11	12[c]
	13	14	15	16	17	18	19
	20	21	22	23	24	25	26
RABĪ' II 1348	27	28	29	30	1	2	3
	4	5	6	7	8	9	10
	11	12	13	14	15	16	17
	18	19	20	21	22	23	24
JUMĀDĀ I 1348	25	26	27	28	29	1	2
	3	4	5	6	7	8	9
	10	11	12	13	14	15	16
	17	18	19	20	21	22	23
	24	25	26	27	28	29	30
JUMĀDĀ II 1348	1	2	3	4	5	6	7
	8	9	10	11	12	13	14
	15	16	17	18	19	20	21
	22	23	24	25	26	27	28
RAJAB 1348	29	30	1	2	3	4	5
	6	7	8	9	10	11	12
	13	14	15	16	17	18	19
	20	21	22	23	24	25	26
	27[d]	28	29	30	1	2	3

‡Leap year
[a]New Year
[b]'Ashūrā'
[c]Prophet's Birthday
[d]Ascent of the Prophet
[e]Start of Ramaḍān
[f]'Īd al-Fiṭr
[g]'Īd al-'Aḍḥā

GREGORIAN 1929

Julian (Sun)	Sun	Mon	Tue	Wed	Thu	Fri	Sat	Month
Dec 17	30	31	1	2	3	4	5	JANUARY 1929
	6	7[a]	8	9	10	11	12	
Dec 31	13	14[b]	15	16	17	18	19	
	20	21	22	23	24	25	26	
Jan 14	27	28	29	30	31	1	2	FEBRUARY 1929
	3	4	5	6	7	8	9	
Jan 28	10	11	12	13[c]	14	15	16	
	17	18	19	20	21	22	23	
Feb 11	24	25	26	27	28	1	2	MARCH 1929
	3	4	5	6	7	8	9	
Feb 25	10	11	12	13	14	15	16	
	17	18	19	20	21	22	23	
Mar 11	24[d]	25	26	27	28	29	30	
	31[e]	1	2	3	4	5	6	APRIL 1929
Mar 25	7	8	9	10	11	12	13	
	14	15	16	17	18	19	20	
Apr 8	21	22	23	24	25	26	27	
	28	29	30	1	2	3	4	MAY 1929
Apr 22	5[f]	6	7	8	9	10	11	
	12	13	14	15	16	17	18	
May 6	19	20	21	22	23	24	25	
	26	27	28	29	30	31	1	JUNE 1929
May 20	2	3	4	5	6	7	8	
	9	10	11	12	13	14	15	
Jun 3	16	17	18	19	20	21	22	
	23	24	25	26	27	28	29	
Jun 17	30	1	2	3	4	5	6	JULY 1929
	7	8	9	10	11	12	13	
Jul 1	14	15	16	17	18	19	20	
	21	22	23	24	25	26	27	
Jul 15	28	29	30	31	1	2	3	AUGUST 1929
	4	5	6	7	8	9	10	
Jul 29	11	12	13	14	15	16	17	
	18	19	20	21	22	23	24	
Aug 12	25	26	27	28	29	30	31	
	1	2	3	4	5	6	7	SEPTEMBER 1929
Aug 26	8	9	10	11	12	13	14	
	15	16	17	18	19	20	21	
Sep 9	22	23	24	25	26	27	28	
	29	30	1	2	3	4	5	OCTOBER 1929
Sep 23	6	7	8	9	10	11	12	
	13	14	15	16	17	18	19	
Oct 7	20	21	22	23	24	25	26	
	27	28	29	30	31	1	2	NOVEMBER 1929
Oct 21	3	4	5	6	7	8	9	
	10	11	12	13	14	15	16	
Nov 4	17	18	19	20	21	22	23	
	24	25	26	27	28	29	30	
Nov 18	1[g]	2	3	4	5	6	7	DECEMBER 1929
	8	9	10	11	12	13	14	
Dec 2	15	16	17	18	19	20	21	
	22	23	24	25[h]	26	27	28	
Dec 16	29	30	31	1	2	3	4	

[a]Orthodox Christmas
[b]Julian New Year
[c]Ash Wednesday
[d]Feast of Orthodoxy
[e]Easter
[f]Orthodox Easter
[g]Advent
[h]Christmas

1930

GREGORIAN 1930	Sun	Mon	Tue	Wed	Thu	Fri	Sat	Lunar Phases	ISO WEEK (Mon)	JULIAN DAY (Sun noon)	HEBREW 5690/5691	Sun	Mon	Tue	Wed	Thu	Fri	Sat	Molad	CHINESE Jǐ-Sì/Gēng-Wǔ‡	Sun	Mon	Tue	Wed	Thu	Fri	Sat	Solar Term	COPTIC 1646/1647‡	Sun	Mon	Tue	Wed	Thu	Fri	Sat	ETHIOPIC 1922/1923‡
JANUARY 1930	29	●	31	1[a]	2	3	4	23:42	1	2425975	TEVETH 5690	27[e]	28[e]	29[e]	1[e]	2[e]	3[e]	4	Tue 6h48m11p	MONTH 12 Jǐ-Sì	29	30	1	2	3	4	5		KOIAK 1646	20	21	22	23	24	25	26	TĀKHŚĀŚ 1922
	5	6	7	◐	9	10	11	3:11	2	2425982		5	6	7	8	9	10	11			6	7	8	9	10	11	12	Xiǎo hán		27	28	29[c]	30	1	2	3	
	12	13	○	15	16	17	18	22:21	3	2425989		12	13	14	15	16	17	18			13	14	15*	16	17	18	19		TŌBE 1646	4	5	6[d]	7	8	9	10	ṬER 1922
	19	20	◑	22	23	24	25	16:07	4	2425996		19	20	21	22	23	24	25	Wed 19h32m12p		20	21	22	23	24	25	26	Dà hán		11[e]	12	13	14	15	16	17	
	26	27	28	●	30	31	1	19:07	5	2426003		26	27	28	29	1	2	3			27	28	29	30	1[a]	2	3			18	19	20	21	22	23	24	
FEBRUARY 1930	2	3	4	5	◐	7	8	17:26	6	2426010	SHEVAT 5690	4	5	6	7	8	9	10		MONTH 1 Gēng-Wǔ	4	5	6	7	8	9	10	Lì chūn		25	26	27	28	29	30	1	
	9	10	11	12	○	14	15	8:38	7	2426017		11	12	13	14	15	16	17			11	12	13	14	15[b]	16	17		MESHIR 1646	2	3	4	5	6	7	8	YAKĀTIT 1922
	16	17	18	19	◑	21	22	8:44	8	2426024		18	19	20	21	22	23	24	Fri 8h16m13p		18	19	20	21	22	23	24	Yǔ shuǐ		9	10	11	12	13	14	15	
	23	24	25	26	27	●	1	13:32	9	2426031		25	26	27	28	29	30	1			25	26	27	28	29	1	2			16	17	18	19	20	21	22	
MARCH 1930	2	3	4	5	6	7	◐	4:00	10	2426038	ADAR 5690	2	3	4	5	6	7	8		MONTH 2 Gēng-Wǔ	3	4	5	6	7	8	9	Jīng zhé		23	24	25	26	27	28	29	
	9	10	11	12	13	○	15	18:58	11	2426045		9	10	11	12	13	14[f]	15			10	11	12	13	14	15	16*			30	1	2	3	4	5	6	
	16	17	18	19	20	21[b]	◑	3:13	12	2426052		16	17	18	19	20	21	22			17	18	19	20	21	22	23	Chūn fēn	PAREMOTEP 1646	7	8	9	10	11	12	13	MAGĀBIT 1922
	23	24	25	26	27	28	29		13	2426059		23	24	25	26	27	28	29			24	25	26	27	28	29	30			14	15	16	17	18	19	20	
	●	31	1	2	3	4	5	5:46	14	2426066	NISAN 5690	1	2	3	4	5	6	7	Sat 21h0m14p	MONTH 3 Gēng-Wǔ	1	2	3	4	5	6	7[c]	Qīng míng		21	22	23	24	25	26	27	
APRIL 1930	◐	7	8	9	10	11	12	11:25	15	2426073		8	9	10	11	12	13	14			8	9	10	11	12	13	14			28	29	30	1	2	3	4	
	○	14	15	16	17	18	19	5:49	16	2426080		15[g]	16	17	18	19	20	21			15	16	17	18	19	20	21		PARMOUTE 1646	5	6	7	8	9	10	11	MIYĀZYĀ 1922
	◑	21	22	23	24	25	26	22:08	17	2426087		22	23	24	25	26	27	28			22	23	24	25	26	27	28	Gǔ yǔ		12[f]	13	14	15	16	17	18	
	27	●	29	30	1	2	3	19:09	18	2426094		29	30	1	2	3	4	5	Mon 9h44m15p		29	30	1	2	3	4	5			19	20	21	22	23	24	25	
MAY 1930	4	◐	6	7	8	9	10	16:53	19	2426101	IYYAR 5690	6	7	8	9	10	11	12		MONTH 4 Gēng-Wǔ	6	7	8	9	10	11	12	Lì xià		26	27	28	29[g]	30	1	2	
	11	○	13	14	15	16	17	17:29	20	2426108		13	14	15	16	17	18	19			13	14	15	16*	17	18	19		PASHONS 1646	3	4	5	6	7	8	9	GENBOT 1922
	18	19	◑	21	22	23	24	16:22	21	2426115		20	21	22	23	24	25	26			20	21	22	23	24	25	26	Xiǎo mǎn		10	11	12	13	14	15	16	
	25	26	27	●	29	30	31	5:37	22	2426122		27	28	29	1	2	3	4	Tue 22h28m16p		27	28	29	1	2	3	4			17	18	19	20	21	22	23	
JUNE 1930	1	2	◐	4	5	6	7	21:56	23	2426129	SIVAN 5690	5	6[h]	7	8	9	10	11		MONTH 5 Gēng-Wǔ	5[d]	6	7	8	9	10	11	Máng zhòng		24	25	26	27	28	29	30	
	8	9	10	○	12	13	14	6:11	24	2426136		12	13	14	15	16	17	18			12	13	14	15	16	17	18			1	2	3	4	5	6	7	
	15	16	17	18	◑	20	21	9:00	25	2426143		19	20	21	22	23	24	25			19	20	21	22	23	24	25		PAŌNE 1646	8	9	10	11	12	13	14	SANĒ 1922
	22[c]	23	24	25	●	27	28	13:47	26	2426150		26	27	28	29	30	1	2	Thu 11h12m17p		26	27	28	29	1	2	3	Xià zhì		15	16	17	18	19	20	21	
	29	30	1	2	◐	4	5	4:03	27	2426157	TAMMUZ 5690	3	4	5	6	7	8	9		MONTH 6 Gēng-Wǔ	4	5	6	7	8	9	10			22	23	24	25	26	27	28	
JULY 1930	6	7	8	9	○	11	12	20:01	28	2426164		10	11	12	13	14	15	16			11	12	13	14	15	16	17	Xiǎo shǔ		29	30	1	2	3	4	5	
	13	14	15	16	17	◑	19	23:29	29	2426171		17	18	19	20	21	22	23			18*	19	20	21	22	23	24		EPĒP 1646	6	7	8	9	10	11	12	
	20	21	22	23	24	●	26	20:42	30	2426178		24	25	26	27	28	29	1	Fri 23h57m0p		25	26	27	28	29	30	1	Dà shǔ		13	14	15	16	17	18	19	ḤAMLĒ 1922
	27	28	29	30	31	◐	2	12:26	31	2426185	AV 5690	2	3	4	5	6	7	8		LEAP MONTH 6 Gēng-Wǔ	2	3	4	5	6	7	8			20	21	22	23	24	25	26	
AUGUST 1930	3	4	5	6	7	8	○	10:57	32	2426192		9[i]	10	11	12	13	14	15			9	10	11	12	13	14	15	Lì qiū		27	28	29	30	1	2	3	
	10	11	12	13	14	15	16		33	2426199		16	17	18	19	20	21	22			16	17	18	19	20	21	22		MESORĒ 1646	4	5	6	7	8	9	10	
	◑	18	19	20	21	22	23	11:30	34	2426206		23	24	25	26	27	28	29			23	24	25	26	27	28	29			11	12	13[h]	14	15	16	17	NAHASĒ 1922
	●	25	26	27	28	29	◐	3:37 23:57	35	2426213		30	1	2	3	4	5	6	Sun 12h41m1p	MONTH 7 Gēng-Wǔ	1	2	3	4	5	6	7[e]	Chǔ shǔ		18	19	20	21	22	23	24	
	31	1	2	3	4	5	6		36	2426220	ELUL 5690	7	8	9	10	11	12	13			8	9	10	11	12	13	14			25	26	27	28	29	30	1	
SEPTEMBER 1930	7	○	9	10	11	12	13	2:48	37	2426227		14	15	16	17	18	19	20			15[f]	16	17	18	19*	20	21	Bái lù	EPAG. 1646	2	3	4	5	1[a]	2	3	PĀG. 1922
	14	◑	16	17	18	19	20	21:13	38	2426234		21	22	23	24	25	26	27			22	23	24	25	26	27	28		THOOUT 1647	4	5	6	7	8	9	10	MASKARAM 1923
	21	●	23[d]	24	25	26	27	11:41	39	2426241		28	29	1[a]	2[a]	3	4	5	Tue 1h25m2p		29	1	2	3	4	5	6	Qiū fēn		11	12	13	14	15	16	17[b]	
	28	◐	30	1	2	3	4	14:58	40	2426248	TISHRI 5691	6	7	8	9	10[b]	11	12		MONTH 8 Gēng-Wǔ	7	8	9	10	11	12	13			18	19	20	21	22	23	24	
OCTOBER 1930	5	6	○	8	9	10	11	18:56	41	2426255		13	14	15[c]	16	17	18	19			14	15[g]	16	17	18	19	20	Hán lù		25	26	27	28	29	30	1	
	12	13	14	◑	16	17	18	5:12	42	2426262		20	21	22	23	24	25	26			21	22	23	24	25	26	27		PAOPE 1647	2	3	4	5	6	7	8	ṬEQEMT 1923
	19	20	●	22	23	24	25	21:47	43	2426269		27	28	29	30	1	2	3	Wed 14h9m3p		28	29	30	1	2	3	4	Shuāng jiàng		9	10	11	12	13	14	15	
	26	27	28	◐	30	31	1	9:22	44	2426276	ḤESHVAN 5691	4	5	6	7	8	9	10		MONTH 9 Gēng-Wǔ	5	6	7	8	9[h]	10	11			16	17	18	19	20	21	22	
NOVEMBER 1930	2	3	4	5	○	7	8	10:28	45	2426283		11	12	13	14	15	16	17			12	13	14	15	16	17	18	Lì dōng		23	24	25	26	27	28	29	
	9	10	11	12	◑	14	15	12:27	46	2426290		18	19	20	21	22	23	24			19	20*	21	22	23	24	25			30	1	2	3	4	5	6	
	16	17	18	19	●	21	22	10:21	47	2426297		25	26	27	28	29	1	2			26	27	28	29	1	2	3		ATHŌR 1647	7	8	9	10	11	12	13	
	23	24	25	26	27	◐	29	6:17	48	2426304	KISLEV 5691	3	4	5	6	7	8	9	Fri 2h53m4p	MONTH 10 Gēng-Wǔ	4	5	6	7	8	9	10	Xiǎo xuě		14	15	16	17	18	19	20	ḪEDĀR 1923
	30	1	2	3	4	5	○	0:40	49	2426311		10	11	12	13	14	15[d]	16			11	12	13	14	15	16	17			21	22	23	24	25	26	27	
DECEMBER 1930	7	8	9	10	11	◑	13	20:07	50	2426318		17	18	19	20	21	22	23			18	19	20	21	22	23	24	Dà xuě		28	29	30	1	2	3	4	
	14	15	16	17	18	19	●	1:24	51	2426325		24	25[e]	26[e]	27[e]	28[e]	29[e]	30[e]			25	26	27	28	29	30	1	Dōng zhì	KOIAK 1647	5	6	7	8	9	10	11	TĀKHŚĀŚ 1923
	21	22[e]	23	24	25	26	27		52	2426332	TEVETH 5691	1[e]	2[e]	3	4	5	6	7	Sat 15h37m5p	MONTH 11 Gēng-Wǔ	2	3[i]	4	5	6	7	8			12	13	14	15	16	17	18	
	◐	29	30	31	1	2	3	3:59	1	2426339		8	9	10	11	12	13	14			9	10	11	12	13	14	15			19	20	21	22	23	24	25	

[a]New Year
[b]Spring (8:29)
[c]Summer (3:53)
[d]Autumn (18:36)
[e]Winter (13:39)
● New moon
◐ First quarter moon
○ Full moon
◑ Last quarter moon

[a]New Year
[b]Yom Kippur
[c]Sukkot
[d]Winter starts
[e]Ḥanukkah
[f]Purim
[g]Passover
[h]Shavuot
[i]Fast of Av

‡Leap year
[a]New Year (4628, Horse)
[b]Lantern Festival
[c]Qīngmíng
[d]Dragon Festival
[e]Qīqiǎo
[f]Hungry Ghosts
[g]Mid-Autumn Festival
[h]Double-Ninth Festival
[i]Dōngzhì
*Start of 60-name cycle

‡Leap year
[a]New Year
[b]Building of the Cross
[c]Christmas
[d]Jesus's Circumcision
[e]Epiphany
[f]Easter
[g]Mary's Announcement
[h]Jesus's Transfiguration

PERSIAN (ASTRONOMICAL) 1308/1309‡

Month	Sun	Mon	Tue	Wed	Thu	Fri	Sat
	8	9	10	11	12	13	14
DEY 1308	15	16	17	18	19	20	21
	22	23	24	25	26	27	28
	29	30	1	2	3	4	5
BAHMAN 1308	6	7	8	9	10	11	12
	13	14	15	16	17	18	19
	20	21	22	23	24	25	26
	27	28	29	30	1	2	3
ESFAND 1308	4	5	6	7	8	9	10
	11	12	13	14	15	16	17
	18	19	20	21	22	23	24
	25	26	27	28	29	1[a]	2*
FARVARDĪN 1309	3	4	5	6	7	8	9
	10	11	12	13[b]	14	15	16
	17	18	19	20	21	22	23
	24	25	26	27	28	29	30
	31	1	2	3	4	5	6
ORDĪBEHEŠT 1309	7	8	9	10	11	12	13
	14	15	16	17	18	19	20
	21	22	23	24	25	26	27
	28	29	30	31	1	2	3
XORDĀD 1309	4	5	6	7	8	9	10
	11	12	13	14	15	16	17
	18	19	20	21	22	23	24
	25	26	27	28	29	30	31
	1	2	3	4	5	6	7
TĪR 1309	8	9	10	11	12	13	14
	15	16	17	18	19	20	21
	22	23	24	25	26	27	28
	29	30	31	1	2	3	4
MORDĀD 1309	5	6	7	8	9	10	11
	12	13	14	15	16	17	18
	19	20	21	22	23	24	25
	26	27	28	29	30	31	1
SHAHRĪVAR 1309	2	3	4	5	6	7	8
	9	10	11	12	13	14	15
	16	17	18	19	20	21	22
	23	24	25	26	27	28	29
	30	31	1	2	3	4	5
MEHR 1309	6	7	8	9	10	11	12
	13	14	15	16	17	18	19
	20	21	22	23	24	25	26
	27	28	29	30	1	2	3
ĀBĀN 1309	4	5	6	7	8	9	10
	11	12	13	14	15	16	17
	18	19	20	21	22	23	24
	25	26	27	28	29	30	1
ĀZAR 1309	2	3	4	5	6	7	8
	9	10	11	12	13	14	15
	16	17	18	19	20	21	22
	23	24	25	26	27	28	29
DEY 1309	30	1	2	3	4	5	6
	7	8	9	10	11	12	13

‡Leap year
[a]New Year (or next day)
*Near New Year: 0′31″
[b]Sizdeh Bedar

HINDU LUNAR 1986/1987

Month	Sun	Mon	Tue	Wed	Thu	Fri	Sat
	29	30	1	2	2	3	4
PAUSHA 1986	5	6	7	8	9	10	11
	12	13	15	16	17	18	19
	20	21	22	23	24	25	26
	27	28	29	30	1	2	3
MĀGHA 1986	4	5	6	7	8	9	10
	11	12	13	14	15	16	17
	18	19	21	22	23	24	24
	25	26	27	28[h]	29	30	1
PHĀLGUNA 1986	2	3	4	5	6	7	8
	9	10	11	12	14	15[i]	16
	17	18	19	20	21	22	23
	24	25	26	27	27	28	29
	30	1[a]	2	3	4	5	6
CHAITRA 1987	8	9[b]	10	11	12	13	14
	15	16	17	18	19	20	21
	22	23	24	25	26	27	28
	29	30	1	2	3	4	5
VAIŚĀKHA 1987	6	7	8	9	11	12	13
	14	15	16	17	18	19	20
	21	22	22	23	24	25	26
	27	28	29	30	1	2	4
JYAISHṬHA 1987	5	6	7	8	9	10	11
	12	13	14	15	16	17	18
	19	20	21	22	23	24	25
	26	27	28	29	30	1	2
ĀSHĀḌHA 1987	3	4	5	7	8	9	10
	11	12	13	14	15	16	17
	18	19	19	20	21	22	23
	24	25	26	27	28	30	1
ŚRĀVAṆA 1987	2	3	4	5	6	7	8
	9	10	11	12	13	14	15
	16	17	18	19	20	21	22
	23[c]	24	25	26	27	28	29
BHĀDRAPADA 1987	30	1	3	4[d]	5	6	7
	8	9	10	11	12	13	14
	15	15	16	17	18	19	20
	21	22	23	24	26	27	28
	29	30	1	2	3	4	5
ĀŚVINA 1987	6	7	8[e]	9[e]	10[e]	11	12
	13	14	15	16	17	18	19
	20	21	22	23	24	25	26
	27	28	30	1[f]	2	3	4
KĀRTTIKA 1987	5	6	7	8	9	10	10
	11	12	13	14	15	16	17
	18	19	20	21	22	24	25
	26	27	28	29	30	1	2
MĀRGAŚIRA 1987	3	4	5	6	7	8	9
	10	11[g]	12	13	14	15	16
	17	18	19	20	21	22	23
	24	25	26	27	29	30	1
PAUSHA 1987	2	2	3	4	5	6	7
	8	9	10	11	12	13	14

[a]New Year (Pramoda)
[b]Birthday of Rāma
[c]Birthday of Krishna
[d]Ganēśa Chaturthī
[e]Dashara
[f]Diwali
[g]Birthday of Vishnu
[h]Night of Śiva
[i]Holi

HINDU SOLAR 1851/1852

Month	Sun	Mon	Tue	Wed	Thu	Fri	Sat
	15	16	17	18	19	20	21
PAUSHA 1851	22	23	24	25	26	27	28
	29	1[b]	2	3	4	5	6
MĀGHA 1851	7	8	9	10	11	12	13
	14	15	16	17	18	19	20
	21	22	23	24	25	26	27
	28	29	30	1	2	3	4
PHĀLGUNA 1851	5	6	7	8	9	10	11
	12	13	14	15	16	17	18
	19	20	21	22	23	24	25
	26	27	28	29	30	1	2
CHAITRA 1851	3	4	5	6	7	8	9
	10	11	12	13	14	15	16
	17	18	19	20	21	22	23
	24	25	26	27	28	29	30
VAIŚĀKHA 1852	1[a]	2	3	4	5	6	7
	8	9	10	11	12	13	14
	15	16	17	18	19	20	21
	22	23	24	25	26	27	28
	29	30	31	1	2	3	4
JYAISHṬHA 1852	5	6	7	8	9	10	11
	12	13	14	15	16	17	18
	19	20	21	22	23	24	25
	26	27	28	29	30	31	1
ĀSHĀḌHA 1852	2	3	4	5	6	7	8
	9	10	11	12	13	14	15
	16	17	18	19	20	21	22
	23	24	25	26	27	28	29
	30	31	32	1	2	3	4
ŚRĀVAṆA 1852	5	6	7	8	9	10	11
	12	13	14	15	16	17	18
	19	20	21	22	23	24	25
	26	27	28	29	30	31	1
BHĀDRAPADA 1852	2	3	4	5	6	7	8
	9	10	11	12	13	14	15
	16	17	18	19	20	21	22
	23	24	25	26	27	28	29
	30	31	1	2	3	4	5
ĀŚVINA 1852	6	7	8	9	10	11	12
	13	14	15	16	17	18	19
	20	21	22	23	24	25	26
	27	28	29	30	31	1	2
KĀRTTIKA 1852	3	4	5	6	7	8	9
	10	11	12	13	14	15	16
	17	18	19	20	21	22	23
	24	25	26	27	28	29	30
	1	2	3	4	5	6	7
MĀRGAŚIRA 1852	8	9	10	11	12	13	14
	15	16	17	18	19	20	21
	22	23	24	25	26	27	28
	29	1	2	3	4	5	6
PAUSHA 1852	7	8	9	10	11	12	13
	14	15	16	17	18	19	20

[a]New Year (Chitrabhānu)
[b]Pongal

ISLAMIC (ASTRONOMICAL) 1348/1349‡

Month	Sun	Mon	Tue	Wed	Thu	Fri	Sat
	27	28	29	30	1	2	3
SHA'BĀN 1348	4	5	6	7	8	9	10
	11	12	13	14	15	16	17
	18	19	20	21	22	23	24
	25	26	27	28	29	1[e]	2
RAMAḌĀN 1348	3	4	5	6	7	8	9
	10	11	12	13	14	15	16
	17	18	19	20	21	22	23
	24	25	26	27	28	29	30
SHAWWĀL 1348	1[f]	2	3	4	5	6	7
	8	9	10	11	12	13	14
	15	16	17	18	19	20	21
	22	23	24	25	26	27	28
	29	30	1	2	3	4	5
DHU AL-QA'DA 1348	6	7	8	9	10	11	12
	13	14	15	16	17	18	19
	20	21	22	23	24	25	26
	27	28	29	1	2	3	4
DHU AL-ḤIJJA 1348	5	6	7	8	9	10[g]	11
	12	13	14	15	16	17	18
	19	20	21	22	23	24	25
	26	27	28	29	1[a]	2	3
MUḤARRAM 1349	4	5	6	7	8	9	10[b]
	11	12	13	14	15	16	17
	18	19	20	21	22	23	24
	25	26	27	28	29	30	1
ṢAFAR 1349	2	3	4	5	6	7	8
	9	10	11	12	13	14	15
	16	17	18	19	20	21	22
	23	24	25	26	27	28	29
RABĪ' I 1349	1	2	3	4	5	6	7
	8	9	10	11	12[c]	13	14
	15	16	17	18	19	20	21
	22	23	24	25	26	27	28
	29	1	2	3	4	5	6
RABĪ' II 1349	7	8	9	10	11	12	13
	14	15	16	17	18	19	20
	21	22	23	24	25	26	27
	28	29	30	1	2	3	4
JUMĀDĀ I 1349	5	6	7	8	9	10	11
	12	13	14	15	16	17	18
	19	20	21	22	23	24	25
	26	27	28	29	30	1	2
JUMĀDĀ II 1349	3	4	5	6	7	8	9
	10	11	12	13	14	15	16
	17	18	19	20	21	22	23
	24	25	26	27	28	29	1
RAJAB 1349	2	3	4	5	6	7	8
	9	10	11	12	13	14	15
	16	17	18	19	20	21	22
	23	24	25	26	27[d]	28	29
SHA'BĀN 1349	30	1	2	3	4	5	6
	7	8	9	10	11	12	13

‡Leap year
[a]New Year
[b]'Ashūrā'
[c]Prophet's Birthday
[d]Ascent of the Prophet
[e]Start of Ramaḍān
[f]'Id al-Fiṭr
[g]'Id al-'Aḍḥā

GREGORIAN 1930

Julian (Sun)	Sun	Mon	Tue	Wed	Thu	Fri	Sat	Month
Dec 16	29	30	31	1	2	3	4	
	5	6	7[a]	8	9	10	11	JANUARY 1930
Dec 30	12	13	14[b]	15	16	17	18	
	19	20	21	22	23	24	25	
Jan 13	26	27	28	29	30	31	1	
	2	3	4	5	6	7	8	FEBRUARY 1930
Jan 27	9	10	11	12	13	14	15	
	16	17	18	19	20	21	22	
Feb 10	23	24	25	26	27	28	1	
	2	3	4	5[c]	6	7	8	MARCH 1930
Feb 24	9[d]	10	11	12	13	14	15	
	16	17	18	19	20	21	22	
Mar 10	23	24	25	26	27	28	29	
	30	31	1	2	3	4	5	
Mar 24	6	7	8	9	10	11	12	APRIL 1930
	13	14	15	16	17	18	19	
Apr 7	20[e]	21	22	23	24	25	26	
	27	28	29	30	1	2	3	
Apr 21	4	5	6	7	8	9	10	MAY 1930
	11	12	13	14	15	16	17	
May 5	18	19	20	21	22	23	24	
	25	26	27	28	29	30	31	
May 19	1	2	3	4	5	6	7	
	8	9	10	11	12	13	14	JUNE 1930
Jun 2	15	16	17	18	19	20	21	
	22	23	24	25	26	27	28	
Jun 16	29	30	1	2	3	4	5	
	6	7	8	9	10	11	12	JULY 1930
Jun 30	13	14	15	16	17	18	19	
	20	21	22	23	24	25	26	
Jul 14	27	28	29	30	31	1	2	
	3	4	5	6	7	8	9	AUGUST 1930
Jul 28	10	11	12	13	14	15	16	
	17	18	19	20	21	22	23	
Aug 11	24	25	26	27	28	29	30	
	31	1	2	3	4	5	6	
Aug 25	7	8	9	10	11	12	13	SEPTEMBER 1930
	14	15	16	17	18	19	20	
Sep 8	21	22	23	24	25	26	27	
	28	29	30	1	2	3	4	
Sep 22	5	6	7	8	9	10	11	OCTOBER 1930
	12	13	14	15	16	17	18	
Oct 6	19	20	21	22	23	24	25	
	26	27	28	29	30	31	1	
Oct 20	2	3	4	5	6	7	8	NOVEMBER 1930
	9	10	11	12	13	14	15	
Nov 3	16	17	18	19	20	21	22	
	23	24	25	26	27	28	29	
Nov 17	30[g]	1	2	3	4	5	6	
	7	8	9	10	11	12	13	DECEMBER 1930
Dec 1	14	15	16	17	18	19	20	
	21	22	23	24	25[h]	26	27	
Dec 15	28	29	30	31	1	2	3	

[a]Orthodox Christmas
[b]Julian New Year
[c]Ash Wednesday
[d]Feast of Orthodoxy
[e]Easter (also Orthodox)
[g]Advent
[h]Christmas

1931

Month	GREGORIAN 1931 (Sun Mon Tue Wed Thu Fri Sat)	Lunar Phases	ISO WEEK (Mon)	JULIAN DAY (Sun noon)	Hebrew month	HEBREW 5691/5692‡ (Sun Mon Tue Wed Thu Fri Sat)	Molad	Chinese month	CHINESE Gēng-Wǔ‡/Xīn-Wèi (Sun Mon Tue Wed Thu Fri Sat)	Solar Term	Coptic month	COPTIC 1647‡/1648 (Sun Mon Tue Wed Thu Fri Sat)	Ethiopic month 1923‡/1924
	◐ 29 30 31 1[a] 2 3	3:59	1	2426339		8 9 10 11 12 13 14			9 10 11 12 13 14 15			19 20 21 22 23 24 25	TĀKHŚĀŚ 1923
	○ 5 6 7 8 9 10	13:15	2	2426346	TEVETH 5691	15 16 17 18 19 20 21		MONTH 11 Gēng-Wǔ	16 17 18 19 20 21* 22	Xiǎo hán	KOIAK 1647	26 27 28 29[c] 30 1 2	
JANUARY 1931	◑ 12 13 14 15 16 17	5:09	3	2426353		22 23 24 25 26 27 28			23 24 25 26 27 28 29			3 4 5 6[d] 7 8 9	
	● 19 20 21 22 23 24	18:36	4	2426360		29 1 2 3 4 5 6	Mon 4h21m16p		30 1 2 3 4 5 6	Dà hán	TŌBE 1647	10 11[e] 12 13 14 15 16	ṬER 1923
	25 26 ◐ 28 29 30 31	0:05	5	2426367		7 8 9 10 11 12 13			7 8 9 10 11 12 13			17 18 19 20 21 22 23	
	1 2 ○ 4 5 6 7	0:26	6	2426374	SHEVAT 5691	14 15 16 17 18 19 20		MONTH 12 Gēng-Wǔ	14 15 16 17 18 19 20	Lì chūn		24 25 26 27 28 29 30	
FEBRUARY 1931	8 ◑ 10 11 12 13 14	16:10	7	2426381		21 22 23 24 25 26 27			21 22 23 24 25 26 27			1 2 3 4 5 6 7	
	15 16 ● 18 19 20 21	13:11	8	2426388		28 29 30 1 2 3 4	Tue 17h5m7p		28 29 1[a] 2 3 4 5	Yǔ shuǐ		8 9 10 11 12 13 14	YAKĀTIT 1923
	22 23 24 ◐ 26 27 28	16:42	9	2426395		5 6 7 8 9 10 11			6 7 8 9 10 11 12		MESHIR 1647	15 16 17 18 19 20 21	
	1 2 3 ○ 5 6 7	10:36	10	2426402	ADAR 5691	12 13 14[f] 15 16 17 18		MONTH 1 Xīn-Wèi	13 14 15[b] 16 17 18 19	Jīng zhé		22 23 24 25 26 27 28	
	8 9 10 ◑ 12 13 14	5:15	11	2426409		19 20 21 22 23 24 25			20 21 22* 23 24 25 26			29 30 1 2 3 4 5	
MARCH 1931	15 16 17 18 ● 20 21[b]	7:50	12	2426416		26 27 28 29 1 2 3	Thu 5h49m8p		27 28 29 30 1 2 3	Chūn fēn		6 7 8 9 10 11 12	
	22 23 24 25 26 ◐ 28	5:04	13	2426423		4 5 6 7 8 9 10			4 5 6 7 8 9 10		PAREMOTEP 1647	13 14 15 16 17 18 19	MAGĀBIT 1923
	29 30 31 1 ○ 3 4	20:05	14	2426430	NISAN 5691	11 12 13 14 15[g] 16 17		MONTH 2 Xīn-Wèi	11 12 13 14 15 16 17			20 21 22 23 24 25 26	
	5 6 7 8 ◑ 10 11	20:15	15	2426437		18 19 20 21 22 23 24			18 19[c] 20 21 22 23 24	Qīng míng		27 28 29 30 1 2 3	
APRIL 1931	12 13 14 15 16 17 ●	1:00	16	2426444		25 26 27 28 29 30 1	Fri 18h33m9p		25 26 27 28 29 30 1	Gǔ yǔ		4[f] 5 6 7 8 9 10	
	19 20 21 22 23 24 ◐	13:40	17	2426451		2 3 4 5 6 7 8			2 3 4 5 6 7 8		PARMOUTE 1647	11 12 13 14 15 16 17	MIYĀZYĀ 1923
	26 27 28 29 30 1 ○	5:14	18	2426458	IYYAR 5691	9 10 11 12 13 14 15		MONTH 3 Xīn-Wèi	9 10 11 12 13 14 15			18 19 20 21 22 23 24	
	3 4 5 6 7 8 ◑	12:48	19	2426465		16 17 18 19 20 21 22			16 17 18 19 20 21 22*	Lì xià		25 26 27 28 29[g] 30 1	
MAY 1931	10 11 12 13 14 15 16		20	2426472		23 24 25 26 27 28 29			23 24 25 26 27 28 29			2 3 4 5 6 7 8	
	● 18 19 20 21 22 23	15:28	21	2426479		1 2 3 4 5 6[h] 7	Sun 7h17m10p		1 2 3 4 5 6 7	Xiǎo mǎn		9 10 11 12 13 14 15	GENBOT 1923
	◐ 25 26 27 28 29 30	19:39	22	2426486		8 9 10 11 12 13 14		MONTH 4 Xīn-Wèi	8 9 10 11 12 13 14		PASHONS 1647	16 17 18 19 20 21 22	
	○ 1 2 3 4 5 6	14:33	23	2426493	SIVAN 5691	15 16 17 18 19 20 21			15 16 17 18 19 20 21			23 24 25 26 27 28 29	
	7 ◑ 9 10 11 12 13	6:18	24	2426500		22 23 24 25 26 27 28			22 23 24 25 26 27 28	Máng zhòng		30 1 2 3 4 5 6	
JUNE 1931	14 15 ● 17 18 19 20	3:02	25	2426507		29 30 1 2 3 4 5	Mon 20h1m11p		29 30 1 2 3 4 5[d]			7 8 9 10 11 12 13	
	21 22[c] ◐ 24 25 26 27	0:23	26	2426514		6 7 8 9 10 11 12			6 7 8 9 10 11 12	Xià zhì	PAŌNE 1647	14 15 16 17 18 19 20	SANĒ 1923
	28 29 ○ 1 2 3 4	0:47	27	2426521	TAMMUZ 5691	13 14 15 16 17 18 19		MONTH 5 Xīn-Wèi	13 14 15 16 17 18 19			21 22 23 24 25 26 27	
	5 6 ◑ 8 9 10 11	23:51	28	2426528		20 21 22 23 24 25 26			20 21 22 23* 24 25 26	Xiǎo shǔ		28 29 30 1 2 3 4	
JULY 1931	12 13 14 ● 16 17 18	12:20	29	2426535		27 28 29 1 2 3 4	Wed 8h45m12p		27 28 29 1 2 3 4			5 6 7 8 9 10 11	
	19 20 21 ◐ 23 24 25	5:16	30	2426542		5 6 7 8 9[i] 10 11			5 6 7 8 9 10 11	Dà shǔ	EPĒP 1647	12 13 14 15 16 17 18	ḤAMLĒ 1923
	26 27 28 ○ 30 31 1	12:47	31	2426549	AV 5691	12 13 14 15 16 17 18		MONTH 6 Xīn-Wèi	12 13 14 15 16 17 18			19 20 21 22 23 24 25	
	2 3 4 5 ◑ 7 8	16:28	32	2426556		19 20 21 22 23 24 25			19 20 21 22 23 24 25	Lì qiū		26 27 28 29 30 1 2	
AUGUST 1931	9 10 11 12 ● 14 15	20:27	33	2426563		26 27 28 29 30 1 2	Thu 21h29m13p		26 27 28 29 30 1 2			3 4 5 6 7 8 9	
	16 17 18 19 ◐ 21 22	11:36	34	2426570		3 4 5 6 7 8 9			3 4 5 6 7[e] 8 9			10 11 12 13[h] 14 15 16	NAḤASĒ 1923
	23 24 25 26 27 ○ 29	3:09	35	2426577	ELUL 5691	10 11 12 13 14 15 16		MONTH 7 Xīn-Wèi	10 11 12 13 14 15[f] 16	Chǔ shǔ	MESORĒ 1647	17 18 19 20 21 22 23	
	30 31 1 2 3 4 ◑	7:21	36	2426584		17 18 19 20 21 22 23			17 18 19 20 21 22 23			24 25 26 27 28 29 30	
	6 7 8 9 10 11 ●	4:26	37	2426591		24 25 26 27 28 29 1[a]	Sat 10h13m14p		24* 25 26 27 28 29 1	Bái lù	EPAG. 1647	1 2 3 4 5 6 1[a]	PĀG. 1923
SEPTEMBER 1931	13 14 15 16 17 ◐ 19	20:37	38	2426598		2[a] 3 4 5 6 7 8			2 3 4 5 6 7 8			2 3 4 5 6 7 8	
	20 21 22 23 24[d] 25 ○	19:45	39	2426605	TISHRI 5692	9 10[b] 11 12 13 14 15[c]		MONTH 8 Xīn-Wèi	9 10 11 12 13 14 15[g]	Qiū fēn	THOOUT 1648	9 10 11 12 13 14 15	MASKARAM 1924
	27 28 29 30 1 2 3		40	2426612		16 17 18 19 20 21 22			16 17 18 19 20 21 22			16 17[b] 18 19 20 21 22	
	◑ 5 6 7 8 9 10	20:15	41	2426619		23 24 25 26 27 28 29			23 24 25 26 27 28 29	Hán lù		23 24 25 26 27 28 29	
OCTOBER 1931	● 12 13 14 15 16 17	13:06	42	2426626		30 1 2 3 4 5 6	Sun 22h57m15p		1 2 3 4 5 6 7			30 1 2 3 4 5 6	
	◐ 19 20 21 22 23 24	9:20	43	2426633		7 8 9 10 11 12 13			8 9[h] 10 11 12 13 14	Shuāng jiàng		7 8 9 10 11 12 13	
	25 ○ 27 28 29 30 31	13:34	44	2426640	ḤESHVAN 5692	14 15 16 17 18 19 20		MONTH 9 Xīn-Wèi	15 16 17 18 19 20 21		PAOPE 1648	14 15 16 17 18 19 20	ṬEQEMT 1924
	1 2 ◑ 4 5 6 7	7:17	45	2426647		21 22 23 24 25 26 27			22 23 24 25 26* 27 28			21 22 23 24 25 26 27	
	8 ● 10 11 12 13 14	22:55	46	2426654		28 29 30 1 2 3 4	Tue 11h41m16p		29 30 1 2 3 4 5	Lì dōng		28 29 30 1 2 3 4	
NOVEMBER 1931	15 16 ◐ 18 19 20 21	2:13	47	2426661		5 6 7 8 9 10 11			6 7 8 9 10 11 12			5 6 7 8 9 10 11	
	22 23 24 ○ 26 27 28	7:10	48	2426668	KISLEV 5692	12 13 14 15 16 17 18		MONTH 10 Xīn-Wèi	13 14 15 16 17 18 19	Xiǎo xuě	ATHŌR 1648	12 13 14 15 16 17 18	HEDĀR 1924
	29 30 1 ◑ 3 4 5	16:50	49	2426675		19 20 21 22 23 24 25[e]			20 21 22 23 24 25 26			19 20 21 22 23 24 25	
	6 7 8 ● 10 11 12	10:16	50	2426682		26[d,e] 27e 28e 29e 30e 1e 2[e]	Thu 0h25m17p		27 28 29 1 2 3 4	Dà xuě		26 27 28 29 30 1 2	
DECEMBER 1931	13 14 15 ◐ 17 18 19	22:43	51	2426689		3 4 5 6 7 8 9			5 6 7 8 9 10 11			3 4 5 6 7 8 9	
	20 21 22[e] 23 ○ 25 26	23:23	52	2426696	TEVETH 5692	10 11 12 13 14 15 16		MONTH 11 Xīn-Wèi	12 13 14 15[i] 16 17 18	Dōng zhì	KOIAK 1648	10 11 12 13 14 15 16	TĀKHŚĀŚ 1924
	27 28 29 30 31 ◑ 2	1:23	53	2426703		17 18 19 20 21 22 23			19 20 21 22 23 24 25			17 18 19 20 21 22 23	

[a]New Year
[b]Spring (14:06)
[c]Summer (9:28)
[d]Autumn (0:23)
[e]Winter (19:29)
● New moon
◐ First quarter moon
○ Full moon
◑ Last quarter moon

‡Leap year
[a]New Year
[b]Yom Kippur
[c]Sukkot
[d]Winter starts
[e]Ḥanukkah
[f]Purim
[g]Passover
[h]Shavuot
[i]Fast of Av

‡Leap year
[a]New Year (4629, Sheep)
[b]Lantern Festival
[c]Qīngmíng
[d]Dragon Festival
[e]Qīqiǎo
[f]Hungry Ghosts
[g]Mid-Autumn Festival
[h]Double-Ninth Festival
[i]Dōngzhì
*Start of 60-name cycle

‡Leap year
[a]New Year
[b]Building of the Cross
[c]Christmas
[d]Jesus's Circumcision
[e]Epiphany
[f]Easter
[g]Mary's Announcement
[h]Jesus's Transfiguration

1931

PERSIAN (ASTRONOMICAL) 1309‡/1310

Month	Sun	Mon	Tue	Wed	Thu	Fri	Sat
DEY 1309	7	8	9	10	11	12	13
	14	15	16	17	18	19	20
	21	22	23	24	25	26	27
BAHMAN 1309	28	29	30	1	2	3	4
	5	6	7	8	9	10	11
	12	13	14	15	16	17	18
	19	20	21	22	23	24	25
ESFAND 1309	26	27	28	29	30	1	2
	3	4	5	6	7	8	9
	10	11	12	13	14	15	16
	17	18	19	20	21	22	23
	24	25	26	27	28	29	30
FARVARDĪN 1310	1[a]	2	3	4	5	6	7
	8	9	10	11	12	13[b]	14
	15	16	17	18	19	20	21
	22	23	24	25	26	27	28
ORDĪBEHEŠT 1310	29	30	31	1	2	3	4
	5	6	7	8	9	10	11
	12	13	14	15	16	17	18
	19	20	21	22	23	24	25
XORDĀD 1310	26	27	28	29	30	31	1
	2	3	4	5	6	7	8
	9	10	11	12	13	14	15
	16	17	18	19	20	21	22
	23	24	25	26	27	28	29
TĪR 1310	30	31	1	2	3	4	5
	6	7	8	9	10	11	12
	13	14	15	16	17	18	19
	20	21	22	23	24	25	26
MORDĀD 1310	27	28	29	30	31	1	2
	3	4	5	6	7	8	9
	10	11	12	13	14	15	16
	17	18	19	20	21	22	23
	24	25	26	27	28	29	30
SHAHRĪVAR 1310	31	1	2	3	4	5	6
	7	8	9	10	11	12	13
	14	15	16	17	18	19	20
	21	22	23	24	25	26	27
MEHR 1310	28	29	30	31	1	2	3
	4	5	6	7	8	9	10
	11	12	13	14	15	16	17
	18	19	20	21	22	23	24
ABĀN 1310	25	26	27	28	29	30	1
	2	3	4	5	6	7	8
	9	10	11	12	13	14	15
	16	17	18	19	20	21	22
	23	24	25	26	27	28	29
ĀZAR 1310	30	1	2	3	4	5	6
	7	8	9	10	11	12	13
	14	15	16	17	18	19	20
	21	22	23	24	25	26	27
DEY 1310	28	29	30	1	2	3	4
	5	6	7	8	9	10	11

‡Leap year
[a]New Year
[b]Sizdeh Bedar

HINDU LUNAR 1987/1988‡

Month	Sun	Mon	Tue	Wed	Thu	Fri	Sat
PAUSHA 1987	8	9	10	11	12	13	14
	15	16	17	18	19	**20**	22
	23	24	25	26	27	28	29
MĀGHA 1987	30	1	2	3	4	5	*5*
	6	7	8	9	10	11	12
	13	**14**	16	17	18	19	20
	21	22	23	24	25	26	27
PHĀLGUNA 1987	28[h]	29	30	1	2	3	4
	5	6	7	8	9	10	11
	12	13	14	15[i]	16	17	18
	19	21	22	23	24	25	26
CHAITRA 1988	27	*27*	28	29	30	1[a]	2
	3	4	5	6	7	8	9[b]
	10	11	12	**13**	15	16	17
	18	19	20	21	22	23	24
VAIŚĀKHA 1988	25	26	27	28	29	30	1
	1	2	3	4	5	**6**	8
	9	10	11	12	13	14	15
	16	17	18	19	20	21	22
	23	24	25	26	27	28	29
JYAISHṬHA 1988	30	1	2	3	4	5	6
	7	8	**9**	11	12	13	14
	15	16	17	18	19	20	21
	22	23	24	25	26	*26*	27
LEAP ĀSHĀḌHA 1988	28	29	30	1	**2**	4	5
	6	7	8	9	10	11	12
	13	**14**	16	17	*17*	18	19
	20	21	22	23	24	25	26
ĀSHĀḌHA 1988	27	28	29	30	1	2	3
	4	**5**	7	8	9	10	11
	12	13	14	15	16	17	18
	19	20	21	22	23	*23*	24
ŚRĀVAṆA 1988	25	26	**27**	29	30	1	2
	3	4	5	6	7	8	**9**
	11	12	13	14	*14*	15	16
	17	18	19	20	21	22	23[c]
	24	25	26	27	28	29	30
BHĀDRAPADA 1988	**1**	3	4[d]	5	6	7	8
	9	10	11	12	13	14	15
	16	17	18	19	*19*	20	21
	22	23	**24**	26	27	28	29
ĀŚVINA 1988	30	1	2	3	4	5	6
	7	8[e]	9[e]	10[e]	11	12	13
	14	15	16	17	18	19	20
	21	22	23	24	25	26	27
KĀRTTIKA 1988	**28**	30	1[f]	2	3	4	5
	6	7	8	9	10	11	12
	13	*13*	14	15	16	17	18
	19	20	21	**22**	24	25	26
MĀRGAŚĪRA 1988	27	28	29	30	1	2	3
	4	5	6	7	8	9	10
	11[g]	12	13	14	15	16	17
	18	19	20	21	22	23	24

‡Leap year
[a]New Year (Prajāpati)
[b]Birthday of Rāma
[c]Birthday of Krishna
[d]Ganēśa Chaturthī
[e]Dashara
[f]Diwali
[g]Birthday of Vishnu
[h]Night of Śiva
[i]Holi

HINDU SOLAR 1852/1853

Month	Sun	Mon	Tue	Wed	Thu	Fri	Sat
PAUSHA 1852	14	15	16	17	18	19	20
	21	22	23	24	25	26	27
MĀGHA 1852	28	29	1[b]	2	3	4	5
	6	7	8	9	10	11	12
	13	14	15	16	17	18	19
	20	21	22	23	24	25	26
PHĀLGUNA 1852	27	28	29	30	1	2	3
	4	5	6	7	8	9	10
	11	12	13	14	15	16	17
	18	19	20	21	22	23	24
CHAITRA 1852	25	26	27	28	29	30	1
	2	3	4	5	6	7	8
	9	10	11	12	13	14	15
	16	17	18	19	20	21	22
	23	24	25	26	27	28	29
VAIŚĀKHA 1853	30	1[a]	2	3	4	5	6
	7	8	9	10	11	12	13
	14	15	16	17	18	19	20
	21	22	23	24	25	26	27
JYAISHṬHA 1853	28	29	30	31	1	2	3
	4	5	6	7	8	9	10
	11	12	13	14	15	16	17
	18	19	20	21	22	23	24
	25	26	27	28	29	30	31
ĀSHĀḌHA 1853	32	1	2	3	4	5	6
	7	8	9	10	11	12	13
	14	15	16	17	18	19	20
	21	22	23	24	25	26	27
ŚRĀVAṆA 1853	28	29	30	31	1	2	3
	4	5	6	7	8	9	10
	11	12	13	14	15	16	17
	18	19	20	21	22	23	24
	25	26	27	28	29	30	31
BHĀDRAPADA 1853	32	1	2	3	4	5	6
	7	8	9	10	11	12	13
	14	15	16	17	18	19	20
	21	22	23	24	25	26	27
ĀŚVINA 1853	28	29	30	31	1	2	3
	4	5	6	7	8	9	10
	11	12	13	14	15	16	17
	18	19	20	21	22	23	24
KĀRTTIKA 1853	25	26	27	28	29	30	1
	2	3	4	5	6	7	8
	9	10	11	12	13	14	15
	16	17	18	19	20	21	22
	23	24	25	26	27	28	29
MĀRGAŚĪRA 1853	30	1	2	3	4	5	6
	7	8	9	10	11	12	13
	14	15	16	17	18	19	20
	21	22	23	24	25	26	27
PAUSHA 1853	28	29	1	2	3	4	5
	6	7	8	9	10	11	12
	13	14	15	16	17	18	19

[a]New Year (Subhānu)
[b]Pongal

ISLAMIC (ASTRONOMICAL) 1349‡/1350

Month	Sun	Mon	Tue	Wed	Thu	Fri	Sat
SHA'BĀN 1349	7	8	9	10	11	12	13
	14	15	16	17	18	19	20
	21	22	23	24	25	26	27
RAMAḌĀN 1349	28	29	1[e]	2	3	4	5
	6	7	8	9	10	11	12
	13	14	15	16	17	18	19
	20	21	22	23	24	25	26
SHAWWĀL 1349	27	28	29	30	1[f]	2	3
	4	5	6	7	8	9	10
	11	12	13	14	15	16	17
	18	19	20	21	22	23	24
DHU AL-QA'DA 1349	25	26	27	28	29	*30*	1
	2	3	4	5	6	7	8
	9	10	11	12	13	14	15
	16	17	18	19	20	21	22
	23	24	25	26	27	28	29
DHU AL-ḤIJJA 1349	*1*	2	3	4	5	6	7
	8	9	10[g]	11	12	13	14
	15	16	17	18	19	20	21
	22	23	24	25	26	27	28
MUḤARRAM 1350	29	30	1[a]	2	3	4	5
	6	7	8	9	10[b]	11	12
	13	14	15	16	17	18	19
	20	21	22	23	24	25	26
ṢAFAR 1350	27	28	29	1	*2*	3	4
	5	6	7	8	9	10	11
	12	13	14	15	16	17	18
	19	20	21	22	23	24	25
RABĪ' I 1350	26	27	28	29	30	*1*	2
	3	4	5	6	7	8	9
	10	11	12[c]	13	14	15	16
	17	18	19	20	21	22	23
RABĪ' II 1350	24	25	26	27	28	29	1
	2	3	4	5	6	7	8
	9	10	11	12	13	14	15
	16	17	18	19	20	21	22
	23	24	25	26	27	28	29
JUMĀDĀ I 1350	30	*1*	2	3	4	5	6
	7	8	9	10	11	12	13
	14	15	16	17	18	19	20
	21	22	23	24	25	26	27
JUMĀDĀ II 1350	28	29	1	*2*	3	4	5
	6	7	8	9	10	11	12
	13	14	15	16	17	18	19
	20	21	22	23	24	25	26
RAJAB 1350	27	28	29	30	*1*	2	3
	4	5	6	7	8	9	10
	11	12	13	14	15	16	17
	18	19	20	21	22	23	24
SHA'BĀN 1350	25	26	27[d]	28	29	1	*2*
	3	4	5	6	7	8	9
	10	11	12	13	14	15	16
	17	18	19	20	21	22	23

‡Leap year
[a]New Year
[b]'Ashūrā'
[c]Prophet's Birthday
[d]Ascent of the Prophet
[e]Start of Ramaḍān
[f]'Id al-Fiṭr
[g]'Id al-'Aḍḥā

GREGORIAN 1931

Julian (Sun)	Sun	Mon	Tue	Wed	Thu	Fri	Sat	Month
Dec 15	*28*	29	30	31	1	2	3	
	4	5	6	7[a]	8	9	10	JANUARY 1931
Dec 29	*11*	12	13	14[b]	15	16	17	
	18	19	20	21	22	23	24	
Jan 12	*25*	26	27	28	29	30	31	
	1	2	3	4	5	6	7	
Jan 26	*8*	9	10	11	12	13	14	FEBRUARY 1931
	15	16	17	18[c]	19	20	21	
Feb 9	*22*	23	24	25	26	27	28	
	1[d]	2	3	4	5	6	7	
Feb 23	*8*	9	10	11	12	13	14	
	15	16	17	18	19	20	21	MARCH 1931
Mar 9	*22*	23	24	25	26	27	28	
	29	30	31	1	2	3	4	
Mar 23	5[e]	6	7	8	9	10	11	
	12[f]	13	14	15	16	17	18	APRIL 1931
Apr 6	*19*	20	21	22	23	24	25	
	26	27	28	29	30	1	2	
Apr 20	*3*	4	5	6	7	8	9	
	10	11	12	13	14	15	16	MAY 1931
May 4	*17*	18	19	20	21	22	23	
	24	25	26	27	28	29	30	
May 18	*31*	1	2	3	4	5	6	
	7	8	9	10	11	12	13	
Jun 1	*14*	15	16	17	18	19	20	JUNE 1931
	21	22	23	24	25	26	27	
Jun 15	*28*	29	30	1	2	3	4	
	5	6	7	8	9	10	11	
Jun 29	*12*	13	14	15	16	17	18	JULY 1931
	19	20	21	22	23	24	25	
Jul 13	*26*	27	28	29	30	31	1	
	2	3	4	5	6	7	8	
Jul 27	*9*	10	11	12	13	14	15	AUGUST 1931
	16	17	18	19	20	21	22	
Aug 10	*23*	24	25	26	27	28	29	
	30	31	1	2	3	4	5	
Aug 24	*6*	7	8	9	10	11	12	
	13	14	15	16	17	18	19	SEPTEMBER 1931
Sep 7	*20*	21	22	23	24	25	26	
	27	28	29	30	1	2	3	
Sep 21	*4*	5	6	7	8	9	10	
	11	12	13	14	15	16	17	OCTOBER 1931
Oct 5	*18*	19	20	21	22	23	24	
	25	26	27	28	29	30	31	
Oct 19	*1*	2	3	4	5	6	7	
	8	9	10	11	12	13	14	NOVEMBER 1931
Nov 2	*15*	16	17	18	19	20	21	
	22	23	24	25	26	27	28	
Nov 16	29[g]	30	1	2	3	4	5	
	6	7	8	9	10	11	12	
Nov 30	*13*	14	15	16	17	18	19	DECEMBER 1931
	20	21	22	23	24	25[h]	26	
Dec 14	*27*	28	29	30	31	1	2	

[a]Orthodox Christmas
[b]Julian New Year
[c]Ash Wednesday
[d]Feast of Orthodoxy
[e]Easter
[f]Orthodox Easter
[g]Advent
[h]Christmas

1932

Gregorian month	GREGORIAN 1932‡ (Sun Mon Tue Wed Thu Fri Sat)	Lunar Phases	ISO WEEK (Mon)	JULIAN DAY (Sun noon)	Hebrew month	HEBREW 5692‡/5693 (Sun Mon Tue Wed Thu Fri Sat)	Molad	Chinese month	CHINESE Xīn-Wèi/Rén-Shēn (Sun Mon Tue Wed Thu Fri Sat)	Solar Term	Coptic month	COPTIC 1648/1649 / ETHIOPIC 1924/1925 (Sun Mon Tue Wed Thu Fri Sat)	Ethiopic month
	27 28 29 30 31 ◑[a] 2	1:23	53	2426703	TEVETH 5692	17 18 19 20 21 22 23		MONTH 11 Xīn-Wèi	19 20 21 22 23 24 25		KOIAK 1648	17 18 19 20 21 22 23	TĀKHŚĀŚ 1924
JANUARY 1932	3 4 5 6 ● 8 9	23:29	1	2426710		24 25 26 27 28 29 1	Fri 13h10m0p	MONTH 12 Xīn-Wèi	26 27* 28 29 30 1 2	Xiǎo hán		24 25 26 27 28 29[c] 30	
	10 11 12 13 14 ◐ 16	20:55	2	2426717		2 3 4 5 6 7 8			3 4 5 6 7 8 9			1 2 3 4 5 6[d] 7	
	17 18 19 20 21 22 ○	13:44	3	2426724	SHEVAT 5692	9 10 11 12 13 14 15			10 11 12 13 14 15 16	Dà hán	TŌBE 1648	8 9 10 11[e] 12 13 14	ṬER 1924
	24 25 26 27 28 29 ◑	9:32	4	2426731		16 17 18 19 20 21 22			17 18 19 20 21 22 23			15 16 17 18 19 20 21	
	31 1 2 3 4 5 ●	14:45	5	2426738		23 24 25 26 27 28 29			24 25 26 27 28 29 1[a]	Lì chūn		22 23 24 25 26 27 28	
FEBRUARY 1932	7 8 9 10 11 12 13		6	2426745		30 1 2 3 4 5 6	Sun 1h54m1p	MONTH 1 Rén-Shēn	2 3 4 5 6 7 8			29 30 1 2 3 4 5	
	◐ 15 16 17 18 19 20	18:16	7	2426752	ADAR I 5692	7 8 9 10 11 12 13			9 10 11 12 13 14 15[b]	Yǔ shuǐ	MESHIR 1648	6 7 8 9 10 11 12	YAKĀTIT 1924
	21 ○ 23 24 25 26 27	2:07	8	2426759		14 15 16 17 18 19 20			16 17 18 19 20 21 22			13 14 15 16 17 18 19	
	◑ 29 1 2 3 4 5	18:03	9	2426766		21 22 23 24 25 26 27			23 24 25 26 27 28* 29			20 21 22 23 24 25 26	
MARCH 1932	6 ● 8 9 10 11 12	7:44	10	2426773		28 29 30 1 2 3 4	Mon 14h38m2p		30 1 2 3 4 5 6	Jīng zhé		27 28 29 30 1 2 3	
	13 14 ◐ 16 17 18 19	12:41	11	2426780	ADAR II 5692	5 6 7 8 9 10 11		MONTH 2 Rén-Shēn	7 8 9 10 11 12 13		PAREMOTEP 1648	4 5 6 7 8 9 10	MAGĀBIT 1924
	20[b] 21 ○ 23 24 25 26	12:37	12	2426787		12 13 14[f] 15 16 17 18			14 15 16 17 18 19 20	Chūn fēn		11 12 13 14 15 16 17	
	27 28 ◑ 30 31 1 2	3:44	13	2426794		19 20 21 22 23 24 25			21 22 23 24 25 26 27			18 19 20 21 22 23 24	
APRIL 1932	3 4 5 ● 7 8 9	1:21	14	2426801		26 27 28 29 1 2 3	Wed 3h22m3p		28 29 30[c] 1 2 3 4	Qīng míng		25 26 27 28 29 30 1	
	10 11 12 13 ◐ 15 16	3:15	15	2426808	NISAN 5692	4 5 6 7 8 9 10		MONTH 3 Rén-Shēn	5 6 7 8 9 10 11		PARMOUTE 1648	2 3 4 5 6 7 8	MIYĀZYĀ 1924
	17 18 19 ○ 21 22 23	21:27	16	2426815		11 12 13 14 15[g] 16 17			12 13 14 15 16 17 18	Gǔ yǔ		9 10 11 12 13 14 15	
	24 25 26 ◑ 28 29 30	15:14	17	2426822		18 19 20 21 22 23 24			19 20 21 22 23 24 25			16 17 18 19 20 21 22	
	1 2 3 4 ● 6 7	18:11	18	2426829		25 26 27 28 29 30 1	Thu 16h6m4p		26 27 28* 29 30 1 2	Lì xià		23[f] 24 25 26 27 28 29[g]	
MAY 1932	8 9 10 11 12 ◐ 14	14:02	19	2426836	IYAR 5692	2 3 4 5 6 7 8		MONTH 4 Rén-Shēn	3 4 5 6 7 8 9			30 1 2 3 4 5 6	
	15 16 17 18 19 ○ 21	5:08	20	2426843		9 10 11 12 13 14 15			10 11 12 13 14 15 16	Xiǎo mǎn	PASHONS 1648	7 8 9 10 11 12 13	GENBOT 1924
	22 23 24 25 26 ◑ 28	4:54	21	2426850		16 17 18 19 20 21 22			17 18 19 20 21 22 23			14 15 16 17 18 19 20	
	29 30 31 1 2 3 ●	9:16	22	2426857		23 24 25 26 27 28 29			24 25 26 27 28 29 1			21 22 23 24 25 26 27	
JUNE 1932	5 6 7 8 9 10 ◐	21:39	23	2426864		1 2 3 4 5 6[h] 7	Sat 4h50m5p	MONTH 5 Rén-Shēn	2 3 4 5[d] 6 7 8	Máng zhòng		28 29 30 1 2 3 4	
	12 13 14 15 16 17 ○	12:38	24	2426871	SIVAN 5692	8 9 10 11 12 13 14			9 10 11 12 13 14 15		PAŌNE 1648	5 6 7 8 9 10 11	SANĒ 1924
	19 20 21[c] 22 23 24 ◑	20:36	25	2426878		15 16 17 18 19 20 21			16 17 18 19 20 21 22	Xià zhì		12 13 14 15 16 17 18	
	26 27 28 29 30 1 2		26	2426885		22 23 24 25 26 27 28			23 24 25 26 27 28 29*			19 20 21 22 23 24 25	
JULY 1932	● 4 5 6 7 8 9	22:20	27	2426892		29 30 1 2 3 4 5	Sun 17h34m6p		30 1 2 3 4 5 6	Xiǎo shǔ		26 27 28 29 30 1 2	
	10 ◐ 12 13 14 15 16	3:07	28	2426899	TAMMUZ 5692	6 7 8 9 10 11 12		MONTH 6 Rén-Shēn	7 8 9 10 11 12 13		EPĒP 1648	3 4 5 6 7 8 9	ḤAMLĒ 1924
	○ 18 19 20 21 22 23	21:06	29	2426906		13 14 15 16 17 18 19			14 15 16 17 18 19 20	Dà shǔ		10 11 12 13 14 15 16	
	24 ◑ 26 27 28 29 30	13:41	30	2426913		20 21 22 23 24 25 26			21 22 23 24 25 26 27			17 18 19 20 21 22 23	
	31 1 ● 3 4 5 6	9:42	31	2426920		27 28 29 1 2 3 4	Tue 6h18m7p		28 29 1 2 3 4 5			24 25 26 27 28 29 30	
AUGUST 1932	7 8 ◐ 10 11 12 13	7:40	32	2426927	AV 5692	5 6 7 8 9[i] 10 11		MONTH 7 Rén-Shēn	6 7[e] 8 9 10 11 12	Lì qiū		1 2 3 4 5 6 7	
	14 15 ○ 17 18 19 20	7:41	33	2426934		12 13 14 15 16 17 18			13 14 15[f] 16 17 18 19		MESORĒ 1648	8 9 10 11 12 13[h] 14	NAḤASĒ 1924
	21 22 23 ◑ 25 26 27	7:21	34	2426941		19 20 21 22 23 24 25			20 21 22 23 24 25 26	Chǔ shǔ		15 16 17 18 19 20 21	
	28 29 30 ● 1 2 3	19:54	35	2426948		26 27 28 29 30 1 2	Wed 19h2m8p		27 28 29 30* 1 2 3			22 23 24 25 26 27 28	
SEPTEMBER 1932	4 5 6 ◐ 8 9 10	12:49	36	2426955	ELUL 5692	3 4 5 6 7 8 9		MONTH 8 Rén-Shēn	4 5 6 7 8 9 10	Bái lù	EPAG. 1648	29 30 1 2 3 4 5	PĀG. 1924
	11 12 13 ○ 15 16 17	21:06	37	2426962		10 11 12 13 14 15 16			11 12 13 14 15[g] 16 17			1[a] 2 3 4 5 6 7	
	18 19 20 21 22 ◑[d] 24	0:47	38	2426969		17 18 19 20 21 22 23			18 19 20 21 22 23 24	Qiū fēn	THOOUT 1649	8 9 10 11 12 13 14	MASKARAM 1925
	25 26 27 28 29 ● 1	5:30	39	2426976		24 25 26 27 28 29 1[a]	Fri 7h46m9p		25 26 27 28 29 1 2			15 16 17[b] 18 19 20 21	
OCTOBER 1932	2 3 4 5 ◐ 7 8	20:05	40	2426983	TISHRI 5693	2[a] 3 4 5 6 7 8		MONTH 9 Rén-Shēn	3 4 5 6 7 8 9[h]	Hán lù		22 23 24 25 26 27 28	
	9 10 11 12 13 ○ 15	13:18	41	2426990		9 10[b] 11 12 13 14 15[c]			10 11 12 13 14 15 16			29 30 1 2 3 4 5	
	16 17 18 19 20 21 ◑	17:14	42	2426997		16 17 18 19 20 21 22			17 18 19 20 21 22 23		PAOPE 1649	6 7 8 9 10 11 12	ṬEQEMT 1925
	23 24 25 26 27 28 ●	14:56	43	2427004		23 24 25 26 27 28 29			24 25 26 27 28 29 1	Shuāng jiàng		13 14 15 16 17 18 19	
	30 31 1 2 3 4 ◐	6:50	44	2427011		30 1 2 3 4 5 6	Sat 20h30m10p		2* 3 4 5 6 7 8			20 21 22 23 24 25 26	
NOVEMBER 1932	6 7 8 9 10 11 12		45	2427018	HESHVAN 5693	7 8 9 10 11 12 13		MONTH 10 Rén-Shēn	9 10 11 12 13 14 15	Lì dōng		27 28 29 30 1 2 3	
	○ 14 15 16 17 18 19	7:28	46	2427025		14 15 16 17 18 19 20			16 17 18 19 20 21 22		ATHŌR 1649	4 5 6 7 8 9 10	ḪEDĀR 1925
	20 ◑ 22 23 24 25 26	7:58	47	2427032		21 22 23 24 25 26 27			23 24 25 26 27 28 29	Xiǎo xuě		11 12 13 14 15 16 17	
	27 ● 29 30 1 2 3	0:43	48	2427039		28 29 30 1 2 3 4	Mon 9h14m11p		30 1 2 3 4 5 6			18 19 20 21 22 23 24	
DECEMBER 1932	◐ 5 6 7 8 9 10	21:45	49	2427046	KISLEV 5693	5 6[d] 7 8 9 10 11		MONTH 11 Rén-Shēn	7 8 9 10 11 12 13	Dà xuě		25 26 27 28 29 30 1	
	11 12 ○ 14 15 16 17	2:21	50	2427053		12 13 14 15 16 17 18			14 15 16 17 18 19 20		KOIAK 1649	2 3 4 5 6 7 8	TĀKHŚĀŚ 1925
	18 19 ◑ 21 22[e] 23 24	20:22	51	2427060		19 20 21 22 23 24 25[e]			21 22 23 24 25[i] 26 27	Dōng zhì		9 10 11 12 13 14 15	
	25 26 ● 28 29 30 31	11:22	52	2427067		26[e] 27[e] 28[e] 29[e] 30[e] 1[e] 2[e]	Tue 21h58m12p		28 29 1 2 3* 4 5			16 17 18 19 20 21 22	

‡Leap year
[a]New Year
[b]Spring (19:54)
[c]Summer (15:23)
[d]Autumn (6:16)
[e]Winter (1:14)
● New moon
◐ First quarter moon
○ Full moon
◑ Last quarter moon

‡Leap year
[a]New Year
[b]Yom Kippur
[c]Sukkot
[d]Winter starts
[e]Ḥanukkah
[f]Purim
[g]Passover
[h]Shavuot
[i]Fast of Av

[a]New Year (4630, Monkey)
[b]Lantern Festival
[c]Qīngmíng
[d]Dragon Festival
[e]Qīqiǎo
[f]Hungry Ghosts
[g]Mid-Autumn Festival
[h]Double-Ninth Festival
[i]Dōngzhì
*Start of 60-name cycle

[a]New Year
[b]Building of the Cross
[c]Christmas
[d]Jesus's Circumcision
[e]Epiphany
[f]Easter
[g]Mary's Announcement
[h]Jesus's Transfiguration

PERSIAN (ASTRONOMICAL) 1310/1311

Month	Sun	Mon	Tue	Wed	Thu	Fri	Sat
DEY 1310	5	6	7	8	9	10	11
	12	13	14	15	16	17	18
	19	20	21	22	23	24	25
BAHMAN 1310	26	27	28	29	30	1	2
	3	4	5	6	7	8	9
	10	11	12	13	14	15	16
	17	18	19	20	21	22	23
	24	25	26	27	28	29	30
ESFAND 1310	1	2	3	4	5	6	7
	8	9	10	11	12	13	14
	15	16	17	18	19	20	21
	22	23	24	25	26	27	28
FARVARDĪN 1311	29	1[a]	2	3	4	5	6
	7	8	9	10	11	12	13[b]
	14	15	16	17	18	19	20
	21	22	23	24	25	26	27
ORDĪBEHEŠT 1311	28	29	30	31	1	2	3
	4	5	6	7	8	9	10
	11	12	13	14	15	16	17
	18	19	20	21	22	23	24
	25	26	27	28	29	30	31
XORDĀD 1311	1	2	3	4	5	6	7
	8	9	10	11	12	13	14
	15	16	17	18	19	20	21
	22	23	24	25	26	27	28
TĪR 1311	29	30	31	1	2	3	4
	5	6	7	8	9	10	11
	12	13	14	15	16	17	18
	19	20	21	22	23	24	25
MORDĀD 1311	26	27	28	29	30	31	1
	2	3	4	5	6	7	8
	9	10	11	12	13	14	15
	16	17	18	19	20	21	22
	23	24	25	26	27	28	29
SHAHRĪVAR 1311	30	31	1	2	3	4	5
	6	7	8	9	10	11	12
	13	14	15	16	17	18	19
	20	21	22	23	24	25	26
MEHR 1311	27	28	29	30	31	1	2
	3	4	5	6	7	8	9
	10	11	12	13	14	15	16
	17	18	19	20	21	22	23
	24	25	26	27	28	29	30
ĀBĀN 1311	1	2	3	4	5	6	7
	8	9	10	11	12	13	14
	15	16	17	18	19	20	21
	22	23	24	25	26	27	28
ĀZAR 1311	29	30	1	2	3	4	5
	6	7	8	9	10	11	12
	13	14	15	16	17	18	19
	20	21	22	23	24	25	26
DEY 1311	27	28	29	30	1	2	3
	4	5	6	7	8	9	10

[a]New Year
[b]Sizdeh Bedar

HINDU LUNAR 1988‡/1989

Month	Sun	Mon	Tue	Wed	Thu	Fri	Sat
MĀRGAŚIRA 1988	18	19	20	21	22	23	24
PAUSHA 1988	25	26	**27**	29	30	1	2
	3	4	5	5	6	7	8
	9	10	11	12	13	14	15
	16	17	18	19	20	**21**	23
	24	25	26	27	28	29	30
MĀGHA 1988	1	2	3	4	5	6	7
	7	8	9	10	11	12	13
	14	**15**	17	18	19	20	21
	22	23	24	25	26	27	28[h]
PHĀLGUNA 1988	29	30	1	2	3	4	5
	6	7	8	9	10	11	12
	13	14	15[i]	16	17	18	19
	20	22	23	24	25	26	27
CHAITRA 1989	28	29	30	1[a]	1	2	3
	4	5	6	7	8	9[b]	10
	11	12	**13**	15	16	17	18
	19	20	21	22	23	24	25
VAIŚĀKHA 1989	26	27	28	29	30	1	2
	3	4	5	6	7	8	9
	10	11	12	13	14	15	16
	17	19	20	21	22	23	24
	25	26	26	27	28	29	30
JYAISHTHA 1989	1	2	3	4	5	6	7
	8	9	**10**	12	13	14	15
	16	17	18	19	20	21	22
	23	24	25	26	27	28	29
ĀSHĀḌHA 1989	30	1	2	3	4	5	6
	7	8	9	10	11	**12**	14
	15	16	17	18	19	20	21
	22	23	23	24	25	26	27
ŚRĀVAṆA 1989	28	29	30	1	2	3	4
	5	7	8	9	10	11	12
	13	14	15	16	17	18	19
	20	21	22	23[c]	24	25	26
BHĀDRAPADA 1989	27	28	29	30	1	2	3
	4[d]	5	6	7	**8**	10	11
	12	13	14	15	16	17	18
	19	19	20	21	22	23	24
ĀŚVINA 1989	25	26	27	28	29	30	1
	2	4	5	6	7	8[e]	9[e]
	10[e]	11	12	13	14	15	16
	17	18	19	20	21	22	23
	24	25	26	27	28	29	30
KĀRTTIKA 1989	1[f]	2	3	4	5	**6**	8
	9	10	11	12	13	13	14
	15	16	17	18	19	20	21
	22	23	24	25	26	27	28
MĀRGAŚIRA 1989	**29**	1	2	3	4	5	6
	7	8	9	10	11[g]	12	13
	14	15	15	16	17	18	19
	20	21	22	**23**	25	26	27
PAUSHA 1989	28	29	30	1	2	3	4

‡Leap year
[a]New Year (Aṅgiras)
[b]Birthday of Rāma
[c]Birthday of Krishna
[d]Ganēśa Chaturthī
[e]Dashara
[f]Diwali
[g]Birthday of Vishnu
[h]Night of Śiva
[i]Holi

HINDU SOLAR 1853/1854‡

Month	Sun	Mon	Tue	Wed	Thu	Fri	Sat
PAUSHA 1853	13	14	15	16	17	18	19
	20	21	22	23	24	25	26
MĀGHA 1853	27	28	29	30	1[b]	2	3
	4	5	6	7	8	9	10
	11	12	13	14	15	16	17
	18	19	20	21	22	23	24
PHĀLGUNA 1853	25	26	27	28	29	1	2
	3	4	5	6	7	8	9
	10	11	12	13	14	15	16
	17	18	19	20	21	22	23
	24	25	26	27	28	29	30
CHAITRA 1853	1	2	3	4	5	6	7
	8	9	10	11	12	13	14
	15	16	17	18	19	20	21
	22	23	24	25	26	27	28
VAIŚĀKHA 1854	29	30	1[a]	2	3	4	5
	6	7	8	9	10	11	12
	13	14	15	16	17	18	19
	20	21	22	23	24	25	26
JYAISHTHA 1854	27	28	29	30	31	1	2
	3	4	5	6	7	8	9
	10	11	12	13	14	15	16
	17	18	19	20	21	22	23
	24	25	26	27	28	29	30
ĀSHĀḌHA 1854	31	32	1	2	3	4	5
	6	7	8	9	10	11	12
	13	14	15	16	17	18	19
	20	21	22	23	24	25	26
ŚRĀVAṆA 1854	27	28	29	30	31	1	2
	3	4	5	6	7	8	9
	10	11	12	13	14	15	16
	17	18	19	20	21	22	23
	24	25	26	27	28	29	30
BHĀDRAPADA 1854	31	32	1	2	3	4	5
	6	7	8	9	10	11	12
	13	14	15	16	17	18	19
	20	21	22	23	24	25	26
ĀŚVINA 1854	27	28	29	30	31	1	2
	3	4	5	6	7	8	9
	10	11	12	13	14	15	16
	17	18	19	20	21	22	23
	24	25	26	27	28	29	30
KĀRTTIKA 1854	1	2	3	4	5	6	7
	8	9	10	11	12	13	14
	15	16	17	18	19	20	21
	22	23	24	25	26	27	28
MĀRGAŚIRA 1854	29	30	1	2	3	4	5
	6	7	8	9	10	11	12
	13	14	15	16	17	18	19
	20	21	22	23	24	25	26
PAUSHA 1854	27	28	29	30	1	2	3
	4	5	6	7	8	9	10
	11	12	13	14	15	16	17

‡Leap year
[a]New Year (Tāraṇa)
[b]Pongal

ISLAMIC (ASTRONOMICAL) 1350/1351

Month	Sun	Mon	Tue	Wed	Thu	Fri	Sat
SHA'BĀN 1350	17	18	19	20	21	22	23
RAMAḌĀN 1350	24	25	26	27	28	29	1[e]
	2	3	4	5	6	7	8
	9	10	11	12	13	14	15
	16	17	18	19	20	21	22
	23	24	25	26	27	28	29
SHAWWĀL 1350	30	1[f]	2	3	4	5	6
	7	8	9	10	11	12	13
	14	15	16	17	18	19	20
	21	22	23	24	25	26	27
DHU AL-QA'DA 1350	28	29	30	1	2	3	4
	5	6	7	8	9	10	11
	12	13	14	15	16	17	18
	19	20	21	22	23	24	25
DHU AL-ḤIJJA 1350	26	27	28	29	1	2	3
	4	5	6	7	8	9	10[g]
	11	12	13	14	15	16	17
	18	19	20	21	22	23	24
MUḤARRAM 1351	25	26	27	28	29	30	1[a]
	2	3	4	5	6	7	8
	9	10[b]	11	12	13	14	15
	16	17	18	19	20	21	22
	23	24	25	26	27	28	29
ṢAFAR 1351	30	1	2	3	4	5	6
	7	8	9	10	11	12	13
	14	15	16	17	18	19	20
	21	22	23	24	25	26	27
RABĪ' I 1351	28	29	1	2	3	4	5
	6	7	8	9	10	11	12[c]
	13	14	15	16	17	18	19
	20	21	22	23	24	25	26
RABĪ' II 1351	27	28	29	30	1	2	3
	4	5	6	7	8	9	10
	11	12	13	14	15	16	17
	18	19	20	21	22	23	24
JUMĀDĀ I 1351	25	26	27	28	29	30	1
	2	3	4	5	6	7	8
	9	10	11	12	13	14	15
	16	17	18	19	20	21	22
	23	24	25	26	27	28	29
JUMĀDĀ II 1351	1	2	3	4	5	6	7
	8	9	10	11	12	13	14
	15	16	17	18	19	20	21
	22	23	24	25	26	27	28
RAJAB 1351	29	30	1	2	3	4	5
	6	7	8	9	10	11	12
	13	14	15	16	17	18	19
	20	21	22	23	24	25	26
SHA'BĀN 1351	27[d]	28	29	1	2	3	4
	5	6	7	8	9	10	11
	12	13	14	15	16	17	18
	19	20	21	22	23	24	25
RAMAḌĀN 1351	26	27	28	29	1[e]	2	3

[a]New Year
[b]'Ashūrā'
[c]Prophet's Birthday
[d]Ascent of the Prophet
[e]Start of Ramaḍān
[f]'Id al-Fiṭr
[g]'Id al-'Aḍḥā

GREGORIAN 1932‡

Julian† (Sun)	Month	Sun	Mon	Tue	Wed	Thu	Fri	Sat
Dec 14		27	28	29	30	31	1	2
	JANUARY 1932	3	4	5	6	7[a]	8	9
Dec 28		10	11	12	13	14[b]	15	16
		17	18	19	20	21	22	23
Jan 11		24	25	26	27	28	29	30
	FEBRUARY 1932	31	1	2	3	4	5	6
Jan 25		7	8	9	10[c]	11	12	13
		14	15	16	17	18	19	20
Feb 8		21	22	23	24	25	26	27
	MARCH 1932	28	29	1	2	3	4	5
Feb 22		6	7	8	9	10	11	12
		13	14	15	16	17	18	19
Mar 7		20[d]	21	22	23	24	25	26
	APRIL 1932	27[e]	28	29	30	31	1	2
Mar 21		3	4	5	6	7	8	9
		10	11	12	13	14	15	16
Apr 4		17	18	19	20	21	22	23
		24	25	26	27	28	29	30
Apr 18	MAY 1932	1[f]	2	3	4	5	6	7
		8	9	10	11	12	13	14
May 2		15	16	17	18	19	20	21
		22	23	24	25	26	27	28
May 16	JUNE 1932	29	30	31	1	2	3	4
		5	6	7	8	9	10	11
May 30		12	13	14	15	16	17	18
		19	20	21	22	23	24	25
Jun 13	JULY 1932	26	27	28	29	30	1	2
		3	4	5	6	7	8	9
Jun 27		10	11	12	13	14	15	16
		17	18	19	20	21	22	23
Jul 11		24	25	26	27	28	29	30
	AUGUST 1932	31	1	2	3	4	5	6
Jul 25		7	8	9	10	11	12	13
		14	15	16	17	18	19	20
Aug 8		21	22	23	24	25	26	27
	SEPTEMBER 1932	28	29	30	31	1	2	3
Aug 22		4	5	6	7	8	9	10
		11	12	13	14	15	16	17
Sep 5		18	19	20	21	22	23	24
	OCTOBER 1932	25	26	27	28	29	30	1
Sep 19		2	3	4	5	6	7	8
		9	10	11	12	13	14	15
Oct 3		16	17	18	19	20	21	22
		23	24	25	26	27	28	29
Oct 17	NOVEMBER 1932	30	31	1	2	3	4	5
		6	7	8	9	10	11	12
Oct 31		13	14	15	16	17	18	19
		20	21	22	23	24	25	26
Nov 14	DECEMBER 1932	27[g]	28	29	30	1	2	3
		4	5	6	7	8	9	10
Nov 28		11	12	13	14	15	16	17
		18	19	20	21	22	23	24
Dec 12		25[h]	26	27	28	29	30	31

‡Leap year
[a]Orthodox Christmas
[b]Julian New Year
[c]Ash Wednesday
[d]Feast of Orthodoxy
[e]Easter
[f]Orthodox Easter
[g]Advent
[h]Christmas

1933

GREGORIAN 1933

ISO Week (Mon)	Month	Sun	Mon	Tue	Wed	Thu	Fri	Sat	Lunar Phases	Julian Day (Sun noon)
1	JANUARY 1933	1[a]	2	◐	4	5	6	7	16:24	2427074
2		8	9	10	○	12	13	14	20:36	2427081
3		15	16	17	18	◑	20	21	6:15	2427088
4		22	23	24	●	26	27	28	23:20	2427095
5		29	30	31	1	◐	3	4	13:16	2427102
6	FEBRUARY 1933	5	6	7	8	9	○	11	13:00	2427109
7		12	13	14	15	16	◑	18	14:08	2427116
8		19	20	21	22	23	●	25	12:44	2427123
9		26	27	28	1	2	3	◐	10:23	2427130
10	MARCH 1933	5	6	7	8	9	10	11		2427137
11		○	13	14	15	16	17	◑	2:46 21:05	2427144
12		19	20	21[b]	22	23	24	25		2427151
13		●	27	28	29	30	31	1	3:20	2427158
14	APRIL 1933	2	◐	4	5	6	7	8	5:56	2427165
15		9	○	11	12	13	14	15	13:38	2427172
16		16	◑	18	19	20	21	22	4:17	2427179
17		23	●	25	26	27	28	29	18:38	2427186
18		30	1	◐	3	4	5	6	22:39	2427193
19	MAY 1933	7	8	○	10	11	12	13	22:04	2427200
20		14	15	◑	17	18	19	20	12:50	2427207
21		21	22	23	●	25	26	27	10:07	2427214
22		28	29	30	31	◐	2	3	11:53	2427221
23	JUNE 1933	4	5	6	7	○	9	10	5:05	2427228
24		11	12	13	◑	15	16	17	23:25	2427235
25		18	19	20	21[c]	22	●	24	1:22	2427242
26		25	26	27	28	29	◐	1	21:41	2427249
27	JULY 1933	2	3	4	5	6	○	8	11:51	2427256
28		9	10	11	12	13	◑	15	12:24	2427263
29		16	17	18	19	20	21	●	16:03	2427270
30		23	24	25	26	27	28	29		2427277
31		◐	31	1	2	3	4	○	4:44 19:32	2427284
32	AUGUST 1933	6	7	8	9	10	11	12		2427291
33		◑	14	15	16	17	18	19	3:49	2427298
34		20	●	22	23	24	25	26	5:48	2427305
35		27	◐	29	30	31	1	2	10:13	2427312
36	SEPTEMBER 1933	3	○	5	6	7	8	9	5:04	2427319
37		10	◑	12	13	14	15	16	21:30	2427326
38		17	18	●	20	21	22	23[d]	18:21	2427333
39		24	25	◐	27	28	29	30	15:36	2427340
40	OCTOBER 1933	1	2	○	4	5	6	7	17:08	2427347
41		8	9	10	◑	12	13	14	16:46	2427354
42		15	16	17	18	●	20	21	5:45	2427361
43		22	23	24	◐	26	27	28	22:21	2427368
44		29	30	31	1	○	3	4	7:59	2427375
45	NOVEMBER 1933	5	6	7	8	9	◑	11	12:18	2427382
46		12	13	14	15	16	●	18	16:24	2427389
47		19	20	21	22	23	◐	25	7:38	2427396
48		26	27	28	29	30	1	○	1:31	2427403
49	DECEMBER 1933	3	4	5	6	7	8	9		2427410
50		◑	11	12	13	14	15	16	6:24	2427417
51		●	18	19	20	21	22[e]	◐	2:53 20:09	2427424
52		24	25	26	27	28	29	30		2427431
1		○	1	2	3	4	5	6	20:54	2427438

HEBREW 5693/5694

ISO Week	Month	Sun	Mon	Tue	Wed	Thu	Fri	Sat	Molad
1	TEVETH 5693	3	4	5	6	7	8	9	
2		10	11	12	13	14	15	16	
3		17	18	19	20	21	22	23	
4		24	25	26	27	28	29	1	Thu $10^h42^m13^p$
5	SHEVAT 5693	2	3	4	5	6	7	8	
6		9	10	11	12	13	14	15	
7		16	17	18	19	20	21	22	
8		23	24	25	26	27	28	29	
9		30	1	2	3	4	5	6	Fri $23^h26^m14^p$
10	ADAR 5693	7	8	9	10	11	12	13	
11		14[f]	15	16	17	18	19	20	
12		21	22	23	24	25	26	27	
13		28	29	1	2	3	4	5	Sun $12^h10^m15^p$
14	NISAN 5693	6	7	8	9	10	11	12	
15		13	14	15[g]	16	17	18	19	
16		20	21	22	23	24	25	26	
17		27	28	29	30	1	2	3	Tue $0^h54^m16^p$
18	IYYAR 5693	4	5	6	7	8	9	10	
19		11	12	13	14	15	16	17	
20		18	19	20	21	22	23	24	
21		25	26	27	28	29	1	2	Wed $13^h38^m17^p$
22	SIVAN 5693	3	4	5	6[h]	7	8	9	
23		10	11	12	13	14	15	16	
24		17	18	19	20	21	22	23	
25		24	25	26	27	28	29	30	
26	TAMMUZ 5693	1	2	3	4	5	6	7	Fri $2^h23^m0^p$
27		8	9	10	11	12	13	14	
28		15	16	17	18	19	20	21	
29		22	23	24	25	26	27	28	
30		29	1	2	3	4	5	6	Sat $15^h7^m1^p$
31	AV 5693	7	8	9[i]	10	11	12	13	
32		14	15	16	17	18	19	20	
33		21	22	23	24	25	26	27	
34		28	29	30	1	2	3	4	Mon $3^h51^m2^p$
35	ELUL 5693	5	6	7	8	9	10	11	
36		12	13	14	15	16	17	18	
37		19	20	21	22	23	24	25	
38		26	27	28	29	1[a]	2[a]	3	Tue $16^h35^m3^p$
39	TISHRI 5694	4	5	6	7	8	9	10[b]	
40		11	12	13	14	15[c]	16	17	
41		18	19	20	21	22	23	24	
42		25	26	27	28	29	30	1	Thu $5^h19^m4^p$
43	HESHVAN 5694	2	3	4	5	6	7	8	
44		9	10	11	12	13	14	15	
45		16	17	18	19	20	21	22	
46		23	24	25	26	27	28	29	
47		1	2	3	4	5	6	7	Fri $18^h3^m5^p$
48	KISLEV 5694	8	9	10	11	12	13	14	
49		15	16	17[d]	18	19	20	21	
50		22	23	24	25[e]	26[e]	27[e]	28[e]	
51		29[e]	30[e]	1[e]	2[e]	3	4	5	Sun $6^h47^m6^p$
52	TEVETH 5694	6	7	8	9	10	11	12	
1		13	14	15	16	17	18	19	

CHINESE Rén-Shēn/Guǐ-Yǒu‡

ISO Week	Month	Sun	Mon	Tue	Wed	Thu	Fri	Sat	Solar Term
1	MONTH 12 Rén-Shēn	6	7	8	9	10	*11*	12	Xiǎo hán
2		13	14	15	16	17	18	19	
3		20	21	22	23	24	**25**	26	Dà hán
4		27	28	29	30	1[a]	2	3	
5	MONTH 1 Guǐ-Yǒu	4	5	6	7	8	9	*10*	Lì chūn
6		11	12	13	14	15[b]	16	17	
7		18	19	20	21	22	23	24	
8		**25**	26	27	28	29	1	2	Yǔ shuǐ
9	MONTH 2 Guǐ-Yǒu	3	4*	5	6	7	8	9	
10		10	*11*	12	13	14	15	16	Jīng zhé
11		17	18	19	20	21	22	23	
12		24	25	**26**	27	28	29	30	Chūn fēn
13		1	2	3	4	5	6	7	
14	MONTH 3 Guǐ-Yǒu	8	9	10	*11*[c]	12	13	14	Qīng míng
15		15	16	17	18	19	20	21	
16		22	23	24	25	**26**	27	28	Gǔ yǔ
17		29	30	1	2	3	4*	5	
18	MONTH 4 Guǐ-Yǒu	6	7	8	9	10	11	*12*	Lì xià
19		13	14	15	16	17	18	19	
20		20	21	22	23	24	25	26	
21		**27**	28	29	1	2	3	4	Xiǎo mǎn
22	MONTH 5 Guǐ-Yǒu	5[d]	6	7	8	9	10	11	
23		12	13	*14*	15	16	17	18	Máng zhòng
24		19	20	21	22	23	24	25	
25		26	27	28	29	**30**	1	2	Xià zhì
26	LEAP MONTH 5 Guǐ-Yǒu	3	4	5*	6	7	8	9	
27		10	11	12	13	14	*15*	16	Xiǎo shǔ
28		17	18	19	20	21	22	23	
29		24	25	26	27	28	29	30	
30		***1***	2	3	4	5	6	7	Dà shǔ
31	MONTH 6 Guǐ-Yǒu	8	9	10	11	12	13	14	
32		15	16	*17*	18	19	20	21	Lì qiū
33		22	23	24	25	26	27	28	
34		29	1	2	**3**	4	5	6*	Chǔ shǔ
35	MONTH 7 Guǐ-Yǒu	7[e]	8	9	10	11	12	13	
36		14	15[f]	16	17	18	*19*	20	Bái lù
37		21	22	23	24	25	26	27	
38		28	29	30	1	2	3	**4**	Qiū fēn
39	MONTH 8 Guǐ-Yǒu	5	6	7	8	9	10	11	
40		12	13	14	15[g]	16	17	18	
41		19	*20*	21	22	23	24	25	Hán lù
42		26	27	28	29	1	2	3	
43	MONTH 9 Guǐ-Yǒu	4	5	**6**	7*	8	9[h]	10	Shuāng jiàng
44		11	12	13	14	15	16	17	
45		18	19	20	*21*	22	23	24	Lì dōng
46		25	26	27	28	29	30	1	
47	MONTH 10 Guǐ-Yǒu	2	3	4	5	**6**	7	8	Xiǎo xuě
48		9	10	11	12	13	14	15	
49		16	17	18	19	*20*	21	22	Dà xuě
50		23	24	25	26	27	28	29	
51	MONTH 11* Guǐ-Yǒu	1	2	3	4	5	**6**[i]	7	Dōng zhì
52		8*	9	10	11	12	13	14	
1		15	16	17	18	19	20	*21*	Xiǎo hán

COPTIC 1649/1650 — ETHIOPIC 1925/1926

ISO Week	Coptic Month	Sun	Mon	Tue	Wed	Thu	Fri	Sat	Ethiopic Month
1	KOIAK 1649	23	24	25	26	27	28	29[c]	TĀKHŚĀŚ 1925
2		30	1	2	3	4	5	6[d]	
3	TŌBE 1649	7	8	9	10	11[e]	12	13	ṬER 1925
4		14	15	16	17	18	19	20	
5		21	22	23	24	25	26	27	
6		28	29	30	1	2	3	4	
7	MESHIR 1649	5	6	7	8	9	10	11	YAKĀTIT 1925
8		12	13	14	15	16	17	18	
9		19	20	21	22	23	24	25	
10		26	27	28	29	30	1	2	
11	PAREMOTEP 1649	3	4	5	6	7	8	9	MAGĀBIT 1925
12		10	11	12	13	14	15	16	
13		17	18	19	20	21	22	23	
14		24	25	26	27	28	29	30	
15	PARMOUTE 1649	1	2	3	4	5	6	7	MIYĀZYĀ 1925
16		8[f]	9	10	11	12	13	14	
17		15	16	17	18	19	20	21	
18		22	23	24	25	26	27	28	
19		29[g]	30	1	2	3	4	5	
20	PASHONS 1649	6	7	8	9	10	11	12	GENBOT 1925
21		13	14	15	16	17	18	19	
22		20	21	22	23	24	25	26	
23		27	28	29	30	1	2	3	
24	PAŌNE 1649	4	5	6	7	8	9	10	SANĒ 1925
25		11	12	13	14	15	16	17	
26		18	19	20	21	22	23	24	
27		25	26	27	28	29	30	1	
28	EPĒP 1649	2	3	4	5	6	7	8	ḤAMLĒ 1925
29		9	10	11	12	13	14	15	
30		16	17	18	19	20	21	22	
31		23	24	25	26	27	28	29	
32		30	1	2	3	4	5	6	
33	MESORĒ 1649	7	8	9	10	11	12	13[h]	NAḤASĒ 1925
34		14	15	16	17	18	19	20	
35		21	22	23	24	25	26	27	
36	EPAG. 1649	28	29	30	1	2	3	4	PĀG. 1925
37		5	1[a]	2	3	4	5	6	
38	THOOUT 1650	7	8	9	10	11	12	13	MASKARAM 1926
39		14	15	16	17[b]	18	19	20	
40		21	22	23	24	25	26	27	
41		28	29	30	1	2	3	4	
42	PAOPE 1650	5	6	7	8	9	10	11	TEQEMT 1926
43		12	13	14	15	16	17	18	
44		19	20	21	22	23	24	25	
45		26	27	28	29	30	1	2	
46	ATHŌR 1650	3	4	5	6	7	8	9	HEDĀR 1926
47		10	11	12	13	14	15	16	
48		17	18	19	20	21	22	23	
49		24	25	26	27	28	29	30	
50		1	2	3	4	5	6	7	
51	KOIAK 1650	8	9	10	11	12	13	14	TĀKHŚĀŚ 1926
52		15	16	17	18	19	20	21	
1		22	23	24	25	26	27	28	

Gregorian notes:
[a] New Year
[b] Spring (1:43)
[c] Summer (21:12)
[d] Autumn (12:00)
[e] Winter (6:57)
● New moon
◐ First quarter moon
○ Full moon
◑ Last quarter moon

Hebrew notes:
[a] New Year
[b] Yom Kippur
[c] Sukkot
[d] Winter starts
[e] Ḥanukkah
[f] Purim
[g] Passover
[h] Shavuot
[i] Fast of Av

Chinese notes:
‡ Leap year
[a] New Year (4631, Fowl)
[b] Lantern Festival
[c] Qīngmíng
[d] Dragon Festival
[e] Qīqiǎo
[f] Hungry Ghosts
[g] Mid-Autumn Festival
[h] Double-Ninth Festival
[i] Dōngzhì
* Start of 60-name cycle

Coptic/Ethiopic notes:
[a] New Year
[b] Building of the Cross
[c] Christmas
[d] Jesus's Circumcision
[e] Epiphany
[f] Easter
[g] Mary's Announcement
[h] Jesus's Transfiguration

1933

PERSIAN (ASTRONOMICAL) 1311/1312

Month	Sun	Mon	Tue	Wed	Thu	Fri	Sat
DEY 1311	11	12	13	14	15	16	17
	18	19	20	21	22	23	24
	25	26	27	28	29	30	1
BAHMAN 1311	2	3	4	5	6	7	8
	9	10	11	12	13	14	15
	16	17	18	19	20	21	22
	23	24	25	26	27	28	29
	30	1	2	3	4	5	6
ESFAND 1311	7	8	9	10	11	12	13
	14	15	16	17	18	19	20
	21	22	23	24	25	26	27
	28	29	1[a]	2	3	4	5
FARVARDIN 1312	6	7	8	9	10	11	12
	13[b]	14	15	16	17	18	19
	20	21	22	23	24	25	26
	27	28	29	30	31	1	2
ORDIBEHESHT 1312	3	4	5	6	7	8	9
	10	11	12	13	14	15	16
	17	18	19	20	21	22	23
	24	25	26	27	28	29	30
	31	1	2	3	4	5	6
XORDAD 1312	7	8	9	10	11	12	13
	14	15	16	17	18	19	20
	21	22	23	24	25	26	27
	28	29	30	31	1	2	3
TIR 1312	4	5	6	7	8	9	10
	11	12	13	14	15	16	17
	18	19	20	21	22	23	24
	25	26	27	28	29	30	31
MORDAD 1312	1	2	3	4	5	6	7
	8	9	10	11	12	13	14
	15	16	17	18	19	20	21
	22	23	24	25	26	27	28
	29	30	31	1	2	3	4
SHAHRIVAR 1312	5	6	7	8	9	10	11
	12	13	14	15	16	17	18
	19	20	21	22	23	24	25
	26	27	28	29	30	31	1
MEHR 1312	2	3	4	5	6	7	8
	9	10	11	12	13	14	15
	16	17	18	19	20	21	22
	23	24	25	26	27	28	29
	30	1	2	3	4	5	6
ABAN 1312	7	8	9	10	11	12	13
	14	15	16	17	18	19	20
	21	22	23	24	25	26	27
	28	29	30	1	2	3	4
AZAR 1312	5	6	7	8	9	10	11
	12	13	14	15	16	17	18
	19	20	21	22	23	24	25
	26	27	28	29	30	1	2
DEY 1312	3	4	5	6	7	8	9
	10	11	12	13	14	15	16

[a]New Year
[b]Sizdeh Bedar

HINDU LUNAR 1989/1990

Month	Sun	Mon	Tue	Wed	Thu	Fri	Sat
PAUSHA 1989	5	6	7	8	9	10	11
	12	13	14	15	16	17	18
	19	20	21	22	23	24	25
MAGHA 1989	26	27	28	30	1	2	3
	4	5	6	7	8	8	9
	10	11	12	13	14	15	16
	17	18	19	20	21	22	24
	25	26	27	28[h]	29	30	1
PHALGUNA 1989	2	3	4	5	6	7	8
	9	10	10	11	12	13	14
	15[i]	16	18	19	20	21	22
	23	24	25	26	27	28	29
CHAITRA 1990	30	1[a]	2	3	4	5	6
	7	8	9[b]	10	11	12	13
	14	15	16	17	18	19	20
	22	23	24	25	26	27	28
VAISAKHA 1990	29	30	1	2	3	4	4
	5	6	7	8	9	10	11
	12	13	14	16	17	18	19
	20	21	22	23	24	25	26
JYAISHTHA 1990	27	28	29	30	1	2	3
	4	5	6	7	8	9	10
	11	12	13	14	15	16	17
	19	20	21	22	23	24	25
ASHADHA 1990	26	27	28	29	30	30	1
	2	3	4	5	6	7	8
	9	11	12	13	14	15	16
	17	18	19	20	21	22	23
	24	25	26	27	28	29	30
SRAVANA 1990	1	2	3	4	5	6	7
	8	9	10	11	12	14	15
	16	17	18	19	20	21	22
	23[c]	24	25	26	27	27	28
BHADRAPADA 1990	29	30	1	2	3[d]	4	5
	7	8	9	10	11	12	13
	14	15	16	17	18	19	20
	21	22	23	24	25	26	27
ASVINA 1990	28	29	30	1	2	3	4
	5	6	7	8[e]	9[e]	11	12
	13	14	15	16	17	18	19
	20	21	22	22	23	24	25
KARTTIKA 1990	26	27	28	29	30	1[f]	2
	4	5	6	7	8	9	10
	11	12	13	14	15	16	17
	18	19	20	21	22	23	24
MARGASIRA 1990	25	26	27	28	29	30	1
	2	3	4	5	6	8	9
	10	11[g]	12	13	14	15	16
	16	17	18	19	20	21	22
	23	24	25	26	27	28	29
PAUSHA 1990	30	2	3	4	5	6	7
	8	9	10	11	12	13	14
	15	16	17	18	18	19	20

[a]New Year (Śrīmukha)
[b]Birthday of Rāma
[c]Birthday of Krishna
[d]Ganēśa Chaturthī
[e]Dashara
[f]Diwali
[g]Birthday of Vishnu
[h]Night of Śiva
[i]Holi

HINDU SOLAR 1854‡/1855

Month	Sun	Mon	Tue	Wed	Thu	Fri	Sat
PAUSHA 1854	18	19	20	21	22	23	24
	25	26	27	28	29	1[b]	2
MAGHA 1854	3	4	5	6	7	8	9
	10	11	12	13	14	15	16
	17	18	19	20	21	22	23
	24	25	26	27	28	29	1
PHALGUNA 1854	2	3	4	5	6	7	8
	9	10	11	12	13	14	15
	16	17	18	19	20	21	22
	23	24	25	26	27	28	29
	30	1	2	3	4	5	6
CHAITRA 1854	7	8	9	10	11	12	13
	14	15	16	17	18	19	20
	21	22	23	24	25	26	27
	28	29	30	31	1[a]	2	3
VAISAKHA 1855	4	5	6	7	8	9	10
	11	12	13	14	15	16	17
	18	19	20	21	22	23	24
	25	26	27	28	29	30	31
JYAISHTHA 1855	1	2	3	4	5	6	7
	8	9	10	11	12	13	14
	15	16	17	18	19	20	21
	22	23	24	25	26	27	28
	29	30	31	1	2	3	4
ASHADHA 1855	5	6	7	8	9	10	11
	12	13	14	15	16	17	18
	19	20	21	22	23	24	25
	26	27	28	29	30	31	32
SRAVANA 1855	1	2	3	4	5	6	7
	8	9	10	11	12	13	14
	15	16	17	18	19	20	21
	22	23	24	25	26	27	28
	29	30	31	1	2	3	4
BHADRAPADA 1855	5	6	7	8	9	10	11
	12	13	14	15	16	17	18
	19	20	21	22	23	24	25
	26	27	28	29	30	31	1
ASVINA 1855	2	3	4	5	6	7	8
	9	10	11	12	13	14	15
	16	17	18	19	20	21	22
	23	24	25	26	27	28	29
	30	31	1	2	3	4	5
KARTTIKA 1855	6	7	8	9	10	11	12
	13	14	15	16	17	18	19
	20	21	22	23	24	25	26
	27	28	29	1	2	3	4
MARGASIRA 1855	5	6	7	8	9	10	11
	12	13	14	15	16	17	18
	19	20	21	22	23	24	25
	26	27	28	29	30	1	2
PAUSHA 1855	3	4	5	6	7	8	9
	10	11	12	13	14	15	16
	17	18	19	20	21	22	23

‡Leap year
[a]New Year (Pārthiva)
[b]Pongal

ISLAMIC (ASTRONOMICAL) 1351/1352

Month	Sun	Mon	Tue	Wed	Thu	Fri	Sat
RAMADAN 1351	4	5	6	7	8	9	10
	11	12	13	14	15	16	17
	18	19	20	21	22	23	24
SHAWWAL 1351	25	26	27	28	29	1[f]	2
	3	4	5	6	7	8	9
	10	11	12	13	14	15	16
	17	18	19	20	21	22	23
	24	25	26	27	28	29	30
DHU AL-QA'DA 1351	1	2	3	4	5	6	7
	8	9	10	11	12	13	14
	15	16	17	18	19	20	21
	22	23	24	25	26	27	28
DHU AL-HIJJA 1351	29	1	2	3	4	5	6
	7	8	9	10[g]	11	12	13
	14	15	16	17	18	19	20
	21	22	23	24	25	26	27
MUHARRAM 1352	28	29	30	1[a]	2	3	4
	5	6	7	8	9	10[b]	11
	12	13	14	15	16	17	18
	19	20	21	22	23	24	25
SAFAR 1352	26	27	28	29	30	1	2
	3	4	5	6	7	8	9
	10	11	12	13	14	15	16
	17	18	19	20	21	22	23
RABI' I 1352	24	25	26	27	28	29	1
	2	3	4	5	6	7	8
	9	10	11	12[c]	13	14	15
	16	17	18	19	20	21	22
	23	24	25	26	27	28	29
RABI' II 1352	30	1	2	3	4	5	6
	7	8	9	10	11	12	13
	14	15	16	17	18	19	20
	21	22	23	24	25	26	27
JUMADA I 1352	28	29	30	1	2	3	4
	5	6	7	8	9	10	11
	12	13	14	15	16	17	18
	19	20	21	22	23	24	25
JUMADA II 1352	26	27	28	29	30	1	2
	3	4	5	6	7	8	9
	10	11	12	13	14	15	16
	17	18	19	20	21	22	23
RAJAB 1352	24	25	26	27	28	29	1
	2	3	4	5	6	7	8
	9	10	11	12	13	14	15
	16	17	18	19	20	21	22
	23	24	25	26	27[d]	28	29
SHA'BAN 1352	1	2	3	4	5	6	7
	8	9	10	11	12	13	14
	15	16	17	18	19	20	21
	22	23	24	25	26	27	28
RAMADAN 1352	29	30	1[e]	2	3	4	5
	6	7	8	9	10	11	12
	13	14	15	16	17	18	19

[a]New Year
[b]'Ashūrā'
[c]Prophet's Birthday
[d]Ascent of the Prophet
[e]Start of Ramaḍān
[f]'Īd al-Fiṭr
[g]'Īd al-'Aḍḥā

GREGORIAN 1933

Julian (Sun)	Sun	Mon	Tue	Wed	Thu	Fri	Sat	Month
Dec 19	1	2	3	4	5	6	7[a]	JANUARY 1933
	8	9	10	11	12	13	14[b]	
Jan 2	15	16	17	18	19	20	21	
	22	23	24	25	26	27	28	
Jan 16	29	30	31	1	2	3	4	FEBRUARY 1933
	5	6	7	8	9	10	11	
Jan 30	12	13	14	15	16	17	18	
	19	20	21	22	23	24	25	
Feb 13	26	27	28	1[c]	2	3	4	MARCH 1933
	5[d]	6	7	8	9	10	11	
Feb 27	12	13	14	15	16	17	18	
	19	20	21	22	23	24	25	
Mar 13	26	27	28	29	30	31	1	APRIL 1933
	2	3	4	5	6	7	8	
Mar 27	9	10	11	12	13	14	15	
	16[e]	17	18	19	20	21	22	
Apr 10	23	24	25	26	27	28	29	
	30	1	2	3	4	5	6	MAY 1933
Apr 24	7	8	9	10	11	12	13	
	14	15	16	17	18	19	20	
May 8	21	22	23	24	25	26	27	
	28	29	30	31	1	2	3	JUNE 1933
May 22	4	5	6	7	8	9	10	
	11	12	13	14	15	16	17	
Jun 5	18	19	20	21	22	23	24	
	25	26	27	28	29	30	1	JULY 1933
Jun 19	2	3	4	5	6	7	8	
	9	10	11	12	13	14	15	
Jul 3	16	17	18	19	20	21	22	
	23	24	25	26	27	28	29	
Jul 17	30	31	1	2	3	4	5	AUGUST 1933
	6	7	8	9	10	11	12	
Jul 31	13	14	15	16	17	18	19	
	20	21	22	23	24	25	26	
Aug 14	27	28	29	30	31	1	2	SEPTEMBER 1933
	3	4	5	6	7	8	9	
Aug 28	10	11	12	13	14	15	16	
	17	18	19	20	21	22	23	
Sep 11	24	25	26	27	28	29	30	
	1	2	3	4	5	6	7	OCTOBER 1933
Sep 25	8	9	10	11	12	13	14	
	15	16	17	18	19	20	21	
Oct 9	22	23	24	25	26	27	28	
	29	30	31	1	2	3	4	NOVEMBER 1933
Oct 23	5	6	7	8	9	10	11	
	12	13	14	15	16	17	18	
Nov 6	19	20	21	22	23	24	25	
	26	27	28	29	30	1	2	DECEMBER 1933
Nov 20	3[g]	4	5	6	7	8	9	
	10	11	12	13	14	15	16	
Dec 4	17	18	19	20	21	22	23	
	24	25[h]	26	27	28	29	30	
Dec 18	31	1	2	3	4	5	6	

[a]Orthodox Christmas
[b]Julian New Year
[c]Ash Wednesday
[d]Feast of Orthodoxy
[e]Easter (also Orthodox)
[g]Advent
[h]Christmas

1934

GREGORIAN 1934								Lunar Phases	ISO WEEK	JULIAN DAY	HEBREW 5694/5695‡								Molad	CHINESE Guǐ-Yǒu‡/Jiǎ-Xū								Solar Term	COPTIC 1650/1651‡								ETHIOPIC 1926/1927‡
	Sun	Mon	Tue	Wed	Thu	Fri	Sat		(Mon)	(Sun noon)		Sun	Mon	Tue	Wed	Thu	Fri	Sat			Sun	Mon	Tue	Wed	Thu	Fri	Sat			Sun	Mon	Tue	Wed	Thu	Fri	Sat	
JANUARY 1934	○	1[a]	2	3	4	5	6	20:54	1	2427438	TEVETH 5694	13	14	15	16	17	18	19		MONTH 11* Guǐ-Yǒu	15	16	17	18	19	20	_21_	Xiǎo hán	KOIAK 1650	22	23	24	25	26	27	28	TĀKHŚĀŚ 1926
	7	◑	9	10	11	12	13	21:36	2	2427445		20	21	22	23	24	25	26			22	23	24	25	26	27	28		TÔBE 1650	29[c]	30	1	2	3	4	5	ṬER 1926
	14	●	16	17	18	19	20	13:37	3	2427452	SHEVAT 5694	27	28	29	1	2	3	4	Mon 19h31m7p	MONTH 12 Guǐ-Yǒu	29	1	2	3	4	5	6			6[d]	7	8	9	10	11[e]	12	
	21	◐	23	24	25	26	27	11:50	4	2427459		5	6	7	8	9	10	11			**7**	8	9	10	11	12	13	Dà hán		13	14	15	16	17	18	19	
FEBRUARY 1934	28	29	○	31	1	2	3	16:31	5	2427466		12	13	14	15	16	17	18			14	15	16	17	18	19	20			20	21	22	23	24	25	26	
	4	5	6	◑	8	9	10	9:22	6	2427473		19	20	21	22	23	24	25			_21_	22	23	24	25	26	27	Lì chūn	MESHIR 1650	27	28	29	30	1	2	3	YAKĀTIT 1926
	11	12	13	●	15	16	17	0:43	7	2427480	ADAR 5694	26	27	28	29	30	1	2	Wed 8h15m8p	MONTH 1 Jiǎ-Xū	28	29	30	1[a]	2	3	4			4	5	6	7	8	9	10	
	18	19	20	◐	22	23	24	6:05	8	2427487		3	4	5	6	7	8	9			5	**6**	7	8	9*	10	11	Yǔ shuǐ		11	12	13	14	15	16	17	
MARCH 1934	25	26	27	28	○	2	3	10:26	9	2427494		10	11	12	13	14[f]	15	16			12	13	14	15[b]	16	17	18			18	19	20	21	22	23	24	
	4	5	6	7	◑	9	10	18:06	10	2427501		17	18	19	20	21	22	23			19	20	_21_	22	23	24	25	Jīng zhé	PAREMOTEP 1650	25	26	27	28	29	30	1	MAGĀBIT 1926
	11	12	13	14	●	16	17	12:08	11	2427508	NISAN 5694	24	25	26	27	28	29	1	Thu 20h59m9p	MONTH 2 Jiǎ-Xū	26	27	28	29	1	2	3			2	3	4	5	6	7	8	
	18	19	20	21[b]	22	◐	24	1:44	12	2427515		2	3	4	5	6	7	8			4	5	6	**7**	8	9	10	Chūn fēn		9	10	11	12	13	14	15	
	25	26	27	28	29	30	○	1:14	13	2427522		9	10	11	12	13	14	15[g]			11	12	13	14	15	16	17			16	17	18	19	20	21	22	
APRIL 1934	1	2	3	4	5	6	◑	0:48	14	2427529		16	17	18	19	20	21	22			18	19	20	21	_22_[c]	23	24	Qīng míng		23	24	25	26	27	28	29	
	8	9	10	11	12	●	14	23:57	15	2427536		23	24	25	26	27	28	29		MONTH 3 Jiǎ-Xū	25	26	27	28	29	30	1		PARMOUTE 1650	30[f]	1	2	3	4	5	6	MIYĀZYĀ 1926
	15	16	17	18	19	20	◐	21:20	16	2427543	IYYAR 5694	30	1	2	3	4	5	6	Sat 9h43m10p		2	3	4	5	6	7	**8**	Gǔ yǔ		7	8	9	10	11	12	13	
	22	23	24	25	26	27	28		17	2427550		7	8	9	10	11	12	13			9	10*	11	12	13	14	15			14	15	16	17	18	19	20	
MAY 1934	○	30	1	2	3	4	5	12:45	18	2427557		14	15	16	17	18	19	20			16	17	18	19	20	21	22			21	22	23	24	25	26	27	
	◑	7	8	9	10	11	12	6:41	19	2427564		21	22	23	24	25	26	27			_23_	24	25	26	27	28	29	Lì xià	PASHONS 1650	28	29[g]	30	1	2	3	4	GENBOT 1926
	●	14	15	16	17	18	19	12:30	20	2427571	SIVAN 5694	28	29	1	2	3	4	5	Sun 22h27m11p	MONTH 4 Jiǎ-Xū	1	2	3	4	5	6	7			5	6	7	8	9	10	11	
	20	◐	22	23	24	25	26	15:20	21	2427578		6[h]	7	8	9	10	11	12			8	9	**10**	11	12	13	14	Xiǎo mǎn		12	13	14	15	16	17	18	
JUNE 1934	27	○	29	30	31	1	2	21:41	22	2427585		13	14	15	16	17	18	19			15	16	17	18	19	20	21			19	20	21	22	23	24	25	
	3	◑	5	6	7	8	9	12:53	23	2427592		20	21	22	23	24	25	26			22	23	24	_25_	26	27	28	Máng zhòng	PAÔNE 1650	26	27	28	29	30	1	2	SANĒ 1926
	10	11	●	13	14	15	16	2:11	24	2427599	TAMMUZ 5694	27	28	29	30	1	2	3	Tue 11h11m12p	MONTH 5 Jiǎ-Xū	29	30	1	2	3	4	5[d]			3	4	5	6	7	8	9	
	17	18	19	◐	21	22[c]	23	6:37	25	2427606		4	5	6	7	8	9	10			6	7	8	9	10	**11***	12	Xià zhì		10	11	12	13	14	15	16	
	24	25	26	○	28	29	30	5:08	26	2427613		11	12	13	14	15	16	17			13	14	15	16	17	18	19			17	18	19	20	21	22	23	
JULY 1934	1	2	◑	4	5	6	7	20:28	27	2427620		18	19	20	21	22	23	24			20	21	22	23	24	25	26			24	25	26	27	28	29	30	
	8	9	10	●	12	13	14	17:06	28	2427627	AV 5694	25	26	27	28	29	1	2	Wed 23h55m13p	MONTH 6 Jiǎ-Xū	_27_	28	29	30	1	2	3	Xiǎo shǔ	EPÊP 1650	1	2	3	4	5	6	7	ḤAMLĒ 1926
	15	16	17	18	◐	20	21	18:53	29	2427634		3	4	5	6	7	8	9			4	5	6	7	8	9	10			8	9	10	11	12	13	14	
	22	23	24	25	○	27	28	12:09	30	2427641		10[i]	11	12	13	14	15	16			11	**12**	13	14	15	16	17	Dà shǔ		15	16	17	18	19	20	21	
AUGUST 1934	29	30	31	1	◑	3	4	6:27	31	2427648		17	18	19	20	21	22	23			18	19	20	21	22	23	24			22	23	24	25	26	27	28	
	5	6	7	8	9	●	11	8:46	32	2427655		24	25	26	27	28	29	30		MONTH 7 Jiǎ-Xū	25	26	27	_28_	29	1	2	Lì qiū	MESORÊ 1650	29	30	1	2	3	4	5	NAḤASĒ 1926
	12	13	14	15	16	17	◐	4:33	33	2427662	ELUL 5694	1	2	3	4	5	6	7	Fri 12h39m14p		3	4	5	6	7[e]	8	9			6	7	8	9	10	11	12	
	19	20	21	22	23	○	25	19:37	34	2427669		8	9	10	11	12	13	14			10	11	12*	13	14	**15**[f]	16	Chǔ shǔ		13[h]	14	15	16	17	18	19	
SEPTEMBER 1934	26	27	28	29	30	◑	1	19:40	35	2427676		15	16	17	18	19	20	21			17	18	19	20	21	22	23			20	21	22	23	24	25	26	
	2	3	4	5	6	7	8		36	2427683		22	23	24	25	26	27	28			24	25	26	27	28	29	_30_	Bái lù	EPAG. 1650	27	28	29	30	1	2	3	PĀG. 1926
	●	10	11	12	13	14	15	0:20	37	2427690	TISHRI 5695	29	1[a]	2[a]	3	4	5	6	Sun 1h23m15p	MONTH 8 Jiǎ-Xū	1	2	3	4	5	6	7		THOOUT 1651	4	5	1[a]	2	3	4	5	MASKARAM 1927
	◐	17	18	19	20	21	22	12:26	38	2427697		7	8	9	10[b]	11	12	13			8	9	10	11	12	13	14			6	7	8	9	10	11	12	
	○[d]	24	25	26	27	28	29	4:19	39	2427704		14	15[c]	16	17	18	19	20			15[g]	**16**	17	18	19	20	21	Qiū fēn		13	14	15	16	17[b]	18	19	
OCTOBER 1934	◑	1	2	3	4	5	6	12:29	40	2427711		21	22	23	24	25	26	27			22	23	24	25	26	27	28			20	21	22	23	24	25	26	
	7	●	9	10	11	12	13	15:05	41	2427718	ḤESHVAN 5695	28	29	30	1	2	3	4	Mon 14h7m16p	MONTH 9 Jiǎ-Xū	29	1	_2_	3	4	5	6	Hán lù	PAOPE 1651	27	28	29	30	1	2	3	ṬEQEMT 1927
	14	◐	16	17	18	19	20	19:29	42	2427725		5	6	7	8	9	10	11			7	8	9[h]	10	11	12	13*			4	5	6	7	8	9	10	
	21	○	23	24	25	26	27	15:01	43	2427732		12	13	14	15	16	17	18			14	15	16	**17**	18	19	20	Shuāng jiàng		11	12	13	14	15	16	17	
NOVEMBER 1934	28	29	◑	31	1	2	3	8:22	44	2427739		19	20	21	22	23	24	25			21	22	23	24	25	26	27			18	19	20	21	22	23	24	
	4	5	6	●	8	9	10	4:43	45	2427746	KISLEV 5695	26	27	28	29	1	2	3	Wed 2h51m17p	MONTH 10 Jiǎ-Xū	28	29	30	1	_2_	3	4	Lì dōng	ATHÔR 1651	25	26	27	28	29	30	1	ḪEDĀR 1927
	11	12	13	◐	15	16	17	2:39	46	2427753		4	5	6	7	8	9	10			5	6	7	8	9	10	11			2	3	4	5	6	7	8	
	18	19	20	○	22	23	24	4:26	47	2427760		11	12	13	14	15	16	17			12	13	14	15	16	**17**	18	Xiǎo xuě		9	10	11	12	13	14	15	
DECEMBER 1934	25	26	27	28	◑	30	1	5:39	48	2427767		18	19	20	21	22	23	24			19	20	21	22	23	24	25			16	17	18	19	20	21	22	
	2	3	4	5	●	7	8	17:25	49	2427774	TEVETH 5695	25[e]	26[e]	27[e]	28[d,e]	29[e]	1[e]	2[e]	Thu 15h36m0p	MONTH 11 Jiǎ-Xū	26	27	28	29	30	1	_2_	Dà xuě		23	24	25	26	27	28	29	
	9	10	11	12	◐	14	15	10:52	50	2427781		3[e]	4	5	6	7	8	9			3	4	5	6	7	8	9		KOIAK 1651	30	1	2	3	4	5	6	TĀKHŚĀŚ 1927
	16	17	18	19	○	21	22[e]	20:53	51	2427788		10	11	12	13	14	15	16			10	11	12	13*	14	15	**16**[i]	Dōng zhì		7	8	9	10	11	12	13	
	23	24	25	26	27	28	◑	2:08	52	2427795		17	18	19	20	21	22	23			17	18	19	20	21	22	23			14	15	16	17	18	19	20	
	30	31	1	2	3	4	●	5:20	1	2427802		24	25	26	27	28	29	1	Sat 4h20m1p		24	25	26	27	28	29	1			21	22	23	24	25	26	27	

[a]New Year
[b]Spring (7:27)
[c]Summer (2:47)
[d]Autumn (17:45)
[e]Winter (12:49)
● New moon
◐ First quarter moon
○ Full moon
◑ Last quarter moon

‡Leap year
[a]New Year
[b]Yom Kippur
[c]Sukkot
[d]Winter starts
[e]Ḥanukkah
[f]Purim
[g]Passover
[h]Shavuot
[i]Fast of Av

‡Leap year
[a]New Year (4632, Dog)
[b]Lantern Festival
[c]Qīngmíng
[d]Dragon Festival
[e]Qīqiǎo
[f]Hungry Ghosts
[g]Mid-Autumn Festival
[h]Double-Ninth Festival
[i]Dōngzhì
*Start of 60-name cycle

‡Leap year
[a]New Year
[b]Building of the Cross
[c]Christmas
[d]Jesus's Circumcision
[e]Epiphany
[f]Easter
[g]Mary's Announcement
[h]Jesus's Transfiguration

1934

PERSIAN (ASTRONOMICAL) 1312/1313‡

Month	Sun	Mon	Tue	Wed	Thu	Fri	Sat
DEY 1312	10	11	12	13	14	15	16
	17	18	19	20	21	22	23
	24	25	26	27	28	29	30
BAHMAN 1312	*1*	2	3	4	5	6	7
	8	9	10	11	12	13	14
	15	16	17	18	19	20	21
	22	23	24	25	26	27	28
	29	30	*1*	2	3	4	5
ESFAND 1312	6	7	8	9	10	11	12
	13	14	15	16	17	18	19
	20	21	22	23	24	25	26
	27	28	29	*1*[a]	2	3	4
FARVARDĪN 1313	5	6	7	8	9	10	11
	12	13[b]	14	15	16	17	18
	19	20	21	22	23	24	25
	26	27	28	29	30	31	*1*
ORDĪBEHEŠT 1313	2	3	4	5	6	7	8
	9	10	11	12	13	14	15
	16	17	18	19	20	21	22
	23	24	25	26	27	28	29
	30	31	*1*	2	3	4	5
XORDĀD 1313	6	7	8	9	10	11	12
	13	14	15	16	17	18	19
	20	21	22	23	24	25	26
	27	28	29	30	31	*1*	2
TĪR 1313	3	4	5	6	7	8	9
	10	11	12	13	14	15	16
	17	18	19	20	21	22	23
	24	25	26	27	28	29	30
	31	*1*	2	3	4	5	6
MORDĀD 1313	7	8	9	10	11	12	13
	14	15	16	17	18	19	20
	21	22	23	24	25	26	27
	28	29	30	31	*1*	2	3
SHAHRĪVAR 1313	4	5	6	7	8	9	10
	11	12	13	14	15	16	17
	18	19	20	21	22	23	24
	25	26	27	28	29	30	31
MEHR 1313	*1*	2	3	4	5	6	7
	8	9	10	11	12	13	14
	15	16	17	18	19	20	21
	22	23	24	25	26	27	28
	29	30	*1*	2	3	4	5
ABĀN 1313	6	7	8	9	10	11	12
	13	14	15	16	17	18	19
	20	21	22	23	24	25	26
	27	28	29	30	*1*	2	3
ĀZAR 1313	4	5	6	7	8	9	10
	11	12	13	14	15	16	17
	18	19	20	21	22	23	24
	25	26	27	28	29	30	*1*
DEY 1313	2	3	4	5	6	7	8
	9	10	11	12	13	14	15

‡Leap year
[a]New Year
[b]Sizdeh Bedar

HINDU LUNAR 1990/1991‡

Month	Sun	Mon	Tue	Wed	Thu	Fri	Sat
PAUSHA 1990	15	16	17	18	*18*	19	20
	21	22	23	**24**	26	27	28
	29	30	1	2	3	4	5
MĀGHA 1990	6	7	8	9	10	11	12
	13	14	15	16	17	18	19
	20	21	22	23	24	25	26
	27	28[h]	**29**	1	2	3	4
PHĀLGUNA 1990	5	6	7	8	9	10	11
	11	12	13	14	15[i]	16	17
	18	19	20	21	22	**23**	25
	26	27	28	29	30	1[a]	2
CHAITRA 1991	3	4	5	6	7	8	9[b]
	10	11	12	13	14	15	*15*
	17	18	19	20	21	22	23
	24	25	26	27	**28**	30	1
LEAP VAIŚĀKHA 1991	2	3	4	*4*	5	6	7
	8	9	10	11	12	13	14
	15	16	17	18	19	20	**21**
	23	24	25	26	27	28	29
	30	1	2	3	4	5	6
VAIŚĀKHA 1991	7	8	*8*	9	10	11	12
	13	15	16	17	18	19	20
	21	22	23	24	**25**	27	28
	29	*29*	30	1	2	3	4
JYAISHṬHA 1991	5	6	7	8	9	10	11
	12	13	14	15	16	**17**	19
	20	21	22	23	24	25	26
	27	28	29	30	1	2	3
ĀSHĀḌHA 1991	4	5	*5*	6	7	**8**	10
	11	12	13	14	15	16	17
	18	19	**20**	22	23	24	25
	26	27	*27*	28	29	30	1
ŚRĀVAṆA 1991	2	3	4	5	6	7	8
	9	10	11	**12**	14	15	16
	17	18	19	20	21	22	23[c]
	24	25	26	27	28	29	30
BHĀDRAPADA 1991	1	2	*2*	3[d]	**4**	6	7
	8	9	10	11	12	13	14
	15	16	**17**	19	20	21	22
	22	23	24	25	26	27	28
	29	30	1	2	3	4	5
ĀŚVINA 1991	6	7	8[e]	**9**[e]	11	12	13
	14	15	16	17	18	19	20
	21	22	23	24	25	26	*26*
	27	28	29	30	**1**[f]	2	**3**
KĀRTTIKA 1991	5	6	7	8	9	10	11
	12	13	14	15	16	17	18
	19	20	21	22	23	24	25
	26	27	28	29	30	1	2
MĀRGAŚĪRA 1991	3	4	5	6	**7**	9	10
	11[g]	12	13	14	15	16	17
	18	19	*19*	20	21	22	23
	24	25	26	27	28	29	30

‡Leap year
[a]New Year (Bhāva)
[b]Birthday of Rāma
[c]Birthday of Krishna
[d]Ganēśa Chaturthī
[e]Dashara
[f]Diwali
[g]Birthday of Vishnu
[h]Night of Śiva
[i]Holi

HINDU SOLAR 1855/1856

Month	Sun	Mon	Tue	Wed	Thu	Fri	Sat
PAUSHA 1855	17	18	19	20	21	22	23
	24	25	26	27	28	29	1[b]
MĀGHA 1855	2	3	4	5	6	7	8
	9	10	11	12	13	14	15
	16	17	18	19	20	21	22
	23	24	25	26	27	28	29
	30	1	2	3	4	5	6
PHĀLGUNA 1855	7	8	9	10	11	12	13
	14	15	16	17	18	19	20
	21	22	23	24	25	26	27
	28	29	30	1	2	3	4
CHAITRA 1855	5	6	7	8	9	10	11
	12	13	14	15	16	17	18
	19	20	21	22	23	24	25
	26	27	28	29	30	1[a]	2
VAIŚĀKHA 1856	3	4	5	6	7	8	9
	10	11	12	13	14	15	16
	17	18	19	20	21	22	23
	24	25	26	27	28	29	30
	31	1	2	3	4	5	6
JYAISHṬHA 1856	7	8	9	10	11	12	13
	14	15	16	17	18	19	20
	21	22	23	24	25	26	27
	28	29	30	31	1	2	3
ĀSHĀḌHA 1856	4	5	6	7	8	9	10
	11	12	13	14	15	16	17
	18	19	20	21	22	23	24
	25	26	27	28	29	30	31
	32	1	2	3	4	5	6
ŚRĀVAṆA 1856	7	8	9	10	11	12	13
	14	15	16	17	18	19	20
	21	22	23	24	25	26	27
	28	29	30	31	1	2	3
BHĀDRAPADA 1856	4	5	6	7	8	9	10
	11	12	13	14	15	16	17
	18	19	20	21	22	23	24
	25	26	27	28	29	30	31
ĀŚVINA 1856	1	2	3	4	5	6	7
	8	9	10	11	12	13	14
	15	16	17	18	19	20	21
	22	23	24	25	26	27	28
	29	30	31	1	2	3	4
KĀRTTIKA 1856	5	6	7	8	9	10	11
	12	13	14	15	16	17	18
	19	20	21	22	23	24	25
	26	27	28	29	30	1	2
MĀRGAŚĪRA 1856	3	4	5	6	7	8	9
	10	11	12	13	14	15	16
	17	18	19	20	21	22	23
	24	25	26	27	28	29	1
PAUSHA 1856	2	3	4	5	6	7	8
	9	10	11	12	13	14	15
	16	17	18	19	20	21	22

[a]New Year (Vyaya)
[b]Pongal

ISLAMIC (ASTRONOMICAL) 1352/1353‡

Month	Sun	Mon	Tue	Wed	Thu	Fri	Sat
RAMAḌĀN 1352	13	14	15	16	17	18	19
	20	21	22	23	24	25	26
	27	28	29	*1*[f]	2	3	4
SHAWWĀL 1352	5	6	7	8	9	10	11
	12	13	14	15	16	17	18
	19	20	21	22	23	24	25
	26	27	28	29	*1*	2	3
DHU AL-QA'DA 1352	4	5	6	7	8	9	10
	11	12	13	14	15	16	17
	18	19	20	21	22	23	24
	25	26	27	28	29	30	*1*
DHU AL-ḤIJJA 1352	2	3	4	5	6	7	8
	9	10[g]	11	12	13	14	15
	16	17	18	19	20	21	22
	23	24	25	26	27	28	29
MUḤARRAM 1353	1[a]	*2*[â]	3	4	5	6	7
	8	9	10[b]	11	12	13	14
	15	16	17	18	19	20	21
	22	23	24	25	26	27	28
	29	30	1	*2*	3	4	5
ṢAFAR 1353	6	7	8	9	10	11	12
	13	14	15	16	17	18	19
	20	21	22	23	24	25	26
	27	28	29	1	*2*	3	4
RABĪ' I 1353	5	6	7	8	9	10	11
	12[c]	13	14	15	16	17	18
	19	20	21	22	23	24	25
	26	27	28	29	30	1	*2*
RABĪ' II 1353	3	4	5	6	7	8	9
	10	11	12	13	14	15	16
	17	18	19	20	21	22	23
	24	25	26	27	28	29	30
JUMĀDĀ I 1353	*1*	2	3	4	5	6	7
	8	9	10	11	12	13	14
	15	16	17	18	19	20	21
	22	23	24	25	26	27	28
	29	30	*1*	2	3	4	5
JUMĀDĀ II 1353	6	7	8	9	10	11	12
	13	14	15	16	17	18	19
	20	21	22	23	24	25	26
	27	28	29	*30*	1	2	3
RAJAB 1353	4	5	6	7	8	9	10
	11	12	13	14	15	16	17
	18	19	20	21	22	23	24
	25	26	27[d]	28	29	*1*	2
SHA'BĀN 1353	3	4	5	6	7	8	9
	10	11	12	13	14	15	16
	17	18	19	20	21	22	23
	24	25	26	27	28	29	*1*[e]
RAMAḌĀN 1353	2	3	4	5	6	7	8
	9	10	11	12	13	14	15
	16	17	18	19	20	21	22
	23	24	25	26	27	28	29

‡Leap year
[a]New Year
[â]New Year (Arithmetic)
[b]'Ashūrā'
[c]Prophet's Birthday
[d]Ascent of the Prophet
[e]Start of Ramaḍān
[f]'Id al-Fiṭr
[g]'Id al-'Aḍḥā

GREGORIAN 1934

Julian (Sun)	Sun	Mon	Tue	Wed	Thu	Fri	Sat	Month
Dec 18	*31*	1	2	3	4	5	6	JANUARY 1934
	7[a]	8	9	10	11	12	13	
Jan 1	*14*[b]	15	16	17	18	19	20	
	21	22	23	24	25	26	27	
Jan 15	*28*	29	30	31	1	2	3	
	4	5	6	7	8	9	10	FEBRUARY 1934
Jan 29	*11*	12	13	14[c]	15	16	17	
	18	19	20	21	22	23	24	
Feb 12	*25*[d]	26	27	28	1	2	3	
	4	5	6	7	8	9	10	MARCH 1934
Feb 26	*11*	12	13	14	15	16	17	
	18	19	20	21	22	23	24	
Mar 12	*25*	26	27	28	29	30	31	
	1[e]	2	3	4	5	6	7	APRIL 1934
Mar 26	*8*[f]	9	10	11	12	13	14	
	15	16	17	18	19	20	21	
Apr 9	*22*	23	24	25	26	27	28	
	29	30	1	2	3	4	5	
Apr 23	*6*	7	8	9	10	11	12	MAY 1934
	13	14	15	16	17	18	19	
May 7	*20*	21	22	23	24	25	26	
	27	28	29	30	31	1	2	
May 21	*3*	4	5	6	7	8	9	JUNE 1934
	10	11	12	13	14	15	16	
Jun 4	*17*	18	19	20	21	22	23	
	24	25	26	27	28	29	30	
Jun 18	*1*	2	3	4	5	6	7	JULY 1934
	8	9	10	11	12	13	14	
Jul 2	*15*	16	17	18	19	20	21	
	22	23	24	25	26	27	28	
Jul 16	*29*	30	31	1	2	3	4	
	5	6	7	8	9	10	11	AUGUST 1934
Jul 30	*12*	13	14	15	16	17	18	
	19	20	21	22	23	24	25	
Aug 13	*26*	27	28	29	30	31	1	
	2	3	4	5	6	7	8	SEPTEMBER 1934
Aug 27	*9*	10	11	12	13	14	15	
	16	17	18	19	20	21	22	
Sep 10	*23*	24	25	26	27	28	29	
	30	1	2	3	4	5	6	
Sep 24	*7*	8	9	10	11	12	13	OCTOBER 1934
	14	15	16	17	18	19	20	
Oct 8	*21*	22	23	24	25	26	27	
	28	29	30	31	1	2	3	
Oct 22	*4*	5	6	7	8	9	10	NOVEMBER 1934
	11	12	13	14	15	16	17	
Nov 5	*18*	19	20	21	22	23	24	
	25	26	27	28	29	30	1	
Nov 19	2[g]	3	4	5	6	7	8	DECEMBER 1934
	9	10	11	12	13	14	15	
Dec 3	*16*	17	18	19	20	21	22	
	23	24	25[h]	26	27	28	29	
Dec 17	*30*	31	1	2	3	4	5	

[a]Orthodox Christmas
[b]Julian New Year
[c]Ash Wednesday
[d]Feast of Orthodoxy
[e]Easter
[f]Orthodox Easter
[g]Advent
[h]Christmas

1935

GREGORIAN 1935	Sun	Mon	Tue	Wed	Thu	Fri	Sat	Lunar Phases	ISO WEEK (Mon)	JULIAN DAY (Sun noon)	HEBREW 5695‡/5696	Sun	Mon	Tue	Wed	Thu	Fri	Sat	Molad	CHINESE Jiǎ-Xū/Yǐ-Hài	Sun	Mon	Tue	Wed	Thu	Fri	Sat	Solar Term	COPTIC 1651‡/1652	Sun	Mon	Tue	Wed	Thu	Fri	Sat	ETHIOPIC 1927‡/1928
JANUARY 1935	30	31	1[a]	2	3	4	●	5:20	1	2427802	SHEVAT 5695	24	25	26	27	28	29	1	Sat 4h20m1p	MONTH 12 Jiǎ-Xū	24	25	26	27	28	29	1		KOIAK 1651	21	22	23	24	25	26	27	TĀKHŚĀŚ 1927
	6	7	8	9	10	◐	12	20:55	2	2427809		2	3	4	5	6	7	8			*2*	3	4	5	6	7	8	Xiǎo hán	TŌBE 1651	28	29[c]	30	1	2	3	4	ṬER 1927
	13	14	15	16	17	18	○	15:44	3	2427816		9	10	11	12	13	14	15			9	10	11	12	13	14	15			5	6[d]	7	8	9	10	11[e]	
	20	21	22	23	24	25	26		4	2427823		16	17	18	19	20	21	22			16	**17**	18	19	20	21	22	Dà hán		12	13	14	15	16	17	18	
FEBRUARY 1935	◑	28	29	30	31	1	2	19:59	5	2427830		23	24	25	26	27	28	29			23	24	25	26	27	28	29			19	20	21	22	23	24	25	
	●	4	5	6	7	8	9	16:27	6	2427837	ADAR I 5695	30	1	2	3	4	5	6	Sun 17h4m2p	MONTH 1 Yǐ-Hài	30	1[a]	2	3	4	5	6	Lì chūn	MESHIR 1651	26	27	28	29	30	1	2	YAKĀTIT 1927
	◐	11	12	13	14	15	16	9:24	7	2427844		7	8	9	10	11	12	13			7	8	9	10	11	12	13			3	4	5	6	7	8	9	
	17	○	19	20	21	22	23	11:17	8	2427851		14	15	16	17	18	19	20			14*	15[b]	**16**	17	18	19	20	Yǔ shuǐ		10	11	12	13	14	15	16	
MARCH 1935	24	25	◑	27	28	1	2	10:14	9	2427858		21	22	23	24	25	26	27			21	22	23	24	25	26	27			17	18	19	20	21	22	23	
	3	4	●	6	7	8	9	2:40	10	2427865	ADAR II 5695	28	29	30	1	2	3	4	Tue 5h48m3p	MONTH 2 Yǐ-Hài	28	29	1	2	3	4	5	Jīng zhé		24	25	26	27	28	29	30	
	10	11	◐	13	14	15	16	0:30	11	2427872		5	6	7	8	9	10	11			6	7	8	9	10	11	12		PAREMOTEP 1651	1	2	3	4	5	6	7	MAGĀBIT 1927
	17	18	19	○	21[b]	22	23	5:31	12	2427879		12	13	14[f]	15	16	17	18			13	14	15	16	**17**	18	19	Chūn fēn		8	9	10	11	12	13	14	
	24	25	26	◑	28	29	30	20:51	13	2427886		19	20	21	22	23	24	25			20	21	22	23	24	25	26			15	16	17	18	19	20	21	
APRIL 1935	31	1	2	●	4	5	6	12:10	14	2427893	NISAN 5695	26	27	28	29	1	2	3	Wed 18h32m4p	MONTH 3 Yǐ-Hài	27	28	29	1	2	3	4[c]	Qīng míng		22	23	24	25	26	27	28	
	7	8	9	◐	11	12	13	17:42	15	2427900		4	5	6	7	8	9	10			5	6	7	8	9	10	11		PARMOUTE 1651	29	30	1	2	3	4	5	MIYĀZYĀ 1927
	14	15	16	17	○	19	20	21:10	16	2427907		11	12	13	14	15[g]	16	17			12	13	14	15	16*	17	18			6	7	8	9	10	11	12	
	21	22	23	24	25	◑	27	4:20	17	2427914		18	19	20	21	22	23	24			**19**	20	21	22	23	24	25	Gǔ yǔ		13	14	15	16	17	18	19	
MAY 1935	28	29	30	1	●	3	4	21:36	18	2427921	IYAR 5695	25	26	27	28	29	30	1	Fri 7h16m5p	MONTH 4 Yǐ-Hài	26	27	28	29	30	1	2			20[f]	21	22	23	24	25	26	
	5	6	7	8	9	◐	11	11:54	19	2427928		2	3	4	5	6	7	8			3	4	5	6	7	8	9	Lì xià	PASHONS 1651	27	28	29[g]	30	1	2	3	GENBOT 1927
	12	13	14	15	16	17	○	9:57	20	2427935		9	10	11	12	13	14	15			10	11	12	13	14	15	16			4	5	6	7	8	9	10	
	19	20	21	22	23	24	◑	9:44	21	2427942		16	17	18	19	20	21	22			17	18	19	**20**	21	22	23	Xiǎo mǎn		11	12	13	14	15	16	17	
JUNE 1935	26	27	28	29	30	31	●	7:52	22	2427949		23	24	25	26	27	28	29		MONTH 5 Yǐ-Hài	24	25	26	27	28	29	1			18	19	20	21	22	23	24	
	2	3	4	5	6	7	8		23	2427956	SIVAN 5695	1	2	3	4	5	6[h]	7	Sat 20h0m6p		2	3	4	5[d]	6	7	8	Máng zhòng	PAÔNE 1651	25	26	27	28	29	30	1	SANÉ 1927
	◐	10	11	12	13	14	15	5:49	24	2427963		8	9	10	11	12	13	14			9	10	11	12	13	14	15			2	3	4	5	6	7	8	
	○	17	18	19	20	21	22[c]	20:20	25	2427970		15	16	17	18	19	20	21			16	17*	18	19	20	21	**22**	Xià zhì		9	10	11	12	13	14	15	
	◑	24	25	26	27	28	29	14:21	26	2427977		22	23	24	25	26	27	28			23	24	25	26	27	28	29			16	17	18	19	20	21	22	
JULY 1935	●	1	2	3	4	5	6	19:44	27	2427984	TAMMUZ 5695	29	30	1	2	3	4	5	Mon 8h44m7p	MONTH 6 Yǐ-Hài	30	1	2	3	4	5	6			23	24	25	26	27	28	29	
	7	◐	9	10	11	12	13	22:28	28	2427991		6	7	8	9	10	11	12			7	*8*	9	10	11	12	13	Xiǎo shǔ	EPÊP 1651	30	1	2	3	4	5	6	ḤAMLÉ 1927
	14	15	○	17	18	19	20	5:00	29	2427998		13	14	15	16	17	18	19			14	15	16	17	18	19	20			7	8	9	10	11	12	13	
	21	◑	23	24	25	26	27	19:42	30	2428005		20	21	22	23	24	25	26			21	22	23	**24**	25	26	27	Dà shǔ		14	15	16	17	18	19	20	
AUGUST 1935	28	29	●	31	1	2	3	9:32	31	2428012	AV 5695	27	28	29	1	2	3	4	Tue 21h28m8p	MONTH 7 Yǐ-Hài	28	29	1	2	3	4	5			21	22	23	24	25	26	27	
	4	5	6	◐	8	9	10	13:23	32	2428019		5	6	7	8	9[i]	10	11			6	7[e]	8	9	*10*	11	12	Lì qiū	MESORÊ 1651	28	29	30	1	2	3	4	NAHASÉ 1927
	11	12	13	○	15	16	17	12:44	33	2428026		12	13	14	15	16	17	18			13	14	15[f]	16	17	18*	19			5	6	7	8	9	10	11	
	18	19	20	◑	22	23	24	3:17	34	2428033		19	20	21	22	23	24	25			20	21	22	23	24	25	**26**	Chǔ shǔ		12	13[h]	14	15	16	17	18	
	25	26	27	28	●	30	31	1:00	35	2428040	ELUL 5695	26	27	28	29	30	1	2	Thu 10h12m9p	MONTH 8 Yǐ-Hài	27	28	29	30	1	2	3			19	20	21	22	23	24	25	
SEPTEMBER 1935	1	2	3	4	5	◐	7	2:26	36	2428047		3	4	5	6	7	8	9			4	5	6	7	8	9	10		EPAG. 1651	26	27	28	29	30	1	2	PĀG. 1927
	8	9	10	11	○	13	14	20:18	37	2428054		10	11	12	13	14	15	16			*11*	12	13	14	15[g]	16	17	Bái lù	THOOUT 1652	3	4	5	6	1[a]	2	3	MASKARAM 1928
	15	16	17	18	◑	20	21	14:23	38	2428061		17	18	19	20	21	22	23			18	19	20	21	22	23	24			4	5	6	7	8	9	10	
	22	23[d]	24	25	26	●	28	17:29	39	2428068	TISHRI 5696	24	25	26	27	28	29	1[a]	Fri 22h56m10p	MONTH 9 Yǐ-Hài	25	26	**27**	28	29	30	1	Qiū fēn		11	12	13	14	15	16	17[b]	
OCTOBER 1935	29	30	1	2	3	4	◐	13:39	40	2428075		2[a]	3	4	5	6	7	8			2	3	4	5	6	7	8			18	19	20	21	22	23	24	
	6	7	8	9	10	11	○	4:39	41	2428082		9	10[b]	11	12	13	14	15[c]			9[h]	10	11	*12*	13	14	15	Hán lù	PAOPE 1652	25	26	27	28	29	30	1	ṬEQEMT 1928
	13	14	15	16	17	18	◑	5:36	42	2428089		16	17	18	19	20	21	22			16	17	18*	19	20	21	22			2	3	4	5	6	7	8	
	20	21	22	23	24	25	26		43	2428096		23	24	25	26	27	28	29			23	24	25	26	**27**	28	29	Shuāng jiàng		9	10	11	12	13	14	15	
NOVEMBER 1935	●	28	29	30	31	1	2	10:15	44	2428103	ḤESHVAN 5696	30	1	2	3	4	5	6	Sun 11h40m11p	MONTH 10 Yǐ-Hài	1	2	3	4	5	6	7			16	17	18	19	20	21	22	
	◐	4	5	6	7	8	9	23:12	45	2428110		7	8	9	10	11	12	13			8	9	10	11	12	*13*	14	Lì dōng		23	24	25	26	27	28	29	
	○	11	12	13	14	15	16	14:42	46	2428117		14	15	16	17	18	19	20			15	16	17	18	19	20	21		ATHŌR 1652	30	1	2	3	4	5	6	ḪEDĀR 1928
	17	◑	19	20	21	22	23	0:36	47	2428124		21	22	23	24	25	26	27			22	23	24	25	26	27	**28**	Xiǎo xuě		7	8	9	10	11	12	13	
	24	25	●	27	28	29	30	2:36	48	2428131	KISLEV 5696	28	29	30	1	2	3	4	Tue 0h24m12p	MONTH 11 Yǐ-Hài	29	30	1	2	3	4	5			14	15	16	17	18	19	20	
DECEMBER 1935	1	2	◐	4	5	6	7	7:28	49	2428138		5	6	7	8	9	10[d]	11			6	7	8	9	10	11	12			21	22	23	24	25	26	27	
	8	9	○	11	12	13	14	3:10	50	2428145		12	13	14	15	16	17	18			*13*	14	15	16	17	18	19*	Dà xuě	KOIAK 1652	28	29	30	1	2	3	4	TĀKHŚĀŚ 1928
	15	16	◑	18	19	20	21	21:57	51	2428152		19	20	21	22	23	24	25[e]			20	21	22	23	24	25	26			5	6	7	8	9	10	11	
	22[e]	23	24	●	26	27	28	17:49	52	2428159	ṬEVETH 5696	26[e]	27[e]	28[e]	29[e]	30[e]	1[e]	2[e]	Wed 13h8m13p	MONTH 12 Yǐ-Hài	27	**28**[i]	29	30	1	2	3	Dōng zhì		12	13	14	15	16	17	18	
	29	30	31	◐	2	3	4	15:15	1	2428166		3	4	5	6	7	8	9			4	5	6	7	8	9	10			19	20	21	22	23	24	25	

[a]New Year
[b]Spring (13:17)
[c]Summer (8:38)
[d]Autumn (23:38)
[e]Winter (18:36)
● New moon
◐ First quarter moon
○ Full moon
◑ Last quarter moon

‡Leap year
[a]New Year
[b]Yom Kippur
[c]Sukkot
[d]Winter starts
[e]Ḥanukkah
[f]Purim
[g]Passover
[h]Shavuot
[i]Fast of Av

[a]New Year (4633, Pig)
[b]Lantern Festival
[c]Qīngmíng
[d]Dragon Festival
[e]Qīqiǎo
[f]Hungry Ghosts
[g]Mid-Autumn Festival
[h]Double-Ninth Festival
[i]Dōngzhì
*Start of 60-name cycle

‡Leap year
[a]New Year
[b]Building of the Cross
[c]Christmas
[d]Jesus's Circumcision
[e]Epiphany
[f]Easter
[g]Mary's Announcement
[h]Jesus's Transfiguration

PERSIAN (ASTRONOMICAL) 1313‡/1314

Month	Sun	Mon	Tue	Wed	Thu	Fri	Sat
	9	10	11	12	13	14	15
DEY 1313	16	17	18	19	20	21	22
	23	24	25	26	27	28	29
	30	1	2	3	4	5	6
BAHMAN 1313	7	8	9	10	11	12	13
	14	15	16	17	18	19	20
	21	22	23	24	25	26	27
	28	29	30	1	2	3	4
ESFAND 1313	5	6	7	8	9	10	11
	12	13	14	15	16	17	18
	19	20	21	22	23	24	25
	26	27	28	29	30	1[a]	2
	3	4	5	6	7	8	9
FARVARDĪN 1314	10	11	12	13[b]	14	15	16
	17	18	19	20	21	22	23
	24	25	26	27	28	29	30
	31	1	2	3	4	5	6
ORDĪBEHEŠT 1314	7	8	9	10	11	12	13
	14	15	16	17	18	19	20
	21	22	23	24	25	26	27
	28	29	30	31	1	2	3
XORDĀD 1314	4	5	6	7	8	9	10
	11	12	13	14	15	16	17
	18	19	20	21	22	23	24
	25	26	27	28	29	30	31
	1	2	3	4	5	6	7
TĪR 1314	8	9	10	11	12	13	14
	15	16	17	18	19	20	21
	22	23	24	25	26	27	28
	29	30	31	1	2	3	4
MORDĀD 1314	5	6	7	8	9	10	11
	12	13	14	15	16	17	18
	19	20	21	22	23	24	25
	26	27	28	29	30	31	1
SHAHRĪVAR 1314	2	3	4	5	6	7	8
	9	10	11	12	13	14	15
	16	17	18	19	20	21	22
	23	24	25	26	27	28	29
	30	31	1	2	3	4	5
MEHR 1314	6	7	8	9	10	11	12
	13	14	15	16	17	18	19
	20	21	22	23	24	25	26
	27	28	29	30	1	2	3
ĀBĀN 1314	4	5	6	7	8	9	10
	11	12	13	14	15	16	17
	18	19	20	21	22	23	24
	25	26	27	28	29	30	1
ĀZAR 1314	2	3	4	5	6	7	8
	9	10	11	12	13	14	15
	16	17	18	19	20	21	22
	23	24	25	26	27	28	29
DEY 1314	30	1	2	3	4	5	6
	7	8	9	10	11	12	13

‡Leap year
[a]New Year
[b]Sizdeh Bedar

HINDU LUNAR 1991‡/1992

Month	Sun	Mon	Tue	Wed	Thu	Fri	Sat
	24	25	26	27	28	29	30
	1	3	4	5	6	7	8
PAUSHA 1991	9	10	11	12	13	14	15
	16	17	18	19	20	21	*21*
	22	23	24	**25**	27	28	29
	30	1	2	3	4	5	6
MĀGHA 1991	7	8	9	10	11	12	13
	14	15	16	17	18	19	20
	21	22	23	24	25	26	27
	28[h]	29	**30**	2	3	4	5
PHĀLGUNA 1991	6	7	8	9	10	11	12
	13	14	*14*	**15**[i]	16	17	18
	19	20	21	22	23	**24**	26
	27	28	29	30	1[a]	2	3
CHAITRA 1992	4	5	6	7	8	9[b]	10
	11	12	13	14	15	16	17
	18	19	20	21	22	23	24
	25	26	27	**28**	30	1	2
VAIŚĀKHA 1992	3	4	5	6	7	8	*8*
	9	10	11	12	13	14	15
	16	17	18	19	20	**21**	23
	24	25	26	27	28	29	30
JYAISHṬHA 1992	1	2	3	4	5	6	7
	8	9	10	11	12	13	14
	15	16	17	18	19	20	21
	22	23	**24**	26	27	28	29
	30	1	2	3	4	5	*5*
ĀSHĀḌHA 1992	6	7	8	9	10	11	12
	13	14	15	16	**17**	19	20
	21	22	23	24	25	26	27
	28	29	30	1	2	3	4
ŚRĀVAṆA 1992	5	6	7	8	9	10	11
	12	13	14	15	16	17	18
	19	**20**	22	23[c]	24	25	26
	27	28	29	30	1	*1*	2
BHĀDRAPADA 1992	3[d]	4	5	6	7	8	9
	10	11	12	**13**	15	16	17
	18	19	20	21	22	23	24
	25	26	27	28	29	30	1
ĀŚVINA 1992	2	3	4	5	6	7	8[e]
	9[e]	10[e]	11	12	13	14	15
	16	18	19	20	21	22	23
	24	25	26	*26*	27	28	29
	30	1[f]	2	3	4	5	6
KĀRTTIKA 1992	7	8	9	**10**	12	13	14
	15	16	17	18	19	20	21
	22	23	24	25	26	27	28
	29	*29*	30	1	2	**3**	5
MĀRGAŚĪRA 1992	6	7	8	9	10	11[g]	12
	13	14	15	16	17	18	19
	20	21	22	23	24	25	26
PAUSHA 1992	27	28	29	30	1	2	3
	4	5	6	7	**8**	10	11

‡Leap year
[a]New Year (Yuvan)
[b]Birthday of Rāma
[c]Birthday of Krishna
[d]Ganēśa Chaturthī
[e]Dashara
[f]Diwali
[g]Birthday of Vishnu
[h]Night of Śiva
[i]Holi

HINDU SOLAR 1856/1857

Month	Sun	Mon	Tue	Wed	Thu	Fri	Sat
	16	17	18	19	20	21	22
PAUSHA 1856	23	24	25	26	27	28	29
	30	1[b]	2	3	4	5	6
	7	8	9	10	11	12	13
MĀGHA 1856	14	15	16	17	18	19	20
	21	22	23	24	25	26	27
	28	29	1	2	3	4	5
PHĀLGUNA 1856	6	7	8	9	10	11	12
	13	14	15	16	17	18	19
	20	21	22	23	24	25	26
	27	28	29	30	1	2	3
CHAITRA 1856	4	5	6	7	8	9	10
	11	12	13	14	15	16	17
	18	19	20	21	22	23	24
	25	26	27	28	29	30	1[a]
VAIŚĀKHA 1857	2	3	4	5	6	7	8
	9	10	11	12	13	14	15
	16	17	18	19	20	21	22
	23	24	25	26	27	28	29
	30	31	1	2	3	4	5
JYAISHṬHA 1857	6	7	8	9	10	11	12
	13	14	15	16	17	18	19
	20	21	22	23	24	25	26
	27	28	29	30	31	32	1
ĀSHĀḌHA 1857	2	3	4	5	6	7	8
	9	10	11	12	13	14	15
	16	17	18	19	20	21	22
	23	24	25	26	27	28	29
	30	31	1	2	3	4	5
ŚRĀVAṆA 1857	6	7	8	9	10	11	12
	13	14	15	16	17	18	19
	20	21	22	23	24	25	26
	27	28	29	30	31	32	1
BHĀDRAPADA 1857	2	3	4	5	6	7	8
	9	10	11	12	13	14	15
	16	17	18	19	20	21	22
	23	24	25	26	27	28	29
	30	31	1	2	3	4	5
ĀŚVINA 1857	6	7	8	9	10	11	12
	13	14	15	16	17	18	19
	20	21	22	23	24	25	26
	27	28	29	30	1	2	3
KĀRTTIKA 1857	4	5	6	7	8	9	10
	11	12	13	14	15	16	17
	18	19	20	21	22	23	24
	25	26	27	28	29	30	1
MĀRGAŚĪRA 1857	2	3	4	5	6	7	8
	9	10	11	12	13	14	15
	16	17	18	19	20	21	22
	23	24	25	26	27	28	29
PAUSHA 1857	1	2	3	4	5	6	7
	8	9	10	11	12	13	14
	15	16	17	18	19	20	21

[a]New Year (Sarvajit)
[b]Pongal

ISLAMIC (ASTRONOMICAL) 1353‡/1354

Month	Sun	Mon	Tue	Wed	Thu	Fri	Sat
	23	24	25	26	27	28	29
SHAWWĀL 1353	1[f]	2	3	4	5	6	7
	8	9	10	11	12	13	14
	15	16	17	18	19	20	21
	22	23	24	25	26	27	28
	29	30	1	2	3	4	5
DHU AL-QA'DA 1353	6	7	8	9	10	11	12
	13	14	15	16	17	18	19
	20	21	22	23	24	25	26
	27	28	29	1	2	3	4
DHU AL-ḤIJJA 1353	5	6	7	8	9	10[g]	11
	12	13	14	15	16	17	18
	19	20	21	22	23	24	25
	26	27	28	29	30	1[a]	2
MUḤARRAM 1354	3	4	5	6	7	8	9
	10[b]	11	12	13	14	15	16
	17	18	19	20	21	22	23
	24	25	26	27	28	29	1
ṢAFAR 1354	2	3	4	5	6	7	8
	9	10	11	12	13	14	15
	16	17	18	19	20	21	22
	23	24	25	26	27	28	29
	30	1	2	3	4	5	6
RABĪ' I 1354	7	8	9	10	11	12[c]	13
	14	15	16	17	18	19	20
	21	22	23	24	25	26	27
	28	29	1	2	3	4	5
RABĪ' II 1354	6	7	8	9	10	11	12
	13	14	15	16	17	18	19
	20	21	22	23	24	25	26
	27	28	29	30	1	2	3
JUMĀDĀ I 1354	4	5	6	7	8	9	10
	11	12	13	14	15	16	17
	18	19	20	21	22	23	24
	25	26	27	28	29	30	*31*
JUMĀDĀ II 1354	1	2	3	4	5	6	7
	8	9	10	11	12	13	14
	15	16	17	18	19	20	21
	22	23	24	25	26	27	28
	29	1	2	3	4	5	6
RAJAB 1354	7	8	9	10	11	12	13
	14	15	16	17	18	19	20
	21	22	23	24	25	26	27[d]
	28	29	30	1	2	3	4
SHA'BĀN 1354	5	6	7	8	9	10	11
	12	13	14	15	16	17	18
	19	20	21	22	23	24	25
	26	27	28	29	1[e]	2	3
RAMAḌĀN 1354	4	5	6	7	8	9	10
	11	12	13	14	15	16	17
	18	19	20	21	22	23	24
SHAWWĀL 1354	25	26	27	28	29	1[f]	2
	3	4	5	6	7	8	9

‡Leap year
[a]New Year
[b]'Ashūrā'
[c]Prophet's Birthday
[d]Ascent of the Prophet
[e]Start of Ramaḍān
[f]'Id al-Fiṭr
[g]'Id al-'Aḍḥā

GREGORIAN 1935

Julian (Sun)	Sun	Mon	Tue	Wed	Thu	Fri	Sat	Month
Dec 17	30	31	1	2	3	4	5	
	6	7[a]	8	9	10	11	12	
Dec 31	13	14[b]	15	16	17	18	19	JANUARY 1935
	20	21	22	23	24	25	26	
Jan 14	27	28	29	30	31	1	2	
	3	4	5	6	7	8	9	
Jan 28	10	11	12	13	14	15	16	FEBRUARY 1935
	17	18	19	20	21	22	23	
Feb 11	24	25	26	27	28	1	2	
	3	4	5	6[c]	7	8	9	
Feb 25	10	11	12	13	14	15	16	MARCH 1935
	17[d]	18	19	20	21	22	23	
Mar 11	24	25	26	27	28	29	30	
	31	1	2	3	4	5	6	
Mar 25	7	8	9	10	11	12	13	
	14	15	16	17	18	19	20	APRIL 1935
Apr 8	21[e]	22	23	24	25	26	27	
	28[f]	29	30	1	2	3	4	
Apr 22	5	6	7	8	9	10	11	
	12	13	14	15	16	17	18	MAY 1935
May 6	19	20	21	22	23	24	25	
	26	27	28	29	30	31	1	
May 20	2	3	4	5	6	7	8	
	9	10	11	12	13	14	15	JUNE 1935
Jun 3	16	17	18	19	20	21	22	
	23	24	25	26	27	28	29	
Jun 17	30	1	2	3	4	5	6	
	7	8	9	10	11	12	13	
Jul 1	14	15	16	17	18	19	20	JULY 1935
	21	22	23	24	25	26	27	
Jul 15	28	29	30	31	1	2	3	
	4	5	6	7	8	9	10	
Jul 29	11	12	13	14	15	16	17	AUGUST 1935
	18	19	20	21	22	23	24	
Aug 12	25	26	27	28	29	30	31	
	1	2	3	4	5	6	7	
Aug 26	8	9	10	11	12	13	14	SEPTEMBER 1935
	15	16	17	18	19	20	21	
Sep 9	22	23	24	25	26	27	28	
	29	30	1	2	3	4	5	
Sep 23	6	7	8	9	10	11	12	
	13	14	15	16	17	18	19	OCTOBER 1935
Oct 7	20	21	22	23	24	25	26	
	27	28	29	30	31	1	2	
Oct 21	3	4	5	6	7	8	9	
	10	11	12	13	14	15	16	NOVEMBER 1935
Nov 4	17	18	19	20	21	22	23	
	24	25	26	27	28	29	30	
Nov 18	1[g]	2	3	4	5	6	7	
	8	9	10	11	12	13	14	DECEMBER 1935
Dec 2	15	16	17	18	19	20	21	
	22	23	24	25[h]	26	27	28	
Dec 16	29	30	31	1	2	3	4	

[a]Orthodox Christmas
[b]Julian New Year
[c]Ash Wednesday
[d]Feast of Orthodoxy
[e]Easter
[f]Orthodox Easter
[g]Advent
[h]Christmas

1936

GREGORIAN 1936‡								Lunar Phases	ISO WEEK	JULIAN DAY	HEBREW 5696/5697								Molad	CHINESE Yǐ-Hài/Bǐng-Zǐ‡								Solar Term	COPTIC 1652/1653								ETHIOPIC 1928/1929
	Sun	Mon	Tue	Wed	Thu	Fri	Sat		(Mon)	(Sun noon)		Sun	Mon	Tue	Wed	Thu	Fri	Sat			Sun	Mon	Tue	Wed	Thu	Fri	Sat			Sun	Mon	Tue	Wed	Thu	Fri	Sat	
JANUARY 1936	29	30	31	◐[a]	2	3	4	15:15	1	2428166	TEVETH 5696	3	4	5	6	7	8	9		MONTH 12 Yǐ-Hài	4	5	6	7	8	9	10		KOIAK 1652	19	20	21	22	23	24	25	TĀKHŚĀŚ 1928
	5	6	7	○	9	10	11	18:14	2	2428173		10	11	12	13	14	15	16			11	*12*	13	14	15	16	17	Xiǎo hán		26	27	28	29[c]	30	1	2	
	12	13	14	15	◑	17	18	19:41	3	2428180		17	18	19	20	21	22	23			18	19	20	21	22	23	24			3	4	5	6[d]	7	8	9	ṬER 1928
	19	20	21	22	23	●	25	7:18	4	2428187		24	25	26	27	28	29	1	Fri 1h52m14p		25	26	**27**	28	29	1[a]	2	**Dà hán**	TŌBE 1652	10	11[e]	12	13	14	15	16	
	26	27	28	29	◐	31	1	23:36	5	2428194	SHEVAT 5696	2	3	4	5	6	7	8		MONTH 1 Bǐng-Zǐ	3	4	5	6	7	8	9			17	18	19	20	21	22	23	
FEBRUARY 1936	2	3	4	5	6	○	8	11:19	6	2428201		9	10	11	12	13	14	15			10	11	12	*13*	14	15[b]	16	Lì chūn		24	25	26	27	28	29	30	
	9	10	11	12	13	14	◑	15:45	7	2428208		16	17	18	19	20	21	22			17	18	19	20*	21	22	23			1	2	3	4	5	6	7	
	16	17	18	19	20	21	●	18:42	8	2428215		23	24	25	26	27	28	29			24	25	26	27	**28**	29	30	**Yǔ shuǐ**	MESHIR 1652	8	9	10	11	12	13	14	YAKĀTIT 1928
	23	24	25	26	27	28	◐	9:28	9	2428222		30	1	2	3	4	5	6	Sat 14h36m15p		1	2	3	4	5	6	7			15	16	17	18	19	20	21	
MARCH 1936	1	2	3	4	5	6	7		10	2428229	ADAR 5696	7	8	9	10	11	12	13		MONTH 2 Bǐng-Zǐ	8	9	10	11	12	*13*	14	Jīng zhé		22	23	24	25	26	27	28	
	○	9	10	11	12	13	14	5:14	11	2428236		14[f]	15	16	17	18	19	20			15	16	17	18	19	20	21			29	30	1	2	3	4	5	
	15	◑	17	18	19	20[b]	21	8:35	12	2428243		21	22	23	24	25	26	27			22	23	24	25	26	27	**28**	**Chūn fēn**	PAREMOTEP 1652	6	7	8	9	10	11	12	MAGĀBIT 1928
	22	●	24	25	26	27	28	4:13	13	2428250		28	29	1	2	3	4	5	Mon 3h20m16p		29	1	2	3	4	5	6			13	14	15	16	17	18	19	
	◐	30	31	1	2	3	4	21:22	14	2428257	NISAN 5696	6	7	8	9	10	11	12		MONTH 3 Bǐng-Zǐ	7	8	9	10	11	12	13			20	21	22	23	24	25	26	
APRIL 1936	5	○	7	8	9	10	11	22:46	15	2428264		13	14	15[g]	16	17	18	19			*14*[c]	15	16	17	18	19	20	Qīng míng		27	28	29	30	1	2	3	
	12	13	◑	15	16	17	18	21:21	16	2428271		20	21	22	23	24	25	26			21*	22	23	24	25	26	27		PARMOUTE 1652	4[f]	5	6	7	8	9	10	MIYĀZYĀ 1928
	19	20	●	22	23	24	25	12:32	17	2428278		27	28	29	30	1	2	3	Tue 16h4m17p		28	**29**	1	2	3	4	5	**Gǔ yǔ**		11	12	13	14	15	16	17	
	26	27	◐	29	30	1	2	11:16	18	2428285	IYYAR 5696	4	5	6	7	8	9	10		*LEAP MONTH 3* Bǐng-Zǐ	6	7	8	9	10	11	12			18	19	20	21	22	23	24	
MAY 1936	3	4	5	○	7	8	9	15:01	19	2428292		11	12	13	14	15	16	17			13	14	15	*16*	17	18	19	Lì xià		25	26	27	28	29[g]	30	1	
	10	11	12	13	◑	15	16	6:12	20	2428299		18	19	20	21	22	23	24			20	21	22	23	24	25	26		PASHONS 1652	2	3	4	5	6	7	8	GENBOT 1928
	17	18	19	●	21	22	23	20:34	21	2428306		25	26	27	28	29	1	2	Thu 4h49m0p		27	28	29	30	*1*	2	3	**Xiǎo mǎn**		9	10	11	12	13	14	15	
	24	25	26	27	◐	29	30	2:46	22	2428313	SIVAN 5696	3	4	5	6[h]	7	8	9		MONTH 4 Bǐng-Zǐ	4	5	6	7	8	9	10			16	17	18	19	20	21	22	
	31	1	2	3	4	○	6	5:22	23	2428320		10	11	12	13	14	15	16			11	12	13	14	15	16	*17*	Máng zhòng		23	24	25	26	27	28	29	
JUNE 1936	7	8	9	10	11	◑	13	12:35	24	2428327		17	18	19	20	21	22	23			18	19	20	21	22*	23	24			30	1	2	3	4	5	6	
	14	15	16	17	18	●	20	5:14	25	2428334		24	25	26	27	28	29	30			25	26	27	28	29	1	2		PAŌNE 1652	7	8	9	10	11	12	13	SANĒ 1928
	21[c]	22	23	24	25	◐	27	19:22	26	2428341	TAMMUZ 5696	1	2	3	4	5	6	7	Fri 17h33m1p	MONTH 5 Bǐng-Zǐ	**3**	4	5[d]	6	7	8	9	**Xià zhì**		14	15	16	17	18	19	20	
	28	29	30	1	2	3	○	17:34	27	2428348		8	9	10	11	12	13	14			10	11	12	13	14	15	16			21	22	23	24	25	26	27	
JULY 1936	5	6	7	8	9	10	◑	16:28	28	2428355		15	16	17	18	19	20	21			17	18	*19*	20	21	22	23	Xiǎo shǔ		28	29	30	1	2	3	4	
	12	13	14	15	16	17	●	15:19	29	2428362		22	23	24	25	26	27	28			24	25	26	27	28	29	1		EPĒP 1652	5	6	7	8	9	10	11	ḤAMLĒ 1928
	19	20	21	22	23	24	25		30	2428369		29	1	2	3	4	5	6	Sun 6h17m2p	MONTH 6 Bǐng-Zǐ	2	3	4	5	**6**	7	8	**Dà shǔ**		12	13	14	15	16	17	18	
	◐	27	28	29	30	31	1	12:36	31	2428376	AV 5696	7	8	9[i]	10	11	12	13			9	10	11	12	13	14	15			19	20	21	22	23	24	25	
AUGUST 1936	2	○	4	5	6	7	8	3:47	32	2428383		14	15	16	17	18	19	20			16	17	18	19	20	21	*22*	Lì qiū		26	27	28	29	30	1	2	
	◑	10	11	12	13	14	15	20:59	33	2428390		21	22	23	24	25	26	27			23	24*	25	26	27	28	29		MESORĒ 1652	3	4	5	6	7	8	9	NAḤASĒ 1928
	16	●	18	19	20	21	22	3:21	34	2428397		28	29	30	1	2	3	4	Mon 19h1m3p		30	1	2	3	4	5	6			10	11	12	13[h]	14	15	16	
	23	24	◐	26	27	28	29	5:49	35	2428404	ELUL 5696	5	6	7	8	9	10	11		MONTH 7 Bǐng-Zǐ	*7*[e]	8	9	10	11	12	13	**Chǔ shǔ**		17	18	19	20	21	22	23	
	30	31	○	2	3	4	5	12:37	36	2428411		12	13	14	15	16	17	18			14	15[f]	16	17	18	19	20			24	25	26	27	28	29	30	
SEPTEMBER 1936	6	7	◑	9	10	11	12	3:14	37	2428418		19	20	21	22	23	24	25			21	22	*23*	24	25	26	27	Bái lù	EPAG. 1652	1	2	3	4	5	1[a]	2	PĀG. 1928
	13	14	●	16	17	18	19	17:41	38	2428425		26	27	28	29	1[a]	2[a]	3	Wed 7h45m4p		28	29	30	1	2	3	4		THOOUT 1653	3	4	5	6	7	8	9	MASKARAM 1929
	20	21	22	◐[d]	24	25	26	22:12	39	2428432	TISHRI 5697	4	5	6	7	8	9	10[b]		MONTH 8 Bǐng-Zǐ	5	6	7	**8**	9	10	11	**Qiū fēn**		10	11	12	13	14	15	16	
	27	28	29	○	1	2	3	21:01	40	2428439		11	12	13	14	15[c]	16	17			12	13	14	15[g]	16	17	18			17[b]	18	19	20	21	22	23	
OCTOBER 1936	4	5	6	◑	8	9	10	12:28	41	2428446		18	19	20	21	22	23	24			19	20	21	22	*23*	24*	25	Hán lù		24	25	26	27	28	29	30	
	11	12	13	14	●	16	17	10:20	42	2428453		25	26	27	28	29	30	1	Thu 20h29m5p		26	27	28	29	1	2	3		PAOPE 1653	1	2	3	4	5	6	7	ṬEQEMT 1929
	18	19	20	21	22	◐	24	12:54	43	2428460	ḤESHVAN 5697	2	3	4	5	6	7	8		MONTH 9 Bǐng-Zǐ	4	5	6	7	8	**9**[h]	10	**Shuāng jiàng**		8	9	10	11	12	13	14	
	25	26	27	28	29	○	31	5:58	44	2428467		9	10	11	12	13	14	15			11	12	13	14	15	16	17			15	16	17	18	19	20	21	
NOVEMBER 1936	1	2	3	4	5	◑	7	1:29	45	2428474		16	17	18	19	20	21	22			18	19	20	21	22	23	*24*	Lì dōng		22	23	24	25	26	27	28	
	8	9	10	11	12	13	●	4:42	46	2428481		23	24	25	26	27	28	29			25	26	27	28	29	30	1			29	30	1	2	3	4	5	
	15	16	17	18	19	20	21		47	2428488	KISLEV 5697	1	2	3	4	5	6	7	Sat 9h13m6p	MONTH 10 Bǐng-Zǐ	2	3	4	5	6	7	8		ATHŌR 1653	6	7	8	9	10	11	12	ḪEDĀR 1929
	◐	23	24	25	26	27	○	1:19 16:12	48	2428495		8	9	10	11	12	13	14			**9**	10	11	12	13	14	15	**Xiǎo xuě**		13	14	15	16	17	18	19	
	29	30	1	2	3	4	◑	18:20	49	2428502		15	16	17	18	19	20	21[d]			16	17	18	19	20	21	22			20	21	22	23	24	25	26	
DECEMBER 1936	6	7	8	9	10	11	12		50	2428509		22	23	24	25[e]	26[e]	27[e]	28[e]			23	*24*	25*	26	27	28	29	Dà xuě		27	28	29	30	1	2	3	
	●	14	15	16	17	18	19	23:25	51	2428516	TEVETH 5697	29[e]	30[e]	1[e]	2[e]	3	4	5	Sun 21h57m7p	MONTH 11 Bǐng-Zǐ	30	1	2	3	4	5	6		KOIAK 1653	4	5	6	7	8	9	10	TĀKHŚĀŚ 1929
	20	◐	22[e]	23	24	25	26	11:30	52	2428523		6	7	8	9	10	11	12			7	8	**9**[i]	10	11	12	13	**Dōng zhì**		11	12	13	14	15	16	17	
	27	○	29	30	31	1	2	4:00	53	2428530		13	14	15	16	17	18	19			14	15	16	17	18	19	20			18	19	20	21	22	23	24	

‡Leap year
[a]New Year
[b]Spring (18:57)
[c]Summer (14:21)
[d]Autumn (5:26)
[e]Winter (0:26)
● New moon
◐ First quarter moon
○ Full moon
◑ Last quarter moon

[a]New Year
[b]Yom Kippur
[c]Sukkot
[d]Winter starts
[e]Ḥanukkah
[f]Purim
[g]Passover
[h]Shavuot
[i]Fast of Av

‡Leap year
[a]New Year (4634, Rat)
[b]Lantern Festival
[c]Qīngmíng
[d]Dragon Festival
[e]Qīqiǎo
[f]Hungry Ghosts
[g]Mid-Autumn Festival
[h]Double-Ninth Festival
[i]Dōngzhì
*Start of 60-name cycle

[a]New Year
[b]Building of the Cross
[c]Christmas
[d]Jesus's Circumcision
[e]Epiphany
[f]Easter
[g]Mary's Announcement
[h]Jesus's Transfiguration

PERSIAN (ASTRONOMICAL) 1314/1315

Month	Sun	Mon	Tue	Wed	Thu	Fri	Sat
DEY 1314	7	8	9	10	11	12	13
	14	15	16	17	18	19	20
	21	22	23	24	25	26	27
	28	29	30	1	2	3	4
BAHMAN 1314	5	6	7	8	9	10	11
	12	13	14	15	16	17	18
	19	20	21	22	23	24	25
	26	27	28	29	30	1	2
ESFAND 1314	3	4	5	6	7	8	9
	10	11	12	13	14	15	16
	17	18	19	20	21	22	23
	24	25	26	27	28	29	1[a]
FARVARDĪN 1315	2	3	4	5	6	7	8
	9	10	11	12	13[b]	14	15
	16	17	18	19	20	21	22
	23	24	25	26	27	28	29
	30	31	1	2	3	4	5
ORDĪBEHEŠT 1315	6	7	8	9	10	11	12
	13	14	15	16	17	18	19
	20	21	22	23	24	25	26
	27	28	29	30	31	1	2
XORDĀD 1315	3	4	5	6	7	8	9
	10	11	12	13	14	15	16
	17	18	19	20	21	22	23
	24	25	26	27	28	29	30
	31	1	2	3	4	5	6
TĪR 1315	7	8	9	10	11	12	13
	14	15	16	17	18	19	20
	21	22	23	24	25	26	27
	28	29	30	31	1	2	3
MORDĀD 1315	4	5	6	7	8	9	10
	11	12	13	14	15	16	17
	18	19	20	21	22	23	24
	25	26	27	28	29	30	31
SHAHRĪVAR 1315	1	2	3	4	5	6	7
	8	9	10	11	12	13	14
	15	16	17	18	19	20	21
	22	23	24	25	26	27	28
	29	30	31	1	2	3	4
MEHR 1315	5	6	7	8	9	10	11
	12	13	14	15	16	17	18
	19	20	21	22	23	24	25
	26	27	28	29	30	1	2
ĀBĀN 1315	3	4	5	6	7	8	9
	10	11	12	13	14	15	16
	17	18	19	20	21	22	23
	24	25	26	27	28	29	30
ĀZAR 1315	1	2	3	4	5	6	7
	8	9	10	11	12	13	14
	15	16	17	18	19	20	21
	22	23	24	25	26	27	28
DEY 1315	29	30	1	2	3	4	5
	6	7	8	9	10	11	12

[a]New Year
[b]Sizdeh Bedar

HINDU LUNAR 1992/1993‡

Month	Sun	Mon	Tue	Wed	Thu	Fri	Sat
PAUSHA 1992	4	5	6	7	**8**	10	11
	12	13	14	15	16	17	18
	19	20	21	21	22	23	24
	25	26	27	28	29	30	1
MĀGHA 1992	2	**3**	5	6	7	8	9
	10	11	12	13	14	15	16
	17	18	19	20	21	22	23
	24	25	26	27	28	29[h]	30
PHĀLGUNA 1992	1	2	3	4	5	6	7
	8	10	11	12	13	14	14
	15[i]	16	17	18	19	20	21
	22	23	24	25	26	27	28
CHAITRA 1993	29	30	1[a]	3	4	5	6
	7	8	9[b]	10	11	12	13
	14	15	16	17	17	18	19
	20	21	22	23	**24**	26	27
VAIŚĀKHA 1993	28	29	30	1	2	3	4
	5	6	7	8	9	10	11
	12	13	14	15	16	17	18
	19	20	21	22	23	24	25
JYAISHṬHA 1993	26	27	**28**	30	1	2	3
	4	5	6	7	8	9	10
	11	12	12	13	14	15	16
	17	18	19	20	**21**	23	24
ĀSHĀḌHA 1993	25	26	27	28	29	30	1
	2	3	4	5	6	7	8
	9	10	11	12	13	14	15
	16	17	18	19	20	21	22
	23	**24**	26	27	28	29	30
ŚRĀVAṆA 1993	1	2	3	4	5	6	7
	8	9	9	10	11	12	13
	14	15	**16**	18	19	20	21
	22	23[c]	24	25	26	27	28
LEAP BHĀDRAPADA 1993	29	30	1	2	3	4	5
	6	7	8	9	10	11	12
	13	14	15	16	17	18	19
	20	22	23	24	25	26	27
BHĀDRAPADA 1993	28	29	30	1	2	3	4[d]
	5	5	6	7	8	9	10
	11	12	**13**	15	16	17	18
	19	20	21	22	23	24	25
ĀŚVINA 1993	26	27	28	29	30	1	2
	3	4	5	6	7	8[e]	9[e]
	10[e]	11	12	13	14	15	16
	17	19	20	21	22	23	24
	25	26	27	28	29	29	30
KĀRTTIKA 1993	1[f]	2	3	4	5	6	7
	8	9	10	**11**	13	14	15
	16	17	18	19	20	21	22
	23	24	25	26	27	28	29
MĀRGAŚĪRA 1993	30	1	2	3	4	5	6
	7	8	9	10	11[g]	12	13
	14	15	**16**	18	19	20	21

‡Leap year
[a]New Year (Dhātṛi)
[b]Birthday of Rāma
[c]Birthday of Krishna
[d]Ganēśa Chaturthī
[e]Dashara
[f]Diwali
[g]Birthday of Vishnu
[h]Night of Śiva
[i]Holi

HINDU SOLAR 1857/1858‡

Month	Sun	Mon	Tue	Wed	Thu	Fri	Sat
PAUSHA 1857	15	16	17	18	19	20	21
	22	23	24	25	26	27	28
	29	30	1[b]	2	3	4	5
MĀGHA 1857	6	7	8	9	10	11	12
	13	14	15	16	17	18	19
	20	21	22	23	24	25	26
	27	28	29	1	2	3	4
PHĀLGUNA 1857	5	6	7	8	9	10	11
	12	13	14	15	16	17	18
	19	20	21	22	23	24	25
	26	27	28	29	30	1	2
CHAITRA 1857	3	4	5	6	7	8	9
	10	11	12	13	14	15	16
	17	18	19	20	21	22	23
	24	25	26	27	28	29	30
VAIŚĀKHA 1858	1[a]	2	3	4	5	6	7
	8	9	10	11	12	13	14
	15	16	17	18	19	20	21
	22	23	24	25	26	27	28
	29	30	31	1	2	3	4
JYAISHṬHA 1858	5	6	7	8	9	10	11
	12	13	14	15	16	17	18
	19	20	21	22	23	24	25
	26	27	28	29	30	31	32
ĀSHĀḌHA 1858	1	2	3	4	5	6	7
	8	9	10	11	12	13	14
	15	16	17	18	19	20	21
	22	23	24	25	26	27	28
	29	30	31	1	2	3	4
ŚRĀVAṆA 1858	5	6	7	8	9	10	11
	12	13	14	15	16	17	18
	19	20	21	22	23	24	25
	26	27	28	29	30	31	32
BHĀDRAPADA 1858	1	2	3	4	5	6	7
	8	9	10	11	12	13	14
	15	16	17	18	19	20	21
	22	23	24	25	26	27	28
	29	30	31	1	2	3	4
ĀŚVINA 1858	5	6	7	8	9	10	11
	12	13	14	15	16	17	18
	19	20	21	22	23	24	25
	26	27	28	29	30	1	2
KĀRTTIKA 1858	3	4	5	6	7	8	9
	10	11	12	13	14	15	16
	17	18	19	20	21	22	23
	24	25	26	27	28	29	30
MĀRGAŚĪRA 1858	1	2	3	4	5	6	7
	8	9	10	11	12	13	14
	15	16	17	18	19	20	21
	22	23	24	25	26	27	28
	29	30	1	2	3	4	5
PAUSHA 1858	6	7	8	9	10	11	12
	13	14	15	16	17	18	19

‡Leap year
[a]New Year (Sarvadhārin)
[b]Pongal

ISLAMIC (ASTRONOMICAL) 1354/1355‡

Month	Sun	Mon	Tue	Wed	Thu	Fri	Sat
SHAWWĀL 1354	3	4	5	6	7	8	9
	10	11	12	13	14	15	16
	17	18	19	20	21	22	23
	24	25	26	27	28	29	30
DHU AL-QA'DA 1354	1	2	3	4	5	6	7
	8	9	10	11	12	13	14
	15	16	17	18	19	20	21
	22	23	24	25	26	27	28
DHU AL-ḤIJJA 1354	29	1	2	3	4	5	6
	7	8	9	10[g]	11	12	13
	14	15	16	17	18	19	20
	21	22	23	24	25	26	27
MUḤARRAM 1355	28	29	1[a]	2	3	4	5
	6	7	8	9	10[b]	11	12
	13	14	15	16	17	18	19
	20	21	22	23	24	25	26
	27	28	29	30	1	2	3
ṢAFAR 1355	4	5	6	7	8	9	10
	11	12	13	14	15	16	17
	18	19	20	21	22	23	24
	25	26	27	28	29	1	2
RABĪ' I 1355	3	4	5	6	7	8	9
	10	11	12[c]	13	14	15	16
	17	18	19	20	21	22	23
	24	25	26	27	28	29	1
RABĪ' II 1355	2	3	4	5	6	7	8
	9	10	11	12	13	14	15
	16	17	18	19	20	21	22
	23	24	25	26	27	28	29
	30	1	2	3	4	5	6
JUMĀDĀ I 1355	7	8	9	10	11	12	13
	14	15	16	17	18	19	20
	21	22	23	24	25	26	27
	28	29	30	31	1	2	3
JUMĀDĀ II 1355	4	5	6	7	8	9	10
	11	12	13	14	15	16	17
	18	19	20	21	22	23	24
	25	26	27	28	29	1	2
RAJAB 1355	3	4	5	6	7	8	9
	10	11	12	13	14	15	16
	17	18	19	20	21	22	23
	24	25	26	27[d]	28	29	30
SHA'BĀN 1355	1	2	3	4	5	6	7
	8	9	10	11	12	13	14
	15	16	17	18	19	20	21
	22	23	24	25	26	27	28
RAMAḌĀN 1355	29	1[e]	2	3	4	5	6
	7	8	9	10	11	12	13
	14	15	16	17	18	19	20
	21	22	23	24	25	26	27
SHAWWĀL 1355	28	29	1[f]	2	3	4	5
	6	7	8	9	10	11	12
	13	14	15	16	17	18	19

‡Leap year
[a]New Year
[b]'Ashūrā'
[c]Prophet's Birthday
[d]Ascent of the Prophet
[e]Start of Ramaḍān
[f]'Id al-Fiṭr
[g]'Id al-'Aḍḥā

GREGORIAN 1936‡

Julian‡ (Sun)	Sun	Mon	Tue	Wed	Thu	Fri	Sat	Month
Dec 16	29	30	31	1	2	3	4	
	5	6	7[a]	8	9	10	11	JANUARY 1936
Dec 30	12	13	14[b]	15	16	17	18	
	19	20	21	22	23	24	25	
Jan 13	26	27	28	29	30	31	1	
	2	3	4	5	6	7	8	FEBRUARY 1936
Jan 27	9	10	11	12	13	14	15	
	16	17	18	19	20	21	22	
Feb 10	23	24	25	26[c]	27	28	29	
	1[d]	2	3	4	5	6	7	MARCH 1936
Feb 24	8	9	10	11	12	13	14	
	15	16	17	18	19	20	21	
Mar 9	22	23	24	25	26	27	28	
	29	30	31	1	2	3	4	
Mar 23	5	6	7	8	9	10	11	APRIL 1936
	12[e]	13	14	15	16	17	18	
Apr 6	19	20	21	22	23	24	25	
	26	27	28	29	30	1	2	
Apr 20	3	4	5	6	7	8	9	MAY 1936
	10	11	12	13	14	15	16	
May 4	17	18	19	20	21	22	23	
	24	25	26	27	28	29	30	
May 18	31	1	2	3	4	5	6	
	7	8	9	10	11	12	13	JUNE 1936
Jun 1	14	15	16	17	18	19	20	
	21	22	23	24	25	26	27	
Jun 15	28	29	30	1	2	3	4	
	5	6	7	8	9	10	11	JULY 1936
Jun 29	12	13	14	15	16	17	18	
	19	20	21	22	23	24	25	
Jul 13	26	27	28	29	30	31	1	
	2	3	4	5	6	7	8	AUGUST 1936
Jul 27	9	10	11	12	13	14	15	
	16	17	18	19	20	21	22	
Aug 10	23	24	25	26	27	28	29	
	30	31	1	2	3	4	5	
Aug 24	6	7	8	9	10	11	12	SEPTEMBER 1936
	13	14	15	16	17	18	19	
Sep 7	20	21	22	23	24	25	26	
	27	28	29	30	1	2	3	
Sep 21	4	5	6	7	8	9	10	OCTOBER 1936
	11	12	13	14	15	16	17	
Oct 5	18	19	20	21	22	23	24	
	25	26	27	28	29	30	31	
Oct 19	1	2	3	4	5	6	7	NOVEMBER 1936
	8	9	10	11	12	13	14	
Nov 2	15	16	17	18	19	20	21	
	22	23	24	25	26	27	28	
Nov 16	29[g]	30	1	2	3	4	5	
	6	7	8	9	10	11	12	DECEMBER 1936
Nov 30	13	14	15	16	17	18	19	
	20	21	22	23	24	25[h]	26	
Dec 14	27	28	29	30	31	1	2	

‡Leap year
[a]Orthodox Christmas
[b]Julian New Year
[c]Ash Wednesday
[d]Feast of Orthodoxy
[e]Easter (also Orthodox)
[g]Advent
[h]Christmas

1937

GREGORIAN 1937	Sun Mon Tue Wed Thu Fri Sat	Lunar Phases	ISO WEEK (Mon)	JULIAN DAY (Sun noon)	HEBREW 5697/5698‡	Sun Mon Tue Wed Thu Fri Sat	Molad	CHINESE Bǐng-Zǐ‡/Dīng-Chǒu	Sun Mon Tue Wed Thu Fri Sat	Solar Term	COPTIC 1653/1654	Sun Mon Tue Wed Thu Fri Sat	ETHIOPIC 1929/1930
JANUARY 1937	27 ○ 29 30 31 1[a] 2	4:00	53	2428530	TEVETH 5697	13 14 15 16 17 18 19		MONTH 11 Bǐng-Zǐ	14 15 16 17 18 19 20		KOIAK 1653	18 19 20 21 22 23 24	TĀKHŚĀŚ 1929
	3 ◑ 5 6 7 8 9	14:22	1	2428537		20 21 22 23 24 25 26			21 22 23 24 25 26 27	Xiǎo hán	TŌBE 1653	25 26 27 28 29[c] 30 1	ṬER 1929
	10 11 ● 13 14 15 16	16:47	2	2428544		27 28 29 1 2 3 4	Tue 10h 41m 8p	MONTH 12 Bǐng-Zǐ	28 29 30 1 2 3 4			2 3 4 5 6[d] 7 8	
	17 18 ◐ 20 21 22 23	20:02	3	2428551	SHEVAT 5697	5 6 7 8 9 10 11			5 6 7 8 9 10 11	Dà hán		9 10 11[e] 12 13 14 15	
	24 25 ○ 27 28 29 30	17:15	4	2428558		12 13 14 15 16 17 18			12 13 14 15 16 17 18			16 17 18 19 20 21 22	
FEBRUARY 1937	31 1 2 ◑ 4 5 6	12:04	5	2428565		19 20 21 22 23 24 25			19 20 21 22 23 24 25*	Lì chūn		23 24 25 26 27 28 29	
	7 8 9 10 ● 12 13	7:34	6	2428572	ADAR 5697	26 27 28 29 30 1 2	Wed 23h 25m 9p	MONTH 1 Dīng-Chǒu	26 27 28 29 1[a] 2 3		MESHIR 1653	30 1 2 3 4 5 6	YAKĀTIT 1929
	14 15 16 17 ◐ 19 20	3:49	7	2428579		3 4 5 6 7 8 9			4 5 6 7 8 9 10	Yǔ shuǐ		7 8 9 10 11 12 13	
	21 22 23 24 ○ 26 27	7:43	8	2428586		10 11 12 13 14[f] 15 16			11 12 13 14 15[b] 16 17			14 15 16 17 18 19 20	
MARCH 1937	28 1 2 3 4 ◑ 6	9:17	9	2428593		17 18 19 20 21 22 23			18 19 20 21 22 23 24	Jīng zhé		21 22 23 24 25 26 27	
	7 8 9 10 11 ● 13	19:32	10	2428600	NISAN 5697	24 25 26 27 28 29 1	Fri 12h 9m 10p	MONTH 2 Dīng-Chǒu	25 26 27 28 29 30 1		PAREMOTEP 1653	28 29 30 1 2 3 4	MAGĀBIT 1929
	14 15 16 17 18 ◐ 20	11:46	11	2428607		2 3 4 5 6 7 8			2 3 4 5 6 7 8			5 6 7 8 9 10 11	
	21[b] 22 23 24 25 ○ 27	23:12	12	2428614		9 10 11 12 13 14 15[g]			9 10 11 12 13 14 15	Chūn fēn		12 13 14 15 16 17 18	
APRIL 1937	28 29 30 31 1 2 3		13	2428621		16 17 18 19 20 21 22			16 17 18 19 20 21 22			19 20 21 22 23 24 25	
	◑ 5 6 7 8 9 10	3:53 5:10	14	2428628		23 24 25 26 27 28 29			23 24[c] 25 26* 27 28 29	Qīng míng	PARMOUTE 1653	26 27 28 29 30 1 2	MIYĀZYĀ 1929
	● 12 13 14 15 16 ◐	20:34	15	2428635	IYYAR 5697	30 1 2 3 4 5 6	Sun 0h 53m 11p	MONTH 3 Dīng-Chǒu	1 2 3 4 5 6 7			3 4 5 6 7 8 9	
	18 19 20 21 22 23 24		16	2428642		7 8 9 10 11 12 13			8 9 10 11 12 13 14	Gǔ yǔ		10 11 12 13 14 15 16	
MAY 1937	○ 26 27 28 29 30 1	15:24	17	2428649		14 15 16 17 18 19 20			15 16 17 18 19 20 21			17 18 19 20 21 22 23	
	2 ◑ 4 5 6 7 8	18:36	18	2428656		21 22 23 24 25 26 27			22 23 24 25 26 27 28	Lì xià		24[f] 25 26 27 28 29[g] 30	
	9 ● 11 12 13 14 15	13:18	19	2428663	SIVAN 5697	28 29 1 2 3 4 5	Mon 13h 37m 12p	MONTH 4 Dīng-Chǒu	29 1 2 3 4 5 6		PASHONS 1653	1 2 3 4 5 6 7	GENBOT 1929
	16 ◐ 18 19 20 21 22	6:49	20	2428670		6[h] 7 8 9 10 11 12			7 8 9 10 11 12 13	Xiǎo mǎn		8 9 10 11 12 13 14	
	23 24 ○ 26 27 28 29	7:38	21	2428677		13 14 15 16 17 18 19			14 15 16 17 18 19 20			15 16 17 18 19 20 21	
JUNE 1937	30 31 1 ◑ 3 4 5	5:24	22	2428684		20 21 22 23 24 25 26			21 22 23 24 25 26 27			22 23 24 25 26 27 28	
	6 7 ● 9 10 11 12	20:43	23	2428691	TAMMUZ 5697	27 28 29 30 1 2 3	Wed 2h 21m 13p	MONTH 5 Dīng-Chǒu	28* 29 30 1 2 3 4	Máng zhòng	PAŌNE 1653	29 30 1 2 3 4 5	SANĒ 1929
	13 14 ◐ 16 17 18 19	19:03	24	2428698		4 5 6 7 8 9 10			5[d] 6 7 8 9 10 11			6 7 8 9 10 11 12	
	20 21[c] 22 ○ 24 25 26	23:00	25	2428705		11 12 13 14 15 16 17			12 13 14 15 16 17 18	Xià zhì		13 14 15 16 17 18 19	
JULY 1937	27 28 29 30 ◑ 2 3	13:03	26	2428712		18 19 20 21 22 23 24			19 20 21 22 23 24 25			20 21 22 23 24 25 26	
	4 5 6 7 ● 9 10	4:12	27	2428719	AV 5697	25 26 27 28 29 1 2	Thu 15h 5m 14p	MONTH 6 Dīng-Chǒu	26 27 28 29 1 2 3	Xiǎo shǔ	EPĒP 1653	27 28 29 30 1 2 3	ḤAMLĒ 1929
	11 12 13 14 ◐ 16 17	9:36	28	2428726		3 4 5 6 7 8 9			4 5 6 7 8 9 10			4 5 6 7 8 9 10	
	18 19 20 21 22 ○ 24	12:45	29	2428733		10[i] 11 12 13 14 15 16			11 12 13 14 15 16 17	Dà shǔ		11 12 13 14 15 16 17	
	25 26 27 28 29 ◑ 31	18:47	30	2428740		17 18 19 20 21 22 23			18 19 20 21 22 23 24			18 19 20 21 22 23 24	
AUGUST 1937	1 2 3 4 5 ● 7	12:37	31	2428747		24 25 26 27 28 29 30		MONTH 7 Dīng-Chǒu	25 26 27 28 29* 1 2		MESORĒ 1653	25 26 27 28 29 30 1	NAḤASĒ 1929
	8 9 10 11 12 13 ◐	2:28	32	2428754	ELUL 5697	1 2 3 4 5 6 7	Sat 3h 49m 15p		3 4 5 6 7[e] 8 9	Lì qiū		2 3 4 5 6 7 8	
	15 16 17 18 19 20 21		33	2428761		8 9 10 11 12 13 14			10 11 12 13 14 15[f] 16			9 10 11 12 13[h] 14 15	
	○ 23 24 25 26 27 ◑	0:47 23:54	34	2428768		15 16 17 18 19 20 21			17 18 19 20 21 22 23	Chǔ shǔ		16 17 18 19 20 21 22	
SEPTEMBER 1937	29 30 31 1 2 3 ●	22:53	35	2428775		22 23 24 25 26 27 28			24 25 26 27 28 29 30			23 24 25 26 27 28 29	
	5 6 7 8 9 10 11		36	2428782	TISHRI 5698	29 1[a] 2[a] 3 4 5 6	Sun 16h 33m 16p	MONTH 8 Dīng-Chǒu	1 2 3 4 5 6 7	Bái lù	EPAG. 1653	30 1 2 3 4 5 1[a]	PĀG. 1929
	◐ 13 14 15 16 17 18	20:57	37	2428789		7 8 9 10[b] 11 12 13			8 9 10 11 12 13 14		THOOUT 1654	2 3 4 5 6 7 8	MASKARAM 1930
	19 ○ 21 22 23[d] 24 25	11:32	38	2428796		14 15[c] 16 17 18 19 20			15[g] 16 17 18 19 20 21	Qiū fēn		9 10 11 12 13 14 15	
OCTOBER 1937	26 ◑ 28 29 30 1 2	5:43	39	2428803		21 22 23 24 25 26 27			22 23 24 25 26 27 28			16 17[b] 18 19 20 21 22	
	3 ● 5 6 7 8 9	11:58	40	2428810	HESHVAN 5698	28 29 30 1 2 3 4	Tue 5h 17m 17p	MONTH 9 Dīng-Chǒu	29 1* 2 3 4 5 6	Hán lù		23 24 25 26 27 28 29	
	10 11 ◐ 13 14 15 16	15:47	41	2428817		5 6 7 8 9 10 11			7 8 9[h] 10 11 12 13		PAOPE 1654	30 1 2 3 4 5 6	ṬEQEMT 1930
	17 18 ○ 20 21 22 23	21:48	42	2428824		12 13 14 15 16 17 18			14 15 16 17 18 19 20			7 8 9 10 11 12 13	
	24 25 ◑ 27 28 29 30	13:26	43	2428831		19 20 21 22 23 24 25			21 22 23 24 25 26 27	Shuāng jiàng		14 15 16 17 18 19 20	
NOVEMBER 1937	31 1 2 ● 4 5 6	4:16	44	2428838	KISLEV 5698	26 27 28 29 30 1 2		MONTH 10 Dīng-Chǒu	28 29 30 1 2 3 4			21 22 23 24 25 26 27	
	7 8 9 10 ◐ 12 13	9:33	45	2428845		3 4 5 6 7 8 9	Wed 18h 2m 0p		5 6 7 8 9 10 11	Lì dōng	ATHŌR 1654	28 29 30 1 2 3 4	ḪEDĀR 1930
	14 15 16 17 ○ 19 20	8:10	46	2428852		10 11 12 13 14 15 16			12 13 14 15 16 17 18			5 6 7 8 9 10 11	
	21 22 23 24 ◑ 26 27	0:04	47	2428859		17 18 19 20 21 22 23			19 20 21 22 23 24 25	Xiǎo xuě		12 13 14 15 16 17 18	
DECEMBER 1937	28 29 30 1 ● 3 4	23:11	48	2428866		24 25e 26e 27e 28e 29e 30[e]		MONTH 11 Dīng-Chǒu	26 27 28 29 30 1* 2			19 20 21 22 23 24 25	
	5 6 7 8 9 10 ◐	1:12	49	2428873	TEVETH 5698	1[d,e] 2e 3 4 5 6 7	Fri 6h 46m 1p		3 4 5 6 7 8 9	Dà xuě	KOIAK 1654	26 27 28 29 30 1 2	TĀKHŚĀŚ 1930
	12 13 14 15 16 ○ 18	18:52	50	2428880		8 9 10 11 12 13 14			10 11 12 13 14 15 16			3 4 5 6 7 8 9	
	19 20 21 22[e] 23 ◑ 25	14:20	51	2428887		15 16 17 18 19 20 21			17 18 19 20[i] 21 22 23	Dōng zhì		10 11 12 13 14 15 16	
	26 27 28 29 30 31 ●	18:58	52	2428894		22 23 24 25 26 27 28			24 25 26 27 28 29 30			17 18 19 20 21 22 23	

[a]New Year
[b]Spring (0:45)
[c]Summer (20:12)
[d]Autumn (11:13)
[e]Winter (6:22)
● New moon
◐ First quarter moon
○ Full moon
◑ Last quarter moon

‡Leap year
[a]New Year
[b]Yom Kippur
[c]Sukkot
[d]Winter starts
[e]Ḥanukkah
[f]Purim
[g]Passover
[h]Shavuot
[i]Fast of Av

‡Leap year
[a]New Year (4635, Ox)
[b]Lantern Festival
[c]Qīngmíng
[d]Dragon Festival
[e]Qīqiǎo
[f]Hungry Ghosts
[g]Mid-Autumn Festival
[h]Double-Ninth Festival
[i]Dōngzhì
*Start of 60-name cycle

[a]New Year
[b]Building of the Cross
[c]Christmas
[d]Jesus's Circumcision
[e]Epiphany
[f]Easter
[g]Mary's Announcement
[h]Jesus's Transfiguration

PERSIAN (ASTRONOMICAL) 1315/1316

Month	Sun	Mon	Tue	Wed	Thu	Fri	Sat
DEY 1315	6	7	8	9	10	11	12
	13	14	15	16	17	18	19
	20	21	22	23	24	25	26
BAHMAN 1315	27	28	29	30	*1*	2	3
	4	5	6	7	8	9	10
	11	12	13	14	15	16	17
	18	19	20	21	22	23	24
ESFAND 1315	25	26	27	28	29	30	*1*
	2	3	4	5	6	7	8
	9	10	11	12	13	14	15
	16	17	18	19	20	21	22
	23	24	25	26	27	28	29
FARVARDĪN 1316	*1*[a]	2	3	4	5	6	7
	8	9	10	11	12	13[b]	14
	15	16	17	18	19	20	21
	22	23	24	25	26	27	28
ORDĪBEHEŠT 1316	29	30	31	*1*	2	3	4
	5	6	7	8	9	10	11
	12	13	14	15	16	17	18
	19	20	21	22	23	24	25
XORDĀD 1316	26	27	28	29	30	31	*1*
	2	3	4	5	6	7	8
	9	10	11	12	13	14	15
	16	17	18	19	20	21	22
	23	24	25	26	27	28	29
TĪR 1316	30	31	*1*	2	3	4	5
	6	7	8	9	10	11	12
	13	14	15	16	17	18	19
	20	21	22	23	24	25	26
MORDĀD 1316	27	28	29	30	31	*1*	2
	3	4	5	6	7	8	9
	10	11	12	13	14	15	16
	17	18	19	20	21	22	23
	24	25	26	27	28	29	30
SHAHRĪVAR 1316	31	*1*	2	3	4	5	6
	7	8	9	10	11	12	13
	14	15	16	17	18	19	20
	21	22	23	24	25	26	27
MEHR 1316	28	29	30	31	*1*	2	3
	4	5	6	7	8	9	10
	11	12	13	14	15	16	17
	18	19	20	21	22	23	24
ĀBĀN 1316	25	26	27	28	29	30	*1*
	2	3	4	5	6	7	8
	9	10	11	12	13	14	15
	16	17	18	19	20	21	22
	23	24	25	26	27	28	29
ĀZAR 1316	30	*1*	2	3	4	5	6
	7	8	9	10	11	12	13
	14	15	16	17	18	19	20
	21	22	23	24	25	26	27
DEY 1316	28	29	30	*1*	2	3	4
	5	6	7	8	9	10	11

[a]New Year
[b]Sizdeh Bedar

HINDU LUNAR 1993‡/1994

Month	Sun	Mon	Tue	Wed	Thu	Fri	Sat
MĀRGAŚĪRA 1993	14	15	**16**	18	19	20	21
	22	*22*	23	24	25	26	27
PAUSHA 1993	28	29	30	1	2	3	4
	5	6	7	8	**9**	11	12
	13	14	15	16	17	18	19
	20	21	22	23	24	*24*	25
MĀGHA 1993	26	27	28	29	30	1	2
	3	**4**	6	7	8	9	10
	11	12	13	14	15	16	17
	18	19	20	21	22	23	24
PHĀLGUNA 1993	25	26	27	28	29[h]	30	1
	2	3	4	5	6	7	**8**
	10	11	12	13	14	15[i]	16
	17	*17*	18	19	20	21	22
	23	24	25	26	27	28	29
CHAITRA 1994	30	1[a]	**2**	4	5	6	7
	8	9[b]	10	11	12	13	14
	15	16	17	18	19	20	21
	21	22	23	**24**	26	27	28
VAIŚĀKHA 1994	29	30	1	2	3	4	5
	6	8	9	10	11	12	*12*
	13	14	15	16	17	18	19
	20	21	22	23	24	25	26
JYAISHṬHA 1994	27	**28**	30	1	2	3	4
	5	6	7	8	9	10	11
	12	13	14	15	16	17	*17*
	18	19	**20**	22	23	24	25
ĀSHĀḌHA 1994	26	27	28	29	30	1	**2**
	4	5	6	7	8	9	*9*
	10	11	12	13	14	15	16
	17	18	19	20	21	22	23
ŚRĀVAṆA 1994	**24**	26	27	28	29	30	1
	2	3	4	5	6	7	8
	9	10	11	12	13	14	15
	16	17	18	19	20	21	22
	23[c]	24	25	26	**27**	29	30
BHĀDRAPADA 1994	1	2	3	4[d]	5	*5*	6
	7	8	9	10	11	12	13
	14	15	16	17	18	19	**20**
	22	23	24	25	26	27	28
ĀŚVINA 1994	29	30	1	2	3	4	5
	6	7	8[e]	9[e]	*9*[e]	10[e]	11
	12	**13**	15	16	17	18	19
	20	21	22	23	24	25	**26**
KĀRTTIKA 1994	28	*28*	29	30	1[f]	2	3
	4	5	6	7	8	9	10
	11	12	13	14	15	16	17
	18	20	21	22	23	24	25
MĀRGAŚĪRA 1994	26	27	28	29	30	1	2
	2	3	4	5	6	7	8
	9	10	11[g]	**12**	14	15	16
	17	18	19	20	21	22	23
	24	25	26	27	28	29	30

‡Leap year
[a]New Year (Īśvara)
[b]Birthday of Rāma
[c]Birthday of Krishna
[d]Ganēśa Chaturthī
[e]Dashara
[f]Diwali
[g]Birthday of Vishnu
[h]Night of Śiva
[i]Holi

HINDU SOLAR 1858‡/1859

Month	Sun	Mon	Tue	Wed	Thu	Fri	Sat
PAUSHA 1858	13	14	15	16	17	18	19
	20	21	22	23	24	25	26
MĀGHA 1858	27	28	29	1[b]	2	3	4
	5	6	7	8	9	10	11
	12	13	14	15	16	17	18
	19	20	21	22	23	24	25
PHĀLGUNA 1858	26	27	28	29	1	2	3
	4	5	6	7	8	9	10
	11	12	13	14	15	16	17
	18	19	20	21	22	23	24
CHAITRA 1858	25	26	27	28	29	30	1
	2	3	4	5	6	7	8
	9	10	11	12	13	14	15
	16	17	18	19	20	21	22
	23	24	25	26	27	28	29
VAIŚĀKHA 1859	30	31	1[a]	2	3	4	5
	6	7	8	9	10	11	12
	13	14	15	16	17	18	19
	20	21	22	23	24	25	26
JYAISHṬHA 1859	27	28	29	30	31	1	2
	3	4	5	6	7	8	9
	10	11	12	13	14	15	16
	17	18	19	20	21	22	23
	24	25	26	27	28	29	30
ĀSHĀḌHA 1859	31	1	2	3	4	5	6
	7	8	9	10	11	12	13
	14	15	16	17	18	19	20
	21	22	23	24	25	26	27
ŚRĀVAṆA 1859	28	29	30	31	32	1	2
	3	4	5	6	7	8	9
	10	11	12	13	14	15	16
	17	18	19	20	21	22	23
	24	25	26	27	28	29	30
BHĀDRAPADA 1859	31	1	2	3	4	5	6
	7	8	9	10	11	12	13
	14	15	16	17	18	19	20
	21	22	23	24	25	26	27
ĀŚVINA 1859	28	29	30	31	1	2	3
	4	5	6	7	8	9	10
	11	12	13	14	15	16	17
	18	19	20	21	22	23	24
	25	26	27	28	29	30	31
KĀRTTIKA 1859	1	2	3	4	5	6	7
	8	9	10	11	12	13	14
	15	16	17	18	19	20	21
	22	23	24	25	26	27	28
MĀRGAŚĪRA 1859	29	1	2	3	4	5	6
	7	8	9	10	11	12	13
	14	15	16	17	18	19	20
	21	22	23	24	25	26	27
PAUSHA 1859	28	29	30	1	2	3	4
	5	6	7	8	9	10	11
	12	13	14	15	16	17	18

‡Leap year
[a]New Year (Virodhin)
[b]Pongal

ISLAMIC (ASTRONOMICAL) 1355‡/1356

Month	Sun	Mon	Tue	Wed	Thu	Fri	Sat
SHAWWĀL 1355	13	14	15	16	17	18	19
	20	21	22	23	24	25	26
DHU AL-QA'DA 1355	27	28	29	30	1	2	3
	4	5	6	7	8	9	10
	11	12	13	14	15	16	17
	18	19	20	21	22	23	24
DHU AL-ḤIJJA 1355	25	26	27	28	29	*1*	2
	3	4	5	6	7	8	9
	10[g]	11	12	13	14	15	16
	17	18	19	20	21	22	23
	24	25	26	27	28	29	30
MUḤARRAM 1356	*1*[a]	2	3	4	5	6	7
	8	9	10[b]	11	12	13	14
	15	16	17	18	19	20	21
	22	23	24	25	26	27	28
ṢAFAR 1356	29	1	2	3	4	5	6
	7	8	9	10	11	12	13
	14	15	16	17	18	19	20
	21	22	23	24	25	26	27
RABĪ' I 1356	28	29	30	*1*	2	3	4
	5	6	7	8	9	10	11
	12[c]	13	14	15	16	17	18
	19	20	21	22	23	24	25
RABĪ' II 1356	26	27	28	29	1	2	3
	4	5	6	7	8	9	10
	11	12	13	14	15	16	17
	18	19	20	21	22	23	24
JUMĀDĀ I 1356	25	26	27	28	29	30	*1*
	2	3	4	5	6	7	8
	9	10	11	12	13	14	15
	16	17	18	19	20	21	22
	23	24	25	26	27	28	29
JUMĀDĀ II 1356	30	*1*	2	3	4	5	6
	7	8	9	10	11	12	13
	14	15	16	17	18	19	20
	21	22	23	24	25	26	27
RAJAB 1356	28	29	*1*	2	3	4	5
	6	7	8	9	10	11	12
	13	14	15	16	17	18	19
	20	21	22	23	24	25	26
SHA'BĀN 1356	27[d]	28	29	30	*1*	2	3
	4	5	6	7	8	9	10
	11	12	13	14	15	16	17
	18	19	20	21	22	23	24
RAMAḌĀN 1356	25	26	27	28	29	1[e]	2
	3	4	5	6	7	8	9
	10	11	12	13	14	15	16
	17	18	19	20	21	22	23
SHAWWĀL 1356	24	25	26	27	28	29	1[f]
	2	3	4	5	6	7	8
	9	10	11	12	13	14	15
	16	17	18	19	20	21	22
	23	24	25	26	27	28	29

‡Leap year
[a]New Year
[b]'Ashūrā'
[c]Prophet's Birthday
[d]Ascent of the Prophet
[e]Start of Ramaḍān
[f]'Id al-Fiṭr
[g]'Id al-'Aḍḥā

GREGORIAN 1937

Julian (Sun)	Sun	Mon	Tue	Wed	Thu	Fri	Sat	Month
Dec 14	*27*	*28*	*29*	*30*	*31*	1	2	JANUARY 1937
	3	4	5	6	7[a]	8	9	
Dec 28	*10*	11	12	13	14[b]	15	16	
	17	18	19	20	21	22	23	
Jan 11	*24*	25	26	27	28	29	30	
	31	1	2	3	4	5	6	FEBRUARY 1937
Jan 25	*7*	8	9	10[c]	11	12	13	
	14	15	16	17	18	19	20	
Feb 8	*21*	22	23	24	25	26	27	
	28	1	2	3	4	5	6	MARCH 1937
Feb 22	*7*	8	9	10	11	12	13	
	14	15	16	17	18	19	20	
Mar 8	*21*[d]	22	23	24	25	26	27	
	28[e]	29	30	31	1	2	3	APRIL 1937
Mar 22	*4*	5	6	7	8	9	10	
	11	12	13	14	15	16	17	
Apr 5	*18*	19	20	21	22	23	24	
	25	26	27	28	29	30	1	MAY 1937
Apr 19	*2*[f]	3	4	5	6	7	8	
	9	10	11	12	13	14	15	
May 3	*16*	17	18	19	20	21	22	
	23	24	25	26	27	28	29	
May 17	*30*	31	1	2	3	4	5	JUNE 1937
	6	7	8	9	10	11	12	
May 31	*13*	14	15	16	17	18	19	
	20	21	22	23	24	25	26	
Jun 14	*27*	28	29	30	1	2	3	JULY 1937
	4	5	6	7	8	9	10	
Jun 28	*11*	12	13	14	15	16	17	
	18	19	20	21	22	23	24	
Jul 12	*25*	26	27	28	29	30	31	
	1	2	3	4	5	6	7	AUGUST 1937
Jul 26	*8*	9	10	11	12	13	14	
	15	16	17	18	19	20	21	
Aug 9	*22*	23	24	25	26	27	28	
	29	30	31	1	2	3	4	SEPTEMBER 1937
Aug 23	*5*	6	7	8	9	10	11	
	12	13	14	15	16	17	18	
Sep 6	*19*	20	21	22	23	24	25	
	26	27	28	29	30	1	2	OCTOBER 1937
Sep 20	*3*	4	5	6	7	8	9	
	10	11	12	13	14	15	16	
Oct 4	*17*	18	19	20	21	22	23	
	24	25	26	27	28	29	30	
Oct 18	*31*	1	2	3	4	5	6	NOVEMBER 1937
	7	8	9	10	11	12	13	
Nov 1	*14*	15	16	17	18	19	20	
	21	22	23	24	25	26	27	
Nov 15	*28*[g]	29	30	1	2	3	4	DECEMBER 1937
	5	6	7	8	9	10	11	
Nov 29	*12*	13	14	15	16	17	18	
	19	20	21	22	23	24	25[h]	
Dec 13	*26*	27	28	29	30	31	1	

[a]Orthodox Christmas
[b]Julian New Year
[c]Ash Wednesday
[d]Feast of Orthodoxy
[e]Easter
[f]Orthodox Easter
[g]Advent
[h]Christmas

1938

Gregorian 1938	Sun Mon Tue Wed Thu Fri Sat	Lunar Phases	ISO Week (Mon)	Julian Day (Sun noon)	Hebrew 5698‡/5699	Sun Mon Tue Wed Thu Fri Sat	Molad	Chinese Dīng-Chǒu/Wù-Yín‡	Sun Mon Tue Wed Thu Fri Sat	Solar Term	Coptic 1654/1655‡	Sun Mon Tue Wed Thu Fri Sat	Ethiopic 1930/1931‡
	26 27 28 29 30 31 ●[a]	18:58	52	2428894	Teveth 5698	22 23 24 25 26 27 28		Month 12 Dīng-Chǒu	24 25 26 27 28 29 30		Koiak 1654	17 18 19 20 21 22 23	Tākhśāś 1930
January 1938	2 3 4 5 6 7 8		1	2428901	Shevat 5698	29 1 2 3 4 5 6	Sat 19h 30m 2p		1 2 3 4 *5* 6 7	Xiǎo hán		24 25 26 27 28 29[c] 30	
	◐ 10 11 12 13 14 15	14:13	2	2428908		7 8 9 10 11 12 13			8 9 10 11 12 13 14		Tôbe 1654	1 2 3 4 5 6[d] 7	Ṭer 1930
	○ 17 18 19 20 21 22	5:53	3	2428915		14 15 16 17 18 19 20			15 16 17 18 19 **20** 21	Dà hán		8 9 10 11[e] 12 13 14	
	◑ 24 25 26 27 28 29	8:09	4	2428922		21 22 23 24 25 26 27			22 23 24 25 26 27 28			15 16 17 18 19 20 21	
February 1938	30 ● 1 2 3 4 5	13:35	5	2428929	Adar I 5698	28 29 30 1 2 3 4	Mon 8h 14m 3p	Month 1 Wù-Yín	29 1[a] 2* 3 4 *5* 6	Lì chūn		22 23 24 25 26 27 28	
	6 7 ◐ 9 10 11 12	0:32	6	2428936		5 6 7 8 9 10 11			7 8 9 10 11 12 13		Meshir 1654	29 30 1 2 3 4 5	Yakātit 1930
	13 ○ 15 16 17 18 19	17:14	7	2428943		12 13 14 15 16 17 18			14 15[b] 16 17 18 19 **20**	Yǔ shuǐ		6 7 8 9 10 11 12	
	20 21 ◑ 23 24 25 26	4:24	8	2428950		19 20 21 22 23 24 25			21 22 23 24 25 26 27			13 14 15 16 17 18 19	
March 1938	27 28 1 ● 3 4 5	5:40	9	2428957	Adar II 5698	26 27 28 29 30 1 2	Tue 20h 58m 4p	Month 2 Wù-Yín	28 29 30 1 2 3 4			20 21 22 23 24 25 26	
	6 7 8 ◐ 10 11 12	8:35	10	2428964		3 4 5 6 7 8 9			*5* 6 7 8 9 10 11	Jīng zhé	Paremotep 1654	27 28 29 30 1 2 3	Magābit 1930
	13 14 15 ○ 17 18 19	5:15	11	2428971		10 11 12 13 14[f] 15 16			12 13 14 15 16 17 18			4 5 6 7 8 9 10	
	20 21[b] 22 23 ◑ 25 26	1:06	12	2428978		17 18 19 20 21 22 23			19 **20** 21 22 23 24 25	Chūn fēn		11 12 13 14 15 16 17	
April 1938	27 28 29 30 ● 1 2	18:52	13	2428985	Nisan 5698	24 25 26 27 28 29 1	Thu 9h 42m 5p	Month 3 Wù-Yín	26 27 28 29 30 1 2*			18 19 20 21 22 23 24	
	3 4 5 6 ◐ 8 9	15:10	14	2428992		2 3 4 5 6 7 8			3 4 5[c] 6 7 8 9	Qīng míng	Parmoute 1654	25 26 27 28 29 30 1	Miyāzyā 1930
	10 11 12 13 ○ 15 16	18:21	15	2428999		9 10 11 12 13 14 15[g]			10 11 12 13 14 15 16			2 3 4 5 6 7 8	
	17 18 19 20 21 ◑ 23	20:14	16	2429006		16 17 18 19 20 21 22			17 18 19 20 **21** 22 23	Gǔ yǔ		9 10 11 12 13 14 15	
	24 25 26 27 28 29 ●	5:28	17	2429013		23 24 25 26 27 28 29		Month 4 Wù-Yín	24 25 26 27 28 29 1			16[f] 17 18 19 20 21 22	
May 1938	1 2 3 4 5 ◐ 7	21:24	18	2429020	Iyar 5698	30 1 2 3 4 5 6	Fri 22h 26m 6p		2 3 4 5 6 *7* 8	Lì xià		23 24 25 26 27 28 29[g]	
	8 9 10 11 12 13 ○	8:39	19	2429027		7 8 9 10 11 12 13			9 10 11 12 13 14 15		Pashons 1654	30 1 2 3 4 5 6	Genbot 1930
	15 16 17 18 19 20 21		20	2429034		14 15 16 17 18 19 20			16 17 18 19 20 21 22			7 8 9 10 11 12 13	
	◑ 23 24 25 26 27 28	12:36	21	2429041		21 22 23 24 25 26 27			**23** 24 25 26 27 28 29	Xiǎo mǎn		14 15 16 17 18 19 20	
June 1938	● 30 31 1 2 3 4	14:00	22	2429048	Sivan 5698	28 29 1 2 3 4 5	Sun 11h 10m 7p	Month 5 Wù-Yín	1 2 3 4* 5[d] 6 7			21 22 23 24 25 26 27	
	◐ 6 7 8 9 10 11	4:32	23	2429055		6[h] 7 8 9 10 11 12			8 *9* 10 11 12 13 14	Máng zhòng	Paône 1654	28 29 30 1 2 3 4	Sanē 1930
	○ 13 14 15 16 17 18	23:47	24	2429062		13 14 15 16 17 18 19			15 16 17 18 19 20 21			5 6 7 8 9 10 11	
	19 20 ◑ 22[c] 23 24 25	1:52	25	2429069		20 21 22 23 24 25 26			22 23 24 **25** 26 27 28	Xià zhì		12 13 14 15 16 17 18	
July 1938	26 ● 28 29 30 1 2	21:10	26	2429076	Tammuz 5698	27 28 29 30 1 2 3	Mon 23h 54m 8p	Month 6 Wù-Yín	29 30 1 2 3 4 5			19 20 21 22 23 24 25	
	3 ◐ 5 6 7 8 9	13:47	27	2429083		4 5 6 7 8 9 10			6 7 8 9 10 *11* 12	Xiǎo shǔ	Epêp 1654	26 27 28 29 30 1 2	Ḥamlē 1930
	10 11 ○ 13 14 15 16	15:05	28	2429090		11 12 13 14 15 16 17			13 14 15 16 17 18 19			3 4 5 6 7 8 9	
	17 18 19 ◑ 21 22 23	12:19	29	2429097		18 19 20 21 22 23 24			20 21 22 23 24 25 **26**	Dà shǔ		10 11 12 13 14 15 16	
	24 25 26 ● 28 29 30	3:53	30	2429104	Av 5698	25 26 27 28 29 1 2	Wed 12h 38m 9p	Month 7 Wù-Yín	27 28 29 1 2 3 4			17 18 19 20 21 22 23	
August 1938	31 1 2 ◐ 4 5 6	2:00	31	2429111		3 4 5 6 7 8 9			5* 6 7[e] 8 9 10 11			24 25 26 27 28 29 30	
	7 8 9 10 ○ 12 13	5:57	32	2429118		10[i] 11 12 13 14 15 16			12 *13* 14 15[f] 16 17 18	Lì qiū	Mesorê 1654	1 2 3 4 5 6 7	Naḥasē 1930
	14 15 16 17 ◑ 19 20	20:30	33	2429125		17 18 19 20 21 22 23			19 20 21 22 23 24 25			8 9 10 11 12 13[h] 14	
	21 22 23 24 ● 26 27	11:17	34	2429132		24 25 26 27 28 29 30		Leap Month 7 Wù-Yín	26 27 28 **29** 1 2 3	Chǔ shǔ		15 16 17 18 19 20 21	
September 1938	28 29 30 31 ◐ 2 3	17:28	35	2429139	Elul 5698	1 2 3 4 5 6 7	Fri 1h 22m 10p		4 5 6 7 8 9 10			22 23 24 25 26 27 28	
	4 5 6 7 8 ○ 10	20:08	36	2429146		8 9 10 11 12 13 14			11 12 13 14 *15* 16 17	Bái lù	Epag. 1654	29 30 1 2 3 4 5	Pāg. 1930
	11 12 13 14 15 16 ◑	3:12	37	2429153		15 16 17 18 19 20 21			18 19 20 21 22 23 24		Thoout 1655	1[a] 2 3 4 5 6 7	Maskaram 1931
	18 19 20 21 22 ●[d] 24	20:34	38	2429160		22 23 24 25 26 27 28		Month 8 Wù-Yín	25 26 27 28 29 30 **1**	Qiū fēn		8 9 10 11 12 13 14	
October 1938	25 26 27 28 29 30 ◐	11:45	39	2429167	Tishri 5699	29 1[a] 2[a] 3 4 5 6	Sat 14h 6m 11p		2 3 4 5 6* 7 8			15 16 17[b] 18 19 20 21	
	2 3 4 5 6 7 8		40	2429174		7 8 9 10[b] 11 12 13			9 10 11 12 13 14 15[g]			22 23 24 25 26 27 28	
	○ 10 11 12 13 14 15	9:37	41	2429181		14 15[c] 16 17 18 19 20			*16* 17 18 19 20 21 22	Hán lù	Paope 1655	29 30 1 2 3 4 5	Teqemt 1931
	◑ 17 18 19 20 21 22	9:24	42	2429188		21 22 23 24 25 26 27			23 24 25 26 27 28 29			6 7 8 9 10 11 12	
	● 24 25 26 27 28 29	8:42	43	2429195	Heshvan 5699	28 29 30 1 2 3 4	Mon 2h 50m 12p	Month 9 Wù-Yín	1 **2** 3 4 5 6 7	Shuāng jiàng		13 14 15 16 17 18 19	
November 1938	30 ◐ 1 2 3 4 5	7:45	44	2429202		5 6 7 8 9 10 11			8 9[h] 10 11 12 13 14			20 21 22 23 24 25 26	
	6 ○ 8 9 10 11 12	22:23	45	2429209		12 13 14 15 16 17 18			15 16 *17* 18 19 20 21	Lì dōng	Athôr 1655	27 28 29 30 1 2 3	Ḥedār 1931
	13 ◑ 15 16 17 18 19	16:20	46	2429216		19 20 21 22 23 24 25			22 23 24 25 26 27 28			4 5 6 7 8 9 10	
	20 21 ● 23 24 25 26	0:05	47	2429223	Kislev 5699	26 27 28 29 1 2 3	Tue 15h 34m 13p	Month 10 Wù-Yín	29 30 1 **2** 3 4 5	Xiǎo xuě		11 12 13 14 15 16 17	
December 1938	27 28 29 ◐ 1 2 3	3:59	48	2429230		4 5 6 7 8 9 10			6 7* 8 9 10 11 12			18 19 20 21 22 23 24	
	4 5 6 ○ 8 9 10	10:22	49	2429237		11 12[d] 13 14 15 16 17			13 14 15 16 *17* 18 19	Dà xuě	Koiak 1655	25 26 27 28 29 30 1	Tākhśāś 1931
	11 12 13 ◑ 15 16 17	1:17	50	2429244		18 19 20 21 22 23 24			20 21 22 23 24 25 26			2 3 4 5 6 7 8	
	18 19 20 ● 22[e] 23 24	18:07	51	2429251	Teveth 5699	25[e] 26[e] 27[e] 28[e] 29[e] 1[e] 2[e]	Thu 4h 18m 14p	Month 11* Wù-Yín	27 28 29 30 **1**[i] 2 3	Dōng zhì		9 10 11 12 13 14 15	
	25 26 27 28 ◐ 30 31	22:53	52	2429258		3[e] 4 5 6 7 8 9			4 5 6 7 8 9 10			16 17 18 19 20 21 22	

[a]New Year
[b]Spring (6:43)
[c]Summer (2:03)
[d]Autumn (17:00)
[e]Winter (12:13)
● New moon
◐ First quarter moon
○ Full moon
◑ Last quarter moon

‡Leap year
[a]New Year
[b]Yom Kippur
[c]Sukkot
[d]Winter starts
[e]Ḥanukkah
[f]Purim
[g]Passover
[h]Shavuot
[i]Fast of Av

‡Leap year
[a]New Year (4636, Tiger)
[b]Lantern Festival
[c]Qīngmíng
[d]Dragon Festival
[e]Qīqiǎo
[f]Hungry Ghosts
[g]Mid-Autumn Festival
[h]Double-Ninth Festival
[i]Dōngzhì
*Start of 60-name cycle

‡Leap year
[a]New Year
[b]Building of the Cross
[c]Christmas
[d]Jesus's Circumcision
[e]Epiphany
[f]Easter
[g]Mary's Announcement
[h]Jesus's Transfiguration

PERSIAN (ASTRONOMICAL) 1316/1317‡

Month	Sun	Mon	Tue	Wed	Thu	Fri	Sat
DEY 1316	5	6	7	8	9	10	11
	12	13	14	15	16	17	18
	19	20	21	22	23	24	25
BAHMAN 1316	26	27	28	29	30	*1*	2
	3	4	5	6	7	8	9
	10	11	12	13	14	15	16
	17	18	19	20	21	22	23
	24	25	26	27	28	29	30
ESFAND 1316	*1*	2	3	4	5	6	7
	8	9	10	11	12	13	14
	15	16	17	18	19	20	21
	22	23	24	25	26	27	28
FARVARDĪN 1317	29	*1*[a]	2	3	4	5	6
	7	8	9	10	11	12	13[b]
	14	15	16	17	18	19	20
	21	22	23	24	25	26	27
ORDĪBEHEŠT 1317	28	29	30	31	*1*	2	3
	4	5	6	7	8	9	10
	11	12	13	14	15	16	17
	18	19	20	21	22	23	24
	25	26	27	28	29	30	31
XORDĀD 1317	*1*	2	3	4	5	6	7
	8	9	10	11	12	13	14
	15	16	17	18	19	20	21
	22	23	24	25	26	27	28
TĪR 1317	29	30	31	*1*	2	3	4
	5	6	7	8	9	10	11
	12	13	14	15	16	17	18
	19	20	21	22	23	24	25
MORDĀD 1317	26	27	28	29	30	31	*1*
	2	3	4	5	6	7	8
	9	10	11	12	13	14	15
	16	17	18	19	20	21	22
	23	24	25	26	27	28	29
SHAHRĪVAR 1317	30	31	*1*	2	3	4	5
	6	7	8	9	10	11	12
	13	14	15	16	17	18	19
	20	21	22	23	24	25	26
MEHR 1317	27	28	29	30	31	*1*	2
	3	4	5	6	7	8	9
	10	11	12	13	14	15	16
	17	18	19	20	21	22	23
	24	25	26	27	28	29	30
ĀBĀN 1317	*1*	2	3	4	5	6	7
	8	9	10	11	12	13	14
	15	16	17	18	19	20	21
	22	23	24	25	26	27	28
ĀZAR 1317	29	30	*1*	2	3	4	5
	6	7	8	9	10	11	12
	13	14	15	16	17	18	19
	20	21	22	23	24	25	26
DEY 1317	27	28	29	30	*1*	2	3
	4	5	6	7	8	9	10

‡Leap year
[a]New Year
[b]Sizdeh Bedar

HINDU LUNAR 1994/1995

Month	Sun	Mon	Tue	Wed	Thu	Fri	Sat
	24	25	26	27	28	29	30
PAUSHA 1994	1	2	3	4	5	6	7
	8	9	10	11	12	13	14
	15	16	**17**	19	20	21	22
	23	24	25	*25*	26	27	28
MĀGHA 1994	29	30	1	2	3	4	5
	6	7	8	9	**10**	12	13
	14	15	16	17	18	19	20
	21	22	23	24	25	26	27
PHĀLGUNA 1994	*27*	28[h]	29	30	1	2	3
	4	6	7	8	9	10	11
	12	13	14	15[i]	16	17	18
	19	20	21	22	23	24	25
CHAITRA 1995	26	27	28	29	30	1[a]	2
	3	4	5	6	7	8[b]	**9**
	11	12	13	14	15	16	17
	18	19	20	21	*21*	22	23
	24	25	26	27	28	29	30
VAIŚĀKHA 1995	1	**2**	4	5	6	7	8
	9	10	11	12	13	14	15
	16	17	18	19	20	21	22
	23	24	25	26	27	28	29
JYAISHṬHA 1995	30	1	2	3	4	**5**	7
	8	9	10	11	12	13	14
	15	16	*16*	17	18	19	20
	21	22	23	24	25	26	27
ĀSHĀḌHA 1995	**28**	30	1	2	3	4	5
	6	7	8	9	10	11	12
	13	14	15	16	17	18	19
	20	21	22	23	24	25	26
ŚRĀVAṆA 1995	27	28	29	30	**1**	3	4
	5	6	7	8	9	10	11
	12	13	*13*	14	15	16	17
	18	19	20	21	22	23[c]	**24**
BHĀDRAPADA 1995	26	27	28	29	30	1	2
	3	4[d]	5	6	7	8	9
	10	11	12	13	14	15	16
	17	18	19	20	21	22	23
ĀŚVINA 1995	24	25	26	**27**	29	30	1
	2	3	4	5	6	7	8[e]
	9[e]	9[e]	10[e]	11	12	13	14
	15	16	17	18	19	20	**21**
	23	24	25	26	27	28	29
KĀRTTIKA 1995	30	1[f]	2	3	4	5	6
	7	8	9	10	11	12	13
	14	15	16	17	18	19	20
	21	22	23	24	**25**	27	28
MĀRGAŚIRA 1995	29	30	1	2	2	3	4
	5	6	7	8	9	10	11[g]
	12	13	14	15	16	17	18
	19	21	22	23	24	25	26
PAUSHA 1995	27	28	29	30	1	2	3
	4	5	5	6	7	8	9

[a]New Year (Bahudhānya)
[b]Birthday of Rāma
[c]Birthday of Krishna
[d]Ganēśa Chaturthī
[e]Dashara
[f]Diwali
[g]Birthday of Vishnu
[h]Night of Śiva
[i]Holi

HINDU SOLAR 1859/1860

Month	Sun	Mon	Tue	Wed	Thu	Fri	Sat
PAUSHA 1859	12	13	14	15	16	17	18
	19	20	21	22	23	24	25
MĀGHA 1859	26	27	28	29	1[b]	2	3
	4	5	6	7	8	9	10
	11	12	13	14	15	16	17
	18	19	20	21	22	23	24
PHĀLGUNA 1859	25	26	27	28	29	30	1
	2	3	4	5	6	7	8
	9	10	11	12	13	14	15
	16	17	18	19	20	21	22
	23	24	25	26	27	28	29
CHAITRA 1859	30	1	2	3	4	5	6
	7	8	9	10	11	12	13
	14	15	16	17	18	19	20
	21	22	23	24	25	26	27
VAIŚĀKHA 1860	28	29	30	1[a]	2	3	4
	5	6	7	8	9	10	11
	12	13	14	15	16	17	18
	19	20	21	22	23	24	25
JYAISHṬHA 1860	26	27	28	29	30	31	1
	2	3	4	5	6	7	8
	9	10	11	12	13	14	15
	16	17	18	19	20	21	22
	23	24	25	26	27	28	29
ĀSHĀḌHA 1860	30	31	1	2	3	4	5
	6	7	8	9	10	11	12
	13	14	15	16	17	18	19
	20	21	22	23	24	25	26
ŚRĀVAṆA 1860	27	28	29	30	31	32	1
	2	3	4	5	6	7	8
	9	10	11	12	13	14	15
	16	17	18	19	20	21	22
	23	24	25	26	27	28	29
BHĀDRAPADA 1860	30	31	1	2	3	4	5
	6	7	8	9	10	11	12
	13	14	15	16	17	18	19
	20	21	22	23	24	25	26
ĀŚVINA 1860	27	28	29	30	31	1	2
	3	4	5	6	7	8	9
	10	11	12	13	14	15	16
	17	18	19	20	21	22	23
	24	25	26	27	28	29	30
KĀRTTIKA 1860	31	1	2	3	4	5	6
	7	8	9	10	11	12	13
	14	15	16	17	18	19	20
	21	22	23	24	25	26	27
MĀRGAŚIRA 1860	28	29	30	1	2	3	4
	5	6	7	8	9	10	11
	12	13	14	15	16	17	18
	19	20	21	22	23	24	25
PAUSHA 1860	26	27	28	29	1	2	3
	4	5	6	7	8	9	10
	11	12	13	14	15	16	17

[a]New Year (Vikṛita)
[b]Pongal

ISLAMIC (ASTRONOMICAL) 1356/1357‡

Month	Sun	Mon	Tue	Wed	Thu	Fri	Sat
SHAWWĀL 1356	23	24	25	26	27	28	29
DHU AL-QA'DA 1356	30	*1*	2	3	4	5	6
	7	8	9	10	11	12	13
	14	15	16	17	18	19	20
	21	22	23	24	25	26	27
DHU AL-ḤIJJA 1356	28	29	30	*1*	2	3	4
	5	6	7	8	9	10[g]	11
	12	13	14	15	16	17	18
	19	20	21	22	23	24	25
MUḤARRAM 1357	26	27	28	29	*1*[a]	2	3
	4	5	6	7	8	9	10[b]
	11	12	13	14	15	16	17
	18	19	20	21	22	23	24
ṢAFAR 1357	25	26	27	28	29	30	*1*
	2	3	4	5	6	7	8
	9	10	11	12	13	14	15
	16	17	18	19	20	21	22
	23	24	25	26	27	28	29
RABĪ' I 1357	*1*	2	3	4	5	6	7
	8	9	10	11	12[c]	13	14
	15	16	17	18	19	20	21
	22	23	24	25	26	27	28
RABĪ' II 1357	29	30	*1*	2	3	4	5
	6	7	8	9	10	11	12
	13	14	15	16	17	18	19
	20	21	22	23	24	25	26
JUMĀDĀ I 1357	27	28	29	*1*	2	3	4
	5	6	7	8	9	10	11
	12	13	14	15	16	17	18
	19	20	21	22	23	24	25
JUMĀDĀ II 1357	26	27	28	29	30	*1*	2
	3	4	5	6	7	8	9
	10	11	12	13	14	15	16
	17	18	19	20	21	22	23
RAJAB 1357	24	25	26	27	28	29	*1*
	2	3	4	5	6	7	8
	9	10	11	12	13	14	15
	16	17	18	19	20	21	22
	23	24	25	26	27[d]	28	29
SHA'BĀN 1357	30	*1*	2	3	4	5	6
	7	8	9	10	11	12	13
	14	15	16	17	18	19	20
	21	22	23	24	25	26	27
RAMAḌĀN 1357	28	29	*1*[e]	2	3	4	5
	6	7	8	9	10	11	12
	13	14	15	16	17	18	19
	20	21	22	23	24	25	26
SHAWWĀL 1357	27	28	29	*1*[f]	2	3	4
	5	6	7	8	9	10	11
	12	13	14	15	16	17	18
	19	20	21	22	23	24	25
DHU AL-QA'DA 1357	26	27	28	29	30	*1*	2
	3	4	5	6	7	8	9

‡Leap year
[a]New Year
[b]'Ashūrā'
[c]Prophet's Birthday
[d]Ascent of the Prophet
[e]Start of Ramaḍān
[f]'Id al-Fiṭr
[g]'Id al-'Aḍḥā

GREGORIAN 1938

Month	Julian (Sun)	Sun	Mon	Tue	Wed	Thu	Fri	Sat
JANUARY 1938	Dec 13	*26*	27	28	29	30	31	1
		2	3	4	5	6	7[a]	8
	Dec 27	*9*	10	11	12	13	14[b]	15
		16	17	18	19	20	21	22
	Jan 10	*23*	24	25	26	27	28	29
FEBRUARY 1938		30	31	1	2	3	4	5
	Jan 24	*6*	7	8	9	10	11	12
		13	14	15	16	17	18	19
	Feb 7	*20*	21	22	23	24	25	26
MARCH 1938		27	28	1	2[c]	3	4	5
	Feb 21	*6*	7	8	9	10	11	12
		13[d]	14	15	16	17	18	19
	Mar 7	*20*	21	22	23	24	25	26
APRIL 1938		27	28	29	30	31	1	2
	Mar 21	*3*	4	5	6	7	8	9
		10	11	12	13	14	15	16
	Apr 4	*17*[e]	18	19	20	21	22	23
		24[f]	25	26	27	28	29	30
MAY 1938	Apr 18	*1*	2	3	4	5	6	7
		8	9	10	11	12	13	14
	May 2	*15*	16	17	18	19	20	21
		22	23	24	25	26	27	28
JUNE 1938	May 16	*29*	30	31	1	2	3	4
		5	6	7	8	9	10	11
	May 30	*12*	13	14	15	16	17	18
		19	20	21	22	23	24	25
JULY 1938	Jun 13	*26*	27	28	29	30	1	2
		3	4	5	6	7	8	9
	Jun 27	*10*	11	12	13	14	15	16
		17	18	19	20	21	22	23
	Jul 11	*24*	25	26	27	28	29	30
AUGUST 1938		31	1	2	3	4	5	6
	Jul 25	*7*	8	9	10	11	12	13
		14	15	16	17	18	19	20
	Aug 8	*21*	22	23	24	25	26	27
SEPTEMBER 1938		28	29	30	31	1	2	3
	Aug 22	*4*	5	6	7	8	9	10
		11	12	13	14	15	16	17
	Sep 5	*18*	19	20	21	22	23	24
OCTOBER 1938		25	26	27	28	29	30	1
	Sep 19	*2*	3	4	5	6	7	8
		9	10	11	12	13	14	15
	Oct 3	*16*	17	18	19	20	21	22
		23	24	25	26	27	28	29
NOVEMBER 1938	Oct 17	*30*	31	1	2	3	4	5
		6	7	8	9	10	11	12
	Oct 31	*13*	14	15	16	17	18	19
		20	21	22	23	24	25	26
DECEMBER 1938	Nov 14	27[g]	28	29	30	1	2	3
		4	5	6	7	8	9	10
	Nov 28	*11*	12	13	14	15	16	17
		18	19	20	21	22	23	24
	Dec 12	25[h]	26	27	28	29	30	31

[a]Orthodox Christmas
[b]Julian New Year
[c]Ash Wednesday
[d]Feast of Orthodoxy
[e]Easter
[f]Orthodox Easter
[g]Advent
[h]Christmas

1939

Month	Sun	Mon	Tue	Wed	Thu	Fri	Sat	Lunar Phases	ISO WEEK (Mon)	JULIAN DAY (Sun noon)
	1[a]	2	3	4	○	6	7	21:30	1	2429265
JANUARY 1939	8	9	10	11	◑	13	14	13:10	2	2429272
	15	16	17	18	19	●	21	13:27	3	2429279
	22	23	24	25	26	27	◐	14:59	4	2429286
	29	30	31	1	2	3	○	7:54	5	2429293
FEBRUARY 1939	5	6	7	8	9	10	◑	4:12	6	2429300
	12	13	14	15	16	17	18		7	2429307
	●	20	21	22	23	24	25	8:28	8	2429314
	26	◐	28	1	2	3	4	3:26	9	2429321
	○	6	7	8	9	10	11	18:00	10	2429328
MARCH 1939	◑	13	14	15	16	17	18	21:37	11	2429335
	19	20	●[b]	22	23	24	25	1:49	12	2429342
	26	27	◐	29	30	31	1	12:15	13	2429349
	2	3	○	5	6	7	8	4:18	14	2429356
APRIL 1939	9	10	◑	12	13	14	15	16:11	15	2429363
	16	17	18	●	20	21	22	16:35	16	2429370
	23	24	25	◐	27	28	29	18:25	17	2429377
	30	1	2	○	4	5	6	15:15	18	2429384
	7	8	9	10	◑	12	13	10:40	19	2429391
MAY 1939	14	15	16	17	18	●	20	4:25	20	2429398
	21	22	23	24	◐	26	27	23:20	21	2429405
	28	29	30	31	1	○	3	3:11	22	2429412
	4	5	6	7	8	9	◑	4:07	23	2429419
JUNE 1939	11	12	13	14	15	16	●	13:37	24	2429426
	18	19	20	21	22[c]	23	◐	4:35	25	2429433
	25	26	27	28	29	30	○	16:16	26	2429440
	2	3	4	5	6	7	8		27	2429447
JULY 1939	◑	10	11	12	13	14	15	19:49	28	2429454
	●	17	18	19	20	21	22	21:03	29	2429461
	◐	24	25	26	27	28	29	11:34	30	2429468
	30	○	1	2	3	4	5	6:37	31	2429475
	6	7	◑	9	10	11	12	9:18	32	2429482
AUGUST 1939	13	14	●	16	17	18	19	3:53	33	2429489
	20	◐	22	23	24	25	26	21:21	34	2429496
	27	28	○	30	31	1	2	22:09	35	2429503
	3	4	5	◑	7	8	9	20:24	36	2429510
SEPTEMBER 1939	10	11	12	●	14	15	16	11:22	37	2429517
	17	18	19	◐	21	22	23[d]	10:34	38	2429524
	24	25	26	27	○	29	30	14:27	39	2429531
	1	2	3	4	5	◑	7	5:27	40	2429538
OCTOBER 1939	8	9	10	11	●	13	14	20:30	41	2429545
	15	16	17	18	19	◐	21	3:24	42	2429552
	22	23	24	25	26	27	○	6:42	43	2429559
	29	30	31	1	2	3	◑	13:12	44	2429566
	5	6	7	8	9	10	●	7:54	45	2429573
NOVEMBER 1939	12	13	14	15	16	17	◐	23:21	46	2429580
	19	20	21	22	23	24	25		47	2429587
	○	27	28	29	30	1	2	21:54	48	2429594
	◑	4	5	6	7	8	9	20:40	49	2429601
DECEMBER 1939	●	11	12	13	14	15	16	21:46	50	2429608
	17	◐	19	20	21	22[e]	23	21:04	51	2429615
	24	25	○	27	28	29	30	11:28	52	2429622
	31	1	◑	3	4	5	6	4:56	1	2429629

JULIAN DAY	HEBREW 5699/5700‡ Month	Sun	Mon	Tue	Wed	Thu	Fri	Sat	Molad	CHINESE Wù-Yín‡/Jǐ-Mǎo Month	Sun	Mon	Tue	Wed	Thu	Fri	Sat	Solar Term
2429265		10	11	12	13	14	15	16			11	12	13	14	15	16	17	Xiǎo hán
2429272	TEVETH 5699	17	18	19	20	21	22	23		MONTH 11* Wù-Yín	18	19	20	21	22	23	24	
2429279		24	25	26	27	28	29	1	Fri 17h2m15p		25	26	27	28	29	1	2	Dà hán
2429286		2	3	4	5	6	7	8			3	4	5	6	7	8*	9	
2429293	SHEVAT 5699	9	10	11	12	13	14	15		MONTH 12 Wù-Yín	10	11	12	13	14	15	16	
2429300		16	17	18	19	20	21	22			17	18	19	20	21	22	23	Lì chūn
2429307		23	24	25	26	27	28	29			24	25	26	27	28	29	30	
2429314		30	1	2	3	4	5	6	Sun 5h46m16p		1[a]	2	3	4	5	6	7	Yǔ shuǐ
2429321		7	8	9	10	11	12	13			8	9	10	11	12	13	14	
2429328	ADAR 5699	14[f]	15	16	17	18	19	20		MONTH 1 Jǐ-Mǎo	15[b]	16	17	18	19	20	21	Jīng zhé
2429335		21	22	23	24	25	26	27			22	23	24	25	26	27	28	
2429342		28	29	1	2	3	4	5	Mon 18h30m17p		29	30	1	2	3	4	5	Chūn fēn
2429349		6	7	8	9	10	11	12			6	7	8*	9	10	11	12	
2429356	NISAN 5699	13	14	15[g]	16	17	18	19		MONTH 2 Jǐ-Mǎo	13	14	15	16	17[c]	18	19	Qīng míng
2429363		20	21	22	23	24	25	26			20	21	22	23	24	25	26	
2429370		27	28	29	30	1	2	3	Wed 7h15m0p		27	28	29	30	1	2	3	Gǔ yǔ
2429377		4	5	6	7	8	9	10			4	5	6	7	8	9	10	
2429384	IYYAR 5699	11	12	13	14	15	16	17		MONTH 3 Jǐ-Mǎo	11	12	13	14	15	16	17	Lì xià
2429391		18	19	20	21	22	23	24			18	19	20	21	22	23	24	
2429398		25	26	27	28	29	1	2	Thu 19h59m1p		25	26	27	28	29	1	2	
2429405		3	4	5	6[h]	7	8	9			3	4	5	6	7	8	9*	Xiǎo mǎn
2429412	SIVAN 5699	10	11	12	13	14	15	16		MONTH 4 Jǐ-Mǎo	10	11	12	13	14	15	16	
2429419		17	18	19	20	21	22	23			17	18	19	20	21	22	23	Máng zhòng
2429426		24	25	26	27	28	29	30			24	25	26	27	28	29	1	
2429433		1	2	3	4	5	6	7	Sat 8h43m2p		2	3	4	5[d]	6	7	8	Xià zhì
2429440		8	9	10	11	12	13	14		MONTH 5 Jǐ-Mǎo	9	10	11	12	13	14	15	
2429447	TAMMUZ 5699	15	16	17	18	19	20	21			16	17	18	19	20	21	22	Xiǎo shǔ
2429454		22	23	24	25	26	27	28			23	24	25	26	27	28	29	
2429461		29	1	2	3	4	5	6	Sun 21h27m3p		30	1	2	3	4	5	6	
2429468		7	8	9[i]	10	11	12	13			7	8	9	10*	11	12	13	Dà shǔ
2429475	AV 5699	14	15	16	17	18	19	20		MONTH 6 Jǐ-Mǎo	14	15	16	17	18	19	20	
2429482		21	22	23	24	25	26	27			21	22	23	24	25	26	27	Lì qiū
2429489		28	29	30	1	2	3	4	Tue 10h11m4p		28	29	1	2	3	4	5	
2429496		5	6	7	8	9	10	11			6	7[e]	8	9	10	11	12	Chǔ shǔ
2429503	ELUL 5699	12	13	14	15	16	17	18		MONTH 7 Jǐ-Mǎo	13	14	15[f]	16	17	18	19	
2429510		19	20	21	22	23	24	25			20	21	22	23	24	25	26	Bái lù
2429517		26	27	28	29	1[a]	2[a]	3	Wed 22h55m5p		27	28	29	1	2	3	4	
2429524		4	5	6	7	8	9	10[b]			5	6	7	8	9	10	11	
2429531	TISHRI 5700	11	12	13	14	15[c]	16	17		MONTH 8 Jǐ-Mǎo	12*	13	14	15[g]	16	17	18	Qiū fēn
2429538		18	19	20	21	22	23	24			19	20	21	22	23	24	25	
2429545		25	26	27	28	29	30	1	Fri 11h39m6p		26	27	28	29	30	1	2	Hán lù
2429552		2	3	4	5	6	7	8			3	4	5	6	7	8	9[h]	
2429559	HESHVAN 5700	9	10	11	12	13	14	15		MONTH 9 Jǐ-Mǎo	10	11	12	13	14	15	16	Shuāng jiàng
2429566		16	17	18	19	20	21	22			17	18	19	20	21	22	23	
2429573		23	24	25	26	27	28	29			24	25	26	27	28	29	1	Lì dōng
2429580		30	1	2	3	4	5	6	Sun 0h23m7p		2	3	4	5	6	7	8	
2429587	KISLEV 5700	7	8	9	10	11	12	13		MONTH 10 Jǐ-Mǎo	9	10	11	12	13*	14	15	Xiǎo xuě
2429594		14	15	16	17	18	19	20			16	17	18	19	20	21	22	
2429601		21	22	23	24[d]	25[e]	26[e]	27[e]			23	24	25	26	27	28	29	Dà xuě
2429608		28[e]	29[e]	30[e]	1[e]	2[e]	3	4	Mon 13h7m8p		30	1	2	3	4	5	6	
2429615	TEVETH 5700	5	6	7	8	9	10	11		MONTH 11 Jǐ-Mǎo	7	8	9	10	11	12	13[i]	Dōng zhì
2429622		12	13	14	15	16	17	18			14	15	16	17	18	19	20	
2429629		19	20	21	22	23	24	25			21	22	23	24	25	26	27	Xiǎo hán

JULIAN DAY	COPTIC 1655‡/1656 Month	Sun	Mon	Tue	Wed	Thu	Fri	Sat	ETHIOPIC 1931‡/1932 Month
2429265	KOIAK 1655	23	24	25	26	27	28	29[c]	TĀKHŚĀŚ 1931
2429272		30	1	2	3	4	5	6[d]	
2429279		7	8	9	10	11[e]	12	13	
2429286	TŌBE 1655	14	15	16	17	18	19	20	ṬER 1931
2429293		21	22	23	24	25	26	27	
2429300		28	29	30	1	2	3	4	
2429307		5	6	7	8	9	10	11	
2429314	MESHIR 1655	12	13	14	15	16	17	18	YAKĀTIT 1931
2429321		19	20	21	22	23	24	25	
2429328		26	27	28	29	30	1	2	
2429335		3	4	5	6	7	8	9	
2429342	PAREMOTEP 1655	10	11	12	13	14	15	16	MAGĀBIT 1931
2429349		17	18	19	20	21	22	23	
2429356		24	25	26	27	28	29	30	
2429363		1[f]	2	3	4	5	6	7	
2429370	PARMOUTE 1655	8	9	10	11	12	13	14	MIYĀZYĀ 1931
2429377		15	16	17	18	19	20	21	
2429384		22	23	24	25	26	27	28	
2429391		29[g]	30	1	2	3	4	5	
2429398	PASHONS 1655	6	7	8	9	10	11	12	GENBOT 1931
2429405		13	14	15	16	17	18	19	
2429412		20	21	22	23	24	25	26	
2429419		27	28	29	30	1	2	3	
2429426	PAŌNE 1655	4	5	6	7	8	9	10	SANĒ 1931
2429433		11	12	13	14	15	16	17	
2429440		18	19	20	21	22	23	24	
2429447		25	26	27	28	29	30	1	
2429454		2	3	4	5	6	7	8	
2429461	EPĒP 1655	9	10	11	12	13	14	15	HAMLĒ 1931
2429468		16	17	18	19	20	21	22	
2429475		23	24	25	26	27	28	29	
2429482		30	1	2	3	4	5	6	
2429489	MESORĒ 1655	7	8	9	10	11	12	13[h]	NAHASĒ 1931
2429496		14	15	16	17	18	19	20	
2429503		21	22	23	24	25	26	27	
2429510	EPAG. 1655	28	29	30	1	2	3	4	PĀG. 1931
2429517		5	6	1[a]	2	3	4	5	
2429524	THOOUT 1656	6	7	8	9	10	11	12	MASKARAM 1932
2429531		13	14	15	16	17[b]	18	19	
2429538		20	21	22	23	24	25	26	
2429545		27	28	29	30	1	2	3	
2429552	PAOPE 1656	4	5	6	7	8	9	10	ṬEQEMT 1932
2429559		11	12	13	14	15	16	17	
2429566		18	19	20	21	22	23	24	
2429573		25	26	27	28	29	30	1	
2429580		2	3	4	5	6	7	8	
2429587	ATHŌR 1656	9	10	11	12	13	14	15	HEDĀR 1932
2429594		16	17	18	19	20	21	22	
2429601		23	24	25	26	27	28	29	
2429608		30	1	2	3	4	5	6	
2429615	KOIAK 1656	7	8	9	10	11	12	13	TĀKHŚĀŚ 1932
2429622		14	15	16	17	18	19	20	
2429629		21	22	23	24	25	26	27	

Gregorian notes:
[a]New Year
[b]Spring (12:28)
[c]Summer (7:39)
[d]Autumn (22:49)
[e]Winter (18:05)
● New moon
◐ First quarter moon
○ Full moon
◑ Last quarter moon

Hebrew notes:
‡Leap year
[a]New Year
[b]Yom Kippur
[c]Sukkot
[d]Winter starts
[e]Ḥanukkah
[f]Purim
[g]Passover
[h]Shavuot
[i]Fast of Av

Chinese notes:
‡Leap year
[a]New Year (4637, Hare)
[b]Lantern Festival
[c]Qīngmíng
[d]Dragon Festival
[e]Qīqiǎo
[f]Hungry Ghosts
[g]Mid-Autumn Festival
[h]Double-Ninth Festival
[i]Dōngzhì
*Start of 60-name cycle

Coptic/Ethiopic notes:
‡Leap year
[a]New Year
[b]Building of the Cross
[c]Christmas
[d]Jesus's Circumcision
[e]Epiphany
[f]Easter
[g]Mary's Announcement
[h]Jesus's Transfiguration

PERSIAN (ASTRONOMICAL) 1317‡/1318

Month	Sun	Mon	Tue	Wed	Thu	Fri	Sat
DEY 1317	11	12	13	14	15	16	17
	18	19	20	21	22	23	24
BAHMAN 1317	25	26	27	28	29	30	1
	2	3	4	5	6	7	8
	9	10	11	12	13	14	15
	16	17	18	19	20	21	22
	23	24	25	26	27	28	29
ESFAND 1317	30	1	2	3	4	5	6
	7	8	9	10	11	12	13
	14	15	16	17	18	19	20
	21	22	23	24	25	26	27
FARVARDIN 1318	28	29	30	1[a]	2	3	4
	5	6	7	8	9	10	11
	12	13[b]	14	15	16	17	18
	19	20	21	22	23	24	25
ORDIBEHEŠT 1318	26	27	28	29	30	31	1
	2	3	4	5	6	7	8
	9	10	11	12	13	14	15
	16	17	18	19	20	21	22
	23	24	25	26	27	28	29
XORDĀD 1318	30	31	1	2	3	4	5
	6	7	8	9	10	11	12
	13	14	15	16	17	18	19
	20	21	22	23	24	25	26
TĪR 1318	27	28	29	30	31	1	2
	3	4	5	6	7	8	9
	10	11	12	13	14	15	16
	17	18	19	20	21	22	23
	24	25	26	27	28	29	30
MORDĀD 1318	31	1	2	3	4	5	6
	7	8	9	10	11	12	13
	14	15	16	17	18	19	20
	21	22	23	24	25	26	27
SHAHRĪVAR 1318	28	29	30	31	1	2	3
	4	5	6	7	8	9	10
	11	12	13	14	15	16	17
	18	19	20	21	22	23	24
	25	26	27	28	29	30	31
MEHR 1318	1	2	3	4	5	6	7
	8	9	10	11	12	13	14
	15	16	17	18	19	20	21
	22	23	24	25	26	27	28
ABĀN 1318	29	30	1	2	3	4	5
	6	7	8	9	10	11	12
	13	14	15	16	17	18	19
	20	21	22	23	24	25	26
ĀZAR 1318	27	28	29	30	1	2	3
	4	5	6	7	8	9	10
	11	12	13	14	15	16	17
	18	19	20	21	22	23	24
DEY 1318	25	26	27	28	29	30	1
	2	3	4	5	6	7	8
	9	10	11	12	13	14	15

‡Leap year
[a]New Year
[b]Sizdeh Bedar

HINDU LUNAR 1995/1996‡

Month	Sun	Mon	Tue	Wed	Thu	Fri	Sat
PAUSHA 1995	10	11	12	**13**	15	16	17
	18	19	20	21	22	23	24
MĀGHA 1995	25	26	27	28	29	30	1
	2	3	4	5	6	7	8
	9	10	11	12	13	14	15
	16	17	**18**	20	21	22	23
	24	25	26	27	27	28[h]	29
PHĀLGUNA 1995	30	1	2	3	4	5	6
	7	8	9	10	11	**12**	14
	15[i]	16	17	18	19	20	21
	22	23	24	25	26	27	28
CHAITRA 1996	29	30	30	1[a]	2	3	4
	5	7	8	9[b]	10	11	12
	13	14	15	16	17	18	19
	20	21	22	23	24	25	26
VAISĀKHA 1996	27	28	29	30	1	2	3
	4	5	6	7	8	**9**	11
	12	13	14	15	16	17	18
	19	20	21	22	23	24	24
JYAISHTHA 1996	25	26	27	28	29	30	1
	2	4	5	6	7	8	9
	10	11	12	13	14	15	16
	17	18	19	20	21	22	23
	24	25	26	27	28	29	30
ĀSHĀDHA 1996	1	2	3	4	**5**	7	8
	9	10	11	12	13	14	15
	16	17	18	19	20	21	21
	22	23	24	25	26	27	**28**
LEAP ŚRĀVAṆA 1996	30	1	2	3	4	5	6
	7	8	9	10	11	12	13
	14	15	16	17	18	19	20
	21	22	23	24	25	26	27
ŚRĀVAṆA 1996	28	29	30	**1**	3	4	5
	6	7	8	9	10	11	12
	13	14	15	16	17	17	18
	19	20	21	22	23[c]	**24**	26
BHĀDRAPADA 1996	27	28	29	30	1	2	3[d]
	4	5	6	7	8	9	10
	11	12	13	14	15	16	17
	18	19	20	21	22	23	24
ĀŚVINA 1996	25	26	27	**28**	30	1	2
	3	4	5	6	7	8[e]	9[e]
	10[e]	11	12	12	13	14	15
	16	17	18	19	20	**21**	23
	24	25	26	27	28	29	30
KĀRTTIKA 1996	1[f]	2	3	4	5	6	7
	8	9	10	11	12	13	14
	15	16	17	18	19	20	21
	22	23	24	25	**26**	28	29
MĀRGAŚĪRA 1996	30	1	2	3	4	5	5
	6	7	8	9	10	11[g]	12
	13	14	15	16	17	18	19
	20	22	23	24	25	26	27

‡Leap year
[a]New Year (Pramāthin)
[b]Birthday of Rāma
[c]Birthday of Krishna
[d]Ganēśa Chaturthī
[e]Dashara
[f]Diwali
[g]Birthday of Vishnu
[h]Night of Śiva
[i]Holi

HINDU SOLAR 1860/1861

Month	Sun	Mon	Tue	Wed	Thu	Fri	Sat
PAUSHA 1860	18	19	20	21	22	23	24
	25	26	27	28	29	30	1[b]
MĀGHA 1860	2	3	4	5	6	7	8
	9	10	11	12	13	14	15
	16	17	18	19	20	21	22
	23	24	25	26	27	28	29
PHĀLGUNA 1860	1	2	3	4	5	6	7
	8	9	10	11	12	13	14
	15	16	17	18	19	20	21
	22	23	24	25	26	27	28
CHAITRA 1860	29	30	1	2	3	4	5
	6	7	8	9	10	11	12
	13	14	15	16	17	18	19
	20	21	22	23	24	25	26
VAIŚĀKHA 1861	27	28	29	30	1[a]	2	3
	4	5	6	7	8	9	10
	11	12	13	14	15	16	17
	18	19	20	21	22	23	24
	25	26	27	28	29	30	31
JYAISHTHA 1861	1	2	3	4	5	6	7
	8	9	10	11	12	13	14
	15	16	17	18	19	20	21
	22	23	24	25	26	27	28
ĀSHĀDHA 1861	29	30	31	32	1	2	3
	4	5	6	7	8	9	10
	11	12	13	14	15	16	17
	18	19	20	21	22	23	24
	25	26	27	28	29	30	31
ŚRĀVAṆA 1861	1	2	3	4	5	6	7
	8	9	10	11	12	13	14
	15	16	17	18	19	20	21
	22	23	24	25	26	27	28
BHĀDRAPADA 1861	29	30	31	32	1	2	3
	4	5	6	7	8	9	10
	11	12	13	14	15	16	17
	18	19	20	21	22	23	24
	25	26	27	28	29	30	31
ĀŚVINA 1861	1	2	3	4	5	6	7
	8	9	10	11	12	13	14
	15	16	17	18	19	20	21
	22	23	24	25	26	27	28
KĀRTTIKA 1861	29	30	1	2	3	4	5
	6	7	8	9	10	11	12
	13	14	15	16	17	18	19
	20	21	22	23	24	25	26
MĀRGAŚĪRA 1861	27	28	29	30	1	2	3
	4	5	6	7	8	9	10
	11	12	13	14	15	16	17
	18	19	20	21	22	23	24
PAUSHA 1861	25	26	27	28	29	1	2
	3	4	5	6	7	8	9
	10	11	12	13	14	15	16
	17	18	19	20	21	22	23

[a]New Year (Khara)
[b]Pongal

ISLAMIC (ASTRONOMICAL) 1357‡/1358

Month	Sun	Mon	Tue	Wed	Thu	Fri	Sat
DHU AL-QA'DA 1357	10	11	12	13	14	15	16
	17	18	19	20	21	22	23
	24	25	26	27	28	29	30
DHU AL-ḤIJJA 1357	1	2	3	4	5	6	7
	8	9	10[g]	11	12	13	14
	15	16	17	18	19	20	21
	22	23	24	25	26	27	28
MUḤARRAM 1358	29	30	1[a]	2	3	4	5
	6	7	8	9	10[b]	11	12
	13	14	15	16	17	18	19
	20	21	22	23	24	25	26
ṢAFAR 1358	27	28	29	1	2	3	4
	5	6	7	8	9	10	11
	12	13	14	15	16	17	18
	19	20	21	22	23	24	25
RABĪ' I 1358	26	27	28	29	30	1	2
	3	4	5	6	7	8	9
	10	11	12[c]	13	14	15	16
	17	18	19	20	21	22	23
RABĪ' II 1358	24	25	26	27	28	29	1
	2	3	4	5	6	7	8
	9	10	11	12	13	14	15
	16	17	18	19	20	21	22
	23	24	25	26	27	28	29
JUMĀDĀ I 1358	30	1	2	3	4	5	6
	7	8	9	10	11	12	13
	14	15	16	17	18	19	20
	21	22	23	24	25	26	27
JUMĀDĀ II 1358	28	29	30	1	2	3	4
	5	6	7	8	9	10	11
	12	13	14	15	16	17	18
	19	20	21	22	23	24	25
RAJAB 1358	26	27	28	29	1	2	3
	4	5	6	7	8	9	10
	11	12	13	14	15	16	17
	18	19	20	21	22	23	24
SHA'BĀN 1358	25	26	27[d]	28	29	1	2
	3	4	5	6	7	8	9
	10	11	12	13	14	15	16
	17	18	19	20	21	22	23
RAMAḌĀN 1358	24	25	26	27	28	29	1[e]
	2	3	4	5	6	7	8
	9	10	11	12	13	14	15
	16	17	18	19	20	21	22
	23	24	25	26	27	28	29
SHAWWĀL 1358	30	1[f]	2	3	4	5	6
	7	8	9	10	11	12	13
	14	15	16	17	18	19	20
	21	22	23	24	25	26	27
DHU AL-QA'DA 1358	28	29	1	2	3	4	5
	6	7	8	9	10	11	12
	13	14	15	16	17	18	19
	20	21	22	23	24	25	26

‡Leap year
[a]New Year
[b]'Ashūrā'
[c]Prophet's Birthday
[d]Ascent of the Prophet
[e]Start of Ramaḍān
[f]'Id al-Fiṭr
[g]'Id al-'Aḍḥā

GREGORIAN 1939

Julian (Sun)	Sun	Mon	Tue	Wed	Thu	Fri	Sat	Month
Dec 19	1	2	3	4	5	6	7[a]	JANUARY 1939
	8	9	10	11	12	13	14[b]	
Jan 2	15	16	17	18	19	20	21	
	22	23	24	25	26	27	28	
Jan 16	29	30	31	1	2	3	4	FEBRUARY 1939
	5	6	7	8	9	10	11	
Jan 30	12	13	14	15	16	17	18	
	19	20	21	22[c]	23	24	25	
Feb 13	26[d]	27	28	1	2	3	4	MARCH 1939
	5	6	7	8	9	10	11	
Feb 27	12	13	14	15	16	17	18	
	19	20	21	22	23	24	25	
Mar 13	26	27	28	29	30	31	1	APRIL 1939
	2	3	4	5	6	7	8	
Mar 27	9[e]	10	11	12	13	14	15	
	16	17	18	19	20	21	22	
Apr 10	23	24	25	26	27	28	29	
	30	1	2	3	4	5	6	MAY 1939
Apr 24	7	8	9	10	11	12	13	
	14	15	16	17	18	19	20	
May 8	21	22	23	24	25	26	27	
	28	29	30	31	1	2	3	JUNE 1939
May 22	4	5	6	7	8	9	10	
	11	12	13	14	15	16	17	
Jun 5	18	19	20	21	22	23	24	
	25	26	27	28	29	30	1	JULY 1939
Jun 19	2	3	4	5	6	7	8	
	9	10	11	12	13	14	15	
Jul 3	16	17	18	19	20	21	22	
	23	24	25	26	27	28	29	
Jul 17	30	31	1	2	3	4	5	AUGUST 1939
	6	7	8	9	10	11	12	
Jul 31	13	14	15	16	17	18	19	
	20	21	22	23	24	25	26	
Aug 14	27	28	29	30	31	1	2	SEPTEMBER 1939
	3	4	5	6	7	8	9	
Aug 28	10	11	12	13	14	15	16	
	17	18	19	20	21	22	23	
Sep 11	24	25	26	27	28	29	30	
	1	2	3	4	5	6	7	OCTOBER 1939
Sep 25	8	9	10	11	12	13	14	
	15	16	17	18	19	20	21	
Oct 9	22	23	24	25	26	27	28	
	29	30	31	1	2	3	4	NOVEMBER 1939
Oct 23	5	6	7	8	9	10	11	
	12	13	14	15	16	17	18	
Nov 6	19	20	21	22	23	24	25	
	26	27	28	29	30	1	2	DECEMBER 1939
Nov 20	3[g]	4	5	6	7	8	9	
	10	11	12	13	14	15	16	
Dec 4	17	18	19	20	21	22	23	
	24	25[h]	26	27	28	29	30	
Dec 18	31	1	2	3	4	5	6	

[a]Orthodox Christmas
[b]Julian New Year
[c]Ash Wednesday
[d]Feast of Orthodoxy
[e]Easter (also Orthodox)
[g]Advent
[h]Christmas

1940

Gregorian month	GREGORIAN 1940‡ Sun	Mon	Tue	Wed	Thu	Fri	Sat	Lunar Phases	ISO WEEK (Mon)	JULIAN DAY (Sun noon)	Hebrew month	HEBREW 5700‡/5701 Sun	Mon	Tue	Wed	Thu	Fri	Sat	Molad	Chinese month	CHINESE Jǐ-Mǎo/Gēng-Chén Sun	Mon	Tue	Wed	Thu	Fri	Sat	Solar Term	Coptic month	COPTIC 1656/1657 / ETHIOPIC 1932/1933 Sun	Mon	Tue	Wed	Thu	Fri	Sat	Ethiopic month
JANUARY 1940	31	1[a]	◑	3	4	5	6	4:56	1	2429629	TEVETH 5700	19	20	21	22	23	24	25		MONTH 11 Jǐ-Mǎo	21	22	23	24	25	26	27	Xiǎo hán	KOIAK 1656	21	22	23	24	25	26	27	TĀKHŚĀŚ 1932
	7	8	●	10	11	12	13	13:53	2	2429636		26	27	28	29	1	2	3	Wed $1^{h}51^{m}9^{p}$	MONTH 12 Jǐ-Mǎo	28	29	1	2	3	4	5		TŌBE 1656	28	29[c]	30	1	2	3	4	TER 1932
	14	15	16	◐	18	19	20	18:21	3	2429643	SHEVAT 5700	4	5	6	7	8	9	10			6	7	8	9	10	11	12			5	6[d]	7	8	9	10	11[e]	
	21	22	23	○	25	26	27	23:22	4	2429650		11	12	13	14	15	16	17			13	14*	15	16	17	18	19	Dà hán		12	13	14	15	16	17	18	
	28	29	30	◑	1	2	3	14:47	5	2429657		18	19	20	21	22	23	24			20	21	22	23	24	25	26			19	20	21	22	23	24	25	
FEBRUARY 1940	4	5	6	7	●	9	10	7:45	6	2429664	ADAR I 5700	25	26	27	28	29	30	1	Thu $14^{h}35^{m}10^{p}$	MONTH 1 Gēng-Chén	27	28	29	30	1[a]	2	3	Lì chūn	MESHIR 1656	26	27	28	29	30	1	2	YAKĀTIT 1932
	11	12	13	14	15	◐	17	12:55	7	2429671		2	3	4	5	6	7	8			4	5	6	7	8	9	10			3	4	5	6	7	8	9	
	18	19	20	21	22	○	24	9:55	8	2429678		9	10	11	12	13	14	15			11	12	13	14	15[b]	16	17	Yǔ shuǐ		10	11	12	13	14	15	16	
	25	26	27	28	29	◑	2	2:35	9	2429685		16	17	18	19	20	21	22			18	19	20	21	22	23	24			17	18	19	20	21	22	23	
MARCH 1940	3	4	5	6	7	8	●	2:23	10	2429692		23	24	25	26	27	28	29	Sat $3^{h}19^{m}11^{p}$	MONTH 2 Gēng-Chén	25	26	27	28	29	30	1	Jīng zhé		24	25	26	27	28	29	30	
	10	11	12	13	14	15	16		11	2429699	ADAR II 5700	30	1	2	3	4	5	6			2	3	4	5	6	7	8		PAREMOTEP 1656	1	2	3	4	5	6	7	MAGĀBIT 1932
	◐	18	19	20[b]	21	22	○	3:25 19:33	12	2429706		7	8	9	10	11	12	13			9	10	11	12	13	14*	15	Chūn fēn		8	9	10	11	12	13	14	
	24	25	26	27	28	29	◑	16:20	13	2429713		14[f]	15	16	17	18	19	20			16	17	18	19	20	21	22			15	16	17	18	19	20	21	
	31	1	2	3	4	5	6		14	2429720		21	22	23	24	25	26	27			23	24	25	26	27	28[c]	29	Qīng míng		22	23	24	25	26	27	28	
APRIL 1940	●	8	9	10	11	12	13	20:18	15	2429727	NISAN 5700	28	29	1	2	3	4	5	Sun $16^{h}3^{m}12^{p}$	MONTH 3 Gēng-Chén	30	1	2	3	4	5	6		PARMOUTE 1656	29	30	1	2	3	4	5	MIYĀZYĀ 1932
	14	◐	16	17	18	19	20	13:45	16	2429734		6	7	8	9	10	11	12			7	8	9	10	11	12	13	Gǔ yǔ		6	7	8	9	10	11	12	
	21	○	23	24	25	26	27	4:37	17	2429741		13	14	15[g]	16	17	18	19			14	15	16	17	18	19	20			13	14	15	16	17	18	19	
	28	◑	30	1	2	3	4	7:49	18	2429748		20	21	22	23	24	25	26			21	22	23	24	25	26	27			20[f]	21	22	23	24	25	26	
MAY 1940	5	6	●	8	9	10	11	12:07	19	2429755	IYAR 5700	27	28	29	30	1	2	3	Tue $4^{h}47^{m}13^{p}$	MONTH 4 Gēng-Chén	28	29	1	2	3	4	5	Lì xià	PASHONS 1656	27	28	29[g]	30	1	2	3	GENBOT 1932
	12	13	◐	15	16	17	18	20:50	20	2429762		4	5	6	7	8	9	10			6	7	8	9	10	11	12			4	5	6	7	8	9	10	
	19	20	○	22	23	24	25	13:33	21	2429769		11	12	13	14	15	16	17			13	14	15*	16	17	18	19	Xiǎo mǎn		11	12	13	14	15	16	17	
	26	27	28	◑	30	31	1	0:40	22	2429776		18	19	20	21	22	23	24			20	21	22	23	24	25	26			18	19	20	21	22	23	24	
JUNE 1940	2	3	4	5	●	7	8	1:05	23	2429783	SIVAN 5700	25	26	27	28	29	1	2	Wed $17^{h}31^{m}14^{p}$	MONTH 5 Gēng-Chén	27	28	29	30	1	2	3	Máng zhòng	PAÔNE 1656	25	26	27	28	29	30	1	SANĒ 1932
	9	10	11	12	◐	14	15	1:59	24	2429790		3	4	5	6[h]	7	8	9			4	5[d]	6	7	8	9	10			2	3	4	5	6	7	8	
	16	17	18	○	20	21[c]	22	23:01	25	2429797		10	11	12	13	14	15	16			11	12	13	14	15	16	17	Xià zhì		9	10	11	12	13	14	15	
	23	24	25	26	◑	28	29	18:13	26	2429804		17	18	19	20	21	22	23			18	19	20	21	22	23	24			16	17	18	19	20	21	22	
	30	1	2	3	4	●	6	11:28	27	2429811		24	25	26	27	28	29	30	Fri $6^{h}15^{m}15^{p}$	MONTH 6 Gēng-Chén	25	26	27	28	29	1	2			23	24	25	26	27	28	29	
JULY 1940	7	8	9	10	11	◐	13	6:35	28	2429818	TAMMUZ 5700	1	2	3	4	5	6	7			3	4	5	6	7	8	9	Xiǎo shǔ	EPĒP 1656	30	1	2	3	4	5	6	HAMLĒ 1932
	14	15	16	17	18	○	20	9:55	29	2429825		8	9	10	11	12	13	14			10	11	12	13	14	15	16*			7	8	9	10	11	12	13	
	21	22	23	24	25	26	◑	11:29	30	2429832		15	16	17	18	19	20	21			17	18	19	20	21	22	23	Dà shǔ		14	15	16	17	18	19	20	
	28	29	30	31	1	2	●	20:09	31	2429839		22	23	24	25	26	27	28	Sat $18^{h}59^{m}16^{p}$		24	25	26	27	28	29	30			21	22	23	24	25	26	27	
AUGUST 1940	4	5	6	7	8	9	◐	12:00	32	2429846	AV 5700	29	1	2	3	4	5	6		MONTH 7 Gēng-Chén	1	2	3	4	5	6	7[e]	Lì qiū	MESORĒ 1656	28	29	30	1	2	3	4	NAHASĒ 1932
	11	12	13	14	15	16	○	23:02	33	2429853		7	8	9[i]	10	11	12	13			8	9	10	11	12	13	14			5	6	7	8	9	10	11	
	18	19	20	21	22	23	24		34	2429860		14	15	16	17	18	19	20			15[f]	16	17	18	19	20	21	Chǔ shǔ		12	13[h]	14	15	16	17	18	
	25	◑	27	28	29	30	31	3:33	35	2429867		21	22	23	24	25	26	27			22	23	24	25	26	27	28			19	20	21	22	23	24	25	
SEPTEMBER 1940	1	●	3	4	5	6	7	4:15	36	2429874	ELUL 5700	28	29	30	1	2	3	4	Mon $7^{h}43^{m}17^{p}$	MONTH 8 Gēng-Chén	29	1	2	3	4	5	6		EPAG. 1656	26	27	28	29	30	1	2	PĀG. 1932
	◐	9	10	11	12	13	14	19:32	37	2429881		5	6	7	8	9	10	11			7	8	9	10	11	12	13	Bái lù	THOOUT 1657	3	4	5	1[a]	2	3	4	MASKARAM 1933
	15	○	17	18	19	20	21	14:41	38	2429888		12	13	14	15	16	17	18			14	15[g]	16	17*	18	19	20			5	6	7	8	9	10	11	
	22	23[d]	◑	25	26	27	28	17:47	39	2429895		19	20	21	22	23	24	25			21	22	23	24	25	26	27	Qiū fēn		12	13	14	15	16	17[b]	18	
	29	30	●	2	3	4	5	12:41	40	2429902	TISHRI 5701	26	27	28	29	1[a]	2[a]	3	Tue $20^{h}28^{m}0^{p}$	MONTH 9 Gēng-Chén	28	29	1	2	3	4	5			19	20	21	22	23	24	25	
OCTOBER 1940	6	7	◐	9	10	11	12	6:18	41	2429909		4	5	6	7	8	9	10[b]			6	7	8	9[h]	10	11	12	Hán lù	PAOPE 1657	26	27	28	29	30	1	2	TEQEMT 1933
	13	14	15	○	17	18	19	8:15	42	2429916		11	12	13	14	15[c]	16	17			13	14	15	16	17	18	19			3	4	5	6	7	8	9	
	20	21	22	23	◑	25	26	6:04	43	2429923		18	19	20	21	22	23	24			20	21	22	23	24	25	26	Shuāng jiàng		10	11	12	13	14	15	16	
	27	28	29	●	31	1	2	22:03	44	2429930	ḤESHVAN 5701	25	26	27	28	29	30	1	Thu $9^{h}12^{m}1^{p}$	MONTH 10 Gēng-Chén	27	28	29	30	1	2	3			17	18	19	20	21	22	23	
NOVEMBER 1940	3	4	5	◐	7	8	9	21:08	45	2429937		2	3	4	5	6	7	8			4	5	6	7	8	9	10	Lì dōng		24	25	26	27	28	29	30	
	10	11	12	13	14	○	16	2:23	46	2429944		9	10	11	12	13	14	15			11	12	13	14	15	16	17		ATHŌR 1657	1	2	3	4	5	6	7	HEDĀR 1933
	17	18	19	20	21	◑	23	16:36	47	2429951		16	17	18	19	20	21	22			18*	19	20	21	22	23	24	Xiǎo xuě		8	9	10	11	12	13	14	
	24	25	26	27	28	●	30	8:42	48	2429958		23	24	25	26	27	28	29		MONTH 11 Gēng-Chén	25	26	27	28	29	1	2			15	16	17	18	19	20	21	
DECEMBER 1940	1	2	3	4	5	◐	7	16:01	49	2429965	KISLEV 5701	1	2	3	4	5[d]	6	7	Fri $21^{h}56^{m}2^{p}$		3	4	5	6	7	8	9	Dà xuě		22	23	24	25	26	27	28	
	8	9	10	11	12	13	○	19:37	50	2429972		8	9	10	11	12	13	14			10	11	12	13	14	15	16		KOIAK 1657	29	30	1	2	3	4	5	TĀKHŚĀŚ 1933
	15	16	17	18	19	20	21[e]		51	2429979		15	16	17	18	19	20	21			17	18	19	20	21	22	23			6	7	8	9	10	11	12	
	◑	23	24	25	26	27	●	1:45 20:56	52	2429986		22	23	24	25[e]	26[e]	27[e]	28[e]			24[i]	25	26	27	28	29	30	Dōng zhì		13	14	15	16	17	18	19	
	29	30	31	1	2	3	4		1	2429993		29[e]	30[e]	1[e]	2[e]	3	4	5	Sun $10^{h}40^{m}3^{p}$		1	2	3	4	5	6	7			20	21	22	23	24	25	26	

‡Leap year
[a]New Year
[b]Spring (18:24)
[c]Summer (13:36)
[d]Autumn (4:45)
[e]Winter (23:54)
● New moon
◐ First quarter moon
○ Full moon
◑ Last quarter moon

‡Leap year
[a]New Year
[b]Yom Kippur
[c]Sukkot
[d]Winter starts
[e]Ḥanukkah
[f]Purim
[g]Passover
[h]Shavuot
[i]Fast of Av

[a]New Year (4638, Dragon)
[b]Lantern Festival
[c]Qīngmíng
[d]Dragon Festival
[e]Qǐqiǎo
[f]Hungry Ghosts
[g]Mid-Autumn Festival
[h]Double-Ninth Festival
[i]Dōngzhì
*Start of 60-name cycle

[a]New Year
[b]Building of the Cross
[c]Christmas
[d]Jesus's Circumcision
[e]Epiphany
[f]Easter
[g]Mary's Announcement
[h]Jesus's Transfiguration

PERSIAN (ASTRONOMICAL) 1318/1319

Month	Sun	Mon	Tue	Wed	Thu	Fri	Sat
DEY 1318	9	10	11	12	13	14	15
	16	17	18	19	20	21	22
	23	24	25	26	27	28	29
	30	1	2	3	4	5	6
BAHMAN 1318	7	8	9	10	11	12	13
	14	15	16	17	18	19	20
	21	22	23	24	25	26	27
	28	29	30	1	2	3	4
ESFAND 1318	5	6	7	8	9	10	11
	12	13	14	15	16	17	18
	19	20	21	22	23	24	25
	26	27	28	29	1[a]	2	3
FARVARDĪN 1319	4	5	6	7	8	9	10
	11	12	13[b]	14	15	16	17
	18	19	20	21	22	23	24
	25	26	27	28	29	30	31
ORDĪBEHEŠT 1319	1	2	3	4	5	6	7
	8	9	10	11	12	13	14
	15	16	17	18	19	20	21
	22	23	24	25	26	27	28
	29	30	31	1	2	3	4
XORDĀD 1319	5	6	7	8	9	10	11
	12	13	14	15	16	17	18
	19	20	21	22	23	24	25
	26	27	28	29	30	31	1
TĪR 1319	2	3	4	5	6	7	8
	9	10	11	12	13	14	15
	16	17	18	19	20	21	22
	23	24	25	26	27	28	29
	30	31	1	2	3	4	5
MORDĀD 1319	6	7	8	9	10	11	12
	13	14	15	16	17	18	19
	20	21	22	23	24	25	26
	27	28	29	30	31	1	2
SHAHRĪVAR 1319	3	4	5	6	7	8	9
	10	11	12	13	14	15	16
	17	18	19	20	21	22	23
	24	25	26	27	28	29	30
	31	1	2	3	4	5	6
MEHR 1319	7	8	9	10	11	12	13
	14	15	16	17	18	19	20
	21	22	23	24	25	26	27
	28	29	30	1	2	3	4
ĀBĀN 1319	5	6	7	8	9	10	11
	12	13	14	15	16	17	18
	19	20	21	22	23	24	25
	26	27	28	29	30	1	2
ĀZAR 1319	3	4	5	6	7	8	9
	10	11	12	13	14	15	16
	17	18	19	20	21	22	23
	24	25	26	27	28	29	30
DEY 1319	1	2	3	4	5	6	7
	8	9	10	11	12	13	14

[a]New Year
[b]Sizdeh Bedar

HINDU LUNAR 1996‡/1997

Month	Sun	Mon	Tue	Wed	Thu	Fri	Sat
MĀRGAŚIRA 1996	20	22	23	24	25	26	27
	28	29	30	1	2	3	4
PAUSHA 1996	5	6	7	8	8	9	10
	11	12	13	15	16	17	18
	19	20	21	22	23	24	25
	26	27	28	29	30	1	2
MĀGHA 1996	3	4	5	6	7	8	9
	10	11	12	13	14	15	16
	17	18	20	21	22	23	24
	25	26	27	28	29[h]	30	30
PHĀLGUNA 1996	1	2	3	4	5	6	7
	8	9	10	11	12	14	15[i]
	16	17	18	19	20	21	22
	23	24	25	26	27	28	29
	30	1[a]	2	3	4	5	6
CHAITRA 1997	7	8	9[b]	10	11	12	13
	14	15	16	17	19	20	21
	22	23	24	24	25	26	27
	28	29	30	1	2	3	4
VAIŚĀKHA 1997	5	6	7	8	9	10	12
	13	14	15	16	17	18	19
	20	21	22	23	24	25	26
	27	28	29	29	30	1	3
JYAISHṬHA 1997	4	5	6	7	8	9	10
	11	12	13	15	16	17	18
	19	20	20	21	22	23	24
	25	26	27	28	29	30	1
ĀSHĀḌHA 1997	2	3	4	5	7	8	9
	10	11	12	13	14	15	16
	17	18	19	20	21	22	23
	24	25	26	27	28	29	30
ŚRĀVAṆA 1997	1	2	3	4	5	6	7
	8	10	11	12	13	14	15
	16	17	17	18	19	20	21
	22	23[c]	24	25	26	27	28
	29	30	1	3	4[d]	5	6
BHĀDRAPADA 1997	7	8	9	10	11	12	13
	14	15	16	17	18	19	20
	21	22	23	24	25	26	27
	28	29	30	1	2	3	4
ĀŚVINA 1997	5	7	8[e]	9[e]	10[e]	11	12
	12	13	14	15	16	17	18
	19	20	21	22	23	24	25
	26	27	28	30	1[f]	2	3
KĀRTTIKA 1997	4	5	6	7	8	9	10
	11	12	13	14	15	15	16
	17	18	19	20	21	22	24
	25	26	27	28	29	30	1
MĀRGAŚIRA 1997	2	3	4	5	6	7	8
	9	10	11[g]	12	13	14	15
	16	17	18	19	20	21	22
	23	24	25	26	27	29	30
	1	2	3	4	5	6	7

‡Leap year
[a]New Year (Vikrama)
[b]Birthday of Rāma
[c]Birthday of Krishna
[d]Ganēśa Chaturthī
[e]Dashara
[f]Diwali
[g]Birthday of Vishnu
[h]Night of Śiva
[i]Holi

HINDU SOLAR 1861/1862‡

Month	Sun	Mon	Tue	Wed	Thu	Fri	Sat
PAUSHA 1861	17	18	19	20	21	22	23
	24	25	26	27	28	29	30
MĀGHA 1861	1[b]	2	3	4	5	6	7
	8	9	10	11	12	13	14
	15	16	17	18	19	20	21
	22	23	24	25	26	27	28
PHĀLGUNA 1861	29	1	2	3	4	5	6
	7	8	9	10	11	12	13
	14	15	16	17	18	19	20
	21	22	23	24	25	26	27
CHAITRA 1861	28	29	30	1	2	3	4
	5	6	7	8	9	10	11
	12	13	14	15	16	17	18
	19	20	21	22	23	24	25
	26	27	28	29	30	1[a]	2
VAIŚĀKHA 1862	3	4	5	6	7	8	9
	10	11	12	13	14	15	16
	17	18	19	20	21	22	23
	24	25	26	27	28	29	30
	31	1	2	3	4	5	6
JYAISHṬHA 1862	7	8	9	10	11	12	13
	14	15	16	17	18	19	20
	21	22	23	24	25	26	27
	28	29	30	31	32	1	2
ĀSHĀḌHA 1862	3	4	5	6	7	8	9
	10	11	12	13	14	15	16
	17	18	19	20	21	22	23
	24	25	26	27	28	29	30
	31	1	2	3	4	5	6
ŚRĀVAṆA 1862	7	8	9	10	11	12	13
	14	15	16	17	18	19	20
	21	22	23	24	25	26	27
	28	29	30	31	32	1	2
BHĀDRAPADA 1862	3	4	5	6	7	8	9
	10	11	12	13	14	15	16
	17	18	19	20	21	22	23
	24	25	26	27	28	29	30
	31	1	2	3	4	5	6
ĀŚVINA 1862	7	8	9	10	11	12	13
	14	15	16	17	18	19	20
	21	22	23	24	25	26	27
	28	29	30	1	2	3	4
KĀRTTIKA 1862	5	6	7	8	9	10	11
	12	13	14	15	16	17	18
	19	20	21	22	23	24	25
	26	27	28	29	30	1	2
MĀRGAŚIRA 1862	3	4	5	6	7	8	9
	10	11	12	13	14	15	16
	17	18	19	20	21	22	23
	24	25	26	27	28	29	30
PAUSHA 1862	1	2	3	4	5	6	7
	8	9	10	11	12	13	14
	15	16	17	18	19	20	21

‡Leap year
[a]New Year (Nandana)
[b]Pongal

ISLAMIC (ASTRONOMICAL) 1358/1359

Month	Sun	Mon	Tue	Wed	Thu	Fri	Sat
DHU AL-QAʿDA 1358	20	21	22	23	24	25	26
	27	28	29	30	1	2	3
DHU AL-ḤIJJA 1358	4	5	6	7	8	9	10[g]
	11	12	13	14	15	16	17
	18	19	20	21	22	23	24
	25	26	27	28	29	30	1[a]
MUḤARRAM 1359	2	3	4	5	6	7	8
	9	10[b]	11	12	13	14	15
	16	17	18	19	20	21	22
	23	24	25	26	27	28	29
ṢAFAR 1359	1	2	3	4	5	6	7
	8	9	10	11	12	13	14
	15	16	17	18	19	20	21
	22	23	24	25	26	27	28
	29	30	1	2	3	4	5
RABĪʿ I 1359	6	7	8	9	10	11	12[c]
	13	14	15	16	17	18	19
	20	21	22	23	24	25	26
	27	28	29	30	1	2	3
RABĪʿ II 1359	4	5	6	7	8	9	10
	11	12	13	14	15	16	17
	18	19	20	21	22	23	24
	25	26	27	28	29	30	1
JUMĀDĀ I 1359	2	3	4	5	6	7	8
	9	10	11	12	13	14	15
	16	17	18	19	20	21	22
	23	24	25	26	27	28	29
JUMĀDĀ II 1359	1	2	3	4	5	6	7
	8	9	10	11	12	13	14
	15	16	17	18	19	20	21
	22	23	24	25	26	27	28
	29	30	1	2	3	4	5
RAJAB 1359	6	7	8	9	10	11	12
	13	14	15	16	17	18	19
	20	21	22	23	24	25	26
	27[d]	28	29	1	2	3	4
SHAʿBĀN 1359	5	6	7	8	9	10	11
	12	13	14	15	16	17	18
	19	20	21	22	23	24	25
	26	27	28	29	1[e]	2	3
RAMAḌĀN 1359	4	5	6	7	8	9	10
	11	12	13	14	15	16	17
	18	19	20	21	22	23	24
	25	26	27	28	29	1[f]	2
SHAWWĀL 1359	3	4	5	6	7	8	9
	10	11	12	13	14	15	16
	17	18	19	20	21	22	23
	24	25	26	27	28	29	30
DHU AL-QAʿDA 1359	1	2	3	4	5	6	7
	8	9	10	11	12	13	14
	15	16	17	18	19	20	21
	22	23	24	25	26	27	28
	29	1	2	3	4	5	6

[a]New Year
[b]ʿAshūrāʾ
[c]Prophet's Birthday
[d]Ascent of the Prophet
[e]Start of Ramaḍān
[f]ʿĪd al-Fiṭr
[g]ʿĪd al-ʾAḍḥā

GREGORIAN 1940‡

Julian‡ (Sun)	Sun	Mon	Tue	Wed	Thu	Fri	Sat	Month
Dec 18	31	1	2	3	4	5	6	JANUARY 1940
	7[a]	8	9	10	11	12	13	
Jan 1	14[b]	15	16	17	18	19	20	
	21	22	23	24	25	26	27	
Jan 15	28	29	30	31	1	2	3	
	4	5	6	7[c]	8	9	10	FEBRUARY 1940
Jan 29	11	12	13	14	15	16	17	
	18	19	20	21	22	23	24	
Feb 12	25	26	27	28	29	1	2	
	3	4	5	6	7	8	9	MARCH 1940
Feb 26	10	11	12	13	14	15	16	
	17[d]	18	19	20	21	22	23	
Mar 11	24[e]	25	26	27	28	29	30	
	31	1	2	3	4	5	6	
Mar 25	7	8	9	10	11	12	13	APRIL 1940
	14	15	16	17	18	19	20	
Apr 8	21	22	23	24	25	26	27	
	28[f]	29	30	1	2	3	4	
Apr 22	5	6	7	8	9	10	11	MAY 1940
	12	13	14	15	16	17	18	
May 6	19	20	21	22	23	24	25	
	26	27	28	29	30	31	1	
May 20	2	3	4	5	6	7	8	JUNE 1940
	9	10	11	12	13	14	15	
Jun 3	16	17	18	19	20	21	22	
	23	24	25	26	27	28	29	
Jun 17	30	1	2	3	4	5	6	
	7	8	9	10	11	12	13	JULY 1940
Jul 1	14	15	16	17	18	19	20	
	21	22	23	24	25	26	27	
Jul 15	28	29	30	31	1	2	3	
	4	5	6	7	8	9	10	AUGUST 1940
Jul 29	11	12	13	14	15	16	17	
	18	19	20	21	22	23	24	
Aug 12	25	26	27	28	29	30	31	
	1	2	3	4	5	6	7	SEPTEMBER 1940
Aug 26	8	9	10	11	12	13	14	
	15	16	17	18	19	20	21	
Sep 9	22	23	24	25	26	27	28	
	29	30	1	2	3	4	5	
Sep 23	6	7	8	9	10	11	12	OCTOBER 1940
	13	14	15	16	17	18	19	
Oct 7	20	21	22	23	24	25	26	
	27	28	29	30	31	1	2	
Oct 21	3	4	5	6	7	8	9	NOVEMBER 1940
	10	11	12	13	14	15	16	
Nov 4	17	18	19	20	21	22	23	
	24	25	26	27	28	29	30	
Nov 18	1[g]	2	3	4	5	6	7	DECEMBER 1940
	8	9	10	11	12	13	14	
Dec 2	15	16	17	18	19	20	21	
	22	23	24	25[h]	26	27	28	
Dec 16	29	30	31	1	2	3	4	

‡Leap year
[a]Orthodox Christmas
[b]Julian New Year
[c]Ash Wednesday
[d]Feast of Orthodoxy
[e]Easter
[f]Orthodox Easter
[g]Advent
[h]Christmas

1941

GREGORIAN 1941

Month	Sun	Mon	Tue	Wed	Thu	Fri	Sat	Lunar Phases	ISO WEEK (Mon)	JULIAN DAY (Sun noon)
JANUARY 1941	29	30	31	1[a]	2	3	4		1	2429993
	◐	6	7	8	9	10	11	13:40	2	2430000
	12	○	14	15	16	17	18	11:04	3	2430007
	19	◑	21	22	23	24	25	10:02	4	2430014
	26	●	28	29	30	31	1	11:03	5	2430021
FEBRUARY 1941	2	3	◐	5	6	7	8	11:42	6	2430028
	9	10	11	○	13	14	15	0:26	7	2430035
	16	17	◑	19	20	21	22	18:07	8	2430042
	23	24	25	●	27	28	1	3:02	9	2430049
MARCH 1941	2	3	4	5	◐	7	8	7:42	10	2430056
	9	10	11	12	○	14	15	11:47	11	2430063
	16	17	18	19	◑	21[b]	22	2:51	12	2430070
	23	24	25	26	●	28	29	20:14	13	2430077
	30	31	1	2	3	4	◐	0:12	14	2430084
APRIL 1941	6	7	8	9	10	○	12	21:15	15	2430091
	13	14	15	16	17	◑	19	13:03	16	2430098
	20	21	22	23	24	25	●	13:24	17	2430105
	27	28	29	30	1	2	3		18	2430112
MAY 1941	◐	5	6	7	8	9	10	12:48	19	2430119
	○	12	13	14	15	16	17	5:15	20	2430126
	◑	19	20	21	22	23	24	1:17	21	2430133
	25	●	27	28	29	30	31	5:18	22	2430140
JUNE 1941	1	◐	3	4	5	6	7	21:56	23	2430147
	8	○	10	11	12	13	14	12:34	24	2430154
	15	◑	17	18	19	20	21[c]	15:45	25	2430161
	22	23	●	25	26	27	28	19:22	26	2430168
	29	30	1	◐	3	4	5	4:24	27	2430175
JULY 1941	6	7	○	9	10	11	12	20:17	28	2430182
	13	14	15	◑	17	18	19	8:07	29	2430189
	20	21	22	23	●	25	26	7:39	30	2430196
	27	28	29	30	◐	1	2	9:19	31	2430203
AUGUST 1941	3	4	5	6	○	8	9	5:38	32	2430210
	10	11	12	13	14	◑	16	1:40	33	2430217
	17	18	19	20	21	●	23	18:34	34	2430224
	24	25	26	27	28	◐	30	14:04	35	2430231
	31	1	2	3	4	○	6	17:36	36	2430238
SEPTEMBER 1941	7	8	9	10	11	12	◑	19:31	37	2430245
	14	15	16	17	18	19	20		38	2430252
	●	22	23[d]	24	25	26	◐	4:38 20:09	39	2430259
	28	29	30	1	2	3	4		40	2430266
OCTOBER 1941	○	6	7	8	9	10	11	8:32	41	2430273
	12	◑	14	15	16	17	18	12:52	42	2430280
	19	●	21	22	23	24	25	14:20	43	2430287
	26	◐	28	29	30	31	1	5:04	44	2430294
NOVEMBER 1941	2	3	○	5	6	7	8	2:00	45	2430301
	9	10	11	◑	13	14	15	4:53	46	2430308
	16	17	18	●	20	21	22	0:04	47	2430315
	23	24	◐	26	27	28	29	17:52	48	2430322
	30	1	2	○	4	5	6	20:51	49	2430329
DECEMBER 1941	7	8	9	10	◑	12	13	18:48	50	2430336
	14	15	16	17	●	19	20	10:18	51	2430343
	21	22[e]	23	24	◐	26	27	10:43	52	2430350
	28	29	30	31	1	○	3	15:42	1	2430357

HEBREW 5701/5702

JULIAN DAY	Month	Sun	Mon	Tue	Wed	Thu	Fri	Sat	Molad
2429993	TEVETH 5701	29[e]	30[e]	1[e]	2[e]	3	4	5	Sun 10h40m3p
2430000		6	7	8	9	10	11	12	
2430007		13	14	15	16	17	18	19	
2430014		20	21	22	23	24	25	26	
2430021	SHEVAT 5701	27	28	29	1	2	3	4	Mon 23h24m4p
2430028		5	6	7	8	9	10	11	
2430035		12	13	14	15	16	17	18	
2430042		19	20	21	22	23	24	25	
2430049	ADAR 5701	26	27	28	29	30	1	2	Wed 12h8m5p
2430056		3	4	5	6	7	8	9	
2430063		10	11	12	13	14[f]	15	16	
2430070		17	18	19	20	21	22	23	
2430077		24	25	26	27	28	29	1	Fri 0h52m6p
2430084	NISAN 5701	2	3	4	5	6	7	8	
2430091		9	10	11	12	13	14	15[g]	
2430098		16	17	18	19	20	21	22	
2430105		23	24	25	26	27	28	29	
2430112	IYYAR 5701	30	1	2	3	4	5	6	Sat 13h36m7p
2430119		7	8	9	10	11	12	13	
2430126		14	15	16	17	18	19	20	
2430133		21	22	23	24	25	26	27	
2430140	SIVAN 5701	28	29	1	2	3	4	5	Mon 2h20m8p
2430147		6[h]	7	8	9	10	11	12	
2430154		13	14	15	16	17	18	19	
2430161		20	21	22	23	24	25	26	
2430168	TAMMUZ 5701	27	28	29	30	1	2	3	Tue 15h4m9p
2430175		4	5	6	7	8	9	10	
2430182		11	12	13	14	15	16	17	
2430189		18	19	20	21	22	23	24	
2430196	AV 5701	25	26	27	28	29	1	2	Thu 3h48m10p
2430203		3	4	5	6	7	8	9	
2430210		10[i]	11	12	13	14	15	16	
2430217		17	18	19	20	21	22	23	
2430224		24	25	26	27	28	29	30	
2430231	ELUL 5701	1	2	3	4	5	6	7	Fri 16h32m11p
2430238		8	9	10	11	12	13	14	
2430245		15	16	17	18	19	20	21	
2430252		22	23	24	25	26	27	28	
2430259	TISHRI 5702	29	1[a]	2[a]	3	4	5	6	Sun 5h16m12p
2430266		7	8	9	10[b]	11	12	13	
2430273		14	15[c]	16	17	18	19	20	
2430280		21	22	23	24	25	26	27	
2430287	HESHVAN 5702	28	29	30	1	2	3	4	Mon 18h0m13p
2430294		5	6	7	8	9	10	11	
2430301		12	13	14	15	16	17	18	
2430308		19	20	21	22	23	24	25	
2430315	KISLEV 5702	26	27	28	29	30	1	2	Wed 6h44m14p
2430322		3	4	5	6	7	8	9	
2430329		10	11	12	13	14	15[d]	16	
2430336		17	18	19	20	21	22	23	
2430343		24	25[e]	26[e]	27[e]	28[e]	29[e]	30[e]	
2430350	TEVETH 5702	1[e]	2[e]	3	4	5	6	7	Thu 19h28m15p
2430357		8	9	10	11	12	13	14	

CHINESE Gēng-Chén/Xīn-Sì‡

JULIAN DAY	Month	Sun	Mon	Tue	Wed	Thu	Fri	Sat	Solar Term
2429993	MONTH 12 Gēng-Chén	1	2	3	4	5	6	7	
2430000		8	9	10	11	12	13	14	Xiǎo hán
2430007		15	16	17	18	19*	20	21	
2430014		22	23	24	25	26	27	28	Dà hán
2430021	MONTH 1 Xīn-Sì	29	1[a]	2	3	4	5	6	
2430028		7	8	9	10	11	12	13	Lì chūn
2430035		14	15[b]	16	17	18	19	20	
2430042		21	22	23	24	25	26	27	Yǔ shuǐ
2430049	MONTH 2 Xīn-Sì	28	29	30	1	2	3	4	
2430056		5	6	7	8	9	10	11	Jīng zhé
2430063		12	13	14	15	16	17	18	
2430070		19	20*	21	22	23	24	25	Chūn fēn
2430077	MONTH 3 Xīn-Sì	26	27	28	29	30	1	2	
2430084		3	4	5	6	7	8	9[c]	Qīng míng
2430091		10	11	12	13	14	15	16	
2430098		17	18	19	20	21	22	23	
2430105	MONTH 4 Xīn-Sì	24	25	26	27	28	29	1	Gǔ yǔ
2430112		2	3	4	5	6	7	8	
2430119		9	10	11	12	13	14	15	Lì xià
2430126		16	17	18	19	20	21*	22	
2430133		23	24	25	26	27	28	29	Xiǎo mǎn
2430140	MONTH 5 Xīn-Sì	30	1	2	3	4	5[d]	6	
2430147		7	8	9	10	11	12	13	Máng zhòng
2430154		14	15	16	17	18	19	20	
2430161		21	22	23	24	25	26	27	Xià zhì
2430168	MONTH 6 Xīn-Sì	28	29	30	1	2	3	4	
2430175		5	6	7	8	9	10	11	
2430182		12	13	14	15	16	17	18	Xiǎo shǔ
2430189		19	20	21*	22	23	24	25	
2430196	LEAP MONTH 6 Xīn-Sì	26	27	28	29	1	2	3	Dà shǔ
2430203		4	5	6	7	8	9	10	
2430210		11	12	13	14	15	16	17	Lì qiū
2430217		18	19	20	21	22	23	24	
2430224	MONTH 7 Xīn-Sì	25	26	27	28	29	30	1	Chǔ shǔ
2430231		2	3	4	5	6	7[e]	8	
2430238		9	10	11	12	13	14	15[f]	
2430245		16	17	18	19	20	21	22*	Bái lù
2430252		23	24	25	26	27	28	29	
2430259	MONTH 8 Xīn-Sì	1	2	3	4	5	6	7	Qiū fēn
2430266		8	9	10	11	12	13	14	
2430273		15[g]	16	17	18	19	20	21	Hán lù
2430280		22	23	24	25	26	27	28	
2430287	MONTH 9 Xīn-Sì	29	1	2	3	4	5	6	Shuāng jiàng
2430294		7	8	9[h]	10	11	12	13	
2430301		14	15	16	17	18	19	20	Lì dōng
2430308		21	22	23	24*	25	26	27	
2430315	MONTH 10 Xīn-Sì	28	29	30	1	2	3	4	
2430322		5	6	7	8	9	10	11	Xiǎo xuě
2430329		12	13	14	15	16	17	18	
2430336		19	20	21	22	23	24	25	Dà xuě
2430343	MONTH 11 Xīn-Sì	26	27	28	29	1	2	3	
2430350		4	5[i]	6	7	8	9	10	Dōng zhì
2430357		11	12	13	14	15	16	17	

COPTIC 1657/1658 — ETHIOPIC 1933/1934

JULIAN DAY	Coptic month	Sun	Mon	Tue	Wed	Thu	Fri	Sat	Ethiopic month
2429993	KOIAK 1657	20	21	22	23	24	25	26	TĀKHŚĀŚ 1933
2430000		27	28	29[c]	30	1	2	3	
2430007	TŌBE 1657	4	5	6[d]	7	8	9	10	ṬER 1933
2430014		11[e]	12	13	14	15	16	17	
2430021		18	19	20	21	22	23	24	
2430028		25	26	27	28	29	30	1	
2430035	MESHIR 1657	2	3	4	5	6	7	8	YAKĀTIT 1933
2430042		9	10	11	12	13	14	15	
2430049		16	17	18	19	20	21	22	
2430056		23	24	25	26	27	28	29	
2430063	PAREMOTEP 1657	30	1	2	3	4	5	6	MAGĀBIT 1933
2430070		7	8	9	10	11	12	13	
2430077		14	15	16	17	18	19	20	
2430084		21	22	23	24	25	26	27	
2430091	PARMOUTE 1657	28	29	30	1	2	3	4	MIYĀZYĀ 1933
2430098		5	6	7	8	9	10	11	
2430105		12[f]	13	14	15	16	17	18	
2430112		19	20	21	22	23	24	25	
2430119	PASHONS 1657	26	27	28	29[g]	30	1	2	GENBOT 1933
2430126		3	4	5	6	7	8	9	
2430133		10	11	12	13	14	15	16	
2430140		17	18	19	20	21	22	23	
2430147		24	25	26	27	28	29	30	
2430154	PAŌNE 1657	1	2	3	4	5	6	7	SANĒ 1933
2430161		8	9	10	11	12	13	14	
2430168		15	16	17	18	19	20	21	
2430175		22	23	24	25	26	27	28	
2430182	EPĒP 1657	29	30	1	2	3	4	5	ḤAMLĒ 1933
2430189		6	7	8	9	10	11	12	
2430196		13	14	15	16	17	18	19	
2430203		20	21	22	23	24	25	26	
2430210	MESORĒ 1657	27	28	29	30	1	2	3	NAḤASĒ 1933
2430217		4	5	6	7	8	9	10	
2430224		11	12	13[h]	14	15	16	17	
2430231		18	19	20	21	22	23	24	
2430238	EPAG. 1657	25	26	27	28	29	30	1	PĀG. 1933
2430245	THOOUT 1658	2	3	4	5	1[a]	2	3	MASKARAM 1934
2430252		4	5	6	7	8	9	10	
2430259		11	12	13	14	15	16	17[b]	
2430266		18	19	20	21	22	23	24	
2430273	PAOPE 1658	25	26	27	28	29	30	1	ṬEQEMT 1934
2430280		2	3	4	5	6	7	8	
2430287		9	10	11	12	13	14	15	
2430294		16	17	18	19	20	21	22	
2430301		23	24	25	26	27	28	29	
2430308	ATHŌR 1658	30	1	2	3	4	5	6	ḪEDĀR 1934
2430315		7	8	9	10	11	12	13	
2430322		14	15	16	17	18	19	20	
2430329		21	22	23	24	25	26	27	
2430336	KOIAK 1658	28	29	30	1	2	3	4	TĀKHŚĀŚ 1934
2430343		5	6	7	8	9	10	11	
2430350		12	13	14	15	16	17	18	
2430357		19	20	21	22	23	24	25	

[a]New Year
[b]Spring (0:20)
[c]Summer (19:33)
[d]Autumn (10:33)
[e]Winter (5:44)
● New moon
◐ First quarter moon
○ Full moon
◑ Last quarter moon

[a]New Year
[b]Yom Kippur
[c]Sukkot
[d]Winter starts
[e]Ḥanukkah
[f]Purim
[g]Passover
[h]Shavuot
[i]Fast of Av

‡Leap year
[a]New Year (4639, Snake)
[b]Lantern Festival
[c]Qīngmíng
[d]Dragon Festival
[e]Qīqiǎo
[f]Hungry Ghosts
[g]Mid-Autumn Festival
[h]Double-Ninth Festival
[i]Dōngzhì
*Start of 60-name cycle

[a]New Year
[b]Building of the Cross
[c]Christmas
[d]Jesus's Circumcision
[e]Epiphany
[f]Easter
[g]Mary's Announcement
[h]Jesus's Transfiguration

PERSIAN (ASTRONOMICAL) 1319/1320

Month	Sun	Mon	Tue	Wed	Thu	Fri	Sat
	8	9	10	11	12	13	14
DEY 1319	15	16	17	18	19	20	21
	22	23	24	25	26	27	28
	29	30	*1*	2	3	4	5
BAHMAN 1319	6	7	8	9	10	11	12
	13	14	15	16	17	18	19
	20	21	22	23	24	25	26
	27	28	29	30	*1*	2	3
ESFAND 1319	4	5	6	7	8	9	10
	11	12	13	14	15	16	17
	18	19	20	21	22	23	24
	25	26	27	28	29	*1*[a]	2
FARVARDĪN 1320	3	4	5	6	7	8	9
	10	11	12	13[b]	14	15	16
	17	18	19	20	21	22	23
	24	25	26	27	28	29	30
	31	*1*	2	3	4	5	6
ORDĪBEHEŠT 1320	7	8	9	10	11	12	13
	14	15	16	17	18	19	20
	21	22	23	24	25	26	27
	28	29	30	31	*1*	2	3
XORDĀD 1320	4	5	6	7	8	9	10
	11	12	13	14	15	16	17
	18	19	20	21	22	23	24
	25	26	27	28	29	30	31
TĪR 1320	*1*	2	3	4	5	6	7
	8	9	10	11	12	13	14
	15	16	17	18	19	20	21
	22	23	24	25	26	27	28
	29	30	31	*1*	2	3	4
MORDĀD 1320	5	6	7	8	9	10	11
	12	13	14	15	16	17	18
	19	20	21	22	23	24	25
	26	27	28	29	30	31	*1*
SHAHRĪVAR 1320	2	3	4	5	6	7	8
	9	10	11	12	13	14	15
	16	17	18	19	20	21	22
	23	24	25	26	27	28	29
	30	31	*1*	2	3	4	5
MEHR 1320	6	7	8	9	10	11	12
	13	14	15	16	17	18	19
	20	21	22	23	24	25	26
	27	28	29	30	*1*	2	3
ĀBĀN 1320	4	5	6	7	8	9	10
	11	12	13	14	15	16	17
	18	19	20	21	22	23	24
	25	26	27	28	29	30	*1*
ĀZAR 1320	2	3	4	5	6	7	8
	9	10	11	12	13	14	15
	16	17	18	19	20	21	22
	23	24	25	26	27	28	29
DEY 1320	30	*1*	2	3	4	5	6
	7	8	9	10	11	12	13

HINDU LUNAR 1997/1998

Month	Sun	Mon	Tue	Wed	Thu	Fri	Sat
	1	2	3	4	5	6	7
PAUSHA 1997	8	*8*	9	10	11	12	13
	14	15	16	17	18	19	20
	21	23	24	25	26	27	28
	29	30	1	2	3	4	5
MĀGHA 1997	6	7	8	9	10	11	*11*
	12	13	**14**	16	17	18	19
	20	21	22	23	24	25	26
	27	28[h]	29	30	1	2	3
PHĀLGUNA 1997	4	5	6	7	8	9	10
	11	12	13	14	15[i]	16	17
	18	**19**	21	22	23	24	25
	26	27	28	29	30	1[a]	2
CHAITRA 1998	3	3	4	5	6	7	8
	9[b]	10	11	12	**13**	15	16
	17	18	19	20	21	22	23
	24	25	26	27	28	29	30
VAIŚĀKHA 1998	1	2	3	4	5	6	7
	8	9	10	11	12	13	14
	15	16	**17**	19	20	21	22
	23	24	25	26	27	28	*28*
	29	30	1	2	3	4	5
JYAISHTHA 1998	6	7	8	9	**10**	12	13
	14	15	16	17	18	19	20
	21	22	23	24	25	26	27
	28	29	30	1	2	3	4
ĀSHĀDHA 1998	5	6	7	8	9	10	11
	12	14	15	16	17	18	19
	20	21	22	23	24	25	*25*
	26	27	28	29	30	1	2
ŚRĀVAṆA 1998	3	4	**5**	7	8	9	10
	11	12	13	14	15	16	17
	18	19	20	21	22	23[c]	24
	25	26	27	28	29	30	1
BHĀDRAPADA 1998	2	3	4[d]	5	6	7	**8**
	10	11	12	13	14	15	16
	17	18	19	20	21	*21*	22
	23	24	25	26	27	28	29
	30	**1**	3	4	5	6	7
ĀŚVINA 1998	8[e]	9[e]	10[e]	11	12	13	14
	15	16	17	18	19	20	21
	22	23	24	25	26	27	28
	29	30	1[f]	2	3	4	**5**
KĀRTTIKA 1998	7	8	9	10	11	12	13
	14	15	16	*16*	17	18	19
	20	21	22	23	24	25	26
	27	28	**29**	1	2	3	4
MĀRGAŚĪRA 1998	5	6	7	8	9	10	11[g]
	12	13	14	15	16	17	18
	19	*19*	20	21	**22**	24	25
	26	27	28	29	30	1	2
PAUSHA 1998	3	4	5	6	7	8	9
	10	11	12	13	14	15	16

HINDU SOLAR 1862[‡]/1863

Month	Sun	Mon	Tue	Wed	Thu	Fri	Sat
	15	16	17	18	19	20	21
PAUSHA 1862	22	23	24	25	26	27	28
	29	1[b]	2	3	4	5	6
	7	8	9	10	11	12	13
MĀGHA 1862	14	15	16	17	18	19	20
	21	22	23	24	25	26	27
	28	29	30	1	2	3	4
PHĀLGUNA 1862	5	6	7	8	9	10	11
	12	13	14	15	16	17	18
	19	20	21	22	23	24	25
	26	27	28	29	1	2	3
CHAITRA 1862	4	5	6	7	8	9	10
	11	12	13	14	15	16	17
	18	19	20	21	22	23	24
	25	26	27	28	29	30	31
	1[a]	2	3	4	5	6	7
VAIŚĀKHA 1863	8	9	10	11	12	13	14
	15	16	17	18	19	20	21
	22	23	24	25	26	27	28
	29	30	31	1	2	3	4
JYAISHTHA 1863	5	6	7	8	9	10	11
	12	13	14	15	16	17	18
	19	20	21	22	23	24	25
	26	27	28	29	30	31	1
ĀSHĀDHA 1863	2	3	4	5	6	7	8
	9	10	11	12	13	14	15
	16	17	18	19	20	21	22
	23	24	25	26	27	28	29
	30	31	32	1	2	3	4
ŚRĀVAṆA 1863	5	6	7	8	9	10	11
	12	13	14	15	16	17	18
	19	20	21	22	23	24	25
	26	27	28	29	30	31	1
BHĀDRAPADA 1863	2	3	4	5	6	7	8
	9	10	11	12	13	14	15
	16	17	18	19	20	21	22
	23	24	25	26	27	28	29
	30	31	1	2	3	4	5
ĀŚVINA 1863	6	7	8	9	10	11	12
	13	14	15	16	17	18	19
	20	21	22	23	24	25	26
	27	28	29	30	31	1	2
KĀRTTIKA 1863	3	4	5	6	7	8	9
	10	11	12	13	14	15	16
	17	18	19	20	21	22	23
	24	25	26	27	28	29	30
MĀRGAŚĪRA 1863	1	2	3	4	5	6	7
	8	9	10	11	12	13	14
	15	16	17	18	19	20	21
	22	23	24	25	26	27	28
PAUSHA 1863	29	1	2	3	4	5	6
	7	8	9	10	11	12	13
	14	15	16	17	18	19	20

ISLAMIC (ASTRONOMICAL) 1359/1360

Month	Sun	Mon	Tue	Wed	Thu	Fri	Sat
	29	1	2	3	4	5	6
DHU AL-ḤIJJA 1359	7	8	9	10[g]	11	12	13
	14	15	16	17	18	19	20
	21	22	23	24	25	26	27
	28	29	30	*1*[a]	2	3	4
MUHARRAM 1360	5	6	7	8	9	10[b]	11
	12	13	14	15	16	17	18
	19	20	21	22	23	24	25
	26	27	28	29	1	2	3
ṢAFAR 1360	4	5	6	7	8	9	10
	11	12	13	14	15	16	17
	18	19	20	21	22	23	24
	25	26	27	28	29	30	*1*
RABĪ' I 1360	2	3	4	5	6	7	8
	9	10	11	12[c]	13	14	15
	16	17	18	19	20	21	22
	23	24	25	26	27	28	29
	30	*1*	2	3	4	5	6
RABĪ' II 1360	7	8	9	10	11	12	13
	14	15	16	17	18	19	20
	21	22	23	24	25	26	27
	28	29	*30*	1	2	3	4
JUMĀDĀ I 1360	5	6	7	8	9	10	11
	12	13	14	15	16	17	18
	19	20	21	22	23	24	25
	26	27	28	29	*30*	1	2
JUMĀDĀ II 1360	3	4	5	6	7	8	9
	10	11	12	13	14	15	16
	17	18	19	20	21	22	23
	24	25	26	27	28	*29*	1
RAJAB 1360	2	3	4	5	6	7	8
	9	10	11	12	13	14	15
	16	17	18	19	20	21	22
	23	24	25	26	27[d]	28	29
SHA'BĀN 1360	*1*	2	3	4	5	6	7
	8	9	10	11	12	13	14
	15	16	17	18	19	20	21
	22	23	24	25	26	27	28
	29	*30*	1[e]	2	3	4	5
RAMAḌĀN 1360	6	7	8	9	10	11	12
	13	14	15	16	17	18	19
	20	21	22	23	24	25	26
	27	28	29	*1*[f]	2	3	4
SHAWWĀL 1360	5	6	7	8	9	10	11
	12	13	14	15	16	17	18
	19	20	21	22	23	24	25
	26	27	28	29	*1*	2	3
DHU AL-QA'DA 1360	4	5	6	7	8	9	10
	11	12	13	14	15	16	17
	18	19	20	21	22	23	24
	25	26	27	28	29	30	*1*
DHU AL-ḤIJJA 1360	2	3	4	5	6	7	8
	9	10[g]	11	12	13	14	15

GREGORIAN 1941

Julian (Sun)	Sun	Mon	Tue	Wed	Thu	Fri	Sat	Month
Dec 16	29	30	31	1	2	3	4	
	5	6	7[a]	8	9	10	11	JANUARY 1941
Dec 30	*12*	13	14[b]	15	16	17	18	
	19	20	21	22	23	24	25	
Jan 13	*26*	27	28	29	30	31	1	
	2	3	4	5	6	7	8	FEBRUARY 1941
Jan 27	*9*	10	11	12	13	14	15	
	16	17	18	19	20	21	22	
Feb 10	*23*	24	25	26[c]	27	28	1	
	2	3	4	5	6	7	8	MARCH 1941
Feb 24	*9*[d]	10	11	12	13	14	15	
	16	17	18	19	20	21	22	
Mar 10	*23*	24	25	26	27	28	29	
	30	31	1	2	3	4	5	
Mar 24	*6*	7	8	9	10	11	12	APRIL 1941
	13[e]	14	15	16	17	18	19	
Apr 7	*20*[f]	21	22	23	24	25	26	
	27	28	29	30	1	2	3	
Apr 21	*4*	5	6	7	8	9	10	MAY 1941
	11	12	13	14	15	16	17	
May 5	*18*	19	20	21	22	23	24	
	25	26	27	28	29	30	31	
May 19	*1*	2	3	4	5	6	7	JUNE 1941
	8	9	10	11	12	13	14	
Jun 2	*15*	16	17	18	19	20	21	
	22	23	24	25	26	27	28	
Jun 16	*29*	30	1	2	3	4	5	
	6	7	8	9	10	11	12	JULY 1941
Jun 30	*13*	14	15	16	17	18	19	
	20	21	22	23	24	25	26	
Jul 14	*27*	28	29	30	31	1	2	
	3	4	5	6	7	8	9	AUGUST 1941
Jul 28	*10*	11	12	13	14	15	16	
	17	18	19	20	21	22	23	
Aug 11	*24*	25	26	27	28	29	30	
	31	1	2	3	4	5	6	
Aug 25	*7*	8	9	10	11	12	13	SEPTEMBER 1941
	14	15	16	17	18	19	20	
Sep 8	*21*	22	23	24	25	26	27	
	28	29	30	1	2	3	4	
Sep 22	*5*	6	7	8	9	10	11	OCTOBER 1941
	12	13	14	15	16	17	18	
Oct 6	*19*	20	21	22	23	24	25	
	26	27	28	29	30	31	1	
Oct 20	*2*	3	4	5	6	7	8	NOVEMBER 1941
	9	10	11	12	13	14	15	
Nov 3	*16*	17	18	19	20	21	22	
	23	24	25	26	27	28	29	
Nov 17	*30*[g]	1	2	3	4	5	6	
	7	8	9	10	11	12	13	DECEMBER 1941
Dec 1	*14*	15	16	17	18	19	20	
	21	22	23	24	25[h]	26	27	
Dec 15	*28*	29	30	31	1	2	3	

Persian: [a]New Year; [b]Sizdeh Bedar

Hindu Lunar: [a]New Year (Vṛisha); [b]Birthday of Rāma; [c]Birthday of Krishna; [d]Ganēśa Chaturthī; [e]Dashara; [f]Diwali; [g]Birthday of Vishnu; [h]Night of Śiva; [i]Holi

Hindu Solar: [‡]Leap year; [a]New Year (Vijaya); [b]Pongal

Islamic: [a]New Year; [b]'Ashūrā'; [c]Prophet's Birthday; [d]Ascent of the Prophet; [e]Start of Ramaḍān; [f]'Īd al-Fiṭr; [g]'Īd al-'Aḍḥā

Gregorian: [a]Orthodox Christmas; [b]Julian New Year; [c]Ash Wednesday; [d]Feast of Orthodoxy; [e]Easter; [f]Orthodox Easter; [g]Advent; [h]Christmas

1942

Gregorian 1942	Sun	Mon	Tue	Wed	Thu	Fri	Sat	Lunar Phases	ISO Week (Mon)	Julian Day (Sun noon)	Hebrew 5702/5703‡	Sun	Mon	Tue	Wed	Thu	Fri	Sat	Molad	Chinese Xīn-Sì‡/Rén-Wǔ	Sun	Mon	Tue	Wed	Thu	Fri	Sat	Solar Term	Coptic 1658/1659‡	Sun	Mon	Tue	Wed	Thu	Fri	Sat	Ethiopic 1934/1935‡
JANUARY 1942	28	29	30	31	1[a]	○	3	15:42	1	2430357	TEVETH 5702	8	9	10	11	12	13	14		MONTH 11 Xīn-Sì	11	12	13	14	15	16	17		KOIAK 1658	19	20	21	22	23	24	25	TĀKHŚĀŚ 1934
	4	5	6	7	8	9	◑	6:05	2	2430364		15	16	17	18	19	20	21			18	19	20	21	22	23	24	Xiǎo hán		26	27	28	29[c]	30	1	2	ṬER 1934
	11	12	13	14	15	●	17	21:32	3	2430371		22	23	24	25	26	27	28	Sat 8h12m16p	MONTH 12 Xīn-Sì	25*	26	27	28	29	30	1		TŌBE 1658	3	4	5	6[d]	7	8	9	
	18	19	20	21	22	23	◐	6:35	4	2430378	SHEVAT 5702	29	1	2	3	4	5	6			2	3	4	5	6	7	8	Dà hán		10	11[e]	12	13	14	15	16	
	25	26	27	28	29	30	31		5	2430385		7	8	9	10	11	12	13			9	10	11	12	13	14	15			17	18	19	20	21	22	23	
FEBRUARY 1942	○	2	3	4	5	6	7	9:12	6	2430392		14	15	16	17	18	19	20			16	17	18	19	20	21	22	Lì chūn		24	25	26	27	28	29	30	
	◑	9	10	11	12	13	14	14:52	7	2430399		21	22	23	24	25	26	27			23	24	25	26	27	28	29		MESHIR 1658	1	2	3	4	5	6	7	YAKĀTIT 1934
	●	16	17	18	19	20	21	10:03	8	2430406	ADAR 5702	28	29	30	1	2	3	4	Sun 20h56m17p	MONTH 1 Rén-Wǔ	1[a]	2	3	4	5	6	7	Yǔ shuǐ		8	9	10	11	12	13	14	
	22	◐	24	25	26	27	28	3:40	9	2430413		5	6	7	8	9	10	11			8	9	10	11	12	13	14			15	16	17	18	19	20	21	
MARCH 1942	1	2	○	4	5	6	7	0:20	10	2430420		12	13	14[f]	15	16	17	18			15[b]	16	17	18	19	20	21	Jīng zhé		22	23	24	25	26	27	28	
	8	◑	10	11	12	13	14	22:00	11	2430427		19	20	21	22	23	24	25			22	23	24	25	26*	27	28		PAREMOTEP 1658	29	30	1	2	3	4	5	MAGĀBIT 1934
	15	●	17	18	19	20	21[b]	23:50	12	2430434	NISAN 5702	26	27	28	29	1	2	3	Tue 9h41m0p	MONTH 2 Rén-Wǔ	29	30	1	2	3	4	5	Chūn fēn		6	7	8	9	10	11	12	
	22	23	24	◐	26	27	28	0:01	13	2430441		4	5	6	7	8	9	10			6	7	8	9	10	11	12			13	14	15	16	17	18	19	
APRIL 1942	29	30	31	○	2	3	4	12:32	14	2430448		11	12	13	14	15[g]	16	17			13	14	15	16	17	18	19			20	21	22	23	24	25	26	
	5	6	7	◑	9	10	11	4:43	15	2430455		18	19	20	21	22	23	24			20[c]	21	22	23	24	25	26	Qīng míng	PARMOUTE 1658	27[f]	28	29	30	1	2	3	MIYĀZYĀ 1934
	12	13	14	●	16	17	18	14:33	16	2430462	IYYAR 5702	25	26	27	28	29	30	1	Wed 22h25m1p	MONTH 3 Rén-Wǔ	27	28	29	1	2	3	4			4	5	6	7	8	9	10	
	19	20	21	22	◐	24	25	18:10	17	2430469		2	3	4	5	6	7	8			5	6	7	8	9	10	11	Gǔ yǔ		11	12	13	14	15	16	17	
MAY 1942	26	27	28	29	○	1	2	21:59	18	2430476		9	10	11	12	13	14	15			12	13	14	15	16	17	18			18	19	20	21	22	23	24	
	3	4	5	6	◑	8	9	12:13	19	2430483		16	17	18	19	20	21	22			19	20	21	22	23	24	25	Lì xià	PASHONS 1658	25	26	27	28	29[g]	30	1	GENBOT 1934
	10	11	12	13	14	●	16	5:45	20	2430490		23	24	25	26	27	28	29	Fri 11h9m2p	MONTH 4 Rén-Wǔ	26	27*	28	29	30	1	2			2	3	4	5	6	7	8	
	17	18	19	20	21	22	◐	9:11	21	2430497	SIVAN 5702	1	2	3	4	5	6[h]	7			3	4	5	6	7	8	9	Xiǎo mǎn		9	10	11	12	13	14	15	
	24	25	26	27	28	29	○	5:29	22	2430504		8	9	10	11	12	13	14			10	11	12	13	14	15	16			16	17	18	19	20	21	22	
JUNE 1942	31	1	2	3	4	◑	6	21:26	23	2430511		15	16	17	18	19	20	21			17	18	19	20	21	22	23	Máng zhòng		23	24	25	26	27	28	29	
	7	8	9	10	11	12	●	21:02	24	2430518		22	23	24	25	26	27	28	Sat 23h53m3p		24	25	26	27	28	29	30		PAŌNE 1658	30	1	2	3	4	5	6	SANĒ 1934
	14	15	16	17	18	19	20		25	2430525	TAMMUZ 5702	29	30	1	2	3	4	5		MONTH 5 Rén-Wǔ	1	2	3	4	5[d]	6	7			7	8	9	10	11	12	13	
	◐	22[c]	23	24	25	26	27	20:45	26	2430532		6	7	8	9	10	11	12			8	9	10	11	12	13	14	Xià zhì		14	15	16	17	18	19	20	
JULY 1942	○	29	30	1	2	3	4	12:09	27	2430539		13	14	15	16	17	18	19			15	16	17	18	19	20	21			21	22	23	24	25	26	27	
	◑	6	7	8	9	10	11	8:58	28	2430546		20	21	22	23	24	25	26			22	23	24	25	26	27*	28	Xiǎo shǔ	EPĒP 1658	28	29	30	1	2	3	4	ḤAMLĒ 1934
	12	●	14	15	16	17	18	12:03	29	2430553	AV 5702	27	28	29	1	2	3	4	Mon 12h37m4p	MONTH 6 Rén-Wǔ	29	1	2	3	4	5	6			5	6	7	8	9	10	11	
	19	20	◐	22	23	24	25	5:13	30	2430560		5	6	7	8	9[i]	10	11			7	8	9	10	11	12	13	Dà shǔ		12	13	14	15	16	17	18	
AUGUST 1942	26	○	28	29	30	31	1	19:14	31	2430567		12	13	14	15	16	17	18			14	15	16	17	18	19	20			19	20	21	22	23	24	25	
	2	◑	4	5	6	7	8	23:04	32	2430574		19	20	21	22	23	24	25			21	22	23	24	25	26	27	Lì qiū	MESORĒ 1658	26	27	28	29	30	1	2	NAHASĒ 1934
	9	10	11	●	13	14	15	2:28	33	2430581	ELUL 5702	26	27	28	29	30	1	2	Wed 1h21m5p	MONTH 7 Rén-Wǔ	28	29	30	1	2	3	4			3	4	5	6	7	8	9	
	16	17	18	◐	20	21	22	11:30	34	2430588		3	4	5	6	7	8	9			5	6	7[e]	8	9	10	11			10	11	12	13[h]	14	15	16	
	23	24	25	○	27	28	29	3:46	35	2430595		10	11	12	13	14	15	16			12	13	14	15[f]	16	17	18	Chǔ shǔ		17	18	19	20	21	22	23	
SEPTEMBER 1942	30	31	1	◑	3	4	5	15:42	36	2430602		17	18	19	20	21	22	23			19	20	21	22	23	24	25			24	25	26	27	28	29	30	
	6	7	8	9	●	11	12	15:53	37	2430609	TISHRI 5703	24	25	26	27	28	29	1[a]	Thu 14h5m6p	MONTH 8 Rén-Wǔ	26	27	28*	29	1	2	3	Bái lù	EPAG. 1658 / THOOUT 1659	1	2	3	4	5	1[a]	2	PĀG. 1934 / MASKARAM 1935
	13	14	15	16	◐	18	19	16:57	38	2430616		2[a]	3	4	5	6	7	8			4	5	6	7	8	9	10			3	4	5	6	7	8	9	
	20	21	22	23[d]	○	25	26	14:34	39	2430623		9	10[b]	11	12	13	14	15[c]			11	12	13	14	15[g]	16	17	Qiū fēn		10	11	12	13	14	15	16	
OCTOBER 1942	27	28	29	30	1	◑	3	10:27	40	2430630		16	17	18	19	20	21	22			18	19	20	21	22	23	24			17[b]	18	19	20	21	22	23	
	4	5	6	7	8	9	●	4:06	41	2430637		23	24	25	26	27	28	29	Sat 2h49m7p	MONTH 9 Rén-Wǔ	25	26	27	28	29	30	1	Hán lù		24	25	26	27	28	29	30	
	11	12	13	14	15	◐	17	22:58	42	2430644	ḤESHVAN 5703	30	1	2	3	4	5	6			2	3	4	5	6	7	8		PAOPE 1659	1	2	3	4	5	6	7	ṬEQEMT 1935
	18	19	20	21	22	23	○	4:05	43	2430651		7	8	9	10	11	12	13			9[h]	10	11	12	13	14	15	Shuāng jiàng		8	9	10	11	12	13	14	
	25	26	27	28	29	30	31		44	2430658		14	15	16	17	18	19	20			16	17	18	19	20	21	22			15	16	17	18	19	20	21	
NOVEMBER 1942	◑	2	3	4	5	6	7	6:18	45	2430665		21	22	23	24	25	26	27			23	24	25	26	27	28	29*			22	23	24	25	26	27	28	
	●	9	10	11	12	13	14	15:19	46	2430672	KISLEV 5703	28	29	1	2	3	4	5	Sun 15h33m8p	MONTH 10 Rén-Wǔ	1	2	3	4	5	6	7	Lì dōng	ATHŌR 1659	29	30	1	2	3	4	5	HEDĀR 1935
	◐	16	17	18	19	20	21	6:57	47	2430679		6	7	8	9	10	11	12			8	9	10	11	12	13	14			6	7	8	9	10	11	12	
	○	23	24	25	26	27	28	20:24	48	2430686		13	14	15	16	17	18	19			15	16	17	18	19	20	21	Xiǎo xuě		13	14	15	16	17	18	19	
DECEMBER 1942	29	30	◑	2	3	4	5	1:37	49	2430693		20	21	22	23	24	25[e]	26[d,e]			22	23	24	25	26	27	28			20	21	22	23	24	25	26	
	6	7	●	9	10	11	12	2:00	50	2430700	TEVETH 5703	27[e]	28[e]	29[e]	1[e]	2[e]	3[e]	4	Tue 4h17m9p	MONTH 11 Rén-Wǔ	29	30	1	2	3	4	5	Dà xuě	KOIAK 1659	27	28	29	30	1	2	3	TĀKHŚĀŚ 1935
	13	◐	15	16	17	18	19	17:47	51	2430707		5	6	7	8	9	10	11			6	7	8	9	10	11	12			4	5	6	7	8	9	10	
	20	21	○[e]	23	24	25	26	15:03	52	2430714		12	13	14	15	16	17	18			13	14	15[i]	16	17	18	19	Dōng zhì		11	12	13	14	15	16	17	
	27	28	29	◑	31	1	2	18:37	53	2430721		19	20	21	22	23	24	25			20	21	22	23	24	25	26			18	19	20	21	22	23	24	

[a]New Year
[b]Spring (6:10)
[c]Summer (1:16)
[d]Autumn (16:16)
[e]Winter (11:39)
● New moon
◐ First quarter moon
○ Full moon
◑ Last quarter moon

‡Leap year
[a]New Year
[b]Yom Kippur
[c]Sukkot
[d]Winter starts
[e]Ḥanukkah
[f]Purim
[g]Passover
[h]Shavuot
[i]Fast of Av

‡Leap year
[a]New Year (4640, Horse)
[b]Lantern Festival
[c]Qīngmíng
[d]Dragon Festival
[e]Qīqiǎo
[f]Hungry Ghosts
[g]Mid-Autumn Festival
[h]Double-Ninth Festival
[i]Dōngzhì
*Start of 60-name cycle

‡Leap year
[a]New Year
[b]Building of the Cross
[c]Christmas
[d]Jesus's Circumcision
[e]Epiphany
[f]Easter
[g]Mary's Announcement
[h]Jesus's Transfiguration

PERSIAN (ASTRONOMICAL) 1320/1321‡

Month	Sun	Mon	Tue	Wed	Thu	Fri	Sat
DEY 1320	7	8	9	10	11	12	13
	14	15	16	17	18	19	20
	21	22	23	24	25	26	27
	28	29	30	1	2	3	4
BAHMAN 1320	5	6	7	8	9	10	11
	12	13	14	15	16	17	18
	19	20	21	22	23	24	25
	26	27	28	29	30	1	2
ESFAND 1320	3	4	5	6	7	8	9
	10	11	12	13	14	15	16
	17	18	19	20	21	22	23
	24	25	26	27	28	29	1[a]
FARVARDĪN 1321	2	3	4	5	6	7	8
	9	10	11	12	13[b]	14	15
	16	17	18	19	20	21	22
	23	24	25	26	27	28	29
	30	31	1	2	3	4	5
ORDĪBEHEŠT 1321	6	7	8	9	10	11	12
	13	14	15	16	17	18	19
	20	21	22	23	24	25	26
	27	28	29	30	31	1	2
XORDĀD 1321	3	4	5	6	7	8	9
	10	11	12	13	14	15	16
	17	18	19	20	21	22	23
	24	25	26	27	28	29	30
	31	1	2	3	4	5	6
TĪR 1321	7	8	9	10	11	12	13
	14	15	16	17	18	19	20
	21	22	23	24	25	26	27
	28	29	30	31	1	2	3
MORDĀD 1321	4	5	6	7	8	9	10
	11	12	13	14	15	16	17
	18	19	20	21	22	23	24
	25	26	27	28	29	30	31
SHAHRĪVAR 1321	1	2	3	4	5	6	7
	8	9	10	11	12	13	14
	15	16	17	18	19	20	21
	22	23	24	25	26	27	28
	29	30	31	1	2	3	4
MEHR 1321	5	6	7	8	9	10	11
	12	13	14	15	16	17	18
	19	20	21	22	23	24	25
	26	27	28	29	30	1	2
ĀBĀN 1321	3	4	5	6	7	8	9
	10	11	12	13	14	15	16
	17	18	19	20	21	22	23
	24	25	26	27	28	29	30
ĀZAR 1321	1	2	3	4	5	6	7
	8	9	10	11	12	13	14
	15	16	17	18	19	20	21
	22	23	24	25	26	27	28
DEY 1321	29	30	1	2	3	4	5
	6	7	8	9	10	11	12

HINDU LUNAR 1998/1999‡

Month	Sun	Mon	Tue	Wed	Thu	Fri	Sat
PAUSHA 1998	10	11	12	13	14	15	16
	17	18	19	20	21	22	23
	24	25	26	27	**28**	30	1
MĀGHA 1998	2	3	4	5	6	7	8
	9	10	11	*11*	12	13	14
	15	16	17	18	19	20	21
	22	24	25	26	27	28[h]	29
	30	1	2	3	4	5	6
PHĀLGUNA 1998	7	8	9	10	11	12	13
	14	15[i]	16	17	18	19	20
	21	22	23	24	25	26	**27**
	29	30	1[a]	2	3	3	4
CHAITRA 1999	5	6	7	8	9[b]	10	11
	12	13	14	15	16	17	18
	19	**20**	22	23	24	25	26
	27	28	29	30	1	2	3
VAIŚĀKHA 1999	4	5	6	7	*7*	8	9
	10	11	12	**13**	15	16	17
	18	19	20	21	22	23	24
	25	26	27	28	29	30	1
LEAP JYAISHṬHA 1999	2	3	4	5	6	7	8
	9	10	11	12	13	14	15
	16	**17**	19	20	21	22	23
	24	25	26	27	28	29	30
JYAISHṬHA 1999	1	2	3	*3*	4	5	6
	7	8	**9**	11	12	13	14
	15	16	17	18	19	20	21
	22	23	24	25	26	27	28
	29	30	1	2	3	4	5
ĀSHĀḌHA 1999	6	7	8	9	10	11	**12**
	14	15	16	17	18	19	20
	21	22	23	24	25	26	27
	28	29	30	*30*	1	2	3
ŚRĀVAṆA 1999	4	**5**	7	8	9	10	11
	12	13	14	15	16	**17**	19
	20	*20*	21	22	23[c]	24	25
	26	27	28	29	30	1	2
BHĀDRAPADA 1999	3	4[d]	5	6	7	8	**9**
	11	12	13	14	15	16	17
	18	19	20	21	22	23	24
	25	*25*	26	27	28	29	30
	1	**2**	4	5	6	7	8[e]
ĀŚVINA 1999	9[e]	10[e]	11	12	13	14	15
	16	17	18	19	20	21	22
	23	24	25	26	27	28	29
	30	1[f]	2	3	4	5	**6**
KĀRTTIKA 1999	8	9	10	11	12	13	14
	15	16	17	18	19	*19*	20
	21	22	23	24	25	26	27
	28	29	**30**	2	3	4	5
MĀRGAŚĪRA 1999	6	7	8	9	10	11[g]	12
	13	14	15	16	17	18	19
	20	21	22	23	24	25	26

HINDU SOLAR 1863/1864

Month	Sun	Mon	Tue	Wed	Thu	Fri	Sat
PAUSHA 1863	14	15	16	17	18	19	20
	21	22	23	24	25	26	27
	28	29	1[b]	2	3	4	5
MĀGHA 1863	6	7	8	9	10	11	12
	13	14	15	16	17	18	19
	20	21	22	23	24	25	26
	27	28	29	30	1	2	3
PHĀLGUNA 1863	4	5	6	7	8	9	10
	11	12	13	14	15	16	17
	18	19	20	21	22	23	24
	25	26	27	28	29	30	1
CHAITRA 1863	2	3	4	5	6	7	8
	9	10	11	12	13	14	15
	16	17	18	19	20	21	22
	23	24	25	26	27	28	29
	30	1[a]	2	3	4	5	6
VAIŚĀKHA 1864	7	8	9	10	11	12	13
	14	15	16	17	18	19	20
	21	22	23	24	25	26	27
	28	29	30	31	1	2	3
JYAISHṬHA 1864	4	5	6	7	8	9	10
	11	12	13	14	15	16	17
	18	19	20	21	22	23	24
	25	26	27	28	29	30	31
ĀSHĀḌHA 1864	1	2	3	4	5	6	7
	8	9	10	11	12	13	14
	15	16	17	18	19	20	21
	22	23	24	25	26	27	28
	29	30	31	32	1	2	3
ŚRĀVAṆA 1864	4	5	6	7	8	9	10
	11	12	13	14	15	16	17
	18	19	20	21	22	23	24
	25	26	27	28	29	30	31
BHĀDRAPADA 1864	1	2	3	4	5	6	7
	8	9	10	11	12	13	14
	15	16	17	18	19	20	21
	22	23	24	25	26	27	28
	29	30	31	1	2	3	4
ĀŚVINA 1864	5	6	7	8	9	10	11
	12	13	14	15	16	17	18
	19	20	21	22	23	24	25
	26	27	28	29	30	31	1
KĀRTTIKA 1864	2	3	4	5	6	7	8
	9	10	11	12	13	14	15
	16	17	18	19	20	21	22
	23	24	25	26	27	28	29
	30	1	2	3	4	5	6
MĀRGAŚĪRA 1864	7	8	9	10	11	12	13
	14	15	16	17	18	19	20
	21	22	23	24	25	26	27
PAUSHA 1864	28	29	1	2	3	4	5
	6	7	8	9	10	11	12
	13	14	15	16	17	18	19

ISLAMIC (ASTRONOMICAL) 1360/1361‡

Month	Sun	Mon	Tue	Wed	Thu	Fri	Sat
DHU AL-ḤIJJA 1360	9	10	11	12	13	14	15
	16	17	18	19	20	21	22
	23	24	25	26	27	28	29
MUḤARRAM 1361	1[a]	2[A]	3	4	5	6	7
	8	9	10[b]	11	12	13	14
	15	16	17	18	19	20	21
	22	23	24	25	26	27	28
	29	30	1	2	3	4	5
ṢAFAR 1361	6	7	8	9	10	11	12
	13	14	15	16	17	18	19
	20	21	22	23	24	25	26
	27	28	29	1	2	3	4
RABĪ' I 1361	5	6	7	8	9	10	11
	12[c]	13	14	15	16	17	18
	19	20	21	22	23	24	25
	26	27	28	29	30	1	2
RABĪ' II 1361	3	4	5	6	7	8	9
	10	11	12	13	14	15	16
	17	18	19	20	21	22	23
	24	25	26	27	28	29	30
JUMĀDĀ I 1361	1	2	3	4	5	6	7
	8	9	10	11	12	13	14
	15	16	17	18	19	20	21
	22	23	24	25	26	27	28
	29	30	1	2	3	4	5
JUMĀDĀ II 1361	6	7	8	9	10	11	12
	13	14	15	16	17	18	19
	20	21	22	23	24	25	26
	27	28	29	1	2	3	4
RAJAB 1361	5	6	7	8	9	10	11
	12	13	14	15	16	17	18
	19	20	21	22	23	24	25
	26	27[d]	28	29	30	1	2
SHA'BĀN 1361	3	4	5	6	7	8	9
	10	11	12	13	14	15	16
	17	18	19	20	21	22	23
	24	25	26	27	28	29	1[e]
RAMAḌĀN 1361	2	3	4	5	6	7	8
	9	10	11	12	13	14	15
	16	17	18	19	20	21	22
	23	24	25	26	27	28	29
	1[f]	2	3	4	5	6	7
SHAWWĀL 1361	8	9	10	11	12	13	14
	15	16	17	18	19	20	21
	22	23	24	25	26	27	28
	29	30	1	2	3	4	5
DHU AL-QA'DA 1361	6	7	8	9	10	11	12
	13	14	15	16	17	18	19
	20	21	22	23	24	25	26
	27	28	29	1	2	3	4
DHU AL-ḤIJJA 1361	5	6	7	8	9	10[g]	11
	12	13	14	15	16	17	18
	19	20	21	22	23	24	25

GREGORIAN 1942

Julian (Sun)	Sun	Mon	Tue	Wed	Thu	Fri	Sat	Month
Dec 15	28	29	30	31	1	2	3	
	4	5	6	7[a]	8	9	10	JANUARY 1942
Dec 29	11	12	13	14[b]	15	16	17	
	18	19	20	21	22	23	24	
Jan 12	25	26	27	28	29	30	31	
	1	2	3	4	5	6	7	
Jan 26	8	9	10	11	12	13	14	FEBRUARY 1942
	15	16	17	18[c]	19	20	21	
Feb 9	22[d]	23	24	25	26	27	28	
	1	2	3	4	5	6	7	
Feb 23	8	9	10	11	12	13	14	
	15	16	17	18	19	20	21	MARCH 1942
Mar 9	22	23	24	25	26	27	28	
	29	30	31	1	2	3	4	
Mar 23	5[e]	6	7	8	9	10	11	
	12	13	14	15	16	17	18	APRIL 1942
Apr 6	19	20	21	22	23	24	25	
	26	27	28	29	30	1	2	
Apr 20	3	4	5	6	7	8	9	
	10	11	12	13	14	15	16	MAY 1942
May 4	17	18	19	20	21	22	23	
	24	25	26	27	28	29	30	
May 18	31	1	2	3	4	5	6	
	7	8	9	10	11	12	13	
Jun 1	14	15	16	17	18	19	20	JUNE 1942
	21	22	23	24	25	26	27	
Jun 15	28	29	30	1	2	3	4	
	5	6	7	8	9	10	11	
Jun 29	12	13	14	15	16	17	18	JULY 1942
	19	20	21	22	23	24	25	
Jul 13	26	27	28	29	30	31	1	
	2	3	4	5	6	7	8	
Jul 27	9	10	11	12	13	14	15	AUGUST 1942
	16	17	18	19	20	21	22	
Aug 10	23	24	25	26	27	28	29	
	30	31	1	2	3	4	5	
Aug 24	6	7	8	9	10	11	12	SEPTEMBER 1942
	13	14	15	16	17	18	19	
Sep 7	20	21	22	23	24	25	26	
	27	28	29	30	1	2	3	
Sep 21	4	5	6	7	8	9	10	OCTOBER 1942
	11	12	13	14	15	16	17	
Oct 5	18	19	20	21	22	23	24	
	25	26	27	28	29	30	31	
Oct 19	1	2	3	4	5	6	7	
	8	9	10	11	12	13	14	NOVEMBER 1942
Nov 2	15	16	17	18	19	20	21	
	22	23	24	25	26	27	28	
Nov 16	29[g]	30	1	2	3	4	5	
	6	7	8	9	10	11	12	DECEMBER 1942
Nov 30	13	14	15	16	17	18	19	
	20	21	22	23	24	25[h]	26	
Dec 14	27	28	29	30	31	1	2	

Persian: ‡Leap year; [a]New Year; [b]Sizdeh Bedar

Hindu lunar: ‡Leap year; [a]New Year (Chitrabhānu); [b]Birthday of Rāma; [c]Birthday of Krishna; [d]Ganēśa Chaturthī; [e]Dashara; [f]Diwali; [g]Birthday of Vishnu; [h]Night of Śiva; [i]Holi

Hindu solar: [a]New Year (Jaya); [b]Pongal

Islamic: ‡Leap year; [a]New Year; [A]New Year (Arithmetic); [b]'Ashūrā'; [c]Prophet's Birthday; [d]Ascent of the Prophet; [e]Start of Ramaḍān; [f]'Id al-Fiṭr; [g]'Id al-'Aḍḥā

Gregorian: [a]Orthodox Christmas; [b]Julian New Year; [c]Ash Wednesday; [d]Feast of Orthodoxy; [e]Easter (also Orthodox); [g]Advent; [h]Christmas

1943

Gregorian 1943	Sun	Mon	Tue	Wed	Thu	Fri	Sat	Lunar Phases	ISO Week (Mon)	Julian Day (Sun noon)
January 1943	27	28	29	◑	31	1[a]	2	18:37	53	2430721
	3	4	5	●	7	8	9	12:38	1	2430728
	10	11	12	◐	14	15	16	7:49	2	2430735
	17	18	19	20	○	22	23	10:48	3	2430742
	24	25	26	27	28	◑	30	8:13	4	2430749
February 1943	31	1	2	3	●	5	6	23:29	5	2430756
	7	8	9	10	11	◐	13	0:40	6	2430763
	14	15	16	17	18	19	○	5:45	7	2430770
	21	22	23	24	25	26	◑	18:22	8	2430777
March 1943	28	1	2	3	4	5	●	10:34	9	2430784
	7	8	9	10	11	12	◐	19:30	10	2430791
	14	15	16	17	18	19	20		11	2430798
	○[b]	22	23	24	25	26	27	22:08	12	2430805
April 1943	28	◑	30	31	1	2	3	1:52	13	2430812
	●	5	6	7	8	9	10	21:53	14	2430819
	11	◐	13	14	15	16	17	15:04	15	2430826
	18	19	○	21	22	23	24	11:10	16	2430833
May 1943	25	26	◑	28	29	30	1	7:51	17	2430840
	2	3	●	5	6	7	8	9:43	18	2430847
	9	10	11	◐	13	14	15	9:52	19	2430854
	16	17	18	○	20	21	22	21:13	20	2430861
	23	24	25	◑	27	28	29	13:34	21	2430868
June 1943	30	31	1	●	3	4	5	22:33	22	2430875
	6	7	8	9	10	◐	12	2:35	23	2430882
	13	14	15	16	17	○	19	5:14	24	2430889
	20	21	22[c]	23	◑	25	26	20:08	25	2430896
July 1943	27	28	29	30	1	●	3	12:44	26	2430903
	4	5	6	7	8	9	◐	16:29	27	2430910
	11	12	13	14	15	16	○	12:22	28	2430917
	18	19	20	21	22	23	◑	4:38	29	2430924
	25	26	27	28	29	30	31		30	2430931
August 1943	●	2	3	4	5	6	7	4:06	31	2430938
	8	◐	10	11	12	13	14	3:36	32	2430945
	○	16	17	18	19	20	21	19:34	33	2430952
	◑	23	24	25	26	27	28	16:04	34	2430959
September 1943	29	●	31	1	2	3	4	19:59	35	2430966
	5	6	◐	8	9	10	11	12:33	36	2430973
	12	13	○	15	16	17	18	3:40	37	2430980
	19	20	◑	22	23[d]	24	25	7:06	38	2430987
October 1943	26	27	28	●	30	1	2	11:29	39	2430994
	3	4	5	◐	7	8	9	20:10	40	2431001
	10	11	12	○	14	15	16	13:23	41	2431008
	17	18	19	20	◑	22	23	1:42	42	2431015
	24	25	26	27	28	●	30	1:59	43	2431022
November 1943	31	1	2	3	4	◐	6	3:22	44	2431029
	7	8	9	10	11	○	13	1:27	45	2431036
	14	15	16	17	18	◑	20	22:43	46	2431043
	21	22	23	24	25	26	●	15:23	47	2431050
December 1943	28	29	30	1	2	3	◐	11:03	48	2431057
	5	6	7	8	9	10	○	16:24	49	2431064
	12	13	14	15	16	17	18		50	2431071
	◑	20	21	22[e]	23	24	25	20:03	51	2431078
	26	●	28	29	30	31	1	3:50	52	2431085

ISO Week	Hebrew 5703‡/5704	Sun	Mon	Tue	Wed	Thu	Fri	Sat	Molad
53	TEVETH 5703	19	20	21	22	23	24	25	
1	SHEVAT 5703	26	27	28	29	1	2	3	Wed $17^h1^m10^p$
2		4	5	6	7	8	9	10	
3		11	12	13	14	15	16	17	
4		18	19	20	21	22	23	24	
5	ADAR I 5703	25	26	27	28	29	30	1	Fri $5^h45^m11^p$
6		2	3	4	5	6	7	8	
7		9	10	11	12	13	14	15	
8		16	17	18	19	20	21	22	
9		23	24	25	26	27	28	29	
10	ADAR II 5703	30	1	2	3	4	5	6	Sat $18^h29^m12^p$
11		7	8	9	10	11	12	13	
12		14[f]	15	16	17	18	19	20	
13		21	22	23	24	25	26	27	
14	NISAN 5703	28	29	1	2	3	4	5	Mon $7^h13^m13^p$
15		6	7	8	9	10	11	12	
16		13	14	15[g]	16	17	18	19	
17		20	21	22	23	24	25	26	
18	IYAR 5703	27	28	29	30	1	2	3	Tue $19^h57^m14^p$
19		4	5	6	7	8	9	10	
20		11	12	13	14	15	16	17	
21		18	19	20	21	22	23	24	
22	SIVAN 5703	25	26	27	28	29	1	2	Thu $8^h41^m15^p$
23		3	4	5	6[h]	7	8	9	
24		10	11	12	13	14	15	16	
25		17	18	19	20	21	22	23	
26		24	25	26	27	28	29	30	
27	TAMMUZ 5703	1	2	3	4	5	6	7	Fri $21^h25^m16^p$
28		8	9	10	11	12	13	14	
29		15	16	17	18	19	20	21	
30		22	23	24	25	26	27	28	
31	AV 5703	29	1	2	3	4	5	6	Sun $10^h9^m17^p$
32		7	8	9[i]	10	11	12	13	
33		14	15	16	17	18	19	20	
34		21	22	23	24	25	26	27	
35	ELUL 5703	28	29	30	1	2	3	4	Mon $22^h54^m0^p$
36		5	6	7	8	9	10	11	
37		12	13	14	15	16	17	18	
38		19	20	21	22	23	24	25	
39	TISHRI 5704	26	27	28	29	1[a]	2[a]	3	Wed $11^h38^m1^p$
40		4	5	6	7	8	9	10[b]	
41		11	12	13	14	15[c]	16	17	
42		18	19	20	21	22	23	24	
43	HESHVAN 5704	25	26	27	28	29	30	1	Fri $0^h22^m2^p$
44		2	3	4	5	6	7	8	
45		9	10	11	12	13	14	15	
46		16	17	18	19	20	21	22	
47		23	24	25	26	27	28	29	
48	KISLEV 5704	1	2	3	4	5	6	7	Sat $13^h6^m3^p$
49		8	9[d]	10	11	12	13	14	
50		15	16	17	18	19	20	21	
51		22	23	24	25[e]	26[e]	27[e]	28[e]	
52		29[e]	30[e]	1[e]	2[e]	3	4	5	Mon $1^h50^m4^p$

ISO Week	Chinese Rén-Wǔ/Guǐ-Wèi	Sun	Mon	Tue	Wed	Thu	Fri	Sat	Solar Term
53	MONTH 11 Rén-Wǔ	20	21	22	23	24	25	26	
1	MONTH 12 Rén-Wǔ	27	28	29	1*	2	3	4	Xiǎo hán
2		5	6	7	8	9	10	11	
3		12	13	14	15	16	17	18	Dà hán
4		19	20	21	22	23	24	25	
5	MONTH 1 Guǐ-Wèi	26	27	28	29	30	1[a]	2	Lì chūn
6		3	4	5	6	7	8	9	
7		10	11	12	13	14	15[b]	16	Yǔ shuǐ
8		17	18	19	20	21	22	23	
9	MONTH 2 Guǐ-Wèi	24	25	26	27	28	29	1	Jīng zhé
10		2*	3	4	5	6	7	8	
11		9	10	11	12	13	14	15	
12		16	17	18	19	20	21	22	Chūn fēn
13		23	24	25	26	27	28	29	
14	MONTH 3 Guǐ-Wèi	30	1	2[c]	3	4	5	6	Qīng míng
15		7	8	9	10	11	12	13	
16		14	15	16	17	18	19	20	Gǔ yǔ
17		21	22	23	24	25	26	27	
18	MONTH 4 Guǐ-Wèi	28	29	1	2	3*	4	5	Lì xià
19		6	7	8	9	10	11	12	
20		13	14	15	16	17	18	19	Xiǎo mǎn
21		20	21	22	23	24	25	26	
22	MONTH 5 Guǐ-Wèi	27	28	29	30	1	2	3	
23		4	5[d]	6	7	8	9	10	Máng zhòng
24		11	12	13	14	15	16	17	
25		18	19	20	21	22	23	24	Xià zhì
26	MONTH 6 Guǐ-Wèi	25	26	27	28	29	1	2	
27		3	4*	5	6	7	8	9	Xiǎo shǔ
28		10	11	12	13	14	15	16	
29		17	18	19	20	21	22	23	Dà shǔ
30		24	25	26	27	28	29	30	
31	MONTH 7 Guǐ-Wèi	1	2	3	4	5	6	7[e]	
32		8	9	10	11	12	13	14	Lì qiū
33		15[f]	16	17	18	19	20	21	
34		22	23	24	25	26	27	28	Chǔ shǔ
35	MONTH 8 Guǐ-Wèi	29	30	1	2	3	4*	5	
36		6	7	8	9	10	11	12	Bái lù
37		13	14	15[g]	16	17	18	19	
38		20	21	22	23	24	25	26	Qiū fēn
39	MONTH 9 Guǐ-Wèi	27	28	29	1	2	3	4	
40		5	6	7	8	9[h]	10	11	Hán lù
41		12	13	14	15	16	17	18	
42		19	20	21	22	23	24	25	
43	MONTH 10 Guǐ-Wèi	26	27	28	29	30	1	2	Shuāng jiàng
44		3	4	5*	6	7	8	9	
45		10	11	12	13	14	15	16	Lì dōng
46		17	18	19	20	21	22	23	
47		24	25	26	27	28	29	1	Xiǎo xuě
48	MONTH 11* Guǐ-Wèi	2	3	4	5	6	7	8	
49		9	10	11	12	13	14	15	Dà xuě
50		16	17	18	19	20	21	22	
51		23	24	25	26	27[i]	28	29	Dōng zhì
52		30	1	2	3	4	5	6	

ISO Week	Coptic 1659‡/1660	Sun	Mon	Tue	Wed	Thu	Fri	Sat	Ethiopic 1935‡/1936
53	KOIAK 1659	18	19	20	21	22	23	24	TĀKHŚĀŚ 1935
1	TÔBE 1659	25	26	27	28	29[c]	30	1	ṬER 1935
2		2	3	4	5	6[d]	7	8	
3		9	10	11[e]	12	13	14	15	
4		16	17	18	19	20	21	22	
5		23	24	25	26	27	28	29	
6	MESHIR 1659	30	1	2	3	4	5	6	YAKĀTIT 1935
7		7	8	9	10	11	12	13	
8		14	15	16	17	18	19	20	
9		21	22	23	24	25	26	27	
10	PAREMOTEP 1659	28	29	30	1	2	3	4	MAGĀBIT 1935
11		5	6	7	8	9	10	11	
12		12	13	14	15	16	17	18	
13		19	20	21	22	23	24	25	
14	PARMOUTE 1659	26	27	28	29	30	1	2	MIYĀZYĀ 1935
15		3	4	5	6	7	8	9	
16		10	11	12	13	14	15	16	
17		17[f]	18	19	20	21	22	23	
18		24	25	26	27	28	29[g]	30	
19	PASHONS 1659	1	2	3	4	5	6	7	GENBOT 1935
20		8	9	10	11	12	13	14	
21		15	16	17	18	19	20	21	
22		22	23	24	25	26	27	28	
23	PAÔNE 1659	29	30	1	2	3	4	5	SANĒ 1935
24		6	7	8	9	10	11	12	
25		13	14	15	16	17	18	19	
26		20	21	22	23	24	25	26	
27	EPÊP 1659	27	28	29	30	1	2	3	ḤAMLĒ 1935
28		4	5	6	7	8	9	10	
29		11	12	13	14	15	16	17	
30		18	19	20	21	22	23	24	
31	MESORÊ 1659	25	26	27	28	29	30	1	NAHASĒ 1935
32		2	3	4	5	6	7	8	
33		9	10	11	12	13[h]	14	15	
34		16	17	18	19	20	21	22	
35		23	24	25	26	27	28	29	
36	EPAG. 1659	30	1	2	3	4	5	6	PĀG. 1935
37	THOOUT 1660	1[a]	2	3	4	5	6	7	MASKARAM 1936
38		8	9	10	11	12	13	14	
39		15	16	17[b]	18	19	20	21	
40		22	23	24	25	26	27	28	
41	PAOPE 1660	29	30	1	2	3	4	5	ṬEQEMT 1936
42		6	7	8	9	10	11	12	
43		13	14	15	16	17	18	19	
44		20	21	22	23	24	25	26	
45	ATHÔR 1660	27	28	29	30	1	2	3	ḪEDĀR 1936
46		4	5	6	7	8	9	10	
47		11	12	13	14	15	16	17	
48		18	19	20	21	22	23	24	
49	KOIAK 1660	25	26	27	28	29	30	1	TĀKHŚĀŚ 1936
50		2	3	4	5	6	7	8	
51		9	10	11	12	13	14	15	
52		16	17	18	19	20	21	22	

[a]New Year
[b]Spring (12:02)
[c]Summer (7:12)
[d]Autumn (22:11)
[e]Winter (17:29)
● New moon
◐ First quarter moon
○ Full moon
◑ Last quarter moon

‡Leap year
[a]New Year
[b]Yom Kippur
[c]Sukkot
[d]Winter starts
[e]Ḥanukkah
[f]Purim
[g]Passover
[h]Shavuot
[i]Fast of Av

[a]New Year (4641, Sheep)
[b]Lantern Festival
[c]Qīngmíng
[d]Dragon Festival
[e]Qīqiǎo
[f]Hungry Ghosts
[g]Mid-Autumn Festival
[h]Double-Ninth Festival
[i]Dōngzhì
*Start of 60-name cycle

‡Leap year
[a]New Year
[b]Building of the Cross
[c]Christmas
[d]Jesus's Circumcision
[e]Epiphany
[f]Easter
[g]Mary's Announcement
[h]Jesus's Transfiguration

1943

PERSIAN (ASTRONOMICAL) 1321‡/1322

Month	Sun	Mon	Tue	Wed	Thu	Fri	Sat
DEY 1321	6	7	8	9	10	11	12
	13	14	15	16	17	18	19
	20	21	22	23	24	25	26
BAHMAN 1321	27	28	29	30	1	2	3
	4	5	6	7	8	9	10
	11	12	13	14	15	16	17
	18	19	20	21	22	23	24
ESFAND 1321	25	26	27	28	29	30	1
	2	3	4	5	6	7	8
	9	10	11	12	13	14	15
	16	17	18	19	20	21	22
	23	24	25	26	27	28	29
FARVARDĪN 1322	30	1[a]	2	3	4	5	6
	7	8	9	10	11	12	13[b]
	14	15	16	17	18	19	20
	21	22	23	24	25	26	27
ORDĪBEHEŠT 1322	28	29	30	31	1	2	3
	4	5	6	7	8	9	10
	11	12	13	14	15	16	17
	18	19	20	21	22	23	24
	25	26	27	28	29	30	31
XORDĀD 1322	1	2	3	4	5	6	7
	8	9	10	11	12	13	14
	15	16	17	18	19	20	21
	22	23	24	25	26	27	28
TĪR 1322	29	30	31	1	2	3	4
	5	6	7	8	9	10	11
	12	13	14	15	16	17	18
	19	20	21	22	23	24	25
MORDĀD 1322	26	27	28	29	30	31	1
	2	3	4	5	6	7	8
	9	10	11	12	13	14	15
	16	17	18	19	20	21	22
	23	24	25	26	27	28	29
SHAHRĪVAR 1322	30	31	1	2	3	4	5
	6	7	8	9	10	11	12
	13	14	15	16	17	18	19
	20	21	22	23	24	25	26
MEHR 1322	27	28	29	30	31	1	2
	3	4	5	6	7	8	9
	10	11	12	13	14	15	16
	17	18	19	20	21	22	23
	24	25	26	27	28	29	30
ĀBĀN 1322	1	2	3	4	5	6	7
	8	9	10	11	12	13	14
	15	16	17	18	19	20	21
	22	23	24	25	26	27	28
ĀZAR 1322	29	30	1	2	3	4	5
	6	7	8	9	10	11	12
	13	14	15	16	17	18	19
	20	21	22	23	24	25	26
DEY 1322	27	28	29	30	1	2	3
	4	5	6	7	8	9	10

‡Leap year
[a]New Year
[b]Sizdeh Bedar

HINDU LUNAR 1999‡/2000

Month	Sun	Mon	Tue	Wed	Thu	Fri	Sat
MĀRGAŚĪRA 1999	20	21	22	23	24	25	26
PAUSHA 1999	27	28	29	30	1	2	3
	4	5	7	8	9	10	11
	11	12	13	14	15	16	17
	18	19	20	21	22	23	24
MĀGHA 1999	25	26	27	28	29	1	2
	3	4	5	6	7	8	9
	10	11	12	13	13	14	15
	16	17	18	19	20	21	22
	23	25	26	27	28[h]	29	30
PHĀLGUNA 1999	1	2	3	4	5	6	7
	8	9	10	11	12	13	14
	15[i]	16	17	18	19	20	21
	22	23	24	25	26	27	29
CHAITRA 2000	30	1[a]	2	3	4	5	6
	7	7	8[b]	9	10	11	12
	13	14	15	16	17	18	19
	20	21	23	24	25	26	27
VAIŚĀKHA 2000	28	29	30	1	2	3	4
	5	6	7	8	9	10	11
	12	13	14	15	16	17	18
	19	20	21	22	23	24	26
JYAISHTHA 2000	27	28	29	30	1	2	2
	3	4	5	6	7	8	9
	10	11	12	13	14	15	16
	17	19	20	21	22	23	24
ĀSHĀDHA 2000	25	26	27	28	29	30	1
	2	3	4	5	6	7	8
	9	10	11	12	13	14	15
	16	17	18	19	20	22	23
	24	25	26	27	28	29	29
ŚRĀVAṆA 2000	30	1	2	3	4	5	6
	7	8	9	10	11	12	14
	15	16	17	18	19	20	21
	22	23[c]	24	25	26	27	28
BHĀDRAPADA 2000	29	30	1	2	3	4[d]	5
	6	7	8	9	10	11	12
	13	14	15	16	18	19	20
	21	22	23	24	25	25	26
ĀŚVINA 2000	27	28	29	30	1	2	3
	4	5	6	7	8[e]	9[e]	11
	12	13	14	15	16	17	18
	19	20	21	22	23	24	25
KĀRTTIKA 2000	26	27	28	29	29	30	1[f]
	3	4	5	6	7	8	9
	10	11	12	13	14	16	17
	18	18	19	20	21	22	23
	24	25	26	27	28	29	30
MĀRGAŚĪRA 2000	1	2	3	4	5	6	7
	9	10	11[g]	12	13	14	15
	16	17	18	19	20	21	22
	22	23	24	25	26	27	28
PAUSHA 2000	29	30	1	3	4	5	6

‡Leap year
[a]New Year (Subhānu)
[b]Birthday of Rāma
[c]Birthday of Krishna
[d]Ganēśa Chaturthī
[e]Dashara
[f]Diwali
[g]Birthday of Vishnu
[h]Night of Śiva
[i]Holi

HINDU SOLAR 1864/1865

Month	Sun	Mon	Tue	Wed	Thu	Fri	Sat
PAUSHA 1864	13	14	15	16	17	18	19
	20	21	22	23	24	25	26
MĀGHA 1864	27	28	29	30	1[b]	2	3
	4	5	6	7	8	9	10
	11	12	13	14	15	16	17
	18	19	20	21	22	23	24
PHĀLGUNA 1864	25	26	27	28	29	1	2
	3	4	5	6	7	8	9
	10	11	12	13	14	15	16
	17	18	19	20	21	22	23
	24	25	26	27	28	29	30
CHAITRA 1864	1	2	3	4	5	6	7
	8	9	10	11	12	13	14
	15	16	17	18	19	20	21
	22	23	24	25	26	27	28
VAIŚĀKHA 1865	29	30	1[a]	2	3	4	5
	6	7	8	9	10	11	12
	13	14	15	16	17	18	19
	20	21	22	23	24	25	26
JYAISHTHA 1865	27	28	29	30	31	1	2
	3	4	5	6	7	8	9
	10	11	12	13	14	15	16
	17	18	19	20	21	22	23
	24	25	26	27	28	29	30
ĀSHĀDHA 1865	31	32	1	2	3	4	5
	6	7	8	9	10	11	12
	13	14	15	16	17	18	19
	20	21	22	23	24	25	26
ŚRĀVAṆA 1865	27	28	29	30	31	1	2
	3	4	5	6	7	8	9
	10	11	12	13	14	15	16
	17	18	19	20	21	22	23
	24	25	26	27	28	29	30
BHĀDRAPADA 1865	31	32	1	2	3	4	5
	6	7	8	9	10	11	12
	13	14	15	16	17	18	19
	20	21	22	23	24	25	26
ĀŚVINA 1865	27	28	29	30	31	1	2
	3	4	5	6	7	8	9
	10	11	12	13	14	15	16
	17	18	19	20	21	22	23
	24	25	26	27	28	29	30
KĀRTTIKA 1865	1	2	3	4	5	6	7
	8	9	10	11	12	13	14
	15	16	17	18	19	20	21
	22	23	24	25	26	27	28
MĀRGAŚĪRA 1865	29	30	1	2	3	4	5
	6	7	8	9	10	11	12
	13	14	15	16	17	18	19
	20	21	22	23	24	25	26
PAUSHA 1865	27	28	29	30	1	2	3
	4	5	6	7	8	9	10
	11	12	13	14	15	16	17

[a]New Year (Durmukha)
[b]Pongal

ISLAMIC (ASTRONOMICAL) 1361‡/1362/1363‡

Month	Sun	Mon	Tue	Wed	Thu	Fri	Sat
DHU AL-ḤIJJA 1361	19	20	21	22	23	24	25
MUḤARRAM 1362	26	27	28	29	30	1[a]	2
	3	4	5	6	7	8	9
	10[b]	11	12	13	14	15	16
	17	18	19	20	21	22	23
ṢAFAR 1362	24	25	26	27	28	29	1
	2	3	4	5	6	7	8
	9	10	11	12	13	14	15
	16	17	18	19	20	21	22
	23	24	25	26	27	28	29
RABĪʿ I 1362	30	1	2	3	4	5	6
	7	8	9	10	11	12[c]	13
	14	15	16	17	18	19	20
	21	22	23	24	25	26	27
RABĪʿ II 1362	28	29	1	2	3	4	5
	6	7	8	9	10	11	12
	13	14	15	16	17	18	19
	20	21	22	23	24	25	26
JUMĀDĀ I 1362	27	28	29	30	1	2	3
	4	5	6	7	8	9	10
	11	12	13	14	15	16	17
	18	19	20	21	22	23	24
JUMĀDĀ II 1362	25	26	27	28	29	1	2
	3	4	5	6	7	8	9
	10	11	12	13	14	15	16
	17	18	19	20	21	22	23
	24	25	26	27	28	29	30
RAJAB 1362	1	2	3	4	5	6	7
	8	9	10	11	12	13	14
	15	16	17	18	19	20	21
	22	23	24	25	26	27[d]	28
SHAʿBĀN 1362	29	30	1	2	3	4	5
	6	7	8	9	10	11	12
	13	14	15	16	17	18	19
	20	21	22	23	24	25	26
RAMAḌĀN 1362	27	28	29	1[e]	2	3	4
	5	6	7	8	9	10	11
	12	13	14	15	16	17	18
	19	20	21	22	23	24	25
SHAWWĀL 1362	26	27	28	29	30	1[f]	2
	3	4	5	6	7	8	9
	10	11	12	13	14	15	16
	17	18	19	20	21	22	23
DHU AL-QAʿDA 1362	24	25	26	27	28	29	1
	2	3	4	5	6	7	8
	9	10	11	12	13	14	15
	16	17	18	19	20	21	22
	23	24	25	26	27	28	29
DHU AL-ḤIJJA 1362	30	1	2	3	4	5	6
	7	8	9	10[g]	11	12	13
	14	15	16	17	18	19	20
	21	22	23	24	25	26	27
	28	29	1[a]	2	3	4	5

‡Leap year
[a]New Year
[b]ʿAshūrāʾ
[c]Prophet's Birthday
[d]Ascent of the Prophet
[e]Start of Ramaḍān
[f]ʿId al-Fiṭr
[g]ʿId al-ʾAḍḥā

GREGORIAN 1943

Julian (Sun)	Sun	Mon	Tue	Wed	Thu	Fri	Sat	Month
Dec 14	27	28	29	30	31	1	2	JANUARY 1943
	3	4	5	6	7[a]	8	9	
Dec 28	10	11	12	13	14[b]	15	16	
	17	18	19	20	21	22	23	
Jan 11	24	25	26	27	28	29	30	
	31	1	2	3	4	5	6	FEBRUARY 1943
Jan 25	7	8	9	10	11	12	13	
	14	15	16	17	18	19	20	
Feb 8	21	22	23	24	25	26	27	
	28	1	2	3	4	5	6	MARCH 1943
Feb 22	7	8	9	10[c]	11	12	13	
	14[d]	15	16	17	18	19	20	
Mar 8	21	22	23	24	25	26	27	
	28	29	30	31	1	2	3	APRIL 1943
Mar 22	4	5	6	7	8	9	10	
	11	12	13	14	15	16	17	
Apr 5	18	19	20	21	22	23	24	
	25[e]	26	27	28	29	30	1	MAY 1943
Apr 19	2	3	4	5	6	7	8	
	9	10	11	12	13	14	15	
May 3	16	17	18	19	20	21	22	
	23	24	25	26	27	28	29	
May 17	30	31	1	2	3	4	5	JUNE 1943
	6	7	8	9	10	11	12	
May 31	13	14	15	16	17	18	19	
	20	21	22	23	24	25	26	
Jun 14	27	28	29	30	1	2	3	JULY 1943
	4	5	6	7	8	9	10	
Jun 28	11	12	13	14	15	16	17	
	18	19	20	21	22	23	24	
Jul 12	25	26	27	28	29	30	31	
	1	2	3	4	5	6	7	AUGUST 1943
Jul 26	8	9	10	11	12	13	14	
	15	16	17	18	19	20	21	
Aug 9	22	23	24	25	26	27	28	
	29	30	31	1	2	3	4	SEPTEMBER 1943
Aug 23	5	6	7	8	9	10	11	
	12	13	14	15	16	17	18	
Sep 6	19	20	21	22	23	24	25	
	26	27	28	29	30	1	2	OCTOBER 1943
Sep 20	3	4	5	6	7	8	9	
	10	11	12	13	14	15	16	
Oct 4	17	18	19	20	21	22	23	
	24	25	26	27	28	29	30	
Oct 18	31	1	2	3	4	5	6	NOVEMBER 1943
	7	8	9	10	11	12	13	
Nov 1	14	15	16	17	18	19	20	
	21	22	23	24	25	26	27	
Nov 15	28[g]	29	30	1	2	3	4	DECEMBER 1943
	5	6	7	8	9	10	11	
Nov 29	12	13	14	15	16	17	18	
	19	20	21	22	23	24	25[h]	
Dec 13	26	27	28	29	30	31	1	

[a]Orthodox Christmas
[b]Julian New Year
[c]Ash Wednesday
[d]Feast of Orthodoxy
[e]Easter (also Orthodox)
[g]Advent
[h]Christmas

1944

Gregorian month	GREGORIAN 1944‡ (Sun Mon Tue Wed Thu Fri Sat)	Lunar Phases	ISO WEEK (Mon)	JULIAN DAY (Sun noon)	Hebrew month	HEBREW 5704/5705 (Sun Mon Tue Wed Thu Fri Sat)	Molad	Chinese month	CHINESE Guǐ-Wèi/Jiǎ-Shēn‡ (Sun Mon Tue Wed Thu Fri Sat)	Solar Term	Coptic month	COPTIC 1660/1661 / ETHIOPIC 1936/1937 (Sun Mon Tue Wed Thu Fri Sat)	Ethiopic month
JANUARY 1944	26 ● 28 29 30 31 | 1[a]	3:50	52	2431085	TEVETH 5704	29[e] 30[e] | 1[e] 2[e] 3 4 5	Mon 1h50m4p	MONTH 12 Guǐ-Wèi	30 | 1 2 3 4 5 6*		KOIAK 1660	16 17 18 19 20 21 22	TĀKHŚĀŚ 1936
	◐ 3 4 5 6 7 8	20:04	1	2431092		6 7 8 9 10 11 12			7 8 9 10 *11* 12 13	Xiǎo hán		23 24 25 26 27 28 29[c]	
	9 ○ 11 12 13 14 15	10:09	2	2431099		13 14 15 16 17 18 19			14 15 16 17 18 19 20		TŌBE 1660	30 | 1 2 3 4 5 6[d]	ṬER 1936
	16 17 ◑ 19 20 21 22	15:32	3	2431106		20 21 22 23 24 25 26			21 22 23 24 25 ***26*** 27	Dà hán		7 8 9 10 11[e] 12 13	
	23 24 ● 26 27 28 29	15:24	4	2431113	SHEVAT 5704	27 28 29 | 1 2 3 4	Tue 14h34m5p	MONTH 1 Jiǎ-Shēn	28 29 | 1[a] 2 3 4 5			14 15 16 17 18 19 20	
FEBRUARY 1944	30 31 | ◐ 2 3 4 5	7:08	5	2431120		5 6 7 8 9 10 11			6 7 8 9 10 11 *12*	Lì chūn		21 22 23 24 25 26 27	
	6 7 8 ○ 10 11 12	5:29	6	2431127		12 13 14 15 16 17 18			13 14 15[b] 16 17 18 19		MESHIR 1660	28 29 30 | 1 2 3 4	YAKĀTIT 1936
	13 14 15 16 ◑ 18 19	7:42	7	2431134		19 20 21 22 23 24 25			20 21 22 23 24 25 26			5 6 7 8 9 10 11	
	20 21 22 23 ● 25 26	1:59	8	2431141	ADAR 5704	26 27 28 29 30 | 1 2	Thu 3h18m6p	MONTH 2 Jiǎ-Shēn	***27*** 28 29 30 | 1 2 3	Yǔ shuǐ		12 13 14 15 16 17 18	
MARCH 1944	27 28 29 | ◐ 2 3 4	20:40	9	2431148		3 4 5 6 7 8 9			4 5 6 7* 8 9 10			19 20 21 22 23 24 25	
	5 6 7 8 9 ○ 11	0:28	10	2431155		10 11 12 13 14[f] 15 16			11 *12* 13 14 15 16 17	Jīng zhé	PAREMOTEP 1660	26 27 28 29 30 | 1 2	MAGĀBIT 1936
	12 13 14 15 16 ◑ 18	20:05	11	2431162		17 18 19 20 21 22 23			18 19 20 21 22 23 24			3 4 5 6 7 8 9	
	19 20[b] 21 22 23 ● 25	11:36	12	2431169	NISAN 5704	24 25 26 27 28 29 | 1	Fri 16h2m7p	MONTH 3 Jiǎ-Shēn	25 26 ***27*** 28 29 | 1 2	Chūn fēn		10 11 12 13 14 15 16	
APRIL 1944	26 27 28 29 30 ◐ | 1	12:34	13	2431176		2 3 4 5 6 7 8			3 4 5 6 7 8 9			17 18 19 20 21 22 23	
	2 3 4 5 6 7 ○	17:21	14	2431183		9 10 11 12 13 14 15[g]			10 11 12 *13*[c] 14 15 16	Qīng míng		24 25 26 27 28 29 30	
	9 10 11 12 13 14 15		15	2431190		16 17 18 19 20 21 22			17 18 19 20 21 22 23		PARMOUTE 1660	1 2 3 4 5 6 7	MIYĀZYĀ 1936
	◑ 17 18 19 20 21 ●	4:59 20:43	16	2431197		23 24 25 26 27 28 29			24 25 26 27 ***28*** 29 30	Gǔ yǔ		8[f] 9 10 11 12 13 14	
	23 24 25 26 27 28 29		17	2431204	IYYAR 5704	30 | 1 2 3 4 5 6	Sun 4h46m8p	MONTH 4 Jiǎ-Shēn	1 2 3 4 5 6 7			15 16 17 18 19 20 21	
MAY 1944	◐ | 1 2 3 4 5 6	6:06	18	2431211		7 8 9 10 11 12 13			8* 9 10 11 12 *13* 14	Lì xià		22 23 24 25 26 27 28	
	7 ○ 9 10 11 12 13	7:28	19	2431218		14 15 16 17 18 19 20			15 16 17 18 19 20 21		PASHONS 1660	29[g] 30 | 1 2 3 4 5	GENBOT 1936
	14 ◑ 16 17 18 19 20	11:12	20	2431225		21 22 23 24 25 26 27			22 23 24 25 26 27 28			6 7 8 9 10 11 12	
	21 ● 23 24 25 26 27	6:12	21	2431232	SIVAN 5704	28 29 | 1 2 3 4 5	Mon 17h30m9p	LEAP MONTH 4 Jiǎ-Shēn	***29*** | 1 2 3 4 5 6	Xiǎo mǎn		13 14 15 16 17 18 19	
JUNE 1944	28 29 ◐ 31 | 1 2 3	0:06	22	2431239		6[h] 7 8 9 10 11 12			7 8 9 10 11 12 13			20 21 22 23 24 25 26	
	4 5 ○ 7 8 9 10	18:58	23	2431246		13 14 15 16 17 18 19			14 15 *16* 17 18 19 20	Máng zhòng	PAŌNE 1660	27 28 29 30 | 1 2 3	SANÉ 1936
	11 12 ◑ 14 15 16 17	15:56	24	2431253		20 21 22 23 24 25 26			21 22 23 24 25 26 27			4 5 6 7 8 9 10	
	18 19 ● 21[c] 22 23 24	16:59	25	2431260	TAMMUZ 5704	27 28 29 30 | 1 2 3	Wed 6h14m10p	MONTH 5 Jiǎ-Shēn	28 29 30 | ***1*** 2 3 4	Xià zhì		11 12 13 14 15 16 17	
JULY 1944	25 26 27 ◐ 29 30 | 1	17:27	26	2431267		4 5 6 7 8 9 10			5[d] 6 7 8 9* 10 11			18 19 20 21 22 23 24	
	2 3 4 5 ○ 7 8	4:27	27	2431274		11 12 13 14 15 16 17			12 13 14 15 16 *17* 18	Xiǎo shǔ	EPĒP 1660	25 26 27 28 29 30 | 1	ḤAMLÉ 1936
	9 10 11 ◑ 13 14 15	20:39	28	2431281		18 19 20 21 22 23 24			19 20 21 22 23 24 25			2 3 4 5 6 7 8	
	16 17 18 19 ● 21 22	5:42	29	2431288	AV 5704	25 26 27 28 29 | 1 2	Thu 18h58m11p	MONTH 6 Jiǎ-Shēn	26 27 28 29 | 1 2 3			9 10 11 12 13 14 15	
	23 24 25 26 27 ◐ 29	9:24	30	2431295		3 4 5 6 7 8 9			***4*** 5 6 7 8 9 10	Dà shǔ		16 17 18 19 20 21 22	
AUGUST 1944	30 31 | 1 2 3 ○ 5	12:39	31	2431302		10[i] 11 12 13 14 15 16			11 12 13 14 15 16 17			23 24 25 26 27 28 29	
	6 7 8 9 10 ◑ 12	2:52	32	2431309		17 18 19 20 21 22 23			18 19 *20* 21 22 23 24	Lì qiū	MESORĒ 1660	30 | 1 2 3 4 5 6	NAHASÉ 1936
	13 14 15 16 17 ● 19	20:25	33	2431316		24 25 26 27 28 29 30		MONTH 7 Jiǎ-Shēn	25 26 27 28 29 30 | 1			7 8 9 10 11 12 13[h]	
	20 21 22 23 24 25 ◐	23:39	34	2431323	ELUL 5704	1 2 3 4 5 6 7	Sat 7h42m12p		2 3 4 ***5*** 6 7[e] 8	Chǔ shǔ		14 15 16 17 18 19 20	
SEPTEMBER 1944	27 28 29 30 31 | 1 ○	20:21	35	2431330		8 9 10 11 12 13 14			9 10* 11 12 13 14 15[f]			21 22 23 24 25 26 27	
	3 4 5 6 7 8 ◑	12:03	36	2431337		15 16 17 18 19 20 21			16 17 18 19 20 *21* 22	Bái lù	EPAG. 1660	28 29 30 | 1 2 3 4	PĀG. 1936
	10 11 12 13 14 15 16		37	2431344		22 23 24 25 26 27 28			23 24 25 26 27 28 29		THOOUT 1661	5 | 1[a] 2 3 4 5 6	MASKARAM 1937
	● 18 19 20 21 22 23[d]	12:37	38	2431351	TISHRI 5705	29 | 1[a] 2[a] 3 4 5 6	Sun 20h26m13p	MONTH 8 Jiǎ-Shēn	1 2 3 4 5 6 ***7***	Qiū fēn		7 8 9 10 11 12 13	
	24 ◐ 26 27 28 29 30	12:07	39	2431358		7 8 9 10[b] 11 12 13			8 9 10 11 12 13 14			14 15 16 17[b] 18 19 20	
OCTOBER 1944	1 ○ 3 4 5 6 7	4:22	40	2431365		14 15[c] 16 17 18 19 20			15[g] 16 17 18 19 20 21			21 22 23 24 25 26 27	
	8 ◑ 10 11 12 13 14	1:12	41	2431372		21 22 23 24 25 26 27			*22* 23 24 25 26 27 28	Hán lù	PAOPE 1661	28 29 30 | 1 2 3 4	TEQEMT 1937
	15 16 ● 18 19 20 21	5:35	42	2431379	HESHVAN 5705	28 29 30 | 1 2 3 4	Tue 9h10m14p	MONTH 9 Jiǎ-Shēn	29 30 | 1 2 3 4 5			5 6 7 8 9 10 11	
	22 23 ◐ 25 26 27 28	22:48	43	2431386		5 6 7 8 9 10 11			6 ***7*** 8 9[h] 10 11* 12	Shuāng jiàng		12 13 14 15 16 17 18	
NOVEMBER 1944	29 30 ○ | 1 2 3 4	13:36	44	2431393		12 13 14 15 16 17 18			13 14 15 16 17 18 19			19 20 21 22 23 24 25	
	5 6 ◑ 8 9 10 11	18:29	45	2431400		19 20 21 22 23 24 25			20 21 *22* 23 24 25 26	Lì dōng	ATHŌR 1661	26 27 28 29 30 | 1 2	ḤEDĀR 1937
	12 13 14 ● 16 17 18	22:29	46	2431407	KISLEV 5705	26 27 28 29 30 | 1 2	Wed 21h54m15p	MONTH 10 Jiǎ-Shēn	27 28 29 30 | 1 2 3			3 4 5 6 7 8 9	
	19 20 21 22 ◐ 24 25	7:53	47	2431414		3 4 5 6 7 8 9			4 5 6 ***7*** 8 9 10	Xiǎo xuě		10 11 12 13 14 15 16	
DECEMBER 1944	26 27 28 29 ○ | 1 2	0:52	48	2431421		10 11 12 13 14 15 16			11 12 13 14 15 16 17			17 18 19 20 21 22 23	
	3 4 5 6 ◑ 8 9	14:57	49	2431428		17 18 19[d] 20 21 22 23			18 19 20 21 *22* 23 24	Dà xuě		24 25 26 27 28 29 30	
	10 11 12 13 14 ● 16	14:35	50	2431435		24 25[e] 26[e] 27[e] 28[e] 29[e] 30[e]		MONTH 11 Jiǎ-Shēn	25 26 27 28 29 | 1 2		KOIAK 1661	1 2 3 4 5 6 7	TĀKHŚĀŚ 1937
	17 18 19 20 21[e] ◐ 23	15:54	51	2431442	TEVETH 5705	1[e] 2[e] 3 4 5 6 7	Fri 10h38m16p		3 4 5 6 7 ***8***[i] 9	Dōng zhì		8 9 10 11 12 13 14	
	24 25 26 27 28 ○ 30	14:38	52	2431449		8 9 10 11 12 13 14			10 11 12* 13 14 15 16			15 16 17 18 19 20 21	
	31 | 1 2 3 4 5 ◑	12:47	1	2431456		15 16 17 18 19 20 21			17 18 19 20 21 22 23	Xiǎo hán		22 23 24 25 26 27 28	

‡Leap year
[a]New Year
[b]Spring (17:48)
[c]Summer (13:02)
[d]Autumn (4:01)
[e]Winter (23:15)
● New moon
◐ First quarter moon
○ Full moon
◑ Last quarter moon

[a]New Year
[b]Yom Kippur
[c]Sukkot
[d]Winter starts
[e]Ḥanukkah
[f]Purim
[g]Passover
[h]Shavuot
[i]Fast of Av

‡Leap year
[a]New Year (4642, Monkey)
[b]Lantern Festival
[c]Qīngmíng
[d]Dragon Festival
[e]Qīqiǎo
[f]Hungry Ghosts
[g]Mid-Autumn Festival
[h]Double-Ninth Festival
[i]Dōngzhì
*Start of 60-name cycle

[a]New Year
[b]Building of the Cross
[c]Christmas
[d]Jesus's Circumcision
[e]Epiphany
[f]Easter
[g]Mary's Announcement
[h]Jesus's Transfiguration

1944

PERSIAN (ASTRONOMICAL) 1322/1323								HINDU LUNAR 2000/2001								HINDU SOLAR 1865/1866‡								ISLAMIC (ASTRONOMICAL) 1362/1363‡/1364								Julian‡ (Sun)	GREGORIAN 1944‡							
	Sun	Mon	Tue	Wed	Thu	Fri	Sat		Sun	Mon	Tue	Wed	Thu	Fri	Sat		Sun	Mon	Tue	Wed	Thu	Fri	Sat		Sun	Mon	Tue	Wed	Thu	Fri	Sat		Sun	Mon	Tue	Wed	Thu	Fri	Sat	
DEY 1322	4	5	6	7	8	9	10	PAUSHA 2000	29	30	1	3	4	5	6	PAUSHA 1865	11	12	13	14	15	16	17	MUHARRAM 1363	28	29	1	2	3	4	5	Dec 13	26	27	28	29	30	31	1	
	11	12	13	14	15	16	17		7	8	9	10	11	12	13		18	19	20	21	22	23	24		6	7	8	9	10[b]	11	12		2	3	4	5	6	7[a]	8	JANUARY 1944
	18	19	20	21	22	23	24		14	15	16	17	18	19	20	MĀGHA 1865	25	26	27	28	29	1[b]	2		13	14	15	16	17	18	19	Dec 27	9	10	11	12	13	14[b]	15	
	25	26	27	28	29	30	1		21	22	23	24	25	26	27		3	4	5	6	7	8	9		20	21	22	23	24	25	26		16	17	18	19	20	21	22	
BAHMAN 1322	2	3	4	5	6	7	8	MĀGHA 2000	28	29	30	1	2	3	4		10	11	12	13	14	15	16	ṢAFAR 1363	27	28	29	30	1	2	3	Jan 10	23	24	25	26	27	28	29	
	9	10	11	12	13	14	15		5	6	8	9	10	11	12		17	18	19	20	21	22	23		4	5	6	7	8	9	10		30	31	1	2	3	4	5	FEBRUARY 1944
	16	17	18	19	20	21	22		13	14	14	15	16	17	18	PHĀLGUNA 1865	24	25	26	27	28	29	1		11	12	13	14	15	16	17	Jan 24	6	7	8	9	10	11	12	
	23	24	25	26	27	28	29		19	20	21	22	23	24	25		2	3	4	5	6	7	8		18	19	20	21	22	23	24		13	14	15	16	17	18	19	
ESFAND 1322	30	1	2	3	4	5	6	PHĀLGUNA 2000	26	27	28[h]	29	30	2	3		9	10	11	12	13	14	15	RABĪʿ I 1363	25	26	27	28	29	1	2	Feb 7	20	21	22	23[c]	24	25	26	
	7	8	9	10	11	12	13		4	5	6	7	8	9	10		16	17	18	19	20	21	22		3	4	5	6	7	8	9		27	28	29	1	2	3	4	MARCH 1944
	14	15	16	17	18	19	20		11	12	13	14	15[i]	16	16		23	24	25	26	27	28	29		10	11	12[c]	13	14	15	16	Feb 21	5[d]	6	7	8	9	10	11	
	21	22	23	24	25	26	27		17	18	19	20	21	22	23	CHAITRA 1865	30	1	2	3	4	5	6		17	18	19	20	21	22	23		12	13	14	15	16	17	18	
FARVARDĪN 1323	28	29	1[a]	2	3	4	5	CHAITRA 2001	24	26	27	28	29	30	1[a]		7	8	9	10	11	12	13		24	25	26	27	28	29	30	Mar 6	19	20	21	22	23	24	25	
	6	7	8	9	10	11	12		2	3	4	5	6	7	8[b]		14	15	16	17	18	19	20	RABĪʿ II 1363	1	2	3	4	5	6	7		26	27	28	29	30	31	1	APRIL 1944
	13[b]	14	15	16	17	18	19		9	10	11	12	13	14	15		21	22	23	24	25	26	27		8	9	10	11	12	13	14	Mar 20	2	3	4	5	6	7	8	
	20	21	22	23	24	25	26		16	17	18	19	20	21	22	VAIŚĀKHA 1866	28	29	30	1[a]	2	3	4		15	16	17	18	19	20	21		9[e]	10	11	12	13	14	15	
ORDĪBEHEŠT 1323	27	28	29	30	31	1	2		23	24	25	26	27	28	30		5	6	7	8	9	10	11		22	23	24	25	26	27	28	Apr 3	16[f]	17	18	19	20	21	22	
	3	4	5	6	7	8	9	VAIŚĀKHA 2001	1	2	3	4	5	6	7		12	13	14	15	16	17	18	JUMĀDĀ I 1363	29	1	2	3	4	5	6		23	24	25	26	27	28	29	
	10	11	12	13	14	15	16		8	9	10	11	11	12	13		19	20	21	22	23	24	25		7	8	9	10	11	12	13	Apr 17	30	1	2	3	4	5	6	MAY 1944
	17	18	19	20	21	22	23		14	15	16	17	18	19	20	JYAISHTHA 1866	26	27	28	29	30	31	1		14	15	16	17	18	19	20		7	8	9	10	11	12	13	
	24	25	26	27	28	29	30		21	23	24	25	26	27	28		2	3	4	5	6	7	8		21	22	23	24	25	26	27	May 1	14	15	16	17	18	19	20	
XORDĀD 1323	31	1	2	3	4	5	6	JYAISHTHA 2001	29	30	1	2	3	4	5		9	10	11	12	13	14	15	JUMĀDĀ II 1363	28	29	30	1	2	3	4		21	22	23	24	25	26	27	
	7	8	9	10	11	12	13		6	7	8	9	10	11	12		16	17	18	19	20	21	22		5	6	7	8	9	10	11	May 15	28	29	30	31	1	2	3	JUNE 1944
	14	15	16	17	18	19	20		13	14	15	16	17	18	19	ĀSHĀḌHA 1866	23	24	25	26	27	28	29		12	13	14	15	16	17	18		4	5	6	7	8	9	10	
	21	22	23	24	25	26	27		20	21	22	23	24	26	27		30	31	32	1	2	3	4		19	20	21	22	23	24	25	May 29	11	12	13	14	15	16	17	
TĪR 1323	28	29	30	31	1	2	3	ĀSHĀḌHA 2001	28	29	30	1	2	3	4		5	6	7	8	9	10	11	RAJAB 1363	26	27	28	29	1	2	3		18	19	20	21	22	23	24	
	4	5	6	7	8	9	10		5	6	7	7	8	9	10		12	13	14	15	16	17	18		4	5	6	7	8	9	10	Jun 12	25	26	27	28	29	30	1	JULY 1944
	11	12	13	14	15	16	17		11	12	13	14	15	16	17		19	20	21	22	23	24	25		11	12	13	14	15	16	17		2	3	4	5	6	7	8	
	18	19	20	21	22	23	24		19	20	21	22	23	24	25		26	27	28	29	30	31	32		18	19	20	21	22	23	24	Jun 26	9	10	11	12	13	14	15	
	25	26	27	28	29	30	31	ŚRĀVAṆA 2001	26	27	28	29	30	1	2	ŚRĀVAṆA 1866	1	2	3	4	5	6	7	SHAʿBĀN 1363	25	26	27[d]	28	29	30	1		16	17	18	19	20	21	22	
MORDĀD 1323	1	2	3	4	5	6	7		3	4	5	6	7	8	9		8	9	10	11	12	13	14		2	3	4	5	6	7	8	Jul 10	23	24	25	26	27	28	29	
	8	9	10	11	12	13	14		10	11	12	13	14	15	16		15	16	17	18	19	20	21		9	10	11	12	13	14	15		30	31	1	2	3	4	5	AUGUST 1944
	15	16	17	18	19	20	21		17	18	19	20	22	23[c]	24		22	23	24	25	26	27	28		16	17	18	19	20	21	22	Jul 24	6	7	8	9	10	11	12	
	22	23	24	25	26	27	28	BHĀDRAPADA 2001	25	26	27	28	29	30	1	BHĀDRAPADA 1866	29	30	31	1	2	3	4		23	24	25	26	27	28	29		13	14	15	16	17	18	19	
SHAHRĪVAR 1323	29	30	31	1	2	3	4		2	3	3[d]	4	5	6	7		5	6	7	8	9	10	11	RAMAḌĀN 1363	1[e]	2	3	4	5	6	7	Aug 7	20	21	22	23	24	25	26	
	5	6	7	8	9	10	11		8	9	10	11	12	13	15		12	13	14	15	16	17	18		8	9	10	11	12	13	14		27	28	29	30	31	1	2	SEPTEMBER 1944
	12	13	14	15	16	17	18		16	17	18	19	20	21	22		19	20	21	22	23	24	25		15	16	17	18	19	20	21	Aug 21	3	4	5	6	7	8	9	
	19	20	21	22	23	24	25		23	24	25	26	27	28	29	ĀŚVINA 1866	26	27	28	29	30	31	1		22	23	24	25	26	27	28		10	11	12	13	14	15	16	
MEHR 1323	26	27	28	29	30	31	1	ĀŚVINA 2001	30	1	2	3	4	5	6		2	3	4	5	6	7	8	SHAWWĀL 1363	29	30	1[f]	2	3	4	5	Sep 4	17	18	19	20	21	22	23	
	2	3	4	5	6	7	8		7	8[e]	9[e]	10[e]	11	12	13		9	10	11	12	13	14	15		6	7	8	9	10	11	12		24	25	26	27	28	29	30	
	9	10	11	12	13	14	15		14	15	16	18	19	20	21		16	17	18	19	20	21	22		13	14	15	16	17	18	19	Sep 18	1	2	3	4	5	6	7	OCTOBER 1944
	16	17	18	19	20	21	22		22	23	24	25	26	27	28	KĀRTTIKA 1866	23	24	25	26	27	28	29		20	21	22	23	24	25	26		8	9	10	11	12	13	14	
ĀBĀN 1323	23	24	25	26	27	28	29	KĀRTTIKA 2001	29	29	30	1[f]	2	3	4		30	1	2	3	4	5	6	DHU AL-QAʿDA 1363	27	28	29	30	1	2	3	Oct 2	15	16	17	18	19	20	21	
	30	1	2	3	4	5	6		5	6	7	8	9	10	12		7	8	9	10	11	12	13		4	5	6	7	8	9	10		22	23	24	25	26	27	28	
	7	8	9	10	11	12	13		13	14	15	16	17	18	19		14	15	16	17	18	19	20		11	12	13	14	15	16	17	Oct 16	29	30	31	1	2	3	4	NOVEMBER 1944
	14	15	16	17	18	19	20		20	21	22	23	24	25	26	MĀRGAŚĪRA 1866	21	22	23	24	25	26	27		18	19	20	21	22	23	24		5	6	7	8	9	10	11	
ĀZAR 1323	21	22	23	24	25	26	27	MĀRGAŚĪRA 2001	27	28	29	30	1	2	3		28	29	30	1	2	3	4	DHU AL-ḤIJJA 1363	25	26	27	28	29	1	2	Oct 30	12	13	14	15	16	17	18	
	28	29	30	1	2	3	4		4	5	6	7	8	9	10		5	6	7	8	9	10	11		3	4	5	6	7	8	9		19	20	21	22	23	24	25	
	5	6	7	8	9	10	11		11[g]	12	13	14	16	17	18		12	13	14	15	16	17	18		10[g]	11	12	13	14	15	16	Nov 13	26	27	28	29	30	1	2	DECEMBER 1944
	12	13	14	15	16	17	18		19	20	21	22	22	23	24	PAUSHA 1866	19	20	21	22	23	24	25		17	18	19	20	21	22	23		3[g]	4	5	6	7	8	9	
DEY 1323	19	20	21	22	23	24	25	PAUSHA 2001	25	26	27	28	29	30	1		26	27	28	29	30	1	2	MUḤARRAM 1364	24	25	26	27	28	29	30	Nov 27	10	11	12	13	14	15	16	
	26	27	28	29	30	1	2		2	3	4	5	6	7	8		3	4	5	6	7	8	9		1[a]	2	3	4	5	6	7		17	18	19	20	21	22	23	
	3	4	5	6	7	8	9		10	11	12	13	14	15	16		10	11	12	13	14	15	16		8	9	10[b]	11	12	13	14	Dec 11	24	25[h]	26	27	28	29	30	
	10	11	12	13	14	15	16		17	18	19	20	21	22	23		17	18	19	20	21	22	23		15	16	17	18	19	20	21		31	1	2	3	4	5	6	

[a]New Year
[b]Sizdeh Bedar

[a]New Year (Tāraṇa)
[b]Birthday of Rāma
[c]Birthday of Krishna
[d]Gaṇēśa Chaturthī
[e]Dashara
[f]Diwali
[g]Birthday of Vishnu
[h]Night of Śiva
[i]Holi

‡Leap year
[a]New Year (Hemalamba)
[b]Pongal

‡Leap year
[a]New Year
[b]ʿĀshūrāʾ
[c]Prophet's Birthday
[d]Ascent of the Prophet
[e]Start of Ramaḍān
[f]ʿId al-Fiṭr
[g]ʿId al-ʾAḍḥā

‡Leap year
[a]Orthodox Christmas
[b]Julian New Year
[c]Ash Wednesday
[d]Feast of Orthodoxy
[e]Easter
[f]Orthodox Easter
[g]Advent
[h]Christmas

1945

Gregorian 1945	Sun	Mon	Tue	Wed	Thu	Fri	Sat	Lunar Phases	ISO Week (Mon)	Julian Day (Sun noon)	Hebrew 5705/5706‡	Sun	Mon	Tue	Wed	Thu	Fri	Sat	Molad	Chinese Jiă-Shēn‡/Yĭ-Yŏu	Sun	Mon	Tue	Wed	Thu	Fri	Sat	Solar Term	Coptic 1661/1662	Sun	Mon	Tue	Wed	Thu	Fri	Sat	Ethiopic 1937/1938
January 1945	31	1[a]	2	3	4	5	◑	12:47	1	2431456	Teveth 5705	15	16	17	18	19	20	21		Month 11 Jiă-Shēn	17	18	19	20	21	22	23	Xiăo hán	Koiak 1661	22	23	24	25	26	27	28	Tākhśāś 1937
	7	8	9	10	11	12	13		2	2431463		22	23	24	25	26	27	28			24	25	26	27	28	29	30			29[c]	30	1	2	3	4	5	
	●	15	16	17	18	19	◐	5:07 23:48	3	2431470		29	1	2	3	4	5	6	Sat 23h22m17p	Month 12 Jiă-Shēn	1	2	3	4	5	6	7	Dà hán	Tôbe 1661	6[d]	7	8	9	10	11[e]	12	Ṭer 1937
	21	22	23	24	25	26	27		4	2431477	Shevat 5705	7	8	9	10	11	12	13			8	9	10	11	12	13	14			13	14	15	16	17	18	19	
	○	29	30	31	1	2	3	6:41	5	2431484		14	15	16	17	18	19	20			15	16	17	18	19	20	21			20	21	22	23	24	25	26	
February 1945	4	◑	6	7	8	9	10	9:55	6	2431491		21	22	23	24	25	26	27			22	23	24	25	26	27	28	Lì chūn		27	28	29	30	1	2	3	
	11	●	13	14	15	16	17	17:33	7	2431498		28	29	30	1	2	3	4	Mon 12h7m0p		29	30	1[a]	2	3	4	5		Meshir 1661	4	5	6	7	8	9	10	Yakātit 1937
	18	◐	20	21	22	23	24	8:38	8	2431505	Adar 5705	5	6	7	8	9	10	11		Month 1 Yĭ-Yŏu	6	7	8	9	10	11	12*	Yŭ shuĭ		11	12	13	14	15	16	17	
	25	26	○	28	1	2	3	0:07	9	2431512		12	13	14[f]	15	16	17	18			13	14	15[b]	16	17	18	19			18	19	20	21	22	23	24	
March 1945	4	5	6	◑	8	9	10	4:30	10	2431519		19	20	21	22	23	24	25			20	21	22	23	24	25	26	Jīng zhé		25	26	27	28	29	30	1	
	11	12	13	●	15	16	17	3:51	11	2431526		26	27	28	29	1	2	3	Wed 0h51m1p		27	28	29	1	2	3	4		Paremotep 1661	2	3	4	5	6	7	8	Magābit 1937
	18	19	◐[b]	21	22	23	24	19:11	12	2431533	Nisan 5705	4	5	6	7	8	9	10		Month 2 Yĭ-Yŏu	5	6	7	8	9	10	11	Chūn fēn		9	10	11	12	13	14	15	
	25	26	27	○	29	30	31	17:44	13	2431540		11	12	13	14	15[g]	16	17			12	13	14	15	16	17	18			16	17	18	19	20	21	22	
	1	2	3	4	◑	6	7	19:18	14	2431547		18	19	20	21	22	23	24			19	20	21	22	23[c]	24	25	Qīng míng		23	24	25	26	27	28	29	
April 1945	8	9	10	11	●	13	14	12:30	15	2431554		25	26	27	28	29	30	1	Thu 13h35m2p		26	27	28	29	1	2	3			30	1	2	3	4	5	6	
	15	16	17	18	◐	20	21	7:46	16	2431561	Iyyar 5705	2	3	4	5	6	7	8		Month 3 Yĭ-Yŏu	4	5	6	7	8	9	10	Gŭ yŭ	Parmoute 1661	7	8	9	10	11	12	13	Miyāzyā 1937
	22	23	24	25	26	○	28	10:33	17	2431568		9	10	11	12	13	14	15			11	12	13	14*	15	16	17			14	15	16	17	18	19	20	
	29	30	1	2	3	4	◑	6:02	18	2431575		16	17	18	19	20	21	22			18	19	20	21	22	23	24			21	22	23	24	25	26	27	
May 1945	6	7	8	9	10	●	12	20:22	19	2431582		23	24	25	26	27	28	29	Sat 2h19m3p		25	26	27	28	29	30	1	Lì xià		28[f]	29[g]	30	1	2	3	4	
	13	14	15	16	17	◐	19	22:12	20	2431589		1	2	3	4	5	6[h]	7		Month 4 Yĭ-Yŏu	2	3	4	5	6	7	8		Pashons 1661	5	6	7	8	9	10	11	Genbot 1937
	20	21	22	23	24	25	26		21	2431596	Sivan 5705	8	9	10	11	12	13	14			9	10	11	12	13	14	15	Xiăo măn		12	13	14	15	16	17	18	
	○	28	29	30	31	1	2	1:49	22	2431603		15	16	17	18	19	20	21			16	17	18	19	20	21	22			19	20	21	22	23	24	25	
June 1945	◑	4	5	6	7	8	9	13:15	23	2431610		22	23	24	25	26	27	28			23	24	25	26	27	28	29	Máng zhòng		26	27	28	29	30	1	2	
	●	11	12	13	14	15	16	4:26	24	2431617		29	30	1	2	3	4	5	Sun 15h3m4p		1	2	3	4	5[d]	6	7		Paĉne 1661	3	4	5	6	7	8	9	Sanē 1937
	◐	18	19	20	21[c]	22	23	14:05	25	2431624	Tammuz 5705	6	7	8	9	10	11	12		Month 5 Yĭ-Yŏu	8	9	10	11	12	13	14	Xià zhì		10	11	12	13	14	15	16	
	24	○	26	27	28	29	30	15:08	26	2431631		13	14	15	16	17	18	19			15*	16	17	18	19	20	21			17	18	19	20	21	22	23	
	1	◑	3	4	5	6	7	18:13	27	2431638		20	21	22	23	24	25	26			22	23	24	25	26	27	28	Xiăo shŭ		24	25	26	27	28	29	30	
July 1945	8	●	10	11	12	13	14	13:35	28	2431645		27	28	29	1	2	3	4	Tue 3h47m5p		29	1	2	3	4	5	6			1	2	3	4	5	6	7	
	15	16	◐	18	19	20	21	7:01	29	2431652	Av 5705	5	6	7	8	9[i]	10	11		Month 6 Yĭ-Yŏu	7	8	9	10	11	12	13		Epêp 1661	8	9	10	11	12	13	14	Ḥamlē 1937
	22	23	24	○	26	27	28	2:26	30	2431659		12	13	14	15	16	17	18			14	15	16	17	18	19	20	Dà shŭ		15	16	17	18	19	20	21	
	29	30	◑	1	2	3	4	22:30	31	2431666		19	20	21	22	23	24	25			21	22	23	24	25	26	27			22	23	24	25	26	27	28	
August 1945	5	6	7	●	9	10	11	0:32	32	2431673		26	27	28	29	30	1	2	Wed 16h31m6p		28	29	30	1	2	3	4	Lì qiū		29	30	1	2	3	4	5	
	12	13	14	15	◐	17	18	0:27	33	2431680	Elul 5705	3	4	5	6	7	8	9		Month 7 Yĭ-Yŏu	5	6	7[e]	8	9	10	11		Mesorê 1661	6	7	8	9	10	11	12	Naḥasē 1937
	19	20	21	22	○	24	25	12:03	34	2431687		10	11	12	13	14	15	16			12	13	14	15[f]	16*	17	18	Chŭ shŭ		13[h]	14	15	16	17	18	19	
	26	27	28	29	◑	31	1	3:44	35	2431694		17	18	19	20	21	22	23			19	20	21	22	23	24	25			20	21	22	23	24	25	26	
September 1945	2	3	4	5	●	7	8	13:44	36	2431701		24	25	26	27	28	29	1[a]	Fri 5h15m7p		26	27	28	29	1	2	3	Bái lù	Epag. 1661	27	28	29	30	1	2	3	Pāg. 1937
	9	10	11	12	13	◐	15	17:38	37	2431708		2[a]	3	4	5	6	7	8		Month 8 Yĭ-Yŏu	4	5	6	7	8	9	10			4	5	1[a]	2	3	4	5	Maskaram 1938
	16	17	18	19	20	○	22	20:46	38	2431715	Tishri 5706	9	10[b]	11	12	13	14	15[c]			11	12	13	14	15[g]	16	17		Thoout 1662	6	7	8	9	10	11	12	
	23[d]	24	25	26	27	◑	29	11:24	39	2431722		16	17	18	19	20	21	22			18	19	20	21	22	23	24	Qiū fēn		13	14	15	16	17[b]	18	19	
	30	1	2	3	4	5	●	5:22	40	2431729		23	24	25	26	27	28	29			25	26	27	28	29	30	1			20	21	22	23	24	25	26	
October 1945	7	8	9	10	11	12	13		41	2431736		30	1	2	3	4	5	6	Sat 17h59m8p		2	3	4	5	6	7	8	Hán lù		27	28	29	30	1	2	3	
	◐	15	16	17	18	19	20	9:38	42	2431743	Ḥeshvan 5706	7	8	9	10	11	12	13		Month 9 Yĭ-Yŏu	9[h]	10	11	12	13	14	15		Paope 1662	4	5	6	7	8	9	10	Teqemt 1938
	○	22	23	24	25	26	◑	5:32 22:30	43	2431750		14	15	16	17	18	19	20			16	17*	18	19	20	21	22	Shuāng jiàng		11	12	13	14	15	16	17	
	28	29	30	31	1	2	3		44	2431757		21	22	23	24	25	26	27			23	24	25	26	27	28	29			18	19	20	21	22	23	24	
November 1945	●	5	6	7	8	9	10	23:10	45	2431764		28	29	1	2	3	4	5	Mon 6h43m9p		30	1	2	3	4	5	6	Lì dōng		25	26	27	28	29	30	1	
	11	◐	13	14	15	16	17	23:34	46	2431771	Kislev 5706	6	7	8	9	10	11	12		Month 10 Yĭ-Yŏu	7	8	9	10	11	12	13		Athôr 1662	2	3	4	5	6	7	8	Ḫedār 1938
	18	○	20	21	22	23	24	15:13	47	2431778		13	14	15	16	17	18	19			14	15	16	17	18	19	20	Xiăo xuĕ		9	10	11	12	13	14	15	
	25	◑	27	28	29	30	1	13:28	48	2431785		20	21	22	23	24	25[e]	26[e]			21	22	23	24	25	26	27			16	17	18	19	20	21	22	
December 1945	2	3	●	5	6	7	8	18:06	49	2431792		27[e]	28[e]	29[e]	1[d][e]	2[e]	3[e]	4	Tue 19h27m10p		28	29	30	1	2	3	4	Dà xuĕ		23	24	25	26	27	28	29	
	9	10	11	◐	13	14	15	11:05	50	2431799	Teveth 5706	5	6	7	8	9	10	11		Month 11 Yĭ-Yŏu	5	6	7	8	9	10	11			30	1	2	3	4	5	6	
	16	17	18	○	20	21	22[e]	2:17	51	2431806		12	13	14	15	16	17	18			12	13	14	15	16	17*	18[i]	Dōng zhì	Koiak 1662	7	8	9	10	11	12	13	Tākhśāś 1938
	23	24	25	◑	27	28	29	8:00	52	2431813		19	20	21	22	23	24	25			19	20	21	22	23	24	25			14	15	16	17	18	19	20	
	30	31	1	2	●	4	5	12:30	1	2431820		26	27	28	29	1	2	3	Thu 8h11m11p		26	27	28	29	1	2	3			21	22	23	24	25	26	27	

[a]New Year
[b]Spring (23:37)
[c]Summer (18:52)
[d]Autumn (9:49)
[e]Winter (5:03)
● New moon
◐ First quarter moon
○ Full moon
◑ Last quarter moon

‡Leap year
[a]New Year
[b]Yom Kippur
[c]Sukkot
[d]Winter starts
[e]Ḥanukkah
[f]Purim
[g]Passover
[h]Shavuot
[i]Fast of Av

‡Leap year
[a]New Year (4643, Fowl)
[b]Lantern Festival
[c]Qīngmíng
[d]Dragon Festival
[e]Qīqiăo
[f]Hungry Ghosts
[g]Mid-Autumn Festival
[h]Double-Ninth Festival
[i]Dōngzhì
*Start of 60-name cycle

[a]New Year
[b]Building of the Cross
[c]Christmas
[d]Jesus's Circumcision
[e]Epiphany
[f]Easter
[g]Mary's Announcement
[h]Jesus's Transfiguration

PERSIAN (ASTRONOMICAL) 1323/1324

Month	Sun	Mon	Tue	Wed	Thu	Fri	Sat
DEY 1323	10	11	12	13	14	15	16
	17	18	19	20	21	22	23
	24	25	26	27	28	29	30
BAHMAN 1323	1	2	3	4	5	6	7
	8	9	10	11	12	13	14
	15	16	17	18	19	20	21
	22	23	24	25	26	27	28
	29	30	1	2	3	4	5
ESFAND 1323	6	7	8	9	10	11	12
	13	14	15	16	17	18	19
	20	21	22	23	24	25	26
	27	28	29	1[a]	2	3	4
FARVARDĪN 1324	5	6	7	8	9	10	11
	12	13[b]	14	15	16	17	18
	19	20	21	22	23	24	25
	26	27	28	29	30	31	1
ORDĪBEHEŠT 1324	2	3	4	5	6	7	8
	9	10	11	12	13	14	15
	16	17	18	19	20	21	22
	23	24	25	26	27	28	29
	30	31	1	2	3	4	5
XORDĀD 1324	6	7	8	9	10	11	12
	13	14	15	16	17	18	19
	20	21	22	23	24	25	26
	27	28	29	30	31	1	2
TĪR 1324	3	4	5	6	7	8	9
	10	11	12	13	14	15	16
	17	18	19	20	21	22	23
	24	25	26	27	28	29	30
	31	1	2	3	4	5	6
MORDĀD 1324	7	8	9	10	11	12	13
	14	15	16	17	18	19	20
	21	22	23	24	25	26	27
	28	29	30	31	1	2	3
SHAHRĪVAR 1324	4	5	6	7	8	9	10
	11	12	13	14	15	16	17
	18	19	20	21	22	23	24
	25	26	27	28	29	30	31
MEHR 1324	1	2	3	4	5	6	7
	8	9	10	11	12	13	14
	15	16	17	18	19	20	21
	22	23	24	25	26	27	28
	29	30	1	2	3	4	5
ĀBĀN 1324	6	7	8	9	10	11	12
	13	14	15	16	17	18	19
	20	21	22	23	24	25	26
	27	28	29	30	1	2	3
ĀZAR 1324	4	5	6	7	8	9	10
	11	12	13	14	15	16	17
	18	19	20	21	22	23	24
	25	26	27	28	29	30	1
DEY 1324	2	3	4	5	6	7	8
	9	10	11	12	13	14	15

HINDU LUNAR 2001/2002‡

Month	Sun	Mon	Tue	Wed	Thu	Fri	Sat
PAUSHA 2001	17	18	19	20	21	22	23
	24	24	25	26	27	28	29
	30	1	2	4	5	6	7
MĀGHA 2001	8	9	10	11	12	13	14
	15	16	17	18	19	20	21
	22	23	24	25	26	27	28
	29[h]	30	1	2	3	4	5
PHĀLGUNA 2001	6	7	9	10	11	12	13
	14	15[i]	16	17	17	18	19
	20	21	22	23	24	25	26
	27	28	29	30	1[a]	3	4
LEAP CHAITRA 2002	5	6	7	8	9	10	11
	12	13	14	15	16	17	18
	19	20	20	21	22	23	24
	26	27	28	29	30	1	2
CHAITRA 2002	3	4	5	6	7	9[b]	10
	10	11	12	13	14	15	16
	17	18	19	20	21	22	23
	24	25	26	27	28	30	1
VAIŚĀKHA 2002	2	3	4	5	6	7	8
	9	10	11	12	13	14	15
	15	16	17	18	19	20	21
	23	24	25	26	27	28	29
	30	1	2	3	4	5	6
JYAISHTHA 2002	7	8	9	10	11	12	13
	14	15	16	17	18	19	20
	21	22	23	24	26	27	28
	29	30	1	2	3	4	5
ĀSHĀḌHA 2002	6	7	8	9	10	11	12
	12	13	14	15	16	18	19
	20	21	22	23	24	25	26
	27	28	30	1	2	3	3
ŚRĀVAṆA 2002	4	5	6	7	8	9	10
	11	12	13	14	15	16	17
	18	19	20	22	23[c]	24	25
	26	27	28	29	30	1	2
BHĀDRAPADA 2002	3	4[d]	5	6	7	8	8
	9	10	11	12	14	15	16
	17	18	19	20	21	22	23
	24	25	27	27	28	29	30
ĀŚVINA 2002	1	2	3	4	5	6	7
	8[e]	9[e]	10[e]	11	12	13	14
	15	16	17	19	20	21	22
	23	24	25	26	27	28	29
	30	1[f]	2	2	3	4	5
KĀRTTIKA 2002	6	7	8	9	10	12	13
	14	15	16	17	18	19	20
	21	22	23	24	25	26	27
	28	29	30	1	2	3	4
MĀRGAŚĪRA 2002	5	6	7	8	9	10	11[g]
	12	13	14	15	17	18	19
	20	21	22	23	24	25	25
	26	27	28	29	30	1	2

HINDU SOLAR 1866‡/1867

Month	Sun	Mon	Tue	Wed	Thu	Fri	Sat
PAUSHA 1866	17	18	19	20	21	22	23
	24	25	26	27	28	29	1[b]
	2	3	4	5	6	7	8
MĀGHA 1866	9	10	11	12	13	14	15
	16	17	18	19	20	21	22
	23	24	25	26	27	28	29
	30	1	2	3	4	5	6
PHĀLGUNA 1866	7	8	9	10	11	12	13
	14	15	16	17	18	19	20
	21	22	23	24	25	26	27
	28	29	1	2	3	4	5
CHAITRA 1866	6	7	8	9	10	11	12
	13	14	15	16	17	18	19
	20	21	22	23	24	25	26
	27	28	29	30	31	1[a]	2
VAIŚĀKHA 1867	3	4	5	6	7	8	9
	10	11	12	13	14	15	16
	17	18	19	20	21	22	23
	24	25	26	27	28	29	30
	31	1	2	3	4	5	6
JYAISHTHA 1867	7	8	9	10	11	12	13
	14	15	16	17	18	19	20
	21	22	23	24	25	26	27
	28	29	30	31	1	2	3
ĀSHĀḌHA 1867	4	5	6	7	8	9	10
	11	12	13	14	15	16	17
	18	19	20	21	22	23	24
	25	26	27	28	29	30	31
	32	1	2	3	4	5	6
ŚRĀVAṆA 1867	7	8	9	10	11	12	13
	14	15	16	17	18	19	20
	21	22	23	24	25	26	27
	28	29	30	31	1	2	3
BHĀDRAPADA 1867	4	5	6	7	8	9	10
	11	12	13	14	15	16	17
	18	19	20	21	22	23	24
	25	26	27	28	29	30	31
	1	2	3	4	5	6	7
ĀŚVINA 1867	8	9	10	11	12	13	14
	15	16	17	18	19	20	21
	22	23	24	25	26	27	28
	29	30	31	1	2	3	4
KĀRTTIKA 1867	5	6	7	8	9	10	11
	12	13	14	15	16	17	18
	19	20	21	22	23	24	25
	26	27	28	29	30	1	2
MĀRGAŚĪRA 1867	3	4	5	6	7	8	9
	10	11	12	13	14	15	16
	17	18	19	20	21	22	23
	24	25	26	27	28	29	1
PAUSHA 1867	2	3	4	5	6	7	8
	9	10	11	12	13	14	15
	16	17	18	19	20	21	22

ISLAMIC (ASTRONOMICAL) 1364/1365

Month	Sun	Mon	Tue	Wed	Thu	Fri	Sat
MUḤARRAM 1364	15	16	17	18	19	20	21
	22	23	24	25	26	27	28
	29	1	2	3	4	5	6
ṢAFAR 1364	7	8	9	10	11	12	13
	14	15	16	17	18	19	20
	21	22	23	24	25	26	27
	28	29	30	1	2	3	4
RABĪ' I 1364	5	6	7	8	9	10	11
	12[c]	13	14	15	16	17	18
	19	20	21	22	23	24	25
	26	27	28	29	1	2	3
RABĪ' II 1364	4	5	6	7	8	9	10
	11	12	13	14	15	16	17
	18	19	20	21	22	23	24
	25	26	27	28	29	30	1
JUMĀDĀ I 1364	2	3	4	5	6	7	8
	9	10	11	12	13	14	15
	16	17	18	19	20	21	22
	23	24	25	26	27	28	29
JUMĀDĀ II 1364	1	2	3	4	5	6	7
	8	9	10	11	12	13	14
	15	16	17	18	19	20	21
	22	23	24	25	26	27	28
	29	1	2	3	4	5	6
RAJAB 1364	7	8	9	10	11	12	13
	14	15	16	17	18	19	20
	21	22	23	24	25	26	27[d]
	28	29	30	1	2	3	4
SHA'BĀN 1364	5	6	7	8	9	10	11
	12	13	14	15	16	17	18
	19	20	21	22	23	24	25
	26	27	28	29	1[e]	2	3
RAMAḌĀN 1364	4	5	6	7	8	9	10
	11	12	13	14	15	16	17
	18	19	20	21	22	23	24
	25	26	27	28	29	30	1[f]
SHAWWĀL 1364	2	3	4	5	6	7	8
	9	10	11	12	13	14	15
	16	17	18	19	20	21	22
	23	24	25	26	27	28	29
	30	1	2	3	4	5	6
DHU AL-QA'DA 1364	7	8	9	10	11	12	13
	14	15	16	17	18	19	20
	21	22	23	24	25	26	27
	28	29	1	2	3	4	5
DHU AL-ḤIJJA 1364	6	7	8	9	10[g]	11	12
	13	14	15	16	17	18	19
	20	21	22	23	24	25	26
	27	28	29	30	1[a]	2	3
MUḤARRAM 1365	4	5	6	7	8	9	10[b]
	11	12	13	14	15	16	17
	18	19	20	21	22	23	24
	25	26	27	28	29	30	1

GREGORIAN 1945

Julian (Sun)	Sun	Mon	Tue	Wed	Thu	Fri	Sat	Month
Dec 18	31	1	2	3	4	5	6	
	7[a]	8	9	10	11	12	13	JANUARY 1945
Jan 1	14[b]	15	16	17	18	19	20	
	21	22	23	24	25	26	27	
Jan 15	28	29	30	31	1	2	3	
	4	5	6	7	8	9	10	FEBRUARY 1945
Jan 29	11	12	13	14[c]	15	16	17	
	18	19	20	21	22	23	24	
Feb 12	25	26	27	28	1	2	3	
	4	5	6	7	8	9	10	MARCH 1945
Feb 26	11	12	13	14	15	16	17	
	18	19	20	21	22	23	24	
Mar 12	25[d]	26	27	28	29	30	31	
	1[e]	2	3	4	5	6	7	APRIL 1945
Mar 26	8	9	10	11	12	13	14	
	15	16	17	18	19	20	21	
Apr 9	22	23	24	25	26	27	28	
	29	30	1	2	3	4	5	
Apr 23	6[f]	7	8	9	10	11	12	MAY 1945
	13	14	15	16	17	18	19	
May 7	20	21	22	23	24	25	26	
	27	28	29	30	31	1	2	
May 21	3	4	5	6	7	8	9	JUNE 1945
	10	11	12	13	14	15	16	
Jun 4	17	18	19	20	21	22	23	
	24	25	26	27	28	29	30	
Jun 18	1	2	3	4	5	6	7	JULY 1945
	8	9	10	11	12	13	14	
Jul 2	15	16	17	18	19	20	21	
	22	23	24	25	26	27	28	
Jul 16	29	30	31	1	2	3	4	
	5	6	7	8	9	10	11	AUGUST 1945
Jul 30	12	13	14	15	16	17	18	
	19	20	21	22	23	24	25	
Aug 13	26	27	28	29	30	31	1	
	2	3	4	5	6	7	8	SEPTEMBER 1945
Aug 27	9	10	11	12	13	14	15	
	16	17	18	19	20	21	22	
Sep 10	23	24	25	26	27	28	29	
	30	1	2	3	4	5	6	
Sep 24	7	8	9	10	11	12	13	OCTOBER 1945
	14	15	16	17	18	19	20	
Oct 8	21	22	23	24	25	26	27	
	28	29	30	31	1	2	3	
Oct 22	4	5	6	7	8	9	10	NOVEMBER 1945
	11	12	13	14	15	16	17	
Nov 5	18	19	20	21	22	23	24	
	25	26	27	28	29	30	1	
Nov 19	2[g]	3	4	5	6	7	8	DECEMBER 1945
	9	10	11	12	13	14	15	
Dec 3	16	17	18	19	20	21	22	
	23	24	25[h]	26	27	28	29	
Dec 17	30	31	1	2	3	4	5	

Persian:
[a]New Year
[b]Sizdeh Bedar

Hindu lunar:
‡Leap year
[a]New Year (Pārthiva)
[b]Birthday of Rāma
[c]Birthday of Krishna
[d]Ganēśa Chaturthī
[e]Dashara
[f]Diwali
[g]Birthday of Vishnu
[h]Night of Śiva
[i]Holi

Hindu solar:
‡Leap year
[a]New Year (Vilamba)
[b]Pongal

Islamic:
[a]New Year
[b]'Ashūrā'
[c]Prophet's Birthday
[d]Ascent of the Prophet
[e]Start of Ramaḍān
[f]'Īd al-Fiṭr
[g]'Īd al-'Aḍḥā

Gregorian:
[a]Orthodox Christmas
[b]Julian New Year
[c]Ash Wednesday
[d]Feast of Orthodoxy
[e]Easter
[f]Orthodox Easter
[g]Advent
[h]Christmas

1946

GREGORIAN 1946	Sun	Mon	Tue	Wed	Thu	Fri	Sat	Lunar Phases	ISO WEEK (Mon)	JULIAN DAY (Sun noon)
JANUARY 1946	30	31	1[a]	2	●	4	5	12:30	1	2431820
	6	7	8	9	◐	11	12	20:27	2	2431827
	13	14	15	16	○	18	19	14:47	3	2431834
	20	21	22	23	24	◑	26	5:00	4	2431841
FEBRUARY 1946	27	28	29	30	31	1	●	4:43	5	2431848
	3	4	5	6	7	8	◐	4:28	6	2431855
	10	11	12	13	14	15	○	4:28	7	2431862
	17	18	19	20	21	22	23		8	2431869
MARCH 1946	◑	25	26	27	28	1	2	2:36	9	2431876
	●	4	5	6	7	8	9	18:01	10	2431883
	◐	11	12	13	14	15	16	12:03	11	2431890
	○	18	19	20	21[b]	22	23	19:11	12	2431897
	24	◑	26	27	28	29	30	22:37	13	2431904
APRIL 1946	31	1	●	3	4	5	6	4:37	14	2431911
	7	◐	9	10	11	12	13	20:04	15	2431918
	14	15	○	17	18	19	20	10:47	16	2431925
	21	22	23	◑	25	26	27	15:18	17	2431932
MAY 1946	28	29	30	●	2	3	4	13:16	18	2431939
	5	6	7	◐	9	10	11	5:13	19	2431946
	12	13	14	15	○	17	18	2:52	20	2431953
	19	20	21	22	23	◑	25	4:02	21	2431960
JUNE 1946	26	27	28	29	●	31	1	20:50	22	2431967
	2	3	4	5	◐	7	8	16:06	23	2431974
	9	10	11	12	13	○	15	18:42	24	2431981
	16	17	18	19	20	21	◑[c]	13:12	25	2431988
	23	24	25	26	27	28	●	4:06	26	2431995
JULY 1946	30	1	2	3	4	5	◐	5:15	27	2432002
	7	8	9	10	11	12	13		28	2432009
	○	15	16	17	18	19	20	9:23	29	2432016
	◑	22	23	24	25	26	27	19:52	30	2432023
AUGUST 1946	●	29	30	31	1	2	3	11:54	31	2432030
	◐	5	6	7	8	9	10	20:55	32	2432037
	11	○	13	14	15	16	17	22:26	33	2432044
	18	19	◑	21	22	23	24	1:17	34	2432051
	25	●	27	28	29	30	31	21:07	35	2432058
SEPTEMBER 1946	1	2	◐	4	5	6	7	14:49	36	2432065
	8	9	10	○	12	13	14	10:00	37	2432072
	15	16	17	◑	19	20	21	6:45	38	2432079
	22	23[d]	24	●	26	27	28	8:45	39	2432086
OCTOBER 1946	29	30	1	2	◐	4	5	9:53	40	2432093
	6	7	8	9	○	11	12	20:41	41	2432100
	13	14	15	16	◑	18	19	13:28	42	2432107
	20	21	22	23	●	25	26	23:32	43	2432114
NOVEMBER 1946	27	28	29	30	31	1	◐	4:40	44	2432121
	3	4	5	6	7	8	○	7:10	45	2432128
	10	11	12	13	14	◑	16	22:35	46	2432135
	17	18	19	20	21	22	●	17:24	47	2432142
	24	25	26	27	28	29	30		48	2432149
DECEMBER 1946	◐	2	3	4	5	6	7	21:48	49	2432156
	○	9	10	11	12	13	14	17:52	50	2432163
	◑	16	17	18	19	20	21	10:57	51	2432170
	22[e]	●	24	25	26	27	28	13:06	52	2432177
	29	30	◐	1	2	3	4	12:23	1	2432184

ISO WEEK	HEBREW 5706‡/5707	Sun	Mon	Tue	Wed	Thu	Fri	Sat	Molad
1		26	27	28	29	1	2	3	Thu 8h11m11p
2	SHEVAT 5706	4	5	6	7	8	9	10	
3		11	12	13	14	15	16	17	
4		18	19	20	21	22	23	24	
5		25	26	27	28	29	30	1	Fri 20h55m12p
6	ADAR I 5706	2	3	4	5	6	7	8	
7		9	10	11	12	13	14	15	
8		16	17	18	19	20	21	22	
9		23	24	25	26	27	28	29	
10		30	1	2	3	4	5	6	Sun 9h39m13p
11	ADAR II 5706	7	8	9	10	11	12	13	
12		14[f]	15	16	17	18	19	20	
13		21	22	23	24	25	26	27	
14		28	29	1	2	3	4	5	Mon 22h23m14p
15	NISAN 5706	6	7	8	9	10	11	12	
16		13	14	15[g]	16	17	18	19	
17		20	21	22	23	24	25	26	
18		27	28	29	30	1	2	3	Wed 11h7m15p
19	IYAR 5706	4	5	6	7	8	9	10	
20		11	12	13	14	15	16	17	
21		18	19	20	21	22	23	24	
22		25	26	27	28	29	1	2	Thu 23h51m16p
23	SIVAN 5706	3	4	5	6[h]	7	8	9	
24		10	11	12	13	14	15	16	
25		17	18	19	20	21	22	23	
26		24	25	26	27	28	29	30	
27		1	2	3	4	5	6	7	Sat 12h35m17p
28	TAMMUZ 5706	8	9	10	11	12	13	14	
29		15	16	17	18	19	20	21	
30		22	23	24	25	26	27	28	
31		29	1	2	3	4	5	6	Mon 1h20m0p
32	AV 5706	7	8	9[i]	10	11	12	13	
33		14	15	16	17	18	19	20	
34		21	22	23	24	25	26	27	
35		28	29	30	1	2	3	4	Tue 14h4m1p
36	ELUL 5706	5	6	7	8	9	10	11	
37		12	13	14	15	16	17	18	
38		19	20	21	22	23	24	25	
39		26	27	28	29	1[a]	2[a]	3	Thu 2h48m2p
40	TISHRI 5707	4	5	6	7	8	9	10[b]	
41		11	12	13	14	15[c]	16	17	
42		18	19	20	21	22	23	24	
43		25	26	27	28	29	30	1	Fri 15h32m3p
44	HESHVAN 5707	2	3	4	5	6	7	8	
45		9	10	11	12	13	14	15	
46		16	17	18	19	20	21	22	
47		23	24	25	26	27	28	29	
48		1	2	3	4	5	6	7	Sun 4h16m4p
49	KISLEV 5707	8	9	10	11	12[d]	13	14	
50		15	16	17	18	19	20	21	
51		22	23	24	25[e]	26[e]	27[e]	28[e]	
52		29[e]	30[e]	1[e]	2[e]	3	4	5	Mon 17h0m5p
1	TEVETH 5707	6	7	8	9	10	11	12	

ISO WEEK	CHINESE Yǐ-Yǒu/Bǐng-Xū	Sun	Mon	Tue	Wed	Thu	Fri	Sat	Solar Term
1		26	27	28	29	1	2	3	
2	MONTH 12 Yǐ-Yǒu	4	5	6	7	8	9	10	Xiǎo hán
3		11	12	13	14	15	16	17	
4		**18**	19	20	21	22	23	24	Dà hán
5		25	26	27	28	29	30	1[a]	
6	MONTH 1 Bǐng-Xū	2	3	4	5	6	7	8	Lì chūn
7		9	10	11	12	13	14	15[b]	
8		16	17	**18***	19	20	21	22	Yǔ shuǐ
9		23	24	25	26	27	28	29	
10		30	1	2	3	4	5	6	Jīng zhé
11	MONTH 2 Bǐng-Xū	7	8	9	10	11	12	13	
12		14	15	16	17	**18**	19	20	Chūn fēn
13		21	22	23	24	25	26	27	
14		28	29	1	2	3	4[c]	5	Qīng míng
15	MONTH 3 Bǐng-Xū	6	7	8	9	10	11	12	
16		13	14	15	16	17	18	19*	Gǔ yǔ
17		**20**	21	22	23	24	25	26	
18		27	28	29	1	2	3	4	
19	MONTH 4 Bǐng-Xū	5	6	7	8	9	10	11	Lì xià
20		12	13	14	15	16	17	18	
21		19	20	21	**22**	23	24	25	Xiǎo mǎn
22		26	27	28	29	30	1	2	
23	MONTH 5 Bǐng-Xū	3	4	5[d]	6	7	8	9	Máng zhòng
24		10	11	12	13	14	15	16	
25		17	18	19	20*	21	22	**23**	Xià zhì
26		24	25	26	27	28	29	1	
27	MONTH 6 Bǐng-Xū	2	3	4	5	6	7	8	
28		9	10	11	12	13	14	15	Xiǎo shǔ
29		16	17	18	19	20	21	22	
30		23	24	**25**	26	27	28	29	Dà shǔ
31		1	2	3	4	5	6	7[e]	
32	MONTH 7 Bǐng-Xū	8	9	10	11	12	13	14	Lì qiū
33		15[f]	16	17	18	19	20	21	
34		22*	23	24	25	26	27	**28**	Chǔ shǔ
35		29	30	1	2	3	4	5	
36	MONTH 8 Bǐng-Xū	6	7	8	9	10	11	12	
37		13	14	15[g]	16	17	18	19	Bái lù
38		20	21	22	23	24	25	26	
39		27	**28**	29	1	2	3	4	Qiū fēn
40	MONTH 9 Bǐng-Xū	5	6	7	8	9[h]	10	11	
41		12	13	14	15	16	17	18	Hán lù
42		19	20	21	22	23*	24	25	
43		26	27	28	29	**30**	1	2	Shuāng jiàng
44	MONTH 10 Bǐng-Xū	3	4	5	6	7	8	9	
45		10	11	12	13	14	15	16	Lì dōng
46		17	18	19	20	21	22	23	
47		24	25	26	27	28	29	**30**	Xiǎo xuě
48		1	2	3	4	5	6	7	
49	MONTH 11 Bǐng-Xū	8	9	10	11	12	13	14	
50		15	16	17	18	19	20	21	Dà xuě
51		22	23*	24	25	26	27	28	
52	MONTH 12 Bǐng-Xū	29[i]	1	2	3	4	5	6	Dōng zhì
1		7	8	9	10	11	12	13	

ISO WEEK	COPTIC 1662/1663‡	Sun	Mon	Tue	Wed	Thu	Fri	Sat	ETHIOPIC 1938/1939‡
1	KOIAK 1662	21	22	23	24	25	26	27	TĀKHŚĀŚ 1938
2		28	29[c]	30	1	2	3	4	
3	TŌBE 1662	5	6[d]	7	8	9	10	11[e]	
4		12	13	14	15	16	17	18	ṬER 1938
5		19	20	21	22	23	24	25	
6		26	27	28	29	30	1	2	
7	MESHIR 1662	3	4	5	6	7	8	9	
8		10	11	12	13	14	15	16	YAKĀTIT 1938
9		17	18	19	20	21	22	23	
10		24	25	26	27	28	29	30	
11	PAREMOTEP 1662	1	2	3	4	5	6	7	
12		8	9	10	11	12	13	14	
13		15	16	17	18	19	20	21	MAGĀBIT 1938
14		22	23	24	25	26	27	28	
15		29	30	1	2	3	4	5	
16	PARMOUTE 1662	6	7	8	9	10	11	12	
17		13[f]	14	15	16	17	18	19	MIYĀZYĀ 1938
18		20	21	22	23	24	25	26	
19		27	28	29[g]	30	1	2	3	
20	PASHONS 1662	4	5	6	7	8	9	10	
21		11	12	13	14	15	16	17	GENBOT 1938
22		18	19	20	21	22	23	24	
23		25	26	27	28	29	30	1	
24	PAŌNE 1662	2	3	4	5	6	7	8	
25		9	10	11	12	13	14	15	SANĒ 1938
26		16	17	18	19	20	21	22	
27		23	24	25	26	27	28	29	
28		30	1	2	3	4	5	6	
29	EPĒP 1662	7	8	9	10	11	12	13	
30		14	15	16	17	18	19	20	HAMLĒ 1938
31		21	22	23	24	25	26	27	
32		28	29	30	1	2	3	4	
33	MESORĒ 1662	5	6	7	8	9	10	11	
34		12	13[h]	14	15	16	17	18	NAHASĒ 1938
35		19	20	21	22	23	24	25	
36	EPAG. 1662	26	27	28	29	30	1	2	PĀG. 1938
37		3	4	5	1[a]	2	3	4	
38	THOOUT 1663	5	6	7	8	9	10	11	MASKARAM 1939
39		12	13	14	15	16	17[b]	18	
40		19	20	21	22	23	24	25	
41		26	27	28	29	30	1	2	
42	PAOPE 1663	3	4	5	6	7	8	9	ṬEQEMT 1939
43		10	11	12	13	14	15	16	
44		17	18	19	20	21	22	23	
45		24	25	26	27	28	29	30	
46		1	2	3	4	5	6	7	
47	ATHŌR 1663	8	9	10	11	12	13	14	
48		15	16	17	18	19	20	21	HEDĀR 1939
49		22	23	24	25	26	27	28	
50		29	30	1	2	3	4	5	
51	KOIAK 1663	6	7	8	9	10	11	12	TĀKHŚĀŚ 1939
52		13	14	15	16	17	18	19	
1		20	21	22	23	24	25	26	

[a]New Year
[b]Spring (5:32)
[c]Summer (0:44)
[d]Autumn (15:41)
[e]Winter (10:53)
● New moon
◐ First quarter moon
○ Full moon
◑ Last quarter moon

‡Leap year
[a]New Year
[b]Yom Kippur
[c]Sukkot
[d]Winter starts
[e]Ḥanukkah
[f]Purim
[g]Passover
[h]Shavuot
[i]Fast of Av

[a]New Year (4644, Dog)
[b]Lantern Festival
[c]Qīngmíng
[d]Dragon Festival
[e]Qīqiǎo
[f]Hungry Ghosts
[g]Mid-Autumn Festival
[h]Double-Ninth Festival
[i]Dōngzhì
*Start of 60-name cycle

‡Leap year
[a]New Year
[b]Building of the Cross
[c]Christmas
[d]Jesus's Circumcision
[e]Epiphany
[f]Easter
[g]Mary's Announcement
[h]Jesus's Transfiguration

PERSIAN (ASTRONOMICAL) 1324/1325‡

Month	Sun	Mon	Tue	Wed	Thu	Fri	Sat
DEY 1324	9	10	11	12	13	14	15
	16	17	18	19	20	21	22
	23	24	25	26	27	28	29
BAHMAN 1324	30	1	2	3	4	5	6
	7	8	9	10	11	12	13
	14	15	16	17	18	19	20
	21	22	23	24	25	26	27
ESFAND 1324	28	29	30	1	2	3	4
	5	6	7	8	9	10	11
	12	13	14	15	16	17	18
	19	20	21	22	23	24	25
FARVARDĪN 1325	26	27	28	29	1[a]	2	3
	4	5	6	7	8	9	10
	11	12	13[b]	14	15	16	17
	18	19	20	21	22	23	24
	25	26	27	28	29	30	31
ORDĪBEHEŠT 1325	1	2	3	4	5	6	7
	8	9	10	11	12	13	14
	15	16	17	18	19	20	21
	22	23	24	25	26	27	28
XORDĀD 1325	29	30	31	1	2	3	4
	5	6	7	8	9	10	11
	12	13	14	15	16	17	18
	19	20	21	22	23	24	25
TĪR 1325	26	27	28	29	30	31	1
	2	3	4	5	6	7	8
	9	10	11	12	13	14	15
	16	17	18	19	20	21	22
	23	24	25	26	27	28	29
MORDĀD 1325	30	31	1	2	3	4	5
	6	7	8	9	10	11	12
	13	14	15	16	17	18	19
	20	21	22	23	24	25	26
SHAHRĪVAR 1325	27	28	29	30	31	1	2
	3	4	5	6	7	8	9
	10	11	12	13	14	15	16
	17	18	19	20	21	22	23
	24	25	26	27	28	29	30
MEHR 1325	31	1	2	3	4	5	6
	7	8	9	10	11	12	13
	14	15	16	17	18	19	20
	21	22	23	24	25	26	27
ĀBĀN 1325	28	29	30	1	2	3	4
	5	6	7	8	9	10	11
	12	13	14	15	16	17	18
	19	20	21	22	23	24	25
ĀZAR 1325	26	27	28	29	30	1	2
	3	4	5	6	7	8	9
	10	11	12	13	14	15	16
	17	18	19	20	21	22	23
	24	25	26	27	28	29	30
DEY 1325	1	2	3	4	5	6	7
	8	9	10	11	12	13	14

‡Leap year
[a]New Year
[b]Sizdeh Bedar

HINDU LUNAR 2002‡/2003

Month	Sun	Mon	Tue	Wed	Thu	Fri	Sat
PAUSHA 2002	26	27	28	29	30	1	2
	3	4	5	6	7	8	**9**
	11	12	13	14	15	16	17
	18	19	20	21	22	23	24
	25	26	27	27	28	29	30
MĀGHA 2002	1	2	**3**	5	6	7	8
	9	10	11	12	13	14	15
	16	17	18	19	20	21	22
	23	24	25	26	27	28	29[h]
PHĀLGUNA 2002	30	1	2	3	4	5	6
	7	**8**	10	11	12	13	14
	15[i]	16	17	18	19	20	20
	21	22	23	24	25	26	27
CHAITRA 2003	28	29	30	1[a]	**2**	4	5
	6	7	8	9[b]	10	11	12
	13	14	15	16	17	18	19
	20	21	22	23	24	25	26
VAIŚĀKHA 2003	27	28	29	30	1	2	3
	4	**5**	7	8	9	10	11
	12	13	14	15	15	16	17
	18	19	20	21	22	23	24
JYAISHTHA 2003	25	26	27	**28**	30	1	2
	3	4	5	6	7	8	9
	10	11	12	13	14	15	16
	17	18	19	20	21	22	23
	24	25	26	27	28	29	30
ĀSHĀDHA 2003	**1**	3	4	5	6	7	8
	9	10	11	11	12	13	14
	15	16	17	18	19	20	21
	22	23	**24**	26	27	28	29
ŚRĀVANA 2003	30	1	2	3	4	5	6
	7	8	9	10	11	12	13
	14	15	16	17	18	19	20
	21	22	23[c]	24	25	26	**27**
BHĀDRAPADA 2003	29	30	1	2	3	4[d]	5
	6	7	8	8	9	10	11
	12	13	14	15	16	17	18
	19	**20**	22	23	24	25	26
ĀŚVINA 2003	27	28	29	30	1	2	3
	4	5	6	7	8[e]	9[e]	10[e]
	11	12	13	14	15	16	17
	18	19	20	21	22	23	**24**
KĀRTTIKA 2003	26	27	28	29	30	1[f]	2
	2	3	4	5	6	7	8
	9	10	11	12	13	14	15
	16	**17**	19	20	21	22	23
	24	25	26	27	28	29	30
MĀRGAŚĪRA 2003	1	2	3	4	5	5	6
	7	8	9	10	**11**[g]	13	14
	15	16	17	18	19	20	21
	22	23	24	25	26	27	28
PAUSHA 2003	29	30	1	2	3	4	5
	6	7	8	9	10	11	12

‡Leap year
[a]New Year (Vyaya)
[b]Birthday of Rāma
[c]Birthday of Krishna
[d]Ganēśa Chaturthī
[e]Dashara
[f]Diwali
[g]Birthday of Vishnu
[h]Night of Śiva
[i]Holi

HINDU SOLAR 1867/1868

Month	Sun	Mon	Tue	Wed	Thu	Fri	Sat
PAUSHA 1867	16	17	18	19	20	21	22
	23	24	25	26	27	28	29
MĀGHA 1867	1[b]	2	3	4	5	6	7
	8	9	10	11	12	13	14
	15	16	17	18	19	20	21
	22	23	24	25	26	27	28
PHĀLGUNA 1867	29	30	1	2	3	4	5
	6	7	8	9	10	11	12
	13	14	15	16	17	18	19
	20	21	22	23	24	25	26
CHAITRA 1867	27	28	29	30	1	2	3
	4	5	6	7	8	9	10
	11	12	13	14	15	16	17
	18	19	20	21	22	23	24
VAIŚĀKHA 1868	25	26	27	28	29	30	1[a]
	2	3	4	5	6	7	8
	9	10	11	12	13	14	15
	16	17	18	19	20	21	22
	23	24	25	26	27	28	29
JYAISHTHA 1868	30	31	1	2	3	4	5
	6	7	8	9	10	11	12
	13	14	15	16	17	18	19
	20	21	22	23	24	25	26
ĀSHĀDHA 1868	27	28	29	30	31	1	2
	3	4	5	6	7	8	9
	10	11	12	13	14	15	16
	17	18	19	20	21	22	23
	24	25	26	27	28	29	30
ŚRĀVANA 1868	31	32	1	2	3	4	5
	6	7	8	9	10	11	12
	13	14	15	16	17	18	19
	20	21	22	23	24	25	26
BHĀDRAPADA 1868	27	28	29	30	31	1	2
	3	4	5	6	7	8	9
	10	11	12	13	14	15	16
	17	18	19	20	21	22	23
	24	25	26	27	28	29	30
ĀŚVINA 1868	31	32	1	2	3	4	5
	6	7	8	9	10	11	12
	13	14	15	16	17	18	19
	20	21	22	23	24	25	26
KĀRTTIKA 1868	27	28	29	30	1	2	3
	4	5	6	7	8	9	10
	11	12	13	14	15	16	17
	18	19	20	21	22	23	24
MĀRGAŚĪRA 1868	25	26	27	28	29	30	1
	2	3	4	5	6	7	8
	9	10	11	12	13	14	15
	16	17	18	19	20	21	22
	23	24	25	26	27	28	29
PAUSHA 1868	1	2	3	4	5	6	7
	8	9	10	11	12	13	14
	15	16	17	18	19	20	21

[a]New Year (Vikārin)
[b]Pongal

ISLAMIC (ASTRONOMICAL) 1365/1366‡

Month	Sun	Mon	Tue	Wed	Thu	Fri	Sat
ṢAFAR 1365	25	26	27	28	29	30	1
	2	3	4	5	6	7	8
	9	10	11	12	13	14	15
	16	17	18	19	20	21	22
	23	24	25	26	27	28	29
RABĪ' I 1365	1	2	3	4	5	6	7
	8	9	10	11	12[c]	13	14
	15	16	17	18	19	20	21
	22	23	24	25	26	27	28
RABĪ' II 1365	29	30	1	2	3	4	5
	6	7	8	9	10	11	12
	13	14	15	16	17	18	19
	20	21	22	23	24	25	26
JUMĀDĀ I 1365	27	28	29	1	2	3	4
	5	6	7	8	9	10	11
	12	13	14	15	16	17	18
	19	20	21	22	23	24	25
JUMĀDĀ II 1365	26	27	28	29	30	1	2
	3	4	5	6	7	8	9
	10	11	12	13	14	15	16
	17	18	19	20	21	22	23
RAJAB 1365	24	25	26	27	28	29	1
	2	3	4	5	6	7	8
	9	10	11	12	13	14	15
	16	17	18	19	20	21	22
	23	24	25	26	27[d]	28	29
SHA'BĀN 1365	1	2	3	4	5	6	7
	8	9	10	11	12	13	14
	15	16	17	18	19	20	21
	22	23	24	25	26	27	28
RAMAḌĀN 1365	29	30	1[e]	2	3	4	5
	6	7	8	9	10	11	12
	13	14	15	16	17	18	19
	20	21	22	23	24	25	26
SHAWWĀL 1365	27	28	29	1[f]	2	3	4
	5	6	7	8	9	10	11
	12	13	14	15	16	17	18
	19	20	21	22	23	24	25
DHU AL-QA'DA 1365	26	27	28	29	30	1	2
	3	4	5	6	7	8	9
	10	11	12	13	14	15	16
	17	18	19	20	21	22	23
DHU AL-ḤIJJA 1365	24	25	26	27	28	29	1
	2	3	4	5	6	7	8
	9	10[g]	11	12	13	14	15
	16	17	18	19	20	21	22
	23	24	25	26	27	28	29
MUḤARRAM 1366	30	1[a]	2	3	4	5	6
	7	8	9	10[b]	11	12	13
	14	15	16	17	18	19	20
	21	22	23	24	25	26	27
ṢAFAR 1366	28	29	30	1	2	3	4
	5	6	7	8	9	10	11

‡Leap year
[a]New Year
[b]'Ashūrā'
[c]Prophet's Birthday
[d]Ascent of the Prophet
[e]Start of Ramaḍān
[f]'Id al-Fiṭr
[g]'Id al-'Aḍḥā

GREGORIAN 1946

Julian (Sun)	Sun	Mon	Tue	Wed	Thu	Fri	Sat	Month
Dec 17	30	31	1	2	3	4	5	JANUARY 1946
	6	7[a]	8	9	10	11	12	
Dec 31	13	14[b]	15	16	17	18	19	
	20	21	22	23	24	25	26	
Jan 14	27	28	29	30	31	1	2	FEBRUARY 1946
	3	4	5	6	7	8	9	
Jan 28	10	11	12	13	14	15	16	
	17	18	19	20	21	22	23	
Feb 11	24	25	26	27	28	1	2	MARCH 1946
	3	4	5	6[c]	7	8	9	
Feb 25	10[d]	11	12	13	14	15	16	
	17	18	19	20	21	22	23	
Mar 11	24	25	26	27	28	29	30	
	31	1	2	3	4	5	6	APRIL 1946
Mar 25	7	8	9	10	11	12	13	
	14	15	16	17	18	19	20	
Apr 8	21[e]	22	23	24	25	26	27	
	28	29	30	1	2	3	4	MAY 1946
Apr 22	5	6	7	8	9	10	11	
	12	13	14	15	16	17	18	
May 6	19	20	21	22	23	24	25	
	26	27	28	29	30	31	1	JUNE 1946
May 20	2	3	4	5	6	7	8	
	9	10	11	12	13	14	15	
Jun 3	16	17	18	19	20	21	22	
	23	24	25	26	27	28	29	
Jun 17	30	1	2	3	4	5	6	JULY 1946
	7	8	9	10	11	12	13	
Jul 1	14	15	16	17	18	19	20	
	21	22	23	24	25	26	27	
Jul 15	28	29	30	31	1	2	3	AUGUST 1946
	4	5	6	7	8	9	10	
Jul 29	11	12	13	14	15	16	17	
	18	19	20	21	22	23	24	
Aug 12	25	26	27	28	29	30	31	
	1	2	3	4	5	6	7	SEPTEMBER 1946
Aug 26	8	9	10	11	12	13	14	
	15	16	17	18	19	20	21	
Sep 9	22	23	24	25	26	27	28	
	29	30	1	2	3	4	5	OCTOBER 1946
Sep 23	6	7	8	9	10	11	12	
	13	14	15	16	17	18	19	
Oct 7	20	21	22	23	24	25	26	
	27	28	29	30	31	1	2	NOVEMBER 1946
Oct 21	3	4	5	6	7	8	9	
	10	11	12	13	14	15	16	
Nov 4	17	18	19	20	21	22	23	
	24	25	26	27	28	29	30	
Nov 18	1[g]	2	3	4	5	6	7	DECEMBER 1946
	8	9	10	11	12	13	14	
Dec 2	15	16	17	18	19	20	21	
	22	23	24	25[h]	26	27	28	
Dec 16	29	30	31	1	2	3	4	

[a]Orthodox Christmas
[b]Julian New Year
[c]Ash Wednesday
[d]Feast of Orthodoxy
[e]Easter (also Orthodox)
[g]Advent
[h]Christmas

1947

GREGORIAN 1947	Sun	Mon	Tue	Wed	Thu	Fri	Sat	Lunar Phases	ISO WEEK (Mon)	JULIAN DAY (Sun noon)	HEBREW 5707/5708‡	Sun	Mon	Tue	Wed	Thu	Fri	Sat	Molad
JANUARY 1947	29	30	◐	1[a]	2	3	4	12:23	1	2432184	TEVETH 5707	6	7	8	9	10	11	12	
	5	6	○	8	9	10	11	4:47	2	2432191		13	14	15	16	17	18	19	
	12	13	◑	15	16	17	18	2:56	3	2432198		20	21	22	23	24	25	26	
	19	20	21	●	23	24	25	8:34	4	2432205	SHEVAT 5707	27	28	29	1	2	3	4	Wed 5h44m6p
FEBRUARY 1947	26	27	28	29	◐	31	1	0:07	5	2432212		5	6	7	8	9	10	11	
	2	3	4	○	6	7	8	15:50	6	2432219		12	13	14	15	16	17	18	
	9	10	11	◑	13	14	15	21:58	7	2432226		19	20	21	22	23	24	25	
	16	17	18	19	20	●	22	2:00	8	2432233	ADAR 5707	26	27	28	29	30	1	2	Thu 18h28m7p
MARCH 1947	23	24	25	26	27	◐	1	9:12	9	2432240		3	4	5	6	7	8	9	
	2	3	4	5	6	○	8	3:15	10	2432247		10	11	12	13	14[f]	15	16	
	9	10	11	12	13	◑	15	18:28	11	2432254		17	18	19	20	21	22	23	
	16	17	18	19	20	21[b]	●	16:34	12	2432261	NISAN 5707	24	25	26	27	28	29	1	Sat 7h12m8p
	23	24	25	26	27	28	◐	16:15	13	2432268		2	3	4	5	6	7	8	
APRIL 1947	30	31	1	2	3	4	○	15:28	14	2432275		9	10	11	12	13	14	15[g]	
	6	7	8	9	10	11	12		15	2432282		16	17	18	19	20	21	22	
	◑	14	15	16	17	18	19	14:23	16	2432289		23	24	25	26	27	28	29	
	20	●	22	23	24	25	26	4:19	17	2432296	IYYAR 5707	30	1	2	3	4	5	6	Sun 19h56m9p
MAY 1947	◐	28	29	30	1	2	3	22:18	18	2432303		7	8	9	10	11	12	13	
	4	○	6	7	8	9	10	4:53	19	2432310		14	15	16	17	18	19	20	
	11	12	◑	14	15	16	17	8:08	20	2432317		21	22	23	24	25	26	27	
	18	19	●	21	22	23	24	13:44	21	2432324	SIVAN 5707	28	29	1	2	3	4	5	Tue 8h40m10p
	25	26	◐	28	29	30	31	4:36	22	2432331		6[h]	7	8	9	10	11	12	
JUNE 1947	1	2	○	4	5	6	7	19:27	23	2432338		13	14	15	16	17	18	19	
	8	9	10	◑	12	13	14	22:58	24	2432345		20	21	22	23	24	25	26	
	15	16	17	●	19	20	21	21:26	25	2432352	TAMMUZ 5707	27	28	29	30	1	2	3	Wed 21h24m11p
	22[c]	23	24	◐	26	27	28	12:25	26	2432359		4	5	6	7	8	9	10	
JULY 1947	29	30	1	2	○	4	5	10:39	27	2432366		11	12	13	14	15	16	17	
	6	7	8	9	10	◑	12	10:54	28	2432373		18	19	20	21	22	23	24	
	13	14	15	16	17	●	19	4:15	29	2432380	AV 5707	25	26	27	28	29	1	2	Fri 10h8m12p
	20	21	22	23	◐	25	26	22:54	30	2432387		3	4	5	6	7	8	9	
AUGUST 1947	27	28	29	30	31	1	○	1:50	31	2432394		10[i]	11	12	13	14	15	16	
	3	4	5	6	7	8	◑	20:22	32	2432401		17	18	19	20	21	22	23	
	10	11	12	13	14	15	●	11:12	33	2432408		24	25	26	27	28	29	30	
	17	18	19	20	21	22	◐	12:40	34	2432415	ELUL 5707	1	2	3	4	5	6	7	Sat 22h52m13p
	24	25	26	27	28	29	30		35	2432422		8	9	10	11	12	13	14	
SEPTEMBER 1947	○	1	2	3	4	5	6	16:34	36	2432429		15	16	17	18	19	20	21	
	7	◑	9	10	11	12	13	3:57	37	2432436		22	23	24	25	26	27	28	
	●	15	16	17	18	19	20	19:28	38	2432443	TISHRI 5708	29	1[a]	2[a]	3	4	5	6	Mon 11h36m14p
	21	◐	23[d]	24	25	26	27	5:42	39	2432450		7	8	9	10[b]	11	12	13	
OCTOBER 1947	28	29	○	1	2	3	4	6:41	40	2432457		14	15[c]	16	17	18	19	20	
	5	6	◑	8	9	10	11	10:29	41	2432464		21	22	23	24	25	26	27	
	12	13	●	15	16	17	18	6:10	42	2432471	ḤESHVAN 5708	28	29	30	1	2	3	4	Wed 0h20m15p
	19	20	21	◐	23	24	25	1:11	43	2432478		5	6	7	8	9	10	11	
NOVEMBER 1947	26	27	28	○	30	31	1	20:07	44	2432485		12	13	14	15	16	17	18	
	2	3	4	◑	6	7	8	17:04	45	2432492		19	20	21	22	23	24	25	
	9	10	11	●	13	14	15	20:01	46	2432499	KISLEV 5708	26	27	28	29	30	1	2	Thu 13h4m16p
	16	17	18	19	◐	21	22	21:44	47	2432506		3	4	5	6	7	8	9	
	23	24	25	26	27	○	29	8:45	48	2432513		10	11	12	13	14	15	16	
DECEMBER 1947	30	1	2	3	4	◑	6	0:55	49	2432520		17	18	19	20	21	22	23[d]	
	7	8	9	10	11	●	13	12:53	50	2432527		24	25[e]	26[e]	27[e]	28[e]	29[e]	30[e]	
	14	15	16	17	18	19	◐	17:44	51	2432534	TEVETH 5708	1[e]	2[e]	3	4	5	6	7	Sat 1h48m17p
	21	22[e]	23	24	25	26	○	20:27	52	2432541		8	9	10	11	12	13	14	
	28	29	30	31	1	2	◑	11:13	1	2432548		15	16	17	18	19	20	21	

ISO WEEK	CHINESE Bǐng-Xū/Dīng-Hài‡	Sun	Mon	Tue	Wed	Thu	Fri	Sat	Solar Term	COPTIC 1663‡/1664	Sun	Mon	Tue	Wed	Thu	Fri	Sat	ETHIOPIC 1939‡/1940
1	MONTH 12 Bǐng-Xū	7	8	9	10	11	12	13		KOIAK 1663	20	21	22	23	24	25	26	TĀKHŚĀŚ 1939
2		14	15	16	17	18	19	20	Xiǎo hán		27	28	29[c]	30	1	2	3	
3		21	22	23	24	25	26	27		TŌBE 1663	4	5	6[d]	7	8	9	10	ṬER 1939
4	MONTH 1 Dīng-Hài	28	29	30	1[a]	2	3	4	Dà hán		11[e]	12	13	14	15	16	17	
5		5	6	7	8	9	10	11			18	19	20	21	22	23	24	
6		12	13	14	15[b]	16	17	18	Lì chūn		25	26	27	28	29	30	1	
7		19	20	21	22	23	24*	25		MESHIR 1663	2	3	4	5	6	7	8	YAKĀTĪT 1939
8	MONTH 2 Dīng-Hài	26	27	28	29	30	1	2	Yǔ shuǐ		9	10	11	12	13	14	15	
9		3	4	5	6	7	8	9			16	17	18	19	20	21	22	
10		10	11	12	13	14	15	16	Jīng zhé		23	24	25	26	27	28	29	
11		17	18	19	20	21	22	23		PAREMOTEP 1663	30	1	2	3	4	5	6	MAGĀBIT 1939
12		24	25	26	27	28	29	30	Chūn fēn		7	8	9	10	11	12	13	
13	LEAP MONTH 2 Dīng-Hài	1	2	3	4	5	6	7			14	15	16	17	18	19	20	
14		8	9	10	11	12	13	14[c]	Qīng míng		21	22	23	24	25	26	27	
15		15	16	17	18	19	20	21		PARMOUTE 1663	28	29	30	1	2	3	4	MIYĀZYĀ 1939
16		22	23	24*	25	26	27	28			5[f]	6	7	8	9	10	11	
17	MONTH 3 Dīng-Hài	29	1	2	3	4	5	6	Gǔ yǔ		12	13	14	15	16	17	18	
18		7	8	9	10	11	12	13			19	20	21	22	23	24	25	
19		14	15	16	17	18	19	20	Lì xià	PASHONS 1663	26	27	28	29[g]	30	1	2	GENBOT 1939
20		21	22	23	24	25	26	27			3	4	5	6	7	8	9	
21	MONTH 4 Dīng-Hài	28	29	1	2	3	4	5	Xiǎo mǎn		10	11	12	13	14	15	16	
22		6	7	8	9	10	11	12			17	18	19	20	21	22	23	
23		13	14	15	16	17	18	19	Máng zhòng		24	25	26	27	28	29	30	
24		20	21	22	23	24	25	26*		PAŌNE 1663	1	2	3	4	5	6	7	SANĒ 1939
25	MONTH 5 Dīng-Hài	27	28	29	30	1	2	3			8	9	10	11	12	13	14	
26		4	5[d]	6	7	8	9	10	Xià zhì		15	16	17	18	19	20	21	
27		11	12	13	14	15	16	17			22	23	24	25	26	27	28	
28		18	19	20	21	22	23	24	Xiǎo shǔ	EPĒP 1663	29	30	1	2	3	4	5	ḤAMLĒ 1939
29	MONTH 6 Dīng-Hài	25	26	27	28	29	1	2			6	7	8	9	10	11	12	
30		3	4	5	6	7	8	9	Dà shǔ		13	14	15	16	17	18	19	
31		10	11	12	13	14	15	16			20	21	22	23	24	25	26	
32		17	18	19	20	21	22	23	Lì qiū	MESORĒ 1663	27	28	29	30	1	2	3	NAḤASĒ 1939
33	MONTH 7 Dīng-Hài	24	25	26	27*	28	29	1			4	5	6	7	8	9	10	
34		2	3	4	5	6	7[e]	8			11	12	13[h]	14	15	16	17	
35		9	10	11	12	13	14	15[f]	Chǔ shǔ		18	19	20	21	22	23	24	
36		16	17	18	19	20	21	22		EPAG. 1663	25	26	27	28	29	30	1	PĀG. 1939
37		23	24	25	26	27	28	29	Bái lù	THOOUT 1664	2	3	4	5	6	1[a]	2	MASKARAM 1940
38	MONTH 8 Dīng-Hài	30	1	2	3	4	5	6			3	4	5	6	7	8	9	
39		7	8	9	10	11	12	13	Qiū fēn		10	11	12	13	14	15	16	
40		14	15[g]	16	17	18	19	20			17[b]	18	19	20	21	22	23	
41		21	22	23	24	25	26	27	Hán lù		24	25	26	27	28	29	30	
42	MONTH 9 Dīng-Hài	28*	29	1	2	3	4	5		PAOPE 1664	1	2	3	4	5	6	7	ṬEQEMT 1940
43		6	7	8	9[h]	10	11	12	Shuāng jiàng		8	9	10	11	12	13	14	
44		13	14	15	16	17	18	19			15	16	17	18	19	20	21	
45		20	21	22	23	24	25	26	Lì dōng		22	23	24	25	26	27	28	
46	MONTH 10 Dīng-Hài	27	28	29	30	1	2	3		ATHŌR 1664	29	30	1	2	3	4	5	ḪEDĀR 1940
47		4	5	6	7	8	9	10			6	7	8	9	10	11	12	
48		11	12	13	14	15	16	17	Xiǎo xuě		13	14	15	16	17	18	19	
49		18	19	20	21	22	23	24			20	21	22	23	24	25	26	
50	MONTH 11 Dīng-Hài	25	26	27	28	29*	1	2	Dà xuě	KOIAK 1664	27	28	29	30	1	2	3	TĀKHŚĀŚ 1940
51		3	4	5	6	7	8	9			4	5	6	7	8	9	10	
52		10	11	12[i]	13	14	15	16	Dōng zhì		11	12	13	14	15	16	17	
1		17	18	19	20	21	22	23			18	19	20	21	22	23	24	

[a]New Year
[b]Spring (11:12)
[c]Summer (6:19)
[d]Autumn (21:28)
[e]Winter (16:42)
● New moon
◐ First quarter moon
○ Full moon
◑ Last quarter moon

‡Leap year
[a]New Year
[b]Yom Kippur
[c]Sukkot
[d]Winter starts
[e]Ḥanukkah
[f]Purim
[g]Passover
[h]Shavuot
[i]Fast of Av

‡Leap year
[a]New Year (4645, Pig)
[b]Lantern Festival
[c]Qīngmíng
[d]Dragon Festival
[e]Qǐqiǎo
[f]Hungry Ghosts
[g]Mid-Autumn Festival
[h]Double-Ninth Festival
[i]Dōngzhì
*Start of 60-name cycle

‡Leap year
[a]New Year
[b]Building of the Cross
[c]Christmas
[d]Jesus's Circumcision
[e]Epiphany
[f]Easter
[g]Mary's Announcement
[h]Jesus's Transfiguration

PERSIAN (ASTRONOMICAL) 1325‡/1326

Month	Sun	Mon	Tue	Wed	Thu	Fri	Sat
DEY 1325	8	9	10	11	12	13	14
	15	16	17	18	19	20	21
	22	23	24	25	26	27	28
BAHMAN 1325	29	30	1	2	3	4	5
	6	7	8	9	10	11	12
	13	14	15	16	17	18	19
	20	21	22	23	24	25	26
ESFAND 1325	27	28	29	30	1	2	3
	4	5	6	7	8	9	10
	11	12	13	14	15	16	17
	18	19	20	21	22	23	24
FARVARDĪN 1326	25	26	27	28	29	30	1[a]
	2	3	4	5	6	7	8
	9	10	11	12	13[b]	14	15
	16	17	18	19	20	21	22
	23	24	25	26	27	28	29
ORDĪBEHEŠT 1326	30	31	1	2	3	4	5
	6	7	8	9	10	11	12
	13	14	15	16	17	18	19
	20	21	22	23	24	25	26
XORDĀD 1326	27	28	29	30	31	1	2
	3	4	5	6	7	8	9
	10	11	12	13	14	15	16
	17	18	19	20	21	22	23
	24	25	26	27	28	29	30
TĪR 1326	31	1	2	3	4	5	6
	7	8	9	10	11	12	13
	14	15	16	17	18	19	20
	21	22	23	24	25	26	27
MORDĀD 1326	28	29	30	31	1	2	3
	4	5	6	7	8	9	10
	11	12	13	14	15	16	17
	18	19	20	21	22	23	24
	25	26	27	28	29	30	31
SHAHRĪVAR 1326	1	2	3	4	5	6	7
	8	9	10	11	12	13	14
	15	16	17	18	19	20	21
	22	23	24	25	26	27	28
MEHR 1326	29	30	31	1	2	3	4
	5	6	7	8	9	10	11
	12	13	14	15	16	17	18
	19	20	21	22	23	24	25
ĀBĀN 1326	26	27	28	29	30	1	2
	3	4	5	6	7	8	9
	10	11	12	13	14	15	16
	17	18	19	20	21	22	23
	24	25	26	27	28	29	30
ĀZAR 1326	1	2	3	4	5	6	7
	8	9	10	11	12	13	14
	15	16	17	18	19	20	21
	22	23	24	25	26	27	28
DEY 1326	29	30	1	2	3	4	5
	6	7	8	9	10	11	12

‡Leap year
[a]New Year
[b]Sizdeh Bedar

HINDU LUNAR 2003/2004‡

Month	Sun	Mon	Tue	Wed	Thu	Fri	Sat
PAUSHA 2003	6	7	8	9	10	11	12
	13	14	15	**16**	18	19	20
	21	22	23	24	25	26	27
MĀGHA 2003	28	*28*	29	30	1	2	3
	4	5	6	7	8	9	**10**
	12	13	14	15	16	17	18
	19	20	21	22	23	24	25
PHĀLGUNA 2003	26	27	28	29[h]	30	*30*	1
	2	**3**	5	6	7	8	9
	10	11	12	13	14	15[i]	16
	17	18	19	20	21	22	23
	24	25	26	27	28	29	30
CHAITRA 2004	1[a]	2	3	4	5	6	7
	8[b]	10	11	12	13	14	15
	16	17	18	19	20	21	22
	23	*23*	24	25	26	27	28
VAIŚĀKHA 2004	29	30	1	**2**	4	5	6
	7	8	9	10	11	12	13
	14	15	16	17	18	19	20
	21	22	23	24	25	26	27
JYAISHTHA 2004	28	29	30	1	2	3	4
	5	7	8	9	10	11	12
	13	14	15	16	17	18	19
	19	20	21	22	23	24	25
ĀSHĀḌHA 2004	26	27	**28**	30	1	2	3
	4	5	6	7	8	9	10
	11	12	13	14	15	16	17
	18	19	20	21	22	23	24
LEAP ŚRĀVAṆA 2004	25	26	27	28	29	30	**1**
	3	4	5	6	7	8	9
	10	11	12	13	14	15	*15*
	16	17	18	19	20	21	22
	23	**24**	26	27	28	29	30
ŚRĀVAṆA 2004	1	2	3	4	5	6	7
	8	9	10	11	12	13	14
	15	16	17	18	19	20	21
	22	23[c]	24	25	26	**27**	29
BHĀDRAPADA 2004	30	1	2	3	4[d]	5	6
	7	8	9	10	11	*11*	12
	13	14	15	16	17	18	19
	20	22	23	24	25	26	27
ĀŚVINA 2004	28	29	30	1	2	3	4
	5	6	7	8[e]	9[e]	10[e]	11
	12	13	14	15	16	17	18
	19	20	21	22	23	**24**	26
KĀRTTIKA 2004	27	28	29	30	1[f]	2	3
	4	5	*5*	6	7	8	9
	10	11	12	13	14	15	16
	17	**18**	20	21	22	23	24
MĀRGAŚĪRA 2004	25	26	27	28	29	30	1
	2	3	4	5	6	7	8
	8	9	10	**11**[g]	13	14	15
	16	17	18	19	20	21	22

‡Leap year
[a]New Year (Sarvajit)
[b]Birthday of Rāma
[c]Birthday of Krishna
[d]Ganēśa Chaturthī
[e]Dashara
[f]Diwali
[g]Birthday of Vishnu
[h]Night of Śiva
[i]Holi

HINDU SOLAR 1868/1869‡

Month	Sun	Mon	Tue	Wed	Thu	Fri	Sat
PAUSHA 1868	15	16	17	18	19	20	21
	22	23	24	25	26	27	28
MĀGHA 1868	29	30	1[b]	2	3	4	5
	6	7	8	9	10	11	12
	13	14	15	16	17	18	19
	20	21	22	23	24	25	26
PHĀLGUNA 1868	27	28	29	1	2	3	4
	5	6	7	8	9	10	11
	12	13	14	15	16	17	18
	19	20	21	22	23	24	25
CHAITRA 1868	26	27	28	29	30	1	2
	3	4	5	6	7	8	9
	10	11	12	13	14	15	16
	17	18	19	20	21	22	23
	24	25	26	27	28	29	30
VAIŚĀKHA 1869	1[a]	2	3	4	5	6	7
	8	9	10	11	12	13	14
	15	16	17	18	19	20	21
	22	23	24	25	26	27	28
JYAISHTHA 1869	29	30	31	1	2	3	4
	5	6	7	8	9	10	11
	12	13	14	15	16	17	18
	19	20	21	22	23	24	25
	26	27	28	29	30	31	32
ĀSHĀḌHA 1869	1	2	3	4	5	6	7
	8	9	10	11	12	13	14
	15	16	17	18	19	20	21
	22	23	24	25	26	27	28
ŚRĀVAṆA 1869	29	30	31	1	2	3	4
	5	6	7	8	9	10	11
	12	13	14	15	16	17	18
	19	20	21	22	23	24	25
	26	27	28	29	30	31	32
BHĀDRAPADA 1869	1	2	3	4	5	6	7
	8	9	10	11	12	13	14
	15	16	17	18	19	20	21
	22	23	24	25	26	27	28
ĀŚVINA 1869	29	30	31	1	2	3	4
	5	6	7	8	9	10	11
	12	13	14	15	16	17	18
	19	20	21	22	23	24	25
KĀRTTIKA 1869	26	27	28	29	30	1	2
	3	4	5	6	7	8	9
	10	11	12	13	14	15	16
	17	18	19	20	21	22	23
	24	25	26	27	28	29	30
MĀRGAŚĪRA 1869	1	2	3	4	5	6	7
	8	9	10	11	12	13	14
	15	16	17	18	19	20	21
	22	23	24	25	26	27	28
PAUSHA 1869	29	30	1	2	3	4	5
	6	7	8	9	10	11	12
	13	14	15	16	17	18	19

‡Leap year
[a]New Year (Śārvari)
[b]Pongal

ISLAMIC (ASTRONOMICAL) 1366‡/1367

Month	Sun	Mon	Tue	Wed	Thu	Fri	Sat
ṢAFAR 1366	5	6	7	8	9	10	11
	12	13	14	15	16	17	18
	19	20	21	22	23	24	25
RABĪ' I 1366	26	27	28	29	30	1	2
	3	4	5	6	7	8	9
	10	11	12[c]	13	14	15	16
	17	18	19	20	21	22	23
RABĪ' II 1366	24	25	26	27	28	29	1
	2	3	4	5	6	7	8
	9	10	11	12	13	14	15
	16	17	18	19	20	21	22
	23	24	25	26	27	28	29
JUMĀDĀ I 1366	30	1	2	3	4	5	6
	7	8	9	10	11	12	13
	14	15	16	17	18	19	20
	21	22	23	24	25	26	27
JUMĀDĀ II 1366	28	29	1	2	3	4	5
	6	7	8	9	10	11	12
	13	14	15	16	17	18	19
	20	21	22	23	24	25	26
RAJAB 1366	27	28	29	30	1	2	3
	4	5	6	7	8	9	10
	11	12	13	14	15	16	17
	18	19	20	21	22	23	24
SHA'BĀN 1366	25	26	27[d]	28	29	1	2
	3	4	5	6	7	8	9
	10	11	12	13	14	15	16
	17	18	19	20	21	22	23
RAMAḌĀN 1366	24	25	26	27	28	29	1[e]
	2	3	4	5	6	7	8
	9	10	11	12	13	14	15
	16	17	18	19	20	21	22
	23	24	25	26	27	28	29
SHAWWĀL 1366	30	1[f]	2	3	4	5	6
	7	8	9	10	11	12	13
	14	15	16	17	18	19	20
	21	22	23	24	25	26	27
DHU AL-QA'DA 1366	28	29	1	2	3	4	5
	6	7	8	9	10	11	12
	13	14	15	16	17	18	19
	20	21	22	23	24	25	26
DHU AL-ḤIJJA 1366	27	28	29	30	1	2	3
	4	5	6	7	8	9	10[g]
	11	12	13	14	15	16	17
	18	19	20	21	22	23	24
MUḤARRAM 1367	25	26	27	28	29	30	1[a]
	2	3	4	5	6	7	8
	9	10[b]	11	12	13	14	15
	16	17	18	19	20	21	22
	23	24	25	26	27	28	29
ṢAFAR 1367	1	2	3	4	5	6	7
	8	9	10	11	12	13	14
	15	16	17	18	19	20	21

‡Leap year
[a]New Year
[b]'Ashūrā'
[c]Prophet's Birthday
[d]Ascent of the Prophet
[e]Start of Ramaḍān
[f]'Id al-Fiṭr
[g]'Id al-'Aḍḥā

GREGORIAN 1947

Julian (Sun)	Sun	Mon	Tue	Wed	Thu	Fri	Sat	Month
Dec 16	29	30	31	1	2	3	4	JANUARY 1947
	5	6	7[a]	8	9	10	11	
Dec 30	12	13	14[b]	15	16	17	18	
	19	20	21	22	23	24	25	
Jan 13	26	27	28	29	30	31	1	FEBRUARY 1947
	2	3	4	5	6	7	8	
Jan 27	9	10	11	12	13	14	15	
	16	17	18	19[c]	20	21	22	
Feb 10	23	24	25	26	27	28	1	MARCH 1947
	2[d]	3	4	5	6	7	8	
Feb 24	9	10	11	12	13	14	15	
	16	17	18	19	20	21	22	
Mar 10	23	24	25	26	27	28	29	
	30	31	1	2	3	4	5	APRIL 1947
Mar 24	6[e]	7	8	9	10	11	12	
	13[f]	14	15	16	17	18	19	
Apr 7	20	21	22	23	24	25	26	
	27	28	29	30	1	2	3	MAY 1947
Apr 21	4	5	6	7	8	9	10	
	11	12	13	14	15	16	17	
May 5	18	19	20	21	22	23	24	
	25	26	27	28	29	30	31	
May 19	1	2	3	4	5	6	7	JUNE 1947
	8	9	10	11	12	13	14	
Jun 2	15	16	17	18	19	20	21	
	22	23	24	25	26	27	28	
Jun 16	29	30	1	2	3	4	5	JULY 1947
	6	7	8	9	10	11	12	
Jun 30	13	14	15	16	17	18	19	
	20	21	22	23	24	25	26	
Jul 14	27	28	29	30	31	1	2	AUGUST 1947
	3	4	5	6	7	8	9	
Jul 28	10	11	12	13	14	15	16	
	17	18	19	20	21	22	23	
Aug 11	24	25	26	27	28	29	30	
	31	1	2	3	4	5	6	SEPTEMBER 1947
Aug 25	7	8	9	10	11	12	13	
	14	15	16	17	18	19	20	
Sep 8	21	22	23	24	25	26	27	
	28	29	30	1	2	3	4	OCTOBER 1947
Sep 22	5	6	7	8	9	10	11	
	12	13	14	15	16	17	18	
Oct 6	19	20	21	22	23	24	25	
	26	27	28	29	30	31	1	NOVEMBER 1947
Oct 20	2	3	4	5	6	7	8	
	9	10	11	12	13	14	15	
Nov 3	16	17	18	19	20	21	22	
	23	24	25	26	27	28	29	
Nov 17	30[g]	1	2	3	4	5	6	DECEMBER 1947
	7	8	9	10	11	12	13	
Dec 1	14	15	16	17	18	19	20	
	21	22	23	24	25[h]	26	27	
Dec 15	28	29	30	31	1	2	3	

[a]Orthodox Christmas
[b]Julian New Year
[c]Ash Wednesday
[d]Feast of Orthodoxy
[e]Easter
[f]Orthodox Easter
[g]Advent
[h]Christmas

1948

GREGORIAN 1948[‡]

Month	Sun	Mon	Tue	Wed	Thu	Fri	Sat	Lunar Phases	ISO WEEK (Mon)	JULIAN DAY (Sun noon)
	28	29	30	31	1[a]	2	◑	11:13	1	2432548
JANUARY 1948	4	5	6	7	8	9	10		2	2432555
	●	12	13	14	15	16	17	7:45	3	2432562
	18	◐	20	21	22	23	24	11:32	4	2432569
	25	○	27	28	29	30	31	7:11	5	2432576
FEBRUARY 1948	1	◑	3	4	5	6	7	0:32	6	2432583
	8	9	●	11	12	13	14	3:02	7	2432590
	15	16	17	◐	19	20	21	1:55	8	2432597
	22	23	○	25	26	27	28	17:15	9	2432604
	29	1	◑	3	4	5	6	16:35	10	2432611
MARCH 1948	7	8	9	●	11	12	13	21:15	11	2432618
	14	15	16	17	◐	19	20[b]	12:27	12	2432625
	21	22	23	24	○	26	27	3:10	13	2432632
	28	29	30	31	◑	2	3	10:25	14	2432639
APRIL 1948	4	5	6	7	8	●	10	13:17	15	2432646
	11	12	13	14	15	◐	17	19:42	16	2432653
	18	19	20	21	22	○	24	13:28	17	2432660
	25	26	27	28	29	30	◑	4:48	18	2432667
MAY 1948	2	3	4	5	6	7	8		19	2432674
	●	10	11	12	13	14	15	2:30	20	2432681
	◐	17	18	19	20	21	22	0:55	21	2432688
	○	24	25	26	27	28	29	0:37	22	2432695
	◑	31	1	2	3	4	5	22:43	23	2432702
JUNE 1948	6	●	8	9	10	11	12	12:56	24	2432709
	13	◐	15	16	17	18	19	5:40	25	2432716
	20	○[c]	22	23	24	25	26	12:54	26	2432723
	27	28	◑	30	1	2	3	15:23	27	2432730
JULY 1948	4	5	●	7	8	9	10	21:09	28	2432737
	11	12	◐	14	15	16	17	11:30	29	2432744
	18	19	20	○	22	23	24	2:31	30	2432751
	25	26	27	28	◑	30	31	6:11	31	2432758
AUGUST 1948	1	2	3	4	●	6	7	4:13	32	2432765
	8	9	10	◐	12	13	14	19:40	33	2432772
	15	16	17	18	○	20	21	17:32	34	2432779
	22	23	24	25	26	◑	28	18:46	35	2432786
	29	30	31	1	2	●	4	11:21	36	2432793
SEPTEMBER 1948	5	6	7	8	9	◐	11	7:05	37	2432800
	12	13	14	15	16	17	○	9:43	38	2432807
	19	20	21	22	23[d]	24	25		39	2432814
	◑	27	28	29	30	1	●	5:07 19:42	40	2432821
OCTOBER 1948	3	4	5	6	7	8	◐	22:10	41	2432828
	10	11	12	13	14	15	16		42	2432835
	17	○	19	20	21	22	23	2:24	43	2432842
	24	◑	26	27	28	29	30	13:41	44	2432849
	31	●	2	3	4	5	6	6:03	45	2432856
NOVEMBER 1948	7	◐	9	10	11	12	13	16:46	46	2432863
	14	15	○	17	18	19	20	18:31	47	2432870
	21	22	◑	24	25	26	27	21:22	48	2432877
	28	29	●	1	2	3	4	18:45	49	2432884
DECEMBER 1948	5	6	7	◐	9	10	11	13:57	50	2432891
	12	13	14	15	○	17	18	9:11	51	2432898
	19	20	21[e]	22	◑	24	25	5:12	52	2432905
	26	27	28	29	●	31	1	9:45	53	2432912

HEBREW 5708[‡]/5709

ISO WEEK	Month	Sun	Mon	Tue	Wed	Thu	Fri	Sat	Molad
1	TEVETH 5708	15	16	17	18	19	20	21	
2		22	23	24	25	26	27	28	
3	SHEVAT 5708	29	1	2	3	4	5	6	Sun 14h33m0p
4		7	8	9	10	11	12	13	
5		14	15	16	17	18	19	20	
6		21	22	23	24	25	26	27	
7	ADAR I 5708	28	29	30	1	2	3	4	Tue 3h17m1p
8		5	6	7	8	9	10	11	
9		12	13	14	15	16	17	18	
10		19	20	21	22	23	24	25	
11	ADAR II 5708	26	27	28	29	30	1	2	Wed 16h1m2p
12		3	4	5	6	7	8	9	
13		10	11	12	13	14[f]	15	16	
14		17	18	19	20	21	22	23	
15	NISAN 5708	24	25	26	27	28	29	1	Fri 4h45m3p
16		2	3	4	5	6	7	8	
17		9	10	11	12	13	14	15[g]	
18		16	17	18	19	20	21	22	
19		23	24	25	26	27	28	29	
20	IYAR 5708	30	1	2	3	4	5	6	Sat 17h29m4p
21		7	8	9	10	11	12	13	
22		14	15	16	17	18	19	20	
23		21	22	23	24	25	26	27	
24	SIVAN 5708	28	29	1	2	3	4	5	Mon 6h13m5p
25		6[h]	7	8	9	10	11	12	
26		13	14	15	16	17	18	19	
27		20	21	22	23	24	25	26	
28	TAMMUZ 5708	27	28	29	30	1	2	3	Tue 18h57m6p
29		4	5	6	7	8	9	10	
30		11	12	13	14	15	16	17	
31		18	19	20	21	22	23	24	
32	AV 5708	25	26	27	28	29	1	2	Thu 7h41m7p
33		3	4	5	6	7	8	9	
34		10[i]	11	12	13	14	15	16	
35		17	18	19	20	21	22	23	
36		24	25	26	27	28	29	30	
37	ELUL 5708	1	2	3	4	5	6	7	Fri 20h25m8p
38		8	9	10	11	12	13	14	
39		15	16	17	18	19	20	21	
40		22	23	24	25	26	27	28	
41	TISHRI 5709	29	1[a]	2[a]	3	4	5	6	Sun 9h9m9p
42		7	8	9	10[b]	11	12	13	
43		14	15[c]	16	17	18	19	20[§]	
44		21	22	23	24	25	26	27	
45	ḤESHVAN 5709	28	29	30	1	2	3	4	Mon 21h53m10p
46		5	6	7	8	9	10	11	
47		12	13	14	15	16	17	18	
48		19	20	21	22	23	24	25	
49	KISLEV 5709	26	27	28	29	30	1	2	Wed 10h37m11p
50		3[d]	4	5	6	7	8	9	
51		10	11	12	13	14	15	16	
52		17	18	19	20	21	22	23	
53		24	25[e]	26[e]	27[e]	28[e]	29[e]	30[e]	

CHINESE Dīng-Hài[‡]/Wù-Zǐ

ISO WEEK	Month	Sun	Mon	Tue	Wed	Thu	Fri	Sat	Solar Term
1	MONTH 11 Dīng-Hài	17	18	19	20	21	22	23	
2		24	25	26	27	28	29	30	Xiǎo hán
3	MONTH 12 Dīng-Hài	1	2	3	4	5	6	7	
4		8	9	10	11	12	13	14	Dà hán
5		15	16	17	18	19	20	21	
6		22	23	24	25	26	27	28	Lì chūn
7	MONTH 1 Wù-Zǐ	29	30*	1[a]	2	3	4	5	
8		6	7	8	9	10	11	12	Yǔ shuǐ
9		13	14	15[b]	16	17	18	19	
10		20	21	22	23	24	25	26	Jīng zhé
11	MONTH 2 Wù-Zǐ	27	28	29	30	1	2	3	
12		4	5	6	7	8	9	10	
13		11	12	13	14	15	16	17	Chūn fēn
14		18	19	20	21	22	23	24	
15	MONTH 3 Wù-Zǐ	25	26[c]	27	28	29	1*	2	Qīng míng
16		3	4	5	6	7	8	9	
17		10	11	12	13	14	15	16	Gǔ yǔ
18		17	18	19	20	21	22	23	
19		24	25	26	27	28	29	30	Lì xià
20	MONTH 4 Wù-Zǐ	1	2	3	4	5	6	7	
21		8	9	10	11	12	13	14	Xiǎo mǎn
22		15	16	17	18	19	20	21	
23		22	23	24	25	26	27	28	
24	MONTH 5 Wù-Zǐ	29	1	2*	3	4	5[d]	6	Máng zhòng
25		7	8	9	10	11	12	13	
26		14	15	16	17	18	19	20	Xià zhì
27		21	22	23	24	25	26	27	
28	MONTH 6 Wù-Zǐ	28	29	30	1	2	3	4	Xiǎo shǔ
29		5	6	7	8	9	10	11	
30		12	13	14	15	16	17	18	Dà shǔ
31		19	20	21	22	23	24	25	
32	MONTH 7 Wù-Zǐ	26	27	28	29	1	2	3*	Lì qiū
33		4	5	6	7[e]	8	9	10	
34		11	12	13	14	15[f]	16	17	
35		18	19	20	21	22	23	24	Chǔ shǔ
36	MONTH 8 Wù-Zǐ	25	26	27	28	29	1	2	
37		3	4	5	6	7	8	9	Bái lù
38		10	11	12	13	14	15[g]	16	
39		17	18	19	20	21	22	23	Qiū fēn
40		24	25	26	27	28	29	30	
41	MONTH 9 Wù-Zǐ	1	2	3	4*	5	6	7	Hán lù
42		8	9[h]	10	11	12	13	14	
43		15	16	17	18	19	20	21	Shuāng jiàng
44		22	23	24	25	26	27	28	
45	MONTH 10 Wù-Zǐ	29	1	2	3	4	5	6	
46		7	8	9	10	11	12	13	Lì dōng
47		14	15	16	17	18	19	20	
48		21	22	23	24	25	26	27	Xiǎo xuě
49	MONTH 11* Wù-Zǐ	28	29	30	1	2	3	4	
50		5*	6	7	8	9	10	11	Dà xuě
51		12	13	14	15	16	17	18	
52		19	20	21	22[i]	23	24	25	Dōng zhì
53		26	27	28	29	1	2	3	

COPTIC 1664/1665 — ETHIOPIC 1940/1941

ISO WEEK	Coptic Month	Sun	Mon	Tue	Wed	Thu	Fri	Sat	Ethiopic Month
1	KOIAK 1664	18	19	20	21	22	23	24	TĀKHŚĀŚ 1940
2		25	26	27	28	29[c]	30	1	
3	TÔBE 1664	2	3	4	5	6[d]	7	8	ṬER 1940
4		9	10	11[e]	12	13	14	15	
5		16	17	18	19	20	21	22	
6		23	24	25	26	27	28	29	
7		30	1	2	3	4	5	6	
8	MESHIR 1664	7	8	9	10	11	12	13	YAKĀTIT 1940
9		14	15	16	17	18	19	20	
10		21	22	23	24	25	26	27	
11		28	29	30	1	2	3	4	
12	PAREMOTEP 1664	5	6	7	8	9	10	11	MAGĀBIT 1940
13		12	13	14	15	16	17	18	
14		19	20	21	22	23	24	25	
15		26	27	28	29	30	1	2	
16	PARMOUTE 1664	3	4	5	6	7	8	9	MIYĀZYĀ 1940
17		10	11	12	13	14	15	16	
18		17	18	19	20	21	22	23	
19		24[f]	25	26	27	28	29[g]	30	
20		1	2	3	4	5	6	7	
21	PASHONS 1664	8	9	10	11	12	13	14	GENBOT 1940
22		15	16	17	18	19	20	21	
23		22	23	24	25	26	27	28	
24		29	30	1	2	3	4	5	
25	PAÔNE 1664	6	7	8	9	10	11	12	SANĒ 1940
26		13	14	15	16	17	18	19	
27		20	21	22	23	24	25	26	
28		27	28	29	30	1	2	3	
29	EPÊP 1664	4	5	6	7	8	9	10	ḤAMLĒ 1940
30		11	12	13	14	15	16	17	
31		18	19	20	21	22	23	24	
32		25	26	27	28	29	30	1	
33		2	3	4	5	6	7	8	
34	MESORÊ 1664	9	10	11	12	13[h]	14	15	NAḤASĒ 1940
35		16	17	18	19	20	21	22	
36		23	24	25	26	27	28	29	
37	EPAG. 1664	30	1	2	3	4	5	1[a]	PĀG. 1940
38		2	3	4	5	6	7	8	
39	THOOUT 1665	9	10	11	12	13	14	15	MASKARAM 1941
40		16	17[b]	18	19	20	21	22	
41		23	24	25	26	27	28	29	
42		30	1	2	3	4	5	6	
43	PAOPE 1665	7	8	9	10	11	12	13	TEQEMT 1941
44		14	15	16	17	18	19	20	
45		21	22	23	24	25	26	27	
46		28	29	30	1	2	3	4	
47	ATHÔR 1665	5	6	7	8	9	10	11	ḪEDĀR 1941
48		12	13	14	15	16	17	18	
49		19	20	21	22	23	24	25	
50		26	27	28	29	30	1	2	
51	KOIAK 1665	3	4	5	6	7	8	9	TĀKHŚĀŚ 1941
52		10	11	12	13	14	15	16	
53		17	18	19	20	21	22	23	

[‡]Leap year
[a]New Year
[b]Spring (16:57)
[c]Summer (12:11)
[d]Autumn (3:21)
[e]Winter (22:33)
● New moon
◐ First quarter moon
○ Full moon
◑ Last quarter moon

[‡]Leap year
[a]New Year
[b]Yom Kippur
[c]Sukkot
[§]רות ריינגולד נולדה בליל שבת
[d]Winter starts
[e]Ḥanukkah
[f]Purim
[g]Passover
[h]Shavuot
[i]Fast of Av

[‡]Leap year
[a]New Year (4646, Rat)
[b]Lantern Festival
[c]Qīngmíng
[d]Dragon Festival
[e]Qīqiǎo
[f]Hungry Ghosts
[g]Mid-Autumn Festival
[h]Double-Ninth Festival
[i]Dōngzhì
*Start of 60-name cycle

[a]New Year
[b]Building of the Cross
[c]Christmas
[d]Jesus's Circumcision
[e]Epiphany
[f]Easter
[g]Mary's Announcement
[h]Jesus's Transfiguration

PERSIAN (ASTRONOMICAL) 1326/1327

Month	Sun	Mon	Tue	Wed	Thu	Fri	Sat
	6	7	8	9	10	11	12
DEY 1326	13	14	15	16	17	18	19
	20	21	22	23	24	25	26
	27	28	29	30	1	2	3
BAHMAN 1326	4	5	6	7	8	9	10
	11	12	13	14	15	16	17
	18	19	20	21	22	23	24
	25	26	27	28	29	30	1
ESFAND 1326	2	3	4	5	6	7	8
	9	10	11	12	13	14	15
	16	17	18	19	20	21	22
	23	24	25	26	27	28	29
	1[a]	2	3	4	5	6	7
FARVARDĪN 1327	8	9	10	11	12	13[b]	14
	15	16	17	18	19	20	21
	22	23	24	25	26	27	28
	29	30	31	1	2	3	4
ORDĪBEHEŠT 1327	5	6	7	8	9	10	11
	12	13	14	15	16	17	18
	19	20	21	22	23	24	25
	26	27	28	29	30	31	1
XORDĀD 1327	2	3	4	5	6	7	8
	9	10	11	12	13	14	15
	16	17	18	19	20	21	22
	23	24	25	26	27	28	29
	30	31	1	2	3	4	5
TĪR 1327	6	7	8	9	10	11	12
	13	14	15	16	17	18	19
	20	21	22	23	24	25	26
	27	28	29	30	31	1	2
MORDĀD 1327	3	4	5	6	7	8	9
	10	11	12	13	14	15	16
	17	18	19	20	21	22	23
	24	25	26	27	28	29	30
	31	1	2	3	4	5	6
SHAHRĪVAR 1327	7	8	9	10	11	12	13
	14	15	16	17	18	19	20
	21	22	23	24	25	26	27
	28	29	30	31	1	2	3
MEHR 1327	4	5	6	7	8	9	10
	11	12	13	14	15	16	17
	18	19	20	21	22	23	24
	25	26	27	28	29	30	1
ĀBĀN 1327	2	3	4	5	6	7	8
	9	10	11	12	13	14	15
	16	17	18	19	20	21	22
	23	24	25	26	27	28	29
	30	1	2	3	4	5	6
ĀZAR 1327	7	8	9	10	11	12	13
	14	15	16	17	18	19	20
	21	22	23	24	25	26	27
DEY 1327	28	29	30	1	2	3	4
	5	6	7	8	9	10	11

[a]New Year
[b]Sizdeh Bedar

HINDU LUNAR 2004‡/2005

Month	Sun	Mon	Tue	Wed	Thu	Fri	Sat
	16	17	18	19	20	21	22
MĀRGAŚĪRA 2004	23	24	25	26	27	28	29
	30	1	2	3	4	5	6
	7	8	9	10	11	12	13
PAUSHA 2004	14	15	16	17	19	20	21
	22	23	24	25	26	27	28
	29	30	30	1	2	3	4
	5	6	7	8	9	10	11
MĀGHA 2004	13	14	15	16	17	18	19
	20	21	22	23	24	25	26
	27	28[h]	29	30	1	2	3
	4	5	6	7	8	9	10
PHĀLGUNA 2004	11	12	13	14	15[i]	16	18
	19	20	21	22	23	23	24
	25	26	27	28	29	30	1[a]
	2	3	4	5	6	7	8[b]
CHAITRA 2005	9	11	12	13	14	15	16
	17	18	19	20	21	22	23
	24	25	26	27	27	28	29
	30	1	2	4	5	6	7
	8	9	10	11	12	13	14
VAIŚĀKHA 2005	16	17	17	18	19	20	21
	22	23	24	25	26	27	28
	29	30	1	2	3	4	5
	7	8	9	10	11	12	13
JYAISHṬHA 2005	14	15	16	17	18	19	20
	21	22	23	23	24	25	26
	27	29	30	1	2	3	4
	5	6	7	8	9	11	12
ĀSHĀḌHA 2005	13	14	15	15	16	17	18
	19	20	21	22	23	24	25
	26	27	28	29	30	1	3
	4	5	6	7	8	9	10
ŚRĀVAṆA 2005	11	12	13	14	15	16	17
	18	19	20	21	21	22	23[c]
	25	26	27	28	29	30	1
	2	3[d]	4	5	7	8	9
BHĀDRAPADA 2005	10	11	11	12	13	14	15
	16	17	18	19	20	21	22
	23	24	25	26	27	29	30
	1	2	3	4	5	6	7
ĀŚVINA 2005	8[e]	9[e]	10[e]	11	12	13	14
	15	15	16	17	18	19	20
	21	23	24	25	26	27	28
	29	30	1[f]	2	3	4	5
	6	7	8	9	10	11	12
KĀRTTIKA 2005	13	14	15	16	17	18	19
	20	21	22	23	24	25	27
	28	29	30	1	2	3	4
	5	6	7	8	8	9	10
MĀRGAŚĪRA 2005	11[g]	12	13	14	15	16	17
	18	19	21	22	23	24	25
	26	27	28	29	30	1	2

‡Leap year
[a]New Year (Sarvadhārin)
[b]Birthday of Rāma
[c]Birthday of Krishna
[d]Gaṇeśa Chaturthī
[e]Dashara
[f]Diwali
[g]Birthday of Vishnu
[h]Night of Śiva
[i]Holi

HINDU SOLAR 1869‡/1870

Month	Sun	Mon	Tue	Wed	Thu	Fri	Sat
	13	14	15	16	17	18	19
PAUSHA 1869	20	21	22	23	24	25	26
	27	28	29	1[b]	2	3	4
	5	6	7	8	9	10	11
MĀGHA 1869	12	13	14	15	16	17	18
	19	20	21	22	23	24	25
	26	27	28	29	1	2	3
	4	5	6	7	8	9	10
PHĀLGUNA 1869	11	12	13	14	15	16	17
	18	19	20	21	22	23	24
	25	26	27	28	29	30	1
	2	3	4	5	6	7	8
CHAITRA 1869	9	10	11	12	13	14	15
	16	17	18	19	20	21	22
	23	24	25	26	27	28	29
	30	31	1[a]	2	3	4	5
	6	7	8	9	10	11	12
VAIŚĀKHA 1870	13	14	15	16	17	18	19
	20	21	22	23	24	25	26
	27	28	29	30	1	2	3
	4	5	6	7	8	9	10
JYAISHṬHA 1870	11	12	13	14	15	16	17
	18	19	20	21	22	23	24
	25	26	27	28	29	30	31
	32	1	2	3	4	5	6
	7	8	9	10	11	12	13
ĀSHĀḌHA 1870	14	15	16	17	18	19	20
	21	22	23	24	25	26	27
	28	29	30	31	32	1	2
	3	4	5	6	7	8	9
ŚRĀVAṆA 1870	10	11	12	13	14	15	16
	17	18	19	20	21	22	23
	24	25	26	27	28	29	30
	31	1	2	3	4	5	6
	7	8	9	10	11	12	13
BHĀDRAPADA 1870	14	15	16	17	18	19	20
	21	22	23	24	25	26	27
	28	29	30	31	1	2	3
	4	5	6	7	8	9	10
ĀŚVINA 1870	11	12	13	14	15	16	17
	18	19	20	21	22	23	24
	25	26	27	28	29	30	1
	2	3	4	5	6	7	8
KĀRTTIKA 1870	9	10	11	12	13	14	15
	16	17	18	19	20	21	22
	23	24	25	26	27	28	29
	30	1	2	3	4	5	6
MĀRGAŚĪRA 1870	7	8	9	10	11	12	13
	14	15	16	17	18	19	20
	21	22	23	24	25	26	27
	28	29	30	1	2	3	4
PAUSHA 1870	5	6	7	8	9	10	11
	12	13	14	15	16	17	18

‡Leap year
[a]New Year (Plava)
[b]Pongal

ISLAMIC (ASTRONOMICAL) 1367/1368‡

Month	Sun	Mon	Tue	Wed	Thu	Fri	Sat
	15	16	17	18	19	20	21
ṢAFAR 1367	22	23	24	25	26	27	28
	29	30	1	2	3	4	5
	6	7	8	9	10	11	12[c]
RABĪ' I 1367	13	14	15	16	17	18	19
	20	21	22	23	24	25	26
	27	28	29	1	2	3	4
	5	6	7	8	9	10	11
RABĪ' II 1367	12	13	14	15	16	17	18
	19	20	21	22	23	24	25
	26	27	28	29	30	1	2
	3	4	5	6	7	8	9
JUMĀDĀ I 1367	10	11	12	13	14	15	16
	17	18	19	20	21	22	23
	24	25	26	27	28	29	30
	1	2	3	4	5	6	7
	8	9	10	11	12	13	14
JUMĀDĀ II 1367	15	16	17	18	19	20	21
	22	23	24	25	26	27	28
	29	1	2	3	4	5	6
	7	8	9	10	11	12	13
RAJAB 1367	14	15	16	17	18	19	20
	21	22	23	24	25	26	27[d]
	28	29	30	1	2	3	4
	5	6	7	8	9	10	11
SHA'BĀN 1367	12	13	14	15	16	17	18
	19	20	21	22	23	24	25
	26	27	28	29	1[e]	2	3
	4	5	6	7	8	9	10
RAMAḌĀN 1367	11	12	13	14	15	16	17
	18	19	20	21	22	23	24
	25	26	27	28	29	1[f]	2
	3	4	5	6	7	8	9
SHAWWĀL 1367	10	11	12	13	14	15	16
	17	18	19	20	21	22	23
	24	25	26	27	28	29	30
	1	2	3	4	5	6	7
DHU AL-QA'DA 1367	8	9	10	11	12	13	14
	15	16	17	18	19	20	21
	22	23	24	25	26	27	28
	29	1	2	3	4	5	6
DHU AL-ḤIJJA 1367	7	8	9	10[g]	11	12	13
	14	15	16	17	18	19	20
	21	22	23	24	25	26	27
	28	29	30	1[a]	2	3	4
	5	6	7	8	9	10[b]	11
MUḤARRAM 1368	12	13	14	15	16	17	18
	19	20	21	22	23	24	25
	26	27	28	29	1	2	3
	4	5	6	7	8	9	10
ṢAFAR 1368	11	12	13	14	15	16	17
	18	19	20	21	22	23	24
	25	26	27	28	29	30	1

‡Leap year
[a]New Year
[b]'Ashūrā'
[c]Prophet's Birthday
[d]Ascent of the Prophet
[e]Start of Ramaḍān
[f]'Id al-Fiṭr
[g]'Id al-'Aḍḥā

GREGORIAN 1948‡

Julian‡ (Sun)	Sun	Mon	Tue	Wed	Thu	Fri	Sat	Month
Dec 15	28	29	30	31	1	2	3	
	4	5	6	7[a]	8	9	10	JANUARY 1948
Dec 29	11	12	13	14[b]	15	16	17	
	18	19	20	21	22	23	24	
Jan 12	25	26	27	28	29	30	31	
	1	2	3	4	5	6	7	
Jan 26	8	9	10	11[c]	12	13	14	FEBRUARY 1948
	15	16	17	18	19	20	21	
Feb 9	22	23	24	25	26	27	28	
	29	1	2	3	4	5	6	
Feb 23	7	8	9	10	11	12	13	MARCH 1948
	14	15	16	17	18	19	20	
Mar 8	21[d]	22	23	24	25	26	27	
	28[e]	29	30	31	1	2	3	
Mar 22	4	5	6	7	8	9	10	APRIL 1948
	11	12	13	14	15	16	17	
Apr 5	18	19	20	21	22	23	24	
	25	26	27	28	29	30	1	
Apr 19	2[f]	3	4	5	6	7	8	
	9	10	11	12	13	14	15	MAY 1948
May 3	16	17	18	19	20	21	22	
	23	24	25	26	27	28	29	
May 17	30	31	1	2	3	4	5	
	6	7	8	9	10	11	12	JUNE 1948
May 31	13	14	15	16	17	18	19	
	20	21	22	23	24	25	26	
Jun 14	27	28	29	30	1	2	3	
	4	5	6	7	8	9	10	JULY 1948
Jun 28	11	12	13	14	15	16	17	
	18	19	20	21	22	23	24	
Jul 12	25	26	27	28	29	30	31	
	1	2	3	4	5	6	7	
Jul 26	8	9	10	11	12	13	14	AUGUST 1948
	15	16	17	18	19	20	21	
Aug 9	22	23	24	25	26	27	28	
	29	30	31	1	2	3	4	
Aug 23	5	6	7	8	9	10	11	SEPTEMBER 1948
	12	13	14	15	16	17	18	
Sep 6	19	20	21	22	23	24	25	
	26	27	28	29	30	1	2	
Sep 20	3	4	5	6	7	8	9	
	10	11	12	13	14	15	16	OCTOBER 1948
Oct 4	17	18	19	20	21	22	23	
	24	25	26	27	28	29	30	
Oct 18	31	1	2	3	4	5	6	
	7	8	9	10	11	12	13	NOVEMBER 1948
Nov 1	14	15	16	17	18	19	20	
	21	22	23	24	25	26	27	
Nov 15	28[g]	29	30	1	2	3	4	
	5	6	7	8	9	10	11	DECEMBER 1948
Nov 29	12	13	14	15	16	17	18	
	19	20	21	22	23	24	25[h]	
Dec 13	26	27	28	29	30	31	1	

‡Leap year
[a]Orthodox Christmas
[b]Julian New Year
[c]Ash Wednesday
[d]Feast of Orthodoxy
[e]Easter
[f]Orthodox Easter
[g]Advent
[h]Christmas

1949

GREGORIAN 1949 — Lunar Phases — ISO WEEK — JULIAN DAY

Month	Sun	Mon	Tue	Wed	Thu	Fri	Sat	Lunar Phases	ISO WEEK (Mon)	JULIAN DAY (Sun noon)
	26	27	28	29	●	31	1[a]	9:45	53	2432912
JANUARY 1949	2	3	4	5	6	◐	8	11:51	1	2432919
	9	10	11	12	13	○	15	21:59	2	2432926
	16	17	18	19	20	◑	22	14:08	3	2432933
	23	24	25	26	27	28	●	2:42	4	2432940
	30	31	1	2	3	4	5		5	2432947
FEBRUARY 1949	◐	7	8	9	10	11	12	8:05	6	2432954
	○	14	15	16	17	18	19	9:08	7	2432961
	◑	21	22	23	24	25	26	0:43	8	2432968
	●	28	1	2	3	4	5	20:55	9	2432975
MARCH 1949	6	7	◐	9	10	11	12	0:42	10	2432982
	13	○	15	16	17	18	19	19:03	11	2432989
	20[b]	◑	22	23	24	25	26	13:10	12	2432996
	27	28	●	30	31	1	2	15:11	13	2433003
APRIL 1949	3	4	5	◐	7	8	9	13:01	14	2433010
	10	11	12	○	14	15	16	4:08	15	2433017
	17	18	19	◑	21	22	23	3:27	16	2433024
	24	25	26	27	●	29	30	8:02	17	2433031
MAY 1949	1	2	3	4	◐	6	7	21:33	18	2433038
	8	9	10	11	○	13	14	12:51	19	2433045
	15	16	17	18	◑	20	21	19:22	20	2433052
	22	23	24	25	26	●	28	22:24	21	2433059
	29	30	31	1	2	3	◐	3:27	22	2433066
JUNE 1949	5	6	7	8	9	○	11	21:45	23	2433073
	12	13	14	15	16	17	◑	12:29	24	2433080
	19	20	21[c]	22	23	24	25		25	2433087
	●	27	28	29	30	1	2	10:02	26	2433094
JULY 1949	◐	4	5	6	7	8	9	8:08	27	2433101
	○	11	12	13	14	15	16	7:41	28	2433108
	17	◑	19	20	21	22	23	6:02	29	2433115
	24	●	26	27	28	29	30	19:33	30	2433122
	31	◐	2	3	4	5	6	12:58	31	2433129
AUGUST 1949	7	○	9	10	11	12	13	19:33	32	2433136
	14	15	◑	17	18	19	20	22:59	33	2433143
	21	22	23	●	25	26	27	3:59	34	2433150
	28	29	◐	31	1	2	3	19:17	35	2433157
SEPTEMBER 1949	4	5	6	○	8	9	10	9:59	36	2433164
	11	12	13	14	◑	16	17	14:29	37	2433171
	18	19	20	21	●	23[d]	24	12:21	38	2433178
	25	26	27	28	◐	30	1	4:18	39	2433185
OCTOBER 1949	2	3	4	5	6	○	8	2:53	40	2433192
	9	10	11	12	13	14	◑	4:06	41	2433199
	16	17	18	19	20	●	22	21:23	42	2433206
	23	24	25	26	27	◐	29	17:04	43	2433213
	30	31	1	2	3	4	○	21:09	44	2433220
NOVEMBER 1949	6	7	8	9	10	11	12		45	2433227
	◑	14	15	16	17	18	19	15:48	46	2433234
	●	21	22	23	24	25	26	7:29	47	2433241
	◐	28	29	30	1	2	3	10:01	48	2433248
DECEMBER 1949	4	○	6	7	8	9	10	15:14	49	2433255
	11	12	◑	14	15	16	17	1:48	50	2433262
	18	●	20	21	22[e]	23	24	18:56	51	2433269
	25	26	◐	28	29	30	31	6:31	52	2433276

HEBREW 5709/5710 — Molad

ISO WEEK	Month	Sun	Mon	Tue	Wed	Thu	Fri	Sat	Molad
53		24	25[e]	26[e]	27[e]	28[e]	29[e]	30[e]	
1	TEVETH 5709	1[e]	2[e]	3	4	5	6	7	Thu 23h21m12p
2		8	9	10	11	12	13	14	
3		15	16	17	18	19	20	21	
4		22	23	24	25	26	27	28	
5		29	1	2	3	4	5	6	Sat 12h5m13p
6	SHEVAT 5709	7	8	9	10	11	12	13	
7		14	15	16	17	18	19	20	
8		21	22	23	24	25	26	27	
9		28	29	30	1	2	3	4	Mon 0h49m14p
10	ADAR 5709	5	6	7	8	9	10	11	
11		12	13	14[f]	15	16	17	18	
12		19	20	21	22	23	24	25	
13		26	27	28	29	1	2	3	Tue 13h33m15p
14	NISAN 5709	4	5	6	7	8	9	10	
15		11	12	13	14	15[g]	16	17	
16		18	19	20	21	22	23	24	
17		25	26	27	28	29	30	1	Thu 2h17m16p
18	IYYAR 5709	2	3	4	5	6	7	8	
19		9	10	11	12	13	14	15	
20		16	17	18	19	20	21	22	
21		23	24	25	26	27	28	29	
22	SIVAN 5709	1	2	3	4	5	6[h]	7	Fri 15h1m17p
23		8	9	10	11	12	13	14	
24		15	16	17	18	19	20	21	
25		22	23	24	25	26	27	28	
26		29	30	1	2	3	4	5	Sun 3h46m0p
27	TAMMUZ 5709	6	7	8	9	10	11	12	
28		13	14	15	16	17	18	19	
29		20	21	22	23	24	25	26	
30		27	28	29	1	2	3	4	Mon 16h30m1p
31	AV 5709	5	6	7	8	9[i]	10	11	
32		12	13	14	15	16	17	18	
33		19	20	21	22	23	24	25	
34		26	27	28	29	30	1	2	Wed 5h14m2p
35	ELUL 5709	3	4	5	6	7	8	9	
36		10	11	12	13	14	15	16	
37		17	18	19	20	21	22	23	
38		24	25	26	27	28	29	1[a]	Thu 17h58m3p
39	TISHRI 5710	2[a]	3	4	5	6	7	8	
40		9	10[b]	11	12	13	14	15[c]	
41		16	17	18	19	20	21	22	
42		23	24	25	26	27	28	29	
43		30	1	2	3	4	5	6	Sat 6h42m4p
44	HESHVAN 5710	7	8	9	10	11	12	13	
45		14	15	16	17	18	19	20	
46		21	22	23	24	25	26	27	
47		28	29	1	2	3	4	5	Sun 19h26m5p
48	KISLEV 5710	6	7	8	9	10	11	12	
49		13	14[d]	15	16	17	18	19	
50		20	21	22	23	24	25[e]	26[e]	
51		27[e]	28[e]	29[e]	1[e]	2[e]	3[e]	4	Tue 8h10m6p
52	TEVETH 5710	5	6	7	8	9	10	11	

CHINESE Wù-Zǐ/Jǐ-Chǒu[‡] — Solar Term

ISO WEEK	Month	Sun	Mon	Tue	Wed	Thu	Fri	Sat	Solar Term
53	MONTH 12 Wù-Zǐ	26	27	28	29	1	2	3	
1		4	5	6	7	8	9	10	Xiǎo hán
2		11	12	13	14	15	16	17	
3		18	19	20	21	22	23	24	Dà hán
4		25	26	27	28	29	30	1[a]	
5	MONTH 1 Jǐ-Chǒu	2	3	4	5	6*	7	8	Lì chūn
6		9	10	11	12	13	14	15[b]	
7		16	17	18	19	20	21	22	Yǔ shuǐ
8		23	24	25	26	27	28	29	
9		30	1	2	3	4	5	6	
10	MONTH 2 Jǐ-Chǒu	7	8	9	10	11	12	13	Jīng zhé
11		14	15	16	17	18	19	20	
12		21	22	23	24	25	26	27	Chūn fēn
13		28	29	1	2	3	4	5	
14	MONTH 3 Jǐ-Chǒu	6	7*	8[c]	9	10	11	12	Qīng míng
15		13	14	15	16	17	18	19	
16		20	21	22	23	24	25	26	Gǔ yǔ
17		27	28	29	30	1	2	3	
18	MONTH 4 Jǐ-Chǒu	4	5	6	7	8	9	10	Lì xià
19		11	12	13	14	15	16	17	
20		18	19	20	21	22	23	24	Xiǎo mǎn
21		25	26	27	28	29	30	1	
22	MONTH 5 Jǐ-Chǒu	2	3	4	5[d]	6	7*	8	
23		9	10	11	12	13	14	15	Máng zhòng
24		16	17	18	19	20	21	22	
25		23	24	25	26	27	28	29	Xià zhì
26	MONTH 6 Jǐ-Chǒu	1	2	3	4	5	6	7	
27		8	9	10	11	12	13	14	Xiǎo shǔ
28		15	16	17	18	19	20	21	
29		22	23	24	25	26	27	28	Dà shǔ
30		29	30	1	2	3	4	5	
31	MONTH 7 Jǐ-Chǒu	6	7[e]	8*	9	10	11	12	
32		13	14	15[f]	16	17	18	19	Lì qiū
33		20	21	22	23	24	25	26	
34		27	28	29	1	2	3	4	Chǔ shǔ
35	LEAP MONTH 7 Jǐ-Chǒu	5	6	7	8	9	10	11	
36		12	13	14	15	16	17	18	Bái lù
37		19	20	21	22	23	24	25	
38		26	27	28	29	1	2	3	Qiū fēn
39	MONTH 8 Jǐ-Chǒu	4	5	6	7	8	9	10*	
40		11	12	13	14	15[g]	16	17	Hán lù
41		18	19	20	21	22	23	24	
42		25	26	27	28	29	30	1	
43	MONTH 9 Jǐ-Chǒu	2	3	4	5	6	7	8	Shuāng jiàng
44		9[h]	10	11	12	13	14	15	
45		16	17	18	19	20	21	22	Lì dōng
46		23	24	25	26	27	28	29	
47	MONTH 10 Jǐ-Chǒu	1	2	3	4	5	6	7	Xiǎo xuě
48		8	9	10	11*	12	13	14	
49		15	16	17	18	19	20	21	Dà xuě
50		22	23	24	25	26	27	28	
51	MONTH 11 Jǐ-Chǒu	29	30	1	2	3[i]	4	5	Dōng zhì
52		6	7	8	9	10	11	12	

COPTIC 1665/1666 — ETHIOPIC 1941/1942

ISO WEEK	Coptic month	Sun	Mon	Tue	Wed	Thu	Fri	Sat	Ethiopic month
53	KOIAK 1665	17	18	19	20	21	22	23	TĀKHŚĀŚ 1941
1		24	25	26	27	28	29[c]	30	
2	TÔBE 1665	1	2	3	4	5	6[d]	7	TER 1941
3		8	9	10	11[e]	12	13	14	
4		15	16	17	18	19	20	21	
5		22	23	24	25	26	27	28	
6	MESHIR 1665	29	30	1	2	3	4	5	YAKĀTIT 1941
7		6	7	8	9	10	11	12	
8		13	14	15	16	17	18	19	
9		20	21	22	23	24	25	26	
10	PAREMOTEP 1665	27	28	29	30	1	2	3	MAGĀBIT 1941
11		4	5	6	7	8	9	10	
12		11	12	13	14	15	16	17	
13		18	19	20	21	22	23	24	
14	PARMOUTE 1665	25	26	27	28	29	30	1	MIYĀZYĀ 1941
15		2	3	4	5	6	7	8	
16		9	10	11	12	13	14	15	
17		16[f]	17	18	19	20	21	22	
18		23	24	25	26	27	28	29[g]	
19	PASHONS 1665	30	1	2	3	4	5	6	GENBOT 1941
20		7	8	9	10	11	12	13	
21		14	15	16	17	18	19	20	
22		21	22	23	24	25	26	27	
23	PAÔNE 1665	28	29	30	1	2	3	4	SANÉ 1941
24		5	6	7	8	9	10	11	
25		12	13	14	15	16	17	18	
26		19	20	21	22	23	24	25	
27	EPÊP 1665	26	27	28	29	30	1	2	HAMLÉ 1941
28		3	4	5	6	7	8	9	
29		10	11	12	13	14	15	16	
30		17	18	19	20	21	22	23	
31		24	25	26	27	28	29	30	
32	MESORÊ 1665	1	2	3	4	5	6	7	NAHASÉ 1941
33		8	9	10	11	12	13[h]	14	
34		15	16	17	18	19	20	21	
35		22	23	24	25	26	27	28	
36	EPAG. 1665	29	30	1	2	3	4	5	PĀG. 1941
37	THOOUT 1666	1[a]	2	3	4	5	6	7	MASKARAM 1942
38		8	9	10	11	12	13	14	
39		15	16	17[b]	18	19	20	21	
40		22	23	24	25	26	27	28	
41	PAOPE 1666	29	30	1	2	3	4	5	TEQEMT 1942
42		6	7	8	9	10	11	12	
43		13	14	15	16	17	18	19	
44		20	21	22	23	24	25	26	
45	ATHÔR 1666	27	28	29	30	1	2	3	HEDĀR 1942
46		4	5	6	7	8	9	10	
47		11	12	13	14	15	16	17	
48		18	19	20	21	22	23	24	
49	KOIAK 1666	25	26	27	28	29	30	1	TĀKHŚĀŚ 1942
50		2	3	4	5	6	7	8	
51		9	10	11	12	13	14	15	
52		16	17	18	19	20	21	22	

[a]New Year
[b]Spring (22:48)
[c]Summer (18:03)
[d]Autumn (9:06)
[e]Winter (4:23)
● New moon
◐ First quarter moon
○ Full moon
◑ Last quarter moon

[a]New Year
[b]Yom Kippur
[c]Sukkot
[d]Winter starts
[e]Ḥanukkah
[f]Purim
[g]Passover
[h]Shavuot
[i]Fast of Av

‡Leap year
[a]New Year (4647, Ox)
[b]Lantern Festival
[c]Qīngmíng
[d]Dragon Festival
[e]Qīqiǎo
[f]Hungry Ghosts
[g]Mid-Autumn Festival
[h]Double-Ninth Festival
[i]Dōngzhì
*Start of 60-name cycle

[a]New Year
[b]Building of the Cross
[c]Christmas
[d]Jesus's Circumcision
[e]Epiphany
[f]Easter
[g]Mary's Announcement
[h]Jesus's Transfiguration

1949

PERSIAN (ASTRONOMICAL) 1327/1328

Month	Sun	Mon	Tue	Wed	Thu	Fri	Sat
DEY 1327	5	6	7	8	9	10	11
	12	13	14	15	16	17	18
	19	20	21	22	23	24	25
	26	27	28	29	30	*1*	2
BAHMAN 1327	3	4	5	6	7	8	9
	10	11	12	13	14	15	16
	17	18	19	20	21	22	23
	24	25	26	27	28	29	30
ESFAND 1327	*1*	2	3	4	5	6	7
	8	9	10	11	12	13	14
	15	16	17	18	19	20	21
	22	23	24	25	26	27	28
	29	*1*[a]	2	3	4	5	6
FARVARDĪN 1328	7	8	9	10	11	12	13[b]
	14	15	16	17	18	19	20
	21	22	23	24	25	26	27
	28	29	30	31	*1*	2	3
ORDĪBEHEŠT 1328	4	5	6	7	8	9	10
	11	12	13	14	15	16	17
	18	19	20	21	22	23	24
	25	26	27	28	29	30	31
XORDĀD 1328	*1*	2	3	4	5	6	7
	8	9	10	11	12	13	14
	15	16	17	18	19	20	21
	22	23	24	25	26	27	28
	29	30	31	*1*	2	3	4
TĪR 1328	5	6	7	8	9	10	11
	12	13	14	15	16	17	18
	19	20	21	22	23	24	25
	26	27	28	29	30	31	*1*
MORDĀD 1328	2	3	4	5	6	7	8
	9	10	11	12	13	14	15
	16	17	18	19	20	21	22
	23	24	25	26	27	28	29
	30	31	*1*	2	3	4	5
SHAHRĪVAR 1328	6	7	8	9	10	11	12
	13	14	15	16	17	18	19
	20	21	22	23	24	25	26
	27	28	29	30	31	*1*	2
MEHR 1328	3	4	5	6	7	8	9
	10	11	12	13	14	15	16
	17	18	19	20	21	22	23
	24	25	26	27	28	29	30
ABĀN 1328	*1*	2	3	4	5	6	7
	8	9	10	11	12	13	14
	15	16	17	18	19	20	21
	22	23	24	25	26	27	28
	29	30	*1*	2	3	4	5
ĀZAR 1328	6	7	8	9	10	11	12
	13	14	15	16	17	18	19
	20	21	22	23	24	25	26
	27	28	29	30	*1*	2	3
DEY 1328	4	5	6	7	8	9	10

[a]New Year
[b]Sizdeh Bedar

HINDU LUNAR 2005/2006

Month	Sun	Mon	Tue	Wed	Thu	Fri	Sat
PAUSHA 2005	26	27	28	29	30	1	2
	3	4	5	6	7	8	9
	10	11	12	13	14	15	16
	17	18	19	20	21	22	23
	24	**25**	27	28	29	30	*30*
MĀGHA 2005	1	2	3	4	5	6	7
	8	9	10	11	12	13	14
	15	16	17	**18**	20	21	22
	23	24	25	26	27	28[h]	29
PHĀLGUNA 2005	30	1	2	3	3	4	5
	6	7	8	9	10	11	**12**
	14	15[i]	16	17	18	19	20
	21	22	23	24	25	26	27
	28	29	30	1[a]	2	3	4
CHAITRA 2006	5	6	7	8	9[b]	10	11
	12	13	14	15	**16**	18	19
	20	21	22	23	24	25	26
	27	*27*	28	29	30	1	2
VAIŚĀKHA 2006	3	4	5	6	7	8	9
	10	12	13	14	15	16	17
	18	19	20	21	22	23	24
	25	26	27	28	29	30	1
JYAISHṬHA 2006	2	3	4	5	6	7	8
	9	10	11	12	**13**	15	16
	17	18	19	20	21	22	23
	23	24	25	26	27	28	29
	30	1	2	3	4	**5**	7
ĀSHĀḌHA 2006	8	9	10	11	12	13	14
	15	16	17	18	19	20	21
	22	23	24	25	26	27	28
	29	30	1	2	3	4	5
ŚRĀVAṆA 2006	6	7	**8**	10	11	12	13
	14	15	16	17	18	19	20
	20	21	22	23[c]	24	25	26
	27	28	29	30	**1**	3	4[d]
BHĀDRAPADA 2006	5	6	7	8	9	10	11
	12	13	14	15	16	17	18
	19	20	21	22	23	24	25
	26	27	28	29	30	1	2
ĀŚVINA 2006	3	4	**5**	7	8[e]	9[e]	10[e]
	11	12	13	14	15	*15*	16
	17	18	19	20	21	22	23
	24	25	26	27	**28**	30	1[f]
KĀRTTIKA 2006	2	3	4	5	6	7	8
	9	10	11	12	13	14	15
	16	17	18	19	20	*20*	22
	23	24	25	26	27	28	29
	30	1	2	**3**	5	6	7
MĀRGAŚĪRA 2006	8	*8*	9	10	11[g]	12	13
	14	15	16	17	18	19	20
	21	22	23	24	25	**26**	28
PAUSHA 2006	29	30	1	2	3	4	5
	6	7	8	9	10	11	*11*

[a]New Year (Virodhin)
[b]Birthday of Rāma
[c]Birthday of Krishna
[d]Ganēśa Chaturthī
[e]Dashara
[f]Diwali
[g]Birthday of Vishnu
[h]Night of Śiva
[i]Holi

HINDU SOLAR 1870/1871

Month	Sun	Mon	Tue	Wed	Thu	Fri	Sat
PAUSHA 1870	12	13	14	15	16	17	18
	19	20	21	22	23	24	25
	26	27	28	29	1[b]	2	3
MĀGHA 1870	4	5	6	7	8	9	10
	11	12	13	14	15	16	17
	18	19	20	21	22	23	24
	25	26	27	28	29	30	1
PHĀLGUNA 1870	2	3	4	5	6	7	8
	9	10	11	12	13	14	15
	16	17	18	19	20	21	22
	23	24	25	26	27	28	29
CHAITRA 1870	1	2	3	4	5	6	7
	8	9	10	11	12	13	14
	15	16	17	18	19	20	21
	22	23	24	25	26	27	28
	29	30	31	1[a]	2	3	4
VAIŚĀKHA 1871	5	6	7	8	9	10	11
	12	13	14	15	16	17	18
	19	20	21	22	23	24	25
	26	27	28	29	30	31	1
JYAISHṬHA 1871	2	3	4	5	6	7	8
	9	10	11	12	13	14	15
	16	17	18	19	20	21	22
	23	24	25	26	27	28	29
	30	31	1	2	3	4	5
ĀSHĀḌHA 1871	6	7	8	9	10	11	12
	13	14	15	16	17	18	19
	20	21	22	23	24	25	26
	27	28	29	30	31	32	1
ŚRĀVAṆA 1871	2	3	4	5	6	7	8
	9	10	11	12	13	14	15
	16	17	18	19	20	21	22
	23	24	25	26	27	28	29
	30	31	1	2	3	4	5
BHĀDRAPADA 1871	6	7	8	9	10	11	12
	13	14	15	16	17	18	19
	20	21	22	23	24	25	26
	27	28	29	30	31	1	2
ĀŚVINA 1871	3	4	5	6	7	8	9
	10	11	12	13	14	15	16
	17	18	19	20	21	22	23
	24	25	26	27	28	29	30
	31	1	2	3	4	5	6
KĀRTTIKA 1871	7	8	9	10	11	12	13
	14	15	16	17	18	19	20
	21	22	23	24	25	26	27
	28	29	30	1	2	3	4
MĀRGAŚĪRA 1871	5	6	7	8	9	10	11
	12	13	14	15	16	17	18
	19	20	21	22	23	24	25
	26	27	28	29	1	2	3
PAUSHA 1871	4	5	6	7	8	9	10
	11	12	13	14	15	16	17

[a]New Year (Śubhakṛit)
[b]Pongal

ISLAMIC (ASTRONOMICAL) 1368‡/1369

Month	Sun	Mon	Tue	Wed	Thu	Fri	Sat
	25	26	27	28	29	30	*1*
RABĪʿ I 1368	2	3	4	5	6	7	8
	9	10	11	12[c]	13	14	15
	16	17	18	19	20	21	22
	23	24	25	26	27	28	29
RABĪʿ II 1368	*1*	2	3	4	5	6	7
	8	9	10	11	12	13	14
	15	16	17	18	19	20	21
	22	23	24	25	26	27	28
	29	30	*1*	2	3	4	5
JUMĀDĀ I 1368	6	7	8	9	10	11	12
	13	14	15	16	17	18	19
	20	21	22	23	24	25	26
	27	28	29	30	*1*	2	3
JUMĀDĀ II 1368	4	5	6	7	8	9	10
	11	12	13	14	15	16	17
	18	19	20	21	22	23	24
	25	26	27	28	29	*30*	1
RAJAB 1368	2	3	4	5	6	7	8
	9	10	11	12	13	14	15
	16	17	18	19	20	21	22
	23	24	25	26	27[d]	28	29
SHAʿBĀN 1368	*1*	2	3	4	5	6	7
	8	9	10	11	12	13	14
	15	16	17	18	19	20	21
	22	23	24	25	26	27	28
	29	*30*	1[e]	2	3	4	5
RAMAḌĀN 1368	6	7	8	9	10	11	12
	13	14	15	16	17	18	19
	20	21	22	23	24	25	26
	27	28	29	*1*[f]	2	3	4
SHAWWĀL 1368	5	6	7	8	9	10	11
	12	13	14	15	16	17	18
	19	20	21	22	23	24	25
	26	27	28	29	*1*	2	3
DHU AL-QAʿDA 1368	4	5	6	7	8	9	10
	11	12	13	14	15	16	17
	18	19	20	21	22	23	24
	25	26	27	28	29	30	*1*
DHU AL-ḤIJJA 1368	2	3	4	5	6	7	8
	9	10[g]	11	12	13	14	15
	16	17	18	19	20	21	22
	23	24	25	26	27	28	29
	30	*1*[a]	2	3	4	5	6
MUḤARRAM 1369	7	8	9	10[b]	11	12	13
	14	15	16	17	18	19	20
	21	22	23	24	25	26	27
	28	29	1	*2*	3	4	5
ṢAFAR 1369	6	7	8	9	10	11	12
	13	14	15	16	17	18	19
	20	21	22	23	24	25	26
	27	28	29	1	*2*	3	4
RABĪʿ I 1369	5	6	7	8	9	10	11

‡Leap year
[a]New Year
[b]ʿAshūrā'
[c]Prophet's Birthday
[d]Ascent of the Prophet
[e]Start of Ramaḍān
[f]ʿId al-Fiṭr
[g]ʿId al-'Aḍḥā

GREGORIAN 1949

Julian (Sun)	Sun	Mon	Tue	Wed	Thu	Fri	Sat	Month
Dec 13	26	27	28	29	30	31	1	
	2	3	4	5	6	7[a]	8	JANUARY 1949
Dec 27	9	10	11	12	13	14[b]	15	
	16	17	18	19	20	21	22	
Jan 10	*23*	24	25	26	27	28	29	
	30	31	1	2	3	4	5	
Jan 24	*6*	7	8	9	10	11	12	FEBRUARY 1949
	13	14	15	16	17	18	19	
Feb 7	*20*	21	22	23	24	25	26	
	27	28	1	2[c]	3	4	5	
Feb 21	*6*	7	8	9	10	11	12	MARCH 1949
	13[d]	14	15	16	17	18	19	
Mar 7	*20*	21	22	23	24	25	26	
	27	28	29	30	31	1	2	
Mar 21	*3*	4	5	6	7	8	9	APRIL 1949
	10	11	12	13	14	15	16	
Apr 4	*17*[e]	18	19	20	21	22	23	
	24[f]	25	26	27	28	29	30	
Apr 18	*1*	2	3	4	5	6	7	MAY 1949
	8	9	10	11	12	13	14	
May 2	*15*	16	17	18	19	20	21	
	22	23	24	25	26	27	28	
May 16	*29*	30	31	1	2	3	4	
	5	6	7	8	9	10	11	JUNE 1949
May 30	*12*	13	14	15	16	17	18	
	19	20	21	22	23	24	25	
Jun 13	*26*	27	28	29	30	1	2	
	3	4	5	6	7	8	9	JULY 1949
Jun 27	*10*	11	12	13	14	15	16	
	17	18	19	20	21	22	23	
Jul 11	*24*	25	26	27	28	29	30	
	31	1	2	3	4	5	6	
Jul 25	*7*	8	9	10	11	12	13	AUGUST 1949
	14	15	16	17	18	19	20	
Aug 8	*21*	22	23	24	25	26	27	
	28	29	30	31	1	2	3	
Aug 22	*4*	5	6	7	8	9	10	SEPTEMBER 1949
	11	12	13	14	15	16	17	
Sep 5	*18*	19	20	21	22	23	24	
	25	26	27	28	29	30	1	
Sep 19	*2*	3	4	5	6	7	8	OCTOBER 1949
	9	10	11	12	13	14	15	
Oct 3	*16*	17	18	19	20	21	22	
	23	24	25	26	27	28	29	
Oct 17	*30*	31	1	2	3	4	5	
	6	7	8	9	10	11	12	NOVEMBER 1949
Oct 31	*13*	14	15	16	17	18	19	
	20	21	22	23	24	25	26	
Nov 14	*27*[g]	28	29	30	1	2	3	
	4	5	6	7	8	9	10	DECEMBER 1949
Nov 28	*11*	12	13	14	15	16	17	
	18	19	20	21	22	23	24	
Dec 12	25[h]	26	27	28	29	30	31	

[a]Orthodox Christmas
[b]Julian New Year
[c]Ash Wednesday
[d]Feast of Orthodoxy
[e]Easter
[f]Orthodox Easter
[g]Advent
[h]Christmas

1950

Gregorian 1950

Month	Sun	Mon	Tue	Wed	Thu	Fri	Sat	Lunar Phases	ISO Week (Mon)	Julian Day (Sun noon)
January 1950	1[a]	2	3	○	5	6	7	7:48	1	2433283
	8	9	10	◑	12	13	14	10:31	2	2433290
	15	16	17	●	19	20	21	8:00	3	2433297
	22	23	24	25	◐	27	28	4:39	4	2433304
February 1950	29	30	31	1	○	3	4	22:16	5	2433311
	5	6	7	8	◑	10	11	18:32	6	2433318
	12	13	14	15	●	17	18	22:53	7	2433325
	19	20	21	22	23	24	◐	1:52	8	2433332
March 1950	26	27	28	1	2	3	○	10:34	9	2433339
	5	6	7	8	9	10	◑	2:38	10	2433346
	12	13	14	15	16	17	●	15:20	11	2433353
	19	20	21[b]	22	23	24	25		12	2433360
April 1950	◐	27	28	29	30	31	1	20:09	13	2433367
	○	3	4	5	6	7	8	20:49	14	2433374
	◑	10	11	12	13	14	15	11:42	15	2433381
	16	●	18	19	20	21	22	8:25	16	2433388
	23	24	◐	26	27	28	29	10:40	17	2433395
May 1950	30	1	○	3	4	5	6	5:19	18	2433402
	7	◑	9	10	11	12	13	22:32	19	2433409
	14	15	16	●	18	19	20	0:54	20	2433416
	21	22	23	◐	25	26	27	21:28	21	2433423
June 1950	28	29	30	○	1	2	3	12:43	22	2433430
	4	5	6	◑	8	9	10	11:35	23	2433437
	11	12	13	14	●	16	17	15:53	24	2433444
	18	19	20	21[c]	22	◐	24	5:13	25	2433451
July 1950	25	26	27	28	○	30	1	19:58	26	2433458
	2	3	4	5	6	◑	8	2:53	27	2433465
	9	10	11	12	13	14	●	5:05	28	2433472
	16	17	18	19	20	21	◐	10:50	29	2433479
	23	24	25	26	27	28	○	4:18	30	2433486
August 1950	30	31	1	2	3	4	◑	19:56	31	2433493
	6	7	8	9	10	11	12		32	2433500
	●	14	15	16	17	18	19	16:48	33	2433507
	◐	21	22	23	24	25	26	15:35	34	2433514
September 1950	○	28	29	30	31	1	2	14:51	35	2433521
	3	◑	5	6	7	8	9	13:53	36	2433528
	10	11	●	13	14	15	16	3:29	37	2433535
	17	◐	19	20	21	22	23[d]	20:54	38	2433542
	24	25	○	27	28	29	30	4:21	39	2433549
October 1950	1	2	3	◑	5	6	7	7:53	40	2433556
	8	9	10	●	12	13	14	13:34	41	2433563
	15	16	17	◐	19	20	21	4:18	42	2433570
	22	23	24	○	26	27	28	20:46	43	2433577
November 1950	29	30	31	1	2	◑	4	1:00	44	2433584
	5	6	7	8	●	10	11	23:26	45	2433591
	12	13	14	15	◐	17	18	15:06	46	2433598
	19	20	21	22	23	○	25	15:14	47	2433605
December 1950	26	27	28	29	30	1	◑	16:22	48	2433612
	3	4	5	6	7	8	●	9:29	49	2433619
	10	11	12	13	14	15	◐	5:57	50	2433626
	17	18	19	20	21	22[e]	23		51	2433633
	○	25	26	27	28	29	30	10:23	52	2433640
	31	◑	2	3	4	5	6	5:11	1	2433647

Hebrew 5710/5711‡

Julian Day	Month	Sun	Mon	Tue	Wed	Thu	Fri	Sat	Molad
2433283	Teveth 5710	12	13	14	15	16	17	18	
2433290		19	20	21	22	23	24	25	
2433297	Shevat 5710	26	27	28	29	1	2	3	Wed 20h54m7p
2433304		4	5	6	7	8	9	10	
2433311		11	12	13	14	15	16	17	
2433318		18	19	20	21	22	23	24	
2433325	Adar 5710	25	26	27	28	29	30	1	Fri 9h38m8p
2433332		2	3	4	5	6	7	8	
2433339		9	10	11	12	13	14[f]	15	
2433346		16	17	18	19	20	21	22	
2433353		23	24	25	26	27	28	29	
2433360	Nisan 5710	1	2	3	4	5	6	7	Sat 22h22m9p
2433367		8	9	10	11	12	13	14	
2433374		15[g]	16	17	18	19	20	21	
2433381		22	23	24	25	26	27	28	
2433388	Iyyar 5710	29	30	1	2	3	4	5	Mon 11h6m10p
2433395		6	7	8	9	10	11	12	
2433402		13	14	15	16	17	18	19	
2433409		20	21	22	23	24	25	26	
2433416	Sivan 5710	27	28	29	1	2	3	4	Tue 23h50m11p
2433423		5	6[h]	7	8	9	10	11	
2433430		12	13	14	15	16	17	18	
2433437		19	20	21	22	23	24	25	
2433444	Tammuz 5710	26	27	28	29	30	1	2	Thu 12h34m12p
2433451		3	4	5	6	7	8	9	
2433458		10	11	12	13	14	15	16	
2433465		17	18	19	20	21	22	23	
2433472	Av 5710	24	25	26	27	28	29	1	Sat 1h18m13p
2433479		2	3	4	5	6	7	8	
2433486		9[i]	10	11	12	13	14	15	
2433493		16	17	18	19	20	21	22	
2433500		23	24	25	26	27	28	29	
2433507	Elul 5710	30	1	2	3	4	5	6	Sun 14h2m14p
2433514		7	8	9	10	11	12	13	
2433521		14	15	16	17	18	19	20	
2433528		21	22	23	24	25	26	27	
2433535	Tishri 5711	28	29	1[a]	2[a]	3	4	5	Tue 2h46m15p
2433542		6	7	8	9	10[b]	11	12	
2433549		13	14	15[c]	16	17	18	19	
2433556		20	21	22	23	24	25	26	
2433563	Heshvan 5711	27	28	29	30	1	2	3	Wed 15h30m16p
2433570		4	5	6	7	8	9	10	
2433577		11	12	13	14	15	16	17	
2433584		18	19	20	21	22	23	24	
2433591	Kislev 5711	25	26	27	28	29	1	2	Fri 4h14m17p
2433598		3	4	5	6	7	8	9	
2433605		10	11	12	13	14	15	16	
2433612		17	18	19	20	21	22	23	
2433619		24	25[e]	26[d][e]	27[e]	28[e]	29[e]	30[e]	
2433626	Teveth 5711	1[e]	2[e]	3	4	5	6	7	Sat 16h59m0p
2433633		8	9	10	11	12	13	14	
2433640		15	16	17	18	19	20	21	
2433647		22	23	24	25	26	27	28	

Chinese Jǐ-Chǒu‡/Gēng-Yín

Julian Day	Month	Sun	Mon	Tue	Wed	Thu	Fri	Sat	Solar Term
2433283	Month 11 Jǐ-Chǒu	13	14	15	16	17	*18*	19	Xiǎo hán
2433290		20	21	22	23	24	25	26	
2433297	Month 12 Jǐ-Chǒu	27	28	29	1	2	**3**	4	Dà hán
2433304		5	6	7	8	9	10	11	
2433311		12*	13	14	15	16	17	*18*	Lì chūn
2433318		19	20	21	22	23	24	25	
2433325	Month 1 Gēng-Yín	26	27	28	29	30	1[a]	2	
2433332		**3**	4	5	6	7	8	9	Yǔ shuǐ
2433339		10	11	12	13	14	15[b]	16	
2433346		17	*18*	19	20	21	22	23	Jīng zhé
2433353	Month 2 Gēng-Yín	24	25	26	27	28	29	1	
2433360		2	3	**4**	5	6	7	8	Chūn fēn
2433367		9	10	11	12	13*	14	15	
2433374		16	17	18	*19*[c]	20	21	22	Qīng míng
2433381		23	24	25	26	27	28	29	
2433388	Month 3 Gēng-Yín	30	1	2	3	**4**	5	6	Gǔ yǔ
2433395		7	8	9	10	11	12	13	
2433402		14	15	16	17	18	19	*20*	Lì xià
2433409		21	22	23	24	25	26	27	
2433416	Month 4 Gēng-Yín	28	29	30	1	2	3	4	
2433423		**5**	6	7	8	9	10	11	Xiǎo mǎn
2433430		12	13*	14	15	16	17	18	
2433437		19	20	*21*	22	23	24	25	Máng zhòng
2433444	Month 5 Gēng-Yín	26	27	28	29	1	2	3	
2433451		4	5[d]	6	7	**8**	9	10	Xià zhì
2433458		11	12	13	14	15	16	17	
2433465		18	19	20	21	22	23	*24*	Xiǎo shǔ
2433472	Month 6 Gēng-Yín	25	26	27	28	29	30	1	
2433479		2	3	4	5	6	7	8	
2433486		**9**	10	11	12	13	14*	15	Dà shǔ
2433493		16	17	18	19	20	21	22	
2433500		23	24	*25*	26	27	28	29	Lì qiū
2433507	Month 7 Gēng-Yín	30	1	2	3	4	5	6	
2433514		7[e]	8	9	10	**11**	12	13	Chǔ shǔ
2433521		14	15[f]	16	17	18	19	20	
2433528		21	22	23	24	25	*26*	27	Bái lù
2433535	Month 8 Gēng-Yín	28	29	1	2	3	4	5	
2433542		6	7	8	9	10	11	**12**	Qiū fēn
2433549		13	14	15[g]*	16	17	18	19	
2433556		20	21	22	23	24	25	26	
2433563	Month 9 Gēng-Yín	27	*28*	29	1	2	3	4	Hán lù
2433570		5	6	7	8	9[h]	10	11	
2433577		12	13	**14**	15	16	17	18	Shuāng jiàng
2433584		19	20	21	22	23	24	25	
2433591	Month 10 Gēng-Yín	26	27	28	29	30	1	2	Lì dōng
2433598		3	4	5	6	7	8	9	
2433605		10	11	12	13	**14**	15	16*	Xiǎo xuě
2433612		17	18	19	20	21	22	23	
2433619	Month 11 Gēng-Yín	24	25	26	27	28	*29*	1	Dà xuě
2433626		2	3	4	5	6	7	8	
2433633		9	10	11	12	13	**14**[i]	15	Dōng zhì
2433640		16	17	18	19	20	21	22	
2433647		23	24	25	26	27	28	*29*	Xiǎo hán

Coptic 1666/1667‡ — Ethiopic 1942/1943‡

Julian Day	Coptic Month	Sun	Mon	Tue	Wed	Thu	Fri	Sat	Ethiopic Month
2433283	Koiak 1666	23	24	25	26	27	28	29[c]	Tākhśāś 1942
2433290	Tōbe 1666	30	1	2	3	4	5	6[d]	Ṭer 1942
2433297		7	8	9	10	11[e]	12	13	
2433304		14	15	16	17	18	19	20	
2433311		21	22	23	24	25	26	27	
2433318	Meshir 1666	28	29	30	1	2	3	4	Yakātit 1942
2433325		5	6	7	8	9	10	11	
2433332		12	13	14	15	16	17	18	
2433339		19	20	21	22	23	24	25	
2433346	Paremotep 1666	26	27	28	29	30	1	2	Magābit 1942
2433353		3	4	5	6	7	8	9	
2433360		10	11	12	13	14	15	16	
2433367		17	18	19	20	21	22	23	
2433374		24	25	26	27	28	29	30	
2433381	Parmoute 1666	1[f]	2	3	4	5	6	7	Miyāzyā 1942
2433388		8	9	10	11	12	13	14	
2433395		15	16	17	18	19	20	21	
2433402		22	23	24	25	26	27	28	
2433409	Pashons 1666	29[g]	30	1	2	3	4	5	Genbot 1942
2433416		6	7	8	9	10	11	12	
2433423		13	14	15	16	17	18	19	
2433430		20	21	22	23	24	25	26	
2433437	Paōne 1666	27	28	29	30	1	2	3	Sanē 1942
2433444		4	5	6	7	8	9	10	
2433451		11	12	13	14	15	16	17	
2433458		18	19	20	21	22	23	24	
2433465	Epēp 1666	25	26	27	28	29	30	1	Hamlē 1942
2433472		2	3	4	5	6	7	8	
2433479		9	10	11	12	13	14	15	
2433486		16	17	18	19	20	21	22	
2433493		23	24	25	26	27	28	29	
2433500	Mesorē 1666	30	1	2	3	4	5	6	Naḥasē 1942
2433507		7	8	9	10	11	12	13[h]	
2433514		14	15	16	17	18	19	20	
2433521		21	22	23	24	25	26	27	
2433528	Epag. 1666	28	29	30	1	2	3	4	Pāg. 1942
2433535	Thoout 1667	5	1[a]	2	3	4	5	6	Maskaram 1943
2433542		7	8	9	10	11	12	13	
2433549		14	15	16	17[b]	18	19	20	
2433556		21	22	23	24	25	26	27	
2433563	Paope 1667	28	29	30	1	2	3	4	Ṭeqemt 1943
2433570		5	6	7	8	9	10	11	
2433577		12	13	14	15	16	17	18	
2433584		19	20	21	22	23	24	25	
2433591	Athōr 1667	26	27	28	29	30	1	2	Hedār 1943
2433598		3	4	5	6	7	8	9	
2433605		10	11	12	13	14	15	16	
2433612		17	18	19	20	21	22	23	
2433619		24	25	26	27	28	29	30	
2433626	Koiak 1667	1	2	3	4	5	6	7	Tākhśāś 1943
2433633		8	9	10	11	12	13	14	
2433640		15	16	17	18	19	20	21	
2433647		22	23	24	25	26	27	28	

[a]New Year
[b]Spring (4:35)
[c]Summer (23:36)
[d]Autumn (14:44)
[e]Winter (10:13)
● New moon
◐ First quarter moon
○ Full moon
◑ Last quarter moon

‡Leap year
[a]New Year
[b]Yom Kippur
[c]Sukkot
[d]Winter starts
[e]Ḥanukkah
[f]Purim
[g]Passover
[h]Shavuot
[i]Fast of Av

‡Leap year
[a]New Year (4648, Tiger)
[b]Lantern Festival
[c]Qīngmíng
[d]Dragon Festival
[e]Qīqiǎo
[f]Hungry Ghosts
[g]Mid-Autumn Festival
[h]Double-Ninth Festival
[i]Dōngzhì
*Start of 60-name cycle

‡Leap year
[a]New Year
[b]Building of the Cross
[c]Christmas
[d]Jesus's Circumcision
[e]Epiphany
[f]Easter
[g]Mary's Announcement
[h]Jesus's Transfiguration

Month	Sun	Mon	Tue	Wed	Thu	Fri	Sat
PERSIAN (ASTRONOMICAL) 1328/1329‡							
DEY 1328	11	12	13	14	15	16	17
	18	19	20	21	22	23	24
	25	26	27	28	29	30	1
BAHMAN 1328	2	3	4	5	6	7	8
	9	10	11	12	13	14	15
	16	17	18	19	20	21	22
	23	24	25	26	27	28	29
ESFAND 1328	30	1	2	3	4	5	6
	7	8	9	10	11	12	13
	14	15	16	17	18	19	20
	21	22	23	24	25	26	27
FARVARDĪN 1329	28	29	1[a]	2	3	4	5
	6	7	8	9	10	11	12
	13[b]	14	15	16	17	18	19
	20	21	22	23	24	25	26
ORDĪBEHEŠT 1329	27	28	29	30	31	1	2
	3	4	5	6	7	8	9
	10	11	12	13	14	15	16
	17	18	19	20	21	22	23
	24	25	26	27	28	29	30
XORDĀD 1329	31	1	2	3	4	5	6
	7	8	9	10	11	12	13
	14	15	16	17	18	19	20
	21	22	23	24	25	26	27
TĪR 1329	28	29	30	31	1	2	3
	4	5	6	7	8	9	10
	11	12	13	14	15	16	17
	18	19	20	21	22	23	24
	25	26	27	28	29	30	31
MORDĀD 1329	1	2	3	4	5	6	7
	8	9	10	11	12	13	14
	15	16	17	18	19	20	21
	22	23	24	25	26	27	28
SHAHRĪVAR 1329	29	30	31	1	2	3	4
	5	6	7	8	9	10	11
	12	13	14	15	16	17	18
	19	20	21	22	23	24	25
MEHR 1329	26	27	28	29	30	31	1
	2	3	4	5	6	7	8
	9	10	11	12	13	14	15
	16	17	18	19	20	21	22
	23	24	25	26	27	28	29
ĀBĀN 1329	30	1	2	3	4	5	6
	7	8	9	10	11	12	13
	14	15	16	17	18	19	20
	21	22	23	24	25	26	27
ĀZAR 1329	28	29	30	1	2	3	4
	5	6	7	8	9	10	11
	12	13	14	15	16	17	18
	19	20	21	22	23	24	25
DEY 1329	26	27	28	29	30	1	2
	3	4	5	6	7	8	9
	10	11	12	13	14	15	16

‡Leap year
[a]New Year
[b]Sizdeh Bedar

Month	Sun	Mon	Tue	Wed	Thu	Fri	Sat
HINDU LUNAR 2006/2007‡							
PAUSHA 2006	12	13	14	15	16	17	18
	19	**20**	22	23	24	25	26
	27	28	29	30	1	2	3
MĀGHA 2006	4	5	6	7	8	9	10
	11	12	13	14	15	16	17
	18	19	20	21	22	23	24
	25	27	28	29[h]	30	1	2
PHĀLGUNA 2006	3	3	4	5	6	7	8
	9	10	11	12	13	14	15[i]
	16	17	18	**19**	21	22	23
	24	25	26	27	28	29	30
CHAITRA 2007	1[a]	2	3	4	5	6	6
	7	8[b]	9	10	11	12	**13**
	15	16	17	18	19	20	21
	22	23	24	25	26	27	28
VAIŚĀKHA 2007	29	30	1	2	3	4	5
	6	7	8	9	10	11	12
	13	14	15	16	**17**	19	20
	21	22	23	24	25	26	27
JYAISHṬHA 2007	28	29	30	1	1	2	3
	4	5	6	7	8	9	**10**
	12	13	14	15	16	17	18
	19	20	21	22	23	24	25
LEAP ĀSHĀḌHA 2007	26	27	28	29	30	1	2
	3	4	5	6	7	8	9
	10	11	12	**13**	15	16	17
	18	19	20	21	22	23	24
	25	26	27	27	28	29	30
ĀSHĀḌHA 2007	1	2	3	4	**5**	7	8
	9	10	11	12	13	14	15
	16	17	18	19	20	21	22
	23	24	25	26	27	28	29
ŚRĀVAṆA 2007	30	1	2	3	4	5	6
	7	**8**	10	11	12	13	14
	15	16	17	18	19	20	21
	22	23[c]	24	24	25	26	27
BHĀDRAPADA 2007	28	29	30	**1**	3	4[d]	5
	6	7	8	9	10	11	12
	13	14	15	16	17	18	19
	20	21	22	23	24	25	26
ĀŚVINA 2007	27	28	29	30	1	2	3
	4	5	7	8[e]	9[e]	10[e]	11
	12	13	14	15	16	17	18
	18	19	20	21	22	23	24
KĀRTTIKA 2007	25	26	27	28	**29**	1[f]	2
	3	4	5	6	7	8	9
	10	11	12	13	14	15	16
	17	18	19	20	21	22	23
	24	25	26	27	28	29	30
MĀRGAŚĪRA 2007	1	2	3	**4**	6	7	8
	9	10	11[g]	12	12	13	14
	15	16	17	18	19	20	21
	22	23	24	25	26	**27**	29

‡Leap year
[a]New Year (Vikṛita)
[b]Birthday of Rāma
[c]Birthday of Krishna
[d]Ganēśa Chaturthī
[e]Dashara
[f]Diwali
[g]Birthday of Vishnu
[h]Night of Śiva
[i]Holi

Month	Sun	Mon	Tue	Wed	Thu	Fri	Sat
HINDU SOLAR 1871/1872							
PAUSHA 1871	18	19	20	21	22	23	24
	25	26	27	28	29	1[b]	2
MĀGHA 1871	3	4	5	6	7	8	9
	10	11	12	13	14	15	16
	17	18	19	20	21	22	23
	24	25	26	27	28	29	30
PHĀLGUNA 1871	1	2	3	4	5	6	7
	8	9	10	11	12	13	14
	15	16	17	18	19	20	21
	22	23	24	25	26	27	28
CHAITRA 1871	29	30	1	2	3	4	5
	6	7	8	9	10	11	12
	13	14	15	16	17	18	19
	20	21	22	23	24	25	26
VAIŚĀKHA 1872	27	28	29	30	1[a]	2	3
	4	5	6	7	8	9	10
	11	12	13	14	15	16	17
	18	19	20	21	22	23	24
	25	26	27	28	29	30	31
JYAISHṬHA 1872	1	2	3	4	5	6	7
	8	9	10	11	12	13	14
	15	16	17	18	19	20	21
	22	23	24	25	26	27	28
ĀSHĀḌHA 1872	29	30	31	1	2	3	4
	5	6	7	8	9	10	11
	12	13	14	15	16	17	18
	19	20	21	22	23	24	25
	26	27	28	29	30	31	32
ŚRĀVAṆA 1872	1	2	3	4	5	6	7
	8	9	10	11	12	13	14
	15	16	17	18	19	20	21
	22	23	24	25	26	27	28
BHĀDRAPADA 1872	29	30	31	32	1	2	3
	4	5	6	7	8	9	10
	11	12	13	14	15	16	17
	18	19	20	21	22	23	24
	25	26	27	28	29	30	31
ĀŚVINA 1872	1	2	3	4	5	6	7
	8	9	10	11	12	13	14
	15	16	17	18	19	20	21
	22	23	24	25	26	27	28
KĀRTTIKA 1872	29	30	1	2	3	4	5
	6	7	8	9	10	11	12
	13	14	15	16	17	18	19
	20	21	22	23	24	25	26
MĀRGAŚĪRA 1872	27	28	29	30	1	2	3
	4	5	6	7	8	9	10
	11	12	13	14	15	16	17
	18	19	20	21	22	23	24
PAUSHA 1872	25	26	27	28	29	1	2
	3	4	5	6	7	8	9
	10	11	12	13	14	15	16
	17	18	19	20	21	22	23

[a]New Year (Śobhana)
[b]Pongal

Month	Sun	Mon	Tue	Wed	Thu	Fri	Sat
ISLAMIC (ASTRONOMICAL) 1369/1370‡							
RABĪ' I 1369	12[c]	13	14	15	16	17	18
	19	20	21	22	23	24	25
RABĪ' II 1369	26	27	28	29	30	1	2
	3	4	5	6	7	8	9
	10	11	12	13	14	15	16
	17	18	19	20	21	22	23
JUMĀDĀ I 1369	24	25	26	27	28	29	1
	2	3	4	5	6	7	8
	9	10	11	12	13	14	15
	16	17	18	19	20	21	22
	23	24	25	26	27	28	29
JUMĀDĀ II 1369	30	1	2	3	4	5	6
	7	8	9	10	11	12	13
	14	15	16	17	18	19	20
	21	22	23	24	25	26	27
RAJAB 1369	28	29	30	1	2	3	4
	5	6	7	8	9	10	11
	12	13	14	15	16	17	18
	19	20	21	22	23	24	25
SHA'BĀN 1369	26	27[d]	28	29	1	2	3
	4	5	6	7	8	9	10
	11	12	13	14	15	16	17
	18	19	20	21	22	23	24
RAMAḌĀN 1369	25	26	27	28	29	30	1[e]
	2	3	4	5	6	7	8
	9	10	11	12	13	14	15
	16	17	18	19	20	21	22
	23	24	25	26	27	28	29
SHAWWĀL 1369	1[f]	2	3	4	5	6	7
	8	9	10	11	12	13	14
	15	16	17	18	19	20	21
	22	23	24	25	26	27	28
DHU AL-QA'DA 1369	29	30	1	2	3	4	5
	6	7	8	9	10	11	12
	13	14	15	16	17	18	19
	20	21	22	23	24	25	26
DHU AL-ḤIJJA 1369	27	28	29	30	1	2	3
	4	5	6	7	8	9	10[g]
	11	12	13	14	15	16	17
	18	19	20	21	22	23	24
MUḤARRAM 1370	25	26	27	28	29	1[a]	2
	3	4	5	6	7	8	9
	10[b]	11	12	13	14	15	16
	17	18	19	20	21	22	23
	24	25	26	27	28	29	30
ṢAFAR 1370	1	2	3	4	5	6	7
	8	9	10	11	12	13	14
	15	16	17	18	19	20	21
	22	23	24	25	26	27	28
RABĪ' I 1370	29	1	2	3	4	5	6
	7	8	9	10	11	12[c]	13
	14	15	16	17	18	19	20
	21	22	23	24	25	26	27

‡Leap year
[a]New Year
[b]'Ashūrā'
[c]Prophet's Birthday
[d]Ascent of the Prophet
[e]Start of Ramaḍān
[f]'Id al-Fiṭr
[g]'Id al-'Aḍḥā

Julian (Sun)	Sun	Mon	Tue	Wed	Thu	Fri	Sat	Month
	GREGORIAN 1950							
Dec 19	1	2	3	4	5	6	7[a]	JANUARY 1950
	8	9	10	11	12	13	14[b]	
Jan 2	15	16	17	18	19	20	21	
	22	23	24	25	26	27	28	
Jan 16	29	30	31	1	2	3	4	FEBRUARY 1950
	5	6	7	8	9	10	11	
Jan 30	12	13	14	15	16	17	18	
	19	20	21	22[c]	23	24	25	
Feb 13	26[d]	27	28	1	2	3	4	MARCH 1950
	5	6	7	8	9	10	11	
Feb 27	12	13	14	15	16	17	18	
	19	20	21	22	23	24	25	
Mar 13	26	27	28	29	30	31	1	APRIL 1950
	2	3	4	5	6	7	8	
Mar 27	9[e]	10	11	12	13	14	15	
	16	17	18	19	20	21	22	
Apr 10	23	24	25	26	27	28	29	
	30	1	2	3	4	5	6	MAY 1950
Apr 24	7	8	9	10	11	12	13	
	14	15	16	17	18	19	20	
May 8	21	22	23	24	25	26	27	
	28	29	30	31	1	2	3	JUNE 1950
May 22	4	5	6	7	8	9	10	
	11	12	13	14	15	16	17	
Jun 5	18	19	20	21	22	23	24	
	25	26	27	28	29	30	1	JULY 1950
Jun 19	2	3	4	5	6	7	8	
	9	10	11	12	13	14	15	
Jul 3	16	17	18	19	20	21	22	
	23	24	25	26	27	28	29	
Jul 17	30	31	1	2	3	4	5	AUGUST 1950
	6	7	8	9	10	11	12	
Jul 31	13	14	15	16	17	18	19	
	20	21	22	23	24	25	26	
Aug 14	27	28	29	30	31	1	2	SEPTEMBER 1950
	3	4	5	6	7	8	9	
Aug 28	10	11	12	13	14	15	16	
	17	18	19	20	21	22	23	
Sep 11	24	25	26	27	28	29	30	
	1	2	3	4	5	6	7	OCTOBER 1950
Sep 25	8	9	10	11	12	13	14	
	15	16	17	18	19	20	21	
Oct 9	22	23	24	25	26	27	28	
	29	30	31	1	2	3	4	NOVEMBER 1950
Oct 23	5	6	7	8	9	10	11	
	12	13	14	15	16	17	18	
Nov 6	19	20	21	22	23	24	25	
	26	27	28	29	30	1	2	DECEMBER 1950
Nov 20	3[g]	4	5	6	7	8	9	
	10	11	12	13	14	15	16	
Dec 4	17	18	19	20	21	22	23	
	24	25[h]	26	27	28	29	30	
Dec 18	31	1	2	3	4	5	6	

[a]Orthodox Christmas
[b]Julian New Year
[c]Ash Wednesday
[d]Feast of Orthodoxy
[e]Easter (also Orthodox)
[g]Advent
[h]Christmas

1951

Month	Sun	Mon	Tue	Wed	Thu	Fri	Sat	Lunar Phases	ISO WEEK (Mon)	JULIAN DAY (Sun noon)	HEBREW 5711‡/5712	Sun	Mon	Tue	Wed	Thu	Fri	Sat	Molad	CHINESE Gēng-Yín/Xīn-Mǎo	Sun	Mon	Tue	Wed	Thu	Fri	Sat	Solar Term	COPTIC 1667‡/1668	Sun	Mon	Tue	Wed	Thu	Fri	Sat	ETHIOPIC 1943‡/1944
JANUARY 1951	31	◑[a]	2	3	4	5	6	5:11	1	2433647	TEVETH 5711	22	23	24	25	26	27	28		MONTH 11 Gēng-Yín	23	24	25	26	27	28	*29*	Xiǎo hán	KOIAK 1667	22	23	24	25	26	27	28	TĀKHŚĀŚ 1943
	●	8	9	10	11	12	13	20:10	2	2433654		29	1	2	3	4	5	6	Mon $5^h43^m1^p$		30	1	2	3	4	5	6			29[c]	30	1	2	3	4	5	
	14	◐	16	17	18	19	20	0:23	3	2433661	SHEVAT 5711	7	8	9	10	11	12	13		MONTH 12 Gēng-Yín	7	8	9	10	11	12	13		TÔBE 1667	6[d]	7	8	9	10	11[e]	12	ṬER 1943
	21	22	○	24	25	26	27	4:47	4	2433668		14	15	16	17	18	19	20			***14***	15	16	17*	18	19	20	Dà hán		13	14	15	16	17	18	19	
	28	29	◑	31	1	2	3	15:14	5	2433675		21	22	23	24	25	26	27			21	22	23	24	25	26	27			20	21	22	23	24	25	26	
FEBRUARY 1951	4	5	●	7	8	9	10	7:54	6	2433682		28	29	30	1	2	3	4	Tue $18^h27^m2^p$		*28*	29	1[a]	2	3	4	5	Lì chūn		27	28	29	30	1	2	3	
	11	12	◐	14	15	16	17	20:55	7	2433689	ADAR I 5711	5	6	7	8	9	10	11		MONTH 1 Xīn-Mǎo	6	7	8	9	10	11	12		MESHIR 1667	4	5	6	7	8	9	10	YAKĀTIT 1943
	18	19	20	○	22	23	24	21:12	8	2433696		12	13	14	15	16	17	18			13	***14***	15[b]	16	17	18	19	Yǔ shuǐ		11	12	13	14	15	16	17	
	25	26	27	◑	1	2	3	22:59	9	2433703		19	20	21	22	23	24	25			20	21	22	23	24	25	26			18	19	20	21	22	23	24	
MARCH 1951	4	5	6	●	8	9	10	20:51	10	2433710		26	27	28	29	30	1	2	Thu $7^h11^m3^p$		27	28	*29*	30	1	2	3	Jīng zhé		25	26	27	28	29	30	1	
	11	12	13	14	◐	16	17	17:40	11	2433717	ADAR II 5711	3	4	5	6	7	8	9		MONTH 2 Xīn-Mǎo	4	5	6	7	8	9	10		PAREMOTEP 1667	2	3	4	5	6	7	8	MAGĀBIT 1943
	18	19	20	21[b]	22	○	24	10:50	12	2433724		10	11	12	13	14[f]	15	16			11	12	13	***14***	15	16	17	Chūn fēn		9	10	11	12	13	14	15	
	25	26	27	28	29	◑	31	5:35	13	2433731		17	18	19	20	21	22	23			18*	19	20	21	22	23	24			16	17	18	19	20	21	22	
APRIL 1951	1	2	3	4	5	●	7	10:52	14	2433738		24	25	26	27	28	29	1	Fri $19^h55^m4^p$		25	26	27	28	*29*[c]	1	2	Qīng míng		23	24	25	26	27	28	29	
	8	9	10	11	12	13	◐	12:55	15	2433745	NISAN 5711	2	3	4	5	6	7	8		MONTH 3 Xīn-Mǎo	3	4	5	6	7	8	9		PARMOUTE 1667	30	1	2	3	4	5	6	MIYĀZYĀ 1943
	15	16	17	18	19	20	○	21:30	16	2433752		9	10	11	12	13	14	15[g]			10	11	12	13	14	15	***16***	Gǔ yǔ		7	8	9	10	11	12	13	
	22	23	24	25	26	27	◑	12:18	17	2433759		16	17	18	19	20	21	22			17	18	19	20	21	22	23			14	15	16	17	18	19	20	
	29	30	1	2	3	4	5		18	2433766		23	24	25	26	27	28	29			24	25	26	27	28	29	30			21[f]	22	23	24	25	26	27	
MAY 1951	●	7	8	9	10	11	12	1:36	19	2433773		30	1	2	3	4	5	6	Sun $8^h39^m5^p$		*1*	2	3	4	5	6	7	Lì xià		28	29[g]	30	1	2	3	4	
	13	◐	15	16	17	18	19	5:32	20	2433780	IYAR 5711	7	8	9	10	11	12	13		MONTH 4 Xīn-Mǎo	8	9	10	11	12	13	14		PASHONS 1667	5	6	7	8	9	10	11	GENBOT 1943
	20	○	22	23	24	25	26	5:45	21	2433787		14	15	16	17	18	19	20			15	16	***17***	18	19*	20	21	Xiǎo mǎn		12	13	14	15	16	17	18	
	◑	28	29	30	31	1	2	20:17	22	2433794		21	22	23	24	25	26	27			22	23	24	25	26	27	28			19	20	21	22	23	24	25	
JUNE 1951	3	●	5	6	7	8	9	16:40	23	2433801		28	29	1	2	3	4	5	Mon $21^h23^m6^p$		29	30	1	*2*	3	4	5[d]	Máng zhòng		26	27	28	29	30	1	2	
	10	11	◐	13	14	15	16	18:52	24	2433808	SIVAN 5711	6[h]	7	8	9	10	11	12		MONTH 5 Xīn-Mǎo	6	7	8	9	10	11	12		PAÔNE 1667	3	4	5	6	7	8	9	SANĒ 1943
	17	18	○	20	21	22[c]	23	12:36	25	2433815		13	14	15	16	17	18	19			13	14	15	16	17	***18***	19	Xià zhì		10	11	12	13	14	15	16	
	24	25	◑	27	28	29	30	6:21	26	2433822		20	21	22	23	24	25	26			20	21	22	23	24	25	26			17	18	19	20	21	22	23	
JULY 1951	1	2	3	●	5	6	7	7:48	27	2433829		27	28	29	30	1	2	3	Wed $10^h7^m7^p$		27	28	29	1	2	3	4			24	25	26	27	28	29	30	
	8	9	10	11	◐	13	14	4:57	28	2433836	TAMMUZ 5711	4	5	6	7	8	9	10		MONTH 6 Xīn-Mǎo	5	6	7	8	9	10	11	Xiǎo shǔ	EPĒP 1667	1	2	3	4	5	6	7	ḤAMLĒ 1943
	15	16	17	○	19	20	21	19:17	29	2433843		11	12	13	14	15	16	17			12	13	14	15	16	17	18			8	9	10	11	12	13	14	
	22	23	24	◑	26	27	28	18:59	30	2433850		18	19	20	21	22	23	24			19	20*	***21***	22	23	24	25	Dà shǔ		15	16	17	18	19	20	21	
	29	30	31	1	●	3	4	22:39	31	2433857		25	26	27	28	29	1	2	Thu $22^h51^m8^p$		26	27	28	29	30	1	2			22	23	24	25	26	27	28	
AUGUST 1951	5	6	7	8	9	◐	11	12:22	32	2433864	AV 5711	3	4	5	6	7	8	9		MONTH 7 Xīn-Mǎo	3	4	5	*6*	7[e]	8	9	Lì qiū		29	30	1	2	3	4	5	
	12	13	14	15	16	○	18	2:59	33	2433871		10[i]	11	12	13	14	15	16			10	11	12	13	14	15[f]	16		MESORĒ 1667	6	7	8	9	10	11	12	NAḤASĒ 1943
	19	20	21	22	23	◑	25	10:20	34	2433878		17	18	19	20	21	22	23			17	18	19	20	21	***22***	23	Chǔ shǔ		13[h]	14	15	16	17	18	19	
	26	27	28	29	30	31	●	12:50	35	2433885		24	25	26	27	28	29	30			24	25	26	27	28	29	1			20	21	22	23	24	25	26	
SEPTEMBER 1951	2	3	4	5	6	7	◐	18:16	36	2433892	ELUL 5711	1	2	3	4	5	6	7	Sat $11^h35^m9^p$	MONTH 8 Xīn-Mǎo	2	3	4	5	6	7	*8*	Bái lù	EPAG. 1667	27	28	29	30	1	2	3	PĀG. 1943
	9	10	11	12	13	14	○	12:38	37	2433899		8	9	10	11	12	13	14			9	10	11	12	13	14	15[g]		THOOUT 1668	4	5	6	1[a]	2	3	4	MASKARAM 1944
	16	17	18	19	20	21	22		38	2433906		15	16	17	18	19	20	21			16	17	18	19	20	21*	22	Qiū fēn		5	6	7	8	9	10	11	
	◑[d]	24	25	26	27	28	29	4:13	39	2433913		22	23	24	25	26	27	28			23	***24***	25	26	27	28	29			12	13	14	15	16	17[b]	18	
OCTOBER 1951	30	●	2	3	4	5	6	1:57	40	2433920		29	1[a]	2[a]	3	4	5	6	Mon $0^h19^m10^p$		30	1	2	3	4	5	6			19	20	21	22	23	24	25	
	7	◐	9	10	11	12	13	0:00	41	2433927	TISHRI 5712	7	8	9	10[b]	11	12	13		MONTH 9 Xīn-Mǎo	7	8	***9***[h]	10	11	12	13	Hán lù		26	27	28	29	30	1	2	
	14	○	16	17	18	19	20	0:51	42	2433934		14	15[c]	16	17	18	19	20			14	15	16	17	18	19	20		PAOPE 1668	3	4	5	6	7	8	9	ṬEQEMT 1944
	21	◑	23	24	25	26	27	23:55	43	2433941		21	22	23	24	25	26	27			21	22	23	***24***	25	26	27	Shuāng jiàng		10	11	12	13	14	15	16	
	28	29	●	31	1	2	3	13:55	44	2433948		28	29	30	1	2	3	4	Tue $13^h3^m11^p$		28	29	1	2	3	4	5			17	18	19	20	21	22	23	
NOVEMBER 1951	4	5	◐	7	8	9	10	6:59	45	2433955	ḤESHVAN 5712	5	6	7	8	9	10	11		MONTH 10 Xīn-Mǎo	6	7	8	9	*10*	11	12	Lì dōng		24	25	26	27	28	29	30	
	11	12	○	14	15	16	17	15:52	46	2433962		12	13	14	15	16	17	18			13	14	15	16	17	18	19		ATHÔR 1668	1	2	3	4	5	6	7	ḪEDĀR 1944
	18	19	20	◑	22	23	24	20:01	47	2433969		19	20	21	22	23	24	25			20	21	22*	23	24	***25***	26	Xiǎo xuě		8	9	10	11	12	13	14	
	25	26	27	28	●	30	1	1:00	48	2433976		26	27	28	29	30	1	2	Thu $1^h47^m12^p$		27	28	29	30	1	2	3			15	16	17	18	19	20	21	
DECEMBER 1951	2	3	4	◐	6	7	8	16:20	49	2433983	KISLEV 5712	3	4	5	6	7[d]	8	9		MONTH 11 Xīn-Mǎo	4	5	6	7	8	9	*10*	Dà xuě		22	23	24	25	26	27	28	
	9	10	11	12	○	14	15	9:30	50	2433990		10	11	12	13	14	15	16			11	12	13	14	15	16	17			29	30	1	2	3	4	5	
	16	17	18	19	20	◑	22[e]	14:37	51	2433997		17	18	19	20	21	22	23			18	19	20	21	22	23	***24***[i]	Dōng zhì	KOIAK 1668	6	7	8	9	10	11	12	TĀKHŚĀŚ 1944
	23	24	25	26	27	●	29	11:44	52	2434004		24	25[e]	26[e]	27[e]	28[e]	29[e]	30[e]		MONTH 12 Xīn-Mǎo	25	26	27	28	29	1	2			13	14	15	16	17	18	19	
	30	31	1	2	3	◐	5	4:42	1	2434011		1[e]	2[e]	3	4	5	6	7	Fri $14^h31^m13^p$		3	4	5	6	7	8	9			20	21	22	23	24	25	26	

[a]New Year
[b]Spring (10:26)
[c]Summer (5:25)
[d]Autumn (20:37)
[e]Winter (16:00)
● New moon
◐ First quarter moon
○ Full moon
◑ Last quarter moon

‡Leap year
[a]New Year
[b]Yom Kippur
[c]Sukkot
[d]Winter starts
[e]Ḥanukkah
[f]Purim
[g]Passover
[h]Shavuot
[i]Fast of Av

[a]New Year (4649, Hare)
[b]Lantern Festival
[c]Qīngmíng
[d]Dragon Festival
[e]Qīqiǎo
[f]Hungry Ghosts
[g]Mid-Autumn Festival
[h]Double-Ninth Festival
[i]Dōngzhì
*Start of 60-name cycle

‡Leap year
[a]New Year
[b]Building of the Cross
[c]Christmas
[d]Jesus's Circumcision
[e]Epiphany
[f]Easter
[g]Mary's Announcement
[h]Jesus's Transfiguration

PERSIAN (ASTRONOMICAL) 1329‡/1330

Month	Sun	Mon	Tue	Wed	Thu	Fri	Sat
DEY 1329	10	11	12	13	14	15	16
	17	18	19	20	21	22	23
	24	25	26	27	28	29	30
BAHMAN 1329	1	2	3	4	5	6	7
	8	9	10	11	12	13	14
	15	16	17	18	19	20	21
	22	23	24	25	26	27	28
	29	30	1	2	3	4	5
ESFAND 1329	6	7	8	9	10	11	12
	13	14	15	16	17	18	19
	20	21	22	23	24	25	26
	27	28	29	30	1[a]	2	3
FARVARDĪN 1330	4	5	6	7	8	9	10
	11	12	13[b]	14	15	16	17
	18	19	20	21	22	23	24
	25	26	27	28	29	30	31
ORDĪBEHEŠT 1330	1	2	3	4	5	6	7
	8	9	10	11	12	13	14
	15	16	17	18	19	20	21
	22	23	24	25	26	27	28
	29	30	31	1	2	3	4
XORDĀD 1330	5	6	7	8	9	10	11
	12	13	14	15	16	17	18
	19	20	21	22	23	24	25
	26	27	28	29	30	31	1
TĪR 1330	2	3	4	5	6	7	8
	9	10	11	12	13	14	15
	16	17	18	19	20	21	22
	23	24	25	26	27	28	29
	30	31	1	2	3	4	5
MORDĀD 1330	6	7	8	9	10	11	12
	13	14	15	16	17	18	19
	20	21	22	23	24	25	26
	27	28	29	30	31	1	2
SHAHRĪVAR 1330	3	4	5	6	7	8	9
	10	11	12	13	14	15	16
	17	18	19	20	21	22	23
	24	25	26	27	28	29	30
	31	1	2	3	4	5	6
MEHR 1330	7	8	9	10	11	12	13
	14	15	16	17	18	19	20
	21	22	23	24	25	26	27
	28	29	30	1	2	3	4
ĀBĀN 1330	5	6	7	8	9	10	11
	12	13	14	15	16	17	18
	19	20	21	22	23	24	25
	26	27	28	29	30	1	2
ĀZAR 1330	3	4	5	6	7	8	9
	10	11	12	13	14	15	16
	17	18	19	20	21	22	23
	24	25	26	27	28	29	30
DEY 1330	1	2	3	4	5	6	7
	8	9	10	11	12	13	14

‡Leap year
[a]New Year
[b]Sizdeh Bedar

HINDU LUNAR 2007‡/2008

Month	Sun	Mon	Tue	Wed	Thu	Fri	Sat
MĀRGAŚĪRA 2007	22	23	24	25	26	**27**	29
PAUSHA 2007	30	1	2	3	4	5	6
	7	8	9	10	11	12	13
	14	14	15	16	17	18	19
	20	**21**	23	24	25	26	27
MĀGHA 2007	28	29	30	1	2	3	4
	5	6	7	8	9	10	11
	12	13	14	15	16	17	18
	19	20	21	22	23	24	25
PHĀLGUNA 2007	**26**	28	29[h]	30	1	2	3
	4	5	6	6	7	8	9
	10	11	12	13	14	15[i]	16
	17	18	19	**20**	22	23	24
CHAITRA 2008	25	26	27	28	29	30	1[a]
	2	3	4	5	6	7	8
	9[b]	10	10	11	**12**	14	15
	16	17	18	19	20	21	22
	23	24	**25**	27	28	29	30
VAIŚĀKHA 2008	30	1	2	3	4	5	6
	7	8	9	10	11	12	13
	14	15	16	**17**	19	20	21
	22	23	24	25	26	27	28
JYAISHṬHA 2008	29	30	1	2	3	4	5
	5	6	7	8	**9**	11	12
	13	14	15	16	17	18	19
	20	**21**	23	24	25	26	27
ĀSHĀḌHA 2008	27	28	29	30	1	2	3
	4	5	6	7	8	9	10
	11	12	**13**	15	16	17	18
	19	20	21	22	23	24	25
ŚRĀVAṆA 2008	26	27	28	29	30	1	2
	3	4	5	6	7	8	9
	10	11	12	13	14	15	**16**
	18	19	20	21	22	23[c]	24
	24	25	26	27	28	29	30
BHĀDRAPADA 2008	1	2	3	4[d]	5	6	7
	8	**9**	11	12	13	14	15
	16	17	18	19	20	21	22
	23	24	25	26	27	28	28
ĀŚVINA 2008	29	30	**1**	3	4	5	6
	7	8[e]	9[e]	10[e]	11	12	**13**
	15	16	17	18	18	19	20
	21	22	23	24	25	26	27
KĀRTTIKA 2008	28	29	30	1[f]	2	3	4
	5	**6**	8	9	10	11	12
	13	14	15	16	17	18	19
	20	21	21	22	23	24	25
MĀRGAŚĪRA 2008	26	27	28	29	**30**	2	3
	4	5	6	7	8	9	10
	11[g]	12	13	14	15	16	17
	18	19	20	21	22	23	24
PAUSHA 2008	25	26	27	28	29	30	1
	2	3	**4**	6	7	8	9

‡Leap year
[a]New Year (Khara)
[b]Birthday of Rāma
[c]Birthday of Krishna
[d]Ganēśa Chaturthī
[e]Dashara
[f]Diwali
[g]Birthday of Vishnu
[h]Night of Śiva
[i]Holi

HINDU SOLAR 1872/1873‡

Month	Sun	Mon	Tue	Wed	Thu	Fri	Sat
PAUSHA 1872	17	18	19	20	21	22	23
	24	25	26	27	28	29	30
MĀGHA 1872	1[b]	2	3	4	5	6	7
	8	9	10	11	12	13	14
	15	16	17	18	19	20	21
	22	23	24	25	26	27	28
PHĀLGUNA 1872	29	1	2	3	4	5	6
	7	8	9	10	11	12	13
	14	15	16	17	18	19	20
	21	22	23	24	25	26	27
CHAITRA 1872	28	29	30	1	2	3	4
	5	6	7	8	9	10	11
	12	13	14	15	16	17	18
	19	20	21	22	23	24	25
VAIŚĀKHA 1873	26	27	28	29	30	1[a]	2
	3	4	5	6	7	8	9
	10	11	12	13	14	15	16
	17	18	19	20	21	22	23
	24	25	26	27	28	29	30
JYAISHṬHA 1873	31	1	2	3	4	5	6
	7	8	9	10	11	12	13
	14	15	16	17	18	19	20
	21	22	23	24	25	26	27
ĀSHĀḌHA 1873	28	29	30	31	32	1	2
	3	4	5	6	7	8	9
	10	11	12	13	14	15	16
	17	18	19	20	21	22	23
	24	25	26	27	28	29	30
ŚRĀVAṆA 1873	31	1	2	3	4	5	6
	7	8	9	10	11	12	13
	14	15	16	17	18	19	20
	21	22	23	24	25	26	27
BHĀDRAPADA 1873	28	29	30	31	32	1	2
	3	4	5	6	7	8	9
	10	11	12	13	14	15	16
	17	18	19	20	21	22	23
	24	25	26	27	28	29	30
ĀŚVINA 1873	31	1	2	3	4	5	6
	7	8	9	10	11	12	13
	14	15	16	17	18	19	20
	21	22	23	24	25	26	27
KĀRTTIKA 1873	28	29	30	1	2	3	4
	5	6	7	8	9	10	11
	12	13	14	15	16	17	18
	19	20	21	22	23	24	25
MĀRGAŚĪRA 1873	26	27	28	29	30	1	2
	3	4	5	6	7	8	9
	10	11	12	13	14	15	16
	17	18	19	20	21	22	23
	24	25	26	27	28	29	30
PAUSHA 1873	1	2	3	4	5	6	7
	8	9	10	11	12	13	14
	15	16	17	18	19	20	21

‡Leap year
[a]New Year (Krodhin)
[b]Pongal

ISLAMIC (ASTRONOMICAL) 1370‡/1371‡

Month	Sun	Mon	Tue	Wed	Thu	Fri	Sat
RABĪ' I 1370	21	22	23	24	25	26	27
RABĪ' II 1370	28	29	1	2	3	4	5
	6	7	8	9	10	11	12
	13	14	15	16	17	18	19
	20	21	22	23	24	25	26
JUMĀDĀ I 1370	27	28	29	30	1	2	3
	4	5	6	7	8	9	10
	11	12	13	14	15	16	17
	18	19	20	21	22	23	24
JUMĀDĀ II 1370	25	26	27	28	29	1	2
	3	4	5	6	7	8	9
	10	11	12	13	14	15	16
	17	18	19	20	21	22	23
	24	25	26	27	28	29	30
RAJAB 1370	1	2	3	4	5	6	7
	8	9	10	11	12	13	14
	15	16	17	18	19	20	21
	22	23	24	25	26	27[d]	28
SHA'BĀN 1370	29	1	2	3	4	5	6
	7	8	9	10	11	12	13
	14	15	16	17	18	19	20
	21	22	23	24	25	26	27
RAMAḌĀN 1370	28	29	30	1[e]	2	3	4
	5	6	7	8	9	10	11
	12	13	14	15	16	17	18
	19	20	21	22	23	24	25
SHAWWĀL 1370	26	27	28	29	30	1[f]	2
	3	4	5	6	7	8	9
	10	11	12	13	14	15	16
	17	18	19	20	21	22	23
DHU AL-QA'DA 1370	24	25	26	27	28	29	1
	2	3	4	5	6	7	8
	9	10	11	12	13	14	15
	16	17	18	19	20	21	22
	23	24	25	26	27	28	29
DHU AL-ḤIJJA 1370	30	1	2	3	4	5	6
	7	8	9	10[g]	11	12	13
	14	15	16	17	18	19	20
	21	22	23	24	25	26	27
MUḤARRAM 1371	28	29	30[ā]	1[a]	2	3	4
	5	6	7	8	9	10[b]	11
	12	13	14	15	16	17	18
	19	20	21	22	23	24	25
ṢAFAR 1371	26	27	28	29	30	1	2
	3	4	5	6	7	8	9
	10	11	12	13	14	15	16
	17	18	19	20	21	22	23
RABĪ' I 1371	24	25	26	27	28	29	1
	2	3	4	5	6	7	8
	9	10	11	12[c]	13	14	15
	16	17	18	19	20	21	22
	23	24	25	26	27	28	29
	1	2	3	4	5	6	7

‡Leap year
[a]New Year
[ā]New Year (Arithmetic)
[b]'Ashūrā'
[c]Prophet's Birthday
[d]Ascent of the Prophet
[e]Start of Ramaḍān
[f]'Īd al-Fiṭr
[g]'Īd al-'Aḍḥā

GREGORIAN 1951

Julian (Sun)	Sun	Mon	Tue	Wed	Thu	Fri	Sat	Month
Dec 18	31	1	2	3	4	5	6	JANUARY 1951
	7[a]	8	9	10	11	12	13	
Jan 1	14[b]	15	16	17	18	19	20	
	21	22	23	24	25	26	27	
Jan 15	28	29	30	31	1	2	3	FEBRUARY 1951
	4	5	6	7[c]	8	9	10	
Jan 29	11	12	13	14	15	16	17	
	18	19	20	21	22	23	24	
Feb 12	25	26	27	28	1	2	3	MARCH 1951
	4	5	6	7	8	9	10	
Feb 26	11	12	13	14	15	16	17	
	18[d]	19	20	21	22	23	24	
Mar 12	25[e]	26	27	28	29	30	31	
	1	2	3	4	5	6	7	APRIL 1951
Mar 26	8	9	10	11	12	13	14	
	15	16	17	18	19	20	21	
Apr 9	22	23	24	25	26	27	28	
	29[f]	30	1	2	3	4	5	MAY 1951
Apr 23	6	7	8	9	10	11	12	
	13	14	15	16	17	18	19	
May 7	20	21	22	23	24	25	26	
	27	28	29	30	31	1	2	JUNE 1951
May 21	3	4	5	6	7	8	9	
	10	11	12	13	14	15	16	
Jun 4	17	18	19	20	21	22	23	
	24	25	26	27	28	29	30	
Jun 18	1	2	3	4	5	6	7	JULY 1951
	8	9	10	11	12	13	14	
Jul 2	15	16	17	18	19	20	21	
	22	23	24	25	26	27	28	
Jul 16	29	30	31	1	2	3	4	AUGUST 1951
	5	6	7	8	9	10	11	
Jul 30	12	13	14	15	16	17	18	
	19	20	21	22	23	24	25	
Aug 13	26	27	28	29	30	31	1	SEPTEMBER 1951
	2	3	4	5	6	7	8	
Aug 27	9	10	11	12	13	14	15	
	16	17	18	19	20	21	22	
Sep 10	23	24	25	26	27	28	29	
	30	1	2	3	4	5	6	OCTOBER 1951
Sep 24	7	8	9	10	11	12	13	
	14	15	16	17	18	19	20	
Oct 8	21	22	23	24	25	26	27	
	28	29	30	31	1	2	3	NOVEMBER 1951
Oct 22	4	5	6	7	8	9	10	
	11	12	13	14	15	16	17	
Nov 5	18	19	20	21	22	23	24	
	25	26	27	28	29	30	1	DECEMBER 1951
Nov 19	2[g]	3	4	5	6	7	8	
	9	10	11	12	13	14	15	
Dec 3	16	17	18	19	20	21	22	
	23	24	25[h]	26	27	28	29	
Dec 17	30	31	1	2	3	4	5	

[a]Orthodox Christmas
[b]Julian New Year
[c]Ash Wednesday
[d]Feast of Orthodoxy
[e]Easter
[f]Orthodox Easter
[g]Advent
[h]Christmas

1952

GREGORIAN 1952‡	Sun	Mon	Tue	Wed	Thu	Fri	Sat	Lunar Phases	ISO WEEK (Mon)	JULIAN DAY (Sun noon)
	30	31	1[a]	2	3	◐	5	4:42	1	2434011
JANUARY 1952	6	7	8	9	10	11	○	4:55	2	2434018
	13	14	15	16	17	18	19		3	2434025
	◑	21	22	23	24	25	●	6:09 22:26	4	2434032
	27	28	29	30	31	1	◐	20:01	5	2434039
	3	4	5	6	7	8	9		6	2434046
FEBRUARY 1952	10	○	12	13	14	15	16	0:28	7	2434053
	17	◑	19	20	21	22	23	18:01	8	2434060
	24	●	26	27	28	29	1	9:16	9	2434067
	2	◐	4	5	6	7	8	13:43	10	2434074
MARCH 1952	9	10	○	12	13	14	15	18:14	11	2434081
	16	17	18	◑	20[b]	21	22	2:40	12	2434088
	23	24	●	26	27	28	29	20:13	13	2434095
	30	31	1	◐	3	4	5	8:48	14	2434102
	6	7	8	9	○	11	12	8:53	15	2434109
APRIL 1952	13	14	15	16	◑	18	19	9:07	16	2434116
	20	21	22	23	●	25	26	7:27	17	2434123
	27	28	29	30	1	◐	3	3:58	18	2434130
	4	5	6	7	8	○	10	20:16	19	2434137
MAY 1952	11	12	13	14	15	◑	17	14:39	20	2434144
	18	19	20	21	22	●	24	19:28	21	2434151
	25	26	27	28	29	30	◐	21:46	22	2434158
	1	2	3	4	5	6	7		23	2434165
	○	9	10	11	12	13	◑	5:07 20:28	24	2434172
JUNE 1952	15	16	17	18	19	20	21[c]		25	2434179
	●	23	24	25	26	27	28	8:45	26	2434186
	29	◐	1	2	3	4	5	13:11	27	2434193
	6	○	8	9	10	11	12	12:34	28	2434200
JULY 1952	13	◑	15	16	17	18	19	3:42	29	2434207
	20	●	22	23	24	25	26	23:30	30	2434214
	27	28	29	◐	31	1	2	1:51	31	2434221
	3	4	○	6	7	8	9	19:40	32	2434228
AUGUST 1952	10	11	◑	13	14	15	16	13:27	33	2434235
	17	18	19	●	21	22	23	15:20	34	2434242
	24	25	26	27	◐	29	30	12:03	35	2434249
	31	1	2	3	○	5	6	3:19	36	2434256
	7	8	9	10	◑	12	13	2:36	37	2434263
SEPTEMBER 1952	14	15	16	17	18	●	20	7:22	38	2434270
	21	22	23[d]	24	25	◐	27	20:31	39	2434277
	28	29	30	1	2	○	4	12:15	40	2434284
	5	6	7	8	9	◑	11	19:33	41	2434291
OCTOBER 1952	12	13	14	15	16	17	●	22:42	42	2434298
	19	20	21	22	23	24	25		43	2434305
	◐	27	28	29	30	31	○	4:04 23:10	44	2434312
	2	3	4	5	6	7	8		45	2434319
NOVEMBER 1952	◑	10	11	12	13	14	15	15:43	46	2434326
	16	●	18	19	20	21	22	12:56	47	2434333
	23	◐	25	26	27	28	29	11:34	48	2434340
	30	○	2	3	4	5	6	12:42	49	2434347
	7	8	◑	10	11	12	13	13:22	50	2434354
DECEMBER 1952	14	15	16	●	18	19	20	2:02	51	2434361
	21[e]	22	◐	24	25	26	27	19:52	52	2434368
	28	29	30	○	1	2	3	5:06	1	2434375

ISO WEEK	HEBREW 5712/5713	Sun	Mon	Tue	Wed	Thu	Fri	Sat	Molad
1		1[e]	2[e]	3	4	5	6	7	Fri $14^h31^m13^p$
2	TEVETH 5712	8	9	10	11	12	13	14	
3		15	16	17	18	19	20	21	
4		22	23	24	25	26	27	28	
5		29	1	2	3	4	5	6	Sun $3^h15^m14^p$
6		7	8	9	10	11	12	13	
7	SHEVAT 5712	14	15	16	17	18	19	20	
8		21	22	23	24	25	26	27	
9		28	29	30	1	2	3	4	Mon $15^h59^m15^p$
10		5	6	7	8	9	10	11	
11	ADAR 5712	12	13	14[f]	15	16	17	18	
12		19	20	21	22	23	24	25	
13		26	27	28	29	1	2	3	Wed $4^h43^m16^p$
14		4	5	6	7	8	9	10	
15	NISAN 5712	11	12	13	14	15[g]	16	17	
16		18	19	20	21	22	23	24	
17		25	26	27	28	29	30	1	Thu $17^h27^m17^p$
18		2	3	4	5	6	7	8	
19	IYYAR 5712	9	10	11	12	13	14	15	
20		16	17	18	19	20	21	22	
21		23	24	25	26	27	28	29	
22		1	2	3	4	5	6[h]	7	Sat $6^h12^m0^p$
23		8	9	10	11	12	13	14	
24	SIVAN 5712	15	16	17	18	19	20	21	
25		22	23	24	25	26	27	28	
26		29	30	1	2	3	4	5	Sun $18^h56^m1^p$
27		6	7	8	9	10	11	12	
28	TAMMUZ 5712	13	14	15	16	17	18	19	
29		20	21	22	23	24	25	26	
30		27	28	29	1	2	3	4	Tue $7^h40^m2^p$
31		5	6	7	8	9[i]	10	11	
32	AV 5712	12	13	14	15	16	17	18	
33		19	20	21	22	23	24	25	
34		26	27	28	29	30	1	2	Wed $20^h24^m3^p$
35		3	4	5	6	7	8	9	
36	ELUL 5712	10	11	12	13	14	15	16	
37		17	18	19	20	21	22	23	
38		24	25	26	27	28	29	1[a]	Fri $9^h8^m4^p$
39		2[a]	3	4	5	6	7	8	
40	TISHRI 5713	9	10[b]	11	12	13	14	15[c]	
41		16	17	18	19	20	21	22	
42		23	24	25	26	27	28	29	
43		30	1	2	3	4	5	6	Sat $21^h52^m5^p$
44		7	8	9	10	11	12	13	
45	ḤESHVAN 5713	14	15	16	17	18	19	20	
46		21	22	23	24	25	26	27	
47		28	29	30	1	2	3	4	Mon $10^h36^m6^p$
48		5	6	7	8	9	10	11	
49	KISLEV 5713	12	13	14	15	16	17[d]	18	
50		19	20	21	22	23	24	25[e]	
51		26[e]	27[e]	28[e]	29[e]	30[e]	1[e]	2[e]	Tue $23^h20^m7^p$
52	TEVETH 5713	3	4	5	6	7	8	9	
1		10	11	12	13	14	15	16	

ISO WEEK	CHINESE Xīn-Mǎo/Rén-Chén‡	Sun	Mon	Tue	Wed	Thu	Fri	Sat	Solar Term
1		3	4	5	6	7	8	9	
2	MONTH 12 Xīn-Mǎo	*10*	11	12	13	14	15	16	Xiǎo hán
3		17	18	19	20	21	22	23*	
4		24	**25**	26	27	28	29	30	**Dà hán**
5		1[a]	2	3	4	5	6	7	
6		8	9	*10*	11	12	13	14	Lì chūn
7	MONTH 1 Rén-Chén	15[b]	16	17	18	19	20	21	
8		22	23	24	**25**	26	27	28	**Yǔ shuǐ**
9		29	1	2	3	4	5	6	
10		7	8	9	*10*	11	12	13	Jīng zhé
11	MONTH 2 Rén-Chén	14	15	16	17	18	19	20	
12		21	22	23	24*	25	**26**	27	**Chūn fēn**
13		28	29	30	1	2	3	4	
14		5	6	7	8	9	10	*11*[c]	Qīng míng
15	MONTH 3 Rén-Chén	12	13	14	15	16	17	18	
16		19	20	21	22	23	24	25	
17		**26**	27	28	29	1	2	3	**Gǔ yǔ**
18		4	5	6	7	8	9	10	
19	MONTH 4 Rén-Chén	11	*12*	13	14	15	16	17	Lì xià
20		18	19	20	21	22	23	24	
21		25*	26	27	**28**	29	30	1	**Xiǎo mǎn**
22		2	3	4	5[d]	6	7	8	
23		9	10	11	12	13	*14*	15	Máng zhòng
24	MONTH 5 Rén-Chén	16	17	18	19	20	21	22	
25		23	24	25	26	27	28	**29**	**Xià zhì**
26		1	2	3	4	5	6	7	
27		8	9	10	11	12	13	14	
28	LEAP MONTH 5 Rén-Chén	15	*16*	17	18	19	20	21	Xiǎo shǔ
29		22	23	24	25	26*	27	28	
30		29	30	1	**2**	3	4	5	**Dà shǔ**
31		6	7	8	9	10	11	12	
32	MONTH 6 Rén-Chén	13	14	15	16	*17*	18	19	Lì qiū
33		20	21	22	23	24	25	26	
34		27	28	29	1	2	3	**4**	**Chǔ shǔ**
35		5	6	7[e]	8	9	10	11	
36	MONTH 7 Rén-Chén	12	13	14	15[f]	16	17	18	
37		19	*20*	21	22	23	24	25	Bái lù
38		26	27*	28	29	30	1	2	
39		3	4	**5**	6	7	8	9	**Qiū fēn**
40	MONTH 8 Rén-Chén	10	11	12	13	14	15[g]	16	
41		17	18	19	*20*	21	22	23	Hán lù
42		24	25	26	27	28	29	30	
43		1	2	3	4	**5**	6	7	**Shuāng jiàng**
44		8	9[h]	10	11	12	13	14	
45	MONTH 9 Rén-Chén	15	16	17	18	19	*20*	21	Lì dōng
46		22	23	24	25	26	27*	28	
47		29	1	2	3	4	5	**6**	**Xiǎo xuě**
48		7	8	9	10	11	12	13	
49	MONTH 10 Rén-Chén	14	15	16	17	18	19	20	
50		*21*	22	23	24	25	26	27	Dà xuě
51		28	29	30	1	2	3	4	
52	MONTH 11 Rén-Chén	5	**6**[i]	7	8	9	10	11	**Dōng zhì**
1		12	13	14	15	16	17	18	

ISO WEEK	COPTIC 1668/1669	Sun	Mon	Tue	Wed	Thu	Fri	Sat	ETHIOPIC 1944/1945
1	KOIAK 1668	20	21	22	23	24	25	26	TĀKHŚĀŚ 1944
2		27	28	29[c]	30	1	2	3	
3	TŌBE 1668	4	5	6[d]	7	8	9	10	
4		11[e]	12	13	14	15	16	17	ṬER 1944
5		18	19	20	21	22	23	24	
6		25	26	27	28	29	30	1	
7		2	3	4	5	6	7	8	
8	MESHIR 1668	9	10	11	12	13	14	15	YAKĀTIT 1944
9		16	17	18	19	20	21	22	
10		23	24	25	26	27	28	29	
11		30	1	2	3	4	5	6	
12	PAREMOTEP 1668	7	8	9	10	11	12	13	MAGĀBIT 1944
13		14	15	16	17	18	19	20	
14		21	22	23	24	25	26	27	
15		28	29	30	1	2	3	4	
16	PARMOUTE 1668	5	6	7	8	9	10	11	MIYĀZYĀ 1944
17		12[f]	13	14	15	16	17	18	
18		19	20	21	22	23	24	25	
19		26	27	28	29[g]	30	1	2	
20		3	4	5	6	7	8	9	
21	PASHONS 1668	10	11	12	13	14	15	16	GENBOT 1944
22		17	18	19	20	21	22	23	
23		24	25	26	27	28	29	30	
24		1	2	3	4	5	6	7	
25	PAŌNE 1668	8	9	10	11	12	13	14	SANĒ 1944
26		15	16	17	18	19	20	21	
27		22	23	24	25	26	27	28	
28		29	30	1	2	3	4	5	
29		6	7	8	9	10	11	12	
30	EPĒP 1668	13	14	15	16	17	18	19	ḤAMLĒ 1944
31		20	21	22	23	24	25	26	
32		27	28	29	30	1	2	3	
33		4	5	6	7	8	9	10	
34	MESORĒ 1668	11	12	13[h]	14	15	16	17	NAḤASĒ 1944
35		18	19	20	21	22	23	24	
36		25	26	27	28	29	30	1	
37	EPAG. 1668	2	3	4	5	1[a]	2	3	PĀG. 1944
38	THOOUT 1669	4	5	6	7	8	9	10	MASKARAM 1945
39		11	12	13	14	15	16	17[b]	
40		18	19	20	21	22	23	24	
41		25	26	27	28	29	30	1	
42		2	3	4	5	6	7	8	
43	PAOPE 1669	9	10	11	12	13	14	15	ṬEQEMT 1945
44		16	17	18	19	20	21	22	
45		23	24	25	26	27	28	29	
46		30	1	2	3	4	5	6	
47		7	8	9	10	11	12	13	
48	ATHŌR 1669	14	15	16	17	18	19	20	ḪEDĀR 1945
49		21	22	23	24	25	26	27	
50		28	29	30	1	2	3	4	
51	KOIAK 1669	5	6	7	8	9	10	11	TĀKHŚĀŚ 1945
52		12	13	14	15	16	17	18	
1		19	20	21	22	23	24	25	

‡Leap year
[a]New Year
[b]Spring (16:13)
[c]Summer (11:12)
[d]Autumn (2:23)
[e]Winter (21:43)
● New moon
◐ First quarter moon
○ Full moon
◑ Last quarter moon

[a]New Year
[b]Yom Kippur
[c]Sukkot
[d]Winter starts
[e]Ḥanukkah
[f]Purim
[g]Passover
[h]Shavuot
[i]Fast of Av

‡Leap year
[a]New Year (4650, Dragon)
[b]Lantern Festival
[c]Qīngmíng
[d]Dragon Festival
[e]Qīqiǎo
[f]Hungry Ghosts
[g]Mid-Autumn Festival
[h]Double-Ninth Festival
[i]Dōngzhì
*Start of 60-name cycle

[a]New Year
[b]Building of the Cross
[c]Christmas
[d]Jesus's Circumcision
[e]Epiphany
[f]Easter
[g]Mary's Announcement
[h]Jesus's Transfiguration

1952

PERSIAN (ASTRONOMICAL) 1330/1331

Month	Sun	Mon	Tue	Wed	Thu	Fri	Sat
DEY 1330	8	9	10	11	12	13	14
	15	16	17	18	19	20	21
	22	23	24	25	26	27	28
	29	30	1	2	3	4	5
BAHMAN 1330	6	7	8	9	10	11	12
	13	14	15	16	17	18	19
	20	21	22	23	24	25	26
	27	28	29	30	1	2	3
ESFAND 1330	4	5	6	7	8	9	10
	11	12	13	14	15	16	17
	18	19	20	21	22	23	24
	25	26	27	28	29	1[a]	2
FARVARDĪN 1331	3	4	5	6	7	8	9
	10	11	12	13[b]	14	15	16
	17	18	19	20	21	22	23
	24	25	26	27	28	29	30
	31	1	2	3	4	5	6
ORDĪBEHEŠT 1331	7	8	9	10	11	12	13
	14	15	16	17	18	19	20
	21	22	23	24	25	26	27
	28	29	30	31	1	2	3
XORDĀD 1331	4	5	6	7	8	9	10
	11	12	13	14	15	16	17
	18	19	20	21	22	23	24
	25	26	27	28	29	30	31
TĪR 1331	1	2	3	4	5	6	7
	8	9	10	11	12	13	14
	15	16	17	18	19	20	21
	22	23	24	25	26	27	28
	29	30	31	1	2	3	4
MORDĀD 1331	5	6	7	8	9	10	11
	12	13	14	15	16	17	18
	19	20	21	22	23	24	25
	26	27	28	29	30	31	1
SHAHRĪVAR 1331	2	3	4	5	6	7	8
	9	10	11	12	13	14	15
	16	17	18	19	20	21	22
	23	24	25	26	27	28	29
	30	31	1	2	3	4	5
MEHR 1331	6	7	8	9	10	11	12
	13	14	15	16	17	18	19
	20	21	22	23	24	25	26
	27	28	29	30	1	2	3
ĀBĀN 1331	4	5	6	7	8	9	10
	11	12	13	14	15	16	17
	18	19	20	21	22	23	24
	25	26	27	28	29	30	1
ĀZAR 1331	2	3	4	5	6	7	8
	9	10	11	12	13	14	15
	16	17	18	19	20	21	22
	23	24	25	26	27	28	29
DEY 1331	30	1	2	3	4	5	6
	7	8	9	10	11	12	13

[a]New Year
[b]Sizdeh Bedar

HINDU LUNAR 2008/2009

Month	Sun	Mon	Tue	Wed	Thu	Fri	Sat
PAUSHA 2008	2	3	4	6	7	8	9
	10	11	12	13	14	14	15
	16	17	18	19	20	21	22
	23	24	25	26	27	28	30
MĀGHA 2008	1	2	3	4	5	6	7
	8	9	10	11	12	13	14
	15	16	16	17	18	19	20
	21	22	24	25	26	27	28[h]
PHĀLGUNA 2008	29	30	1	2	3	4	5
	6	7	8	9	10	11	12
	13	14	15[i]	16	17	18	19
	20	21	22	23	24	25	26
CHAITRA 2009	27	29	30	1[a]	2	3	4
	5	6	7	8	9[b]	10	10
	11	12	13	14	15	16	17
	18	19	20	21	23	24	25
	26	27	28	29	30	1	2
VAIŚĀKHA 2009	3	4	5	6	7	8	9
	10	11	12	13	14	15	16
	17	18	19	20	21	22	23
	24	26	27	28	29	30	1
JYAISHTHA 2009	2	3	4	5	5	6	7
	8	9	10	11	12	13	14
	15	16	17	19	20	21	22
	23	24	25	26	27	28	29
ĀSHĀDHA 2009	30	1	2	3	4	5	6
	7	8	9	10	11	12	13
	14	15	16	17	18	19	20
	22	23	24	25	26	27	28
ŚRĀVAṆA 2009	29	30	1	2	2	3	4
	5	6	7	8	9	10	11
	12	13	15	16	17	18	19
	20	21	22	23[c]	24	25	26
	27	28	29	30	1	2	3
BHĀDRAPADA 2009	4[d]	5	6	7	8	9	10
	11	12	13	14	15	16	18
	19	20	21	22	23	24	25
	26	27	28	28	29	30	1
ĀŚVINA 2009	2	3	4	5	6	7	8[e]
	9[e]	11	12	13	14	15	16
	17	18	19	20	21	22	23
	24	25	26	27	28	29	30
KĀRTTIKA 2009	1[f]	2	3	4	5	6	7
	8	9	10	11	12	13	15
	16	17	18	19	20	21	22
	22	23	24	25	26	27	28
MĀRGAŚĪRA 2009	29	30	1	2	3	4	5
	6	7	9	10	11[g]	12	13
	14	15	16	17	18	19	20
	21	22	23	24	24	25	26
PAUSHA 2009	27	28	29	30	2	3	4
	5	6	7	8	9	10	11
	12	13	14	15	16	17	18

[a]New Year (Nandana)
[b]Birthday of Rāma
[c]Birthday of Krishna
[d]Ganēśa Chaturthī
[e]Dashara
[f]Diwali
[g]Birthday of Vishnu
[h]Night of Śiva
[i]Holi

HINDU SOLAR 1873‡/1874

Month	Sun	Mon	Tue	Wed	Thu	Fri	Sat
PAUSHA 1873	15	16	17	18	19	20	21
	22	23	24	25	26	27	28
MĀGHA 1873	29	1[b]	2	3	4	5	6
	7	8	9	10	11	12	13
	14	15	16	17	18	19	20
	21	22	23	24	25	26	27
PHĀLGUNA 1873	28	29	1	2	3	4	5
	6	7	8	9	10	11	12
	13	14	15	16	17	18	19
	20	21	22	23	24	25	26
CHAITRA 1873	27	28	29	30	1	2	3
	4	5	6	7	8	9	10
	11	12	13	14	15	16	17
	18	19	20	21	22	23	24
	25	26	27	28	29	30	31
VAIŚĀKHA 1874	1[a]	2	3	4	5	6	7
	8	9	10	11	12	13	14
	15	16	17	18	19	20	21
	22	23	24	25	26	27	28
JYAISHTHA 1874	29	30	31	1	2	3	4
	5	6	7	8	9	10	11
	12	13	14	15	16	17	18
	19	20	21	22	23	24	25
ĀSHĀDHA 1874	26	27	28	29	30	31	1
	2	3	4	5	6	7	8
	9	10	11	12	13	14	15
	16	17	18	19	20	21	22
	23	24	25	26	27	28	29
ŚRĀVAṆA 1874	30	31	32	1	2	3	4
	5	6	7	8	9	10	11
	12	13	14	15	16	17	18
	19	20	21	22	23	24	25
BHĀDRAPADA 1874	26	27	28	29	30	31	1
	2	3	4	5	6	7	8
	9	10	11	12	13	14	15
	16	17	18	19	20	21	22
	23	24	25	26	27	28	29
ĀŚVINA 1874	30	31	1	2	3	4	5
	6	7	8	9	10	11	12
	13	14	15	16	17	18	19
	20	21	22	23	24	25	26
KĀRTTIKA 1874	27	28	29	30	1	2	3
	4	5	6	7	8	9	10
	11	12	13	14	15	16	17
	18	19	20	21	22	23	24
MĀRGAŚĪRA 1874	25	26	27	28	29	30	1
	2	3	4	5	6	7	8
	9	10	11	12	13	14	15
	16	17	18	19	20	21	22
	23	24	25	26	27	28	29
PAUSHA 1874	30	1	2	3	4	5	6
	7	8	9	10	11	12	13
	14	15	16	17	18	19	20

‡Leap year
[a]New Year (Viśvāvasu)
[b]Pongal

ISLAMIC (ASTRONOMICAL) 1371‡/1372

Month	Sun	Mon	Tue	Wed	Thu	Fri	Sat
RABĪ' II 1371	1	2	3	4	5	6	7
	8	9	10	11	12	13	14
	15	16	17	18	19	20	21
	22	23	24	25	26	27	28
JUMĀDĀ I 1371	29	1	2	3	4	5	6
	7	8	9	10	11	12	13
	14	15	16	17	18	19	20
	21	22	23	24	25	26	27
JUMĀDĀ II 1371	28	29	30	1	2	3	4
	5	6	7	8	9	10	11
	12	13	14	15	16	17	18
	19	20	21	22	23	24	25
RAJAB 1371	26	27	28	29	1	2	3
	4	5	6	7	8	9	10
	11	12	13	14	15	16	17
	18	19	20	21	22	23	24
SHA'BĀN 1371	25	26	27[d]	28	29	1	2
	3	4	5	6	7	8	9
	10	11	12	13	14	15	16
	17	18	19	20	21	22	23
	24	25	26	27	28	29	30
RAMAḌĀN 1371	1[e]	2	3	4	5	6	7
	8	9	10	11	12	13	14
	15	16	17	18	19	20	21
	22	23	24	25	26	27	28
SHAWWĀL 1371	29	30	1[f]	2	3	4	5
	6	7	8	9	10	11	12
	13	14	15	16	17	18	19
	20	21	22	23	24	25	26
DHU AL-QA'DA 1371	27	28	29	30	1	2	3
	4	5	6	7	8	9	10
	11	12	13	14	15	16	17
	18	19	20	21	22	23	24
DHU AL-ḤIJJA 1371	25	26	27	28	29	30	1
	2	3	4	5	6	7	8
	9	10[g]	11	12	13	14	15
	16	17	18	19	20	21	22
	23	24	25	26	27	28	29
MUḤARRAM 1372	30[d]	1[a]	2	3	4	5	6
	7	8	9	10[b]	11	12	13
	14	15	16	17	18	19	20
	21	22	23	24	25	26	27
ṢAFAR 1372	28	29	1	2	3	4	5
	6	7	8	9	10	11	12
	13	14	15	16	17	18	19
	20	21	22	23	24	25	26
RABĪ' I 1372	27	28	29	1	2	3	4
	5	6	7	8	9	10	11
	12[c]	13	14	15	16	17	18
	19	20	21	22	23	24	25
RABĪ' II 1372	26	27	28	29	30	1	2
	3	4	5	6	7	8	9
	10	11	12	13	14	15	16

‡Leap year
[a]New Year
[d]New Year (Arithmetic)
[b]'Ashūrā'
[c]Prophet's Birthday
[d]Ascent of the Prophet
[e]Start of Ramaḍān
[f]'Id al-Fiṭr
[g]'Id al-'Aḍḥā

GREGORIAN 1952‡

Julian‡ (Sun)	Sun	Mon	Tue	Wed	Thu	Fri	Sat	Month
Dec 17	30	31	1	2	3	4	5	JANUARY 1952
	6	7[a]	8	9	10	11	12	
Dec 31	13	14[b]	15	16	17	18	19	
	20	21	22	23	24	25	26	
Jan 14	27	28	29	30	31	1	2	FEBRUARY 1952
	3	4	5	6	7	8	9	
Jan 28	10	11	12	13	14	15	16	
	17	18	19	20	21	22	23	
Feb 11	24	25	26	27[c]	28	29	1	MARCH 1952
	2	3	4	5	6	7	8	
Feb 25	9[d]	10	11	12	13	14	15	
	16	17	18	19	20	21	22	
Mar 10	23	24	25	26	27	28	29	
	30	31	1	2	3	4	5	APRIL 1952
Mar 24	6	7	8	9	10	11	12	
	13[e]	14	15	16	17	18	19	
Apr 7	20[f]	21	22	23	24	25	26	
	27	28	29	30	1	2	3	MAY 1952
Apr 21	4	5	6	7	8	9	10	
	11	12	13	14	15	16	17	
May 5	18	19	20	21	22	23	24	
	25	26	27	28	29	30	31	
May 19	1	2	3	4	5	6	7	JUNE 1952
	8	9	10	11	12	13	14	
Jun 2	15	16	17	18	19	20	21	
	22	23	24	25	26	27	28	
Jun 16	29	30	1	2	3	4	5	JULY 1952
	6	7	8	9	10	11	12	
Jun 30	13	14	15	16	17	18	19	
	20	21	22	23	24	25	26	
Jul 14	27	28	29	30	31	1	2	AUGUST 1952
	3	4	5	6	7	8	9	
Jul 28	10	11	12	13	14	15	16	
	17	18	19	20	21	22	23	
Aug 11	24	25	26	27	28	29	30	
	31	1	2	3	4	5	6	SEPTEMBER 1952
Aug 25	7	8	9	10	11	12	13	
	14	15	16	17	18	19	20	
Sep 8	21	22	23	24	25	26	27	
	28	29	30	1	2	3	4	OCTOBER 1952
Sep 22	5	6	7	8	9	10	11	
	12	13	14	15	16	17	18	
Oct 6	19	20	21	22	23	24	25	
	26	27	28	29	30	31	1	NOVEMBER 1952
Oct 20	2	3	4	5	6	7	8	
	9	10	11	12	13	14	15	
Nov 3	16	17	18	19	20	21	22	
	23	24	25	26	27	28	29	
Nov 17	30[g]	1	2	3	4	5	6	DECEMBER 1952
	7	8	9	10	11	12	13	
Dec 1	14	15	16	17	18	19	20	
	21	22	23	24	25[h]	26	27	
Dec 15	28	29	30	31	1	2	3	

‡Leap year
[a]Orthodox Christmas
[b]Julian New Year
[c]Ash Wednesday
[d]Feast of Orthodoxy
[e]Easter
[f]Orthodox Easter
[g]Advent
[h]Christmas

1953

Gregorian 1953

Month	Sun	Mon	Tue	Wed	Thu	Fri	Sat	Lunar Phases	ISO Week (Mon)	Julian Day (Sun noon)
January 1953	28	29	30	○	1a	2	3	5:06	1	2434375
	4	5	6	7	◑	9	10	10:09	2	2434382
	11	12	13	14	●	16	17	14:08	3	2434389
	18	19	20	21	◐	23	24	5:43	4	2434396
	25	26	27	28	○	30	31	23:44	5	2434403
February 1953	1	2	3	4	5	6	◑	4:09	6	2434410
	8	9	10	11	12	13	●	1:10	7	2434417
	15	16	17	18	19	◐	21	17:44	8	2434424
	22	23	24	25	26	27	○	18:59	9	2434431
March 1953	1	2	3	4	5	6	7		10	2434438
	◑	9	10	11	12	13	14	18:26	11	2434445
	●	16	17	18	19	20b	21	11:05	12	2434452
	◐	23	24	25	26	27	28	8:11	13	2434459
April 1953	29	○	31	1	2	3	4	12:55	14	2434466
	5	6	◑	8	9	10	11	4:58	15	2434473
	12	●	14	15	16	17	18	20:09	16	2434480
	19	20	◐	22	23	24	25	0:41	17	2434487
	26	27	28	○	30	1	2	4:20	18	2434494
May 1953	3	4	5	◑	7	8	9	12:21	19	2434501
	10	11	12	●	14	15	16	5:06	20	2434508
	17	18	19	◐	21	22	23	18:20	21	2434515
	24	25	26	27	○	29	30	17:03	22	2434522
June 1953	31	1	2	3	◑	5	6	17:36	23	2434529
	7	8	9	10	●	12	13	14:55	24	2434536
	14	15	16	17	18	◐	20	12:01	25	2434543
	21c	22	23	24	25	26	○	3:29	26	2434550
July 1953	28	29	30	1	2	◑	4	22:03	27	2434557
	5	6	7	8	9	10	●	2:28	28	2434564
	12	13	14	15	16	17	18		29	2434571
	◐	20	21	22	23	24	25	4:47	30	2434578
	○	27	28	29	30	31	1	12:21	31	2434585
August 1953	◑	3	4	5	6	7	8	3:16	32	2434592
	●	10	11	12	13	14	15	16:10	33	2434599
	16	◐	18	19	20	21	22	20:08	34	2434606
	23	○	25	26	27	28	29	20:21	35	2434613
September 1953	30	◑	1	2	3	4	5	10:46	36	2434620
	6	7	●	9	10	11	12	7:48	37	2434627
	13	14	15	◐	17	18	19	9:49	38	2434634
	20	21	22	○d	24	25	26	4:16	39	2434641
October 1953	27	28	◑	30	1	2	3	21:51	40	2434648
	4	5	6	7	●	9	10	0:40	41	2434655
	11	12	13	14	◐	16	17	21:44	42	2434662
	18	19	20	21	○	23	24	12:56	43	2434669
	25	26	27	28	◑	30	31	13:09	44	2434676
November 1953	1	2	3	4	5	●	7	17:58	45	2434683
	8	9	10	11	12	13	◐	7:52	46	2434690
	15	16	17	18	19	○	21	23:12	47	2434697
	22	23	24	25	26	27	◑	8:16	48	2434704
December 1953	29	30	1	2	3	4	5		49	2434711
	●	7	8	9	10	11	12	10:48	50	2434718
	◐	14	15	16	17	18	19	16:30	51	2434725
	○	21	22e	23	24	25	26	11:44	52	2434732
	27	◑	29	30	31	1	2	5:43	53	2434739

Hebrew 5713/5714‡

ISO Week	Month	Sun	Mon	Tue	Wed	Thu	Fri	Sat	Molad
1	Teveth 5713	10	11	12	13	14	15	16	
2		17	18	19	20	21	22	23	
3		24	25	26	27	28	29	1	Thu 12h4m8p
4	Shevat 5713	2	3	4	5	6	7	8	
5		9	10	11	12	13	14	15	
6		16	17	18	19	20	21	22	
7		23	24	25	26	27	28	29	
8		30	1	2	3	4	5	6	Sat 0h48m9p
9	Adar 5713	7	8	9	10	11	12	13	
10		14f	15	16	17	18	19	20	
11		21	22	23	24	25	26	27	
12		28	29	1	2	3	4	5	Sun 13h32m10p
13	Nisan 5713	6	7	8	9	10	11	12	
14		13	14	15g	16	17	18	19	
15		20	21	22	23*	24	25	26	
16		27	28	29	30	1	2	3	Tue 2h16m11p
17	Iyyar 5713	4	5	6	7	8	9	10	
18		11	12	13	14	15	16	17	
19		18	19	20	21	22	23	24	
20		25	26	27	28	29	1	2	Wed 15h0m12p
21	Sivan 5713	3	4	5	6h	7	8	9	
22		10	11	12	13	14	15	16	
23		17	18	19	20	21	22	23	
24		24	25	26	27	28	29	30	
25	Tammuz 5713	1	2	3	4	5	6	7	Fri 3h44m13p
26		8	9	10	11	12	13	14	
27		15	16	17	18	19	20	21	
28		22	23	24	25	26	27	28	
29	Av 5713	29	1	2	3	4	5	6	Sat 16h28m14p
30		7	8	9i	10	11	12	13	
31		14	15	16	17	18	19	20	
32		21	22	23	24	25	26	27	
33	Elul 5713	28	29	30	1	2	3	4	Mon 5h12m15p
34		5	6	7	8	9	10	11	
35		12	13	14	15	16	17	18	
36		19	20	21	22	23	24	25	
37	Tishri 5714	26	27	28	29	1a	2a	3	Tue 17h56m16p
38		4	5	6	7	8	9	10b	
39		11	12	13	14	15c	16	17	
40		18	19	20	21	22	23	24	
41	Heshvan 5714	25	26	27	28	29	30	1	Thu 6h40m17p
42		2	3	4	5	6	7	8	
43		9	10	11	12	13	14	15	
44		16	17	18	19	20	21	22	
45		23	24	25	26	27	28	29	
46	Kislev 5714	1	2	3	4	5	6	7	Fri 19h25m0p
47		8	9	10	11	12	13	14	
48		15	16	17	18	19	20	21	
49		22	23	24	25e	26e	27e	28de	
50	Teveth 5714	29e	1e	2e	3e	4	5	6	Sun 8h9m1p
51		7	8	9	10	11	12	13	
52		14	15	16	17	18	19	20	
53		21	22	23	24	25	26	27	

Chinese Rén-Chén‡/Guǐ-Sì

ISO Week	Month	Sun	Mon	Tue	Wed	Thu	Fri	Sat	Solar Term
1	Month 11 Rén-Chén	12	13	14	15	16	17	18	
2		19	20	21	22	23	24	25	Xiǎo hán
3	Month 12 Rén-Chén	26	27	28*	29	1	2	3	
4		4	5	6	7	8	9	10	Dà hán
5		11	12	13	14	15	16	17	
6		18	19	20	21	22	23	24	Lì chūn
7	Month 1 Guǐ-Sì	25	26	27	28	29	30	1a	
8		2	3	4	5	6	7	8	Yǔ shuǐ
9		9	10	11	12	13	14	15b	
10		16	17	18	19	20	21	22	Jīng zhé
11		23	24	25	26	27	28	29*	
12	Month 2 Guǐ-Sì	1	2	3	4	5	6	7	Chūn fēn
13		8	9	10	11	12	13	14	
14		15	16	17	18	19	20	21	
15		22c	23	24	25	26	27	28	Qīng míng
16	Month 3 Guǐ-Sì	29	30	1	2	3	4	5	
17		6	7	8	9	10	11	12	Gǔ yǔ
18		13	14	15	16	17	18	19	
19		20	21	22	23	24	25	26	Lì xià
20	Month 4 Guǐ-Sì	27	28	29	1*	2	3	4	
21		5	6	7	8	9	10	11	Xiǎo mǎn
22		12	13	14	15	16	17	18	
23		19	20	21	22	23	24	25	Máng zhòng
24	Month 5 Guǐ-Sì	26	27	28	29	1	2	3	
25		4	5d	6	7	8	9	10	Xià zhì
26		11	12	13	14	15	16	17	
27		18	19	20	21	22	23	24	
28	Month 6 Guǐ-Sì	25	26	27	28	29	30	1	Xiǎo shǔ
29		2*	3	4	5	6	7	8	
30		9	10	11	12	13	14	15	Dà shǔ
31		16	17	18	19	20	21	22	
32		23	24	25	26	27	28	29	Lì qiū
33	Month 7 Guǐ-Sì	30	1	2	3	4	5	6	
34		7e	8	9	10	11	12	13	Chǔ shǔ
35		14	15f	16	17	18	19	20	
36		21	22	23	24	25	26	27	
37	Month 8 Guǐ-Sì	28	29	1	2	3*	4	5	Bái lù
38		6	7	8	9	10	11	12	
39		13	14	15g	16	17	18	19	Qiū fēn
40		20	21	22	23	24	25	26	
41	Month 9 Guǐ-Sì	27	28	29	30	1	2	3	Hán lù
42		4	5	6	7	8	9h	10	
43		11	12	13	14	15	16	17	Shuāng jiàng
44		18	19	20	21	22	23	24	
45	Month 10 Guǐ-Sì	25	26	27	28	29	30	1	
46		2	3*	4	5	6	7	8	Lì dōng
47		9	10	11	12	13	14	15	
48		16	17	18	19	20	21	22	Xiǎo xuě
49		23	24	25	26	27	28	29	
50	Month 11* Guǐ-Sì	1	2	3	4	5	6	7	Dà xuě
51		8	9	10	11	12	13	14	
52		15	16	17i	18	19	20	21	Dōng zhì
53		22	23	24	25	26	27	28	

Coptic 1669/1670 — Ethiopic 1945/1946

ISO Week	Coptic Month	Sun	Mon	Tue	Wed	Thu	Fri	Sat	Ethiopic Month
1	Koiak 1669	19	20	21	22	23	24	25	Tākhśāś 1945
2	Tôbe 1669	26	27	28	29c	30	1	2	Ṭer 1945
3		3	4	5	6d	7	8	9	
4		10	11e	12	13	14	15	16	
5		17	18	19	20	21	22	23	
6		24	25	26	27	28	29	30	
7	Meshir 1669	1	2	3	4	5	6	7	Yakātit 1945
8		8	9	10	11	12	13	14	
9		15	16	17	18	19	20	21	
10		22	23	24	25	26	27	28	
11	Paremotep 1669	29	30	1	2	3	4	5	Magābit 1945
12		6	7	8	9	10	11	12	
13		13	14	15	16	17	18	19	
14		20	21	22	23	24	25	26	
15	Parmoute 1669	27f	28	29	30	1	2	3	Miyāzyā 1945
16		4	5	6	7	8	9	10	
17		11	12	13	14	15	16	17	
18		18	19	20	21	22	23	24	
19	Pashons 1669	25	26	27	28	29g	30	1	Genbot 1945
20		2	3	4	5	6	7	8	
21		9	10	11	12	13	14	15	
22		16	17	18	19	20	21	22	
23		23	24	25	26	27	28	29	
24	Paône 1669	30	1	2	3	4	5	6	Sanê 1945
25		7	8	9	10	11	12	13	
26		14	15	16	17	18	19	20	
27		21	22	23	24	25	26	27	
28	Epêp 1669	28	29	30	1	2	3	4	Ḥamlê 1945
29		5	6	7	8	9	10	11	
30		12	13	14	15	16	17	18	
31		19	20	21	22	23	24	25	
32	Mesorê 1669	26	27	28	29	30	1	2	Naḥasê 1945
33		3	4	5	6	7	8	9	
34		10	11	12	13h	14	15	16	
35		17	18	19	20	21	22	23	
36		24	25	26	27	28	29	30	
37	Epag. 1669 / Thout 1670	1	2	3	4	5	1a	2	Pāg. 1945 / Maskaram 1946
38		3	4	5	6	7	8	9	
39		10	11	12	13	14	15	16	
40		17b	18	19	20	21	22	23	
41		24	25	26	27	28	29	30	
42	Paope 1670	1	2	3	4	5	6	7	Ṭeqemt 1946
43		8	9	10	11	12	13	14	
44		15	16	17	18	19	20	21	
45		22	23	24	25	26	27	28	
46	Athôr 1670	29	30	1	2	3	4	5	Hedār 1946
47		6	7	8	9	10	11	12	
48		13	14	15	16	17	18	19	
49		20	21	22	23	24	25	26	
50	Koiak 1670	27	28	29	30	1	2	3	Tākhśāś 1946
51		4	5	6	7	8	9	10	
52		11	12	13	14	15	16	17	
53		18	19	20	21	22	23	24	

Gregorian notes:
[a]New Year
[b]Spring (22:00)
[c]Summer (16:59)
[d]Autumn (8:06)
[e]Winter (3:31)
● New moon
◐ First quarter moon
○ Full moon
◑ Last quarter moon

Hebrew notes:
‡Leap year
[a]New Year
[b]Yom Kippur
[c]Sukkot
[d]Winter starts
[e]Ḥanukkah
[f]Purim
[g]Passover
[h]Shavuot
[i]Fast of Av
*New solar cycle

Chinese notes:
‡Leap year
[a]New Year (4651, Snake)
[b]Lantern Festival
[c]Qīngmíng
[d]Dragon Festival
[e]Qīqiǎo
[f]Hungry Ghosts
[g]Mid-Autumn Festival
[h]Double-Ninth Festival
[i]Dōngzhì
*Start of 60-name cycle

Coptic/Ethiopic notes:
[a]New Year
[b]Building of the Cross
[c]Christmas
[d]Jesus's Circumcision
[e]Epiphany
[f]Easter
[g]Mary's Announcement
[h]Jesus's Transfiguration

PERSIAN (ASTRONOMICAL) 1331/1332

Month	Sun	Mon	Tue	Wed	Thu	Fri	Sat
DEY 1331	7	8	9	10	11	12	13
	14	15	16	17	18	19	20
	21	22	23	24	25	26	27
BAHMAN 1331	28	29	30	1	2	3	4
	5	6	7	8	9	10	11
	12	13	14	15	16	17	18
	19	20	21	22	23	24	25
ESFAND 1331	26	27	28	29	30	1	2
	3	4	5	6	7	8	9
	10	11	12	13	14	15	16
	17	18	19	20	21	22	23
FARVARDĪN 1332	24	25	26	27	28	29	1[a]
	2	3	4	5	6	7	8
	9	10	11	12	13[b]	14	15
	16	17	18	19	20	21	22
	23	24	25	26	27	28	29
ORDĪBEHEŠT 1332	30	31	1	2	3	4	5
	6	7	8	9	10	11	12
	13	14	15	16	17	18	19
	20	21	22	23	24	25	26
XORDĀD 1332	27	28	29	30	31	1	2
	3	4	5	6	7	8	9
	10	11	12	13	14	15	16
	17	18	19	20	21	22	23
	24	25	26	27	28	29	30
TĪR 1332	31	1	2	3	4	5	6
	7	8	9	10	11	12	13
	14	15	16	17	18	19	20
	21	22	23	24	25	26	27
MORDĀD 1332	28	29	30	31	1	2	3
	4	5	6	7	8	9	10
	11	12	13	14	15	16	17
	18	19	20	21	22	23	24
	25	26	27	28	29	30	31
SHAHRĪVAR 1332	1	2	3	4	5	6	7
	8	9	10	11	12	13	14
	15	16	17	18	19	20	21
	22	23	24	25	26	27	28
MEHR 1332	29	30	31	1	2	3	4
	5	6	7	8	9	10	11
	12	13	14	15	16	17	18
	19	20	21	22	23	24	25
ĀBĀN 1332	26	27	28	29	30	1	2
	3	4	5	6	7	8	9
	10	11	12	13	14	15	16
	17	18	19	20	21	22	23
	24	25	26	27	28	29	30
ĀZAR 1332	1	2	3	4	5	6	7
	8	9	10	11	12	13	14
	15	16	17	18	19	20	21
	22	23	24	25	26	27	28
DEY 1332	29	30	1	2	3	4	5
	6	7	8	9	10	11	12

[a]New Year
[b]Sizdeh Bedar

HINDU LUNAR 2009/2010‡

Month	Sun	Mon	Tue	Wed	Thu	Fri	Sat
PAUSHA 2009	12	13	14	15	16	17	18
	19	20	21	22	23	24	25
MĀGHA 2009	26	27	28	29	30	1	2
	3	4	5	7	8	9	10
	11	12	13	14	15	16	17
	17	18	19	20	21	22	23
PHĀLGUNA 2009	24	25	26	27	28[h]	29	1
	2	3	4	5	6	7	8
	9	10	11	12	13	14	15[i]
	16	17	18	19	20	20	21
	22	24	25	26	27	28	29
CHAITRA 2010	30	1[a]	2	3	4	5	7
	8	9[b]	9	10	11	12	13
	14	15	16	17	18	19	20
	21	22	23	24	25	26	27
LEAP VAIŚĀKHA 2010	28	30	1	2	3	4	5
	6	7	8	9	10	11	12
	13	13	14	15	16	17	18
	19	20	21	23	24	25	26
VAIŚĀKHA 2010	27	28	29	30	1	2	3
	4	5	6	7	8	9	10
	11	12	13	14	15	16	17
	18	19	20	21	22	23	24
JYAISHTHA 2010	26	27	28	29	30	1	2
	3	4	5	6	7	8	9
	9	10	11	12	13	14	15
	16	17	19	20	21	22	23
	24	25	26	27	28	29	30
ĀSHĀḌHA 2010	1	2	3	4	5	6	7
	8	9	10	11	12	13	14
	15	16	17	18	19	20	22
	23	24	25	26	27	28	29
ŚRĀVAṆA 2010	30	1	2	3	4	5	6
	6	7	8	9	10	11	12
	14	15	16	17	18	19	20
	21	22	23[c]	24	25	26	27
BHĀDRAPADA 2010	28	29	30	1	2	3	4[d]
	5	6	7	8	9	10	11
	12	13	14	15	16	18	19
	20	21	22	23	24	25	26
ĀŚVINA 2010	27	28	29	30	1	1	2
	3	4	5	6	7	8[e]	9[e]
	11	12	13	14	15	16	17
	18	19	20	21	22	23	24
KĀRTTIKA 2010	25	26	27	28	29	30	1[f]
	2	3	4	5	6	7	8
	9	10	11	12	13	14	16
	17	18	19	20	21	22	23
	24	25	25	26	27	28	29
MĀRGAŚIRA 2010	30	1	2	3	4	5	6
	7	8	10	11[g]	12	13	14
	15	16	17	18	19	20	21
	22	23	24	25	26	27	28

‡Leap year
[a]New Year (Vijaya)
[b]Birthday of Rāma
[c]Birthday of Krishna
[d]Gaṇēśa Chaturthī
[e]Dashara
[f]Diwali
[g]Birthday of Vishnu
[h]Night of Śiva
[i]Holi

HINDU SOLAR 1874/1875

Month	Sun	Mon	Tue	Wed	Thu	Fri	Sat
PAUSHA 1874	14	15	16	17	18	19	20
	21	22	23	24	25	26	27
MĀGHA 1874	28	29	1[b]	2	3	4	5
	6	7	8	9	10	11	12
	13	14	15	16	17	18	19
	20	21	22	23	24	25	26
PHĀLGUNA 1874	27	28	29	30	1	2	3
	4	5	6	7	8	9	10
	11	12	13	14	15	16	17
	18	19	20	21	22	23	24
CHAITRA 1874	25	26	27	28	29	1	2
	3	4	5	6	7	8	9
	10	11	12	13	14	15	16
	17	18	19	20	21	22	23
	24	25	26	27	28	29	30
VAIŚĀKHA 1875	31	1[a]	2	3	4	5	6
	7	8	9	10	11	12	13
	14	15	16	17	18	19	20
	21	22	23	24	25	26	27
JYAISHTHA 1875	28	29	30	31	1	2	3
	4	5	6	7	8	9	10
	11	12	13	14	15	16	17
	18	19	20	21	22	23	24
	25	26	27	28	29	30	31
ĀSHĀḌHA 1875	1	2	3	4	5	6	7
	8	9	10	11	12	13	14
	15	16	17	18	19	20	21
	22	23	24	25	26	27	28
ŚRĀVAṆA 1875	29	30	31	32	1	2	3
	4	5	6	7	8	9	10
	11	12	13	14	15	16	17
	18	19	20	21	22	23	24
	25	26	27	28	29	30	31
BHĀDRAPADA 1875	1	2	3	4	5	6	7
	8	9	10	11	12	13	14
	15	16	17	18	19	20	21
	22	23	24	25	26	27	28
ĀŚVINA 1875	29	30	31	1	2	3	4
	5	6	7	8	9	10	11
	12	13	14	15	16	17	18
	19	20	21	22	23	24	25
KĀRTTIKA 1875	26	27	28	29	30	31	1
	2	3	4	5	6	7	8
	9	10	11	12	13	14	15
	16	17	18	19	20	21	22
	23	24	25	26	27	28	29
MĀRGAŚIRA 1875	30	1	2	3	4	5	6
	7	8	9	10	11	12	13
	14	15	16	17	18	19	20
	21	22	23	24	25	26	27
PAUSHA 1875	28	29	1	2	3	4	5
	6	7	8	9	10	11	12
	13	14	15	16	17	18	19

[a]New Year (Parābhava)
[b]Pongal

ISLAMIC (ASTRONOMICAL) 1372/1373

Month	Sun	Mon	Tue	Wed	Thu	Fri	Sat
RABĪʿ II 1372	10	11	12	13	14	15	16
	17	18	19	20	21	22	23
JUMĀDĀ I 1372	24	25	26	27	28	29	1
	2	3	4	5	6	7	8
	9	10	11	12	13	14	15
	16	17	18	19	20	21	22
	23	24	25	26	27	28	29
JUMĀDĀ II 1372	1	2	3	4	5	6	7
	8	9	10	11	12	13	14
	15	16	17	18	19	20	21
	22	23	24	25	26	27	28
RAJAB 1372	29	30	1	2	3	4	5
	6	7	8	9	10	11	12
	13	14	15	16	17	18	19
	20	21	22	23	24	25	26
SHAʿBĀN 1372	27[d]	28	29	1	2	3	4
	5	6	7	8	9	10	11
	12	13	14	15	16	17	18
	19	20	21	22	23	24	25
RAMAḌĀN 1372	26	27	28	29	1[e]	2	3
	4	5	6	7	8	9	10
	11	12	13	14	15	16	17
	18	19	20	21	22	23	24
SHAWWĀL 1372	25	26	27	28	29	30	1[f]
	2	3	4	5	6	7	8
	9	10	11	12	13	14	15
	16	17	18	19	20	21	22
	23	24	25	26	27	28	29
DHU AL-QAʿDA 1372	30	1	2	3	4	5	6
	7	8	9	10	11	12	13
	14	15	16	17	18	19	20
	21	22	23	24	25	26	27
DHU AL-ḤIJJA 1372	28	29	30	1	2	3	4
	5	6	7	8	9	10[g]	11
	12	13	14	15	16	17	18
	19	20	21	22	23	24	25
MUḤARRAM 1373	26	27	28	29	30[A]	1[a]	2
	3	4	5	6	7	8	9
	10[b]	11	12	13	14	15	16
	17	18	19	20	21	22	23
	24	25	26	27	28	29	30
ṢAFAR 1373	1	2	3	4	5	6	7
	8	9	10	11	12	13	14
	15	16	17	18	19	20	21
	22	23	24	25	26	27	28
RABĪʿ I 1373	29	1	2	3	4	5	6
	7	8	9	10	11	12[c]	13
	14	15	16	17	18	19	20
	21	22	23	24	25	26	27
RABĪʿ II 1373	28	29	1	2	3	4	5
	6	7	8	9	10	11	12
	13	14	15	16	17	18	19
	20	21	22	23	24	25	26

[a]New Year
[A]New Year (Arithmetic)
[b]ʿAshūrāʾ
[c]Prophet's Birthday
[d]Ascent of the Prophet
[e]Start of Ramaḍān
[f]ʿĪd al-Fiṭr
[g]ʿĪd al-ʾAḍḥā

GREGORIAN 1953

Julian (Sun)	Month	Sun	Mon	Tue	Wed	Thu	Fri	Sat
Dec 15	JANUARY 1953	28	29	30	31	1	2	3
		4	5	6	7[a]	8	9	10
Dec 29		11	12	13	14[b]	15	16	17
		18	19	20	21	22	23	24
Jan 12		25	26	27	28	29	30	31
	FEBRUARY 1953	1	2	3	4	5	6	7
Jan 26		8	9	10	11	12	13	14
		15	16	17	18[c]	19	20	21
Feb 9		22[d]	23	24	25	26	27	28
	MARCH 1953	1	2	3	4	5	6	7
Feb 23		8	9	10	11	12	13	14
		15	16	17	18	19	20	21
Mar 9		22	23	24	25	26	27	28
	APRIL 1953	29	30	31	1	2	3	4
Mar 23		5[e]	6	7	8	9	10	11
		12	13	14	15	16	17	18
Apr 6		19	20	21	22	23	24	25
	MAY 1953	26	27	28	29	30	1	2
Apr 20		3	4	5	6	7	8	9
		10	11	12	13	14	15	16
May 4		17	18	19	20	21	22	23
		24	25	26	27	28	29	30
May 18	JUNE 1953	31	1	2	3	4	5	6
		7	8	9	10	11	12	13
Jun 1		14	15	16	17	18	19	20
		21	22	23	24	25	26	27
Jun 15	JULY 1953	28	29	30	1	2	3	4
		5	6	7	8	9	10	11
Jun 29		12	13	14	15	16	17	18
		19	20	21	22	23	24	25
Jul 13	AUGUST 1953	26	27	28	29	30	31	1
		2	3	4	5	6	7	8
Jul 27		9	10	11	12	13	14	15
		16	17	18	19	20	21	22
Aug 10		23	24	25	26	27	28	29
	SEPTEMBER 1953	30	31	1	2	3	4	5
Aug 24		6	7	8	9	10	11	12
		13	14	15	16	17	18	19
Sep 7		20	21	22	23	24	25	26
	OCTOBER 1953	27	28	29	30	1	2	3
Sep 21		4	5	6	7	8	9	10
		11	12	13	14	15	16	17
Oct 5		18	19	20	21	22	23	24
		25	26	27	28	29	30	31
Oct 19	NOVEMBER 1953	1	2	3	4	5	6	7
		8	9	10	11	12	13	14
Nov 2		15	16	17	18	19	20	21
		22	23	24	25	26	27	28
Nov 16	DECEMBER 1953	29[g]	30	1	2	3	4	5
		6	7	8	9	10	11	12
Nov 30		13	14	15	16	17	18	19
		20	21	22	23	24	25[h]	26
Dec 14		27	28	29	30	31	1	2

[a]Orthodox Christmas
[b]Julian New Year
[c]Ash Wednesday
[d]Feast of Orthodoxy
[e]Easter (also Orthodox)
[g]Advent
[h]Christmas

1954

GREGORIAN 1954	Sun	Mon	Tue	Wed	Thu	Fri	Sat	Lunar Phases	ISO WEEK (Mon)	JULIAN DAY (Sun noon)
	27	◑	29	30	31	1[a]	2	5:43	53	2434739
JANUARY 1954	3	4	●	6	7	8	9	2:21	1	2434746
	10	11	◐	13	14	15	16	0:22	2	2434753
	17	18	○	20	21	22	23	2:37	3	2434760
	24	25	26	◑	28	29	30	3:28	4	2434767
	31	1	2	●	4	5	6	15:55	5	2434774
FEBRUARY 1954	7	8	9	◐	11	12	13	8:29	6	2434781
	14	15	16	○	18	19	20	19:17	7	2434788
	21	22	23	24	◑	26	27	23:29	8	2434795
	28	1	2	3	4	●	6	3:11	9	2434802
MARCH 1954	7	8	9	10	◐	12	13	17:52	10	2434809
	14	15	16	17	18	○	20	12:43	11	2434816
	21[b]	22	23	24	25	26	◑	16:14	12	2434823
	28	29	30	31	1	2	●	12:25	13	2434830
APRIL 1954	4	5	6	7	8	9	◐	5:05	14	2434837
	11	12	13	14	15	16	17		15	2434844
	○	19	20	21	22	23	24	5:49	16	2434851
	25	◑	27	28	29	30	1	4:57	17	2434858
	●	3	4	5	6	7	8	20:22	18	2434865
MAY 1954	◐	10	11	12	13	14	15	18:17	19	2434872
	16	○	18	19	20	21	22	21:47	20	2434879
	23	24	◑	26	27	28	29	13:49	21	2434886
	30	31	●	2	3	4	5	4:03	22	2434893
JUNE 1954	6	7	◐	9	10	11	12	9:14	23	2434900
	13	14	15	○	17	18	19	12:06	24	2434907
	20	21[c]	22	◑	24	25	26	19:46	25	2434914
	27	28	29	●	1	2	3	12:26	26	2434921
JULY 1954	4	5	6	7	◐	9	10	1:33	27	2434928
	11	12	13	14	15	○	17	0:29	28	2434935
	18	19	20	21	22	◑	24	0:14	29	2434942
	25	26	27	28	●	30	31	22:20	30	2434949
AUGUST 1954	1	2	3	4	5	◐	7	18:51	31	2434956
	8	9	10	11	12	13	○	11:03	32	2434963
	15	16	17	18	19	20	◑	4:51	33	2434970
	22	23	24	25	26	27	●	10:21	34	2434977
	29	30	31	1	2	3	4		35	2434984
SEPTEMBER 1954	◐	6	7	8	9	10	11	12:28	36	2434991
	○	13	14	15	16	17	18	20:19	37	2434998
	◑	20	21	22	23[d]	24	25	11:11	38	2435005
	26	●	28	29	30	1	2	0:50	39	2435012
OCTOBER 1954	3	4	◐	6	7	8	9	5:31	40	2435019
	10	11	○	13	14	15	16	5:10	41	2435026
	17	◑	19	20	21	22	23	20:30	42	2435033
	24	25	●	27	28	29	30	17:47	43	2435040
	31	1	2	◐	4	5	6	20:55	44	2435047
NOVEMBER 1954	7	8	9	○	11	12	13	14:29	45	2435054
	14	15	16	◑	18	19	20	9:33	46	2435061
	21	22	23	24	●	26	27	12:30	47	2435068
	28	29	30	1	2	◐	4	9:56	48	2435075
DECEMBER 1954	5	6	7	8	9	○	11	0:57	49	2435082
	12	13	14	15	16	◑	18	2:21	50	2435089
	19	20	21	22[e]	23	24	●	7:33	51	2435096
	26	27	28	29	30	31	◐	20:29	52	2435103

ISO WEEK	HEBREW 5714‡/5715	Sun	Mon	Tue	Wed	Thu	Fri	Sat	Molad
53	TEVETH 5714	21	22	23	24	25	26	27	
1		28	29	1	2	3	4	5	Mon 20h53m2p
2	SHEVAT 5714	6	7	8	9	10	11	12	
3		13	14	15	16	17	18	19	
4		20	21	22	23	24	25	26	
5		27	28	29	30	1	2	3	Wed 9h37m3p
6	ADAR I 5714	4	5	6	7	8	9	10	
7		11	12	13	14	15	16	17	
8		18	19	20	21	22	23	24	
9		25	26	27	28	29	30	1	Thu 22h21m4p
10	ADAR II 5714	2	3	4	5	6	7	8	
11		9	10	11	12	13	14[f]	15	
12		16	17	18	19	20	21	22	
13		23	24	25	26	27	28	29	
14		1	2	3	4	5	6	7	Sat 11h5m5p
15	NISAN 5714	8	9	10	11	12	13	14	
16		15[g]	16	17	18	19	20	21	
17		22	23	24	25	26	27	28	
18		29	30	1	2	3	4	5	Sun 23h49m6p
19	IYAR 5714	6	7	8	9	10	11	12	
20		13	14	15	16	17	18	19	
21		20	21	22	23	24	25	26	
22		27	28	29	1	2	3	4	Tue 12h33m7p
23	SIVAN 5714	5	6[h]	7	8	9	10	11	
24		12	13	14	15	16	17	18	
25		19	20	21	22	23	24	25	
26		26	27	28	29	30	1	2	Thu 1h17m8p
27	TAMMUZ 5714	3	4	5	6	7	8	9	
28		10	11	12	13	14	15	16	
29		17	18	19	20	21	22	23	
30		24	25	26	27	28	29	1	Fri 14h1m9p
31	AV 5714	2	3	4	5	6	7	8	
32		9[i]	10	11	12	13	14	15	
33		16	17	18	19	20	21	22	
34		23	24	25	26	27	28	29	
35		30	1	2	3	4	5	6	Sun 2h45m10p
36	ELUL 5714	7	8	9	10	11	12	13	
37		14	15	16	17	18	19	20	
38		21	22	23	24	25	26	27	
39		28	29	1[a]	2[a]	3	4	5	Mon 15h29m11p
40	TISHRI 5715	6	7	8	9	10[b]	11	12	
41		13	14	15[c]	16	17	18	19	
42		20	21	22	23	24	25	26	
43		27	28	29	30	1	2	3	Wed 4h13m12p
44	HESHVAN 5715	4	5	6	7	8	9	10	
45		11	12	13	14	15	16	17	
46		18	19	20	21	22	23	24	
47		25	26	27	28	29	1	2	Thu 16h57m13p
48	KISLEV 5715	3	4	5	6	7	8	9	
49		10[d]	11	12	13	14	15	16	
50		17	18	19	20	21	22	23	
51		24	25[e]	26[e]	27[e]	28[e]	29[e]	30[e]	
52		1[e]	2[e]	3	4	5	6	7	Sat 5h41m14p

ISO WEEK	CHINESE Guǐ-Sì/Jiǎ-Wǔ	Sun	Mon	Tue	Wed	Thu	Fri	Sat	Solar Term
53	MONTH 11* Guǐ-Sì	22	23	24	25	26	27	28	
1	MONTH 12 Guǐ-Sì	29	30	1	2	3	4*	5	Xiǎo hán
2		6	7	8	9	10	11	12	
3		13	14	15	**16**	17	18	19	Dà hán
4		20	21	22	23	24	25	26	
5		27	28	29	1[a]	2	3	4	Lì chūn
6	MONTH 1 Jiǎ-Wǔ	5	6	7	8	9	10	11	
7		12	13	14	15[b]	16	**17**	18	Yǔ shuǐ
8		19	20	21	22	23	24	25	
9		26	27	28	29	30	1	2	Jīng zhé
10	MONTH 2 Jiǎ-Wǔ	3	4	5*	6	7	8	9	
11		10	11	12	13	14	15	16	
12		**17**	18	19	20	21	22	23	Chūn fēn
13		24	25	26	27	28	29	1	
14	MONTH 3 Jiǎ-Wǔ	2	3[c]	4	5	6	7	8	Qīng míng
15		9	10	11	12	13	14	15	
16		16	17	**18**	19	20	21	22	Gǔ yǔ
17		23	24	25	26	27	28	29	
18		30	1	2	3	4	5	6*	Lì xià
19	MONTH 4 Jiǎ-Wǔ	7	8	9	10	11	12	13	
20		14	15	16	17	18	**19**	20	Xiǎo mǎn
21		21	22	23	24	25	26	27	
22		28	29	1	2	3	4	5[d]	
23	MONTH 5 Jiǎ-Wǔ	6	7	8	9	10	11	12	Máng zhòng
24		13	14	15	16	17	18	19	
25		20	21	**22**	23	24	25	26	Xià zhì
26		27	28	29	1	2	3	4	
27	MONTH 6 Jiǎ-Wǔ	5	6	7	8*	9	10	11	Xiǎo shǔ
28		12	13	14	15	16	17	18	
29		19	20	21	22	23	**24**	25	Dà shǔ
30		26	27	28	29	30	1	2	
31	MONTH 7 Jiǎ-Wǔ	3	4	5	6	7[e]	8	9	
32		*10*	11	12	13	14	15[f]	16	Lì qiū
33		17	18	19	20	21	22	23	
34		24	25	**26**	27	28	29	1	Chǔ shǔ
35	MONTH 8 Jiǎ-Wǔ	2	3	4	5	6	7	8	
36		9*	10	11	*12*	13	14	15[g]	Bái lù
37		16	17	18	19	20	21	22	
38		23	24	25	26	**27**	28	29	Qiū fēn
39		30	1	2	3	4	5	6	
40	MONTH 9 Jiǎ-Wǔ	7	8	9[h]	10	11	12	*13*	Hán lù
41		14	15	16	17	18	19	20	
42		21	22	23	24	25	26	27	
43		**28**	29	30	1	2	3	4	Shuāng jiàng
44	MONTH 10 Jiǎ-Wǔ	5	6	7	8	9*	10	11	
45		12	*13*	14	15	16	17	18	Lì dōng
46		19	20	21	22	23	24	25	
47		26	27	**28**	29	1	2	3	Xiǎo xuě
48	MONTH 11 Jiǎ-Wǔ	4	5	6	7	8	9	10	
49		11	12	*13*	14	15	16	17	Dà xuě
50		18	19	20	21	22	23	24	
51		25	26	27	28[i]	29	30	1	Dōng zhì
52	MONTH 12 Jiǎ-Wǔ	2	3	4	5	6	7	8	

ISO WEEK	COPTIC 1670/1671‡	Sun	Mon	Tue	Wed	Thu	Fri	Sat	ETHIOPIC 1946/1947‡
53	KOIAK 1670	18	19	20	21	22	23	24	TĀKHŚĀŚ 1946
1		25	26	27	28	29[c]	30	1	
2		2	3	4	5	6[d]	7	8	
3	TŌBE 1670	9	10	11[e]	12	13	14	15	ṬER 1946
4		16	17	18	19	20	21	22	
5		23	24	25	26	27	28	29	
6		30	1	2	3	4	5	6	
7	MESHIR 1670	7	8	9	10	11	12	13	YAKĀTIT 1946
8		14	15	16	17	18	19	20	
9		21	22	23	24	25	26	27	
10		28	29	30	1	2	3	4	
11	PAREMOTEP 1670	5	6	7	8	9	10	11	MAGĀBIT 1946
12		12	13	14	15	16	17	18	
13		19	20	21	22	23	24	25	
14		26	27	28	29	30	1	2	
15	PARMOUTE 1670	3	4	5	6	7	8	9	MIYĀZYĀ 1946
16		10	11	12	13	14	15	16	
17		17[f]	18	19	20	21	22	23	
18		24	25	26	27	28	29[g]	30	
19		1	2	3	4	5	6	7	
20	PASHONS 1670	8	9	10	11	12	13	14	GENBOT 1946
21		15	16	17	18	19	20	21	
22		22	23	24	25	26	27	28	
23		29	30	1	2	3	4	5	
24	PAŌNE 1670	6	7	8	9	10	11	12	SANĒ 1946
25		13	14	15	16	17	18	19	
26		20	21	22	23	24	25	26	
27		27	28	29	30	1	2	3	
28	EPĒP 1670	4	5	6	7	8	9	10	HAMLĒ 1946
29		11	12	13	14	15	16	17	
30		18	19	20	21	22	23	24	
31		25	26	27	28	29	30	1	
32	MESORĒ 1670	2	3	4	5	6	7	8	NAḤASĒ 1946
33		9	10	11	12	13[h]	14	15	
34		16	17	18	19	20	21	22	
35		23	24	25	26	27	28	29	
36	EPAG. 1670	30	1	2	3	4	5	1[a]	PĀG. 1946
37		2	3	4	5	6	7	8	
38	THOOUT 1671	9	10	11	12	13	14	15	MASKARAM 1947
39		16	17[b]	18	19	20	21	22	
40		23	24	25	26	27	28	29	
41		30	1	2	3	4	5	6	
42	PAOPE 1671	7	8	9	10	11	12	13	ṬEQEMT 1947
43		14	15	16	17	18	19	20	
44		21	22	23	24	25	26	27	
45		28	29	30	1	2	3	4	
46	ATHŌR 1671	5	6	7	8	9	10	11	HEDĀR 1947
47		12	13	14	15	16	17	18	
48		19	20	21	22	23	24	25	
49		26	27	28	29	30	1	2	
50	KOIAK 1671	3	4	5	6	7	8	9	TĀKHŚĀŚ 1947
51		10	11	12	13	14	15	16	
52		17	18	19	20	21	22	23	

[a]New Year
[b]Spring (3:53)
[c]Summer (22:54)
[d]Autumn (13:56)
[e]Winter (9:24)
● New moon
◐ First quarter moon
○ Full moon
◑ Last quarter moon

‡Leap year
[a]New Year
[b]Yom Kippur
[c]Sukkot
[d]Winter starts
[e]Ḥanukkah
[f]Purim
[g]Passover
[h]Shavuot
[i]Fast of Av

[a]New Year (4652, Horse)
[b]Lantern Festival
[c]Qīngmíng
[d]Dragon Festival
[e]Qīqiǎo
[f]Hungry Ghosts
[g]Mid-Autumn Festival
[h]Double-Ninth Festival
[i]Dōngzhì
*Start of 60-name cycle

‡Leap year
[a]New Year
[b]Building of the Cross
[c]Christmas
[d]Jesus's Circumcision
[e]Epiphany
[f]Easter
[g]Mary's Announcement
[h]Jesus's Transfiguration

PERSIAN (ASTRONOMICAL) 1332/1333‡

Month	Sun	Mon	Tue	Wed	Thu	Fri	Sat
DEY 1332	6	7	8	9	10	11	12
	13	14	15	16	17	18	19
	20	21	22	23	24	25	26
	27	28	29	30	1	2	3
BAHMAN 1332	4	5	6	7	8	9	10
	11	12	13	14	15	16	17
	18	19	20	21	22	23	24
	25	26	27	28	29	30	1
ESFAND 1332	2	3	4	5	6	7	8
	9	10	11	12	13	14	15
	16	17	18	19	20	21	22
	23	24	25	26	27	28	29
FARVARDĪN 1333	1[a]	2	3	4	5	6	7
	8	9	10	11	12	13[b]	14
	15	16	17	18	19	20	21
	22	23	24	25	26	27	28
	29	30	31	1	2	3	4
ORDĪBEHEŠT 1333	5	6	7	8	9	10	11
	12	13	14	15	16	17	18
	19	20	21	22	23	24	25
	26	27	28	29	30	31	1
XORDĀD 1333	2	3	4	5	6	7	8
	9	10	11	12	13	14	15
	16	17	18	19	20	21	22
	23	24	25	26	27	28	29
	30	31	1	2	3	4	5
TĪR 1333	6	7	8	9	10	11	12
	13	14	15	16	17	18	19
	20	21	22	23	24	25	26
	27	28	29	30	31	1	2
MORDĀD 1333	3	4	5	6	7	8	9
	10	11	12	13	14	15	16
	17	18	19	20	21	22	23
	24	25	26	27	28	29	30
	31	1	2	3	4	5	6
SHAHRĪVAR 1333	7	8	9	10	11	12	13
	14	15	16	17	18	19	20
	21	22	23	24	25	26	27
	28	29	30	31	1	2	3
MEHR 1333	4	5	6	7	8	9	10
	11	12	13	14	15	16	17
	18	19	20	21	22	23	24
	25	26	27	28	29	30	1
ĀBĀN 1333	2	3	4	5	6	7	8
	9	10	11	12	13	14	15
	16	17	18	19	20	21	22
	23	24	25	26	27	28	29
	30	1	2	3	4	5	6
ĀZAR 1333	7	8	9	10	11	12	13
	14	15	16	17	18	19	20
	21	22	23	24	25	26	27
	28	29	30	1	2	3	4
DEY 1333	5	6	7	8	9	10	11

‡Leap year
[a]New Year
[b]Sizdeh Bedar

HINDU LUNAR 2010‡/2011

Month	Sun	Mon	Tue	Wed	Thu	Fri	Sat
MĀRGAŚĪRA 2010	22	23	24	25	26	27	28
	28	29	30	**1**	3	4	5
PAUSHA 2010	6	7	8	9	10	11	12
	13	14	15	16	17	18	19
	20	21	22	23	24	25	26
	27	28	29	30	1	2	3
MĀGHA 2010	4	5	**6**	8	9	10	11
	12	13	14	15	16	17	18
	19	20	20	21	22	23	24
	25	26	27	28[h]	29	**30**	2
PHĀLGUNA 2010	3	4	5	6	7	8	9
	10	11	12	13	14	15[i]	16
	17	18	19	20	21	22	23
	24	25	26	27	28	29	30
CHAITRA 2011	1[a]	2	3	4	**5**	7	8
	9[b]	10	11	12	13	13	14
	15	16	17	18	19	20	21
	22	23	24	25	26	27	**28**
	30	1	2	3	4	5	6
VAIŚĀKHA 2011	7	8	9	10	11	12	13
	14	15	16	17	18	18	19
	20	22	23	24	25	26	27
	28	29	30	1	**2**	4	5
JYAISHTHA 2011	6	7	8	9	9	10	11
	12	13	14	15	16	17	18
	19	20	21	22	23	**24**	26
	27	28	29	30	1	2	3
ĀSHĀDHA 2011	4	5	6	7	8	9	10
	11	12	13	14	15	16	17
	18	19	20	21	22	23	24
	25	26	**27**	29	30	1	2
ŚRĀVAṆA 2011	3	4	5	6	6	7	8
	9	10	11	12	13	14	15
	16	17	18	19	**20**	22	23[c]
	24	25	26	27	28	29	30
BHĀDRAPADA 2011	1	2	3	4[d]	5	6	7
	8	9	10	11	12	13	14
	15	16	17	18	19	20	21
	22	**23**	25	26	27	28	29
	30	1	1	2	3	4	5
ĀŚVINA 2011	6	7	8[e]	9[e]	10[e]	11	12
	13	14	15	**16**	18	19	20
	21	22	23	24	25	26	27
	28	29	30	1[f]	2	3	4
KĀRTTIKA 2011	5	5	6	7	8	9	**10**
	12	13	14	15	16	17	18
	19	20	21	22	23	24	25
	26	27	28	29	30	1	2
MĀRGAŚĪRA 2011	3	4	5	6	7	8	9
	10	11[g]	12	13	**14**	16	17
	18	19	20	21	22	23	24
	25	26	27	28	28	29	30
	1	2	3	4	5	6	7

‡Leap year
[a]New Year (Jaya)
[b]Birthday of Rāma
[c]Birthday of Krishna
[d]Ganēśa Chaturthī
[e]Dashara
[f]Diwali
[g]Birthday of Vishnu
[h]Night of Śiva
[i]Holi

HINDU SOLAR 1875/1876

Month	Sun	Mon	Tue	Wed	Thu	Fri	Sat
PAUSHA 1875	13	14	15	16	17	18	19
	20	21	22	23	24	25	26
MĀGHA 1875	27	28	29	1[b]	2	3	4
	5	6	7	8	9	10	11
	12	13	14	15	16	17	18
	19	20	21	22	23	24	25
PHĀLGUNA 1875	26	27	28	29	30	1	2
	3	4	5	6	7	8	9
	10	11	12	13	14	15	16
	17	18	19	20	21	22	23
	24	25	26	27	28	29	30
CHAITRA 1875	1	2	3	4	5	6	7
	8	9	10	11	12	13	14
	15	16	17	18	19	20	21
	22	23	24	25	26	27	28
VAIŚĀKHA 1876	29	30	1[a]	2	3	4	5
	6	7	8	9	10	11	12
	13	14	15	16	17	18	19
	20	21	22	23	24	25	26
JYAISHTHA 1876	27	28	29	30	31	1	2
	3	4	5	6	7	8	9
	10	11	12	13	14	15	16
	17	18	19	20	21	22	23
	24	25	26	27	28	29	30
ĀSHĀḌHA 1876	31	1	2	3	4	5	6
	7	8	9	10	11	12	13
	14	15	16	17	18	19	20
	21	22	23	24	25	26	27
ŚRĀVAṆA 1876	28	29	30	31	32	1	2
	3	4	5	6	7	8	9
	10	11	12	13	14	15	16
	17	18	19	20	21	22	23
	24	25	26	27	28	29	30
BHĀDRAPADA 1876	31	32	1	2	3	4	5
	6	7	8	9	10	11	12
	13	14	15	16	17	18	19
	20	21	22	23	24	25	26
ĀŚVINA 1876	27	28	29	30	31	1	2
	3	4	5	6	7	8	9
	10	11	12	13	14	15	16
	17	18	19	20	21	22	23
	24	25	26	27	28	29	30
KĀRTTIKA 1876	1	2	3	4	5	6	7
	8	9	10	11	12	13	14
	15	16	17	18	19	20	21
	22	23	24	25	26	27	28
MĀRGAŚĪRA 1876	29	30	1	2	3	4	5
	6	7	8	9	10	11	12
	13	14	15	16	17	18	19
	20	21	22	23	24	25	26
PAUSHA 1876	27	28	29	1	2	3	4
	5	6	7	8	9	10	11
	12	13	14	15	16	17	18

[a]New Year (Plavaṅga)
[b]Pongal

ISLAMIC (ASTRONOMICAL) 1373/1374

Month	Sun	Mon	Tue	Wed	Thu	Fri	Sat
RABĪʿ II 1373	20	21	22	23	24	25	26
JUMĀDĀ I 1373	27	28	29	1	2	3	4
	5	6	7	8	9	10	11
	12	13	14	15	16	17	18
	19	20	21	22	23	24	25
JUMĀDĀ II 1373	26	27	28	29	30	1	2
	3	4	5	6	7	8	9
	10	11	12	13	14	15	16
	17	18	19	20	21	22	23
RAJAB 1373	24	25	26	27	28	29	1
	2	3	4	5	6	7	8
	9	10	11	12	13	14	15
	16	17	18	19	20	21	22
	23	24	25	26	27[d]	28	29
SHAʿBĀN 1373	30	1	2	3	4	5	6
	7	8	9	10	11	12	13
	14	15	16	17	18	19	20
	21	22	23	24	25	26	27
RAMAḌĀN 1373	28	29	1[e]	2	3	4	5
	6	7	8	9	10	11	12
	13	14	15	16	17	18	19
	20	21	22	23	24	25	26
SHAWWĀL 1373	27	28	29	1[f]	2	3	4
	5	6	7	8	9	10	11
	12	13	14	15	16	17	18
	19	20	21	22	23	24	25
DHU AL-QAʿDA 1373	26	27	28	29	30	1	2
	3	4	5	6	7	8	9
	10	11	12	13	14	15	16
	17	18	19	20	21	22	23
	24	25	26	27	28	29	30
DHU AL-ḤIJJA 1373	1	2	3	4	5	6	7
	8	9	10[g]	11	12	13	14
	15	16	17	18	19	20	21
	22	23	24	25	26	27	28
MUḤARRAM 1374	29	30[d]	1[a]	2	3	4	5
	6	7	8	9	10[b]	11	12
	13	14	15	16	17	18	19
	20	21	22	23	24	25	26
ṢAFAR 1374	27	28	29	30	1	2	3
	4	5	6	7	8	9	10
	11	12	13	14	15	16	17
	18	19	20	21	22	23	24
RABĪʿ I 1374	25	26	27	28	29	1	2
	3	4	5	6	7	8	9
	10	11	12[c]	13	14	15	16
	17	18	19	20	21	22	23
RABĪʿ II 1374	24	25	26	27	28	29	1
	2	3	4	5	6	7	8
	9	10	11	12	13	14	15
	16	17	18	19	20	21	22
	23	24	25	26	27	28	29
	30	1	2	3	4	5	6

[a]New Year
[d]New Year (Arithmetic)
[b]ʿAshūrāʾ
[c]Prophet's Birthday
[d]Ascent of the Prophet
[e]Start of Ramaḍān
[f]ʿĪd al-Fiṭr
[g]ʿĪd al-ʾAḍḥā

GREGORIAN 1954

Julian (Sun)	Sun	Mon	Tue	Wed	Thu	Fri	Sat	Month
Dec 14	27	28	29	30	31	1	2	
	3	4	5	6	7[a]	8	9	JANUARY 1954
Dec 28	10	11	12	13	14[b]	15	16	
	17	18	19	20	21	22	23	
Jan 11	24	25	26	27	28	29	30	
	31	1	2	3	4	5	6	
Jan 25	7	8	9	10	11	12	13	FEBRUARY 1954
	14	15	16	17	18	19	20	
Feb 8	21	22	23	24	25	26	27	
	28	1	2	3[c]	4	5	6	
Feb 22	7	8	9	10	11	12	13	MARCH 1954
	14[d]	15	16	17	18	19	20	
Mar 8	21	22	23	24	25	26	27	
	28	29	30	31	1	2	3	
Mar 22	4	5	6	7	8	9	10	APRIL 1954
	11	12	13	14	15	16	17	
Apr 5	18[e]	19	20	21	22	23	24	
	25[f]	26	27	28	29	30	1	
Apr 19	2	3	4	5	6	7	8	MAY 1954
	9	10	11	12	13	14	15	
May 3	16	17	18	19	20	21	22	
	23	24	25	26	27	28	29	
May 17	30	31	1	2	3	4	5	
	6	7	8	9	10	11	12	JUNE 1954
May 31	13	14	15	16	17	18	19	
	20	21	22	23	24	25	26	
Jun 14	27	28	29	30	1	2	3	
	4	5	6	7	8	9	10	JULY 1954
Jun 28	11	12	13	14	15	16	17	
	18	19	20	21	22	23	24	
Jul 12	25	26	27	28	29	30	31	
	1	2	3	4	5	6	7	AUGUST 1954
Jul 26	8	9	10	11	12	13	14	
	15	16	17	18	19	20	21	
Aug 9	22	23	24	25	26	27	28	
	29	30	31	1	2	3	4	
Aug 23	5	6	7	8	9	10	11	SEPTEMBER 1954
	12	13	14	15	16	17	18	
Sep 6	19	20	21	22	23	24	25	
	26	27	28	29	30	1	2	
Sep 20	3	4	5	6	7	8	9	OCTOBER 1954
	10	11	12	13	14	15	16	
Oct 4	17	18	19	20	21	22	23	
	24	25	26	27	28	29	30	
Oct 18	31	1	2	3	4	5	6	
	7	8	9	10	11	12	13	NOVEMBER 1954
Nov 1	14	15	16	17	18	19	20	
	21	22	23	24	25	26	27	
Nov 15	28[g]	29	30	1	2	3	4	
	5	6	7	8	9	10	11	DECEMBER 1954
Nov 29	12	13	14	15	16	17	18	
	19	20	21	22	23	24	25[h]	
Dec 13	26	27	28	29	30	31	1	

[a]Orthodox Christmas
[b]Julian New Year
[c]Ash Wednesday
[d]Feast of Orthodoxy
[e]Easter
[f]Orthodox Easter
[g]Advent
[h]Christmas

1955

Gregorian 1955	Sun	Mon	Tue	Wed	Thu	Fri	Sat	Lunar Phases	ISO Week (Mon)	Julian Day (Sun noon)	Hebrew 5715/5716	Sun	Mon	Tue	Wed	Thu	Fri	Sat	Molad	Chinese Jiă-Wŭ/Yĭ-Wèi‡	Sun	Mon	Tue	Wed	Thu	Fri	Sat	Solar Term	Coptic 1671‡/1672	Sun	Mon	Tue	Wed	Thu	Fri	Sat	Ethiopic 1947‡/1948
January 1955	26	27	28	29	30	31	◐[a]	20:29	52	2435103	Teveth 5715	1[e]	2[e]	3	4	5	6	7	Sat 5h41m14p	Month 12 Jiă-Wŭ	2	3	4	5	6	7	8		Koiak 1671	17	18	19	20	21	22	23	Tākhśāś 1947
	2	3	4	5	6	7	○	12:44	1	2435110		8	9	10	11	12	13	14			9	10*	11	12	13	14	15	Xiăo hán		24	25	26	27	28	29[c]	30	
	9	10	11	12	13	14	◑	22:13	2	2435117		15	16	17	18	19	20	21			16	17	18	19	20	21	22			1	2	3	4	5	6[d]	7	
	16	17	18	19	20	21	22		3	2435124		22	23	24	25	26	27	28			23	24	25	26	27	28	29	Dà hán	Tōbe 1671	8	9	10	11[e]	12	13	14	Ṭer 1947
	23	●	25	26	27	28	29	1:07	4	2435131	Shevat 5715	29	1	2	3	4	5	6	Sun 18h25m15p	Month 1 Yĭ-Wèi	30	1[a]	2	3	4	5	6			15	16	17	18	19	20	21	
February 1955	30	◐	1	2	3	4	5	5:05	5	2435138		7	8	9	10	11	12	13			7	8	9	10	11	12	13	Lì chūn		22	23	24	25	26	27	28	
	6	○	8	9	10	11	12	1:43	6	2435145		14	15	16	17	18	19	20			14	15[b]	16	17	18	19	20		Meshir 1671	29	30	1	2	3	4	5	Yakātit 1947
	13	◑	15	16	17	18	19	19:40	7	2435152		21	22	23	24	25	26	27			21	22	23	24	25	26	27	Yŭ shuĭ		6	7	8	9	10	11	12	
	20	21	●	23	24	25	26	15:54	8	2435159	Adar 5715	28	29	30	1	2	3	4	Tue 7h9m16p	Month 2 Yĭ-Wèi	28	29	1	2	3	4	5			13	14	15	16	17	18	19	
March 1955	27	28	◐	2	3	4	5	12:40	9	2435166		5	6	7	8	9	10	11			6	7	8	9	10	11*	12			20	21	22	23	24	25	26	
	6	7	○	9	10	11	12	15:41	10	2435173		12	13	14[f]	15	16	17	18			13	14	15	16	17	18	19	Jīng zhé	Paremotep 1671	27	28	29	30	1	2	3	Magābit 1947
	13	14	15	◑	17	18	19	16:36	11	2435180		19	20	21	22	23	24	25			20	21	22	23	24	25	26			4	5	6	7	8	9	10	
	20	21[b]	22	23	●	25	26	3:43	12	2435187	Nisan 5715	26	27	28	29	1	2	3	Wed 19h53m17p	Month 3 Yĭ-Wèi	27	28	29	30	1	2	3	Chūn fēn		11	12	13	14	15	16	17	
April 1955	27	28	29	◐	31	1	2	20:10	13	2435194		4	5	6	7	8	9	10			4	5	6	7	8	9	10			18	19	20	21	22	23	24	
	3	4	5	6	○	8	9	6:35	14	2435201		11	12	13[§]	14	15[g]	16	17			11	12	13[c]	14	15	16	17	Qīng míng	Parmoute 1671	25	26	27	28	29	30	1	Miyāzyā 1947
	10	11	12	13	14	◑	16	11:01	15	2435208		18	19	20	21	22	23	24			18	19	20	21	22	23	24	Gŭ yŭ		2	3	4	5	6	7	8	
	17	18	19	20	21	●	23	13:06	16	2435215	Iyyar 5715	25	26	27	28	29	30	1	Fri 8h38m0p	Leap Month 3 Yĭ-Wèi	25	26	27	28	29	1	2			9[f]	10	11	12	13	14	15	
May 1955	24	25	26	27	28	◐	30	4:23	17	2435222		2	3	4	5	6	7	8			3	4	5	6	7	8	9			16	17	18	19	20	21	22	
	1	2	3	4	5	○	7	22:14	18	2435229		9	10	11	12	13	14	15			10	11	12*	13	14	15	16	Lì xià	Pashons 1671	23	24	25	26	27	28	29[g]	Genbot 1947
	8	9	10	11	12	13	14		19	2435236		16	17	18	19	20	21	22			17	18	19	20	21	22	23			30	1	2	3	4	5	6	
	◑	16	17	18	19	20	●	1:42 20:59	20	2435243	Sivan 5715	23	24	25	26	27	28	29	Sat 21h22m1p	Month 4 Yĭ-Wèi	24	25	26	27	28	29	30			7	8	9	10	11	12	13	
June 1955	22	23	24	25	26	27	◐	14:01	21	2435250		1	2	3	4	5	6[h]	7			1	2	3	4	5	6	7	Xiăo măn		14	15	16	17	18	19	20	
	29	30	31	1	2	3	4		22	2435257		8	9	10	11	12	13	14			8	9	10	11	12	13	14			21	22	23	24	25	26	27	
	○	6	7	8	9	10	11	14:08	23	2435264		15	16	17	18	19	20	21			15	16	17	18	19	20	21	Máng zhòng	Paōne 1671	28	29	30	1	2	3	4	Sanē 1947
	12	◑	14	15	16	17	18	12:37	24	2435271	Tammuz 5715	22	23	24	25	26	27	28	Mon 10h6m2p	Month 5 Yĭ-Wèi	22	23	24	25	26	27	28			5	6	7	8	9	10	11	
	19	●	21	22[c]	23	24	25	4:12	25	2435278		29	30	1	2	3	4	5			29	1	2	3	4	5[d]	6	Xià zhì		12	13	14	15	16	17	18	
July 1955	26	◐	28	29	30	1	2	1:44	26	2435285		6	7	8	9	10	11	12			7	8	9	10	11	12	13*			19	20	21	22	23	24	25	
	3	4	○	6	7	8	9	5:29	27	2435292		13	14	15	16	17	18	19			14	15	16	17	18	19	20	Xiăo shŭ	Epēp 1671	26	27	28	29	30	1	2	Ḥamlē 1947
	10	11	◑	13	14	15	16	20:31	28	2435299	Av 5715	20	21	22	23	24	25	26	Tue 22h50m3p	Month 6 Yĭ-Wèi	21	22	23	24	25	26	27			3	4	5	6	7	8	9	
	17	18	●	20	21	22	23	11:34	29	2435306		27	28	29	1	2	3	4			28	29	1	2	3	4	5	Dà shŭ		10	11	12	13	14	15	16	
August 1955	24	25	◐	27	28	29	30	15:59	30	2435313		5	6	7	8	9[i]	10	11			6	7	8	9	10	11	12			17	18	19	20	21	22	23	
	31	1	2	○	4	5	6	19:30	31	2435320		12	13	14	15	16	17	18			13	14	15	16	17	18	19		Mesorē 1671	24	25	26	27	28	29	30	Naḥasē 1947
	7	8	9	10	◑	12	13	2:33	32	2435327	Elul 5715	19	20	21	22	23	24	25	Thu 11h34m4p	Month 7 Yĭ-Wèi	20	21	22	23	24	25	26	Lì qiū		1	2	3	4	5	6	7	
	14	15	16	●	18	19	20	19:58	33	2435334		26	27	28	29	30	1	2			27	28	29	30	1	2	3			8	9	10	11	12	13[h]	14	
	21	22	23	24	◐	26	27	8:52	34	2435341		3	4	5	6	7	8	9			4	5	6	7[e]	8	9	10	Chŭ shŭ		15	16	17	18	19	20	21	
September 1955	28	29	30	31	1	○	3	7:59	35	2435348		10	11	12	13	14	15	16			11	12	13	14*	15[f]	16	17		Epag. 1671	22	23	24	25	26	27	28	Pāg. 1947
	4	5	6	7	8	◑	10	7:59	36	2435355	Tishri 5716	17	18	19	20	21	22	23	Sat 0h18m5p	Month 8 Yĭ-Wèi	18	19	20	21	22	23	24	Bái lù	Thoout 1672	29	30	1	2	3	4	5	Maskaram 1948
	11	12	13	14	15	●	17	6:19	37	2435362		24	25	26	27	28	29	1[a]			25	26	27	28	29	1	2			6	1[a]	2	3	4	5	6	
	18	19	20	21	22	23[d]	◐	3:40	38	2435369		2[a]	3	4	5	6	7	8			3	4	5	6	7	8	9	Qiū fēn		7	8	9	10	11	12	13	
October 1955	25	26	27	28	29	30	○	19:17	39	2435376		9	10[b]	11	12	13	14	15[c]			10	11	12	13	14	15[g]	16			14	15	16	17[b]	18	19	20	
	2	3	4	5	6	7	◑	14:04	40	2435383		16	17	18	19	20	21	22			17	18	19	20	21	22	23			21	22	23	24	25	26	27	
	9	10	11	12	13	14	●	19:32	41	2435390	Heshvan 5716	23	24	25	26	27	28	29	Sun 13h2m6p	Month 9 Yĭ-Wèi	24	25	26	27	28	29	30	Hán lù	Paope 1672	28	29	30	1	2	3	4	Ṭeqemt 1948
	16	17	18	19	20	21	22		42	2435397		30	1	2	3	4	5	6			1	2	3	4	5	6	7			5	6	7	8	9	10	11	
	◐	24	25	26	27	28	29	23:05	43	2435404		7	8	9	10	11	12	13			8	9[h]	10	11	12	13	14	Shuāng jiàng		12	13	14	15	16	17	18	
November 1955	30	○	1	2	3	4	5	6:04	44	2435411		14	15	16	17	18	19	20			15*	16	17	18	19	20	21			19	20	21	22	23	24	25	
	◑	7	8	9	10	11	12	21:56	45	2435418	Kislev 5716	21	22	23	24	25	26	27	Tue 1h46m7p	Month 10 Yĭ-Wèi	22	23	24	25	26	27	28	Lì dōng	Athōr 1672	26	27	28	29	30	1	2	Ḫedār 1948
	13	●	15	16	17	18	19	12:01	46	2435425		28	29	30	1	2	3	4			29	1	2	3	4	5	6			3	4	5	6	7	8	9	
	20	21	◐	23	24	25	26	17:29	47	2435432		5	6	7	8	9	10	11			7	8	9	10	11	12	13	Xiăo xuě		10	11	12	13	14	15	16	
December 1955	27	28	○	30	1	2	3	16:50	48	2435439		12	13	14	15	16	17	18			14	15	16	17	18	19	20			17	18	19	20	21	22	23	
	4	5	◑	7	8	9	10	8:35	49	2435446	Teveth 5716	19	20	21[d]	22	23	24	25[e]	Wed 14h30m8p	Month 11 Yĭ-Wèi	21	22	23	24	25	26	27	Dà xuě	Koiak 1672	24	25	26	27	28	29	30	Tākhśāś 1948
	11	12	13	●	15	16	17	7:07	50	2435453		26[e]	27[e]	28[e]	29[e]	30[e]	1[e]	2[e]			28	29	30	1	2	3	4			1	2	3	4	5	6	7	
	18	19	20	21	◐[e]	23	24	9:39	51	2435460		3	4	5	6	7	8	9			5	6	7	8	9[i]	10	11	Dōng zhì		8	9	10	11	12	13	14	
	25	26	27	28	○	30	31	3:44	52	2435467		10	11	12	13	14	15	16			12	13	14	15	16*	17	18			15	16	17	18	19	20	21	

[a]New Year
[b]Spring (9:35)
[c]Summer (4:32)
[d]Autumn (19:41)
[e]Winter (15:11)
● New moon
◐ First quarter moon
○ Full moon
◑ Last quarter moon

[a]New Year
[b]Yom Kippur
[c]Sukkot
[d]Winter starts
[e]Ḥanukkah
§שולמית חוה הלוי נולדה
[f]Purim
[g]Passover
[h]Shavuot
[i]Fast of Av

‡Leap year
[a]New Year (4653, Sheep)
[b]Lantern Festival
[c]Qīngmíng
[d]Dragon Festival
[e]Qīqiăo
[f]Hungry Ghosts
[g]Mid-Autumn Festival
[h]Double-Ninth Festival
[i]Dōngzhì
*Start of 60-name cycle

‡Leap year
[a]New Year
[b]Building of the Cross
[c]Christmas
[d]Jesus's Circumcision
[e]Epiphany
[f]Easter
[g]Mary's Announcement
[h]Jesus's Transfiguration

PERSIAN (ASTRONOMICAL) 1333‡/1334

Month	Sun	Mon	Tue	Wed	Thu	Fri	Sat
DEY 1333	5	6	7	8	9	10	11
	12	13	14	15	16	17	18
	19	20	21	22	23	24	25
BAHMAN 1333	26	27	28	29	30	1	2
	3	4	5	6	7	8	9
	10	11	12	13	14	15	16
	17	18	19	20	21	22	23
	24	25	26	27	28	29	30
ESFAND 1333	1	2	3	4	5	6	7
	8	9	10	11	12	13	14
	15	16	17	18	19	20	21
	22	23	24	25	26	27	28
FARVARDĪN 1334	29	30	1[a]	2	3	4	5
	6	7	8	9	10	11	12
	13[b]	14	15	16	17	18	19
	20	21	22	23	24	25	26
ORDĪBEHEŠT 1334	27	28	29	30	31	1	2
	3	4	5	6	7	8	9
	10	11	12	13	14	15	16
	17	18	19	20	21	22	23
	24	25	26	27	28	29	30
XORDĀD 1334	31	1	2	3	4	5	6
	7	8	9	10	11	12	13
	14	15	16	17	18	19	20
	21	22	23	24	25	26	27
TĪR 1334	28	29	30	31	1	2	3
	4	5	6	7	8	9	10
	11	12	13	14	15	16	17
	18	19	20	21	22	23	24
	25	26	27	28	29	30	31
MORDĀD 1334	1	2	3	4	5	6	7
	8	9	10	11	12	13	14
	15	16	17	18	19	20	21
	22	23	24	25	26	27	28
SHAHRĪVAR 1334	29	30	31	1	2	3	4
	5	6	7	8	9	10	11
	12	13	14	15	16	17	18
	19	20	21	22	23	24	25
MEHR 1334	26	27	28	29	30	31	1
	2	3	4	5	6	7	8
	9	10	11	12	13	14	15
	16	17	18	19	20	21	22
	23	24	25	26	27	28	29
ĀBĀN 1334	30	1	2	3	4	5	6
	7	8	9	10	11	12	13
	14	15	16	17	18	19	20
	21	22	23	24	25	26	27
ĀZAR 1334	28	29	30	1	2	3	4
	5	6	7	8	9	10	11
	12	13	14	15	16	17	18
	19	20	21	22	23	24	25
DEY 1334	26	27	28	29	30	1	2
	3	4	5	6	7	8	9

‡Leap year
[a]New Year
[b]Sizdeh Bedar

HINDU LUNAR 2011/2012‡

Month	Sun	Mon	Tue	Wed	Thu	Fri	Sat
PAUSHA 2011	1	2	3	4	5	6	7
	8	9	11	12	13	14	15
	16	17	18	19	20	21	22
	23	24	25	26	27	28	29
MĀGHA 2011	30	1	2	3	4	5	6
	7	8	9	10	11	12	13
	14	16	17	18	19	20	20
	21	22	23	24	25	26	27
PHĀLGUNA 2011	28[h]	29	30	1	2	3	4
	5	6	7	9	10	11	12
	13	14	15[i]	16	17	18	19
	20	21	22	22	23	24	25
CHAITRA 2012	26	27	28	29	30	1[a]	3
	4	5	6	7	8	9[b]	10
	11	12	13	14	15	16	17
	18	19	20	21	22	23	24
VAIŚĀKHA 2012	25	26	27	28	29	30	1
	2	3	4	5	7	8	9
	10	11	12	13	14	15	16
	17	17	18	19	20	21	22
	23	24	25	26	27	28	30
JYAISHTHA 2012	1	2	3	4	5	6	7
	8	9	10	11	12	13	14
	15	16	17	18	19	20	21
	22	23	24	25	26	27	28
ĀSHĀDHA 2012	29	30	1	3	4	5	6
	7	8	9	10	11	12	13
	13	14	15	16	17	18	19
	20	21	22	23	24	26	27
ŚRĀVAṆA 2012	28	29	30	1	2	3	4
	5	6	7	8	9	10	11
	12	13	14	15	16	17	18
	19	20	21	22	23[c]	24	25
LEAP BHĀDRAPADA 2012	26	27	29	30	1	2	3
	4	5	6	7	8	9	10
	10	11	12	13	14	15	16
	17	18	19	20	22	23	24
BHĀDRAPADA 2012	25	26	27	28	29	30	1
	2	3	4[d]	5	6	7	8
	9	10	11	12	13	14	15
	16	17	18	19	20	21	22
	23	24	26	27	28	29	30
ĀŚVINA 2012	1	2	3	4	5	5	6
	7	8[e]	9[e]	10[e]	11	12	13
	14	15	16	17	19	20	21
	22	23	24	25	26	27	28
KĀRTTIKA 2012	29	30	1[f]	2	3	4	5
	6	7	8	9	10	11	12
	13	14	15	16	17	18	19
	20	21	22	24	25	26	27
MĀRGAŚĪRA 2012	28	28	29	30	1	2	3
	4	5	6	7	8	9	10
	11[g]	12	13	14	15	17	18

‡Leap year
[a]New Year (Manmatha)
[b]Birthday of Rāma
[c]Birthday of Krishna
[d]Ganēśa Chaturthī
[e]Dashara
[f]Diwali
[g]Birthday of Vishnu
[h]Night of Śiva
[i]Holi

HINDU SOLAR 1876/1877‡

Month	Sun	Mon	Tue	Wed	Thu	Fri	Sat
PAUSHA 1876	12	13	14	15	16	17	18
	19	20	21	22	23	24	25
MĀGHA 1876	26	27	28	29	30	1[b]	2
	3	4	5	6	7	8	9
	10	11	12	13	14	15	16
	17	18	19	20	21	22	23
PHĀLGUNA 1876	24	25	26	27	28	29	1
	2	3	4	5	6	7	8
	9	10	11	12	13	14	15
	16	17	18	19	20	21	22
	23	24	25	26	27	28	29
CHAITRA 1876	30	1	2	3	4	5	6
	7	8	9	10	11	12	13
	14	15	16	17	18	19	20
	21	22	23	24	25	26	27
VAIŚĀKHA 1877	28	29	30	1[a]	2	3	4
	5	6	7	8	9	10	11
	12	13	14	15	16	17	18
	19	20	21	22	23	24	25
JYAISHTHA 1877	26	27	28	29	30	31	1
	2	3	4	5	6	7	8
	9	10	11	12	13	14	15
	16	17	18	19	20	21	22
	23	24	25	26	27	28	29
ĀSHĀDHA 1877	30	31	32	1	2	3	4
	5	6	7	8	9	10	11
	12	13	14	15	16	17	18
	19	20	21	22	23	24	25
ŚRĀVAṆA 1877	26	27	28	29	30	31	1
	2	3	4	5	6	7	8
	9	10	11	12	13	14	15
	16	17	18	19	20	21	22
	23	24	25	26	27	28	29
BHĀDRAPADA 1877	30	31	32	1	2	3	4
	5	6	7	8	9	10	11
	12	13	14	15	16	17	18
	19	20	21	22	23	24	25
ĀŚVINA 1877	26	27	28	29	30	31	1
	2	3	4	5	6	7	8
	9	10	11	12	13	14	15
	16	17	18	19	20	21	22
	23	24	25	26	27	28	29
KĀRTTIKA 1877	30	1	2	3	4	5	6
	7	8	9	10	11	12	13
	14	15	16	17	18	19	20
	21	22	23	24	25	26	27
MĀRGAŚĪRA 1877	28	29	30	1	2	3	4
	5	6	7	8	9	10	11
	12	13	14	15	16	17	18
	19	20	21	22	23	24	25
PAUSHA 1877	26	27	28	29	30	1	2
	3	4	5	6	7	8	9
	10	11	12	13	14	15	16

‡Leap year
[a]New Year (Kīlaka)
[b]Pongal

ISLAMIC (ASTRONOMICAL) 1374/1375

Month	Sun	Mon	Tue	Wed	Thu	Fri	Sat
JUMĀDĀ I 1374	30	1	2	3	4	5	6
	7	8	9	10	11	12	13
	14	15	16	17	18	19	20
	21	22	23	24	25	26	27
JUMĀDĀ II 1374	28	29	1	2	3	4	5
	6	7	8	9	10	11	12
	13	14	15	16	17	18	19
	20	21	22	23	24	25	26
RAJAB 1374	27	28	29	30	1	2	3
	4	5	6	7	8	9	10
	11	12	13	14	15	16	17
	18	19	20	21	22	23	24
SHA'BĀN 1374	25	26	27[d]	28	29	1	2
	3	4	5	6	7	8	9
	10	11	12	13	14	15	16
	17	18	19	20	21	22	23
	24	25	26	27	28	29	30
RAMAḌĀN 1374	1[e]	2	3	4	5	6	7
	8	9	10	11	12	13	14
	15	16	17	18	19	20	21
	22	23	24	25	26	27	28
SHAWWĀL 1374	29	1[f]	2	3	4	5	6
	7	8	9	10	11	12	13
	14	15	16	17	18	19	20
	21	22	23	24	25	26	27
DHU AL-QA'DA 1374	28	29	1	2	3	4	5
	6	7	8	9	10	11	12
	13	14	15	16	17	18	19
	20	21	22	23	24	25	26
DHU AL-ḤIJJA 1374	27	28	29	30	1	2	3
	4	5	6	7	8	9	10[g]
	11	12	13	14	15	16	17
	18	19	20	21	22	23	24
MUḤARRAM 1375	25	26	27	28	29	30	1[a]
	2	3	4	5	6	7	8
	9	10[b]	11	12	13	14	15
	16	17	18	19	20	21	22
	23	24	25	26	27	28	29
ṢAFAR 1375	30	1	2	3	4	5	6
	7	8	9	10	11	12	13
	14	15	16	17	18	19	20
	21	22	23	24	25	26	27
RABĪ' I 1375	28	29	1	2	3	4	5
	6	7	8	9	10	11	12[c]
	13	14	15	16	17	18	19
	20	21	22	23	24	25	26
RABĪ' II 1375	27	28	29	1	2	3	4
	5	6	7	8	9	10	11
	12	13	14	15	16	17	18
	19	20	21	22	23	24	25
JUMĀDĀ I 1375	26	27	28	29	30	1	2
	3	4	5	6	7	8	9
	10	11	12	13	14	15	16

[a]New Year
[b]'Ashūrā'
[c]Prophet's Birthday
[d]Ascent of the Prophet
[e]Start of Ramaḍān
[f]'Īd al-Fiṭr
[g]'Īd al-'Aḍḥā

GREGORIAN 1955

Julian (Sun)	Month	Sun	Mon	Tue	Wed	Thu	Fri	Sat
Dec 13	JANUARY 1955	26	27	28	29	30	31	1
		2	3	4	5	6	7[a]	8
Dec 27		9	10	11	12	13	14[b]	15
		16	17	18	19	20	21	22
Jan 10		23	24	25	26	27	28	29
	FEBRUARY 1955	30	31	1	2	3	4	5
Jan 24		6	7	8	9	10	11	12
		13	14	15	16	17	18	19
Feb 7		20	21	22	23[c]	24	25	26
	MARCH 1955	27	28	1	2	3	4	5
Feb 21		6[d]	7	8	9	10	11	12
		13	14	15	16	17	18	19
Mar 7		20	21	22	23	24	25	26
	APRIL 1955	27	28	29	30	31	1	2
Mar 21		3	4	5	6	7	8	9
		10[e]	11	12	13	14	15	16
Apr 4		17[f]	18	19	20	21	22	23
		24	25	26	27	28	29	30
Apr 18	MAY 1955	1	2	3	4	5	6	7
		8	9	10	11	12	13	14
May 2		15	16	17	18	19	20	21
		22	23	24	25	26	27	28
May 16	JUNE 1955	29	30	31	1	2	3	4
		5	6	7	8	9	10	11
May 30		12	13	14	15	16	17	18
		19	20	21	22	23	24	25
Jun 13	JULY 1955	26	27	28	29	30	1	2
		3	4	5	6	7	8	9
Jun 27		10	11	12	13	14	15	16
		17	18	19	20	21	22	23
Jul 11		24	25	26	27	28	29	30
	AUGUST 1955	31	1	2	3	4	5	6
Jul 25		7	8	9	10	11	12	13
		14	15	16	17	18	19	20
Aug 8		21	22	23	24	25	26	27
	SEPTEMBER 1955	28	29	30	31	1	2	3
Aug 22		4	5	6	7	8	9	10
		11	12	13	14	15	16	17
Sep 5		18	19	20	21	22	23	24
	OCTOBER 1955	25	26	27	28	29	30	1
Sep 19		2	3	4	5	6	7	8
		9	10	11	12	13	14	15
Oct 3		16	17	18	19	20	21	22
		23	24	25	26	27	28	29
Oct 17	NOVEMBER 1955	30	31	1	2	3	4	5
		6	7	8	9	10	11	12
Oct 31		13	14	15	16	17	18	19
		20	21	22	23	24	25	26
Nov 14	DECEMBER 1955	27[g]	28	29	30	1	2	3
		4	5	6	7	8	9	10
Nov 28		11	12	13	14	15	16	17
		18	19	20	21	22	23	24
Dec 12		25[h]	26	27	28	29	30	31

[a]Orthodox Christmas
[b]Julian New Year
[c]Ash Wednesday
[d]Feast of Orthodoxy
[e]Easter
[f]Orthodox Easter
[g]Advent
[h]Christmas

1956

GREGORIAN 1956‡

Month	Sun	Mon	Tue	Wed	Thu	Fri	Sat	Lunar Phases	ISO WEEK (Mon)	JULIAN DAY (Sun noon)
JANUARY 1956	1[a]	2	3	◑	5	6	7	22:41	1	2435474
	8	9	10	11	12	●	14	3:01	2	2435481
	15	16	17	18	19	◐	21	22:58	3	2435488
	22	23	24	25	26	○	28	14:40	4	2435495
	29	30	31	1	2	◑	4	16:08	5	2435502
FEBRUARY 1956	5	6	7	8	9	10	●	21:38	6	2435509
	12	13	14	15	16	17	18		7	2435516
	◐	20	21	22	23	24	25	9:21	8	2435523
	○	27	28	29	1	2	3	1:42	9	2435530
MARCH 1956	◑	5	6	7	8	9	10	11:53	10	2435537
	11	●	13	14	15	16	17	13:37	11	2435544
	18	◐	20[b]	21	22	23	24	17:13	12	2435551
	25	○	27	28	29	30	31	13:11	13	2435558
APRIL 1956	1	2	◑	4	5	6	7	8:06	14	2435565
	8	9	10	●	12	13	14	2:39	15	2435572
	15	16	◐	18	19	20	21	23:28	16	2435579
	22	23	24	○	26	27	28	1:40	17	2435586
	29	30	1	2	◑	4	5	2:55	18	2435593
MAY 1956	6	7	8	9	●	11	12	13:05	19	2435600
	13	14	15	16	◐	18	19	5:15	20	2435607
	20	21	22	23	○	25	26	15:26	21	2435614
	27	28	29	30	31	◑	2	19:13	22	2435621
JUNE 1956	3	4	5	6	7	●	9	21:29	23	2435628
	10	11	12	13	14	◐	16	11:56	24	2435635
	17	18	19	20	21[c]	22	○	6:13	25	2435642
	24	25	26	27	28	29	30		26	2435649
JULY 1956	◑	2	3	4	5	6	7	8:41 4:38	27	2435656
	●	9	10	11	12	13	◐	20:46	28	2435663
	15	16	17	18	19	20	21		29	2435670
	○	23	24	25	26	27	28	21:29	30	2435677
	29	◑	31	1	2	3	4	19:31	31	2435684
AUGUST 1956	5	●	7	8	9	10	11	11:25	32	2435691
	12	◐	14	15	16	17	18	8:45	33	2435698
	19	20	○	22	23	24	25	12:38	34	2435705
	26	27	28	◑	30	31	1	4:13	35	2435712
SEPTEMBER 1956	2	3	●	5	6	7	8	18:57	36	2435719
	9	10	11	◐	13	14	15	0:13	37	2435726
	16	17	18	19	○	21	22	3:19	38	2435733
	23[d]	24	25	26	◑	28	29	11:25	39	2435740
	30	1	2	3	●	5	6	4:24	40	2435747
OCTOBER 1956	7	8	9	10	◐	12	13	18:44	41	2435754
	14	15	16	17	18	○	20	17:25	42	2435761
	21	22	23	24	25	◑	27	18:02	43	2435768
	28	29	30	31	1	●	3	16:43	44	2435775
NOVEMBER 1956	4	5	6	7	8	9	◐	15:09	45	2435782
	11	12	13	14	15	16	17		46	2435789
	○	19	20	21	22	23	24	6:44	47	2435796
	◑	26	27	28	29	30	1	1:13	48	2435803
DECEMBER 1956	●	3	4	5	6	7	8	8:12	49	2435810
	9	◐	11	12	13	14	15	11:51	50	2435817
	16	○	18	19	20	21[e]	22	19:06	51	2435824
	23	◑	25	26	27	28	29	10:10	52	2435831
	30	31	●	2	3	4	5	2:14	1	2435838

HEBREW 5716/5717‡

ISO WEEK	Month	Sun	Mon	Tue	Wed	Thu	Fri	Sat	Molad
1	TEVETH 5716	17	18	19	20	21	22	23	Fri 3h14m9p
2		24	25	26	27	28	29	1	
3	SHEVAT 5716	2	3	4	5	6	7	8	
4		9	10	11	12	13	14	15	
5		16	17	18	19	20	21	22	
6		23	24	25	26	27	28	29	
7		30	1	2	3	4	5	6	Sat 15h58m10p
8	ADAR 5716	7	8	9	10	11	12	13	
9		14[f]	15	16	17	18	19	20	
10		21	22	23	24	25	26	27	
11		28	29	1	2	3	4	5	Mon 4h42m11p
12	NISAN 5716	6	7	8	9	10	11	12	
13		13	14	15[g]	16	17	18	19	
14		20	21	22	23	24	25	26	
15		27	28	29	30	1	2	3	Tue 17h26m12p
16	IYYAR 5716	4	5	6	7	8	9	10	
17		11	12	13	14	15	16	17	
18		18	19	20	21	22	23	24	
19		25	26	27	28	29	1	2	Thu 6h10m13p
20	SIVAN 5716	3	4	5	6[h]	7	8	9	
21		10	11	12	13	14	15	16	
22		17	18	19	20	21	22	23	
23		24	25	26	27	28	29	30	Fri 18h54m14p
24	TAMMUZ 5716	1	2	3	4	5	6	7	
25		8	9	10	11	12	13	14	
26		15	16	17	18	19	20	21	
27		22	23	24	25	26	27	28	
28		29	1	2	3	4	5	6	Sun 7h38m15p
29	AV 5716	7	8	9[i]	10	11	12	13	
30		14	15	16	17	18	19	20	
31		21	22	23	24	25	26	27	
32		28	29	30	1	2	3	4	Mon 20h22m16p
33	ELUL 5716	5	6	7	8	9	10	11	
34		12	13	14	15	16	17	18	
35		19	20	21	22	23	24	25	
36		26	27	28	29	1[a]	2[a]	3	Wed 9h6m17p
37	TISHRI 5717	4	5	6	7	8	9	10[b]	
38		11	12	13	14	15[c]	16	17	
39		18	19	20	21	22	23	24	
40		25	26	27	28	29	30	1	Thu 21h51m0p
41	HESHVAN 5717	2	3	4	5	6	7	8	
42		9	10	11	12	13	14	15	
43		16	17	18	19	20	21	22	
44		23	24	25	26	27	28	29	
45		30	1	2	3	4	5	6	Sat 10h35m1p
46	KISLEV 5717	7	8	9	10	11	12	13	
47		14	15	16	17	18	19	20	
48		21	22	23	24	25[e]	26[e]	27[e]	
49		28[e]	29[e]	30[e]	1[d][e]	2[e]	3	4	Sun 23h19m2p
50	TEVETH 5717	5	6	7	8	9	10	11	
51		12	13	14	15	16	17	18	
52		19	20	21	22	23	24	25	
53		26	27	28	29	1	2	3	Tue 12h3m3p

CHINESE Yǐ-Wèi‡/Bǐng-Shēn

ISO WEEK	Month	Sun	Mon	Tue	Wed	Thu	Fri	Sat	Solar Term
1	MONTH 11 Yǐ-Wèi	19	20	21	22	23	24	25	Xiǎo hán
2		26	27	28	29	30	1	2	
3	MONTH 12 Yǐ-Wèi	3	4	5	6	7	8	9	Dà hán
4		10	11	12	13	14	15	16	
5		17	18	19	20	21	22	23	
6		24	25	26	27	28	29	30	Lì chūn
7	MONTH 1 Bǐng-Shēn	1[a]	2	3	4	5	6	7	
8		8	9	10	11	12	13	14	Yǔ shuǐ
9		15[b]	16*	17	18	19	20	21	
10		22	23	24	25	26	27	28	Jīng zhé
11		29	1	2	3	4	5	6	
12	MONTH 2 Bǐng-Shēn	7	8	9	10	11	12	13	Chūn fēn
13		14	15	16	17	18	19	20	
14		21	22	23	24	25[c]	26	27	Qīng míng
15		28	29	30	1	2	3	4	
16	MONTH 3 Bǐng-Shēn	5	6	7	8	9	10	11	Gǔ yǔ
17		12	13	14	15	16	17*	18	
18		19	20	21	22	23	24	25	Lì xià
19		26	27	28	29	1	2	3	
20	MONTH 4 Bǐng-Shēn	4	5	6	7	8	9	10	
21		11	12	13	14	15	16	17	Xiǎo mǎn
22		18	19	20	21	22	23	24	
23		25	26	27	28	29	30	1	Máng zhòng
24	MONTH 5 Bǐng-Shēn	2	3	4	5[d]	6	7	8	
25		9	10	11	12	13	14	15	Xià zhì
26		16	17	18*	19	20	21	22	
27		23	24	25	26	27	28	29	Xiǎo shǔ
28		1	2	3	4	5	6	7	
29	MONTH 6 Bǐng-Shēn	8	9	10	11	12	13	14	
30		15	16	17	18	19	20	21	Dà shǔ
31		22	23	24	25	26	27	28	
32		29	1	2	3	4	5	6	Lì qiū
33	MONTH 7 Bǐng-Shēn	7[e]	8	9	10	11	12	13	
34		14	15[f]	16	17	18	19	20*	Chǔ shǔ
35		21	22	23	24	25	26	27	
36		28	29	30	1	2	3	4	Bái lù
37	MONTH 8 Bǐng-Shēn	5	6	7	8	9	10	11	
38		12	13	14	15[g]	16	17	18	
39		19	20	21	22	23	24	25	Qiū fēn
40		26	27	28	29	1	2	3	
41	MONTH 9 Bǐng-Shēn	4	5	6	7	8	9[h]	10	Hán lù
42		11	12	13	14	15	16	17	
43		18	19	20	21*	22	23	24	Shuāng jiàng
44		25	26	27	28	29	30	1	
45	MONTH 10 Bǐng-Shēn	2	3	4	5	6	7	8	Lì dōng
46		9	10	11	12	13	14	15	
47		16	17	18	19	20	21	22	Xiǎo xuě
48		23	24	25	26	27	28	29	
49		1	2	3	4	5	6	7	Dà xuě
50	MONTH 11 Bǐng-Shēn	8	9	10	11	12	13	14	
51		15	16	17	18	19	20	21[i]	Dōng zhì
52		22*	23	24	25	26	27	28	
53		29	30	1	2	3	4	5	Xiǎo hán

COPTIC 1672/1673 — ETHIOPIC 1948/1949

ISO WEEK	Coptic Month	Sun	Mon	Tue	Wed	Thu	Fri	Sat	Ethiopic Month
1	KOIAK 1672	22	23	24	25	26	27	28	TĀKHŚĀŚ 1948
2		29[c]	30	1	2	3	4	5	
3	TŌBE 1672	6[d]	7	8	9	10	11[e]	12	ṬER 1948
4		13	14	15	16	17	18	19	
5		20	21	22	23	24	25	26	
6		27	28	29	30	1	2	3	
7	MESHIR 1672	4	5	6	7	8	9	10	YAKĀTIT 1948
8		11	12	13	14	15	16	17	
9		18	19	20	21	22	23	24	
10		25	26	27	28	29	30	1	
11	PAREMOTEP 1672	2	3	4	5	6	7	8	MAGĀBIT 1948
12		9	10	11	12	13	14	15	
13		16	17	18	19	20	21	22	
14		23	24	25	26	27	28	29	
15		30	1	2	3	4	5	6	
16	PARMOUTE 1672	7	8	9	10	11	12	13	MIYĀZYĀ 1948
17		14	15	16	17	18	19	20	
18		21	22	23	24	25	26	27	
19		28[f]	29[g]	30	1	2	3	4	
20	PASHONS 1672	5	6	7	8	9	10	11	GENBOT 1948
21		12	13	14	15	16	17	18	
22		19	20	21	22	23	24	25	
23		26	27	28	29	30	1	2	
24	PAŌNE 1672	3	4	5	6	7	8	9	SANĒ 1948
25		10	11	12	13	14	15	16	
26		17	18	19	20	21	22	23	
27		24	25	26	27	28	29	30	
28	EPĒP 1672	1	2	3	4	5	6	7	ḤAMLĒ 1948
29		8	9	10	11	12	13	14	
30		15	16	17	18	19	20	21	
31		22	23	24	25	26	27	28	
32		29	30	1	2	3	4	5	
33	MESORĒ 1672	6	7	8	9	10	11	12	NAHASĒ 1948
34		13[h]	14	15	16	17	18	19	
35		20	21	22	23	24	25	26	
36		27	28	29	30	1	2	3	
37	EPAG. 1672	4	5	1[a]	2	3	4	5	PĀG. 1948
38	THOOUT 1673	6	7	8	9	10	11	12	MASKARAM 1949
39		13	14	15	16	17[b]	18	19	
40		20	21	22	23	24	25	26	
41		27	28	29	30	1	2	3	
42	PAOPE 1673	4	5	6	7	8	9	10	ṬEQEMT 1949
43		11	12	13	14	15	16	17	
44		18	19	20	21	22	23	24	
45		25	26	27	28	29	30	1	
46	ATHŌR 1673	2	3	4	5	6	7	8	ḤEDĀR 1949
47		9	10	11	12	13	14	15	
48		16	17	18	19	20	21	22	
49		23	24	25	26	27	28	29	
50		30	1	2	3	4	5	6	
51	KOIAK 1673	7	8	9	10	11	12	13	TĀKHŚĀŚ 1949
52		14	15	16	17	18	19	20	
53		21	22	23	24	25	26	27	

Gregorian notes:
‡Leap year
[a]New Year
[b]Spring (15:21)
[c]Summer (10:24)
[d]Autumn (1:35)
[e]Winter (21:00)
● New moon
◐ First quarter moon
○ Full moon
◑ Last quarter moon

Hebrew notes:
‡Leap year
[a]New Year
[b]Yom Kippur
[c]Sukkot
[d]Winter starts
[e]Ḥanukkah
[f]Purim
[g]Passover
[h]Shavuot
[i]Fast of Av

Chinese notes:
‡Leap year
[a]New Year (4654, Monkey)
[b]Lantern Festival
[c]Qīngmíng
[d]Dragon Festival
[e]Qīqiǎo
[f]Hungry Ghosts
[g]Mid-Autumn Festival
[h]Double-Ninth Festival
[i]Dōngzhì
*Start of 60-name cycle

Coptic/Ethiopic notes:
[a]New Year
[b]Building of the Cross
[c]Christmas
[d]Jesus's Circumcision
[e]Epiphany
[f]Easter
[g]Mary's Announcement
[h]Jesus's Transfiguration

PERSIAN (ASTRONOMICAL) 1334/1335

Month	Sun	Mon	Tue	Wed	Thu	Fri	Sat
DEY 1334	10	11	12	13	14	15	16
	17	18	19	20	21	22	23
	24	25	26	27	28	29	30
BAHMAN 1334	1	2	3	4	5	6	7
	8	9	10	11	12	13	14
	15	16	17	18	19	20	21
	22	23	24	25	26	27	28
ESFAND 1334	29	30	1	2	3	4	5
	6	7	8	9	10	11	12
	13	14	15	16	17	18	19
	20	21	22	23	24	25	26
FARVARDĪN 1335	27	28	29	1[a]	2	3	4
	5	6	7	8	9	10	11
	12	13[b]	14	15	16	17	18
	19	20	21	22	23	24	25
ORDĪBEHEŠT 1335	26	27	28	29	30	31	1
	2	3	4	5	6	7	8
	9	10	11	12	13	14	15
	16	17	18	19	20	21	22
	23	24	25	26	27	28	29
XORDĀD 1335	30	31	1	2	3	4	5
	6	7	8	9	10	11	12
	13	14	15	16	17	18	19
	20	21	22	23	24	25	26
TĪR 1335	27	28	29	30	31	1	2
	3	4	5	6	7	8	9
	10	11	12	13	14	15	16
	17	18	19	20	21	22	23
	24	25	26	27	28	29	30
MORDĀD 1335	31	1	2	3	4	5	6
	7	8	9	10	11	12	13
	14	15	16	17	18	19	20
	21	22	23	24	25	26	27
SHAHRĪVAR 1335	28	29	30	31	1	2	3
	4	5	6	7	8	9	10
	11	12	13	14	15	16	17
	18	19	20	21	22	23	24
	25	26	27	28	29	30	31
MEHR 1335	1	2	3	4	5	6	7
	8	9	10	11	12	13	14
	15	16	17	18	19	20	21
	22	23	24	25	26	27	28
ĀBĀN 1335	29	30	1	2	3	4	5
	6	7	8	9	10	11	12
	13	14	15	16	17	18	19
	20	21	22	23	24	25	26
ĀZAR 1335	27	28	29	30	1	2	3
	4	5	6	7	8	9	10
	11	12	13	14	15	16	17
	18	19	20	21	22	23	24
DEY 1335	25	26	27	28	29	30	1
	2	3	4	5	6	7	8
	9	10	11	12	13	14	15

[a]New Year
[b]Sizdeh Bedar

HINDU LUNAR 2012‡/2013

Month	Sun	Mon	Tue	Wed	Thu	Fri	Sat
MĀRGAŚĪRA 2012	19	20	21	22	23	24	25
PAUSHA 2012	26	27	28	29	30	30	1
	2	3	4	5	6	7	8
	9	**10**	12	13	14	15	16
	17	18	19	20	21	22	23
	24	25	26	27	28	29	30
MĀGHA 2012	1	2	3	4	5	6	7
	8	9	10	11	12	13	14
	15	17	18	19	20	21	22
	23	23	24	25	26	27	28[h]
PHĀLGUNA 2012	29	30	1	2	3	4	5
	6	7	**8**	10	11	12	13
	14	15[i]	16	17	18	19	20
	21	22	23	24	25	26	26
CHAITRA 2013	27	28	29	30	1[a]	3	4
	5	6	7	8	9[b]	10	11
	12	13	14	15	16	17	18
	19	20	21	22	23	24	25
VAIŚĀKHA 2013	26	27	28	29	30	1	2
	3	4	**5**	7	8	9	10
	11	12	13	14	15	16	17
	18	19	20	21	21	22	23
JYAISHTHA 2013	24	25	26	27	**28**	30	1
	2	3	4	5	6	7	8
	9	10	11	12	13	14	15
	16	17	18	19	20	21	22
	23	24	25	26	27	28	29
ĀSHĀDHA 2013	30	**1**	3	4	5	6	7
	8	9	10	11	12	13	14
	15	16	17	18	18	19	20
	21	22	23	**24**	26	27	28
ŚRĀVAṆA 2013	29	30	1	2	3	4	5
	6	8	8	9	10	11	12
	13	14	15	16	17	18	19
	20	21	22	23[c]	24	25	26
BHĀDRAPADA 2013	**27**	29	30	1	2	3	4[d]
	5	6	7	8	9	10	11
	12	13	14	14	15	16	17
	18	19	**20**	22	23	24	25
ĀŚVINA 2013	26	27	28	29	30	1	2
	3	4	5	6	7	8[e]	9[e]
	10[e]	11	12	13	14	15	16
	17	18	19	20	21	22	23
KĀRTTIKA 2013	**24**	26	27	28	29	30	1[f]
	2	3	4	5	6	7	8
	8	9	10	11	12	13	14
	15	16	17	**18**	20	21	22
	23	24	25	26	27	28	29
MĀRGAŚĪRA 2013	30	1	2	3	4	5	6
	7	8	9	10	11[g]	12	13
	14	15	16	17	18	19	20
	21	22	**23**	25	26	27	28
	29	30	1	1	2	3	4

‡Leap year
[a]New Year (Durmukha)
[b]Birthday of Rāma
[c]Birthday of Krishna
[d]Ganēśa Chaturthī
[e]Dashara
[f]Diwali
[g]Birthday of Vishnu
[h]Night of Śiva
[i]Holi

HINDU SOLAR 1877‡/1878

Month	Sun	Mon	Tue	Wed	Thu	Fri	Sat
PAUSHA 1877	17	18	19	20	21	22	23
MĀGHA 1877	24	25	26	27	28	29	1[b]
	2	3	4	5	6	7	8
	9	10	11	12	13	14	15
	16	17	18	19	20	21	22
	23	24	25	26	27	28	29
PHĀLGUNA 1877	1	2	3	4	5	6	7
	8	9	10	11	12	13	14
	15	16	17	18	19	20	21
	22	23	24	25	26	27	28
CHAITRA 1877	29	30	1	2	3	4	5
	6	7	8	9	10	11	12
	13	14	15	16	17	18	19
	20	21	22	23	24	25	26
VAIŚĀKHA 1878	27	28	29	30	31	1[a]	2
	3	4	5	6	7	8	9
	10	11	12	13	14	15	16
	17	18	19	20	21	22	23
	24	25	26	27	28	29	30
JYAISHTHA 1878	31	1	2	3	4	5	6
	7	8	9	10	11	12	13
	14	15	16	17	18	19	20
	21	22	23	24	25	26	27
ĀSHĀDHA 1878	28	29	30	31	1	2	3
	4	5	6	7	8	9	10
	11	12	13	14	15	16	17
	18	19	20	21	22	23	24
	25	26	27	28	29	30	31
ŚRĀVAṆA 1878	32	1	2	3	4	5	6
	7	8	9	10	11	12	13
	14	15	16	17	18	19	20
	21	22	23	24	25	26	27
BHĀDRAPADA 1878	28	29	30	31	1	2	3
	4	5	6	7	8	9	10
	11	12	13	14	15	16	17
	18	19	20	21	22	23	24
	25	26	27	28	29	30	31
ĀŚVINA 1878	1	2	3	4	5	6	7
	8	9	10	11	12	13	14
	15	16	17	18	19	20	21
	22	23	24	25	26	27	28
KĀRTTIKA 1878	29	30	31	1	2	3	4
	5	6	7	8	9	10	11
	12	13	14	15	16	17	18
	19	20	21	22	23	24	25
MĀRGAŚĪRA 1878	26	27	28	29	1	2	3
	4	5	6	7	8	9	10
	11	12	13	14	15	16	17
	18	19	20	21	22	23	24
PAUSHA 1878	25	26	27	28	29	30	1
	2	3	4	5	6	7	8
	9	10	11	12	13	14	15
	16	17	18	19	20	21	22

‡Leap year
[a]New Year (Saumya)
[b]Pongal

ISLAMIC (ASTRONOMICAL) 1375/1376‡

Month	Sun	Mon	Tue	Wed	Thu	Fri	Sat
JUMĀDĀ I 1375	17	18	19	20	21	22	23
JUMĀDĀ II 1375	24	25	26	27	28	29	1
	2	3	4	5	6	7	8
	9	10	11	12	13	14	15
	16	17	18	19	20	21	22
	23	24	25	26	27	28	29
RAJAB 1375	30	1	2	3	4	5	6
	7	8	9	10	11	12	13
	14	15	16	17	18	19	20
	21	22	23	24	25	26	27[d]
SHA'BĀN 1375	28	29	30	1	2	3	4
	5	6	7	8	9	10	11
	12	13	14	15	16	17	18
	19	20	21	22	23	24	25
RAMAḌĀN 1375	26	27	28	29	1[e]	2	3
	4	5	6	7	8	9	10
	11	12	13	14	15	16	17
	18	19	20	21	22	23	24
SHAWWĀL 1375	25	26	27	28	29	30	1[f]
	2	3	4	5	6	7	8
	9	10	11	12	13	14	15
	16	17	18	19	20	21	22
	23	24	25	26	27	28	29
DHU AL-QA'DA 1375	1	2	3	4	5	6	7
	8	9	10	11	12	13	14
	15	16	17	18	19	20	21
	22	23	24	25	26	27	28
DHU AL-ḤIJJA 1375	29	30	1	2	3	4	5
	6	7	8	9	10[g]	11	12
	13	14	15	16	17	18	19
	20	21	22	23	24	25	26
MUHARRAM 1376	27	28	29	1[a]	2	3	4
	5	6	7	8	9	10[b]	11
	12	13	14	15	16	17	18
	19	20	21	22	23	24	25
ṢAFAR 1376	26	27	28	29	30	1	2
	3	4	5	6	7	8	9
	10	11	12	13	14	15	16
	17	18	19	20	21	22	23
RABĪ' I 1376	24	25	26	27	28	29	1
	2	3	4	5	6	7	8
	9	10	11	12[c]	13	14	15
	16	17	18	19	20	21	22
	23	24	25	26	27	28	29
RABĪ' II 1376	1	2	3	4	5	6	7
	8	9	10	11	12	13	14
	15	16	17	18	19	20	21
	22	23	24	25	26	27	28
JUMĀDĀ I 1376	29	30	1	2	3	4	5
	6	7	8	9	10	11	12
	13	14	15	16	17	18	19
	20	21	22	23	24	25	26
	27	28	29	1	2	3	4

‡Leap year
[a]New Year
[b]'Āshūrā'
[c]Prophet's Birthday
[d]Ascent of the Prophet
[e]Start of Ramaḍān
[f]'Īd al-Fiṭr
[g]'Īd al-'Aḍḥā

GREGORIAN 1956‡

Julian‡ (Sun)	Sun	Mon	Tue	Wed	Thu	Fri	Sat	Month
Dec 19	1	2	3	4	5	6	7[a]	JANUARY 1956
	8	9	10	11	12	13	14[b]	
Jan 2	15	16	17	18	19	20	21	
	22	23	24	25	26	27	28	
Jan 16	29	30	31	1	2	3	4	FEBRUARY 1956
	5	6	7	8	9	10	11	
Jan 30	12	13	14	15[c]	16	17	18	
	19	20	21	22	23	24	25	
Feb 13	26	27	28	29	1	2	3	MARCH 1956
	4	5	6	7	8	9	10	
Feb 27	11	12	13	14	15	16	17	
	18	19	20	21	22	23	24	
Mar 12	25[d]	26	27	28	29	30	31	
	1[e]	2	3	4	5	6	7	APRIL 1956
Mar 26	8	9	10	11	12	13	14	
	15	16	17	18	19	20	21	
Apr 9	22	23	24	25	26	27	28	
	29	30	1	2	3	4	5	MAY 1956
Apr 23	6[f]	7	8	9	10	11	12	
	13	14	15	16	17	18	19	
May 7	20	21	22	23	24	25	26	
	27	28	29	30	31	1	2	JUNE 1956
May 21	3	4	5	6	7	8	9	
	10	11	12	13	14	15	16	
Jun 4	17	18	19	20	21	22	23	
	24	25	26	27	28	29	30	
Jun 18	1	2	3	4	5	6	7	JULY 1956
	8	9	10	11	12	13	14	
Jul 2	15	16	17	18	19	20	21	
	22	23	24	25	26	27	28	
Jul 16	29	30	31	1	2	3	4	AUGUST 1956
	5	6	7	8	9	10	11	
Jul 30	12	13	14	15	16	17	18	
	19	20	21	22	23	24	25	
Aug 13	26	27	28	29	30	31	1	SEPTEMBER 1956
	2	3	4	5	6	7	8	
Aug 27	9	10	11	12	13	14	15	
	16	17	18	19	20	21	22	
Sep 10	23	24	25	26	27	28	29	
	30	1	2	3	4	5	6	OCTOBER 1956
Sep 24	7	8	9	10	11	12	13	
	14	15	16	17	18	19	20	
Oct 8	21	22	23	24	25	26	27	
	28	29	30	31	1	2	3	NOVEMBER 1956
Oct 22	4	5	6	7	8	9	10	
	11	12	13	14	15	16	17	
Nov 5	18	19	20	21	22	23	24	
	25	26	27	28	29	30	1	DECEMBER 1956
Nov 19	2[g]	3	4	5	6	7	8	
	9	10	11	12	13	14	15	
Dec 3	16	17	18	19	20	21	22	
	23	24	25[h]	26	27	28	29	
Dec 17	30	31	1	2	3	4	5	

‡Leap year
[a]Orthodox Christmas
[b]Julian New Year
[c]Ash Wednesday
[d]Feast of Orthodoxy
[e]Easter
[f]Orthodox Easter
[g]Advent
[h]Christmas

1957

GREGORIAN 1957 / Lunar Phases / ISO WEEK / JULIAN DAY

Month	Sun	Mon	Tue	Wed	Thu	Fri	Sat	Lunar Phases	ISO WEEK (Mon)	JULIAN DAY (Sun noon)
JANUARY 1957	30	31	●[a]	2	3	4	5	2:14	1	2435838
	6	7	8	◐	10	11	12	7:06	2	2435845
	13	14	15	○	17	18	19	6:21	3	2435852
	20	21	◑	23	24	25	26	21:48	4	2435859
	27	28	29	●	31	1	2	21:25	5	2435866
FEBRUARY 1957	3	4	5	6	◐	8	9	23:23	6	2435873
	10	11	12	13	○	15	16	16:38	7	2435880
	17	18	19	20	◑	22	23	12:19	8	2435887
	24	25	26	27	28	●	2	16:12	9	2435894
MARCH 1957	3	4	5	6	7	8	◐	11:50	10	2435901
	10	11	12	13	14	15	○	2:22	11	2435908
	17	18	19	20[b]	21	22	◑	5:04	12	2435915
	24	25	26	27	28	29	30		13	2435922
	●	1	2	3	4	5	6	9:19	14	2435929
APRIL 1957	◐	8	9	10	11	12	13	20:32	15	2435936
	○	15	16	17	18	19	20	12:09	16	2435943
	◑	22	23	24	25	26	27	23:00	17	2435950
	28	●	30	1	2	3	4	23:54	18	2435957
MAY 1957	5	6	◐	8	9	10	11	2:29	19	2435964
	12	○	14	15	16	17	18	22:34	20	2435971
	19	20	◑	22	23	24	25	17:03	21	2435978
	26	27	28	●	30	31	1	11:39	22	2435985
JUNE 1957	2	3	4	◐	6	7	8	7:10	23	2435992
	9	10	11	○	13	14	15	10:02	24	2435999
	16	17	18	19	◑	21[c]	22	10:22	25	2436006
	23	24	25	26	●	28	29	20:54	26	2436013
	30	1	2	3	◐	5	6	12:09	27	2436020
JULY 1957	7	8	9	10	○	12	13	22:50	28	2436027
	14	15	16	17	18	19	◑	2:17	29	2436034
	21	22	23	24	25	26	●	4:28	30	2436041
	28	29	30	31	1	◐	3	18:55	31	2436048
AUGUST 1957	4	5	6	7	8	9	○	13:08	32	2436055
	11	12	13	14	15	16	17		33	2436062
	◑	19	20	21	22	23	24	16:16	34	2436069
	●	26	27	28	29	30	31	11:33	35	2436076
SEPTEMBER 1957	◐	2	3	4	5	6	7	4:35	36	2436083
	8	○	10	11	12	13	14	4:55	37	2436090
	15	16	◑	18	19	20	21	4:02	38	2436097
	22	●[d]	24	25	26	27	28	19:19	39	2436104
	29	◐	1	2	3	4	5	17:49	40	2436111
OCTOBER 1957	6	7	○	9	10	11	12	21:42	41	2436118
	13	14	15	◑	17	18	19	13:44	42	2436125
	20	21	22	●	24	25	26	4:43	43	2436132
	27	28	29	◐	31	1	2	10:48	44	2436139
NOVEMBER 1957	3	4	5	6	○	8	9	14:32	45	2436146
	10	11	12	13	◑	15	16	21:59	46	2436153
	17	18	19	20	●	22	23	16:19	47	2436160
	24	25	26	27	28	◐	30	6:58	48	2436167
DECEMBER 1957	1	2	3	4	5	6	○	6:16	49	2436174
	8	9	10	11	12	13	◑	5:45	50	2436181
	15	16	17	18	19	20	●	6:12	51	2436188
	22[e]	23	24	25	26	27	28		52	2436195
	◐	30	31	1	2	3	4	4:52	1	2436202

HEBREW 5717‡/5718

JULIAN DAY	Month	Sun	Mon	Tue	Wed	Thu	Fri	Sat	Molad
2435838		26	27	28	29	1	2	3	Tue 12h3m3p
2435845	SHEVAT 5717	4	5	6	7	8	9	10	
2435852		11	12	13	14	15	16	17	
2435859		18	19	20	21	22	23	24	
2435866		25	26	27	28	29	30	1	Thu 0h47m4p
2435873	ADAR I 5717	2	3	4	5	6	7	8	
2435880		9	10	11	12	13	14	15	
2435887		16	17	18	19	20	21	22	
2435894		23	24	25	26	27	28	29	
2435901	ADAR II 5717	30	1	2	3	4	5	6	Fri 13h31m5p
2435908		7	8	9	10	11	12	13	
2435915		14[f]	15	16	17	18	19	20	
2435922		21	22	23	24	25	26	27	
2435929	NISAN 5717	28	29	1	2	3	4	5	Sun 2h15m6p
2435936		6	7	8	9	10	11	12	
2435943		13	14	15[g]	16	17	18	19	
2435950		20	21	22	23	24	25	26	
2435957	IYAR 5717	27	28	29	30	1	2	3	Mon 14h59m7p
2435964		4	5	6	7	8	9	10	
2435971		11	12	13	14	15	16	17	
2435978		18	19	20	21	22	23	24	
2435985	SIVAN 5717	25	26	27	28	29	1	2	Wed 3h43m8p
2435992		3	4	5	6[h]	7	8	9	
2435999		10	11	12	13	14	15	16	
2436006		17	18	19	20	21	22	23	
2436013		24	25	26	27	28	29	30	
2436020	TAMMUZ 5717	1	2	3	4	5	6	7	Thu 16h27m9p
2436027		8	9	10	11	12	13	14	
2436034		15	16	17	18	19	20	21	
2436041		22	23	24	25	26	27	28	
2436048	AV 5717	29	1	2	3	4	5	6	Sat 5h11m10p
2436055		7	8	9[i]	10	11	12	13	
2436062		14	15	16	17	18	19	20	
2436069		21	22	23	24	25	26	27	
2436076	ELUL 5717	28	29	30	1	2	3	4	Sun 17h55m11p
2436083		5	6	7	8	9	10	11	
2436090		12	13	14	15	16	17	18	
2436097		19	20	21	22	23	24	25	
2436104	TISHRI 5718	26	27	28	29	1[a]	2[a]	3	Tue 6h39m12p
2436111		4	5	6	7	8	9	10[b]	
2436118		11	12	13	14	15[c]	16	17	
2436125		18	19	20	21	22	23	24	
2436132	HESHVAN 5718	25	26	27	28	29	30	1	Wed 19h23m13p
2436139		2	3	4	5	6	7	8	
2436146		9	10	11	12	13	14	15	
2436153		16	17	18	19	20	21	22	
2436160		23	24	25	26	27	28	29	
2436167	KISLEV 5718	1	2	3	4	5	6	7	Fri 8h7m14p
2436174		8	9	10	11	12[d]	13	14	
2436181		15	16	17	18	19	20	21	
2436188		22	23	24	25[e]	26[e]	27[e]	28[e]	
2436195	TEVETH 5718	29[e]	30[e]	1[e]	2[e]	3	4	5	Sat 20h51m15p
2436202		6	7	8	9	10	11	12	

CHINESE Bǐng-Shēn/Dīng-Yǒu‡

JULIAN DAY	Month	Sun	Mon	Tue	Wed	Thu	Fri	Sat	Solar Term
2435838	MONTH 12 Bǐng-Shēn	29	30	1	2	3	4	5	Xiǎo hán
2435845		6	7	8	9	10	11	12	
2435852		13	14	15	16	17	18	19	
2435859		20	21	22	23	24	25	26	Dà hán
2435866	MONTH 1 Dīng-Yǒu	27	28	29	30	1[a]	2	3	
2435873		4	5	6	7	8	9	10	
2435880		11	12	13	14	15[b]	16	17	Lì chūn
2435887		18	19	20	21	22*	23	24	Yǔ shuǐ
2435894		25	26	27	28	29	30	1	
2435901	MONTH 2 Dīng-Yǒu	2	3	4	5	6	7	8	Jīng zhé
2435908		9	10	11	12	13	14	15	
2435915		16	17	18	19	20	21	22	Chūn fēn
2435922		23	24	25	26	27	28	29	
2435929	MONTH 3 Dīng-Yǒu	1	2	3	4	5	6[c]	7	Qīng míng
2435936		8	9	10	11	12	13	14	
2435943		15	16	17	18	19	20	21	Gǔ yǔ
2435950		22	23*	24	25	26	27	28	
2435957	MONTH 4 Dīng-Yǒu	29	30	1	2	3	4	5	
2435964		6	7	8	9	10	11	12	Lì xià
2435971		13	14	15	16	17	18	19	
2435978		20	21	22	23	24	25	26	Xiǎo mǎn
2435985	MONTH 5 Dīng-Yǒu	27	28	29	1	2	3	4	
2435992		5[d]	6	7	8	9	10	11	Máng zhòng
2435999		12	13	14	15	16	17	18	
2436006		19	20	21	22	23	24*	25	Xià zhì
2436013	MONTH 6 Dīng-Yǒu	26	27	28	29	30	1	2	
2436020		3	4	5	6	7	8	9	
2436027		10	11	12	13	14	15	16	Xiǎo shǔ
2436034		17	18	19	20	21	22	23	
2436041	MONTH 7 Dīng-Yǒu	24	25	26	27	28	29	1	Dà shǔ
2436048		2	3	4	5	6	7[e]	8	
2436055		9	10	11	12	13	14	15[f]	Lì qiū
2436062		16	17	18	19	20	21	22	
2436069		23	24	25*	26	27	28	29	Chǔ shǔ
2436076	MONTH 8 Dīng-Yǒu	1	2	3	4	5	6	7	
2436083		8	9	10	11	12	13	14	
2436090		15[g]	16	17	18	19	20	21	Bái lù
2436097		22	23	24	25	26	27	28	
2436104	LEAP MONTH 8 Dīng-Yǒu	29	30	1	2	3	4	5	Qiū fēn
2436111		6	7	8	9	10	11	12	
2436118		13	14	15	16	17	18	19	Hán lù
2436125		20	21	22	23	24	25	26*	
2436132	MONTH 9 Dīng-Yǒu	27	28	29	1	2	3	4	Shuāng jiàng
2436139		5	6	7	8	9[h]	10	11	
2436146		12	13	14	15	16	17	18	Lì dōng
2436153		19	20	21	22	23	24	25	
2436160	MONTH 10 Dīng-Yǒu	26	27	28	29	30	1	2	Xiǎo xuě
2436167		3	4	5	6	7	8	9	
2436174		10	11	12	13	14	15	16	Dà xuě
2436181		17	18	19	20	21	22	23	
2436188	MONTH 11 Dīng-Yǒu	24	25	26	27*	28	29	1	
2436195		2[i]	3	4	5	6	7	8	Dōng zhì
2436202		9	10	11	12	13	14	15	

COPTIC 1673/1674 — ETHIOPIC 1949/1950

JULIAN DAY	Coptic Month	Sun	Mon	Tue	Wed	Thu	Fri	Sat	Ethiopic Month
2435838	KOIAK 1673	21	22	23	24	25	26	27	TĀKHŚĀŚ 1949
2435845		28	29[c]	30	1	2	3	4	
2435852	TŌBE 1673	5	6[d]	7	8	9	10	11[e]	ṬER 1949
2435859		12	13	14	15	16	17	18	
2435866		19	20	21	22	23	24	25	
2435873		26	27	28	29	30	1	2	
2435880	MESHIR 1673	3	4	5	6	7	8	9	YAKĀTIT 1949
2435887		10	11	12	13	14	15	16	
2435894		17	18	19	20	21	22	23	
2435901		24	25	26	27	28	29	30	
2435908	PAREMOTEP 1673	1	2	3	4	5	6	7	MAGĀBIT 1949
2435915		8	9	10	11	12	13	14	
2435922		15	16	17	18	19	20	21	
2435929		22	23	24	25	26	27	28	
2435936	PARMOUTE 1673	29	30	1	2	3	4	5	MIYĀZYĀ 1949
2435943		6	7	8	9	10	11	12	
2435950		13[f]	14	15	16	17	18	19	
2435957		20	21	22	23	24	25	26	
2435964	PASHONS 1673	27	28	29[g]	30	1	2	3	GENBOT 1949
2435971		4	5	6	7	8	9	10	
2435978		11	12	13	14	15	16	17	
2435985		18	19	20	21	22	23	24	
2435992		25	26	27	28	29	30	1	
2435999	PAŌNE 1673	2	3	4	5	6	7	8	SANĒ 1949
2436006		9	10	11	12	13	14	15	
2436013		16	17	18	19	20	21	22	
2436020		23	24	25	26	27	28	29	
2436027	EPĒP 1673	30	1	2	3	4	5	6	HAMLĒ 1949
2436034		7	8	9	10	11	12	13	
2436041		14	15	16	17	18	19	20	
2436048		21	22	23	24	25	26	27	
2436055	MESORĒ 1673	28	29	30	1	2	3	4	NAḤASĒ 1949
2436062		5	6	7	8	9	10	11	
2436069		12	13[h]	14	15	16	17	18	
2436076		19	20	21	22	23	24	25	
2436083	EPAG. 1673	26	27	28	29	30	1	2	PĀG. 1949
2436090	THOOUT 1674	3	4	5	1[a]	2	3	4	MASKARAM 1950
2436097		5	6	7	8	9	10	11	
2436104		12	13	14	15	16	17[b]	18	
2436111		19	20	21	22	23	24	25	
2436118	PAOPE 1674	26	27	28	29	30	1	2	ṬEQEMT 1950
2436125		3	4	5	6	7	8	9	
2436132		10	11	12	13	14	15	16	
2436139		17	18	19	20	21	22	23	
2436146		24	25	26	27	28	29	30	
2436153	ATHŌR 1674	1	2	3	4	5	6	7	HEDĀR 1950
2436160		8	9	10	11	12	13	14	
2436167		15	16	17	18	19	20	21	
2436174		22	23	24	25	26	27	28	
2436181	KOIAK 1674	29	30	1	2	3	4	5	TĀKHŚĀŚ 1950
2436188		6	7	8	9	10	11	12	
2436195		13	14	15	16	17	18	19	
2436202		20	21	22	23	24	25	26	

Gregorian notes:
[a]New Year
[b]Spring (21:16)
[c]Summer (16:21)
[d]Autumn (7:26)
[e]Winter (2:49)
● New moon
◐ First quarter moon
○ Full moon
◑ Last quarter moon

Hebrew notes:
‡Leap year
[a]New Year
[b]Yom Kippur
[c]Sukkot
[d]Winter starts
[e]Ḥanukkah
[f]Purim
[g]Passover
[h]Shavuot
[i]Fast of Av

Chinese notes:
‡Leap year
[a]New Year (4655, Fowl)
[b]Lantern Festival
[c]Qīngmíng
[d]Dragon Festival
[e]Qīqiǎo
[f]Hungry Ghosts
[g]Mid-Autumn Festival
[h]Double-Ninth Festival
[i]Dōngzhì
*Start of 60-name cycle

Coptic/Ethiopic notes:
[a]New Year
[b]Building of the Cross
[c]Christmas
[d]Jesus's Circumcision
[e]Epiphany
[f]Easter
[g]Mary's Announcement
[h]Jesus's Transfiguration

PERSIAN (ASTRONOMICAL) 1335/1336

Month	Sun	Mon	Tue	Wed	Thu	Fri	Sat
DEY 1335	9	10	11	12	13	14	15
	16	17	18	19	20	21	22
	23	24	25	26	27	28	29
	30	1	2	3	4	5	6
BAHMAN 1335	7	8	9	10	11	12	13
	14	15	16	17	18	19	20
	21	22	23	24	25	26	27
	28	29	30	1	2	3	4
ESFAND 1335	5	6	7	8	9	10	11
	12	13	14	15	16	17	18
	19	20	21	22	23	24	25
	26	27	28	29	1[a]	2	3
FARVARDĪN 1336	4	5	6	7	8	9	10
	11	12	13[b]	14	15	16	17
	18	19	20	21	22	23	24
	25	26	27	28	29	30	31
ORDĪBEHEŠT 1336	1	2	3	4	5	6	7
	8	9	10	11	12	13	14
	15	16	17	18	19	20	21
	22	23	24	25	26	27	28
	29	30	31	1	2	3	4
XORDĀD 1336	5	6	7	8	9	10	11
	12	13	14	15	16	17	18
	19	20	21	22	23	24	25
	26	27	28	29	30	31	1
TĪR 1336	2	3	4	5	6	7	8
	9	10	11	12	13	14	15
	16	17	18	19	20	21	22
	23	24	25	26	27	28	29
	30	31	1	2	3	4	5
MORDĀD 1336	6	7	8	9	10	11	12
	13	14	15	16	17	18	19
	20	21	22	23	24	25	26
	27	28	29	30	31	1	2
SHAHRĪVAR 1336	3	4	5	6	7	8	9
	10	11	12	13	14	15	16
	17	18	19	20	21	22	23
	24	25	26	27	28	29	30
	31	1	2	3	4	5	6
MEHR 1336	7	8	9	10	11	12	13
	14	15	16	17	18	19	20
	21	22	23	24	25	26	27
	28	29	30	1	2	3	4
ĀBĀN 1336	5	6	7	8	9	10	11
	12	13	14	15	16	17	18
	19	20	21	22	23	24	25
	26	27	28	29	30	1	2
ĀZAR 1336	3	4	5	6	7	8	9
	10	11	12	13	14	15	16
	17	18	19	20	21	22	23
	24	25	26	27	28	29	30
DEY 1336	1	2	3	4	5	6	7
	8	9	10	11	12	13	14

[a]New Year
[b]Sizdeh Bedar

HINDU LUNAR 2013/2014

Month	Sun	Mon	Tue	Wed	Thu	Fri	Sat
	29	30	1	1	2	3	4
PAUSHA 2013	5	6	7	8	9	10	11
	12	13	14	15	16	17	19
	20	21	22	23	24	25	26
	27	28	29	30	1	2	3
MĀGHA 2013	3	4	5	6	7	8	9
	10	11	13	14	15	16	17
	18	19	20	21	22	23	24
	25	26	27	28[h]	29	30	1
PHĀLGUNA 2013	2	3	4	5	6	7	8
	9	10	11	12	13	14	15[i]
	17	18	19	20	21	22	23
	24	25	26	26	27	28	29
	30	1[a]	2	3	4	5	6
CHAITRA 2014	7	8[b]	9	11	12	13	14
	15	16	17	18	19	20	21
	22	23	24	25	26	27	28
	29	30	1	2	3	4	5
VAIŚĀKHA 2014	6	7	8	9	10	11	12
	13	15	16	17	18	19	20
	21	21	22	23	24	25	26
	27	28	29	30	1	2	3
JYAISHṬHA 2014	4	5	6	8	9	10	11
	12	13	14	15	16	17	18
	19	20	21	22	23	24	25
	26	27	28	29	30	1	2
ĀSHĀḌHA 2014	3	4	5	6	7	8	9
	11	12	13	14	15	16	17
	18	18	19	20	21	22	23
	24	25	26	27	28	29	30
ŚRĀVAṆA 2014	1	3	4	5	6	7	8
	9	10	11	12	13	14	15
	16	17	18	19	20	21	22
	23[c]	24	25	26	27	28	29
BHĀDRAPADA 2014	30	1	2	3[d]	4	6	7
	8	9	10	11	12	13	14
	14	15	16	17	18	19	20
	21	22	23	24	25	26	27
	29	30	1	2	3	4	5
ĀŚVINA 2014	6	7	8[e]	9[e]	10[e]	11	12
	13	14	15	16	17	18	19
	20	21	22	23	24	25	26
	27	28	29	30	1[f]	2	4
KĀRTTIKA 2014	5	6	7	8	8	9	10
	11	12	13	14	15	16	17
	18	19	20	21	22	23	24
	25	27	28	29	30	1	2
MĀRGAŚIRA 2014	3	4	5	6	7	8	9
	10	11	11[g]	12	13	14	15
	16	17	18	19	21	22	23
	24	25	26	27	28	29	30
PAUSHA 2014	1	2	3	4	5	6	7
	8	9	10	11	12	13	14

[a]New Year (Hemalamba)
[b]Birthday of Rāma
[c]Birthday of Krishna
[d]Ganēśa Chaturthī
[e]Dashara
[f]Diwali
[g]Birthday of Vishnu
[h]Night of Śiva
[i]Holi

HINDU SOLAR 1878/1879

Month	Sun	Mon	Tue	Wed	Thu	Fri	Sat
PAUSHA 1878	16	17	18	19	20	21	22
	23	24	25	26	27	28	29
	1[b]	2	3	4	5	6	7
MĀGHA 1878	8	9	10	11	12	13	14
	15	16	17	18	19	20	21
	22	23	24	25	26	27	28
	29	30	1	2	3	4	5
PHĀLGUNA 1878	6	7	8	9	10	11	12
	13	14	15	16	17	18	19
	20	21	22	23	24	25	26
	27	28	29	1	2	3	4
CHAITRA 1878	5	6	7	8	9	10	11
	12	13	14	15	16	17	18
	19	20	21	22	23	24	25
	26	27	28	29	30	31	1[a]
VAIŚĀKHA 1879	2	3	4	5	6	7	8
	9	10	11	12	13	14	15
	16	17	18	19	20	21	22
	23	24	25	26	27	28	29
	30	31	1	2	3	4	5
JYAISHṬHA 1879	6	7	8	9	10	11	12
	13	14	15	16	17	18	19
	20	21	22	23	24	25	26
	27	28	29	30	31	1	2
ĀSHĀḌHA 1879	3	4	5	6	7	8	9
	10	11	12	13	14	15	16
	17	18	19	20	21	22	23
	24	25	26	27	28	29	30
	31	32	1	2	3	4	5
ŚRĀVAṆA 1879	6	7	8	9	10	11	12
	13	14	15	16	17	18	19
	20	21	22	23	24	25	26
	27	28	29	30	31	1	2
BHĀDRAPADA 1879	3	4	5	6	7	8	9
	10	11	12	13	14	15	16
	17	18	19	20	21	22	23
	24	25	26	27	28	29	30
	31	1	2	3	4	5	6
ĀŚVINA 1879	7	8	9	10	11	12	13
	14	15	16	17	18	19	20
	21	22	23	24	25	26	27
	28	29	30	31	1	2	3
KĀRTTIKA 1879	4	5	6	7	8	9	10
	11	12	13	14	15	16	17
	18	19	20	21	22	23	24
	25	26	27	28	29	30	1
MĀRGAŚIRA 1879	2	3	4	5	6	7	8
	9	10	11	12	13	14	15
	16	17	18	19	20	21	22
	23	24	25	26	27	28	29
PAUSHA 1879	1	2	3	4	5	6	7
	8	9	10	11	12	13	14
	15	16	17	18	19	20	21

[a]New Year (Sādhāraṇa)
[b]Pongal

ISLAMIC (ASTRONOMICAL) 1376‡/1377‡

Month	Sun	Mon	Tue	Wed	Thu	Fri	Sat
	27	28	29	1	2	3	4
JUMĀDĀ II 1376	5	6	7	8	9	10	11
	12	13	14	15	16	17	18
	19	20	21	22	23	24	25
	26	27	28	29	30	1	2
RAJAB 1376	3	4	5	6	7	8	9
	10	11	12	13	14	15	16
	17	18	19	20	21	22	23
	24	25	26	27[d]	28	29	30
SHA'BĀN 1376	1	2	3	4	5	6	7
	8	9	10	11	12	13	14
	15	16	17	18	19	20	21
	22	23	24	25	26	27	28
	29	30	1[e]	2	3	4	5
RAMAḌĀN 1376	6	7	8	9	10	11	12
	13	14	15	16	17	18	19
	20	21	22	23	24	25	26
	27	28	29	1[f]	2	3	4
SHAWWĀL 1376	5	6	7	8	9	10	11
	12	13	14	15	16	17	18
	19	20	21	22	23	24	25
	26	27	28	29	30	1	2
DHU AL-QA'DA 1376	3	4	5	6	7	8	9
	10	11	12	13	14	15	16
	17	18	19	20	21	22	23
	24	25	26	27	28	29	1
DHU AL-ḤIJJA 1376	2	3	4	5	6	7	8
	9	10[g]	11	12	13	14	15
	16	17	18	19	20	21	22
	23	24	25	26	27	28	29
MUḤARRAM 1377	30	1[a]	2	3	4	5	6
	7	8	9	10[b]	11	12	13
	14	15	16	17	18	19	20
	21	22	23	24	25	26	27
ṢAFAR 1377	28	29	1	2	3	4	5
	6	7	8	9	10	11	12
	13	14	15	16	17	18	19
	20	21	22	23	24	25	26
	27	28	29	30	1	2	3
RABĪ' I 1377	4	5	6	7	8	9	10
	11	12[c]	13	14	15	16	17
	18	19	20	21	22	23	24
	25	26	27	28	29	1	2
RABĪ' II 1377	3	4	5	6	7	8	9
	10	11	12	13	14	15	16
	17	18	19	20	21	22	23
	24	25	26	27	28	29	1
JUMĀDĀ I 1377	2	3	4	5	6	7	8
	9	10	11	12	13	14	15
	16	17	18	19	20	21	22
	23	24	25	26	27	28	29
JUMĀDĀ II 1377	30	1	2	3	4	5	6
	7	8	9	10	11	12	13

‡Leap year
[a]New Year
[b]'Ashūrā'
[c]Prophet's Birthday
[d]Ascent of the Prophet
[e]Start of Ramaḍān
[f]'Id al-Fiṭr
[g]'Id al-'Aḍḥā

GREGORIAN 1957

Julian (Sun)	Sun	Mon	Tue	Wed	Thu	Fri	Sat	Month
Dec 17	30	31	1	2	3	4	5	JANUARY 1957
	6	7[a]	8	9	10	11	12	
Dec 31	13	14[b]	15	16	17	18	19	
	20	21	22	23	24	25	26	
Jan 14	27	28	29	30	31	1	2	FEBRUARY 1957
	3	4	5	6	7	8	9	
Jan 28	10	11	12	13	14	15	16	
	17	18	19	20	21	22	23	
Feb 11	24	25	26	27	28	1	2	MARCH 1957
	3	4	5	6[c]	7	8	9	
Feb 25	10[d]	11	12	13	14	15	16	
	17	18	19	20	21	22	23	
Mar 11	24	25	26	27	28	29	30	
	31	1	2	3	4	5	6	APRIL 1957
Mar 25	7	8	9	10	11	12	13	
	14	15	16	17	18	19	20	
Apr 8	21[e]	22	23	24	25	26	27	
	28	29	30	1	2	3	4	MAY 1957
Apr 22	5	6	7	8	9	10	11	
	12	13	14	15	16	17	18	
May 6	19	20	21	22	23	24	25	
	26	27	28	29	30	31	1	JUNE 1957
May 20	2	3	4	5	6	7	8	
	9	10	11	12	13	14	15	
Jun 3	16	17	18	19	20	21	22	
	23	24	25	26	27	28	29	
Jun 17	30	1	2	3	4	5	6	JULY 1957
	7	8	9	10	11	12	13	
Jul 1	14	15	16	17	18	19	20	
	21	22	23	24	25	26	27	
Jul 15	28	29	30	31	1	2	3	AUGUST 1957
	4	5	6	7	8	9	10	
Jul 29	11	12	13	14	15	16	17	
	18	19	20	21	22	23	24	
Aug 12	25	26	27	28	29	30	31	
	1	2	3	4	5	6	7	SEPTEMBER 1957
Aug 26	8	9	10	11	12	13	14	
	15	16	17	18	19	20	21	
Sep 9	22	23	24	25	26	27	28	
	29	30	1	2	3	4	5	OCTOBER 1957
Sep 23	6	7	8	9	10	11	12	
	13	14	15	16	17	18	19	
Oct 7	20	21	22	23	24	25	26	
	27	28	29	30	31	1	2	NOVEMBER 1957
Oct 21	3	4	5	6	7	8	9	
	10	11	12	13	14	15	16	
Nov 4	17	18	19	20	21	22	23	
	24	25	26	27	28	29	30	
Nov 18	1[g]	2	3	4	5	6	7	DECEMBER 1957
	8	9	10	11	12	13	14	
Dec 2	15	16	17	18	19	20	21	
	22	23	24	25[h]	26	27	28	
Dec 16	29	30	31	1	2	3	4	

[a]Orthodox Christmas
[b]Julian New Year
[c]Ash Wednesday
[d]Feast of Orthodoxy
[e]Easter (also Orthodox)
[g]Advent
[h]Christmas

1958

Gregorian 1958 (month)	Gregorian: Sun Mon Tue Wed Thu Fri Sat	Lunar Phases	ISO Week (Mon)	Julian Day (Sun noon)	Hebrew 5718/5719‡ (month)	Hebrew: Sun Mon Tue Wed Thu Fri Sat	Molad	Chinese Dīng-Yǒu‡/Wù-Xū (month)	Chinese: Sun Mon Tue Wed Thu Fri Sat	Solar Term	Coptic 1674/1675‡ (month)	Coptic/Ethiopic: Sun Mon Tue Wed Thu Fri Sat	Ethiopic 1950/1951‡ (month)
	◐ 30 31 1[a] 2 3 4	4:52	1	2436202		6 7 8 9 10 11 12			9 10 11 12 13 14 15			20 21 22 23 24 25 26	TĀKHŚĀŚ 1950
JANUARY 1958	○ 6 7 8 9 10 11	20:09	2	2436209	TEVETH 5718	13 14 15 16 17 18 19		MONTH 11 Dīng-Yǒu	16 17 18 19 20 21 22	Xiǎo hán	KOIAK 1674	27 28 29[c] 30 1 2 3	
	◑ 13 14 15 16 17 18	14:01	3	2436216		20 21 22 23 24 25 26			23 24 25 26 27 28 29			4 5 6[d] 7 8 9 10	
	● 20 21 22 23 24 25	22:08	4	2436223		27 28 29 1 2 3 4	Mon 9h35m16p		30 1 2 3 4 5 6	Dà hán	TŌBE 1674	11[e] 12 13 14 15 16 17	TER 1950
	26 27 ◐ 29 30 31 1	2:16	5	2436230	SHEVAT 5718	5 6 7 8 9 10 11		MONTH 12 Dīng-Yǒu	7 8 9 10 11 12 13			18 19 20 21 22 23 24	
FEBRUARY 1958	2 3 ○ 5 6 7 8	8:05	6	2436237		12 13 14 15 16 17 18			14 15 16 17 18 19 20	Lì chūn		25 26 27 28 29 30 1	
	9 ◑ 11 12 13 14 15	23:34	7	2436244		19 20 21 22 23 24 25			21 22 23 24 25 26 27			2 3 4 5 6 7 8	
	16 17 ● 19 20 21 22	15:38	8	2436251		26 27 28 29 30 1 2	Tue 22h19m17p		28* 29 1[a] 2 3 4 5	Yǔ shuǐ	MESHIR 1674	9 10 11 12 13 14 15	YAKĀTIT 1950
	23 24 25 ◐ 27 28 1	20:52	9	2436258	ADAR 5718	3 4 5 6 7 8 9		MONTH 1 Wù-Xū	6 7 8 9 10 11 12			16 17 18 19 20 21 22	
MARCH 1958	2 3 4 ○ 6 7 8	18:28	10	2436265		10 11 12 13 14[f] 15 16			13 14 15[b] 16 17 18 19	Jīng zhé		23 24 25 26 27 28 29	
	9 10 11 ◑ 13 14 15	10:48	11	2436272		17 18 19 20 21 22 23			20 21 22 23 24 25 26			30 1 2 3 4 5 6	
	16 17 18 19 ● 21[b] 22	9:50	12	2436279		24 25 26 27 28 29 1	Thu 11h4m0p		27 28 29 30 1 2 3	Chūn fēn	PAREMOTEP 1674	7 8 9 10 11 12 13	MAGĀBIT 1950
	23 24 25 26 27 ◐ 29	11:19	13	2436286		2 3 4 5 6 7 8		MONTH 2 Wù-Xū	4 5 6 7 8 9 10			14 15 16 17 18 19 20	
	30 31 1 2 3 ○ 5	3:45	14	2436293	NISAN 5718	9 10 11 12 13 14 15[g]			11 12 13 14 15 16 17[c]	Qīng míng		21 22 23 24 25 26 27	
APRIL 1958	6 7 8 9 ◑ 11 12	23:50	15	2436300		16 17 18 19 20 21 22			18 19 20 21 22 23 24			28 29 30 1 2 3 4	
	13 14 15 16 17 18 ●	3:23	16	2436307		23 24 25 26 27 28 29	Fri 23h48m1p		25 26 27 28 29* 30 1		PARMOUTE 1674	5[f] 6 7 8 9 10 11	MIYĀZYĀ 1950
	20 21 22 23 24 25 ◐	21:36	17	2436314		30 1 2 3 4 5 6		MONTH 3 Wù-Xū	2 3 4 5 6 7 8	Gǔ yǔ		12 13 14 15 16 17 18	
	27 28 29 30 1 2 ○	12:23	18	2436321	IYYAR 5718	7 8 9 10 11 12 13			9 10 11 12 13 14 15			19 20 21 22 23 24 25	
MAY 1958	4 5 6 7 8 9 ◑	14:38	19	2436328		14 15 16 17 18 19 20			16 17 18 19 20 21 22	Lì xià		26 27 28 29[g] 30 1 2	
	11 12 13 14 15 16 17		20	2436335		21 22 23 24 25 26 27			23 24 25 26 27 28 29			3 4 5 6 7 8 9	
	● 19 20 21 22 23 24	19:00	21	2436342		28 29 1 2 3 4 5	Sun 12h32m2p		30 1 2 3 4 5 6	Xiǎo mǎn	PASHONS 1674	10 11 12 13 14 15 16	GENBOT 1950
	25 ◐ 27 28 29 30 31	4:38	22	2436349	SIVAN 5718	6[h] 7 8 9 10 11 12		MONTH 4 Wù-Xū	7 8 9 10 11 12 13			17 18 19 20 21 22 23	
	○ 2 3 4 5 6 7	20:55	23	2436356		13 14 15 16 17 18 19			14 15 16 17 18 19 20	Máng zhòng		24 25 26 27 28 29 30	
JUNE 1958	8 ◑ 10 11 12 13 14	6:59	24	2436363		20 21 22 23 24 25 26			21 22 23 24 25 26 27			1 2 3 4 5 6 7	
	15 16 ● 18 19 20 21[c]	7:59	25	2436370		27 28 29 30 1 2 3	Tue 1h16m3p		28 29* 1 2 3 4 5[d]		PAÔNE 1674	8 9 10 11 12 13 14	SANĒ 1950
	22 23 ◐ 25 26 27 28	9:45	26	2436377	TAMMUZ 5718	4 5 6 7 8 9 10		MONTH 5 Wù-Xū	6 7 8 9 10 11 12	Xià zhì		15 16 17 18 19 20 21	
	29 30 ○ 2 3 4 5	6:04	27	2436384		11 12 13 14 15 16 17			13 14 15 16 17 18 19			22 23 24 25 26 27 28	
JULY 1958	6 7 8 ◑ 10 11 12	0:21	28	2436391		18 19 20 21 22 23 24			20 21 22 23 24 25 26	Xiǎo shǔ		29 30 1 2 3 4 5	
	13 14 15 ● 17 18 19	18:33	29	2436398		25 26 27 28 29 1 2	Wed 14h0m4p		27 28 29 30 1 2 3		EPĒP 1674	6 7 8 9 10 11 12	
	20 21 22 ◐ 24 25 26	14:20	30	2436405	AV 5718	3 4 5 6 7 8 9		MONTH 6 Wù-Xū	4 5 6 7 8 9 10	Dà shǔ		13 14 15 16 17 18 19	HAMLĒ 1950
	27 28 29 ○ 31 1 2	16:47	31	2436412		10[i] 11 12 13 14 15 16			11 12 13 14 15 16 17			20 21 22 23 24 25 26	
AUGUST 1958	3 4 5 6 ◑ 8 9	17:49	32	2436419		17 18 19 20 21 22 23			18 19 20 21 22 23 24	Lì qiū		27 28 29 30 1 2 3	
	10 11 12 13 14 ● 16	3:33	33	2436426		24 25 26 27 28 29 30			25 26 27 28 29 1* 2		MESORĒ 1674	4 5 6 7 8 9 10	NAHASĒ 1950
	17 18 19 20 ◐ 22 23	19:45	34	2436433		1 2 3 4 5 6 7	Fri 2h44m5p	MONTH 7 Wù-Xū	3 4 5 6 7[e] 8 9	Chǔ shǔ		11 12 13[h] 14 15 16 17	
	24 25 26 27 28 ○ 30	5:53	35	2436440	ELUL 5718	8 9 10 11 12 13 14			10 11 12 13 14 15[f] 16			18 19 20 21 22 23 24	
	31 1 2 3 4 5 ◑	10:24	36	2436447		15 16 17 18 19 20 21			17 18 19 20 21 22 23		EPAG. 1674	25 26 27 28 29 30 1	PĀG. 1950
SEPTEMBER 1958	7 8 9 10 11 12 ●	12:02	37	2436454		22 23 24 25 26 27 28			24 25 26 27 28 29 1	Bái lù		2 3 4 5 1[a] 2 3	
	14 15 16 17 18 19 ◐	3:18	38	2436461		29 1[a] 2[a] 3 4 5 6	Sat 15h28m6p	MONTH 8 Wù-Xū	2 3 4 5 6 7 8		THOOUT 1675	4 5 6 7 8 9 10	MASKARAM 1951
	21 22 23[d] 24 25 26 ○	21:44	39	2436468	TISHRI 5719	7 8 9 10[b] 11 12 13			9 10 11 12 13 14 15[g]	Qiū fēn		11 12 13 14 15 16 17[b]	
	28 29 30 1 2 3 4		40	2436475		14 15[c] 16 17 18 19 20			16 17 18 19 20 21 22			18 19 20 21 22 23 24	
OCTOBER 1958	5 ◑ 7 8 9 10 11	1:20	41	2436482		21 22 23 24 25 26 27			23 24 25 26 27 28 29	Hán lù		25 26 27 28 29 30 1	
	● 13 14 15 16 17 18	20:52	42	2436489		28 29 30 1 2 3 4	Mon 4h12m7p		30 1 2* 3 4 5 6			2 3 4 5 6 7 8	
	◐ 20 21 22 23 24 25	14:07	43	2436496	HESHVAN 5719	5 6 7 8 9 10 11		MONTH 9 Wù-Xū	7 8 9[h] 10 11 12 13	Shuāng jiàng	PAOPE 1675	9 10 11 12 13 14 15	TEQEMT 1951
	26 ○ 28 29 30 31 1	15:41	44	2436503		12 13 14 15 16 17 18			14 15 16 17 18 19 20			16 17 18 19 20 21 22	
NOVEMBER 1958	2 3 ◑ 5 6 7 8	14:19	45	2436510		19 20 21 22 23 24 25			21 22 23 24 25 26 27	Lì dōng		23 24 25 26 27 28 29	
	9 10 ● 12 13 14 15	6:34	46	2436517		26 27 28 29 1 2 3	Tue 16h56m8p		28 29 1 2 3 4 5			30 1 2 3 4 5 6	
	16 17 ◐ 19 20 21 22	4:59	47	2436524	KISLEV 5719	4 5 6 7 8 9 10		MONTH 10 Wù-Xū	6 7 8 9 10 11 12	Xiǎo xuě	ATHŌR 1675	7 8 9 10 11 12 13	HEDĀR 1951
	23 24 25 ○ 27 28 29	10:17	48	2436531		11 12 13 14 15 16 17			13 14 15 16 17 18 19			14 15 16 17 18 19 20	
	30 1 2 3 ◑ 5 6	1:24	49	2436538		18 19 20 21 22 23[d] 24			20 21 22 23 24 25 26			21 22 23 24 25 26 27	
DECEMBER 1958	7 8 9 ● 11 12 13	17:23	50	2436545		25[e] 26[e] 27[e] 28[e] 29[e] 1[e] 2[e]	Thu 5h40m9p		27 28 29 30 1 2 3*	Dà xuě		28 29 30 1 2 3 4	
	14 15 16 ◐ 18 19 20	23:52	51	2436552	TEVETH 5719	3[e] 4 5 6 7 8 9		MONTH 11* Wù-Xū	4 5 6 7 8 9 10		KOIAK 1675	5 6 7 8 9 10 11	TĀKHŚĀŚ 1951
	21 22[e] 23 24 25 ○ 27	3:54	52	2436559		10 11 12 13 14 15 16			11 12[i] 13 14 15 16 17	Dōng zhì		12 13 14 15 16 17 18	
	28 29 30 31 1 ◑ 3	10:50	1	2436566		17 18 19 20 21 22 23			18 19 20 21 22 23 24			19 20 21 22 23 24 25	

[a]New Year
[b]Spring (3:05)
[c]Summer (21:57)
[d]Autumn (13:09)
[e]Winter (8:40)
● New moon
◐ First quarter moon
○ Full moon
◑ Last quarter moon

‡Leap year
[a]New Year
[b]Yom Kippur
[c]Sukkot
[d]Winter starts
[e]Ḥanukkah
[f]Purim
[g]Passover
[h]Shavuot
[i]Fast of Av

‡Leap year
[a]New Year (4656, Dog)
[b]Lantern Festival
[c]Qīngmíng
[d]Dragon Festival
[e]Qīqiǎo
[f]Hungry Ghosts
[g]Mid-Autumn Festival
[h]Double-Ninth Festival
[i]Dōngzhì
*Start of 60-name cycle

‡Leap year
[a]New Year
[b]Building of the Cross
[c]Christmas
[d]Jesus's Circumcision
[e]Epiphany
[f]Easter
[g]Mary's Announcement
[h]Jesus's Transfiguration

PERSIAN (ASTRONOMICAL) 1336/1337‡

Month	Sun	Mon	Tue	Wed	Thu	Fri	Sat
DEY 1336	8	9	10	11	12	13	14
	15	16	17	18	19	20	21
	22	23	24	25	26	27	28
BAHMAN 1336	29	30	1	2	3	4	5
	6	7	8	9	10	11	12
	13	14	15	16	17	18	19
	20	21	22	23	24	25	26
ESFAND 1336	27	28	29	30	1	2	3
	4	5	6	7	8	9	10
	11	12	13	14	15	16	17
	18	19	20	21	22	23	24
FARVARDĪN 1337	25	26	27	28	29	1[a]	2
	3	4	5	6	7	8	9
	10	11	12	13[b]	14	15	16
	17	18	19	20	21	22	23
	24	25	26	27	28	29	30
ORDĪBEHEŠT 1337	31	1	2	3	4	5	6
	7	8	9	10	11	12	13
	14	15	16	17	18	19	20
	21	22	23	24	25	26	27
XORDĀD 1337	28	29	30	31	1	2	3
	4	5	6	7	8	9	10
	11	12	13	14	15	16	17
	18	19	20	21	22	23	24
	25	26	27	28	29	30	31
TĪR 1337	1	2	3	4	5	6	7
	8	9	10	11	12	13	14
	15	16	17	18	19	20	21
	22	23	24	25	26	27	28
MORDĀD 1337	29	30	31	1	2	3	4
	5	6	7	8	9	10	11
	12	13	14	15	16	17	18
	19	20	21	22	23	24	25
SHAHRĪVAR 1337	26	27	28	29	30	31	1
	2	3	4	5	6	7	8
	9	10	11	12	13	14	15
	16	17	18	19	20	21	22
	23	24	25	26	27	28	29
MEHR 1337	30	31	1	2	3	4	5
	6	7	8	9	10	11	12
	13	14	15	16	17	18	19
	20	21	22	23	24	25	26
ĀBĀN 1337	27	28	29	30	1	2	3
	4	5	6	7	8	9	10
	11	12	13	14	15	16	17
	18	19	20	21	22	23	24
ĀZAR 1337	25	26	27	28	29	30	1
	2	3	4	5	6	7	8
	9	10	11	12	13	14	15
	16	17	18	19	20	21	22
	23	24	25	26	27	28	29
DEY 1337	30	1	2	3	4	5	6
	7	8	9	10	11	12	13

‡Leap year
[a]New Year
[b]Sizdeh Bedar

HINDU LUNAR 2014/2015‡

Month	Sun	Mon	Tue	Wed	Thu	Fri	Sat
PAUSHA 2014	8	9	10	11	12	13	14
	15	16	17	18	19	20	21
	22	23	**24**	26	27	28	29
MĀGHA 2014	30	1	2	3	4	4	5
	6	7	8	9	10	11	12
	13	14	15	16	17	**18**	20
	21	22	23	24	25	26	27
PHĀLGUNA 2014	28[h]	29	30	1	2	3	4
	5	6	6	7	8	9	10
	11	13	14	15[i]	16	17	18
	19	20	21	22	23	24	25
CHAITRA 2015	26	27	28	29	30	1[a]	2
	3	4	5	6	7	8	9[b]
	10	11	12	13	14	15	**16**
	18	19	20	21	22	23	24
	25	26	27	28	29	29	30
VAIŚĀKHA 2015	1	2	3	4	5	6	7
	8	**9**	11	12	13	14	15
	16	17	18	19	20	21	22
	23	24	25	26	27	28	29
JYAISHṬHA 2015	30	1	2	3	4	5	6
	7	8	9	10	11	12	**13**
	15	16	17	18	19	20	21
	22	23	24	25	25	26	27
ĀSHĀḌHA 2015	28	29	30	1	2	3	4
	5	**6**	8	9	10	11	12
	13	14	15	16	17	18	19
	20	21	22	23	24	25	26
LEAP ŚRĀVAṆA 2015	27	28	29	30	1	2	3
	4	5	6	7	**8**	10	11
	12	13	14	15	16	17	18
	19	20	21	22	22	23	24
ŚRĀVAṆA 2015	25	26	27	28	29	30	**1**
	3	4	5	6	7	8	9
	10	11	12	13	14	15	16
	17	18	19	20	21	22	23[c]
	24	25	26	27	28	29	30
BHĀDRAPADA 2015	1	2	3[d]	**4**	6	7	8
	9	10	11	12	13	14	15
	16	17	18	18	19	20	21
	22	23	24	25	26	27	**28**
ĀŚVINA 2015	30	1	2	3	4	5	6
	7	8[e]	9[e]	10[e]	11	12	13
	14	15	16	17	18	19	20
	21	22	23	24	25	26	27
KĀRTTIKA 2015	28	29	30	1[f]	**2**	4	5
	6	7	8	9	10	11	12
	12	13	14	15	16	17	18
	19	20	21	22	23	24	25
MĀRGAŚĪRA 2015	**26**	28	29	30	1	2	3
	4	5	6	7	8	9	10
	11[g]	12	13	14	14	15	16
	17	18	19	**20**	22	23	24

‡Leap year
[a]New Year (Vilamba)
[b]Birthday of Rāma
[c]Birthday of Krishna
[d]Ganēśa Chaturthī
[e]Dashara
[f]Diwali
[g]Birthday of Vishnu
[h]Night of Śiva
[i]Holi

HINDU SOLAR 1879/1880

Month	Sun	Mon	Tue	Wed	Thu	Fri	Sat
PAUSHA 1879	15	16	17	18	19	20	21
	22	23	24	25	26	27	28
MĀGHA 1879	29	1[b]	2	3	4	5	6
	7	8	9	10	11	12	13
	14	15	16	17	18	19	20
	21	22	23	24	25	26	27
PHĀLGUNA 1879	28	29	30	1	2	3	4
	5	6	7	8	9	10	11
	12	13	14	15	16	17	18
	19	20	21	22	23	24	25
CHAITRA 1879	26	27	28	29	30	1	2
	3	4	5	6	7	8	9
	10	11	12	13	14	15	16
	17	18	19	20	21	22	23
	24	25	26	27	28	29	30
VAIŚĀKHA 1880	1[a]	2	3	4	5	6	7
	8	9	10	11	12	13	14
	15	16	17	18	19	20	21
	22	23	24	25	26	27	28
JYAISHṬHA 1880	29	30	31	1	2	3	4
	5	6	7	8	9	10	11
	12	13	14	15	16	17	18
	19	20	21	22	23	24	25
ĀSHĀḌHA 1880	26	27	28	29	30	31	1
	2	3	4	5	6	7	8
	9	10	11	12	13	14	15
	16	17	18	19	20	21	22
	23	24	25	26	27	28	29
ŚRĀVAṆA 1880	30	31	32	1	2	3	4
	5	6	7	8	9	10	11
	12	13	14	15	16	17	18
	19	20	21	22	23	24	25
	26	27	28	29	30	31	32
BHĀDRAPADA 1880	1	2	3	4	5	6	7
	8	9	10	11	12	13	14
	15	16	17	18	19	20	21
	22	23	24	25	26	27	28
ĀŚVINA 1880	29	30	31	1	2	3	4
	5	6	7	8	9	10	11
	12	13	14	15	16	17	18
	19	20	21	22	23	24	25
KĀRTTIKA 1880	26	27	28	29	30	1	2
	3	4	5	6	7	8	9
	10	11	12	13	14	15	16
	17	18	19	20	21	22	23
	24	25	26	27	28	29	30
MĀRGAŚĪRA 1880	1	2	3	4	5	6	7
	8	9	10	11	12	13	14
	15	16	17	18	19	20	21
	22	23	24	25	26	27	28
PAUSHA 1880	29	1	2	3	4	5	6
	7	8	9	10	11	12	13
	14	15	16	17	18	19	20

[a]New Year (Virodhakṛit)
[b]Pongal

ISLAMIC (ASTRONOMICAL) 1377‡/1378

Month	Sun	Mon	Tue	Wed	Thu	Fri	Sat
JUMĀDĀ II 1377	7	8	9	10	11	12	13
	14	15	16	17	18	19	20
	21	22	23	24	25	26	27
RAJAB 1377	28	29	1	2	3	4	5
	6	7	8	9	10	11	12
	13	14	15	16	17	18	19
	20	21	22	23	24	25	26
SHA'BĀN 1377	27[d]	28	29	30	1	2	3
	4	5	6	7	8	9	10
	11	12	13	14	15	16	17
	18	19	20	21	22	23	24
RAMAḌĀN 1377	25	26	27	28	29	30	1[e]
	2	3	4	5	6	7	8
	9	10	11	12	13	14	15
	16	17	18	19	20	21	22
	23	24	25	26	27	28	29
SHAWWĀL 1377	1[f]	2	3	4	5	6	7
	8	9	10	11	12	13	14
	15	16	17	18	19	20	21
	22	23	24	25	26	27	28
DHU AL-QA'DA 1377	29	30	1	2	3	4	5
	6	7	8	9	10	11	12
	13	14	15	16	17	18	19
	20	21	22	23	24	25	26
DHU AL-ḤIJJA 1377	27	28	29	30	1	2	3
	4	5	6	7	8	9	10[g]
	11	12	13	14	15	16	17
	18	19	20	21	22	23	24
MUḤARRAM 1378	25	26	27	28	29	30[ȧ]	1[a]
	2	3	4	5	6	7	8
	9	10[b]	11	12	13	14	15
	16	17	18	19	20	21	22
	23	24	25	26	27	28	29
ṢAFAR 1378	1	2	3	4	5	6	7
	8	9	10	11	12	13	14
	15	16	17	18	19	20	21
	22	23	24	25	26	27	28
RABĪ' I 1378	29	1	2	3	4	5	6
	7	8	9	10	11	12[c]	13
	14	15	16	17	18	19	20
	21	22	23	24	25	26	27
RABĪ' II 1378	28	29	1	2	3	4	5
	6	7	8	9	10	11	12
	13	14	15	16	17	18	19
	20	21	22	23	24	25	26
JUMĀDĀ I 1378	27	28	29	1	2	3	4
	5	6	7	8	9	10	11
	12	13	14	15	16	17	18
	19	20	21	22	23	24	25
JUMĀDĀ II 1378	26	27	28	29	30	1	2
	3	4	5	6	7	8	9
	10	11	12	13	14	15	16
	17	18	19	20	21	22	23

‡Leap year
[a]New Year
[ȧ]New Year (Arithmetic)
[b]'Ashūrā'
[c]Prophet's Birthday
[d]Ascent of the Prophet
[e]Start of Ramaḍān
[f]'Id al-Fiṭr
[g]'Id al-'Aḍḥā

GREGORIAN 1958

Julian (Sun)	Sun	Mon	Tue	Wed	Thu	Fri	Sat	Month
Dec 16	29	30	31	1	2	3	4	JANUARY 1958
	5	6	7[a]	8	9	10	11	
Dec 30	12	13	14[b]	15	16	17	18	
	19	20	21	22	23	24	25	
Jan 13	26	27	28	29	30	31	1	FEBRUARY 1958
	2	3	4	5	6	7	8	
Jan 27	9	10	11	12	13	14	15	
	16	17	18	19[c]	20	21	22	
Feb 10	23	24	25	26	27	28	1	MARCH 1958
	2[d]	3	4	5	6	7	8	
Feb 24	9	10	11	12	13	14	15	
	16	17	18	19	20	21	22	
Mar 10	23	24	25	26	27	28	29	
	30	31	1	2	3	4	5	APRIL 1958
Mar 24	6[e]	7	8	9	10	11	12	
	13[f]	14	15	16	17	18	19	
Apr 7	20	21	22	23	24	25	26	
	27	28	29	30	1	2	3	MAY 1958
Apr 21	4	5	6	7	8	9	10	
	11	12	13	14	15	16	17	
May 5	18	19	20	21	22	23	24	
	25	26	27	28	29	30	31	
May 19	1	2	3	4	5	6	7	JUNE 1958
	8	9	10	11	12	13	14	
Jun 2	15	16	17	18	19	20	21	
	22	23	24	25	26	27	28	
Jun 16	29	30	1	2	3	4	5	JULY 1958
	6	7	8	9	10	11	12	
Jun 30	13	14	15	16	17	18	19	
	20	21	22	23	24	25	26	
Jul 14	27	28	29	30	31	1	2	AUGUST 1958
	3	4	5	6	7	8	9	
Jul 28	10	11	12	13	14	15	16	
	17	18	19	20	21	22	23	
Aug 11	24	25	26	27	28	29	30	
	31	1	2	3	4	5	6	SEPTEMBER 1958
Aug 25	7	8	9	10	11	12	13	
	14	15	16	17	18	19	20	
Sep 8	21	22	23	24	25	26	27	
	28	29	30	1	2	3	4	OCTOBER 1958
Sep 22	5	6	7	8	9	10	11	
	12	13	14	15	16	17	18	
Oct 6	19	20	21	22	23	24	25	
	26	27	28	29	30	31	1	NOVEMBER 1958
Oct 20	2	3	4	5	6	7	8	
	9	10	11	12	13	14	15	
Nov 3	16	17	18	19	20	21	22	
	23	24	25	26	27	28	29	
Nov 17	30[g]	1	2	3	4	5	6	DECEMBER 1958
	7	8	9	10	11	12	13	
Dec 1	14	15	16	17	18	19	20	
	21	22	23	24	25[h]	26	27	
Dec 15	28	29	30	31	1	2	3	

[a]Orthodox Christmas
[b]Julian New Year
[c]Ash Wednesday
[d]Feast of Orthodoxy
[e]Easter
[f]Orthodox Easter
[g]Advent
[h]Christmas

1959

	GREGORIAN 1959							Lunar Phases	ISO WEEK	JULIAN DAY		HEBREW 5719‡/5720							Molad		CHINESE Wù-Xū/Jǐ-Hài							Solar Term		COPTIC 1675‡/1676 / ETHIOPIC 1951‡/1952							
	Sun	Mon	Tue	Wed	Thu	Fri	Sat		(Mon)	(Sun noon)		Sun	Mon	Tue	Wed	Thu	Fri	Sat			Sun	Mon	Tue	Wed	Thu	Fri	Sat			Sun	Mon	Tue	Wed	Thu	Fri	Sat	
JANUARY 1959	28	29	30	31	1[a]	◑	3	10:50	1	2436566	TEVETH 5719	17	18	19	20	21	22	23		MONTH 11* Wù-Xū	18	19	20	21	22	23	24			19	20	21	22	23	24	25	TĀKHŚĀŚ 1951
	4	5	6	7	8	●	10	5:34	2	2436573		24	25	26	27	28	29	1	Fri 18h24m10p		25	26	27	28	29	1	2	Xiǎo hán	KOIAK 1675	26	27	28	29[c]	30	1	2	
	11	12	13	14	15	◐	17	21:27	3	2436580	SHEVAT 5719	2	3	4	5	6	7	8		MONTH 12 Wù-Xū	3	4	5	6	7	8	9			3	4	5	6[d]	7	8	9	ṬER 1951
	18	19	20	21	22	23	○	19:32	4	2436587		9	10	11	12	13	14	15			10	11	12	**13**	14	15	16	Dà hán	TŌBE 1675	10	11[e]	12	13	14	15	16	
	25	26	27	28	29	30	◑	19:07	5	2436594		16	17	18	19	20	21	22			17	18	19	20	21	22	23			17	18	19	20	21	22	23	
FEBRUARY 1959	1	2	3	4	5	6	●	19:22	6	2436601		23	24	25	26	27	28	29			24	25	26	27	28	29	30	Lì chūn		24	25	26	27	28	29	30	
	8	9	10	11	12	13	14		7	2436608		30	1	2	3	4	5	6	Sun 7h8m11p		1[a]	2	3	4*	5	6	7			1	2	3	4	5	6	7	
	◐	16	17	18	19	20	21	19:20	8	2436615	ADAR I 5719	7	8	9	10	11	12	13		MONTH 1 Jǐ-Hài	8	9	10	11	**12**	13	14	Yǔ shuǐ	MESHIR 1675	8	9	10	11	12	13	14	YAKĀTIT 1951
	22	○	24	25	26	27	28	8:54	9	2436622		14	15	16	17	18	19	20			15[b]	16	17	18	19	20	21			15	16	17	18	19	20	21	
MARCH 1959	1	◑	3	4	5	6	7	2:54	10	2436629		21	22	23	24	25	26	27			22	23	24	25	26	27	28	Jīng zhé		22	23	24	25	26	27	28	
	8	●	10	11	12	13	14	10:51	11	2436636		28	29	30	1	2	3	4	Mon 19h52m12p		29	1	2	3	4	5	6			29	30	1	2	3	4	5	
	15	16	◐	18	19	20	21[b]	15:10	12	2436643	ADAR II 5719	5	6	7	8	9	10	11		MONTH 2 Jǐ-Hài	7	8	9	10	11	12	**13**	Chūn fēn	PAREMOTEP 1675	6	7	8	9	10	11	12	MAGĀBIT 1951
	22	23	○	25	26	27	28	20:03	13	2436650		12	13	14[f]	15	16	17	18			14	15	16	17	18	19	20			13	14	15	16	17	18	19	
	29	30	◑	1	2	3	4	11:07	14	2436657		19	20	21	22	23	24	25			21	22	23	24	25	26	27			20	21	22	23	24	25	26	
APRIL 1959	5	6	7	●	9	10	11	3:29	15	2436664		26	27	28	29	1	2	3	Wed 8h36m13p		28[c]	29	30	1	2	3	4	Qīng míng		27	28	29	30	1	2	3	
	12	13	14	15	◐	17	18	7:33	16	2436671	NISAN 5719	4	5	6	7	8	9	10		MONTH 3 Jǐ-Hài	5*	6	7	8	9	10	11		PARMOUTE 1675	4	5	6	7	8	9	10	MIYĀZYĀ 1951
	19	20	21	22	○	24	25	5:13	17	2436678		11	12	13	14	15[g]	16	17			12	13	**14**	15	16	17	18	Gǔ yǔ		11	12	13	14	15	16	17	
	26	27	28	◑	30	1	2	20:38	18	2436685		18	19	20	21	22	23	24			19	20	21	22	23	24	25			18	19	20	21	22	23	24	
MAY 1959	3	4	5	6	●	8	9	20:12	19	2436692		25	26	27	28	29	30	1	Thu 21h20m14p		26	27	28	29	30	1	2	Lì xià		25[f]	26	27	28	29[g]	30	1	
	10	11	12	13	14	◐	16	20:09	20	2436699	IYAR 5719	2	3	4	5	6	7	8		MONTH 4 Jǐ-Hài	3	4	5	6	7	8	9			2	3	4	5	6	7	8	GENBOT 1951
	17	18	19	20	21	○	23	12:56	21	2436706		9	10	11	12	13	14	15			10	11	12	13	14	**15**	16	Xiǎo mǎn	PASHONS 1675	9	10	11	12	13	14	15	
	24	25	26	27	28	◑	30	8:14	22	2436713		16	17	18	19	20	21	22			17	18	19	20	21	22	23			16	17	18	19	20	21	22	
JUNE 1959	31	1	2	3	4	5	●	11:53	23	2436720		23	24	25	26	27	28	29			24	25	26	27	28	29	1	Máng zhòng		23	24	25	26	27	28	29	
	7	8	9	10	11	12	13		24	2436727		1	2	3	4	5	6[h]	7	Sat 10h4m15p		2	3	4	5[d]	6*	7	8			30	1	2	3	4	5	6	
	◐	15	16	17	18	19	○	5:23 20:00	25	2436734	SIVAN 5719	8	9	10	11	12	13	14		MONTH 5 Jǐ-Hài	9	10	11	12	13	14	15		PAŌNE 1675	7	8	9	10	11	12	13	SANÉ 1951
	21	22[c]	23	24	25	26	◑	22:12	26	2436741		15	16	17	18	19	20	21			16	**17**	18	19	20	21	22	Xià zhì		14	15	16	17	18	19	20	
	28	29	30	1	2	3	4		27	2436748		22	23	24	25	26	27	28			23	24	25	26	27	28	29			21	22	23	24	25	26	27	
JULY 1959	5	●	7	8	9	10	11	2:00	28	2436755		29	30	1	2	3	4	5	Sun 22h48m16p		30	1	2	3	4	5	6	Xiǎo shǔ		28	29	30	1	2	3	4	
	12	◐	14	15	16	17	18	12:01	29	2436762	TAMMUZ 5719	6	7	8	9	10	11	12		MONTH 6 Jǐ-Hài	7	8	9	10	11	12	13		EPĒP 1675	5	6	7	8	9	10	11	HAMLÉ 1951
	19	○	21	22	23	24	25	3:33	30	2436769		13	14	15	16	17	18	19			14	15	16	17	**18**	19	20	Dà shǔ		12	13	14	15	16	17	18	
	26	◑	28	29	30	31	1	14:22	31	2436776		20	21	22	23	24	25	26			21	22	23	24	25	26	27			19	20	21	22	23	24	25	
AUGUST 1959	2	3	●	5	6	7	8	14:34	32	2436783		27	28	29	1	2	3	4	Tue 11h32m17p		28	29	1	2	3	4	5	Lì qiū		26	27	28	29	30	1	2	
	9	10	◐	12	13	14	15	17:10	33	2436790	AV 5719	5	6	7	8	9[i]	10	11		MONTH 7 Jǐ-Hài	6	7[e]*	8	9	10	11	12			3	4	5	6	7	8	9	NAHASÉ 1951
	16	17	○	19	20	21	22	12:51	34	2436797		12	13	14	15	16	17	18			13	14	15[f]	16	17	18	19		MESORĒ 1675	10	11	12	13[h]	14	15	16	
	23	24	25	◑	27	28	29	8:03	35	2436804		19	20	21	22	23	24	25			20	**21**	22	23	24	25	26	Chǔ shǔ		17	18	19	20	21	22	23	
SEPTEMBER 1959	30	31	1	2	●	4	5	1:56	36	2436811		26	27	28	29	30	1	2	Thu 0h17m0p		27	28	29	30	1	2	3			24	25	26	27	28	29	30	
	6	7	8	◐	10	11	12	22:07	37	2436818	ELUL 5719	3	4	5	6	7	8	9			4	5	6	7	8	9	10	Bái lù	EPAG. 1675	1	2	3	4	5	6	1[a]	PĀG. 1951
	13	14	15	16	○	18	19	0:52	38	2436825		10	11	12	13	14	15	16		MONTH 8 Jǐ-Hài	11	12	13	14	15[g]	16	17			2	3	4	5	6	7	8	MASKARAM 1952
	20	21	22	23[d]	24	◑	26	2:22	39	2436832		17	18	19	20	21	22	23			18	19	20	21	**22**	23	24	Qiū fēn	THOOUT 1676	9	10	11	12	13	14	15	
	27	28	29	30	1	●	3	12:31	40	2436839		24	25	26	27	28	29	1[a]	Fri 13h1m1p		25	26	27	28	29	1	2			16	17[b]	18	19	20	21	22	
OCTOBER 1959	4	5	6	7	8	◐	10	4:23	41	2436846		2[a]	3	4	5	6	7	8			3	4	5	6	7	8*	9[h]	Hán lù		23	24	25	26	27	28	29	
	11	12	13	14	15	○	17	15:58	42	2436853	TISHRI 5720	9	10[b]	11	12	13	14	15[c]		MONTH 9 Jǐ-Hài	10	11	12	13	14	15	16			30	1	2	3	4	5	6	
	18	19	20	21	22	23	◑	20:22	43	2436860		16	17	18	19	20	21	22			17	18	19	20	21	22	**23**	Shuāng jiàng	PAOPE 1676	7	8	9	10	11	12	13	ṬEQEMT 1952
	25	26	27	28	29	30	●	22:41	44	2436867		23	24	25	26	27	28	29			24	25	26	27	28	29	30			14	15	16	17	18	19	20	
NOVEMBER 1959	1	2	3	4	5	6	◐	13:23	45	2436874		30	1	2	3	4	5	6	Sun 1h45m2p		1	2	3	4	5	6	7			21	22	23	24	25	26	27	
	8	9	10	11	12	13	14		46	2436881		7	8	9	10	11	12	13			8	9	10	11	12	13	14	Lì dōng		28	29	30	1	2	3	4	
	○	16	17	18	19	20	21	9:42	47	2436888	HESHVAN 5720	14	15	16	17	18	19	20		MONTH 10 Jǐ-Hài	15	16	17	18	19	20	21		ATHŌR 1676	5	6	7	8	9	10	11	HEDĀR 1952
	22	◑	24	25	26	27	28	13:03	48	2436895		21	22	23	24	25	26	27			22	**23**	24	25	26	27	28	Xiǎo xuě		12	13	14	15	16	17	18	
	29	●	1	2	3	4	5	8:46	49	2436902		28	29	30	1	2	3	4	Mon 14h29m3p		29	1	2	3	4	5	6			19	20	21	22	23	24	25	
DECEMBER 1959	6	◐	8	9	10	11	12	2:12	50	2436909		5[d]	6	7	8	9	10	11			7	8	9*	10	11	12	13	Dà xuě		26	27	28	29	30	1	2	
	13	14	○	16	17	18	19	4:49	51	2436916	KISLEV 5720	12	13	14	15	16	17	18		MONTH 11 Jǐ-Hài	14	15	16	17	18	19	20		KOIAK 1676	3	4	5	6	7	8	9	TĀKHŚĀŚ 1952
	20	21	22[e]	◑	24	25	26	3:28	52	2436923		19	20	21	22	23	24	25[e]			21	22	**23**[i]	24	25	26	27	Dōng zhì		10	11	12	13	14	15	16	
	27	28	●	30	31	1	2	19:09	53	2436930		26[e]	27[e]	28[e]	29[e]	30[e]	1[e]	2[e]	Wed 3h13m4p		28	29	30	1	2	3	4			17	18	19	20	21	22	23	

[a]New Year
[b]Spring (8:55)
[c]Summer (3:50)
[d]Autumn (19:08)
[e]Winter (14:34)
● New moon
◐ First quarter moon
○ Full moon
◑ Last quarter moon

‡Leap year
[a]New Year
[b]Yom Kippur
[c]Sukkot
[d]Winter starts
[e]Ḥanukkah
[f]Purim
[g]Passover
[h]Shavuot
[i]Fast of Av

[a]New Year (4657, Pig)
[b]Lantern Festival
[c]Qīngmíng
[d]Dragon Festival
[e]Qīqiǎo
[f]Hungry Ghosts
[g]Mid-Autumn Festival
[h]Double-Ninth Festival
[i]Dōngzhì
*Start of 60-name cycle

‡Leap year
[a]New Year
[b]Building of the Cross
[c]Christmas
[d]Jesus's Circumcision
[e]Epiphany
[f]Easter
[g]Mary's Announcement
[h]Jesus's Transfiguration

1959

PERSIAN (ASTRONOMICAL) 1337‡/1338

Month	Sun	Mon	Tue	Wed	Thu	Fri	Sat
DEY 1337	7	8	9	10	11	12	13
	14	15	16	17	18	19	20
	21	22	23	24	25	26	27
BAHMAN 1337	28	29	30	1	2	3	4
	5	6	7	8	9	10	11
	12	13	14	15	16	17	18
	19	20	21	22	23	24	25
ESFAND 1337	26	27	28	29	30	1	2
	3	4	5	6	7	8	9
	10	11	12	13	14	15	16
	17	18	19	20	21	22	23
	24	25	26	27	28	29	30*
FARVARDIN 1338	1[a]	2	3	4	5	6	7
	8	9	10	11	12	13[b]	14
	15	16	17	18	19	20	21
	22	23	24	25	26	27	28
ORDIBEHEST 1338	29	30	31	1	2	3	4
	5	6	7	8	9	10	11
	12	13	14	15	16	17	18
	19	20	21	22	23	24	25
XORDAD 1338	26	27	28	29	30	31	1
	2	3	4	5	6	7	8
	9	10	11	12	13	14	15
	16	17	18	19	20	21	22
	23	24	25	26	27	28	29
TIR 1338	30	31	1	2	3	4	5
	6	7	8	9	10	11	12
	13	14	15	16	17	18	19
	20	21	22	23	24	25	26
MORDAD 1338	27	28	29	30	31	1	2
	3	4	5	6	7	8	9
	10	11	12	13	14	15	16
	17	18	19	20	21	22	23
	24	25	26	27	28	29	30
SHAHRIVAR 1338	31	1	2	3	4	5	6
	7	8	9	10	11	12	13
	14	15	16	17	18	19	20
	21	22	23	24	25	26	27
MEHR 1338	28	29	30	31	1	2	3
	4	5	6	7	8	9	10
	11	12	13	14	15	16	17
	18	19	20	21	22	23	24
ABAN 1338	25	26	27	28	29	30	1
	2	3	4	5	6	7	8
	9	10	11	12	13	14	15
	16	17	18	19	20	21	22
	23	24	25	26	27	28	29
AZAR 1338	30	1	2	3	4	5	6
	7	8	9	10	11	12	13
	14	15	16	17	18	19	20
	21	22	23	24	25	26	27
DEY 1338	28	29	30	1	2	3	4
	5	6	7	8	9	10	11

‡Leap year
[a]New Year (or prior day)
*Near New Year: −0′32″
[b]Sizdeh Bedar

HINDU LUNAR 2015‡/2016

Month	Sun	Mon	Tue	Wed	Thu	Fri	Sat
MĀRGAŚĪRA 2015	17	18	19	**20**	22	23	24
PAUSHA 2015	25	26	27	28	29	30	1
	2	3	4	5	6	7	8
	9	10	11	12	13	14	15
	16	17	18	19	20	21	22
	23	24	**25**	27	28	29	30
MĀGHA 2015	1	2	3	4	5	6	6
	7	8	9	10	11	12	13
	14	15	16	17	18	**19**	21
	22	23	24	25	26	27	28[h]
PHĀLGUNA 2015	29	30	1	2	3	4	5
	6	7	8	9	10	10	**11**
	13	14	15[i]	16	17	18	19
	20	21	22	23	**24**	26	27
CHAITRA 2016	28	29	29	30	1[a]	2	3
	4	5	6	7	8	9[b]	10
	11	12	13	14	15	16	**17**
	19	20	21	22	23	24	25
VAIŚĀKHA 2016	26	27	28	29	30	1	2
	3	3	4	5	6	7	8
	9	11	12	13	14	15	16
	17	18	19	20	21	22	23
	24	25	26	27	28	29	30
JYAISHTHA 2016	1	2	3	4	5	6	7
	8	9	10	11	12	**13**	15
	16	17	18	19	20	21	22
	23	24	25	26	27	28	29
ĀSHĀḌHA 2016	30	30	1	2	3	4	**5**
	7	8	9	10	11	12	13
	14	15	16	**17**	19	20	21
	21	22	23	24	25	26	27
ŚRĀVAṆA 2016	28	29	30	1	2	3	4
	5	6	7	**8**	10	11	12
	13	14	15	16	17	18	19
	20	21	22	23[c]	24	25	26
BHĀDRAPADA 2016	26	27	28	29	30	**1**	3
	4[d]	5	6	7	8	9	10
	11	12	**13**	15	16	17	17
	18	19	20	21	22	23	24
ĀŚVINA 2016	25	26	27	28	29	30	1
	2	3	4	5	7	8[e]	9[e]
	10[e]	11	12	13	14	15	16
	17	18	19	20	21	21	22
	23	24	25	26	27	**28**	30
KĀRTTIKA 2016	1[f]	2	3	4	5	6	7
	8	9	10	11	12	13	14
	15	16	17	18	19	20	21
	22	23	24	25	26	27	28
MĀRGAŚĪRA 2016	29	30	1	2	**3**	5	6
	7	8	9	10	11[g]	12	13
	14	14	15	16	17	18	19
	20	21	22	23	24	25	26
PAUSHA	**27**	29	30	1	2	3	4

‡Leap year
[a]New Year (Vikārin)
[b]Birthday of Rāma
[c]Birthday of Krishna
[d]Gaṇēśa Chaturthī
[e]Dashara
[f]Diwali
[g]Birthday of Vishnu
[h]Night of Śiva
[i]Holi

HINDU SOLAR 1880/1881‡

Month	Sun	Mon	Tue	Wed	Thu	Fri	Sat
PAUSHA 1880	14	15	16	17	18	19	20
	21	22	23	24	25	26	27
MĀGHA 1880	28	29	30	1[b]	2	3	4
	5	6	7	8	9	10	11
	12	13	14	15	16	17	18
	19	20	21	22	23	24	25
PHĀLGUNA 1880	26	27	28	29	1	2	3
	4	5	6	7	8	9	10
	11	12	13	14	15	16	17
	18	19	20	21	22	23	24
CHAITRA 1880	25	26	27	28	29	30	1
	2	3	4	5	6	7	8
	9	10	11	12	13	14	15
	16	17	18	19	20	21	22
	23	24	25	26	27	28	29
VAIŚĀKHA 1881	30	1[a]	2	3	4	5	6
	7	8	9	10	11	12	13
	14	15	16	17	18	19	20
	21	22	23	24	25	26	27
JYAISHTHA 1881	28	29	30	31	1	2	3
	4	5	6	7	8	9	10
	11	12	13	14	15	16	17
	18	19	20	21	22	23	24
	25	26	27	28	29	30	31
ĀSHĀḌHA 1881	32	1	2	3	4	5	6
	7	8	9	10	11	12	13
	14	15	16	17	18	19	20
	21	22	23	24	25	26	27
ŚRĀVAṆA 1881	28	29	30	31	1	2	3
	4	5	6	7	8	9	10
	11	12	13	14	15	16	17
	18	19	20	21	22	23	24
	25	26	27	28	29	30	31
BHĀDRAPADA 1881	32	1	2	3	4	5	6
	7	8	9	10	11	12	13
	14	15	16	17	18	19	20
	21	22	23	24	25	26	27
ĀŚVINA 1881	28	29	30	31	1	2	3
	4	5	6	7	8	9	10
	11	12	13	14	15	16	17
	18	19	20	21	22	23	24
KĀRTTIKA 1881	25	26	27	28	29	30	1
	2	3	4	5	6	7	8
	9	10	11	12	13	14	15
	16	17	18	19	20	21	22
	23	24	25	26	27	28	29
MĀRGAŚĪRA 1881	30	1	2	3	4	5	6
	7	8	9	10	11	12	13
	14	15	16	17	18	19	20
	21	22	23	24	25	26	27
PAUSHA 1881	28	29	30	1	2	3	4
	5	6	7	8	9	10	11
	12	13	14	15	16	17	18

‡Leap year
[a]New Year (Paridhāvin)
[b]Pongal

ISLAMIC (ASTRONOMICAL) 1378/1379

Month	Sun	Mon	Tue	Wed	Thu	Fri	Sat
JUMĀDĀ II 1378	17	18	19	20	21	22	23
RAJAB 1378	24	25	26	27	28	29	1
	2	3	4	5	6	7	8
	9	10	11	12	13	14	15
	16	17	18	19	20	21	22
	23	24	25	26	27[d]	28	29
SHA'BĀN 1378	30	1	2	3	4	5	6
	7	8	9	10	11	12	13
	14	15	16	17	18	19	20
	21	22	23	24	25	26	27
RAMAḌĀN 1378	28	29	30	1[e]	2	3	4
	5	6	7	8	9	10	11
	12	13	14	15	16	17	18
	19	20	21	22	23	24	25
SHAWWĀL 1378	26	27	28	29	1[f]	2	3
	4	5	6	7	8	9	10
	11	12	13	14	15	16	17
	18	19	20	21	22	23	24
DHU AL-QA'DA 1378	25	26	27	28	29	30	1
	2	3	4	5	6	7	8
	9	10	11	12	13	14	15
	16	17	18	19	20	21	22
	23	24	25	26	27	28	29
DHU AL-ḤIJJA 1378	30	1	2	3	4	5	6
	7	8	9	10[g]	11	12	13
	14	15	16	17	18	19	20
	21	22	23	24	25	26	27
MUḤARRAM 1379	28	29	30[d]	1[a]	2	3	4
	5	6	7	8	9	10[b]	11
	12	13	14	15	16	17	18
	19	20	21	22	23	24	25
ṢAFAR 1379	26	27	28	29	1	2	3
	4	5	6	7	8	9	10
	11	12	13	14	15	16	17
	18	19	20	21	22	23	24
RABĪ' I 1379	25	26	27	28	29	30	1
	2	3	4	5	6	7	8
	9	10	11	12[c]	13	14	15
	16	17	18	19	20	21	22
	23	24	25	26	27	28	29
RABĪ' II 1379	1	2	3	4	5	6	7
	8	9	10	11	12	13	14
	15	16	17	18	19	20	21
	22	23	24	25	26	27	28
JUMĀDĀ I 1379	29	1	2	3	4	5	6
	7	8	9	10	11	12	13
	14	15	16	17	18	19	20
	21	22	23	24	25	26	27
JUMĀDĀ II 1379	28	29	1	2	3	4	5
	6	7	8	9	10	11	12
	13	14	15	16	17	18	19
	20	21	22	23	24	25	26
	27	28	29	30	1	2	3

[a]New Year
[d]New Year (Arithmetic)
[b]'Ashūrā'
[c]Prophet's Birthday
[d]Ascent of the Prophet
[e]Start of Ramaḍān
[f]'Īd al-Fiṭr
[g]'Īd al-'Aḍḥā

GREGORIAN 1959

Julian (Sun)	Sun	Mon	Tue	Wed	Thu	Fri	Sat	Month
Dec 15	28	29	30	31	1	2	3	JANUARY 1959
	4	5	6	7[a]	8	9	10	
Dec 29	11	12	13	14[b]	15	16	17	
	18	19	20	21	22	23	24	
Jan 12	25	26	27	28	29	30	31	
	1	2	3	4	5	6	7	FEBRUARY 1959
Jan 26	8	9	10	11[c]	12	13	14	
	15	16	17	18	19	20	21	
Feb 9	22	23	24	25	26	27	28	
	1	2	3	4	5	6	7	MARCH 1959
Feb 23	8	9	10	11	12	13	14	
	15	16	17	18	19	20	21	
Mar 9	22[d]	23	24	25	26	27	28	
	29[e]	30	31	1	2	3	4	APRIL 1959
Mar 23	5	6	7	8	9	10	11	
	12	13	14	15	16	17	18	
Apr 6	19	20	21	22	23	24	25	
	26	27	28	29	30	1	2	MAY 1959
Apr 20	3[f]	4	5	6	7	8	9	
	10	11	12	13	14	15	16	
May 4	17	18	19	20	21	22	23	
	24	25	26	27	28	29	30	
May 18	31	1	2	3	4	5	6	JUNE 1959
	7	8	9	10	11	12	13	
Jun 1	14	15	16	17	18	19	20	
	21	22	23	24	25	26	27	
Jun 15	28	29	30	1	2	3	4	JULY 1959
	5	6	7	8	9	10	11	
Jun 29	12	13	14	15	16	17	18	
	19	20	21	22	23	24	25	
Jul 13	26	27	28	29	30	31	1	AUGUST 1959
	2	3	4	5	6	7	8	
Jul 27	9	10	11	12	13	14	15	
	16	17	18	19	20	21	22	
Aug 10	23	24	25	26	27	28	29	
	30	31	1	2	3	4	5	SEPTEMBER 1959
Aug 24	6	7	8	9	10	11	12	
	13	14	15	16	17	18	19	
Sep 7	20	21	22	23	24	25	26	
	27	28	29	30	1	2	3	OCTOBER 1959
Sep 21	4	5	6	7	8	9	10	
	11	12	13	14	15	16	17	
Oct 5	18	19	20	21	22	23	24	
	25	26	27	28	29	30	31	
Oct 19	1	2	3	4	5	6	7	NOVEMBER 1959
	8	9	10	11	12	13	14	
Nov 2	15	16	17	18	19	20	21	
	22	23	24	25	26	27	28	
Nov 16	29[g]	30	1	2	3	4	5	DECEMBER 1959
	6	7	8	9	10	11	12	
Nov 30	13	14	15	16	17	18	19	
	20	21	22	23	24	25[h]	26	
Dec 14	27	28	29	30	31	1	2	

[a]Orthodox Christmas
[b]Julian New Year
[c]Ash Wednesday
[d]Feast of Orthodoxy
[e]Easter
[f]Orthodox Easter
[g]Advent
[h]Christmas

1960

Gregorian month	Sun	Mon	Tue	Wed	Thu	Fri	Sat	Lunar Phases	ISO WEEK (Mon)	JULIAN DAY (Sun noon)	Hebrew month	Sun	Mon	Tue	Wed	Thu	Fri	Sat	Molad
	27	28	●	30	31	1[a]	2	19:09	53	2436930		26[e]	27[e]	28[e]	29[e]	30[e]	1[e]	2[e]	Wed 3h13m4p
JANUARY 1960	3	4	◐	6	7	8	9	18:53	1	2436937	TEVETH 5720	3	4	5	6	7	8	9	
	10	11	12	○	14	15	16	23:50	2	2436944		10	11	12	13	14	15	16	
	17	18	19	20	◑	22	23	15:01	3	2436951		17	18	19	20	21	22	23	
	24	25	26	27	●	29	30	6:15	4	2436958		24	25	26	27	28	29	1	Thu 15h57m5p
	31	1	2	3	◐	5	6	14:26	5	2436965		2	3	4	5	6	7	8	
FEBRUARY 1960	7	8	9	10	11	○	13	17:24	6	2436972	SHEVAT 5720	9	10	11	12	13	14	15	
	14	15	16	17	18	◑	20	23:47	7	2436979		16	17	18	19	20	21	22	
	21	22	23	24	25	●	27	18:24	8	2436986		23	24	25	26	27	28	29	
	28	29	1	2	3	4	◐	11:05	9	2436993		30	1	2	3	4	5	6	Sat 4h41m6p
MARCH 1960	6	7	8	9	10	11	12		10	2437000		7	8	9	10	11	12	13	
	○	14	15	16	17	18	19	8:26	11	2437007	ADAR 5720	14[f]	15	16	17	18	19	20	
	◑[b]	21	22	23	24	25	26	6:40	12	2437014		21	22	23	24	25	26	27	
	●	28	29	30	31	1	2	7:37	13	2437021		28	29	1	2	3	4	5	Sun 17h25m7p
APRIL 1960	3	◐	5	6	7	8	9	7:04	14	2437028		6	7	8	9	10	11	12	
	10	○	12	13	14	15	16	20:27	15	2437035	NISAN 5720	13	14	15[g]	16	17	18	19	
	17	◑	19	20	21	22	23	12:57	16	2437042		20	21	22	23	24	25	26	
	24	●	26	27	28	29	30	21:44	17	2437049		27	28	29	30	1	2	3	Tue 6h9m8p
	1	2	3	◐	5	6	7	1:00	18	2437056		4	5	6	7	8	9	10	
MAY 1960	8	9	10	○	12	13	14	5:42	19	2437063	IYYAR 5720	11	12	13	14	15	16	17	
	15	16	◑	18	19	20	21	19:54	20	2437070		18	19	20	21	22	23	24	
	22	23	24	●	26	27	28	12:26	21	2437077		25	26	27	28	29	1	2	Wed 18h53m9p
	29	30	31	1	◐	3	4	16:01	22	2437084		3	4	5	6[h]	7	8	9	
JUNE 1960	5	6	7	8	○	10	11	13:02	23	2437091	SIVAN 5720	10	11	12	13	14	15	16	
	12	13	14	15	◑	17	18	4:35	24	2437098		17	18	19	20	21	22	23	
	19	20	21[c]	22	23	●	25	3:27	25	2437105		24	25	26	27	28	29	30	
	26	27	28	29	30	1	◐	3:48	26	2437112		1	2	3	4	5	6	7	Fri 7h37m10p
JULY 1960	3	4	5	6	7	○	9	19:37	27	2437119	TAMMUZ 5720	8	9	10	11	12	13	14	
	10	11	12	13	14	◑	16	15:43	28	2437126		15	16	17	18	19	20	21	
	17	18	19	20	21	22	●	18:31	29	2437133		22	23	24	25	26	27	28	
	24	25	26	27	28	29	30		30	2437140		29	1	2	3	4	5	6	Sat 20h21m11p
	◐	1	2	3	4	5	6	12:38	31	2437147		7	8	9[i]	10	11	12	13	
AUGUST 1960	○	8	9	10	11	12	13	2:41	32	2437154	AV 5720	14	15	16	17	18	19	20	
	◑	15	16	17	18	19	20	5:37	33	2437161		21	22	23	24	25	26	27	
	21	●	23	24	25	26	27	9:15	34	2437168		28	29	30	1	2	3	4	Mon 9h5m12p
	28	◐	30	31	1	2	3	19:22	35	2437175		5	6	7	8	9	10	11	
SEPTEMBER 1960	4	○	6	7	8	9	10	11:19	36	2437182	ELUL 5720	12	13	14	15	16	17	18	
	11	◑	13	14	15	16	17	22:19	37	2437189		19	20	21	22	23	24	25	
	18	19	●	21	22	23[d]	24	23:13	38	2437196		26	27	28	29	1[a]	2[a]	3	Tue 21h49m13p
	25	26	27	◐	29	30	1	1:13	39	2437203		4	5	6	7	8	9	10[b]	
OCTOBER 1960	2	3	○	5	6	7	8	22:16	40	2437210	TISHRI 5721	11	12	13	14	15[c]	16	17	
	9	10	11	◑	13	14	15	17:25	41	2437217		18	19	20	21	22	23	24	
	16	17	18	19	●	21	22	12:02	42	2437224		25	26	27	28	29	30	1	Thu 10h33m14p
	23	24	25	26	◐	28	29	7:34	43	2437231		2	3	4	5	6	7	8	
	30	31	1	2	○	4	5	11:58	44	2437238	HESHVAN 5721	9	10	11	12	13	14	15	
NOVEMBER 1960	6	7	8	9	10	◑	12	13:48	45	2437245		16	17	18	19	20	21	22	
	13	14	15	16	17	●	19	23:46	46	2437252		23	24	25	26	27	28	29	
	20	21	22	23	24	◐	26	15:42	47	2437259		1	2	3	4	5	6	7	Fri 23h17m15p
	27	28	29	30	1	2	○	4:24	48	2437266		8	9	10	11	12	13	14	
DECEMBER 1960	4	5	6	7	8	9	10		49	2437273	KISLEV 5721	15	16[d]	17	18	19	20	21	
	◑	12	13	14	15	16	17	9:38	50	2437280		22	23	24	25[e]	26[e]	27[e]	28[e]	
	●	19	20	21[e]	22	23	24	10:47	51	2437287		29[e]	30[e]	1[e]	2[e]	3	4	5	Sun 12h1m16p
	◐	26	27	28	29	30	31	2:30	52	2437294	TEVETH 5721	6	7	8	9	10	11	12	

ISO WEEK	Chinese month (Jĭ-Hài/Gēng-Zĭ‡)	Sun	Mon	Tue	Wed	Thu	Fri	Sat	Solar Term	Coptic month (1676/1677)	Sun	Mon	Tue	Wed	Thu	Fri	Sat	Ethiopic month (1952/1953)
53		28	29	30	1	2	3	4		KOIAK 1676	17	18	19	20	21	22	23	TĀKHŚĀŚ 1952
1	MONTH 12 Jĭ-Hài	5	6	7	*8*	9	10	11	Xiǎo hán		24	25	26	27	28	29[c]	30	
2		12	13	14	15	16	17	18			1	2	3	4	5	6[d]	7	
3		19	20	21	22	***23***	24	25	Dà hán	TÔBE 1676	8	9	10	11[e]	12	13	14	
4		26	27	28	29	1[a]	2	3			15	16	17	18	19	20	21	ṬER 1952
5	MONTH 1 Gēng-Zĭ	4	5	6	7	8	*9*	10*	Lì chūn		22	23	24	25	26	27	28	
6		11	12	13	14	15[b]	16	17			29	30	1	2	3	4	5	
7		18	19	20	21	22	***23***	24	Yǔ shuǐ	MESHIR 1676	6	7	8	9	10	11	12	YAKĀTIT 1952
8		25	26	27	28	29	30	1			13	14	15	16	17	18	19	
9	MONTH 2 Gēng-Zĭ	2	3	4	5	6	7	*8*	Jīng zhé		20	21	22	23	24	25	26	
10		9	10	11	12	13	14	15			27	28	29	30	1	2	3	
11		16	17	18	19	20	21	22		PAREMOTEP 1676	4	5	6	7	8	9	10	MAGĀBIT 1952
12		***23***	24	25	26	27	28	29	Chūn fēn		11	12	13	14	15	16	17	
13		1	2	3	4	5	6	7			18	19	20	21	22	23	24	
14	MONTH 3 Gēng-Zĭ	8	9	*10*[c]	11*	12	13	14	Qīng míng		25	26	27	28	29	30	1	
15		15	16	17	18	19	20	21		PARMOUTE 1676	2	3	4	5	6	7	8	MIYĀZYĀ 1952
16		22	23	24	***25***	26	27	28	Gǔ yǔ		9[f]	10	11	12	13	14	15	
17		29	30	1	2	3	4	5			16	17	18	19	20	21	22	
18	MONTH 4 Gēng-Zĭ	6	7	8	9	*10*	11	12	Lì xià		23	24	25	26	27	28	29[g]	
19		13	14	15	16	17	18	19			30	1	2	3	4	5	6	
20		20	21	22	23	24	25	***26***	Xiǎo mǎn	PASHONS 1676	7	8	9	10	11	12	13	GENBOT 1952
21		27	28	29	1	2	3	4			14	15	16	17	18	19	20	
22	MONTH 5 Gēng-Zĭ	5[d]	6	7	8	9	10	11			21	22	23	24	25	26	27	
23		12*	*13*	14	15	16	17	18	Máng zhòng		28	29	30	1	2	3	4	
24		19	20	21	22	23	24	25		PAÔNE 1676	5	6	7	8	9	10	11	SANĒ 1952
25		26	27	***28***	29	30	1	2	Xià zhì		12	13	14	15	16	17	18	
26	MONTH 6 Gēng-Zĭ	3	4	5	6	7	8	9			19	20	21	22	23	24	25	
27		10	11	12	13	*14*	15	16	Xiǎo shǔ		26	27	28	29	30	1	2	
28		17	18	19	20	21	22	23		EPÊP 1676	3	4	5	6	7	8	9	ḤAMLĒ 1952
29		24	25	26	27	28	29	***30***	Dà shǔ		10	11	12	13	14	15	16	
30		1	2	3	4	5	6	7			17	18	19	20	21	22	23	
31	LEAP MONTH 6 Gēng-Zĭ	8	9	10	11	12*	13	14			24	25	26	27	28	29	30	
32		*15*	16	17	18	19	20	21	Lì qiū		1	2	3	4	5	6	7	
33		22	23	24	25	26	27	28		MESORÊ 1676	8	9	10	11	12	13[h]	14	NAḤASĒ 1952
34		29	1	***2***	3	4	5	6	Chǔ shǔ		15	16	17	18	19	20	21	
35	MONTH 7 Gēng-Zĭ	7[e]	8	9	10	11	12	13			22	23	24	25	26	27	28	
36		14	15[f]	16	*17*	18	19	20	Bái lù	EPAG. 1676	29	30	1	2	3	4	5	PĀG. 1952
37		21	22	23	24	25	26	27			1[a]	2	3	4	5	6	7	
38		28	29	30	1	2	***3***	4	Qiū fēn	THOOUT 1677	8	9	10	11	12	13	14	MASKARAM 1953
39	MONTH 8 Gēng-Zĭ	5	6	7	8	9	10	11			15	16	17[b]	18	19	20	21	
40		12	13*	14	15[g]	16	17	*18*	Hán lù		22	23	24	25	26	27	28	
41		19	20	21	22	23	24	25			29	30	1	2	3	4	5	
42		26	27	28	29	1	2	3			6	7	8	9	10	11	12	
43	MONTH 9 Gēng-Zĭ	***4***	5	6	7	8	9[h]	10	Shuāng jiàng	PAOPE 1677	13	14	15	16	17	18	19	ṬEQEMT 1953
44		11	12	13	14	15	16	17			20	21	22	23	24	25	26	
45		18	*19*	20	21	22	23	24	Lì dōng		27	28	29	30	1	2	3	
46		25	26	27	28	29	30	1			4	5	6	7	8	9	10	
47	MONTH 10 Gēng-Zĭ	2	3	***4***	5	6	7	8	Xiǎo xuě	ATHÔR 1677	11	12	13	14	15	16	17	ḪEDĀR 1953
48		9	10	11	12	13	14*	15			18	19	20	21	22	23	24	
49		16	17	18	*19*	20	21	22	Dà xuě		25	26	27	28	29	30	1	
50		23	24	25	26	27	28	29		KOIAK 1677	2	3	4	5	6	7	8	TĀKHŚĀŚ 1953
51	MONTH 11 Gēng-Zĭ	1	2	3	4	***5***[i]	6	7	Dōng zhì		9	10	11	12	13	14	15	
52		8	9	10	11	12	13	14			16	17	18	19	20	21	22	

‡Leap year
[a]New Year
[b]Spring (14:42)
[c]Summer (9:42)
[d]Autumn (0:59)
[e]Winter (20:26)
● New moon
◐ First quarter moon
○ Full moon
◑ Last quarter moon

[a]New Year
[b]Yom Kippur
[c]Sukkot
[d]Winter starts
[e]Ḥanukkah
[f]Purim
[g]Passover
[h]Shavuot
[i]Fast of Av

‡Leap year
[a]New Year (4658, Rat)
[b]Lantern Festival
[c]Qīngmíng
[d]Dragon Festival
[e]Qīqiǎo
[f]Hungry Ghosts
[g]Mid-Autumn Festival
[h]Double-Ninth Festival
[i]Dōngzhì
*Start of 60-name cycle

[a]New Year
[b]Building of the Cross
[c]Christmas
[d]Jesus's Circumcision
[e]Epiphany
[f]Easter
[g]Mary's Announcement
[h]Jesus's Transfiguration

PERSIAN (ASTRONOMICAL) 1338/1339

Month	Sun	Mon	Tue	Wed	Thu	Fri	Sat
DEY 1338	5	6	7	8	9	10	11
	12	13	14	15	16	17	18
	19	20	21	22	23	24	25
	26	27	28	29	30	*1*	2
BAHMAN 1338	3	4	5	6	7	8	9
	10	11	12	13	14	15	16
	17	18	19	20	21	22	23
	24	25	26	27	28	29	30
ESFAND 1338	*1*	2	3	4	5	6	7
	8	9	10	11	12	13	14
	15	16	17	18	19	20	21
	22	23	24	25	26	27	28
	29	*1*[a]	2	3	4	5	6
FARVARDĪN 1339	7	8	9	10	11	12	13[b]
	14	15	16	17	18	19	20
	21	22	23	24	25	26	27
	28	29	30	31	*1*	2	3
ORDĪBEHEŠT 1339	4	5	6	7	8	9	10
	11	12	13	14	15	16	17
	18	19	20	21	22	23	24
	25	26	27	28	29	30	31
XORDĀD 1339	*1*	2	3	4	5	6	7
	8	9	10	11	12	13	14
	15	16	17	18	19	20	21
	22	23	24	25	26	27	28
	29	30	31	*1*	2	3	4
TĪR 1339	5	6	7	8	9	10	11
	12	13	14	15	16	17	18
	19	20	21	22	23	24	25
	26	27	28	29	30	31	*1*
MORDĀD 1339	2	3	4	5	6	7	8
	9	10	11	12	13	14	15
	16	17	18	19	20	21	22
	23	24	25	26	27	28	29
	30	31	*1*	2	3	4	5
SHAHRĪVAR 1339	6	7	8	9	10	11	12
	13	14	15	16	17	18	19
	20	21	22	23	24	25	26
	27	28	29	30	31	*1*	2
MEHR 1339	3	4	5	6	7	8	9
	10	11	12	13	14	15	16
	17	18	19	20	21	22	23
	24	25	26	27	28	29	30
ĀBĀN 1339	*1*	2	3	4	5	6	7
	8	9	10	11	12	13	14
	15	16	17	18	19	20	21
	22	23	24	25	26	27	28
	29	30	*1*	2	3	4	5
ĀZAR 1339	6	7	8	9	10	11	12
	13	14	15	16	17	18	19
	20	21	22	23	24	25	26
	27	28	29	30	*1*	2	3
DEY 1339	4	5	6	7	8	9	10

[a]New Year
[b]Sizdeh Bedar

HINDU LUNAR 2016/2017

Month	Sun	Mon	Tue	Wed	Thu	Fri	Sat
	27	29	30	1	2	3	4
PAUSHA 2016	5	6	7	8	9	10	11
	12	13	14	15	16	17	*17*
	18	19	**20**	22	23	24	25
	26	27	28	29	30	1	2
MĀGHA 2016	3	4	5	6	7	8	9
	10	11	12	13	14	15	16
	17	18	19	20	21	22	23
	24	25	**26**	28	29[h]	30	1
PHĀLGUNA 2016	2	3	4	5	6	7	8
	9	*9*	10	11	12	13	14
	15[i]	16	17	18	19	**20**	22
	23	24	25	26	27	28	29
	30	1[a]	2	3	4	5	6
CHAITRA 2017	7	8	9[b]	10	11	12	13
	14	15	16	17	18	19	20
	21	22	23	**24**	26	27	28
	29	30	1	2	3	*3*	4
VAIŚĀKHA 2017	5	6	7	8	9	10	11
	12	13	14	15	16	**17**	19
	20	21	22	23	24	25	26
	27	28	29	30	1	2	3
JYAISHTHA 2017	4	5	6	7	8	9	10
	11	12	13	14	15	16	17
	18	19	**20**	22	23	24	25
	26	27	28	29	*29*	30	1
ĀSHĀḌHA 2017	2	3	4	5	6	7	8
	9	10	11	12	**13**	15	16
	17	18	19	20	21	22	23
	24	25	26	27	28	29	30
	1	2	3	4	5	6	7
ŚRĀVAṆA 2017	8	9	10	11	12	13	14
	15	**16**	18	19	20	21	22
	23[c]	24	25	26	*26*	27	28
	29	30	1	2	3	4[d]	5
BHĀDRAPADA 2017	6	7	8	**9**	11	12	13
	14	15	16	17	18	19	20
	21	22	23	24	25	26	27
	28	29	30	1	2	3	4
ĀŚVINA 2017	5	6	7	8[e]	9[e]	10[e]	11
	12	14	15	16	17	18	19
	20	21	*21*	22	23	24	25
	26	27	28	29	30	1[f]	2
KĀRTTIKA 2017	3	4	5	**6**	8	9	10
	11	12	13	14	15	16	17
	18	19	20	21	22	23	24
	25	*25*	26	27	28	**29**	1
MĀRGAŚĪRA 2017	2	3	4	5	6	7	8
	9	10	11[g]	12	13	14	15
	16	17	18	19	20	21	22
	23	24	25	26	27	28	29
PAUSHA 2017	30	1	2	3	**4**	6	7
	8	9	10	11	12	13	14

[a]New Year (Śārvari)
[b]Birthday of Rāma
[c]Birthday of Krishna
[d]Ganēśa Chaturthī
[e]Dashara
[f]Diwali
[g]Birthday of Vishnu
[h]Night of Śiva
[i]Holi

HINDU SOLAR 1881‡/1882

Month	Sun	Mon	Tue	Wed	Thu	Fri	Sat
PAUSHA 1881	12	13	14	15	16	17	18
	19	20	21	22	23	24	25
	26	27	28	29	1[b]	2	3
MĀGHA 1881	4	5	6	7	8	9	10
	11	12	13	14	15	16	17
	18	19	20	21	22	23	24
	25	26	27	28	29	1	2
PHĀLGUNA 1881	3	4	5	6	7	8	9
	10	11	12	13	14	15	16
	17	18	19	20	21	22	23
	24	25	26	27	28	29	30
	1	2	3	4	5	6	7
CHAITRA 1881	8	9	10	11	12	13	14
	15	16	17	18	19	20	21
	22	23	24	25	26	27	28
	29	30	31	1[a]	2	3	4
VAIŚĀKHA 1882	5	6	7	8	9	10	11
	12	13	14	15	16	17	18
	19	20	21	22	23	24	25
	26	27	28	29	30	31	1
JYAISHTHA 1882	2	3	4	5	6	7	8
	9	10	11	12	13	14	15
	16	17	18	19	20	21	22
	23	24	25	26	27	28	29
	30	31	1	2	3	4	5
ĀSHĀḌHA 1882	6	7	8	9	10	11	12
	13	14	15	16	17	18	19
	20	21	22	23	24	25	26
	27	28	29	30	31	32	1
ŚRĀVAṆA 1882	2	3	4	5	6	7	8
	9	10	11	12	13	14	15
	16	17	18	19	20	21	22
	23	24	25	26	27	28	29
	30	31	1	2	3	4	5
BHĀDRAPADA 1882	6	7	8	9	10	11	12
	13	14	15	16	17	18	19
	20	21	22	23	24	25	26
	27	28	29	30	31	1	2
ĀŚVINA 1882	3	4	5	6	7	8	9
	10	11	12	13	14	15	16
	17	18	19	20	21	22	23
	24	25	26	27	28	29	30
	31	1	2	3	4	5	6
KĀRTTIKA 1882	7	8	9	10	11	12	13
	14	15	16	17	18	19	20
	21	22	23	24	25	26	27
	28	29	1	2	3	4	5
MĀRGAŚĪRA 1882	6	7	8	9	10	11	12
	13	14	15	16	17	18	19
	20	21	22	23	24	25	26
	27	28	29	30	1	2	3
PAUSHA 1882	4	5	6	7	8	9	10
	11	12	13	14	15	16	17

‡Leap year
[a]New Year (Pramādin)
[b]Pongal

ISLAMIC (ASTRONOMICAL) 1379/1380

Month	Sun	Mon	Tue	Wed	Thu	Fri	Sat
	27	28	29	30	*1*	2	3
RAJAB 1379	4	5	6	7	8	9	10
	11	12	13	14	15	16	17
	18	19	20	21	22	23	24
	25	26	27[d]	28	29	*1*	2
SHA'BĀN 1379	3	4	5	6	7	8	9
	10	11	12	13	14	15	16
	17	18	19	20	21	22	23
	24	25	26	27	28	29	30
RAMAḌĀN 1379	*1*[e]	2	3	4	5	6	7
	8	9	10	11	12	13	14
	15	16	17	18	19	20	21
	22	23	24	25	26	27	28
	29	30	*1*[f]	2	3	4	5
SHAWWĀL 1379	6	7	8	9	10	11	12
	13	14	15	16	17	18	19
	20	21	22	23	24	25	26
	27	28	29	*1*	2	3	4
DHU AL-QA'DA 1379	5	6	7	8	9	10	11
	12	13	14	15	16	17	18
	19	20	21	22	23	24	25
	26	27	28	29	30	*1*	2
DHU AL-ḤIJJA 1379	3	4	5	6	7	8	9
	10[g]	11	12	13	14	15	16
	17	18	19	20	21	22	23
	24	25	26	27	28	29	30
MUḤARRAM 1380	*1*[a]	2	3	4	5	6	7
	8	9	10[b]	11	12	13	14
	15	16	17	18	19	20	21
	22	23	24	25	26	27	28
	29	30	*1*	2	3	4	5
ṢAFAR 1380	6	7	8	9	10	11	12
	13	14	15	16	17	18	19
	20	21	22	23	24	25	26
	27	28	29	*1*	2	3	4
RABĪ' I 1380	5	6	7	8	9	10	11
	12[c]	13	14	15	16	17	18
	19	20	21	22	23	24	25
	26	27	28	29	1	*2*	3
RABĪ' II 1380	4	5	6	7	8	9	10
	11	12	13	14	15	16	17
	18	19	20	21	22	23	24
	25	26	27	28	29	30	*1*
JUMĀDĀ I 1380	2	3	4	5	6	7	8
	9	10	11	12	13	14	15
	16	17	18	19	20	21	22
	23	24	25	26	27	28	29
JUMĀDĀ II 1380	*1*	2	3	4	5	6	7
	8	9	10	11	12	13	14
	15	16	17	18	19	20	21
	22	23	24	25	26	27	28
	29	30	*1*	2	3	4	5
RAJAB 1380	6	7	8	9	10	11	12

[a]New Year
[b]'Ashūrā'
[c]Prophet's Birthday
[d]Ascent of the Prophet
[e]Start of Ramaḍān
[f]'Id al-Fiṭr
[g]'Id al-'Aḍḥā

GREGORIAN 1960‡

Julian‡ (Sun)	Month	Sun	Mon	Tue	Wed	Thu	Fri	Sat
Dec 14		*27*	28	29	30	31	1	2
	JANUARY 1960	3	4	5	6	7[a]	8	9
Dec 28		*10*	11	12	13	14[b]	15	16
		17	18	19	20	21	22	23
Jan 11		*24*	25	26	27	28	29	30
	FEBRUARY 1960	31	1	2	3	4	5	6
Jan 25		*7*	8	9	10	11	12	13
		14	15	16	17	18	19	20
Feb 8		*21*	22	23	24	25	26	27
	MARCH 1960	28	29	1	2[c]	3	4	5
Feb 22		*6*[d]	7	8	9	10	11	12
		13	14	15	16	17	18	19
Mar 7		*20*	21	22	23	24	25	26
	APRIL 1960	27	28	29	30	31	1	2
Mar 21		*3*	4	5	6	7	8	9
		10	11	12	13	14	15	16
Apr 4		*17*[e]	18	19	20	21	22	23
		24	25	26	27	28	29	30
Apr 18	MAY 1960	*1*	2	3	4	5	6	7
		8	9	10	11	12	13	14
May 2		*15*	16	17	18	19	20	21
		22	23	24	25	26	27	28
May 16	JUNE 1960	*29*	30	31	1	2	3	4
		5	6	7	8	9	10	11
May 30		*12*	13	14	15	16	17	18
		19	20	21	22	23	24	25
Jun 13	JULY 1960	*26*	27	28	29	30	1	2
		3	4	5	6	7	8	9
Jun 27		*10*	11	12	13	14	15	16
		17	18	19	20	21	22	23
Jul 11		*24*	25	26	27	28	29	30
	AUGUST 1960	31	1	2	3	4	5	6
Jul 25		*7*	8	9	10	11	12	13
		14	15	16	17	18	19	20
Aug 8		*21*	22	23	24	25	26	27
	SEPTEMBER 1960	28	29	30	31	1	2	3
Aug 22		*4*	5	6	7	8	9	10
		11	12	13	14	15	16	17
Sep 5		*18*	19	20	21	22	23	24
	OCTOBER 1960	25	26	27	28	29	30	1
Sep 19		*2*	3	4	5	6	7	8
		9	10	11	12	13	14	15
Oct 3		*16*	17	18	19	20	21	22
		23	24	25	26	27	28	29
Oct 17	NOVEMBER 1960	*30*	31	1	2	3	4	5
		6	7	8	9	10	11	12
Oct 31		*13*	14	15	16	17	18	19
		20	21	22	23	24	25	26
Nov 14	DECEMBER 1960	*27*[g]	28	29	30	1	2	3
		4	5	6	7	8	9	10
Nov 28		*11*	12	13	14	15	16	17
		18	19	20	21	22	23	24
Dec 12		*25*[h]	26	27	28	29	30	31

‡Leap year
[a]Orthodox Christmas
[b]Julian New Year
[c]Ash Wednesday
[d]Feast of Orthodoxy
[e]Easter (also Orthodox)
[g]Advent
[h]Christmas

1961

Gregorian 1961	Sun	Mon	Tue	Wed	Thu	Fri	Sat	Lunar Phases	ISO Week (Mon)	Julian Day (Sun noon)	Hebrew 5721/5722‡	Sun	Mon	Tue	Wed	Thu	Fri	Sat	Molad	Chinese Gēng-Zǐ‡/Xīn-Chǒu	Sun	Mon	Tue	Wed	Thu	Fri	Sat	Solar Term	Coptic 1677/1678	Sun	Mon	Tue	Wed	Thu	Fri	Sat	Ethiopic 1953/1954
January 1961	○[a]	2	3	4	5	6	7	23:06	1	2437301	Tevet 5721	13	14	15	16	17	18	19	Tue 0h45m17p	Month 11 Gēng-Zǐ	15	16	17	18	19	20	21	Xiǎo hán	Koiak 1677	23	24	25	26	27	28	29[c]	Tāḫśāś 1953
	8	9	◑	11	12	13	14	3:02	2	2437308		20	21	22	23	24	25	26			22	23	24	25	26	27	28		Ṭōbe 1677	30	1	2	3	4	5	6[d]	Ṭer 1953
	15	●	17	18	19	20	21	21:30	3	2437315	Shevat 5721	27	28	29	1	2	3	4		Month 12 Gēng-Zǐ	29	30	1	2	3	4	5	Dà hán		7	8	9	10	11[e]	12	13	
	22	◐	24	25	26	27	28	16:13	4	2437322		5	6	7	8	9	10	11			6	7	8	9	10	11	12			14	15	16	17	18	19	20	
February 1961	29	30	○	1	2	3	4	18:47	5	2437329		12	13	14	15	16	17	18			13	14	15*	16	17	18	19	Lì chūn		21	22	23	24	25	26	27	
	5	6	7	◑	9	10	11	16:49	6	2437336		19	20	21	22	23	24	25			20	21	22	23	24	25	26		Meshir 1677	28	29	30	1	2	3	4	Yakātit 1953
	12	13	14	●	16	17	18	8:10	7	2437343	Adar 5721	26	27	28	29	30	1	2	Wed 13h30m0p	Month 1 Xīn-Chǒu	27	28	29	1[a]	2	3	4			5	6	7	8	9	10	11	
	19	20	21	◐	23	24	25	8:34	8	2437350		3	4	5	6	7	8	9			5	6	7	8	9	10	11	Yǔ shuǐ		12	13	14	15	16	17	18	
March 1961	26	27	28	1	○	3	4	13:35	9	2437357		10	11	12	13	14[f]	15	16			12	13	14	15[b]	16	17	18			19	20	21	22	23	24	25	
	5	6	7	8	9	◑	11	2:57	10	2437364		17	18	19	20	21	22	23			19	20	21	22	23	24	25	Jīng zhé	Paremotep 1677	26	27	28	29	30	1	2	Magābit 1953
	12	13	14	15	●	17	18	18:51	11	2437371	Nisan 5721	24	25	26	27	28	29	1	Fri 2h14m1p	Month 2 Xīn-Chǒu	26	27	28	29	30	1	2			3	4	5	6	7	8	9	
	19	20[b]	21	22	23	◐	25	2:48	12	2437378		2	3	4	5	6	7	8			3	4	5	6	7	8	9	Chūn fēn		10	11	12	13	14	15	16	
April 1961	26	27	28	29	30	31	○	5:47	13	2437385		9	10	11	12	13	14	15[g]			10	11	12	13	14	15	16*			17	18	19	20	21	22	23	
	2	3	4	5	6	7	◑	10:16	14	2437392		16	17	18	19	20	21	22			17	18	19	20[c]	21	22	23	Qīng míng		24	25	26	27	28	29	30	
	9	10	11	12	13	14	●	5:38	15	2437399		23	24	25	26	27	28	29		Month 3 Xīn-Chǒu	24	25	26	27	28	29	1		Parmoute 1677	1[f]	2	3	4	5	6	7	Miyāzyā 1953
	16	17	18	19	20	21	◐	21:49	16	2437406	Iyyar 5721	30	1	2	3	4	5	6	Sat 14h58m2p		2	3	4	5	6	7	8	Gǔ yǔ		8	9	10	11	12	13	14	
	23	24	25	26	27	28	29		17	2437413		7	8	9	10	11	12	13			9	10	11	12	13	14	15			15	16	17	18	19	20	21	
May 1961	○	1	2	3	4	5	6	18:40	18	2437420		14	15	16	17	18	19	20			16	17	18	19	20	21	22	Lì xià		22	23	24	25	26	27	28	
	◑	8	9	10	11	12	13	15:57	19	2437427		21	22	23	24	25	26	27			23	24	25	26	27	28	29		Pashons 1677	29[g]	30	1	2	3	4	5	Genbot 1953
	●	15	16	17	18	19	20	16:54	20	2437434	Sivan 5721	28	29	1	2	3	4	5	Mon 3h42m3p	Month 4 Xīn-Chǒu	30	1	2	3	4	5	6			6	7	8	9	10	11	12	
	21	◐	23	24	25	26	27	16:18	21	2437441		6[h]	7	8	9	10	11	12			7	8	9	10	11	12	13	Xiǎo mǎn		13	14	15	16	17	18	19	
June 1961	28	29	○	31	1	2	3	4:37	22	2437448		13	14	15	16	17	18	19			14	15	16	17*	18	19	20			20	21	22	23	24	25	26	
	4	◑	6	7	8	9	10	21:19	23	2437455		20	21	22	23	24	25	26			21	22	23	24	25	26	27	Máng zhòng	Paōne 1677	27	28	29	30	1	2	3	Sanē 1953
	11	12	●	14	15	16	17	5:15	24	2437462	Tammuz 5721	27	28	29	30	1	2	3	Tue 16h26m4p	Month 5 Xīn-Chǒu	28	29	1	2	3	4	5[d]			4	5	6	7	8	9	10	
	18	19	20	◐[c]	22	23	24	9:01	25	2437469		4	5	6	7	8	9	10			6	7	8	9	10	11	12	Xià zhì		11	12	13	14	15	16	17	
July 1961	25	26	27	○	29	30	1	12:38	26	2437476		11	12	13	14	15	16	17			13	14	15	16	17	18	19			18	19	20	21	22	23	24	
	2	3	4	◑	6	7	8	3:32	27	2437483		18	19	20	21	22	23	24			20	21	22	23	24	25	26	Xiǎo shǔ	Epēp 1677	25	26	27	28	29	30	1	Hamlē 1953
	9	10	11	●	13	14	15	19:11	28	2437490	Av 5721	25	26	27	28	29	1	2	Thu 5h10m5p	Month 6 Xīn-Chǒu	27	28	29	30	1	2	3			2	3	4	5	6	7	8	
	16	17	18	19	◐	21	22	23:13	29	2437497		3	4	5	6	7	8	9			4	5	6	7	8	9	10			9	10	11	12	13	14	15	
	23	24	25	26	○	28	29	19:50	30	2437504		10[i]	11	12	13	14	15	16			11	12	13	14	15	16	17	Dà shǔ		16	17	18	19	20	21	22	
August 1961	30	31	1	2	◑	4	5	11:47	31	2437511		17	18	19	20	21	22	23			18*	19	20	21	22	23	24			23	24	25	26	27	28	29	
	6	7	8	9	10	●	12	10:36	32	2437518	Elul 5721	24	25	26	27	28	29	30	Fri 17h54m6p	Month 7 Xīn-Chǒu	25	26	27	28	29	1	2	Lì qiū	Mesorē 1677	30	1	2	3	4	5	6	Naḥasē 1953
	13	14	15	16	17	18	◐	10:51	33	2437525		1	2	3	4	5	6	7			3	4	5	6	7[e]	8	9			7	8	9	10	11	12	13[h]	
	20	21	22	23	24	25	○	3:13	34	2437532		8	9	10	11	12	13	14			10	11	12	13	14	15[f]	16	Chǔ shǔ		14	15	16	17	18	19	20	
September 1961	27	28	29	30	31	◑	2	23:05	35	2437539		15	16	17	18	19	20	21			17	18	19	20	21	22	23			21	22	23	24	25	26	27	
	3	4	5	6	7	8	9		36	2437546		22	23	24	25	26	27	28			24	25	26	27	28	29	30	Bái lù	Epag. 1677	28	29	30	1	2	3	4	Pāg. 1953
	●	11	12	13	14	15	16	2:49	37	2437553	Tishri 5722	29	1[a]	2[a]	3	4	5	6	Sun 6h38m7p	Month 8 Xīn-Chǒu	1	2	3	4	5	6	7		Thoout 1678	5	1[a]	2	3	4	5	6	Maskaram 1954
	◐	18	19	20	21	22	23[d]	20:23	38	2437560		7	8	9	10[b]	11	12	13			8	9	10	11	12	13	14	Qiū fēn		7	8	9	10	11	12	13	
	○	25	26	27	28	29	30	11:33	39	2437567		14	15[c]	16	17	18	19	20			15[g]	16	17	18	19*	20	21			14	15	16	17[g]	18	19	20	
October 1961	◑	2	3	4	5	6	7	14:10	40	2437574		21	22	23	24	25	26	27			22	23	24	25	26	27	28			21	22	23	24	25	26	27	
	8	●	10	11	12	13	14	18:52	41	2437581	Heshvan 5722	28	29	30	1	2	3	4	Mon 19h22m8p	Month 9 Xīn-Chǒu	29	30	1	2	3	4	5	Hán lù	Paope 1678	28	29	30	1	2	3	4	Ṭeqemt 1954
	15	16	◐	18	19	20	21	4:34	42	2437588		5	6	7	8	9	10	11			6	7	8	9[h]	10	11	12			5	6	7	8	9	10	11	
	22	○	24	25	26	27	28	21:31	43	2437595		12	13	14	15	16	17	18			13	14	15	16	17	18	19	Shuāng jiàng		12	13	14	15	16	17	18	
November 1961	29	30	◑	1	2	3	4	8:58	44	2437602		19	20	21	22	23	24	25			20	21	22	23	24	25	26			19	20	21	22	23	24	25	
	5	6	7	●	9	10	11	9:58	45	2437609	Kislev 5722	26	27	28	29	1	2	3	Wed 8h6m9p	Month 10 Xīn-Chǒu	27	28	29	1	2	3	4	Lì dōng	Athōr 1678	26	27	28	29	30	1	2	Ḫedār 1954
	12	13	14	◐	16	17	18	12:12	46	2437616		4	5	6	7	8	9	10			5	6	7	8	9	10	11			3	4	5	6	7	8	9	
	19	20	21	○	23	24	25	9:44	47	2437623		11	12	13	14	15	16	17			12	13	14	15	16	17	18	Xiǎo xuě		10	11	12	13	14	15	16	
December 1961	26	27	28	29	◑	1	2	6:18	48	2437630		18	19	20	21	22	23	24			19	20*	21	22	23	24	25			17	18	19	20	21	22	23	
	3	4	5	6	●	8	9	23:52	49	2437637	Tevet 5722	25[e]	26[e]	27[d][e]	28[e]	29[e]	1[e]	2[e]	Thu 20h50m10p	Month 11 Xīn-Chǒu	26	27	28	29	30	1	2	Dà xuě		24	25	26	27	28	29	30	
	10	11	12	13	◐	15	16	20:06	50	2437644		3[e]	4	5	6	7	8	9			3	4	5	6	7	8	9		Koiak 1678	1	2	3	4	5	6	7	Tāḫśāś 1954
	17	18	19	20	21	○[e]	23	0:42	51	2437651		10	11	12	13	14	15	16			10	11	12	13	14	15[i]	16	Dōng zhì		8	9	10	11	12	13	14	
	24	25	26	27	28	29	◑	3:57	52	2437658		17	18	19	20	21	22	23	Sat 9h34m11p		17	18	19	20	21	22	23			15	16	17	18	19	20	21	
	31	1	2	3	4	5	●	12:35	1	2437665		24	25	26	27	28	29	1			24	25	26	27	28	29	1	Xiǎo hán		22	23	24	25	26	27	28	

[a] New Year
[b] Spring (20:32)
[c] Summer (15:30)
[d] Autumn (6:42)
[e] Winter (2:19)
● New moon
◐ First quarter moon
○ Full moon
◑ Last quarter moon

‡ Leap year
[a] New Year
[b] Yom Kippur
[c] Sukkot
[d] Winter starts
[e] Ḥanukkah
[f] Purim
[g] Passover
[h] Shavuot
[i] Fast of Av

‡ Leap year
[a] New Year (4659, Ox)
[b] Lantern Festival
[c] Qīngmíng
[d] Dragon Festival
[e] Qīqiǎo
[f] Hungry Ghosts
[g] Mid-Autumn Festival
[h] Double-Ninth Festival
[i] Dōngzhì
* Start of 60-name cycle

[a] New Year
[b] Building of the Cross
[c] Christmas
[d] Jesus's Circumcision
[e] Epiphany
[f] Easter
[g] Mary's Announcement
[h] Jesus's Transfiguration

PERSIAN (ASTRONOMICAL) 1339/1340	Sun	Mon	Tue	Wed	Thu	Fri	Sat
DEY 1339	11	12	13	14	15	16	17
	18	19	20	21	22	23	24
	25	26	27	28	29	30	1
BAHMAN 1339	2	3	4	5	6	7	8
	9	10	11	12	13	14	15
	16	17	18	19	20	21	22
	23	24	25	26	27	28	29
ESFAND 1339	30	1	2	3	4	5	6
	7	8	9	10	11	12	13
	14	15	16	17	18	19	20
	21	22	23	24	25	26	27
FARVARDĪN 1340	28	29	1[a]	2	3	4	5
	6	7	8	9	10	11	12
	13[b]	14	15	16	17	18	19
	20	21	22	23	24	25	26
ORDĪBEHEŠT 1340	27	28	29	30	31	1	2
	3	4	5	6	7	8	9
	10	11	12	13	14	15	16
	17	18	19	20	21	22	23
	24	25	26	27	28	29	30
XORDĀD 1340	31	1	2	3	4	5	6
	7	8	9	10	11	12	13
	14	15	16	17	18	19	20
	21	22	23	24	25	26	27
TĪR 1340	28	29	30	31	1	2	3
	4	5	6	7	8	9	10
	11	12	13	14	15	16	17
	18	19	20	21	22	23	24
	25	26	27	28	29	30	31
MORDĀD 1340	1	2	3	4	5	6	7
	8	9	10	11	12	13	14
	15	16	17	18	19	20	21
	22	23	24	25	26	27	28
SHAHRĪVAR 1340	29	30	31	1	2	3	4
	5	6	7	8	9	10	11
	12	13	14	15	16	17	18
	19	20	21	22	23	24	25
MEHR 1340	26	27	28	29	30	31	1
	2	3	4	5	6	7	8
	9	10	11	12	13	14	15
	16	17	18	19	20	21	22
	23	24	25	26	27	28	29
ĀBĀN 1340	30	1	2	3	4	5	6
	7	8	9	10	11	12	13
	14	15	16	17	18	19	20
	21	22	23	24	25	26	27
ĀZAR 1340	28	29	30	1	2	3	4
	5	6	7	8	9	10	11
	12	13	14	15	16	17	18
	19	20	21	22	23	24	25
DEY 1340	26	27	28	29	30	1	2
	3	4	5	6	7	8	9
	10	11	12	13	14	15	16

HINDU LUNAR 2017/2018‡	Sun	Mon	Tue	Wed	Thu	Fri	Sat
PAUSHA 2017	15	16	17	17	18	19	20
	21	22	23	24	25	26	27
MĀGHA 2017	28	30	1	2	3	4	5
	6	7	8	9	10	11	12
	13	14	15	16	17	18	19
	20	21	22	23	24	25	26
PHĀLGUNA 2017	27	28[h]	29	30	1	2	3
	5	6	7	8	9	9	10
	11	12	13	14	15[i]	16	17
	18	19	20	21	22	23	24
CHAITRA 2018	25	26	27	29	30	1[a]	2
	3	4	5	6	7	8	9[b]
	10	11	12	12	13	14	15
	16	17	18	19	20	22	23
	24	25	26	27	28	29	30
VAIŚĀKHA 2018	1	2	3	4	5	6	7
	8	9	10	11	12	13	14
	15	16	17	18	19	20	21
	22	23	24	26	27	28	29
LEAP JYAISHTHA 2018	30	1	2	3	4	5	6
	7	7	8	9	10	11	12
	13	14	15	16	17	19	20
	21	22	23	24	25	26	27
JYAISHTHA 2018	28	29	30	1	2	3	4
	5	6	7	8	9	10	11
	12	13	14	15	16	17	18
	19	20	22	23	24	25	26
ĀSHĀḌHA 2018	27	28	29	30	1	2	3
	4	4	5	6	7	8	9
	10	11	12	13	15	16	17
	18	19	20	21	22	23	24
ŚRĀVAṆA 2018	25	26	27	28	29	30	1
	2	3	4	5	6	7	8
	9	10	11	12	13	14	15
	16	18	19	20	21	22	23[c]
	24	25	26	27	28	29	30
BHĀDRAPADA 2018	30	1	2	3[d]	4	5	6
	7	8	9	11	12	13	14
	15	16	17	18	19	20	21
	22	23	24	25	26	27	28
ĀŚVINA 2018	29	30	1	2	3	4	5
	6	7	8[e]	9[e]	10[e]	11	12
	13	15	16	17	18	19	20
	21	22	23	24	25	25	26
KĀRTTIKA 2018	27	28	29	30	1[f]	2	3
	4	5	6	8	9	10	11
	12	13	14	15	16	17	18
	19	20	21	22	23	24	25
MĀRGAŚĪRA 2018	26	27	28	29	30	1	2
	3	4	5	6	7	8	9
	10	11[g]	12	14	15	16	17
	17	18	19	20	21	22	23
	24	25	26	27	28	29	30

HINDU SOLAR 1882/1883	Sun	Mon	Tue	Wed	Thu	Fri	Sat
PAUSHA 1882	18	19	20	21	22	23	24
	25	26	27	28	29	1[b]	2
MĀGHA 1882	3	4	5	6	7	8	9
	10	11	12	13	14	15	16
	17	18	19	20	21	22	23
	24	25	26	27	28	29	30
PHĀLGUNA 1882	1	2	3	4	5	6	7
	8	9	10	11	12	13	14
	15	16	17	18	19	20	21
	22	23	24	25	26	27	28
CHAITRA 1882	29	30	1	2	3	4	5
	6	7	8	9	10	11	12
	13	14	15	16	17	18	19
	20	21	22	23	24	25	26
VAIŚĀKHA 1883	27	28	29	30	1[a]	2	3
	4	5	6	7	8	9	10
	11	12	13	14	15	16	17
	18	19	20	21	22	23	24
	25	26	27	28	29	30	31
JYAISHTHA 1883	1	2	3	4	5	6	7
	8	9	10	11	12	13	14
	15	16	17	18	19	20	21
	22	23	24	25	26	27	28
ĀSHĀḌHA 1883	29	30	31	1	2	3	4
	5	6	7	8	9	10	11
	12	13	14	15	16	17	18
	19	20	21	22	23	24	25
	26	27	28	29	30	31	32
ŚRĀVAṆA 1883	1	2	3	4	5	6	7
	8	9	10	11	12	13	14
	15	16	17	18	19	20	21
	22	23	24	25	26	27	28
BHĀDRAPADA 1883	29	30	31	1	2	3	4
	5	6	7	8	9	10	11
	12	13	14	15	16	17	18
	19	20	21	22	23	24	25
ĀŚVINA 1883	26	27	28	29	30	31	1
	2	3	4	5	6	7	8
	9	10	11	12	13	14	15
	16	17	18	19	20	21	22
	23	24	25	26	27	28	29
KĀRTTIKA 1883	30	31	1	2	3	4	5
	6	7	8	9	10	11	12
	13	14	15	16	17	18	19
	20	21	22	23	24	25	26
MĀRGAŚĪRA 1883	27	28	29	30	1	2	3
	4	5	6	7	8	9	10
	11	12	13	14	15	16	17
	18	19	20	21	22	23	24
PAUSHA 1883	25	26	27	28	29	1	2
	3	4	5	6	7	8	9
	10	11	12	13	14	15	16
	17	18	19	20	21	22	23

ISLAMIC (ASTRONOMICAL) 1380/1381	Sun	Mon	Tue	Wed	Thu	Fri	Sat
RAJAB 1380	13	14	15	16	17	18	19
	20	21	22	23	24	25	26
SHA'BĀN 1380	27[d]	28	29	1	2	3	4
	5	6	7	8	9	10	11
	12	13	14	15	16	17	18
	19	20	21	22	23	24	25
RAMAḌĀN 1380	26	27	28	29	30	1[e]	2
	3	4	5	6	7	8	9
	10	11	12	13	14	15	16
	17	18	19	20	21	22	23
SHAWWĀL 1380	24	25	26	27	28	29	1[f]
	2	3	4	5	6	7	8
	9	10	11	12	13	14	15
	16	17	18	19	20	21	22
	23	24	25	26	27	28	29
DHU AL-QA'DA 1380	1	2	3	4	5	6	7
	8	9	10	11	12	13	14
	15	16	17	18	19	20	21
	22	23	24	25	26	27	28
DHU AL-ḤIJJA 1380	29	30	1	2	3	4	5
	6	7	8	9	10[g]	11	12
	13	14	15	16	17	18	19
	20	21	22	23	24	25	26
MUḤARRAM 1381	27	28	29	30	1[a]	2	3
	4	5	6	7	8	9	10[b]
	11	12	13	14	15	16	17
	18	19	20	21	22	23	24
ṢAFAR 1381	25	26	27	28	29	30	1
	2	3	4	5	6	7	8
	9	10	11	12	13	14	15
	16	17	18	19	20	21	22
	23	24	25	26	27	28	29
RABĪ' I 1381	1	2	3	4	5	6	7
	8	9	10	11	12[c]	13	14
	15	16	17	18	19	20	21
	22	23	24	25	26	27	28
RABĪ' II 1381	29	30	1	2	3	4	5
	6	7	8	9	10	11	12
	13	14	15	16	17	18	19
	20	21	22	23	24	25	26
JUMĀDĀ I 1381	27	28	29	1	2	3	4
	5	6	7	8	9	10	11
	12	13	14	15	16	17	18
	19	20	21	22	23	24	25
JUMĀDĀ II 1381	26	27	28	29	30	1	2
	3	4	5	6	7	8	9
	10	11	12	13	14	15	16
	17	18	19	20	21	22	23
RAJAB 1381	24	25	26	27	28	29	1
	2	3	4	5	6	7	8
	9	10	11	12	13	14	15
	16	17	18	19	20	21	22
	23	24	25	26	27	28	29

Julian (Sun)	Sun	Mon	Tue	Wed	Thu	Fri	Sat	GREGORIAN 1961
Dec 19	1	2	3	4	5	6	7[a]	JANUARY 1961
	8	9	10	11	12	13	14[b]	
Jan 2	15	16	17	18	19	20	21	
	22	23	24	25	26	27	28	
Jan 16	29	30	31	1	2	3	4	FEBRUARY 1961
	5	6	7	8	9	10	11	
Jan 30	12	13	14	15[c]	16	17	18	
	19	20	21	22	23	24	25	
Feb 13	26[d]	27	28	1	2	3	4	MARCH 1961
	5	6	7	8	9	10	11	
Feb 27	12	13	14	15	16	17	18	
	19	20	21	22	23	24	25	
Mar 13	26	27	28	29	30	31	1	APRIL 1961
	2[e]	3	4	5	6	7	8	
Mar 27	9[f]	10	11	12	13	14	15	
	16	17	18	19	20	21	22	
Apr 10	23	24	25	26	27	28	29	
	30	1	2	3	4	5	6	MAY 1961
Apr 24	7	8	9	10	11	12	13	
	14	15	16	17	18	19	20	
May 8	21	22	23	24	25	26	27	
	28	29	30	31	1	2	3	JUNE 1961
May 22	4	5	6	7	8	9	10	
	11	12	13	14	15	16	17	
Jun 5	18	19	20	21	22	23	24	
	25	26	27	28	29	30	1	JULY 1961
Jun 19	2	3	4	5	6	7	8	
	9	10	11	12	13	14	15	
Jul 3	16	17	18	19	20	21	22	
	23	24	25	26	27	28	29	
Jul 17	30	31	1	2	3	4	5	AUGUST 1961
	6	7	8	9	10	11	12	
Jul 31	13	14	15	16	17	18	19	
	20	21	22	23	24	25	26	
Aug 14	27	28	29	30	31	1	2	SEPTEMBER 1961
	3	4	5	6	7	8	9	
Aug 28	10	11	12	13	14	15	16	
	17	18	19	20	21	22	23	
Sep 11	24	25	26	27	28	29	30	
	1	2	3	4	5	6	7	OCTOBER 1961
Sep 25	8	9	10	11	12	13	14	
	15	16	17	18	19	20	21	
Oct 9	22	23	24	25	26	27	28	
	29	30	31	1	2	3	4	NOVEMBER 1961
Oct 23	5	6	7	8	9	10	11	
	12	13	14	15	16	17	18	
Nov 6	19	20	21	22	23	24	25	
	26	27	28	29	30	1	2	DECEMBER 1961
Nov 20	3[g]	4	5	6	7	8	9	
	10	11	12	13	14	15	16	
Dec 4	17	18	19	20	21	22	23	
	24	25[h]	26	27	28	29	30	
Dec 18	31	1	2	3	4	5	6	

Persian: [a]New Year; [b]Sizdeh Bedar

Hindu Lunar: ‡Leap year; [a]New Year (Plava); [b]Birthday of Rāma; [c]Birthday of Krishna; [d]Ganēśa Chaturthī; [e]Dashara; [f]Diwali; [g]Birthday of Vishnu; [h]Night of Śiva; [i]Holi

Hindu Solar: [a]New Year (Ānanda); [b]Pongal

Islamic: [a]New Year; [b]'Āshūrā'; [c]Prophet's Birthday; [d]Ascent of the Prophet; [e]Start of Ramaḍān; [f]'Id al-Fiṭr; [g]'Id al-'Aḍḥā

Gregorian: [a]Orthodox Christmas; [b]Julian New Year; [c]Ash Wednesday; [d]Feast of Orthodoxy; [e]Easter; [f]Orthodox Easter; [g]Advent; [h]Christmas

1962

Gregorian month	Sun	Mon	Tue	Wed	Thu	Fri	Sat	Lunar Phases	ISO WEEK (Mon)	JULIAN DAY (Sun noon)	Hebrew month	Sun	Mon	Tue	Wed	Thu	Fri	Sat	Molad	Chinese month	Sun	Mon	Tue	Wed	Thu	Fri	Sat	Solar Term	Coptic month	Sun	Mon	Tue	Wed	Thu	Fri	Sat	Ethiopic month
JANUARY 1962	31	1[a]	2	3	4	5	●	12:35	1	2437665	SHEVAT 5722	24	25	26	27	28	29	1	Sat 9h34m1p	MONTH 12 Xīn-Chǒu	24	25	26	27	28	29	1	Xiǎo hán	KOIAK 1678	22	23	24	25	26	27	28	TĀKHŚĀŚ 1954
	7	8	9	10	11	12	◐	5:01	2	2437672		2	3	4	5	6	7	8			2	3	4	5	6	7	8			29[c]	30	1	2	3	4	5	ṬER 1954
	14	15	16	17	18	19	○	18:16	3	2437679		9	10	11	12	13	14	15			9	10	11	12	13	14	15	Dà hán	TŌBE 1678	6[d]	7	8	9	10	11[e]	12	
	21	22	23	24	25	26	27		4	2437686		16	17	18	19	20	21	22			16	17	18	19	20	21*	22			13	14	15	16	17	18	19	
	◑	29	30	31	1	2	3	23:36	5	2437693		23	24	25	26	27	28	29			23	24	25	26	27	28	29			20	21	22	23	24	25	26	
FEBRUARY 1962	4	●	6	7	8	9	10	0:10	6	2437700	ADAR I 5722	30	1	2	3	4	5	6	Sun 22h18m1p	MONTH 1 Rén-Yín	30	1[a]	2	3	4	5	6	Lì chūn		27	28	29	30	1	2	3	
	◐	12	13	14	15	16	17	15:43	7	2437707		7	8	9	10	11	12	13			7	8	9	10	11	12	13		MESHIR 1678	4	5	6	7	8	9	10	YAKĀTIT 1954
	18	○	20	21	22	23	24	13:18	8	2437714		14	15	16	17	18	19	20			14	15[b]	16	17	18	19	20	Yǔ shuǐ		11	12	13	14	15	16	17	
	25	26	◑	28	1	2	3	15:50	9	2437721		21	22	23	24	25	26	27			21	22	23	24	25	26	27			18	19	20	21	22	23	24	
MARCH 1962	4	5	●	7	8	9	10	10:31	10	2437728	ADAR II 5722	28	29	30	1	2	3	4	Tue 11h2m1p	MONTH 2 Rén-Yín	28	29	1	2	3	4	5	Jīng zhé		25	26	27	28	29	30	1	
	11	12	◐	14	15	16	17	4:39	11	2437735		5	6	7	8	9	10	11			6	7	8	9	10	11	12		PAREMOTEP 1678	2	3	4	5	6	7	8	MAGĀBIT 1954
	18	19	20	○[b]	22	23	24	7:55	12	2437742		12	13	14[f]	15	16	17	18			13	14	15	16	17	18	19	Chūn fēn		9	10	11	12	13	14	15	
	25	26	27	28	◑	30	31	4:11	13	2437749		19	20	21	22	23	24	25			20	21	22*	23	24	25	26			16	17	18	19	20	21	22	
APRIL 1962	1	2	3	●	5	6	7	19:45	14	2437756	NISAN 5722	26	27	28	29	1	2	3	Wed 23h46m14p	MONTH 3 Rén-Yín	27	28	29	30	1[c]	2	3	Qīng míng		23	24	25	26	27	28	29	
	8	9	10	◐	12	13	14	19:50	15	2437763		4	5	6	7	8	9	10			4	5	6	7	8	9	10		PARMOUTE 1678	30	1	2	3	4	5	6	MIYĀZYĀ 1954
	15	16	17	18	19	○	21	0:33	16	2437770		11	12	13	14	15[g]	16	17			11	12	13	14	15	16	17	Gǔ yǔ		7	8	9	10	11	12	13	
	22	23	24	25	26	◑	28	12:59	17	2437777		18	19	20	21	22	23	24			18	19	20	21	22	23	24			14	15	16	17	18	19	20	
	29	30	1	2	3	●	5	4:25	18	2437784		25	26	27	28	29	30	1	Fri 12h30m15p		25	26	27	28	29	1	2			21[f]	22	23	24	25	26	27	
MAY 1962	6	7	8	9	10	◐	12	12:44	19	2437791	IYAR 5722	2	3	4	5	6	7	8		MONTH 4 Rén-Yín	3	4	5	6	7	8	9	Lì xià		28	29[g]	30	1	2	3	4	
	13	14	15	16	17	18	○	14:32	20	2437798		9	10	11	12	13	14	15			10	11	12	13	14	15	16		PASHONS 1678	5	6	7	8	9	10	11	GENBOT 1954
	20	21	22	23	24	25	◑	19:05	21	2437805		16	17	18	19	20	21	22			17	18	19	20	21	22	23*	Xiǎo mǎn		12	13	14	15	16	17	18	
	27	28	29	30	31	1	●	13:27	22	2437812		23	24	25	26	27	28	29	Sun 1h14m16p		24	25	26	27	28	29	1			19	20	21	22	23	24	25	
JUNE 1962	3	4	5	6	7	8	9		23	2437819	SIVAN 5722	1	2	3	4	5	6[h]	7		MONTH 5 Rén-Yín	2	3	4	5[d]	6	7	8	Máng zhòng		26	27	28	29	30	1	2	
	◐	11	12	13	14	15	16	6:21	24	2437826		8	9	10	11	12	13	14			9	10	11	12	13	14	15		PAŌNE 1678	3	4	5	6	7	8	9	SANĒ 1954
	17	○	19	20	21[c]	22	23	2:02	25	2437833		15	16	17	18	19	20	21			16	17	18	19	20	21	22	Xià zhì		10	11	12	13	14	15	16	
	◑	25	26	27	28	29	30	23:43	26	2437840		22	23	24	25	26	27	28	Mon 13h58m17p		23	24	25	26	27	28	29			17	18	19	20	21	22	23	
JULY 1962	●	2	3	4	5	6	7	23:52	27	2437847	TAMMUZ 5722	29	30	1	2	3	4	5		MONTH 6 Rén-Yín	30	1	2	3	4	5	6	Xiǎo shǔ		24	25	26	27	28	29	30	
	8	◐	10	11	12	13	14	23:39	28	2437854		6	7	8	9	10	11	12			7	8	9	10	11	12	13		EPĒP 1678	1	2	3	4	5	6	7	HAMLĒ 1954
	15	16	○	18	19	20	21	11:41	29	2437861		13	14	15	16	17	18	19			14	15	16	17	18	19	20			8	9	10	11	12	13	14	
	22	23	◑	25	26	27	28	4:18	30	2437868		20	21	22	23	24	25	26	Wed 2h43m0p		21	22	23	24*	25	26	27	Dà shǔ		15	16	17	18	19	20	21	
	29	30	●	1	2	3	4	12:24	31	2437875		27	28	29	1	2	3	4			28	29	1	2	3	4	5			22	23	24	25	26	27	28	
AUGUST 1962	5	6	7	◐	9	10	11	15:55	32	2437882	AV 5722	5	6	7	8	9[i]	10	11		MONTH 7 Rén-Yín	6	7[e]	8	9	10	11	12	Lì qiū		29	30	1	2	3	4	5	
	12	13	14	○	16	17	18	20:09	33	2437889		12	13	14	15	16	17	18			13	14	15[f]	16	17	18	19		MESORĒ 1678	6	7	8	9	10	11	12	NAḤASĒ 1954
	19	20	21	◑	23	24	25	10:26	34	2437896		19	20	21	22	23	24	25	Thu 15h27m1p		20	21	22	23	24	25	26	Chǔ shǔ		13[h]	14	15	16	17	18	19	
	26	27	28	29	●	31	1	3:09	35	2437903		26	27	28	29	30	1	2			27	28	29	30	1	2	3			20	21	22	23	24	25	26	
SEPTEMBER 1962	2	3	4	5	6	◐	8	6:44	36	2437910	ELUL 5722	3	4	5	6	7	8	9		MONTH 8 Rén-Yín	4	5	6	7	8	9	10	Bái lù	EPAG. 1678	27	28	29	30	1	2	3	PĀG. 1954
	9	10	11	12	13	○	15	4:11	37	2437917		10	11	12	13	14	15	16			11	12	13	14	15[g]	16	17			4	5	1[a]	2	3	4	5	
	16	17	18	19	◑	21	22	19:36	38	2437924		17	18	19	20	21	22	23	Sat 4h11m2p		18	19	20	21	22	23	24		THOOUT 1679	6	7	8	9	10	11	12	MASKARAM 1955
	23[d]	24	25	26	27	●	29	19:39	39	2437931		24	25	26	27	28	29	1[a]			25*	26	27	28	29	30	1	Qiū fēn		13	14	15	16	17[b]	18	19	
OCTOBER 1962	30	1	2	3	4	5	◐	19:54	40	2437938	TISHRI 5723	2[a]	3	4	5	6	7	8		MONTH 9 Rén-Yín	2	3	4	5	6	7	8			20	21	22	23	24	25	26	
	7	8	9	10	11	12	○	12:33	41	2437945		9	10[b]	11	12	13	14	15[c]			9[h]	10	11	12	13	14	15	Hán lù		27	28	29	30	1	2	3	
	14	15	16	17	18	19	◑	8:47	42	2437952		16	17	18	19	20	21	22			16	17	18	19	20	21	22		PAOPE 1679	4	5	6	7	8	9	10	TEQEMT 1955
	21	22	23	24	25	26	27		43	2437959		23	24	25	26	27	28	29	Sun 16h55m3p		23	24	25	26	27	28	29	Shuāng jiàng		11	12	13	14	15	16	17	
NOVEMBER 1962	●	29	30	31	1	2	3	13:04	44	2437966	HESHVAN 5723	30	1	2	3	4	5	6		MONTH 10 Rén-Yín	1	2	3	4	5	6	7			18	19	20	21	22	23	24	
	4	◐	6	7	8	9	10	7:15	45	2437973		7	8	9	10	11	12	13			8	9	10	11	12	13	14	Lì dōng		25	26	27	28	29	30	1	
	○	12	13	14	15	16	17	22:04	46	2437980		14	15	16	17	18	19	20			15	16	17	18	19	20	21		ATHŌR 1679	2	3	4	5	6	7	8	HEDĀR 1955
	18	◑	20	21	22	23	24	2:09	47	2437987		21	22	23	24	25	26	27	Tue 5h39m4p		22	23	24	25	26*	27	28	Xiǎo xuě		9	10	11	12	13	14	15	
	25	26	●	28	29	30	1	6:29	48	2437994		28	29	30	1	2	3	4			29	30	1	2	3	4	5			16	17	18	19	20	21	22	
DECEMBER 1962	2	3	◐	5	6	7	8	16:48	49	2438001	KISLEV 5723	5	6	7	8[d]	9	10	11		MONTH 11 Rén-Yín	6	7	8	9	10	11	12	Dà xuě		23	24	25	26	27	28	29	
	9	10	○	12	13	14	15	9:28	50	2438008		12	13	14	15	16	17	18			13	14	15	16	17	18	19			30	1	2	3	4	5	6	
	16	17	◑	19	20	21	22[e]	22:42	51	2438015		19	20	21	22	23	24	25[e]	Wed 18h23m5p		20	21	22	23	24	25	26[i]	Dōng zhì	KOIAK 1679	7	8	9	10	11	12	13	TĀKHŚĀŚ 1955
	23	24	25	●	27	28	29	22:59	52	2438022		26[e]	27[e]	28[e]	29[e]	30[e]	1[e]	2[e]			27	28	29	30	1	2	3			14	15	16	17	18	19	20	
	30	31	1	2	◐	4	5	1:02	1	2438029	TEVETH 5723	3	4	5	6	7	8	9		MONTH 12 Rén-Yín	4	5	6	7	8	9	10			21	22	23	24	25	26	27	

Gregorian 1962; Hebrew 5722‡/5723; Chinese Xīn-Chǒu/Rén-Yín; Coptic 1678/1679‡; Ethiopic 1954/1955‡

[a]New Year
[b]Spring (2:29)
[c]Summer (21:24)
[d]Autumn (12:36)
[e]Winter (8:15)
● New moon
◐ First quarter moon
○ Full moon
◑ Last quarter moon

‡Leap year
[a]New Year
[b]Yom Kippur
[c]Sukkot
[d]Winter starts
[e]Ḥanukkah
[f]Purim
[g]Passover
[h]Shavuot
[i]Fast of Av

[a]New Year (4660, Tiger)
[b]Lantern Festival
[c]Qīngmíng
[d]Dragon Festival
[e]Qīqiǎo
[f]Hungry Ghosts
[g]Mid-Autumn Festival
[h]Double-Ninth Festival
[i]Dōngzhì
*Start of 60-name cycle

‡Leap year
[a]New Year
[b]Building of the Cross
[c]Christmas
[d]Jesus's Circumcision
[e]Epiphany
[f]Easter
[g]Mary's Announcement
[h]Jesus's Transfiguration

PERSIAN (ASTRONOMICAL) 1340/1341

Month	Sun	Mon	Tue	Wed	Thu	Fri	Sat
DEY 1340	10	11	12	13	14	15	16
	17	18	19	20	21	22	23
	24	25	26	27	28	29	30
BAHMAN 1340	1	2	3	4	5	6	7
	8	9	10	11	12	13	14
	15	16	17	18	19	20	21
	22	23	24	25	26	27	28
ESFAND 1340	29	30	1	2	3	4	5
	6	7	8	9	10	11	12
	13	14	15	16	17	18	19
	20	21	22	23	24	25	26
FARVARDĪN 1341	27	28	29	1[a]	2	3	4
	5	6	7	8	9	10	11
	12	13[b]	14	15	16	17	18
	19	20	21	22	23	24	25
ORDĪBEHEŠT 1341	26	27	28	29	30	31	1
	2	3	4	5	6	7	8
	9	10	11	12	13	14	15
	16	17	18	19	20	21	22
	23	24	25	26	27	28	29
XORDĀD 1341	30	31	1	2	3	4	5
	6	7	8	9	10	11	12
	13	14	15	16	17	18	19
	20	21	22	23	24	25	26
TĪR 1341	27	28	29	30	31	1	2
	3	4	5	6	7	8	9
	10	11	12	13	14	15	16
	17	18	19	20	21	22	23
	24	25	26	27	28	29	30
MORDĀD 1341	31	1	2	3	4	5	6
	7	8	9	10	11	12	13
	14	15	16	17	18	19	20
	21	22	23	24	25	26	27
SHAHRĪVAR 1341	28	29	30	31	1	2	3
	4	5	6	7	8	9	10
	11	12	13	14	15	16	17
	18	19	20	21	22	23	24
	25	26	27	28	29	30	31
MEHR 1341	1	2	3	4	5	6	7
	8	9	10	11	12	13	14
	15	16	17	18	19	20	21
	22	23	24	25	26	27	28
ĀBĀN 1341	29	30	1	2	3	4	5
	6	7	8	9	10	11	12
	13	14	15	16	17	18	19
	20	21	22	23	24	25	26
ĀZAR 1341	27	28	29	30	1	2	3
	4	5	6	7	8	9	10
	11	12	13	14	15	16	17
	18	19	20	21	22	23	24
DEY 1341	25	26	27	28	29	30	1
	2	3	4	5	6	7	8
	9	10	11	12	13	14	15

[a]New Year
[b]Sizdeh Bedar

HINDU LUNAR 2018‡/2019

Month	Sun	Mon	Tue	Wed	Thu	Fri	Sat
PAUSHA 2018	24	25	26	27	28	29	30
	1	2	3	4	**5**	7	8
	9	10	11	12	13	14	15
	16	17	18	19	20	20	21
	22	23	24	25	26	27	28
MĀGHA 2018	**29**	1	2	3	4	5	6
	7	8	9	10	11	12	13
	14	15	16	17	18	19	20
	21	22	23	24	25	26	27
PHĀLGUNA 2018	28[h]	29	30	1	2	3	**4**
	6	7	8	9	10	11	12
	13	13	14	15[i]	16	17	18
	19	20	21	22	23	24	25
CHAITRA 2019	26	**27**	29	30	1[a]	2	3
	4	5	6	7	8	9[b]	10
	11	12	13	14	15	16	16
	17	18	19	**20**	22	23	24
VAIŚĀKHA 2019	25	26	27	28	29	30	1
	2	**3**	5	6	6	7	8
	9	10	11	12	13	14	15
	16	17	18	19	20	21	22
	23	**24**	26	27	28	29	30
JYAISHTHA 2019	1	2	3	4	5	6	7
	8	9	10	11	12	12	13
	14	15	**16**	18	19	20	21
	22	23	24	25	26	27	**28**
ĀSHĀḌHA 2019	30	1	2	3	3	4	5
	6	7	8	9	10	11	12
	13	14	15	16	17	18	19
	20	22	23	24	25	26	27
ŚRĀVAṆA 2019	28	29	30	1	2	3	4
	5	6	7	8	9	9	10
	11	13	14	15	16	17	18
	19	20	21	22	23[c]	**24**	26
BHĀDRAPADA 2019	27	28	29	30	30	1	2
	3	4[d]	5	6	7	8	9
	10	11	12	13	14	15	**16**
	18	19	20	21	22	23	24
ĀŚVINA 2019	25	26	27	28	29	30	1
	2	3	4	4	5	6	7
	8[e]	**9**[e]	11	12	13	14	15
	16	17	18	19	20	21	22
	23	24	25	26	27	28	29
KĀRTTIKA 2019	30	1[f]	2	3	4	5	6
	7	8	9	10	11	12	**13**
	15	16	17	18	19	20	21
	22	23	24	25	26	27	28
MĀRGAŚIRA 2019	28	29	30	1	2	3	4
	5	6	**7**	9	10	11[g]	12
	13	14	15	16	17	18	19
	20	21	22	23	24	25	26
PAUSHA 2019	27	28	29	30	1	2	3
	4	5	6	7	8	9	10

‡Leap year
[a]New Year (Śubhakṛt)
[b]Birthday of Rāma
[c]Birthday of Krishna
[d]Ganēśa Chaturthī
[e]Dashara
[f]Diwali
[g]Birthday of Vishnu
[h]Night of Śiva
[i]Holi

HINDU SOLAR 1883/1884

Month	Sun	Mon	Tue	Wed	Thu	Fri	Sat
PAUSHA 1883	17	18	19	20	21	22	23
MĀGHA 1883	24	25	26	27	28	29	1[b]
	2	3	4	5	6	7	8
	9	10	11	12	13	14	15
	16	17	18	19	20	21	22
	23	24	25	26	27	28	29
PHĀLGUNA 1883	30	1	2	3	4	5	6
	7	8	9	10	11	12	13
	14	15	16	17	18	19	20
	21	22	23	24	25	26	27
CHAITRA 1883	28	29	30	1	2	3	4
	5	6	7	8	9	10	11
	12	13	14	15	16	17	18
	19	20	21	22	23	24	25
VAIŚĀKHA 1884	26	27	28	29	30	1[a]	2
	3	4	5	6	7	8	9
	10	11	12	13	14	15	16
	17	18	19	20	21	22	23
	24	25	26	27	28	29	30
JYAISHTHA 1884	31	1	2	3	4	5	6
	7	8	9	10	11	12	13
	14	15	16	17	18	19	20
	21	22	23	24	25	26	27
ĀSHĀḌHA 1884	28	29	30	31	32	1	2
	3	4	5	6	7	8	9
	10	11	12	13	14	15	16
	17	18	19	20	21	22	23
	24	25	26	27	28	29	30
ŚRĀVAṆA 1884	31	1	2	3	4	5	6
	7	8	9	10	11	12	13
	14	15	16	17	18	19	20
	21	22	23	24	25	26	27
BHĀDRAPADA 1884	28	29	30	31	32	1	2
	3	4	5	6	7	8	9
	10	11	12	13	14	15	16
	17	18	19	20	21	22	23
	24	25	26	27	28	29	30
ĀŚVINA 1884	31	1	2	3	4	5	6
	7	8	9	10	11	12	13
	14	15	16	17	18	19	20
	21	22	23	24	25	26	27
KĀRTTIKA 1884	28	29	30	1	2	3	4
	5	6	7	8	9	10	11
	12	13	14	15	16	17	18
	19	20	21	22	23	24	25
MĀRGAŚIRA 1884	26	27	28	29	30	1	2
	3	4	5	6	7	8	9
	10	11	12	13	14	15	16
	17	18	19	20	21	22	23
PAUSHA 1884	24	25	26	27	28	29	1
	2	3	4	5	6	7	8
	9	10	11	12	13	14	15
	16	17	18	19	20	21	22

[a]New Year (Rākshasa)
[b]Pongal

ISLAMIC (ASTRONOMICAL) 1381/1382

Month	Sun	Mon	Tue	Wed	Thu	Fri	Sat
RAJAB 1381	23	24	25	26	27[d]	28	29
SHA'BĀN 1381	30	1	2	3	4	5	6
	7	8	9	10	11	12	13
	14	15	16	17	18	19	20
	21	22	23	24	25	26	27
RAMAḌĀN 1381	28	29	1[e]	2	3	4	5
	6	7	8	9	10	11	12
	13	14	15	16	17	18	19
	20	21	22	23	24	25	26
SHAWWĀL 1381	27	28	29	30	1[f]	2	3
	4	5	6	7	8	9	10
	11	12	13	14	15	16	17
	18	19	20	21	22	23	24
DHU AL-QA'DA 1381	25	26	27	28	29	1	2
	3	4	5	6	7	8	9
	10	11	12	13	14	15	16
	17	18	19	20	21	22	23
DHU AL-ḤIJJA 1381	24	25	26	27	28	29	1
	2	3	4	5	6	7	8
	9	10[g]	11	12	13	14	15
	16	17	18	19	20	21	22
	23	24	25	26	27	28	29
MUḤARRAM 1382	30	1[a]	2	3	4	5	6
	7	8	9	10[b]	11	12	13
	14	15	16	17	18	19	20
	21	22	23	24	25	26	27
ṢAFAR 1382	28	29	1	2	3	4	5
	6	7	8	9	10	11	12
	13	14	15	16	17	18	19
	20	21	22	23	24	25	26
RABĪ' I 1382	27	28	29	30	1	2	3
	4	5	6	7	8	9	10
	11	12[c]	13	14	15	16	17
	18	19	20	21	22	23	24
RABĪ' II 1382	25	26	27	28	29	30	1
	2	3	4	5	6	7	8
	9	10	11	12	13	14	15
	16	17	18	19	20	21	22
	23	24	25	26	27	28	29
JUMĀDĀ I 1382	1	2	3	4	5	6	7
	8	9	10	11	12	13	14
	15	16	17	18	19	20	21
	22	23	24	25	26	27	28
JUMĀDĀ II 1382	29	30	1	2	3	4	5
	6	7	8	9	10	11	12
	13	14	15	16	17	18	19
	20	21	22	23	24	25	26
RAJAB 1382	27	28	29	30	1	2	3
	4	5	6	7	8	9	10
	11	12	13	14	15	16	17
	18	19	20	21	22	23	24
SHA'BĀN 1382	25	26	27[d]	28	29	1	2
	3	4	5	6	7	8	9

[a]New Year
[b]'Ashūrā'
[c]Prophet's Birthday
[d]Ascent of the Prophet
[e]Start of Ramaḍān
[f]'Id al-Fiṭr
[g]'Id al-'Aḍḥā

GREGORIAN 1962

Julian (Sun)	Sun	Mon	Tue	Wed	Thu	Fri	Sat	Month
Dec 18	31	1	2	3	4	5	6	JANUARY 1962
	7[a]	8	9	10	11	12	13	
Jan 1	14[b]	15	16	17	18	19	20	
	21	22	23	24	25	26	27	
Jan 15	28	29	30	31	1	2	3	FEBRUARY 1962
	4	5	6	7	8	9	10	
Jan 29	11	12	13	14	15	16	17	
	18	19	20	21	22	23	24	
Feb 12	25	26	27	28	1	2	3	MARCH 1962
	4	5	6	7[c]	8	9	10	
Feb 26	11	12	13	14	15	16	17	
	18[d]	19	20	21	22	23	24	
Mar 12	25	26	27	28	29	30	31	
	1	2	3	4	5	6	7	APRIL 1962
Mar 26	8	9	10	11	12	13	14	
	15	16	17	18	19	20	21	
Apr 9	22[e]	23	24	25	26	27	28	
	29[f]	30	1	2	3	4	5	MAY 1962
Apr 23	6	7	8	9	10	11	12	
	13	14	15	16	17	18	19	
May 7	20	21	22	23	24	25	26	
	27	28	29	30	31	1	2	JUNE 1962
May 21	3	4	5	6	7	8	9	
	10	11	12	13	14	15	16	
Jun 4	17	18	19	20	21	22	23	
	24	25	26	27	28	29	30	
Jun 18	1	2	3	4	5	6	7	JULY 1962
	8	9	10	11	12	13	14	
Jul 2	15	16	17	18	19	20	21	
	22	23	24	25	26	27	28	
Jul 16	29	30	31	1	2	3	4	AUGUST 1962
	5	6	7	8	9	10	11	
Jul 30	12	13	14	15	16	17	18	
	19	20	21	22	23	24	25	
Aug 13	26	27	28	29	30	31	1	SEPTEMBER 1962
	2	3	4	5	6	7	8	
Aug 27	9	10	11	12	13	14	15	
	16	17	18	19	20	21	22	
Sep 10	23	24	25	26	27	28	29	
	30	1	2	3	4	5	6	OCTOBER 1962
Sep 24	7	8	9	10	11	12	13	
	14	15	16	17	18	19	20	
Oct 8	21	22	23	24	25	26	27	
	28	29	30	31	1	2	3	NOVEMBER 1962
Oct 22	4	5	6	7	8	9	10	
	11	12	13	14	15	16	17	
Nov 5	18	19	20	21	22	23	24	
	25	26	27	28	29	30	1	DECEMBER 1962
Nov 19	2[g]	3	4	5	6	7	8	
	9	10	11	12	13	14	15	
Dec 3	16	17	18	19	20	21	22	
	23	24	25[h]	26	27	28	29	
Dec 17	30	31	1	2	3	4	5	

[a]Orthodox Christmas
[b]Julian New Year
[c]Ash Wednesday
[d]Feast of Orthodoxy
[e]Easter
[f]Orthodox Easter
[g]Advent
[h]Christmas

1963

GREGORIAN 1963	Sun	Mon	Tue	Wed	Thu	Fri	Sat	Lunar Phases	ISO WEEK (Mon)	JULIAN DAY (Sun noon)	HEBREW 5723/5724	Sun	Mon	Tue	Wed	Thu	Fri	Sat	Molad	CHINESE Rén-Yín/Guǐ-Mǎo‡	Sun	Mon	Tue	Wed	Thu	Fri	Sat	Solar Term	COPTIC 1679‡/1680	Sun	Mon	Tue	Wed	Thu	Fri	Sat	ETHIOPIC 1955‡/1956
JANUARY 1963	30	31	1[a]	2	◐	4	5	1:02	1	2438029	TEVETH 5723	3	4	5	6	7	8	9		MONTH 12 Rén-Yín	4	5	6	7	8	9	10		KOIAK 1679	21	22	23	24	25	26	27	TĀḪŚĀŚ 1955
	6	7	8	○	10	11	12	23:08	2	2438036		10	11	12	13	14	15	16			11	12	13	14	15	16	17	Xiǎo hán	TŌBE 1679	28	29[c]	30	1	2	3	4	ṬER 1955
	13	14	15	16	◑	18	19	20:34	3	2438043		17	18	19	20	21	22	23	Fri 7h7m6p		18	19	20	21	22	23	24			5	6[d]	7	8	9	10	11[e]	
	20	21	22	23	24	●	26	13:42	4	2438050	SHEVAT 5723	24	25	26	27	28	29	1		MONTH 1 Guǐ-Mǎo	25	26*	27	28	29	1[a]	2	Dà hán		12	13	14	15	16	17	18	
FEBRUARY 1963	27	28	29	30	31	◐	2	8:50	5	2438057		2	3	4	5	6	7	8			3	4	5	6	7	8	9			19	20	21	22	23	24	25	
	3	4	5	6	7	○	9	14:52	6	2438064		9	10	11	12	13	14	15			10	11	12	13	14	15[b]	16	Lì chūn	MESHIR 1679	26	27	28	29	30	1	2	YAKĀTIT 1955
	10	11	12	13	14	15	◑	17:38	7	2438071		16	17	18	19	20	21	22			17	18	19	20	21	22	23			3	4	5	6	7	8	9	
	17	18	19	20	21	22	23		8	2438078		23	24	25	26	27	28	29	Sat 19h51m7p		24	25	26	27	28	29	30	Yǔ shuǐ		10	11	12	13	14	15	16	
MARCH 1963	●	25	26	27	28	1	◐	2:06 17:17	9	2438085	ADAR 5723	30	1	2	3	4	5	6		MONTH 2 Guǐ-Mǎo	1	2	3	4	5	6	7			17	18	19	20	21	22	23	
	3	4	5	6	7	8	9		10	2438092		7	8	9	10	11	12	13			8	9	10	11	12	13	14	Jīng zhé		24	25	26	27	28	29	30	
	○	11	12	13	14	15	16	7:48	11	2438099		14[f]	15	16	17	18	19	20			15	16	17	18	19	20	21		PAREMOTEP 1679	1	2	3	4	5	6	7	MAGĀBIT 1955
	17	◑	19	20	21[b]	22	23	12:07	12	2438106		21	22	23	24	25	26	27	Mon 8h35m8p		22	23	24	25	26	27*	28	Chūn fēn		8	9	10	11	12	13	14	
	24	●	26	27	28	29	30	12:10	13	2438113	NISAN 5723	28	29	1	2	3	4	5		MONTH 3 Guǐ-Mǎo	29	1	2	3	4	5	6			15	16	17	18	19	20	21	
APRIL 1963	31	◐	2	3	4	5	6	3:15	14	2438120		6	7	8	9	10	11	12			7	8	9	10	11	12[c]	13	Qīng míng		22	23	24	25	26	27	28	
	7	8	○	10	11	12	13	0:57	15	2438127		13	14	15[g]	16	17	18	19			14	15	16	17	18	19	20		PARMOUTE 1679	29	30	1	2	3	4	5	MIYĀZYĀ 1955
	14	15	16	◑	18	19	20	2:52	16	2438134		20	21	22	23	24	25	26	Tue 21h19m9p		21	22	23	24	25	26	27			6[f]	7	8	9	10	11	12	
	21	22	●	24	25	26	27	20:29	17	2438141	IYYAR 5723	27	28	29	30	1	2	3		MONTH 4 Guǐ-Mǎo	28	29	30	1	2	3	4	Gǔ yǔ		13	14	15	16	17	18	19	
MAY 1963	28	29	◐	1	2	3	4	15:08	18	2438148		4	5	6	7	8	9	10			5	6	7	8	9	10	11			20	21	22	23	24	25	26	
	5	6	7	○	9	10	11	17:23	19	2438155		11	12	13	14	15	16	17			12	13	14	15	16	17	18	Lì xià	PASHONS 1679	27	28	29[g]	30	1	2	3	GENBOT 1955
	12	13	14	15	◑	17	18	13:36	20	2438162		18	19	20	21	22	23	24	Thu 10h3m10p		19	20	21	22	23	24	25			4	5	6	7	8	9	10	
	19	20	21	22	●	24	25	4:00	21	2438169	SIVAN 5723	25	26	27	28	29	1	2		LEAP MONTH 4 Guǐ-Mǎo	26	27	28*	29	1	2	3	Xiǎo mǎn		11	12	13	14	15	16	17	
JUNE 1963	26	27	28	29	◐	31	1	4:55	22	2438176		3	4	5	6[h]	7	8	9			4	5	6	7	8	9	10			18	19	20	21	22	23	24	
	2	3	4	5	6	○	8	8:30	23	2438183		10	11	12	13	14	15	16			11	12	13	14	15	16	17	Máng zhòng	PAŌNE 1679	25	26	27	28	29	30	1	SANĒ 1955
	9	10	11	12	13	◑	15	20:53	24	2438190		17	18	19	20	21	22	23			18	19	20	21	22	23	24			2	3	4	5	6	7	8	
	16	17	18	19	20	●	22[c]	11:46	25	2438197		24	25	26	27	28	29	30	Fri 22h47m11p	MONTH 5 Guǐ-Mǎo	25	26	27	28	29	1	2	Xià zhì		9	10	11	12	13	14	15	
	23	24	25	26	27	◐	29	20:23	26	2438204	TAMMUZ 5723	1	2	3	4	5	6	7			3	4	5[d]	6	7	8	9			16	17	18	19	20	21	22	
JULY 1963	30	1	2	3	4	5	○	21:55	27	2438211		8	9	10	11	12	13	14			10	11	12	13	14	15	16			23	24	25	26	27	28	29	
	7	8	9	10	11	12	13		28	2438218		15	16	17	18	19	20	21			17	18	19	20	21	22	23	Xiǎo shǔ	EPĒP 1679	30	1	2	3	4	5	6	ḤAMLĒ 1955
	◑	15	16	17	18	19	●	1:57 20:43	29	2438225		22	23	24	25	26	27	28	Sun 11h31m12p		24	25	26	27	28	29	30*			7	8	9	10	11	12	13	
	21	22	23	24	25	26	27		30	2438232	AV 5723	29	1	2	3	4	5	6		MONTH 6 Guǐ-Mǎo	1	2	3	4	5	6	7	Dà shǔ		14	15	16	17	18	19	20	
AUGUST 1963	◐	29	30	31	1	2	3	13:12	31	2438239		7	8	9[i]	10	11	12	13			8	9	10	11	12	13	14			21	22	23	24	25	26	27	
	4	○	6	7	8	9	10	9:31	32	2438246		14	15	16	17	18	19	20			15	16	17	18	19	20	21	Lì qiū	MESORĒ 1679	28	29	30	1	2	3	4	NAḤASĒ 1955
	11	◑	13	14	15	16	17	6:21	33	2438253		21	22	23	24	25	26	27	Tue 0h15m13p		22	23	24	25	26	27	28			5	6	7	8	9	10	11	
	18	●	20	21	22	23	24	7:34	34	2438260	ELUL 5723	28	29	30	1	2	3	4		MONTH 7 Guǐ-Mǎo	29	1	2	3	4	5	6	Chǔ shǔ		12	13[h]	14	15	16	17	18	
SEPTEMBER 1963	25	26	◐	28	29	30	31	6:54	35	2438267		5	6	7	8	9	10	11			7[e]	8	9	10	11	12	13			19	20	21	22	23	24	25	
	1	2	○	4	5	6	7	19:33	36	2438274		12	13	14	15	16	17	18			14	15[f]	16	17	18	19	20		EPAG. 1679	26	27	28	29	30	1	2	PĀG. 1955
	8	9	◑	11	12	13	14	11:42	37	2438281		19	20	21	22	23	24	25	Wed 12h59m14p		21	22	23	24	25	26	27	Bái lù	THOOUT 1680	3	4	5	6	1[a]	2	3	MASKARAM 1956
	15	16	●	18	19	20	21	20:51	38	2438288	TISHRI 5724	26	27	28	29	1[a]	2[a]	3		MONTH 8 Guǐ-Mǎo	28	29	30	1*	2	3	4			4	5	6	7	8	9	10	
	22	23[d]	24	25	◐	27	28	0:38	39	2438295		4	5	6	7	8	9	10[b]			5	6	7	8	9	10	11	Qiū fēn		11	12	13	14	15	16	17[b]	
OCTOBER 1963	29	30	1	2	○	4	5	4:44	40	2438302		11	12	13	14	15[c]	16	17			12	13	14	15[g]	16	17	18			18	19	20	21	22	23	24	
	6	7	8	◑	10	11	12	19:27	41	2438309		18	19	20	21	22	23	24	Fri 1h43m15p		19	20	21	22	23	24	25	Hán lù	PAOPE 1680	25	26	27	28	29	30	1	ṬEQEMT 1956
	13	14	15	16	●	18	19	12:43	42	2438316	HESHVAN 5724	25	26	27	28	29	30	1		MONTH 9 Guǐ-Mǎo	26	27	28	29	1	2	3			2	3	4	5	6	7	8	
	20	21	22	23	24	◐	26	17:20	43	2438323		2	3	4	5	6	7	8			4	5	6	7	8	9[h]	10	Shuāng jiàng		9	10	11	12	13	14	15	
NOVEMBER 1963	27	28	29	30	31	○	2	13:56	44	2438330		9	10	11	12	13	14	15			11	12	13	14	15	16	17			16	17	18	19	20	21	22	
	3	4	5	6	7	◑	9	6:37	45	2438337		16	17	18	19	20	21	22			18	19	20	21	22	23	24	Lì dōng		23	24	25	26	27	28	29	
	10	11	12	13	14	15	●	6:50	46	2438344		23	24	25	26	27	28	29	Sat 14h27m16p	MONTH 10 Guǐ-Mǎo	25	26	27	28	29	30	1		ATHŌR 1680	30	1	2	3	4	5	6	ḪEDĀR 1956
	17	18	19	20	21	22	23		47	2438351	KISLEV 5724	1	2	3	4	5	6	7			2*	3	4	5	6	7	8	Xiǎo xuě		7	8	9	10	11	12	13	
DECEMBER 1963	◐	25	26	27	28	29	○	7:56 23:54	48	2438358		8	9	10	11	12	13	14			9	10	11	12	13	14	15			14	15	16	17	18	19	20	
	1	2	3	4	5	6	◑	21:34	49	2438365		15	16	17	18	19	20[d]	21			16	17	18	19	20	21	22			21	22	23	24	25	26	27	
	8	9	10	11	12	13	14		50	2438372		22	23	24	25[e]	26[e]	27[e]	28[e]			23	24	25	26	27	28	29	Dà xuě	KOIAK 1680	28	29	30	1	2	3	4	TĀḪŚĀŚ 1956
	15	●	17	18	19	20	21	2:06	51	2438379	TEVETH 5724	29[e]	30[e]	1[e]	2[e]	3	4	5	Mon 3h11m17p	MONTH 11* Guǐ-Mǎo	30	1	2	3	4	5	6			5	6	7	8	9	10	11	
	22[e]	◐	24	25	26	27	28	19:54	52	2438386		6	7	8	9	10	11	12			7[i]	8	9	10	11	12	13	Dōng zhì		12	13	14	15	16	17	18	
	29	○	31	1	2	3	4	11:04	1	2438393		13	14	15	16	17	18	19			14	15	16	17	18	19	20			19	20	21	22	23	24	25	

[a]New Year
[b]Spring (8:20)
[c]Summer (3:04)
[d]Autumn (18:23)
[e]Winter (14:02)
● New moon
◐ First quarter moon
○ Full moon
◑ Last quarter moon

[a]New Year
[b]Yom Kippur
[c]Sukkot
[d]Winter starts
[e]Ḥanukkah
[f]Purim
[g]Passover
[h]Shavuot
[i]Fast of Av

‡Leap year
[a]New Year (4661, Hare)
[b]Lantern Festival
[c]Qīngmíng
[d]Dragon Festival
[e]Qīqiǎo
[f]Hungry Ghosts
[g]Mid-Autumn Festival
[h]Double-Ninth Festival
[i]Dōngzhì
*Start of 60-name cycle

‡Leap year
[a]New Year
[b]Building of the Cross
[c]Christmas
[d]Jesus's Circumcision
[e]Epiphany
[f]Easter
[g]Mary's Announcement
[h]Jesus's Transfiguration

PERSIAN (ASTRONOMICAL) 1341/1342‡

Month	Sun	Mon	Tue	Wed	Thu	Fri	Sat
	9	10	11	12	13	14	15
DEY 1341	16	17	18	19	20	21	22
	23	24	25	26	27	28	29
	30	1	2	3	4	5	6
BAHMAN 1341	7	8	9	10	11	12	13
	14	15	16	17	18	19	20
	21	22	23	24	25	26	27
	28	29	30	1	2	3	4
ESFAND 1341	5	6	7	8	9	10	11
	12	13	14	15	16	17	18
	19	20	21	22	23	24	25
	26	27	28	29	1[a]	2*	3
FARVARDĪN 1342	4	5	6	7	8	9	10
	11	12	13[b]	14	15	16	17
	18	19	20	21	22	23	24
	25	26	27	28	29	30	31
	1	2	3	4	5	6	7
ORDĪBEHEŠT 1342	8	9	10	11	12	13	14
	15	16	17	18	19	20	21
	22	23	24	25	26	27	28
	29	30	31	1	2	3	4
XORDĀD 1342	5	6	7	8	9	10	11
	12	13	14	15	16	17	18
	19	20	21	22	23	24	25
	26	27	28	29	30	31	1
	2	3	4	5	6	7	8
TĪR 1342	9	10	11	12	13	14	15
	16	17	18	19	20	21	22
	23	24	25	26	27	28	29
	30	31	1	2	3	4	5
MORDĀD 1342	6	7	8	9	10	11	12
	13	14	15	16	17	18	19
	20	21	22	23	24	25	26
	27	28	29	30	31	1	2
SHAHRĪVAR 1342	3	4	5	6	7	8	9
	10	11	12	13	14	15	16
	17	18	19	20	21	22	23
	24	25	26	27	28	29	30
	31	1	2	3	4	5	6
MEHR 1342	7	8	9	10	11	12	13
	14	15	16	17	18	19	20
	21	22	23	24	25	26	27
	28	29	30	1	2	3	4
ĀBĀN 1342	5	6	7	8	9	10	11
	12	13	14	15	16	17	18
	19	20	21	22	23	24	25
	26	27	28	29	30	1	2
ĀZAR 1342	3	4	5	6	7	8	9
	10	11	12	13	14	15	16
	17	18	19	20	21	22	23
	24	25	26	27	28	29	30
DEY 1342	1	2	3	4	5	6	7
	8	9	10	11	12	13	14

‡Leap year
[a]New Year (or next day)
*Near New Year: 0′55″
[b]Sizdeh Bedar

HINDU LUNAR 2019/2020

Month	Sun	Mon	Tue	Wed	Thu	Fri	Sat
	4	5	6	7	8	9	10
PAUSHA 2019	11	**12**	14	15	16	17	18
	19	20	20	21	22	23	24
	25	26	27	28	29	30	1
MĀGHA 2019	2	3	4	5	**6**	8	9
	10	11	12	13	14	15	16
	17	18	19	20	21	22	22
	23	24	25	26	27	28[h]	29
PHĀLGUNA 2019	**30**	2	3	4	5	6	7
	8	9	10	11	12	13	14
	15[i]	16	17	18	19	20	21
	22	23	24	25	26	27	28
	29	30	1[a]	2	3	**4**	6
CHAITRA 2020	7	8	9[b]	10	11	12	13
	14	15	16	16	17	18	19
	20	21	22	23	24	25	26
	27	**28**	30	1	2	3	4
VAIŚĀKHA 2020	5	6	7	8	9	10	11
	12	13	14	15	16	17	18
	19	20	21	22	23	24	25
	26	27	28	29	30	1	**2**
JYAISHTHA 2020	4	5	6	7	8	9	10
	11	11	12	13	14	15	16
	17	18	19	20	21	22	23
	24	26	27	28	29	30	1
ĀSHĀDHA 2020	2	3	4	5	6	7	8
	9	10	11	12	13	14	15
	16	17	18	19	20	21	22
	23	24	25	26	**27**	29	30
	1	2	3	4	5	6	7
ŚRĀVAṆA 2020	8	8	9	10	11	12	13
	14	15	16	17	18	19	**20**
	22	23[c]	24	25	26	27	28
	29	30	1	2	3	4[d]	5
BHĀDRAPADA 2020	6	7	8	9	10	11	12
	13	14	15	16	17	18	19
	20	21	22	**23**	25	26	27
	28	29	30	1	2	3	4
LEAP ĀŚVINA 2020	4	5	6	7	8	9	10
	11	12	13	14	15	**16**	18
	19	20	21	22	23	24	25
	26	27	28	29	30	1	2
ĀŚVINA 2020	3	4	5	6	7	8[e]	9[e]
	10[e]	11	12	13	14	15	16
	17	18	19	20	**21**	23	24
	25	26	27	28	28	29	30
	1[f]	2	3	4	5	6	7
KĀRTTIKA 2020	8	9	10	11	12	13	**14**
	16	17	18	19	20	21	22
	23	24	25	26	27	28	29
	30	1	1	2	3	4	5
MĀRGAŚĪRA 2020	6	7	**8**	10	11[g]	12	13
	14	15	16	17	18	19	20

[a]New Year (Śobhana)
[b]Birthday of Rāma
[c]Birthday of Krishna
[d]Ganēśa Chaturthī
[e]Dashara
[f]Diwali
[g]Birthday of Vishnu
[h]Night of Śiva
[i]Holi

HINDU SOLAR 1884/1885‡

Month	Sun	Mon	Tue	Wed	Thu	Fri	Sat
	16	17	18	19	20	21	22
PAUSHA 1884	23	24	25	26	27	28	29
	30	1[b]	2	3	4	5	6
MĀGHA 1884	7	8	9	10	11	12	13
	14	15	16	17	18	19	20
	21	22	23	24	25	26	27
	28	29	1	2	3	4	5
PHĀLGUNA 1884	6	7	8	9	10	11	12
	13	14	15	16	17	18	19
	20	21	22	23	24	25	26
	27	28	29	30	1	2	3
CHAITRA 1884	4	5	6	7	8	9	10
	11	12	13	14	15	16	17
	18	19	20	21	22	23	24
	25	26	27	28	29	30	1[a]
VAIŚĀKHA 1885	2	3	4	5	6	7	8
	9	10	11	12	13	14	15
	16	17	18	19	20	21	22
	23	24	25	26	27	28	29
	30	31	1	2	3	4	5
JYAISHTHA 1885	6	7	8	9	10	11	12
	13	14	15	16	17	18	19
	20	21	22	23	24	25	26
	27	28	29	30	31	32	1
ĀSHĀDHA 1885	2	3	4	5	6	7	8
	9	10	11	12	13	14	15
	16	17	18	19	20	21	22
	23	24	25	26	27	28	29
	30	31	1	2	3	4	5
ŚRĀVAṆA 1885	6	7	8	9	10	11	12
	13	14	15	16	17	18	19
	20	21	22	23	24	25	26
	27	28	29	30	31	32	1
BHĀDRAPADA 1885	2	3	4	5	6	7	8
	9	10	11	12	13	14	15
	16	17	18	19	20	21	22
	23	24	25	26	27	28	29
	30	31	1	2	3	4	5
ĀŚVINA 1885	6	7	8	9	10	11	12
	13	14	15	16	17	18	19
	20	21	22	23	24	25	26
	27	28	29	30	1	2	3
KĀRTTIKA 1885	4	5	6	7	8	9	10
	11	12	13	14	15	16	17
	18	19	20	21	22	23	24
	25	26	27	28	29	30	1
MĀRGAŚĪRA 1885	2	3	4	5	6	7	8
	9	10	11	12	13	14	15
	16	17	18	19	20	21	22
	23	24	25	26	27	28	29
PAUSHA 1885	30	1	2	3	4	5	6
	7	8	9	10	11	12	13
	14	15	16	17	18	19	20

‡Leap year
[a]New Year (Anala)
[b]Pongal

ISLAMIC (ASTRONOMICAL) 1382/1383‡

Month	Sun	Mon	Tue	Wed	Thu	Fri	Sat
	3	4	5	6	7	8	9
SHA'BĀN 1382	10	11	12	13	14	15	16
	17	18	19	20	21	22	23
	24	25	26	27	28	29	30
RAMAḌĀN 1382	1[e]	2	3	4	5	6	7
	8	9	10	11	12	13	14
	15	16	17	18	19	20	21
	22	23	24	25	26	27	28
SHAWWĀL 1382	29	1[f]	2	3	4	5	6
	7	8	9	10	11	12	13
	14	15	16	17	18	19	20
	21	22	23	24	25	26	27
	28	29	30	1	2	3	4
DHU AL-QA'DA 1382	5	6	7	8	9	10	11
	12	13	14	15	16	17	18
	19	20	21	22	23	24	25
	26	27	28	29	1	2	3
DHU AL-ḤIJJA 1382	4	5	6	7	8	9	10[g]
	11	12	13	14	15	16	17
	18	19	20	21	22	23	24
	25	26	27	28	29	1[a]	2[d]
MUḤARRAM 1383	3	4	5	6	7	8	9
	10[b]	11	12	13	14	15	16
	17	18	19	20	21	22	23
	24	25	26	27	28	29	30
	1	2	3	4	5	6	7
ṢAFAR 1383	8	9	10	11	12	13	14
	15	16	17	18	19	20	21
	22	23	24	25	26	27	28
	29	1	2	3	4	5	6
RABĪ' I 1383	7	8	9	10	11	12[c]	13
	14	15	16	17	18	19	20
	21	22	23	24	25	26	27
	28	29	30	1	2	3	4
RABĪ' II 1383	5	6	7	8	9	10	11
	12	13	14	15	16	17	18
	19	20	21	22	23	24	25
	26	27	28	29	1	2	3
JUMĀDĀ I 1383	4	5	6	7	8	9	10
	11	12	13	14	15	16	17
	18	19	20	21	22	23	24
	25	26	27	28	29	30	1
JUMĀDĀ II 1383	2	3	4	5	6	7	8
	9	10	11	12	13	14	15
	16	17	18	19	20	21	22
	23	24	25	26	27	28	29
	30	1	2	3	4	5	6
RAJAB 1383	7	8	9	10	11	12	13
	14	15	16	17	18	19	20
	21	22	23	24	25	26	27[d]
	28	29	30	1	2	3	4
SHA'BĀN 1383	5	6	7	8	9	10	11
	12	13	14	15	16	17	18

‡Leap year
[a]New Year
[d]New Year (Arithmetic)
[b]'Āshūrā'
[c]Prophet's Birthday
[d]Ascent of the Prophet
[e]Start of Ramaḍān
[f]'Īd al-Fiṭr
[g]'Īd al-'Aḍḥā

GREGORIAN 1963

Julian (Sun)	Sun	Mon	Tue	Wed	Thu	Fri	Sat	Month
Dec 17	30	31	1	2	3	4	5	
	6	7[a]	8	9	10	11	12	JANUARY 1963
Dec 31	13	14[b]	15	16	17	18	19	
	20	21	22	23	24	25	26	
Jan 14	27	28	29	30	31	1	2	
	3	4	5	6	7	8	9	FEBRUARY 1963
Jan 28	10	11	12	13	14	15	16	
	17	18	19	20	21	22	23	
Feb 11	24	25	26	27[c]	28	1	2	
	3[d]	4	5	6	7	8	9	
Feb 25	10	11	12	13	14	15	16	MARCH 1963
	17	18	19	20	21	22	23	
Mar 11	24	25	26	27	28	29	30	
	31	1	2	3	4	5	6	
Mar 25	7	8	9	10	11	12	13	
	14[e]	15	16	17	18	19	20	APRIL 1963
Apr 8	21	22	23	24	25	26	27	
	28	29	30	1	2	3	4	
Apr 22	5	6	7	8	9	10	11	MAY 1963
	12	13	14	15	16	17	18	
May 6	19	20	21	22	23	24	25	
	26	27	28	29	30	31	1	
May 20	2	3	4	5	6	7	8	
	9	10	11	12	13	14	15	JUNE 1963
Jun 3	16	17	18	19	20	21	22	
	23	24	25	26	27	28	29	
Jun 17	30	1	2	3	4	5	6	
	7	8	9	10	11	12	13	
Jul 1	14	15	16	17	18	19	20	JULY 1963
	21	22	23	24	25	26	27	
Jul 15	28	29	30	31	1	2	3	
	4	5	6	7	8	9	10	
Jul 29	11	12	13	14	15	16	17	AUGUST 1963
	18	19	20	21	22	23	24	
Aug 12	25	26	27	28	29	30	31	
	1	2	3	4	5	6	7	
Aug 26	8	9	10	11	12	13	14	SEPTEMBER 1963
	15	16	17	18	19	20	21	
Sep 9	22	23	24	25	26	27	28	
	29	30	1	2	3	4	5	
Sep 23	6	7	8	9	10	11	12	OCTOBER 1963
	13	14	15	16	17	18	19	
Oct 7	20	21	22	23	24	25	26	
	27	28	29	30	31	1	2	
Oct 21	3	4	5	6	7	8	9	NOVEMBER 1963
	10	11	12	13	14	15	16	
Nov 4	17	18	19	20	21	22	23	
	24	25	26	27	28	29	30	
Nov 18	1[g]	2	3	4	5	6	7	
	8	9	10	11	12	13	14	DECEMBER 1963
Dec 2	15	16	17	18	19	20	21	
	22	23	24	25[h]	26	27	28	
Dec 16	29	30	31	1	2	3	4	

[a]Orthodox Christmas
[b]Julian New Year
[c]Ash Wednesday
[d]Feast of Orthodoxy
[e]Easter (also Orthodox)
[g]Advent
[h]Christmas

1964

Gregorian 1964[‡], Lunar Phases, ISO Week, Julian Day

Month	Sun	Mon	Tue	Wed	Thu	Fri	Sat	Lunar Phases	ISO WEEK (Mon)	JULIAN DAY (Sun noon)
JANUARY 1964	29	○	31	1[a]	2	3	4	11:04	1	2438393
	5	◑	7	8	9	10	11	15:58	2	2438400
	12	13	●	15	16	17	18	20:44	3	2438407
	19	20	21	◐	23	24	25	5:29	4	2438414
	26	27	○	29	30	31	1	23:23	5	2438421
FEBRUARY 1964	2	3	4	◑	6	7	8	12:42	6	2438428
	9	10	11	12	●	14	15	13:01	7	2438435
	16	17	18	19	◐	21	22	13:24	8	2438442
	23	24	25	26	○	28	29	12:39	9	2438449
MARCH 1964	1	2	3	4	5	◑	7	10:00	10	2438456
	8	9	10	11	12	13	●	2:14	11	2438463
	15	16	17	18	19	◐[b]	21	20:39	12	2438470
	22	23	24	25	26	27	○	2:48	13	2438477
	29	30	31	1	2	3	4		14	2438484
APRIL 1964	◑	6	7	8	9	10	11	5:45	15	2438491
	●	13	14	15	16	17	18	12:38	16	2438498
	◐	20	21	22	23	24	25	4:09	17	2438505
	○	27	28	29	30	1	2	17:49	18	2438512
MAY 1964	3	◑	5	6	7	8	9	22:20	19	2438519
	10	●	12	13	14	15	16	21:02	20	2438526
	17	◐	19	20	21	22	23	12:42	21	2438533
	24	25	○	27	28	29	30	9:29	22	2438540
	31	1	2	◑	4	5	6	11:07	23	2438547
JUNE 1964	7	8	9	●	11	12	13	4:22	24	2438554
	14	15	◐	17	18	19	20	23:02	25	2438561
	21[c]	22	23	24	○	26	27	1:08	26	2438568
	28	29	30	1	◑	3	4	20:31	27	2438575
JULY 1964	5	6	7	8	●	10	11	11:31	28	2438582
	12	13	14	15	◐	17	18	11:47	29	2438589
	19	20	21	22	23	○	25	15:58	30	2438596
	26	27	28	29	30	31	◑	3:29	31	2438603
AUGUST 1964	2	3	4	5	6	●	8	19:17	32	2438610
	9	10	11	12	13	14	◐	3:19	33	2438617
	16	17	18	19	20	21	22		34	2438624
	○	24	25	26	27	28	29	5:25	35	2438631
	◑	31	1	2	3	4	5	9:15	36	2438638
SEPTEMBER 1964	●	7	8	9	10	11	12	4:34	37	2438645
	◐	14	15	16	17	18	19	21:23	38	2438652
	20	○	22	23[d]	24	25	26	17:31	39	2438659
	27	◑	29	30	1	2	3	15:02	40	2438666
OCTOBER 1964	4	●	6	7	8	9	10	16:20	41	2438673
	11	12	◐	14	15	16	17	16:56	42	2438680
	18	19	20	○	22	23	24	4:45	43	2438687
	25	26	◑	28	29	30	31	21:59	44	2438694
NOVEMBER 1964	1	2	3	●	5	6	7	7:16	45	2438701
	8	9	10	11	◐	13	14	12:20	46	2438708
	15	16	17	18	○	20	21	15:43	47	2438715
	22	23	24	25	◑	27	28	7:11	48	2438722
	29	30	1	2	3	●	5	1:18	49	2438729
DECEMBER 1964	6	7	8	9	10	11	◐	6:01	50	2438736
	13	14	15	16	17	18	○	2:41	51	2438743
	20	21[e]	22	23	24	◑	26	19:27	52	2438750
	27	28	29	30	31	1	●	21:07	53	2438757

Hebrew 5724/5725[‡]

ISO Week	Month	Sun	Mon	Tue	Wed	Thu	Fri	Sat	Molad
1	TEVETH 5724	13	14	15	16	17	18	19	
2		20	21	22	23	24	25	26	
3		27	28	29	1	2	3	4	Tue 15h56m0p
4	SHEVAT 5724	5	6	7	8	9	10	11	
5		12	13	14	15	16	17	18	
6		19	20	21	22	23	24	25	
7		26	27	28	29	30	1	2	Thu 4h40m1p
8	ADAR 5724	3	4	5	6	7	8	9	
9		10	11	12	13	14[f]	15	16	
10		17	18	19	20	21	22	23	
11		24	25	26	27	28	29	1	Fri 17h24m2p
12	NISAN 5724	2	3	4	5	6	7	8	
13		9	10	11	12	13	14	15[g]	
14		16	17	18	19	20	21	22	
15		23	24	25	26	27	28	29	
16		30	1	2	3	4	5	6	Sun 6h8m3p
17	IYYAR 5724	7	8	9	10	11	12	13	
18		14	15	16	17	18	19	20	
19		21	22	23	24	25	26	27	
20		28	29	1	2	3	4	5	Mon 18h52m4p
21	SIVAN 5724	6[h]	7	8	9	10	11	12	
22		13	14	15	16	17	18	19	
23		20	21	22	23	24	25	26	
24		27	28	29	30	1	2	3	Wed 7h36m5p
25	TAMMUZ 5724	4	5	6	7	8	9	10	
26		11	12	13	14	15	16	17	
27		18	19	20	21	22	23	24	
28		25	26	27	28	29	1	2	Thu 20h20m6p
29	AV 5724	3	4	5	6	7	8	9	
30		10[i]	11	12	13	14	15	16	
31		17	18	19	20	21	22	23	
32		24	25	26	27	28	29	30	
33	ELUL 5724	1	2	3	4	5	6	7	Sat 9h4m7p
34		8	9	10	11	12	13	14	
35		15	16	17	18	19	20	21	
36		22	23	24	25	26	27	28	
37		29	1[a]	2[a]	3	4	5	6	Sun 21h48m8p
38	TISHRI 5725	7	8	9	10[b]	11	12	13	
39		14	15[c]	16	17	18	19	20	
40		21	22	23	24	25	26	27	
41		28	29	30	1	2	3	4	Tue 10h32m9p
42	HESHVAN 5725	5	6	7	8	9	10	11	
43		12	13	14	15	16	17	18	
44		19	20	21	22	23	24	25	
45		26	27	28	29	30	1	2	Wed 23h16m10p
46	KISLEV 5725	3	4	5	6	7	8	9	
47		10	11	12	13	14	15	16	
48		17	18	19	20	21	22	23	
49		24	25[e]	26[e]	27[e]	28[e]	29[e]	30[d,e]	
50	TEVETH 5725	1[e]	2[e]	3	4	5	6	7	Fri 12h0m11p
51		8	9	10	11	12	13	14	
52		15	16	17	18	19	20	21	
53		22	23	24	25	26	27	28	

Chinese Guǐ-Mǎo[‡]/Jiǎ-Chén

ISO Week	Month	Sun	Mon	Tue	Wed	Thu	Fri	Sat	Solar Term
1	MONTH 11* Guǐ-Mǎo	14	15	16	17	18	19	20	
2		21	22	23	24	25	26	27	Xiǎo hán
3		28	29	30	1	2*	3	4	
4	MONTH 12 Guǐ-Mǎo	5	6	7	8	9	10	11	Dà hán
5		12	13	14	15	16	17	18	
6		19	20	21	22	23	24	25	Lì chūn
7		26	27	28	29	1[a]	2	3	
8	MONTH 1 Jiǎ-Chén	4	5	6	7	8	9	10	Yǔ shuǐ
9		11	12	13	14	15[b]	16	17	
10		18	19	20	21	22	23	24	Jīng zhé
11		25	26	27	28	29	30	1	
12	MONTH 2 Jiǎ-Chén	2	3*	4	5	6	7	8	Chūn fēn
13		9	10	11	12	13	14	15	
14		16	17	18	19	20	21	22	
15		23[c]	24	25	26	27	28	29	Qīng míng
16	MONTH 3 Jiǎ-Chén	1	2	3	4	5	6	7	
17		8	9	10	11	12	13	14	Gǔ yǔ
18		15	16	17	18	19	20	21	
19		22	23	24	25	26	27	28	Lì xià
20		29	30	1	2	3	4*	5	
21	MONTH 4 Jiǎ-Chén	6	7	8	9	10	11	12	Xiǎo mǎn
22		13	14	15	16	17	18	19	
23		20	21	22	23	24	25	26	Máng zhòng
24		27	28	29	1	2	3	4	
25	MONTH 5 Jiǎ-Chén	5[d]	6	7	8	9	10	11	
26		12	13	14	15	16	17	18	Xià zhì
27		19	20	21	22	23	24	25	
28		26	27	28	29	1	2	3	Xiǎo shǔ
29	MONTH 6 Jiǎ-Chén	4	5	6*	7	8	9	10	
30		11	12	13	14	15	16	17	Dà shǔ
31		18	19	20	21	22	23	24	
32		25	26	27	28	29	30	1	Lì qiū
33	MONTH 7 Jiǎ-Chén	2	3	4	5	6	7[e]	8	
34		9	10	11	12	13	14	15[f]	
35		16	17	18	19	20	21	22	Chǔ shǔ
36		23	24	25	26	27	28	29	
37		1	2	3	4	5	6	7*	Bái lù
38	MONTH 8 Jiǎ-Chén	8	9	10	11	12	13	14	
39		15[g]	16	17	18	19	20	21	Qiū fēn
40		22	23	24	25	26	27	28	
41		29	30	1	2	3	4	5	Hán lù
42	MONTH 9 Jiǎ-Chén	6	7	8	9[h]	10	11	12	
43		13	14	15	16	17	18	19	Shuāng jiàng
44		20	21	22	23	24	25	26	
45		27	28	29	1	2	3	4	Lì dōng
46	MONTH 10 Jiǎ-Chén	5	6	7	8*	9	10	11	
47		12	13	14	15	16	17	18	
48		19	20	21	22	23	24	25	Xiǎo xuě
49		26	27	28	29	30	1	2	
50	MONTH 11 Jiǎ-Chén	3	4	5	6	7	8	9	Dà xuě
51		10	11	12	13	14	15	16	
52		17	18	19[i]	20	21	22	23	Dōng zhì
53		24	25	26	27	28	29	30	

Coptic 1680/1681 and Ethiopic 1956/1957

ISO Week	Coptic Month	Sun	Mon	Tue	Wed	Thu	Fri	Sat	Ethiopic Month
1	KOIAK 1680	19	20	21	22	23	24	25	TĀKHŚĀŚ 1956
2		26	27	28	29[c]	30	1	2	
3	TÔBE 1680	3	4	5	6[d]	7	8	9	ṬER 1956
4		10	11[e]	12	13	14	15	16	
5		17	18	19	20	21	22	23	
6		24	25	26	27	28	29	30	
7	MESHIR 1680	1	2	3	4	5	6	7	YAKĀTIT 1956
8		8	9	10	11	12	13	14	
9		15	16	17	18	19	20	21	
10		22	23	24	25	26	27	28	
11		29	30	1	2	3	4	5	
12	PAREMOTEP 1680	6	7	8	9	10	11	12	MAGĀBIT 1956
13		13	14	15	16	17	18	19	
14		20	21	22	23	24	25	26	
15		27	28	29	30	1	2	3	
16	PARMOUTE 1680	4	5	6	7	8	9	10	MIYĀZYĀ 1956
17		11	12	13	14	15	16	17	
18		18	19	20	21	22	23	24	
19		25[f]	26	27	28	29[g]	30	1	
20	PASHONS 1680	2	3	4	5	6	7	8	GENBOT 1956
21		9	10	11	12	13	14	15	
22		16	17	18	19	20	21	22	
23		23	24	25	26	27	28	29	
24		30	1	2	3	4	5	6	
25	PAÔNE 1680	7	8	9	10	11	12	13	SANÉ 1956
26		14	15	16	17	18	19	20	
27		21	22	23	24	25	26	27	
28		28	29	30	1	2	3	4	
29	EPÊP 1680	5	6	7	8	9	10	11	ḤAMLÉ 1956
30		12	13	14	15	16	17	18	
31		19	20	21	22	23	24	25	
32		26	27	28	29	30	1	2	
33	MESORÊ 1680	3	4	5	6	7	8	9	NAHASÉ 1956
34		10	11	12	13[h]	14	15	16	
35		17	18	19	20	21	22	23	
36		24	25	26	27	28	29	30	
37	EPAG. 1680	1	2	3	4	5	1[a]	2	PĀG. 1956
38	THOOUT 1681	3	4	5	6	7	8	9	MASKARAM 1957
39		10	11	12	13	14	15	16	
40		17[b]	18	19	20	21	22	23	
41		24	25	26	27	28	29	30	
42	PAOPE 1681	1	2	3	4	5	6	7	ṬEQEMT 1957
43		8	9	10	11	12	13	14	
44		15	16	17	18	19	20	21	
45		22	23	24	25	26	27	28	
46		29	30	1	2	3	4	5	
47	ATHÔR 1681	6	7	8	9	10	11	12	HEDĀR 1957
48		13	14	15	16	17	18	19	
49		20	21	22	23	24	25	26	
50		27	28	29	30	1	2	3	
51	KOIAK 1681	4	5	6	7	8	9	10	TĀKHŚĀŚ 1957
52		11	12	13	14	15	16	17	
53		18	19	20	21	22	23	24	

Gregorian notes:
‡Leap year
[a]New Year
[b]Spring (14:10)
[c]Summer (8:56)
[d]Autumn (0:16)
[e]Winter (19:49)
● New moon
◐ First quarter moon
○ Full moon
◑ Last quarter moon

Hebrew notes:
‡Leap year
[a]New Year
[b]Yom Kippur
[c]Sukkot
[d]Winter starts
[e]Ḥanukkah
[f]Purim
[g]Passover
[h]Shavuot
[i]Fast of Av

Chinese notes:
‡Leap year
[a]New Year (4662, Dragon)
[b]Lantern Festival
[c]Qīngmíng
[d]Dragon Festival
[e]Qīqiǎo
[f]Hungry Ghosts
[g]Mid-Autumn Festival
[h]Double-Ninth Festival
[i]Dōngzhì
*Start of 60-name cycle

Coptic/Ethiopic notes:
[a]New Year
[b]Building of the Cross
[c]Christmas
[d]Jesus's Circumcision
[e]Epiphany
[f]Easter
[g]Mary's Announcement
[h]Jesus's Transfiguration

1964

PERSIAN (ASTRONOMICAL) 1342‡/1343

Month	Sun	Mon	Tue	Wed	Thu	Fri	Sat
DEY 1342	8	9	10	11	12	13	14
	15	16	17	18	19	20	21
	22	23	24	25	26	27	28
	29	30	1	2	3	4	5
BAHMAN 1342	6	7	8	9	10	11	12
	13	14	15	16	17	18	19
	20	21	22	23	24	25	26
	27	28	29	30	1	2	3
ESFAND 1342	4	5	6	7	8	9	10
	11	12	13	14	15	16	17
	18	19	20	21	22	23	24
	25	26	27	28	29	30	1[a]
FARVARDĪN 1343	2	3	4	5	6	7	8
	9	10	11	12	13[b]	14	15
	16	17	18	19	20	21	22
	23	24	25	26	27	28	29
	30	31	1	2	3	4	5
ORDĪBEHEŠT 1343	6	7	8	9	10	11	12
	13	14	15	16	17	18	19
	20	21	22	23	24	25	26
	27	28	29	30	31	1	2
XORDĀD 1343	3	4	5	6	7	8	9
	10	11	12	13	14	15	16
	17	18	19	20	21	22	23
	24	25	26	27	28	29	30
	31	1	2	3	4	5	6
TĪR 1343	7	8	9	10	11	12	13
	14	15	16	17	18	19	20
	21	22	23	24	25	26	27
	28	29	30	31	1	2	3
MORDĀD 1343	4	5	6	7	8	9	10
	11	12	13	14	15	16	17
	18	19	20	21	22	23	24
	25	26	27	28	29	30	31
SHAHRĪVAR 1343	1	2	3	4	5	6	7
	8	9	10	11	12	13	14
	15	16	17	18	19	20	21
	22	23	24	25	26	27	28
	29	30	31	1	2	3	4
MEHR 1343	5	6	7	8	9	10	11
	12	13	14	15	16	17	18
	19	20	21	22	23	24	25
	26	27	28	29	30	1	2
ĀBĀN 1343	3	4	5	6	7	8	9
	10	11	12	13	14	15	16
	17	18	19	20	21	22	23
	24	25	26	27	28	29	30
ĀZAR 1343	1	2	3	4	5	6	7
	8	9	10	11	12	13	14
	15	16	17	18	19	20	21
	22	23	24	25	26	27	28
	29	30	1	2	3	4	5
DEY 1343	6	7	8	9	10	11	12

‡Leap year
[a]New Year
[b]Sizdeh Bedar

HINDU LUNAR 2020/2021‡

Month	Sun	Mon	Tue	Wed	Thu	Fri	Sat
MĀRGAŚĪRA 2020	14	15	16	17	18	19	20
	21	22	23	24	25	26	27
	28	29	30	1	2	3	4
MĀGHA 2020	5	6	7	8	9	10	11
	12	13	15	16	17	18	19
	20	21	22	23	23	24	25
	26	27	28[h]	29	30	1	2
PHĀLGUNA 2020	3	4	5	6	7	9	10
	11	12	13	14	15[i]	16	17
	18	19	20	21	22	23	24
	25	25	26	27	28	29	30[a]
LEAP CHAITRA 2021	2	3	4	5	6	7	8
	9	10	11	12	13	14	15
	16	17	18	19	20	21	22
	23	24	25	26	27	28	29
CHAITRA 2021	30	1	2	3	4	5	7
	8	9[b]	10	11	12	13	14
	15	16	17	18	19	19	20
	21	22	23	24	25	26	27
	28	30	1	2	3	4	5
VAIŚĀKHA 2021	6	7	8	9	10	11	12
	13	14	15	16	17	18	19
	20	21	22	23	24	25	26
	27	28	29	30	1	3	4
JYAISHTHA 2021	5	6	7	8	9	10	11
	12	13	14	15	16	16	17
	18	19	20	21	22	23	24
	26	27	28	29	30	1	2
ĀSHĀDHA 2021	3	4	5	6	7	8	9
	10	11	12	13	14	15	16
	17	18	19	20	21	22	23
	24	25	26	27	29	30	1
ŚRĀVAṆA 2021	2	3	4	5	6	7	8
	9	10	11	12	12	13	14
	15	16	17	18	19	20	22
	23[c]	24	25	26	27	28	29
BHĀDRAPADA 2021	30	1	2	3[d]	4	5	6
	7	8	9	10	11	12	13
	14	15	16	17	18	19	20
	21	22	23	25	26	27	28
	29	30	1	2	3	4	5
ĀŚVINA 2021	6	7	8	8[e]	9[e]	10[e]	11
	12	13	14	15	16	17	19
	20	21	22	23	24	25	26
	27	28	29	30	1[f]	2	3
KĀRTTIKA 2021	4	5	6	7	8	9	10
	11	12	13	14	15	16	17
	18	19	20	21	23	24	25
	26	27	28	29	30	1	1
MĀRGAŚĪRA 2021	2	3	4	5	6	7	8
	9	10	11[g]	12	13	14	15
	17	18	19	20	21	22	23
	24	25	26	27	28	29	30

‡Leap year
[a]New Year (Krodhin)
[b]Birthday of Rāma
[c]Birthday of Krishna
[d]Ganēśa Chaturthī
[e]Dashara
[f]Diwali
[g]Birthday of Vishnu
[h]Night of Śiva
[i]Holi

HINDU SOLAR 1885‡/1886

Month	Sun	Mon	Tue	Wed	Thu	Fri	Sat
PAUSHA 1885	14	15	16	17	18	19	20
	21	22	23	24	25	26	27
MĀGHA 1885	28	29	1[b]	2	3	4	5
	6	7	8	9	10	11	12
	13	14	15	16	17	18	19
	20	21	22	23	24	25	26
PHĀLGUNA 1885	27	28	29	1	2	3	4
	5	6	7	8	9	10	11
	12	13	14	15	16	17	18
	19	20	21	22	23	24	25
CHAITRA 1885	26	27	28	29	30	1	2
	3	4	5	6	7	8	9
	10	11	12	13	14	15	16
	17	18	19	20	21	22	23
	24	25	26	27	28	29	30
VAIŚĀKHA 1886	31	1[a]	2	3	4	5	6
	7	8	9	10	11	12	13
	14	15	16	17	18	19	20
	21	22	23	24	25	26	27
JYAISHTHA 1886	28	29	30	31	1	2	3
	4	5	6	7	8	9	10
	11	12	13	14	15	16	17
	18	19	20	21	22	23	24
	25	26	27	28	29	30	31
ĀSHĀDHA 1886	1	2	3	4	5	6	7
	8	9	10	11	12	13	14
	15	16	17	18	19	20	21
	22	23	24	25	26	27	28
ŚRĀVAṆA 1886	29	30	31	32	1	2	3
	4	5	6	7	8	9	10
	11	12	13	14	15	16	17
	18	19	20	21	22	23	24
	25	26	27	28	29	30	31
BHĀDRAPADA 1886	1	2	3	4	5	6	7
	8	9	10	11	12	13	14
	15	16	17	18	19	20	21
	22	23	24	25	26	27	28
ĀŚVINA 1886	29	30	31	1	2	3	4
	5	6	7	8	9	10	11
	12	13	14	15	16	17	18
	19	20	21	22	23	24	25
KĀRTTIKA 1886	26	27	28	29	30	31	1
	2	3	4	5	6	7	8
	9	10	11	12	13	14	15
	16	17	18	19	20	21	22
	23	24	25	26	27	28	29
MĀRGAŚĪRA 1886	1	2	3	4	5	6	7
	8	9	10	11	12	13	14
	15	16	17	18	19	20	21
	22	23	24	25	26	27	28
PAUSHA 1886	29	30	1	2	3	4	5
	6	7	8	9	10	11	12
	13	14	15	16	17	18	19

‡Leap year
[a]New Year (Piṅgala)
[b]Pongal

ISLAMIC (ASTRONOMICAL) 1383‡/1384‡

Month	Sun	Mon	Tue	Wed	Thu	Fri	Sat
SHA'BĀN 1383	12	13	14	15	16	17	18
	19	20	21	22	23	24	25
RAMAḌĀN 1383	26	27	28	29	1[e]	2	3
	4	5	6	7	8	9	10
	11	12	13	14	15	16	17
	18	19	20	21	22	23	24
SHAWWĀL 1383	25	26	27	28	29	30	1[f]
	2	3	4	5	6	7	8
	9	10	11	12	13	14	15
	16	17	18	19	20	21	22
	23	24	25	26	27	28	29
DHU AL-QA'DA 1383	1	2	3	4	5	6	7
	8	9	10	11	12	13	14
	15	16	17	18	19	20	21
	22	23	24	25	26	27	28
DHU AL-HIJJA 1383	29	30	1	2	3	4	5
	6	7	8	9	10[g]	11	12
	13	14	15	16	17	18	19
	20	21	22	23	24	25	26
MUHARRAM 1384	27	28	29	1[a]	2	3	4
	5	6	7	8	9	10[b]	11
	12	13	14	15	16	17	18
	19	20	21	22	23	24	25
ṢAFAR 1384	26	27	28	29	1	2	3
	4	5	6	7	8	9	10
	11	12	13	14	15	16	17
	18	19	20	21	22	23	24
RABĪ' I 1384	25	26	27	28	29	30	1
	2	3	4	5	6	7	8
	9	10	11	12[c]	13	14	15
	16	17	18	19	20	21	22
	23	24	25	26	27	28	29
RABĪ' II 1384	1	2	3	4	5	6	7
	8	9	10	11	12	13	14
	15	16	17	18	19	20	21
	22	23	24	25	26	27	28
JUMĀDĀ I 1384	29	1	2	3	4	5	6
	7	8	9	10	11	12	13
	14	15	16	17	18	19	20
	21	22	23	24	25	26	27
JUMĀDĀ II 1384	28	29	30	1	2	3	4
	5	6	7	8	9	10	11
	12	13	14	15	16	17	18
	19	20	21	22	23	24	25
RAJAB 1384	26	27	28	29	30	1	2
	3	4	5	6	7	8	9
	10	11	12	13	14	15	16
	17	18	19	20	21	22	23
	24	25	26	27[d]	28	29	30
SHA'BĀN 1384	1	2	3	4	5	6	7
	8	9	10	11	12	13	14
	15	16	17	18	19	20	21
	22	23	24	25	26	27	28

‡Leap year
[a]New Year
[b]'Ashūrā'
[c]Prophet's Birthday
[d]Ascent of the Prophet
[e]Start of Ramaḍān
[f]'Īd al-Fiṭr
[g]'Īd al-'Aḍḥā

GREGORIAN 1964‡

Julian‡ (Sun)	Sun	Mon	Tue	Wed	Thu	Fri	Sat	Month
Dec 16	29	30	31	1	2	3	4	
	5	6	7[a]	8	9	10	11	JANUARY 1964
Dec 30	12	13	14[b]	15	16	17	18	
	19	20	21	22	23	24	25	
Jan 13	26	27	28	29	30	31	1	
	2	3	4	5	6	7	8	FEBRUARY 1964
Jan 27	9	10	11	12[c]	13	14	15	
	16	17	18	19	20	21	22	
Feb 10	23	24	25	26	27	28	29	
	1	2	3	4	5	6	7	MARCH 1964
Feb 24	8	9	10	11	12	13	14	
	15	16	17	18	19	20	21	
Mar 9	22[d]	23	24	25	26	27	28	
	29[e]	30	31	1	2	3	4	
Mar 23	5	6	7	8	9	10	11	APRIL 1964
	12	13	14	15	16	17	18	
Apr 6	19	20	21	22	23	24	25	
	26	27	28	29	30	1	2	
Apr 20	3[f]	4	5	6	7	8	9	
	10	11	12	13	14	15	16	MAY 1964
May 4	17	18	19	20	21	22	23	
	24	25	26	27	28	29	30	
May 18	31	1	2	3	4	5	6	
	7	8	9	10	11	12	13	
Jun 1	14	15	16	17	18	19	20	JUNE 1964
	21	22	23	24	25	26	27	
Jun 15	28	29	30	1	2	3	4	
	5	6	7	8	9	10	11	
Jun 29	12	13	14	15	16	17	18	JULY 1964
	19	20	21	22	23	24	25	
Jul 13	26	27	28	29	30	31	1	
	2	3	4	5	6	7	8	
Jul 27	9	10	11	12	13	14	15	AUGUST 1964
	16	17	18	19	20	21	22	
Aug 10	23	24	25	26	27	28	29	
	30	31	1	2	3	4	5	
Aug 24	6	7	8	9	10	11	12	SEPTEMBER 1964
	13	14	15	16	17	18	19	
Sep 7	20	21	22	23	24	25	26	
	27	28	29	30	1	2	3	
Sep 21	4	5	6	7	8	9	10	OCTOBER 1964
	11	12	13	14	15	16	17	
Oct 5	18	19	20	21	22	23	24	
	25	26	27	28	29	30	31	
Oct 19	1	2	3	4	5	6	7	
	8	9	10	11	12	13	14	NOVEMBER 1964
Nov 2	15	16	17	18	19	20	21	
	22	23	24	25	26	27	28	
Nov 16	29[g]	30	1	2	3	4	5	
	6	7	8	9	10	11	12	DECEMBER 1964
Nov 30	13	14	15	16	17	18	19	
	20	21	22	23	24	25[h]	26	
Dec 14	27	28	29	30	31	1	2	

‡Leap year
[a]Orthodox Christmas
[b]Julian New Year
[c]Ash Wednesday
[d]Feast of Orthodoxy
[e]Easter
[f]Orthodox Easter
[g]Advent
[h]Christmas

1965

GREGORIAN 1965 — Lunar Phases — ISO WEEK — JULIAN DAY

GREGORIAN 1965	Sun	Mon	Tue	Wed	Thu	Fri	Sat	Lunar Phases	ISO WEEK (Mon)	JULIAN DAY (Sun noon)
JANUARY 1965	27	28	29	30	31	1[a]	●	21:07	53	2438757
	3	4	5	6	7	8	9		1	2438764
	◐	11	12	13	14	15	16	20:59	2	2438771
	○	18	19	20	21	22	23	13:37	3	2438778
	◑	25	26	27	28	29	30	11:07	4	2438785
FEBRUARY 1965	31	●	2	3	4	5	6	16:35	5	2438792
	7	8	◐	10	11	12	13	8:53	6	2438799
	14	15	○	17	18	19	20	0:27	7	2438806
	21	22	◑	24	25	26	27	5:39	8	2438813
MARCH 1965	28	1	2	●	4	5	6	9:56	9	2438820
	7	8	9	◐	11	12	13	17:52	10	2438827
	14	15	16	○	18	19	20[b]	11:24	11	2438834
	21	22	23	24	◑	26	27	1:37	12	2438841
APRIL 1965	28	29	30	31	1	●	3	0:21	13	2438848
	4	5	6	7	8	◐	10	0:40	14	2438855
	11	12	13	14	○	16	17	23:02	15	2438862
	18	19	20	21	22	◑	24	21:07	16	2438869
MAY 1965	25	26	27	28	29	30	●	11:56	17	2438876
	2	3	4	5	6	7	◐	6:20	18	2438883
	9	10	11	12	13	14	○	11:52	19	2438890
	16	17	18	19	20	21	22		20	2438897
	◑	24	25	26	27	28	29	14:40	21	2438904
JUNE 1965	●	31	1	2	3	4	5	21:13	22	2438911
	◐	7	8	9	10	11	12	12:11	23	2438918
	13	○	15	16	17	18	19	1:59	24	2438925
	20	21[c]	◑	23	24	25	26	5:36	25	2438932
JULY 1965	27	28	●	30	1	2	3	4:53	26	2438939
	4	◐	6	7	8	9	10	19:36	27	2438946
	11	12	○	14	15	16	17	17:01	28	2438953
	18	19	20	◑	22	23	24	17:53	29	2438960
	25	26	27	●	29	30	31	11:45	30	2438967
AUGUST 1965	1	2	3	◐	5	6	7	5:47	31	2438974
	8	9	10	11	○	13	14	8:22	32	2438981
	15	16	17	18	19	◑	21	3:50	33	2438988
	22	23	24	25	●	27	28	18:51	34	2438995
SEPTEMBER 1965	29	30	31	1	◐	3	4	19:27	35	2439002
	5	6	7	8	9	○	11	23:32	36	2439009
	12	13	14	15	16	17	◑	11:58	37	2439016
	19	20	21	22	23[d]	24	●	3:18	38	2439023
OCTOBER 1965	26	27	28	29	30	1	◐	12:37	39	2439030
	3	4	5	6	7	8	9		40	2439037
	○	11	12	13	14	15	16	14:14	41	2439044
	◑	18	19	20	21	22	23	19:00	42	2439051
	●	25	26	27	28	29	30	14:11	43	2439058
NOVEMBER 1965	31	◐	2	3	4	5	6	8:26	44	2439065
	7	8	○	10	11	12	13	4:15	45	2439072
	14	15	◑	17	18	19	20	1:54	46	2439079
	21	22	●	24	25	26	27	4:10	47	2439086
DECEMBER 1965	28	29	30	◐	2	3	4	5:24	48	2439093
	5	6	7	○	9	10	11	17:21	49	2439100
	12	13	14	◑	16	17	18	9:52	50	2439107
	19	20	21	●[e]	23	24	25	21:03	51	2439114
	26	27	28	29	30	◐	1	1:46	52	2439121

HEBREW 5725‡/5726

ISO WEEK	Month	Sun	Mon	Tue	Wed	Thu	Fri	Sat	Molad
53	TEVETH 5725	22	23	24	25	26	27	28	
1	SHEVAT 5725	29	1	2	3	4	5	6	Sun 0h44m12p
2		7	8	9	10	11	12	13	
3		14	15	16	17	18	19	20	
4		21	22	23	24	25	26	27	
5	ADAR I 5725	28	29	30	1	2	3	4	Mon 13h28m13p
6		5	6	7	8	9	10	11	
7		12	13	14	15	16	17	18	
8		19	20	21	22	23	24	25	
9	ADAR II 5725	26	27	28	29	30	1	2	Wed 2h12m14p
10		3	4	5	6	7	8	9	
11		10	11	12	13	14[f]	15	16	
12		17	18	19	20	21	22	23	
13	NISAN 5725	24	25	26	27	28	29	1	Thu 14h56m15p
14		2	3	4	5	6	7	8	
15		9	10	11	12	13	14	15[g]	
16		16	17	18	19	20	21	22	
17		23	24	25	26	27	28	29	
18	IYAR 5725	30	1	2	3	4	5	6	Sat 3h40m16p
19		7	8	9	10	11	12	13	
20		14	15	16	17	18	19	20	
21		21	22	23	24	25	26	27	
22	SIVAN 5725	28	29	1	2	3	4	5	Sun 16h24m17p
23		6[h]	7	8	9	10	11	12	
24		13	14	15	16	17	18	19	
25		20	21	22	23	24	25	26	
26	TAMMUZ 5725	27	28	29	30	1	2	3	Tue 5h9m0p
27		4	5	6	7	8	9	10	
28		11	12	13	14	15	16	17	
29		18	19	20	21	22	23	24	
30	AV 5725	25	26	27	28	29	1	2	Wed 17h53m1p
31		3	4	5	6	7	8	9	
32		10[i]	11	12	13	14	15	16	
33		17	18	19	20	21	22	23	
34		24	25	26	27	28	29	30	
35	ELUL 5725	1	2	3	4	5	6	7	Fri 6h37m2p
36		8	9	10	11	12	13	14	
37		15	16	17	18	19	20	21	
38		22	23	24	25	26	27	28	
39	TISHRI 5726	29	1[a]	2[a]	3	4	5	6	Sat 19h21m3p
40		7	8	9	10[b]	11	12	13	
41		14	15[c]	16	17	18	19	20	
42		21	22	23	24	25	26	27	
43	ḤESHVAN 5726	28	29	30	1	2	3	4	Mon 8h5m4p
44		5	6	7	8	9	10	11	
45		12	13	14	15	16	17	18	
46		19	20	21	22	23	24	25	
47	KISLEV 5726	26	27	28	29	1	2	3	Tue 20h49m5p
48		4	5	6	7	8	9	10	
49		11[d]	12	13	14	15	16	17	
50		18	19	20	21	22	23	24	
51	TEVETH 5726	25[e]	26[e]	27[e]	28[e]	29[e]	1[e]	2[e]	Thu 9h33m6p
52		3[e]	4	5	6	7	8	9	

CHINESE Jiă-Chén/Yĭ-Sì

ISO WEEK	Month	Sun	Mon	Tue	Wed	Thu	Fri	Sat	Solar Term
53		24	25	26	27	28	29	30	
1	MONTH 12 Jiă-Chén	1	2	3	4	5	6	7	Xiǎo hán
2		8*	9	10	11	12	13	14	
3		15	16	17	**18**	19	20	21	Dà hán
4		22	23	24	25	26	27	28	
5	MONTH 1 Yĭ-Sì	29	30	1[a]	2	3	4	5	Lì chūn
6		6	7	8	9	10	11	12	
7		13	14	15[b]	16	17	**18**	19	Yǔ shuǐ
8		20	21	22	23	24	25	26	
9	MONTH 2 Yĭ-Sì	27	28	29	1	2	3	4	Jīng zhé
10		5	6	7	8	9*	10	11	
11		12	13	14	15	16	17	18	
12		**19**	20	21	22	23	24	25	Chūn fēn
13	MONTH 3 Yĭ-Sì	26	27	28	29	30	1	2	
14		3	4[c]	5	6	7	8	9	Qīng míng
15		10	11	12	13	14	15	16	
16		17	18	**19**	20	21	22	23	Gǔ yǔ
17	MONTH 4 Yĭ-Sì	24	25	26	27	28	29	1	
18		2	3	4	5	6	7	8	Lì xià
19		9	10*	11	12	13	14	15	
20		16	17	18	19	20	**21**	22	Xiǎo mǎn
21		23	24	25	26	27	28	29	
22	MONTH 5 Yĭ-Sì	30	1	2	3	4	5[d]	6	
23		7	8	9	10	11	12	13	Máng zhòng
24		14	15	16	17	18	19	20	
25		21	**22**	23	24	25	26	27	Xià zhì
26	MONTH 6 Yĭ-Sì	28	29	1	2	3	4	5	
27		6	7	8	9	10	11*	12	Xiǎo shǔ
28		13	14	15	16	17	18	19	
29		20	21	22	23	24	**25**	26	Dà shǔ
30	MONTH 7 Yĭ-Sì	27	28	29	1	2	3	4	
31		5	6	7[e]	8	9	10	11	
32		*12*	13	14	15[f]	16	17	18	Lì qiū
33		19	20	21	22	23	24	25	
34	MONTH 8 Yĭ-Sì	26	**27**	28	29	30	1	2	Chǔ shǔ
35		3	4	5	6	7	8	9	
36		10	11	12*	*13*	14	15[g]	16	Bái lù
37		17	18	19	20	21	22	23	
38	MONTH 9 Yĭ-Sì	24	25	26	27	**28**	29	1	Qiū fēn
39		2	3	4	5	6	7	8	
40		9[h]	10	11	12	13	*14*	15	Hán lù
41		16	17	18	19	20	21	22	
42		23	24	25	26	27	28	**29**	Shuāng jiàng
43	MONTH 10 Yĭ-Sì	1	2	3	4	5	6	7	
44		8	9	10	11	12	13	14*	
45		*15*	16	17	18	19	20	21	Lì dōng
46		22	23	24	25	26	27	28	
47	MONTH 11 Yĭ-Sì	29	**30**	1	2	3	4	5	Xiǎo xuě
48		6	7	8	9	10	11	12	
49		13	14	*15*	16	17	18	19	Dà xuě
50		20	21	22	23	24	25	26	
51	MONTH 12 Yĭ-Sì	27	28	29	**30**[i]	1	2	3	Dōng zhì
52		4	5	6	7	8	9	10	

COPTIC 1681/1682 — ETHIOPIC 1957/1958

ISO WEEK	Coptic Month	Sun	Mon	Tue	Wed	Thu	Fri	Sat	Ethiopic Month
53	KOIAK 1681	18	19	20	21	22	23	24	TĀKHŚĀŚ 1957
1	TŌBE 1681	25	26	27	28	29[c]	30	1	ṬER 1957
2		2	3	4	5	6[d]	7	8	
3		9	10	11[e]	12	13	14	15	
4		16	17	18	19	20	21	22	
5		23	24	25	26	27	28	29	
6	MESHIR 1681	30	1	2	3	4	5	6	YAKĀTIT 1957
7		7	8	9	10	11	12	13	
8		14	15	16	17	18	19	20	
9		21	22	23	24	25	26	27	
10	PAREMOTEP 1681	28	29	30	1	2	3	4	MAGĀBIT 1957
11		5	6	7	8	9	10	11	
12		12	13	14	15	16	17	18	
13		19	20	21	22	23	24	25	
14	PARMOUTE 1681	26	27	28	29	30	1	2	MIYĀZYĀ 1957
15		3	4	5	6	7	8	9	
16		10	11	12	13	14	15	16	
17		17[f]	18	19	20	21	22	23	
18		24	25	26	27	28	29[g]	30	
19	PASHONS 1681	1	2	3	4	5	6	7	GENBOT 1957
20		8	9	10	11	12	13	14	
21		15	16	17	18	19	20	21	
22		22	23	24	25	26	27	28	
23	PAŌNE 1681	29	30	1	2	3	4	5	SANĒ 1957
24		6	7	8	9	10	11	12	
25		13	14	15	16	17	18	19	
26		20	21	22	23	24	25	26	
27	EPĒP 1681	27	28	29	30	1	2	3	ḤAMLĒ 1957
28		4	5	6	7	8	9	10	
29		11	12	13	14	15	16	17	
30		18	19	20	21	22	23	24	
31	MESORĒ 1681	25	26	27	28	29	30	1	NAḤASĒ 1957
32		2	3	4	5	6	7	8	
33		9	10	11	12	13[h]	14	15	
34		16	17	18	19	20	21	22	
35		23	24	25	26	27	28	29	
36	EPAG. 1681	30	1	2	3	4	5	1[a]	PĀG. 1957
37	THOOUT 1682	2	3	4	5	6	7	8	MASKARAM 1958
38		9	10	11	12	13	14	15	
39		16	17[b]	18	19	20	21	22	
40		23	24	25	26	27	28	29	
41	PAOPE 1682	30	1	2	3	4	5	6	ṬEQEMT 1958
42		7	8	9	10	11	12	13	
43		14	15	16	17	18	19	20	
44		21	22	23	24	25	26	27	
45	ATHŌR 1682	28	29	30	1	2	3	4	ḪEDĀR 1958
46		5	6	7	8	9	10	11	
47		12	13	14	15	16	17	18	
48		19	20	21	22	23	24	25	
49	KOIAK 1682	26	27	28	29	30	1	2	TĀKHŚĀŚ 1958
50		3	4	5	6	7	8	9	
51		10	11	12	13	14	15	16	
52		17	18	19	20	21	22	23	

[a] New Year
[b] Spring (20:04)
[c] Summer (14:55)
[d] Autumn (6:06)
[e] Winter (1:40)
● New moon
◐ First quarter moon
○ Full moon
◑ Last quarter moon

‡ Leap year
[a] New Year
[b] Yom Kippur
[c] Sukkot
[d] Winter starts
[e] Ḥanukkah
[f] Purim
[g] Passover
[h] Shavuot
[i] Fast of Av

[a] New Year (4663, Snake)
[b] Lantern Festival
[c] Qīngmíng
[d] Dragon Festival
[e] Qīqiǎo
[f] Hungry Ghosts
[g] Mid-Autumn Festival
[h] Double-Ninth Festival
[i] Dōngzhì
* Start of 60-name cycle

[a] New Year
[b] Building of the Cross
[c] Christmas
[d] Jesus's Circumcision
[e] Epiphany
[f] Easter
[g] Mary's Announcement
[h] Jesus's Transfiguration

PERSIAN (ASTRONOMICAL) 1343/1344

Month	Sun	Mon	Tue	Wed	Thu	Fri	Sat
	6	7	8	9	10	11	12
DEY 1343	13	14	15	16	17	18	19
	20	21	22	23	24	25	26
	27	28	29	30	1	2	3
BAHMAN 1343	4	5	6	7	8	9	10
	11	12	13	14	15	16	17
	18	19	20	21	22	23	24
	25	26	27	28	29	30	1
ESFAND 1343	2	3	4	5	6	7	8
	9	10	11	12	13	14	15
	16	17	18	19	20	21	22
	23	24	25	26	27	28	29
	1[a]	2	3	4	5	6	7
FARVARDĪN 1344	8	9	10	11	12	13[b]	14
	15	16	17	18	19	20	21
	22	23	24	25	26	27	28
	29	30	31	1	2	3	4
ORDĪBEHEŠT 1344	5	6	7	8	9	10	11
	12	13	14	15	16	17	18
	19	20	21	22	23	24	25
	26	27	28	29	30	31	1
	2	3	4	5	6	7	8
XORDĀD 1344	9	10	11	12	13	14	15
	16	17	18	19	20	21	22
	23	24	25	26	27	28	29
	30	31	1	2	3	4	5
TĪR 1344	6	7	8	9	10	11	12
	13	14	15	16	17	18	19
	20	21	22	23	24	25	26
	27	28	29	30	31	1	2
	3	4	5	6	7	8	9
MORDĀD 1344	10	11	12	13	14	15	16
	17	18	19	20	21	22	23
	24	25	26	27	28	29	30
	31	1	2	3	4	5	6
	7	8	9	10	11	12	13
SHAHRĪVAR 1344	14	15	16	17	18	19	20
	21	22	23	24	25	26	27
	28	29	30	31	1	2	3
MEHR 1344	4	5	6	7	8	9	10
	11	12	13	14	15	16	17
	18	19	20	21	22	23	24
	25	26	27	28	29	30	1
ĀBĀN 1344	2	3	4	5	6	7	8
	9	10	11	12	13	14	15
	16	17	18	19	20	21	22
	23	24	25	26	27	28	29
	30	1	2	3	4	5	6
ĀZAR 1344	7	8	9	10	11	12	13
	14	15	16	17	18	19	20
	21	22	23	24	25	26	27
DEY 1344	28	29	30	1	2	3	4
	5	6	7	8	9	10	11

[a]New Year
[b]Sizdeh Bedar

HINDU LUNAR 2021‡/2022

Month	Sun	Mon	Tue	Wed	Thu	Fri	Sat
	24	25	26	27	28	29	30
	1	2	3	3	4	5	6
PAUSHA 2021	7	8	**9**	11	12	13	14
	15	16	17	18	19	20	21
	22	23	24	25	26	27	28
	29	30	1	2	3	4	5
	6	7	8	9	10	11	12
MĀGHA 2021	13	**14**	16	17	18	19	20
	21	22	23	24	25	26	26
	27	28[h]	29	30	1	2	3
	4	5	6	7	**8**	10	11
PHĀLGUNA 2021	12	13	14	15[i]	16	17	18
	19	20	21	22	23	24	25
	26	27	28	29	30	1[a]	2
	3	4	5	6	7	8	9[b]
CHAITRA 2022	10	11	12	**13**	15	16	17
	18	19	19	20	21	22	23
	24	25	26	27	28	29	30
	1	2	3	4	**5**	7	8
	9	10	11	12	13	14	15
VAIŚĀKHA 2022	16	17	18	19	20	21	22
	23	24	24	25	26	27	**28**
	30	1	2	3	4	5	6
	7	8	9	**10**	12	13	14
JYAISHTHA 2022	15	15	16	17	18	19	20
	21	22	23	24	25	26	27
	28	29	30	**1**	3	4	5
	6	7	8	9	10	11	12
ĀSHĀDHA 2022	13	14	15	16	17	18	19
	20	21	21	22	**23**	25	26
	27	28	29	30	1	2	3
	4	**5**	7	8	9	10	11
ŚRĀVANA 2022	12	12	13	14	15	16	17
	18	19	20	21	22	23[c]	24
	25	26	**27**	29	30	1	2
	3	4[d]	5	6	7	8	9
BHĀDRAPADA 2022	10	11	12	13	14	15	16
	17	18	18	20	21	22	23
	24	25	26	27	28	29	30
	1	3	4	5	6	7	8
ĀŚVINA 2022	8[e]	9[e]	10[e]	11	12	13	14
	15	16	17	18	19	20	21
	22	23	**24**	26	27	28	29
	30	1[f]	2	3	4	5	6
KĀRTTIKA 2022	7	8	9	10	11	11	12
	13	14	15	16	**17**	19	20
	21	22	23	24	25	26	27
	28	29	30	1	2	3	4
	5	6	7	8	9	10	11[g]
MĀRGAŚĪRA 2022	12	13	14	15	16	17	18
	19	20	21	**22**	24	25	26
PAUSHA 2022	27	28	29	30	1	2	3
	4	4	5	6	7	8	9

‡Leap year
[a]New Year (Viśvāvasu)
[b]Birthday of Rāma
[c]Birthday of Krishna
[d]Ganēśa Chaturthī
[e]Dashara
[f]Diwali
[g]Birthday of Vishnu
[h]Night of Śiva
[i]Holi

HINDU SOLAR 1886/1887

Month	Sun	Mon	Tue	Wed	Thu	Fri	Sat
	13	14	15	16	17	18	19
PAUSHA 1886	20	21	22	23	24	25	26
	27	28	29	1[b]	2	3	4
	5	6	7	8	9	10	11
MĀGHA 1886	12	13	14	15	16	17	18
	19	20	21	22	23	24	25
	26	27	28	29	30	1	2
	3	4	5	6	7	8	9
PHĀLGUNA 1886	10	11	12	13	14	15	16
	17	18	19	20	21	22	23
	24	25	26	27	28	29	30
	1	2	3	4	5	6	7
	8	9	10	11	12	13	14
CHAITRA 1886	15	16	17	18	19	20	21
	22	23	24	25	26	27	28
	29	30	1[a]	2	3	4	5
	6	7	8	9	10	11	12
VAIŚĀKHA 1887	13	14	15	16	17	18	19
	20	21	22	23	24	25	26
	27	28	29	30	31	1	2
	3	4	5	6	7	8	9
JYAISHTHA 1887	10	11	12	13	14	15	16
	17	18	19	20	21	22	23
	24	25	26	27	28	29	30
	31	1	2	3	4	5	6
ĀSHĀDHA 1887	7	8	9	10	11	12	13
	14	15	16	17	18	19	20
	21	22	23	24	25	26	27
	28	29	30	31	32	1	2
	3	4	5	6	7	8	9
ŚRĀVANA 1887	10	11	12	13	14	15	16
	17	18	19	20	21	22	23
	24	25	26	27	28	29	30
	31	1	2	3	4	5	6
	7	8	9	10	11	12	13
BHĀDRAPADA 1887	14	15	16	17	18	19	20
	21	22	23	24	25	26	27
	28	29	30	31	1	2	3
	4	5	6	7	8	9	10
ĀŚVINA 1887	11	12	13	14	15	16	17
	18	19	20	21	22	23	24
	25	26	27	28	29	30	31
	1	2	3	4	5	6	7
	8	9	10	11	12	13	14
KĀRTTIKA 1887	15	16	17	18	19	20	21
	22	23	24	25	26	27	28
	29	30	1	2	3	4	5
	6	7	8	9	10	11	12
MĀRGAŚĪRA 1887	13	14	15	16	17	18	19
	20	21	22	23	24	25	26
	27	28	29	1	2	3	4
PAUSHA 1887	5	6	7	8	9	10	11
	12	13	14	15	16	17	18

[a]New Year (Kālayukta)
[b]Pongal

ISLAMIC (ASTRONOMICAL) 1384‡/1385

Month	Sun	Mon	Tue	Wed	Thu	Fri	Sat
SHA'BĀN 1384	22	23	24	25	26	27	28
	29	1[e]	2	3	4	5	6
RAMAḌĀN 1384	7	8	9	10	11	12	13
	14	15	16	17	18	19	20
	21	22	23	24	25	26	27
	28	29	30	1[f]	2	3	4
SHAWWĀL 1384	5	6	7	8	9	10	11
	12	13	14	15	16	17	18
	19	20	21	22	23	24	25
	26	27	28	29	30	1	2
	3	4	5	6	7	8	9
DHU AL-QA'DA 1384	10	11	12	13	14	15	16
	17	18	19	20	21	22	23
	24	25	26	27	28	29	1
	2	3	4	5	6	7	8
DHU AL-ḤIJJA 1384	9	10[g]	11	12	13	14	15
	16	17	18	19	20	21	22
	23	24	25	26	27	28	29
	30[d]	1[a]	2	3	4	5	6
MUḤARRAM 1385	7	8	9	10[b]	11	12	13
	14	15	16	17	18	19	20
	21	22	23	24	25	26	27
	28	29	1	2	3	4	5
ṢAFAR 1385	6	7	8	9	10	11	12
	13	14	15	16	17	18	19
	20	21	22	23	24	25	26
	27	28	29	1	2	3	4
RABĪ' I 1385	5	6	7	8	9	10	11
	12[c]	13	14	15	16	17	18
	19	20	21	22	23	24	25
	26	27	28	29	30	1	2
	3	4	5	6	7	8	9
RABĪ' II 1385	10	11	12	13	14	15	16
	17	18	19	20	21	22	23
	24	25	26	27	28	29	1
	2	3	4	5	6	7	8
JUMĀDĀ I 1385	9	10	11	12	13	14	15
	16	17	18	19	20	21	22
	23	24	25	26	27	28	29
	1	2	3	4	5	6	7
JUMĀDĀ II 1385	8	9	10	11	12	13	14
	15	16	17	18	19	20	21
	22	23	24	25	26	27	28
	29	30	1	2	3	4	5
RAJAB 1385	6	7	8	9	10	11	12
	13	14	15	16	17	18	19
	20	21	22	23	24	25	26
	27[d]	28	29	30	1	2	3
SHA'BĀN 1385	4	5	6	7	8	9	10
	11	12	13	14	15	16	17
	18	19	20	21	22	23	24
RAMAḌĀN 1385	25	26	27	28	29	1[e]	2
	3	4	5	6	7	8	9

‡Leap year
[a]New Year
[d]New Year (Arithmetic)
[b]'Ashūrā'
[c]Prophet's Birthday
[d]Ascent of the Prophet
[e]Start of Ramaḍān
[f]'Īd al-Fiṭr
[g]'Īd al-'Aḍḥā

GREGORIAN 1965

Julian (Sun)	Sun	Mon	Tue	Wed	Thu	Fri	Sat	Month
Dec 14	27	28	29	30	31	1	2	
	3	4	5	6	7[a]	8	9	
Dec 28	10	11	12	13	14[b]	15	16	JANUARY 1965
	17	18	19	20	21	22	23	
Jan 11	24	25	26	27	28	29	30	
	31	1	2	3	4	5	6	
Jan 25	7	8	9	10	11	12	13	
	14	15	16	17	18	19	20	FEBRUARY 1965
Feb 8	21	22	23	24	25	26	27	
	28	1	2	3[c]	4	5	6	
Feb 22	7	8	9	10	11	12	13	
	14[d]	15	16	17	18	19	20	MARCH 1965
Mar 8	21	22	23	24	25	26	27	
	28	29	30	31	1	2	3	
Mar 22	4	5	6	7	8	9	10	
	11	12	13	14	15	16	17	APRIL 1965
Apr 5	18[e]	19	20	21	22	23	24	
	25[f]	26	27	28	29	30	1	
Apr 19	2	3	4	5	6	7	8	
	9	10	11	12	13	14	15	MAY 1965
May 3	16	17	18	19	20	21	22	
	23	24	25	26	27	28	29	
May 17	30	31	1	2	3	4	5	
	6	7	8	9	10	11	12	JUNE 1965
May 31	13	14	15	16	17	18	19	
	20	21	22	23	24	25	26	
Jun 14	27	28	29	30	1	2	3	
	4	5	6	7	8	9	10	JULY 1965
Jun 28	11	12	13	14	15	16	17	
	18	19	20	21	22	23	24	
Jul 12	25	26	27	28	29	30	31	
	1	2	3	4	5	6	7	
Jul 26	8	9	10	11	12	13	14	AUGUST 1965
	15	16	17	18	19	20	21	
Aug 9	22	23	24	25	26	27	28	
	29	30	31	1	2	3	4	
Aug 23	5	6	7	8	9	10	11	SEPTEMBER 1965
	12	13	14	15	16	17	18	
Sep 6	19	20	21	22	23	24	25	
	26	27	28	29	30	1	2	
Sep 20	3	4	5	6	7	8	9	
	10	11	12	13	14	15	16	OCTOBER 1965
Oct 4	17	18	19	20	21	22	23	
	24	25	26	27	28	29	30	
Oct 18	31	1	2	3	4	5	6	
	7	8	9	10	11	12	13	NOVEMBER 1965
Nov 1	14	15	16	17	18	19	20	
	21	22	23	24	25	26	27	
Nov 15	28[g]	29	30	1	2	3	4	
	5	6	7	8	9	10	11	DECEMBER 1965
Nov 29	12	13	14	15	16	17	18	
	19	20	21	22	23	24	25[h]	
Dec 13	26	27	28	29	30	31	1	

[a]Orthodox Christmas
[b]Julian New Year
[c]Ash Wednesday
[d]Feast of Orthodoxy
[e]Easter
[f]Orthodox Easter
[g]Advent
[h]Christmas

1966

Month	Sun	Mon	Tue	Wed	Thu	Fri	Sat	Lunar Phases	ISO Week (Mon)	Julian Day (Sun noon)
JANUARY 1966	26	27	28	29	30	◐	1[a]	1:46	52	2439121
	2	3	4	5	6	○	8	5:16	1	2439128
	9	10	11	12	◑	14	15	20:00	2	2439135
	16	17	18	19	20	●	22	15:46	3	2439142
	23	24	25	26	27	28	◐	19:48	4	2439149
FEBRUARY 1966	30	31	1	2	3	4	○	15:58	5	2439156
	6	7	8	9	10	11	◑	8:53	6	2439163
	13	14	15	16	17	18	19		7	2439170
	●	21	22	23	24	25	26	10:49	8	2439177
MARCH 1966	27	◐	1	2	3	4	5	10:15	9	2439184
	6	○	8	9	10	11	12	1:45	10	2439191
	13	◑	15	16	17	18	19	0:19	11	2439198
	20	21[b]	●	23	24	25	26	4:46	12	2439205
APRIL 1966	27	28	◐	30	31	1	2	20:43	13	2439212
	3	4	○	6	7	8	9	11:13	14	2439219
	10	11	◑	13	14	15	16	17:28	15	2439226
	17	18	19	●	21	22	23	20:35	16	2439233
	24	25	26	27	◐	29	30	3:49	17	2439240
MAY 1966	1	2	3	○	5	6	7	21:01	18	2439247
	8	9	10	11	◑	13	14	11:19	19	2439254
	15	16	17	18	19	●	21	9:42	20	2439261
	22	23	24	25	26	◐	28	8:50	21	2439268
JUNE 1966	29	30	31	1	2	○	4	7:40	22	2439275
	5	6	7	8	9	10	◑	4:58	23	2439282
	12	13	14	15	16	17	●	20:09	24	2439289
	19	20	21[c]	22	23	24	◐	13:22	25	2439296
JULY 1966	26	27	28	29	30	1	○	19:36	26	2439303
	3	4	5	6	7	8	9		27	2439310
	◑	11	12	13	14	15	16	21:43	28	2439317
	17	●	19	20	21	22	23	4:30	29	2439324
	◐	25	26	27	28	29	30	19:00	30	2439331
AUGUST 1966	31	○	2	3	4	5	6	9:05	31	2439338
	7	8	◑	10	11	12	13	12:55	32	2439345
	14	15	●	17	18	19	20	11:48	33	2439352
	21	22	◐	24	25	26	27	3:02	34	2439359
SEPTEMBER 1966	28	29	30	○	1	2	3	0:13	35	2439366
	4	5	6	7	◑	9	10	2:07	36	2439373
	11	12	13	●	15	16	17	19:13	37	2439380
	18	19	20	◐	22	23[d]	24	14:25	38	2439387
OCTOBER 1966	25	26	27	28	○	30	1	16:47	39	2439394
	2	3	4	5	6	◑	8	13:08	40	2439401
	9	10	11	12	13	●	15	3:52	41	2439408
	16	17	18	19	20	◐	22	5:34	42	2439415
	23	24	25	26	27	28	○	10:00	43	2439422
NOVEMBER 1966	30	31	1	2	3	4	◑	22:18	44	2439429
	6	7	8	9	10	11	●	14:26	45	2439436
	13	14	15	16	17	18	19		46	2439443
	◐	21	22	23	24	25	26	0:20	47	2439450
DECEMBER 1966	27	○	29	30	1	2	3	2:40	48	2439457
	4	◑	6	7	8	9	10	6:22	49	2439464
	11	●	13	14	15	16	17	3:13	50	2439471
	18	◐	20	21	22[e]	23	24	21:41	51	2439478
	25	26	○	28	29	30	31	17:43	52	2439485

ISO Week	Hebrew 5726/5727‡	Sun	Mon	Tue	Wed	Thu	Fri	Sat	Molad
52	TEVETH 5726	3[e]	4	5	6	7	8	9	
1		10	11	12	13	14	15	16	
2		17	18	19	20	21	22	23	
3		24	25	26	27	28	29	1	Fri $22^h17^m7^p$
4	SHEVAT 5726	2	3	4	5	6	7	8	
5		9	10	11	12	13	14	15	
6		16	17	18	19	20	21	22	
7		23	24	25	26	27	28	29	
8		30	1	2	3	4	5	6	Sun $11^h1^m8^p$
9	ADAR 5726	7	8	9	10	11	12	13	
10		14[f]	15	16	17	18	19	20	
11		21	22	23	24	25	26	27	
12		28	29	1	2	3	4	5	Mon $23^h45^m9^p$
13	NISAN 5726	6	7	8	9	10	11	12	
14		13	14	15[g]	16	17	18	19	
15		20	21	22	23	24	25	26	
16		27	28	29	30	1	2	3	Wed $12^h29^m10^p$
17	IYYAR 5726	4	5	6	7	8	9	10	
18		11	12	13	14	15	16	17	
19		18	19	20	21	22	23	24	
20		25	26	27	28	29	1	2	Fri $1^h13^m11^p$
21	SIVAN 5726	3	4	5	6[h]	7	8	9	
22		10	11	12	13	14	15	16	
23		17	18	19	20	21	22	23	
24		24	25	26	27	28	29	30	
25	TAMMUZ 5726	1	2	3	4	5	6	7	Sat $13^h57^m12^p$
26		8	9	10	11	12	13	14	
27		15	16	17	18	19	20	21	
28		22	23	24	25	26	27	28	
29		29	1	2	3	4	5	6	Mon $2^h41^m13^p$
30	AV 5726	7	8	9[i]	10	11	12	13	
31		14	15	16	17	18	19	20	
32		21	22	23	24	25	26	27	
33		28	29	30	1	2	3	4	Tue $15^h25^m14^p$
34	ELUL 5726	5	6	7	8	9	10	11	
35		12	13	14	15	16	17	18	
36		19	20	21	22	23	24	25	
37		26	27	28	29	1[a]	2[a]	3	Thu $4^h9^m15^p$
38	TISHRI 5727	4	5	6	7	8	9	10[b]	
39		11	12	13	14	15[c]	16	17	
40		18	19	20	21	22	23	24	
41		25	26	27	28	29	30	1	Fri $16^h53^m16^p$
42	ḤESHVAN 5727	2	3	4	5	6	7	8	
43		9	10	11	12	13	14	15	
44		16	17	18	19	20	21	22	
45		23	24	25	26	27	28	29	
46		30	1	2	3	4	5	6	Sun $5^h37^m17^p$
47	KISLEV 5727	7	8	9	10	11	12	13	
48		14	15	16	17	18	19	20	
49		21	22[d]	23	24	25[e]	26[e]	27[e]	
50		28[e]	29[e]	30[e]	1[e]	2[e]	3	4	Mon $18^h22^m0^p$
51	TEVETH 5727	5	6	7	8	9	10	11	
52		12	13	14	15	16	17	18	

ISO Week	Chinese Yǐ-Sì/Bǐng-Wǔ‡	Sun	Mon	Tue	Wed	Thu	Fri	Sat	Solar Term
52	MONTH 12 Yǐ-Sì	4	5	6	7	8	9	10	
1		11	12	13	14*	15	16	17	Xiǎo hán
2		18	19	20	21	22	23	24	
3		25	26	27	28	29	1[a]	2	Dà hán
4	MONTH 1 Bǐng-Wǔ	3	4	5	6	7	8	9	
5		10	11	12	13	14	15[b]	16	Lì chūn
6		17	18	19	20	21	22	23	
7		24	25	26	27	28	29	30	Yǔ shuǐ
8	MONTH 2 Bǐng-Wǔ	1	2	3	4	5	6	7	
9		8	9	10	11	12	13	14	
10		15*	16	17	18	19	20	21	Jīng zhé
11		22	23	24	25	26	27	28	
12		29	30	1	2	3	4	5	Chūn fēn
13	MONTH 3 Bǐng-Wǔ	6	7	8	9	10	11	12	
14		13	14	15[c]	16	17	18	19	Qīng míng
15		20	21	22	23	24	25	26	
16		27	28	29	30	1	2	3	Gǔ yǔ
17	LEAP MONTH 3 Bǐng-Wǔ	4	5	6	7	8	9	10	
18		11	12	13	14	15*	16	17	Lì xià
19		18	19	20	21	22	23	24	
20		25	26	27	28	29	1	2	Xiǎo mǎn
21	MONTH 4 Bǐng-Wǔ	3	4	5	6	7	8	9	
22		10	11	12	13	14	15	16	
23		17	18	19	20	21	22	23	Máng zhòng
24		24	25	26	27	28	29	30	
25	MONTH 5 Bǐng-Wǔ	1	2	3	4	5[d]	6	7	Xià zhì
26		8	9	10	11	12	13	14	
27		15	16*	17	18	19	20	21	Xiǎo shǔ
28		22	23	24	25	26	27	28	
29		29	1	2	3	4	5	6	Dà shǔ
30	MONTH 6 Bǐng-Wǔ	7	8	9	10	11	12	13	
31		14	15	16	17	18	19	20	
32		21	22	23	24	25	26	27	Lì qiū
33		28	29	1	2	3	4	5	
34	MONTH 7 Bǐng-Wǔ	6	7[e]	8	9	10	11	12	Chǔ shǔ
35		13	14	15[f]	16	17	18*	19	
36		20	21	22	23	24	25	26	Bái lù
37		27	28	29	30	1	2	3	
38	MONTH 8 Bǐng-Wǔ	4	5	6	7	8	9	10	Qiū fēn
39		11	12	13	14	15[g]	16	17	
40		18	19	20	21	22	23	24	
41		25	26	27	28	29	1	2	Hán lù
42	MONTH 9 Bǐng-Wǔ	3	4	5	6	7	8	9[h]	
43		10	11	12	13	14	15	16	Shuāng jiàng
44		17	18	19*	20	21	22	23	
45		24	25	26	27	28	29	1	Lì dōng
46	MONTH 10 Bǐng-Wǔ	2	3	4	5	6	7	8	
47		9	10	11	12	13	14	15	Xiǎo xuě
48		16	17	18	19	20	21	22	
49		23	24	25	26	27	28	29	Dà xuě
50		30	1	2	3	4	5	6	
51	MONTH 11 Bǐng-Wǔ	7	8	9	10	11[i]	12	13	Dōng zhì
52		14	15	16	17	18	19	20*	

ISO Week	Coptic 1682/1683‡	Sun	Mon	Tue	Wed	Thu	Fri	Sat	Ethiopic 1958/1959‡
52	KOIAK 1682	17	18	19	20	21	22	23	TĀKHŚĀŚ 1958
1		24	25	26	27	28	29[c]	30	
2	TÔBE 1682	1	2	3	4	5	6[d]	7	ṬER 1958
3		8	9	10	11[e]	12	13	14	
4		15	16	17	18	19	20	21	
5		22	23	24	25	26	27	28	
6		29	30	1	2	3	4	5	
7	MESHIR 1682	6	7	8	9	10	11	12	YAKĀTIT 1958
8		13	14	15	16	17	18	19	
9		20	21	22	23	24	25	26	
10		27	28	29	30	1	2	3	
11	PAREMOTEP 1682	4	5	6	7	8	9	10	MAGĀBIT 1958
12		11	12	13	14	15	16	17	
13		18	19	20	21	22	23	24	
14		25	26	27	28	29	30	1	
15	PARMOUTE 1682	2[f]	3	4	5	6	7	8	MIYĀZYĀ 1958
16		9	10	11	12	13	14	15	
17		16	17	18	19	20	21	22	
18		23	24	25	26	27	28	29[g]	
19		30	1	2	3	4	5	6	
20	PASHONS 1682	7	8	9	10	11	12	13	GENBOT 1958
21		14	15	16	17	18	19	20	
22		21	22	23	24	25	26	27	
23		28	29	30	1	2	3	4	
24	PAÔNE 1682	5	6	7	8	9	10	11	SANĒ 1958
25		12	13	14	15	16	17	18	
26		19	20	21	22	23	24	25	
27		26	27	28	29	30	1	2	
28	EPÊP 1682	3	4	5	6	7	8	9	ḤAMLĒ 1958
29		10	11	12	13	14	15	16	
30		17	18	19	20	21	22	23	
31		24	25	26	27	28	29	30	
32	MESORĒ 1682	1	2	3	4	5	6	7	NAḤASĒ 1958
33		8	9	10	11	12	13[h]	14	
34		15	16	17	18	19	20	21	
35		22	23	24	25	26	27	28	
36	EPAG. 1682	29	30	1	2	3	4	5	PĀG. 1958
37	THOOUT 1683	1[a]	2	3	4	5	6	7	MASKARAM 1959
38		8	9	10	11	12	13	14	
39		15	16	17[b]	18	19	20	21	
40		22	23	24	25	26	27	28	
41		29	30	1	2	3	4	5	
42	PAOPE 1683	6	7	8	9	10	11	12	ṬEQEMT 1959
43		13	14	15	16	17	18	19	
44		20	21	22	23	24	25	26	
45		27	28	29	30	1	2	3	
46	ATHÔR 1683	4	5	6	7	8	9	10	ḤEDĀR 1959
47		11	12	13	14	15	16	17	
48		18	19	20	21	22	23	24	
49		25	26	27	28	29	30	1	
50	KOIAK 1683	2	3	4	5	6	7	8	TĀKHŚĀŚ 1959
51		9	10	11	12	13	14	15	
52		16	17	18	19	20	21	22	

[a]New Year
[b]Spring (1:52)
[c]Summer (20:33)
[d]Autumn (11:43)
[e]Winter (7:28)
● New moon
◐ First quarter moon
○ Full moon
◑ Last quarter moon

‡Leap year
[a]New Year
[b]Yom Kippur
[c]Sukkot
[d]Winter starts
[e]Ḥanukkah
[f]Purim
[g]Passover
[h]Shavuot
[i]Fast of Av

‡Leap year
[a]New Year (4664, Horse)
[b]Lantern Festival
[c]Qīngmíng
[d]Dragon Festival
[e]Qīqiǎo
[f]Hungry Ghosts
[g]Mid-Autumn Festival
[h]Double-Ninth Festival
[i]Dōngzhì
*Start of 60-name cycle

‡Leap year
[a]New Year
[b]Building of the Cross
[c]Christmas
[d]Jesus's Circumcision
[e]Epiphany
[f]Easter
[g]Mary's Announcement
[h]Jesus's Transfiguration

PERSIAN (ASTRONOMICAL) 1344/1345

Month	Sun	Mon	Tue	Wed	Thu	Fri	Sat
DEY 1344	5	6	7	8	9	10	11
	12	13	14	15	16	17	18
	19	20	21	22	23	24	25
	26	27	28	29	30	1	2
BAHMAN 1344	3	4	5	6	7	8	9
	10	11	12	13	14	15	16
	17	18	19	20	21	22	23
	24	25	26	27	28	29	30
ESFAND 1344	1	2	3	4	5	6	7
	8	9	10	11	12	13	14
	15	16	17	18	19	20	21
	22	23	24	25	26	27	28
	29	1[a]	2	3	4	5	6
FARVARDIN 1345	7	8	9	10	11	12	13[b]
	14	15	16	17	18	19	20
	21	22	23	24	25	26	27
	28	29	30	31	1	2	3
ORDIBEHEŠT 1345	4	5	6	7	8	9	10
	11	12	13	14	15	16	17
	18	19	20	21	22	23	24
	25	26	27	28	29	30	31
XORDĀD 1345	1	2	3	4	5	6	7
	8	9	10	11	12	13	14
	15	16	17	18	19	20	21
	22	23	24	25	26	27	28
	29	30	31	1	2	3	4
TĪR 1345	5	6	7	8	9	10	11
	12	13	14	15	16	17	18
	19	20	21	22	23	24	25
	26	27	28	29	30	31	1
MORDĀD 1345	2	3	4	5	6	7	8
	9	10	11	12	13	14	15
	16	17	18	19	20	21	22
	23	24	25	26	27	28	29
	30	31	1	2	3	4	5
SHAHRĪVAR 1345	6	7	8	9	10	11	12
	13	14	15	16	17	18	19
	20	21	22	23	24	25	26
	27	28	29	30	31	1	2
MEHR 1345	3	4	5	6	7	8	9
	10	11	12	13	14	15	16
	17	18	19	20	21	22	23
	24	25	26	27	28	29	30
ĀBĀN 1345	1	2	3	4	5	6	7
	8	9	10	11	12	13	14
	15	16	17	18	19	20	21
	22	23	24	25	26	27	28
	29	30	1	2	3	4	5
ĀZAR 1345	6	7	8	9	10	11	12
	13	14	15	16	17	18	19
	20	21	22	23	24	25	26
	27	28	29	30	1	2	3
DEY 1345	4	5	6	7	8	9	10

HINDU LUNAR 2022/2023‡

Month	Sun	Mon	Tue	Wed	Thu	Fri	Sat
PAUSHA 2022	4	4	5	6	7	8	9
	10	11	12	13	14	15	**16**
	18	19	20	21	22	23	24
	25	26	27	28	29	30	1
MĀGHA 2022	2	3	4	5	6	6	7
	8	**9**	11	12	13	14	15
	16	17	18	19	20	21	22
	23	24	25	26	27	28[h]	29
	30	1	2	3	4	5	6
PHĀLGUNA 2022	7	8	9	10	11	12	13
	14	15[i]	17	18	19	20	21
	22	23	24	25	26	27	28
	29	29	30	1[a]	2	3	4
CHAITRA 2023	5	6	7	8[b]	**9**	11	12
	13	14	15	16	17	18	19
	20	21	22	23	24	25	26
	27	28	29	30	1	2	3
VAIŚĀKHA 2023	4	5	6	7	8	9	10
	11	12	**13**	15	16	17	18
	19	20	21	22	23	23	24
	25	26	27	28	29	30	1
JYAISHṬHA 2023	2	3	4	5	**6**	8	9
	10	11	12	13	14	15	16
	17	18	19	20	21	22	23
	24	25	26	27	28	29	30
ĀSHĀḌHA 2023	1	2	3	4	5	6	7
	8	**9**	11	12	13	14	15
	16	17	18	19	20	20	21
	22	23	24	25	26	27	28
	29	30	**1**	3	4	5	6
LEAP ŚRĀVAṆA 2023	7	8	9	10	11	12	13
	14	15	16	17	18	19	20
	21	22	23	24	25	26	27
	28	29	30	1	2	3	**4**
ŚRĀVAṆA 2023	6	7	8	9	10	11	12
	13	14	15	16	16	17	18
	19	20	21	22	23[c]	24	25
	26	**27**	29	30	1	2	3
BHĀDRAPADA 2023	4[d]	5	6	7	8	9	10
	11	12	13	14	15	16	17
	18	19	20	21	22	23	24
	25	26	27	28	29	30	**1**
ĀŚVINA 2023	3	4	5	6	7	8[e]	9[e]
	10[e]	11	11	12	13	14	15
	16	17	18	19	20	21	22
	23	24	**25**	27	28	29	30
KĀRTTIKA 2023	1[f]	2	3	4	5	6	7
	8	9	10	11	12	13	14
	14	15	16	17	**18**	20	21
	22	23	24	25	26	27	28
	29	30	1	2	3	4	5
MĀRGAŚĪRA 2023	6	7	8	9	10	11[g]	12
	13	14	15	16	17	18	19

HINDU SOLAR 1887/1888

Month	Sun	Mon	Tue	Wed	Thu	Fri	Sat
PAUSHA 1887	12	13	14	15	16	17	18
	19	20	21	22	23	24	25
	26	27	28	29	30	1[b]	2
MĀGHA 1887	3	4	5	6	7	8	9
	10	11	12	13	14	15	16
	17	18	19	20	21	22	23
	24	25	26	27	28	29	1
PHĀLGUNA 1887	2	3	4	5	6	7	8
	9	10	11	12	13	14	15
	16	17	18	19	20	21	22
	23	24	25	26	27	28	29
	30	1	2	3	4	5	6
CHAITRA 1887	7	8	9	10	11	12	13
	14	15	16	17	18	19	20
	21	22	23	24	25	26	27
	28	29	30	1[a]	2	3	4
VAIŚĀKHA 1888	5	6	7	8	9	10	11
	12	13	14	15	16	17	18
	19	20	21	22	23	24	25
	26	27	28	29	30	31	1
JYAISHṬHA 1888	2	3	4	5	6	7	8
	9	10	11	12	13	14	15
	16	17	18	19	20	21	22
	23	24	25	26	27	28	29
	30	31	32	1	2	3	4
ĀSHĀḌHA 1888	5	6	7	8	9	10	11
	12	13	14	15	16	17	18
	19	20	21	22	23	24	25
	26	27	28	29	30	31	1
ŚRĀVAṆA 1888	2	3	4	5	6	7	8
	9	10	11	12	13	14	15
	16	17	18	19	20	21	22
	23	24	25	26	27	28	29
	30	31	32	1	2	3	4
BHĀDRAPADA 1888	5	6	7	8	9	10	11
	12	13	14	15	16	17	18
	19	20	21	22	23	24	25
	26	27	28	29	30	31	1
ĀŚVINA 1888	2	3	4	5	6	7	8
	9	10	11	12	13	14	15
	16	17	18	19	20	21	22
	23	24	25	26	27	28	29
	30	1	2	3	4	5	6
KĀRTTIKA 1888	7	8	9	10	11	12	13
	14	15	16	17	18	19	20
	21	22	23	24	25	26	27
	28	29	30	1	2	3	4
MĀRGAŚĪRA 1888	5	6	7	8	9	10	11
	12	13	14	15	16	17	18
	19	20	21	22	23	24	25
	26	27	28	29	1	2	3
PAUSHA 1888	4	5	6	7	8	9	10
	11	12	13	14	15	16	17

ISLAMIC (ASTRONOMICAL) 1385/1386

Month	Sun	Mon	Tue	Wed	Thu	Fri	Sat
RAMAḌĀN 1385	3	4	5	6	7	8	9
	10	11	12	13	14	15	16
	17	18	19	20	21	22	23
	24	25	26	27	28	29	30
SHAWWĀL 1385	1[f]	2	3	4	5	6	7
	8	9	10	11	12	13	14
	15	16	17	18	19	20	21
	22	23	24	25	26	27	28
	29	30	1	2	3	4	5
DHU AL-QA'DA 1385	6	7	8	9	10	11	12
	13	14	15	16	17	18	19
	20	21	22	23	24	25	26
	27	28	29	1	2	3	4
DHU AL-ḤIJJA 1385	5	6	7	8	9	10[g]	11
	12	13	14	15	16	17	18
	19	20	21	22	23	24	25
	26	27	28	29	30	1[a]	2
MUḤARRAM 1386	3	4	5	6	7	8	9
	10[b]	11	12	13	14	15	16
	17	18	19	20	21	22	23
	24	25	26	27	28	29	30
ṢAFAR 1386	1	2	3	4	5	6	7
	8	9	10	11	12	13	14
	15	16	17	18	19	20	21
	22	23	24	25	26	27	28
	29	1	2	3	4	5	6
RABĪ' I 1386	7	8	9	10	11	12[c]	13
	14	15	16	17	18	19	20
	21	22	23	24	25	26	27
	28	29	1	2	3	4	5
RABĪ' II 1386	6	7	8	9	10	11	12
	13	14	15	16	17	18	19
	20	21	22	23	24	25	26
	27	28	29	30	1	2	3
JUMĀDĀ I 1386	4	5	6	7	8	9	10
	11	12	13	14	15	16	17
	18	19	20	21	22	23	24
	25	26	27	28	29	1	2
JUMĀDĀ II 1386	3	4	5	6	7	8	9
	10	11	12	13	14	15	16
	17	18	19	20	21	22	23
	24	25	26	27	28	29	30
RAJAB 1386	1	2	3	4	5	6	7
	8	9	10	11	12	13	14
	15	16	17	18	19	20	21
	22	23	24	25	26	27[d]	28
	29	1	2	3	4	5	6
SHA'BĀN 1386	7	8	9	10	11	12	13
	14	15	16	17	18	19	20
	21	22	23	24	25	26	27
	28	29	30	1[e]	2	3	4
RAMAḌĀN 1386	5	6	7	8	9	10	11
	12	13	14	15	16	17	18

GREGORIAN 1966

Julian (Sun)	Sun	Mon	Tue	Wed	Thu	Fri	Sat	Month
Dec 13	26	27	28	29	30	31	1	JANUARY 1966
	2	3	4	5	6	7[a]	8	
Dec 27	9	10	11	12	13	14[b]	15	
	16	17	18	19	20	21	22	
Jan 10	23	24	25	26	27	28	29	
	30	31	1	2	3	4	5	FEBRUARY 1966
Jan 24	6	7	8	9	10	11	12	
	13	14	15	16	17	18	19	
Feb 7	20	21	22	23[c]	24	25	26	
	27[d]	28	1	2	3	4	5	MARCH 1966
Feb 21	6	7	8	9	10	11	12	
	13	14	15	16	17	18	19	
Mar 7	20	21	22	23	24	25	26	
	27	28	29	30	31	1	2	APRIL 1966
Mar 21	3	4	5	6	7	8	9	
	10[e]	11	12	13	14	15	16	
Apr 4	17	18	19	20	21	22	23	
	24	25	26	27	28	29	30	
Apr 18	1	2	3	4	5	6	7	MAY 1966
	8	9	10	11	12	13	14	
May 2	15	16	17	18	19	20	21	
	22	23	24	25	26	27	28	
May 16	29	30	31	1	2	3	4	JUNE 1966
	5	6	7	8	9	10	11	
May 30	12	13	14	15	16	17	18	
	19	20	21	22	23	24	25	
Jun 13	26	27	28	29	30	1	2	JULY 1966
	3	4	5	6	7	8	9	
Jun 27	10	11	12	13	14	15	16	
	17	18	19	20	21	22	23	
Jul 11	24	25	26	27	28	29	30	
	31	1	2	3	4	5	6	AUGUST 1966
Jul 25	7	8	9	10	11	12	13	
	14	15	16	17	18	19	20	
Aug 8	21	22	23	24	25	26	27	
	28	29	30	31	1	2	3	SEPTEMBER 1966
Aug 22	4	5	6	7	8	9	10	
	11	12	13	14	15	16	17	
Sep 5	18	19	20	21	22	23	24	
	25	26	27	28	29	30	1	OCTOBER 1966
Sep 19	2	3	4	5	6	7	8	
	9	10	11	12	13	14	15	
Oct 3	16	17	18	19	20	21	22	
	23	24	25	26	27	28	29	
Oct 17	30	31	1	2	3	4	5	NOVEMBER 1966
	6	7	8	9	10	11	12	
Oct 31	13	14	15	16	17	18	19	
	20	21	22	23	24	25	26	
Nov 14	27[g]	28	29	30	1	2	3	DECEMBER 1966
	4	5	6	7	8	9	10	
Nov 28	11	12	13	14	15	16	17	
	18	19	20	21	22	23	24	
Dec 12	25[h]	26	27	28	29	30	31	

Persian: [a]New Year; [b]Sizdeh Bedar

Hindu Lunar: ‡Leap year; [a]New Year (Parābhava); [b]Birthday of Rāma; [c]Birthday of Krishna; [d]Ganēśa Chaturthī; [e]Dashara; [f]Diwali; [g]Birthday of Vishnu; [h]Night of Śiva; [i]Holi

Hindu Solar: [a]New Year (Siddhārthin); [b]Pongal

Islamic: [a]New Year; [b]'Ashūrā'; [c]Prophet's Birthday; [d]Ascent of the Prophet; [e]Start of Ramaḍān; [f]'Īd al-Fiṭr; [g]'Īd al-'Aḍḥā

Gregorian: [a]Orthodox Christmas; [b]Julian New Year; [c]Ash Wednesday; [d]Feast of Orthodoxy; [e]Easter (also Orthodox); [g]Advent; [h]Christmas

1967

Month	Sun	Mon	Tue	Wed	Thu	Fri	Sat	Lunar Phases	ISO WEEK (Mon)	JULIAN DAY (Sun noon)
JANUARY 1967	1[a]	2	◑	4	5	6	7	14:19	1	2439492
	8	9	●	11	12	13	14	18:06	2	2439499
	15	16	17	◐	19	20	21	19:41	3	2439506
	22	23	24	25	○	27	28	6:40	4	2439513
	29	30	31	◑	2	3	4	23:03	5	2439520
FEBRUARY 1967	5	6	7	8	●	10	11	10:44	6	2439527
	12	13	14	15	16	◐	18	15:56	7	2439534
	19	20	21	22	23	○	25	17:43	8	2439541
	26	27	28	1	2	◑	4	9:10	9	2439548
MARCH 1967	5	6	7	8	9	10	●	4:30	10	2439555
	12	13	14	15	16	17	18		11	2439562
	◐	20	21[b]	22	23	24	25	8:31	12	2439569
	○	27	28	29	30	31	◑	3:21 20:58	13	2439576
APRIL 1967	2	3	4	5	6	7	8		14	2439583
	●	10	11	12	13	14	15	22:20	15	2439590
	16	◐	18	19	20	21	22	20:48	16	2439597
	23	○	25	26	27	28	29	12:03	17	2439604
	30	◑	2	3	4	5	6	10:32	18	2439611
MAY 1967	7	8	●	10	11	12	13	14:55	19	2439618
	14	15	16	◐	18	19	20	5:18	20	2439625
	21	22	○	24	25	26	27	20:22	21	2439632
	28	29	30	◑	1	2	3	1:52	22	2439639
JUNE 1967	4	5	6	7	●	9	10	5:13	23	2439646
	11	12	13	14	◐	16	17	11:12	24	2439653
	18	19	20	21	○[c]	23	24	4:57	25	2439660
	25	26	27	28	◑	30	1	18:39	26	2439667
JULY 1967	2	3	4	5	6	●	8	17:00	27	2439674
	9	10	11	12	13	◐	15	15:53	28	2439681
	16	17	18	19	20	○	22	14:39	29	2439688
	23	24	25	26	27	28	◑	12:14	30	2439695
	30	31	1	2	3	4	5		31	2439702
AUGUST 1967	●	7	8	9	10	11	◐	2:48 20:44	32	2439709
	13	14	15	16	17	18	19		33	2439716
	○	21	22	23	24	25	26	2:27	34	2439723
	27	◑	29	30	31	1	2	5:35	35	2439730
SEPTEMBER 1967	3	●	5	6	7	8	9	11:37	36	2439737
	10	◐	12	13	14	15	16	3:06	37	2439744
	17	○	19	20	21	22	23[d]	16:59	38	2439751
	24	25	◑	27	28	29	30	21:44	39	2439758
OCTOBER 1967	1	2	●	4	5	6	7	20:24	40	2439765
	8	9	◐	11	12	13	14	12:11	41	2439772
	15	16	17	○	19	20	21	10:11	42	2439779
	22	23	24	25	◑	27	28	12:04	43	2439786
	29	30	31	1	●	3	4	5:48	44	2439793
NOVEMBER 1967	5	6	7	8	◐	10	11	0:59	45	2439800
	12	13	14	15	16	○	18	4:53	46	2439807
	19	20	21	22	23	24	◑	0:23	47	2439814
	26	27	28	29	30	●	2	16:10	48	2439821
DECEMBER 1967	3	4	5	6	7	◐	9	17:57	49	2439828
	10	11	12	13	14	15	○	23:21	50	2439835
	17	18	19	20	21	22[e]	23		51	2439842
	◑	25	26	27	28	29	30	10:48	52	2439849
	●	1	2	3	4	5	6	3:38	1	2439856

HEBREW 5727‡/5728

ISO WEEK	Month	Sun	Mon	Tue	Wed	Thu	Fri	Sat	Molad
1	TEVETH 5727	19	20	21	22	23	24	25	
2		26	27	28	29	1	2	3	Wed 7h6m1p
3	SHEVAT 5727	4	5	6	7	8	9	10	
4		11	12	13	14	15	16	17	
5		18	19	20	21	22	23	24	
6		25	26	27	28	29	30	1	Thu 19h50m2p
7		2	3	4	5	6	7	8	
8	ADAR I 5727	9	10	11	12	13	14	15	
9		16	17	18	19	20	21	22	
10		23	24	25	26	27	28	29	Sat 8h34m3p
11		30	1	2	3	4	5	6	
12	ADAR II 5727	7	8	9	10	11	12	13	
13		14[f]	15	16	17	18	19	20	
14		21	22	23	24	25	26	27	Sun 21h18m4p
15		28	29	1	2	3	4	5	
16	NISAN 5727	6	7	8	9	10	11	12	
17		13	14	15[g]	16	17	18	19	
18		20	21	22	23	24	25	26	
19		27	28	29	30	1	2	3	Tue 10h2m5p
20		4	5	6	7	8	9	10	
21	IYAR 5727	11	12	13	14	15	16	17	
22		18	19	20	21	22	23	24	
23		25	26	27	28	29	1	2	Wed 22h46m6p
24		3	4	5	6[h]	7	8	9	
25	SIVAN 5727	10	11	12	13	14	15	16	
26		17	18	19	20	21	22	23	
27		24	25	26	27	28	29	30	Fri 11h30m7p
28		1	2	3	4	5	6	7	
29	TAMMUZ 5727	8	9	10	11	12	13	14	
30		15	16	17	18	19	20	21	
31		22	23	24	25	26	27	28	
32		29	1	2	3	4	5	6	Sun 0h14m8p
33		7	8	9[i]	10	11	12	13	
34	AV 5727	14	15	16	17	18	19	20	
35		21	22	23	24	25	26	27	
36		28	29	30	1	2	3	4	Mon 12h58m9p
37		5	6	7	8	9	10	11	
38	ELUL 5727	12	13	14	15	16	17	18	
39		19	20	21	22	23	24	25	
40		26	27	28	29	1[a]	2[a]	3	Wed 1h42m10p
41		4	5	6	7	8	9	10[b]	
42	TISHRI 5728	11	12	13	14	15[c]	16	17	
43		18	19	20	21	22	23	24	
44		25	26	27	28	29	30	1	Thu 14h26m11p
45		2	3	4	5	6	7	8	
46	HESHVAN 5728	9	10	11	12	13	14	15	
47		16	17	18	19	20	21	22	
48		23	24	25	26	27	28	29	
49		1	2	3	4[d]	5	6	7	Sat 3h10m12p
50	KISLEV 5728	8	9	10	11	12	13	14	
51		15	16	17	18	19	20	21	
52		22	23	24	25[e]	26[e]	27[e]	28[e]	
1		29[e]	30[e]	1[e]	2[e]	3	4	5	Sun 15h54m13p

CHINESE Bǐng-Wǔ‡/Dīng-Wèi

ISO WEEK	Month	Sun	Mon	Tue	Wed	Thu	Fri	Sat	Solar Term
1	MONTH 11 Bǐng-Wǔ	21	22	23	24	25	26	27	Xiǎo hán
2		28	29	30	1	2	3	4	
3	MONTH 12 Bǐng-Wǔ	5	6	7	8	9	10	***11***	**Dà hán**
4		12	13	14	15	16	17	18	
5		19	20	21	22	23	24	*25*	Lì chūn
6		26	27	28	29	1[a]	2	3	
7	MONTH 1 Dīng-Wèi	4	5	6	7	8	9	10	
8		***11***	12	13	14	15[b]	16	17	**Yǔ shuǐ**
9		18	19	20	21*	22	23	24	
10		25	26	27	28	29	30	1	Jīng zhé
11	MONTH 2 Dīng-Wèi	2	3	4	5	6	7	8	
12		9	10	***11***	12	13	14	15	**Chūn fēn**
13		16	17	18	19	20	21	22	
14		23	24	25	26[c]	27	28	29	Qīng míng
15		30	1	2	3	4	5	6	
16	MONTH 3 Dīng-Wèi	7	8	9	10	11	***12***	13	**Gǔ yǔ**
17		14	15	16	17	18	19	20	
18		21*	22	23	24	25	26	*27*	Lì xià
19		28	29	1	2	3	4	5	
20	MONTH 4 Dīng-Wèi	6	7	8	9	10	11	12	
21		13	***14***	15	16	17	18	19	**Xiǎo mǎn**
22		20	21	22	23	24	25	26	
23		27	28	29	30	1	2	3	Máng zhòng
24	MONTH 5 Dīng-Wèi	4	5[d]	6	7	8	9	10	
25		11	12	13	14	***15***	16	17	**Xià zhì**
26		18	19	20	21	22*	23	24	
27		25	26	27	28	29	30	*1*	Xiǎo shǔ
28	MONTH 6 Dīng-Wèi	2	3	4	5	6	7	8	
29		9	10	11	12	13	14	15	**Dà shǔ**
30		***16***	17	18	19	20	21	22	
31		23	24	25	26	27	28	29	
32	MONTH 7 Dīng-Wèi	1	2	3	4	5	6	7[e]	Lì qiū
33		8	9	10	11	12	13	14	
34		15[f]	16	17	18	***19***	20	21	**Chǔ shǔ**
35		22	23*	24	25	26	27	28	
36		29	1	2	3	4	5	6	Bái lù
37	MONTH 8 Dīng-Wèi	7	8	9	10	11	12	13	
38		14	15[g]	16	17	18	19	20	**Qiū fēn**
39		***21***	22	23	24	25	26	27	
40		28	29	30	1	2	3	4	
41	MONTH 9 Dīng-Wèi	5	6	7	8	9[h]	10	11	Hán lù
42		12	13	14	15	16	17	18	
43		19	20	***21***	22	23	24*	25	**Shuāng jiàng**
44		26	27	28	29	1	2	3	
45	MONTH 10 Dīng-Wèi	4	5	6	7	8	9	10	Lì dōng
46		11	12	13	14	15	16	17	
47		18	19	20	21	***22***	23	24	**Xiǎo xuě**
48		25	26	27	28	29	30	1	
49	MONTH 11 Dīng-Wèi	2	3	4	5	6	7	8	Dà xuě
50		9	10	11	12	13	14	15	
51		16	17	18	19	20	***21***[i]	22	**Dōng zhì**
52		23	24	25*	26	27	28	29	
1		1	2	3	4	5	6	7	Xiǎo hán

COPTIC 1683‡/1684 — ETHIOPIC 1959‡/1960

ISO WEEK	Coptic Month	Sun	Mon	Tue	Wed	Thu	Fri	Sat	Ethiopic Month
1	KOIAK 1683	23	24	25	26	27	28	29[c]	TĀKHŚĀŚ 1959
2		30	1	2	3	4	5	6[d]	
3	TŌBE 1683	7	8	9	10	11[e]	12	13	TER 1959
4		14	15	16	17	18	19	20	
5		21	22	23	24	25	26	27	
6		28	29	30	1	2	3	4	
7	MESHIR 1683	5	6	7	8	9	10	11	YAKĀTIT 1959
8		12	13	14	15	16	17	18	
9		19	20	21	22	23	24	25	
10		26	27	28	29	30	1	2	
11	PAREMOTEP 1683	3	4	5	6	7	8	9	MAGĀBIT 1959
12		10	11	12	13	14	15	16	
13		17	18	19	20	21	22	23	
14		24	25	26	27	28	29	30	
15		1	2	3	4	5	6	7	
16	PARMOUTE 1683	8	9	10	11	12	13	14	MIYĀZYĀ 1959
17		15	16	17	18	19	20	21	
18		22[f]	23	24	25	26	27	28	
19		29[g]	30	1	2	3	4	5	
20	PASHONS 1683	6	7	8	9	10	11	12	GENBOT 1959
21		13	14	15	16	17	18	19	
22		20	21	22	23	24	25	26	
23		27	28	29	30	1	2	3	
24	PAŌNE 1683	4	5	6	7	8	9	10	SANĒ 1959
25		11	12	13	14	15	16	17	
26		18	19	20	21	22	23	24	
27		25	26	27	28	29	30	1	
28	EPĒP 1683	2	3	4	5	6	7	8	HAMLĒ 1959
29		9	10	11	12	13	14	15	
30		16	17	18	19	20	21	22	
31		23	24	25	26	27	28	29	
32		30	1	2	3	4	5	6	
33	MESORĒ 1683	7	8	9	10	11	12	13[h]	NAHASĒ 1959
34		14	15	16	17	18	19	20	
35		21	22	23	24	25	26	27	
36	EPAG. 1683	28	29	30	1	2	3	4	PĀG. 1959
37		5	6	1[a]	2	3	4	5	
38	THOOUT 1684	6	7	8	9	10	11	12	MASKARAM 1960
39		13	14	15	16	17[b]	18	19	
40		20	21	22	23	24	25	26	
41		27	28	29	30	1	2	3	
42	PAOPE 1684	4	5	6	7	8	9	10	TEQEMT 1960
43		11	12	13	14	15	16	17	
44		18	19	20	21	22	23	24	
45		25	26	27	28	29	30	1	
46	ATHŌR 1684	2	3	4	5	6	7	8	HEDĀR 1960
47		9	10	11	12	13	14	15	
48		16	17	18	19	20	21	22	
49		23	24	25	26	27	28	29	
50		30	1	2	3	4	5	6	
51	KOIAK 1684	7	8	9	10	11	12	13	TĀKHŚĀŚ 1960
52		14	15	16	17	18	19	20	
1		21	22	23	24	25	26	27	

[a]New Year
[b]Spring (7:37)
[c]Summer (2:23)
[d]Autumn (17:38)
[e]Winter (13:16)
● New moon
◐ First quarter moon
○ Full moon
◑ Last quarter moon

‡Leap year
[a]New Year
[b]Yom Kippur
[c]Sukkot
[d]Winter starts
[e]Ḥanukkah
[f]Purim
[g]Passover
[h]Shavuot
[i]Fast of Av

‡Leap year
[a]New Year (4665, Sheep)
[b]Lantern Festival
[c]Qīngmíng
[d]Dragon Festival
[e]Qīqiǎo
[f]Hungry Ghosts
[g]Mid-Autumn Festival
[h]Double-Ninth Festival
[i]Dōngzhì
*Start of 60-name cycle

‡Leap year
[a]New Year
[b]Building of the Cross
[c]Christmas
[d]Jesus's Circumcision
[e]Epiphany
[f]Easter
[g]Mary's Announcement
[h]Jesus's Transfiguration

PERSIAN (ASTRONOMICAL) 1345/1346‡

Month	Sun	Mon	Tue	Wed	Thu	Fri	Sat
DEY 1345	11	12	13	14	15	16	17
	18	19	20	21	22	23	24
	25	26	27	28	29	30	1
BAHMAN 1345	2	3	4	5	6	7	8
	9	10	11	12	13	14	15
	16	17	18	19	20	21	22
	23	24	25	26	27	28	29
	30	1	2	3	4	5	6
ESFAND 1345	7	8	9	10	11	12	13
	14	15	16	17	18	19	20
	21	22	23	24	25	26	27
	28	29	1[a]	2	3	4	5
FARVARDĪN 1346	6	7	8	9	10	11	12
	13[b]	14	15	16	17	18	19
	20	21	22	23	24	25	26
	27	28	29	30	31	1	2
ORDĪBEHEŠT 1346	3	4	5	6	7	8	9
	10	11	12	13	14	15	16
	17	18	19	20	21	22	23
	24	25	26	27	28	29	30
	31	1	2	3	4	5	6
XORDĀD 1346	7	8	9	10	11	12	13
	14	15	16	17	18	19	20
	21	22	23	24	25	26	27
	28	29	30	31	1	2	3
TĪR 1346	4	5	6	7	8	9	10
	11	12	13	14	15	16	17
	18	19	20	21	22	23	24
	25	26	27	28	29	30	31
MORDĀD 1346	1	2	3	4	5	6	7
	8	9	10	11	12	13	14
	15	16	17	18	19	20	21
	22	23	24	25	26	27	28
	29	30	31	1	2	3	4
SHAHRĪVAR 1346	5	6	7	8	9	10	11
	12	13	14	15	16	17	18
	19	20	21	22	23	24	25
	26	27	28	29	30	31	1
MEHR 1346	2	3	4	5	6	7	8
	9	10	11	12	13	14	15
	16	17	18	19	20	21	22
	23	24	25	26	27	28	29
	30	1	2	3	4	5	6
ĀBĀN 1346	7	8	9	10	11	12	13
	14	15	16	17	18	19	20
	21	22	23	24	25	26	27
	28	29	30	1	2	3	4
ĀZAR 1346	5	6	7	8	9	10	11
	12	13	14	15	16	17	18
	19	20	21	22	23	24	25
	26	27	28	29	30	1	2
DEY 1346	3	4	5	6	7	8	9
	10	11	12	13	14	15	16

‡Leap year
[a]New Year
[b]Sizdeh Bedar

HINDU LUNAR 2023‡/2024

Month	Sun	Mon	Tue	Wed	Thu	Fri	Sat
MĀRGAŚĪRA 2023	20	21	22	**23**	25	26	27
	28	29	30	1	2	3	4
PAUSHA 2023	5	6	6	7	8	9	10
	11	12	13	14	15	16	**17**
	19	20	21	22	23	24	25
	26	27	28	29	30	1	2
MĀGHA 2023	3	4	5	6	7	8	9
	10	11	12	13	14	15	16
	17	18	19	20	21	22	**23**
	25	26	27	28	29[h]	29	30
PHĀLGUNA 2023	1	2	3	4	5	6	7
	8	9	10	11	12	13	14
	15[i]	**16**	18	19	20	21	22
	23	24	25	26	27	28	29
	30	1[a]	2	2	3	4	5
CHAITRA 2024	6	7	8[b]	**9**	11	12	13
	14	15	16	17	18	19	20
	21	22	23	24	25	26	27
	28	29	30	1	2	3	4
VAIŚĀKHA 2024	5	6	7	8	9	10	11
	12	**13**	15	16	17	18	19
	20	21	22	23	24	25	26
	27	27	28	29	30	1	2
JYAISHTHA 2024	3	4	5	**6**	8	9	10
	11	12	13	14	15	16	17
	18	19	20	21	22	23	24
	25	26	27	28	29	30	1
ĀSHĀḌHA 2024	2	3	4	5	6	7	**8**
	10	11	12	13	14	15	16
	17	18	19	20	21	22	23
	24	24	25	26	27	28	29
	30	**1**	3	4	5	6	7
ŚRĀVAṆA 2024	8	9	10	11	12	13	14
	15	16	17	18	19	20	21
	22	23[c]	24	25	26	27	28
	29	30	1	2	3[d]	**4**	6
BHĀDRAPADA 2024	7	8	9	10	11	12	13
	14	15	16	17	18	19	20
	20	21	22	23	24	25	26
	27	**28**	30	1	2	3	4
ĀŚVINA 2024	5	6	7	8[e]	9[e]	10[e]	11
	12	13	14	15	16	17	18
	19	20	21	22	23	24	25
	26	27	28	29	30	1[f]	**2**
KĀRTTIKA 2024	4	5	6	7	8	9	10
	11	12	13	14	14	15	16
	17	18	19	20	21	22	23
	24	25	**26**	28	29	30	1
MĀRGAŚĪRA 2024	2	3	4	5	6	7	8
	9	10	11[g]	12	13	14	15
	16	17	18	19	20	21	22
	23	24	25	26	27	28	29
PAUSHA 2024	30	**1**	3	4	5	6	7

‡Leap year
[a]New Year (Plavaṅga)
[b]Birthday of Rāma
[c]Birthday of Krishna
[d]Ganēśa Chaturthī
[e]Dashara
[f]Diwali
[g]Birthday of Vishnu
[h]Night of Śiva
[i]Holi

HINDU SOLAR 1888/1889‡

Month	Sun	Mon	Tue	Wed	Thu	Fri	Sat
PAUSHA 1888	18	19	20	21	22	23	24
	25	26	27	28	29	30	1[b]
MĀGHA 1888	2	3	4	5	6	7	8
	9	10	11	12	13	14	15
	16	17	18	19	20	21	22
	23	24	25	26	27	28	29
PHĀLGUNA 1888	1	2	3	4	5	6	7
	8	9	10	11	12	13	14
	15	16	17	18	19	20	21
	22	23	24	25	26	27	28
	29	30	1	2	3	4	5
CHAITRA 1888	6	7	8	9	10	11	12
	13	14	15	16	17	18	19
	20	21	22	23	24	25	26
	27	28	29	30	1[a]	2	3
VAIŚĀKHA 1889	4	5	6	7	8	9	10
	11	12	13	14	15	16	17
	18	19	20	21	22	23	24
	25	26	27	28	29	30	31
JYAISHTHA 1889	1	2	3	4	5	6	7
	8	9	10	11	12	13	14
	15	16	17	18	19	20	21
	22	23	24	25	26	27	28
	29	30	31	32	1	2	3
ĀSHĀḌHA 1889	4	5	6	7	8	9	10
	11	12	13	14	15	16	17
	18	19	20	21	22	23	24
	25	26	27	28	29	30	31
ŚRĀVAṆA 1889	1	2	3	4	5	6	7
	8	9	10	11	12	13	14
	15	16	17	18	19	20	21
	22	23	24	25	26	27	28
	29	30	31	32	1	2	3
BHĀDRAPADA 1889	4	5	6	7	8	9	10
	11	12	13	14	15	16	17
	18	19	20	21	22	23	24
	25	26	27	28	29	30	31
ĀŚVINA 1889	1	2	3	4	5	6	7
	8	9	10	11	12	13	14
	15	16	17	18	19	20	21
	22	23	24	25	26	27	28
	29	30	1	2	3	4	5
KĀRTTIKA 1889	6	7	8	9	10	11	12
	13	14	15	16	17	18	19
	20	21	22	23	24	25	26
	27	28	29	30	1	2	3
MĀRGAŚĪRA 1889	4	5	6	7	8	9	10
	11	12	13	14	15	16	17
	18	19	20	21	22	23	24
	25	26	27	28	29	30	1
PAUSHA 1889	2	3	4	5	6	7	8
	9	10	11	12	13	14	15
	16	17	18	19	20	21	22

‡Leap year
[a]New Year (Rāudra)
[b]Pongal

ISLAMIC (ASTRONOMICAL) 1386/1387

Month	Sun	Mon	Tue	Wed	Thu	Fri	Sat
RAMAḌĀN 1386	19	20	21	22	23	24	25
	26	27	28	29	1[f]	2	3
SHAWWĀL 1386	4	5	6	7	8	9	10
	11	12	13	14	15	16	17
	18	19	20	21	22	23	24
	25	26	27	28	29	30	1
DHU AL-QA'DA 1386	2	3	4	5	6	7	8
	9	10	11	12	13	14	15
	16	17	18	19	20	21	22
	23	24	25	26	27	28	29
	30	1	2	3	4	5	6
DHU AL-ḤIJJA 1386	7	8	9	10[g]	11	12	13
	14	15	16	17	18	19	20
	21	22	23	24	25	26	27
	28	29	1[a]	2	3	4	5
MUḤARRAM 1387	6	7	8	9	10[b]	11	12
	13	14	15	16	17	18	19
	20	21	22	23	24	25	26
	27	28	29	30	1	2	3
ṢAFAR 1387	4	5	6	7	8	9	10
	11	12	13	14	15	16	17
	18	19	20	21	22	23	24
	25	26	27	28	29	1	2
RABĪ' I 1387	3	4	5	6	7	8	9
	10	11	12[c]	13	14	15	16
	17	18	19	20	21	22	23
	24	25	26	27	28	29	30
RABĪ' II 1387	1	2	3	4	5	6	7
	8	9	10	11	12	13	14
	15	16	17	18	19	20	21
	22	23	24	25	26	27	28
	29	1	2	3	4	5	6
JUMĀDĀ I 1387	7	8	9	10	11	12	13
	14	15	16	17	18	19	20
	21	22	23	24	25	26	27
	28	29	30	1	2	3	4
JUMĀDĀ II 1387	5	6	7	8	9	10	11
	12	13	14	15	16	17	18
	19	20	21	22	23	24	25
	26	27	28	29	1	2	3
RAJAB 1387	4	5	6	7	8	9	10
	11	12	13	14	15	16	17
	18	19	20	21	22	23	24
	25	26	27[d]	28	29	30	1
SHA'BĀN 1387	2	3	4	5	6	7	8
	9	10	11	12	13	14	15
	16	17	18	19	20	21	22
	23	24	25	26	27	28	29
RAMAḌĀN 1387	1[e]	2	3	4	5	6	7
	8	9	10	11	12	13	14
	15	16	17	18	19	20	21
	22	23	24	25	26	27	28
	29	30	1	2	3	4	5

[a]New Year
[b]'Ashūrā'
[c]Prophet's Birthday
[d]Ascent of the Prophet
[e]Start of Ramaḍān
[f]'Id al-Fiṭr
[g]'Id al-'Aḍḥā

GREGORIAN 1967

Julian (Sun)	Sun	Mon	Tue	Wed	Thu	Fri	Sat	Month
Dec 19	1	2	3	4	5	6	7[a]	JANUARY 1967
	8	9	10	11	12	13	14[b]	
Jan 2	15	16	17	18	19	20	21	
	22	23	24	25	26	27	28	
Jan 16	29	30	31	1	2	3	4	FEBRUARY 1967
	5	6	7	8[c]	9	10	11	
Jan 30	12	13	14	15	16	17	18	
	19	20	21	22	23	24	25	
Feb 13	26	27	28	1	2	3	4	MARCH 1967
	5	6	7	8	9	10	11	
Feb 27	12	13	14	15	16	17	18	
	19[d]	20	21	22	23	24	25	
Mar 13	26[e]	27	28	29	30	31	1	APRIL 1967
	2	3	4	5	6	7	8	
Mar 27	9	10	11	12	13	14	15	
	16	17	18	19	20	21	22	
Apr 10	23	24	25	26	27	28	29	
	30[f]	1	2	3	4	5	6	MAY 1967
Apr 24	7	8	9	10	11	12	13	
	14	15	16	17	18	19	20	
May 8	21	22	23	24	25	26	27	
	28	29	30	31	1	2	3	JUNE 1967
May 22	4	5	6	7	8	9	10	
	11	12	13	14	15	16	17	
Jun 5	18	19	20	21	22	23	24	
	25	26	27	28	29	30	1	JULY 1967
Jun 19	2	3	4	5	6	7	8	
	9	10	11	12	13	14	15	
Jul 3	16	17	18	19	20	21	22	
	23	24	25	26	27	28	29	
Jul 17	30	31	1	2	3	4	5	AUGUST 1967
	6	7	8	9	10	11	12	
Jul 31	13	14	15	16	17	18	19	
	20	21	22	23	24	25	26	
Aug 14	27	28	29	30	31	1	2	SEPTEMBER 1967
	3	4	5	6	7	8	9	
Aug 28	10	11	12	13	14	15	16	
	17	18	19	20	21	22	23	
Sep 11	24	25	26	27	28	29	30	
	1	2	3	4	5	6	7	OCTOBER 1967
Sep 25	8	9	10	11	12	13	14	
	15	16	17	18	19	20	21	
Oct 9	22	23	24	25	26	27	28	
	29	30	31	1	2	3	4	NOVEMBER 1967
Oct 23	5	6	7	8	9	10	11	
	12	13	14	15	16	17	18	
Nov 6	19	20	21	22	23	24	25	
	26	27	28	29	30	1	2	DECEMBER 1967
Nov 20	3[g]	4	5	6	7	8	9	
	10	11	12	13	14	15	16	
Dec 4	17	18	19	20	21	22	23	
	24	25[h]	26	27	28	29	30	
Dec 18	31	1	2	3	4	5	6	

[a]Orthodox Christmas
[b]Julian New Year
[c]Ash Wednesday
[d]Feast of Orthodoxy
[e]Easter
[f]Orthodox Easter
[g]Advent
[h]Christmas

1968

GREGORIAN 1968‡ — Lunar Phases — ISO WEEK — JULIAN DAY

Month	Sun	Mon	Tue	Wed	Thu	Fri	Sat	Lunar Phases	ISO WEEK (Mon)	JULIAN DAY (Sun noon)
JANUARY 1968	●	1[a]	2	3	4	5	6	3:38	1	2439856
	◐	8	9	10	11	12	13	14:23	2	2439863
	14	○	16	17	18	19	20	16:11	3	2439870
	21	◑	23	24	25	26	27	19:38	4	2439877
	28	●	30	31	1	2	3	16:29	5	2439884
FEBRUARY 1968	4	5	◐	7	8	9	10	12:20	6	2439891
	11	12	13	○	15	16	17	6:43	7	2439898
	18	19	20	◑	22	23	24	3:28	8	2439905
	25	26	27	●	29	1	2	6:55	9	2439912
MARCH 1968	3	4	5	6	◐	8	9	9:20	10	2439919
	10	11	12	13	○	15	16	18:52	11	2439926
	17	18	19	20[b]	◑	22	23	11:08	12	2439933
	24	25	26	27	●	29	30	22:48	13	2439940
	31	1	2	3	4	5	◐	3:27	14	2439947
APRIL 1968	7	8	9	10	11	12	○	4:52	15	2439954
	14	15	16	17	18	◑	20	19:35	16	2439961
	21	22	23	24	25	26	●	15:21	17	2439968
	28	29	30	1	2	3	4		18	2439975
MAY 1968	◐	6	7	8	9	10	11	17:54	19	2439982
	○	13	14	15	16	17	18	13:05	20	2439989
	◑	20	21	22	23	24	25	5:44	21	2439996
	26	●	28	29	30	31	1	7:30	22	2440003
JUNE 1968	2	3	◐	5	6	7	8	4:47	23	2440010
	9	○	11	12	13	14	15	20:13	24	2440017
	16	◑	18	19	20	21[c]	22	18:14	25	2440024
	23	24	●	26	27	28	29	22:24	26	2440031
	30	1	2	◐	4	5	6	12:42	27	2440038
JULY 1968	7	8	9	○	11	12	13	3:18	28	2440045
	14	15	16	◑	18	19	20	9:11	29	2440052
	21	22	23	24	●	26	27	11:49	30	2440059
	28	29	30	31	◐	2	3	18:34	31	2440066
AUGUST 1968	4	5	6	7	○	9	10	11:32	32	2440073
	11	12	13	14	15	◑	17	2:13	33	2440080
	18	19	20	21	22	●	24	23:57	34	2440087
	25	26	27	28	29	◐	31	23:35	35	2440094
SEPTEMBER 1968	1	2	3	4	5	○	7	22:07	36	2440101
	8	9	10	11	12	13	◑	20:31	37	2440108
	15	16	17	18	19	20	21		38	2440115
	●[d]	23	24	25	26	27	28	11:08	39	2440122
	◐	30	1	2	3	4	5	5:07	40	2440129
OCTOBER 1968	○	7	8	9	10	11	12	11:46	41	2440136
	13	◑	15	16	17	18	19	15:05	42	2440143
	20	●	22	23	24	25	26	21:44	43	2440150
	27	◐	29	30	31	1	2	12:40	44	2440157
NOVEMBER 1968	3	4	○	6	7	8	9	4:25	45	2440164
	10	11	12	◑	14	15	16	8:53	46	2440171
	17	18	19	●	21	22	23	8:02	47	2440178
	24	25	◐	27	28	29	30	23:30	48	2440185
DECEMBER 1968	1	2	3	○	5	6	7	23:07	49	2440192
	8	9	10	11	12	◑	14	0:49	50	2440199
	15	16	17	18	●	20	21[e]	18:19	51	2440206
	22	23	24	25	◐	27	28	14:14	52	2440213
	29	30	31	1	2	○	4	18:2	1	2440220

HEBREW 5728/5729 — Molad

ISO WEEK	Month	Sun	Mon	Tue	Wed	Thu	Fri	Sat	Molad
1	TEVETH 5728	29[e]	30[e]	1[e]	2[e]	3	4	5	Sun 15h54m13p
2		6	7	8	9	10	11	12	
3		13	14	15	16	17	18	19	
4		20	21	22	23	24	25	26	
5		27	28	29	1	2	3	4	Tue 4h38m14p
6	SHEVAT 5728	5	6	7	8	9	10	11	
7		12	13	14	15	16	17	18	
8		19	20	21	22	23	24	25	
9		26	27	28	29	30	1	2	Wed 17h22m15p
10	ADAR 5728	3	4	5	6	7	8	9	
11		10	11	12	13	14[f]	15	16	
12		17	18	19	20	21	22	23	
13		24	25	26	27	28	29	1	Fri 6h6m16p
14	NISAN 5728	2	3	4	5	6	7	8	
15		9	10	11	12	13	14	15[g]	
16		16	17	18	19	20	21	22	
17		23	24	25	26	27	28	29	
18		30	1	2	3	4	5	6	Sat 18h50m17p
19	IYYAR 5728	7	8	9	10	11	12	13	
20		14	15	16	17	18	19	20	
21		21	22	23	24	25	26	27	
22		28	29	1	2	3	4	5	Mon 7h35m0p
23	SIVAN 5728	6[h]	7	8	9	10	11	12	
24		13	14	15	16	17	18	19	
25		20	21	22	23	24	25	26	
26		27	28	29	30	1	2	3	Tue 20h19m1p
27	TAMMUZ 5728	4	5	6	7	8	9	10	
28		11	12	13	14	15	16	17	
29		18	19	20	21	22	23	24	
30		25	26	27	28	29	1	2	Thu 9h3m2p
31	AV 5728	3	4	5	6	7	8	9	
32		10[i]	11	12	13	14	15	16	
33		17	18	19	20	21	22	23	
34		24	25	26	27	28	29	30	
35	ELUL 5728	1	2	3	4	5	6	7	Fri 21h47m3p
36		8	9	10	11	12	13	14	
37		15	16	17	18	19	20	21	
38		22	23	24	25	26	27	28	
39		29	1[a]	2[a]	3	4	5	6	Sun 10h31m4p
40	TISHRI 5729	7	8	9	10[b]	11	12	13	
41		14	15[c]	16	17	18	19	20	
42		21	22	23	24	25	26	27	
43		28	29	30	1	2	3	4	Mon 23h15m5p
44	HESHVAN 5729	5	6	7	8	9	10	11	
45		12	13	14	15	16	17	18	
46		19	20	21	22	23	24	25	
47		26	27	28	29	30	1	2	Wed 11h59m6p
48	KISLEV 5729	3	4	5	6	7	8	9	
49		10	11	12	13	14[d]	15	16	
50		17	18	19	20	21	22	23	
51		24	25[e]	26[e]	27[e]	28[e]	29[e]	30[e]	
52	TEVETH 5729	1[e]	2[e]	3	4	5	6	7	Fri 0h43m7p
1		8	9	10	11	12	13	14	

CHINESE Dīng-Wèi/Wù-Shēn‡ — Solar Term

ISO WEEK	Month	Sun	Mon	Tue	Wed	Thu	Fri	Sat	Solar Term
1	MONTH 12 Dīng-Wèi	1	2	3	4	5	6	7	Xiǎo hán
2		8	9	10	11	12	13	14	
3		15	16	17	18	19	20	21	
4		22	23	24	25	26	27	28	Dà hán
5		29	30	1[a]	2	3	4	5	
6	MONTH 1 Wù-Shēn	6	7	8	9	10	11	12	Lì chūn
7		13	14	15[b]	16	17	18	19	
8		20	21	22	23	24	25	26*	Yǔ shuǐ
9		27	28	29	1	2	3	4	
10	MONTH 2 Wù-Shēn	5	6	7	8	9	10	11	Jīng zhé
11		12	13	14	15	16	17	18	
12		19	20	21	22	23	24	25	Chūn fēn
13		26	27	28	29	30	1	2	
14	MONTH 3 Wù-Shēn	3	4	5	6	7	8[c]	9	Qīng míng
15		10	11	12	13	14	15	16	
16		17	18	19	20	21	22	23	Gǔ yǔ
17		24	25	26	27*	28	29	1	
18	MONTH 4 Wù-Shēn	2	3	4	5	6	7	8	
19		9	10	11	12	13	14	15	Lì xià
20		16	17	18	19	20	21	22	
21		23	24	25	26	27	28	29	Xiǎo mǎn
22		30	1	2	3	4	5[d]	6	
23	MONTH 5 Wù-Shēn	7	8	9	10	11	12	13	Máng zhòng
24		14	15	16	17	18	19	20	
25		21	22	23	24	25	26	27	Xià zhì
26		28*	29	30	1	2	3	4	
27	MONTH 6 Wù-Shēn	5	6	7	8	9	10	11	
28		12	13	14	15	16	17	18	Xiǎo shǔ
29		19	20	21	22	23	24	25	
30		26	27	28	29	1	2	3	Dà shǔ
31	MONTH 7 Wù-Shēn	4	5	6	7[e]	8	9	10	
32		11	12	13	14	15[f]	16	17	Lì qiū
33		18	19	20	21	22	23	24	
34		25	26	27	28	29*	30	1	Chǔ shǔ
35	LEAP MONTH 7 Wù-Shēn	2	3	4	5	6	7	8	
36		9	10	11	12	13	14	15	Bái lù
37		16	17	18	19	20	21	22	
38		23	24	25	26	27	28	29	
39	MONTH 8 Wù-Shēn	1	2	3	4	5	6	7	Qiū fēn
40		8	9	10	11	12	13	14	
41		15[g]	16	17	18	19	20	21	Hán lù
42		22	23	24	25	26	27	28	
43		29	30*	1	2	3	4	5	Shuāng jiàng
44	MONTH 9 Wù-Shēn	6	7	8	9[h]	10	11	12	
45		13	14	15	16	17	18	19	Lì dōng
46		20	21	22	23	24	25	26	
47		27	28	29	1	2	3	4	Xiǎo xuě
48	MONTH 10 Wù-Shēn	5	6	7	8	9	10	11	
49		12	13	14	15	16	17	18	Dà xuě
50		19	20	21	22	23	24	25	
51		26	27	28	29	30	1*	2	
52	MONTH 11* Wù-Shēn	3[i]	4	5	6	7	8	9	Dōng zhì
1		10	11	12	13	14	15	16	

COPTIC 1684/1685 — ETHIOPIC 1960/1961

ISO WEEK	Coptic Month	Sun	Mon	Tue	Wed	Thu	Fri	Sat	Ethiopic Month
1	KOIAK 1684	21	22	23	24	25	26	27	TĀKHŚĀŚ 1960
2		28	29[c]	30	1	2	3	4	
3	TŌBE 1684	5	6[d]	7	8	9	10	11[e]	TER 1960
4		12	13	14	15	16	17	18	
5		19	20	21	22	23	24	25	
6		26	27	28	29	30	1	2	
7	MESHIR 1684	3	4	5	6	7	8	9	YAKĀTIT 1960
8		10	11	12	13	14	15	16	
9		17	18	19	20	21	22	23	
10		24	25	26	27	28	29	30	
11	PAREMOTEP 1684	1	2	3	4	5	6	7	MAGĀBIT 1960
12		8	9	10	11	12	13	14	
13		15	16	17	18	19	20	21	
14		22	23	24	25	26	27	28	
15		29	30	1	2	3	4	5	
16	PARMOUTE 1684	6	7	8	9	10	11	12	MIYĀZYĀ 1960
17		13[f]	14	15	16	17	18	19	
18		20	21	22	23	24	25	26	
19		27	28	29[g]	30	1	2	3	
20	PASHONS 1684	4	5	6	7	8	9	10	GENBOT 1960
21		11	12	13	14	15	16	17	
22		18	19	20	21	22	23	24	
23		25	26	27	28	29	30	1	
24	PAŌNE 1684	2	3	4	5	6	7	8	SANĒ 1960
25		9	10	11	12	13	14	15	
26		16	17	18	19	20	21	22	
27		23	24	25	26	27	28	29	
28		30	1	2	3	4	5	6	
29	EPĒP 1684	7	8	9	10	11	12	13	HAMLĒ 1960
30		14	15	16	17	18	19	20	
31		21	22	23	24	25	26	27	
32		28	29	30	1	2	3	4	
33	MESORĒ 1684	5	6	7	8	9	10	11	NAHASĒ 1960
34		12	13[h]	14	15	16	17	18	
35		19	20	21	22	23	24	25	
36		26	27	28	29	30	1	2	
37	EPAG. 1684	3	4	5	1[a]	2	3	4	PĀG. 1960
38	THOOUT 1685	5	6	7	8	9	10	11	MASKARAM 1961
39		12	13	14	15	16	17[b]	18	
40		19	20	21	22	23	24	25	
41		26	27	28	29	30	1	2	
42	PAOPE 1685	3	4	5	6	7	8	9	TEQEMT 1961
43		10	11	12	13	14	15	16	
44		17	18	19	20	21	22	23	
45		24	25	26	27	28	29	30	
46	ATHŌR 1685	1	2	3	4	5	6	7	HEDĀR 1961
47		8	9	10	11	12	13	14	
48		15	16	17	18	19	20	21	
49		22	23	24	25	26	27	28	
50		29	30	1	2	3	4	5	
51	KOIAK 1685	6	7	8	9	10	11	12	TĀKHŚĀŚ 1961
52		13	14	15	16	17	18	19	
1		20	21	22	23	24	25	26	

‡Leap year
[a]New Year
[b]Spring (13:22)
[c]Summer (8:13)
[d]Autumn (23:26)
[e]Winter (19:00)
● New moon
◐ First quarter moon
○ Full moon
◑ Last quarter moon

[a]New Year
[b]Yom Kippur
[c]Sukkot
[d]Winter starts
[e]Ḥanukkah
[f]Purim
[g]Passover
[h]Shavuot
[i]Fast of Av

‡Leap year
[a]New Year (4666, Monkey)
[b]Lantern Festival
[c]Qīngmíng
[d]Dragon Festival
[e]Qǐqiǎo
[f]Hungry Ghosts
[g]Mid-Autumn Festival
[h]Double-Ninth Festival
[i]Dōngzhì
*Start of 60-name cycle

[a]New Year
[b]Building of the Cross
[c]Christmas
[d]Jesus's Circumcision
[e]Epiphany
[f]Easter
[g]Mary's Announcement
[h]Jesus's Transfiguration

PERSIAN (ASTRONOMICAL) 1346‡/1347

Month	Sun	Mon	Tue	Wed	Thu	Fri	Sat
DEY 1346	10	11	12	13	14	15	16
	17	18	19	20	21	22	23
	24	25	26	27	28	29	30
BAHMAN 1346	1	2	3	4	5	6	7
	8	9	10	11	12	13	14
	15	16	17	18	19	20	21
	22	23	24	25	26	27	28
ESFAND 1346	29	30	1	2	3	4	5
	6	7	8	9	10	11	12
	13	14	15	16	17	18	19
	20	21	22	23	24	25	26
FARVARDĪN 1347	27	28	29	30	1[a]	2	3
	4	5	6	7	8	9	10
	11	12	13[b]	14	15	16	17
	18	19	20	21	22	23	24
	25	26	27	28	29	30	31
ORDĪBEHEŠT 1347	1	2	3	4	5	6	7
	8	9	10	11	12	13	14
	15	16	17	18	19	20	21
	22	23	24	25	26	27	28
XORDĀD 1347	29	30	31	1	2	3	4
	5	6	7	8	9	10	11
	12	13	14	15	16	17	18
	19	20	21	22	23	24	25
TĪR 1347	26	27	28	29	30	31	1
	2	3	4	5	6	7	8
	9	10	11	12	13	14	15
	16	17	18	19	20	21	22
	23	24	25	26	27	28	29
MORDĀD 1347	30	31	1	2	3	4	5
	6	7	8	9	10	11	12
	13	14	15	16	17	18	19
	20	21	22	23	24	25	26
SHAHRĪVAR 1347	27	28	29	30	31	1	2
	3	4	5	6	7	8	9
	10	11	12	13	14	15	16
	17	18	19	20	21	22	23
	24	25	26	27	28	29	30
MEHR 1347	31	1	2	3	4	5	6
	7	8	9	10	11	12	13
	14	15	16	17	18	19	20
	21	22	23	24	25	26	27
ĀBĀN 1347	28	29	30	1	2	3	4
	5	6	7	8	9	10	11
	12	13	14	15	16	17	18
	19	20	21	22	23	24	25
ĀZAR 1347	26	27	28	29	30	1	2
	3	4	5	6	7	8	9
	10	11	12	13	14	15	16
	17	18	19	20	21	22	23
	24	25	26	27	28	29	30
DEY 1347	1	2	3	4	5	6	7
	8	9	10	11	12	13	14

‡Leap year
[a]New Year
[b]Sizdeh Bedar

HINDU LUNAR 2024/2025

Month	Sun	Mon	Tue	Wed	Thu	Fri	Sat
PAUSHA 2024	30	**1**	3	4	5	6	7
	7	8	9	10	11	12	13
	14	15	16	17	18	19	20
	21	22	23	**24**	26	27	28
MĀGHA 2024	29	30	1	2	3	4	5
	6	7	8	9	9	10	11
	12	13	14	15	16	17	**18**
	20	21	22	23	24	25	26
PHĀLGUNA 2024	27	28[h]	29	30	1	2	3
	4	5	6	7	8	9	10
	11	12	13	14	15[i]	16	17
	18	19	20	21	22	**23**	25
CHAITRA 2025	26	27	28	29	30	1[a]	2
	2	3	4	5	6	7	8
	9[b]	10	11	12	13	14	15
	16	18	19	20	21	22	23
	24	25	26	27	28	29	30
VAIŚĀKHA 2025	1	2	3	4	5	6	7
	7	**8**	10	11	12	13	14
	15	16	17	18	19	20	**21**
	23	24	25	26	27	27	28
JYAISHTHA 2025	29	30	1	2	3	4	5
	6	7	8	9	10	11	12
	13	15	16	17	18	19	20
	21	22	23	24	25	26	27
ĀSHĀDHA 2025	28	29	30	1	2	3	3
	4	6	7	8	9	10	11
	12	13	14	15	**16**	18	19
	20	21	22	23	24	24	25
ŚRĀVANA 2025	26	27	28	29	30	1	2
	3	4	5	6	7	8	**9**
	11	12	13	14	15	16	17
	18	19	20	21	22	23[c]	24
BHĀDRAPADA 2025	25	26	27	28	29	30	1
	2	3	4[d]	5	6	7	8
	9	10	11	**12**	14	15	16
	17	18	19	20	20	21	22
	23	24	25	26	27	28	29
ĀŚVINA 2025	30	1	2	3	4	**5**	7
	8[e]	9[e]	10[e]	11	12	13	14
	15	16	17	18	19	20	21
	22	23	24	24	25	26	**27**
KĀRTTIKA 2025	29	30	1[f]	2	3	4	5
	6	7	8	9	**10**	12	13
	14	14	15	16	17	18	19
	20	21	22	23	24	25	26
MĀRGAŚĪRA 2025	27	28	29	30	1	**2**	4
	5	6	7	8	9	10	11[g]
	12	13	14	15	16	17	17
	18	19	20	21	22	23	24
PAUSHA 2025	25	**26**	28	29	30	1	2
	3	4	5	6	7	8	9
	10	11	12	13	14	15	16

[a]New Year (Kīlaka)
[b]Birthday of Rāma
[c]Birthday of Krishna
[d]Ganēśa Chaturthī
[e]Dashara
[f]Diwali
[g]Birthday of Vishnu
[h]Night of Śiva
[i]Holi

HINDU SOLAR 1889‡/1890

Month	Sun	Mon	Tue	Wed	Thu	Fri	Sat
PAUSHA 1889	16	17	18	19	20	21	22
	23	24	25	26	27	28	29
MĀGHA 1889	1[b]	2	3	4	5	6	7
	8	9	10	11	12	13	14
	15	16	17	18	19	20	21
	22	23	24	25	26	27	28
PHĀLGUNA 1889	29	1	2	3	4	5	6
	7	8	9	10	11	12	13
	14	15	16	17	18	19	20
	21	22	23	24	25	26	27
CHAITRA 1889	28	29	30	1	2	3	4
	5	6	7	8	9	10	11
	12	13	14	15	16	17	18
	19	20	21	22	23	24	25
VAIŚĀKHA 1890	26	27	28	29	30	31	1[a]
	2	3	4	5	6	7	8
	9	10	11	12	13	14	15
	16	17	18	19	20	21	22
	23	24	25	26	27	28	29
JYAISHTHA 1890	30	31	1	2	3	4	5
	6	7	8	9	10	11	12
	13	14	15	16	17	18	19
	20	21	22	23	24	25	26
ĀSHĀDHA 1890	27	28	29	30	31	1	2
	3	4	5	6	7	8	9
	10	11	12	13	14	15	16
	17	18	19	20	21	22	23
	24	25	26	27	28	29	30
ŚRĀVANA 1890	31	32	1	2	3	4	5
	6	7	8	9	10	11	12
	13	14	15	16	17	18	19
	20	21	22	23	24	25	26
BHĀDRAPADA 1890	27	28	29	30	31	1	2
	3	4	5	6	7	8	9
	10	11	12	13	14	15	16
	17	18	19	20	21	22	23
	24	25	26	27	28	29	30
ĀŚVINA 1890	31	1	2	3	4	5	6
	7	8	9	10	11	12	13
	14	15	16	17	18	19	20
	21	22	23	24	25	26	27
KĀRTTIKA 1890	28	29	30	31	1	2	3
	4	5	6	7	8	9	10
	11	12	13	14	15	16	17
	18	19	20	21	22	23	24
MĀRGAŚĪRA 1890	25	26	27	28	29	30	1
	2	3	4	5	6	7	8
	9	10	11	12	13	14	15
	16	17	18	19	20	21	22
	23	24	25	26	27	28	29
PAUSHA 1890	1	2	3	4	5	6	7
	8	9	10	11	12	13	14
	15	16	17	18	19	20	21

‡Leap year
[a]New Year (Durmati)
[b]Pongal

ISLAMIC (ASTRONOMICAL) 1387/1388

Month	Sun	Mon	Tue	Wed	Thu	Fri	Sat
SHAWWĀL 1387	29	30	1[f]	2	3	4	5
	6	7	8	9	10	11	12
	13	14	15	16	17	18	19
	20	21	22	23	24	25	26
DHU AL-QA'DA 1387	27	28	29	1	2	3	4
	5	6	7	8	9	10	11
	12	13	14	15	16	17	18
	19	20	21	22	23	24	25
DHU AL-ḤIJJA 1387	26	27	28	29	30	1	2
	3	4	5	6	7	8	9
	10[g]	11	12	13	14	15	16
	17	18	19	20	21	22	23
MUḤARRAM 1388	24	25	26	27	28	29	1[a]
	2[d]	3	4	5	6	7	8
	9	10[b]	11	12	13	14	15
	16	17	18	19	20	21	22
	23	24	25	26	27	28	29
ṢAFAR 1388	30	1	2	3	4	5	6
	7	8	9	10	11	12	13
	14	15	16	17	18	19	20
	21	22	23	24	25	26	27
RABĪ' I 1388	28	29	30	1	2	3	4
	5	6	7	8	9	10	11
	12[c]	13	14	15	16	17	18
	19	20	21	22	23	24	25
RABĪ' II 1388	26	27	28	29	1	2	3
	4	5	6	7	8	9	10
	11	12	13	14	15	16	17
	18	19	20	21	22	23	24
JUMĀDĀ I 1388	25	26	27	28	29	30	1
	2	3	4	5	6	7	8
	9	10	11	12	13	14	15
	16	17	18	19	20	21	22
	23	24	25	26	27	28	29
JUMĀDĀ II 1388	1	2	3	4	5	6	7
	8	9	10	11	12	13	14
	15	16	17	18	19	20	21
	22	23	24	25	26	27	28
RAJAB 1388	29	30	1	2	3	4	5
	6	7	8	9	10	11	12
	13	14	15	16	17	18	19
	20	21	22	23	24	25	26
SHA'BĀN 1388	27[d]	28	29	30	1	2	3
	4	5	6	7	8	9	10
	11	12	13	14	15	16	17
	18	19	20	21	22	23	24
RAMAḌĀN 1388	25	26	27	28	29	1[e]	2
	3	4	5	6	7	8	9
	10	11	12	13	14	15	16
	17	18	19	20	21	22	23
SHAWWĀL 1388	24	25	26	27	28	29	1[f]
	2	3	4	5	6	7	8
	9	10	11	12	13	14	15

[a]New Year
[d]New Year (Arithmetic)
[b]'Ashūrā'
[c]Prophet's Birthday
[d]Ascent of the Prophet
[e]Start of Ramaḍān
[f]'Īd al-Fiṭr
[g]'Īd al-'Aḍḥā

GREGORIAN 1968‡

Julian† (Sun)	Month	Sun	Mon	Tue	Wed	Thu	Fri	Sat
Dec 18	JANUARY 1968	31	1	2	3	4	5	6
		7[a]	8	9	10	11	12	13
Jan 1		14[b]	15	16	17	18	19	20
		21	22	23	24	25	26	27
Jan 15	FEBRUARY 1968	28	29	30	31	1	2	3
		4	5	6	7	8	9	10
Jan 29		11	12	13	14	15	16	17
		18	19	20	21	22	23	24
Feb 12	MARCH 1968	25	26	27	28[c]	29	1	2
		3	4	5	6	7	8	9
Feb 26		10[d]	11	12	13	14	15	16
		17	18	19	20	21	22	23
Mar 11		24	25	26	27	28	29	30
	APRIL 1968	31	1	2	3	4	5	6
Mar 25		7	8	9	10	11	12	13
		14[e]	15	16	17	18	19	20
Apr 8		21[f]	22	23	24	25	26	27
	MAY 1968	28	29	30	1	2	3	4
Apr 22		5	6	7	8	9	10	11
		12	13	14	15	16	17	18
May 6		19	20	21	22	23	24	25
	JUNE 1968	26	27	28	29	30	31	1
May 20		2	3	4	5	6	7	8
		9	10	11	12	13	14	15
Jun 3		16	17	18	19	20	21	22
		23	24	25	26	27	28	29
Jun 17	JULY 1968	30	1	2	3	4	5	6
		7	8	9	10	11	12	13
Jul 1		14	15	16	17	18	19	20
		21	22	23	24	25	26	27
Jul 15	AUGUST 1968	28	29	30	31	1	2	3
		4	5	6	7	8	9	10
Jul 29		11	12	13	14	15	16	17
		18	19	20	21	22	23	24
Aug 12		25	26	27	28	29	30	31
	SEPTEMBER 1968	1	2	3	4	5	6	7
Aug 26		8	9	10	11	12	13	14
		15	16	17	18	19	20	21
Sep 9		22	23	24	25	26	27	28
	OCTOBER 1968	29	30	1	2	3	4	5
Sep 23		6	7	8	9	10	11	12
		13	14	15	16	17	18	19
Oct 7		20	21	22	23	24	25	26
	NOVEMBER 1968	27	28	29	30	31	1	2
Oct 21		3	4	5	6	7	8	9
		10	11	12	13	14	15	16
Nov 4		17	18	19	20	21	22	23
		24	25	26	27	28	29	30
Nov 18	DECEMBER 1968	1[g]	2	3	4	5	6	7
		8	9	10	11	12	13	14
Dec 2		15	16	17	18	19	20	21
		22	23	24	25[h]	26	27	28
Dec 16		29	30	31	1	2	3	4

‡Leap year
[a]Orthodox Christmas
[b]Julian New Year
[c]Ash Wednesday
[d]Feast of Orthodoxy
[e]Easter
[f]Orthodox Easter
[g]Advent
[h]Christmas

1969

GREGORIAN 1969	Sun Mon Tue Wed Thu Fri Sat	Lunar Phases	ISO WEEK (Mon)	JULIAN DAY (Sun noon)	HEBREW 5729/5730‡	Sun Mon Tue Wed Thu Fri Sat	Molad	CHINESE Wù-Shēn‡/Jĭ-Yŏu	Sun Mon Tue Wed Thu Fri Sat	Solar Term	COPTIC 1685/1686	Sun Mon Tue Wed Thu Fri Sat	ETHIOPIC 1961/1962
JANUARY 1969	29 30 31 1[a] 2 ○ 4	18:27	1	2440220	TEVETH 5729	8 9 10 11 12 13 14		MONTH 11* Wù-Shēn	10 11 12 13 14 15 16		KOIAK 1685	20 21 22 23 24 25 26	TĀKHŚĀŚ 1961
	5 6 7 8 9 10 ◑	14:00	2	2440227		15 16 17 18 19 20 21			17 18 19 20 21 22 23	Xiǎo hán		27 28 29[c] 30 1 2 3	
	12 13 14 15 16 17 ●	4:59	3	2440234		22 23 24 25 26 27 28		MONTH 12 Wù-Shēn	24 25 26 27 28 29 1		TÔBE 1685	4 5 6[d] 7 8 9 10	ṬER 1961
	19 20 21 22 23 24 ◐	8:23	4	2440241	SHEVAT 5729	29 1 2 3 4 5 6	Sat 13h27m8p		2 3 4 5 6 7 8	Dà hán		11[e] 12 13 14 15 16 17	
	26 27 28 29 30 31 1		5	2440248		7 8 9 10 11 12 13			9 10 11 12 13 14 15			18 19 20 21 22 23 24	
FEBRUARY 1969	○ 3 4 5 6 7 8	12:56	6	2440255		14 15 16 17 18 19 20			16 17 18 19 20 21 22	Lì chūn	MESHIR 1685	25 26 27 28 29 30 1	YAKĀTIT 1961
	9 ◑ 11 12 13 14 15	0:08	7	2440262		21 22 23 24 25 26 27			23 24 25 26 27 28 29			2 3 4 5 6 7 8	
	● 17 18 19 20 21 22	16:25	8	2440269	ADAR 5729	28 29 30 1 2 3 4	Mon 2h11m9p	MONTH 1 Jĭ-Yŏu	30 1[a] 2* 3 4 5 6	Yǔ shuǐ		9 10 11 12 13 14 15	
	23 ◐ 25 26 27 28 1	4:30	9	2440276		5 6 7 8 9 10 11			7 8 9 10 11 12 13			16 17 18 19 20 21 22	
MARCH 1969	2 3 ○ 5 6 7 8	5:17	10	2440283		12 13 14[f] 15 16 17 18			14 15[b] 16 17 18 19 20	Jīng zhé		23 24 25 26 27 28 29	
	9 10 ◑ 12 13 14 15	7:44	11	2440290		19 20 21 22 23 24 25			21 22 23 24 25 26 27		PAREMOTEP 1685	30 1 2 3 4 5 6	MAGĀBIT 1961
	16 17 ● 19 20[b] 21 22	4:51	12	2440297	NISAN 5729	26 27 28 29 1 2 3	Tue 14h55m10p	MONTH 2 Jĭ-Yŏu	28 29 1 2 3 4 5	Chūn fēn		7 8 9 10 11 12 13	
	23 24 25 ◐ 27 28 29	0:48	13	2440304		4 5 6 7 8 9 10			6 7 8 9 10 11 12			14 15 16 17 18 19 20	
	30 31 1 ○ 3 4 5	18:45	14	2440311		11 12 13 14 15[g] 16 17			13 14 15 16 17 18 19[c]	Qīng míng		21 22 23 24 25 26 27	
APRIL 1969	6 7 8 ◑ 10 11 12	13:58	15	2440318		18 19 20 21 22 23 24			20 21 22 23 24 25 26		PARMOUTE 1685	28 29 30 1 2 3 4	MIYĀZYĀ 1961
	13 14 15 ● 17 18 19	18:16	16	2440325	IYYAR 5729	25 26 27 28 29 30 1	Thu 3h39m11p	MONTH 3 Jĭ-Yŏu	27 28 29 30 1 2 3*			5[f] 6 7 8 9 10 11	
	20 21 22 23 ◐ 25 26	19:44	17	2440332		2 3 4 5 6 7 8			4 5 6 7 8 9 10	Gǔ yǔ		12 13 14 15 16 17 18	
	27 28 29 30 1 ○ 3	5:13	18	2440339		9 10 11 12 13 14 15			11 12 13 14 15 16 17			19 20 21 22 23 24 25	
MAY 1969	4 5 6 7 ◑ 9 10	20:12	19	2440346		16 17 18 19 20 21 22			18 19 20 21 22 23 24	Lì xià	PASHONS 1685	26 27 28 29[g] 30 1 2	GENBOT 1961
	11 12 13 14 15 ● 17	8:26	20	2440353		23 24 25 26 27 28 29		MONTH 4 Jĭ-Yŏu	25 26 27 28 29 1 2			3 4 5 6 7 8 9	
	18 19 20 21 22 23 ◐	12:15	21	2440360	SIVAN 5729	1 2 3 4 5 6[h] 7	Fri 16h23m12p		3 4 5 6 7 8 9	Xiǎo mǎn		10 11 12 13 14 15 16	
	25 26 27 28 29 30 ○	13:18	22	2440367		8 9 10 11 12 13 14			10 11 12 13 14 15 16			17 18 19 20 21 22 23	
JUNE 1969	1 2 3 4 5 6 ◑	3:39	23	2440374		15 16 17 18 19 20 21			17 18 19 20 21 22 23	Máng zhòng		24 25 26 27 28 29 30	
	8 9 10 11 12 13 ●	23:C9	24	2440381		22 23 24 25 26 27 28			24 25 26 27 28 29 30		PAÔNE 1685	1 2 3 4 5 6 7	SANĒ 1961
	15 16 17 18 19 20 21[c]		25	2440388	TAMMUZ 5729	29 30 1 2 3 4 5	Sun 5h7m13p	MONTH 5 Jĭ-Yŏu	1 2 3 4* 5[d] 6 7	Xià zhì		8 9 10 11 12 13 14	
	22 ◐ 24 25 26 27 28	1:44	26	2440395		6 7 8 9 10 11 12			8 9 10 11 12 13 14			15 16 17 18 19 20 21	
	○ 30 1 2 3 4 5	20:04	27	2440402		13 14 15 16 17 18 19			15 16 17 18 19 20 21			22 23 24 25 26 27 28	
JULY 1969	◑ 7 8 9 10 11 12	13:17	28	2440409		20 21 22 23 24 25 26			22 23 24 25 26 27 28	Xiǎo shǔ	EPÊP 1685	29 30 1 2 3 4 5	ḤAMLĒ 1961
	13 ● 15 16 17 18 19	14:11	29	2440416	AV 5729	27 28 29 1 2 3 4	Mon 17h51m14p	MONTH 6 Jĭ-Yŏu	29 1 2 3 4 5 6			6 7 8 9 10 11 12	
	20 21 ◐ 23 24 25 26	12:10	30	2440423		5 6 7 8 9[i] 10 11			7 8 9 10 11 12 13	Dà shǔ		13 14 15 16 17 18 19	
	27 28 ○ 30 31 1 2	2:45	31	2440430		12 13 14 15 16 17 18			14 15 16 17 18 19 20			20 21 22 23 24 25 26	
AUGUST 1969	3 4 ◑ 6 7 8 9	1:38	32	2440437		19 20 21 22 23 24 25			21 22 23 24 25 26 27	Lì qiū	MESORÊ 1685	27 28 29 30 1 2 3	NAḤASĒ 1961
	10 11 12 ● 14 15 16	5:16	33	2440444	ELUL 5729	26 27 28 29 30 1 2	Wed 6h35m15p	MONTH 7 Jĭ-Yŏu	28 29 30 1 2 3 4			4 5 6 7 8 9 10	
	17 18 19 ◐ 21 22 23	20:03	34	2440451		3 4 5 6 7 8 9			5* 6 7[e] 8 9 10 11	Chǔ shǔ		11 12 13[h] 14 15 16 17	
	24 25 26 ○ 28 29 30	10:32	35	2440458		10 11 12 13 14 15 16			12 13 14 15[f] 16 17 18			18 19 20 21 22 23 24	
SEPTEMBER 1969	31 1 2 ◑ 4 5 6	16:58	36	2440465		17 18 19 20 21 22 23			19 20 21 22 23 24 25		EPAG. 1685	25 26 27 28 29 30 1	PĀG. 1961
	7 8 9 10 ● 12 13	19:56	37	2440472	TISHRI 5730	24 25 26 27 28 29 1[a]	Thu 19h19m16p	MONTH 8 Jĭ-Yŏu	26 27 28 29 30 1 2	Bái lù	THOOUT 1686	2 3 4 5 1[a] 2 3	MASKARAM 1962
	14 15 16 17 18 ◐ 20	2:24	38	2440479		2[a] 3 4 5 6 7 8			3 4 5 6 7 8 9			4 5 6 7 8 9 10	
	21 22 23[d] 24 ○ 26 27	20:21	39	2440486		9 10[b] 11 12 13 14 15[c]			10 11 12 13 14 15[g] 16	Qiū fēn		11 12 13 14 15 16 17[b]	
OCTOBER 1969	28 29 30 1 2 ◑ 4	11:05	40	2440493		16 17 18 19 20 21 22			17 18 19 20 21 22 23			18 19 20 21 22 23 24	
	5 6 7 8 9 10 ●	9:39	41	2440500		23 24 25 26 27 28 29		MONTH 9 Jĭ-Yŏu	24 25 26 27 28 29 1	Hán lù	PAOPE 1686	25 26 27 28 29 30 1	ṬEQEMT 1962
	12 13 14 15 16 17 ◐	8:32	42	2440507	HESHVAN 5730	30 1 2 3 4 5 6	Sat 8h3m17p		2 3 4 5 6* 7 8			2 3 4 5 6 7 8	
	19 20 21 22 23 24 ○	8:44	43	2440514		7 8 9 10 11 12 13			9[h] 10 11 12 13 14 15	Shuāng jiàng		9 10 11 12 13 14 15	
	26 27 28 29 30 31 1		44	2440521		14 15 16 17 18 19 20			16 17 18 19 20 21 22			16 17 18 19 20 21 22	
NOVEMBER 1969	◑ 3 4 5 6 7 8	7:14	45	2440528		21 22 23 24 25 26 27			23 24 25 26 27 28 29	Lì dōng		23 24 25 26 27 28 29	
	● 10 11 12 13 14 15	22:11	46	2440535	KISLEV 5730	28 29 1 2 3 4 5	Sun 20h48m0p	MONTH 10 Jĭ-Yŏu	30 1 2 3 4 5 6		ATHÔR 1686	30 1 2 3 4 5 6	ḪEDĀR 1962
	◐ 17 18 19 20 21 22	15:45	47	2440542		6 7 8 9 10 11 12			7 8 9 10 11 12 13	Xiǎo xuě		7 8 9 10 11 12 13	
	○ 24 25 26 27 28 29	23:54	48	2440549		13 14 15 16 17 18 19			14 15 16 17 18 19 20			14 15 16 17 18 19 20	
DECEMBER 1969	30 1 ◑ 3 4 5 6	3:50	49	2440556		20 21 22 23 24 25[d,e] 26[e]			21 22 23 24 25 26 27			21 22 23 24 25 26 27	
	7 8 ● 10 11 12 13	9:42	50	2440563	TEVETH 5730	27e 28e 29e 1e 2e 3e 4	Tue 9h32m1p	MONTH 11 Jĭ-Yŏu	28 29 1 2 3 4 5	Dà xuě	KOIAK 1686	28 29 30 1 2 3 4	TĀKHŚĀŚ 1962
	14 15 ◐ 17 18 19 20	1:09	51	2440570		5 6 7 8 9 10 11			6 7* 8 9 10 11 12			5 6 7 8 9 10 11	
	21 22[e] ○ 24 25 26 27	17:35	52	2440577		12 13 14 15 16 17 18			13 14[i] 15 16 17 18 19	Dōng zhì		12 13 14 15 16 17 18	
	28 29 30 ◑ 1 2 3	22:52	1	2440584		19 20 21 22 23 24 25			20 21 22 23 24 25 26			19 20 21 22 23 24 25	

[a]New Year
[b]Spring (19:08)
[c]Summer (13:55)
[d]Autumn (5:07)
[e]Winter (0:43)
● New moon
◐ First quarter moon
○ Full moon
◑ Last quarter moon

‡Leap year
[a]New Year
[b]Yom Kippur
[c]Sukkot
[d]Winter starts
[e]Ḥanukkah
[f]Purim
[g]Passover
[h]Shavuot
[i]Fast of Av

‡Leap year
[a]New Year (4667, Fowl)
[b]Lantern Festival
[c]Qīngmíng
[d]Dragon Festival
[e]Qīqiǎo
[f]Hungry Ghosts
[g]Mid-Autumn Festival
[h]Double-Ninth Festival
[i]Dōngzhì
*Start of 60-name cycle

[a]New Year
[b]Building of the Cross
[c]Christmas
[d]Jesus's Circumcision
[e]Epiphany
[f]Easter
[g]Mary's Announcement
[h]Jesus's Transfiguration

PERSIAN (ASTRONOMICAL) 1347/1348

Month	Sun	Mon	Tue	Wed	Thu	Fri	Sat
DEY 1347	8	9	10	11	12	13	14
	15	16	17	18	19	20	21
	22	23	24	25	26	27	28
BAHMAN 1347	29	30	1	2	3	4	5
	6	7	8	9	10	11	12
	13	14	15	16	17	18	19
	20	21	22	23	24	25	26
ESFAND 1347	27	28	29	30	1	2	3
	4	5	6	7	8	9	10
	11	12	13	14	15	16	17
	18	19	20	21	22	23	24
FARVARDĪN 1348	25	26	27	28	29	1[a]	2
	3	4	5	6	7	8	9
	10	11	12	13[b]	14	15	16
	17	18	19	20	21	22	23
	24	25	26	27	28	29	30
ORDĪBEHEŠT 1348	31	1	2	3	4	5	6
	7	8	9	10	11	12	13
	14	15	16	17	18	19	20
	21	22	23	24	25	26	27
XORDĀD 1348	28	29	30	31	1	2	3
	4	5	6	7	8	9	10
	11	12	13	14	15	16	17
	18	19	20	21	22	23	24
	25	26	27	28	29	30	31
TĪR 1348	1	2	3	4	5	6	7
	8	9	10	11	12	13	14
	15	16	17	18	19	20	21
	22	23	24	25	26	27	28
MORDĀD 1348	29	30	31	1	2	3	4
	5	6	7	8	9	10	11
	12	13	14	15	16	17	18
	19	20	21	22	23	24	25
SHAHRĪVAR 1348	26	27	28	29	30	31	1
	2	3	4	5	6	7	8
	9	10	11	12	13	14	15
	16	17	18	19	20	21	22
	23	24	25	26	27	28	29
MEHR 1348	30	31	1	2	3	4	5
	6	7	8	9	10	11	12
	13	14	15	16	17	18	19
	20	21	22	23	24	25	26
ABĀN 1348	27	28	29	30	1	2	3
	4	5	6	7	8	9	10
	11	12	13	14	15	16	17
	18	19	20	21	22	23	24
ĀZAR 1348	25	26	27	28	29	30	1
	2	3	4	5	6	7	8
	9	10	11	12	13	14	15
	16	17	18	19	20	21	22
	23	24	25	26	27	28	29
DEY 1348	30	1	2	3	4	5	6
	7	8	9	10	11	12	13

[a]New Year
[b]Sizdeh Bedar

HINDU LUNAR 2025/2026‡

Month	Sun	Mon	Tue	Wed	Thu	Fri	Sat
PAUSHA 2025	10	11	12	13	14	15	16
	17	18	19	20	21	22	23
	24	25	26	27	28	29	30
MĀGHA 2025	**1**	3	4	5	6	7	8
	9	10	10	11	12	13	14
	15	16	17	18	19	20	21
	22	23	24	**25**	27	28	29[h]
PHĀLGUNA 2025	30	1	2	3	4	5	6
	7	8	9	10	11	12	12
	13	14	15[i]	16	17	18	**19**
	21	22	23	24	25	26	27
CHAITRA 2026	28	29	30	1[a]	2	3	4
	5	6	7	8	9[b]	10	11
	12	13	14	15	16	17	18
	19	20	21	22	**23**	25	26
VAIŚĀKHA 2026	27	28	29	30	1	2	3
	4	5	6	6	7	8	9
	10	11	12	13	14	15	16
	17	19	20	21	22	23	24
JYAISHTHA 2026	25	26	27	28	29	30	1
	2	3	4	5	6	7	8
	9	10	11	12	13	14	15
	16	17	18	19	**20**	22	23
	24	25	26	27	28	29	30
LEAP ĀSHĀDHA 2026	1	2	2	3	4	5	6
	7	8	9	10	11	12	**13**
	15	16	17	18	19	20	21
	22	23	24	25	26	27	28
ĀSHĀDHA 2026	29	30	1	2	3	4	5
	6	7	8	9	10	11	12
	13	14	15	**16**	18	19	20
	21	22	23	24	25	26	27
ŚRĀVANA 2026	28	28	29	30	1	2	3
	4	5	6	7	8	**9**	11
	12	13	14	15	16	17	18
	19	20	21	22	23[c]	24	25
BHĀDRAPADA 2026	26	27	28	29	30	1	2
	3	4[d]	5	6	7	8	9
	10	11	**12**	14	15	16	17
	18	19	20	21	22	23	24
	24	25	26	27	28	29	30
ĀŚVINA 2026	1	2	3	4	**5**	7	8[e]
	9[e]	10[e]	11	12	13	14	15
	16	17	18	19	20	21	22
	23	24	25	26	27	28	29
KĀRTTIKA 2026	30	1[f]	2	3	4	5	6
	7	8	9	**10**	12	13	14
	15	16	17	18	18	19	20
	21	22	23	24	25	26	27
MĀRGAŚĪRA 2026	28	29	30	1	2	**3**	5
	6	7	8	9	10	11[g]	12
	13	14	15	16	17	18	19
	20	20	21	22	23	24	25

‡Leap year
[a]New Year (Saumya)
[b]Birthday of Rāma
[c]Birthday of Krishna
[d]Ganēśa Chaturthī
[e]Dashara
[f]Diwali
[g]Birthday of Vishnu
[h]Night of Śiva
[i]Holi

HINDU SOLAR 1890/1891

Month	Sun	Mon	Tue	Wed	Thu	Fri	Sat
PAUSHA 1890	15	16	17	18	19	20	21
	22	23	24	25	26	27	28
MĀGHA 1890	29	1[b]	2	3	4	5	6
	7	8	9	10	11	12	13
	14	15	16	17	18	19	20
	21	22	23	24	25	26	27
PHĀLGUNA 1890	28	29	30	1	2	3	4
	5	6	7	8	9	10	11
	12	13	14	15	16	17	18
	19	20	21	22	23	24	25
CHAITRA 1890	26	27	28	29	30	1	2
	3	4	5	6	7	8	9
	10	11	12	13	14	15	16
	17	18	19	20	21	22	23
	24	25	26	27	28	29	30
VAIŚĀKHA 1891	1[a]	2	3	4	5	6	7
	8	9	10	11	12	13	14
	15	16	17	18	19	20	21
	22	23	24	25	26	27	28
JYAISHTHA 1891	29	30	31	1	2	3	4
	5	6	7	8	9	10	11
	12	13	14	15	16	17	18
	19	20	21	22	23	24	25
ĀSHĀDHA 1891	26	27	28	29	30	31	1
	2	3	4	5	6	7	8
	9	10	11	12	13	14	15
	16	17	18	19	20	21	22
	23	24	25	26	27	28	29
ŚRĀVANA 1891	30	31	32	1	2	3	4
	5	6	7	8	9	10	11
	12	13	14	15	16	17	18
	19	20	21	22	23	24	25
BHĀDRAPADA 1891	26	27	28	29	30	31	1
	2	3	4	5	6	7	8
	9	10	11	12	13	14	15
	16	17	18	19	20	21	22
	23	24	25	26	27	28	29
ĀŚVINA 1891	30	31	1	2	3	4	5
	6	7	8	9	10	11	12
	13	14	15	16	17	18	19
	20	21	22	23	24	25	26
KĀRTTIKA 1891	27	28	29	30	31	1	2
	3	4	5	6	7	8	9
	10	11	12	13	14	15	16
	17	18	19	20	21	22	23
	24	25	26	27	28	29	30
MĀRGAŚĪRA 1891	1	2	3	4	5	6	7
	8	9	10	11	12	13	14
	15	16	17	18	19	20	21
	22	23	24	25	26	27	28
PAUSHA 1891	29	1	2	3	4	5	6
	7	8	9	10	11	12	13
	14	15	16	17	18	19	20

[a]New Year (Dundubhi)
[b]Pongal

ISLAMIC (ASTRONOMICAL) 1388/1389‡

Month	Sun	Mon	Tue	Wed	Thu	Fri	Sat
SHAWWĀL 1388	9	10	11	12	13	14	15
	16	17	18	19	20	21	22
	23	24	25	26	27	28	29
DHU AL-QA'DA 1388	1	2	3	4	5	6	7
	8	9	10	11	12	13	14
	15	16	17	18	19	20	21
	22	23	24	25	26	27	28
DHU AL-ḤIJJA 1388	29	30	1	2	3	4	5
	6	7	8	9	10[g]	11	12
	13	14	15	16	17	18	19
	20	21	22	23	24	25	26
MUḤARRAM 1389	27	28	29	1[a]	2[d]	3	4
	5	6	7	8	9	10[b]	11
	12	13	14	15	16	17	18
	19	20	21	22	23	24	25
ṢAFAR 1389	26	27	28	29	30	1	2
	3	4	5	6	7	8	9
	10	11	12	13	14	15	16
	17	18	19	20	21	22	23
	24	25	26	27	28	29	30
RABĪ' I 1389	1	2	3	4	5	6	7
	8	9	10	11	12[c]	13	14
	15	16	17	18	19	20	21
	22	23	24	25	26	27	28
RABĪ' II 1389	29	1	2	3	4	5	6
	7	8	9	10	11	12	13
	14	15	16	17	18	19	20
	21	22	23	24	25	26	27
JUMĀDĀ I 1389	28	29	30	1	2	3	4
	5	6	7	8	9	10	11
	12	13	14	15	16	17	18
	19	20	21	22	23	24	25
JUMĀDĀ II 1389	26	27	28	29	30	1	2
	3	4	5	6	7	8	9
	10	11	12	13	14	15	16
	17	18	19	20	21	22	23
	24	25	26	27	28	29	30
RAJAB 1389	1	2	3	4	5	6	7
	8	9	10	11	12	13	14
	15	16	17	18	19	20	21
	22	23	24	25	26	27[d]	28
SHA'BĀN 1389	29	30	1	2	3	4	5
	6	7	8	9	10	11	12
	13	14	15	16	17	18	19
	20	21	22	23	24	25	26
RAMAḌĀN 1389	27	28	29	1[e]	2	3	4
	5	6	7	8	9	10	11
	12	13	14	15	16	17	18
	19	20	21	22	23	24	25
SHAWWĀL 1389	26	27	28	29	1[f]	2	3
	4	5	6	7	8	9	10
	11	12	13	14	15	16	17
	18	19	20	21	22	23	24

‡Leap year
[a]New Year
[d]New Year (Arithmetic)
[b]'Ashūrā'
[c]Prophet's Birthday
[d]Ascent of the Prophet
[e]Start of Ramaḍān
[f]'Id al-Fiṭr
[g]'Id al-'Aḍḥā

GREGORIAN 1969

Julian (Sun)	Month	Sun	Mon	Tue	Wed	Thu	Fri	Sat
Dec 16	JANUARY 1969	29	30	31	1	2	3	4
		5	6	7[a]	8	9	10	11
Dec 30		12	13	14[b]	15	16	17	18
		19	20	21	22	23	24	25
Jan 13	FEBRUARY 1969	26	27	28	29	30	31	1
		2	3	4	5	6	7	8
Jan 27		9	10	11	12	13	14	15
		16	17	18	19[c]	20	21	22
Feb 10	MARCH 1969	23	24	25	26	27	28	1
		2[d]	3	4	5	6	7	8
Feb 24		9	10	11	12	13	14	15
		16	17	18	19	20	21	22
Mar 10		23	24	25	26	27	28	29
	APRIL 1969	30	31	1	2	3	4	5
Mar 24		6[e]	7	8	9	10	11	12
		13[f]	14	15	16	17	18	19
Apr 7		20	21	22	23	24	25	26
	MAY 1969	27	28	29	30	1	2	3
Apr 21		4	5	6	7	8	9	10
		11	12	13	14	15	16	17
May 5		18	19	20	21	22	23	24
		25	26	27	28	29	30	31
May 19	JUNE 1969	1	2	3	4	5	6	7
		8	9	10	11	12	13	14
Jun 2		15	16	17	18	19	20	21
		22	23	24	25	26	27	28
Jun 16	JULY 1969	29	30	1	2	3	4	5
		6	7	8	9	10	11	12
Jun 30		13	14	15	16	17	18	19
		20	21	22	23	24	25	26
Jul 14	AUGUST 1969	27	28	29	30	31	1	2
		3	4	5	6	7	8	9
Jul 28		10	11	12	13	14	15	16
		17	18	19	20	21	22	23
Aug 11		24	25	26	27	28	29	30
	SEPTEMBER 1969	31	1	2	3	4	5	6
Aug 25		7	8	9	10	11	12	13
		14	15	16	17	18	19	20
Sep 8		21	22	23	24	25	26	27
	OCTOBER 1969	28	29	30	1	2	3	4
Sep 22		5	6	7	8	9	10	11
		12	13	14	15	16	17	18
Oct 6		19	20	21	22	23	24	25
	NOVEMBER 1969	26	27	28	29	30	31	1
Oct 20		2	3	4	5	6	7	8
		9	10	11	12	13	14	15
Nov 3		16	17	18	19	20	21	22
		23	24	25	26	27	28	29
Nov 17	DECEMBER 1969	30[g]	1	2	3	4	5	6
		7	8	9	10	11	12	13
Dec 1		14	15	16	17	18	19	20
		21	22	23	24	25[h]	26	27
Dec 15		28	29	30	31	1	2	3

[a]Orthodox Christmas
[b]Julian New Year
[c]Ash Wednesday
[d]Feast of Orthodoxy
[e]Easter
[f]Orthodox Easter
[g]Advent
[h]Christmas

1970

	GREGORIAN 1970							Lunar Phases	ISO WEEK	JULIAN DAY		HEBREW 5730‡/5731							Molad		CHINESE Jǐ-Yǒu/Gēng-Xū							Solar Term		COPTIC 1686/1687‡ ETHIOPIC 1962/1963‡							
	Sun	Mon	Tue	Wed	Thu	Fri	Sat		(Mon)	(Sun noon)		Sun	Mon	Tue	Wed	Thu	Fri	Sat			Sun	Mon	Tue	Wed	Thu	Fri	Sat			Sun	Mon	Tue	Wed	Thu	Fri	Sat	
JANUARY 1970	28	29	30	◑	1[a]	2	3	22:52	1	2440584	TEVETH 5730	19	20	21	22	23	24	25		MONTH 11 Jǐ-Yǒu	20	21	22	23	24	25	26		KOIAK 1686	19	20	21	22	23	24	25	TĀKHŚĀŚ 1962
	4	5	6	●	8	9	10	20:36	2	2440591	SHEVAT 5730	26	27	28	29	1	2	3	Wed 22h16m2p	MONTH 12 Jǐ-Yǒu	27	28	29	30	1	2	3	Xiǎo hán	TŌBE 1686	26	27	28	29[c]	30	1	2	ṬER 1962
	11	12	13	◐	15	16	17	13:18	3	2440598		4	5	6	7	8	9	10			4	5	6	7	8	9	10			3	4	5	6[d]	7	8	9	
	18	19	20	21	○	23	24	12:55	4	2440605		11	12	13	14	15	16	17			11	12	13	14	15	16	17	Dà hán		10	11[e]	12	13	14	15	16	
	25	26	27	28	29	◑	31	14:39	5	2440612		18	19	20	21	22	23	24			18	19	20	21	22	23	24			17	18	19	20	21	22	23	
FEBRUARY 1970	1	2	3	4	5	●	7	7:13	6	2440619	ADAR I 5730	25	26	27	28	29	30	1	Fri 11h0m3p	MONTH 1 Gēng-Xū	25	26	27	28	29	1[a]	2	Lì chūn		24	25	26	27	28	29	30	
	8	9	10	11	12	◐	14	4:10	7	2440626		2	3	4	5	6	7	8			3	4	5	6	7	8*	9		MESHIR 1686	1	2	3	4	5	6	7	YAKĀTIT 1962
	15	16	17	18	19	20	○	8:19	8	2440633		9	10	11	12	13	14	15			10	11	12	13	14	15[b]	16	Yǔ shuǐ		8	9	10	11	12	13	14	
	22	23	24	25	26	27	28		9	2440640		16	17	18	19	20	21	22			17	18	19	20	21	22	23			15	16	17	18	19	20	21	
MARCH 1970	◑	2	3	4	5	6	●	2:33 17:43	10	2440647		23	24	25	26	27	28	29	Sat 23h44m4p		24	25	26	27	28	29	30	Jīng zhé		22	23	24	25	26	27	28	
	8	9	10	11	12	13	◐	21:16	11	2440654	ADAR II 5730	30	1	2	3	4	5	6		MONTH 2 Gēng-Xū	1	2	3	4	5	6	7		PAREMOTEP 1686	29	30	1	2	3	4	5	MAGĀBIT 1962
	15	16	17	18	19	20	21[b]		12	2440661		7	8	9	10	11	12	13			8	9	10	11	12	13	14	Chūn fēn		6	7	8	9	10	11	12	
	22	○	24	25	26	27	28	1:52	13	2440668		14[f]	15	16	17	18	19	20			15	16	17	18	19	20	21			13	14	15	16	17	18	19	
APRIL 1970	29	◑	31	1	2	3	4	11:04	14	2440675		21	22	23	24	25	26	27	Mon 12h28m5p		22	23	24	25	26	27	28			20	21	22	23	24	25	26	
	5	●	7	8	9	10	11	4:10	15	2440682	NISAN 5730	28	29	1	2	3	4	5		MONTH 3 Gēng-Xū	29[c]	1	2	3	4	5	6	Qīng míng	PARMOUTE 1686	27	28	29	30	1	2	3	MIYĀZYĀ 1962
	12	◐	14	15	16	17	18	15:44	16	2440689		6	7	8	9	10	11	12			7	8	9*	10	11	12	13			4	5	6	7	8	9	10	
	19	20	○	22	23	24	25	16:21	17	2440696		13	14	15[g]	16	17	18	19			14	15	16	17	18	19	20	Gǔ yǔ		11	12	13	14	15	16	17	
	26	27	◑	29	30	1	2	17:18	18	2440703		20	21	22	23	24	25	26			21	22	23	24	25	26	27			18[f]	19	20	21	22	23	24	
MAY 1970	3	4	●	6	7	8	9	14:51	19	2440710	IYAR 5730	27	28	29	30	1	2	3	Wed 1h12m6p	MONTH 4 Gēng-Xū	28	29	1	2	3	4	5	Lì xià	PASHONS 1686	25	26	27	28	29[g]	30	1	GENBOT 1962
	10	11	12	◐	14	15	16	10:26	20	2440717		4	5	6	7	8	9	10			6	7	8	9	10	11	12			2	3	4	5	6	7	8	
	17	18	19	20	○	22	23	3:38	21	2440724		11	12	13	14	15	16	17			13	14	15	16	17	18	19	Xiǎo mǎn		9	10	11	12	13	14	15	
	24	25	26	◑	28	29	30	22:32	22	2440731		18	19	20	21	22	23	24			20	21	22	23	24	25	26			16	17	18	19	20	21	22	
JUNE 1970	31	1	2	3	●	5	6	2:21	23	2440738	SIVAN 5730	25	26	27	28	29	1	2	Thu 13h56m7p	MONTH 5 Gēng-Xū	27	28	29	30	1	2	3			23	24	25	26	27	28	29	
	7	8	9	10	11	◐	13	4:06	24	2440745		3	4	5	6[h]	7	8	9			4	5[d]	6	7	8	9	10*	Máng zhòng	PAŌNE 1686	30	1	2	3	4	5	6	SANĒ 1962
	14	15	16	17	18	○	20	12:27	25	2440752		10	11	12	13	14	15	16			11	12	13	14	15	16	17			7	8	9	10	11	12	13	
	21[c]	22	23	24	25	◑	27	4:01	26	2440759		17	18	19	20	21	22	23			18	19	20	21	22	23	24	Xià zhì		14	15	16	17	18	19	20	
JULY 1970	28	29	30	1	2	●	4	15:18	27	2440766		24	25	26	27	28	29	30		MONTH 6 Gēng-Xū	25	26	27	28	29	1	2			21	22	23	24	25	26	27	
	5	6	7	8	9	10	◐	19:43	28	2440773	TAMMUZ 5730	1	2	3	4	5	6	7	Sat 2h40m8p		3	4	5	6	7	8	9	Xiǎo shǔ	EPĒP 1686	28	29	30	1	2	3	4	ḤAMLĒ 1962
	12	13	14	15	16	17	○	19:59	29	2440780		8	9	10	11	12	13	14			10	11	12	13	14	15	16			5	6	7	8	9	10	11	
	19	20	21	22	23	24	◑	11:00	30	2440787		15	16	17	18	19	20	21			17	18	19	20	21	22	23	Dà shǔ		12	13	14	15	16	17	18	
AUGUST 1970	26	27	28	29	30	31	1		31	2440794		22	23	24	25	26	27	28			24	25	26	27	28	29	30			19	20	21	22	23	24	25	
	●	3	4	5	6	7	8	5:58	32	2440801	AV 5730	29	1	2	3	4	5	6	Sun 15h24m9p	MONTH 7 Gēng-Xū	1	2	3	4	5	6	7[e]	Lì qiū	MESORĒ 1686	26	27	28	29	30	1	2	NAHASĒ 1962
	9	◐	11	12	13	14	15	8:50	33	2440808		7	8	9[i]	10	11	12	13			8	9	10	11*	12	13	14			3	4	5	6	7	8	9	
	16	○	18	19	20	21	22	3:15	34	2440815		14	15	16	17	18	19	20			15[f]	16	17	18	19	20	21			10	11	12	13[h]	14	15	16	
	◑	24	25	26	27	28	29	20:34	35	2440822		21	22	23	24	25	26	27			22	23	24	25	26	27	28	Chǔ shǔ		17	18	19	20	21	22	23	
SEPTEMBER 1970	30	●	1	2	3	4	5	22:01	36	2440829	ELUL 5730	28	29	30	1	2	3	4	Tue 4h8m10p	MONTH 8 Gēng-Xū	29	30	1	2	3	4	5			24	25	26	27	28	29	30	
	6	7	◐	9	10	11	12	19:38	37	2440836		5	6	7	8	9	10	11			6	7	8	9	10	11	12	Bái lù	EPAG. 1686 / THOOUT 1687	1	2	3	4	5	1[a]	2	PĀG. 1962 / MASKARAM 1963
	13	14	○	16	17	18	19	11:09	38	2440843		12	13	14	15	16	17	18			13	14	15[g]	16	17	18	19			3	4	5	6	7	8	9	
	20	21	◑	23[d]	24	25	26	9:42	39	2440850		19	20	21	22	23	24	25			20	21	22	23	24	25	26	Qiū fēn		10	11	12	13	14	15	16	
OCTOBER 1970	27	28	29	●	1	2	3	14:32	40	2440857	TISHRI 5731	26	27	28	29	1[a]	2[a]	3	Wed 16h52m11p	MONTH 9 Gēng-Xū	27	28	29	1	2	3	4			17[b]	18	19	20	21	22	23	
	4	5	6	7	◐	9	10	4:43	41	2440864		4	5	6	7	8	9	10[b]			5	6	7	8	9[h]	10	11	Hán lù		24	25	26	27	28	29	30	
	11	12	13	○	15	16	17	20:21	42	2440871		11	12	13	14	15[c]	16	17			12*	13	14	15	16	17	18		PAOPE 1687	1	2	3	4	5	6	7	ṬEQEMT 1963
	18	19	20	21	◑	23	24	2:47	43	2440878		18	19	20	21	22	23	24			19	20	21	22	23	24	25	Shuāng jiàng		8	9	10	11	12	13	14	
	25	26	27	28	29	●	31	6:28	44	2440885	ḤESHVAN 5731	25	26	27	28	29	30	1	Fri 5h36m12p	MONTH 10 Gēng-Xū	26	27	28	29	30	1	2			15	16	17	18	19	20	21	
NOVEMBER 1970	1	2	3	4	5	◐	7	12:47	45	2440892		2	3	4	5	6	7	8			3	4	5	6	7	8	9	Lì dōng		22	23	24	25	26	27	28	
	8	9	10	11	12	○	14	7:28	46	2440899		9	10	11	12	13	14	15			10	11	12	13	14	15	16		ATHŌR 1687	29	30	1	2	3	4	5	ḤEDĀR 1963
	15	16	17	18	19	◑	21	23:13	47	2440906		16	17	18	19	20	21	22			17	18	19	20	21	22	23			6	7	8	9	10	11	12	
	22	23	24	25	26	27	●	21:14	48	2440913		23	24	25	26	27	28	29			24	25	26	27	28	29	30	Xiǎo xuě		13	14	15	16	17	18	19	
DECEMBER 1970	29	30	1	2	3	4	◐	20:36	49	2440920	KISLEV 5731	1	2	3	4	5	6	7[d]	Sat 18h20m13p	MONTH 11 Gēng-Xū	1	2	3	4	5	6	7			20	21	22	23	24	25	26	
	6	7	8	9	10	11	○	21:03	50	2440927		8	9	10	11	12	13	14			8	9	10	11	12*	13	14	Dà xuě	KOIAK 1687	27	28	29	30	1	2	3	TĀKHŚĀŚ 1963
	13	14	15	16	17	18	19		51	2440934		15	16	17	18	19	20	21			15	16	17	18	19	20	21			4	5	6	7	8	9	10	
	◑	21	22[e]	23	24	25	26	21:09	52	2440941		22	23	24	25[e]	26[e]	27[e]	28[e]	Mon 7h4m14p		22	23	24[i]	25	26	27	28	Dōng zhì		11	12	13	14	15	16	17	
	27	●	29	30	31	1	2	10:43	53	2440948		29[e]	30[e]	1[e]	2[e]	3	4	5			29	1	2	3	4	5	6			18	19	20	21	22	23	24	

[a]New Year
[b]Spring (0:56)
[c]Summer (19:43)
[d]Autumn (10:59)
[e]Winter (6:35)
● New moon
◐ First quarter moon
○ Full moon
◑ Last quarter moon

‡Leap year
[a]New Year
[b]Yom Kippur
[c]Sukkot
[d]Winter starts
[e]Ḥanukkah
[f]Purim
[g]Passover
[h]Shavuot
[i]Fast of Av

[a]New Year (4668, Dog)
[b]Lantern Festival
[c]Qīngmíng
[d]Dragon Festival
[e]Qīqiǎo
[f]Hungry Ghosts
[g]Mid-Autumn Festival
[h]Double-Ninth Festival
[i]Dōngzhì
*Start of 60-name cycle

‡Leap year
[a]New Year
[b]Building of the Cross
[c]Christmas
[d]Jesus's Circumcision
[e]Epiphany
[f]Easter
[g]Mary's Announcement
[h]Jesus's Transfiguration

PERSIAN (ASTRONOMICAL) 1348/1349

Month	Sun	Mon	Tue	Wed	Thu	Fri	Sat
DEY 1348	7	8	9	10	11	12	13
	14	15	16	17	18	19	20
	21	22	23	24	25	26	27
BAHMAN 1348	28	29	30	1	2	3	4
	5	6	7	8	9	10	11
	12	13	14	15	16	17	18
	19	20	21	22	23	24	25
ESFAND 1348	26	27	28	29	30	1	2
	3	4	5	6	7	8	9
	10	11	12	13	14	15	16
	17	18	19	20	21	22	23
FARVARDĪN 1349	24	25	26	27	28	29	1[a]
	2	3	4	5	6	7	8
	9	10	11	12	13[b]	14	15
	16	17	18	19	20	21	22
	23	24	25	26	27	28	29
ORDĪBEHEŠT 1349	30	31	1	2	3	4	5
	6	7	8	9	10	11	12
	13	14	15	16	17	18	19
	20	21	22	23	24	25	26
XORDĀD 1349	27	28	29	30	31	1	2
	3	4	5	6	7	8	9
	10	11	12	13	14	15	16
	17	18	19	20	21	22	23
	24	25	26	27	28	29	30
TĪR 1349	31	1	2	3	4	5	6
	7	8	9	10	11	12	13
	14	15	16	17	18	19	20
	21	22	23	24	25	26	27
MORDĀD 1349	28	29	30	31	1	2	3
	4	5	6	7	8	9	10
	11	12	13	14	15	16	17
	18	19	20	21	22	23	24
	25	26	27	28	29	30	31
SHAHRĪVAR 1349	1	2	3	4	5	6	7
	8	9	10	11	12	13	14
	15	16	17	18	19	20	21
	22	23	24	25	26	27	28
MEHR 1349	29	30	31	1	2	3	4
	5	6	7	8	9	10	11
	12	13	14	15	16	17	18
	19	20	21	22	23	24	25
ĀBĀN 1349	26	27	28	29	30	1	2
	3	4	5	6	7	8	9
	10	11	12	13	14	15	16
	17	18	19	20	21	22	23
	24	25	26	27	28	29	30
ĀZAR 1349	1	2	3	4	5	6	7
	8	9	10	11	12	13	14
	15	16	17	18	19	20	21
	22	23	24	25	26	27	28
DEY 1349	29	30	1	2	3	4	5
	6	7	8	9	10	11	12

[a]New Year
[b]Sizdeh Bedar

HINDU LUNAR 2026‡/2027

Month	Sun	Mon	Tue	Wed	Thu	Fri	Sat
MĀRGAŚĪRA 2026	20	20	21	22	23	24	25
PAUSHA 2026	26	**27**	29	30	1	2	3
	4	5	6	7	8	9	10
	11	12	13	14	15	16	17
	18	19	20	21	22	23	24
MĀGHA 2026	25	26	27	28	29	30	1
	2	4	5	6	7	8	9
	10	11	12	12	13	14	15
	16	17	18	19	20	21	22
	23	24	25	**26**	28	29[h]	30
PHĀLGUNA 2026	1	2	3	4	5	6	7
	8	9	10	11	12	13	14
	15	15[i]	16	17	18	**19**	21
	22	23	24	25	26	27	28
CHAITRA 2027	29	30	1[a]	2	3	4	5
	6	7	8[b]	9	10	11	12
	13	14	15	16	17	18	19
	20	21	22	23	**24**	26	27
VAIŚĀKHA 2027	28	29	30	1	2	3	4
	5	6	7	8	9	10	10
	11	12	13	14	15	16	**17**
	19	20	21	22	23	24	25
JYAISHTHA 2027	26	27	28	29	30	1	2
	3	4	5	6	7	8	9
	10	11	12	13	14	15	16
	17	18	19	**20**	22	23	24
ĀSHĀḌHA 2027	25	26	27	28	29	30	1
	2	3	4	5	6	6	7
	8	9	10	11	**12**	14	15
	16	17	18	19	20	21	22
	23	24	25	26	27	28	29
ŚRĀVAṆA 2027	30	1	2	3	4	5	6
	7	8	9	10	11	12	13
	14	15	**16**	18	19	20	21
	22	23[c]	24	25	26	27	28
BHĀDRAPADA 2027	29	30	1	2	3	3[d]	4
	5	6	7	**8**	10	11	12
	13	14	15	16	17	18	19
	20	21	22	23	24	25	26
ĀŚVINA 2027	27	28	29	30	1	2	3
	4	5	6	7	8[e]	9[e]	10[e]
	11	**12**	14	15	16	17	18
	19	20	21	22	23	24	25
KĀRTTIKA 2027	26	27	27	28	29	30	1[f]
	2	3	4	5	**6**	8	9
	10	11	12	13	14	15	16
	17	18	19	20	21	22	23
	24	25	26	27	28	29	30
MĀRGAŚĪRA 2027	1	2	3	4	5	6	7
	8	9	**10**[g]	12	13	14	15
	16	17	18	19	20	21	21
	22	23	24	25	26	27	28
PAUSHA 2027	29	30	1	2	3	**4**	6

‡Leap year
[a]New Year (Sādhāraṇa)
[b]Birthday of Rāma
[c]Birthday of Krishna
[d]Ganēśa Chaturthī
[e]Dashara
[f]Diwali
[g]Birthday of Vishnu
[h]Night of Śiva
[i]Holi

HINDU SOLAR 1891/1892

Month	Sun	Mon	Tue	Wed	Thu	Fri	Sat
PAUSHA 1891	14	15	16	17	18	19	20
	21	22	23	24	25	26	27
MĀGHA 1891	28	29	30	1[b]	2	3	4
	5	6	7	8	9	10	11
	12	13	14	15	16	17	18
	19	20	21	22	23	24	25
PHĀLGUNA 1891	26	27	28	29	1	2	3
	4	5	6	7	8	9	10
	11	12	13	14	15	16	17
	18	19	20	21	22	23	24
CHAITRA 1891	25	26	27	28	29	30	1
	2	3	4	5	6	7	8
	9	10	11	12	13	14	15
	16	17	18	19	20	21	22
	23	24	25	26	27	28	29
VAIŚĀKHA 1892	30	1[a]	2	3	4	5	6
	7	8	9	10	11	12	13
	14	15	16	17	18	19	20
	21	22	23	24	25	26	27
JYAISHTHA 1892	28	29	30	31	1	2	3
	4	5	6	7	8	9	10
	11	12	13	14	15	16	17
	18	19	20	21	22	23	24
	25	26	27	28	29	30	31
ĀSHĀḌHA 1892	32	1	2	3	4	5	6
	7	8	9	10	11	12	13
	14	15	16	17	18	19	20
	21	22	23	24	25	26	27
ŚRĀVAṆA 1892	28	29	30	31	1	2	3
	4	5	6	7	8	9	10
	11	12	13	14	15	16	17
	18	19	20	21	22	23	24
	25	26	27	28	29	30	31
BHĀDRAPADA 1892	32	1	2	3	4	5	6
	7	8	9	10	11	12	13
	14	15	16	17	18	19	20
	21	22	23	24	25	26	27
ĀŚVINA 1892	28	29	30	31	1	2	3
	4	5	6	7	8	9	10
	11	12	13	14	15	16	17
	18	19	20	21	22	23	24
KĀRTTIKA 1892	25	26	27	28	29	30	1
	2	3	4	5	6	7	8
	9	10	11	12	13	14	15
	16	17	18	19	20	21	22
	23	24	25	26	27	28	29
MĀRGAŚĪRA 1892	30	1	2	3	4	5	6
	7	8	9	10	11	12	13
	14	15	16	17	18	19	20
	21	22	23	24	25	26	27
PAUSHA 1892	28	29	30	1	2	3	4
	5	6	7	8	9	10	11
	12	13	14	15	16	17	18

[a]New Year (Rudhirodgārin)
[b]Pongal

ISLAMIC (ASTRONOMICAL) 1389‡/1390‡

Month	Sun	Mon	Tue	Wed	Thu	Fri	Sat
SHAWWĀL 1389	18	19	20	21	22	23	24
DHU AL-QA'DAH 1389	25	26	27	28	29	1	2
	3	4	5	6	7	8	9
	10	11	12	13	14	15	16
	17	18	19	20	21	22	23
DHU AL-ḤIJJA 1389	24	25	26	27	28	29	1
	2	3	4	5	6	7	8
	9	10[g]	11	12	13	14	15
	16	17	18	19	20	21	22
	23	24	25	26	27	28	29
MUḤARRAM 1390	30	1[a]	2	3	4	5	6
	7	8	9	10[b]	11	12	13
	14	15	16	17	18	19	20
	21	22	23	24	25	26	27
ṢAFAR 1390	28	29	1	2	3	4	5
	6	7	8	9	10	11	12
	13	14	15	16	17	18	19
	20	21	22	23	24	25	26
RABĪ' I 1390	27	28	29	30	1	2	3
	4	5	6	7	8	9	10
	11	12[c]	13	14	15	16	17
	18	19	20	21	22	23	24
RABĪ' II 1390	25	26	27	28	29	1	2
	3	4	5	6	7	8	9
	10	11	12	13	14	15	16
	17	18	19	20	21	22	23
	24	25	26	27	28	29	30
JUMĀDĀ I 1390	1	2	3	4	5	6	7
	8	9	10	11	12	13	14
	15	16	17	18	19	20	21
	22	23	24	25	26	27	28
JUMĀDĀ II 1390	29	30	1	2	3	4	5
	6	7	8	9	10	11	12
	13	14	15	16	17	18	19
	20	21	22	23	24	25	26
RAJAB 1390	27	28	29	30	1	2	3
	4	5	6	7	8	9	10
	11	12	13	14	15	16	17
	18	19	20	21	22	23	24
SHA'BĀN 1390	25	26	27[d]	28	29	30	1
	2	3	4	5	6	7	8
	9	10	11	12	13	14	15
	16	17	18	19	20	21	22
	23	24	25	26	27	28	29
RAMAḌĀN 1390	1[e]	2	3	4	5	6	7
	8	9	10	11	12	13	14
	15	16	17	18	19	20	21
	22	23	24	25	26	27	28
SHAWWĀL 1390	29	30	1[f]	2	3	4	5
	6	7	8	9	10	11	12
	13	14	15	16	17	18	19
	20	21	22	23	24	25	26
DHU AL-QA'DAH 1390	27	28	29	1	2	3	4

‡Leap year
[a]New Year
[b]'Ashūrā'
[c]Prophet's Birthday
[d]Ascent of the Prophet
[e]Start of Ramaḍān
[f]'Īd al-Fiṭr
[g]'Īd al-'Aḍḥā

GREGORIAN 1970

Julian (Sun)	Month	Sun	Mon	Tue	Wed	Thu	Fri	Sat
Dec 15		28	29	30	31	1	2	3
	JANUARY 1970	4	5	6	7[a]	8	9	10
Dec 29		11	12	13	14[b]	15	16	17
		18	19	20	21	22	23	24
Jan 12		25	26	27	28	29	30	31
	FEBRUARY 1970	1	2	3	4	5	6	7
Jan 26		8	9	10	11[c]	12	13	14
		15	16	17	18	19	20	21
Feb 9		22	23	24	25	26	27	28
	MARCH 1970	1	2	3	4	5	6	7
Feb 23		8	9	10	11	12	13	14
		15[d]	16	17	18	19	20	21
Mar 9		22	23	24	25	26	27	28
		29[e]	30	31	1	2	3	4
Mar 23	APRIL 1970	5	6	7	8	9	10	11
		12	13	14	15	16	17	18
Apr 6		19	20	21	22	23	24	25
		26[f]	27	28	29	30	1	2
Apr 20	MAY 1970	3	4	5	6	7	8	9
		10	11	12	13	14	15	16
May 4		17	18	19	20	21	22	23
		24	25	26	27	28	29	30
May 18		31	1	2	3	4	5	6
	JUNE 1970	7	8	9	10	11	12	13
Jun 1		14	15	16	17	18	19	20
		21	22	23	24	25	26	27
Jun 15		28	29	30	1	2	3	4
	JULY 1970	5	6	7	8	9	10	11
Jun 29		12	13	14	15	16	17	18
		19	20	21	22	23	24	25
Jul 13		26	27	28	29	30	31	1
	AUGUST 1970	2	3	4	5	6	7	8
Jul 27		9	10	11	12	13	14	15
		16	17	18	19	20	21	22
Aug 10		23	24	25	26	27	28	29
		30	31	1	2	3	4	5
Aug 24	SEPTEMBER 1970	6	7	8	9	10	11	12
		13	14	15	16	17	18	19
Sep 7		20	21	22	23	24	25	26
		27	28	29	30	1	2	3
Sep 21	OCTOBER 1970	4	5	6	7	8	9	10
		11	12	13	14	15	16	17
Oct 5		18	19	20	21	22	23	24
		25	26	27	28	29	30	31
Oct 19	NOVEMBER 1970	1	2	3	4	5	6	7
		8	9	10	11	12	13	14
Nov 2		15	16	17	18	19	20	21
		22	23	24	25	26	27	28
Nov 16		29[g]	30	1	2	3	4	5
	DECEMBER 1970	6	7	8	9	10	11	12
Nov 30		13	14	15	16	17	18	19
		20	21	22	23	24	25[h]	26
Dec 14		27	28	29	30	31	1	2

[a]Orthodox Christmas
[b]Julian New Year
[c]Ash Wednesday
[d]Feast of Orthodoxy
[e]Easter
[f]Orthodox Easter
[g]Advent
[h]Christmas

1971

GREGORIAN 1971	Sun Mon Tue Wed Thu Fri Sat	Lunar Phases	ISO WEEK (Mon)	JULIAN DAY (Sun noon)	HEBREW 5731/5732	Sun Mon Tue Wed Thu Fri Sat	Molad	CHINESE Gēng-Xū/Xīn-Hài‡	Sun Mon Tue Wed Thu Fri Sat	Solar Term	COPTIC 1687‡/1688	Sun Mon Tue Wed Thu Fri Sat	ETHIOPIC 1963‡/1964
JANUARY 1971	27 ● 29 30 31 1[a] 2	10:43	53	2440948	TEVETH 5731	29[e] 30[e] 1[e] 2[e] 3 4 5	Mon 7h14m14p	MONTH 12 Gēng-Xū	29 1 2 3 4 5 6		KOIAK 1687	18 19 20 21 22 23 24	TĀKHŚĀŚ 1963
	3 ◐ 5 6 7 8 9	4:55	1	2440955		6 7 8 9 10 11 12			7 8 9 10 11 12 13	Xiǎo hán	TŌBE 1687	25 26 27 28 29[c] 30 1	ṬER 1963
	10 ○ 12 13 14 15 16	13:20	2	2440962		13 14 15 16 17 18 19			14 15 16 17 18 19 20			2 3 4 5 6[d] 7 8	
	17 18 ◑ 20 21 22 23	18:08	3	2440969		20 21 22 23 24 25 26			21 22 23 24 **25** 26 27	Dà hán		9 10 11[e] 12 13 14 15	
	24 25 ● 27 28 29 30	22:55	4	2440976	SHEVAT 5731	27 28 29 1 2 3 4	Tue 19h48m15p	MONTH 1 Xīn-Hài	28 29 30 1[a] 2 3 4			16 17 18 19 20 21 22	
FEBRUARY 1971	31 1 ◐ 3 4 5 6	14:31	5	2440983		5 6 7 8 9 10 11			5 6 7 8 9 10 11	Lì chūn		23 24 25 26 27 28 29	
	7 8 9 ○ 11 12 13	7:41	6	2440990		12 13 14 15 16 17 18			12 13* 14 15[b] 16 17 18		MESHIR 1687	30 1 2 3 4 5 6	YAKĀTIT 1963
	14 15 16 17 ◑ 19 20	12:13	7	2440997		19 20 21 22 23 24 25			19 20 21 22 23 **24** 25	Yǔ shuǐ		7 8 9 10 11 12 13	
	21 22 23 24 ● 26 27	9:48	8	2441004	ADAR 5731	26 27 28 29 30 1 2	Thu 8h32m16p	MONTH 2 Xīn-Hài	26 27 28 29 1 2 3			14 15 16 17 18 19 20	
MARCH 1971	28 1 2 3 ◐ 5 6	2:01	9	2441011		3 4 5 6 7 8 9			4 5 6 7 8 9 *10*	Jīng zhé		21 22 23 24 25 26 27	
	7 8 9 10 11 ○ 13	2:34	10	2441018		10 11 12 13 14[f] 15 16			11 12 13 14 15 16 17		PAREMOTEP 1687	28 29 30 1 2 3 4	MAGĀBIT 1963
	14 15 16 17 18 19 ◑	2:30	11	2441025		17 18 19 20 21 22 23			18 19 20 21 22 23 24			5 6 7 8 9 10 11	
	21[b] 22 23 24 25 ● 27	19:23	12	2441032	NISAN 5731	24 25 26 27 28 29 1	Fri 21h16m17p	MONTH 3 Xīn-Hài	*25* 26 27 28 29 30 1	Chūn fēn		12 13 14 15 16 17 18	
APRIL 1971	28 29 30 31 1 ◐ 3	15:46	13	2441039		2 3 4 5 6 7 8			2 3 4 5 6 7 8			19 20 21 22 23 24 25	
	4 5 6 7 8 9 ○	20:10	14	2441046		9 10 11 12 13 14 15[g]			9 *10*[c] 11 12 13 14* 15	Qīng míng	PARMOUTE 1687	26 27 28 29 30 1 2	MIYĀZYĀ 1963
	11 12 13 14 15 16 17		15	2441053		16 17 18 19 20 21 22			16 17 18 19 20 21 22			3 4 5 6 7 8 9	
	◑ 19 20 21 22 23 24	12:58	16	2441060		23 24 25 26 27 28 29			23 24 25 **26** 27 28 29	Gǔ yǔ		10[f] 11 12 13 14 15 16	
MAY 1971	● 26 27 28 29 30 1	4:02	17	2441067	IYYAR 5731	30 1 2 3 4 5 6	Sun 10h1m0p	MONTH 4 Xīn-Hài	1 2 3 4 5 6 7			17 18 19 20 21 22 23	
	◐ 3 4 5 6 7 8	7:34	18	2441074		7 8 9 10 11 12 13			8 9 10 11 *12* 13 14	Lì xià		24 25 26 27 28 29[g] 30	
	9 ○ 11 12 13 14 15	11:23	19	2441081		14 15 16 17 18 19 20			15 16 17 18 19 20 21		PASHONS 1687	1 2 3 4 5 6 7	GENBOT 1963
	16 ◑ 18 19 20 21 22	20:15	20	2441088		21 22 23 24 25 26 27			22 23 24 25 26 27 **28**			8 9 10 11 12 13 14	
	23 ● 25 26 27 28 29	12:32	21	2441095	SIVAN 5731	28 29 1 2 3 4 5	Mon 22h45m1p	MONTH 5 Xīn-Hài	29 1 2 3 4 5[d] 6	Xiǎo mǎn		15 16 17 18 19 20 21	
JUNE 1971	30 31 ◐ 2 3 4 5	0:42	22	2441102		6[h] 7 8 9 10 11 12			7 8 9 10 11 12 13			22 23 24 25 26 27 28	
	6 7 8 ○ 10 11 12	0:04	23	2441109		13 14 15 16 17 18 19			*14* 15 16* 17 18 19 20	Máng zhòng	PAŌNE 1687	29 30 1 2 3 4 5	SANĒ 1963
	13 14 15 ◑ 17 18 19	1:24	24	2441116		20 21 22 23 24 25 26			21 22 23 24 25 26 27			6 7 8 9 10 11 12	
	20 21 ●[c] 23 24 25 26	21:57	25	2441123	TAMMUZ 5731	27 28 29 30 1 2 3	Wed 11h29m2p	LEAP MONTH 5 Xīn-Hài	28 29 **30** 1 2 3 4	Xià zhì		13 14 15 16 17 18 19	
JULY 1971	27 28 29 ◐ 1 2 3	18:11	26	2441130		4 5 6 7 8 9 10			5 6 7 8 9 10 11			20 21 22 23 24 25 26	
	4 5 6 7 ○ 9 10	10:37	27	2441137		11 12 13 14 15 16 17			12 13 14 15 *16* 17 18	Xiǎo shǔ	EPĒP 1687	27 28 29 30 1 2 3	HAMLĒ 1963
	11 12 13 14 ◑ 16 17	5:47	28	2441144		18 19 20 21 22 23 24			19 20 21 22 23 24 25			4 5 6 7 8 9 10	
	18 19 20 21 ● 23 24	9:15	29	2441151	AV 5731	25 26 27 28 29 1 2	Fri 0h13m3p	MONTH 6 Xīn-Hài	26 27 28 29 1 **2** 3	Dà shǔ		11 12 13 14 15 16 17	
	25 26 27 28 29 ◐ 31	11:07	30	2441158		3 4 5 6 7 8 9			4 5 6 7 8 9 10			18 19 20 21 22 23 24	
AUGUST 1971	1 2 3 4 5 ○ 7	19:42	31	2441165		10[i] 11 12 13 14 15 16			11 12 13 14 15 16 17*		MESORĒ 1687	25 26 27 28 29 30 1	NAḤASĒ 1963
	8 9 10 11 12 ◑ 14	10:55	32	2441172		17 18 19 20 21 22 23			*18* 19 20 21 22 23 24	Lì qiū		2 3 4 5 6 7 8	
	15 16 17 18 19 ● 21	22:53	33	2441179		24 25 26 27 28 29 30		MONTH 7 Xīn-Hài	25 26 27 28 29 30 1			9 10 11 12 13[h] 14 15	
	22 23 24 25 26 27 28		34	2441186	ELUL 5731	1 2 3 4 5 6 7	Sat 12h57m4p		2 3 **4** 5 6 7[e] 8	Chǔ shǔ		16 17 18 19 20 21 22	
SEPTEMBER 1971	◐ 30 31 1 2 3 4	2:56	35	2441193		8 9 10 11 12 13 14			9 10 11 12 13 14 15[f]			23 24 25 26 27 28 29	
	○ 6 7 8 9 10 ◑	4:03 18:23	36	2441200		15 16 17 18 19 20 21			16 17 18 *19* 20 21 22	Bái lù	EPAG. 1687	30 1 2 3 4 5 6	PĀG. 1963
	12 13 14 15 16 17 18		37	2441207		22 23 24 25 26 27 28			23 24 25 26 27 28 29		THOOUT 1688	1[a] 2 3 4 5 6 7	MASKARAM 1964
	● 20 21 22 23[d] 24 25	14:42	38	2441214	TISHRI 5732	29 1[a] 2[a] 3 4 5 6	Mon 1h41m5p	MONTH 8 Xīn-Hài	1 2 3 4 5 **6** 7	Qiū fēn		8 9 10 11 12 13 14	
OCTOBER 1971	26 ◐ 28 29 30 1 2	17:17	39	2441221		7 8 9 10[b] 11 12 13			8 9 10 11 12 13 14			15 16 17[b] 18 19 20 21	
	3 ○ 5 6 7 8 9	12:20	40	2441228		14 15[c] 16 17 18 19 20			15[g] 16 17 18* 19 20 *21*	Hán lù		22 23 24 25 26 27 28	
	10 ◑ 12 13 14 15 16	5:29	41	2441235		21 22 23 24 25 26 27			22 23 24 25 26 27 28		PAOPE 1688	29 30 1 2 3 4 5	ṬEQEMT 1964
	17 18 ● 20 21 22 23	7:59	42	2441242	ḤESHVAN 5732	28 29 30 1 2 3 4	Tue 14h25m6p	MONTH 9 Xīn-Hài	29 30 1 2 3 4 5			6 7 8 9 10 11 12	
	24 25 26 ◐ 28 29 30	5:54	43	2441249		5 6 7 8 9 10 11			**6** 7 8 9[h] 10 11 12	Shuāng jiàng		13 14 15 16 17 18 19	
NOVEMBER 1971	31 1 ○ 3 4 5 6	21:20	44	2441256		12 13 14 15 16 17 18			13 14 15 16 17 18 19			20 21 22 23 24 25 26	
	7 8 ◑ 10 11 12 13	20:51	45	2441263		19 20 21 22 23 24 25			20 *21* 22 23 24 25 26	Lì dōng	ATHŌR 1688	27 28 29 30 1 2 3	HEDĀR 1964
	14 15 16 17 ● 19 20	1:46	46	2441270	KISLEV 5732	26 27 28 29 30 1 2	Thu 3h9m7p	MONTH 10 Xīn-Hài	27 28 29 30 1 2 3			4 5 6 7 8 9 10	
	21 22 23 24 ◐ 26 27	16:37	47	2441277		3 4 5 6 7 8 9			4 5 **6** 7 8 9 10	Xiǎo xuě		11 12 13 14 15 16 17	
DECEMBER 1971	28 29 30 1 ○ 3 4	7:48	48	2441284		10 11 12 13 14 15 16			11 12 13 14 15 16 17			18 19 20 21 22 23 24	
	5 6 7 8 ◑ 10 11	16:02	49	2441291		17 18[d] 19 20 21 22 23			18* 19 20 *21* 22 23 24	Dà xuě	KOIAK 1688	25 26 27 28 29 30 1	TĀKHŚĀŚ 1964
	12 13 14 15 16 ● 18	19:03	50	2441298		24 25[e] 26[e] 27[e] 28[e] 29[e] 30[e]		MONTH 11 Xīn-Hài	25 26 27 28 29 30 1			2 3 4 5 6 7 8	
	19 20 21 22[e] 23 24 ◐	1:35	51	2441305	TEVETH 5732	1[e] 2[e] 3 4 5 6 7	Fri 15h53m8p		2 3 4 5[i] 6 7 8	Dōng zhì		9 10 11 12 13 14 15	
	26 27 28 29 30 ○ 1	20:20	52	2441312		8 9 10 11 12 13 14			9 10 11 12 13 14 15			16 17 18 19 20 21 22	

[a]New Year
[b]Spring (6:38)
[c]Summer (1:19)
[d]Autumn (16:44)
[e]Winter (12:23)
● New moon
◐ First quarter moon
○ Full moon
◑ Last quarter moon

[a]New Year
[b]Yom Kippur
[c]Sukkot
[d]Winter starts
[e]Ḥanukkah
[f]Purim
[g]Passover
[h]Shavuot
[i]Fast of Av

‡Leap year
[a]New Year (4669, Pig)
[b]Lantern Festival
[c]Qīngmíng
[d]Dragon Festival
[e]Qīqiǎo
[f]Hungry Ghosts
[g]Mid-Autumn Festival
[h]Double-Ninth Festival
[i]Dōngzhì
*Start of 60-name cycle

‡Leap year
[a]New Year
[b]Building of the Cross
[c]Christmas
[d]Jesus's Circumcision
[e]Epiphany
[f]Easter
[g]Mary's Announcement
[h]Jesus's Transfiguration

PERSIAN (ASTRONOMICAL) 1349/1350‡

Month	Sun	Mon	Tue	Wed	Thu	Fri	Sat
	6	7	8	9	10	11	12
DEY 1349	13	14	15	16	17	18	19
	20	21	22	23	24	25	26
	27	28	29	30	1	2	3
BAHMAN 1349	4	5	6	7	8	9	10
	11	12	13	14	15	16	17
	18	19	20	21	22	23	24
	25	26	27	28	29	30	1
ESFAND 1349	2	3	4	5	6	7	8
	9	10	11	12	13	14	15
	16	17	18	19	20	21	22
	23	24	25	26	27	28	29
	1[a]	2	3	4	5	6	7
FARVARDĪN 1350	8	9	10	11	12	13[b]	14
	15	16	17	18	19	20	21
	22	23	24	25	26	27	28
	29	30	31	1	2	3	4
ORDĪBEHEŠT 1350	5	6	7	8	9	10	11
	12	13	14	15	16	17	18
	19	20	21	22	23	24	25
	26	27	28	29	30	31	1
XORDĀD 1350	2	3	4	5	6	7	8
	9	10	11	12	13	14	15
	16	17	18	19	20	21	22
	23	24	25	26	27	28	29
	30	31	1	2	3	4	5
TĪR 1350	6	7	8	9	10	11	12
	13	14	15	16	17	18	19
	20	21	22	23	24	25	26
	27	28	29	30	31	1	2
MORDĀD 1350	3	4	5	6	7	8	9
	10	11	12	13	14	15	16
	17	18	19	20	21	22	23
	24	25	26	27	28	29	30
	31	1	2	3	4	5	6
SHAHRĪVAR 1350	7	8	9	10	11	12	13
	14	15	16	17	18	19	20
	21	22	23	24	25	26	27
	28	29	30	31	1	2	3
MEHR 1350	4	5	6	7	8	9	10
	11	12	13	14	15	16	17
	18	19	20	21	22	23	24
	25	26	27	28	29	30	1
ĀBĀN 1350	2	3	4	5	6	7	8
	9	10	11	12	13	14	15
	16	17	18	19	20	21	22
	23	24	25	26	27	28	29
	30	1	2	3	4	5	6
ĀZAR 1350	7	8	9	10	11	12	13
	14	15	16	17	18	19	20
	21	22	23	24	25	26	27
	28	29	30	1	2	3	4
DEY 1350	5	6	7	8	9	10	11

‡Leap year
[a]New Year
[b]Sizdeh Bedar

HINDU LUNAR 2027/2028

Month	Sun	Mon	Tue	Wed	Thu	Fri	Sat
	29	30	1	2	3	4	6
PAUSHA 2027	7	8	9	10	11	12	13
	14	15	16	17	18	19	20
	21	22	23	23	24	25	26
	27	28	30	1	2	3	4
MĀGHA 2027	5	6	7	8	9	10	11
	12	13	14	15	16	17	18
	19	20	21	22	23	24	25
	26	27	28[h]	29	30	1	2
PHĀLGUNA 2027	3	5	6	7	8	9	10
	11	12	13	14	15	15[i]	16
	17	18	19	20	21	22	23
	24	25	26	27	29	30	1[a]
CHAITRA 2028	2	3	4	5	6	7	8
	9[b]	10	11	12	13	14	15
	16	17	18	19	20	21	22
	23	24	25	26	27	28	29
	30	1	3	4	5	6	7
VAIŚĀKHA 2028	8	9	10	10	11	12	13
	14	15	16	17	18	19	20
	21	22	23	24	26	27	28
	29	30	1	2	3	4	5
JYAISHTHA 2028	6	7	8	9	10	11	12
	13	14	15	16	17	18	19
	20	21	22	23	24	25	26
	27	28	30	1	2	3	4
ĀSHĀḌHA 2028	5	6	6	7	8	9	10
	11	12	13	14	15	16	17
	18	19	20	22	23	24	25
	26	27	28	29	30	1	2
ŚRĀVAṆA 2028	3	4	5	6	7	8	9
	10	11	12	13	14	15	16
	17	18	19	20	21	22	23[c]
	25	26	27	28	29	30	1
BHĀDRAPADA 2028	2	3	3[d]	4	5	6	7
	8	9	10	11	12	13	14
	15	16	18	19	20	21	22
	23	24	25	26	27	28	29
	30	1	2	3	4	5	6
ĀŚVINA 2028	7	8[e]	9[e]	10[e]	11	12	13
	14	15	16	17	18	19	20
	22	23	24	25	26	27	28
	28	29	30	1[f]	2	3	4
KĀRTTIKA 2028	5	6	7	8	9	10	11
	12	13	15	16	17	18	19
	20	21	22	23	24	25	26
	27	28	29	30	1	1	2
MĀRGAŚĪRA 2028	3	4	5	6	7	9	10
	11[g]	12	13	14	15	16	17
	18	19	20	21	22	23	24
	25	26	27	28	29	30	1
PAUSHA 2028	2	3	4	5	6	7	8
	9	10	11	13	14	15	16

[a]New Year (Virodhakṛit)
[b]Birthday of Rāma
[c]Birthday of Krishna
[d]Ganēśa Chaturthī
[e]Dashara
[f]Diwali
[g]Birthday of Vishnu
[h]Night of Śiva
[i]Holi

HINDU SOLAR 1892/1893‡

Month	Sun	Mon	Tue	Wed	Thu	Fri	Sat
PAUSHA 1892	12	13	14	15	16	17	18
	19	20	21	22	23	24	25
	26	27	28	29	1[b]	2	3
MĀGHA 1892	4	5	6	7	8	9	10
	11	12	13	14	15	16	17
	18	19	20	21	22	23	24
	25	26	27	28	29	1	2
PHĀLGUNA 1892	3	4	5	6	7	8	9
	10	11	12	13	14	15	16
	17	18	19	20	21	22	23
	24	25	26	27	28	29	30
	1	2	3	4	5	6	7
CHAITRA 1892	8	9	10	11	12	13	14
	15	16	17	18	19	20	21
	22	23	24	25	26	27	28
	29	30	1[a]	2	3	4	5
VAIŚĀKHA 1893	6	7	8	9	10	11	12
	13	14	15	16	17	18	19
	20	21	22	23	24	25	26
	27	28	29	30	31	1	2
JYAISHTHA 1893	3	4	5	6	7	8	9
	10	11	12	13	14	15	16
	17	18	19	20	21	22	23
	24	25	26	27	28	29	30
	31	32	1	2	3	4	5
ĀSHĀḌHA 1893	6	7	8	9	10	11	12
	13	14	15	16	17	18	19
	20	21	22	23	24	25	26
	27	28	29	30	31	1	2
ŚRĀVAṆA 1893	3	4	5	6	7	8	9
	10	11	12	13	14	15	16
	17	18	19	20	21	22	23
	24	25	26	27	28	29	30
	31	32	1	2	3	4	5
BHĀDRAPADA 1893	6	7	8	9	10	11	12
	13	14	15	16	17	18	19
	20	21	22	23	24	25	26
	27	28	29	30	31	1	2
ĀŚVINA 1893	3	4	5	6	7	8	9
	10	11	12	13	14	15	16
	17	18	19	20	21	22	23
	24	25	26	27	28	29	30
	1	2	3	4	5	6	7
KĀRTTIKA 1893	8	9	10	11	12	13	14
	15	16	17	18	19	20	21
	22	23	24	25	26	27	28
	29	30	1	2	3	4	5
MĀRGAŚĪRA 1893	6	7	8	9	10	11	12
	13	14	15	16	17	18	19
	20	21	22	23	24	25	26
	27	28	29	30	1	2	3
PAUSHA 1893	4	5	6	7	8	9	10
	11	12	13	14	15	16	17

‡Leap year
[a]New Year (Raktāksha)
[b]Pongal

ISLAMIC (ASTRONOMICAL) 1390‡/1391

Month	Sun	Mon	Tue	Wed	Thu	Fri	Sat
	27	28	29	1	2	3	4
DHU AL-QA'DA 1390	5	6	7	8	9	10	11
	12	13	14	15	16	17	18
	19	20	21	22	23	24	25
	26	27	28	29	1	2	3
DHU AL-ḤIJJA 1390	4	5	6	7	8	9	10[g]
	11	12	13	14	15	16	17
	18	19	20	21	22	23	24
	25	26	27	28	29	30	1[a]
MUḤARRAM 1391	2	3	4	5	6	7	8
	9	10[b]	11	12	13	14	15
	16	17	18	19	20	21	22
	23	24	25	26	27	28	29
	1	2	3	4	5	6	7
ṢAFAR 1391	8	9	10	11	12	13	14
	15	16	17	18	19	20	21
	22	23	24	25	26	27	28
	29	1	2	3	4	5	6
RABĪ' I 1391	7	8	9	10	11	12[c]	13
	14	15	16	17	18	19	20
	21	22	23	24	25	26	27
	28	29	30	1	2	3	4
RABĪ' II 1391	5	6	7	8	9	10	11
	12	13	14	15	16	17	18
	19	20	21	22	23	24	25
	26	27	28	29	1	2	3
JUMĀDĀ I 1391	4	5	6	7	8	9	10
	11	12	13	14	15	16	17
	18	19	20	21	22	23	24
	25	26	27	28	29	30	1
JUMĀDĀ II 1391	2	3	4	5	6	7	8
	9	10	11	12	13	14	15
	16	17	18	19	20	21	22
	23	24	25	26	27	28	29
	30	1	2	3	4	5	6
RAJAB 1391	7	8	9	10	11	12	13
	14	15	16	17	18	19	20
	21	22	23	24	25	26	27[d]
	28	29	30	1	2	3	4
SHA'BĀN 1391	5	6	7	8	9	10	11
	12	13	14	15	16	17	18
	19	20	21	22	23	24	25
	26	27	28	29	30	1[e]	2
RAMAḌĀN 1391	3	4	5	6	7	8	9
	10	11	12	13	14	15	16
	17	18	19	20	21	22	23
	24	25	26	27	28	29	1[f]
SHAWWĀL 1391	2	3	4	5	6	7	8
	9	10	11	12	13	14	15
	16	17	18	19	20	21	22
	23	24	25	26	27	28	29
DHU AL-QA'DA 1391	1	2	3	4	5	6	7
	8	9	10	11	12	13	14

‡Leap year
[a]New Year
[b]'Ashūrā'
[c]Prophet's Birthday
[d]Ascent of the Prophet
[e]Start of Ramaḍān
[f]'Īd al-Fiṭr
[g]'Īd al-'Aḍḥā

GREGORIAN 1971

Julian (Sun)	Sun	Mon	Tue	Wed	Thu	Fri	Sat	Month
Dec 14	27	28	29	30	31	1	2	
	3	4	5	6	7[a]	8	9	JANUARY 1971
Dec 28	10	11	12	13	14[b]	15	16	
	17	18	19	20	21	22	23	
Jan 11	24	25	26	27	28	29	30	
	31	1	2	3	4	5	6	
Jan 25	7	8	9	10	11	12	13	FEBRUARY 1971
	14	15	16	17	18	19	20	
Feb 8	21	22	23	24[c]	25	26	27	
	28	1	2	3	4	5	6	
Feb 22	7[d]	8	9	10	11	12	13	MARCH 1971
	14	15	16	17	18	19	20	
Mar 8	21	22	23	24	25	26	27	
	28	29	30	31	1	2	3	
Mar 22	4	5	6	7	8	9	10	APRIL 1971
	11[e]	12	13	14	15	16	17	
Apr 5	18[f]	19	20	21	22	23	24	
	25	26	27	28	29	30	1	
Apr 19	2	3	4	5	6	7	8	MAY 1971
	9	10	11	12	13	14	15	
May 3	16	17	18	19	20	21	22	
	23	24	25	26	27	28	29	
May 17	30	31	1	2	3	4	5	
	6	7	8	9	10	11	12	JUNE 1971
May 31	13	14	15	16	17	18	19	
	20	21	22	23	24	25	26	
Jun 14	27	28	29	30	1	2	3	
	4	5	6	7	8	9	10	JULY 1971
Jun 28	11	12	13	14	15	16	17	
	18	19	20	21	22	23	24	
Jul 12	25	26	27	28	29	30	31	
	1	2	3	4	5	6	7	AUGUST 1971
Jul 26	8	9	10	11	12	13	14	
	15	16	17	18	19	20	21	
Aug 9	22	23	24	25	26	27	28	
	29	30	31	1	2	3	4	
Aug 23	5	6	7	8	9	10	11	SEPTEMBER 1971
	12	13	14	15	16	17	18	
Sep 6	19	20	21	22	23	24	25	
	26	27	28	29	30	1	2	
Sep 20	3	4	5	6	7	8	9	OCTOBER 1971
	10	11	12	13	14	15	16	
Oct 4	17	18	19	20	21	22	23	
	24	25	26	27	28	29	30	
Oct 18	31	1	2	3	4	5	6	
	7	8	9	10	11	12	13	NOVEMBER 1971
Nov 1	14	15	16	17	18	19	20	
	21	22	23	24	25	26	27	
Nov 15	28[g]	29	30	1	2	3	4	
	5	6	7	8	9	10	11	DECEMBER 1971
Nov 29	12	13	14	15	16	17	18	
	19	20	21	22	23	24	25[h]	
Dec 13	26	27	28	29	30	31	1	

[a]Orthodox Christmas
[b]Julian New Year
[c]Ash Wednesday
[d]Feast of Orthodoxy
[e]Easter
[f]Orthodox Easter
[g]Advent
[h]Christmas

1972

Month	Sun	Mon	Tue	Wed	Thu	Fri	Sat	Lunar Phases	ISO WEEK (Mon)	JULIAN DAY (Sun noon)
	26	27	28	29	30	○	1[a]	20:20	52	2441312
JANUARY 1972	2	3	4	5	6	7	◑	13:31	1	2441319
	9	10	11	12	13	14	15		2	2441326
	●	17	18	19	20	21	22	10:52	3	2441333
	◐	24	25	26	27	28	29	9:29	4	2441340
	○	31	1	2	3	4	5	10:58	5	2441347
FEBRUARY 1972	6	◑	8	9	10	11	12	11:12	6	2441354
	13	14	●	16	17	18	19	0:29	7	2441361
	20	◐	22	23	24	25	26	17:20	8	2441368
	27	28	○	1	2	3	4	3:12	9	2441375
MARCH 1972	5	6	7	◑	9	10	11	7:05	10	2441382
	12	13	14	●	16	17	18	11:35	11	2441389
	19	20[b]	21	◐	23	24	25	2:12	12	2441396
	26	27	28	○	30	31	1	20:06	13	2441403
APRIL 1972	2	3	4	5	◑	7	8	23:44	14	2441410
	9	10	11	12	●	14	15	20:31	15	2441417
	16	17	18	19	◐	21	22	12:45	16	2441424
	23	24	25	26	27	○	29	12:44	17	2441431
	30	1	2	3	4	5	◑	12:26	18	2441438
MAY 1972	7	8	9	10	11	12	●	4:08	19	2441445
	14	15	16	17	18	19	◐	1:16	20	2441452
	21	22	23	24	25	26	27		21	2441459
	○	29	30	31	1	2	3	4:28	22	2441466
JUNE 1972	◑	5	6	7	8	9	10	21:22	23	2441473
	●	12	13	14	15	16	17	11:30	24	2441480
	◐	19	20	21[c]	22	23	24	15:41	25	2441487
	25	○	27	28	29	30	1	18:46	26	2441494
JULY 1972	2	3	◑	5	6	7	8	3:25	27	2441501
	9	●	11	12	13	14	15	19:39	28	2441508
	16	17	◐	19	20	21	22	7:46	29	2441515
	23	24	25	○	27	28	29	7:24	30	2441522
	30	31	1	◑	3	4	5	8:02	31	2441529
AUGUST 1972	6	7	8	●	10	11	12	5:26	32	2441536
	13	14	15	16	◐	18	19	1:09	33	2441543
	20	21	22	23	○	25	26	18:22	34	2441550
	27	28	29	30	◑	1	2	12:48	35	2441557
SEPTEMBER 1972	3	4	5	6	●	8	9	17:28	36	2441564
	10	11	12	13	14	◐	16	19:13	37	2441571
	17	18	19	20	21	22[d]	○	4:07	38	2441578
	24	25	26	27	28	◑	30	19:16	39	2441585
OCTOBER 1972	1	2	3	4	5	6	●	8:08	40	2441592
	8	9	10	11	12	13	14		41	2441599
	◐	16	17	18	19	20	21	12:55	42	2441606
	○	23	24	25	26	27	28	13:25	43	2441613
	◑	30	31	1	2	3	4	4:41	44	2441620
NOVEMBER 1972	5	●	7	8	9	10	11	1:21	45	2441627
	12	13	◐	15	16	17	18	5:01	46	2441634
	19	○	21	22	23	24	25	23:07	47	2441641
	26	◑	28	29	30	1	2	17:45	48	2441648
DECEMBER 1972	3	4	●	6	7	8	9	20:24	49	2441655
	10	11	12	◐	14	15	16	18:36	50	2441662
	17	18	19	○	21[e]	22	23	9:45	51	2441669
	24	25	26	◑	28	29	30	10:27	52	2441676
	31	1	2	3	●	5	6	15:42	1	2441683

GREGORIAN 1972‡

‡Leap year
[a]New Year
[b]Spring (12:21)
[c]Summer (7:06)
[d]Autumn (22:32)
[e]Winter (18:13)
● New moon
◐ First quarter moon
○ Full moon
◑ Last quarter moon

HEBREW 5732/5733‡

JULIAN DAY	Month	Sun	Mon	Tue	Wed	Thu	Fri	Sat	Molad
2441312	TEVETH 5732	8	9	10	11	12	13	14	
2441319		15	16	17	18	19	20	21	
2441326		22	23	24	25	26	27	28	
2441333	SHEVAT 5732	29	1	2	3	4	5	6	Sun 4h37m9p
2441340		7	8	9	10	11	12	13	
2441347		14	15	16	17	18	19	20	
2441354		21	22	23	24	25	26	27	
2441361	ADAR 5732	28	29	30	1	2	3	4	Mon 17h21m10p
2441368		5	6	7	8	9	10	11	
2441375		12	13	14[f]	15	16	17	18	
2441382		19	20	21	22	23	24	25	
2441389	NISAN 5732	26	27	28	29	1	2	3	Wed 6h5m11p
2441396		4	5	6	7	8	9	10	
2441403		11	12	13	14	15[g]	16	17	
2441410		18	19	20	21	22	23	24	
2441417	IYYAR 5732	25	26	27	28	29	30	1	Thu 18h49m12p
2441424		2	3	4	5	6	7	8	
2441431		9	10	11	12	13	14	15	
2441438		16	17	18	19	20	21	22	
2441445		23	24	25	26	27	28	29	
2441452	SIVAN 5732	1	2	3	4	5	6[h]	7	Sat 7h33m13p
2441459		8	9	10	11	12	13	14	
2441466		15	16	17	18	19	20	21	
2441473		22	23	24	25	26	27	28	
2441480	TAMMUZ 5732	29	30	1	2	3	4	5	Sun 20h17m14p
2441487		6	7	8	9	10	11	12	
2441494		13	14	15	16	17	18	19	
2441501		20	21	22	23	24	25	26	
2441508	AV 5732	27	28	29	1	2	3	4	Tue 9h1m15p
2441515		5	6	7	8	9[i]	10	11	
2441522		12	13	14	15	16	17	18	
2441529		19	20	21	22	23	24	25	
2441536	ELUL 5732	26	27	28	29	30	1	2	Wed 21h45m16p
2441543		3	4	5	6	7	8	9	
2441550		10	11	12	13	14	15	16	
2441557		17	18	19	20	21	22	23	
2441564	TISHRI 5733	24	25	26	27	28	29	1[a]	Fri 10h29m17p
2441571		2[a]	3	4	5	6	7	8	
2441578		9	10[b]	11	12	13	14	15[c]	
2441585		16	17	18	19	20	21	22	
2441592		23	24	25	26	27	28	29	
2441599	HESHVAN 5733	30	1	2	3	4	5	6	Sat 23h14m0p
2441606		7	8	9	10	11	12	13	
2441613		14	15	16	17	18	19	20	
2441620		21	22	23	24	25	26	27	
2441627	KISLEV 5733	28	29	1	2	3	4	5	Mon 11h58m1p
2441634		6	7	8	9	10	11	12	
2441641		13	14	15	16	17	18	19	
2441648		20	21	22	23	24	25[e]	26[e]	
2441655	TEVETH 5733	27[e]	28[e]	29[d][e]	1[e]	2[e]	3[e]	4	Wed 0h42m2p
2441662		5	6	7	8	9	10	11	
2441669		12	13	14	15	16	17	18	
2441676		19	20	21	22	23	24	25	
2441683		26	27	28	29	1	2	3	Thu 13h26m3p

‡Leap year
[a]New Year
[b]Yom Kippur
[c]Sukkot
[d]Winter starts
[e]Ḥanukkah
[f]Purim
[g]Passover
[h]Shavuot
[i]Fast of Av

CHINESE Xīn-Hài‡/Rén-Zǐ

JULIAN DAY	Month	Sun	Mon	Tue	Wed	Thu	Fri	Sat	Solar Term
2441312	MONTH 11 Xīn-Hài	9	10	11	12	13	14	15	
2441319		16	17	18	19	20	21	22	Xiǎo hán
2441326		23	24	25	26	27	28	29	
2441333	MONTH 12 Xīn-Hài	1	2	3	4	5	6	7	Dà hán
2441340		8	9	10	11	12	13	14	
2441347		15	16	17	18	19*	20	21	Lì chūn
2441354		22	23	24	25	26	27	28	
2441361	MONTH 1 Rén-Zǐ	29	30	1[a]	2	3	4	5	Yǔ shuǐ
2441368		6	7	8	9	10	11	12	
2441375		13	14	15[b]	16	17	18	19	
2441382		20	21	22	23	24	25	26	Jīng zhé
2441389	MONTH 2 Rén-Zǐ	27	28	29	1	2	3	4	
2441396		5	6	7	8	9	10	11	Chūn fēn
2441403		12	13	14	15	16	17	18	
2441410		19	20*	21	22[c]	23	24	25	Qīng míng
2441417	MONTH 3 Rén-Zǐ	26	27	28	29	30	1	2	
2441424		3	4	5	6	7	8	9	Gǔ yǔ
2441431		10	11	12	13	14	15	16	
2441438		17	18	19	20	21	22	23	Lì xià
2441445	MONTH 4 Rén-Zǐ	24	25	26	27	28	29	1	
2441452		2	3	4	5	6	7	8	
2441459		9	10	11	12	13	14	15	Xiǎo mǎn
2441466		16	17	18	19	20	21*	22	
2441473		23	24	25	26	27	28	29	Máng zhòng
2441480	MONTH 5 Rén-Zǐ	1	2	3	4	5[d]	6	7	
2441487		8	9	10	11	12	13	14	Xià zhì
2441494		15	16	17	18	19	20	21	
2441501		22	23	24	25	26	27	28	Xiǎo shǔ
2441508	MONTH 6 Rén-Zǐ	29	30	1	2	3	4	5	
2441515		6	7	8	9	10	11	12	
2441522		13	14	15	16	17	18	19	Dà shǔ
2441529		20	21	22*	23	24	25	26	
2441536	MONTH 7 Rén-Zǐ	27	28	29	1	2	3	4	Lì qiū
2441543		5	6	7[e]	8	9	10	11	
2441550		12	13	14	15[f]	16	17	18	Chǔ shǔ
2441557		19	20	21	22	23	24	25	
2441564	MONTH 8 Rén-Zǐ	26	27	28	29	30	1	2	Bái lù
2441571		3	4	5	6	7	8	9	
2441578		10	11	12	13	14	15[g]	16	Qiū fēn
2441585		17	18	19	20	21	22	23*	
2441592	MONTH 9 Rén-Zǐ	24	25	26	27	28	29	1	
2441599		2	3	4	5	6	7	8	Hán lù
2441606		9[h]	10	11	12	13	14	15	
2441613		16	17	18	19	20	21	22	Shuāng jiàng
2441620		23	24	25	26	27	28	29	
2441627	MONTH 10 Rén-Zǐ	30	1	2	3	4	5	6	Lì dōng
2441634		7	8	9	10	11	12	13	
2441641		14	15	16	17	18	19	20	Xiǎo xuě
2441648		21	22	23	24*	25	26	27	
2441655	MONTH 11 Rén-Zǐ	28	29	30	1	2	3	4	Dà xuě
2441662		5	6	7	8	9	10	11	
2441669		12	13	14	15	16	17[i]	18	Dōng zhì
2441676		19	20	21	22	23	24	25	
2441683		26	27	28	29	1	2	3	Xiǎo hán

‡Leap year
[a]New Year (4670, Rat)
[b]Lantern Festival
[c]Qīngmíng
[d]Dragon Festival
[e]Qīqiǎo
[f]Hungry Ghosts
[g]Mid-Autumn Festival
[h]Double-Ninth Festival
[i]Dōngzhì
*Start of 60-name cycle

COPTIC 1688/1689 — ETHIOPIC 1964/1965

JULIAN DAY	Coptic Month	Sun	Mon	Tue	Wed	Thu	Fri	Sat	Ethiopic Month
2441312	KOIAK 1688	16	17	18	19	20	21	22	TĀKHŚĀŚ 1964
2441319		23	24	25	26	27	28	29[c]	
2441326	TŌBE 1688	30	1	2	3	4	5	6[d]	ṬER 1964
2441333		7	8	9	10	11[e]	12	13	
2441340		14	15	16	17	18	19	20	
2441347		21	22	23	24	25	26	27	
2441354	MESHIR 1688	28	29	30	1	2	3	4	YAKĀTIT 1964
2441361		5	6	7	8	9	10	11	
2441368		12	13	14	15	16	17	18	
2441375		19	20	21	22	23	24	25	
2441382	PAREMOTEP 1688	26	27	28	29	30	1	2	MAGĀBIT 1964
2441389		3	4	5	6	7	8	9	
2441396		10	11	12	13	14	15	16	
2441403		17	18	19	20	21	22	23	
2441410		24	25	26	27	28	29	30	
2441417	PARMOUTE 1688	1[f]	2	3	4	5	6	7	MIYĀZYĀ 1964
2441424		8	9	10	11	12	13	14	
2441431		15	16	17	18	19	20	21	
2441438		22	23	24	25	26	27	28	
2441445	PASHONS 1688	29[g]	30	1	2	3	4	5	GENBOT 1964
2441452		6	7	8	9	10	11	12	
2441459		13	14	15	16	17	18	19	
2441466		20	21	22	23	24	25	26	
2441473	PAŌNE 1688	27	28	29	30	1	2	3	SANĒ 1964
2441480		4	5	6	7	8	9	10	
2441487		11	12	13	14	15	16	17	
2441494		18	19	20	21	22	23	24	
2441501	EPĒP 1688	25	26	27	28	29	30	1	ḤAMLĒ 1964
2441508		2	3	4	5	6	7	8	
2441515		9	10	11	12	13	14	15	
2441522		16	17	18	19	20	21	22	
2441529		23	24	25	26	27	28	29	
2441536	MESORĒ 1688	30	1	2	3	4	5	6	NAḤASĒ 1964
2441543		7	8	9	10	11	12	13[h]	
2441550		14	15	16	17	18	19	20	
2441557		21	22	23	24	25	26	27	
2441564	EPAG. 1688	28	29	30	1	2	3	4	PĀG. 1964
2441571	THOOUT 1689	5	1[a]	2	3	4	5	6	MASKARAM 1965
2441578		7	8	9	10	11	12	13	
2441585		14	15	16	17[b]	18	19	20	
2441592		21	22	23	24	25	26	27	
2441599	PAOPE 1689	28	29	30	1	2	3	4	ṬEQEMT 1965
2441606		5	6	7	8	9	10	11	
2441613		12	13	14	15	16	17	18	
2441620		19	20	21	22	23	24	25	
2441627	ATHŌR 1689	26	27	28	29	30	1	2	ḪEDĀR 1965
2441634		3	4	5	6	7	8	9	
2441641		10	11	12	13	14	15	16	
2441648		17	18	19	20	21	22	23	
2441655		24	25	26	27	28	29	30	
2441662	KOIAK 1689	1	2	3	4	5	6	7	TĀKHŚĀŚ 1965
2441669		8	9	10	11	12	13	14	
2441676		15	16	17	18	19	20	21	
2441683		22	23	24	25	26	27	28	

[a]New Year
[b]Building of the Cross
[c]Christmas
[d]Jesus's Circumcision
[e]Epiphany
[f]Easter
[g]Mary's Announcement
[h]Jesus's Transfiguration

PERSIAN (ASTRONOMICAL) 1350‡/1351

Month	Sun	Mon	Tue	Wed	Thu	Fri	Sat
DEY 1350	5	6	7	8	9	10	11
	12	13	14	15	16	17	18
	19	20	21	22	23	24	25
	26	27	28	29	30	1	2
BAHMAN 1350	3	4	5	6	7	8	9
	10	11	12	13	14	15	16
	17	18	19	20	21	22	23
	24	25	26	27	28	29	30
ESFAND 1350	1	2	3	4	5	6	7
	8	9	10	11	12	13	14
	15	16	17	18	19	20	21
	22	23	24	25	26	27	28
	29	30	1[a]	2	3	4	5
FARVARDĪN 1351	6	7	8	9	10	11	12
	13[b]	14	15	16	17	18	19
	20	21	22	23	24	25	26
	27	28	29	30	31	1	2
ORDĪBEHEŠT 1351	3	4	5	6	7	8	9
	10	11	12	13	14	15	16
	17	18	19	20	21	22	23
	24	25	26	27	28	29	30
	31	1	2	3	4	5	6
XORDĀD 1351	7	8	9	10	11	12	13
	14	15	16	17	18	19	20
	21	22	23	24	25	26	27
	28	29	30	31	1	2	3
TĪR 1351	4	5	6	7	8	9	10
	11	12	13	14	15	16	17
	18	19	20	21	22	23	24
	25	26	27	28	29	30	31
MORDĀD 1351	1	2	3	4	5	6	7
	8	9	10	11	12	13	14
	15	16	17	18	19	20	21
	22	23	24	25	26	27	28
	29	30	31	1	2	3	4
SHAHRĪVAR 1351	5	6	7	8	9	10	11
	12	13	14	15	16	17	18
	19	20	21	22	23	24	25
	26	27	28	29	30	31	1
MEHR 1351	2	3	4	5	6	7	8
	9	10	11	12	13	14	15
	16	17	18	19	20	21	22
	23	24	25	26	27	28	29
	30	1	2	3	4	5	6
ĀBĀN 1351	7	8	9	10	11	12	13
	14	15	16	17	18	19	20
	21	22	23	24	25	26	27
	28	29	30	1	2	3	4
ĀZAR 1351	5	6	7	8	9	10	11
	12	13	14	15	16	17	18
	19	20	21	22	23	24	25
	26	27	28	29	30	1	2
DEY 1351	3	4	5	6	7	8	9
	10	11	12	13	14	15	16

‡Leap year
[a]New Year
[b]Sizdeh Bedar

HINDU LUNAR 2028/2029‡

Month	Sun	Mon	Tue	Wed	Thu	Fri	Sat
PAUSHA 2028	9	10	**11**	13	14	15	16
	17	18	19	20	21	22	23
	23	24	25	26	27	28	29
	30	1	2	3	4	5	**6**
MĀGHA 2028	8	9	10	11	12	13	14
	15	16	17	18	19	20	21
	22	23	24	25	26	26	27
	28[h]	**29**	1	2	3	4	5
PHĀLGUNA 2028	6	7	8	9	10	11	12
	13	14	15[i]	16	17	18	19
	20	21	22	23	24	25	26
	27	28	29	30	1[a]	2	3
CHAITRA 2029	**4**	6	7	8	9[b]	10	11
	12	13	14	15	16	17	18
	18	19	20	21	22	23	24
	25	26	27	**28**	30	1	2
LEAP VAIŚĀKHA 2029	3	4	5	6	7	8	9
	10	11	12	13	14	15	16
	17	18	19	20	21	22	23
	24	25	26	27	28	29	30
VAIŚĀKHA 2029	**1**	3	4	5	6	7	8
	9	10	11	12	13	14	14
	15	16	17	18	19	20	21
	22	23	**24**	26	27	28	29
JYAISHTHA 2029	30	1	2	3	4	5	6
	7	8	9	10	11	12	13
	14	15	16	17	18	19	20
	21	22	23	24	25	26	**27**
ĀSHĀDHA 2029	29	30	1	2	3	4	5
	6	7	8	9	10	10	11
	12	13	14	15	16	17	18
	19	**20**	22	23	24	25	26
ŚRĀVAṆA 2029	27	28	29	30	1	2	3
	4	5	6	7	8	9	10
	11	12	13	14	15	16	17
	18	19	20	21	22	**23**[c]	25
BHĀDRAPADA 2029	26	27	28	29	30	1	2
	3	**4**[d]	5	6	6	7	8
	9	10	11	12	13	14	15
	16	18	19	20	21	22	23
	24	25	26	27	28	29	30
ĀŚVINA 2029	1	2	3	4	5	6	7
	8[e]	9[e]	10[e]	11	12	13	14
	15	16	17	18	19	**20**	22
	23	24	25	26	27	28	29
KĀRTTIKA 2029	30	1	1[f]	2	3	4	5
	6	7	8	9	10	11	12
	13	**14**	16	17	18	19	20
	21	22	23	24	25	26	27
MĀRGAŚĪRA 2029	28	29	30	1	2	3	4
	4	5	6	**7**	9	10	11[g]
	12	13	14	15	16	17	18
	19	20	21	22	23	24	25
	26	27	28	29	30	1	2

‡Leap year
[a]New Year (Paridhāvin)
[b]Birthday of Rāma
[c]Birthday of Krishna
[d]Ganēśa Chaturthī
[e]Dashara
[f]Diwali
[g]Birthday of Vishnu
[h]Night of Śiva
[i]Holi

HINDU SOLAR 1893‡/1894

Month	Sun	Mon	Tue	Wed	Thu	Fri	Sat
PAUSHA 1893	11	12	13	14	15	16	17
	18	19	20	21	22	23	24
	25	26	27	28	29	1[b]	2
MĀGHA 1893	3	4	5	6	7	8	9
	10	11	12	13	14	15	16
	17	18	19	20	21	22	23
	24	25	26	27	28	29	30
PHĀLGUNA 1893	1	2	3	4	5	6	7
	8	9	10	11	12	13	14
	15	16	17	18	19	20	21
	22	23	24	25	26	27	28
	29	1	2	3	4	5	6
CHAITRA 1893	7	8	9	10	11	12	13
	14	15	16	17	18	19	20
	21	22	23	24	25	26	27
	28	29	30	31	1[a]	2	3
VAIŚĀKHA 1894	4	5	6	7	8	9	10
	11	12	13	14	15	16	17
	18	19	20	21	22	23	24
	25	26	27	28	29	30	31
JYAISHTHA 1894	1	2	3	4	5	6	7
	8	9	10	11	12	13	14
	15	16	17	18	19	20	21
	22	23	24	25	26	27	28
	29	30	31	1	2	3	4
ĀSHĀDHA 1894	5	6	7	8	9	10	11
	12	13	14	15	16	17	18
	19	20	21	22	23	24	25
	26	27	28	29	30	31	32
ŚRĀVAṆA 1894	1	2	3	4	5	6	7
	8	9	10	11	12	13	14
	15	16	17	18	19	20	21
	22	23	24	25	26	27	28
	29	30	31	1	2	3	4
BHĀDRAPADA 1894	5	6	7	8	9	10	11
	12	13	14	15	16	17	18
	19	20	21	22	23	24	25
	26	27	28	29	30	31	1
ĀŚVINA 1894	2	3	4	5	6	7	8
	9	10	11	12	13	14	15
	16	17	18	19	20	21	22
	23	24	25	26	27	28	29
	30	31	1	2	3	4	5
KĀRTTIKA 1894	6	7	8	9	10	11	12
	13	14	15	16	17	18	19
	20	21	22	23	24	25	26
	27	28	29	30	1	2	3
MĀRGAŚĪRA 1894	4	5	6	7	8	9	10
	11	12	13	14	15	16	17
	18	19	20	21	22	23	24
	25	26	27	28	29	1	2
PAUSHA 1894	3	4	5	6	7	8	9
	10	11	12	13	14	15	16
	17	18	19	20	21	22	23

‡Leap year
[a]New Year (Krodhana)
[b]Pongal

ISLAMIC (ASTRONOMICAL) 1391/1392‡

Month	Sun	Mon	Tue	Wed	Thu	Fri	Sat
DHU AL-QA'DA 1391	8	9	10	11	12	13	14
	15	16	17	18	19	20	21
	22	23	24	25	26	27	28
	29	30	1	2	3	4	5
DHU AL-ḤIJJA 1391	6	7	8	9	10[g]	11	12
	13	14	15	16	17	18	19
	20	21	22	23	24	25	26
	27	28	29	1[a]	2	3	4
MUḤARRAM 1392	5	6	7	8	9	10[b]	11
	12	13	14	15	16	17	18
	19	20	21	22	23	24	25
	26	27	28	29	30	1	2
ṢAFAR 1392	3	4	5	6	7	8	9
	10	11	12	13	14	15	16
	17	18	19	20	21	22	23
	24	25	26	27	28	29	1
RABĪ' I 1392	2	3	4	5	6	7	8
	9	10	11	12[c]	13	14	15
	16	17	18	19	20	21	22
	23	24	25	26	27	28	29
RABĪ' II 1392	1	2	3	4	5	6	7
	8	9	10	11	12	13	14
	15	16	17	18	19	20	21
	22	23	24	25	26	27	28
	29	30	1	2	3	4	5
JUMĀDĀ I 1392	6	7	8	9	10	11	12
	13	14	15	16	17	18	19
	20	21	22	23	24	25	26
	27	28	29	1	2	3	4
JUMĀDĀ II 1392	5	6	7	8	9	10	11
	12	13	14	15	16	17	18
	19	20	21	22	23	24	25
	26	27	28	29	30	1	2
RAJAB 1392	3	4	5	6	7	8	9
	10	11	12	13	14	15	16
	17	18	19	20	21	22	23
	24	25	26	27[d]	28	29	30
SHA'BĀN 1392	1	2	3	4	5	6	7
	8	9	10	11	12	13	14
	15	16	17	18	19	20	21
	22	23	24	25	26	27	28
	29	30	1[e]	2	3	4	5
RAMAḌĀN 1392	6	7	8	9	10	11	12
	13	14	15	16	17	18	19
	20	21	22	23	24	25	26
	27	28	29	1[f]	2	3	4
SHAWWĀL 1392	5	6	7	8	9	10	11
	12	13	14	15	16	17	18
	19	20	21	22	23	24	25
	26	27	28	29	1	2	3
DHU AL-QA'DA 1392	4	5	6	7	8	9	10
	11	12	13	14	15	16	17
	18	19	20	21	22	23	24
	25	26	27	28	29	30	1

‡Leap year
[a]New Year
[b]'Ashūrā'
[c]Prophet's Birthday
[d]Ascent of the Prophet
[e]Start of Ramaḍān
[f]'Id al-Fiṭr
[g]'Id al-'Aḍḥā

GREGORIAN 1972‡

Julian‡ (Sun)	Sun	Mon	Tue	Wed	Thu	Fri	Sat	Month
Dec 13	26	27	28	29	30	31	1	
	2	3	4	5	6	7[a]	8	JANUARY 1972
Dec 27	9	10	11	12	13	14[b]	15	
	16	17	18	19	20	21	22	
Jan 10	23	24	25	26	27	28	29	
	30	31	1	2	3	4	5	
Jan 24	6	7	8	9	10	11	12	FEBRUARY 1972
	13	14	15	16[c]	17	18	19	
Feb 7	20	21	22	23	24	25	26	
	27[d]	28	29	1	2	3	4	
Feb 21	5	6	7	8	9	10	11	MARCH 1972
	12	13	14	15	16	17	18	
Mar 6	19	20	21	22	23	24	25	
	26	27	28	29	30	31	1	
Mar 20	2[e]	3	4	5	6	7	8	APRIL 1972
	9[f]	10	11	12	13	14	15	
Apr 3	16	17	18	19	20	21	22	
	23	24	25	26	27	28	29	
Apr 17	30	1	2	3	4	5	6	
	7	8	9	10	11	12	13	MAY 1972
May 1	14	15	16	17	18	19	20	
	21	22	23	24	25	26	27	
May 15	28	29	30	31	1	2	3	
	4	5	6	7	8	9	10	JUNE 1972
May 29	11	12	13	14	15	16	17	
	18	19	20	21	22	23	24	
Jun 12	25	26	27	28	29	30	1	
	2	3	4	5	6	7	8	JULY 1972
Jun 26	9	10	11	12	13	14	15	
	16	17	18	19	20	21	22	
Jul 10	23	24	25	26	27	28	29	
	30	31	1	2	3	4	5	
Jul 24	6	7	8	9	10	11	12	AUGUST 1972
	13	14	15	16	17	18	19	
Aug 7	20	21	22	23	24	25	26	
	27	28	29	30	31	1	2	
Aug 21	3	4	5	6	7	8	9	SEPTEMBER 1972
	10	11	12	13	14	15	16	
Sep 4	17	18	19	20	21	22	23	
	24	25	26	27	28	29	30	
Sep 18	1	2	3	4	5	6	7	OCTOBER 1972
	8	9	10	11	12	13	14	
Oct 2	15	16	17	18	19	20	21	
	22	23	24	25	26	27	28	
Oct 16	29	30	31	1	2	3	4	
	5	6	7	8	9	10	11	NOVEMBER 1972
Oct 30	12	13	14	15	16	17	18	
	19	20	21	22	23	24	25	
Nov 13	26	27	28	29	30	1	2	
	3[g]	4	5	6	7	8	9	DECEMBER 1972
Nov 27	10	11	12	13	14	15	16	
	17	18	19	20	21	22	23	
Dec 11	24	25[h]	26	27	28	29	30	
	31	1	2	3	4	5	6	

‡Leap year
[a]Orthodox Christmas
[b]Julian New Year
[c]Ash Wednesday
[d]Feast of Orthodoxy
[e]Easter
[f]Orthodox Easter
[g]Advent
[h]Christmas

1973

	GREGORIAN 1973							Lunar Phases	ISO WEEK	JULIAN DAY		HEBREW 5733‡/5734							Molad		CHINESE Rén-Zǐ/Guǐ-Chǒu							Solar Term		COPTIC 1689/1690 — ETHIOPIC 1965/1966							
	Sun	Mon	Tue	Wed	Thu	Fri	Sat		(Mon)	(Sun noon)		Sun	Mon	Tue	Wed	Thu	Fri	Sat			Sun	Mon	Tue	Wed	Thu	Fri	Sat			Sun	Mon	Tue	Wed	Thu	Fri	Sat	
	31	1[a]	2	3	●	5	6	15:42	1	2441683		26	27	28	29	1	2	3	Thu 13h26m3p		26	27	28	29	1	2	3	Xiǎo hán	KOIAK 1689	22	23	24	25	26	27	28	TĀKHŚĀŚ 1965
JANUARY 1973	7	8	9	10	11	◐	13	5:27	2	2441690	SHEVAT 5733	4	5	6	7	8	9	10		MONTH 12 Rén-Zǐ	4	5	6	7	8	9	10			29[c]	30	1	2	3	4	5	
	14	15	16	17	○	19	20	21:28	3	2441697		11	12	13	14	15	16	17			11	12	13	14	15	16	**17**	Dà hán	TŌBE 1689	6[d]	7	8	9	10	11[e]	12	TER 1965
	21	22	23	24	25	◑	27	6:05	4	2441704		18	19	20	21	22	23	24			18	19	20	21	22	23	24			13	14	15	16	17	18	19	
	28	29	30	31	1	2	●	9:23	5	2441711		25	26	27	28	29	30	1	Sat 2h10m4p		25*	26	27	28	29	30	1[a]			20	21	22	23	24	25	26	
	4	5	6	7	8	9	◐	14:05	6	2441718		2	3	4	5	6	7	8			2	3	4	5	6	7	8	Lì chūn		27	28	29	30	1	2	3	
FEBRUARY 1973	11	12	13	14	15	16	○	10:07	7	2441725	ADAR I 5733	9	10	11	12	13	14	15		MONTH 1 Guǐ-Chǒu	9	10	11	12	13	14	15[b]		MESHIR 1689	4	5	6	7	8	9	10	YAKĀTĪT 1965
	18	19	20	21	22	23	24		8	2441732		16	17	18	19	20	21	22			16	**17**	18	19	20	21	22	Yǔ shuǐ		11	12	13	14	15	16	17	
	◑	26	27	28	1	2	3	3:10	9	2441739		23	24	25	26	27	28	29			23	24	25	26	27	28	29			18	19	20	21	22	23	24	
	4	●	6	7	8	9	10	0:07	10	2441746		30	1	2	3	4	5	6	Sun 14h54m5p		30	1	2	3	4	5	6	Jīng zhé		25	26	27	28	29	30	1	
MARCH 1973	◐	12	13	14	15	16	17	21:26	11	2441753		7	8	9	10	11	12	13			7	8	9	10	11	12	13			2	3	4	5	6	7	8	
	○	19	20[b]	21	22	23	24	23:33	12	2441760	ADAR II 5733	14[f]	15	16	17	18	19	20		MONTH 2 Guǐ-Chǒu	14	15	16	**17**	18	19	20	Chūn fēn	PAREMOTEP 1689	9	10	11	12	13	14	15	MAGABIT 1965
	25	◑	27	28	29	30	31	23:46	13	2441767		21	22	23	24	25	26	27			21	22	23	24	25*	26	27			16	17	18	19	20	21	22	
	1	2	●	4	5	6	7	11:45	14	2441774		28	29	1	2	3	4	5	Tue 3h38m6p		28	29	1	2	3[c]	4	5	Qīng míng		23	24	25	26	27	28	29	
APRIL 1973	8	9	◐	11	12	13	14	4:28	15	2441781		6	7	8	9	10	11	12		MONTH 3 Guǐ-Chǒu	6	7	8	9	10	11	12			30	1	2	3	4	5	6	
	15	16	○	18	19	20	21	13:50	16	2441788	NISAN 5733	13	14	15[g]	16	17	18	19			13	14	15	16	17	**18**	19	Gǔ yǔ	PARMOUTE 1689	7	8	9	10	11	12	13	MIYĀZYĀ 1965
	22	23	24	◑	26	27	28	17:58	17	2441795		20	21	22	23	24	25	26			20	21	22	23	24	25	26			14	15	16	17	18	19	20	
	29	30	1	●	3	4	5	20:55	18	2441802		27	28	29	30	1	2	3	Wed 16h22m7p		27	28	29	30	1	2	3	Lì xià		21[f]	22	23	24	25	26	27	
	6	7	8	◐	10	11	12	12:07	19	2441809		4	5	6	7	8	9	10		MONTH 4 Guǐ-Chǒu	4	5	6	7	8	9	10			28	29[g]	30	1	2	3	4	
MAY 1973	13	14	15	16	○	18	19	4:58	20	2441816	IYAR 5733	11	12	13	14	15	16	17			11	12	13	14	15	16	17		PASHONS 1689	5	6	7	8	9	10	11	GENBOT 1965
	20	21	22	23	24	◑	26	8:40	21	2441823		18	19	20	21	22	23	24			18	**19**	20	21	22	23	24	Xiǎo mǎn		12	13	14	15	16	17	18	
	27	28	29	30	31	●	2	4:34	22	2441830		25	26	27	28	29	1	2	Fri 5h6m8p		25	26*	27	28	29	1	2			19	20	21	22	23	24	25	
	3	4	5	6	◐	8	9	21:11	23	2441837		3	4	5	6[h]	7	8	9			3	4	5[d]	6	7	8	9	Máng zhòng		26	27	28	29	30	1	2	
JUNE 1973	10	11	12	13	14	○	16	20:35	24	2441844	SIVAN 5733	10	11	12	13	14	15	16		MONTH 5 Guǐ-Chǒu	10	11	12	13	14	15	16			3	4	5	6	7	8	9	
	17	18	19	20	21[c]	22	◑	19:45	25	2441851		17	18	19	20	21	22	23			17	18	19	20	**21**	22	23	Xià zhì	PAŌNE 1689	10	11	12	13	14	15	16	SANĒ 1965
	24	25	26	27	28	29	●	11:39	26	2441858		24	25	26	27	28	29	30	Sat 17h50m9p		24	25	26	27	28	29	1			17	18	19	20	21	22	23	
	1	2	3	4	5	6	◐	8:26	27	2441865		1	2	3	4	5	6	7			2	3	4	5	6	7	8	Xiǎo shǔ		24	25	26	27	28	29	30	
JULY 1973	8	9	10	11	12	13	14		28	2441872		8	9	10	11	12	13	14		MONTH 6 Guǐ-Chǒu	9	10	11	12	13	14	15			1	2	3	4	5	6	7	
	○	16	17	18	19	20	21	11:56	29	2441879	TAMMUZ 5733	15	16	17	18	19	20	21			16	17	18	19	20	21	22		EPĒP 1689	8	9	10	11	12	13	14	HAMLĒ 1965
	22	◑	24	25	26	27	28	3:58	30	2441886		22	23	24	25	26	27	28			23	**24**	25	26	27	28*	29	Dà shǔ		15	16	17	18	19	20	21	
	●	30	31	1	2	3	4	18:59	31	2441893		29	1	2	3	4	5	6	Mon 6h34m10p		30	1	2	3	4	5	6			22	23	24	25	26	27	28	
AUGUST 1973	◐	6	7	8	9	10	11	22:27	32	2441900		7	8	9[i]	10	11	12	13		MONTH 7 Guǐ-Chǒu	7[e]	8	9	10	11	12	13	Lì qiū		29	30	1	2	3	4	5	
	12	13	○	15	16	17	18	2:17	33	2441907	AV 5733	14	15	16	17	18	19	20			14	15[f]	16	17	18	19	20		MESORĒ 1689	6	7	8	9	10	11	12	NAHASĒ 1965
	19	20	◑	22	23	24	25	10:22	34	2441914		21	22	23	24	25	26	27			21	22	23	24	**25**	26	27	Chǔ shǔ		13[h]	14	15	16	17	18	19	
	26	27	●	29	30	31	1	3:25	35	2441921		28	29	30	1	2	3	4	Tue 19h18m11p		28	29	1	2	3	4	5			20	21	22	23	24	25	26	
	2	3	◐	5	6	7	8	15:22	36	2441928		5	6	7	8	9	10	11		MONTH 8 Guǐ-Chǒu	6	7	8	9	10	11	12	Bái lù	EPAG. 1689	27	28	29	30	1	2	3	PĀG. 1965
SEPTEMBER 1973	9	10	11	○	13	14	15	15:16	37	2441935	ELUL 5733	12	13	14	15	16	17	18			13	14	15[g]	16	17	18	19			4	5	1[a]	2	3	4	5	
	16	17	18	◑	20	21	22	16:11	38	2441942		19	20	21	22	23	24	25			20	21	22	23	24	25	26		THOOUT 1690	6	7	8	9	10	11	12	MASKARAM 1966
	23[d]	24	25	●	27	28	29	13:54	39	2441949		26	27	28	29	1[a]	2[a]	3	Thu 8h2m12p		**27**	28	29*	1	2	3	4	Qiū fēn		13	14	15	16	17[b]	18	19	
	30	1	2	3	◐	5	6	10:32	40	2441956		4	5	6	7	8	9	10[b]		MONTH 9 Guǐ-Chǒu	5	6	7	8	9[h]	10	11			20	21	22	23	24	25	26	
OCTOBER 1973	7	8	9	10	11	○	13	3:09	41	2441963	TISHRI 5734	11	12	13	14	15[c]	16	17			12	13	14	15	16	17	18	Hán lù		27	28	29	30	1	2	3	
	14	15	16	17	◑	19	20	22:33	42	2441970		18	19	20	21	22	23	24			19	20	21	22	23	24	25		PAOPE 1690	4	5	6	7	8	9	10	TEQEMT 1966
	21	22	23	24	25	●	27	3:17	43	2441977		25	26	27	28	29	30	1	Fri 20h46m13p		26	27	**28**	29	30	1	2	Shuāng jiàng		11	12	13	14	15	16	17	
	28	29	30	31	1	2	◐	6:29	44	2441984		2	3	4	5	6	7	8		MONTH 10 Guǐ-Chǒu	3	4	5	6	7	8	9			18	19	20	21	22	23	24	
NOVEMBER 1973	4	5	6	7	8	9	○	14:27	45	2441991	HESHVAN 5734	9	10	11	12	13	14	15			10	11	12	13	14	15	16	Lì dōng		25	26	27	28	29	30	1	
	11	12	13	14	15	16	◑	6:35	46	2441998		16	17	18	19	20	21	22			17	18	19	20	21	22	23			2	3	4	5	6	7	8	
	18	19	20	21	22	23	●	19:55	47	2442005		23	24	25	26	27	28	29			24	25	26	27	**28**	29	30*	Xiǎo xuě	ATHŌR 1690	9	10	11	12	13	14	15	HEDĀR 1966
	25	26	27	28	29	30	1		48	2442012		30	1	2	3	4	5	6	Sun 9h30m14p		1	2	3	4	5	6	7			16	17	18	19	20	21	22	
	2	◐	4	5	6	7	8	1:29	49	2442019		7	8	9	10[d]	11	12	13		MONTH 11* Guǐ-Chǒu	8	9	10	11	12	13	14	Dà xuě		23	24	25	26	27	28	29	
DECEMBER 1973	9	○	11	12	13	14	15	1:35	50	2442026	KISLEV 5734	14	15	16	17	18	19	20			15	16	17	18	19	20	21			30	1	2	3	4	5	6	
	◑	17	18	19	20	21	22[e]	17:13	51	2442033		21	22	23	24	25[e]	26[e]	27[e]			22	23	24	25	26	27	**28**[i]	Dōng zhì	KOIAK 1690	7	8	9	10	11	12	13	TĀKHŚĀŚ 1966
	23	●	25	26	27	28	29	15:07	52	2442040	TEVETH 5734	28[e]	29[e]	30[e]	1[e]	2[e]	3	4	Mon 22h14m15p	MONTH 12 Guǐ-Chǒu	29	1	2	3	4	5	6			14	15	16	17	18	19	20	
	30	31	◐	2	3	4	5	18:06	1	2442047		5	6	7	8	9	10	11			7	8	9	10	11	12	13			21	22	23	24	25	26	27	

[a]New Year
[b]Spring (18:12)
[c]Summer (13:00)
[d]Autumn (4:21)
[e]Winter (0:08)
● New moon
◐ First quarter moon
○ Full moon
◑ Last quarter moon

‡Leap year
[a]New Year
[b]Yom Kippur
[c]Sukkot
[d]Winter starts
[e]Ḥanukkah
[f]Purim
[g]Passover
[h]Shavuot
[i]Fast of Av

[a]New Year (4671, Ox)
[b]Lantern Festival
[c]Qīngmíng
[d]Dragon Festival
[e]Qīqiǎo
[f]Hungry Ghosts
[g]Mid-Autumn Festival
[h]Double-Ninth Festival
[i]Dōngzhì
*Start of 60-name cycle

[a]New Year
[b]Building of the Cross
[c]Christmas
[d]Jesus's Circumcision
[e]Epiphany
[f]Easter
[g]Mary's Announcement
[h]Jesus's Transfiguration

PERSIAN (ASTRONOMICAL) 1351/1352

Month	Sun	Mon	Tue	Wed	Thu	Fri	Sat
DEY 1351	10	11	12	13	14	15	16
	17	18	19	20	21	22	23
	24	25	26	27	28	29	30
BAHMAN 1351	*1*	2	3	4	5	6	7
	8	9	10	11	12	13	14
	15	16	17	18	19	20	21
	22	23	24	25	26	27	28
ESFAND 1351	29	30	*1*	2	3	4	5
	6	7	8	9	10	11	12
	13	14	15	16	17	18	19
	20	21	22	23	24	25	26
FARVARDĪN 1352	27	28	29	*1*[a]	2	3	4
	5	6	7	8	9	10	11
	12	13[b]	14	15	16	17	18
	19	20	21	22	23	24	25
ORDĪBEHEŠT 1352	26	27	28	29	30	31	*1*
	2	3	4	5	6	7	8
	9	10	11	12	13	14	15
	16	17	18	19	20	21	22
	23	24	25	26	27	28	29
XORDĀD 1352	30	31	*1*	2	3	4	5
	6	7	8	9	10	11	12
	13	14	15	16	17	18	19
	20	21	22	23	24	25	26
TĪR 1352	27	28	29	30	31	*1*	2
	3	4	5	6	7	8	9
	10	11	12	13	14	15	16
	17	18	19	20	21	22	23
	24	25	26	27	28	29	30
MORDĀD 1352	31	*1*	2	3	4	5	6
	7	8	9	10	11	12	13
	14	15	16	17	18	19	20
	21	22	23	24	25	26	27
SHAHRĪVAR 1352	28	29	30	31	*1*	2	3
	4	5	6	7	8	9	10
	11	12	13	14	15	16	17
	18	19	20	21	22	23	24
	25	26	27	28	29	30	31
MEHR 1352	*1*	2	3	4	5	6	7
	8	9	10	11	12	13	14
	15	16	17	18	19	20	21
	22	23	24	25	26	27	28
ĀBĀN 1352	29	30	*1*	2	3	4	5
	6	7	8	9	10	11	12
	13	14	15	16	17	18	19
	20	21	22	23	24	25	26
ĀZAR 1352	27	28	29	30	*1*	2	3
	4	5	6	7	8	9	10
	11	12	13	14	15	16	17
	18	19	20	21	22	23	24
DEY 1352	25	26	27	28	29	30	*1*
	2	3	4	5	6	7	8
	9	10	11	12	13	14	15

[a]New Year
[b]Sizdeh Bedar

HINDU LUNAR 2029‡/2030

Month	Sun	Mon	Tue	Wed	Thu	Fri	Sat
PAUSHA 2029	26	27	28	29	30	1	2
	3	4	5	6	7	8	9
	10	11	**12**	14	15	16	17
	18	19	20	21	22	23	24
	25	26	*26*	27	28	29	30
MĀGHA 2029	1	2	3	4	5	6	**7**
	9	10	11	12	13	14	15
	16	17	18	19	20	21	22
	23	24	25	26	27	28	29[h]
PHĀLGUNA 2029	30	1	2	3	4	5	6
	7	8	9	10	11	**12**	14
	15[i]	16	17	18	19	*19*	20
	21	22	23	24	25	26	27
CHAITRA 2030	28	29	30	1[a]	2	3	4
	5	7	8	9[b]	10	11	12
	13	14	15	16	17	18	19
	20	21	22	*22*	23	24	25
VAIŚĀKHA 2030	26	27	**28**	30	1	2	3
	4	5	6	7	8	9	10
	11	12	13	14	15	16	17
	18	19	20	21	22	23	24
JYAISHTHA 2030	25	26	27	28	29	30	1
	2	4	5	6	7	8	9
	10	11	12	13	14	15	16
	17	18	*18*	19	20	21	22
	23	**24**	26	27	28	29	30
ĀSHĀDHA 2030	1	2	3	4	5	6	7
	8	9	10	11	12	13	14
	15	16	17	18	19	20	21
	22	23	24	25	26	**27**	29
ŚRĀVAṆA 2030	30	1	2	3	4	5	6
	7	8	9	10	11	12	13
	14	15	*15*	16	17	18	**19**
	21	22	23[c]	24	25	26	27
BHĀDRAPADA 2030	28	29	30	**1**	3	4[d]	5
	6	*6*	7	8	9	10	11
	12	13	14	15	16	17	18
	19	20	21	22	**23**	25	26
ĀŚVINA 2030	27	28	29	30	1	2	3
	4	5	6	7	8[e]	9[e]	10[e]
	10[e]	11	12	13	14	15	**16**
	18	19	20	21	22	23	24
KĀRTTIKA 2030	25	26	27	28	29	30	1[f]
	2	3	4	5	6	7	8
	9	10	11	12	13	14	15
	16	17	18	19	20	**21**	23
	24	25	26	27	28	29	30
MĀRGAŚĪRA 2030	1	2	3	4	*4*	5	6
	7	8	9	10	11[g]	12	13
	14	**15**	17	18	19	20	21
	22	23	24	25	26	27	28
PAUSHA 2030	29	30	1	2	3	4	5
	6	7	8	9	10	11	12

‡Leap year
[a]New Year (Pramādin)
[b]Birthday of Rāma
[c]Birthday of Krishna
[d]Ganēśa Chaturthī
[e]Dashara
[f]Diwali
[g]Birthday of Vishnu
[h]Night of Śiva
[i]Holi

HINDU SOLAR 1894/1895

Month	Sun	Mon	Tue	Wed	Thu	Fri	Sat
PAUSHA 1894	17	18	19	20	21	22	23
MĀGHA 1894	24	25	26	27	28	29	1[b]
	2	3	4	5	6	7	8
	9	10	11	12	13	14	15
	16	17	18	19	20	21	22
	23	24	25	26	27	28	29
PHĀLGUNA 1894	30	1	2	3	4	5	6
	7	8	9	10	11	12	13
	14	15	16	17	18	19	20
	21	22	23	24	25	26	27
CHAITRA 1894	28	29	30	1	2	3	4
	5	6	7	8	9	10	11
	12	13	14	15	16	17	18
	19	20	21	22	23	24	25
VAIŚĀKHA 1895	26	27	28	29	30	1[a]	2
	3	4	5	6	7	8	9
	10	11	12	13	14	15	16
	17	18	19	20	21	22	23
	24	25	26	27	28	29	30
JYAISHTHA 1895	31	1	2	3	4	5	6
	7	8	9	10	11	12	13
	14	15	16	17	18	19	20
	21	22	23	24	25	26	27
ĀSHĀDHA 1895	28	29	30	31	1	2	3
	4	5	6	7	8	9	10
	11	12	13	14	15	16	17
	18	19	20	21	22	23	24
	25	26	27	28	29	30	31
ŚRĀVAṆA 1895	32	1	2	3	4	5	6
	7	8	9	10	11	12	13
	14	15	16	17	18	19	20
	21	22	23	24	25	26	27
BHĀDRAPADA 1895	28	29	30	31	1	2	3
	4	5	6	7	8	9	10
	11	12	13	14	15	16	17
	18	19	20	21	22	23	24
	25	26	27	28	29	30	31
ĀŚVINA 1895	1	2	3	4	5	6	7
	8	9	10	11	12	13	14
	15	16	17	18	19	20	21
	22	23	24	25	26	27	28
KĀRTTIKA 1895	29	30	31	1	2	3	4
	5	6	7	8	9	10	11
	12	13	14	15	16	17	18
	19	20	21	22	23	24	25
MĀRGAŚĪRA 1895	26	27	28	29	30	1	2
	3	4	5	6	7	8	9
	10	11	12	13	14	15	16
	17	18	19	20	21	22	23
PAUSHA 1895	24	25	26	27	28	29	1
	2	3	4	5	6	7	8
	9	10	11	12	13	14	15
	16	17	18	19	20	21	22

[a]New Year (Kshaya)
[b]Pongal

ISLAMIC (ASTRONOMICAL) 1392‡/1393

Month	Sun	Mon	Tue	Wed	Thu	Fri	Sat
DHU AL-ḤIJJA 1392	25	26	27	28	29	30	*1*
	2	3	4	5	6	7	8
	9	10[g]	11	12	13	14	15
	16	17	18	19	20	21	22
	23	24	25	26	27	28	29
MUḤARRAM 1393	30[d]	1[a]	2	3	4	5	6
	7	8	9	10[b]	11	12	13
	14	15	16	17	18	19	20
	21	22	23	24	25	26	27
ṢAFAR 1393	28	29	*1*	2	3	4	5
	6	7	8	9	10	11	12
	13	14	15	16	17	18	19
	20	21	22	23	24	25	26
RABĪʿ I 1393	27	28	29	*30*	1	2	3
	4	5	6	7	8	9	10
	11	12[c]	13	14	15	16	17
	18	19	20	21	22	23	24
RABĪʿ II 1393	25	26	27	28	29	*1*	2
	3	4	5	6	7	8	9
	10	11	12	13	14	15	16
	17	18	19	20	21	22	23
JUMĀDĀ I 1393	24	25	26	27	28	29	*1*
	2	3	4	5	6	7	8
	9	10	11	12	13	14	15
	16	17	18	19	20	21	22
	23	24	25	26	27	28	29
JUMĀDĀ II 1393	30	*1*	2	3	4	5	6
	7	8	9	10	11	12	13
	14	15	16	17	18	19	20
	21	22	23	24	25	26	27
RAJAB 1393	28	29	*30*	1	2	3	4
	5	6	7	8	9	10	11
	12	13	14	15	16	17	18
	19	20	21	22	23	24	25
SHAʿBĀN 1393	26	27[d]	28	29	*1*	2	3
	4	5	6	7	8	9	10
	11	12	13	14	15	16	17
	18	19	20	21	22	23	24
RAMAḌĀN 1393	25	26	27	28	29	*30*	1[e]
	2	3	4	5	6	7	8
	9	10	11	12	13	14	15
	16	17	18	19	20	21	22
	23	24	25	26	27	28	29
SHAWWĀL 1393	*1*[f]	2	3	4	5	6	7
	8	9	10	11	12	13	14
	15	16	17	18	19	20	21
	22	23	24	25	26	27	28
DHU AL-QAʿDA 1393	29	*1*	2	3	4	5	6
	7	8	9	10	11	12	13
	14	15	16	17	18	19	20
	21	22	23	24	25	26	27
DHU AL-ḤIJJA 1393	28	29	30	*1*	2	3	4
	5	6	7	8	9	10	11

‡Leap year
[a]New Year
[d]New Year (Arithmetic)
[b]ʿAshūrā'
[c]Prophet's Birthday
[d]Ascent of the Prophet
[e]Start of Ramaḍān
[f]ʿId al-Fiṭr
[g]ʿId al-'Aḍḥā

GREGORIAN 1973

Julian (Sun)	Sun	Mon	Tue	Wed	Thu	Fri	Sat	Month
Dec 18	31	1	2	3	4	5	6	JANUARY 1973
	7[a]	8	9	10	11	12	13	
Jan 1	*14*[b]	15	16	17	18	19	20	
	21	22	23	24	25	26	27	
Jan 15	*28*	29	30	31	1	2	3	FEBRUARY 1973
	4	5	6	7	8	9	10	
Jan 29	*11*	12	13	14	15	16	17	
	18	19	20	21	22	23	24	
Feb 12	*25*	26	27	28	1	2	3	MARCH 1973
	4	5	6	7[c]	8	9	10	
Feb 26	*11*	12	13	14	15	16	17	
	18[d]	19	20	21	22	23	24	
Mar 12	*25*	26	27	28	29	30	31	
	1	2	3	4	5	6	7	APRIL 1973
Mar 26	*8*	9	10	11	12	13	14	
	15	16	17	18	19	20	21	
Apr 9	*22*[e]	23	24	25	26	27	28	
	29[f]	30	1	2	3	4	5	MAY 1973
Apr 23	*6*	7	8	9	10	11	12	
	13	14	15	16	17	18	19	
May 7	*20*	21	22	23	24	25	26	
	27	28	29	30	31	1	2	JUNE 1973
May 21	*3*	4	5	6	7	8	9	
	10	11	12	13	14	15	16	
Jun 4	*17*	18	19	20	21	22	23	
	24	25	26	27	28	29	30	
Jun 18	*1*	2	3	4	5	6	7	JULY 1973
	8	9	10	11	12	13	14	
Jul 2	*15*	16	17	18	19	20	21	
	22	23	24	25	26	27	28	
Jul 16	*29*	30	31	1	2	3	4	AUGUST 1973
	5	6	7	8	9	10	11	
Jul 30	*12*	13	14	15	16	17	18	
	19	20	21	22	23	24	25	
Aug 13	*26*	27	28	29	30	31	1	SEPTEMBER 1973
	2	3	4	5	6	7	8	
Aug 27	*9*	10	11	12	13	14	15	
	16	17	18	19	20	21	22	
Sep 10	*23*	24	25	26	27	28	29	
	30	1	2	3	4	5	6	OCTOBER 1973
Sep 24	*7*	8	9	10	11	12	13	
	14	15	16	17	18	19	20	
Oct 8	*21*	22	23	24	25	26	27	
	28	29	30	31	1	2	3	NOVEMBER 1973
Oct 22	*4*	5	6	7	8	9	10	
	11	12	13	14	15	16	17	
Nov 5	*18*	19	20	21	22	23	24	
	25	26	27	28	29	30	1	DECEMBER 1973
Nov 19	*2*[g]	3	4	5	6	7	8	
	9	10	11	12	13	14	15	
Dec 3	*16*	17	18	19	20	21	22	
	23	24	25[h]	26	27	28	29	
Dec 17	*30*	31	1	2	3	4	5	

[a]Orthodox Christmas
[b]Julian New Year
[c]Ash Wednesday
[d]Feast of Orthodoxy
[e]Easter
[f]Orthodox Easter
[g]Advent
[h]Christmas

1974

Month	Sun	Mon	Tue	Wed	Thu	Fri	Sat	Lunar Phases	ISO WEEK (Mon)	JULIAN DAY (Sun noon)	Hebrew month	Sun	Mon	Tue	Wed	Thu	Fri	Sat	Molad
GREGORIAN 1974											HEBREW 5734/5735								
	30	31	◐[a]	2	3	4	5	18:06	1	2442047		5	6	7	8	9	10	11	
JANUARY 1974	6	7	○	9	10	11	12	12:36	2	2442054	TEVETH 5734	12	13	14	15	16	17	18	
	13	14	◑	16	17	18	19	7:04	3	2442061		19	20	21	22	23	24	25	
	20	21	22	●	24	25	26	11:02	4	2442068		26	27	28	29	1	2	3	Wed 10h58m16p
	27	28	29	30	◐	1	2	7:39	5	2442075		4	5	6	7	8	9	10	
FEBRUARY 1974	3	4	5	○	7	8	9	23:24	6	2442082	SHEVAT 5734	11	12	13	14	15	16	17	
	10	11	12	13	◑	15	16	0:04	7	2442089		18	19	20	21	22	23	24	
	17	18	19	20	21	●	23	5:34	8	2442096		25	26	27	28	29	30	1	Thu 23h42m17p
	24	25	26	27	28	◐	2	18:02	9	2442103		2	3	4	5	6	7	8	
	3	4	5	6	7	○	9	10:03	10	2442110	ADAR 5734	9	10	11	12	13	14[f]	15	
MARCH 1974	10	11	12	13	14	◑	16	19:15	11	2442117		16	17	18	19	20	21	22	
	17	18	19	20	21[b]	22	●	21:24	12	2442124		23	24	25	26	27	28	29	Sat 12h27m0p
	24	25	26	27	28	29	30		13	2442131		1	2	3	4	5	6	7	
	◐	1	2	3	4	5	○	1:44 21:00	14	2442138		8	9	10	11	12	13	14	
APRIL 1974	7	8	9	10	11	12	13		15	2442145	NISAN 5734	15[g]	16	17	18	19	20	21	
	◑	15	16	17	18	19	20	14:57	16	2442152		22	23	24	25	26	27	28	
	21	●	23	24	25	26	27	10:17	17	2442159		29	30	1	2	3	4	5	Mon 1h11m1p
	28	◐	30	1	2	3	4	7:39	18	2442166		6	7	8	9	10	11	12	
MAY 1974	5	○	7	8	9	10	11	8:54	19	2442173	IYYAR 5734	13	14	15	16	17	18	19	
	12	13	◑	15	16	17	18	9:29	20	2442180		20	21	22	23	24	25	26	
	19	20	●	22	23	24	25	20:34	21	2442187		27	28	29	1	2	3	4	Tue 13h55m2p
	26	27	◐	29	30	31	1	13:03	22	2442194		5	6[h]	7	8	9	10	11	
	2	3	○	5	6	7	8	22:09	23	2442201	SIVAN 5734	12	13	14	15	16	17	18	
JUNE 1974	9	10	11	12	◑	14	15	1:45	24	2442208		19	20	21	22	23	24	25	
	16	17	18	19	●	21[c]	22	4:56	25	2442215		26	27	28	29	30	1	2	Thu 2h39m3p
	23	24	25	◐	27	28	29	19:20	26	2442222		3	4	5	6	7	8	9	
	30	1	2	3	○	5	6	12:40	27	2442229	TAMMUZ 5734	10	11	12	13	14	15	16	
JULY 1974	7	8	9	10	11	◑	13	15:28	28	2442236		17	18	19	20	21	22	23	
	14	15	16	17	18	●	20	12:06	29	2442243		24	25	26	27	28	29	1	Fri 15h23m4p
	21	22	23	24	25	◐	27	3:51	30	2442250		2	3	4	5	6	7	8	
	28	29	30	31	1	2	○	3:57	31	2442257	AV 5734	9[i]	10	11	12	13	14	15	
AUGUST 1974	4	5	6	7	8	9	10		32	2442264		16	17	18	19	20	21	22	
	◑	12	13	14	15	16	●	2:46 19:01	33	2442271		23	24	25	26	27	28	29	
	18	19	20	21	22	23	◐	15:38	34	2442278		30	1	2	3	4	5	6	Sun 4h7m5p
	25	26	27	28	29	30	31		35	2442285		7	8	9	10	11	12	13	
	○	2	3	4	5	6	7	19:25	36	2442292	ELUL 5734	14	15	16	17	18	19	20	
SEPTEMBER 1974	8	◑	10	11	12	13	14	12:01	37	2442299		21	22	23	24	25	26	27	
	15	●	17	18	19	20	21	2:45	38	2442306		28	29	1[a]	2[a]	3	4	5	Mon 16h51m6p
	22	◐[d]	24	25	26	27	28	7:08	39	2442313		6	7	8	9	10[b]	11	12	
	29	30	○	2	3	4	5	10:38	40	2442320	TISHRI 5735	13	14	15[c]	16	17	18	19	
OCTOBER 1974	6	7	◑	9	10	11	12	19:46	41	2442327		20	21	22	23	24	25	26	
	13	14	●	16	17	18	19	12:25	42	2442334		27	28	29	30	1	2	3	Wed 5h35m7p
	20	21	22	◐	24	25	26	1:53	43	2442341		4	5	6	7	8	9	10	
	27	28	29	30	○	1	2	1:19	44	2442348	HESHVAN 5735	11	12	13	14	15	16	17	
	3	4	5	6	◑	8	9	2:47	45	2442355		18	19	20	21	22	23	24	
NOVEMBER 1974	10	11	12	13	●	15	16	0:53	46	2442362		25	26	27	28	29	1	2	Thu 18h19m8p
	17	18	19	20	◐	22	23	22:39	47	2442369		3	4	5	6	7	8	9	
	24	25	26	27	28	○	30	15:10	48	2442376	KISLEV 5735	10	11	12	13	14	15	16	
	1	2	3	4	5	◑	7	10:10	49	2442383		17	18	19	20	21[d]	22	23	
DECEMBER 1974	8	9	10	11	12	●	14	16:25	50	2442390		24	25[e]	26[e]	27[e]	28[e]	29[e]	30[e]	
	15	16	17	18	19	20	◐	19:43	51	2442397		1[e]	2[e]	3	4	5	6	7	Sat 7h3m9p
	22[e]	23	24	25	26	27	28		52	2442404	TEVETH 5735	8	9	10	11	12	13	14	
	○	30	31	1	2	3	◑	3:51 19:04	1	2442411		15	16	17	18	19	20	21	

ISO WEEK	Chinese month	Sun	Mon	Tue	Wed	Thu	Fri	Sat	Solar Term	Coptic month	Sun	Mon	Tue	Wed	Thu	Fri	Sat	Ethiopic month
	CHINESE Guǐ-Chǒu/Jiǎ-Yín‡									COPTIC 1690/1691‡								ETHIOPIC 1966/1967‡
1		7	8	9	10	11	12	13		KOIAK 1690	21	22	23	24	25	26	27	TĀKHŚĀŚ 1966
2	MONTH 12 Guǐ-Chǒu	*14*	15	16	17	18	19	20	Xiǎo hán		28	29[c]	30	1	2	3	4	
3		21	22	23	24	25	26	27		TŌBE 1690	5	6[d]	7	8	9	10	11[e]	ṬER 1966
4		***28***	29	30	1[a]*	2	3	4	Dà hán		12	13	14	15	16	17	18	
5		5	6	7	8	9	10	11			19	20	21	22	23	24	25	
6	MONTH 1 Jiǎ-Yín	12	*13*	14	15[b]	16	17	18	Lì chūn		26	27	28	29	30	1	2	
7		19	20	21	22	23	24	25		MESHIR 1690	3	4	5	6	7	8	9	YAKĀTIT 1966
8		26	27	**28**	29	30	1	2	Yǔ shuǐ		10	11	12	13	14	15	16	
9		3	4	5	6	7	8	9			17	18	19	20	21	22	23	
10	MONTH 2 Jiǎ-Yín	10	11	12	*13*	14	15	16	Jīng zhé		24	25	26	27	28	29	30	
11		17	18	19	20	21	22	23			1	2	3	4	5	6	7	
12		24	25	26	27	***28***	29	30	Chūn fēn	PAREMOTEP 1690	8	9	10	11	12	13	14	MAGĀBIT 1966
13		1*	2	3	4	5	6	7			15	16	17	18	19	20	21	
14		8	9	10	11	12	*13*[c]	14	Qīng míng		22	23	24	25	26	27	28	
15	MONTH 3 Jiǎ-Yín	15	16	17	18	19	20	21			29	30	1	2	3	4	5	
16		22	23	24	25	26	27	***28***	Gǔ yǔ		6[f]	7	8	9	10	11	12	
17		29	1	2	3	4	5	6		PARMOUTE 1690	13	14	15	16	17	18	19	MIYĀZYĀ 1966
18		7	8	9	10	11	12	13			20	21	22	23	24	25	26	
19	MONTH 4 Jiǎ-Yín	14	*15*	16	17	18	19	20	Lì xià		27	28	29[g]	30	1	2	3	
20		21	22	23	24	25	26	27			4	5	6	7	8	9	10	GENBOT 1966
21		28	29	***30***	1	2*	3	4	Xiǎo mǎn	PASHONS 1690	11	12	13	14	15	16	17	
22		5	6	7	8	9	10	11			18	19	20	21	22	23	24	
23	LEAP MONTH 4 Jiǎ-Yín	12	13	14	15	*16*	17	18	Máng zhòng		25	26	27	28	29	30	1	
24		19	20	21	22	23	24	25			2	3	4	5	6	7	8	
25		26	27	28	29	1	2	***3***	Xià zhì	PAŌNE 1690	9	10	11	12	13	14	15	SANĒ 1966
26		4	5[d]	6	7	8	9	10			16	17	18	19	20	21	22	
27	MONTH 5 Jiǎ-Yín	11	12	13	14	15	16	17			23	24	25	26	27	28	29	
28		*18*	19	20	21	22	23	24	Xiǎo shǔ		30	1	2	3	4	5	6	
29		25	26	27	28	29	1	2			7	8	9	10	11	12	13	
30	MONTH 6 Jiǎ-Yín	3	4*	**5**	6	7	8	9	Dà shǔ	EPĒP 1690	14	15	16	17	18	19	20	ḤAMLĒ 1966
31		10	11	12	13	14	15	16			21	22	23	24	25	26	27	
32		17	18	19	20	*21*	22	23	Lì qiū		28	29	30	1	2	3	4	
33		24	25	26	27	28	29	30			5	6	7	8	9	10	11	
34		1	2	3	4	5	**6**	7[e]	Chǔ shǔ	MESORĒ 1690	12	13[h]	14	15	16	17	18	NAHASĒ 1966
35	MONTH 7 Jiǎ-Yín	8	9	10	11	12	13	14			19	20	21	22	23	24	25	
36		15[f]	16	17	18	19	20	21		EPAG. 1690	26	27	28	29	30	1	2	PĀG. 1966
37		*22*	23	24	25	26	27	28	Bái lù		3	4	5	1[a]	2	3	4	
38		29	1	2	3	4	5*	6		THOOUT 1691	5	6	7	8	9	10	11	MASKARAM 1967
39	MONTH 8 Jiǎ-Yín	7	**8**	9	10	11	12	13	Qiū fēn		12	13	14	15	16	17[b]	18	
40		14	15[g]	16	17	18	19	20			19	20	21	22	23	24	25	
41		21	22	23	*24*	25	26	27	Hán lù		26	27	28	29	30	1	2	
42		28	29	1	2	3	4	5		PAOPE 1691	3	4	5	6	7	8	9	ṬEQEMT 1967
43	MONTH 9 Jiǎ-Yín	6	7	8	9[h]	***10***	11	12	Shuāng jiàng		10	11	12	13	14	15	16	
44		13	14	15	16	17	18	19			17	18	19	20	21	22	23	
45		20	21	22	23	24	*25*	26	Lì dōng		24	25	26	27	28	29	30	
46		27	28	29	30	1	2	3			1	2	3	4	5	6	7	
47	MONTH 10 Jiǎ-Yín	4	5	6*	7	8	9	***10***	Xiǎo xuě	ATHŌR 1691	8	9	10	11	12	13	14	ḪEDĀR 1967
48		11	12	13	14	15	16	17			15	16	17	18	19	20	21	
49		18	19	20	21	22	23	*24*	Dà xuě		22	23	24	25	26	27	28	
50		25	26	27	28	29	30	1			29	30	1	2	3	4	5	
51	MONTH 11 Jiǎ-Yín	2	3	4	5	6	7	8		KOIAK 1691	6	7	8	9	10	11	12	TĀKHŚĀŚ 1967
52		**9**[i]	10	11	12	13	14	15	Dōng zhì		13	14	15	16	17	18	19	
1		16	17	18	19	20	21	22			20	21	22	23	24	25	26	

[a]New Year
[b]Spring (0:06)
[c]Summer (18:37)
[d]Autumn (9:59)
[e]Winter (5:55)
● New moon
◐ First quarter moon
○ Full moon
◑ Last quarter moon

[a]New Year
[b]Yom Kippur
[c]Sukkot
[d]Winter starts
[e]Ḥanukkah
[f]Purim
[g]Passover
[h]Shavuot
[i]Fast of Av

‡Leap year
[a]New Year (4672, Tiger)
[b]Lantern Festival
[c]Qīngmíng
[d]Dragon Festival
[e]Qīqiǎo
[f]Hungry Ghosts
[g]Mid-Autumn Festival
[h]Double-Ninth Festival
[i]Dōngzhì
*Start of 60-name cycle

‡Leap year
[a]New Year
[b]Building of the Cross
[c]Christmas
[d]Jesus's Circumcision
[e]Epiphany
[f]Easter
[g]Mary's Announcement
[h]Jesus's Transfiguration

1974

PERSIAN (ASTRONOMICAL) 1352/1353

Month	Sun	Mon	Tue	Wed	Thu	Fri	Sat
DEY 1352	9	10	11	12	13	14	15
	16	17	18	19	20	21	22
	23	24	25	26	27	28	29
BAHMAN 1352	30	*1*	2	3	4	5	6
	7	8	9	10	11	12	13
	14	15	16	17	18	19	20
	21	22	23	24	25	26	27
ESFAND 1352	28	29	30	*1*	2	3	4
	5	6	7	8	9	10	11
	12	13	14	15	16	17	18
	19	20	21	22	23	24	25
FARVARDĪN 1353	26	27	28	29	*1*[a]	2	3
	4	5	6	7	8	9	10
	11	12	13[b]	14	15	16	17
	18	19	20	21	22	23	24
	25	26	27	28	29	30	31
ORDĪBEHEŠT 1353	*1*	2	3	4	5	6	7
	8	9	10	11	12	13	14
	15	16	17	18	19	20	21
	22	23	24	25	26	27	28
XORDĀD 1353	29	30	31	*1*	2	3	4
	5	6	7	8	9	10	11
	12	13	14	15	16	17	18
	19	20	21	22	23	24	25
TĪR 1353	26	27	28	29	30	31	*1*
	2	3	4	5	6	7	8
	9	10	11	12	13	14	15
	16	17	18	19	20	21	22
	23	24	25	26	27	28	29
MORDĀD 1353	30	31	*1*	2	3	4	5
	6	7	8	9	10	11	12
	13	14	15	16	17	18	19
	20	21	22	23	24	25	26
SHAHRĪVAR 1353	27	28	29	30	31	*1*	2
	3	4	5	6	7	8	9
	10	11	12	13	14	15	16
	17	18	19	20	21	22	23
	24	25	26	27	28	29	30
MEHR 1353	31	*1*	2	3	4	5	6
	7	8	9	10	11	12	13
	14	15	16	17	18	19	20
	21	22	23	24	25	26	27
ABĀN 1353	28	29	30	*1*	2	3	4
	5	6	7	8	9	10	11
	12	13	14	15	16	17	18
	19	20	21	22	23	24	25
ĀZAR 1353	26	27	28	29	30	*1*	2
	3	4	5	6	7	8	9
	10	11	12	13	14	15	16
	17	18	19	20	21	22	23
	24	25	26	27	28	29	30
DEY 1353	*1*	2	3	4	5	6	7
	8	9	10	11	12	13	14

[a]New Year
[b]Sizdeh Bedar

HINDU LUNAR 2030/2031‡

Month	Sun	Mon	Tue	Wed	Thu	Fri	Sat
PAUSHA 2030	6	7	8	9	10	11	12
	13	14	15	16	17	18	19
	20	22	23	24	25	26	*26*
MĀGHA 2030	27	28	29	30	1	2	3
	4	5	6	7	8	9	10
	11	12	13	**14**	16	17	18
	19	20	21	22	23	24	25
PHĀLGUNA 2030	26	27	28	29[h]	*29*	30	1
	2	3	4	5	6	7	**8**
	10	11	12	13	14	15[i]	16
	17	18	19	20	21	22	23
	24	25	26	27	28	29	30
CHAITRA 2031	1[a]	2	3	4	5	6	7
	8	9[b]	10	11	**12**	14	15
	16	17	18	19	20	21	22
	22	23	24	25	26	27	28
VAIŚĀKHA 2031	29	30	1	2	3	4	**5**
	7	8	9	10	11	12	13
	14	15	16	17	18	19	20
	21	22	23	24	25	26	27
JYAISHṬHA 2031	28	29	30	1	2	3	4
	5	6	7	8	**9**	11	12
	13	14	15	16	17	18	*18*
	19	20	21	22	23	24	25
ĀSHĀḌHA 2031	26	27	28	29	30	1	**2**
	4	5	6	7	8	9	10
	11	12	13	14	15	16	17
	18	19	20	21	22	23	24
ŚRĀVAṆA 2031	25	26	27	28	29	30	1
	2	3	**4**	6	7	8	9
	10	11	12	13	14	15	*15*
	16	17	18	19	20	21	22
	23[c]	24	25	26	**27**	29	30
LEAP BHĀDRAPADA 2031	1	2	3	4	5	6	7
	8	9	10	11	12	13	14
	15	16	17	18	19	20	21
	22	23	24	25	26	27	28
BHĀDRAPADA 2031	29	30	**1**	3	4[d]	5	6
	7	8	9	10	*10*	11	12
	13	14	15	16	17	18	19
	20	21	22	23	**24**	26	27
ĀŚVINA 2031	28	29	30	1	2	3	4
	5	6	7	8[e]	9[e]	10[e]	11
	12	13	14	15	*15*	**16**	18
	19	20	21	22	23	24	25
KĀRTTIKA 2031	26	27	28	**29**	1[f]	2	3
	4	*4*	5	6	7	8	9
	10	11	12	13	14	15	16
	17	18	19	20	21	**22**	24
MĀRGAŚĪRA 2031	25	26	27	28	29	30	1
	2	3	4	5	6	7	*7*
	8	9	10	11[g]	12	13	14
	15	**16**	18	19	20	21	22

‡Leap year
[a]New Year (Ānanda)
[b]Birthday of Rāma
[c]Birthday of Krishna
[d]Ganēśa Chaturthī
[e]Dashara
[f]Diwali
[g]Birthday of Vishnu
[h]Night of Śiva
[i]Holi

HINDU SOLAR 1895/1896‡

Month	Sun	Mon	Tue	Wed	Thu	Fri	Sat
PAUSHA 1895	16	17	18	19	20	21	22
	23	24	25	26	27	28	29
MĀGHA 1895	30	1[b]	2	3	4	5	6
	7	8	9	10	11	12	13
	14	15	16	17	18	19	20
	21	22	23	24	25	26	27
PHĀLGUNA 1895	28	29	1	2	3	4	5
	6	7	8	9	10	11	12
	13	14	15	16	17	18	19
	20	21	22	23	24	25	26
CHAITRA 1895	27	28	29	30	1	2	3
	4	5	6	7	8	9	10
	11	12	13	14	15	16	17
	18	19	20	21	22	23	24
VAIŚĀKHA 1896	25	26	27	28	29	30	1[a]
	2	3	4	5	6	7	8
	9	10	11	12	13	14	15
	16	17	18	19	20	21	22
	23	24	25	26	27	28	29
JYAISHṬHA 1896	30	31	1	2	3	4	5
	6	7	8	9	10	11	12
	13	14	15	16	17	18	19
	20	21	22	23	24	25	26
ĀSHĀḌHA 1896	27	28	29	30	31	32	1
	2	3	4	5	6	7	8
	9	10	11	12	13	14	15
	16	17	18	19	20	21	22
	23	24	25	26	27	28	29
ŚRĀVAṆA 1896	30	31	1	2	3	4	5
	6	7	8	9	10	11	12
	13	14	15	16	17	18	19
	20	21	22	23	24	25	26
BHĀDRAPADA 1896	27	28	29	30	31	32	1
	2	3	4	5	6	7	8
	9	10	11	12	13	14	15
	16	17	18	19	20	21	22
	23	24	25	26	27	28	29
ĀŚVINA 1896	30	31	1	2	3	4	5
	6	7	8	9	10	11	12
	13	14	15	16	17	18	19
	20	21	22	23	24	25	26
KĀRTTIKA 1896	27	28	29	30	1	2	3
	4	5	6	7	8	9	10
	11	12	13	14	15	16	17
	18	19	20	21	22	23	24
MĀRGAŚĪRA 1896	25	26	27	28	29	30	1
	2	3	4	5	6	7	8
	9	10	11	12	13	14	15
	16	17	18	19	20	21	22
	23	24	25	26	27	28	29
PAUSHA 1896	30	1	2	3	4	5	6
	7	8	9	10	11	12	13
	14	15	16	17	18	19	20

‡Leap year
[a]New Year (Prabhava)
[b]Pongal

ISLAMIC (ASTRONOMICAL) 1393/1394

Month	Sun	Mon	Tue	Wed	Thu	Fri	Sat
DHU AL-ḤIJJA 1393	5	6	7	8	9	10[g]	11
	12	13	14	15	16	17	18
	19	20	21	22	23	24	25
MUḤARRAM 1394	26	27	28	29	30	*1*[a]	2
	3	4	5	6	7	8	9
	10[b]	11	12	13	14	15	16
	17	18	19	20	21	22	23
ṢAFAR 1394	24	25	26	27	28	29	1
	2	3	4	5	6	7	8
	9	10	11	12	13	14	15
	16	17	18	19	20	21	22
	23	24	25	26	27	28	29
RABĪʿ I 1394	30	*1*	2	3	4	5	6
	7	8	9	10	11	12[c]	13
	14	15	16	17	18	19	20
	21	22	23	24	25	26	27
RABĪʿ II 1394	28	29	30	*1*	2	3	4
	5	6	7	8	9	10	11
	12	13	14	15	16	17	18
	19	20	21	22	23	24	25
JUMĀDĀ I 1394	26	27	28	29	*1*	2	3
	4	5	6	7	8	9	10
	11	12	13	14	15	16	17
	18	19	20	21	22	23	24
JUMĀDĀ II 1394	25	26	27	28	29	1	*2*
	3	4	5	6	7	8	9
	10	11	12	13	14	15	16
	17	18	19	20	21	22	23
	24	25	26	27	28	29	30
RAJAB 1394	*1*	2	3	4	5	6	7
	8	9	10	11	12	13	14
	15	16	17	18	19	20	21
	22	23	24	25	26	27[d]	28
SHAʿBĀN 1394	29	30	*1*	2	3	4	5
	6	7	8	9	10	11	12
	13	14	15	16	17	18	19
	20	21	22	23	24	25	26
RAMAḌĀN 1394	27	28	29	*1*[e]	2	3	4
	5	6	7	8	9	10	11
	12	13	14	15	16	17	18
	19	20	21	22	23	24	25
SHAWWĀL 1394	26	27	28	29	1[f]	*2*	3
	4	5	6	7	8	9	10
	11	12	13	14	15	16	17
	18	19	20	21	22	23	24
DHU AL-QAʿDA 1394	25	26	27	28	29	30	*1*
	2	3	4	5	6	7	8
	9	10	11	12	13	14	15
	16	17	18	19	20	21	22
	23	24	25	26	27	28	29
DHU AL-ḤIJJA 1394	1	*2*	3	4	5	6	7
	8	9	10[g]	11	12	13	14
	15	16	17	18	19	20	21

[a]New Year
[b]ʿAshūrāʾ
[c]Prophet's Birthday
[d]Ascent of the Prophet
[e]Start of Ramaḍān
[f]ʿId al-Fiṭr
[g]ʿId al-ʾAḍḥā

GREGORIAN 1974

Julian (Sun)	Sun	Mon	Tue	Wed	Thu	Fri	Sat	Month
Dec 17	*30*	31	1	2	3	4	5	JANUARY 1974
	6	7[a]	8	9	10	11	12	
Dec 31	*13*	14[b]	15	16	17	18	19	
	20	21	22	23	24	25	26	
Jan 14	*27*	28	29	30	31	1	2	FEBRUARY 1974
	3	4	5	6	7	8	9	
Jan 28	*10*	11	12	13	14	15	16	
	17	18	19	20	21	22	23	
Feb 11	*24*	25	26	27[c]	28	1	2	MARCH 1974
	3[d]	4	5	6	7	8	9	
Feb 25	*10*	11	12	13	14	15	16	
	17	18	19	20	21	22	23	
Mar 11	*24*	25	26	27	28	29	30	
	31	1	2	3	4	5	6	APRIL 1974
Mar 25	*7*	8	9	10	11	12	13	
	14[e]	15	16	17	18	19	20	
Apr 8	*21*	22	23	24	25	26	27	
	28	29	30	1	2	3	4	MAY 1974
Apr 22	*5*	6	7	8	9	10	11	
	12	13	14	15	16	17	18	
May 6	*19*	20	21	22	23	24	25	
	26	27	28	29	30	31	1	JUNE 1974
May 20	*2*	3	4	5	6	7	8	
	9	10	11	12	13	14	15	
Jun 3	*16*	17	18	19	20	21	22	
	23	24	25	26	27	28	29	
Jun 17	*30*	1	2	3	4	5	6	JULY 1974
	7	8	9	10	11	12	13	
Jul 1	*14*	15	16	17	18	19	20	
	21	22	23	24	25	26	27	
Jul 15	*28*	29	30	31	1	2	3	AUGUST 1974
	4	5	6	7	8	9	10	
Jul 29	*11*	12	13	14	15	16	17	
	18	19	20	21	22	23	24	
Aug 12	*25*	26	27	28	29	30	31	
	1	2	3	4	5	6	7	SEPTEMBER 1974
Aug 26	*8*	9	10	11	12	13	14	
	15	16	17	18	19	20	21	
Sep 9	*22*	23	24	25	26	27	28	
	29	30	1	2	3	4	5	OCTOBER 1974
Sep 23	*6*	7	8	9	10	11	12	
	13	14	15	16	17	18	19	
Oct 7	*20*	21	22	23	24	25	26	
	27	28	29	30	31	1	2	NOVEMBER 1974
Oct 21	*3*	4	5	6	7	8	9	
	10	11	12	13	14	15	16	
Nov 4	*17*	18	19	20	21	22	23	
	24	25	26	27	28	29	30	
Nov 18	*1*[g]	2	3	4	5	6	7	DECEMBER 1974
	8	9	10	11	12	13	14	
Dec 2	*15*	16	17	18	19	20	21	
	22	23	24	25[h]	26	27	28	
Dec 16	*29*	30	31	1	2	3	4	

[a]Orthodox Christmas
[b]Julian New Year
[c]Ash Wednesday
[d]Feast of Orthodoxy
[e]Easter (also Orthodox)
[g]Advent
[h]Christmas

1975

GREGORIAN 1975

Month	Sun	Mon	Tue	Wed	Thu	Fri	Sat	Lunar Phases	ISO WEEK (Mon)	JULIAN DAY (Sun noon)
	○	30	31	1[a]	2	3	◑	3:51 19:04	1	2442411
	5	6	7	8	9	10	11		2	2442418
JANUARY 1975	●	13	14	15	16	17	18	10:20	3	2442425
	19	◐	21	22	23	24	25	15:14	4	2442432
	26	○	28	29	30	31	1	15:09	5	2442439
	2	◑	4	5	6	7	8	6:23	6	2442446
FEBRUARY 1975	9	10	●	12	13	14	15	5:17	7	2442453
	16	17	18	◐	20	21	22	7:38	8	2442460
	23	24	25	○	27	28	1	1:14	9	2442467
	2	3	◑	5	6	7	8	20:20	10	2442474
MARCH 1975	9	10	11	●	13	14	15	23:47	11	2442481
	16	17	18	19	◐	21[b]	22	20:05	12	2442488
	23	24	25	26	○	28	29	10:36	13	2442495
	30	31	1	2	◑	4	5	12:25	14	2442502
	6	7	8	9	10	●	12	16:39	15	2442509
APRIL 1975	13	14	15	16	17	18	◐	4:41	16	2442516
	20	21	22	23	24	○	26	19:55	17	2442523
	27	28	29	30	1	2	◑	5:44	18	2442530
	4	5	6	7	8	9	10		19	2442537
MAY 1975	●	12	13	14	15	16	17	7:05	20	2442544
	◐	19	20	21	22	23	24	10:29	21	2442551
	○	26	27	28	29	30	31	5:51	22	2442558
	◑	2	3	4	5	6	7	23:23	23	2442565
	8	●	10	11	12	13	14	18:49	24	2442572
JUNE 1975	15	◐	17	18	19	20	21	14:58	25	2442579
	22[c]	○	24	25	26	27	28	16:54	26	2442586
	29	30	◑	2	3	4	5	16:37	27	2442593
	6	7	8	●	10	11	12	4:10	28	2442600
JULY 1975	13	14	◐	16	17	18	19	19:47	29	2442607
	20	21	22	○	24	25	26	5:28	30	2442614
	27	28	29	30	◑	1	2	8:48	31	2442621
	3	4	5	6	●	8	9	11:57	32	2442628
AUGUST 1975	10	11	12	13	◐	15	16	2:23	33	2442635
	17	18	19	20	○	22	23	19:48	34	2442642
	24	25	26	27	28	◑	30	23:19	35	2442649
	31	1	2	3	4	●	6	19:19	36	2442656
	7	8	9	10	11	◐	13	11:59	37	2442663
SEPTEMBER 1975	14	15	16	17	18	19	○	11:50	38	2442670
	21	22	23[d]	24	25	26	27		39	2442677
	◑	29	30	1	2	3	4	11:46	40	2442684
	●	6	7	8	9	10	11	3:23	41	2442691
OCTOBER 1975	◐	13	14	15	16	17	18	1:15	42	2442698
	19	○	21	22	23	24	25	5:06	43	2442705
	26	◑	28	29	30	31	1	22:07	44	2442712
	2	●	4	5	6	7	8	13:05	45	2442719
NOVEMBER 1975	9	◐	11	12	13	14	15	18:21	46	2442726
	16	17	○	19	20	21	22	22:28	47	2442733
	23	24	25	◑	27	28	29	6:52	48	2442740
	30	1	2	●	4	5	6	0:50	49	2442747
	7	8	9	◐	11	12	13	14:39	50	2442754
DECEMBER 1975	14	15	16	17	○	19	20	14:39	51	2442761
	21	22[e]	23	24	◑	26	27	14:52	52	2442768
	28	29	30	31	●	2	3	14:40	1	2442775

HEBREW 5735/5736‡

ISO WEEK	Month	Sun	Mon	Tue	Wed	Thu	Fri	Sat	Molad
1		15	16	17	18	19	20	21	
2	TEVETH 5735	22	23	24	25	26	27	28	
3		29	1	2	3	4	5	6	Sun 19h47m10p
4		7	8	9	10	11	12	13	
5	SHEVAT 5735	14	15	16	17	18	19	20	
6		21	22	23	24	25	26	27	
7		28	29	30	1	2	3	4	Tue 8h31m11p
8	ADAR 5735	5	6	7	8	9	10	11	
9		12	13	14[f]	15	16	17	18	
10		19	20	21	22	23	24	25	
11		26	27	28	29	1	2	3	Wed 21h15m12p
12	NISAN 5735	4	5	6	7	8	9	10	
13		11	12	13	14	15[g]	16	17	
14		18	19	20	21	22	23	24	
15		25	26	27	28	29	30	1	Fri 9h59m13p
16		2	3	4	5	6	7	8	
17	IYYAR 5735	9	10	11	12	13	14	15	
18		16	17	18	19	20	21	22	
19		23	24	25	26	27	28	29	
20		1	2	3	4	5	6[h]	7	Sat 22h43m14p
21	SIVAN 5735	8	9	10	11	12	13	14	
22		15	16	17	18	19	20	21	
23		22	23	24	25	26	27	28	
24		29	30	1	2	3	4	5	Mon 11h27m15p
25		6	7	8	9	10	11	12	
26	TAMMUZ 5735	13	14	15	16	17	18	19	
27		20	21	22	23	24	25	26	
28		27	28	29	1	2	3	4	Wed 0h11m16p
29	AV 5735	5	6	7	8	9[i]	10	11	
30		12	13	14	15	16	17	18	
31		19	20	21	22	23	24	25	
32		26	27	28	29	30	1	2	Thu 12h55m17p
33		3	4	5	6	7	8	9	
34	ELUL 5735	10	11	12	13	14	15	16	
35		17	18	19	20	21	22	23	
36		24	25	26	27	28	29	1[a]	Sat 1h40m0p
37		2[a]	3	4	5	6	7	8	
38	TISHRI 5736	9	10[b]	11	12	13	14	15[c]	
39		16	17	18	19	20	21	22	
40		23	24	25	26	27	28	29	
41		30	1	2	3	4	5	6	Sun 14h24m1p
42	HESHVAN 5736	7	8	9	10	11	12	13	
43		14	15	16	17	18	19	20	
44		21	22	23	24	25	26	27	
45		28	29	30	1	2	3	4	Tue 3h8m2p
46		5	6	7	8	9	10	11	
47	KISLEV 5736	12	13	14	15	16	17	18	
48		19	20	21	22	23	24	25[e]	
49		26[e]	27[e]	28[e]	29[e]	30[e]	1[e]	2[d][e]	Wed 15h52m3p
50		3	4	5	6	7	8	9	
51	TEVETH 5736	10	11	12	13	14	15	16	Fri 4h36m4p
52		17	18	19	20	21	22	23	
1		24	25	26	27	28	29	1	

CHINESE Jiă-Yín‡/Yĭ-Măo

ISO WEEK	Month	Sun	Mon	Tue	Wed	Thu	Fri	Sat	Solar Term
1		16	17	18	19	20	21	22	
2	MONTH 11 Jiă-Yín	23	*24*	25	26	27	28	29	*Xiǎo hán*
3		1	2	3	4	5	6	7*	
4		8	9	**10**	11	12	13	14	**Dà hán**
5	MONTH 12 Jiă-Yín	15	16	17	18	19	20	21	
6		22	23	*24*	25	26	27	28	*Lì chūn*
7		29	30	1[a]	2	3	4	5	
8	MONTH 1 Yĭ-Măo	6	7	8	**9**	10	11	12	**Yǔ shuǐ**
9		13	14	15[b]	16	17	18	19	
10		20	21	22	23	*24*	25	26	*Jīng zhé*
11		27	28	29	30	1	2	3	
12	MONTH 2 Yĭ-Măo	4	5	6	7*	8	**9**	10	**Chūn fēn**
13		11	12	13	14	15	16	17	
14		18	19	20	21	22	23	*24*[c]	*Qīng míng*
15		25	26	27	28	29	30	1	
16	MONTH 3 Yĭ-Măo	2	3	4	5	6	7	8	
17		9	**10**	11	12	13	14	15	**Gǔ yǔ**
18		16	17	18	19	20	21	22	
19		23	24	*25*	26	27	28	29	*Lì xià*
20		1	2	3	4	5	6	7	
21	MONTH 4 Yĭ-Măo	8*	9	10	11	***12***	13	14	**Xiǎo mǎn**
22		15	16	17	18	19	20	21	
23		22	23	24	25	26	*27*	28	*Máng zhòng*
24		29	30	1	2	3	4	5[d]	
25		6	7	8	9	10	11	12	
26	MONTH 5 Yĭ-Măo	***13***	14	15	16	17	18	19	**Xià zhì**
27		20	21	22	23	24	25	26	
28		27	28	*29*	1	2	3	4	*Xiǎo shǔ*
29		5	6	7	8	9*	10	11	
30	MONTH 6 Yĭ-Măo	12	13	14	**15**	16	17	18	**Dà shǔ**
31		19	20	21	22	23	24	25	
32		26	27	28	29	1	*2*	3	*Lì qiū*
33		4	5	6	7[e]	8	9	10	
34	MONTH 7 Yĭ-Măo	11	12	13	14	15[f]	16	17	
35		**18**	19	20	21	22	23	24	**Chǔ shǔ**
36		25	26	27	28	29	30	1	
37		2	3	4	5	6	7	8	*Bái lù*
38	MONTH 8 Yĭ-Măo	9	10*	11	12	13	14	15[g]	
39		16	17	**18**	19	20	21	22	**Qiū fēn**
40		23	24	25	26	27	28	29	
41		1	2	3	4	5	6	7	*Hán lù*
42		8	9[h]	10	11	12	13	14	
43	MONTH 9 Yĭ-Măo	15	16	17	18	19	**20**	21	**Shuāng jiàng**
44		22	23	24	25	26	27	28	
45		29	1	2	3	4	5	6	*Lì dōng*
46		7	8	9	10	11	12*	13	
47	MONTH 10 Yĭ-Măo	14	15	16	17	18	19	20	
48		**21**	22	23	24	25	26	27	**Xiǎo xuě**
49		28	29	30	1	2	3	4	
50		5	6	7	8	9	10	11	*Dà xuě*
51	MONTH 11 Yĭ-Măo	12	13	14	15	16	17	18	
52		19	**20**[i]	21	22	23	24	25	**Dōng zhì**
1		26	27	28	29	1	2	3	

COPTIC 1691‡/1692 — ETHIOPIC 1967‡/1968

ISO WEEK	Coptic Month	Sun	Mon	Tue	Wed	Thu	Fri	Sat	Ethiopic Month
1		20	21	22	23	24	25	26	
2	KOIAK 1691	27	28	29[c]	30	1	2	3	TĀKHŚĀŚ 1967
3		4	5	6[d]	7	8	9	10	
4	TŌBE 1691	11[e]	12	13	14	15	16	17	ṬER 1967
5		18	19	20	21	22	23	24	
6		25	26	27	28	29	30	1	
7		2	3	4	5	6	7	8	
8	MESHIR 1691	9	10	11	12	13	14	15	YAKĀTIT 1967
9		16	17	18	19	20	21	22	
10		23	24	25	26	27	28	29	
11		30	1	2	3	4	5	6	
12	PAREMOTEP 1691	7	8	9	10	11	12	13	MAGĀBIT 1967
13		14	15	16	17	18	19	20	
14		21	22	23	24	25	26	27	
15		28	29	30	1	2	3	4	
16	PARMOUTE 1691	5	6	7	8	9	10	11	MIYĀZYĀ 1967
17		12	13	14	15	16	17	18	
18		19	20	21	22	23	24	25	
19		26[f]	27	28	29[g]	30	1	2	
20		3	4	5	6	7	8	9	
21	PASHONS 1691	10	11	12	13	14	15	16	GENBOT 1967
22		17	18	19	20	21	22	23	
23		24	25	26	27	28	29	30	
24		1	2	3	4	5	6	7	
25		8	9	10	11	12	13	14	
26	PAŌNE 1691	15	16	17	18	19	20	21	SANÉ 1967
27		22	23	24	25	26	27	28	
28		29	30	1	2	3	4	5	
29		6	7	8	9	10	11	12	
30	EPĒP 1691	13	14	15	16	17	18	19	HAMLĒ 1967
31		20	21	22	23	24	25	26	
32		27	28	29	30	1	2	3	
33		4	5	6	7	8	9	10	
34	MESORĒ 1691	11	12	13[h]	14	15	16	17	NAHASĒ 1967
35		18	19	20	21	22	23	24	
36	EPAG. 1691	25	26	27	28	29	30	1	PĀG. 1967
37		2	3	4	5	6	1[a]	2	
38	THOOUT 1692	3	4	5	6	7	8	9	MASKARAM 1968
39		10	11	12	13	14	15	16	
40		17[b]	18	19	20	21	22	23	
41		24	25	26	27	28	29	30	
42		1	2	3	4	5	6	7	
43	PAOPE 1692	8	9	10	11	12	13	14	ṬEQEMT 1968
44		15	16	17	18	19	20	21	
45		22	23	24	25	26	27	28	
46		29	30	1	2	3	4	5	
47	ATHŌR 1692	6	7	8	9	10	11	12	HEDĀR 1968
48		13	14	15	16	17	18	19	
49		20	21	22	23	24	25	26	
50		27	28	29	30	1	2	3	
51	KOIAK 1692	4	5	6	7	8	9	10	TĀKHŚĀŚ 1968
52		11	12	13	14	15	16	17	
1		18	19	20	21	22	23	24	

[a]New Year
[b]Spring (5:57)
[c]Summer (0:26)
[d]Autumn (15:55)
[e]Winter (11:45)
● New moon
◐ First quarter moon
○ Full moon
◑ Last quarter moon

‡Leap year
[a]New Year
[b]Yom Kippur
[c]Sukkot
[d]Winter starts
[e]Ḥanukkah
[f]Purim
[g]Passover
[h]Shavuot
[i]Fast of Av

‡Leap year
[a]New Year (4673, Hare)
[b]Lantern Festival
[c]Qīngmíng
[d]Dragon Festival
[e]Qīqiǎo
[f]Hungry Ghosts
[g]Mid-Autumn Festival
[h]Double-Ninth Festival
[i]Dōngzhì
*Start of 60-name cycle

‡Leap year
[a]New Year
[b]Building of the Cross
[c]Christmas
[d]Jesus's Circumcision
[e]Epiphany
[f]Easter
[g]Mary's Announcement
[h]Jesus's Transfiguration

PERSIAN (ASTRONOMICAL) 1353/1354‡

Month	Sun	Mon	Tue	Wed	Thu	Fri	Sat
DEY 1353	8	9	10	11	12	13	14
	15	16	17	18	19	20	21
	22	23	24	25	26	27	28
	29	30	1	2	3	4	5
BAHMAN 1353	6	7	8	9	10	11	12
	13	14	15	16	17	18	19
	20	21	22	23	24	25	26
	27	28	29	30	1	2	3
ESFAND 1353	4	5	6	7	8	9	10
	11	12	13	14	15	16	17
	18	19	20	21	22	23	24
	25	26	27	28	29	1[a]	2
FARVARDĪN 1354	3	4	5	6	7	8	9
	10	11	12	13[b]	14	15	16
	17	18	19	20	21	22	23
	24	25	26	27	28	29	30
	31	1	2	3	4	5	6
ORDĪBEHEŠT 1354	7	8	9	10	11	12	13
	14	15	16	17	18	19	20
	21	22	23	24	25	26	27
	28	29	30	31	1	2	3
XORDĀD 1354	4	5	6	7	8	9	10
	11	12	13	14	15	16	17
	18	19	20	21	22	23	24
	25	26	27	28	29	30	31
TĪR 1354	1	2	3	4	5	6	7
	8	9	10	11	12	13	14
	15	16	17	18	19	20	21
	22	23	24	25	26	27	28
	29	30	31	1	2	3	4
MORDĀD 1354	5	6	7	8	9	10	11
	12	13	14	15	16	17	18
	19	20	21	22	23	24	25
	26	27	28	29	30	31	1
SHAHRĪVAR 1354	2	3	4	5	6	7	8
	9	10	11	12	13	14	15
	16	17	18	19	20	21	22
	23	24	25	26	27	28	29
	30	31	1	2	3	4	5
MEHR 1354	6	7	8	9	10	11	12
	13	14	15	16	17	18	19
	20	21	22	23	24	25	26
	27	28	29	30	1	2	3
ĀBĀN 1354	4	5	6	7	8	9	10
	11	12	13	14	15	16	17
	18	19	20	21	22	23	24
	25	26	27	28	29	30	1
ĀZAR 1354	2	3	4	5	6	7	8
	9	10	11	12	13	14	15
	16	17	18	19	20	21	22
	23	24	25	26	27	28	29
DEY 1354	30	1	2	3	4	5	6
	7	8	9	10	11	12	13

‡Leap year
[a]New Year
[b]Sizdeh Bedar

HINDU LUNAR 2031‡/2032

Month	Sun	Mon	Tue	Wed	Thu	Fri	Sat
MĀRGAŚIRA 2031	15	**16**	18	19	20	21	22
	23	24	25	26	27	28	29
	30	1	2	3	4	5	6
PAUSHA 2031	7	8	9	10	11	12	13
	14	15	16	17	18	19	20
	21	23	24	25	26	27	28
	29	29	30	1	2	3	4
MĀGHA 2031	5	6	7	8	9	10	11
	12	13	14	**15**	17	18	19
	20	21	22	23	24	25	26
	27	28	29[h]	30	1	1	2
PHĀLGUNA 2031	3	4	5	6	7	**8**	10
	11	12	13	14	15[i]	16	17
	18	19	20	21	22	23	24
	25	26	27	28	29	30	1[a]
CHAITRA 2032	2	3	4	5	6	7	8
	9[b]	10	11	**12**	14	15	16
	17	18	19	20	21	22	23
	24	25	26	26	27	28	29
	30	1	2	3	4	5	**6**
VAIŚĀKHA 2032	8	9	10	11	12	13	14
	15	16	17	18	19	20	21
	22	23	24	25	26	27	28
	29	30	1	2	3	4	5
JYAISHTHA 2032	6	7	8	**9**	11	12	13
	14	15	16	17	18	19	20
	21	22	22	23	24	25	26
	27	28	29	30	**1**	3	4
ĀSHĀḌHA 2032	5	6	7	8	9	10	11
	12	13	14	15	16	17	18
	19	20	21	22	23	24	25
	26	27	28	29	30	1	2
ŚRĀVAṆA 2032	3	**4**	6	7	8	9	10
	11	12	13	14	15	16	17
	18	19	19	20	21	22	23[c]
	24	25	26	**27**	29	30	1
BHĀDRAPADA 2032	2	3	4[d]	5	6	7	8
	9	10	11	12	13	14	15
	16	17	18	19	20	21	22
	23	24	25	26	27	28	29
	30	**1**	3	4	5	6	7
ĀŚVINA 2032	8[e]	9[e]	10[e]	11	12	13	14
	14	15	16	17	18	19	20
	21	22	23	**24**	26	27	28
	29	30	1[f]	2	3	4	5
KĀRTTIKA 2032	6	7	8	9	10	11	12
	13	14	15	16	17	18	19
	20	21	22	23	24	25	26
	27	28	**29**	1	2	3	4
MĀRGAŚIRA 2032	5	6	7	7	8	9	10
	11[g]	12	13	14	15	16	17
	18	19	20	21	22	**23**	25
	26	27	28	29	30	1	2

‡Leap year
[a]New Year (Rākshasa)
[b]Birthday of Rāma
[c]Birthday of Krishna
[d]Ganēśa Chaturthī
[e]Dashara
[f]Diwali
[g]Birthday of Vishnu
[h]Night of Śiva
[i]Holi

HINDU SOLAR 1896‡/1897

Month	Sun	Mon	Tue	Wed	Thu	Fri	Sat
PAUSHA 1896	14	15	16	17	18	19	20
	21	22	23	24	25	26	27
	28	29	1[b]	2	3	4	5
MĀGHA 1896	6	7	8	9	10	11	12
	13	14	15	16	17	18	19
	20	21	22	23	24	25	26
	27	28	29	1	2	3	4
PHĀLGUNA 1896	5	6	7	8	9	10	11
	12	13	14	15	16	17	18
	19	20	21	22	23	24	25
	26	27	28	29	30	1	2
CHAITRA 1896	3	4	5	6	7	8	9
	10	11	12	13	14	15	16
	17	18	19	20	21	22	23
	24	25	26	27	28	29	30
	31	1[a]	2	3	4	5	6
VAIŚĀKHA 1897	7	8	9	10	11	12	13
	14	15	16	17	18	19	20
	21	22	23	24	25	26	27
	28	29	30	1	2	3	4
JYAISHTHA 1897	5	6	7	8	9	10	11
	12	13	14	15	16	17	18
	19	20	21	22	23	24	25
	26	27	28	29	30	31	32
ĀSHĀḌHA 1897	1	2	3	4	5	6	7
	8	9	10	11	12	13	14
	15	16	17	18	19	20	21
	22	23	24	25	26	27	28
	29	30	31	32	1	2	3
ŚRĀVAṆA 1897	4	5	6	7	8	9	10
	11	12	13	14	15	16	17
	18	19	20	21	22	23	24
	25	26	27	28	29	30	31
BHĀDRAPADA 1897	1	2	3	4	5	6	7
	8	9	10	11	12	13	14
	15	16	17	18	19	20	21
	22	23	24	25	26	27	28
	29	30	31	1	2	3	4
ĀŚVINA 1897	5	6	7	8	9	10	11
	12	13	14	15	16	17	18
	19	20	21	22	23	24	25
	26	27	28	29	30	1	2
KĀRTTIKA 1897	3	4	5	6	7	8	9
	10	11	12	13	14	15	16
	17	18	19	20	21	22	23
	24	25	26	27	28	29	30
MĀRGAŚIRA 1897	1	2	3	4	5	6	7
	8	9	10	11	12	13	14
	15	16	17	18	19	20	21
	22	23	24	25	26	27	28
	29	30	1	2	3	4	5
PAUSHA 1897	6	7	8	9	10	11	12
	13	14	15	16	17	18	19

‡Leap year
[a]New Year (Vibhava)
[b]Pongal

ISLAMIC (ASTRONOMICAL) 1394/1395/1396

Month	Sun	Mon	Tue	Wed	Thu	Fri	Sat
DHU AL-ḤIJJA 1394	15	16	17	18	19	20	21
	22	23	24	25	26	27	28
	29	30	1[a]	2	3	4	5
MUḤARRAM 1395	6	7	8	9	10[b]	11	12
	13	14	15	16	17	18	19
	20	21	22	23	24	25	26
	27	28	29	30	1	2	3
ṢAFAR 1395	4	5	6	7	8	9	10
	11	12	13	14	15	16	17
	18	19	20	21	22	23	24
	25	26	27	28	29	1	2
RABĪʿ I 1395	3	4	5	6	7	8	9
	10	11	12[c]	13	14	15	16
	17	18	19	20	21	22	23
	24	25	26	27	28	29	30
RABĪʿ II 1395	1	2	3	4	5	6	7
	8	9	10	11	12	13	14
	15	16	17	18	19	20	21
	22	23	24	25	26	27	28
	29	30	1	2	3	4	5
JUMĀDĀ I 1395	6	7	8	9	10	11	12
	13	14	15	16	17	18	19
	20	21	22	23	24	25	26
	27	28	29	1	2	3	4
JUMĀDĀ II 1395	5	6	7	8	9	10	11
	12	13	14	15	16	17	18
	19	20	21	22	23	24	25
	26	27	28	29	30	1	2
RAJAB 1395	3	4	5	6	7	8	9
	10	11	12	13	14	15	16
	17	18	19	20	21	22	23
	24	25	26	27[d]	28	29	1
SHAʿBĀN 1395	2	3	4	5	6	7	8
	9	10	11	12	13	14	15
	16	17	18	19	20	21	22
	23	24	25	26	27	28	29
	30	1[e]	2	3	4	5	6
RAMAḌĀN 1395	7	8	9	10	11	12	13
	14	15	16	17	18	19	20
	21	22	23	24	25	26	27
	28	29	1[f]	2	3	4	5
SHAWWĀL 1395	6	7	8	9	10	11	12
	13	14	15	16	17	18	19
	20	21	22	23	24	25	26
	27	28	29	1	2	3	4
DHU AL-QAʿDA 1395	5	6	7	8	9	10	11
	12	13	14	15	16	17	18
	19	20	21	22	23	24	25
	26	27	28	29	1	2	3
DHU AL-ḤIJJA 1395	4	5	6	7	8	9	10[g]
	11	12	13	14	15	16	17
	18	19	20	21	22	23	24
	25	26	27	28	29	30	1

[a]New Year
[b]ʿAshūrāʾ
[c]Prophet's Birthday
[d]Ascent of the Prophet
[e]Start of Ramaḍān
[f]ʿId al-Fiṭr
[g]ʿId al-ʾAḍḥā

GREGORIAN 1975

Julian (Sun)	Sun	Mon	Tue	Wed	Thu	Fri	Sat	Month
Dec 16	29	30	31	1	2	3	4	
	5	6	7[a]	8	9	10	11	JANUARY 1975
Dec 30	12	13	14[b]	15	16	17	18	
	19	20	21	22	23	24	25	
Jan 13	26	27	28	29	30	31	1	
	2	3	4	5	6	7	8	FEBRUARY 1975
Jan 27	9	10	11	12[c]	13	14	15	
	16	17	18	19	20	21	22	
Feb 10	23	24	25	26	27	28	1	
	2	3	4	5	6	7	8	MARCH 1975
Feb 24	9	10	11	12	13	14	15	
	16	17	18	19	20	21	22	
Mar 10	23[d]	24	25	26	27	28	29	
	30[e]	31	1	2	3	4	5	
Mar 24	6	7	8	9	10	11	12	APRIL 1975
	13	14	15	16	17	18	19	
Apr 7	20	21	22	23	24	25	26	
	27	28	29	30	1	2	3	
Apr 21	4[f]	5	6	7	8	9	10	MAY 1975
	11	12	13	14	15	16	17	
May 5	18	19	20	21	22	23	24	
	25	26	27	28	29	30	31	
May 19	1	2	3	4	5	6	7	JUNE 1975
	8	9	10	11	12	13	14	
Jun 2	15	16	17	18	19	20	21	
	22	23	24	25	26	27	28	
Jun 16	29	30	1	2	3	4	5	
	6	7	8	9	10	11	12	JULY 1975
Jun 30	13	14	15	16	17	18	19	
	20	21	22	23	24	25	26	
Jul 14	27	28	29	30	31	1	2	
	3	4	5	6	7	8	9	AUGUST 1975
Jul 28	10	11	12	13	14	15	16	
	17	18	19	20	21	22	23	
Aug 11	24	25	26	27	28	29	30	
	31	1	2	3	4	5	6	
Aug 25	7	8	9	10	11	12	13	SEPTEMBER 1975
	14	15	16	17	18	19	20	
Sep 8	21	22	23	24	25	26	27	
	28	29	30	1	2	3	4	
Sep 22	5	6	7	8	9	10	11	OCTOBER 1975
	12	13	14	15	16	17	18	
Oct 6	19	20	21	22	23	24	25	
	26	27	28	29	30	31	1	
Oct 20	2	3	4	5	6	7	8	NOVEMBER 1975
	9	10	11	12	13	14	15	
Nov 3	16	17	18	19	20	21	22	
	23	24	25	26	27	28	29	
Nov 17	30[g]	1	2	3	4	5	6	
	7	8	9	10	11	12	13	DECEMBER 1975
Dec 1	14	15	16	17	18	19	20	
	21	22	23	24	25[h]	26	27	
Dec 15	28	29	30	31	1	2	3	

[a]Orthodox Christmas
[b]Julian New Year
[c]Ash Wednesday
[d]Feast of Orthodoxy
[e]Easter
[f]Orthodox Easter
[g]Advent
[h]Christmas

1976

GREGORIAN 1976‡ / Lunar Phases / ISO WEEK / JULIAN DAY

Month	Sun	Mon	Tue	Wed	Thu	Fri	Sat	Lunar Phases	ISO WEEK (Mon)	JULIAN DAY (Sun noon)
	28	29	30	31	●[a]	2	3	14:40	1	2442775
JANUARY 1976	4	5	6	7	8	◐	10	12:40	2	2442782
	11	12	13	14	15	16	○	4:47	3	2442789
	18	19	20	21	22	◑	24	23:04	4	2442796
	25	26	27	28	29	30	●	6:20	5	2442803
	1	2	3	4	5	6	7		6	2442810
FEBRUARY 1976	◐	9	10	11	12	13	14	10:05	7	2442817
	○	16	17	18	19	20	21	16:43	8	2442824
	◑	23	24	25	26	27	28	8:16	9	2442831
	●	1	2	3	4	5	6	23:25	10	2442838
MARCH 1976	7	8	◐	10	11	12	13	4:38	11	2442845
	14	15	○	17	18	19	20[b]	2:53	12	2442852
	21	◑	23	24	25	26	27	18:54	13	2442859
	28	29	●	31	1	2	3	17:08	14	2442866
APRIL 1976	4	5	6	◐	8	9	10	19:02	15	2442873
	11	12	13	○	15	16	17	11:49	16	2442880
	18	19	20	◑	22	23	24	7:14	17	2442887
	25	26	27	28	●	30	1	10:20	18	2442894
	2	3	4	5	6	◐	8	5:17	19	2442901
MAY 1976	9	10	11	12	○	14	15	20:04	20	2442908
	16	17	18	19	◑	21	22	21:22	21	2442915
	23	24	25	26	27	28	●	1:47	22	2442922
	30	31	1	2	3	4	◐	12:20	23	2442929
JUNE 1976	6	7	8	9	10	11	○	4:15	24	2442936
	13	14	15	16	17	18	◑	13:15	25	2442943
	20	21[c]	22	23	24	25	26		26	2442950
	●	28	29	30	1	2	3	14:50	27	2442957
JULY 1976	◐	5	6	7	8	9	10	17:28	28	2442964
	○	12	13	14	15	16	17	13:09	29	2442971
	18	◑	20	21	22	23	24	6:29	30	2442978
	25	26	●	28	29	30	31	1:39	31	2442985
AUGUST 1976	1	◐	3	4	5	6	7	22:06	32	2442992
	8	○	10	11	12	13	14	23:44	33	2442999
	15	16	17	◑	19	20	21	0:12	34	2443006
	22	23	24	●	26	27	28	11:01	35	2443013
	29	30	31	◐	2	3	4	3:35	36	2443020
SEPTEMBER 1976	5	6	7	○	9	10	11	12:52	37	2443027
	12	13	14	15	◑	17	18	17:20	38	2443034
	19	20	21	22[d]	●	24	25	19:55	39	2443041
	26	27	28	29	◐	1	2	11:12	40	2443048
OCTOBER 1976	3	4	5	6	7	○	9	4:55	41	2443055
	10	11	12	13	14	15	◑	8:59	42	2443062
	17	18	19	20	21	22	●	5:10	43	2443069
	24	25	26	27	28	◐	30	22:05	44	2443076
	31	1	2	3	4	5	○	23:15	45	2443083
NOVEMBER 1976	7	8	9	10	11	12	13		46	2443090
	◑	15	16	17	18	19	20	22:39	47	2443097
	●	22	23	24	25	26	27	15:11	48	2443104
	◐	29	30	1	2	3	4	12:59	49	2443111
DECEMBER 1976	5	○	7	8	9	10	11	18:15	50	2443118
	12	13	◑	15	16	17	18	10:14	51	2443125
	19	20	●[e]	22	23	24	25	2:08	52	2443132
	26	27	◐	29	30	31	1	7:48	53	2443139

‡Leap year
[a]New Year
[b]Spring (11:49)
[c]Summer (6:24)
[d]Autumn (21:48)
[e]Winter (17:35)
● New moon
◐ First quarter moon
○ Full moon
◑ Last quarter moon

HEBREW 5736‡/5737

ISO WEEK	Month	Sun	Mon	Tue	Wed	Thu	Fri	Sat	Molad
1		24	25	26	27	28	29	1	Fri 4h36m4p
2	SHEVAT 5736	2	3	4	5	6	7	8	
3		9	10	11	12	13	14	15	
4		16	17	18	19	20	21	22	
5		23	24	25	26	27	28	29	
6		30	1	2	3	4	5	6	Sat 17h20m5p
7	ADAR I 5736	7	8	9	10	11	12	13	
8		14	15	16	17	18	19	20	
9		21	22	23	24	25	26	27	
10		28	29	30	1	2	3	4	Mon 6h4m6p
11	ADAR II 5736	5	6	7	8	9	10	11	
12		12	13	14[f]	15	16	17	18	
13		19	20	21	22	23	24	25	
14		26	27	28	29	1	2	3	Tue 18h48m7p
15	NISAN 5736	4	5	6	7	8	9	10	
16		11	12	13	14	15[g]	16	17	
17		18	19	20	21	22	23	24	
18		25	26	27	28	29	30	1	Thu 7h32m8p
19	IYAR 5736	2	3	4	5	6	7	8	
20		9	10	11	12	13	14	15	
21		16	17	18	19	20	21	22	
22		23	24	25	26	27	28	29	
23		1	2	3	4	5	6[h]	7	Fri 20h16m9p
24	SIVAN 5736	8	9	10	11	12	13	14	
25		15	16	17	18	19	20	21	
26		22	23	24	25	26	27	28	
27		29	30	1	2	3	4	5	Sun 9h0m10p
28	TAMMUZ 5736	6	7	8	9	10	11	12	
29		13	14	15	16	17	18	19	
30		20	21	22	23	24	25	26	
31		27	28	29	1	2	3	4	Mon 21h44m11p
32	AV 5736	5	6	7	8	9[i]	10	11	
33		12	13	14	15	16	17	18	
34		19	20	21	22	23	24	25	
35		26	27	28	29	30	1	2	Wed 10h28m12p
36	ELUL 5736	3	4	5	6	7	8	9	
37		10	11	12	13	14	15	16	
38		17	18	19	20	21	22	23	
39		24	25	26	27	28	29	1[a]	Thu 23h12m13p
40		2[a]	3	4	5	6	7	8	
41	TISHRI 5737	9	10[b]	11	12	13	14	15[c]	
42		16	17	18	19	20	21	22	
43		23	24	25	26	27	28	29	
44		30	1	2	3	4	5	6	Sat 11h56m14p
45	HESHVAN 5737	7	8	9	10	11	12	13	
46		14	15	16	17	18	19	20	
47		21	22	23	24	25	26	27	
48		28	29	1	2	3	4	5	Mon 0h40m15p
49	KISLEV 5737	6	7	8	9	10	11	12	
50		13[d]	14	15	16	17	18	19	
51		20	21	22	23	24	25[e]	26[e]	
52		27[e]	28[e]	29[e]	1[e]	2[e]	3[e]	4	Tue 13h24m16p
53	TEVETH 5737	5	6	7	8	9	10	11	

‡Leap year
[a]New Year
[b]Yom Kippur
[c]Sukkot
[d]Winter starts
[e]Ḥanukkah
[f]Purim
[g]Passover
[h]Shavuot
[i]Fast of Av

CHINESE Yǐ-Mǎo/Bǐng-Chén‡

ISO WEEK	Month	Sun	Mon	Tue	Wed	Thu	Fri	Sat	Solar Term
1		26	27	28	29	1	2	3	
2	MONTH 12 Yǐ-Mǎo	4	5	6	7	8	9	10	Xiǎo hán
3		11	12	13*	14	15	16	17	
4		18	19	20	21	22	23	24	Dà hán
5		25	26	27	28	29	30	1[a]	
6		2	3	4	5	6	7	8	Lì chūn
7	MONTH 1 Bǐng-Chén	9	10	11	12	13	14	15[b]	
8		16	17	18	19	20	21	22	Yǔ shuǐ
9		23	24	25	26	27	28	29	
10		30	1	2	3	4	5	6	Jīng zhé
11	MONTH 2 Bǐng-Chén	7	8	9	10	11	12	13*	
12		14	15	16	17	18	19	20	Chūn fēn
13		21	22	23	24	25	26	27	
14		28	29	30	1	2	3	4	
15	MONTH 3 Bǐng-Chén	5[c]	6	7	8	9	10	11	Qīng míng
16		12	13	14	15	16	17	18	
17		19	20	21	22	23	24	25	Gǔ yǔ
18		26	27	28	29	1	2	3	
19	MONTH 4 Bǐng-Chén	4	5	6	7	8	9	10	Lì xià
20		11	12	13	14*	15	16	17	
21		18	19	20	21	22	23	24	Xiǎo mǎn
22		25	26	27	28	29	30	1	
23	MONTH 5 Bǐng-Chén	2	3	4	5[d]	6	7	8	Máng zhòng
24		9	10	11	12	13	14	15	
25		16	17	18	19	20	21	22	Xià zhì
26		23	24	25	26	27	28	29	
27		1	2	3	4	5	6	7	
28	MONTH 6 Bǐng-Chén	8	9	10	11	12	13	14	Xiǎo shǔ
29		15*	16	17	18	19	20	21	
30		22	23	24	25	26	27	28	Dà shǔ
31		29	30	1	2	3	4	5	
32	MONTH 7 Bǐng-Chén	6	7[e]	8	9	10	11	12	Lì qiū
33		13	14	15[f]	16	17	18	19	
34		20	21	22	23	24	25	26	Chǔ shǔ
35		27	28	29	1	2	3	4	
36	MONTH 8 Bǐng-Chén	5	6	7	8	9	10	11	
37		12	13	14	15[g]	16*	17	18	Bái lù
38		19	20	21	22	23	24	25	
39		26	27	28	29	30	1	2	Qiū fēn
40	LEAP MONTH 8 Bǐng-Chén	3	4	5	6	7	8	9	
41		10	11	12	13	14	15	16	Hán lù
42		17	18	19	20	21	22	23	
43		24	25	26	27	28	29	1	Shuāng jiàng
44	MONTH 9 Bǐng-Chén	2	3	4	5	6	7	8	
45		9[h]	10	11	12	13	14	15	
46		16	17*	18	19	20	21	22	Lì dōng
47		23	24	25	26	27	28	29	
48		1	2	3	4	5	6	7	Xiǎo xuě
49	MONTH 10 Bǐng-Chén	8	9	10	11	12	13	14	
50		15	16	17	18	19	20	21	Dà xuě
51		22	23	24	25	26	27	28	
52	MONTH 11 Bǐng-Chén	29	30	1	2[i]	3	4	5	Dōng zhì
53		6	7	8	9	10	11	12	

‡Leap year
[a]New Year (4674, Dragon)
[b]Lantern Festival
[c]Qīngmíng
[d]Dragon Festival
[e]Qīqiǎo
[f]Hungry Ghosts
[g]Mid-Autumn Festival
[h]Double-Ninth Festival
[i]Dōngzhì
*Start of 60-name cycle

COPTIC 1692/1693 — ETHIOPIC 1968/1969

ISO WEEK	Coptic Month	Sun	Mon	Tue	Wed	Thu	Fri	Sat	Ethiopic Month
1	KOIAK 1692	18	19	20	21	22	23	24	TĀKHŚĀŚ 1968
2		25	26	27	28	29[c]	30	1	
3		2	3	4	5	6[d]	7	8	
4	TŌBE 1692	9	10	11[e]	12	13	14	15	ṬER 1968
5		16	17	18	19	20	21	22	
6		23	24	25	26	27	28	29	
7		30	1	2	3	4	5	6	
8	MESHIR 1692	7	8	9	10	11	12	13	YAKĀTIT 1968
9		14	15	16	17	18	19	20	
10		21	22	23	24	25	26	27	
11		28	29	30	1	2	3	4	
12	PAREMOTEP 1692	5	6	7	8	9	10	11	MAGĀBIT 1968
13		12	13	14	15	16	17	18	
14		19	20	21	22	23	24	25	
15		26	27	28	29	30	1	2	
16	PARMOUTE 1692	3	4	5	6	7	8	9	MIYĀZYĀ 1968
17		10	11	12	13	14	15	16	
18		17[f]	18	19	20	21	22	23	
19		24	25	26	27	28	29[g]	30	
20		1	2	3	4	5	6	7	
21	PASHONS 1692	8	9	10	11	12	13	14	GENBOT 1968
22		15	16	17	18	19	20	21	
23		22	23	24	25	26	27	28	
24		29	30	1	2	3	4	5	
25	PAŌNE 1692	6	7	8	9	10	11	12	SANĒ 1968
26		13	14	15	16	17	18	19	
27		20	21	22	23	24	25	26	
28		27	28	29	30	1	2	3	
29	EPĒP 1692	4	5	6	7	8	9	10	ḤAMLĒ 1968
30		11	12	13	14	15	16	17	
31		18	19	20	21	22	23	24	
32		25	26	27	28	29	30	1	
33	MESORĒ 1692	2	3	4	5	6	7	8	NAHASĒ 1968
34		9	10	11	12	13[h]	14	15	
35		16	17	18	19	20	21	22	
36		23	24	25	26	27	28	29	
37	EPAG. 1692	30	1	2	3	4	5	1[a]	PĀG. 1968
38	THOOUT 1693	2	3	4	5	6	7	8	MASKARAM 1969
39		9	10	11	12	13	14	15	
40		16	17[b]	18	19	20	21	22	
41		23	24	25	26	27	28	29	
42		30	1	2	3	4	5	6	
43	PAOPE 1693	7	8	9	10	11	12	13	TEQEMT 1969
44		14	15	16	17	18	19	20	
45		21	22	23	24	25	26	27	
46		28	29	30	1	2	3	4	
47	ATHŌR 1693	5	6	7	8	9	10	11	HEDĀR 1969
48		12	13	14	15	16	17	18	
49		19	20	21	22	23	24	25	
50		26	27	28	29	30	1	2	
51	KOIAK 1693	3	4	5	6	7	8	9	TĀKHŚĀŚ 1969
52		10	11	12	13	14	15	16	
53		17	18	19	20	21	22	23	

[a]New Year
[b]Building of the Cross
[c]Christmas
[d]Jesus's Circumcision
[e]Epiphany
[f]Easter
[g]Mary's Announcement
[h]Jesus's Transfiguration

1976

PERSIAN (ASTRONOMICAL) 1354‡/1355

Month	Sun	Mon	Tue	Wed	Thu	Fri	Sat
	7	8	9	10	11	12	13
DEY 1354	14	15	16	17	18	19	20
	21	22	23	24	25	26	27
	28	29	30	1	2	3	4
BAHMAN 1354	5	6	7	8	9	10	11
	12	13	14	15	16	17	18
	19	20	21	22	23	24	25
	26	27	28	29	30	1	2
ESFAND 1354	3	4	5	6	7	8	9
	10	11	12	13	14	15	16
	17	18	19	20	21	22	23
	24	25	26	27	28	29	30
FARVARDĪN 1355	1[a]	2	3	4	5	6	7
	8	9	10	11	12	13[b]	14
	15	16	17	18	19	20	21
	22	23	24	25	26	27	28
	29	30	31	1	2	3	4
ORDĪBEHEŠT 1355	5	6	7	8	9	10	11
	12	13	14	15	16	17	18
	19	20	21	22	23	24	25
	26	27	28	29	30	31	1
XORDĀD 1355	2	3	4	5	6	7	8
	9	10	11	12	13	14	15
	16	17	18	19	20	21	22
	23	24	25	26	27	28	29
	30	31	1	2	3	4	5
TĪR 1355	6	7	8	9	10	11	12
	13	14	15	16	17	18	19
	20	21	22	23	24	25	26
	27	28	29	30	31	1	2
MORDĀD 1355	3	4	5	6	7	8	9
	10	11	12	13	14	15	16
	17	18	19	20	21	22	23
	24	25	26	27	28	29	30
	31	1	2	3	4	5	6
SHAHRĪVAR 1355	7	8	9	10	11	12	13
	14	15	16	17	18	19	20
	21	22	23	24	25	26	27
	28	29	30	31	1	2	3
MEHR 1355	4	5	6	7	8	9	10
	11	12	13	14	15	16	17
	18	19	20	21	22	23	24
	25	26	27	28	29	30	1
ĀBĀN 1355	2	3	4	5	6	7	8
	9	10	11	12	13	14	15
	16	17	18	19	20	21	22
	23	24	25	26	27	28	29
	30	1	2	3	4	5	6
ĀZAR 1355	7	8	9	10	11	12	13
	14	15	16	17	18	19	20
	21	22	23	24	25	26	27
	28	29	30	1	2	3	4
DEY 1355	5	6	7	8	9	10	11

‡Leap year
[a]New Year
[b]Sizdeh Bedar

HINDU LUNAR 2032/2033

Month	Sun	Mon	Tue	Wed	Thu	Fri	Sat
	26	27	28	29	30	1	2
PAUSHA 2032	3	4	5	6	7	8	9
	9	10	11	12	13	14	15
	16	**17**	19	20	21	22	23
	24	25	26	27	28	29	30
MĀGHA 2032	1	2	3	4	5	6	7
	8	9	10	11	12	13	14
	15	16	17	18	19	20	21
	22	24	25	26	27	28	29[h]
	30	1	2	*2*	3	4	5
PHĀLGUNA 2032	6	7	8	9	10	11	12
	13	14	15[i]	**16**	18	19	20
	21	22	23	24	25	26	27
	28	29	30	1[a]	2	3	4
CHAITRA 2033	5	*5*	6	7	**8**[b]	10	11
	12	13	14	15	16	17	18
	19	20	**21**	23	24	25	*25*
	26	27	28	29	30	1	2
VAIŚĀKHA 2033	3	4	5	6	7	8	9
	10	11	12	**13**	15	16	17
	18	19	20	21	22	23	24
	25	26	27	28	29	30	*30*
JYAISHṬHA 2033	1	2	3	4	**5**	7	8
	9	10	11	12	13	14	15
	16	17	**18**	20	21	*21*	22
	23	24	25	26	27	28	29
	30	1	2	3	4	5	6
ĀSHĀḌHA 2033	7	8	**9**	11	12	13	14
	15	16	17	18	19	20	21
	22	23	24	25	26	27	*27*
	28	29	**30**	2	3	4	5
ŚRĀVAṆA 2033	6	7	8	9	10	11	**12**
	14	15	16	17	18	*18*	19
	20	21	22	23[c]	24	25	26
	27	28	29	30	1	2	3[d]
BHĀDRAPADA 2033	**4**	6	7	8	9	10	11
	12	13	14	15	16	17	18
	19	20	21	22	23	*23*	24
	25	26	**27**	29	30	1	2
ĀŚVINA 2033	3	4	5	6	7	8[e]	**9**[e]
	11	12	13	*13*	14	15	16
	17	18	19	20	21	22	23
	24	25	26	27	28	29	30
KĀRTTIKA 2033	**1**[f]	3	4	5	6	7	8
	9	10	11	12	13	14	15
	16	17	*17*	18	19	20	21
	22	23	24	**25**	27	28	29
	30	1	2	3	4	5	6
MĀRGAŚĪRA 2033	7	8	9	10	**11**[g]	12	13
	14	15	16	17	18	19	20
	21	22	23	24	25	26	27
PAUSHA 2033	28	29	**30**	2	3	4	5
	6	7	8	9	10	*10*	11

[a]New Year (Anala)
[b]Birthday of Rāma
[c]Birthday of Krishna
[d]Ganēśa Chaturthī
[e]Dashara
[f]Diwali
[g]Birthday of Vishnu
[h]Night of Śiva
[i]Holi

HINDU SOLAR 1897/1898

Month	Sun	Mon	Tue	Wed	Thu	Fri	Sat
PAUSHA 1897	13	14	15	16	17	18	19
	20	21	22	23	24	25	26
	27	28	29	1[b]	2	3	4
MĀGHA 1897	5	6	7	8	9	10	11
	12	13	14	15	16	17	18
	19	20	21	22	23	24	25
	26	27	28	29	30	1	2
PHĀLGUNA 1897	3	4	5	6	7	8	9
	10	11	12	13	14	15	16
	17	18	19	20	21	22	23
	24	25	26	27	28	29	1
CHAITRA 1897	2	3	4	5	6	7	8
	9	10	11	12	13	14	15
	16	17	18	19	20	21	22
	23	24	25	26	27	28	29
	30	31	1[a]	2	3	4	5
VAIŚĀKHA 1898	6	7	8	9	10	11	12
	13	14	15	16	17	18	19
	20	21	22	23	24	25	26
	27	28	29	30	31	1	2
JYAISHṬHA 1898	3	4	5	6	7	8	9
	10	11	12	13	14	15	16
	17	18	19	20	21	22	23
	24	25	26	27	28	29	30
	31	1	2	3	4	5	6
ĀSHĀḌHA 1898	7	8	9	10	11	12	13
	14	15	16	17	18	19	20
	21	22	23	24	25	26	27
	28	29	30	31	32	1	2
ŚRĀVAṆA 1898	3	4	5	6	7	8	9
	10	11	12	13	14	15	16
	17	18	19	20	21	22	23
	24	25	26	27	28	29	30
	31	1	2	3	4	5	6
BHĀDRAPADA 1898	7	8	9	10	11	12	13
	14	15	16	17	18	19	20
	21	22	23	24	25	26	27
	28	29	30	31	1	2	3
ĀŚVINA 1898	4	5	6	7	8	9	10
	11	12	13	14	15	16	17
	18	19	20	21	22	23	24
	25	26	27	28	29	30	31
KĀRTTIKA 1898	1	2	3	4	5	6	7
	8	9	10	11	12	13	14
	15	16	17	18	19	20	21
	22	23	24	25	26	27	28
	29	30	1	2	3	4	5
MĀRGAŚĪRA 1898	6	7	8	9	10	11	12
	13	14	15	16	17	18	19
	20	21	22	23	24	25	26
	27	28	29	1	2	3	4
PAUSHA 1898	5	6	7	8	9	10	11
	12	13	14	15	16	17	18

[a]New Year (Śukla)
[b]Pongal

ISLAMIC (ASTRONOMICAL) 1395/1396/1397‡

Month	Sun	Mon	Tue	Wed	Thu	Fri	Sat
	25	26	27	28	29	30	1[a]
MUḤARRAM 1396	2	3	4	5	6	7	8
	9	10[b]	11	12	13	14	15
	16	17	18	19	20	21	22
	23	24	25	26	27	28	29
	30	1	2	3	4	5	6
ṢAFAR 1396	7	8	9	10	11	12	13
	14	15	16	17	18	19	20
	21	22	23	24	25	26	27
	28	29	1	2	3	4	5
RABĪ' I 1396	6	7	8	9	10	11	12[c]
	13	14	15	16	17	18	19
	20	21	22	23	24	25	26
	27	28	29	30	1	2	3
RABĪ' II 1396	4	5	6	7	8	9	10
	11	12	13	14	15	16	17
	18	19	20	21	22	23	24
	25	26	27	28	29	30	1
JUMĀDĀ I 1396	2	3	4	5	6	7	8
	9	10	11	12	13	14	15
	16	17	18	19	20	21	22
	23	24	25	26	27	28	29
JUMĀDĀ II 1396	1	2	3	4	5	6	7
	8	9	10	11	12	13	14
	15	16	17	18	19	20	21
	22	23	24	25	26	27	28
	29	30	1	2	3	4	5
RAJAB 1396	6	7	8	9	10	11	12
	13	14	15	16	17	18	19
	20	21	22	23	24	25	26
	27[d]	28	29	30	1	2	3
SHA'BĀN 1396	4	5	6	7	8	9	10
	11	12	13	14	15	16	17
	18	19	20	21	22	23	24
	25	26	27	28	29	1[e]	2
RAMAḌĀN 1396	3	4	5	6	7	8	9
	10	11	12	13	14	15	16
	17	18	19	20	21	22	23
	24	25	26	27	28	29	30
SHAWWĀL 1396	1[f]	2	3	4	5	6	7
	8	9	10	11	12	13	14
	15	16	17	18	19	20	21
	22	23	24	25	26	27	28
	29	1	2	3	4	5	6
DHU AL-QA'DA 1396	7	8	9	10	11	12	13
	14	15	16	17	18	19	20
	21	22	23	24	25	26	27
	28	29	1	2	3	4	5
DHU AL-ḤIJJA 1396	6	7	8	9	10[g]	11	12
	13	14	15	16	17	18	19
	20	21	22	23	24	25	26
MUḤARRAM 1397	27	28	29	1[a]	2[A]	3	4
	5	6	7	8	9	10[b]	11

‡Leap year
[a]New Year
[A]New Year (Arithmetic)
[b]'Ashūrā'
[c]Prophet's Birthday
[d]Ascent of the Prophet
[e]Start of Ramaḍān
[f]'Īd al-Fiṭr
[g]'Īd al-'Aḍḥā

GREGORIAN 1976‡

Julian‡ (Sun)	Sun	Mon	Tue	Wed	Thu	Fri	Sat	Month
Dec 15	28	29	30	31	1	2	3	
	4	5	6	7[a]	8	9	10	JANUARY 1976
Dec 29	11	12	13	14[b]	15	16	17	
	18	19	20	21	22	23	24	
Jan 12	25	26	27	28	29	30	31	
	1	2	3	4	5	6	7	
Jan 26	8	9	10	11	12	13	14	FEBRUARY 1976
	15	16	17	18	19	20	21	
Feb 9	22	23	24	25	26	27	28	
	29	1	2	3[c]	4	5	6	
Feb 23	7	8	9	10	11	12	13	MARCH 1976
	14[d]	15	16	17	18	19	20	
Mar 8	21	22	23	24	25	26	27	
	28	29	30	31	1	2	3	
Mar 22	4	5	6	7	8	9	10	APRIL 1976
	11	12	13	14	15	16	17	
Apr 5	18[e]	19	20	21	22	23	24	
	25[f]	26	27	28	29	30	1	
Apr 19	2	3	4	5	6	7	8	
	9	10	11	12	13	14	15	MAY 1976
May 3	16	17	18	19	20	21	22	
	23	24	25	26	27	28	29	
May 17	30	31	1	2	3	4	5	
	6	7	8	9	10	11	12	JUNE 1976
May 31	13	14	15	16	17	18	19	
	20	21	22	23	24	25	26	
Jun 14	27	28	29	30	1	2	3	
	4	5	6	7	8	9	10	JULY 1976
Jun 28	11	12	13	14	15	16	17	
	18	19	20	21	22	23	24	
Jul 12	25	26	27	28	29	30	31	
	1	2	3	4	5	6	7	
Jul 26	8	9	10	11	12	13	14	AUGUST 1976
	15	16	17	18	19	20	21	
Aug 9	22	23	24	25	26	27	28	
	29	30	31	1	2	3	4	
Aug 23	5	6	7	8	9	10	11	SEPTEMBER 1976
	12	13	14	15	16	17	18	
Sep 6	19	20	21	22	23	24	25	
	26	27	28	29	30	1	2	
Sep 20	3	4	5	6	7	8	9	OCTOBER 1976
	10	11	12	13	14	15	16	
Oct 4	17	18	19	20	21	22	23	
	24	25	26	27	28	29	30	
Oct 18	31	1	2	3	4	5	6	
	7	8	9	10	11	12	13	NOVEMBER 1976
Nov 1	14	15	16	17	18	19	20	
	21	22	23	24	25	26	27	
Nov 15	28[g]	29	30	1	2	3	4	
	5	6	7	8	9	10	11	DECEMBER 1976
Nov 29	12	13	14	15	16	17	18	
	19	20	21	22	23	24	25[h]	
Dec 13	26	27	28	29	30	31	1	

‡Leap year
[a]Orthodox Christmas
[b]Julian New Year
[c]Ash Wednesday
[d]Feast of Orthodoxy
[e]Easter
[f]Orthodox Easter
[g]Advent
[h]Christmas

1977

GREGORIAN 1977 — Lunar Phases — ISO WEEK (Mon) — JULIAN DAY (Sun noon)

Month	Sun	Mon	Tue	Wed	Thu	Fri	Sat	Lunar Phases	ISO Week	Julian Day
	26	27	◐	29	30	31	1[a]	7:48	53	2443139
JANUARY 1977	2	3	4	○	6	7	8	12:10	1	2443146
	9	10	11	◑	13	14	15	19:55	2	2443153
	16	17	18	●	20	21	22	14:11	3	2443160
	23	24	25	26	◐	28	29	5:11	4	2443167
	30	31	1	2	3	○	5	3:56	5	2443174
FEBRUARY 1977	6	7	8	9	10	◑	12	4:07	6	2443181
	13	14	15	16	17	●	19	3:37	7	2443188
	20	21	22	23	24	25	◐	2:50	8	2443195
	27	28	1	2	3	4	○	17:13	9	2443202
MARCH 1977	6	7	8	9	10	11	◑	11:35	10	2443209
	13	14	15	16	17	18	●	18:33	11	2443216
	20[b]	21	22	23	24	25	26		12	2443223
	◐	28	29	30	31	1	2	22:27	13	2443230
APRIL 1977	3	○	5	6	7	8	9	4:09	14	2443237
	◑	11	12	13	14	15	16	19:15	15	2443244
	17	●	19	20	21	22	23	10:35	16	2443251
	24	25	◐	27	28	29	30	14:42	17	2443258
MAY 1977	1	2	○	4	5	6	7	13:03	18	2443265
	8	9	◑	11	12	13	14	4:08	19	2443272
	15	16	17	●	19	20	21	2:52	20	2443279
	22	23	24	25	◐	27	28	3:20	21	2443286
	29	30	31	○	2	3	4	20:31	22	2443293
JUNE 1977	5	6	7	◑	9	10	11	15:07	23	2443300
	12	13	14	15	●	17	18	18:23	24	2443307
	19	20	21[c]	22	23	◐	25	12:44	25	2443314
	26	27	28	29	30	○	2	3:24	26	2443321
JULY 1977	3	4	5	6	7	◑	9	4:39	27	2443328
	10	11	12	13	14	15	●	8:36	28	2443335
	17	18	19	20	21	22	◐	19:38	29	2443342
	24	25	26	27	28	29	○	10:52	30	2443349
	31	1	2	3	4	5	◑	20:40	31	2443356
AUGUST 1977	7	8	9	10	11	12	13		32	2443363
	●	15	16	17	18	19	20	21:31	33	2443370
	21	◐	23	24	25	26	27	1:04	34	2443377
	○	29	30	31	1	2	3	20:10	35	2443384
SEPTEMBER 1977	4	◑	6	7	8	9	10	14:33	36	2443391
	11	12	●	14	15	16	17	9:23	37	2443398
	18	19	◐	21	22	23[d]	24	6:18	38	2443405
	25	26	○	28	29	30	1	8:17	39	2443412
OCTOBER 1977	2	3	4	◑	6	7	8	9:21	40	2443419
	9	10	11	●	13	14	15	20:31	41	2443426
	16	17	18	◐	20	21	22	12:46	42	2443433
	23	24	25	○	27	28	29	23:35	43	2443440
	30	31	1	2	3	◑	5	3:58	44	2443447
NOVEMBER 1977	6	7	8	9	10	●	12	7:09	45	2443454
	13	14	15	16	◐	18	19	21:52	46	2443461
	20	21	22	23	24	○	26	17:31	47	2443468
	27	28	29	30	1	2	◑	21:16	48	2443475
DECEMBER 1977	4	5	6	7	8	9	●	17:33	49	2443482
	11	12	13	14	15	16	◐	10:37	50	2443489
	18	19	20	21[e]	22	23	24		51	2443496
	○	26	27	28	29	30	31	12:49	52	2443503

HEBREW 5737/5738‡ — Molad

ISO Week	Month	Sun	Mon	Tue	Wed	Thu	Fri	Sat	Molad
53		5	6	7	8	9	10	11	
1	TEVETH 5737	12	13	14	15	16	17	18	
2		19	20	21	22	23	24	25	
3		26	27	28	29	1	2	3	Thu 2h8m17p
4	SHEVAT 5737	4	5	6	7	8	9	10	
5		11	12	13	14	15	16	17	
6		18	19	20	21	22	23	24	
7		25	26	27	28	29	30	1	Fri 14h53m0p
8	ADAR 5737	2	3	4	5	6	7	8	
9		9	10	11	12	13	14[f]	15	
10		16	17	18	19	20	21	22	
11		23	24	25	26	27	28	29	
12		1	2	3	4	5	6	7	Sun 3h37m1p
13	NISAN 5737	8	9	10	11	12	13	14	
14		15[g]	16	17	18	19	20	21	
15		22	23	24	25	26	27	28	
16		29	30	1	2	3	4	5	Mon 16h21m2p
17	IYYAR 5737	6	7	8	9	10	11	12	
18		13	14	15	16	17	18	19	
19		20	21	22	23	24	25	26	
20		27	28	29	1	2	3	4	Wed 5h5m3p
21	SIVAN 5737	5	6[h]	7	8	9	10	11	
22		12	13	14	15	16	17	18	
23		19	20	21	22	23	24	25	
24		26	27	28	29	30	1	2	Thu 17h49m4p
25	TAMMUZ 5737	3	4	5	6	7	8	9	
26		10	11	12	13	14	15	16	
27		17	18	19	20	21	22	23	
28		24	25	26	27	28	29	1	Sat 6h33m5p
29	AV 5737	2	3	4	5	6	7	8	
30		9[i]	10	11	12	13	14	15	
31		16	17	18	19	20	21	22	
32		23	24	25	26	27	28	29	
33		30	1	2	3	4	5	6	Sun 19h17m6p
34	ELUL 5737	7	8	9	10	11	12	13	
35		14	15	16	17	18	19	20	
36		21	22	23	24	25	26	27	
37		28	29	1[a]	2[a]	3	4	5	Tue 8h1m7p
38	TISHRI 5738	6	7	8	9	10[b]	11	12	
39		13	14	15[c]	16	17	18	19	
40		20	21	22	23	24	25	26	
41		27	28	29	30	1	2	3	Wed 20h45m8p
42	HESHVAN 5738	4	5	6	7	8	9	10	
43		11	12	13	14	15	16	17	
44		18	19	20	21	22	23	24	
45		25	26	27	28	29	1	2	Fri 9h29m9p
46	KISLEV 5738	3	4	5	6	7	8	9	
47		10	11	12	13	14	15	16	
48		17	18	19	20	21	22	23	
49		24	25[d]	26[e]	27[e]	28[e]	29[e]	30[e]	Sat 22h13m10p
50	TEVETH 5738	1[e]	2[e]	3	4	5	6	7	
51		8	9	10	11	12	13	14	
52		15	16	17	18	19	20	21	

CHINESE Bǐng-Chén‡/Dīng-Sì — Solar Term

ISO Week	Month	Sun	Mon	Tue	Wed	Thu	Fri	Sat	Solar Term
53		6	7	8	9	10	11	12	
1	MONTH 11 Bǐng-Chén	13	14	15	*16*	17	18*	19	Xiǎo hán
2		20	21	22	23	24	25	26	
3		27	28	29	1	*2*	3	4	Dà hán
4	MONTH 12 Bǐng-Chén	5	6	7	8	9	10	11	
5		12	13	14	15	16	*17*	18	Lì chūn
6		19	20	21	22	23	24	25	
7		26	27	28	29	30	1[a]	2	Yǔ shuǐ
8	MONTH 1 Dīng-Sì	3	4	5	6	7	8	9	
9		10	11	12	13	14	15[b]	16	
10		*17*	18	19*	20	21	22	23	Jīng zhé
11		24	25	26	27	28	29	30	Chūn fēn
12		1	*2*	3	4	5	6	7	
13	MONTH 2 Dīng-Sì	8	9	10	11	12	13	14	
14		15	16	*17*[c]	18	19	20	21	Qīng míng
15		22	23	24	25	26	27	28	
16		29	1	2	*3*	4	5	6	Gǔ yǔ
17	MONTH 3 Dīng-Sì	7	8	9	10	11	12	13	
18		14	15	16	17	*18*	19	20*	Lì xià
19		21	22	23	24	25	26	27	
20		28	29	30	1	2	3	*4*	Xiǎo mǎn
21	MONTH 4 Dīng-Sì	5	6	7	8	9	10	11	
22		12	13	14	15	16	17	18	
23		19	*20*	21	22	23	24	25	Máng zhòng
24		26	27	28	29	30	1	2	
25	MONTH 5 Dīng-Sì	3	4	*5*[d]	6	7	8	9	Xià zhì
26		10	11	12	13	14	15	16	
27		17	18	19	20*	*21*	22	23	Xiǎo shǔ
28		24	25	26	27	28	29	1	
29	MONTH 6 Dīng-Sì	2	3	4	5	6	7	*8*	Dà shǔ
30		9	10	11	12	13	14	15	
31		16	17	18	19	20	21	22	
32		*23*	24	25	26	27	28	29	Lì qiū
33		30	1	2	3	4	5	6	
34	MONTH 7 Dīng-Sì	7[e]	8	*9*	10	11	12	13	Chǔ shǔ
35		14	15[f]	16	17	18	19	20	
36		21*	22	23	24	*25*	26	27	Bái lù
37		28	29	1	2	3	4	5	
38	MONTH 8 Dīng-Sì	6	7	8	9	10	*11*	12	Qiū fēn
39		13	14	15[g]	16	17	18	19	
40		20	21	22	23	24	25	*26*	Hán lù
41		27	28	29	30	1	2	3	
42	MONTH 9 Dīng-Sì	4	5	6	7	8	9[h]	10	
43		*11*	12	13	14	15	16	17	Shuāng jiàng
44		18	19	20	21	22*	23	24	
45		25	*26*	27	28	29	1	2	Lì dōng
46	MONTH 10 Dīng-Sì	3	4	5	6	7	8	9	
47		10	11	*12*	13	14	15	16	Xiǎo xuě
48		17	18	19	20	21	22	23	
49		24	25	26	*27*	28	29	30	Dà xuě
50	MONTH 11 Dīng-Sì	1	2	3	4	5	6	7	
51		8	9	10	11	*12*[i]	13	14	Dōng zhì
52		15	16	17	18	19	20	21	

COPTIC 1693/1694 — ETHIOPIC 1969/1970

ISO Week	Coptic Month	Sun	Mon	Tue	Wed	Thu	Fri	Sat	Ethiopic Month
53	KOIAK 1693	17	18	19	20	21	22	23	TĀKHŚĀŚ 1969
1		24	25	26	27	28	29[c]	30	
2	TŌBE 1693	1	2	3	4	5	6[d]	7	ṬER 1969
3		8	9	10	11[e]	12	13	14	
4		15	16	17	18	19	20	21	
5		22	23	24	25	26	27	28	
6		29	30	1	2	3	4	5	
7	MESHIR 1693	6	7	8	9	10	11	12	YAKĀTIT 1969
8		13	14	15	16	17	18	19	
9		20	21	22	23	24	25	26	
10		27	28	29	30	1	2	3	
11	PAREMOTEP 1693	4	5	6	7	8	9	10	MAGĀBIT 1969
12		11	12	13	14	15	16	17	
13		18	19	20	21	22	23	24	
14		25	26	27	28	29	30	1	
15	PARMOUTE 1693	2[f]	3	4	5	6	7	8	MIYĀZYĀ 1969
16		9	10	11	12	13	14	15	
17		16	17	18	19	20	21	22	
18		23	24	25	26	27	28	29[g]	
19		30	1	2	3	4	5	6	
20	PASHONS 1693	7	8	9	10	11	12	13	GENBOT 1969
21		14	15	16	17	18	19	20	
22		21	22	23	24	25	26	27	
23		28	29	30	1	2	3	4	
24	PAŌNE 1693	5	6	7	8	9	10	11	SANĒ 1969
25		12	13	14	15	16	17	18	
26		19	20	21	22	23	24	25	
27		26	27	28	29	30	1	2	
28	EPĒP 1693	3	4	5	6	7	8	9	HAMLĒ 1969
29		10	11	12	13	14	15	16	
30		17	18	19	20	21	22	23	
31		24	25	26	27	28	29	30	
32	MESORĒ 1693	1	2	3	4	5	6	7	NAHASĒ 1969
33		8	9	10	11	12	13[h]	14	
34		15	16	17	18	19	20	21	
35		22	23	24	25	26	27	28	
36	EPAG. 1693	29	30	1	2	3	4	5	PĀG. 1969
37	THOOUT 1694	1[a]	2	3	4	5	6	7	MASKARAM 1970
38		8	9	10	11	12	13	14	
39		15	16	17[b]	18	19	20	21	
40		22	23	24	25	26	27	28	
41		29	30	1	2	3	4	5	
42	PAOPE 1694	6	7	8	9	10	11	12	ṬEQEMT 1970
43		13	14	15	16	17	18	19	
44		20	21	22	23	24	25	26	
45		27	28	29	30	1	2	3	
46	ATHŌR 1694	4	5	6	7	8	9	10	HEDĀR 1970
47		11	12	13	14	15	16	17	
48		18	19	20	21	22	23	24	
49		25	26	27	28	29	30	1	
50	KOIAK 1694	2	3	4	5	6	7	8	TĀKHŚĀŚ 1970
51		9	10	11	12	13	14	15	
52		16	17	18	19	20	21	22	

Gregorian notes:
[a]New Year
[b]Spring (17:42)
[c]Summer (12:14)
[d]Autumn (3:29)
[e]Winter (23:23)
● New moon
◐ First quarter moon
○ Full moon
◑ Last quarter moon

Hebrew notes:
‡Leap year
[a]New Year
[b]Yom Kippur
[c]Sukkot
[d]Winter starts
[e]Ḥanukkah
[f]Purim
[g]Passover
[h]Shavuot
[i]Fast of Av

Chinese notes:
‡Leap year
[a]New Year (4675, Snake)
[b]Lantern Festival
[c]Qīngmíng
[d]Dragon Festival
[e]Qīqiǎo
[f]Hungry Ghosts
[g]Mid-Autumn Festival
[h]Double-Ninth Festival
[i]Dōngzhì
*Start of 60-name cycle

Coptic/Ethiopic notes:
[a]New Year
[b]Building of the Cross
[c]Christmas
[d]Jesus's Circumcision
[e]Epiphany
[f]Easter
[g]Mary's Announcement
[h]Jesus's Transfiguration

PERSIAN (ASTRONOMICAL) 1355/1356								HINDU LUNAR 2033/2034‡								HINDU SOLAR 1898/1899								ISLAMIC (ASTRONOMICAL) 1397‡/1398								Julian (Sun)	GREGORIAN 1977							
	Sun	Mon	Tue	Wed	Thu	Fri	Sat		Sun	Mon	Tue	Wed	Thu	Fri	Sat		Sun	Mon	Tue	Wed	Thu	Fri	Sat		Sun	Mon	Tue	Wed	Thu	Fri	Sat		Sun	Mon	Tue	Wed	Thu	Fri	Sat	
DEY 1355	5	6	7	8	9	10	11	PAUSHA 2033	6	7	8	9	10	*10*	11	PAUSHA 1898	12	13	14	15	16	17	18	MUHARRAM 1397	5	6	7	8	9	10	11	Dec 13	26	27	28	29	30	31	1	JANUARY 1977
	12	13	14	15	16	17	18		12	13	14	15	16	17	18		19	20	21	22	23	24	25		12	13	14	15	16	17	18		2	3	4	5	6	7[a]	8	
	19	20	21	22	23	24	25		19	20	21	22	23	**24**	26	MĀGHA 1898	26	27	28	29	1[b]	2	3		19	20	21	22	23	24	25	Dec 27	9	10	11	12	13	14[b]	15	
BAHMAN 1355	26	27	28	29	30	*1*	2	MĀGHA 2033	27	28	29	30	1	2	3		4	5	6	7	8	9	10	ṢAFAR 1397	26	27	28	29	30	1	2		16	17	18	19	20	21	22	
	3	4	5	6	7	8	9		4	5	6	7	8	9	10		11	12	13	14	15	16	17		3	4	5	6	7	8	9	Jan 10	23	24	25	26	27	28	29	
	10	11	12	13	14	15	16		11	12	*12*	13	14	15	16		18	19	20	21	22	23	24		10	11	12	13	14	15	16		30	31	1	2	3	4	5	FEBRUARY 1977
	17	18	19	20	21	22	23		17	**18**	20	21	22	23	24	PHĀLGUNA 1898	25	26	27	28	29	30	1		17	18	19	20	21	22	23	Jan 24	6	7	8	9	10	11	12	
	24	25	26	27	28	29	30	PHĀLGUNA 2033	25	26	27	28[h]	29	30	1		2	3	4	5	6	7	8	RABĪʿ I 1397	24	25	26	27	28	29	1		13	14	15	16	17	18	19	
ESFAND 1355	*1*	2	3	4	5	6	7		2	3	4	5	6	7	8		9	10	11	12	13	14	15		2	3	4	5	6	7	8	Feb 7	20	21	22	23[c]	24	25	26	
	8	9	10	11	12	13	14		9	10	11	12	13	14	15[i]		16	17	18	19	20	21	22		9	10	11	12[c]	13	14	15		27[d]	28	1	2	3	4	5	MARCH 1977
	15	16	17	18	19	20	21		16	17	18	19	20	21	**22**	CHAITRA 1898	23	24	25	26	27	28	29		16	17	18	19	20	21	22	Feb 21	6	7	8	9	10	11	12	
	22	23	24	25	26	27	28		24	25	26	27	28	29	30		30	1	2	3	4	5	6	RABĪʿ II 1397	23	24	25	26	27	28	29		13	14	15	16	17	18	19	
FARVARDĪN 1356	29	*1*[a]	2	3	4	5	6	CHAITRA 2034	1[a]	2	3	4	5	5	6		7	8	9	10	11	12	13		30	1	2	3	4	5	6	Mar 7	20	21	22	23	24	25	26	
	7	8	9	10	11	12	13[b]		7	8	9[b]	10	11	12	13		14	15	16	17	18	19	20		7	8	9	10	11	12	13		27	28	29	30	31	1	2	APRIL 1977
	14	15	16	17	18	19	20		14	15	**16**	18	19	20	21	VAIŚĀKHA 1899	21	22	23	24	25	26	27		14	15	16	17	18	19	20	Mar 21	3	4	5	6	7	8	9	
	21	22	23	24	25	26	27		22	23	24	25	26	27	28		28	29	30	1[a]	2	3	4	JUMĀDĀ I 1397	21	22	23	24	25	26	27		10[e]	11	12	13	14	15	16	
ORDĪBEHEŠT 1356	28	29	30	31	*1*	2	3	VAIŚĀKHA 2034	29	30	1	2	3	4	5		5	6	7	8	9	10	11		28	29	30	*1*	2	3	4	Apr 4	17	18	19	20	21	22	23	
	4	5	6	7	8	9	10		6	7	8	9	10	11	12		12	13	14	15	16	17	18		5	6	7	8	9	10	11		24	25	26	27	28	29	30	
	11	12	13	14	15	16	17		13	14	15	16	17	18	19		19	20	21	22	23	24	25		12	13	14	15	16	17	18	Apr 18	*1*	2	3	4	5	6	7	MAY 1977
	18	19	20	21	22	23	24		**20**	22	23	24	25	26	27	JYAISHTHA 1899	26	27	28	29	30	31	1		19	20	21	22	23	24	25		8	9	10	11	12	13	14	
	25	26	27	28	29	30	31	JYAISHTHA 2034	28	29	30	*30*	1	2	3		2	3	4	5	6	7	8	JUMĀDĀ II 1397	26	27	28	29	30	*1*	2	May 2	15	16	17	18	19	20	21	
XORDĀD 1356	*1*	2	3	4	5	6	7		4	5	6	7	8	9	10		9	10	11	12	13	14	15		3	4	5	6	7	8	9		22	23	24	25	26	27	28	
	8	9	10	11	12	13	14		11	12	**13**	15	16	17	18		16	17	18	19	20	21	22		10	11	12	13	14	15	16	May 16	29	30	31	1	2	3	4	JUNE 1977
	15	16	17	18	19	20	21		19	20	21	22	23	24	25		23	24	25	26	27	28	29		17	18	19	20	21	22	23		5	6	7	8	9	10	11	
	22	23	24	25	26	27	28	LEAP ĀSHĀḌHA 2034	26	27	28	29	30	1	2	ĀSHĀḌHA 1899	30	31	1	2	3	4	5	RAJAB 1397	24	25	26	27	28	29	*1*	May 30	12	13	14	15	16	17	18	
TĪR 1356	29	30	31	*1*	2	3	4		3	4	5	6	7	8	9		6	7	8	9	10	11	12		2	3	4	5	6	7	8		19	20	21	22	23	24	25	
	5	6	7	8	9	10	11		10	11	12	13	14	15	**16**		13	14	15	16	17	18	19		9	10	11	12	13	14	15	Jun 13	26	27	28	29	30	1	2	JULY 1977
	12	13	14	15	16	17	18		18	19	20	21	22	23	24		20	21	22	23	24	25	26		16	17	18	19	20	21	22		3	4	5	6	7	8	9	
	19	20	21	22	23	24	25		25	26	*26*	27	28	29	30	ŚRĀVAṆA 1899	27	28	29	30	31	32	1		23	24	25	26	27[d]	28	29	Jun 27	10	11	12	13	14	15	16	
MORDĀD 1356	26	27	28	29	30	31	*1*	ĀSHĀḌHA 2034	1	2	3	4	5	6	7		2	3	4	5	6	7	8	SHAʿBĀN 1397	30	*1*	2	3	4	5	6		17	18	19	20	21	22	23	
	2	3	4	5	6	7	8		8	**9**	11	12	13	14	15		9	10	11	12	13	14	15		7	8	9	10	11	12	13	Jul 11	24	25	26	27	28	29	30	
	9	10	11	12	13	14	15		16	17	18	19	20	21	22		16	17	18	19	20	21	22		14	15	16	17	18	19	20		31	1	2	3	4	5	6	AUGUST 1977
	16	17	18	19	20	21	22		23	24	25	26	27	28	29		23	24	25	26	27	28	29		21	22	23	24	25	26	27	Jul 25	7	8	9	10	11	12	13	
	23	24	25	26	27	28	29	ŚRĀVAṆA 2034	30	1	2	3	4	5	6	BHĀDRAPADA 1899	30	31	32	1	2	3	4	RAMAḌĀN 1397	28	29	*30*	1[e]	2	3	4		14	15	16	17	18	19	20	
SHAHRĪVAR 1356	30	31	*1*	2	3	4	5		7	8	9	10	11	**12**	14		5	6	7	8	9	10	11		5	6	7	8	9	10	11	Aug 8	21	22	23	24	25	26	27	
	6	7	8	9	10	11	12		15	16	17	18	19	20	21		12	13	14	15	16	17	18		12	13	14	15	16	17	18		28	29	30	31	1	2	3	SEPTEMBER 1977
	13	14	15	16	17	18	19		22	23	*23*[c]	24	25	26	27		19	20	21	22	23	24	25		19	20	21	22	23	24	25	Aug 22	4	5	6	7	8	9	10	
	20	21	22	23	24	25	26	BHĀDRAPADA 2034	28	29	30	1	2	3[d]	4	ĀŚVINA 1899	26	27	28	29	30	31	1	SHAWWĀL 1397	26	27	28	29	*1*[f]	2	3		11	12	13	14	15	16	17	
MEHR 1356	27	28	29	30	31	*1*	2		**5**	7	8	9	10	11	12		2	3	4	5	6	7	8		4	5	6	7	8	9	10	Sep 5	18	19	20	21	22	23	24	
	3	4	5	6	7	8	9		13	14	15	16	17	18	19		9	10	11	12	13	14	15		11	12	13	14	15	16	17		25	26	27	28	29	30	1	OCTOBER 1977
	10	11	12	13	14	15	16		20	21	22	23	24	25	26		16	17	18	19	20	21	22		18	19	20	21	22	23	24	Sep 19	2	3	4	5	6	7	8	
	17	18	19	20	21	22	23	ĀŚVINA 2034	27	28	29	30	1	2	3	KĀRTTIKA 1899	23	24	25	26	27	28	29	DHU AL-QAʿDA 1397	25	26	27	28	29	*1*	2		9	10	11	12	13	14	15	
ABĀN 1356	24	25	26	27	28	29	30		4	5	6	7	8[e]	9[e]	11		30	1	2	3	4	5	6		3	4	5	6	7	8	9	Oct 3	16	17	18	19	20	21	22	
	1	2	3	4	5	6	7		12	13	14	15	16	17	*17*		7	8	9	10	11	12	13		10	11	12	13	14	15	16		23	24	25	26	27	28	29	
	8	9	10	11	12	13	14		18	19	20	21	22	23	24		14	15	16	17	18	19	20		17	18	19	20	21	22	23	Oct 17	30	31	1	2	3	4	5	NOVEMBER 1977
	15	16	17	18	19	20	21	KĀRTTIKA 2034	25	26	27	28	29	30	*1*[f]		21	22	23	24	25	26	27	DHU AL-ḤIJJA 1397	24	25	26	27	28	29	1		6	7	8	9	10	11	12	
	22	23	24	25	26	27	28		**2**	4	5	6	7	8	9	MĀRGAŚIRA 1899	28	29	30	1	2	3	4		2	3	4	5	6	7	8	Oct 31	13	14	15	16	17	18	19	
ĀZAR 1356	29	30	*1*	2	3	4	5		10	11	12	13	14	15	16		5	6	7	8	9	10	11		9	10[g]	11	12	13	14	15		20	21	22	23	24	25	26	
	6	7	8	9	10	11	12		17	18	19	20	*20*	21	22		12	13	14	15	16	17	18		16	17	18	19	20	21	22	Nov 14	27[g]	28	29	30	1	2	3	DECEMBER 1977
	13	14	15	16	17	18	19		23	24	25	**26**	28	29	30		19	20	21	22	23	24	25		23	24	25	26	27	28	29		4	5	6	7	8	9	10	
	20	21	22	23	24	25	26	MĀRGAŚIRA 2034	1	2	3	4	5	6	7	PAUSHA 1899	26	27	28	29	1	2	3	MUHARRAM 1398	30	1[a]	2	3	4	5	6	Nov 28	11	12	13	14	15	16	17	
DEY 1356	27	28	29	30	*1*	2	3		8	9	10	11[g]	12	13	14		4	5	6	7	8	9	10		7	8	9	10[b]	11	12	13		18	19	20	21	22	23	24	
	4	5	6	7	8	9	10		15	16	17	18	19	20	21		11	12	13	14	15	16	17		14	15	16	17	18	19	20	Dec 12	25[h]	26	27	28	29	30	31	

Persian: [a]New Year; [b]Sizdeh Bedar

Hindu Lunar: ‡Leap year; [a]New Year (Piṅgala); [b]Birthday of Rāma; [c]Birthday of Krishna; [d]Ganēśa Chaturthī; [e]Dashara; [f]Diwali; [g]Birthday of Vishnu; [h]Night of Śiva; [i]Holi

Hindu Solar: [a]New Year (Pramoda); [b]Pongal

Islamic: ‡Leap year; [a]New Year; [b]ʿAshūrā'; [c]Prophet's Birthday; [d]Ascent of the Prophet; [e]Start of Ramaḍān; [f]ʿId al-Fiṭr; [g]ʿId al-'Aḍḥā

Gregorian: [a]Orthodox Christmas; [b]Julian New Year; [c]Ash Wednesday; [d]Feast of Orthodoxy; [e]Easter (also Orthodox); [g]Advent; [h]Christmas

1978

GREGORIAN 1978	Sun	Mon	Tue	Wed	Thu	Fri	Sat	Lunar Phases	ISO WEEK (Mon)	JULIAN DAY (Sun noon)	HEBREW 5738‡/5739	Sun	Mon	Tue	Wed	Thu	Fri	Sat	Molad	CHINESE Dīng-Sì/Wù-Wǔ	Sun	Mon	Tue	Wed	Thu	Fri	Sat	Solar Term	COPTIC 1694/1695‡	Sun	Mon	Tue	Wed	Thu	Fri	Sat	ETHIOPIC 1970/1971‡
JANUARY 1978	1[a]	◑	3	4	5	6	7	12:07	1	2443510	TEVETH 5738	22	23	24	25	26	27	28		MONTH 11 Dīng-Sì	22	23*	24	25	26	27	28	Xiǎo hán	KOIAK 1694	23	24	25	26	27	28	29[c]	TĀKHŚĀŚ 1970
	8	●	10	11	12	13	14	4:00	2	2443517		29	1	2	3	4	5	6	Mon 10h57m11p		29	1	2	3	4	5	6			30	1	2	3	4	5	6[d]	
	15	◐	17	18	19	20	21	3:03	3	2443524	SHEVAT 5738	7	8	9	10	11	12	13		MONTH 12 Dīng-Sì	7	8	9	10	11	12	13	Dà hán	TŌBE 1694	7	8	9	10	11[e]	12	13	ṬER 1970
	22	23	○	25	26	27	28	7:55	4	2443531		14	15	16	17	18	19	20			14	15	16	17	18	19	20			14	15	16	17	18	19	20	
	29	30	◑	1	2	3	4	23:51	5	2443538		21	22	23	24	25	26	27			21	22	23	24	25	26	27	Lì chūn		21	22	23	24	25	26	27	
FEBRUARY 1978	5	6	●	8	9	10	11	14:54	6	2443545		28	29	30	1	2	3	4	Tue 23h41m12p		28	29	1[a]	2	3	4	5			28	29	30	1	2	3	4	
	12	13	◐	15	16	17	18	22:11	7	2443552	ADAR I 5738	5	6	7	8	9	10	11		MONTH 1 Wù-Wǔ	6	7	8	9	10	11	12		MESHIR 1694	5	6	7	8	9	10	11	YAKĀTIT 1970
	19	20	21	22	○	24	25	1:26	8	2443559		12	13	14	15	16	17	18			13	14	15[b]	16	17	18	19	Yǔ shuǐ		12	13	14	15	16	17	18	
	26	27	28	1	◑	3	4	8:34	9	2443566		19	20	21	22	23	24	25			20	21	22	23	24	25*	26			19	20	21	22	23	24	25	
MARCH 1978	5	6	7	8	●	10	11	2:36	10	2443573		26	27	28	29	30	1	2	Thu 12h25m13p		27	28	29	30	1	2	3	Jīng zhé		26	27	28	29	30	1	2	
	12	13	14	15	◐	17	18	18:21	11	2443580	ADAR II 5738	3	4	5	6	7	8	9		MONTH 2 Wù-Wǔ	4	5	6	7	8	9	10		PAREMOTEP 1694	3	4	5	6	7	8	9	MAGĀBIT 1970
	19	20[b]	21	22	23	○	25	16:20	12	2443587		10	11	12	13	14[f]	15	16			11	12	13	14	15	16	17	Chūn fēn		10	11	12	13	14	15	16	
	26	27	28	29	30	◑	1	15:11	13	2443594		17	18	19	20	21	22	23			18	19	20	21	22	23	24			17	18	19	20	21	22	23	
	2	3	4	5	6	●	8	15:15	14	2443601		24	25	26	27	28	29	1	Sat 1h9m14p		25	26	27	28[c]	29	1	2	Qīng míng		24	25	26	27	28	29	30	
APRIL 1978	9	10	11	12	13	14	◐	13:56	15	2443608		2	3	4	5	6	7	8		MONTH 3 Wù-Wǔ	3	4	5	6	7	8	9			1	2	3	4	5	6	7	
	16	17	18	19	20	21	22		16	2443615	NISAN 5738	9	10	11	12	13	14	15[g]			10	11	12	13	14	15	16	Gǔ yǔ	PARMOUTE 1694	8	9	10	11	12	13	14	MIYĀZYĀ 1970
	○	24	25	26	27	28	◑	4:11 21:02	17	2443622		16	17	18	19	20	21	22			17	18	19	20	21	22	23			15	16	17	18	19	20	21	
	30	1	2	3	4	5	6		18	2443629		23	24	25	26	27	28	29			24	25	26*	27	28	29	30	Lì xià		22[f]	23	24	25	26	27	28	
MAY 1978	●	8	9	10	11	12	13	4:47	19	2443636		30	1	2	3	4	5	6	Sun 13h53m15p		1	2	3	4	5	6	7			29[g]	30	1	2	3	4	5	
	14	◐	16	17	18	19	20	7:39	20	2443643	IYAR 5738	7	8	9	10	11	12	13		MONTH 4 Wù-Wǔ	8	9	10	11	12	13	14		PASHONS 1694	6	7	8	9	10	11	12	GENBOT 1970
	21	○	23	24	25	26	27	13:17	21	2443650		14	15	16	17	18	19	20			15	16	17	18	19	20	21	Xiǎo mǎn		13	14	15	16	17	18	19	
	28	◑	30	31	1	2	3	3:30	22	2443657		21	22	23	24	25	26	27			22	23	24	25	26	27	28			20	21	22	23	24	25	26	
JUNE 1978	4	●	6	7	8	9	10	19:02	23	2443664		28	29	1	2	3	4	5	Tue 2h37m16p		29	30	1	2	3	4	5[d]	Máng zhòng		27	28	29	30	1	2	3	
	11	12	◐	14	15	16	17	22:44	24	2443671	SIVAN 5738	6[h]	7	8	9	10	11	12		MONTH 5 Wù-Wǔ	6	7	8	9	10	11	12		PAŌNE 1694	4	5	6	7	8	9	10	SANĒ 1970
	18	19	○	21[c]	22	23	24	20:31	25	2443678		13	14	15	16	17	18	19			13	14	15	16	17	18	19	Xià zhì		11	12	13	14	15	16	17	
	25	26	◑	28	29	30	1	11:44	26	2443685		20	21	22	23	24	25	26			20	21	22	23	24	25	26*			18	19	20	21	22	23	24	
	2	3	4	●	6	7	8	9:50	27	2443692		27	28	29	30	1	2	3	Wed 15h21m17p		27	28	29	1	2	3	4	Xiǎo shǔ		25	26	27	28	29	30	1	
JULY 1978	9	10	11	12	◐	14	15	10:49	28	2443699	TAMMUZ 5738	4	5	6	7	8	9	10		MONTH 6 Wù-Wǔ	5	6	7	8	9	10	11			2	3	4	5	6	7	8	
	16	17	18	19	○	21	22	3:05	29	2443706		11	12	13	14	15	16	17			12	13	14	15	16	17	18		EPĒP 1694	9	10	11	12	13	14	15	ḤAMLĒ 1970
	23	24	25	◑	27	28	29	22:31	30	2443713		18	19	20	21	22	23	24			19	20	21	22	23	24	25	Dà shǔ		16	17	18	19	20	21	22	
	30	31	1	2	3	●	5	1:01	31	2443720		25	26	27	28	29	1	2	Fri 4h6m0p		26	27	28	29	30	1	2			23	24	25	26	27	28	29	
AUGUST 1978	6	7	8	9	10	◐	12	20:06	32	2443727		3	4	5	6	7	8	9		MONTH 7 Wù-Wǔ	3	4	5	6	7[e]	8	9	Lì qiū		30	1	2	3	4	5	6	
	13	14	15	16	17	○	19	10:14	33	2443734	AV 5738	10[i]	11	12	13	14	15	16			10	11	12	13	14	15[f]	16		MESORĒ 1694	7	8	9	10	11	12	13[h]	NAHASĒ 1970
	20	21	22	23	24	◑	26	12:18	34	2443741		17	18	19	20	21	22	23			17	18	19	20	21	22	23	Chǔ shǔ		14	15	16	17	18	19	20	
	27	28	29	30	31	1	●	16:09	35	2443748		24	25	26	27	28	29	30			24	25	26	27*	28	29	30			21	22	23	24	25	26	27	
SEPTEMBER 1978	3	4	5	6	7	8	9		36	2443755		1	2	3	4	5	6	7	Sat 16h50m1p		1	2	3	4	5	6	7	Bái lù		28	29	30	1	2	3	4	
	◐	11	12	13	14	15	○	3:20 19:01	37	2443762	ELUL 5738	8	9	10	11	12	13	14		MONTH 8 Wù-Wǔ	8	9	10	11	12	13	14		EPAG. 1694	5	1[a]	2	3	4	5	6	PĀG. 1970
	17	18	19	20	21	22	23[d]		38	2443769		15	16	17	18	19	20	21			15[g]	16	17	18	19	20	21	Qiū fēn	THOOUT 1695	7	8	9	10	11	12	13	MASKARAM 1971
	◑	25	26	27	28	29	30	5:07	39	2443776		22	23	24	25	26	27	28			22	23	24	25	26	27	28			14	15	16	17[b]	18	19	20	
OCTOBER 1978	1	●	3	4	5	6	7	6:41	40	2443783		29	1[a]	2[a]	3	4	5	6	Mon 5h34m2p		29	1	2	3	4	5	6			21	22	23	24	25	26	27	
	8	◐	10	11	12	13	14	9:38	41	2443790	TISHRI 5739	7	8	9	10[b]	11	12	13		MONTH 9 Wù-Wǔ	7	8	9[h]	10	11	12	13	Hán lù		28	29	30	1	2	3	4	
	15	○	17	18	19	20	21	6:09	42	2443797		14	15[c]	16	17	18	19	20			14	15	16	17	18	19	20		PAOPE 1695	5	6	7	8	9	10	11	ṬEQEMT 1971
	22	23	◑	25	26	27	28	0:34	43	2443804		21	22	23	24	25	26	27			21	22	23	24	25	26	27	Shuāng jiàng		12	13	14	15	16	17	18	
	29	30	●	1	2	3	4	20:06	44	2443811		28	29	30	1	2	3	4	Tue 18h18m3p		28*	29	30	1	2	3	4			19	20	21	22	23	24	25	
NOVEMBER 1978	5	6	◐	8	9	10	11	16:18	45	2443818	HESHVAN 5739	5	6	7	8	9	10	11		MONTH 10 Wù-Wǔ	5	6	7	8	9	10	11	Lì dōng		26	27	28	29	30	1	2	
	12	13	○	15	16	17	18	20:00	46	2443825		12	13	14	15	16	17	18			12	13	14	15	16	17	18		ATHŌR 1695	3	4	5	6	7	8	9	HEDĀR 1971
	19	20	21	◑	23	24	25	21:24	47	2443832		19	20	21	22	23	24	25			19	20	21	22	23	24	25	Xiǎo xuě		10	11	12	13	14	15	16	
	26	27	28	29	●	1	2	8:19	48	2443839		26	27	28	29	30	1	2	Thu 7h2m4p		26	27	28	29	1	2	3			17	18	19	20	21	22	23	
DECEMBER 1978	3	4	5	6	◐	8	9	0:34	49	2443846	KISLEV 5739	3	4	5[d]	6	7	8	9		MONTH 11* Wù-Wǔ	4	5	6	7	8	9	10	Dà xuě		24	25	26	27	28	29	30	
	10	11	12	13	○	15	16	12:31	50	2443853		10	11	12	13	14	15	16			11	12	13	14	15	16	17			1	2	3	4	5	6	7	
	17	18	19	20	21	◑[e]	23	17:42	51	2443860		17	18	19	20	21	22	23			18	19	20	21	22	23[i]	24	Dōng zhì	KOIAK 1695	8	9	10	11	12	13	14	TĀKHŚĀŚ 1971
	24	25	26	27	28	●	30	19:36	52	2443867		24	25[e]	26[e]	27[e]	28[e]	29[e]	30[e]	Fri 19h46m5p	MONTH 12 Wù-Wǔ	25	26	27	28	29*	30	1			15	16	17	18	19	20	21	
	31	1	2	3	4	◐	6	11:1	1	2443874		1[e]	2[e]	3	4	5	6	7			2	3	4	5	6	7	8	Xiǎo hán		22	23	24	25	26	27	28	

[a]New Year
[b]Spring (23:33)
[c]Summer (18:10)
[d]Autumn (9:25)
[e]Winter (5:20)
● New moon
◐ First quarter moon
○ Full moon
◑ Last quarter moon

‡Leap year
[a]New Year
[b]Yom Kippur
[c]Sukkot
[d]Winter starts
[e]Ḥanukkah
[f]Purim
[g]Passover
[h]Shavuot
[i]Fast of Av

[a]New Year (4676, Horse)
[b]Lantern Festival
[c]Qīngmíng
[d]Dragon Festival
[e]Qīqiǎo
[f]Hungry Ghosts
[g]Mid-Autumn Festival
[h]Double-Ninth Festival
[i]Dōngzhì
*Start of 60-name cycle

‡Leap year
[a]New Year
[b]Building of the Cross
[c]Christmas
[d]Jesus's Circumcision
[e]Epiphany
[f]Easter
[g]Mary's Announcement
[h]Jesus's Transfiguration

PERSIAN (ASTRONOMICAL) 1356/1357

Month	Sun	Mon	Tue	Wed	Thu	Fri	Sat
DEY 1356	11	12	13	14	15	16	17
	18	19	20	21	22	23	24
	25	26	27	28	29	30	1
BAHMAN 1356	2	3	4	5	6	7	8
	9	10	11	12	13	14	15
	16	17	18	19	20	21	22
	23	24	25	26	27	28	29
	30	1	2	3	4	5	6
ESFAND 1356	7	8	9	10	11	12	13
	14	15	16	17	18	19	20
	21	22	23	24	25	26	27
	28	29	1[a]	2	3	4	5
FARVARDĪN 1357	6	7	8	9	10	11	12
	13[b]	14	15	16	17	18	19
	20	21	22	23	24	25	26
	27	28	29	30	31	1	2
ORDĪBEHEŠT 1357	3	4	5	6	7	8	9
	10	11	12	13	14	15	16
	17	18	19	20	21	22	23
	24	25	26	27	28	29	30
	31	1	2	3	4	5	6
XORDĀD 1357	7	8	9	10	11	12	13
	14	15	16	17	18	19	20
	21	22	23	24	25	26	27
	28	29	30	31	1	2	3
TĪR 1357	4	5	6	7	8	9	10
	11	12	13	14	15	16	17
	18	19	20	21	22	23	24
	25	26	27	28	29	30	31
MORDĀD 1357	1	2	3	4	5	6	7
	8	9	10	11	12	13	14
	15	16	17	18	19	20	21
	22	23	24	25	26	27	28
	29	30	31	1	2	3	4
SHAHRĪVAR 1357	5	6	7	8	9	10	11
	12	13	14	15	16	17	18
	19	20	21	22	23	24	25
	26	27	28	29	30	31	1
MEHR 1357	2	3	4	5	6	7	8
	9	10	11	12	13	14	15
	16	17	18	19	20	21	22
	23	24	25	26	27	28	29
	30	1	2	3	4	5	6
ĀBĀN 1357	7	8	9	10	11	12	13
	14	15	16	17	18	19	20
	21	22	23	24	25	26	27
	28	29	30	1	2	3	4
ĀZAR 1357	5	6	7	8	9	10	11
	12	13	14	15	16	17	18
	19	20	21	22	23	24	25
	26	27	28	29	30	1	2
DEY 1357	3	4	5	6	7	8	9
	10	11	12	13	14	15	16

[a]New Year
[b]Sizdeh Bedar

HINDU LUNAR 2034‡/2035

Month	Sun	Mon	Tue	Wed	Thu	Fri	Sat
MĀRGAŚIRA 2034	22	23	24	25	26	27	28
PAUSHA 2034	29	30	**1**	3	4	5	6
	7	8	9	10	11	12	13
	13	14	15	16	17	18	19
	20	21	22	23	24	**25**	27
MĀGHA 2034	28	29	30	1	2	3	4
	5	6	7	8	9	10	11
	12	13	14	15	15	16	17
	18	20	21	22	23	24	25
PHĀLGUNA 2034	26	27	28[h]	29	30	**1**	3
	4	4	5	6	7	8	9
	10	11	12	13	14	15[i]	16
	17	18	19	20	21	22	**23**
CHAITRA 2035	25	26	27	28	29	30	1[a]
	2	3	4	5	6	7	8
	8[b]	9	10	11	12	13	14
	15	16	**17**	19	20	21	22
	23	24	25	26	27	28	29
VAIŚĀKHA 2035	30	1	2	3	4	5	6
	7	8	9	10	11	12	13
	14	15	16	17	18	19	**20**
	22	23	24	25	26	27	28
JYAISHTHA 2035	29	30	1	2	3	4	4
	5	6	7	8	9	10	11
	12	**13**	15	16	17	18	19
	20	21	22	23	24	25	26
ĀSHĀDHA 2035	27	28	29	30	1	2	3
	4	5	6	7	8	9	10
	11	12	13	14	15	**16**	18
	19	20	21	22	23	24	25
ŚRĀVANA 2035	26	27	28	29	30	1	1
	2	3	4	5	6	7	**8**
	10	11	12	13	14	15	16
	17	18	19	20	21	22	23[c]
	24	25	26	27	28	29	30
BHĀDRAPADA 2035	1	2	3	4[d]	5	6	7
	8	9	10	11	**12**	14	15
	16	17	18	19	20	21	22
	23	24	25	26	27	27	28
ĀŚVINA 2035	29	30	1	2	3	4	**5**
	7	8[e]	9[e]	10[e]	11	12	13
	14	15	16	17	18	19	20
	21	22	23	24	25	26	27
KĀRTTIKA 2035	28	29	30	1[f]	2	3	4
	5	6	7	8	**9**	11	12
	13	14	15	16	17	18	19
	20	21	21	22	23	24	25
MĀRGAŚIRA 2035	26	27	28	29	30	1	2
	3	5	6	7	8	9	10
	11[g]	12	13	14	15	16	17
	18	19	20	21	22	23	24
PAUSHA 2035	24	25	**26**	28	29	30	1
	2	3	4	5	6	7	8

‡Leap year
[a]New Year (Kālayukta)
[b]Birthday of Rāma
[c]Birthday of Krishna
[d]Ganēśa Chaturthī
[e]Dashara
[f]Diwali
[g]Birthday of Vishnu
[h]Night of Śiva
[i]Holi

HINDU SOLAR 1899/1900‡

Month	Sun	Mon	Tue	Wed	Thu	Fri	Sat
PAUSHA 1899	18	19	20	21	22	23	24
MĀGHA 1899	25	26	27	28	29	30	1[b]
	2	3	4	5	6	7	8
	9	10	11	12	13	14	15
	16	17	18	19	20	21	22
	23	24	25	26	27	28	29
PHĀLGUNA 1899	1	2	3	4	5	6	7
	8	9	10	11	12	13	14
	15	16	17	18	19	20	21
	22	23	24	25	26	27	28
CHAITRA 1899	29	30	1	2	3	4	5
	6	7	8	9	10	11	12
	13	14	15	16	17	18	19
	20	21	22	23	24	25	26
VAIŚĀKHA 1900	27	28	29	30	1[a]	2	3
	4	5	6	7	8	9	10
	11	12	13	14	15	16	17
	18	19	20	21	22	23	24
	25	26	27	28	29	30	31
JYAISHTHA 1900	1	2	3	4	5	6	7
	8	9	10	11	12	13	14
	15	16	17	18	19	20	21
	22	23	24	25	26	27	28
ĀSHĀDHA 1900	29	30	31	32	1	2	3
	4	5	6	7	8	9	10
	11	12	13	14	15	16	17
	18	19	20	21	22	23	24
	25	26	27	28	29	30	31
ŚRĀVANA 1900	1	2	3	4	5	6	7
	8	9	10	11	12	13	14
	15	16	17	18	19	20	21
	22	23	24	25	26	27	28
BHĀDRAPADA 1900	29	30	31	32	1	2	3
	4	5	6	7	8	9	10
	11	12	13	14	15	16	17
	18	19	20	21	22	23	24
	25	26	27	28	29	30	31
ĀŚVINA 1900	1	2	3	4	5	6	7
	8	9	10	11	12	13	14
	15	16	17	18	19	20	21
	22	23	24	25	26	27	28
KĀRTTIKA 1900	29	30	1	2	3	4	5
	6	7	8	9	10	11	12
	13	14	15	16	17	18	19
	20	21	22	23	24	25	26
MĀRGAŚIRA 1900	27	28	29	30	1	2	3
	4	5	6	7	8	9	10
	11	12	13	14	15	16	17
	18	19	20	21	22	23	24
PAUSHA 1900	25	26	27	28	29	30	1
	2	3	4	5	6	7	8
	9	10	11	12	13	14	15
	16	17	18	19	20	21	22

‡Leap year
[a]New Year (Prajāpati)
[b]Pongal

ISLAMIC (ASTRONOMICAL) 1398/1399‡

Month	Sun	Mon	Tue	Wed	Thu	Fri	Sat
MUḤARRAM 1398	21	22	23	24	25	26	27
ṢAFAR 1398	28	29	1	2	3	4	5
	6	7	8	9	10	11	12
	13	14	15	16	17	18	19
	20	21	22	23	24	25	26
RABĪ' I 1398	27	28	29	30	1	2	3
	4	5	6	7	8	9	10
	11	12[c]	13	14	15	16	17
	18	19	20	21	22	23	24
RABĪ' II 1398	25	26	27	28	29	1	2
	3	4	5	6	7	8	9
	10	11	12	13	14	15	16
	17	18	19	20	21	22	23
	24	25	26	27	28	29	30
JUMĀDĀ I 1398	1	2	3	4	5	6	7
	8	9	10	11	12	13	14
	15	16	17	18	19	20	21
	22	23	24	25	26	27	28
JUMĀDĀ II 1398	29	30	1	2	3	4	5
	6	7	8	9	10	11	12
	13	14	15	16	17	18	19
	20	21	22	23	24	25	26
RAJAB 1398	27	28	29	1	2	3	4
	5	6	7	8	9	10	11
	12	13	14	15	16	17	18
	19	20	21	22	23	24	25
SHA'BĀN 1398	26	27[d]	28	29	30	1	2
	3	4	5	6	7	8	9
	10	11	12	13	14	15	16
	17	18	19	20	21	22	23
	24	25	26	27	28	29	30
RAMAḌĀN 1398	1[e]	2	3	4	5	6	7
	8	9	10	11	12	13	14
	15	16	17	18	19	20	21
	22	23	24	25	26	27	28
SHAWWĀL 1398	29	1[f]	2	3	4	5	6
	7	8	9	10	11	12	13
	14	15	16	17	18	19	20
	21	22	23	24	25	26	27
DHU AL-QA'DA 1398	28	29	30	1	2	3	4
	5	6	7	8	9	10	11
	12	13	14	15	16	17	18
	19	20	21	22	23	24	25
DHU AL-ḤIJJA 1398	26	27	28	29	1	2	3
	4	5	6	7	8	9	10[g]
	11	12	13	14	15	16	17
	18	19	20	21	22	23	24
MUḤARRAM 1399	25	26	27	28	29	1[a]	2[A]
	3	4	5	6	7	8	9
	10[b]	11	12	13	14	15	16
	17	18	19	20	21	22	23
	24	25	26	27	28	29	30
	1	2	3	4	5	6	7

‡Leap year
[a]New Year
[A]New Year (Arithmetic)
[b]'Ashūrā'
[c]Prophet's Birthday
[d]Ascent of the Prophet
[e]Start of Ramaḍān
[f]'Īd al-Fiṭr
[g]'Īd al-'Aḍḥā

GREGORIAN 1978

Julian (Sun)	Sun	Mon	Tue	Wed	Thu	Fri	Sat	Month
Dec 19	1	2	3	4	5	6	7[a]	JANUARY 1978
	8	9	10	11	12	13	14[b]	
Jan 2	15	16	17	18	19	20	21	
	22	23	24	25	26	27	28	
Jan 16	29	30	31	1	2	3	4	FEBRUARY 1978
	5	6	7	8[c]	9	10	11	
Jan 30	12	13	14	15	16	17	18	
	19	20	21	22	23	24	25	
Feb 13	26	27	28	1	2	3	4	MARCH 1978
	5	6	7	8	9	10	11	
Feb 27	12	13	14	15	16	17	18	
	19[d]	20	21	22	23	24	25	
Mar 13	26[e]	27	28	29	30	31	1	APRIL 1978
	2	3	4	5	6	7	8	
Mar 27	9	10	11	12	13	14	15	
	16	17	18	19	20	21	22	
Apr 10	23	24	25	26	27	28	29	
	30[f]	1	2	3	4	5	6	MAY 1978
Apr 24	7	8	9	10	11	12	13	
	14	15	16	17	18	19	20	
May 8	21	22	23	24	25	26	27	
	28	29	30	31	1	2	3	JUNE 1978
May 22	4	5	6	7	8	9	10	
	11	12	13	14	15	16	17	
Jun 5	18	19	20	21	22	23	24	
	25	26	27	28	29	30	1	JULY 1978
Jun 19	2	3	4	5	6	7	8	
	9	10	11	12	13	14	15	
Jul 3	16	17	18	19	20	21	22	
	23	24	25	26	27	28	29	
Jul 17	30	31	1	2	3	4	5	AUGUST 1978
	6	7	8	9	10	11	12	
Jul 31	13	14	15	16	17	18	19	
	20	21	22	23	24	25	26	
Aug 14	27	28	29	30	31	1	2	SEPTEMBER 1978
	3	4	5	6	7	8	9	
Aug 28	10	11	12	13	14	15	16	
	17	18	19	20	21	22	23	
Sep 11	24	25	26	27	28	29	30	
	1	2	3	4	5	6	7	OCTOBER 1978
Sep 25	8	9	10	11	12	13	14	
	15	16	17	18	19	20	21	
Oct 9	22	23	24	25	26	27	28	
	29	30	31	1	2	3	4	NOVEMBER 1978
Oct 23	5	6	7	8	9	10	11	
	12	13	14	15	16	17	18	
Nov 6	19	20	21	22	23	24	25	
	26	27	28	29	30	1	2	DECEMBER 1978
Nov 20	3[g]	4	5	6	7	8	9	
	10	11	12	13	14	15	16	
Dec 4	17	18	19	20	21	22	23	
	24	25[h]	26	27	28	29	30	
Dec 18	31	1	2	3	4	5	6	

[a]Orthodox Christmas
[b]Julian New Year
[c]Ash Wednesday
[d]Feast of Orthodoxy
[e]Easter
[f]Orthodox Easter
[g]Advent
[h]Christmas

1979

Gregorian 1979	Sun	Mon	Tue	Wed	Thu	Fri	Sat	Lunar Phases	ISO Week (Mon)	Julian Day (Sun noon)	Hebrew 5739/5740	Sun	Mon	Tue	Wed	Thu	Fri	Sat	Molad	Chinese Wù-Wǔ/Jǐ-Wèi‡	Sun	Mon	Tue	Wed	Thu	Fri	Sat	Solar Term	Coptic 1695‡/1696	Sun	Mon	Tue	Wed	Thu	Fri	Sat	Ethiopic 1971‡/1972
JANUARY 1979	31	1[a]	2	3	4	◐	6	11:15	1	2443874	TEVETH 5739	1[e]	2[e]	3	4	5	6	7	Fri $19^{h}46^{m}5^{p}$	MONTH 12 Wù-Wǔ	2	3	4	5	6	7	*8*	Xiǎo hán	KOIAK 1695	22	23	24	25	26	27	28	TĀḪŚĀŚ 1971
	7	8	9	10	11	12	○	7:09	2	2443881		8	9	10	11	12	13	14			9	10	11	12	13	14	15		TŌBE 1695	29[c]	30	1	2	3	4	5	ṬER 1971
	14	15	16	17	18	19	20		3	2443888		15	16	17	18	19	20	21			16	17	18	19	20	21	**22**	Dà hán		6[d]	7	8	9	10	11[e]	12	
	◑	22	23	24	25	26	27	11:23	4	2443895		22	23	24	25	26	27	28			23	24	25	26	27	28	29			13	14	15	16	17	18	19	
FEBRUARY 1979	●	29	30	31	1	2	3	6:20	5	2443902	SHEVAT 5739	29	1	2	3	4	5	6	Sun $8^{h}30^{m}6^{p}$	MONTH 1 Jǐ-Wèi	1[a]	2	3	4	5	6	7			20	21	22	23	24	25	26	
	◐	5	6	7	8	9	10	0:36	6	2443909		7	8	9	10	11	12	13			*8*	9	10	11	12	13	14	Lì chūn	MESHIR 1695	27	28	29	30	1	2	3	YAKĀTIT 1971
	11	○	13	14	15	16	17	2:39	7	2443916		14	15	16	17	18	19	20			15[b]	16	17	18	19	20	21			4	5	6	7	8	9	10	
	18	19	◑	21	22	23	24	1:17	8	2443923		21	22	23	24	25	26	27			22	**23**	24	25	26	27	28	Yǔ shuǐ		11	12	13	14	15	16	17	
MARCH 1979	25	●	27	28	1	2	3	16:45	9	2443930	ADAR 5739	28	29	30	1	2	3	4	Mon $21^{h}14^{m}7^{p}$	MONTH 2 Jǐ-Wèi	29	30*	1	2	3	4	5			18	19	20	21	22	23	24	
	4	◐	6	7	8	9	10	16:23	10	2443937		5	6	7	8	9	10	11			6	7	*8*	9	10	11	12	Jīng zhé	PAREMOTEP 1695	25	26	27	28	29	30	1	MAGĀBIT 1971
	11	12	○	14	15	16	17	21:14	11	2443944		12	13	14[f]	15	16	17	18			13	14	15	16	17	18	19			2	3	4	5	6	7	8	
	18	19	20	◑[b]	22	23	24	11:22	12	2443951		19	20	21	22	23	24	25			20	21	22	**23**	24	25	26	Chūn fēn		9	10	11	12	13	14	15	
	25	26	27	●	29	30	31	3:00	13	2443958	NISAN 5739	26	27	28	29	1	2	3	Wed $9^{h}58^{m}8^{p}$	MONTH 3 Jǐ-Wèi	27	28	29	1	2	3	4			16	17	18	19	20	21	22	
APRIL 1979	1	2	3	◐	5	6	7	9:57	14	2443965		4	5	6	7	8	9	10			5	6	7	8	9[c]	10	11	Qīng míng		23	24	25	26	27	28	29	
	8	9	10	11	○	13	14	13:15	15	2443972		11	12	13	14	15[g]	16	17			12	13	14	15	16	17	18		PARMOUTE 1695	30	1	2	3	4	5	6	MIYĀZYĀ 1971
	15	16	17	18	◑	20	21	18:30	16	2443979		18	19	20	21	22	23	24			19	20	21	22	23	24	**25**	Gǔ yǔ		7	8	9	10	11	12	13	
	22	23	24	25	●	27	28	13:15	17	2443986	IYYAR 5739	25	26	27	28	29	30	1	Thu $22^{h}42^{m}9^{p}$	MONTH 4 Jǐ-Wèi	26	27	28	29	1	2*	3			14[f]	15	16	17	18	19	20	
MAY 1979	29	30	1	2	3	◐	5	4:25	18	2443993		2	3	4	5	6	7	8			4	5	6	7	8	9	10			21	22	23	24	25	26	27	
	6	7	8	9	10	11	○	2:01	19	2444000		9	10	11	12	13	14	15			*11*	12	13	14	15	16	17	Lì xià	PASHONS 1695	28	29[g]	30	1	2	3	4	GENBOT 1971
	13	14	15	16	17	◑	19	23:57	20	2444007		16	17	18	19	20	21	22			18	19	20	21	22	23	24			5	6	7	8	9	10	11	
	20	21	22	23	24	25	●	0:00	21	2444014		23	24	25	26	27	28	29		MONTH 5 Jǐ-Wèi	25	**26**	27	28	29	30	1	Xiǎo mǎn		12	13	14	15	16	17	18	
JUNE 1979	27	28	29	30	31	1	◐	22:37	22	2444021	SIVAN 5739	1	2	3	4	5	6[h]	7	Sat $11^{h}26^{m}10^{p}$		2	3	4	5[d]	6	7	8			19	20	21	22	23	24	25	
	3	4	5	6	7	8	9		23	2444028		8	9	10	11	12	13	14			9	10	11	*12*	13	14	15	Máng zhòng	PAŌNE 1695	26	27	28	29	30	1	2	SANĒ 1971
	○	11	12	13	14	15	16	11:55	24	2444035		15	16	17	18	19	20	21			16	17	18	19	20	21	22			3	4	5	6	7	8	9	
	◑	18	19	20	21[c]	22	23	5:01	25	2444042		22	23	24	25	26	27	28			23	24	25	26	27	**28**	29	Xià zhì		10	11	12	13	14	15	16	
	●	25	26	27	28	29	30	11:58	26	2444049	TAMMUZ 5739	29	30	1	2	3	4	5	Mon $0^{h}10^{m}11^{p}$	MONTH 6 Jǐ-Wèi	1	2	3*	4	5	6	7			17	18	19	20	21	22	23	
JULY 1979	1	◐	3	4	5	6	7	15:24	27	2444056		6	7	8	9	10	11	12			8	9	10	11	12	13	14			24	25	26	27	28	29	30	
	8	○	10	11	12	13	14	19:59	28	2444063		13	14	15	16	17	18	19			*15*	16	17	18	19	20	21	Xiǎo shǔ	EPĒP 1695	1	2	3	4	5	6	7	ḤAMLĒ 1971
	15	◑	17	18	19	20	21	10:59	29	2444070		20	21	22	23	24	25	26			22	23	24	25	26	27	28			8	9	10	11	12	13	14	
	22	23	●	25	26	27	28	1:41	30	2444077	AV 5739	27	28	29	1	2	3	4	Tue $12^{h}54^{m}12^{p}$	LEAP MONTH 6 Jǐ-Wèi	29	**30**	1	2	3	4	5	Dà shǔ		15	16	17	18	19	20	21	
AUGUST 1979	29	30	31	◐	2	3	4	5:57	31	2444084		5	6	7	8	9[i]	10	11			6	7	8	9	10	11	12			22	23	24	25	26	27	28	
	5	6	7	○	9	10	11	3:21	32	2444091		12	13	14	15	16	17	18			13	14	15	*16*	17	18	19	Lì qiū	MESORĒ 1695	29	30	1	2	3	4	5	NAḤASĒ 1971
	12	13	◑	15	16	17	18	19:02	33	2444098		19	20	21	22	23	24	25			20	21	22	23	24	25	26			6	7	8	9	10	11	12	
	19	20	21	●	23	24	25	17:10	34	2444105	ELUL 5739	26	27	28	29	30	1	2	Thu $1^{h}38^{m}13^{p}$	MONTH 7 Jǐ-Wèi	27	28	29	30	1	**2**	3*	Chǔ shǔ		13[h]	14	15	16	17	18	19	
SEPTEMBER 1979	26	27	28	29	◐	31	1	18:09	35	2444112		3	4	5	6	7	8	9			4	5	6	7[e]	8	9	10			20	21	22	23	24	25	26	
	2	3	4	5	○	7	8	10:59	36	2444119		10	11	12	13	14	15	16			11	12	13	14	15[f]	16	*17*	Bái lù	EPAG. 1695	27	28	29	30	1	2	3	PĀG. 1971
	9	10	11	12	◑	14	15	6:15	37	2444126		17	18	19	20	21	22	23			18	19	20	21	22	23	24		THOOUT 1696	4	5	6	1[a]	2	3	4	MASKARAM 1972
	16	17	18	19	20	●	22	9:47	38	2444133	TISHRI 5740	24	25	26	27	28	29	1[a]	Fri $14^{h}22^{m}14^{p}$	MONTH 8 Jǐ-Wèi	25	26	27	28	29	1	2			5	6	7	8	9	10	11	
	23[d]	24	25	26	27	28	◐	4:20	39	2444140		2[a]	3	4	5	6	7	8			**3**	4	5	6	7	8	9	Qiū fēn		12	13	14	15	16	17[b]	18	
OCTOBER 1979	30	1	2	3	4	○	6	19:35	40	2444147		9	10[b]	11	12	13	14	15[c]			10	11	12	13	14	15[g]	16			19	20	21	22	23	24	25	
	7	8	9	10	11	◑	13	21:24	41	2444154		16	17	18	19	20	21	22			17	18	*19*	20	21	22	23	Hán lù	PAOPE 1696	26	27	28	29	30	1	2	ṬEQEMT 1972
	14	15	16	17	18	19	20		42	2444161		23	24	25	26	27	28	29			24	25	26	27	28	29	30			3	4	5	6	7	8	9	
	●	22	23	24	25	26	27	2:23	43	2444168	HESHVAN 5740	30	1	2	3	4	5	6	Sun $3^{h}6^{m}15^{p}$	MONTH 9 Jǐ-Wèi	1	2	3	**4***	5	6	7	Shuāng jiàng		10	11	12	13	14	15	16	
NOVEMBER 1979	◐	29	30	31	1	2	3	13:06	44	2444175		7	8	9	10	11	12	13			8	9[h]	10	11	12	13	14			17	18	19	20	21	22	23	
	○	5	6	7	8	9	10	5:47	45	2444182		14	15	16	17	18	19	20			15	16	17	18	*19*	20	21	Lì dōng		24	25	26	27	28	29	30	
	◑	12	13	14	15	16	17	16:24	46	2444189		21	22	23	24	25	26	27			22	23	24	25	26	27	28		ATHŌR 1696	1	2	3	4	5	6	7	ḪEDĀR 1972
	18	●	20	21	22	23	24	18:04	47	2444196	KISLEV 5740	28	29	30	1	2	3	4	Mon $15^{h}50^{m}16^{p}$	MONTH 10 Jǐ-Wèi	29	30	1	2	3	**4**	5	Xiǎo xuě		8	9	10	11	12	13	14	
DECEMBER 1979	25	◐	27	28	29	30	1	21:09	48	2444203		5	6	7	8	9	10	11			6	7	8	9	10	11	12			15	16	17	18	19	20	21	
	2	○	4	5	6	7	8	18:08	49	2444210		12	13	14	15	16[d]	17	18			13	14	15	16	17	18	*19*	Dà xuě		22	23	24	25	26	27	28	
	9	10	◑	12	13	14	15	13:59	50	2444217		19	20	21	22	23	24	25[e]			20	21	22	23	24	25	26		KOIAK 1696	29	30	1	2	3	4	5	TĀḪŚĀŚ 1972
	16	17	18	●	20	21	22[e]	8:23	51	2444224	TEVETH 5740	26[e]	27[e]	28[e]	29[e]	30[e]	1[e]	2[e]	Wed $4^{h}34^{m}17^{p}$	MONTH 11 Jǐ-Wèi	27	28	29	1	2	3	4[i]	Dōng zhì		6	7	8	9	10	11	12	
	23	24	25	◐	27	28	29	5:11	52	2444231		3	4	5	6	7	8	9			5*	6	7	8	9	10	11			13	14	15	16	17	18	19	
	30	31	1	○	3	4	5	9:02	1	2444238		10	11	12	13	14	15	16			12	13	14	15	16	17	18			20	21	22	23	24	25	26	

[a]New Year
[b]Spring (5:22)
[c]Summer (23:56)
[d]Autumn (15:16)
[e]Winter (11:09)
● New moon
◐ First quarter moon
○ Full moon
◑ Last quarter moon

[a]New Year
[b]Yom Kippur
[c]Sukkot
[d]Winter starts
[e]Ḥanukkah
[f]Purim
[g]Passover
[h]Shavuot
[i]Fast of Av

‡Leap year
[a]New Year (4677, Sheep)
[b]Lantern Festival
[c]Qīngmíng
[d]Dragon Festival
[e]Qīqiǎo
[f]Hungry Ghosts
[g]Mid-Autumn Festival
[h]Double-Ninth Festival
[i]Dōngzhì
*Start of 60-name cycle

‡Leap year
[a]New Year
[b]Building of the Cross
[c]Christmas
[d]Jesus's Circumcision
[e]Epiphany
[f]Easter
[g]Mary's Announcement
[h]Jesus's Transfiguration

PERSIAN (ASTRONOMICAL) 1357/1358‡

Month	Sun	Mon	Tue	Wed	Thu	Fri	Sat
DEY 1357	10	11	12	13	14	15	16
	17	18	19	20	21	22	23
	24	25	26	27	28	29	30
BAHMAN 1357	*1*	2	3	4	5	6	7
	8	9	10	11	12	13	14
	15	16	17	18	19	20	21
	22	23	24	25	26	27	28
ESFAND 1357	29	30	*1*	2	3	4	5
	6	7	8	9	10	11	12
	13	14	15	16	17	18	19
	20	21	22	23	24	25	26
FARVARDIN 1358	27	28	29	*1*[a]	2	3	4
	5	6	7	8	9	10	11
	12	13[b]	14	15	16	17	18
	19	20	21	22	23	24	25
ORDIBEHEŠT 1358	26	27	28	29	30	31	*1*
	2	3	4	5	6	7	8
	9	10	11	12	13	14	15
	16	17	18	19	20	21	22
	23	24	25	26	27	28	29
XORDĀD 1358	30	31	*1*	2	3	4	5
	6	7	8	9	10	11	12
	13	14	15	16	17	18	19
	20	21	22	23	24	25	26
TĪR 1358	27	28	29	30	31	*1*	2
	3	4	5	6	7	8	9
	10	11	12	13	14	15	16
	17	18	19	20	21	22	23
	24	25	26	27	28	29	30
MORDĀD 1358	31	*1*	2	3	4	5	6
	7	8	9	10	11	12	13
	14	15	16	17	18	19	20
	21	22	23	24	25	26	27
SHAHRĪVAR 1358	28	29	30	31	*1*	2	3
	4	5	6	7	8	9	10
	11	12	13	14	15	16	17
	18	19	20	21	22	23	24
	25	26	27	28	29	30	31
MEHR 1358	*1*	2	3	4	5	6	7
	8	9	10	11	12	13	14
	15	16	17	18	19	20	21
	22	23	24	25	26	27	28
ĀBĀN 1358	29	30	*1*	2	3	4	5
	6	7	8	9	10	11	12
	13	14	15	16	17	18	19
	20	21	22	23	24	25	26
ĀZAR 1358	27	28	29	30	*1*	2	3
	4	5	6	7	8	9	10
	11	12	13	14	15	16	17
	18	19	20	21	22	23	24
DEY 1358	25	26	27	28	29	30	*1*
	2	3	4	5	6	7	8
	9	10	11	12	13	14	15

HINDU LUNAR 2035/2036

Month	Sun	Mon	Tue	Wed	Thu	Fri	Sat
PAUSHA 2035	2	3	4	5	6	7	8
	9	10	11	12	13	14	15
	16	17	18	19	20	21	22
	23	24	25	26	27	28	29
MĀGHA 2035	30	1	**2**	4	5	6	7
	8	9	10	11	12	13	14
	15	*15*	16	17	18	19	20
	21	22	23	24	25	**26**	28
PHĀLGUNA 2035	29[h]	30	1	2	3	4	5
	6	7	8	9	10	11	12
	13	14	15[i]	16	17	18	19
	20	21	22	23	24	25	26
CHAITRA 2036	27	28	29	30	**1**[a]	3	4
	5	6	7	8	*8*[b]	9	10
	11	12	13	14	15	16	17
	18	19	20	21	22	23	**24**
VAIŚĀKHA 2036	26	27	28	29	30	1	2
	3	4	5	6	7	8	9
	10	11	12	*12*	13	14	15
	16	18	19	20	21	22	23
JYAISHTHA 2036	24	25	26	27	28	**29**	1
	2	3	3	4	5	6	7
	8	9	10	11	12	13	14
	15	16	17	18	19	**20**	22
	23	24	25	26	27	28	29
ĀSHĀDHA 2036	30	1	2	3	4	5	6
	7	8	9	9	10	11	**12**
	14	15	16	17	18	19	20
	21	22	23	**24**	26	27	28
ŚRĀVANA 2036	29	30	*30*	1	2	3	4
	5	6	7	8	9	10	11
	12	13	14	15	**16**	18	19
	20	21	22	23[c]	24	25	26
BHĀDRAPADA 2036	27	28	29	30	1	2	3
	4[d]	5	6	*6*	**7**	9	10
	11	12	13	14	15	16	17
	18	19	**20**	22	23	24	25
ĀŚVINA 2036	26	*26*	27	28	29	30	1
	2	3	4	5	6	7	**8**[e]
	9[e]	10[e]	11	**12**	14	15	16
	17	18	19	20	21	22	23
	24	25	26	27	28	29	30
KĀRTTIKA 2036	*30*	1[f]	2	3	4	**5**	7
	8	9	10	11	12	13	14
	15	16	17	18	19	20	21
	22	23	24	25	26	27	28
MĀRGAŚĪRA 2036	29	30	1	2	3	4	5
	6	7	8	9	**10**[g]	12	13
	14	15	16	17	18	19	20
	21	22	23	*23*	24	25	26
PAUSHA 2036	27	28	29	30	1	2	3
	4	6	7	8	9	10	11
	12	13	14	15	16	17	18

HINDU SOLAR 1900‡/1901

Month	Sun	Mon	Tue	Wed	Thu	Fri	Sat
PAUSHA 1900	16	17	18	19	20	21	22
	23	24	25	26	27	28	29
MĀGHA 1900	1[b]	2	3	4	5	6	7
	8	9	10	11	12	13	14
	15	16	17	18	19	20	21
	22	23	24	25	26	27	28
PHĀLGUNA 1900	29	1	2	3	4	5	6
	7	8	9	10	11	12	13
	14	15	16	17	18	19	20
	21	22	23	24	25	26	27
CHAITRA 1900	28	29	30	1	2	3	4
	5	6	7	8	9	10	11
	12	13	14	15	16	17	18
	19	20	21	22	23	24	25
VAIŚĀKHA 1901	26	27	28	29	30	31	1[a]
	2	3	4	5	6	7	8
	9	10	11	12	13	14	15
	16	17	18	19	20	21	22
	23	24	25	26	27	28	29
JYAISHTHA 1901	30	31	1	2	3	4	5
	6	7	8	9	10	11	12
	13	14	15	16	17	18	19
	20	21	22	23	24	25	26
ĀSHĀDHA 1901	27	28	29	30	31	1	2
	3	4	5	6	7	8	9
	10	11	12	13	14	15	16
	17	18	19	20	21	22	23
	24	25	26	27	28	29	30
ŚRĀVAṆA 1901	31	32	1	2	3	4	5
	6	7	8	9	10	11	12
	13	14	15	16	17	18	19
	20	21	22	23	24	25	26
BHĀDRAPADA 1901	27	28	29	30	31	1	2
	3	4	5	6	7	8	9
	10	11	12	13	14	15	16
	17	18	19	20	21	22	23
	24	25	26	27	28	29	30
ĀŚVINA 1901	31	1	2	3	4	5	6
	7	8	9	10	11	12	13
	14	15	16	17	18	19	20
	21	22	23	24	25	26	27
KĀRTTIKA 1901	28	29	30	1	2	3	4
	5	6	7	8	9	10	11
	12	13	14	15	16	17	18
	19	20	21	22	23	24	25
MĀRGAŚĪRA 1901	26	27	28	29	30	1	2
	3	4	5	6	7	8	9
	10	11	12	13	14	15	16
	17	18	19	20	21	22	23
	24	25	26	27	28	29	30
PAUSHA 1901	1	2	3	4	5	6	7
	8	9	10	11	12	13	14
	15	16	17	18	19	20	21

ISLAMIC (ASTRONOMICAL) 1399‡/1400

Month	Sun	Mon	Tue	Wed	Thu	Fri	Sat
ṢAFAR 1399	*1*	2	3	4	5	6	7
	8	9	10	11	12	13	14
	15	16	17	18	19	20	21
	22	23	24	25	26	27	28
RABĪ' I 1399	29	*1*	2	3	4	5	6
	7	8	9	10	11	12[c]	13
	14	15	16	17	18	19	20
	21	22	23	24	25	26	27
RABĪ' II 1399	28	29	30	*1*	2	3	4
	5	6	7	8	9	10	11
	12	13	14	15	16	17	18
	19	20	21	22	23	24	25
JUMĀDĀ I 1399	26	27	28	29	*1*	2	3
	4	5	6	7	8	9	10
	11	12	13	14	15	16	17
	18	19	20	21	22	23	24
JUMĀDĀ II 1399	25	26	27	28	29	30	*1*
	2	3	4	5	6	7	8
	9	10	11	12	13	14	15
	16	17	18	19	20	21	22
	23	24	25	26	27	28	29
RAJAB 1399	*1*	2	3	4	5	6	7
	8	9	10	11	12	13	14
	15	16	17	18	19	20	21
	22	23	24	25	26	27[d]	28
SHA'BĀN 1399	29	30	*1*	2	3	4	5
	6	7	8	9	10	11	12
	13	14	15	16	17	18	19
	20	21	22	23	24	25	26
RAMAḌĀN 1399	27	28	29	30	*1*[e]	2	3
	4	5	6	7	8	9	10
	11	12	13	14	15	16	17
	18	19	20	21	22	23	24
SHAWWĀL 1399	25	26	27	28	29	*1*[f]	2
	3	4	5	6	7	8	9
	10	11	12	13	14	15	16
	17	18	19	20	21	22	23
	24	25	26	27	28	29	30
DHU AL-QA'DA 1399	*1*	2	3	4	5	6	7
	8	9	10	11	12	13	14
	15	16	17	18	19	20	21
	22	23	24	25	26	27	28
DHU AL-ḤIJJA 1399	29	*1*	2	3	4	5	6
	7	8	9	10[g]	11	12	13
	14	15	16	17	18	19	20
	21	22	23	24	25	26	27
MUḤARRAM 1400	28	29	30	*1*[a]	2	3	4
	5	6	7	8	9	10[b]	11
	12	13	14	15	16	17	18
	19	20	21	22	23	24	25
ṢAFAR 1400	26	27	28	29	30	*1*	2
	3	4	5	6	7	8	9
	10	11	12	13	14	15	16

GREGORIAN 1979

Julian (Sun)	Sun	Mon	Tue	Wed	Thu	Fri	Sat	Month
Dec 18	*31*	1	2	3	4	5	6	JANUARY 1979
	7[a]	8	9	10	11	12	13	
Jan 1	*14*[b]	15	16	17	18	19	20	
	21	22	23	24	25	26	27	
Jan 15	*28*	29	30	31	1	2	3	FEBRUARY 1979
	4	5	6	7	8	9	10	
Jan 29	*11*	12	13	14	15	16	17	
	18	19	20	21	22	23	24	
Feb 12	*25*	26	27	28[c]	1	2	3	MARCH 1979
	4	5	6	7	8	9	10	
Feb 26	*11*[d]	12	13	14	15	16	17	
	18	19	20	21	22	23	24	
Mar 12	*25*	26	27	28	29	30	31	
	1	2	3	4	5	6	7	APRIL 1979
Mar 26	*8*	9	10	11	12	13	14	
	15[e]	16	17	18	19	20	21	
Apr 9	*22*[f]	23	24	25	26	27	28	
	29	30	1	2	3	4	5	MAY 1979
Apr 23	*6*	7	8	9	10	11	12	
	13	14	15	16	17	18	19	
May 7	*20*	21	22	23	24	25	26	
	27	28	29	30	31	1	2	JUNE 1979
May 21	*3*	4	5	6	7	8	9	
	10	11	12	13	14	15	16	
Jun 4	*17*	18	19	20	21	22	23	
	24	25	26	27	28	29	30	
Jun 18	*1*	2	3	4	5	6	7	JULY 1979
	8	9	10	11	12	13	14	
Jul 2	*15*	16	17	18	19	20	21	
	22	23	24	25	26	27	28	
Jul 16	*29*	30	31	1	2	3	4	AUGUST 1979
	5	6	7	8	9	10	11	
Jul 30	*12*	13	14	15	16	17	18	
	19	20	21	22	23	24	25	
Aug 13	*26*	27	28	29	30	31	1	SEPTEMBER 1979
	2	3	4	5	6	7	8	
Aug 27	*9*	10	11	12	13	14	15	
	16	17	18	19	20	21	22	
Sep 10	*23*	24	25	26	27	28	29	
	30	1	2	3	4	5	6	OCTOBER 1979
Sep 24	*7*	8	9	10	11	12	13	
	14	15	16	17	18	19	20	
Oct 8	*21*	22	23	24	25	26	27	
	28	29	30	31	1	2	3	NOVEMBER 1979
Oct 22	*4*	5	6	7	8	9	10	
	11	12	13	14	15	16	17	
Nov 5	*18*	19	20	21	22	23	24	
	25	26	27	28	29	30	1	DECEMBER 1979
Nov 19	*2*[g]	3	4	5	6	7	8	
	9	10	11	12	13	14	15	
Dec 3	*16*	17	18	19	20	21	22	
	23	24	25[h]	26	27	28	29	
Dec 17	*30*	31	1	2	3	4	5	

Persian: ‡Leap year; [a]New Year; [b]Sizdeh Bedar

Hindu Lunar: [a]New Year (Siddhārthin); [b]Birthday of Rāma; [c]Birthday of Krishna; [d]Ganēśa Chaturthī; [e]Dashara; [f]Diwali; [g]Birthday of Vishnu; [h]Night of Śiva; [i]Holi

Hindu Solar: ‡Leap year; [a]New Year (Aṅgiras); [b]Pongal

Islamic: ‡Leap year; [a]New Year; [b]'Āshūrā'; [c]Prophet's Birthday; [d]Ascent of the Prophet; [e]Start of Ramaḍān; [f]'Īd al-Fiṭr; [g]'Īd al-'Aḍḥā

Gregorian: [a]Orthodox Christmas; [b]Julian New Year; [c]Ash Wednesday; [d]Feast of Orthodoxy; [e]Easter; [f]Orthodox Easter; [g]Advent; [h]Christmas

1980

Month	Sun	Mon	Tue	Wed	Thu	Fri	Sat	Lunar Phases	ISO WEEK (Mon)	JULIAN DAY (Sun noon)
GREGORIAN 1980‡										
JANUARY 1980	30	31	1[a]	○	3	4	5	9:02	1	2444238
	6	7	8	9	◑	11	12	11:50	2	2444245
	13	14	15	16	●	18	19	21:20	3	2444252
	20	21	22	23	◐	25	26	13:58	4	2444259
	27	28	29	30	31	○	2	2:21	5	2444266
FEBRUARY 1980	3	4	5	6	7	8	◑	7:35	6	2444273
	10	11	12	13	14	15	●	8:51	7	2444280
	17	18	19	20	21	22	◐	0:14	8	2444287
	24	25	26	27	28	29	○	21:00	9	2444294
MARCH 1980	2	3	4	5	6	7	8		10	2444301
	◑	10	11	12	13	14	15	23:49	11	2444308
	●	17	18	19	20[b]	21	22	18:56	12	2444315
	◐	24	25	26	27	28	29	12:31	13	2444322
	30	○	1	2	3	4	5	15:14	14	2444329
APRIL 1980	6	7	◑	9	10	11	12	12:06	15	2444336
	13	14	●	16	17	18	19	3:46	16	2444343
	20	21	◐	23	24	25	26	3:00	17	2444350
	27	28	29	○	1	2	3	7:35	18	2444357
MAY 1980	4	5	6	◑	8	9	10	20:51	19	2444364
	11	12	13	●	15	16	17	12:00	20	2444371
	18	19	20	◐	22	23	24	19:16	21	2444378
	25	26	27	28	○	30	31	21:28	22	2444385
JUNE 1980	1	2	3	4	5	◑	7	2:53	23	2444392
	8	9	10	11	●	13	14	20:38	24	2444399
	15	16	17	18	19	◐	21[c]	12:32	25	2444406
	22	23	24	25	26	27	○	9:02	26	2444413
	29	30	1	2	3	4	◑	7:27	27	2444420
JULY 1980	6	7	8	9	10	11	●	6:46	28	2444427
	13	14	15	16	17	18	19		29	2444434
	◐	21	22	23	24	25	26	5:50	30	2444441
	○	28	29	30	31	1	2	18:54	31	2444448
AUGUST 1980	◑	4	5	6	7	8	9	12:00	32	2444455
	●	11	12	13	14	15	16	19:09	33	2444462
	17	◐	19	20	21	22	23	22:28	34	2444469
	24	25	○	27	28	29	30	3:42	35	2444476
	31	◑	2	3	4	5	6	18:08	36	2444483
SEPTEMBER 1980	7	8	●	10	11	12	13	10:00	37	2444490
	14	15	16	◐	18	19	20	13:54	38	2444497
	21	22[d]	23	○	25	26	27	12:08	39	2444504
	28	29	30	◑	2	3	4	3:18	40	2444511
OCTOBER 1980	5	6	7	8	●	10	11	2:50	41	2444518
	12	13	14	15	16	◐	18	3:47	42	2444525
	19	20	21	22	○	24	25	20:52	43	2444532
	26	27	28	29	◑	31	1	16:33	44	2444539
NOVEMBER 1980	2	3	4	5	6	●	8	20:42	45	2444546
	9	10	11	12	13	14	◐	15:47	46	2444553
	16	17	18	19	20	21	○	6:39	47	2444560
	23	24	25	26	27	28	◑	9:59	48	2444567
	30	1	2	3	4	5	6		49	2444574
DECEMBER 1980	●	8	9	10	11	12	13	14:35	50	2444581
	14	◐	16	17	18	19	20	1:47	51	2444588
	○[e]	22	23	24	25	26	27	18:08	52	2444595
	28	◑	30	31	1	2	3	6:32	1	2444602

ISO WEEK	Month	Sun	Mon	Tue	Wed	Thu	Fri	Sat	Molad
	HEBREW 5740/5741‡								
1	TEVETH 5740	10	11	12	13	14	15	16	
2		17	18	19	20	21	22	23	
3		24	25	26	27	28	29	1	Thu $17^h19^m0^p$
4	SHEVAT 5740	2	3	4	5	6	7	8	
5		9	10	11	12	13	14	15	
6		16	17	18	19	20	21	22	
7		23	24	25	26	27	28	29	
8		30	1	2	3	4	5	6	Sat $6^h3^m1^p$
9	ADAR 5740	7	8	9	10	11	12	13	
10		14[f]	15	16	17	18	19	20	
11		21	22	23	24	25	26	27	
12		28	29	1	2	3	4	5	Sun $18^h47^m2^p$
13	NISAN 5740	6	7	8	9	10	11	12	
14		13	14	15[g]	16	17	18	19	
15		20	21	22	23	24	25	26	
16		27	28	29	30	1	2	3	Tue $7^h31^m3^p$
17	IYYAR 5740	4	5	6	7	8	9	10	
18		11	12	13	14	15	16	17	
19		18	19	20	21	22	23	24	
20		25	26	27	28	29	1	2	Wed $20^h15^m4^p$
21	SIVAN 5740	3	4	5	6[h]	7	8	9	
22		10	11	12	13	14	15	16	
23		17	18	19	20	21	22	23	
24		24	25	26	27	28	29	30	
25	TAMMUZ 5740	1	2	3	4	5	6	7	Fri $8^h59^m5^p$
26		8	9	10	11	12	13	14	
27		15	16	17	18	19	20	21	
28		22	23	24	25	26	27	28	
29		29	1	2	3	4	5	6	Sat $21^h43^m6^p$
30	AV 5740	7	8	9[i]	10	11	12	13	
31		14	15	16	17	18	19	20	
32		21	22	23	24	25	26	27	
33		28	29	30	1	2	3	4	Mon $10^h27^m7^p$
34	ELUL 5740	5	6	7	8	9	10	11	
35		12	13	14	15	16	17	18	
36		19	20	21	22	23	24	25	
37		26	27	28	29	1[a]	2[a]	3	Tue $23^h11^m8^p$
38	TISHRI 5741	4	5	6	7	8	9	10[b]	
39		11	12	13	14	15[c]	16	17	
40		18	19	20	21	22	23	24	
41		25	26	27	28	29	30	1	Thu $11^h55^m9^p$
42	ḤESHVAN 5741	2	3	4	5	6	7	8	
43		9	10	11	12	13	14	15	
44		16	17	18	19	20	21	22	
45		23	24	25	26	27	28	29	
46	KISLEV 5741	1	2	3	4	5	6	7	Sat $0^h39^m10^p$
47		8	9	10	11	12	13	14	
48		15	16	17	18	19	20	21	
49		22	23	24	25[e]	26[e]	27[d,e]	28[e]	
50		29[e]	1[e]	2[e]	3[e]	4	5	6	Sun $13^h23^m11^p$
51	TEVETH 5741	7	8	9	10	11	12	13	
52		14	15	16	17	18	19	20	
1		21	22	23	24	25	26	27	

ISO WEEK	Month	Sun	Mon	Tue	Wed	Thu	Fri	Sat	Solar Term
	CHINESE Jǐ-Wèi‡/Gēng-Shēn								
1	MONTH 11 Jǐ-Wèi	12	13	14	15	16	17	18	
2		*19*	20	21	22	23	24	25	*Xiǎo hán*
3		26	27	28	29	30	1	2	
4	MONTH 12 Jǐ-Wèi	3	**4**	5	6	7	8	9	**Dà hán**
5		10	11	12	13	14	15	16	
6		17	18	*19*	20	21	22	23	*Lì chūn*
7		24	25	26	27	28	29	1[a]	
8	MONTH 1 Gēng-Shēn	2	3	**4**	5	6*	7	8	**Yǔ shuǐ**
9		9	10	11	12	13	14	15[b]	
10		16	17	18	*19*	20	21	22	*Jīng zhé*
11		23	24	25	26	27	28	29	
12		30	1	2	3	**4**	5	6	**Chūn fēn**
13	MONTH 2 Gēng-Shēn	7	8	9	10	11	12	13	
14		14	15	16	17	18	*19*[c]	20	*Qīng míng*
15		21	22	23	24	25	26	27	
16		28	29	1	2	3	4	5	
17	MONTH 3 Gēng-Shēn	***6***	7*	8	9	10	11	12	**Gǔ yǔ**
18		13	14	15	16	17	18	19	
19		20	*21*	22	23	24	25	26	*Lì xià*
20		27	28	29	1	2	3	4	
21	MONTH 4 Gēng-Shēn	5	6	7	**8**	9	10	11	**Xiǎo mǎn**
22		12	13	14	15	16	17	18	
23		19	20	21	22	*23*	24	25	*Máng zhòng*
24		26	27	28	29	30	1	2	
25	MONTH 5 Gēng-Shēn	3	4	5[d]	6	7	8*	**9**	**Xià zhì**
26		10	11	12	13	14	15	16	
27		17	18	19	20	21	22	23	
28		24	*25*	26	27	28	29	1	*Xiǎo shǔ*
29	MONTH 6 Gēng-Shēn	2	3	4	5	6	7	8	
30		9	10	11	**12**	13	14	15	**Dà shǔ**
31		16	17	18	19	20	21	22	
32		23	24	25	26	*27*	28	29	*Lì qiū*
33		30	1	2	3	4	5	6	
34	MONTH 7 Gēng-Shēn	7[e]	8	9*	10	11	12	***13***	**Chǔ shǔ**
35		14	15[f]	16	17	18	19	20	
36		21	22	23	24	25	26	27	
37		*28*	29	1	2	3	4	5	*Bái lù*
38	MONTH 8 Gēng-Shēn	6	7	8	9	10	11	12	
39		13	14	***15***[g]	16	17	18	19	**Qiū fēn**
40		20	21	22	23	24	25	26	
41		27	28	29	*30*	1	2	3	*Hán lù*
42	MONTH 9 Gēng-Shēn	4	5	6	7	8	9[h]	10*	
43		11	12	13	14	***15***	16	17	**Shuāng jiàng**
44		18	19	20	21	22	23	24	
45		25	26	27	28	29	*30*	1	*Lì dōng*
46	MONTH 10 Gēng-Shēn	2	3	4	5	6	7	8	
47		9	10	11	12	13	14	***15***	**Xiǎo xuě**
48		16	17	18	19	20	21	22	
49		23	24	25	26	27	28	29	
50		*1*	2	3	4	5	6	7	*Dà xuě*
51	MONTH 11 Gēng-Shēn	8	9	10	11*	12	13	14	
52		15	***16***[i]	17	18	19	20	21	**Dōng zhì**
1		22	23	24	25	26	27	28	

ISO WEEK	Coptic month	Sun	Mon	Tue	Wed	Thu	Fri	Sat	Ethiopic month
	COPTIC 1696/1697								ETHIOPIC 1972/1973
1	KOIAK 1696	20	21	22	23	24	25	26	TĀKHŚĀŚ 1972
2		27	28	29[c]	30	1	2	3	
3	TÔBE 1696	4	5	6[d]	7	8	9	10	ṬER 1972
4		11[e]	12	13	14	15	16	17	
5		18	19	20	21	22	23	24	
6		25	26	27	28	29	30	1	
7	MESHIR 1696	2	3	4	5	6	7	8	YAKĀTIT 1972
8		9	10	11	12	13	14	15	
9		16	17	18	19	20	21	22	
10		23	24	25	26	27	28	29	
11		30	1	2	3	4	5	6	
12	PAREMOTEP 1696	7	8	9	10	11	12	13	MAGĀBIT 1972
13		14	15	16	17	18	19	20	
14		21	22	23	24	25	26	27	
15		28[f]	29	30	1	2	3	4	
16	PARMOUTE 1696	5	6	7	8	9	10	11	MIYĀZYĀ 1972
17		12	13	14	15	16	17	18	
18		19	20	21	22	23	24	25	
19		26	27	28	29[g]	30	1	2	
20	PASHONS 1696	3	4	5	6	7	8	9	GENBOT 1972
21		10	11	12	13	14	15	16	
22		17	18	19	20	21	22	23	
23		24	25	26	27	28	29	30	
24	PAÔNE 1696	1	2	3	4	5	6	7	SANĒ 1972
25		8	9	10	11	12	13	14	
26		15	16	17	18	19	20	21	
27		22	23	24	25	26	27	28	
28		29	30	1	2	3	4	5	
29	EPÊP 1696	6	7	8	9	10	11	12	ḤAMLĒ 1972
30		13	14	15	16	17	18	19	
31		20	21	22	23	24	25	26	
32		27	28	29	30	1	2	3	
33	MESORÊ 1696	4	5	6	7	8	9	10	NAḤASĒ 1972
34		11	12	13[h]	14	15	16	17	
35		18	19	20	21	22	23	24	
36		25	26	27	28	29	30	1	
37	EPAG. 1696 / THOOUT 1697	2	3	4	5	1[a]	2	3	PĀG. 1972 / MASKARAM 1973
38		4	5	6	7	8	9	10	
39		11	12	13	14	15	16	17[b]	
40		18	19	20	21	22	23	24	
41		25	26	27	28	29	30	1	
42	PAOPE 1697	2	3	4	5	6	7	8	ṬEQEMT 1973
43		9	10	11	12	13	14	15	
44		16	17	18	19	20	21	22	
45		23	24	25	26	27	28	29	
46		30	1	2	3	4	5	6	
47	ATHÔR 1697	7	8	9	10	11	12	13	ḤEDĀR 1973
48		14	15	16	17	18	19	20	
49		21	22	23	24	25	26	27	
50		28	29	30	1	2	3	4	
51	KOIAK 1697	5	6	7	8	9	10	11	TĀKHŚĀŚ 1973
52		12	13	14	15	16	17	18	
1		19	20	21	22	23	24	25	

‡Leap year
[a]New Year
[b]Spring (11:09)
[c]Summer (5:47)
[d]Autumn (21:08)
[e]Winter (16:56)
● New moon
◐ First quarter moon
○ Full moon
◑ Last quarter moon

‡Leap year
[a]New Year
[b]Yom Kippur
[c]Sukkot
[d]Winter starts
[e]Ḥanukkah
[f]Purim
[g]Passover
[h]Shavuot
[i]Fast of Av

‡Leap year
[a]New Year (4678, Monkey)
[b]Lantern Festival
[c]Qīngmíng
[d]Dragon Festival
[e]Qīqiǎo
[f]Hungry Ghosts
[g]Mid-Autumn Festival
[h]Double-Ninth Festival
[i]Dōngzhì
*Start of 60-name cycle

[a]New Year
[b]Building of the Cross
[c]Christmas
[d]Jesus's Circumcision
[e]Epiphany
[f]Easter
[g]Mary's Announcement
[h]Jesus's Transfiguration

1980

PERSIAN (ASTRONOMICAL) 1358‡/1359

Month	Sun	Mon	Tue	Wed	Thu	Fri	Sat
DEY 1358	9	10	11	12	13	14	15
	16	17	18	19	20	21	22
	23	24	25	26	27	28	29
BAHMAN 1358	30	1	2	3	4	5	6
	7	8	9	10	11	12	13
	14	15	16	17	18	19	20
	21	22	23	24	25	26	27
ESFAND 1358	28	29	30	1	2	3	4
	5	6	7	8	9	10	11
	12	13	14	15	16	17	18
	19	20	21	22	23	24	25
	26	27	28	29	30	1[a]	2
FARVARDĪN 1359	3	4	5	6	7	8	9
	10	11	12	13[b]	14	15	16
	17	18	19	20	21	22	23
	24	25	26	27	28	29	30
ORDĪBEHEŠT 1359	31	1	2	3	4	5	6
	7	8	9	10	11	12	13
	14	15	16	17	18	19	20
	21	22	23	24	25	26	27
XORDĀD 1359	28	29	30	31	1	2	3
	4	5	6	7	8	9	10
	11	12	13	14	15	16	17
	18	19	20	21	22	23	24
	25	26	27	28	29	30	31
TĪR 1359	1	2	3	4	5	6	7
	8	9	10	11	12	13	14
	15	16	17	18	19	20	21
	22	23	24	25	26	27	28
MORDĀD 1359	29	30	31	1	2	3	4
	5	6	7	8	9	10	11
	12	13	14	15	16	17	18
	19	20	21	22	23	24	25
SHAHRĪVAR 1359	26	27	28	29	30	31	1
	2	3	4	5	6	7	8
	9	10	11	12	13	14	15
	16	17	18	19	20	21	22
	23	24	25	26	27	28	29
MEHR 1359	30	31	1	2	3	4	5
	6	7	8	9	10	11	12
	13	14	15	16	17	18	19
	20	21	22	23	24	25	26
ĀBĀN 1359	27	28	29	30	1	2	3
	4	5	6	7	8	9	10
	11	12	13	14	15	16	17
	18	19	20	21	22	23	24
ĀZAR 1359	25	26	27	28	29	30	1
	2	3	4	5	6	7	8
	9	10	11	12	13	14	15
	16	17	18	19	20	21	22
	23	24	25	26	27	28	29
DEY 1359	30	1	2	3	4	5	6
	7	8	9	10	11	12	13

HINDU LUNAR 2036/2037‡

Month	Sun	Mon	Tue	Wed	Thu	Fri	Sat
PAUSHA 2036	12	13	14	15	16	17	18
	19	20	21	22	23	24	25
	26	27	28	29	30	1	2
MĀGHA 2036	3	4	5	6	7	8	9
	10	12	13	14	15	16	16
	17	18	19	20	21	22	23
	24	25	26	27	28[h]	29	30
PHĀLGUNA 2036	1	2	3	5	6	7	8
	9	10	11	12	13	14	15[i]
	16	17	18	18	19	20	21
	22	23	24	25	26	27	29
CHAITRA 2037	30	1[a]	2	3	4	5	6
	7	8[b]	9	10	11	12	13
	14	15	16	17	18	19	20
	21	22	23	24	25	26	27
VAIŚĀKHA 2037	28	29	30	1	3	4	5
	6	7	8	9	10	11	12
	12	13	14	15	16	17	18
	19	20	21	22	23	24	26
LEAP JYAISHTHA 2037	27	28	29	30	1	2	3
	4	5	6	7	8	9	10
	11	12	13	14	15	16	17
	18	19	20	21	22	23	24
JYAISHTHA 2037	25	26	27	29	30	1	2
	3	4	5	6	7	8	8
	9	10	11	12	13	14	15
	16	17	18	19	20	22	23
	24	25	26	27	28	29	30
ĀSHĀḌHA 2037	1	2	3	4	5	6	7
	8	9	10	11	12	13	14
	15	16	17	18	19	20	21
	22	23	25	26	27	28	29
ŚRĀVAṆA 2037	30	1	2	3	4	5	5
	6	7	8	9	10	11	12
	13	14	15	16	18	19	20
	21	22	23[c]	24	25	26	27
BHĀDRAPADA 2037	28	29	30	1	2	3	4[d]
	5	6	7	8	9	10	11
	12	13	14	15	16	17	18
	19	21	22	23	24	25	26
ĀŚVINA 2037	27	28	29	30	30	1	2
	3	4	5	6	7	8[e]	9[e]
	10[e]	11	12	13	15	16	17
	18	19	20	21	22	23	24
KĀRTTIKA 2037	25	26	27	28	29	30	1[f]
	2	3	4	5	6	7	8
	9	10	11	12	13	14	15
	16	17	18	20	21	22	23
	23	24	25	26	27	28	29
MĀRGAŚĪRA 2037	30	1	2	3	4	5	6
	7	8	9	10	11[g]	13	14
	15	16	17	18	19	20	21
	22	23	24	25	26	26	27

HINDU SOLAR 1901/1902

Month	Sun	Mon	Tue	Wed	Thu	Fri	Sat
PAUSHA 1901	15	16	17	18	19	20	21
	22	23	24	25	26	27	28
MĀGHA 1901	29	1[b]	2	3	4	5	6
	7	8	9	10	11	12	13
	14	15	16	17	18	19	20
	21	22	23	24	25	26	27
PHĀLGUNA 1901	28	29	30	1	2	3	4
	5	6	7	8	9	10	11
	12	13	14	15	16	17	18
	19	20	21	22	23	24	25
CHAITRA 1901	26	27	28	29	1	2	3
	4	5	6	7	8	9	10
	11	12	13	14	15	16	17
	18	19	20	21	22	23	24
	25	26	27	28	29	30	31
VAIŚĀKHA 1902	1[a]	2	3	4	5	6	7
	8	9	10	11	12	13	14
	15	16	17	18	19	20	21
	22	23	24	25	26	27	28
JYAISHTHA 1902	29	30	31	1	2	3	4
	5	6	7	8	9	10	11
	12	13	14	15	16	17	18
	19	20	21	22	23	24	25
ĀSHĀḌHA 1902	26	27	28	29	30	31	1
	2	3	4	5	6	7	8
	9	10	11	12	13	14	15
	16	17	18	19	20	21	22
	23	24	25	26	27	28	29
ŚRĀVAṆA 1902	30	31	32	1	2	3	4
	5	6	7	8	9	10	11
	12	13	14	15	16	17	18
	19	20	21	22	23	24	25
BHĀDRAPADA 1902	26	27	28	29	30	31	1
	2	3	4	5	6	7	8
	9	10	11	12	13	14	15
	16	17	18	19	20	21	22
	23	24	25	26	27	28	29
ĀŚVINA 1902	30	31	1	2	3	4	5
	6	7	8	9	10	11	12
	13	14	15	16	17	18	19
	20	21	22	23	24	25	26
KĀRTTIKA 1902	27	28	29	30	31	1	2
	3	4	5	6	7	8	9
	10	11	12	13	14	15	16
	17	18	19	20	21	22	23
	24	25	26	27	28	29	30
MĀRGAŚĪRA 1902	1	2	3	4	5	6	7
	8	9	10	11	12	13	14
	15	16	17	18	19	20	21
	22	23	24	25	26	27	28
PAUSHA 1902	29	1	2	3	4	5	6
	7	8	9	10	11	12	13
	14	15	16	17	18	19	20

ISLAMIC (ASTRONOMICAL) 1400/1401

Month	Sun	Mon	Tue	Wed	Thu	Fri	Sat
ṢAFAR 1400	10	11	12	13	14	15	16
	17	18	19	20	21	22	23
RABĪ' I 1400	24	25	26	27	28	29	1
	2	3	4	5	6	7	8
	9	10	11	12[c]	13	14	15
	16	17	18	19	20	21	22
	23	24	25	26	27	28	29
RABĪ' II 1400	30	1	2	3	4	5	6
	7	8	9	10	11	12	13
	14	15	16	17	18	19	20
	21	22	23	24	25	26	27
JUMĀDĀ I 1400	28	29	1	2	3	4	5
	6	7	8	9	10	11	12
	13	14	15	16	17	18	19
	20	21	22	23	24	25	26
JUMĀDĀ II 1400	27	28	29	1	2	3	4
	5	6	7	8	9	10	11
	12	13	14	15	16	17	18
	19	20	21	22	23	24	25
RAJAB 1400	26	27	28	29	30	1	2
	3	4	5	6	7	8	9
	10	11	12	13	14	15	16
	17	18	19	20	21	22	23
SHA'BĀN 1400	24	25	26	27[d]	28	29	1
	2	3	4	5	6	7	8
	9	10	11	12	13	14	15
	16	17	18	19	20	21	22
	23	24	25	26	27	28	29
RAMAḌĀN 1400	30	1[e]	2	3	4	5	6
	7	8	9	10	11	12	13
	14	15	16	17	18	19	20
	21	22	23	24	25	26	27
SHAWWĀL 1400	28	29	1[f]	2	3	4	5
	6	7	8	9	10	11	12
	13	14	15	16	17	18	19
	20	21	22	23	24	25	26
DHU AL-QA'DA 1400	27	28	29	30	1	2	3
	4	5	6	7	8	9	10
	11	12	13	14	15	16	17
	18	19	20	21	22	23	24
DHU AL-ḤIJJA 1400	25	26	27	28	29	1	2
	3	4	5	6	7	8	9
	10[g]	11	12	13	14	15	16
	17	18	19	20	21	22	23
	24	25	26	27	28	29	30
MUḤARRAM 1401	1[a]	2	3	4	5	6	7
	8	9	10[b]	11	12	13	14
	15	16	17	18	19	20	21
	22	23	24	25	26	27	28
ṢAFAR 1401	29	30	1	2	3	4	5
	6	7	8	9	10	11	12
	13	14	15	16	17	18	19
	20	21	22	23	24	25	26

GREGORIAN 1980‡

Julian‡ (Sun)	Sun	Mon	Tue	Wed	Thu	Fri	Sat	Month
Dec 17	30	31	1	2	3	4	5	JANUARY 1980
	6	7[a]	8	9	10	11	12	
Dec 31	13	14[b]	15	16	17	18	19	
	20	21	22	23	24	25	26	
Jan 14	27	28	29	30	31	1	2	FEBRUARY 1980
	3	4	5	6	7	8	9	
Jan 28	10	11	12	13	14	15	16	
	17	18	19	20[c]	21	22	23	
Feb 11	24[d]	25	26	27	28	29	1	MARCH 1980
	2	3	4	5	6	7	8	
Feb 25	9	10	11	12	13	14	15	
	16	17	18	19	20	21	22	
Mar 10	23	24	25	26	27	28	29	
	30	31	1	2	3	4	5	APRIL 1980
Mar 24	6[e]	7	8	9	10	11	12	
	13	14	15	16	17	18	19	
Apr 7	20	21	22	23	24	25	26	
	27	28	29	30	1	2	3	MAY 1980
Apr 21	4	5	6	7	8	9	10	
	11	12	13	14	15	16	17	
May 5	18	19	20	21	22	23	24	
	25	26	27	28	29	30	31	
May 19	1	2	3	4	5	6	7	JUNE 1980
	8	9	10	11	12	13	14	
Jun 2	15	16	17	18	19	20	21	
	22	23	24	25	26	27	28	
Jun 16	29	30	1	2	3	4	5	JULY 1980
	6	7	8	9	10	11	12	
Jun 30	13	14	15	16	17	18	19	
	20	21	22	23	24	25	26	
Jul 14	27	28	29	30	31	1	2	AUGUST 1980
	3	4	5	6	7	8	9	
Jul 28	10	11	12	13	14	15	16	
	17	18	19	20	21	22	23	
Aug 11	24	25	26	27	28	29	30	
	31	1	2	3	4	5	6	SEPTEMBER 1980
Aug 25	7	8	9	10	11	12	13	
	14	15	16	17	18	19	20	
Sep 8	21	22	23	24	25	26	27	
	28	29	30	1	2	3	4	OCTOBER 1980
Sep 22	5	6	7	8	9	10	11	
	12	13	14	15	16	17	18	
Oct 6	19	20	21	22	23	24	25	
	26	27	28	29	30	31	1	NOVEMBER 1980
Oct 20	2	3	4	5	6	7	8	
	9	10	11	12	13	14	15	
Nov 3	16	17	18	19	20	21	22	
	23	24	25	26	27	28	29	
Nov 17	30[g]	1	2	3	4	5	6	DECEMBER 1980
	7	8	9	10	11	12	13	
Dec 1	14	15	16	17	18	19	20	
	21	22	23	24	25[h]	26	27	
Dec 15	28	29	30	31	1	2	3	

Persian: ‡Leap year; [a]New Year; [b]Sizdeh Bedar

Hindu Lunar: ‡Leap year; [a]New Year (Rāudra); [b]Birthday of Rāma; [c]Birthday of Krishna; [d]Ganēśa Chaturthī; [e]Dashara; [f]Diwali; [g]Birthday of Vishnu; [h]Night of Śiva; [i]Holi

Hindu Solar: [a]New Year (Śrīmukha); [b]Pongal

Islamic: [a]New Year; [b]'Ashūrā'; [c]Prophet's Birthday; [d]Ascent of the Prophet; [e]Start of Ramaḍān; [f]'Id al-Fiṭr; [g]'Id al-'Aḍḥā

Gregorian: ‡Leap year; [a]Orthodox Christmas; [b]Julian New Year; [c]Ash Wednesday; [d]Feast of Orthodoxy; [e]Easter (also Orthodox); [g]Advent; [h]Christmas

1981

GREGORIAN 1981	Sun	Mon	Tue	Wed	Thu	Fri	Sat	Lunar Phases	ISO WEEK (Mon)	JULIAN DAY (Sun noon)	HEBREW 5741‡/5742	Sun	Mon	Tue	Wed	Thu	Fri	Sat	Molad	CHINESE Gēng-Shēn/Xīn-Yǒu	Sun	Mon	Tue	Wed	Thu	Fri	Sat	Solar Term	COPTIC 1697/1698	Sun	Mon	Tue	Wed	Thu	Fri	Sat	ETHIOPIC 1973/1974
JANUARY 1981	28	◑	30	31	1[a]	2	3	6:32	1	2444602	TEVETH 5741	21	22	23	24	25	26	27		MONTH 11 Gēng-Shēn	22	23	24	25	26	27	28		KOIAK 1697	19	20	21	22	23	24	25	TĀKHŚĀŚ 1973
	4	5	●	7	8	9	10	7:24	2	2444609		28	29	1	2	3	4	5	Tue 2h7m12p	MONTH 12 Gēng-Shēn	29	30	1	2	3	4	5	Xiǎo hán		26	27	28	29[c]	30	1	2	
	11	12	◐	14	15	16	17	10:10	3	2444616	SHEVAT 5741	6	7	8	9	10	11	12			6	7	8	9	10	11	12		TŌBE 1697	3	4	5	6[d]	7	8	9	ṬER 1973
	18	19	○	21	22	23	24	7:39	4	2444623		13	14	15	16	17	18	19			13	14	15	16	17	18	19	Dà hán		10	11[e]	12	13	14	15	16	
	25	26	27	◑	29	30	31	4:19	5	2444630		20	21	22	23	24	25	26			20	21	22	23	24	25	26			17	18	19	20	21	22	23	
FEBRUARY 1981	1	2	3	●	5	6	7	22:14	6	2444637		27	28	29	30	1	2	3	Wed 14h51m13p		27	28	29	30	1[a]	2	3	Lì chūn		24	25	26	27	28	29	30	
	8	9	10	◐	12	13	14	17:49	7	2444644	ADAR I 5741	4	5	6	7	8	9	10		MONTH 1 Xīn-Yǒu	4	5	6	7	8	9	10		MESHIR 1697	1	2	3	4	5	6	7	YAKĀTĪT 1973
	15	16	17	○	19	20	21	22:58	8	2444651		11	12	13	14	15	16	17			11*	12	13	14	15[b]	16	17	Yǔ shuǐ		8	9	10	11	12	13	14	
	22	23	24	25	26	◑	28	1:14	9	2444658		18	19	20	21	22	23	24			18	19	20	21	22	23	24			15	16	17	18	19	20	21	
MARCH 1981	1	2	3	4	5	●	7	10:31	10	2444665		25	26	27	28	29	30	1	Fri 3h35m14p		25	26	27	28	29	1	2	Jīng zhé		22	23	24	25	26	27	28	
	8	9	10	11	12	◐	14	1:51	11	2444672	ADAR II 5741	2	3	4	5	6	7	8		MONTH 2 Xīn-Yǒu	3	4	5	6	7	8	9		PAREMOTEP 1697	29	30	1	2	3	4	5	MAGĀBĪT 1973
	15	16	17	18	19	○[b]	21	15:22	12	2444679		9	10	11	12	13	14[f]	15			10	11	12	13	14	15	16	Chūn fēn		6	7	8	9	10	11	12	
	22	23	24	25	26	27	◑	19:34	13	2444686		16	17	18	19	20	21	22			17	18	19	20	21	22	23			13	14	15	16	17	18	19	
	29	30	31	1	2	3	●	20:20	14	2444693		23	24	25	26	27	28	29	Sat 16h19m15p		24	25	26	27	28	29	30			20	21	22	23	24	25	26	
APRIL 1981	5	6	7	8	9	10	◐	11:11	15	2444700	NISAN 5741	1	2	3	4*	5	6	7		MONTH 3 Xīn-Yǒu	1[c]	2	3	4	5	6	7	Qīng míng	PARMOUTE 1697	27	28	29	30	1	2	3	MIYĀZYĀ 1973
	12	13	14	15	16	17	18		16	2444707		8	9	10	11	12	13	14			8	9	10	11	12*	13	14			4	5	6	7	8	9	10	
	○	20	21	22	23	24	25	7:59	17	2444714		15[g]	16	17	18	19	20	21			15	16	17	18	19	20	21	Gǔ yǔ		11	12	13	14	15	16	17	
	26	◑	28	29	30	1	2	10:14	18	2444721		22	23	24	25	26	27	28			22	23	24	25	26	27	28			18[f]	19	20	21	22	23	24	
MAY 1981	3	●	5	6	7	8	9	4:19	19	2444728		29	30	1	2	3	4	5	Mon 5h3m16p		29	1	2	3	4	5	6	Lì xià		25	26	27	28	29[g]	30	1	
	◐	11	12	13	14	15	16	22:22	20	2444735	IYAR 5741	6	7	8	9	10	11	12		MONTH 4 Xīn-Yǒu	7	8	9	10	11	12	13		PASHONS 1697	2	3	4	5	6	7	8	GENBOT 1973
	17	18	○	20	21	22	23	0:04	21	2444742		13	14	15	16	17	18	19			14	15	16	17	18	19	20	Xiǎo mǎn		9	10	11	12	13	14	15	
	24	25	◑	27	28	29	30	21:00	22	2444749		20	21	22	23	24	25	26			21	22	23	24	25	26	27			16	17	18	19	20	21	22	
	31	1	●	3	4	5	6	11:32	23	2444756		27	28	29	1	2	3	4	Tue 17h47m17p		28	29	1	2	3	4	5[d]	Máng zhòng		23	24	25	26	27	28	29	
JUNE 1981	7	8	◐	10	11	12	13	11:33	24	2444763	SIVAN 5741	5	6[h]	7	8	9	10	11		MONTH 5 Xīn-Yǒu	6	7	8	9	10	11	12		PAŌNE 1697	30	1	2	3	4	5	6	SANĒ 1973
	14	15	16	○	18	19	20	15:04	25	2444770		12	13	14	15	16	17	18			13	14*	15	16	17	18	19			7	8	9	10	11	12	13	
	21[c]	22	23	24	◑	26	27	4:25	26	2444777		19	20	21	22	23	24	25			20	21	22	23	24	25	26	Xià zhì		14	15	16	17	18	19	20	
	28	29	30	●	2	3	4	19:03	27	2444784		26	27	28	29	30	1	2	Thu 6h32m0p		27	28	29	30	1	2	3			21	22	23	24	25	26	27	
JULY 1981	5	6	7	8	◐	10	11	2:39	28	2444791	TAMMUZ 5741	3	4	5	6	7	8	9		MONTH 6 Xīn-Yǒu	4	5	6	7	8	9	10	Xiǎo shǔ	EPĒP 1697	28	29	30	1	2	3	4	ḪAMLĒ 1973
	12	13	14	15	16	○	18	4:39	29	2444798		10	11	12	13	14	15	16			11	12	13	14	15	16	17			5	6	7	8	9	10	11	
	19	20	21	22	23	◑	25	9:40	30	2444805		17	18	19	20	21	22	23			18	19	20	21	22	23	24	Dà shǔ		12	13	14	15	16	17	18	
	26	27	28	29	30	●	1	3:52	31	2444812		24	25	26	27	28	29	1	Fri 19h16m1p		25	26	27	28	29	1	2			19	20	21	22	23	24	25	
AUGUST 1981	2	3	4	5	6	◐	8	19:26	32	2444819	AV 5741	2	3	4	5	6	7	8		MONTH 7 Xīn-Yǒu	3	4	5	6	7[e]	8	9	Lì qiū	MESORĒ 1697	26	27	28	29	30	1	2	NAḤASĒ 1973
	9	10	11	12	13	14	○	16:37	33	2444826		9[i]	10	11	12	13	14	15			10	11	12	13	14	15[f]*	16			3	4	5	6	7	8	9	
	16	17	18	19	20	21	◑	14:16	34	2444833		16	17	18	19	20	21	22			17	18	19	20	21	22	23	Chù shǔ		10	11	12	13[h]	14	15	16	
	23	24	25	26	27	28	●	14:43	35	2444840		23	24	25	26	27	28	29			24	25	26	27	28	29	1			17	18	19	20	21	22	23	
	30	31	1	2	3	4	5		36	2444847		30	1	2	3	4	5	6	Sun 8h0m2p	MONTH 8 Xīn-Yǒu	2	3	4	5	6	7	8			24	25	26	27	28	29	30	
SEPTEMBER 1981	◐	7	8	9	10	11	12	13:26	37	2444854	ELUL 5741	7	8	9	10	11	12	13			9	10	11	12	13	14	15[g]	Bái lù	EPAG. 1697 / THOOUT 1698	1	2	3	4	5	1[a]	2	PĀG. 1973 / MASKARAM 1974
	13	○	15	16	17	18	19	3:09	38	2444861		14	15	16	17	18	19	20			16	17	18	19	20	21	22			3	4	5	6	7	8	9	
	◑	21	22	23[d]	24	25	26	19:48	39	2444868		21	22	23	24	25	26	27			23	24	25	26	27	28	29	Qiū fēn		10	11	12	13	14	15	16	
	27	●	29	30	1	2	3	4:07	40	2444875		28	29	1[a]	2[a]	3	4	5	Mon 20h44m3p		30	1	2	3	4	5	6			17[b]	18	19	20	21	22	23	
OCTOBER 1981	4	5	◐	7	8	9	10	7:45	41	2444882	TISHRI 5742	6	7	8	9	10[b]	11	12		MONTH 9 Xīn-Yǒu	7	8	9[h]	10	11	12	13	Hán lù	PAOPE 1698	24	25	26	27	28	29	30	ṬEQEMT 1974
	11	12	○	14	15	16	17	12:50	42	2444889		13	14	15[c]	16	17	18	19			14	15	16*	17	18	19	20			1	2	3	4	5	6	7	
	18	19	◑	21	22	23	24	3:41	43	2444896		20	21	22	23	24	25	26			21	22	23	24	25	26	27	Shuāng jiàng		8	9	10	11	12	13	14	
	25	26	●	28	29	30	31	20:13	44	2444903		27	28	29	30	1	2	3	Wed 9h28m4p		28	29	30	1	2	3	4			15	16	17	18	19	20	21	
NOVEMBER 1981	1	2	3	4	◐	6	7	1:09	45	2444910	ḤESHVAN 5742	4	5	6	7	8	9	10		MONTH 10 Xīn-Yǒu	5	6	7	8	9	10	11	Lì dōng	ATHŌR 1698	22	23	24	25	26	27	28	ḪEDĀR 1974
	8	9	10	○	12	13	14	22:27	46	2444917		11	12	13	14	15	16	17			12	13	14	15	16	17	18			29	30	1	2	3	4	5	
	15	16	17	◑	19	20	21	14:54	47	2444924		18	19	20	21	22	23	24			19	20	21	22	23	24	25	Xiǎo xuě		6	7	8	9	10	11	12	
	22	23	24	25	●	27	28	14:38	48	2444931		25	26	27	28	29	1	2	Thu 22h12m5p		26	27	28	29	1	2	3			13	14	15	16	17	18	19	
	29	30	1	2	3	◐	5	16:22	49	2444938	KISLEV 5742	3	4	5	6	7	8	9[d]		MONTH 11 Xīn-Yǒu	4	5	6	7	8	9	10			20	21	22	23	24	25	26	
DECEMBER 1981	6	7	8	9	10	○	12	8:42	50	2444945		10	11	12	13	14	15	16			11	12	13	14	15	16	17*	Dà xuě	KOIAK 1698	27	28	29	30	1	2	3	TĀKHŚĀŚ 1974
	13	14	15	16	17	◑	19	5:47	51	2444952		17	18	19	20	21	22	23			18	19	20	21	22	23	24			4	5	6	7	8	9	10	
	20	21[e]	22	23	24	25	●	10:10	52	2444959		24	25[e]	26[e]	27[e]	28[e]	29[e]	30[e]	Sat 10h56m6p	MONTH 12 Xīn-Yǒu	25	26	27[i]	28	29	30	1	Dōng zhì		11	12	13	14	15	16	17	
	27	28	29	30	31	1	2		53	2444966		1[e]	2[e]	3	4	5	6	7			2	3	4	5	6	7	8			18	19	20	21	22	23	24	

[a]New Year
[b]Spring (17:02)
[c]Summer (11:44)
[d]Autumn (3:05)
[e]Winter (22:50)
● New moon
◐ First quarter moon
○ Full moon
◑ Last quarter moon

‡Leap year
[a]New Year
[b]Yom Kippur
[c]Sukkot
[d]Winter starts
[e]Ḥanukkah
[f]Purim
[g]Passover
[h]Shavuot
[i]Fast of Av
*New solar cycle

[a]New Year (4679, Fowl)
[b]Lantern Festival
[c]Qīngmíng
[d]Dragon Festival
[e]Qīqiǎo
[f]Hungry Ghosts
[g]Mid-Autumn Festival
[h]Double-Ninth Festival
[i]Dōngzhì
*Start of 60-name cycle

[a]New Year
[b]Building of the Cross
[c]Christmas
[d]Jesus's Circumcision
[e]Epiphany
[f]Easter
[g]Mary's Announcement
[h]Jesus's Transfiguration

1981

PERSIAN (ASTRONOMICAL) 1359/1360

Month	Sun	Mon	Tue	Wed	Thu	Fri	Sat
DEY 1359	7	8	9	10	11	12	13
	14	15	16	17	18	19	20
	21	22	23	24	25	26	27
	28	29	30	1	2	3	4
BAHMAN 1359	5	6	7	8	9	10	11
	12	13	14	15	16	17	18
	19	20	21	22	23	24	25
	26	27	28	29	30	1	2
ESFAND 1359	3	4	5	6	7	8	9
	10	11	12	13	14	15	16
	17	18	19	20	21	22	23
	24	25	26	27	28	29	1[a]
FARVARDĪN 1360	2	3	4	5	6	7	8
	9	10	11	12	13[b]	14	15
	16	17	18	19	20	21	22
	23	24	25	26	27	28	29
	30	31	1	2	3	4	5
ORDĪBEHEŠT 1360	6	7	8	9	10	11	12
	13	14	15	16	17	18	19
	20	21	22	23	24	25	26
	27	28	29	30	31	1	2
XORDĀD 1360	3	4	5	6	7	8	9
	10	11	12	13	14	15	16
	17	18	19	20	21	22	23
	24	25	26	27	28	29	30
	31	1	2	3	4	5	6
TĪR 1360	7	8	9	10	11	12	13
	14	15	16	17	18	19	20
	21	22	23	24	25	26	27
	28	29	30	31	1	2	3
MORDĀD 1360	4	5	6	7	8	9	10
	11	12	13	14	15	16	17
	18	19	20	21	22	23	24
	25	26	27	28	29	30	31
SHAHRĪVAR 1360	1	2	3	4	5	6	7
	8	9	10	11	12	13	14
	15	16	17	18	19	20	21
	22	23	24	25	26	27	28
	29	30	31	1	2	3	4
MEHR 1360	5	6	7	8	9	10	11
	12	13	14	15	16	17	18
	19	20	21	22	23	24	25
	26	27	28	29	30	1	2
ĀBĀN 1360	3	4	5	6	7	8	9
	10	11	12	13	14	15	16
	17	18	19	20	21	22	23
	24	25	26	27	28	29	30
ĀZAR 1360	1	2	3	4	5	6	7
	8	9	10	11	12	13	14
	15	16	17	18	19	20	21
	22	23	24	25	26	27	28
DEY 1360	29	30	1	2	3	4	5
	6	7	8	9	10	11	12

HINDU LUNAR 2037‡/2038

Month	Sun	Mon	Tue	Wed	Thu	Fri	Sat
MĀRGAŚIRA 2037	22	23	24	25	26	*26*	27
	28	29	30	1	2	3	4
PAUSHA 2037	**5**	7	8	9	10	11	12
	13	14	15	16	17	18	19
	20	21	22	23	24	25	26
	27	28	29	30	1	2	3
MĀGHA 2037	4	5	6	7	8	9	**10**
	12	13	14	15	16	17	18
	19	*19*	20	21	22	23	24
	25	26	27	28[h]	29	30	1
PHĀLGUNA 2037	2	3	**4**	6	7	8	9
	10	11	12	13	14	15[i]	16
	17	18	19	20	21	*21*	22
	23	24	25	26	**27**	29	30
CHAITRA 2038	1[a]	2	3	4	5	6	7
	8[b]	9	10	11	12	13	14
	15	16	17	18	19	20	21
	22	23	24	25	26	27	28
	29	30	**1**	3	4	5	6
VAIŚĀKHA 2038	7	8	9	10	11	12	13
	14	15	16	*16*	17	18	19
	20	21	22	23	**24**	26	27
	28	29	30	1	2	3	4
JYAISHTHA 2038	5	6	7	8	9	10	11
	12	13	14	15	16	17	18
	19	20	21	22	23	24	25
	26	**27**	29	30	1	2	3
ĀSHĀDHA 2038	4	5	6	7	8	9	10
	11	12	13	*13*	14	15	16
	17	18	19	**20**	22	23	24
	25	26	27	28	29	30	1
ŚRĀVAṆA 2038	2	3	4	5	6	7	8
	9	10	11	12	13	14	15
	16	17	18	19	20	21	22
	23[c]	25	26	27	28	29	30
BHĀDRAPADA 2038	1	2	3	4[d]	5	6	7
	8	9	*9*	10	11	12	13
	14	15	**16**	18	19	20	21
	22	23	24	25	26	27	28
	29	30	1	2	3	4	5
ĀŚVINA 2038	6	7	8[e]	9[e]	10[e]	11	12
	13	14	15	16	17	18	19
	20	22	23	24	25	26	27
	28	29	30	1[f]	2	3	4
KĀRTTIKA 2038	*4*	5	6	7	8	9	10
	11	12	13	**14**	16	17	18
	19	20	21	22	23	24	25
	26	27	28	29	30	1	2
MĀRGAŚIRA 2038	3	4	5	6	7	8	9
	10	11[g]	12	13	14	15	16
	17	**18**	20	21	22	23	24
	25	26	27	*27*	28	29	30
	1	2	3	4	5	6	7

HINDU SOLAR 1902/1903

Month	Sun	Mon	Tue	Wed	Thu	Fri	Sat
PAUSHA 1902	14	15	16	17	18	19	20
	21	22	23	24	25	26	27
	28	29	1[b]	2	3	4	5
MĀGHA 1902	6	7	8	9	10	11	12
	13	14	15	16	17	18	19
	20	21	22	23	24	25	26
	27	28	29	30	1	2	3
PHĀLGUNA 1902	4	5	6	7	8	9	10
	11	12	13	14	15	16	17
	18	19	20	21	22	23	24
	25	26	27	28	29	30	1
CHAITRA 1902	2	3	4	5	6	7	8
	9	10	11	12	13	14	15
	16	17	18	19	20	21	22
	23	24	25	26	27	28	29
	30	1[a]	2	3	4	5	6
VAIŚĀKHA 1903	7	8	9	10	11	12	13
	14	15	16	17	18	19	20
	21	22	23	24	25	26	27
	28	29	30	31	1	2	3
JYAISHTHA 1903	4	5	6	7	8	9	10
	11	12	13	14	15	16	17
	18	19	20	21	22	23	24
	25	26	27	28	29	30	31
ĀSHĀDHA 1903	1	2	3	4	5	6	7
	8	9	10	11	12	13	14
	15	16	17	18	19	20	21
	22	23	24	25	26	27	28
	29	30	31	32	1	2	3
ŚRĀVAṆA 1903	4	5	6	7	8	9	10
	11	12	13	14	15	16	17
	18	19	20	21	22	23	24
	25	26	27	28	29	30	31
	32	1	2	3	4	5	6
BHĀDRAPADA 1903	7	8	9	10	11	12	13
	14	15	16	17	18	19	20
	21	22	23	24	25	26	27
	28	29	30	31	1	2	3
ĀŚVINA 1903	4	5	6	7	8	9	10
	11	12	13	14	15	16	17
	18	19	20	21	22	23	24
	25	26	27	28	29	30	1
KĀRTTIKA 1903	2	3	4	5	6	7	8
	9	10	11	12	13	14	15
	16	17	18	19	20	21	22
	23	24	25	26	27	28	29
	30	1	2	3	4	5	6
MĀRGAŚIRA 1903	7	8	9	10	11	12	13
	14	15	16	17	18	19	20
	21	22	23	24	25	26	27
	28	29	1	2	3	4	5
PAUSHA 1903	6	7	8	9	10	11	12
	13	14	15	16	17	18	19

ISLAMIC (ASTRONOMICAL) 1401/1402

Month	Sun	Mon	Tue	Wed	Thu	Fri	Sat
SAFAR 1401	20	21	22	23	24	25	26
	27	28	29	30	1	2	3
RABĪʿ I 1401	4	5	6	7	8	9	10
	11	12[c]	13	14	15	16	17
	18	19	20	21	22	23	24
	25	26	27	28	29	1	2
RABĪʿ II 1401	3	4	5	6	7	8	9
	10	11	12	13	14	15	16
	17	18	19	20	21	22	23
	24	25	26	27	28	29	30
JUMĀDĀ I 1401	1	2	3	4	5	6	7
	8	9	10	11	12	13	14
	15	16	17	18	19	20	21
	22	23	24	25	26	27	28
	29	1	2	3	4	5	6
JUMĀDĀ II 1401	7	8	9	10	11	12	13
	14	15	16	17	18	19	20
	21	22	23	24	25	26	27
	28	29	1	2	3	4	5
RAJAB 1401	6	7	8	9	10	11	12
	13	14	15	16	17	18	19
	20	21	22	23	24	25	26
	27[d]	28	29	30	1	2	3
SHAʿBĀN 1401	4	5	6	7	8	9	10
	11	12	13	14	15	16	17
	18	19	20	21	22	23	24
	25	26	27	28	29	1[e]	2
RAMAḌĀN 1401	3	4	5	6	7	8	9
	10	11	12	13	14	15	16
	17	18	19	20	21	22	23
	24	25	26	27	28	29	1[f]
SHAWWĀL 1401	2	3	4	5	6	7	8
	9	10	11	12	13	14	15
	16	17	18	19	20	21	22
	23	24	25	26	27	28	29
	30	1	2	3	4	5	6
DHU AL-QAʿDA 1401	7	8	9	10	11	12	13
	14	15	16	17	18	19	20
	21	22	23	24	25	26	27
	28	29	1	2	3	4	5
DHU AL-HIJJA 1401	6	7	8	9	10[g]	11	12
	13	14	15	16	17	18	19
	20	21	22	23	24	25	26
	27	28	29	30	1[a]	2[a]	3
MUḤARRAM 1402	4	5	6	7	8	9	10[b]
	11	12	13	14	15	16	17
	18	19	20	21	22	23	24
	25	26	27	28	29	30	1
SAFAR 1402	2	3	4	5	6	7	8
	9	10	11	12	13	14	15
	16	17	18	19	20	21	22
	23	24	25	26	27	28	29
	30	1	2	3	4	5	6

GREGORIAN 1981

Julian (Sun)	Sun	Mon	Tue	Wed	Thu	Fri	Sat	Month
Dec 15	28	29	30	31	1	2	3	
	4	5	6	7[a]	8	9	10	JANUARY 1981
Dec 29	11	12	13	14[b]	15	16	17	
	18	19	20	21	22	23	24	
Jan 12	25	26	27	28	29	30	31	
	1	2	3	4	5	6	7	
Jan 26	8	9	10	11	12	13	14	FEBRUARY 1981
	15	16	17	18	19	20	21	
Feb 9	22	23	24	25	26	27	28	
	1	2	3	4[c]	5	6	7	
Feb 23	8	9	10	11	12	13	14	MARCH 1981
	15[d]	16	17	18	19	20	21	
Mar 9	22	23	24	25	26	27	28	
	29	30	31	1	2	3	4	
Mar 23	5	6	7	8	9	10	11	
	12	13	14	15	16	17	18	APRIL 1981
Apr 6	19[e]	20	21	22	23	24	25	
	26[f]	27	28	29	30	1	2	
Apr 20	3	4	5	6	7	8	9	
	10	11	12	13	14	15	16	MAY 1981
May 4	17	18	19	20	21	22	23	
	24	25	26	27	28	29	30	
May 18	31	1	2	3	4	5	6	
	7	8	9	10	11	12	13	JUNE 1981
Jun 1	14	15	16	17	18	19	20	
	21	22	23	24	25	26	27	
Jun 15	28	29	30	1	2	3	4	
	5	6	7	8	9	10	11	
Jun 29	12	13	14	15	16	17	18	JULY 1981
	19	20	21	22	23	24	25	
Jul 13	26	27	28	29	30	31	1	
	2	3	4	5	6	7	8	
Jul 27	9	10	11	12	13	14	15	AUGUST 1981
	16	17	18	19	20	21	22	
Aug 10	23	24	25	26	27	28	29	
	30	31	1	2	3	4	5	
Aug 24	6	7	8	9	10	11	12	SEPTEMBER 1981
	13	14	15	16	17	18	19	
Sep 7	20	21	22	23	24	25	26	
	27	28	29	30	1	2	3	
Sep 21	4	5	6	7	8	9	10	OCTOBER 1981
	11	12	13	14	15	16	17	
Oct 5	18	19	20	21	22	23	24	
	25	26	27	28	29	30	31	
Oct 19	1	2	3	4	5	6	7	NOVEMBER 1981
	8	9	10	11	12	13	14	
Nov 2	15	16	17	18	19	20	21	
	22	23	24	25	26	27	28	
Nov 16	29[g]	30	1	2	3	4	5	
	6	7	8	9	10	11	12	DECEMBER 1981
Nov 30	13	14	15	16	17	18	19	
	20	21	22	23	24	25[h]	26	
Dec 14	27	28	29	30	31	1	2	

Persian: [a]New Year; [b]Sizdeh Bedar

Hindu Lunar: ‡Leap year; [a]New Year (Durmati); [b]Birthday of Rāma; [c]Birthday of Krishna; [d]Ganēśa Chaturthī; [e]Dashara; [f]Diwali; [g]Birthday of Vishnu; [h]Night of Śiva; [i]Holi

Hindu Solar: [a]New Year (Bhāva); [b]Pongal

Islamic: [a]New Year; [a]New Year (Arithmetic); [b]ʿAshūrāʾ; [c]Prophet's Birthday; [d]Ascent of the Prophet; [e]Start of Ramaḍān; [f]ʿĪd al-Fiṭr; [g]ʿĪd al-ʾAḍḥā

Gregorian: [a]Orthodox Christmas; [b]Julian New Year; [c]Ash Wednesday; [d]Feast of Orthodoxy; [e]Easter; [f]Orthodox Easter; [g]Advent; [h]Christmas

1982

	GREGORIAN 1982							Lunar Phases	ISO WEEK	JULIAN DAY		HEBREW 5742/5743							Molad		CHINESE Xīn-Yǒu/Rén-Xū‡							Solar Term		COPTIC 1698/1699‡							ETHIOPIC 1974/1975‡
	Sun	Mon	Tue	Wed	Thu	Fri	Sat		(Mon)	(Sun noon)		Sun	Mon	Tue	Wed	Thu	Fri	Sat			Sun	Mon	Tue	Wed	Thu	Fri	Sat			Sun	Mon	Tue	Wed	Thu	Fri	Sat	
JANUARY 1982	27	28	29	30	31	1[a]	2		53	2444966	TEVETH 5742	1[e]	2[e]	3	4	5	6	7	Sat 10h56m6p	MONTH 12 Xīn-Yǒu	2	3	4	5	6	7	8		KOIAK 1698	18	19	20	21	22	23	24	TĀKHŚĀŚ 1974
	◐	4	5	6	7	8	○	4:45 19:53	1	2444973		8	9	10	11	12	13	14			9	10	11	*12*	13	14	15	*Xiǎo hán*	TÔBE 1698	25	26	27	28	29[c]	30	1	ṬER 1974
	10	11	12	13	14	15	◑	23:58	2	2444980		15	16	17	18	19	20	21			16	17	18	19	20	21	22			2	3	4	5	6[d]	7	8	
	17	18	19	20	21	22	23		3	2444987		22	23	24	25	26	27	28			23	24	25	***26***	27	28	29	***Dà hán***		9	10	11[e]	12	13	14	15	
	24	●	26	27	28	29	30	4:56	4	2444994	SHEVAT 5742	29	1	2	3	4	5	6	Sun 23h40m7p	MONTH 1 Rén-Xū	30	1[a]	2	3	4	5	6			16	17	18	19	20	21	22	
FEBRUARY 1982	31	◐	2	3	4	5	6	14:28	5	2445001		7	8	9	10	11	12	13			7	8	9	10	*11*	12	13	*Lì chūn*		23	24	25	26	27	28	29	
	7	○	9	10	11	12	13	7:57	6	2445008		14	15	16	17	18	19	20			14	15[b]	16	17*	18	19	20		MESHIR 1698	30	1	2	3	4	5	6	YAKĀTIT 1974
	14	◑	16	17	18	19	20	20:21	7	2445015		21	22	23	24	25	26	27			21	22	23	24	25	***26***	27	***Yǔ shuǐ***		7	8	9	10	11	12	13	
	21	22	●	24	25	26	27	21:13	8	2445022	ADAR 5742	28	29	30	1	2	3	4	Tue 12h24m8p	MONTH 2 Rén-Xū	28	29	30	1	2	3	4			14	15	16	17	18	19	20	
MARCH 1982	28	1	◐	3	4	5	6	22:15	9	2445029		5	6	7	8	9	10	11			5	6	7	8	9	10	*11*	*Jīng zhé*		21	22	23	24	25	26	27	
	7	8	○	10	11	12	13	20:45	10	2445036		12	13	14[f]	15	16	17	18			12	13	14	15	16	17	18		PAREMOTEP 1698	28	29	30	1	2	3	4	MAGĀBIT 1974
	14	15	16	◑	18	19	20[b]	17:15	11	2445043		19	20	21	22	23	24	25			19	20	21	22	23	24	25			5	6	7	8	9	10	11	
	21	22	23	24	●	26	27	10:18	12	2445050	NISAN 5742	26	27	28	29	1	2	3	Thu 1h8m9p	MONTH 3 Rén-Xū	***26***	27	28	29	1	2	3	***Chūn fēn***		12	13	14	15	16	17	18	
APRIL 1982	28	29	30	31	◐	2	3	5:08	13	2445057		4	5	6	7	8	9	10			4	5	6	7	8	9	10			19	20	21	22	23	24	25	
	4	5	6	7	○	9	10	10:18	14	2445064		11	12	13	14	15[g]	16	17			11	*12*[c]	13	14	15	16	17	*Qīng míng*	PARMOUTE 1698	26	27	28	29	30	1	2	MIYĀZYĀ 1974
	11	12	13	14	15	◑	17	12:42	15	2445071		18	19	20	21	22	23	24			18*	19	20	21	22	23	24			3	4	5	6	7	8	9	
	18	19	20	21	22	●	24	20:29	16	2445078	IYYAR 5742	25	26	27	28	29	30	1	Fri 13h52m10p	MONTH 4 Rén-Xū	25	26	***27***	28	29	30	1	***Gǔ yǔ***		10[f]	11	12	13	14	15	16	
MAY 1982	25	26	27	28	29	◐	1	12:07	17	2445085		2	3	4	5	6	7	8			2	3	4	5	6	7	8			17	18	19	20	21	22	23	
	2	3	4	5	6	7	○	0:45	18	2445092		9	10	11	12	13	14	15			9	10	11	12	*13*	14	15	*Lì xià*		24	25	26	27	28	29[g]	30	
	9	10	11	12	13	14	15		19	2445099		16	17	18	19	20	21	22			16	17	18	19	20	21	22		PASHONS 1698	1	2	3	4	5	6	7	GENBOT 1974
	◑	17	18	19	20	21	22	5:11	20	2445106		23	24	25	26	27	28	29			23	24	25	26	27	***28***	29	***Xiǎo mǎn***		8	9	10	11	12	13	14	
	●	24	25	26	27	28	◐	4:41 20:07	21	2445113	SIVAN 5742	1	2	3	4	5	6[h]	7	Sun 2h36m11p	*LEAP MONTH 4* Rén-Xū	1	2	3	4	5	6	7			15	16	17	18	19	20	21	
JUNE 1982	30	31	1	2	3	4	5		22	2445120		8	9	10	11	12	13	14			8	9	10	11	12	13	14			22	23	24	25	26	27	28	
	○	7	8	9	10	11	12	15:59	23	2445127		15	16	17	18	19	20	21			*15*	16	17	18	19*	20	21	*Máng zhòng*	PAÔNE 1698	29	30	1	2	3	4	5	SANĒ 1974
	13	◑	15	16	17	18	19	18:06	24	2445134		22	23	24	25	26	27	28			22	23	24	25	26	27	28			6	7	8	9	10	11	12	
	20	●[c]	22	23	24	25	26	11:52	25	2445141	TAMMUZ 5742	29	30	1	2	3	4	5	Mon 15h20m12p	MONTH 5 Rén-Xū	29	1	***2***	3	4	5[d]	6	***Xià zhì***		13	14	15	16	17	18	19	
JULY 1982	27	◐	29	30	1	2	3	5:56	26	2445148		6	7	8	9	10	11	12			7	8	9	10	11	12	13			20	21	22	23	24	25	26	
	4	5	○	7	8	9	10	7:32	27	2445155		13	14	15	16	17	18	19			14	15	16	*17*	18	19	20	*Xiǎo shǔ*	EPÊP 1698	27	28	29	30	1	2	3	ḤAMLĒ 1974
	11	12	13	◑	15	16	17	3:47	28	2445162		20	21	22	23	24	25	26			21	22	23	24	25	26	27			4	5	6	7	8	9	10	
	18	19	●	21	22	23	24	18:57	29	2445169	AV 5742	27	28	29	1	2	3	4	Wed 4h4m13p	MONTH 6 Rén-Xū	28	29	30	1	2	***3***	4	***Dà shǔ***		11	12	13	14	15	16	17	
	25	26	◐	28	29	30	31	18:22	30	2445176		5	6	7	8	9[i]	10	11			5	6	7	8	9	10	11			18	19	20	21	22	23	24	
AUGUST 1982	1	2	3	○	5	6	7	22:34	31	2445183		12	13	14	15	16	17	18			12	13	14	15	16	17	18		MESORÊ 1698	25	26	27	28	29	30	1	NAḤASĒ 1974
	8	9	10	11	◑	13	14	11:09	32	2445190		19	20	21	22	23	24	25			*19*	20*	21	22	23	24	25	*Lì qiū*		2	3	4	5	6	7	8	
	15	16	17	18	●	20	21	2:45	33	2445197	ELUL 5742	26	27	28	29	30	1	2	Thu 16h48m14p	MONTH 7 Rén-Xū	26	27	28	29	1	2	3			9	10	11	12	13[h]	14	15	
	22	23	24	25	◐	27	28	9:49	34	2445204		3	4	5	6	7	8	9			4	***5***	6	7[e]	8	9	10	***Chǔ shǔ***		16	17	18	19	20	21	22	
SEPTEMBER 1982	29	30	31	1	2	○	4	12:28	35	2445211		10	11	12	13	14	15	16			11	12	13	14	15[f]	16	17			23	24	25	26	27	28	29	
	5	6	7	8	9	◑	11	17:19	36	2445218		17	18	19	20	21	22	23			18	19	20	*21*	22	23	24	*Bái lù*	EPAG. 1698	30	1	2	3	4	5	1[a]	PĀG. 1974
	12	13	14	15	16	●	18	12:09	37	2445225	TISHRI 5743	24	25	26	27	28	29	1[a]	Sat 5h32m15p	MONTH 8 Rén-Xū	25	26	27	28	29	1	2		THOOUT 1699	2	3	4	5	6	7	8	MASKARAM 1975
	19	20	21	22	23[d]	24	◐	4:07	38	2445232		2[a]	3	4	5	6	7	8			3	4	5	6	***7***	8	9	***Qiū fēn***		9	10	11	12	13	14	15	
OCTOBER 1982	26	27	28	29	30	1	2		39	2445239		9	10[b]	11	12	13	14	15[c]			10	11	12	13	14	15[g]	16			16	17[b]	18	19	20	21	22	
	○	4	5	6	7	8	◑	1:09 23:27	40	2445246		16	17	18	19	20	21	22			17	18	19	20	21	*22**	23	*Hán lù*		23	24	25	26	27	28	29	
	10	11	12	13	14	15	16		41	2445253		23	24	25	26	27	28	29			24	25	26	27	28	29	30		PAOPE 1699	30	1	2	3	4	5	6	TEQEMT 1975
	●	18	19	20	21	22	23	0:04	42	2445260	ḤESHVAN 5743	30	1	2	3	4	5	6	Sun 18h16m16p	MONTH 9 Rén-Xū	1	2	3	4	5	6	7			7	8	9	10	11	12	13	
	24	◐	26	27	28	29	30	0:08	43	2445267		7	8	9	10	11	12	13			***8***	9[h]	10	11	12	13	14	***Shuāng jiàng***		14	15	16	17	18	19	20	
NOVEMBER 1982	31	○	2	3	4	5	6	12:57	44	2445274		14	15	16	17	18	19	20			15	16	17	18	19	20	21			21	22	23	24	25	26	27	
	7	◑	9	10	11	12	13	6:38	45	2445281		21	22	23	24	25	26	27			22	*23*	24	25	26	27	28	*Lì dōng*	ATHÔR 1699	28	29	30	1	2	3	4	ḪEDĀR 1975
	14	●	16	17	18	19	20	15:10	46	2445288	KISLEV 5743	28	29	30	1	2	3	4	Tue 7h0m17p	MONTH 10 Rén-Xū	29	1	2	3	4	5	6			5	6	7	8	9	10	11	
	21	22	◐	24	25	26	27	20:06	47	2445295		5	6	7	8	9	10	11			7	***8***	9	10	11	12	13	***Xiǎo xuě***		12	13	14	15	16	17	18	
DECEMBER 1982	28	29	30	○	2	3	4	0:21	48	2445302		12	13	14	15	16	17	18			14	15	16	17	18	19	20			19	20	21	22	23	24	25	
	5	6	◑	8	9	10	11	15:53	49	2445309		19[d]	20	21	22	23	24	25[e]			21	22	*23**	24	25	26	27	*Dà xuě*	KOIAK 1699	26	27	28	29	30	1	2	TĀKHŚĀŚ 1975
	12	13	14	●	16	17	18	9:18	50	2445316	TEVETH 5743	26[e]	27[e]	28[e]	29[e]	30[e]	1[e]	2[e]	Wed 19h45m0p	MONTH 11 Rén-Xū	28	29	30	1	2	3	4			3	4	5	6	7	8	9	
	19	20	21	22[e]	◐	24	25	14:17	51	2445323		3	4	5	6	7	8	9			5	6	7	***8***[i]	9	10	11	***Dōng zhì***		10	11	12	13	14	15	16	
	26	27	28	29	○	31	1	11:33	52	2445330		10	11	12	13	14	15	16			12	13	14	15	16	17	18			17	18	19	20	21	22	23	

[a]New Year
[b]Spring (22:55)
[c]Summer (17:23)
[d]Autumn (8:46)
[e]Winter (4:38)
● New moon
◐ First quarter moon
○ Full moon
◑ Last quarter moon

[a]New Year
[b]Yom Kippur
[c]Sukkot
[d]Winter starts
[e]Ḥanukkah
[f]Purim
[g]Passover
[h]Shavuot
[i]Fast of Av

‡Leap year
[a]New Year (4680, Dog)
[b]Lantern Festival
[c]Qīngmíng
[d]Dragon Festival
[e]Qīqiǎo
[f]Hungry Ghosts
[g]Mid-Autumn Festival
[h]Double-Ninth Festival
[i]Dōngzhì
*Start of 60-name cycle

‡Leap year
[a]New Year
[b]Building of the Cross
[c]Christmas
[d]Jesus's Circumcision
[e]Epiphany
[f]Easter
[g]Mary's Announcement
[h]Jesus's Transfiguration

PERSIAN (ASTRONOMICAL) 1360/1361

Month	Sun	Mon	Tue	Wed	Thu	Fri	Sat
DEY 1360	6	7	8	9	10	11	12
	13	14	15	16	17	18	19
	20	21	22	23	24	25	26
	27	28	29	30	1	2	3
BAHMAN 1360	4	5	6	7	8	9	10
	11	12	13	14	15	16	17
	18	19	20	21	22	23	24
	25	26	27	28	29	30	1
ESFAND 1360	2	3	4	5	6	7	8
	9	10	11	12	13	14	15
	16	17	18	19	20	21	22
	23	24	25	26	27	28	29
FARVARDĪN 1361	1[a]	2	3	4	5	6	7
	8	9	10	11	12	13[b]	14
	15	16	17	18	19	20	21
	22	23	24	25	26	27	28
	29	30	31	1	2	3	4
ORDĪBEHEŠT 1361	5	6	7	8	9	10	11
	12	13	14	15	16	17	18
	19	20	21	22	23	24	25
	26	27	28	29	30	31	1
XORDĀD 1361	2	3	4	5	6	7	8
	9	10	11	12	13	14	15
	16	17	18	19	20	21	22
	23	24	25	26	27	28	29
	30	31	1	2	3	4	5
TĪR 1361	6	7	8	9	10	11	12
	13	14	15	16	17	18	19
	20	21	22	23	24	25	26
	27	28	29	30	31	1	2
MORDĀD 1361	3	4	5	6	7	8	9
	10	11	12	13	14	15	16
	17	18	19	20	21	22	23
	24	25	26	27	28	29	30
	31	1	2	3	4	5	6
SHAHRĪVAR 1361	7	8	9	10	11	12	13
	14	15	16	17	18	19	20
	21	22	23	24	25	26	27
	28	29	30	31	1	2	3
MEHR 1361	4	5	6	7	8	9	10
	11	12	13	14	15	16	17
	18	19	20	21	22	23	24
	25	26	27	28	29	30	1
ĀBĀN 1361	2	3	4	5	6	7	8
	9	10	11	12	13	14	15
	16	17	18	19	20	21	22
	23	24	25	26	27	28	29
	30	1	2	3	4	5	6
ĀZAR 1361	7	8	9	10	11	12	13
	14	15	16	17	18	19	20
	21	22	23	24	25	26	27
DEY 1361	28	29	30	1	2	3	4
	5	6	7	8	9	10	11

[a]New Year
[b]Sizdeh Bedar

HINDU LUNAR 2038/2039‡

Month	Sun	Mon	Tue	Wed	Thu	Fri	Sat
PAUSHA 2038	1	2	3	4	5	6	7
	8	9	10	11	**12**	14	15
	16	17	18	19	20	21	22
	23	24	25	26	27	28	29
MĀGHA 2038	29	30	1	2	3	4	5
	6	8	9	10	11	12	13
	14	15	16	17	18	19	20
	21	22	23	24	25	26	27
PHĀLGUNA 2038	28	29[h]	30	1	2	3	4
	5	6	7	8	9	10	**11**
	13	14	15[i]	16	17	18	19
	20	21	22	*22*	23	24	25
CHAITRA 2039	26	27	28	29	30	1[a]	2
	3	4	**5**	7	8	9[b]	10
	11	12	13	14	15	16	17
	18	19	20	21	22	23	24
	25	26	*26*	28	29	30	1
VAIŚĀKHA 2039	2	3	4	5	6	7	8
	9	11	12	13	14	15	16
	16	17	18	19	20	21	22
	23	24	25	26	27	28	29
JYAISHTHA 2039	30	1	**2**	4	5	6	7
	8	9	10	11	12	13	14
	15	16	17	18	19	20	21
	21	22	**23**	25	26	27	28
ĀSHĀḌHA 2039	29	30	1	2	3	4	**5**
	7	8	9	10	11	12	*12*
	13	14	15	16	17	18	19
	20	21	22	23	24	25	26
ŚRĀVAṆA 2039	**27**	29	30	1	2	3	4
	5	6	7	8	9	10	11
	12	13	14	15	16	17	18
	19	20	21	22	23[c]	24	25
BHĀDRAPADA 2039	26	27	28	29	30	**1**	3
	4[d]	5	6	7	8	9	9
	10	11	12	13	14	15	16
	17	18	19	20	21	22	**23**
LEAP ĀŚVINA 2039	25	26	27	28	29	30	1
	2	3	4	5	6	7	8
	9	10	11	12	13	14	*14*
	15	17	18	19	20	21	22
	23	24	25	26	27	**28**	30
ĀŚVINA 2039	1	2	3	4	*4*	5	6
	7	8[e]	9[e]	10[e]	11	12	13
	14	15	16	17	18	19	20
	21	23	24	25	26	27	28
KĀRTTIKA 2039	29	30	1[f]	2	3	4	5
	6	7	*7*	8	9	10	11
	12	13	**14**	16	17	18	19
	20	21	22	23	24	25	26
MĀRGAŚĪRA 2039	27	28	29	30	1	2	3
	4	5	6	7	8	9	10
	11[g]	12	13	14	15	16	17

‡Leap year
[a]New Year (Dundubhi)
[b]Birthday of Rāma
[c]Birthday of Krishna
[d]Ganēśa Chaturthī
[e]Dashara
[f]Diwali
[g]Birthday of Vishnu
[h]Night of Śiva
[i]Holi

HINDU SOLAR 1903/1904‡

Month	Sun	Mon	Tue	Wed	Thu	Fri	Sat
PAUSHA 1903	13	14	15	16	17	18	19
	20	21	22	23	24	25	26
	27	28	29	30	1[b]	2	3
MĀGHA 1903	4	5	6	7	8	9	10
	11	12	13	14	15	16	17
	18	19	20	21	22	23	24
	25	26	27	28	29	1	2
PHĀLGUNA 1903	3	4	5	6	7	8	9
	10	11	12	13	14	15	16
	17	18	19	20	21	22	23
	24	25	26	27	28	29	30
CHAITRA 1903	1	2	3	4	5	6	7
	8	9	10	11	12	13	14
	15	16	17	18	19	20	21
	22	23	24	25	26	27	28
	29	30	1[a]	2	3	4	5
VAIŚĀKHA 1904	6	7	8	9	10	11	12
	13	14	15	16	17	18	19
	20	21	22	23	24	25	26
	27	28	29	30	31	1	2
JYAISHTHA 1904	3	4	5	6	7	8	9
	10	11	12	13	14	15	16
	17	18	19	20	21	22	23
	24	25	26	27	28	29	30
	31	32	1	2	3	4	5
ĀSHĀḌHA 1904	6	7	8	9	10	11	12
	13	14	15	16	17	18	19
	20	21	22	23	24	25	26
	27	28	29	30	31	1	2
ŚRĀVAṆA 1904	3	4	5	6	7	8	9
	10	11	12	13	14	15	16
	17	18	19	20	21	22	23
	24	25	26	27	28	29	30
	31	32	1	2	3	4	5
BHĀDRAPADA 1904	6	7	8	9	10	11	12
	13	14	15	16	17	18	19
	20	21	22	23	24	25	26
	27	28	29	30	31	1	2
ĀŚVINA 1904	3	4	5	6	7	8	9
	10	11	12	13	14	15	16
	17	18	19	20	21	22	23
	24	25	26	27	28	29	30
KĀRTTIKA 1904	1	2	3	4	5	6	7
	8	9	10	11	12	13	14
	15	16	17	18	19	20	21
	22	23	24	25	26	27	28
	29	30	1	2	3	4	5
MĀRGAŚĪRA 1904	6	7	8	9	10	11	12
	13	14	15	16	17	18	19
	20	21	22	23	24	25	26
	27	28	29	30	1	2	3
PAUSHA 1904	4	5	6	7	8	9	10
	11	12	13	14	15	16	17

‡Leap year
[a]New Year (Yuvan)
[b]Pongal

ISLAMIC (ASTRONOMICAL) 1402/1403‡

Month	Sun	Mon	Tue	Wed	Thu	Fri	Sat
RABĪ' I 1402	30	1	2	3	4	5	6
	7	8	9	10	11	12[c]	13
	14	15	16	17	18	19	20
	21	22	23	24	25	26	27
RABĪ' II 1402	28	29	30	1	2	3	4
	5	6	7	8	9	10	11
	12	13	14	15	16	17	18
	19	20	21	22	23	24	25
JUMĀDĀ I 1402	26	27	28	29	1	2	3
	4	5	6	7	8	9	10
	11	12	13	14	15	16	17
	18	19	20	21	22	23	24
JUMĀDĀ II 1402	25	26	27	28	29	30	1
	2	3	4	5	6	7	8
	9	10	11	12	13	14	15
	16	17	18	19	20	21	22
	23	24	25	26	27	28	29
RAJAB 1402	1	2	3	4	5	6	7
	8	9	10	11	12	13	14
	15	16	17	18	19	20	21
	22	23	24	25	26	27[d]	28
SHA'BĀN 1402	29	1	2	3	4	5	6
	7	8	9	10	11	12	13
	14	15	16	17	18	19	20
	21	22	23	24	25	26	27
RAMAḌĀN 1402	28	29	30	1[e]	2	3	4
	5	6	7	8	9	10	11
	12	13	14	15	16	17	18
	19	20	21	22	23	24	25
SHAWWĀL 1402	26	27	28	29	1[f]	2	3
	4	5	6	7	8	9	10
	11	12	13	14	15	16	17
	18	19	20	21	22	23	24
DHU AL-QA'DA 1402	25	26	27	28	29	1	2
	3	4	5	6	7	8	9
	10	11	12	13	14	15	16
	17	18	19	20	21	22	23
	24	25	26	27	28	29	30
DHU AL-ḤIJJA 1402	1	2	3	4	5	6	7
	8	9	10[g]	11	12	13	14
	15	16	17	18	19	20	21
	22	23	24	25	26	27	28
MUḤARRAM 1403	29	1[a]	2[â]	3	4	5	6
	7	8	9	10[b]	11	12	13
	14	15	16	17	18	19	20
	21	22	23	24	25	26	27
ṢAFAR 1403	28	29	30	1	2	3	4
	5	6	7	8	9	10	11
	12	13	14	15	16	17	18
	19	20	21	22	23	24	25
RABĪ' I 1403	26	27	28	29	30	1	2
	3	4	5	6	7	8	9
	10	11	12[c]	13	14	15	16

‡Leap year
[a]New Year
[â]New Year (Arithmetic)
[b]'Ashūrā'
[c]Prophet's Birthday
[d]Ascent of the Prophet
[e]Start of Ramaḍān
[f]'Id al-Fiṭr
[g]'Id al-'Aḍḥā

GREGORIAN 1982

Julian (Sun)	Sun	Mon	Tue	Wed	Thu	Fri	Sat	Month
Dec 14	27	28	29	30	31	1	2	JANUARY 1982
	3	4	5	6	7[a]	8	9	
Dec 28	10	11	12	13	14[b]	15	16	
	17	18	19	20	21	22	23	
Jan 11	24	25	26	27	28	29	30	
	31	1	2	3	4	5	6	FEBRUARY 1982
Jan 25	7	8	9	10	11	12	13	
	14	15	16	17	18	19	20	
Feb 8	21	22	23	24[c]	25	26	27	
	28	1	2	3	4	5	6	MARCH 1982
Feb 22	7[d]	8	9	10	11	12	13	
	14	15	16	17	18	19	20	
Mar 8	21	22	23	24	25	26	27	
	28	29	30	31	1	2	3	APRIL 1982
Mar 22	4	5	6	7	8	9	10	
	11[e]	12	13	14	15	16	17	
Apr 5	18[f]	19	20	21	22	23	24	
	25	26	27	28	29	30	1	MAY 1982
Apr 19	2	3	4	5	6	7	8	
	9	10	11	12	13	14	15	
May 3	16	17	18	19	20	21	22	
	23	24	25	26	27	28	29	
May 17	30	31	1	2	3	4	5	JUNE 1982
	6	7	8	9	10	11	12	
May 31	13	14	15	16	17	18	19	
	20	21	22	23	24	25	26	
Jun 14	27	28	29	30	1	2	3	JULY 1982
	4	5	6	7	8	9	10	
Jun 28	11	12	13	14	15	16	17	
	18	19	20	21	22	23	24	
Jul 12	25	26	27	28	29	30	31	
	1	2	3	4	5	6	7	AUGUST 1982
Jul 26	8	9	10	11	12	13	14	
	15	16	17	18	19	20	21	
Aug 9	22	23	24	25	26	27	28	
	29	30	31	1	2	3	4	SEPTEMBER 1982
Aug 23	5	6	7	8	9	10	11	
	12	13	14	15	16	17	18	
Sep 6	19	20	21	22	23	24	25	
	26	27	28	29	30	1	2	OCTOBER 1982
Sep 20	3	4	5	6	7	8	9	
	10	11	12	13	14	15	16	
Oct 4	17	18	19	20	21	22	23	
	24	25	26	27	28	29	30	
Oct 18	31	1	2	3	4	5	6	NOVEMBER 1982
	7	8	9	10	11	12	13	
Nov 1	14	15	16	17	18	19	20	
	21	22	23	24	25	26	27	
Nov 15	28[g]	29	30	1	2	3	4	DECEMBER 1982
	5	6	7	8	9	10	11	
Nov 29	12	13	14	15	16	17	18	
	19	20	21	22	23	24	25[h]	
Dec 13	26	27	28	29	30	31	1	

[a]Orthodox Christmas
[b]Julian New Year
[c]Ash Wednesday
[d]Feast of Orthodoxy
[e]Easter
[f]Orthodox Easter
[g]Advent
[h]Christmas

1983

	GREGORIAN 1983							Lunar Phases	ISO WEEK	JULIAN DAY	HEBREW 5743/5744‡								Molad	CHINESE Rén-Xū‡/Guǐ-Hài								Solar Term	COPTIC 1699‡/1700 ETHIOPIC 1975‡/1976								
	Sun	Mon	Tue	Wed	Thu	Fri	Sat		(Mon)	(Sun noon)		Sun	Mon	Tue	Wed	Thu	Fri	Sat			Sun	Mon	Tue	Wed	Thu	Fri	Sat			Sun	Mon	Tue	Wed	Thu	Fri	Sat	
JANUARY 1983	26	27	28	29	○	31	1[a]	11:33	52	2445330	TEVETH 5743	10	11	12	13	14	15	16		MONTH 11 Rén-Xū	12	13	14	15	16	17	18		KOIAK 1699	17	18	19	20	21	22	23	TĀKHŚĀŚ 1975
	2	3	4	5	◑	7	8	4:00	1	2445337		17	18	19	20	21	22	23			19	20	21	22	23	24	25	Xiǎo hán		24	25	26	27	28	29[c]	30	
	9	10	11	12	13	●	15	5:08	2	2445344	SHEVAT 5743	24	25	26	27	28	29	1	Fri 8h29m1p	MONTH 12 Rén-Xū	26	27	28	29	30	1	2		TŌBE 1699	1	2	3	4	5	6[d]	7	ṬER 1975
	16	17	18	19	20	21	◐	5:33	3	2445351		2	3	4	5	6	7	8			3	4	5	6	7	8	9	Dà hán		8	9	10	11[e]	12	13	14	
	23	24	25	26	27	○	29	22:26	4	2445358		9	10	11	12	13	14	15			10	11	12	13	14	15	16			15	16	17	18	19	20	21	
FEBRUARY 1983	30	31	1	2	3	◑	5	19:17	5	2445365		16	17	18	19	20	21	22			17	18	19	20	21	22	23*	Lì chūn		22	23	24	25	26	27	28	
	6	7	8	9	10	11	12		6	2445372		23	24	25	26	27	28	29			24	25	26	27	28	29	30		MESHIR 1699	29	30	1	2	3	4	5	YAKĀTIT 1975
	●	14	15	16	17	18	19	0:32	7	2445379	ADAR 5743	30	1	2	3	4	5	6	Sat 21h13m2p	MONTH 1 Guǐ-Hài	1[a]	2	3	4	5	6	7	Yǔ shuǐ		6	7	8	9	10	11	12	
	◐	21	22	23	24	25	26	17:32	8	2445386		7	8	9	10	11	12	13			8	9	10	11	12	13	14			13	14	15	16	17	18	19	
MARCH 1983	○	28	1	2	3	4	5	8:58	9	2445393		14[f]	15	16	17	18	19	20			15[b]	16	17	18	19	20	21			20	21	22	23	24	25	26	
	◑	7	8	9	10	11	12	13:16	10	2445400		21	22	23	24	25	26	27			22	23	24	25	26	27	28	Jīng zhé	PAREMOTEP 1699	27	28	29	30	1	2	3	MAGĀBIT 1975
	13	●	15	16	17	18	19	17:43	11	2445407	NISAN 5743	28	29	1	2	3	4	5		MONTH 2 Guǐ-Hài	29	30	1	2	3	4	5			4	5	6	7	8	9	10	
	20	21[b]	◐	23	24	25	26	2:25	12	2445414		6	7	8	9	10	11	12	Mon 9h57m3p		6	7	8	9	10	11	12	Chūn fēn		11	12	13	14	15	16	17	
APRIL 1983	27	○	29	30	31	1	2	19:27	13	2445421		13	14	15[g]	16	17	18	19			13	14	15	16	17	18	19			18	19	20	21	22	23	24	
	3	4	◑	6	7	8	9	8:38	14	2445428		20	21	22	23	24	25	26			20	21	22[c]	23*	24	25	26	Qīng míng	PARMOUTE 1699	25	26	27	28	29	30	1	MIYĀZYĀ 1975
	10	11	12	●	14	15	16	7:58	15	2445435	IYYAR 5743	27	28	29	30	1	2	3	Tue 22h41m4p	MONTH 3 Guǐ-Hài	27	28	29	1	2	3	4			2	3	4	5	6	7	8	
	17	18	19	◐	21	22	23	8:58	16	2445442		4	5	6	7	8	9	10			5	6	7	8	9	10	11	Gǔ yǔ		9	10	11	12	13	14	15	
	24	25	26	○	28	29	30	6:31	17	2445449		11	12	13	14	15	16	17			12	13	14	15	16	17	18			16	17	18	19	20	21	22	
MAY 1983	1	2	3	4	◑	6	7	3:43	18	2445456		18	19	20	21	22	23	24	Thu 11h25m5p		19	20	21	22	23	24	25	Lì xià		23	24	25	26	27	28	29[g]	
	8	9	10	11	●	13	14	19:25	19	2445463	SIVAN 5743	25	26	27	28	29	1	2		MONTH 4 Guǐ-Hài	26	27	28	29	30	1	2		PASHONS 1699	30[f]	1	2	3	4	5	6	GENBOT 1975
	15	16	17	18	◐	20	21	14:17	20	2445470		3	4	5	6[h]	7	8	9			3	4	5	6	7	8	9	Xiǎo mǎn		7	8	9	10	11	12	13	
	22	23	24	25	○	27	28	18:48	21	2445477		10	11	12	13	14	15	16			10	11	12	13	14	15	16			14	15	16	17	18	19	20	
JUNE 1983	29	30	31	1	2	◑	4	21:07	22	2445484		17	18	19	20	21	22	23			17	18	19	20	21	22	23			21	22	23	24	25	26	27	
	5	6	7	8	9	10	●	4:38	23	2445491		24	25	26	27	28	29	30		MONTH 5 Guǐ-Hài	24*	25	26	27	28	29	1	Máng zhòng	PAÔNE 1699	28	29	30	1	2	3	4	SANĒ 1975
	12	13	14	15	16	◐	18	19:46	24	2445498	TAMMUZ 5743	1	2	3	4	5	6	7	Sat 0h9m6p		2	3	4	5[d]	6	7	8			5	6	7	8	9	10	11	
	19	20	21[c]	22	23	24	○	8:32	25	2445505		8	9	10	11	12	13	14			9	10	11	12	13	14	15	Xià zhì		12	13	14	15	16	17	18	
JULY 1983	26	27	28	29	30	1	2		26	2445512		15	16	17	18	19	20	21			16	17	18	19	20	21	22			19	20	21	22	23	24	25	
	◑	4	5	6	7	8	9	12:12	27	2445519		22	23	24	25	26	27	28			23	24	25	26	27	28	29	Xiǎo shǔ	EPĒP 1699	26	27	28	29	30	1	2	ḤAMLĒ 1975
	●	11	12	13	14	15	16	12:19	28	2445526	AV 5743	29	1	2	3	4	5	6	Sun 12h53m7p	MONTH 6 Guǐ-Hài	1	2	3	4	5	6	7			3	4	5	6	7	8	9	
	◐	18	19	20	21	22	23	2:50	29	2445533		7	8	9[i]	10	11	12	13			8	9	10	11	12	13	14	Dà shǔ		10	11	12	13	14	15	16	
	○	25	26	27	28	29	30	23:27	30	2445540		14	15	16	17	18	19	20			15	16	17	18	19	20	21			17	18	19	20	21	22	23	
AUGUST 1983	31	1	◑	3	4	5	6	0:52	31	2445547		21	22	23	24	25	26	27	Tue 1h37m8p		22	23	24	25	26*	27	28			24	25	26	27	28	29	30	
	7	●	9	10	11	12	13	19:18	32	2445554	ELUL 5743	28	29	30	1	2	3	4		MONTH 7 Guǐ-Hài	29	30	1	2	3	4	5	Lì qiū	MESORĒ 1699	1	2	3	4	5	6	7	NAHASĒ 1975
	14	◐	16	17	18	19	20	12:47	33	2445561		5	6	7	8	9	10	11			6	7[e]	8	9	10	11	12			8	9	10	11	12	13[h]	14	
	21	22	○	24	25	26	27	14:59	34	2445568		12	13	14	15	16	17	18			13	14	15[f]	16	17	18	19	Chǔ shǔ		15	16	17	18	19	20	21	
SEPTEMBER 1983	28	29	30	◑	1	2	3	11:22	35	2445575		19	20	21	22	23	24	25	Wed 14h21m9p		20	21	22	23	24	25	26			22	23	24	25	26	27	28	
	4	5	6	●	8	9	10	2:35	36	2445582	TISHRI 5744	26	27	28	29	1[a]	2[a]	3		MONTH 8 Guǐ-Hài	27	28	29	1	2	3	4	Bái lù	EPAG. 1699	29	30	1	2	3	4	5	PĀG. 1975
	11	12	13	◐	15	16	17	2:24	37	2445589		4	5	6	7	8	9	10[b]			5	6	7	8	9	10	11		THOOUT 1700	6	1[a]	2	3	4	5	6	MASKARAM 1976
	18	19	20	21	○	23[d]	24	6:36	38	2445596		11	12	13	14	15[c]	16	17			12	13	14	15[g]	16	17	18	Qiū fēn		7	8	9	10	11	12	13	
OCTOBER 1983	25	26	27	28	◑	30	1	20:05	39	2445603		18	19	20	21	22	23	24	Fri 3h5m10p		19	20	21	22	23	24	25			14	15	16	17[b]	18	19	20	
	2	3	4	5	●	7	8	11:16	40	2445610	ḤESHVAN 5744	25	26	27	28	29	30	1		MONTH 9 Guǐ-Hài	26	27*	28	29	1	2	3			21	22	23	24	25	26	27	
	9	10	11	12	◐	14	15	19:42	41	2445617		2	3	4	5	6	7	8			4	5	6	7	8	9[h]	10	Hán lù	PAOPE 1700	28	29	30	1	2	3	4	ṬEQEMT 1976
	16	17	18	19	20	○	22	21:53	42	2445624		9	10	11	12	13	14	15			11	12	13	14	15	16	17			5	6	7	8	9	10	11	
	23	24	25	26	27	28	◑	3:37	43	2445631		16	17	18	19	20	21	22			18	19	20	21	22	23	24	Shuāng jiàng		12	13	14	15	16	17	18	
NOVEMBER 1983	30	31	1	2	3	●	5	22:21	44	2445638		23	24	25	26	27	28	29		MONTH 10 Guǐ-Hài	25	26	27	28	29	30	1			19	20	21	22	23	24	25	
	6	7	8	9	10	11	◐	15:49	45	2445645	KISLEV 5744	30	1	2	3	4	5	6	Sat 15h49m11p		2	3	4	5	6	7	8	Lì dōng	ATHŌR 1700	26	27	28	29	30	1	2	ḤEDĀR 1976
	13	14	15	16	17	18	19		46	2445652		7	8	9	10	11	12	13			9	10	11	12	13	14	15			3	4	5	6	7	8	9	
	○	21	22	23	24	25	26	12:29	47	2445659		14	15	16	17	18	19	20			16	17	18	19	20	21	22	Xiǎo xuě		10	11	12	13	14	15	16	
DECEMBER 1983	◑	28	29	30	1	2	3	10:50	48	2445666		21	22	23	24	25[e]	26[e]	27[e]			23	24	25	26	27	28*	29			17	18	19	20	21	22	23	
	●	5	6	7	8	9	10	12:26	49	2445673	TEVETH 5744	28[e]	29[e]	30[d,e]	1[e]	2[e]	3	4	Mon 4h33m12p	MONTH 11* Guǐ-Hài	1	2	3	4	5	6	7	Dà xuě		24	25	26	27	28	29	30	
	11	◐	13	14	15	16	17	13:09	50	2445680		5	6	7	8	9	10	11			8	9	10	11	12	13	14		KOIAK 1700	1	2	3	4	5	6	7	TĀKHŚĀŚ 1976
	18	19	○	21	22[e]	23	24	2:00	51	2445687		12	13	14	15	16	17	18			15	16	17	18	19[i]	20	21	Dōng zhì		8	9	10	11	12	13	14	
	25	◑	27	28	29	30	31	18:53	52	2445694		19	20	21	22	23	24	25			22	23	24	25	26	27	28			15	16	17	18	19	20	21	

[a]New Year
[b]Spring (4:38)
[c]Summer (23:08)
[d]Autumn (14:41)
[e]Winter (10:30)
● New moon
◐ First quarter moon
○ Full moon
◑ Last quarter moon

‡Leap year
[a]New Year
[b]Yom Kippur
[c]Sukkot
[d]Winter starts
[e]Ḥanukkah
[f]Purim
[g]Passover
[h]Shavuot
[i]Fast of Av

‡Leap year
[a]New Year (4681, Pig)
[b]Lantern Festival
[c]Qīngmíng
[d]Dragon Festival
[e]Qīqiǎo
[f]Hungry Ghosts
[g]Mid-Autumn Festival
[h]Double-Ninth Festival
[i]Dōngzhì
*Start of 60-name cycle

‡Leap year
[a]New Year
[b]Building of the Cross
[c]Christmas
[d]Jesus's Circumcision
[e]Epiphany
[f]Easter
[g]Mary's Announcement
[h]Jesus's Transfiguration

PERSIAN (ASTRONOMICAL) 1361/1362‡

Month	Sun	Mon	Tue	Wed	Thu	Fri	Sat
DEY 1361	5	6	7	8	9	10	11
	12	13	14	15	16	17	18
	19	20	21	22	23	24	25
BAHMAN 1361	26	27	28	29	30	*1*	2
	3	4	5	6	7	8	9
	10	11	12	13	14	15	16
	17	18	19	20	21	22	23
	24	25	26	27	28	29	30
ESFAND 1361	*1*	2	3	4	5	6	7
	8	9	10	11	12	13	14
	15	16	17	18	19	20	21
	22	23	24	25	26	27	28
FARVARDĪN 1362	29	*1*[a]	2	3	4	5	6
	7	8	9	10	11	12	13[b]
	14	15	16	17	18	19	20
	21	22	23	24	25	26	27
ORDĪBEHEŠT 1362	28	29	30	31	*1*	2	3
	4	5	6	7	8	9	10
	11	12	13	14	15	16	17
	18	19	20	21	22	23	24
	25	26	27	28	29	30	31
XORDĀD 1362	*1*	2	3	4	5	6	7
	8	9	10	11	12	13	14
	15	16	17	18	19	20	21
	22	23	24	25	26	27	28
TĪR 1362	29	30	31	*1*	2	3	4
	5	6	7	8	9	10	11
	12	13	14	15	16	17	18
	19	20	21	22	23	24	25
MORDĀD 1362	26	27	28	29	30	31	*1*
	2	3	4	5	6	7	8
	9	10	11	12	13	14	15
	16	17	18	19	20	21	22
	23	24	25	26	27	28	29
SHAHRĪVAR 1362	30	31	*1*	2	3	4	5
	6	7	8	9	10	11	12
	13	14	15	16	17	18	19
	20	21	22	23	24	25	26
MEHR 1362	27	28	29	30	31	*1*	2
	3	4	5	6	7	8	9
	10	11	12	13	14	15	16
	17	18	19	20	21	22	23
	24	25	26	27	28	29	30
ABĀN 1362	*1*	2	3	4	5	6	7
	8	9	10	11	12	13	14
	15	16	17	18	19	20	21
	22	23	24	25	26	27	28
ĀZAR 1362	29	30	*1*	2	3	4	5
	6	7	8	9	10	11	12
	13	14	15	16	17	18	19
	20	21	22	23	24	25	26
DEY 1362	27	28	29	30	*1*	2	3
	4	5	6	7	8	9	10

HINDU LUNAR 2039‡/2040

Month	Sun	Mon	Tue	Wed	Thu	Fri	Sat
MĀRGAŚĪRA 2039	11	12	13	14	15	16	17
	18	**19**	21	22	23	24	25
	26	27	28	29	*29*	30	1
PAUSHA 2039	2	3	4	5	6	7	8
	9	10	11	12	**13**	15	16
	17	18	19	20	21	22	23
	24	25	26	27	28	29	30
LEAP PHĀLGUNA 2039	1	2	*2*	3	4	5	6
	7	9	10	11	12	13	14
	15	16	17	18	19	20	21
	22	23	24	25	26	27	28[h]
PHĀLGUNA 2039	29	30	1	2	3	4	5
	6	7	8	9	10	11	**12**
	14	15[i]	16	17	18	19	20
	21	22	23	24	25	*25*	26
CHAITRA 2040	27	28	29	30	1[a]	2	3
	4	**5**	7	8	9[b]	10	11
	12	13	14	15	16	17	18
	19	20	21	22	23	24	25
VAIŚĀKHA 2040	26	27	28	29	30	1	2
	3	4	5	6	7	8	**9**
	11	12	13	14	15	16	17
	18	19	20	*20*	21	22	23
	24	25	26	27	28	29	30
JYAISHTHA 2040	1	**2**	4	5	6	7	8
	9	10	11	12	13	14	15
	16	17	18	19	20	21	22
	23	24	25	26	27	28	29
ĀSHĀDHA 2040	30	1	2	3	**4**	6	7
	8	9	10	11	12	13	14
	15	16	17	*17*	18	19	20
	21	22	23	24	25	26	**27**
ŚRĀVAṆA 2040	29	30	1	2	3	4	5
	6	7	8	9	10	11	12
	13	14	15	16	17	18	19
	20	21	22	23[c]	24	25	26
BHĀDRAPADA 2040	27	28	29	**30**	2	3	4[d]
	5	6	7	8	9	10	11
	12	13	*13*	14	15	16	17
	18	19	20	21	22	23	**24**
ĀŚVINA 2040	26	27	28	29	30	1	2
	3	4	5	6	7	8[e]	9[e]
	10[e]	11	12	13	14	15	16
	17	18	19	20	21	22	23
KĀRTTIKA 2040	24	25	26	27	**28**	30	1[f]
	2	3	4	5	6	7	*7*
	8	9	10	11	12	13	14
	15	16	17	18	19	20	**21**
	23	24	25	26	27	28	29
MĀRGAŚĪRA 2040	30	1	2	3	4	5	6
	7	8	9	10	*10*	11[g]	12
	13	14	**15**	17	18	19	20
	21	22	23	24	25	26	27

HINDU SOLAR 1904‡/1905

Month	Sun	Mon	Tue	Wed	Thu	Fri	Sat
PAUSHA 1904	11	12	13	14	15	16	17
	18	19	20	21	22	23	24
MĀGHA 1904	25	26	27	28	29	1[b]	2
	3	4	5	6	7	8	9
	10	11	12	13	14	15	16
	17	18	19	20	21	22	23
PHĀLGUNA 1904	24	25	26	27	28	29	1
	2	3	4	5	6	7	8
	9	10	11	12	13	14	15
	16	17	18	19	20	21	22
	23	24	25	26	27	28	29
CHAITRA 1904	30	1	2	3	4	5	6
	7	8	9	10	11	12	13
	14	15	16	17	18	19	20
	21	22	23	24	25	26	27
VAIŚĀKHA 1905	28	29	30	31	1[a]	2	3
	4	5	6	7	8	9	10
	11	12	13	14	15	16	17
	18	19	20	21	22	23	24
	25	26	27	28	29	30	31
JYAISHTHA 1905	1	2	3	4	5	6	7
	8	9	10	11	12	13	14
	15	16	17	18	19	20	21
	22	23	24	25	26	27	28
ĀSHĀDHA 1905	29	30	31	1	2	3	4
	5	6	7	8	9	10	11
	12	13	14	15	16	17	18
	19	20	21	22	23	24	25
	26	27	28	29	30	31	32
ŚRĀVAṆA 1905	1	2	3	4	5	6	7
	8	9	10	11	12	13	14
	15	16	17	18	19	20	21
	22	23	24	25	26	27	28
BHĀDRAPADA 1905	29	30	31	1	2	3	4
	5	6	7	8	9	10	11
	12	13	14	15	16	17	18
	19	20	21	22	23	24	25
ĀŚVINA 1905	26	27	28	29	30	31	1
	2	3	4	5	6	7	8
	9	10	11	12	13	14	15
	16	17	18	19	20	21	22
	23	24	25	26	27	28	29
KĀRTTIKA 1905	30	31	1	2	3	4	5
	6	7	8	9	10	11	12
	13	14	15	16	17	18	19
	20	21	22	23	24	25	26
MĀRGAŚĪRA 1905	27	28	29	1	2	3	4
	5	6	7	8	9	10	11
	12	13	14	15	16	17	18
	19	20	21	22	23	24	25
PAUSHA 1905	26	27	28	29	30	1	2
	3	4	5	6	7	8	9
	10	11	12	13	14	15	16

ISLAMIC (ASTRONOMICAL) 1403‡/1404

Month	Sun	Mon	Tue	Wed	Thu	Fri	Sat
RABĪʿ I 1403	10	11	12	13	14	15	16
	17	18	19	20	21	22	23
	24	25	26	27	28	29	30
RABĪʿ II 1403	*1*	2	3	4	5	6	7
	8	9	10	11	12	13	14
	15	16	17	18	19	20	21
	22	23	24	25	26	27	28
JUMĀDĀ I 1403	29	*1*	2	3	4	5	6
	7	8	9	10	11	12	13
	14	15	16	17	18	19	20
	21	22	23	24	25	26	27
JUMĀDĀ II 1403	28	29	30	*1*	2	3	4
	5	6	7	8	9	10	11
	12	13	14	15	16	17	18
	19	20	21	22	23	24	25
RAJAB 1403	26	27	28	29	*30*	1	2
	3	4	5	6	7	8	9
	10	11	12	13	14	15	16
	17	18	19	20	21	22	23
SHAʿBĀN 1403	24	25	26	27[d]	28	29	*1*
	2	3	4	5	6	7	8
	9	10	11	12	13	14	15
	16	17	18	19	20	21	22
	23	24	25	26	27	28	29
RAMAḌĀN 1403	*1*[e]	2	3	4	5	6	7
	8	9	10	11	12	13	14
	15	16	17	18	19	20	21
	22	23	24	25	26	27	28
SHAWWĀL 1403	29	30	*1*[f]	2	3	4	5
	6	7	8	9	10	11	12
	13	14	15	16	17	18	19
	20	21	22	23	24	25	26
DHU AL-QAʿDA 1403	27	28	29	*1*	2	3	4
	5	6	7	8	9	10	11
	12	13	14	15	16	17	18
	19	20	21	22	23	24	25
DHU AL-ḤIJJA 1403	26	27	28	29	1	2	3
	4	5	6	7	8	9	10[g]
	11	12	13	14	15	16	17
	18	19	20	21	22	23	24
MUḤARRAM 1404	25	26	27	28	29	30	*1*[a]
	2	3	4	5	6	7	8
	9	10[b]	11	12	13	14	15
	16	17	18	19	20	21	22
	23	24	25	26	27	28	29
ṢAFAR 1404	1	2	3	4	5	6	7
	8	9	10	11	12	13	14
	15	16	17	18	19	20	21
	22	23	24	25	26	27	28
RABĪʿ I 1404	29	30	*1*	2	3	4	5
	6	7	8	9	10	11	12[c]
	13	14	15	16	17	18	19
	20	21	22	23	24	25	26

GREGORIAN 1983

Julian (Sun)	Sun	Mon	Tue	Wed	Thu	Fri	Sat	Month
Dec 13	26	27	28	29	30	31	1	JANUARY 1983
	2	3	4	5	6	7[a]	8	
Dec 27	9	10	11	12	13	14[b]	15	
	16	17	18	19	20	21	22	
Jan 10	23	24	25	26	27	28	29	
	30	31	1	2	3	4	5	FEBRUARY 1983
Jan 24	6	7	8	9	10	11	12	
	13	14	15	16[c]	17	18	19	
Feb 7	20	21	22	23	24	25	26	
	27	28	1	2	3	4	5	MARCH 1983
Feb 21	6	7	8	9	10	11	12	
	13	14	15	16	17	18	19	
Mar 7	20	21	22	23	24	25	26	
	27[d]	28	29	30	31	1	2	APRIL 1983
Mar 21	3[e]	4	5	6	7	8	9	
	10	11	12	13	14	15	16	
Apr 4	17	18	19	20	21	22	23	
	24	25	26	27	28	29	30	
Apr 18	1	2	3	4	5	6	7	MAY 1983
	8[f]	9	10	11	12	13	14	
May 2	15	16	17	18	19	20	21	
	22	23	24	25	26	27	28	
May 16	29	30	31	1	2	3	4	JUNE 1983
	5	6	7	8	9	10	11	
May 30	12	13	14	15	16	17	18	
	19	20	21	22	23	24	25	
Jun 13	26	27	28	29	30	1	2	JULY 1983
	3	4	5	6	7	8	9	
Jun 27	10	11	12	13	14	15	16	
	17	18	19	20	21	22	23	
Jul 11	24	25	26	27	28	29	30	
	31	1	2	3	4	5	6	AUGUST 1983
Jul 25	7	8	9	10	11	12	13	
	14	15	16	17	18	19	20	
Aug 8	21	22	23	24	25	26	27	
	28	29	30	31	1	2	3	SEPTEMBER 1983
Aug 22	4	5	6	7	8	9	10	
	11	12	13	14	15	16	17	
Sep 5	18	19	20	21	22	23	24	
	25	26	27	28	29	30	1	OCTOBER 1983
Sep 19	2	3	4	5	6	7	8	
	9	10	11	12	13	14	15	
Oct 3	16	17	18	19	20	21	22	
	23	24	25	26	27	28	29	
Oct 17	30	31	1	2	3	4	5	NOVEMBER 1983
	6	7	8	9	10	11	12	
Oct 31	13	14	15	16	17	18	19	
	20	21	22	23	24	25	26	
Nov 14	27[g]	28	29	30	1	2	3	DECEMBER 1983
	4	5	6	7	8	9	10	
Nov 28	11	12	13	14	15	16	17	
	18	19	20	21	22	23	24	
Dec 12	25[h]	26	27	28	29	30	31	

Persian: ‡Leap year; [a]New Year; [b]Sizdeh Bedar

Hindu Lunar: ‡Leap year; [a]New Year (Rudhirodgārin); [b]Birthday of Rāma; [c]Birthday of Krishna; [d]Ganēśa Chaturthī; [e]Dashara; [f]Diwali; [g]Birthday of Vishnu; [h]Night of Śiva; [i]Holi

Hindu Solar: ‡Leap year; [a]New Year (Dhātṛi); [b]Pongal

Islamic: ‡Leap year; [a]New Year; [b]ʿAshūrāʾ; [c]Prophet's Birthday; [d]Ascent of the Prophet; [e]Start of Ramaḍān; [f]ʿId al-Fiṭr; [g]ʿId al-ʾAḍḥā

Gregorian: [a]Orthodox Christmas; [b]Julian New Year; [c]Ash Wednesday; [d]Feast of Orthodoxy; [e]Easter; [f]Orthodox Easter; [g]Advent; [h]Christmas

1984

Gregorian 1984[‡]	Sun	Mon	Tue	Wed	Thu	Fri	Sat	Lunar Phases	ISO WEEK (Mon)	JULIAN DAY (Sun noon)
January 1984	1[a]	2	●	4	5	6	7	5:16	1	2445701
	8	9	10	◐	12	13	14	9:48	2	2445708
	15	16	17	○	19	20	21	14:05	3	2445715
	22	23	24	◑	26	27	28	4:48	4	2445722
	29	30	31	●	2	3	4	23:46	5	2445729
February 1984	5	6	7	8	9	◐	11	3:59	6	2445736
	12	13	14	15	16	○	18	0:41	7	2445743
	19	20	21	22	◑	24	25	17:12	8	2445750
	26	27	28	29	1	●	3	18:31	9	2445757
March 1984	4	5	6	7	8	9	◐	18:28	10	2445764
	11	12	13	14	15	16	○	10:10	11	2445771
	18	19	20[b]	21	22	23	◑	7:58	12	2445778
	25	26	27	28	29	30	31		13	2445785
April 1984	●	2	3	4	5	6	7	12:09	14	2445792
	8	◐	10	11	12	13	14	4:51	15	2445799
	○	16	17	18	19	20	21	19:11	16	2445806
	22	◑	24	25	26	27	28	0:26	17	2445813
	29	30	●	2	3	4	5	3:45	18	2445820
May 1984	6	7	◐	9	10	11	12	11:50	19	2445827
	13	14	○	16	17	18	19	4:29	20	2445834
	20	21	◑	23	24	25	26	17:45	21	2445841
	27	28	29	●	31	1	2	16:48	22	2445848
June 1984	3	4	5	◐	7	8	9	16:42	23	2445855
	10	11	12	○	14	15	16	14:42	24	2445862
	17	18	19	20	◑[c]	22	23	11:10	25	2445869
	24	25	26	27	28	●	30	3:19	26	2445876
July 1984	1	2	3	4	◐	6	7	21:04	27	2445883
	8	9	10	11	12	○	14	2:20	28	2445890
	15	16	17	18	19	20	◑	4:01	29	2445897
	22	23	24	25	26	27	●	11:51	30	2445904
	29	30	31	1	2	3	◐	2:33	31	2445911
August 1984	5	6	7	8	9	10	○	15:43	32	2445918
	12	13	14	15	16	17	18		33	2445925
	◑	20	21	22	23	24	25	19:40	34	2445932
	●	27	28	29	30	31	1	19:26	35	2445939
September 1984	◐	3	4	5	6	7	8	10:30	36	2445946
	9	○	11	12	13	14	15	7:01	37	2445953
	16	17	◑	19	20	21	22[d]	9:31	38	2445960
	23	24	●	26	27	28	29	3:11	39	2445967
	30	◐	2	3	4	5	6	21:53	40	2445974
October 1984	7	8	○	10	11	12	13	23:58	41	2445981
	14	15	16	◑	18	19	20	21:14	42	2445988
	21	22	23	●	25	26	27	12:08	43	2445995
	28	29	30	◐	1	2	3	13:07	44	2446002
November 1984	4	5	6	7	○	9	10	17:43	45	2446009
	11	12	13	14	15	◑	17	6:59	46	2446016
	18	19	20	21	●	23	24	22:57	47	2446023
	25	26	27	28	29	◐	1	8:00	48	2446030
December 1984	2	3	4	5	6	7	○	10:53	49	2446037
	9	10	11	12	13	14	◑	15:25	50	2446044
	16	17	18	19	20	21[e]	●	11:47	51	2446051
	23	24	25	26	27	28	29		52	2446058
	◐	31	1	2	3	4	5	5:27	1	2446065

ISO WEEK	Hebrew 5744[‡]/5745	Sun	Mon	Tue	Wed	Thu	Fri	Sat	Molad
1		26	27	28	29	1	2	3	Tue 17h17m13p
2		4	5	6	7	8	9	10	
3	Shevat 5744	11	12	13	14	15	16	17	
4		18	19	20	21	22	23	24	
5		25	26	27	28	29	30	1	Thu 6h1m14p
6		2	3	4	5	6	7	8	
7	Adar I 5744	9	10	11	12	13	14	15	
8		16	17	18	19	20	21	22	
9		23	24	25	26	27	28	29	
10		30	1	2	3	4	5	6	Fri 18h45m15p
11		7	8	9	10	11	12	13	
12	Adar II 5744	14[f]	15	16	17	18	19	20	
13		21	22	23	24	25	26	27	
14		28	29	1	2	3	4	5	Sun 7h29m16p
15		6	7	8	9	10	11	12	
16	Nisan 5744	13	14	15[g]	16	17	18	19	
17		20	21	22	23	24	25	26	
18		27	28	29	30	1	2	3	Mon 20h13m17p
19		4	5	6	7	8	9	10	
20	Iyar 5744	11	12	13	14	15	16	17	
21		18	19	20	21	22	23	24	
22		25	26	27	28	29	1	2	Wed 8h58m0p
23		3	4	5	6[h]	7	8	9	
24	Sivan 5744	10	11	12	13	14	15	16	
25		17	18	19	20	21	22	23	
26		24	25	26	27	28	29	30	
27		1	2	3	4	5	6	7	Thu 21h42m1p
28		8	9	10	11	12	13	14	
29	Tammuz 5744	15	16	17	18	19	20	21	
30		22	23	24	25	26	27	28	
31		29	1	2	3	4	5	6	Sat 10h26m2p
32		7	8	9[i]	10	11	12	13	
33	Av 5744	14	15	16	17	18	19	20	
34		21	22	23	24	25	26	27	
35		28	29	30	1	2	3	4	Sun 23h10m3p
36		5	6	7	8	9	10	11	
37	Elul 5744	12	13	14	15	16	17	18	
38		19	20	21	22	23	24	25	
39		26	27	28	29	1[a]	2[a]	3	Tue 11h54m4p
40		4	5	6	7	8	9	10[b]	
41	Tishri 5745	11	12	13	14	15[c]	16	17	
42		18	19	20	21	22	23	24	
43		25	26	27	28	29	30	1	Thu 0h38m5p
44		2	3	4	5	6	7	8	
45	Heshvan 5745	9	10	11	12	13	14	15	
46		16	17	18	19	20	21	22	
47		23	24	25	26	27	28	29	
48		1	2	3	4	5	6	7	Fri 13h22m6p
49		8	9	10	11[d]	12	13	14	
50	Kislev 5745	15	16	17	18	19	20	21	
51		22	23	24	25[e]	26[e]	27[e]	28[e]	
52	Teveth 5745	29[e]	30[e]	1[e]	2[e]	3	4	5	Sun 2h6m7p
1		6	7	8	9	10	11	12	

ISO WEEK	Chinese Guĭ-Hài/Jiă-Zĭ[‡]	Sun	Mon	Tue	Wed	Thu	Fri	Sat	Solar Term
1		29	30	1	2	3	4	5	Xiăo hán
2		6	7	8	9	10	11	12	
3	Month 12 Guĭ-Hài	13	14	15	16	17	18	**19**	Dà hán
4		20	21	22	23	24	25	26	
5		27	28	29*	30	1[a]	2	3	Lì chūn
6		4	5	6	7	8	9	10	
7	Month 1 Jiă-Zĭ	11	12	13	14	15[b]	16	17	
8		**18**	19	20	21	22	23	24	Yŭ shuĭ
9		25	26	27	28	29	30	1	
10		2	3	4	5	6	7	8	Jīng zhé
11	Month 2 Jiă-Zĭ	9	10	11	12	13	14	15	
12		16	17	**18**	19	20	21	22	Chūn fēn
13		23	24	25	26	27	28	29*	
14		1	2	3	4[c]	5	6	7	Qīng míng
15	Month 3 Jiă-Zĭ	8	9	10	11	12	13	14	
16		15	16	17	18	19	**20**	21	Gŭ yŭ
17		22	23	24	25	26	27	28	
18		29	30	1	2	3	4	5	Lì xià
19	Month 4 Jiă-Zĭ	6	7	8	9	10	11	12	
20		13	14	15	16	17	18	19	
21		20	**21**	22	23	24	25	26	Xiăo măn
22		27	28	29	30*	1	2	3	
23		4	5[d]	6	7	8	9	10	Máng zhòng
24	Month 5 Jiă-Zĭ	11	12	13	14	15	16	17	
25		18	19	20	21	**22**	23	24	Xià zhì
26		25	26	27	28	29	1	2	
27		3	4	5	6	7	8	9	Xiăo shŭ
28	Month 6 Jiă-Zĭ	10	11	12	13	14	15	16	
29		17	18	19	20	21	22	23	
30		**24**	25	26	27	28	29	1	Dà shŭ
31		2*	3	4	5	6	7[e]	8	
32	Month 7 Jiă-Zĭ	9	10	*11*	12	13	14	15[f]	Lì qiū
33		16	17	18	19	20	21	22	
34		23	24	25	26	**27**	28	29	Chŭ shŭ
35		30	1	2	3	4	5	6	
36		7	8	9	10	11	*12*	13	Bái lù
37	Month 8 Jiă-Zĭ	14	15[g]	16	17	18	19	20	
38		21	22	23	24	25	26	27	
39		**28**	29	1	2	3*	4	5	Qiū fēn
40		6	7	8	9[h]	10	11	12	
41	Month 9 Jiă-Zĭ	13	*14*	15	16	17	18	19	Hán lù
42		20	21	22	23	24	25	26	
43		27	28	**29**	1	2	3	4	Shuāng jiàng
44		5	6	7	8	9	10	11	
45	Month 10 Jiă-Zĭ	12	13	14	*15*	16	17	18	Lì dōng
46		19	20	21	22	23	24	25	
47		26	27	28	29	**30**	1	2	Xiăo xuě
48		3	4*	5	6	7	8	9	
49	Leap Month 10 Jiă-Zĭ	10	11	12	13	14	*15*	16	Dà xuě
50		17	18	19	20	21	22	23	
51		24	25	26	27	28	29	1[i]	Dōng zhì
52	Month 11 Jiă-Zĭ	2	3	4	5	6	7	8	
1		9	10	11	12	13	14	*15*	Xiăo hán

ISO WEEK	Coptic 1700/1701	Sun	Mon	Tue	Wed	Thu	Fri	Sat	Ethiopic 1976/1977
1		22	23	24	25	26	27	28	Tākhśāś 1976
2	Koiak 1700	29[c]	30	1	2	3	4	5	
3		6[d]	7	8	9	10	11[e]	12	
4	Tōbe 1700	13	14	15	16	17	18	19	Ter 1976
5		20	21	22	23	24	25	26	
6		27	28	29	30	1	2	3	
7		4	5	6	7	8	9	10	
8	Meshir 1700	11	12	13	14	15	16	17	Yakātit 1976
9		18	19	20	21	22	23	24	
10		25	26	27	28	29	30	1	
11		2	3	4	5	6	7	8	
12	Paremotep 1700	9	10	11	12	13	14	15	Magābit 1976
13		16	17	18	19	20	21	22	
14		23	24	25	26	27	28	29	
15		30	1	2	3	4	5	6	
16		7	8	9	10	11	12	13	
17	Parmoute 1700	14[f]	15	16	17	18	19	20	Miyāzyā 1976
18		21	22	23	24	25	26	27	
19		28	29[g]	30	1	2	3	4	
20		5	6	7	8	9	10	11	
21	Pashons 1700	12	13	14	15	16	17	18	Genbot 1976
22		19	20	21	22	23	24	25	
23		26	27	28	29	30	1	2	
24		3	4	5	6	7	8	9	
25	Paōne 1700	10	11	12	13	14	15	16	Sanē 1976
26		17	18	19	20	21	22	23	
27		24	25	26	27	28	29	30	
28		1	2	3	4	5	6	7	
29		8	9	10	11	12	13	14	
30	Epēp 1700	15	16	17	18	19	20	21	Hamlē 1976
31		22	23	24	25	26	27	28	
32		29	30	1	2	3	4	5	
33		6	7	8	9	10	11	12	
34	Mesorē 1700	13[h]	14	15	16	17	18	19	Naḥasē 1976
35		20	21	22	23	24	25	26	
36		27	28	29	30	1	2	3	
37	Epag. 1700	4	5	1[a]	2	3	4	5	Pāg. 1976
38		6	7	8	9	10	11	12	
39	Thoout 1701	13	14	15	16	17[b]	18	19	Maskaram 1977
40		20	21	22	23	24	25	26	
41		27	28	29	30	1	2	3	
42		4	5	6	7	8	9	10	
43	Paope 1701	11	12	13	14	15	16	17	Teqemt 1977
44		18	19	20	21	22	23	24	
45		25	26	27	28	29	30	1	
46		2	3	4	5	6	7	8	
47	Athōr 1701	9	10	11	12	13	14	15	Hedār 1977
48		16	17	18	19	20	21	22	
49		23	24	25	26	27	28	29	
50		30	1	2	3	4	5	6	
51	Koiak 1701	7	8	9	10	11	12	13	Tākhśāś 1977
52		14	15	16	17	18	19	20	
1		21	22	23	24	25	26	27	

[‡]Leap year
[a]New Year
[b]Spring (10:24)
[c]Summer (5:02)
[d]Autumn (20:33)
[e]Winter (16:23)
● New moon
◐ First quarter moon
○ Full moon
◑ Last quarter moon

[‡]Leap year
[a]New Year
[b]Yom Kippur
[c]Sukkot
[d]Winter starts
[e]Ḥanukkah
[f]Purim
[g]Passover
[h]Shavuot
[i]Fast of Av

[‡]Leap year
[a]New Year (4682, Rat)
[b]Lantern Festival
[c]Qīngmíng
[d]Dragon Festival
[e]Qīqiǎo
[f]Hungry Ghosts
[g]Mid-Autumn Festival
[h]Double-Ninth Festival
[i]Dōngzhì
*Start of 60-name cycle

[a]New Year
[b]Building of the Cross
[c]Christmas
[d]Jesus's Circumcision
[e]Epiphany
[f]Easter
[g]Mary's Announcement
[h]Jesus's Transfiguration

PERSIAN (ASTRONOMICAL) 1362‡/1363

Month	Sun	Mon	Tue	Wed	Thu	Fri	Sat
DEY 1362	11	12	13	14	15	16	17
	18	19	20	21	22	23	24
	25	26	27	28	29	30	1
BAHMAN 1362	2	3	4	5	6	7	8
	9	10	11	12	13	14	15
	16	17	18	19	20	21	22
	23	24	25	26	27	28	29
ESFAND 1362	30	1	2	3	4	5	6
	7	8	9	10	11	12	13
	14	15	16	17	18	19	20
	21	22	23	24	25	26	27
FARVARDIN 1363	28	29	30	1[a]	2	3	4
	5	6	7	8	9	10	11
	12	13[b]	14	15	16	17	18
	19	20	21	22	23	24	25
ORDIBEHEŠT 1363	26	27	28	29	30	31	1
	2	3	4	5	6	7	8
	9	10	11	12	13	14	15
	16	17	18	19	20	21	22
	23	24	25	26	27	28	29
XORDĀD 1363	30	31	1	2	3	4	5
	6	7	8	9	10	11	12
	13	14	15	16	17	18	19
	20	21	22	23	24	25	26
TĪR 1363	27	28	29	30	31	1	2
	3	4	5	6	7	8	9
	10	11	12	13	14	15	16
	17	18	19	20	21	22	23
	24	25	26	27	28	29	30
MORDĀD 1363	31	1	2	3	4	5	6
	7	8	9	10	11	12	13
	14	15	16	17	18	19	20
	21	22	23	24	25	26	27
SHAHRĪVAR 1363	28	29	30	31	1	2	3
	4	5	6	7	8	9	10
	11	12	13	14	15	16	17
	18	19	20	21	22	23	24
	25	26	27	28	29	30	31
MEHR 1363	1	2	3	4	5	6	7
	8	9	10	11	12	13	14
	15	16	17	18	19	20	21
	22	23	24	25	26	27	28
ĀBĀN 1363	29	30	1	2	3	4	5
	6	7	8	9	10	11	12
	13	14	15	16	17	18	19
	20	21	22	23	24	25	26
ĀZAR 1363	27	28	29	30	1	2	3
	4	5	6	7	8	9	10
	11	12	13	14	15	16	17
	18	19	20	21	22	23	24
DEY 1363	25	26	27	28	29	30	1
	2	3	4	5	6	7	8
	9	10	11	12	13	14	15

‡Leap year
[a]New Year
[b]Sizdeh Bedar

HINDU LUNAR 2040/2041

Month	Sun	Mon	Tue	Wed	Thu	Fri	Sat
PAUSHA 2040	28	29	30	1	2	3	4
	5	6	7	8	9	10	11
	12	13	14	15	16	17	18
	19	20	22	23	24	25	26
MĀGHA 2040	27	28	29	30	1	2	2
	3	4	5	6	7	8	9
	10	11	12	13	14	16	17
	18	19	20	21	22	23	24
PHĀLGUNA 2040	25	26	27	28[h]	29	30	1
	2	3	4	5	5	6	7
	9	10	11	12	13	14	15[i]
	16	17	18	19	20	22	23
	24	24	25	26	27	28	29
CHAITRA 2041	30	1[a]	2	3	4	5	6
	7	8	9[b]	10	11	12	14
	15	16	17	18	19	20	21
	22	23	24	25	26	27	28
VAIŚĀKHA 2041	28	29	30	1	2	3	4
	5	7	8	9	10	11	12
	13	14	15	16	17	18	19
	20	21	22	23	24	25	26
JYAISHTHA 2041	27	28	29	30	1	2	3
	4	5	6	7	8	9	11
	12	13	14	15	16	17	18
	19	20	21	22	23	24	24
ĀSHĀDHA 2041	25	26	27	28	29	30	1
	3	4	5	6	7	8	9
	10	11	12	13	14	15	16
	17	18	19	20	21	22	23
	24	25	26	27	28	29	30
ŚRĀVANA 2041	1	2	3	4	6	7	8
	9	10	11	12	13	14	15
	16	17	18	19	20	21	21
	22	23[c]	24	25	26	27	29
BHĀDRAPADA 2041	30	1	2	3	4[d]	5	6
	7	8	9	10	11	12	13
	14	15	16	17	18	19	20
	21	22	23	24	25	26	27
ĀŚVINA 2041	28	29	30	1	3	4	5
	6	7	8[e]	9[e]	10[e]	11	12
	13	14	15	16	16	17	18
	19	20	21	22	23	24	26
KĀRTTIKA 2041	27	28	29	30	1[f]	2	3
	4	5	6	7	8	9	10
	11	12	13	14	15	16	17
	18	19	20	21	22	23	24
MĀRGAŚIRA 2041	25	26	27	28	30	1	2
	3	4	5	6	7	8	9
	10	10	11[g]	12	13	14	15
	16	17	18	19	20	21	22
PAUSHA 2041	24	25	26	27	28	29	30
	1	2	3	4	5	6	7
	8	9	10	11	12	13	13

[a]New Year (Raktāksha)
[b]Birthday of Rāma
[c]Birthday of Krishna
[d]Ganēśa Chaturthī
[e]Dashara
[f]Diwali
[g]Birthday of Vishnu
[h]Night of Śiva
[i]Holi

HINDU SOLAR 1905/1906

Month	Sun	Mon	Tue	Wed	Thu	Fri	Sat
PAUSHA 1905	17	18	19	20	21	22	23
	24	25	26	27	28	29	1[b]
MĀGHA 1905	2	3	4	5	6	7	8
	9	10	11	12	13	14	15
	16	17	18	19	20	21	22
	23	24	25	26	27	28	29
PHĀLGUNA 1905	30	1	2	3	4	5	6
	7	8	9	10	11	12	13
	14	15	16	17	18	19	20
	21	22	23	24	25	26	27
CHAITRA 1905	28	29	1	2	3	4	5
	6	7	8	9	10	11	12
	13	14	15	16	17	18	19
	20	21	22	23	24	25	26
VAIŚĀKHA 1906	27	28	29	30	31	1[a]	2
	3	4	5	6	7	8	9
	10	11	12	13	14	15	16
	17	18	19	20	21	22	23
	24	25	26	27	28	29	30
JYAISHTHA 1906	31	1	2	3	4	5	6
	7	8	9	10	11	12	13
	14	15	16	17	18	19	20
	21	22	23	24	25	26	27
ĀSHĀDHA 1906	28	29	30	31	1	2	3
	4	5	6	7	8	9	10
	11	12	13	14	15	16	17
	18	19	20	21	22	23	24
	25	26	27	28	29	30	31
ŚRĀVAṆA 1906	32	1	2	3	4	5	6
	7	8	9	10	11	12	13
	14	15	16	17	18	19	20
	21	22	23	24	25	26	27
BHĀDRAPADA 1906	28	29	30	31	1	2	3
	4	5	6	7	8	9	10
	11	12	13	14	15	16	17
	18	19	20	21	22	23	24
	25	26	27	28	29	30	31
ĀŚVINA 1906	1	2	3	4	5	6	7
	8	9	10	11	12	13	14
	15	16	17	18	19	20	21
	22	23	24	25	26	27	28
KĀRTTIKA 1906	29	30	31	1	2	3	4
	5	6	7	8	9	10	11
	12	13	14	15	16	17	18
	19	20	21	22	23	24	25
MĀRGAŚIRA 1906	26	27	28	29	30	1	2
	3	4	5	6	7	8	9
	10	11	12	13	14	15	16
	17	18	19	20	21	22	23
PAUSHA 1906	24	25	26	27	28	29	1
	2	3	4	5	6	7	8
	9	10	11	12	13	14	15
	16	17	18	19	20	21	22

[a]New Year (Īśvara)
[b]Pongal

ISLAMIC (ASTRONOMICAL) 1404/1405‡

Month	Sun	Mon	Tue	Wed	Thu	Fri	Sat
	27	28	29	30	1	2	3
RABĪ' II 1404	4	5	6	7	8	9	10
	11	12	13	14	15	16	17
	18	19	20	21	22	23	24
JUMĀDĀ I 1404	25	26	27	28	29	1	2
	3	4	5	6	7	8	9
	10	11	12	13	14	15	16
	17	18	19	20	21	22	23
	24	25	26	27	28	29	30
JUMĀDĀ II 1404	1	2	3	4	5	6	7
	8	9	10	11	12	13	14
	15	16	17	18	19	20	21
	22	23	24	25	26	27	28
RAJAB 1404	29	30	1	2	3	4	5
	6	7	8	9	10	11	12
	13	14	15	16	17	18	19
	20	21	22	23	24	25	26
SHA'BĀN 1404	27[d]	28	29	1	2	3	4
	5	6	7	8	9	10	11
	12	13	14	15	16	17	18
	19	20	21	22	23	24	25
RAMAḌĀN 1404	26	27	28	29	30	1[e]	2
	3	4	5	6	7	8	9
	10	11	12	13	14	15	16
	17	18	19	20	21	22	23
SHAWWĀL 1404	24	25	26	27	28	29	1[f]
	2	3	4	5	6	7	8
	9	10	11	12	13	14	15
	16	17	18	19	20	21	22
	23	24	25	26	27	28	29
DHU AL-QA'DA 1404	30	1	2	3	4	5	6
	7	8	9	10	11	12	13
	14	15	16	17	18	19	20
	21	22	23	24	25	26	27
DHU AL-ḤIJJA 1404	28	29	1	2	3	4	5
	6	7	8	9	10[g]	11	12
	13	14	15	16	17	18	19
	20	21	22	23	24	25	26
MUḤARRAM 1405	27	28	29	1[a]	2[å]	3	4
	5	6	7	8	9	10[b]	11
	12	13	14	15	16	17	18
	19	20	21	22	23	24	25
ṢAFAR 1405	26	27	28	29	30	1	2
	3	4	5	6	7	8	9
	10	11	12	13	14	15	16
	17	18	19	20	21	22	23
RABĪ' I 1405	24	25	26	27	28	29	1
	2	3	4	5	6	7	8
	9	10	11	12[c]	13	14	15
	16	17	18	19	20	21	22
	23	24	25	26	27	28	29
RABĪ' II 1405	30	1	2	3	4	5	6
	7	8	9	10	11	12	13

‡Leap year
[a]New Year
[å]New Year (Arithmetic)
[b]'Ashūrā'
[c]Prophet's Birthday
[d]Ascent of the Prophet
[e]Start of Ramaḍān
[f]'Īd al-Fiṭr
[g]'Īd al-'Aḍḥā

GREGORIAN 1984‡

Julian‡ (Sun)	Sun	Mon	Tue	Wed	Thu	Fri	Sat	Month
Dec 19	1	2	3	4	5	6	7[a]	
	8	9	10	11	12	13	14[b]	JANUARY 1984
Jan 2	15	16	17	18	19	20	21	
	22	23	24	25	26	27	28	
Jan 16	29	30	31	1	2	3	4	
	5	6	7	8	9	10	11	FEBRUARY 1984
Jan 30	12	13	14	15	16	17	18	
	19	20	21	22	23	24	25	
Feb 13	26	27	28	29	1	2	3	
	4	5	6	7[c]	8	9	10	MARCH 1984
Feb 27	11[d]	12	13	14	15	16	17	
	18	19	20	21	22	23	24	
Mar 12	25	26	27	28	29	30	31	
	1	2	3	4	5	6	7	
Mar 26	8	9	10	11	12	13	14	APRIL 1984
	15	16	17	18	19	20	21	
Apr 9	22[e]	23	24	25	26	27	28	
	29	30	1	2	3	4	5	
Apr 23	6	7	8	9	10	11	12	MAY 1984
	13	14	15	16	17	18	19	
May 7	20	21	22	23	24	25	26	
	27	28	29	30	31	1	2	
May 21	3	4	5	6	7	8	9	JUNE 1984
	10	11	12	13	14	15	16	
Jun 4	17	18	19	20	21	22	23	
	24	25	26	27	28	29	30	
Jun 18	1	2	3	4	5	6	7	
	8	9	10	11	12	13	14	JULY 1984
Jul 2	15	16	17	18	19	20	21	
	22	23	24	25	26	27	28	
Jul 16	29	30	31	1	2	3	4	
	5	6	7	8	9	10	11	AUGUST 1984
Jul 30	12	13	14	15	16	17	18	
	19	20	21	22	23	24	25	
Aug 13	26	27	28	29	30	31	1	
	2	3	4	5	6	7	8	
Aug 27	9	10	11	12	13	14	15	SEPTEMBER 1984
	16	17	18	19	20	21	22	
Sep 10	23	24	25	26	27	28	29	
	30	1	2	3	4	5	6	
Sep 24	7	8	9	10	11	12	13	OCTOBER 1984
	14	15	16	17	18	19	20	
Oct 8	21	22	23	24	25	26	27	
	28	29	30	31	1	2	3	
Oct 22	4	5	6	7	8	9	10	NOVEMBER 1984
	11	12	13	14	15	16	17	
Nov 5	18	19	20	21	22	23	24	
	25	26	27	28	29	30	1	
Nov 19	2[g]	3	4	5	6	7	8	DECEMBER 1984
	9	10	11	12	13	14	15	
Dec 3	16	17	18	19	20	21	22	
	23	24	25[h]	26	27	28	29	
Dec 17	30	31	1	2	3	4	5	

‡Leap year
[a]Orthodox Christmas
[b]Julian New Year
[c]Ash Wednesday
[d]Feast of Orthodoxy
[e]Easter (also Orthodox)
[g]Advent
[h]Christmas

1985

GREGORIAN 1985

Month	Sun	Mon	Tue	Wed	Thu	Fri	Sat	Lunar Phases	ISO WEEK (Mon)	JULIAN DAY (Sun noon)
JANUARY 1985	◐	31	1[a]	2	3	4	5	5:27	1	2446065
	6	○	8	9	10	11	12	2:16	2	2446072
	◑	14	15	16	17	18	19	23:27	3	2446079
	20	●	22	23	24	25	26	2:28	4	2446086
FEBRUARY 1985	27	28	◐	30	31	1	2	3:29	5	2446093
	3	4	○	6	7	8	9	15:19	6	2446100
	10	11	◑	13	14	15	16	7:57	7	2446107
	17	18	●	20	21	22	23	18:43	8	2446114
MARCH 1985	24	25	26	◐	28	1	2	23:41	9	2446121
	3	4	5	6	○	8	9	2:13	10	2446128
	10	11	12	◑	14	15	16	17:34	11	2446135
	17	18	19	20[b]	●	22	23	11:59	12	2446142
	24	25	26	27	28	◐	30	16:11	13	2446149
APRIL 1985	31	1	2	3	4	○	6	11:32	14	2446156
	7	8	9	10	11	◑	13	4:41	15	2446163
	14	15	16	17	18	19	●	5:22	16	2446170
	21	22	23	24	25	26	27		17	2446177
MAY 1985	◐	29	30	1	2	3	○	4:25 19:53	18	2446184
	5	6	7	8	9	10	◑	17:34	19	2446191
	12	13	14	15	16	17	18		20	2446198
	●	20	21	22	23	24	25	21:41	21	2446205
JUNE 1985	26	◐	28	29	30	31	1	12:56	22	2446212
	2	○	4	5	6	7	8	3:50	23	2446219
	9	◑	11	12	13	14	15	8:19	24	2446226
	16	17	●	19	20	21[c]	22	11:58	25	2446233
	23	24	◐	26	27	28	29	18:53	26	2446240
JULY 1985	30	1	○	3	4	5	6	12:08	27	2446247
	7	8	9	◑	11	12	13	0:49	28	2446254
	14	15	16	●	18	19	20	23:56	29	2446261
	21	22	23	◐	25	26	27	23:39	30	2446268
AUGUST 1985	28	29	30	○	1	2	3	21:41	31	2446275
	4	5	6	7	◑	9	10	18:29	32	2446282
	11	12	13	14	15	●	17	10:06	33	2446289
	18	19	20	21	22	◐	24	4:36	34	2446296
	25	26	27	28	29	○	31	9:27	35	2446303
SEPTEMBER 1985	1	2	3	4	5	6	◑	12:16	36	2446310
	8	9	10	11	12	13	●	19:20	37	2446317
	15	16	17	18	19	20	◐	11:03	38	2446324
	22	23[d]	24	25	26	27	28		39	2446331
OCTOBER 1985	○	30	1	2	3	4	5	0:08	40	2446338
	6	◑	8	9	10	11	12	5:04	41	2446345
	13	●	15	16	17	18	19	4:33	42	2446352
	◐	21	22	23	24	25	26	20:13	43	2446359
NOVEMBER 1985	27	○	29	30	31	1	2	17:37	44	2446366
	3	4	◑	6	7	8	9	20:07	45	2446373
	10	11	●	13	14	15	16	14:21	46	2446380
	17	18	◐	20	21	22	23	9:03	47	2446387
	24	25	26	○	28	29	30	12:42	48	2446394
DECEMBER 1985	1	2	3	4	◑	6	7	9:01	49	2446401
	8	9	10	11	●	13	14	0:55	50	2446408
	15	16	17	18	◐	20	21[e]	1:58	51	2446415
	22	23	24	25	26	○	28	7:30	52	2446422
	29	30	31	1	2	◑	4	19:47	1	2446429

HEBREW 5745/5746‡

ISO WEEK	Month	Sun	Mon	Tue	Wed	Thu	Fri	Sat	Molad
1	TEVETH 5745	6	7	8	9	10	11	12	
2		13	14	15	16	17	18	19	
3		20	21	22	23	24	25	26	
4	SHEVAT 5745	27	28	29	1	2	3	4	Mon $14^h50^m8^p$
5		5	6	7	8	9	10	11	
6		12	13	14	15	16	17	18	
7		19	20	21	22	23	24	25	
8	ADAR 5745	26	27	28	29	30	1	2	Wed $3^h34^m9^p$
9		3	4	5	6	7	8	9	
10		10	11	12	13	14[f]	15	16	
11		17	18	19	20	21	22	23	
12	NISAN 5745	24	25	26	27	28	29	1	Thu $16^h18^m10^p$
13		2	3	4	5	6	7	8	
14		9	10	11	12	13	14	15[g]	
15		16	17	18	19	20	21	22	
16		23	24	25	26	27	28	29	Sat $5^h2^m11^p$
17	IYYAR 5745	30	1	2	3	4	5	6	
18		7	8	9	10	11	12	13	
19		14	15	16	17	18	19	20	
20		21	22	23	24	25	26	27	
21	SIVAN 5745	28	29	1	2	3	4	5	Sun $17^h46^m12^p$
22		6[h]	7	8	9	10	11	12	
23		13	14	15	16	17	18	19	
24		20	21	22	23	24	25	26	
25	TAMMUZ 5745	27	28	29	30	1	2	3	Tue $6^h30^m13^p$
26		4	5	6	7	8	9	10	
27		11	12	13	14	15	16	17	
28		18	19	20	21	22	23	24	
29	AV 5745	25	26	27	28	29	1	2	Wed $19^h14^m14^p$
30		3	4	5	6	7	8	9	
31		10[i]	11	12	13	14	15	16	
32		17	18	19	20	21	22	23	
33		24	25	26	27	28	29	30	Fri $7^h58^m15^p$
34	ELUL 5745	1	2	3	4	5	6	7	
35		8	9	10	11	12	13	14	
36		15	16	17	18	19	20	21	
37		22	23	24	25	26	27	28	
38	TISHRI 5746	29	1[a]	2[a]	3	4	5	6	Sat $20^h42^m16^p$
39		7	8	9	10[b]	11	12	13	
40		14	15[c]	16	17	18	19	20	
41		21	22	23	24	25	26	27	
42	HESHVAN 5746	28	29	30	1	2	3	4	Mon $9^h26^m17^p$
43		5	6	7	8	9	10	11	
44		12	13	14	15	16	17	18	
45		19	20	21	22	23	24	25	
46	KISLEV 5746	26	27	28	29	1	2	3	Tue $22^h11^m0^p$
47		4	5	6	7	8	9	10	
48		11	12	13	14	15	16	17	
49		18	19	20	21	22[d]	23	24	
50	TEVETH 5746	25[e]	26[e]	27[e]	28[e]	29[e]	1[e]	2[e]	Thu $10^h55^m1^p$
51		3[e]	4	5	6	7	8	9	
52		10	11	12	13	14	15	16	
1		17	18	19	20	21	22	23	

CHINESE Jiǎ-Zǐ‡/Yǐ-Chǒu

ISO WEEK	Month	Sun	Mon	Tue	Wed	Thu	Fri	Sat	Solar Term
1	MONTH 11 Jiǎ-Zǐ	9	10	11	12	13	14	15	Xiǎo hán
2		16	17	18	19	20	21	22	
3		23	24	25	26	27	28	29	
4	MONTH 12 Jiǎ-Zǐ	30	1	2	3	4	5*	6	Dà hán
5		7	8	9	10	11	12	13	
6		14	15	16	17	18	19	20	Lì chūn
7		21	22	23	24	25	26	27	
8	MONTH 1 Yǐ-Chǒu	28	29	30	1[a]	2	3	4	Yǔ shuǐ
9		5	6	7	8	9	10	11	
10		12	13	14	15[b]	16	17	18	Jīng zhé
11		19	20	21	22	23	24	25	
12	MONTH 2 Yǐ-Chǒu	26	27	28	29	1	2	3	Chūn fēn
13		4	5	6*	7	8	9	10	
14		11	12	13	14	15	16[c]	17	Qīng míng
15		18	19	20	21	22	23	24	
16	MONTH 3 Yǐ-Chǒu	25	26	27	28	29	30	1	Gǔ yǔ
17		2	3	4	5	6	7	8	
18		9	10	11	12	13	14	15	
19		16	17	18	19	20	21	22	Lì xià
20		23	24	25	26	27	28	29	
21	MONTH 4 Yǐ-Chǒu	30	1	2	3	4	5	6*	Xiǎo mǎn
22		7	8	9	10	11	12	13	
23		14	15	16	17	18	19	20	Máng zhòng
24		21	22	23	24	25	26	27	
25	MONTH 5 Yǐ-Chǒu	28	29	1	2	3	4	5[d]	Xià zhì
26		6	7	8	9	10	11	12	
27		13	14	15	16	17	18	19	
28		20	21	22	23	24	25	26	Xiǎo shǔ
29	MONTH 6 Yǐ-Chǒu	27	28	29	30	1	2	3	
30		4	5	6	7*	8	9	10	Dà shǔ
31		11	12	13	14	15	16	17	
32		18	19	20	21	22	23	24	Lì qiū
33	MONTH 7 Yǐ-Chǒu	25	26	27	28	29	1	2	
34		3	4	5	6	7[e]	8	9	Chǔ shǔ
35		10	11	12	13	14	15[f]	16	
36		17	18	19	20	21	22	23	
37		24	25	26	27	28	29	30	Bái lù
38	MONTH 8 Yǐ-Chǒu	1	2	3	4	5	6	7	
39		8*	9	10	11	12	13	14	Qiū fēn
40		15[g]	16	17	18	19	20	21	
41		22	23	24	25	26	27	28	Hán lù
42	MONTH 9 Yǐ-Chǒu	29	1	2	3	4	5	6	
43		7	8	9[h]	10	11	12	13	Shuāng jiàng
44		14	15	16	17	18	19	20	
45		21	22	23	24	25	26	27	Lì dōng
46	MONTH 10 Yǐ-Chǒu	28	29	1	2	3	4	5	
47		6	7	8	9	10*	11	12	Xiǎo xuě
48		13	14	15	16	17	18	19	
49		20	21	22	23	24	25	26	Dà xuě
50	MONTH 11 Yǐ-Chǒu	27	28	29	30	1	2	3	
51		4	5	6	7	8	9	10	Dōng zhì
52		11[i]	12	13	14	15	16	17	
1		18	19	20	21	22	23	24	

COPTIC 1701/1702 — ETHIOPIC 1977/1978

ISO WEEK	Coptic Month	Sun	Mon	Tue	Wed	Thu	Fri	Sat	Ethiopic Month
1	KOIAK 1701	21	22	23	24	25	26	27	TĀKHŚĀŚ 1977
2	TŌBE 1701	28	29[c]	30	1	2	3	4	
3		5	6[d]	7	8	9	10	11[e]	
4		12	13	14	15	16	17	18	ṬER 1977
5		19	20	21	22	23	24	25	
6	MESHIR 1701	26	27	28	29	30	1	2	
7		3	4	5	6	7	8	9	YAKĀTIT 1977
8		10	11	12	13	14	15	16	
9		17	18	19	20	21	22	23	
10		24	25	26	27	28	29	30	
11	PAREMOTEP 1701	1	2	3	4	5	6	7	MAGĀBIT 1977
12		8	9	10	11	12	13	14	
13		15	16	17	18	19	20	21	
14		22	23	24	25	26	27	28	
15	PARMOUTE 1701	29	30	1	2	3	4	5	MIYĀZYĀ 1977
16		6[f]	7	8	9	10	11	12	
17		13	14	15	16	17	18	19	
18		20	21	22	23	24	25	26	
19	PASHONS 1701	27	28	29[g]	30	1	2	3	GENBOT 1977
20		4	5	6	7	8	9	10	
21		11	12	13	14	15	16	17	
22		18	19	20	21	22	23	24	
23	PAŌNE 1701	25	26	27	28	29	30	1	SANĒ 1977
24		2	3	4	5	6	7	8	
25		9	10	11	12	13	14	15	
26		16	17	18	19	20	21	22	
27		23	24	25	26	27	28	29	
28	EPĒP 1701	30	1	2	3	4	5	6	ḤAMLĒ 1977
29		7	8	9	10	11	12	13	
30		14	15	16	17	18	19	20	
31		21	22	23	24	25	26	27	
32	MESORĒ 1701	28	29	30	1	2	3	4	NAḤASĒ 1977
33		5	6	7	8	9	10	11	
34		12	13[h]	14	15	16	17	18	
35		19	20	21	22	23	24	25	
36	EPAG. 1701	26	27	28	29	30	1	2	PĀG. 1977
37	THOOUT 1702	3	4	5	1[a]	2	3	4	MASKARAM 1978
38		5	6	7	8	9	10	11	
39		12	13	14	15	16	17[b]	18	
40		19	20	21	22	23	24	25	
41	PAOPE 1702	26	27	28	29	30	1	2	ṬEQEMT 1978
42		3	4	5	6	7	8	9	
43		10	11	12	13	14	15	16	
44		17	18	19	20	21	22	23	
45		24	25	26	27	28	29	30	
46	ATHŌR 1702	1	2	3	4	5	6	7	ḪEDĀR 1978
47		8	9	10	11	12	13	14	
48		15	16	17	18	19	20	21	
49		22	23	24	25	26	27	28	
50	KOIAK 1702	29	30	1	2	3	4	5	TĀKHŚĀŚ 1978
51		6	7	8	9	10	11	12	
52		13	14	15	16	17	18	19	
1		20	21	22	23	24	25	26	

[a]New Year
[b]Spring (16:14)
[c]Summer (10:44)
[d]Autumn (2:07)
[e]Winter (22:07)
● New moon
◐ First quarter moon
○ Full moon
◑ Last quarter moon

‡Leap year
[a]New Year
[b]Yom Kippur
[c]Sukkot
[d]Winter starts
[e]Ḥanukkah
[f]Purim
[g]Passover
[h]Shavuot
[i]Fast of Av

‡Leap year
[a]New Year (4683, Ox)
[b]Lantern Festival
[c]Qīngmíng
[d]Dragon Festival
[e]Qīqiǎo
[f]Hungry Ghosts
[g]Mid-Autumn Festival
[h]Double-Ninth Festival
[i]Dōngzhì
*Start of 60-name cycle

[a]New Year
[b]Building of the Cross
[c]Christmas
[d]Jesus's Circumcision
[e]Epiphany
[f]Easter
[g]Mary's Announcement
[h]Jesus's Transfiguration

1985

Persian month	PERSIAN (ASTRONOMICAL) 1363/1364 Sun Mon Tue Wed Thu Fri Sat	Hindu lunar month	HINDU LUNAR 2041/2042‡ Sun Mon Tue Wed Thu Fri Sat	Hindu solar month	HINDU SOLAR 1906/1907 Sun Mon Tue Wed Thu Fri Sat	Islamic month	ISLAMIC (ASTRONOMICAL) 1405‡/1406‡ Sun Mon Tue Wed Thu Fri Sat	Julian (Sun)	GREGORIAN 1985 Sun Mon Tue Wed Thu Fri Sat	Gregorian month
DEY 1363	9 10 11 12 13 14 15	PAUSHA 2041	8 9 10 11 12 13 *13*	PAUSHA 1906	16 17 18 19 20 21 22	RABĪʿ II 1405	7 8 9 10 11 12 13	*Dec 17*	*30 31* 1 2 3 4 5	JANUARY 1985
	16 17 18 19 20 21 22		14 **15** 17 18 19 20 21		23 24 25 26 27 28 29		14 15 16 17 18 19 20		6 7[a] 8 9 10 11 12	
	23 24 25 26 27 28 29		22 23 24 25 26 27 28		1[b] 2 3 4 5 6 7		21 22 23 24 25 26 27	*Dec 31*	*13* 14[b] 15 16 17 18 19	
	30 *1* 2 3 4 5 6		29 30 1 2 3 4 5	MĀGHA 1906	8 9 10 11 12 13 14		28 29 1 2 3 4 5		20 21 22 23 24 25 26	
BAHMAN 1363	7 8 9 10 11 12 13	MĀGHA 2041	6 7 8 9 10 11 12		15 16 17 18 19 20 21	JUMĀDĀ I 1405	6 7 8 9 10 11 12	*Jan 14*	*27* 28 29 30 31 1 2	FEBRUARY 1985
	14 15 16 17 18 19 20		13 14 15 16 17 18 19		22 23 24 25 26 27 28		13 14 15 16 17 18 19		3 4 5 6 7 8 9	
	21 22 23 24 25 26 27		20 **21** 23 24 25 26 27		29 30 1 2 3 4 5		20 21 22 23 24 25 26	*Jan 28*	*10* 11 12 13 14 15 16	
	28 29 30 *1* 2 3 4		28[h] 29 30 1 2 3 4	PHĀLGUNA 1906	6 7 8 9 10 11 12		27 28 29 30 1 2 3		17 18 19 20[c] 21 22 23	
ESFAND 1363	5 6 7 8 9 10 11	PHĀLGUNA 2041	5 5 6 7 8 9 10		13 14 15 16 17 18 19	JUMĀDĀ II 1405	4 5 6 7 8 9 10	*Feb 11*	*24* 25 26 27 28 1 2	MARCH 1985
	12 13 14 15 16 17 18		11 12 13 14 **15**[i] 17 18		20 21 22 23 24 25 26		11 12 13 14 15 16 17		3[d] 4 5 6 7 8 9	
	19 20 21 22 23 24 25		19 20 21 22 23 24 25		27 28 29 30 1 2 3		18 19 20 21 22 23 24	*Feb 25*	*10* 11 12 13 14 15 16	
	26 27 28 29 *1*[a] 2 3		26 27 28 29 30 1[a] 2	CHAITRA 1906	4 5 6 7 8 9 10		25 26 27 28 29 30 *1*		17 18 19 20 21 22 23	
FARVARDĪN 1364	4 5 6 7 8 9 10	CHAITRA 2042	3 4 5 6 7 8 9[b]		11 12 13 14 15 16 17	RAJAB 1405	2 3 4 5 6 7 8	*Mar 11*	*24* 25 26 27 28 29 30	APRIL 1985
	11 12 13[b] 14 15 16 17		10 11 12 13 14 15 16		18 19 20 21 22 23 24		9 10 11 12 13 14 15		31 1 2 3 4 5 6	
	18 19 20 21 22 23 24		17 18 19 **20** 22 23 24		25 26 27 28 29 30 1[a]		16 17 18 19 20 21 22	*Mar 25*	*7*[e] 8 9 10 11 12 13	
	25 26 27 28 29 30 31		25 26 27 28 *28* 29 30	VAIŚĀKHA 1907	2 3 4 5 6 7 8		23 24 25 26 27[d] 28 29		14[f] 15 16 17 18 19 20	
ORDĪBEHEŠT 1364	*1* 2 3 4 5 6 7	VAIŚĀKHA 2042	1 2 3 4 5 6 7		9 10 11 12 13 14 15	SHAʿBĀN 1405	30 *1* 2 3 4 5 6	*Apr 8*	*21* 22 23 24 25 26 27	MAY 1985
	8 9 10 11 12 13 14		8 9 10 11 12 **13** 15		16 17 18 19 20 21 22		7 8 9 10 11 12 13		28 29 30 1 2 3 4	
	15 16 17 18 19 20 21		16 17 18 19 20 21 22		23 24 25 26 27 28 29		14 15 16 17 18 19 20	*Apr 22*	*5* 6 7 8 9 10 11	
	22 23 24 25 26 27 28		23 24 25 26 27 28 29		30 31 1 2 3 4 5		21 22 23 24 25 26 27		12 13 14 15 16 17 18	
	29 30 31 *1* 2 3 4		30 1 2 3 4 *4* 6	JYAISHTHA 1907	6 7 8 9 10 11 12		28 29 *1*[e] 2 3 4 5	*May 6*	*19* 20 21 22 23 24 25	
XORDĀD 1364	5 6 7 8 9 10 11	JYAISHTHA 2042	7 8 9 10 11 12 13		13 14 15 16 17 18 19	RAMAḌĀN 1405	6 7 8 9 10 11 12		26 27 28 29 30 31 1	JUNE 1985
	12 13 14 15 16 17 18		14 15 16 **17** 19 20 21		20 21 22 23 24 25 26		13 14 15 16 17 18 19	*May 20*	*2* 3 4 5 6 7 8	
	19 20 21 22 23 24 25		22 23 24 *24* 25 26 27		27 28 29 30 31 1 2		20 21 22 23 24 25 26		9 10 11 12 13 14 15	
	26 27 28 29 30 31 *1*		28 29 30 1 2 3 4	ĀSHĀDHA 1907	3 4 5 6 7 8 9		27 28 29 30 *1*[f] 2 3	*Jun 3*	*16* 17 18 19 20 21 22	
TĪR 1364	2 3 4 5 6 7 8	ĀSHĀDHA 2042	5 6 7 8 **9** 11 12		10 11 12 13 14 15 16	SHAWWĀL 1405	4 5 6 7 8 9 10		23 24 25 26 27 28 29	JULY 1985
	9 10 11 12 13 14 15		13 14 15 16 17 18 19		17 18 19 20 21 22 23		11 12 13 14 15 16 17	*Jun 17*	*30* 1 2 3 4 5 6	
	16 17 18 19 20 21 22		20 21 22 23 24 25 26		24 25 26 27 28 29 30		18 19 20 21 22 23 24		7 8 9 10 11 12 13	
	23 24 25 26 27 28 29		27 28 29 30 1 2 3		31 32 1 2 3 4 5		25 26 27 28 29 *1* 2	*Jul 1*	*14* 15 16 17 18 19 20	
MORDĀD 1364	30 31 *1* 2 3 4 5	*LEAP ŚRĀVANA* 2042	4 5 6 7 8 9 10	ŚRĀVANA 1907	6 7 8 9 10 11 12	DHU AL-QAʿDA 1405	3 4 5 6 7 8 9		21 22 23 24 25 26 27	AUGUST 1985
	6 7 8 9 10 11 12		11 **12** 14 15 16 17 18		13 14 15 16 17 18 19		10 11 12 13 14 15 16	*Jul 15*	*28* 29 30 31 1 2 3	
	13 14 15 16 17 18 19		19 20 21 *21* 22 23 24		20 21 22 23 24 25 26		17 18 19 20 21 22 23		4 5 6 7 8 9 10	
	20 21 22 23 24 25 26		25 26 27 28 29 30 1		27 28 29 30 31 32 1		24 25 26 27 28 29 30	*Jul 29*	*11* 12 13 14 15 16 17	
SHAHRĪVAR 1364	27 28 29 30 31 *1* 2	ŚRĀVANA 2042	2 3 4 **5** 7 8 9	BHĀDRAPADA 1907	2 3 4 5 6 7 8	DHU AL-ḤIJJA 1405	*1* 2 3 4 5 6 7		18 19 20 21 22 23 24	SEPTEMBER 1985
	3 4 5 6 7 8 9		10 11 12 13 14 15 16		9 10 11 12 13 14 15		8 9 10[g] 11 12 13 14	*Aug 12*	*25* 26 27 28 29 30 31	
	10 11 12 13 14 15 16		17 18 19 20 21 22 23[c]		16 17 18 19 20 21 22		15 16 17 18 19 20 21		1 2 3 4 5 6 7	
	17 18 19 20 21 22 23		24 25 26 27 28 29 30		23 24 25 26 27 28 29		22 23 24 25 26 27 28	*Aug 26*	*8* 9 10 11 12 13 14	
MEHR 1364	24 25 26 27 28 29 30	BHĀDRAPADA 2042	1 2 3 4[d] 5 6 7		30 31 1 2 3 4 5	MUHARRAM 1406	29 *1*[a] 2 3 4 5 6		15 16 17 18 19 20 21	OCTOBER 1985
	31 *1* 2 3 4 5 6		**8** 10 11 12 13 14 15	ĀŚVINA 1907	6 7 8 9 10 11 12		7 8 9 10[b] 11 12 13	*Sep 9*	*22* 23 24 25 26 27 28	
	7 8 9 10 11 12 13		16 17 *17* 18 19 20 21		13 14 15 16 17 18 19		14 15 16 17 18 19 20		29 30 1 2 3 4 5	
	14 15 16 17 18 19 20		22 23 24 25 26 27 28		20 21 22 23 24 25 26		21 22 23 24 25 26 27	*Sep 23*	*6* 7 8 9 10 11 12	
	21 22 23 24 25 26 27		29 30 **1** 3 4 5 6		27 28 29 30 1 2 3		28 29 30 *1* 2 3 4		13 14 15 16 17 18 19	
ĀBĀN 1364	28 29 30 *1* 2 3 4	ĀŚVINA 2042	7 8[e] 9[e] 10[e] 11 12 13	KĀRTTIKA 1907	4 5 6 7 8 9 10	ṢAFAR 1406	5 6 7 8 9 10 11	*Oct 7*	*20* 21 22 23 24 25 26	NOVEMBER 1985
	5 6 7 8 9 10 11		14 15 16 17 18 19 20		11 12 13 14 15 16 17		12 13 14 15 16 17 18		27 28 29 30 31 1 2	
	12 13 14 15 16 17 18		*20* 21 22 23 **24** 26 27		18 19 20 21 22 23 24		19 20 21 22 23 24 25	*Oct 21*	*3* 4 5 6 7 8 9	
	19 20 21 22 23 24 25		28 29 30 *1*[f] 2 3 4		25 26 27 28 29 30 1		26 27 28 29 *1* 2 3		10 11 12 13 14 15 16	
ĀZAR 1364	26 27 28 29 30 *1* 2	KĀRTTIKA 2042	5 6 7 8 9 10 11	MĀRGAŚĪRA 1907	2 3 4 5 6 7 8	RABĪʿ I 1406	4 5 6 7 8 9 10	*Nov 4*	*17* 18 19 20 21 22 23	DECEMBER 1985
	3 4 5 6 7 8 9		12 13 14 15 16 17 18		9 10 11 12 13 14 15		11 12[c] 13 14 15 16 17		24 25 26 27 28 29 30	
	10 11 12 13 14 15 16		19 20 21 22 23 24 25		16 17 18 19 20 21 22		18 19 20 21 22 23 24	*Nov 18*	*1*[g] 2 3 4 5 6 7	
	17 18 19 20 21 22 23		26 27 28 **29** 1 2 3		23 24 25 26 27 28 29		25 26 27 28 29 30 *1*		8 9 10 11 12 13 14	
	24 25 26 27 28 29 30	MĀRGAŚĪRA 2042	4 5 6 7 8 9 10	PAUSHA 1907	1 2 3 4 5 6 7	RABĪʿ II 1406	2 3 4 5 6 7 8	*Dec 2*	*15* 16 17 18 19 20 21	
DEY 1364	*1* 2 3 4 5 6 7		11[g] 12 13 *13* 14 15 16		8 9 10 11 12 13 14		9 10 11 12 13 14 15		22 23 24 25[h] 26 27 28	
	8 9 10 11 12 13 14		17 18 19 20 21 22 **23**		15 16 17 18 19 20 21		16 17 18 19 20 21 22	*Dec 16*	*29* 30 31 1 2 3 4	

Persian:
[a] New Year
[b] Sizdeh Bedar

Hindu lunar:
‡ Leap year
[a] New Year (Krodhana)
[b] Birthday of Rāma
[c] Birthday of Krishna
[d] Ganēśa Chaturthī
[e] Dashara
[f] Diwali
[g] Birthday of Vishnu
[h] Night of Śiva
[i] Holi

Hindu solar:
[a] New Year (Bahudhānya)
[b] Pongal

Islamic:
‡ Leap year
[a] New Year
[b] ʿAshūrāʾ
[c] Prophet's Birthday
[d] Ascent of the Prophet
[e] Start of Ramaḍān
[f] ʿId al-Fiṭr
[g] ʿId al-ʾAḍḥā

Gregorian:
[a] Orthodox Christmas
[b] Julian New Year
[c] Ash Wednesday
[d] Feast of Orthodoxy
[e] Easter
[f] Orthodox Easter
[g] Advent
[h] Christmas

1986

Gregorian 1986	Sun	Mon	Tue	Wed	Thu	Fri	Sat	Lunar Phases	ISO WEEK (Mon)	JULIAN DAY (Sun noon)	Hebrew 5746‡/5747	Sun	Mon	Tue	Wed	Thu	Fri	Sat	Molad	Chinese Yǐ-Chǒu/Bǐng-Yín	Sun	Mon	Tue	Wed	Thu	Fri	Sat	Solar Term	Coptic 1702/1703‡	Sun	Mon	Tue	Wed	Thu	Fri	Sat	Ethiopic 1978/1979‡
	29	30	31	1[a]	2	◑	4	19:47	1	2446429	TEVETH 5746	17	18	19	20	21	22	23	Fri 23h39m2p	MONTH 11 Yǐ-Chǒu	18	19	20	21	22	23	24		KOIAK 1702	20	21	22	23	24	25	26	TĀḪŚĀŚ 1978
JANUARY 1986	5	6	7	8	9	●	11	12:22	2	2446436		24	25	26	27	28	29	1		MONTH 12 Yǐ-Chǒu	25	26	27	28	29	1	2	Xiǎo hán		27	28	29[c]	30	1	2	3	
	12	13	14	15	16	◐	18	22:13	3	2446443	SHEVAT 5746	2	3	4	5	6	7	8			3	4	5	6	7	8	9		TŌBE 1702	4	5	6[d]	7	8	9	10	ṬER 1978
	19	20	21	22	23	24	25		4	2446450		9	10	11	12	13	14	15			10	11*	12	13	14	15	16	Dà hán		11[e]	12	13	14	15	16	17	
	○	27	28	29	30	31	1	0:31	5	2446457		16	17	18	19	20	21	22			17	18	19	20	21	22	23			18	19	20	21	22	23	24	
FEBRUARY 1986	◑	3	4	5	6	7	8	4:41	6	2446464		23	24	25	26	27	28	29			24	25	26	27	28	29	30	Lì chūn		25	26	27	28	29	30	1	
	●	10	11	12	13	14	15	0:55	7	2446471	ADAR I 5746	30	1	2	3	4	5	6	Sun 12h23m3p	MONTH 1 Bǐng-Yín	1[a]	2	3	4	5	6	7		MESHIR 1702	2	3	4	5	6	7	8	YAKĀTIT 1978
	◐	17	18	19	20	21	22	19:55	8	2446478		7	8	9	10	11	12	13			8	9	10	11	12	13	14	Yǔ shuǐ		9	10	11	12	13	14	15	
	23	○	25	26	27	28	1	15:02	9	2446485		14	15	16	17	18	19	20			15[b]	16	17	18	19	20	21			16	17	18	19	20	21	22	
MARCH 1986	2	◑	4	5	6	7	8	12:17	10	2446492		21	22	23	24	25	26	27			22	23	24	25	26	27	28	Jīng zhé		23	24	25	26	27	28	29	
	9	●	11	12	13	14	15	14:51	11	2446499	ADAR II 5746	28	29	30	1	2	3	4	Tue 1h7m4p	MONTH 2 Bǐng-Yín	29	1	2	3	4	5	6		PAREMOTEP 1702	30	1	2	3	4	5	6	MAGĀBIT 1978
	16	17	◐	19	20[b]	21	22	16:39	12	2446506		5	6	7	8	9	10	11			7	8	9	10	11	12*	13	Chūn fēn		7	8	9	10	11	12	13	
	23	24	25	○	27	28	29	3:02	13	2446513		12	13	14[f]	15	16	17	18			14	15	16	17	18	19	20			14	15	16	17	18	19	20	
	30	31	◑	2	3	4	5	19:30	14	2446520		19	20	21	22	23	24	25			21	22	23	24	25	26	27[c]	Qīng míng		21	22	23	24	25	26	27	
APRIL 1986	6	7	8	●	10	11	12	6:08	15	2446527	NISAN 5746	26	27	28	29	1	2	3	Wed 13h51m5p	MONTH 3 Bǐng-Yín	28	29	30	1	2	3	4		PARMOUTE 1702	28	29	30	1	2	3	4	MIYĀZYĀ 1978
	13	14	15	16	◐	18	19	10:35	16	2446534		4	5	6	7	8	9	10			5	6	7	8	9	10	11	Gǔ yǔ		5	6	7	8	9	10	11	
	20	21	22	23	○	25	26	12:47	17	2446541		11	12	13	14	15[g]	16	17			12	13	14	15	16	17	18			12	13	14	15	16	17	18	
	27	28	29	30	◑	2	3	3:22	18	2446548		18	19	20	21	22	23	24			19	20	21	22	23	24	25			19	20	21	22	23	24	25	
MAY 1986	4	5	6	7	●	9	10	22:10	19	2446555	IYAR 5746	25	26	27	28	29	30	1	Fri 2h35m6p	MONTH 4 Bǐng-Yín	26	27	28	29	30	1	2	Lì xià	PASHONS 1702	26[f]	27	28	29[g]	30	1	2	GENBOT 1978
	11	12	13	14	15	16	◐	1:00	20	2446562		2	3	4	5	6	7	8			3	4	5	6	7	8	9			3	4	5	6	7	8	9	
	18	19	20	21	22	○	24	20:45	21	2446569		9	10	11	12	13	14	15			10	11	12*	13	14	15	16	Xiǎo mǎn		10	11	12	13	14	15	16	
	25	26	27	28	29	◑	31	12:54	22	2446576		16	17	18	19	20	21	22			17	18	19	20	21	22	23			17	18	19	20	21	22	23	
JUNE 1986	1	2	3	4	5	6	●	14:01	23	2446583		23	24	25	26	27	28	29			24	25	26	27	28	29	1	Máng zhòng		24	25	26	27	28	29	30	
	8	9	10	11	12	13	14		24	2446590	SIVAN 5746	1	2	3	4	5	6[h]	7	Sat 15h19m7p	MONTH 5 Bǐng-Yín	2	3	4	5[d]	6	7	8		PAŌNE 1702	1	2	3	4	5	6	7	SANĒ 1978
	◐	16	17	18	19	20	21[c]	12:00	25	2446597		8	9	10	11	12	13	14			9	10	11	12	13	14	15			8	9	10	11	12	13	14	
	○	23	24	25	26	27	28	3:42	26	2446604		15	16	17	18	19	20	21			16	17	18	19	20	21	22	Xià zhì		15	16	17	18	19	20	21	
	◑	30	1	2	3	4	5	0:53	27	2446611		22	23	24	25	26	27	28			23	24	25	26	27	28	29			22	23	24	25	26	27	28	
JULY 1986	6	●	8	9	10	11	12	4:55	28	2446618	TAMMUZ 5746	29	30	1	2	3	4	5	Mon 4h3m8p	MONTH 6 Bǐng-Yín	30	1	2	3	4	5	6	Xiǎo shǔ	EPĒP 1702	29	30	1	2	3	4	5	ḤAMLĒ 1978
	13	◐	15	16	17	18	19	20:10	29	2446625		6	7	8	9	10	11	12			7	8	9	10	11	12	13*			6	7	8	9	10	11	12	
	20	○	22	23	24	25	26	10:40	30	2446632		13	14	15	16	17	18	19			14	15	16	17	18	19	20	Dà shǔ		13	14	15	16	17	18	19	
	27	◑	29	30	31	1	2	15:34	31	2446639		20	21	22	23	24	25	26			21	22	23	24	25	26	27			20	21	22	23	24	25	26	
AUGUST 1986	3	4	●	6	7	8	9	18:36	32	2446646	AV 5746	27	28	29	1	2	3	4	Tue 16h47m9p	MONTH 7 Bǐng-Yín	28	29	30	1	2	3	4	Lì qiū	MESORĒ 1702	27	28	29	30	1	2	3	NAḤASĒ 1978
	10	11	12	◐	14	15	16	2:21	33	2446653		5	6	7	8	9[i]	10	11			5	6	7[e]	8	9	10	11			4	5	6	7	8	9	10	
	17	18	○	20	21	22	23	18:54	34	2446660		12	13	14	15	16	17	18			12	13	14	15[f]	16	17	18	Chǔ shǔ		11	12	13[h]	14	15	16	17	
	24	25	26	◑	28	29	30	8:38	35	2446667		19	20	21	22	23	24	25			19	20	21	22	23	24	25			18	19	20	21	22	23	24	
SEPTEMBER 1986	31	1	2	3	●	5	6	7:10	36	2446674	ELUL 5746	26	27	28	29	30	1	2	Thu 5h31m10p	MONTH 8 Bǐng-Yín	26	27	28	29	1	2	3		EPAG. 1702	25	26	27	28	29	30	1	PĀG. 1978
	7	8	9	10	◐	12	13	7:41	37	2446681		3	4	5	6	7	8	9			4	5	6	7	8	9	10	Bái lù	THOOUT 1703	2	3	4	5	1[a]	2	3	MASKARAM 1979
	14	15	16	17	○	19	20	5:34	38	2446688		10	11	12	13	14	15	16			11	12	13	14*	15[g]	16	17			4	5	6	7	8	9	10	
	21	22	23[d]	24	25	◑	27	3:17	39	2446695		17	18	19	20	21	22	23			18	19	20	21	22	23	24	Qiū fēn		11	12	13	14	15	16	17[b]	
	28	29	30	1	2	●	4	18:55	40	2446702		24	25	26	27	28	29	1[a]	Fri 18h15m11p		25	26	27	28	29	30	1			18	19	20	21	22	23	24	
OCTOBER 1986	5	6	7	8	9	◐	11	13:28	41	2446709	TISHRI 5747	2[a]	3	4	5	6	7	8		MONTH 9 Bǐng-Yín	2	3	4	5	6	7	8	Hán lù	PAOPE 1703	25	26	27	28	29	30	1	ṬEQEMT 1979
	12	13	14	15	16	○	18	19:22	42	2446716		9	10[b]	11	12	13	14	15[c]			9[h]	10	11	12	13	14	15			2	3	4	5	6	7	8	
	19	20	21	22	23	24	◑	22:26	43	2446723		16	17	18	19	20	21	22			16	17	18	19	20	21	22	Shuāng jiàng		9	10	11	12	13	14	15	
	26	27	28	29	30	31	1		44	2446730		23	24	25	26	27	28	29			23	24	25	26	27	28	29			16	17	18	19	20	21	22	
NOVEMBER 1986	●	3	4	5	6	7	◐	6:02 21:11	45	2446737	HESHVAN 5747	30	1	2	3	4	5	6	Sun 6h59m12p	MONTH 10 Bǐng-Yín	1	2	3	4	5	6	7	Lì dōng	ATHŌR 1703	23	24	25	26	27	28	29	ḪEDĀR 1979
	9	10	11	12	13	14	15		46	2446744		7	8	9	10	11	12	13			8	9	10	11	12	13	14			30	1	2	3	4	5	6	
	○	17	18	19	20	21	22	12:12	47	2446751		14	15	16	17	18	19	20			15*	16	17	18	19	20	21	Xiǎo xuě		7	8	9	10	11	12	13	
	23	◑	25	26	27	28	29	16:50	48	2446758		21	22	23	24	25	26	27			22	23	24	25	26	27	28			14	15	16	17	18	19	20	
DECEMBER 1986	30	●	2	3	4	5	6	16:43	49	2446765	KISLEV 5747	28	29	30	1	2	3[d]	4	Mon 19h43m13p		29	30	1	2	3	4	5		KOIAK 1703	21	22	23	24	25	26	27	TĀḪŚĀŚ 1979
	7	◐	9	10	11	12	13	8:01	50	2446772		5	6	7	8	9	10	11		MONTH 11 Bǐng-Yín	6	7	8	9	10	11	12	Dà xuě		28	29	30	1	2	3	4	
	14	15	○	17	18	19	20	7:04	51	2446779		12	13	14	15	16	17	18			13	14	15	16	17	18	19			5	6	7	8	9	10	11	
	21	22[e]	23	◑	25	26	27	9:17	52	2446786		19	20	21	22	23	24	25[e]			20	21[i]	22	23	24	25	26	Dōng zhì		12	13	14	15	16	17	18	
	28	29	30	●	1	2	3	3:10	1	2446793		26[e]	27[e]	28[e]	29[e]	30[e]	1[e]	2[e]	Wed 8h27m14p		27	28	29	1	2	3	4			19	20	21	22	23	24	25	

[a]New Year
[b]Spring (22:02)
[c]Summer (16:30)
[d]Autumn (7:59)
[e]Winter (4:02)
● New moon
◐ First quarter moon
○ Full moon
◑ Last quarter moon

‡Leap year
[a]New Year
[b]Yom Kippur
[c]Sukkot
[d]Winter starts
[e]Ḥanukkah
[f]Purim
[g]Passover
[h]Shavuot
[i]Fast of Av

[a]New Year (4684, Tiger)
[b]Lantern Festival
[c]Qīngmíng
[d]Dragon Festival
[e]Qīqiǎo
[f]Hungry Ghosts
[g]Mid-Autumn Festival
[h]Double-Ninth Festival
[i]Dōngzhì
*Start of 60-name cycle

‡Leap year
[a]New Year
[b]Building of the Cross
[c]Christmas
[d]Jesus's Circumcision
[e]Epiphany
[f]Easter
[g]Mary's Announcement
[h]Jesus's Transfiguration

1986

PERSIAN (ASTRONOMICAL) 1364/1365

Month	Sun	Mon	Tue	Wed	Thu	Fri	Sat
DEY 1364	8	9	10	11	12	13	14
	15	16	17	18	19	20	21
	22	23	24	25	26	27	28
BAHMAN 1364	29	30	1	2	3	4	5
	6	7	8	9	10	11	12
	13	14	15	16	17	18	19
	20	21	22	23	24	25	26
ESFAND 1364	27	28	29	30	1	2	3
	4	5	6	7	8	9	10
	11	12	13	14	15	16	17
	18	19	20	21	22	23	24
FARVARDĪN 1365	25	26	27	28	29	1[a]	2
	3	4	5	6	7	8	9
	10	11	12	13[b]	14	15	16
	17	18	19	20	21	22	23
	24	25	26	27	28	29	30
ORDĪBEHEŠT 1365	31	1	2	3	4	5	6
	7	8	9	10	11	12	13
	14	15	16	17	18	19	20
	21	22	23	24	25	26	27
XORDĀD 1365	28	29	30	31	1	2	3
	4	5	6	7	8	9	10
	11	12	13	14	15	16	17
	18	19	20	21	22	23	24
	25	26	27	28	29	30	31
TĪR 1365	1	2	3	4	5	6	7
	8	9	10	11	12	13	14
	15	16	17	18	19	20	21
	22	23	24	25	26	27	28
MORDĀD 1365	29	30	31	1	2	3	4
	5	6	7	8	9	10	11
	12	13	14	15	16	17	18
	19	20	21	22	23	24	25
SHAHRĪVAR 1365	26	27	28	29	30	31	1
	2	3	4	5	6	7	8
	9	10	11	12	13	14	15
	16	17	18	19	20	21	22
	23	24	25	26	27	28	29
MEHR 1365	30	31	1	2	3	4	5
	6	7	8	9	10	11	12
	13	14	15	16	17	18	19
	20	21	22	23	24	25	26
ĀBĀN 1365	27	28	29	30	1	2	3
	4	5	6	7	8	9	10
	11	12	13	14	15	16	17
	18	19	20	21	22	23	24
ĀZAR 1365	25	26	27	28	29	30	1
	2	3	4	5	6	7	8
	9	10	11	12	13	14	15
	16	17	18	19	20	21	22
	23	24	25	26	27	28	29
DEY 1365	30	1	2	3	4	5	6
	7	8	9	10	11	12	13

[a]New Year
[b]Sizdeh Bedar

HINDU LUNAR 2042‡/2043

Month	Sun	Mon	Tue	Wed	Thu	Fri	Sat
MĀRGAŚĪRA 2042	17	18	19	20	21	22	**23**
PAUSHA 2042	25	26	27	28	29	30	1
	2	3	4	5	6	7	8
	9	10	11	12	13	14	15
	16	17	18	19	20	21	22
	23	24	25	26	27	28	**29**
MĀGHA 2042	1	2	3	4	5	5	6
	7	8	9	10	11	12	13
	14	15	16	17	18	19	20
	21	**22**	24	25	26	27	28[h]
PHĀLGUNA 2042	29	30	1	2	3	4	5
	6	7	8	8	9	10	11
	12	13	14	15[i]	**16**	18	19
	20	21	22	23	24	25	26
CHAITRA 2043	27	28	29	30	1[a]	2	3
	4	5	6	7	8	9[b]	10
	11	12	13	14	15	16	17
	18	19	**20**	22	23	24	25
VAIŚĀKHA 2043	26	27	28	29	30	1	2
	2	3	4	5	6	7	8
	9	10	11	12	**13**	15	16
	17	18	19	20	21	22	23
	24	25	26	27	28	29	30
JYAISHṬHA 2043	1	2	3	4	5	6	7
	8	9	10	11	12	13	14
	15	**16**	18	19	20	21	22
	23	24	25	26	27	28	29
ĀSHĀḌHA 2043	29	30	1	2	3	4	5
	6	7	8	**9**	11	12	13
	14	15	16	17	18	19	20
	21	22	23	24	25	26	27
ŚRĀVAṆA 2043	28	29	30	1	2	3	4
	5	6	7	8	9	10	11
	12	14	15	16	17	18	19
	20	21	22	23[c]	24	25	25
BHĀDRAPADA 2043	26	27	28	29	30	1	2
	3[d]	4	**5**	7	8	9	10
	11	12	13	14	15	16	17
	18	19	20	21	22	23	24
ĀŚVINA 2043	25	26	27	28	29	30	1
	2	3	4	5	6	7	**8**[e]
	10[e]	11	12	13	14	15	16
	17	18	19	20	20	21	22
	23	24	25	26	27	28	29
KĀRTTIKA 2043	30	1[f]	**2**	4	5	6	7
	8	9	10	11	12	13	14
	15	16	17	18	19	20	21
	22	23	24	25	26	27	28
MĀRGAŚĪRA 2043	29	30	1	2	3	4	5
	6	**7**	9	10	11[g]	12	13
	13	14	15	16	17	18	19
	20	21	22	23	24	25	26
	27	28	29	**30**	2	3	4

‡Leap year
[a]New Year (Kshaya)
[b]Birthday of Rāma
[c]Birthday of Krishna
[d]Ganēśa Chaturthī
[e]Dashara
[f]Diwali
[g]Birthday of Vishnu
[h]Night of Śiva
[i]Holi

HINDU SOLAR 1907/1908‡

Month	Sun	Mon	Tue	Wed	Thu	Fri	Sat
PAUSHA 1907	15	16	17	18	19	20	21
	22	23	24	25	26	27	28
MĀGHA 1907	29	30	1[b]	2	3	4	5
	6	7	8	9	10	11	12
	13	14	15	16	17	18	19
	20	21	22	23	24	25	26
PHĀLGUNA 1907	27	28	29	1	2	3	4
	5	6	7	8	9	10	11
	12	13	14	15	16	17	18
	19	20	21	22	23	24	25
CHAITRA 1907	26	27	28	29	30	1	2
	3	4	5	6	7	8	9
	10	11	12	13	14	15	16
	17	18	19	20	21	22	23
	24	25	26	27	28	29	30
VAIŚĀKHA 1908	1[a]	2	3	4	5	6	7
	8	9	10	11	12	13	14
	15	16	17	18	19	20	21
	22	23	24	25	26	27	28
JYAISHṬHA 1908	29	30	31	1	2	3	4
	5	6	7	8	9	10	11
	12	13	14	15	16	17	18
	19	20	21	22	23	24	25
	26	27	28	29	30	31	32
ĀSHĀḌHA 1908	1	2	3	4	5	6	7
	8	9	10	11	12	13	14
	15	16	17	18	19	20	21
	22	23	24	25	26	27	28
ŚRĀVAṆA 1908	29	30	31	1	2	3	4
	5	6	7	8	9	10	11
	12	13	14	15	16	17	18
	19	20	21	22	23	24	25
	26	27	28	29	30	31	32
BHĀDRAPADA 1908	1	2	3	4	5	6	7
	8	9	10	11	12	13	14
	15	16	17	18	19	20	21
	22	23	24	25	26	27	28
ĀŚVINA 1908	29	30	31	1	2	3	4
	5	6	7	8	9	10	11
	12	13	14	15	16	17	18
	19	20	21	22	23	24	25
KĀRTTIKA 1908	26	27	28	29	30	1	2
	3	4	5	6	7	8	9
	10	11	12	13	14	15	16
	17	18	19	20	21	22	23
	24	25	26	27	28	29	30
MĀRGAŚĪRA 1908	1	2	3	4	5	6	7
	8	9	10	11	12	13	14
	15	16	17	18	19	20	21
	22	23	24	25	26	27	28
PAUSHA 1908	29	30	1	2	3	4	5
	6	7	8	9	10	11	12
	13	14	15	16	17	18	19

‡Leap year
[a]New Year (Pramāthin)
[b]Pongal

ISLAMIC (ASTRONOMICAL) 1406‡/1407

Month	Sun	Mon	Tue	Wed	Thu	Fri	Sat
RABĪʿ II 1406	16	17	18	19	20	21	22
	23	24	25	26	27	28	29
JUMĀDĀ I 1406	1	2	3	4	5	6	7
	8	9	10	11	12	13	14
	15	16	17	18	19	20	21
	22	23	24	25	26	27	28
JUMĀDĀ II 1406	29	1	2	3	4	5	6
	7	8	9	10	11	12	13
	14	15	16	17	18	19	20
	21	22	23	24	25	26	27
RAJAB 1406	28	29	30	1	2	3	4
	5	6	7	8	9	10	11
	12	13	14	15	16	17	18
	19	20	21	22	23	24	25
SHAʿBĀN 1406	26	27[d]	28	29	30	1	2
	3	4	5	6	7	8	9
	10	11	12	13	14	15	16
	17	18	19	20	21	22	23
RAMAḌĀN 1406	24	25	26	27	28	29	1[e]
	2	3	4	5	6	7	8
	9	10	11	12	13	14	15
	16	17	18	19	20	21	22
	23	24	25	26	27	28	29
SHAWWĀL 1406	30	1[f]	2	3	4	5	6
	7	8	9	10	11	12	13
	14	15	16	17	18	19	20
	21	22	23	24	25	26	27
DHU AL-QAʿDA 1406	28	29	1	2	3	4	5
	6	7	8	9	10	11	12
	13	14	15	16	17	18	19
	20	21	22	23	24	25	26
DHU AL-ḤIJJA 1406	27	28	29	30	1	2	3
	4	5	6	7	8	9	10[g]
	11	12	13	14	15	16	17
	18	19	20	21	22	23	24
MUḤARRAM 1407	25	26	27	28	29	30	1[a]
	2	3	4	5	6	7	8
	9	10[b]	11	12	13	14	15
	16	17	18	19	20	21	22
	23	24	25	26	27	28	29
ṢAFAR 1407	1	2	3	4	5	6	7
	8	9	10	11	12	13	14
	15	16	17	18	19	20	21
	22	23	24	25	26	27	28
RABĪʿ I 1407	29	30	1	2	3	4	5
	6	7	8	9	10	11	12[c]
	13	14	15	16	17	18	19
	20	21	22	23	24	25	26
RABĪʿ II 1407	27	28	29	1	2	3	4
	5	6	7	8	9	10	11
	12	13	14	15	16	17	18
	19	20	21	22	23	24	25
	26	27	28	29	1	2	3

‡Leap year
[a]New Year
[b]ʿAshūrāʾ
[c]Prophet's Birthday
[d]Ascent of the Prophet
[e]Start of Ramaḍān
[f]ʿId al-Fiṭr
[g]ʿId al-ʾAḍḥā

GREGORIAN 1986

Julian (Sun)	Sun	Mon	Tue	Wed	Thu	Fri	Sat	Month
Dec 16	29	30	31	1	2	3	4	JANUARY 1986
	5	6	7[a]	8	9	10	11	
Dec 30	12	13	14[b]	15	16	17	18	
	19	20	21	22	23	24	25	
Jan 13	26	27	28	29	30	31	1	FEBRUARY 1986
	2	3	4	5	6	7	8	
Jan 27	9	10	11	12[c]	13	14	15	
	16	17	18	19	20	21	22	
Feb 10	23	24	25	26	27	28	1	MARCH 1986
	2	3	4	5	6	7	8	
Feb 24	9	10	11	12	13	14	15	
	16	17	18	19	20	21	22	
Mar 10	23[d]	24	25	26	27	28	29	
	30[e]	31	1	2	3	4	5	APRIL 1986
Mar 24	6	7	8	9	10	11	12	
	13	14	15	16	17	18	19	
Apr 7	20	21	22	23	24	25	26	
	27	28	29	30	1	2	3	MAY 1986
Apr 21	4[f]	5	6	7	8	9	10	
	11	12	13	14	15	16	17	
May 5	18	19	20	21	22	23	24	
	25	26	27	28	29	30	31	
May 19	1	2	3	4	5	6	7	JUNE 1986
	8	9	10	11	12	13	14	
Jun 2	15	16	17	18	19	20	21	
	22	23	24	25	26	27	28	
Jun 16	29	30	1	2	3	4	5	JULY 1986
	6	7	8	9	10	11	12	
Jun 30	13	14	15	16	17	18	19	
	20	21	22	23	24	25	26	
Jul 14	27	28	29	30	31	1	2	AUGUST 1986
	3	4	5	6	7	8	9	
Jul 28	10	11	12	13	14	15	16	
	17	18	19	20	21	22	23	
Aug 11	24	25	26	27	28	29	30	
	31	1	2	3	4	5	6	SEPTEMBER 1986
Aug 25	7	8	9	10	11	12	13	
	14	15	16	17	18	19	20	
Sep 8	21	22	23	24	25	26	27	
	28	29	30	1	2	3	4	OCTOBER 1986
Sep 22	5	6	7	8	9	10	11	
	12	13	14	15	16	17	18	
Oct 6	19	20	21	22	23	24	25	
	26	27	28	29	30	31	1	NOVEMBER 1986
Oct 20	2	3	4	5	6	7	8	
	9	10	11	12	13	14	15	
Nov 3	16	17	18	19	20	21	22	
	23	24	25	26	27	28	29	
Nov 17	30[g]	1	2	3	4	5	6	DECEMBER 1986
	7	8	9	10	11	12	13	
Dec 1	14	15	16	17	18	19	20	
	21	22	23	24	25[h]	26	27	
Dec 15	28	29	30	31	1	2	3	

[a]Orthodox Christmas
[b]Julian New Year
[c]Ash Wednesday
[d]Feast of Orthodoxy
[e]Easter
[f]Orthodox Easter
[g]Advent
[h]Christmas

1987

GREGORIAN 1987	Sun	Mon	Tue	Wed	Thu	Fri	Sat	Lunar Phases	ISO WEEK (Mon)	JULIAN DAY (Sun noon)	HEBREW 5747/5748	Sun	Mon	Tue	Wed	Thu	Fri	Sat	Molad
JANUARY 1987	28	29	30	●	1[a]	2	3	3:10	1	2446793		26[e]	27[e]	28[e]	29[e]	30[e]	1[e]	2[e]	Wed $8^{h}27^{m}14^{p}$
	4	5	◐	7	8	9	10	22:34	2	2446800	TEVETH 5747	3	4	5	6	7	8	9	
	11	12	13	14	○	16	17	2:30	3	2446807		10	11	12	13	14	15	16	
	18	19	20	21	◑	23	24	22:45	4	2446814		17	18	19	20	21	22	23	
	25	26	27	28	●	30	31	13:44	5	2446821		24	25	26	27	28	29	1	Thu $21^{h}11^{m}15^{p}$
FEBRUARY 1987	1	2	3	4	◐	6	7	16:21	6	2446828	SHEVAT 5747	2	3	4	5	6	7	8	
	8	9	10	11	12	○	14	20:58	7	2446835		9	10	11	12	13	14	15	
	15	16	17	18	19	20	◑	8:56	8	2446842		16	17	18	19	20	21	22	
	22	23	24	25	26	27	●	0:51	9	2446849		23	24	25	26	27	28	29	Sat $9^{h}55^{m}16^{p}$
MARCH 1987	1	2	3	4	5	6	◐	11:58	10	2446856		30	1	2	3	4	5	6	
	8	9	10	11	12	13	14		11	2446863	ADAR 5747	7	8	9	10	11	12	13	
	○	16	17	18	19	20	21[b]	13:13	12	2446870		14[f]	15	16	17	18	19	20	
	◑	23	24	25	26	27	28	16:22	13	2446877		21	22	23	24	25	26	27	
	●	30	31	1	2	3	4	12:46	14	2446884		28	29	1	2	3	4	5	Sun $22^{h}39^{m}17^{p}$
APRIL 1987	5	◐	7	8	9	10	11	7:48	15	2446891	NISAN 5747	6	7	8	9	10	11	12	
	12	13	○	15	16	17	18	2:31	16	2446898		13	14	15[g]	16	17	18	19	
	19	◑	21	22	23	24	25	22:15	17	2446905		20	21	22	23	24	25	26	
	26	27	●	29	30	1	2	1:34	18	2446912		27	28	29	30	1	2	3	Tue $11^{h}24^{m}0^{p}$
MAY 1987	3	4	5	◐	7	8	9	2:26	19	2446919	IYYAR 5747	4	5	6	7	8	9	10	
	10	11	12	○	14	15	16	12:50	20	2446926		11	12	13	14	15	16	17	
	17	18	19	◑	21	22	23	4:02	21	2446933		18	19	20	21	22	23	24	
	24	25	26	●	28	29	30	15:13	22	2446940		25	26	27	28	29	1	2	Thu $0^{h}8^{m}1^{p}$
	31	1	2	3	◐	5	6	18:53	23	2446947	SIVAN 5747	3	4	5	6[h]	7	8	9	
JUNE 1987	7	8	9	10	○	12	13	20:49	24	2446954		10	11	12	13	14	15	16	
	14	15	16	17	◑	19	20	11:02	25	2446961		17	18	19	20	21	22	23	
	21[c]	22	23	24	25	●	27	5:37	26	2446968		24	25	26	27	28	29	30	
	28	29	30	1	2	3	◐	8:34	27	2446975	TAMMUZ 5747	1	2	3	4	5	6	7	Fri $12^{h}52^{m}2^{p}$
JULY 1987	5	6	7	8	9	10	○	3:33	28	2446982		8	9	10	11	12	13	14	
	12	13	14	15	16	◑	18	20:17	29	2446989		15	16	17	18	19	20	21	
	19	20	21	22	23	24	●	20:37	30	2446996		22	23	24	25	26	27	28	
	26	27	28	29	30	31	1		31	2447003		29	1	2	3	4	5	6	Sun $1^{h}36^{m}3^{p}$
AUGUST 1987	◐	3	4	5	6	7	8	19:24	32	2447010	AV 5747	7	8	9[i]	10	11	12	13	
	○	10	11	12	13	14	15	10:17	33	2447017		14	15	16	17	18	19	20	
	◑	17	18	19	20	21	22	8:25	34	2447024		21	22	23	24	25	26	27	
	23	●	25	26	27	28	29	11:58	35	2447031		28	29	30	1	2	3	4	Mon $14^{h}20^{m}4^{p}$
	30	31	◐	2	3	4	5	3:48	36	2447038	ELUL 5747	5	6	7	8	9	10	11	
SEPTEMBER 1987	6	○	8	9	10	11	12	18:13	37	2447045		12	13	14	15	16	17	18	
	13	◑	15	16	17	18	19	23:44	38	2447052		19	20	21	22	23	24	25	
	20	21	22	●[d]	24	25	26	3:08	39	2447059		26	27	28	29	1[a]	2[a]	3	Wed $3^{h}4^{m}5^{p}$
	27	28	29	◐	1	2	3	10:39	40	2447066	TISHRI 5748	4	5	6	7	8	9	10[b]	
OCTOBER 1987	4	5	6	○	8	9	10	4:12	41	2447073		11	12	13	14	15[c]	16	17	
	11	12	13	◑	15	16	17	18:06	42	2447080		18	19	20	21	22	23	24	
	18	19	20	21	●	23	24	17:28	43	2447087		25	26	27	28	29	30	1	Thu $15^{h}48^{m}6^{p}$
	25	26	27	28	◐	30	31	17:10	44	2447094	HESHVAN 5748	2	3	4	5	6	7	8	
NOVEMBER 1987	1	2	3	4	○	6	7	16:46	45	2447101		9	10	11	12	13	14	15	
	8	9	10	11	12	◑	14	14:38	46	2447108		16	17	18	19	20	21	22	
	15	16	17	18	19	20	●	6:33	47	2447115		23	24	25	26	27	28	29	
	22	23	24	25	26	27	◐	0:37	48	2447122	KISLEV 5748	1	2	3	4	5	6	7	Sat $4^{h}32^{m}7^{p}$
	29	30	1	2	3	4	○	8:01	49	2447129		8	9	10	11	12	13	14	
DECEMBER 1987	6	7	8	9	10	11	12		50	2447136		15[d]	16	17	18	19	20	21	
	◑	14	15	16	17	18	19	11:41	51	2447143		22	23	24	25[e]	26[e]	27[e]	28[e]	
	●	21	22[e]	23	24	25	26	18:25	52	2447150	TEVETH 5748	29[e]	30[e]	1[e]	2[e]	3	4	5	Sun $17^{h}16^{m}8^{p}$
	◐	28	29	30	31	1	2	10:01	53	2447157		6	7	8	9	10	11	12	

ISO WEEK	CHINESE Bǐng-Yín/Dīng-Mǎo‡	Sun	Mon	Tue	Wed	Thu	Fri	Sat	Solar Term	COPTIC 1703‡/1704	Sun	Mon	Tue	Wed	Thu	Fri	Sat	ETHIOPIC 1979‡/1980
1		27	28	29	1	2	3	4		KOIAK 1703	19	20	21	22	23	24	25	TĀKHŚĀŚ 1979
2	MONTH 12 Bǐng-Yín	5	6	*7*	8	9	10	11	Xiǎo hán		26	27	28	29[c]	30	1	2	
3		12	13	14	15	16*	17	18		TÔBE 1703	3	4	5	6[d]	7	8	9	ṬER 1979
4		19	20	***21***	22	23	24	25	**Dà hán**		10	11[e]	12	13	14	15	16	
5		26	27	28	29	1[a]	2	3			17	18	19	20	21	22	23	
6	MONTH 1 Dīng-Mǎo	4	5	6	*7*	8	9	10	Lì chūn		24	25	26	27	28	29	30	
7		11	12	13	14	15[b]	16	17			1	2	3	4	5	6	7	
8		18	19	20	21	***22***	23	24	**Yǔ shuǐ**	MESHIR 1703	8	9	10	11	12	13	14	YAKĀTIT 1979
9		25	26	27	28	29	30	1			15	16	17	18	19	20	21	
10	MONTH 2 Dīng-Mǎo	2	3	4	5	6	*7*	8	Jīng zhé		22	23	24	25	26	27	28	
11		9	10	11	12	13	14	15			29	30	1	2	3	4	5	
12		16	17*	18	19	20	21	***22***	**Chūn fēn**	PAREMOTEP 1703	6	7	8	9	10	11	12	MAGĀBIT 1979
13		23	24	25	26	27	28	29			13	14	15	16	17	18	19	
14		1	2	3	4	5	6	7			20	21	22	23	24	25	26	
15	MONTH 3 Dīng-Mǎo	*8*[c]	9	10	11	12	13	14	Qīng míng		27	28	29	30	1	2	3	
16		15	16	17	18	19	20	21		PARMOUTE 1703	4	5	6	7	8	9	10	MIYĀZYĀ 1979
17		22	***23***	24	25	26	27	28	**Gǔ yǔ**		11[f]	12	13	14	15	16	17	
18		29	30	1	2	3	4	5			18	19	20	21	22	23	24	
19	MONTH 4 Dīng-Mǎo	6	7	8	*9*	10	11	12	Lì xià		25	26	27	28	29[g]	30	1	
20		13	14	15	16	17	18*	19			2	3	4	5	6	7	8	
21		20	21	22	23	***24***	25	26	**Xiǎo mǎn**	PASHONS 1703	9	10	11	12	13	14	15	GENBOT 1979
22		27	28	29	1	2	3	4			16	17	18	19	20	21	22	
23	MONTH 5 Dīng-Mǎo	5[d]	6	7	8	9	10	*11*	Máng zhòng		23	24	25	26	27	28	29	
24		12	13	14	15	16	17	18			30	1	2	3	4	5	6	
25		19	20	21	22	23	24	25		PAÔNE 1703	7	8	9	10	11	12	13	SANÉ 1979
26		26	***27***	28	29	30	1	2	**Xià zhì**		14	15	16	17	18	19	20	
27	MONTH 6 Dīng-Mǎo	3	4	5	6	7	8	9			21	22	23	24	25	26	27	
28		10	11	*12*	13	14	15	16	Xiǎo shǔ		28	29	30	1	2	3	4	
29		17	18	19*	20	21	22	23		EPÊP 1703	5	6	7	8	9	10	11	ḤAMLĒ 1979
30		24	25	26	27	***28***	29	30	**Dà shǔ**		12	13	14	15	16	17	18	
31	LEAP MONTH 6 Dīng-Mǎo	1	2	3	4	5	6	7			19	20	21	22	23	24	25	
32		8	9	10	11	12	13	*14*	Lì qiū		26	27	28	29	30	1	2	
33		15	16	17	18	19	20	21		MESORÊ 1703	3	4	5	6	7	8	9	NAHASÉ 1979
34		22	23	24	25	26	27	28			10	11	12	13[h]	14	15	16	
35		29	***1***	2	3	4	5	6	**Chǔ shǔ**		17	18	19	20	21	22	23	
36	MONTH 7 Dīng-Mǎo	7[e]	8	9	10	11	12	13			24	25	26	27	28	29	30	
37		14	15[f]	*16*	17	18	19	20*	Bái lù	EPAG. 1703	1	2	3	4	5	6	1[a]	PĀG. 1979
38		21	22	23	24	25	26	27		THOOUT 1704	2	3	4	5	6	7	8	MASKARAM 1980
39		28	29	30	***1***	2	3	4	**Qiū fēn**		9	10	11	12	13	14	15	
40	MONTH 8 Dīng-Mǎo	5	6	7	8	9	10	11			16	17[b]	18	19	20	21	22	
41		12	13	14	15[g]	16	*17*	18	Hán lù		23	24	25	26	27	28	29	
42		19	20	21	22	23	24	25		PAOPE 1704	30	1	2	3	4	5	6	ṬEQEMT 1980
43		26	27	28	29	30	1	***2***	**Shuāng jiàng**		7	8	9	10	11	12	13	
44	MONTH 9 Dīng-Mǎo	3	4	5	6	7	8	9[h]			14	15	16	17	18	19	20	
45		10	11	12	13	14	15	16			21	22	23	24	25	26	27	
46		*17*	18	19	20*	21	22	23	Lì dōng	ATHÔR 1704	28	29	30	1	2	3	4	HEDĀR 1980
47		24	25	26	27	28	29	1			5	6	7	8	9	10	11	
48	MONTH 10 Dīng-Mǎo	2	***3***	4	5	6	7	8	**Xiǎo xuě**		12	13	14	15	16	17	18	
49		9	10	11	12	13	14	15			19	20	21	22	23	24	25	
50		16	*17*	18	19	20	21	22	Dà xuě	KOIAK 1704	26	27	28	29	30	1	2	TĀKHŚĀŚ 1980
51		23	24	25	26	27	28	29			3	4	5	6	7	8	9	
52	MONTH 11 Dīng-Mǎo	30	1	***2***[i]	3	4	5	6	**Dōng zhì**		10	11	12	13	14	15	16	
53		7	8	9	10	11	12	13			17	18	19	20	21	22	23	

[a]New Year
[b]Spring (3:52)
[c]Summer (22:11)
[d]Autumn (13:45)
[e]Winter (9:46)
● New moon
◐ First quarter moon
○ Full moon
◑ Last quarter moon

[a]New Year
[b]Yom Kippur
[c]Sukkot
[d]Winter starts
[e]Ḥanukkah
[f]Purim
[g]Passover
[h]Shavuot
[i]Fast of Av

‡Leap year
[a]New Year (4685, Hare)
[b]Lantern Festival
[c]Qīngmíng
[d]Dragon Festival
[e]Qīqiǎo
[f]Hungry Ghosts
[g]Mid-Autumn Festival
[h]Double-Ninth Festival
[i]Dōngzhì
*Start of 60-name cycle

‡Leap year
[a]New Year
[b]Building of the Cross
[c]Christmas
[d]Jesus's Circumcision
[e]Epiphany
[f]Easter
[g]Mary's Announcement
[h]Jesus's Transfiguration

1987

PERSIAN (ASTRONOMICAL) 1365/1366‡

Month	Sun	Mon	Tue	Wed	Thu	Fri	Sat
DEY 1365	7	8	9	10	11	12	13
	14	15	16	17	18	19	20
	21	22	23	24	25	26	27
	28	29	30	1	2	3	4
BAHMAN 1365	5	6	7	8	9	10	11
	12	13	14	15	16	17	18
	19	20	21	22	23	24	25
	26	27	28	29	30	1	2
ESFAND 1365	3	4	5	6	7	8	9
	10	11	12	13	14	15	16
	17	18	19	20	21	22	23
	24	25	26	27	28	29	1[a]
FARVARDĪN 1366	2	3	4	5	6	7	8
	9	10	11	12	13[b]	14	15
	16	17	18	19	20	21	22
	23	24	25	26	27	28	29
	30	31	1	2	3	4	5
ORDĪBEHEŠT 1366	6	7	8	9	10	11	12
	13	14	15	16	17	18	19
	20	21	22	23	24	25	26
	27	28	29	30	31	1	2
XORDĀD 1366	3	4	5	6	7	8	9
	10	11	12	13	14	15	16
	17	18	19	20	21	22	23
	24	25	26	27	28	29	30
	31	1	2	3	4	5	6
TĪR 1366	7	8	9	10	11	12	13
	14	15	16	17	18	19	20
	21	22	23	24	25	26	27
	28	29	30	31	1	2	3
MORDĀD 1366	4	5	6	7	8	9	10
	11	12	13	14	15	16	17
	18	19	20	21	22	23	24
	25	26	27	28	29	30	31
SHAHRĪVAR 1366	1	2	3	4	5	6	7
	8	9	10	11	12	13	14
	15	16	17	18	19	20	21
	22	23	24	25	26	27	28
	29	30	31	1	2	3	4
MEHR 1366	5	6	7	8	9	10	11
	12	13	14	15	16	17	18
	19	20	21	22	23	24	25
	26	27	28	29	30	1	2
ABĀN 1366	3	4	5	6	7	8	9
	10	11	12	13	14	15	16
	17	18	19	20	21	22	23
	24	25	26	27	28	29	30
ĀZAR 1366	1	2	3	4	5	6	7
	8	9	10	11	12	13	14
	15	16	17	18	19	20	21
	22	23	24	25	26	27	28
DEY 1366	29	30	1	2	3	4	5
	6	7	8	9	10	11	12

‡Leap year
[a]New Year
[b]Sizdeh Bedar

HINDU LUNAR 2043/2044

Month	Sun	Mon	Tue	Wed	Thu	Fri	Sat
	27	28	29	**30**	2	3	4
PAUSHA 2043	5	6	7	8	9	10	11
	12	13	14	15	15	16	17
	18	19	20	21	22	23	**24**
	26	27	28	29	30	1	2
MĀGHA 2043	3	4	5	6	7	8	9
	10	11	12	13	14	15	16
	17	18	19	20	21	22	23
	24	25	26	27	28[h]	**29**	1
PHĀLGUNA 2043	2	3	4	5	6	7	8
	8	9	10	11	12	13	14
	15[i]	16	17	18	19	20	21
	22	**23**	25	26	27	28	29
	30	1[a]	2	3	4	5	6
CHAITRA 2044	7	8	9[b]	10	11	11	12
	13	14	15	**16**	18	19	20
	21	22	23	24	25	26	27
	28	29	30	1	2	3	4
VAIŚĀKHA 2044	5	6	7	8	9	10	11
	12	13	14	15	16	17	18
	19	**20**	22	23	24	25	26
	27	28	29	30	1	2	3
JYAISHTHA 2044	4	5	6	6	7	8	9
	10	11	12	**13**	15	16	17
	18	19	20	21	22	23	24
	25	26	27	28	29	30	1
ĀSHĀDHA 2044	2	3	4	5	6	7	8
	9	10	11	12	13	14	15
	16	18	19	20	21	22	23
	24	25	26	27	28	29	30
ŚRĀVAṆA 2044	1	2	3	3	4	5	6
	7	**8**	10	11	12	13	14
	15	16	17	18	19	**20**	22
	23[c]	24	24	25	26	27	28
BHĀDRAPADA 2044	29	30	1	2	3	4[d]	5
	6	7	8	9	10	11	**12**
	14	15	16	17	18	19	20
	21	22	23	24	25	26	27
	28	29	29	30	1	2	3
ĀŚVINA 2044	4	**5**	7	8[e]	9[e]	10[e]	11
	12	13	14	15	16	17	18
	19	20	21	22	23	24	25
	26	27	28	29	30	1[f]	2
KĀRTTIKA 2044	3	4	5	6	7	8	**9**
	11	12	13	14	15	16	17
	18	19	20	21	22	23	23
	24	25	26	27	28	29	30
MĀRGAŚĪRA 2044	1	2	**3**	5	6	7	8
	9	10	11[g]	12	13	14	15
	16	17	18	19	20	21	22
	23	24	25	26	27	28	29
PAUSHA 2044	30	1	2	3	4	5	6
	7	**8**	10	11	12	13	14

[a]New Year (Prabhava)
[b]Birthday of Rāma
[c]Birthday of Krishna
[d]Ganēśa Chaturthī
[e]Dashara
[f]Diwali
[g]Birthday of Vishnu
[h]Night of Śiva
[i]Holi

HINDU SOLAR 1908‡/1909

Month	Sun	Mon	Tue	Wed	Thu	Fri	Sat
PAUSHA 1908	13	14	15	16	17	18	19
	20	21	22	23	24	25	26
	27	28	29	1[b]	2	3	4
MĀGHA 1908	5	6	7	8	9	10	11
	12	13	14	15	16	17	18
	19	20	21	22	23	24	25
	26	27	28	29	1	2	3
PHĀLGUNA 1908	4	5	6	7	8	9	10
	11	12	13	14	15	16	17
	18	19	20	21	22	23	24
	25	26	27	28	29	30	1
CHAITRA 1908	2	3	4	5	6	7	8
	9	10	11	12	13	14	15
	16	17	18	19	20	21	22
	23	24	25	26	27	28	29
	30	31	1[a]	2	3	4	5
VAIŚĀKHA 1909	6	7	8	9	10	11	12
	13	14	15	16	17	18	19
	20	21	22	23	24	25	26
	27	28	29	30	31	1	2
JYAISHTHA 1909	3	4	5	6	7	8	9
	10	11	12	13	14	15	16
	17	18	19	20	21	22	23
	24	25	26	27	28	29	30
	31	1	2	3	4	5	6
ĀSHĀDHA 1909	7	8	9	10	11	12	13
	14	15	16	17	18	19	20
	21	22	23	24	25	26	27
	28	29	30	31	32	1	2
ŚRĀVAṆA 1909	3	4	5	6	7	8	9
	10	11	12	13	14	15	16
	17	18	19	20	21	22	23
	24	25	26	27	28	29	30
	31	1	2	3	4	5	6
BHĀDRAPADA 1909	7	8	9	10	11	12	13
	14	15	16	17	18	19	20
	21	22	23	24	25	26	27
	28	29	30	31	1	2	3
ĀŚVINA 1909	4	5	6	7	8	9	10
	11	12	13	14	15	16	17
	18	19	20	21	22	23	24
	25	26	27	28	29	30	31
KĀRTTIKA 1909	1	2	3	4	5	6	7
	8	9	10	11	12	13	14
	15	16	17	18	19	20	21
	22	23	24	25	26	27	28
	29	1	2	3	4	5	6
MĀRGAŚĪRA 1909	7	8	9	10	11	12	13
	14	15	16	17	18	19	20
	21	22	23	24	25	26	27
	28	29	30	1	2	3	4
PAUSHA 1909	5	6	7	8	9	10	11
	12	13	14	15	16	17	18

‡Leap year
[a]New Year (Vikrama)
[b]Pongal

ISLAMIC (ASTRONOMICAL) 1407/1408

Month	Sun	Mon	Tue	Wed	Thu	Fri	Sat
	26	27	28	29	1	2	3
JUMĀDĀ I 1407	4	5	6	7	8	9	10
	11	12	13	14	15	16	17
	18	19	20	21	22	23	24
	25	26	27	28	29	30	1
JUMĀDĀ II 1407	2	3	4	5	6	7	8
	9	10	11	12	13	14	15
	16	17	18	19	20	21	22
	23	24	25	26	27	28	29
RAJAB 1407	1	2	3	4	5	6	7
	8	9	10	11	12	13	14
	15	16	17	18	19	20	21
	22	23	24	25	26	27[d]	28
	29	30	1	2	3	4	5
SHA'BĀN 1407	6	7	8	9	10	11	12
	13	14	15	16	17	18	19
	20	21	22	23	24	25	26
	27	28	29	1[e]	2	3	4
RAMAḌĀN 1407	5	6	7	8	9	10	11
	12	13	14	15	16	17	18
	19	20	21	22	23	24	25
	26	27	28	29	30	1[f]	2
SHAWWĀL 1407	3	4	5	6	7	8	9
	10	11	12	13	14	15	16
	17	18	19	20	21	22	23
	24	25	26	27	28	29	1
DHU AL-QA'DA 1407	2	3	4	5	6	7	8
	9	10	11	12	13	14	15
	16	17	18	19	20	21	22
	23	24	25	26	27	28	29
DHU AL-ḤIJJA 1407	30	1	2	3	4	5	6
	7	8	9	10[g]	11	12	13
	14	15	16	17	18	19	20
	21	22	23	24	25	26	27
MUḤARRAM 1408	28	29	30	1[a]	2	3	4
	5	6	7	8	9	10[b]	11
	12	13	14	15	16	17	18
	19	20	21	22	23	24	25
ṢAFAR 1408	26	27	28	29	30	1	2
	3	4	5	6	7	8	9
	10	11	12	13	14	15	16
	17	18	19	20	21	22	23
	24	25	26	27	28	29	30
RABĪ' I 1408	1	2	3	4	5	6	7
	8	9	10	11	12[c]	13	14
	15	16	17	18	19	20	21
	22	23	24	25	26	27	28
RABĪ' II 1408	29	1	2	3	4	5	6
	7	8	9	10	11	12	13
	14	15	16	17	18	19	20
	21	22	23	24	25	26	27
JUMĀDĀ I 1408	28	29	1	2	3	4	5
	6	7	8	9	10	11	12

[a]New Year
[b]'Ashūrā'
[c]Prophet's Birthday
[d]Ascent of the Prophet
[e]Start of Ramaḍān
[f]'Id al-Fiṭr
[g]'Id al-'Aḍḥā

GREGORIAN 1987

Julian (Sun)	Sun	Mon	Tue	Wed	Thu	Fri	Sat	Month
Dec 15	28	29	30	31	1	2	3	
	4	5	6	7[a]	8	9	10	JANUARY 1987
Dec 29	11	12	13	14[b]	15	16	17	
	18	19	20	21	22	23	24	
Jan 12	25	26	27	28	29	30	31	
	1	2	3	4	5	6	7	FEBRUARY 1987
Jan 26	8	9	10	11	12	13	14	
	15	16	17	18	19	20	21	
Feb 9	22	23	24	25	26	27	28	
	1	2	3	4[c]	5	6	7	MARCH 1987
Feb 23	8[d]	9	10	11	12	13	14	
	15	16	17	18	19	20	21	
Mar 9	22	23	24	25	26	27	28	
	29	30	31	1	2	3	4	
Mar 23	5	6	7	8	9	10	11	APRIL 1987
	12	13	14	15	16	17	18	
Apr 6	19[e]	20	21	22	23	24	25	
	26	27	28	29	30	1	2	
Apr 20	3	4	5	6	7	8	9	MAY 1987
	10	11	12	13	14	15	16	
May 4	17	18	19	20	21	22	23	
	24	25	26	27	28	29	30	
May 18	31	1	2	3	4	5	6	
	7	8	9	10	11	12	13	JUNE 1987
Jun 1	14	15	16	17	18	19	20	
	21	22	23	24	25	26	27	
Jun 15	28	29	30	1	2	3	4	
	5	6	7	8	9	10	11	JULY 1987
Jun 29	12	13	14	15	16	17	18	
	19	20	21	22	23	24	25	
Jul 13	26	27	28	29	30	31	1	
	2	3	4	5	6	7	8	AUGUST 1987
Jul 27	9	10	11	12	13	14	15	
	16	17	18	19	20	21	22	
Aug 10	23	24	25	26	27	28	29	
	30	31	1	2	3	4	5	
Aug 24	6	7	8	9	10	11	12	SEPTEMBER 1987
	13	14	15	16	17	18	19	
Sep 7	20	21	22	23	24	25	26	
	27	28	29	30	1	2	3	
Sep 21	4	5	6	7	8	9	10	OCTOBER 1987
	11	12	13	14	15	16	17	
Oct 5	18	19	20	21	22	23	24	
	25	26	27	28	29	30	31	
Oct 19	1	2	3	4	5	6	7	NOVEMBER 1987
	8	9	10	11	12	13	14	
Nov 2	15	16	17	18	19	20	21	
	22	23	24	25	26	27	28	
Nov 16	29[g]	30	1	2	3	4	5	DECEMBER 1987
	6	7	8	9	10	11	12	
Nov 30	13	14	15	16	17	18	19	
	20	21	22	23	24	25[h]	26	
Dec 14	27	28	29	30	31	1	2	

[a]Orthodox Christmas
[b]Julian New Year
[c]Ash Wednesday
[d]Feast of Orthodoxy
[e]Easter (also Orthodox)
[g]Advent
[h]Christmas

1988

Gregorian 1988‡	Sun	Mon	Tue	Wed	Thu	Fri	Sat	Lunar Phases	ISO WEEK (Mon)	JULIAN DAY (Sun noon)
	◐	28	29	30	31	1[a]	2	10:01	53	2447157
JANUARY 1988	3	○	5	6	7	8	9	1:40	1	2447164
	10	11	◑	13	14	15	16	7:04	2	2447171
	17	18	●	20	21	22	23	5:26	3	2447178
	24	◐	26	27	28	29	30	21:54	4	2447185
	31	1	○	3	4	5	6	20:51	5	2447192
FEBRUARY 1988	7	8	9	◑	11	12	13	23:01	6	2447199
	14	15	16	●	18	19	20	15:54	7	2447206
	21	22	23	◐	25	26	27	12:15	8	2447213
	28	29	1	2	○	4	5	16:01	9	2447220
MARCH 1988	6	7	8	9	10	◑	12	10:56	10	2447227
	13	14	15	16	17	●	19	2:02	11	2447234
	20[b]	21	22	23	24	◐	26	4:41	12	2447241
	27	28	29	30	31	1	○	9:21	13	2447248
APRIL 1988	3	4	5	6	7	8	◑	19:21	14	2447255
	10	11	12	13	14	15	●	12:00	15	2447262
	17	18	19	20	21	22	◐	22:32	16	2447269
	24	25	26	27	28	29	30		17	2447276
MAY 1988	○	2	3	4	5	6	7	23:41	18	2447283
	8	◑	10	11	12	13	14	1:23	19	2447290
	●	16	17	18	19	20	21	22:11	20	2447297
	22	◐	24	25	26	27	28	16:49	21	2447304
	29	30	○	1	2	3	4	10:53	22	2447311
JUNE 1988	5	6	◑	8	9	10	11	6:22	23	2447318
	12	13	●	15	16	17	18	9:14	24	2447325
	19	20	21[c]	◐	23	24	25	10:23	25	2447332
	26	27	28	○	30	1	2	19:46	26	2447339
JULY 1988	3	4	5	◑	7	8	9	11:36	27	2447346
	10	11	12	●	14	15	16	21:53	28	2447353
	17	18	19	20	21	◐	23	2:14	29	2447360
	24	25	26	27	28	○	30	3:25	30	2447367
	31	1	2	3	◑	5	6	18:22	31	2447374
AUGUST 1988	7	8	9	10	11	●	13	12:31	32	2447381
	14	15	16	17	18	19	◐	15:51	33	2447388
	21	22	23	24	25	26	○	10:56	34	2447395
	28	29	30	31	1	2	◑	3:50	35	2447402
SEPTEMBER 1988	4	5	6	7	8	9	10		36	2447409
	●	12	13	14	15	16	17	4:49	37	2447416
	18	◐	20	21	22[d]	23	24	3:18	38	2447423
	○	26	27	28	29	30	1	19:07	39	2447430
OCTOBER 1988	◑	3	4	5	6	7	8	16:58	40	2447437
	9	●	11	12	13	14	15	21:49	41	2447444
	16	17	◐	19	20	21	22	13:01	42	2447451
	23	24	○	26	27	28	29	4:36	43	2447458
	30	31	◑	2	3	4	5	10:11	44	2447465
NOVEMBER 1988	6	7	8	●	10	11	12	14:20	45	2447472
	13	14	15	◐	17	18	19	21:35	46	2447479
	20	21	22	○	24	25	26	15:53	47	2447486
	27	28	29	30	◑	2	3	6:49	48	2447493
DECEMBER 1988	4	5	6	7	8	●	10	5:36	49	2447500
	11	12	13	14	15	◐	17	5:40	50	2447507
	18	19	20	21[e]	22	○	24	5:29	51	2447514
	25	26	27	28	29	30	◑	4:57	52	2447521

ISO WEEK	Hebrew 5748/5749‡	Sun	Mon	Tue	Wed	Thu	Fri	Sat	Molad
53		6	7	8	9	10	11	12	
1	TEVETH 5748	13	14	15	16	17	18	19	
2		20	21	22	23	24	25	26	
3		27	28	29	1	2	3	4	Tue 6h0m0p
4	SHEVAT 5748	5	6	7	8	9	10	11	
5		12	13	14	15	16	17	18	
6		19	20	21	22	23	24	25	
7		26	27	28	29	30	1	2	Wed 18h44m1p
8	ADAR 5748	3	4	5	6	7	8	9	
9		10	11	12	13	14[f]	15	16	
10		17	18	19	20	21	22	23	
11		24	25	26	27	28	29	1	Fri 7h28m11p
12	NISAN 5748	2	3	4	5	6	7	8	
13		9	10	11	12	13	14	15[g]	
14		16	17	18	19	20	21	22	
15		23	24	25	26	27	28	29	
16		30	1	2	3	4	5	6	Sat 20h12m12p
17	IYYAR 5748	7	8	9	10	11	12	13	
18		14	15	16	17	18	19	20	
19		21	22	23	24	25	26	27	
20		28	29	1	2	3	4	5	Mon 8h56m13p
21	SIVAN 5748	6[h]	7	8	9	10	11	12	
22		13	14	15	16	17	18	19	
23		20	21	22	23	24	25	26	
24		27	28	29	30	1	2	3	Tue 21h40m14p
25	TAMMUZ 5748	4	5	6	7	8	9	10	
26		11	12	13	14	15	16	17	
27		18	19	20	21	22	23	24	
28		25	26	27	28	29	1	2	Thu 10h24m15p
29	AV 5748	3	4	5	6	7	8	9	
30		10[i]	11	12	13	14	15	16	
31		17	18	19	20	21	22	23	
32		24	25	26	27	28	29	30	
33		1	2	3	4	5	6	7	Fri 23h8m16p
34	ELUL 5748	8	9	10	11	12	13	14	
35		15	16	17	18	19	20	21	
36		22	23	24	25	26	27	28	
37		29	1[a]	2[a]	3	4	5	6	Sun 11h52m17p
38	TISHRI 5749	7	8	9	10[b]	11	12	13	
39		14	15[c]	16	17	18	19	20	
40		21	22	23	24	25	26	27	
41		28	29	30	1	2	3	4	Tue 0h37m0p
42	ḤESHVAN 5749	5	6	7	8	9	10	11	
43		12	13	14	15	16	17	18	
44		19	20	21	22	23	24	25	
45		26	27	28	29	1	2	3	Wed 13h21m1p
46	KISLEV 5749	4	5	6	7	8	9	10	
47		11	12	13	14	15	16	17	
48		18	19	20	21	22	23	24	
49		25[e]	26[d][e]	27[e]	28[e]	29[e]	1[e]	2[e]	Fri 2h5m2p
50	TEVETH 5749	3[e]	4	5	6	7	8	9	
51		10	11	12	13	14	15	16	
52		17	18	19	20	21	22	23	

ISO WEEK	Chinese Dīng-Mǎo‡/Wù-Chén	Sun	Mon	Tue	Wed	Thu	Fri	Sat	Solar Term
53		7	8	9	10	11	12	13	
1	MONTH 11 Dīng-Mǎo	14	15	16	17	18	19	20	Xiǎo hán
2		21*	22	23	24	25	26	27	
3		28	29	1	2	3	4	5	Dà hán
4	MONTH 12 Dīng-Mǎo	6	7	8	9	10	11	12	
5		13	14	15	16	17	18	19	Lì chūn
6		20	21	22	23	24	25	26	
7		27	28	29	1[a]	2	3	4	Yǔ shuǐ
8	MONTH 1 Wù-Chén	5	6	7	8	9	10	11	
9		12	13	14	15[b]	16	17	18	Jīng zhé
10		19	20	21	22	23*	24	25	
11		26	27	28	29	30	1	2	
12	MONTH 2 Wù-Chén	3	4	5	6	7	8	9	Chūn fēn
13		10	11	12	13	14	15	16	
14		17	18[c]	19	20	21	22	23	Qīng míng
15		24	25	26	27	28	29	1	
16	MONTH 3 Wù-Chén	2	3	4	5	6	7	8	Gǔ yǔ
17		9	10	11	12	13	14	15	
18		16	17	18	19	20	21	22	Lì xià
19		23	24*	25	26	27	28	29	
20		30	1	2	3	4	5	6	Xiǎo mǎn
21	MONTH 4 Wù-Chén	7	8	9	10	11	12	13	
22		14	15	16	17	18	19	20	
23		21	22	23	24	25	26	27	Máng zhòng
24		28	29	1	2	3	4	5[d]	
25	MONTH 5 Wù-Chén	6	7	8	9	10	11	12	Xià zhì
26		13	14	15	16	17	18	19	
27		20	21	22	23	24	25*	26	Xiǎo shǔ
28		27	28	29	30	1	2	3	
29	MONTH 6 Wù-Chén	4	5	6	7	8	9	10	Dà shǔ
30		11	12	13	14	15	16	17	
31		18	19	20	21	22	23	24	
32		25	26	27	28	29	1	2	Lì qiū
33	MONTH 7 Wù-Chén	3	4	5	6	7[e]	8	9	
34		10	11	12	13	14	15[f]	16	Chǔ shǔ
35		17	18	19	20	21	22	23	
36		24	25	26*	27	28	29	30	Bái lù
37		1	2	3	4	5	6	7	
38	MONTH 8 Wù-Chén	8	9	10	11	12	13	14	Qiū fēn
39		15[g]	16	17	18	19	20	21	
40		22	23	24	25	26	27	28	Hán lù
41		29	30	1	2	3	4	5	
42	MONTH 9 Wù-Chén	6	7	8	9[h]	10	11	12	
43		13	14	15	16	17	18	19	Shuāng jiàng
44		20	21	22	23	24	25	26*	
45		27	28	29	1	2	3	4	Lì dōng
46	MONTH 10 Wù-Chén	5	6	7	8	9	10	11	
47		12	13	14	15	16	17	18	Xiǎo xuě
48		19	20	21	22	23	24	25	
49		26	27	28	29	30	1	2	Dà xuě
50	MONTH 11* Wù-Chén	3	4	5	6	7	8	9	
51		10	11	12	13[i]	14	15	16	Dōng zhì
52		17	18	19	20	21	22	23	

ISO WEEK	Coptic 1704/1705	Sun	Mon	Tue	Wed	Thu	Fri	Sat	Ethiopic 1980/1981
53	KOIAK 1704	17	18	19	20	21	22	23	TĀḪŚĀŚ 1980
1		24	25	26	27	28	29[c]	30	
2		1	2	3	4	5	6[d]	7	
3	TŌBE 1704	8	9	10	11[e]	12	13	14	ṬER 1980
4		15	16	17	18	19	20	21	
5		22	23	24	25	26	27	28	
6		29	30	1	2	3	4	5	
7	MESHIR 1704	6	7	8	9	10	11	12	YAKĀTIT 1980
8		13	14	15	16	17	18	19	
9		20	21	22	23	24	25	26	
10		27	28	29	30	1	2	3	
11	PAREMOTEP 1704	4	5	6	7	8	9	10	MAGĀBIT 1980
12		11	12	13	14	15	16	17	
13		18	19	20	21	22	23	24	
14		25	26	27	28	29	30	1	
15	PARMOUTE 1704	2[f]	3	4	5	6	7	8	MIYĀZYĀ 1980
16		9	10	11	12	13	14	15	
17		16	17	18	19	20	21	22	
18		23	24	25	26	27	28	29[g]	
19	PASHONS 1704	30	1	2	3	4	5	6	
20		7	8	9	10	11	12	13	GENBOT 1980
21		14	15	16	17	18	19	20	
22		21	22	23	24	25	26	27	
23		28	29	30	1	2	3	4	
24	PAŌNE 1704	5	6	7	8	9	10	11	SANĒ 1980
25		12	13	14	15	16	17	18	
26		19	20	21	22	23	24	25	
27		26	27	28	29	30	1	2	
28	EPĒP 1704	3	4	5	6	7	8	9	ḤAMLĒ 1980
29		10	11	12	13	14	15	16	
30		17	18	19	20	21	22	23	
31		24	25	26	27	28	29	30	
32	MESORĒ 1704	1	2	3	4	5	6	7	
33		8	9	10	11	12	13[h]	14	NAḤASĒ 1980
34		15	16	17	18	19	20	21	
35		22	23	24	25	26	27	28	
36	EPAG. 1704	29	30	1	2	3	4	5	PĀG. 1980
37	THOOUT 1705	1[a]	2	3	4	5	6	7	
38		8	9	10	11	12	13	14	MASKARAM 1981
39		15	16	17[b]	18	19	20	21	
40		22	23	24	25	26	27	28	
41		29	30	1	2	3	4	5	
42	PAOPE 1705	6	7	8	9	10	11	12	ṬEQEMT 1981
43		13	14	15	16	17	18	19	
44		20	21	22	23	24	25	26	
45		27	28	29	30	1	2	3	
46	ATHŌR 1705	4	5	6	7	8	9	10	ḪEDĀR 1981
47		11	12	13	14	15	16	17	
48		18	19	20	21	22	23	24	
49		25	26	27	28	29	30	1	
50	KOIAK 1705	2	3	4	5	6	7	8	TĀḪŚĀŚ 1981
51		9	10	11	12	13	14	15	
52		16	17	18	19	20	21	22	

Gregorian:
‡Leap year
[a]New Year
[b]Spring (9:39)
[c]Summer (3:56)
[d]Autumn (19:29)
[e]Winter (15:28)
● New moon
◐ First quarter moon
○ Full moon
◑ Last quarter moon

Hebrew:
‡Leap year
[a]New Year
[b]Yom Kippur
[c]Sukkot
[d]Winter starts
[e]Ḥanukkah
[f]Purim
[g]Passover
[h]Shavuot
[i]Fast of Av

Chinese:
‡Leap year
[a]New Year (4686, Dragon)
[b]Lantern Festival
[c]Qīngmíng
[d]Dragon Festival
[e]Qīqiǎo
[f]Hungry Ghosts
[g]Mid-Autumn Festival
[h]Double-Ninth Festival
[i]Dōngzhì
*Start of 60-name cycle

Coptic/Ethiopic:
[a]New Year
[b]Building of the Cross
[c]Christmas
[d]Jesus's Circumcision
[e]Epiphany
[f]Easter
[g]Mary's Announcement
[h]Jesus's Transfiguration

1988

PERSIAN (ASTRONOMICAL) 1366‡/1367

Month	Sun	Mon	Tue	Wed	Thu	Fri	Sat
	6	7	8	9	10	11	12
DEY 1366	13	14	15	16	17	18	19
	20	21	22	23	24	25	26
	27	28	29	30	1	2	3
BAHMAN 1366	4	5	6	7	8	9	10
	11	12	13	14	15	16	17
	18	19	20	21	22	23	24
	25	26	27	28	29	30	1
ESFAND 1366	2	3	4	5	6	7	8
	9	10	11	12	13	14	15
	16	17	18	19	20	21	22
	23	24	25	26	27	28	29
	30	1[a]	2	3	4	5	6
FARVARDĪN 1367	7	8	9	10	11	12	13[b]
	14	15	16	17	18	19	20
	21	22	23	24	25	26	27
	28	29	30	31	1	2	3
ORDĪBEHEŠT 1367	4	5	6	7	8	9	10
	11	12	13	14	15	16	17
	18	19	20	21	22	23	24
	25	26	27	28	29	30	31
	1	2	3	4	5	6	7
XORDĀD 1367	8	9	10	11	12	13	14
	15	16	17	18	19	20	21
	22	23	24	25	26	27	28
	29	30	31	1	2	3	4
TĪR 1367	5	6	7	8	9	10	11
	12	13	14	15	16	17	18
	19	20	21	22	23	24	25
	26	27	28	29	30	31	1
MORDĀD 1367	2	3	4	5	6	7	8
	9	10	11	12	13	14	15
	16	17	18	19	20	21	22
	23	24	25	26	27	28	29
	30	31	1	2	3	4	5
SHAHRĪVAR 1367	6	7	8	9	10	11	12
	13	14	15	16	17	18	19
	20	21	22	23	24	25	26
	27	28	29	30	31	1	2
MEHR 1367	3	4	5	6	7	8	9
	10	11	12	13	14	15	16
	17	18	19	20	21	22	23
	24	25	26	27	28	29	30
	1	2	3	4	5	6	7
ABĀN 1367	8	9	10	11	12	13	14
	15	16	17	18	19	20	21
	22	23	24	25	26	27	28
	29	30	1	2	3	4	5
ĀZAR 1367	6	7	8	9	10	11	12
	13	14	15	16	17	18	19
	20	21	22	23	24	25	26
DEY 1367	27	28	29	30	1	2	3
	4	5	6	7	8	9	10

‡Leap year
[a]New Year
[b]Sizdeh Bedar

HINDU LUNAR 2044/2045‡

Month	Sun	Mon	Tue	Wed	Thu	Fri	Sat
	7	**8**	10	11	12	13	14
PAUSHA 2044	15	16	*16*	17	18	19	20
	21	22	23	24	25	26	27
	28	29	30	**1**	3	4	5
MĀGHA 2044	6	7	8	9	10	11	12
	13	14	15	16	17	18	*18*
	19	20	21	22	23	24	**25**
	27	28	29[h]	30	1	2	3
PHĀLGUNA 2044	4	5	6	7	8	9	10
	11	12	13	14	15[i]	16	17
	18	19	20	21	22	23	24
	25	26	27	28	29	**30**[a]	2
CHAITRA 2045	3	4	5	6	7	8	9[b]
	10	11	*11*	12	13	14	15
	16	17	18	19	20	21	22
	23	**24**	26	27	28	29	30
	1	2	3	4	5	6	7
VAIŚĀKHA 2045	8	9	10	11	12	13	14
	15	16	17	18	19	20	21
	22	23	24	25	26	27	**28**
	30	1	2	3	4	5	6
LEAP JYAISHTHA 2045	6	7	8	9	10	11	12
	13	14	15	16	17	18	19
	20	22	23	24	25	26	27
	28	29	30	1	2	3	4
JYAISHTHA 2045	5	6	7	8	9	10	11
	12	13	14	15	16	17	18
	19	20	21	22	**23**	25	26
	27	28	29	30	1	2	3
ĀSHĀḌHA 2045	3	4	5	6	7	8	9
	10	11	12	13	14	15	**16**
	18	19	20	21	22	23	24
	25	26	27	28	29	30	1
	2	3	4	5	6	7	8
ŚRĀVAṆA 2045	9	10	11	12	13	14	15
	16	17	18	**19**	21	22	23[c]
	24	25	26	27	28	29	*29*
	30	1	2	3	4[d]	5	6
BHĀDRAPADA 2045	7	8	9	10	11	**12**	14
	15	16	17	18	19	20	21
	22	23	24	25	26	27	28
	29	30	1	2	3	4	5
	6	7	8[e]	9[e]	10[e]	11	12
ĀŚVINA 2045	13	14	15	16	**17**	19	20
	21	22	23	*23*	24	25	26
	27	28	29	30	1[f]	2	3
	4	5	6	7	8	9	**10**
KĀRTTIKA 2045	12	13	14	15	16	17	18
	19	20	21	22	23	24	25
	26	*26*	27	28	29	30	1
MĀRGAŚIRA 2045	2	3	**4**	6	7	8	9
	10	11[g]	12	13	14	15	16
	17	18	19	20	21	22	23

‡Leap year
[a]New Year (Vibhava)
[b]Birthday of Rāma
[c]Birthday of Krishna
[d]Gaṇēśa Chaturthī
[e]Dashara
[f]Diwali
[g]Birthday of Vishnu
[h]Night of Śiva
[i]Holi

HINDU SOLAR 1909/1910

Month	Sun	Mon	Tue	Wed	Thu	Fri	Sat
	12	13	14	15	16	17	18
PAUSHA 1909	19	20	21	22	23	24	25
	26	27	28	29	1[b]	2	3
	4	5	6	7	8	9	10
MĀGHA 1909	11	12	13	14	15	16	17
	18	19	20	21	22	23	24
	25	26	27	28	29	30	1
	2	3	4	5	6	7	8
PHĀLGUNA 1909	9	10	11	12	13	14	15
	16	17	18	19	20	21	22
	23	24	25	26	27	28	29
	30	1	2	3	4	5	6
CHAITRA 1909	7	8	9	10	11	12	13
	14	15	16	17	18	19	20
	21	22	23	24	25	26	27
	28	29	30	1[a]	2	3	4
VAIŚĀKHA 1910	5	6	7	8	9	10	11
	12	13	14	15	16	17	18
	19	20	21	22	23	24	25
	26	27	28	29	30	31	1
	2	3	4	5	6	7	8
JYAISHTHA 1910	9	10	11	12	13	14	15
	16	17	18	19	20	21	22
	23	24	25	26	27	28	29
	30	31	1	2	3	4	5
ĀSHĀḌHA 1910	6	7	8	9	10	11	12
	13	14	15	16	17	18	19
	20	21	22	23	24	25	26
	27	28	29	30	31	32	1
	2	3	4	5	6	7	8
ŚRĀVAṆA 1910	9	10	11	12	13	14	15
	16	17	18	19	20	21	22
	23	24	25	26	27	28	29
	30	31	1	2	3	4	5
BHĀDRAPADA 1910	6	7	8	9	10	11	12
	13	14	15	16	17	18	19
	20	21	22	23	24	25	26
	27	28	29	30	31	1	2
	3	4	5	6	7	8	9
ĀŚVINA 1910	10	11	12	13	14	15	16
	17	18	19	20	21	22	23
	24	25	26	27	28	29	30
	31	1	2	3	4	5	6
KĀRTTIKA 1910	7	8	9	10	11	12	13
	14	15	16	17	18	19	20
	21	22	23	24	25	26	27
	28	29	30	1	2	3	4
MĀRGAŚIRA 1910	5	6	7	8	9	10	11
	12	13	14	15	16	17	18
	19	20	21	22	23	24	25
	26	27	28	29	1	2	3
PAUSHA 1910	4	5	6	7	8	9	10
	11	12	13	14	15	16	17

[a]New Year (Vṛisha)
[b]Pongal

ISLAMIC (ASTRONOMICAL) 1408/1409

Month	Sun	Mon	Tue	Wed	Thu	Fri	Sat
	6	7	8	9	10	11	12
JUMĀDĀ I 1408	13	14	15	16	17	18	19
	20	21	22	23	24	25	26
	27	28	29	1	2	3	4
JUMĀDĀ II 1408	5	6	7	8	9	10	11
	12	13	14	15	16	17	18
	19	20	21	22	23	24	25
	26	27	28	29	30	1	2
	3	4	5	6	7	8	9
RAJAB 1408	10	11	12	13	14	15	16
	17	18	19	20	21	22	23
	24	25	26	27[d]	28	29	1
	2	3	4	5	6	7	8
SHA'BĀN 1408	9	10	11	12	13	14	15
	16	17	18	19	20	21	22
	23	24	25	26	27	28	29
	30	1[e]	2	3	4	5	6
RAMAḌĀN 1408	7	8	9	10	11	12	13
	14	15	16	17	18	19	20
	21	22	23	24	25	26	27
	28	29	1[f]	2	3	4	5
SHAWWĀL 1408	6	7	8	9	10	11	12
	13	14	15	16	17	18	19
	20	21	22	23	24	25	26
	27	28	29	30	1	2	3
DHU AL-QA'DA 1408	4	5	6	7	8	9	10
	11	12	13	14	15	16	17
	18	19	20	21	22	23	24
	25	26	27	28	29	1	2
DHU AL-ḤIJJA 1408	3	4	5	6	7	8	9
	10[g]	11	12	13	14	15	16
	17	18	19	20	21	22	23
	24	25	26	27	28	29	30
	1[a]	2	3	4	5	6	7
MUḤARRAM 1409	8	9	10[b]	11	12	13	14
	15	16	17	18	19	20	21
	22	23	24	25	26	27	28
	29	30	1	2	3	4	5
ṢAFAR 1409	6	7	8	9	10	11	12
	13	14	15	16	17	18	19
	20	21	22	23	24	25	26
	27	28	29	30	1	2	3
RABĪ' I 1409	4	5	6	7	8	9	10
	11	12[c]	13	14	15	16	17
	18	19	20	21	22	23	24
	25	26	27	28	29	30	1
RABĪ' II 1409	2	3	4	5	6	7	8
	9	10	11	12	13	14	15
	16	17	18	19	20	21	22
	23	24	25	26	27	28	29
JUMĀDĀ I 1409	1	2	3	4	5	6	7
	8	9	10	11	12	13	14
	15	16	17	18	19	20	21

[a]New Year
[b]'Ashūrā'
[c]Prophet's Birthday
[d]Ascent of the Prophet
[e]Start of Ramaḍān
[f]'Id al-Fiṭr
[g]'Id al-'Aḍḥā

GREGORIAN 1988‡

Julian‡ (Sun)	Sun	Mon	Tue	Wed	Thu	Fri	Sat	Month
Dec 14	27	28	29	30	31	1	2	
	3	4	5	6	7[a]	8	9	
Dec 28	10	11	12	13	14[b]	15	16	JANUARY 1988
	17	18	19	20	21	22	23	
Jan 11	24	25	26	27	28	29	30	
	31	1	2	3	4	5	6	
Jan 25	7	8	9	10	11	12	13	
	14	15	16	17[c]	18	19	20	FEBRUARY 1988
Feb 8	21	22	23	24	25	26	27	
	28[d]	29	1	2	3	4	5	
Feb 22	6	7	8	9	10	11	12	
	13	14	15	16	17	18	19	MARCH 1988
Mar 7	20	21	22	23	24	25	26	
	27	28	29	30	31	1	2	
Mar 21	3[e]	4	5	6	7	8	9	
	10[f]	11	12	13	14	15	16	APRIL 1988
Apr 4	17	18	19	20	21	22	23	
	24	25	26	27	28	29	30	
Apr 18	1	2	3	4	5	6	7	
	8	9	10	11	12	13	14	MAY 1988
May 2	15	16	17	18	19	20	21	
	22	23	24	25	26	27	28	
May 16	29	30	31	1	2	3	4	
	5	6	7	8	9	10	11	JUNE 1988
May 30	12	13	14	15	16	17	18	
	19	20	21	22	23	24	25	
Jun 13	26	27	28	29	30	1	2	
	3	4	5	6	7	8	9	
Jun 27	10	11	12	13	14	15	16	JULY 1988
	17	18	19	20	21	22	23	
Jul 11	24	25	26	27	28	29	30	
	31	1	2	3	4	5	6	
Jul 25	7	8	9	10	11	12	13	AUGUST 1988
	14	15	16	17	18	19	20	
Aug 8	21	22	23	24	25	26	27	
	28	29	30	31	1	2	3	
Aug 22	4	5	6	7	8	9	10	SEPTEMBER 1988
	11	12	13	14	15	16	17	
Sep 5	18	19	20	21	22	23	24	
	25	26	27	28	29	30	1	
Sep 19	2	3	4	5	6	7	8	
	9	10	11	12	13	14	15	OCTOBER 1988
Oct 3	16	17	18	19	20	21	22	
	23	24	25	26	27	28	29	
Oct 17	30	31	1	2	3	4	5	
	6	7	8	9	10	11	12	NOVEMBER 1988
Oct 31	13	14	15	16	17	18	19	
	20	21	22	23	24	25	26	
Nov 14	27[g]	28	29	30	1	2	3	
	4	5	6	7	8	9	10	DECEMBER 1988
Nov 28	11	12	13	14	15	16	17	
	18	19	20	21	22	23	24	
Dec 12	25[h]	26	27	28	29	30	31	

‡Leap year
[a]Orthodox Christmas
[b]Julian New Year
[c]Ash Wednesday
[d]Feast of Orthodoxy
[e]Easter
[f]Orthodox Easter
[g]Advent
[h]Christmas

1989

Gregorian 1989, Lunar Phases, ISO Week, Julian Day

Month	Sun	Mon	Tue	Wed	Thu	Fri	Sat	Lunar Phases	ISO WEEK (Mon)	JULIAN DAY (Sun noon)
JANUARY 1989	1[a]	2	3	4	5	6	●	19:22	1	2447528
	8	9	10	11	12	13	◐	13:58	2	2447535
	15	16	17	18	19	20	○	21:33	3	2447542
	22	23	24	25	26	27	28		4	2447549
	29	◑	31	1	2	3	4	2:02	5	2447556
FEBRUARY 1989	5	●	7	8	9	10	11	7:37	6	2447563
	◐	13	14	15	16	17	18	23:15	7	2447570
	19	○	21	22	23	24	25	15:32	8	2447577
	26	27	◑	1	2	3	4	20:08	9	2447584
MARCH 1989	5	6	●	8	9	10	11	18:19	10	2447591
	12	13	◐	15	16	17	18	10:11	11	2447598
	19	20[b]	21	○	23	24	25	9:58	12	2447605
	26	27	28	29	◑	31	1	10:21	13	2447612
APRIL 1989	2	3	4	5	●	7	8	3:33	14	2447619
	9	10	11	◐	13	14	15	23:13	15	2447626
	16	17	18	19	20	○	22	3:13	16	2447633
	23	24	25	26	27	◑	29	20:46	17	2447640
	30	1	2	3	4	●	6	11:46	18	2447647
MAY 1989	7	8	9	10	11	◐	13	14:20	19	2447654
	14	15	16	17	18	19	○	18:16	20	2447661
	21	22	23	24	25	26	27		21	2447668
	◑	29	30	31	1	2	●	4:01 19:53	22	2447675
JUNE 1989	4	5	6	7	8	9	10		23	2447682
	◐	12	13	14	15	16	17	6:59	24	2447689
	18	○	20	21[c]	22	23	24	6:57	25	2447696
	25	◑	27	28	29	30	1	9:09	26	2447703
JULY 1989	2	●	4	5	6	7	8	4:59	27	2447710
	9	10	◐	12	13	14	15	0:19	28	2447717
	16	17	○	19	20	21	22	17:42	29	2447724
	23	24	◑	26	27	28	29	13:31	30	2447731
	30	31	●	2	3	4	5	16:06	31	2447738
AUGUST 1989	6	7	8	◐	10	11	12	17:29	32	2447745
	13	14	15	16	○	18	19	3:07	33	2447752
	20	21	22	◑	24	25	26	18:40	34	2447759
	27	28	29	30	●	1	2	5:44	35	2447766
SEPTEMBER 1989	3	4	5	6	7	◐	9	9:49	36	2447773
	10	11	12	13	14	○	16	11:51	37	2447780
	17	18	19	20	21	◑	23[d]	2:10	38	2447787
	24	25	26	27	28	●	30	21:47	39	2447794
OCTOBER 1989	1	2	3	4	5	6	7		40	2447801
	◐	9	10	11	12	13	○	0:52 20:32	41	2447808
	15	16	17	18	19	20	◑	13:19	42	2447815
	22	23	24	25	26	27	28		43	2447822
	●	30	31	1	2	3	4	15:27	44	2447829
NOVEMBER 1989	5	◐	7	8	9	10	11	14:11	45	2447836
	12	○	14	15	16	17	18	5:52	46	2447843
	19	◑	21	22	23	24	25	4:44	47	2447850
	26	27	●	29	30	1	2	9:41	48	2447857
DECEMBER 1989	3	4	5	◐	7	8	9	1:26	49	2447864
	10	11	○	13	14	15	16	16:30	50	2447871
	17	18	◑	20	21[e]	22	23	23:55	51	2447878
	24	25	26	27	●	29	30	3:20	52	2447885
	31	1	2	3	◐	5	6	10:40	1	2447892

Hebrew 5749‡/5750

Month	Sun	Mon	Tue	Wed	Thu	Fri	Sat	Molad
	24	25	26	27	28	29	1	Sat 14h49m3p
SHEVAT 5749	2	3	4	5	6	7	8	
	9	10	11	12	13	14	15	
	16	17	18	19	20	21	22	
	23	24	25	26	27	28	29	
	30	1	2	3	4	5	6	Mon 3h33m4p
ADAR I 5749	7	8	9	10	11	12	13	
	14	15	16	17	18	19	20	
	21	22	23	24	25	26	27	
	28	29	30	1	2	3	4	Tue 16h17m5p
ADAR II 5749	5	6	7	8	9	10	11	
	12	13	14[f]	15	16	17	18	
	19	20	21	22	23	24	25	
	26	27	28	29	1	2	3	Thu 5h1m6p
NISAN 5749	4	5	6	7	8	9	10	
	11	12	13	14	15[g]	16	17	
	18	19	20	21	22	23	24	
	25	26	27	28	29	30	1	Fri 17h45m7p
IYAR 5749	2	3	4	5	6	7	8	
	9	10	11	12	13	14	15	
	16	17	18	19	20	21	22	
	23	24	25	26	27	28	29	
SIVAN 5749	1	2	3	4	5	6[h]	7	Sun 6h29m8p
	8	9	10	11	12	13	14	
	15	16	17	18	19	20	21	
	22	23	24	25	26	27	28	
	29	30	1	2	3	4	5	Mon 19h13m9p
TAMMUZ 5749	6	7	8	9	10	11	12	
	13	14	15	16	17	18	19	
	20	21	22	23	24	25	26	
	27	28	29	1	2	3	4	Wed 7h57m10p
AV 5749	5	6	7	8	9[i]	10	11	
	12	13	14	15	16	17	18	
	19	20	21	22	23	24	25	
	26	27	28	29	30	1	2	Thu 20h41m11p
ELUL 5749	3	4	5	6	7	8	9	
	10	11	12	13	14	15	16	
	17	18	19	20	21	22	23	
	24	25	26	27	28	29	1[a]	Sat 9h25m12p
	2[a]	3	4	5	6	7	8	
TISHRI 5750	9	10[b]	11	12	13	14	15[c]	
	16	17	18	19	20	21	22	
	23	24	25	26	27	28	29	
	30	1	2	3	4	5	6	Sun 22h9m13p
HESHVAN 5750	7	8	9	10	11	12	13	
	14	15	16	17	18	19	20	
	21	22	23	24	25	26	27	
	28	29	30	1	2	3	4	Tue 10h53m14p
KISLEV 5750	5	6	7[d]	8	9	10	11	
	12	13	14	15	16	17	18	
	19	20	21	22	23	24	25[e]	
	26[e]	27[e]	28[e]	29[e]	30[e]	1[e]	2[e]	Wed 23h37m15p
TEVETH 5750	3	4	5	6	7	8	9	

Chinese Wù-Chén/Jĭ-Sì

Month	Sun	Mon	Tue	Wed	Thu	Fri	Sat	Solar Term
	24	25	26	27*	*28*	29	30	Xiǎo hán
MONTH 12 Wù-Chén	1	2	3	4	5	6	7	
	8	9	10	11	12	***13***	14	**Dà hán**
	15	16	17	18	19	20	21	
	22	23	24	25	26	27	*28*	Lì chūn
	29	1[a]	2	3	4	5	6	
MONTH 1 Jĭ-Sì	7	8	9	10	11	12	13	
	14	15[b]	16	17	18	19	20	**Yǔ shuǐ**
	21	22	23	24	25	26	27	
	*28**	29	30	1	2	3	4	Jīng zhé
MONTH 2 Jĭ-Sì	5	6	7	8	9	10	11	
	12	***13***	14	15	16	17	18	**Chūn fēn**
	19	20	21	22	23	24	25	
	26	27	28	*29*[c]	1	2	3	Qīng míng
MONTH 3 Jĭ-Sì	4	5	6	7	8	9	10	
	11	12	13	14	***15***	16	17	**Gǔ yǔ**
	18	19	20	21	22	23	24	
	25	26	27	28	29*	*1*	2	Lì xià
MONTH 4 Jĭ-Sì	3	4	5	6	7	8	9	
	10	11	12	13	14	15	16	
	17	18	19	20	21	22	23	**Xiǎo mǎn**
	24	25	26	27	28	29	30	
MONTH 5 Jĭ-Sì	1	2	3	4	5[d]	6	7	Máng zhòng
	8	9	10	11	12	13	14	
	15	16	17	***18***	19	20	21	**Xià zhì**
	22	23	24	25	26	27	28	
	29	1*	2	3	4	5	6	Xiǎo shǔ
MONTH 6 Jĭ-Sì	7	8	9	10	11	12	13	
	14	15	16	17	18	19	20	
	21	22	23	24	25	26	27	**Dà shǔ**
	28	29	30	1	2	3	4	
MONTH 7 Jĭ-Sì	5	6	7[e]	8	9	10	11	Lì qiū
	12	13	14	15[f]	16	17	18	
	19	20	21	***22***	23	24	25	**Chǔ shǔ**
	26	27	28	29	1	2*	3	
MONTH 8 Jĭ-Sì	4	5	6	7	*8*	9	10	Bái lù
	11	12	13	14	15[g]	16	17	
	18	19	20	21	22	23	***24***	**Qiū fēn**
	25	26	27	28	29	30	1	
MONTH 9 Jĭ-Sì	2	3	4	5	6	7	8	
	9[h]	10	11	12	13	14	15	Hán lù
	16	17	18	19	20	21	22	
	23	***24***	25	26	27	28	29	**Shuāng jiàng**
MONTH 10 Jĭ-Sì	1	2	3*	4	5	6	7	Lì dōng
	8	9	*10*	11	12	13	14	
	15	16	17	18	19	20	21	
	22	23	24	***25***	26	27	28	**Xiǎo xuě**
	29	30	1	2	3	4	5	
MONTH 11 Jĭ-Sì	6	7	8	9	*10*	11	12	Dà xuě
	13	14	15	16	17	18	19	
	20	21	22	23	24	***25***[i]	26	**Dōng zhì**
	27	28	29	30	1	2	3*	
MONTH 12 Jĭ-Sì	4	5	6	7	8	9	10	Xiǎo hán

Coptic 1705/1706, Ethiopic 1981/1982

Coptic Month	Sun	Mon	Tue	Wed	Thu	Fri	Sat	Ethiopic Month
KOIAK 1705	23	24	25	26	27	28	29[c]	TĀKHŠĀŠ 1981
	30	1	2	3	4	5	6[d]	
TŌBE 1705	7	8	9	10	11[e]	12	13	TER 1981
	14	15	16	17	18	19	20	
	21	22	23	24	25	26	27	
	28	29	30	1	2	3	4	
MESHIR 1705	5	6	7	8	9	10	11	YAKĀTIT 1981
	12	13	14	15	16	17	18	
	19	20	21	22	23	24	25	
	26	27	28	29	30	1	2	
PAREMOTEP 1705	3	4	5	6	7	8	9	MAGĀBIT 1981
	10	11	12	13	14	15	16	
	17	18	19	20	21	22	23	
	24	25	26	27	28	29	30	
	1	2	3	4	5	6	7	
PARMOUTE 1705	8	9	10	11	12	13	14	MIYĀZYĀ 1981
	15	16	17	18	19	20	21	
	22[f]	23	24	25	26	27	28	
	29[g]	30	1	2	3	4	5	
PASHONS 1705	6	7	8	9	10	11	12	GENBOT 1981
	13	14	15	16	17	18	19	
	20	21	22	23	24	25	26	
	27	28	29	30	1	2	3	
PAŌNE 1705	4	5	6	7	8	9	10	SANĒ 1981
	11	12	13	14	15	16	17	
	18	19	20	21	22	23	24	
	25	26	27	28	29	30	1	
EPĒP 1705	2	3	4	5	6	7	8	HAMLĒ 1981
	9	10	11	12	13	14	15	
	16	17	18	19	20	21	22	
	23	24	25	26	27	28	29	
	30	1	2	3	4	5	6	
MESORĒ 1705	7	8	9	10	11	12	13[h]	NAHASĒ 1981
	14	15	16	17	18	19	20	
	21	22	23	24	25	26	27	
EPAG. 1705	28	29	30	1	2	3	4	PĀG. 1981
	5	1[a]	2	3	4	5	6	
THOOUT 1706	7	8	9	10	11	12	13	MASKARAM 1982
	14	15	16	17[b]	18	19	20	
	21	22	23	24	25	26	27	
	28	29	30	1	2	3	4	
PAOPE 1706	5	6	7	8	9	10	11	TEQEMT 1982
	12	13	14	15	16	17	18	
	19	20	21	22	23	24	25	
	26	27	28	29	30	1	2	
ATHŌR 1706	3	4	5	6	7	8	9	HEDĀR 1982
	10	11	12	13	14	15	16	
	17	18	19	20	21	22	23	
	24	25	26	27	28	29	30	
KOIAK 1706	1	2	3	4	5	6	7	TĀKHŠĀŠ 1982
	8	9	10	11	12	13	14	
	15	16	17	18	19	20	21	
	22	23	24	25	26	27	28	

[a]New Year
[b]Spring (15:28)
[c]Summer (9:53)
[d]Autumn (1:20)
[e]Winter (21:22)
● New moon
◐ First quarter moon
○ Full moon
◑ Last quarter moon

‡Leap year
[a]New Year
[b]Yom Kippur
[c]Sukkot
[d]Winter starts
[e]Ḥanukkah
[f]Purim
[g]Passover
[h]Shavuot
[i]Fast of Av

[a]New Year (4687, Snake)
[b]Lantern Festival
[c]Qīngmíng
[d]Dragon Festival
[e]Qīqiǎo
[f]Hungry Ghosts
[g]Mid-Autumn Festival
[h]Double-Ninth Festival
[i]Dōngzhì
*Start of 60-name cycle

[a]New Year
[b]Building of the Cross
[c]Christmas
[d]Jesus's Circumcision
[e]Epiphany
[f]Easter
[g]Mary's Announcement
[h]Jesus's Transfiguration

1989

PERSIAN (ASTRONOMICAL) 1367/1368

Month	Sun	Mon	Tue	Wed	Thu	Fri	Sat
DEY 1367	11	12	13	14	15	16	17
	18	19	20	21	22	23	24
	25	26	27	28	29	30	*1*
BAHMAN 1367	2	3	4	5	6	7	8
	9	10	11	12	13	14	15
	16	17	18	19	20	21	22
	23	24	25	26	27	28	29
	30	*1*	2	3	4	5	6
ESFAND 1367	7	8	9	10	11	12	13
	14	15	16	17	18	19	20
	21	22	23	24	25	26	27
	28	29	*1*[a]	2	3	4	5
FARVARDĪN 1368	6	7	8	9	10	11	12
	13[b]	14	15	16	17	18	19
	20	21	22	23	24	25	26
	27	28	29	30	31	*1*	2
ORDĪBEHEŠT 1368	3	4	5	6	7	8	9
	10	11	12	13	14	15	16
	17	18	19	20	21	22	23
	24	25	26	27	28	29	30
	31	*1*	2	3	4	5	6
XORDĀD 1368	7	8	9	10	11	12	13
	14	15	16	17	18	19	20
	21	22	23	24	25	26	27
	28	29	30	31	*1*	2	3
TĪR 1368	4	5	6	7	8	9	10
	11	12	13	14	15	16	17
	18	19	20	21	22	23	24
	25	26	27	28	29	30	31
MORDĀD 1368	*1*	2	3	4	5	6	7
	8	9	10	11	12	13	14
	15	16	17	18	19	20	21
	22	23	24	25	26	27	28
	29	30	31	*1*	2	3	4
SHAHRĪVAR 1368	5	6	7	8	9	10	11
	12	13	14	15	16	17	18
	19	20	21	22	23	24	25
	26	27	28	29	30	31	*1*
MEHR 1368	2	3	4	5	6	7	8
	9	10	11	12	13	14	15
	16	17	18	19	20	21	22
	23	24	25	26	27	28	29
	30	*1*	2	3	4	5	6
ABĀN 1368	7	8	9	10	11	12	13
	14	15	16	17	18	19	20
	21	22	23	24	25	26	27
	28	29	30	*1*	2	3	4
ĀZAR 1368	5	6	7	8	9	10	11
	12	13	14	15	16	17	18
	19	20	21	22	23	24	25
	26	27	28	29	30	*1*	2
DEY 1368	3	4	5	6	7	8	9
	10	11	12	13	14	15	16

[a]New Year
[b]Sizdeh Bedar

HINDU LUNAR 2045‡/2046

Month	Sun	Mon	Tue	Wed	Thu	Fri	Sat
	24	25	26	27	28	29	30
	1	2	3	4	5	6	7
PAUSHA 2045	**8**	10	11	12	13	14	15
	16	17	18	19	*19*	20	21
	22	23	24	25	26	27	28
	29	30	1	2	**3**	5	6
MĀGHA 2045	7	8	9	10	11	12	13
	14	15	16	17	18	19	20
	21	*21*	22	23	24	25	**26**
	28	29[h]	30	1	2	3	4
PHĀLGUNA 2045	5	6	7	8	9	10	11
	12	13	14	15[i]	16	17	18
	19	20	21	22	23	24	25
	26	27	28	29	30	**1**[a]	3
CHAITRA 2046	4	5	6	7	8	9[b]	10
	11	12	13	14	15	*15*	16
	17	18	19	20	21	22	23
	24	26	27	28	29	30	1
VAIŚĀKHA 2046	2	3	4	5	6	7	8
	9	10	11	12	13	14	15
	16	17	18	19	20	21	22
	23	24	25	26	**27**	29	30
JYAISHṬHA 2046	1	2	3	4	5	6	7
	8	9	10	*10*	11	12	13
	14	15	16	17	18	19	**20**
	22	23	24	25	26	27	28
	29	30	1	2	3	4	5
ĀSHĀḌHA 2046	6	7	8	9	10	11	12
	13	14	15	16	17	18	19
	20	21	22	**23**	25	26	27
	28	29	30	1	2	3	4
ŚRĀVAṆA 2046	5	6	7	*7*	8	9	10
	11	12	13	14	15	**16**	18
	19	20	21	22	23[c]	24	25
	26	27	28	29	30	1	2
BHĀDRAPADA 2046	3	4[d]	5	6	7	8	9
	10	11	12	13	14	15	16
	17	18	**19**	21	22	23	24
	25	26	27	28	29	30	1
ĀŚVINA 2046	2	3	*3*	4	5	6	7
	8[e]	9[e]	10[e]	11	12	**13**	15
	16	17	18	19	20	21	22
	23	24	25	26	27	28	29
	30	1[f]	2	3	4	5	6
KĀRTTIKA 2046	7	8	9	10	11	12	13
	14	15	16	**17**	19	20	21
	22	23	24	25	26	27	*27*
	28	29	30	1	2	3	4
MĀRGAŚĪRA 2046	5	6	7	8	9	10	**11**[g]
	13	14	15	16	17	18	19
	20	21	22	23	24	25	26
PAUSHA 2046	27	28	29	*29*	30	1	2
	3	**4**	6	7	8	9	10

‡Leap year
[a]New Year (Śukla)
[b]Birthday of Rāma
[c]Birthday of Krishna
[d]Ganēśa Chaturthī
[e]Dashara
[f]Diwali
[g]Birthday of Vishnu
[h]Night of Śiva
[i]Holi

HINDU SOLAR 1910/1911

Month	Sun	Mon	Tue	Wed	Thu	Fri	Sat
PAUSHA 1910	18	19	20	21	22	23	24
	25	26	27	28	29	1[b]	2
MĀGHA 1910	3	4	5	6	7	8	9
	10	11	12	13	14	15	16
	17	18	19	20	21	22	23
	24	25	26	27	28	29	30
PHĀLGUNA 1910	1	2	3	4	5	6	7
	8	9	10	11	12	13	14
	15	16	17	18	19	20	21
	22	23	24	25	26	27	28
	29	30	1	2	3	4	5
CHAITRA 1910	6	7	8	9	10	11	12
	13	14	15	16	17	18	19
	20	21	22	23	24	25	26
	27	28	29	30	1[a]	2	3
VAIŚĀKHA 1911	4	5	6	7	8	9	10
	11	12	13	14	15	16	17
	18	19	20	21	22	23	24
	25	26	27	28	29	30	31
JYAISHṬHA 1911	1	2	3	4	5	6	7
	8	9	10	11	12	13	14
	15	16	17	18	19	20	21
	22	23	24	25	26	27	28
	29	30	31	32	1	2	3
ĀSHĀḌHA 1911	4	5	6	7	8	9	10
	11	12	13	14	15	16	17
	18	19	20	21	22	23	24
	25	26	27	28	29	30	31
ŚRĀVAṆA 1911	1	2	3	4	5	6	7
	8	9	10	11	12	13	14
	15	16	17	18	19	20	21
	22	23	24	25	26	27	28
	29	30	31	32	1	2	3
BHĀDRAPADA 1911	4	5	6	7	8	9	10
	11	12	13	14	15	16	17
	18	19	20	21	22	23	24
	25	26	27	28	29	30	31
ĀŚVINA 1911	1	2	3	4	5	6	7
	8	9	10	11	12	13	14
	15	16	17	18	19	20	21
	22	23	24	25	26	27	28
	29	30	1	2	3	4	5
KĀRTTIKA 1911	6	7	8	9	10	11	12
	13	14	15	16	17	18	19
	20	21	22	23	24	25	26
	27	28	29	30	1	2	3
MĀRGAŚĪRA 1911	4	5	6	7	8	9	10
	11	12	13	14	15	16	17
	18	19	20	21	22	23	24
	25	26	27	28	29	1	2
PAUSHA 1911	3	4	5	6	7	8	9
	10	11	12	13	14	15	16
	17	18	19	20	21	22	23

[a]New Year (Chitrabhānu)
[b]Pongal

ISLAMIC (ASTRONOMICAL) 1409/1410‡

Month	Sun	Mon	Tue	Wed	Thu	Fri	Sat
JUMĀDĀ I 1409	22	23	24	25	26	27	28
JUMĀDĀ II 1409	29	*1*	2	3	4	5	6
	7	8	9	10	11	12	13
	14	15	16	17	18	19	20
	21	22	23	24	25	26	27
	28	29	*30*	1	2	3	4
RAJAB 1409	5	6	7	8	9	10	11
	12	13	14	15	16	17	18
	19	20	21	22	23	24	25
	26	27[d]	28	29	*1*	2	3
SHA'BĀN 1409	4	5	6	7	8	9	10
	11	12	13	14	15	16	17
	18	19	20	21	22	23	24
	25	26	27	28	29	*1*[e]	2
RAMAḌĀN 1409	3	4	5	6	7	8	9
	10	11	12	13	14	15	16
	17	18	19	20	21	22	23
	24	25	26	27	28	29	30
SHAWWĀL 1409	*1*[f]	2	3	4	5	6	7
	8	9	10	11	12	13	14
	15	16	17	18	19	20	21
	22	23	24	25	26	27	28
	29	*1*	2	3	4	5	6
DHU AL-QA'DA 1409	7	8	9	10	11	12	13
	14	15	16	17	18	19	20
	21	22	23	24	25	26	27
	28	29	1	*2*	3	4	5
DHU AL-ḤIJJA 1409	6	7	8	9	10[g]	11	12
	13	14	15	16	17	18	19
	20	21	22	23	24	25	26
	27	28	29	30	1[a]	*2*[â]	3
MUḤARRAM 1410	4	5	6	7	8	9	10[b]
	11	12	13	14	15	16	17
	18	19	20	21	22	23	24
	25	26	27	28	29	30	1
ṢAFAR 1410	*2*	3	4	5	6	7	8
	9	10	11	12	13	14	15
	16	17	18	19	20	21	22
	23	24	25	26	27	28	29
	30	*1*	2	3	4	5	6
RABĪ' I 1410	7	8	9	10	11	12[c]	13
	14	15	16	17	18	19	20
	21	22	23	24	25	26	27
	28	29	30	*1*	2	3	4
RABĪ' II 1410	5	6	7	8	9	10	11
	12	13	14	15	16	17	18
	19	20	21	22	23	24	25
	26	27	28	29	*1*	2	3
JUMĀDĀ I 1410	4	5	6	7	8	9	10
	11	12	13	14	15	16	17
	18	19	20	21	22	23	24
	25	26	27	28	29	30	*1*
JUMĀDĀ II 1410	2	3	4	5	6	7	8

‡Leap year
[a]New Year
[â]New Year (Arithmetic)
[b]‘Āshūrā’
[c]Prophet's Birthday
[d]Ascent of the Prophet
[e]Start of Ramaḍān
[f]‘Id al-Fiṭr
[g]‘Id al-’Aḍḥā

GREGORIAN 1989

Julian (Sun)	Sun	Mon	Tue	Wed	Thu	Fri	Sat	Month
Dec 19	*1*	2	3	4	5	6	7[a]	JANUARY 1989
	8	9	10	11	12	13	14[b]	
Jan 2	*15*	16	17	18	19	20	21	
	22	23	24	25	26	27	28	
Jan 16	*29*	30	31	1	2	3	4	
	5	6	7	8[c]	9	10	11	FEBRUARY 1989
Jan 30	*12*	13	14	15	16	17	18	
	19	20	21	22	23	24	25	
Feb 13	*26*	27	28	1	2	3	4	
	5	6	7	8	9	10	11	MARCH 1989
Feb 27	*12*	13	14	15	16	17	18	
	19[d]	20	21	22	23	24	25	
Mar 13	*26*[e]	27	28	29	30	31	1	
	2	3	4	5	6	7	8	APRIL 1989
Mar 27	*9*	10	11	12	13	14	15	
	16	17	18	19	20	21	22	
Apr 10	*23*	24	25	26	27	28	29	
	30[f]	1	2	3	4	5	6	
Apr 24	*7*	8	9	10	11	12	13	MAY 1989
	14	15	16	17	18	19	20	
May 8	*21*	22	23	24	25	26	27	
	28	29	30	31	1	2	3	
May 22	*4*	5	6	7	8	9	10	JUNE 1989
	11	12	13	14	15	16	17	
Jun 5	*18*	19	20	21	22	23	24	
	25	26	27	28	29	30	1	
Jun 19	*2*	3	4	5	6	7	8	JULY 1989
	9	10	11	12	13	14	15	
Jul 3	*16*	17	18	19	20	21	22	
	23	24	25	26	27	28	29	
Jul 17	*30*	31	1	2	3	4	5	
	6	7	8	9	10	11	12	AUGUST 1989
Jul 31	*13*	14	15	16	17	18	19	
	20	21	22	23	24	25	26	
Aug 14	*27*	28	29	30	31	1	2	
	3	4	5	6	7	8	9	SEPTEMBER 1989
Aug 28	*10*	11	12	13	14	15	16	
	17	18	19	20	21	22	23	
Sep 11	*24*	25	26	27	28	29	30	
	1	2	3	4	5	6	7	OCTOBER 1989
Sep 25	*8*	9	10	11	12	13	14	
	15	16	17	18	19	20	21	
Oct 9	*22*	23	24	25	26	27	28	
	29	30	31	1	2	3	4	
Oct 23	*5*	6	7	8	9	10	11	NOVEMBER 1989
	12	13	14	15	16	17	18	
Nov 6	*19*	20	21	22	23	24	25	
	26	27	28	29	30	1	2	
Nov 20	*3*[g]	4	5	6	7	8	9	DECEMBER 1989
	10	11	12	13	14	15	16	
Dec 4	*17*	18	19	20	21	22	23	
	24	25[h]	26	27	28	29	30	
Dec 18	*31*	1	2	3	4	5	6	

[a]Orthodox Christmas
[b]Julian New Year
[c]Ash Wednesday
[d]Feast of Orthodoxy
[e]Easter
[f]Orthodox Easter
[g]Advent
[h]Christmas

1990

GREGORIAN 1990								Lunar Phases	ISO WEEK	JULIAN DAY	HEBREW 5750/5751								Molad	CHINESE Jǐ-Sì/Gēng-Wǔ‡								Solar Term	COPTIC 1706/1707‡								ETHIOPIC 1982/1983‡
	Sun	Mon	Tue	Wed	Thu	Fri	Sat		(Mon)	(Sun noon)		Sun	Mon	Tue	Wed	Thu	Fri	Sat			Sun	Mon	Tue	Wed	Thu	Fri	Sat			Sun	Mon	Tue	Wed	Thu	Fri	Sat	
	31	1[a]	2	3	◐	5	6	10:40	1	2447892		3	4	5	6	7	8	9			4	5	6	7	8	9	10	Xiǎo hán		22	23	24	25	26	27	28	TĀKHŚĀŚ 1982
	7	8	9	10	○	12	13	4:57	2	2447899	TEVETH 5750	10	11	12	13	14	15	16		MONTH 12 Jǐ-Sì	11	12	13	14	15	16	17		KOIAK 1706	29[c]	30	1	2	3	4	5	
JANUARY 1990	14	15	16	17	◑	19	20	21:17	3	2447906		17	18	19	20	21	22	23			18	19	20	21	22	23	**24**	Dà hán		6[d]	7	8	9	10	11[e]	12	
	21	22	23	24	25	●	27	19:20	4	2447913		24	25	26	27	28	29	1	Fri 12h21m16p		25	26	27	28	29	30	1[a]		ṬŌBE 1706	13	14	15	16	17	18	19	ṬER 1982
	28	29	30	31	1	◐	3	18:32	5	2447920		2	3	4	5	6	7	8			2	3	4	5	6	7	8			20	21	22	23	24	25	26	
	4	5	6	7	8	○	10	19:16	6	2447927	SHEVAT 5750	9	10	11	12	13	14	15		MONTH 1 Gēng-Wǔ	9	10	11	12	13	14	15[b]	Lì chūn		27	28	29	30	1	2	3	
FEBRUARY 1990	11	12	13	14	15	16	◑	18:48	7	2447934		16	17	18	19	20	21	22			16	17	18	19	20	21	22			4	5	6	7	8	9	10	
	18	19	20	21	22	23	24		8	2447941		23	24	25	26	27	28	29			23	**24**	25	26	27	28	29	Yǔ shuǐ	MESHIR 1706	11	12	13	14	15	16	17	YAKĀTIT 1982
	●	26	27	28	1	2	3	8:55	9	2447948		30	1	2	3	4	5	6	Sun 1h5m17p		1	2	3	4*	5	6	7			18	19	20	21	22	23	24	
	◐	5	6	7	8	9	10	2:05	10	2447955		7	8	9	10	11	12	13		MONTH 2 Gēng-Wǔ	8	9	_10_	11	12	13	14	Jīng zhé		25	26	27	28	29	30	1	
MARCH 1990	○	12	13	14	15	16	17	10:58	11	2447962	ADAR 5750	14[f]	15	16	17	18	19	20			15	16	17	18	19	20	21			2	3	4	5	6	7	8	
	18	◑	20[b]	21	22	23	24	14:30	12	2447969		21	22	23	24	25	26	27			22	23	24	**25**	26	27	28	Chūn fēn	PAREMOTEP 1706	9	10	11	12	13	14	15	MAGĀBIT 1982
	25	●	27	28	29	30	31	19:48	13	2447976		28	29	1	2	3	4	5	Mon 13h50m0p		29	30	1	2	3	4	5			16	17	18	19	20	21	22	
	1	◐	3	4	5	6	7	10:24	14	2447983		6	7	8	9	10	11	12		MONTH 3 Gēng-Wǔ	6	7	8	9	_10_[c]	11	12	Qīng míng		23	24	25	26	27	28	29	
	8	9	○	11	12	13	14	3:19	15	2447990	NISAN 5750	13	14	15[g]	16	17	18	19			13	14	15	16	17	18	19			30	1	2	3	4	5	6	
APRIL 1990	15	16	17	◑	19	20	21	7:02	16	2447997		20	21	22	23	24	25	26			20	21	22	23	24	**25**	26	Gǔ yǔ	PARMOUTE 1706	7[f]	8	9	10	11	12	13	MIYĀZYĀ 1982
	22	23	24	●	26	27	28	4:28	17	2448004		27	28	29	30	1	2	3	Wed 2h34m1p		27	28	29	1	2	3	4			14	15	16	17	18	19	20	
	29	30	◐	2	3	4	5	20:18	18	2448011		4	5	6	7	8	9	10			5*	6	7	8	9	10	11			21	22	23	24	25	26	27	
	6	7	8	○	10	11	12	19:31	19	2448018	IYYAR 5750	11	12	13	14	15	16	17		MONTH 4 Gēng-Wǔ	_12_	13	14	15	16	17	18	Lì xià		28	29[g]	30	1	2	3	4	
MAY 1990	13	14	15	16	◑	18	19	19:45	20	2448025		18	19	20	21	22	23	24			19	20	21	22	23	24	25			5	6	7	8	9	10	11	
	20	21	22	23	●	25	26	11:47	21	2448032		25	26	27	28	29	1	2	Thu 15h18m2p		26	**27**	28	29	1	2	3	Xiǎo mǎn	PASHONS 1706	12	13	14	15	16	17	18	GENBOT 1982
	27	28	29	30	◐	1	2	8:11	22	2448039		3	4	5	6[h]	7	8	9			4	5[d]	6	7	8	9	10			19	20	21	22	23	24	25	
	3	4	5	6	7	○	9	11:01	23	2448046	SIVAN 5750	10	11	12	13	14	15	16		MONTH 5 Gēng-Wǔ	11	12	13	_14_	15	16	17	Máng zhòng		26	27	28	29	30	1	2	
JUNE 1990	10	11	12	13	14	15	◑	4:48	24	2448053		17	18	19	20	21	22	23			18	19	20	21	22	23	24			3	4	5	6	7	8	9	
	17	18	19	20	21[c]	●	23	18:55	25	2448060		24	25	26	27	28	29	30			25	26	27	28	**29**	30	1	Xià zhì	PAŌNE 1706	10	11	12	13	14	15	16	SANĒ 1982
	24	25	26	27	28	◐	30	22:07	26	2448067		1	2	3	4	5	6	7	Sat 4h2m3p		2	3	4	5	6*	7	8			17	18	19	20	21	22	23	
	1	2	3	4	5	6	7		27	2448074		8	9	10	11	12	13	14		LEAP MONTH 5 Gēng-Wǔ	9	10	11	12	13	14	_15_	Xiǎo shǔ		24	25	26	27	28	29	30	
	○	9	10	11	12	13	14	1:23	28	2448081	TAMMUZ 5750	15	16	17	18	19	20	21			16	17	18	19	20	21	22			1	2	3	4	5	6	7	
JULY 1990	◑	16	17	18	19	20	21	11:04	29	2448088		22	23	24	25	26	27	28			23	24	25	26	27	28	29			8	9	10	11	12	13	14	
	●	23	24	25	26	27	28	2:54	30	2448095		29	1	2	3	4	5	6	Sun 16h46m4p		1	**2**	3	4	5	6	7	Dà shǔ	EPĒP 1706	15	16	17	18	19	20	21	ḤAMLĒ 1982
	◐	30	31	1	2	3	4	14:01	31	2448102		7	8	9[i]	10	11	12	13		MONTH 6 Gēng-Wǔ	8	9	10	11	12	13	14			22	23	24	25	26	27	28	
	5	○	7	8	9	10	11	14:19	32	2448109	AV 5750	14	15	16	17	18	19	20			15	16	17	_18_	19	20	21	Lì qiū		29	30	1	2	3	4	5	
AUGUST 1990	12	◑	14	15	16	17	18	15:54	33	2448116		21	22	23	24	25	26	27			22	23	24	25	26	27	28			6	7	8	9	10	11	12	
	19	●	21	22	23	24	25	12:39	34	2448123		28	29	30	1	2	3	4	Tue 5h30m5p		29	1	2	3	**4**	5	6	Chǔ shǔ	MESORĒ 1706	13[h]	14	15	16	17	18	19	NAḤASĒ 1982
	26	27	◐	29	30	31	1	7:34	35	2448130		5	6	7	8	9	10	11			7[e]	8*	9	10	11	12	13			20	21	22	23	24	25	26	
	2	3	4	○	6	7	8	1:46	36	2448137	ELUL 5750	12	13	14	15	16	17	18		MONTH 7 Gēng-Wǔ	14	15[f]	16	17	18	19	_20_	Bái lù	EPAG. 1706	27	28	29	30	1	2	3	
SEPTEMBER 1990	9	10	◑	12	13	14	15	20:53	37	2448144		19	20	21	22	23	24	25			21	22	23	24	25	26	27			4	5	1[a]	2	3	4	5	PĀG. 1982
	16	17	18	●	20	21	22	0:46	38	2448151		26	27	28	29	1[a]	2[a]	3	Wed 18h14m6p		28	29	30	1	2	3	4		THOOUT 1707	6	7	8	9	10	11	12	MASKARAM 1983
	23[d]	24	25	26	◐	28	29	2:06	39	2448158		4	5	6	7	8	9	10[b]			**5**	6	7	8	9	10	11	Qiū fēn		13	14	15	16	17[b]	18	19	
	30	1	2	3	○	5	6	12:02	40	2448165	TISHRI 5751	11	12	13	14	15[c]	16	17		MONTH 8 Gēng-Wǔ	12	13	14	15[g]	16	17	18			20	21	22	23	24	25	26	
	7	8	9	10	◑	12	13	3:31	41	2448172		18	19	20	21	22	23	24			19	_20_	21	22	23	24	25	Hán lù		27	28	29	30	1	2	3	
OCTOBER 1990	14	15	16	17	●	19	20	15:37	42	2448179		25	26	27	28	29	30	1	Fri 6h58m7p		26	27	28	29	1	2	3		PAOPE 1707	4	5	6	7	8	9	10	ṬEQEMT 1983
	21	22	23	24	25	◐	27	20:26	43	2448186		2	3	4	5	6	7	8			4	5	6	**7**	8	9[h]*	10	Shuāng jiàng		11	12	13	14	15	16	17	
	28	29	30	31	1	○	3	21:49	44	2448193	HESHVAN 5751	9	10	11	12	13	14	15		MONTH 9 Gēng-Wǔ	11	12	13	14	15	16	17			18	19	20	21	22	23	24	
	4	5	6	7	8	◑	10	13:02	45	2448200		16	17	18	19	20	21	22			18	19	20	21	_22_	23	24	Lì dōng		25	26	27	28	29	30	1	
NOVEMBER 1990	11	12	13	14	15	16	●	9:05	46	2448207		23	24	25	26	27	28	29			25	26	27	28	29	30	1			2	3	4	5	6	7	8	
	18	19	20	21	22	23	24		47	2448214		1	2	3	4	5	6	7	Sat 19h42m8p		2	3	4	5	**6**	7	8	Xiǎo xuě	ATHŌR 1707	9	10	11	12	13	14	15	ḪEDĀR 1983
	◐	26	27	28	29	30	1	13:11	48	2448221		8	9	10	11	12	13	14		MONTH 10 Gēng-Wǔ	9	10	11	12	13	14	15			16	17	18	19	20	21	22	
	○	3	4	5	6	7	8	7:50	49	2448228	KISLEV 5751	15	16	17	18[d]	19	20	21			16	17	18	19	20	_21_	22	Dà xuě		23	24	25	26	27	28	29	
DECEMBER 1990	◑	10	11	12	13	14	15	2:04	50	2448235		22	23	24	25[e]	26[e]	27[e]	28[e]			23	24	25	26	27	28	29			30	1	2	3	4	5	6	
	16	●	18	19	20	21	22[e]	4:22	51	2448242		29[e]	30[e]	1[e]	2[e]	3	4	5	Mon 8h26m9p		30	1	2	3	4	5	**6**[i]	Dōng zhì	KOIAK 1707	7	8	9	10	11	12	13	TĀKHŚĀŚ 1983
	23	24	◐	26	27	28	29	3:16	52	2448249	TEVETH 5751	6	7	8	9	10	11	12		MONTH 11 Gēng-Wǔ	7	8	9*	10	11	12	13			14	15	16	17	18	19	20	
	30	○	1	2	3	4	5	18:35	1	2448256		13	14	15	16	17	18	19			14	15	16	17	18	19	20			21	22	23	24	25	26	27	

[a]New Year
[b]Spring (21:19)
[c]Summer (15:32)
[d]Autumn (6:55)
[e]Winter (3:07)
● New moon
◐ First quarter moon
○ Full moon
◑ Last quarter moon

[a]New Year
[b]Yom Kippur
[c]Sukkot
[d]Winter starts
[e]Ḥanukkah
[f]Purim
[g]Passover
[h]Shavuot
[i]Fast of Av

‡Leap year
[a]New Year (4688, Horse)
[b]Lantern Festival
[c]Qīngmíng
[d]Dragon Festival
[e]Qīqiǎo
[f]Hungry Ghosts
[g]Mid-Autumn Festival
[h]Double-Ninth Festival
[i]Dōngzhì
*Start of 60-name cycle

‡Leap year
[a]New Year
[b]Building of the Cross
[c]Christmas
[d]Jesus's Circumcision
[e]Epiphany
[f]Easter
[g]Mary's Announcement
[h]Jesus's Transfiguration

PERSIAN (ASTRONOMICAL) 1368/1369

Month	Sun	Mon	Tue	Wed	Thu	Fri	Sat
DEY 1368	10	11	12	13	14	15	16
	17	18	19	20	21	22	23
	24	25	26	27	28	29	30
BAHMAN 1368	1	2	3	4	5	6	7
	8	9	10	11	12	13	14
	15	16	17	18	19	20	21
	22	23	24	25	26	27	28
ESFAND 1368	29	30	1	2	3	4	5
	6	7	8	9	10	11	12
	13	14	15	16	17	18	19
	20	21	22	23	24	25	26
FARVARDĪN 1369	27	28	29	1[a]	2	3	4
	5	6	7	8	9	10	11
	12	13[b]	14	15	16	17	18
	19	20	21	22	23	24	25
ORDĪBEHEŠT 1369	26	27	28	29	30	31	1
	2	3	4	5	6	7	8
	9	10	11	12	13	14	15
	16	17	18	19	20	21	22
	23	24	25	26	27	28	29
XORDĀD 1369	30	31	1	2	3	4	5
	6	7	8	9	10	11	12
	13	14	15	16	17	18	19
	20	21	22	23	24	25	26
TĪR 1369	27	28	29	30	31	1	2
	3	4	5	6	7	8	9
	10	11	12	13	14	15	16
	17	18	19	20	21	22	23
	24	25	26	27	28	29	30
MORDĀD 1369	31	1	2	3	4	5	6
	7	8	9	10	11	12	13
	14	15	16	17	18	19	20
	21	22	23	24	25	26	27
SHAHRĪVAR 1369	28	29	30	31	1	2	3
	4	5	6	7	8	9	10
	11	12	13	14	15	16	17
	18	19	20	21	22	23	24
	25	26	27	28	29	30	31
MEHR 1369	1	2	3	4	5	6	7
	8	9	10	11	12	13	14
	15	16	17	18	19	20	21
	22	23	24	25	26	27	28
ĀBĀN 1369	29	30	1	2	3	4	5
	6	7	8	9	10	11	12
	13	14	15	16	17	18	19
	20	21	22	23	24	25	26
ĀZAR 1369	27	28	29	30	1	2	3
	4	5	6	7	8	9	10
	11	12	13	14	15	16	17
	18	19	20	21	22	23	24
DEY 1369	25	26	27	28	29	30	1
	2	3	4	5	6	7	8
	9	10	11	12	13	14	15

[a]New Year
[b]Sizdeh Bedar

HINDU LUNAR 2046/2047

Month	Sun	Mon	Tue	Wed	Thu	Fri	Sat
	3	4	6	7	8	9	10
PAUSHA 2046	11	12	13	14	15	16	17
	18	19	20	21	22	23	24
	25	26	27	28	29	30	1
MĀGHA 2046	2	3	4	5	6	7	8
	9	11	12	13	14	15	16
	17	18	19	20	21	21	22
	23	24	25	26	27	28[h]	29
	30	1	2	3	4	6	7
PHĀLGUNA 2046	8	9	10	11	12	13	14
	15[i]	16	17	18	19	20	21
	22	23	24	25	26	27	28
	29	30	1[a]	2	3	4	5
CHAITRA 2047	6	7	8[b]	9	11	12	13
	14	14	15	16	17	18	19
	20	21	22	23	24	25	26
	27	28	29	30	1	3	4
VAIŚĀKHA 2047	5	6	7	8	9	10	11
	12	13	14	15	16	17	18
	18	19	20	21	22	23	24
	26	27	28	29	30	1	2
JYAISHTHA 2047	3	4	5	6	7	8	9
	10	11	12	13	14	15	16
	17	18	19	20	21	22	23
	24	25	26	27	29	30	1
ĀSHĀḌHA 2047	2	3	4	5	6	7	8
	9	10	11	12	13	14	15
	15	16	17	18	19	20	22
	23	24	25	26	27	28	29
	30	1	3	4	5	6	7
ŚRĀVAṆA 2047	7	8	9	10	11	12	13
	14	15	16	17	18	19	20
	21	22	23[c]	25	26	27	28
	29	30	1	2	3	4[d]	5
BHĀDRAPADA 2047	6	7	8	9	10	11	12
	12	13	14	15	17	18	19
	20	21	22	23	24	25	26
	27	29	30	1	2	3	3
ĀŚVINA 2047	4	5	6	7	8[e]	9[e]	10[e]
	11	12	13	14	15	16	17
	18	19	20	22	23	24	25
	26	27	28	29	30	1[f]	2
KĀRTTIKA 2047	3	4	5	6	6	7	8
	9	10	11	12	13	15	16
	17	18	19	20	21	22	23
	24	25	26	27	28	29	30
MĀRGAŚĪRA 2047	1	2	3	4	5	6	7
	8	9	10	11[g]	12	13	14
	15	16	17	18	20	21	22
	23	24	25	26	27	28	29
PAUSHA 2047	30	30	1	2	3	4	5
	6	7	8	9	10	11	12
	14	15	16	17	18	19	20

[a]New Year (Pramoda)
[b]Birthday of Rāma
[c]Birthday of Krishna
[d]Ganēśa Chaturthī
[e]Dashara
[f]Diwali
[g]Birthday of Vishnu
[h]Night of Śiva
[i]Holi

HINDU SOLAR 1911/1912‡

Month	Sun	Mon	Tue	Wed	Thu	Fri	Sat
PAUSHA 1911	17	18	19	20	21	22	23
	24	25	26	27	28	29	30
	1[b]	2	3	4	5	6	7
MĀGHA 1911	8	9	10	11	12	13	14
	15	16	17	18	19	20	21
	22	23	24	25	26	27	28
	29	1	2	3	4	5	6
PHĀLGUNA 1911	7	8	9	10	11	12	13
	14	15	16	17	18	19	20
	21	22	23	24	25	26	27
	28	29	30	1	2	3	4
CHAITRA 1911	5	6	7	8	9	10	11
	12	13	14	15	16	17	18
	19	20	21	22	23	24	25
	26	27	28	29	30	1[a]	2
VAIŚĀKHA 1912	3	4	5	6	7	8	9
	10	11	12	13	14	15	16
	17	18	19	20	21	22	23
	24	25	26	27	28	29	30
	31	1	2	3	4	5	6
JYAISHTHA 1912	7	8	9	10	11	12	13
	14	15	16	17	18	19	20
	21	22	23	24	25	26	27
	28	29	30	31	32	1	2
ĀSHĀḌHA 1912	3	4	5	6	7	8	9
	10	11	12	13	14	15	16
	17	18	19	20	21	22	23
	24	25	26	27	28	29	30
	31	1	2	3	4	5	6
ŚRĀVAṆA 1912	7	8	9	10	11	12	13
	14	15	16	17	18	19	20
	21	22	23	24	25	26	27
	28	29	30	31	32	1	2
BHĀDRAPADA 1912	3	4	5	6	7	8	9
	10	11	12	13	14	15	16
	17	18	19	20	21	22	23
	24	25	26	27	28	29	30
	31	1	2	3	4	5	6
ĀŚVINA 1912	7	8	9	10	11	12	13
	14	15	16	17	18	19	20
	21	22	23	24	25	26	27
	28	29	30	1	2	3	4
KĀRTTIKA 1912	5	6	7	8	9	10	11
	12	13	14	15	16	17	18
	19	20	21	22	23	24	25
	26	27	28	29	30	1	2
MĀRGAŚĪRA 1912	3	4	5	6	7	8	9
	10	11	12	13	14	15	16
	17	18	19	20	21	22	23
	24	25	26	27	28	29	30
PAUSHA 1912	1	2	3	4	5	6	7
	8	9	10	11	12	13	14
	15	16	17	18	19	20	21

‡Leap year
[a]New Year (Subhānu)
[b]Pongal

ISLAMIC (ASTRONOMICAL) 1410‡/1411

Month	Sun	Mon	Tue	Wed	Thu	Fri	Sat
JUMĀDĀ II 1410	2	3	4	5	6	7	8
	9	10	11	12	13	14	15
	16	17	18	19	20	21	22
	23	24	25	26	27	28	29
RAJAB 1410	1	2	3	4	5	6	7
	8	9	10	11	12	13	14
	15	16	17	18	19	20	21
	22	23	24	25	26	27[d]	28
SHA'BĀN 1410	29	30	1	2	3	4	5
	6	7	8	9	10	11	12
	13	14	15	16	17	18	19
	20	21	22	23	24	25	26
RAMAḌĀN 1410	27	28	29	1[e]	2	3	4
	5	6	7	8	9	10	11
	12	13	14	15	16	17	18
	19	20	21	22	23	24	25
SHAWWĀL 1410	26	27	28	29	1[f]	2	3
	4	5	6	7	8	9	10
	11	12	13	14	15	16	17
	18	19	20	21	22	23	24
DHU AL-QA'DA 1410	25	26	27	28	29	30	1
	2	3	4	5	6	7	8
	9	10	11	12	13	14	15
	16	17	18	19	20	21	22
	23	24	25	26	27	28	29
DHU AL-ḤIJJA 1410	1	2	3	4	5	6	7
	8	9	10[g]	11	12	13	14
	15	16	17	18	19	20	21
	22	23	24	25	26	27	28
MUḤARRAM 1411	29	30	1[a]	2	3	4	5
	6	7	8	9	10[b]	11	12
	13	14	15	16	17	18	19
	20	21	22	23	24	25	26
ṢAFAR 1411	27	28	29	30	1	2	3
	4	5	6	7	8	9	10
	11	12	13	14	15	16	17
	18	19	20	21	22	23	24
RABĪ' I 1411	25	26	27	28	29	1	2
	3	4	5	6	7	8	9
	10	11	12[c]	13	14	15	16
	17	18	19	20	21	22	23
	24	25	26	27	28	29	30
RABĪ' II 1411	1	2	3	4	5	6	7
	8	9	10	11	12	13	14
	15	16	17	18	19	20	21
	22	23	24	25	26	27	28
JUMĀDĀ I 1411	29	1	2	3	4	5	6
	7	8	9	10	11	12	13
	14	15	16	17	18	19	20
	21	22	23	24	25	26	27
JUMĀDĀ II 1411	28	29	30	1	2	3	4
	5	6	7	8	9	10	11
	12	13	14	15	16	17	18

‡Leap year
[a]New Year
[b]'Ashūrā'
[c]Prophet's Birthday
[d]Ascent of the Prophet
[e]Start of Ramaḍān
[f]'Id al-Fiṭr
[g]'Id al-'Aḍḥā

GREGORIAN 1990

Julian (Sun)	Sun	Mon	Tue	Wed	Thu	Fri	Sat	Month
Dec 18	31	1	2	3	4	5	6	
	7[a]	8	9	10	11	12	13	JANUARY 1990
Jan 1	14[b]	15	16	17	18	19	20	
	21	22	23	24	25	26	27	
Jan 15	28	29	30	31	1	2	3	
	4	5	6	7	8	9	10	FEBRUARY 1990
Jan 29	11	12	13	14	15	16	17	
	18	19	20	21	22	23	24	
Feb 12	25	26	27	28[c]	1	2	3	
	4[d]	5	6	7	8	9	10	MARCH 1990
Feb 26	11	12	13	14	15	16	17	
	18	19	20	21	22	23	24	
Mar 12	25	26	27	28	29	30	31	
	1	2	3	4	5	6	7	APRIL 1990
Mar 26	8	9	10	11	12	13	14	
	15[e]	16	17	18	19	20	21	
Apr 9	22	23	24	25	26	27	28	
	29	30	1	2	3	4	5	MAY 1990
Apr 23	6	7	8	9	10	11	12	
	13	14	15	16	17	18	19	
May 7	20	21	22	23	24	25	26	
	27	28	29	30	31	1	2	
May 21	3	4	5	6	7	8	9	JUNE 1990
	10	11	12	13	14	15	16	
Jun 4	17	18	19	20	21	22	23	
	24	25	26	27	28	29	30	
Jun 18	1	2	3	4	5	6	7	JULY 1990
	8	9	10	11	12	13	14	
Jul 2	15	16	17	18	19	20	21	
	22	23	24	25	26	27	28	
Jul 16	29	30	31	1	2	3	4	
	5	6	7	8	9	10	11	AUGUST 1990
Jul 30	12	13	14	15	16	17	18	
	19	20	21	22	23	24	25	
Aug 13	26	27	28	29	30	31	1	
	2	3	4	5	6	7	8	SEPTEMBER 1990
Aug 27	9	10	11	12	13	14	15	
	16	17	18	19	20	21	22	
Sep 10	23	24	25	26	27	28	29	
	30	1	2	3	4	5	6	OCTOBER 1990
Sep 24	7	8	9	10	11	12	13	
	14	15	16	17	18	19	20	
Oct 8	21	22	23	24	25	26	27	
	28	29	30	31	1	2	3	
Oct 22	4	5	6	7	8	9	10	NOVEMBER 1990
	11	12	13	14	15	16	17	
Nov 5	18	19	20	21	22	23	24	
	25	26	27	28	29	30	1	
Nov 19	2[g]	3	4	5	6	7	8	DECEMBER 1990
	9	10	11	12	13	14	15	
Dec 3	16	17	18	19	20	21	22	
	23	24	25[h]	26	27	28	29	
Dec 17	30	31	1	2	3	4	5	

[a]Orthodox Christmas
[b]Julian New Year
[c]Ash Wednesday
[d]Feast of Orthodoxy
[e]Easter (also Orthodox)
[g]Advent
[h]Christmas

1991

Gregorian 1991 — Lunar Phases — ISO Week — Julian Day

Month	Sun	Mon	Tue	Wed	Thu	Fri	Sat	Lunar Phases	ISO WEEK (Mon)	JULIAN DAY (Sun noon)
JANUARY 1991	30	○	1[a]	2	3	4	5	18:35	1	2448256
	6	◑	8	9	10	11	12	18:35	2	2448263
	13	14	●	16	17	18	19	23:50	3	2448270
	20	21	22	◐	24	25	26	14:21	4	2448277
	27	28	29	○	31	1	2	6:10	5	2448284
FEBRUARY 1991	3	4	5	◑	7	8	9	13:52	6	2448291
	10	11	12	13	●	15	16	17:32	7	2448298
	17	18	19	20	◐	22	23	22:58	8	2448305
	24	25	26	27	○	1	2	18:25	9	2448312
MARCH 1991	3	4	5	6	7	◑	9	10:32	10	2448319
	10	11	12	13	14	15	●	8:11	11	2448326
	17	18	19	20	21[b]	22	◐	6:03	12	2448333
	24	25	26	27	28	29	○	7:17	13	2448340
	31	1	2	3	4	5	6		14	2448347
APRIL 1991	◑	8	9	10	11	12	13	6:45	15	2448354
	●	15	16	17	18	19	20	19:38	16	2448361
	◐	22	23	24	25	26	27	12:39	17	2448368
	○	29	30	1	2	3	4	20:58	18	2448375
MAY 1991	5	6	◑	8	9	10	11	0:46	19	2448382
	12	13	●	15	16	17	18	4:36	20	2448389
	19	◐	21	22	23	24	25	19:46	21	2448396
	26	27	○	29	30	31	1	11:37	22	2448403
JUNE 1991	2	3	4	◑	6	7	8	15:30	23	2448410
	9	10	11	●	13	14	15	12:06	24	2448417
	16	17	18	◐	20	21[c]	22	4:19	25	2448424
	23	24	25	26	○	28	29	2:58	26	2448431
	30	1	2	3	4	◑	6	2:50	27	2448438
JULY 1991	7	8	9	10	●	12	13	19:06	28	2448445
	14	15	16	17	◐	19	20	15:11	29	2448452
	21	22	23	24	25	○	27	18:24	30	2448459
	28	29	30	31	1	2	◑	11:26	31	2448466
AUGUST 1991	4	5	6	7	8	9	●	2:28	32	2448473
	11	12	13	14	15	16	◐	5:01	33	2448480
	18	19	20	21	22	23	24		34	2448487
	○	26	27	28	29	30	31	9:07	35	2448494
SEPTEMBER 1991	◑	2	3	4	5	6	7	18:16	36	2448501
	●	9	10	11	12	13	14	11:01	37	2448508
	◐	16	17	18	19	20	21	22:01	38	2448515
	22	○[d]	24	25	26	27	28	22:40	39	2448522
	29	30	◑	2	3	4	5	0:30	40	2448529
OCTOBER 1991	6	●	8	9	10	11	12	21:39	41	2448536
	13	14	◐	16	17	18	19	17:33	42	2448543
	20	21	22	○	24	25	26	11:08	43	2448550
	27	28	29	◑	31	1	2	7:11	44	2448557
NOVEMBER 1991	3	4	5	●	7	8	9	11:11	45	2448564
	10	11	12	13	◐	15	16	14:01	46	2448571
	17	18	19	20	○	22	23	22:56	47	2448578
	24	25	26	27	◑	29	30	15:21	48	2448585
DECEMBER 1991	1	2	3	4	5	●	7	3:56	49	2448592
	8	9	10	11	12	13	◐	9:32	50	2448599
	15	16	17	18	19	20	○	10:23	51	2448606
	22[e]	23	24	25	26	27	◑	1:55	52	2448613
	29	30	31	1	2	3	●	23:10	1	2448620

Hebrew 5751/5752‡

ISO Week	Month	Sun	Mon	Tue	Wed	Thu	Fri	Sat	Molad
1	TEVETH 5751	13	14	15	16	17	18	19	
2		20	21	22	23	24	25	26	Tue $21^h10^m10^p$
3	SHEVAT 5751	27	28	29	1	2	3	4	
4		5	6	7	8	9	10	11	
5		12	13	14	15	16	17	18	
6		19	20	21	22	23	24	25	Thu $9^h54^m11^p$
7	ADAR 5751	26	27	28	29	30	1	2	
8		3	4	5	6	7	8	9	
9		10	11	12	13	14[f]	15	16	
10		17	18	19	20	21	22	23	Fri $22^h38^m12^p$
11	NISAN 5751	24	25	26	27	28	29	1	
12		2	3	4	5	6	7	8	
13		9	10	11	12	13	14	15[g]	
14		16	17	18	19	20	21	22	
15		23	24	25	26	27	28	29	Sun $11^h22^m13^p$
16	IYYAR 5751	30	1	2	3	4	5	6	
17		7	8	9	10	11	12	13	
18		14	15	16	17	18	19	20	
19		21	22	23	24	25	26	27	Tue $0^h6^m14^p$
20	SIVAN 5751	28	29	1	2	3	4	5	
21		6[h]	7	8	9	10	11	12	
22		13	14	15	16	17	18	19	
23		20	21	22	23	24	25	26	Wed $12^h50^m15^p$
24	TAMMUZ 5751	27	28	29	30	1	2	3	
25		4	5	6	7	8	9	10	
26		11	12	13	14	15	16	17	
27		18	19	20	21	22	23	24	
28	AV 5751	25	26	27	28	29	1	2	Fri $1^h34^m16^p$
29		3	4	5	6	7	8	9	
30		10[i]	11	12	13	14	15	16	
31		17	18	19	20	21	22	23	
32		24	25	26	27	28	29	30	Sat $14^h18^m17^p$
33	ELUL 5751	1	2	3	4	5	6	7	
34		8	9	10	11	12	13	14	
35		15	16	17	18	19	20	21	
36		22	23	24	25	26	27	28	Mon $3^h3^m0^p$
37	TISHRI 5752	29	1[a]	2[a]	3	4	5	6	
38		7	8	9	10[b]	11	12	13	
39		14	15[c]	16	17	18	19	20	
40		21	22	23	24	25	26	27	Tue $15^h47^m1^p$
41	HESHVAN 5752	28	29	30	1	2	3	4	
42		5	6	7	8	9	10	11	
43		12	13	14	15	16	17	18	
44		19	20	21	22	23	24	25	Thu $4^h31^m2^p$
45	KISLEV 5752	26	27	28	29	30	1	2	
46		3	4	5	6	7	8	9	
47		10	11	12	13	14	15	16	
48		17	18	19	20	21	22	23	
49		24	25[e]	26[e]	27[e]	28[e]	29[d,e]	30[e]	Fri $17^h15^m3^p$
50	TEVETH 5752	1[e]	2[e]	3	4	5	6	7	
51		8	9	10	11	12	13	14	
52		15	16	17	18	19	20	21	
1		22	23	24	25	26	27	28	

Chinese Gēng-Wǔ‡/Xīn-Wèi

ISO Week	Month	Sun	Mon	Tue	Wed	Thu	Fri	Sat	Solar Term
1	MONTH 11 Gēng-Wǔ	14	15	16	17	18	19	20	
2		*21*	22	23	24	25	26	27	*Xiǎo hán*
3	MONTH 12 Gēng-Wǔ	28	29	30	1	2	3	4	
4		***5***	6	7	8	9	10	11	**Dà hán**
5		12	13	14	15	16	17	18	
6		19	*20*	21	22	23	24	25	*Lì chūn*
7	MONTH 1 Xīn-Wèi	26	27	28	29	30	1[a]	2	
8		3	4	***5***	6	7	8	9*	**Yǔ shuǐ**
9		10	11	12	13	14	15[b]	16	
10		17	18	19	*20*	21	22	23	*Jīng zhé*
11	MONTH 2 Xīn-Wèi	24	25	26	27	28	29	1	
12		2	3	4	5	***6***	7	8	**Chūn fēn**
13		9	10	11	12	13	14	15	
14		16	17	18	19	20	*21*[c]	22	*Qīng míng*
15		23	24	25	26	27	28	29	
16	MONTH 3 Xīn-Wèi	30	1	2	3	4	5	***6***	**Gǔ yǔ**
17		7	8	9	10*	11	12	13	
18		14	15	16	17	18	19	20	
19		21	*22*	23	24	25	26	27	*Lì xià*
20	MONTH 4 Xīn-Wèi	28	29	1	2	3	4	5	
21		6	7	***8***	9	10	11	12	**Xiǎo mǎn**
22		13	14	15	16	17	18	19	
23		20	21	22	23	*24*	25	26	*Máng zhòng*
24	MONTH 5 Xīn-Wèi	27	28	29	1	2	3	4	
25		5[d]	6	7	8	9	10	***11***	**Xià zhì**
26		12*	13	14	15	16	17	18	
27		19	20	21	22	23	24	25	
28	MONTH 6 Xīn-Wèi	*26*	27	28	29	30	1	2	*Xiǎo shǔ*
29		3	4	5	6	7	8	9	
30		10	11	***12***	13	14	15	16	**Dà shǔ**
31		17	18	19	20	21	22	23	
32	MONTH 7 Xīn-Wèi	24	25	26	27	*28*	29	1	*Lì qiū*
33		2	3	4	5	6	7[e]	8	
34		9	10	11	12	13*	***14***	15[f]	**Chǔ shǔ**
35		16	17	18	19	20	21	22	
36		23	24	25	26	27	28	29	
37	MONTH 8 Xīn-Wèi	*1*	2	3	4	5	6	7	*Bái lù*
38		8	9	10	11	12	13	14	
39		15[g]	***16***	17	18	19	20	21	**Qiū fēn**
40		22	23	24	25	26	27	28	
41	MONTH 9 Xīn-Wèi	29	30	1	2	3	4	5	*Hán lù*
42		6	7	8	9[h]	10	11	12	
43		13	14*	15	16	***17***	18	19	**Shuāng jiàng**
44		20	21	22	23	24	25	26	
45	MONTH 10 Xīn-Wèi	27	28	29	1	2	3	4	*Lì dōng*
46		5	6	7	8	9	10	11	
47		12	13	14	15	16	17	***18***	**Xiǎo xuě**
48		19	20	21	22	23	24	25	
49	MONTH 11 Xīn-Wèi	26	27	28	29	30	1	2	*Dà xuě*
50		3	4	5	6	7	8	9	
51		10	11	12	13	14	15*	16	
52		***17***[i]	18	19	20	21	22	23	**Dōng zhì**
1		24	25	26	27	28	29	30	

Coptic 1707‡/1708 — Ethiopic 1983‡/1984

ISO Week	Coptic Month	Sun	Mon	Tue	Wed	Thu	Fri	Sat	Ethiopic Month
1	KOIAK 1707	21	22	23	24	25	26	27	TĀKŚĀŚ 1983
2		28	29[c]	30	1	2	3	4	
3	TŌBE 1707	5	6[d]	7	8	9	10	11[e]	
4		12	13	14	15	16	17	18	ṬER 1983
5		19	20	21	22	23	24	25	
6		26	27	28	29	30	1	2	
7	MESHIR 1707	3	4	5	6	7	8	9	
8		10	11	12	13	14	15	16	YAKĀTIT 1983
9		17	18	19	20	21	22	23	
10		24	25	26	27	28	29	30	
11	PAREMOTEP 1707	1	2	3	4	5	6	7	
12		8	9	10	11	12	13	14	MAGĀBIT 1983
13		15	16	17	18	19	20	21	
14		22	23	24	25	26	27	28	
15		29[f]	30	1	2	3	4	5	
16	PARMOUTE 1707	6	7	8	9	10	11	12	MIYĀZYĀ 1983
17		13	14	15	16	17	18	19	
18		20	21	22	23	24	25	26	
19		27	28	29[g]	30	1	2	3	
20	PASHONS 1707	4	5	6	7	8	9	10	GENBOT 1983
21		11	12	13	14	15	16	17	
22		18	19	20	21	22	23	24	
23		25	26	27	28	29	30	1	
24	PAŌNE 1707	2	3	4	5	6	7	8	
25		9	10	11	12	13	14	15	SANĒ 1983
26		16	17	18	19	20	21	22	
27		23	24	25	26	27	28	29	
28		30	1	2	3	4	5	6	
29	EPĒP 1707	7	8	9	10	11	12	13	ḤAMLĒ 1983
30		14	15	16	17	18	19	20	
31		21	22	23	24	25	26	27	
32		28	29	30	1	2	3	4	
33	MESORĒ 1707	5	6	7	8	9	10	11	NAḤASĒ 1983
34		12	13[h]	14	15	16	17	18	
35		19	20	21	22	23	24	25	
36	EPAG. 1707	26	27	28	29	30	1	2	PĀG. 1983
37		3	4	5	6	1[a]	2	3	
38	THOOUT 1708	4	5	6	7	8	9	10	MASKARAM 1984
39		11	12	13	14	15	16	17[b]	
40		18	19	20	21	22	23	24	
41		25	26	27	28	29	30	1	
42	PAOPE 1708	2	3	4	5	6	7	8	ṬEQEMT 1984
43		9	10	11	12	13	14	15	
44		16	17	18	19	20	21	22	
45		23	24	25	26	27	28	29	
46		30	1	2	3	4	5	6	
47	ATHŌR 1708	7	8	9	10	11	12	13	ḪEDĀR 1984
48		14	15	16	17	18	19	20	
49		21	22	23	24	25	26	27	
50		28	29	30	1	2	3	4	
51	KOIAK 1708	5	6	7	8	9	10	11	TĀKŚĀŚ 1984
52		12	13	14	15	16	17	18	
1		19	20	21	22	23	24	25	

[a]New Year
[b]Spring (3:02)
[c]Summer (21:18)
[d]Autumn (12:48)
[e]Winter (8:53)
● New moon
◐ First quarter moon
○ Full moon
◑ Last quarter moon

‡Leap year
[a]New Year
[b]Yom Kippur
[c]Sukkot
[d]Winter starts
[e]Ḥanukkah
[f]Purim
[g]Passover
[h]Shavuot
[i]Fast of Av

‡Leap year
[a]New Year (4689, Sheep)
[b]Lantern Festival
[c]Qīngmíng
[d]Dragon Festival
[e]Qǐqiǎo
[f]Hungry Ghosts
[g]Mid-Autumn Festival
[h]Double-Ninth Festival
[i]Dōngzhì
*Start of 60-name cycle

‡Leap year
[a]New Year
[b]Building of the Cross
[c]Christmas
[d]Jesus's Circumcision
[e]Epiphany
[f]Easter
[g]Mary's Announcement
[h]Jesus's Transfiguration

PERSIAN (ASTRONOMICAL) 1369/1370‡

Month	Sun	Mon	Tue	Wed	Thu	Fri	Sat
DEY 1369	9	10	11	12	13	14	15
	16	17	18	19	20	21	22
	23	24	25	26	27	28	29
BAHMAN 1369	30	1	2	3	4	5	6
	7	8	9	10	11	12	13
	14	15	16	17	18	19	20
	21	22	23	24	25	26	27
ESFAND 1369	28	29	30	1	2	3	4
	5	6	7	8	9	10	11
	12	13	14	15	16	17	18
	19	20	21	22	23	24	25
FARVARDĪN 1370	26	27	28	29	1[a]	2	3
	4	5	6	7	8	9	10
	11	12	13[b]	14	15	16	17
	18	19	20	21	22	23	24
	25	26	27	28	29	30	31
ORDĪBEHEŠT 1370	1	2	3	4	5	6	7
	8	9	10	11	12	13	14
	15	16	17	18	19	20	21
	22	23	24	25	26	27	28
XORDĀD 1370	29	30	31	1	2	3	4
	5	6	7	8	9	10	11
	12	13	14	15	16	17	18
	19	20	21	22	23	24	25
TĪR 1370	26	27	28	29	30	31	1
	2	3	4	5	6	7	8
	9	10	11	12	13	14	15
	16	17	18	19	20	21	22
	23	24	25	26	27	28	29
MORDĀD 1370	30	31	1	2	3	4	5
	6	7	8	9	10	11	12
	13	14	15	16	17	18	19
	20	21	22	23	24	25	26
SHAHRĪVAR 1370	27	28	29	30	31	1	2
	3	4	5	6	7	8	9
	10	11	12	13	14	15	16
	17	18	19	20	21	22	23
	24	25	26	27	28	29	30
MEHR 1370	31	1	2	3	4	5	6
	7	8	9	10	11	12	13
	14	15	16	17	18	19	20
	21	22	23	24	25	26	27
ABĀN 1370	28	29	30	1	2	3	4
	5	6	7	8	9	10	11
	12	13	14	15	16	17	18
	19	20	21	22	23	24	25
ĀZAR 1370	26	27	28	29	30	1	2
	3	4	5	6	7	8	9
	10	11	12	13	14	15	16
	17	18	19	20	21	22	23
	24	25	26	27	28	29	30
DEY 1370	1	2	3	4	5	6	7
	8	9	10	11	12	13	14

‡Leap year
[a]New Year
[b]Sizdeh Bedar

HINDU LUNAR 2047/2048‡

Month	Sun	Mon	Tue	Wed	Thu	Fri	Sat
PAUSHA 2047	14	15	16	17	18	19	20
	21	22	23	24	25	26	27
MĀGHA 2047	28	29	30	1	2	2	3
	4	**5**	7	8	9	10	11
	12	13	14	15	16	17	18
	19	20	21	22	23	24	25
PHĀLGUNA 2047	26	27	28[h]	29	30	1	2
	3	4	5	6	7	8	9
	10	12	13	14	15[i]	16	17
	18	19	20	21	22	23	24
	24	25	26	27	28	29	30
CHAITRA 2048	1[a]	2	3	**4**	6	7	8
	9[b]	10	11	12	13	14	15
	16	17	18	19	20	21	22
	23	24	25	26	27	28	29
LEAP VAIŚĀKHA 2048	30	1	2	3	4	5	6
	7	8	**9**	11	12	13	14
	15	16	17	18	*18*	19	20
	21	22	23	24	25	26	27
VAIŚĀKHA 2048	28	29	30	1	**2**	4	5
	6	7	8	9	10	11	12
	13	14	15	16	17	18	19
	20	21	22	23	24	25	26
JYAISHṬHA 2048	27	28	29	30	1	2	3
	4	**5**	7	8	9	10	11
	12	13	14	15	*15*	16	17
	18	19	20	21	22	23	24
ĀSHĀḌHA 2048	25	26	**27**	29	30	1	2
	3	4	5	6	7	8	9
	10	11	12	13	14	15	16
	17	18	19	20	21	22	23
	24	25	26	27	28	29	**30**
ŚRĀVAṆA 2048	2	3	4	5	6	7	8
	9	10	11	*11*	12	13	14
	15	16	17	18	19	20	21
	22	**23**[c]	25	26	27	28	29
BHĀDRAPADA 2048	30	1	2	3	4[d]	5	6
	7	8	9	10	11	12	13
	14	15	16	17	18	19	20
	21	22	23	24	25	26	**27**
ĀŚVINA 2048	29	30	1	2	3	4	5
	6	7	7	8[e]	9[e]	10[e]	11
	12	13	14	15	16	17	18
	19	**20**	22	23	24	25	26
KĀRTTIKA 2048	27	28	29	30	1[f]	2	3
	4	5	6	7	8	9	10
	10	11	12	**13**	15	16	17
	18	19	20	21	22	23	24
MĀRGAŚĪRA 2048	25	26	27	28	29	30	1
	2	3	4	5	6	7	8
	9	10	11[g]	12	13	14	15
	16	17	18	**19**	21	22	23
	24	25	26	27	28	29	30

‡Leap year
[a]New Year (Prajāpati)
[b]Birthday of Rāma
[c]Birthday of Krishna
[d]Ganēśa Chaturthī
[e]Dashara
[f]Diwali
[g]Birthday of Vishnu
[h]Night of Śiva
[i]Holi

HINDU SOLAR 1912‡/1913

Month	Sun	Mon	Tue	Wed	Thu	Fri	Sat
PAUSHA 1912	15	16	17	18	19	20	21
	22	23	24	25	26	27	28
MĀGHA 1912	29	1[b]	2	3	4	5	6
	7	8	9	10	11	12	13
	14	15	16	17	18	19	20
	21	22	23	24	25	26	27
PHĀLGUNA 1912	28	29	1	2	3	4	5
	6	7	8	9	10	11	12
	13	14	15	16	17	18	19
	20	21	22	23	24	25	26
CHAITRA 1912	27	28	29	30	1	2	3
	4	5	6	7	8	9	10
	11	12	13	14	15	16	17
	18	19	20	21	22	23	24
	25	26	27	28	29	30	31
VAIŚĀKHA 1913	1[a]	2	3	4	5	6	7
	8	9	10	11	12	13	14
	15	16	17	18	19	20	21
	22	23	24	25	26	27	28
JYAISHṬHA 1913	29	30	31	1	2	3	4
	5	6	7	8	9	10	11
	12	13	14	15	16	17	18
	19	20	21	22	23	24	25
ĀSHĀḌHA 1913	26	27	28	29	30	31	1
	2	3	4	5	6	7	8
	9	10	11	12	13	14	15
	16	17	18	19	20	21	22
	23	24	25	26	27	28	29
ŚRĀVAṆA 1913	30	31	32	1	2	3	4
	5	6	7	8	9	10	11
	12	13	14	15	16	17	18
	19	20	21	22	23	24	25
BHĀDRAPADA 1913	26	27	28	29	30	31	1
	2	3	4	5	6	7	8
	9	10	11	12	13	14	15
	16	17	18	19	20	21	22
	23	24	25	26	27	28	29
ĀŚVINA 1913	30	31	1	2	3	4	5
	6	7	8	9	10	11	12
	13	14	15	16	17	18	19
	20	21	22	23	24	25	26
KĀRTTIKA 1913	27	28	29	30	31	1	2
	3	4	5	6	7	8	9
	10	11	12	13	14	15	16
	17	18	19	20	21	22	23
MĀRGAŚĪRA 1913	24	25	26	27	28	29	1
	2	3	4	5	6	7	8
	9	10	11	12	13	14	15
	16	17	18	19	20	21	22
	23	24	25	26	27	28	29
PAUSHA 1913	30	1	2	3	4	5	6
	7	8	9	10	11	12	13
	14	15	16	17	18	19	20

‡Leap year
[a]New Year (Tāraṇa)
[b]Pongal

ISLAMIC (ASTRONOMICAL) 1411/1412‡

Month	Sun	Mon	Tue	Wed	Thu	Fri	Sat
JUMĀDĀ II 1411	12	13	14	15	16	17	18
	19	20	21	22	23	24	25
RAJAB 1411	26	27	28	29	1	2	3
	4	5	6	7	8	9	10
	11	12	13	14	15	16	17
	18	19	20	21	22	23	24
SHA'BĀN 1411	25	26	27[d]	28	29	30	1
	2	3	4	5	6	7	8
	9	10	11	12	13	14	15
	16	17	18	19	20	21	22
	23	24	25	26	27	28	29
RAMAḌĀN 1411	1[e]	2	3	4	5	6	7
	8	9	10	11	12	13	14
	15	16	17	18	19	20	21
	22	23	24	25	26	27	28
SHAWWĀL 1411	29	30	1[f]	2	3	4	5
	6	7	8	9	10	11	12
	13	14	15	16	17	18	19
	20	21	22	23	24	25	26
DHU AL-QA'DA 1411	27	28	29	1	2	3	4
	5	6	7	8	9	10	11
	12	13	14	15	16	17	18
	19	20	21	22	23	24	25
DHU AL-ḤIJJA 1411	26	27	28	29	30	1	2
	3	4	5	6	7	8	9
	10[g]	11	12	13	14	15	16
	17	18	19	20	21	22	23
MUḤARRAM 1412	24	25	26	27	28	29	1[a]
	2	3	4	5	6	7	8
	9	10[b]	11	12	13	14	15
	16	17	18	19	20	21	22
	23	24	25	26	27	28	29
ṢAFAR 1412	30	1	2	3	4	5	6
	7	8	9	10	11	12	13
	14	15	16	17	18	19	20
	21	22	23	24	25	26	27
RABĪ' I 1412	28	29	30	1	2	3	4
	5	6	7	8	9	10	11
	12[c]	13	14	15	16	17	18
	19	20	21	22	23	24	25
RABĪ' II 1412	26	27	28	29	1	2	3
	4	5	6	7	8	9	10
	11	12	13	14	15	16	17
	18	19	20	21	22	23	24
JUMĀDĀ I 1412	25	26	27	28	29	1	2
	3	4	5	6	7	8	9
	10	11	12	13	14	15	16
	17	18	19	20	21	22	23
	24	25	26	27	28	29	30
JUMĀDĀ II 1412	1	2	3	4	5	6	7
	8	9	10	11	12	13	14
	15	16	17	18	19	20	21
	22	23	24	25	26	27	28

‡Leap year
[a]New Year
[b]'Ashūrā'
[c]Prophet's Birthday
[d]Ascent of the Prophet
[e]Start of Ramaḍān
[f]'Id al-Fiṭr
[g]'Id al-'Aḍḥā

GREGORIAN 1991

Julian (Sun)	Sun	Mon	Tue	Wed	Thu	Fri	Sat	Month
Dec 17	30	31	1	2	3	4	5	JANUARY 1991
	6	7[a]	8	9	10	11	12	
Dec 31	13	14[b]	15	16	17	18	19	
	20	21	22	23	24	25	26	
Jan 14	27	28	29	30	31	1	2	FEBRUARY 1991
	3	4	5	6	7	8	9	
Jan 28	10	11	12	13[c]	14	15	16	
	17	18	19	20	21	22	23	
Feb 11	24[d]	25	26	27	28	1	2	MARCH 1991
	3	4	5	6	7	8	9	
Feb 25	10	11	12	13	14	15	16	
	17	18	19	20	21	22	23	
Mar 11	24	25	26	27	28	29	30	
	31[e]	1	2	3	4	5	6	APRIL 1991
Mar 25	7[f]	8	9	10	11	12	13	
	14	15	16	17	18	19	20	
Apr 8	21	22	23	24	25	26	27	
	28	29	30	1	2	3	4	MAY 1991
Apr 22	5	6	7	8	9	10	11	
	12	13	14	15	16	17	18	
May 6	19	20	21	22	23	24	25	
	26	27	28	29	30	31	1	JUNE 1991
May 20	2	3	4	5	6	7	8	
	9	10	11	12	13	14	15	
Jun 3	16	17	18	19	20	21	22	
	23	24	25	26	27	28	29	
Jun 17	30	1	2	3	4	5	6	JULY 1991
	7	8	9	10	11	12	13	
Jul 1	14	15	16	17	18	19	20	
	21	22	23	24	25	26	27	
Jul 15	28	29	30	31	1	2	3	AUGUST 1991
	4	5	6	7	8	9	10	
Jul 29	11	12	13	14	15	16	17	
	18	19	20	21	22	23	24	
Aug 12	25	26	27	28	29	30	31	
	1	2	3	4	5	6	7	SEPTEMBER 1991
Aug 26	8	9	10	11	12	13	14	
	15	16	17	18	19	20	21	
Sep 9	22	23	24	25	26	27	28	
	29	30	1	2	3	4	5	OCTOBER 1991
Sep 23	6	7	8	9	10	11	12	
	13	14	15	16	17	18	19	
Oct 7	20	21	22	23	24	25	26	
	27	28	29	30	31	1	2	NOVEMBER 1991
Oct 21	3	4	5	6	7	8	9	
	10	11	12	13	14	15	16	
Nov 4	17	18	19	20	21	22	23	
	24	25	26	27	28	29	30	
Nov 18	1[g]	2	3	4	5	6	7	DECEMBER 1991
	8	9	10	11	12	13	14	
Dec 2	15	16	17	18	19	20	21	
	22	23	24	25[h]	26	27	28	
Dec 16	29	30	31	1	2	3	4	

[a]Orthodox Christmas
[b]Julian New Year
[c]Ash Wednesday
[d]Feast of Orthodoxy
[e]Easter
[f]Orthodox Easter
[g]Advent
[h]Christmas

1992

Gregorian 1992‡	Sun Mon Tue Wed Thu Fri Sat	Lunar Phases	ISO Week (Mon)	Julian Day (Sun noon)	Hebrew 5752‡/5753	Sun Mon Tue Wed Thu Fri Sat	Molad	Chinese Xīn-Wèi/Rén-Shēn	Sun Mon Tue Wed Thu Fri Sat	Solar Term	Coptic 1708/1709	Sun Mon Tue Wed Thu Fri Sat	Ethiopic 1984/1985
	29 30 31 1[a] 2 3 ●	23:10	1	2448620	Teveth 5752	22 23 24 25 26 27 28			24 25 26 27 28 29 30		Koiak 1708	19 20 21 22 23 24 25	Tākhśāś 1984
January 1992	5 6 7 8 9 10 11		2	2448627		29 1 2 3 4 5 6	Sun $5^h59^m4^p$	Month 12 Xīn-Wèi	1 *2* 3 4 5 6 7	Xiǎo hán		26 27 28 29[c] 30 1 2	
	12 ◐ 14 15 16 17 18	2:32	3	2448634	Shevat 5752	7 8 9 10 11 12 13			8 9 10 11 12 13 14		Tôbe 1708	3 4 5 6[d] 7 8 9	
	○ 20 21 22 23 24 25	21:28	4	2448641		14 15 16 17 18 19 20			15 16 ***17*** 18 19 20 21	Dà hán		10 11[e] 12 13 14 15 16	Ṭer 1984
	◑ 27 28 29 30 31 1	15:27	5	2448648		21 22 23 24 25 26 27			22 23 24 25 26 27 28			17 18 19 20 21 22 23	
	2 ● 4 5 6 7 8	19:00	6	2448655		28 29 30 1 2 3 4	Mon $18^h43^m5^p$		29 30 *1*[a] 2 3 4 5	Lì chūn		24 25 26 27 28 29 30	
February 1992	9 10 ◐ 12 13 14 15	16:15	7	2448662	Adar I 5752	5 6 7 8 9 10 11		Month 1 Rén-Shēn	6 7 8 9 10 11 12			1 2 3 4 5 6 7	
	16 17 ○ 19 20 21 22	8:04	8	2448669		12 13 14 15 16 17 18			13 14 15[b]* ***16*** 17 18 19	Yǔ shuǐ	Meshir 1708	8 9 10 11 12 13 14	
	23 24 ◑ 26 27 28 29	7:56	9	2448676		19 20 21 22 23 24 25			20 21 22 23 24 25 26			15 16 17 18 19 20 21	Yakātit 1984
	1 2 3 ● 5 6 7	13:22	10	2448683		26 27 28 29 30 1 2	Wed $7^h27^m6^p$		27 28 29 1 *2* 3 4	Jīng zhé		22 23 24 25 26 27 28	
	8 9 10 11 ◐ 13 14	2:36	11	2448690	Adar II 5752	3 4 5 6 7 8 9		Month 2 Rén-Shēn	5 6 7 8 9 10 11			29 30 1 2 3 4 5	
March 1992	15 16 17 ○ 19 20[b] 21	18:18	12	2448697		10 11 12 13 14[f] 15 16			12 13 14 15 16 ***17*** 18	Chūn fēn	Paremotep 1708	6 7 8 9 10 11 12	
	22 23 24 25 ◑ 27 28	2:30	13	2448704		17 18 19 20 21 22 23			19 20 21 22 23 24 25			13 14 15 16 17 18 19	Magābit 1984
	29 30 31 1 2 ● 4	5:01	14	2448711		24 25 26 27 28 29 1	Thu $20^h11^m7^p$		26 27 28 29 30 1 *2*[c]	Qīng míng		20 21 22 23 24 25 26	
April 1992	5 6 7 8 9 ◐ 11	10:06	15	2448718	Nisan 5752	2 3 4 5 6 7 8		Month 3 Rén-Shēn	3 4 5 6 7 8 9			27 28 29 30 1 2 3	
	12 13 14 15 16 ○ 18	4:43	16	2448725		9 10 11 12 13 14 15[g]			10 11 12 13 14 15 16*		Parmoute 1708	4 5 6 7 8 9 10	
	19 20 21 22 23 ◑ 25	21:40	17	2448732		16 17 18 19 20 21 22			17 ***18*** 19 20 21 22 23	Gǔ yǔ		11 12 13 14 15 16 17	Miyāzyā 1984
	26 27 28 29 30 1 ●	17:45	18	2448739		23 24 25 26 27 28 29			24 25 26 27 28 29 30			18[f] 19 20 21 22 23 24	
	3 4 5 6 7 8 ◐	15:43	19	2448746		30 1 2 3 4 5 6	Sat $8^h55^m8^p$		1 2 *3* 4 5 6 7	Lì xià		25 26 27 28 29[g] 30 1	
May 1992	10 11 12 13 14 15 ○	16:02	20	2448753	Iyar 5752	7 8 9 10 11 12 13		Month 4 Rén-Shēn	8 9 10 11 12 13 14		Pashons 1708	2 3 4 5 6 7 8	
	17 18 19 20 21 22 23		21	2448760		14 15 16 17 18 19 20			15 16 17 18 ***19*** 20 21	Xiǎo mǎn		9 10 11 12 13 14 15	Genbot 1984
	◑ 25 26 27 28 29 30	15:53	22	2448767		21 22 23 24 25 26 27			22 23 24 25 26 27 28			16 17 18 19 20 21 22	
	31 ● 2 3 4 5 6	3:57	23	2448774		28 29 1 2 3 4 5	Sun $21^h39^m9^p$		29 1 2 3 4 *5*[d] 6	Máng zhòng		23 24 25 26 27 28 29	
June 1992	◐ 8 9 10 11 12 13	20:47	24	2448781	Sivan 5752	6[h] 7 8 9 10 11 12		Month 5 Rén-Shēn	7 8 9 10 11 12 13			30 1 2 3 4 5 6	
	14 ○ 16 17 18 19 20	4:50	25	2448788		13 14 15 16 17 18 19			14 15 16 17* 18 19 20		Paône 1708	7 8 9 10 11 12 13	
	21[c] 22 ◑ 24 25 26 27	8:11	26	2448795		20 21 22 23 24 25 26			***21*** 22 23 24 25 26 27	Xià zhì		14 15 16 17 18 19 20	Sanē 1984
	28 29 ● 1 2 3 4	12:18	27	2448802		27 28 29 30 1 2 3	Tue $10^h23^m10^p$		28 29 1 2 3 4 5			21 22 23 24 25 26 27	
July 1992	5 6 ◐ 8 9 10 11	2:43	28	2448809	Tammuz 5752	4 5 6 7 8 9 10		Month 6 Rén-Shēn	6 7 *8* 9 10 11 12	Xiǎo shǔ		28 29 30 1 2 3 4	
	12 13 ○ 15 16 17 18	19:06	29	2448816		11 12 13 14 15 16 17			13 14 15 16 17 18 19		Epêp 1708	5 6 7 8 9 10 11	
	19 20 21 ◑ 23 24 25	22:12	30	2448823		18 19 20 21 22 23 24			20 21 22 ***23*** 24 25 26	Dà shǔ		12 13 14 15 16 17 18	Ḥamlē 1984
	26 27 28 ● 30 31 1	19:35	31	2448830		25 26 27 28 29 1 2	Wed $23^h7^m11^p$		27 28 29 30 1 2 3			19 20 21 22 23 24 25	
August 1992	2 3 4 ◐ 6 7 8	10:58	32	2448837	Av 5752	3 4 5 6 7 8 9		Month 7 Rén-Shēn	4 5 6 *7*[e] 8 9 10	Lì qiū		26 27 28 29 30 1 2	
	9 10 11 12 ○ 14 15	10:27	33	2448844		10[i] 11 12 13 14 15 16			11 12 13 14 15[f] 16 17		Mesorê 1708	3 4 5 6 7 8 9	
	16 17 18 19 20 ◑ 22	10:01	34	2448851		17 18 19 20 21 22 23			18* 19 20 21 22 23 24			10 11 12 13[h] 14 15 16	Nahasē 1984
	23 24 25 26 27 ● 29	2:42	35	2448858		24 25 26 27 28 29 30	Fri $11^h51^m12^p$		***25*** 26 27 28 29 1 2	Chǔ shǔ		17 18 19 20 21 22 23	
	30 31 1 2 ◐ 4 5	22:39	36	2448865	Elul 5752	1 2 3 4 5 6 7		Month 8 Rén-Shēn	3 4 5 6 7 8 9			24 25 26 27 28 29 30	
September 1992	6 7 8 9 10 11 ○	2:17	37	2448872		8 9 10 11 12 13 14			10 *11* 12 13 14 15[g] 16	Bái lù	Epag. 1708	1 2 3 4 5 1[a] 2	Pāg. 1984
	13 14 15 16 17 18 ◑	19:53	38	2448879		15 16 17 18 19 20 21			17 18 19 20 21 22 23		Thoout 1709	3 4 5 6 7 8 9	Maskaram 1985
	20 21 22[d] 23 24 25 ●	10:40	39	2448886		22 23 24 25 26 27 28			24 25 26 ***27*** 28 29 1	Qiū fēn		10 11 12 13 14 15 16	
	27 28 29 30 1 2 ◐	14:12	40	2448893		29 1[a] 2[a] 3 4 5 6	Sun $0^h35^m13^p$		2 3 4 5 6 7 8			17[b] 18 19 20 21 22 23	
October 1992	4 5 6 7 8 9 10		41	2448900	Tishri 5753	7 8 9 10[b] 11 12 13		Month 9 Rén-Shēn	9[h] 10 11 12 *13* 14 15	Hán lù		24 25 26 27 28 29 30	
	○ 12 13 14 15 16 17	18:03	42	2448907		14 15[c] 16 17 18 19 20			16 17 18 19 20* 21 22			1 2 3 4 5 6 7	
	18 ◑ 20 21 22 23 24	4:12	43	2448914		21 22 23 24 25 26 27			23 24 25 26 27 ***28*** 29	Shuāng jiàng	Paope 1709	8 9 10 11 12 13 14	Ṭeqemt 1985
	● 26 27 28 29 30 31	20:34	44	2448921		28 29 30 1 2 3 4	Mon $13^h19^m14^p$		30 1 2 3 4 5 6			15 16 17 18 19 20 21	
	1 ◐ 3 4 5 6 7	9:11	45	2448928	Heshvan 5753	5 6 7 8 9 10 11		Month 10 Rén-Shēn	7 8 9 10 11 12 *13*	Lì dōng		22 23 24 25 26 27 28	
November 1992	8 9 ○ 11 12 13 14	9:20	46	2448935		12 13 14 15 16 17 18			14 15 16 17 18 19 20			29 30 1 2 3 4 5	
	15 16 ◑ 18 19 20 21	11:39	47	2448942		19 20 21 22 23 24 25			21 22 23 24 25 26 27		Athôr 1709	6 7 8 9 10 11 12	
	22 23 ● 25 26 27 28	9:11	48	2448949		26 27 28 29 1 2 3	Wed $2^h3^m15^p$		***28*** 29 1 2 3 4 5	Xiǎo xuě		13 14 15 16 17 18 19	Ḥedār 1985
	29 30 1 ◐ 3 4 5	6:17	49	2448956	Kislev 5753	4 5 6 7 8 9 10[d]		Month 11 Rén-Shēn	6 7 8 9 10 11 12			20 21 22 23 24 25 26	
December 1992	6 7 8 ○ 10 11 12	23:41	50	2448963		11 12 13 14 15 16 17			13 *14* 15 16 17 18 19	Dà xuě		27 28 29 30 1 2 3	
	13 14 15 ◑ 17 18 19	19:13	51	2448970		18 19 20 21 22 23 24			20 21* 22 23 24 25 26		Koiak 1709	4 5 6 7 8 9 10	
	20 21e 22 23 ● 25 26	0:43	52	2448977	Teveth 5753	25[e] 26[e] 27[e] 28[e] 29[e] 1[e] 2[e]	Thu $14^h47^m16^p$	Month 12 Rén-Shēn	27 ***28***[i] 29 30 1 2 3	Dōng zhì		11 12 13 14 15 16 17	Tākhśāś 1985
	27 28 29 30 31 ◐ 2	3:38	53	2448984		3[e] 4 5 6 7 8 9			4 5 6 7 8 9 10			18 19 20 21 22 23 24	

‡Leap year
[a]New Year
[b]Spring (8:48)
[c]Summer (3:14)
[d]Autumn (18:43)
[e]Winter (14:43)
● New moon
◐ First quarter moon
○ Full moon
◑ Last quarter moon

‡Leap year
[a]New Year
[b]Yom Kippur
[c]Sukkot
[d]Winter starts
[e]Ḥanukkah
[f]Purim
[g]Passover
[h]Shavuot
[i]Fast of Av

[a]New Year (4690, Monkey)
[b]Lantern Festival
[c]Qīngmíng
[d]Dragon Festival
[e]Qīqiǎo
[f]Hungry Ghosts
[g]Mid-Autumn Festival
[h]Double-Ninth Festival
[i]Dōngzhì
*Start of 60-name cycle

[a]New Year
[b]Building of the Cross
[c]Christmas
[d]Jesus's Circumcision
[e]Epiphany
[f]Easter
[g]Mary's Announcement
[h]Jesus's Transfiguration

PERSIAN (ASTRONOMICAL) 1370‡/1371

Month	Sun	Mon	Tue	Wed	Thu	Fri	Sat
DEY 1370	8	9	10	11	12	13	14
	15	16	17	18	19	20	21
	22	23	24	25	26	27	28
BAHMAN 1370	29	30	*1*	2	3	4	5
	6	7	8	9	10	11	12
	13	14	15	16	17	18	19
	20	21	22	23	24	25	26
ESFAND 1370	27	28	29	30	*1*	2	3
	4	5	6	7	8	9	10
	11	12	13	14	15	16	17
	18	19	20	21	22	23	24
FARVARDĪN 1371	25	26	27	28	29	30*	*1*[a]
	2	3	4	5	6	7	8
	9	10	11	12	13[b]	14	15
	16	17	18	19	20	21	22
	23	24	25	26	27	28	29
ORDĪBEHEŠT 1371	30	31	*1*	2	3	4	5
	6	7	8	9	10	11	12
	13	14	15	16	17	18	19
	20	21	22	23	24	25	26
XORDĀD 1371	27	28	29	30	31	*1*	2
	3	4	5	6	7	8	9
	10	11	12	13	14	15	16
	17	18	19	20	21	22	23
	24	25	26	27	28	29	30
TĪR 1371	31	*1*	2	3	4	5	6
	7	8	9	10	11	12	13
	14	15	16	17	18	19	20
	21	22	23	24	25	26	27
MORDĀD 1371	28	29	30	31	*1*	2	3
	4	5	6	7	8	9	10
	11	12	13	14	15	16	17
	18	19	20	21	22	23	24
	25	26	27	28	29	30	31
SHAHRĪVAR 1371	*1*	2	3	4	5	6	7
	8	9	10	11	12	13	14
	15	16	17	18	19	20	21
	22	23	24	25	26	27	28
MEHR 1371	29	30	31	*1*	2	3	4
	5	6	7	8	9	10	11
	12	13	14	15	16	17	18
	19	20	21	22	23	24	25
ĀBĀN 1371	26	27	28	29	30	*1*	2
	3	4	5	6	7	8	9
	10	11	12	13	14	15	16
	17	18	19	20	21	22	23
	24	25	26	27	28	29	30
ĀZAR 1371	*1*	2	3	4	5	6	7
	8	9	10	11	12	13	14
	15	16	17	18	19	20	21
	22	23	24	25	26	27	28
DEY 1371	29	30	*1*	2	3	4	5
	6	7	8	9	10	11	12

‡Leap year
[a]New Year (or prior day)
*Near New Year: −0′15″
[b]Sizdeh Bedar

HINDU LUNAR 2048‡/2049

Month	Sun	Mon	Tue	Wed	Thu	Fri	Sat
PAUSHA 2048	24	25	26	27	28	29	30
	1	2	2	3	4	5	6
	7	8	9	10	11	12	**13**
	15	16	17	18	19	20	21
	22	23	24	25	26	27	28
MĀGHA 2048	29	30	1	2	3	4	5
	6	7	8	9	10	11	12
	13	14	15	16	17	**18**	20
	21	22	23	24	*24*	25	26
PHĀLGUNA 2048	27	28[h]	29	30	1	2	3
	4	5	6	7	8	9	10
	11	13	14	15[i]	16	17	18
	19	20	21	22	23	24	25
CHAITRA 2049	26	27	*27*	28	29	30	1[a]
	2	3	4	**5**	7	8	9[b]
	10	11	12	13	14	15	16
	17	18	19	20	21	22	23
	24	25	26	27	28	29	30
VAIŚĀKHA 2049	1	2	3	4	5	6	7
	8	**9**	11	12	13	14	15
	16	17	18	19	20	21	22
	22	23	24	25	26	27	28
JYAISHTHA 2049	29	30	1	**2**	4	5	6
	7	8	9	10	11	12	13
	14	15	16	17	18	19	20
	21	22	23	24	25	26	27
ĀSHĀḌHA 2049	28	29	30	1	2	3	4
	5	7	8	9	10	11	12
	13	14	15	16	17	18	19
	19	20	21	22	23	24	25
ŚRĀVAṆA 2049	26	**27**	29	30	1	2	3
	4	5	6	7	8	9	10
	11	12	13	14	15	16	17
	18	19	20	21	22	23[c]	24
BHĀDRAPADA 2049	25	26	27	28	29	**30**	2
	3	4[d]	5	6	7	8	9
	10	11	12	13	14	15	*15*
	16	17	18	19	20	21	22
	23	25	26	27	28	29	30
ĀŚVINA 2049	1	2	3	4	5	6	7
	8[e]	9[e]	10[e]	11	12	13	14
	15	16	17	18	19	20	21
	22	23	24	25	26	**27**	29
KĀRTTIKA 2049	30	1[f]	2	3	4	5	6
	7	8	9	10	*10*	11	12
	13	14	15	16	17	18	19
	20	**21**	23	24	25	26	27
MĀRGAŚĪRA 2049	28	29	30	1	2	3	4
	5	6	7	8	9	10	11[g]
	12	13	14	15	16	17	18
	19	20	21	22	23	24	25
PAUSHA 2049	**26**	28	29	30	1	2	3
	3	4	5	6	7	8	9

‡Leap year
[a]New Year (Aṅgiras)
[b]Birthday of Rāma
[c]Birthday of Krishna
[d]Gaṇēśa Chaturthī
[e]Dashara
[f]Diwali
[g]Birthday of Vishnu
[h]Night of Śiva
[i]Holi

HINDU SOLAR 1913/1914

Month	Sun	Mon	Tue	Wed	Thu	Fri	Sat
PAUSHA 1913	14	15	16	17	18	19	20
	21	22	23	24	25	26	27
MĀGHA 1913	28	29	1[b]	2	3	4	5
	6	7	8	9	10	11	12
	13	14	15	16	17	18	19
	20	21	22	23	24	25	26
PHĀLGUNA 1913	27	28	29	30	1	2	3
	4	5	6	7	8	9	10
	11	12	13	14	15	16	17
	18	19	20	21	22	23	24
CHAITRA 1913	25	26	27	28	29	30	1
	2	3	4	5	6	7	8
	9	10	11	12	13	14	15
	16	17	18	19	20	21	22
	23	24	25	26	27	28	29
VAIŚĀKHA 1914	30	1[a]	2	3	4	5	6
	7	8	9	10	11	12	13
	14	15	16	17	18	19	20
	21	22	23	24	25	26	27
JYAISHTHA 1914	28	29	30	31	1	2	3
	4	5	6	7	8	9	10
	11	12	13	14	15	16	17
	18	19	20	21	22	23	24
	25	26	27	28	29	30	31
ĀSHĀḌHA 1914	1	2	3	4	5	6	7
	8	9	10	11	12	13	14
	15	16	17	18	19	20	21
	22	23	24	25	26	27	28
ŚRĀVAṆA 1914	29	30	31	32	1	2	3
	4	5	6	7	8	9	10
	11	12	13	14	15	16	17
	18	19	20	21	22	23	24
	25	26	27	28	29	30	31
BHĀDRAPADA 1914	1	2	3	4	5	6	7
	8	9	10	11	12	13	14
	15	16	17	18	19	20	21
	22	23	24	25	26	27	28
ĀŚVINA 1914	29	30	31	1	2	3	4
	5	6	7	8	9	10	11
	12	13	14	15	16	17	18
	19	20	21	22	23	24	25
KĀRTTIKA 1914	26	27	28	29	30	31	1
	2	3	4	5	6	7	8
	9	10	11	12	13	14	15
	16	17	18	19	20	21	22
	23	24	25	26	27	28	29
MĀRGAŚĪRA • 1914	30	1	2	3	4	5	6
	7	8	9	10	11	12	13
	14	15	16	17	18	19	20
	21	22	23	24	25	26	27
PAUSHA 1914	28	29	1	2	3	4	5
	6	7	8	9	10	11	12
	13	14	15	16	17	18	19

[a]New Year (Pārthiva)
[b]Pongal

ISLAMIC (ASTRONOMICAL) 1412‡/1413‡

Month	Sun	Mon	Tue	Wed	Thu	Fri	Sat
JUMĀDĀ II 1412	22	23	24	25	26	27	28
RAJAB 1412	29	*1*	2	3	4	5	6
	7	8	9	10	11	12	13
	14	15	16	17	18	19	20
	21	22	23	24	25	26	27[d]
SHA'BĀN 1412	28	29	30	*1*	2	3	4
	5	6	7	8	9	10	11
	12	13	14	15	16	17	18
	19	20	21	22	23	24	25
RAMAḌĀN 1412	26	27	28	29	*30*	1[e]	2
	3	4	5	6	7	8	9
	10	11	12	13	14	15	16
	17	18	19	20	21	22	23
SHAWWĀL 1412	24	25	26	27	28	29	*1*[f]
	2	3	4	5	6	7	8
	9	10	11	12	13	14	15
	16	17	18	19	20	21	22
	23	24	25	26	27	28	29
DHU AL-QA'DA 1412	*30*	1	2	3	4	5	6
	7	8	9	10	11	12	13
	14	15	16	17	18	19	20
	21	22	23	24	25	26	27
DHU AL-ḤIJJA 1412	28	29	*1*	2	3	4	5
	6	7	8	9	10[g]	11	12
	13	14	15	16	17	18	19
	20	21	22	23	24	25	26
MUḤARRAM 1413	27	28	29	30	*1*[a]	2	3
	4	5	6	7	8	9	10[b]
	11	12	13	14	15	16	17
	18	19	20	21	22	23	24
ṢAFAR 1413	25	26	27	28	29	30	*1*
	2	3	4	5	6	7	8
	9	10	11	12	13	14	15
	16	17	18	19	20	21	22
	23	24	25	26	27	28	29
RABĪ' I 1413	*1*	2	3	4	5	6	7
	8	9	10	11	12[c]	13	14
	15	16	17	18	19	20	21
	22	23	24	25	26	27	28
RABĪ' II 1413	29	1	2	3	4	5	6
	7	8	9	10	11	12	13
	14	15	16	17	18	19	20
	21	22	23	24	25	26	27
JUMĀDĀ I 1413	28	29	30	*1*	2	3	4
	5	6	7	8	9	10	11
	12	13	14	15	16	17	18
	19	20	21	22	23	24	25
JUMĀDĀ II 1413	26	27	28	29	1	2	3
	4	5	6	7	8	9	10
	11	12	13	14	15	16	17
	18	19	20	21	22	23	24
RAJAB 1413	25	26	27	28	29	1	2
	3	4	5	6	7	8	9

‡Leap year
[a]New Year
[b]'Ashūrā'
[c]Prophet's Birthday
[d]Ascent of the Prophet
[e]Start of Ramaḍān
[f]'Id al-Fiṭr
[g]'Id al-'Aḍḥā

GREGORIAN 1992‡

Julian‡ (Sun)	Sun	Mon	Tue	Wed	Thu	Fri	Sat	Month
Dec 16	*29*	30	31	1	2	3	4	JANUARY 1992
	5	6	7[a]	8	9	10	11	
Dec 30	*12*	13	14[b]	15	16	17	18	
	19	20	21	22	23	24	25	
Jan 13	*26*	27	28	29	30	31	1	FEBRUARY 1992
	2	3	4	5	6	7	8	
Jan 27	*9*	10	11	12	13	14	15	
	16	17	18	19	20	21	22	
Feb 10	*23*	24	25	26	27	28	29	
	1	2	3	4[c]	5	6	7	MARCH 1992
Feb 24	*8*	9	10	11	12	13	14	
	15[d]	16	17	18	19	20	21	
Mar 9	*22*	23	24	25	26	27	28	
	29	30	31	1	2	3	4	APRIL 1992
Mar 23	*5*	6	7	8	9	10	11	
	12	13	14	15	16	17	18	
Apr 6	*19*[e]	20	21	22	23	24	25	
	26[f]	27	28	29	30	1	2	MAY 1992
Apr 20	*3*	4	5	6	7	8	9	
	10	11	12	13	14	15	16	
May 4	*17*	18	19	20	21	22	23	
	24	25	26	27	28	29	30	
May 18	*31*	1	2	3	4	5	6	JUNE 1992
	7	8	9	10	11	12	13	
Jun 1	*14*	15	16	17	18	19	20	
	21	22	23	24	25	26	27	
Jun 15	*28*	29	30	1	2	3	4	JULY 1992
	5	6	7	8	9	10	11	
Jun 29	*12*	13	14	15	16	17	18	
	19	20	21	22	23	24	25	
Jul 13	*26*	27	28	29	30	31	1	AUGUST 1992
	2	3	4	5	6	7	8	
Jul 27	*9*	10	11	12	13	14	15	
	16	17	18	19	20	21	22	
Aug 10	*23*	24	25	26	27	28	29	
	30	31	1	2	3	4	5	SEPTEMBER 1992
Aug 24	*6*	7	8	9	10	11	12	
	13	14	15	16	17	18	19	
Sep 7	*20*	21	22	23	24	25	26	
	27	28	29	30	1	2	3	OCTOBER 1992
Sep 21	*4*	5	6	7	8	9	10	
	11	12	13	14	15	16	17	
Oct 5	*18*	19	20	21	22	23	24	
	25	26	27	28	29	30	31	
Oct 19	*1*	2	3	4	5	6	7	NOVEMBER 1992
	8	9	10	11	12	13	14	
Nov 2	*15*	16	17	18	19	20	21	
	22	23	24	25	26	27	28	
Nov 16	*29*[g]	30	1	2	3	4	5	DECEMBER 1992
	6	7	8	9	10	11	12	
Nov 30	*13*	14	15	16	17	18	19	
	20	21	22	23	24	25[h]	26	
Dec 14	*27*	28	29	30	31	1	2	

‡Leap year
[a]Orthodox Christmas
[b]Julian New Year
[c]Ash Wednesday
[d]Feast of Orthodoxy
[e]Easter
[f]Orthodox Easter
[g]Advent
[h]Christmas

1993

Month	Sun	Mon	Tue	Wed	Thu	Fri	Sat	Lunar Phases	ISO WEEK (Mon)	JULIAN DAY (Sun noon)	Hebrew month	Sun	Mon	Tue	Wed	Thu	Fri	Sat	Molad	Chinese month	Sun	Mon	Tue	Wed	Thu	Fri	Sat	Solar Term	Coptic month	Sun	Mon	Tue	Wed	Thu	Fri	Sat	Ethiopic month
GREGORIAN 1993											HEBREW 5753/5754									CHINESE Rén-Shēn/Guǐ-Yǒu‡									COPTIC 1709/1710								ETHIOPIC 1985/1986
	27	28	29	30	31	◐[a]	2	3:38	53	2448984		3[e]	4	5	6	7	8	9			4	5	6	7	8	9	10			18	19	20	21	22	23	24	TĀKHŚĀŚ 1985
JANUARY 1993	3	4	5	6	7	○	9	12:37	1	2448991	TEVETH 5753	10	11	12	13	14	15	16		MONTH 12 Rén-Shēn	11	12	13	14	15	16	17	Xiǎo hán	KOIAK 1709	25	26	27	28	29[c]	30	1	
	10	11	12	13	14	◑	16	4:01	2	2448998		17	18	19	20	21	22	23			18	19	20	21	22	23	24			2	3	4	5	6[d]	7	8	
	17	18	19	20	21	●	23	18:27	3	2449005		24	25	26	27	28	29	1	Sat 3h31m17p		25	26	27	28	29	30	1[a]	Dà hán	TŌBE 1709	9	10	11[e]	12	13	14	15	ṬER 1985
	24	25	26	27	28	29	◐	23:20	4	2449012		2	3	4	5	6	7	8			2	3	4	5	6	7	8			16	17	18	19	20	21	22	
	31	1	2	3	4	5	○	23:55	5	2449019	SHEVAT 5753	9	10	11	12	13	14	15		MONTH 1 Guǐ-Yǒu	9	10	11	12	13	14	15[b]	Lì chūn		23	24	25	26	27	28	29	
FEBRUARY 1993	7	8	9	10	11	12	◑	14:57	6	2449026		16	17	18	19	20	21	22			16	17	18	19	20	21*	22			30	1	2	3	4	5	6	
	14	15	16	17	18	19	20		7	2449033		23	24	25	26	27	28	29			23	24	25	26	27	28	29	Yǔ shuǐ	MESHIR 1709	7	8	9	10	11	12	13	YAKĀTIT 1985
	●	22	23	24	25	26	27	13:05	8	2449040		30	1	2	3	4	5	6	Sun 16h16m0p		1	2	3	4	5	6	7			14	15	16	17	18	19	20	
	28	◐	2	3	4	5	6	15:47	9	2449047	ADAR 5753	7	8	9	10	11	12	13		MONTH 2 Guǐ-Yǒu	8	9	10	11	12	13	14	Jīng zhé		21	22	23	24	25	26	27	
MARCH 1993	7	○	9	10	11	12	13	9:46	10	2449054		14[f]	15	16	17	18	19	20			15	16	17	18	19	20	21			28	29	30	1	2	3	4	
	14	◑	16	17	18	19	20[b]	4:17	11	2449061		21	22	23	24	25	26	27			22	23	24	25	26	27	28	Chūn fēn	PAREMOTEP 1709	5	6	7	8	9	10	11	MAGĀBIT 1985
	21	22	●	24	25	26	27	7:14	12	2449068		28	29	1	2	3	4	5	Tue 5h0m1p		29	30	1	2	3	4	5			12	13	14	15	16	17	18	
	28	29	30	◐	1	2	3	4:10	13	2449075	NISAN 5753	6	7	8	9	10	11	12		MONTH 3 Guǐ-Yǒu	6	7	8	9	10	11	12			19	20	21	22	23	24	25	
APRIL 1993	4	5	○	7	8	9	10	18:43	14	2449082		13	14	15[g]	16	17	18	19			13	14[c]	15	16	17	18	19	Qīng míng		26	27	28	29	30	1	2	
	11	12	◑	14	15	16	17	19:39	15	2449089		20	21	22	23	24	25	26			20	21	22*	23	24	25	26		PARMOUTE 1709	3	4	5	6	7	8	9	MIYĀZYĀ 1985
	18	19	20	●	22	23	24	23:49	16	2449096		27	28	29	30	1	2	3	Wed 17h44m2p		27	28	29	30	1	2	3	Gǔ yǔ		10[f]	11	12	13	14	15	16	
	25	26	27	28	◐	30	1	12:41	17	2449103		4	5	6	7	8	9	10		LEAP MONTH 3 Guǐ-Yǒu	4	5	6	7	8	9	10			17	18	19	20	21	22	23	
MAY 1993	2	3	4	5	○	7	8	3:34	18	2449110	IYYAR 5753	11	12	13	14	15	16	17			11	12	13	14	15	16	17	Lì xià		24	25	26	27	28	29[g]	30	
	9	10	11	12	◑	14	15	12:20	19	2449117		18	19	20	21	22	23	24			18	19	20	21	22	23	24			1	2	3	4	5	6	7	
	16	17	18	19	20	●	22	14:07	20	2449124		25	26	27	28	29	1	2	Fri 6h28m3p		25	26	27	28	29	1	2	Xiǎo mǎn	PASHONS 1709	8	9	10	11	12	13	14	GENBOT 1985
	23	24	25	26	27	◐	29	18:21	21	2449131		3	4	5	6[h]	7	8	9		MONTH 4 Guǐ-Yǒu	3	4	5	6	7	8	9			15	16	17	18	19	20	21	
	30	31	1	2	3	○	5	13:02	22	2449138	SIVAN 5753	10	11	12	13	14	15	16			10	11	12	13	14	15	16			22	23	24	25	26	27	28	
JUNE 1993	6	7	8	9	10	11	◑	5:35	23	2449145		17	18	19	20	21	22	23			17	18	19	20	21	22	23*	Máng zhòng		29	30	1	2	3	4	5	
	13	14	15	16	17	18	19		24	2449152		24	25	26	27	28	29	30			24	25	26	27	28	29	30		PAŌNE 1709	6	7	8	9	10	11	12	SANĒ 1985
	●	21[c]	22	23	24	25	◐	1:53 22:43	25	2449159		1	2	3	4	5	6	7	Sat 19h12m4p		1	2	3	4	5[d]	6	7	Xià zhì		13	14	15	16	17	18	19	
	27	28	29	30	1	2	○	23:45	26	2449166	TAMMUZ 5753	8	9	10	11	12	13	14		MONTH 5 Guǐ-Yǒu	8	9	10	11	12	13	14			20	21	22	23	24	25	26	
JULY 1993	4	5	6	7	8	9	10		27	2449173		15	16	17	18	19	20	21			15	16	17	18	19	20	21	Xiǎo shǔ		27	28	29	30	1	2	3	
	◑	12	13	14	15	16	17	22:49	28	2449180		22	23	24	25	26	27	28			22	23	24	25	26	27	28		EPĒP 1709	4	5	6	7	8	9	10	HAMLĒ 1985
	18	●	20	21	22	23	24	11:24	29	2449187		29	1	2	3	4	5	6	Mon 7h56m5p		29	1	2	3	4	5	6	Dà shǔ		11	12	13	14	15	16	17	
	25	◐	27	28	29	30	31	3:25	30	2449194		7	8	9[i]	10	11	12	13		MONTH 6 Guǐ-Yǒu	7	8	9	10	11	12	13			18	19	20	21	22	23	24	
AUGUST 1993	1	○	3	4	5	6	7	12:10	31	2449201	AV 5753	14	15	16	17	18	19	20			14	15	16	17	18	19	20	Lì qiū		25	26	27	28	29	30	1	
	8	9	◑	11	12	13	14	15:19	32	2449208		21	22	23	24	25	26	27			21	22	23	24*	25	26	27		MESORĒ 1709	2	3	4	5	6	7	8	NAHASĒ 1985
	15	16	●	18	19	20	21	19:28	33	2449215		28	29	30	1	2	3	4	Tue 20h40m6p		28	29	30	1	2	3	4			9	10	11	12	13[h]	14	15	
	22	23	◐	25	26	27	28	9:57	34	2449222		5	6	7	8	9	10	11		MONTH 7 Guǐ-Yǒu	5	6	7[e]	8	9	10	11	Chǔ shǔ		16	17	18	19	20	21	22	
	29	30	31	○	2	3	4	2:33	35	2449229	ELUL 5753	12	13	14	15	16	17	18			12	13	14	15[f]	16	17	18			23	24	25	26	27	28	29	
SEPTEMBER 1993	5	6	7	8	◑	10	11	6:26	36	2449236		19	20	21	22	23	24	25			19	20	21	22	23	24	25	Bái lù	EPAG. 1709	30	1	2	3	4	5	1[a]	PĀG. 1985
	12	13	14	15	●	17	18	3:10	37	2449243		26	27	28	29	1[a]	2[a]	3	Thu 9h24m7p		26	27	28	29	1	2	3			2	3	4	5	6	7	8	
	19	20	21	◐	23[d]	24	25	19:32	38	2449250		4	5	6	7	8	9	10[b]		MONTH 8 Guǐ-Yǒu	4	5	6	7	8	9	10	Qiū fēn	THOOUT 1710	9	10	11	12	13	14	15	MASKARAM 1986
	26	27	28	29	○	1	2	18:54	39	2449257	TISHRI 5754	11	12	13	14	15[c]	16	17			11	12	13	14	15[g]	16	17			16	17[b]	18	19	20	21	22	
OCTOBER 1993	3	4	5	6	7	◑	9	19:35	40	2449264		18	19	20	21	22	23	24			18	19	20	21	22	23	24	Hán lù		23	24	25	26	27	28	29	
	10	11	12	13	14	●	16	11:36	41	2449271		25	26	27	28	29	30	1	Fri 22h8m8p		25*	26	27	28	29	1	2			30	1	2	3	4	5	6	
	17	18	19	20	21	◐	23	8:52	42	2449278		2	3	4	5	6	7	8		MONTH 9 Guǐ-Yǒu	3	4	5	6	7	8	9[h]	Shuāng jiàng	PAOPE 1710	7	8	9	10	11	12	13	TEQEMT 1986
	24	25	26	27	28	29	○	12:38	43	2449285	HESHVAN 5754	9	10	11	12	13	14	15			10	11	12	13	14	15	16			14	15	16	17	18	19	20	
	31	1	2	3	4	5	6		44	2449292		16	17	18	19	20	21	22			17	18	19	20	21	22	23			21	22	23	24	25	26	27	
NOVEMBER 1993	◑	8	9	10	11	12	●	6:36 21:34	45	2449299		23	24	25	26	27	28	29			24	25	26	27	28	29	30	Lì dōng		28	29	30	1	2	3	4	
	14	15	16	17	18	19	20		46	2449306		30	1	2	3	4	5	6	Sun 10h52m9p		1	2	3	4	5	6	7		ATHŌR 1710	5	6	7	8	9	10	11	HEDĀR 1986
	◐	22	23	24	25	26	27	2:03	47	2449313		7	8	9	10	11	12	13		MONTH 10 Guǐ-Yǒu	8	9	10	11	12	13	14	Xiǎo xuě		12	13	14	15	16	17	18	
	28	○	30	1	2	3	4	6:31	48	2449320	KISLEV 5754	14	15	16	17	18	19	20			15	16	17	18	19	20	21			19	20	21	22	23	24	25	
DECEMBER 1993	5	◑	7	8	9	10	11	15:49	49	2449327		21[d]	22	23	24	25[e]	26[e]	27[e]			22	23	24	25	26*	27	28	Dà xuě		26	27	28	29	30	1	2	
	12	●	14	15	16	17	18	9:27	50	2449334		28[e]	29[e]	30[e]	1[e]	2[e]	3	4	Mon 23h36m10p		29	1	2	3	4	5	6		KOIAK 1710	3	4	5	6	7	8	9	TĀKHŚĀŚ 1986
	19	◐	21[e]	22	23	24	25	22:26	51	2449341	TEVETH 5754	5	6	7	8	9	10	11		MONTH 11* Guǐ-Yǒu	7	8	9	10[i]	11	12	13	Dōng zhì		10	11	12	13	14	15	16	
	26	27	○	29	30	31	1	23:05	52	2449348		12	13	14	15	16	17	18			14	15	16	17	18	19	20			17	18	19	20	21	22	23	

[a]New Year
[b]Spring (14:41)
[c]Summer (9:00)
[d]Autumn (0:22)
[e]Winter (20:26)
● New moon
◐ First quarter moon
○ Full moon
◑ Last quarter moon

[a]New Year
[b]Yom Kippur
[c]Sukkot
[d]Winter starts
[e]Ḥanukkah
[f]Purim
[g]Passover
[h]Shavuot
[i]Fast of Av

‡Leap year
[a]New Year (4691, Fowl)
[b]Lantern Festival
[c]Qīngmíng
[d]Dragon Festival
[e]Qīqiǎo
[f]Hungry Ghosts
[g]Mid-Autumn Festival
[h]Double-Ninth Festival
[i]Dōngzhì
*Start of 60-name cycle

[a]New Year
[b]Building of the Cross
[c]Christmas
[d]Jesus's Circumcision
[e]Epiphany
[f]Easter
[g]Mary's Announcement
[h]Jesus's Transfiguration

PERSIAN (ASTRONOMICAL) 1371/1372

Month	Sun	Mon	Tue	Wed	Thu	Fri	Sat
DEY 1371	6	7	8	9	10	11	12
	13	14	15	16	17	18	19
	20	21	22	23	24	25	26
BAHMAN 1371	27	28	29	30	1	2	3
	4	5	6	7	8	9	10
	11	12	13	14	15	16	17
	18	19	20	21	22	23	24
ESFAND 1371	25	26	27	28	29	30	1
	2	3	4	5	6	7	8
	9	10	11	12	13	14	15
	16	17	18	19	20	21	22
	23	24	25	26	27	28	29
FARVARDIN 1372	1[a]	2	3	4	5	6	7
	8	9	10	11	12	13[b]	14
	15	16	17	18	19	20	21
	22	23	24	25	26	27	28
ORDIBEHEŠT 1372	29	30	31	1	2	3	4
	5	6	7	8	9	10	11
	12	13	14	15	16	17	18
	19	20	21	22	23	24	25
XORDĀD 1372	26	27	28	29	30	31	1
	2	3	4	5	6	7	8
	9	10	11	12	13	14	15
	16	17	18	19	20	21	22
	23	24	25	26	27	28	29
TĪR 1372	30	31	1	2	3	4	5
	6	7	8	9	10	11	12
	13	14	15	16	17	18	19
	20	21	22	23	24	25	26
MORDĀD 1372	27	28	29	30	31	1	2
	3	4	5	6	7	8	9
	10	11	12	13	14	15	16
	17	18	19	20	21	22	23
	24	25	26	27	28	29	30
SHAHRĪVAR 1372	31	1	2	3	4	5	6
	7	8	9	10	11	12	13
	14	15	16	17	18	19	20
	21	22	23	24	25	26	27
MEHR 1372	28	29	30	31	1	2	3
	4	5	6	7	8	9	10
	11	12	13	14	15	16	17
	18	19	20	21	22	23	24
ĀBĀN 1372	25	26	27	28	29	30	1
	2	3	4	5	6	7	8
	9	10	11	12	13	14	15
	16	17	18	19	20	21	22
	23	24	25	26	27	28	29
ĀZAR 1372	30	1	2	3	4	5	6
	7	8	9	10	11	12	13
	14	15	16	17	18	19	20
	21	22	23	24	25	26	27
DEY 1372	28	29	30	1	2	3	4
	5	6	7	8	9	10	11

[a]New Year
[b]Sizdeh Bedar

HINDU LUNAR 2049/2050‡

Month	Sun	Mon	Tue	Wed	Thu	Fri	Sat
PAUSHA 2049	3	4	5	6	7	8	9
	10	11	12	13	14	15	16
	17	18	19	**20**	22	23	24
MĀGHA 2049	25	26	27	28	29	30	1
	2	3	4	5	*5*	6	7
	8	9	10	11	12	13	**14**
	16	17	18	19	20	21	22
	23	24	25	26	27	28[h]	29
PHĀLGUNA 2049	30	1	2	3	4	5	6
	7	8	9	10	11	12	13
	14	15[i]	16	17	18	**19**	21
	22	23	24	25	26	27	28
CHAITRA 2050	*28*	29	30	1[a]	2	3	4
	5	6	7	8	9[b]	10	11
	12	14	15	16	17	18	19
	20	21	22	23	24	25	26
VAIŚĀKHA 2050	27	28	29	30	1	*1*	2
	3	4	**5**	7	8	9	10
	11	12	13	14	15	16	**17**
	19	20	21	22	*22*	23	24
JYAISHṬHA 2050	25	26	27	28	29	30	1
	2	3	4	5	6	7	8
	9	11	12	13	14	15	16
	17	18	19	20	21	22	23
	24	25	26	27	*27*	28	29
ĀSHĀḌHA 2050	30	**1**	3	4	5	6	7
	8	9	10	11	12	**13**	15
	16	17	18	19	*19*	20	21
	22	23	24	25	26	27	28
ŚRĀVAṆA 2050	29	30	1	2	3	4	**5**
	7	8	9	10	11	12	13
	14	15	16	17	18	19	20
	21	22	23[c]	24	25	*25*	**26**
LEAP BHĀDRAPADA 2050	28	29	30	1	2	3	4
	5	6	7	**8**	10	11	12
	13	14	15	*15*	16	17	18
	19	20	21	22	23	24	25
BHĀDRAPADA 2050	26	27	28	29	30	**1**	3
	4[d]	5	6	7	8	9	10
	11	12	13	14	15	16	17
	18	19	*19*	20	21	22	**23**
ĀŚVINA 2050	25	26	27	28	29	30	1
	2	3	4	5	**6**	8[e]	9[e]
	9[e]	10[e]	11	12	13	14	15
	16	17	18	19	20	21	22
	23	24	25	26	27	**28**	30
KĀRTTIKA 2050	1[f]	2	3	4	5	6	7
	8	9	10	11	12	13	*13*
	14	15	16	17	18	19	20
	21	**22**	24	25	26	27	28
MĀRGAŚIRA 2050	29	30	1	2	3	4	5
	6	7	8	9	10	11[g]	12
	13	14	15	16	17	18	19

‡Leap year
[a]New Year (Śrīmukha)
[b]Birthday of Rāma
[c]Birthday of Krishna
[d]Ganēśa Chaturthī
[e]Dashara
[f]Diwali
[g]Birthday of Vishnu
[h]Night of Śiva
[i]Holi

HINDU SOLAR 1914/1915

Month	Sun	Mon	Tue	Wed	Thu	Fri	Sat
PAUSHA 1914	13	14	15	16	17	18	19
	20	21	22	23	24	25	26
MĀGHA 1914	27	28	29	30	1[b]	2	3
	4	5	6	7	8	9	10
	11	12	13	14	15	16	17
	18	19	20	21	22	23	24
PHĀLGUNA 1914	25	26	27	28	29	1	2
	3	4	5	6	7	8	9
	10	11	12	13	14	15	16
	17	18	19	20	21	22	23
	24	25	26	27	28	29	30
CHAITRA 1914	1	2	3	4	5	6	7
	8	9	10	11	12	13	14
	15	16	17	18	19	20	21
	22	23	24	25	26	27	28
VAIŚĀKHA 1915	29	30	1[a]	2	3	4	5
	6	7	8	9	10	11	12
	13	14	15	16	17	18	19
	20	21	22	23	24	25	26
JYAISHṬHA 1915	27	28	29	30	31	1	2
	3	4	5	6	7	8	9
	10	11	12	13	14	15	16
	17	18	19	20	21	22	23
	24	25	26	27	28	29	30
ĀSHĀḌHA 1915	31	32	1	2	3	4	5
	6	7	8	9	10	11	12
	13	14	15	16	17	18	19
	20	21	22	23	24	25	26
ŚRĀVAṆA 1915	27	28	29	30	31	1	2
	3	4	5	6	7	8	9
	10	11	12	13	14	15	16
	17	18	19	20	21	22	23
	24	25	26	27	28	29	30
BHĀDRAPADA 1915	31	32	1	2	3	4	5
	6	7	8	9	10	11	12
	13	14	15	16	17	18	19
	20	21	22	23	24	25	26
ĀŚVINA 1915	27	28	29	30	31	1	2
	3	4	5	6	7	8	9
	10	11	12	13	14	15	16
	17	18	19	20	21	22	23
	24	25	26	27	28	29	30
KĀRTTIKA 1915	1	2	3	4	5	6	7
	8	9	10	11	12	13	14
	15	16	17	18	19	20	21
	22	23	24	25	26	27	28
MĀRGAŚIRA 1915	29	30	1	2	3	4	5
	6	7	8	9	10	11	12
	13	14	15	16	17	18	19
	20	21	22	23	24	25	26
PAUSHA 1915	27	28	29	1	2	3	4
	5	6	7	8	9	10	11
	12	13	14	15	16	17	18

[a]New Year (Vyaya)
[b]Pongal

ISLAMIC (ASTRONOMICAL) 1413‡/1414

Month	Sun	Mon	Tue	Wed	Thu	Fri	Sat
RAJAB 1413	3	4	5	6	7	8	9
	10	11	12	13	14	15	16
	17	18	19	20	21	22	23
	24	25	26	27[d]	28	29	30
SHA'BĀN 1413	1	2	3	4	5	6	7
	8	9	10	11	12	13	14
	15	16	17	18	19	20	21
	22	23	24	25	26	27	28
RAMAḌĀN 1413	29	30	1[e]	2	3	4	5
	6	7	8	9	10	11	12
	13	14	15	16	17	18	19
	20	21	22	23	24	25	26
SHAWWĀL 1413	27	28	29	30	1[f]	2	3
	4	5	6	7	8	9	10
	11	12	13	14	15	16	17
	18	19	20	21	22	23	24
DHU AL-QA'DA 1413	25	26	27	28	29	1	2
	3	4	5	6	7	8	9
	10	11	12	13	14	15	16
	17	18	19	20	21	22	23
	24	25	26	27	28	29	30
DHU AL-ḤIJJA 1413	1	2	3	4	5	6	7
	8	9	10[g]	11	12	13	14
	15	16	17	18	19	20	21
	22	23	24	25	26	27	28
MUḤARRAM 1414	29	30[d]	1[a]	2	3	4	5
	6	7	8	9	10[b]	11	12
	13	14	15	16	17	18	19
	20	21	22	23	24	25	26
ṢAFAR 1414	27	28	29	1	2	3	4
	5	6	7	8	9	10	11
	12	13	14	15	16	17	18
	19	20	21	22	23	24	25
RABĪ' I 1414	26	27	28	29	30	1	2
	3	4	5	6	7	8	9
	10	11	12[c]	13	14	15	16
	17	18	19	20	21	22	23
RABĪ' II 1414	24	25	26	27	28	29	1
	2	3	4	5	6	7	8
	9	10	11	12	13	14	15
	16	17	18	19	20	21	22
	23	24	25	26	27	28	29
JUMĀDĀ I 1414	1	2	3	4	5	6	7
	8	9	10	11	12	13	14
	15	16	17	18	19	20	21
	22	23	24	25	26	27	28
JUMĀDĀ II 1414	29	1	2	3	4	5	6
	7	8	9	10	11	12	13
	14	15	16	17	18	19	20
	21	22	23	24	25	26	27
RAJAB 1414	28	29	30	1	2	3	4
	5	6	7	8	9	10	11
	12	13	14	15	16	17	18

‡Leap year
[a]New Year
[d]New Year (Arithmetic)
[b]'Ashūrā'
[c]Prophet's Birthday
[d]Ascent of the Prophet
[e]Start of Ramaḍān
[f]'Id al-Fiṭr
[g]'Id al-'Aḍḥā

GREGORIAN 1993

Julian (Sun)	Sun	Mon	Tue	Wed	Thu	Fri	Sat	Month
Dec 14	27	28	29	30	31	1	2	JANUARY 1993
	3	4	5	6	7[a]	8	9	
Dec 28	10	11	12	13	14[b]	15	16	
	17	18	19	20	21	22	23	
Jan 11	24	25	26	27	28	29	30	
	31	1	2	3	4	5	6	FEBRUARY 1993
Jan 25	7	8	9	10	11	12	13	
	14	15	16	17	18	19	20	
Feb 8	21	22	23	24[c]	25	26	27	
	28	1	2	3	4	5	6	MARCH 1993
Feb 22	7[d]	8	9	10	11	12	13	
	14	15	16	17	18	19	20	
Mar 8	21	22	23	24	25	26	27	
	28	29	30	31	1	2	3	APRIL 1993
Mar 22	4	5	6	7	8	9	10	
	11[e]	12	13	14	15	16	17	
Apr 5	18[f]	19	20	21	22	23	24	
	25	26	27	28	29	30	1	MAY 1993
Apr 19	2	3	4	5	6	7	8	
	9	10	11	12	13	14	15	
May 3	16	17	18	19	20	21	22	
	23	24	25	26	27	28	29	
May 17	30	31	1	2	3	4	5	JUNE 1993
	6	7	8	9	10	11	12	
May 31	13	14	15	16	17	18	19	
	20	21	22	23	24	25	26	
Jun 14	27	28	29	30	1	2	3	JULY 1993
	4	5	6	7	8	9	10	
Jun 28	11	12	13	14	15	16	17	
	18	19	20	21	22	23	24	
Jul 12	25	26	27	28	29	30	31	
	1	2	3	4	5	6	7	AUGUST 1993
Jul 26	8	9	10	11	12	13	14	
	15	16	17	18	19	20	21	
Aug 9	22	23	24	25	26	27	28	
	29	30	31	1	2	3	4	SEPTEMBER 1993
Aug 23	5	6	7	8	9	10	11	
	12	13	14	15	16	17	18	
Sep 6	19	20	21	22	23	24	25	
	26	27	28	29	30	1	2	OCTOBER 1993
Sep 20	3	4	5	6	7	8	9	
	10	11	12	13	14	15	16	
Oct 4	17	18	19	20	21	22	23	
	24	25	26	27	28	29	30	
Oct 18	31	1	2	3	4	5	6	NOVEMBER 1993
	7	8	9	10	11	12	13	
Nov 1	14	15	16	17	18	19	20	
	21	22	23	24	25	26	27	
Nov 15	28[g]	29	30	1	2	3	4	DECEMBER 1993
	5	6	7	8	9	10	11	
Nov 29	12	13	14	15	16	17	18	
	19	20	21	22	23	24	25[h]	
Dec 13	26	27	28	29	30	31	1	

[a]Orthodox Christmas
[b]Julian New Year
[c]Ash Wednesday
[d]Feast of Orthodoxy
[e]Easter
[f]Orthodox Easter
[g]Advent
[h]Christmas

1994

GREGORIAN 1994

Month	Sun	Mon	Tue	Wed	Thu	Fri	Sat	Lunar Phases	ISO WEEK (Mon)	JULIAN DAY (Sun noon)
	26	27	○	29	30	31	1[a]	23:05	52	2449348
JANUARY 1994	2	3	4	◑	6	7	8	0:01	1	2449355
	9	10	●	12	13	14	15	23:10	2	2449362
	16	17	18	◐	20	21	22	20:27	3	2449369
	23	24	25	26	○	28	29	13:23	4	2449376
FEBRUARY 1994	30	31	1	2	◑	4	5	8:06	5	2449383
	6	7	8	9	●	11	12	14:30	6	2449390
	13	14	15	16	17	◐	19	17:47	7	2449397
	20	21	22	23	24	25	○	1:15	8	2449404
MARCH 1994	27	28	1	2	3	◑	5	16:53	9	2449411
	6	7	8	9	10	11	●	7:05	10	2449418
	13	14	15	16	17	18	19		11	2449425
	◐[b]	21	22	23	24	25	26	12:14	12	2449432
APRIL 1994	○	28	29	30	31	1	2	11:10	13	2449439
	◑	4	5	6	7	8	9	2:55	14	2449446
	10	●	12	13	14	15	16	0:17	15	2449453
	17	18	◐	20	21	22	23	2:34	16	2449460
	24	○	26	27	28	29	30	19:45	17	2449467
MAY 1994	1	◑	3	4	5	6	7	14:32	18	2449474
	8	9	●	11	12	13	14	17:07	19	2449481
	15	16	17	◐	19	20	21	12:50	20	2449488
	22	23	24	○	26	27	28	3:39	21	2449495
JUNE 1994	29	30	31	◑	2	3	4	4:02	22	2449502
	5	6	7	8	●	10	11	8:27	23	2449509
	12	13	14	15	◐	17	18	19:57	24	2449516
	19	20	21[c]	22	○	24	25	11:33	25	2449523
JULY 1994	26	27	28	29	◑	1	2	19:31	26	2449530
	3	4	5	6	7	●	9	21:37	27	2449537
	10	11	12	13	14	15	◐	1:12	28	2449544
	17	18	19	20	21	○	23	20:16	29	2449551
	24	25	26	27	28	29	◑	12:40	30	2449558
AUGUST 1994	31	1	2	3	4	5	6		31	2449565
	●	8	9	10	11	12	13	8:45	32	2449572
	◐	15	16	17	18	19	20	5:57	33	2449579
	○	22	23	24	25	26	27	6:47	34	2449586
SEPTEMBER 1994	28	◑	30	31	1	2	3	6:41	35	2449593
	4	●	6	7	8	9	10	18:33	36	2449600
	11	◐	13	14	15	16	17	11:34	37	2449607
	18	○	20	21	22	23[d]	24	20:01	38	2449614
OCTOBER 1994	25	26	27	◑	29	30	1	0:23	39	2449621
	2	3	4	●	6	7	8	3:55	40	2449628
	9	10	◐	12	13	14	15	19:17	41	2449635
	16	17	18	○	20	21	22	12:18	42	2449642
	23	24	25	26	◑	28	29	16:44	43	2449649
NOVEMBER 1994	30	31	1	2	●	4	5	13:36	44	2449656
	6	7	8	9	◐	11	12	6:14	45	2449663
	13	14	15	16	17	○	19	6:57	46	2449670
	20	21	22	23	24	25	◑	7:04	47	2449677
DECEMBER 1994	27	28	29	30	1	●	3	23:54	48	2449684
	4	5	6	7	8	◐	10	21:06	49	2449691
	11	12	13	14	15	16	17		50	2449698
	○	19	20	21	22[e]	23	24	2:17	51	2449705
	◑	26	27	28	29	30	31	19:06	52	2449712

HEBREW 5754/5755‡

ISO WEEK	Month	Sun	Mon	Tue	Wed	Thu	Fri	Sat	Molad
52	TEVETH 5754	12	13	14	15	16	17	18	
1		19	20	21	22	23	24	25	
2	SHEVAT 5754	26	27	28	29	1	2	3	Wed $12^{h}20^{m}1^{p}$
3		4	5	6	7	8	9	10	
4		11	12	13	14	15	16	17	
5		18	19	20	21	22	23	24	
6	ADAR 5754	25	26	27	28	29	30	1	Fri $1^{h}4^{m}2^{p}$
7		2	3	4	5	6	7	8	
8		9	10	11	12	13	14[f]	15	
9		16	17	18	19	20	21	22	
10		23	24	25	26	27	28	29	Sat $13^{h}48^{m}3^{p}$
11	NISAN 5754	1	2	3	4	5	6	7	
12		8	9	10	11	12	13	14	
13		15[g]	16	17	18	19	20	21	
14		22	23	24	25	26	27	28	
15	IYYAR 5754	29	30	1	2	3	4	5	Mon $2^{h}32^{m}4^{p}$
16		6	7	8	9	10	11	12	
17		13	14	15	16	17	18	19	
18		20	21	22	23	24	25	26	
19	SIVAN 5754	27	28	29	1	2	3	4	Tue $15^{h}16^{m}5^{p}$
20		5	6[h]	7	8	9	10	11	
21		12	13	14	15	16	17	18	
22		19	20	21	22	23	24	25	
23	TAMMUZ 5754	26	27	28	29	30	1	2	Thu $4^{h}0^{m}6^{p}$
24		3	4	5	6	7	8	9	
25		10	11	12	13	14	15	16	
26		17	18	19	20	21	22	23	
27	AV 5754	24	25	26	27	28	29	1	Fri $16^{h}44^{m}7^{p}$
28		2	3	4	5	6	7	8	
29		9[i]	10	11	12	13	14	15	
30		16	17	18	19	20	21	22	
31		23	24	25	26	27	28	29	
32	ELUL 5754	30	1	2	3	4	5	6	Sun $5^{h}29^{m}0^{p}$
33		7	8	9	10	11	12	13	
34		14	15	16	17	18	19	20	
35		21	22	23	24	25	26	27	
36	TISHRI 5755	28	29	1[a]	2[a]	3	4	5	Mon $18^{h}13^{m}1^{p}$
37		6	7	8	9	10[b]	11	12	
38		13	14	15[c]	16	17	18	19	
39		20	21	22	23	24	25	26	
40	HESHVAN 5755	27	28	29	30	1	2	3	Wed $6^{h}57^{m}2^{p}$
41		4	5	6	7	8	9	10	
42		11	12	13	14	15	16	17	
43		18	19	20	21	22	23	24	
44	KISLEV 5755	25	26	27	28	29	1	2	Thu $19^{h}41^{m}3^{p}$
45		3	4	5	6	7	8	9	
46		10	11	12	13	14	15	16	
47		17	18	19	20	21	22	23	
48		24	25[e]	26[e]	27[e]	28[e]	29[e]	30[e]	Sat $8^{h}25^{m}4^{p}$
49	TEVETH 5755	1[e]	2[d][e]	3	4	5	6	7	
50		8	9	10	11	12	13	14	
51		15	16	17	18	19	20	21	
52		22	23	24	25	26	27	28	

CHINESE Guǐ-Yǒu‡/Jiǎ-Xū

ISO WEEK	Month	Sun	Mon	Tue	Wed	Thu	Fri	Sat	Solar Term
52	MONTH 11* Guǐ-Yǒu	14	15	16	17	18	19	20	
1		21	22	23	24	25	26	27	Xiǎo hán
2	MONTH 12 Guǐ-Yǒu	28	29	30	1	2	3	4	
3		5	6	7	8	9	10	11	Dà hán
4		12	13	14	15	16	17	18	
5		19	20	21	22	23	24	25	Lì chūn
6	MONTH 1 Jiǎ-Xū	26	27*	28	29	1[a]	2	3	
7		4	5	6	7	8	9	10	Yǔ shuǐ
8		11	12	13	14	15[b]	16	17	
9		18	19	20	21	22	23	24	
10	MONTH 2 Jiǎ-Xū	25	26	27	28	29	30	1	Jīng zhé
11		2	3	4	5	6	7	8	
12		9	10	11	12	13	14	15	Chūn fēn
13		16	17	18	19	20	21	22	
14		23	24	25[c]	26	27	28*	29	Qīng míng
15	MONTH 3 Jiǎ-Xū	30	1	2	3	4	5	6	
16		7	8	9	10	11	12	13	Gǔ yǔ
17		14	15	16	17	18	19	20	
18		21	22	23	24	25	26	27	Lì xià
19	MONTH 4 Jiǎ-Xū	28	29	30	1	2	3	4	
20		5	6	7	8	9	10	11	Xiǎo mǎn
21		12	13	14	15	16	17	18	
22		19	20	21	22	23	24	25	
23	MONTH 5 Jiǎ-Xū	26	27	28*	29	1	2	3	Máng zhòng
24		4	5[d]	6	7	8	9	10	
25		11	12	13	14	15	16	17	Xià zhì
26		18	19	20	21	22	23	24	
27	MONTH 6 Jiǎ-Xū	25	26	27	28	29	30	1	Xiǎo shǔ
28		2	3	4	5	6	7	8	
29		9	10	11	12	13	14	15	Dà shǔ
30		16	17	18	19	20	21	22	
31		23	24	25	26	27	28	29*	
32	MONTH 7 Jiǎ-Xū	1	2	3	4	5	6	7[e]	Lì qiū
33		8	9	10	11	12	13	14	
34		15[f]	16	17	18	19	20	21	Chǔ shǔ
35		22	23	24	25	26	27	28	
36	MONTH 8 Jiǎ-Xū	29	30	1	2	3	4	5	Bái lù
37		6	7	8	9	10	11	12	
38		13	14	15[g]	16	17	18	19	Qiū fēn
39		20	21	22	23	24	25	26	
40	MONTH 9 Jiǎ-Xū	27	28	29	1*	2	3	4	Hán lù
41		5	6	7	8	9[h]	10	11	
42		12	13	14	15	16	17	18	
43		19	20	21	22	23	24	25	Shuāng jiàng
44	MONTH 10 Jiǎ-Xū	26	27	28	29	1	2	3	
45		4	5	6	7	8	9	10	Lì dōng
46		11	12	13	14	15	16	17	
47		18	19	20	21	22	23	24	Xiǎo xuě
48	MONTH 11 Jiǎ-Xū	25	26	27	28	29	30	1	
49		2*	3	4	5	6	7	8	Dà xuě
50		9	10	11	12	13	14	15	
51		16	17	18	19	20[i]	21	22	Dōng zhì
52		23	24	25	26	27	28	29	

COPTIC 1710/1711‡ — ETHIOPIC 1986/1987‡

ISO WEEK	Coptic Month	Sun	Mon	Tue	Wed	Thu	Fri	Sat	Ethiopic Month
52	KOIAK 1710	17	18	19	20	21	22	23	TĀKHŚĀŚ 1986
1		24	25	26	27	28	29[c]	30	
2	TŌBE 1710	1	2	3	4	5	6[d]	7	ṬER 1986
3		8	9	10	11[e]	12	13	14	
4		15	16	17	18	19	20	21	
5		22	23	24	25	26	27	28	
6	MESHIR 1710	29	30	1	2	3	4	5	YAKĀTIT 1986
7		6	7	8	9	10	11	12	
8		13	14	15	16	17	18	19	
9		20	21	22	23	24	25	26	
10	PAREMOTEP 1710	27	28	29	30	1	2	3	MAGĀBIT 1986
11		4	5	6	7	8	9	10	
12		11	12	13	14	15	16	17	
13		18	19	20	21	22	23	24	
14	PARMOUTE 1710	25	26	27	28	29	30	1	MIYĀZYĀ 1986
15		2	3	4	5	6	7	8	
16		9	10	11	12	13	14	15	
17		16	17	18	19	20	21	22	
18		23[f]	24	25	26	27	28	29[g]	
19	PASHONS 1710	30	1	2	3	4	5	6	GENBOT 1986
20		7	8	9	10	11	12	13	
21		14	15	16	17	18	19	20	
22		21	22	23	24	25	26	27	
23	PAŌNE 1710	28	29	30	1	2	3	4	SANĒ 1986
24		5	6	7	8	9	10	11	
25		12	13	14	15	16	17	18	
26		19	20	21	22	23	24	25	
27	EPĒP 1710	26	27	28	29	30	1	2	ḤAMLĒ 1986
28		3	4	5	6	7	8	9	
29		10	11	12	13	14	15	16	
30		17	18	19	20	21	22	23	
31		24	25	26	27	28	29	30	
32	MESORĒ 1710	1	2	3	4	5	6	7	NAḤASĒ 1986
33		8	9	10	11	12	13[h]	14	
34		15	16	17	18	19	20	21	
35		22	23	24	25	26	27	28	
36	EPAG. 1710	29	30	1	2	3	4	5	PĀG. 1986
37	THOOUT 1711	1[a]	2	3	4	5	6	7	MASKARAM 1987
38		8	9	10	11	12	13	14	
39		15	16	17[b]	18	19	20	21	
40		22	23	24	25	26	27	28	
41	PAOPE 1711	29	30	1	2	3	4	5	ṬEQEMT 1987
42		6	7	8	9	10	11	12	
43		13	14	15	16	17	18	19	
44		20	21	22	23	24	25	26	
45	ATHŌR 1711	27	28	29	30	1	2	3	ḪEDĀR 1987
46		4	5	6	7	8	9	10	
47		11	12	13	14	15	16	17	
48		18	19	20	21	22	23	24	
49	KOIAK 1711	25	26	27	28	29	30	1	TĀKHŚĀŚ 1987
50		2	3	4	5	6	7	8	
51		9	10	11	12	13	14	15	
52		16	17	18	19	20	21	22	

[a]New Year
[b]Spring (20:28)
[c]Summer (14:48)
[d]Autumn (6:19)
[e]Winter (2:23)
● New moon
◐ First quarter moon
○ Full moon
◑ Last quarter moon

‡Leap year
[a]New Year
[b]Yom Kippur
[c]Sukkot
[d]Winter starts
[e]Ḥanukkah
[f]Purim
[g]Passover
[h]Shavuot
[i]Fast of Av

‡Leap year
[a]New Year (4692, Dog)
[b]Lantern Festival
[c]Qīngmíng
[d]Dragon Festival
[e]Qīqiǎo
[f]Hungry Ghosts
[g]Mid-Autumn Festival
[h]Double-Ninth Festival
[i]Dōngzhì
*Start of 60-name cycle

‡Leap year
[a]New Year
[b]Building of the Cross
[c]Christmas
[d]Jesus's Circumcision
[e]Epiphany
[f]Easter
[g]Mary's Announcement
[h]Jesus's Transfiguration

1994

PERSIAN (ASTRONOMICAL) 1372/1373

Month	Sun	Mon	Tue	Wed	Thu	Fri	Sat
DEY 1372	5	6	7	8	9	10	11
	12	13	14	15	16	17	18
	19	20	21	22	23	24	25
	26	27	28	29	30	*1*	*2*
BAHMAN 1372	3	4	5	6	7	8	9
	10	11	12	13	14	15	16
	17	18	19	20	21	22	23
	24	25	26	27	28	29	30
ESFAND 1372	*1*	*2*	*3*	*4*	*5*	*6*	*7*
	8	9	10	11	12	13	14
	15	16	17	18	19	20	21
	22	23	24	25	26	27	28
FARVARDĪN 1373	29	*1*[a]	2	3	4	5	6
	7	8	9	10	11	12	13[b]
	14	15	16	17	18	19	20
	21	22	23	24	25	26	27
ORDĪBEHEŠT 1373	28	29	30	31	*1*	2	3
	4	5	6	7	8	9	10
	11	12	13	14	15	16	17
	18	19	20	21	22	23	24
	25	26	27	28	29	30	31
XORDĀD 1373	*1*	2	3	4	5	6	7
	8	9	10	11	12	13	14
	15	16	17	18	19	20	21
	22	23	24	25	26	27	28
TĪR 1373	29	30	31	*1*	2	3	4
	5	6	7	8	9	10	11
	12	13	14	15	16	17	18
	19	20	21	22	23	24	25
MORDĀD 1373	26	27	28	29	30	31	*1*
	2	3	4	5	6	7	8
	9	10	11	12	13	14	15
	16	17	18	19	20	21	22
	23	24	25	26	27	28	29
SHAHRĪVAR 1373	30	31	*1*	2	3	4	5
	6	7	8	9	10	11	12
	13	14	15	16	17	18	19
	20	21	22	23	24	25	26
MEHR 1373	27	28	29	30	31	*1*	2
	3	4	5	6	7	8	9
	10	11	12	13	14	15	16
	17	18	19	20	21	22	23
	24	25	26	27	28	29	30
ĀBĀN 1373	*1*	2	3	4	5	6	7
	8	9	10	11	12	13	14
	15	16	17	18	19	20	21
	22	23	24	25	26	27	28
ĀZAR 1373	29	30	*1*	2	3	4	5
	6	7	8	9	10	11	12
	13	14	15	16	17	18	19
	20	21	22	23	24	25	26
DEY 1373	27	28	29	30	*1*	2	3
	4	5	6	7	8	9	10

[a]New Year
[b]Sizdeh Bedar

HINDU LUNAR 2050‡/2051

Month	Sun	Mon	Tue	Wed	Thu	Fri	Sat
MĀRGAŚĪRA 2050	13	14	15	16	17	18	19
	20	21	22	23	24	25	26
	27	29	30	1	2	3	4
PAUSHA 2050	5	5	6	7	8	9	10
	11	12	13	14	15	16	17
	18	19	20	**21**	23	24	25
	26	27	28	29	30	1	2
MĀGHA 2050	3	4	5	6	7	8	*8*
	9	10	11	12	13	14	**15**
	17	18	19	20	21	22	23
	24	25	26	27	28[h]	29	30
PHĀLGUNA 2050	1	2	3	4	5	6	7
	8	9	10	11	12	13	14
	15[i]	16	17	18	**19**	21	22
	23	24	25	26	27	28	29
CHAITRA 2051	30	1[a]	*1*	2	3	4	5
	6	7	8	9[b]	10	11	12
	13	15	16	17	18	19	20
	21	22	23	24	25	26	27
	28	29	30	1	2	3	4
VAIŚĀKHA 2051	5	6	7	8	9	10	11
	12	13	14	15	**16**	18	19
	20	21	22	23	24	25	26
	27	*27*	28	29	30	1	2
JYAISHTHA 2051	3	4	5	6	7	8	**9**
	11	12	13	14	15	16	17
	18	19	20	21	22	23	24
	25	26	27	28	29	30	1
ĀSHĀḌHA 2051	2	3	4	5	6	7	8
	9	10	11	**12**	14	15	16
	17	18	19	20	21	22	23
	23	24	25	26	27	28	29
	30	1	2	3	4	**5**	7
ŚRĀVAṆA 2051	8	9	10	11	12	13	14
	15	16	17	18	19	20	21
	22	23[c]	24	25	26	27	28
	29	30	1	2	3	4[d]	5
BHĀDRAPADA 2051	6	7	**8**	10	11	12	13
	14	15	16	17	18	19	*19*
	20	21	22	23	24	25	26
	27	28	29	30	**1**	3	4
ĀŚVINA 2051	5	6	7	8[e]	9[e]	10[e]	11
	12	13	14	15	16	17	18
	19	20	21	22	23	24	25
	26	27	28	29	30	1[f]	2
KĀRTTIKA 2051	3	4	**5**	7	8	9	10
	11	12	13	*13*	14	15	16
	17	18	19	20	21	22	23
	24	25	26	27	28	**29**	1
MĀRGAŚĪRA 2051	2	3	4	5	6	7	8
	9	10	11[g]	12	13	14	15
	16	*16*	17	18	19	20	21
	22	**23**	25	26	27	28	29

‡Leap year
[a]New Year (Bhāva)
[b]Birthday of Rāma
[c]Birthday of Krishna
[d]Ganēśa Chaturthī
[e]Dashara
[f]Diwali
[g]Birthday of Vishnu
[h]Night of Śiva
[i]Holi

HINDU SOLAR 1915/1916‡

Month	Sun	Mon	Tue	Wed	Thu	Fri	Sat
PAUSHA 1915	12	13	14	15	16	17	18
	19	20	21	22	23	24	25
	26	27	28	29	30	1[b]	2
MĀGHA 1915	3	4	5	6	7	8	9
	10	11	12	13	14	15	16
	17	18	19	20	21	22	23
	24	25	26	27	28	29	1
PHĀLGUNA 1915	2	3	4	5	6	7	8
	9	10	11	12	13	14	15
	16	17	18	19	20	21	22
	23	24	25	26	27	28	29
CHAITRA 1915	30	1	2	3	4	5	6
	7	8	9	10	11	12	13
	14	15	16	17	18	19	20
	21	22	23	24	25	26	27
VAIŚĀKHA 1916	28	29	30	1[a]	2	3	4
	5	6	7	8	9	10	11
	12	13	14	15	16	17	18
	19	20	21	22	23	24	25
	26	27	28	29	30	31	1
JYAISHTHA 1916	2	3	4	5	6	7	8
	9	10	11	12	13	14	15
	16	17	18	19	20	21	22
	23	24	25	26	27	28	29
ĀSHĀḌHA 1916	30	31	32	1	2	3	4
	5	6	7	8	9	10	11
	12	13	14	15	16	17	18
	19	20	21	22	23	24	25
ŚRĀVAṆA 1916	26	27	28	29	30	31	1
	2	3	4	5	6	7	8
	9	10	11	12	13	14	15
	16	17	18	19	20	21	22
	23	24	25	26	27	28	29
BHĀDRAPADA 1916	30	31	32	1	2	3	4
	5	6	7	8	9	10	11
	12	13	14	15	16	17	18
	19	20	21	22	23	24	25
	26	27	28	29	30	31	1
ĀŚVINA 1916	2	3	4	5	6	7	8
	9	10	11	12	13	14	15
	16	17	18	19	20	21	22
	23	24	25	26	27	28	29
KĀRTTIKA 1916	30	1	2	3	4	5	6
	7	8	9	10	11	12	13
	14	15	16	17	18	19	20
	21	22	23	24	25	26	27
MĀRGAŚĪRA 1916	28	29	30	1	2	3	4
	5	6	7	8	9	10	11
	12	13	14	15	16	17	18
	19	20	21	22	23	24	25
PAUSHA 1916	26	27	28	29	30	1	2
	3	4	5	6	7	8	9
	10	11	12	13	14	15	16

‡Leap year
[a]New Year (Sarvajit)
[b]Pongal

ISLAMIC (ASTRONOMICAL) 1414/1415

Month	Sun	Mon	Tue	Wed	Thu	Fri	Sat
RAJAB 1414	12	13	14	15	16	17	18
	19	20	21	22	23	24	25
	26	27[d]	28	29	*1*	*2*	*3*
SHA'BĀN 1414	4	5	6	7	8	9	10
	11	12	13	14	15	16	17
	18	19	20	21	22	23	24
RAMAḌĀN 1414	25	26	27	28	29	30	*1*[e]
	2	3	4	5	6	7	8
	9	10	11	12	13	14	15
	16	17	18	19	20	21	22
	23	24	25	26	27	28	29
SHAWWĀL 1414	30	*1*[f]	2	3	4	5	6
	7	8	9	10	11	12	13
	14	15	16	17	18	19	20
	21	22	23	24	25	26	27
DHU AL-QA'DA 1414	28	29	*1*	2	3	4	5
	6	7	8	9	10	11	12
	13	14	15	16	17	18	19
	20	21	22	23	24	25	26
DHU AL-ḤIJJA 1414	27	28	29	30	*1*	2	3
	4	5	6	7	8	9	10[g]
	11	12	13	14	15	16	17
	18	19	20	21	22	23	24
	25	26	27	28	29	30[d]	1[a]
MUḤARRAM 1415	2	3	4	5	6	7	8
	9	10[b]	11	12	13	14	15
	16	17	18	19	20	21	22
	23	24	25	26	27	28	29
ṢAFAR 1415	30	1	2	3	4	5	6
	7	8	9	10	11	12	13
	14	15	16	17	18	19	20
	21	22	23	24	25	26	27
RABĪ' I 1415	28	29	1	2	3	4	5
	6	7	8	9	10	11	12[c]
	13	14	15	16	17	18	19
	20	21	22	23	24	25	26
RABĪ' II 1415	27	28	29	30	1	2	3
	4	5	6	7	8	9	10
	11	12	13	14	15	16	17
	18	19	20	21	22	23	24
JUMĀDĀ I 1415	25	26	27	28	29	1	2
	3	4	5	6	7	8	9
	10	11	12	13	14	15	16
	17	18	19	20	21	22	23
JUMĀDĀ II 1415	24	25	26	27	28	29	*1*
	2	3	4	5	6	7	8
	9	10	11	12	13	14	15
	16	17	18	19	20	21	22
	23	24	25	26	27	28	29
RAJAB 1415	*1*	2	3	4	5	6	7
	8	9	10	11	12	13	14
	15	16	17	18	19	20	21
	22	23	24	25	26	27[d]	28

[a]New Year
[d]New Year (Arithmetic)
[b]'Ashūrā'
[c]Prophet's Birthday
[d]Ascent of the Prophet
[e]Start of Ramaḍān
[f]'Īd al-Fiṭr
[g]'Īd al-'Aḍḥā

GREGORIAN 1994

Julian (Sun)	Sun	Mon	Tue	Wed	Thu	Fri	Sat	Month
Dec 13	26	27	28	29	30	31	1	JANUARY 1994
	2	3	4	5	6	7[a]	8	
Dec 27	9	10	11	12	13	14[b]	15	
	16	17	18	19	20	21	22	
Jan 10	23	24	25	26	27	28	29	
	30	31	1	2	3	4	5	FEBRUARY 1994
Jan 24	6	7	8	9	10	11	12	
	13	14	15	16[c]	17	18	19	
Feb 7	20	21	22	23	24	25	26	
	27	28	1	2	3	4	5	MARCH 1994
Feb 21	6	7	8	9	10	11	12	
	13	14	15	16	17	18	19	
Mar 7	20[d]	21	22	23	24	25	26	
	27	28	29	30	31	1	2	APRIL 1994
Mar 21	3[e]	4	5	6	7	8	9	
	10	11	12	13	14	15	16	
Apr 4	17	18	19	20	21	22	23	
	24	25	26	27	28	29	30	
Apr 18	1[f]	2	3	4	5	6	7	MAY 1994
	8	9	10	11	12	13	14	
May 2	15	16	17	18	19	20	21	
	22	23	24	25	26	27	28	
May 16	29	30	31	1	2	3	4	JUNE 1994
	5	6	7	8	9	10	11	
May 30	12	13	14	15	16	17	18	
	19	20	21	22	23	24	25	
Jun 13	26	27	28	29	30	1	2	JULY 1994
	3	4	5	6	7	8	9	
Jun 27	10	11	12	13	14	15	16	
	17	18	19	20	21	22	23	
Jul 11	24	25	26	27	28	29	30	
	31	1	2	3	4	5	6	AUGUST 1994
Jul 25	7	8	9	10	11	12	13	
	14	15	16	17	18	19	20	
Aug 8	21	22	23	24	25	26	27	
	28	29	30	31	1	2	3	SEPTEMBER 1994
Aug 22	4	5	6	7	8	9	10	
	11	12	13	14	15	16	17	
Sep 5	18	19	20	21	22	23	24	
	25	26	27	28	29	30	1	OCTOBER 1994
Sep 19	2	3	4	5	6	7	8	
	9	10	11	12	13	14	15	
Oct 3	16	17	18	19	20	21	22	
	23	24	25	26	27	28	29	
Oct 17	30	31	1	2	3	4	5	NOVEMBER 1994
	6	7	8	9	10	11	12	
Oct 31	13	14	15	16	17	18	19	
	20	21	22	23	24	25	26	
Nov 14	27[g]	28	29	30	1	2	3	DECEMBER 1994
	4	5	6	7	8	9	10	
Nov 28	11	12	13	14	15	16	17	
	18	19	20	21	22	23	24	
Dec 12	25[h]	26	27	28	29	30	31	

[a]Orthodox Christmas
[b]Julian New Year
[c]Ash Wednesday
[d]Feast of Orthodoxy
[e]Easter
[f]Orthodox Easter
[g]Advent
[h]Christmas

1995

Month	Sun	Mon	Tue	Wed	Thu	Fri	Sat	Lunar Phases	ISO WEEK (Mon)	JULIAN DAY (Sun noon)
GREGORIAN 1995										
JANUARY 1995	●[a]	2	3	4	5	6	7	10:56	1	2449719
	◐	9	10	11	12	13	14	15:46	2	2449726
	15	○	17	18	19	20	21	20:26	3	2449733
	22	23	◑	25	26	27	28	4:58	4	2449740
	29	●	31	1	2	3	4	22:48	5	2449747
FEBRUARY 1995	5	6	◐	8	9	10	11	12:54	6	2449754
	12	13	14	○	16	17	18	12:15	7	2449761
	19	20	21	◑	23	24	25	13:04	8	2449768
	26	27	28	●	2	3	4	11:48	9	2449775
MARCH 1995	5	6	7	8	◐	10	11	10:14	10	2449782
	12	13	14	15	16	○	18	1:26	11	2449789
	19	20	21[b]	22	◑	24	25	20:10	12	2449796
	26	27	28	29	30	●	1	2:08	13	2449803
APRIL 1995	2	3	4	5	6	7	◐	5:35	14	2449810
	9	10	11	12	13	14	○	12:08	15	2449817
	16	17	18	19	20	21	◑	3:18	16	2449824
	23	24	25	26	27	28	●	17:36	17	2449831
	30	1	2	3	4	5	6		18	2449838
MAY 1995	◐	8	9	10	11	12	13	21:44	19	2449845
	○	15	16	17	18	19	20	20:48	20	2449852
	◑	22	23	24	25	26	27	11:36	21	2449859
	28	●	30	31	1	2	3	9:27	22	2449866
JUNE 1995	4	5	◐	7	8	9	10	10:26	23	2449873
	11	12	○	14	15	16	17	4:03	24	2449880
	18	◑	20	21[c]	22	23	24	22:01	25	2449887
	25	26	27	●	29	30	1	0:50	26	2449894
JULY 1995	2	3	4	◐	6	7	8	20:03	27	2449901
	9	10	11	○	13	14	15	10:49	28	2449908
	16	17	18	◑	20	21	22	11:10	29	2449915
	23	24	25	26	●	28	29	15:13	30	2449922
	30	31	1	2	3	◐	5	3:16	31	2449929
AUGUST 1995	6	7	8	9	○	11	12	18:16	32	2449936
	13	14	15	16	17	◑	19	3:04	33	2449943
	20	21	22	23	24	25	●	4:31	34	2449950
	27	28	29	30	31	1	◐	9:03	35	2449957
SEPTEMBER 1995	3	4	5	6	7	8	○	3:37	36	2449964
	10	11	12	13	14	15	◑	21:09	37	2449971
	17	18	19	20	21	22	23[d]		38	2449978
	●	25	26	27	28	29	30	16:55	39	2449985
OCTOBER 1995	◐	2	3	4	5	6	7	14:36	40	2449992
	○	9	10	11	12	13	14	15:52	41	2449999
	15	◑	17	18	19	20	21	16:26	42	2450006
	22	23	●	25	26	27	28	4:36	43	2450013
	29	◐	31	1	2	3	4	21:17	44	2450020
NOVEMBER 1995	5	6	○	8	9	10	11	7:20	45	2450027
	12	13	14	◑	16	17	18	11:40	46	2450034
	19	20	21	●	23	24	25	15:43	47	2450041
	26	27	28	◐	30	1	2	6:28	48	2450048
DECEMBER 1995	3	4	5	6	○	8	9	1:27	49	2450055
	10	11	12	13	14	◑	16	5:31	50	2450062
	17	18	19	20	21	●[e]	23	2:23	51	2450069
	24	25	26	27	◐	29	30	19:06	52	2450076
	31	1	2	3	4	○	6	20:5	1	2450083

Month	Sun	Mon	Tue	Wed	Thu	Fri	Sat	Molad
HEBREW 5755‡/5756								
SHEVAT 5755	29	1	2	3	4	5	6	Sun 21h9m5p
	7	8	9	10	11	12	13	
	14	15	16	17	18	19	20	
	21	22	23	24	25	26	27	
	28	29	30	1	2	3	4	Tue 9h53m6p
ADAR I 5755	5	6	7	8	9	10	11	
	12	13	14	15	16	17	18	
	19	20	21	22	23	24	25	
	26	27	28	29	30	1	2	Wed 22h37m7p
ADAR II 5755	3	4	5	6	7	8	9	
	10	11	12	13	14[f]	15	16	
	17	18	19	20	21	22	23	
	24	25	26	27	28	29	1	Fri 11h21m8p
NISAN 5755	2	3	4	5	6	7	8	
	9	10	11	12	13	14	15[g]	
	16	17	18	19	20	21	22	
	23	24	25	26	27	28	29	
	30	1	2	3	4	5	6	Sun 0h5m9p
IYAR 5755	7	8	9	10	11	12	13	
	14	15	16	17	18	19	20	
	21	22	23	24	25	26	27	
	28	29	1	2	3	4	5	Mon 12h49m10p
SIVAN 5755	6[h]	7	8	9	10	11	12	
	13	14	15	16	17	18	19	
	20	21	22	23	24	25	26	
	27	28	29	30	1	2	3	Wed 1h33m11p
TAMMUZ 5755	4	5	6	7	8	9	10	
	11	12	13	14	15	16	17	
	18	19	20	21	22	23	24	
	25	26	27	28	29	1	2	Thu 14h17m12p
AV 5755	3	4	5	6	7	8	9	
	10[i]	11	12	13	14	15	16	
	17	18	19	20	21	22	23	
	24	25	26	27	28	29	30	
ELUL 5755	1	2	3	4	5	6	7	Sat 3h1m13p
	8	9	10	11	12	13	14	
	15	16	17	18	19	20	21	
	22	23	24	25	26	27	28	
TISHRI 5756	29	1[a]	2[a]	3	4	5	6	Sun 15h45m14p
	7	8	9	10[b]	11	12	13	
	14	15[c]	16	17	18	19	20	
	21	22	23	24	25	26	27	
	28	29	30	1	2	3	4	Tue 4h29m15p
HESHVAN 5756	5	6	7	8	9	10	11	
	12	13	14	15	16	17	18	
	19	20	21	22	23	24	25	
	26	27	28	29	30	1	2	Wed 17h13m16p
KISLEV 5756	3	4	5	6	7	8	9	
	10	11	12	13[d]	14	15	16	
	17	18	19	20	21	22	23	
	24	25[e]	26[e]	27[e]	28[e]	29[e]	30[e]	
TEVETH 5756	1[e]	2[e]	3	4	5	6	7	Fri 5h57m17p
	8	9	10	11	12	13	14	

Month	Sun	Mon	Tue	Wed	Thu	Fri	Sat	Solar Term
CHINESE Jiă-Xū/Yĭ-Hài‡								
MONTH 12 Jiă-Xū	1	2	3	4	5	6	7	Xiăo hán
	8	9	10	11	12	13	14	
	15	16	17	18	19	**20**	21	Dà hán
	22	23	24	25	26	27	28	
MONTH 1 Yĭ-Hài	29	30	1[a]	2	3*	4	5	Lì chūn
	6	7	8	9	10	11	12	
	13	14	15[b]	16	17	18	19	
	20	21	22	23	24	25	26	Yŭ shuĭ
MONTH 2 Yĭ-Hài	27	28	29	1	2	3	4	
	5	6	7	8	9	10	11	Jīng zhé
	12	13	14	15	16	17	18	
	19	20	**21**	22	23	24	25	Chūn fēn
MONTH 3 Yĭ-Hài	26	27	28	29	30	1	2	
	3	4*	5	6[c]	7	8	9	Qīng míng
	10	11	12	13	14	15	16	
	17	18	19	20	**21**	22	23	Gŭ yŭ
	24	25	26	27	28	29	30	
MONTH 4 Yĭ-Hài	1	2	3	4	5	6	7	Lì xià
	8	9	10	11	12	13	14	
	15	16	17	18	19	20	21	
	22	23	24	25	26	27	28	Xiăo măn
MONTH 5 Yĭ-Hài	29	1	2	3	4	5[d]*	6	
	7	8	9	10	11	12	13	Máng zhòng
	14	15	16	17	18	19	20	
	21	22	23	24	**25**	26	27	Xià zhì
MONTH 6 Yĭ-Hài	28	29	30	1	2	3	4	
	5	6	7	8	9	*10*	11	Xiăo shŭ
	12	13	14	15	16	17	18	
	19	20	21	22	23	24	25	
MONTH 7 Yĭ-Hài	**26**	27	28	29	1	2	3	Dà shŭ
	4	5	6*	7[e]	8	9	10	
	11	12	*13*	14	15[f]	16	17	Lì qiū
	18	19	20	21	22	23	24	
MONTH 8 Yĭ-Hài	25	26	27	**28**	29	30	1	Chŭ shŭ
	2	3	4	5	6	7	8	
	9	10	11	12	13	*14*	15[g]	Bái lù
	16	17	18	19	20	21	22	
	23	24	25	26	27	28	**29**	Qiū fēn
LEAP MONTH 8 Yĭ-Hài	30	1	2	3	4	5	6*	
	7	8	9	10	11	12	13	
	14	*15*	16	17	18	19	20	Hán lù
	21	22	23	24	25	26	27	
MONTH 9 Yĭ-Hài	28	29	***1***	2	3	4	5	Shuāng jiàng
	6	7	8	9[h]	10	11	12	
	13	14	15	*16*	17	18	19	Lì dōng
	20	21	22	23	24	25	26	
MONTH 10 Yĭ-Hài	27	28	29	1	**2**	3	4	Xiăo xuě
	5	6	7	8*	9	10	11	
	12	13	14	15	*16*	17	18	Dà xuě
	19	20	21	22	23	24	25	
MONTH 11 Yĭ-Hài	26	27	28	29	30	***1***[i]	2	Dōng zhì
	3	4	5	6	7	8	9	
	10	11	12	13	14	15	*16*	Xiăo hán

Coptic Month	Sun	Mon	Tue	Wed	Thu	Fri	Sat	Ethiopic Month
COPTIC 1711‡/1712								ETHIOPIC 1987‡/1988
KOIAK 1711	23	24	25	26	27	28	29[c]	TĀKHŚĀŚ 1987
TŌBE 1711	30	1	2	3	4	5	6[d]	
	7	8	9	10	11[e]	12	13	ṬER 1987
	14	15	16	17	18	19	20	
	21	22	23	24	25	26	27	
MESHIR 1711	28	29	30	1	2	3	4	YAKĀTIT 1987
	5	6	7	8	9	10	11	
	12	13	14	15	16	17	18	
	19	20	21	22	23	24	25	
PAREMOTEP 1711	26	27	28	29	30	1	2	MAGĀBIT 1987
	3	4	5	6	7	8	9	
	10	11	12	13	14	15	16	
	17	18	19	20	21	22	23	
	24	25	26	27	28	29	30	
PARMOUTE 1711	1	2	3	4	5	6	7	MIYĀZYĀ 1987
	8	9	10	11	12	13	14	
	15[f]	16	17	18	19	20	21	
	22	23	24	25	26	27	28	
PASHONS 1711	29[g]	30	1	2	3	4	5	GENBOT 1987
	6	7	8	9	10	11	12	
	13	14	15	16	17	18	19	
	20	21	22	23	24	25	26	
PAŌNE 1711	27	28	29	30	1	2	3	SANĒ 1987
	4	5	6	7	8	9	10	
	11	12	13	14	15	16	17	
	18	19	20	21	22	23	24	
EPĒP 1711	25	26	27	28	29	30	1	ḤAMLĒ 1987
	2	3	4	5	6	7	8	
	9	10	11	12	13	14	15	
	16	17	18	19	20	21	22	
	23	24	25	26	27	28	29	
MESORĒ 1711	30	1	2	3	4	5	6	NAHASĒ 1987
	7	8	9	10	11	12	13[h]	
	14	15	16	17	18	19	20	
	21	22	23	24	25	26	27	
EPAG. 1711	28	29	30	1	2	3	4	PĀG. 1987
THOOUT 1712	5	6	1[a]	2	3	4	5	MASKARAM 1988
	6	7	8	9	10	11	12	
	13	14	15	16	17[b]	18	19	
	20	21	22	23	24	25	26	
PAOPE 1712	27	28	29	30	1	2	3	ṬEQEMT 1988
	4	5	6	7	8	9	10	
	11	12	13	14	15	16	17	
	18	19	20	21	22	23	24	
ATHŌR 1712	25	26	27	28	29	30	1	HEDĀR 1988
	2	3	4	5	6	7	8	
	9	10	11	12	13	14	15	
	16	17	18	19	20	21	22	
	23	24	25	26	27	28	29	
KOIAK 1712	30	1	2	3	4	5	6	TĀKHŚĀŚ 1988
	7	8	9	10	11	12	13	
	14	15	16	17	18	19	20	
	21	22	23	24	25	26	27	

[a]New Year
[b]Spring (2:14)
[c]Summer (20:34)
[d]Autumn (12:13)
[e]Winter (8:17)
● New moon
◐ First quarter moon
○ Full moon
◑ Last quarter moon

‡Leap year
[a]New Year
[b]Yom Kippur
[c]Sukkot
[d]Winter starts
[e]Ḥanukkah
[f]Purim
[g]Passover
[h]Shavuot
[i]Fast of Av

‡Leap year
[a]New Year (4693, Pig)
[b]Lantern Festival
[c]Qīngmíng
[d]Dragon Festival
[e]Qīqiăo
[f]Hungry Ghosts
[g]Mid-Autumn Festival
[h]Double-Ninth Festival
[i]Dōngzhì
*Start of 60-name cycle

‡Leap year
[a]New Year
[b]Building of the Cross
[c]Christmas
[d]Jesus's Circumcision
[e]Epiphany
[f]Easter
[g]Mary's Announcement
[h]Jesus's Transfiguration

PERSIAN (ASTRONOMICAL) 1373/1374

Month	Sun	Mon	Tue	Wed	Thu	Fri	Sat
DEY 1373	11	12	13	14	15	16	17
	18	19	20	21	22	23	24
	25	26	27	28	29	30	1
BAHMAN 1373	2	3	4	5	6	7	8
	9	10	11	12	13	14	15
	16	17	18	19	20	21	22
	23	24	25	26	27	28	29
	30	1	2	3	4	5	6
ESFAND 1373	7	8	9	10	11	12	13
	14	15	16	17	18	19	20
	21	22	23	24	25	26	27
	28	29	1[a]	2	3	4	5
FARVARDĪN 1374	6	7	8	9	10	11	12
	13[b]	14	15	16	17	18	19
	20	21	22	23	24	25	26
	27	28	29	30	31	1	2
ORDĪBEHEŠT 1374	3	4	5	6	7	8	9
	10	11	12	13	14	15	16
	17	18	19	20	21	22	23
	24	25	26	27	28	29	30
	31	1	2	3	4	5	6
XORDĀD 1374	7	8	9	10	11	12	13
	14	15	16	17	18	19	20
	21	22	23	24	25	26	27
	28	29	30	31	1	2	3
TĪR 1374	4	5	6	7	8	9	10
	11	12	13	14	15	16	17
	18	19	20	21	22	23	24
	25	26	27	28	29	30	31
MORDĀD 1374	1	2	3	4	5	6	7
	8	9	10	11	12	13	14
	15	16	17	18	19	20	21
	22	23	24	25	26	27	28
	29	30	31	1	2	3	4
SHAHRĪVAR 1374	5	6	7	8	9	10	11
	12	13	14	15	16	17	18
	19	20	21	22	23	24	25
	26	27	28	29	30	31	1
MEHR 1374	2	3	4	5	6	7	8
	9	10	11	12	13	14	15
	16	17	18	19	20	21	22
	23	24	25	26	27	28	29
	30	1	2	3	4	5	6
ĀBĀN 1374	7	8	9	10	11	12	13
	14	15	16	17	18	19	20
	21	22	23	24	25	26	27
	28	29	30	1	2	3	4
ĀZAR 1374	5	6	7	8	9	10	11
	12	13	14	15	16	17	18
	19	20	21	22	23	24	25
	26	27	28	29	30	1	2
DEY 1374	3	4	5	6	7	8	9
	10	11	12	13	14	15	16

HINDU LUNAR 2051/2052

Month	Sun	Mon	Tue	Wed	Thu	Fri	Sat
	30	1	2	3	4	5	6
PAUSHA 2051	7	8	9	10	11	12	13
	14	15	16	17	18	19	20
	21	22	23	24	25	26	27
	28	30	1	2	3	4	5
MĀGHA 2051	6	7	8	8	9	10	11
	12	13	14	15	16	17	18
	19	20	21	**22**	24	25	26
	27	28[h]	29	30	1	2	3
PHĀLGUNA 2051	4	5	6	7	8	9	10
	11	11	12	13	14	**15**[i]	17
	18	19	20	21	22	23	24
	25	26	27	28	29	30	1[a]
CHAITRA 2052	2	3	4	5	6	7	8
	9[b]	10	11	12	13	14	15
	16	17	18	19	**20**	22	23
	24	25	26	27	28	29	30
VAIŚĀKHA 2052	1	2	3	4	5	5	6
	7	8	9	10	11	12	**13**
	15	16	17	18	19	20	21
	22	23	24	25	26	27	28
	29	30	1	2	3	4	5
JYAISHTHA 2052	6	7	8	9	10	11	12
	13	14	15	**16**	18	19	20
	21	22	23	24	25	26	27
	28	29	30	1	1	2	3
ĀSHĀḌHA 2052	4	5	6	7	8	**9**	11
	12	13	14	15	16	17	18
	19	20	21	22	23	24	25
	26	27	28	29	30	1	2
ŚRĀVAṆA 2052	3	4	5	6	7	8	9
	10	11	**12**	14	15	16	17
	18	19	20	21	22	23[c]	24
	25	26	27	28	28	29	30
BHĀDRAPADA 2052	1	2	3[d]	**4**	6	7	8
	9	10	11	12	13	14	15
	16	17	18	19	20	21	22
	23	24	25	26	27	28	29
	30	1	2	3	4	5	6
ĀŚVINA 2052	7	**8**[e]	10[e]	11	12	13	14
	15	16	17	18	19	20	21
	22	23	23	24	25	26	27
	28	29	30	1[f]	**2**	4	5
KĀRTTIKA 2052	6	7	8	9	10	11	12
	13	14	15	16	17	18	19
	20	21	22	23	24	25	26
	27	28	29	30	1	2	3
MĀRGAŚĪRA 2052	4	5	**6**	8	9	10	11[g]
	12	13	14	15	16	16	17
	18	19	20	21	22	23	24
	25	26	27	28	29	**30**	2
PAUSHA 2052	3	4	5	6	7	8	9
	10	11	12	13	14	15	16

HINDU SOLAR 1916‡/1917

Month	Sun	Mon	Tue	Wed	Thu	Fri	Sat
PAUSHA 1916	17	18	19	20	21	22	23
	24	25	26	27	28	29	1[b]
MĀGHA 1916	2	3	4	5	6	7	8
	9	10	11	12	13	14	15
	16	17	18	19	20	21	22
	23	24	25	26	27	28	29
PHĀLGUNA 1916	1	2	3	4	5	6	7
	8	9	10	11	12	13	14
	15	16	17	18	19	20	21
	22	23	24	25	26	27	28
	29	30	1	2	3	4	5
CHAITRA 1916	6	7	8	9	10	11	12
	13	14	15	16	17	18	19
	20	21	22	23	24	25	26
	27	28	29	30	31	1[a]	2
VAIŚĀKHA 1917	3	4	5	6	7	8	9
	10	11	12	13	14	15	16
	17	18	19	20	21	22	23
	24	25	26	27	28	29	30
	31	1	2	3	4	5	6
JYAISHTHA 1917	7	8	9	10	11	12	13
	14	15	16	17	18	19	20
	21	22	23	24	25	26	27
	28	29	30	31	1	2	3
ĀSHĀḌHA 1917	4	5	6	7	8	9	10
	11	12	13	14	15	16	17
	18	19	20	21	22	23	24
	25	26	27	28	29	30	31
	32	1	2	3	4	5	6
ŚRĀVAṆA 1917	7	8	9	10	11	12	13
	14	15	16	17	18	19	20
	21	22	23	24	25	26	27
	28	29	30	31	1	2	3
BHĀDRAPADA 1917	4	5	6	7	8	9	10
	11	12	13	14	15	16	17
	18	19	20	21	22	23	24
	25	26	27	28	29	30	31
ĀŚVINA 1917	1	2	3	4	5	6	7
	8	9	10	11	12	13	14
	15	16	17	18	19	20	21
	22	23	24	25	26	27	28
	29	30	31	1	2	3	4
KĀRTTIKA 1917	5	6	7	8	9	10	11
	12	13	14	15	16	17	18
	19	20	21	22	23	24	25
	26	27	28	29	1	2	3
MĀRGAŚĪRA 1917	4	5	6	7	8	9	10
	11	12	13	14	15	16	17
	18	19	20	21	22	23	24
	25	26	27	28	29	30	1
PAUSHA 1917	2	3	4	5	6	7	8
	9	10	11	12	13	14	15
	16	17	18	19	20	21	22

ISLAMIC (ASTRONOMICAL) 1415/1416

Month	Sun	Mon	Tue	Wed	Thu	Fri	Sat
	29	30	1	2	3	4	5
SHA'BĀN 1415	6	7	8	9	10	11	12
	13	14	15	16	17	18	19
	20	21	22	23	24	25	26
	27	28	29	1[e]	2	3	4
RAMAḌĀN 1415	5	6	7	8	9	10	11
	12	13	14	15	16	17	18
	19	20	21	22	23	24	25
	26	27	28	29	30	1[f]	2
SHAWWĀL 1415	3	4	5	6	7	8	9
	10	11	12	13	14	15	16
	17	18	19	20	21	22	23
	24	25	26	27	28	29	1
DHU AL-QA'DA 1415	2	3	4	5	6	7	8
	9	10	11	12	13	14	15
	16	17	18	19	20	21	22
	23	24	25	26	27	28	29
	30	1	2	3	4	5	6
DHU AL-ḤIJJA 1415	7	8	9	10[g]	11	12	13
	14	15	16	17	18	19	20
	21	22	23	24	25	26	27
	28	29	30	1[a]	2	3	4
MUḤARRAM 1416	5	6	7	8	9	10[b]	11
	12	13	14	15	16	17	18
	19	20	21	22	23	24	25
	26	27	28	29	30	1	2
ṢAFAR 1416	3	4	5	6	7	8	9
	10	11	12	13	14	15	16
	17	18	19	20	21	22	23
	24	25	26	27	28	29	30
RABĪ' I 1416	1	2	3	4	5	6	7
	8	9	10	11	12[c]	13	14
	15	16	17	18	19	20	21
	22	23	24	25	26	27	28
	29	1	2	3	4	5	6
RABĪ' II 1416	7	8	9	10	11	12	13
	14	15	16	17	18	19	20
	21	22	23	24	25	26	27
	28	29	1	2	3	4	5
JUMĀDĀ I 1416	6	7	8	9	10	11	12
	13	14	15	16	17	18	19
	20	21	22	23	24	25	26
	27	28	29	30	1	2	3
JUMĀDĀ II 1416	4	5	6	7	8	9	10
	11	12	13	14	15	16	17
	18	19	20	21	22	23	24
	25	26	27	28	29	1	2
RAJAB 1416	3	4	5	6	7	8	9
	10	11	12	13	14	15	16
	17	18	19	20	21	22	23
	24	25	26	27[d]	28	29	1
SHA'BĀN 1416	2	3	4	5	6	7	8
	9	10	11	12	13	14	15

GREGORIAN 1995

Julian (Sun)	Sun	Mon	Tue	Wed	Thu	Fri	Sat	Month
Dec 19	1	2	3	4	5	6	7[a]	
	8	9	10	11	12	13	14[b]	JANUARY 1995
Jan 2	15	16	17	18	19	20	21	
	22	23	24	25	26	27	28	
Jan 16	29	30	31	1	2	3	4	
	5	6	7	8	9	10	11	FEBRUARY 1995
Jan 30	12	13	14	15	16	17	18	
	19	20	21	22	23	24	25	
Feb 13	26	27	28	1[c]	2	3	4	
	5	6	7	8	9	10	11	
Feb 27	12[d]	13	14	15	16	17	18	MARCH 1995
	19	20	21	22	23	24	25	
Mar 13	26	27	28	29	30	31	1	
	2	3	4	5	6	7	8	
Mar 27	9	10	11	12	13	14	15	APRIL 1995
	16[e]	17	18	19	20	21	22	
Apr 10	23[f]	24	25	26	27	28	29	
	30	1	2	3	4	5	6	
Apr 24	7	8	9	10	11	12	13	MAY 1995
	14	15	16	17	18	19	20	
May 8	21	22	23	24	25	26	27	
	28	29	30	31	1	2	3	
May 22	4	5	6	7	8	9	10	JUNE 1995
	11	12	13	14	15	16	17	
Jun 5	18	19	20	21	22	23	24	
	25	26	27	28	29	30	1	
Jun 19	2	3	4	5	6	7	8	JULY 1995
	9	10	11	12	13	14	15	
Jul 3	16	17	18	19	20	21	22	
	23	24	25	26	27	28	29	
Jul 17	30	31	1	2	3	4	5	
	6	7	8	9	10	11	12	AUGUST 1995
Jul 31	13	14	15	16	17	18	19	
	20	21	22	23	24	25	26	
Aug 14	27	28	29	30	31	1	2	
	3	4	5	6	7	8	9	SEPTEMBER 1995
Aug 28	10	11	12	13	14	15	16	
	17	18	19	20	21	22	23	
Sep 11	24	25	26	27	28	29	30	
	1	2	3	4	5	6	7	
Sep 25	8	9	10	11	12	13	14	OCTOBER 1995
	15	16	17	18	19	20	21	
Oct 9	22	23	24	25	26	27	28	
	29	30	31	1	2	3	4	
Oct 23	5	6	7	8	9	10	11	NOVEMBER 1995
	12	13	14	15	16	17	18	
Nov 6	19	20	21	22	23	24	25	
	26	27	28	29	30	1	2	
Nov 20	3[g]	4	5	6	7	8	9	DECEMBER 1995
	10	11	12	13	14	15	16	
Dec 4	17	18	19	20	21	22	23	
	24	25[h]	26	27	28	29	30	
Dec 18	31	1	2	3	4	5	6	

Persian: [a]New Year; [b]Sizdeh Bedar

Hindu Lunar: [a]New Year (Yuvan); [b]Birthday of Rāma; [c]Birthday of Krishna; [d]Ganēśa Chaturthī; [e]Dashara; [f]Diwali; [g]Birthday of Vishnu; [h]Night of Śiva; [i]Holi

Hindu Solar: ‡Leap year; [a]New Year (Sarvadhārin); [b]Pongal

Islamic: [a]New Year; [b]'Ashūrā'; [c]Prophet's Birthday; [d]Ascent of the Prophet; [e]Start of Ramaḍān; [f]'Id al-Fiṭr; [g]'Id al-'Aḍḥā

Gregorian: [a]Orthodox Christmas; [b]Julian New Year; [c]Ash Wednesday; [d]Feast of Orthodoxy; [e]Easter; [f]Orthodox Easter; [g]Advent; [h]Christmas

1996

Month	Sun	Mon	Tue	Wed	Thu	Fri	Sat	Lunar Phases	ISO WEEK (Mon)	JULIAN DAY (Sun noon)
GREGORIAN 1996‡										
	31	1[a]	2	3	4	○	6	20:51	1	2450083
JANUARY 1996	7	8	9	10	11	12	◑	20:45	2	2450090
	14	15	16	17	18	19	●	12:50	3	2450097
	21	22	23	24	25	26	◐	11:14	4	2450104
	28	29	30	31	1	2	3		5	2450111
FEBRUARY 1996	○	5	6	7	8	9	10	15:58	6	2450118
	11	◑	13	14	15	16	17	8:37	7	2450125
	●	19	20	21	22	23	24	23:30	8	2450132
	25	◐	27	28	29	1	2	5:52	9	2450139
MARCH 1996	3	4	○	6	7	8	9	9:23	10	2450146
	10	11	◑	13	14	15	16	17:15	11	2450153
	17	18	●	20[b]	21	22	23	10:45	12	2450160
	24	25	26	◐	28	29	30	1:31	13	2450167
	31	1	2	3	○	5	6	0:07	14	2450174
APRIL 1996	7	8	9	◑	11	12	13	23:36	15	2450181
	14	15	16	●	18	19	20	22:49	16	2450188
	21	22	23	24	◐	26	27	20:40	17	2450195
	28	29	30	1	2	○	4	11:48	18	2450202
MAY 1996	5	6	7	8	9	◑	11	5:04	19	2450209
	12	13	14	15	16	●	18	11:46	20	2450216
	19	20	21	22	23	24	◐	14:13	21	2450223
	26	27	28	29	30	31	○	20:47	22	2450230
JUNE 1996	2	3	4	5	6	7	◑	11:05	23	2450237
	9	10	11	12	13	14	15		24	2450244
	●	17	18	19	20	21[c]	22	1:36	25	2450251
	23	◐	25	26	27	28	29	5:23	26	2450258
	30	○	2	3	4	5	6	3:58	27	2450265
JULY 1996	◑	8	9	10	11	12	13	18:55	28	2450272
	14	●	16	17	18	19	20	16:15	29	2450279
	21	22	◐	24	25	26	27	17:49	30	2450286
	28	29	○	31	1	2	3	10:35	31	2450293
AUGUST 1996	4	5	◑	7	8	9	10	5:25	32	2450300
	11	12	13	●	15	16	17	7:34	33	2450307
	18	19	20	21	◐	23	24	3:37	34	2450314
	25	26	27	○	29	30	31	17:52	35	2450321
SEPTEMBER 1996	1	2	3	◑	5	6	7	19:06	36	2450328
	8	9	10	11	●	13	14	23:07	37	2450335
	15	16	17	18	19	◐	21	11:23	38	2450342
	22[d]	23	24	25	26	○	28	2:51	39	2450349
	29	30	1	2	3	◑	5	12:04	40	2450356
OCTOBER 1996	6	7	8	9	10	11	●	14:15	41	2450363
	13	14	15	16	17	18	◐	18:09	42	2450370
	20	21	22	23	24	25	○	14:11	43	2450377
	27	28	29	30	31	1	2		44	2450384
NOVEMBER 1996	◑	4	5	6	7	8	9	7:50	45	2450391
	10	●	12	13	14	15	16	4:16	46	2450398
	17	◐	19	20	21	22	23	1:09	47	2450405
	24	○	26	27	28	29	30	4:10	48	2450412
DECEMBER 1996	1	2	◑	4	5	6	7	5:06	49	2450419
	8	9	●	11	12	13	14	16:56	50	2450426
	15	16	◐	18	19	20	21[e]	9:31	51	2450433
	22	23	○	25	26	27	28	20:41	52	2450440
	29	30	31	1	◑	3	4	1:45	1	2450447

JULIAN DAY	HEBREW 5756/5757‡	Sun	Mon	Tue	Wed	Thu	Fri	Sat	Molad
2450083		8	9	10	11	12	13	14	
2450090	TEVETH 5756	15	16	17	18	19	20	21	
2450097		22	23	24	25	26	27	28	
2450104		29	1	2	3	4	5	6	Sat 18h42m0p
2450111		7	8	9	10	11	12	13	
2450118	SHEVAT 5756	14	15	16	17	18	19	20	
2450125		21	22	23	24	25	26	27	
2450132		28	29	30	1	2	3	4	Mon 7h26m1p
2450139		5	6	7	8	9	10	11	
2450146	ADAR 5756	12	13	14[f]	15	16	17	18	
2450153		19	20	21	22	23	24	25	
2450160		26	27	28	29	1	2	3	Tue 20h10m2p
2450167		4	5	6	7	8	9	10	
2450174	NISAN 5756	11	12	13	14	15[g]	16	17	
2450181		18	19	20	21	22	23	24	
2450188		25	26	27	28	29	30	1	Thu 8h54m3p
2450195		2	3	4	5	6	7	8	
2450202	IYYAR 5756	9	10	11	12	13	14	15	
2450209		16	17	18	19	20	21	22	
2450216		23	24	25	26	27	28	29	
2450223		1	2	3	4	5	6[h]	7	Fri 21h38m4p
2450230		8	9	10	11	12	13	14	
2450237	SIVAN 5756	15	16	17	18	19	20	21	
2450244		22	23	24	25	26	27	28	
2450251		29	30	1	2	3	4	5	Sun 10h22m5p
2450258		6	7	8	9	10	11	12	
2450265	TAMMUZ 5756	13	14	15	16	17	18	19	
2450272		20	21	22	23	24	25	26	
2450279		27	28	29	1	2	3	4	Mon 23h6m6p
2450286		5	6	7	8	9[i]	10	11	
2450293	AV 5756	12	13	14	15	16	17	18	
2450300		19	20	21	22	23	24	25	
2450307		26	27	28	29	30	1	2	Wed 11h50m7p
2450314		3	4	5	6	7	8	9	
2450321	ELUL 5756	10	11	12	13	14	15	16	
2450328		17	18	19	20	21	22	23	
2450335		24	25	26	27	28	29	1[a]	Fri 0h34m8p
2450342		2[a]	3	4	5	6	7	8	
2450349	TISHRI 5757	9	10[b]	11	12	13	14	15[c]	
2450356		16	17	18	19	20	21	22	
2450363		23	24	25	26	27	28	29	
2450370		30	1	2	3	4	5	6	Sat 13h18m9p
2450377	HESHVAN 5757	7	8	9	10	11	12	13	
2450384		14	15	16	17	18	19	20	
2450391		21	22	23	24	25	26	27	
2450398		28	29	1	2	3	4	5	Mon 2h2m10p
2450405		6	7	8	9	10	11	12	
2450412	KISLEV 5757	13	14	15	16	17	18	19	
2450419		20	21	22	23	24[d]	25[e]	26[e]	
2450426		27[e]	28[e]	29[e]	1[e]	2[e]	3[e]	4	Tue 14h46m11p
2450433	TEVETH 5757	5	6	7	8	9	10	11	
2450440		12	13	14	15	16	17	18	
2450447		19	20	21	22	23	24	25	

JULIAN DAY	CHINESE Yǐ-Hài‡/Bǐng-Zǐ	Sun	Mon	Tue	Wed	Thu	Fri	Sat	Solar Term
2450083		10	11	12	13	14	15	16	Xiǎo hán
2450090	MONTH 11 Yǐ-Hài	17	18	19	20	21	22	23	
2450097		24	25	26	27	28	29	1	
2450104		2	3	4	5	6	7	8	Dà hán
2450111	MONTH 12 Yǐ-Hài	9*	10	11	12	13	14	15	
2450118		16	17	18	19	20	21	22	Lì chūn
2450125		23	24	25	26	27	28	29	
2450132		30	1[a]	2	3	4	5	6	Yǔ shuǐ
2450139		7	8	9	10	11	12	13	
2450146	MONTH 1 Bǐng-Zǐ	14	15[b]	16	17	18	19	20	Jīng zhé
2450153		21	22	23	24	25	26	27	
2450160		28	29	1	2	3	4	5	Chūn fēn
2450167	MONTH 2 Bǐng-Zǐ	6	7	8	9	10*	11	12	
2450174		13	14	15	16	17[c]	18	19	Qīng míng
2450181		20	21	22	23	24	25	26	
2450188		27	28	29	30	1	2	3	Gǔ yǔ
2450195	MONTH 3 Bǐng-Zǐ	4	5	6	7	8	9	10	
2450202		11	12	13	14	15	16	17	
2450209		18	19	20	21	22	23	24	Lì xià
2450216		25	26	27	28	29	1	2	
2450223	MONTH 4 Bǐng-Zǐ	3	4	5	6	7	8	9	Xiǎo mǎn
2450230		10	11*	12	13	14	15	16	
2450237		17	18	19	20	21	22	23	Máng zhòng
2450244		24	25	26	27	28	29	30	
2450251		1	2	3	4	5[d]	6	7	Xià zhì
2450258	MONTH 5 Bǐng-Zǐ	8	9	10	11	12	13	14	
2450265		15	16	17	18	19	20	21	
2450272		22	23	24	25	26	27	28	Xiǎo shǔ
2450279		29	30	1	2	3	4	5	
2450286	MONTH 6 Bǐng-Zǐ	6	7	8	9	10	11*	12	Dà shǔ
2450293		13	14	15	16	17	18	19	
2450300		20	21	22	23	24	25	26	Lì qiū
2450307		27	28	29	1	2	3	4	
2450314	MONTH 7 Bǐng-Zǐ	5	6	7[e]	8	9	10	11	Chǔ shǔ
2450321		12	13	14	15[f]	16	17	18	
2450328		19	20	21	22	23	24	25	Bái lù
2450335		26	27	28	29	30	1	2	
2450342	MONTH 8 Bǐng-Zǐ	3	4	5	6	7	8	9	Qiū fēn
2450349		10	11	12*	13	14	15[g]	16	
2450356		17	18	19	20	21	22	23	
2450363		24	25	26	27	28	29	1	Hán lù
2450370	MONTH 9 Bǐng-Zǐ	2	3	4	5	6	7	8	
2450377		9[h]	10	11	12	13	14	15	Shuāng jiàng
2450384		16	17	18	19	20	21	22	
2450391		23	24	25	26	27	28	29	Lì dōng
2450398		30	1	2	3	4	5	6	
2450405	MONTH 10 Bǐng-Zǐ	7	8	9	10	11	12	13*	Xiǎo xuě
2450412		14	15	16	17	18	19	20	
2450419		21	22	23	24	25	26	27	Dà xuě
2450426		28	29	30	1	2	3	4	
2450433	MONTH 11 Bǐng-Zǐ	5	6	7	8	9	10	11[i]	Dōng zhì
2450440		12	13	14	15	16	17	18	
2450447		19	20	21	22	23	24	25	

JULIAN DAY	COPTIC 1712/1713	Sun	Mon	Tue	Wed	Thu	Fri	Sat	ETHIOPIC 1988/1989
2450083	KOIAK 1712	21	22	23	24	25	26	27	TĀKHŚĀŚ 1988
2450090		28	29[c]	30	1	2	3	4	
2450097		5	6[d]	7	8	9	10	11[e]	
2450104	TŌBE 1712	12	13	14	15	16	17	18	ṬER 1988
2450111		19	20	21	22	23	24	25	
2450118		26	27	28	29	30	1	2	
2450125		3	4	5	6	7	8	9	
2450132	MESHIR 1712	10	11	12	13	14	15	16	YAKĀTIT 1988
2450139		17	18	19	20	21	22	23	
2450146		24	25	26	27	28	29	30	
2450153		1	2	3	4	5	6	7	
2450160	PAREMOTEP 1712	8	9	10	11	12	13	14	MAGĀBIT 1988
2450167		15	16	17	18	19	20	21	
2450174		22	23	24	25	26	27	28	
2450181		29	30	1	2	3	4	5	
2450188	PARMOUTE 1712	6[f]	7	8	9	10	11	12	MIYĀZYĀ 1988
2450195		13	14	15	16	17	18	19	
2450202		20	21	22	23	24	25	26	
2450209		27	28	29[g]	30	1	2	3	
2450216	PASHONS 1712	4	5	6	7	8	9	10	GENBOT 1988
2450223		11	12	13	14	15	16	17	
2450230		18	19	20	21	22	23	24	
2450237		25	26	27	28	29	30	1	
2450244		2	3	4	5	6	7	8	
2450251	PAŌNE 1712	9	10	11	12	13	14	15	SANĒ 1988
2450258		16	17	18	19	20	21	22	
2450265		23	24	25	26	27	28	29	
2450272		30	1	2	3	4	5	6	
2450279		7	8	9	10	11	12	13	
2450286	EPĒP 1712	14	15	16	17	18	19	20	HAMLĒ 1988
2450293		21	22	23	24	25	26	27	
2450300		28	29	30	1	2	3	4	
2450307		5	6	7	8	9	10	11	
2450314	MESORĒ 1712	12	13[h]	14	15	16	17	18	NAḤASĒ 1988
2450321		19	20	21	22	23	24	25	
2450328	EPAG. 1712	26	27	28	29	30	1	2	PĀG. 1988
2450335		3	4	5	1[a]	2	3	4	
2450342		5	6	7	8	9	10	11	
2450349	THOOUT 1713	12	13	14	15	16	17[b]	18	MASKARAM 1989
2450356		19	20	21	22	23	24	25	
2450363		26	27	28	29	30	1	2	
2450370		3	4	5	6	7	8	9	
2450377	PAOPE 1713	10	11	12	13	14	15	16	ṬEQEMT 1989
2450384		17	18	19	20	21	22	23	
2450391		24	25	26	27	28	29	30	
2450398		1	2	3	4	5	6	7	
2450405	ATHŌR 1713	8	9	10	11	12	13	14	HEDĀR 1989
2450412		15	16	17	18	19	20	21	
2450419		22	23	24	25	26	27	28	
2450426		29	30	1	2	3	4	5	
2450433	KOIAK 1713	6	7	8	9	10	11	12	TĀKHŚĀŚ 1989
2450440		13	14	15	16	17	18	19	
2450447		20	21	22	23	24	25	26	

‡Leap year
[a]New Year
[b]Spring (8:03)
[c]Summer (2:24)
[d]Autumn (18:00)
[e]Winter (14:06)
● New moon
◐ First quarter moon
○ Full moon
◑ Last quarter moon

‡Leap year
[a]New Year
[b]Yom Kippur
[c]Sukkot
[d]Winter starts
[e]Ḥanukkah
[f]Purim
[g]Passover
[h]Shavuot
[i]Fast of Av

‡Leap year
[a]New Year (4694, Rat)
[b]Lantern Festival
[c]Qīngmíng
[d]Dragon Festival
[e]Qīqiǎo
[f]Hungry Ghosts
[g]Mid-Autumn Festival
[h]Double-Ninth Festival
[i]Dōngzhì
*Start of 60-name cycle

[a]New Year
[b]Building of the Cross
[c]Christmas
[d]Jesus's Circumcision
[e]Epiphany
[f]Easter
[g]Mary's Announcement
[h]Jesus's Transfiguration

1996

PERSIAN (ASTRONOMICAL) 1374/1375‡

Month	Sun	Mon	Tue	Wed	Thu	Fri	Sat
DEY 1374	10	11	12	13	14	15	16
	17	18	19	20	21	22	23
	24	25	26	27	28	29	30
BAHMAN 1374	1	2	3	4	5	6	7
	8	9	10	11	12	13	14
	15	16	17	18	19	20	21
	22	23	24	25	26	27	28
ESFAND 1374	29	30	1	2	3	4	5
	6	7	8	9	10	11	12
	13	14	15	16	17	18	19
	20	21	22	23	24	25	26
FARVARDĪN 1375	27	28	29	1[a]	2*	3	4
	5	6	7	8	9	10	11
	12	13[b]	14	15	16	17	18
	19	20	21	22	23	24	25
ORDĪBEHEŠT 1375	26	27	28	29	30	31	1
	2	3	4	5	6	7	8
	9	10	11	12	13	14	15
	16	17	18	19	20	21	22
	23	24	25	26	27	28	29
XORDĀD 1375	30	31	1	2	3	4	5
	6	7	8	9	10	11	12
	13	14	15	16	17	18	19
	20	21	22	23	24	25	26
TĪR 1375	27	28	29	30	31	1	2
	3	4	5	6	7	8	9
	10	11	12	13	14	15	16
	17	18	19	20	21	22	23
	24	25	26	27	28	29	30
MORDĀD 1375	31	1	2	3	4	5	6
	7	8	9	10	11	12	13
	14	15	16	17	18	19	20
	21	22	23	24	25	26	27
SHAHRĪVAR 1375	28	29	30	31	1	2	3
	4	5	6	7	8	9	10
	11	12	13	14	15	16	17
	18	19	20	21	22	23	24
	25	26	27	28	29	30	31
MEHR 1375	1	2	3	4	5	6	7
	8	9	10	11	12	13	14
	15	16	17	18	19	20	21
	22	23	24	25	26	27	28
ĀBĀN 1375	29	30	1	2	3	4	5
	6	7	8	9	10	11	12
	13	14	15	16	17	18	19
	20	21	22	23	24	25	26
ĀZAR 1375	27	28	29	30	1	2	3
	4	5	6	7	8	9	10
	11	12	13	14	15	16	17
	18	19	20	21	22	23	24
DEY 1375	25	26	27	28	29	30	1
	2	3	4	5	6	7	8
	9	10	11	12	13	14	15

‡Leap year
[a]New Year (or next day)
*Near New Year: 1′36″
[b]Sizdeh Bedar

HINDU LUNAR 2052/2053‡

Month	Sun	Mon	Tue	Wed	Thu	Fri	Sat
PAUSHA 2052	10	11	12	13	14	15	16
	17	18	19	19	20	21	22
	23	**24**	26	27	28	29	30
MĀGHA 2052	1	2	3	4	5	6	7
	8	9	10	11	12	13	14
	15	16	17	18	19	20	21
	22	23	24	25	26	27	28[h]
PHĀLGUNA 2052	**29**	1	2	3	4	5	6
	7	8	9	10	11	11	12
	13	14	15[i]	16	17	18	19
	20	21	22	**23**	25	26	27
CHAITRA 2053	28	29	30	1[a]	2	3	4
	5	6	7	8	9[b]	10	11
	12	13	14	15	16	17	18
	19	20	21	22	23	24	25
VAIŚĀKHA 2053	26	**27**	29	30	1	2	3
	4	5	5	6	7	8	9
	10	11	12	13	14	15	16
	17	18	19	**20**	22	23	24
JYAISHTHA 2053	25	26	27	28	29	30	1
	2	3	4	5	6	7	8
	9	9	10	11	**12**	14	15
	16	17	18	19	20	21	22
	23	**24**	26	27	28	29	30
LEAP ĀSHĀDHA 2053	30	1	2	3	4	5	6
	7	8	9	10	11	12	13
	14	15	**16**	18	19	20	21
	22	23	24	25	26	27	28
ĀSHĀDHA 2053	29	30	1	2	3	4	5
	6	7	8	9	10	11	12
	13	14	15	16	17	18	**19**
	21	22	23	24	25	26	27
ŚRĀVANA 2053	27	28	29	30	1	2	3
	4	5	6	7	8	9	10
	11	**12**	14	15	16	17	18
	19	20	21	22	23[c]	24	25
BHĀDRAPADA 2053	26	27	28	29	30	1	2
	3	4[d]	5	6	7	8	9
	10	11	12	13	14	15	**16**
	18	19	20	21	22	23	23
	24	25	26	27	28	29	30
ĀŚVINA 2053	1	2	3	4	5	6	7
	8[e]	**9**[e]	11	12	13	14	15
	16	17	18	19	20	21	22
	23	24	25	26	26	27	28
KĀRTTIKA 2053	29	30	1[f]	**2**	4	5	6
	7	8	9	10	11	12	13
	14	15	16	17	18	19	20
	21	22	23	24	25	26	27
MĀRGAŚĪRA 2053	28	29	30	1	2	3	4
	5	6	**7**	9	10	11[g]	12
	13	14	15	16	17	18	19
	19	20	21	22	23	24	25

‡Leap year
[a]New Year (Dhātṛi)
[b]Birthday of Rāma
[c]Birthday of Krishna
[d]Ganēśa Chaturthī
[e]Dashara
[f]Diwali
[g]Birthday of Vishnu
[h]Night of Śiva
[i]Holi

HINDU SOLAR 1917/1918

Month	Sun	Mon	Tue	Wed	Thu	Fri	Sat
PAUSHA 1917	16	17	18	19	20	21	22
	23	24	25	26	27	28	29
MĀGHA 1917	1[b]	2	3	4	5	6	7
	8	9	10	11	12	13	14
	15	16	17	18	19	20	21
	22	23	24	25	26	27	28
PHĀLGUNA 1917	29	30	1	2	3	4	5
	6	7	8	9	10	11	12
	13	14	15	16	17	18	19
	20	21	22	23	24	25	26
CHAITRA 1917	27	28	29	30	1	2	3
	4	5	6	7	8	9	10
	11	12	13	14	15	16	17
	18	19	20	21	22	23	24
VAIŚĀKHA 1918	25	26	27	28	29	30	1[a]
	2	3	4	5	6	7	8
	9	10	11	12	13	14	15
	16	17	18	19	20	21	22
	23	24	25	26	27	28	29
JYAISHTHA 1918	30	31	1	2	3	4	5
	6	7	8	9	10	11	12
	13	14	15	16	17	18	19
	20	21	22	23	24	25	26
ĀSHĀDHA 1918	27	28	29	30	31	1	2
	3	4	5	6	7	8	9
	10	11	12	13	14	15	16
	17	18	19	20	21	22	23
	24	25	26	27	28	29	30
ŚRĀVANA 1918	31	32	1	2	3	4	5
	6	7	8	9	10	11	12
	13	14	15	16	17	18	19
	20	21	22	23	24	25	26
BHĀDRAPADA 1918	27	28	29	30	31	1	2
	3	4	5	6	7	8	9
	10	11	12	13	14	15	16
	17	18	19	20	21	22	23
	24	25	26	27	28	29	30
ĀŚVINA 1918	31	1	2	3	4	5	6
	7	8	9	10	11	12	13
	14	15	16	17	18	19	20
	21	22	23	24	25	26	27
KĀRTTIKA 1918	28	29	30	31	1	2	3
	4	5	6	7	8	9	10
	11	12	13	14	15	16	17
	18	19	20	21	22	23	24
MĀRGAŚĪRA 1918	25	26	27	28	29	30	1
	2	3	4	5	6	7	8
	9	10	11	12	13	14	15
	16	17	18	19	20	21	22
	23	24	25	26	27	28	29
PAUSHA 1918	1	2	3	4	5	6	7
	8	9	10	11	12	13	14
	15	16	17	18	19	20	21

[a]New Year (Virodhin)
[b]Pongal

ISLAMIC (ASTRONOMICAL) 1416/1417

Month	Sun	Mon	Tue	Wed	Thu	Fri	Sat
SHA'BĀN 1416	9	10	11	12	13	14	15
	16	17	18	19	20	21	22
	23	24	25	26	27	28	29
RAMAḌĀN 1416	30	1[e]	2	3	4	5	6
	7	8	9	10	11	12	13
	14	15	16	17	18	19	20
	21	22	23	24	25	26	27
SHAWWĀL 1416	28	29	1[f]	2	3	4	5
	6	7	8	9	10	11	12
	13	14	15	16	17	18	19
	20	21	22	23	24	25	26
DHU AL-QA'DA 1416	27	28	29	30	1	2	3
	4	5	6	7	8	9	10
	11	12	13	14	15	16	17
	18	19	20	21	22	23	24
DHU AL-ḤIJJA 1416	25	26	27	28	29	1	2
	3	4	5	6	7	8	9
	10[g]	11	12	13	14	15	16
	17	18	19	20	21	22	23
	24	25	26	27	28	29	30
MUḤARRAM 1417	1[a]	2	3	4	5	6	7
	8	9	10[b]	11	12	13	14
	15	16	17	18	19	20	21
	22	23	24	25	26	27	28
ṢAFAR 1417	29	30	1	2	3	4	5
	6	7	8	9	10	11	12
	13	14	15	16	17	18	19
	20	21	22	23	24	25	26
RABĪ' I 1417	27	28	29	30	1	2	3
	4	5	6	7	8	9	10
	11	12[c]	13	14	15	16	17
	18	19	20	21	22	23	24
RABĪ' II 1417	25	26	27	28	29	1	2
	3	4	5	6	7	8	9
	10	11	12	13	14	15	16
	17	18	19	20	21	22	23
	24	25	26	27	28	29	30
JUMĀDĀ I 1417	1	2	3	4	5	6	7
	8	9	10	11	12	13	14
	15	16	17	18	19	20	21
	22	23	24	25	26	27	28
JUMĀDĀ II 1417	29	1	2	3	4	5	6
	7	8	9	10	11	12	13
	14	15	16	17	18	19	20
	21	22	23	24	25	26	27
RAJAB 1417	28	29	1	2	3	4	5
	6	7	8	9	10	11	12
	13	14	15	16	17	18	19
	20	21	22	23	24	25	26
SHA'BĀN 1417	27[d]	28	29	30	1	2	3
	4	5	6	7	8	9	10
	11	12	13	14	15	16	17
	18	19	20	21	22	23	24

[a]New Year
[b]'Ashūrā'
[c]Prophet's Birthday
[d]Ascent of the Prophet
[e]Start of Ramaḍān
[f]'Id al-Fiṭr
[g]'Id al-'Aḍḥā

GREGORIAN 1996‡

Julian‡ (Sun)	Sun	Mon	Tue	Wed	Thu	Fri	Sat	Month
Dec 18	31	1	2	3	4	5	6	JANUARY 1996
	7[a]	8	9	10	11	12	13	
Jan 1	14[b]	15	16	17	18	19	20	
	21	22	23	24	25	26	27	
Jan 15	28	29	30	31	1	2	3	FEBRUARY 1996
	4	5	6	7	8	9	10	
Jan 29	11	12	13	14	15	16	17	
	18	19	20	21[c]	22	23	24	
Feb 12	25	26	27	28	29	1	2	MARCH 1996
	3[d]	4	5	6	7	8	9	
Feb 26	10	11	12	13	14	15	16	
	17	18	19	20	21	22	23	
Mar 11	24	25	26	27	28	29	30	
	31	1	2	3	4	5	6	APRIL 1996
Mar 25	7[e]	8	9	10	11	12	13	
	14[f]	15	16	17	18	19	20	
Apr 8	21	22	23	24	25	26	27	
	28	29	30	1	2	3	4	MAY 1996
Apr 22	5	6	7	8	9	10	11	
	12	13	14	15	16	17	18	
May 6	19	20	21	22	23	24	25	
	26	27	28	29	30	31	1	JUNE 1996
May 20	2	3	4	5	6	7	8	
	9	10	11	12	13	14	15	
Jun 3	16	17	18	19	20	21	22	
	23	24	25	26	27	28	29	
Jun 17	30	1	2	3	4	5	6	JULY 1996
	7	8	9	10	11	12	13	
Jul 1	14	15	16	17	18	19	20	
	21	22	23	24	25	26	27	
Jul 15	28	29	30	31	1	2	3	AUGUST 1996
	4	5	6	7	8	9	10	
Jul 29	11	12	13	14	15	16	17	
	18	19	20	21	22	23	24	
Aug 12	25	26	27	28	29	30	31	
	1	2	3	4	5	6	7	SEPTEMBER 1996
Aug 26	8	9	10	11	12	13	14	
	15	16	17	18	19	20	21	
Sep 9	22	23	24	25	26	27	28	
	29	30	1	2	3	4	5	OCTOBER 1996
Sep 23	6	7	8	9	10	11	12	
	13	14	15	16	17	18	19	
Oct 7	20	21	22	23	24	25	26	
	27	28	29	30	31	1	2	NOVEMBER 1996
Oct 21	3	4	5	6	7	8	9	
	10	11	12	13	14	15	16	
Nov 4	17	18	19	20	21	22	23	
	24	25	26	27	28	29	30	
Nov 18	1[g]	2	3	4	5	6	7	DECEMBER 1996
	8	9	10	11	12	13	14	
Dec 2	15	16	17	18	19	20	21	
	22	23	24	25[h]	26	27	28	
Dec 16	29	30	31	1	2	3	4	

‡Leap year
[a]Orthodox Christmas
[b]Julian New Year
[c]Ash Wednesday
[d]Feast of Orthodoxy
[e]Easter
[f]Orthodox Easter
[g]Advent
[h]Christmas

1997

Gregorian 1997 Month	Sun	Mon	Tue	Wed	Thu	Fri	Sat	Lunar Phases	ISO Week (Mon)	Julian Day (Sun noon)	Hebrew 5757‡/5758 Month	Sun	Mon	Tue	Wed	Thu	Fri	Sat	Molad
JANUARY 1997	29	30	31	1[a]	◑	3	4	1:45	1	2450447	TEVETH 5757	19	20	21	22	23	24	25	
	5	6	7	8	●	10	11	4:26	2	2450454		26	27	28	29	1	2	3	Thu 3h30m12p
	12	13	14	◐	16	17	18	20:02	3	2450461	SHEVAT 5757	4	5	6	7	8	9	10	
	19	20	21	22	○	24	25	15:11	4	2450468		11	12	13	14	15	16	17	
	26	27	28	29	30	◑	1	19:40	5	2450475		18	19	20	21	22	23	24	
FEBRUARY 1997	2	3	4	5	6	●	8	15:06	6	2450482		25	26	27	28	29	30	1	Fri 16h14m13p
	9	10	11	12	13	◐	15	8:57	7	2450489	ADAR I 5757	2	3	4	5	6	7	8	
	16	17	18	19	20	21	○	10:27	8	2450496		9	10	11	12	13	14	15	
	23	24	25	26	27	28	1		9	2450503		16	17	18	19	20	21	22	
MARCH 1997	◑	3	4	5	6	7	8	9:38	10	2450510		23	24	25	26	27	28	29	
	●	10	11	12	13	14	15	1:15	11	2450517	ADAR II 5757	30	1	2	3	4	5	6	Sun 4h58m14p
	◐	17	18	19	20[b]	21	22	0:06	12	2450524		7	8	9	10	11	12	13	
	23	○	25	26	27	28	29	4:45	13	2450531		14[f]	15	16	17	18	19	20	
	30	◑	1	2	3	4	5	19:38	14	2450538		21	22	23	24	25	26	27	
APRIL 1997	6	●	8	9	10	11	12	11:02	15	2450545	NISAN 5757	28	29	1	2	3	4	5	Mon 17h42m15p
	13	◐	15	16	17	18	19	17:00	16	2450552		6	7	8	9	10	11	12	
	20	21	○	23	24	25	26	20:33	17	2450559		13	14	15[g]	16	17	18	19	
	27	28	29	◑	1	2	3	2:37	18	2450566		20	21	22	23	24	25	26	
MAY 1997	4	5	●	7	8	9	10	20:47	19	2450573	IYAR 5757	27	28	29	30	1	2	3	Wed 6h26m16p
	11	12	13	◐	15	16	17	10:55	20	2450580		4	5	6	7	8	9	10	
	18	19	20	21	○	23	24	9:13	21	2450587		11	12	13	14	15	16	17	
	25	26	27	28	◑	30	31	7:51	22	2450594		18	19	20	21	22	23	24	
JUNE 1997	1	2	3	4	●	6	7	7:04	23	2450601	SIVAN 5757	25	26	27	28	29	1	2	Thu 19h10m17p
	8	9	10	11	12	◐	14	4:52	24	2450608		3	4	5	6[h]	7	8	9	
	15	16	17	18	19	○	21[c]	19:09	25	2450615		10	11	12	13	14	15	16	
	22	23	24	25	26	◑	28	12:42	26	2450622		17	18	19	20	21	22	23	
	29	30	1	2	3	●	5	18:40	27	2450629		24	25	26	27	28	29	30	
JULY 1997	6	7	8	9	10	11	◐	21:44	28	2450636	TAMMUZ 5757	1	2	3	4	5	6	7	Sat 7h55m0p
	13	14	15	16	17	18	19		29	2450643		8	9	10	11	12	13	14	
	○	21	22	23	24	25	◑	3:21 18:28	30	2450650		15	16	17	18	19	20	21	
	27	28	29	30	31	1	2		31	2450657		22	23	24	25	26	27	28	
AUGUST 1997	●	4	5	6	7	8	9	8:14	32	2450664	AV 5757	29	1	2	3	4	5	6	Sun 20h39m1p
	10	◐	12	13	14	15	16	12:42	33	2450671		7	8	9[i]	10	11	12	13	
	17	○	19	20	21	22	23	10:56	34	2450678		14	15	16	17	18	19	20	
	24	◑	26	27	28	29	30	2:24	35	2450685		21	22	23	24	25	26	27	
	31	●	2	3	4	5	6	23:51	36	2450692		28	29	30	1	2	3	4	Tue 9h23m2p
SEPTEMBER 1997	7	8	9	◐	11	12	13	1:31	37	2450699	ELUL 5757	5	6	7	8	9	10	11	
	14	15	○	17	18	19	20	18:51	38	2450706		12	13	14	15	16	17	18	
	21	22[d]	◑	24	25	26	27	13:35	39	2450713		19	20	21	22	23	24	25	
	28	29	30	●	2	3	4	16:52	40	2450720		26	27	28	29	1[a]	2[a]	3	Wed 22h7m3p
OCTOBER 1997	5	6	7	8	◐	10	11	12:22	41	2450727	TISHRI 5758	4	5	6	7	8	9	10[b]	
	12	13	14	15	○	17	18	3:46	42	2450734		11	12	13	14	15[c]	16	17	
	19	20	21	22	◑	24	25	4:48	43	2450741		18	19	20	21	22	23	24	
	26	27	28	29	30	●	1	10:01	44	2450748		25	26	27	28	29	30	1	Fri 10h51m4p
NOVEMBER 1997	2	3	4	5	6	◐	8	21:43	45	2450755	HESHVAN 5758	2	3	4	5	6	7	8	
	9	10	11	12	13	○	15	14:12	46	2450762		9	10	11	12	13	14	15	
	16	17	18	19	20	◑	22	23:58	47	2450769		16	17	18	19	20	21	22	
	23	24	25	26	27	28	29		48	2450776		23	24	25	26	27	28	29	
DECEMBER 1997	●	1	2	3	4	5	6	2:14	49	2450783	KISLEV 5758	1	2	3	4	5	6[d]	7	Sat 23h35m5p
	◐	8	9	10	11	12	13	6:09	50	2450790		8	9	10	11	12	13	14	
	○	15	16	17	18	19	20	2:37	51	2450797		15	16	17	18	19	20	21	
	◑[e]	22	23	24	25	26	27	21:43	52	2450804		22	23	24	25[e]	26[e]	27[e]	28[e]	
	28	●	30	31	1	2	3	16:57	1	2450811		29[e]	30[e]	1[e]	2[e]	3	4	5	Mon 12h19m6p

Julian Day	Chinese Bǐng-Zǐ/Dīng-Chǒu Month	Sun	Mon	Tue	Wed	Thu	Fri	Sat	Solar Term	Coptic 1713/1714 Month	Sun	Mon	Tue	Wed	Thu	Fri	Sat	Ethiopic 1989/1990 Month
2450447	MONTH 11 Bǐng-Zǐ	19	20	21	22	23	24	25		KOIAK 1713	20	21	22	23	24	25	26	TĀKHŚĀŚ 1989
2450454	MONTH 12 Bǐng-Zǐ	26	27	28	29	1	2	3	Xiǎo hán		27	28	29[c]	30	1	2	3	
2450461		4	5	6	7	8	9	10		TÔBE 1713	4	5	6[d]	7	8	9	10	ṬER 1989
2450468		11	12	13	14*	15	16	17	Dà hán		11[e]	12	13	14	15	16	17	
2450475		18	19	20	21	22	23	24			18	19	20	21	22	23	24	
2450482	MONTH 1 Dīng-Chǒu	25	26	27	28	29	1[a]	2	Lì chūn	MESHIR 1713	25	26	27	28	29	30	1	YAKĀTIT 1989
2450489		3	4	5	6	7	8	9			2	3	4	5	6	7	8	
2450496		10	11	12	13	14	15[b]	16	Yǔ shuǐ		9	10	11	12	13	14	15	
2450503		17	18	19	20	21	22	23			16	17	18	19	20	21	22	
2450510		24	25	26	27	28	29	30	Jīng zhé		23	24	25	26	27	28	29	
2450517	MONTH 2 Dīng-Chǒu	1	2	3	4	5	6	7		PAREMOTEP 1713	30	1	2	3	4	5	6	MAGĀBIT 1989
2450524		8	9	10	11	12	13	14	Chūn fēn		7	8	9	10	11	12	13	
2450531		15*	16	17	18	19	20	21			14	15	16	17	18	19	20	
2450538		22	23	24	25	26	27	28[c]	Qīng míng		21	22	23	24	25	26	27	
2450545	MONTH 3 Dīng-Chǒu	29	1	2	3	4	5	6		PARMOUTE 1713	28	29	30	1	2	3	4	MIYĀZYĀ 1989
2450552		7	8	9	10	11	12	13			5	6	7	8	9	10	11	
2450559		14	15	16	17	18	19	20	Gǔ yǔ		12	13	14	15	16	17	18	
2450566		21	22	23	24	25	26	27			19[f]	20	21	22	23	24	25	
2450573	MONTH 4 Dīng-Chǒu	28	29	30	1	2	3	4	Lì xià	PASHONS 1713	26	27	28	29[g]	30	1	2	GENBOT 1989
2450580		5	6	7	8	9	10	11			3	4	5	6	7	8	9	
2450587		12	13	14	15	16*	17	18	Xiǎo mǎn		10	11	12	13	14	15	16	
2450594		19	20	21	22	23	24	25			17	18	19	20	21	22	23	
2450601	MONTH 5 Dīng-Chǒu	26	27	28	29	1	2	3	Máng zhòng		24	25	26	27	28	29	30	
2450608		4	5[d]	6	7	8	9	10		PAÔNE 1713	1	2	3	4	5	6	7	SANĒ 1989
2450615		11	12	13	14	15	16	17	Xià zhì		8	9	10	11	12	13	14	
2450622		18	19	20	21	22	23	24			15	16	17	18	19	20	21	
2450629		25	26	27	28	29	30	1			22	23	24	25	26	27	28	
2450636	MONTH 6 Dīng-Chǒu	2	3	4	5	6	7	8	Xiǎo shǔ	EPÊP 1713	29	30	1	2	3	4	5	ḤAMLĒ 1989
2450643		9	10	11	12	13	14	15			6	7	8	9	10	11	12	
2450650		16	17*	18	19	20	21	22	Dà shǔ		13	14	15	16	17	18	19	
2450657		23	24	25	26	27	28	29			20	21	22	23	24	25	26	
2450664	MONTH 7 Dīng-Chǒu	1	2	3	4	5	6	7[e]	Lì qiū	MESORĒ 1713	27	28	29	30	1	2	3	NAḤASĒ 1989
2450671		8	9	10	11	12	13	14			4	5	6	7	8	9	10	
2450678		15[f]	16	17	18	19	20	21	Chǔ shǔ		11	12	13[h]	14	15	16	17	
2450685		22	23	24	25	26	27	28			18	19	20	21	22	23	24	
2450692	MONTH 8 Dīng-Chǒu	29	30	1	2	3	4	5	Bái lù	EPAG. 1713	25	26	27	28	29	30	1	PĀG. 1989
2450699		6	7	8	9	10	11	12		THOOUT 1714	2	3	4	5	1[a]	2	3	MASKARAM 1990
2450706		13	14	15[g]	16	17	18*	19	Qiū fēn		4	5	6	7	8	9	10	
2450713		20	21	22	23	24	25	26			11	12	13	14	15	16	17[b]	
2450720	MONTH 9 Dīng-Chǒu	27	28	29	30	1	2	3			18	19	20	21	22	23	24	
2450727		4	5	6	7	8	9[h]	10	Hán lù	PAOPE 1714	25	26	27	28	29	30	1	ṬEQEMT 1990
2450734		11	12	13	14	15	16	17			2	3	4	5	6	7	8	
2450741		18	19	20	21	22	23	24	Shuāng jiàng		9	10	11	12	13	14	15	
2450748	MONTH 10 Dīng-Chǒu	25	26	27	28	29	1	2			16	17	18	19	20	21	22	
2450755		3	4	5	6	7	8	9	Lì dōng	ATHÔR 1714	23	24	25	26	27	28	29	HEDĀR 1990
2450762		10	11	12	13	14	15	16			30	1	2	3	4	5	6	
2450769		17	18	19*	20	21	22	23	Xiǎo xuě		7	8	9	10	11	12	13	
2450776		24	25	26	27	28	29	30			14	15	16	17	18	19	20	
2450783	MONTH 11 Dīng-Chǒu	1	2	3	4	5	6	7		KOIAK 1714	21	22	23	24	25	26	27	TĀKHŚĀŚ 1990
2450790		8	9	10	11	12	13	14	Dà xuě		28	29	30	1	2	3	4	
2450797		15	16	17	18	19	20	21			5	6	7	8	9	10	11	
2450804		22	23[i]	24	25	26	27	28	Dōng zhì		12	13	14	15	16	17	18	
2450811		29	30	1	2	3	4	5			19	20	21	22	23	24	25	

[a]New Year
[b]Spring (13:55)
[c]Summer (8:20)
[d]Autumn (23:55)
[e]Winter (20:07)
● New moon
◐ First quarter moon
○ Full moon
◑ Last quarter moon

‡Leap year
[a]New Year
[b]Yom Kippur
[c]Sukkot
[d]Winter starts
[e]Ḥanukkah
[f]Purim
[g]Passover
[h]Shavuot
[i]Fast of Av

[a]New Year (4695, Ox)
[b]Lantern Festival
[c]Qīngmíng
[d]Dragon Festival
[e]Qǐqiǎo
[f]Hungry Ghosts
[g]Mid-Autumn Festival
[h]Double-Ninth Festival
[i]Dōngzhì
*Start of 60-name cycle

[a]New Year
[b]Building of the Cross
[c]Christmas
[d]Jesus's Circumcision
[e]Epiphany
[f]Easter
[g]Mary's Announcement
[h]Jesus's Transfiguration

PERSIAN (ASTRONOMICAL) 1375‡/1376

Month	Sun	Mon	Tue	Wed	Thu	Fri	Sat
DEY 1375	9	10	11	12	13	14	15
	16	17	18	19	20	21	22
	23	24	25	26	27	28	29
BAHMAN 1375	30	1	2	3	4	5	6
	7	8	9	10	11	12	13
	14	15	16	17	18	19	20
	21	22	23	24	25	26	27
ESFAND 1375	28	29	30	1	2	3	4
	5	6	7	8	9	10	11
	12	13	14	15	16	17	18
	19	20	21	22	23	24	25
FARVARDIN 1376	26	27	28	29	30	1[a]	2
	3	4	5	6	7	8	9
	10	11	12	13[b]	14	15	16
	17	18	19	20	21	22	23
	24	25	26	27	28	29	30
ORDĪBEHEŠT 1376	31	1	2	3	4	5	6
	7	8	9	10	11	12	13
	14	15	16	17	18	19	20
	21	22	23	24	25	26	27
XORDĀD 1376	28	29	30	31	1	2	3
	4	5	6	7	8	9	10
	11	12	13	14	15	16	17
	18	19	20	21	22	23	24
	25	26	27	28	29	30	31
TĪR 1376	1	2	3	4	5	6	7
	8	9	10	11	12	13	14
	15	16	17	18	19	20	21
	22	23	24	25	26	27	28
MORDĀD 1376	29	30	31	1	2	3	4
	5	6	7	8	9	10	11
	12	13	14	15	16	17	18
	19	20	21	22	23	24	25
SHAHRĪVAR 1376	26	27	28	29	30	31	1
	2	3	4	5	6	7	8
	9	10	11	12	13	14	15
	16	17	18	19	20	21	22
	23	24	25	26	27	28	29
MEHR 1376	30	31	1	2	3	4	5
	6	7	8	9	10	11	12
	13	14	15	16	17	18	19
	20	21	22	23	24	25	26
ĀBĀN 1376	27	28	29	30	1	2	3
	4	5	6	7	8	9	10
	11	12	13	14	15	16	17
	18	19	20	21	22	23	24
ĀZAR 1376	25	26	27	28	29	30	1
	2	3	4	5	6	7	8
	9	10	11	12	13	14	15
	16	17	18	19	20	21	22
	23	24	25	26	27	28	29
DEY 1376	30	1	2	3	4	5	6
	7	8	9	10	11	12	13

‡Leap year
[a]New Year
[b]Sizdeh Bedar

HINDU LUNAR 2053‡/2054

Month	Sun	Mon	Tue	Wed	Thu	Fri	Sat
MĀRGAŚIRA 2053	19	20	21	22	23	24	25
PAUSHA 2053	26	27	28	29	30	1	3
	4	5	6	7	8	9	10
	11	12	13	14	15	16	17
	18	19	20	21	22	22	23
MĀGHA 2053	24	26	27	28	29	30	1
	2	3	4	5	6	7	8
	10	10	11	12	13	14	15
	16	17	18	19	20	21	22
	23	24	25	26	27	28[h]	29
PHĀLGUNA 2053	30	2	3	4	5	6	7
	8	9	10	11	12	13	14
	14	15[i]	16	17	18	19	20
	21	22	23	24	26	27	28
CHAITRA 2054	29	30	1[a]	2	3	4	5
	6	7	8	9[b]	10	11	12
	13	14	15	16	17	18	19
	20	21	22	23	24	25	26
VAIŚĀKHA 2054	27	29	30	1	2	3	4
	5	6	7	8	9	9	10
	11	12	13	14	15	16	17
	18	19	20	22	23	24	25
JYAISHTHA 2054	26	27	28	29	30	1	2
	3	4	5	6	7	8	9
	10	11	12	13	14	15	16
	17	18	19	20	21	22	23
ĀSHĀDHA 2054	25	26	27	28	29	30	1
	2	3	4	5	5	6	7
	8	9	10	11	12	13	14
	15	16	18	19	20	21	22
	23	24	25	26	27	28	29
ŚRĀVANA 2054	30	1	2	3	4	5	6
	7	8	9	10	11	12	13
	14	15	16	17	18	19	21
	22	23[c]	24	25	26	27	28
BHĀDRAPADA 2054	29	30	1	2	2	3[d]	4
	5	6	7	8	9	10	11
	12	14	15	16	17	18	19
	20	21	22	23	24	25	26
ĀŚVINA 2054	27	28	29	30	1	2	3
	4	5	6	7	8[e]	9[e]	10[e]
	11	12	13	14	15	16	18
	19	20	21	22	23	24	25
KĀRTTIKA 2054	26	26	27	28	29	30	1[f]
	2	3	4	5	6	7	8
	9	11	12	13	14	15	16
	17	18	19	20	21	22	23
	24	25	26	27	28	29	30
MĀRGAŚIRA 2054	30	1	2	4	5	6	7
	8	9	10	11[g]	12	13	14
	15	16	18	18	19	20	21
	22	23	24	25	26	27	28
	29	30	1	2	3	4	5

‡Leap year
[a]New Year (Īśvara)
[b]Birthday of Rāma
[c]Birthday of Krishna
[d]Ganēśa Chaturthī
[e]Dashara
[f]Diwali
[g]Birthday of Vishnu
[h]Night of Śiva
[i]Holi

HINDU SOLAR 1918/1919

Month	Sun	Mon	Tue	Wed	Thu	Fri	Sat
PAUSHA 1918	15	16	17	18	19	20	21
	22	23	24	25	26	27	28
MĀGHA 1918	29	30	1[b]	2	3	4	5
	6	7	8	9	10	11	12
	13	14	15	16	17	18	19
	20	21	22	23	24	25	26
PHĀLGUNA 1918	27	28	29	1	2	3	4
	5	6	7	8	9	10	11
	12	13	14	15	16	17	18
	19	20	21	22	23	24	25
CHAITRA 1918	26	27	28	29	30	1	2
	3	4	5	6	7	8	9
	10	11	12	13	14	15	16
	17	18	19	20	21	22	23
	24	25	26	27	28	29	30
VAIŚĀKHA 1919	1[a]	2	3	4	5	6	7
	8	9	10	11	12	13	14
	15	16	17	18	19	20	21
	22	23	24	25	26	27	28
JYAISHTHA 1919	29	30	31	1	2	3	4
	5	6	7	8	9	10	11
	12	13	14	15	16	17	18
	19	20	21	22	23	24	25
	26	27	28	29	30	31	32
ĀSHĀDHA 1919	1	2	3	4	5	6	7
	8	9	10	11	12	13	14
	15	16	17	18	19	20	21
	22	23	24	25	26	27	28
ŚRĀVANA 1919	29	30	31	1	2	3	4
	5	6	7	8	9	10	11
	12	13	14	15	16	17	18
	19	20	21	22	23	24	25
	26	27	28	29	30	31	32
BHĀDRAPADA 1919	1	2	3	4	5	6	7
	8	9	10	11	12	13	14
	15	16	17	18	19	20	21
	22	23	24	25	26	27	28
ĀŚVINA 1919	29	30	31	1	2	3	4
	5	6	7	8	9	10	11
	12	13	14	15	16	17	18
	19	20	21	22	23	24	25
KĀRTTIKA 1919	26	27	28	29	30	1	2
	3	4	5	6	7	8	9
	10	11	12	13	14	15	16
	17	18	19	20	21	22	23
	24	25	26	27	28	29	30
MĀRGAŚIRA 1919	1	2	3	4	5	6	7
	8	9	10	11	12	13	14
	15	16	17	18	19	20	21
	22	23	24	25	26	27	28
PAUSHA 1919	29	1	2	3	4	5	6
	7	8	9	10	11	12	13
	14	15	16	17	18	19	20

[a]New Year (Vikṛita)
[b]Pongal

ISLAMIC (ASTRONOMICAL) 1417/1418‡

Month	Sun	Mon	Tue	Wed	Thu	Fri	Sat
SHA'BĀN 1417	18	19	20	21	22	23	24
RAMAḌĀN 1417	25	26	27	28	29	1[e]	2
	3	4	5	6	7	8	9
	10	11	12	13	14	15	16
	17	18	19	20	21	22	23
	24	25	26	27	28	29	30
SHAWWĀL 1417	1[f]	2	3	4	5	6	7
	8	9	10	11	12	13	14
	15	16	17	18	19	20	21
	22	23	24	25	26	27	28
DHU AL-QA'DA 1417	29	1	2	3	4	5	6
	7	8	9	10	11	12	13
	14	15	16	17	18	19	20
	21	22	23	24	25	26	27
DHU AL-ḤIJJA 1417	28	29	30	1	2	3	4
	5	6	7	8	9	10[g]	11
	12	13	14	15	16	17	18
	19	20	21	22	23	24	25
MUḤARRAM 1418	26	27	28	29	1[a]	2[d]	3
	4	5	6	7	8	9	10[b]
	11	12	13	14	15	16	17
	18	19	20	21	22	23	24
ṢAFAR 1418	25	26	27	28	29	30	1
	2	3	4	5	6	7	8
	9	10	11	12	13	14	15
	16	17	18	19	20	21	22
	23	24	25	26	27	28	29
RABĪ' I 1418	30	1	2	3	4	5	6
	7	8	9	10	11	12[c]	13
	14	15	16	17	18	19	20
	21	22	23	24	25	26	27
RABĪ' II 1418	28	29	1	2	3	4	5
	6	7	8	9	10	11	12
	13	14	15	16	17	18	19
	20	21	22	23	24	25	26
JUMĀDĀ I 1418	27	28	29	30	1	2	3
	4	5	6	7	8	9	10
	11	12	13	14	15	16	17
	18	19	20	21	22	23	24
JUMĀDĀ II 1418	25	26	27	28	29	1	2
	3	4	5	6	7	8	9
	10	11	12	13	14	15	16
	17	18	19	20	21	22	23
	24	25	26	27	28	29	30
RAJAB 1418	1	2	3	4	5	6	7
	8	9	10	11	12	13	14
	15	16	17	18	19	20	21
	22	23	24	25	26	27[d]	28
SHA'BĀN 1418	29	1	2	3	4	5	6
	7	8	9	10	11	12	13
	14	15	16	17	18	19	20
	21	22	23	24	25	26	27
	28	29	30	1[e]	2	3	4

‡Leap year
[a]New Year
[d]New Year (Arithmetic)
[b]'Ashūrā'
[c]Prophet's Birthday
[d]Ascent of the Prophet
[e]Start of Ramaḍān
[f]'Īd al-Fiṭr
[g]'Īd al-'Aḍḥā

GREGORIAN 1997

Julian (Sun)	Month	Sun	Mon	Tue	Wed	Thu	Fri	Sat
Dec 16	JANUARY 1997	29	30	31	1	2	3	4
		5	6	7[a]	8	9	10	11
Dec 30		12	13	14[b]	15	16	17	18
		19	20	21	22	23	24	25
Jan 13	FEBRUARY 1997	26	27	28	29	30	31	1
		2	3	4	5	6	7	8
Jan 27		9	10	11	12[c]	13	14	15
		16	17	18	19	20	21	22
Feb 10	MARCH 1997	23	24	25	26	27	28	1
		2	3	4	5	6	7	8
Feb 24		9	10	11	12	13	14	15
		16[d]	17	18	19	20	21	22
Mar 10		23	24	25	26	27	28	29
	APRIL 1997	30[e]	31	1	2	3	4	5
Mar 24		6	7	8	9	10	11	12
		13	14	15	16	17	18	19
Apr 7		20	21	22	23	24	25	26
	MAY 1997	27[f]	28	29	30	1	2	3
Apr 21		4	5	6	7	8	9	10
		11	12	13	14	15	16	17
May 5		18	19	20	21	22	23	24
		25	26	27	28	29	30	31
May 19	JUNE 1997	1	2	3	4	5	6	7
		8	9	10	11	12	13	14
Jun 2		15	16	17	18	19	20	21
		22	23	24	25	26	27	28
Jun 16	JULY 1997	29	30	1	2	3	4	5
		6	7	8	9	10	11	12
Jun 30		13	14	15	16	17	18	19
		20	21	22	23	24	25	26
Jul 14	AUGUST 1997	27	28	29	30	31	1	2
		3	4	5	6	7	8	9
Jul 28		10	11	12	13	14	15	16
		17	18	19	20	21	22	23
Aug 11		24	25	26	27	28	29	30
	SEPTEMBER 1997	31	1	2	3	4	5	6
Aug 25		7	8	9	10	11	12	13
		14	15	16	17	18	19	20
Sep 8		21	22	23	24	25	26	27
	OCTOBER 1997	28	29	30	1	2	3	4
Sep 22		5	6	7	8	9	10	11
		12	13	14	15	16	17	18
Oct 6		19	20	21	22	23	24	25
	NOVEMBER 1997	26	27	28	29	30	31	1
Oct 20		2	3	4	5	6	7	8
		9	10	11	12	13	14	15
Nov 3		16	17	18	19	20	21	22
		23	24	25	26	27	28	29
Nov 17	DECEMBER 1997	30[g]	1	2	3	4	5	6
		7	8	9	10	11	12	13
Dec 1		14	15	16	17	18	19	20
		21	22	23	24	25[h]	26	27
Dec 15		28	29	30	31	1	2	3

[a]Orthodox Christmas
[b]Julian New Year
[c]Ash Wednesday
[d]Feast of Orthodoxy
[e]Easter
[f]Orthodox Easter
[g]Advent
[h]Christmas

1998

Gregorian 1998	Sun	Mon	Tue	Wed	Thu	Fri	Sat	Lunar Phases	ISO Week (Mon)	Julian Day (Sun noon)	Hebrew 5758/5759	Sun	Mon	Tue	Wed	Thu	Fri	Sat	Molad	Chinese Dīng-Chǒu/Wù-Yín‡	Sun	Mon	Tue	Wed	Thu	Fri	Sat	Solar Term	Coptic 1714/1715‡	Sun	Mon	Tue	Wed	Thu	Fri	Sat	Ethiopic 1990/1991‡
	28	●	30	31	1[a]	2	3	16:57	1	2450811		29[e]	30[e]	1[e]	2[e]	3	4	5	Mon $12^h19^m6^p$	Month 12 Dīng-Chǒu	29	30	1	2	3	4	5		Koiak 1714	19	20	21	22	23	24	25	Tākhšāš 1990
January 1998	4	◐	6	7	8	9	10	14:18	2	2450818	Teveth 5758	6	7	8	9	10	11	12			6	*7*	8	9	10	11	12	*Xiǎo hán*		26	27	28	29[c]	30	1	2	
	11	○	13	14	15	16	17	17:24	3	2450825		13	14	15	16	17	18	19			13	14	15	16	17	18	19*		Tōbe 1714	3	4	5	6[d]	7	8	9	Ṭer 1990
	18	19	◑	21	22	23	24	19:40	4	2450832		20	21	22	23	24	25	26			20	21	**22**	23	24	25	26	**Dà hán**		10	11[e]	12	13	14	15	16	
	25	26	27	●	29	30	31	6:01	5	2450839		27	28	29	1	2	3	4	Wed $1^h3^m7^p$		27	28	29	1[a]	2	3	4			17	18	19	20	21	22	23	
February 1998	1	2	◐	4	5	6	7	22:54	6	2450846	Shevat 5758	5	6	7	8	9	10	11		Month 1 Wù-Yín	5	6	7	*8*	9	10	11	*Lì chūn*		24	25	26	27	28	29	30	
	8	9	10	○	12	13	14	10:23	7	2450853		12	13	14	15	16	17	18			12	13	14	15[b]	16	17	18		Meshir 1714	1	2	3	4	5	6	7	Yakātit 1990
	15	16	17	18	◑	20	21	15:27	8	2450860		19	20	21	22	23	24	25			19	20	21	22	**23**	24	25	**Yǔ shuǐ**		8	9	10	11	12	13	14	
	22	23	24	25	●	27	28	17:26	9	2450867		26	27	28	29	30	1	2	Thu $13^h47^m8^p$		26	27	28	29	30	1	2			15	16	17	18	19	20	21	
March 1998	1	2	3	4	◐	6	7	8:41	10	2450874	Adar 5758	3	4	5	6	7	8	9		Month 2 Wù-Yín	3	4	5	6	7	*8*	9	*Jīng zhé*		22	23	24	25	26	27	28	
	8	9	10	11	12	○	14	4:34	11	2450881		10	11	12	13	14[f]	15	16			10	11	12	13	14	15	16			29	30	1	2	3	4	5	
	15	16	17	18	19	20[b]	◑	7:38	12	2450888		17	18	19	20	21	22	23			17	18	19	20*	21	22	**23**	**Chūn fēn**	Paremotep 1714	6	7	8	9	10	11	12	Magābit 1990
	22	23	24	25	26	27	●	3:14	13	2450895		24	25	26	27	28	29	1	Sat $2^h31^m9^p$		24	25	26	27	28	29	1			13	14	15	16	17	18	19	
	29	30	31	1	2	◐	4	20:18	14	2450902	Nisan 5758	2	3	4	5	6	7	8		Month 3 Wù-Yín	2	3	4	5	6	7	8			20	21	22	23	24	25	26	
April 1998	5	6	7	8	9	10	○	22:23	15	2450909		9	10	11	12	13	14	15[g]			9[c]	10	11	12	13	14	15	*Qīng míng*		27	28	29	30	1	2	3	
	12	13	14	15	16	17	18		16	2450916		16	17	18	19	20	21	22			16	17	18	19	20	21	22		Parmoute 1714	4	5	6	7	8	9	10	Miyāzyā 1990
	◑	20	21	22	23	24	25	19:53	17	2450923		23	24	25	26	27	28	29			23	**24**	25	26	27	28	29	**Gǔ yǔ**		11[f]	12	13	14	15	16	17	
	●	27	28	29	30	1	2	11:41	18	2450930		30	1	2	3	4	5	6	Sun $15^h15^m10^p$	Month 4 Wù-Yín	1	2	3	4	5	6	7			18	19	20	21	22	23	24	
May 1998	◐	4	5	6	7	8	9	10:04	19	2450937	Iyyar 5758	7	8	9	10	11	12	13			8	9	10	*11*	12	13	14	*Lì xià*		25	26	27	28	29[g]	30	1	
	10	○	12	13	14	15	16	14:29	20	2450944		14	15	16	17	18	19	20			15	16	17	18	19	20	21		Pashons 1714	2	3	4	5	6	7	8	Genbot 1990
	17	18	◑	20	21	22	23	4:35	21	2450951		21	22	23	24	25	26	27			22*	23	24	25	**26**	27	28	**Xiǎo mǎn**		9	10	11	12	13	14	15	
	24	●	26	27	28	29	30	19:32	22	2450958		28	29	1	2	3	4	5	Tue $3^h59^m11^p$		29	30	1	2	3	4	5[d]			16	17	18	19	20	21	22	
	31	1	◐	3	4	5	6	1:45	23	2450965	Sivan 5758	6[h]	7	8	9	10	11	12		Month 5 Wù-Yín	6	7	8	9	10	11	*12*	*Máng zhòng*		23	24	25	26	27	28	29	
June 1998	7	8	9	○	11	12	13	4:18	24	2450972		13	14	15	16	17	18	19			13	14	15	16	17	18	19			30	1	2	3	4	5	6	
	14	15	16	◑	18	19	20	10:38	25	2450979		20	21	22	23	24	25	26			20	21	22	23	24	25	26		Paōne 1714	7	8	9	10	11	12	13	Sanē 1990
	21[c]	22	23	●	25	26	27	3:50	26	2450986		27	28	29	30	1	2	3	Wed $16^h43^m12^p$		**27**	28	29	1	2	3	4	**Xià zhì**		14	15	16	17	18	19	20	
	28	29	30	◐	2	3	4	18:42	27	2450993	Tammuz 5758	4	5	6	7	8	9	10		*Leap Month 5* Wù-Yín	5	6	7	8	9	10	11			21	22	23	24	25	26	27	
July 1998	5	6	7	8	○	10	11	16:01	28	2451000		11	12	13	14	15	16	17			12	13	*14*	15	16	17	18	*Xiǎo shǔ*		28	29	30	1	2	3	4	
	12	13	14	15	◑	17	18	15:13	29	2451007		18	19	20	21	22	23	24			19	20	21	22	23*	24	25		Epēp 1714	5	6	7	8	9	10	11	Ḥamlē 1990
	19	20	21	22	●	24	25	13:44	30	2451014		25	26	27	28	29	1	2	Fri $5^h27^m13^p$		26	27	28	29	**1**	2	3	**Dà shǔ**		12	13	14	15	16	17	18	
	26	27	28	29	30	◐	1	12:05	31	2451021	Av 5758	3	4	5	6	7	8	9		Month 6 Wù-Yín	4	5	6	7	8	9	10			19	20	21	22	23	24	25	
August 1998	2	3	4	5	6	7	○	2:10	32	2451028		10[i]	11	12	13	14	15	16			11	12	13	14	15	16	*17*	*Lì qiū*		26	27	28	29	30	1	2	
	9	10	11	12	13	◑	15	19:49	33	2451035		17	18	19	20	21	22	23			18	19	20	21	22	23	24		Mesorē 1714	3	4	5	6	7	8	9	Naḥasē 1990
	16	17	18	19	20	21	●	2:03	34	2451042		24	25	26	27	28	29	30			25	26	27	28	29	30	1			10	11	12	13[h]	14	15	16	
	23	24	25	26	27	28	29		35	2451049	Elul 5758	1	2	3	4	5	6	7	Sat $18^h11^m14^p$	Month 7 Wù-Yín	**2**	3	4	5	6	7[e]	8	**Chǔ shǔ**		17	18	19	20	21	22	23	
	◐	31	1	2	3	4	5	5:06	36	2451056		8	9	10	11	12	13	14			9	10	11	12	13	14	15[f]			24	25	26	27	28	29	30	
September 1998	○	7	8	9	10	11	12	11:21	37	2451063		15	16	17	18	19	20	21			16	17	*18*	19	20	21	22	*Bái lù*	Epag. 1714	1	2	3	4	5	1[a]	2	Pāg. 1990
	◑	14	15	16	17	18	19	1:58	38	2451070		22	23	24	25	26	27	28			23	24*	25	26	27	28	29		Thoout 1715	3	4	5	6	7	8	9	Maskaram 1991
	●	21	22	23[d]	24	25	26	17:01	39	2451077		29	1[a]	2[a]	3	4	5	6	Mon $6^h55^m15^p$		30	1	2	**3**	4	5	6	**Qiū fēn**		10	11	12	13	14	15	16	
	27	◐	29	30	1	2	3	21:11	40	2451084	Tishri 5759	7	8	9	10[b]	11	12	13		Month 8 Wù-Yín	7	8	9	10	11	12	13			17[b]	18	19	20	21	22	23	
October 1998	4	○	6	7	8	9	10	20:12	41	2451091		14	15[c]	16	17	18	19	20			14	15[g]	16	17	*18*	19	20	*Hán lù*		24	25	26	27	28	29	30	
	11	◑	13	14	15	16	17	11:11	42	2451098		21	22	23	24	25	26	27			21	22	23	24	25	26	27		Paope 1715	1	2	3	4	5	6	7	Ṭeqemt 1991
	18	19	●	21	22	23	24	10:09	43	2451105		28	29	30	1	2	3	4	Tue $19^h39^m16^p$		28	29	1	2	3	**4**	5	**Shuāng jiàng**		8	9	10	11	12	13	14	
	25	26	27	◐	29	30	31	11:46	44	2451112	Heshvan 5759	5	6	7	8	9	10	11		Month 9 Wù-Yín	6	7	8	9[h]	10	11	12			15	16	17	18	19	20	21	
November 1998	1	2	3	○	5	6	7	5:18	45	2451119		12	13	14	15	16	17	18			13	14	15	16	17	18	*19*	*Lì dōng*		22	23	24	25	26	27	28	
	8	9	10	◑	12	13	14	0:28	46	2451126		19	20	21	22	23	24	25			20	21	22	23	24	25*	26			29	30	1	2	3	4	5	
	15	16	17	18	●	20	21	4:27	47	2451133		26	27	28	29	30	1	2	Thu $8^h23^m17^p$		27	28	29	30	1	2	3		Athōr 1715	6	7	8	9	10	11	12	Hedār 1991
	22	23	24	25	26	◐	28	0:23	48	2451140	Kislev 5759	3	4	5	6	7	8	9		Month 10 Wù-Yín	**4**	5	6	7	8	9	10	**Xiǎo xuě**		13	14	15	16	17	18	19	
	29	30	1	2	○	4	5	15:19	49	2451147		10	11	12	13	14	15	16[d]			11	12	13	14	15	16	17			20	21	22	23	24	25	26	
December 1998	6	7	8	9	◑	11	12	17:54	50	2451154		17	18	19	20	21	22	23			18	*19*	20	21	22	23	24	*Dà xuě*		27	28	29	30	1	2	3	
	13	14	15	16	17	●	19	22:42	51	2451161		24	25[e]	26[e]	27[e]	28[e]	29[e]	30[e]			25	26	27	28	29	30	1		Koiak 1715	4	5	6	7	8	9	10	Tākhšāš 1991
	20	21	22[e]	23	24	25	◐	10:46	52	2451168	Teveth 5759	1[e]	2[e]	3	4	5	6	7	Fri $21^h8^m0^p$	Month 11* Wù-Yín	2	3	**4**[i]	5	6	7	8	**Dōng zhì**		11	12	13	14	15	16	17	
	27	28	29	30	31	1	○	2:50	53	2451175		8	9	10	11	12	13	14			9	10	11	12	13	14	15			18	19	20	21	22	23	24	

Gregorian:
- [a]New Year
- [b]Spring (19:54)
- [c]Summer (14:02)
- [d]Autumn (5:37)
- [e]Winter (1:56)
- ● New moon
- ◐ First quarter moon
- ○ Full moon
- ◑ Last quarter moon

Hebrew:
- [a]New Year
- [b]Yom Kippur
- [c]Sukkot
- [d]Winter starts
- [e]Ḥanukkah
- [f]Purim
- [g]Passover
- [h]Shavuot
- [i]Fast of Av

Chinese:
- ‡Leap year
- [a]New Year (4696, Tiger)
- [b]Lantern Festival
- [c]Qīngmíng
- [d]Dragon Festival
- [e]Qīqiǎo
- [f]Hungry Ghosts
- [g]Mid-Autumn Festival
- [h]Double-Ninth Festival
- [i]Dōngzhì
- *Start of 60-name cycle

Coptic/Ethiopic:
- ‡Leap year
- [a]New Year
- [b]Building of the Cross
- [c]Christmas
- [d]Jesus's Circumcision
- [e]Epiphany
- [f]Easter
- [g]Mary's Announcement
- [h]Jesus's Transfiguration

PERSIAN (ASTRONOMICAL) 1376/1377

Month	Sun	Mon	Tue	Wed	Thu	Fri	Sat
	7	8	9	10	11	12	13
DEY 1376	14	15	16	17	18	19	20
	21	22	23	24	25	26	27
	28	29	30	1	2	3	4
BAHMAN 1376	5	6	7	8	9	10	11
	12	13	14	15	16	17	18
	19	20	21	22	23	24	25
	26	27	28	29	30	1	2
ESFAND 1376	3	4	5	6	7	8	9
	10	11	12	13	14	15	16
	17	18	19	20	21	22	23
	24	25	26	27	28	29	1[a]
FARVARDIN 1377	2	3	4	5	6	7	8
	9	10	11	12	13[b]	14	15
	16	17	18	19	20	21	22
	23	24	25	26	27	28	29
	30	31	1	2	3	4	5
ORDIBEHEŠT 1377	6	7	8	9	10	11	12
	13	14	15	16	17	18	19
	20	21	22	23	24	25	26
	27	28	29	30	31	1	2
XORDĀD 1377	3	4	5	6	7	8	9
	10	11	12	13	14	15	16
	17	18	19	20	21	22	23
	24	25	26	27	28	29	30
	31	1	2	3	4	5	6
TĪR 1377	7	8	9	10	11	12	13
	14	15	16	17	18	19	20
	21	22	23	24	25	26	27
	28	29	30	31	1	2	3
MORDĀD 1377	4	5	6	7	8	9	10
	11	12	13	14	15	16	17
	18	19	20	21	22	23	24
	25	26	27	28	29	30	31
SHAHRĪVAR 1377	1	2	3	4	5	6	7
	8	9	10	11	12	13	14
	15	16	17	18	19	20	21
	22	23	24	25	26	27	28
	29	30	31	1	2	3	4
MEHR 1377	5	6	7	8	9	10	11
	12	13	14	15	16	17	18
	19	20	21	22	23	24	25
	26	27	28	29	30	1	2
ĀBĀN 1377	3	4	5	6	7	8	9
	10	11	12	13	14	15	16
	17	18	19	20	21	22	23
	24	25	26	27	28	29	30
ĀZAR 1377	1	2	3	4	5	6	7
	8	9	10	11	12	13	14
	15	16	17	18	19	20	21
	22	23	24	25	26	27	28
DEY 1377	29	30	1	2	3	4	5
	6	7	8	9	10	11	12

[a]New Year
[b]Sizdeh Bedar

HINDU LUNAR 2054/2055

Month	Sun	Mon	Tue	Wed	Thu	Fri	Sat
	29	30	1	2	3	4	5
PAUSHA 2054	6	7	8	10	11	12	13
	14	15	16	17	18	19	20
	21	22	22	23	24	25	26
	27	28	29	30	1	2	4
MĀGHA 2054	5	6	7	8	9	10	11
	12	13	14	15	16	17	18
	19	20	21	22	23	24	25
	26	27	28	29[h]	30	1	2
PHĀLGUNA 2054	3	4	5	6	7	9	10
	11	12	13	14	14	15[i]	16
	17	18	19	20	21	22	23
	24	25	26	27	28	29	30
	1[a]	3	4	5	6	7	8
CHAITRA 2055	9[b]	10	11	12	13	14	15
	16	17	17	18	19	20	21
	22	23	24	26	27	28	29
	30	1	2	3	4	5	6
VAIŚĀKHA 2055	7	8	9	10	11	12	13
	14	15	16	17	18	19	20
	21	22	23	24	25	26	27
	29	30	1	2	3	4	5
JYAISHTHA 2055	6	7	8	9	10	11	12
	13	13	14	15	16	17	18
	19	20	22	23	24	25	26
	27	28	29	30	1	2	3
ĀSHĀDHA 2055	4	5	6	7	8	9	10
	11	12	13	14	15	16	17
	18	19	20	21	22	23	25
	26	27	28	29	30	1	2
ŚRĀVANA 2055	3	4	5	6	7	8	9
	10	10	11	12	13	14	15
	16	18	19	20	21	22	23[c]
	24	25	26	27	28	29	30
	1	2	3[d]	4	5	6	7
BHĀDRAPADA 2055	8	9	10	11	12	13	14
	15	16	17	18	19	21	22
	23	24	25	26	27	28	29
	30	1	2	3	4	5	5
ĀŚVINA 2055	6	7	8[e]	9[e]	10[e]	11	12
	14	15	16	17	18	19	20
	21	22	23	24	25	26	27
	28	29	30	1[f]	2	3	4
KĀRTTIKA 2055	5	6	7	8	9	10	11
	12	13	14	15	16	18	19
	20	21	22	23	24	25	26
	27	28	29	29	30	1	2
MĀRGAŚIRA 2055	3	4	5	6	7	8	9
	10[g]	12	13	14	15	16	17
	18	19	20	21	22	23	24
	25	26	27	28	29	30	1
PAUSHA 2055	2	3	4	5	6	7	8
	9	10	11	12	13	14	15

[a]New Year (Bahudhānya)
[b]Birthday of Rāma
[c]Birthday of Krishna
[d]Ganēśa Chaturthī
[e]Dashara
[f]Diwali
[g]Birthday of Vishnu
[h]Night of Śiva
[i]Holi

HINDU SOLAR 1919/1920‡

Month	Sun	Mon	Tue	Wed	Thu	Fri	Sat
	14	15	16	17	18	19	20
PAUSHA 1919	21	22	23	24	25	26	27
	28	29	30	1[b]	2	3	4
MĀGHA 1919	5	6	7	8	9	10	11
	12	13	14	15	16	17	18
	19	20	21	22	23	24	25
	26	27	28	29	1	2	3
PHĀLGUNA 1919	4	5	6	7	8	9	10
	11	12	13	14	15	16	17
	18	19	20	21	22	23	24
	25	26	27	28	29	30	1
CHAITRA 1919	2	3	4	5	6	7	8
	9	10	11	12	13	14	15
	16	17	18	19	20	21	22
	23	24	25	26	27	28	29
	30	1[a]	2	3	4	5	6
VAIŚĀKHA 1920	7	8	9	10	11	12	13
	14	15	16	17	18	19	20
	21	22	23	24	25	26	27
	28	29	30	31	1	2	3
JYAISHTHA 1920	4	5	6	7	8	9	10
	11	12	13	14	15	16	17
	18	19	20	21	22	23	24
	25	26	27	28	29	30	31
	32	1	2	3	4	5	6
ĀSHĀDHA 1920	7	8	9	10	11	12	13
	14	15	16	17	18	19	20
	21	22	23	24	25	26	27
	28	29	30	31	1	2	3
ŚRĀVANA 1920	4	5	6	7	8	9	10
	11	12	13	14	15	16	17
	18	19	20	21	22	23	24
	25	26	27	28	29	30	31
	32	1	2	3	4	5	6
BHĀDRAPADA 1920	7	8	9	10	11	12	13
	14	15	16	17	18	19	20
	21	22	23	24	25	26	27
	28	29	30	31	1	2	3
ĀŚVINA 1920	4	5	6	7	8	9	10
	11	12	13	14	15	16	17
	18	19	20	21	22	23	24
	25	26	27	28	29	30	1
KĀRTTIKA 1920	2	3	4	5	6	7	8
	9	10	11	12	13	14	15
	16	17	18	19	20	21	22
	23	24	25	26	27	28	29
	30	1	2	3	4	5	6
MĀRGAŚIRA 1920	7	8	9	10	11	12	13
	14	15	16	17	18	19	20
	21	22	23	24	25	26	27
	28	29	30	1	2	3	4
PAUSHA 1920	5	6	7	8	9	10	11
	12	13	14	15	16	17	18

‡Leap year
[a]New Year (Khara)
[b]Pongal

ISLAMIC (ASTRONOMICAL) 1418‡/1419

Month	Sun	Mon	Tue	Wed	Thu	Fri	Sat
	28	29	30	1	2	3	4
RAMAḌĀN 1418	5	6	7	8	9	10	11
	12	13	14	15	16	17	18
	19	20	21	22	23	24	25
	26	27	28	29	1[f]	2	3
SHAWWĀL 1418	4	5	6	7	8	9	10
	11	12	13	14	15	16	17
	18	19	20	21	22	23	24
	25	26	27	28	29	30	1
DHU AL-QA'DA 1418	2	3	4	5	6	7	8
	9	10	11	12	13	14	15
	16	17	18	19	20	21	22
	23	24	25	26	27	28	29
	1	2	3	4	5	6	7
DHU AL-ḤIJJA 1418	8	9	10[g]	11	12	13	14
	15	16	17	18	19	20	21
	22	23	24	25	26	27	28
	29	30	1[a]	2	3	4	5
MUḤARRAM 1419	6	7	8	9	10[b]	11	12
	13	14	15	16	17	18	19
	20	21	22	23	24	25	26
	27	28	29	1	2	3	4
ṢAFAR 1419	5	6	7	8	9	10	11
	12	13	14	15	16	17	18
	19	20	21	22	23	24	25
	26	27	28	29	30	1	2
RABĪ' I 1419	3	4	5	6	7	8	9
	10	11	12[c]	13	14	15	16
	17	18	19	20	21	22	23
	24	25	26	27	28	29	1
RABĪ' II 1419	2	3	4	5	6	7	8
	9	10	11	12	13	14	15
	16	17	18	19	20	21	22
	23	24	25	26	27	28	29
	30	1	2	3	4	5	6
JUMĀDĀ I 1419	7	8	9	10	11	12	13
	14	15	16	17	18	19	20
	21	22	23	24	25	26	27
	28	29	1	2	3	4	5
JUMĀDĀ II 1419	6	7	8	9	10	11	12
	13	14	15	16	17	18	19
	20	21	22	23	24	25	26
	27	28	29	30	1	2	3
RAJAB 1419	4	5	6	7	8	9	10
	11	12	13	14	15	16	17
	18	19	20	21	22	23	24
	25	26	27[d]	28	29	1	2
SHA'BĀN 1419	3	4	5	6	7	8	9
	10	11	12	13	14	15	16
	17	18	19	20	21	22	23
	24	25	26	27	28	29	30
RAMAḌĀN 1419	1[e]	2	3	4	5	6	7
	8	9	10	11	12	13	14

‡Leap year
[a]New Year
[b]'Ashūrā'
[c]Prophet's Birthday
[d]Ascent of the Prophet
[e]Start of Ramaḍān
[f]'Id al-Fiṭr
[g]'Id al-'Aḍḥā

GREGORIAN 1998

Julian (Sun)	Sun	Mon	Tue	Wed	Thu	Fri	Sat	Month
Dec 15	28	29	30	31	1	2	3	
	4	5	6	7[a]	8	9	10	JANUARY 1998
Dec 29	11	12	13	14[b]	15	16	17	
	18	19	20	21	22	23	24	
Jan 12	25	26	27	28	29	30	31	
	1	2	3	4	5	6	7	
Jan 26	8	9	10	11	12	13	14	FEBRUARY 1998
	15	16	17	18	19	20	21	
Feb 9	22	23	24	25[c]	26	27	28	
	1	2	3	4	5	6	7	
Feb 23	8[d]	9	10	11	12	13	14	MARCH 1998
	15	16	17	18	19	20	21	
Mar 9	22	23	24	25	26	27	28	
	29	30	31	1	2	3	4	
Mar 23	5	6	7	8	9	10	11	APRIL 1998
	12[e]	13	14	15	16	17	18	
Apr 6	19[f]	20	21	22	23	24	25	
	26	27	28	29	30	1	2	
Apr 20	3	4	5	6	7	8	9	
	10	11	12	13	14	15	16	MAY 1998
May 4	17	18	19	20	21	22	23	
	24	25	26	27	28	29	30	
May 18	31	1	2	3	4	5	6	
	7	8	9	10	11	12	13	JUNE 1998
Jun 1	14	15	16	17	18	19	20	
	21	22	23	24	25	26	27	
Jun 15	28	29	30	1	2	3	4	
	5	6	7	8	9	10	11	JULY 1998
Jun 29	12	13	14	15	16	17	18	
	19	20	21	22	23	24	25	
Jul 13	26	27	28	29	30	31	1	
	2	3	4	5	6	7	8	
Jul 27	9	10	11	12	13	14	15	AUGUST 1998
	16	17	18	19	20	21	22	
Aug 10	23	24	25	26	27	28	29	
	30	31	1	2	3	4	5	
Aug 24	6	7	8	9	10	11	12	SEPTEMBER 1998
	13	14	15	16	17	18	19	
Sep 7	20	21	22	23	24	25	26	
	27	28	29	30	1	2	3	
Sep 21	4	5	6	7	8	9	10	OCTOBER 1998
	11	12	13	14	15	16	17	
Oct 5	18	19	20	21	22	23	24	
	25	26	27	28	29	30	31	
Oct 19	1	2	3	4	5	6	7	
	8	9	10	11	12	13	14	NOVEMBER 1998
Nov 2	15	16	17	18	19	20	21	
	22	23	24	25	26	27	28	
Nov 16	29[g]	30	1	2	3	4	5	
	6	7	8	9	10	11	12	DECEMBER 1998
Nov 30	13	14	15	16	17	18	19	
	20	21	22	23	24	25[h]	26	
Dec 14	27	28	29	30	31	1	2	

[a]Orthodox Christmas
[b]Julian New Year
[c]Ash Wednesday
[d]Feast of Orthodoxy
[e]Easter
[f]Orthodox Easter
[g]Advent
[h]Christmas

1999

Month	Sun	Mon	Tue	Wed	Thu	Fri	Sat	Lunar Phases	ISO WEEK (Mon)	JULIAN DAY (Sun noon)
GREGORIAN 1999										
	27	28	29	30	31	1[a]	○	2:50	53	2451175
JANUARY 1999	3	4	5	6	7	8	◑	14:22	1	2451182
	10	11	12	13	14	15	16		2	2451189
	●	18	19	20	21	22	23	15:46	3	2451196
	◐	25	26	27	28	29	30	19:15	4	2451203
	○	1	2	3	4	5	6	16:07	5	2451210
FEBRUARY 1999	7	◑	9	10	11	12	13	11:58	6	2451217
	14	15	●	17	18	19	20	6:39	7	2451224
	21	22	◐	24	25	26	27	2:43	8	2451231
	28	1	○	3	4	5	6	6:58	9	2451238
MARCH 1999	7	8	9	◑	11	12	13	8:40	10	2451245
	14	15	16	●	18	19	20	18:48	11	2451252
	21[b]	22	23	◐	25	26	27	10:18	12	2451259
	28	29	30	○	1	2	3	22:49	13	2451266
APRIL 1999	4	5	6	7	8	◑	10	2:50	14	2451273
	11	12	13	14	15	●	17	4:22	15	2451280
	18	19	20	21	◐	23	24	19:02	16	2451287
	25	26	27	28	29	○	1	14:55	17	2451294
MAY 1999	2	3	4	5	6	7	◑	17:28	18	2451301
	9	10	11	12	13	14	●	12:05	19	2451308
	16	17	18	19	20	21	◐	5:34	20	2451315
	23	24	25	26	27	28	29		21	2451322
	○	31	1	2	3	4	5	6:40	22	2451329
JUNE 1999	6	◑	8	9	10	11	12	4:20	23	2451336
	●	14	15	16	17	18	19	19:03	24	2451343
	◐	21[c]	22	23	24	25	26	18:13	25	2451350
	27	○	29	30	1	2	3	21:37	26	2451357
JULY 1999	4	5	◑	7	8	9	10	11:57	27	2451364
	11	12	●	14	15	16	17	2:24	28	2451371
	18	19	◐	21	22	23	24	9:00	29	2451378
	25	26	27	○	29	30	31	11:25	30	2451385
AUGUST 1999	1	2	3	◑	5	6	7	17:27	31	2451392
	8	9	10	●	12	13	14	11:08	32	2451399
	15	16	17	18	◐	20	21	1:47	33	2451406
	22	23	24	25	○	27	28	23:48	34	2451413
	29	30	31	1	◑	3	4	22:17	35	2451420
SEPTEMBER 1999	5	6	7	8	●	10	11	22:02	36	2451427
	12	13	14	15	16	◐	18	20:06	37	2451434
	19	20	21	22	23[d]	24	○	10:51	38	2451441
	26	27	28	29	30	1	◑	4:02	39	2451448
OCTOBER 1999	3	4	5	6	7	8	●	11:34	40	2451455
	10	11	12	13	14	15	16		41	2451462
	◐	18	19	20	21	22	23	15:00	42	2451469
	○	25	26	27	28	29	30	21:03	43	2451476
	◑	1	2	3	4	5	6	12:04	44	2451483
NOVEMBER 1999	7	●	9	10	11	12	13	3:53	45	2451490
	14	15	◐	17	18	19	20	9:03	46	2451497
	21	22	○	24	25	26	27	7:04	47	2451504
	28	◑	30	1	2	3	4	23:19	48	2451511
DECEMBER 1999	5	6	●	8	9	10	11	22:31	49	2451518
	12	13	14	15	◐	17	18	0:50	50	2451525
	19	20	21	○[e]	23	24	25	17:32	51	2451532
	26	27	28	◑	30	31	1	14:04	52	2451539

ISO WEEK	HEBREW 5759/5760‡	Sun	Mon	Tue	Wed	Thu	Fri	Sat	Molad
53		8	9	10	11	12	13	14	
1	TEVETH 5759	15	16	17	18	19	20	21	
2		22	23	24	25	26	27	28	
3		29	1	2	3	4	5	6	Sun $9^{h}52^{m}1^{p}$
4	SHEVAT 5759	7	8	9	10	11	12	13	
5		14	15	16	17	18	19	20	
6		21	22	23	24	25	26	27	
7		28	29	30	1	2	3	4	Mon $22^{h}36^{m}2^{p}$
8	ADAR 5759	5	6	7	8	9	10	11	
9		12	13	14[f]	15	16	17	18	
10		19	20	21	22	23	24	25	
11		26	27	28	29	1	2	3	Wed $11^{h}20^{m}3^{p}$
12	NISAN 5759	4	5	6	7	8	9	10	
13		11	12	13	14	15[g]	16	17	
14		18	19	20	21	22	23	24	
15		25	26	27	28	29	30	1	Fri $0^{h}4^{m}4^{p}$
16	IYYAR 5759	2	3	4	5	6	7	8	
17		9	10	11	12	13	14	15	
18		16	17	18	19	20	21	22	
19		23	24	25	26	27	28	29	
20		1	2	3	4	5	6[h]	7	Sat $12^{h}48^{m}5^{p}$
21	SIVAN 5759	8	9	10	11	12	13	14	
22		15	16	17	18	19	20	21	
23		22	23	24	25	26	27	28	
24		29	30	1	2	3	4	5	Mon $1^{h}32^{m}6^{p}$
25	TAMMUZ 5759	6	7	8	9	10	11	12	
26		13	14	15	16	17	18	19	
27		20	21	22	23	24	25	26	
28		27	28	29	1	2	3	4	Tue $14^{h}16^{m}7^{p}$
29	AV 5759	5	6	7	8	9[i]	10	11	
30		12	13	14	15	16	17	18	
31		19	20	21	22	23	24	25	
32		26	27	28	29	30	1	2	Thu $3^{h}0^{m}8^{p}$
33	ELUL 5759	3	4	5	6	7	8	9	
34		10	11	12	13	14	15	16	
35		17	18	19	20	21	22	23	
36		24	25	26	27	28	29	1[a]	Fri $15^{h}44^{m}9^{p}$
37	TISHRI 5760	2[a]	3	4	5	6	7	8	
38		9	10[b]	11	12	13	14	15[c]	
39		16	17	18	19	20	21	22	
40		23	24	25	26	27	28	29	
41		30	1	2	3	4	5	6	Sun $4^{h}28^{m}10^{p}$
42	HESHVAN 5760	7	8	9	10	11	12	13	
43		14	15	16	17	18	19	20	
44		21	22	23	24	25	26	27	
45		28	29	30	1	2	3	4	Mon $17^{h}12^{m}11^{p}$
46	KISLEV 5760	5	6	7	8	9	10	11	
47		12	13	14	15	16	17	18	
48		19	20	21	22	23	24	25[e]	
49		26[e]	27[d,e]	28[e]	29[e]	30[e]	1[e]	2[e]	Wed $5^{h}56^{m}12^{p}$
50	TEVETH 5760	3	4	5	6	7	8	9	
51		10	11	12	13	14	15	16	
52		17	18	19	20	21	22	23	

ISO WEEK	CHINESE Wù-Yín‡/Jǐ-Mǎo	Sun	Mon	Tue	Wed	Thu	Fri	Sat	Solar Term
53	MONTH 11* Wù-Yín	9	10	11	12	13	14	15	
1		16	17	18	*19*	20	21	22	Xiǎo hán
2		23	24	25*	26	27	28	29	
3	MONTH 12 Wù-Yín	1	2	3	**4**	5	6	7	**Dà hán**
4		8	9	10	11	12	13	14	
5		15	16	17	18	*19*	20	21	Lì chūn
6		22	23	24	25	26	27	28	
7		29	30	1[a]	2	3	**4**	5	**Yǔ shuǐ**
8	MONTH 1 Jǐ-Mǎo	6	7	8	9	10	11	12	
9		13	14	15[b]	16	17	18	*19*	Jīng zhé
10		20	21	22	23	24	25	26*	
11		27	28	29	30	1	2	3	
12	MONTH 2 Jǐ-Mǎo	**4**	5	6	7	8	9	10	**Chūn fēn**
13		11	12	13	14	15	16	17	
14		18	*19*[c]	20	21	22	23	24	Qīng míng
15		25	26	27	28	29	1	2	
16	MONTH 3 Jǐ-Mǎo	3	4	**5**	6	7	8	9	**Gǔ yǔ**
17		10	11	12	13	14	15	16	
18		17	18	19	20	*21*	22	23	Lì xià
19		24	25	26	27*	28	29	1	
20	MONTH 4 Jǐ-Mǎo	2	3	4	5	6	**7**	8	**Xiǎo mǎn**
21		9	10	11	12	13	14	15	
22		16	17	18	19	20	21	22	
23		*23*	24	25	26	27	28	29	Máng zhòng
24		30	1	2	3	4	5[d]	6	
25	MONTH 5 Jǐ-Mǎo	7	8	**9**	10	11	12	13	**Xià zhì**
26		14	15	16	17	18	19	20	
27		21	22	23	*24*	25	26	27	Xiǎo shǔ
28		28*	29	1	2	3	4	5	
29	MONTH 6 Jǐ-Mǎo	6	7	8	9	10	**11**	12	**Dà shǔ**
30		13	14	15	16	17	18	19	
31		20	21	22	23	24	25	26	
32		*27*	28	29	1	2	3	4	Lì qiū
33	MONTH 7 Jǐ-Mǎo	5	6	7[e]	8	9	10	11	
34		12	**13**	14	15[f]	16	17	18	**Chǔ shǔ**
35		19	20	21	22	23	24	25	
36		26	27	28	29	30*	1	2	Bái lù
37	MONTH 8 Jǐ-Mǎo	3	4	5	6	7	8	9	
38		10	11	12	13	**14**	15[g]	16	**Qiū fēn**
39		17	18	19	20	21	22	23	
40		24	25	26	27	28	29	*1*	Hán lù
41	MONTH 9 Jǐ-Mǎo	2	3	4	5	6	7	8	
42		9[h]	10	11	12	13	14	15	
43		**16**	17	18	19	20	21	22	**Shuāng jiàng**
44		23	24	25	26	27	28	29	
45		30	*1**	2	3	4	5	6	Lì dōng
46	MONTH 10 Jǐ-Mǎo	7	8	9	10	11	12	13	
47		14	15	**16**	17	18	19	20	**Xiǎo xuě**
48		21	22	23	24	25	26	27	
49		28	29	*30*	1	2	3	4	Dà xuě
50	MONTH 11 Jǐ-Mǎo	5	6	7	8	9	10	11	
51		12	13	14	**15**[i]	16	17	18	**Dōng zhì**
52		19	20	21	22	23	24	25	

ISO WEEK	COPTIC 1715‡/1716	Sun	Mon	Tue	Wed	Thu	Fri	Sat	ETHIOPIC 1991‡/1992
53		18	19	20	21	22	23	24	TĀKHŚĀŚ 1991
1	KOIAK 1715	25	26	27	28	29[c]	30	1	
2		2	3	4	5	6[d]	7	8	
3	TŌBE 1715	9	10	11[e]	12	13	14	15	ṬER 1991
4		16	17	18	19	20	21	22	
5		23	24	25	26	27	28	29	
6		30	1	2	3	4	5	6	
7	MESHIR 1715	7	8	9	10	11	12	13	YAKĀTIT 1991
8		14	15	16	17	18	19	20	
9		21	22	23	24	25	26	27	
10		28	29	30	1	2	3	4	
11	PAREMOTEP 1715	5	6	7	8	9	10	11	MAGĀBIT 1991
12		12	13	14	15	16	17	18	
13		19	20	21	22	23	24	25	
14		26	27	28	29	30	1	2	
15	PARMOUTE 1715	3[f]	4	5	6	7	8	9	MIYĀZYĀ 1991
16		10	11	12	13	14	15	16	
17		17	18	19	20	21	22	23	
18		24	25	26	27	28	29[g]	30	
19		1	2	3	4	5	6	7	
20	PASHONS 1715	8	9	10	11	12	13	14	GENBOT 1991
21		15	16	17	18	19	20	21	
22		22	23	24	25	26	27	28	
23		29	30	1	2	3	4	5	
24	PAŌNE 1715	6	7	8	9	10	11	12	SANĒ 1991
25		13	14	15	16	17	18	19	
26		20	21	22	23	24	25	26	
27		27	28	29	30	1	2	3	
28	EPĒP 1715	4	5	6	7	8	9	10	ḤAMLĒ 1991
29		11	12	13	14	15	16	17	
30		18	19	20	21	22	23	24	
31		25	26	27	28	29	30	1	
32	MESORĒ 1715	2	3	4	5	6	7	8	NAḤASĒ 1991
33		9	10	11	12	13[h]	14	15	
34		16	17	18	19	20	21	22	
35		23	24	25	26	27	28	29	
36	EPAG. 1715	30	1	2	3	4	5	6	PĀG. 1991
37	THOOUT 1716	1[a]	2	3	4	5	6	7	MASKARAM 1992
38		8	9	10	11	12	13	14	
39		15	16	17[b]	18	19	20	21	
40		22	23	24	25	26	27	28	
41		29	30	1	2	3	4	5	
42	PAOPE 1716	6	7	8	9	10	11	12	ṬEQEMT 1992
43		13	14	15	16	17	18	19	
44		20	21	22	23	24	25	26	
45		27	28	29	30	1	2	3	
46	ATHŌR 1716	4	5	6	7	8	9	10	ḪEDĀR 1992
47		11	12	13	14	15	16	17	
48		18	19	20	21	22	23	24	
49		25	26	27	28	29	30	1	
50	KOIAK 1716	2	3	4	5	6	7	8	TĀKHŚĀŚ 1992
51		9	10	11	12	13	14	15	
52		16	17	18	19	20	21	22	

Gregorian notes:
[a]New Year
[b]Spring (1:46)
[c]Summer (19:49)
[d]Autumn (11:31)
[e]Winter (7:44)
● New moon
◐ First quarter moon
○ Full moon
◑ Last quarter moon

Hebrew notes:
‡Leap year
[a]New Year
[b]Yom Kippur
[c]Sukkot
[d]Winter starts
[e]Ḥanukkah
[f]Purim
[g]Passover
[h]Shavuot
[i]Fast of Av

Chinese notes:
‡Leap year
[a]New Year (4697, Hare)
[b]Lantern Festival
[c]Qīngmíng
[d]Dragon Festival
[e]Qīqiǎo
[f]Hungry Ghosts
[g]Mid-Autumn Festival
[h]Double-Ninth Festival
[i]Dōngzhì
*Start of 60-name cycle

Coptic/Ethiopic notes:
‡Leap year
[a]New Year
[b]Building of the Cross
[c]Christmas
[d]Jesus's Circumcision
[e]Epiphany
[f]Easter
[g]Mary's Announcement
[h]Jesus's Transfiguration

PERSIAN (ASTRONOMICAL) 1377/1378

Month	Sun	Mon	Tue	Wed	Thu	Fri	Sat
	6	7	8	9	10	11	12
DEY 1377	13	14	15	16	17	18	19
	20	21	22	23	24	25	26
	27	28	29	30	1	2	3
BAHMAN 1377	4	5	6	7	8	9	10
	11	12	13	14	15	16	17
	18	19	20	21	22	23	24
	25	26	27	28	29	30	1
ESFAND 1377	2	3	4	5	6	7	8
	9	10	11	12	13	14	15
	16	17	18	19	20	21	22
	23	24	25	26	27	28	29
FARVARDĪN 1378	1[a]	2	3	4	5	6	7
	8	9	10	11	12	13[b]	14
	15	16	17	18	19	20	21
	22	23	24	25	26	27	28
	29	30	31	1	2	3	4
ORDĪBEHEŠT 1378	5	6	7	8	9	10	11
	12	13	14	15	16	17	18
	19	20	21	22	23	24	25
	26	27	28	29	30	31	1
XORDĀD 1378	2	3	4	5	6	7	8
	9	10	11	12	13	14	15
	16	17	18	19	20	21	22
	23	24	25	26	27	28	29
	30	31	1	2	3	4	5
TĪR 1378	6	7	8	9	10	11	12
	13	14	15	16	17	18	19
	20	21	22	23	24	25	26
	27	28	29	30	31	1	2
MORDĀD 1378	3	4	5	6	7	8	9
	10	11	12	13	14	15	16
	17	18	19	20	21	22	23
	24	25	26	27	28	29	30
	31	1	2	3	4	5	6
SHAHRĪVAR 1378	7	8	9	10	11	12	13
	14	15	16	17	18	19	20
	21	22	23	24	25	26	27
	28	29	30	31	1	2	3
MEHR 1378	4	5	6	7	8	9	10
	11	12	13	14	15	16	17
	18	19	20	21	22	23	24
	25	26	27	28	29	30	1
ABĀN 1378	2	3	4	5	6	7	8
	9	10	11	12	13	14	15
	16	17	18	19	20	21	22
	23	24	25	26	27	28	29
	30	1	2	3	4	5	6
ĀZAR 1378	7	8	9	10	11	12	13
	14	15	16	17	18	19	20
	21	22	23	24	25	26	27
	28	29	30	1	2	3	4
DEY 1378	5	6	7	8	9	10	11

[a]New Year
[b]Sizdeh Bedar

HINDU LUNAR 2055/2056‡

Month	Sun	Mon	Tue	Wed	Thu	Fri	Sat
	9	10	11	12	13	14	15
PAUSHA 2055	**16**	18	19	20	21	22	*22*
	23	24	25	26	27	28	29
	30	1	2	3	4	5	6
MĀGHA 2055	7	8	**9**	11	12	13	14
	15	16	17	18	19	20	21
	22	23	24	*24*	25	26	27
	28[h]	29	30	1	2	**3**	5
PHĀLGUNA 2055	6	7	8	9	10	11	12
	13	14	15[i]	16	17	18	19
	20	21	22	23	24	25	26
	27	28	29	30	1[a]	2	3
CHAITRA 2056	4	5	6	7	8[b]	10	11
	12	13	14	15	16	17	*17*
	18	19	20	21	22	23	24
	25	26	27	28	29	30	**1**
VAIŚĀKHA 2056	3	4	5	6	7	8	9
	10	11	12	13	14	15	16
	17	18	19	20	21	22	23
	24	25	26	27	28	29	30
LEAP JYAISHṬHA 2056	1	2	3	4	**5**	7	8
	9	10	11	12	*12*	13	14
	15	16	17	18	19	20	21
	22	23	24	25	26	27	**28**
	30	1	2	3	4	5	6
JYAISHṬHA 2056	7	8	9	10	11	12	13
	14	15	16	17	18	19	20
	21	22	23	24	25	26	27
	28	29	30	**1**	3	4	5
ĀSHĀḌHA 2056	6	7	8	9	*9*	10	11
	12	13	14	15	16	17	18
	19	20	21	22	**23**	25	26
	27	28	29	30	1	2	3
ŚRĀVAṆA 2056	4	5	6	7	8	9	10
	11	12	13	14	15	16	17
	18	19	20	21	22	23[c]	24
	25	26	**27**	29	30	1	2
BHĀDRAPADA 2056	3	4[d]	5	6	*6*	7	8
	9	10	11	12	13	14	15
	16	17	18	19	**20**	22	23
	24	25	26	27	28	29	30
ĀŚVINA 2056	1	2	3	4	5	6	7
	8[e]	9[e]	10[e]	*10*[e]	11	**12**	14
	15	16	17	18	19	20	21
	22	23	24	**25**	27	28	29
	29	30	1[f]	2	3	4	5
KĀRTTIKA 2056	6	7	8	9	10	11	12
	13	14	15	16	**17**	19	20
	21	22	23	24	25	26	27
	28	29	30	1	2	*2*	3
MĀRGAŚĪRA 2056	4	5	6	7	8	9	10
	11[g]	13	14	15	16	17	18
	19	20	21	22	23	24	25

‡Leap year
[a]New Year (Pramāthin)
[b]Birthday of Rāma
[c]Birthday of Krishna
[d]Gaṇēśa Chaturthī
[e]Dashara
[f]Diwali
[g]Birthday of Vishnu
[h]Night of Śiva
[i]Holi

HINDU SOLAR 1920‡/1921

Month	Sun	Mon	Tue	Wed	Thu	Fri	Sat
PAUSHA 1920	12	13	14	15	16	17	18
	19	20	21	22	23	24	25
	26	27	28	29	1[b]	2	3
MĀGHA 1920	4	5	6	7	8	9	10
	11	12	13	14	15	16	17
	18	19	20	21	22	23	24
	25	26	27	28	29	30	1
PHĀLGUNA 1920	2	3	4	5	6	7	8
	9	10	11	12	13	14	15
	16	17	18	19	20	21	22
	23	24	25	26	27	28	29
	1	2	3	4	5	6	7
CHAITRA 1920	8	9	10	11	12	13	14
	15	16	17	18	19	20	21
	22	23	24	25	26	27	28
	29	30	31	1[a]	2	3	4
VAIŚĀKHA 1921	5	6	7	8	9	10	11
	12	13	14	15	16	17	18
	19	20	21	22	23	24	25
	26	27	28	29	30	31	1
JYAISHṬHA 1921	2	3	4	5	6	7	8
	9	10	11	12	13	14	15
	16	17	18	19	20	21	22
	23	24	25	26	27	28	29
	30	31	1	2	3	4	5
ĀSHĀḌHA 1921	6	7	8	9	10	11	12
	13	14	15	16	17	18	19
	20	21	22	23	24	25	26
	27	28	29	30	31	32	1
ŚRĀVAṆA 1921	2	3	4	5	6	7	8
	9	10	11	12	13	14	15
	16	17	18	19	20	21	22
	23	24	25	26	27	28	29
	30	31	1	2	3	4	5
BHĀDRAPADA 1921	6	7	8	9	10	11	12
	13	14	15	16	17	18	19
	20	21	22	23	24	25	26
	27	28	29	30	31	1	2
ĀŚVINA 1921	3	4	5	6	7	8	9
	10	11	12	13	14	15	16
	17	18	19	20	21	22	23
	24	25	26	27	28	29	30
	31	1	2	3	4	5	6
KĀRTTIKA 1921	7	8	9	10	11	12	13
	14	15	16	17	18	19	20
	21	22	23	24	25	26	27
	28	29	30	1	2	3	4
MĀRGAŚĪRA 1921	5	6	7	8	9	10	11
	12	13	14	15	16	17	18
	19	20	21	22	23	24	25
	26	27	28	29	1	2	3
PAUSHA 1921	4	5	6	7	8	9	10
	11	12	13	14	15	16	17

‡Leap year
[a]New Year (Nandana)
[b]Pongal

ISLAMIC (ASTRONOMICAL) 1419/1420‡

Month	Sun	Mon	Tue	Wed	Thu	Fri	Sat
RAMAḌĀN 1419	8	9	10	11	12	13	14
	15	16	17	18	19	20	21
	22	23	24	25	26	27	28
	29	30	1[f]	2	3	4	5
SHAWWĀL 1419	6	7	8	9	10	11	12
	13	14	15	16	17	18	19
	20	21	22	23	24	25	26
	27	28	29	30	1	2	3
DHU AL-QA'DA 1419	4	5	6	7	8	9	10
	11	12	13	14	15	16	17
	18	19	20	21	22	23	24
	25	26	27	28	29	1	2
DHU AL-ḤIJJA 1419	3	4	5	6	7	8	9
	10[g]	11	12	13	14	15	16
	17	18	19	20	21	22	23
	24	25	26	27	28	29	1[a]
MUḤARRAM 1420	2	3	4	5	6	7	8
	9	10[b]	11	12	13	14	15
	16	17	18	19	20	21	22
	23	24	25	26	27	28	29
	30	1	2	3	4	5	6
ṢAFAR 1420	7	8	9	10	11	12	13
	14	15	16	17	18	19	20
	21	22	23	24	25	26	27
	28	29	1	2	3	4	5
RABĪ' I 1420	6	7	8	9	10	11	12[c]
	13	14	15	16	17	18	19
	20	21	22	23	24	25	26
	27	28	29	1	2	3	4
RABĪ' II 1420	5	6	7	8	9	10	11
	12	13	14	15	16	17	18
	19	20	21	22	23	24	25
	26	27	28	29	30	1	2
JUMĀDĀ I 1420	3	4	5	6	7	8	9
	10	11	12	13	14	15	16
	17	18	19	20	21	22	23
	24	25	26	27	28	29	1
JUMĀDĀ II 1420	2	3	4	5	6	7	8
	9	10	11	12	13	14	15
	16	17	18	19	20	21	22
	23	24	25	26	27	28	29
	30	1	2	3	4	5	6
RAJAB 1420	7	8	9	10	11	12	13
	14	15	16	17	18	19	20
	21	22	23	24	25	26	27[d]
	28	29	1	2	3	4	5
SHA'BĀN 1420	6	7	8	9	10	11	12
	13	14	15	16	17	18	19
	20	21	22	23	24	25	26
	27	28	29	30	1[e]	2	3
RAMAḌĀN 1420	4	5	6	7	8	9	10
	11	12	13	14	15	16	17
	18	19	20	21	22	23	24

‡Leap year
[a]New Year
[b]'Ashūrā'
[c]Prophet's Birthday
[d]Ascent of the Prophet
[e]Start of Ramaḍān
[f]'Id al-Fiṭr
[g]'Id al-'Aḍḥā

GREGORIAN 1999

Julian (Sun)	Sun	Mon	Tue	Wed	Thu	Fri	Sat	Month
Dec 14	27	28	29	30	31	1	2	
	3	4	5	6	7[a]	8	9	JANUARY 1999
Dec 28	10	11	12	13	14[b]	15	16	
	17	18	19	20	21	22	23	
Jan 11	24	25	26	27	28	29	30	
	31	1	2	3	4	5	6	
Jan 25	7	8	9	10	11	12	13	FEBRUARY 1999
	14	15	16	17[c]	18	19	20	
Feb 8	21	22	23	24	25	26	27	
	28[d]	1	2	3	4	5	6	
Feb 22	7	8	9	10	11	12	13	MARCH 1999
	14	15	16	17	18	19	20	
Mar 8	21	22	23	24	25	26	27	
	28	29	30	31	1	2	3	
Mar 22	4[e]	5	6	7	8	9	10	APRIL 1999
	11[f]	12	13	14	15	16	17	
Apr 5	18	19	20	21	22	23	24	
	25	26	27	28	29	30	1	
Apr 19	2	3	4	5	6	7	8	MAY 1999
	9	10	11	12	13	14	15	
May 3	16	17	18	19	20	21	22	
	23	24	25	26	27	28	29	
May 17	30	31	1	2	3	4	5	
	6	7	8	9	10	11	12	JUNE 1999
May 31	13	14	15	16	17	18	19	
	20	21	22	23	24	25	26	
Jun 14	27	28	29	30	1	2	3	
	4	5	6	7	8	9	10	JULY 1999
Jun 28	11	12	13	14	15	16	17	
	18	19	20	21	22	23	24	
Jul 12	25	26	27	28	29	30	31	
	1	2	3	4	5	6	7	AUGUST 1999
Jul 26	8	9	10	11	12	13	14	
	15	16	17	18	19	20	21	
Aug 9	22	23	24	25	26	27	28	
	29	30	31	1	2	3	4	
Aug 23	5	6	7	8	9	10	11	SEPTEMBER 1999
	12	13	14	15	16	17	18	
Sep 6	19	20	21	22	23	24	25	
	26	27	28	29	30	1	2	
Sep 20	3	4	5	6	7	8	9	OCTOBER 1999
	10	11	12	13	14	15	16	
Oct 4	17	18	19	20	21	22	23	
	24	25	26	27	28	29	30	
Oct 18	31	1	2	3	4	5	6	
	7	8	9	10	11	12	13	NOVEMBER 1999
Nov 1	14	15	16	17	18	19	20	
	21	22	23	24	25	26	27	
Nov 15	28[g]	29	30	1	2	3	4	
	5	6	7	8	9	10	11	DECEMBER 1999
Nov 29	12	13	14	15	16	17	18	
	19	20	21	22	23	24	25[h]	
Dec 13	26	27	28	29	30	31	1	

[a]Orthodox Christmas
[b]Julian New Year
[c]Ash Wednesday
[d]Feast of Orthodoxy
[e]Easter
[f]Orthodox Easter
[g]Advent
[h]Christmas

2000

GREGORIAN 2000‡	Sun Mon Tue Wed Thu Fri Sat	Lunar Phases	ISO WEEK (Mon)	JULIAN DAY (Sun noon)	HEBREW 5760‡/5761	Sun Mon Tue Wed Thu Fri Sat	Molad	CHINESE Jǐ-Mǎo/Gēng-Chén	Sun Mon Tue Wed Thu Fri Sat	Solar Term	COPTIC 1716/1717	Sun Mon Tue Wed Thu Fri Sat	ETHIOPIC 1992/1993
JANUARY 2000	26 27 28 ◑ 30 31 1[a]	14:04	52	2451539	TEVETH 5760	17 18 19 20 21 22 23		MONTH 11 Jǐ-Mǎo	19 20 21 22 23 24 25		KOIAK 1716	16 17 18 19 20 21 22	TĀḪŚĀŚ 1992
	2 3 4 5 ● 7 8	18:13	1	2451546	SHEVAT 5760	24 25 26 27 28 29 1	Thu 18h40m13p	MONTH 12 Jǐ-Mǎo	26 27 28 29 30 1* 2	Xiǎo hán		23 24 25 26 27 28 29[c]	
	9 10 11 12 13 ◐ 15	13:34	2	2451553		2 3 4 5 6 7 8			3 4 5 6 7 8 9		TŌBE 1716	30 1 2 3 4 5 6[d]	ṬER 1992
	16 17 18 19 20 ○ 22	4:41	3	2451560		9 10 11 12 13 14 15			10 11 12 13 14 15 16	Dà hán		7 8 9 10 11[e] 12 13	
	23 24 25 26 27 ◑ 29	7:57	4	2451567		16 17 18 19 20 21 22			17 18 19 20 21 22 23			14 15 16 17 18 19 20	
FEBRUARY 2000	30 31 1 2 3 4 ●	13:03	5	2451574		23 24 25 26 27 28 29		MONTH 1 Gēng-Chén	24 25 26 27 28 29 1[a]	Lì chūn		21 22 23 24 25 26 27	
	6 7 8 9 10 11 ◐	23:21	6	2451581	ADAR I 5760	30 1 2 3 4 5 6	Sat 7h24m14p		2 3 4 5 6 7 8		MESHIR 1716	28 29 30 1 2 3 4	YAKĀTIT 1992
	13 14 15 16 17 18 ○	16:27	7	2451588		7 8 9 10 11 12 13			9 10 11 12 13 14 15[b]	Yǔ shuǐ		5 6 7 8 9 10 11	
	20 21 22 23 24 25 26		8	2451595		14 15 16 17 18 19 20			16 17 18 19 20 21 22			12 13 14 15 16 17 18	
MARCH 2000	◑ 28 29 1 2 3 4	3:53	9	2451602		21 22 23 24 25 26 27			23 24 25 26 27 28 29			19 20 21 22 23 24 25	
	5 ● 7 8 9 10 11	5:17	10	2451609	ADAR II 5760	28 29 30 1 2 3 4	Sun 20h8m15p	MONTH 2 Gēng-Chén	30 1 2* 3 4 5 6	Jīng zhé	PAREMOTEP 1716	26 27 28 29 30 1 2	MAGĀBIT 1992
	12 ◐ 14 15 16 17 18	6:59	11	2451616		5 6 7 8 9 10 11			7 8 9 10 11 12 13			3 4 5 6 7 8 9	
	19 ○[b] 21 22 23 24 25	4:44	12	2451623		12 13 14[f] 15 16 17 18			14 15 16 17 18 19 20	Chūn fēn		10 11 12 13 14 15 16	
APRIL 2000	26 27 ◑ 29 30 31 1	0:21	13	2451630		19 20 21 22 23 24 25			21 22 23 24 25 26 27			17 18 19 20 21 22 23	
	2 3 ● 5 6 7 8	18:12	14	2451637	NISAN 5760	26 27 28 29 1 2 3	Tue 8h52m16p	MONTH 3 Gēng-Chén	28 29 30[c] 1 2 3 4	Qīng míng		24 25 26 27 28 29 30	
	9 10 ◐ 12 13 14 15	13:30	15	2451644		4 5 6 7 8 9 10			5 6 7 8 9 10 11		PARMOUTE 1716	1 2 3 4 5 6 7	MIYĀZYĀ 1992
	16 17 ○ 19 20 21 22	17:41	16	2451651		11 12 13 14 15[g] 16 17			12 13 14 15 16 17 18	Gǔ yǔ		8 9 10 11 12 13 14	
	23 24 25 ◑ 27 28 29	19:30	17	2451658		18 19 20 21 22 23 24			19 20 21 22 23 24 25			15 16 17 18 19 20 21	
MAY 2000	30 1 2 3 ● 5 6	4:12	18	2451665	IYAR 5760	25 26 27 28 29 30 1	Wed 21h36m17p	MONTH 4 Gēng-Chén	26 27 28 29 1 2 3*	Lì xià		22[f] 23 24 25 26 27 28	
	7 8 9 ◐ 11 12 13	20:01	19	2451672		2 3 4 5 6 7 8			4 5 6 7 8 9 10		PASHONS 1716	29[g] 30 1 2 3 4 5	GENBOT 1992
	14 15 16 17 ○ 19 20	7:34	20	2451679		9 10 11 12 13 14 15			11 12 13 14 15 16 17			6 7 8 9 10 11 12	
	21 22 23 24 25 ◑ 27	11:55	21	2451686		16 17 18 19 20 21 22			18 19 20 21 22 23 24	Xiǎo mǎn		13 14 15 16 17 18 19	
JUNE 2000	28 29 30 31 1 ● 3	12:14	22	2451693		23 24 25 26 27 28 29		MONTH 5 Gēng-Chén	25 26 27 28 29 1 2			20 21 22 23 24 25 26	
	4 5 6 7 8 ◐ 10	3:29	23	2451700	SIVAN 5760	1 2 3 4 5 6[h] 7	Fri 10h21m0p		3 4 5[d] 6 7 8 9	Máng zhòng	PAŌNE 1716	27 28 29 30 1 2 3	SANĒ 1992
	11 12 13 14 15 ○ 17	22:27	24	2451707		8 9 10 11 12 13 14			10 11 12 13 14 15 16			4 5 6 7 8 9 10	
	18 19 20 21[c] 22 23 24		25	2451714		15 16 17 18 19 20 21			17 18 19 20 21 22 23	Xià zhì		11 12 13 14 15 16 17	
JULY 2000	◑ 26 27 28 29 30 ●	1:00 19:20	26	2451721		22 23 24 25 26 27 28			24 25 26 27 28 29 30			18 19 20 21 22 23 24	
	2 3 4 5 6 7 ◐	12:53	27	2451728	TAMMUZ 5760	29 30 1 2 3 4 5	Sat 23h5m1p	MONTH 6 Gēng-Chén	1 2 3 4* 5 6 7	Xiǎo shǔ	EPĒP 1716	25 26 27 28 29 30 1	ḤAMLĒ 1992
	9 10 11 12 13 14 15		28	2451735		6 7 8 9 10 11 12			8 9 10 11 12 13 14			2 3 4 5 6 7 8	
	○ 17 18 19 20 21 22	13:55	29	2451742		13 14 15 16 17 18 19			15 16 17 18 19 20 21	Dà shǔ		9 10 11 12 13 14 15	
	23 ◑ 25 26 27 28 29	11:02	30	2451749		20 21 22 23 24 25 26			22 23 24 25 26 27 28			16 17 18 19 20 21 22	
AUGUST 2000	30 ● 1 2 3 4 5	2:25	31	2451756	AV 5760	27 28 29 1 2 3 4	Mon 11h49m2p	MONTH 7 Gēng-Chén	29 1 2 3 4 5 6			23 24 25 26 27 28 29	
	6 ◐ 8 9 10 11 12	1:02	32	2451763		5 6 7 8 9[i] 10 11			7[e] 8 9 10 11 12 13	Lì qiū	MESORĒ 1716	30 1 2 3 4 5 6	NAḤASĒ 1992
	13 14 ○ 16 17 18 19	5:13	33	2451770		12 13 14 15 16 17 18			14 15[f] 16 17 18 19 20			7 8 9 10 11 12 13[h]	
	20 21 ◑ 23 24 25 26	18:51	34	2451777		19 20 21 22 23 24 25			21 22 23 24 25 26 27	Chǔ shǔ		14 15 16 17 18 19 20	
SEPTEMBER 2000	27 28 ● 30 31 1 2	10:19	35	2451784	ELUL 5760	26 27 28 29 30 1 2	Wed 0h33m3p	MONTH 8 Gēng-Chén	28 29 1 2 3 4 5			21 22 23 24 25 26 27	
	3 4 ◐ 6 7 8 9	16:27	36	2451791		3 4 5 6 7 8 9			6* 7 8 9 10 11 12	Bái lù	EPAG. 1716	28 29 30 1 2 3 4	PĀG. 1992
	10 11 12 ○ 14 15 16	19:37	37	2451798		10 11 12 13 14 15 16			13 14 15[g] 16 17 18 19		THOOUT 1717	5 1[a] 2 3 4 5 6	MASKARAM 1993
	17 18 19 20 ◑ 22[d] 23	1:28	38	2451805		17 18 19 20 21 22 23			20 21 22 23 24 25 26	Qiū fēn		7 8 9 10 11 12 13	
	24 25 26 ● 28 29 30	19:53	39	2451812	TISHRI 5761	24 25 26 27 28 29 1[a]	Thu 13h17m4p	MONTH 9 Gēng-Chén	27 28 29 30 1 2 3			14 15 16 17[b] 18 19 20	
OCTOBER 2000	1 2 3 4 ◐ 6 7	10:59	40	2451819		2[a] 3 4 5 6 7 8			4 5 6 7 8 9[h] 10			21 22 23 24 25 26 27	
	8 9 10 11 12 ○ 14	8:53	41	2451826		9 10[b] 11 12 13 14 15[c]			11 12 13 14 15 16 17	Hán lù	PAOPE 1717	28 29 30 1 2 3 4	ṬEQEMT 1993
	15 16 17 18 19 ◑ 21	7:59	42	2451833		16 17 18 19 20 21 22			18 19 20 21 22 23 24			5 6 7 8 9 10 11	
	22 23 24 25 26 ● 28	7:58	43	2451840		23 24 25 26 27 28 29		MONTH 10 Gēng-Chén	25 26 27 28 29 1 2	Shuāng jiàng		12 13 14 15 16 17 18	
NOVEMBER 2000	29 30 31 1 2 3 ◐	7:27	44	2451847	HESHVAN 5761	30 1 2 3 4 5 6	Sat 2h1m5p		3 4 5 6 7* 8 9			19 20 21 22 23 24 25	
	5 6 7 8 9 10 ○	21:15	45	2451854		7 8 9 10 11 12 13			10 11 12 13 14 15 16	Lì dōng	ATHŌR 1717	26 27 28 29 30 1 2	ḪEDĀR 1993
	12 13 14 15 16 17 ◑	15:25	46	2451861		14 15 16 17 18 19 20			17 18 19 20 21 22 23			3 4 5 6 7 8 9	
	19 20 21 22 23 24 ●	23:11	47	2451868		21 22 23 24 25 26 27			24 25 26 27 28 29 30	Xiǎo xuě		10 11 12 13 14 15 16	
DECEMBER 2000	26 27 28 29 30 1 2		48	2451875	KISLEV 5761	28 29 1 2 3 4 5	Sun 14h45m6p	MONTH 11 Gēng-Chén	1 2 3 4 5 6 7			17 18 19 20 21 22 23	
	3 ◐ 5 6 7 8 9	3:55	49	2451882		6 7 8[d] 9 10 11 12			8 9 10 11 12 13 14	Dà xuě		24 25 26 27 28 29 30	
	10 ○ 12 13 14 15 16	9:03	50	2451889		13 14 15 16 17 18 19			15 16 17 18 19 20 21		KOIAK 1717	1 2 3 4 5 6 7	TĀḪŚĀŚ 1993
	17 ◑ 19 20 21[e] 22 23	0:41	51	2451896		20 21 22 23 24 25[e] 26[e]			22 23 24 25 26[i] 27 28	Dōng zhì		8 9 10 11 12 13 14	
	24 ● 26 27 28 29 30	17:21	52	2451903	TEVETH 5761	27[e] 28[e] 29[e] 1[e] 2[e] 3[e] 4	Tue 3h29m7p	MONTH 12 Gēng-Chén	29 30 1 2 3 4 5			15 16 17 18 19 20 21	
	31 1 ◐ 3 4 5 6	22:31	1	2451910		5 6 7 8 9 10 11			6 7 8 9 10 11 12	Xiǎo hán		22 23 24 25 26 27 28	

‡Leap year
[a]New Year
[b]Spring (7:35)
[c]Summer (1:48)
[d]Autumn (17:27)
[e]Winter (13:37)
● New moon
◐ First quarter moon
○ Full moon
◑ Last quarter moon

‡Leap year
[a]New Year
[b]Yom Kippur
[c]Sukkot
[d]Winter starts
[e]Ḥanukkah
[f]Purim
[g]Passover
[h]Shavuot
[i]Fast of Av

[a]New Year (4698, Dragon)
[b]Lantern Festival
[c]Qīngmíng
[d]Dragon Festival
[e]Qīqiǎo
[f]Hungry Ghosts
[g]Mid-Autumn Festival
[h]Double-Ninth Festival
[i]Dōngzhì
*Start of 60-name cycle

[a]New Year
[b]Building of the Cross
[c]Christmas
[d]Jesus's Circumcision
[e]Epiphany
[f]Easter
[g]Mary's Announcement
[h]Jesus's Transfiguration

PERSIAN (ASTRONOMICAL) 1378/1379‡

Month	Sun	Mon	Tue	Wed	Thu	Fri	Sat
DEY 1378	5	6	7	8	9	10	11
	12	13	14	15	16	17	18
	19	20	21	22	23	24	25
	26	27	28	29	30	1	2
BAHMAN 1378	3	4	5	6	7	8	9
	10	11	12	13	14	15	16
	17	18	19	20	21	22	23
	24	25	26	27	28	29	30
ESFAND 1378	1	2	3	4	5	6	7
	8	9	10	11	12	13	14
	15	16	17	18	19	20	21
	22	23	24	25	26	27	28
FARVARDĪN 1379	29	1[a]	2	3	4	5	6
	7	8	9	10	11	12	13[b]
	14	15	16	17	18	19	20
	21	22	23	24	25	26	27
ORDĪBEHEŠT 1379	28	29	30	31	1	2	3
	4	5	6	7	8	9	10
	11	12	13	14	15	16	17
	18	19	20	21	22	23	24
	25	26	27	28	29	30	31
XORDĀD 1379	1	2	3	4	5	6	7
	8	9	10	11	12	13	14
	15	16	17	18	19	20	21
	22	23	24	25	26	27	28
TĪR 1379	29	30	31	1	2	3	4
	5	6	7	8	9	10	11
	12	13	14	15	16	17	18
	19	20	21	22	23	24	25
MORDĀD 1379	26	27	28	29	30	31	1
	2	3	4	5	6	7	8
	9	10	11	12	13	14	15
	16	17	18	19	20	21	22
	23	24	25	26	27	28	29
SHAHRĪVAR 1379	30	31	1	2	3	4	5
	6	7	8	9	10	11	12
	13	14	15	16	17	18	19
	20	21	22	23	24	25	26
MEHR 1379	27	28	29	30	31	1	2
	3	4	5	6	7	8	9
	10	11	12	13	14	15	16
	17	18	19	20	21	22	23
	24	25	26	27	28	29	30
ĀBĀN 1379	1	2	3	4	5	6	7
	8	9	10	11	12	13	14
	15	16	17	18	19	20	21
	22	23	24	25	26	27	28
ĀZAR 1379	29	30	1	2	3	4	5
	6	7	8	9	10	11	12
	13	14	15	16	17	18	19
	20	21	22	23	24	25	26
DEY 1379	27	28	29	30	1	2	3
	4	5	6	7	8	9	10
	11	12	13	14	15	16	17

‡Leap year
[a]New Year
[b]Sizdeh Bedar

HINDU LUNAR 2056‡/2057

Month	Sun	Mon	Tue	Wed	Thu	Fri	Sat
MĀRGAŚĪRA 2056	19	20	21	22	23	24	25
PAUSHA 2056	26	27	28	29	30	1	2
	3	4	5	6	7	8	9
	10	11	12	13	14	15	**16**
	18	19	20	21	22	23	24
	25	25	26	27	28	29	30
MĀGHA 2056	1	2	3	4	5	6	7
	8	9	**10**	12	13	14	15
	16	17	18	19	20	21	22
	23	24	25	26	27	27	28[h]
PHĀLGUNA 2056	29	30	1	2	3	**4**	6
	7	8	9	10	11	12	13
	14	15[i]	16	17	18	19	20
	21	22	23	24	25	26	27
CHAITRA 2057	28	29	30	1[a]	2	3	4
	5	6	7	**8**[b]	10	11	12
	13	14	15	16	17	18	19
	20	21	21	22	23	24	25
VAIŚĀKHA 2057	26	27	28	29	30	1	**2**
	4	5	6	7	8	9	10
	11	12	13	14	15	16	17
	18	19	20	21	22	23	24
JYAISHTHA 2057	25	26	27	28	29	30	1
	2	3	4	**5**	7	8	9
	10	11	12	13	14	15	16
	17	17	18	19	20	21	22
	23	24	25	26	27	**28**	30
ĀSHĀDHA 2057	1	2	3	4	5	6	7
	8	9	10	11	12	13	14
	15	16	17	18	19	20	21
	22	23	24	25	26	27	28
ŚRĀVAṆA 2057	29	**30**	2	3	4	5	6
	7	8	9	10	11	12	13
	14	14	15	16	17	18	19
	20	21	22	**23**[c]	25	26	27
BHĀDRAPADA 2057	28	29	30	1	2	3[d]	4
	5	6	7	8	9	10	11
	12	13	14	15	16	17	18
	19	20	21	22	23	24	25
ĀŚVINA 2057	26	**27**	29	30	1	2	3
	4	5	6	7	8[e]	9[e]	9[e]
	10[e]	11	12	13	14	15	16
	17	18	19	**20**	22	23	24
KĀRTTIKA 2057	25	26	27	28	29	30	1[f]
	2	3	4	5	6	7	8
	9	10	11	12	13	14	15
	16	17	18	19	20	21	22
	23	24	**25**	27	28	29	30
MĀRGAŚĪRA 2057	1	2	3	3	4	5	6
	7	8	9	10	11[g]	12	13
	14	15	16	17	**18**	20	21
	22	23	24	25	26	27	28
PAUSHA 2057	29	30	1	2	3	4	5
	5	6	7	8	9	10	11

‡Leap year
[a]New Year (Vikrama)
[b]Birthday of Rāma
[c]Birthday of Krishna
[d]Ganēśa Chaturthī
[e]Dashara
[f]Diwali
[g]Birthday of Vishnu
[h]Night of Śiva
[i]Holi

HINDU SOLAR 1921/1922

Month	Sun	Mon	Tue	Wed	Thu	Fri	Sat
PAUSHA 1921	11	12	13	14	15	16	17
	18	19	20	21	22	23	24
MĀGHA 1921	25	26	27	28	29	1[b]	2
	3	4	5	6	7	8	9
	10	11	12	13	14	15	16
	17	18	19	20	21	22	23
	24	25	26	27	28	29	30
PHĀLGUNA 1921	1	2	3	4	5	6	7
	8	9	10	11	12	13	14
	15	16	17	18	19	20	21
	22	23	24	25	26	27	28
CHAITRA 1921	29	30	1	2	3	4	5
	6	7	8	9	10	11	12
	13	14	15	16	17	18	19
	20	21	22	23	24	25	26
VAIŚĀKHA 1922	27	28	29	30	1[a]	2	3
	4	5	6	7	8	9	10
	11	12	13	14	15	16	17
	18	19	20	21	22	23	24
	25	26	27	28	29	30	31
JYAISHTHA 1922	1	2	3	4	5	6	7
	8	9	10	11	12	13	14
	15	16	17	18	19	20	21
	22	23	24	25	26	27	28
ĀSHĀDHA 1922	29	30	31	1	2	3	4
	5	6	7	8	9	10	11
	12	13	14	15	16	17	18
	19	20	21	22	23	24	25
	26	27	28	29	30	31	32
ŚRĀVAṆA 1922	1	2	3	4	5	6	7
	8	9	10	11	12	13	14
	15	16	17	18	19	20	21
	22	23	24	25	26	27	28
BHĀDRAPADA 1922	29	30	31	1	2	3	4
	5	6	7	8	9	10	11
	12	13	14	15	16	17	18
	19	20	21	22	23	24	25
ĀŚVINA 1922	26	27	28	29	30	31	1
	2	3	4	5	6	7	8
	9	10	11	12	13	14	15
	16	17	18	19	20	21	22
	23	24	25	26	27	28	29
KĀRTTIKA 1922	30	31	1	2	3	4	5
	6	7	8	9	10	11	12
	13	14	15	16	17	18	19
	20	21	22	23	24	25	26
MĀRGAŚĪRA 1922	27	28	29	30	1	2	3
	4	5	6	7	8	9	10
	11	12	13	14	15	16	17
	18	19	20	21	22	23	24
PAUSHA 1922	25	26	27	28	29	1	2
	3	4	5	6	7	8	9
	10	11	12	13	14	15	16
	17	18	19	20	21	22	23

[a]New Year (Vijaya)
[b]Pongal

ISLAMIC (ASTRONOMICAL) 1420‡/1421

Month	Sun	Mon	Tue	Wed	Thu	Fri	Sat
RAMAḌĀN 1420	18	19	20	21	22	23	24
SHAWWĀL 1420	25	26	27	28	29	30	1[f]
	2	3	4	5	6	7	8
	9	10	11	12	13	14	15
	16	17	18	19	20	21	22
	23	24	25	26	27	28	29
DHU AL-QA'DA 1420	30	1	2	3	4	5	6
	7	8	9	10	11	12	13
	14	15	16	17	18	19	20
	21	22	23	24	25	26	27
DHU AL-ḤIJJA 1420	28	29	1	2	3	4	5
	6	7	8	9	10[g]	11	12
	13	14	15	16	17	18	19
	20	21	22	23	24	25	26
MUḤARRAM 1421	27	28	29	30	1[a]	2	3
	4	5	6	7	8	9	10[b]
	11	12	13	14	15	16	17
	18	19	20	21	22	23	24
ṢAFAR 1421	25	26	27	28	29	1	2
	3	4	5	6	7	8	9
	10	11	12	13	14	15	16
	17	18	19	20	21	22	23
	24	25	26	27	28	29	30
RABĪ' I 1421	1	2	3	4	5	6	7
	8	9	10	11	12[c]	13	14
	15	16	17	18	19	20	21
	22	23	24	25	26	27	28
RABĪ' II 1421	29	1	2	3	4	5	6
	7	8	9	10	11	12	13
	14	15	16	17	18	19	20
	21	22	23	24	25	26	27
JUMĀDĀ I 1421	28	29	1	2	3	4	5
	6	7	8	9	10	11	12
	13	14	15	16	17	18	19
	20	21	22	23	24	25	26
JUMĀDĀ II 1421	27	28	29	30	1	2	3
	4	5	6	7	8	9	10
	11	12	13	14	15	16	17
	18	19	20	21	22	23	24
RAJAB 1421	25	26	27	28	29	1	2
	3	4	5	6	7	8	9
	10	11	12	13	14	15	16
	17	18	19	20	21	22	23
	24	25	26	27[d]	28	29	30
SHA'BĀN 1421	1	2	3	4	5	6	7
	8	9	10	11	12	13	14
	15	16	17	18	19	20	21
	22	23	24	25	26	27	28
RAMAḌĀN 1421	29	1[e]	2	3	4	5	6
	7	8	9	10	11	12	13
	14	15	16	17	18	19	20
	21	22	23	24	25	26	27
SHAWWĀL 1421	28	29	30	1[f]	2	3	4
	5	6	7	8	9	10	11

‡Leap year
[a]New Year
[b]'Ashūrā'
[c]Prophet's Birthday
[d]Ascent of the Prophet
[e]Start of Ramaḍān
[f]'Id al-Fiṭr
[g]'Id al-'Aḍḥā

GREGORIAN 2000‡

Julian‡ (Sun)	Sun	Mon	Tue	Wed	Thu	Fri	Sat	Month
Dec 13	26	27	28	29	30	31	1	JANUARY 2000
	2	3	4	5	6	7[a]	8	
Dec 27	9	10	11	12	13	14[b]	15	
	16	17	18	19	20	21	22	
Jan 10	23	24	25	26	27	28	29	
	30	31	1	2	3	4	5	FEBRUARY 2000
Jan 24	6	7	8	9	10	11	12	
	13	14	15	16	17	18	19	
Feb 7	20	21	22	23	24	25	26	
	27	28	29	1	2	3	4	MARCH 2000
Feb 21	5	6	7	8[c]	9	10	11	
	12	13	14	15	16	17	18	
Mar 6	19[d]	20	21	22	23	24	25	
	26	27	28	29	30	31	1	APRIL 2000
Mar 20	2	3	4	5	6	7	8	
	9	10	11	12	13	14	15	
Apr 3	16	17	18	19	20	21	22	
	23[e]	24	25	26	27	28	29	
Apr 17	30[f]	1	2	3	4	5	6	MAY 2000
	7	8	9	10	11	12	13	
May 1	14	15	16	17	18	19	20	
	21	22	23	24	25	26	27	
May 15	28	29	30	31	1	2	3	JUNE 2000
	4	5	6	7	8	9	10	
May 29	11	12	13	14	15	16	17	
	18	19	20	21	22	23	24	
Jun 12	25	26	27	28	29	30	1	JULY 2000
	2	3	4	5	6	7	8	
Jun 26	9	10	11	12	13	14	15	
	16	17	18	19	20	21	22	
Jul 10	23	24	25	26	27	28	29	
	30	31	1	2	3	4	5	AUGUST 2000
Jul 24	6	7	8	9	10	11	12	
	13	14	15	16	17	18	19	
Aug 7	20	21	22	23	24	25	26	
	27	28	29	30	31	1	2	SEPTEMBER 2000
Aug 21	3	4	5	6	7	8	9	
	10	11	12	13	14	15	16	
Sep 4	17	18	19	20	21	22	23	
	24	25	26	27	28	29	30	
Sep 18	1	2	3	4	5	6	7	OCTOBER 2000
	8	9	10	11	12	13	14	
Oct 2	15	16	17	18	19	20	21	
	22	23	24	25	26	27	28	
Oct 16	29	30	31	1	2	3	4	NOVEMBER 2000
	5	6	7	8	9	10	11	
Oct 30	12	13	14	15	16	17	18	
	19	20	21	22	23	24	25	
Nov 13	26	27	28	29	30	1	2	DECEMBER 2000
	3[g]	4	5	6	7	8	9	
Nov 27	10	11	12	13	14	15	16	
	17	18	19	20	21	22	23	
Dec 11	24	25[h]	26	27	28	29	30	
	31	1	2	3	4	5	6	

‡Leap year
[a]Orthodox Christmas
[b]Julian New Year
[c]Ash Wednesday
[d]Feast of Orthodoxy
[e]Easter
[f]Orthodox Easter
[g]Advent
[h]Christmas

2001

Month	Sun	Mon	Tue	Wed	Thu	Fri	Sat	Lunar Phases	ISO Week (Mon)	Julian Day (Sun noon)
JANUARY 2001	31	1[a]	◐	3	4	5	6	22:31	1	2451910
	7	8	○	10	11	12	13	20:25	2	2451917
	14	15	◑	17	18	19	20	12:35	3	2451924
	21	22	23	●	25	26	27	13:07	4	2451931
FEBRUARY 2001	28	29	30	31	◐	2	3	14:02	5	2451938
	4	5	6	7	○	9	10	7:12	6	2451945
	11	12	13	14	◑	16	17	3:24	7	2451952
	18	19	20	21	22	●	24	8:21	8	2451959
MARCH 2001	25	26	27	28	1	2	◐	2:03	9	2451966
	4	5	6	7	8	○	10	17:23	10	2451973
	11	12	13	14	15	◑	17	20:45	11	2451980
	18	19	20[b]	21	22	23	24		12	2451987
	●	26	27	28	29	30	31	1:21	13	2451994
APRIL 2001	◐	2	3	4	5	6	7	10:49	14	2452001
	○	9	10	11	12	13	14	3:22	15	2452008
	◑	16	17	18	19	20	21	15:31	16	2452015
	22	●	24	25	26	27	28	15:26	17	2452022
MAY 2001	29	◐	1	2	3	4	5	17:07	18	2452029
	6	○	8	9	10	11	12	13:53	19	2452036
	13	14	◑	16	17	18	19	10:10	20	2452043
	20	21	22	●	24	25	26	2:46	21	2452050
JUNE 2001	27	28	◐	30	31	1	2	22:09	22	2452057
	3	4	5	○	7	8	9	1:39	23	2452064
	10	11	12	13	◑	15	16	3:28	24	2452071
	17	18	19	20	●[c]	22	23	11:58	25	2452078
	24	25	26	27	◐	29	30	3:20	26	2452085
JULY 2001	1	2	3	4	○	6	7	15:04	27	2452092
	8	9	10	11	12	◑	14	18:45	28	2452099
	15	16	17	18	19	●	21	19:45	29	2452106
	22	23	24	25	26	◐	28	10:08	30	2452113
AUGUST 2001	29	30	31	1	2	3	○	5:56	31	2452120
	5	6	7	8	9	10	11		32	2452127
	◑	13	14	15	16	17	18	7:53	33	2452134
	●	20	21	22	23	24	◐	2:55 19:55	34	2452141
SEPTEMBER 2001	26	27	28	29	30	31	1		35	2452148
	○	3	4	5	6	7	8	21:43	36	2452155
	9	◑	11	12	13	14	15	18:59	37	2452162
	16	●	18	19	20	21	22[d]	10:27	38	2452169
	23	◐	25	26	27	28	29	9:31	39	2452176
OCTOBER 2001	30	1	○	3	4	5	6	13:49	40	2452183
	7	8	9	◑	11	12	13	4:20	41	2452190
	14	15	●	17	18	19	20	19:23	42	2452197
	21	22	23	◐	25	26	27	2:58	43	2452204
NOVEMBER 2001	28	29	30	31	○	2	3	5:41	44	2452211
	4	5	6	7	◑	9	10	12:21	45	2452218
	11	12	13	14	●	16	17	6:40	46	2452225
	18	19	20	21	◐	23	24	23:20	47	2452232
DECEMBER 2001	25	26	27	28	29	○	1	20:49	48	2452239
	2	3	4	5	6	◑	8	19:52	49	2452246
	9	10	11	12	13	●	15	20:47	50	2452253
	16	17	18	19	20	21[e]	◐	20:56	51	2452260
	23	24	25	26	27	28	29		52	2452267
	○	31	1	2	3	4	5	10:41	1	2452274

HEBREW 5761/5762

ISO Week	Month	Sun	Mon	Tue	Wed	Thu	Fri	Sat	Molad
1	TEVETH 5761	5	6	7	8	9	10	11	
2		12	13	14	15	16	17	18	
3		19	20	21	22	23	24	25	
4	SHEVAT 5761	26	27	28	29	1	2	3	Wed $16^h13^m8^p$
5		4	5	6	7	8	9	10	
6		11	12	13	14	15	16	17	
7		18	19	20	21	22	23	24	
8	ADAR 5761	25	26	27	28	29	30	1	Fri $4^h57^m9^p$
9		2	3	4	5	6	7	8	
10		9	10	11	12	13	14[f]	15	
11		16	17	18	19	20	21	22	
12		23	24	25	26	27	28	29	Sat $17^h41^m10^p$
13	NISAN 5761	1	2	3	4	5	6	7	
14		8	9	10	11	12	13	14	
15		15[g]	16	17	18	19	20	21	
16		22	23	24	25	26	27	28	
17	IYYAR 5761	29	30	1	2	3	4	5	Mon $6^h25^m11^p$
18		6	7	8	9	10	11	12	
19		13	14	15	16	17	18	19	
20		20	21	22	23	24	25	26	
21	SIVAN 5761	27	28	29	1	2	3	4	Tue $19^h9^m12^p$
22		5	6[h]	7	8	9	10	11	
23		12	13	14	15	16	17	18	
24		19	20	21	22	23	24	25	
25	TAMMUZ 5761	26	27	28	29	30	1	2	Thu $7^h53^m13^p$
26		3	4	5	6	7	8	9	
27		10	11	12	13	14	15	16	
28		17	18	19	20	21	22	23	
29	AV 5761	24	25	26	27	28	29	1	Fri $20^h37^m14^p$
30		2	3	4	5	6	7	8	
31		9[i]	10	11	12	13	14	15	
32		16	17	18	19	20	21	22	
33		23	24	25	26	27	28	29	
34	ELUL 5761	30	1	2	3	4	5	6	Sun $9^h21^m15^p$
35		7	8	9	10	11	12	13	
36		14	15	16	17	18	19	20	
37		21	22	23	24	25	26	27	
38	TISHRI 5762	28	29	1[a]	2[a]	3	4	5	Mon $22^h5^m16^p$
39		6	7	8	9	10[b]	11	12	
40		13	14	15[c]	16	17	18	19	
41		20	21	22	23	24	25	26	
42	ḤESHVAN 5762	27	28	29	30	1	2	3	Wed $10^h49^m17^p$
43		4	5	6	7	8	9	10	
44		11	12	13	14	15	16	17	
45		18	19	20	21	22	23	24	
46	KISLEV 5762	25	26	27	28	29	1	2	Thu $23^h34^m0^p$
47		3	4	5	6	7	8	9	
48		10	11	12	13	14	15	16	
49		17	18	19	20[d]	21	22	23	
50		24	25[e]	26[e]	27[e]	28[e]	29[e]	30[e]	Sat $12^h18^m1^p$
51	TEVETH 5762	1[e]	2[e]	3	4	5	6	7	
52		8	9	10	11	12	13	14	
1		15	16	17	18	19	20	21	

CHINESE Gēng-Chén/Xīn-Sì[‡]

ISO Week	Month	Sun	Mon	Tue	Wed	Thu	Fri	Sat	Solar Term
1	MONTH 12 Gēng-Chén	6	7*	8	9	10	11	12	Xiǎo hán
2		13	14	15	16	17	18	19	
3		20	21	22	23	24	25	26	Dà hán
4	MONTH 1 Xīn-Sì	27	28	29	1[a]	2	3	4	
5		5	6	7	8	9	10	11	
6		12	13	14	15[b]	16	17	18	Lì chūn
7		19	20	21	22	23	24	25	
8	MONTH 2 Xīn-Sì	26	27	28	29	30	1	2	Yǔ shuǐ
9		3	4	5	6	7	8*	9	
10		10	11	12	13	14	15	16	Jīng zhé
11		17	18	19	20	21	22	23	
12		24	25	26	27	28	29	30	Chūn fēn
13	MONTH 3 Xīn-Sì	1	2	3	4	5	6	7	
14		8	9	10	11	12[c]	13	14	Qīng míng
15		15	16	17	18	19	20	21	
16		22	23	24	25	26	27	28	Gǔ yǔ
17	MONTH 4 Xīn-Sì	29	1	2	3	4	5	6	
18		7	8	9*	10	11	12	13	Lì xià
19		14	15	16	17	18	19	20	
20		21	22	23	24	25	26	27	
21	LEAP MONTH 4 Xīn-Sì	28	29	30	1	2	3	4	Xiǎo mǎn
22		5	6	7	8	9	10	11	
23		12	13	14	15	16	17	18	Máng zhòng
24		19	20	21	22	23	24	25	
25	MONTH 5 Xīn-Sì	26	27	28	29	1	2	3	Xià zhì
26		4	5[d]	6	7	8	9	10*	
27		11	12	13	14	15	16	17	Xiǎo shǔ
28		18	19	20	21	22	23	24	
29	MONTH 6 Xīn-Sì	25	26	27	28	29	30	1	
30		2	3	4	5	6	7	8	Dà shǔ
31		9	10	11	12	13	14	15	
32		16	17	18	19	20	21	22	Lì qiū
33		23	24	25	26	27	28	29	
34	MONTH 7 Xīn-Sì	1	2	3	4	5	6	7[e]	Chǔ shǔ
35		8	9	10	11*	12	13	14	
36		15[f]	16	17	18	19	20	21	Bái lù
37		22	23	24	25	26	27	28	
38	MONTH 8 Xīn-Sì	29	1	2	3	4	5	6	
39		7	8	9	10	11	12	13	Qiū fēn
40		14	15[g]	16	17	18	19	20	
41		21	22	23	24	25	26	27	Hán lù
42	MONTH 9 Xīn-Sì	28	29	30	1	2	3	4	
43		5	6	7	8	9[h]	10	11	Shuāng jiàng
44		12*	13	14	15	16	17	18	
45		19	20	21	22	23	24	25	Lì dōng
46	MONTH 10 Xīn-Sì	26	27	28	29	1	2	3	
47		4	5	6	7	8	9	10	Xiǎo xuě
48		11	12	13	14	15	16	17	
49		18	19	20	21	22	23	24	Dà xuě
50	MONTH 11 Xīn-Sì	25	26	27	28	29	30	1	
51		2	3	4	5	6	7	8[i]	Dōng zhì
52		9	10	11	12	13*	14	15	
1		16	17	18	19	20	21	22	Xiǎo hán

COPTIC 1717/1718 — ETHIOPIC 1993/1994

ISO Week	Coptic Month	Sun	Mon	Tue	Wed	Thu	Fri	Sat	Ethiopic Month
1	KOIAK 1717	22	23	24	25	26	27	28	TĀKHŚĀŚ 1993
2	TÔBE 1717	29[c]	30	1	2	3	4	5	ṬER 1993
3		6[d]	7	8	9	10	11[e]	12	
4		13	14	15	16	17	18	19	
5		20	21	22	23	24	25	26	
6	MESHIR 1717	27	28	29	30	1	2	3	YAKĀTIT 1993
7		4	5	6	7	8	9	10	
8		11	12	13	14	15	16	17	
9		18	19	20	21	22	23	24	
10	PAREMOTEP 1717	25	26	27	28	29	30	1	MAGĀBIT 1993
11		2	3	4	5	6	7	8	
12		9	10	11	12	13	14	15	
13		16	17	18	19	20	21	22	
14		23	24	25	26	27	28	29	
15	PARMOUTE 1717	30	1	2	3	4	5	6	MIYĀZYĀ 1993
16		7[f]	8	9	10	11	12	13	
17		14	15	16	17	18	19	20	
18		21	22	23	24	25	26	27	
19	PASHONS 1717	28	29[g]	30	1	2	3	4	GENBOT 1993
20		5	6	7	8	9	10	11	
21		12	13	14	15	16	17	18	
22		19	20	21	22	23	24	25	
23	PAÔNE 1717	26	27	28	29	30	1	2	SANÉ 1993
24		3	4	5	6	7	8	9	
25		10	11	12	13	14	15	16	
26		17	18	19	20	21	22	23	
27		24	25	26	27	28	29	30	
28	EPÊP 1717	1	2	3	4	5	6	7	ḤAMLÉ 1993
29		8	9	10	11	12	13	14	
30		15	16	17	18	19	20	21	
31		22	23	24	25	26	27	28	
32	MESORÊ 1717	29	30	1	2	3	4	5	NAḤASÉ 1993
33		6	7	8	9	10	11	12	
34		13[h]	14	15	16	17	18	19	
35		20	21	22	23	24	25	26	
36	EPAG. 1717	27	28	29	30	1	2	3	PĀG. 1993
37	THOOUT 1718	4	5	1[a]	2	3	4	5	MASKARAM 1994
38		6	7	8	9	10	11	12	
39		13	14	15	16	17[b]	18	19	
40		20	21	22	23	24	25	26	
41	PAOPE 1718	27	28	29	30	1	2	3	ṬEQEMT 1994
42		4	5	6	7	8	9	10	
43		11	12	13	14	15	16	17	
44		18	19	20	21	22	23	24	
45	ATHÔR 1718	25	26	27	28	29	30	1	ḪEDĀR 1994
46		2	3	4	5	6	7	8	
47		9	10	11	12	13	14	15	
48		16	17	18	19	20	21	22	
49		23	24	25	26	27	28	29	
50	KOIAK 1718	30	1	2	3	4	5	6	TĀKHŚĀŚ 1994
51		7	8	9	10	11	12	13	
52		14	15	16	17	18	19	20	
1		21	22	23	24	25	26	27	

Gregorian:
- [a] New Year
- [b] Spring (13:30)
- [c] Summer (7:37)
- [d] Autumn (23:04)
- [e] Winter (19:21)
- ● New moon
- ◐ First quarter moon
- ○ Full moon
- ◑ Last quarter moon

Hebrew:
- [a] New Year
- [b] Yom Kippur
- [c] Sukkot
- [d] Winter starts
- [e] Ḥanukkah
- [f] Purim
- [g] Passover
- [h] Shavuot
- [i] Fast of Av

Chinese:
- ‡ Leap year
- [a] New Year (4699, Snake)
- [b] Lantern Festival
- [c] Qīngmíng
- [d] Dragon Festival
- [e] Qīqiǎo
- [f] Hungry Ghosts
- [g] Mid-Autumn Festival
- [h] Double-Ninth Festival
- [i] Dōngzhì
- * Start of 60-name cycle

Coptic/Ethiopic:
- [a] New Year
- [b] Building of the Cross
- [c] Christmas
- [d] Jesus's Circumcision
- [e] Epiphany
- [f] Easter
- [g] Mary's Announcement
- [h] Jesus's Transfiguration

PERSIAN (ASTRONOMICAL) 1379‡/1380

Month	Sun	Mon	Tue	Wed	Thu	Fri	Sat
	11	12	13	14	15	16	17
DEY 1379	18	19	20	21	22	23	24
	25	26	27	28	29	30	*1*
	2	3	4	5	6	7	8
BAHMAN 1379	9	10	11	12	13	14	15
	16	17	18	19	20	21	22
	23	24	25	26	27	28	29
	30	*1*	2	3	4	5	6
	7	8	9	10	11	12	13
ESFAND 1379	14	15	16	17	18	19	20
	21	22	23	24	25	26	27
	28	29	30	*1*[a]	2	3	4
	5	6	7	8	9	10	11
FARVARDĪN 1380	12	13[b]	14	15	16	17	18
	19	20	21	22	23	24	25
	26	27	28	29	30	31	*1*
	2	3	4	5	6	7	8
ORDĪBEHEŠT 1380	9	10	11	12	13	14	15
	16	17	18	19	20	21	22
	23	24	25	26	27	28	29
	30	31	*1*	2	3	4	5
	6	7	8	9	10	11	12
XORDĀD 1380	13	14	15	16	17	18	19
	20	21	22	23	24	25	26
	27	28	29	30	31	*1*	2
	3	4	5	6	7	8	9
TĪR 1380	10	11	12	13	14	15	16
	17	18	19	20	21	22	23
	24	25	26	27	28	29	30
	31	*1*	2	3	4	5	6
	7	8	9	10	11	12	13
MORDĀD 1380	14	15	16	17	18	19	20
	21	22	23	24	25	26	27
	28	29	30	31	*1*	2	3
	4	5	6	7	8	9	10
SHAHRĪVAR 1380	11	12	13	14	15	16	17
	18	19	20	21	22	23	24
	25	26	27	28	29	30	31
	1	2	3	4	5	6	7
MEHR 1380	8	9	10	11	12	13	14
	15	16	17	18	19	20	21
	22	23	24	25	26	27	28
	29	30	*1*	2	3	4	5
	6	7	8	9	10	11	12
ABĀN 1380	13	14	15	16	17	18	19
	20	21	22	23	24	25	26
	27	28	29	30	*1*	2	3
	4	5	6	7	8	9	10
ĀZAR 1380	11	12	13	14	15	16	17
	18	19	20	21	22	23	24
	25	26	27	28	29	30	*1*
DEY 1380	2	3	4	5	6	7	8
	9	10	11	12	13	14	15

‡Leap year
[a]New Year
[b]Sizdeh Bedar

HINDU LUNAR 2057/2058‡

Month	Sun	Mon	Tue	Wed	Thu	Fri	Sat
	5	6	7	8	9	10	11
PAUSHA 2057	**12**	14	15	16	17	18	19
	20	21	22	23	24	25	26
	27	28	29	30	1	2	3
MĀGHA 2057	4	5	6	7	8	9	10
	11	12	13	14	15	16	**17**
	19	20	21	22	23	24	25
	26	27	28	*28*[h]	29	30	1
	2	3	4	5	6	7	8
PHĀLGUNA 2057	9	10	**11**	13	14	15[i]	16
	17	18	19	20	21	22	23
	24	25	26	27	28	29	30
	30	1[a]	2	3	**4**	6	7
CHAITRA 2058	8	9[b]	10	11	12	13	14
	15	16	**17**	19	20	*20*	21
	22	23	24	25	26	27	28
	29	30	1	2	3	4	5
VAIŚĀKHA 2058	6	7	8	**9**	11	12	13
	14	15	16	17	18	19	20
	21	22	23	24	25	*25*	26
	27	28	29	30	1	**2**	4
	5	6	7	8	9	10	11
JYAISHTHA 2058	12	13	14	15	16	17	18
	19	20	21	22	23	24	25
	26	27	28	29	30	1	2
	3	4	**5**	7	8	9	10
ĀSHĀḌHA 2058	11	12	13	14	15	16	17
	18	19	20	21	*21*	22	23
	24	25	26	**27**	29	30	1
	2	3	4	5	6	7	8
ŚRĀVAṆA 2058	**9**	11	12	*12*	13	14	15
	16	17	18	19	20	21	22
	23[c]	24	25	26	27	28	29
	30	2	3	4[d]	5	6	7
	8	9	10	11	12	13	14
BHĀDRAPADA 2058	15	16	17	18	*18*	19	20
	21	22	**23**	25	26	27	28
	29	30	1	2	3	4	5
	6	7	8	9	10	11	12
LEAP ĀŚVINA 2058	13	14	15	16	17	18	19
	20	21	22	23	24	25	26
	27	29	30	1	2	3	4
	5	6	7	8[e]	9[e]	10[e]	11
ĀŚVINA 2058	12	*12*	13	14	15	16	17
	18	19	20	**21**	23	24	25
	26	27	28	29	30	1[f]	2
	3	4	5	6	7	8	9
KĀRTTIKA 2058	10	11	12	13	14	15	16
	17	18	19	20	21	22	23
	24	**25**	27	28	29	30	1
	2	3	4	5	6	*6*	7
MĀRGAŚIRA 2058	8	9	10	11[g]	12	13	14
	15	16	17	18	**19**	21	22

‡Leap year
[a]New Year (Vṛisha)
[b]Birthday of Rāma
[c]Birthday of Krishna
[d]Ganēśa Chaturthī
[e]Dashara
[f]Diwali
[g]Birthday of Vishnu
[h]Night of Śiva
[i]Holi

HINDU SOLAR 1922/1923‡

Month	Sun	Mon	Tue	Wed	Thu	Fri	Sat
	17	18	19	20	21	22	23
PAUSHA 1922	24	25	26	27	28	29	30
	1[b]	2	3	4	5	6	7
MĀGHA 1922	8	9	10	11	12	13	14
	15	16	17	18	19	20	21
	22	23	24	25	26	27	28
	29	1	2	3	4	5	6
PHĀLGUNA 1922	7	8	9	10	11	12	13
	14	15	16	17	18	19	20
	21	22	23	24	25	26	27
	28	29	30	1	2	3	4
CHAITRA 1922	5	6	7	8	9	10	11
	12	13	14	15	16	17	18
	19	20	21	22	23	24	25
	26	27	28	29	30	1[a]	2
VAIŚĀKHA 1923	3	4	5	6	7	8	9
	10	11	12	13	14	15	16
	17	18	19	20	21	22	23
	24	25	26	27	28	29	30
	31	1	2	3	4	5	6
JYAISHTHA 1923	7	8	9	10	11	12	13
	14	15	16	17	18	19	20
	21	22	23	24	25	26	27
	28	29	30	31	32	1	2
ĀSHĀḌHA 1923	3	4	5	6	7	8	9
	10	11	12	13	14	15	16
	17	18	19	20	21	22	23
	24	25	26	27	28	29	30
	31	1	2	3	4	5	6
ŚRĀVAṆA 1923	7	8	9	10	11	12	13
	14	15	16	17	18	19	20
	21	22	23	24	25	26	27
	28	29	30	31	32	1	2
BHĀDRAPADA 1923	3	4	5	6	7	8	9
	10	11	12	13	14	15	16
	17	18	19	20	21	22	23
	24	25	26	27	28	29	30
	31	1	2	3	4	5	6
ĀŚVINA 1923	7	8	9	10	11	12	13
	14	15	16	17	18	19	20
	21	22	23	24	25	26	27
	28	29	30	1	2	3	4
KĀRTTIKA 1923	5	6	7	8	9	10	11
	12	13	14	15	16	17	18
	19	20	21	22	23	24	25
	26	27	28	29	30	1	2
MĀRGAŚIRA 1923	3	4	5	6	7	8	9
	10	11	12	13	14	15	16
	17	18	19	20	21	22	23
	24	25	26	27	28	29	30
	1	2	3	4	5	6	7
PAUSHA 1923	8	9	10	11	12	13	14
	15	16	17	18	19	20	21

‡Leap year
[a]New Year (Jaya)
[b]Pongal

ISLAMIC (ASTRONOMICAL) 1421/1422

Month	Sun	Mon	Tue	Wed	Thu	Fri	Sat
	5	6	7	8	9	10	11
SHAWWĀL 1421	12	13	14	15	16	17	18
	19	20	21	22	23	24	25
	26	27	28	29	30	*1*	2
DHU AL-QA'DA 1421	3	4	5	6	7	8	9
	10	11	12	13	14	15	16
	17	18	19	20	21	22	23
	24	25	26	27	28	29	30
	1	2	3	4	5	6	7
DHU AL-ḤIJJA 1421	8	9	10[g]	11	12	13	14
	15	16	17	18	19	20	21
	22	23	24	25	26	27	28
	29	*1*[a]	2	3	4	5	6
MUḤARRAM 1422	7	8	9	10[b]	11	12	13
	14	15	16	17	18	19	20
	21	22	23	24	25	26	27
	28	29	30	*1*	2	3	4
ṢAFAR 1422	5	6	7	8	9	10	11
	12	13	14	15	16	17	18
	19	20	21	22	23	24	25
	26	27	28	29	*1*	2	3
RABĪ' I 1422	4	5	6	7	8	9	10
	11	12[c]	13	14	15	16	17
	18	19	20	21	22	23	24
	25	26	27	28	29	30	*1*
RABĪ' II 1422	2	3	4	5	6	7	8
	9	10	11	12	13	14	15
	16	17	18	19	20	21	22
	23	24	25	26	27	28	29
	1	2	3	4	5	6	7
JUMĀDĀ I 1422	8	9	10	11	12	13	14
	15	16	17	18	19	20	21
	22	23	24	25	26	27	28
	29	1	2	3	4	5	6
JUMĀDĀ II 1422	7	8	9	10	11	12	13
	14	15	16	17	18	19	20
	21	22	23	24	25	26	27
	28	29	30	*1*	2	3	4
RAJAB 1422	5	6	7	8	9	10	11
	12	13	14	15	16	17	18
	19	20	21	22	23	24	25
	26	27[d]	28	29	1	2	3
SHA'BĀN 1422	4	5	6	7	8	9	10
	11	12	13	14	15	16	17
	18	19	20	21	22	23	24
	25	26	27	28	29	30	*1*[e]
RAMAḌĀN 1422	2	3	4	5	6	7	8
	9	10	11	12	13	14	15
	16	17	18	19	20	21	22
	23	24	25	26	27	28	29
SHAWWĀL 1422	*1*[f]	2	3	4	5	6	7
	8	9	10	11	12	13	14
	15	16	17	18	19	20	21

[a]New Year
[b]'Ashūrā'
[c]Prophet's Birthday
[d]Ascent of the Prophet
[e]Start of Ramaḍān
[f]'Īd al-Fiṭr
[g]'Īd al-'Aḍḥā

GREGORIAN 2001

Julian (Sun)	Sun	Mon	Tue	Wed	Thu	Fri	Sat	Month
Dec 18	31	1	2	3	4	5	6	
	7[a]	8	9	10	11	12	13	JANUARY 2001
Jan 1	14[b]	15	16	17	18	19	20	
	21	22	23	24	25	26	27	
Jan 15	28	29	30	31	1	2	3	
	4	5	6	7	8	9	10	FEBRUARY 2001
Jan 29	11	12	13	14	15	16	17	
	18	19	20	21	22	23	24	
Feb 12	25	26	27	28[c]	1	2	3	
	4[d]	5	6	7	8	9	10	MARCH 2001
Feb 26	11	12	13	14	15	16	17	
	18	19	20	21	22	23	24	
Mar 12	25	26	27	28	29	30	31	
	1	2	3	4	5	6	7	
Mar 26	8	9	10	11	12	13	14	APRIL 2001
	15[e]	16	17	18	19	20	21	
Apr 9	22	23	24	25	26	27	28	
	29	30	1	2	3	4	5	
Apr 23	6	7	8	9	10	11	12	MAY 2001
	13	14	15	16	17	18	19	
May 7	20	21	22	23	24	25	26	
	27	28	29	30	31	1	2	
May 21	3	4	5	6	7	8	9	JUNE 2001
	10	11	12	13	14	15	16	
Jun 4	17	18	19	20	21	22	23	
	24	25	26	27	28	29	30	
Jun 18	1	2	3	4	5	6	7	
	8	9	10	11	12	13	14	JULY 2001
Jul 2	15	16	17	18	19	20	21	
	22	23	24	25	26	27	28	
Jul 16	29	30	31	1	2	3	4	
	5	6	7	8	9	10	11	AUGUST 2001
Jul 30	12	13	14	15	16	17	18	
	19	20	21	22	23	24	25	
Aug 13	26	27	28	29	30	31	1	
	2	3	4	5	6	7	8	SEPTEMBER 2001
Aug 27	9	10	11	12	13	14	15	
	16	17	18	19	20	21	22	
Sep 10	23	24	25	26	27	28	29	
	30	1	2	3	4	5	6	
Sep 24	7	8	9	10	11	12	13	OCTOBER 2001
	14	15	16	17	18	19	20	
Oct 8	21	22	23	24	25	26	27	
	28	29	30	31	1	2	3	
Oct 22	4	5	6	7	8	9	10	NOVEMBER 2001
	11	12	13	14	15	16	17	
Nov 5	18	19	20	21	22	23	24	
	25	26	27	28	29	30	1	
Nov 19	2[g]	3	4	5	6	7	8	DECEMBER 2001
	9	10	11	12	13	14	15	
Dec 3	16	17	18	19	20	21	22	
	23	24	25[h]	26	27	28	29	
Dec 17	30	31	1	2	3	4	5	

[a]Orthodox Christmas
[b]Julian New Year
[c]Ash Wednesday
[d]Feast of Orthodoxy
[e]Easter (also Orthodox)
[g]Advent
[h]Christmas

2002

Month	Sun	Mon	Tue	Wed	Thu	Fri	Sat	Lunar Phases	ISO WEEK (Mon)	JULIAN DAY (Sun noon)	Hebrew Month	Sun	Mon	Tue	Wed	Thu	Fri	Sat	Molad	Chinese Month	Sun	Mon	Tue	Wed	Thu	Fri	Sat	Solar Term	Coptic Month	Sun	Mon	Tue	Wed	Thu	Fri	Sat	Ethiopic Month
GREGORIAN 2002											HEBREW 5762/5763‡									CHINESE Xīn-Sì‡/Rén-Wǔ									COPTIC 1718/1719‡								ETHIOPIC 1994/1995‡
	○	31	1[a]	2	3	4	5	10:41	1	2452274		15	16	17	18	19	20	21			16	17	18	19	20	21	22	Xiǎo hán	KOIAK 1718	21	22	23	24	25	26	27	TĀKHŠĀŠ 1994
JANUARY 2002	◑	7	8	9	10	11	12	3:55	2	2452281	TEVETH 5762	22	23	24	25	26	27	28		MONTH 11 Xīn-Sì	23	24	25	26	27	28	29			28	29[c]	30	1	2	3	4	
	●	14	15	16	17	18	19	13:29	3	2452288		29	1	2	3	4	5	6	Mon $1^h29^m0^p$		1	2	3	4	5	6	7			5	6[d]	7	8	9	10	11[e]	
	20	◐	22	23	24	25	26	17:46	4	2452295		7	8	9	10	11	12	13			8	9	10	11	12	13	14	Dà hán	TŌBE 1718	12	13	14	15	16	17	18	TER 1994
	27	○	29	30	31	1	2	22:50	5	2452302	SHEVAT 5762	14	15	16	17	18	19	20		MONTH 12 Xīn-Sì	15	16	17	18	19	20	21			19	20	21	22	23	24	25	
	3	◑	5	6	7	8	9	13:33	6	2452309		21	22	23	24	25	26	27			22	23	24	25	26	27	28	Lì chūn		26	27	28	29	30	1	2	
FEBRUARY 2002	10	11	●	13	14	15	16	7:41	7	2452316		28	29	30	1	2	3	4	Tue $13^h46^m3^p$		29	30	1[a]	2	3	4	5			3	4	5	6	7	8	9	
	17	18	19	◐	21	22	23	12:02	8	2452323		5	6	7	8	9	10	11			6	7	8	9	10	11	12	Yǔ shuǐ	MESHIR 1718	10	11	12	13	14	15	16	YAKĀTIT 1994
	24	25	26	○	28	1	2	9:17	9	2452330	ADAR 5762	12	13	14[f]	15	16	17	18		MONTH 1 Rén-Wǔ	13	14*	15[b]	16	17	18	19			17	18	19	20	21	22	23	
	3	4	5	◑	7	8	9	1:25	10	2452337		19	20	21	22	23	24	25			20	21	22	23	24	25	26	Jīng zhé		24	25	26	27	28	29	30	
MARCH 2002	10	11	12	13	●	15	16	2:02	11	2452344		26	27	28	29	1	2	3	Thu $2^h30^m4^p$		27	28	29	30	1	2	3			1	2	3	4	5	6	7	
	17	18	19	20[b]	21	◐	23	2:28	12	2452351		4	5	6	7	8	9	10			4	5	6	7	8	9	10	Chūn fēn	PAREMOTEP 1718	8	9	10	11	12	13	14	MAGĀBIT 1994
	24	25	26	27	○	29	30	18:25	13	2452358	NISAN 5762	11	12	13	14	15[g]	16	17		MONTH 2 Rén-Wǔ	11	12	13	14	15	16	17			15	16	17	18	19	20	21	
	31	1	2	3	◑	5	6	15:29	14	2452365		18	19	20	21	22	23	24			18	19	20	21	22	23[c]	24	Qīng míng		22	23	24	25	26	27	28	
	7	8	9	10	11	●	13	19:21	15	2452372		25	26	27	28	29	30	1	Fri $15^h14^m5^p$		25	26	27	28	29	30	1			29	30	1	2	3	4	5	
APRIL 2002	14	15	16	17	18	19	◐	12:48	16	2452379		2	3	4	5	6	7	8			2	3	4	5	6	7	8	Gǔ yǔ	PARMOUTE 1718	6	7	8	9	10	11	12	MIYĀZYĀ 1994
	21	22	23	24	25	26	○	3:00	17	2452386	IYYAR 5762	9	10	11	12	13	14	15		MONTH 3 Rén-Wǔ	9	10	11	12	13	14*	15			13	14	15	16	17	18	19	
	28	29	30	1	2	3	◑	7:16	18	2452393		16	17	18	19	20	21	22			16	17	18	19	20	21	22			20	21	22	23	24	25	26	
	5	6	7	8	9	10	11		19	2452400		23	24	25	26	27	28	29			23	24	25	26	27	28	29	Lì xià		27[f]	28	29[g]	30	1	2	3	
MAY 2002	●	13	14	15	16	17	18	10:45	20	2452407		1	2	3	4	5	6[h]	7	Sun $3^h58^m6^p$		1	2	3	4	5	6	7			4	5	6	7	8	9	10	
	◐	20	21	22	23	24	25	19:42	21	2452414	SIVAN 5762	8	9	10	11	12	13	14		MONTH 4 Rén-Wǔ	8	9	10	11	12	13	14	Xiǎo mǎn	PASHONS 1718	11	12	13	14	15	16	17	GENBOT 1994
	○	27	28	29	30	31	1	11:51	22	2452421		15	16	17	18	19	20	21			15	16	17	18	19	20	21			18	19	20	21	22	23	24	
	2	◑	4	5	6	7	8	0:05	23	2452428		22	23	24	25	26	27	28			22	23	24	25	26	27	28	Máng zhòng		25	26	27	28	29	30	1	
JUNE 2002	9	●	11	12	13	14	15	23:47	24	2452435		29	30	1	2	3	4	5	Mon $16^h42^m7^p$		29	30	1	2	3	4	5[d]			2	3	4	5	6	7	8	
	16	17	◐	19	20	21[c]	22	0:29	25	2452442	TAMMUZ 5762	6	7	8	9	10	11	12		MONTH 5 Rén-Wǔ	6	7	8	9	10	11	12	Xià zhì	PAŌNE 1718	9	10	11	12	13	14	15	SANĒ 1994
	23	○	25	26	27	28	29	21:42	26	2452449		13	14	15	16	17	18	19			13	14	15*	16	17	18	19			16	17	18	19	20	21	22	
	30	1	◑	3	4	5	6	17:19	27	2452456		20	21	22	23	24	25	26			20	21	22	23	24	25	26	Xiǎo shǔ		23	24	25	26	27	28	29	
JULY 2002	7	8	9	●	11	12	13	10:26	28	2452463		27	28	29	1	2	3	4	Wed $5^h26^m8^p$		27	28	29	1	2	3	4			30	1	2	3	4	5	6	
	14	15	16	◐	18	19	20	4:47	29	2452470		5	6	7	8	9[i]	10	11			5	6	7	8	9	10	11		EPĒP 1718	7	8	9	10	11	12	13	HAMLĒ 1994
	21	22	23	○	25	26	27	9:07	30	2452477	AV 5762	12	13	14	15	16	17	18		MONTH 6 Rén-Wǔ	12	13	14	15	16	17	18	Dà shǔ		14	15	16	17	18	19	20	
	28	29	30	31	◑	2	3	10:22	31	2452484		19	20	21	22	23	24	25			19	20	21	22	23	24	25			21	22	23	24	25	26	27	
	4	5	6	7	●	9	10	19:15	32	2452491		26	27	28	29	30	1	2			26	27	28	29	30	1	2	Lì qiū		28	29	30	1	2	3	4	
AUGUST 2002	11	12	13	14	◐	16	17	10:12	33	2452498		3	4	5	6	7	8	9	Thu $18^h10^m9^p$		3	4	5	6	7[e]	8	9			5	6	7	8	9	10	11	
	18	19	20	21	○	23	24	22:29	34	2452505	ELUL 5762	10	11	12	13	14	15	16		MONTH 7 Rén-Wǔ	10	11	12	13	14	15[f]	16*	Chǔ shǔ	MESORĒ 1718	12	13[h]	14	15	16	17	18	NAHASĒ 1994
	25	26	27	28	29	30	◑	2:31	35	2452512		17	18	19	20	21	22	23			17	18	19	20	21	22	23			19	20	21	22	23	24	25	
	1	2	3	4	5	6	●	3:10	36	2452519		24	25	26	27	28	29	1[a]	Sat $6^h54^m10^p$		24	25	26	27	28	29	1			26	27	28	29	30	1	2	
SEPTEMBER 2002	8	9	10	11	12	◐	14	18:08	37	2452526		2[a]	3	4	5	6	7	8			2	3	4	5	6	7	8	Bái lù	EPAG. 1718	3	4	5	1[a]	2	3	4	PĀG. 1994
	15	16	17	18	19	20	○	13:59	38	2452533	TISHRI 5763	9	10[b]	11	12	13	14	15[c]		MONTH 8 Rén-Wǔ	9	10	11	12	13	14	15[g]			5	6	7	8	9	10	11	
	22	23[d]	24	25	26	27	28		39	2452540		16	17	18	19	20	21	22			16	17	18	19	20	21	22	Qiū fēn	THOOUT 1719	12	13	14	15	16	17[b]	18	MASKARAM 1995
	◑	30	1	2	3	4	5	17:03	40	2452547		23	24	25	26	27	28	29			23	24	25	26	27	28	29			19	20	21	22	23	24	25	
	●	7	8	9	10	11	12	11:18	41	2452554		30	1	2	3	4	5	6	Sun $19^h38^m11^p$		1	2	3	4	5	6	7	Hán lù		26	27	28	29	30	1	2	
OCTOBER 2002	◐	14	15	16	17	18	19	5:33	42	2452561	HESHVAN 5763	7	8	9	10	11	12	13		MONTH 9 Rén-Wǔ	8	9[h]	10	11	12	13	14			3	4	5	6	7	8	9	
	20	○	22	23	24	25	26	7:20	43	2452568		14	15	16	17	18	19	20			15	16	17	18*	19	20	21	Shuāng jiàng	PAOPE 1719	10	11	12	13	14	15	16	TEQEMT 1995
	27	28	◑	30	31	1	2	5:28	44	2452575		21	22	23	24	25	26	27			22	23	24	25	26	27	28			17	18	19	20	21	22	23	
	3	●	5	6	7	8	9	20:34	45	2452582		28	29	30	1	2	3	4	Tue $8^h22^m12^p$		29	30	1	2	3	4	5	Lì dōng		24	25	26	27	28	29	30	
NOVEMBER 2002	10	◐	12	13	14	15	16	20:52	46	2452589	KISLEV 5763	5	6	7	8	9	10	11		MONTH 10 Rén-Wǔ	6	7	8	9	10	11	12			1	2	3	4	5	6	7	
	17	18	19	○	21	22	23	1:34	47	2452596		12	13	14	15	16	17	18			13	14	15	16	17	18	19	Xiǎo xuě	ATHŌR 1719	8	9	10	11	12	13	14	HEDĀR 1995
	24	25	26	◑	28	29	30	15:46	48	2452603		19	20	21	22	23	24	25[e]			20	21	22	23	24	25	26			15	16	17	18	19	20	21	
	1	2	3	●	5	6	7	7:34	49	2452610		26[e]	27[e]	28[e]	29[e]	30[d][e]	1[e]	2[e]			27	28	29	1	2	3	4	Dà xuě		22	23	24	25	26	27	28	
DECEMBER 2002	8	9	10	◐	12	13	14	15:48	50	2452617		3	4	5	6	7	8	9	Wed $21^h6^m13^p$		5	6	7	8	9	10	11			29	30	1	2	3	4	5	
	15	16	17	18	○	20	21	19:10	51	2452624	TEVETH 5763	10	11	12	13	14	15	16		MONTH 11 Rén-Wǔ	12	13	14	15	16	17	18	Dōng zhì	KOIAK 1719	6	7	8	9	10	11	12	TĀKHŠĀŠ 1995
	22[e]	23	24	25	26	◑	28	0:31	52	2452631		17	18	19	20	21	22	23			19[i]*	20	21	22	23	24	25			13	14	15	16	17	18	19	
	29	30	31	1	●	3	4	20:23	1	2452638		24	25	26	27	28	29	1	Fri $9^h50^m14^p$		26	27	28	29	30	1	2			20	21	22	23	24	25	26	

[a]New Year
[b]Spring (19:16)
[c]Summer (13:25)
[d]Autumn (4:55)
[e]Winter (1:14)
● New moon
◐ First quarter moon
○ Full moon
◑ Last quarter moon

‡Leap year
[a]New Year
[b]Yom Kippur
[c]Sukkot
[d]Winter starts
[e]Hanukkah
[f]Purim
[g]Passover
[h]Shavuot
[i]Fast of Av

‡Leap year
[a]New Year (4700, Horse)
[b]Lantern Festival
[c]Qīngmíng
[d]Dragon Festival
[e]Qīqiǎo
[f]Hungry Ghosts
[g]Mid-Autumn Festival
[h]Double-Ninth Festival
[i]Dōngzhì
*Start of 60-name cycle

‡Leap year
[a]New Year
[b]Building of the Cross
[c]Christmas
[d]Jesus's Circumcision
[e]Epiphany
[f]Easter
[g]Mary's Announcement
[h]Jesus's Transfiguration

2002

PERSIAN (ASTRONOMICAL) 1380/1381

Month	Sun	Mon	Tue	Wed	Thu	Fri	Sat
DEY 1380	9	10	11	12	13	14	15
	16	17	18	19	20	21	22
	23	24	25	26	27	28	29
	30	1	2	3	4	5	6
BAHMAN 1380	7	8	9	10	11	12	13
	14	15	16	17	18	19	20
	21	22	23	24	25	26	27
	28	29	30	1	2	3	4
ESFAND 1380	5	6	7	8	9	10	11
	12	13	14	15	16	17	18
	19	20	21	22	23	24	25
	26	27	28	29	1[a]	2	3
FARVARDIN 1381	4	5	6	7	8	9	10
	11	12	13[b]	14	15	16	17
	18	19	20	21	22	23	24
	25	26	27	28	29	30	31
ORDIBEHEST 1381	1	2	3	4	5	6	7
	8	9	10	11	12	13	14
	15	16	17	18	19	20	21
	22	23	24	25	26	27	28
	29	30	31	1	2	3	4
XORDAD 1381	5	6	7	8	9	10	11
	12	13	14	15	16	17	18
	19	20	21	22	23	24	25
	26	27	28	29	30	31	1
TIR 1381	2	3	4	5	6	7	8
	9	10	11	12	13	14	15
	16	17	18	19	20	21	22
	23	24	25	26	27	28	29
	30	31	1	2	3	4	5
MORDAD 1381	6	7	8	9	10	11	12
	13	14	15	16	17	18	19
	20	21	22	23	24	25	26
	27	28	29	30	31	1	2
SHAHRIVAR 1381	3	4	5	6	7	8	9
	10	11	12	13	14	15	16
	17	18	19	20	21	22	23
	24	25	26	27	28	29	30
	31	1	2	3	4	5	6
MEHR 1381	7	8	9	10	11	12	13
	14	15	16	17	18	19	20
	21	22	23	24	25	26	27
	28	29	30	1	2	3	4
ABAN 1381	5	6	7	8	9	10	11
	12	13	14	15	16	17	18
	19	20	21	22	23	24	25
	26	27	28	29	30	1	2
AZAR 1381	3	4	5	6	7	8	9
	10	11	12	13	14	15	16
	17	18	19	20	21	22	23
	24	25	26	27	28	29	30
DEY 1381	1	2	3	4	5	6	7
	8	9	10	11	12	13	14

[a]New Year
[b]Sizdeh Bedar

HINDU LUNAR 2058‡/2059

Month	Sun	Mon	Tue	Wed	Thu	Fri	Sat
MARGASIRA 2058	15	16	17	18	**19**	21	22
	23	24	25	26	27	28	29
	30	1	2	3	4	5	6
PAUSHA 2058	7	8	8	9	10	11	12
	13	15	16	17	18	19	20
	21	22	23	24	25	26	27
	28	29	30	1	2	3	4
MAGHA 2058	5	6	7	8	9	10	11
	12	13	14	15	16	17	**18**
	20	21	22	23	24	25	26
	27	28	29[h]	30	30	1	2
PHALGUNA 2058	3	4	5	6	7	8	9
	10	11	**12**	14	15[i]	16	17
	18	19	20	21	22	23	24
	25	26	27	28	29	30	1[a]
CHAITRA 2059	2	3	4	5	6	7	8
	9[b]	10	11	12	13	14	15
	16	18	19	20	21	22	23
	24	25	25	26	27	28	29
	30	1	2	3	4	5	6
VAISAKHA 2059	7	8	**9**	11	12	13	14
	15	16	17	18	19	20	21
	22	23	24	25	26	27	28
	29	30	1	2	3	4	5
JYAISHTHA 2059	6	7	8	9	10	11	**12**
	14	15	16	17	18	19	20
	21	21	22	23	24	25	26
	27	28	29	30	1	2	3
ASHADHA 2059	4	**5**	7	8	9	10	11
	12	13	14	15	16	17	18
	19	20	21	22	23	24	25
	26	27	28	29	30	1	2
SRAVANA 2059	3	4	5	6	7	**8**	10
	11	12	13	14	15	16	17
	18	18	19	20	21	22	23[c]
	24	25	26	27	28	29	30
BHADRAPADA 2059	**1**	3	4[d]	5	6	7	8
	9	10	11	12	13	14	15
	16	17	18	19	20	21	22
	23	24	25	26	27	28	29
	30	1	2	3	4	**5**	7
ASVINA 2059	8[e]	9[e]	10[e]	11	12	13	13
	14	15	16	17	18	19	20
	21	22	23	24	25	26	27
	28	30	1[f]	2	3	4	5
KARTTIKA 2059	6	7	8	9	10	11	12
	13	14	15	16	16	17	18
	19	20	**21**	23	24	25	26
	27	28	29	30	1	2	3
MARGASIRA 2059	4	5	6	7	8	9	10
	11[g]	12	13	14	15	16	17
	18	19	20	21	22	23	24
	25	**26**	28	29	30	1	2

‡Leap year
[a]New Year (Chitrabhānu)
[b]Birthday of Rāma
[c]Birthday of Krishna
[d]Ganēśa Chaturthī
[e]Dashara
[f]Diwali
[g]Birthday of Vishnu
[h]Night of Śiva
[i]Holi

HINDU SOLAR 1923‡/1924

Month	Sun	Mon	Tue	Wed	Thu	Fri	Sat
PAUSHA 1923	15	16	17	18	19	20	21
	22	23	24	25	26	27	28
	29	1[b]	2	3	4	5	6
MAGHA 1923	7	8	9	10	11	12	13
	14	15	16	17	18	19	20
	21	22	23	24	25	26	27
	28	29	1	2	3	4	5
PHALGUNA 1923	6	7	8	9	10	11	12
	13	14	15	16	17	18	19
	20	21	22	23	24	25	26
	27	28	29	30	1	2	3
CHAITRA 1923	4	5	6	7	8	9	10
	11	12	13	14	15	16	17
	18	19	20	21	22	23	24
	25	26	27	28	29	30	31
VAISAKHA 1924	1[a]	2	3	4	5	6	7
	8	9	10	11	12	13	14
	15	16	17	18	19	20	21
	22	23	24	25	26	27	28
	29	30	1	2	3	4	5
JYAISHTHA 1924	6	7	8	9	10	11	12
	13	14	15	16	17	18	19
	20	21	22	23	24	25	26
	27	28	29	30	31	32	1
ASHADHA 1924	2	3	4	5	6	7	8
	9	10	11	12	13	14	15
	16	17	18	19	20	21	22
	23	24	25	26	27	28	29
	30	31	32	1	2	3	4
SRAVANA 1924	5	6	7	8	9	10	11
	12	13	14	15	16	17	18
	19	20	21	22	23	24	25
	26	27	28	29	30	31	1
BHADRAPADA 1924	2	3	4	5	6	7	8
	9	10	11	12	13	14	15
	16	17	18	19	20	21	22
	23	24	25	26	27	28	29
	30	31	1	2	3	4	5
ASVINA 1924	6	7	8	9	10	11	12
	13	14	15	16	17	18	19
	20	21	22	23	24	25	26
	27	28	29	30	1	2	3
KARTTIKA 1924	4	5	6	7	8	9	10
	11	12	13	14	15	16	17
	18	19	20	21	22	23	24
	25	26	27	28	29	30	1
MARGASIRA 1924	2	3	4	5	6	7	8
	9	10	11	12	13	14	15
	16	17	18	19	20	21	22
	23	24	25	26	27	28	29
PAUSHA 1924	30	1	2	3	4	5	6
	7	8	9	10	11	12	13
	14	15	16	17	18	19	20

‡Leap year
[a]New Year (Manmatha)
[b]Pongal

ISLAMIC (ASTRONOMICAL) 1422/1423

Month	Sun	Mon	Tue	Wed	Thu	Fri	Sat
SHAWWAL 1422	15	16	17	18	19	20	21
	22	23	24	25	26	27	28
	29	30	1	2	3	4	5
DHU AL-QA'DA 1422	6	7	8	9	10	11	12
	13	14	15	16	17	18	19
	20	21	22	23	24	25	26
	27	28	29	30	1	2	3
DHU AL-HIJJA 1422	4	5	6	7	8	9	10[g]
	11	12	13	14	15	16	17
	18	19	20	21	22	23	24
	25	26	27	28	29	1[a]	2
MUHARRAM 1423	3	4	5	6	7	8	9
	10[b]	11	12	13	14	15	16
	17	18	19	20	21	22	23
	24	25	26	27	28	29	30
SAFAR 1423	1	2	3	4	5	6	7
	8	9	10	11	12	13	14
	15	16	17	18	19	20	21
	22	23	24	25	26	27	28
	29	30	1	2	3	4	5
RABI' I 1423	6	7	8	9	10	11	12[c]
	13	14	15	16	17	18	19
	20	21	22	23	24	25	26
	27	28	29	1	2	3	4
RABI' II 1423	5	6	7	8	9	10	11
	12	13	14	15	16	17	18
	19	20	21	22	23	24	25
	26	27	28	29	30	1	2
JUMADA I 1423	3	4	5	6	7	8	9
	10	11	12	13	14	15	16
	17	18	19	20	21	22	23
	24	25	26	27	28	29	1
JUMADA II 1423	2	3	4	5	6	7	8
	9	10	11	12	13	14	15
	16	17	18	19	20	21	22
	23	24	25	26	27	28	29
RAJAB 1423	1	2	3	4	5	6	7
	8	9	10	11	12	13	14
	15	16	17	18	19	20	21
	22	23	24	25	26	27[d]	28
	29	30	1	2	3	4	5
SHA'BAN 1423	6	7	8	9	10	11	12
	13	14	15	16	17	18	19
	20	21	22	23	24	25	26
	27	28	29	1[e]	2	3	4
RAMADAN 1423	5	6	7	8	9	10	11
	12	13	14	15	16	17	18
	19	20	21	22	23	24	25
	26	27	28	29	30	1[f]	2
SHAWWAL 1423	3	4	5	6	7	8	9
	10	11	12	13	14	15	16
	17	18	19	20	21	22	23
	24	25	26	27	28	29	1

[a]New Year
[b]'Ashūrā'
[c]Prophet's Birthday
[d]Ascent of the Prophet
[e]Start of Ramaḍān
[f]'Id al-Fiṭr
[g]'Id al-'Aḍḥā

GREGORIAN 2002

Julian (Sun)	Sun	Mon	Tue	Wed	Thu	Fri	Sat	Month
Dec 17	30	31	1	2	3	4	5	JANUARY 2002
	6	7[a]	8	9	10	11	12	
Dec 31	13	14[b]	15	16	17	18	19	
	20	21	22	23	24	25	26	
Jan 14	27	28	29	30	31	1	2	
	3	4	5	6	7	8	9	FEBRUARY 2002
Jan 28	10	11	12	13[c]	14	15	16	
	17	18	19	20	21	22	23	
Feb 11	24	25	26	27	28	1	2	
	3	4	5	6	7	8	9	MARCH 2002
Feb 25	10	11	12	13	14	15	16	
	17	18	19	20	21	22	23	
Mar 11	24[d]	25	26	27	28	29	30	
	31[e]	1	2	3	4	5	6	
Mar 25	7	8	9	10	11	12	13	APRIL 2002
	14	15	16	17	18	19	20	
Apr 8	21	22	23	24	25	26	27	
	28	29	30	1	2	3	4	
Apr 22	5[f]	6	7	8	9	10	11	MAY 2002
	12	13	14	15	16	17	18	
May 6	19	20	21	22	23	24	25	
	26	27	28	29	30	31	1	
May 20	2	3	4	5	6	7	8	JUNE 2002
	9	10	11	12	13	14	15	
Jun 3	16	17	18	19	20	21	22	
	23	24	25	26	27	28	29	
Jun 17	30	1	2	3	4	5	6	
	7	8	9	10	11	12	13	JULY 2002
Jul 1	14	15	16	17	18	19	20	
	21	22	23	24	25	26	27	
Jul 15	28	29	30	31	1	2	3	
	4	5	6	7	8	9	10	AUGUST 2002
Jul 29	11	12	13	14	15	16	17	
	18	19	20	21	22	23	24	
Aug 12	25	26	27	28	29	30	31	
	1	2	3	4	5	6	7	SEPTEMBER 2002
Aug 26	8	9	10	11	12	13	14	
	15	16	17	18	19	20	21	
Sep 9	22	23	24	25	26	27	28	
	29	30	1	2	3	4	5	
Sep 23	6	7	8	9	10	11	12	OCTOBER 2002
	13	14	15	16	17	18	19	
Oct 7	20	21	22	23	24	25	26	
	27	28	29	30	31	1	2	
Oct 21	3	4	5	6	7	8	9	NOVEMBER 2002
	10	11	12	13	14	15	16	
Nov 4	17	18	19	20	21	22	23	
	24	25	26	27	28	29	30	
Nov 18	1[g]	2	3	4	5	6	7	DECEMBER 2002
	8	9	10	11	12	13	14	
Dec 2	15	16	17	18	19	20	21	
	22	23	24	25[h]	26	27	28	
Dec 16	29	30	31	1	2	3	4	

[a]Orthodox Christmas
[b]Julian New Year
[c]Ash Wednesday
[d]Feast of Orthodoxy
[e]Easter
[f]Orthodox Easter
[g]Advent
[h]Christmas

2003

GREGORIAN 2003	Sun	Mon	Tue	Wed	Thu	Fri	Sat	Lunar Phases	ISO WEEK (Mon)	JULIAN DAY (Sun noon)
JANUARY 2003	29	30	31	1[a]	●	3	4	20:23	1	2452638
	5	6	7	8	9	◐	11	13:15	2	2452645
	12	13	14	15	16	17	○	10:47	3	2452652
	19	20	21	22	23	24	◑	8:33	4	2452659
	26	27	28	29	30	31	●	10:48	5	2452666
FEBRUARY 2003	2	3	4	5	6	7	8		6	2452673
	◐	10	11	12	13	14	15	11:11	7	2452680
	○	17	18	19	20	21	22	23:51	8	2452687
	◑	24	25	26	27	28	1	16:46	9	2452694
MARCH 2003	2	●	4	5	6	7	8	2:35	10	2452701
	9	10	◐	12	13	14	15	7:15	11	2452708
	16	17	○	19	20	21[b]	22	10:34	12	2452715
	23	24	◑	26	27	28	29	1:51	13	2452722
	30	31	●	2	3	4	5	19:18	14	2452729
APRIL 2003	6	7	8	◐	10	11	12	23:40	15	2452736
	13	14	15	○	17	18	19	19:36	16	2452743
	20	21	22	◑	24	25	26	12:18	17	2452750
	27	28	29	30	●	2	3	12:15	18	2452757
MAY 2003	4	5	6	7	8	◐	10	11:53	19	2452764
	11	12	13	14	15	○	17	3:36	20	2452771
	18	19	20	21	22	◑	24	0:30	21	2452778
	25	26	27	28	29	30	●	4:20	22	2452785
JUNE 2003	1	2	3	4	5	6	◐	20:28	23	2452792
	8	9	10	11	12	13	○	11:16	24	2452799
	15	16	17	18	19	20	◑[c]	14:45	25	2452806
	22	23	24	25	26	27	28		26	2452813
	●	30	1	2	3	4	5	18:39	27	2452820
JULY 2003	6	◐	8	9	10	11	12	2:32	28	2452827
	○	14	15	16	17	18	19	19:21	29	2452834
	20	◑	22	23	24	25	26	7:01	30	2452841
	27	28	●	30	31	1	2	6:53	31	2452848
AUGUST 2003	3	4	◐	6	7	8	9	7:28	32	2452855
	10	11	○	13	14	15	16	4:48	33	2452862
	17	18	19	◑	21	22	23	0:48	34	2452869
	24	25	26	●	28	29	30	17:26	35	2452876
	31	1	2	◐	4	5	6	12:34	36	2452883
SEPTEMBER 2003	7	8	9	○	11	12	13	16:36	37	2452890
	14	15	16	17	◑	19	20	19:03	38	2452897
	21	22	23[d]	24	25	●	27	3:09	39	2452904
	28	29	30	1	◐	3	4	19:09	40	2452911
OCTOBER 2003	5	6	7	8	9	○	11	7:27	41	2452918
	12	13	14	15	16	17	◑	12:31	42	2452925
	19	20	21	22	23	24	●	12:50	43	2452932
	26	27	28	29	30	31	◐	4:25	44	2452939
NOVEMBER 2003	2	3	4	5	6	7	8		45	2452946
	○	10	11	12	13	14	15	1:13	46	2452953
	16	◑	18	19	20	21	22	4:15	47	2452960
	●	24	25	26	27	28	29	22:59	48	2452967
	◐	1	2	3	4	5	6	17:16	49	2452974
DECEMBER 2003	7	○	9	10	11	12	13	20:37	50	2452981
	14	15	◑	17	18	19	20	17:42	51	2452988
	21	22[e]	●	24	25	26	27	9:43	52	2452995
	28	29	◐	31	1	2	3	10:03	1	2453002

JULIAN DAY	HEBREW 5763‡/5764	Sun	Mon	Tue	Wed	Thu	Fri	Sat	Molad
2452638	SHEVAT 5763	24	25	26	27	28	29	1	Fri $9^{h}50^{m}14^{p}$
2452645		2	3	4	5	6	7	8	
2452652		9	10	11	12	13	14	15	
2452659		16	17	18	19	20	21	22	
2452666		23	24	25	26	27	28	29	
2452673	ADAR I 5763	30	1	2	3	4	5	6	Sat $22^{h}34^{m}15^{p}$
2452680		7	8	9	10	11	12	13	
2452687		14	15	16	17	18	19	20	
2452694		21	22	23	24	25	26	27	
2452701	ADAR II 5763	28	29	30	1	2	3	4	Mon $11^{h}18^{m}16^{p}$
2452708		5	6	7	8	9	10	11	
2452715		12	13	14[f]	15	16	17	18	
2452722		19	20	21	22	23	24	25	
2452729	NISAN 5763	26	27	28	29	1	2	3	Wed $0^{h}2^{m}17^{p}$
2452736		4	5	6	7	8	9	10	
2452743		11	12	13	14	15[g]	16	17	
2452750		18	19	20	21	22	23	24	
2452757	IYAR 5763	25	26	27	28	29	30	1	Thu $12^{h}47^{m}0^{p}$
2452764		2	3	4	5	6	7	8	
2452771		9	10	11	12	13	14	15	
2452778		16	17	18	19	20	21	22	
2452785		23	24	25	26	27	28	29	
2452792	SIVAN 5763	1	2	3	4	5	6[h]	7	Sat $1^{h}31^{m}1^{p}$
2452799		8	9	10	11	12	13	14	
2452806		15	16	17	18	19	20	21	
2452813		22	23	24	25	26	27	28	
2452820	TAMMUZ 5763	29	30	1	2	3	4	5	Sun $14^{h}15^{m}2^{p}$
2452827		6	7	8	9	10	11	12	
2452834		13	14	15	16	17	18	19	
2452841		20	21	22	23	24	25	26	
2452848	AV 5763	27	28	29	1	2	3	4	Tue $2^{h}59^{m}3^{p}$
2452855		5	6	7	8	9[i]	10	11	
2452862		12	13	14	15	16	17	18	
2452869		19	20	21	22	23	24	25	
2452876	ELUL 5763	26	27	28	29	30	1	2	Wed $15^{h}43^{m}4^{p}$
2452883		3	4	5	6	7	8	9	
2452890		10	11	12	13	14	15	16	
2452897		17	18	19	20	21	22	23	
2452904	TISHRI 5764	24	25	26	27	28	29	1[a]	Fri $4^{h}27^{m}5^{p}$
2452911		2[a]	3	4	5	6	7	8	
2452918		9	10[b]	11	12	13	14	15[c]	
2452925		16	17	18	19	20	21	22	
2452932		23	24	25	26	27	28	29	
2452939	ḤESHVAN 5764	30	1	2	3	4	5	6	Sat $17^{h}11^{m}6^{p}$
2452946		7	8	9	10	11	12	13	
2452953		14	15	16	17	18	19	20	
2452960		21	22	23	24	25	26	27	
2452967	KISLEV 5764	28	29	30	1	2	3	4	Mon $5^{h}55^{m}7^{p}$
2452974		5	6	7	8	9	10	11[d]	
2452981		12	13	14	15	16	17	18	
2452988		19	20	21	22	23	24	25[e]	
2452995	TEVETH 5764	26[e]	27[e]	28[e]	29[e]	30[e]	1[e]	2[e]	Tue $18^{h}39^{m}8^{p}$
2453002		3	4	5	6	7	8	9	

JULIAN DAY	CHINESE Rén-Wǔ/Guǐ-Wèi	Sun	Mon	Tue	Wed	Thu	Fri	Sat	Solar Term
2452638	MONTH 12 Rén-Wǔ	26	27	28	29	30	1	2	
2452645		3	*4*	5	6	7	8	9	*Xiǎo hán*
2452652		10	11	12	13	14	15	16	
2452659		17	***18***	19	20	21	22	23	***Dà hán***
2452666	MONTH 1 Guǐ-Wèi	24	25	26	27	28	29	1[a]	
2452673		2	3	*4*	5	6	7	8	*Lì chūn*
2452680		9	10	11	12	13	14	15[b]	
2452687		16	17	18	***19***	20*	21	22	***Yǔ shuǐ***
2452694		23	24	25	26	27	28	29	
2452701	MONTH 2 Guǐ-Wèi	30	1	2	3	*4*	5	6	*Jīng zhé*
2452708		7	8	9	10	11	12	13	
2452715		14	15	16	17	18	***19***	20	***Chūn fēn***
2452722		21	22	23	24	25	26	27	
2452729	MONTH 3 Guǐ-Wèi	28	29	30	1	2	3	*4*[c]	*Qīng míng*
2452736		5	6	7	8	9	10	11	
2452743		12	13	14	15	16	17	18	
2452750		***19***	20*	21	22	23	24	25	***Gǔ yǔ***
2452757	MONTH 4 Guǐ-Wèi	26	27	28	29	1	2	3	
2452764		4	5	6	7	8	9	10	*Lì xià*
2452771		11	12	13	14	15	16	17	
2452778		18	19	20	***21***	22	23	24	***Xiǎo mǎn***
2452785	MONTH 5 Guǐ-Wèi	25	26	27	28	29	30	1	
2452792		2	3	4	5[d]	6	*7*	8	*Máng zhòng*
2452799		9	10	11	12	13	14	15	
2452806		16	17	18	19	20	21*	22	
2452813		***23***	24	25	26	27	28	29	***Xià zhì***
2452820	MONTH 6 Guǐ-Wèi	30	1	2	3	4	5	6	
2452827		7	*8*	9	10	11	12	13	*Xiǎo shǔ*
2452834		14	15	16	17	18	19	20	
2452841		21	22	23	***24***	25	26	27	***Dà shǔ***
2452848	MONTH 7 Guǐ-Wèi	28	29	1	2	3	4	5	
2452855		6	7[e]	8	9	10	*11*	12	*Lì qiū*
2452862		13	14	15[f]	16	17	18	19	
2452869		20	21	22*	23	24	25	***26***	***Chǔ shǔ***
2452876	MONTH 8 Guǐ-Wèi	27	28	29	30	1	2	3	
2452883		4	5	6	7	8	9	10	
2452890		11	*12*	13	14	15[g]	16	17	*Bái lù*
2452897		18	19	20	21	22	23	24	
2452904	MONTH 9 Guǐ-Wèi	25	26	***27***	28	29	1	2	***Qiū fēn***
2452911		3	4	5	6	7	8	9[h]	
2452918		10	11	12	13	*14*	15	16	*Hán lù*
2452925		17	18	19	20	21	22	23*	
2452932	MONTH 10 Guǐ-Wèi	24	25	26	27	28	***29***	1	***Shuāng jiàng***
2452939		2	3	4	5	6	7	8	
2452946		9	10	11	12	13	14	*15*	*Lì dōng*
2452953		16	17	18	19	20	21	22	
2452960		23	24	25	26	27	28	29	
2452967	MONTH 11* Guǐ-Wèi	***30***	1	2	3	4	5	6	***Xiǎo xuě***
2452974		7	8	9	10	11	12	13	
2452981		*14*	15	16	17	18	19	20	*Dà xuě*
2452988		21	22	23	24*	25	26	27	
2452995	MONTH 12 Guǐ-Wèi	28	***29***[i]	1	2	3	4	5	***Dōng zhì***
2453002		6	7	8	9	10	11	12	

JULIAN DAY	COPTIC 1719‡/1720	Sun	Mon	Tue	Wed	Thu	Fri	Sat	ETHIOPIC 1995‡/1996
2452638	KOIAK 1719	20	21	22	23	24	25	26	TĀKHŚĀŚ 1995
2452645	TÔBE 1719	27	28	29[c]	30	1	2	3	ṬER 1995
2452652		4	5	6[d]	7	8	9	10	
2452659		11[e]	12	13	14	15	16	17	
2452666		18	19	20	21	22	23	24	
2452673	MESHIR 1719	25	26	27	28	29	30	1	YAKĀTIT 1995
2452680		2	3	4	5	6	7	8	
2452687		9	10	11	12	13	14	15	
2452694		16	17	18	19	20	21	22	
2452701		23	24	25	26	27	28	29	
2452708	PAREMOTEP 1719	30	1	2	3	4	5	6	MAGĀBIT 1995
2452715		7	8	9	10	11	12	13	
2452722		14	15	16	17	18	19	20	
2452729		21	22	23	24	25	26	27	
2452736	PARMOUTE 1719	28	29	30	1	2	3	4	MIYĀZYĀ 1995
2452743		5	6	7	8	9	10	11	
2452750		12	13	14	15	16	17	18	
2452757		19[f]	20	21	22	23	24	25	
2452764	PASHONS 1719	26	27	28	29[g]	30	1	2	GENBOT 1995
2452771		3	4	5	6	7	8	9	
2452778		10	11	12	13	14	15	16	
2452785		17	18	19	20	21	22	23	
2452792		24	25	26	27	28	29	30	
2452799	PAÔNE 1719	1	2	3	4	5	6	7	SANĒ 1995
2452806		8	9	10	11	12	13	14	
2452813		15	16	17	18	19	20	21	
2452820		22	23	24	25	26	27	28	
2452827	EPÊP 1719	29	30	1	2	3	4	5	ḤAMLĒ 1995
2452834		6	7	8	9	10	11	12	
2452841		13	14	15	16	17	18	19	
2452848		20	21	22	23	24	25	26	
2452855	MESORÊ 1719	27	28	29	30	1	2	3	NAḤASĒ 1995
2452862		4	5	6	7	8	9	10	
2452869		11	12	13[h]	14	15	16	17	
2452876		18	19	20	21	22	23	24	
2452883	EPAG. 1719	25	26	27	28	29	30	1	PĀG. 1995
2452890	THOOUT 1720	2	3	4	5	6	1[a]	2	MASKARAM 1996
2452897		3	4	5	6	7	8	9	
2452904		10	11	12	13	14	15	16	
2452911		17[b]	18	19	20	21	22	23	
2452918		24	25	26	27	28	29	30	
2452925	PAOPE 1720	1	2	3	4	5	6	7	ṬEQEMT 1996
2452932		8	9	10	11	12	13	14	
2452939		15	16	17	18	19	20	21	
2452946		22	23	24	25	26	27	28	
2452953	ATHÔR 1720	29	30	1	2	3	4	5	ḪEDĀR 1996
2452960		6	7	8	9	10	11	12	
2452967		13	14	15	16	17	18	19	
2452974		20	21	22	23	24	25	26	
2452981	KOIAK 1720	27	28	29	30	1	2	3	TĀKHŚĀŚ 1996
2452988		4	5	6	7	8	9	10	
2452995		11	12	13	14	15	16	17	
2453002		18	19	20	21	22	23	24	

[a]New Year
[b]Spring (1:00)
[c]Summer (19:10)
[d]Autumn (10:47)
[e]Winter (7:03)
● New moon
◐ First quarter moon
○ Full moon
◑ Last quarter moon

‡Leap year
[a]New Year
[b]Yom Kippur
[c]Sukkot
[d]Winter starts
[e]Ḥanukkah
[f]Purim
[g]Passover
[h]Shavuot
[i]Fast of Av

[a]New Year (4701, Sheep)
[b]Lantern Festival
[c]Qīngmíng
[d]Dragon Festival
[e]Qīqiǎo
[f]Hungry Ghosts
[g]Mid-Autumn Festival
[h]Double-Ninth Festival
[i]Dōngzhì
*Start of 60-name cycle

‡Leap year
[a]New Year
[b]Building of the Cross
[c]Christmas
[d]Jesus's Circumcision
[e]Epiphany
[f]Easter
[g]Mary's Announcement
[h]Jesus's Transfiguration

PERSIAN (ASTRONOMICAL) 1381/1382

Month	Sun	Mon	Tue	Wed	Thu	Fri	Sat
DEY 1381	8	9	10	11	12	13	14
	15	16	17	18	19	20	21
	22	23	24	25	26	27	28
	29	30	1	2	3	4	5
BAHMAN 1381	6	7	8	9	10	11	12
	13	14	15	16	17	18	19
	20	21	22	23	24	25	26
	27	28	29	30	1	2	3
ESFAND 1381	4	5	6	7	8	9	10
	11	12	13	14	15	16	17
	18	19	20	21	22	23	24
	25	26	27	28	29	1[a]	2
FARVARDĪN 1382	3	4	5	6	7	8	9
	10	11	12	13[b]	14	15	16
	17	18	19	20	21	22	23
	24	25	26	27	28	29	30
ORDĪBEHEŠT 1382	31	1	2	3	4	5	6
	7	8	9	10	11	12	13
	14	15	16	17	18	19	20
	21	22	23	24	25	26	27
XORDĀD 1382	28	29	30	31	1	2	3
	4	5	6	7	8	9	10
	11	12	13	14	15	16	17
	18	19	20	21	22	23	24
	25	26	27	28	29	30	31
TĪR 1382	1	2	3	4	5	6	7
	8	9	10	11	12	13	14
	15	16	17	18	19	20	21
	22	23	24	25	26	27	28
MORDĀD 1382	29	30	31	1	2	3	4
	5	6	7	8	9	10	11
	12	13	14	15	16	17	18
	19	20	21	22	23	24	25
SHAHRĪVAR 1382	26	27	28	29	30	31	1
	2	3	4	5	6	7	8
	9	10	11	12	13	14	15
	16	17	18	19	20	21	22
	23	24	25	26	27	28	29
MEHR 1382	30	31	1	2	3	4	5
	6	7	8	9	10	11	12
	13	14	15	16	17	18	19
	20	21	22	23	24	25	26
ĀBĀN 1382	27	28	29	30	1	2	3
	4	5	6	7	8	9	10
	11	12	13	14	15	16	17
	18	19	20	21	22	23	24
ĀZAR 1382	25	26	27	28	29	30	1
	2	3	4	5	6	7	8
	9	10	11	12	13	14	15
	16	17	18	19	20	21	22
	23	24	25	26	27	28	29
DEY 1382	30	1	2	3	4	5	6
	7	8	9	10	11	12	13

[a]New Year
[b]Sizdeh Bedar

HINDU LUNAR 2059/2060

Month	Sun	Mon	Tue	Wed	Thu	Fri	Sat
PAUSHA 2059	25	**26**	28	29	30	1	2
	3	4	5	6	7	8	8
	9	10	11	12	13	14	15
	16	17	18	19	**20**	22	23
	24	25	26	27	28	29	30
MĀGHA 2059	1	2	3	4	5	6	7
	8	9	10	11	*11*	12	**13**
	15	16	17	18	19	20	21
	22	23	24	25	26	**27**	29[h]
	30	*30*	1	2	3	4	5
PHĀLGUNA 2059	6	7	8	9	10	11	12
	13	14	15[i]	16	17	18	**19**
	21	22	23	24	25	26	27
CHAITRA 2060	28	29	30	1[a]	2	3	4
	4	5	6	7	8[b]	9	10
	11	12	**13**	15	16	17	18
	19	20	21	22	23	24	25
VAIŚĀKHA 2060	26	27	28	29	30	1	2
	3	4	5	6	7	8	9
	10	11	12	13	14	15	**16**
	18	19	20	21	22	23	24
	25	26	27	28	29	29	30
JYAISHTHA 2060	1	2	3	4	5	6	7
	8	**9**	11	12	13	14	15
	16	17	18	19	20	21	22
	23	24	25	26	27	28	29
ĀSHĀDHA 2060	30	1	2	3	4	5	6
	7	8	9	10	11	**12**	14
	15	16	17	18	19	20	21
	22	23	24	25	26	*26*	27
ŚRĀVANA 2060	28	29	30	1	2	3	4
	5	7	8	9	10	11	12
	13	14	15	16	17	18	19
	20	21	22	23[c]	24	25	26
BHĀDRAPADA 2060	27	28	29	30	1	2	3
	4[d]	5	6	7	**8**	10	11
	12	13	14	15	16	17	18
	19	20	21	22	*22*	23	24
ĀŚVINA 2060	25	26	27	28	29	30	**1**
	3	4	5	6	7	8[e]	9[e]
	10[e]	11	12	13	14	15	16
	17	18	19	20	21	22	23
	24	25	26	27	28	29	30
KĀRTTIKA 2060	1[f]	2	3	4	**5**	7	8
	9	10	11	12	13	14	15
	16	*16*	17	18	19	20	21
	22	23	24	25	26	27	28
MĀRGAŚIRA 2060	**29**	1	2	3	4	5	6
	7	8	9	10	11[g]	12	13
	14	15	16	17	18	19	*19*
	20	**21**	23	24	25	26	27
PAUSHA 2060	28	29	30	1	2	3	4
	5	7	8	*8*	9	10	11

[a]New Year (Subhānu)
[b]Birthday of Rāma
[c]Birthday of Krishna
[d]Ganēśa Chaturthī
[e]Dashara
[f]Diwali
[g]Birthday of Vishnu
[h]Night of Śiva
[i]Holi

HINDU SOLAR 1924/1925

Month	Sun	Mon	Tue	Wed	Thu	Fri	Sat
PAUSHA 1924	14	15	16	17	18	19	20
	21	22	23	24	25	26	27
MĀGHA 1924	28	29	1[b]	2	3	4	5
	6	7	8	9	10	11	12
	13	14	15	16	17	18	19
	20	21	22	23	24	25	26
PHĀLGUNA 1924	27	28	29	30	1	2	3
	4	5	6	7	8	9	10
	11	12	13	14	15	16	17
	18	19	20	21	22	23	24
CHAITRA 1924	25	26	27	28	29	1	2
	3	4	5	6	7	8	9
	10	11	12	13	14	15	16
	17	18	19	20	21	22	23
	24	25	26	27	28	29	30
VAIŚĀKHA 1925	31	1[a]	2	3	4	5	6
	7	8	9	10	11	12	13
	14	15	16	17	18	19	20
	21	22	23	24	25	26	27
JYAISHTHA 1925	28	29	30	31	1	2	3
	4	5	6	7	8	9	10
	11	12	13	14	15	16	17
	18	19	20	21	22	23	24
	25	26	27	28	29	30	31
ĀSHĀDHA 1925	1	2	3	4	5	6	7
	8	9	10	11	12	13	14
	15	16	17	18	19	20	21
	22	23	24	25	26	27	28
ŚRĀVANA 1925	29	30	31	32	1	2	3
	4	5	6	7	8	9	10
	11	12	13	14	15	16	17
	18	19	20	21	22	23	24
	25	26	27	28	29	30	31
BHĀDRAPADA 1925	1	2	3	4	5	6	7
	8	9	10	11	12	13	14
	15	16	17	18	19	20	21
	22	23	24	25	26	27	28
ĀŚVINA 1925	29	30	31	1	2	3	4
	5	6	7	8	9	10	11
	12	13	14	15	16	17	18
	19	20	21	22	23	24	25
KĀRTTIKA 1925	26	27	28	29	30	31	1
	2	3	4	5	6	7	8
	9	10	11	12	13	14	15
	16	17	18	19	20	21	22
	23	24	25	26	27	28	29
MĀRGAŚIRA 1925	30	1	2	3	4	5	6
	7	8	9	10	11	12	13
	14	15	16	17	18	19	20
	21	22	23	24	25	26	27
PAUSHA 1925	28	29	1	2	3	4	5
	6	7	8	9	10	11	12
	13	14	15	16	17	18	19

[a]New Year (Durmukha)
[b]Pongal

ISLAMIC (ASTRONOMICAL) 1423/1424‡

Month	Sun	Mon	Tue	Wed	Thu	Fri	Sat
DHU AL-QA'DA 1423	24	25	26	27	28	29	1
	2	3	4	5	6	7	8
	9	10	11	12	13	14	15
	16	17	18	19	20	21	22
	23	24	25	26	27	28	29
DHU AL-HIJJA 1423	30	1	2	3	4	5	6
	7	8	9	10[g]	11	12	13
	14	15	16	17	18	19	20
	21	22	23	24	25	26	27
MUHARRAM 1424	28	29	1[a]	2[d]	3	4	5
	6	7	8	9	10[b]	11	12
	13	14	15	16	17	18	19
	20	21	22	23	24	25	26
ṢAFAR 1424	27	28	29	30	1	2	3
	4	5	6	7	8	9	10
	11	12	13	14	15	16	17
	18	19	20	21	22	23	24
RABĪ' I 1424	25	26	27	28	29	30	1
	2	3	4	5	6	7	8
	9	10	11	12[c]	13	14	15
	16	17	18	19	20	21	22
	23	24	25	26	27	28	29
RABĪ' II 1424	1	2	3	4	5	6	7
	8	9	10	11	12	13	14
	15	16	17	18	19	20	21
	22	23	24	25	26	27	28
JUMĀDĀ I 1424	29	30	1	2	3	4	5
	6	7	8	9	10	11	12
	13	14	15	16	17	18	19
	20	21	22	23	24	25	26
JUMĀDĀ II 1424	27	28	29	1	2	3	4
	5	6	7	8	9	10	11
	12	13	14	15	16	17	18
	19	20	21	22	23	24	25
RAJAB 1424	26	27	28	29	30	1	2
	3	4	5	6	7	8	9
	10	11	12	13	14	15	16
	17	18	19	20	21	22	23
SHA'BĀN 1424	24	25	26	27[d]	28	29	1
	2	3	4	5	6	7	8
	9	10	11	12	13	14	15
	16	17	18	19	20	21	22
	23	24	25	26	27	28	29
RAMAḌĀN 1424	30	1[e]	2	3	4	5	6
	7	8	9	10	11	12	13
	14	15	16	17	18	19	20
	21	22	23	24	25	26	27
SHAWWĀL 1424	28	29	1[f]	2	3	4	5
	6	7	8	9	10	11	12
	13	14	15	16	17	18	19
	20	21	22	23	24	25	26
DHU AL-QA'DA 1424	27	28	29	30	1	2	3
	4	5	6	7	8	9	10

‡Leap year
[a]New Year
[d]New Year (Arithmetic)
[b]'Ashūrā'
[c]Prophet's Birthday
[d]Ascent of the Prophet
[e]Start of Ramaḍān
[f]'Īd al-Fiṭr
[g]'Īd al-'Aḍḥā

GREGORIAN 2003

Julian (Sun)	Sun	Mon	Tue	Wed	Thu	Fri	Sat	Month
Dec 16	29	30	31	1	2	3	4	
	5	6	7[a]	8	9	10	11	JANUARY 2003
Dec 30	12	13	14[b]	15	16	17	18	
	19	20	21	22	23	24	25	
Jan 13	26	27	28	29	30	31	1	
	2	3	4	5	6	7	8	FEBRUARY 2003
Jan 27	9	10	11	12	13	14	15	
	16	17	18	19	20	21	22	
Feb 10	23	24	25	26	27	28	1	
	2	3	4	5[c]	6	7	8	MARCH 2003
Feb 24	9	10	11	12	13	14	15	
	16[d]	17	18	19	20	21	22	
Mar 10	23	24	25	26	27	28	29	
	30	31	1	2	3	4	5	
Mar 24	6	7	8	9	10	11	12	APRIL 2003
	13	14	15	16	17	18	19	
Apr 7	20[e]	21	22	23	24	25	26	
	27[f]	28	29	30	1	2	3	
Apr 21	4	5	6	7	8	9	10	MAY 2003
	11	12	13	14	15	16	17	
May 5	18	19	20	21	22	23	24	
	25	26	27	28	29	30	31	
May 19	1	2	3	4	5	6	7	
	8	9	10	11	12	13	14	JUNE 2003
Jun 2	15	16	17	18	19	20	21	
	22	23	24	25	26	27	28	
Jun 16	29	30	1	2	3	4	5	
	6	7	8	9	10	11	12	JULY 2003
Jun 30	13	14	15	16	17	18	19	
	20	21	22	23	24	25	26	
Jul 14	27	28	29	30	31	1	2	
	3	4	5	6	7	8	9	AUGUST 2003
Jul 28	10	11	12	13	14	15	16	
	17	18	19	20	21	22	23	
Aug 11	24	25	26	27	28	29	30	
	31	1	2	3	4	5	6	
Aug 25	7	8	9	10	11	12	13	SEPTEMBER 2003
	14	15	16	17	18	19	20	
Sep 8	21	22	23	24	25	26	27	
	28	29	30	1	2	3	4	
Sep 22	5	6	7	8	9	10	11	OCTOBER 2003
	12	13	14	15	16	17	18	
Oct 6	19	20	21	22	23	24	25	
	26	27	28	29	30	31	1	
Oct 20	2	3	4	5	6	7	8	NOVEMBER 2003
	9	10	11	12	13	14	15	
Nov 3	16	17	18	19	20	21	22	
	23	24	25	26	27	28	29	
Nov 17	30[g]	1	2	3	4	5	6	
	7	8	9	10	11	12	13	DECEMBER 2003
Dec 1	14	15	16	17	18	19	20	
	21	22	23	24	25[h]	26	27	
Dec 15	28	29	30	31	1	2	3	

[a]Orthodox Christmas
[b]Julian New Year
[c]Ash Wednesday
[d]Feast of Orthodoxy
[e]Easter
[f]Orthodox Easter
[g]Advent
[h]Christmas

2004

GREGORIAN 2004‡								Lunar Phases	ISO WEEK	JULIAN DAY	HEBREW 5764/5765‡								Molad	CHINESE Guǐ-Wèi/Jiǎ-Shēn‡								Solar Term	COPTIC 1720/1721								ETHIOPIC 1996/1997
	Sun	Mon	Tue	Wed	Thu	Fri	Sat		(Mon)	(Sun noon)		Sun	Mon	Tue	Wed	Thu	Fri	Sat			Sun	Mon	Tue	Wed	Thu	Fri	Sat			Sun	Mon	Tue	Wed	Thu	Fri	Sat	
JANUARY 2004	28	29	◐	31	1[a]	2	3	10:03	1	2453002	TEVETH 5764	3	4	5	6	7	8	9		MONTH 12 Guǐ-Wèi	6	7	8	9	10	11	12		KOIAK 1720	18	19	20	21	22	23	24	TÂKHŚÂŚ 1996
	4	5	6	○	8	9	10	15:40	2	2453009		10	11	12	13	14	15	16			13	14	15	16	17	18	19	Xiǎo hán		25	26	27	28	29[c]	30	1	
	11	12	13	14	◑	16	17	4:46	3	2453016		17	18	19	20	21	22	23			20	21	22	23	24	25	26		TÔBE 1720	2	3	4	5	6[d]	7	8	ṬER 1996
	18	19	20	●	22	23	24	21:05	4	2453023	SHEVAT 5764	24	25	26	27	28	29	1	Thu 7h23m9p	MONTH 1 Jiǎ-Shēn	27	28	29	30	1[a]	2	3	Dà hán		9	10	11[e]	12	13	14	15	
	25	26	27	28	◐	30	31	6:03	5	2453030		2	3	4	5	6	7	8			4	5	6	7	8	9	10			16	17	18	19	20	21	22	
FEBRUARY 2004	1	2	3	4	5	○	7	8:47	6	2453037		9	10	11	12	13	14	15			11	12	13	14	15[b]	16	17	Lì chūn		23	24	25	26	27	28	29	
	8	9	10	11	12	◑	14	13:40	7	2453044		16	17	18	19	20	21	22			18	19	20	21	22	23	24		MESHIR 1720	30	1	2	3	4	5	6	YAKÂTIT 1996
	15	16	17	18	19	●	21	9:18	8	2453051		23	24	25	26	27	28	29		MONTH 2 Jiǎ-Shēn	25*	26	27	28	29	1	2	Yǔ shuǐ		7	8	9	10	11	12	13	
	22	23	24	25	26	27	◐	3:24	9	2453058	ADAR 5764	30	1	2	3	4	5	6	Fri 20h7m10p		3	4	5	6	7	8	9			14	15	16	17	18	19	20	
MARCH 2004	29	1	2	3	4	5	○	23:14	10	2453065		7	8	9	10	11	12	13			10	11	12	13	14	15	16	Jīng zhé		21	22	23	24	25	26	27	
	7	8	9	10	11	12	◑	21:01	11	2453072		14[f]	15	16	17	18	19	20			17	18	19	20	21	22	23		PAREMOTEP 1720	28	29	30	1	2	3	4	MAGÂBIT 1996
	14	15	16	17	18	19	●[b]	22:41	12	2453079		21	22	23	24	25	26	27			24	25	26	27	28	29	30	Chūn fēn		5	6	7	8	9	10	11	
	21	22	23	24	25	26	27		13	2453086	NISAN 5764	28	29	1	2	3	4	5	Sun 8h51m11p	LEAP MONTH 2 Jiǎ-Shēn	1	2	3	4	5	6	7			12	13	14	15	16	17	18	
APRIL 2004	◐	29	30	31	1	2	3	23:48	14	2453093		6	7	8	9	10	11	12			8	9	10	11	12	13	14	Qīng míng		19	20	21	22	23	24	25	
	4	○	6	7	8	9	10	11:03	15	2453100		13	14	15[g]	16	17	18	19			15[c]	16	17	18	19	20	21		PARMOUTE 1720	26	27	28	29	30	1	2	MIYÂZYÂ 1996
	11	◑	13	14	15	16	17	3:46	16	2453107		20	21	22	23	24	25	26			22	23	24	25	26*	27	28	Gǔ yǔ		3[f]	4	5	6	7	8	9	
	18	●	20	21	22	23	24	13:21	17	2453114	IYYAR 5764	27	28	29	30	1	2	3	Mon 21h35m12p	MONTH 3 Jiǎ-Shēn	29	1	2	3	4	5	6			10	11	12	13	14	15	16	
MAY 2004	25	26	◐	28	29	30	1	17:32	18	2453121		4	5	6	7	8	9	10			7	8	9	10	11	12	13			17	18	19	20	21	22	23	
	2	3	○	5	6	7	8	20:34	19	2453128		11	12	13	14	15	16	17			14	15	16	17	18	19	20	Lì xià		24	25	26	27	28	29[g]	30	
	9	10	◑	12	13	14	15	11:04	20	2453135		18	19	20	21	22	23	24			21	22	23	24	25	26	27		PASHONS 1720	1	2	3	4	5	6	7	GENBOT 1996
	16	17	18	●	20	21	22	4:52	21	2453142	SIVAN 5764	25	26	27	28	29	1	2	Wed 10h19m13p	MONTH 4 Jiǎ-Shēn	28	29	30	1	2	3	4	Xiǎo mǎn		8	9	10	11	12	13	14	
	23	24	25	26	◐	28	29	7:57	22	2453149		3	4	5	6[h]	7	8	9			5	6	7	8	9	10	11			15	16	17	18	19	20	21	
JUNE 2004	30	31	1	2	○	4	5	4:20	23	2453156		10	11	12	13	14	15	16			12	13	14	15	16	17	18	Máng zhòng		22	23	24	25	26	27	28	
	6	7	8	◑	10	11	12	20:02	24	2453163		17	18	19	20	21	22	23			19	20	21	22	23	24	25		PAÔNE 1720	29	30	1	2	3	4	5	SANÊ 1996
	13	14	15	16	●	18	19	20:27	25	2453170		24	25	26	27	28	29	30		MONTH 5 Jiǎ-Shēn	26	27*	28	29	30	1	2	Xià zhì		6	7	8	9	10	11	12	
	20	21[c]	22	23	24	◐	26	19:08	26	2453177	TAMMUZ 5764	1	2	3	4	5	6	7	Thu 23h3m14p		3	4	5[d]	6	7	8	9			13	14	15	16	17	18	19	
JULY 2004	27	28	29	30	1	○	3	11:09	27	2453184		8	9	10	11	12	13	14			10	11	12	13	14	15	16	Xiǎo shǔ		20	21	22	23	24	25	26	
	4	5	6	7	8	◑	10	7:33	28	2453191		15	16	17	18	19	20	21			17	18	19	20	21	22	23		EPÊP 1720	27	28	29	30	1	2	3	ḤAMLÊ 1996
	11	12	13	14	15	16	●	11:24	29	2453198		22	23	24	25	26	27	28		MONTH 6 Jiǎ-Shēn	24	25	26	27	28	29	1	Dà shǔ		4	5	6	7	8	9	10	
	18	19	20	21	22	23	24		30	2453205	AV 5764	29	1	2	3	4	5	6	Sat 11h47m15p		2	3	4	5	6	7	8			11	12	13	14	15	16	17	
	◐	26	27	28	29	30	○	3:37 18:05	31	2453212		7	8	9[i]	10	11	12	13			9	10	11	12	13	14	15			18	19	20	21	22	23	24	
AUGUST 2004	1	2	3	4	5	6	◑	22:01	32	2453219		14	15	16	17	18	19	20			16	17	18	19	20	21	22	Lì qiū	MESORÊ 1720	25	26	27	28	29	30	1	NAHASÊ 1996
	8	9	10	11	12	13	14		33	2453226		21	22	23	24	25	26	27			23	24	25	26	27	28*	29			2	3	4	5	6	7	8	
	15	●	17	18	19	20	21	1:24	34	2453233	ELUL 5764	28	29	30	1	2	3	4	Mon 0h31m16p	MONTH 7 Jiǎ-Shēn	30	1	2	3	4	5	6	Chǔ shǔ		9	10	11	12	13[h]	14	15	
	22	◐	24	25	26	27	28	10:12	35	2453240		5	6	7	8	9	10	11			7[e]	8	9	10	11	12	13			16	17	18	19	20	21	22	
SEPTEMBER 2004	29	○	31	1	2	3	4	2:22	36	2453247		12	13	14	15	16	17	18			14	15[f]	16	17	18	19	20			23	24	25	26	27	28	29	
	5	◑	7	8	9	10	11	15:10	37	2453254		19	20	21	22	23	24	25			21	22	23	24	25	26	27	Bái lù	EPAG. 1720	30	1	2	3	4	5	1[a]	PÂG. 1996
	12	13	●	15	16	17	18	14:29	38	2453261	TISHRI 5765	26	27	28	29	1[a]	2[a]	3	Tue 13h15m17p	MONTH 8 Jiǎ-Shēn	28	29	1	2	3	4	5		THOOUT 1721	2	3	4	5	6	7	8	MASKARAM 1997
	19	20	◐	22[d]	23	24	25	15:53	39	2453268		4	5	6	7	8	9	10[b]			6	7	8	9	10	11	12	Qiū fēn		9	10	11	12	13	14	15	
OCTOBER 2004	26	27	○	29	30	1	2	13:09	40	2453275		11	12	13	14	15[c]	16	17			13	14	15[g]	16	17	18	19			16	17[b]	18	19	20	21	22	
	3	4	5	◑	7	8	9	10:12	41	2453282		18	19	20	21	22	23	24			20	21	22	23	24	25	26	Hán lù		23	24	25	26	27	28	29	
	10	11	12	13	●	15	16	2:48	42	2453289	ḤESHVAN 5765	25	26	27	28	29	30	1	Thu 2h0m0p	MONTH 9 Jiǎ-Shēn	27	28	29*	30	1	2	3		PAOPE 1721	30	1	2	3	4	5	6	TEQEMT 1997
	17	18	19	◐	21	22	23	21:59	43	2453296		2	3	4	5	6	7	8			4	5	6	7	8	9[h]	10	Shuāng jiàng		7	8	9	10	11	12	13	
	24	25	26	27	○	29	30	3:07	44	2453303		9	10	11	12	13	14	15			11	12	13	14	15	16	17			14	15	16	17	18	19	20	
NOVEMBER 2004	31	1	2	3	4	◑	6	5:53	45	2453310		16	17	18	19	20	21	22			18	19	20	21	22	23	24	Lì dōng		21	22	23	24	25	26	27	
	7	8	9	10	11	●	13	14:27	46	2453317		23	24	25	26	27	28	29		MONTH 10 Jiǎ-Shēn	25	26	27	28	29	1	2		ATHÔR 1721	28	29	30	1	2	3	4	HEDÂR 1997
	14	15	16	17	18	◐	20	5:50	47	2453324	KISLEV 5765	1	2	3	4	5	6	7	Fri 14h44m1p		3	4	5	6	7	8	9	Xiǎo xuě		5	6	7	8	9	10	11	
	21	22	23	24	25	○	27	20:07	48	2453331		8	9	10	11	12	13	14			10	11	12	13	14	15	16			12	13	14	15	16	17	18	
DECEMBER 2004	28	29	30	1	2	3	4		49	2453338		15	16	17	18	19	20	21			17	18	19	20	21	22	23			19	20	21	22	23	24	25	
	◑	6	7	8	9	10	11	0:53	50	2453345		22[d]	23	24	25[e]	26[e]	27[e]	28[e]			24	25	26	27	28	29	30*	Dà xuě	KOIAK 1721	26	27	28	29	30	1	2	TÂKHŚÂŚ 1997
	●	13	14	15	16	17	◐	1:29 16:39	51	2453352	TEVETH 5765	29[e]	1[e]	2[e]	3[e]	4	5	6	Sun 3h28m2p	MONTH 11 Jiǎ-Shēn	1	2	3	4	5	6	7			3	4	5	6	7	8	9	
	19	20	21[e]	22	23	24	25		52	2453359		7	8	9	10	11	12	13			8	9	10[i]	11	12	13	14	Dōng zhì		10	11	12	13	14	15	16	
	○	27	28	29	30	31	1	15:06	53	2453366		14	15	16	17	18	19	20			15	16	17	18	19	20	21			17	18	19	20	21	22	23	

‡Leap year
[a]New Year
[b]Spring (6:48)
[c]Summer (0:57)
[d]Autumn (16:30)
[e]Winter (12:41)
● New moon
◐ First quarter moon
○ Full moon
◑ Last quarter moon

‡Leap year
[a]New Year
[b]Yom Kippur
[c]Sukkot
[d]Winter starts
[e]Ḥanukkah
[f]Purim
[g]Passover
[h]Shavuot
[i]Fast of Av

‡Leap year
[a]New Year (4702, Monkey)
[b]Lantern Festival
[c]Qīngmíng
[d]Dragon Festival
[e]Qǐqiǎo
[f]Hungry Ghosts
[g]Mid-Autumn Festival
[h]Double-Ninth Festival
[i]Dōngzhì
*Start of 60-name cycle

[a]New Year
[b]Building of the Cross
[c]Christmas
[d]Jesus's Circumcision
[e]Epiphany
[f]Easter
[g]Mary's Announcement
[h]Jesus's Transfiguration

PERSIAN (ASTRONOMICAL) 1382/1383‡

Month	Sun	Mon	Tue	Wed	Thu	Fri	Sat
DEY 1382	7	8	9	10	11	12	13
	14	15	16	17	18	19	20
	21	22	23	24	25	26	27
BAHMAN 1382	28	29	30	1	2	3	4
	5	6	7	8	9	10	11
	12	13	14	15	16	17	18
	19	20	21	22	23	24	25
ESFAND 1382	26	27	28	29	30	1	2
	3	4	5	6	7	8	9
	10	11	12	13	14	15	16
	17	18	19	20	21	22	23
FARVARDĪN 1383	24	25	26	27	28	29	1[a]
	2	3	4	5	6	7	8
	9	10	11	12	13[b]	14	15
	16	17	18	19	20	21	22
	23	24	25	26	27	28	29
ORDĪBEHEŠT 1383	30	31	1	2	3	4	5
	6	7	8	9	10	11	12
	13	14	15	16	17	18	19
	20	21	22	23	24	25	26
XORDĀD 1383	27	28	29	30	31	1	2
	3	4	5	6	7	8	9
	10	11	12	13	14	15	16
	17	18	19	20	21	22	23
	24	25	26	27	28	29	30
TĪR 1383	31	1	2	3	4	5	6
	7	8	9	10	11	12	13
	14	15	16	17	18	19	20
	21	22	23	24	25	26	27
MORDĀD 1383	28	29	30	31	1	2	3
	4	5	6	7	8	9	10
	11	12	13	14	15	16	17
	18	19	20	21	22	23	24
	25	26	27	28	29	30	31
SHAHRĪVAR 1383	1	2	3	4	5	6	7
	8	9	10	11	12	13	14
	15	16	17	18	19	20	21
	22	23	24	25	26	27	28
MEHR 1383	29	30	31	1	2	3	4
	5	6	7	8	9	10	11
	12	13	14	15	16	17	18
	19	20	21	22	23	24	25
ĀBĀN 1383	26	27	28	29	30	1	2
	3	4	5	6	7	8	9
	10	11	12	13	14	15	16
	17	18	19	20	21	22	23
	24	25	26	27	28	29	30
ĀZAR 1383	1	2	3	4	5	6	7
	8	9	10	11	12	13	14
	15	16	17	18	19	20	21
	22	23	24	25	26	27	28
DEY 1383	29	30	1	2	3	4	5
	6	7	8	9	10	11	12

‡Leap year
[a]New Year
[b]Sizdeh Bedar

HINDU LUNAR 2060/2061‡

Month	Sun	Mon	Tue	Wed	Thu	Fri	Sat
PAUSHA 2060	5	7	8	8	9	10	11
	12	13	14	15	16	17	18
	19	20	21	22	23	24	25
MĀGHA 2060	26	**27**	29	30	1	2	3
	4	5	6	7	8	9	10
	11	11	12	13	14	15	16
	17	18	19	20	**21**	23	24
PHĀLGUNA 2060	25	26	27	28[h]	29	30	1
	2	3	4	5	6	7	8
	9	10	11	12	13	14	15[i]
	16	17	18	19	20	21	22
	23	24	25	**26**	28	29	30
CHAITRA 2061	1[a]	2	3	4	4	5	6
	7	8	9[b]	10	11	12	13
	14	15	16	17	18	19	**20**
	22	23	24	25	26	27	28
VAIŚĀKHA 2061	29	30	1	2	3	4	5
	6	7	7	8	9	10	11
	12	**13**	15	16	17	18	19
	20	21	22	23	24	25	26
JYAISHTHA 2061	27	28	29	30	1	2	3
	4	5	6	7	8	9	10
	11	12	13	14	15	**16**	18
	19	20	21	22	23	24	25
ĀSHĀḌHA 2061	26	27	28	29	30	1	2
	3	3	4	5	6	7	8
	9	11	12	13	14	15	16
	17	18	19	20	**21**	23	24
	25	25	26	27	28	29	30
LEAP ŚRĀVAṆA 2061	1	2	3	4	5	6	7
	8	9	10	11	**12**	14	15
	16	17	18	19	20	21	22
	23	24	25	26	27	28	29
ŚRĀVAṆA 2061	30	30	1	2	3	**4**	6
	7	8	9	10	11	12	13
	14	15	**16**	18	19	20	21
	21	22	23[c]	24	25	26	27
BHĀDRAPADA 2061	28	29	30	1	2	3	4[d]
	5	6	7	**8**	10	11	12
	13	14	15	16	17	18	19
	20	21	22	23	24	25	25
ĀŚVINA 2061	26	27	28	29	30	**1**	3
	4	5	6	7	8[e]	9[e]	10[e]
	11	12	13	14	15	16	17
	18	19	20	21	22	23	24
KĀRTTIKA 2061	25	26	27	28	29	30	1[f]
	2	3	4	5	**6**	8	9
	10	11	12	13	14	15	16
	17	18	19	19	20	21	22
	23	24	25	26	27	28	29
MĀRGAŚĪRA 2061	**30**	2	3	4	5	6	7
	8	9	10	11[g]	12	13	14
	15	16	17	18	19	20	21

‡Leap year
[a]New Year (Tāraṇa)
[b]Birthday of Rāma
[c]Birthday of Krishna
[d]Ganēśa Chaturthī
[e]Dashara
[f]Diwali
[g]Birthday of Vishnu
[h]Night of Śiva
[i]Holi

HINDU SOLAR 1925/1926

Month	Sun	Mon	Tue	Wed	Thu	Fri	Sat
PAUSHA 1925	13	14	15	16	17	18	19
	20	21	22	23	24	25	26
MĀGHA 1925	27	28	29	1[b]	2	3	4
	5	6	7	8	9	10	11
	12	13	14	15	16	17	18
	19	20	21	22	23	24	25
PHĀLGUNA 1925	26	27	28	29	30	1	2
	3	4	5	6	7	8	9
	10	11	12	13	14	15	16
	17	18	19	20	21	22	23
	24	25	26	27	28	29	30
CHAITRA 1925	1	2	3	4	5	6	7
	8	9	10	11	12	13	14
	15	16	17	18	19	20	21
	22	23	24	25	26	27	28
VAIŚĀKHA 1926	29	30	1[a]	2	3	4	5
	6	7	8	9	10	11	12
	13	14	15	16	17	18	19
	20	21	22	23	24	25	26
JYAISHTHA 1926	27	28	29	30	31	1	2
	3	4	5	6	7	8	9
	10	11	12	13	14	15	16
	17	18	19	20	21	22	23
	24	25	26	27	28	29	30
ĀSHĀḌHA 1926	31	1	2	3	4	5	6
	7	8	9	10	11	12	13
	14	15	16	17	18	19	20
	21	22	23	24	25	26	27
ŚRĀVAṆA 1926	28	29	30	31	32	1	2
	3	4	5	6	7	8	9
	10	11	12	13	14	15	16
	17	18	19	20	21	22	23
	24	25	26	27	28	29	30
BHĀDRAPADA 1926	31	1	2	3	4	5	6
	7	8	9	10	11	12	13
	14	15	16	17	18	19	20
	21	22	23	24	25	26	27
ĀŚVINA 1926	28	29	30	31	32	1	2
	3	4	5	6	7	8	9
	10	11	12	13	14	15	16
	17	18	19	20	21	22	23
	24	25	26	27	28	29	30
KĀRTTIKA 1926	1	2	3	4	5	6	7
	8	9	10	11	12	13	14
	15	16	17	18	19	20	21
	22	23	24	25	26	27	28
MĀRGAŚĪRA 1926	29	30	1	2	3	4	5
	6	7	8	9	10	11	12
	13	14	15	16	17	18	19
	20	21	22	23	24	25	26
PAUSHA 1926	27	28	29	1	2	3	4
	5	6	7	8	9	10	11
	12	13	14	15	16	17	18

[a]New Year (Hemalamba)
[b]Pongal

ISLAMIC (ASTRONOMICAL) 1424‡/1425

Month	Sun	Mon	Tue	Wed	Thu	Fri	Sat
DHU AL-QA'DA 1424	4	5	6	7	8	9	10
	11	12	13	14	15	16	17
	18	19	20	21	22	23	24
DHU AL-ḤIJJA 1424	25	26	27	28	29	1	2
	3	4	5	6	7	8	9
	10[g]	11	12	13	14	15	16
	17	18	19	20	21	22	23
	24	25	26	27	28	29	30
MUḤARRAM 1425	1[a]	2	3	4	5	6	7
	8	9	10[b]	11	12	13	14
	15	16	17	18	19	20	21
	22	23	24	25	26	27	28
ṢAFAR 1425	29	1	2	3	4	5	6
	7	8	9	10	11	12	13
	14	15	16	17	18	19	20
	21	22	23	24	25	26	27
RABĪ' I 1425	28	29	30	1	2	3	4
	5	6	7	8	9	10	11
	12[c]	13	14	15	16	17	18
	19	20	21	22	23	24	25
RABĪ' II 1425	26	27	28	29	30	1	2
	3	4	5	6	7	8	9
	10	11	12	13	14	15	16
	17	18	19	20	21	22	23
JUMĀDĀ I 1425	24	25	26	27	28	29	1
	2	3	4	5	6	7	8
	9	10	11	12	13	14	15
	16	17	18	19	20	21	22
	23	24	25	26	27	28	29
JUMĀDĀ II 1425	30	1	2	3	4	5	6
	7	8	9	10	11	12	13
	14	15	16	17	18	19	20
	21	22	23	24	25	26	27
RAJAB 1425	28	29	1	2	3	4	5
	6	7	8	9	10	11	12
	13	14	15	16	17	18	19
	20	21	22	23	24	25	26
SHA'BĀN 1425	27[d]	28	29	30	1	2	3
	4	5	6	7	8	9	10
	11	12	13	14	15	16	17
	18	19	20	21	22	23	24
RAMAḌĀN 1425	25	26	27	28	29	30	1[e]
	2	3	4	5	6	7	8
	9	10	11	12	13	14	15
	16	17	18	19	20	21	22
	23	24	25	26	27	28	29
SHAWWĀL 1425	1[f]	2	3	4	5	6	7
	8	9	10	11	12	13	14
	15	16	17	18	19	20	21
	22	23	24	25	26	27	28
DHU AL-QA'DA 1425	29	30	1	2	3	4	5
	6	7	8	9	10	11	12
	13	14	15	16	17	18	19

‡Leap year
[a]New Year
[b]'Ashūrā'
[c]Prophet's Birthday
[d]Ascent of the Prophet
[e]Start of Ramaḍān
[f]'Id al-Fiṭr
[g]'Id al-'Aḍḥā

GREGORIAN 2004‡

Julian‡ (Sun)	Sun	Mon	Tue	Wed	Thu	Fri	Sat	Month
Dec 15	28	29	30	31	1	2	3	JANUARY 2004
	4	5	6	7[a]	8	9	10	
Dec 29	11	12	13	14[b]	15	16	17	
	18	19	20	21	22	23	24	
Jan 12	25	26	27	28	29	30	31	
	1	2	3	4	5	6	7	FEBRUARY 2004
Jan 26	8	9	10	11	12	13	14	
	15	16	17	18	19	20	21	
Feb 9	22	23	24	25[c]	26	27	28	
	29[d]	1	2	3	4	5	6	MARCH 2004
Feb 23	7	8	9	10	11	12	13	
	14	15	16	17	18	19	20	
Mar 8	21	22	23	24	25	26	27	
	28	29	30	31	1	2	3	APRIL 2004
Mar 22	4	5	6	7	8	9	10	
	11[e]	12	13	14	15	16	17	
Apr 5	18	19	20	21	22	23	24	
	25	26	27	28	29	30	1	MAY 2004
Apr 19	2	3	4	5	6	7	8	
	9	10	11	12	13	14	15	
May 3	16	17	18	19	20	21	22	
	23	24	25	26	27	28	29	
May 17	30	31	1	2	3	4	5	JUNE 2004
	6	7	8	9	10	11	12	
May 31	13	14	15	16	17	18	19	
	20	21	22	23	24	25	26	
Jun 14	27	28	29	30	1	2	3	JULY 2004
	4	5	6	7	8	9	10	
Jun 28	11	12	13	14	15	16	17	
	18	19	20	21	22	23	24	
Jul 12	25	26	27	28	29	30	31	
	1	2	3	4	5	6	7	AUGUST 2004
Jul 26	8	9	10	11	12	13	14	
	15	16	17	18	19	20	21	
Aug 9	22	23	24	25	26	27	28	
	29	30	31	1	2	3	4	SEPTEMBER 2004
Aug 23	5	6	7	8	9	10	11	
	12	13	14	15	16	17	18	
Sep 6	19	20	21	22	23	24	25	
	26	27	28	29	30	1	2	OCTOBER 2004
Sep 20	3	4	5	6	7	8	9	
	10	11	12	13	14	15	16	
Oct 4	17	18	19	20	21	22	23	
	24	25	26	27	28	29	30	
Oct 18	31	1	2	3	4	5	6	NOVEMBER 2004
	7	8	9	10	11	12	13	
Nov 1	14	15	16	17	18	19	20	
	21	22	23	24	25	26	27	
Nov 15	28[g]	29	30	1	2	3	4	DECEMBER 2004
	5	6	7	8	9	10	11	
Nov 29	12	13	14	15	16	17	18	
	19	20	21	22	23	24	25[h]	
Dec 13	26	27	28	29	30	31	1	

‡Leap year
[a]Orthodox Christmas
[b]Julian New Year
[c]Ash Wednesday
[d]Feast of Orthodoxy
[e]Easter (also Orthodox)
[g]Advent
[h]Christmas

2005

GREGORIAN 2005

Month	Sun	Mon	Tue	Wed	Thu	Fri	Sat	Lunar Phases	ISO WEEK (Mon)	JULIAN DAY (Sun noon)
	○	27	28	29	30	31	1[a]	15:06	53	2453366
JANUARY 2005	2	◑	4	5	6	7	8	17:46	1	2453373
	9	●	11	12	13	14	15	12:03	2	2453380
	16	◐	18	19	20	21	22	6:57	3	2453387
	23	24	○	26	27	28	29	10:32	4	2453394
	30	31	1	◑	3	4	5	7:27	5	2453401
FEBRUARY 2005	6	7	●	9	10	11	12	22:28	6	2453408
	13	14	15	◐	17	18	19	0:16	7	2453415
	20	21	22	23	○	25	26	4:54	8	2453422
	27	28	1	2	◑	4	5	17:36	9	2453429
MARCH 2005	6	7	8	9	●	11	12	9:10	10	2453436
	13	14	15	16	◐	18	19	19:19	11	2453443
	20[b]	21	22	23	24	○	26	20:59	12	2453450
	27	28	29	30	31	1	◑	0:50	13	2453457
APRIL 2005	3	4	5	6	7	●	9	20:32	14	2453464
	10	11	12	13	14	15	◐	14:37	15	2453471
	17	18	19	20	21	22	23		16	2453478
	○	25	26	27	28	29	30	10:06	17	2453485
	◑	2	3	4	5	6	7	6:24	18	2453492
MAY 2005	●	9	10	11	12	13	14	8:45	19	2453499
	15	◐	17	18	19	20	21	8:57	20	2453506
	22	○	24	25	26	27	28	20:18	21	2453513
	29	◑	31	1	2	3	4	11:47	22	2453520
JUNE 2005	5	●	7	8	9	10	11	21:55	23	2453527
	12	13	14	◐	16	17	18	1:22	24	2453534
	19	20	21[c]	○	23	24	25	4:14	25	2453541
	26	27	◑	29	30	1	2	18:23	26	2453548
JULY 2005	3	4	5	●	7	8	9	12:03	27	2453555
	10	11	12	13	◐	15	16	15:20	28	2453562
	17	18	19	20	○	22	23	11:00	29	2453569
	24	25	26	27	◑	29	30	3:19	30	2453576
	31	1	2	3	4	●	6	3:05	31	2453583
AUGUST 2005	7	8	9	10	11	12	◐	2:39	32	2453590
	14	15	16	17	18	○	20	17:53	33	2453597
	21	22	23	24	25	◑	27	15:18	34	2453604
	28	29	30	31	1	2	●	18:45	35	2453611
SEPTEMBER 2005	4	5	6	7	8	9	10		36	2453618
	◐	12	13	14	15	16	17	11:37	37	2453625
	○	19	20	21	22[d]	23	24	2:01	38	2453632
	◑	26	27	28	29	30	1	6:41	39	2453639
OCTOBER 2005	2	●	4	5	6	7	8	10:28	40	2453646
	9	◐	11	12	13	14	15	19:01	41	2453653
	16	○	18	19	20	21	22	12:14	42	2453660
	23	24	◑	26	27	28	29	1:17	43	2453667
	30	31	1	●	3	4	5	1:25	44	2453674
NOVEMBER 2005	6	7	8	◐	10	11	12	1:57	45	2453681
	13	14	15	○	17	18	19	0:57	46	2453688
	20	21	22	◑	24	25	26	22:11	47	2453695
	27	28	29	30	●	2	3	15:01	48	2453702
DECEMBER 2005	4	5	6	7	◐	9	10	9:36	49	2453709
	11	12	13	14	○	16	17	16:15	50	2453716
	18	19	20	21[e]	22	◑	24	19:36	51	2453723
	25	26	27	28	29	30	●	3:12	52	2453730

HEBREW 5765‡/5766

ISO WEEK	Month	Sun	Mon	Tue	Wed	Thu	Fri	Sat	Molad
53	TEVETH 5765	14	15	16	17	18	19	20	
1		21	22	23	24	25	26	27	
2		28	29	1	2	3	4	5	Mon 16h12m3p
3	SHEVAT 5765	6	7	8	9	10	11	12	
4		13	14	15	16	17	18	19	
5		20	21	22	23	24	25	26	
6		27	28	29	30	1	2	3	Wed 4h56m4p
7	ADAR I 5765	4	5	6	7	8	9	10	
8		11	12	13	14	15	16	17	
9		18	19	20	21	22	23	24	
10		25	26	27	28	29	30	1	Thu 17h40m5p
11	ADAR II 5765	2	3	4	5	6	7	8	
12		9	10	11	12	13	14[f]	15	
13		16	17	18	19	20	21	22	
14		23	24	25	26	27	28	29	
15		1	2	3	4	5	6	7	Sat 6h24m6p
16	NISAN 5765	8	9	10	11	12	13	14	
17		15[g]	16	17	18	19	20	21	
18		22	23	24	25	26	27	28	
19		29	30	1	2	3	4	5	Sun 19h8m7p
20	IYAR 5765	6	7	8	9	10	11	12	
21		13	14	15	16	17	18	19	
22		20	21	22	23	24	25	26	
23		27	28	29	1	2	3	4	Tue 7h52m8p
24	SIVAN 5765	5	6[h]	7	8	9	10	11	
25		12	13	14	15	16	17	18	
26		19	20	21	22	23	24	25	
27		26	27	28	29	30	1	2	Wed 20h36m9p
28	TAMMUZ 5765	3	4	5	6	7	8	9	
29		10	11	12	13	14	15	16	
30		17	18	19	20	21	22	23	
31		24	25	26	27	28	29	1	Fri 9h20m10p
32	AV 5765	2	3	4	5	6	7	8	
33		9[i]	10	11	12	13	14	15	
34		16	17	18	19	20	21	22	
35		23	24	25	26	27	28	29	
36		30	1	2	3	4	5	6	Sat 22h4m11p
37	ELUL 5765	7	8	9	10	11	12	13	
38		14	15	16	17	18	19	20	
39		21	22	23	24	25	26	27	
40		28	29	1[a]	2[a]	3	4	5	Mon 10h48m12p
41	TISHRI 5766	6	7	8	9	10[b]	11	12	
42		13	14	15[c]	16	17	18	19	
43		20	21	22	23	24	25	26	
44		27	28	29	30	1	2	3	Tue 23h32m13p
45	HESHVAN 5766	4	5	6	7	8	9	10	
46		11	12	13	14	15	16	17	
47		18	19	20	21	22	23	24	
48		25	26	27	28	29	1	2	Thu 12h16m14p
49	KISLEV 5766	3	4[d]	5	6	7	8	9	
50		10	11	12	13	14	15	16	
51		17	18	19	20	21	22	23	
52		24	25[e]	26[e]	27[e]	28[e]	29[e]	30[e]	

CHINESE Jiă-Shēn‡/Yĭ-Yŏu

ISO WEEK	Month	Sun	Mon	Tue	Wed	Thu	Fri	Sat	Solar Term
53	MONTH 11 Jiă-Shēn	15	16	17	18	19	20	21	
1		22	23	24	25	26	27	28	Xiăo hán
2		29	1	2	3	4	5	6	
3	MONTH 12 Jiă-Shēn	7	8	9	10	**11**	12	13	Dà hán
4		14	15	16	17	18	19	20	
5		21	22	23	24	25	26	27	Lì chūn
6		28	29	30	1[a]*	2	3	4	
7	MONTH 1 Yĭ-Yŏu	5	6	7	8	9	**10**	11	Yŭ shuĭ
8		12	13	14	15[b]	16	17	18	
9		19	20	21	22	23	24	25	Jīng zhé
10		26	27	28	29	1	2	3	
11	MONTH 2 Yĭ-Yŏu	4	5	6	7	8	9	10	
12		**11**	12	13	14	15	16	17	Chūn fēn
13		18	19	20	21	22	23	24	
14		25	26	27[c]	28	29	30	1	Qīng míng
15	MONTH 3 Yĭ-Yŏu	2*	3	4	5	6	7	8	
16		9	10	11	**12**	13	14	15	Gŭ yŭ
17		16	17	18	19	20	21	22	
18		23	24	25	26	27	28	29	Lì xià
19		1	2	3	4	5	6	7	
20	MONTH 4 Yĭ-Yŏu	8	9	10	11	12	13	**14**	Xiăo măn
21		15	16	17	18	19	20	21	
22		22	23	24	25	26	27	28	
23		29	30	1	2	3*	4	5[d]	Máng zhòng
24	MONTH 5 Yĭ-Yŏu	6	7	8	9	10	11	12	
25		13	14	**15**	16	17	18	19	Xià zhì
26		20	21	22	23	24	25	26	
27		27	28	29	1	2	3	4	Xiăo shŭ
28	MONTH 6 Yĭ-Yŏu	5	6	7	8	9	10	11	
29		12	13	14	15	16	17	**18**	Dà shŭ
30		19	20	21	22	23	24	25	
31		26	27	28	29	30	1	2	
32	MONTH 7 Yĭ-Yŏu	3	4*	5	6	7[e]	8	9	Lì qiū
33		10	11	12	13	14	15[f]	16	
34		17	18	**19**	20	21	22	23	Chŭ shŭ
35		24	25	26	27	28	29	30	
36		1	2	3	4	5	6	7	Bái lù
37	MONTH 8 Yĭ-Yŏu	8	9	10	11	12	13	14	
38		15[g]	16	17	18	19	**20**	21	Qiū fēn
39		22	23	24	25	26	27	28	
40		29	1	2	3	4	5*	6	Hán lù
41	MONTH 9 Yĭ-Yŏu	7	8	9[h]	10	11	12	13	
42		14	15	16	17	18	19	20	Shuāng jiàng
43		**21**	22	23	24	25	26	27	
44		28	29	30	1	2	3	4	
45	MONTH 10 Yĭ-Yŏu	5	6	7	8	9	10	11	Lì dōng
46		12	13	14	15	16	17	18	
47		19	20	**21**	22	23	24	25	Xiăo xuě
48		26	27	28	29	1	2	3	
49	MONTH 11 Yĭ-Yŏu	4	5	6*	7	8	9	10	Dà xuě
50		11	12	13	14	15	16	17	
51		18	19	20	21	**22**[i]	23	24	Dōng zhì
52		25	26	27	28	29	30	1	

COPTIC 1721/1722 — ETHIOPIC 1997/1998

ISO WEEK	Coptic Month	Sun	Mon	Tue	Wed	Thu	Fri	Sat	Ethiopic Month
53	KOIAK 1721	17	18	19	20	21	22	23	TĀKHŚĀŚ 1997
1		24	25	26	27	28	29[c]	30	
2		1	2	3	4	5	6[d]	7	
3	TŌBE 1721	8	9	10	11[e]	12	13	14	ṬER 1997
4		15	16	17	18	19	20	21	
5		22	23	24	25	26	27	28	
6		29	30	1	2	3	4	5	
7	MESHIR 1721	6	7	8	9	10	11	12	YAKĀTIT 1997
8		13	14	15	16	17	18	19	
9		20	21	22	23	24	25	26	
10		27	28	29	30	1	2	3	
11	PAREMOTEP 1721	4	5	6	7	8	9	10	MAGĀBIT 1997
12		11	12	13	14	15	16	17	
13		18	19	20	21	22	23	24	
14		25	26	27	28	29	30	1	
15	PARMOUTE 1721	2	3	4	5	6	7	8	MIYĀZYĀ 1997
16		9	10	11	12	13	14	15	
17		16	17	18	19	20	21	22	
18		23[f]	24	25	26	27	28	29[g]	
19		30	1	2	3	4	5	6	
20	PASHONS 1721	7	8	9	10	11	12	13	GENBOT 1997
21		14	15	16	17	18	19	20	
22		21	22	23	24	25	26	27	
23		28	29	30	1	2	3	4	
24	PAŌNE 1721	5	6	7	8	9	10	11	SANĒ 1997
25		12	13	14	15	16	17	18	
26		19	20	21	22	23	24	25	
27		26	27	28	29	30	1	2	
28	EPĒP 1721	3	4	5	6	7	8	9	ḤAMLĒ 1997
29		10	11	12	13	14	15	16	
30		17	18	19	20	21	22	23	
31		24	25	26	27	28	29	30	
32	MESORĒ 1721	1	2	3	4	5	6	7	NAḤASĒ 1997
33		8	9	10	11	12	13[h]	14	
34		15	16	17	18	19	20	21	
35		22	23	24	25	26	27	28	
36	EPAG. 1721	29	30	1	2	3	4	5	PĀG. 1997
37		1[a]	2	3	4	5	6	7	
38	THOOUT 1722	8	9	10	11	12	13	14	MASKARAM 1998
39		15	16	17[b]	18	19	20	21	
40		22	23	24	25	26	27	28	
41		29	30	1	2	3	4	5	
42	PAOPE 1722	6	7	8	9	10	11	12	ṬEQEMT 1998
43		13	14	15	16	17	18	19	
44		20	21	22	23	24	25	26	
45		27	28	29	30	1	2	3	
46	ATHŌR 1722	4	5	6	7	8	9	10	HEDĀR 1998
47		11	12	13	14	15	16	17	
48		18	19	20	21	22	23	24	
49		25	26	27	28	29	30	1	
50	KOIAK 1722	2	3	4	5	6	7	8	TĀKHŚĀŚ 1998
51		9	10	11	12	13	14	15	
52		16	17	18	19	20	21	22	

[a]New Year
[b]Spring (12:33)
[c]Summer (6:46)
[d]Autumn (22:22)
[e]Winter (18:35)
● New moon
◐ First quarter moon
○ Full moon
◑ Last quarter moon

‡Leap year
[a]New Year
[b]Yom Kippur
[c]Sukkot
[d]Winter starts
[e]Ḥanukkah
[f]Purim
[g]Passover
[h]Shavuot
[i]Fast of Av

‡Leap year
[a]New Year (4703, Fowl)
[b]Lantern Festival
[c]Qīngmíng
[d]Dragon Festival
[e]Qīqiǎo
[f]Hungry Ghosts
[g]Mid-Autumn Festival
[h]Double-Ninth Festival
[i]Dōngzhì
*Start of 60-name cycle

[a]New Year
[b]Building of the Cross
[c]Christmas
[d]Jesus's Circumcision
[e]Epiphany
[f]Easter
[g]Mary's Announcement
[h]Jesus's Transfiguration

PERSIAN (ASTRONOMICAL) 1383‡/1384

Month	Sun	Mon	Tue	Wed	Thu	Fri	Sat
DEY 1383	6	7	8	9	10	11	12
	13	14	15	16	17	18	19
	20	21	22	23	24	25	26
BAHMAN 1383	27	28	29	30	*1*	2	3
	4	5	6	7	8	9	10
	11	12	13	14	15	16	17
	18	19	20	21	22	23	24
ESFAND 1383	25	26	27	28	29	30	*1*
	2	3	4	5	6	7	8
	9	10	11	12	13	14	15
	16	17	18	19	20	21	22
	23	24	25	26	27	28	29
FARVARDĪN 1384	30	*1*[a]	2	3	4	5	6
	7	8	9	10	11	12	13[b]
	14	15	16	17	18	19	20
	21	22	23	24	25	26	27
ORDĪBEHEŠT 1384	28	29	30	31	*1*	2	3
	4	5	6	7	8	9	10
	11	12	13	14	15	16	17
	18	19	20	21	22	23	24
	25	26	27	28	29	30	31
XORDĀD 1384	*1*	2	3	4	5	6	7
	8	9	10	11	12	13	14
	15	16	17	18	19	20	21
	22	23	24	25	26	27	28
TĪR 1384	29	30	31	*1*	2	3	4
	5	6	7	8	9	10	11
	12	13	14	15	16	17	18
	19	20	21	22	23	24	25
MORDĀD 1384	26	27	28	29	30	31	*1*
	2	3	4	5	6	7	8
	9	10	11	12	13	14	15
	16	17	18	19	20	21	22
	23	24	25	26	27	28	29
SHAHRĪVAR 1384	30	31	*1*	2	3	4	5
	6	7	8	9	10	11	12
	13	14	15	16	17	18	19
	20	21	22	23	24	25	26
MEHR 1384	27	28	29	30	31	*1*	2
	3	4	5	6	7	8	9
	10	11	12	13	14	15	16
	17	18	19	20	21	22	23
	24	25	26	27	28	29	30
ĀBĀN 1384	*1*	2	3	4	5	6	7
	8	9	10	11	12	13	14
	15	16	17	18	19	20	21
	22	23	24	25	26	27	28
ĀZAR 1384	29	30	*1*	2	3	4	5
	6	7	8	9	10	11	12
	13	14	15	16	17	18	19
	20	21	22	23	24	25	26
DEY 1384	27	28	29	30	*1*	2	3
	4	5	6	7	8	9	10

‡Leap year
[a]New Year
[b]Sizdeh Bedar

HINDU LUNAR 2061‡/2062

Month	Sun	Mon	Tue	Wed	Thu	Fri	Sat
MĀRGAŚĪRA 2061	15	16	17	18	19	20	21
	22	23	24	25	26	27	28
PAUSHA 2061	29	30	1	2	3	4	**5**
	7	8	9	10	11	*11*	12
	13	14	15	16	17	18	19
	20	21	22	23	24	25	26
MĀGHA 2061	27	**28**	30	1	2	3	4
	5	6	7	8	9	10	11
	12	13	14	*14*	15	16	17
	18	19	20	21	**22**	24	25
PHĀLGUNA 2061	26	27	28[h]	29	30	1	2
	3	4	5	6	7	8	9
	10	11	12	13	14	15[i]	16
	17	18	19	20	21	22	23
CHAITRA 2062	24	25	26	**27**	29	30	1[a]
	2	3	4	5	6	7	*7*
	8[b]	9	10	11	12	13	14
	15	16	17	18	19	**20**	22
	23	24	25	26	27	28	29
VAIŚĀKHA 2062	30	1	2	3	4	5	6
	7	8	9	10	11	12	13
	14	15	16	17	18	19	20
	21	22	23	**24**	26	27	28
JYAISHṬHA 2062	29	30	1	2	3	*3*	4
	5	6	7	8	9	10	11
	12	13	14	15	**16**	18	19
	20	21	22	23	24	25	26
ĀSHĀḌHA 2062	27	28	29	30	1	2	3
	4	5	6	7	8	9	10
	11	12	13	14	15	16	17
	18	**19**	21	22	23	24	25
ŚRĀVAṆA 2062	26	27	28	29	30	*30*	1
	2	3	4	5	6	7	8
	9	10	11	**12**	14	15	16
	17	18	19	20	21	22	23[c]
	24	25	26	27	28	29	30
BHĀDRAPADA 2062	1	2	3	4[d]	5	6	7
	8	9	10	11	12	13	14
	15	17	18	19	20	21	22
	23	24	25	26	*26*	27	28
ĀŚVINA 2062	29	30	1	2	3	4	5
	6	7	8[e]	**9**[e]	11	12	13
	14	15	16	17	18	19	20
	21	22	23	24	25	26	27
KĀRTTIKA 2062	28	29	30	1[f]	2	3	4
	5	6	7	8	9	10	11
	12	**13**	15	16	17	18	19
	19	20	21	22	23	24	25
MĀRGAŚĪRA 2062	26	27	28	29	30	1	2
	3	4	5	**6**	8	9	10
	11[g]	12	13	14	15	16	17
	18	19	20	21	22	*22*	23
	24	25	26	27	28	29	30

‡Leap year
[a]New Year (Pārthiva)
[b]Birthday of Rāma
[c]Birthday of Krishna
[d]Ganēśa Chaturthī
[e]Dashara
[f]Diwali
[g]Birthday of Vishnu
[h]Night of Śiva
[i]Holi

HINDU SOLAR 1926/1927‡

Month	Sun	Mon	Tue	Wed	Thu	Fri	Sat
PAUSHA 1926	12	13	14	15	16	17	18
	19	20	21	22	23	24	25
MĀGHA 1926	26	27	28	29	30	1[b]	2
	3	4	5	6	7	8	9
	10	11	12	13	14	15	16
	17	18	19	20	21	22	23
PHĀLGUNA 1926	24	25	26	27	28	29	1
	2	3	4	5	6	7	8
	9	10	11	12	13	14	15
	16	17	18	19	20	21	22
	23	24	25	26	27	28	29
CHAITRA 1926	30	1	2	3	4	5	6
	7	8	9	10	11	12	13
	14	15	16	17	18	19	20
	21	22	23	24	25	26	27
VAIŚĀKHA 1927	28	29	30	1[a]	2	3	4
	5	6	7	8	9	10	11
	12	13	14	15	16	17	18
	19	20	21	22	23	24	25
JYAISHṬHA 1927	26	27	28	29	30	31	1
	2	3	4	5	6	7	8
	9	10	11	12	13	14	15
	16	17	18	19	20	21	22
	23	24	25	26	27	28	29
ĀSHĀḌHA 1927	30	31	32	1	2	3	4
	5	6	7	8	9	10	11
	12	13	14	15	16	17	18
	19	20	21	22	23	24	25
ŚRĀVAṆA 1927	26	27	28	29	30	31	1
	2	3	4	5	6	7	8
	9	10	11	12	13	14	15
	16	17	18	19	20	21	22
	23	24	25	26	27	28	29
BHĀDRAPADA 1927	30	31	32	1	2	3	4
	5	6	7	8	9	10	11
	12	13	14	15	16	17	18
	19	20	21	22	23	24	25
ĀŚVINA 1927	26	27	28	29	30	31	1
	2	3	4	5	6	7	8
	9	10	11	12	13	14	15
	16	17	18	19	20	21	22
	23	24	25	26	27	28	29
KĀRTTIKA 1927	30	1	2	3	4	5	6
	7	8	9	10	11	12	13
	14	15	16	17	18	19	20
	21	22	23	24	25	26	27
MĀRGAŚĪRA 1927	28	29	30	1	2	3	4
	5	6	7	8	9	10	11
	12	13	14	15	16	17	18
	19	20	21	22	23	24	25
PAUSHA 1927	26	27	28	29	30	1	2
	3	4	5	6	7	8	9
	10	11	12	13	14	15	16

‡Leap year
[a]New Year (Vilamba)
[b]Pongal

ISLAMIC (ASTRONOMICAL) 1425/1426‡

Month	Sun	Mon	Tue	Wed	Thu	Fri	Sat
DHU AL-QA'DA 1425	13	14	15	16	17	18	19
	20	21	22	23	24	25	26
DHU AL-ḤIJJA 1425	27	28	29	*1*	2	3	4
	5	6	7	8	9	10[g]	11
	12	13	14	15	16	17	18
	19	20	21	22	23	24	25
MUḤARRAM 1426	26	27	28	29	*1*[a]	2	3
	4	5	6	7	8	9	10[b]
	11	12	13	14	15	16	17
	18	19	20	21	22	23	24
ṢAFAR 1426	25	26	27	28	29	30	*1*
	2	3	4	5	6	7	8
	9	10	11	12	13	14	15
	16	17	18	19	20	21	22
	23	24	25	26	27	28	29
RABĪ' I 1426	*1*	2	3	4	5	6	7
	8	9	10	11	12[c]	13	14
	15	16	17	18	19	20	21
	22	23	24	25	26	27	28
RABĪ' II 1426	29	30	*1*	2	3	4	5
	6	7	8	9	10	11	12
	13	14	15	16	17	18	19
	20	21	22	23	24	25	26
JUMĀDĀ I 1426	27	28	29	*1*	2	3	4
	5	6	7	8	9	10	11
	12	13	14	15	16	17	18
	19	20	21	22	23	24	25
JUMĀDĀ II 1426	26	27	28	29	30	*1*	2
	3	4	5	6	7	8	9
	10	11	12	13	14	15	16
	17	18	19	20	21	22	23
RAJAB 1426	24	25	26	27	28	29	*1*
	2	3	4	5	6	7	8
	9	10	11	12	13	14	15
	16	17	18	19	20	21	22
	23	24	25	26	27[d]	28	29
SHA'BĀN 1426	30	*1*	2	3	4	5	6
	7	8	9	10	11	12	13
	14	15	16	17	18	19	20
	21	22	23	24	25	26	27
RAMAḌĀN 1426	28	29	*30*	1[e]	2	3	4
	5	6	7	8	9	10	11
	12	13	14	15	16	17	18
	19	20	21	22	23	24	25
SHAWWĀL 1426	26	27	28	29	*30*	1[f]	2
	3	4	5	6	7	8	9
	10	11	12	13	14	15	16
	17	18	19	20	21	22	23
DHU AL-QA'DA 1426	24	25	26	27	28	*29*	1
	2	3	4	5	6	7	8
	9	10	11	12	13	14	15
	16	17	18	19	20	21	22
	23	24	25	26	27	28	29

‡Leap year
[a]New Year
[b]'Ashūrā'
[c]Prophet's Birthday
[d]Ascent of the Prophet
[e]Start of Ramaḍān
[f]'Id al-Fiṭr
[g]'Id al-'Aḍḥā

GREGORIAN 2005

Julian (Sun)	Sun	Mon	Tue	Wed	Thu	Fri	Sat	Month
Dec 13	26	27	28	29	30	31	1	JANUARY 2005
	2	3	4	5	6	7[a]	8	
Dec 27	9	10	11	12	13	14[b]	15	
	16	17	18	19	20	21	22	
Jan 10	23	24	25	26	27	28	29	
	30	31	1	2	3	4	5	FEBRUARY 2005
Jan 24	6	7	8	9[c]	10	11	12	
	13	14	15	16	17	18	19	
Feb 7	20	21	22	23	24	25	26	
	27	28	1	2	3	4	5	MARCH 2005
Feb 21	6	7	8	9	10	11	12	
	13	14	15	16	17	18	19	
Mar 7	20[d]	21	22	23	24	25	26	
	27[e]	28	29	30	31	1	2	APRIL 2005
Mar 21	3	4	5	6	7	8	9	
	10	11	12	13	14	15	16	
Apr 4	17	18	19	20	21	22	23	
	24	25	26	27	28	29	30	
Apr 18	1[f]	2	3	4	5	6	7	MAY 2005
	8	9	10	11	12	13	14	
May 2	15	16	17	18	19	20	21	
	22	23	24	25	26	27	28	
May 16	29	30	31	1	2	3	4	JUNE 2005
	5	6	7	8	9	10	11	
May 30	12	13	14	15	16	17	18	
	19	20	21	22	23	24	25	
Jun 13	26	27	28	29	30	1	2	JULY 2005
	3	4	5	6	7	8	9	
Jun 27	10	11	12	13	14	15	16	
	17	18	19	20	21	22	23	
Jul 11	24	25	26	27	28	29	30	
	31	1	2	3	4	5	6	AUGUST 2005
Jul 25	7	8	9	10	11	12	13	
	14	15	16	17	18	19	20	
Aug 8	21	22	23	24	25	26	27	
	28	29	30	31	1	2	3	SEPTEMBER 2005
Aug 22	4	5	6	7	8	9	10	
	11	12	13	14	15	16	17	
Sep 5	18	19	20	21	22	23	24	
	25	26	27	28	29	30	1	OCTOBER 2005
Sep 19	2	3	4	5	6	7	8	
	9	10	11	12	13	14	15	
Oct 3	16	17	18	19	20	21	22	
	23	24	25	26	27	28	29	
Oct 17	30	31	1	2	3	4	5	NOVEMBER 2005
	6	7	8	9	10	11	12	
Oct 31	13	14	15	16	17	18	19	
	20	21	22	23	24	25	26	
Nov 14	27[g]	28	29	30	1	2	3	DECEMBER 2005
	4	5	6	7	8	9	10	
Nov 28	11	12	13	14	15	16	17	
	18	19	20	21	22	23	24	
Dec 12	25[h]	26	27	28	29	30	31	

[a]Orthodox Christmas
[b]Julian New Year
[c]Ash Wednesday
[d]Feast of Orthodoxy
[e]Easter
[f]Orthodox Easter
[g]Advent
[h]Christmas

2006

GREGORIAN 2006 / Lunar Phases / ISO WEEK / JULIAN DAY

Month	Sun	Mon	Tue	Wed	Thu	Fri	Sat	Lunar Phases	ISO WEEK (Mon)	JULIAN DAY (Sun noon)
JANUARY 2006	1[a]	2	3	4	5	◐	7	18:56	1	2453737
	8	9	10	11	12	13	○	9:48	2	2453744
	15	16	17	18	19	20	21		3	2453751
	◑	23	24	25	26	27	28	15:14	4	2453758
FEBRUARY 2006	●	30	31	1	2	3	4	14:15	5	2453765
	◐	6	7	8	9	10	11	6:29	6	2453772
	12	○	14	15	16	17	18	4:44	7	2453779
	19	20	◑	22	23	24	25	7:17	8	2453786
MARCH 2006	26	27	●	1	2	3	4	0:31	9	2453793
	5	◐	7	8	9	10	11	20:16	10	2453800
	12	13	○	15	16	17	18	23:35	11	2453807
	19	20[b]	21	◑	23	24	25	19:10	12	2453814
	26	27	28	●	30	31	1	10:15	13	2453821
APRIL 2006	2	3	4	◐	6	7	8	12:01	14	2453828
	9	10	11	12	○	14	15	16:40	15	2453835
	16	17	18	19	20	◑	22	3:28	16	2453842
	23	24	25	26	●	28	29	19:44	17	2453849
MAY 2006	30	1	2	3	4	◐	6	5:13	18	2453856
	7	8	9	10	11	12	○	6:51	19	2453863
	14	15	16	17	18	19	◑	9:20	20	2453870
	21	22	23	24	25	26	●	5:26	21	2453877
JUNE 2006	28	29	30	31	1	2	◐	23:06	22	2453884
	4	5	6	7	8	9	10		23	2453891
	○	12	13	14	15	16	17	18:03	24	2453898
	◑	19	20	21[c]	22	23	24	14:08	25	2453905
JULY 2006	●	26	27	28	29	30	1	16:05	26	2453912
	2	◐	4	5	6	7	8	16:37	27	2453919
	9	10	○	12	13	14	15	3:02	28	2453926
	16	◑	18	19	20	21	22	19:12	29	2453933
	23	24	●	26	27	28	29	4:31	30	2453940
AUGUST 2006	30	31	1	◐	3	4	5	8:46	31	2453947
	6	7	8	○	10	11	12	10:54	32	2453954
	13	14	15	◑	17	18	19	1:51	33	2453961
	20	21	22	●	24	25	26	19:10	34	2453968
SEPTEMBER 2006	27	28	29	30	◐	1	2	22:56	35	2453975
	3	4	5	6	○	8	9	18:42	36	2453982
	10	11	12	13	◑	15	16	11:15	37	2453989
	17	18	19	20	21	●	23[d]	11:45	38	2453996
	24	25	26	27	28	29	◐	11:04	39	2454003
OCTOBER 2006	1	2	3	4	5	6	○	3:13	40	2454010
	8	9	10	11	12	13	◑	0:25	41	2454017
	15	16	17	18	19	20	21		42	2454024
	●	23	24	25	26	27	28	5:14	43	2454031
NOVEMBER 2006	◐	30	31	1	2	3	4	21:25	44	2454038
	○	6	7	8	9	10	11	12:58	45	2454045
	◑	13	14	15	16	17	18	17:45	46	2454052
	19	●	21	22	23	24	25	22:18	47	2454059
DECEMBER 2006	26	27	◐	29	30	1	2	6:29	48	2454066
	3	4	○	6	7	8	9	0:25	49	2454073
	10	11	◑	13	14	15	16	14:32	50	2454080
	17	18	19	●	21	22[e]	23	14:01	51	2454087
	24	25	26	◐	28	29	30	14:48	52	2454094
	31	1	2	○	4	5	6	13:57	1	2454101

HEBREW 5766/5767

ISO WEEK	Month	Sun	Mon	Tue	Wed	Thu	Fri	Sat	Molad
1	TEVETH 5766	1[e]	2[e]	3	4	5	6	7	Sat 1h0m15p
2		8	9	10	11	12	13	14	
3		15	16	17	18	19	20	21	
4		22	23	24	25	26	27	28	
5	SHEVAT 5766	29	1	2	3	4	5	6	Sun 13h44m16p
6		7	8	9	10	11	12	13	
7		14	15	16	17	18	19	20	
8		21	22	23	24	25	26	27	
9	ADAR 5766	28	29	30	1	2	3	4	Tue 2h28m17p
10		5	6	7	8	9	10	11	
11		12	13	14[f]	15	16	17	18	
12		19	20	21	22	23	24	25	
13	NISAN 5766	26	27	28	29	1	2	3	Wed 15h13m0p
14		4	5	6	7	8	9	10	
15		11	12	13	14	15[g]	16	17	
16		18	19	20	21	22	23	24	
17	IYYAR 5766	25	26	27	28	29	30	1	Fri 3h57m1p
18		2	3	4	5	6	7	8	
19		9	10	11	12	13	14	15	
20		16	17	18	19	20	21	22	
21		23	24	25	26	27	28	29	
22	SIVAN 5766	1	2	3	4	5	6[h]	7	Sat 16h41m2p
23		8	9	10	11	12	13	14	
24		15	16	17	18	19	20	21	
25		22	23	24	25	26	27	28	
26	TAMMUZ 5766	29	30	1	2	3	4	5	Mon 5h25m3p
27		6	7	8	9	10	11	12	
28		13	14	15	16	17	18	19	
29		20	21	22	23	24	25	26	
30	AV 5766	27	28	29	1	2	3	4	Tue 18h9m4p
31		5	6	7	8	9[i]	10	11	
32		12	13	14	15	16	17	18	
33		19	20	21	22	23	24	25	
34	ELUL 5766	26	27	28	29	30	1	2	Thu 6h53m5p
35		3	4	5	6	7	8	9	
36		10	11	12	13	14	15	16	
37		17	18	19	20	21	22	23	
38	TISHRI 5767	24	25	26	27	28	29	1[a]	Fri 19h37m6p
39		2[a]	3	4	5	6	7	8	
40		9	10[b]	11	12	13	14	15[c]	
41		16	17	18	19	20	21	22	
42		23	24	25	26	27	28	29	
43	HESHVAN 5767	30	1	2	3	4	5	6	Sun 8h21m7p
44		7	8	9	10	11	12	13	
45		14	15	16	17	18	19	20	
46		21	22	23	24	25	26	27	
47	KISLEV 5767	28	29	30	1	2	3	4	Mon 21h5m8p
48		5	6	7	8	9	10	11	
49		12	13	14[d]	15	16	17	18	
50		19	20	21	22	23	24	25[e]	
51	TEVETH 5767	26[e]	27[e]	28[e]	29[e]	30[e]	1[e]	2[e]	Wed 9h49m9p
52		3	4	5	6	7	8	9	
1		10	11	12	13	14	15	16	

CHINESE Yǐ-Yǒu/Bǐng-Xū‡

ISO WEEK	Month	Sun	Mon	Tue	Wed	Thu	Fri	Sat	Solar Term
1	MONTH 12 Yǐ-Yǒu	2	3	4	5	6	7	8	Xiǎo hán
2		9	10	11	12	13	14	15	
3		16	17	18	19	20	21	22	Dà hán
4		23	24	25	26	27	28	29	
5	MONTH 1 Bǐng-Xū	1[a]	2	3	4	5	6	7*	Lì chūn
6		8	9	10	11	12	13	14	
7		15[b]	16	17	18	19	20	21	
8		22	23	24	25	26	27	28	Yǔ shuǐ
9	MONTH 2 Bǐng-Xū	29	30	1	2	3	4	5	
10		6	7	8	9	10	11	12	Jīng zhé
11		13	14	15	16	17	18	19	
12		20	21	22	23	24	25	26	Chūn fēn
13	MONTH 3 Bǐng-Xū	27	28	29	1	2	3	4	
14		5	6	7	8[c]*	9	10	11	Qīng míng
15		12	13	14	15	16	17	18	
16		19	20	21	22	23	24	25	Gǔ yǔ
17	MONTH 4 Bǐng-Xū	26	27	28	29	30	1	2	
18		3	4	5	6	7	8	9	Lì xià
19		10	11	12	13	14	15	16	
20		17	18	19	20	21	22	23	
21	MONTH 5 Bǐng-Xū	24	25	26	27	28	29	1	Xiǎo mǎn
22		2	3	4	5[d]	6	7	8	
23		9*	10	11	12	13	14	15	Máng zhòng
24		16	17	18	19	20	21	22	
25		23	24	25	26	27	28	29	Xià zhì
26	MONTH 6 Bǐng-Xū	30	1	2	3	4	5	6	
27		7	8	9	10	11	12	13	Xiǎo shǔ
28		14	15	16	17	18	19	20	
29		21	22	23	24	25	26	27	
30	MONTH 7 Bǐng-Xū	28	29	1	2	3	4	5	Dà shǔ
31		6	7[e]	8	9	10*	11	12	
32		13	14	15[f]	16	17	18	19	Lì qiū
33		20	21	22	23	24	25	26	
34	LEAP MONTH 7 Bǐng-Xū	27	28	29	30	1	2	3	Chǔ shǔ
35		4	5	6	7	8	9	10	
36		11	12	13	14	15	16	17	Bái lù
37		18	19	20	21	22	23	24	
38	MONTH 8 Bǐng-Xū	25	26	27	28	29	1	2	Qiū fēn
39		3	4	5	6	7	8	9	
40		10	11*	12	13	14	15[g]	16	
41		17	18	19	20	21	22	23	Hán lù
42		24	25	26	27	28	29	30	
43	MONTH 9 Bǐng-Xū	1	2	3	4	5	6	7	Shuāng jiàng
44		8	9[h]	10	11	12	13	14	
45		15	16	17	18	19	20	21	Lì dōng
46		22	23	24	25	26	27	28	
47	MONTH 10 Bǐng-Xū	29	30	1	2	3	4	5	Xiǎo xuě
48		6	7	8	9	10	11*	12	
49		13	14	15	16	17	18	19	Dà xuě
50		20	21	22	23	24	25	26	
51	MONTH 11 Bǐng-Xū	27	28	29	1	2	3[i]	4	Dōng zhì
52		5	6	7	8	9	10	11	
1		12	13	14	15	16	17	18	Xiǎo hán

COPTIC 1722/1723‡ — ETHIOPIC 1998/1999‡

ISO WEEK	Coptic Month	Sun	Mon	Tue	Wed	Thu	Fri	Sat	Ethiopic Month
1	KOIAK 1722	23	24	25	26	27	28	29[c]	TĀKHŚĀŚ 1998
2	TŌBE 1722	30	1	2	3	4	5	6[d]	ṬER 1998
3		7	8	9	10	11[e]	12	13	
4		14	15	16	17	18	19	20	
5		21	22	23	24	25	26	27	
6	MESHIR 1722	28	29	30	1	2	3	4	YAKĀTIT 1998
7		5	6	7	8	9	10	11	
8		12	13	14	15	16	17	18	
9		19	20	21	22	23	24	25	
10	PAREMOTEP 1722	26	27	28	29	30	1	2	MAGĀBIT 1998
11		3	4	5	6	7	8	9	
12		10	11	12	13	14	15	16	
13		17	18	19	20	21	22	23	
14		24	25	26	27	28	29	30	
15	PARMOUTE 1722	1	2	3	4	5	6	7	MIYĀZYĀ 1998
16		8	9	10	11	12	13	14	
17		15[f]	16	17	18	19	20	21	
18		22	23	24	25	26	27	28	
19	PASHONS 1722	29[g]	30	1	2	3	4	5	GENBOT 1998
20		6	7	8	9	10	11	12	
21		13	14	15	16	17	18	19	
22		20	21	22	23	24	25	26	
23	PAŌNE 1722	27	28	29	30	1	2	3	SANĒ 1998
24		4	5	6	7	8	9	10	
25		11	12	13	14	15	16	17	
26		18	19	20	21	22	23	24	
27	EPĒP 1722	25	26	27	28	29	30	1	ḤAMLĒ 1998
28		2	3	4	5	6	7	8	
29		9	10	11	12	13	14	15	
30		16	17	18	19	20	21	22	
31		23	24	25	26	27	28	29	
32	MESORĒ 1722	30	1	2	3	4	5	6	NAḤASĒ 1998
33		7	8	9	10	11	12	13[h]	
34		14	15	16	17	18	19	20	
35		21	22	23	24	25	26	27	
36	EPAG. 1722	28	29	30	1	2	3	4	PĀG. 1998
37	THOOUT 1723	5	1[a]	2	3	4	5	6	MASKARAM 1999
38		7	8	9	10	11	12	13	
39		14	15	16	17[b]	18	19	20	
40		21	22	23	24	25	26	27	
41	PAOPE 1723	28	29	30	1	2	3	4	ṬEQEMT 1999
42		5	6	7	8	9	10	11	
43		12	13	14	15	16	17	18	
44		19	20	21	22	23	24	25	
45	ATHŌR 1723	26	27	28	29	30	1	2	ḪEDĀR 1999
46		3	4	5	6	7	8	9	
47		10	11	12	13	14	15	16	
48		17	18	19	20	21	22	23	
49		24	25	26	27	28	29	30	
50	KOIAK 1723	1	2	3	4	5	6	7	TĀKHŚĀŚ 1999
51		8	9	10	11	12	13	14	
52		15	16	17	18	19	20	21	
1		22	23	24	25	26	27	28	

Gregorian notes:
[a]New Year
[b]Spring (18:25)
[c]Summer (12:25)
[d]Autumn (4:03)
[e]Winter (0:22)
● New moon
◐ First quarter moon
○ Full moon
◑ Last quarter moon

Hebrew notes:
[a]New Year
[b]Yom Kippur
[c]Sukkot
[d]Winter starts
[e]Hanukkah
[f]Purim
[g]Passover
[h]Shavuot
[i]Fast of Av

Chinese notes:
‡Leap year
[a]New Year (4704, Dog)
[b]Lantern Festival
[c]Qīngmíng
[d]Dragon Festival
[e]Qīqiǎo
[f]Hungry Ghosts
[g]Mid-Autumn Festival
[h]Double-Ninth Festival
[i]Dōngzhì
*Start of 60-name cycle

Coptic/Ethiopic notes:
‡Leap year
[a]New Year
[b]Building of the Cross
[c]Christmas
[d]Jesus's Circumcision
[e]Epiphany
[f]Easter
[g]Mary's Announcement
[h]Jesus's Transfiguration

2006

PERSIAN (ASTRONOMICAL) 1384/1385

Month	Sun	Mon	Tue	Wed	Thu	Fri	Sat
DEY 1384	11	12	13	14	15	16	17
	18	19	20	21	22	23	24
	25	26	27	28	29	30	1
BAHMAN 1384	2	3	4	5	6	7	8
	9	10	11	12	13	14	15
	16	17	18	19	20	21	22
	23	24	25	26	27	28	29
	30	1	2	3	4	5	6
ESFAND 1384	7	8	9	10	11	12	13
	14	15	16	17	18	19	20
	21	22	23	24	25	26	27
	28	29	1[a]	2	3	4	5
FARVARDĪN 1385	6	7	8	9	10	11	12
	13[b]	14	15	16	17	18	19
	20	21	22	23	24	25	26
	27	28	29	30	31	1	2
ORDĪBEHEŠT 1385	3	4	5	6	7	8	9
	10	11	12	13	14	15	16
	17	18	19	20	21	22	23
	24	25	26	27	28	29	30
	31	1	2	3	4	5	6
XORDĀD 1385	7	8	9	10	11	12	13
	14	15	16	17	18	19	20
	21	22	23	24	25	26	27
	28	29	30	31	1	2	3
TĪR 1385	4	5	6	7	8	9	10
	11	12	13	14	15	16	17
	18	19	20	21	22	23	24
	25	26	27	28	29	30	31
MORDĀD 1385	1	2	3	4	5	6	7
	8	9	10	11	12	13	14
	15	16	17	18	19	20	21
	22	23	24	25	26	27	28
	29	30	31	1	2	3	4
SHAHRĪVAR 1385	5	6	7	8	9	10	11
	12	13	14	15	16	17	18
	19	20	21	22	23	24	25
	26	27	28	29	30	31	1
MEHR 1385	2	3	4	5	6	7	8
	9	10	11	12	13	14	15
	16	17	18	19	20	21	22
	23	24	25	26	27	28	29
	30	1	2	3	4	5	6
ĀBĀN 1385	7	8	9	10	11	12	13
	14	15	16	17	18	19	20
	21	22	23	24	25	26	27
	28	29	30	1	2	3	4
ĀZAR 1385	5	6	7	8	9	10	11
	12	13	14	15	16	17	18
	19	20	21	22	23	24	25
	26	27	28	29	30	1	2
DEY 1385	3	4	5	6	7	8	9
	10	11	12	13	14	15	16

[a]New Year
[b]Sizdeh Bedar

HINDU LUNAR 2062/2063

Month	Sun	Mon	Tue	Wed	Thu	Fri	Sat
PAUSHA 2062	1	3	4	5	6	7	8
	9	10	11	12	13	14	15
	16	17	18	19	20	21	22
	23	24	25	26	27	28	29
MĀGHA 2062	30	1	2	3	4	5	6
	8	9	10	11	12	13	14
	14	15	16	17	18	19	20
	21	22	23	24	25	26	27
PHĀLGUNA 2062	28[h]	29	1	2	3	4	5
	6	7	8	9	10	11	12
	13	14	15[i]	16	17	17	18
	19	20	21	22	23	25	26
CHAITRA 2063	27	28	29	30	1[a]	2	3
	4	5	6	7	8[b]	9	10
	11	12	13	14	15	16	17
	18	19	20	21	22	23	24
VAIŚĀKHA 2063	25	26	27	29	30	1	2
	3	4	5	6	7	8	9
	10	11	11	12	13	14	15
	16	17	18	19	20	22	23
	24	25	26	27	28	29	30
JYAISHṬHA 2063	1	2	3	4	5	6	7
	8	9	10	11	12	13	14
	15	16	17	18	19	20	21
	22	23	25	26	27	28	29
ĀSHĀḌHA 2063	30	1	2	3	4	5	6
	7	7	8	9	10	11	12
	13	14	15	16	18	19	20
	21	22	23	24	25	26	27
ŚRĀVAṆA 2063	28	29	30	1	2	3	4
	5	6	7	8	9	10	11
	12	13	14	15	16	17	18
	19	21	22	23[c]	24	25	26
BHĀDRAPADA 2063	27	28	29	30	1	2	3
	4[d]	4	5	6	7	8	9
	10	11	12	14	15	16	17
	18	19	20	21	22	23	24
ĀŚVINA 2063	25	26	27	28	29	30	1
	2	3	4	5	6	7	8[e]
	9[e]	10[e]	11	12	13	14	15
	16	18	19	20	21	22	23
	24	25	26	27	28	29	29
KĀRTTIKA 2063	30	1[f]	2	3	4	5	6
	7	8	9	11	12	13	14
	15	16	17	18	19	20	21
	22	23	24	25	26	27	28
MĀRGAŚĪRA 2063	29	30	1	2	3	4	5
	6	7	8	9	10	11[g]	12
	13	14	16	17	18	19	20
	21	22	22	23	24	25	26
PAUSHA 2063	27	28	29	30	1	2	3
	4	5	6	7	8	10	11
	12	13	14	15	16	17	18

[a]New Year (Vyaya)
[b]Birthday of Rāma
[c]Birthday of Krishna
[d]Ganēśa Chaturthī
[e]Dashara
[f]Diwali
[g]Birthday of Vishnu
[h]Night of Śiva
[i]Holi

HINDU SOLAR 1927‡/1928

Month	Sun	Mon	Tue	Wed	Thu	Fri	Sat
PAUSHA 1927	17	18	19	20	21	22	23
	24	25	26	27	28	29	1[b]
MĀGHA 1927	2	3	4	5	6	7	8
	9	10	11	12	13	14	15
	16	17	18	19	20	21	22
	23	24	25	26	27	28	29
PHĀLGUNA 1927	1	2	3	4	5	6	7
	8	9	10	11	12	13	14
	15	16	17	18	19	20	21
	22	23	24	25	26	27	28
	29	30	1	2	3	4	5
CHAITRA 1927	6	7	8	9	10	11	12
	13	14	15	16	17	18	19
	20	21	22	23	24	25	26
	27	28	29	30	31	1[a]	2
VAIŚĀKHA 1928	3	4	5	6	7	8	9
	10	11	12	13	14	15	16
	17	18	19	20	21	22	23
	24	25	26	27	28	29	30
JYAISHṬHA 1928	1	2	3	4	5	6	7
	8	9	10	11	12	13	14
	15	16	17	18	19	20	21
	22	23	24	25	26	27	28
	29	30	31	32	1	2	3
ĀSHĀḌHA 1928	4	5	6	7	8	9	10
	11	12	13	14	15	16	17
	18	19	20	21	22	23	24
	25	26	27	28	29	30	31
	32	1	2	3	4	5	6
ŚRĀVAṆA 1928	7	8	9	10	11	12	13
	14	15	16	17	18	19	20
	21	22	23	24	25	26	27
	28	29	30	31	1	2	3
BHĀDRAPADA 1928	4	5	6	7	8	9	10
	11	12	13	14	15	16	17
	18	19	20	21	22	23	24
	25	26	27	28	29	30	31
ĀŚVINA 1928	1	2	3	4	5	6	7
	8	9	10	11	12	13	14
	15	16	17	18	19	20	21
	22	23	24	25	26	27	28
	29	30	1	2	3	4	5
KĀRTTIKA 1928	6	7	8	9	10	11	12
	13	14	15	16	17	18	19
	20	21	22	23	24	25	26
	27	28	29	30	1	2	3
MĀRGAŚĪRA 1928	4	5	6	7	8	9	10
	11	12	13	14	15	16	17
	18	19	20	21	22	23	24
	25	26	27	28	29	30	1
PAUSHA 1928	2	3	4	5	6	7	8
	9	10	11	12	13	14	15
	16	17	18	19	20	21	22

‡Leap year
[a]New Year (Vikārin)
[b]Pongal

ISLAMIC (ASTRONOMICAL) 1426‡/1427

Month	Sun	Mon	Tue	Wed	Thu	Fri	Sat	Julian (Sun)
DHU AL-ḤIJJA 1426	30	1	2	3	4	5	6	Dec 19
	7	8	9	10[g]	11	12	13	
	14	15	16	17	18	19	20	Jan 2
	21	22	23	24	25	26	27	
MUḤARRAM 1427	28	29	1[a]	2	3	4	5	Jan 16
	6	7	8	9	10[b]	11	12	
	13	14	15	16	17	18	19	Jan 30
	20	21	22	23	24	25	26	
ṢAFAR 1427	27	28	29	1	2	3	4	Feb 13
	5	6	7	8	9	10	11	
	12	13	14	15	16	17	18	Feb 27
	19	20	21	22	23	24	25	
RABĪ' I 1427	26	27	28	29	30	1	2	Mar 13
	3	4	5	6	7	8	9	
	10	11	12[c]	13	14	15	16	Mar 27
	17	18	19	20	21	22	23	
RABĪ' II 1427	24	25	26	27	28	29	1	Apr 10
	2	3	4	5	6	7	8	
	9	10	11	12	13	14	15	Apr 24
	16	17	18	19	20	21	22	
	23	24	25	26	27	28	29	May 8
JUMĀDĀ I 1427	1	2	3	4	5	6	7	
	8	9	10	11	12	13	14	May 22
	15	16	17	18	19	20	21	
	22	23	24	25	26	27	28	Jun 5
JUMĀDĀ II 1427	29	30	1	2	3	4	5	
	6	7	8	9	10	11	12	Jun 19
	13	14	15	16	17	18	19	
	20	21	22	23	24	25	26	Jul 3
RAJAB 1427	27	28	29	1	2	3	4	
	5	6	7	8	9	10	11	Jul 17
	12	13	14	15	16	17	18	
	19	20	21	22	23	24	25	Jul 31
SHA'BĀN 1427	26	27[d]	28	29	30	31	1	
	2	3	4	5	6	7	8	Aug 14
	9	10	11	12	13	14	15	
	16	17	18	19	20	21	22	Aug 28
	23	24	25	26	27	28	29	
RAMAḌĀN 1427	30	1[e]	2	3	4	5	6	Sep 11
	7	8	9	10	11	12	13	
	14	15	16	17	18	19	20	Sep 25
	21	22	23	24	25	26	27	
SHAWWĀL 1427	28	29	30	1[f]	2	3	4	Oct 9
	5	6	7	8	9	10	11	
	12	13	14	15	16	17	18	Oct 23
	19	20	21	22	23	24	25	
DHU AL-QA'DA 1427	26	27	28	29	1	2	3	Nov 6
	4	5	6	7	8	9	10	
	11	12	13	14	15	16	17	Nov 20
	18	19	20	21	22	23	24	
DHU AL-ḤIJJA 1427	25	26	27	28	29	1	2	Dec 4
	3	4	5	6	7	8	9	
	10[g]	11	12	13	14	15	16	Dec 18

‡Leap year
[a]New Year
[b]'Ashūrā'
[c]Prophet's Birthday
[d]Ascent of the Prophet
[e]Start of Ramaḍān
[f]'Id al-Fiṭr
[g]'Id al-'Aḍḥā

GREGORIAN 2006

Sun	Mon	Tue	Wed	Thu	Fri	Sat	Month
1	2	3	4	5	6	7[a]	JANUARY 2006
8	9	10	11	12	13	14[b]	
15	16	17	18	19	20	21	
22	23	24	25	26	27	28	
29	30	31	1	2	3	4	FEBRUARY 2006
5	6	7	8	9	10	11	
12	13	14	15	16	17	18	
19	20	21	22	23	24	25	
26	27	28	1[c]	2	3	4	MARCH 2006
5	6	7	8	9	10	11	
12[d]	13	14	15	16	17	18	
19	20	21	22	23	24	25	
26	27	28	29	30	31	1	APRIL 2006
2	3	4	5	6	7	8	
9	10	11	12	13	14	15	
16[e]	17	18	19	20	21	22	
23[f]	24	25	26	27	28	29	
30	1	2	3	4	5	6	MAY 2006
7	8	9	10	11	12	13	
14	15	16	17	18	19	20	
21	22	23	24	25	26	27	
28	29	30	31	1	2	3	JUNE 2006
4	5	6	7	8	9	10	
11	12	13	14	15	16	17	
18	19	20	21	22	23	24	
25	26	27	28	29	30	1	JULY 2006
2	3	4	5	6	7	8	
9	10	11	12	13	14	15	
16	17	18	19	20	21	22	
23	24	25	26	27	28	29	
30	31	1	2	3	4	5	AUGUST 2006
6	7	8	9	10	11	12	
13	14	15	16	17	18	19	
20	21	22	23	24	25	26	
27	28	29	30	31	1	2	SEPTEMBER 2006
3	4	5	6	7	8	9	
10	11	12	13	14	15	16	
17	18	19	20	21	22	23	
24	25	26	27	28	29	30	
1	2	3	4	5	6	7	OCTOBER 2006
8	9	10	11	12	13	14	
15	16	17	18	19	20	21	
22	23	24	25	26	27	28	
29	30	31	1	2	3	4	NOVEMBER 2006
5	6	7	8	9	10	11	
12	13	14	15	16	17	18	
19	20	21	22	23	24	25	
26	27	28	29	30	1	2	DECEMBER 2006
3[g]	4	5	6	7	8	9	
10	11	12	13	14	15	16	
17	18	19	20	21	22	23	
24	25[h]	26	27	28	29	30	
31	1	2	3	4	5	6	

[a]Orthodox Christmas
[b]Julian New Year
[c]Ash Wednesday
[d]Feast of Orthodoxy
[e]Easter
[f]Orthodox Easter
[g]Advent
[h]Christmas

2007

GREGORIAN 2007

Month	Sun	Mon	Tue	Wed	Thu	Fri	Sat	Lunar Phases	ISO WEEK (Mon)	JULIAN DAY (Sun noon)
JANUARY 2007	31	1[a]	2	○	4	5	6	13:57	1	2454101
	7	8	9	10	◑	12	13	12:45	2	2454108
	14	15	16	17	18	●	20	4:01	3	2454115
	21	22	23	24	◐	26	27	23:01	4	2454122
FEBRUARY 2007	28	29	30	31	1	○	3	5:45	5	2454129
	4	5	6	7	8	9	◑	9:51	6	2454136
	11	12	13	14	15	16	●	16:14	7	2454143
	18	19	20	21	22	23	◐	7:56	8	2454150
MARCH 2007	25	26	27	28	1	2	○	23:17	9	2454157
	4	5	6	7	8	9	10		10	2454164
	11	◑	13	14	15	16	17	3:54	11	2454171
	18	●	20	21[b]	22	23	24	2:43	12	2454178
	◐	26	27	28	29	30	31	18:16	13	2454185
APRIL 2007	1	○	3	4	5	6	7	17:15	14	2454192
	8	9	◑	11	12	13	14	18:04	15	2454199
	15	16	●	18	19	20	21	11:36	16	2454206
	22	23	◐	25	26	27	28	6:35	17	2454213
MAY 2007	29	30	1	○	3	4	5	10:09	18	2454220
	6	7	8	9	◑	11	12	4:27	19	2454227
	13	14	15	●	17	18	19	19:27	20	2454234
	20	21	22	◐	24	25	26	21:02	21	2454241
JUNE 2007	27	28	29	30	31	○	2	1:03	22	2454248
	3	4	5	6	7	◑	9	11:43	23	2454255
	10	11	12	13	14	●	16	3:13	24	2454262
	17	18	19	20	21[c]	◐	23	13:15	25	2454269
	24	25	26	27	28	29	○	13:49	26	2454276
JULY 2007	1	2	3	4	5	6	◑	16:53	27	2454283
	8	9	10	11	12	13	●	12:04	28	2454290
	15	16	17	18	19	20	21		29	2454297
	◐	23	24	25	26	27	28	6:29	30	2454304
AUGUST 2007	29	○	31	1	2	3	4	0:48	31	2454311
	◑	6	7	8	9	10	11	21:20	32	2454318
	●	13	14	15	16	17	18	23:02	33	2454325
	19	◐	21	22	23	24	25	23:54	34	2454332
SEPTEMBER 2007	26	27	○	29	30	31	1	10:35	35	2454339
	2	3	◑	5	6	7	8	2:32	36	2454346
	9	10	●	12	13	14	15	12:44	37	2454353
	16	17	18	◐	20	21	22	16:48	38	2454360
	23[d]	24	25	○	27	28	29	19:45	39	2454367
OCTOBER 2007	30	1	2	◑	4	5	6	10:06	40	2454374
	7	8	9	10	●	12	13	5:01	41	2454381
	14	15	16	17	18	◐	20	8:33	42	2454388
	21	22	23	24	25	○	27	4:52	43	2454395
NOVEMBER 2007	28	29	30	31	◑	2	3	21:18	44	2454402
	4	5	6	7	8	●	10	23:03	45	2454409
	11	12	13	14	15	16	◐	22:32	46	2454416
	18	19	20	21	22	23	○	14:30	47	2454423
DECEMBER 2007	25	26	27	28	29	30	◑	12:44	48	2454430
	2	3	4	5	6	7	8		49	2454437
	●	10	11	12	13	14	15	17:40	50	2454444
	16	◐	18	19	20	21	22[e]	10:17	51	2454451
	23	○	25	26	27	28	29	1:16	52	2454458
	30	◑	1	2	3	4	5	7:51	1	2454465

HEBREW 5767/5768‡

JULIAN DAY	Month	Sun	Mon	Tue	Wed	Thu	Fri	Sat	Molad
2454101	TEVETH 5767	10	11	12	13	14	15	16	
2454108		17	18	19	20	21	22	23	
2454115		24	25	26	27	28	29	1	Thu 22h 33m 10p
2454122	SHEVAT 5767	2	3	4	5	6	7	8	
2454129		9	10	11	12	13	14	15	
2454136		16	17	18	19	20	21	22	
2454143		23	24	25	26	27	28	29	Sat 11h 17m 11p
2454150	ADAR 5767	30	1	2	3	4	5	6	
2454157		7	8	9	10	11	12	13	
2454164		14[f]	15	16	17	18	19	20	
2454171		21	22	23	24	25	26	27	
2454178	NISAN 5767	28	29	1	2	3	4	5	Mon 0h 1m 12p
2454185		6	7	8	9	10	11	12	
2454192		13	14	15[g]	16	17	18	19	
2454199		20	21	22	23	24	25	26	
2454206	IYYAR 5767	27	28	29	30	1	2	3	Tue 12h 45m 13p
2454213		4	5	6	7	8	9	10	
2454220		11	12	13	14	15	16	17	
2454227		18	19	20	21	22	23	24	
2454234	SIVAN 5767	25	26	27	28	29	1	2	Thu 1h 29m 14p
2454241		3	4	5	6[h]	7	8	9	
2454248		10	11	12	13	14	15	16	
2454255		17	18	19	20	21	22	23	
2454262		24	25	26	27	28	29	30	Fri 14h 13m 15p
2454269	TAMMUZ 5767	1	2	3	4	5	6	7	
2454276		8	9	10	11	12	13	14	
2454283		15	16	17	18	19	20	21	
2454290		22	23	24	25	26	27	28	
2454297	AV 5767	29	1	2	3	4	5	6	Sun 2h 57m 16p
2454304		7	8	9[i]	10	11	12	13	
2454311		14	15	16	17	18	19	20	
2454318		21	22	23	24	25	26	27	
2454325	ELUL 5767	28	29	30	1	2	3	4	Mon 15h 41m 17p
2454332		5	6	7	8	9	10	11	
2454339		12	13	14	15	16	17	18	
2454346		19	20	21	22	23	24	25	
2454353	TISHRI 5768	26	27	28	29	1[a]	2[a]	3	Wed 4h 25m 0p
2454360		4	5	6	7	8	9	10[b]	
2454367		11	12	13	14	15[c]	16	17	
2454374		18	19	20	21	22	23	24	
2454381	HESHVAN 5768	25	26	27	28	29	30	1	Thu 17h 10m 1p
2454388		2	3	4	5	6	7	8	
2454395		9	10	11	12	13	14	15	
2454402		16	17	18	19	20	21	22	
2454409		23	24	25	26	27	28	29	Sat 5h 54m 2p
2454416	KISLEV 5768	1	2	3	4	5	6	7	
2454423		8	9	10	11	12	13	14	
2454430		15	16	17	18	19	20	21	
2454437		22	23	24	25[e]	26[d,e]	27[e]	28[e]	
2454444	TEVETH 5768	29[e]	1[e]	2[e]	3[e]	4	5	6	Sun 18h 38m 3p
2454451		7	8	9	10	11	12	13	
2454458		14	15	16	17	18	19	20	
2454465		21	22	23	24	25	26	27	

CHINESE Bǐng-Xū‡/Dīng-Hài

JULIAN DAY	Month	Sun	Mon	Tue	Wed	Thu	Fri	Sat	Solar Term
2454101	MONTH 11 Bǐng-Xū	12	13	14	15	16	17	18	Xiǎo hán
2454108		19	20	21	22	23	24	25	
2454115	MONTH 12 Bǐng-Xū	26	27	28	29	30	1	2	Dà hán
2454122		3	4	5	6	7	8	9	
2454129		10	11	12*	13	14	15	16	
2454136		17	18	19	20	21	22	23	Lì chūn
2454143		24	25	26	27	28	29	30	
2454150	MONTH 1 Dīng-Hài	1[a]	2	3	4	5	6	7	Yǔ shuǐ
2454157		8	9	10	11	12	13	14	
2454164		15[b]	16	17	18	19	20	21	Jīng zhé
2454171		22	23	24	25	26	27	28	
2454178	MONTH 2 Dīng-Hài	29	1	2	3	4	5	6	Chūn fēn
2454185		7	8	9	10	11	12	13*	
2454192		14	15	16	17	18[c]	19	20	Qīng míng
2454199		21	22	23	24	25	26	27	
2454206	MONTH 3 Dīng-Hài	28	29	1	2	3	4	5	Gǔ yǔ
2454213		6	7	8	9	10	11	12	
2454220		13	14	15	16	17	18	19	
2454227		20	21	22	23	24	25	26	Lì xià
2454234	MONTH 4 Dīng-Hài	27	28	29	30	1	2	3	
2454241		4	5	6	7	8	9	10	Xiǎo mǎn
2454248		11	12	13	14*	15	16	17	
2454255		18	19	20	21	22	23	24	Máng zhòng
2454262	MONTH 5 Dīng-Hài	25	26	27	28	29	1	2	
2454269		3	4	5[d]	6	7	8	9	Xià zhì
2454276		10	11	12	13	14	15	16	
2454283		17	18	19	20	21	22	23	Xiǎo shǔ
2454290	MONTH 6 Dīng-Hài	24	25	26	27	28	29	1	
2454297		2	3	4	5	6	7	8	
2454304		9	10	11	12	13	14	15	Dà shǔ
2454311		16*	17	18	19	20	21	22	
2454318		23	24	25	26	27	28	29	Lì qiū
2454325	MONTH 7 Dīng-Hài	30	1	2	3	4	5	6	
2454332		7[e]	8	9	10	11	12	13	Chǔ shǔ
2454339		14	15[f]	16	17	18	19	20	
2454346		21	22	23	24	25	26	27	Bái lù
2454353	MONTH 8 Dīng-Hài	28	29	1	2	3	4	5	
2454360		6	7	8	9	10	11	12	
2454367		13	14	15[g]	16	17*	18	19	Qiū fēn
2454374		20	21	22	23	24	25	26	
2454381	MONTH 9 Dīng-Hài	27	28	29	30	1	2	3	Hán lù
2454388		4	5	6	7	8	9[h]	10	
2454395		11	12	13	14	15	16	17	Shuāng jiàng
2454402		18	19	20	21	22	23	24	
2454409	MONTH 10 Dīng-Hài	25	26	27	28	29	30	1	Lì dōng
2454416		2	3	4	5	6	7	8	
2454423		9	10	11	12	13	14	15	Xiǎo xuě
2454430		16	17*	18	19	20	21	22	
2454437		23	24	25	26	27	28	29	Dà xuě
2454444	MONTH 11 Dīng-Hài	30	1	2	3	4	5	6	
2454451		7	8	9	10	11	12	13[i]	Dōng zhì
2454458		14	15	16	17	18	19	20	
2454465		21	22	23	24	25	26	27	

COPTIC 1723‡/1724 — ETHIOPIC 1999‡/2000

JULIAN DAY	Coptic Month	Sun	Mon	Tue	Wed	Thu	Fri	Sat	Ethiopic Month
2454101	KOIAK 1723	22	23	24	25	26	27	28	TĀKHŚĀŚ 1999
2454108	TŌBE 1723	29[c]	30	1	2	3	4	5	ṬER 1999
2454115		6[d]	7	8	9	10	11[e]	12	
2454122		13	14	15	16	17	18	19	
2454129		20	21	22	23	24	25	26	
2454136	MESHIR 1723	27	28	29	30	1	2	3	YAKĀTIT 1999
2454143		4	5	6	7	8	9	10	
2454150		11	12	13	14	15	16	17	
2454157		18	19	20	21	22	23	24	
2454164	PAREMOTEP 1723	25	26	27	28	29	30	1	MAGĀBIT 1999
2454171		2	3	4	5	6	7	8	
2454178		9	10	11	12	13	14	15	
2454185		16	17	18	19	20	21	22	
2454192		23	24	25	26	27	28	29	
2454199	PARMOUTE 1723	30[f]	1	2	3	4	5	6	MIYĀZYĀ 1999
2454206		7	8	9	10	11	12	13	
2454213		14	15	16	17	18	19	20	
2454220		21	22	23	24	25	26	27	
2454227	PASHONS 1723	28	29[g]	30	1	2	3	4	GENBOT 1999
2454234		5	6	7	8	9	10	11	
2454241		12	13	14	15	16	17	18	
2454248		19	20	21	22	23	24	25	
2454255	PAŌNE 1723	26	27	28	29	30	1	2	SANĒ 1999
2454262		3	4	5	6	7	8	9	
2454269		10	11	12	13	14	15	16	
2454276		17	18	19	20	21	22	23	
2454283		24	25	26	27	28	29	30	
2454290	EPĒP 1723	1	2	3	4	5	6	7	ḤAMLĒ 1999
2454297		8	9	10	11	12	13	14	
2454304		15	16	17	18	19	20	21	
2454311		22	23	24	25	26	27	28	
2454318	MESORĒ 1723	29	30	1	2	3	4	5	NAHASĒ 1999
2454325		6	7	8	9	10	11	12	
2454332		13[h]	14	15	16	17	18	19	
2454339		20	21	22	23	24	25	26	
2454346	EPAG. 1723	27	28	29	30	1	2	3	PĀG. 1999
2454353	THOOUT 1724	4	5	6	1[a]	2	3	4	MASKARAM 2000
2454360		5	6	7	8	9	10	11	
2454367		12	13	14	15	16	17[b]	18	
2454374		19	20	21	22	23	24	25	
2454381	PAOPE 1724	26	27	28	29	30	1	2	ṬEQEMT 2000
2454388		3	4	5	6	7	8	9	
2454395		10	11	12	13	14	15	16	
2454402		17	18	19	20	21	22	23	
2454409		24	25	26	27	28	29	30	
2454416	ATHŌR 1724	1	2	3	4	5	6	7	ḤEDĀR 2000
2454423		8	9	10	11	12	13	14	
2454430		15	16	17	18	19	20	21	
2454437		22	23	24	25	26	27	28	
2454444	KOIAK 1724	29	30	1	2	3	4	5	TĀKHŚĀŚ 2000
2454451		6	7	8	9	10	11	12	
2454458		13	14	15	16	17	18	19	
2454465		20	21	22	23	24	25	26	

[a]New Year
[b]Spring (0:07)
[c]Summer (18:06)
[d]Autumn (9:51)
[e]Winter (6:07)
● New moon
◐ First quarter moon
○ Full moon
◑ Last quarter moon

‡Leap year
[a]New Year
[b]Yom Kippur
[c]Sukkot
[d]Winter starts
[e]Ḥanukkah
[f]Purim
[g]Passover
[h]Shavuot
[i]Fast of Av

‡Leap year
[a]New Year (4705, Pig)
[b]Lantern Festival
[c]Qīngmíng
[d]Dragon Festival
[e]Qīqiǎo
[f]Hungry Ghosts
[g]Mid-Autumn Festival
[h]Double-Ninth Festival
[i]Dōngzhì
*Start of 60-name cycle

‡Leap year
[a]New Year
[b]Building of the Cross
[c]Christmas
[d]Jesus's Circumcision
[e]Epiphany
[f]Easter
[g]Mary's Announcement
[h]Jesus's Transfiguration

PERSIAN (ASTRONOMICAL) 1385/1386

Month	Sun	Mon	Tue	Wed	Thu	Fri	Sat
DEY 1385	10	11	12	13	14	15	16
	17	18	19	20	21	22	23
	24	25	26	27	28	29	30
BAHMAN 1385	1	2	3	4	5	6	7
	8	9	10	11	12	13	14
	15	16	17	18	19	20	21
	22	23	24	25	26	27	28
ESFAND 1385	29	30	1	2	3	4	5
	6	7	8	9	10	11	12
	13	14	15	16	17	18	19
	20	21	22	23	24	25	26
FARVARDĪN 1386	27	28	29	1[a]	2	3	4
	5	6	7	8	9	10	11
	12	13[b]	14	15	16	17	18
	19	20	21	22	23	24	25
ORDĪBEHEŠT 1386	26	27	28	29	30	31	1
	2	3	4	5	6	7	8
	9	10	11	12	13	14	15
	16	17	18	19	20	21	22
	23	24	25	26	27	28	29
XORDĀD 1386	30	31	1	2	3	4	5
	6	7	8	9	10	11	12
	13	14	15	16	17	18	19
	20	21	22	23	24	25	26
TĪR 1386	27	28	29	30	31	1	2
	3	4	5	6	7	8	9
	10	11	12	13	14	15	16
	17	18	19	20	21	22	23
	24	25	26	27	28	29	30
MORDĀD 1386	31	1	2	3	4	5	6
	7	8	9	10	11	12	13
	14	15	16	17	18	19	20
	21	22	23	24	25	26	27
SHAHRĪVAR 1386	28	29	30	31	1	2	3
	4	5	6	7	8	9	10
	11	12	13	14	15	16	17
	18	19	20	21	22	23	24
	25	26	27	28	29	30	31
MEHR 1386	1	2	3	4	5	6	7
	8	9	10	11	12	13	14
	15	16	17	18	19	20	21
	22	23	24	25	26	27	28
ĀBĀN 1386	29	30	1	2	3	4	5
	6	7	8	9	10	11	12
	13	14	15	16	17	18	19
	20	21	22	23	24	25	26
ĀZAR 1386	27	28	29	30	1	2	3
	4	5	6	7	8	9	10
	11	12	13	14	15	16	17
	18	19	20	21	22	23	24
DEY 1386	25	26	27	28	29	30	1
	2	3	4	5	6	7	8
	9	10	11	12	13	14	15

[a]New Year
[b]Sizdeh Bedar

HINDU LUNAR 2063/2064‡

Month	Sun	Mon	Tue	Wed	Thu	Fri	Sat
PAUSHA 2063	12	13	14	15	16	17	18
	19	20	21	22	23	24	24
MĀGHA 2063	25	26	27	28	29	30	1
	2	4	5	6	7	8	9
	10	11	12	13	14	15	16
	17	18	19	20	21	22	23
	24	25	26	27	28	29[h]	30
PHĀLGUNA 2063	1	2	3	4	5	**6**	8
	9	10	11	12	13	14	15[i]
	16	17	17	18	19	20	21
	22	23	24	25	26	27	28
CHAITRA 2064	29	**30**[a]	2	3	4	5	6
	7	8	9[b]	10	11	12	13
	14	15	16	17	18	19	20
	21	21	22	**23**	25	26	27
VAIŚĀKHA 2064	28	29	30	1	2	3	4
	5	7	8	9	10	11	11
	12	13	14	15	16	17	18
	19	20	21	22	23	24	25
LEAP JYAISHTHA 2064	26	27	**28**	30	1	2	3
	4	5	6	7	8	9	10
	11	12	13	14	15	15	16
	17	18	19	**20**	22	23	24
JYAISHTHA 2064	25	26	27	28	29	30	1
	2	4	5	6	7	7	8
	9	10	11	12	13	14	15
	16	17	18	19	20	21	22
	23	25	26	27	28	29	30
ĀSHĀDHA 2064	1	2	3	4	5	6	7
	8	9	10	11	12	13	13
	14	**15**	17	18	19	20	21
	22	23	24	25	26	**27**	29
ŚRĀVANA 2064	30	1	2	3	4	4	5
	6	7	8	9	10	11	12
	13	14	15	16	17	18	**19**
	21	22	23[c]	24	25	26	27
BHĀDRAPADA 2064	28	29	30	1	2	3	4[d]
	5	6	7	8	9	9	10
	11	13	14	15	16	17	18
	19	20	21	22	23	**24**	26
ĀŚVINA 2064	27	28	29	29	30	1	2
	3	4	5	6	7	8[e]	9[e]
	10[e]	11	12	13	14	15	**16**
	18	19	20	21	22	23	24
KĀRTTIKA 2064	25	26	27	28	29	30	1[f]
	2	2	3	4	5	6	7
	8	9	**10**	12	13	14	15
	16	17	18	19	20	21	22
	23	24	25	26	27	28	29
MĀRGAŚĪRA 2064	30	1	2	3	4	5	6
	7	8	9	10	11[g]	12	13
	14	**15**	17	18	19	20	21
	22	23	24	25	25	26	27

‡Leap year
[a]New Year (Sarvajit)
[b]Birthday of Rāma
[c]Birthday of Krishna
[d]Ganēśa Chaturthī
[e]Dashara
[f]Diwali
[g]Birthday of Vishnu
[h]Night of Śiva
[i]Holi

HINDU SOLAR 1928/1929

Month	Sun	Mon	Tue	Wed	Thu	Fri	Sat
PAUSHA 1928	16	17	18	19	20	21	22
	23	24	25	26	27	28	29
MĀGHA 1928	1[b]	2	3	4	5	6	7
	8	9	10	11	12	13	14
	15	16	17	18	19	20	21
	22	23	24	25	26	27	28
PHĀLGUNA 1928	29	30	1	2	3	4	5
	6	7	8	9	10	11	12
	13	14	15	16	17	18	19
	20	21	22	23	24	25	26
CHAITRA 1928	27	28	29	1	2	3	4
	5	6	7	8	9	10	11
	12	13	14	15	16	17	18
	19	20	21	22	23	24	25
VAIŚĀKHA 1929	26	27	28	29	30	31	1[a]
	2	3	4	5	6	7	8
	9	10	11	12	13	14	15
	16	17	18	19	20	21	22
	23	24	25	26	27	28	29
JYAISHṬHA 1929	30	31	1	2	3	4	5
	6	7	8	9	10	11	12
	13	14	15	16	17	18	19
	20	21	22	23	24	25	26
ĀSHĀDHA 1929	27	28	29	30	31	1	2
	3	4	5	6	7	8	9
	10	11	12	13	14	15	16
	17	18	19	20	21	22	23
	24	25	26	27	28	29	30
ŚRĀVAṆA 1929	31	32	1	2	3	4	5
	6	7	8	9	10	11	12
	13	14	15	16	17	18	19
	20	21	22	23	24	25	26
BHĀDRAPADA 1929	27	28	29	30	31	1	2
	3	4	5	6	7	8	9
	10	11	12	13	14	15	16
	17	18	19	20	21	22	23
	24	25	26	27	28	29	30
ĀŚVINA 1929	31	1	2	3	4	5	6
	7	8	9	10	11	12	13
	14	15	16	17	18	19	20
	21	22	23	24	25	26	27
KĀRTTIKA 1929	28	29	30	31	1	2	3
	4	5	6	7	8	9	10
	11	12	13	14	15	16	17
	18	19	20	21	22	23	24
MĀRGAŚĪRA 1929	25	26	27	28	29	30	1
	2	3	4	5	6	7	8
	9	10	11	12	13	14	15
	16	17	18	19	20	21	22
	23	24	25	26	27	28	29
PAUSHA 1929	1	2	3	4	5	6	7
	8	9	10	11	12	13	14
	15	16	17	18	19	20	21

[a]New Year (Śārvari)
[b]Pongal

ISLAMIC (ASTRONOMICAL) 1427/1428‡

Month	Sun	Mon	Tue	Wed	Thu	Fri	Sat
DHU AL-ḤIJJA 1427	10	11	12	13	14	15	16
	17	18	19	20	21	22	23
MUḤARRAM 1428	24	25	26	27	28	29	1[a]
	2	3	4	5	6	7	8
	9	10[b]	11	12	13	14	15
	16	17	18	19	20	21	22
	23	24	25	26	27	28	29
ṢAFAR 1428	30	1	2	3	4	5	6
	7	8	9	10	11	12	13
	14	15	16	17	18	19	20
	21	22	23	24	25	26	27
RABĪ' I 1428	28	29	1	2	3	4	5
	6	7	8	9	10	11	12[c]
	13	14	15	16	17	18	19
	20	21	22	23	24	25	26
RABĪ' II 1428	27	28	29	30	1	2	3
	4	5	6	7	8	9	10
	11	12	13	14	15	16	17
	18	19	20	21	22	23	24
JUMĀDĀ I 1428	25	26	27	28	29	1	2
	3	4	5	6	7	8	9
	10	11	12	13	14	15	16
	17	18	19	20	21	22	23
JUMĀDĀ II 1428	24	25	26	27	28	29	1
	2	3	4	5	6	7	8
	9	10	11	12	13	14	15
	16	17	18	19	20	21	22
	23	24	25	26	27	28	29
RAJAB 1428	30	1	2	3	4	5	6
	7	8	9	10	11	12	13
	14	15	16	17	18	19	20
	21	22	23	24	25	26	27[d]
SHA'BĀN 1428	28	29	30	1	2	3	4
	5	6	7	8	9	10	11
	12	13	14	15	16	17	18
	19	20	21	22	23	24	25
RAMAḌĀN 1428	26	27	28	29	30	1[e]	2
	3	4	5	6	7	8	9
	10	11	12	13	14	15	16
	17	18	19	20	21	22	23
	24	25	26	27	28	29	30
SHAWWĀL 1428	1[f]	2	3	4	5	6	7
	8	9	10	11	12	13	14
	15	16	17	18	19	20	21
	22	23	24	25	26	27	28
DHU AL-QA'DA 1428	29	1	2	3	4	5	6
	7	8	9	10	11	12	13
	14	15	16	17	18	19	20
	21	22	23	24	25	26	27
DHU AL-ḤIJJA 1428	28	29	30	1	2	3	4
	5	6	7	8	9	10[g]	11
	12	13	14	15	16	17	18
	19	20	21	22	23	24	25

‡Leap year
[a]New Year
[b]'Ashūrā'
[c]Prophet's Birthday
[d]Ascent of the Prophet
[e]Start of Ramaḍān
[f]'Id al-Fiṭr
[g]'Id al-'Aḍḥā

GREGORIAN 2007

Julian (Sun)	Sun	Mon	Tue	Wed	Thu	Fri	Sat	Month
Dec 18	31	1	2	3	4	5	6	JANUARY 2007
	7[a]	8	9	10	11	12	13	
Jan 1	14[b]	15	16	17	18	19	20	
	21	22	23	24	25	26	27	
Jan 15	28	29	30	31	1	2	3	FEBRUARY 2007
	4	5	6	7	8	9	10	
Jan 29	11	12	13	14	15	16	17	
	18	19	20	21[c]	22	23	24	
Feb 12	25[d]	26	27	28	1	2	3	MARCH 2007
	4	5	6	7	8	9	10	
Feb 26	11	12	13	14	15	16	17	
	18	19	20	21	22	23	24	
Mar 12	25	26	27	28	29	30	31	
	1	2	3	4	5	6	7	APRIL 2007
Mar 26	8[e]	9	10	11	12	13	14	
	15	16	17	18	19	20	21	
Apr 9	22	23	24	25	26	27	28	
	29	30	1	2	3	4	5	MAY 2007
Apr 23	6	7	8	9	10	11	12	
	13	14	15	16	17	18	19	
May 7	20	21	22	23	24	25	26	
	27	28	29	30	31	1	2	JUNE 2007
May 21	3	4	5	6	7	8	9	
	10	11	12	13	14	15	16	
Jun 4	17	18	19	20	21	22	23	
	24	25	26	27	28	29	30	
Jun 18	1	2	3	4	5	6	7	JULY 2007
	8	9	10	11	12	13	14	
Jul 2	15	16	17	18	19	20	21	
	22	23	24	25	26	27	28	
Jul 16	29	30	31	1	2	3	4	AUGUST 2007
	5	6	7	8	9	10	11	
Jul 30	12	13	14	15	16	17	18	
	19	20	21	22	23	24	25	
Aug 13	26	27	28	29	30	31	1	SEPTEMBER 2007
	2	3	4	5	6	7	8	
Aug 27	9	10	11	12	13	14	15	
	16	17	18	19	20	21	22	
Sep 10	23	24	25	26	27	28	29	
	30	1	2	3	4	5	6	OCTOBER 2007
Sep 24	7	8	9	10	11	12	13	
	14	15	16	17	18	19	20	
Oct 8	21	22	23	24	25	26	27	
	28	29	30	31	1	2	3	NOVEMBER 2007
Oct 22	4	5	6	7	8	9	10	
	11	12	13	14	15	16	17	
Nov 5	18	19	20	21	22	23	24	
	25	26	27	28	29	30	1	DECEMBER 2007
Nov 19	2[g]	3	4	5	6	7	8	
	9	10	11	12	13	14	15	
Dec 3	16	17	18	19	20	21	22	
	23	24	25[h]	26	27	28	29	
Dec 17	30	31	1	2	3	4	5	

[a]Orthodox Christmas
[b]Julian New Year
[c]Ash Wednesday
[d]Feast of Orthodoxy
[e]Easter (also Orthodox)
[g]Advent
[h]Christmas

2008

GREGORIAN 2008‡	Sun	Mon	Tue	Wed	Thu	Fri	Sat	Lunar Phases	ISO WEEK (Mon)	JULIAN DAY (Sun noon)
	30	◑	1[a]	2	3	4	5	7:51	1	2454465
	6	7	●	9	10	11	12	11:37	2	2454472
JANUARY 2008	13	14	◐	16	17	18	19	19:45	3	2454479
	20	21	○	23	24	25	26	13:35	4	2454486
	27	28	29	◑	31	1	2	5:03	5	2454493
	3	4	5	6	●	8	9	3:44	6	2454500
FEBRUARY 2008	10	11	12	13	◐	15	16	3:33	7	2454507
	17	18	19	20	○	22	23	3:30	8	2454514
	24	25	26	27	28	◑	1	2:18	9	2454521
	2	3	4	5	6	●	8	17:14	10	2454528
MARCH 2008	9	10	11	12	13	◐	15	10:45	11	2454535
	16	17	18	19	20[b]	○	22	18:40	12	2454542
	23	24	25	26	27	28	◑	21:47	13	2454549
	30	31	1	2	3	4	5		14	2454556
	●	7	8	9	10	11	◐	3:55 18:32	15	2454563
APRIL 2008	13	14	15	16	17	18	19		16	2454570
	○	21	22	23	24	25	26	10:25	17	2454577
	27	◑	29	30	1	2	3	14:12	18	2454584
	4	●	6	7	8	9	10	12:18	19	2454591
MAY 2008	11	◐	13	14	15	16	17	3:47	20	2454598
	18	19	○	21	22	23	24	2:11	21	2454605
	25	26	27	◑	29	30	31	2:56	22	2454612
	1	2	●	4	5	6	7	19:22	23	2454619
	8	9	◐	11	12	13	14	15:04	24	2454626
JUNE 2008	15	16	17	○	19	20[c]	21	17:30	25	2454633
	22	23	24	25	◑	27	28	12:10	26	2454640
	29	30	1	2	●	4	5	2:18	27	2454647
	6	7	8	9	◐	11	12	4:35	28	2454654
JULY 2008	13	14	15	16	17	○	19	7:59	29	2454661
	20	21	22	23	24	◑	26	18:41	30	2454668
	27	28	29	30	31	●	2	10:12	31	2454675
	3	4	5	6	7	◐	9	20:20	32	2454682
AUGUST 2008	10	11	12	13	14	15	○	21:16	33	2454689
	17	18	19	20	21	22	◑	23:49	34	2454696
	24	25	26	27	28	29	●	19:58	35	2454703
	31	1	2	3	4	5	6		36	2454710
	◐	8	9	10	11	12	13	14:04	37	2454717
SEPTEMBER 2008	14	○	16	17	18	19	20	9:13	38	2454724
	21	◑[d]	23	24	25	26	27	5:04	39	2454731
	28	●	30	1	2	3	4	8:12	40	2454738
	5	6	◐	8	9	10	11	9:04	41	2454745
OCTOBER 2008	12	13	○	15	16	17	18	20:02	42	2454752
	19	20	◑	22	23	24	25	11:55	43	2454759
	26	27	●	29	30	31	1	23:14	44	2454766
	2	3	4	5	◐	7	8	4:03	45	2454773
NOVEMBER 2008	9	10	11	12	○	14	15	6:18	46	2454780
	16	17	18	◑	20	21	22	21:31	47	2454787
	23	24	25	26	●	28	29	16:54	48	2454794
	30	1	2	3	4	◐	6	21:25	49	2454801
	7	8	9	10	11	○	13	16:37	50	2454808
DECEMBER 2008	14	15	16	17	18	◑	20	10:29	51	2454815
	21[e]	22	23	24	25	26	●	12:22	52	2454822
	28	29	30	31	1	2	3		1	2454829

ISO WEEK	HEBREW 5768‡/5769	Sun	Mon	Tue	Wed	Thu	Fri	Sat	Molad
1		21	22	23	24	25	26	27	
2	TEVETH 5768	28	29	1	2	3	4	5	Tue $7^{h}22^{m}4^{p}$
3		6	7	8	9	10	11	12	
4	SHEVAT 5768	13	14	15	16	17	18	19	
5		20	21	22	23	24	25	26	
6		27	28	29	30	1	2	3	Wed $20^{h}6^{m}5^{p}$
7		4	5	6	7	8	9	10	
8	ADAR I 5768	11	12	13	14	15	16	17	
9		18	19	20	21	22	23	24	
10		25	26	27	28	29	30	1	Fri $8^{h}50^{m}6^{p}$
11		2	3	4	5	6	7	8	
12	ADAR II 5768	9	10	11	12	13	14[f]	15	
13		16	17	18	19	20	21	22	
14		23	24	25	26	27	28	29	
15		1	2	3	4	5	6	7	Sat $21^{h}34^{m}7^{p}$
16		8	9	10	11	12	13	14	
17	NISAN 5768	15[g]	16	17	18	19	20	21	
18		22	23	24	25	26	27	28	
19		29	30	1	2	3	4	5	Mon $10^{h}18^{m}8^{p}$
20		6	7	8	9	10	11	12	
21	IYAR 5768	13	14	15	16	17	18	19	
22		20	21	22	23	24	25	26	
23		27	28	29	1	2	3	4	Tue $23^{h}2^{m}9^{p}$
24		5	6[h]	7	8	9	10	11	
25	SIVAN 5768	12	13	14	15	16	17	18	
26		19	20	21	22	23	24	25	
27		26	27	28	29	30	1	2	Thu $11^{h}46^{m}10^{p}$
28		3	4	5	6	7	8	9	
29	TAMMUZ 5768	10	11	12	13	14	15	16	
30		17	18	19	20	21	22	23	
31		24	25	26	27	28	29	1	Sat $0^{h}30^{m}11^{p}$
32		2	3	4	5	6	7	8	
33	AV 5768	9[i]	10	11	12	13	14	15	
34		16	17	18	19	20	21	22	
35		23	24	25	26	27	28	29	
36		30	1	2	3	4	5	6	Sun $13^{h}14^{m}12^{p}$
37		7	8	9	10	11	12	13	
38	ELUL 5768	14	15	16	17	18	19	20	
39		21	22	23	24	25	26	27	
40		28	29	1[a]	2[a]	3	4	5	Tue $1^{h}58^{m}13^{p}$
41		6	7	8	9	10[b]	11	12	
42	TISHRI 5769	13	14	15[c]	16	17	18	19	
43		20	21	22	23	24	25	26	
44		27	28	29	30	1	2	3	Wed $14^{h}42^{m}14^{p}$
45		4	5	6	7	8	9	10	
46	HESHVAN 5769	11	12	13	14	15	16	17	
47		18	19	20	21	22	23	24	
48		25	26	27	28	29	1	2	Fri $3^{h}26^{m}15^{p}$
49		3	4	5	6	7	8[d]	9	
50	KISLEV 5769	10	11	12	13	14	15	16	
51		17	18	19	20	21	22	23	
52		24	25[e]	26[e]	27[e]	28[e]	29[e]	30[e]	Sat $16^{h}10^{m}16^{p}$
1		1[e]	2[e]	3	4	5	6	7	

ISO WEEK	CHINESE Dīng-Hài/Wù-Zǐ	Sun	Mon	Tue	Wed	Thu	Fri	Sat	Solar Term
1	MONTH 11 Dīng-Hài	21	22	23	24	25	26	27	
2		*28*	29	1	2	3	4	5	*Xiǎo hán*
3	MONTH 12 Dīng-Hài	6	7	8	9	10	11	12	
4		13	***14***	15	16	17	18*	19	***Dà hán***
5		20	21	22	23	24	25	26	
6		27	*28*	29	30	1[a]	2	3	*Lì chūn*
7		4	5	6	7	8	9	10	
8	MONTH 1 Wù-Zǐ	11	12	***13***	14	15[b]	16	17	***Yǔ shuǐ***
9		18	19	20	21	22	23	24	
10		25	26	27	*28*	29	30	1	*Jīng zhé*
11		2	3	4	5	6	7	8	
12	MONTH 2 Wù-Zǐ	9	10	11	12	***13***	14	15	***Chūn fēn***
13		16	17	18*	19	20	21	22	
14		23	24	25	26	27	28[c]	29	*Qīng míng*
15		1	2	3	4	5	6	7	
16		8	9	10	11	12	13	14	
17	MONTH 3 Wù-Zǐ	***15***	16	17	18	19	20	21	***Gǔ yǔ***
18		22	23	24	25	26	27	28	
19		29	*1*	2	3	4	5	6	*Lì xià*
20		7	8	9	10	11	12	13	
21	MONTH 4 Wù-Zǐ	14	15	16	***17***	18	19	20*	***Xiǎo mǎn***
22		21	22	23	24	25	26	27	
23		28	29	30	1	*2*	3	4	*Máng zhòng*
24		5[d]	6	7	8	9	10	11	
25	MONTH 5 Wù-Zǐ	12	13	14	15	16	17	***18***	***Xià zhì***
26		19	20	21	22	23	24	25	
27		26	27	28	29	1	2	3	
28		4	5	6	7	8	9	10	*Xiǎo shǔ*
29	MONTH 6 Wù-Zǐ	11	12	13	14	15	16	17	
30		18	19	***20***	21*	22	23	24	***Dà shǔ***
31		25	26	27	28	29	1	2	
32		3	4	5	6	*7*[e]	8	9	*Lì qiū*
33	MONTH 7 Wù-Zǐ	10	11	12	13	14	15[f]	16	
34		17	18	19	20	21	22	***23***	***Chǔ shǔ***
35		24	25	26	27	28	29	30	
36		1	2	3	4	5	6	7	
37		*8*	9	10	11	12	13	14	*Bái lù*
38	MONTH 8 Wù-Zǐ	15[g]	16	17	18	19	20	21	
39		22*	***23***	24	25	26	27	28	***Qiū fēn***
40		29	1	2	3	4	5	6	
41		7	8	9[h]	*10*	11	12	13	*Hán lù*
42	MONTH 9 Wù-Zǐ	14	15	16	17	18	19	20	
43		21	22	23	24	***25***	26	27	***Shuāng jiàng***
44		28	29	30	1	2	3	4	
45		5	6	7	8	9	*10*	11	*Lì dōng*
46	MONTH 10 Wù-Zǐ	12	13	14	15	16	17	18	
47		19	20	21	22	23*	24	***25***	***Xiǎo xuě***
48		26	27	28	29	30	1	2	
49		3	4	5	6	7	8	9	
50	MONTH 11* Wù-Zǐ	*10*	11	12	13	14	15	16	*Dà xuě*
51		17	18	19	20	21	22	23	
52		***24***[i]	25	26	27	28	29	1	***Dōng zhì***
1	MONTH 12 Wù-Zǐ	2	3	4	5	6	7	8	

ISO WEEK	COPTIC 1724/1725	Sun	Mon	Tue	Wed	Thu	Fri	Sat	ETHIOPIC 2000/2001
1	KOIAK 1724	20	21	22	23	24	25	26	TĀKHŚĀŚ 2000
2		27	28	29[c]	30	1	2	3	
3	TÔBE 1724	4	5	6[d]	7	8	9	10	ṬER 2000
4		11[e]	12	13	14	15	16	17	
5		18	19	20	21	22	23	24	
6		25	26	27	28	29	30	1	
7		2	3	4	5	6	7	8	
8	MESHIR 1724	9	10	11	12	13	14	15	YAKĀTIT 2000
9		16	17	18	19	20	21	22	
10		23	24	25	26	27	28	29	
11		30	1	2	3	4	5	6	
12	PAREMOTEP 1724	7	8	9	10	11	12	13	MAGĀBIT 2000
13		14	15	16	17	18	19	20	
14		21	22	23	24	25	26	27	
15		28	29	30	1	2	3	4	
16	PARMOUTE 1724	5	6	7	8	9	10	11	
17		12	13	14	15	16	17	18	MIYĀZYĀ 2000
18		19[f]	20	21	22	23	24	25	
19		26	27	28	29[g]	30	1	2	
20		3	4	5	6	7	8	9	
21	PASHONS 1724	10	11	12	13	14	15	16	GENBOT 2000
22		17	18	19	20	21	22	23	
23		24	25	26	27	28	29	30	
24		1	2	3	4	5	6	7	
25	PAÔNE 1724	8	9	10	11	12	13	14	SANĒ 2000
26		15	16	17	18	19	20	21	
27		22	23	24	25	26	27	28	
28		29	30	1	2	3	4	5	
29	EPÊP 1724	6	7	8	9	10	11	12	
30		13	14	15	16	17	18	19	ḤAMLĒ 2000
31		20	21	22	23	24	25	26	
32		27	28	29	30	1	2	3	
33	MESORÊ 1724	4	5	6	7	8	9	10	
34		11	12	13[h]	14	15	16	17	NAḤASĒ 2000
35		18	19	20	21	22	23	24	
36		25	26	27	28	29	30	1	
37	EPAG. 1724	2	3	4	5	1[a]	2	3	PĀG. 2000
38	THOOUT 1725	4	5	6	7	8	9	10	MASKARAM 2001
39		11	12	13	14	15	16	17[b]	
40		18	19	20	21	22	23	24	
41		25	26	27	28	29	30	1	
42		2	3	4	5	6	7	8	
43	PAOPE 1725	9	10	11	12	13	14	15	ṬEQEMT 2001
44		16	17	18	19	20	21	22	
45		23	24	25	26	27	28	29	
46		30	1	2	3	4	5	6	
47	ATHÔR 1725	7	8	9	10	11	12	13	ḤEDĀR 2001
48		14	15	16	17	18	19	20	
49		21	22	23	24	25	26	27	
50		28	29	30	1	2	3	4	
51	KOIAK 1725	5	6	7	8	9	10	11	
52		12	13	14	15	16	17	18	TĀKHŚĀŚ 2001
1		19	20	21	22	23	24	25	

‡Leap year
[a]New Year
[b]Spring (5:48)
[c]Summer (23:59)
[d]Autumn (15:44)
[e]Winter (12:03)
● New moon
◐ First quarter moon
○ Full moon
◑ Last quarter moon

‡Leap year
[a]New Year
[b]Yom Kippur
[c]Sukkot
[d]Winter starts
[e]Ḥanukkah
[f]Purim
[g]Passover
[h]Shavuot
[i]Fast of Av

[a]New Year (4706, Rat)
[b]Lantern Festival
[c]Qīngmíng
[d]Dragon Festival
[e]Qīqiǎo
[f]Hungry Ghosts
[g]Mid-Autumn Festival
[h]Double-Ninth Festival
[i]Dōngzhì
*Start of 60-name cycle

[a]New Year
[b]Building of the Cross
[c]Christmas
[d]Jesus's Circumcision
[e]Epiphany
[f]Easter
[g]Mary's Announcement
[h]Jesus's Transfiguration

2008

PERSIAN (ASTRONOMICAL) 1386/1387‡

Month	Sun	Mon	Tue	Wed	Thu	Fri	Sat
DEY 1386	9	10	11	12	13	14	15
	16	17	18	19	20	21	22
	23	24	25	26	27	28	29
BAHMAN 1386	30	1	2	3	4	5	6
	7	8	9	10	11	12	13
	14	15	16	17	18	19	20
	21	22	23	24	25	26	27
ESFAND 1386	28	29	30	1	2	3	4
	5	6	7	8	9	10	11
	12	13	14	15	16	17	18
	19	20	21	22	23	24	25
FARVARDĪN 1387	26	27	28	29	1[a]	2	3
	4	5	6	7	8	9	10
	11	12	13[b]	14	15	16	17
	18	19	20	21	22	23	24
	25	26	27	28	29	30	31
ORDĪBEHEŠT 1387	1	2	3	4	5	6	7
	8	9	10	11	12	13	14
	15	16	17	18	19	20	21
	22	23	24	25	26	27	28
XORDĀD 1387	29	30	31	1	2	3	4
	5	6	7	8	9	10	11
	12	13	14	15	16	17	18
	19	20	21	22	23	24	25
TĪR 1387	26	27	28	29	30	31	1
	2	3	4	5	6	7	8
	9	10	11	12	13	14	15
	16	17	18	19	20	21	22
	23	24	25	26	27	28	29
MORDĀD 1387	30	31	1	2	3	4	5
	6	7	8	9	10	11	12
	13	14	15	16	17	18	19
	20	21	22	23	24	25	26
SHAHRĪVAR 1387	27	28	29	30	31	1	2
	3	4	5	6	7	8	9
	10	11	12	13	14	15	16
	17	18	19	20	21	22	23
	24	25	26	27	28	29	30
MEHR 1387	31	1	2	3	4	5	6
	7	8	9	10	11	12	13
	14	15	16	17	18	19	20
	21	22	23	24	25	26	27
ĀBĀN 1387	28	29	30	1	2	3	4
	5	6	7	8	9	10	11
	12	13	14	15	16	17	18
	19	20	21	22	23	24	25
ĀZAR 1387	26	27	28	29	30	1	2
	3	4	5	6	7	8	9
	10	11	12	13	14	15	16
	17	18	19	20	21	22	23
	24	25	26	27	28	29	30
DEY 1387	1	2	3	4	5	6	7
	8	9	10	11	12	13	14

‡Leap year
[a]New Year
[b]Sizdeh Bedar

HINDU LUNAR 2064‡/2065

Month	Sun	Mon	Tue	Wed	Thu	Fri	Sat
MĀRGAŚĪRA 2064	22	23	24	25	25	26	27
PAUSHA 2064	28	29	30	1	2	3	4
	5	6	7	8	**9**	11	12
	13	14	15	16	17	18	19
	20	21	22	23	24	25	26
MĀGHA 2064	27	27	28	29	30	1	**2**
	4	5	6	7	8	9	10
	11	12	13	14	15	16	17
	18	19	20	21	22	23	24
PHĀLGUNA 2064	25	26	27	28[h]	29	30	1
	2	3	4	5	6	**7**	9
	10	11	12	13	14	15[i]	16
	17	18	19	20	20	21	22
	23	24	25	26	27	28	29
CHAITRA 2065	30	**1**[a]	3	4	5	6	7
	8	9[b]	10	11	12	13	14
	15	16	17	18	19	20	21
	22	23	24	25	26	27	28
VAIŚĀKHA 2065	29	30	1	2	3	4	**5**
	7	8	9	10	11	12	13
	14	15	15	16	17	18	19
	20	21	22	23	24	25	26
JYAISHTHA 2065	27	**28**	30	1	2	3	4
	5	6	7	8	9	10	11
	12	13	14	15	16	17	18
	19	20	21	22	23	24	25
ĀSHĀDHA 2065	26	27	28	29	30	**1**	3
	4	5	6	7	8	9	10
	11	12	12	13	14	15	16
	17	18	19	20	21	22	**23**
ŚRĀVANA 2065	25	26	27	28	29	30	1
	2	3	4	5	6	7	8
	9	10	11	12	13	14	15
	16	17	18	19	20	21	22
	23[c]	24	25	**26**	28	29	30
BHĀDRAPADA 2065	1	2	3	4[d]	5	6	7
	8	8	9	10	11	12	13
	14	15	16	17	18	19	**20**
	22	23	24	25	26	27	28
ĀŚVINA 2065	29	30	1	2	3	4	5
	6	7	8[e]	9[e]	10[e]	11	12
	13	14	15	16	17	18	19
	20	21	22	**23**	25	26	27
KĀRTTIKA 2065	28	29	30	1[f]	2	3	3
	4	5	6	7	8	9	10
	11	12	13	14	15	16	**17**
	19	20	21	22	23	24	25
MĀRGAŚĪRA 2065	26	27	28	29	30	1	2
	3	4	5	5	6	7	8
	9	**10**[g]	12	13	14	15	16
	17	18	19	20	21	22	23
	24	25	26	27	28	29	30
	1	2	3	4	5	6	7

‡Leap year
[a]New Year (Sarvadhārin)
[b]Birthday of Rāma
[c]Birthday of Krishna
[d]Ganēśa Chaturthī
[e]Dashara
[f]Diwali
[g]Birthday of Vishnu
[h]Night of Śiva
[i]Holi

HINDU SOLAR 1929/1930

Month	Sun	Mon	Tue	Wed	Thu	Fri	Sat
PAUSHA 1929	15	16	17	18	19	20	21
	22	23	24	25	26	27	28
MĀGHA 1929	29	1[b]	2	3	4	5	6
	7	8	9	10	11	12	13
	14	15	16	17	18	19	20
	21	22	23	24	25	26	27
PHĀLGUNA 1929	28	29	30	1	2	3	4
	5	6	7	8	9	10	11
	12	13	14	15	16	17	18
	19	20	21	22	23	24	25
CHAITRA 1929	26	27	28	29	30	1	2
	3	4	5	6	7	8	9
	10	11	12	13	14	15	16
	17	18	19	20	21	22	23
	24	25	26	27	28	29	30
VAIŚĀKHA 1930	1[a]	2	3	4	5	6	7
	8	9	10	11	12	13	14
	15	16	17	18	19	20	21
	22	23	24	25	26	27	28
JYAISHTHA 1930	29	30	31	1	2	3	4
	5	6	7	8	9	10	11
	12	13	14	15	16	17	18
	19	20	21	22	23	24	25
ĀSHĀDHA 1930	26	27	28	29	30	31	1
	2	3	4	5	6	7	8
	9	10	11	12	13	14	15
	16	17	18	19	20	21	22
	23	24	25	26	27	28	29
ŚRĀVANA 1930	30	31	32	1	2	3	4
	5	6	7	8	9	10	11
	12	13	14	15	16	17	18
	19	20	21	22	23	24	25
	26	27	28	29	30	31	32
BHĀDRAPADA 1930	1	2	3	4	5	6	7
	8	9	10	11	12	13	14
	15	16	17	18	19	20	21
	22	23	24	25	26	27	28
ĀŚVINA 1930	29	30	31	1	2	3	4
	5	6	7	8	9	10	11
	12	13	14	15	16	17	18
	19	20	21	22	23	24	25
KĀRTTIKA 1930	26	27	28	29	30	1	2
	3	4	5	6	7	8	9
	10	11	12	13	14	15	16
	17	18	19	20	21	22	23
	24	25	26	27	28	29	30
MĀRGAŚĪRA 1930	1	2	3	4	5	6	7
	8	9	10	11	12	13	14
	15	16	17	18	19	20	21
	22	23	24	25	26	27	28
PAUSHA 1930	29	1	2	3	4	5	6
	7	8	9	10	11	12	13
	14	15	16	17	18	19	20

[a]New Year (Plava)
[b]Pongal

ISLAMIC (ASTRONOMICAL) 1428‡/1429/1430

Month	Sun	Mon	Tue	Wed	Thu	Fri	Sat
DHU AL-HIJJA 1428	19	20	21	22	23	24	25
MUHARRAM 1429	26	27	28	29	1[a]	2	3
	4	5	6	7	8	9	10[b]
	11	12	13	14	15	16	17
	18	19	20	21	22	23	24
SAFAR 1429	25	26	27	28	29	1	2
	3	4	5	6	7	8	9
	10	11	12	13	14	15	16
	17	18	19	20	21	22	23
	24	25	26	27	28	29	30
RABĪ' I 1429	1	2	3	4	5	6	7
	8	9	10	11	12[c]	13	14
	15	16	17	18	19	20	21
	22	23	24	25	26	27	28
RABĪ' II 1429	29	1	2	3	4	5	6
	7	8	9	10	11	12	13
	14	15	16	17	18	19	20
	21	22	23	24	25	26	27
JUMĀDĀ I 1429	28	29	30	1	2	3	4
	5	6	7	8	9	10	11
	12	13	14	15	16	17	18
	19	20	21	22	23	24	25
JUMĀDĀ II 1429	26	27	28	29	1	2	3
	4	5	6	7	8	9	10
	11	12	13	14	15	16	17
	18	19	20	21	22	23	24
RAJAB 1429	25	26	27	28	29	1	2
	3	4	5	6	7	8	9
	10	11	12	13	14	15	16
	17	18	19	20	21	22	23
	24	25	26	27[d]	28	29	30
SHA'BĀN 1429	1	2	3	4	5	6	7
	8	9	10	11	12	13	14
	15	16	17	18	19	20	21
	22	23	24	25	26	27	28
RAMADĀN 1429	29	30	1[e]	2	3	4	5
	6	7	8	9	10	11	12
	13	14	15	16	17	18	19
	20	21	22	23	24	25	26
SHAWWĀL 1429	27	28	29	30	1[f]	2	3
	4	5	6	7	8	9	10
	11	12	13	14	15	16	17
	18	19	20	21	22	23	24
DHU AL-QA'DA 1429	25	26	27	28	29	1	2
	3	4	5	6	7	8	9
	10	11	12	13	14	15	16
	17	18	19	20	21	22	23
	24	25	26	27	28	29	30
DHU AL-HIJJA 1429	1	2	3	4	5	6	7
	8	9	10[g]	11	12	13	14
	15	16	17	18	19	20	21
	22	23	24	25	26	27	28
	29	1[a]	2	3	4	5	6

‡Leap year
[a]New Year
[b]'Ashūrā'
[c]Prophet's Birthday
[d]Ascent of the Prophet
[e]Start of Ramaḍān
[f]'Id al-Fiṭr
[g]'Id al-'Aḍḥā

GREGORIAN 2008‡

Julian‡ (Sun)	Sun	Mon	Tue	Wed	Thu	Fri	Sat	Month
Dec 17	30	31	1	2	3	4	5	
	6	7[a]	8	9	10	11	12	JANUARY 2008
Dec 31	13	14[b]	15	16	17	18	19	
	20	21	22	23	24	25	26	
Jan 14	27	28	29	30	31	1	2	
	3	4	5	6[c]	7	8	9	FEBRUARY 2008
Jan 28	10	11	12	13	14	15	16	
	17	18	19	20	21	22	23	
Feb 11	24	25	26	27	28	29	1	
	2	3	4	5	6	7	8	MARCH 2008
Feb 25	9	10	11	12	13	14	15	
	16[d]	17	18	19	20	21	22	
Mar 10	23[e]	24	25	26	27	28	29	
	30	31	1	2	3	4	5	
Mar 24	6	7	8	9	10	11	12	APRIL 2008
	13	14	15	16	17	18	19	
Apr 7	20	21	22	23	24	25	26	
	27[f]	28	29	30	1	2	3	
Apr 21	4	5	6	7	8	9	10	MAY 2008
	11	12	13	14	15	16	17	
May 5	18	19	20	21	22	23	24	
	25	26	27	28	29	30	31	
May 19	1	2	3	4	5	6	7	
	8	9	10	11	12	13	14	JUNE 2008
Jun 2	15	16	17	18	19	20	21	
	22	23	24	25	26	27	28	
Jun 16	29	30	1	2	3	4	5	
	6	7	8	9	10	11	12	JULY 2008
Jun 30	13	14	15	16	17	18	19	
	20	21	22	23	24	25	26	
Jul 14	27	28	29	30	31	1	2	
	3	4	5	6	7	8	9	AUGUST 2008
Jul 28	10	11	12	13	14	15	16	
	17	18	19	20	21	22	23	
Aug 11	24	25	26	27	28	29	30	
	31	1	2	3	4	5	6	
Aug 25	7	8	9	10	11	12	13	SEPTEMBER 2008
	14	15	16	17	18	19	20	
Sep 8	21	22	23	24	25	26	27	
	28	29	30	1	2	3	4	
Sep 22	5	6	7	8	9	10	11	OCTOBER 2008
	12	13	14	15	16	17	18	
Oct 6	19	20	21	22	23	24	25	
	26	27	28	29	30	31	1	
Oct 20	2	3	4	5	6	7	8	NOVEMBER 2008
	9	10	11	12	13	14	15	
Nov 3	16	17	18	19	20	21	22	
	23	24	25	26	27	28	29	
Nov 17	30[g]	1	2	3	4	5	6	
	7	8	9	10	11	12	13	DECEMBER 2008
Dec 1	14	15	16	17	18	19	20	
	21	22	23	24	25[h]	26	27	
Dec 15	28	29	30	31	1	2	3	

‡Leap year
[a]Orthodox Christmas
[b]Julian New Year
[c]Ash Wednesday
[d]Feast of Orthodoxy
[e]Easter
[f]Orthodox Easter
[g]Advent
[h]Christmas

2009

GREGORIAN 2009

Month	Sun	Mon	Tue	Wed	Thu	Fri	Sat	Lunar Phases	ISO WEEK (Mon)	JULIAN DAY (Sun noon)
JANUARY 2009	28	29	30	31	1[a]	2	3		1	2454829
	◐	5	6	7	8	9	10	11:56	2	2454836
	○	12	13	14	15	16	17	3:27	3	2454843
	◑	19	20	21	22	23	24	2:46	4	2454850
	25	●	27	28	29	30	31	7:55	5	2454857
FEBRUARY 2009	1	◐	3	4	5	6	7	23:13	6	2454864
	8	○	10	11	12	13	14	14:49	7	2454871
	15	◑	17	18	19	20	21	21:37	8	2454878
	22	23	24	●	26	27	28	1:35	9	2454885
MARCH 2009	1	2	3	◐	5	6	7	7:45	10	2454892
	8	9	10	○	12	13	14	2:38	11	2454899
	15	16	17	◑	19	20[b]	21	17:47	12	2454906
	22	23	24	25	●	27	28	16:06	13	2454913
	29	30	31	1	◐	3	4	14:33	14	2454920
APRIL 2009	5	6	7	8	○	10	11	14:56	15	2454927
	12	13	14	15	16	◑	18	13:36	16	2454934
	19	20	21	22	23	24	●	3:22	17	2454941
	26	27	28	29	30	◐	2	20:44	18	2454948
MAY 2009	3	4	5	6	7	8	○	4:01	19	2454955
	10	11	12	13	14	15	16		20	2454962
	◑	18	19	20	21	22	23	7:26	21	2454969
	●	25	26	27	28	29	30	12:11	22	2454976
	◐	1	2	3	4	5	6	3:22	23	2454983
JUNE 2009	○	8	9	10	11	12	13	18:12	24	2454990
	14	◑	16	17	18	19	20	22:14	25	2454997
	21[c]	●	23	24	25	26	27	19:35	26	2455004
	28	◐	30	1	2	3	4	11:28	27	2455011
JULY 2009	5	6	○	8	9	10	11	9:21	28	2455018
	12	13	14	◑	16	17	18	9:53	29	2455025
	19	20	21	●	23	24	25	2:34	30	2455032
	26	27	◐	29	30	31	1	22:00	31	2455039
AUGUST 2009	2	3	4	5	○	7	8	0:55	32	2455046
	9	10	11	12	◑	14	15	18:55	33	2455053
	16	17	18	19	●	21	22	10:01	34	2455060
	23	24	25	26	◐	28	29	11:42	35	2455067
	30	31	1	2	3	○	5	16:02	36	2455074
SEPTEMBER 2009	6	7	8	9	10	11	◑	2:16	37	2455081
	13	14	15	16	17	●	19	18:44	38	2455088
	20	21	22[d]	23	24	25	◐	4:49	39	2455095
	27	28	29	30	1	2	3		40	2455102
OCTOBER 2009	○	5	6	7	8	9	10	6:10	41	2455109
	◑	12	13	14	15	16	17	8:56	42	2455116
	●	19	20	21	22	23	24	5:33	43	2455123
	25	◐	27	28	29	30	31	0:42	44	2455130
NOVEMBER 2009	1	○	3	4	5	6	7	19:14	45	2455137
	8	◑	10	11	12	13	14	15:56	46	2455144
	15	●	17	18	19	20	21	19:14	47	2455151
	22	23	◐	25	26	27	28	21:39	48	2455158
	29	30	1	○	3	4	5	7:30	49	2455165
DECEMBER 2009	6	7	8	◑	10	11	12	0:13	50	2455172
	13	14	15	●	17	18	19	12:02	51	2455179
	20	21[e]	22	23	◐	25	26	17:36	52	2455186
	27	28	29	30	○	1	2	19:13	53	2455193

HEBREW 5769/5770

ISO WEEK	Month	Sun	Mon	Tue	Wed	Thu	Fri	Sat	Molad
1		1[e]	2[e]	3	4	5	6	7	Sat 16h 10m 16p
2	TEVETH 5769	8	9	10	11	12	13	14	
3		15	16	17	18	19	20	21	
4		22	23	24	25	26	27	28	
5		29	1	2	3	4	5	6	Mon 4h 54m 17p
6	SHEVAT 5769	7	8	9	10	11	12	13	
7		14	15	16	17	18	19	20	
8		21	22	23	24	25	26	27	
9		28	29	30	1	2	3	4	Tue 17h 39m 0p
10	ADAR 5769	5	6	7	8	9	10	11	
11		12	13	14[f]	15	16	17	18	
12		19	20	21	22	23	24	25	
13		26	27	28	29	1	2	3	Thu 6h 23m 1p
14	NISAN 5769	4	5	6	7	8	9	10	
15		11	12	13	14*	15[g]	16	17	
16		18	19	20	21	22	23	24	
17		25	26	27	28	29	30	1	Fri 19h 7m 2p
18	IYYAR 5769	2	3	4	5	6	7	8	
19		9	10	11	12	13	14	15	
20		16	17	18	19	20	21	22	
21		23	24	25	26	27	28	29	
22		1	2	3	4	5	6[h]	7	Sun 7h 51m 3p
23	SIVAN 5769	8	9	10	11	12	13	14	
24		15	16	17	18	19	20	21	
25		22	23	24	25	26	27	28	
26		29	30	1	2	3	4	5	Mon 20h 35m 4p
27	TAMMUZ 5769	6	7	8	9	10	11	12	
28		13	14	15	16	17	18	19	
29		20	21	22	23	24	25	26	
30		27	28	29	1	2	3	4	Wed 9h 19m 5p
31	AV 5769	5	6	7	8	9[i]	10	11	
32		12	13	14	15	16	17	18	
33		19	20	21	22	23	24	25	
34		26	27	28	29	30	1	2	Thu 22h 3m 6p
35	ELUL 5769	3	4	5	6	7	8	9	
36		10	11	12	13	14	15	16	
37		17	18	19	20	21	22	23	
38		24	25	26	27	28	29	1[a]	Sat 10h 47m 7p
39	TISHRI 5770	2[a]	3	4	5	6	7	8	
40		9	10[b]	11	12	13	14	15[c]	
41		16	17	18	19	20	21	22	
42		23	24	25	26	27	28	29	
43		30	1	2	3	4	5	6	Sun 23h 31m 8p
44	ḤESHVAN 5770	7	8	9	10	11	12	13	
45		14	15	16	17	18	19	20	
46		21	22	23	24	25	26	27	
47		28	29	30	1	2	3	4	Tue 12h 15m 9p
48	KISLEV 5770	5	6	7	8	9	10	11	
49		12	13	14	15	16	17	18[d]	
50		19	20	21	22	23	24	25[e]	
51		26[e]	27[e]	28[e]	29[e]	30[e]	1[e]	2[e]	Thu 0h 59m 10p
52	TEVETH 5770	3	4	5	6	7	8	9	
53		10	11	12	13	14	15	16	

CHINESE Wù-Zǐ/Jǐ-Chǒu‡

ISO WEEK	Month	Sun	Mon	Tue	Wed	Thu	Fri	Sat	Solar Term
1		2	3	4	5	6	7	8	
2	MONTH 12 Wù-Zǐ	9	10	11	12	13	14	15	Xiǎo hán
3		16	17	18	19	20	21	22	
4		23	24*	25	26	27	28	29	Dà hán
5		30	1[a]	2	3	4	5	6	
6	MONTH 1 Jǐ-Chǒu	7	8	9	10	11	12	13	Lì chūn
7		14	15[b]	16	17	18	19	20	
8		21	22	23	24	25	26	27	Yǔ shuǐ
9		28	29	30	1	2	3	4	
10	MONTH 2 Jǐ-Chǒu	5	6	7	8	9	10	11	Jīng zhé
11		12	13	14	15	16	17	18	
12		19	20	21	22	23	24*	25	Chūn fēn
13		26	27	28	29	30	1	2	
14	MONTH 3 Jǐ-Chǒu	3	4	5	6	7	8	9[c]	Qīng míng
15		10	11	12	13	14	15	16	
16		17	18	19	20	21	22	23	
17		24	25	26	27	28	29	1	Gǔ yǔ
18	MONTH 4 Jǐ-Chǒu	2	3	4	5	6	7	8	
19		9	10	11	12	13	14	15	Lì xià
20		16	17	18	19	20	21	22	
21		23	24	25*	26	27	28	29	Xiǎo mǎn
22		1	2	3	4	5[d]	6	7	
23	MONTH 5 Jǐ-Chǒu	8	9	10	11	12	13	14	Máng zhòng
24		15	16	17	18	19	20	21	
25		22	23	24	25	26	27	28	
26		29	30	1	2	3	4	5	Xià zhì
27	LEAP MONTH 5 Jǐ-Chǒu	6	7	8	9	10	11	12	
28		13	14	15	16	17	18	19	Xiǎo shǔ
29		20	21	22	23	24	25	26*	
30		27	28	29	1	2	3	4	Dà shǔ
31	MONTH 6 Jǐ-Chǒu	5	6	7	8	9	10	11	
32		12	13	14	15	16	17	18	Lì qiū
33		19	20	21	22	23	24	25	
34		26	27	28	29	1	2	3	
35	MONTH 7 Jǐ-Chǒu	4	5	6	7[e]	8	9	10	Chǔ shǔ
36		11	12	13	14	15[f]	16	17	
37		18	19	20	21	22	23	24	Bái lù
38		25	26	27	28*	29	30	1	
39	MONTH 8 Jǐ-Chǒu	2	3	4	5	6	7	8	Qiū fēn
40		9	10	11	12	13	14	15[g]	
41		16	17	18	19	20	21	22	Hán lù
42		23	24	25	26	27	28	29	
43		1	2	3	4	5	6	7	Shuāng jiàng
44	MONTH 9 Jǐ-Chǒu	8	9[h]	10	11	12	13	14	
45		15	16	17	18	19	20	21	Lì dōng
46		22	23	24	25	26	27	28	
47		29*	30	1	2	3	4	5	
48	MONTH 10 Jǐ-Chǒu	6	7	8	9	10	11	12	Xiǎo xuě
49		13	14	15	16	17	18	19	
50		20	21	22	23	24	25	26	Dà xuě
51		27	28	29	1	2	3	4	
52	MONTH 11 Jǐ-Chǒu	5	6	7[i]	8	9	10	11	Dōng zhì
53		12	13	14	15	16	17	18	

COPTIC 1725/1726 — ETHIOPIC 2001/2002

ISO WEEK	Coptic Month	Sun	Mon	Tue	Wed	Thu	Fri	Sat	Ethiopic Month
1	KOIAK 1725	19	20	21	22	23	24	25	TĀKHŚĀŚ 2001
2		26	27	28	29[c]	30	1	2	
3	TŌBE 1725	3	4	5	6[d]	7	8	9	ṬER 2001
4		10	11[e]	12	13	14	15	16	
5		17	18	19	20	21	22	23	
6		24	25	26	27	28	29	30	
7	MESHIR 1725	1	2	3	4	5	6	7	YAKĀTIT 2001
8		8	9	10	11	12	13	14	
9		15	16	17	18	19	20	21	
10		22	23	24	25	26	27	28	
11		29	30	1	2	3	4	5	
12	PAREMOTEP 1725	6	7	8	9	10	11	12	MAGĀBIT 2001
13		13	14	15	16	17	18	19	
14		20	21	22	23	24	25	26	
15		27	28	29	30	1	2	3	
16	PARMOUTE 1725	4	5	6	7	8	9	10	MIYĀZYĀ 2001
17		11[f]	12	13	14	15	16	17	
18		18	19	20	21	22	23	24	
19		25	26	27	28	29[g]	30	1	
20	PASHONS 1725	2	3	4	5	6	7	8	GENBOT 2001
21		9	10	11	12	13	14	15	
22		16	17	18	19	20	21	22	
23		23	24	25	26	27	28	29	
24		30	1	2	3	4	5	6	
25	PAŌNE 1725	7	8	9	10	11	12	13	SANĒ 2001
26		14	15	16	17	18	19	20	
27		21	22	23	24	25	26	27	
28		28	29	30	1	2	3	4	
29	EPĒP 1725	5	6	7	8	9	10	11	ḤAMLĒ 2001
30		12	13	14	15	16	17	18	
31		19	20	21	22	23	24	25	
32		26	27	28	29	30	1	2	
33	MESORĒ 1725	3	4	5	6	7	8	9	NAHASĒ 2001
34		10	11	12	13[h]	14	15	16	
35		17	18	19	20	21	22	23	
36		24	25	26	27	28	29	30	
37	EPAG. 1725	1	2	3	4	5	1[a]	2	PĀG. 2001 / MASKARAM 2002
38	THOOUT 1726	3	4	5	6	7	8	9	
39		10	11	12	13	14	15	16	
40		17[b]	18	19	20	21	22	23	
41		24	25	26	27	28	29	30	
42	PAOPE 1726	1	2	3	4	5	6	7	ṬEQEMT 2002
43		8	9	10	11	12	13	14	
44		15	16	17	18	19	20	21	
45		22	23	24	25	26	27	28	
46		29	30	1	2	3	4	5	
47	ATHŌR 1726	6	7	8	9	10	11	12	ḤEDĀR 2002
48		13	14	15	16	17	18	19	
49		20	21	22	23	24	25	26	
50		27	28	29	30	1	2	3	
51	KOIAK 1726	4	5	6	7	8	9	10	TĀKHŚĀŚ 2002
52		11	12	13	14	15	16	17	
53		18	19	20	21	22	23	24	

Gregorian:
[a]New Year
[b]Spring (11:43)
[c]Summer (5:45)
[d]Autumn (21:18)
[e]Winter (17:46)
● New moon
◐ First quarter moon
○ Full moon
◑ Last quarter moon

Hebrew:
[a]New Year
[b]Yom Kippur
[c]Sukkot
[d]Winter starts
[e]Ḥanukkah
[f]Purim
[g]Passover
[h]Shavuot
[i]Fast of Av
*New solar cycle

Chinese:
‡Leap year
[a]New Year (4707, Ox)
[b]Lantern Festival
[c]Qīngmíng
[d]Dragon Festival
[e]Qīqiǎo
[f]Hungry Ghosts
[g]Mid-Autumn Festival
[h]Double-Ninth Festival
[i]Dōngzhì
*Start of 60-name cycle

Coptic/Ethiopic:
[a]New Year
[b]Building of the Cross
[c]Christmas
[d]Jesus's Circumcision
[e]Epiphany
[f]Easter
[g]Mary's Announcement
[h]Jesus's Transfiguration

PERSIAN (ASTRONOMICAL) 1387‡/1388

Month	Sun	Mon	Tue	Wed	Thu	Fri	Sat
DEY 1387	8	9	10	11	12	13	14
	15	16	17	18	19	20	21
	22	23	24	25	26	27	28
BAHMAN 1387	29	30	1	2	3	4	5
	6	7	8	9	10	11	12
	13	14	15	16	17	18	19
	20	21	22	23	24	25	26
ESFAND 1387	27	28	29	30	1	2	3
	4	5	6	7	8	9	10
	11	12	13	14	15	16	17
	18	19	20	21	22	23	24
FARVARDIN 1388	25	26	27	28	29	30	1[a]
	2	3	4	5	6	7	8
	9	10	11	12	13[b]	14	15
	16	17	18	19	20	21	22
	23	24	25	26	27	28	29
ORDIBEHEŠT 1388	30	31	1	2	3	4	5
	6	7	8	9	10	11	12
	13	14	15	16	17	18	19
	20	21	22	23	24	25	26
XORDĀD 1388	27	28	29	30	31	1	2
	3	4	5	6	7	8	9
	10	11	12	13	14	15	16
	17	18	19	20	21	22	23
	24	25	26	27	28	29	30
TĪR 1388	31	1	2	3	4	5	6
	7	8	9	10	11	12	13
	14	15	16	17	18	19	20
	21	22	23	24	25	26	27
MORDĀD 1388	28	29	30	31	1	2	3
	4	5	6	7	8	9	10
	11	12	13	14	15	16	17
	18	19	20	21	22	23	24
	25	26	27	28	29	30	31
SHAHRĪVAR 1388	1	2	3	4	5	6	7
	8	9	10	11	12	13	14
	15	16	17	18	19	20	21
	22	23	24	25	26	27	28
MEHR 1388	29	30	31	1	2	3	4
	5	6	7	8	9	10	11
	12	13	14	15	16	17	18
	19	20	21	22	23	24	25
ĀBĀN 1388	26	27	28	29	30	1	2
	3	4	5	6	7	8	9
	10	11	12	13	14	15	16
	17	18	19	20	21	22	23
	24	25	26	27	28	29	30
ĀZAR 1388	1	2	3	4	5	6	7
	8	9	10	11	12	13	14
	15	16	17	18	19	20	21
	22	23	24	25	26	27	28
DEY 1388	29	30	1	2	3	4	5
	6	7	8	9	10	11	12

‡Leap year
[a]New Year
[b]Sizdeh Bedar

HINDU LUNAR 2065/2066

Month	Sun	Mon	Tue	Wed	Thu	Fri	Sat
PAUSHA 2065	1	2	3	4	5	6	7
	8	9	10	11	12	13	14
	15	**16**	18	19	20	21	22
	23	24	25	26	27	28	*28*
MĀGHA 2065	29	30	1	2	3	4	5
	6	7	8	9	**10**	12	13
	14	15	16	17	18	19	20
	21	22	23	24	25	26	27
PHĀLGUNA 2065	28	29[h]	30	1	*1*	**2**	4
	5	6	7	8	9	10	11
	12	13	14	15[i]	**16**	18	19
	20	*20*	21	22	23	24	25
CHAITRA 2066	26	27	28	29	30	1[a]	2
	3	4	5	6	7	**8**[b]	10
	11	12	13	14	15	16	17
	18	19	20	21	22	23	*23*
	24	25	26	27	28	29	30
VAIŚĀKHA 2066	**1**	3	4	5	6	7	8
	9	10	11	12	13	14	15
	16	17	18	19	20	21	22
	23	24	25	26	27	28	29
JYAISHTHA 2066	30	1	2	3	4	**5**	7
	8	9	10	11	12	13	14
	15	16	17	18	19	*19*	20
	21	22	23	24	25	26	27
ĀSHĀDHA 2066	**28**	30	1	2	3	4	5
	6	7	8	9	10	11	12
	13	14	15	16	17	18	19
	20	21	22	23	24	25	26
ŚRĀVAṆA 2066	27	28	29	**30**	2	3	4
	5	6	7	8	9	10	11
	12	13	14	15	16	*16*	17
	18	19	20	21	22	**23**[c]	25
BHĀDRAPADA 2066	26	27	28	29	30	1	2
	3[d]	4	5	6	7	8	9
	10	11	12	13	14	15	16
	17	18	19	20	21	22	23
ĀŚVINA 2066	24	25	26	**27**	29	30	1
	2	3	4	5	6	7	8[e]
	9[e]	10[e]	11	12	*12*	13	14
	15	16	17	18	19	**20**	22
	23	24	25	26	27	28	29
KĀRTTIKA 2066	30	1[f]	2	3	4	5	6
	7	8	9	10	11	12	13
	14	15	16	17	18	19	20
	21	22	23	**24**	26	27	28
MĀRGAŚĪRA 2066	29	30	1	2	3	4	5
	6	*6*	7	8	9	10	11[g]
	12	13	14	15	16	17	**18**
	20	21	22	23	24	25	26
PAUSHA 2066	27	28	29	30	1	2	3
	4	5	6	7	8	9	*9*
	10	12	13	14	15	16	17

[a]New Year (Virodhin)
[b]Birthday of Rāma
[c]Birthday of Krishna
[d]Ganēśa Chaturthī
[e]Dashara
[f]Diwali
[g]Birthday of Vishnu
[h]Night of Śiva
[i]Holi

HINDU SOLAR 1930/1931‡

Month	Sun	Mon	Tue	Wed	Thu	Fri	Sat
PAUSHA 1930	14	15	16	17	18	19	20
	21	22	23	24	25	26	27
MĀGHA 1930	28	29	30	1[b]	2	3	4
	5	6	7	8	9	10	11
	12	13	14	15	16	17	18
	19	20	21	22	23	24	25
PHĀLGUNA 1930	26	27	28	29	1	2	3
	4	5	6	7	8	9	10
	11	12	13	14	15	16	17
	18	19	20	21	22	23	24
CHAITRA 1930	25	26	27	28	29	30	1
	2	3	4	5	6	7	8
	9	10	11	12	13	14	15
	16	17	18	19	20	21	22
	23	24	25	26	27	28	29
VAIŚĀKHA 1931	30	1[a]	2	3	4	5	6
	7	8	9	10	11	12	13
	14	15	16	17	18	19	20
	21	22	23	24	25	26	27
JYAISHTHA 1931	28	29	30	31	1	2	3
	4	5	6	7	8	9	10
	11	12	13	14	15	16	17
	18	19	20	21	22	23	24
	25	26	27	28	29	30	31
ĀSHĀDHA 1931	32	1	2	3	4	5	6
	7	8	9	10	11	12	13
	14	15	16	17	18	19	20
	21	22	23	24	25	26	27
ŚRĀVAṆA 1931	28	29	30	31	1	2	3
	4	5	6	7	8	9	10
	11	12	13	14	15	16	17
	18	19	20	21	22	23	24
	25	26	27	28	29	30	31
BHĀDRAPADA 1931	32	1	2	3	4	5	6
	7	8	9	10	11	12	13
	14	15	16	17	18	19	20
	21	22	23	24	25	26	27
ĀŚVINA 1931	28	29	30	31	1	2	3
	4	5	6	7	8	9	10
	11	12	13	14	15	16	17
	18	19	20	21	22	23	24
KĀRTTIKA 1931	25	26	27	28	29	30	1
	2	3	4	5	6	7	8
	9	10	11	12	13	14	15
	16	17	18	19	20	21	22
	23	24	25	26	27	28	29
MĀRGAŚĪRA 1931	30	1	2	3	4	5	6
	7	8	9	10	11	12	13
	14	15	16	17	18	19	20
	21	22	23	24	25	26	27
PAUSHA 1931	28	29	30	1	2	3	4
	5	6	7	8	9	10	11
	12	13	14	15	16	17	18

‡Leap year
[a]New Year (Śubhakṛit)
[b]Pongal

ISLAMIC (ASTRONOMICAL) 1429/1430/1431

Month	Sun	Mon	Tue	Wed	Thu	Fri	Sat
MUHARRAM 1430	29	1	2	3	4	5	6
	7	8	9	10[b]	11	12	13
	14	15	16	17	18	19	20
	21	22	23	24	25	26	27
SAFAR 1430	28	29	30	1	2	3	4
	5	6	7	8	9	10	11
	12	13	14	15	16	17	18
	19	20	21	22	23	24	25
RABĪ' I 1430	26	27	28	29	1	2	3
	4	5	6	7	8	9	10
	11	12[c]	13	14	15	16	17
	18	19	20	21	22	23	24
RABĪ' II 1430	25	26	27	28	29	30	1
	2	3	4	5	6	7	8
	9	10	11	12	13	14	15
	16	17	18	19	20	21	22
	23	24	25	26	27	28	29
JUMĀDĀ I 1430	1	2	3	4	5	6	7
	8	9	10	11	12	13	14
	15	16	17	18	19	20	21
	22	23	24	25	26	27	28
JUMĀDĀ II 1430	29	30	1	2	3	4	5
	6	7	8	9	10	11	12
	13	14	15	16	17	18	19
	20	21	22	23	24	25	26
RAJAB 1430	27	28	29	1	2	3	4
	5	6	7	8	9	10	11
	12	13	14	15	16	17	18
	19	20	21	22	23	24	25
SHA'BĀN 1430	26	27[d]	28	29	30	1	2
	3	4	5	6	7	8	9
	10	11	12	13	14	15	16
	17	18	19	20	21	22	23
RAMAḌĀN 1430	24	25	26	27	28	29	1[e]
	2	3	4	5	6	7	8
	9	10	11	12	13	14	15
	16	17	18	19	20	21	22
	23	24	25	26	27	28	29
SHAWWĀL 1430	30	1[f]	2	3	4	5	6
	7	8	9	10	11	12	13
	14	15	16	17	18	19	20
	21	22	23	24	25	26	27
DHU AL-QA'DA 1430	28	29	1	2	3	4	5
	6	7	8	9	10	11	12
	13	14	15	16	17	18	19
	20	21	22	23	24	25	26
DHU AL-ḤIJJA 1430	27	28	29	30	1	2	3
	4	5	6	7	8	9	10[g]
	11	12	13	14	15	16	17
	18	19	20	21	22	23	24
MUHARRAM 1431	25	26	27	28	29	1[a]	2
	3	4	5	6	7	8	9
	10[b]	11	12	13	14	15	16

[a]New Year
[b]'Ashūrā'
[c]Prophet's Birthday
[d]Ascent of the Prophet
[e]Start of Ramaḍān
[f]'Id al-Fiṭr
[g]'Id al-'Aḍḥā

GREGORIAN 2009

Julian (Sun)	Sun	Mon	Tue	Wed	Thu	Fri	Sat	Month
Dec 15	28	29	30	31	1	2	3	JANUARY 2009
	4	5	6	7[a]	8	9	10	
Dec 29	11	12	13	14[b]	15	16	17	
	18	19	20	21	22	23	24	
Jan 12	25	26	27	28	29	30	31	
	1	2	3	4	5	6	7	FEBRUARY 2009
Jan 26	8	9	10	11	12	13	14	
	15	16	17	18	19	20	21	
Feb 9	22	23	24	25[c]	26	27	28	
	1	2	3	4	5	6	7	MARCH 2009
Feb 23	8[d]	9	10	11	12	13	14	
	15	16	17	18	19	20	21	
Mar 9	22	23	24	25	26	27	28	
	29	30	31	1	2	3	4	APRIL 2009
Mar 23	5	6	7	8	9	10	11	
	12[e]	13	14	15	16	17	18	
Apr 6	19[f]	20	21	22	23	24	25	
	26	27	28	29	30	1	2	MAY 2009
Apr 20	3	4	5	6	7	8	9	
	10	11	12	13	14	15	16	
May 4	17	18	19	20	21	22	23	
	24	25	26	27	28	29	30	
May 18	31	1	2	3	4	5	6	JUNE 2009
	7	8	9	10	11	12	13	
Jun 1	14	15	16	17	18	19	20	
	21	22	23	24	25	26	27	
Jun 15	28	29	30	1	2	3	4	JULY 2009
	5	6	7	8	9	10	11	
Jun 29	12	13	14	15	16	17	18	
	19	20	21	22	23	24	25	
Jul 13	26	27	28	29	30	31	1	AUGUST 2009
	2	3	4	5	6	7	8	
Jul 27	9	10	11	12	13	14	15	
	16	17	18	19	20	21	22	
Aug 10	23	24	25	26	27	28	29	
	30	31	1	2	3	4	5	SEPTEMBER 2009
Aug 24	6	7	8	9	10	11	12	
	13	14	15	16	17	18	19	
Sep 7	20	21	22	23	24	25	26	
	27	28	29	30	1	2	3	OCTOBER 2009
Sep 21	4	5	6	7	8	9	10	
	11	12	13	14	15	16	17	
Oct 5	18	19	20	21	22	23	24	
	25	26	27	28	29	30	31	
Oct 19	1	2	3	4	5	6	7	NOVEMBER 2009
	8	9	10	11	12	13	14	
Nov 2	15	16	17	18	19	20	21	
	22	23	24	25	26	27	28	
Nov 16	29[g]	30	1	2	3	4	5	DECEMBER 2009
	6	7	8	9	10	11	12	
Nov 30	13	14	15	16	17	18	19	
	20	21	22	23	24	25[h]	26	
Dec 14	27	28	29	30	31	1	2	

[a]Orthodox Christmas
[b]Julian New Year
[c]Ash Wednesday
[d]Feast of Orthodoxy
[e]Easter
[f]Orthodox Easter
[g]Advent
[h]Christmas

2010

Gregorian 2010	Sun	Mon	Tue	Wed	Thu	Fri	Sat	Lunar Phases	ISO WEEK (Mon)	JULIAN DAY (Sun noon)
	27	28	29	30	○	1[a]	2	19:13	53	2455193
	3	4	5	6	◑	8	9	10:39	1	2455200
JANUARY 2010	10	11	12	13	14	●	16	7:11	2	2455207
	17	18	19	20	21	22	◐	10:53	3	2455214
	24	25	26	27	28	29	○	6:17	4	2455221
	31	1	2	3	4	◑	6	23:48	5	2455228
	7	8	9	10	11	12	13		6	2455235
FEBRUARY 2010	●	15	16	17	18	19	20	2:51	7	2455242
	21	◐	23	24	25	26	27	0:42	8	2455249
	○	1	2	3	4	5	6	16:38	9	2455256
	◑	8	9	10	11	12	13	15:42	10	2455263
MARCH 2010	14	●	16	17	18	19	20[b]	21:01	11	2455270
	21	22	◐	24	25	26	27	11:00	12	2455277
	28	29	○	31	1	2	3	2:25	13	2455284
	4	5	◑	7	8	9	10	9:37	14	2455291
APRIL 2010	11	12	13	●	15	16	17	12:29	15	2455298
	18	19	20	◐	22	23	24	18:19	16	2455305
	25	26	27	○	29	30	1	12:18	17	2455312
	2	3	4	5	◑	7	8	4:15	18	2455319
MAY 2010	9	10	11	12	13	●	15	1:04	19	2455326
	16	17	18	19	◐	21	22	23:42	20	2455333
	23	24	25	26	○	28	29	23:07	21	2455340
	30	31	1	2	3	◑	5	22:13	22	2455347
	6	7	8	9	10	11	●	11:14	23	2455354
JUNE 2010	13	14	15	16	17	18	◐	4:29	24	2455361
	20	21[c]	22	23	24	25	○	11:30	25	2455368
	27	28	29	30	1	2	3		26	2455375
	◑	5	6	7	8	9	10	14:35	27	2455382
JULY 2010	●	12	13	14	15	16	17	19:40	28	2455389
	◐	19	20	21	22	23	24	10:10	29	2455396
	25	○	27	28	29	30	31	1:36	30	2455403
	1	2	◑	4	5	6	7	4:58	31	2455410
	8	9	●	11	12	13	14	3:08	32	2455417
AUGUST 2010	15	◐	17	18	19	20	21	18:14	33	2455424
	22	23	○	25	26	27	28	17:04	34	2455431
	29	30	31	◑	2	3	4	17:21	35	2455438
	5	6	7	●	9	10	11	10:30	36	2455445
SEPTEMBER 2010	12	13	14	◐	16	17	18	5:50	37	2455452
	19	20	21	22	○[d]	24	25	9:17	38	2455459
	26	27	28	29	30	◑	2	3:52	39	2455466
	3	4	5	6	●	8	9	18:44	40	2455473
OCTOBER 2010	10	11	12	13	◐	15	16	21:27	41	2455480
	17	18	19	20	21	22	○	1:36	42	2455487
	24	25	26	27	28	29	◑	12:46	43	2455494
	31	1	2	3	4	5	●	4:52	44	2455501
	7	8	9	10	11	12	◐	16:38	45	2455508
NOVEMBER 2010	14	15	16	17	18	19	20		46	2455515
	○	22	23	24	25	26	27	17:27	47	2455522
	◑	29	30	1	2	3	4	20:36	48	2455529
	●	6	7	8	9	10	11	17:36	49	2455536
DECEMBER 2010	12	◐	14	15	16	17	18	13:58	50	2455543
	19	20	○[e]	22	23	24	25	8:13	51	2455550
	26	27	◑	29	30	31	1	4:18	52	2455557

ISO WEEK	Hebrew 5770/5771‡	Sun	Mon	Tue	Wed	Thu	Fri	Sat	Molad
53		10	11	12	13	14	15	16	
1	TEVETH 5770	17	18	19	20	21	22	23	
2		24	25	26	27	28	29	1	Fri 13h43m11p
3		2	3	4	5	6	7	8	
4	SHEVAT 5770	9	10	11	12	13	14	15	
5		16	17	18	19	20	21	22	
6		23	24	25	26	27	28	29	
7		30	1	2	3	4	5	6	Sun 2h27m12p
8		7	8	9	10	11	12	13	
9	ADAR 5770	14[f]	15	16	17	18	19	20	
10		21	22	23	24	25	26	27	
11		28	29	1	2	3	4	5	Mon 15h11m13p
12		6	7	8	9	10	11	12	
13	NISAN 5770	13	14	15[g]	16	17	18	19	
14		20	21	22	23	24	25	26	
15		27	28	29	30	1	2	3	Wed 3h55m14p
16		4	5	6	7	8	9	10	
17	IYYAR 5770	11	12	13	14	15	16	17	
18		18	19	20	21	22	23	24	
19		25	26	27	28	29	1	2	Thu 16h39m15p
20		3	4	5	6[h]	7	8	9	
21	SIVAN 5770	10	11	12	13	14	15	16	
22		17	18	19	20	21	22	23	
23		24	25	26	27	28	29	30	
24		1	2	3	4	5	6	7	Sat 5h23m16p
25		8	9	10	11	12	13	14	
26	TAMMUZ 5770	15	16	17	18	19	20	21	
27		22	23	24	25	26	27	28	
28		29	1	2	3	4	5	6	Sun 18h7m17p
29		7	8	9[i]	10	11	12	13	
30	AV 5770	14	15	16	17	18	19	20	
31		21	22	23	24	25	26	27	
32		28	29	30	1	2	3	4	Tue 6h52m0p
33		5	6	7	8	9	10	11	
34	ELUL 5770	12	13	14	15	16	17	18	
35		19	20	21	22	23	24	25	
36		26	27	28	29	1[a]	2[a]	3	
37		4	5	6	7	8	9	10[b]	Wed 19h36m1p
38	TISHRI 5771	11	12	13	14	15[c]	16	17	
39		18	19	20	21	22	23	24	
40		25	26	27	28	29	30	1	Fri 8h20m2p
41		2	3	4	5	6	7	8	
42	HESHVAN 5771	9	10	11	12	13	14	15	
43		16	17	18	19	20	21	22	
44		23	24	25	26	27	28	29	
45		30	1	2	3	4	5	6	Sat 21h4m3p
46		7	8	9	10	11	12	13	
47	KISLEV 5771	14	15	16	17	18	19	20	
48		21	22	23	24	25[e]	26[e]	27[e]	
49		28[e]	29[e]	30[e]	1[e]	2[e]	3	4	Mon 9h48m4p
50		5	6	7	8	9	10	11	
51	TEVETH 5771	12	13	14	15	16	17	18	
52		19	20	21	22	23	24	25	

ISO WEEK	Chinese Jǐ-Chǒu‡/Gēng-Yín	Sun	Mon	Tue	Wed	Thu	Fri	Sat	Solar Term
53		12	13	14	15	16	17	18	
1	MONTH 11 Jǐ-Chǒu	19	20	*21*	22	23	24	25	*Xiǎo hán*
2		26	27	28	29	30*	1	2	
3		3	4	5	**6**	7	8	9	**Dà hán**
4	MONTH 12 Jǐ-Chǒu	10	11	12	13	14	15	16	
5		17	18	19	20	*21*	22	23	*Lì chūn*
6		24	25	26	27	28	29	30	
7		1[a]	2	3	4	5	**6**	7	**Yǔ shuǐ**
8		8	9	10	11	12	13	14	
9	MONTH 1 Gēng-Yín	15[b]	16	17	18	19	20	*21*	*Jīng zhé*
10		22	23	24	25	26	27	28	
11		29	30*	1	2	3	4	5	**Chūn fēn**
12		**6**	7	8	9	10	11	12	
13	MONTH 2 Gēng-Yín	13	14	15	16	17	18	19	
14		20	*21*[c]	22	23	24	25	26	*Qīng míng*
15		27	28	29	1	2	3	4	
16		5	6	**7**	8	9	10	11	**Gǔ yǔ**
17	MONTH 3 Gēng-Yín	12	13	14	15	16	17	18	
18		19	20	21	*22*	23	24	25	*Lì xià*
19		26	27	28	29	30	1*	2	
20		3	4	5	6	7	**8**	9	**Xiǎo mǎn**
21	MONTH 4 Gēng-Yín	10	11	12	13	14	15	16	
22		17	18	19	20	21	22	23	
23		*24*	25	26	27	28	29	1	*Máng zhòng*
24		2	3	4	5[d]	6	7	8	
25	MONTH 5 Gēng-Yín	9	**10**	11	12	13	14	15	**Xià zhì**
26		16	17	18	19	20	21	22	
27		23	24	25	*26*	27	28	29	*Xiǎo shǔ*
28		30	1	2*	3	4	5	6	
29	MONTH 6 Gēng-Yín	7	8	9	10	11	**12**	13	**Dà shǔ**
30		14	15	16	17	18	19	20	
31		21	22	23	24	25	26	*27*	*Lì qiū*
32		28	29	1	2	3	4	5	
33		6	7[e]	8	9	10	11	12	**Chǔ shǔ**
34	MONTH 7 Gēng-Yín	13	**14**	15[f]	16	17	18	19	
35		20	21	22	23	24	25	26	
36		27	28	29	*1*	2	3	4*	*Bái lù*
37		5	6	7	8	9	10	11	
38	MONTH 8 Gēng-Yín	12	13	14	15[g]	**16**	17	18	**Qiū fēn**
39		19	20	21	22	23	24	25	
40		26	27	28	29	30	*1*	2	*Hán lù*
41		3	4	5	6	7	8	9[h]	
42	MONTH 9 Gēng-Yín	10	11	12	13	14	15	**16**	**Shuāng jiàng**
43		17	18	19	20	21	22	23	
44		24	25	26	27	28	29	1	
45		*2*	3	4	5*	6	7	8	*Lì dōng*
46		9	10	11	12	13	14	15	
47	MONTH 10 Gēng-Yín	16	**17**	18	19	20	21	22	**Xiǎo xuě**
48		23	24	25	26	27	28	29	
49		30	1	*2*	3	4	5	6	*Dà xuě*
50		7	8	9	10	11	12	13	
51	MONTH 11 Gēng-Yín	14	15	16	**17**[i]	18	19	20	**Dōng zhì**
52		21	22	23	24	25	26	27	

ISO WEEK	Coptic 1726/1727‡	Sun	Mon	Tue	Wed	Thu	Fri	Sat	Ethiopic 2002/2003‡
53		18	19	20	21	22	23	24	TĀKHŚĀŚ 2002
1	KOIAK 1726	25	26	27	28	29[c]	30	1	
2		2	3	4	5	6[d]	7	8	
3	TŌBE 1726	9	10	11[e]	12	13	14	15	ṬER 2002
4		16	17	18	19	20	21	22	
5		23	24	25	26	27	28	29	
6		30	1	2	3	4	5	6	
7		7	8	9	10	11	12	13	
8	MESHIR 1726	14	15	16	17	18	19	20	YAKĀTIT 2002
9		21	22	23	24	25	26	27	
10		28	29	30	1	2	3	4	
11		5	6	7	8	9	10	11	
12	PAREMOTEP 1726	12	13	14	15	16	17	18	MAGĀBIT 2002
13		19	20	21	22	23	24	25	
14		26[f]	27	28	29	30	1	2	
15		3	4	5	6	7	8	9	
16	PARMOUTE 1726	10	11	12	13	14	15	16	MIYĀZYĀ 2002
17		17	18	19	20	21	22	23	
18		24	25	26	27	28	29[g]	30	
19		1	2	3	4	5	6	7	
20		8	9	10	11	12	13	14	
21	PASHONS 1726	15	16	17	18	19	20	21	GENBOT 2002
22		22	23	24	25	26	27	28	
23		29	30	1	2	3	4	5	
24		6	7	8	9	10	11	12	
25	PAŌNE 1726	13	14	15	16	17	18	19	SANĒ 2002
26		20	21	22	23	24	25	26	
27		27	28	29	30	1	2	3	
28		4	5	6	7	8	9	10	
29	EPĒP 1726	11	12	13	14	15	16	17	ḤAMLĒ 2002
30		18	19	20	21	22	23	24	
31		25	26	27	28	29	30	1	
32		2	3	4	5	6	7	8	
33	MESORĒ 1726	9	10	11	12	13[h]	14	15	NAHASĒ 2002
34		16	17	18	19	20	21	22	
35		23	24	25	26	27	28	29	
36	EPAG. 1726	30	1	2	3	4	5	1[a]	PĀG. 2002
37		2	3	4	5	6	7	8	
38	THOOUT 1727	9	10	11	12	13	14	15	MASKARAM 2003
39		16	17[b]	18	19	20	21	22	
40		23	24	25	26	27	28	29	
41		30	1	2	3	4	5	6	
42	PAOPE 1727	7	8	9	10	11	12	13	ṬEQEMT 2003
43		14	15	16	17	18	19	20	
44		21	22	23	24	25	26	27	
45		28	29	30	1	2	3	4	
46		5	6	7	8	9	10	11	
47	ATHŌR 1727	12	13	14	15	16	17	18	ḪEDĀR 2003
48		19	20	21	22	23	24	25	
49		26	27	28	29	30	1	2	
50		3	4	5	6	7	8	9	
51	KOIAK 1727	10	11	12	13	14	15	16	TĀKHŚĀŚ 2003
52		17	18	19	20	21	22	23	

Gregorian:
[a]New Year
[b]Spring (17:31)
[c]Summer (11:28)
[d]Autumn (3:09)
[e]Winter (23:38)
● New moon
◐ First quarter moon
○ Full moon
◑ Last quarter moon

Hebrew:
‡Leap year
[a]New Year
[b]Yom Kippur
[c]Sukkot
[d]Winter starts
[e]Ḥanukkah
[f]Purim
[g]Passover
[h]Shavuot
[i]Fast of Av

Chinese:
‡Leap year
[a]New Year (4708, Tiger)
[b]Lantern Festival
[c]Qīngmíng
[d]Dragon Festival
[e]Qīqiǎo
[f]Hungry Ghosts
[g]Mid-Autumn Festival
[h]Double-Ninth Festival
[i]Dōngzhì
*Start of 60-name cycle

Coptic/Ethiopic:
‡Leap year
[a]New Year
[b]Building of the Cross
[c]Christmas
[d]Jesus's Circumcision
[e]Epiphany
[f]Easter
[g]Mary's Announcement
[h]Jesus's Transfiguration

2010

PERSIAN (ASTRONOMICAL) 1388/1389

Month	Sun	Mon	Tue	Wed	Thu	Fri	Sat
DEY 1388	6	7	8	9	10	11	12
	13	14	15	16	17	18	19
	20	21	22	23	24	25	26
BAHMAN 1388	27	28	29	30	1	2	3
	4	5	6	7	8	9	10
	11	12	13	14	15	16	17
	18	19	20	21	22	23	24
ESFAND 1388	25	26	27	28	29	30	1
	2	3	4	5	6	7	8
	9	10	11	12	13	14	15
	16	17	18	19	20	21	22
	23	24	25	26	27	28	29
FARVARDĪN 1389	1[a]	2	3	4	5	6	7
	8	9	10	11	12	13[b]	14
	15	16	17	18	19	20	21
	22	23	24	25	26	27	28
ORDĪBEHEŠT 1389	29	30	31	1	2	3	4
	5	6	7	8	9	10	11
	12	13	14	15	16	17	18
	19	20	21	22	23	24	25
XORDĀD 1389	26	27	28	29	30	31	1
	2	3	4	5	6	7	8
	9	10	11	12	13	14	15
	16	17	18	19	20	21	22
	23	24	25	26	27	28	29
TĪR 1389	30	31	1	2	3	4	5
	6	7	8	9	10	11	12
	13	14	15	16	17	18	19
	20	21	22	23	24	25	26
MORDĀD 1389	27	28	29	30	31	1	2
	3	4	5	6	7	8	9
	10	11	12	13	14	15	16
	17	18	19	20	21	22	23
	24	25	26	27	28	29	30
SHAHRĪVAR 1389	31	1	2	3	4	5	6
	7	8	9	10	11	12	13
	14	15	16	17	18	19	20
	21	22	23	24	25	26	27
MEHR 1389	28	29	30	31	1	2	3
	4	5	6	7	8	9	10
	11	12	13	14	15	16	17
	18	19	20	21	22	23	24
ĀBĀN 1389	25	26	27	28	29	30	1
	2	3	4	5	6	7	8
	9	10	11	12	13	14	15
	16	17	18	19	20	21	22
	23	24	25	26	27	28	29
ĀZAR 1389	30	1	2	3	4	5	6
	7	8	9	10	11	12	13
	14	15	16	17	18	19	20
	21	22	23	24	25	26	27
DEY 1389	28	29	30	1	2	3	4
	5	6	7	8	9	10	11

[a]New Year
[b]Sizdeh Bedar

HINDU LUNAR 2066/2067‡

Month	Sun	Mon	Tue	Wed	Thu	Fri	Sat
PAUSHA 2066	**10**	12	13	14	15	16	17
	18	19	20	21	22	23	**24**
MĀGHA 2066	26	27	*27*	28	29	30	1
	2	3	4	5	6	7	8
	9	10	11	12	13	14	15
	16	**17**	19	20	21	22	23
	24	25	26	27	28	29[h]	30
PHĀLGUNA 2066	30	1	2	3	4	5	6
	7	8	9	10	**11**	13	14
	15[i]	16	17	18	19	20	21
	22	23	24	25	26	27	28
CHAITRA 2067	29	30	1[a]	2	3	4	5
	6	7	8	9[b]	10	11	12
	13	14	**15**	17	18	19	20
	21	22	23	24	*24*	25	26
LEAP VAIŚĀKHA 2067	27	28	29	30	1	2	3
	4	5	6	7	8	**9**	11
	12	13	14	15	16	17	18
	19	20	21	22	23	24	25
VAIŚĀKHA 2067	26	27	28	*28*	29	30	**1**
	3	4	5	6	7	8	9
	10	11	12	**13**	15	16	17
	18	19	*19*	20	21	22	23
	24	25	26	27	28	29	30
JYAISHTHA 2067	1	2	3	4	**5**	7	8
	9	10	11	12	13	14	15
	16	17	18	19	20	21	22
	23	24	25	*25*	**26**	28	29
ĀSHĀDHA 2067	30	1	2	3	4	5	6
	7	**8**	10	11	12	13	14
	15	16	*16*	17	18	19	20
	21	22	23	24	25	26	27
ŚRĀVAṆA 2067	28	29	30	**1**	3	4	5
	6	7	8	9	10	11	12
	13	14	15	16	17	18	19
	20	21	22	23[c]	24	25	26
BHĀDRAPADA 2067	27	28	29	30	1	2	3[d]
	4	6	7	8	9	10	11
	12	*12*	13	14	15	16	17
	18	19	20	21	22	23	24
ĀŚVINA 2067	25	26	**27**	29	30	1	2
	3	4	5	6	7	8[e]	9[e]
	10[e]	11	12	13	14	15	*15*
	16	17	18	19	**20**	22	23
	24	25	26	27	28	29	30
KĀRTTIKA 2067	1[f]	2	3	4	5	6	7
	8	9	10	11	12	13	14
	15	16	17	18	19	20	21
	22	23	24	**25**	27	28	29
MĀRGAŚĪRA 2067	30	1	2	3	4	5	6
	7	8	*8*	9	10	11[g]	12
	13	14	15	16	17	18	**19**
	21	22	23	24	25	26	27

‡Leap year
[a]New Year (Vikṛita)
[b]Birthday of Rāma
[c]Birthday of Krishna
[d]Ganēśa Chaturthī
[e]Dashara
[f]Diwali
[g]Birthday of Vishnu
[h]Night of Śiva
[i]Holi

HINDU SOLAR 1931‡/1932

Month	Sun	Mon	Tue	Wed	Thu	Fri	Sat
PAUSHA 1931	12	13	14	15	16	17	18
	19	20	21	22	23	24	25
MĀGHA 1931	26	27	28	29	1[b]	2	3
	4	5	6	7	8	9	10
	11	12	13	14	15	16	17
	18	19	20	21	22	23	24
PHĀLGUNA 1931	25	26	27	28	29	1	2
	3	4	5	6	7	8	9
	10	11	12	13	14	15	16
	17	18	19	20	21	22	23
	24	25	26	27	28	29	30
CHAITRA 1931	1	2	3	4	5	6	7
	8	9	10	11	12	13	14
	15	16	17	18	19	20	21
	22	23	24	25	26	27	28
VAIŚĀKHA 1932	29	30	31	1[a]	2	3	4
	5	6	7	8	9	10	11
	12	13	14	15	16	17	18
	19	20	21	22	23	24	25
JYAISHTHA 1932	26	27	28	29	30	31	1
	2	3	4	5	6	7	8
	9	10	11	12	13	14	15
	16	17	18	19	20	21	22
	23	24	25	26	27	28	29
ĀSHĀḌHA 1932	30	31	1	2	3	4	5
	6	7	8	9	10	11	12
	13	14	15	16	17	18	19
	20	21	22	23	24	25	26
ŚRĀVAṆA 1932	27	28	29	30	31	32	1
	2	3	4	5	6	7	8
	9	10	11	12	13	14	15
	16	17	18	19	20	21	22
	23	24	25	26	27	28	29
BHĀDRAPADA 1932	30	31	1	2	3	4	5
	6	7	8	9	10	11	12
	13	14	15	16	17	18	19
	20	21	22	23	24	25	26
ĀŚVINA 1932	27	28	29	30	31	1	2
	3	4	5	6	7	8	9
	10	11	12	13	14	15	16
	17	18	19	20	21	22	23
	24	25	26	27	28	29	30
KĀRTTIKA 1932	1	2	3	4	5	6	7
	8	9	10	11	12	13	14
	15	16	17	18	19	20	21
	22	23	24	25	26	27	28
MĀRGAŚĪRA 1932	29	30	1	2	3	4	5
	6	7	8	9	10	11	12
	13	14	15	16	17	18	19
	20	21	22	23	24	25	26
PAUSHA 1932	27	28	29	30	1	2	3
	4	5	6	7	8	9	10
	11	12	13	14	15	16	17

‡Leap year
[a]New Year (Śobhana)
[b]Pongal

ISLAMIC (ASTRONOMICAL) 1431/1432‡

Month	Sun	Mon	Tue	Wed	Thu	Fri	Sat
MUḤARRAM 1431	10	11	12	13	14	15	16
	17	18	19	20	21	22	23
	24	25	26	27	28	29	30
ṢAFAR 1431	1	2	3	4	5	6	7
	8	9	10	11	12	13	14
	15	16	17	18	19	20	21
	22	23	24	25	26	27	28
RABĪ' I 1431	29	1	2	3	4	5	6
	7	8	9	10	11	12[c]	13
	14	15	16	17	18	19	20
	21	22	23	24	25	26	27
RABĪ' II 1431	28	29	30	1	2	3	4
	5	6	7	8	9	10	11
	12	13	14	15	16	17	18
	19	20	21	22	23	24	25
JUMĀDĀ I 1431	26	27	28	29	30	1	2
	3	4	5	6	7	8	9
	10	11	12	13	14	15	16
	17	18	19	20	21	22	23
JUMĀDĀ II 1431	24	25	26	27	28	29	1
	2	3	4	5	6	7	8
	9	10	11	12	13	14	15
	16	17	18	19	20	21	22
	23	24	25	26	27	28	29
RAJAB 1431	30	1	2	3	4	5	6
	7	8	9	10	11	12	13
	14	15	16	17	18	19	20
	21	22	23	24	25	26	27[d]
SHA'BĀN 1431	28	29	1	2	3	4	5
	6	7	8	9	10	11	12
	13	14	15	16	17	18	19
	20	21	22	23	24	25	26
RAMAḌĀN 1431	27	28	29	30	1[e]	2	3
	4	5	6	7	8	9	10
	11	12	13	14	15	16	17
	18	19	20	21	22	23	24
SHAWWĀL 1431	25	26	27	28	29	30	1[f]
	2	3	4	5	6	7	8
	9	10	11	12	13	14	15
	16	17	18	19	20	21	22
	23	24	25	26	27	28	29
DHU AL-QA'DA 1431	1	2	3	4	5	6	7
	8	9	10	11	12	13	14
	15	16	17	18	19	20	21
	22	23	24	25	26	27	28
DHU AL-ḤIJJA 1431	29	1	2	3	4	5	6
	7	8	9	10[g]	11	12	13
	14	15	16	17	18	19	20
	21	22	23	24	25	26	27
MUḤARRAM 1432	28	29	1[a]	2[d]	3	4	5
	6	7	8	9	10[b]	11	12
	13	14	15	16	17	18	19
	20	21	22	23	24	25	26

‡Leap year
[a]New Year
[d]New Year (Arithmetic)
[b]'Āshūrā'
[c]Prophet's Birthday
[d]Ascent of the Prophet
[e]Start of Ramaḍān
[f]'Īd al-Fiṭr
[g]'Īd al-'Aḍḥā

GREGORIAN 2010

Julian (Sun)	Sun	Mon	Tue	Wed	Thu	Fri	Sat	Month
Dec 14	27	28	29	30	31	1	2	JANUARY 2010
	3	4	5	6	7[a]	8	9	
Dec 28	10	11	12	13	14[b]	15	16	
	17	18	19	20	21	22	23	
Jan 11	24	25	26	27	28	29	30	
	31	1	2	3	4	5	6	FEBRUARY 2010
Jan 25	7	8	9	10	11	12	13	
	14	15	16	17[c]	18	19	20	
Feb 8	21[d]	22	23	24	25	26	27	
	28	1	2	3	4	5	6	MARCH 2010
Feb 22	7	8	9	10	11	12	13	
	14	15	16	17	18	19	20	
Mar 8	21	22	23	24	25	26	27	
	28	29	30	31	1	2	3	APRIL 2010
Mar 22	4[e]	5	6	7	8	9	10	
	11	12	13	14	15	16	17	
Apr 5	18	19	20	21	22	23	24	
	25	26	27	28	29	30	1	MAY 2010
Apr 19	2	3	4	5	6	7	8	
	9	10	11	12	13	14	15	
May 3	16	17	18	19	20	21	22	
	23	24	25	26	27	28	29	
May 17	30	31	1	2	3	4	5	JUNE 2010
	6	7	8	9	10	11	12	
May 31	13	14	15	16	17	18	19	
	20	21	22	23	24	25	26	
Jun 14	27	28	29	30	1	2	3	JULY 2010
	4	5	6	7	8	9	10	
Jun 28	11	12	13	14	15	16	17	
	18	19	20	21	22	23	24	
Jul 12	25	26	27	28	29	30	31	
	1	2	3	4	5	6	7	AUGUST 2010
Jul 26	8	9	10	11	12	13	14	
	15	16	17	18	19	20	21	
Aug 9	22	23	24	25	26	27	28	
	29	30	31	1	2	3	4	SEPTEMBER 2010
Aug 23	5	6	7	8	9	10	11	
	12	13	14	15	16	17	18	
Sep 6	19	20	21	22	23	24	25	
	26	27	28	29	30	1	2	OCTOBER 2010
Sep 20	3	4	5	6	7	8	9	
	10	11	12	13	14	15	16	
Oct 4	17	18	19	20	21	22	23	
	24	25	26	27	28	29	30	
Oct 18	31	1	2	3	4	5	6	NOVEMBER 2010
	7	8	9	10	11	12	13	
Nov 1	14	15	16	17	18	19	20	
	21	22	23	24	25	26	27	
Nov 15	28[g]	29	30	1	2	3	4	DECEMBER 2010
	5	6	7	8	9	10	11	
Nov 29	12	13	14	15	16	17	18	
	19	20	21	22	23	24	25[h]	
Dec 13	26	27	28	29	30	31	1	

[a]Orthodox Christmas
[b]Julian New Year
[c]Ash Wednesday
[d]Feast of Orthodoxy
[e]Easter (also Orthodox)
[g]Advent
[h]Christmas

2011

	GREGORIAN 2011							Lunar Phases	ISO WEEK	JULIAN DAY		HEBREW 5771[‡]/5772							Molad		CHINESE Gēng-Yín/Xīn-Mǎo							Solar Term		COPTIC 1727[‡]/1728							ETHIOPIC 2003[‡]/2004
	Sun	Mon	Tue	Wed	Thu	Fri	Sat		(Mon)	(Sun noon)		Sun	Mon	Tue	Wed	Thu	Fri	Sat			Sun	Mon	Tue	Wed	Thu	Fri	Sat			Sun	Mon	Tue	Wed	Thu	Fri	Sat	
	26	27	◑	29	30	31	1[a]	4:18	52	2455557	TEVETH 5771	19	20	21	22	23	24	25		MONTH 11 Gēng-Yín	21	22	23	24	25	26	27		KOIAK 1727	17	18	19	20	21	22	23	TĀKHŚĀŚ 2003
JANUARY 2011	2	3	●	5	6	7	8	9:02	1	2455564	SHEVAT 5771	26	27	28	29	1	2	3	Tue 22h32m5p	MONTH 12 Gēng-Yín	28	29	1	2	*3*	4	5	Xiǎo hán		24	25	26	27	28	29[c]	30	
	9	10	11	◐	13	14	15	11:31	2	2455571		4	5	6	7	8	9	10			6*	7	8	9	10	11	12		TÔBE 1727	1	2	3	4	5	6[d]	7	ṬER 2003
	16	17	18	○	20	21	22	21:21	3	2455578		11	12	13	14	15	16	17			13	14	15	16	**17**	18	19	**Dà hán**		8	9	10	11[e]	12	13	14	
	23	24	25	◑	27	28	29	12:57	4	2455585		18	19	20	21	22	23	24			20	21	22	23	24	25	26			15	16	17	18	19	20	21	
FEBRUARY 2011	30	31	1	2	●	4	5	2:31	5	2455592	ADAR I 5771	25	26	27	28	29	30	1	Thu 11h16m6p	MONTH 1 Xīn-Mǎo	27	28	29	30	1[a]	*2*	3	Lì chūn		22	23	24	25	26	27	28	
	6	7	8	9	10	◐	12	7:18	6	2455599		2	3	4	5	6	7	8			4	5	6	7	8	9	10		MESHIR 1727	29	30	1	2	3	4	5	YAKĀTIT 2003
	13	14	15	16	17	○	19	8:35	7	2455606		9	10	11	12	13	14	15			11	12	13	14	15[b]	16	**17**	**Yǔ shuǐ**		6	7	8	9	10	11	12	
	20	21	22	23	◑	25	26	23:26	8	2455613		16	17	18	19	20	21	22			18	19	20	21	22	23	24			13	14	15	16	17	18	19	
MARCH 2011	27	28	1	2	3	●	5	20:46	9	2455620		23	24	25	26	27	28	29		MONTH 2 Xīn-Mǎo	25	26	27	28	29	30	1			20	21	22	23	24	25	26	
	6	7	8	9	10	11	◐	23:45	10	2455627	ADAR II 5771	30	1	2	3	4	5	6	Sat 0h0m7p		*2*	3	4	5	6*	7	8	Jīng zhé	PAREMOTEP 1727	27	28	29	30	1	2	3	MAGĀBIT 2003
	13	14	15	16	17	18	○	18:10	11	2455634		7	8	9	10	11	12	13			9	10	11	12	13	14	15			4	5	6	7	8	9	10	
	20[b]	21	22	23	24	25	◑	12:07	12	2455641		14[f]	15	16	17	18	19	20			16	**17**	18	19	20	21	22	**Chūn fēn**		11	12	13	14	15	16	17	
APRIL 2011	27	28	29	30	31	1	2		13	2455648		21	22	23	24	25	26	27			23	24	25	26	27	28	29			18	19	20	21	22	23	24	
	●	4	5	6	7	8	9	14:32	14	2455655	NISAN 5771	28	29	1	2	3	4	5	Sun 12h44m8p	MONTH 3 Xīn-Mǎo	1	2	*3[c]*	4	5	6	7	Qīng míng	PARMOUTE 1727	25	26	27	28	29	30	1	MIYĀZYĀ 2003
	10	◐	12	13	14	15	16	12:05	15	2455662		6	7	8	9	10	11	12			8	9	10	11	12	13	14			2	3	4	5	6	7	8	
	17	○	19	20	21	22	23	2:44	16	2455669		13	14	15[g]	16	17	18	19			15	16	17	**18**	19	20	21	**Gǔ yǔ**		9	10	11	12	13	14	15	
	24	◑	26	27	28	29	30	2:47	17	2455676		20	21	22	23	24	25	26			22	23	24	25	26	27	28			16[f]	17	18	19	20	21	22	
MAY 2011	1	2	●	4	5	6	7	6:50	18	2455683	IYAR 5771	27	28	29	30	1	2	3	Tue 1h28m9p	MONTH 4 Xīn-Mǎo	29	30	1	2	3	*4*	5	Lì xià		23	24	25	26	27	28	29[g]	
	8	9	◐	11	12	13	14	20:33	19	2455690		4	5	6	7	8	9	10			6	7*	8	9	10	11	12		PASHONS 1727	30	1	2	3	4	5	6	GENBOT 2003
	15	16	○	18	19	20	21	11:08	20	2455697		11	12	13	14	15	16	17			13	14	15	16	17	18	**19**	**Xiǎo mǎn**		7	8	9	10	11	12	13	
	22	23	◑	25	26	27	28	18:52	21	2455704		18	19	20	21	22	23	24			20	21	22	23	24	25	26			14	15	16	17	18	19	20	
JUNE 2011	29	30	31	●	2	3	4	21:02	22	2455711	SIVAN 5771	25	26	27	28	29	1	2	Wed 14h12m10p	MONTH 5 Xīn-Mǎo	27	28	29	30	1	2	3			21	22	23	24	25	26	27	
	5	6	7	8	◐	10	11	2:10	23	2455718		3	4	5	6[h]	7	8	9			4	*5[d]*	6	7	8	9	10	Máng zhòng	PAÔNE 1727	28	29	30	1	2	3	4	SANĒ 2003
	12	13	14	○	16	17	18	20:13	24	2455725		10	11	12	13	14	15	16			11	12	13	14	15	16	17			5	6	7	8	9	10	11	
	19	20	21[c]	22	◑	24	25	11:48	25	2455732		17	18	19	20	21	22	23			18	19	20	**21**	22	23	24	**Xià zhì**		12	13	14	15	16	17	18	
JULY 2011	26	27	28	29	30	●	2	8:54	26	2455739		24	25	26	27	28	29	30		MONTH 6 Xīn-Mǎo	25	26	27	28	29	1	2			19	20	21	22	23	24	25	
	3	4	5	6	7	◐	9	6:29	27	2455746	TAMMUZ 5771	1	2	3	4	5	6	7	Fri 2h56m11p		3	4	5	6	*7*	8*	9	Xiǎo shǔ	EPÊP 1727	26	27	28	29	30	1	2	ḤAMLĒ 2003
	10	11	12	13	14	○	16	6:39	28	2455753		8	9	10	11	12	13	14			10	11	12	13	14	15	16			3	4	5	6	7	8	9	
	17	18	19	20	21	22	◑	5:02	29	2455760		15	16	17	18	19	20	21			17	18	19	20	21	22	**23**	**Dà shǔ**		10	11	12	13	14	15	16	
	24	25	26	27	28	29	●	18:40	30	2455767		22	23	24	25	26	27	28			24	25	26	27	28	29	30			17	18	19	20	21	22	23	
AUGUST 2011	31	1	2	3	4	5	◐	11:08	31	2455774	AV 5771	29	1	2	3	4	5	6	Sat 15h40m12p	MONTH 7 Xīn-Mǎo	1	2	3	4	5	6	7[e]			24	25	26	27	28	29	30	
	7	8	9	10	11	12	○	18:57	32	2455781		7	8	9[i]	10	11	12	13			8	*9*	10	11	12	13	14	Lì qiū	MESORÊ 1727	1	2	3	4	5	6	7	NAHASĒ 2003
	14	15	16	17	18	19	20		33	2455788		14	15	16	17	18	19	20			15[f]	16	17	18	19	20	21			8	9	10	11	12	13[h]	14	
	◑	22	23	24	25	26	27	21:54	34	2455795		21	22	23	24	25	26	27			22	23	**24**	25	26	27	28	**Chǔ shǔ**		15	16	17	18	19	20	21	
SEPTEMBER 2011	28	●	30	31	1	2	3	3:04	35	2455802	ELUL 5771	28	29	30	1	2	3	4	Mon 4h24m13p	MONTH 8 Xīn-Mǎo	29	1	2	3	4	5	6			22	23	24	25	26	27	28	
	◐	5	6	7	8	9	10	17:39	36	2455809		5	6	7	8	9	10	11			7	8	9*	10	*11*	12	13	Bái lù	EPAG. 1727	29	30	1	2	3	4	5	PĀG. 2003
	11	○	13	14	15	16	17	9:27	37	2455816		12	13	14	15	16	17	18			14	15[g]	16	17	18	19	20		THOOUT 1728	6	1[a]	2	3	4	5	6	MASKARAM 2004
	18	19	◑	21	22	23[d]	24	13:38	38	2455823		19	20	21	22	23	24	25			21	22	23	24	25	**26**	27	**Qiū fēn**		7	8	9	10	11	12	13	
OCTOBER 2011	25	26	●	28	29	30	1	11:09	39	2455830	TISHRI 5772	26	27	28	29	1[a]	2[a]	3	Tue 17h8m14p	MONTH 9 Xīn-Mǎo	28	29	1	2	3	4	5			14	15	16	17[b]	18	19	20	
	2	3	◐	5	6	7	8	3:15	40	2455837		4	5	6	7	8	9	10[b]			6	7	8	9[h]	10	11	*12*	Hán lù		21	22	23	24	25	26	27	
	9	10	11	○	13	14	15	2:05	41	2455844		11	12	13	14	15[c]	16	17			13	14	15	16	17	18	19		PAOPE 1728	28	29	30	1	2	3	4	ṬEQEMT 2004
	16	17	18	19	◑	21	22	3:30	42	2455851		18	19	20	21	22	23	24			20	21	22	23	24	25	26			5	6	7	8	9	10	11	
	23	24	25	●	27	28	29	19:56	43	2455858	HESHVAN 5772	25	26	27	28	29	30	1		MONTH 10 Xīn-Mǎo	27	**28**	29	30	1	2	3	**Shuāng jiàng**		12	13	14	15	16	17	18	
NOVEMBER 2011	30	31	1	◐	3	4	5	16:38	44	2455865		2	3	4	5	6	7	8	Thu 5h52m15p		4	5	6	7	8	9	10*			19	20	21	22	23	24	25	
	6	7	8	9	○	11	12	20:16	45	2455872		9	10	11	12	13	14	15			11	12	*13*	14	15	16	17	Lì dōng	ATHÔR 1728	26	27	28	29	30	1	2	ḪEDĀR 2004
	13	14	15	16	17	◑	19	15:09	46	2455879		16	17	18	19	20	21	22			18	19	20	21	22	23	24			3	4	5	6	7	8	9	
	20	21	22	23	24	●	26	6:10	47	2455886		23	24	25	26	27	28	29		MONTH 11 Xīn-Mǎo	25	26	27	**28**	29	1	2	**Xiǎo xuě**		10	11	12	13	14	15	16	
DECEMBER 2011	27	28	29	30	1	◐	3	9:52	48	2455893	KISLEV 5772	1	2	3	4	5	6	7	Fri 18h36m16p		3	4	5	6	7	8	9			17	18	19	20	21	22	23	
	4	5	6	7	8	9	○	14:36	49	2455900		8	9	10[d]	11	12	13	14			10	11	12	*13*	14	15	16	Dà xuě		24	25	26	27	28	29	30	
	11	12	13	14	15	16	17		50	2455907		15	16	17	18	19	20	21			17	18	19	20	21	22	23		KOIAK 1728	1	2	3	4	5	6	7	TĀKHŚĀŚ 2004
	◑	19	20	21	22[e]	23	●	0:47 18:06	51	2455914		22	23	24	25[e]	26[e]	27[e]	28[e]			24	25	26	27	**28[i]**	29	30	**Dōng zhì**		8	9	10	11	12	13	14	
	25	26	27	28	29	30	31		52	2455921		29[e]	30[e]	1[e]	2[e]	3	4	5	Sun 7h20m17p		1	2	3	4	5	6	7			15	16	17	18	19	20	21	

[a]New Year
[b]Spring (23:20)
[c]Summer (17:16)
[d]Autumn (9:04)
[e]Winter (5:29)
● New moon
◐ First quarter moon
○ Full moon
◑ Last quarter moon

[‡]Leap year
[a]New Year
[b]Yom Kippur
[c]Sukkot
[d]Winter starts
[e]Ḥanukkah
[f]Purim
[g]Passover
[h]Shavuot
[i]Fast of Av

[a]New Year (4709, Hare)
[b]Lantern Festival
[c]Qīngmíng
[d]Dragon Festival
[e]Qīqiǎo
[f]Hungry Ghosts
[g]Mid-Autumn Festival
[h]Double-Ninth Festival
[i]Dōngzhì
*Start of 60-name cycle

[‡]Leap year
[a]New Year
[b]Building of the Cross
[c]Christmas
[d]Jesus's Circumcision
[e]Epiphany
[f]Easter
[g]Mary's Announcement
[h]Jesus's Transfiguration

PERSIAN (ASTRONOMICAL) 1389/1390

Month	Sun	Mon	Tue	Wed	Thu	Fri	Sat
DEY 1389	5	6	7	8	9	10	11
	12	13	14	15	16	17	18
	19	20	21	22	23	24	25
	26	27	28	29	30	1	2
BAHMAN 1389	3	4	5	6	7	8	9
	10	11	12	13	14	15	16
	17	18	19	20	21	22	23
	24	25	26	27	28	29	30
ESFAND 1389	1	2	3	4	5	6	7
	8	9	10	11	12	13	14
	15	16	17	18	19	20	21
	22	23	24	25	26	27	28
	29	1[a]	2	3	4	5	6
FARVARDĪN 1390	7	8	9	10	11	12	13[b]
	14	15	16	17	18	19	20
	21	22	23	24	25	26	27
	28	29	30	31	1	2	3
ORDĪBEHEŠT 1390	4	5	6	7	8	9	10
	11	12	13	14	15	16	17
	18	19	20	21	22	23	24
	25	26	27	28	29	30	31
XORDĀD 1390	1	2	3	4	5	6	7
	8	9	10	11	12	13	14
	15	16	17	18	19	20	21
	22	23	24	25	26	27	28
	29	30	31	1	2	3	4
TĪR 1390	5	6	7	8	9	10	11
	12	13	14	15	16	17	18
	19	20	21	22	23	24	25
	26	27	28	29	30	31	1
MORDĀD 1390	2	3	4	5	6	7	8
	9	10	11	12	13	14	15
	16	17	18	19	20	21	22
	23	24	25	26	27	28	29
	30	31	1	2	3	4	5
SHAHRĪVAR 1390	6	7	8	9	10	11	12
	13	14	15	16	17	18	19
	20	21	22	23	24	25	26
	27	28	29	30	31	1	2
MEHR 1390	3	4	5	6	7	8	9
	10	11	12	13	14	15	16
	17	18	19	20	21	22	23
	24	25	26	27	28	29	30
ĀBĀN 1390	1	2	3	4	5	6	7
	8	9	10	11	12	13	14
	15	16	17	18	19	20	21
	22	23	24	25	26	27	28
	29	30	1	2	3	4	5
ĀZAR 1390	6	7	8	9	10	11	12
	13	14	15	16	17	18	19
	20	21	22	23	24	25	26
	27	28	29	30	1	2	3
DEY 1390	4	5	6	7	8	9	10

[a]New Year
[b]Sizdeh Bedar

HINDU LUNAR 2067‡/2068

Month	Sun	Mon	Tue	Wed	Thu	Fri	Sat
MĀRGAŚĪRA 2067	21	22	23	24	25	26	27
	28	29	30	1	2	3	4
PAUSHA 2067	5	6	7	8	9	10	11
	12	13	14	15	16	17	18
	19	20	21	22	23	**24**	26
	27	28	29	30	1	1	2
MĀGHA 2067	3	4	5	6	7	8	9
	10	11	12	13	14	15	16
	17	**18**	20	21	22	23	24
	25	26	27	28[h]	29	30	1
	2	3	3	4	5	6	7
PHĀLGUNA 2067	8	9	10	11	**12**	14	15[i]
	16	17	18	19	20	21	22
	23	24	25	26	27	28	29
	30	1[a]	2	3	4	5	6
CHAITRA 2068	7	8	9[b]	10	11	12	13
	14	15	**16**	18	19	20	21
	22	23	24	25	26	27	27
	28	29	30	1	2	3	4
VAIŚĀKHA 2068	5	6	7	8	**9**	11	12
	13	14	15	16	17	18	19
	20	21	22	23	24	25	26
	27	28	29	30	1	2	3
JYAISHTHA 2068	4	5	6	7	8	9	10
	11	**12**	14	15	16	17	18
	19	20	21	22	23	23	24
	25	26	27	28	29	30	1
ĀSHĀDHA 2068	2	3	4	**5**	7	8	9
	10	11	12	13	14	15	16
	17	18	19	20	21	22	23
	24	25	26	27	28	29	30
	1	2	3	4	5	6	7
ŚRĀVAṆA 2068	**8**	10	11	12	13	14	15
	16	17	18	19	20	20	21
	22	23[c]	24	25	26	27	28
	29	30	**1**	3	4[d]	5	6
BHĀDRAPADA 2068	7	8	9	10	11	12	13
	14	15	16	17	18	19	20
	21	22	23	24	25	26	27
	28	29	30	1	2	3	**4**
ĀŚVINA 2068	6	7	8[e]	9[e]	10[e]	11	12
	13	14	15	15	16	17	18
	19	20	21	22	23	24	25
	26	27	**28**	30	1[f]	2	3
KĀRTTIKA 2068	4	5	6	7	8	9	10
	11	12	13	14	15	16	17
	18	19	20	21	22	23	24
	25	26	27	28	29	30	1
MĀRGAŚĪRA 2068	2	**3**	5	6	7	8	9
	9	10	11[g]	12	13	14	15
	16	17	18	19	20	21	22
	23	24	25	**26**	28	29	30
	1	2	3	4	5	6	7

‡Leap year
[a]New Year (Khara)
[b]Birthday of Rāma
[c]Birthday of Krishna
[d]Ganēśa Chaturthī
[e]Dashara
[f]Diwali
[g]Birthday of Vishnu
[h]Night of Śiva
[i]Holi

HINDU SOLAR 1932/1933

Month	Sun	Mon	Tue	Wed	Thu	Fri	Sat
PAUSHA 1932	11	12	13	14	15	16	17
	18	19	20	21	22	23	24
	25	26	27	28	29	1[b]	2
MĀGHA 1932	3	4	5	6	7	8	9
	10	11	12	13	14	15	16
	17	18	19	20	21	22	23
	24	25	26	27	28	29	30
PHĀLGUNA 1932	1	2	3	4	5	6	7
	8	9	10	11	12	13	14
	15	16	17	18	19	20	21
	22	23	24	25	26	27	28
	29	1	2	3	4	5	6
CHAITRA 1932	7	8	9	10	11	12	13
	14	15	16	17	18	19	20
	21	22	23	24	25	26	27
	28	29	30	31	1[a]	2	3
VAIŚĀKHA 1933	4	5	6	7	8	9	10
	11	12	13	14	15	16	17
	18	19	20	21	22	23	24
	25	26	27	28	29	30	31
JYAISHTHA 1933	1	2	3	4	5	6	7
	8	9	10	11	12	13	14
	15	16	17	18	19	20	21
	22	23	24	25	26	27	28
	29	30	31	1	2	3	4
ĀSHĀDHA 1933	5	6	7	8	9	10	11
	12	13	14	15	16	17	18
	19	20	21	22	23	24	25
	26	27	28	29	30	31	32
ŚRĀVAṆA 1933	1	2	3	4	5	6	7
	8	9	10	11	12	13	14
	15	16	17	18	19	20	21
	22	23	24	25	26	27	28
	29	30	31	1	2	3	4
BHĀDRAPADA 1933	5	6	7	8	9	10	11
	12	13	14	15	16	17	18
	19	20	21	22	23	24	25
	26	27	28	29	30	31	1
ĀŚVINA 1933	2	3	4	5	6	7	8
	9	10	11	12	13	14	15
	16	17	18	19	20	21	22
	23	24	25	26	27	28	29
	30	31	1	2	3	4	5
KĀRTTIKA 1933	6	7	8	9	10	11	12
	13	14	15	16	17	18	19
	20	21	22	23	24	25	26
	27	28	29	30	1	2	3
MĀRGAŚĪRA 1933	4	5	6	7	8	9	10
	11	12	13	14	15	16	17
	18	19	20	21	22	23	24
	25	26	27	28	29	1	2
PAUSHA 1933	3	4	5	6	7	8	9
	10	11	12	13	14	15	16

[a]New Year (Krodhin)
[b]Pongal

ISLAMIC (ASTRONOMICAL) 1432‡/1433

Month	Sun	Mon	Tue	Wed	Thu	Fri	Sat
MUHARRAM 1432	20	21	22	23	24	25	26
	27	28	29	30	1	2	3
ṢAFAR 1432	4	5	6	7	8	9	10
	11	12	13	14	15	16	17
	18	19	20	21	22	23	24
	25	26	27	28	29	1	2
RABĪ' I 1432	3	4	5	6	7	8	9
	10	11	12[c]	13	14	15	16
	17	18	19	20	21	22	23
	24	25	26	27	28	29	30
	1	2	3	4	5	6	7
RABĪ' II 1432	8	9	10	11	12	13	14
	15	16	17	18	19	20	21
	22	23	24	25	26	27	28
	29	30	1	2	3	4	5
JUMĀDĀ I 1432	6	7	8	9	10	11	12
	13	14	15	16	17	18	19
	20	21	22	23	24	25	26
	27	28	29	30	1	2	3
JUMĀDĀ II 1432	4	5	6	7	8	9	10
	11	12	13	14	15	16	17
	18	19	20	21	22	23	24
	25	26	27	28	29	1	2
RAJAB 1432	3	4	5	6	7	8	9
	10	11	12	13	14	15	16
	17	18	19	20	21	22	23
	24	25	26	27[d]	28	29	30
	1	2	3	4	5	6	7
SHA'BĀN 1432	8	9	10	11	12	13	14
	15	16	17	18	19	20	21
	22	23	24	25	26	27	28
	29	30	1[e]	2	3	4	5
RAMAḌĀN 1432	6	7	8	9	10	11	12
	13	14	15	16	17	18	19
	20	21	22	23	24	25	26
	27	28	29	1[f]	2	3	4
SHAWWĀL 1432	5	6	7	8	9	10	11
	12	13	14	15	16	17	18
	19	20	21	22	23	24	25
	26	27	28	29	1	2	3
DHU AL-QA'DA 1432	4	5	6	7	8	9	10
	11	12	13	14	15	16	17
	18	19	20	21	22	23	24
	25	26	27	28	29	1	2
DHU AL-ḤIJJA 1432	3	4	5	6	7	8	9
	10[g]	11	12	13	14	15	16
	17	18	19	20	21	22	23
	24	25	26	27	28	29	30
	1[a]	2	3	4	5	6	7
MUHARRAM 1433	8	9	10[b]	11	12	13	14
	15	16	17	18	19	20	21
	22	23	24	25	26	27	28
	29	1	2	3	4	5	6

‡Leap year
[a]New Year
[b]'Ashūrā'
[c]Prophet's Birthday
[d]Ascent of the Prophet
[e]Start of Ramaḍān
[f]'Id al-Fiṭr
[g]'Id al-'Aḍḥā

GREGORIAN 2011

Julian (Sun)	Sun	Mon	Tue	Wed	Thu	Fri	Sat	Month
Dec 13	26	27	28	29	30	31	1	
	2	3	4	5	6	7[a]	8	JANUARY 2011
Dec 27	9	10	11	12	13	14[b]	15	
	16	17	18	19	20	21	22	
Jan 10	23	24	25	26	27	28	29	
	30	31	1	2	3	4	5	
Jan 24	6	7	8	9	10	11	12	FEBRUARY 2011
	13	14	15	16	17	18	19	
Feb 7	20	21	22	23	24	25	26	
	27	28	1	2	3	4	5	
Feb 21	6	7	8	9[c]	10	11	12	MARCH 2011
	13[d]	14	15	16	17	18	19	
Mar 7	20	21	22	23	24	25	26	
	27	28	29	30	31	1	2	
Mar 21	3	4	5	6	7	8	9	APRIL 2011
	10	11	12	13	14	15	16	
Apr 4	17	18	19	20	21	22	23	
	24[e]	25	26	27	28	29	30	
Apr 18	1	2	3	4	5	6	7	MAY 2011
	8	9	10	11	12	13	14	
May 2	15	16	17	18	19	20	21	
	22	23	24	25	26	27	28	
May 16	29	30	31	1	2	3	4	
	5	6	7	8	9	10	11	JUNE 2011
May 30	12	13	14	15	16	17	18	
	19	20	21	22	23	24	25	
Jun 13	26	27	28	29	30	1	2	
	3	4	5	6	7	8	9	JULY 2011
Jun 27	10	11	12	13	14	15	16	
	17	18	19	20	21	22	23	
Jul 11	24	25	26	27	28	29	30	
	31	1	2	3	4	5	6	
Jul 25	7	8	9	10	11	12	13	AUGUST 2011
	14	15	16	17	18	19	20	
Aug 8	21	22	23	24	25	26	27	
	28	29	30	31	1	2	3	
Aug 22	4	5	6	7	8	9	10	SEPTEMBER 2011
	11	12	13	14	15	16	17	
Sep 5	18	19	20	21	22	23	24	
	25	26	27	28	29	30	1	
Sep 19	2	3	4	5	6	7	8	OCTOBER 2011
	9	10	11	12	13	14	15	
Oct 3	16	17	18	19	20	21	22	
	23	24	25	26	27	28	29	
Oct 17	30	31	1	2	3	4	5	
	6	7	8	9	10	11	12	NOVEMBER 2011
Oct 31	13	14	15	16	17	18	19	
	20	21	22	23	24	25	26	
Nov 14	27[g]	28	29	30	1	2	3	
	4	5	6	7	8	9	10	DECEMBER 2011
Nov 28	11	12	13	14	15	16	17	
	18	19	20	21	22	23	24	
Dec 12	25[h]	26	27	28	29	30	31	

[a]Orthodox Christmas
[b]Julian New Year
[c]Ash Wednesday
[d]Feast of Orthodoxy
[e]Easter (also Orthodox)
[g]Advent
[h]Christmas

2012

Gregorian 2012[‡]

Month	Sun	Mon	Tue	Wed	Thu	Fri	Sat	Lunar Phases	ISO Week (Mon)	Julian Day (Sun noon)
January 2012	◐[a]	2	3	4	5	6	7	6:14	1	2455928
	8	○	10	11	12	13	14	7:30	2	2455935
	15	◑	17	18	19	20	21	9:08	3	2455942
	22	●	24	25	26	27	28	7:39	4	2455949
February 2012	29	30	◐	1	2	3	4	4:09	5	2455956
	5	6	○	8	9	10	11	21:53	6	2455963
	12	13	◑	15	16	17	18	17:04	7	2455970
	19	20	●	22	23	24	25	22:35	8	2455977
March 2012	26	27	28	29	◐	2	3	1:21	9	2455984
	4	5	6	7	○	9	10	9:39	10	2455991
	11	12	13	14	◑	16	17	1:25	11	2455998
	18	19	20[b]	21	●	23	24	14:37	12	2456005
	25	26	27	28	29	◐	31	19:40	13	2456012
April 2012	1	2	3	4	5	○	7	19:19	14	2456019
	8	9	10	11	12	◑	14	10:49	15	2456026
	15	16	17	18	19	20	●	7:18	16	2456033
	22	23	24	25	26	27	28		17	2456040
May 2012	◐	30	1	2	3	4	5	9:57	18	2456047
	○	7	8	9	10	11	◑	3:35 21:46	19	2456054
	13	14	15	16	17	18	19		20	2456061
	●	21	22	23	24	25	26	23:47	21	2456068
June 2012	27	◐	29	30	31	1	2	20:16	22	2456075
	3	○	5	6	7	8	9	11:11	23	2456082
	10	◑	12	13	14	15	16	10:41	24	2456089
	17	18	●	20[c]	21	22	23	15:02	25	2456096
	24	25	26	◐	28	29	30	3:30	26	2456103
July 2012	1	2	○	4	5	6	7	18:52	27	2456110
	8	9	10	◑	12	13	14	1:48	28	2456117
	15	16	17	18	●	20	21	4:24	29	2456124
	22	23	24	25	◐	27	28	8:56	30	2456131
August 2012	29	30	31	1	○	3	4	3:27	31	2456138
	5	6	7	8	◑	10	11	18:55	32	2456145
	12	13	14	15	16	●	18	15:54	33	2456152
	19	20	21	22	23	◐	25	13:53	34	2456159
September 2012	26	27	28	29	30	○	1	13:58	35	2456166
	2	3	4	5	6	7	◑	13:15	36	2456173
	9	10	11	12	13	14	15		37	2456180
	●	17	18	19	20	21	◐[d]	2:10 19:41	38	2456187
	23	24	25	26	27	28	29		39	2456194
October 2012	○	1	2	3	4	5	6	3:19	40	2456201
	7	◑	9	10	11	12	13	7:33	41	2456208
	14	●	16	17	18	19	20	12:02	42	2456215
	21	◐	23	24	25	26	27	3:32	43	2456222
November 2012	28	○	30	31	1	2	3	19:49	44	2456229
	4	5	6	◑	8	9	10	0:36	45	2456236
	11	12	●	14	15	16	17	22:08	46	2456243
	18	19	◐	21	22	23	24	14:31	47	2456250
December 2012	25	26	27	○	29	30	1	14:46	48	2456257
	2	3	4	5	◑	7	8	15:31	49	2456264
	9	10	11	12	●	14	15	8:41	50	2456271
	16	17	18	19	◐	21[e]	22	5:19	51	2456278
	23	24	25	26	27	○	29	10:21	52	2456285
	30	31	1	2	3	4	◑	3:58	1	2456292

Hebrew 5772/5773

Month	Sun	Mon	Tue	Wed	Thu	Fri	Sat	Molad
Teveth 5772	6	7	8	9	10	11	12	
	13	14	15	16	17	18	19	
	20	21	22	23	24	25	26	
Shevat 5772	27	28	29	1	2	3	4	Mon $20^h5^m0^p$
	5	6	7	8	9	10	11	
	12	13	14	15	16	17	18	
	19	20	21	22	23	24	25	
Adar 5772	26	27	28	29	30	1	2	Wed $8^h49^m1^p$
	3	4	5	6	7	8	9	
	10	11	12	13	14[f]	15	16	
	17	18	19	20	21	22	23	
Nisan 5772	24	25	26	27	28	29	1	Thu $21^h33^m2^p$
	2	3	4	5	6	7	8	
	9	10	11	12	13	14	15[g]	
	16	17	18	19	20	21	22	
	23	24	25	26	27	28	29	
Iyyar 5772	30	1	2	3	4	5	6	Sat $10^h17^m3^p$
	7	8	9	10	11	12	13	
	14	15	16	17	18	19	20	
	21	22	23	24	25	26	27	
Sivan 5772	28	29	1	2	3	4	5	Sun $23^h1^m4^p$
	6[h]	7	8	9	10	11	12	
	13	14	15	16	17	18	19	
	20	21	22	23	24	25	26	
Tammuz 5772	27	28	29	30	1	2	3	Tue $11^h45^m5^p$
	4	5	6	7	8	9	10	
	11	12	13	14	15	16	17	
	18	19	20	21	22	23	24	
Av 5772	25	26	27	28	29	1	2	Thu $0^h29^m6^p$
	3	4	5	6	7	8	9	
	10[i]	11	12	13	14	15	16	
	17	18	19	20	21	22	23	
	24	25	26	27	28	29	30	
Elul 5772	1	2	3	4	5	6	7	Fri $13^h13^m7^p$
	8	9	10	11	12	13	14	
	15	16	17	18	19	20	21	
	22	23	24	25	26	27	28	
Tishri 5773	29	1[a]	2[a]	3	4	5	6	Sun $1^h57^m8^p$
	7	8	9	10[b]	11	12	13	
	14	15[c]	16	17	18	19	20	
	21	22	23	24	25	26	27	
Heshvan 5773	28	29	30	1	2	3	4	Mon $14^h41^m9^p$
	5	6	7	8	9	10	11	
	12	13	14	15	16	17	18	
	19	20	21	22	23	24	25	
Kislev 5773	26	27	28	29	1	2	3	Wed $3^h25^m10^p$
	4	5	6	7	8	9	10	
	11	12	13	14	15	16	17	
	18	19	20	21[d]	22	23	24	
Teveth 5773	25[e]	26[e]	27[e]	28[e]	29[e]	1[e]	2[e]	Thu $16^h9^m11^p$
	3[e]	4	5	6	7	8	9	
	10	11	12	13	14	15	16	
	17	18	19	20	21	22	23	

Chinese Xīn-Mǎo/Rén-Chén[‡]

Month	Sun	Mon	Tue	Wed	Thu	Fri	Sat	Solar Term
Month 12 Xīn-Mǎo	8	9	10	11*	12	13	14	Xiǎo hán
	15	16	17	18	19	20	21	
	22	23	24	25	26	27	**28**	Dà hán
Month 1 Rén-Chén	29	1[a]	2	3	4	5	6	
	7	8	9	10	11	12	*13*	Lì chūn
	14	15[b]	16	17	18	19	20	
	21	22	23	24	25	26	27	
Month 2 Rén-Chén	**28**	29	30	1	2	3	4	Yǔ shuǐ
	5	6	7	8	9	10	11	
	12*	*13*	14	15	16	17	18	Jīng zhé
	19	20	21	22	23	24	25	
Month 3 Rén-Chén	26	27	**28**	29	1	2	3	Chūn fēn
	4	5	6	7	8	9	10	
	11	12	13	*14*[c]	15	16	17	Qīng míng
	18	19	20	21	22	23	24	
Month 4 Rén-Chén	25	26	27	28	29	**30**	1	Gǔ yǔ
	2	3	4	5	6	7	8	
	9	10	11	12	13*	14	*15*	Lì xià
	16	17	18	19	20	21	22	
	23	24	25	26	27	28	29	
Leap Month 4 Rén-Chén	**30**	1	2	3	4	5	6	Xiǎo mǎn
	7	8	9	10	11	12	13	
	14	15	*16*	17	18	19	20	Máng zhòng
	21	22	23	24	25	26	27	
Month 5 Rén-Chén	28	29	1	2	**3**	4	5[d]	Xià zhì
	6	7	8	9	10	11	12	
	13	14*	15	16	17	18	*19*	Xiǎo shǔ
	20	21	22	23	24	25	26	
Month 6 Rén-Chén	27	28	29	30	1	2	3	
	4	5	6	7	8	9	10	Dà shǔ
	11	12	13	14	15	16	17	
	18	19	*20*	21	22	23	24	Lì qiū
Month 7 Rén-Chén	25	26	27	28	29	1	2	
	3	4	5	6	**7**[e]	8	9	Chǔ shǔ
	10	11	12	13	14	15[f]*	16	
	17	18	19	20	21	*22*	23	Bái lù
	24	25	26	27	28	29	30	
Month 8 Rén-Chén	1	2	3	4	5	6	**7**	Qiū fēn
	8	9	10	11	12	13	14	
	15[g]	16	17	18	19	20	21	
	22	*23*	24	25	26	27	28	Hán lù
Month 9 Rén-Chén	29	1	2	3	4	5	6	
	7	8	**9**[h]	10	11	12	13	Shuāng jiàng
	14	15	16*	17	18	19	20	
	21	22	23	*24*	25	26	27	Lì dōng
Month 10 Rén-Chén	28	29	30	1	2	3	4	
	5	6	7	8	**9**	10	11	Xiǎo xuě
	12	13	14	15	16	17	18	
	19	20	21	22	23	*24*	25	Dà xuě
Month 11 Rén-Chén	26	27	28	29	1	2	3	
	4	5	6	7	8	**9**[i]	10	Dōng zhì
	11	12	13	14	15	16	17*	
	18	19	20	21	22	23	*24*	Xiǎo hán

Coptic 1728/1729 — Ethiopic 2004/2005

Coptic Month	Sun	Mon	Tue	Wed	Thu	Fri	Sat	Ethiopic Month
Koiak 1728	22	23	24	25	26	27	28	Tākhśāś 2004
Tōbe 1728	29[c]	30	1	2	3	4	5	Ṭer 2004
	6[d]	7	8	9	10	11[e]	12	
	13	14	15	16	17	18	19	
	20	21	22	23	24	25	26	
Meshir 1728	27	28	29	30	1	2	3	Yakātit 2004
	4	5	6	7	8	9	10	
	11	12	13	14	15	16	17	
	18	19	20	21	22	23	24	
Paremotep 1728	25	26	27	28	29	30	1	Magābit 2004
	2	3	4	5	6	7	8	
	9	10	11	12	13	14	15	
	16	17	18	19	20	21	22	
	23	24	25	26	27	28	29	
Parmoute 1728	30	1	2	3	4	5	6	Miyāzyā 2004
	7[f]	8	9	10	11	12	13	
	14	15	16	17	18	19	20	
	21	22	23	24	25	26	27	
Pashons 1728	28	29[g]	30	1	2	3	4	Genbot 2004
	5	6	7	8	9	10	11	
	12	13	14	15	16	17	18	
	19	20	21	22	23	24	25	
Paōne 1728	26	27	28	29	30	1	2	Sanē 2004
	3	4	5	6	7	8	9	
	10	11	12	13	14	15	16	
	17	18	19	20	21	22	23	
	24	25	26	27	28	29	30	
Epēp 1728	1	2	3	4	5	6	7	Ḥamlē 2004
	8	9	10	11	12	13	14	
	15	16	17	18	19	20	21	
	22	23	24	25	26	27	28	
Mesorē 1728	29	30	1	2	3	4	5	Naḥasē 2004
	6	7	8	9	10	11	12	
	13[h]	14	15	16	17	18	19	
	20	21	22	23	24	25	26	
Epag. 1728	27	28	29	30	1	2	3	Pāg. 2004
Thoout 1729	4	5	1[a]	2	3	4	5	Maskaram 2005
	6	7	8	9	10	11	12	
	13	14	15	16	17[b]	18	19	
	20	21	22	23	24	25	26	
Paope 1729	27	28	29	30	1	2	3	Ṭeqemt 2005
	4	5	6	7	8	9	10	
	11	12	13	14	15	16	17	
	18	19	20	21	22	23	24	
Athōr 1729	25	26	27	28	29	30	1	Ḫedār 2005
	2	3	4	5	6	7	8	
	9	10	11	12	13	14	15	
	16	17	18	19	20	21	22	
	23	24	25	26	27	28	29	
Koiak 1729	30	1	2	3	4	5	6	Tākhśāś 2005
	7	8	9	10	11	12	13	
	14	15	16	17	18	19	20	
	21	22	23	24	25	26	27	

‡Leap year
[a]New Year
[b]Spring (5:14)
[c]Summer (23:08)
[d]Autumn (14:49)
[e]Winter (11:11)
● New moon
◐ First quarter moon
○ Full moon
◑ Last quarter moon

[a]New Year
[b]Yom Kippur
[c]Sukkot
[d]Winter starts
[e]Ḥanukkah
[f]Purim
[g]Passover
[h]Shavuot
[i]Fast of Av

‡Leap year
[a]New Year (4710, Dragon)
[b]Lantern Festival
[c]Qīngmíng
[d]Dragon Festival
[e]Qīqiǎo
[f]Hungry Ghosts
[g]Mid-Autumn Festival
[h]Double-Ninth Festival
[i]Dōngzhì
*Start of 60-name cycle

[a]New Year
[b]Building of the Cross
[c]Christmas
[d]Jesus's Circumcision
[e]Epiphany
[f]Easter
[g]Mary's Announcement
[h]Jesus's Transfiguration

PERSIAN (ASTRONOMICAL) 1390/1391‡

Month	Sun	Mon	Tue	Wed	Thu	Fri	Sat
DEY 1390	11	12	13	14	15	16	17
	18	19	20	21	22	23	24
	25	26	27	28	29	30	1
BAHMAN 1390	2	3	4	5	6	7	8
	9	10	11	12	13	14	15
	16	17	18	19	20	21	22
	23	24	25	26	27	28	29
	30	1	2	3	4	5	6
ESFAND 1390	7	8	9	10	11	12	13
	14	15	16	17	18	19	20
	21	22	23	24	25	26	27
	28	29	1[a]	2	3	4	5
FARVARDĪN 1391	6	7	8	9	10	11	12
	13[b]	14	15	16	17	18	19
	20	21	22	23	24	25	26
	27	28	29	30	31	1	2
ORDĪBEHEŠT 1391	3	4	5	6	7	8	9
	10	11	12	13	14	15	16
	17	18	19	20	21	22	23
	24	25	26	27	28	29	30
	31	1	2	3	4	5	6
XORDĀD 1391	7	8	9	10	11	12	13
	14	15	16	17	18	19	20
	21	22	23	24	25	26	27
	28	29	30	31	1	2	3
TĪR 1391	4	5	6	7	8	9	10
	11	12	13	14	15	16	17
	18	19	20	21	22	23	24
	25	26	27	28	29	30	31
MORDĀD 1391	1	2	3	4	5	6	7
	8	9	10	11	12	13	14
	15	16	17	18	19	20	21
	22	23	24	25	26	27	28
	29	30	31	1	2	3	4
SHAHRĪVAR 1391	5	6	7	8	9	10	11
	12	13	14	15	16	17	18
	19	20	21	22	23	24	25
	26	27	28	29	30	31	1
MEHR 1391	2	3	4	5	6	7	8
	9	10	11	12	13	14	15
	16	17	18	19	20	21	22
	23	24	25	26	27	28	29
	30	1	2	3	4	5	6
ĀBĀN 1391	7	8	9	10	11	12	13
	14	15	16	17	18	19	20
	21	22	23	24	25	26	27
	28	29	30	1	2	3	4
ĀZAR 1391	5	6	7	8	9	10	11
	12	13	14	15	16	17	18
	19	20	21	22	23	24	25
	26	27	28	29	30	1	2
DEY 1391	3	4	5	6	7	8	9
	10	11	12	13	14	15	16

‡Leap year
[a]New Year
[b]Sizdeh Bedar

HINDU LUNAR 2068/2069‡

Month	Sun	Mon	Tue	Wed	Thu	Fri	Sat
PAUSHA 2068	8	9	10	11	*11*	12	13
	14	15	16	17	18	19	**20**
	22	23	24	25	26	27	28
MĀGHA 2068	29	30	1	2	3	4	5
	6	7	8	9	10	11	12
	13	14	15	16	17	18	19
	20	21	22	23	24	**25**	27
PHĀLGUNA 2068	28	29[h]	30	1	2	3	4
	4	5	6	7	8	9	10
	11	12	13	14	15[i]	16	17
	18	**19**	21	22	23	24	25
CHAITRA 2069	26	27	28	29	30	1[a]	2
	3	4	5	6	*6*	7	8[b]
	9	10	11	**12**	14	15	16
	17	18	19	20	21	22	23
	24	25	26	27	28	29	30
VAIŚĀKHA 2069	1	2	3	4	5	6	7
	8	9	10	11	12	13	14
	15	**16**	18	19	20	21	22
	23	24	25	26	27	28	29
JYAISHTHA 2069	30	1	*1*	2	3	4	5
	6	7	8	**9**	11	12	13
	14	15	16	17	18	19	20
	21	22	23	24	25	26	27
ĀSHĀDHA 2069	28	29	30	1	2	3	4
	5	6	7	8	9	10	11
	12	14	15	16	17	18	19
	20	21	22	23	24	25	26
ŚRĀVAṆA 2069	27	28	*28*	29	30	1	2
	3	**4**	6	7	8	9	10
	11	12	13	14	15	16	17
	18	19	20	21	22	23[c]	24
LEAP BHĀDRAPADA 2069	25	26	27	28	29	30	1
	2	3	4	5	6	7	**8**
	10	11	12	13	14	15	16
	17	18	19	20	21	22	23
	24	*24*	25	26	27	28	29
BHĀDRAPADA 2069	30	**1**	3	4[d]	5	6	7
	8	9	10	11	12	13	14
	15	16	17	18	19	20	21
	22	23	24	25	26	27	28
ĀŚVINA 2069	29	30	1	2	3	4	**5**
	7	8[e]	9[e]	10[e]	11	12	13
	14	15	16	17	18	19	*19*
	20	21	22	23	24	25	26
KĀRTTIKA 2069	27	**28**	30	1[f]	2	3	4
	5	6	7	8	9	10	11
	12	13	14	15	16	17	18
	19	20	21	22	23	24	25
MĀRGAŚĪRA 2069	26	27	28	29	30	1	2
	3	5	6	7	8	9	10
	11[g]	12	*12*	13	14	15	16
	17	18	19	20	21	22	23

‡Leap year
[a]New Year (Nandana)
[b]Birthday of Rāma
[c]Birthday of Krishna
[d]Ganēśa Chaturthī
[e]Dashara
[f]Diwali
[g]Birthday of Vishnu
[h]Night of Śiva
[i]Holi

HINDU SOLAR 1933/1934

Month	Sun	Mon	Tue	Wed	Thu	Fri	Sat
PAUSHA 1933	17	18	19	20	21	22	23
	24	25	26	27	28	29	1[b]
MĀGHA 1933	2	3	4	5	6	7	8
	9	10	11	12	13	14	15
	16	17	18	19	20	21	22
	23	24	25	26	27	28	29
PHĀLGUNA 1933	30	1	2	3	4	5	6
	7	8	9	10	11	12	13
	14	15	16	17	18	19	20
	21	22	23	24	25	26	27
CHAITRA 1933	28	29	30	1	2	3	4
	5	6	7	8	9	10	11
	12	13	14	15	16	17	18
	19	20	21	22	23	24	25
VAIŚĀKHA 1934	26	27	28	29	30	1[a]	2
	3	4	5	6	7	8	9
	10	11	12	13	14	15	16
	17	18	19	20	21	22	23
	24	25	26	27	28	29	30
JYAISHTHA 1934	31	1	2	3	4	5	6
	7	8	9	10	11	12	13
	14	15	16	17	18	19	20
	21	22	23	24	25	26	27
ĀSHĀDHA 1934	28	29	30	31	1	2	3
	4	5	6	7	8	9	10
	11	12	13	14	15	16	17
	18	19	20	21	22	23	24
	25	26	27	28	29	30	31
ŚRĀVAṆA 1934	32	1	2	3	4	5	6
	7	8	9	10	11	12	13
	14	15	16	17	18	19	20
	21	22	23	24	25	26	27
BHĀDRAPADA 1934	28	29	30	31	32	1	2
	3	4	5	6	7	8	9
	10	11	12	13	14	15	16
	17	18	19	20	21	22	23
	24	25	26	27	28	29	30
ĀŚVINA 1934	31	1	2	3	4	5	6
	7	8	9	10	11	12	13
	14	15	16	17	18	19	20
	21	22	23	24	25	26	27
KĀRTTIKA 1934	28	29	30	1	2	3	4
	5	6	7	8	9	10	11
	12	13	14	15	16	17	18
	19	20	21	22	23	24	25
MĀRGAŚĪRA 1934	26	27	28	29	30	1	2
	3	4	5	6	7	8	9
	10	11	12	13	14	15	16
	17	18	19	20	21	22	23
PAUSHA 1934	24	25	26	27	28	29	1
	2	3	4	5	6	7	8
	9	10	11	12	13	14	15
	16	17	18	19	20	21	22

[a]New Year (Viśvāvasu)
[b]Pongal

ISLAMIC (ASTRONOMICAL) 1433/1434‡

Month	Sun	Mon	Tue	Wed	Thu	Fri	Sat
ṢAFAR 1433	7	8	9	10	11	12	13
	14	15	16	17	18	19	20
	21	22	23	24	25	26	27
RABĪʿ I 1433	28	29	30	1	2	3	4
	5	6	7	8	9	10	11
	12[c]	13	14	15	16	17	18
	19	20	21	22	23	24	25
RABĪʿ II 1433	26	27	28	29	1	2	3
	4	5	6	7	8	9	10
	11	12	13	14	15	16	17
	18	19	20	21	22	23	24
JUMĀDĀ I 1433	25	26	27	28	29	30	1
	2	3	4	5	6	7	8
	9	10	11	12	13	14	15
	16	17	18	19	20	21	22
	23	24	25	26	27	28	29
JUMĀDĀ II 1433	30	1	2	3	4	5	6
	7	8	9	10	11	12	13
	14	15	16	17	18	19	20
	21	22	23	24	25	26	27
RAJAB 1433	28	29	1	2	3	4	5
	6	7	8	9	10	11	12
	13	14	15	16	17	18	19
	20	21	22	23	24	25	26
SHAʿBĀN 1433	27[d]	28	29	30	1	2	3
	4	5	6	7	8	9	10
	11	12	13	14	15	16	17
	18	19	20	21	22	23	24
RAMAḌĀN 1433	25	26	27	28	29	30	1[e]
	2	3	4	5	6	7	8
	9	10	11	12	13	14	15
	16	17	18	19	20	21	22
	23	24	25	26	27	28	29
SHAWWĀL 1433	30	1[f]	2	3	4	5	6
	7	8	9	10	11	12	13
	14	15	16	17	18	19	20
	21	22	23	24	25	26	27
DHU AL-QAʿDA 1433	28	29	1	2	3	4	5
	6	7	8	9	10	11	12
	13	14	15	16	17	18	19
	20	21	22	23	24	25	26
DHU AL-ḤIJJA 1433	27	28	29	1	2	3	4
	5	6	7	8	9	10[g]	11
	12	13	14	15	16	17	18
	19	20	21	22	23	24	25
MUḤARRAM 1434	26	27	28	29	1[a]	2	3
	4	5	6	7	8	9	10[b]
	11	12	13	14	15	16	17
	18	19	20	21	22	23	24
ṢAFAR 1434	25	26	27	28	29	30	1
	2	3	4	5	6	7	8
	9	10	11	12	13	14	15
	16	17	18	19	20	21	22

‡Leap year
[a]New Year
[b]ʿAshūrāʾ
[c]Prophet's Birthday
[d]Ascent of the Prophet
[e]Start of Ramaḍān
[f]ʿĪd al-Fiṭr
[g]ʿĪd al-ʾAḍḥā

GREGORIAN 2012‡

Julian‡ (Sun)	Sun	Mon	Tue	Wed	Thu	Fri	Sat	Month
Dec 19	1	2	3	4	5	6	7[a]	JANUARY 2012
	8	9	10	11	12	13	14[b]	
Jan 2	15	16	17	18	19	20	21	
	22	23	24	25	26	27	28	
Jan 16	29	30	31	1	2	3	4	FEBRUARY 2012
	5	6	7	8	9	10	11	
Jan 30	12	13	14	15	16	17	18	
	19	20	21	22[c]	23	24	25	
Feb 13	26	27	28	29	1	2	3	MARCH 2012
	4[d]	5	6	7	8	9	10	
Feb 27	11	12	13	14	15	16	17	
	18	19	20	21	22	23	24	
Mar 12	25	26	27	28	29	30	31	
	1	2	3	4	5	6	7	APRIL 2012
Mar 26	8[e]	9	10	11	12	13	14	
	15[f]	16	17	18	19	20	21	
Apr 9	22	23	24	25	26	27	28	
	29	30	1	2	3	4	5	MAY 2012
Apr 23	6	7	8	9	10	11	12	
	13	14	15	16	17	18	19	
May 7	20	21	22	23	24	25	26	
	27	28	29	30	31	1	2	JUNE 2012
May 21	3	4	5	6	7	8	9	
	10	11	12	13	14	15	16	
Jun 4	17	18	19	20	21	22	23	
	24	25	26	27	28	29	30	
Jun 18	1	2	3	4	5	6	7	JULY 2012
	8	9	10	11	12	13	14	
Jul 2	15	16	17	18	19	20	21	
	22	23	24	25	26	27	28	
Jul 16	29	30	31	1	2	3	4	AUGUST 2012
	5	6	7	8	9	10	11	
Jul 30	12	13	14	15	16	17	18	
	19	20	21	22	23	24	25	
Aug 13	26	27	28	29	30	31	1	SEPTEMBER 2012
	2	3	4	5	6	7	8	
Aug 27	9	10	11	12	13	14	15	
	16	17	18	19	20	21	22	
Sep 10	23	24	25	26	27	28	29	
	30	1	2	3	4	5	6	OCTOBER 2012
Sep 24	7	8	9	10	11	12	13	
	14	15	16	17	18	19	20	
Oct 8	21	22	23	24	25	26	27	
	28	29	30	31	1	2	3	NOVEMBER 2012
Oct 22	4	5	6	7	8	9	10	
	11	12	13	14	15	16	17	
Nov 5	18	19	20	21	22	23	24	
	25	26	27	28	29	30	1	DECEMBER 2012
Nov 19	2[g]	3	4	5	6	7	8	
	9	10	11	12	13	14	15	
Dec 3	16	17	18	19	20	21	22	
	23	24	25[h]	26	27	28	29	
Dec 17	30	31	1	2	3	4	5	

‡Leap year
[a]Orthodox Christmas
[b]Julian New Year
[c]Ash Wednesday
[d]Feast of Orthodoxy
[e]Easter
[f]Orthodox Easter
[g]Advent
[h]Christmas

2013

Gregorian 2013

Month	Sun	Mon	Tue	Wed	Thu	Fri	Sat	Lunar Phases	ISO WEEK (Mon)	JULIAN DAY (Sun noon)
JANUARY 2013	30	31	1[a]	2	3	4	◑	3:58	1	2456292
	6	7	8	9	10	●	12	19:43	2	2456299
	13	14	15	16	17	◐	19	23:45	3	2456306
	20	21	22	23	24	25	26		4	2456313
FEBRUARY 2013	○	28	29	30	31	1	2	4:38	5	2456320
	◑	4	5	6	7	8	9	13:56	6	2456327
	●	11	12	13	14	15	16	7:20	7	2456334
	◐	18	19	20	21	22	23	20:30	8	2456341
MARCH 2013	24	○	26	27	28	1	2	20:26	9	2456348
	3	◑	5	6	7	8	9	21:53	10	2456355
	10	●	12	13	14	15	16	19:51	11	2456362
	17	18	◐	20[b]	21	22	23	17:26	12	2456369
	24	25	26	○	28	29	30	9:27	13	2456376
APRIL 2013	31	1	2	◑	4	5	6	4:36	14	2456383
	7	8	9	●	11	12	13	9:35	15	2456390
	14	15	16	17	◐	19	20	12:31	16	2456397
	21	22	23	24	○	26	27	19:57	17	2456404
MAY 2013	28	29	30	1	◑	3	4	11:14	18	2456411
	5	6	7	8	9	●	11	0:28	19	2456418
	12	13	14	15	16	17	◐	4:34	20	2456425
	19	20	21	22	23	24	○	4:25	21	2456432
JUNE 2013	26	27	28	29	30	◑	1	18:58	22	2456439
	2	3	4	5	6	7	●	15:56	23	2456446
	9	10	11	12	13	14	15		24	2456453
	◐	17	18	19	20	21[c]	22	17:24	25	2456460
	○	24	25	26	27	28	29	11:32	26	2456467
JULY 2013	◑	1	2	3	4	5	6	4:53	27	2456474
	7	●	9	10	11	12	13	7:14	28	2456481
	14	15	◐	17	18	19	20	3:18	29	2456488
	21	○	23	24	25	26	27	18:15	30	2456495
AUGUST 2013	28	◑	30	31	1	2	3	17:43	31	2456502
	4	5	●	7	8	9	10	21:50	32	2456509
	11	12	13	◐	15	16	17	10:56	33	2456516
	18	19	20	○	22	23	24	1:45	34	2456523
	25	26	27	◑	29	30	31	9:35	35	2456530
SEPTEMBER 2013	1	2	3	4	●	6	7	11:36	36	2456537
	8	9	10	11	◐	13	14	17:08	37	2456544
	15	16	17	18	○	20	21	11:13	38	2456551
	22[d]	23	24	25	26	◑	28	3:55	39	2456558
OCTOBER 2013	29	30	1	2	3	4	●	0:34	40	2456565
	6	7	8	9	10	◐	12	23:02	41	2456572
	13	14	15	16	17	○	19	23:37	42	2456579
	20	21	22	23	24	25	◑	23:40	43	2456586
NOVEMBER 2013	27	28	29	30	31	1	2		44	2456593
	●	4	5	6	7	8	9	12:50	45	2456600
	◐	11	12	13	14	15	16	5:57	46	2456607
	○	18	19	20	21	22	23	15:15	47	2456614
	24	◑	26	27	28	29	30	19:28	48	2456621
DECEMBER 2013	1	2	●	4	5	6	7	0:22	49	2456628
	8	◐	10	11	12	13	14	15:11	50	2456635
	15	16	○	18	19	20	21[e]	9:28	51	2456642
	22	23	24	◑	26	27	28	13:48	52	2456649
	29	30	31	●	2	3	4	11:14	1	2456656

Hebrew 5773/5774‡

ISO WEEK	Month	Sun	Mon	Tue	Wed	Thu	Fri	Sat	Molad
1	TEVETH 5773	17	18	19	20	21	22	23	
2	SHEVAT 5773	24	25	26	27	28	29	1	Sat 4h53m12p
3		2	3	4	5	6	7	8	
4		9	10	11	12	13	14	15	
5		16	17	18	19	20	21	22	
6		23	24	25	26	27	28	29	
7	ADAR 5773	30	1	2	3	4	5	6	Sun 17h37m13p
8		7	8	9	10	11	12	13	
9		14[f]	15	16	17	18	19	20	
10		21	22	23	24	25	26	27	
11	NISAN 5773	28	29	1	2	3	4	5	Tue 6h21m14p
12		6	7	8	9	10	11	12	
13		13	14	15[g]	16	17	18	19	
14		20	21	22	23	24	25	26	
15	IYYAR 5773	27	28	29	30	1	2	3	Wed 19h5m15p
16		4	5	6	7	8	9	10	
17		11	12	13	14	15	16	17	
18		18	19	20	21	22	23	24	
19	SIVAN 5773	25	26	27	28	29	1	2	Fri 7h49m16p
20		3	4	5	6[h]	7	8	9	
21		10	11	12	13	14	15	16	
22		17	18	19	20	21	22	23	
23		24	25	26	27	28	29	30	
24	TAMMUZ 5773	1	2	3	4	5	6	7	Sat 20h33m17p
25		8	9	10	11	12	13	14	
26		15	16	17	18	19	20	21	
27		22	23	24	25	26	27	28	
28	AV 5773	29	1	2	3	4	5	6	Mon 9h18m0p
29		7	8	9[i]	10	11	12	13	
30		14	15	16	17	18	19	20	
31		21	22	23	24	25	26	27	
32	ELUL 5773	28	29	30	1	2	3	4	Tue 22h2m1p
33		5	6	7	8	9	10	11	
34		12	13	14	15	16	17	18	
35		19	20	21	22	23	24	25	
36	TISHRI 5774	26	27	28	29	1[a]	2[a]	3	Thu 10h46m2p
37		4	5	6	7	8	9	10[b]	
38		11	12	13	14	15[c]	16	17	
39		18	19	20	21	22	23	24	
40	ḤESHVAN 5774	25	26	27	28	29	30	1	Fri 23h30m3p
41		2	3	4	5	6	7	8	
42		9	10	11	12	13	14	15	
43		16	17	18	19	20	21	22	
44		23	24	25	26	27	28	29	
45	KISLEV 5774	30	1	2	3	4	5	6	Sun 12h14m4p
46		7	8	9	10	11	12	13	
47		14	15	16	17	18	19	20	
48		21	22	23	24	25[e]	26[e]	27[e]	
49	TEVETH 5774	28[e]	29[e]	30[e]	1[e]	2[d,e]	3	4	Tue 0h58m5p
50		5	6	7	8	9	10	11	
51		12	13	14	15	16	17	18	
52		19	20	21	22	23	24	25	
1		26	27	28	29	1	2	3	Wed 13h42m6p

Chinese Rén-Chén‡/Guǐ-Sì

ISO WEEK	Month	Sun	Mon	Tue	Wed	Thu	Fri	Sat	Solar Term
1	MONTH 11 Rén-Chén	18	19	20	21	22	23	*24*	*Xiǎo hán*
2	MONTH 12 Rén-Chén	25	26	27	28	29	30	1	
3		2	3	4	5	6	7	8	
4		**9**	10	11	12	13	14	15	**Dà hán**
5		16	17	18	19	20	21	22	
6		23	*24*	25	26	27	28	29	*Lì chūn*
7	MONTH 1 Guǐ-Sì	1[a]	2	3	4	5	6	7	
8		8	**9**	10	11	12	13	14	**Yǔ shuǐ**
9		15[b]	16	17	18*	19	20	21	
10		22	23	*24*	25	26	27	28	*Jīng zhé*
11	MONTH 2 Guǐ-Sì	29	30	1	2	3	4	5	
12		6	7	8	**9**	10	11	12	**Chūn fēn**
13		13	14	15	16	17	18	19	
14		20	21	22	23	*24*[c]	25	26	*Qīng míng*
15	MONTH 3 Guǐ-Sì	27	28	29	1	2	3	4	
16		5	6	7	8	9	10	***11***	**Gǔ yǔ**
17		12	13	14	15	16	17	18	
18		19*	20	21	22	23	24	25	
19	MONTH 4 Guǐ-Sì	*26*	27	28	29	30	1	2	*Lì xià*
20		3	4	5	6	7	8	9	
21		10	11	**12**	13	14	15	16	**Xiǎo mǎn**
22		17	18	19	20	21	22	23	
23	MONTH 5 Guǐ-Sì	24	25	26	*27*	28	29	1	*Máng zhòng*
24		2	3	4	5[d]	6	7	8	
25		9	10	11	12	13	**14**	15	**Xià zhì**
26		16	17	18	19	20*	21	22	
27		23	24	25	26	27	28	29	
28	MONTH 6 Guǐ-Sì	*30*	1	2	3	4	5	6	*Xiǎo shǔ*
29		7	8	9	10	11	12	13	
30		14	**15**	16	17	18	19	20	**Dà shǔ**
31		21	22	23	24	25	26	27	
32	MONTH 7 Guǐ-Sì	28	29	30	*1*	2	3	4	*Lì qiū*
33		5	6	7[e]	8	9	10	11	
34		12	13	14	15[f]	16	**17**	18	**Chǔ shǔ**
35		19	20*	21	22	23	24	25	
36	MONTH 8 Guǐ-Sì	26	27	28	29	1	2	3	*Bái lù*
37		4	5	6	7	8	9	10	
38		11	12	13	14	15[g]	16	17	
39		18	**19**	20	21	22	23	24	**Qiū fēn**
40	MONTH 9 Guǐ-Sì	25	26	27	28	29	30	1	
41		2	3	*4*	5	6	7	8	*Hán lù*
42		9[h]	10	11	12	13	14	15	
43		16	17	18	**19**	20	21*	22	**Shuāng jiàng**
44		23	24	25	26	27	28	29	
45	MONTH 10 Guǐ-Sì	1	2	3	4	5	6	7	*Lì dōng*
46		8	9	10	11	12	13	14	
47		15	16	17	18	19	**20**	21	**Xiǎo xuě**
48		22	23	24	25	26	27	28	
49	MONTH 11* Guǐ-Sì	29	30	1	2	3	4	5	*Dà xuě*
50		6	7	8	9	10	11	12	
51		13	14	15	16	17	18	19	
52		**20**[i]	21	22*	23	24	25	26	**Dōng zhì**
1		27	28	29	1	2	3	4	

Coptic 1729/1730 — Ethiopic 2005/2006

ISO WEEK	Coptic Month	Sun	Mon	Tue	Wed	Thu	Fri	Sat	Ethiopic Month
1	KOIAK 1729	21	22	23	24	25	26	27	TĀKHŚĀŚ 2005
2	TÔBE 1729	28	29[c]	30	1	2	3	4	ṬER 2005
3		5	6[d]	7	8	9	10	11[e]	
4		12	13	14	15	16	17	18	
5		19	20	21	22	23	24	25	
6	MESHIR 1729	26	27	28	29	30	1	2	YAKĀTIT 2005
7		3	4	5	6	7	8	9	
8		10	11	12	13	14	15	16	
9		17	18	19	20	21	22	23	
10		24	25	26	27	28	29	30	
11	PAREMOTEP 1729	1	2	3	4	5	6	7	MAGĀBIT 2005
12		8	9	10	11	12	13	14	
13		15	16	17	18	19	20	21	
14		22	23	24	25	26	27	28	
15	PARMOUTE 1729	29	30	1	2	3	4	5	MIYĀZYĀ 2005
16		6	7	8	9	10	11	12	
17		13	14	15	16	17	18	19	
18		20	21	22	23	24	25	26	
19	PASHONS 1729	27[f]	28	29[g]	30	1	2	3	GENBOT 2005
20		4	5	6	7	8	9	10	
21		11	12	13	14	15	16	17	
22		18	19	20	21	22	23	24	
23	PAÔNE 1729	25	26	27	28	29	30	1	SANĒ 2005
24		2	3	4	5	6	7	8	
25		9	10	11	12	13	14	15	
26		16	17	18	19	20	21	22	
27		23	24	25	26	27	28	29	
28	EPÊP 1729	30	1	2	3	4	5	6	ḤAMLĒ 2005
29		7	8	9	10	11	12	13	
30		14	15	16	17	18	19	20	
31		21	22	23	24	25	26	27	
32	MESORĒ 1729	28	29	30	1	2	3	4	NAHASĒ 2005
33		5	6	7	8	9	10	11	
34		12	13[h]	14	15	16	17	18	
35		19	20	21	22	23	24	25	
36	EPAG. 1729	26	27	28	29	30	1	2	PĀG. 2005
37	THOOUT 1730	3	4	5	1[a]	2	3	4	MASKARAM 2006
38		5	6	7	8	9	10	11	
39		12	13	14	15	16	17[b]	18	
40		19	20	21	22	23	24	25	
41	PAOPE 1730	26	27	28	29	30	1	2	ṬEQEMT 2006
42		3	4	5	6	7	8	9	
43		10	11	12	13	14	15	16	
44		17	18	19	20	21	22	23	
45		24	25	26	27	28	29	30	
46	ATHÔR 1730	1	2	3	4	5	6	7	ḪEDĀR 2006
47		8	9	10	11	12	13	14	
48		15	16	17	18	19	20	21	
49		22	23	24	25	26	27	28	
50	KOIAK 1730	29	30	1	2	3	4	5	TĀKHŚĀŚ 2006
51		6	7	8	9	10	11	12	
52		13	14	15	16	17	18	19	
1		20	21	22	23	24	25	26	

Gregorian notes:

[a]New Year
[b]Spring (11:01)
[c]Summer (5:03)
[d]Autumn (20:43)
[e]Winter (17:11)
● New moon
◐ First quarter moon
○ Full moon
◑ Last quarter moon

Hebrew notes:

‡Leap year
[a]New Year
[b]Yom Kippur
[c]Sukkot
[d]Winter starts
[e]Ḥanukkah
[f]Purim
[g]Passover
[h]Shavuot
[i]Fast of Av

Chinese notes:

‡Leap year
[a]New Year (4711, Snake)
[b]Lantern Festival
[c]Qīngmíng
[d]Dragon Festival
[e]Qīqiǎo
[f]Hungry Ghosts
[g]Mid-Autumn Festival
[h]Double-Ninth Festival
[i]Dōngzhì
*Start of 60-name cycle

Coptic/Ethiopic notes:

[a]New Year
[b]Building of the Cross
[c]Christmas
[d]Jesus's Circumcision
[e]Epiphany
[f]Easter
[g]Mary's Announcement
[h]Jesus's Transfiguration

2013

PERSIAN (ASTRONOMICAL) 1391‡/1392

Month	Sun	Mon	Tue	Wed	Thu	Fri	Sat
DEY 1391	10	11	12	13	14	15	16
	17	18	19	20	21	22	23
	24	25	26	27	28	29	30
BAHMAN 1391	1	2	3	4	5	6	7
	8	9	10	11	12	13	14
	15	16	17	18	19	20	21
	22	23	24	25	26	27	28
	29	30	1	2	3	4	5
ESFAND 1391	6	7	8	9	10	11	12
	13	14	15	16	17	18	19
	20	21	22	23	24	25	26
	27	28	29	30	1[a]	2	3
FARVARDĪN 1392	4	5	6	7	8	9	10
	11	12	13[b]	14	15	16	17
	18	19	20	21	22	23	24
	25	26	27	28	29	30	31
ORDĪBEHEŠT 1392	1	2	3	4	5	6	7
	8	9	10	11	12	13	14
	15	16	17	18	19	20	21
	22	23	24	25	26	27	28
	29	30	31	1	2	3	4
XORDĀD 1392	5	6	7	8	9	10	11
	12	13	14	15	16	17	18
	19	20	21	22	23	24	25
	26	27	28	29	30	31	1
TĪR 1392	2	3	4	5	6	7	8
	9	10	11	12	13	14	15
	16	17	18	19	20	21	22
	23	24	25	26	27	28	29
	30	31	1	2	3	4	5
MORDĀD 1392	6	7	8	9	10	11	12
	13	14	15	16	17	18	19
	20	21	22	23	24	25	26
	27	28	29	30	31	1	2
SHAHRĪVAR 1392	3	4	5	6	7	8	9
	10	11	12	13	14	15	16
	17	18	19	20	21	22	23
	24	25	26	27	28	29	30
	31	1	2	3	4	5	6
MEHR 1392	7	8	9	10	11	12	13
	14	15	16	17	18	19	20
	21	22	23	24	25	26	27
	28	29	30	1	2	3	4
ĀBĀN 1392	5	6	7	8	9	10	11
	12	13	14	15	16	17	18
	19	20	21	22	23	24	25
	26	27	28	29	30	1	2
ĀZAR 1392	3	4	5	6	7	8	9
	10	11	12	13	14	15	16
	17	18	19	20	21	22	23
	24	25	26	27	28	29	30
DEY 1392	1	2	3	4	5	6	7
	8	9	10	11	12	13	14

‡Leap year
[a]New Year
[b]Sizdeh Bedar

HINDU LUNAR 2069‡/2070

Month	Sun	Mon	Tue	Wed	Thu	Fri	Sat
MĀRGAŚĪRA 2069	17	18	19	20	21	22	23
	24	25	26	27	29	30	1
PAUSHA 2069	2	3	4	5	6	7	8
	9	10	11	12	13	14	14
	15	16	17	18	19	20	21
	23	24	25	26	27	28	29
	30	1	2	3	4	5	6
MĀGHA 2069	7	8	9	10	11	12	13
	14	15	16	17	18	19	20
	21	22	23	24	25	26	28
	29[h]	30	1	2	3	4	5
PHĀLGUNA 2069	6	7	7	8	9	10	11
	12	13	14	15[i]	16	17	18
	19	20	22	23	24	25	26
	27	28	29	30	1[a]	2	3
CHAITRA 2070	4	5	6	7	8	9[b]	10
	11	12	13	14	15	16	17
	18	19	20	21	22	23	24
	26	27	28	29	30	1	1
VAIŚĀKHA 2070	2	3	4	5	6	7	8
	9	10	11	12	13	14	15
	16	18	19	20	21	22	23
	24	25	26	27	28	29	30
	1	2	3	4	5	6	7
JYAISHṬHA 2070	7	9	10	11	12	13	14
	15	16	17	18	19	20	22
	23	24	25	26	27	28	28
	29	30	1	2	3	4	5
ĀSHĀḌHA 2070	6	7	8	9	10	11	12
	14	15	16	17	18	19	20
	21	22	23	24	25	26	27
	28	29	30	1	2	3	4
ŚRĀVAṆA 2070	5	6	7	8	9	10	11
	12	13	14	15	17	18	19
	20	21	22	23[c]	24	24	25
	26	27	28	29	30	1	2
BHĀDRAPADA 2070	3	4[d]	5	6	7	8	10
	11	12	13	14	15	16	17
	18	19	20	21	22	23	24
	25	26	27	28	29	30	1
ĀŚVINA 2070	2	3	4	5	6	7	8[e]
	9[e]	10[e]	11	12	14	15	16
	17	18	19	19	20	21	22
	23	24	25	26	27	28	29
	30	1[f]	2	3	4	5	7
KĀRTTIKA 2070	8	9	10	11	12	13	14
	15	16	17	18	19	20	21
	22	22	23	24	25	26	27
	28	29	1	2	3	4	5
MĀRGAŚĪRA 2070	6	7	8	9	10	11[g]	12
	13	14	15	16	17	18	19
	20	21	22	23	24	25	26
	27	28	29	30	1	2	3

‡Leap year
[a]New Year (Vijaya)
[b]Birthday of Rāma
[c]Birthday of Krishna
[d]Gaṇēśa Chaturthī
[e]Dashara
[f]Diwali
[g]Birthday of Vishnu
[h]Night of Śiva
[i]Holi

HINDU SOLAR 1934/1935‡

Month	Sun	Mon	Tue	Wed	Thu	Fri	Sat
PAUSHA 1934	16	17	18	19	20	21	22
	23	24	25	26	27	28	29
	30	1[b]	2	3	4	5	6
MĀGHA 1934	7	8	9	10	11	12	13
	14	15	16	17	18	19	20
	21	22	23	24	25	26	27
	28	29	1	2	3	4	5
PHĀLGUNA 1934	6	7	8	9	10	11	12
	13	14	15	16	17	18	19
	20	21	22	23	24	25	26
	27	28	29	30	1	2	3
CHAITRA 1934	4	5	6	7	8	9	10
	11	12	13	14	15	16	17
	18	19	20	21	22	23	24
	25	26	27	28	29	30	1[a]
VAIŚĀKHA 1935	2	3	4	5	6	7	8
	9	10	11	12	13	14	15
	16	17	18	19	20	21	22
	23	24	25	26	27	28	29
	30	31	1	2	3	4	5
JYAISHṬHA 1935	6	7	8	9	10	11	12
	13	14	15	16	17	18	19
	20	21	22	23	24	25	26
	27	28	29	30	31	32	1
ĀSHĀḌHA 1935	2	3	4	5	6	7	8
	9	10	11	12	13	14	15
	16	17	18	19	20	21	22
	23	24	25	26	27	28	29
	30	31	1	2	3	4	5
ŚRĀVAṆA 1935	6	7	8	9	10	11	12
	13	14	15	16	17	18	19
	20	21	22	23	24	25	26
	27	28	29	30	31	32	1
BHĀDRAPADA 1935	2	3	4	5	6	7	8
	9	10	11	12	13	14	15
	16	17	18	19	20	21	22
	23	24	25	26	27	28	29
	30	31	1	2	3	4	5
ĀŚVINA 1935	6	7	8	9	10	11	12
	13	14	15	16	17	18	19
	20	21	22	23	24	25	26
	27	28	29	30	1	2	3
KĀRTTIKA 1935	4	5	6	7	8	9	10
	11	12	13	14	15	16	17
	18	19	20	21	22	23	24
	25	26	27	28	29	30	1
MĀRGAŚĪRA 1935	2	3	4	5	6	7	8
	9	10	11	12	13	14	15
	16	17	18	19	20	21	22
	23	24	25	26	27	28	29
	30	1	2	3	4	5	6
PAUSHA 1935	7	8	9	10	11	12	13
	14	15	16	17	18	19	20

‡Leap year
[a]New Year (Parābhava)
[b]Pongal

ISLAMIC (ASTRONOMICAL) 1434‡/1435

Month	Sun	Mon	Tue	Wed	Thu	Fri	Sat
ṢAFAR 1434	16	17	18	19	20	21	22
	23	24	25	26	27	28	29
	1	2	3	4	5	6	7
RABĪʿ I 1434	8	9	10	11	12[c]	13	14
	15	16	17	18	19	20	21
	22	23	24	25	26	27	28
	29	1	2	3	4	5	6
RABĪʿ II 1434	7	8	9	10	11	12	13
	14	15	16	17	18	19	20
	21	22	23	24	25	26	27
	28	29	30	1	2	3	4
JUMĀDĀ I 1434	5	6	7	8	9	10	11
	12	13	14	15	16	17	18
	19	20	21	22	23	24	25
	26	27	28	29	30	1	2
JUMĀDĀ II 1434	3	4	5	6	7	8	9
	10	11	12	13	14	15	16
	17	18	19	20	21	22	23
	24	25	26	27	28	29	1
RAJAB 1434	2	3	4	5	6	7	8
	9	10	11	12	13	14	15
	16	17	18	19	20	21	22
	23	24	25	26	27[d]	28	29
	30	1	2	3	4	5	6
SHAʿBĀN 1434	7	8	9	10	11	12	13
	14	15	16	17	18	19	20
	21	22	23	24	25	26	27
	28	29	30	1[e]	2	3	4
RAMAḌĀN 1434	5	6	7	8	9	10	11
	12	13	14	15	16	17	18
	19	20	21	22	23	24	25
	26	27	28	29	30	1[f]	2
SHAWWĀL 1434	3	4	5	6	7	8	9
	10	11	12	13	14	15	16
	17	18	19	20	21	22	23
	24	25	26	27	28	29	30
DHU AL-QAʿDA 1434	1	2	3	4	5	6	7
	8	9	10	11	12	13	14
	15	16	17	18	19	20	21
	22	23	24	25	26	27	28
	29	1	2	3	4	5	6
DHU AL-ḤIJJA 1434	7	8	9	10[g]	11	12	13
	14	15	16	17	18	19	20
	21	22	23	24	25	26	27
	28	29	1[a]	2	3	4	5
MUḤARRAM 1435	6	7	8	9	10[b]	11	12
	13	14	15	16	17	18	19
	20	21	22	23	24	25	26
	27	28	29	1	2	3	4
ṢAFAR 1435	5	6	7	8	9	10	11
	12	13	14	15	16	17	18
	19	20	21	22	23	24	25
	26	27	28	29	30	1	2

‡Leap year
[a]New Year
[b]ʿAshūrāʾ
[c]Prophet's Birthday
[d]Ascent of the Prophet
[e]Start of Ramaḍān
[f]ʿĪd al-Fiṭr
[g]ʿĪd al-ʾAḍḥā

GREGORIAN 2013

Julian (Sun)	Sun	Mon	Tue	Wed	Thu	Fri	Sat	Month
Dec 17	30	31	1	2	3	4	5	
	6	7[a]	8	9	10	11	12	JANUARY 2013
Dec 31	13	14[b]	15	16	17	18	19	
	20	21	22	23	24	25	26	
Jan 14	27	28	29	30	31	1	2	
	3	4	5	6	7	8	9	FEBRUARY 2013
Jan 28	10	11	12	13[c]	14	15	16	
	17	18	19	20	21	22	23	
Feb 11	24	25	26	27	28	1	2	
	3	4	5	6	7	8	9	MARCH 2013
Feb 25	10	11	12	13	14	15	16	
	17	18	19	20	21	22	23	
Mar 11	24[d]	25	26	27	28	29	30	
	31[e]	1	2	3	4	5	6	
Mar 25	7	8	9	10	11	12	13	APRIL 2013
	14	15	16	17	18	19	20	
Apr 8	21	22	23	24	25	26	27	
	28	29	30	1	2	3	4	
Apr 22	5[f]	6	7	8	9	10	11	MAY 2013
	12	13	14	15	16	17	18	
May 6	19	20	21	22	23	24	25	
	26	27	28	29	30	31	1	
May 20	2	3	4	5	6	7	8	JUNE 2013
	9	10	11	12	13	14	15	
Jun 3	16	17	18	19	20	21	22	
	23	24	25	26	27	28	29	
Jun 17	30	1	2	3	4	5	6	
	7	8	9	10	11	12	13	JULY 2013
Jul 1	14	15	16	17	18	19	20	
	21	22	23	24	25	26	27	
Jul 15	28	29	30	31	1	2	3	
	4	5	6	7	8	9	10	AUGUST 2013
Jul 29	11	12	13	14	15	16	17	
	18	19	20	21	22	23	24	
Aug 12	25	26	27	28	29	30	31	
	1	2	3	4	5	6	7	SEPTEMBER 2013
Aug 26	8	9	10	11	12	13	14	
	15	16	17	18	19	20	21	
Sep 9	22	23	24	25	26	27	28	
	29	30	1	2	3	4	5	
Sep 23	6	7	8	9	10	11	12	OCTOBER 2013
	13	14	15	16	17	18	19	
Oct 7	20	21	22	23	24	25	26	
	27	28	29	30	31	1	2	
Oct 21	3	4	5	6	7	8	9	NOVEMBER 2013
	10	11	12	13	14	15	16	
Nov 4	17	18	19	20	21	22	23	
	24	25	26	27	28	29	30	
Nov 18	1[g]	2	3	4	5	6	7	DECEMBER 2013
	8	9	10	11	12	13	14	
Dec 2	15	16	17	18	19	20	21	
	22	23	24	25[h]	26	27	28	
Dec 16	29	30	31	1	2	3	4	

[a]Orthodox Christmas
[b]Julian New Year
[c]Ash Wednesday
[d]Feast of Orthodoxy
[e]Easter
[f]Orthodox Easter
[g]Advent
[h]Christmas

2014

Gregorian 2014, Lunar Phases, ISO Week, Julian Day

Month	Sun	Mon	Tue	Wed	Thu	Fri	Sat	Lunar Phases	ISO WEEK (Mon)	JULIAN DAY (Sun noon)
January 2014	29	30	31	●[a]	2	3	4	11:14	1	2456656
	5	6	7	◐	9	10	11	3:39	2	2456663
	12	13	14	15	○	17	18	4:52	3	2456670
	19	20	21	22	23	◑	25	5:19	4	2456677
	26	27	28	29	●	31	1	21:38	5	2456684
February 2014	2	3	4	5	◐	7	8	19:22	6	2456691
	9	10	11	12	13	○	15	23:53	7	2456698
	16	17	18	19	20	21	◑	17:15	8	2456705
	23	24	25	26	27	28	●	7:59	9	2456712
March 2014	2	3	4	5	6	7	◐	13:26	10	2456719
	9	10	11	12	13	14	15		11	2456726
	○	17	18	19	20[b]	21	22	17:08	12	2456733
	23	◑	25	26	27	28	29	1:46	13	2456740
	●	31	1	2	3	4	5	18:45	14	2456747
April 2014	6	◐	8	9	10	11	12	8:30	15	2456754
	13	14	○	16	17	18	19	7:42	16	2456761
	20	21	◑	23	24	25	26	7:51	17	2456768
	27	28	●	30	1	2	3	6:14	18	2456775
May 2014	4	5	6	◐	8	9	10	3:15	19	2456782
	11	12	13	○	15	16	17	19:16	20	2456789
	18	19	20	◑	22	23	24	12:59	21	2456796
	25	26	27	●	29	30	31	18:40	22	2456803
June 2014	1	2	3	4	◐	6	7	20:39	23	2456810
	8	9	10	11	12	○	14	4:11	24	2456817
	15	16	17	18	◑	20	21[c]	18:38	25	2456824
	22	23	24	25	26	●	28	8:08	26	2456831
July 2014	29	30	1	2	3	4	◐	11:59	27	2456838
	6	7	8	9	10	11	○	11:25	28	2456845
	13	14	15	16	17	18	◑	2:08	29	2456852
	20	21	22	23	24	25	●	22:42	30	2456859
	27	28	29	30	31	1	2		31	2456866
August 2014	3	◐	5	6	7	8	9	0:49	32	2456873
	○	11	12	13	14	15	16	18:09	33	2456880
	◑	18	19	20	21	22	23	12:26	34	2456887
	24	●	26	27	28	29	30	14:12	35	2456894
September 2014	31	1	◐	3	4	5	6	11:11	36	2456901
	7	8	○	10	11	12	13	1:38	37	2456908
	14	15	◑	17	18	19	20	2:05	38	2456915
	21	22	23[d]	●	25	26	27	6:14	39	2456922
October 2014	28	29	30	◐	2	3	4	19:32	40	2456929
	5	6	7	○	9	10	11	10:50	41	2456936
	12	13	14	◑	16	17	18	19:12	42	2456943
	19	20	21	22	●	24	25	21:57	43	2456950
	26	27	28	29	30	◐	1	2:48	44	2456957
November 2014	2	3	4	5	○	7	8	22:23	45	2456964
	9	10	11	12	13	◑	15	15:15	46	2456971
	16	17	18	19	20	21	●	12:32	47	2456978
	23	24	25	26	27	28	◐	10:06	48	2456985
December 2014	30	1	2	3	4	5	○	12:27	49	2456992
	7	8	9	10	11	12	13		50	2456999
	◑	15	16	17	18	19	20	12:51	51	2457006
	21[e]	●	23	24	25	26	27	1:36	52	2457013
	◐	29	30	31	1	2	3	18:31	1	2457020

Hebrew 5774‡/5775

ISO WEEK	Month	Sun	Mon	Tue	Wed	Thu	Fri	Sat	Molad
1	Shevat 5774	26	27	28	29	1	2	3	Wed 13h42m6p
2		4	5	6	7	8	9	10	
3		11	12	13	14	15	16	17	
4		18	19	20	21	22	23	24	
5	Adar I 5774	25	26	27	28	29	30	1	Fri 2h26m7p
6		2	3	4	5	6	7	8	
7		9	10	11	12	13	14	15	
8		16	17	18	19	20	21	22	
9		23	24	25	26	27	28	29	
10	Adar II 5774	30	1	2	3	4	5	6	Sat 15h10m8p
11		7	8	9	10	11	12	13	
12		14[f]	15	16	17	18	19	20	
13		21	22	23	24	25	26	27	
14	Nisan 5774	28	29	1	2	3	4	5	Mon 3h54m9p
15		6	7	8	9	10	11	12	
16		13	14	15[g]	16	17	18	19	
17		20	21	22	23	24	25	26	
18	Iyar 5774	27	28	29	30	1	2	3	Tue 16h38m10p
19		4	5	6	7	8	9	10	
20		11	12	13	14	15	16	17	
21		18	19	20	21	22	23	24	
22	Sivan 5774	25	26	27	28	29	1	2	Thu 5h22m11p
23		3	4	5	6[h]	7	8	9	
24		10	11	12	13	14	15	16	
25		17	18	19	20	21	22	23	
26		24	25	26	27	28	29	30	
27	Tammuz 5774	1	2	3	4	5	6	7	Fri 18h6m12p
28		8	9	10	11	12	13	14	
29		15	16	17	18	19	20	21	
30		22	23	24	25	26	27	28	
31	Av 5774	29	1	2	3	4	5	6	Sun 6h50m13p
32		7	8	9[i]	10	11	12	13	
33		14	15	16	17	18	19	20	
34		21	22	23	24	25	26	27	
35	Elul 5774	28	29	30	1	2	3	4	Mon 19h34m14p
36		5	6	7	8	9	10	11	
37		12	13	14	15	16	17	18	
38		19	20	21	22	23	24	25	
39	Tishri 5775	26	27	28	29	1[a]	2[a]	3	Wed 8h18m15p
40		4	5	6	7	8	9	10[b]	
41		11	12	13	14	15[c]	16	17	
42		18	19	20	21	22	23	24	
43	Heshvan 5775	25	26	27	28	29	30	1	Thu 21h2m16p
44		2	3	4	5	6	7	8	
45		9	10	11	12	13	14	15	
46		16	17	18	19	20	21	22	
47		23	24	25	26	27	28	29	
48	Kislev 5775	1	2	3	4	5	6	7	Sat 9h46m17p
49		8	9	10	11	12	13[d]	14	
50		15	16	17	18	19	20	21	
51		22	23	24	25[e]	26[e]	27[e]	28[e]	
52	Teveth 5775	29[e]	30[e]	1[e]	2[e]	3	4	5	Sun 22h31m0p
1		6	7	8	9	10	11	12	

Chinese Guǐ-Sì/Jiă-Wǔ‡

ISO WEEK	Month	Sun	Mon	Tue	Wed	Thu	Fri	Sat	Solar Term
1	Month 12 Guǐ-Sì	27	28	29	1	2	3	4	
2		5	6	7	8	9	10	11	Xiǎo hán
3		12	13	14	15	16	17	18	
4		19	**20**	21	22	23	24	25	**Dà hán**
5	Month 1 Jiă-Wǔ	26	27	28	29	30	1[a]	2	
6		3	4	5	6	7	8	9	Lì chūn
7		10	11	12	13	14	15[b]	16	
8		17	18	19	**20**	21	22	23*	**Yǔ shuǐ**
9	Month 2 Jiă-Wǔ	24	25	26	27	28	29	1	
10		2	3	4	5	*6*	7	8	Jīng zhé
11		9	10	11	12	13	14	15	
12		16	17	18	19	20	**21**	22	**Chūn fēn**
13		23	24	25	26	27	28	29	
14	Month 3 Jiă-Wǔ	30	1	2	3	4	5	6[c]	Qīng míng
15		7	8	9	10	11	12	13	
16		14	15	16	17	18	19	20	
17		**21**	22	23	24*	25	26	27	**Gǔ yǔ**
18	Month 4 Jiă-Wǔ	28	29	1	2	3	4	5	
19		6	7	8	9	10	11	12	Lì xià
20		13	14	15	16	17	18	19	
21		20	21	22	**23**	24	25	26	**Xiǎo mǎn**
22	Month 5 Jiă-Wǔ	27	28	29	30	1	2	3	
23		4	5[d]	6	7	8	*9*	10	Máng zhòng
24		11	12	13	14	15	16	17	
25		18	19	20	21	22	23	**24**	**Xià zhì**
26	Month 6 Jiă-Wǔ	25*	26	27	28	29	1	2	
27		3	4	5	6	7	8	9	
28		10	*11*	12	13	14	15	16	Xiǎo shǔ
29		17	18	19	20	21	22	23	
30		24	25	26	**27**	28	29	30	**Dà shǔ**
31	Month 7 Jiă-Wǔ	1	2	3	4	5	6	7[e]	
32		8	9	10	11	*12*	13	14	Lì qiū
33		15[f]	16	17	18	19	20	21	
34		22	23	24	25	26*	27	**28**	**Chǔ shǔ**
35	Month 8 Jiă-Wǔ	29	1	2	3	4	5	6	
36		7	8	9	10	11	12	13	
37		14	15[g]	16	17	18	19	20	Bái lù
38		21	22	23	24	25	26	27	
39	Month 9 Jiă-Wǔ	28	29	**30**	1	2	3	4	**Qiū fēn**
40		5	6	7	8	9[h]	10	11	
41		12	13	14	*15*	16	17	18	Hán lù
42		19	20	21	22	23	24	25	
43	Leap Month 9 Jiă-Wǔ	26	27*	28	29	**30**	1	2	**Shuāng jiàng**
44		3	4	5	6	7	8	9	
45		10	11	12	13	14	*15*	16	Lì dōng
46		17	18	19	20	21	22	23	
47	Month 10 Jiă-Wǔ	24	25	26	27	28	29	*1*	**Xiǎo xuě**
48		2	3	4	5	6	7	8	
49		9	10	11	12	13	14	15	
50		*16*	17	18	19	20	21	22	Dà xuě
51		23	24	25	26	27	28*	29	
52	Month 11 Jiă-Wǔ	30	*1*[i]	2	3	4	5	6	**Dōng zhì**
1		7	8	9	10	11	12	13	

Coptic 1730/1731‡ — Ethiopic 2006/2007‡

ISO WEEK	Coptic Month	Sun	Mon	Tue	Wed	Thu	Fri	Sat	Ethiopic Month
1	Koiak 1730	20	21	22	23	24	25	26	Tākhśāś 2006
2	Tōbe 1730	27	28	29[c]	30	1	2	3	Ṭer 2006
3		4	5	6[d]	7	8	9	10	
4		11[e]	12	13	14	15	16	17	
5		18	19	20	21	22	23	24	
6	Meshir 1730	25	26	27	28	29	30	1	Yakātit 2006
7		2	3	4	5	6	7	8	
8		9	10	11	12	13	14	15	
9		16	17	18	19	20	21	22	
10		23	24	25	26	27	28	29	
11	Paremotep 1730	30	1	2	3	4	5	6	Magābit 2006
12		7	8	9	10	11	12	13	
13		14	15	16	17	18	19	20	
14		21	22	23	24	25	26	27	
15	Parmoute 1730	28	29	30	1	2	3	4	Miyāzyā 2006
16		5	6	7	8	9	10	11	
17		12[f]	13	14	15	16	17	18	
18		19	20	21	22	23	24	25	
19	Pashons 1730	26	27	28	29[g]	30	1	2	Genbot 2006
20		3	4	5	6	7	8	9	
21		10	11	12	13	14	15	16	
22		17	18	19	20	21	22	23	
23		24	25	26	27	28	29	30	
24	Paōne 1730	1	2	3	4	5	6	7	Sanē 2006
25		8	9	10	11	12	13	14	
26		15	16	17	18	19	20	21	
27		22	23	24	25	26	27	28	
28	Epēp 1730	29	30	1	2	3	4	5	Ḥamlē 2006
29		6	7	8	9	10	11	12	
30		13	14	15	16	17	18	19	
31		20	21	22	23	24	25	26	
32	Mesorē 1730	27	28	29	30	1	2	3	Naḥasē 2006
33		4	5	6	7	8	9	10	
34		11	12	13[h]	14	15	16	17	
35		18	19	20	21	22	23	24	
36	Epag. 1730	25	26	27	28	29	30	1	Pāg. 2006
37	Thoout 1731	2	3	4	5	1[a]	2	3	Maskaram 2007
38		4	5	6	7	8	9	10	
39		11	12	13	14	15	16	17[b]	
40		18	19	20	21	22	23	24	
41	Paope 1731	25	26	27	28	29	30	1	Ṭeqemt 2007
42		2	3	4	5	6	7	8	
43		9	10	11	12	13	14	15	
44		16	17	18	19	20	21	22	
45		23	24	25	26	27	28	29	
46	Athōr 1731	30	1	2	3	4	5	6	Ḫedār 2007
47		7	8	9	10	11	12	13	
48		14	15	16	17	18	19	20	
49		21	22	23	24	25	26	27	
50	Koiak 1731	28	29	30	1	2	3	4	Tākhśāś 2007
51		5	6	7	8	9	10	11	
52		12	13	14	15	16	17	18	
1		19	20	21	22	23	24	25	

[a]New Year
[b]Spring (16:56)
[c]Summer (10:51)
[d]Autumn (2:29)
[e]Winter (23:02)
● New moon
◐ First quarter moon
○ Full moon
◑ Last quarter moon

‡Leap year
[a]New Year
[b]Yom Kippur
[c]Sukkot
[d]Winter starts
[e]Ḥanukkah
[f]Purim
[g]Passover
[h]Shavuot
[i]Fast of Av

‡Leap year
[a]New Year (4712, Horse)
[b]Lantern Festival
[c]Qīngmíng
[d]Dragon Festival
[e]Qīqiǎo
[f]Hungry Ghosts
[g]Mid-Autumn Festival
[h]Double-Ninth Festival
[i]Dōngzhì
*Start of 60-name cycle

‡Leap year
[a]New Year
[b]Building of the Cross
[c]Christmas
[d]Jesus's Circumcision
[e]Epiphany
[f]Easter
[g]Mary's Announcement
[h]Jesus's Transfiguration

2014

PERSIAN (ASTRONOMICAL) 1392/1393

Month	Sun	Mon	Tue	Wed	Thu	Fri	Sat
DEY 1392	8	9	10	11	12	13	14
	15	16	17	18	19	20	21
	22	23	24	25	26	27	28
	29	30	*1*	2	3	4	5
BAHMAN 1392	6	7	8	9	10	11	12
	13	14	15	16	17	18	19
	20	21	22	23	24	25	26
	27	28	29	30	*1*	2	3
ESFAND 1392	4	5	6	7	8	9	10
	11	12	13	14	15	16	17
	18	19	20	21	22	23	24
	25	26	27	28	29	*1*[a]	2
FARVARDĪN 1393	3	4	5	6	7	8	9
	10	11	12	13[b]	14	15	16
	17	18	19	20	21	22	23
	24	25	26	27	28	29	30
	31	*1*	2	3	4	5	6
ORDĪBEHEŠT 1393	7	8	9	10	11	12	13
	14	15	16	17	18	19	20
	21	22	23	24	25	26	27
	28	29	30	31	*1*	2	3
XORDĀD 1393	4	5	6	7	8	9	10
	11	12	13	14	15	16	17
	18	19	20	21	22	23	24
	25	26	27	28	29	30	31
TĪR 1393	*1*	2	3	4	5	6	7
	8	9	10	11	12	13	14
	15	16	17	18	19	20	21
	22	23	24	25	26	27	28
	29	30	31	*1*	2	3	4
MORDĀD 1393	5	6	7	8	9	10	11
	12	13	14	15	16	17	18
	19	20	21	22	23	24	25
	26	27	28	29	30	31	*1*
SHAHRĪVAR 1393	2	3	4	5	6	7	8
	9	10	11	12	13	14	15
	16	17	18	19	20	21	22
	23	24	25	26	27	28	29
	30	31	*1*	2	3	4	5
MEHR 1393	6	7	8	9	10	11	12
	13	14	15	16	17	18	19
	20	21	22	23	24	25	26
	27	28	29	30	*1*	2	3
ĀBĀN 1393	4	5	6	7	8	9	10
	11	12	13	14	15	16	17
	18	19	20	21	22	23	24
	25	26	27	28	29	30	*1*
ĀZAR 1393	2	3	4	5	6	7	8
	9	10	11	12	13	14	15
	16	17	18	19	20	21	22
	23	24	25	26	27	28	29
DEY 1393	30	*1*	2	3	4	5	6
	7	8	9	10	11	12	13

HINDU LUNAR 2070/2071

Month	Sun	Mon	Tue	Wed	Thu	Fri	Sat
	27	28	29	30	1	2	3
PAUSHA 2070	**4**	6	7	8	9	10	11
	12	13	14	*14*	15	16	17
	18	19	20	21	22	23	24
	25	26	27	**28**	30	1	2
MĀGHA 2070	3	4	5	6	7	8	9
	10	11	12	13	14	15	16
	17	*17*	18	19	20	21	**22**
	24	25	26	27	28[h]	29	30
	1	2	3	4	5	6	7
PHĀLGUNA 2070	8	9	10	11	12	13	14
	15[i]	16	17	18	19	20	21
	22	23	24	25	**26**	28	29
	30	1[a]	2	3	4	5	6
CHAITRA 2071	7	8	9[b]	10	*10*	11	12
	13	14	15	16	17	18	19
	20	22	23	24	25	26	27
	28	29	30	1	2	3	4
VAIŚĀKHA 2071	5	6	7	8	9	10	11
	12	13	14	15	16	17	18
	19	20	21	22	**23**	25	26
	27	28	29	30	1	2	3
JYAISHTHA 2071	4	5	*5*	6	7	8	9
	10	11	12	13	14	15	**16**
	18	19	20	21	22	23	24
	25	26	27	28	29	30	1
ĀSHĀDHA 2071	2	3	4	5	6	7	8
	9	10	11	12	13	14	15
	16	17	18	**19**	21	22	23
	24	25	26	27	28	29	30
	1	2	*2*	3	4	5	6
ŚRĀVANA 2071	7	8	9	10	11	**12**	14
	15	16	17	18	19	20	21
	22	23[c]	24	25	26	27	28
	29	30	1	2	3	4[d]	5
BHĀDRAPADA 2071	6	7	8	9	10	11	12
	13	14	**15**	17	18	19	20
	21	22	23	24	25	26	27
	28	*28*	29	30	1	2	3
ĀŚVINA 2071	4	5	6	7	**8**[e]	10[e]	11
	12	13	14	15	16	17	18
	19	20	21	22	23	24	25
	26	27	28	29	30	1[f]	2
KĀRTTIKA 2071	3	4	5	6	7	8	9
	10	11	**12**	14	15	16	17
	18	19	20	21	22	*22*	23
	24	25	26	27	28	29	30
	1	2	3	4	5	**6**	8
MĀRGAŚĪRA 2071	9	10	11[g]	12	13	14	15
	16	17	18	19	20	21	22
	23	24	25	*25*	26	27	28
	29	**30**	2	3	4	5	6
PAUSHA 2071	7	8	9	10	11	12	13

HINDU SOLAR 1935‡/1936

Month	Sun	Mon	Tue	Wed	Thu	Fri	Sat
PAUSHA 1935	14	15	16	17	18	19	20
	21	22	23	24	25	26	27
	28	29	1[b]	2	3	4	5
MĀGHA 1935	6	7	8	9	10	11	12
	13	14	15	16	17	18	19
	20	21	22	23	24	25	26
	27	28	29	1	2	3	4
PHĀLGUNA 1935	5	6	7	8	9	10	11
	12	13	14	15	16	17	18
	19	20	21	22	23	24	25
	26	27	28	29	30	1	2
CHAITRA 1935	3	4	5	6	7	8	9
	10	11	12	13	14	15	16
	17	18	19	20	21	22	23
	24	25	26	27	28	29	30
	31	1[a]	2	3	4	5	6
VAIŚĀKHA 1936	7	8	9	10	11	12	13
	14	15	16	17	18	19	20
	21	22	23	24	25	26	27
	28	29	30	31	1	2	3
JYAISHTHA 1936	4	5	6	7	8	9	10
	11	12	13	14	15	16	17
	18	19	20	21	22	23	24
	25	26	27	28	29	30	31
	1	2	3	4	5	6	7
ĀSHĀDHA 1936	8	9	10	11	12	13	14
	15	16	17	18	19	20	21
	22	23	24	25	26	27	28
	29	30	31	32	1	2	3
ŚRĀVANA 1936	4	5	6	7	8	9	10
	11	12	13	14	15	16	17
	18	19	20	21	22	23	24
	25	26	27	28	29	30	31
	1	2	3	4	5	6	7
BHĀDRAPADA 1936	8	9	10	11	12	13	14
	15	16	17	18	19	20	21
	22	23	24	25	26	27	28
	29	30	31	1	2	3	4
ĀŚVINA 1936	5	6	7	8	9	10	11
	12	13	14	15	16	17	18
	19	20	21	22	23	24	25
	26	27	28	29	30	31	1
KĀRTTIKA 1936	2	3	4	5	6	7	8
	9	10	11	12	13	14	15
	16	17	18	19	20	21	22
	23	24	25	26	27	28	29
	1	2	3	4	5	6	7
MĀRGAŚĪRA 1936	8	9	10	11	12	13	14
	15	16	17	18	19	20	21
	22	23	24	25	26	27	28
	29	30	1	2	3	4	5
PAUSHA 1936	6	7	8	9	10	11	12
	13	14	15	16	17	18	19

ISLAMIC (ASTRONOMICAL) 1435/1436

Month	Sun	Mon	Tue	Wed	Thu	Fri	Sat
	26	27	28	29	30	*1*	2
RABĪ' I 1435	3	4	5	6	7	8	9
	10	11	12[c]	13	14	15	16
	17	18	19	20	21	22	23
	24	25	26	27	28	29	*1*
RABĪ' II 1435	2	3	4	5	6	7	8
	9	10	11	12	13	14	15
	16	17	18	19	20	21	22
	23	24	25	26	27	28	29
JUMĀDĀ I 1435	1	2	3	4	5	6	7
	8	9	10	11	12	13	14
	15	16	17	18	19	20	21
	22	23	24	25	26	27	28
	29	30	*1*	2	3	4	5
JUMĀDĀ II 1435	6	7	8	9	10	11	12
	13	14	15	16	17	18	19
	20	21	22	23	24	25	26
	27	28	29	*1*	2	3	4
RAJAB 1435	5	6	7	8	9	10	11
	12	13	14	15	16	17	18
	19	20	21	22	23	24	25
	26	27[d]	28	29	30	*1*	2
SHA'BĀN 1435	3	4	5	6	7	8	9
	10	11	12	13	14	15	16
	17	18	19	20	21	22	23
	24	25	26	27	28	29	30
	1[e]	2	3	4	5	6	7
RAMAḌĀN 1435	8	9	10	11	12	13	14
	15	16	17	18	19	20	21
	22	23	24	25	26	27	28
	29	30	*1*[f]	2	3	4	5
SHAWWĀL 1435	6	7	8	9	10	11	12
	13	14	15	16	17	18	19
	20	21	22	23	24	25	26
	27	28	29	30	1	2	3
DHU AL-QA'DA 1435	4	5	6	7	8	9	10
	11	12	13	14	15	16	17
	18	19	20	21	22	23	24
	25	26	27	28	29	*1*	2
DHU AL-HIJJA 1435	3	4	5	6	7	8	9
	10[g]	11	12	13	14	15	16
	17	18	19	20	21	22	23
	24	25	26	27	28	29	1[a]
MUHARRAM 1436	2	3	4	5	6	7	8
	9	10[b]	11	12	13	14	15
	16	17	18	19	20	21	22
	23	24	25	26	27	28	29
	30	*1*	2	3	4	5	6
SAFAR 1436	7	8	9	10	11	12	13
	14	15	16	17	18	19	20
	21	22	23	24	25	26	27
	28	29	*1*	2	3	4	5
RABĪ' I 1436	6	7	8	9	10	11	12

GREGORIAN 2014

Julian (Sun)	Sun	Mon	Tue	Wed	Thu	Fri	Sat	Month
Dec 16	29	30	31	1	2	3	4	
	5	6	7[a]	8	9	10	11	JANUARY 2014
Dec 30	12	13	14[b]	15	16	17	18	
	19	20	21	22	23	24	25	
Jan 13	26	27	28	29	30	31	1	
	2	3	4	5	6	7	8	FEBRUARY 2014
Jan 27	9	10	11	12	13	14	15	
	16	17	18	19	20	21	22	
Feb 10	23	24	25	26	27	28	1	
	2	3	4	5[c]	6	7	8	
Feb 24	9[d]	10	11	12	13	14	15	MARCH 2014
	16	17	18	19	20	21	22	
Mar 10	23	24	25	26	27	28	29	
	30	31	1	2	3	4	5	
Mar 24	6	7	8	9	10	11	12	APRIL 2014
	13	14	15	16	17	18	19	
Apr 7	20[e]	21	22	23	24	25	26	
	27	28	29	30	1	2	3	
Apr 21	4	5	6	7	8	9	10	MAY 2014
	11	12	13	14	15	16	17	
May 5	18	19	20	21	22	23	24	
	25	26	27	28	29	30	31	
May 19	1	2	3	4	5	6	7	
	8	9	10	11	12	13	14	JUNE 2014
Jun 2	15	16	17	18	19	20	21	
	22	23	24	25	26	27	28	
Jun 16	29	30	1	2	3	4	5	
	6	7	8	9	10	11	12	JULY 2014
Jun 30	13	14	15	16	17	18	19	
	20	21	22	23	24	25	26	
Jul 14	27	28	29	30	31	1	2	
	3	4	5	6	7	8	9	
Jul 28	10	11	12	13	14	15	16	AUGUST 2014
	17	18	19	20	21	22	23	
Aug 11	24	25	26	27	28	29	30	
	31	1	2	3	4	5	6	
Aug 25	7	8	9	10	11	12	13	SEPTEMBER 2014
	14	15	16	17	18	19	20	
Sep 8	21	22	23	24	25	26	27	
	28	29	30	1	2	3	4	
Sep 22	5	6	7	8	9	10	11	OCTOBER 2014
	12	13	14	15	16	17	18	
Oct 6	19	20	21	22	23	24	25	
	26	27	28	29	30	31	1	
Oct 20	2	3	4	5	6	7	8	NOVEMBER 2014
	9	10	11	12	13	14	15	
Nov 3	16	17	18	19	20	21	22	
	23	24	25	26	27	28	29	
Nov 17	30[g]	1	2	3	4	5	6	
	7	8	9	10	11	12	13	DECEMBER 2014
Dec 1	14	15	16	17	18	19	20	
	21	22	23	24	25[h]	26	27	
Dec 15	28	29	30	31	1	2	3	

Persian: [a]New Year; [b]Sizdeh Bedar

Hindu Lunar: [a]New Year (Jaya); [b]Birthday of Rāma; [c]Birthday of Krishna; [d]Ganēśa Chaturthī; [e]Dashara; [f]Diwali; [g]Birthday of Vishnu; [h]Night of Śiva; [i]Holi

Hindu Solar: ‡Leap year; [a]New Year (Plavaṅga); [b]Pongal

Islamic: [a]New Year; [b]'Ashūrā'; [c]Prophet's Birthday; [d]Ascent of the Prophet; [e]Start of Ramaḍān; [f]'Īd al-Fiṭr; [g]'Īd al-'Aḍḥā

Gregorian: [a]Orthodox Christmas; [b]Julian New Year; [c]Ash Wednesday; [d]Feast of Orthodoxy; [e]Easter (also Orthodox); [g]Advent; [h]Christmas

2015

Gregorian 2015	Sun Mon Tue Wed Thu Fri Sat	Lunar Phases	ISO Week (Mon)	Julian Day (Sun noon)	Hebrew 5775/5776‡	Sun Mon Tue Wed Thu Fri Sat	Molad	Chinese Jiă-Wŭ‡/Yĭ-Wèi	Sun Mon Tue Wed Thu Fri Sat	Solar Term	Coptic 1731‡/1732	Sun Mon Tue Wed Thu Fri Sat	Ethiopic 2007‡/2008
JANUARY 2015	◐ 29 30 31 1[a] 2 3	18:31	1	2457020	TEVETH 5775	6 7 8 9 10 11 12		MONTH 11 Jiă-Wŭ	7 8 9 10 11 12 13		KOIAK 1731	19 20 21 22 23 24 25	TĀKHŚĀŚ 2007
	4 ○ 6 7 8 9 10	4:53	2	2457027		13 14 15 16 17 18 19			14 15 16 17 18 19 20	*Xiăo hán*	TÔBE 1731	26 27 28 29[c] 30 1 2	ṬER 2007
	11 12 ◑ 14 15 16 17	9:46	3	2457034		20 21 22 23 24 25 26			21 22 23 24 25 26 27			3 4 5 6[d] 7 8 9	
	18 19 ● 21 22 23 24	13:14	4	2457041	SHEVAT 5775	27 28 29 1 2 3 4	Tue 11h15m1p	MONTH 12 Jiă-Wŭ	28 29 1 2 3 4 5	**Dà hán**		10 11[e] 12 13 14 15 16	
	25 26 ◐ 28 29 30 31	4:48	5	2457048		5 6 7 8 9 10 11			6 7 8 9 10 11 12			17 18 19 20 21 22 23	
FEBRUARY 2015	1 2 ○ 4 5 6 7	23:09	6	2457055		12 13 14 15 16 17 18			13 14 15 16 17 18 19	*Lì chūn*		24 25 26 27 28 29 30	
	8 9 10 11 ◑ 13 14	3:50	7	2457062		19 20 21 22 23 24 25			20 21 22 23 24 25 26		MESHIR 1731	1 2 3 4 5 6 7	YAKĀTIT 2007
	15 16 17 ● 19 20 21	23:47	8	2457069	ADAR 5775	26 27 28 29 30 1 2	Wed 23h59m2p	MONTH 1 Yĭ-Wèi	27 28 29* 30 1[a] 2 3	**Yŭ shuĭ**		8 9 10 11 12 13 14	
	22 23 24 ◐ 26 27 28	17:14	9	2457076		3 4 5 6 7 8 9			4 5 6 7 8 9 10			15 16 17 18 19 20 21	
MARCH 2015	1 2 3 4 ○ 6 7	18:05	10	2457083		10 11 12 13 14[f] 15 16			11 12 13 14 15[b] 16 17	*Jīng zhé*		22 23 24 25 26 27 28	
	8 9 10 11 12 ◑ 14	17:48	11	2457090		17 18 19 20 21 22 23			18 19 20 21 22 23 24		PAREMOTEP 1731	29 30 1 2 3 4 5	MAGĀBIT 2007
	15 16 17 18 19 ●[b] 21	9:36	12	2457097	NISAN 5775	24 25 26 27 28 29 1	Fri 12h43m3p	MONTH 2 Yĭ-Wèi	25 26 27 28 29 1 2	**Chūn fēn**		6 7 8 9 10 11 12	
	22 23 24 25 26 ◐ 28	7:42	13	2457104		2 3 4 5 6 7 8			3 4 5 6 7 8 9			13 14 15 16 17 18 19	
APRIL 2015	29 30 31 1 2 3 ○	12:05	14	2457111		9 10 11 12 13 14 15[g]			10 11 12 13 14 15 16			20 21 22 23 24 25 26	
	5 6 7 8 9 10 11		15	2457118		16 17 18 19 20 21 22			17[c] 18 19 20 21 22 23	*Qīng míng*	PARMOUTE 1731	27 28 29 30 1 2 3	MIYĀZYĀ 2007
	◑ 13 14 15 16 17 ●	3:44 18:57	16	2457125		23 24 25 26 27 28 29			24 25 26 27 28 29 30*			4[f] 5 6 7 8 9 10	
	19 20 21 22 23 24 ◐	23:55	17	2457132	IYYAR 5775	30 1 2 3 4 5 6	Sun 1h27m4p	MONTH 3 Yĭ-Wèi	1 2 3 4 5 6 7	**Gŭ yŭ**		11 12 13 14 15 16 17	
MAY 2015	26 27 28 29 30 1 2		18	2457139		7 8 9 10 11 12 13			8 9 10 11 12 13 14			18 19 20 21 22 23 24	
	3 ○ 5 6 7 8 9	3:42	19	2457146		14 15 16 17 18 19 20			15 16 17 18 19 20 21	*Lì xià*	PASHONS 1731	25 26 27 28 29[g] 30 1	GENBOT 2007
	10 ◑ 12 13 14 15 16	10:36	20	2457153		21 22 23 24 25 26 27			22 23 24 25 26 27 28			2 3 4 5 6 7 8	
	17 ● 19 20 21 22 23	4:13	21	2457160	SIVAN 5775	28 29 1 2 3 4 5	Mon 14h11m5p	MONTH 4 Yĭ-Wèi	29 1 2 3 4 5 6	**Xiăo măn**		9 10 11 12 13 14 15	
	24 ◐ 26 27 28 29 30	17:19	22	2457167		6[h] 7 8 9 10 11 12			7 8 9 10 11 12 13			16 17 18 19 20 21 22	
JUNE 2015	31 1 ○ 3 4 5 6	16:19	23	2457174		13 14 15 16 17 18 19			14 15 16 17 18 19 20	*Máng zhòng*		23 24 25 26 27 28 29	
	7 8 ◑ 10 11 12 13	15:42	24	2457181		20 21 22 23 24 25 26			21 22 23 24 25 26 27		PAÔNE 1731	30 1 2 3 4 5 6	SANĒ 2007
	14 15 ● 17 18 19 20	14:05	25	2457188	TAMMUZ 5775	27 28 29 30 1 2 3	Wed 2h55m6p	MONTH 5 Yĭ-Wèi	28 29 1 2* 3 4 5[d]			7 8 9 10 11 12 13	
	21[c] 22 23 ◐ 25 26 27	11:02	26	2457195		4 5 6 7 8 9 10			6 7 8 9 10 11 12	**Xià zhì**		14 15 16 17 18 19 20	
JULY 2015	28 29 30 1 ○ 3 4	2:19	27	2457202		11 12 13 14 15 16 17			13 14 15 16 17 18 19			21 22 23 24 25 26 27	
	5 6 7 ◑ 9 10 11	20:24	28	2457209		18 19 20 21 22 23 24			20 21 22 23 24 25 26	*Xiăo shŭ*	EPÊP 1731	28 29 30 1 2 3 4	ḤAMLĒ 2007
	12 13 14 15 ● 17 18	1:24	29	2457216	AV 5775	25 26 27 28 29 1 2	Thu 15h39m7p	MONTH 6 Yĭ-Wèi	27 28 29 30 1 2 3			5 6 7 8 9 10 11	
	19 20 21 22 23 ◐ 25	4:04	30	2457223		3 4 5 6 7 8 9			4 5 6 7 8 9 10	**Dà shŭ**		12 13 14 15 16 17 18	
AUGUST 2015	26 27 28 29 30 ○ 1	10:43	31	2457230		10[i] 11 12 13 14 15 16			11 12 13 14 15 16 17			19 20 21 22 23 24 25	
	2 3 4 5 6 ◑ 8	2:02	32	2457237		17 18 19 20 21 22 23			18 19 20 21 22 23 24	*Lì qiū*	MESORÊ 1731	26 27 28 29 30 1 2	NAḤASĒ 2007
	9 10 11 12 13 ● 15	14:53	33	2457244		24 25 26 27 28 29 30		MONTH 7 Yĭ-Wèi	25 26 27 28 29 1 2			3 4 5 6 7 8 9	
	16 17 18 19 20 21 ◐	19:31	34	2457251	ELUL 5775	1 2 3 4 5 6 7	Sat 4h23m8p		3* 4 5 6 7[e] 8 9			10 11 12 13[h] 14 15 16	
	23 24 25 26 27 28 ○	18:35	35	2457258		8 9 10 11 12 13 14			10 11 12 13 14 15[f] 16	**Chŭ shŭ**		17 18 19 20 21 22 23	
SEPTEMBER 2015	30 31 1 2 3 4 ◑	9:54	36	2457265		15 16 17 18 19 20 21			17 18 19 20 21 22 23			24 25 26 27 28 29 30	
	6 7 8 9 10 11 12		37	2457272		22 23 24 25 26 27 28			24 25 26 27 28 29 30	*Bái lù*	EPAG. 1731 / THOOUT 1732	1 2 3 4 5 6 1[a]	PĀG. 2007 / MASKARAM 2008
	● 14 15 16 17 18 19	6:41	38	2457279	TISHRI 5776	29 1[a] 2[a] 3 4 5 6	Sun 17h7m9p	MONTH 8 Yĭ-Wèi	1 2 3 4 5 6 7			2 3 4 5 6 7 8	
	20 ◐ 22 23[d] 24 25 26	8:59	39	2457286		7 8 9 10[b] 11 12 13			8 9 10 11 12 13 14	**Qiū fēn**		9 10 11 12 13 14 15	
OCTOBER 2015	27 ○ 29 30 1 2 3	2:50	40	2457293		14 15[c] 16 17 18 19 20			15[g] 16 17 18 19 20 21			16 17[b] 18 19 20 21 22	
	◑ 5 6 7 8 9 10	21:06	41	2457300		21 22 23 24 25 26 27			22 23 24 25 26 27 28	*Hán lù*		23 24 25 26 27 28 29	
	11 12 ● 14 15 16 17	0:05	42	2457307	HESHVAN 5776	28 29 30 1 2 3 4	Tue 5h51m10p	MONTH 9 Yĭ-Wèi	29 30 1 2 3* 4 5		PAOPE 1732	30 1 2 3 4 5 6	ṬEQEMT 2008
	18 19 ◐ 21 22 23 24	20:31	43	2457314		5 6 7 8 9 10 11			6 7 8 9[h] 10 11 12	**Shuāng jiàng**		7 8 9 10 11 12 13	
	25 26 ○ 28 29 30 31	12:05	44	2457321		12 13 14 15 16 17 18			13 14 15 16 17 18 19			14 15 16 17 18 19 20	
NOVEMBER 2015	1 2 ◑ 4 5 6 7	12:24	45	2457328		19 20 21 22 23 24 25			20 21 22 23 24 25 26			21 22 23 24 25 26 27	
	8 9 10 ● 12 13 14	17:47	46	2457335	KISLEV 5776	26 27 28 29 30 1 2	Wed 18h35m11p	MONTH 10 Yĭ-Wèi	27 28 29 30 1 2 3	*Lì dōng*	ATHÔR 1732	28 29 30 1 2 3 4	ḪEDĀR 2008
	15 16 17 18 ◐ 20 21	6:27	47	2457342		3 4 5 6 7 8 9			4 5 6 7 8 9 10			5 6 7 8 9 10 11	
	22 23 24 ○ 26 27 28	22:44	48	2457349		10 11 12 13 14 15 16			11 12 13 14 15 16 17	**Xiăo xuĕ**		12 13 14 15 16 17 18	
DECEMBER 2015	29 30 1 2 ◑ 4 5	7:40	49	2457356		17 18 19 20 21 22 23			18 19 20 21 22 23 24			19 20 21 22 23 24 25	
	6 7 8 9 10 ● 12	10:29	50	2457363		24[d] 25[e] 26[e] 27[e] 28[e] 29[e] 30[e]		MONTH 11 Yĭ-Wèi	25 26 27 28 29 1 2	*Dà xuĕ*	KOIAK 1732	26 27 28 29 30 1 2	TĀKHŚĀŚ 2008
	13 14 15 16 17 ◐ 19	15:14	51	2457370	TEVETH 5776	1[e] 2[e] 3 4 5 6 7	Fri 7h19m12p		3 4* 5 6 7 8 9			3 4 5 6 7 8 9	
	20 21 22[e] 23 24 ○ 26	11:11	52	2457377		8 9 10 11 12 13 14			10 11 12[i] 13 14 15 16	**Dōng zhì**		10 11 12 13 14 15 16	
	27 28 29 30 31 1 ◑	5:30	53	2457384		15 16 17 18 19 20 21			17 18 19 20 21 22 23			17 18 19 20 21 22 23	

[a]New Year
[b]Spring (22:45)
[c]Summer (16:37)
[d]Autumn (8:20)
[e]Winter (4:47)
● New moon
◐ First quarter moon
○ Full moon
◑ Last quarter moon

‡Leap year
[a]New Year
[b]Yom Kippur
[c]Sukkot
[d]Winter starts
[e]Ḥanukkah
[f]Purim
[g]Passover
[h]Shavuot
[i]Fast of Av

‡Leap year
[a]New Year (4713, Sheep)
[b]Lantern Festival
[c]Qīngmíng
[d]Dragon Festival
[e]Qīqiăo
[f]Hungry Ghosts
[g]Mid-Autumn Festival
[h]Double-Ninth Festival
[i]Dōngzhì
*Start of 60-name cycle

‡Leap year
[a]New Year
[b]Building of the Cross
[c]Christmas
[d]Jesus's Circumcision
[e]Epiphany
[f]Easter
[g]Mary's Announcement
[h]Jesus's Transfiguration

PERSIAN (ASTRONOMICAL) 1393/1394

Month	Sun	Mon	Tue	Wed	Thu	Fri	Sat
DEY 1393	7	8	9	10	11	12	13
	14	15	16	17	18	19	20
	21	22	23	24	25	26	27
	28	29	30	*1*	2	3	4
BAHMAN 1393	5	6	7	8	9	10	11
	12	13	14	15	16	17	18
	19	20	21	22	23	24	25
	26	27	28	29	30	*1*	2
ESFAND 1393	3	4	5	6	7	8	9
	10	11	12	13	14	15	16
	17	18	19	20	21	22	23
	24	25	26	27	28	29	*1*[a]
FARVARDĪN 1394	2	3	4	5	6	7	8
	9	10	11	12	13[b]	14	15
	16	17	18	19	20	21	22
	23	24	25	26	27	28	29
ORDĪBEHEŠT 1394	30	31	*1*	2	3	4	5
	6	7	8	9	10	11	12
	13	14	15	16	17	18	19
	20	21	22	23	24	25	26
	27	28	29	30	31	*1*	2
XORDĀD 1394	3	4	5	6	7	8	9
	10	11	12	13	14	15	16
	17	18	19	20	21	22	23
	24	25	26	27	28	29	30
TĪR 1394	31	*1*	2	3	4	5	6
	7	8	9	10	11	12	13
	14	15	16	17	18	19	20
	21	22	23	24	25	26	27
MORDĀD 1394	28	29	30	31	*1*	2	3
	4	5	6	7	8	9	10
	11	12	13	14	15	16	17
	18	19	20	21	22	23	24
	25	26	27	28	29	30	31
SHAHRĪVAR 1394	*1*	2	3	4	5	6	7
	8	9	10	11	12	13	14
	15	16	17	18	19	20	21
	22	23	24	25	26	27	28
MEHR 1394	29	30	31	*1*	2	3	4
	5	6	7	8	9	10	11
	12	13	14	15	16	17	18
	19	20	21	22	23	24	25
ĀBĀN 1394	26	27	28	29	30	*1*	2
	3	4	5	6	7	8	9
	10	11	12	13	14	15	16
	17	18	19	20	21	22	23
	24	25	26	27	28	29	30
ĀZAR 1394	*1*	2	3	4	5	6	7
	8	9	10	11	12	13	14
	15	16	17	18	19	20	21
	22	23	24	25	26	27	28
DEY 1394	29	30	*1*	2	3	4	5
	6	7	8	9	10	11	12

HINDU LUNAR 2071/2072‡

Month	Sun	Mon	Tue	Wed	Thu	Fri	Sat
PAUSHA 2071	7	8	9	10	11	12	13
	14	15	16	17	18	19	20
	21	22	23	24	25	26	27
	28	29	30	1	2	3	4
MĀGHA 2071	**5**	7	8	9	10	11	12
	13	14	15	16	17	*17*	18
	19	20	21	22	23	24	25
	26	27	28[h]	**29**	1	2	3
PHĀLGUNA 2071	4	5	6	7	8	9	10
	11	12	13	14	15[i]	16	17
	18	19	20	21	*21*	23	24
	25	26	27	28	29	30	1[a]
CHAITRA 2072	2	3	**4**	6	7	8	9[b]
	10	*10*	11	12	13	14	15
	16	17	18	19	20	21	22
	23	24	25	26	**27**	29	30
VAIŚĀKHA 2072	1	2	3	4	5	6	7
	8	9	10	11	12	13	14
	14	15	16	17	18	19	**20**
	22	23	24	25	26	27	28
JYAISHṬHA 2072	29	30	1	2	3	4	5
	6	7	8	9	10	11	12
	13	14	15	16	17	18	19
	20	21	22	23	**24**	26	27
LEAP ĀSHĀḌHA 2072	28	29	30	1	2	3	4
	5	6	7	8	9	10	*10*
	11	12	13	14	15	**16**	18
	19	20	21	22	23	24	25
ĀSHĀḌHA 2072	26	27	28	29	30	1	2
	3	4	5	6	7	8	9
	10	11	12	13	14	15	16
	17	18	**19**	21	22	23	24
ŚRĀVAṆA 2072	25	26	27	28	29	30	1
	2	3	4	5	6	7	*7*
	8	9	10	**11**	13	14	15
	16	17	18	19	20	21	22
	23[c]	**24**	26	27	*27*	28	29
BHĀDRAPADA 2072	30	1	2	3	4[d]	5	6
	7	8	9	10	11	12	13
	14	**15**	17	18	19	20	21
	22	23	24	25	26	27	28
ĀŚVINA 2072	29	30	1	2	*2*	3	4
	5	6	7	**8**[e]	**9**[e]	11	12
	13	14	15	16	17	18	19
	20	21	22	23	24	25	26
KĀRTTIKA 2072	27	28	29	30	1[f]	2	3
	4	5	6	7	8	9	10
	11	12	**13**	15	16	17	18
	19	20	21	22	23	24	25
MĀRGAŚĪRA 2072	*25*	26	27	28	29	30	1
	2	3	4	5	6	**7**	9
	10	11[g]	12	13	14	15	16
	17	18	19	20	21	22	23

HINDU SOLAR 1936/1937

Month	Sun	Mon	Tue	Wed	Thu	Fri	Sat
PAUSHA 1936	13	14	15	16	17	18	19
	20	21	22	23	24	25	26
MĀGHA 1936	27	28	29	1[b]	2	3	4
	5	6	7	8	9	10	11
	12	13	14	15	16	17	18
	19	20	21	22	23	24	25
PHĀLGUNA 1936	26	27	28	29	30	1	2
	3	4	5	6	7	8	9
	10	11	12	13	14	15	16
	17	18	19	20	21	22	23
CHAITRA 1936	24	25	26	27	28	29	1
	2	3	4	5	6	7	8
	9	10	11	12	13	14	15
	16	17	18	19	20	21	22
	23	24	25	26	27	28	29
VAIŚĀKHA 1937	30	31	1[a]	2	3	4	5
	6	7	8	9	10	11	12
	13	14	15	16	17	18	19
	20	21	22	23	24	25	26
JYAISHṬHA 1937	27	28	29	30	31	1	2
	3	4	5	6	7	8	9
	10	11	12	13	14	15	16
	17	18	19	20	21	22	23
	24	25	26	27	28	29	30
ĀSHĀḌHA 1937	31	1	2	3	4	5	6
	7	8	9	10	11	12	13
	14	15	16	17	18	19	20
	21	22	23	24	25	26	27
ŚRĀVAṆA 1937	28	29	30	31	32	1	2
	3	4	5	6	7	8	9
	10	11	12	13	14	15	16
	17	18	19	20	21	22	23
	24	25	26	27	28	29	30
BHĀDRAPADA 1937	31	1	2	3	4	5	6
	7	8	9	10	11	12	13
	14	15	16	17	18	19	20
	21	22	23	24	25	26	27
ĀŚVINA 1937	28	29	30	31	1	2	3
	4	5	6	7	8	9	10
	11	12	13	14	15	16	17
	18	19	20	21	22	23	24
	25	26	27	28	29	30	31
KĀRTTIKA 1937	1	2	3	4	5	6	7
	8	9	10	11	12	13	14
	15	16	17	18	19	20	21
	22	23	24	25	26	27	28
MĀRGAŚĪRA 1937	29	30	1	2	3	4	5
	6	7	8	9	10	11	12
	13	14	15	16	17	18	19
	20	21	22	23	24	25	26
PAUSHA 1937	27	28	29	1	2	3	4
	5	6	7	8	9	10	11
	12	13	14	15	16	17	18

ISLAMIC (ASTRONOMICAL) 1436/1437

Month	Sun	Mon	Tue	Wed	Thu	Fri	Sat
RABĪ' I 1436	6	7	8	9	10	11	12[c]
	13	14	15	16	17	18	19
	20	21	22	23	24	25	26
RABĪ' II 1436	27	28	29	30	*1*	2	3
	4	5	6	7	8	9	10
	11	12	13	14	15	16	17
	18	19	20	21	22	23	24
JUMĀDĀ I 1436	25	26	27	28	29	*1*	2
	3	4	5	6	7	8	9
	10	11	12	13	14	15	16
	17	18	19	20	21	22	23
	24	25	26	27	28	29	30
JUMĀDĀ II 1436	*1*	2	3	4	5	6	7
	8	9	10	11	12	13	14
	15	16	17	18	19	20	21
	22	23	24	25	26	27	28
RAJAB 1436	29	*1*	2	3	4	5	6
	7	8	9	10	11	12	13
	14	15	16	17	18	19	20
	21	22	23	24	25	26	27[d]
SHA'BĀN 1436	28	29	1	*2*	3	4	5
	6	7	8	9	10	11	12
	13	14	15	16	17	18	19
	20	21	22	23	24	25	26
RAMAḌĀN 1436	27	28	29	30	*1*[e]	2	3
	4	5	6	7	8	9	10
	11	12	13	14	15	16	17
	18	19	20	21	22	23	24
SHAWWĀL 1436	25	26	27	28	29	30	*1*[f]
	2	3	4	5	6	7	8
	9	10	11	12	13	14	15
	16	17	18	19	20	21	22
	23	24	25	26	27	28	29
DHU AL-QA'DA 1436	30	1	2	3	4	5	6
	7	8	9	10	11	12	13
	14	15	16	17	18	19	20
	21	22	23	24	25	26	27
DHU AL-ḤIJJA 1436	28	29	*1*	2	3	4	5
	6	7	8	9	10[g]	11	12
	13	14	15	16	17	18	19
	20	21	22	23	24	25	26
MUḤARRAM 1437	27	28	29	1[a]	2[â]	3	4
	5	6	7	8	9	10[b]	11
	12	13	14	15	16	17	18
	19	20	21	22	23	24	25
ṢAFAR 1437	26	27	28	29	30	1	2
	3	4	5	6	7	8	9
	10	11	12	13	14	15	16
	17	18	19	20	21	22	23
	24	25	26	27	28	29	30
RABĪ' I 1437	*1*	2	3	4	5	6	7
	8	9	10	11	12[c]	13	14
	15	16	17	18	19	20	21

GREGORIAN 2015

Julian (Sun)	Sun	Mon	Tue	Wed	Thu	Fri	Sat	Month
Dec 15	28	29	30	31	1	2	3	JANUARY 2015
	4	5	6	7[a]	8	9	10	
Dec 29	*11*	12	13	14[b]	15	16	17	
	18	19	20	21	22	23	24	
Jan 12	25	26	27	28	29	30	31	
	1	2	3	4	5	6	7	FEBRUARY 2015
Jan 26	8	9	10	11	12	13	14	
	15	16	17	18[c]	19	20	21	
Feb 9	22	23	24	25	26	27	28	
	1[d]	2	3	4	5	6	7	MARCH 2015
Feb 23	8	9	10	11	12	13	14	
	15	16	17	18	19	20	21	
Mar 9	22	23	24	25	26	27	28	
	29	30	31	1	2	3	4	APRIL 2015
Mar 23	5[e]	6	7	8	9	10	11	
	12[f]	13	14	15	16	17	18	
Apr 6	19	20	21	22	23	24	25	
	26	27	28	29	30	1	2	MAY 2015
Apr 20	3	4	5	6	7	8	9	
	10	11	12	13	14	15	16	
May 4	17	18	19	20	21	22	23	
	24	25	26	27	28	29	30	
May 18	31	1	2	3	4	5	6	JUNE 2015
	7	8	9	10	11	12	13	
Jun 1	14	15	16	17	18	19	20	
	21	22	23	24	25	26	27	
Jun 15	28	29	30	1	2	3	4	JULY 2015
	5	6	7	8	9	10	11	
Jun 29	12	13	14	15	16	17	18	
	19	20	21	22	23	24	25	
Jul 13	26	27	28	29	30	31	1	AUGUST 2015
	2	3	4	5	6	7	8	
Jul 27	9	10	11	12	13	14	15	
	16	17	18	19	20	21	22	
Aug 10	23	24	25	26	27	28	29	
	30	31	1	2	3	4	5	SEPTEMBER 2015
Aug 24	6	7	8	9	10	11	12	
	13	14	15	16	17	18	19	
Sep 7	20	21	22	23	24	25	26	
	27	28	29	30	1	2	3	OCTOBER 2015
Sep 21	4	5	6	7	8	9	10	
	11	12	13	14	15	16	17	
Oct 5	18	19	20	21	22	23	24	
	25	26	27	28	29	30	31	
Oct 19	1	2	3	4	5	6	7	NOVEMBER 2015
	8	9	10	11	12	13	14	
Nov 2	15	16	17	18	19	20	21	
	22	23	24	25	26	27	28	
Nov 16	29[g]	30	1	2	3	4	5	DECEMBER 2015
	6	7	8	9	10	11	12	
Nov 30	13	14	15	16	17	18	19	
	20	21	22	23	24	25[h]	26	
Dec 14	27	28	29	30	31	1	2	

Persian: [a]New Year; [b]Sizdeh Bedar

Hindu Lunar: ‡Leap year; [a]New Year (Manmatha); [b]Birthday of Rāma; [c]Birthday of Krishna; [d]Ganēśa Chaturthī; [e]Dashara; [f]Diwali; [g]Birthday of Vishnu; [h]Night of Śiva; [i]Holi

Hindu Solar: [a]New Year (Kīlaka); [b]Pongal

Islamic: [a]New Year; [â]New Year (Arithmetic); [b]'Ashūrā'; [c]Prophet's Birthday; [d]Ascent of the Prophet; [e]Start of Ramaḍān; [f]'Īd al-Fiṭr; [g]'Īd al-'Aḍḥā

Gregorian: [a]Orthodox Christmas; [b]Julian New Year; [c]Ash Wednesday; [d]Feast of Orthodoxy; [e]Easter; [f]Orthodox Easter; [g]Advent; [h]Christmas

2016

GREGORIAN 2016‡ · Lunar Phases · ISO WEEK · JULIAN DAY

Month	Sun	Mon	Tue	Wed	Thu	Fri	Sat	Lunar Phases	ISO WEEK (Mon)	JULIAN DAY (Sun noon)
	27	28	29	30	31	1[a]	◑	5:30	53	2457384
JANUARY 2016	3	4	5	6	7	8	9		1	2457391
	●	11	12	13	14	15	◐	1:30 23:26	2	2457398
	17	18	19	20	21	22	23		3	2457405
	○	25	26	27	28	29	30	1:46	4	2457412
	31	◑	2	3	4	5	6	3:28	5	2457419
FEBRUARY 2016	7	●	9	10	11	12	13	14:39	6	2457426
	14	◐	16	17	18	19	20	7:46	7	2457433
	21	○	23	24	25	26	27	18:20	8	2457440
	28	29	◑	2	3	4	5	23:10	9	2457447
MARCH 2016	6	7	8	●	10	11	12	1:54	10	2457454
	13	14	◐	16	17	18	19	17:03	11	2457461
	20[b]	21	22	○	24	25	26	12:01	12	2457468
	27	28	29	30	◑	1	2	15:17	13	2457475
APRIL 2016	3	4	5	6	●	8	9	11:24	14	2457482
	10	11	12	13	◐	15	16	3:59	15	2457489
	17	18	19	20	21	○	23	5:23	16	2457496
	24	25	26	27	28	29	◑	3:28	17	2457503
	1	2	3	4	5	●	7	19:29	18	2457510
MAY 2016	8	9	10	11	12	◐	14	17:02	19	2457517
	15	16	17	18	19	20	○	21:14	20	2457524
	22	23	24	25	26	27	28		21	2457531
	◑	30	31	1	2	3	4	12:12	22	2457538
JUNE 2016	●	6	7	8	9	10	11	2:59	23	2457545
	◐	13	14	15	16	17	18	8:10	24	2457552
	19	○[c]	21	22	23	24	25	11:02	25	2457559
	26	◑	28	29	30	1	2	18:18	26	2457566
JULY 2016	3	●	5	6	7	8	9	11:01	27	2457573
	10	11	◐	13	14	15	16	0:52	28	2457580
	17	18	○	20	21	22	23	22:56	29	2457587
	24	25	◑	27	28	29	30	22:59	30	2457594
	31	1	●	3	4	5	6	20:44	31	2457601
AUGUST 2016	7	8	9	◐	11	12	13	18:21	32	2457608
	14	15	16	17	○	19	20	9:26	33	2457615
	21	22	23	24	◑	26	27	3:41	34	2457622
	28	29	30	31	●	2	3	9:03	35	2457629
SEPTEMBER 2016	4	5	6	7	8	◐	10	11:49	36	2457636
	11	12	13	14	15	○	17	19:05	37	2457643
	18	19	20	21	22[d]	◑	24	9:56	38	2457650
	25	26	27	28	29	30	●	0:11	39	2457657
OCTOBER 2016	2	3	4	5	6	7	8		40	2457664
	◐	10	11	12	13	14	15	4:33	41	2457671
	○	17	18	19	20	21	◑	4:23 19:14	42	2457678
	23	24	25	26	27	28	29		43	2457685
	●	31	1	2	3	4	5	17:38	44	2457692
NOVEMBER 2016	6	◐	8	9	10	11	12	19:51	45	2457699
	13	○	15	16	17	18	19	13:52	46	2457706
	20	◑	22	23	24	25	26	8:33	47	2457713
	27	28	●	30	1	2	3	12:18	48	2457720
DECEMBER 2016	4	5	6	◐	8	9	10	9:03	49	2457727
	11	12	13	○	15	16	17	0:06	50	2457734
	18	19	20	◑[e]	22	23	24	1:56	51	2457741
	25	26	27	28	●	30	31	6:53	52	2457748

HEBREW 5776‡/5777

ISO WEEK	Month	Sun	Mon	Tue	Wed	Thu	Fri	Sat	Molad
53		15	16	17	18	19	20	21	
1	TEVETH 5776	22	23	24	25	26	27	28	
2		29	1	2	3	4	5	6	Sat 20h3m13p
3	SHEVAT 5776	7	8	9	10	11	12	13	
4		14	15	16	17	18	19	20	
5		21	22	23	24	25	26	27	
6		28	29	30	1	2	3	4	Mon 8h47m14p
7	ADAR I 5776	5	6	7	8	9	10	11	
8		12	13	14	15	16	17	18	
9		19	20	21	22	23	24	25	
10		26	27	28	29	30	1	2	Tue 21h31m15p
11	ADAR II 5776	3	4	5	6	7	8	9	
12		10	11	12	13	14[f]	15	16	
13		17	18	19	20	21	22	23	
14		24	25	26	27	28	29	1	Thu 10h15m16p
15		2	3	4	5	6	7	8	
16	NISAN 5776	9	10	11	12	13	14	15[g]	
17		16	17	18	19	20	21	22	
18		23	24	25	26	27	28	29	Fri 22h59m17p
19		30	1	2	3	4	5	6	
20		7	8	9	10	11	12	13	
21	IYAR 5776	14	15	16	17	18	19	20	
22		21	22	23	24	25	26	27	
23		28	29	1	2	3	4	5	Sun 11h44m0p
24		6[h]	7	8	9	10	11	12	
25	SIVAN 5776	13	14	15	16	17	18	19	
26		20	21	22	23	24	25	26	
27		27	28	29	30	1	2	3	Tue 0h28m1p
28	TAMMUZ 5776	4	5	6	7	8	9	10	
29		11	12	13	14	15	16	17	
30		18	19	20	21	22	23	24	
31		25	26	27	28	29	1	2	Wed 13h12m2p
32	AV 5776	3	4	5	6	7	8	9	
33		10[i]	11	12	13	14	15	16	
34		17	18	19	20	21	22	23	
35		24	25	26	27	28	29	30	Fri 1h56m3p
36		1	2	3	4	5	6	7	
37	ELUL 5776	8	9	10	11	12	13	14	
38		15	16	17	18	19	20	21	
39		22	23	24	25	26	27	28	Sat 14h40m4p
40		29	1[a]	2[a]	3	4	5	6	
41	TISHRI 5777	7	8	9	10[b]	11	12	13	
42		14	15[c]	16	17	18	19	20	
43		21	22	23	24	25	26	27	
44		28	29	30	1	2	3	4	Mon 3h24m5p
45	HESHVAN 5777	5	6	7	8	9	10	11	
46		12	13	14	15	16	17	18	
47		19	20	21	22	23	24	25	
48		26	27	28	29	1	2	3	Tue 16h8m6p
49		4	5[d]	6	7	8	9	10	
50	KISLEV 5777	11	12	13	14	15	16	17	
51		18	19	20	21	22	23	24	
52		25[e]	26[e]	27[e]	28[e]	29[e]	1[e]	2[e]	Thu 4h52m7p

CHINESE Yǐ-Wèi/Bǐng-Shēn

ISO WEEK	Month	Sun	Mon	Tue	Wed	Thu	Fri	Sat	Solar Term
53	MONTH 11 Yǐ-Wèi	17	18	19	20	21	22	23	
1		24	25	26	27	28	29	30	Xiǎo hán
2		1	2	3	4	5	6	7	
3	MONTH 12 Yǐ-Wèi	8	9	10	11	12	13	14	Dà hán
4		15	16	17	18	19	20	21	
5		22	23	24	25	26	27	28	Lì chūn
6		29	1[a]	2	3	4	5*	6	
7	MONTH 1 Bǐng-Shēn	7	8	9	10	11	12	13	Yǔ shuǐ
8		14	15[b]	16	17	18	19	20	
9		21	22	23	24	25	26	27	Jīng zhé
10		28	29	30	1	2	3	4	
11	MONTH 2 Bǐng-Shēn	5	6	7	8	9	10	11	
12		12	13	14	15	16	17	18	Chūn fēn
13		19	20	21	22	23	24	25	
14		26	27[c]	28	29	1	2	3	Qīng míng
15	MONTH 3 Bǐng-Shēn	4	5	6*	7	8	9	10	
16		11	12	13	14	15	16	17	Gǔ yǔ
17		18	19	20	21	22	23	24	
18		25	26	27	28	29	30	1	Lì xià
19	MONTH 4 Bǐng-Shēn	2	3	4	5	6	7	8	
20		9	10	11	12	13	14	15	Xiǎo mǎn
21		16	17	18	19	20	21	22	
22		23	24	25	26	27	28	29	
23		1	2	3	4	5[d]	6	7*	Máng zhòng
24	MONTH 5 Bǐng-Shēn	8	9	10	11	12	13	14	
25		15	16	17	18	19	20	21	Xià zhì
26		22	23	24	25	26	27	28	
27		29	1	2	3	4	5	6	Xiǎo shǔ
28	MONTH 6 Bǐng-Shēn	7	8	9	10	11	12	13	
29		14	15	16	17	18	19	20	Dà shǔ
30		21	22	23	24	25	26	27	
31		28	29	30	1	2	3	4	
32	MONTH 7 Bǐng-Shēn	5	6	7[e]	8*	9	10	11	Lì qiū
33		12	13	14	15[f]	16	17	18	
34		19	20	21	22	23	24	25	Chǔ shǔ
35		26	27	28	29	1	2	3	
36	MONTH 8 Bǐng-Shēn	4	5	6	7	8	9	10	Bái lù
37		11	12	13	14	15[g]	16	17	
38		18	19	20	21	22	23	24	Qiū fēn
39		25	26	27	28	29	30	1	
40	MONTH 9 Bǐng-Shēn	2	3	4	5	6	7	8	Hán lù
41		9[h]*	10	11	12	13	14	15	
42		16	17	18	19	20	21	22	
43		23	24	25	26	27	28	29	Shuāng jiàng
44		30	1	2	3	4	5	6	
45	MONTH 10 Bǐng-Shēn	7	8	9	10	11	12	13	Lì dōng
46		14	15	16	17	18	19	20	
47		21	22	23	24	25	26	27	Xiǎo xuě
48		28	29	1	2	3	4	5	
49	MONTH 11 Bǐng-Shēn	6	7	8	9	10*	11	12	Dà xuě
50		13	14	15	16	17	18	19	
51		20	21	22	23[i]	24	25	26	Dōng zhì
52		27	28	29	30	1	2	3	

COPTIC 1732/1733 · ETHIOPIC 2008/2009

ISO WEEK	Coptic Month	Sun	Mon	Tue	Wed	Thu	Fri	Sat	Ethiopic Month
53	KOIAK 1732	17	18	19	20	21	22	23	TĀKHŚĀŚ 2008
1		24	25	26	27	28	29[c]	30	
2		1	2	3	4	5	6[d]	7	
3	TŌBE 1732	8	9	10	11[e]	12	13	14	ṬER 2008
4		15	16	17	18	19	20	21	
5		22	23	24	25	26	27	28	
6		29	30	1	2	3	4	5	
7	MESHIR 1732	6	7	8	9	10	11	12	YAKĀTIT 2008
8		13	14	15	16	17	18	19	
9		20	21	22	23	24	25	26	
10		27	28	29	30	1	2	3	
11	PAREMOTEP 1732	4	5	6	7	8	9	10	MAGĀBIT 2008
12		11	12	13	14	15	16	17	
13		18	19	20	21	22	23	24	
14		25	26	27	28	29	30	1	
15		2	3	4	5	6	7	8	
16	PARMOUTE 1732	9	10	11	12	13	14	15	MIYĀZYĀ 2008
17		16	17	18	19	20	21	22	
18		23[f]	24	25	26	27	28	29[g]	
19		30	1	2	3	4	5	6	
20		7	8	9	10	11	12	13	
21	PASHONS 1732	14	15	16	17	18	19	20	GENBOT 2008
22		21	22	23	24	25	26	27	
23		28	29	30	1	2	3	4	
24		5	6	7	8	9	10	11	
25	PAŌNE 1732	12	13	14	15	16	17	18	SANĒ 2008
26		19	20	21	22	23	24	25	
27		26	27	28	29	30	1	2	
28		3	4	5	6	7	8	9	
29	EPĒP 1732	10	11	12	13	14	15	16	HAMLĒ 2008
30		17	18	19	20	21	22	23	
31		24	25	26	27	28	29	30	
32		1	2	3	4	5	6	7	
33	MESORĒ 1732	8	9	10	11	12	13[h]	14	NAḤASĒ 2008
34		15	16	17	18	19	20	21	
35		22	23	24	25	26	27	28	
36	EPAG. 1732	29	30	1	2	3	4	5	PĀG. 2008
37		1[a]	2	3	4	5	6	7	
38	THOOUT 1733	8	9	10	11	12	13	14	MASKARAM 2009
39		15	16	17[b]	18	19	20	21	
40		22	23	24	25	26	27	28	
41		29	30	1	2	3	4	5	
42	PAOPE 1733	6	7	8	9	10	11	12	ṬEQEMT 2009
43		13	14	15	16	17	18	19	
44		20	21	22	23	24	25	26	
45		27	28	29	30	1	2	3	
46	ATHŌR 1733	4	5	6	7	8	9	10	HEDĀR 2009
47		11	12	13	14	15	16	17	
48		18	19	20	21	22	23	24	
49		25	26	27	28	29	30	1	
50	KOIAK 1733	2	3	4	5	6	7	8	TĀKHŚĀŚ 2009
51		9	10	11	12	13	14	15	
52		16	17	18	19	20	21	22	

‡Leap year
[a]New Year
[b]Spring (4:30)
[c]Summer (22:34)
[d]Autumn (14:21)
[e]Winter (10:44)
● New moon
◐ First quarter moon
○ Full moon
◑ Last quarter moon

‡Leap year
[a]New Year
[b]Yom Kippur
[c]Sukkot
[d]Winter starts
[e]Ḥanukkah
[f]Purim
[g]Passover
[h]Shavuot
[i]Fast of Av

[a]New Year (4714, Monkey)
[b]Lantern Festival
[c]Qīngmíng
[d]Dragon Festival
[e]Qīqiǎo
[f]Hungry Ghosts
[g]Mid-Autumn Festival
[h]Double-Ninth Festival
[i]Dōngzhì
*Start of 60-name cycle

[a]New Year
[b]Building of the Cross
[c]Christmas
[d]Jesus's Circumcision
[e]Epiphany
[f]Easter
[g]Mary's Announcement
[h]Jesus's Transfiguration

2016

PERSIAN (ASTRONOMICAL) 1394/1395‡

Month	Sun	Mon	Tue	Wed	Thu	Fri	Sat
DEY 1394	6	7	8	9	10	11	12
	13	14	15	16	17	18	19
	20	21	22	23	24	25	26
	27	28	29	30	*1*	2	3
BAHMAN 1394	4	5	6	7	8	9	10
	11	12	13	14	15	16	17
	18	19	20	21	22	23	24
	25	26	27	28	29	30	*1*
ESFAND 1394	2	3	4	5	6	7	8
	9	10	11	12	13	14	15
	16	17	18	19	20	21	22
	23	24	25	26	27	28	29
FARVARDĪN 1395	1[a]	2	3	4	5	6	7
	8	9	10	11	12	13[b]	14
	15	16	17	18	19	20	21
	22	23	24	25	26	27	28
	29	30	31	*1*	2	3	4
ORDĪBEHEŠT 1395	5	6	7	8	9	10	11
	12	13	14	15	16	17	18
	19	20	21	22	23	24	25
	26	27	28	29	30	31	*1*
XORDĀD 1395	2	3	4	5	6	7	8
	9	10	11	12	13	14	15
	16	17	18	19	20	21	22
	23	24	25	26	27	28	29
	30	31	*1*	2	3	4	5
TĪR 1395	6	7	8	9	10	11	12
	13	14	15	16	17	18	19
	20	21	22	23	24	25	26
	27	28	29	30	31	*1*	2
MORDĀD 1395	3	4	5	6	7	8	9
	10	11	12	13	14	15	16
	17	18	19	20	21	22	23
	24	25	26	27	28	29	30
	31	*1*	2	3	4	5	6
SHAHRĪVAR 1395	7	8	9	10	11	12	13
	14	15	16	17	18	19	20
	21	22	23	24	25	26	27
	28	29	30	31	*1*	2	3
MEHR 1395	4	5	6	7	8	9	10
	11	12	13	14	15	16	17
	18	19	20	21	22	23	24
	25	26	27	28	29	30	*1*
ĀBĀN 1395	2	3	4	5	6	7	8
	9	10	11	12	13	14	15
	16	17	18	19	20	21	22
	23	24	25	26	27	28	29
	30	*1*	2	3	4	5	6
ĀZAR 1395	7	8	9	10	11	12	13
	14	15	16	17	18	19	20
	21	22	23	24	25	26	27
	28	29	30	*1*	2	3	4
DEY 1395	5	6	7	8	9	10	11

HINDU LUNAR 2072‡/2073

Month	Sun	Mon	Tue	Wed	Thu	Fri	Sat
MĀRGAŚĪRA 2072	17	18	19	20	21	22	23
	24	25	26	27	28	*28*	29
	30	2	3	4	5	6	7
PAUSHA 2072	8	9	10	11	12	13	**14**
	16	*16*	17	18	19	20	21
	22	23	24	25	26	27	28
	29	30	1	2	3	4	5
MĀGHA 2072	**6**	8	9	10	11	12	13
	14	15	16	17	18	19	20
	20	21	22	23	24	25	26
	27	28[h]	29	**30**	2	3	4
PHĀLGUNA 2072	5	6	7	8	9	10	11
	12	13	14	15[i]	16	17	18
	19	20	21	22	23	24	25
	26	27	28	29	30	1[a]	2
CHAITRA 2073	3	**4**	6	7	8	9[b]	10
	11	12	13	14	*14*	15	16
	17	18	19	20	21	22	23
	24	25	26	27	**28**	30	1
VAIŚĀKHA 2073	2	3	4	5	6	7	8
	9	10	11	12	13	14	15
	16	17	18	19	20	21	22
	23	24	25	26	27	28	29
	30	**1**	3	4	5	6	7
JYAISHṬHA 2073	8	9	*9*	10	11	12	13
	14	15	16	17	18	19	20
	21	22	23	**24**	26	27	28
	29	30	1	2	3	4	5
ĀSHĀḌHA 2073	6	7	8	9	10	11	12
	13	14	15	16	17	18	19
	20	21	22	23	24	25	26
	27	29	30	1	2	3	4
ŚRĀVAṆA 2073	5	6	*6*	7	8	9	10
	11	12	13	14	15	16	17
	18	**19**	21	22	23[c]	24	25
	26	27	28	29	30	1	2
BHĀDRAPADA 2073	3	4[d]	5	6	7	8	9
	10	11	12	13	14	15	16
	17	18	19	20	21	22	**23**
	25	26	27	28	29	30	1
ĀŚVINA 2073	2	2	3	4	5	6	7
	8[e]	9[e]	10[e]	11	12	13	14
	15	**16**	18	19	20	21	22
	23	24	25	26	27	28	29
	30	1[f]	2	3	4	5	5
KĀRTTIKA 2073	6	7	8	**9**	11	12	13
	14	15	16	17	18	19	20
	21	22	23	24	25	26	27
	28	29	30	1	2	3	4
MĀRGAŚĪRA 2073	5	6	7	8	9	10	11[g]
	12	13	**14**	16	17	18	19
	20	21	22	23	24	25	26
	27	28	*28*	29	30	1	2

HINDU SOLAR 1937/1938

Month	Sun	Mon	Tue	Wed	Thu	Fri	Sat
PAUSHA 1937	12	13	14	15	16	17	18
	19	20	21	22	23	24	25
	26	27	28	29	1[b]	2	3
MĀGHA 1937	4	5	6	7	8	9	10
	11	12	13	14	15	16	17
	18	19	20	21	22	23	24
	25	26	27	28	29	30	1
PHĀLGUNA 1937	2	3	4	5	6	7	8
	9	10	11	12	13	14	15
	16	17	18	19	20	21	22
	23	24	25	26	27	28	29
	30	1	2	3	4	5	6
CHAITRA 1937	7	8	9	10	11	12	13
	14	15	16	17	18	19	20
	21	22	23	24	25	26	27
	28	29	30	1[a]	2	3	4
VAIŚĀKHA 1938	5	6	7	8	9	10	11
	12	13	14	15	16	17	18
	19	20	21	22	23	24	25
	26	27	28	29	30	31	1
JYAISHṬHA 1938	2	3	4	5	6	7	8
	9	10	11	12	13	14	15
	16	17	18	19	20	21	22
	23	24	25	26	27	28	29
	30	31	1	2	3	4	5
ĀSHĀḌHA 1938	6	7	8	9	10	11	12
	13	14	15	16	17	18	19
	20	21	22	23	24	25	26
	27	28	29	30	31	32	1
ŚRĀVAṆA 1938	2	3	4	5	6	7	8
	9	10	11	12	13	14	15
	16	17	18	19	20	21	22
	23	24	25	26	27	28	29
	30	31	32	1	2	3	4
BHĀDRAPADA 1938	5	6	7	8	9	10	11
	12	13	14	15	16	17	18
	19	20	21	22	23	24	25
	26	27	28	29	30	31	1
ĀŚVINA 1938	2	3	4	5	6	7	8
	9	10	11	12	13	14	15
	16	17	18	19	20	21	22
	23	24	25	26	27	28	29
	30	1	2	3	4	5	6
KĀRTTIKA 1938	7	8	9	10	11	12	13
	14	15	16	17	18	19	20
	21	22	23	24	25	26	27
	28	29	30	1	2	3	4
MĀRGAŚĪRA 1938	5	6	7	8	9	10	11
	12	13	14	15	16	17	18
	19	20	21	22	23	24	25
	26	27	28	29	1	2	3
PAUSHA 1938	4	5	6	7	8	9	10
	11	12	13	14	15	16	17

ISLAMIC (ASTRONOMICAL) 1437/1438

Month	Sun	Mon	Tue	Wed	Thu	Fri	Sat
RABĪ' I 1437	15	16	17	18	19	20	21
	22	23	24	25	26	27	28
	29	*1*	2	3	4	5	6
RABĪ' II 1437	7	8	9	10	11	12	13
	14	15	16	17	18	19	20
	21	22	23	24	25	26	27
	28	29	30	*1*	2	3	4
JUMĀDĀ I 1437	5	6	7	8	9	10	11
	12	13	14	15	16	17	18
	19	20	21	22	23	24	25
	26	27	28	29	*1*	2	3
JUMĀDĀ II 1437	4	5	6	7	8	9	10
	11	12	13	14	15	16	17
	18	19	20	21	22	23	24
	25	26	27	28	29	30	*1*
RAJAB 1437	2	3	4	5	6	7	8
	9	10	11	12	13	14	15
	16	17	18	19	20	21	22
	23	24	25	26	27[d]	28	29
SHA'BĀN 1437	1	2	3	4	5	6	7
	8	9	10	11	12	13	14
	15	16	17	18	19	20	21
	22	23	24	25	26	27	28
	29	1[e]	2	3	4	5	6
RAMAḌĀN 1437	7	8	9	10	11	12	13
	14	15	16	17	18	19	20
	21	22	23	24	25	26	27
	28	29	30	1[f]	2	3	4
SHAWWĀL 1437	5	6	7	8	9	10	11
	12	13	14	15	16	17	18
	19	20	21	22	23	24	25
	26	27	28	29	30	*1*	2
DHU AL-QA'DA 1437	3	4	5	6	7	8	9
	10	11	12	13	14	15	16
	17	18	19	20	21	22	23
	24	25	26	27	28	29	1
DHU AL-HIJJA 1437	2	3	4	5	6	7	8
	9	10[g]	11	12	13	14	15
	16	17	18	19	20	21	22
	23	24	25	26	27	28	29
MUḤARRAM 1438	1[a]	2[a]	3	4	5	6	7
	8	9	10[b]	11	12	13	14
	15	16	17	18	19	20	21
	22	23	24	25	26	27	28
	29	30	1	2	3	4	5
ṢAFAR 1438	6	7	8	9	10	11	12
	13	14	15	16	17	18	19
	20	21	22	23	24	25	26
	27	28	29	30	*1*	2	3
RABĪ' I 1438	4	5	6	7	8	9	10
	11	12[c]	13	14	15	16	17
	18	19	20	21	22	23	24
	25	26	27	28	29	30	*1*

GREGORIAN 2016‡

Julian† (Sun)	Sun	Mon	Tue	Wed	Thu	Fri	Sat	Month
Dec 14	27	28	29	30	31	1	2	
	3	4	5	6	7[a]	8	9	JANUARY 2016
Dec 28	10	11	12	13	14[b]	15	16	
	17	18	19	20	21	22	23	
Jan 11	24	25	26	27	28	29	30	
	31	1	2	3	4	5	6	
Jan 25	7	8	9	10[c]	11	12	13	FEBRUARY 2016
	14	15	16	17	18	19	20	
Feb 8	21	22	23	24	25	26	27	
	28	29	1	2	3	4	5	
Feb 22	6	7	8	9	10	11	12	MARCH 2016
	13	14	15	16	17	18	19	
Mar 7	20[d]	21	22	23	24	25	26	
	27[e]	28	29	30	31	1	2	
Mar 21	3	4	5	6	7	8	9	APRIL 2016
	10	11	12	13	14	15	16	
Apr 4	17	18	19	20	21	22	23	
	24	25	26	27	28	29	30	
Apr 18	1[f]	2	3	4	5	6	7	
	8	9	10	11	12	13	14	MAY 2016
May 2	15	16	17	18	19	20	21	
	22	23	24	25	26	27	28	
May 16	29	30	31	1	2	3	4	
	5	6	7	8	9	10	11	JUNE 2016
May 30	12	13	14	15	16	17	18	
	19	20	21	22	23	24	25	
Jun 13	26	27	28	29	30	1	2	
	3	4	5	6	7	8	9	
Jun 27	10	11	12	13	14	15	16	JULY 2016
	17	18	19	20	21	22	23	
Jul 11	24	25	26	27	28	29	30	
	31	1	2	3	4	5	6	
Jul 25	7	8	9	10	11	12	13	AUGUST 2016
	14	15	16	17	18	19	20	
Aug 8	21	22	23	24	25	26	27	
	28	29	30	31	1	2	3	
Aug 22	4	5	6	7	8	9	10	SEPTEMBER 2016
	11	12	13	14	15	16	17	
Sep 5	18	19	20	21	22	23	24	
	25	26	27	28	29	30	1	
Sep 19	2	3	4	5	6	7	8	
	9	10	11	12	13	14	15	OCTOBER 2016
Oct 3	16	17	18	19	20	21	22	
	23	24	25	26	27	28	29	
Oct 17	30	31	1	2	3	4	5	
	6	7	8	9	10	11	12	NOVEMBER 2016
Oct 31	13	14	15	16	17	18	19	
	20	21	22	23	24	25	26	
Nov 14	27[g]	28	29	30	1	2	3	
	4	5	6	7	8	9	10	DECEMBER 2016
Nov 28	11	12	13	14	15	16	17	
	18	19	20	21	22	23	24	
Dec 12	25[h]	26	27	28	29	30	31	

Persian: ‡Leap year; [a]New Year; [b]Sizdeh Bedar

Hindu lunar: ‡Leap year; [a]New Year (Durmukha); [b]Birthday of Rāma; [c]Birthday of Krishna; [d]Ganēśa Chaturthī; [e]Dashara; [f]Diwali; [g]Birthday of Vishnu; [h]Night of Śiva; [i]Holi

Hindu solar: [a]New Year (Saumya); [b]Pongal

Islamic: [a]New Year; [a]New Year (Arithmetic); [b]'Ashūrā'; [c]Prophet's Birthday; [d]Ascent of the Prophet; [e]Start of Ramaḍān; [f]'Id al-Fiṭr; [g]'Id al-'Aḍḥā

Gregorian: ‡Leap year; [a]Orthodox Christmas; [b]Julian New Year; [c]Ash Wednesday; [d]Feast of Orthodoxy; [e]Easter; [f]Orthodox Easter; [g]Advent; [h]Christmas

2017

Month	Sun	Mon	Tue	Wed	Thu	Fri	Sat	Lunar Phases	ISO WEEK (Mon)	JULIAN DAY (Sun noon)
JANUARY 2017	1[a]	2	3	4	◐	6	7	19:47	1	2457755
	8	9	10	11	○	13	14	11:34	2	2457762
	15	16	17	18	◑	20	21	22:13	3	2457769
	22	23	24	25	26	27	●	0:07	4	2457776
FEBRUARY 2017	29	30	31	1	2	3	◐	4:18	5	2457783
	5	6	7	8	9	10	○	0:33	6	2457790
	12	13	14	15	16	17	◑	19:33	7	2457797
	19	20	21	22	23	24	25		8	2457804
MARCH 2017	●	27	28	1	2	3	4	14:58	9	2457811
	◐	6	7	8	9	10	11	11:32	10	2457818
	○	13	14	15	16	17	18	14:54	11	2457825
	19	◑[b]	21	22	23	24	25	15:58	12	2457832
APRIL 2017	26	27	●	29	30	31	1	2:57	13	2457839
	2	◐	4	5	6	7	8	18:39	14	2457846
	9	10	○	12	13	14	15	6:08	15	2457853
	16	17	18	◑	20	21	22	9:56	16	2457860
	23	24	25	●	27	28	29	12:16	17	2457867
MAY 2017	30	1	2	◐	4	5	6	2:47	18	2457874
	7	8	9	○	11	12	13	21:42	19	2457881
	14	15	16	17	18	◑	20	0:32	20	2457888
	21	22	23	24	●	26	27	19:44	21	2457895
JUNE 2017	28	29	30	31	◐	2	3	12:42	22	2457902
	4	5	6	7	8	○	10	13:09	23	2457909
	11	12	13	14	15	16	◑	11:33	24	2457916
	18	19	20	21[c]	22	23	●	2:31	25	2457923
JULY 2017	25	26	27	28	29	30	◐	0:51	26	2457930
	2	3	4	5	6	7	8		27	2457937
	○	10	11	12	13	14	15	4:06	28	2457944
	◑	17	18	19	20	21	22	19:25	29	2457951
	●	24	25	26	27	28	29	9:45	30	2457958
AUGUST 2017	◐	31	1	2	3	4	5	15:23	31	2457965
	6	○	8	9	10	11	12	18:11	32	2457972
	13	14	◑	16	17	18	19	1:15	33	2457979
	20	●	22	23	24	25	26	18:30	34	2457986
SEPTEMBER 2017	27	28	◐	30	31	1	2	8:13	35	2457993
	3	4	5	○	7	8	9	7:03	36	2458000
	10	11	12	◑	14	15	16	6:25	37	2458007
	17	18	19	●	21	22[d]	23	5:30	38	2458014
	24	25	26	27	◐	29	30	2:53	39	2458021
OCTOBER 2017	1	2	3	4	○	6	7	18:40	40	2458028
	8	9	10	11	◑	13	14	12:25	41	2458035
	15	16	17	18	●	20	21	19:12	42	2458042
	22	23	24	25	26	◐	28	22:22	43	2458049
NOVEMBER 2017	29	30	31	1	2	3	○	5:23	44	2458056
	5	6	7	8	9	◑	11	20:36	45	2458063
	12	13	14	15	16	17	●	11:42	46	2458070
	19	20	21	22	23	24	25		47	2458077
DECEMBER 2017	◐	27	28	29	30	1	2	17:03	48	2458084
	○	4	5	6	7	8	9	15:47	49	2458091
	◑	11	12	13	14	15	16	7:51	50	2458098
	17	●	19	20	21[e]	22	23	6:30	51	2458105
	24	25	◐	27	28	29	30	9:20	52	2458112
	31	1	○	3	4	5	6	2:24	1	2458119

ISO WEEK	HEBREW 5777/5778	Sun	Mon	Tue	Wed	Thu	Fri	Sat	Molad
1	TEVETH 5777	3[e]	4	5	6	7	8	9	
2		10	11	12	13	14	15	16	
3		17	18	19	20	21	22	23	
4	SHEVAT 5777	24	25	26	27	28	29	1	Fri $17^h36^m8^p$
5		2	3	4	5	6	7	8	
6		9	10	11	12	13	14	15	
7		16	17	18	19	20	21	22	
8		23	24	25	26	27	28	29	
9	ADAR 5777	30	1	2	3	4	5	6	Sun $6^h20^m9^p$
10		7	8	9	10	11	12	13	
11		14[f]	15	16	17	18	19	20	
12		21	22	23	24	25	26	27	
13	NISAN 5777	28	29	1	2	3	4	5	Mon $19^h4^m10^p$
14		6	7	8	9	10	11	12	
15		13	14	15[g]	16	17	18	19	
16		20	21	22	23	24	25	26	
17	IYYAR 5777	27	28	29	30	1	2	3	Wed $7^h48^m11^p$
18		4	5	6	7	8	9	10	
19		11	12	13	14	15	16	17	
20		18	19	20	21	22	23	24	
21	SIVAN 5777	25	26	27	28	29	1	2	Thu $20^h32^m12^p$
22		3	4	5	6[h]	7	8	9	
23		10	11	12	13	14	15	16	
24		17	18	19	20	21	22	23	
25		24	25	26	27	28	29	30	Sat $9^h16^m13^p$
26	TAMMUZ 5777	1	2	3	4	5	6	7	
27		8	9	10	11	12	13	14	
28		15	16	17	18	19	20	21	
29		22	23	24	25	26	27	28	
30	AV 5777	29	1	2	3	4	5	6	Sun $22^h0^m14^p$
31		7	8	9[i]	10	11	12	13	
32		14	15	16	17	18	19	20	
33		21	22	23	24	25	26	27	
34	ELUL 5777	28	29	30	1	2	3	4	Tue $10^h44^m15^p$
35		5	6	7	8	9	10	11	
36		12	13	14	15	16	17	18	
37		19	20	21	22	23	24	25	
38	TISHRI 5778	26	27	28	29	1[a]	2[a]	3	Wed $23^h28^m16^p$
39		4	5	6	7	8	9	10[b]	
40		11	12	13	14	15[c]	16	17	
41		18	19	20	21	22	23	24	
42	HESHVAN 5778	25	26	27	28	29	30	1	Fri $12^h12^m17^p$
43		2	3	4	5	6	7	8	
44		9	10	11	12	13	14	15	
45		16	17	18	19	20	21	22	
46		23	24	25	26	27	28	29	
47	KISLEV 5778	1	2	3	4	5	6	7	Sun $0^h57^m0^p$
48		8	9	10	11	12	13	14	
49		15	16	17[d]	18	19	20	21	
50		22	23	24	25[e]	26[e]	27[e]	28[e]	
51	TEVETH 5778	29[e]	30[e]	1[e]	2[e]	3	4	5	Mon $13^h41^m1^p$
52		6	7	8	9	10	11	12	
1		13	14	15	16	17	18	19	

ISO WEEK	CHINESE Bǐng-Shēn/Dīng-Yǒu‡	Sun	Mon	Tue	Wed	Thu	Fri	Sat	Solar Term
1	MONTH 12 Bǐng-Shēn	4	5	6	7	*8*	9	10	*Xiǎo hán*
2		11	12	13	14	15	16	17	
3		18	19	20	21	22	***23***	24	**Dà hán**
4	MONTH 1 Dīng-Yǒu	25	26	27	28	29	30	1[a]	
5		2	3	4	5	6	*7*	8	*Lì chūn*
6		9	10*	11	12	13	14	15[b]	
7		16	17	18	19	20	21	***22***	**Yǔ shuǐ**
8		23	24	25	26	27	28	29	
9	MONTH 2 Dīng-Yǒu	1	2	3	4	5	6	7	
10		*8*	9	10	11	12	13	14	*Jīng zhé*
11		15	16	17	18	19	20	21	
12		22	***23***	24	25	26	27	28	**Chūn fēn**
13	MONTH 3 Dīng-Yǒu	29	30	1	2	3	4	5	
14		6	7	*8*[c]	9	10	11*	12	*Qīng míng*
15		13	14	15	16	17	18	19	
16		20	21	22	23	***24***	25	26	**Gǔ yǔ**
17	MONTH 4 Dīng-Yǒu	27	28	29	1	2	3	4	
18		5	6	7	8	9	*10*	11	*Lì xià*
19		12	13	14	15	16	17	18	
20		19	20	21	22	23	24	25	
21	MONTH 5 Dīng-Yǒu	***26***	27	28	29	30	1	2	**Xiǎo mǎn**
22		3	4	5[d]	6	7	8	9	
23		10	*11*	12*	13	14	15	16	*Máng zhòng*
24		17	18	19	20	21	22	23	
25	MONTH 6 Dīng-Yǒu	24	25	26	***27***	28	29	1	**Xià zhì**
26		2	3	4	5	6	7	8	
27		9	10	11	12	13	*14*	15	*Xiǎo shǔ*
28		16	17	18	19	20	21	22	
29		23	24	25	26	27	28	***29***	**Dà shǔ**
30	*LEAP MONTH 6* Dīng-Yǒu	1	2	3	4	5	6	7	
31		8	9	10	11	12	13	14*	
32		15	*16*	17	18	19	20	21	*Lì qiū*
33		22	23	24	25	26	27	28	
34	MONTH 7 Dīng-Yǒu	29	30	1	***2***	3	4	5	**Chǔ shǔ**
35		6	7[e]	8	9	10	11	12	
36		13	14	15[f]	16	*17*	18	19	*Bái lù*
37		20	21	22	23	24	25	26	
38	MONTH 8 Dīng-Yǒu	27	28	29	1	2	3	***4***	**Qiū fēn**
39		5	6	7	8	9	10	11	
40		12	13	14	15[g]*	16	17	18	
41		*19*	20	21	22	23	24	25	*Hán lù*
42	MONTH 9 Dīng-Yǒu	26	27	28	29	30	1	2	
43		3	***4***	5	6	7	8	9[h]	**Shuāng jiàng**
44		10	11	12	13	14	15	16	
45		17	18	*19*	20	21	22	23	*Lì dōng*
46	MONTH 10 Dīng-Yǒu	24	25	26	27	28	29	1	
47		2	3	4	***5***	6	7	8	**Xiǎo xuě**
48		9	10	11	12	13	14	15	
49		16*	17	18	19	*20*	21	22	*Dà xuě*
50		23	24	25	26	27	28	29	
51	MONTH 11 Dīng-Yǒu	30	1	2	3	4	***5***[i]	6	**Dōng zhì**
52		7	8	9	10	11	12	13	
1		14	15	16	17	18	*19*	20	*Xiǎo hán*

ISO WEEK	COPTIC 1733/1734	Sun	Mon	Tue	Wed	Thu	Fri	Sat	ETHIOPIC 2009/2010
1	KOIAK 1733	23	24	25	26	27	28	29[c]	TĀKHŚĀŚ 2009
2	TÔBE 1733	30	1	2	3	4	5	6[d]	ṬER 2009
3		7	8	9	10	11[e]	12	13	
4		14	15	16	17	18	19	20	
5		21	22	23	24	25	26	27	
6	MESHIR 1733	28	29	30	1	2	3	4	YAKĀTIT 2009
7		5	6	7	8	9	10	11	
8		12	13	14	15	16	17	18	
9		19	20	21	22	23	24	25	
10	PAREMOTEP 1733	26	27	28	29	30	1	2	MAGĀBIT 2009
11		3	4	5	6	7	8	9	
12		10	11	12	13	14	15	16	
13		17	18	19	20	21	22	23	
14		24	25	26	27	28	29	30	
15	PARMOUTE 1733	1	2	3	4	5	6	7	MIYĀZYĀ 2009
16		8[f]	9	10	11	12	13	14	
17		15	16	17	18	19	20	21	
18		22	23	24	25	26	27	28	
19	PASHONS 1733	29[g]	30	1	2	3	4	5	GENBOT 2009
20		6	7	8	9	10	11	12	
21		13	14	15	16	17	18	19	
22		20	21	22	23	24	25	26	
23	PAÔNE 1733	27	28	29	30	1	2	3	SANÉ 2009
24		4	5	6	7	8	9	10	
25		11	12	13	14	15	16	17	
26		18	19	20	21	22	23	24	
27	EPĒP 1733	25	26	27	28	29	30	1	ḤAMLĒ 2009
28		2	3	4	5	6	7	8	
29		9	10	11	12	13	14	15	
30		16	17	18	19	20	21	22	
31		23	24	25	26	27	28	29	
32	MESORĒ 1733	30	1	2	3	4	5	6	NAHASĒ 2009
33		7	8	9	10	11	12	13[h]	
34		14	15	16	17	18	19	20	
35		21	22	23	24	25	26	27	
36	EPAG. 1733	28	29	30	1	2	3	4	PĀG. 2009
37	THOOUT 1734	5	1[a]	2	3	4	5	6	MASKARAM 2010
38		7	8	9	10	11	12	13	
39		14	15	16	17[b]	18	19	20	
40		21	22	23	24	25	26	27	
41	PAOPE 1734	28	29	30	1	2	3	4	TEQEMT 2010
42		5	6	7	8	9	10	11	
43		12	13	14	15	16	17	18	
44		19	20	21	22	23	24	25	
45	ATHÔR 1734	26	27	28	29	30	1	2	HEDĀR 2010
46		3	4	5	6	7	8	9	
47		10	11	12	13	14	15	16	
48		17	18	19	20	21	22	23	
49		24	25	26	27	28	29	30	
50	KOIAK 1734	1	2	3	4	5	6	7	TĀKHŚĀŚ 2010
51		8	9	10	11	12	13	14	
52		15	16	17	18	19	20	21	
1		22	23	24	25	26	27	28	

[a]New Year
[b]Spring (10:28)
[c]Summer (4:23)
[d]Autumn (20:01)
[e]Winter (16:27)
● New moon
◐ First quarter moon
○ Full moon
◑ Last quarter moon

[a]New Year
[b]Yom Kippur
[c]Sukkot
[d]Winter starts
[e]Ḥanukkah
[f]Purim
[g]Passover
[h]Shavuot
[i]Fast of Av

‡Leap year
[a]New Year (4715, Fowl)
[b]Lantern Festival
[c]Qīngmíng
[d]Dragon Festival
[e]Qīqiǎo
[f]Hungry Ghosts
[g]Mid-Autumn Festival
[h]Double-Ninth Festival
[i]Dōngzhì
*Start of 60-name cycle

[a]New Year
[b]Building of the Cross
[c]Christmas
[d]Jesus's Circumcision
[e]Epiphany
[f]Easter
[g]Mary's Announcement
[h]Jesus's Transfiguration

PERSIAN (ASTRONOMICAL) 1395‡/1396

Month	Sun	Mon	Tue	Wed	Thu	Fri	Sat
DEY 1395	12	13	14	15	16	17	18
	19	20	21	22	23	24	25
	26	27	28	29	30	1	2
BAHMAN 1395	3	4	5	6	7	8	9
	10	11	12	13	14	15	16
	17	18	19	20	21	22	23
	24	25	26	27	28	29	30
ESFAND 1395	1	2	3	4	5	6	7
	8	9	10	11	12	13	14
	15	16	17	18	19	20	21
	22	23	24	25	26	27	28
	29	30	1[a]	2	3	4	5
FARVARDĪN 1396	6	7	8	9	10	11	12
	13[b]	14	15	16	17	18	19
	20	21	22	23	24	25	26
	27	28	29	30	31	1	2
ORDĪBEHEŠT 1396	3	4	5	6	7	8	9
	10	11	12	13	14	15	16
	17	18	19	20	21	22	23
	24	25	26	27	28	29	30
	31	1	2	3	4	5	6
XORDĀD 1396	7	8	9	10	11	12	13
	14	15	16	17	18	19	20
	21	22	23	24	25	26	27
	28	29	30	31	1	2	3
TĪR 1396	4	5	6	7	8	9	10
	11	12	13	14	15	16	17
	18	19	20	21	22	23	24
	25	26	27	28	29	30	31
	1	2	3	4	5	6	7
MORDĀD 1396	8	9	10	11	12	13	14
	15	16	17	18	19	20	21
	22	23	24	25	26	27	28
	29	30	31	1	2	3	4
SHAHRĪVAR 1396	5	6	7	8	9	10	11
	12	13	14	15	16	17	18
	19	20	21	22	23	24	25
	26	27	28	29	30	31	1
MEHR 1396	2	3	4	5	6	7	8
	9	10	11	12	13	14	15
	16	17	18	19	20	21	22
	23	24	25	26	27	28	29
	30	1	2	3	4	5	6
ĀBĀN 1396	7	8	9	10	11	12	13
	14	15	16	17	18	19	20
	21	22	23	24	25	26	27
	28	29	30	1	2	3	4
ĀZAR 1396	5	6	7	8	9	10	11
	12	13	14	15	16	17	18
	19	20	21	22	23	24	25
	26	27	28	29	30	1	2
DEY 1396	3	4	5	6	7	8	9
	10	11	12	13	14	15	16

HINDU LUNAR 2073/2074

Month	Sun	Mon	Tue	Wed	Thu	Fri	Sat
	3	4	5	6	7	**8**	10
PAUSHA 2073	11	12	13	14	15	16	17
	18	19	20	21	22	23	24
	25	26	27	28	29	30	1
	2	3	4	5	6	7	8
MĀGHA 2073	9	10	11	12	13	**14**	16
	17	18	19	20	20	21	22
	23	24	25	26	27	28[h]	29
	30	1	2	3	4	5	6
PHĀLGUNA 2073	7	9	10	11	12	13	14
	15[i]	16	17	18	19	20	21
	22	23	23	24	25	26	27
	28	29	30	1[a]	3	4	5
CHAITRA 2074	6	7	8	9[b]	10	11	12
	13	14	15	16	17	18	19
	20	21	22	23	24	25	26
	27	28	29	30	1	2	3
VAIŚĀKHA 2074	4	**5**	7	8	9	10	11
	12	13	14	15	16	17	17
	18	19	20	21	22	23	24
	25	26	27	**28**	30	1	2
JYAISHṬHA 2074	3	4	5	6	7	8	9
	10	11	12	13	14	15	16
	17	18	19	20	21	22	23
	24	25	26	27	28	29	30
	1	3	4	5	6	7	8
ĀSHĀḌHA 2074	9	10	11	12	13	14	14
	15	16	17	18	19	20	21
	22	**23**	25	26	27	28	29
	30	1	2	3	4	5	6
ŚRĀVAṆA 2074	7	8	9	10	11	12	13
	14	15	16	17	18	19	20
	21	22	23[c]	24	25	**26**	28
	29	30	1	2	3	4[d]	5
BHĀDRAPADA 2074	6	7	8	9	10	10	11
	12	13	14	15	16	17	18
	19	21	22	23	24	25	26
	27	28	29	30	1	2	3
	4	5	6	7	8[e]	9[e]	10[e]
ĀŚVINA 2074	11	12	13	14	15	16	17
	18	19	20	21	22	**23**	25
	26	27	28	29	30	1[f]	2
KĀRTTIKA 2074	3	4	5	5	6	7	8
	9	10	11	12	13	14	15
	16	**17**	19	20	21	22	23
	24	25	26	27	28	29	30
	1	2	3	4	5	6	7
MĀRGAŚIRA 2074	8	9	10	11[g]	12	13	14
	15	16	17	18	19	20	21
	22	24	25	26	27	28	28
	29	30	1	2	3	4	5
PAUSHA 2074	6	7	8	9	10	11	12
	13	14	**15**	17	18	19	20

HINDU SOLAR 1938/1939‡

Month	Sun	Mon	Tue	Wed	Thu	Fri	Sat
PAUSHA 1938	18	19	20	21	22	23	24
	25	26	27	28	29	30	1[b]
	2	3	4	5	6	7	8
MĀGHA 1938	9	10	11	12	13	14	15
	16	17	18	19	20	21	22
	23	24	25	26	27	28	29
	1	2	3	4	5	6	7
PHĀLGUNA 1938	8	9	10	11	12	13	14
	15	16	17	18	19	20	21
	22	23	24	25	26	27	28
	29	30	1	2	3	4	5
	6	7	8	9	10	11	12
CHAITRA 1938	13	14	15	16	17	18	19
	20	21	22	23	24	25	26
	27	28	29	30	1[a]	2	3
VAIŚĀKHA 1939	4	5	6	7	8	9	10
	11	12	13	14	15	16	17
	18	19	20	21	22	23	24
	25	26	27	28	29	30	31
	1	2	3	4	5	6	7
JYAISHṬHA 1939	8	9	10	11	12	13	14
	15	16	17	18	19	20	21
	22	23	24	25	26	27	28
	29	30	31	32	1	2	3
ĀSHĀḌHA 1939	4	5	6	7	8	9	10
	11	12	13	14	15	16	17
	18	19	20	21	22	23	24
	25	26	27	28	29	30	31
	1	2	3	4	5	6	7
ŚRĀVAṆA 1939	8	9	10	11	12	13	14
	15	16	17	18	19	20	21
	22	23	24	25	26	27	28
	29	30	31	32	1	2	3
BHĀDRAPADA 1939	4	5	6	7	8	9	10
	11	12	13	14	15	16	17
	18	19	20	21	22	23	24
	25	26	27	28	29	30	31
	1	2	3	4	5	6	7
ĀŚVINA 1939	8	9	10	11	12	13	14
	15	16	17	18	19	20	21
	22	23	24	25	26	27	28
	29	30	1	2	3	4	5
KĀRTTIKA 1939	6	7	8	9	10	11	12
	13	14	15	16	17	18	19
	20	21	22	23	24	25	26
	27	28	29	30	1	2	3
MĀRGAŚIRA 1939	4	5	6	7	8	9	10
	11	12	13	14	15	16	17
	18	19	20	21	22	23	24
	25	26	27	28	29	30	1
PAUSHA 1939	2	3	4	5	6	7	8
	9	10	11	12	13	14	15
	16	17	18	19	20	21	22

ISLAMIC (ASTRONOMICAL) 1438/1439‡

Month	Sun	Mon	Tue	Wed	Thu	Fri	Sat
	2	3	4	5	6	7	8
RABĪ' II 1438	9	10	11	12	13	14	15
	16	17	18	19	20	21	22
	23	24	25	26	27	28	29
	1	2	3	4	5	6	7
JUMĀDĀ I 1438	8	9	10	11	12	13	14
	15	16	17	18	19	20	21
	22	23	24	25	26	27	28
	29	30	1	2	3	4	5
JUMĀDĀ II 1438	6	7	8	9	10	11	12
	13	14	15	16	17	18	19
	20	21	22	23	24	25	26
	27	28	29	1	2	3	4
RAJAB 1438	5	6	7	8	9	10	11
	12	13	14	15	16	17	18
	19	20	21	22	23	24	25
	26	27[d]	28	29	30	1	2
SHA'BĀN 1438	3	4	5	6	7	8	9
	10	11	12	13	14	15	16
	17	18	19	20	21	22	23
	24	25	26	27	28	29	1[e]
RAMAḌĀN 1438	2	3	4	5	6	7	8
	9	10	11	12	13	14	15
	16	17	18	19	20	21	22
	23	24	25	26	27	28	29
	1[f]	2	3	4	5	6	7
SHAWWĀL 1438	8	9	10	11	12	13	14
	15	16	17	18	19	20	21
	22	23	24	25	26	27	28
	29	30	1	2	3	4	5
DHU AL-QA'DA 1438	6	7	8	9	10	11	12
	13	14	15	16	17	18	19
	20	21	22	23	24	25	26
	27	28	29	1	2	3	4
DHU AL-ḤIJJA 1438	5	6	7	8	9	10[g]	11
	12	13	14	15	16	17	18
	19	20	21	22	23	24	25
	26	27	28	29	1[a]	2[d]	3
MUḤARRAM 1439	4	5	6	7	8	9	10[b]
	11	12	13	14	15	16	17
	18	19	20	21	22	23	24
	25	26	27	28	29	30	1
	2	3	4	5	6	7	8
ṢAFAR 1439	9	10	11	12	13	14	15
	16	17	18	19	20	21	22
	23	24	25	26	27	28	29
	30	1	2	3	4	5	6
RABĪ' I 1439	7	8	9	10	11	12[c]	13
	14	15	16	17	18	19	20
	21	22	23	24	25	26	27
	28	29	30	1	2	3	4
RABĪ' II 1439	5	6	7	8	9	10	11
	12	13	14	15	16	17	18

GREGORIAN 2017

Julian (Sun)	Sun	Mon	Tue	Wed	Thu	Fri	Sat	Month
Dec 19	1	2	3	4	5	6	7[a]	JANUARY 2017
	8	9	10	11	12	13	14[b]	
Jan 2	15	16	17	18	19	20	21	
	22	23	24	25	26	27	28	
Jan 16	29	30	31	1	2	3	4	FEBRUARY 2017
	5	6	7	8	9	10	11	
Jan 30	12	13	14	15	16	17	18	
	19	20	21	22	23	24	25	
Feb 13	26	27	28	1[c]	2	3	4	MARCH 2017
	5[d]	6	7	8	9	10	11	
Feb 27	12	13	14	15	16	17	18	
	19	20	21	22	23	24	25	
Mar 13	26	27	28	29	30	31	1	APRIL 2017
	2	3	4	5	6	7	8	
Mar 27	9	10	11	12	13	14	15	
	16[e]	17	18	19	20	21	22	
Apr 10	23	24	25	26	27	28	29	
	30	1	2	3	4	5	6	MAY 2017
Apr 24	7	8	9	10	11	12	13	
	14	15	16	17	18	19	20	
May 8	21	22	23	24	25	26	27	
	28	29	30	31	1	2	3	JUNE 2017
May 22	4	5	6	7	8	9	10	
	11	12	13	14	15	16	17	
Jun 5	18	19	20	21	22	23	24	
	25	26	27	28	29	30	1	JULY 2017
Jun 19	2	3	4	5	6	7	8	
	9	10	11	12	13	14	15	
Jul 3	16	17	18	19	20	21	22	
	23	24	25	26	27	28	29	
Jul 17	30	31	1	2	3	4	5	AUGUST 2017
	6	7	8	9	10	11	12	
Jul 31	13	14	15	16	17	18	19	
	20	21	22	23	24	25	26	
Aug 14	27	28	29	30	31	1	2	SEPTEMBER 2017
	3	4	5	6	7	8	9	
Aug 28	10	11	12	13	14	15	16	
	17	18	19	20	21	22	23	
Sep 11	24	25	26	27	28	29	30	
	1	2	3	4	5	6	7	OCTOBER 2017
Sep 25	8	9	10	11	12	13	14	
	15	16	17	18	19	20	21	
Oct 9	22	23	24	25	26	27	28	
	29	30	31	1	2	3	4	NOVEMBER 2017
Oct 23	5	6	7	8	9	10	11	
	12	13	14	15	16	17	18	
Nov 6	19	20	21	22	23	24	25	
	26	27	28	29	30	1	2	DECEMBER 2017
Nov 20	3[g]	4	5	6	7	8	9	
	10	11	12	13	14	15	16	
Dec 4	17	18	19	20	21	22	23	
	24	25[h]	26	27	28	29	30	
Dec 18	31	1	2	3	4	5	6	

Persian:
‡Leap year
[a]New Year
[b]Sizdeh Bedar

Hindu lunar:
[a]New Year (Hemalamba)
[b]Birthday of Rāma
[c]Birthday of Krishna
[d]Ganēśa Chaturthī
[e]Dashara
[f]Diwali
[g]Birthday of Vishnu
[h]Night of Śiva
[i]Holi

Hindu solar:
‡Leap year
[a]New Year (Sādhāraṇa)
[b]Pongal

Islamic:
‡Leap year
[a]New Year
[d]New Year (Arithmetic)
[b]'Ashūrā'
[c]Prophet's Birthday
[d]Ascent of the Prophet
[e]Start of Ramaḍān
[f]'Id al-Fiṭr
[g]'Id al-'Aḍḥā

Gregorian:
[a]Orthodox Christmas
[b]Julian New Year
[c]Ash Wednesday
[d]Feast of Orthodoxy
[e]Easter (also Orthodox)
[g]Advent
[h]Christmas

2018

GREGORIAN 2018

Month	Sun	Mon	Tue	Wed	Thu	Fri	Sat	Lunar Phases	ISO WEEK (Mon)	JULIAN DAY (Sun noon)
JANUARY 2018	31	1[a]	○	3	4	5	6	2:24	1	2458119
	7	◑	9	10	11	12	13	22:25	2	2458126
	14	15	16	●	18	19	20	2:17	3	2458133
	21	22	23	◐	25	26	27	22:20	4	2458140
FEBRUARY 2018	28	29	30	○	1	2	3	13:26	5	2458147
	4	5	6	◑	8	9	10	15:54	6	2458154
	11	12	13	14	●	16	17	21:05	7	2458161
	18	19	20	21	22	◐	24	8:09	8	2458168
MARCH 2018	25	26	27	28	1	○	3	0:51	9	2458175
	4	5	6	7	8	◑	10	11:20	10	2458182
	11	12	13	14	15	16	●	13:11	11	2458189
	18	19	20[b]	21	22	23	◐	15:35	12	2458196
	25	26	27	28	29	30	○	12:37	13	2458203
APRIL 2018	1	2	3	4	5	6	7		14	2458210
	◑	9	10	11	12	13	14	7:17	15	2458217
	15	●	17	18	19	20	21	1:57	16	2458224
	◐	23	24	25	26	27	28	21:45	17	2458231
MAY 2018	29	○	1	2	3	4	5	0:58	18	2458238
	6	7	◑	9	10	11	12	2:08	19	2458245
	13	14	●	16	17	18	19	11:48	20	2458252
	20	21	◐	23	24	25	26	3:49	21	2458259
JUNE 2018	27	28	○	30	31	1	2	14:19	22	2458266
	3	4	5	◑	7	8	9	18:31	23	2458273
	10	11	12	●	14	15	16	19:43	24	2458280
	17	18	19	◐	21[c]	22	23	10:51	25	2458287
	24	25	26	27	○	29	30	4:53	26	2458294
JULY 2018	1	2	3	4	5	◑	7	7:50	27	2458301
	8	9	10	11	12	●	14	2:48	28	2458308
	15	16	17	18	◐	20	21	19:52	29	2458315
	22	23	24	25	26	○	28	20:20	30	2458322
AUGUST 2018	29	30	31	1	2	3	◑	18:18	31	2458329
	5	6	7	8	9	10	●	9:58	32	2458336
	12	13	14	15	16	17	◐	7:48	33	2458343
	19	20	21	22	23	24	25		34	2458350
SEPTEMBER 2018	○	27	28	29	30	31	1	11:56	35	2458357
	2	◑	4	5	6	7	8	2:37	36	2458364
	●	10	11	12	13	14	15	18:01	37	2458371
	◐	17	18	19	20	21	22	23:15	38	2458378
	23[d]	24	○	26	27	28	29	2:52	39	2458385
OCTOBER 2018	30	1	◑	3	4	5	6	9:45	40	2458392
	7	8	●	10	11	12	13	3:47	41	2458399
	14	15	◐	17	18	19	20	18:01	42	2458406
	21	22	23	○	25	26	27	16:45	43	2458413
NOVEMBER 2018	28	29	30	◑	1	2	3	16:40	44	2458420
	4	5	6	●	8	9	10	16:02	45	2458427
	11	12	13	14	◐	16	17	14:54	46	2458434
	18	19	20	21	22	○	24	5:39	47	2458441
DECEMBER 2018	25	26	27	28	29	◑	1	0:19	48	2458448
	2	3	4	5	6	●	8	7:20	49	2458455
	9	10	11	12	13	14	◐	11:49	50	2458462
	16	17	18	19	20	21[e]	○	17:48	51	2458469
	23	24	25	26	27	28	◑	9:34	52	2458476
	30	31	1	2	3	4	5		1	2458483

HEBREW 5778/5779‡

ISO Week	Month	Sun	Mon	Tue	Wed	Thu	Fri	Sat	Molad
1	TEVETH 5778	13	14	15	16	17	18	19	
2		20	21	22	23	24	25	26	
3	SHEVAT 5778	27	28	29	1	2	3	4	Wed $2^h25^m2^p$
4		5	6	7	8	9	10	11	
5		12	13	14	15	16	17	18	
6		19	20	21	22	23	24	25	
7	ADAR 5778	26	27	28	29	30	1	2	Thu $15^h9^m3^p$
8		3	4	5	6	7	8	9	
9		10	11	12	13	14[f]	15	16	
10		17	18	19	20	21	22	23	
11	NISAN 5778	24	25	26	27	28	29	1	Sat $3^h53^m4^p$
12		2	3	4	5	6	7	8	
13		9	10	11	12	13	14	15[g]	
14		16	17	18	19	20	21	22	
15		23	24	25	26	27	28	29	
16	IYYAR 5778	30	1	2	3	4	5	6	Sun $16^h37^m5^p$
17		7	8	9	10	11	12	13	
18		14	15	16	17	18	19	20	
19		21	22	23	24	25	26	27	
20	SIVAN 5778	28	29	1	2	3	4	5	Tue $5^h21^m6^p$
21		6[h]	7	8	9	10	11	12	
22		13	14	15	16	17	18	19	
23		20	21	22	23	24	25	26	
24	TAMMUZ 5778	27	28	29	30	1	2	3	Wed $18^h5^m7^p$
25		4	5	6	7	8	9	10	
26		11	12	13	14	15	16	17	
27		18	19	20	21	22	23	24	
28	AV 5778	25	26	27	28	29	1	2	Fri $6^h49^m8^p$
29		3	4	5	6	7	8	9	
30		10[i]	11	12	13	14	15	16	
31		17	18	19	20	21	22	23	
32		24	25	26	27	28	29	30	Sat $19^h33^m9^p$
33	ELUL 5778	1	2	3	4	5	6	7	
34		8	9	10	11	12	13	14	
35		15	16	17	18	19	20	21	
36		22	23	24	25	26	27	28	
37	TISHRI 5779	29	1[a]	2[a]	3	4	5	6	Mon $8^h17^m10^p$
38		7	8	9	10[b]	11	12	13	
39		14	15[c]	16	17	18	19	20	
40		21	22	23	24	25	26	27	
41	HESHVAN 5779	28	29	30	1	2	3	4	Tue $21^h1^m11^p$
42		5	6	7	8	9	10	11	
43		12	13	14	15	16	17	18	
44		19	20	21	22	23	24	25	
45	KISLEV 5779	26	27	28	29	30	1	2	Thu $9^h45^m12^p$
46		3	4	5	6	7	8	9	
47		10	11	12	13	14	15	16	
48		17	18	19	20	21	22	23	
49		24	25[e]	26[e]	27[d,e]	28[e]	29[e]	30[e]	Fri $22^h29^m13^p$
50	TEVETH 5779	1[e]	2[e]	3	4	5	6	7	
51		8	9	10	11	12	13	14	
52		15	16	17	18	19	20	21	
1		22	23	24	25	26	27	28	

CHINESE Dīng-Yǒu‡/Wù-Xū

ISO Week	Month	Sun	Mon	Tue	Wed	Thu	Fri	Sat	Solar Term
1	MONTH 11 Dīng-Yǒu	14	15	16	17	18	19	20	Xiǎo hán
2		21	22	23	24	25	26	27	
3	MONTH 12 Dīng-Yǒu	28	29	30	1	2	3	4	Dà hán
4		5	6	7	8	9	10	11	
5		12	13	14	15	16*	17	18	
6		19	20	21	22	23	24	25	Lì chūn
7	MONTH 1 Wù-Xū	26	27	28	29	30	1[a]	2	
8		3	4	5	6	7	8	9	Yǔ shuǐ
9		10	11	12	13	14	15[b]	16	
10		17	18	19	20	21	22	23	Jīng zhé
11	MONTH 2 Wù-Xū	24	25	26	27	28	29	1	
12		2	3	4	5	6	7	8	Chūn fēn
13		9	10	11	12	13	14	15	
14		16	17*	18	19	20[c]	21	22	Qīng míng
15		23	24	25	26	27	28	29	
16	MONTH 3 Wù-Xū	30	1	2	3	4	5	6	Gǔ yǔ
17		7	8	9	10	11	12	13	
18		14	15	16	17	18	19	20	Lì xià
19		21	22	23	24	25	26	27	
20	MONTH 4 Wù-Xū	28	29	1	2	3	4	5	
21		6	7	8	9	10	11	12	Xiǎo mǎn
22		13	14	15	16	17	18*	19	
23		20	21	22	23	24	25	26	Máng zhòng
24	MONTH 5 Wù-Xū	27	28	29	30	1	2	3	
25		4	5[d]	6	7	8	9	10	Xià zhì
26		11	12	13	14	15	16	17	
27		18	19	20	21	22	23	24	Xiǎo shǔ
28	MONTH 6 Wù-Xū	25	26	27	28	29	1	2	
29		3	4	5	6	7	8	9	
30		10	11	12	13	14	15	16	Dà shǔ
31		17	18	19*	20	21	22	23	
32	MONTH 7 Wù-Xū	24	25	26	27	28	29	1	Lì qiū
33		2	3	4	5	6	7[e]	8	
34		9	10	11	12	13	14	15[f]	Chǔ shǔ
35		16	17	18	19	20	21	22	
36		23	24	25	26	27	28	29	Bái lù
37	MONTH 8 Wù-Xū	30	1	2	3	4	5	6	
38		7	8	9	10	11	12	13	
39		14	15[g]	16	17	18	19	20*	Qiū fēn
40		21	22	23	24	25	26	27	
41	MONTH 9 Wù-Xū	28	29	1	2	3	4	5	Hán lù
42		6	7	8	9[h]	10	11	12	
43		13	14	15	16	17	18	19	Shuāng jiàng
44		20	21	22	23	24	25	26	
45	MONTH 10 Wù-Xū	27	28	29	30	1	2	3	Lì dōng
46		4	5	6	7	8	9	10	
47		11	12	13	14	15	16	17	Xiǎo xuě
48		18	19	20	21*	22	23	24	
49	MONTH 11* Wù-Xū	25	26	27	28	29	1	2	Dà xuě
50		3	4	5	6	7	8	9	
51		10	11	12	13	14	15	16[i]	Dōng zhì
52		17	18	19	20	21	22	23	
1		24	25	26	27	28	29	30	Xiǎo hán

COPTIC 1734/1735‡ — ETHIOPIC 2010/2011‡

ISO Week	Coptic Month	Sun	Mon	Tue	Wed	Thu	Fri	Sat	Ethiopic Month
1	KOIAK 1734	22	23	24	25	26	27	28	TĀKHŚĀŚ 2010
2	TÔBE 1734	29[c]	30	1	2	3	4	5	ṬER 2010
3		6[d]	7	8	9	10	11[e]	12	
4		13	14	15	16	17	18	19	
5		20	21	22	23	24	25	26	
6	MESHIR 1734	27	28	29	30	1	2	3	YAKĀTIT 2010
7		4	5	6	7	8	9	10	
8		11	12	13	14	15	16	17	
9		18	19	20	21	22	23	24	
10	PAREMOTEP 1734	25	26	27	28	29	30	1	MAGABIT 2010
11		2	3	4	5	6	7	8	
12		9	10	11	12	13	14	15	
13		16	17	18	19	20	21	22	
14		23	24	25	26	27	28	29	
15	PARMOUTE 1734	30[f]	1	2	3	4	5	6	MIYĀZYĀ 2010
16		7	8	9	10	11	12	13	
17		14	15	16	17	18	19	20	
18		21	22	23	24	25	26	27	
19	PASHONS 1734	28	29[g]	30	1	2	3	4	GENBOT 2010
20		5	6	7	8	9	10	11	
21		12	13	14	15	16	17	18	
22		19	20	21	22	23	24	25	
23	PAĈNE 1734	26	27	28	29	30	1	2	SANĒ 2010
24		3	4	5	6	7	8	9	
25		10	11	12	13	14	15	16	
26		17	18	19	20	21	22	23	
27		24	25	26	27	28	29	30	
28	EPÊP 1734	1	2	3	4	5	6	7	ḤAMLĒ 2010
29		8	9	10	11	12	13	14	
30		15	16	17	18	19	20	21	
31		22	23	24	25	26	27	28	
32	MESORÊ 1734	29	30	1	2	3	4	5	NAHASĒ 2010
33		6	7	8	9	10	11	12	
34		13[h]	14	15	16	17	18	19	
35		20	21	22	23	24	25	26	
36	EPAG. 1734	27	28	29	30	1	2	3	PĀG. 2010
37	THOOUT 1735	4	5	1[a]	2	3	4	5	MASKARAM 2011
38		6	7	8	9	10	11	12	
39		13	14	15	16	17[b]	18	19	
40		20	21	22	23	24	25	26	
41	PAOPE 1735	27	28	29	30	1	2	3	TEQEMT 2011
42		4	5	6	7	8	9	10	
43		11	12	13	14	15	16	17	
44		18	19	20	21	22	23	24	
45	ATHÔR 1735	25	26	27	28	29	30	1	HEDAR 2011
46		2	3	4	5	6	7	8	
47		9	10	11	12	13	14	15	
48		16	17	18	19	20	21	22	
49		23	24	25	26	27	28	29	
50	KOIAK 1735	30	1	2	3	4	5	6	TĀKHŚĀŚ 2011
51		7	8	9	10	11	12	13	
52		14	15	16	17	18	19	20	
1		21	22	23	24	25	26	27	

Gregorian:
[a] New Year
[b] Spring (16:14)
[c] Summer (10:07)
[d] Autumn (1:53)
[e] Winter (22:22)
● New moon
◐ First quarter moon
○ Full moon
◑ Last quarter moon

Hebrew:
‡ Leap year
[a] New Year
[b] Yom Kippur
[c] Sukkot
[d] Winter starts
[e] Ḥanukkah
[f] Purim
[g] Passover
[h] Shavuot
[i] Fast of Av

Chinese:
‡ Leap year
[a] New Year (4716, Dog)
[b] Lantern Festival
[c] Qīngmíng
[d] Dragon Festival
[e] Qīqiǎo
[f] Hungry Ghosts
[g] Mid-Autumn Festival
[h] Double-Ninth Festival
[i] Dōngzhì
* Start of 60-name cycle

Coptic/Ethiopic:
‡ Leap year
[a] New Year
[b] Building of the Cross
[c] Christmas
[d] Jesus's Circumcision
[e] Epiphany
[f] Easter
[g] Mary's Announcement
[h] Jesus's Transfiguration

PERSIAN (ASTRONOMICAL) 1396/1397

Month	Sun	Mon	Tue	Wed	Thu	Fri	Sat
	10	11	12	13	14	15	16
DEY 1396	17	18	19	20	21	22	23
	24	25	26	27	28	29	30
	1	2	3	4	5	6	7
BAHMAN 1396	8	9	10	11	12	13	14
	15	16	17	18	19	20	21
	22	23	24	25	26	27	28
	29	30	1	2	3	4	5
ESFAND 1396	6	7	8	9	10	11	12
	13	14	15	16	17	18	19
	20	21	22	23	24	25	26
	27	28	29	1[a]	2	3	4
	5	6	7	8	9	10	11
FARVARDĪN 1397	12	13[b]	14	15	16	17	18
	19	20	21	22	23	24	25
	26	27	28	29	30	31	1
	2	3	4	5	6	7	8
ORDĪBEHEŠT 1397	9	10	11	12	13	14	15
	16	17	18	19	20	21	22
	23	24	25	26	27	28	29
	30	31	1	2	3	4	5
XORDĀD 1397	6	7	8	9	10	11	12
	13	14	15	16	17	18	19
	20	21	22	23	24	25	26
	27	28	29	30	31	1	2
	3	4	5	6	7	8	9
TĪR 1397	10	11	12	13	14	15	16
	17	18	19	20	21	22	23
	24	25	26	27	28	29	30
	31	1	2	3	4	5	6
MORDĀD 1397	7	8	9	10	11	12	13
	14	15	16	17	18	19	20
	21	22	23	24	25	26	27
	28	29	30	31	1	2	3
SHAHRĪVAR 1397	4	5	6	7	8	9	10
	11	12	13	14	15	16	17
	18	19	20	21	22	23	24
	25	26	27	28	29	30	31
	1	2	3	4	5	6	7
MEHR 1397	8	9	10	11	12	13	14
	15	16	17	18	19	20	21
	22	23	24	25	26	27	28
	29	30	1	2	3	4	5
ĀBĀN 1397	6	7	8	9	10	11	12
	13	14	15	16	17	18	19
	20	21	22	23	24	25	26
	27	28	29	30	1	2	3
ĀZAR 1397	4	5	6	7	8	9	10
	11	12	13	14	15	16	17
	18	19	20	21	22	23	24
	25	26	27	28	29	30	1
DEY 1397	2	3	4	5	6	7	8
	9	10	11	12	13	14	15

HINDU LUNAR 2074/2075‡

Month	Sun	Mon	Tue	Wed	Thu	Fri	Sat
	13	14	15	17	18	19	20
PAUSHA 2074	21	22	23	24	25	26	27
	28	29	30	1	1	2	3
MĀGHA 2074	4	5	6	7	8	9	11
	12	13	14	15	16	17	18
	19	20	21	22	23	24	25
	26	27	28[h]	29	30	1	2
PHĀLGUNA 2074	3	4	5	6	7	8	9
	10	11	12	13	14[i]	16	17
	18	19	20	21	22	23	23
	24	25	26	27	28	29	30
	1[a]	2	3	4	5	6	7
CHAITRA 2075	8[b]	10	11	12	13	14	15
	16	17	18	19	20	21	22
	23	24	25	26	26	27	28
	29	30	1	3	4	5	6
VAIŚĀKHA 2075	7	8	9	10	11	12	13
	14	16	16	17	18	19	20
	21	22	23	24	25	26	27
	28	29	30	1	2	3	4
LEAP JYAISHTHA 2075	5	7	8	9	10	11	12
	13	14	15	16	17	18	19
	20	21	22	22	23	24	25
	26	27	29	30	1	2	3
JYAISHTHA 2075	4	5	6	7	8	9	10
	12	12	13	14	15	16	17
	18	19	20	21	22	23	24
	25	26	27	28	29	30	1
ĀSHĀḌHA 2075	3	4	5	6	7	8	9
	10	11	12	13	14	15	16
	17	18	19	19	20	21	22
	23	25	26	27	28	29	30
	1	2	3	4	5	7	8
ŚRĀVAṆA 2075	9	10	10	11	12	13	14
	15	16	17	18	19	20	21
	22	23[c]	24	25	26	27	29
	30	1	2	3	4[d]	5	6
BHĀDRAPADA 2075	7	8	9	10	11	12	13
	14	15	15	16	17	18	19
	21	22	23	24	25	26	27
	28	29	30	1	2	3	4
ĀŚVINA 2075	5	6	7	8[e]	9[e]	10[e]	11
	12	13	14	15	16	17	18
	19	20	21	22	23	24	26
	27	28	29	30	1[f]	2	3
KĀRTTIKA 2075	4	5	6	7	8	8	9
	10	11	12	13	14	15	16
	17	18	20	21	22	23	24
	25	26	27	28	29	30	1
MĀRGAŚĪRA 2075	2	3	4	5	6	7	8
	9	10	11[g]	12	13	14	15
	16	17	18	19	20	21	22
	24	25	26	27	28	29	30

HINDU SOLAR 1939‡/1940

Month	Sun	Mon	Tue	Wed	Thu	Fri	Sat
PAUSHA 1939	16	17	18	19	20	21	22
	23	24	25	26	27	28	29
	1[b]	2	3	4	5	6	7
MĀGHA 1939	8	9	10	11	12	13	14
	15	16	17	18	19	20	21
	22	23	24	25	26	27	28
	29	1	2	3	4	5	6
PHĀLGUNA 1939	7	8	9	10	11	12	13
	14	15	16	17	18	19	20
	21	22	23	24	25	26	27
	28	29	30	1	2	3	4
CHAITRA 1939	5	6	7	8	9	10	11
	12	13	14	15	16	17	18
	19	20	21	22	23	24	25
	26	27	28	29	30	31	1[a]
VAIŚĀKHA 1940	2	3	4	5	6	7	8
	9	10	11	12	13	14	15
	16	17	18	19	20	21	22
	23	24	25	26	27	28	29
	30	31	1	2	3	4	5
JYAISHTHA 1940	6	7	8	9	10	11	12
	13	14	15	16	17	18	19
	20	21	22	23	24	25	26
	27	28	29	30	31	1	2
ĀSHĀḌHA 1940	3	4	5	6	7	8	9
	10	11	12	13	14	15	16
	17	18	19	20	21	22	23
	24	25	26	27	28	29	30
	31	32	1	2	3	4	5
ŚRĀVAṆA 1940	6	7	8	9	10	11	12
	13	14	15	16	17	18	19
	20	21	22	23	24	25	26
	27	28	29	30	31	1	2
BHĀDRAPADA 1940	3	4	5	6	7	8	9
	10	11	12	13	14	15	16
	17	18	19	20	21	22	23
	24	25	26	27	28	29	30
	31	1	2	3	4	5	6
ĀŚVINA 1940	7	8	9	10	11	12	13
	14	15	16	17	18	19	20
	21	22	23	24	25	26	27
	28	29	30	31	1	2	3
KĀRTTIKA 1940	4	5	6	7	8	9	10
	11	12	13	14	15	16	17
	18	19	20	21	22	23	24
	25	26	27	28	29	1	2
MĀRGAŚĪRA 1940	3	4	5	6	7	8	9
	10	11	12	13	14	15	16
	17	18	19	20	21	22	23
	24	25	26	27	28	29	30
PAUSHA 1940	1	2	3	4	5	6	7
	8	9	10	11	12	13	14
	15	16	17	18	19	20	21

ISLAMIC (ASTRONOMICAL) 1439‡/1440‡

Month	Sun	Mon	Tue	Wed	Thu	Fri	Sat
RABĪʿ II 1439	12	13	14	15	16	17	18
	19	20	21	22	23	24	25
	26	27	28	29	30	1	2
JUMĀDĀ I 1439	3	4	5	6	7	8	9
	10	11	12	13	14	15	16
	17	18	19	20	21	22	23
	24	25	26	27	28	29	1
JUMĀDĀ II 1439	2	3	4	5	6	7	8
	9	10	11	12	13	14	15
	16	17	18	19	20	21	22
	23	24	25	26	27	28	29
	30	1	2	3	4	5	6
RAJAB 1439	7	8	9	10	11	12	13
	14	15	16	17	18	19	20
	21	22	23	24	25	26	27[d]
	28	29	1	2	3	4	5
SHAʿBĀN 1439	6	7	8	9	10	11	12
	13	14	15	16	17	18	19
	20	21	22	23	24	25	26
	27	28	29	30	1[e]	2	3
RAMAḌĀN 1439	4	5	6	7	8	9	10
	11	12	13	14	15	16	17
	18	19	20	21	22	23	24
	25	26	27	28	29	1[f]	2
SHAWWĀL 1439	3	4	5	6	7	8	9
	10	11	12	13	14	15	16
	17	18	19	20	21	22	23
	24	25	26	27	28	29	1
DHU AL-QAʿDA 1439	2	3	4	5	6	7	8
	9	10	11	12	13	14	15
	16	17	18	19	20	21	22
	23	24	25	26	27	28	29
	30	1	2	3	4	5	6
DHU AL-ḤIJJA 1439	7	8	9	10[g]	11	12	13
	14	15	16	17	18	19	20
	21	22	23	24	25	26	27
	28	29	1[a]	2[a]	3	4	5
MUḤARRAM 1440	6	7	8	9	10[b]	11	12
	13	14	15	16	17	18	19
	20	21	22	23	24	25	26
	27	28	29	1	2	3	4
ṢAFAR 1440	5	6	7	8	9	10	11
	12	13	14	15	16	17	18
	19	20	21	22	23	24	25
	26	27	28	29	30	1	2
RABĪʿ I 1440	3	4	5	6	7	8	9
	10	11	12[c]	13	14	15	16
	17	18	19	20	21	22	23
	24	25	26	27	28	29	30
RABĪʿ II 1440	1	2	3	4	5	6	7
	8	9	10	11	12	13	14
	15	16	17	18	19	20	21
	22	23	24	25	26	27	28

GREGORIAN 2018

Julian (Sun)	Sun	Mon	Tue	Wed	Thu	Fri	Sat	Month
Dec 18	31	1	2	3	4	5	6	
	7[a]	8	9	10	11	12	13	JANUARY 2018
Jan 1	14[b]	15	16	17	18	19	20	
	21	22	23	24	25	26	27	
Jan 15	28	29	30	31	1	2	3	
	4	5	6	7	8	9	10	FEBRUARY 2018
Jan 29	11	12	13	14[c]	15	16	17	
	18	19	20	21	22	23	24	
Feb 12	25[d]	26	27	28	1	2	3	
	4	5	6	7	8	9	10	MARCH 2018
Feb 26	11	12	13	14	15	16	17	
	18	19	20	21	22	23	24	
Mar 12	25	26	27	28	29	30	31	
	1[e]	2	3	4	5	6	7	
Mar 26	8[f]	9	10	11	12	13	14	APRIL 2018
	15	16	17	18	19	20	21	
Apr 9	22	23	24	25	26	27	28	
	29	30	1	2	3	4	5	
Apr 23	6	7	8	9	10	11	12	MAY 2018
	13	14	15	16	17	18	19	
May 7	20	21	22	23	24	25	26	
	27	28	29	30	31	1	2	
May 21	3	4	5	6	7	8	9	JUNE 2018
	10	11	12	13	14	15	16	
Jun 4	17	18	19	20	21	22	23	
	24	25	26	27	28	29	30	
Jun 18	1	2	3	4	5	6	7	
	8	9	10	11	12	13	14	JULY 2018
Jul 2	15	16	17	18	19	20	21	
	22	23	24	25	26	27	28	
Jul 16	29	30	31	1	2	3	4	
	5	6	7	8	9	10	11	AUGUST 2018
Jul 30	12	13	14	15	16	17	18	
	19	20	21	22	23	24	25	
Aug 13	26	27	28	29	30	31	1	
	2	3	4	5	6	7	8	SEPTEMBER 2018
Aug 27	9	10	11	12	13	14	15	
	16	17	18	19	20	21	22	
Sep 10	23	24	25	26	27	28	29	
	30	1	2	3	4	5	6	
Sep 24	7	8	9	10	11	12	13	OCTOBER 2018
	14	15	16	17	18	19	20	
Oct 8	21	22	23	24	25	26	27	
	28	29	30	31	1	2	3	
Oct 22	4	5	6	7	8	9	10	NOVEMBER 2018
	11	12	13	14	15	16	17	
Nov 5	18	19	20	21	22	23	24	
	25	26	27	28	29	30	1	
Nov 19	2[g]	3	4	5	6	7	8	DECEMBER 2018
	9	10	11	12	13	14	15	
Dec 3	16	17	18	19	20	21	22	
	23	24	25[h]	26	27	28	29	
Dec 17	30	31	1	2	3	4	5	

Persian: [a]New Year; [b]Sizdeh Bedar

Hindu lunar: ‡Leap year; [a]New Year (Vilamba); [b]Birthday of Rāma; [c]Birthday of Krishna; [d]Ganēśa Chaturthī; [e]Dashara; [f]Diwali; [g]Birthday of Vishnu; [h]Night of Śiva; [i]Holi

Hindu solar: ‡Leap year; [a]New Year (Virodhakṛit); [b]Pongal

Islamic: ‡Leap year; [a]New Year; [a]New Year (Arithmetic); [b]ʿAshūrā'; [c]Prophet's Birthday; [d]Ascent of the Prophet; [e]Start of Ramaḍān; [f]ʿId al-Fiṭr; [g]ʿId al-'Aḍḥā

Gregorian: [a]Orthodox Christmas; [b]Julian New Year; [c]Ash Wednesday; [d]Feast of Orthodoxy; [e]Easter; [f]Orthodox Easter; [g]Advent; [h]Christmas

2019

	GREGORIAN 2019							Lunar Phases	ISO WEEK	JULIAN DAY		HEBREW 5779‡/5780							Molad		CHINESE Wù-Xū/Jǐ-Hài							Solar Term		COPTIC 1735‡/1736 / ETHIOPIC 2011‡/2012							
	Sun	Mon	Tue	Wed	Thu	Fri	Sat		(Mon)	(Sun noon)		Sun	Mon	Tue	Wed	Thu	Fri	Sat			Sun	Mon	Tue	Wed	Thu	Fri	Sat			Sun	Mon	Tue	Wed	Thu	Fri	Sat	
	30	31	1[a]	2	3	4	5		1	2458483	TEVETH 5779	22	23	24	25	26	27	28			24	25	26	27	28	29	30	Xiǎo hán	KOIAK 1735	21	22	23	24	25	26	27	TĀHŚĀŚ 2011
JANUARY 2019	●	7	8	9	10	11	12	1:28	2	2458490		29	1	2	3	4	5	6	Sun 11h 13m 14p		1	2	3	4	5	6	7			28	29[c]	30	1	2	3	4	
	13	◐	15	16	17	18	19	6:45	3	2458497	SHEVAT 5779	7	8	9	10	11	12	13		MONTH 12 Wù-Xū	8	9	10	11	12	13	14		TŌBE 1735	5	6[d]	7	8	9	10	11[e]	ṬER 2011
	20	○	22	23	24	25	26	5:16	4	2458504		14	15	16	17	18	19	20			15	16	17	18	19	20	21	Dà hán		12	13	14	15	16	17	18	
	◑	28	29	30	31	1	2	21:10	5	2458511		21	22	23	24	25	26	27	Mon 23h 57m 15p		22*	23	24	25	26	27	28			19	20	21	22	23	24	25	
	3	●	5	6	7	8	9	21:03	6	2458518		28	29	30	1	2	3	4			29	30	1[a]	2	3	4	5	Lì chūn		26	27	28	29	30	1	2	
FEBRUARY 2019	10	11	◐	13	14	15	16	22:26	7	2458525	ADAR I 5779	5	6	7	8	9	10	11		MONTH 1 Jǐ-Hài	6	7	8	9	10	11	12		MESHIR 1735	3	4	5	6	7	8	9	YAKĀTIT 2011
	17	18	○	20	21	22	23	15:53	8	2458532		12	13	14	15	16	17	18			13	14	15[b]	16	17	18	19	Yǔ shuǐ		10	11	12	13	14	15	16	
	24	25	◑	27	28	1	2	11:27	9	2458539		19	20	21	22	23	24	25	Wed 12h 41m 16p		20	21	22	23	24	25	26			17	18	19	20	21	22	23	
	3	4	5	●	7	8	9	16:04	10	2458546		26	27	28	29	30	1	2			27	28	29	30	1	2	3	Jīng zhé		24	25	26	27	28	29	30	
MARCH 2019	10	11	12	13	◐	15	16	10:27	11	2458553	ADAR II 5779	3	4	5	6	7	8	9		MONTH 2 Jǐ-Hài	4	5	6	7	8	9	10		PAREMHOTEP 1735	1	2	3	4	5	6	7	MAGĀBIT 2011
	17	18	19	20[b]	○	22	23	1:42	12	2458560		10	11	12	13	14[f]	15	16			11	12	13	14	15	16	17	Chūn fēn		8	9	10	11	12	13	14	
	24	25	26	27	◑	29	30	4:09	13	2458567		17	18	19	20	21	22	23			18	19	20	21	22*	23	24			15	16	17	18	19	20	21	
	31	1	2	3	4	●	6	8:50	14	2458574		24	25	26	27	28	29	1	Fri 1h 25m 17p		25	26	27	28	29	1[c]	2	Qīng míng		22	23	24	25	26	27	28	
APRIL 2019	7	8	9	10	11	◐	13	19:05	15	2458581	NISAN 5779	2	3	4	5	6	7	8		MONTH 3 Jǐ-Hài	3	4	5	6	7	8	9		PARMOUTE 1735	29	30	1	2	3	4	5	MIYĀZYĀ 2011
	14	15	16	17	18	○	20	11:12	16	2458588		9	10	11	12	13	14	15[g]			10	11	12	13	14	15	16	Gǔ yǔ		6	7	8	9	10	11	12	
	21	22	23	24	25	◑	27	22:18	17	2458595		16	17	18	19	20	21	22			17	18	19	20	21	22	23			13	14	15	16	17	18	19	
	28	29	30	1	2	3	●	22:45	18	2458602		23	24	25	26	27	28	29	Sat 14h 10m 0p		24	25	26	27	28	29	30			20[f]	21	22	23	24	25	26	
MAY 2019	5	6	7	8	9	10	11		19	2458609	IYAR 5779	30	1	2	3	4	5	6		MONTH 4 Jǐ-Hài	1	2	3	4	5	6	7	Lì xià	PASHONS 1735	27	28	29[g]	30	1	2	3	GENBOT 2011
	◐	13	14	15	16	17	○	21:12 21:11	20	2458616		7	8	9	10	11	12	13			8	9	10	11	12	13	14			4	5	6	7	8	9	10	
	19	20	21	22	23	24	25		21	2458623		14	15	16	17	18	19	20			15	16	17	18	19	20	21	Xiǎo mǎn		11	12	13	14	15	16	17	
	◑	27	28	29	30	31	1	16:33	22	2458630		21	22	23	24	25	26	27			22	23*	24	25	26	27	28			18	19	20	21	22	23	24	
	2	●	4	5	6	7	8	10:02	23	2458637		28	29	1	2	3	4	5	Mon 2h 54m 1p		29	1	2	3	4	5[d]	6	Máng zhòng		25	26	27	28	29	30	1	
JUNE 2019	9	◐	11	12	13	14	15	5:59	24	2458644	SIVAN 5779	6[h]	7	8	9	10	11	12		MONTH 5 Jǐ-Hài	7	8	9	10	11	12	13		PAŌNE 1735	2	3	4	5	6	7	8	SANĒ 2011
	16	○	18	19	20	21[c]	22	8:30	25	2458651		13	14	15	16	17	18	19			14	15	16	17	18	19	20	Xià zhì		9	10	11	12	13	14	15	
	23	24	◑	26	27	28	29	9:46	26	2458658		20	21	22	23	24	25	26			21	22	23	24	25	26	27			16	17	18	19	20	21	22	
	30	1	●	3	4	5	6	19:16	27	2458665		27	28	29	30	1	2	3	Tue 15h 38m 2p		28	29	30	1	2	3	4			23	24	25	26	27	28	29	
JULY 2019	7	8	◐	10	11	12	13	10:55	28	2458672	TAMMUZ 5779	4	5	6	7	8	9	10		MONTH 6 Jǐ-Hài	5	6	7	8	9	10	11	Xiǎo shǔ	EPĒP 1735	30	1	2	3	4	5	6	ḤAMLĒ 2011
	14	15	○	17	18	19	20	21:38	29	2458679		11	12	13	14	15	16	17			12	13	14	15	16	17	18			7	8	9	10	11	12	13	
	21	22	23	24	◑	26	27	1:18	30	2458686		18	19	20	21	22	23	24			19	20	21	22	23	24*	25	Dà shǔ		14	15	16	17	18	19	20	
	28	29	30	31	●	2	3	3:12	31	2458693		25	26	27	28	29	1	2	Thu 4h 22m 3p		26	27	28	29	1	2	3			21	22	23	24	25	26	27	
AUGUST 2019	4	5	6	◐	8	9	10	17:31	32	2458700	AV 5779	3	4	5	6	7	8	9		MONTH 7 Jǐ-Hài	4	5	6	7[e]	8	9	10	Lì qiū	MESORĒ 1735	28	29	30	1	2	3	4	NAḤASĒ 2011
	11	12	13	14	○	16	17	12:29	33	2458707		10[i]	11	12	13	14	15	16			11	12	13	14	15[f]	16	17			5	6	7	8	9	10	11	
	18	19	20	21	22	◑	24	14:56	34	2458714		17	18	19	20	21	22	23			18	19	20	21	22	23	24	Chǔ shǔ		12	13[h]	14	15	16	17	18	
	25	26	27	28	29	●	31	10:37	35	2458721		24	25	26	27	28	29	30	Fri 17h 6m 4p		25	26	27	28	29	1	2			19	20	21	22	23	24	25	
	1	2	3	4	5	◐	7	3:10	36	2458728	ELUL 5779	1	2	3	4	5	6	7		MONTH 8 Jǐ-Hài	3	4	5	6	7	8	9		EPAG. 1735	26	27	28	29	30	1	2	PĀG. 2011
SEPTEMBER 2019	8	9	10	11	12	13	○	4:32	37	2458735		8	9	10	11	12	13	14			10	11	12	13	14	15[g]	16	Bái lù		3	4	5	6	1[a]	2	3	
	15	16	17	18	19	20	21		38	2458742		15	16	17	18	19	20	21			17	18	19	20	21	22	23		THOOUT 1736	4	5	6	7	8	9	10	MASKARAM 2012
	◑	23[d]	24	25	26	27	●	2:41 18:26	39	2458749		22	23	24	25	26	27	28			24	25	26*	27	28	29	30	Qiū fēn		11	12	13	14	15	16	17[b]	
	29	30	1	2	3	4	◐	16:47	40	2458756		29	1[a]	2[a]	3	4	5	6	Sun 5h 50m 5p		1	2	3	4	5	6	7			18	19	20	21	22	23	24	
OCTOBER 2019	6	7	8	9	10	11	12		41	2458763	TISHRI 5780	7	8	9	10[b]	11	12	13		MONTH 9 Jǐ-Hài	8	9[h]	10	11	12	13	14	Hán lù		25	26	27	28	29	30	1	
	○	14	15	16	17	18	19	21:08	42	2458770		14	15[c]	16	17	18	19	20			15	16	17	18	19	20	21		PAOPE 1736	2	3	4	5	6	7	8	ṬEQEMT 2012
	20	◑	22	23	24	25	26	12:39	43	2458777		21	22	23	24	25	26	27			22	23	24	25	26	27	28	Shuāng jiàng		9	10	11	12	13	14	15	
	27	●	29	30	31	1	2	3:38	44	2458784		28	29	30	1	2	3	4	Mon 18h 34m 6p		29	1	2	3	4	5	6			16	17	18	19	20	21	22	
NOVEMBER 2019	3	◐	5	6	7	8	9	10:23	45	2458791	ḤESHVAN 5780	5	6	7	8	9	10	11		MONTH 10 Jǐ-Hài	7	8	9	10	11	12	13	Lì dōng		23	24	25	26	27	28	29	
	10	11	○	13	14	15	16	13:34	46	2458798		12	13	14	15	16	17	18			14	15	16	17	18	19	20		ATHŌR 1736	30	1	2	3	4	5	6	ḪEDĀR 2012
	17	18	◑	20	21	22	23	21:11	47	2458805		19	20	21	22	23	24	25			21	22	23	24	25	26	27*	Xiǎo xuě		7	8	9	10	11	12	13	
	24	25	●	27	28	29	30	15:05	48	2458812		26	27	28	29	30	1	2	Wed 7h 18m 7p		28	29	1	2	3	4	5			14	15	16	17	18	19	20	
	1	2	3	◐	5	6	7	6:58	49	2458819	KISLEV 5780	3	4	5	6	7	8[d]	9		MONTH 11 Jǐ-Hài	6	7	8	9	10	11	12	Dà xuě		21	22	23	24	25	26	27	
DECEMBER 2019	8	9	10	11	○	13	14	5:12	50	2458826		10	11	12	13	14	15	16			13	14	15	16	17	18	19			28	29	30	1	2	3	4	
	15	16	17	18	◑	20	21	4:57	51	2458833		17	18	19	20	21	22	23			20	21	22	23	24	25	26		KOIAK 1736	5	6	7	8	9	10	11	TĀHŚĀŚ 2012
	22[e]	23	24	25	●	27	28	5:13	52	2458840		24	25[e]	26[e]	27[e]	28[e]	29[e]	30[e]	Thu 20h 2m 8p	MONTH 12 Jǐ-Hài	27[i]	28	29	30	1	2	3	Dōng zhì		12	13	14	15	16	17	18	
	29	30	31	1	2	◐	4	4:44	1	2458847		1[e]	2[e]	3	4	5	6	7			4	5	6	7	8	9	10			19	20	21	22	23	24	25	

[a]New Year
[b]Spring (21:58)
[c]Summer (15:54)
[d]Autumn (7:49)
[e]Winter (4:18)
● New moon
◐ First quarter moon
○ Full moon
◑ Last quarter moon

‡Leap year
[a]New Year
[b]Yom Kippur
[c]Sukkot
[d]Winter starts
[e]Ḥanukkah
[f]Purim
[g]Passover
[h]Shavuot
[i]Fast of Av

[a]New Year (4717, Pig)
[b]Lantern Festival
[c]Qīngmíng
[d]Dragon Festival
[e]Qǐqiǎo
[f]Hungry Ghosts
[g]Mid-Autumn Festival
[h]Double-Ninth Festival
[i]Dōngzhì
*Start of 60-name cycle

‡Leap year
[a]New Year
[b]Building of the Cross
[c]Christmas
[d]Jesus's Circumcision
[e]Epiphany
[f]Easter
[g]Mary's Announcement
[h]Jesus's Transfiguration

PERSIAN (ASTRONOMICAL) 1397/1398

Month	Sun	Mon	Tue	Wed	Thu	Fri	Sat
DEY 1397	9	10	11	12	13	14	15
	16	17	18	19	20	21	22
	23	24	25	26	27	28	29
	30	1	2	3	4	5	6
BAHMAN 1397	7	8	9	10	11	12	13
	14	15	16	17	18	19	20
	21	22	23	24	25	26	27
	28	29	30	1	2	3	4
ESFAND 1397	5	6	7	8	9	10	11
	12	13	14	15	16	17	18
	19	20	21	22	23	24	25
	26	27	28	29	1[a]	2	3
FARVARDĪN 1398	4	5	6	7	8	9	10
	11	12	13[b]	14	15	16	17
	18	19	20	21	22	23	24
	25	26	27	28	29	30	31
ORDĪBEHEŠT 1398	1	2	3	4	5	6	7
	8	9	10	11	12	13	14
	15	16	17	18	19	20	21
	22	23	24	25	26	27	28
	29	30	31	1	2	3	4
XORDĀD 1398	5	6	7	8	9	10	11
	12	13	14	15	16	17	18
	19	20	21	22	23	24	25
	26	27	28	29	30	31	1
TĪR 1398	2	3	4	5	6	7	8
	9	10	11	12	13	14	15
	16	17	18	19	20	21	22
	23	24	25	26	27	28	29
	30	31	1	2	3	4	5
MORDĀD 1398	6	7	8	9	10	11	12
	13	14	15	16	17	18	19
	20	21	22	23	24	25	26
	27	28	29	30	31	1	2
SHAHRĪVAR 1398	3	4	5	6	7	8	9
	10	11	12	13	14	15	16
	17	18	19	20	21	22	23
	24	25	26	27	28	29	30
	31	1	2	3	4	5	6
MEHR 1398	7	8	9	10	11	12	13
	14	15	16	17	18	19	20
	21	22	23	24	25	26	27
	28	29	30	1	2	3	4
ĀBĀN 1398	5	6	7	8	9	10	11
	12	13	14	15	16	17	18
	19	20	21	22	23	24	25
	26	27	28	29	30	1	2
ĀZAR 1398	3	4	5	6	7	8	9
	10	11	12	13	14	15	16
	17	18	19	20	21	22	23
	24	25	26	27	28	29	30
DEY 1398	1	2	3	4	5	6	7
	8	9	10	11	12	13	14

HINDU LUNAR 2075‡/2076

Month	Sun	Mon	Tue	Wed	Thu	Fri	Sat
	24	25	26	27	28	29	30
PAUSHA 2075	1	1	2	3	4	5	6
	7	8	9	10	11	12	13
	14	15	16	18	19	20	21
	22	23	24	25	26	27	28
MĀGHA 2075	29	30	1	2	3	3	4
	5	6	7	8	9	10	12
	13	14	15	16	17	18	19
	20	21	22	23	24	25	26
PHĀLGUNA 2075	27	28[h]	29	30	1	2	3
	4	5	6	7	8	9	10
	11	12	13	14	15[i]	17	18
	19	20	21	22	23	24	25
CHAITRA 2076	26	26	27	28	29	30	1[a]
	2	3	4	5	6	7	8[b]
	9	11	12	13	14	15	16
	17	18	19	20	21	22	23
	24	25	26	27	28	29	30
VAIŚĀKHA 2076	1	2	3	4	5	6	7
	8	9	10	11	12	14	15
	16	17	18	19	20	21	21
	22	23	24	25	26	27	28
JYAISHTHA 2076	29	30	1	2	3	4	5
	7	8	9	10	11	12	13
	14	15	16	17	18	19	20
	21	22	23	24	25	26	27
ĀSHĀDHA 2076	28	29	30	1	2	3	4
	5	6	7	8	10	11	12
	13	14	15	16	17	18	18
	19	20	21	22	23	24	25
ŚRĀVANA 2076	26	27	28	29	30	1	3
	4	5	6	7	8	9	10
	11	12	13	14	15	16	17
	18	19	20	21	22	23[c]	24
BHĀDRAPADA 2076	25	26	27	28	29	30	1
	2	3[d]	4	6	7	8	9
	10	11	12	13	14	14	15
	16	17	18	19	20	21	22
	23	24	25	26	27	29	30
ĀŚVINA 2076	1	2	3	4	5	6	7
	8[e]	9[e]	10[e]	11	12	13	14
	15	16	17	18	19	20	21
	22	23	24	25	26	27	28
KĀRTTIKA 2076	29	30	1[f]	3	4	5	6
	7	8	9	9	10	11	12
	13	14	15	16	17	18	19
	20	21	22	23	24	25	27
MĀRGAŚĪRA 2076	28	29	30	1	2	3	4
	5	6	7	8	9	10	11
	11[g]	12	13	14	15	16	17
	18	20	21	22	23	24	25
PAUSHA 2076	26	27	28	29	30	1	2
	3	4	5	6	7	8	9

HINDU SOLAR 1940/1941

Month	Sun	Mon	Tue	Wed	Thu	Fri	Sat
PAUSHA 1940	15	16	17	18	19	20	21
	22	23	24	25	26	27	28
MĀGHA 1940	29	1[b]	2	3	4	5	6
	7	8	9	10	11	12	13
	14	15	16	17	18	19	20
	21	22	23	24	25	26	27
PHĀLGUNA 1940	28	29	30	1	2	3	4
	5	6	7	8	9	10	11
	12	13	14	15	16	17	18
	19	20	21	22	23	24	25
CHAITRA 1940	26	27	28	29	30	1	2
	3	4	5	6	7	8	9
	10	11	12	13	14	15	16
	17	18	19	20	21	22	23
	24	25	26	27	28	29	30
VAIŚĀKHA 1941	1[a]	2	3	4	5	6	7
	8	9	10	11	12	13	14
	15	16	17	18	19	20	21
	22	23	24	25	26	27	28
JYAISHTHA 1941	29	30	31	1	2	3	4
	5	6	7	8	9	10	11
	12	13	14	15	16	17	18
	19	20	21	22	23	24	25
ĀSHĀDHA 1941	26	27	28	29	30	31	1
	2	3	4	5	6	7	8
	9	10	11	12	13	14	15
	16	17	18	19	20	21	22
	23	24	25	26	27	28	29
ŚRĀVANA 1941	30	31	32	1	2	3	4
	5	6	7	8	9	10	11
	12	13	14	15	16	17	18
	19	20	21	22	23	24	25
BHĀDRAPADA 1941	26	27	28	29	30	31	1
	2	3	4	5	6	7	8
	9	10	11	12	13	14	15
	16	17	18	19	20	21	22
	23	24	25	26	27	28	29
ĀŚVINA 1941	30	31	1	2	3	4	5
	6	7	8	9	10	11	12
	13	14	15	16	17	18	19
	20	21	22	23	24	25	26
KĀRTTIKA 1941	27	28	29	30	31	1	2
	3	4	5	6	7	8	9
	10	11	12	13	14	15	16
	17	18	19	20	21	22	23
	24	25	26	27	28	29	30
MĀRGAŚĪRA 1941	1	2	3	4	5	6	7
	8	9	10	11	12	13	14
	15	16	17	18	19	20	21
	22	23	24	25	26	27	28
PAUSHA 1941	29	1	2	3	4	5	6
	7	8	9	10	11	12	13
	14	15	16	17	18	19	20

ISLAMIC (ASTRONOMICAL) 1440‡/1441

Month	Sun	Mon	Tue	Wed	Thu	Fri	Sat
RABĪ' II 1440	22	23	24	25	26	27	28
JUMĀDĀ I 1440	29	1	2	3	4	5	6
	7	8	9	10	11	12	13
	14	15	16	17	18	19	20
	21	22	23	24	25	26	27
JUMĀDĀ II 1440	28	29	30	1	2	3	4
	5	6	7	8	9	10	11
	12	13	14	15	16	17	18
	19	20	21	22	23	24	25
RAJAB 1440	26	27	28	29	30	1	2
	3	4	5	6	7	8	9
	10	11	12	13	14	15	16
	17	18	19	20	21	22	23
	24	25	26	27[d]	28	29	30
SHA'BĀN 1440	1	2	3	4	5	6	7
	8	9	10	11	12	13	14
	15	16	17	18	19	20	21
	22	23	24	25	26	27	28
RAMAḌĀN 1440	29	1[e]	2	3	4	5	6
	7	8	9	10	11	12	13
	14	15	16	17	18	19	20
	21	22	23	24	25	26	27
SHAWWĀL 1440	28	29	30	1[f]	2	3	4
	5	6	7	8	9	10	11
	12	13	14	15	16	17	18
	19	20	21	22	23	24	25
DHU AL-QA'DA 1440	26	27	28	29	1	2	3
	4	5	6	7	8	9	10
	11	12	13	14	15	16	17
	18	19	20	21	22	23	24
DHU AL-HIJJA 1440	25	26	27	28	29	1	2
	3	4	5	6	7	8	9
	10[g]	11	12	13	14	15	16
	17	18	19	20	21	22	23
	24	25	26	27	28	29	30
MUHARRAM 1441	1[a]	2	3	4	5	6	7
	8	9	10[b]	11	12	13	14
	15	16	17	18	19	20	21
	22	23	24	25	26	27	28
SAFAR 1441	29	1	2	3	4	5	6
	7	8	9	10	11	12	13
	14	15	16	17	18	19	20
	21	22	23	24	25	26	27
RABĪ' I 1441	28	29	1	2	3	4	5
	6	7	8	9	10	11	12[c]
	13	14	15	16	17	18	19
	20	21	22	23	24	25	26
RABĪ' II 1441	27	28	29	30	1	2	3
	4	5	6	7	8	9	10
	11	12	13	14	15	16	17
	18	19	20	21	22	23	24
JUMĀDĀ I 1441	25	26	27	28	29	30	1
	2	3	4	5	6	7	8

GREGORIAN 2019

Julian (Sun)	Sun	Mon	Tue	Wed	Thu	Fri	Sat	Month
Dec 17	30	31	1	2	3	4	5	JANUARY 2019
	6	7[a]	8	9	10	11	12	
Dec 31	13	14[b]	15	16	17	18	19	
	20	21	22	23	24	25	26	
Jan 14	27	28	29	30	31	1	2	FEBRUARY 2019
	3	4	5	6	7	8	9	
Jan 28	10	11	12	13	14	15	16	
	17	18	19	20	21	22	23	
Feb 11	24	25	26	27	28	1	2	MARCH 2019
	3	4	5	6[c]	7	8	9	
Feb 25	10	11	12	13	14	15	16	
	17[d]	18	19	20	21	22	23	
Mar 11	24	25	26	27	28	29	30	
	31	1	2	3	4	5	6	APRIL 2019
Mar 25	7	8	9	10	11	12	13	
	14	15	16	17	18	19	20	
Apr 8	21[e]	22	23	24	25	26	27	
	28[f]	29	30	1	2	3	4	MAY 2019
Apr 22	5	6	7	8	9	10	11	
	12	13	14	15	16	17	18	
May 6	19	20	21	22	23	24	25	
	26	27	28	29	30	31	1	JUNE 2019
May 20	2	3	4	5	6	7	8	
	9	10	11	12	13	14	15	
Jun 3	16	17	18	19	20	21	22	
	23	24	25	26	27	28	29	
Jun 17	30	1	2	3	4	5	6	JULY 2019
	7	8	9	10	11	12	13	
Jul 1	14	15	16	17	18	19	20	
	21	22	23	24	25	26	27	
Jul 15	28	29	30	31	1	2	3	AUGUST 2019
	4	5	6	7	8	9	10	
Jul 29	11	12	13	14	15	16	17	
	18	19	20	21	22	23	24	
Aug 12	25	26	27	28	29	30	31	
	1	2	3	4	5	6	7	SEPTEMBER 2019
Aug 26	8	9	10	11	12	13	14	
	15	16	17	18	19	20	21	
Sep 9	22	23	24	25	26	27	28	
	29	30	1	2	3	4	5	OCTOBER 2019
Sep 23	6	7	8	9	10	11	12	
	13	14	15	16	17	18	19	
Oct 7	20	21	22	23	24	25	26	
	27	28	29	30	31	1	2	NOVEMBER 2019
Oct 21	3	4	5	6	7	8	9	
	10	11	12	13	14	15	16	
Nov 4	17	18	19	20	21	22	23	
	24	25	26	27	28	29	30	
Nov 18	1[g]	2	3	4	5	6	7	DECEMBER 2019
	8	9	10	11	12	13	14	
Dec 2	15	16	17	18	19	20	21	
	22	23	24	25[h]	26	27	28	
Dec 16	29	30	31	1	2	3	4	

Persian:
[a]New Year
[b]Sizdeh Bedar

Hindu Lunar:
‡Leap year
[a]New Year (Vikārin)
[b]Birthday of Rāma
[c]Birthday of Krishna
[d]Ganēśa Chaturthī
[e]Dashara
[f]Diwali
[g]Birthday of Vishnu
[h]Night of Śiva
[i]Holi

Hindu Solar:
[a]New Year (Paridhāvin)
[b]Pongal

Islamic:
‡Leap year
[a]New Year
[b]'Ashūrā'
[c]Prophet's Birthday
[d]Ascent of the Prophet
[e]Start of Ramaḍān
[f]'Id al-Fiṭr
[g]'Id al-'Aḍḥā

Gregorian:
[a]Orthodox Christmas
[b]Julian New Year
[c]Ash Wednesday
[d]Feast of Orthodoxy
[e]Easter
[f]Orthodox Easter
[g]Advent
[h]Christmas

2020

GREGORIAN 2020‡ — Lunar Phases — ISO WEEK — JULIAN DAY

Month	Sun	Mon	Tue	Wed	Thu	Fri	Sat	Lunar Phases	ISO WEEK (Mon)	JULIAN DAY (Sun noon)
JANUARY 2020	29	30	31	1[a]	2	◐	4	4:44	1	2458847
	5	6	7	8	9	○	11	19:20	2	2458854
	12	13	14	15	16	◑	18	12:58	3	2458861
	19	20	21	22	23	●	25	21:41	4	2458868
	26	27	28	29	30	31	1		5	2458875
FEBRUARY 2020	◐	3	4	5	6	7	8	1:41	6	2458882
	○	10	11	12	13	14	◑	7:32 22:16	7	2458889
	16	17	18	19	20	21	22		8	2458896
	●	24	25	26	27	28	29	15:31	9	2458903
MARCH 2020	1	◐	3	4	5	6	7	19:56	10	2458910
	8	○	10	11	12	13	14	17:47	11	2458917
	15	◑	17	18	19	20[b]	21	9:33	12	2458924
	22	23	●	25	26	27	28	9:27	13	2458931
APRIL 2020	29	30	31	◐	2	3	4	10:20	14	2458938
	5	6	7	○	9	10	11	2:34	15	2458945
	12	13	◑	15	16	17	18	22:55	16	2458952
	19	20	21	22	●	24	25	2:25	17	2458959
MAY 2020	26	27	28	29	◐	1	2	20:37	18	2458966
	3	4	5	6	○	8	9	10:44	19	2458973
	10	11	12	13	◑	15	16	14:02	20	2458980
	17	18	19	20	21	●	23	17:38	21	2458987
	24	25	26	27	28	29	◐	3:29	22	2458994
JUNE 2020	31	1	2	3	4	○	6	19:11	23	2459001
	7	8	9	10	11	12	◑	6:23	24	2459008
	14	15	16	17	18	19	20[c]		25	2459015
	●	22	23	24	25	26	27	6:41	26	2459022
JULY 2020	◐	29	30	1	2	3	4	8:15	27	2459029
	○	6	7	8	9	10	11	4:43	28	2459036
	◑	13	14	15	16	17	18	23:28	29	2459043
	19	●	21	22	23	24	25	17:32	30	2459050
AUGUST 2020	26	◐	28	29	30	31	1	12:32	31	2459057
	2	○	4	5	6	7	8	15:58	32	2459064
	9	10	◑	12	13	14	15	16:44	33	2459071
	16	17	18	●	20	21	22	2:41	34	2459078
	23	24	◐	26	27	28	29	17:57	35	2459085
SEPTEMBER 2020	30	31	1	○	3	4	5	5:21	36	2459092
	6	7	8	9	◑	11	12	9:25	37	2459099
	13	14	15	16	●	18	19	10:59	38	2459106
	20	21	22[d]	23	◐	25	26	1:54	39	2459113
OCTOBER 2020	27	28	29	30	○	2	3	21:04	40	2459120
	4	5	6	7	8	9	◑	0:38	41	2459127
	11	12	13	14	15	●	17	19:30	42	2459134
	18	19	20	21	22	◐	24	13:22	43	2459141
	25	26	27	28	29	30	○	14:48	44	2459148
NOVEMBER 2020	1	2	3	4	5	6	7		45	2459155
	◑	9	10	11	12	13	14	13:45	46	2459162
	●	16	17	18	19	20	21	5:06	47	2459169
	◐	23	24	25	26	27	28	4:44	48	2459176
DECEMBER 2020	29	○	1	2	3	4	5	9:29	49	2459183
	6	7	◑	9	10	11	12	0:36	50	2459190
	13	●	15	16	17	18	19	16:16	51	2459197
	20	◐[e]	22	23	24	25	26	23:40	52	2459204
	27	28	29	○	31	1	2	3:27	53	2459211

HEBREW 5780/5781 — Molad

ISO WEEK	Month	Sun	Mon	Tue	Wed	Thu	Fri	Sat	Molad
1	TEVETH 5780	1[e]	2[e]	3	4	5	6	7	Thu 20h2m8p
2		8	9	10	11	12	13	14	
3		15	16	17	18	19	20	21	
4		22	23	24	25	26	27	28	Sat 8h46m9p
5	SHEVAT 5780	29	1	2	3	4	5	6	
6		7	8	9	10	11	12	13	
7		14	15	16	17	18	19	20	
8		21	22	23	24	25	26	27	
9	ADAR 5780	28	29	30	1	2	3	4	Sun 21h30m10p
10		5	6	7	8	9	10	11	
11		12	13	14[f]	15	16	17	18	
12		19	20	21	22	23	24	25	
13	NISAN 5780	26	27	28	29	1	2	3	Tue 10h14m11p
14		4	5	6	7	8	9	10	
15		11	12	13	14	15[g]	16	17	
16		18	19	20	21	22	23	24	
17	IYYAR 5780	25	26	27	28	29	30	1	Wed 22h58m12p
18		2	3	4	5	6	7	8	
19		9	10	11	12	13	14	15	
20		16	17	18	19	20	21	22	
21		23	24	25	26	27	28	29	Fri 11h42m13p
22	SIVAN 5780	1	2	3	4	5	6[h]	7	
23		8	9	10	11	12	13	14	
24		15	16	17	18	19	20	21	
25		22	23	24	25	26	27	28	
26	TAMMUZ 5780	29	30	1	2	3	4	5	Sun 0h26m14p
27		6	7	8	9	10	11	12	
28		13	14	15	16	17	18	19	
29		20	21	22	23	24	25	26	
30	AV 5780	27	28	29	1	2	3	4	Mon 13h10m15p
31		5	6	7	8	9[i]	10	11	
32		12	13	14	15	16	17	18	
33		19	20	21	22	23	24	25	
34	ELUL 5780	26	27	28	29	30	1	2	Wed 1h54m16p
35		3	4	5	6	7	8	9	
36		10	11	12	13	14	15	16	
37		17	18	19	20	21	22	23	
38	TISHRI 5781	24	25	26	27	28	29	1[a]	Thu 14h38m17p
39		2[a]	3	4	5	6	7	8	
40		9	10[b]	11	12	13	14	15[c]	
41		16	17	18	19	20	21	22	
42		23	24	25	26	27	28	29	
43	HESHVAN 5781	30	1	2	3	4	5	6	Sat 3h23m0p
44		7	8	9	10	11	12	13	
45		14	15	16	17	18	19	20	
46		21	22	23	24	25	26	27	
47	KISLEV 5781	28	29	1	2	3	4	5	Sun 16h7m1p
48		6	7	8	9	10	11	12	
49		13	14	15	16	17	18	19[d]	
50		20	21	22	23	24	25[e]	26[e]	
51	TEVETH 5781	27[e]	28[e]	29[e]	1[e]	2[e]	3[e]	4	Tue 4h51m2p
52		5	6	7	8	9	10	11	
53		12	13	14	15	16	17	18	

CHINESE Jǐ-Hài/Gēng-Zǐ‡ — Solar Term

ISO WEEK	Month	Sun	Mon	Tue	Wed	Thu	Fri	Sat	Solar Term
1	MONTH 12 Jǐ-Hài	4	5	6	7	8	9	10	
2		11	12	13	14	15	16	17	Xiǎo hán
3		18	19	20	21	22	23	24	
4	MONTH 1 Gēng-Zǐ	25	26	27	28*	29	30	1[a]	Dà hán
5		2	3	4	5	6	7	8	
6		9	10	11	12	13	14	15[b]	Lì chūn
7		16	17	18	19	20	21	22	
8		23	24	25	26	27	28	29	Yǔ shuǐ
9	MONTH 2 Gēng-Zǐ	1	2	3	4	5	6	7	
10		8	9	10	11	12	13	14	Jīng zhé
11		15	16	17	18	19	20	21	
12		22	23	24	25	26	27	28	Chūn fēn
13	MONTH 3 Gēng-Zǐ	29*	30	1	2	3	4	5	
14		6	7	8	9	10	11	12[c]	Qīng míng
15		13	14	15	16	17	18	19	
16		20	21	22	23	24	25	26	
17	MONTH 4 Gēng-Zǐ	27	28	29	30	1	2	3	Gǔ yǔ
18		4	5	6	7	8	9	10	
19		11	12	13	14	15	16	17	Lì xià
20		18	19	20	21	22	23	24	
21	LEAP MONTH 4 Gēng-Zǐ	25	26	27	28	29*	30	1	Xiǎo mǎn
22		2	3	4	5	6	7	8	
23		9	10	11	12	13	14	15	Máng zhòng
24		16	17	18	19	20	21	22	
25		23	24	25	26	27	28	29	
26	MONTH 5 Gēng-Zǐ	1	2	3	4	5[d]	6	7	Xià zhì
27		8	9	10	11	12	13	14	
28		15	16	17	18	19	20	21	Xiǎo shǔ
29		22	23	24	25	26	27	28	
30	MONTH 6 Gēng-Zǐ	29	30*	1	2	3	4	5	Dà shǔ
31		6	7	8	9	10	11	12	
32		13	14	15	16	17	18	19	Lì qiū
33		20	21	22	23	24	25	26	
34	MONTH 7 Gēng-Zǐ	27	28	29	1	2	3	4	Chǔ shǔ
35		5	6	7[e]	8	9	10	11	
36		12	13	14	15[f]	16	17	18	
37		19	20	21	22	23	24	25	Bái lù
38	MONTH 8 Gēng-Zǐ	26	27	28	29	1	2*	3	
39		4	5	6	7	8	9	10	Qiū fēn
40		11	12	13	14	15[g]	16	17	
41		18	19	20	21	22	23	24	Hán lù
42	MONTH 9 Gēng-Zǐ	25	26	27	28	29	30	1	
43		2	3	4	5	6	7	8	Shuāng jiàng
44		9[h]	10	11	12	13	14	15	
45		16	17	18	19	20	21	22	Lì dōng
46		23	24	25	26	27	28	29	
47	MONTH 10 Gēng-Zǐ	1	2	3*	4	5	6	7	Xiǎo xuě
48		8	9	10	11	12	13	14	
49		15	16	17	18	19	20	21	
50		22	23	24	25	26	27	28	Dà xuě
51	MONTH 11 Gēng-Zǐ	29	30	1	2	3	4	5	
52		6	7[i]	8	9	10	11	12	Dōng zhì
53		13	14	15	16	17	18	19	

COPTIC 1736/1737 — ETHIOPIC 2012/2013

ISO WEEK	Coptic month	Sun	Mon	Tue	Wed	Thu	Fri	Sat	Ethiopic month
1	KOIAK 1736	19	20	21	22	23	24	25	TĀKHŚĀŚ 2012
2	TŌBE 1736	26	27	28	29[c]	30	1	2	ṬER 2012
3		3	4	5	6[d]	7	8	9	
4		10	11[e]	12	13	14	15	16	
5		17	18	19	20	21	22	23	
6		24	25	26	27	28	29	30	
7	MESHIR 1736	1	2	3	4	5	6	7	YAKĀTIT 2012
8		8	9	10	11	12	13	14	
9		15	16	17	18	19	20	21	
10		22	23	24	25	26	27	28	
11	PAREMOTEP 1736	29	30	1	2	3	4	5	MAGĀBIT 2012
12		6	7	8	9	10	11	12	
13		13	14	15	16	17	18	19	
14		20	21	22	23	24	25	26	
15	PARMOUTE 1736	27	28	29	30	1	2	3	MIYĀZYĀ 2012
16		4	5	6	7	8	9	10	
17		11[f]	12	13	14	15	16	17	
18		18	19	20	21	22	23	24	
19	PASHONS 1736	25	26	27	28	29[g]	30	1	GENBOT 2012
20		2	3	4	5	6	7	8	
21		9	10	11	12	13	14	15	
22		16	17	18	19	20	21	22	
23		23	24	25	26	27	28	29	
24	PAŌNE 1736	30	1	2	3	4	5	6	SANĒ 2012
25		7	8	9	10	11	12	13	
26		14	15	16	17	18	19	20	
27		21	22	23	24	25	26	27	
28	EPĒP 1736	28	29	30	1	2	3	4	ḤAMLĒ 2012
29		5	6	7	8	9	10	11	
30		12	13	14	15	16	17	18	
31		19	20	21	22	23	24	25	
32	MESORĒ 1736	26	27	28	29	30	1	2	NAḤASĒ 2012
33		3	4	5	6	7	8	9	
34		10	11	12	13[h]	14	15	16	
35		17	18	19	20	21	22	23	
36		24	25	26	27	28	29	30	
37	EPAG. 1736 / THOOUT 1737	1	2	3	4	5	1[a]	2	PĀG. 2012 / MASKARAM 2013
38		3	4	5	6	7	8	9	
39		10	11	12	13	14	15	16	
40		17[b]	18	19	20	21	22	23	
41		24	25	26	27	28	29	30	
42	PAOPE 1737	1	2	3	4	5	6	7	ṬEQEMT 2013
43		8	9	10	11	12	13	14	
44		15	16	17	18	19	20	21	
45		22	23	24	25	26	27	28	
46	ATHŌR 1737	29	30	1	2	3	4	5	ḪEDĀR 2013
47		6	7	8	9	10	11	12	
48		13	14	15	16	17	18	19	
49		20	21	22	23	24	25	26	
50	KOIAK 1737	27	28	29	30	1	2	3	TĀKHŚĀŚ 2013
51		4	5	6	7	8	9	10	
52		11	12	13	14	15	16	17	
53		18	19	20	21	22	23	24	

‡Leap year
[a]New Year
[b]Spring (3:49)
[c]Summer (21:42)
[d]Autumn (13:30)
[e]Winter (10:01)
● New moon
◐ First quarter moon
○ Full moon
◑ Last quarter moon

[a]New Year
[b]Yom Kippur
[c]Sukkot
[d]Winter starts
[e]Ḥanukkah
[f]Purim
[g]Passover
[h]Shavuot
[i]Fast of Av

‡Leap year
[a]New Year (4718, Rat)
[b]Lantern Festival
[c]Qīngmíng
[d]Dragon Festival
[e]Qǐqiǎo
[f]Hungry Ghosts
[g]Mid-Autumn Festival
[h]Double-Ninth Festival
[i]Dōngzhì
*Start of 60-name cycle

[a]New Year
[b]Building of the Cross
[c]Christmas
[d]Jesus's Circumcision
[e]Epiphany
[f]Easter
[g]Mary's Announcement
[h]Jesus's Transfiguration

2020

PERSIAN (ASTRONOMICAL) 1398/1399‡

Month	Sun	Mon	Tue	Wed	Thu	Fri	Sat
DEY 1398	8	9	10	11	12	13	14
	15	16	17	18	19	20	21
	22	23	24	25	26	27	28
	29	30	1	2	3	4	5
BAHMAN 1398	6	7	8	9	10	11	12
	13	14	15	16	17	18	19
	20	21	22	23	24	25	26
	27	28	29	30	1	2	3
ESFAND 1398	4	5	6	7	8	9	10
	11	12	13	14	15	16	17
	18	19	20	21	22	23	24
	25	26	27	28	29	1[a]	2
FARVARDĪN 1399	3	4	5	6	7	8	9
	10	11	12	13[b]	14	15	16
	17	18	19	20	21	22	23
	24	25	26	27	28	29	30
	31	1	2	3	4	5	6
ORDĪBEHEŠT 1399	7	8	9	10	11	12	13
	14	15	16	17	18	19	20
	21	22	23	24	25	26	27
	28	29	30	31	1	2	3
XORDĀD 1399	4	5	6	7	8	9	10
	11	12	13	14	15	16	17
	18	19	20	21	22	23	24
	25	26	27	28	29	30	31
TĪR 1399	1	2	3	4	5	6	7
	8	9	10	11	12	13	14
	15	16	17	18	19	20	21
	22	23	24	25	26	27	28
	29	30	31	1	2	3	4
MORDĀD 1399	5	6	7	8	9	10	11
	12	13	14	15	16	17	18
	19	20	21	22	23	24	25
	26	27	28	29	30	31	1
SHAHRĪVAR 1399	2	3	4	5	6	7	8
	9	10	11	12	13	14	15
	16	17	18	19	20	21	22
	23	24	25	26	27	28	29
	30	31	1	2	3	4	5
MEHR 1399	6	7	8	9	10	11	12
	13	14	15	16	17	18	19
	20	21	22	23	24	25	26
	27	28	29	30	1	2	3
ĀBĀN 1399	4	5	6	7	8	9	10
	11	12	13	14	15	16	17
	18	19	20	21	22	23	24
	25	26	27	28	29	30	1
ĀZAR 1399	2	3	4	5	6	7	8
	9	10	11	12	13	14	15
	16	17	18	19	20	21	22
	23	24	25	26	27	28	29
DEY 1399	30	1	2	3	4	5	6
	7	8	9	10	11	12	13

HINDU LUNAR 2076/2077‡

Month	Sun	Mon	Tue	Wed	Thu	Fri	Sat
	3	4	5	6	7	8	9
PAUSHA 2076	10	11	12	13	14	15	16
	17	18	19	20	21	22	**23**
	25	26	27	28	29	30	1
MĀGHA 2076	2	3	4	4	5	6	7
	8	9	10	11	12	13	14
	15	16	**17**	19	20	21	22
	23	24	25	26	27	28[h]	29
	30	1	2	3	4	5	6
PHĀLGUNA 2076	6	7	8	9	10	**11**	13
	14	15[i]	16	17	18	19	20
	21	22	23	24	25	26	27
	28	29	30	1[a]	2	3	4
CHAITRA 2077	5	6	7	8	9[b]	10	11
	12	13	14	15	**16**	18	19
	20	21	22	23	24	25	26
	27	28	29	30	30	1	2
VAIŚĀKHA 2077	3	4	5	6	7	8	**9**
	11	12	13	14	15	16	17
	18	19	20	21	22	23	24
	25	26	27	28	29	30	1
JYAISHTHA 2077	2	3	4	5	6	7	8
	9	10	11	**12**	14	15	16
	17	18	19	20	21	22	23
	24	25	26	26	27	28	29
	30	1	2	3	4	**5**	7
ĀSHĀDHA 2077	8	9	10	11	12	13	14
	15	16	17	18	19	20	21
	22	23	24	25	26	27	28
	29	30	1	2	3	4	5
ŚRĀVAṆA 2077	6	7	**8**	10	11	12	13
	14	15	16	17	18	19	20
	21	22	22	23[c]	24	25	26
	27	28	29	30	**1**	3	4[d]
BHĀDRAPADA 2077	5	6	7	8	9	10	11
	12	13	14	15	16	17	18
	19	20	21	22	23	24	25
	26	27	28	29	30	1	2
LEAP ĀŚVINA 2077	3	**4**	6	7	8	9	10
	11	12	13	14	15	16	17
	18	18	19	20	21	22	23
	24	25	26	**27**	29	30	1
	2	3	4	5	6	7	8[e]
ĀŚVINA 2077	9[e]	10[e]	11	12	13	14	15
	16	17	18	19	20	21	22
	23	24	25	26	27	28	29
	30	1[f]	**2**	4	5	6	7
	8	9	10	11	12	12	13
KĀRTTIKA 2077	14	15	16	17	18	19	20
	21	22	23	24	**25**	27	28
	29	30	1	2	3	4	5
MĀRGAŚIRA 2077	6	7	8	9	10	11[g]	12
	13	14	14	15	16	17	18

HINDU SOLAR 1941/1942

Month	Sun	Mon	Tue	Wed	Thu	Fri	Sat
PAUSHA 1941	14	15	16	17	18	19	20
	21	22	23	24	25	26	27
	28	29	1[b]	2	3	4	5
MĀGHA 1941	6	7	8	9	10	11	12
	13	14	15	16	17	18	19
	20	21	22	23	24	25	26
	27	28	29	30	1	2	3
PHĀLGUNA 1941	4	5	6	7	8	9	10
	11	12	13	14	15	16	17
	18	19	20	21	22	23	24
	25	26	27	28	29	30	1
CHAITRA 1941	2	3	4	5	6	7	8
	9	10	11	12	13	14	15
	16	17	18	19	20	21	22
	23	24	25	26	27	28	29
	30	1[a]	2	3	4	5	6
VAIŚĀKHA 1942	7	8	9	10	11	12	13
	14	15	16	17	18	19	20
	21	22	23	24	25	26	27
	28	29	30	31	1	2	3
JYAISHTHA 1942	4	5	6	7	8	9	10
	11	12	13	14	15	16	17
	18	19	20	21	22	23	24
	25	26	27	28	29	30	31
	32	1	2	3	4	5	6
ĀSHĀDHA 1942	7	8	9	10	11	12	13
	14	15	16	17	18	19	20
	21	22	23	24	25	26	27
	28	29	30	31	1	2	3
ŚRĀVAṆA 1942	4	5	6	7	8	9	10
	11	12	13	14	15	16	17
	18	19	20	21	22	23	24
	25	26	27	28	29	30	31
	32	1	2	3	4	5	6
BHĀDRAPADA 1942	7	8	9	10	11	12	13
	14	15	16	17	18	19	20
	21	22	23	24	25	26	27
	28	29	30	31	1	2	3
ĀŚVINA 1942	4	5	6	7	8	9	10
	11	12	13	14	15	16	17
	18	19	20	21	22	23	24
	25	26	27	28	29	30	1
KĀRTTIKA 1942	2	3	4	5	6	7	8
	9	10	11	12	13	14	15
	16	17	18	19	20	21	22
	23	24	25	26	27	28	29
	30	1	2	3	4	5	6
MĀRGAŚIRA 1942	7	8	9	10	11	12	13
	14	15	16	17	18	19	20
	21	22	23	24	25	26	27
	28	29	1	2	3	4	5
PAUSHA 1942	6	7	8	9	10	11	12
	13	14	15	16	17	18	19

ISLAMIC (ASTRONOMICAL) 1441/1442‡

Month	Sun	Mon	Tue	Wed	Thu	Fri	Sat
JUMĀDĀ I 1441	2	3	4	5	6	7	8
	9	10	11	12	13	14	15
	16	17	18	19	20	21	22
	23	24	25	26	27	28	29
JUMĀDĀ II 1441	1	2	3	4	5	6	7
	8	9	10	11	12	13	14
	15	16	17	18	19	20	21
	22	23	24	25	26	27	28
RAJAB 1441	29	30	1	2	3	4	5
	6	7	8	9	10	11	12
	13	14	15	16	17	18	19
	20	21	22	23	24	25	26
SHA'BĀN 1441	27[d]	28	29	30	1	2	3
	4	5	6	7	8	9	10
	11	12	13	14	15	16	17
	18	19	20	21	22	23	24
RAMAḌĀN 1441	25	26	27	28	29	1[e]	2
	3	4	5	6	7	8	9
	10	11	12	13	14	15	16
	17	18	19	20	21	22	23
	24	25	26	27	28	29	30
SHAWWĀL 1441	1[f]	2	3	4	5	6	7
	8	9	10	11	12	13	14
	15	16	17	18	19	20	21
	22	23	24	25	26	27	28
DHU AL-QA'DA 1441	29	30	1	2	3	4	5
	6	7	8	9	10	11	12
	13	14	15	16	17	18	19
	20	21	22	23	24	25	26
DHU AL-ḤIJJA 1441	27	28	29	1	2	3	4
	5	6	7	8	9	10[g]	11
	12	13	14	15	16	17	18
	19	20	21	22	23	24	25
MUḤARRAM 1442	26	27	28	29	1[a]	2	3
	4	5	6	7	8	9	10[b]
	11	12	13	14	15	16	17
	18	19	20	21	22	23	24
	25	26	27	28	29	30	1
ṢAFAR 1442	2	3	4	5	6	7	8
	9	10	11	12	13	14	15
	16	17	18	19	20	21	22
	23	24	25	26	27	28	29
RABĪ' I 1442	1	2	3	4	5	6	7
	8	9	10	11	12[c]	13	14
	15	16	17	18	19	20	21
	22	23	24	25	26	27	28
RABĪ' II 1442	29	1	2	3	4	5	6
	7	8	9	10	11	12	13
	14	15	16	17	18	19	20
	21	22	23	24	25	26	27
JUMĀDĀ I 1442	28	29	30	1	2	3	4
	5	6	7	8	9	10	11
	12	13	14	15	16	17	18

GREGORIAN 2020‡

Julian‡ (Sun)	Sun	Mon	Tue	Wed	Thu	Fri	Sat	Month
Dec 16	29	30	31	1	2	3	4	JANUARY 2020
	5	6	7[a]	8	9	10	11	
Dec 30	12	13	14[b]	15	16	17	18	
	19	20	21	22	23	24	25	
Jan 13	26	27	28	29	30	31	1	FEBRUARY 2020
	2	3	4	5	6	7	8	
Jan 27	9	10	11	12	13	14	15	
	16	17	18	19	20	21	22	
Feb 10	23	24	25	26[c]	27	28	29	
	1	2	3	4	5	6	7	MARCH 2020
Feb 24	8[d]	9	10	11	12	13	14	
	15	16	17	18	19	20	21	
Mar 9	22	23	24	25	26	27	28	
	29	30	31	1	2	3	4	APRIL 2020
Mar 23	5	6	7	8	9	10	11	
	12[e]	13	14	15	16	17	18	
Apr 6	19[f]	20	21	22	23	24	25	
	26	27	28	29	30	1	2	MAY 2020
Apr 20	3	4	5	6	7	8	9	
	10	11	12	13	14	15	16	
May 4	17	18	19	20	21	22	23	
	24	25	26	27	28	29	30	
May 18	31	1	2	3	4	5	6	JUNE 2020
	7	8	9	10	11	12	13	
Jun 1	14	15	16	17	18	19	20	
	21	22	23	24	25	26	27	
Jun 15	28	29	30	1	2	3	4	JULY 2020
	5	6	7	8	9	10	11	
Jun 29	12	13	14	15	16	17	18	
	19	20	21	22	23	24	25	
Jul 13	26	27	28	29	30	31	1	AUGUST 2020
	2	3	4	5	6	7	8	
Jul 27	9	10	11	12	13	14	15	
	16	17	18	19	20	21	22	
Aug 10	23	24	25	26	27	28	29	
	30	31	1	2	3	4	5	SEPTEMBER 2020
Aug 24	6	7	8	9	10	11	12	
	13	14	15	16	17	18	19	
Sep 7	20	21	22	23	24	25	26	
	27	28	29	30	1	2	3	OCTOBER 2020
Sep 21	4	5	6	7	8	9	10	
	11	12	13	14	15	16	17	
Oct 5	18	19	20	21	22	23	24	
	25	26	27	28	29	30	31	
Oct 19	1	2	3	4	5	6	7	NOVEMBER 2020
	8	9	10	11	12	13	14	
Nov 2	15	16	17	18	19	20	21	
	22	23	24	25	26	27	28	
Nov 16	29[g]	30	1	2	3	4	5	DECEMBER 2020
	6	7	8	9	10	11	12	
Nov 30	13	14	15	16	17	18	19	
	20	21	22	23	24	25[h]	26	
Dec 14	27	28	29	30	31	1	2	

Persian:
‡Leap year
[a]New Year
[b]Sizdeh Bedar

Hindu Lunar:
‡Leap year
[a]New Year (Śārvari)
[b]Birthday of Rāma
[c]Birthday of Krishna
[d]Ganēśa Chaturthī
[e]Dashara
[f]Diwali
[g]Birthday of Vishnu
[h]Night of Śiva
[i]Holi

Hindu Solar:
[a]New Year (Pramādin)
[b]Pongal

Islamic:
‡Leap year
[a]New Year
[b]'Ashūrā'
[c]Prophet's Birthday
[d]Ascent of the Prophet
[e]Start of Ramaḍān
[f]'Īd al-Fiṭr
[g]'Īd al-'Aḍḥā

Gregorian:
‡Leap year
[a]Orthodox Christmas
[b]Julian New Year
[c]Ash Wednesday
[d]Feast of Orthodoxy
[e]Easter
[f]Orthodox Easter
[g]Advent
[h]Christmas

2021

Gregorian 2021 (with Lunar Phases, ISO Week, Julian Day)

Month	Sun	Mon	Tue	Wed	Thu	Fri	Sat	Lunar Phases	ISO WEEK (Mon)	JULIAN DAY (Sun noon)
JANUARY 2021	27	28	29	○	31	1[a]	2	3:27	53	2459211
	3	4	5	◑	7	8	9	9:36	1	2459218
	10	11	12	●	14	15	16	4:59	2	2459225
	17	18	19	◐	21	22	23	21:00	3	2459232
	24	25	26	27	○	29	30	19:15	4	2459239
FEBRUARY 2021	31	1	2	3	◑	5	6	17:36	5	2459246
	7	8	9	10	●	12	13	19:05	6	2459253
	14	15	16	17	18	◐	20	18:46	7	2459260
	21	22	23	24	25	26	○	8:16	8	2459267
MARCH 2021	28	1	2	3	4	5	◑	1:29	9	2459274
	7	8	9	10	11	12	●	10:20	10	2459281
	14	15	16	17	18	19	20[b]		11	2459288
	◐	22	23	24	25	26	27	14:39	12	2459295
APRIL 2021	○	29	30	31	1	2	3	18:47	13	2459302
	◑	5	6	7	8	9	10	10:02	14	2459309
	11	●	13	14	15	16	17	2:30	15	2459316
	18	19	◐	21	22	23	24	6:58	16	2459323
MAY 2021	25	26	○	28	29	30	1	3:31	17	2459330
	2	◑	4	5	6	7	8	19:49	18	2459337
	9	10	●	12	13	14	15	18:59	19	2459344
	16	17	18	◐	20	21	22	19:12	20	2459351
	23	24	25	○	27	28	29	11:13	21	2459358
JUNE 2021	30	31	1	◑	3	4	5	7:23	22	2459365
	6	7	8	9	●	11	12	10:52	23	2459372
	13	14	15	16	17	◐	19	3:53	24	2459379
	20	21[c]	22	23	○	25	26	18:39	25	2459386
JULY 2021	27	28	29	30	◑	2	3	21:10	26	2459393
	4	5	6	7	8	9	●	1:16	27	2459400
	11	12	13	14	15	16	◐	10:10	28	2459407
	18	19	20	21	22	23	○	2:36	29	2459414
	25	26	27	28	29	30	◑	13:15	30	2459421
AUGUST 2021	1	2	3	4	5	6	7		31	2459428
	●	9	10	11	12	13	14	13:49	32	2459435
	◐	16	17	18	19	20	21	15:19	33	2459442
	○	23	24	25	26	27	28	12:01	34	2459449
SEPTEMBER 2021	29	◑	31	1	2	3	4	7:12	35	2459456
	5	6	●	8	9	10	11	0:51	36	2459463
	12	◐	14	15	16	17	18	20:39	37	2459470
	19	○	21	22[d]	23	24	25	23:54	38	2459477
OCTOBER 2021	26	27	28	◑	30	1	2	1:56	39	2459484
	3	4	5	●	7	8	9	11:04	40	2459491
	10	11	12	◐	14	15	16	3:24	41	2459498
	17	18	19	○	21	22	23	14:56	42	2459505
	24	25	26	27	◑	29	30	20:04	43	2459512
NOVEMBER 2021	31	1	2	3	●	5	6	21:14	44	2459519
	7	8	9	10	◐	12	13	12:45	45	2459526
	14	15	16	17	18	○	20	8:56	46	2459533
	21	22	23	24	25	26	◑	12:27	47	2459540
DECEMBER 2021	28	29	30	1	2	3	●	7:42	48	2459547
	5	6	7	8	9	10	◐	1:34	49	2459554
	12	13	14	15	16	17	18		50	2459561
	○	20	21[e]	22	23	24	25	4:35	51	2459568
	26	◑	28	29	30	31	1	2:23	52	2459575

Hebrew 5781/5782‡

ISO WEEK	Month	Sun	Mon	Tue	Wed	Thu	Fri	Sat	Molad
53	TEVETH 5781	12	13	14	15	16	17	18	
1		19	20	21	22	23	24	25	Wed 17h35m9p
2	SHEVAT 5781	26	27	28	29	1	2	3	
3		4	5	6	7	8	9	10	
4		11	12	13	14	15	16	17	
5		18	19	20	21	22	23	24	
6	ADAR 5781	25	26	27	28	29	30	1	Fri 6h19m10p
7		2	3	4	5	6	7	8	
8		9	10	11	12	13	14[f]	15	
9		16	17	18	19	20	21	22	
10		23	24	25	26	27	28	29	Sat 19h3m11p
11	NISAN 5781	1	2	3	4	5	6	7	
12		8	9	10	11	12	13	14	
13		15[g]	16	17	18	19	20	21	
14		22	23	24	25	26	27	28	Mon 7h47m0p
15	IYYAR 5781	29	30	1	2	3	4	5	
16		6	7	8	9	10	11	12	
17		13	14	15	16	17	18	19	
18		20	21	22	23	24	25	26	Tue 20h31m1p
19	SIVAN 5781	27	28	29	1	2	3	4	
20		5	6[h]	7	8	9	10	11	
21		12	13	14	15	16	17	18	
22		19	20	21	22	23	24	25	
23	TAMMUZ 5781	26	27	28	29	30	1	2	Thu 9h15m2p
24		3	4	5	6	7	8	9	
25		10	11	12	13	14	15	16	
26		17	18	19	20	21	22	23	Fri 21h59m3p
27	AV 5781	24	25	26	27	28	29	1	
28		2	3	4	5	6	7	8	
29		9[i]	10	11	12	13	14	15	
30		16	17	18	19	20	21	22	
31		23	24	25	26	27	28	29	Sun 10h43m4p
32	ELUL 5781	30	1	2	3	4	5	6	
33		7	8	9	10	11	12	13	
34		14	15	16	17	18	19	20	
35		21	22	23	24	25	26	27	Mon 23h27m5p
36	TISHRI 5782	28	29	1[a]	2[a]	3	4	5	
37		6	7	8	9	10[b]	11	12	
38		13	14	15[c]	16	17	18	19	
39		20	21	22	23	24	25	26	Wed 12h11m6p
40	HESHVAN 5782	27	28	29	30	1	2	3	
41		4	5	6	7	8	9	10	
42		11	12	13	14	15	16	17	
43		18	19	20	21	22	23	24	Fri 0h55m7p
44	KISLEV 5782	25	26	27	28	29	1	2	
45		3	4	5	6	7	8	9	
46		10	11	12	13	14	15	16	
47		17	18	19	20	21	22	23	
48		24	25[e]	26[e]	27[e]	28[e]	29[e]	30[e]	Sat 13h39m8p
49	TEVETH 5782	1[d][e]	2[e]	3	4	5	6	7	
50		8	9	10	11	12	13	14	
51		15	16	17	18	19	20	21	
52		22	23	24	25	26	27	28	

Chinese Gēng-Zǐ‡/Xīn-Chǒu

ISO WEEK	Month	Sun	Mon	Tue	Wed	Thu	Fri	Sat	Solar Term
53	MONTH 11 Gēng-Zǐ	13	14	15	16	17	18	19	
1		20	21	22	23	24	25	26	Xiǎo hán
2	MONTH 12 Gēng-Zǐ	27	28	29	1	2	3	4*	
3		5	6	7	**8**	9	10	11	Dà hán
4		12	13	14	15	16	17	18	
5		19	20	21	22	23	24	25	Lì chūn
6	MONTH 1 Xīn-Chǒu	26	27	28	29	30	1[a]	2	
7		3	4	5	6	**7**	8	9	Yǔ shuǐ
8		10	11	12	13	14	15[b]	16	
9		17	18	19	20	21	22	23	Jīng zhé
10	MONTH 2 Xīn-Chǒu	24	25	26	27	28	29	1	
11		2	3	4	5*	6	7	**8**	Chūn fēn
12		9	10	11	12	13	14	15	
13		16	17	18	19	20	21	22	
14		23[c]	24	25	26	27	28	29	Qīng míng
15	MONTH 3 Xīn-Chǒu	30	1	2	3	4	5	6	
16		7	8	**9**	10	11	12	13	Gǔ yǔ
17		14	15	16	17	18	19	20	
18		21	22	23	24	25	26	27	Lì xià
19	MONTH 4 Xīn-Chǒu	28	29	30	1	2	3	4	
20		5*	6	7	8	9	**10**	11	Xiǎo mǎn
21		12	13	14	15	16	17	18	
22		19	20	21	22	23	24	25	Máng zhòng
23	MONTH 5 Xīn-Chǒu	26	27	28	29	1	2	3	
24		4	5[d]	6	7	8	9	10	
25		11	**12**	13	14	15	16	17	Xià zhì
26		18	19	20	21	22	23	24	
27	MONTH 6 Xīn-Chǒu	25	26	27	28	29	30	1	Xiǎo shǔ
28		2	3	4	5	6*	7	8	
29		9	10	11	12	**13**	14	15	Dà shǔ
30		16	17	18	19	20	21	22	
31		23	24	25	26	27	28	29	Lì qiū
32	MONTH 7 Xīn-Chǒu	1	2	3	4	5	6	7[e]	
33		8	9	10	11	12	13	14	
34		15[f]	**16**	17	18	19	20	21	Chǔ shǔ
35		22	23	24	25	26	27	28	
36	MONTH 8 Xīn-Chǒu	29	30	1	2	3	4	5	Bái lù
37		6	7*	8	9	10	11	12	
38		13	14	15[g]	16	**17**	18	19	Qiū fēn
39		20	21	22	23	24	25	26	
40	MONTH 9 Xīn-Chǒu	27	28	29	1	2	3	4	Hán lù
41		5	6	7	8	9[h]	10	11	
42		12	13	14	15	16	17	**18**	Shuāng jiàng
43		19	20	21	22	23	24	25	
44	MONTH 10 Xīn-Chǒu	26	27	28	29	30	1	2	
45		3	4	5	6	7	8*	9	Lì dōng
46		10	11	12	13	14	15	16	
47		17	**18**	19	20	21	22	23	Xiǎo xuě
48	MONTH 11 Xīn-Chǒu	24	25	26	27	28	29	1	
49		2	3	4	5	6	7	8	Dà xuě
50		9	10	11	12	13	14	15	
51		16	17	**18**[i]	19	20	21	22	Dōng zhì
52		23	24	25	26	27	28	29	

Coptic 1737/1738 — Ethiopic 2013/2014

ISO WEEK	Coptic Month	Sun	Mon	Tue	Wed	Thu	Fri	Sat	Ethiopic Month
53	KOIAK 1737	18	19	20	21	22	23	24	TĀKHŚĀŚ 2013
1	TŌBE 1737	25	26	27	28	29[c]	30	1	ṬER 2013
2		2	3	4	5	6[d]	7	8	
3		9	10	11[e]	12	13	14	15	
4		16	17	18	19	20	21	22	
5		23	24	25	26	27	28	29	
6	MESHIR 1737	30	1	2	3	4	5	6	YAKĀTIT 2013
7		7	8	9	10	11	12	13	
8		14	15	16	17	18	19	20	
9		21	22	23	24	25	26	27	
10	PAREMOTEP 1737	28	29	30	1	2	3	4	MAGĀBIT 2013
11		5	6	7	8	9	10	11	
12		12	13	14	15	16	17	18	
13		19	20	21	22	23	24	25	
14	PARMOUTE 1737	26	27	28	29	30	1	2	MIYĀZYĀ 2013
15		3	4	5	6	7	8	9	
16		10	11	12	13	14	15	16	
17		17	18	19	20	21	22	23	
18		24[f]	25	26	27	28	29[g]	30	
19	PASHONS 1737	1	2	3	4	5	6	7	GENBOT 2013
20		8	9	10	11	12	13	14	
21		15	16	17	18	19	20	21	
22		22	23	24	25	26	27	28	
23	PAŌNE 1737	29	30	1	2	3	4	5	SANĒ 2013
24		6	7	8	9	10	11	12	
25		13	14	15	16	17	18	19	
26		20	21	22	23	24	25	26	
27	EPĒP 1737	27	28	29	30	1	2	3	ḤAMLĒ 2013
28		4	5	6	7	8	9	10	
29		11	12	13	14	15	16	17	
30		18	19	20	21	22	23	24	
31	MESORĒ 1737	25	26	27	28	29	30	1	NAḤASĒ 2013
32		2	3	4	5	6	7	8	
33		9	10	11	12	13[h]	14	15	
34		16	17	18	19	20	21	22	
35		23	24	25	26	27	28	29	
36	EPAG. 1737 / THOOUT 1738	30	1	2	3	4	5	1[a]	PĀG. 2013 / MASKARAM 2014
37		2	3	4	5	6	7	8	
38		9	10	11	12	13	14	15	
39		16	17[b]	18	19	20	21	22	
40		23	24	25	26	27	28	29	
41	PAOPE 1738	30	1	2	3	4	5	6	ṬEQEMT 2014
42		7	8	9	10	11	12	13	
43		14	15	16	17	18	19	20	
44		21	22	23	24	25	26	27	
45	ATHŌR 1738	28	29	30	1	2	3	4	ḪEDĀR 2014
46		5	6	7	8	9	10	11	
47		12	13	14	15	16	17	18	
48		19	20	21	22	23	24	25	
49	KOIAK 1738	26	27	28	29	30	1	2	TĀKHŚĀŚ 2014
50		3	4	5	6	7	8	9	
51		10	11	12	13	14	15	16	
52		17	18	19	20	21	22	23	

Gregorian notes:
[a]New Year
[b]Spring (9:36)
[c]Summer (3:31)
[d]Autumn (19:20)
[e]Winter (15:58)
● New moon
◐ First quarter moon
○ Full moon
◑ Last quarter moon

Hebrew notes:
‡Leap year
[a]New Year
[b]Yom Kippur
[c]Sukkot
[d]Winter starts
[e]Ḥanukkah
[f]Purim
[g]Passover
[h]Shavuot
[i]Fast of Av

Chinese notes:
‡Leap year
[a]New Year (4719, Ox)
[b]Lantern Festival
[c]Qīngmíng
[d]Dragon Festival
[e]Qīqiǎo
[f]Hungry Ghosts
[g]Mid-Autumn Festival
[h]Double-Ninth Festival
[i]Dōngzhì
*Start of 60-name cycle

Coptic/Ethiopic notes:
[a]New Year
[b]Building of the Cross
[c]Christmas
[d]Jesus's Circumcision
[e]Epiphany
[f]Easter
[g]Mary's Announcement
[h]Jesus's Transfiguration

2021

PERSIAN (ASTRONOMICAL) 1399‡/1400

Month	Sun	Mon	Tue	Wed	Thu	Fri	Sat
DEY 1399	7	8	9	10	11	12	13
	14	15	16	17	18	19	20
	21	22	23	24	25	26	27
BAHMAN 1399	28	29	30	*1*	2	3	4
	5	6	7	8	9	10	11
	12	13	14	15	16	17	18
	19	20	21	22	23	24	25
ESFAND 1399	26	27	28	29	30	*1*	2
	3	4	5	6	7	8	9
	10	11	12	13	14	15	16
	17	18	19	20	21	22	23
	24	25	26	27	28	29	30
FARVARDĪN 1400	*1*[a]	2	3	4	5	6	7
	8	9	10	11	12	13[b]	14
	15	16	17	18	19	20	21
	22	23	24	25	26	27	28
ORDĪBEHEŠT 1400	29	30	31	*1*	2	3	4
	5	6	7	8	9	10	11
	12	13	14	15	16	17	18
	19	20	21	22	23	24	25
XORDĀD 1400	26	27	28	29	30	31	*1*
	2	3	4	5	6	7	8
	9	10	11	12	13	14	15
	16	17	18	19	20	21	22
	23	24	25	26	27	28	29
TĪR 1400	30	31	*1*	2	3	4	5
	6	7	8	9	10	11	12
	13	14	15	16	17	18	19
	20	21	22	23	24	25	26
MORDĀD 1400	27	28	29	30	31	*1*	2
	3	4	5	6	7	8	9
	10	11	12	13	14	15	16
	17	18	19	20	21	22	23
	24	25	26	27	28	29	30
SHAHRĪVAR 1400	31	*1*	2	3	4	5	6
	7	8	9	10	11	12	13
	14	15	16	17	18	19	20
	21	22	23	24	25	26	27
MEHR 1400	28	29	30	31	*1*	2	3
	4	5	6	7	8	9	10
	11	12	13	14	15	16	17
	18	19	20	21	22	23	24
ĀBĀN 1400	25	26	27	28	29	30	*1*
	2	3	4	5	6	7	8
	9	10	11	12	13	14	15
	16	17	18	19	20	21	22
	23	24	25	26	27	28	29
ĀZAR 1400	30	*1*	2	3	4	5	6
	7	8	9	10	11	12	13
	14	15	16	17	18	19	20
	21	22	23	24	25	26	27
DEY 1400	28	29	30	*1*	2	3	4
	5	6	7	8	9	10	11

‡Leap year
[a]New Year
[b]Sizdeh Bedar

HINDU LUNAR 2077‡/2078

Month	Sun	Mon	Tue	Wed	Thu	Fri	Sat
MĀRGAŚĪRA 2077	13	14	*14*	15	16	17	18
	19	21	22	23	24	25	26
PAUSHA 2077	27	28	29	30	1	2	3
	4	5	6	7	8	9	10
	11	12	13	14	15	16	17
	18	19	20	21	22	23	**24**
MĀGHA 2077	26	27	28	29	30	1	2
	3	4	5	6	7	*7*	8
	9	10	11	12	13	14	15
	16	17	**18**	20	21	22	23
	24	25	26	27	28[h]	29	30
PHĀLGUNA 2077	1	2	3	4	5	6	7
	8	9	10	11	12	13	14
	15[i]	16	17	18	19	20	21
	22	**23**	25	26	27	28	29
CHAITRA 2078	30	*30*	1[a]	2	3	4	5
	6	7	8	9[b]	10	11	12
	13	14	15	**16**	18	19	20
	21	22	23	24	25	26	27
VAIŚĀKHA 2078	28	29	30	1	2	3	4
	4	5	6	7	8	**9**	11
	12	13	14	15	16	17	18
	19	20	**21**	23	24	25	*25*
JYAISHTHA 2078	26	27	28	29	30	1	2
	3	4	5	6	7	8	9
	10	11	**12**	14	15	16	17
	18	19	20	21	22	23	24
ĀSHĀḌHA 2078	25	26	27	28	29	30	1
	1	2	3	**4**	6	7	8
	9	10	11	12	13	14	15
	16	18	19	20	21	22	*22*
	23	24	25	26	27	28	29
ŚRĀVAṆA 2078	30	1	2	3	4	5	6
	7	**8**	10	11	12	13	14
	15	16	17	18	19	20	21
	22	23[c]	24	25	26	27	*27*
BHĀDRAPADA 2078	28	**29**	1	2	3	4[d]	5
	6	7	8	9	10	11	**12**
	14	15	16	17	18	*18*	19
	20	21	22	23	24	25	26
ĀŚVINA 2078	27	28	29	30	1	2	3
	4	6	7	8[e]	9[e]	10[e]	11
	12	13	14	15	16	17	18
	19	20	21	*21*	22	23	24
KĀRTTIKA 2078	25	26	27	**28**	30	1[f]	2
	3	4	5	6	7	8	9
	10	11	12	13	14	15	16
	17	18	19	20	21	22	23
	24	25	26	27	28	29	30
MĀRGAŚĪRA 2078	1	**2**	4	5	6	7	8
	9	10	11[g]	12	13	14	15
	15	16	17	18	19	20	21
	22	23	24	25	26	**27**	29

‡Leap year
[a]New Year (Plava)
[b]Birthday of Rāma
[c]Birthday of Krishna
[d]Ganēśa Chaturthī
[e]Dashara
[f]Diwali
[g]Birthday of Vishnu
[h]Night of Śiva
[i]Holi

HINDU SOLAR 1942/1943‡

Month	Sun	Mon	Tue	Wed	Thu	Fri	Sat
PAUSHA 1942	13	14	15	16	17	18	19
	20	21	22	23	24	25	26
MĀGHA 1942	27	28	29	30	1[b]	2	3
	4	5	6	7	8	9	10
	11	12	13	14	15	16	17
	18	19	20	21	22	23	24
PHĀLGUNA 1942	25	26	27	28	29	1	2
	3	4	5	6	7	8	9
	10	11	12	13	14	15	16
	17	18	19	20	21	22	23
	24	25	26	27	28	29	30
CHAITRA 1942	1	2	3	4	5	6	7
	8	9	10	11	12	13	14
	15	16	17	18	19	20	21
	22	23	24	25	26	27	28
VAIŚĀKHA 1943	29	30	1[a]	2	3	4	5
	6	7	8	9	10	11	12
	13	14	15	16	17	18	19
	20	21	22	23	24	25	26
JYAISHTHA 1943	27	28	29	30	31	1	2
	3	4	5	6	7	8	9
	10	11	12	13	14	15	16
	17	18	19	20	21	22	23
	24	25	26	27	28	29	30
ĀSHĀḌHA 1943	31	32	1	2	3	4	5
	6	7	8	9	10	11	12
	13	14	15	16	17	18	19
	20	21	22	23	24	25	26
ŚRĀVAṆA 1943	27	28	29	30	31	1	2
	3	4	5	6	7	8	9
	10	11	12	13	14	15	16
	17	18	19	20	21	22	23
	24	25	26	27	28	29	30
BHĀDRAPADA 1943	31	32	1	2	3	4	5
	6	7	8	9	10	11	12
	13	14	15	16	17	18	19
	20	21	22	23	24	25	26
ĀŚVINA 1943	27	28	29	30	31	1	2
	3	4	5	6	7	8	9
	10	11	12	13	14	15	16
	17	18	19	20	21	22	23
	24	25	26	27	28	29	30
KĀRTTIKA 1943	1	2	3	4	5	6	7
	8	9	10	11	12	13	14
	15	16	17	18	19	20	21
	22	23	24	25	26	27	28
MĀRGAŚĪRA 1943	29	30	1	2	3	4	5
	6	7	8	9	10	11	12
	13	14	15	16	17	18	19
	20	21	22	23	24	25	26
PAUSHA 1943	27	28	29	30	1	2	3
	4	5	6	7	8	9	10
	11	12	13	14	15	16	17

‡Leap year
[a]New Year (Ānanda)
[b]Pongal

ISLAMIC (ASTRONOMICAL) 1442‡/1443

Month	Sun	Mon	Tue	Wed	Thu	Fri	Sat
JUMĀDĀ I 1442	12	13	14	15	16	17	18
	19	20	21	22	23	24	25
JUMĀDĀ II 1442	26	27	28	29	30	*1*	2
	3	4	5	6	7	8	9
	10	11	12	13	14	15	16
	17	18	19	20	21	22	23
RAJAB 1442	24	25	26	27	28	29	*1*
	2	3	4	5	6	7	8
	9	10	11	12	13	14	15
	16	17	18	19	20	21	22
	23	24	25	26	27[d]	28	29
SHA'BĀN 1442	30	*1*	2	3	4	5	6
	7	8	9	10	11	12	13
	14	15	16	17	18	19	20
	21	22	23	24	25	26	27
RAMAḌĀN 1442	28	29	*1*[e]	2	3	4	5
	6	7	8	9	10	11	12
	13	14	15	16	17	18	19
	20	21	22	23	24	25	26
SHAWWĀL 1442	27	28	29	30	*1*[f]	2	3
	4	5	6	7	8	9	10
	11	12	13	14	15	16	17
	18	19	20	21	22	23	24
DHU AL-QA'DA 1442	25	26	27	28	29	*30*	1
	2	3	4	5	6	7	8
	9	10	11	12	13	14	15
	16	17	18	19	20	21	22
	23	24	25	26	27	28	29
DHU AL-ḤIJJA 1442	*1*	2	3	4	5	6	7
	8	9	10[g]	11	12	13	14
	15	16	17	18	19	20	21
	22	23	24	25	26	27	28
MUḤARRAM 1443	29	30	*1*[a]	2	3	4	5
	6	7	8	9	10[b]	11	12
	13	14	15	16	17	18	19
	20	21	22	23	24	25	26
ṢAFAR 1443	27	28	29	1	2	3	4
	5	6	7	8	9	10	11
	12	13	14	15	16	17	18
	19	20	21	22	23	24	25
RABĪ' I 1443	26	27	28	29	30	*1*	2
	3	4	5	6	7	8	9
	10	11	12[c]	13	14	15	16
	17	18	19	20	21	22	23
RABĪ' II 1443	24	25	26	27	28	29	1
	2	3	4	5	6	7	8
	9	10	11	12	13	14	15
	16	17	18	19	20	21	22
	23	24	25	26	27	28	29
JUMĀDĀ I 1443	30	*1*	2	3	4	5	6
	7	8	9	10	11	12	13
	14	15	16	17	18	19	20
	21	22	23	24	25	26	27

‡Leap year
[a]New Year
[b]'Ashūrā'
[c]Prophet's Birthday
[d]Ascent of the Prophet
[e]Start of Ramaḍān
[f]'Īd al-Fiṭr
[g]'Īd al-'Aḍḥā

GREGORIAN 2021

Julian (Sun)	Month	Sun	Mon	Tue	Wed	Thu	Fri	Sat
Dec 14	JANUARY 2021	27	28	29	30	31	1	2
		3	4	5	6	7[a]	8	9
Dec 28		10	11	12	13	14[b]	15	16
		17	18	19	20	21	22	23
Jan 11		24	25	26	27	28	29	30
	FEBRUARY 2021	31	1	2	3	4	5	6
Jan 25		7	8	9	10	11	12	13
		14	15	16	17[c]	18	19	20
Feb 8		21	22	23	24	25	26	27
	MARCH 2021	28	1	2	3	4	5	6
Feb 22		7	8	9	10	11	12	13
		14	15	16	17	18	19	20
Mar 8		21[d]	22	23	24	25	26	27
	APRIL 2021	28	29	30	31	1	2	3
Mar 22		4[e]	5	6	7	8	9	10
		11	12	13	14	15	16	17
Apr 5		18	19	20	21	22	23	24
	MAY 2021	25	26	27	28	29	30	1
Apr 19		2[f]	3	4	5	6	7	8
		9	10	11	12	13	14	15
May 3		16	17	18	19	20	21	22
		23	24	25	26	27	28	29
May 17	JUNE 2021	30	31	1	2	3	4	5
		6	7	8	9	10	11	12
May 31		13	14	15	16	17	18	19
		20	21	22	23	24	25	26
Jun 14	JULY 2021	27	28	29	30	1	2	3
		4	5	6	7	8	9	10
Jun 28		11	12	13	14	15	16	17
		18	19	20	21	22	23	24
Jul 12		25	26	27	28	29	30	31
	AUGUST 2021	1	2	3	4	5	6	7
Jul 26		8	9	10	11	12	13	14
		15	16	17	18	19	20	21
Aug 9		22	23	24	25	26	27	28
	SEPTEMBER 2021	29	30	31	1	2	3	4
Aug 23		5	6	7	8	9	10	11
		12	13	14	15	16	17	18
Sep 6		19	20	21	22	23	24	25
	OCTOBER 2021	26	27	28	29	30	1	2
Sep 20		3	4	5	6	7	8	9
		10	11	12	13	14	15	16
Oct 4		17	18	19	20	21	22	23
		24	25	26	27	28	29	30
Oct 18	NOVEMBER 2021	31	1	2	3	4	5	6
		7	8	9	10	11	12	13
Nov 1		14	15	16	17	18	19	20
		21	22	23	24	25	26	27
Nov 15	DECEMBER 2021	28[g]	29	30	1	2	3	4
		5	6	7	8	9	10	11
Nov 29		12	13	14	15	16	17	18
		19	20	21	22	23	24	25[h]
Dec 13		26	27	28	29	30	31	1

[a]Orthodox Christmas
[b]Julian New Year
[c]Ash Wednesday
[d]Feast of Orthodoxy
[e]Easter
[f]Orthodox Easter
[g]Advent
[h]Christmas

2022

Month	Sun	Mon	Tue	Wed	Thu	Fri	Sat	Lunar Phases	ISO WEEK (Mon)	JULIAN DAY (Sun noon)
	26	◑	28	29	30	31	1[a]	2:23	52	2459575
JANUARY 2022	●	3	4	5	6	7	8	18:33	1	2459582
	◐	10	11	12	13	14	15	18:10	2	2459589
	16	○	18	19	20	21	22	23:47	3	2459596
	23	24	◑	26	27	28	29	13:40	4	2459603
	30	31	●	2	3	4	5	5:45	5	2459610
FEBRUARY 2022	6	7	◐	9	10	11	12	13:49	6	2459617
	13	14	15	○	17	18	19	16:55	7	2459624
	20	21	22	◑	24	25	26	22:31	8	2459631
	27	28	1	●	3	4	5	17:34	9	2459638
MARCH 2022	6	7	8	9	◐	11	12	10:44	10	2459645
	13	14	15	16	17	○	19	7:17	11	2459652
	20[b]	21	22	23	24	◑	26	5:36	12	2459659
	27	28	29	30	31	●	2	6:23	13	2459666
APRIL 2022	3	4	5	6	7	8	◐	6:47	14	2459673
	10	11	12	13	14	15	○	18:54	15	2459680
	17	18	19	20	21	22	◑	11:55	16	2459687
	24	25	26	27	28	29	●	20:27	17	2459694
	1	2	3	4	5	6	7		18	2459701
MAY 2022	8	◐	10	11	12	13	14	0:20	19	2459708
	15	○	17	18	19	20	21	4:13	20	2459715
	◑	23	24	25	26	27	28	18:42	21	2459722
	29	●	31	1	2	3	4	11:29	22	2459729
JUNE 2022	5	6	◐	8	9	10	11	14:47	23	2459736
	12	13	○	15	16	17	18	11:51	24	2459743
	19	20	◑[c]	22	23	24	25	3:10	25	2459750
	26	27	28	●	30	1	2	2:51	26	2459757
JULY 2022	3	4	5	6	◐	8	9	2:13	27	2459764
	10	11	12	○	14	15	16	18:36	28	2459771
	17	18	19	◑	21	22	23	14:17	29	2459778
	24	25	26	27	●	29	30	17:54	30	2459785
	31	1	2	3	4	◐	6	11:06	31	2459792
AUGUST 2022	7	8	9	10	11	○	13	1:35	32	2459799
	14	15	16	17	18	◑	20	4:35	33	2459806
	21	22	23	24	25	26	●	8:16	34	2459813
	28	29	30	31	1	2	◐	18:07	35	2459820
SEPTEMBER 2022	4	5	6	7	8	9	○	9:58	36	2459827
	11	12	13	14	15	16	◑	21:51	37	2459834
	18	19	20	21	22	23[d]	24		38	2459841
	●	26	27	28	29	30	1	21:54	39	2459848
OCTOBER 2022	2	◐	4	5	6	7	8	0:13	40	2459855
	○	10	11	12	13	14	15	20:54	41	2459862
	16	◑	18	19	20	21	22	17:14	42	2459869
	23	24	●	26	27	28	29	10:48	43	2459876
	30	31	◐	2	3	4	5	6:36	44	2459883
NOVEMBER 2022	6	7	○	9	10	11	12	11:01	45	2459890
	13	14	15	◑	17	18	19	13:26	46	2459897
	20	21	22	●	24	25	26	22:56	47	2459904
	27	28	29	◐	1	2	3	14:36	48	2459911
DECEMBER 2022	4	5	6	7	○	9	10	4:07	49	2459918
	11	12	13	14	15	◑	17	8:55	50	2459925
	18	19	20	21[e]	22	●	24	10:16	51	2459932
	25	26	27	28	29	◐	31	1:19	52	2459939

HEBREW 5782‡/5783

ISO WEEK	Month	Sun	Mon	Tue	Wed	Thu	Fri	Sat	Molad
52	TEVETH 5782	22	23	24	25	26	27	28	
1		29	1	2	3	4	5	6	Mon $2^h23^m15^p$
2		7	8	9	10	11	12	13	
3	SHEVAT 5782	14	15	16	17	18	19	20	
4		21	22	23	24	25	26	27	
5		28	29	30	1	2	3	4	Tue $15^h7^m16^p$
6		5	6	7	8	9	10	11	
7	ADAR I 5782	12	13	14	15	16	17	18	
8		19	20	21	22	23	24	25	
9		26	27	28	29	30	1	2	Thu $3^h51^m17^p$
10	ADAR II 5782	3	4	5	6	7	8	9	
11		10	11	12	13	14[f]	15	16	
12		17	18	19	20	21	22	23	
13		24	25	26	27	28	29	1	Fri $16^h36^m0^p$
14		2	3	4	5	6	7	8	
15	NISAN 5782	9	10	11	12	13	14	15[g]	
16		16	17	18	19	20	21	22	
17		23	24	25	26	27	28	29	
18		30	1	2	3	4	5	6	Sun $5^h20^m1^p$
19		7	8	9	10	11	12	13	
20	IYAR 5782	14	15	16	17	18	19	20	
21		21	22	23	24	25	26	27	
22		28	29	1	2	3	4	5	Mon $18^h4^m2^p$
23		6[h]	7	8	9	10	11	12	
24	SIVAN 5782	13	14	15	16	17	18	19	
25		20	21	22	23	24	25	26	
26		27	28	29	30	1	2	3	Wed $6^h48^m3^p$
27		4	5	6	7	8	9	10	
28	TAMMUZ 5782	11	12	13	14	15	16	17	
29		18	19	20	21	22	23	24	
30		25	26	27	28	29	1	2	Thu $19^h32^m4^p$
31		3	4	5	6	7	8	9	
32	AV 5782	10[i]	11	12	13	14	15	16	
33		17	18	19	20	21	22	23	
34		24	25	26	27	28	29	30	Sat $8^h16^m5^p$
35		1	2	3	4	5	6	7	
36	ELUL 5782	8	9	10	11	12	13	14	
37		15	16	17	18	19	20	21	
38		22	23	24	25	26	27	28	Sun $21^h0^m6^p$
39		29	1[a]	2[a]	3	4	5	6	
40		7	8	9	10[b]	11	12	13	
41	TISHRI 5783	14	15[c]	16	17	18	19	20	
42		21	22	23	24	25	26	27	
43		28	29	30	1	2	3	4	Tue $9^h44^m7^p$
44	HESHVAN 5783	5	6	7	8	9	10	11	
45		12	13	14	15	16	17	18	
46		19	20	21	22	23	24	25	
47		26	27	28	29	30	1	2	Wed $22^h28^m8^p$
48	KISLEV 5783	3	4	5	6	7	8	9	
49		10	11[d]	12	13	14	15	16	
50		17	18	19	20	21	22	23	
51		24	25[e]	26[e]	27[e]	28[e]	29[e]	30[e]	Fri $11^h12^m9^p$
52		1[e]	2[e]	3	4	5	6	7	

CHINESE Xīn-Chǒu/Rén-Yín

ISO WEEK	Month	Sun	Mon	Tue	Wed	Thu	Fri	Sat	Solar Term
52	MONTH 11 Xīn-Chǒu	23	24	25	26	27	28	29	
1	MONTH 12 Xīn-Chǒu	30	1	2	3	4	5	6	Xiǎo hán
2		7	8	9*	10	11	12	13	
3		14	15	16	17	**18**	19	20	Dà hán
4		21	22	23	24	25	26	27	
5		28	29	1[a]	2	3	*4*	5	Lì chūn
6	MONTH 1 Rén-Yín	6	7	8	9	10	11	12	
7		13	14	15[b]	16	17	18	**19**	Yǔ shuǐ
8		20	21	22	23	24	25	26	
9		27	28	29	30	1	2	3	Jīng zhé
10	MONTH 2 Rén-Yín	4	5	6	7	8	9	10*	
11		11	12	13	14	15	16	17	
12		**18**	19	20	21	22	23	24	Chūn fēn
13		25	26	27	28	29	1	2	
14	MONTH 3 Rén-Yín	3	4	5[c]	6	7	8	9	Qīng míng
15		10	11	12	13	14	15	16	
16		17	18	19	**20**	21	22	23	Gǔ yǔ
17		24	25	26	27	28	29	30	
18		1	2	3	4	5	6	7	Lì xià
19	MONTH 4 Rén-Yín	8	9	10	11*	12	13	14	
20		15	16	17	18	19	20	**21**	Xiǎo mǎn
21		22	23	24	25	26	27	28	
22		29	1	2	3	4	5[d]	6	
23	MONTH 5 Rén-Yín	7	*8*	9	10	11	12	13	Máng zhòng
24		14	15	16	17	18	19	20	
25		21	22	**23**	24	25	26	27	Xià zhì
26		28	29	30	1	2	3	4	
27	MONTH 6 Rén-Yín	5	6	7	8	9	10	11	Xiǎo shǔ
28		12*	13	14	15	16	17	18	
29		19	20	21	22	23	24	**25**	Dà shǔ
30		26	27	28	29	30	1	2	
31	MONTH 7 Rén-Yín	3	4	5	6	7[e]	8	9	
32		*10*	11	12	13	14	15[f]	16	Lì qiū
33		17	18	19	20	21	22	23	
34		24	25	**26**	27	28	29	1	Chǔ shǔ
35		2	3	4	5	6	7	8	
36	MONTH 8 Rén-Yín	9	10	11	*12*	13*	14	15[g]	Bái lù
37		16	17	18	19	20	21	22	
38		23	24	25	26	27	**28**	29	Qiū fēn
39		30	1	2	3	4	5	6	
40	MONTH 9 Rén-Yín	7	8	9[h]	10	11	12	*13*	Hán lù
41		14	15	16	17	18	19	20	
42		21	22	23	24	25	26	27	
43		*28*	29	1	2	3	4	5	Shuāng jiàng
44	MONTH 10 Rén-Yín	6	7	8	9	10	11	12	
45		13	*14**	15	16	17	18	19	Lì dōng
46		20	21	22	23	24	25	26	
47		27	28	**29**	30	1	2	3	Xiǎo xuě
48	MONTH 11 Rén-Yín	4	5	6	7	8	9	10	
49		11	12	13	*14*	15	16	17	Dà xuě
50		18	19	20	21	22	23	24	
51		25	26	27	28	**29**[i]	1	2	Dōng zhì
52	MONTH 12 Rén-Yín	3	4	5	6	7	8	9	

COPTIC 1738/1739‡ — ETHIOPIC 2014/2015‡

ISO WEEK	Coptic Month	Sun	Mon	Tue	Wed	Thu	Fri	Sat	Ethiopic Month
52	KOIAK 1738	17	18	19	20	21	22	23	TĀKHŚĀŚ 2014
1		24	25	26	27	28	29[c]	30	
2		1	2	3	4	5	6[d]	7	
3	TŌBE 1738	8	9	10	11[e]	12	13	14	TER 2014
4		15	16	17	18	19	20	21	
5		22	23	24	25	26	27	28	
6		29	30	1	2	3	4	5	
7	MESHIR 1738	6	7	8	9	10	11	12	YAKĀTIT 2014
8		13	14	15	16	17	18	19	
9		20	21	22	23	24	25	26	
10		27	28	29	30	1	2	3	
11	PAREMOTEP 1738	4	5	6	7	8	9	10	MAGĀBIT 2014
12		11	12	13	14	15	16	17	
13		18	19	20	21	22	23	24	
14		25	26	27	28	29	30	1	
15	PARMOUTE 1738	2	3	4	5	6	7	8	MIYĀZYĀ 2014
16		9	10	11	12	13	14	15	
17		16[f]	17	18	19	20	21	22	
18		23	24	25	26	27	28	29[g]	
19		30	1	2	3	4	5	6	
20	PASHONS 1738	7	8	9	10	11	12	13	GENBOT 2014
21		14	15	16	17	18	19	20	
22		21	22	23	24	25	26	27	
23		28	29	30	1	2	3	4	
24	PAŌNE 1738	5	6	7	8	9	10	11	SANĒ 2014
25		12	13	14	15	16	17	18	
26		19	20	21	22	23	24	25	
27		26	27	28	29	30	1	2	
28	EPĒP 1738	3	4	5	6	7	8	9	ḤAMLĒ 2014
29		10	11	12	13	14	15	16	
30		17	18	19	20	21	22	23	
31		24	25	26	27	28	29	30	
32		1	2	3	4	5	6	7	
33	MESORĒ 1738	8	9	10	11	12	13[h]	14	NAḤASĒ 2014
34		15	16	17	18	19	20	21	
35		22	23	24	25	26	27	28	
36	EPAG. 1738	29	30	1	2	3	4	5	PĀG. 2014
37		1[a]	2	3	4	5	6	7	
38	THOOUT 1739	8	9	10	11	12	13	14	MASKARAM 2015
39		15	16	17[b]	18	19	20	21	
40		22	23	24	25	26	27	28	
41		29	30	1	2	3	4	5	
42	PAOPE 1739	6	7	8	9	10	11	12	ṬEQEMT 2015
43		13	14	15	16	17	18	19	
44		20	21	22	23	24	25	26	
45		27	28	29	30	1	2	3	
46	ATHŌR 1739	4	5	6	7	8	9	10	ḪEDĀR 2015
47		11	12	13	14	15	16	17	
48		18	19	20	21	22	23	24	
49		25	26	27	28	29	30	1	
50	KOIAK 1739	2	3	4	5	6	7	8	TĀKHŚĀŚ 2015
51		9	10	11	12	13	14	15	
52		16	17	18	19	20	21	22	

[a]New Year
[b]Spring (15:32)
[c]Summer (9:13)
[d]Autumn (1:03)
[e]Winter (21:47)
● New moon
◐ First quarter moon
○ Full moon
◑ Last quarter moon

‡Leap year
[a]New Year
[b]Yom Kippur
[c]Sukkot
[d]Winter starts
[e]Ḥanukkah
[f]Purim
[g]Passover
[h]Shavuot
[i]Fast of Av

[a]New Year (4720, Tiger)
[b]Lantern Festival
[c]Qīngmíng
[d]Dragon Festival
[e]Qīqiǎo
[f]Hungry Ghosts
[g]Mid-Autumn Festival
[h]Double-Ninth Festival
[i]Dōngzhì
*Start of 60-name cycle

‡Leap year
[a]New Year
[b]Building of the Cross
[c]Christmas
[d]Jesus's Circumcision
[e]Epiphany
[f]Easter
[g]Mary's Announcement
[h]Jesus's Transfiguration

PERSIAN (ASTRONOMICAL) 1400/1401

Month	Sun	Mon	Tue	Wed	Thu	Fri	Sat
DEY 1400	5	6	7	8	9	10	11
	12	13	14	15	16	17	18
	19	20	21	22	23	24	25
	26	27	28	29	30	1	2
BAHMAN 1400	3	4	5	6	7	8	9
	10	11	12	13	14	15	16
	17	18	19	20	21	22	23
	24	25	26	27	28	29	30
ESFAND 1400	1	2	3	4	5	6	7
	8	9	10	11	12	13	14
	15	16	17	18	19	20	21
	22	23	24	25	26	27	28
FARVARDĪN 1401	29	1[a]	2	3	4	5	6
	7	8	9	10	11	12	13[b]
	14	15	16	17	18	19	20
	21	22	23	24	25	26	27
ORDĪBEHEŠT 1401	28	29	30	31	1	2	3
	4	5	6	7	8	9	10
	11	12	13	14	15	16	17
	18	19	20	21	22	23	24
	25	26	27	28	29	30	31
XORDĀD 1401	1	2	3	4	5	6	7
	8	9	10	11	12	13	14
	15	16	17	18	19	20	21
	22	23	24	25	26	27	28
TĪR 1401	29	30	31	1	2	3	4
	5	6	7	8	9	10	11
	12	13	14	15	16	17	18
	19	20	21	22	23	24	25
MORDĀD 1401	26	27	28	29	30	31	1
	2	3	4	5	6	7	8
	9	10	11	12	13	14	15
	16	17	18	19	20	21	22
	23	24	25	26	27	28	29
SHAHRĪVAR 1401	30	31	1	2	3	4	5
	6	7	8	9	10	11	12
	13	14	15	16	17	18	19
	20	21	22	23	24	25	26
MEHR 1401	27	28	29	30	31	1	2
	3	4	5	6	7	8	9
	10	11	12	13	14	15	16
	17	18	19	20	21	22	23
	24	25	26	27	28	29	30
ABĀN 1401	1	2	3	4	5	6	7
	8	9	10	11	12	13	14
	15	16	17	18	19	20	21
	22	23	24	25	26	27	28
ĀZAR 1401	29	30	1	2	3	4	5
	6	7	8	9	10	11	12
	13	14	15	16	17	18	19
	20	21	22	23	24	25	26
DEY 1401	27	28	29	30	1	2	3
	4	5	6	7	8	9	10

HINDU LUNAR 2078/2079

Month	Sun	Mon	Tue	Wed	Thu	Fri	Sat
MĀRGAŚIRA 2078	22	23	24	25	26	27	29
PAUSHA 2078	30	1	2	3	4	5	6
	7	8	9	10	11	12	13
	14	15	16	17	18	18	19
	21	22	23	24	25	26	27
MĀGHA 2078	28	29	30	1	2	3	5
	6	6	7	8	9	10	11
	12	13	14	15	16	17	18
	19	20	21	22	23	24	25
PHĀLGUNA 2078	27	28	29[h]	30	1	2	3
	4	5	6	7	8	9	9
	10	11	12	13	14	15[i]	16
	17	18	19	21	22	23	24
CHAITRA 2079	25	26	27	28	29	30	1[a]
	2	3	4	5	6	7	8
	9[b]	10	11	12	13	14	15
	16	17	18	19	20	21	22
	23	25	26	27	28	29	30
VAIŚĀKHA 2079	1	2	3	4	4	5	6
	7	8	9	10	11	12	13
	14	15	16	18	19	20	21
	22	23	24	25	26	27	28
JYAISHTHA 2079	29	30	1	2	3	4	5
	6	7	8	9	10	11	12
	13	14	15	16	17	18	19
	20	22	23	24	25	26	27
ĀSHĀDHA 2079	28	29	30	30	1	2	3
	4	5	6	7	8	9	10
	11	12	14	15	16	17	18
	19	20	21	22	23	24	25
ŚRĀVAṆA 2079	26	27	28	29	30	1	2
	3	4	5	6	7	8	9
	10	11	12	13	14	15	17
	18	19	20	21	22	23[c]	24
	25	26	27	27	28	29	30
BHĀDRAPADA 2079	1	2	3	4[d]	5	6	7
	8	10	11	12	13	14	15
	16	17	18	19	20	21	22
	23	24	25	26	27	28	29
ĀŚVINA 2079	30	1	2	3	4	5	6
	7	8[e]	9[e]	10[e]	11	12	14
	15	16	17	18	19	20	21
	22	22	23	24	25	26	27
KĀRTTIKA 2079	28	29	30	1[f]	2	3	4
	5	7	8	9	10	11	12
	13	14	15	16	17	18	19
	20	21	22	23	24	25	25
MĀRGAŚIRA 2079	26	27	28	30	1	2	3
	4	5	6	7	8	9	10
	11[g]	13	14	14	15	16	17
	18	19	20	21	22	23	24
PAUSHA 2079	25	26	27	28	29	30	1
	2	3	5	6	7	8	9

HINDU SOLAR 1943‡/1944

Month	Sun	Mon	Tue	Wed	Thu	Fri	Sat
PAUSHA 1943	11	12	13	14	15	16	17
	18	19	20	21	22	23	24
MĀGHA 1943	25	26	27	28	29	1[b]	2
	3	4	5	6	7	8	9
	10	11	12	13	14	15	16
	17	18	19	20	21	22	23
PHĀLGUNA 1943	24	25	26	27	28	29	1
	2	3	4	5	6	7	8
	9	10	11	12	13	14	15
	16	17	18	19	20	21	22
	23	24	25	26	27	28	29
CHAITRA 1943	30	1	2	3	4	5	6
	7	8	9	10	11	12	13
	14	15	16	17	18	19	20
	21	22	23	24	25	26	27
VAIŚĀKHA 1944	28	29	30	31	1[a]	2	3
	4	5	6	7	8	9	10
	11	12	13	14	15	16	17
	18	19	20	21	22	23	24
	25	26	27	28	29	30	31
JYAISHTHA 1944	1	2	3	4	5	6	7
	8	9	10	11	12	13	14
	15	16	17	18	19	20	21
	22	23	24	25	26	27	28
ĀSHĀDHA 1944	29	30	31	1	2	3	4
	5	6	7	8	9	10	11
	12	13	14	15	16	17	18
	19	20	21	22	23	24	25
	26	27	28	29	30	31	32
ŚRĀVAṆA 1944	1	2	3	4	5	6	7
	8	9	10	11	12	13	14
	15	16	17	18	19	20	21
	22	23	24	25	26	27	28
BHĀDRAPADA 1944	29	30	31	1	2	3	4
	5	6	7	8	9	10	11
	12	13	14	15	16	17	18
	19	20	21	22	23	24	25
ĀŚVINA 1944	26	27	28	29	30	31	1
	2	3	4	5	6	7	8
	9	10	11	12	13	14	15
	16	17	18	19	20	21	22
	23	24	25	26	27	28	29
KĀRTTIKA 1944	30	31	1	2	3	4	5
	6	7	8	9	10	11	12
	13	14	15	16	17	18	19
	20	21	22	23	24	25	26
MĀRGAŚIRA 1944	27	28	29	1	2	3	4
	5	6	7	8	9	10	11
	12	13	14	15	16	17	18
	19	20	21	22	23	24	25
PAUSHA 1944	26	27	28	29	30	1	2
	3	4	5	6	7	8	9
	10	11	12	13	14	15	16

ISLAMIC (ASTRONOMICAL) 1443/1444

Month	Sun	Mon	Tue	Wed	Thu	Fri	Sat
JUMĀDĀ I 1443	21	22	23	24	25	26	27
JUMĀDĀ II 1443	28	29	1	2	3	4	5
	6	7	8	9	10	11	12
	13	14	15	16	17	18	19
	20	21	22	23	24	25	26
RAJAB 1443	27	28	29	1	2	3	4
	5	6	7	8	9	10	11
	12	13	14	15	16	17	18
	19	20	21	22	23	24	25
SHA'BĀN 1443	26	27[d]	28	29	30	1	2
	3	4	5	6	7	8	9
	10	11	12	13	14	15	16
	17	18	19	20	21	22	23
	24	25	26	27	28	29	30
RAMAḌĀN 1443	1[e]	2	3	4	5	6	7
	8	9	10	11	12	13	14
	15	16	17	18	19	20	21
	22	23	24	25	26	27	28
SHAWWĀL 1443	29	1[f]	2	3	4	5	6
	7	8	9	10	11	12	13
	14	15	16	17	18	19	20
	21	22	23	24	25	26	27
DHU AL-QA'DA 1443	28	29	30	1	2	3	4
	5	6	7	8	9	10	11
	12	13	14	15	16	17	18
	19	20	21	22	23	24	25
DHU AL-ḤIJJA 1443	26	27	28	29	1	2	3
	4	5	6	7	8	9	10[g]
	11	12	13	14	15	16	17
	18	19	20	21	22	23	24
MUḤARRAM 1444	25	26	27	28	29	30	1[a]
	2	3	4	5	6	7	8
	9	10[b]	11	12	13	14	15
	16	17	18	19	20	21	22
	23	24	25	26	27	28	29
ṢAFAR 1444	30	1	2	3	4	5	6
	7	8	9	10	11	12	13
	14	15	16	17	18	19	20
	21	22	23	24	25	26	27
RABĪ' I 1444	28	29	1	2	3	4	5
	6	7	8	9	10	11	12[c]
	13	14	15	16	17	18	19
	20	21	22	23	24	25	26
RABĪ' II 1444	27	28	29	30	1	2	3
	4	5	6	7	8	9	10
	11	12	13	14	15	16	17
	18	19	20	21	22	23	24
JUMĀDĀ I 1444	25	26	27	28	29	30	1
	2	3	4	5	6	7	8
	9	10	11	12	13	14	15
	16	17	18	19	20	21	22
	23	24	25	26	27	28	29
	1	2	3	4	5	6	7

GREGORIAN 2022

Julian (Sun)	Sun	Mon	Tue	Wed	Thu	Fri	Sat	Month
Dec 13	26	27	28	29	30	31	1	JANUARY 2022
	2	3	4	5	6	7[a]	8	
Dec 27	9	10	11	12	13	14[b]	15	
	16	17	18	19	20	21	22	
Jan 10	23	24	25	26	27	28	29	
	30	31	1	2	3	4	5	FEBRUARY 2022
Jan 24	6	7	8	9	10	11	12	
	13	14	15	16	17	18	19	
Feb 7	20	21	22	23	24	25	26	
	27	28	1	2[c]	3	4	5	MARCH 2022
Feb 21	6	7	8	9	10	11	12	
	13[d]	14	15	16	17	18	19	
Mar 7	20	21	22	23	24	25	26	
	27	28	29	30	31	1	2	APRIL 2022
Mar 21	3	4	5	6	7	8	9	
	10	11	12	13	14	15	16	
Apr 4	17[e]	18	19	20	21	22	23	
	24[f]	25	26	27	28	29	30	
Apr 18	1	2	3	4	5	6	7	MAY 2022
	8	9	10	11	12	13	14	
May 2	15	16	17	18	19	20	21	
	22	23	24	25	26	27	28	
May 16	29	30	31	1	2	3	4	JUNE 2022
	5	6	7	8	9	10	11	
May 30	12	13	14	15	16	17	18	
	19	20	21	22	23	24	25	
Jun 13	26	27	28	29	30	1	2	JULY 2022
	3	4	5	6	7	8	9	
Jun 27	10	11	12	13	14	15	16	
	17	18	19	20	21	22	23	
Jul 11	24	25	26	27	28	29	30	
	31	1	2	3	4	5	6	AUGUST 2022
Jul 25	7	8	9	10	11	12	13	
	14	15	16	17	18	19	20	
Aug 8	21	22	23	24	25	26	27	
	28	29	30	31	1	2	3	SEPTEMBER 2022
Aug 22	4	5	6	7	8	9	10	
	11	12	13	14	15	16	17	
Sep 5	18	19	20	21	22	23	24	
	25	26	27	28	29	30	1	OCTOBER 2022
Sep 19	2	3	4	5	6	7	8	
	9	10	11	12	13	14	15	
Oct 3	16	17	18	19	20	21	22	
	23	24	25	26	27	28	29	
Oct 17	30	31	1	2	3	4	5	NOVEMBER 2022
	6	7	8	9	10	11	12	
Oct 31	13	14	15	16	17	18	19	
	20	21	22	23	24	25	26	
Nov 14	27[g]	28	29	30	1	2	3	DECEMBER 2022
	4	5	6	7	8	9	10	
Nov 28	11	12	13	14	15	16	17	
	18	19	20	21	22	23	24	
Dec 12	25[h]	26	27	28	29	30	31	

Persian:
[a]New Year
[b]Sizdeh Bedar

Hindu Lunar:
[a]New Year (Śubhakṛt)
[b]Birthday of Rāma
[c]Birthday of Krishna
[d]Ganēśa Chaturthī
[e]Dashara
[f]Diwali
[g]Birthday of Vishnu
[h]Night of Śiva
[i]Holi

Hindu Solar:
‡Leap year
[a]New Year (Rākshasa)
[b]Pongal

Islamic:
[a]New Year
[b]'Ashūrā'
[c]Prophet's Birthday
[d]Ascent of the Prophet
[e]Start of Ramaḍān
[f]'Id al-Fiṭr
[g]'Id al-'Aḍḥā

Gregorian:
[a]Orthodox Christmas
[b]Julian New Year
[c]Ash Wednesday
[d]Feast of Orthodoxy
[e]Easter
[f]Orthodox Easter
[g]Advent
[h]Christmas

2023

Gregorian 2023	Sun	Mon	Tue	Wed	Thu	Fri	Sat	Lunar Phases	ISO Week (Mon)	Julian Day (Sun noon)
	1[a]	2	3	4	5	○	7	23:07	1	2459946
	8	9	10	11	12	13	14		2	2459953
JANUARY 2023	◑	16	17	18	19	20	●	2:09 20:52	3	2459960
	22	23	24	25	26	27	◐	15:18	4	2459967
	29	30	31	1	2	3	4		5	2459974
	○	6	7	8	9	10	11	18:27	6	2459981
FEBRUARY 2023	12	◑	14	15	16	17	18	16:00	7	2459988
	19	●	21	22	23	24	25	7:05	8	2459995
	26	◐	28	1	2	3	4	8:05	9	2460002
	5	6	○	8	9	10	11	12:39	10	2460009
MARCH 2023	12	13	14	◑	16	17	18	2:07	11	2460016
	19	20[b]	●	22	23	24	25	17:22	12	2460023
	26	27	28	◐	30	31	1	2:31	13	2460030
	2	3	4	5	○	7	8	4:34	14	2460037
APRIL 2023	9	10	11	12	◑	14	15	9:10	15	2460044
	16	17	18	19	●	21	22	4:12	16	2460051
	23	24	25	26	◐	28	29	21:19	17	2460058
	30	1	2	3	4	○	6	17:33	18	2460065
	7	8	9	10	11	◑	13	14:27	19	2460072
MAY 2023	14	15	16	17	18	●	20	15:52	20	2460079
	21	22	23	24	25	26	◐	15:21	21	2460086
	28	29	30	31	1	2	3		22	2460093
	○	5	6	7	8	9	◑	3:41 19:30	23	2460100
JUNE 2023	11	12	13	14	15	16	17		24	2460107
	●	19	20	21[c]	22	23	24	4:36	25	2460114
	25	◐	27	28	29	30	1	7:49	26	2460121
	2	○	4	5	6	7	8	11:38	27	2460128
JULY 2023	9	◑	11	12	13	14	15	1:47	28	2460135
	16	●	18	19	20	21	22	18:31	29	2460142
	23	24	◐	26	27	28	29	22:06	30	2460149
	30	31	○	2	3	4	5	18:31	31	2460156
	6	7	◑	9	10	11	12	10:27	32	2460163
AUGUST 2023	13	14	15	●	17	18	19	9:37	33	2460170
	20	21	22	23	◐	25	26	9:56	34	2460177
	27	28	29	30	○	1	2	1:35	35	2460184
	3	4	5	◑	7	8	9	22:20	36	2460191
SEPTEMBER 2023	10	11	12	13	14	●	16	1:39	37	2460198
	17	18	19	20	21	◐	23[d]	19:31	38	2460205
	24	25	26	27	28	○	30	9:56	39	2460212
	1	2	3	4	5	◑	7	13:47	40	2460219
OCTOBER 2023	8	9	10	11	12	13	●	17:54	41	2460226
	15	16	17	18	19	20	21		42	2460233
	◐	23	24	25	26	27	○	3:28 20:23	43	2460240
	29	30	31	1	2	3	4		44	2460247
	◑	6	7	8	9	10	11	8:36	45	2460254
NOVEMBER 2023	12	●	14	15	16	17	18	9:26	46	2460261
	19	◐	21	22	23	24	25	10:49	47	2460268
	26	○	28	29	30	1	2	9:15	48	2460275
	3	4	◑	6	7	8	9	5:48	49	2460282
DECEMBER 2023	10	11	●	13	14	15	16	23:31	50	2460289
	17	18	◐	20	21	22[e]	23	18:38	51	2460296
	24	25	26	○	28	29	30	0:32	52	2460303
	31	1	2	3	◑	5	6	3:29	1	2460310

Julian Day	Hebrew 5783/5784‡	Sun	Mon	Tue	Wed	Thu	Fri	Sat	Molad
2459946		8	9	10	11	12	13	14	
2459953	TEVETH 5783	15	16	17	18	19	20	21	
2459960		22	23	24	25	26	27	28	
2459967		29	1	2	3	4	5	6	Sat 23h56m10p
2459974		7	8	9	10	11	12	13	
2459981	SHEVAT 5783	14	15	16	17	18	19	20	
2459988		21	22	23	24	25	26	27	
2459995		28	29	30	1	2	3	4	Mon 12h40m11p
2460002		5	6	7	8	9	10	11	
2460009	ADAR 5783	12	13	14[f]	15	16	17	18	
2460016		19	20	21	22	23	24	25	
2460023		26	27	28	29	1	2	3	Wed 1h24m12p
2460030		4	5	6	7	8	9	10	
2460037	NISAN 5783	11	12	13	14	15[g]	16	17	
2460044		18	19	20	21	22	23	24	
2460051		25	26	27	28	29	30	1	Thu 14h8m13p
2460058		2	3	4	5	6	7	8	
2460065	IYYAR 5783	9	10	11	12	13	14	15	
2460072		16	17	18	19	20	21	22	
2460079		23	24	25	26	27	28	29	
2460086		1	2	3	4	5	6[h]	7	Sat 2h52m14p
2460093		8	9	10	11	12	13	14	
2460100	SIVAN 5783	15	16	17	18	19	20	21	
2460107		22	23	24	25	26	27	28	
2460114		29	30	1	2	3	4	5	Sun 15h36m15p
2460121		6	7	8	9	10	11	12	
2460128	TAMMUZ 5783	13	14	15	16	17	18	19	
2460135		20	21	22	23	24	25	26	
2460142		27	28	29	1	2	3	4	Tue 4h20m16p
2460149		5	6	7	8	9[i]	10	11	
2460156	AV 5783	12	13	14	15	16	17	18	
2460163		19	20	21	22	23	24	25	
2460170		26	27	28	29	30	1	2	Wed 17h4m17p
2460177		3	4	5	6	7	8	9	
2460184	ELUL 5783	10	11	12	13	14	15	16	
2460191		17	18	19	20	21	22	23	
2460198		24	25	26	27	28	29	1[a]	Fri 5h49m0p
2460205		2[a]	3	4	5	6	7	8	
2460212	TISHRI 5784	9	10[b]	11	12	13	14	15[c]	
2460219		16	17	18	19	20	21	22	
2460226		23	24	25	26	27	28	29	
2460233		30	1	2	3	4	5	6	Sat 18h33m1p
2460240		7	8	9	10	11	12	13	
2460247	ḤESHVAN 5784	14	15	16	17	18	19	20	
2460254		21	22	23	24	25	26	27	
2460261		28	29	1	2	3	4	5	Mon 7h17m2p
2460268		6	7	8	9	10	11	12	
2460275	KISLEV 5784	13	14	15	16	17	18	19	
2460282		20	21	22	23[d]	24	25[e]	26[e]	
2460289		27[e]	28[e]	29[e]	1[e]	2[e]	3[e]	4	Tue 20h1m3p
2460296		5	6	7	8	9	10	11	
2460303	TEVETH 5784	12	13	14	15	16	17	18	
2460310		19	20	21	22	23	24	25	

Julian Day	Chinese Rén-Yín/Guǐ-Mǎo‡	Sun	Mon	Tue	Wed	Thu	Fri	Sat	Solar Term
2459946		10	11	12	13	*14*	15*	16	Xiǎo hán
2459953	MONTH 12 Rén-Yín	17	18	19	20	21	22	23	
2459960		24	25	26	27	28	**29**	30	**Dà hán**
2459967		1[a]	2	3	4	5	6	7	
2459974		8	9	10	11	12	13	*14*	Lì chūn
2459981	MONTH 1 Guǐ-Mǎo	15[b]	16	17	18	19	20	21	
2459988		22	23	24	25	26	27	28	
2459995		**29**	1	2	3	4	5	6	**Yǔ shuǐ**
2460002		7	8	9	10	11	12	13	
2460009	MONTH 2 Guǐ-Mǎo	14	*15*	16*	17	18	19	20	Jīng zhé
2460016		21	22	23	24	25	26	27	
2460023		28	29	**30**	1	2	3	4	**Chūn fēn**
2460030		5	6	7	8	9	10	11	
2460037	LEAP MONTH 2 Guǐ-Mǎo	12	13	14	*15*[c]	16	17	18	Qīng míng
2460044		19	20	21	22	23	24	25	
2460051		26	27	28	29	*1*	2	3	**Gǔ yǔ**
2460058		4	5	6	7	8	9	10	
2460065	MONTH 3 Guǐ-Mǎo	11	12	13	14	15	16	17*	Lì xià
2460072		18	19	20	21	22	23	24	
2460079		25	26	27	28	29	1	2	
2460086		**3**	4	5	6	7	8	9	**Xiǎo mǎn**
2460093	MONTH 4 Guǐ-Mǎo	10	11	12	13	14	15	16	
2460100		17	18	*19*	20	21	22	23	Máng zhòng
2460107		24	25	26	27	28	29	30	
2460114		1	2	3	**4**	5[d]	6	7	**Xià zhì**
2460121		8	9	10	11	12	13	14	
2460128	MONTH 5 Guǐ-Mǎo	15	16	17	18*	19	*20*	21	Xiǎo shǔ
2460135		22	23	24	25	26	27	28	
2460142		29	30	1	2	3	4	5	
2460149		**6**	7	8	9	10	11	12	**Dà shǔ**
2460156	MONTH 6 Guǐ-Mǎo	13	14	15	16	17	18	19	
2460163		20	21	*22*	23	24	25	26	Lì qiū
2460170		27	28	29	1	2	3	4	
2460177		5	6	7[e]	**8**	9	10	11	**Chǔ shǔ**
2460184	MONTH 7 Guǐ-Mǎo	12	13	14	15[f]	16	17	18	
2460191		19*	20	21	22	23	*24*	25	Bái lù
2460198		26	27	28	29	30	1	2	
2460205		3	4	5	6	7	8	**9**	**Qiū fēn**
2460212	MONTH 8 Guǐ-Mǎo	10	11	12	13	14	15[g]	16	
2460219		17	18	19	20	21	22	23	
2460226		*24*	25	26	27	28	29	30	Hán lù
2460233		1	2	3	4	5	6	7	
2460240		8	9[h]	**10**	11	12	13	14	**Shuāng jiàng**
2460247	MONTH 9 Guǐ-Mǎo	15	16	17	18	19*	20	21	
2460254		22	23	24	*25*	26	27	28	Lì dōng
2460261		29	1	2	3	4	5	6	
2460268		7	8	9	**10**	11	12	13	**Xiǎo xuě**
2460275	MONTH 10 Guǐ-Mǎo	14	15	16	17	18	19	20	
2460282		21	22	23	24	*25*	26	27	Dà xuě
2460289		28	29	30	1	2	3	4	
2460296		5	6	7	8	9	**10**[i]	11	**Dōng zhì**
2460303	MONTH 11* Guǐ-Mǎo	12	13	14	15	16	17	18	
2460310		19	20	21	22	23	24	*25*	Xiǎo hán

Julian Day	Coptic 1739‡/1740	Sun	Mon	Tue	Wed	Thu	Fri	Sat	Ethiopic 2015‡/2016
2459946	KOIAK 1739	23	24	25	26	27	28	29[c]	TĀKHŚĀŚ 2015
2459953		30	1	2	3	4	5	6[d]	
2459960	TÔBE 1739	7	8	9	10	11[e]	12	13	ṬER 2015
2459967		14	15	16	17	18	19	20	
2459974		21	22	23	24	25	26	27	
2459981		28	29	30	1	2	3	4	
2459988		5	6	7	8	9	10	11	
2459995	MESHIR 1739	12	13	14	15	16	17	18	YAKĀTIT 2015
2460002		19	20	21	22	23	24	25	
2460009		26	27	28	29	30	1	2	
2460016		3	4	5	6	7	8	9	
2460023	PAREMOTEP 1739	10	11	12	13	14	15	16	MAGĀBIT 2015
2460030		17	18	19	20	21	22	23	
2460037		24	25	26	27	28	29	30	
2460044		1	2	3	4	5	6	7	
2460051	PARMOUTE 1739	8[f]	9	10	11	12	13	14	MIYĀZYĀ 2015
2460058		15	16	17	18	19	20	21	
2460065		22	23	24	25	26	27	28	
2460072		29[g]	30	1	2	3	4	5	
2460079		6	7	8	9	10	11	12	
2460086	PASHONS 1739	13	14	15	16	17	18	19	GENBOT 2015
2460093		20	21	22	23	24	25	26	
2460100		27	28	29	30	1	2	3	
2460107		4	5	6	7	8	9	10	
2460114	PAÔNE 1739	11	12	13	14	15	16	17	SANĒ 2015
2460121		18	19	20	21	22	23	24	
2460128		25	26	27	28	29	30	1	
2460135		2	3	4	5	6	7	8	
2460142	EPÊP 1739	9	10	11	12	13	14	15	ḤAMLĒ 2015
2460149		16	17	18	19	20	21	22	
2460156		23	24	25	26	27	28	29	
2460163		30	1	2	3	4	5	6	
2460170		7	8	9	10	11	12	13[h]	
2460177	MESORÊ 1739	14	15	16	17	18	19	20	NAḤASĒ 2015
2460184		21	22	23	24	25	26	27	
2460191	EPAG. 1739	28	29	30	1	2	3	4	
2460198		5	6	1[a]	2	3	4	5	PĀG. 2015
2460205	THOOUT 1740	6	7	8	9	10	11	12	MASKARAM 2016
2460212		13	14	15	16	17[b]	18	19	
2460219		20	21	22	23	24	25	26	
2460226		27	28	29	30	1	2	3	
2460233		4	5	6	7	8	9	10	ṬEQEMT 2016
2460240	PAOPE 1740	11	12	13	14	15	16	17	
2460247		18	19	20	21	22	23	24	
2460254		25	26	27	28	29	30	1	
2460261		2	3	4	5	6	7	8	
2460268	ATHÔR 1740	9	10	11	12	13	14	15	ḪEDĀR 2016
2460275		16	17	18	19	20	21	22	
2460282		23	24	25	26	27	28	29	
2460289		30	1	2	3	4	5	6	
2460296	KOIAK 1740	7	8	9	10	11	12	13	TĀKHŚĀŚ 2016
2460303		14	15	16	17	18	19	20	
2460310		21	22	23	24	25	26	27	

[a]New Year
[b]Spring (21:23)
[c]Summer (14:56)
[d]Autumn (6:49)
[e]Winter (3:26)
● New moon
◐ First quarter moon
○ Full moon
◑ Last quarter moon

‡Leap year
[a]New Year
[b]Yom Kippur
[c]Sukkot
[d]Winter starts
[e]Ḥanukkah
[f]Purim
[g]Passover
[h]Shavuot
[i]Fast of Av

‡Leap year
[a]New Year (4721, Hare)
[b]Lantern Festival
[c]Qīngmíng
[d]Dragon Festival
[e]Qīqiǎo
[f]Hungry Ghosts
[g]Mid-Autumn Festival
[h]Double-Ninth Festival
[i]Dōngzhì
*Start of 60-name cycle

‡Leap year
[a]New Year
[b]Building of the Cross
[c]Christmas
[d]Jesus's Circumcision
[e]Epiphany
[f]Easter
[g]Mary's Announcement
[h]Jesus's Transfiguration

PERSIAN (ASTRONOMICAL) 1401/1402

Month	Sun	Mon	Tue	Wed	Thu	Fri	Sat
DEY 1401	11	12	13	14	15	16	17
	18	19	20	21	22	23	24
	25	26	27	28	29	30	1
BAHMAN 1401	2	3	4	5	6	7	8
	9	10	11	12	13	14	15
	16	17	18	19	20	21	22
	23	24	25	26	27	28	29
	30	1	2	3	4	5	6
ESFAND 1401	7	8	9	10	11	12	13
	14	15	16	17	18	19	20
	21	22	23	24	25	26	27
	28	29	1[a]	2	3	4	5
FARVARDĪN 1402	6	7	8	9	10	11	12
	13[b]	14	15	16	17	18	19
	20	21	22	23	24	25	26
	27	28	29	30	31	1	2
ORDĪBEHEŠT 1402	3	4	5	6	7	8	9
	10	11	12	13	14	15	16
	17	18	19	20	21	22	23
	24	25	26	27	28	29	30
	31	1	2	3	4	5	6
XORDĀD 1402	7	8	9	10	11	12	13
	14	15	16	17	18	19	20
	21	22	23	24	25	26	27
	28	29	30	31	1	2	3
TĪR 1402	4	5	6	7	8	9	10
	11	12	13	14	15	16	17
	18	19	20	21	22	23	24
	25	26	27	28	29	30	31
MORDĀD 1402	1	2	3	4	5	6	7
	8	9	10	11	12	13	14
	15	16	17	18	19	20	21
	22	23	24	25	26	27	28
	29	30	31	1	2	3	4
SHAHRĪVAR 1402	5	6	7	8	9	10	11
	12	13	14	15	16	17	18
	19	20	21	22	23	24	25
	26	27	28	29	30	31	1
MEHR 1402	2	3	4	5	6	7	8
	9	10	11	12	13	14	15
	16	17	18	19	20	21	22
	23	24	25	26	27	28	29
	30	1	2	3	4	5	6
ĀBĀN 1402	7	8	9	10	11	12	13
	14	15	16	17	18	19	20
	21	22	23	24	25	26	27
	28	29	30	1	2	3	4
ĀZAR 1402	5	6	7	8	9	10	11
	12	13	14	15	16	17	18
	19	20	21	22	23	24	25
	26	27	28	29	30	1	2
DEY 1402	3	4	5	6	7	8	9
	10	11	12	13	14	15	16

[a]New Year
[b]Sizdeh Bedar

HINDU LUNAR 2079/2080‡

Month	Sun	Mon	Tue	Wed	Thu	Fri	Sat
PAUSHA 2079	10	11	12	13	14	15	16
	17	17	18	19	20	21	22
	23	24	25	26	27	**28**	30
MĀGHA 2079	1	2	3	4	5	6	7
	8	9	10	11	12	13	14
	15	16	17	18	19	20	21
	22	23	24	25	26	27	28[h]
PHĀLGUNA 2079	29	30	1	2	**3**	5	6
	7	8	9	10	10	11	12
	13	14	15[i]	16	17	18	19
	20	21	22	23	24	25	**26**
	28	29	30	1[a]	2	3	4
CHAITRA 2080	5	6	7	8	9[b]	10	11
	12	13	13	14	15	16	17
	18	19	**20**	22	23	24	25
	26	27	28	29	30	1	2
VAIŚĀKHA 2080	3	4	5	6	7	8	9
	10	11	12	13	14	15	16
	17	18	19	20	21	22	**23**
	25	26	27	28	29	30	1
JYAISHṬHA 2080	2	3	4	5	6	7	8
	8	9	10	11	12	13	14
	15	**16**	18	19	20	21	22
	23	24	25	26	27	28	29
	30	1	2	3	4	5	6
ĀSHĀḌHA 2080	7	8	9	10	11	12	13
	14	15	16	17	18	**19**	21
	22	23	24	25	26	27	28
	29	30	1	2	3	4	4
LEAP ŚRĀVAṆA 2080	5	6	7	8	9	10	11
	12	14	15	16	17	18	19
	20	21	22	23	24	25	26
	27	28	29	30	1	2	3
ŚRĀVAṆA 2080	4	5	6	7	8	9	10
	11	12	13	14	**15**	17	18
	19	20	21	22	23[c]	24	25
	26	27	28	29	30	1	1
BHĀDRAPADA 2080	2	3[d]	4	5	6	7	**8**
	10	11	12	13	14	15	16
	17	18	19	20	21	22	23
	24	25	26	27	28	29	30
ĀŚVINA 2080	1	2	3	4	5	6	7
	8[e]	9[e]	10[e]	11	**12**	14	15
	16	17	18	19	20	21	22
	23	24	25	25	26	27	28
	29	30	1[f]	2	3	4	5
KĀRTTIKA 2080	**6**	8	9	10	11	12	13
	14	15	16	17	18	19	20
	21	22	23	24	25	26	27
	28	29	30	1	2	3	4
MĀRGAŚĪRA 2080	5	6	7	8	9	10	**11**[g]
	13	14	15	16	17	18	18
	19	20	21	22	23	24	25

‡Leap year
[a]New Year (Śobhana)
[b]Birthday of Rāma
[c]Birthday of Krishna
[d]Ganēśa Chaturthī
[e]Dashara
[f]Diwali
[g]Birthday of Vishnu
[h]Night of Śiva
[i]Holi

HINDU SOLAR 1944/1945

Month	Sun	Mon	Tue	Wed	Thu	Fri	Sat
PAUSHA 1944	17	18	19	20	21	22	23
	24	25	26	27	28	29	1[b]
MĀGHA 1944	2	3	4	5	6	7	8
	9	10	11	12	13	14	15
	16	17	18	19	20	21	22
	23	24	25	26	27	28	29
PHĀLGUNA 1944	30	1	2	3	4	5	6
	7	8	9	10	11	12	13
	14	15	16	17	18	19	20
	21	22	23	24	25	26	27
CHAITRA 1944	28	29	30	1	2	3	4
	5	6	7	8	9	10	11
	12	13	14	15	16	17	18
	19	20	21	22	23	24	25
VAIŚĀKHA 1945	26	27	28	29	30	1[a]	2
	3	4	5	6	7	8	9
	10	11	12	13	14	15	16
	17	18	19	20	21	22	23
	24	25	26	27	28	29	30
JYAISHṬHA 1945	31	1	2	3	4	5	6
	7	8	9	10	11	12	13
	14	15	16	17	18	19	20
	21	22	23	24	25	26	27
ĀSHĀḌHA 1945	28	29	30	31	1	2	3
	4	5	6	7	8	9	10
	11	12	13	14	15	16	17
	18	19	20	21	22	23	24
	25	26	27	28	29	30	31
ŚRĀVAṆA 1945	32	1	2	3	4	5	6
	7	8	9	10	11	12	13
	14	15	16	17	18	19	20
	21	22	23	24	25	26	27
BHĀDRAPADA 1945	28	29	30	31	1	2	3
	4	5	6	7	8	9	10
	11	12	13	14	15	16	17
	18	19	20	21	22	23	24
	25	26	27	28	29	30	31
ĀŚVINA 1945	1	2	3	4	5	6	7
	8	9	10	11	12	13	14
	15	16	17	18	19	20	21
	22	23	24	25	26	27	28
KĀRTTIKA 1945	29	30	31	1	2	3	4
	5	6	7	8	9	10	11
	12	13	14	15	16	17	18
	19	20	21	22	23	24	25
MĀRGAŚĪRA 1945	26	27	28	29	30	1	2
	3	4	5	6	7	8	9
	10	11	12	13	14	15	16
	17	18	19	20	21	22	23
PAUSHA 1945	24	25	26	27	28	29	1
	2	3	4	5	6	7	8
	9	10	11	12	13	14	15
	16	17	18	19	20	21	22

[a]New Year (Anala)
[b]Pongal

ISLAMIC (ASTRONOMICAL) 1444/1445

Month	Sun	Mon	Tue	Wed	Thu	Fri	Sat
JUMĀDĀ II 1444	8	9	10	11	12	13	14
	15	16	17	18	19	20	21
	22	23	24	25	26	27	28
RAJAB 1444	29	1	2	3	4	5	6
	7	8	9	10	11	12	13
	14	15	16	17	18	19	20
	21	22	23	24	25	26	27[d]
SHA'BĀN 1444	28	29	1	2	3	4	5
	6	7	8	9	10	11	12
	13	14	15	16	17	18	19
	20	21	22	23	24	25	26
RAMAḌĀN 1444	27	28	29	30	1[e]	2	3
	4	5	6	7	8	9	10
	11	12	13	14	15	16	17
	18	19	20	21	22	23	24
SHAWWĀL 1444	25	26	27	28	29	1[f]	2
	3	4	5	6	7	8	9
	10	11	12	13	14	15	16
	17	18	19	20	21	22	23
	24	25	26	27	28	29	30
DHU AL-QA'DA 1444	1	2	3	4	5	6	7
	8	9	10	11	12	13	14
	15	16	17	18	19	20	21
	22	23	24	25	26	27	28
DHU AL-ḤIJJA 1444	29	1	2	3	4	5	6
	7	8	9	10[g]	11	12	13
	14	15	16	17	18	19	20
	21	22	23	24	25	26	27
MUḤARRAM 1445	28	29	30	1[a]	2	3	4
	5	6	7	8	9	10[b]	11
	12	13	14	15	16	17	18
	19	20	21	22	23	24	25
ṢAFAR 1445	26	27	28	29	30	1	2
	3	4	5	6	7	8	9
	10	11	12	13	14	15	16
	17	18	19	20	21	22	23
	24	25	26	27	28	29	30
RABĪ' I 1445	1	2	3	4	5	6	7
	8	9	10	11	12[c]	13	14
	15	16	17	18	19	20	21
	22	23	24	25	26	27	28
RABĪ' II 1445	29	30	1	2	3	4	5
	6	7	8	9	10	11	12
	13	14	15	16	17	18	19
	20	21	22	23	24	25	26
JUMĀDĀ I 1445	27	28	29	1	2	3	4
	5	6	7	8	9	10	11
	12	13	14	15	16	17	18
	19	20	21	22	23	24	25
JUMĀDĀ II 1445	26	27	28	29	30	1	2
	3	4	5	6	7	8	9
	10	11	12	13	14	15	16
	17	18	19	20	21	22	23

[a]New Year
[b]'Ashūrā'
[c]Prophet's Birthday
[d]Ascent of the Prophet
[e]Start of Ramaḍān
[f]'Id al-Fiṭr
[g]'Id al-'Aḍḥā

GREGORIAN 2023

Julian (Sun)	Sun	Mon	Tue	Wed	Thu	Fri	Sat	Month
Dec 19	1	2	3	4	5	6	7[a]	JANUARY 2023
	8	9	10	11	12	13	14[b]	
Jan 2	15	16	17	18	19	20	21	
	22	23	24	25	26	27	28	
Jan 16	29	30	31	1	2	3	4	
	5	6	7	8	9	10	11	FEBRUARY 2023
Jan 30	12	13	14	15	16	17	18	
	19	20	21	22[c]	23	24	25	
Feb 13	26	27	28	1	2	3	4	
	5[d]	6	7	8	9	10	11	MARCH 2023
Feb 27	12	13	14	15	16	17	18	
	19	20	21	22	23	24	25	
Mar 13	26	27	28	29	30	31	1	
	2	3	4	5	6	7	8	APRIL 2023
Mar 27	9[e]	10	11	12	13	14	15	
	16[f]	17	18	19	20	21	22	
Apr 10	23	24	25	26	27	28	29	
	30	1	2	3	4	5	6	
Apr 24	7	8	9	10	11	12	13	MAY 2023
	14	15	16	17	18	19	20	
May 8	21	22	23	24	25	26	27	
	28	29	30	31	1	2	3	
May 22	4	5	6	7	8	9	10	JUNE 2023
	11	12	13	14	15	16	17	
Jun 5	18	19	20	21	22	23	24	
	25	26	27	28	29	30	1	
Jun 19	2	3	4	5	6	7	8	JULY 2023
	9	10	11	12	13	14	15	
Jul 3	16	17	18	19	20	21	22	
	23	24	25	26	27	28	29	
Jul 17	30	31	1	2	3	4	5	
	6	7	8	9	10	11	12	AUGUST 2023
Jul 31	13	14	15	16	17	18	19	
	20	21	22	23	24	25	26	
Aug 14	27	28	29	30	31	1	2	
	3	4	5	6	7	8	9	SEPTEMBER 2023
Aug 28	10	11	12	13	14	15	16	
	17	18	19	20	21	22	23	
Sep 11	24	25	26	27	28	29	30	
	1	2	3	4	5	6	7	OCTOBER 2023
Sep 25	8	9	10	11	12	13	14	
	15	16	17	18	19	20	21	
Oct 9	22	23	24	25	26	27	28	
	29	30	31	1	2	3	4	
Oct 23	5	6	7	8	9	10	11	NOVEMBER 2023
	12	13	14	15	16	17	18	
Nov 6	19	20	21	22	23	24	25	
	26	27	28	29	30	1	2	
Nov 20	3[g]	4	5	6	7	8	9	DECEMBER 2023
	10	11	12	13	14	15	16	
Dec 4	17	18	19	20	21	22	23	
	24	25[h]	26	27	28	29	30	
Dec 18	31	1	2	3	4	5	6	

[a]Orthodox Christmas
[b]Julian New Year
[c]Ash Wednesday
[d]Feast of Orthodoxy
[e]Easter
[f]Orthodox Easter
[g]Advent
[h]Christmas

2024

Gregorian 2024‡

Month	Sun	Mon	Tue	Wed	Thu	Fri	Sat	Lunar Phases	ISO Week (Mon)	Julian Day (Sun noon)
January 2024	31	1[a]	2	3	◑	5	6	3:29	1	2460310
	7	8	9	10	●	12	13	11:56	2	2460317
	14	15	16	17	◐	19	20	3:52	3	2460324
	21	22	23	24	○	26	27	17:53	4	2460331
	28	29	30	31	1	◑	3	23:17	5	2460338
February 2024	4	5	6	7	8	●	10	22:58	6	2460345
	11	12	13	14	15	◐	17	15:00	7	2460352
	18	19	20	21	22	23	○	12:29	8	2460359
	25	26	27	28	29	1	2		9	2460366
March 2024	◑	4	5	6	7	8	9	15:23	10	2460373
	●	11	12	13	14	15	16	8:59	11	2460380
	◐	18	19	20[b]	21	22	23	4:10	12	2460387
	24	○	26	27	28	29	30	6:59	13	2460394
	31	1	◑	3	4	5	6	3:14	14	2460401
April 2024	7	●	9	10	11	12	13	18:20	15	2460408
	14	◐	16	17	18	19	20	19:12	16	2460415
	21	22	○	24	25	26	27	23:48	17	2460422
	28	29	30	◑	2	3	4	11:26	18	2460429
May 2024	5	6	7	●	9	10	11	3:21	19	2460436
	12	13	14	◐	16	17	18	11:47	20	2460443
	19	20	21	22	○	24	25	13:52	21	2460450
	26	27	28	29	◑	31	1	17:12	22	2460457
June 2024	2	3	4	5	●	7	8	12:37	23	2460464
	9	10	11	12	13	◐	15	5:17	24	2460471
	16	17	18	19	20[c]	21	○	1:07	25	2460478
	23	24	25	26	27	◑	29	21:52	26	2460485
	30	1	2	3	4	●	6	22:56	27	2460492
July 2024	7	8	9	10	11	12	◐	22:48	28	2460499
	14	15	16	17	18	19	20		29	2460506
	○	22	23	24	25	26	27	10:16	30	2460513
	◑	29	30	31	1	2	3	2:50	31	2460520
August 2024	●	5	6	7	8	9	10	11:12	32	2460527
	11	◐	13	14	15	16	17	15:18	33	2460534
	18	○	20	21	22	23	24	18:25	34	2460541
	25	◑	27	28	29	30	31	9:25	35	2460548
September 2024	1	2	●	4	5	6	7	1:54	36	2460555
	8	9	10	◐	12	13	14	6:05	37	2460562
	15	16	17	○	19	20	21	2:34	38	2460569
	22[d]	23	◑	25	26	27	28	18:49	39	2460576
	29	30	1	●	3	4	5	18:48	40	2460583
October 2024	6	7	8	9	◐	11	12	18:54	41	2460590
	13	14	15	16	○	18	19	11:25	42	2460597
	20	21	22	23	◑	25	26	8:02	43	2460604
	27	28	29	30	31	●	2	12:46	44	2460611
November 2024	3	4	5	6	7	8	◐	5:54	45	2460618
	10	11	12	13	14	○	16	21:28	46	2460625
	17	18	19	20	21	22	◑	1:27	47	2460632
	24	25	26	27	28	29	30		48	2460639
December 2024	●	2	3	4	5	6	7	6:20	49	2460646
	◐	9	10	11	12	13	14	15:25	50	2460653
	○	16	17	18	19	20	21[e]	9:01	51	2460660
	◑	23	24	25	26	27	28	22:17	52	2460667
	29	●	31	1	2	3	4	22:26	1	2460674

Hebrew 5784‡/5785

ISO Week	Month	Sun	Mon	Tue	Wed	Thu	Fri	Sat	Molad
1	Teveth 5784	19	20	21	22	23	24	25	
2		26	27	28	29	1	2	3	Thu 8h 45m 4p
3	Shevat 5784	4	5	6	7	8	9	10	
4		11	12	13	14	15	16	17	
5		18	19	20	21	22	23	24	
6		25	26	27	28	29	30	1	Fri 21h 29m 5p
7	Adar I 5784	2	3	4	5	6	7	8	
8		9	10	11	12	13	14	15	
9		16	17	18	19	20	21	22	
10		23	24	25	26	27	28	29	
11		30	1	2	3	4	5	6	Sun 10h 13m 6p
12	Adar II 5784	7	8	9	10	11	12	13	
13		14[f]	15	16	17	18	19	20	
14		21	22	23	24	25	26	27	
15		28	29	1	2	3	4	5	Mon 22h 57m 7p
16	Nisan 5784	6	7	8	9	10	11	12	
17		13	14	15[g]	16	17	18	19	
18		20	21	22	23	24	25	26	
19		27	28	29	30	1	2	3	Wed 11h 41m 8p
20	Iyar 5784	4	5	6	7	8	9	10	
21		11	12	13	14	15	16	17	
22		18	19	20	21	22	23	24	
23		25	26	27	28	29	1	2	Fri 0h 25m 9p
24	Sivan 5784	3	4	5	6[h]	7	8	9	
25		10	11	12	13	14	15	16	
26		17	18	19	20	21	22	23	
27		24	25	26	27	28	29	30	
28		1	2	3	4	5	6	7	Sat 13h 9m 10p
29	Tammuz 5784	8	9	10	11	12	13	14	
30		15	16	17	18	19	20	21	
31		22	23	24	25	26	27	28	
32		29	1	2	3	4	5	6	Mon 1h 53m 11p
33	Av 5784	7	8	9[i]	10	11	12	13	
34		14	15	16	17	18	19	20	
35		21	22	23	24	25	26	27	
36		28	29	30	1	2	3	4	Tue 14h 37m 12p
37	Elul 5784	5	6	7	8	9	10	11	
38		12	13	14	15	16	17	18	
39		19	20	21	22	23	24	25	
40		26	27	28	29	1[a]	2[a]	3	Thu 3h 21m 13p
41	Tishri 5785	4	5	6	7	8	9	10[b]	
42		11	12	13	14	15[c]	16	17	
43		18	19	20	21	22	23	24	
44		25	26	27	28	29	30	1	Fri 16h 5m 14p
45	Ḥeshvan 5785	2	3	4	5	6	7	8	
46		9	10	11	12	13	14	15	
47		16	17	18	19	20	21	22	
48		23	24	25	26	27	28	29	
49		30	1	2	3	4[d]	5	6	Sun 4h 49m 15p
50	Kislev 5785	7	8	9	10	11	12	13	
51		14	15	16	17	18	19	20	
52		21	22	23	24	25[e]	26[e]	27[e]	
1		28[e]	29[e]	30[e]	1[e]	2[e]	3	4	Mon 17h 33m 16p

Chinese Guǐ-Mǎo‡/Jiǎ-Chén

ISO Week	Month	Sun	Mon	Tue	Wed	Thu	Fri	Sat	Solar Term
1	Month 11* Guǐ-Mǎo	19	20*	21	22	23	24	25	Xiǎo hán
2	Month 12 Guǐ-Mǎo	26	27	28	29	1	2	3	
3		4	5	6	7	8	9	10	Dà hán
4		11	12	13	14	15	16	17	
5		18	19	20	21	22	23	24	
6		25	26	27	28	29	30	1[a]	Lì chūn
7	Month 1 Jiǎ-Chén	2	3	4	5	6	7	8	
8		9	10	11	12	13	14	15[b]	Yǔ shuǐ
9		16	17	18	19	20	21*	22	
10		23	24	25	26	27	28	29	Jīng zhé
11	Month 2 Jiǎ-Chén	1	2	3	4	5	6	7	
12		8	9	10	11	12	13	14	Chūn fēn
13		15	16	17	18	19	20	21	
14		22	23	24	25	26[c]	27	28	Qīng míng
15		29	30	1	2	3	4	5	
16	Month 3 Jiǎ-Chén	6	7	8	9	10	11	12	Gǔ yǔ
17		13	14	15	16	17	18	19	
18		20	21	22*	23	24	25	26	
19		27	28	29	1	2	3	4	Lì xià
20	Month 4 Jiǎ-Chén	5	6	7	8	9	10	11	
21		12	13	14	15	16	17	18	Xiǎo mǎn
22		19	20	21	22	23	24	25	
23		26	27	28	29	1	2	3	Máng zhòng
24	Month 5 Jiǎ-Chén	4	5[d]	6	7	8	9	10	
25		11	12	13	14	15	16	17	Xià zhì
26		18	19	20	21	22	23	24*	
27		25	26	27	28	29	30	1	Xiǎo shǔ
28	Month 6 Jiǎ-Chén	2	3	4	5	6	7	8	
29		9	10	11	12	13	14	15	
30		16	17	18	19	20	21	22	Dà shǔ
31		23	24	25	26	27	28	29	
32	Month 7 Jiǎ-Chén	1	2	3	4	5	6	7[e]	Lì qiū
33		8	9	10	11	12	13	14	
34		15[f]	16	17	18	19	20	21	Chǔ shǔ
35		22	23	24	25*	26	27	28	
36		29	30	1	2	3	4	5	Bái lù
37	Month 8 Jiǎ-Chén	6	7	8	9	10	11	12	
38		13	14	15[g]	16	17	18	19	
39		20	21	22	23	24	25	26	Qiū fēn
40		27	28	29	30	1	2	3	
41	Month 9 Jiǎ-Chén	4	5	6	7	8	9[h]	10	Hán lù
42		11	12	13	14	15	16	17	
43		18	19	20	21	22	23	24	Shuāng jiàng
44		25*	26	27	28	29	1	2	
45	Month 10 Jiǎ-Chén	3	4	5	6	7	8	9	Lì dōng
46		10	11	12	13	14	15	16	
47		17	18	19	20	21	22	23	Xiǎo xuě
48		24	25	26	27	28	29	30	
49	Month 11 Jiǎ-Chén	1	2	3	4	5	6	7	Dà xuě
50		8	9	10	11	12	13	14	
51		15	16	17	18	19	20	21[i]	Dōng zhì
52		22	23	24	25	26*	27	28	
1		29	30	1	2	3	4	5	

Coptic 1740/1741 — Ethiopic 2016/2017

ISO Week	Coptic Month	Sun	Mon	Tue	Wed	Thu	Fri	Sat	Ethiopic Month
1	Koiak 1740	21	22	23	24	25	26	27	Tâkhśâś 2016
2		28	29[c]	30	1	2	3	4	
3	Tôbe 1740	5	6[d]	7	8	9	10	11[e]	Ṭer 2016
4		12	13	14	15	16	17	18	
5		19	20	21	22	23	24	25	
6		26	27	28	29	30	1	2	
7	Meshir 1740	3	4	5	6	7	8	9	Yakâtit 2016
8		10	11	12	13	14	15	16	
9		17	18	19	20	21	22	23	
10		24	25	26	27	28	29	30	
11	Paremotep 1740	1	2	3	4	5	6	7	Magâbit 2016
12		8	9	10	11	12	13	14	
13		15	16	17	18	19	20	21	
14		22	23	24	25	26	27	28	
15		29	30	1	2	3	4	5	
16	Parmoute 1740	6	7	8	9	10	11	12	Miyâzyâ 2016
17		13	14	15	16	17	18	19	
18		20	21	22	23	24	25	26	
19		27[f]	28	29[g]	30	1	2	3	
20	Pashons 1740	4	5	6	7	8	9	10	Genbot 2016
21		11	12	13	14	15	16	17	
22		18	19	20	21	22	23	24	
23		25	26	27	28	29	30	1	
24	Paône 1740	2	3	4	5	6	7	8	Sanê 2016
25		9	10	11	12	13	14	15	
26		16	17	18	19	20	21	22	
27		23	24	25	26	27	28	29	
28		30	1	2	3	4	5	6	
29	Epêp 1740	7	8	9	10	11	12	13	Ḥamlê 2016
30		14	15	16	17	18	19	20	
31		21	22	23	24	25	26	27	
32		28	29	30	1	2	3	4	
33	Mesorê 1740	5	6	7	8	9	10	11	Naḥasê 2016
34		12	13[h]	14	15	16	17	18	
35		19	20	21	22	23	24	25	
36	Epag. 1740	26	27	28	29	30	1	2	Pâg. 2016
37		3	4	5	1[a]	2	3	4	
38	Thoout 1741	5	6	7	8	9	10	11	Maskaram 2017
39		12	13	14	15	16	17[b]	18	
40		19	20	21	22	23	24	25	
41		26	27	28	29	30	1	2	
42	Paope 1741	3	4	5	6	7	8	9	Ṭeqemt 2017
43		10	11	12	13	14	15	16	
44		17	18	19	20	21	22	23	
45		24	25	26	27	28	29	30	
46	Athôr 1741	1	2	3	4	5	6	7	Ḫedâr 2017
47		8	9	10	11	12	13	14	
48		15	16	17	18	19	20	21	
49		22	23	24	25	26	27	28	
50		29	30	1	2	3	4	5	
51	Koiak 1741	6	7	8	9	10	11	12	Tâkhśâś 2017
52		13	14	15	16	17	18	19	
1		20	21	22	23	24	25	26	

Gregorian notes:
‡Leap year
[a]New Year
[b]Spring (3:05)
[c]Summer (20:50)
[d]Autumn (12:42)
[e]Winter (9:19)
● New moon
◐ First quarter moon
○ Full moon
◑ Last quarter moon

Hebrew notes:
‡Leap year
[a]New Year
[b]Yom Kippur
[c]Sukkot
[d]Winter starts
[e]Ḥanukkah
[f]Purim
[g]Passover
[h]Shavuot
[i]Fast of Av

Chinese notes:
‡Leap year
[a]New Year (4722, Dragon)
[b]Lantern Festival
[c]Qīngmíng
[d]Dragon Festival
[e]Qīqiǎo
[f]Hungry Ghosts
[g]Mid-Autumn Festival
[h]Double-Ninth Festival
[i]Dōngzhì
*Start of 60-name cycle

Coptic/Ethiopic notes:
[a]New Year
[b]Building of the Cross
[c]Christmas
[d]Jesus's Circumcision
[e]Epiphany
[f]Easter
[g]Mary's Announcement
[h]Jesus's Transfiguration

PERSIAN (ASTRONOMICAL) 1402/1403‡

Month	Sun	Mon	Tue	Wed	Thu	Fri	Sat
DEY 1402	10	11	12	13	14	15	16
	17	18	19	20	21	22	23
	24	25	26	27	28	29	30
BAHMAN 1402	1	2	3	4	5	6	7
	8	9	10	11	12	13	14
	15	16	17	18	19	20	21
	22	23	24	25	26	27	28
ESFAND 1402	29	30	1	2	3	4	5
	6	7	8	9	10	11	12
	13	14	15	16	17	18	19
	20	21	22	23	24	25	26
FARVARDĪN 1403	27	28	29	1[a]	2	3	4
	5	6	7	8	9	10	11
	12	13[b]	14	15	16	17	18
	19	20	21	22	23	24	25
ORDĪBEHEŠT 1403	26	27	28	29	30	31	1
	2	3	4	5	6	7	8
	9	10	11	12	13	14	15
	16	17	18	19	20	21	22
	23	24	25	26	27	28	29
XORDĀD 1403	30	31	1	2	3	4	5
	6	7	8	9	10	11	12
	13	14	15	16	17	18	19
	20	21	22	23	24	25	26
TĪR 1403	27	28	29	30	31	1	2
	3	4	5	6	7	8	9
	10	11	12	13	14	15	16
	17	18	19	20	21	22	23
	24	25	26	27	28	29	30
MORDĀD 1403	31	1	2	3	4	5	6
	7	8	9	10	11	12	13
	14	15	16	17	18	19	20
	21	22	23	24	25	26	27
SHAHRĪVAR 1403	28	29	30	31	1	2	3
	4	5	6	7	8	9	10
	11	12	13	14	15	16	17
	18	19	20	21	22	23	24
	25	26	27	28	29	30	31
MEHR 1403	1	2	3	4	5	6	7
	8	9	10	11	12	13	14
	15	16	17	18	19	20	21
	22	23	24	25	26	27	28
ĀBĀN 1403	29	30	1	2	3	4	5
	6	7	8	9	10	11	12
	13	14	15	16	17	18	19
	20	21	22	23	24	25	26
ĀZAR 1403	27	28	29	30	1	2	3
	4	5	6	7	8	9	10
	11	12	13	14	15	16	17
	18	19	20	21	22	23	24
DEY 1403	25	26	27	28	29	30	1
	2	3	4	5	6	7	8
	9	10	11	12	13	14	15

HINDU LUNAR 2080‡/2081

Month	Sun	Mon	Tue	Wed	Thu	Fri	Sat
MĀRGAŚĪRA 2080	19	20	21	22	23	24	25
PAUSHA 2080	26	27	28	29	30	1	2
	3	4	6	7	8	9	10
	11	12	13	14	15	16	17
	18	19	20	20	21	22	23
MĀGHA 2080	24	25	26	27	28	29	1
	2	3	4	5	6	7	8
	9	10	11	12	13	14	15
	16	17	18	19	20	21	22
	23	24	25	26	27	28[h]	29
PHĀLGUNA 2080	30	1	2	3	5	6	7
	8	9	10	11	12	13	13
	14	15[i]	16	17	18	19	20
	21	22	23	24	25	26	27
CHAITRA 2081	29	30	1[a]	2	3	4	5
	6	7	8	9[b]	10	11	12
	13	14	15	16	17	17	18
	19	21	22	23	24	25	26
VAIŚĀKHA 2081	27	28	29	30	1	2	4
	5	6	7	7	8	9	10
	11	12	13	14	15	16	17
	18	19	20	21	22	23	24
JYAISHṬHA 2081	26	27	28	29	30	1	2
	3	4	5	6	7	8	9
	10	11	12	13	13	14	15
	17	18	19	20	21	22	23
ĀSHĀḌHA 2081	24	25	26	27	29	30	1
	2	3	4	4	5	6	7
	8	9	10	11	12	13	14
	15	16	17	18	19	21	22
	23	24	25	26	27	28	29
ŚRĀVAṆA 2081	30	1	2	3	4	5	6
	7	8	9	10	11	12	13
	14	15	16	17	18	19	20
	21	22	23[c]	25	26	27	28
BHĀDRAPADA 2081	29	30	1	1	2	3	4[d]
	5	6	7	8	9	10	11
	12	13	14	15	17	18	19
	20	21	22	23	24	25	26
ĀŚVINA 2081	27	28	29	30	1	2	3
	4	5	5	6	7	8[e]	10[e]
	11	12	13	14	15	16	17
	18	19	20	22	23	24	25
KĀRTTIKA 2081	25	26	27	28	29	30	1[f]
	2	3	4	5	6	7	8
	9	10	11	12	13	15	16
	17	18	19	20	21	22	23
	24	25	26	27	28	28	29
MĀRGAŚĪRA 2081	30	1	2	3	4	5	6
	7	9	10	11[g]	12	13	14
	15	16	17	18	19	20	21
	22	23	24	25	26	27	28
PAUSHA 2081	29	30	1	2	3	4	5

HINDU SOLAR 1945/1946

Month	Sun	Mon	Tue	Wed	Thu	Fri	Sat
PAUSHA 1945	16	17	18	19	20	21	22
	23	24	25	26	27	28	29
MĀGHA 1945	30	1[b]	2	3	4	5	6
	7	8	9	10	11	12	13
	14	15	16	17	18	19	20
	21	22	23	24	25	26	27
PHĀLGUNA 1945	28	29	1	2	3	4	5
	6	7	8	9	10	11	12
	13	14	15	16	17	18	19
	20	21	22	23	24	25	26
CHAITRA 1945	27	28	29	30	1	2	3
	4	5	6	7	8	9	10
	11	12	13	14	15	16	17
	18	19	20	21	22	23	24
VAIŚĀKHA 1946	25	26	27	28	29	30	1[a]
	2	3	4	5	6	7	8
	9	10	11	12	13	14	15
	16	17	18	19	20	21	22
	23	24	25	26	27	28	29
JYAISHṬHA 1946	30	31	1	2	3	4	5
	6	7	8	9	10	11	12
	13	14	15	16	17	18	19
	20	21	22	23	24	25	26
ĀSHĀḌHA 1946	27	28	29	30	31	32	1
	2	3	4	5	6	7	8
	9	10	11	12	13	14	15
	16	17	18	19	20	21	22
	23	24	25	26	27	28	29
ŚRĀVAṆA 1946	30	31	1	2	3	4	5
	6	7	8	9	10	11	12
	13	14	15	16	17	18	19
	20	21	22	23	24	25	26
BHĀDRAPADA 1946	27	28	29	30	31	32	1
	2	3	4	5	6	7	8
	9	10	11	12	13	14	15
	16	17	18	19	20	21	22
	23	24	25	26	27	28	29
ĀŚVINA 1946	30	31	1	2	3	4	5
	6	7	8	9	10	11	12
	13	14	15	16	17	18	19
	20	21	22	23	24	25	26
KĀRTTIKA 1946	27	28	29	30	1	2	3
	4	5	6	7	8	9	10
	11	12	13	14	15	16	17
	18	19	20	21	22	23	24
MĀRGAŚĪRA 1946	25	26	27	28	29	30	1
	2	3	4	5	6	7	8
	9	10	11	12	13	14	15
	16	17	18	19	20	21	22
	23	24	25	26	27	28	29
PAUSHA 1946	1	2	3	4	5	6	7
	8	9	10	11	12	13	14
	15	16	17	18	19	20	21

ISLAMIC (ASTRONOMICAL) 1445/1446‡

Month	Sun	Mon	Tue	Wed	Thu	Fri	Sat
JUMĀDĀ II 1445	17	18	19	20	21	22	23
RAJAB 1445	24	25	26	27	28	29	1
	2	3	4	5	6	7	8
	9	10	11	12	13	14	15
	16	17	18	19	20	21	22
	23	24	25	26	27[d]	28	29
SHA'BĀN 1445	1	2	3	4	5	6	7
	8	9	10	11	12	13	14
	15	16	17	18	19	20	21
	22	23	24	25	26	27	28
RAMAḌĀN 1445	29	30	1[e]	2	3	4	5
	6	7	8	9	10	11	12
	13	14	15	16	17	18	19
	20	21	22	23	24	25	26
SHAWWĀL 1445	27	28	29	1[f]	2	3	4
	5	6	7	8	9	10	11
	12	13	14	15	16	17	18
	19	20	21	22	23	24	25
DHU AL-QA'DA 1445	26	27	28	29	1	2	3
	4	5	6	7	8	9	10
	11	12	13	14	15	16	17
	18	19	20	21	22	23	24
DHU AL-ḤIJJA 1445	25	26	27	28	29	30	1
	2	3	4	5	6	7	8
	9	10[g]	11	12	13	14	15
	16	17	18	19	20	21	22
	23	24	25	26	27	28	29
MUḤARRAM 1446	1[a]	2[d]	3	4	5	6	7
	8	9	10[b]	11	12	13	14
	15	16	17	18	19	20	21
	22	23	24	25	26	27	28
ṢAFAR 1446	29	30	1	2	3	4	5
	6	7	8	9	10	11	12
	13	14	15	16	17	18	19
	20	21	22	23	24	25	26
RABĪ' I 1446	27	28	29	30	1	2	3
	4	5	6	7	8	9	10
	11	12[c]	13	14	15	16	17
	18	19	20	21	22	23	24
RABĪ' II 1446	25	26	27	28	29	30	1
	2	3	4	5	6	7	8
	9	10	11	12	13	14	15
	16	17	18	19	20	21	22
	23	24	25	26	27	28	29
JUMĀDĀ I 1446	30	1	2	3	4	5	6
	7	8	9	10	11	12	13
	14	15	16	17	18	19	20
	21	22	23	24	25	26	27
JUMĀDĀ II 1446	28	29	1	2	3	4	5
	6	7	8	9	10	11	12
	13	14	15	16	17	18	19
	20	21	22	23	24	25	26
	27	28	29	1	2	3	4

GREGORIAN 2024‡

Julian‡ (Sun)	Sun	Mon	Tue	Wed	Thu	Fri	Sat	Month
Dec 18	31	1	2	3	4	5	6	JANUARY 2024
	7[a]	8	9	10	11	12	13	
Jan 1	14[b]	15	16	17	18	19	20	
	21	22	23	24	25	26	27	
Jan 15	28	29	30	31	1	2	3	FEBRUARY 2024
	4	5	6	7	8	9	10	
Jan 29	11	12	13	14[c]	15	16	17	
	18	19	20	21	22	23	24	
Feb 12	25	26	27	28	29	1	2	MARCH 2024
	3	4	5	6	7	8	9	
Feb 26	10	11	12	13	14	15	16	
	17	18	19	20	21	22	23	
Mar 11	24[d]	25	26	27	28	29	30	
	31[e]	1	2	3	4	5	6	APRIL 2024
Mar 25	7	8	9	10	11	12	13	
	14	15	16	17	18	19	20	
Apr 8	21	22	23	24	25	26	27	
	28	29	30	1	2	3	4	MAY 2024
Apr 22	5[f]	6	7	8	9	10	11	
	12	13	14	15	16	17	18	
May 6	19	20	21	22	23	24	25	
	26	27	28	29	30	31	1	JUNE 2024
May 20	2	3	4	5	6	7	8	
	9	10	11	12	13	14	15	
Jun 3	16	17	18	19	20	21	22	
	23	24	25	26	27	28	29	
Jun 17	30	1	2	3	4	5	6	JULY 2024
	7	8	9	10	11	12	13	
Jul 1	14	15	16	17	18	19	20	
	21	22	23	24	25	26	27	
Jul 15	28	29	30	31	1	2	3	AUGUST 2024
	4	5	6	7	8	9	10	
Jul 29	11	12	13	14	15	16	17	
	18	19	20	21	22	23	24	
Aug 12	25	26	27	28	29	30	31	
	1	2	3	4	5	6	7	SEPTEMBER 2024
Aug 26	8	9	10	11	12	13	14	
	15	16	17	18	19	20	21	
Sep 9	22	23	24	25	26	27	28	
	29	30	1	2	3	4	5	OCTOBER 2024
Sep 23	6	7	8	9	10	11	12	
	13	14	15	16	17	18	19	
Oct 7	20	21	22	23	24	25	26	
	27	28	29	30	31	1	2	NOVEMBER 2024
Oct 21	3	4	5	6	7	8	9	
	10	11	12	13	14	15	16	
Nov 4	17	18	19	20	21	22	23	
	24	25	26	27	28	29	30	
Nov 18	1[g]	2	3	4	5	6	7	DECEMBER 2024
	8	9	10	11	12	13	14	
Dec 2	15	16	17	18	19	20	21	
	22	23	24	25[h]	26	27	28	
Dec 16	29	30	31	1	2	3	4	

Persian: ‡Leap year; [a]New Year; [b]Sizdeh Bedar

Hindu lunar: ‡Leap year; [a]New Year (Krodhin); [b]Birthday of Rāma; [c]Birthday of Krishna; [d]Ganēśa Chaturthī; [e]Dashara; [f]Diwali; [g]Birthday of Vishnu; [h]Night of Śiva; [i]Holi

Hindu solar: [a]New Year (Piṅgala); [b]Pongal

Islamic: ‡Leap year; [a]New Year; [d]New Year (Arithmetic); [b]'Ashūrā'; [c]Prophet's Birthday; [d]Ascent of the Prophet; [e]Start of Ramaḍān; [f]'Īd al-Fiṭr; [g]'Īd al-'Aḍḥā

Gregorian: ‡Leap year; [a]Orthodox Christmas; [b]Julian New Year; [c]Ash Wednesday; [d]Feast of Orthodoxy; [e]Easter; [f]Orthodox Easter; [g]Advent; [h]Christmas

2025

GREGORIAN 2025 · Lunar Phases · ISO WEEK · JULIAN DAY

Month	Sun	Mon	Tue	Wed	Thu	Fri	Sat	Lunar Phases	ISO WEEK (Mon)	JULIAN DAY (Sun noon)
JANUARY 2025	29	●	31	1[a]	2	3	4	22:26	1	2460674
	5	◐	7	8	9	10	11	23:55	2	2460681
	12	○	14	15	16	17	18	22:26	3	2460688
	19	20	◑	22	23	24	25	20:30	4	2460695
	26	27	28	●	30	31	1	12:35	5	2460702
FEBRUARY 2025	2	3	4	◐	6	7	8	8:01	6	2460709
	9	10	11	○	13	14	15	13:52	7	2460716
	16	17	18	19	◑	21	22	17:32	8	2460723
	23	24	25	26	27	●	1	0:44	9	2460730
MARCH 2025	2	3	4	5	◐	7	8	16:31	10	2460737
	9	10	11	12	13	○	15	6:53	11	2460744
	16	17	18	19	20[b]	21	◑	11:28	12	2460751
	23	24	25	26	27	28	●	10:57	13	2460758
	30	31	1	2	3	4	◐	2:14	14	2460765
APRIL 2025	6	7	8	9	10	11	12		15	2460772
	○	14	15	16	17	18	19	0:21	16	2460779
	20	◑	22	23	24	25	26	1:34	17	2460786
	●	28	29	30	1	2	3	19:30	18	2460793
MAY 2025	◐	5	6	7	8	9	10	13:51	19	2460800
	11	○	13	14	15	16	17	16:55	20	2460807
	18	19	◑	21	22	23	24	11:58	21	2460814
	25	26	●	28	29	30	31	3:01	22	2460821
JUNE 2025	1	2	◐	4	5	6	7	3:40	23	2460828
	8	9	10	○	12	13	14	7:43	24	2460835
	15	16	17	◑	19	20	21[c]	19:18	25	2460842
	22	23	24	●	26	27	28	10:31	26	2460849
	29	30	1	◐	3	4	5	19:29	27	2460856
JULY 2025	6	7	8	9	○	11	12	20:36	28	2460863
	13	14	15	16	17	◑	19	0:37	29	2460870
	20	21	22	23	●	25	26	19:10	30	2460877
	27	28	29	30	31	◐	2	12:40	31	2460884
AUGUST 2025	3	4	5	6	7	8	○	7:54	32	2460891
	10	11	12	13	14	15	◑	5:11	33	2460898
	17	18	19	20	21	22	●	6:05	34	2460905
	24	25	26	27	28	29	30		35	2460912
SEPTEMBER 2025	◐	1	2	3	4	5	6	6:24	36	2460919
	○	8	9	10	11	12	13	18:08	37	2460926
	◑	15	16	17	18	19	20	10:32	38	2460933
	●	22[d]	23	24	25	26	27	19:53	39	2460940
	28	◐	30	1	2	3	4	23:53	40	2460947
OCTOBER 2025	5	6	○	8	9	10	11	3:46	41	2460954
	12	◑	14	15	16	17	18	18:11	42	2460961
	19	20	●	22	23	24	25	12:24	43	2460968
	26	27	28	◐	30	31	1	16:20	44	2460975
NOVEMBER 2025	2	3	4	○	6	7	8	13:18	45	2460982
	9	10	11	◑	13	14	15	5:27	46	2460989
	16	17	18	19	●	21	22	6:46	47	2460996
	23	24	25	26	27	◐	29	6:58	48	2461003
	30	1	2	3	○	5	6	23:13	49	2461010
DECEMBER 2025	7	8	9	10	◑	12	13	20:51	50	2461017
	14	15	16	17	18	19	●	1:42	51	2461024
	21[e]	22	23	24	25	26	◐	19:09	52	2461031
	28	29	30	31	1	2	○	10:02	1	2461038

HEBREW 5785/5786 · Molad

ISO WEEK	Month	Sun	Mon	Tue	Wed	Thu	Fri	Sat	Molad
1		28[e]	29[e]	30[e]	1[e]	2[e]	3	4	Mon 17h33m16p
2	TEVETH 5785	5	6	7	8	9	10	11	
3		12	13	14	15	16	17	18	
4		19	20	21	22	23	24	25	Wed 6h17m17p
5		26	27	28	29	1	2	3	
6	SHEVAT 5785	4	5	6	7	8	9	10	
7		11	12	13	14	15	16	17	
8		18	19	20	21	22	23	24	
9		25	26	27	28	29	30	1	Thu 19h2m0p
10	ADAR 5785	2	3	4	5	6	7	8	
11		9	10	11	12	13	14[f]	15	
12		16	17	18	19	20	21	22	
13		23	24	25	26	27	28	29	Sat 7h46m1p
14		1	2	3	4	5	6	7	
15		8	9	10	11	12	13	14	
16	NISAN 5785	15[g]	16	17	18	19	20	21	
17		22	23	24	25	26	27	28	Sun 20h30m2p
18		29	30	1	2	3	4	5	
19	IYYAR 5785	6	7	8	9	10	11	12	
20		13	14	15	16	17	18	19	
21		20	21	22	23	24	25	26	
22		27	28	29	1	2	3	4	Tue 9h14m3p
23	SIVAN 5785	5	6[h]	7	8	9	10	11	
24		12	13	14	15	16	17	18	
25		19	20	21	22	23	24	25	
26		26	27	28	29	30	1	2	Wed 21h58m4p
27	TAMMUZ 5785	3	4	5	6	7	8	9	
28		10	11	12	13	14	15	16	
29		17	18	19	20	21	22	23	
30		24	25	26	27	28	29	1	Fri 10h42m5p
31		2	3	4	5	6	7	8	
32	AV 5785	9[i]	10	11	12	13	14	15	
33		16	17	18	19	20	21	22	
34		23	24	25	26	27	28	29	
35		30	1	2	3	4	5	6	Sat 23h26m6p
36	ELUL 5785	7	8	9	10	11	12	13	
37		14	15	16	17	18	19	20	
38		21	22	23	24	25	26	27	
39		28	29	1[a]	2[a]	3	4	5	Mon 12h10m7p
40	TISHRI 5786	6	7	8	9	10[b]	11	12	
41		13	14	15[c]	16	17	18	19	
42		20	21	22	23	24	25	26	
43		27	28	29	30	1	2	3	Wed 0h54m8p
44	ḤESHVAN 5786	4	5	6	7	8	9	10	
45		11	12	13	14	15	16	17	
46		18	19	20	21	22	23	24	
47		25	26	27	28	29	1	2	Thu 13h38m9p
48	KISLEV 5786	3	4	5	6	7	8	9	
49		10	11	12	13	14	15[d]	16	
50		17	18	19	20	21	22	23	
51		24	25[e]	26[e]	27[e]	28[e]	29[e]	30[e]	
52	TEVETH 5786	1[e]	2[e]	3	4	5	6	7	Sat 2h22m10p
1		8	9	10	11	12	13	14	

CHINESE Jiă-Chén/Yĭ-Sì‡ · Solar Term

ISO WEEK	Month	Sun	Mon	Tue	Wed	Thu	Fri	Sat	Solar Term
1		29	30	1	2	3	4	5	
2	MONTH 12 Jiă-Chén	6	7	8	9	10	11	12	Xiǎo hán
3		13	14	15	16	17	18	19	
4		20	**21**	22	23	24	25	26	**Dà hán**
5		27	28	29	1[a]	2	3	4	
6	MONTH 1 Yĭ-Sì	5	6	7	8	9	10	11	Lì chūn
7		12	13	14	15[b]	16	17	18	
8		19	20	**21**	22	23	24	25	**Yǔ shuǐ**
9		26	27*	28	29	30	1	2	
10	MONTH 2 Yĭ-Sì	3	4	5	*6*	7	8	9	Jīng zhé
11		10	11	12	13	14	15	16	
12		17	18	19	20	**21**	22	23	**Chūn fēn**
13		24	25	26	27	28	29	1	
14	MONTH 3 Yĭ-Sì	2	3	4	5	6	7[c]	8	Qīng míng
15		9	10	11	12	13	14	15	
16		16	17	18	19	20	21	22	
17		**23**	24	25	26	27	28*	29	**Gǔ yǔ**
18		30	1	2	3	4	5	6	
19	MONTH 4 Yĭ-Sì	7	*8*	9	10	11	12	13	Lì xià
20		14	15	16	17	18	19	20	
21		21	22	23	**24**	25	26	27	**Xiǎo mǎn**
22		28	29	1	2	3	4	5[d]	
23	MONTH 5 Yĭ-Sì	6	7	8	9	*10*	11	12	Máng zhòng
24		13	14	15	16	17	18	19	
25		20	21	22	23	24	25	**26**	**Xià zhì**
26		27	28	29*	1	2	3	4	
27	MONTH 6 Yĭ-Sì	5	6	7	8	9	10	11	
28		12	*13*	14	15	16	17	18	Xiǎo shǔ
29		19	20	21	22	23	24	25	
30		26	27	**28**	29	30	1	2	**Dà shǔ**
31	LEAP MONTH 6 Yĭ-Sì	3	4	5	6	7	8	9	
32		10	11	12	13	*14*	15	16	Lì qiū
33		17	18	19	20	21	22	23	
34		24	25	26	27	28	29	**1***	**Chǔ shǔ**
35	MONTH 7 Yĭ-Sì	2	3	4	5	6	7[e]	8	
36		9	10	11	12	13	14	15[f]	
37		*16*	17	18	19	20	21	22	Bái lù
38		23	24	25	26	27	28	29	
39		30	1	**2**	3	4	5	6	**Qiū fēn**
40	MONTH 8 Yĭ-Sì	7	8	9	10	11	12	13	
41		14	15[g]	16	*17*	18	19	20	Hán lù
42		21	22	23	24	25	26	27	
43		28	29	1	2*	**3**	4	5	**Shuāng jiàng**
44	MONTH 9 Yĭ-Sì	6	7	8	9[h]	10	11	12	
45		13	14	15	16	17	*18*	19	Lì dōng
46		20	21	22	23	24	25	26	
47		27	28	29	30	1	2	**3**	**Xiǎo xuě**
48	MONTH 10 Yĭ-Sì	4	5	6	7	8	9	10	
49		11	12	13	14	15	16	17	
50		*18*	19	20	21	22	23	24	Dà xuě
51		25	26	27	28	29	30	1	
52	MONTH 11 Yĭ-Sì	**2[i]***	3	4	5	6	7	8	**Dōng zhì**
1		9	10	11	12	13	14	15	

COPTIC 1741/1742 · ETHIOPIC 2017/2018

ISO WEEK	Coptic Month	Sun	Mon	Tue	Wed	Thu	Fri	Sat	Ethiopic Month
1	KOIAK 1741	20	21	22	23	24	25	26	TĀKHŚĀŚ 2017
2		27	28	29[c]	30	1	2	3	
3	TÔBE 1741	4	5	6[d]	7	8	9	10	
4		11[e]	12	13	14	15	16	17	ṬER 2017
5		18	19	20	21	22	23	24	
6		25	26	27	28	29	30	1	
7	MESHIR 1741	2	3	4	5	6	7	8	
8		9	10	11	12	13	14	15	YAKĀTIT 2017
9		16	17	18	19	20	21	22	
10		23	24	25	26	27	28	29	
11		30	1	2	3	4	5	6	
12	PAREMOTEP 1741	7	8	9	10	11	12	13	MAGĀBIT 2017
13		14	15	16	17	18	19	20	
14		21	22	23	24	25	26	27	
15		28	29	30	1	2	3	4	
16	PARMOUTE 1741	5	6	7	8	9	10	11	MIYĀZYĀ 2017
17		12[f]	13	14	15	16	17	18	
18		19	20	21	22	23	24	25	
19		26	27	28	29[g]	30	1	2	
20	PASHONS 1741	3	4	5	6	7	8	9	
21		10	11	12	13	14	15	16	GENBOT 2017
22		17	18	19	20	21	22	23	
23		24	25	26	27	28	29	30	
24		1	2	3	4	5	6	7	
25	PAÔNE 1741	8	9	10	11	12	13	14	SANĒ 2017
26		15	16	17	18	19	20	21	
27		22	23	24	25	26	27	28	
28		29	30	1	2	3	4	5	
29	EPÊP 1741	6	7	8	9	10	11	12	
30		13	14	15	16	17	18	19	ḤAMLĒ 2017
31		20	21	22	23	24	25	26	
32		27	28	29	30	1	2	3	
33	MESORÊ 1741	4	5	6	7	8	9	10	
34		11	12	13[h]	14	15	16	17	NAHASĒ 2017
35		18	19	20	21	22	23	24	
36		25	26	27	28	29	30	1	
37	EPAG. 1741	2	3	4	5	1[a]	2	3	PĀG. 2017
38	THOOUT 1742	4	5	6	7	8	9	10	MASKARAM 2018
39		11	12	13	14	15	16	17[b]	
40		18	19	20	21	22	23	24	
41		25	26	27	28	29	30	1	
42	PAOPE 1742	2	3	4	5	6	7	8	
43		9	10	11	12	13	14	15	ṬEQEMT 2018
44		16	17	18	19	20	21	22	
45		23	24	25	26	27	28	29	
46		30	1	2	3	4	5	6	
47	ATHÔR 1742	7	8	9	10	11	12	13	HEDĀR 2018
48		14	15	16	17	18	19	20	
49		21	22	23	24	25	26	27	
50		28	29	30	1	2	3	4	
51	KOIAK 1742	5	6	7	8	9	10	11	TĀKHŚĀŚ 2018
52		12	13	14	15	16	17	18	
1		19	20	21	22	23	24	25	

[a]New Year
[b]Spring (9:00)
[c]Summer (2:41)
[d]Autumn (18:18)
[e]Winter (15:02)
● New moon
◐ First quarter moon
○ Full moon
◑ Last quarter moon

[a]New Year
[b]Yom Kippur
[c]Sukkot
[d]Winter starts
[e]Ḥanukkah
[f]Purim
[g]Passover
[h]Shavuot
[i]Fast of Av

‡Leap year
[a]New Year (4723, Snake)
[b]Lantern Festival
[c]Qīngmíng
[d]Dragon Festival
[e]Qīqiǎo
[f]Hungry Ghosts
[g]Mid-Autumn Festival
[h]Double-Ninth Festival
[i]Dōngzhì
*Start of 60-name cycle

[a]New Year
[b]Building of the Cross
[c]Christmas
[d]Jesus's Circumcision
[e]Epiphany
[f]Easter
[g]Mary's Announcement
[h]Jesus's Transfiguration

PERSIAN (ASTRONOMICAL) 1403‡/1404

Month	Sun	Mon	Tue	Wed	Thu	Fri	Sat
	9	10	11	12	13	14	15
DEY 1403	16	17	18	19	20	21	22
	23	24	25	26	27	28	29
	30	*1*	2	3	4	5	6
	7	8	9	10	11	12	13
BAHMAN 1403	14	15	16	17	18	19	20
	21	22	23	24	25	26	27
	28	29	30	*1*	2	3	4
	5	6	7	8	9	10	11
ESFAND 1403	12	13	14	15	16	17	18
	19	20	21	22	23	24	25
	26	27	28	29	*30*[*][ǎ]	1[a]	2
	3	4	5	6	7	8	9
FARVARDĪN 1404	10	11	12	13[b]	14	15	16
	17	18	19	20	21	22	23
	24	25	26	27	28	29	30
	31	1	2	3	4	5	6
	7	8	9	10	11	12	13
ORDĪBEHEŠT 1404	14	15	16	17	18	19	20
	21	22	23	24	25	26	27
	28	29	30	*31*	1	2	3
	4	5	6	7	8	9	10
XORDĀD 1404	11	12	13	14	15	16	17
	18	19	20	21	22	23	24
	25	26	27	28	29	30	*31*
	1	2	3	4	5	6	7
	8	9	10	11	12	13	14
TĪR 1404	15	16	17	18	19	20	21
	22	23	24	25	26	27	28
	29	30	*31*	1	2	3	4
MORDĀD 1404	5	6	7	8	9	10	11
	12	13	14	15	16	17	18
	19	20	21	22	23	24	25
	26	27	28	29	30	*31*	1
	2	3	4	5	6	7	8
SHAHRĪVAR 1404	9	10	11	12	13	14	15
	16	17	18	19	20	21	22
	23	24	25	26	27	28	29
	30	*31*	1	2	3	4	5
MEHR 1404	6	7	8	9	10	11	12
	13	14	15	16	17	18	19
	20	21	22	23	24	25	26
	27	28	29	*30*	1	2	3
ĀBĀN 1404	4	5	6	7	8	9	10
	11	12	13	14	15	16	17
	18	19	20	21	22	23	24
	25	26	27	28	29	*30*	1
	2	3	4	5	6	7	8
ĀZAR 1404	9	10	11	12	13	14	15
	16	17	18	19	20	21	22
	23	24	25	26	27	28	29
DEY 1404	*30*	1	2	3	4	5	6
	7	8	9	10	11	12	13

‡Leap year
[a]New Year (or prior day)
*Near New Year: −0′46″
[ǎ]New Year (Arithmetic)
[b]Sizdeh Bedar

HINDU LUNAR 2081/2082

Month	Sun	Mon	Tue	Wed	Thu	Fri	Sat
	29	30	1	2	3	4	5
PAUSHA 2081	6	7	8	9	10	11	**12**
	14	15	16	17	18	19	20
	21	*21*	22	23	24	25	26
	27	28	29	30	1	2	3
	4	5	**6**	8	9	10	11
MĀGHA 2081	12	13	14	15	16	17	18
	19	20	21	22	23	*23*	24
	25	26	27	28[h]**29**	1	2	
	3	4	5	6	7	8	9
PHĀLGUNA 2081	10	11	12	13	14	15[i]	16
	17	18	19	20	21	22	23
	24	25	26	27	28	29	30
	1[a]	2	3	**4**	6	7	8
	9[b]	10	11	12	13	14	15
CHAITRA 2082	16	*16*	17	18	19	20	21
	22	23	24	25	26	27	**28**
	30	1	2	3	4	5	6
	7	8	9	10	11	12	13
VAIŚĀKHA 2082	14	15	16	17	18	19	20
	21	22	23	24	25	26	27
	28	29	30	**1**	3	4	5
JYAISHṬHA 2082	6	7	8	9	10	11	12
	12	13	14	15	16	17	18
	19	20	21	22	23	**24**	26
	27	28	29	30	1	2	3
	4	5	6	7	8	9	10
ĀSHĀḌHA 2082	11	12	13	14	15	16	17
	18	19	20	21	22	23	24
	25	**26**	28	29	30	1	2
ŚRĀVAṆA 2082	3	4	5	6	7	8	9
	9	10	11	12	13	14	15
	16	17	18	**19**	21	22	23[c]
	24	25	26	27	28	29	30
	1	2	3	4[d]	5	6	7
BHĀDRAPADA 2082	8	9	10	11	12	13	14
	15	16	17	18	19	20	21
	22	**23**	25	26	27	28	29
	30	1	2	3	4	*4*	5
ĀŚVINA 2082	6	7	8[e]	9[e]	10[e]	11	12
	13	14	15	**16**	18	19	20
	21	22	23	24	25	26	27
	28	29	30	1[f]	2	3	4
KĀRTTIKA 2082	5	6	7	8	9	10	11
	12	13	14	15	16	17	18
	19	**20**	22	23	24	25	26
	27	28	*28*	29	30	1	2
MĀRGAŚIRA 2082	3	4	5	6	7	8	9
	10	11[g]	12	13	**14**	16	17
	18	19	20	21	22	23	24
	25	26	27	28	29	30	1
PAUSHA 2082	*1*	2	3	4	5	6	7
	8	10	11	12	13	14	15

[a]New Year (Viśvāvasu)
[b]Birthday of Rāma
[c]Birthday of Krishna
[d]Ganēśa Chaturthī
[e]Dashara
[f]Diwali
[g]Birthday of Vishnu
[h]Night of Śiva
[i]Holi

HINDU SOLAR 1946/1947‡

Month	Sun	Mon	Tue	Wed	Thu	Fri	Sat
PAUSHA 1946	15	16	17	18	19	20	21
	22	23	24	25	26	27	28
	29	30	1[b]	2	3	4	5
MĀGHA 1946	6	7	8	9	10	11	12
	13	14	15	16	17	18	19
	20	21	22	23	24	25	26
	27	28	29	1	2	3	4
PHĀLGUNA 1946	5	6	7	8	9	10	11
	12	13	14	15	16	17	18
	19	20	21	22	23	24	25
	26	27	28	29	30	1	2
	3	4	5	6	7	8	9
CHAITRA 1946	10	11	12	13	14	15	16
	17	18	19	20	21	22	23
	24	25	26	27	28	29	30
	1[a]	2	3	4	5	6	7
VAIŚĀKHA 1947	8	9	10	11	12	13	14
	15	16	17	18	19	20	21
	22	23	24	25	26	27	28
	29	30	31	1	2	3	4
JYAISHṬHA 1947	5	6	7	8	9	10	11
	12	13	14	15	16	17	18
	19	20	21	22	23	24	25
	26	27	28	29	30	31	32
	1	2	3	4	5	6	7
ĀSHĀḌHA 1947	8	9	10	11	12	13	14
	15	16	17	18	19	20	21
	22	23	24	25	26	27	28
	29	30	31	1	2	3	4
ŚRĀVAṆA 1947	5	6	7	8	9	10	11
	12	13	14	15	16	17	18
	19	20	21	22	23	24	25
	26	27	28	29	30	31	32
	1	2	3	4	5	6	7
BHĀDRAPADA 1947	8	9	10	11	12	13	14
	15	16	17	18	19	20	21
	22	23	24	25	26	27	28
	29	30	31	1	2	3	4
ĀŚVINA 1947	5	6	7	8	9	10	11
	12	13	14	15	16	17	18
	19	20	21	22	23	24	25
	26	27	28	29	30	1	2
KĀRTTIKA 1947	3	4	5	6	7	8	9
	10	11	12	13	14	15	16
	17	18	19	20	21	22	23
	24	25	26	27	28	29	30
	1	2	3	4	5	6	7
MĀRGAŚIRA 1947	8	9	10	11	12	13	14
	15	16	17	18	19	20	21
	22	23	24	25	26	27	28
	29	30	1	2	3	4	5
PAUSHA 1947	6	7	8	9	10	11	12
	13	14	15	16	17	18	19

‡Leap year
[a]New Year (Kālayukta)
[b]Pongal

ISLAMIC (ASTRONOMICAL) 1446‡/1447

Month	Sun	Mon	Tue	Wed	Thu	Fri	Sat
	27	28	29	*1*	2	3	4
RAJAB 1446	5	6	7	8	9	10	11
	12	13	14	15	16	17	18
	19	20	21	22	23	24	25
	26	27[d]	28	29	30	*1*	2
	3	4	5	6	7	8	9
SHA'BĀN 1446	10	11	12	13	14	15	16
	17	18	19	20	21	22	23
	24	25	26	27	28	29	*1*[e]
	2	3	4	5	6	7	8
RAMAḌĀN 1446	9	10	11	12	13	14	15
	16	17	18	19	20	21	22
	23	24	25	26	27	28	29
	30	*1*[f]	2	3	4	5	6
SHAWWĀL 1446	7	8	9	10	11	12	13
	14	15	16	17	18	19	20
	21	22	23	24	25	26	27
	28	29	*1*	2	3	4	5
DHU AL-QA'DA 1446	6	7	8	9	10	11	12
	13	14	15	16	17	18	19
	20	21	22	23	24	25	26
	27	28	29	1	*2*	3	4
DHU AL-ḤIJJA 1446	5	6	7	8	9	10[g]	11
	12	13	14	15	16	17	18
	19	20	21	22	23	24	25
	26	27	28	29	30	*1*[a]	2
	3	4	5	6	7	8	9
MUḤARRAM 1447	10[b]	11	12	13	14	15	16
	17	18	19	20	21	22	23
	24	25	26	27	28	29	1
	2	3	4	5	6	7	8
ṢAFAR 1447	9	10	11	12	13	14	15
	16	17	18	19	20	21	22
	23	24	25	26	27	28	29
	30	*1*	2	3	4	5	6
RABĪ' I 1447	7	8	9	10	11	12[c]	13
	14	15	16	17	18	19	20
	21	22	23	24	25	26	27
	28	29	30	*1*	2	3	4
RABĪ' II 1447	5	6	7	8	9	10	11
	12	13	14	15	16	17	18
	19	20	21	22	23	24	25
	26	27	28	29	*30*	1	2
JUMĀDĀ I 1447	3	4	5	6	7	8	9
	10	11	12	13	14	15	16
	17	18	19	20	21	22	23
	24	25	26	27	28	29	*1*
JUMĀDĀ II 1447	2	3	4	5	6	7	8
	9	10	11	12	13	14	15
	16	17	18	19	20	21	22
	23	24	25	26	27	28	29
RAJAB 1447	*30*	1	2	3	4	5	6
	7	8	9	10	11	12	13

‡Leap year
[a]New Year
[b]'Ashūrā'
[c]Prophet's Birthday
[d]Ascent of the Prophet
[e]Start of Ramaḍān
[f]'Id al-Fiṭr
[g]'Id al-'Aḍḥā

GREGORIAN 2025

Julian (Sun)	Sun	Mon	Tue	Wed	Thu	Fri	Sat	Month
Dec 16	29	30	31	1	2	3	4	
	5	6	7[a]	8	9	10	11	JANUARY 2025
Dec 30	*12*	13	14[b]	15	16	17	18	
	19	20	21	22	23	24	25	
Jan 13	*26*	27	28	29	30	31	1	
	2	3	4	5	6	7	8	FEBRUARY 2025
Jan 27	*9*	10	11	12	13	14	15	
	16	17	18	19	20	21	22	
Feb 10	*23*	24	25	26	27	28	1	
	2	3	4	5[c]	6	7	8	
Feb 24	*9*[d]	10	11	12	13	14	15	MARCH 2025
	16	17	18	19	20	21	22	
Mar 10	*23*	24	25	26	27	28	29	
	30	31	1	2	3	4	5	
Mar 24	*6*	7	8	9	10	11	12	APRIL 2025
	13	14	15	16	17	18	19	
Apr 7	*20*[e]	21	22	23	24	25	26	
	27	28	29	30	1	2	3	
Apr 21	*4*	5	6	7	8	9	10	MAY 2025
	11	12	13	14	15	16	17	
May 5	*18*	19	20	21	22	23	24	
	25	26	27	28	29	30	31	
May 19	*1*	2	3	4	5	6	7	
	8	9	10	11	12	13	14	JUNE 2025
Jun 2	*15*	16	17	18	19	20	21	
	22	23	24	25	26	27	28	
Jun 16	*29*	30	1	2	3	4	5	
	6	7	8	9	10	11	12	JULY 2025
Jun 30	*13*	14	15	16	17	18	19	
	20	21	22	23	24	25	26	
Jul 14	*27*	28	29	30	31	1	2	
	3	4	5	6	7	8	9	AUGUST 2025
Jul 28	*10*	11	12	13	14	15	16	
	17	18	19	20	21	22	23	
Aug 11	*24*	25	26	27	28	29	30	
	31	1	2	3	4	5	6	
Aug 25	*7*	8	9	10	11	12	13	SEPTEMBER 2025
	14	15	16	17	18	19	20	
Sep 8	*21*	22	23	24	25	26	27	
	28	29	30	1	2	3	4	
Sep 22	*5*	6	7	8	9	10	11	OCTOBER 2025
	12	13	14	15	16	17	18	
Oct 6	*19*	20	21	22	23	24	25	
	26	27	28	29	30	31	1	
Oct 20	*2*	3	4	5	6	7	8	NOVEMBER 2025
	9	10	11	12	13	14	15	
Nov 3	*16*	17	18	19	20	21	22	
	23	24	25	26	27	28	29	
Nov 17	*30*[g]	1	2	3	4	5	6	
	7	8	9	10	11	12	13	DECEMBER 2025
Dec 1	*14*	15	16	17	18	19	20	
	21	22	23	24	25[h]	26	27	
Dec 15	*28*	29	30	31	1	2	3	

[a]Orthodox Christmas
[b]Julian New Year
[c]Ash Wednesday
[d]Feast of Orthodoxy
[e]Easter (also Orthodox)
[g]Advent
[h]Christmas

2026

	GREGORIAN 2026							Lunar Phases	ISO WEEK	JULIAN DAY		HEBREW 5786/5787‡							Molad		CHINESE Yǐ-Sì‡/Bǐng-Wǔ							Solar Term		COPTIC 1742/1743‡ / ETHIOPIC 2018/2019‡							
	Sun	Mon	Tue	Wed	Thu	Fri	Sat		(Mon)	(Sun noon)		Sun	Mon	Tue	Wed	Thu	Fri	Sat			Sun	Mon	Tue	Wed	Thu	Fri	Sat			Sun	Mon	Tue	Wed	Thu	Fri	Sat	
JANUARY 2026	28	29	30	31	1[a]	2	○	10:02	1	2461038	TEVETH 5786	8	9	10	11	12	13	14		MONTH 11 Yǐ-Sì	9	10	11	12	13	14	15		KOIAK 1742	19	20	21	22	23	24	25	TĀḪŚĀŚ 2018
	4	5	6	7	8	9	◑	15:47	2	2461045		15	16	17	18	19	20	21			16	17	18	19	20	21	22	Xiǎo hán	TŌBE 1742	26	27	28	29[c]	30	1	2	
	11	12	13	14	15	16	17		3	2461052		22	23	24	25	26	27	28			23	24	25	26	27	28	29			3	4	5	6[d]	7	8	9	ṬER 2018
	●	19	20	21	22	23	24	19:51	4	2461059	SHEVAT 5786	29	1	2	3	4	5	6	Sun 15h 6m 11p	MONTH 12 Yǐ-Sì	30	1	2	3	4	5	6	Dà hán		10	11[e]	12	13	14	15	16	
	25	◐	27	28	29	30	31	4:46	5	2461066		7	8	9	10	11	12	13			7	8	9	10	11	12	13			17	18	19	20	21	22	23	
FEBRUARY 2026	○	2	3	4	5	6	7	22:08	6	2461073		14	15	16	17	18	19	20			14	15	16	17	18	19	20	Lì chūn		24	25	26	27	28	29	30	
	8	◑	10	11	12	13	14	12:42	7	2461080		21	22	23	24	25	26	27			21	22	23	24	25	26	27		MESHIR 1742	1	2	3	4	5	6	7	YAKĀTIT 2018
	15	16	●	18	19	20	21	12:00	8	2461087	ADAR 5786	28	29	30	1	2	3	4	Tue 3h 50m 12p	MONTH 1 Bǐng-Wǔ	28	29	1[a]	2	3*	4	5	Yǔ shuǐ		8	9	10	11	12	13	14	
	22	23	◐	25	26	27	28	12:26	9	2461094		5	6	7	8	9	10	11			6	7	8	9	10	11	12			15	16	17	18	19	20	21	
MARCH 2026	1	2	○	4	5	6	7	11:37	10	2461101		12	13	14[f]	15	16	17	18			13	14	15[b]	16	17	18	19	Jīng zhé		22	23	24	25	26	27	28	
	8	9	10	◑	12	13	14	9:38	11	2461108		19	20	21	22	23	24	25			20	21	22	23	24	25	26		PAREMOTEP 1742	29	30	1	2	3	4	5	
	15	16	17	18	●	20[b]	21	1:23	12	2461115	NISAN 5786	26	27	28	29	1	2	3	Wed 16h 34m 13p	MONTH 2 Bǐng-Wǔ	27	28	29	30	1	2	3	Chūn fēn		6	7	8	9	10	11	12	MAGĀBIT 2018
	22	23	24	◐	26	27	28	19:17	13	2461122		4	5	6	7	8	9	10			4	5	6	7	8	9	10			13	14	15	16	17	18	19	
APRIL 2026	29	30	31	1	○	3	4	2:11	14	2461129		11	12	13	14	15[g]	16	17			11	12	13	14	15	16	17			20	21	22	23	24	25	26	
	5	6	7	8	9	◑	11	4:51	15	2461136		18	19	20	21	22	23	24			18[c]	19	20	21	22	23	24	Qīng míng	PARMOUTE 1742	27	28	29	30	1	2	3	
	12	13	14	15	16	●	18	11:51	16	2461143	IYYAR 5786	25	26	27	28	29	30	1	Fri 5h 18m 14p	MONTH 3 Bǐng-Wǔ	25	26	27	28	29	1	2			4[f]	5	6	7	8	9	10	MIYĀZYĀ 2018
	19	20	21	22	23	◐	25	2:31	17	2461150		2	3	4	5	6	7	8			3	4*	5	6	7	8	9	Gǔ yǔ		11	12	13	14	15	16	17	
MAY 2026	26	27	28	29	30	○	2	17:22	18	2461157		9	10	11	12	13	14	15			10	11	12	13	14	15	16			18	19	20	21	22	23	24	
	3	4	5	6	7	8	◑	21:09	19	2461164		16	17	18	19	20	21	22			17	18	19	20	21	22	23	Lì xià	PASHONS 1742	25	26	27	28	29[g]	30	1	
	10	11	12	13	14	15	●	20:00	20	2461171		23	24	25	26	27	28	29			24	25	26	27	28	29	30			2	3	4	5	6	7	8	GENBOT 2018
	17	18	19	20	21	22	◐	11:10	21	2461178	SIVAN 5786	1	2	3	4	5	6[h]	7	Sat 18h 2m 15p	MONTH 4 Bǐng-Wǔ	1	2	3	4	5	6	7	Xiǎo mǎn		9	10	11	12	13	14	15	
	24	25	26	27	28	29	30		22	2461185		8	9	10	11	12	13	14			8	9	10	11	12	13	14			16	17	18	19	20	21	22	
JUNE 2026	○	1	2	3	4	5	6	8:44	23	2461192		15	16	17	18	19	20	21			15	16	17	18	19	20	21	Máng zhòng		23	24	25	26	27	28	29	
	7	◑	9	10	11	12	13	9:59	24	2461199		22	23	24	25	26	27	28			22	23	24	25	26	27	28		PAŌNE 1742	30	1	2	3	4	5	6	
	14	●	16	17	18	19	20	2:53	25	2461206	TAMMUZ 5786	29	30	1	2	3	4	5	Mon 6h 46m 16p	MONTH 5 Bǐng-Wǔ	29	1	2	3	4	5[d]*	6			7	8	9	10	11	12	13	SANĒ 2018
	◐[c]	22	23	24	25	26	27	21:54	26	2461213		6	7	8	9	10	11	12			7	8	9	10	11	12	13	Xià zhì		14	15	16	17	18	19	20	
	28	○	30	1	2	3	4	23:56	27	2461220		13	14	15	16	17	18	19			14	15	16	17	18	19	20			21	22	23	24	25	26	27	
JULY 2026	5	6	◑	8	9	10	11	19:28	28	2461227		20	21	22	23	24	25	26			21	22	23	24	25	26	27	Xiǎo shǔ	EPĒP 1742	28	29	30	1	2	3	4	
	12	13	●	15	16	17	18	9:42	29	2461234	AV 5786	27	28	29	1	2	3	4	Tue 19h 30m 17p	MONTH 6 Bǐng-Wǔ	28	29	1	2	3	4	5			5	6	7	8	9	10	11	ḤAMLĒ 2018
	19	20	◐	22	23	24	25	11:04	30	2461241		5	6	7	8	9[i]	10	11			6	7	8	9	10	11	12	Dà shǔ		12	13	14	15	16	17	18	
	26	27	28	○	30	31	1	14:35	31	2461248		12	13	14	15	16	17	18			13	14	15	16	17	18	19			19	20	21	22	23	24	25	
AUGUST 2026	2	3	4	5	◑	7	8	2:20	32	2461255		19	20	21	22	23	24	25			20	21	22	23	24	25	26	Lì qiū	MESORĒ 1742	26	27	28	29	30	1	2	
	9	10	11	●	13	14	15	17:35	33	2461262	ELUL 5786	26	27	28	29	30	1	2	Thu 8h 15m 0p	MONTH 7 Bǐng-Wǔ	27	28	29	30	1	2	3			3	4	5	6	7	8	9	NAḤASĒ 2018
	16	17	18	19	◐	21	22	2:45	34	2461269		3	4	5	6	7	8	9			4	5	6*	7[e]	8	9	10			10	11	12	13[h]	14	15	16	
	23	24	25	26	27	○	29	4:18	35	2461276		10	11	12	13	14	15	16			11	12	13	14	15[f]	16	17	Chǔ shǔ		17	18	19	20	21	22	23	
SEPTEMBER 2026	30	31	1	2	3	◑	5	7:50	36	2461283		17	18	19	20	21	22	23			18	19	20	21	22	23	24			24	25	26	27	28	29	30	
	6	7	8	9	10	●	12	3:26	37	2461290	TISHRI 5787	24	25	26	27	28	29	1[a]	Fri 20h 59m 1p	MONTH 8 Bǐng-Wǔ	25	26	27	28	29	1	2	Bái lù	EPAG. 1742 / THOOUT 1743	1	2	3	4	5	1[a]	2	PĀG. 2018 / MASKARAM 2019
	13	14	15	16	17	◐	19	20:43	38	2461297		2[a]	3	4	5	6	7	8			3	4	5	6	7	8	9			3	4	5	6	7	8	9	
	20	21	22	23[d]	24	25	○	16:48	39	2461304		9	10[b]	11	12	13	14	15[c]			10	11	12	13	14	15[g]	16	Qiū fēn		10	11	12	13	14	15	16	
OCTOBER 2026	27	28	29	30	1	2	◑	13:24	40	2461311		16	17	18	19	20	21	22			17	18	19	20	21	22	23			17[b]	18	19	20	21	22	23	
	4	5	6	7	8	9	●	15:49	41	2461318		23	24	25	26	27	28	29		MONTH 9 Bǐng-Wǔ	24	25	26	27	28	29	1	Hán lù		24	25	26	27	28	29	30	
	11	12	13	14	15	16	17		42	2461325	HESHVAN 5787	30	1	2	3	4	5	6	Sun 9h 43m 2p		2	3	4	5	6	7	8*		PAOPE 1743	1	2	3	4	5	6	7	ṬEQEMT 2019
	◐	19	20	21	22	23	24	16:12	43	2461332		7	8	9	10	11	12	13			9[h]	10	11	12	13	14	15	Shuāng jiàng		8	9	10	11	12	13	14	
	25	○	27	28	29	30	31	4:11	44	2461339		14	15	16	17	18	19	20			16	17	18	19	20	21	22			15	16	17	18	19	20	21	
NOVEMBER 2026	◑	2	3	4	5	6	7	20:27	45	2461346		21	22	23	24	25	26	27			23	24	25	26	27	28	29	Lì dōng		22	23	24	25	26	27	28	
	8	●	10	11	12	13	14	7:01	46	2461353	KISLEV 5787	28	29	30	1	2	3	4	Mon 22h 27m 3p	MONTH 10 Bǐng-Wǔ	30	1	2	3	4	5	6		ATHŌR 1743	29	30	1	2	3	4	5	ḪEDĀR 2019
	15	16	◐	18	19	20	21	11:47	47	2461360		5	6	7	8	9	10	11			7	8	9	10	11	12	13			6	7	8	9	10	11	12	
	22	23	○	25	26	27	28	14:53	48	2461367		12	13	14	15	16	17	18			14	15	16	17	18	19	20	Xiǎo xuě		13	14	15	16	17	18	19	
DECEMBER 2026	29	30	◑	2	3	4	5	6:08	49	2461374		19	20	21	22	23	24	25[d][e]			21	22	23	24	25	26	27			20	21	22	23	24	25	26	
	6	7	8	●	10	11	12	0:51	50	2461381	TEVETH 5787	26[e]	27[e]	28[e]	29[e]	30[e]	1[e]	2[e]	Wed 11h 11m 4p	MONTH 11 Bǐng-Wǔ	28	29	30	1	2	3	4	Dà xuě	KOIAK 1743	27	28	29	30	1	2	3	TĀḪŚĀŚ 2019
	13	14	15	16	◐	18	19	5:42	51	2461388		3	4	5	6	7	8	9			5	6	7	8*	9	10	11			4	5	6	7	8	9	10	
	20	21[e]	22	23	○	25	26	1:27	52	2461395		10	11	12	13	14	15	16			12	13	14[i]	15	16	17	18	Dōng zhì		11	12	13	14	15	16	17	
	27	28	29	◑	31	1	2	18:58	53	2461402		17	18	19	20	21	22	23			19	20	21	22	23	24	25			18	19	20	21	22	23	24	

[a]New Year
[b]Spring (14:44)
[c]Summer (8:24)
[d]Autumn (0:04)
[e]Winter (20:49)
● New moon
◐ First quarter moon
○ Full moon
◑ Last quarter moon

‡Leap year
[a]New Year
[b]Yom Kippur
[c]Sukkot
[d]Winter starts
[e]Ḥanukkah
[f]Purim
[g]Passover
[h]Shavuot
[i]Fast of Av

‡Leap year
[a]New Year (4724, Horse)
[b]Lantern Festival
[c]Qīngmíng
[d]Dragon Festival
[e]Qīqiǎo
[f]Hungry Ghosts
[g]Mid-Autumn Festival
[h]Double-Ninth Festival
[i]Dōngzhì
*Start of 60-name cycle

‡Leap year
[a]New Year
[b]Building of the Cross
[c]Christmas
[d]Jesus's Circumcision
[e]Epiphany
[f]Easter
[g]Mary's Announcement
[h]Jesus's Transfiguration

PERSIAN (ASTRONOMICAL) 1404/1405

Month	Sun	Mon	Tue	Wed	Thu	Fri	Sat
DEY 1404	7	8	9	10	11	12	13
	14	15	16	17	18	19	20
	21	22	23	24	25	26	27
BAHMAN 1404	28	29	*30*	1	2	3	4
	5	6	7	8	9	10	11
	12	13	14	15	16	17	18
	19	20	21	22	23	24	25
ESFAND 1404	26	27	28	29	*30*	1	2
	3	4	5	6	7	8	9
	10	11	12	13	14	15	16
	17	18	19	20	21	22	23
FARVARDĪN 1405	24	25	26	27	28	29	*1*[a]
	2	3	4	5	6	7	8
	9	10	11	12	13[b]	14	15
	16	17	18	19	20	21	22
	23	24	25	26	27	28	29
ORDĪBEHEŠT 1405	30	31	*1*	2	3	4	5
	6	7	8	9	10	11	12
	13	14	15	16	17	18	19
	20	21	22	23	24	25	26
XORDĀD 1405	27	28	29	30	31	*1*	2
	3	4	5	6	7	8	9
	10	11	12	13	14	15	16
	17	18	19	20	21	22	23
	24	25	26	27	28	29	30
TĪR 1405	31	*1*	2	3	4	5	6
	7	8	9	10	11	12	13
	14	15	16	17	18	19	20
	21	22	23	24	25	26	27
MORDĀD 1405	28	29	30	31	*1*	2	3
	4	5	6	7	8	9	10
	11	12	13	14	15	16	17
	18	19	20	21	22	23	24
	25	26	27	28	29	30	31
SHAHRĪVAR 1405	*1*	2	3	4	5	6	7
	8	9	10	11	12	13	14
	15	16	17	18	19	20	21
	22	23	24	25	26	27	28
MEHR 1405	29	30	31	*1*	2	3	4
	5	6	7	8	9	10	11
	12	13	14	15	16	17	18
	19	20	21	22	23	24	25
ĀBĀN 1405	26	27	28	29	30	*1*	2
	3	4	5	6	7	8	9
	10	11	12	13	14	15	16
	17	18	19	20	21	22	23
	24	25	26	27	28	29	30
ĀZAR 1405	*1*	2	3	4	5	6	7
	8	9	10	11	12	13	14
	15	16	17	18	19	20	21
	22	23	24	25	26	27	28
DEY 1405	29	30	*1*	2	3	4	5
	6	7	8	9	10	11	12

[a]New Year
[b]Sizdeh Bedar

HINDU LUNAR 2082/2083‡

Month	Sun	Mon	Tue	Wed	Thu	Fri	Sat
PAUSHA 2082	**8**	10	11	12	13	14	15
	16	17	18	19	20	21	22
	23	24	25	26	27	28	29
MĀGHA 2082	30	1	2	3	4	5	6
	7	8	9	10	11	12	**13**
	15	16	17	18	19	20	21
	22	23	*23*	24	25	26	27
PHĀLGUNA 2082	28[h]	29	30	1	2	3	4
	5	6	**7**	9	10	11	12
	13	14	15[i]	16	17	18	19
	20	21	22	23	24	25	26
CHAITRA 2083	*26*	27	28	29	**30**[a]	2	3
	4	5	6	7	8	**9**[b]	10
	11	12	13	14	15	16	17
	18	19	20	21	22	23	24
VAIŚĀKHA 2083	25	26	27	28	29	30	1
	2	3	4	**5**	7	8	9
	10	11	12	13	14	15	16
	17	18	19	20	*20*	21	22
	23	24	25	26	27	**28**	30
LEAP JYAISHṬHA 2083	1	2	3	4	5	6	7
	8	9	10	11	12	13	14
	15	16	17	18	19	20	21
	22	23	24	25	26	27	28
JYAISHṬHA 2083	29	30	**1**	3	4	5	6
	7	8	9	10	11	12	13
	14	15	16	*16*	17	18	19
	20	21	22	**23**	25	26	27
ĀSHĀḌHA 2083	28	29	30	1	2	3	4
	5	6	7	8	9	10	11
	12	13	14	15	16	17	18
	19	20	21	22	23	24	25
ŚRĀVAṆA 2083	**26**	28	29	30	1	2	3
	4	5	6	7	8	9	10
	11	12	13	*13*	14	15	16
	17	18	**19**	21	22	23[c]	24
BHĀDRAPADA 2083	25	26	27	28	29	30	1
	2	**3**[d]	4	5	6	7	8
	9	10	11	12	13	14	15
	16	17	18	19	20	21	22
	23	25	26	27	28	29	30
ĀŚVINA 2083	1	2	3	4	5	6	7
	8	*8*[e]	9[e]	10[e]	11	12	13
	14	15	**16**	18	19	20	21
	22	23	24	25	26	27	28
KĀRTTIKA 2083	29	30	1[f]	2	3	4	5
	6	7	8	9	10	11	12
	13	14	15	16	17	18	19
	20	**21**	23	24	25	26	27
MĀRGAŚIRA 2083	28	29	30	1	*1*	2	3
	4	5	6	7	8	9	10
	11[g]	12	13	14	**15**	17	18
	19	20	21	22	23	24	25

‡Leap year
[a]New Year (Parābhava)
[b]Birthday of Rāma
[c]Birthday of Krishna
[d]Ganēśa Chaturthī
[e]Dashara
[f]Diwali
[g]Birthday of Vishnu
[h]Night of Śiva
[i]Holi

HINDU SOLAR 1947‡/1948

Month	Sun	Mon	Tue	Wed	Thu	Fri	Sat
PAUSHA 1947	13	14	15	16	17	18	19
	20	21	22	23	24	25	26
MĀGHA 1947	27	28	29	1[b]	2	3	4
	5	6	7	8	9	10	11
	12	13	14	15	16	17	18
	19	20	21	22	23	24	25
PHĀLGUNA 1947	26	27	28	29	30	1	2
	3	4	5	6	7	8	9
	10	11	12	13	14	15	16
	17	18	19	20	21	22	23
CHAITRA 1947	24	25	26	27	28	29	1
	2	3	4	5	6	7	8
	9	10	11	12	13	14	15
	16	17	18	19	20	21	22
	23	24	25	26	27	28	29
VAIŚĀKHA 1948	30	31	1[a]	2	3	4	5
	6	7	8	9	10	11	12
	13	14	15	16	17	18	19
	20	21	22	23	24	25	26
JYAISHṬHA 1948	27	28	29	30	31	1	2
	3	4	5	6	7	8	9
	10	11	12	13	14	15	16
	17	18	19	20	21	22	23
	24	25	26	27	28	29	30
ĀSHĀḌHA 1948	31	1	2	3	4	5	6
	7	8	9	10	11	12	13
	14	15	16	17	18	19	20
	21	22	23	24	25	26	27
ŚRĀVAṆA 1948	28	29	30	31	32	1	2
	3	4	5	6	7	8	9
	10	11	12	13	14	15	16
	17	18	19	20	21	22	23
	24	25	26	27	28	29	30
BHĀDRAPADA 1948	31	1	2	3	4	5	6
	7	8	9	10	11	12	13
	14	15	16	17	18	19	20
	21	22	23	24	25	26	27
ĀŚVINA 1948	28	29	30	31	1	2	3
	4	5	6	7	8	9	10
	11	12	13	14	15	16	17
	18	19	20	21	22	23	24
	25	26	27	28	29	30	31
KĀRTTIKA 1948	1	2	3	4	5	6	7
	8	9	10	11	12	13	14
	15	16	17	18	19	20	21
	22	23	24	25	26	27	28
MĀRGAŚIRA 1948	29	30	1	2	3	4	5
	6	7	8	9	10	11	12
	13	14	15	16	17	18	19
	20	21	22	23	24	25	26
PAUSHA 1948	27	28	29	1	2	3	4
	5	6	7	8	9	10	11
	12	13	14	15	16	17	18

‡Leap year
[a]New Year (Siddhārthin)
[b]Pongal

ISLAMIC (ASTRONOMICAL) 1447/1448‡

Month	Sun	Mon	Tue	Wed	Thu	Fri	Sat
RAJAB 1447	7	8	9	10	11	12	13
	14	15	16	17	18	19	20
	21	22	23	24	25	26	27[d]
SHA'BĀN 1447	28	29	*1*	2	3	4	5
	6	7	8	9	10	11	12
	13	14	15	16	17	18	19
	20	21	22	23	24	25	26
RAMAḌĀN 1447	27	28	29	*30*	1[e]	2	3
	4	5	6	7	8	9	10
	11	12	13	14	15	16	17
	18	19	20	21	22	23	24
SHAWWĀL 1447	25	26	27	28	29	1[f]	2
	3	4	5	6	7	8	9
	10	11	12	13	14	15	16
	17	18	19	20	21	22	23
	24	25	26	27	28	29	*30*
DHU AL-QA'DA 1447	1	2	3	4	5	6	7
	8	9	10	11	12	13	14
	15	16	17	18	19	20	21
	22	23	24	25	26	27	28
DHU AL-ḤIJJA 1447	29	*1*	2	3	4	5	6
	7	8	9	10[g]	11	12	13
	14	15	16	17	18	19	20
	21	22	23	24	25	26	27
MUḤARRAM 1448	28	29	1[a]	2[ä]	3	4	5
	6	7	8	9	10[b]	11	12
	13	14	15	16	17	18	19
	20	21	22	23	24	25	26
ṢAFAR 1448	27	28	29	30	1	2	3
	4	5	6	7	8	9	10
	11	12	13	14	15	16	17
	18	19	20	21	22	23	24
RABĪ' I 1448	25	26	27	28	29	1	2
	3	4	5	6	7	8	9
	10	11	12[c]	13	14	15	16
	17	18	19	20	21	22	23
	24	25	26	27	28	29	30
RABĪ' II 1448	1	2	3	4	5	6	7
	8	9	10	11	12	13	14
	15	16	17	18	19	20	21
	22	23	24	25	26	27	28
JUMĀDĀ I 1448	29	30	*1*	2	3	4	5
	6	7	8	9	10	11	12
	13	14	15	16	17	18	19
	20	21	22	23	24	25	26
JUMĀDĀ II 1448	27	28	29	1	2	3	4
	5	6	7	8	9	10	11
	12	13	14	15	16	17	18
	19	20	21	22	23	24	25
RAJAB 1448	26	27	28	29	30	*1*	2
	3	4	5	6	7	8	9
	10	11	12	13	14	15	16
	17	18	19	20	21	22	23

‡Leap year
[a]New Year
[ä]New Year (Arithmetic)
[b]'Āshūrā'
[c]Prophet's Birthday
[d]Ascent of the Prophet
[e]Start of Ramaḍān
[f]'Id al-Fiṭr
[g]'Id al-'Aḍḥā

GREGORIAN 2026

Julian (Sun)	Sun	Mon	Tue	Wed	Thu	Fri	Sat	Month
Dec 15	*28*	29	30	31	1	2	3	
	4	5	6	7[a]	8	9	10	JANUARY 2026
Dec 29	*11*	12	13	14[b]	15	16	17	
	18	19	20	21	22	23	24	
Jan 12	*25*	26	27	28	29	30	31	
	1	2	3	4	5	6	7	FEBRUARY 2026
Jan 26	*8*	9	10	11	12	13	14	
	15	16	17	18[c]	19	20	21	
Feb 9	*22*	23	24	25	26	27	28	
	1[d]	2	3	4	5	6	7	MARCH 2026
Feb 23	*8*	9	10	11	12	13	14	
	15	16	17	18	19	20	21	
Mar 9	*22*	23	24	25	26	27	28	
	29	30	31	1	2	3	4	APRIL 2026
Mar 23	*5*[e]	6	7	8	9	10	11	
	12[f]	13	14	15	16	17	18	
Apr 6	*19*	20	21	22	23	24	25	
	26	27	28	29	30	1	2	MAY 2026
Apr 20	*3*	4	5	6	7	8	9	
	10	11	12	13	14	15	16	
May 4	*17*	18	19	20	21	22	23	
	24	25	26	27	28	29	30	
May 18	*31*	1	2	3	4	5	6	JUNE 2026
	7	8	9	10	11	12	13	
Jun 1	*14*	15	16	17	18	19	20	
	21	22	23	24	25	26	27	
Jun 15	*28*	29	30	1	2	3	4	JULY 2026
	5	6	7	8	9	10	11	
Jun 29	*12*	13	14	15	16	17	18	
	19	20	21	22	23	24	25	
Jul 13	*26*	27	28	29	30	31	1	AUGUST 2026
	2	3	4	5	6	7	8	
Jul 27	*9*	10	11	12	13	14	15	
	16	17	18	19	20	21	22	
Aug 10	*23*	24	25	26	27	28	29	
	30	31	1	2	3	4	5	SEPTEMBER 2026
Aug 24	*6*	7	8	9	10	11	12	
	13	14	15	16	17	18	19	
Sep 7	*20*	21	22	23	24	25	26	
	27	28	29	30	1	2	3	OCTOBER 2026
Sep 21	*4*	5	6	7	8	9	10	
	11	12	13	14	15	16	17	
Oct 5	*18*	19	20	21	22	23	24	
	25	26	27	28	29	30	31	
Oct 19	*1*	2	3	4	5	6	7	NOVEMBER 2026
	8	9	10	11	12	13	14	
Nov 2	*15*	16	17	18	19	20	21	
	22	23	24	25	26	27	28	
Nov 16	29[g]	30	1	2	3	4	5	DECEMBER 2026
	6	7	8	9	10	11	12	
Nov 30	*13*	14	15	16	17	18	19	
	20	21	22	23	24	25[h]	26	
Dec 14	*27*	28	29	30	31	1	2	

[a]Orthodox Christmas
[b]Julian New Year
[c]Ash Wednesday
[d]Feast of Orthodoxy
[e]Easter
[f]Orthodox Easter
[g]Advent
[h]Christmas

2027

Month	Sun	Mon	Tue	Wed	Thu	Fri	Sat	Lunar Phases	ISO Week (Mon)	Julian Day (Sun noon)
	27	28	29	◑	31	1[a]	2	18:58	53	2461402
JANUARY 2027	3	4	5	6	●	8	9	20:23	1	2461409
	10	11	12	13	14	◐	16	20:33	2	2461416
	17	18	19	20	21	○	23	12:16	3	2461423
	24	25	26	27	28	◑	30	10:54	4	2461430
	31	1	2	3	4	5	●	15:55	5	2461437
FEBRUARY 2027	7	8	9	10	11	12	13		6	2461444
	◐	15	16	17	18	19	○	7:57 23:22	7	2461451
	21	22	23	24	25	26	27		8	2461458
	◑	1	2	3	4	5	6	5:15	9	2461465
MARCH 2027	7	●	9	10	11	12	13	9:28	10	2461472
	14	◐	16	17	18	19	20[b]	16:24	11	2461479
	21	○	23	24	25	26	27	10:43	12	2461486
	28	29	◑	31	1	2	3	0:53	13	2461493
APRIL 2027	4	5	●	7	8	9	10	23:50	14	2461500
	11	12	◐	14	15	16	17	22:55	15	2461507
	18	19	○	21	22	23	24	22:26	16	2461514
	25	26	27	◑	29	30	1	20:17	17	2461521
MAY 2027	2	3	4	5	●	7	8	10:58	18	2461528
	9	10	11	12	◐	14	15	4:43	19	2461535
	16	17	18	19	○	21	22	10:58	20	2461542
	23	24	25	26	27	◑	29	13:57	21	2461549
	30	31	1	2	3	●	5	19:39	22	2461556
JUNE 2027	6	7	8	9	10	◐	12	10:55	23	2461563
	13	14	15	16	17	18	○	0:43	24	2461570
	20	21[c]	22	23	24	25	26		25	2461577
	◑	28	29	30	1	2	3	4:53	26	2461584
JULY 2027	●	5	6	7	8	9	◐	3:01 18:38	27	2461591
	11	12	13	14	15	16	17		28	2461598
	○	19	20	21	22	23	24	15:44	29	2461605
	25	◑	27	28	29	30	31	16:54	30	2461612
AUGUST 2027	1	●	3	4	5	6	7	10:04	31	2461619
	8	◐	10	11	12	13	14	4:53	32	2461626
	15	16	○	18	19	20	21	7:28	33	2461633
	22	23	24	◑	26	27	28	2:26	34	2461640
	29	30	●	1	2	3	4	17:40	35	2461647
SEPTEMBER 2027	5	6	◐	8	9	10	11	18:30	36	2461654
	12	13	14	○	16	17	18	23:02	37	2461661
	19	20	21	22	◑[d]	24	25	10:19	38	2461668
	26	27	28	29	●	1	2	2:35	39	2461675
OCTOBER 2027	3	4	5	6	◐	8	9	11:46	40	2461682
	10	11	12	13	14	○	16	13:46	41	2461689
	17	18	19	20	21	◑	23	17:28	42	2461696
	24	25	26	27	28	●	30	13:35	43	2461703
	31	1	2	3	4	5	◐	7:59	44	2461710
NOVEMBER 2027	7	8	9	10	11	12	13		45	2461717
	○	15	16	17	18	19	20	3:25	46	2461724
	◑	22	23	24	25	26	27	0:47	47	2461731
	●	29	30	1	2	3	4	3:23	48	2461738
DECEMBER 2027	5	◐	7	8	9	10	11	5:21	49	2461745
	12	○	14	15	16	17	18	16:08	50	2461752
	19	◑	21	22[e]	23	24	25	9:10	51	2461759
	26	●	28	29	30	31	1	20:11	52	2461766

HEBREW 5787‡/5788

ISO Week	Month	Sun	Mon	Tue	Wed	Thu	Fri	Sat	Molad
53	TEVETH 5787	17	18	19	20	21	22	23	
1		24	25	26	27	28	29	1	Thu 23h55m5p
2		2	3	4	5	6	7	8	
3	SHEVAT 5787	9	10	11	12	13	14	15	
4		16	17	18	19	20	21	22	
5		23	24	25	26	27	28	29	
6		30	1	2	3	4	5	6	Sat 12h39m6p
7	ADAR I 5787	7	8	9	10	11	12	13	
8		14	15	16	17	18	19	20	
9		21	22	23	24	25	26	27	
10		28	29	30	1	2	3	4	Mon 1h23m7p
11	ADAR II 5787	5	6	7	8	9	10	11	
12		12	13	14[f]	15	16	17	18	
13		19	20	21	22	23	24	25	
14		26	27	28	29	1	2	3	Tue 14h7m8p
15	NISAN 5787	4	5	6	7	8	9	10	
16		11	12	13	14	15[g]	16	17	
17		18	19	20	21	22	23	24	
18		25	26	27	28	29	30	1	Thu 2h51m9p
19	IYAR 5787	2	3	4	5	6	7	8	
20		9	10	11	12	13	14	15	
21		16	17	18	19	20	21	22	
22		23	24	25	26	27	28	29	
23		1	2	3	4	5	6[h]	7	Fri 15h35m10p
24	SIVAN 5787	8	9	10	11	12	13	14	
25		15	16	17	18	19	20	21	
26		22	23	24	25	26	27	28	
27		29	30	1	2	3	4	5	Sun 4h19m11p
28	TAMMUZ 5787	6	7	8	9	10	11	12	
29		13	14	15	16	17	18	19	
30		20	21	22	23	24	25	26	
31		27	28	29	1	2	3	4	Mon 17h3m12p
32	AV 5787	5	6	7	8	9[i]	10	11	
33		12	13	14	15	16	17	18	
34		19	20	21	22	23	24	25	
35		26	27	28	29	30	1	2	
36	ELUL 5787	3	4	5	6	7	8	9	Wed 5h47m13p
37		10	11	12	13	14	15	16	
38		17	18	19	20	21	22	23	
39		24	25	26	27	28	29	1[a]	Thu 18h31m14p
40	TISHRI 5788	2[a]	3	4	5	6	7	8	
41		9	10[b]	11	12	13	14	15[c]	
42		16	17	18	19	20	21	22	
43		23	24	25	26	27	28	29	
44		30	1	2	3	4	5	6	Sat 7h15m15p
45	ḤESHVAN 5788	7	8	9	10	11	12	13	
46		14	15	16	17	18	19	20	
47		21	22	23	24	25	26	27	
48		28	29	30	1	2	3	4	Sun 19h59m16p
49	KISLEV 5788	5	6[d]	7	8	9	10	11	
50		12	13	14	15	16	17	18	
51		19	20	21	22	23	24	25[e]	Tue 8h43m17p
52		26[e]	27[e]	28[e]	29[e]	30[e]	1[e]	2[e]	

CHINESE Bǐng-Wǔ/Dīng-Wèi

ISO Week	Month	Sun	Mon	Tue	Wed	Thu	Fri	Sat	Solar Term
53	MONTH 11 Bǐng-Wǔ	19	20	21	22	23	24	25	
1	MONTH 12 Bǐng-Wǔ	26	27	28	29	30	1	2	Xiǎo hán
2		3	4	5	6	7	8	9	
3		10	11	12	*13*	14	15	16	Dà hán
4		17	18	19	20	21	22	23	
5		24	25	26	27	*28*	29	1[a]	Lì chūn
6	MONTH 1 Dīng-Wèi	2	3	4	5	6	7	8	
7		9*	10	11	12	13	*14*	15[b]	Yǔ shuǐ
8		16	17	18	19	20	21	22	
9		23	24	25	26	27	28	*29*	Jīng zhé
10		30	1	2	3	4	5	6	
11	MONTH 2 Dīng-Wèi	7	8	9	10	11	12	13	
12		*14*	15	16	17	18	19	20	Chūn fēn
13		21	22	23	24	25	26	27	
14		28	29[c]	30	1	2	3	4	Qīng míng
15	MONTH 3 Dīng-Wèi	5	6	7	8	9*	10	11	
16		12	13	*14*	15	16	17	18	Gǔ yǔ
17		19	20	21	22	23	24	25	
18		26	27	28	29	*1*	2	3	Lì xià
19	MONTH 4 Dīng-Wèi	4	5	6	7	8	9	10	
20		11	12	13	14	15	*16*	17	Xiǎo mǎn
21		18	19	20	21	22	23	24	
22		25	26	27	28	29	30	1	
23	MONTH 5 Dīng-Wèi	2	3	4	5[d]	6	7	8	Máng zhòng
24		9	10*	11	12	13	14	15	
25		16	*17*	18	19	20	21	22	Xià zhì
26		23	24	25	26	27	28	29	
27	MONTH 6 Dīng-Wèi	1	2	3	*4*	5	6	7	Xiǎo shǔ
28		8	9	10	11	12	13	14	
29		15	16	17	18	19	*20*	21	Dà shǔ
30		22	23	24	25	26	27	28	
31		29	1	2	3	4	5	6	
32	MONTH 7 Dīng-Wèi	7[e]	8	9	10	11	12*	13	Lì qiū
33		14	15[f]	16	17	18	19	20	
34		21	*22*	23	24	25	26	27	Chǔ shǔ
35		28	29	30	1	2	3	4	
36	MONTH 8 Dīng-Wèi	5	6	7	*8*	9	10	11	Bái lù
37		12	13	14	15[g]	16	17	18	
38		19	20	21	22	*23*	24	25	Qiū fēn
39		26	27	28	29	1	2	3	
40	MONTH 9 Dīng-Wèi	4	5	6	7	8	9[h]	10	Hán lù
41		11	12	13*	14	15	16	17	
42		18	19	20	21	22	23	*24*	Shuāng jiàng
43		25	26	27	28	29	1	2	
44	MONTH 10 Dīng-Wèi	3	4	5	6	7	8	9	
45		*10*	11	12	13	14	15	16	Lì dōng
46		17	18	19	20	21	22	23	
47		24	*25*	26	27	28	29	30	Xiǎo xuě
48		1	2	3	4	5	6	7	
49	MONTH 11 Dīng-Wèi	8	9	*10*	11	12	13	14*	Dà xuě
50		15	16	17	18	19	20	21	
51		22	23	24	25[i]	26	27	28	Dōng zhì
52		29	30	1	2	3	4	5	

COPTIC 1743‡/1744 — ETHIOPIC 2019‡/2020

ISO Week	Coptic Month	Sun	Mon	Tue	Wed	Thu	Fri	Sat	Ethiopic Month
53	KOIAK 1743	18	19	20	21	22	23	24	TĀḪŚĀŚ 2019
1		25	26	27	28	29[c]	30	1	
2		2	3	4	5	6[d]	7	8	
3	TŌBE 1743	9	10	11[e]	12	13	14	15	ṬER 2019
4		16	17	18	19	20	21	22	
5		23	24	25	26	27	28	29	
6		30	1	2	3	4	5	6	
7	MESHIR 1743	7	8	9	10	11	12	13	YAKĀTIT 2019
8		14	15	16	17	18	19	20	
9		21	22	23	24	25	26	27	
10		28	29	30	1	2	3	4	
11	PAREMOTEP 1743	5	6	7	8	9	10	11	MAGĀBIT 2019
12		12	13	14	15	16	17	18	
13		19	20	21	22	23	24	25	
14		26	27	28	29	30	1	2	
15	PARMOUTE 1743	3	4	5	6	7	8	9	MIYĀZYĀ 2019
16		10	11	12	13	14	15	16	
17		17	18	19	20	21	22	23	
18		24[f]	25	26	27	28	29[g]	30	
19		1	2	3	4	5	6	7	
20	PASHONS 1743	8	9	10	11	12	13	14	GENBOT 2019
21		15	16	17	18	19	20	21	
22		22	23	24	25	26	27	28	
23		29	30	1	2	3	4	5	
24	PAŌNE 1743	6	7	8	9	10	11	12	SANĒ 2019
25		13	14	15	16	17	18	19	
26		20	21	22	23	24	25	26	
27		27	28	29	30	1	2	3	
28	EPĒP 1743	4	5	6	7	8	9	10	ḤAMLĒ 2019
29		11	12	13	14	15	16	17	
30		18	19	20	21	22	23	24	
31		25	26	27	28	29	30	1	
32	MESORĒ 1743	2	3	4	5	6	7	8	NAḤASĒ 2019
33		9	10	11	12	13[h]	14	15	
34		16	17	18	19	20	21	22	
35		23	24	25	26	27	28	29	
36	EPAG. 1743	30	1	2	3	4	5	6	PĀG. 2019
37		1[a]	2	3	4	5	6	7	
38	THOOUT 1744	8	9	10	11	12	13	14	MASKARAM 2020
39		15	16	17[b]	18	19	20	21	
40		22	23	24	25	26	27	28	
41		29	30	1	2	3	4	5	
42	PAOPE 1744	6	7	8	9	10	11	12	ṬEQEMT 2020
43		13	14	15	16	17	18	19	
44		20	21	22	23	24	25	26	
45		27	28	29	30	1	2	3	
46	ATHŌR 1744	4	5	6	7	8	9	10	ḪEDĀR 2020
47		11	12	13	14	15	16	17	
48		18	19	20	21	22	23	24	
49		25	26	27	28	29	30	1	
50	KOIAK 1744	2	3	4	5	6	7	8	TĀḪŚĀŚ 2020
51		9	10	11	12	13	14	15	
52		16	17	18	19	20	21	22	

Gregorian notes:
[a]New Year
[b]Spring (20:23)
[c]Summer (14:09)
[d]Autumn (6:00)
[e]Winter (2:41)
● New moon
◐ First quarter moon
○ Full moon
◑ Last quarter moon

Hebrew notes:
‡Leap year
[a]New Year
[b]Yom Kippur
[c]Sukkot
[d]Winter starts
[e]Ḥanukkah
[f]Purim
[g]Passover
[h]Shavuot
[i]Fast of Av

Chinese notes:
[a]New Year (4725, Sheep)
[b]Lantern Festival
[c]Qīngmíng
[d]Dragon Festival
[e]Qīqiǎo
[f]Hungry Ghosts
[g]Mid-Autumn Festival
[h]Double-Ninth Festival
[i]Dōngzhì
*Start of 60-name cycle

Coptic/Ethiopic notes:
‡Leap year
[a]New Year
[b]Building of the Cross
[c]Christmas
[d]Jesus's Circumcision
[e]Epiphany
[f]Easter
[g]Mary's Announcement
[h]Jesus's Transfiguration

2027

PERSIAN (ASTRONOMICAL) 1405/1406

Month	Sun	Mon	Tue	Wed	Thu	Fri	Sat
DEY 1405	6	7	8	9	10	11	12
	13	14	15	16	17	18	19
	20	21	22	23	24	25	26
	27	28	29	30	1	2	3
BAHMAN 1405	4	5	6	7	8	9	10
	11	12	13	14	15	16	17
	18	19	20	21	22	23	24
	25	26	27	28	29	30	1
ESFAND 1405	2	3	4	5	6	7	8
	9	10	11	12	13	14	15
	16	17	18	19	20	21	22
	23	24	25	26	27	28	29
FARVARDĪN 1406	1[a]	2	3	4	5	6	7
	8	9	10	11	12	13[b]	14
	15	16	17	18	19	20	21
	22	23	24	25	26	27	28
	29	30	31	1	2	3	4
ORDĪBEHEŠT 1406	5	6	7	8	9	10	11
	12	13	14	15	16	17	18
	19	20	21	22	23	24	25
	26	27	28	29	30	31	1
XORDĀD 1406	2	3	4	5	6	7	8
	9	10	11	12	13	14	15
	16	17	18	19	20	21	22
	23	24	25	26	27	28	29
	30	31	1	2	3	4	5
TĪR 1406	6	7	8	9	10	11	12
	13	14	15	16	17	18	19
	20	21	22	23	24	25	26
	27	28	29	30	31	1	2
MORDĀD 1406	3	4	5	6	7	8	9
	10	11	12	13	14	15	16
	17	18	19	20	21	22	23
	24	25	26	27	28	29	30
	31	1	2	3	4	5	6
SHAHRĪVAR 1406	7	8	9	10	11	12	13
	14	15	16	17	18	19	20
	21	22	23	24	25	26	27
	28	29	30	31	1	2	3
MEHR 1406	4	5	6	7	8	9	10
	11	12	13	14	15	16	17
	18	19	20	21	22	23	24
	25	26	27	28	29	30	1
ĀBĀN 1406	2	3	4	5	6	7	8
	9	10	11	12	13	14	15
	16	17	18	19	20	21	22
	23	24	25	26	27	28	29
	30	1	2	3	4	5	6
ĀZAR 1406	7	8	9	10	11	12	13
	14	15	16	17	18	19	20
	21	22	23	24	25	26	27
	28	29	30	1	2	3	4
DEY 1406	5	6	7	8	9	10	11

[a]New Year
[b]Sizdeh Bedar

HINDU LUNAR 2083‡/2084

Month	Sun	Mon	Tue	Wed	Thu	Fri	Sat
MĀRGAŚĪRA 2083	19	20	21	22	23	24	25
	26	27	28	29	30	1	2
PAUSHA 2083	3	4	*4*	5	6	7	**8**
	10	11	12	13	14	15	16
	17	18	19	20	21	22	23
	24	25	26	27	28	29	30
MĀGHA 2083	1	2	3	4	5	6	7
	8	9	10	11	12	13	**14**
	16	17	18	19	20	21	22
	23	24	25	26	*26*	27	28[h]
PHĀLGUNA 2083	29	30	1	2	3	4	5
	6	7	**8**	10	11	12	13
	14	15[i]	16	17	18	19	20
	21	22	23	24	25	26	27
CHAITRA 2084	28	29	30	1[a]	2	3	4
	5	6	7	8	9[b]	10	11
	12	14	15	16	17	18	19
	20	*20*	21	22	23	24	25
VAIŚĀKHA 2084	26	27	28	29	30	1	2
	3	4	**5**	7	8	9	10
	11	12	13	14	15	16	17
	18	19	20	21	22	23	24
JYAISHTHA 2084	25	*25*	**26**	28	29	30	1
	2	3	4	5	6	7	8
	9	11	12	13	14	15	16
	16	17	18	19	20	21	22
	23	24	25	26	27	28	29
ĀSHĀDHA 2084	30	**1**	3	4	5	6	7
	8	9	10	11	12	13	14
	15	16	17	18	19	20	21
	22	23	24	25	26	27	28
ŚRĀVANA 2084	29	30	1	2	3	**4**	6
	7	8	9	10	11	12	13
	13	14	15	16	17	18	19
	20	21	22	23[c]	24	25	26
BHĀDRAPADA 2084	**27**	29	30	1	2	3	4[d]
	5	6	7	8	9	10	11
	12	13	14	15	16	17	18
	19	20	21	22	23	24	25
ĀŚVINA 2084	26	27	28	29	**30**	2	3
	4	5	6	7	8	*8*[e]	9[e]
	10[e]	11	12	13	14	15	16
	17	18	19	20	21	22	23
KĀRTTIKA 2084	**24**	26	27	28	29	30	1[f]
	2	3	4	5	6	7	8
	9	10	11	*11*	12	13	14
	15	16	**17**	19	20	21	22
	23	24	25	26	27	28	29
MĀRGAŚĪRA 2084	30	1	2	3	4	5	6
	7	8	9	10	11[g]	12	13
	14	15	16	17	18	19	20
	21	**22**	24	25	26	27	28
	29	30	1	2	3	4	*4*

‡Leap year
[a]New Year (Plavaṅga)
[b]Birthday of Rāma
[c]Birthday of Krishna
[d]Ganēśa Chaturthī
[e]Dashara
[f]Diwali
[g]Birthday of Vishnu
[h]Night of Śiva
[i]Holi

HINDU SOLAR 1948/1949

Month	Sun	Mon	Tue	Wed	Thu	Fri	Sat
PAUSHA 1948	12	13	14	15	16	17	18
	19	20	21	22	23	24	25
	26	27	28	29	1[b]	2	3
MĀGHA 1948	4	5	6	7	8	9	10
	11	12	13	14	15	16	17
	18	19	20	21	22	23	24
	25	26	27	28	29	30	1
PHĀLGUNA 1948	2	3	4	5	6	7	8
	9	10	11	12	13	14	15
	16	17	18	19	20	21	22
	23	24	25	26	27	28	29
	30	1	2	3	4	5	6
CHAITRA 1948	7	8	9	10	11	12	13
	14	15	16	17	18	19	20
	21	22	23	24	25	26	27
	28	29	30	1[a]	2	3	4
VAIŚĀKHA 1949	5	6	7	8	9	10	11
	12	13	14	15	16	17	18
	19	20	21	22	23	24	25
	26	27	28	29	30	31	1
JYAISHTHA 1949	2	3	4	5	6	7	8
	9	10	11	12	13	14	15
	16	17	18	19	20	21	22
	23	24	25	26	27	28	29
	30	31	1	2	3	4	5
ĀSHĀDHA 1949	6	7	8	9	10	11	12
	13	14	15	16	17	18	19
	20	21	22	23	24	25	26
	27	28	29	30	31	32	1
ŚRĀVANA 1949	2	3	4	5	6	7	8
	9	10	11	12	13	14	15
	16	17	18	19	20	21	22
	23	24	25	26	27	28	29
	30	31	1	2	3	4	5
BHĀDRAPADA 1949	6	7	8	9	10	11	12
	13	14	15	16	17	18	19
	20	21	22	23	24	25	26
	27	28	29	30	31	1	2
ĀŚVINA 1949	3	4	5	6	7	8	9
	10	11	12	13	14	15	16
	17	18	19	20	21	22	23
	24	25	26	27	28	29	30
	31	1	2	3	4	5	6
KĀRTTIKA 1949	7	8	9	10	11	12	13
	14	15	16	17	18	19	20
	21	22	23	24	25	26	27
	28	29	30	1	2	3	4
MĀRGAŚĪRA 1949	5	6	7	8	9	10	11
	12	13	14	15	16	17	18
	19	20	21	22	23	24	25
	26	27	28	29	1	2	3
PAUSHA 1949	4	5	6	7	8	9	10
	11	12	13	14	15	16	17

[a]New Year (Rāudra)
[b]Pongal

ISLAMIC (ASTRONOMICAL) 1448‡/1449‡

Month	Sun	Mon	Tue	Wed	Thu	Fri	Sat
RAJAB 1448	17	18	19	20	21	22	23
	24	25	26	27[d]	28	29	1
SHA'BĀN 1448	2	3	4	5	6	7	8
	9	10	11	12	13	14	15
	16	17	18	19	20	21	22
	23	24	25	26	27	28	29
RAMAḌĀN 1448	30	1[e]	2	3	4	5	6
	7	8	9	10	11	12	13
	14	15	16	17	18	19	20
	21	22	23	24	25	26	27
SHAWWĀL 1448	28	29	30	1[f]	2	3	4
	5	6	7	8	9	10	11
	12	13	14	15	16	17	18
	19	20	21	22	23	24	25
DHU AL-QA'DA 1448	26	27	28	29	1	2	3
	4	5	6	7	8	9	10
	11	12	13	14	15	16	17
	18	19	20	21	22	23	24
DHU AL-HIJJA 1448	25	26	27	28	29	30	1
	2	3	4	5	6	7	8
	9	10[g]	11	12	13	14	15
	16	17	18	19	20	21	22
	23	24	25	26	27	28	29
MUHARRAM 1449	1[a]	2	3	4	5	6	7
	8	9	10[b]	11	12	13	14
	15	16	17	18	19	20	21
	22	23	24	25	26	27	28
ṢAFAR 1449	29	1	2	3	4	5	6
	7	8	9	10	11	12	13
	14	15	16	17	18	19	20
	21	22	23	24	25	26	27
RABĪ' I 1449	28	29	30	1	2	3	4
	5	6	7	8	9	10	11
	12[c]	13	14	15	16	17	18
	19	20	21	22	23	24	25
RABĪ' II 1449	26	27	28	29	30	1	2
	3	4	5	6	7	8	9
	10	11	12	13	14	15	16
	17	18	19	20	21	22	23
JUMĀDĀ I 1449	24	25	26	27	28	29	1
	2	3	4	5	6	7	8
	9	10	11	12	13	14	15
	16	17	18	19	20	21	22
	23	24	25	26	27	28	29
JUMĀDĀ II 1449	30	1	2	3	4	5	6
	7	8	9	10	11	12	13
	14	15	16	17	18	19	20
	21	22	23	24	25	26	27
RAJAB 1449	28	29	1	2	3	4	5
	6	7	8	9	10	11	12
	13	14	15	16	17	18	19
	20	21	22	23	24	25	26
	27[d]	28	29	1	2	3	4

‡Leap year
[a]New Year
[b]'Āshūrā'
[c]Prophet's Birthday
[d]Ascent of the Prophet
[e]Start of Ramaḍān
[f]'Id al-Fiṭr
[g]'Id al-'Aḍḥā

GREGORIAN 2027

Julian (Sun)	Sun	Mon	Tue	Wed	Thu	Fri	Sat	Month
Dec 14	27	28	29	30	31	1	2	
	3	4	5	6	7[a]	8	9	JANUARY 2027
Dec 28	10	11	12	13	14[b]	15	16	
	17	18	19	20	21	22	23	
Jan 11	24	25	26	27	28	29	30	
	31	1	2	3	4	5	6	
Jan 25	7	8	9	10[c]	11	12	13	FEBRUARY 2027
	14	15	16	17	18	19	20	
Feb 8	21	22	23	24	25	26	27	
	28	1	2	3	4	5	6	
Feb 22	7	8	9	10	11	12	13	MARCH 2027
	14	15	16	17	18	19	20	
Mar 8	21[d]	22	23	24	25	26	27	
	28[e]	29	30	31	1	2	3	
Mar 22	4	5	6	7	8	9	10	APRIL 2027
	11	12	13	14	15	16	17	
Apr 5	18	19	20	21	22	23	24	
	25	26	27	28	29	30	1	
Apr 19	2[f]	3	4	5	6	7	8	
	9	10	11	12	13	14	15	MAY 2027
May 3	16	17	18	19	20	21	22	
	23	24	25	26	27	28	29	
May 17	30	31	1	2	3	4	5	
	6	7	8	9	10	11	12	
May 31	13	14	15	16	17	18	19	JUNE 2027
	20	21	22	23	24	25	26	
Jun 14	27	28	29	30	1	2	3	
	4	5	6	7	8	9	10	
Jun 28	11	12	13	14	15	16	17	JULY 2027
	18	19	20	21	22	23	24	
Jul 12	25	26	27	28	29	30	31	
	1	2	3	4	5	6	7	
Jul 26	8	9	10	11	12	13	14	AUGUST 2027
	15	16	17	18	19	20	21	
Aug 9	22	23	24	25	26	27	28	
	29	30	31	1	2	3	4	
Aug 23	5	6	7	8	9	10	11	SEPTEMBER 2027
	12	13	14	15	16	17	18	
Sep 6	19	20	21	22	23	24	25	
	26	27	28	29	30	1	2	
Sep 20	3	4	5	6	7	8	9	OCTOBER 2027
	10	11	12	13	14	15	16	
Oct 4	17	18	19	20	21	22	23	
	24	25	26	27	28	29	30	
Oct 18	31	1	2	3	4	5	6	
	7	8	9	10	11	12	13	NOVEMBER 2027
Nov 1	14	15	16	17	18	19	20	
	21	22	23	24	25	26	27	
Nov 15	28[g]	29	30	1	2	3	4	
	5	6	7	8	9	10	11	DECEMBER 2027
Nov 29	12	13	14	15	16	17	18	
	19	20	21	22	23	24	25[h]	
Dec 13	26	27	28	29	30	31	1	

[a]Orthodox Christmas
[b]Julian New Year
[c]Ash Wednesday
[d]Feast of Orthodoxy
[e]Easter
[f]Orthodox Easter
[g]Advent
[h]Christmas

2028

Gregorian 2028‡ month	Sun	Mon	Tue	Wed	Thu	Fri	Sat	Lunar Phases	ISO WEEK (Mon)	JULIAN DAY (Sun noon)
	26	●	28	29	30	31	1[a]	20:11	52	2461766
JANUARY 2028	2	3	4	◐	6	7	8	1:39	1	2461773
	9	10	11	○	13	14	15	4:02	2	2461780
	16	17	◑	19	20	21	22	19:25	3	2461787
	23	24	25	●	27	28	29	15:11	4	2461794
	30	31	1	2	◐	4	5	19:09	5	2461801
FEBRUARY 2028	6	7	8	9	○	11	12	15:02	6	2461808
	13	14	15	16	◑	18	19	8:07	7	2461815
	20	21	22	23	24	●	26	10:36	8	2461822
	27	28	29	1	2	3	◐	9:01	9	2461829
MARCH 2028	5	6	7	8	9	10	○	1:05	10	2461836
	12	13	14	15	16	◑	18	23:22	11	2461843
	19	20[b]	21	22	23	24	25		12	2461850
	●	27	28	29	30	31	1	4:30	13	2461857
APRIL 2028	◐	3	4	5	6	7	8	19:14	14	2461864
	○	10	11	12	13	14	15	10:25	15	2461871
	◑	17	18	19	20	21	22	16:36	16	2461878
	23	●	25	26	27	28	29	19:46	17	2461885
	30	1	◐	3	4	5	6	2:25	18	2461892
MAY 2028	7	○	9	10	11	12	13	19:48	19	2461899
	14	15	◑	17	18	19	20	10:42	20	2461906
	21	22	23	●	25	26	27	8:15	21	2461913
	28	29	30	◐	1	2	3	7:35	22	2461920
JUNE 2028	4	5	6	○	8	9	10	6:08	23	2461927
	11	12	13	14	◑	16	17	4:26	24	2461934
	18	19	20[c]	21	●	23	24	18:26	25	2461941
	25	26	27	28	◐	30	1	12:09	26	2461948
JULY 2028	2	3	4	5	○	7	8	18:10	27	2461955
	9	10	11	12	13	◑	15	20:56	28	2461962
	16	17	18	19	20	21	●	3:01	29	2461969
	23	24	25	26	27	◐	29	17:39	30	2461976
	30	31	1	2	3	4	○	8:09	31	2461983
AUGUST 2028	6	7	8	9	10	11	12		32	2461990
	◑	14	15	16	17	18	19	11:44	33	2461997
	●	21	22	23	24	25	26	10:43	34	2462004
	◐	28	29	30	31	1	2	1:35	35	2462011
SEPTEMBER 2028	○	4	5	6	7	8	9	23:46	36	2462018
	10	11	◑	13	14	15	16	0:45	37	2462025
	17	●	19	20	21	22[d]	23	18:23	38	2462032
	24	◐	26	27	28	29	30	13:09	39	2462039
OCTOBER 2028	1	2	○	4	5	6	7	16:24	40	2462046
	8	9	10	◑	12	13	14	11:56	41	2462053
	15	16	17	●	19	20	21	2:56	42	2462060
	22	23	24	◐	26	27	28	4:52	43	2462067
	29	30	31	1	○	3	4	9:16	44	2462074
NOVEMBER 2028	5	6	7	8	◑	10	11	21:25	45	2462081
	12	13	14	15	●	17	18	13:17	46	2462088
	19	20	21	22	23	◐	25	0:13	47	2462095
	26	27	28	29	30	1	○	1:39	48	2462102
DECEMBER 2028	3	4	5	6	7	8	◑	5:38	49	2462109
	10	11	12	13	14	15	●	2:05	50	2462116
	17	18	19	20	21[e]	22	◐	21:44	51	2462123
	24	25	26	27	28	29	30		52	2462130
	○	1	2	3	4	5	6	16:47	1	2462137

ISO WEEK	Hebrew 5788/5789 month	Sun	Mon	Tue	Wed	Thu	Fri	Sat	Molad
52		26[e]	27[e]	28[e]	29[e]	30[e]	1[e]	2[e]	Tue 8h43m11p
1	TEVETH 5788	3	4	5	6	7	8	9	
2		10	11	12	13	14	15	16	
3		17	18	19	20	21	22	23	
4		24	25	26	27	28	29	1	Wed 21h28m0p
5	SHEVAT 5788	2	3	4	5	6	7	8	
6		9	10	11	12	13	14	15	
7		16	17	18	19	20	21	22	
8		23	24	25	26	27	28	29	
9		30	1	2	3	4	5	6	Fri 10h12m1p
10	ADAR 5788	7	8	9	10	11	12	13	
11		14[f]	15	16	17	18	19	20	
12		21	22	23	24	25	26	27	
13		28	29	1	2	3	4	5	Sat 22h56m2p
14	NISAN 5788	6	7	8	9	10	11	12	
15		13	14	15[g]	16	17	18	19	
16		20	21	22	23	24	25	26	
17		27	28	29	30	1	2	3	Mon 11h40m3p
18	IYYAR 5788	4	5	6	7	8	9	10	
19		11	12	13	14	15	16	17	
20		18	19	20	21	22	23	24	
21		25	26	27	28	29	1	2	Wed 0h24m4p
22	SIVAN 5788	3	4	5	6[h]	7	8	9	
23		10	11	12	13	14	15	16	
24		17	18	19	20	21	22	23	
25		24	25	26	27	28	29	30	
26		1	2	3	4	5	6	7	Thu 13h8m5p
27	TAMMUZ 5788	8	9	10	11	12	13	14	
28		15	16	17	18	19	20	21	
29		22	23	24	25	26	27	28	
30		29	1	2	3	4	5	6	Sat 1h52m6p
31	AV 5788	7	8	9[i]	10	11	12	13	
32		14	15	16	17	18	19	20	
33		21	22	23	24	25	26	27	
34		28	29	30	1	2	3	4	Sun 14h36m7p
35	ELUL 5788	5	6	7	8	9	10	11	
36		12	13	14	15	16	17	18	
37		19	20	21	22	23	24	25	
38		26	27	28	29	1[a]	2[a]	3	Tue 3h20m8p
39	TISHRI 5789	4	5	6	7	8	9	10[b]	
40		11	12	13	14	15[c]	16	17	
41		18	19	20	21	22	23	24	
42		25	26	27	28	29	30	1	Wed 16h4m9p
43	HESHVAN 5789	2	3	4	5	6	7	8	
44		9	10	11	12	13	14	15	
45		16	17	18	19	20	21	22	
46		23	24	25	26	27	28	29	
47		1	2	3	4	5	6	7	Fri 4h48m10p
48	KISLEV 5789	8	9	10	11	12	13	14	
49		15	16	17[d]	18	19	20	21	
50		22	23	24	25[e]	26[e]	27[e]	28[e]	
51		29[e]	30[e]	1[e]	2[e]	3	4	5	Sat 17h32m11p
52	TEVETH 5789	6	7	8	9	10	11	12	
1		13	14	15	16	17	18	19	

ISO WEEK	Chinese Dīng-Wèi/Wù-Shēn‡ month	Sun	Mon	Tue	Wed	Thu	Fri	Sat	Solar Term
52		29	30	1	2	3	4	5	
1	MONTH 12 Dīng-Wèi	6	7	8	9	10	11	12	Xiǎo hán
2		13	14	15	16	17	18	19	
3		20	21	22	23	24	25	26	Dà hán
4		27	28	29	1[a]	2	3	4	
5	MONTH 1 Wù-Shēn	5	6	7	8	9	10	11	Lì chūn
6		12	13	14	15[b]*	16	17	18	
7		19	20	21	22	23	24	25	Yǔ shuǐ
8		26	27	28	29	30	1	2	
9	MONTH 2 Wù-Shēn	3	4	5	6	7	8	9	
10		10	11	12	13	14	15	16	Jīng zhé
11		17	18	19	20	21	22	23	
12		24	25	26	27	28	29	30	Chūn fēn
13		1	2	3	4	5	6	7	
14	MONTH 3 Wù-Shēn	8	9	10[c]	11	12	13	14	Qīng míng
15		15*	16	17	18	19	20	21	
16		22	23	24	25	26	27	28	Gǔ yǔ
17		29	30	1	2	3	4	5	
18	MONTH 4 Wù-Shēn	6	7	8	9	10	11	12	Lì xià
19		13	14	15	16	17	18	19	
20		20	21	22	23	24	25	26	Xiǎo mǎn
21		27	28	29	1	2	3	4	
22	MONTH 5 Wù-Shēn	5[d]	6	7	8	9	10	11	
23		12	13	14	15	16*	17	18	Máng zhòng
24		19	20	21	22	23	24	25	
25		26	27	28	29	30	1	2	Xià zhì
26	LEAP MONTH 5 Wù-Shēn	3	4	5	6	7	8	9	
27		10	11	12	13	14	15	16	Xiǎo shǔ
28		17	18	19	20	21	22	23	
29		24	25	26	27	28	29	1	Dà shǔ
30	MONTH 6 Wù-Shēn	2	3	4	5	6	7	8	
31		9	10	11	12	13	14	15	
32		16	17*	18	19	20	21	22	Lì qiū
33		23	24	25	26	27	28	29	
34		1	2	3	4	5	6	7[e]	Chǔ shǔ
35	MONTH 7 Wù-Shēn	8	9	10	11	12	13	14	
36		15[f]	16	17	18	19	20	21	Bái lù
37		22	23	24	25	26	27	28	
38		29	30	1	2	3	4	5	Qiū fēn
39	MONTH 8 Wù-Shēn	6	7	8	9	10	11	12	
40		13	14	15[g]	16	17	18*	19	
41		20	21	22	23	24	25	26	Hán lù
42		27	28	29	1	2	3	4	
43	MONTH 9 Wù-Shēn	5	6	7	8	9[h]	10	11	Shuāng jiàng
44		12	13	14	15	16	17	18	
45		19	20	21	22	23	24	25	Lì dōng
46		26	27	28	29	1	2	3	
47	MONTH 10 Wù-Shēn	4	5	6	7	8	9	10	Xiǎo xuě
48		11	12	13	14	15	16	17	
49		18	19	20*	21	22	23	24	Dà xuě
50		25	26	27	28	29	30	1	
51	MONTH 11* Wù-Shēn	2	3	4	5	6[i]	7	8	Dōng zhì
52		9	10	11	12	13	14	15	
1		16	17	18	19	20	21	22	Xiǎo hán

ISO WEEK	Coptic 1744/1745 month	Sun	Mon	Tue	Wed	Thu	Fri	Sat	Ethiopic 2020/2021 month
52	KOIAK 1744	16	17	18	19	20	21	22	TĀKHŚĀŚ 2020
1		23	24	25	26	27	28	29[c]	
2		30	1	2	3	4	5	6[d]	
3	TŌBE 1744	7	8	9	10	11[e]	12	13	ṬER 2020
4		14	15	16	17	18	19	20	
5		21	22	23	24	25	26	27	
6		28	29	30	1	2	3	4	
7	MESHIR 1744	5	6	7	8	9	10	11	YAKĀTIT 2020
8		12	13	14	15	16	17	18	
9		19	20	21	22	23	24	25	
10		26	27	28	29	30	1	2	
11	PAREMOTEP 1744	3	4	5	6	7	8	9	MAGĀBIT 2020
12		10	11	12	13	14	15	16	
13		17	18	19	20	21	22	23	
14		24	25	26	27	28	29	30	
15	PARMOUTE 1744	1	2	3	4	5	6	7	MIYĀZYĀ 2020
16		8[f]	9	10	11	12	13	14	
17		15	16	17	18	19	20	21	
18		22	23	24	25	26	27	28	
19		29[g]	30	1	2	3	4	5	
20	PASHONS 1744	6	7	8	9	10	11	12	GENBOT 2020
21		13	14	15	16	17	18	19	
22		20	21	22	23	24	25	26	
23		27	28	29	30	1	2	3	
24	PAŌNE 1744	4	5	6	7	8	9	10	SANĒ 2020
25		11	12	13	14	15	16	17	
26		18	19	20	21	22	23	24	
27		25	26	27	28	29	30	1	
28	EPĒP 1744	2	3	4	5	6	7	8	ḤAMLĒ 2020
29		9	10	11	12	13	14	15	
30		16	17	18	19	20	21	22	
31		23	24	25	26	27	28	29	
32		30	1	2	3	4	5	6	
33	MESORĒ 1744	7	8	9	10	11	12	13[h]	NAḤASĒ 2020
34		14	15	16	17	18	19	20	
35		21	22	23	24	25	26	27	
36		28	29	30	1	2	3	4	
37	EPAG. 1744	5	1[a]	2	3	4	5	6	PĀG. 2020
38	THOOUT 1745	7	8	9	10	11	12	13	MASKARAM 2021
39		14	15	16	17[b]	18	19	20	
40		21	22	23	24	25	26	27	
41		28	29	30	1	2	3	4	
42	PAOPE 1745	5	6	7	8	9	10	11	ṬEQEMT 2021
43		12	13	14	15	16	17	18	
44		19	20	21	22	23	24	25	
45		26	27	28	29	30	1	2	
46	ATHŌR 1745	3	4	5	6	7	8	9	ḪEDĀR 2021
47		10	11	12	13	14	15	16	
48		17	18	19	20	21	22	23	
49		24	25	26	27	28	29	30	
50	KOIAK 1745	1	2	3	4	5	6	7	TĀKHŚĀŚ 2021
51		8	9	10	11	12	13	14	
52		15	16	17	18	19	20	21	
1		22	23	24	25	26	27	28	

‡Leap year
[a]New Year
[b]Spring (2:16)
[c]Summer (20:00)
[d]Autumn (11:44)
[e]Winter (8:19)
● New moon
◐ First quarter moon
○ Full moon
◑ Last quarter moon

[a]New Year
[b]Yom Kippur
[c]Sukkot
[d]Winter starts
[e]Ḥanukkah
[f]Purim
[g]Passover
[h]Shavuot
[i]Fast of Av

‡Leap year
[a]New Year (4726, Monkey)
[b]Lantern Festival
[c]Qīngmíng
[d]Dragon Festival
[e]Qīqiǎo
[f]Hungry Ghosts
[g]Mid-Autumn Festival
[h]Double-Ninth Festival
[i]Dōngzhì
*Start of 60-name cycle

[a]New Year
[b]Building of the Cross
[c]Christmas
[d]Jesus's Circumcision
[e]Epiphany
[f]Easter
[g]Mary's Announcement
[h]Jesus's Transfiguration

PERSIAN (ASTRONOMICAL) 1406/1407

Month	Sun	Mon	Tue	Wed	Thu	Fri	Sat
DEY 1406	5	6	7	8	9	10	11
	12	13	14	15	16	17	18
	19	20	21	22	23	24	25
	26	27	28	29	30	1	2
BAHMAN 1406	3	4	5	6	7	8	9
	10	11	12	13	14	15	16
	17	18	19	20	21	22	23
	24	25	26	27	28	29	30
ESFAND 1406	1	2	3	4	5	6	7
	8	9	10	11	12	13	14
	15	16	17	18	19	20	21
	22	23	24	25	26	27	28
FARVARDĪN 1407	29	1[a]	2	3	4	5	6
	7	8	9	10	11	12	13[b]
	14	15	16	17	18	19	20
	21	22	23	24	25	26	27
ORDĪBEHEŠT 1407	28	29	30	31	1	2	3
	4	5	6	7	8	9	10
	11	12	13	14	15	16	17
	18	19	20	21	22	23	24
	25	26	27	28	29	30	31
XORDĀD 1407	1	2	3	4	5	6	7
	8	9	10	11	12	13	14
	15	16	17	18	19	20	21
	22	23	24	25	26	27	28
TĪR 1407	29	30	31	1	2	3	4
	5	6	7	8	9	10	11
	12	13	14	15	16	17	18
	19	20	21	22	23	24	25
MORDĀD 1407	26	27	28	29	30	31	1
	2	3	4	5	6	7	8
	9	10	11	12	13	14	15
	16	17	18	19	20	21	22
	23	24	25	26	27	28	29
SHAHRĪVAR 1407	30	31	1	2	3	4	5
	6	7	8	9	10	11	12
	13	14	15	16	17	18	19
	20	21	22	23	24	25	26
MEHR 1407	27	28	29	30	31	1	2
	3	4	5	6	7	8	9
	10	11	12	13	14	15	16
	17	18	19	20	21	22	23
	24	25	26	27	28	29	30
ABĀN 1407	1	2	3	4	5	6	7
	8	9	10	11	12	13	14
	15	16	17	18	19	20	21
	22	23	24	25	26	27	28
ĀZAR 1407	29	30	1	2	3	4	5
	6	7	8	9	10	11	12
	13	14	15	16	17	18	19
	20	21	22	23	24	25	26
DEY 1407	27	28	29	30	1	2	3
	4	5	6	7	8	9	10
	11	12	13	14	15	16	17

[a]New Year
[b]Sizdeh Bedar

HINDU LUNAR 2084/2085

Month	Sun	Mon	Tue	Wed	Thu	Fri	Sat
PAUSHA 2084	29	30	1	2	3	4	4
	5	6	7	8	9	10	11
	12	13	14	15	**16**	18	19
	20	21	22	23	24	25	26
MĀGHA 2084	27	28	29	30	1	2	3
	4	5	6	7	7	**8**	10
	11	12	13	14	15	16	17
	18	19	20	21	**22**	24	25
PHĀLGUNA 2084	26	26	27	28[h]	29	30	1
	2	3	4	5	6	7	8
	9	10	11	12	13	14	**15**[i]
	17	18	19	20	21	22	23
	24	25	26	27	28	29	29
CHAITRA 2085	30	1[a]	2	3	4	5	6
	7	**8**[b]	10	11	12	13	14
	15	16	17	18	19	20	21
	22	23	24	25	26	27	28
VAIŚĀKHA 2085	29	30	1	2	3	4	5
	6	7	8	9	10	11	**12**
	14	15	16	17	18	19	20
	21	22	23	24	24	25	26
JYAISHṬHA 2085	27	28	29	30	1	2	3
	4	**5**	7	8	9	10	11
	12	13	14	15	16	17	18
	19	20	21	22	23	24	25
ĀSHĀḌHA 2085	26	27	28	29	30	1	2
	3	4	5	6	7	**8**	10
	11	12	13	14	15	16	17
	18	19	20	20	21	22	23
	24	25	26	27	28	29	30
ŚRĀVAṆA 2085	**1**	3	4	5	6	7	8
	9	10	11	12	13	14	15
	16	17	18	19	20	21	22
	23[c]	24	25	26	27	28	29
BHĀDRAPADA 2085	30	1	2	3[d]	**4**	6	7
	8	9	10	11	12	13	14
	15	16	17	17	18	19	20
	21	22	23	24	25	26	**27**
ĀŚVINA 2085	29	30	1	2	3	4	5
	6	7	8[e]	9[e]	10[e]	11	12
	13	14	15	16	17	18	19
	20	21	22	23	24	25	26
LEAP KĀRTTIKA 2085	27	28	29	30	**1**	3	4
	5	6	7	8	9	10	11
	12	12	13	14	15	16	17
	18	19	20	21	22	23	**24**
KĀRTTIKA 2085	26	27	28	29	30	1[f]	2
	3	4	5	6	7	8	9
	10	11	12	13	14	15	15
	16	**17**	19	20	21	22	23
	24	25	26	27	28	29	**30**
MĀRGAŚĪRA 2085	2	3	4	4	5	6	7
	8	9	10	11[g]	12	13	14
	15	16	17	18	19	20	21

[a]New Year (Kīlaka)
[b]Birthday of Rāma
[c]Birthday of Krishna
[d]Ganēśa Chaturthī
[e]Dashara
[f]Diwali
[g]Birthday of Vishnu
[h]Night of Śiva
[i]Holi

HINDU SOLAR 1949/1950

Month	Sun	Mon	Tue	Wed	Thu	Fri	Sat
PAUSHA 1949	11	12	13	14	15	16	17
	18	19	20	21	22	23	24
	25	26	27	28	29	30	1[b]
MĀGHA 1949	2	3	4	5	6	7	8
	9	10	11	12	13	14	15
	16	17	18	19	20	21	22
	23	24	25	26	27	28	29
PHĀLGUNA 1949	1	2	3	4	5	6	7
	8	9	10	11	12	13	14
	15	16	17	18	19	20	21
	22	23	24	25	26	27	28
	29	30	1	2	3	4	5
CHAITRA 1949	6	7	8	9	10	11	12
	13	14	15	16	17	18	19
	20	21	22	23	24	25	26
	27	28	29	30	1[a]	2	3
VAIŚĀKHA 1950	4	5	6	7	8	9	10
	11	12	13	14	15	16	17
	18	19	20	21	22	23	24
	25	26	27	28	29	30	31
JYAISHṬHA 1950	1	2	3	4	5	6	7
	8	9	10	11	12	13	14
	15	16	17	18	19	20	21
	22	23	24	25	26	27	28
	29	30	31	32	1	2	3
ĀSHĀḌHA 1950	4	5	6	7	8	9	10
	11	12	13	14	15	16	17
	18	19	20	21	22	23	24
	25	26	27	28	29	30	31
ŚRĀVAṆA 1950	1	2	3	4	5	6	7
	8	9	10	11	12	13	14
	15	16	17	18	19	20	21
	22	23	24	25	26	27	28
	29	30	31	32	1	2	3
BHĀDRAPADA 1950	4	5	6	7	8	9	10
	11	12	13	14	15	16	17
	18	19	20	21	22	23	24
	25	26	27	28	29	30	31
ĀŚVINA 1950	1	2	3	4	5	6	7
	8	9	10	11	12	13	14
	15	16	17	18	19	20	21
	22	23	24	25	26	27	28
	29	30	1	2	3	4	5
KĀRTTIKA 1950	6	7	8	9	10	11	12
	13	14	15	16	17	18	19
	20	21	22	23	24	25	26
	27	28	29	30	1	2	3
MĀRGAŚĪRA 1950	4	5	6	7	8	9	10
	11	12	13	14	15	16	17
	18	19	20	21	22	23	24
	25	26	27	28	29	30	1
PAUSHA 1950	2	3	4	5	6	7	8
	9	10	11	12	13	14	15
	16	17	18	19	20	21	22

[a]New Year (Dundubhi)
[b]Pongal

ISLAMIC (ASTRONOMICAL) 1449‡/1450

Month	Sun	Mon	Tue	Wed	Thu	Fri	Sat
SHA'BĀN 1449	27	28	29	1	2	3	4
	5	6	7	8	9	10	11
	12	13	14	15	16	17	18
	19	20	21	22	23	24	25
RAMAḌĀN 1449	26	27	28	29	30	1[e]	2
	3	4	5	6	7	8	9
	10	11	12	13	14	15	16
	17	18	19	20	21	22	23
	24	25	26	27	28	29	30
SHAWWĀL 1449	1[f]	2	3	4	5	6	7
	8	9	10	11	12	13	14
	15	16	17	18	19	20	21
	22	23	24	25	26	27	28
DHU AL-QA'DA 1449	29	1	2	3	4	5	6
	7	8	9	10	11	12	13
	14	15	16	17	18	19	20
	21	22	23	24	25	26	27
DHU AL-ḤIJJA 1449	28	29	30	1	2	3	4
	5	6	7	8	9	10[g]	11
	12	13	14	15	16	17	18
	19	20	21	22	23	24	25
MUḤARRAM 1450	26	27	28	29	30[â]	1[a]	2
	3	4	5	6	7	8	9
	10[b]	11	12	13	14	15	16
	17	18	19	20	21	22	23
	24	25	26	27	28	29	1
ṢAFAR 1450	2	3	4	5	6	7	8
	9	10	11	12	13	14	15
	16	17	18	19	20	21	22
	23	24	25	26	27	28	29
RABĪ' I 1450	30	1	2	3	4	5	6
	7	8	9	10	11	12[c]	13
	14	15	16	17	18	19	20
	21	22	23	24	25	26	27
RABĪ' II 1450	28	29	1	2	3	4	5
	6	7	8	9	10	11	12
	13	14	15	16	17	18	19
	20	21	22	23	24	25	26
JUMĀDĀ I 1450	27	28	29	30	1	2	3
	4	5	6	7	8	9	10
	11	12	13	14	15	16	17
	18	19	20	21	22	23	24
	25	26	27	28	29	1	2
JUMĀDĀ II 1450	3	4	5	6	7	8	9
	10	11	12	13	14	15	16
	17	18	19	20	21	22	23
	24	25	26	27	28	29	1
RAJAB 1450	2	3	4	5	6	7	8
	9	10	11	12	13	14	15
	16	17	18	19	20	21	22
	23	24	25	26	27[d]	28	29
SHA'BĀN 1450	1	2	3	4	5	6	7
	8	9	10	11	12	13	14
	15	16	17	18	19	20	21

‡Leap year
[a]New Year
[â]New Year (Arithmetic)
[b]'Ashūrā'
[c]Prophet's Birthday
[d]Ascent of the Prophet
[e]Start of Ramaḍān
[f]'Īd al-Fiṭr
[g]'Īd al-'Aḍḥā

GREGORIAN 2028‡

Julian‡ (Sun)	Sun	Mon	Tue	Wed	Thu	Fri	Sat	Month
Dec 13	26	27	28	29	30	31	1	JANUARY 2028
	2	3	4	5	6	7[a]	8	
Dec 27	9	10	11	12	13	14[b]	15	
	16	17	18	19	20	21	22	
Jan 10	23	24	25	26	27	28	29	
	30	31	1	2	3	4	5	FEBRUARY 2028
Jan 24	6	7	8	9	10	11	12	
	13	14	15	16	17	18	19	
Feb 7	20	21	22	23	24	25	26	
	27	28	29	1[c]	2	3	4	MARCH 2028
Feb 21	5[d]	6	7	8	9	10	11	
	12	13	14	15	16	17	18	
Mar 6	19	20	21	22	23	24	25	
	26	27	28	29	30	31	1	APRIL 2028
Mar 20	2	3	4	5	6	7	8	
	9	10	11	12	13	14	15	
Apr 3	16[e]	17	18	19	20	21	22	
	23	24	25	26	27	28	29	
Apr 17	30	1	2	3	4	5	6	MAY 2028
	7	8	9	10	11	12	13	
May 1	14	15	16	17	18	19	20	
	21	22	23	24	25	26	27	
May 15	28	29	30	31	1	2	3	JUNE 2028
	4	5	6	7	8	9	10	
May 29	11	12	13	14	15	16	17	
	18	19	20	21	22	23	24	
Jun 12	25	26	27	28	29	30	1	JULY 2028
	2	3	4	5	6	7	8	
Jun 26	9	10	11	12	13	14	15	
	16	17	18	19	20	21	22	
Jul 10	23	24	25	26	27	28	29	
	30	31	1	2	3	4	5	AUGUST 2028
Jul 24	6	7	8	9	10	11	12	
	13	14	15	16	17	18	19	
Aug 7	20	21	22	23	24	25	26	
	27	28	29	30	31	1	2	SEPTEMBER 2028
Aug 21	3	4	5	6	7	8	9	
	10	11	12	13	14	15	16	
Sep 4	17	18	19	20	21	22	23	
	24	25	26	27	28	29	30	
Sep 18	1	2	3	4	5	6	7	OCTOBER 2028
	8	9	10	11	12	13	14	
Oct 2	15	16	17	18	19	20	21	
	22	23	24	25	26	27	28	
Oct 16	29	30	31	1	2	3	4	NOVEMBER 2028
	5	6	7	8	9	10	11	
Oct 30	12	13	14	15	16	17	18	
	19	20	21	22	23	24	25	
Nov 13	26	27	28	29	30	1	2	DECEMBER 2028
	3[g]	4	5	6	7	8	9	
Nov 27	10	11	12	13	14	15	16	
	17	18	19	20	21	22	23	
Dec 11	24	25[h]	26	27	28	29	30	
	31	1	2	3	4	5	6	

‡Leap year
[a]Orthodox Christmas
[b]Julian New Year
[c]Ash Wednesday
[d]Feast of Orthodoxy
[e]Easter (also Orthodox)
[g]Advent
[h]Christmas

2029

GREGORIAN 2029 / ISO WEEK / JULIAN DAY

	Sun	Mon	Tue	Wed	Thu	Fri	Sat	Lunar Phases	ISO WEEK (Mon)	JULIAN DAY (Sun noon)
JANUARY 2029	○	1[a]	2	3	4	5	6	16:47	1	2462137
	◑	8	9	10	11	12	13	13:25	2	2462144
	●	15	16	17	18	19	20	17:23	3	2462151
	21	◐	23	24	25	26	27	19:22	4	2462158
	28	29	○	31	1	2	3	6:02	5	2462165
FEBRUARY 2029	4	◑	6	7	8	9	10	21:51	6	2462172
	11	12	●	14	15	16	17	10:30	7	2462179
	18	19	20	◐	22	23	24	15:09	8	2462186
	25	26	27	○	1	2	3	17:09	9	2462193
MARCH 2029	4	5	6	◑	8	9	10	7:51	10	2462200
	11	12	13	14	●	16	17	4:18	11	2462207
	18	19	20[b]	21	22	◐	24	7:32	12	2462214
	25	26	27	28	29	○	31	2:25	13	2462221
APRIL 2029	1	2	3	4	◑	6	7	19:51	14	2462228
	8	9	10	11	12	●	14	21:39	15	2462235
	15	16	17	18	19	20	◐	19:49	16	2462242
	22	23	24	25	26	27	○	10:36	17	2462249
	29	30	1	2	3	4	◑	9:47	18	2462256
MAY 2029	6	7	8	9	10	11	12		19	2462263
	●	14	15	16	17	18	19	13:41	20	2462270
	20	◐	22	23	24	25	26	4:15	21	2462277
	○	28	29	30	31	1	2	18:36	22	2462284
JUNE 2029	3	◑	5	6	7	8	9	1:18	23	2462291
	10	11	●	13	14	15	16	3:49	24	2462298
	17	18	◐	20	21[c]	22	23	9:53	25	2462305
	24	25	○	27	28	29	30	3:21	26	2462312
JULY 2029	1	2	◑	4	5	6	7	17:56	27	2462319
	8	9	10	●	12	13	14	15:50	28	2462326
	15	16	17	◐	19	20	21	14:13	29	2462333
	22	23	24	○	26	27	28	13:35	30	2462340
	29	30	31	1	◑	3	4	11:14	31	2462347
AUGUST 2029	5	6	7	8	9	●	11	1:55	32	2462354
	12	13	14	15	◐	17	18	18:54	33	2462361
	19	20	21	22	23	○	25	1:50	34	2462368
	26	27	28	29	30	31	◑	4:32	35	2462375
SEPTEMBER 2029	2	3	4	5	6	7	●	10:43	36	2462382
	9	10	11	12	13	14	◐	1:28	37	2462389
	16	17	18	19	20	21	○[d]	16:28	38	2462396
	23	24	25	26	27	28	29		39	2462403
OCTOBER 2029	◑	1	2	3	4	5	6	20:56	40	2462410
	●	8	9	10	11	12	13	19:14	41	2462417
	◐	15	16	17	18	19	20	11:08	42	2462424
	21	○	23	24	25	26	27	9:26	43	2462431
	28	29	◑	31	1	2	3	11:31	44	2462438
NOVEMBER 2029	4	5	●	7	8	9	10	4:23	45	2462445
	11	12	◐	14	15	16	17	0:34	46	2462452
	18	19	20	○	22	23	24	4:02	47	2462459
	25	26	27	◑	29	30	1	23:47	48	2462466
DECEMBER 2029	2	3	4	●	6	7	8	14:51	49	2462473
	9	10	11	◐	13	14	15	17:48	50	2462480
	16	17	18	19	○	21[e]	22	22:45	51	2462487
	23	24	25	26	27	◑	29	9:48	52	2462494
	30	31	1	2	3	●	5	2:48	1	2462501

HEBREW 5789/5790‡

ISO WEEK	Month	Sun	Mon	Tue	Wed	Thu	Fri	Sat	Molad
1	TEVETH 5789	13	14	15	16	17	18	19	
2		20	21	22	23	24	25	26	Mon $6^h16^m12^p$
3	SHEVAT 5789	27	28	29	1	2	3	4	
4		5	6	7	8	9	10	11	
5		12	13	14	15	16	17	18	
6		19	20	21	22	23	24	25	
7		26	27	28	29	30	1	2	Tue $19^h0^m13^p$
8	ADAR 5789	3	4	5	6	7	8	9	
9		10	11	12	13	14[f]	15	16	
10		17	18	19	20	21	22	23	
11		24	25	26	27	28	29	1	Thu $7^h4^m14^p$
12	NISAN 5789	2	3	4	5	6	7	8	
13		9	10	11	12	13	14	15[g]	
14		16	17	18	19	20	21	22	
15		23	24	25	26	27	28	29	
16		30	1	2	3	4	5	6	Fri $20^h28^m15^p$
17	IYYAR 5789	7	8	9	10	11	12	13	
18		14	15	16	17	18	19	20	
19		21	22	23	24	25	26	27	
20		28	29	1	2	3	4	5	Sun $9^h12^m16^p$
21	SIVAN 5789	6[h]	7	8	9	10	11	12	
22		13	14	15	16	17	18	19	
23		20	21	22	23	24	25	26	
24		27	28	29	30	1	2	3	Mon $21^h56^m17^p$
25	TAMMUZ 5789	4	5	6	7	8	9	10	
26		11	12	13	14	15	16	17	
27		18	19	20	21	22	23	24	
28		25	26	27	28	29	1	2	Wed $10^h41^m0^p$
29	AV 5789	3	4	5	6	7	8	9	
30		10[i]	11	12	13	14	15	16	
31		17	18	19	20	21	22	23	
32		24	25	26	27	28	29	30	
33	ELUL 5789	1	2	3	4	5	6	7	Thu $23^h25^m1^p$
34		8	9	10	11	12	13	14	
35		15	16	17	18	19	20	21	
36		22	23	24	25	26	27	28	
37	TISHRI 5790	29	1[a]	2[a]	3	4	5	6	Sat $12^h9^m2^p$
38		7	8	9	10[b]	11	12	13	
39		14	15[c]	16	17	18	19	20	
40		21	22	23	24	25	26	27	
41	HESHVAN 5790	28	29	30	1	2	3	4	Mon $0^h53^m3^p$
42		5	6	7	8	9	10	11	
43		12	13	14	15	16	17	18	
44		19	20	21	22	23	24	25	
45	KISLEV 5790	26	27	28	29	1	2	3	
46		4	5	6	7	8	9	10	Tue $13^h37^m4^p$
47		11	12	13	14	15	16	17	
48		18	19	20	21	22	23	24	
49		25[e]	26[e]	27[e]	28[d][e]	29[e]	1[e]	2[e]	
50	TEVETH 5790	3[e]	4	5	6	7	8	9	Thu $2^h21^m5^p$
51		10	11	12	13	14	15	16	
52		17	18	19	20	21	22	23	Fri $15^h5^m6^p$
1		24	25	26	27	28	29	1	

CHINESE Wù-Shēn‡/Jǐ-Yǒu

ISO WEEK	Month	Sun	Mon	Tue	Wed	Thu	Fri	Sat	Solar Term
1	MONTH 11* Wù-Shēn	16	17	18	19	20	21	22	Xiǎo hán
2		23	24	25	26	27	28	29	
3	MONTH 12 Wù-Shēn	30	1	2	3	4	5	6	Dà hán
4		7	8	9	10	11	12	13	
5		14	15	16	17	18	19	20*	Lì chūn
6		21	22	23	24	25	26	27	
7	MONTH 1 Jǐ-Yǒu	28	29	1[a]	2	3	4	5	Yǔ shuǐ
8		6	7	8	9	10	11	12	
9		13	14	15[b]	16	17	18	19	Jīng zhé
10		20	21	22	23	24	25	26	
11	MONTH 2 Jǐ-Yǒu	27	28	29	30	1	2	3	
12		4	5	6	7	8	9	10	Chūn fēn
13		11	12	13	14	15	16	17	
14		18	19	20	21[c]*	22	23	24	Qīng míng
15	MONTH 3 Jǐ-Yǒu	25	26	27	28	29	30	1	
16		2	3	4	5	6	7	8	Gǔ yǔ
17		9	10	11	12	13	14	15	
18		16	17	18	19	20	21	22	Lì xià
19		23	24	25	26	27	28	29	
20	MONTH 4 Jǐ-Yǒu	1	2	3	4	5	6	7	Xiǎo mǎn
21		8	9	10	11	12	13	14	
22		15	16	17	18	19	20	21	
23		22*	23	24	25	26	27	28	Máng zhòng
24	MONTH 5 Jǐ-Yǒu	29	30	1	2	3	4	5[d]	
25		6	7	8	9	10	11	12	Xià zhì
26		13	14	15	16	17	18	19	
27		20	21	22	23	24	25	26	Xiǎo shǔ
28	MONTH 6 Jǐ-Yǒu	27	28	29	1	2	3	4	
29		5	6	7	8	9	10	11	Dà shǔ
30		12	13	14	15	16	17	18	
31		19	20	21	22	23*	24	25	Lì qiū
32	MONTH 7 Jǐ-Yǒu	26	27	28	29	30	1	2	
33		3	4	5	6	7[e]	8	9	Chǔ shǔ
34		10	11	12	13	14	15[f]	16	
35		17	18	19	20	21	22	23	
36	MONTH 8 Jǐ-Yǒu	24	25	26	27	28	29	1	Bái lù
37		2	3	4	5	6	7	8	
38		9	10	11	12	13	14	15[g]	Qiū fēn
39		16	17	18	19	20	21	22	
40		23	24*	25	26	27	28	29	Hán lù
41	MONTH 9 Jǐ-Yǒu	30	1	2	3	4	5	6	
42		7	8	9[h]	10	11	12	13	Shuāng jiàng
43		14	15	16	17	18	19	20	
44		21	22	23	24	25	26	27	Lì dōng
45	MONTH 10 Jǐ-Yǒu	28	29	1	2	3	4	5	
46		6	7	8	9	10	11	12	
47		13	14	15	16	17	18	19	Xiǎo xuě
48		20	21	22	23	24	25*	26	
49	MONTH 11 Jǐ-Yǒu	27	28	29	1	2	3	4	Dà xuě
50		5	6	7	8	9	10	11	
51		12	13	14	15	16	17[i]	18	Dōng zhì
52		19	20	21	22	23	24	25	
1		26	27	28	29	30	1	2	Xiǎo hán

COPTIC 1745/1746 / ETHIOPIC 2021/2022

ISO WEEK	Coptic Month	Sun	Mon	Tue	Wed	Thu	Fri	Sat	Ethiopic Month
1	KOIAK 1745	22	23	24	25	26	27	28	TĀKHŚĀŚ 2021
2	TŌBE 1745	29[c]	30	1	2	3	4	5	ṬER 2021
3		6[d]	7	8	9	10	11[e]	12	
4		13	14	15	16	17	18	19	
5		20	21	22	23	24	25	26	
6	MESHIR 1745	27	28	29	30	1	2	3	YAKĀTIT 2021
7		4	5	6	7	8	9	10	
8		11	12	13	14	15	16	17	
9		18	19	20	21	22	23	24	
10	PAREMOTEP 1745	25	26	27	28	29	30	1	MAGĀBIT 2021
11		2	3	4	5	6	7	8	
12		9	10	11	12	13	14	15	
13		16	17	18	19	20	21	22	
14		23	24	25	26	27	28	29	
15	PARMOUTE 1745	30[f]	1	2	3	4	5	6	MIYĀZYĀ 2021
16		7	8	9	10	11	12	13	
17		14	15	16	17	18	19	20	
18		21	22	23	24	25	26	27	
19	PASHONS 1745	28	29[g]	30	1	2	3	4	GENBOT 2021
20		5	6	7	8	9	10	11	
21		12	13	14	15	16	17	18	
22		19	20	21	22	23	24	25	
23	PAŌNE 1745	26	27	28	29	30	1	2	SANĒ 2021
24		3	4	5	6	7	8	9	
25		10	11	12	13	14	15	16	
26		17	18	19	20	21	22	23	
27		24	25	26	27	28	29	30	
28	EPĒP 1745	1	2	3	4	5	6	7	ḤAMLĒ 2021
29		8	9	10	11	12	13	14	
30		15	16	17	18	19	20	21	
31		22	23	24	25	26	27	28	
32	MESORĒ 1745	29	30	1	2	3	4	5	NAḤASĒ 2021
33		6	7	8	9	10	11	12	
34		13[h]	14	15	16	17	18	19	
35		20	21	22	23	24	25	26	
36	EPAG. 1745	27	28	29	30	1	2	3	PĀG. 2021
37	THOOUT 1746	4	5	1[a]	2	3	4	5	MASKARAM 2022
38		6	7	8	9	10	11	12	
39		13	14	15	16	17[b]	18	19	
40		20	21	22	23	24	25	26	
41	PAOPE 1746	27	28	29	30	1	2	3	ṬEQEMT 2022
42		4	5	6	7	8	9	10	
43		11	12	13	14	15	16	17	
44		18	19	20	21	22	23	24	
45	ATHŌR 1746	25	26	27	28	29	30	1	ḪEDĀR 2022
46		2	3	4	5	6	7	8	
47		9	10	11	12	13	14	15	
48		16	17	18	19	20	21	22	
49		23	24	25	26	27	28	29	
50	KOIAK 1746	30	1	2	3	4	5	6	TĀKHŚĀŚ 2022
51		7	8	9	10	11	12	13	
52		14	15	16	17	18	19	20	
1		21	22	23	24	25	26	27	

[a]New Year
[b]Spring (8:00)
[c]Summer (1:47)
[d]Autumn (17:37)
[e]Winter (14:13)
● New moon
◐ First quarter moon
○ Full moon
◑ Last quarter moon

‡Leap year
[a]New Year
[b]Yom Kippur
[c]Sukkot
[d]Winter starts
[e]Ḥanukkah
[f]Purim
[g]Passover
[h]Shavuot
[i]Fast of Av

‡Leap year
[a]New Year (4727, Fowl)
[b]Lantern Festival
[c]Qīngmíng
[d]Dragon Festival
[e]Qīqiǎo
[f]Hungry Ghosts
[g]Mid-Autumn Festival
[h]Double-Ninth Festival
[i]Dōngzhì
*Start of 60-name cycle

[a]New Year
[b]Building of the Cross
[c]Christmas
[d]Jesus's Circumcision
[e]Epiphany
[f]Easter
[g]Mary's Announcement
[h]Jesus's Transfiguration

2029

PERSIAN (ASTRONOMICAL) 1407/1408‡

Month	Sun	Mon	Tue	Wed	Thu	Fri	Sat
DEY 1407	11	12	13	14	15	16	17
	18	19	20	21	22	23	24
	25	26	27	28	29	30	*1*
BAHMAN 1407	2	3	4	5	6	7	8
	9	10	11	12	13	14	15
	16	17	18	19	20	21	22
	23	24	25	26	27	28	29
ESFAND 1407	30	*1*	2	3	4	5	6
	7	8	9	10	11	12	13
	14	15	16	17	18	19	20
	21	22	23	24	25	26	27
FARVARDĪN 1408	28	29	*1*[a]	2*	3	4	5
	6	7	8	9	10	11	12
	13[b]	14	15	16	17	18	19
	20	21	22	23	24	25	26
ORDĪBEHEŠT 1408	27	28	29	30	31	*1*	2
	3	4	5	6	7	8	9
	10	11	12	13	14	15	16
	17	18	19	20	21	22	23
	24	25	26	27	28	29	30
XORDĀD 1408	31	*1*	2	3	4	5	6
	7	8	9	10	11	12	13
	14	15	16	17	18	19	20
	21	22	23	24	25	26	27
TĪR 1408	28	29	30	31	*1*	2	3
	4	5	6	7	8	9	10
	11	12	13	14	15	16	17
	18	19	20	21	22	23	24
	25	26	27	28	29	30	31
MORDĀD 1408	*1*	2	3	4	5	6	7
	8	9	10	11	12	13	14
	15	16	17	18	19	20	21
	22	23	24	25	26	27	28
SHAHRĪVAR 1408	29	30	31	*1*	2	3	4
	5	6	7	8	9	10	11
	12	13	14	15	16	17	18
	19	20	21	22	23	24	25
MEHR 1408	26	27	28	29	30	31	*1*
	2	3	4	5	6	7	8
	9	10	11	12	13	14	15
	16	17	18	19	20	21	22
	23	24	25	26	27	28	29
ĀBĀN 1408	30	*1*	2	3	4	5	6
	7	8	9	10	11	12	13
	14	15	16	17	18	19	20
	21	22	23	24	25	26	27
ĀZAR 1408	28	29	30	*1*	2	3	4
	5	6	7	8	9	10	11
	12	13	14	15	16	17	18
	19	20	21	22	23	24	25
DEY 1408	26	27	28	29	30	*1*	2
	3	4	5	6	7	8	9
	10	11	12	13	14	15	16

‡Leap year
[a]New Year (or next day)
*Near New Year: 1′44″
[b]Sizdeh Bedar

HINDU LUNAR 2085/2086‡

Month	Sun	Mon	Tue	Wed	Thu	Fri	Sat
MĀRGAŚĪRA 2085	15	16	17	18	19	20	21
	22	**23**	25	26	27	28	29
	30	1	2	3	4	5	6
MĀGHA 2085	7	7	8	9	10	11	12
	13	14	15	16	**17**	19	20
	21	22	23	24	25	26	27
	28[h]	29	30	1	2	3	4
PHĀLGUNA 2085	5	6	7	8	9	10	11
	12	13	14	15[i]	16	17	18
	19	20	21	**22**	24	25	26
	27	28	29	*29*	30	1[a]	2
LEAP CHAITRA 2086	3	4	5	6	7	8	9
	10	11	12	13	14	**15**	17
	18	19	20	21	22	23	24
	25	26	27	28	29	30	1
CHAITRA 2086	2	2	3	4	5	6	7
	8[b]	**9**	11	12	13	14	15
	16	17	18	19	20	21	22
	23	24	25	26	27	28	29
	30	1	2	3	4	5	6
VAIŚĀKHA 2086	7	8	9	10	11	**12**	14
	15	16	17	18	19	20	21
	22	23	24	25	26	27	28
	28	29	30	1	2	3	4
JYAISHṬHA 2086	**5**	7	8	9	10	11	12
	13	14	15	16	17	18	19
	20	21	22	23	24	25	26
	27	28	29	30	1	2	3
ĀSHĀḌHA 2086	4	5	6	7	**8**	10	11
	12	13	14	15	16	17	18
	19	20	21	22	23	24	25
	25	26	27	28	29	**30**	2
ŚRĀVAṆA 2086	3	4	5	6	7	8	9
	10	11	12	**13**	15	16	*16*
	17	18	19	20	21	22	23[c]
	24	25	26	27	28	29	30
BHĀDRAPADA 2086	1	2	3[d]	**4**	6	7	8
	9	10	11	12	13	14	15
	16	17	18	19	20	21	*21*
	22	23	24	25	26	**27**	29
	30	1	2	3	4	5	6
ĀŚVINA 2086	7	8[e]	9[e]	10[e]	11	12	13
	14	15	16	17	18	19	20
	21	22	23	24	25	26	27
	28	29	30	1[f]	3	4	5
KĀRTTIKA 2086	6	7	8	9	10	11	12
	13	14	15	*15*	16	17	18
	19	20	21	22	23	24	**25**
	27	28	29	30	1	2	3
MĀRGAŚĪRA 2086	4	5	6	7	8	9	10
	11[g]	12	13	14	15	16	17
	18	19	20	21	22	23	24
	25	26	27	28	29	**30**	2

‡Leap year
[a]New Year (Saumya)
[b]Birthday of Rāma
[c]Birthday of Krishna
[d]Ganēśa Chaturthī
[e]Dashara
[f]Diwali
[g]Birthday of Vishnu
[h]Night of Śiva
[i]Holi

HINDU SOLAR 1950/1951‡

Month	Sun	Mon	Tue	Wed	Thu	Fri	Sat
PAUSHA 1950	16	17	18	19	20	21	22
	23	24	25	26	27	28	29
MĀGHA 1950	1[b]	2	3	4	5	6	7
	8	9	10	11	12	13	14
	15	16	17	18	19	20	21
	22	23	24	25	26	27	28
PHĀLGUNA 1950	29	1	2	3	4	5	6
	7	8	9	10	11	12	13
	14	15	16	17	18	19	20
	21	22	23	24	25	26	27
CHAITRA 1950	28	29	30	1	2	3	4
	5	6	7	8	9	10	11
	12	13	14	15	16	17	18
	19	20	21	22	23	24	25
VAIŚĀKHA 1951	26	27	28	29	30	1[a]	2
	3	4	5	6	7	8	9
	10	11	12	13	14	15	16
	17	18	19	20	21	22	23
	24	25	26	27	28	29	30
JYAISHṬHA 1951	31	1	2	3	4	5	6
	7	8	9	10	11	12	13
	14	15	16	17	18	19	20
	21	22	23	24	25	26	27
ĀSHĀḌHA 1951	28	29	30	31	32	1	2
	3	4	5	6	7	8	9
	10	11	12	13	14	15	16
	17	18	19	20	21	22	23
	24	25	26	27	28	29	30
ŚRĀVAṆA 1951	31	1	2	3	4	5	6
	7	8	9	10	11	12	13
	14	15	16	17	18	19	20
	21	22	23	24	25	26	27
BHĀDRAPADA 1951	28	29	30	31	32	1	2
	3	4	5	6	7	8	9
	10	11	12	13	14	15	16
	17	18	19	20	21	22	23
	24	25	26	27	28	29	30
ĀŚVINA 1951	31	1	2	3	4	5	6
	7	8	9	10	11	12	13
	14	15	16	17	18	19	20
	21	22	23	24	25	26	27
KĀRTTIKA 1951	28	29	30	1	2	3	4
	5	6	7	8	9	10	11
	12	13	14	15	16	17	18
	19	20	21	22	23	24	25
MĀRGAŚĪRA 1951	26	27	28	29	30	1	2
	3	4	5	6	7	8	9
	10	11	12	13	14	15	16
	17	18	19	20	21	22	23
	24	25	26	27	28	29	30
PAUSHA 1951	1	2	3	4	5	6	7
	8	9	10	11	12	13	14
	15	16	17	18	19	20	21

‡Leap year
[a]New Year (Rudhirodgārin)
[b]Pongal

ISLAMIC (ASTRONOMICAL) 1450/1451

Month	Sun	Mon	Tue	Wed	Thu	Fri	Sat
SHA'BĀN 1450	15	16	17	18	19	20	21
	22	23	24	25	26	27	28
RAMAḌĀN 1450	29	30	*1*[e]	2	3	4	5
	6	7	8	9	10	11	12
	13	14	15	16	17	18	19
	20	21	22	23	24	25	26
SHAWWĀL 1450	27	28	29	30	*1*[f]	2	3
	4	5	6	7	8	9	10
	11	12	13	14	15	16	17
	18	19	20	21	22	23	24
DHU AL-QA'DA 1450	25	26	27	28	29	*1*	2
	3	4	5	6	7	8	9
	10	11	12	13	14	15	16
	17	18	19	20	21	22	23
	24	25	26	27	28	29	30
DHU AL-ḤIJJA 1450	*1*	2	3	4	5	6	7
	8	9	10[g]	11	12	13	14
	15	16	17	18	19	20	21
	22	23	24	25	26	27	28
MUḤARRAM 1451	29	30	*1*[a]	2	3	4	5
	6	7	8	9	10[b]	11	12
	13	14	15	16	17	18	19
	20	21	22	23	24	25	26
ṢAFAR 1451	27	28	29	1	2	3	4
	5	6	7	8	9	10	11
	12	13	14	15	16	17	18
	19	20	21	22	23	24	25
RABĪ' I 1451	26	27	28	29	30	*1*	2
	3	4	5	6	7	8	9
	10	11	12[c]	13	14	15	16
	17	18	19	20	21	22	23
	24	25	26	27	28	29	30
RABĪ' II 1451	*1*	2	3	4	5	6	7
	8	9	10	11	12	13	14
	15	16	17	18	19	20	21
	22	23	24	25	26	27	28
JUMĀDĀ I 1451	29	*30*	1	2	3	4	5
	6	7	8	9	10	11	12
	13	14	15	16	17	18	19
	20	21	22	23	24	25	26
JUMĀDĀ II 1451	27	28	29	*1*	2	3	4
	5	6	7	8	9	10	11
	12	13	14	15	16	17	18
	19	20	21	22	23	24	25
RAJAB 1451	26	27	28	29	*1*	2	3
	4	5	6	7	8	9	10
	11	12	13	14	15	16	17
	18	19	20	21	22	23	24
SHA'BĀN 1451	25	26	27[d]	28	29	*1*	2
	3	4	5	6	7	8	9
	10	11	12	13	14	15	16
	17	18	19	20	21	22	23
	24	25	26	27	28	29	1

[a]New Year
[b]'Ashūrā'
[c]Prophet's Birthday
[d]Ascent of the Prophet
[e]Start of Ramaḍān
[f]'Id al-Fiṭr
[g]'Id al-'Aḍḥā

GREGORIAN 2029

Julian (Sun)	Sun	Mon	Tue	Wed	Thu	Fri	Sat	Month
Dec 18	31	1	2	3	4	5	6	JANUARY 2029
	7[a]	8	9	10	11	12	13	
Jan 1	14[b]	15	16	17	18	19	20	
	21	22	23	24	25	26	27	
Jan 15	28	29	30	31	1	2	3	FEBRUARY 2029
	4	5	6	7	8	9	10	
Jan 29	*11*	12	13	14[c]	15	16	17	
	18	19	20	21	22	23	24	
Feb 12	25[d]	26	27	28	1	2	3	MARCH 2029
	4	5	6	7	8	9	10	
Feb 26	*11*	12	13	14	15	16	17	
	18	19	20	21	22	23	24	
Mar 12	25	26	27	28	29	30	31	
	1[e]	2	3	4	5	6	7	APRIL 2029
Mar 26	8[f]	9	10	11	12	13	14	
	15	16	17	18	19	20	21	
Apr 9	22	23	24	25	26	27	28	
	29	30	1	2	3	4	5	MAY 2029
Apr 23	6	7	8	9	10	11	12	
	13	14	15	16	17	18	19	
May 7	*20*	21	22	23	24	25	26	
	27	28	29	30	31	1	2	JUNE 2029
May 21	3	4	5	6	7	8	9	
	10	11	12	13	14	15	16	
Jun 4	*17*	18	19	20	21	22	23	
	24	25	26	27	28	29	30	
Jun 18	*1*	2	3	4	5	6	7	JULY 2029
	8	9	10	11	12	13	14	
Jul 2	*15*	16	17	18	19	20	21	
	22	23	24	25	26	27	28	
Jul 16	*29*	30	31	1	2	3	4	AUGUST 2029
	5	6	7	8	9	10	11	
Jul 30	*12*	13	14	15	16	17	18	
	19	20	21	22	23	24	25	
Aug 13	*26*	27	28	29	30	31	1	SEPTEMBER 2029
	2	3	4	5	6	7	8	
Aug 27	9	10	11	12	13	14	15	
	16	17	18	19	20	21	22	
Sep 10	23	24	25	26	27	28	29	
	30	1	2	3	4	5	6	OCTOBER 2029
Sep 24	7	8	9	10	11	12	13	
	14	15	16	17	18	19	20	
Oct 8	*21*	22	23	24	25	26	27	
	28	29	30	31	1	2	3	NOVEMBER 2029
Oct 22	4	5	6	7	8	9	10	
	11	12	13	14	15	16	17	
Nov 5	*18*	19	20	21	22	23	24	
	25	26	27	28	29	30	1	DECEMBER 2029
Nov 19	2[g]	3	4	5	6	7	8	
	9	10	11	12	13	14	15	
Dec 3	*16*	17	18	19	20	21	22	
	23	24	25[h]	26	27	28	29	
Dec 17	*30*	31	1	2	3	4	5	

[a]Orthodox Christmas
[b]Julian New Year
[c]Ash Wednesday
[d]Feast of Orthodoxy
[e]Easter
[f]Orthodox Easter
[g]Advent
[h]Christmas

2030

GREGORIAN 2030	Sun	Mon	Tue	Wed	Thu	Fri	Sat	Lunar Phases	ISO WEEK (Mon)	JULIAN DAY (Sun noon)
JANUARY 2030	30	31	1[a]	2	3	●	5	2:48	1	2462501
	6	7	8	9	10	◐	12	14:05	2	2462508
	13	14	15	16	17	18	○	15:53	3	2462515
	20	21	22	23	24	25	◑	18:13	4	2462522
	27	28	29	30	31	1	●	16:06	5	2462529
FEBRUARY 2030	3	4	5	6	7	8	9		6	2462536
	◐	11	12	13	14	15	16	11:48	7	2462543
	17	○	19	20	21	22	23	6:19	8	2462550
	24	◑	26	27	28	1	2	1:57	9	2462557
MARCH 2030	3	●	5	6	7	8	9	6:34	10	2462564
	10	11	◐	13	14	15	16	8:46	11	2462571
	17	18	○	20[b]	21	22	23	17:55	12	2462578
	24	25	◑	27	28	29	30	9:50	13	2462585
	31	1	●	3	4	5	6	22:01	14	2462592
APRIL 2030	7	8	9	10	◐	12	13	2:56	15	2462599
	14	15	16	17	○	19	20	3:19	16	2462606
	21	22	23	◑	25	26	27	18:38	17	2462613
	28	29	30	1	●	3	4	14:11	18	2462620
MAY 2030	5	6	7	8	9	◐	11	17:10	19	2462627
	12	13	14	15	16	○	18	11:18	20	2462634
	19	20	21	22	23	◑	25	4:56	21	2462641
	26	27	28	29	30	31	●	6:20	22	2462648
JUNE 2030	2	3	4	5	6	7	8		23	2462655
	◐	10	11	12	13	14	○	3:35 18:40	24	2462662
	16	17	18	19	20	21[c]	◑	17:18	25	2462669
	23	24	25	26	27	28	29		26	2462676
	●	1	2	3	4	5	6	21:33	27	2462683
JULY 2030	7	◐	9	10	11	12	13	11:01	28	2462690
	14	○	16	17	18	19	20	2:11	29	2462697
	21	◑	23	24	25	26	27	8:06	30	2462704
	28	29	●	31	1	2	3	11:10	31	2462711
AUGUST 2030	4	5	◐	7	8	9	10	16:42	32	2462718
	11	12	○	14	15	16	17	10:43	33	2462725
	18	19	20	◑	22	23	24	1:14	34	2462732
	25	26	27	●	29	30	31	23:06	35	2462739
SEPTEMBER 2030	1	2	3	◐	5	6	7	21:54	36	2462746
	8	9	10	○	12	13	14	21:17	37	2462753
	15	16	17	18	◑	20	21	19:55	38	2462760
	22[d]	23	24	25	26	●	28	9:53	39	2462767
	29	30	1	2	3	◐	5	3:55	40	2462774
OCTOBER 2030	6	7	8	9	10	○	12	10:46	41	2462781
	13	14	15	16	17	18	◑	14:49	42	2462788
	20	21	22	23	24	25	●	20:16	43	2462795
	27	28	29	30	31	1	◐	11:55	44	2462802
NOVEMBER 2030	3	4	5	6	7	8	9		45	2462809
	○	11	12	13	14	15	16	3:29	46	2462816
	17	◑	19	20	21	22	23	8:31	47	2462823
	24	●	26	27	28	29	30	6:45	48	2462830
DECEMBER 2030	◐	2	3	4	5	6	7	22:56	49	2462837
	8	○	10	11	12	13	14	22:39	50	2462844
	15	16	17	◑	19	20	21[e]	0:00	51	2462851
	22	23	●	25	26	27	28	17:31	52	2462858
	29	30	◐	1	2	3	4	13:35	1	2462865

ISO WEEK	HEBREW 5790‡/5791	Sun	Mon	Tue	Wed	Thu	Fri	Sat	Molad
1	SHEVAT 5790	24	25	26	27	28	29	1	Fri 15h5m6p
2		2	3	4	5	6	7	8	
3		9	10	11	12	13	14	15	
4		16	17	18	19	20	21	22	
5		23	24	25	26	27	28	29	
6	ADAR I 5790	30	1	2	3	4	5	6	Sun 3h49m7p
7		7	8	9	10	11	12	13	
8		14	15	16	17	18	19	20	
9		21	22	23	24	25	26	27	
10	ADAR II 5790	28	29	30	1	2	3	4	Mon 16h33m8p
11		5	6	7	8	9	10	11	
12		12	13	14[f]	15	16	17	18	
13		19	20	21	22	23	24	25	
14	NISAN 5790	26	27	28	29	1	2	3	Wed 5h17m9p
15		4	5	6	7	8	9	10	
16		11	12	13	14	15[g]	16	17	
17		18	19	20	21	22	23	24	
18	IYAR 5790	25	26	27	28	29	30	1	Thu 18h1m10p
19		2	3	4	5	6	7	8	
20		9	10	11	12	13	14	15	
21		16	17	18	19	20	21	22	
22		23	24	25	26	27	28	29	
23	SIVAN 5790	1	2	3	4	5	6[h]	7	Sat 6h45m11p
24		8	9	10	11	12	13	14	
25		15	16	17	18	19	20	21	
26		22	23	24	25	26	27	28	
27	TAMMUZ 5790	29	30	1	2	3	4	5	Sun 19h29m12p
28		6	7	8	9	10	11	12	
29		13	14	15	16	17	18	19	
30		20	21	22	23	24	25	26	
31	AV 5790	27	28	29	1	2	3	4	Tue 8h13m13p
32		5	6	7	8	9[i]	10	11	
33		12	13	14	15	16	17	18	
34		19	20	21	22	23	24	25	
35	ELUL 5790	26	27	28	29	30	1	2	Wed 20h57m14p
36		3	4	5	6	7	8	9	
37		10	11	12	13	14	15	16	
38		17	18	19	20	21	22	23	
39	TISHRI 5791	24	25	26	27	28	29	1[a]	Fri 9h41m15p
40		2[a]	3	4	5	6	7	8	
41		9	10[b]	11	12	13	14	15[c]	
42		16	17	18	19	20	21	22	
43		23	24	25	26	27	28	29	
44	HESHVAN 5791	30	1	2	3	4	5	6	Sat 22h25m16p
45		7	8	9	10	11	12	13	
46		14	15	16	17	18	19	20	
47		21	22	23	24	25	26	27	
48	KISLEV 5791	28	29	30	1	2	3	4	Mon 11h9m17p
49		5	6	7	8	9[d]	10	11	
50		12	13	14	15	16	17	18	
51		19	20	21	22	23	24	25[e]	
52	TEVETH 5791	26[e]	27[e]	28[e]	29[e]	30[e]	1[e]	2[e]	Tue 23h54m0p
1		3	4	5	6	7	8	9	

ISO WEEK	CHINESE Jǐ-Yǒu/Gēng-Xū	Sun	Mon	Tue	Wed	Thu	Fri	Sat	Solar Term
1	MONTH 12 Jǐ-Yǒu	26	27	28	29	30	1	2	*Xiǎo hán*
2		3	4	5	6	7	8	9	
3		10	11	12	13	14	15	16	
4		***17***	18	19	20	21	22	23	**Dà hán**
5		24	25	26*	27	28	29	30	
6	MONTH 1 Gēng-Xū	1[a]	2	3	4	5	6	7	*Lì chūn*
7		8	9	10	11	12	13	14	
8		15[b]	***16***	17	18	19	20	21	**Yǔ shuǐ**
9		22	23	24	25	26	27	28	
10	MONTH 2 Gēng-Xū	29	1	2	3	4	5	6	*Jīng zhé*
11		7	8	9	10	11	12	13	
12		14	15	16	***17***	18	19	20	**Chūn fēn**
13		21	22	23	24	25	26	27*	
14	MONTH 3 Gēng-Xū	28	29	30	1	2	3[c]	4	*Qīng míng*
15		5	6	7	8	9	10	11	
16		12	13	14	15	16	17	***18***	**Gǔ yǔ**
17		19	20	21	22	23	24	25	
18	MONTH 4 Gēng-Xū	26	27	28	29	1	2	3	
19		4	5	6	7	8	9	10	*Lì xià*
20		11	12	13	14	15	16	17	
21		18	19	***20***	21	22	23	24	**Xiǎo mǎn**
22	MONTH 5 Gēng-Xū	25	26	27	28*	29	30	1	
23		2	3	4	5[d]	6	7	8	*Máng zhòng*
24		9	10	11	12	13	14	15	
25		16	17	18	19	20	***21***	22	**Xià zhì**
26		23	24	25	26	27	28	29	
27	MONTH 6 Gēng-Xū	30	1	2	3	4	5	6	
28		7	8	9	10	11	12	13	*Xiǎo shǔ*
29		14	15	16	17	18	19	20	
30		21	22	***23***	24	25	26	27	**Dà shǔ**
31	MONTH 7 Gēng-Xū	28*	29	1	2	3	4	5	
32		6	7[e]	8	9	10	11	12	*Lì qiū*
33		13	14	15[f]	16	17	18	19	
34		20	21	22	23	24	***25***	26	**Chǔ shǔ**
35	MONTH 8 Gēng-Xū	27	28	29	30	1	2	3	
36		4	5	6	7	8	9	*10*	*Bái lù*
37		11	12	13	14	15[g]	16	17	
38		18	19	20	21	22	23	24	**Qiū fēn**
39	MONTH 9 Gēng-Xū	25	***26***	27	28	29*	1	2	
40		3	4	5	6	7	8	9[h]	
41		10	11	*12*	13	14	15	16	*Hán lù*
42		17	18	19	20	21	22	23	
43		24	25	26	***27***	28	29	30	**Shuāng jiàng**
44	MONTH 10 Gēng-Xū	1	2	3	4	5	6	7	
45		8	9	10	11	*12*	13	14	*Lì dōng*
46		15	16	17	18	19	20	21	
47		22	23	24	25	26	***27***	28	**Xiǎo xuě**
48	MONTH 11 Gēng-Xū	29	1*	2	3	4	5	6	
49		7	8	9	10	11	12	*13*	*Dà xuě*
50		14	15	16	17	18	19	20	
51		21	22	23	24	25	26	27	**Dōng zhì**
52	MONTH 12 Gēng-Xū	***28***[i]	29	30	1	2	3	4	
1		5	6	7	8	9	10	11	

ISO WEEK	COPTIC 1746/1747‡	Sun	Mon	Tue	Wed	Thu	Fri	Sat	ETHIOPIC 2022/2023‡
1	KOIAK 1746	21	22	23	24	25	26	27	TÁKHŚÁŚ 2022
2		28	29[c]	30	1	2	3	4	
3	TŌBE 1746	5	6[d]	7	8	9	10	11[e]	ṬER 2022
4		12	13	14	15	16	17	18	
5		19	20	21	22	23	24	25	
6		26	27	28	29	30	1	2	
7	MESHIR 1746	3	4	5	6	7	8	9	YAKĀTIT 2022
8		10	11	12	13	14	15	16	
9		17	18	19	20	21	22	23	
10		24	25	26	27	28	29	30	
11	PAREMOTEP 1746	1	2	3	4	5	6	7	MAGĀBIT 2022
12		8	9	10	11	12	13	14	
13		15	16	17	18	19	20	21	
14		22	23	24	25	26	27	28	
15	PARMOUTE 1746	29	30	1	2	3	4	5	MIYĀZYĀ 2022
16		6	7	8	9	10	11	12	
17		13	14	15	16	17	18	19	
18		20[f]	21	22	23	24	25	26	
19	PASHONS 1746	27	28	29[g]	30	1	2	3	GENBOT 2022
20		4	5	6	7	8	9	10	
21		11	12	13	14	15	16	17	
22		18	19	20	21	22	23	24	
23	PAŌNE 1746	25	26	27	28	29	30	1	SANĒ 2022
24		2	3	4	5	6	7	8	
25		9	10	11	12	13	14	15	
26		16	17	18	19	20	21	22	
27		23	24	25	26	27	28	29	
28	EPĒP 1746	30	1	2	3	4	5	6	HAMLĒ 2022
29		7	8	9	10	11	12	13	
30		14	15	16	17	18	19	20	
31		21	22	23	24	25	26	27	
32	MESORĒ 1746	28	29	30	1	2	3	4	NAḤASĒ 2022
33		5	6	7	8	9	10	11	
34		12	13[h]	14	15	16	17	18	
35		19	20	21	22	23	24	25	
36	EPAG. 1746	26	27	28	29	30	1	2	PĀG. 2022
37	THOOUT 1747	3	4	5	1[a]	2	3	4	MASKARAM 2023
38		5	6	7	8	9	10	11	
39		12	13	14	15	16	17[b]	18	
40		19	20	21	22	23	24	25	
41	PAOPE 1747	26	27	28	29	30	1	2	ṬEQEMT 2023
42		3	4	5	6	7	8	9	
43		10	11	12	13	14	15	16	
44		17	18	19	20	21	22	23	
45		24	25	26	27	28	29	30	
46	ATHŌR 1747	1	2	3	4	5	6	7	HEDĀR 2023
47		8	9	10	11	12	13	14	
48		15	16	17	18	19	20	21	
49		22	23	24	25	26	27	28	
50	KOIAK 1747	29	30	1	2	3	4	5	TĀKHŚĀŚ 2023
51		6	7	8	9	10	11	12	
52		13	14	15	16	17	18	19	
1		20	21	22	23	24	25	26	

Gregorian:
[a]New Year
[b]Spring (13:50)
[c]Summer (7:30)
[d]Autumn (23:26)
[e]Winter (20:08)
● New moon
◐ First quarter moon
○ Full moon
◑ Last quarter moon

Hebrew:
‡Leap year
[a]New Year
[b]Yom Kippur
[c]Sukkot
[d]Winter starts
[e]Ḥanukkah
[f]Purim
[g]Passover
[h]Shavuot
[i]Fast of Av

Chinese:
[a]New Year (4728, Dog)
[b]Lantern Festival
[c]Qīngmíng
[d]Dragon Festival
[e]Qīqiǎo
[f]Hungry Ghosts
[g]Mid-Autumn Festival
[h]Double-Ninth Festival
[i]Dōngzhì
*Start of 60-name cycle

Coptic/Ethiopic:
‡Leap year
[a]New Year
[b]Building of the Cross
[c]Christmas
[d]Jesus's Circumcision
[e]Epiphany
[f]Easter
[g]Mary's Announcement
[h]Jesus's Transfiguration

PERSIAN (ASTRONOMICAL) 1408‡/1409

Month	Sun	Mon	Tue	Wed	Thu	Fri	Sat
DEY 1408	10	11	12	13	14	15	16
	17	18	19	20	21	22	23
	24	25	26	27	28	29	30
	1	2	3	4	5	6	7
BAHMAN 1408	8	9	10	11	12	13	14
	15	16	17	18	19	20	21
	22	23	24	25	26	27	28
	29	30	1	2	3	4	5
ESFAND 1408	6	7	8	9	10	11	12
	13	14	15	16	17	18	19
	20	21	22	23	24	25	26
	27	28	29	30	1[a]	2	3
FARVARDĪN 1409	4	5	6	7	8	9	10
	11	12	13[b]	14	15	16	17
	18	19	20	21	22	23	24
	25	26	27	28	29	30	31
	1	2	3	4	5	6	7
ORDĪBEHEŠT 1409	8	9	10	11	12	13	14
	15	16	17	18	19	20	21
	22	23	24	25	26	27	28
	29	30	31	1	2	3	4
XORDĀD 1409	5	6	7	8	9	10	11
	12	13	14	15	16	17	18
	19	20	21	22	23	24	25
	26	27	28	29	30	31	1
TĪR 1409	2	3	4	5	6	7	8
	9	10	11	12	13	14	15
	16	17	18	19	20	21	22
	23	24	25	26	27	28	29
	30	31	1	2	3	4	5
MORDĀD 1409	6	7	8	9	10	11	12
	13	14	15	16	17	18	19
	20	21	22	23	24	25	26
	27	28	29	30	31	1	2
SHAHRĪVAR 1409	3	4	5	6	7	8	9
	10	11	12	13	14	15	16
	17	18	19	20	21	22	23
	24	25	26	27	28	29	30
	31	1	2	3	4	5	6
MEHR 1409	7	8	9	10	11	12	13
	14	15	16	17	18	19	20
	21	22	23	24	25	26	27
	28	29	30	1	2	3	4
ĀBĀN 1409	5	6	7	8	9	10	11
	12	13	14	15	16	17	18
	19	20	21	22	23	24	25
	26	27	28	29	30	1	2
ĀZAR 1409	3	4	5	6	7	8	9
	10	11	12	13	14	15	16
	17	18	19	20	21	22	23
	24	25	26	27	28	29	30
DEY 1409	1	2	3	4	5	6	7
	8	9	10	11	12	13	14

‡Leap year
[a]New Year
[b]Sizdeh Bedar

HINDU LUNAR 2086‡/2087

Month	Sun	Mon	Tue	Wed	Thu	Fri	Sat
	25	26	27	28	29	**30**	2
PAUSHA 2086	3	4	5	6	7	*7*	8
	9	10	11	12	13	14	15
	16	17	18	19	20	21	22
	23	**24**	26	27	28	29	30
	1	2	3	4	5	6	7
MĀGHA 2086	8	9	*9*	10	11	12	13
	14	15	16	17	**18**	20	21
	22	23	24	25	26	27	28[h]
	29	30	1	2	3	4	5
PHĀLGUNA 2086	6	7	8	9	10	11	12
	13	14	15[i]	16	17	18	19
	20	21	**22**	24	25	26	27
	28	29	30	1[a]	2	3	*3*
CHAITRA 2087	4	5	6	7	8	9[b]	10
	11	12	13	14	15	**16**	18
	19	20	21	22	23	24	25
	26	27	28	29	30	1	2
VAIŚĀKHA 2087	3	4	5	6	7	8	9
	10	11	12	13	14	15	16
	17	18	19	**20**	22	23	24
	25	26	27	28	*28*	29	30
	1	2	3	4	5	6	7
JYAISHṬHA 2087	8	9	10	11	**12**	14	15
	16	17	18	19	20	21	22
	23	24	25	26	27	28	29
	30	1	2	3	4	5	6
ĀSHĀḌHA 2087	7	8	9	10	11	12	13
	14	**15**	17	18	19	20	21
	22	23	24	25	*25*	26	27
	28	29	30	1	2	3	4
ŚRĀVAṆA 2087	5	6	7	**8**	10	11	12
	13	14	15	16	17	18	19
	20	21	22	23[c]	24	25	26
	27	28	29	30	1	2	3
BHĀDRAPADA 2087	4[d]	5	6	7	8	9	10
	11	13	14	15	16	17	18
	19	20	21	*21*	22	23	24
	25	26	27	28	29	30	1
ĀŚVINA 2087	2	3	**4**	6	7	8[e]	9[e]
	10[e]	11	12	13	14	15	16
	17	18	19	20	21	22	23
	24	25	26	*26*	28	29	30
	1[f]	2	3	4	5	6	7
KĀRTTIKA 2087	8	**9**	11	12	13	14	15
	15	16	17	18	19	20	21
	22	23	24	25	26	27	28
	29	30	1	**2**	4	5	6
MĀRGAŚĪRA 2087	7	8	9	10	11[g]	12	13
	14	15	16	17	*17*	18	19
	20	21	22	23	24	25	**26**
PAUSHA 2087	28	29	30	1	2	3	4
	5	6	7	8	9	10	11

‡Leap year
[a]New Year (Sādhāraṇa)
[b]Birthday of Rāma
[c]Birthday of Krishna
[d]Ganēśa Chaturthī
[e]Dashara
[f]Diwali
[g]Birthday of Vishnu
[h]Night of Śiva
[i]Holi

HINDU SOLAR 1951‡/1952

Month	Sun	Mon	Tue	Wed	Thu	Fri	Sat
PAUSHA 1951	15	16	17	18	19	20	21
	22	23	24	25	26	27	28
	29	1[b]	2	3	4	5	6
MĀGHA 1951	7	8	9	10	11	12	13
	14	15	16	17	18	19	20
	21	22	23	24	25	26	27
	28	29	30	1	2	3	4
PHĀLGUNA 1951	5	6	7	8	9	10	11
	12	13	14	15	16	17	18
	19	20	21	22	23	24	25
	26	27	28	29	1	2	3
CHAITRA 1951	4	5	6	7	8	9	10
	11	12	13	14	15	16	17
	18	19	20	21	22	23	24
	25	26	27	28	29	30	31
	1[a]	2	3	4	5	6	7
VAIŚĀKHA 1952	8	9	10	11	12	13	14
	15	16	17	18	19	20	21
	22	23	24	25	26	27	28
	29	30	31	1	2	3	4
JYAISHṬHA 1952	5	6	7	8	9	10	11
	12	13	14	15	16	17	18
	19	20	21	22	23	24	25
	26	27	28	29	30	31	1
ĀSHĀḌHA 1952	2	3	4	5	6	7	8
	9	10	11	12	13	14	15
	16	17	18	19	20	21	22
	23	24	25	26	27	28	29
	30	31	32	1	2	3	4
ŚRĀVAṆA 1952	5	6	7	8	9	10	11
	12	13	14	15	16	17	18
	19	20	21	22	23	24	25
	26	27	28	29	30	31	1
BHĀDRAPADA 1952	2	3	4	5	6	7	8
	9	10	11	12	13	14	15
	16	17	18	19	20	21	22
	23	24	25	26	27	28	29
	30	31	1	2	3	4	5
ĀŚVINA 1952	6	7	8	9	10	11	12
	13	14	15	16	17	18	19
	20	21	22	23	24	25	26
	27	28	29	30	31	1	2
KĀRTTIKA 1952	3	4	5	6	7	8	9
	10	11	12	13	14	15	16
	17	18	19	20	21	22	23
	24	25	26	27	28	29	30
	1	2	3	4	5	6	7
MĀRGAŚĪRA 1952	8	9	10	11	12	13	14
	15	16	17	18	19	20	21
	22	23	24	25	26	27	28
	29	1	2	3	4	5	6
PAUSHA 1952	7	8	9	10	11	12	13
	14	15	16	17	18	19	20

‡Leap year
[a]New Year (Raktāksha)
[b]Pongal

ISLAMIC (ASTRONOMICAL) 1451/1452

Month	Sun	Mon	Tue	Wed	Thu	Fri	Sat
	24	25	26	27	28	29	1[e]
RAMAḌĀN 1451	2	3	4	5	6	7	8
	9	10	11	12	13	14	15
	16	17	18	19	20	21	22
	23	24	25	26	27	28	29
	30	1[f]	2	3	4	5	6
SHAWWĀL 1451	7	8	9	10	11	12	13
	14	15	16	17	18	19	20
	21	22	23	24	25	26	27
	28	29	1	2	3	4	5
DHU AL-QA'DA 1451	6	7	8	9	10	11	12
	13	14	15	16	17	18	19
	20	21	22	23	24	25	26
	27	28	29	30	1	2	3
DHU AL-ḤIJJA 1451	4	5	6	7	8	9	10[g]
	11	12	13	14	15	16	17
	18	19	20	21	22	23	24
	25	26	27	28	29	30	1[a]
MUḤARRAM 1452	2	3	4	5	6	7	8
	9	10[b]	11	12	13	14	15
	16	17	18	19	20	21	22
	23	24	25	26	27	28	29
	30	1	2	3	4	5	6
ṢAFAR 1452	7	8	9	10	11	12	13
	14	15	16	17	18	19	20
	21	22	23	24	25	26	27
	28	29	30	1	2	3	4
RABĪ' I 1452	5	6	7	8	9	10	11
	12[c]	13	14	15	16	17	18
	19	20	21	22	23	24	25
	26	27	28	29	30	1	2
RABĪ' II 1452	3	4	5	6	7	8	9
	10	11	12	13	14	15	16
	17	18	19	20	21	22	23
	24	25	26	27	28	29	1
JUMĀDĀ I 1452	2	3	4	5	6	7	8
	9	10	11	12	13	14	15
	16	17	18	19	20	21	22
	23	24	25	26	27	28	29
JUMĀDĀ II 1452	1	2	3	4	5	6	7
	8	9	10	11	12	13	14
	15	16	17	18	19	20	21
	22	23	24	25	26	27	28
	29	1	2	3	4	5	6
RAJAB 1452	7	8	9	10	11	12	13
	14	15	16	17	18	19	20
	21	22	23	24	25	26	27[d]
	28	29	30	1	2	3	4
SHA'BĀN 1452	5	6	7	8	9	10	11
	12	13	14	15	16	17	18
	19	20	21	22	23	24	25
	26	27	28	29	1[e]	2	3
RAMAḌĀN 1452	4	5	6	7	8	9	10

[a]New Year
[b]'Ashūrā'
[c]Prophet's Birthday
[d]Ascent of the Prophet
[e]Start of Ramaḍān
[f]'Id al-Fiṭr
[g]'Id al-'Aḍḥā

GREGORIAN 2030

Julian (Sun)	Sun	Mon	Tue	Wed	Thu	Fri	Sat	Month
Dec 17	30	31	1	2	3	4	5	JANUARY 2030
	6	7[a]	8	9	10	11	12	
Dec 31	13	14[b]	15	16	17	18	19	
	20	21	22	23	24	25	26	
Jan 14	27	28	29	30	31	1	2	
	3	4	5	6	7	8	9	FEBRUARY 2030
Jan 28	10	11	12	13	14	15	16	
	17	18	19	20	21	22	23	
Feb 11	24	25	26	27	28	1	2	
	3	4	5	6[c]	7	8	9	MARCH 2030
Feb 25	10	11	12	13	14	15	16	
	17[d]	18	19	20	21	22	23	
Mar 11	24	25	26	27	28	29	30	
	31	1	2	3	4	5	6	
Mar 25	7	8	9	10	11	12	13	APRIL 2030
	14	15	16	17	18	19	20	
Apr 8	21[e]	22	23	24	25	26	27	
	28[f]	29	30	1	2	3	4	
Apr 22	5	6	7	8	9	10	11	MAY 2030
	12	13	14	15	16	17	18	
May 6	19	20	21	22	23	24	25	
	26	27	28	29	30	31	1	
May 20	2	3	4	5	6	7	8	JUNE 2030
	9	10	11	12	13	14	15	
Jun 3	16	17	18	19	20	21	22	
	23	24	25	26	27	28	29	
Jun 17	30	1	2	3	4	5	6	
	7	8	9	10	11	12	13	JULY 2030
Jul 1	14	15	16	17	18	19	20	
	21	22	23	24	25	26	27	
Jul 15	28	29	30	31	1	2	3	
	4	5	6	7	8	9	10	AUGUST 2030
Jul 29	11	12	13	14	15	16	17	
	18	19	20	21	22	23	24	
Aug 12	25	26	27	28	29	30	31	
	1	2	3	4	5	6	7	SEPTEMBER 2030
Aug 26	8	9	10	11	12	13	14	
	15	16	17	18	19	20	21	
Sep 9	22	23	24	25	26	27	28	
	29	30	1	2	3	4	5	
Sep 23	6	7	8	9	10	11	12	OCTOBER 2030
	13	14	15	16	17	18	19	
Oct 7	20	21	22	23	24	25	26	
	27	28	29	30	31	1	2	
Oct 21	3	4	5	6	7	8	9	NOVEMBER 2030
	10	11	12	13	14	15	16	
Nov 4	17	18	19	20	21	22	23	
	24	25	26	27	28	29	30	
Nov 18	1[g]	2	3	4	5	6	7	DECEMBER 2030
	8	9	10	11	12	13	14	
Dec 2	15	16	17	18	19	20	21	
	22	23	24	25[h]	26	27	28	
Dec 16	29	30	31	1	2	3	4	

[a]Orthodox Christmas
[b]Julian New Year
[c]Ash Wednesday
[d]Feast of Orthodoxy
[e]Easter
[f]Orthodox Easter
[g]Advent
[h]Christmas

2031

GREGORIAN 2031	Sun	Mon	Tue	Wed	Thu	Fri	Sat	Lunar Phases	ISO WEEK (Mon)	JULIAN DAY (Sun noon)	HEBREW 5791/5792	Sun	Mon	Tue	Wed	Thu	Fri	Sat	Molad	CHINESE Gēng-Xū/Xīn-Hài‡	Sun	Mon	Tue	Wed	Thu	Fri	Sat	Solar Term	COPTIC 1747‡/1748	Sun	Mon	Tue	Wed	Thu	Fri	Sat	ETHIOPIC 2023‡/2024
JANUARY 2031	29	30	◐	1[a]	2	3	4	13:35	1	2462865		3	4	5	6	7	8	9			5	6	7	8	9	10	11		KOIAK 1747	20	21	22	23	24	25	26	TĀKHŚĀŚ 2023
	5	6	7	○	9	10	11	18:25	2	2462872	TEVETH 5791	10	11	12	13	14	15	16		MONTH 12 Gēng-Xū	12	13	14	15	16	17	18	Xiǎo hán		27	28	29[c]	30	1	2	3	
	12	13	14	15	◑	17	18	12:46	3	2462879		17	18	19	20	21	22	23	Thu 12h38m1p		19	20	21	22	23	24	25		TŌBE 1747	4	5	6[d]	7	8	9	10	ṬER 2023
	19	20	21	22	●	24	25	4:30	4	2462886		24	25	26	27	28	29	1			26	27	28	29	1[a]	2*	3	Dà hán		11[e]	12	13	14	15	16	17	
	26	27	28	29	◐	31	1	7:42	5	2462893		2	3	4	5	6	7	8		MONTH 1 Xīn-Hài	4	5	6	7	8	9	10			18	19	20	21	22	23	24	
FEBRUARY 2031	2	3	4	5	6	○	8	12:45	6	2462900	SHEVAT 5791	9	10	11	12	13	14	15			11	12	13	14	15[b]	16	17	Lì chūn		25	26	27	28	29	30	1	
	9	10	11	12	13	◑	15	22:49	7	2462907		16	17	18	19	20	21	22			18	19	20	21	22	23	24		MESHIR 1747	2	3	4	5	6	7	8	YAKĀTIT 2023
	16	17	18	19	20	●	22	15:48	8	2462914		23	24	25	26	27	28	29			25	26	27	28	29	1	2	Yǔ shuǐ		9	10	11	12	13	14	15	
	23	24	25	26	27	28	◐	4:01	9	2462921		30	1	2	3	4	5	6	Sat 1h22m2p	MONTH 2 Xīn-Hài	3	4	5	6	7	8	9			16	17	18	19	20	21	22	
MARCH 2031	2	3	4	5	6	7	8		10	2462928	ADAR 5791	7	8	9	10	11	12	13			10	11	12	13	14	15	16	Jīng zhé		23	24	25	26	27	28	29	
	○	10	11	12	13	14	15	4:28	11	2462935		14[f]	15	16	17	18	19	20			17	18	19	20	21	22	23			30	1	2	3	4	5	6	
	◑	17	18	19	20[b]	21	22	6:35	12	2462942		21	22	23	24	25	26	27			24	25	26	27	28	29	30	Chūn fēn	PAREMOTEP 1747	7	8	9	10	11	12	13	MAGĀBIT 2023
	●	24	25	26	27	28	29	3:48	13	2462949		28	29	1	2	3	4	5	Sun 14h6m3p		1	2	3*	4	5	6	7			14	15	16	17	18	19	20	
	30	◐	1	2	3	4	5	0:31	14	2462956	NISAN 5791	6	7	8	9	10	11	12		MONTH 3 Xīn-Hài	8	9	10	11	12	13	14[c]	Qīng míng		21	22	23	24	25	26	27	
APRIL 2031	6	○	8	9	10	11	12	17:20	15	2462963		13	14	15[g]	16	17	18	19			15	16	17	18	19	20	21			28	29	30	1	2	3	4	
	13	◑	15	16	17	18	19	12:57	16	2462970		20	21	22	23	24	25	26			22	23	24	25	26	27	28		PARMOUTE 1747	5[f]	6	7	8	9	10	11	MIYĀZYĀ 2023
	20	●	22	23	24	25	26	16:56	17	2462977		27	28	29	30	1	2	3	Tue 2h50m4p		29	30	1	2	3	4	5	Gǔ yǔ		12	13	14	15	16	17	18	
	27	28	◐	30	1	2	3	19:18	18	2462984	IYYAR 5791	4	5	6	7	8	9	10		LEAP MONTH 3 Xīn-Hài	6	7	8	9	10	11	12			19	20	21	22	23	24	25	
MAY 2031	4	5	6	○	8	9	10	3:39	19	2462991		11	12	13	14	15	16	17			13	14	15	16	17	18	19	Lì xià		26	27	28	29[g]	30	1	2	
	11	12	◑	14	15	16	17	19:06	20	2462998		18	19	20	21	22	23	24			20	21	22	23	24	25	26		PASHONS 1747	3	4	5	6	7	8	9	GENBOT 2023
	18	19	20	●	22	23	24	7:16	21	2463005		25	26	27	28	29	1	2	Wed 15h34m5p		27	28	29	1	2	3	4*	Xiǎo mǎn		10	11	12	13	14	15	16	
	25	26	27	28	◐	30	31	11:18	22	2463012	SIVAN 5791	3	4	5	6[h]	7	8	9		MONTH 4 Xīn-Hài	5	6	7	8	9	10	11			17	18	19	20	21	22	23	
JUNE 2031	1	2	3	4	○	6	7	11:57	23	2463019		10	11	12	13	14	15	16			12	13	14	15	16	17	18	Máng zhòng		24	25	26	27	28	29	30	
	8	9	10	11	◑	13	14	2:19	24	2463026		17	18	19	20	21	22	23			19	20	21	22	23	24	25			1	2	3	4	5	6	7	
	15	16	17	18	●	20	21[c]	22:24	25	2463033		24	25	26	27	28	29	30			26	27	28	29	30	1	2	Xià zhì	PAŌNE 1747	8	9	10	11	12	13	14	SANĒ 2023
	22	23	24	25	26	27	◐	0:18	26	2463040		1	2	3	4	5	6	7	Fri 4h18m6p	MONTH 5 Xīn-Hài	3	4	5[d]	6	7	8	9			15	16	17	18	19	20	21	
	29	30	1	2	3	○	5	19:00	27	2463047	TAMMUZ 5791	8	9	10	11	12	13	14			10	11	12	13	14	15	16			22	23	24	25	26	27	28	
JULY 2031	6	7	8	9	10	◑	12	11:49	28	2463054		15	16	17	18	19	20	21			17	18	19	20	21	22	23	Xiǎo shǔ		29	30	1	2	3	4	5	
	13	14	15	16	17	18	●	13:39	29	2463061		22	23	24	25	26	27	28			24	25	26	27	28	29	1		EPĒP 1747	6	7	8	9	10	11	12	ḤAMLĒ 2023
	20	21	22	23	24	25	26		30	2463068		29	1	2	3	4	5	6	Sat 17h2m7p	MONTH 6 Xīn-Hài	2	3	4	5*	6	7	8	Dà shǔ		13	14	15	16	17	18	19	
	◐	28	29	30	31	1	2	10:34	31	2463075	AV 5791	7	8	9[i]	10	11	12	13			9	10	11	12	13	14	15			20	21	22	23	24	25	26	
AUGUST 2031	○	4	5	6	7	8	9	1:44	32	2463082		14	15	16	17	18	19	20			16	17	18	19	20	21	22	Lì qiū		27	28	29	30	1	2	3	
	◑	11	12	13	14	15	16	0:22	33	2463089		21	22	23	24	25	26	27			23	24	25	26	27	28	29		MESORĒ 1747	4	5	6	7	8	9	10	NAḤASĒ 2023
	17	●	19	20	21	22	23	4:31	34	2463096		28	29	30	1	2	3	4	Mon 5h46m8p		30	1	2	3	4	5	6	Chǔ shǔ		11	12	13[h]	14	15	16	17	
	24	◐	26	27	28	29	30	18:39	35	2463103	ELUL 5791	5	6	7	8	9	10	11		MONTH 7 Xīn-Hài	7[e]	8	9	10	11	12	13			18	19	20	21	22	23	24	
	31	○	2	3	4	5	6	9:19	36	2463110		12	13	14	15	16	17	18			14	15[f]	16	17	18	19	20		EPAG. 1747	25	26	27	28	29	30	1	
SEPTEMBER 2031	7	◑	9	10	11	12	13	16:13	37	2463117		19	20	21	22	23	24	25			21	22	23	24	25	26	27	Bái lù		2	3	4	5	6	1[a]	2	PĀG. 2023
	14	15	●	17	18	19	20	18:46	38	2463124		26	27	28	29	1[a]	2[a]	3	Tue 18h30m9p		28	29	30	1	2	3	4		THOOUT 1748	3	4	5	6	7	8	9	MASKARAM 2024
	21	22	23[d]	◐	25	26	27	1:19	39	2463131	TISHRI 5792	4	5	6	7	8	9	10[b]		MONTH 8 Xīn-Hài	5*	6	7	8	9	10	11	Qiū fēn		10	11	12	13	14	15	16	
	28	29	○	1	2	3	4	18:57	40	2463138		11	12	13	14	15[c]	16	17			12	13	14	15[g]	16	17	18			17[b]	18	19	20	21	22	23	
OCTOBER 2031	5	6	7	◑	9	10	11	10:49	41	2463145		18	19	20	21	22	23	24			19	20	21	22	23	24	25	Hán lù		24	25	26	27	28	29	30	
	12	13	14	15	●	17	18	8:20	42	2463152		25	26	27	28	29	30	1	Thu 7h14m10p		26	27	28	29	1	2	3			1	2	3	4	5	6	7	
	19	20	21	22	◐	24	25	7:35	43	2463159	ḤESHVAN 5792	2	3	4	5	6	7	8		MONTH 9 Xīn-Hài	4	5	6	7	8	9[h]	10	Shuāng jiàng	PAOPE 1748	8	9	10	11	12	13	14	TEQEMT 2024
	26	27	28	29	○	31	1	7:32	44	2463166		9	10	11	12	13	14	15			11	12	13	14	15	16	17			15	16	17	18	19	20	21	
NOVEMBER 2031	2	3	4	5	6	◑	8	7:01	45	2463173		16	17	18	19	20	21	22			18	19	20	21	22	23	24	Lì dōng		22	23	24	25	26	27	28	
	9	10	11	12	13	●	15	21:08	46	2463180		23	24	25	26	27	28	29			25	26	27	28	29	30	1			29	30	1	2	3	4	5	
	16	17	18	19	20	◐	22	14:44	47	2463187	KISLEV 5792	1	2	3	4	5	6	7	Fri 19h58m11p	MONTH 10 Xīn-Hài	2	3	4	5	6*	7	8	Xiǎo xuě	ATHŌR 1748	6	7	8	9	10	11	12	ḪEDĀR 2024
	23	24	25	26	27	○	29	23:17	48	2463194		8	9	10	11	12	13	14			9	10	11	12	13	14	15			13	14	15	16	17	18	19	
	30	1	2	3	4	5	6		49	2463201		15	16	17	18	19	20	21[d]			16	17	18	19	20	21	22			20	21	22	23	24	25	26	
DECEMBER 2031	◑	8	9	10	11	12	13	3:19	50	2463208		22	23	24	25[e]	26[e]	27[e]	28[e]			23	24	25	26	27	28	29	Dà xuě		27	28	29	30	1	2	3	
	●	15	16	17	18	19	◐	9:05 23:59	51	2463215		29[e]	30[e]	1[e]	2[e]	3	4	5	Sun 8h42m12p	MONTH 11 Xīn-Hài	1	2	3	4	5	6	7		KOIAK 1748	4	5	6	7	8	9	10	TĀKHŚĀŚ 2024
	21	22[e]	23	24	25	26	27		52	2463222	TEVETH 5792	6	7	8	9	10	11	12			8	9[i]	10	11	12	13	14	Dōng zhì		11	12	13	14	15	16	17	
	○	29	30	31	1	2	3	17:3	1	2463229		13	14	15	16	17	18	19			15	16	17	18	19	20	21			18	19	20	21	22	23	24	

Gregorian:
[a]New Year
[b]Spring (19:40)
[c]Summer (13:16)
[d]Autumn (5:14)
[e]Winter (1:54)
● New moon
◐ First quarter moon
○ Full moon
◑ Last quarter moon

Hebrew:
[a]New Year
[b]Yom Kippur
[c]Sukkot
[d]Winter starts
[e]Ḥanukkah
[f]Purim
[g]Passover
[h]Shavuot
[i]Fast of Av

Chinese:
‡Leap year
[a]New Year (4729, Pig)
[b]Lantern Festival
[c]Qīngmíng
[d]Dragon Festival
[e]Qīqiǎo
[f]Hungry Ghosts
[g]Mid-Autumn Festival
[h]Double-Ninth Festival
[i]Dōngzhì
*Start of 60-name cycle

Coptic/Ethiopic:
‡Leap year
[a]New Year
[b]Building of the Cross
[c]Christmas
[d]Jesus's Circumcision
[e]Epiphany
[f]Easter
[g]Mary's Announcement
[h]Jesus's Transfiguration

PERSIAN (ASTRONOMICAL) 1409/1410

Month	Sun	Mon	Tue	Wed	Thu	Fri	Sat
DEY 1409	8	9	10	11	12	13	14
	15	16	17	18	19	20	21
	22	23	24	25	26	27	28
BAHMAN 1409	29	30	1	2	3	4	5
	6	7	8	9	10	11	12
	13	14	15	16	17	18	19
	20	21	22	23	24	25	26
ESFAND 1409	27	28	29	30	1	2	3
	4	5	6	7	8	9	10
	11	12	13	14	15	16	17
	18	19	20	21	22	23	24
FARVARDĪN 1410	25	26	27	28	29	1[a]	2
	3	4	5	6	7	8	9
	10	11	12	13[b]	14	15	16
	17	18	19	20	21	22	23
	24	25	26	27	28	29	30
ORDĪBEHEŠT 1410	31	1	2	3	4	5	6
	7	8	9	10	11	12	13
	14	15	16	17	18	19	20
	21	22	23	24	25	26	27
XORDĀD 1410	28	29	30	31	1	2	3
	4	5	6	7	8	9	10
	11	12	13	14	15	16	17
	18	19	20	21	22	23	24
	25	26	27	28	29	30	31
TĪR 1410	1	2	3	4	5	6	7
	8	9	10	11	12	13	14
	15	16	17	18	19	20	21
	22	23	24	25	26	27	28
MORDĀD 1410	29	30	31	1	2	3	4
	5	6	7	8	9	10	11
	12	13	14	15	16	17	18
	19	20	21	22	23	24	25
SHAHRĪVAR 1410	26	27	28	29	30	31	1
	2	3	4	5	6	7	8
	9	10	11	12	13	14	15
	16	17	18	19	20	21	22
	23	24	25	26	27	28	29
MEHR 1410	30	31	1	2	3	4	5
	6	7	8	9	10	11	12
	13	14	15	16	17	18	19
	20	21	22	23	24	25	26
ĀBĀN 1410	27	28	29	30	1	2	3
	4	5	6	7	8	9	10
	11	12	13	14	15	16	17
	18	19	20	21	22	23	24
ĀZAR 1410	25	26	27	28	29	30	1
	2	3	4	5	6	7	8
	9	10	11	12	13	14	15
	16	17	18	19	20	21	22
	23	24	25	26	27	28	29
DEY 1410	30	1	2	3	4	5	6
	7	8	9	10	11	12	13

HINDU LUNAR 2087/2088‡

Month	Sun	Mon	Tue	Wed	Thu	Fri	Sat
PAUSHA 2087	5	6	7	8	9	10	11
	12	13	14	15	16	17	18
	19	20	21	22	23	24	25
	26	27	28	29	30	**1**	3
MĀGHA 2087	4	5	6	7	8	9	10
	10	11	12	13	14	15	16
	17	18	19	20	21	22	23
	24	**25**	27	28	29[h]	30	1
PHĀLGUNA 2087	2	3	4	5	6	7	8
	9	10	11	12	*12*	13	14
	15[i]	16	17	18	**19**	21	22
	23	24	25	26	27	28	29
CHAITRA 2088	30	1[a]	2	3	4	5	6
	7	8	9[b]	10	11	12	13
	14	15	16	17	18	19	20
	21	22	**23**	25	26	27	28
VAIŚĀKHA 2088	29	30	1	2	3	4	5
	6	*6*	7	8	9	10	11
	12	13	14	15	**16**	18	19
	20	21	22	23	24	25	26
JYAISHṬHA 2088	27	28	29	30	1	2	3
	4	5	6	7	8	9	10
	11	12	13	14	15	16	17
	18	**19**	21	22	23	24	25
ĀSHĀḌHA 2088	26	27	28	29	30	1	2
	2	3	4	5	6	7	8
	9	10	11	**12**	14	15	16
	17	18	19	20	21	22	23
	24	25	26	27	28	29	30
ŚRĀVAṆA 2088	1	2	3	4	5	6	7
	8	9	10	11	12	13	14
	15	17	18	19	20	21	22
	23[c]	24	25	26	27	28	29
LEAP BHĀDRAPADA 2088	*29*	30	1	2	3	4	5
	6	7	**8**	10	11	12	13
	14	15	16	17	18	19	20
	21	22	23	24	25	26	27
BHĀDRAPADA 2088	28	29	30	1	2	3	4[d]
	5	6	7	8	9	10	**11**
	13	14	15	16	17	18	19
	20	21	22	23	24	*24*	25
ĀŚVINA 2088	26	27	28	29	30	1	2
	3	4	**5**	7	8[e]	9[e]	10[e]
	11	12	13	14	15	16	17
	18	19	20	21	22	23	24
KĀRTTIKA 2088	25	26	27	28	29	30	1[f]
	2	3	4	5	6	7	8
	9	11	12	13	14	15	16
	17	18	*18*	19	20	21	22
	23	24	25	26	27	28	29
MĀRGAŚĪRA 2088	30	1	2	**3**	5	6	7
	8	9	10	11[g]	12	13	14
	15	16	17	18	19	20	*20*

HINDU SOLAR 1952/1953

Month	Sun	Mon	Tue	Wed	Thu	Fri	Sat
PAUSHA 1952	14	15	16	17	18	19	20
	21	22	23	24	25	26	27
MĀGHA 1952	28	29	1[b]	2	3	4	5
	6	7	8	9	10	11	12
	13	14	15	16	17	18	19
	20	21	22	23	24	25	26
PHĀLGUNA 1952	27	28	29	30	1	2	3
	4	5	6	7	8	9	10
	11	12	13	14	15	16	17
	18	19	20	21	22	23	24
CHAITRA 1952	25	26	27	28	29	30	1
	2	3	4	5	6	7	8
	9	10	11	12	13	14	15
	16	17	18	19	20	21	22
	23	24	25	26	27	28	29
VAIŚĀKHA 1953	30	1[a]	2	3	4	5	6
	7	8	9	10	11	12	13
	14	15	16	17	18	19	20
	21	22	23	24	25	26	27
JYAISHṬHA 1953	28	29	30	31	1	2	3
	4	5	6	7	8	9	10
	11	12	13	14	15	16	17
	18	19	20	21	22	23	24
	25	26	27	28	29	30	31
ĀSHĀḌHA 1953	1	2	3	4	5	6	7
	8	9	10	11	12	13	14
	15	16	17	18	19	20	21
	22	23	24	25	26	27	28
ŚRĀVAṆA 1953	29	30	31	32	1	2	3
	4	5	6	7	8	9	10
	11	12	13	14	15	16	17
	18	19	20	21	22	23	24
	25	26	27	28	29	30	31
BHĀDRAPADA 1953	1	2	3	4	5	6	7
	8	9	10	11	12	13	14
	15	16	17	18	19	20	21
	22	23	24	25	26	27	28
ĀŚVINA 1953	29	30	31	1	2	3	4
	5	6	7	8	9	10	11
	12	13	14	15	16	17	18
	19	20	21	22	23	24	25
KĀRTTIKA 1953	26	27	28	29	30	31	1
	2	3	4	5	6	7	8
	9	10	11	12	13	14	15
	16	17	18	19	20	21	22
	23	24	25	26	27	28	29
MĀRGAŚĪRA 1953	30	1	2	3	4	5	6
	7	8	9	10	11	12	13
	14	15	16	17	18	19	20
	21	22	23	24	25	26	27
PAUSHA 1953	28	29	1	2	3	4	5
	6	7	8	9	10	11	12
	13	14	15	16	17	18	19

ISLAMIC (ASTRONOMICAL) 1452/1453

Month	Sun	Mon	Tue	Wed	Thu	Fri	Sat
RAMAḌĀN 1452	4	5	6	7	8	9	10
	11	12	13	14	15	16	17
	18	19	20	21	22	23	24
SHAWWĀL 1452	25	26	27	28	29	1[f]	2
	3	4	5	6	7	8	9
	10	11	12	13	14	15	16
	17	18	19	20	21	22	23
	24	25	26	27	28	29	30
DHU AL-QA'DA 1452	1	2	3	4	5	6	7
	8	9	10	11	12	13	14
	15	16	17	18	19	20	21
	22	23	24	25	26	27	28
DHU AL-ḤIJJA 1452	29	1	2	3	4	5	6
	7	8	9	10[g]	11	12	13
	14	15	16	17	18	19	20
	21	22	23	24	25	26	27
MUḤARRAM 1453	28	29	30	1[a]	2	3	4
	5	6	7	8	9	10[b]	11
	12	13	14	15	16	17	18
	19	20	21	22	23	24	25
ṢAFAR 1453	26	27	28	29	30	1	2
	3	4	5	6	7	8	9
	10	11	12	13	14	15	16
	17	18	19	20	21	22	23
	24	25	26	27	28	29	30
RABĪ' I 1453	1	2	3	4	5	6	7
	8	9	10	11	12[c]	13	14
	15	16	17	18	19	20	21
	22	23	24	25	26	27	28
RABĪ' II 1453	29	30	1	2	3	4	5
	6	7	8	9	10	11	12
	13	14	15	16	17	18	19
	20	21	22	23	24	25	26
JUMĀDĀ I 1453	27	28	29	30	1	2	3
	4	5	6	7	8	9	10
	11	12	13	14	15	16	17
	18	19	20	21	22	23	24
JUMĀDĀ II 1453	25	26	27	28	29	1	2
	3	4	5	6	7	8	9
	10	11	12	13	14	15	16
	17	18	19	20	21	22	23
RAJAB 1453	24	25	26	27	28	29	1
	2	3	4	5	6	7	8
	9	10	11	12	13	14	15
	16	17	18	19	20	21	22
	23	24	25	26	27[d]	28	29
SHA'BĀN 1453	1	2	3	4	5	6	7
	8	9	10	11	12	13	14
	15	16	17	18	19	20	21
	22	23	24	25	26	27	28
RAMAḌĀN 1453	29	30	1[e]	2	3	4	5
	6	7	8	9	10	11	12
	13	14	15	16	17	18	19

GREGORIAN 2031

Julian (Sun)	Sun	Mon	Tue	Wed	Thu	Fri	Sat	Month
Dec 16	29	30	31	1	2	3	4	JANUARY 2031
	5	6	7[a]	8	9	10	11	
Dec 30	12	13	14[b]	15	16	17	18	
	19	20	21	22	23	24	25	
Jan 13	26	27	28	29	30	31	1	FEBRUARY 2031
	2	3	4	5	6	7	8	
Jan 27	9	10	11	12	13	14	15	
	16	17	18	19	20	21	22	
Feb 10	23	24	25	26[c]	27	28	1	MARCH 2031
	2[d]	3	4	5	6	7	8	
Feb 24	9	10	11	12	13	14	15	
	16	17	18	19	20	21	22	
Mar 10	23	24	25	26	27	28	29	
	30	31	1	2	3	4	5	APRIL 2031
Mar 24	6	7	8	9	10	11	12	
	13[e]	14	15	16	17	18	19	
Apr 7	20	21	22	23	24	25	26	
	27	28	29	30	1	2	3	MAY 2031
Apr 21	4	5	6	7	8	9	10	
	11	12	13	14	15	16	17	
May 5	18	19	20	21	22	23	24	
	25	26	27	28	29	30	31	
May 19	1	2	3	4	5	6	7	JUNE 2031
	8	9	10	11	12	13	14	
Jun 2	15	16	17	18	19	20	21	
	22	23	24	25	26	27	28	
Jun 16	29	30	1	2	3	4	5	JULY 2031
	6	7	8	9	10	11	12	
Jun 30	13	14	15	16	17	18	19	
	20	21	22	23	24	25	26	
Jul 14	27	28	29	30	31	1	2	AUGUST 2031
	3	4	5	6	7	8	9	
Jul 28	10	11	12	13	14	15	16	
	17	18	19	20	21	22	23	
Aug 11	24	25	26	27	28	29	30	
	31	1	2	3	4	5	6	SEPTEMBER 2031
Aug 25	7	8	9	10	11	12	13	
	14	15	16	17	18	19	20	
Sep 8	21	22	23	24	25	26	27	
	28	29	30	1	2	3	4	OCTOBER 2031
Sep 22	5	6	7	8	9	10	11	
	12	13	14	15	16	17	18	
Oct 6	19	20	21	22	23	24	25	
	26	27	28	29	30	31	1	NOVEMBER 2031
Oct 20	2	3	4	5	6	7	8	
	9	10	11	12	13	14	15	
Nov 3	16	17	18	19	20	21	22	
	23	24	25	26	27	28	29	
Nov 17	30[g]	1	2	3	4	5	6	DECEMBER 2031
	7	8	9	10	11	12	13	
Dec 1	14	15	16	17	18	19	20	
	21	22	23	24	25[h]	26	27	
Dec 15	28	29	30	31	1	2	3	

Persian: [a]New Year; [b]Sizdeh Bedar

Hindu Lunar: ‡Leap year; [a]New Year (Virodhakṛit); [b]Birthday of Rāma; [c]Birthday of Krishna; [d]Ganēśa Chaturthī; [e]Dashara; [f]Diwali; [g]Birthday of Vishnu; [h]Night of Śiva; [i]Holi

Hindu Solar: [a]New Year (Krodhana); [b]Pongal

Islamic: [a]New Year; [b]'Ashūrā'; [c]Prophet's Birthday; [d]Ascent of the Prophet; [e]Start of Ramaḍān; [f]'Id al-Fiṭr; [g]'Id al-'Aḍḥā

Gregorian: [a]Orthodox Christmas; [b]Julian New Year; [c]Ash Wednesday; [d]Feast of Orthodoxy; [e]Easter (also Orthodox); [g]Advent; [h]Christmas

2032

Month	Sun	Mon	Tue	Wed	Thu	Fri	Sat	Lunar Phases	ISO WEEK (Mon)	JULIAN DAY (Sun noon)	HEBREW 5792/5793‡	Sun	Mon	Tue	Wed	Thu	Fri	Sat	Molad	CHINESE Xīn-Hài‡/Rén-Zǐ	Sun	Mon	Tue	Wed	Thu	Fri	Sat	Solar Term	COPTIC 1748/1749	Sun	Mon	Tue	Wed	Thu	Fri	Sat	ETHIOPIC 2024/2025
GREGORIAN 2032‡	○	29	30	31	1[a]	2	3	17:32	1	2463229		13	14	15	16	17	18	19			15	16	17	18	19	20	21			18	19	20	21	22	23	24	
	4	◑	6	7	8	9	10	22:03	2	2463236	TEVETH 5792	20	21	22	23	24	25	26		MONTH 11 Xīn-Hài	22	23	24	25	26	27	28		KOIAK 1748	25	26	27	28	29[c]	30	1	TĀKHŚĀŚ 2024
JANUARY 2032	11	●	13	14	15	16	17	20:05	3	2463243		27	28	29	1	2	3	4	Mon 21h 28m 13p		29	30	1	2	3	4	5	Xiǎo hán		2	3	4	5	6[d]	7	8	
	18	◐	20	21	22	23	24	12:13	4	2463250		5	6	7	8	9	10	11		MONTH 12 Xīn-Hài	6	7*	**8**	9	10	11	12	Dà hán	TÔBE 1748	9	10	11[e]	12	13	14	15	ṬER 2024
	25	26	○	28	29	30	31	12:51	5	2463257	SHEVAT 5792	12	13	14	15	16	17	18			13	14	15	16	17	18	19			16	17	18	19	20	21	22	
	1	2	3	◑	5	6	7	13:48	6	2463264		19	20	21	22	23	24	25			20	21	22	23	24	25	26	Lì chūn		23	24	25	26	27	28	29	
	8	9	10	●	12	13	14	6:23	7	2463271		26	27	28	29	30	1	2	Wed 10h 10m 14p		27	28	29	1[a]	2	3	4			30	1	2	3	4	5	6	
FEBRUARY 2032	15	16	17	◐	19	20	21	3:28	8	2463278		3	4	5	6	7	8	9		MONTH 1 Rén-Zǐ	5	6	7	8	**9**	10	11	Yǔ shuǐ	MESHIR 1748	7	8	9	10	11	12	13	YAKĀTIT 2024
	22	23	24	25	○	27	28	7:42	9	2463285	ADAR 5792	10	11	12	13	14[f]	15	16			12	13	14	15[b]	16	17	18			14	15	16	17	18	19	20	
	29	1	2	3	4	◑	6	1:46	10	2463292		17	18	19	20	21	22	23			19	20	21	22	23	24	25	Jīng zhé		21	22	23	24	25	26	27	
	7	8	9	10	●	12	13	16:23	11	2463299		24	25	26	27	28	29	1	Thu 22h 54m 15p		26	27	28	29	30	1	2			28	29	30	1	2	3	4	
MARCH 2032	14	15	16	17	◐	19	20[b]	20:55	12	2463306		2	3	4	5	6	7	8		MONTH 2 Rén-Zǐ	3	4	5	6	7	8*	**9**	Chūn fēn	PAREMOTEP 1748	5	6	7	8	9	10	11	MAGĀBIT 2024
	21	22	23	24	25	26	○	0:45	13	2463313	NISAN 5792	9	10	11	12	13	14	15[g]			10	11	12	13	14	15	16			12	13	14	15	16	17	18	
	28	29	30	31	1	2	◑	10:09	14	2463320		16	17	18	19	20	21	22			17	18	19	20	21	22	23			19	20	21	22	23	24	25	
	4	5	6	7	8	9	●	2:38	15	2463327		23	24	25	26	27	28	29			24[c]	25	26	27	28	29	1	Qīng míng		26	27	28	29	30	1	2	
APRIL 2032	11	12	13	14	15	16	◐	15:23	16	2463334		30	1	2	3	4	5	6	Sat 11h 38m 16p	MONTH 3 Rén-Zǐ	2	3	4	5	6	7	8		PARMOUTE 1748	3	4	5	6	7	8	9	MIYĀZYĀ 2024
	18	19	20	21	22	23	24		17	2463341		7	8	9	10	11	12	13			9	**10**	11	12	13	14	15	Gǔ yǔ		10	11	12	13	14	15	16	
	○	26	27	28	29	30	1	15:09	18	2463348	IYYAR 5792	14	15	16	17	18	19	20			16	17	18	19	20	21	22			17	18	19	20	21	22	23	
	◑	3	4	5	6	7	8	16:01	19	2463355		21	22	23	24	25	26	27			23	24	25	26	27	28	29	Lì xià		24[f]	25	26	27	28	29[g]	30	
MAY 2032	●	10	11	12	13	14	15	13:34	20	2463362		28	29	1	2	3	4	5	Mon 0h 22m 17p		1	2	3	4	5	6	7			1	2	3	4	5	6	7	
	16	◐	18	19	20	21	22	9:42	21	2463369		6[h]	7	8	9	10	11	12		MONTH 4 Rén-Zǐ	8	9	10*	11	**12**	13	14	Xiǎo mǎn	PASHONS 1748	8	9	10	11	12	13	14	GENBOT 2024
	23	24	○	26	27	28	29	2:36	22	2463376	SIVAN 5792	13	14	15	16	17	18	19			15	16	17	18	19	20	21			15	16	17	18	19	20	21	
	30	◑	1	2	3	4	5	20:50	23	2463383		20	21	22	23	24	25	26			22	23	24	25	26	27	28	Máng zhòng		22	23	24	25	26	27	28	
	6	7	●	9	10	11	12	1:31	24	2463390		27	28	29	30	1	2	3			29	30	1	2	3	4	5[d]			29	30	1	2	3	4	5	
JUNE 2032	13	14	15	◐	17	18	19	2:59	25	2463397		4	5	6	7	8	9	10	Tue 13h 7m 0p	MONTH 5 Rén-Zǐ	6	7	8	9	10	11	12		PAÔNE 1748	6	7	8	9	10	11	12	SANĒ 2024
	20[c]	21	22	○	24	25	26	11:31	26	2463404	TAMMUZ 5792	11	12	13	14	15	16	17			13	**14**	15	16	17	18	19	Xià zhì		13	14	15	16	17	18	19	
	27	28	29	◑	1	2	3	2:11	27	2463411		18	19	20	21	22	23	24			20	21	22	23	24	25	26			20	21	22	23	24	25	26	
	4	5	6	●	8	9	10	14:40	28	2463418		25	26	27	28	29	1	2			27	28	29	1	2	3	4	Xiǎo shǔ		27	28	29	30	1	2	3	
JULY 2032	11	12	13	14	◐	16	17	18:31	29	2463425		3	4	5	6	7	8	9	Thu 1h 51m 1p	MONTH 6 Rén-Zǐ	5	6	7	8	9	10	11*		EPÊP 1748	4	5	6	7	8	9	10	ḤAMLĒ 2024
	18	19	20	21	○	23	24	18:51	30	2463432	AV 5792	10[i]	11	12	13	14	15	16			12	13	14	15	**16**	17	18	Dà shǔ		11	12	13	14	15	16	17	
	25	26	27	28	◑	30	31	9:24	31	2463439		17	18	19	20	21	22	23			19	20	21	22	23	24	25			18	19	20	21	22	23	24	
	1	2	3	4	5	●	7	5:10	32	2463446		24	25	26	27	28	29	30			26	27	28	29	30	1	2	Lì qiū		25	26	27	28	29	30	1	
AUGUST 2032	8	9	10	11	12	13	◐	7:50	33	2463453		1	2	3	4	5	6	7	Fri 14h 35m 2p	MONTH 7 Rén-Zǐ	3	4	5	6	7[e]	8	9		MESORÊ 1748	2	3	4	5	6	7	8	NAHASĒ 2024
	15	16	17	18	19	20	○	1:46	34	2463460	ELUL 5792	8	9	10	11	12	13	14			10	11	12	13	14	15[f]	16			9	10	11	12	13[h]	14	15	
	22	23	24	25	26	◑	28	19:32	35	2463467		15	16	17	18	19	20	21			**17**	18	19	20	21	22	23	Chǔ shǔ		16	17	18	19	20	21	22	
	29	30	31	1	2	3	●	20:55	36	2463474		22	23	24	25	26	27	28			24	25	26	27	28	29	30			23	24	25	26	27	28	29	
	5	6	7	8	9	10	11		37	2463481		29	1[a]	2[a]	3	4	5	6	Sun 3h 19m 3p		1	2	3	4	5	6	7	Bái lù	EPAG. 1748	30	1	2	3	4	5	1[a]	PĀG. 2024
SEPTEMBER 2032	◐	13	14	15	16	17	18	18:48	38	2463488		7	8	9	10[b]	11	12	13		MONTH 8 Rén-Zǐ	8	9	10	11*	12	13	14			2	3	4	5	6	7	8	
	○	20	21	22[d]	23	24	25	9:29	39	2463495	TISHRI 5793	14	15[c]	16	17	18	19	20			15[g]	16	17	**18**	19	20	21	Qiū fēn	THOOUT 1749	9	10	11	12	13	14	15	MASKARAM 2025
	◑	27	28	29	30	1	2	9:11	40	2463502		21	22	23	24	25	26	27			22	23	24	25	26	27	28			16	17[b]	18	19	20	21	22	
	3	●	5	6	7	8	9	13:25	41	2463509		28	29	30	1	2	3	4			29	1	2	3	4	5	6	Hán lù		23	24	25	26	27	28	29	
OCTOBER 2032	10	11	◐	13	14	15	16	3:46	42	2463516	HESHVAN 5793	5	6	7	8	9	10	11	Mon 16h 3m 4p	MONTH 9 Rén-Zǐ	7	8	9[h]	10	11	12	13			30	1	2	3	4	5	6	
	17	○	19	20	21	22	23	18:57	43	2463523		12	13	14	15	16	17	18			14	15	16	17	18	19	**20**	Shuāng jiàng	PAOPE 1749	7	8	9	10	11	12	13	TEQEMT 2025
	24	25	◑	27	28	29	30	2:28	44	2463530		19	20	21	22	23	24	25			21	22	23	24	25	26	27			14	15	16	17	18	19	20	
	31	1	2	●	4	5	6	5:44	45	2463537		26	27	28	29	1	2	3			28	29	30	1	2	3	4			21	22	23	24	25	26	27	
	7	8	9	◐	11	12	13	11:32	46	2463544		4	5	6	7	8	9	10	Wed 4h 47m 5p	MONTH 10 Rén-Zǐ	5	6	7	8	9	10	11	Lì dōng		28	29	30	1	2	3	4	
NOVEMBER 2032	14	15	16	○	18	19	20	6:41	47	2463551	KISLEV 5793	11	12	13	14	15	16	17			12*	13	14	15	16	17	18		ATHÔR 1749	5	6	7	8	9	10	11	HEDĀR 2025
	21	22	23	◑	25	26	27	22:47	48	2463558		18	19	20	21	22	23	24			19	**20**	21	22	23	24	25	Xiǎo xuě		12	13	14	15	16	17	18	
	28	29	30	1	●	3	4	20:52	49	2463565		25[e]	26[e]	27[e]	28[e]	29[e]	1[e]	2[e]			26	27	28	29	30	1	2			19	20	21	22	23	24	25	
	5	6	7	8	◐	10	11	19:07	50	2463572		3[d][e]	4	5	6	7	8	9	Thu 17h 31m 6p		3	4	5	6	7	8	9	Dà xuě		26	27	28	29	30	1	2	
DECEMBER 2032	12	13	14	15	○	17	18	20:48	51	2463579	TEVETH 5793	10	11	12	13	14	15	16		MONTH 11 Rén-Zǐ	10	11	12	13	14	15	16		KOIAK 1749	3	4	5	6	7	8	9	TĀKHŚĀŚ 2025
	19	20	21[e]	22	23	◑	25	20:38	52	2463586		17	18	19	20	21	22	23	Sat 6h 15m 7p		17	18	**19**[i]	20	21	22	23	Dōngzhì		10	11	12	13	14	15	16	
	26	27	28	29	30	31	●	10:16	53	2463593		24	25	26	27	28	29	1			24	25	26	27	28	29	1			17	18	19	20	21	22	23	

‡Leap year
[a]New Year
[b]Spring (1:20)
[c]Summer (19:07)
[d]Autumn (11:09)
[e]Winter (7:55)
● New moon
◐ First quarter moon
○ Full moon
◑ Last quarter moon

‡Leap year
[a]New Year
[b]Yom Kippur
[c]Sukkot
[d]Winter starts
[e]Ḥanukkah
[f]Purim
[g]Passover
[h]Shavuot
[i]Fast of Av

‡Leap year
[a]New Year (4730, Rat)
[b]Lantern Festival
[c]Qīngmíng
[d]Dragon Festival
[e]Qīqiǎo
[f]Hungry Ghosts
[g]Mid-Autumn Festival
[h]Double-Ninth Festival
[i]Dōngzhì
*Start of 60-name cycle

[a]New Year
[b]Building of the Cross
[c]Christmas
[d]Jesus's Circumcision
[e]Epiphany
[f]Easter
[g]Mary's Announcement
[h]Jesus's Transfiguration

2032

PERSIAN (ASTRONOMICAL) 1410/1411

Month	Sun	Mon	Tue	Wed	Thu	Fri	Sat
DEY 1410	7	8	9	10	11	12	13
	14	15	16	17	18	19	20
	21	22	23	24	25	26	27
BAHMAN 1410	28	29	30	1	2	3	4
	5	6	7	8	9	10	11
	12	13	14	15	16	17	18
	19	20	21	22	23	24	25
ESFAND 1410	26	27	28	29	30	1	2
	3	4	5	6	7	8	9
	10	11	12	13	14	15	16
	17	18	19	20	21	22	23
FARVARDĪN 1411	24	25	26	27	28	29	1[a]
	2	3	4	5	6	7	8
	9	10	11	12	13[b]	14	15
	16	17	18	19	20	21	22
	23	24	25	26	27	28	29
ORDĪBEHEŠT 1411	30	31	1	2	3	4	5
	6	7	8	9	10	11	12
	13	14	15	16	17	18	19
	20	21	22	23	24	25	26
XORDĀD 1411	27	28	29	30	31	1	2
	3	4	5	6	7	8	9
	10	11	12	13	14	15	16
	17	18	19	20	21	22	23
	24	25	26	27	28	29	30
TĪR 1411	31	1	2	3	4	5	6
	7	8	9	10	11	12	13
	14	15	16	17	18	19	20
	21	22	23	24	25	26	27
MORDĀD 1411	28	29	30	31	1	2	3
	4	5	6	7	8	9	10
	11	12	13	14	15	16	17
	18	19	20	21	22	23	24
	25	26	27	28	29	30	31
SHAHRĪVAR 1411	1	2	3	4	5	6	7
	8	9	10	11	12	13	14
	15	16	17	18	19	20	21
	22	23	24	25	26	27	28
MEHR 1411	29	30	31	1	2	3	4
	5	6	7	8	9	10	11
	12	13	14	15	16	17	18
	19	20	21	22	23	24	25
ĀBĀN 1411	26	27	28	29	30	1	2
	3	4	5	6	7	8	9
	10	11	12	13	14	15	16
	17	18	19	20	21	22	23
	24	25	26	27	28	29	30
ĀZAR 1411	1	2	3	4	5	6	7
	8	9	10	11	12	13	14
	15	16	17	18	19	20	21
	22	23	24	25	26	27	28
DEY 1411	29	30	1	2	3	4	5
	6	7	8	9	10	11	12

[a]New Year
[b]Sizdeh Bedar

HINDU LUNAR 2088‡/2089

Month	Sun	Mon	Tue	Wed	Thu	Fri	Sat
MĀRGAŚĪRA 2088	15	16	17	18	19	20	20
	21	22	23	24	25	26	**27**
PAUSHA 2088	29	30	1	2	3	4	5
	6	7	8	9	10	11	12
	13	14	15	16	17	18	19
	20	21	22	23	24	25	26
MĀGHA 2088	27	28	29	30	1	**2**	4
	5	6	7	8	9	10	11
	12	13	13	14	15	16	17
	18	19	20	21	22	23	24
PHĀLGUNA 2088	25	**26**	28	29[h]	30	1	2
	3	4	5	6	7	8	9
	10	11	12	13	14	15[i]	16
	16	17	18	**19**	21	22	23
	24	25	26	27	28	29	30
CHAITRA 2089	1[a]	3	4	5	6	6	7
	8[b]	9	10	11	12	13	14
	15	16	17	18	19	20	21
	22	**23**	25	26	27	28	29
VAIŚĀKHA 2089	30	1	2	3	4	5	6
	7	8	9	10	10	11	12
	13	14	15	**16**	18	19	20
	21	22	23	24	25	26	27
JYAISHTHA 2089	28	29	30	1	2	3	4
	5	6	7	8	9	10	11
	12	13	14	15	16	17	18
	19	21	22	23	24	25	26
ĀSHĀḌHA 2089	27	28	29	30	1	2	3
	4	5	6	7	7	8	9
	10	11	**12**	14	15	16	17
	18	19	20	21	22	**23**	25
ŚRĀVAṆA 2089	26	27	28	28	29	30	1
	2	3	4	5	6	7	8
	9	10	11	12	13	14	**15**
	17	18	19	20	21	22	23[c]
	24	25	26	27	28	29	30
BHĀDRAPADA 2089	1	2	3	3[d]	4	5	6
	7	9	10	11	12	13	14
	15	16	17	18	19	**20**	22
	23	24	24	25	26	27	28
ĀŚVINA 2089	29	30	1	2	3	4	5
	6	7	8[e]	9[e]	10[e]	11	**12**
	14	15	16	17	18	19	20
	21	22	23	24	25	26	27
KĀRTTIKA 2089	28	28	29	30	1[f]	2	3
	4	**5**	7	8	9	10	11
	12	13	14	15	16	17	18
	19	20	21	22	23	24	25
MĀRGAŚĪRA 2089	26	27	28	29	30	1	2
	3	4	5	6	7	8	9
	10[g]	12	13	14	15	16	17
	18	19	20	21	21	22	23
	24	25	26	27	28	29	30

‡Leap year
[a]New Year (Paridhāvin)
[b]Birthday of Rāma
[c]Birthday of Krishna
[d]Ganēśa Chaturthī
[e]Dashara
[f]Diwali
[g]Birthday of Vishnu
[h]Night of Śiva
[i]Holi

HINDU SOLAR 1953/1954‡

Month	Sun	Mon	Tue	Wed	Thu	Fri	Sat
PAUSHA 1953	13	14	15	16	17	18	19
	20	21	22	23	24	25	26
MĀGHA 1953	27	28	29	30	1[b]	2	3
	4	5	6	7	8	9	10
	11	12	13	14	15	16	17
	18	19	20	21	22	23	24
PHĀLGUNA 1953	25	26	27	28	29	1	2
	3	4	5	6	7	8	9
	10	11	12	13	14	15	16
	17	18	19	20	21	22	23
	24	25	26	27	28	29	30
CHAITRA 1953	1	2	3	4	5	6	7
	8	9	10	11	12	13	14
	15	16	17	18	19	20	21
	22	23	24	25	26	27	28
VAIŚĀKHA 1954	29	30	1[a]	2	3	4	5
	6	7	8	9	10	11	12
	13	14	15	16	17	18	19
	20	21	22	23	24	25	26
JYAISHTHA 1954	27	28	29	30	31	1	2
	3	4	5	6	7	8	9
	10	11	12	13	14	15	16
	17	18	19	20	21	22	23
	24	25	26	27	28	29	30
ĀSHĀḌHA 1954	31	32	1	2	3	4	5
	6	7	8	9	10	11	12
	13	14	15	16	17	18	19
	20	21	22	23	24	25	26
ŚRĀVAṆA 1954	27	28	29	30	31	1	2
	3	4	5	6	7	8	9
	10	11	12	13	14	15	16
	17	18	19	20	21	22	23
	24	25	26	27	28	29	30
BHĀDRAPADA 1954	31	32	1	2	3	4	5
	6	7	8	9	10	11	12
	13	14	15	16	17	18	19
	20	21	22	23	24	25	26
ĀŚVINA 1954	27	28	29	30	31	1	2
	3	4	5	6	7	8	9
	10	11	12	13	14	15	16
	17	18	19	20	21	22	23
	24	25	26	27	28	29	30
KĀRTTIKA 1954	1	2	3	4	5	6	7
	8	9	10	11	12	13	14
	15	16	17	18	19	20	21
	22	23	24	25	26	27	28
MĀRGAŚĪRA 1954	29	30	1	2	3	4	5
	6	7	8	9	10	11	12
	13	14	15	16	17	18	19
	20	21	22	23	24	25	26
PAUSHA 1954	27	28	29	30	1	2	3
	4	5	6	7	8	9	10
	11	12	13	14	15	16	17

‡Leap year
[a]New Year (Kshaya)
[b]Pongal

ISLAMIC (ASTRONOMICAL) 1453/1454‡

Month	Sun	Mon	Tue	Wed	Thu	Fri	Sat
RAMAḌĀN 1453	13	14	15	16	17	18	19
	20	21	22	23	24	25	26
SHAWWĀL 1453	27	28	29	1[f]	2	3	4
	5	6	7	8	9	10	11
	12	13	14	15	16	17	18
	19	20	21	22	23	24	25
DHU AL-QA'DA 1453	26	27	28	29	1	2	3
	4	5	6	7	8	9	10
	11	12	13	14	15	16	17
	18	19	20	21	22	23	24
DHU AL-ḤIJJA 1453	25	26	27	28	29	30	1
	2	3	4	5	6	7	8
	9	10[g]	11	12	13	14	15
	16	17	18	19	20	21	22
	23	24	25	26	27	28	29
MUḤARRAM 1454	1[a]	2[A]	3	4	5	6	7
	8	9	10[b]	11	12	13	14
	15	16	17	18	19	20	21
	22	23	24	25	26	27	28
ṢAFAR 1454	29	30	1	2	3	4	5
	6	7	8	9	10	11	12
	13	14	15	16	17	18	19
	20	21	22	23	24	25	26
RABĪ' I 1454	27	28	29	30	1	2	3
	4	5	6	7	8	9	10
	11	12[c]	13	14	15	16	17
	18	19	20	21	22	23	24
RABĪ' II 1454	25	26	27	28	29	30	1
	2	3	4	5	6	7	8
	9	10	11	12	13	14	15
	16	17	18	19	20	21	22
	23	24	25	26	27	28	29
JUMĀDĀ I 1454	1	2	3	4	5	6	7
	8	9	10	11	12	13	14
	15	16	17	18	19	20	21
	22	23	24	25	26	27	28
JUMĀDĀ II 1454	29	30	1	2	3	4	5
	6	7	8	9	10	11	12
	13	14	15	16	17	18	19
	20	21	22	23	24	25	26
RAJAB 1454	27	28	29	1	2	3	4
	5	6	7	8	9	10	11
	12	13	14	15	16	17	18
	19	20	21	22	23	24	25
SHA'BĀN 1454	26	27[d]	28	29	30	1	2
	3	4	5	6	7	8	9
	10	11	12	13	14	15	16
	17	18	19	20	21	22	23
RAMAḌĀN 1454	24	25	26	27	28	29	1[e]
	2	3	4	5	6	7	8
	9	10	11	12	13	14	15
	16	17	18	19	20	21	22
	23	24	25	26	27	28	29

‡Leap year
[a]New Year
[A]New Year (Arithmetic)
[b]'Ashūrā'
[c]Prophet's Birthday
[d]Ascent of the Prophet
[e]Start of Ramaḍān
[f]'Id al-Fiṭr
[g]'Id al-'Aḍḥā

GREGORIAN 2032‡

Julian‡ (Sun)	Sun	Mon	Tue	Wed	Thu	Fri	Sat	Month
Dec 15	28	29	30	31	1	2	3	JANUARY 2032
	4	5	6	7[a]	8	9	10	
Dec 29	11	12	13	14[b]	15	16	17	
	18	19	20	21	22	23	24	
Jan 12	25	26	27	28	29	30	31	
	1	2	3	4	5	6	7	FEBRUARY 2032
Jan 26	8	9	10	11[c]	12	13	14	
	15	16	17	18	19	20	21	
Feb 9	22	23	24	25	26	27	28	
	29	1	2	3	4	5	6	MARCH 2032
Feb 23	7	8	9	10	11	12	13	
	14	15	16	17	18	19	20	
Mar 8	21[d]	22	23	24	25	26	27	
	28[e]	29	30	31	1	2	3	APRIL 2032
Mar 22	4	5	6	7	8	9	10	
	11	12	13	14	15	16	17	
Apr 5	18	19	20	21	22	23	24	
	25	26	27	28	29	30	1	MAY 2032
Apr 19	2[f]	3	4	5	6	7	8	
	9	10	11	12	13	14	15	
May 3	16	17	18	19	20	21	22	
	23	24	25	26	27	28	29	
May 17	30	31	1	2	3	4	5	JUNE 2032
	6	7	8	9	10	11	12	
May 31	13	14	15	16	17	18	19	
	20	21	22	23	24	25	26	
Jun 14	27	28	29	30	1	2	3	JULY 2032
	4	5	6	7	8	9	10	
Jun 28	11	12	13	14	15	16	17	
	18	19	20	21	22	23	24	
Jul 12	25	26	27	28	29	30	31	
	1	2	3	4	5	6	7	AUGUST 2032
Jul 26	8	9	10	11	12	13	14	
	15	16	17	18	19	20	21	
Aug 9	22	23	24	25	26	27	28	
	29	30	31	1	2	3	4	SEPTEMBER 2032
Aug 23	5	6	7	8	9	10	11	
	12	13	14	15	16	17	18	
Sep 6	19	20	21	22	23	24	25	
	26	27	28	29	30	1	2	OCTOBER 2032
Sep 20	3	4	5	6	7	8	9	
	10	11	12	13	14	15	16	
Oct 4	17	18	19	20	21	22	23	
	24	25	26	27	28	29	30	
Oct 18	31	1	2	3	4	5	6	NOVEMBER 2032
	7	8	9	10	11	12	13	
Nov 1	14	15	16	17	18	19	20	
	21	22	23	24	25	26	27	
Nov 15	28[g]	29	30	1	2	3	4	DECEMBER 2032
	5	6	7	8	9	10	11	
Nov 29	12	13	14	15	16	17	18	
	19	20	21	22	23	24	25[h]	
Dec 13	26	27	28	29	30	31	1	

‡Leap year
[a]Orthodox Christmas
[b]Julian New Year
[c]Ash Wednesday
[d]Feast of Orthodoxy
[e]Easter
[f]Orthodox Easter
[g]Advent
[h]Christmas

2033

Gregorian 2033	Sun	Mon	Tue	Wed	Thu	Fri	Sat	Lunar Phases	ISO WEEK (Mon)	JULIAN DAY (Sun noon)	Hebrew 5793‡/5794	Sun	Mon	Tue	Wed	Thu	Fri	Sat	Molad	Chinese Rén-Zǐ/Guǐ-Chǒu‡	Sun	Mon	Tue	Wed	Thu	Fri	Sat	Solar Term	Coptic 1749/1750	Sun	Mon	Tue	Wed	Thu	Fri	Sat	Ethiopic 2025/2026
	26	27	28	29	30	31	●[a]	10:16	53	2463593		24	25	26	27	28	29	1	Sat 6h15m7p		24	25	26	27	28	29	1		Koiak 1749	17	18	19	20	21	22	23	Tāḫśāś 2025
January 2033	2	3	4	5	6	7	◐	3:33	1	2463600		2	3	4	5	6	7	8			2	3	4	5	6	7	8	Xiǎo hán		24	25	26	27	28	29[c]	30	
	9	10	11	12	13	14	○	13:06	2	2463607	Shevat 5793	9	10	11	12	13	14	15		Month 12 Rén-Zǐ	9	10	11	12	13*	14	15		Tōbe 1749	1	2	3	4	5	6[d]	7	
	16	17	18	19	20	21	22		3	2463614		16	17	18	19	20	21	22			16	17	18	19	**20**	21	22	Dà hán		8	9	10	11[e]	12	13	14	Ṭer 2025
	◑	24	25	26	27	28	29	17:45	4	2463621		23	24	25	26	27	28	29			23	24	25	26	27	28	29			15	16	17	18	19	20	21	
	●	31	1	2	3	4	5	21:59	5	2463628		30	1	2	3	4	5	6	Sun 18h59m8p		30	1[a]	2	3	*4*	5	6	Lì chūn		22	23	24	25	26	27	28	
February 2033	◐	7	8	9	10	11	12	13:33	6	2463635	Adar I 5793	7	8	9	10	11	12	13		Month 1 Guǐ-Chǒu	7	8	9	10	11	12	13			29	30	1	2	3	4	5	
	13	○	15	16	17	18	19	7:03	7	2463642		14	15	16	17	18	19	20			14	15[b]	16	17	18	**19**	20	Yǔ shuǐ	Meshir 1749	6	7	8	9	10	11	12	Yakātit 2025
	20	21	◑	23	24	25	26	11:52	8	2463649		21	22	23	24	25	26	27			21	22	23	24	25	26	27			13	14	15	16	17	18	19	
	27	28	●	2	3	4	5	8:22	9	2463656		28	29	30	1	2	3	4	Tue 7h43m9p		28	29	1	2	3	4	5	Jīng zhé		20	21	22	23	24	25	26	
March 2033	6	7	◐	9	10	11	12	1:26	10	2463663	Adar II 5793	5	6	7	8	9	10	11		Month 2 Guǐ-Chǒu	6	7	8	9	10	11	12		Paremotep 1749	27	28	29	30	1	2	3	
	13	14	15	○	17	18	19	1:36	11	2463670		12	13	14[f]	15	16	17	18			13	14*	15	16	17	18	19			4	5	6	7	8	9	10	Magābit 2025
	20[b]	21	22	23	◑	25	26	1:49	12	2463677		19	20	21	22	23	24	25			**20**	21	22	23	24	25	26	Chūn fēn		11	12	13	14	15	16	17	
	27	28	29	●	31	1	2	17:50	13	2463684		26	27	28	29	1	2	3	Wed 20h27m10p		27	28	29	30	1	2	3			18	19	20	21	22	23	24	
April 2033	3	4	5	◐	7	8	9	15:13	14	2463691	Nisan 5793	4	5	6	7	8	9	10		Month 3 Guǐ-Chǒu	4	5[c]	6	7	8	9	10	Qīng míng		25	26	27	28	29	30	1	
	10	11	12	13	○	15	16	19:16	15	2463698		11	12	13	14	15[g]	16	17			11	12	13	14	15	16	17		Parmoute 1749	2	3	4	5	6	7	8	Miyāzyā 2025
	17	18	19	20	21	◑	23	11:41	16	2463705		18	19	20	21	22	23	24			18	19	20	**21**	22	23	24	Gǔ yǔ		9	10	11	12	13	14	15	
	24	25	26	27	28	●	30	2:45	17	2463712		25	26	27	28	29	30	1	Fri 9h11m11p		25	26	27	28	29	1	2			16[f]	17	18	19	20	21	22	
May 2033	1	2	3	4	5	◐	7	6:44	18	2463719	Iyar 5793	2	3	4	5	6	7	8		Month 4 Guǐ-Chǒu	3	4	5	6	*7*	8	9	Lì xià		23	24	25	26	27	28	29[g]	
	8	9	10	11	12	13	○	10:41	19	2463726		9	10	11	12	13	14	15			10	11	12	13	14	15*	16			30	1	2	3	4	5	6	
	15	16	17	18	19	20	◑	18:28	20	2463733		16	17	18	19	20	21	22			17	18	19	20	21	22	**23**	Xiǎo mǎn	Pashons 1749	7	8	9	10	11	12	13	Genbot 2025
	22	23	24	25	26	27	●	11:35	21	2463740		23	24	25	26	27	28	29			24	25	26	27	28	29	1			14	15	16	17	18	19	20	
	29	30	31	1	2	3	◐	23:38	22	2463747		1	2	3	4	5	6[h]	7	Sat 21h55m12p		2	3	4	5[d]	6	7	8			21	22	23	24	25	26	27	
June 2033	5	6	7	8	9	10	11		23	2463754	Sivan 5793	8	9	10	11	12	13	14		Month 5 Guǐ-Chǒu	9	10	11	12	13	14	15	Máng zhòng		28	29	30	1	2	3	4	
	○	13	14	15	16	17	18	23:18	24	2463761		15	16	17	18	19	20	21			16	17	18	19	20	21	22		Paōne 1749	5	6	7	8	9	10	11	Sanē 2025
	◑	20	21[c]	22	23	24	25	23:28	25	2463768		22	23	24	25	26	27	28			23	24	**25**	26	27	28	29	Xià zhì		12	13	14	15	16	17	18	
	●	27	28	29	30	1	2	21:06	26	2463775		29	30	1	2	3	4	5	Mon 10h39m13p		30	1	2	3	4	5	6			19	20	21	22	23	24	25	
July 2033	3	◐	5	6	7	8	9	17:11	27	2463782	Tammuz 5793	6	7	8	9	10	11	12		Month 6 Guǐ-Chǒu	7	8	9	10	*11*	12	13	Xiǎo shǔ		26	27	28	29	30	1	2	
	10	11	○	13	14	15	16	9:27	28	2463789		13	14	15	16	17	18	19			14	15	16*	17	18	19	20		Epēp 1749	3	4	5	6	7	8	9	Ḥamlē 2025
	17	18	◑	20	21	22	23	4:06	29	2463796		20	21	22	23	24	25	26			21	22	23	24	25	**26**	27	Dà shǔ		10	11	12	13	14	15	16	
	24	25	●	27	28	29	30	8:11	30	2463803		27	28	29	1	2	3	4	Tue 23h23m14p		28	29	1	2	3	4	5			17	18	19	20	21	22	23	
	31	1	2	◐	4	5	6	10:24	31	2463810	Av 5793	5	6	7	8	9[i]	10	11		Month 7 Guǐ-Chǒu	6	7[e]	8	9	10	11	12			24	25	26	27	28	29	30	
August 2033	7	8	9	○	11	12	13	18:07	32	2463817		12	13	14	15	16	17	18			*13*	14	15[f]	16	17	18	19	Lì qiū		1	2	3	4	5	6	7	
	14	15	16	◑	18	19	20	9:42	33	2463824		19	20	21	22	23	24	25			20	21	22	23	24	25	26		Mesorē 1749	8	9	10	11	12	13[h]	14	Naḥasē 2025
	21	22	23	●	25	26	27	21:39	34	2463831		26	27	28	29	30	1	2	Thu 12h7m15p		27	28	**29**	30	1	2	3	Chǔ shǔ		15	16	17	18	19	20	21	
	28	29	30	31	1	◐	3	2:22	35	2463838	Elul 5793	3	4	5	6	7	8	9		Month 8 Guǐ-Chǒu	4	5	6	7	8	9	10			22	23	24	25	26	27	28	
September 2033	4	5	6	7	8	○	10	2:19	36	2463845		10	11	12	13	14	15	16			11	12	13	*14*	15[g]	16	17*	Bái lù	Epag. 1749	29	30	1	2	3	4	5	Pāg. 2025
	11	12	13	14	◑	16	17	17:32	37	2463852		17	18	19	20	21	22	23			18	19	20	21	22	23	24			1[a]	2	3	4	5	6	7	
	18	19	20	21	22[d]	●	24	13:38	38	2463859		24	25	26	27	28	29	1[a]	Sat 0h51m16p		25	26	27	28	29	***1***	2	Qiū fēn	Thoout 1750	8	9	10	11	12	13	14	Maskaram 2026
	25	26	27	28	29	30	◐	16:32	39	2463866	Tishri 5794	2[a]	3	4	5	6	7	8		Month 9 Guǐ-Chǒu	3	4	5	6	7	8	9[h]			15	16	17[b]	18	19	20	21	
October 2033	2	3	4	5	6	7	○	10:57	40	2463873		9	10[b]	11	12	13	14	15[c]			10	11	12	13	14	15	*16*	Hán lù		22	23	24	25	26	27	28	
	9	10	11	12	13	14	◑	4:46	41	2463880		16	17	18	19	20	21	22			17	18	19	20	21	22	23			29	30	1	2	3	4	5	
	16	17	18	19	20	21	22		42	2463887		23	24	25	26	27	28	29			24	25	26	27	28	29	30		Paope 1750	6	7	8	9	10	11	12	Ṭeqemt 2026
	●	24	25	26	27	28	29	7:27	43	2463894		30	1	2	3	4	5	6	Sun 13h35m17p		***1***	2	3	4	5	6	7	Shuāng jiàng		13	14	15	16	17	18	19	
	30	◐	1	2	3	4	5	4:45	44	2463901	Heshvan 5794	7	8	9	10	11	12	13		Month 10 Guǐ-Chǒu	8	9	10	11	12	13	14			20	21	22	23	24	25	26	
November 2033	○	7	8	9	10	11	12	20:31	45	2463908		14	15	16	17	18	19	20			15	*16*	17	18*	19	20	21	Lì dōng		27	28	29	30	1	2	3	
	◑	14	15	16	17	18	19	20:08	46	2463915		21	22	23	24	25	26	27			22	23	24	25	26	27	28		Athōr 1750	4	5	6	7	8	9	10	Ḫedār 2026
	20	21	●	23	24	25	26	1:38	47	2463922		28	29	30	1	2	3	4	Tue 2h20m0p		29	30	*1*	2	3	4	5	Xiǎo xuě		11	12	13	14	15	16	17	
	27	28	◐	30	1	2	3	15:14	48	2463929	Kislev 5794	5	6	7	8	9	10	11		Month 11* Guǐ-Chǒu	6	7	8	9	10	11	12			18	19	20	21	22	23	24	
December 2033	4	5	○	7	8	9	10	7:21	49	2463936		12	13[d]	14	15	16	17	18			13	14	15	*16*	17	18	19	Dà xuě		25	26	27	28	29	30	1	
	11	12	◑	14	15	16	17	15:27	50	2463943		19	20	21	22	23	24	25[e]			20	21	22	23	24	25	26		Koiak 1750	2	3	4	5	6	7	8	Tāḫśāś 2026
	18	19	20	●[e]	22	23	24	18:45	51	2463950		26[e]	27[e]	28[e]	29[e]	30[e]	1[e]	2[e]	Wed 15h4m1p		27	28	29	**30**[i]	1	2	3	Dōng zhì		9	10	11	12	13	14	15	
	25	26	27	28	◐	30	31	0:19	52	2463957	Tevet 5794	3	4	5	6	7	8	9		Leap Month 11 Guǐ-Chǒu	4	5	6	7	8	9	10			16	17	18	19	20	21	22	

[a]New Year
[b]Spring (7:21)
[c]Summer (1:00)
[d]Autumn (16:51)
[e]Winter (13:44)
● New moon
◐ First quarter moon
○ Full moon
◑ Last quarter moon

‡Leap year
[a]New Year
[b]Yom Kippur
[c]Sukkot
[d]Winter starts
[e]Ḥanukkah
[f]Purim
[g]Passover
[h]Shavuot
[i]Fast of Av

‡Leap year
[a]New Year (4731, Ox)
[b]Lantern Festival
[c]Qīngmíng
[d]Dragon Festival
[e]Qīqiǎo
[f]Hungry Ghosts
[g]Mid-Autumn Festival
[h]Double-Ninth Festival
[i]Dōngzhì
*Start of 60-name cycle

[a]New Year
[b]Building of the Cross
[c]Christmas
[d]Jesus's Circumcision
[e]Epiphany
[f]Easter
[g]Mary's Announcement
[h]Jesus's Transfiguration

2033

PERSIAN (ASTRONOMICAL) 1411/1412‡

Month	Sun	Mon	Tue	Wed	Thu	Fri	Sat
DEY 1411	6	7	8	9	10	11	12
	13	14	15	16	17	18	19
	20	21	22	23	24	25	26
	27	28	29	30	1	2	3
BAHMAN 1411	4	5	6	7	8	9	10
	11	12	13	14	15	16	17
	18	19	20	21	22	23	24
	25	26	27	28	29	30	1
ESFAND 1411	2	3	4	5	6	7	8
	9	10	11	12	13	14	15
	16	17	18	19	20	21	22
	23	24	25	26	27	28	29
FARVARDĪN 1412	1[a]	2	3	4	5	6	7
	8	9	10	11	12	13[b]	14
	15	16	17	18	19	20	21
	22	23	24	25	26	27	28
	29	30	31	1	2	3	4
ORDĪBEHEŠT 1412	5	6	7	8	9	10	11
	12	13	14	15	16	17	18
	19	20	21	22	23	24	25
	26	27	28	29	30	31	1
XORDĀD 1412	2	3	4	5	6	7	8
	9	10	11	12	13	14	15
	16	17	18	19	20	21	22
	23	24	25	26	27	28	29
	30	31	1	2	3	4	5
TĪR 1412	6	7	8	9	10	11	12
	13	14	15	16	17	18	19
	20	21	22	23	24	25	26
	27	28	29	30	31	1	2
MORDĀD 1412	3	4	5	6	7	8	9
	10	11	12	13	14	15	16
	17	18	19	20	21	22	23
	24	25	26	27	28	29	30
	31	1	2	3	4	5	6
SHAHRĪVAR 1412	7	8	9	10	11	12	13
	14	15	16	17	18	19	20
	21	22	23	24	25	26	27
	28	29	30	31	1	2	3
MEHR 1412	4	5	6	7	8	9	10
	11	12	13	14	15	16	17
	18	19	20	21	22	23	24
	25	26	27	28	29	30	1
ĀBĀN 1412	2	3	4	5	6	7	8
	9	10	11	12	13	14	15
	16	17	18	19	20	21	22
	23	24	25	26	27	28	29
	30	1	2	3	4	5	6
ĀZAR 1412	7	8	9	10	11	12	13
	14	15	16	17	18	19	20
	21	22	23	24	25	26	27
	28	29	30	1	2	3	4
DEY 1412	5	6	7	8	9	10	11

‡Leap year
[a]New Year
[b]Sizdeh Bedar

HINDU LUNAR 2089/2090

Month	Sun	Mon	Tue	Wed	Thu	Fri	Sat
	24	25	26	27	28	29	30
PAUSHA 2089	1	2	3	**4**	6	7	8
	9	10	11	12	13	14	15
	16	17	18	19	20	21	22
	23	23	24	25	26	27	**28**
	30	1	2	3	4	5	6
MĀGHA 2089	7	8	9	10	11	12	13
	14	15	16	17	18	19	20
	21	22	23	24	25	26	27
	28[h]	29	30	1	2	**3**	5
PHĀLGUNA 2089	6	7	8	9	10	11	12
	13	14	15[i]	16	16	17	18
	19	20	21	22	23	24	25
	26	**27**	29	30	1[a]	2	3
CHAITRA 2090	4	5	6	7	8	9[b]	10
	11	12	13	14	15	16	17
	18	19	20	21	22	23	24
	25	26	27	28	29	30	**1**
VAIŚĀKHA 2090	3	4	5	6	7	8	9
	10	10	11	12	13	14	15
	16	17	18	19	20	21	22
	23	**24**	26	27	28	29	30
JYAISHTHA 2090	1	2	3	4	5	6	7
	8	9	10	11	12	13	14
	15	16	17	18	19	20	21
	22	23	24	25	26	**27**	29
	30	1	2	3	4	5	6
ĀSHĀDHA 2090	6	7	8	9	10	11	12
	13	14	15	16	17	18	**19**
	21	22	23	24	25	26	27
	28	29	30	1	2	3	4
ŚRĀVANA 2090	5	6	7	8	9	10	11
	12	13	14	15	16	17	18
	19	20	21	**22**[c]	24	25	26
	27	28	29	30	1	2	3
BHĀDRAPADA 2090	3[d]	4	5	6	7	8	9
	10	11	12	13	14	**15**	17
	18	19	20	21	22	23	24
	25	26	27	28	29	30	1
ĀŚVINA 2090	2	3	4	5	6	7	8[e]
	9[e]	10[e]	11	12	13	14	15
	16	17	18	**19**	21	22	23
	24	25	26	27	28	28	29
	30	1[f]	2	3	4	5	6
KĀRTTIKA 2090	7	8	9	10	11	12	**13**
	15	16	17	18	19	20	21
	22	23	24	25	26	27	28
	29	30	1	1	2	3	4
MĀRGAŚĪRA 2090	5	**6**	8	9	10	11[g]	12
	13	14	15	16	17	18	19
	20	21	22	23	24	25	26
	27	28	29	30	1	2	3
PAUSHA 2090	4	5	6	7	8	9	10

[a]New Year (Pramādin)
[b]Birthday of Rāma
[c]Birthday of Krishna
[d]Ganēśa Chaturthī
[e]Dashara
[f]Diwali
[g]Birthday of Vishnu
[h]Night of Śiva
[i]Holi

HINDU SOLAR 1954‡/1955

Month	Sun	Mon	Tue	Wed	Thu	Fri	Sat
PAUSHA 1954	11	12	13	14	15	16	17
	18	19	20	21	22	23	24
	25	26	27	28	29	1[b]	2
MĀGHA 1954	3	4	5	6	7	8	9
	10	11	12	13	14	15	16
	17	18	19	20	21	22	23
	24	25	26	27	28	29	1
PHĀLGUNA 1954	2	3	4	5	6	7	8
	9	10	11	12	13	14	15
	16	17	18	19	20	21	22
	23	24	25	26	27	28	29
	30	1	2	3	4	5	6
CHAITRA 1954	7	8	9	10	11	12	13
	14	15	16	17	18	19	20
	21	22	23	24	25	26	27
	28	29	30	31	1[a]	2	3
VAIŚĀKHA 1955	4	5	6	7	8	9	10
	11	12	13	14	15	16	17
	18	19	20	21	22	23	24
	25	26	27	28	29	30	1
JYAISHTHA 1955	2	3	4	5	6	7	8
	9	10	11	12	13	14	15
	16	17	18	19	20	21	22
	23	24	25	26	27	28	29
	30	31	32	1	2	3	4
ĀSHĀDHA 1955	5	6	7	8	9	10	11
	12	13	14	15	16	17	18
	19	20	21	22	23	24	25
	26	27	28	29	30	31	32
	1	2	3	4	5	6	7
ŚRĀVANA 1955	8	9	10	11	12	13	14
	15	16	17	18	19	20	21
	22	23	24	25	26	27	28
	29	30	31	1	2	3	4
BHĀDRAPADA 1955	5	6	7	8	9	10	11
	12	13	14	15	16	17	18
	19	20	21	22	23	24	25
	26	27	28	29	30	31	1
ĀŚVINA 1955	2	3	4	5	6	7	8
	9	10	11	12	13	14	15
	16	17	18	19	20	21	22
	23	24	25	26	27	28	29
	30	1	2	3	4	5	6
KĀRTTIKA 1955	7	8	9	10	11	12	13
	14	15	16	17	18	19	20
	21	22	23	24	25	26	27
	28	29	30	1	2	3	4
MĀRGAŚĪRA 1955	5	6	7	8	9	10	11
	12	13	14	15	16	17	18
	19	20	21	22	23	24	25
	26	27	28	29	30	1	2
PAUSHA 1955	3	4	5	6	7	8	9
	10	11	12	13	14	15	16

‡Leap year
[a]New Year (Prabhava)
[b]Pongal

ISLAMIC (ASTRONOMICAL) 1454‡/1455‡

Month	Sun	Mon	Tue	Wed	Thu	Fri	Sat
RAMAḌĀN 1454	23	24	25	26	27	28	29
SHAWWĀL 1454	30	1[f]	2	3	4	5	6
	7	8	9	10	11	12	13
	14	15	16	17	18	19	20
	21	22	23	24	25	26	27
DHU AL-QA'DA 1454	28	29	1	2	3	4	5
	6	7	8	9	10	11	12
	13	14	15	16	17	18	19
	20	21	22	23	24	25	26
DHU AL-ḤIJJA 1454	27	28	29	1	2	3	4
	5	6	7	8	9	10[g]	11
	12	13	14	15	16	17	18
	19	20	21	22	23	24	25
MUḤARRAM 1455	26	27	28	29	30	1[a]	2
	3	4	5	6	7	8	9
	10[b]	11	12	13	14	15	16
	17	18	19	20	21	22	23
	24	25	26	27	28	29	1
ṢAFAR 1455	2	3	4	5	6	7	8
	9	10	11	12	13	14	15
	16	17	18	19	20	21	22
	23	24	25	26	27	28	29
RABĪ' I 1455	30	1	2	3	4	5	6
	7	8	9	10	11	12[c]	13
	14	15	16	17	18	19	20
	21	22	23	24	25	26	27
RABĪ' II 1455	28	29	30	1	2	3	4
	5	6	7	8	9	10	11
	12	13	14	15	16	17	18
	19	20	21	22	23	24	25
JUMĀDĀ I 1455	26	27	28	29	1	2	3
	4	5	6	7	8	9	10
	11	12	13	14	15	16	17
	18	19	20	21	22	23	24
	25	26	27	28	29	30	1
JUMĀDĀ II 1455	2	3	4	5	6	7	8
	9	10	11	12	13	14	15
	16	17	18	19	20	21	22
	23	24	25	26	27	28	29
RAJAB 1455	1	2	3	4	5	6	7
	8	9	10	11	12	13	14
	15	16	17	18	19	20	21
	22	23	24	25	26	27[d]	28
SHA'BĀN 1455	29	30	1	2	3	4	5
	6	7	8	9	10	11	12
	13	14	15	16	17	18	19
	20	21	22	23	24	25	26
RAMAḌĀN 1455	27	28	29	1[e]	2	3	4
	5	6	7	8	9	10	11
	12	13	14	15	16	17	18
	19	20	21	22	23	24	25
SHAWWĀL 1455	26	27	28	29	30	1[f]	2
	3	4	5	6	7	8	9

‡Leap year
[a]New Year
[b]'Ashūrā'
[c]Prophet's Birthday
[d]Ascent of the Prophet
[e]Start of Ramaḍān
[f]'Id al-Fiṭr
[g]'Id al-'Aḍḥā

GREGORIAN 2033

Julian (Sun)	Sun	Mon	Tue	Wed	Thu	Fri	Sat	Month
Dec 13	26	27	28	29	30	31	1	JANUARY 2033
	2	3	4	5	6	7[a]	8	
Dec 27	9	10	11	12	13	14[b]	15	
	16	17	18	19	20	21	22	
Jan 10	23	24	25	26	27	28	29	
	30	31	1	2	3	4	5	FEBRUARY 2033
Jan 24	6	7	8	9	10	11	12	
	13	14	15	16	17	18	19	
Feb 7	20	21	22	23	24	25	26	
	27	28	1	2[c]	3	4	5	MARCH 2033
Feb 21	6	7	8	9	10	11	12	
	13[d]	14	15	16	17	18	19	
Mar 7	20	21	22	23	24	25	26	
	27	28	29	30	31	1	2	APRIL 2033
Mar 21	3	4	5	6	7	8	9	
	10	11	12	13	14	15	16	
Apr 4	17[e]	18	19	20	21	22	23	
	24[f]	25	26	27	28	29	30	
Apr 18	1	2	3	4	5	6	7	MAY 2033
	8	9	10	11	12	13	14	
May 2	15	16	17	18	19	20	21	
	22	23	24	25	26	27	28	
May 16	29	30	31	1	2	3	4	JUNE 2033
	5	6	7	8	9	10	11	
May 30	12	13	14	15	16	17	18	
	19	20	21	22	23	24	25	
Jun 13	26	27	28	29	30	1	2	JULY 2033
	3	4	5	6	7	8	9	
Jun 27	10	11	12	13	14	15	16	
	17	18	19	20	21	22	23	
Jul 11	24	25	26	27	28	29	30	
	31	1	2	3	4	5	6	AUGUST 2033
Jul 25	7	8	9	10	11	12	13	
	14	15	16	17	18	19	20	
Aug 8	21	22	23	24	25	26	27	
	28	29	30	31	1	2	3	SEPTEMBER 2033
Aug 22	4	5	6	7	8	9	10	
	11	12	13	14	15	16	17	
Sep 5	18	19	20	21	22	23	24	
	25	26	27	28	29	30	1	OCTOBER 2033
Sep 19	2	3	4	5	6	7	8	
	9	10	11	12	13	14	15	
Oct 3	16	17	18	19	20	21	22	
	23	24	25	26	27	28	29	
Oct 17	30	31	1	2	3	4	5	NOVEMBER 2033
	6	7	8	9	10	11	12	
Oct 31	13	14	15	16	17	18	19	
	20	21	22	23	24	25	26	
Nov 14	27[g]	28	29	30	1	2	3	DECEMBER 2033
	4	5	6	7	8	9	10	
Nov 28	11	12	13	14	15	16	17	
	18	19	20	21	22	23	24	
Dec 12	25[h]	26	27	28	29	30	31	

[a]Orthodox Christmas
[b]Julian New Year
[c]Ash Wednesday
[d]Feast of Orthodoxy
[e]Easter
[f]Orthodox Easter
[g]Advent
[h]Christmas

2034

Gregorian 2034	Sun	Mon	Tue	Wed	Thu	Fri	Sat	Lunar Phases	ISO Week (Mon)	Julian Day (Sun noon)
	1[a]	2	3	○	5	6	7	19:46	1	2463964
JANUARY 2034	8	9	10	11	◑	13	14	13:16	2	2463971
	15	16	17	18	19	●	21	10:00	3	2463978
	22	23	24	25	26	◐	28	8:31	4	2463985
	29	30	31	1	2	○	4	10:03	5	2463992
	5	6	7	8	9	10	◑	11:08	6	2463999
FEBRUARY 2034	12	13	14	15	16	17	●	23:09	7	2464006
	19	20	21	22	23	24	◐	16:33	8	2464013
	26	27	28	1	2	3	4		9	2464020
	○	6	7	8	9	10	11	2:09	10	2464027
MARCH 2034	12	◑	14	15	16	17	18	6:43	11	2464034
	19	●[b]	21	22	23	24	25	10:14	12	2464041
	26	◐	28	29	30	31	1	1:17	13	2464048
	2	○	4	5	6	7	8	19:18	14	2464055
APRIL 2034	9	10	◑	12	13	14	15	22:44	15	2464062
	16	17	●	19	20	21	22	19:25	16	2464069
	23	24	◐	26	27	28	29	11:33	17	2464076
	30	1	2	○	4	5	6	12:14	18	2464083
MAY 2034	7	8	9	10	◑	12	13	10:55	19	2464090
	14	15	16	17	●	19	20	3:11	20	2464097
	21	22	23	◐	25	26	27	23:56	21	2464104
	28	29	30	31	1	○	3	3:53	22	2464111
JUNE 2034	4	5	6	7	8	◑	10	19:43	23	2464118
	11	12	13	14	15	●	17	10:25	24	2464125
	18	19	20	21[c]	22	◐	24	4:34	25	2464132
	25	26	27	28	29	30	○	17:43	26	2464139
	2	3	4	5	6	7	8		27	2464146
JULY 2034	◑	10	11	12	13	14	●	1:58 18:14	28	2464153
	16	17	18	19	20	21	22		29	2464160
	◐	24	25	26	27	28	29	7:04	30	2464167
	30	○	1	2	3	4	5	5:53	31	2464174
	6	◑	8	9	10	11	12	6:49	32	2464181
AUGUST 2034	13	●	15	16	17	18	19	3:52	33	2464188
	20	21	◐	23	24	25	26	0:42	34	2464195
	27	28	○	30	31	1	2	16:48	35	2464202
	3	4	◑	6	7	8	9	11:40	36	2464209
SEPTEMBER 2034	10	11	●	13	14	15	16	16:12	37	2464216
	17	18	19	◐	21	22[d]	23	18:38	38	2464223
	24	25	26	27	○	29	30	2:56	39	2464230
	1	2	3	◑	5	6	7	18:04	40	2464237
OCTOBER 2034	8	9	10	11	●	13	14	7:31	41	2464244
	15	16	17	18	19	◐	21	12:02	42	2464251
	22	23	24	25	26	○	28	12:41	43	2464258
	29	30	31	1	2	◑	4	3:26	44	2464265
	5	6	7	8	9	10	●	1:15	45	2464272
NOVEMBER 2034	12	13	14	15	16	17	18		46	2464279
	◐	20	21	22	23	24	○	4:00 22:31	47	2464286
	26	27	28	29	30	1	◑	16:45	48	2464293
	3	4	5	6	7	8	9		49	2464300
DECEMBER 2034	●	11	12	13	14	15	16	20:13	50	2464307
	17	◐	19	20	21[e]	22	23	17:44	51	2464314
	24	○	26	27	28	29	30	8:53	52	2464321
	31	◑	2	3	4	5	6	10:00	1	2464328

ISO Week	Hebrew 5794/5795‡	Sun	Mon	Tue	Wed	Thu	Fri	Sat	Molad
1		10	11	12	13	14	15	16	
2	TEVETH 5794	17	18	19	20	21	22	23	
3		24	25	26	27	28	29	1	Fri 3h48m2p
4		2	3	4	5	6	7	8	
5	SHEVAT 5794	9	10	11	12	13	14	15	
6		16	17	18	19	20	21	22	
7		23	24	25	26	27	28	29	
8		30	1	2	3	4	5	6	Sat 16h32m3p
9	ADAR 5794	7	8	9	10	11	12	13	
10		14[f]	15	16	17	18	19	20	
11		21	22	23	24	25	26	27	
12		28	29	1	2	3	4	5	Mon 5h16m4p
13	NISAN 5794	6	7	8	9	10	11	12	
14		13	14	15[g]	16	17	18	19	
15		20	21	22	23	24	25	26	
16		27	28	29	30	1	2	3	Tue 18h0m5p
17	IYYAR 5794	4	5	6	7	8	9	10	
18		11	12	13	14	15	16	17	
19		18	19	20	21	22	23	24	
20		25	26	27	28	29	1	2	Thu 6h44m6p
21	SIVAN 5794	3	4	5	6[h]	7	8	9	
22		10	11	12	13	14	15	16	
23		17	18	19	20	21	22	23	
24		24	25	26	27	28	29	30	
25		1	2	3	4	5	6	7	Fri 19h28m7p
26	TAMMUZ 5794	8	9	10	11	12	13	14	
27		15	16	17	18	19	20	21	
28		22	23	24	25	26	27	28	
29		29	1	2	3	4	5	6	Sun 8h12m8p
30	AV 5794	7	8	9[i]	10	11	12	13	
31		14	15	16	17	18	19	20	
32		21	22	23	24	25	26	27	
33		28	29	30	1	2	3	4	Mon 20h56m9p
34	ELUL 5794	5	6	7	8	9	10	11	
35		12	13	14	15	16	17	18	
36		19	20	21	22	23	24	25	
37		26	27	28	29	1[a]	2[a]	3	Wed 9h40m10p
38	TISHRI 5795	4	5	6	7	8	9	10[b]	
39		11	12	13	14	15[c]	16	17	
40		18	19	20	21	22	23	24	
41		25	26	27	28	29	30	1	Thu 22h24m11p
42	ḤESHVAN 5795	2	3	4	5	6	7	8	
43		9	10	11	12	13	14	15	
44		16	17	18	19	20	21	22	
45		23	24	25	26	27	28	29	
46		30	1	2	3	4	5	6	Sat 11h8m12p
47	KISLEV 5795	7	8	9	10	11	12	13	
48		14	15	16	17	18	19	20	
49		21	22	23[d]	24	25[e]	26[e]	27[e]	
50		28[e]	29[e]	30[e]	1[e]	2[e]	3	4	Sun 23h52m13p
51	TEVETH 5795	5	6	7	8	9	10	11	
52		12	13	14	15	16	17	18	
53		19	20	21	22	23	24	25	

ISO Week	Chinese Guǐ-Chǒu‡/Jiǎ-Yín	Sun	Mon	Tue	Wed	Thu	Fri	Sat	Solar Term
1	LEAP MONTH 11 Guǐ-Chǒu	11	12	13	14	15	16	17	Xiǎo hán
2		18*	19	20	21	22	23	24	
3		25	26	27	28	29	1	2	Dà hán
4	MONTH 12 Guǐ-Chǒu	3	4	5	6	7	8	9	
5		10	11	12	13	14	15	16	Lì chūn
6		17	18	19	20	21	22	23	
7		24	25	26	27	28	29	30	Yǔ shuǐ
8		1[a]	2	3	4	5	6	7	
9	MONTH 1 Jiǎ-Yín	8	9	10	11	12	13	14	
10		15[b]	16	17	18	19*	20	21	Jīng zhé
11		22	23	24	25	26	27	28	
12		29	1	2	3	4	5	6	Chūn fēn
13	MONTH 2 Jiǎ-Yín	7	8	9	10	11	12	13	
14		14	15	16	17[c]	18	19	20	Qīng míng
15		21	22	23	24	25	26	27	
16		28	29	30	1	2	3	4	Gǔ yǔ
17	MONTH 3 Jiǎ-Yín	5	6	7	8	9	10	11	
18		12	13	14	15	16	17	18	Lì xià
19		19	20*	21	22	23	24	25	
20		26	27	28	29	1	2	3	
21	MONTH 4 Jiǎ-Yín	4	5	6	7	8	9	10	Xiǎo mǎn
22		11	12	13	14	15	16	17	
23		18	19	20	21	22	23	24	Máng zhòng
24		25	26	27	28	29	1	2	
25	MONTH 5 Jiǎ-Yín	3	4	5[d]	6	7	8	9	Xià zhì
26		10	11	12	13	14	15	16	
27		17	18	19	20	21	22*	23	Xiǎo shǔ
28		24	25	26	27	28	29	30	
29		1	2	3	4	5	6	7	
30	MONTH 6 Jiǎ-Yín	8	9	10	11	12	13	14	Dà shǔ
31		15	16	17	18	19	20	21	
32		22	23	24	25	26	27	28	Lì qiū
33		29	1	2	3	4	5	6	
34	MONTH 7 Jiǎ-Yín	7[e]	8	9	10	11	12	13	Chǔ shǔ
35		14	15[f]	16	17	18	19	20	
36		21	22	23*	24	25	26	27	Bái lù
37		28	29	30	1	2	3	4	
38	MONTH 8 Jiǎ-Yín	5	6	7	8	9	10	11	Qiū fēn
39		12	13	14	15[g]	16	17	18	
40		19	20	21	22	23	24	25	
41		26	27	28	29	1	2	3	Hán lù
42	MONTH 9 Jiǎ-Yín	4	5	6	7	8	9[h]	10	
43		11	12	13	14	15	16	17	Shuāng jiàng
44		18	19	20	21	22	23	24*	
45		25	26	27	28	29	30	1	Lì dōng
46	MONTH 10 Jiǎ-Yín	2	3	4	5	6	7	8	
47		9	10	11	12	13	14	15	Xiǎo xuě
48		16	17	18	19	20	21	22	
49		23	24	25	26	27	28	29	Dà xuě
50		30	1	2	3	4	5	6	
51	MONTH 11 Jiǎ-Yín	7	8	9	10	11	12[i]	13	Dōng zhì
52		14	15	16	17	18	19	20	
53		21	22	23	24	25	26	27	Xiǎo hán

ISO Week	Coptic 1750/1751‡	Sun	Mon	Tue	Wed	Thu	Fri	Sat	Ethiopic 2026/2027‡
1	KOIAK 1750	23	24	25	26	27	28	29[c]	TĀKHŚĀŚ 2026
2		30	1	2	3	4	5	6[d]	
3	TÔBE 1750	7	8	9	10	11[e]	12	13	ṬER 2026
4		14	15	16	17	18	19	20	
5		21	22	23	24	25	26	27	
6		28	29	30	1	2	3	4	
7	MESHIR 1750	5	6	7	8	9	10	11	YAKĀTIT 2026
8		12	13	14	15	16	17	18	
9		19	20	21	22	23	24	25	
10		26	27	28	29	30	1	2	
11	PAREMOTEP 1750	3	4	5	6	7	8	9	MAGĀBIT 2026
12		10	11	12	13	14	15	16	
13		17	18	19	20	21	22	23	
14		24	25	26	27	28	29	30	
15		1[f]	2	3	4	5	6	7	
16	PARMOUTE 1750	8	9	10	11	12	13	14	MIYĀZYĀ 2026
17		15	16	17	18	19	20	21	
18		22	23	24	25	26	27	28	
19		29[g]	30	1	2	3	4	5	
20	PASHONS 1750	6	7	8	9	10	11	12	GENBOT 2026
21		13	14	15	16	17	18	19	
22		20	21	22	23	24	25	26	
23		27	28	29	30	1	2	3	
24	PAÔNE 1750	4	5	6	7	8	9	10	SANĒ 2026
25		11	12	13	14	15	16	17	
26		18	19	20	21	22	23	24	
27		25	26	27	28	29	30	1	
28	EPÊP 1750	2	3	4	5	6	7	8	ḤAMLĒ 2026
29		9	10	11	12	13	14	15	
30		16	17	18	19	20	21	22	
31		23	24	25	26	27	28	29	
32		30	1	2	3	4	5	6	
33	MESORÊ 1750	7	8	9	10	11	12	13[h]	NAḤASĒ 2026
34		14	15	16	17	18	19	20	
35		21	22	23	24	25	26	27	
36	EPAG. 1750	28	29	30	1	2	3	4	PĀG. 2026
37		5	1[a]	2	3	4	5	6	
38	THOOUT 1751	7	8	9	10	11	12	13	MASKARAM 2027
39		14	15	16	17[b]	18	19	20	
40		21	22	23	24	25	26	27	
41		28	29	30	1	2	3	4	
42	PAOPE 1751	5	6	7	8	9	10	11	TEQEMT 2027
43		12	13	14	15	16	17	18	
44		19	20	21	22	23	24	25	
45		26	27	28	29	30	1	2	
46	ATHÔR 1751	3	4	5	6	7	8	9	ḪEDĀR 2027
47		10	11	12	13	14	15	16	
48		17	18	19	20	21	22	23	
49		24	25	26	27	28	29	30	
50	KOIAK 1751	1	2	3	4	5	6	7	TĀKHŚĀŚ 2027
51		8	9	10	11	12	13	14	
52		15	16	17	18	19	20	21	
53		22	23	24	25	26	27	28	

[a]New Year
[b]Spring (13:16)
[c]Summer (6:43)
[d]Autumn (22:38)
[e]Winter (19:32)
● New moon
◐ First quarter moon
○ Full moon
◑ Last quarter moon

‡Leap year
[a]New Year
[b]Yom Kippur
[c]Sukkot
[d]Winter starts
[e]Ḥanukkah
[f]Purim
[g]Passover
[h]Shavuot
[i]Fast of Av

‡Leap year
[a]New Year (4732, Tiger)
[b]Lantern Festival
[c]Qīngmíng
[d]Dragon Festival
[e]Qīqiǎo
[f]Hungry Ghosts
[g]Mid-Autumn Festival
[h]Double-Ninth Festival
[i]Dōngzhì
*Start of 60-name cycle

‡Leap year
[a]New Year
[b]Building of the Cross
[c]Christmas
[d]Jesus's Circumcision
[e]Epiphany
[f]Easter
[g]Mary's Announcement
[h]Jesus's Transfiguration

PERSIAN (ASTRONOMICAL) 1412‡/1413

Month	Sun	Mon	Tue	Wed	Thu	Fri	Sat
DEY 1412	12	13	14	15	16	17	18
	19	20	21	22	23	24	25
	26	27	28	29	30	1	2
BAHMAN 1412	3	4	5	6	7	8	9
	10	11	12	13	14	15	16
	17	18	19	20	21	22	23
	24	25	26	27	28	29	30
ESFAND 1412	1	2	3	4	5	6	7
	8	9	10	11	12	13	14
	15	16	17	18	19	20	21
	22	23	24	25	26	27	28
	29	30	1[a]	2	3	4	5
FARVARDĪN 1413	6	7	8	9	10	11	12
	13[b]	14	15	16	17	18	19
	20	21	22	23	24	25	26
	27	28	29	30	31	1	2
ORDĪBEHEŠT 1413	3	4	5	6	7	8	9
	10	11	12	13	14	15	16
	17	18	19	20	21	22	23
	24	25	26	27	28	29	30
	31	1	2	3	4	5	6
XORDĀD 1413	7	8	9	10	11	12	13
	14	15	16	17	18	19	20
	21	22	23	24	25	26	27
	28	29	30	31	1	2	3
TĪR 1413	4	5	6	7	8	9	10
	11	12	13	14	15	16	17
	18	19	20	21	22	23	24
	25	26	27	28	29	30	31
MORDĀD 1413	1	2	3	4	5	6	7
	8	9	10	11	12	13	14
	15	16	17	18	19	20	21
	22	23	24	25	26	27	28
	29	30	31	1	2	3	4
SHAHRĪVAR 1413	5	6	7	8	9	10	11
	12	13	14	15	16	17	18
	19	20	21	22	23	24	25
	26	27	28	29	30	31	1
MEHR 1413	2	3	4	5	6	7	8
	9	10	11	12	13	14	15
	16	17	18	19	20	21	22
	23	24	25	26	27	28	29
	30	1	2	3	4	5	6
ĀBĀN 1413	7	8	9	10	11	12	13
	14	15	16	17	18	19	20
	21	22	23	24	25	26	27
	28	29	30	1	2	3	4
ĀZAR 1413	5	6	7	8	9	10	11
	12	13	14	15	16	17	18
	19	20	21	22	23	24	25
	26	27	28	29	30	1	2
DEY 1413	3	4	5	6	7	8	9
	10	11	12	13	14	15	16

‡Leap year
[a]New Year
[b]Sizdeh Bedar

HINDU LUNAR 2090/2091‡

Month	Sun	Mon	Tue	Wed	Thu	Fri	Sat
PAUSHA 2090	11	13	14	15	16	17	18
	19	20	21	22	23	23	24
	25	26	27	28	29	30	1
MĀGHA 2090	2	3	4	5	7	8	9
	10	11	12	13	14	15	16
	17	18	19	20	21	22	23
	24	25	26	27	27	28[h]	30
PHĀLGUNA 2090	1	2	3	4	5	6	7
	8	9	10	11	13	14	15
	15[i]	16	17	18	19	20	21
	22	23	24	25	26	27	28
	29	30	1[a]	2	3	4	6
CHAITRA 2091	7	8	9[b]	10	11	12	13
	14	15	16	17	18	19	19
	20	21	22	23	24	25	26
	27	29	30	1	2	3	4
VAIŚĀKHA 2091	5	6	7	8	9	10	11
	12	13	14	15	16	17	18
	19	20	21	22	23	24	25
	26	27	28	29	30	1	3
JYAISHṬHA 2091	4	5	6	7	8	9	10
	11	12	13	14	14	15	16
	17	18	19	20	21	22	23
	24	26	27	28	29	30	1
LEAP ĀSHĀḌHA 2091	2	3	4	5	6	7	8
	9	10	11	12	13	14	15
	16	17	18	19	20	21	22
	23	24	25	26	27	29	30
ĀSHĀḌHA 2091	1	2	3	4	5	6	7
	8	9	10	11	11	12	13
	14	15	16	17	18	19	21
	22	23	24	25	26	27	28
	29	30	1	2	3	4	5
ŚRĀVAṆA 2091	6	7	8	9	10	11	12
	13	14	15	16	17	18	19
	20	21	22[c]	24	25	26	27
	28	29	30	1	2	3	4[d]
BHĀDRAPADA 2091	5	6	7	7	8	9	10
	11	12	13	14	15	16	18
	19	20	21	22	23	24	25
	26	27	28	29	30	1	2
ĀŚVINA 2091	3	4	5	6	7	8[e]	9[e]
	10[e]	11	12	13	14	15	16
	17	18	19	20	22	23	24
	25	26	27	28	29	30	1
KĀRTTIKA 2091	1[f]	2	3	4	5	6	7
	8	9	10	11	12	13	15
	16	17	18	19	20	21	22
	23	24	25	26	27	28	29
	30	1	2	3	4	5	5
MĀRGAŚIRA 2091	6	8	9	10	11[g]	12	13
	14	15	16	17	18	19	21
	22	23	23	24	25	26	27

‡Leap year
[a]New Year (Ānanda)
[b]Birthday of Rāma
[c]Birthday of Krishna
[d]Ganēśa Chaturthī
[e]Dashara
[f]Diwali
[g]Birthday of Vishnu
[h]Night of Śiva
[i]Holi

HINDU SOLAR 1955/1956

Month	Sun	Mon	Tue	Wed	Thu	Fri	Sat
PAUSHA 1955	17	18	19	20	21	22	23
	24	25	26	27	28	29	1[b]
MĀGHA 1955	2	3	4	5	6	7	8
	9	10	11	12	13	14	15
	16	17	18	19	20	21	22
	23	24	25	26	27	28	29
	30	1	2	3	4	5	6
PHĀLGUNA 1955	7	8	9	10	11	12	13
	14	15	16	17	18	19	20
	21	22	23	24	25	26	27
	28	29	1	2	3	4	5
CHAITRA 1955	6	7	8	9	10	11	12
	13	14	15	16	17	18	19
	20	21	22	23	24	25	26
	27	28	29	30	31	1[a]	2
VAIŚĀKHA 1956	3	4	5	6	7	8	9
	10	11	12	13	14	15	16
	17	18	19	20	21	22	23
	24	25	26	27	28	29	30
	31	1	2	3	4	5	6
JYAISHṬHA 1956	7	8	9	10	11	12	13
	14	15	16	17	18	19	20
	21	22	23	24	25	26	27
	28	29	30	31	1	2	3
ĀSHĀḌHA 1956	4	5	6	7	8	9	10
	11	12	13	14	15	16	17
	18	19	20	21	22	23	24
	25	26	27	28	29	30	31
	32	1	2	3	4	5	6
ŚRĀVAṆA 1956	7	8	9	10	11	12	13
	14	15	16	17	18	19	20
	21	22	23	24	25	26	27
	28	29	30	31	1	2	3
BHĀDRAPADA 1956	4	5	6	7	8	9	10
	11	12	13	14	15	16	17
	18	19	20	21	22	23	24
	25	26	27	28	29	30	31
	1	2	3	4	5	6	7
ĀŚVINA 1956	8	9	10	11	12	13	14
	15	16	17	18	19	20	21
	22	23	24	25	26	27	28
	29	30	31	1	2	3	4
KĀRTTIKA 1956	5	6	7	8	9	10	11
	12	13	14	15	16	17	18
	19	20	21	22	23	24	25
	26	27	28	29	30	1	2
MĀRGAŚIRA 1956	3	4	5	6	7	8	9
	10	11	12	13	14	15	16
	17	18	19	20	21	22	23
	24	25	26	27	28	29	1
PAUSHA 1956	2	3	4	5	6	7	8
	9	10	11	12	13	14	15
	16	17	18	19	20	21	22

[a]New Year (Vibhava)
[b]Pongal

ISLAMIC (ASTRONOMICAL) 1455‡/1456

Month	Sun	Mon	Tue	Wed	Thu	Fri	Sat
SHAWWĀL 1455	10	11	12	13	14	15	16
	17	18	19	20	21	22	23
	24	25	26	27	28	29	30
DHU AL-QA'DA 1455	1	2	3	4	5	6	7
	8	9	10	11	12	13	14
	15	16	17	18	19	20	21
	22	23	24	25	26	27	28
	29	1	2	3	4	5	6
DHU AL-ḤIJJA 1455	7	8	9	10[g]	11	12	13
	14	15	16	17	18	19	20
	21	22	23	24	25	26	27
	28	29	30[d]	1[a]	2	3	4
MUḤARRAM 1456	5	6	7	8	9	10[b]	11
	12	13	14	15	16	17	18
	19	20	21	22	23	24	25
	26	27	28	29	1	2	3
ṢAFAR 1456	4	5	6	7	8	9	10
	11	12	13	14	15	16	17
	18	19	20	21	22	23	24
	25	26	27	28	29	1	2
RABĪʿ I 1456	3	4	5	6	7	8	9
	10	11	12[c]	13	14	15	16
	17	18	19	20	21	22	23
	24	25	26	27	28	29	30
RABĪʿ II 1456	1	2	3	4	5	6	7
	8	9	10	11	12	13	14
	15	16	17	18	19	20	21
	22	23	24	25	26	27	28
	29	1	2	3	4	5	6
JUMĀDĀ I 1456	7	8	9	10	11	12	13
	14	15	16	17	18	19	20
	21	22	23	24	25	26	27
	28	29	30	1	2	3	4
JUMĀDĀ II 1456	5	6	7	8	9	10	11
	12	13	14	15	16	17	18
	19	20	21	22	23	24	25
	26	27	28	29	1	2	3
RAJAB 1456	4	5	6	7	8	9	10
	11	12	13	14	15	16	17
	18	19	20	21	22	23	24
	25	26	27[d]	28	29	30	1
SHAʿBĀN 1456	2	3	4	5	6	7	8
	9	10	11	12	13	14	15
	16	17	18	19	20	21	22
	23	24	25	26	27	28	29
	1[e]	2	3	4	5	6	7
RAMAḌĀN 1456	8	9	10	11	12	13	14
	15	16	17	18	19	20	21
	22	23	24	25	26	27	28
	29	30	1[f]	2	3	4	5
SHAWWĀL 1456	6	7	8	9	10	11	12
	13	14	15	16	17	18	19
	20	21	22	23	24	25	26

‡Leap year
[a]New Year
[d]New Year (Arithmetic)
[b]ʿAshūrā'
[c]Prophet's Birthday
[d]Ascent of the Prophet
[e]Start of Ramaḍān
[f]ʿId al-Fiṭr
[g]ʿId al-'Aḍḥā

GREGORIAN 2034

Julian (Sun)	Sun	Mon	Tue	Wed	Thu	Fri	Sat	Month
Dec 19	1	2	3	4	5	6	7[a]	JANUARY 2034
	8	9	10	11	12	13	14[b]	
Jan 2	15	16	17	18	19	20	21	
	22	23	24	25	26	27	28	
Jan 16	29	30	31	1	2	3	4	FEBRUARY 2034
	5	6	7	8	9	10	11	
Jan 30	12	13	14	15	16	17	18	
	19	20	21	22[c]	23	24	25	
Feb 13	26[d]	27	28	1	2	3	4	MARCH 2034
	5	6	7	8	9	10	11	
Feb 27	12	13	14	15	16	17	18	
	19	20	21	22	23	24	25	
Mar 13	26	27	28	29	30	31	1	APRIL 2034
	2	3	4	5	6	7	8	
Mar 27	9[e]	10	11	12	13	14	15	
	16	17	18	19	20	21	22	
Apr 10	23	24	25	26	27	28	29	
	30	1	2	3	4	5	6	MAY 2034
Apr 24	7	8	9	10	11	12	13	
	14	15	16	17	18	19	20	
May 8	21	22	23	24	25	26	27	
	28	29	30	31	1	2	3	JUNE 2034
May 22	4	5	6	7	8	9	10	
	11	12	13	14	15	16	17	
Jun 5	18	19	20	21	22	23	24	
	25	26	27	28	29	30	1	JULY 2034
Jun 19	2	3	4	5	6	7	8	
	9	10	11	12	13	14	15	
Jul 3	16	17	18	19	20	21	22	
	23	24	25	26	27	28	29	
Jul 17	30	31	1	2	3	4	5	AUGUST 2034
	6	7	8	9	10	11	12	
Jul 31	13	14	15	16	17	18	19	
	20	21	22	23	24	25	26	
Aug 14	27	28	29	30	31	1	2	SEPTEMBER 2034
	3	4	5	6	7	8	9	
Aug 28	10	11	12	13	14	15	16	
	17	18	19	20	21	22	23	
Sep 11	24	25	26	27	28	29	30	
	1	2	3	4	5	6	7	OCTOBER 2234
Sep 25	8	9	10	11	12	13	14	
	15	16	17	18	19	20	21	
Oct 9	22	23	24	25	26	27	28	
	29	30	31	1	2	3	4	NOVEMBER 2034
Oct 23	5	6	7	8	9	10	11	
	12	13	14	15	16	17	18	
Nov 6	19	20	21	22	23	24	25	
	26	27	28	29	30	1	2	DECEMBER 2034
Nov 20	3[g]	4	5	6	7	8	9	
	10	11	12	13	14	15	16	
Dec 4	17	18	19	20	21	22	23	
	24	25[h]	26	27	28	29	30	
Dec 18	31	1	2	3	4	5	6	

[a]Orthodox Christmas
[b]Julian New Year
[c]Ash Wednesday
[d]Feast of Orthodoxy
[e]Easter (also Orthodox)
[g]Advent
[h]Christmas

2035

GREGORIAN 2035								Lunar Phases	ISO WEEK	JULIAN DAY	HEBREW 5795‡/5796								Molad	CHINESE Jiă-Yín/Yĭ-Măo								Solar Term	COPTIC 1751‡/1752								ETHIOPIC 2027‡/2028
	Sun	Mon	Tue	Wed	Thu	Fri	Sat		(Mon)	(Sun noon)		Sun	Mon	Tue	Wed	Thu	Fri	Sat			Sun	Mon	Tue	Wed	Thu	Fri	Sat			Sun	Mon	Tue	Wed	Thu	Fri	Sat	
	31	◑[a]	2	3	4	5	6	10:00	1	2464328	TEVETH 5795	19	20	21	22	23	24	25		MONTH 11 Jiă-Yín	21	22	23	24*	25	26	27	Xiăo hán	KOIAK 1751	22	23	24	25	26	27	28	TĀKHŚĀŚ 2027
JANUARY 2035	7	8	●	10	11	12	13	15:02	2	2464335		26	27	28	29	1	2	3	Tue 12h36m14p		28	29	1	2	3	4	5			29[c]	30	1	2	3	4	5	
	14	15	16	◐	18	19	20	4:44	3	2464342	SHEVAT 5795	4	5	6	7	8	9	10		MONTH 12 Jiă-Yín	6	7	8	9	10	11	12	Dà hán	TÔBE 1751	6[d]	7	8	9	10	11[e]	12	ṬER 2027
	21	22	○	24	25	26	27	20:15	4	2464349		11	12	13	14	15	16	17			13	14	15	16	17	18	19			13	14	15	16	17	18	19	
	28	29	30	◑	1	2	3	6:01	5	2464356		18	19	20	21	22	23	24			20	21	22	23	24	25	26			20	21	22	23	24	25	26	
FEBRUARY 2035	4	5	6	7	●	9	10	8:21	6	2464363		25	26	27	28	29	30	1	Thu 1h20m15p		27	28	29	30	1[a]	2	3	Lì chūn		27	28	29	30	1	2	3	
	11	12	13	14	◐	16	17	13:16	7	2464370	ADAR I 5795	2	3	4	5	6	7	8		MONTH 1 Yĭ-Măo	4	5	6	7	8	9	10		MESHIR 1751	4	5	6	7	8	9	10	YAKĀTIT 2027
	18	19	20	21	○	23	24	8:53	8	2464377		9	10	11	12	13	14	15			11	12	13	14	15[b]	16	17	Yŭ shuĭ		11	12	13	14	15	16	17	
	25	26	27	28	1	◑	3	3:00	9	2464384		16	17	18	19	20	21	22			18	19	20	21	22	23	24			18	19	20	21	22	23	24	
MARCH 2035	4	5	6	7	8	●	10	23:08	10	2464391		23	24	25	26	27	28	29			25*	26	27	28	29	30	1	Jīng zhé		25	26	27	28	29	30	1	
	11	12	13	14	15	◐	17	20:14	11	2464398	ADAR II 5795	30	1	2	3	4	5	6	Fri 14h4m16p	MONTH 2 Yĭ-Măo	2	3	4	5	6	7	8		PAREMOTEP 1751	2	3	4	5	6	7	8	MAGĀBIT 2027
	18	19	20[b]	21	22	○	24	22:41	12	2464405		7	8	9	10	11	12	13			9	10	11	12	13	14	15	Chūn fēn		9	10	11	12	13	14	15	
	25	26	27	28	29	30	◑	23:05	13	2464412		14[f]	15	16	17	18	19	20			16	17	18	19	20	21	22			16	17	18	19	20	21	22	
	1	2	3	4	5	6	7		14	2464419		21	22	23	24	25	26	27			23	24	25	26	27[c]	28	29	Qīng míng		23	24	25	26	27	28	29	
APRIL 2035	●	9	10	11	12	13	14	10:57	15	2464426		28	29	1	2	3	4	5	Sun 2h48m17p		1	2	3	4	5	6	7			30	1	2	3	4	5	6	
	◐	16	17	18	19	20	21	2:54	16	2464433	NISAN 5795	6	7	8	9	10	11	12		MONTH 3 Yĭ-Măo	8	9	10	11	12	13	14	Gŭ yŭ	PARMOUTE 1751	7	8	9	10	11	12	13	MIYĀZYĀ 2027
	○	23	24	25	26	27	28	13:19	17	2464440		13	14	15[g]	16	17	18	19			15	16	17	18	19	20	21			14	15	16	17	18	19	20	
	29	◑	1	2	3	4	5	16:53	18	2464447		20	21	22	23	24	25	26			22	23	24	25	26*	27	28	Lì xià		21[f]	22	23	24	25	26	27	
MAY 2035	6	●	8	9	10	11	12	20:03	19	2464454		27	28	29	30	1	2	3	Mon 15h33m0p		29	30	1	2	3	4	5			28	29[g]	30	1	2	3	4	
	13	◐	15	16	17	18	19	10:27	20	2464461	IYAR 5795	4	5	6	7	8	9	10		MONTH 4 Yĭ-Măo	6	7	8	9	10	11	12		PASHONS 1751	5	6	7	8	9	10	11	GENBOT 2027
	20	21	○	23	24	25	26	4:25	21	2464468		11	12	13	14	15	16	17			13	14	15	16	17	18	19	Xiăo măn		12	13	14	15	16	17	18	
	27	28	29	◑	31	1	2	7:29	22	2464475		18	19	20	21	22	23	24			20	21	22	23	24	25	26			19	20	21	22	23	24	25	
JUNE 2035	3	4	5	●	7	8	9	3:19	23	2464482		25	26	27	28	29	1	2	Wed 4h17m1p		27	28	29	1	2	3	4	Máng zhòng		26	27	28	29	30	1	2	
	10	11	◐	13	14	15	16	19:49	24	2464489	SIVAN 5795	3	4	5	6[h]	7	8	9		MONTH 5 Yĭ-Măo	5[d]	6	7	8	9	10	11		PAŌNE 1751	3	4	5	6	7	8	9	SANÉ 2027
	17	18	19	○	21[c]	22	23	19:36	25	2464496		10	11	12	13	14	15	16			12	13	14	15	16	17	18	Xià zhì		10	11	12	13	14	15	16	
	24	25	26	27	◑	29	30	18:42	26	2464503		17	18	19	20	21	22	23			19	20	21	22	23	24	25			17	18	19	20	21	22	23	
	1	2	3	4	●	6	7	9:58	27	2464510		24	25	26	27	28	29	30			26	27*	28	29	1	2	3	Xiăo shŭ		24	25	26	27	28	29	30	
JULY 2035	8	9	10	11	◐	13	14	7:32	28	2464517	TAMMUZ 5795	1	2	3	4	5	6	7	Thu 17h1m2p	MONTH 6 Yĭ-Măo	4	5	6	7	8	9	10		EPĒP 1751	1	2	3	4	5	6	7	ḤAMLĒ 2027
	15	16	17	18	19	○	21	10:36	29	2464524		8	9	10	11	12	13	14			11	12	13	14	15	16	17			8	9	10	11	12	13	14	
	22	23	24	25	26	27	◑	2:54	30	2464531		15	16	17	18	19	20	21			18	19	20	21	22	23	24	Dà shŭ		15	16	17	18	19	20	21	
	29	30	31	1	2	●	4	17:10	31	2464538		22	23	24	25	26	27	28			25	26	27	28	29	30	1			22	23	24	25	26	27	28	
AUGUST 2035	5	6	7	8	9	◐	11	21:51	32	2464545	AV 5795	29	1	2	3	4	5	6	Sat 5h45m3p	MONTH 7 Yĭ-Măo	2	3	4	5	6	7[e]	8	Lì qiū	MESORĒ 1751	29	30	1	2	3	4	5	NAHASĒ 2027
	12	13	14	15	16	17	18		33	2464552		7	8	9[i]	10	11	12	13			9	10	11	12	13	14	15[f]			6	7	8	9	10	11	12	
	○	20	21	22	23	24	25	0:59	34	2464559		14	15	16	17	18	19	20			16	17	18	19	20	21	22	Chŭ shŭ		13[h]	14	15	16	17	18	19	
	◑	27	28	29	30	31	1	9:07	35	2464566		21	22	23	24	25	26	27			23	24	25	26	27	28*	29			20	21	22	23	24	25	26	
SEPTEMBER 2035	●	3	4	5	6	7	8	1:58	36	2464573	ELUL 5795	28	29	30	1	2	3	4	Sun 18h29m4p	MONTH 8 Yĭ-Măo	1	2	3	4	5	6	7	Bái lù	EPAG. 1751	27	28	29	30	1	2	3	PĀG. 2027
	◐	10	11	12	13	14	15	14:46	37	2464580		5	6	7	8	9	10	11			8	9	10	11	12	13	14		THOOUT 1752	4	5	6	1[a]	2	3	4	MASKARAM 2028
	16	○	18	19	20	21	22	14:22	38	2464587		12	13	14	15	16	17	18			15[g]	16	17	18	19	20	21			5	6	7	8	9	10	11	
	23[d]	◑	25	26	27	28	29	14:38	39	2464594		19	20	21	22	23	24	25			22	23	24	25	26	27	28	Qiū fēn		12	13	14	15	16	17[b]	18	
	30	●	2	3	4	5	6	13:05	40	2464601		26	27	28	29	1[a]	2[a]	3	Tue 7h13m5p		29	1	2	3	4	5	6			19	20	21	22	23	24	25	
OCTOBER 2035	7	8	◐	10	11	12	13	9:48	41	2464608	TISHRI 5796	4	5	6	7	8	9	10[b]		MONTH 9 Yĭ-Măo	7	8	9[h]	10	11	12	13	Hán lù	PAOPE 1752	26	27	28	29	30	1	2	ṬEQEMT 2028
	14	15	16	○	18	19	20	2:34	42	2464615		11	12	13	14	15[c]	16	17			14	15	16	17	18	19	20			3	4	5	6	7	8	9	
	21	22	◑	24	25	26	27	20:56	43	2464622		18	19	20	21	22	23	24			21	22	23	24	25	26	27	Shuāng jiàng		10	11	12	13	14	15	16	
	28	29	30	●	1	2	3	2:57	44	2464629		25	26	27	28	29	30	1	Wed 19h57m6p		28	29	30*	1	2	3	4			17	18	19	20	21	22	23	
NOVEMBER 2035	4	5	6	7	◐	9	10	5:49	45	2464636	ḤESHVAN 5796	2	3	4	5	6	7	8		MONTH 10 Yĭ-Măo	5	6	7	8	9	10	11	Lì dōng		24	25	26	27	28	29	30	
	11	12	13	14	○	16	17	13:48	46	2464643		9	10	11	12	13	14	15			12	13	14	15	16	17	18		ATHŌR 1752	1	2	3	4	5	6	7	ḪEDĀR 2028
	18	19	20	21	◑	23	24	5:15	47	2464650		16	17	18	19	20	21	22			19	20	21	22	23	24	25	Xiăo xuě		8	9	10	11	12	13	14	
	25	26	27	28	●	30	1	19:36	48	2464657		23	24	25	26	27	28	29			26	27	28	29	30	1	2			15	16	17	18	19	20	21	
DECEMBER 2035	2	3	4	5	6	7	◐	1:04	49	2464664	KISLEV 5796	1	2	3	4	5[d]	6	7	Fri 8h41m7p	MONTH 11 Yĭ-Măo	3	4	5	6	7	8	9	Dà xuě		22	23	24	25	26	27	28	
	9	10	11	12	13	14	○	0:32	50	2464671		8	9	10	11	12	13	14			10	11	12	13	14	15	16		KOIAK 1752	29	30	1	2	3	4	5	TĀKHŚĀŚ 2028
	16	17	18	19	20	◑	22[e]	16:27	51	2464678		15	16	17	18	19	20	21			17	18	19	20	21	22	23[i]	Dōng zhì		6	7	8	9	10	11	12	
	23	24	25	26	27	28	●	14:30	52	2464685		22	23	24	25[e]	26[e]	27[e]	28[e]	Sat 21h25m8p	MONTH 12 Yĭ-Măo	24	25	26	27	28	29	1*			13	14	15	16	17	18	19	
	30	31	1	2	3	4	5		1	2464692		29[e]	30[e]	1[e]	2[e]	3	4	5			2	3	4	5	6	7	8			20	21	22	23	24	25	26	

[a]New Year
[b]Spring (19:02)
[c]Summer (12:31)
[d]Autumn (4:37)
[e]Winter (1:29)
● New moon
◐ First quarter moon
○ Full moon
◑ Last quarter moon

‡Leap year
[a]New Year
[b]Yom Kippur
[c]Sukkot
[d]Winter starts
[e]Ḥanukkah
[f]Purim
[g]Passover
[h]Shavuot
[i]Fast of Av

[a]New Year (4733, Hare)
[b]Lantern Festival
[c]Qīngmíng
[d]Dragon Festival
[e]Qīqiăo
[f]Hungry Ghosts
[g]Mid-Autumn Festival
[h]Double-Ninth Festival
[i]Dōngzhì
*Start of 60-name cycle

‡Leap year
[a]New Year
[b]Building of the Cross
[c]Christmas
[d]Jesus's Circumcision
[e]Epiphany
[f]Easter
[g]Mary's Announcement
[h]Jesus's Transfiguration

2035

PERSIAN (ASTRONOMICAL) 1413/1414

Month	Sun	Mon	Tue	Wed	Thu	Fri	Sat
DEY 1413	10	11	12	13	14	15	16
	17	18	19	20	21	22	23
	24	25	26	27	28	29	30
BAHMAN 1413	*1*	2	3	4	5	6	7
	8	9	10	11	12	13	14
	15	16	17	18	19	20	21
	22	23	24	25	26	27	28
	29	30	*1*	2	3	4	5
ESFAND 1413	6	7	8	9	10	11	12
	13	14	15	16	17	18	19
	20	21	22	23	24	25	26
	27	28	29	*1*[a]	2	3	4
FARVARDĪN 1414	5	6	7	8	9	10	11
	12	13[b]	14	15	16	17	18
	19	20	21	22	23	24	25
	26	27	28	29	30	31	*1*
ORDĪBEHEŠT 1414	2	3	4	5	6	7	8
	9	10	11	12	13	14	15
	16	17	18	19	20	21	22
	23	24	25	26	27	28	29
	30	31	*1*	2	3	4	5
XORDĀD 1414	6	7	8	9	10	11	12
	13	14	15	16	17	18	19
	20	21	22	23	24	25	26
	27	28	29	30	31	*1*	2
TĪR 1414	3	4	5	6	7	8	9
	10	11	12	13	14	15	16
	17	18	19	20	21	22	23
	24	25	26	27	28	29	30
	31	*1*	2	3	4	5	6
MORDĀD 1414	7	8	9	10	11	12	13
	14	15	16	17	18	19	20
	21	22	23	24	25	26	27
	28	29	30	31	*1*	2	3
SHAHRĪVAR 1414	4	5	6	7	8	9	10
	11	12	13	14	15	16	17
	18	19	20	21	22	23	24
	25	26	27	28	29	30	31
MEHR 1414	*1*	2	3	4	5	6	7
	8	9	10	11	12	13	14
	15	16	17	18	19	20	21
	22	23	24	25	26	27	28
	29	30	*1*	2	3	4	5
ĀBĀN 1414	6	7	8	9	10	11	12
	13	14	15	16	17	18	19
	20	21	22	23	24	25	26
	27	28	29	30	*1*	2	3
ĀZAR 1414	4	5	6	7	8	9	10
	11	12	13	14	15	16	17
	18	19	20	21	22	23	24
	25	26	27	28	29	30	*1*
DEY 1414	2	3	4	5	6	7	8
	9	10	11	12	13	14	15

HINDU LUNAR 2091‡/2092

Month	Sun	Mon	Tue	Wed	Thu	Fri	Sat
MĀRGAŚĪRA 2091	22	23	*23*	24	25	26	27
	28	29	30	1	2	3	4
PAUSHA 2091	5	6	7	8	9	10	11
	12	14	15	16	17	18	19
	20	21	22	23	24	25	26
	26	27	28	29	30	1	2
MĀGHA 2091	3	4	5	**6**	8	9	10
	11	12	13	14	15	16	17
	18	19	20	21	22	23	24
	25	26	27	28	29[h]	30	1
PHĀLGUNA 2091	2	3	4	5	6	7	8
	9	10	**11**	13	14	15[i]	16
	17	18	19	*19*	20	21	22
	23	24	25	26	27	28	29
CHAITRA 2092	30	1[a]	2	3	**4**	6	7
	8	9[b]	10	11	12	13	14
	15	16	17	18	19	20	21
	22	23	*23*	24	25	26	**27**
	29	30	1	2	3	4	5
VAIŚĀKHA 2092	6	7	8	9	**10**	12	13
	13	14	15	16	17	18	19
	20	21	22	23	24	25	26
	27	28	29	30	**1**	3	4
JYAISHTHA 2092	5	6	7	8	9	10	11
	12	13	14	15	16	17	18
	19	*19*	20	21	22	**23**	25
	26	27	28	29	30	1	2
ĀSHĀDHA 2092	3	4	**5**	7	8	9	10
	10	11	12	13	14	15	16
	17	18	19	20	21	22	23
	24	25	26	**27**	29	30	1
ŚRĀVAṆA 2092	2	3	4	5	6	7	8
	9	10	11	12	13	14	15
	16	*16*	17	**18**	20	21	22
	23[c]	24	25	26	27	28	29
	30	2	3	4[d]	5	6	7
BHĀDRAPADA 2092	7	8	9	10	11	12	13
	14	15	16	17	18	19	20
	21	22	**23**	25	26	27	28
	29	30	1	2	3	4	5
ĀŚVINA 2092	6	7	8[e]	9[e]	10[e]	11	*11*
	12	13	14	15	**16**	18	19
	20	21	22	23	24	25	26
	27	28	29	30	1[f]	2	3
KĀRTTIKA 2092	4	5	6	7	8	9	10
	11	12	13	14	15	16	17
	18	19	**20**	22	23	24	25
	26	27	28	29	30	1	2
MĀRGAŚĪRA 2092	3	4	*4*	5	6	7	8
	9	10	11[g]	12	13	**14**	16
	17	18	19	20	21	22	23
	24	25	26	27	28	29	30
	1	2	3	4	5	6	7

HINDU SOLAR 1956/1957

Month	Sun	Mon	Tue	Wed	Thu	Fri	Sat
PAUSHA 1956	16	17	18	19	20	21	22
	23	24	25	26	27	28	29
	1[b]	2	3	4	5	6	7
MĀGHA 1956	8	9	10	11	12	13	14
	15	16	17	18	19	20	21
	22	23	24	25	26	27	28
	29	30	1	2	3	4	5
PHĀLGUNA 1956	6	7	8	9	10	11	12
	13	14	15	16	17	18	19
	20	21	22	23	24	25	26
	27	28	29	30	1	2	3
CHAITRA 1956	4	5	6	7	8	9	10
	11	12	13	14	15	16	17
	18	19	20	21	22	23	24
	25	26	27	28	29	30	1[a]
VAIŚĀKHA 1957	2	3	4	5	6	7	8
	9	10	11	12	13	14	15
	16	17	18	19	20	21	22
	23	24	25	26	27	28	29
	30	31	1	2	3	4	5
JYAISHTHA 1957	6	7	8	9	10	11	12
	13	14	15	16	17	18	19
	20	21	22	23	24	25	26
	27	28	29	30	31	1	2
ĀSHĀDHA 1957	3	4	5	6	7	8	9
	10	11	12	13	14	15	16
	17	18	19	20	21	22	23
	24	25	26	27	28	29	30
	31	32	1	2	3	4	5
ŚRĀVAṆA 1957	6	7	8	9	10	11	12
	13	14	15	16	17	18	19
	20	21	22	23	24	25	26
	27	28	29	30	31	32	1
BHĀDRAPADA 1957	2	3	4	5	6	7	8
	9	10	11	12	13	14	15
	16	17	18	19	20	21	22
	23	24	25	26	27	28	29
	30	31	1	2	3	4	5
ĀŚVINA 1957	6	7	8	9	10	11	12
	13	14	15	16	17	18	19
	20	21	22	23	24	25	26
	27	28	29	30	1	2	3
KĀRTTIKA 1957	4	5	6	7	8	9	10
	11	12	13	14	15	16	17
	18	19	20	21	22	23	24
	25	26	27	28	29	30	1
MĀRGAŚĪRA 1957	2	3	4	5	6	7	8
	9	10	11	12	13	14	15
	16	17	18	19	20	21	22
	23	24	25	26	27	28	29
PAUSHA 1957	1	2	3	4	5	6	7
	8	9	10	11	12	13	14
	15	16	17	18	19	20	21

ISLAMIC (ASTRONOMICAL) 1456/1457‡

Month	Sun	Mon	Tue	Wed	Thu	Fri	Sat
SHAWWĀL 1456	20	21	22	23	24	25	26
	27	28	29	*30*	1	2	3
DHU AL-QA'DA 1456	4	5	6	7	8	9	10
	11	12	13	14	15	16	17
	18	19	20	21	22	23	24
	25	26	27	28	29	*30*	1
DHU AL-ḤIJJA 1456	2	3	4	5	6	7	8
	9	10[g]	11	12	13	14	15
	16	17	18	19	20	21	22
	23	24	25	26	27	28	29
MUḤARRAM 1457	*1*[a]	2	3	4	5	6	7
	8	9	10[b]	11	12	13	14
	15	16	17	18	19	20	21
	22	23	24	25	26	27	28
	29	30	*1*	2	3	4	5
ṢAFAR 1457	6	7	8	9	10	11	12
	13	14	15	16	17	18	19
	20	21	22	23	24	25	26
	27	28	29	*1*	2	3	4
RABĪ' I 1457	5	6	7	8	9	10	11
	12[c]	13	14	15	16	17	18
	19	20	21	22	23	24	25
	26	27	28	29	1	*2*	3
RABĪ' II 1457	4	5	6	7	8	9	10
	11	12	13	14	15	16	17
	18	19	20	21	22	23	24
	25	26	27	28	29	30	*1*
JUMĀDĀ I 1457	2	3	4	5	6	7	8
	9	10	11	12	13	14	15
	16	17	18	19	20	21	22
	23	24	25	26	27	28	29
JUMĀDĀ II 1457	1	2	3	4	5	6	7
	8	9	10	11	12	13	14
	15	16	17	18	19	20	21
	22	23	24	25	26	27	28
	29	30	*1*	2	3	4	5
RAJAB 1457	6	7	8	9	10	11	12
	13	14	15	16	17	18	19
	20	21	22	23	24	25	26
	27[d]	28	29	1	*2*	3	4
SHA'BĀN 1457	5	6	7	8	9	10	11
	12	13	14	15	16	17	18
	19	20	21	22	23	24	25
	26	27	28	29	1[e]	2	3
RAMAḌĀN 1457	4	5	6	7	8	9	10
	11	12	13	14	15	16	17
	18	19	20	21	22	23	24
	25	26	27	28	29	30	1[f]
SHAWWĀL 1457	2	3	4	5	6	7	8
	9	10	11	12	13	14	15
	16	17	18	19	20	21	22
	23	24	25	26	27	28	29
	30	*1*	2	3	4	5	6

GREGORIAN 2035

Julian (Sun)	Sun	Mon	Tue	Wed	Thu	Fri	Sat	Month
Dec 18	31	1	2	3	4	5	6	JANUARY 2035
	7[a]	8	9	10	11	12	13	
Jan 1	14[b]	15	16	17	18	19	20	
	21	22	23	24	25	26	27	
Jan 15	28	29	30	31	1	2	3	FEBRUARY 2035
	4	5	6	7[c]	8	9	10	
Jan 29	*11*	12	13	14	15	16	17	
	18	19	20	21	22	23	24	
Feb 12	25	26	27	28	1	2	3	MARCH 2035
	4	5	6	7	8	9	10	
Feb 26	*11*	12	13	14	15	16	17	
	18[d]	19	20	21	22	23	24	
Mar 12	25[e]	26	27	28	29	30	31	
	1	2	3	4	5	6	7	APRIL 2035
Mar 26	*8*	9	10	11	12	13	14	
	15	16	17	18	19	20	21	
Apr 9	*22*	23	24	25	26	27	28	
	29[f]	30	1	2	3	4	5	MAY 2035
Apr 23	*6*	7	8	9	10	11	12	
	13	14	15	16	17	18	19	
May 7	*20*	21	22	23	24	25	26	
	27	28	29	30	31	1	2	JUNE 2035
May 21	*3*	4	5	6	7	8	9	
	10	11	12	13	14	15	16	
Jun 4	*17*	18	19	20	21	22	23	
	24	25	26	27	28	29	30	
Jun 18	*1*	2	3	4	5	6	7	JULY 2035
	8	9	10	11	12	13	14	
Jul 2	*15*	16	17	18	19	20	21	
	22	23	24	25	26	27	28	
Jul 16	29	30	31	1	2	3	4	AUGUST 2035
	5	6	7	8	9	10	11	
Jul 30	*12*	13	14	15	16	17	18	
	19	20	21	22	23	24	25	
Aug 13	26	27	28	29	30	31	1	SEPTEMBER 2035
	2	3	4	5	6	7	8	
Aug 27	9	10	11	12	13	14	15	
	16	17	18	19	20	21	22	
Sep 10	*23*	24	25	26	27	28	29	
	30	1	2	3	4	5	6	OCTOBER 2035
Sep 24	*7*	8	9	10	11	12	13	
	14	15	16	17	18	19	20	
Oct 8	*21*	22	23	24	25	26	27	
	28	29	30	31	1	2	3	NOVEMBER 2035
Oct 22	*4*	5	6	7	8	9	10	
	11	12	13	14	15	16	17	
Nov 5	*18*	19	20	21	22	23	24	
	25	26	27	28	29	30	1	DECEMBER 2035
Nov 19	2[g]	3	4	5	6	7	8	
	9	10	11	12	13	14	15	
Dec 3	*16*	17	18	19	20	21	22	
	23	24	25[h]	26	27	28	29	
Dec 17	*30*	31	1	2	3	4	5	

Persian: [a]New Year; [b]Sizdeh Bedar

Hindu Lunar: ‡Leap year; [a]New Year (Rākshasa); [b]Birthday of Rāma; [c]Birthday of Krishna; [d]Ganēśa Chaturthī; [e]Dashara; [f]Diwali; [g]Birthday of Vishnu; [h]Night of Śiva; [i]Holi

Hindu Solar: [a]New Year (Śukla); [b]Pongal

Islamic: ‡Leap year; [a]New Year; [b]'Ashūrā'; [c]Prophet's Birthday; [d]Ascent of the Prophet; [e]Start of Ramaḍān; [f]'Id al-Fiṭr; [g]'Id al-'Aḍḥā

Gregorian: [a]Orthodox Christmas; [b]Julian New Year; [c]Ash Wednesday; [d]Feast of Orthodoxy; [e]Easter; [f]Orthodox Easter; [g]Advent; [h]Christmas

2036

Gregorian 2036‡	Sun	Mon	Tue	Wed	Thu	Fri	Sat	Lunar Phases	ISO Week (Mon)	Julian Day (Sun noon)
JANUARY 2036	30	31	1[a]	2	3	4	5		1	2464692
	◐	7	8	9	10	11	12	17:47	2	2464699
	○	14	15	16	17	18	19	11:15	3	2464706
	◑	21	22	23	24	25	26	6:45	4	2464713
FEBRUARY 2036	27	●	29	30	31	1	2	10:16	5	2464720
	3	4	◐	6	7	8	9	7:00	6	2464727
	10	○	12	13	14	15	16	22:07	7	2464734
	17	◑	19	20	21	22	23	23:46	8	2464741
MARCH 2036	24	25	26	●	28	29	1	4:58	9	2464748
	2	3	4	◐	6	7	8	16:48	10	2464755
	9	10	11	○	13	14	15	9:08	11	2464762
	16	17	18	◑	20[b]	21	22	18:37	12	2464769
	23	24	25	26	●	28	29	20:56	13	2464776
APRIL 2036	30	31	1	2	3	◐	5	0:02	14	2464783
	6	7	8	9	○	11	12	20:21	15	2464790
	13	14	15	16	17	◑	19	14:05	16	2464797
	20	21	22	23	24	25	●	9:32	17	2464804
MAY 2036	27	28	29	30	1	2	◐	5:53	18	2464811
	4	5	6	7	8	9	○	8:08	19	2464818
	11	12	13	14	15	16	17		20	2464825
	◑	19	20	21	22	23	24	8:38	21	2464832
	●	26	27	28	29	30	31	19:16	22	2464839
JUNE 2036	◐	2	3	4	5	6	7	11:33	23	2464846
	○	9	10	11	12	13	14	21:01	24	2464853
	15	16	◑	18	19	20[c]	21	1:02	25	2464860
	22	23	●	25	26	27	28	3:08	26	2464867
JULY 2036	29	◐	1	2	3	4	5	18:12	27	2464874
	6	7	○	9	10	11	12	11:18	28	2464881
	13	14	15	◑	17	18	19	14:38	29	2464888
	20	21	22	●	24	25	26	10:16	30	2464895
AUGUST 2036	27	28	29	◐	31	1	2	2:55	31	2464902
	3	4	5	6	○	8	9	2:48	32	2464909
	10	11	12	13	14	◑	16	1:35	33	2464916
	17	18	19	20	●	22	23	17:34	34	2464923
	24	25	26	27	◐	29	30	14:42	35	2464930
SEPTEMBER 2036	31	1	2	3	4	○	6	18:44	36	2464937
	7	8	9	10	11	12	◑	10:28	37	2464944
	14	15	16	17	18	19	●	1:50	38	2464951
	21	22[d]	23	24	25	26	◐	6:11	39	2464958
OCTOBER 2036	28	29	30	1	2	3	4		40	2464965
	○	6	7	8	9	10	11	10:14	41	2464972
	◑	13	14	15	16	17	18	18:08	42	2464979
	●	20	21	22	23	24	25	11:49	43	2464986
NOVEMBER 2036	26	◐	28	29	30	31	1	1:12	44	2464993
	2	3	○	5	6	7	8	0:43	45	2465000
	9	10	◑	12	13	14	15	1:27	46	2465007
	16	17	●	19	20	21	22	0:13	47	2465014
	23	24	◐	26	27	28	29	22:27	48	2465021
DECEMBER 2036	30	1	2	○	4	5	6	14:07	49	2465028
	7	8	9	◑	11	12	13	9:17	50	2465035
	14	15	16	●	18	19	20	15:33	51	2465042
	21[e]	22	23	24	◐	26	27	19:43	52	2465049
	28	29	30	31	1	○	3	2:34	1	2465056

Julian Day	Hebrew 5796/5797	Sun	Mon	Tue	Wed	Thu	Fri	Sat	Molad
2464692	TEVETH 5796	29[e]	30[e]	1[e]	2[e]	3	4	5	Sat 21h25m8p
2464699		6	7	8	9	10	11	12	
2464706		13	14	15	16	17	18	19	
2464713		20	21	22	23	24	25	26	
2464720	SHEVAT 5796	27	28	29	1	2	3	4	Mon 10h9m9p
2464727		5	6	7	8	9	10	11	
2464734		12	13	14	15	16	17	18	
2464741		19	20	21	22	23	24	25	
2464748	ADAR 5796	26	27	28	29	30	1	2	Tue 22h53m10p
2464755		3	4	5	6	7	8	9	
2464762		10	11	12	13	14[f]	15	16	
2464769		17	18	19	20	21	22	23	
2464776	NISAN 5796	24	25	26	27	28	29	1	Thu 11h37m11p
2464783		2	3	4	5	6	7	8	
2464790		9	10	11	12	13	14	15[g]	
2464797		16	17	18	19	20	21	22	
2464804		23	24	25	26	27	28	29	Sat 0h21m12p
2464811	IYYAR 5796	30	1	2	3	4	5	6	
2464818		7	8	9	10	11	12	13	
2464825		14	15	16	17	18	19	20	
2464832		21	22	23	24	25	26	27	
2464839	SIVAN 5796	28	29	1	2	3	4	5	Sun 13h5m13p
2464846		6[h]	7	8	9	10	11	12	
2464853		13	14	15	16	17	18	19	
2464860		20	21	22	23	24	25	26	
2464867	TAMMUZ 5796	27	28	29	30	1	2	3	Tue 1h49m14p
2464874		4	5	6	7	8	9	10	
2464881		11	12	13	14	15	16	17	
2464888		18	19	20	21	22	23	24	
2464895	AV 5796	25	26	27	28	29	1	2	Wed 14h33m15p
2464902		3	4	5	6	7	8	9	
2464909		10[i]	11	12	13	14	15	16	
2464916		17	18	19	20	21	22	23	
2464923		24	25	26	27	28	29	30	
2464930	ELUL 5796	1	2	3	4	5	6	7	Fri 3h17m16p
2464937		8	9	10	11	12	13	14	
2464944		15	16	17	18	19	20	21	
2464951		22	23	24	25	26	27	28	
2464958	TISHRI 5797	29	1[a]	2[a]	3	4	5	6	Sat 16h1m17p
2464965		7	8	9	10[b]	11	12	13	
2464972		14	15[c]	16	17	18	19	20	
2464979		21	22	23	24	25	26	27	
2464986	HESHVAN 5797	28	29	30	1	2	3	4	Mon 4h46m0p
2464993		5	6	7	8	9	10	11	
2465000		12	13	14	15	16	17	18	
2465007		19	20	21	22	23	24	25	
2465014	KISLEV 5797	26	27	28	29	1	2	3	Tue 17h30m1p
2465021		4	5	6	7	8	9	10	
2465028		11	12	13	14	15	16[d]	17	
2465035		18	19	20	21	22	23	24	
2465042	TEVETH 5797	25[e]	26[e]	27[e]	28[e]	29[e]	1[e]	2[e]	Thu 6h14m2p
2465049		3[e]	4	5	6	7	8	9	
2465056		10	11	12	13	14	15	16	

Julian Day	Chinese Yǐ-Mǎo/Bǐng-Chén‡	Sun	Mon	Tue	Wed	Thu	Fri	Sat	Solar Term
2464692	MONTH 12 Yǐ-Mǎo	2	3	4	5	6	7	8	
2464699		*9*	10	11	12	13	14	15	*Xiǎo hán*
2464706		16	17	18	19	20	21	22	
2464713		**23**	24	25	26	27	28	29	**Dà hán**
2464720	MONTH 1 Bǐng-Chén	30	1[a]	2	3	4	5	6	
2464727		7	*8*	9	10	11	12	13	*Lì chūn*
2464734		14	15[b]	16	17	18	19	20	
2464741		21	22	**23**	24	25	26	27	**Yǔ shuǐ**
2464748	MONTH 2 Bǐng-Chén	28	29	30	1*	2	3	4	
2464755		5	6	7	*8*	9	10	11	*Jīng zhé*
2464762		12	13	14	15	16	17	18	
2464769		19	20	21	22	**23**	24	25	**Chūn fēn**
2464776	MONTH 3 Bǐng-Chén	26	27	28	29	30	1	2	
2464783		3	4	5	6	7	*8*[c]	9	*Qīng míng*
2464790		10	11	12	13	14	15	16	
2464797		17	18	19	20	21	22	**23**	**Gǔ yǔ**
2464804	MONTH 4 Bǐng-Chén	24	25	26	27	28	29	1	
2464811		2*	3	4	5	6	7	8	
2464818		9	*10*	11	12	13	14	15	*Lì xià*
2464825		16	17	18	19	20	21	22	
2464832		23	24	**25**	26	27	28	29	**Xiǎo mǎn**
2464839	MONTH 5 Bǐng-Chén	30	1	2	3	4	5[d]	6	
2464846		7	8	9	10	*11*	12	13	*Máng zhòng*
2464853		14	15	16	17	18	19	20	
2464860		21	22	23	24	25	26	**27**	**Xià zhì**
2464867	MONTH 6 Bǐng-Chén	28	29	1	2	3*	4	5	
2464874		6	7	8	9	10	11	12	
2464881		*13*	14	15	16	17	18	19	*Xiǎo shǔ*
2464888		20	21	22	23	24	25	26	
2464895	LEAP MONTH 6 Bǐng-Chén	27	28	**29**	1	2	3	4	**Dà shǔ**
2464902		5	6	7	8	9	10	11	
2464909		12	13	14	15	*16*	17	18	*Lì qiū*
2464916		19	20	21	22	23	24	25	
2464923	MONTH 7 Bǐng-Chén	26	27	28	29	30	**1**	2	**Chǔ shǔ**
2464930		3	4*	5	6	7[e]	8	9	
2464937		10	11	12	13	14	15[f]	16	
2464944		*17*	18	19	20	21	22	23	*Bái lù*
2464951	MONTH 8 Bǐng-Chén	24	25	26	27	28	29	1	
2464958		2	**3**	4	5	6	7	8	**Qiū fēn**
2464965		9	10	11	12	13	14	15[g]	
2464972		16	17	18	*19*	20	21	22	*Hán lù*
2464979		23	24	25	26	27	28	29	
2464986	MONTH 9 Bǐng-Chén	1	2	3	4	**5**	6*	7	**Shuāng jiàng**
2464993		8	9[h]	10	11	12	13	14	
2465000		15	16	17	18	19	*20*	21	*Lì dōng*
2465007		22	23	24	25	26	27	28	
2465014	MONTH 10 Bǐng-Chén	29	30	1	2	3	4	**5**	**Xiǎo xuě**
2465021		6	7	8	9	10	11	12	
2465028		13	14	15	16	17	18	*19*	*Dà xuě*
2465035		20	21	22	23	24	25	26	
2465042	MONTH 11 Bǐng-Chén	27	28	29	1	2	3	4	
2465049		**5**[i]	6	7*	8	9	10	11	**Dōng zhì**
2465056		12	13	14	15	16	17	18	

Julian Day	Coptic 1752/1753	Sun	Mon	Tue	Wed	Thu	Fri	Sat	Ethiopic 2028/2029
2464692	KOIAK 1752	20	21	22	23	24	25	26	TĀKHŚĀŚ 2028
2464699	TÔBE 1752	27	28	29[c]	30	1	2	3	ṬER 2028
2464706		4	5	6[d]	7	8	9	10	
2464713		11[e]	12	13	14	15	16	17	
2464720		18	19	20	21	22	23	24	
2464727	MESHIR 1752	25	26	27	28	29	30	1	YAKĀTIT 2028
2464734		2	3	4	5	6	7	8	
2464741		9	10	11	12	13	14	15	
2464748		16	17	18	19	20	21	22	
2464755		23	24	25	26	27	28	29	
2464762	PAREMOTEP 1752	30	1	2	3	4	5	6	MAGĀBIT 2028
2464769		7	8	9	10	11	12	13	
2464776		14	15	16	17	18	19	20	
2464783		21	22	23	24	25	26	27	
2464790	PARMOUTE 1752	28	29	30	1	2	3	4	MIYĀZYĀ 2028
2464797		5	6	7	8	9	10	11	
2464804		12[f]	13	14	15	16	17	18	
2464811		19	20	21	22	23	24	25	
2464818	PASHONS 1752	26	27	28	29[g]	30	1	2	GENBOT 2028
2464825		3	4	5	6	7	8	9	
2464832		10	11	12	13	14	15	16	
2464839		17	18	19	20	21	22	23	
2464846		24	25	26	27	28	29	30	
2464853	PAÔNE 1752	1	2	3	4	5	6	7	SANĒ 2028
2464860		8	9	10	11	12	13	14	
2464867		15	16	17	18	19	20	21	
2464874		22	23	24	25	26	27	28	
2464881	EPÊP 1752	29	30	1	2	3	4	5	ḤAMLĒ 2028
2464888		6	7	8	9	10	11	12	
2464895		13	14	15	16	17	18	19	
2464902		20	21	22	23	24	25	26	
2464909	MESORÊ 1752	27	28	29	30	1	2	3	NAHASĒ 2028
2464916		4	5	6	7	8	9	10	
2464923		11	12	13[h]	14	15	16	17	
2464930		18	19	20	21	22	23	24	
2464937	EPAG. 1752	25	26	27	28	29	30	1	PĀG. 2028
2464944	THOOUT 1753	2	3	4	5	1[a]	2	3	MASKARAM 2029
2464951		4	5	6	7	8	9	10	
2464958		11	12	13	14	15	16	17[b]	
2464965		18	19	20	21	22	23	24	
2464972	PAOPE 1753	25	26	27	28	29	30	1	ṬEQEMT 2029
2464979		2	3	4	5	6	7	8	
2464986		9	10	11	12	13	14	15	
2464993		16	17	18	19	20	21	22	
2465000		23	24	25	26	27	28	29	
2465007	ATHÔR 1753	30	1	2	3	4	5	6	ḤEDĀR 2029
2465014		7	8	9	10	11	12	13	
2465021		14	15	16	17	18	19	20	
2465028		21	22	23	24	25	26	27	
2465035	KOIAK 1753	28	29	30	1	2	3	4	TĀKHŚĀŚ 2029
2465042		5	6	7	8	9	10	11	
2465049		12	13	14	15	16	17	18	
2465056		19	20	21	22	23	24	25	

Gregorian notes:
‡Leap year
[a]New Year
[b]Spring (1:01)
[c]Summer (18:30)
[d]Autumn (10:22)
[e]Winter (7:11)
● New moon
◐ First quarter moon
○ Full moon
◑ Last quarter moon

Hebrew notes:
[a]New Year
[b]Yom Kippur
[c]Sukkot
[d]Winter starts
[e]Ḥanukkah
[f]Purim
[g]Passover
[h]Shavuot
[i]Fast of Av

Chinese notes:
‡Leap year
[a]New Year (4734, Dragon)
[b]Lantern Festival
[c]Qīngmíng
[d]Dragon Festival
[e]Qīqiǎo
[f]Hungry Ghosts
[g]Mid-Autumn Festival
[h]Double-Ninth Festival
[i]Dōngzhì
*Start of 60-name cycle

Coptic/Ethiopic notes:
[a]New Year
[b]Building of the Cross
[c]Christmas
[d]Jesus's Circumcision
[e]Epiphany
[f]Easter
[g]Mary's Announcement
[h]Jesus's Transfiguration

PERSIAN (ASTRONOMICAL) 1414/1415

Month	Sun	Mon	Tue	Wed	Thu	Fri	Sat
	9	10	11	12	13	14	15
DEY 1414	16	17	18	19	20	21	22
	23	24	25	26	27	28	29
	30	1	2	3	4	5	6
	7	8	9	10	11	12	13
BAHMAN 1414	14	15	16	17	18	19	20
	21	22	23	24	25	26	27
	28	29	30	1	2	3	4
	5	6	7	8	9	10	11
ESFAND 1414	12	13	14	15	16	17	18
	19	20	21	22	23	24	25
	26	27	28	29	1[a]	2	3
	4	5	6	7	8	9	10
FARVARDĪN 1415	11	12	13[b]	14	15	16	17
	18	19	20	21	22	23	24
	25	26	27	28	29	30	31
	1	2	3	4	5	6	7
ORDĪBEHEŠT 1415	8	9	10	11	12	13	14
	15	16	17	18	19	20	21
	22	23	24	25	26	27	28
	29	30	31	1	2	3	4
	5	6	7	8	9	10	11
XORDĀD 1415	12	13	14	15	16	17	18
	19	20	21	22	23	24	25
	26	27	28	29	30	31	1
	2	3	4	5	6	7	8
TĪR 1415	9	10	11	12	13	14	15
	16	17	18	19	20	21	22
	23	24	25	26	27	28	29
	30	31	1	2	3	4	5
MORDĀD 1415	6	7	8	9	10	11	12
	13	14	15	16	17	18	19
	20	21	22	23	24	25	26
	27	28	29	30	31	1	2
SHAHRĪVAR 1415	3	4	5	6	7	8	9
	10	11	12	13	14	15	16
	17	18	19	20	21	22	23
	24	25	26	27	28	29	30
	31	1	2	3	4	5	6
MEHR 1415	7	8	9	10	11	12	13
	14	15	16	17	18	19	20
	21	22	23	24	25	26	27
	28	29	30	1	2	3	4
ĀBĀN 1415	5	6	7	8	9	10	11
	12	13	14	15	16	17	18
	19	20	21	22	23	24	25
	26	27	28	29	30	1	2
ĀZAR 1415	3	4	5	6	7	8	9
	10	11	12	13	14	15	16
	17	18	19	20	21	22	23
	24	25	26	27	28	29	30
DEY 1415	1	2	3	4	5	6	7
	8	9	10	11	12	13	14

[a]New Year
[b]Sizdeh Bedar

HINDU LUNAR 2092/2093

Month	Sun	Mon	Tue	Wed	Thu	Fri	Sat
	1	2	3	4	5	6	7
PAUSHA 2092	8	9	10	11	12	13	14
	15	16	17	18	19	**20**	22
	23	24	25	26	26	27	28
	29	30	1	2	3	4	5
MĀGHA 2092	6	7	8	9	10	11	12
	13	15	16	17	18	19	20
	21	22	23	24	25	26	27
	28	29[h]	29	30	1	2	3
PHĀLGUNA 2092	4	5	6	**7**	9	10	11
	12	13	14	15[i]	16	17	18
	19	20	21	22	23	24	25
	26	27	28	29	30	1[a]	2
CHAITRA 2093	3	4	5	6	7	8	9[b]
	10	11	**12**	14	15	16	17
	18	19	20	21	22	23	23
	24	25	26	27	28	29	30
	1	2	3	4	**5**	7	8
VAIŚĀKHA 2093	9	10	11	12	13	14	15
	16	17	18	19	20	21	22
	23	24	25	26	27	28	29
	30	1	2	3	4	5	6
JYAISHTHA 2093	7	**8**	10	11	12	13	14
	15	16	17	18	18	19	20
	21	22	23	24	25	26	27
	28	29	30	**1**	3	4	5
ĀSHĀDHA 2093	6	7	8	9	10	11	12
	13	14	15	16	17	18	19
	20	21	22	23	24	25	26
	27	28	29	30	1	2	3
ŚRĀVAṆA 2093	**4**	6	7	8	9	10	11
	12	13	14	15	15	16	17
	18	19	20	21	22	23[c]	24
	25	26	**27**	29	30	1	2
BHĀDRAPADA 2093	3	4[d]	5	6	7	8	9
	10	11	12	13	14	15	16
	17	18	19	20	21	22	23
	24	25	26	27	28	29	**30**
	2	3	4	5	6	7	8[e]
ĀŚVINA 2093	9[e]	10[e]	11	11	12	13	14
	15	16	17	18	19	20	21
	22	**23**	25	26	27	28	29
	30	1[f]	2	3	4	5	6
KĀRTTIKA 2093	7	8	9	10	11	12	13
	14	15	16	17	18	19	20
	21	22	23	24	25	26	27
	28	30	1	2	3	4	4
MĀRGAŚĪRA 2093	5	6	7	8	9	10	11[g]
	12	13	14	15	16	17	18
	19	20	**21**	23	24	25	26
	27	28	29	30	1	2	3
PAUSHA 2093	4	5	6	7	7	8	9
	10	11	12	13	14	**15**	17

[a]New Year (Anala)
[b]Birthday of Rāma
[c]Birthday of Krishna
[d]Ganēśa Chaturthī
[e]Dashara
[f]Diwali
[g]Birthday of Vishnu
[h]Night of Śiva
[i]Holi

HINDU SOLAR 1957/1958‡

Month	Sun	Mon	Tue	Wed	Thu	Fri	Sat
	15	16	17	18	19	20	21
PAUSHA 1957	22	23	24	25	26	27	28
	29	30	1[b]	2	3	4	5
	6	7	8	9	10	11	12
MĀGHA 1957	13	14	15	16	17	18	19
	20	21	22	23	24	25	26
	27	28	29	1	2	3	4
	5	6	7	8	9	10	11
PHĀLGUNA 1957	12	13	14	15	16	17	18
	19	20	21	22	23	24	25
	26	27	28	29	30	1	2
	3	4	5	6	7	8	9
CHAITRA 1957	10	11	12	13	14	15	16
	17	18	19	20	21	22	23
	24	25	26	27	28	29	30
	1[a]	2	3	4	5	6	7
VAIŚĀKHA 1958	8	9	10	11	12	13	14
	15	16	17	18	19	20	21
	22	23	24	25	26	27	28
	29	30	31	1	2	3	4
JYAISHTHA 1958	5	6	7	8	9	10	11
	12	13	14	15	16	17	18
	19	20	21	22	23	24	25
	26	27	28	29	30	31	32
	1	2	3	4	5	6	7
ĀSHĀDHA 1958	8	9	10	11	12	13	14
	15	16	17	18	19	20	21
	22	23	24	25	26	27	28
	29	30	31	1	2	3	4
ŚRĀVAṆA 1958	5	6	7	8	9	10	11
	12	13	14	15	16	17	18
	19	20	21	22	23	24	25
	26	27	28	29	30	31	32
	1	2	3	4	5	6	7
BHĀDRAPADA 1958	8	9	10	11	12	13	14
	15	16	17	18	19	20	21
	22	23	24	25	26	27	28
	29	30	31	1	2	3	4
ĀŚVINA 1958	5	6	7	8	9	10	11
	12	13	14	15	16	17	18
	19	20	21	22	23	24	25
	26	27	28	29	30	1	2
KĀRTTIKA 1958	3	4	5	6	7	8	9
	10	11	12	13	14	15	16
	17	18	19	20	21	22	23
	24	25	26	27	28	29	30
	1	2	3	4	5	6	7
MĀRGAŚĪRA 1958	8	9	10	11	12	13	14
	15	16	17	18	19	20	21
	22	23	24	25	26	27	28
	29	30	1	2	3	4	5
PAUSHA 1958	6	7	8	9	10	11	12
	13	14	15	16	17	18	19

‡Leap year
[a]New Year (Pramoda)
[b]Pongal

ISLAMIC (ASTRONOMICAL) 1457‡/1458

Month	Sun	Mon	Tue	Wed	Thu	Fri	Sat
	30	1	2	3	4	5	6
DHU AL-QA'DA 1457	7	8	9	10	11	12	13
	14	15	16	17	18	19	20
	21	22	23	24	25	26	27
	28	29	30	1	2	3	4
DHU AL-ḤIJJA 1457	5	6	7	8	9	10[g]	11
	12	13	14	15	16	17	18
	19	20	21	22	23	24	25
	26	27	28	29	30[a]	1[a]	2
MUḤARRAM 1458	3	4	5	6	7	8	9
	10[b]	11	12	13	14	15	16
	17	18	19	20	21	22	23
	24	25	26	27	28	29	1
	2	3	4	5	6	7	8
ṢAFAR 1458	9	10	11	12	13	14	15
	16	17	18	19	20	21	22
	23	24	25	26	27	28	29
	30	1	2	3	4	5	6
RABĪ' I 1458	7	8	9	10	11	12[c]	13
	14	15	16	17	18	19	20
	21	22	23	24	25	26	27
	28	29	1	2	3	4	5
RABĪ' II 1458	6	7	8	9	10	11	12
	13	14	15	16	17	18	19
	20	21	22	23	24	25	26
	27	28	29	1	2	3	4
JUMĀDĀ I 1458	5	6	7	8	9	10	11
	12	13	14	15	16	17	18
	19	20	21	22	23	24	25
	26	27	28	29	30	1	2
JUMĀDĀ II 1458	3	4	5	6	7	8	9
	10	11	12	13	14	15	16
	17	18	19	20	21	22	23
	24	25	26	27	28	29	1
RAJAB 1458	2	3	4	5	6	7	8
	9	10	11	12	13	14	15
	16	17	18	19	20	21	22
	23	24	25	26	27[d]	28	29
	1	2	3	4	5	6	7
SHA'BĀN 1458	8	9	10	11	12	13	14
	15	16	17	18	19	20	21
	22	23	24	25	26	27	28
	29	30	1[e]	2	3	4	5
RAMAḌĀN 1458	6	7	8	9	10	11	12
	13	14	15	16	17	18	19
	20	21	22	23	24	25	26
	27	28	29	1[f]	2	3	4
SHAWWĀL 1458	5	6	7	8	9	10	11
	12	13	14	15	16	17	18
	19	20	21	22	23	24	25
	26	27	28	29	30	1	2
DHU AL-QA'DA 1458	3	4	5	6	7	8	9
	10	11	12	13	14	15	16

‡Leap year
[a]New Year
[ā]New Year (Arithmetic)
[b]'Ashūrā'
[c]Prophet's Birthday
[d]Ascent of the Prophet
[e]Start of Ramaḍān
[f]'Id al-Fiṭr
[g]'Id al-'Aḍḥā

GREGORIAN 2036‡

Julian‡ (Sun)	Sun	Mon	Tue	Wed	Thu	Fri	Sat	Month
Dec 17	30	31	1	2	3	4	5	
	6	7[a]	8	9	10	11	12	JANUARY 2036
Dec 31	13	14[b]	15	16	17	18	19	
	20	21	22	23	24	25	26	
Jan 14	27	28	29	30	31	1	2	
	3	4	5	6	7	8	9	FEBRUARY 2036
Jan 28	10	11	12	13	14	15	16	
	17	18	19	20	21	22	23	
Feb 11	24	25	26	27[c]	28	29	1	
	2	3	4	5	6	7	8	
Feb 25	9[d]	10	11	12	13	14	15	MARCH 2036
	16	17	18	19	20	21	22	
Mar 10	23	24	25	26	27	28	29	
	30	31	1	2	3	4	5	
Mar 24	6	7	8	9	10	11	12	APRIL 2036
	13[e]	14	15	16	17	18	19	
Apr 7	20[f]	21	22	23	24	25	26	
	27	28	29	30	1	2	3	
Apr 21	4	5	6	7	8	9	10	MAY 2036
	11	12	13	14	15	16	17	
May 5	18	19	20	21	22	23	24	
	25	26	27	28	29	30	31	
May 19	1	2	3	4	5	6	7	
	8	9	10	11	12	13	14	JUNE 2036
Jun 2	15	16	17	18	19	20	21	
	22	23	24	25	26	27	28	
Jun 16	29	30	1	2	3	4	5	
	6	7	8	9	10	11	12	JULY 2036
Jun 30	13	14	15	16	17	18	19	
	20	21	22	23	24	25	26	
Jul 14	27	28	29	30	31	1	2	
	3	4	5	6	7	8	9	
Jul 28	10	11	12	13	14	15	16	AUGUST 2036
	17	18	19	20	21	22	23	
Aug 11	24	25	26	27	28	29	30	
	31	1	2	3	4	5	6	
Aug 25	7	8	9	10	11	12	13	SEPTEMBER 2036
	14	15	16	17	18	19	20	
Sep 8	21	22	23	24	25	26	27	
	28	29	30	1	2	3	4	
Sep 22	5	6	7	8	9	10	11	OCTOBER 2036
	12	13	14	15	16	17	18	
Oct 6	19	20	21	22	23	24	25	
	26	27	28	29	30	31	1	
Oct 20	2	3	4	5	6	7	8	NOVEMBER 2036
	9	10	11	12	13	14	15	
Nov 3	16	17	18	19	20	21	22	
	23	24	25	26	27	28	29	
Nov 17	30[g]	1	2	3	4	5	6	
	7	8	9	10	11	12	13	DECEMBER 2036
Dec 1	14	15	16	17	18	19	20	
	21	22	23	24	25[h]	26	27	
Dec 15	28	29	30	31	1	2	3	

‡Leap year
[a]Orthodox Christmas
[b]Julian New Year
[c]Ash Wednesday
[d]Feast of Orthodoxy
[e]Easter
[f]Orthodox Easter
[g]Advent
[h]Christmas

2037

GREGORIAN 2037								Lunar Phases	ISO WEEK	JULIAN DAY	HEBREW 5797/5798‡								Molad	CHINESE Bǐng-Chén‡/Dīng-Sì								Solar Term	COPTIC 1753/1754								ETHIOPIC 2029/2030
	Sun	Mon	Tue	Wed	Thu	Fri	Sat		(Mon)	(Sun noon)		Sun	Mon	Tue	Wed	Thu	Fri	Sat			Sun	Mon	Tue	Wed	Thu	Fri	Sat			Sun	Mon	Tue	Wed	Thu	Fri	Sat	
JANUARY 2037	28	29	30	31	1[a]	○	3	2:34	1	2465056	TEVET 5797	10	11	12	13	14	15	16		MONTH 11 Bǐng-Chén	12	13	14	15	16	17	18		KOIAK 1753	19	20	21	22	23	24	25	TĀKHŚĀŚ 2029
	4	5	6	7	◑	9	10	18:28	2	2465063		17	18	19	20	21	22	23	Fri 18h58m3p		19	20	21	22	23	24	25	Xiǎo hán	TÔBE 1753	26	27	28	29[c]	30	1	2	ṬER 2029
	11	12	13	14	15	●	17	9:33	3	2465070	SHEVAT 5797	24	25	26	27	28	29	1		MONTH 12 Bǐng-Chén	26	27	28	29	30	1	2			3	4	5	6[d]	7	8	9	
	18	19	20	21	22	23	◐	14:54	4	2465077		2	3	4	5	6	7	8			3	4	5	6	7	8	9	Dà hán		10	11[e]	12	13	14	15	16	
	25	26	27	28	29	30	○	14:03	5	2465084		9	10	11	12	13	14	15			10	11	12	13	14	15	16			17	18	19	20	21	22	23	
FEBRUARY 2037	1	2	3	4	5	6	◑	5:42	6	2465091		16	17	18	19	20	21	22			17	18	19	20	21	22	23	Lì chūn		24	25	26	27	28	29	30	
	8	9	10	11	12	13	14		7	2465098		23	24	25	26	27	28	29			24	25	26	27	28	29	30		MESHIR 1753	1	2	3	4	5	6	7	YAKĀTIT 2029
	●	16	17	18	19	20	21	4:53	8	2465105	ADAR 5797	30	1	2	3	4	5	6	Sun 7h42m4p	MONTH 1 Dīng-Sì	1[a]	2	3	4	5	6	7*	Yǔ shuǐ		8	9	10	11	12	13	14	
	22	◐	24	25	26	27	28	6:40	9	2465112		7	8	9	10	11	12	13			8	9	10	11	12	13	14			15	16	17	18	19	20	21	
MARCH 2037	1	○	3	4	5	6	7	0:27	10	2465119		14[f]	15	16	17	18	19	20			15[b]	16	17	18	19	20	21	Jīng zhé		22	23	24	25	26	27	28	
	◑	9	10	11	12	13	14	19:24	11	2465126		21	22	23	24	25	26	27			22	23	24	25	26	27	28		PAREMOTEP 1753	29	30	1	2	3	4	5	MAGĀBIT 2029
	15	●	17	18	19	20[b]	21	23:35	12	2465133	NISAN 5797	28	29	1	2	3	4	5	Mon 20h26m5p	MONTH 2 Dīng-Sì	29	30	1	2	3	4	5	Chūn fēn		6	7	8	9	10	11	12	
	22	23	◐	25	26	27	28	18:38	13	2465140		6	7	8	9	10	11	12			6	7	8	9	10	11	12			13	14	15	16	17	18	19	
	29	30	○	1	2	3	4	9:52	14	2465147		13	14	15[g]	16	17	18	19			13	14	15	16	17	18	19[c]	Qīng míng		20	21	22	23	24	25	26	
APRIL 2037	5	6	◑	8	9	10	11	11:24	15	2465154		20	21	22	23*	24	25	26			20	21	22	23	24	25	26		PARMOUTE 1753	27[f]	28	29	30	1	2	3	MIYĀZYĀ 2029
	12	13	14	●	16	17	18	16:06	16	2465161	IYYAR 5797	27	28	29	30	1	2	3	Wed 9h10m6p	MONTH 3 Dīng-Sì	27	28	29	30	1	2	3			4	5	6	7	8	9	10	
	19	20	21	22	◐	24	25	3:10	17	2465168		4	5	6	7	8	9	10			4	5	6	7*	8	9	10	Gǔ yǔ		11	12	13	14	15	16	17	
	26	27	28	○	30	1	2	18:53	18	2465175		11	12	13	14	15	16	17			11	12	13	14	15	16	17			18	19	20	21	22	23	24	
MAY 2037	3	4	5	6	◑	8	9	4:55	19	2465182		18	19	20	21	22	23	24			18	19	20	21	22	23	24	Lì xià		25	26	27	28	29[g]	30	1	
	10	11	12	13	14	●	16	5:53	20	2465189	SIVAN 5797	25	26	27	28	29	1	2	Thu 21h54m7p	MONTH 4 Dīng-Sì	25	26	27	28	29	1	2		PASHONS 1753	2	3	4	5	6	7	8	GENBOT 2029
	17	18	19	20	21	◐	23	9:07	21	2465196		3	4	5	6[h]	7	8	9			3	4	5	6	7	8	9	Xiǎo mǎn		9	10	11	12	13	14	15	
	24	25	26	27	28	○	30	4:23	22	2465203		10	11	12	13	14	15	16			10	11	12	13	14	15	16			16	17	18	19	20	21	22	
JUNE 2037	31	1	2	3	4	◑	6	22:48	23	2465210		17	18	19	20	21	22	23			17	18	19	20	21	22	23	Máng zhòng		23	24	25	26	27	28	29	
	7	8	9	10	11	12	●	17:09	24	2465217		24	25	26	27	28	29	30			24	25	26	27	28	29	30		PAÔNE 1753	30	1	2	3	4	5	6	SANÉ 2029
	14	15	16	17	18	19	◐	13:44	25	2465224	TAMMUZ 5797	1	2	3	4	5	6	7	Sat 10h38m8p	MONTH 5 Dīng-Sì	1	2	3	4	5[d]	6	7	Xià zhì		7	8	9	10	11	12	13	
	21[c]	22	23	24	25	26	○	15:19	26	2465231		8	9	10	11	12	13	14			8*	9	10	11	12	13	14			14	15	16	17	18	19	20	
JULY 2037	28	29	30	1	2	3	4		27	2465238		15	16	17	18	19	20	21			15	16	17	18	19	20	21			21	22	23	24	25	26	27	
	◑	6	7	8	9	10	11	15:59	28	2465245		22	23	24	25	26	27	28			22	23	24	25	26	27	28	Xiǎo shǔ	EPÊP 1753	28	29	30	1	2	3	4	ḤAMLÉ 2029
	12	●	14	15	16	17	18	2:31	29	2465252	AV 5797	29	1	2	3	4	5	6	Sun 23h22m9p	MONTH 6 Dīng-Sì	29	1	2	3	4	5	6			5	6	7	8	9	10	11	
	◐	20	21	22	23	24	25	18:30	30	2465259		7	8	9[i]	10	11	12	13			7	8	9	10	11	12	13	Dà shǔ		12	13	14	15	16	17	18	
AUGUST 2037	26	○	28	29	30	31	1	4:14	31	2465266		14	15	16	17	18	19	20			14	15	16	17	18	19	20			19	20	21	22	23	24	25	
	2	3	◑	5	6	7	8	7:50	32	2465273		21	22	23	24	25	26	27			21	22	23	24	25	26	27	Lì qiū	MESORÊ 1753	26	27	28	29	30	1	2	NAḤASÉ 2029
	9	10	●	12	13	14	15	10:40	33	2465280	ELUL 5797	28	29	30	1	2	3	4	Tue 12h6m10p	MONTH 7 Dīng-Sì	28	29	1	2	3	4	5			3	4	5	6	7	8	9	
	16	17	◐	19	20	21	22	0:58	34	2465287		5	6	7	8	9	10	11			6	7[e]	8	9	10*	11	12			10	11	12	13[h]	14	15	16	
	23	24	○	26	27	28	29	19:08	35	2465294		12	13	14	15	16	17	18			13	14	15[f]	16	17	18	19	Chǔ shǔ		17	18	19	20	21	22	23	
SEPTEMBER 2037	30	31	1	◑	3	4	5	22:02	36	2465301		19	20	21	22	23	24	25			20	21	22	23	24	25	26			24	25	26	27	28	29	30	
	6	7	8	●	10	11	12	18:24	37	2465308	TISHRI 5798	26	27	28	29	1[a]	2[a]	3	Thu 0h50m11p	MONTH 8 Dīng-Sì	27	28	29	30	1	2	3	Bái lù	EPAG. 1753 / THOOUT 1754	1	2	3	4	5	1[a]	2	PĀG. 2029 / MASKARAM 2030
	13	14	15	◐	17	18	19	10:35	38	2465315		4	5	6	7	8	9	10[b]			4	5	6	7	8	9	10			3	4	5	6	7	8	9	
	20	21	22[d]	23	○	25	26	11:30	39	2465322		11	12	13	14	15[c]	16	17			11	12	13	14	15[g]	16	17	Qiū fēn		10	11	12	13	14	15	16	
OCTOBER 2037	27	28	29	30	1	◑	3	10:28	40	2465329		18	19	20	21	22	23	24			18	19	20	21	22	23	24			17[b]	18	19	20	21	22	23	
	4	5	6	7	8	●	10	2:33	41	2465336	HESHVAN 5798	25	26	27	28	29	30	1	Fri 13h34m12p	MONTH 9 Dīng-Sì	25	26	27	28	29	1	2	Hán lù		24	25	26	27	28	29	30	
	11	12	13	14	15	◐	17	0:14	42	2465343		2	3	4	5	6	7	8			3	4	5	6	7	8	9[h]		PAOPE 1754	1	2	3	4	5	6	7	ṬEQEMT 2030
	18	19	20	21	22	23	○	4:35	43	2465350		9	10	11	12	13	14	15			10	11*	12	13	14	15	16	Shuāng jiàng		8	9	10	11	12	13	14	
	25	26	27	28	29	30	◑	21:05	44	2465357		16	17	18	19	20	21	22			17	18	19	20	21	22	23			15	16	17	18	19	20	21	
NOVEMBER 2037	1	2	3	4	5	6	●	12:02	45	2465364		23	24	25	26	27	28	29		MONTH 10 Dīng-Sì	24	25	26	27	28	29	1	Lì dōng		22	23	24	25	26	27	28	
	8	9	10	11	12	13	◐	17:57	46	2465371	KISLEV 5798	30	1	2	3	4	5	6	Sun 2h18m13p		2	3	4	5	6	7	8		ATHÔR 1754	29	30	1	2	3	4	5	ḪEDĀR 2030
	15	16	17	18	19	20	21		47	2465378		7	8	9	10	11	12	13			9	10	11	12	13	14	15			6	7	8	9	10	11	12	
	○	23	24	25	26	27	28	21:34	48	2465385		14	15	16	17	18	19	20			16	17	18	19	20	21	22	Xiǎo xuě		13	14	15	16	17	18	19	
DECEMBER 2037	29	◑	1	2	3	4	5	6:05	49	2465392		21	22	23	24	25[e]	26[e]	27[d][e]			23	24	25	26	27	28	29			20	21	22	23	24	25	26	
	●	7	8	9	10	11	12	23:37	50	2465399	TEVET 5798	28[e]	29[e]	30[e]	1[e]	2[e]	3	4	Mon 15h2m14p	MONTH 11 Dīng-Sì	30	1	2	3	4	5	6	Dà xuě	KOIAK 1754	27	28	29	30	1	2	3	TĀKHŚĀŚ 2030
	13	◐	15	16	17	18	19	14:41	51	2465406		5	6	7	8	9	10	11			7	8	9	10	11	12*	13			4	5	6	7	8	9	10	
	20	21[e]	○	23	24	25	26	13:37	52	2465413		12	13	14	15	16	17	18			14	15[i]	16	17	18	19	20	Dōng zhì		11	12	13	14	15	16	17	
	27	28	◑	30	31	1	2	14:04	53	2465420		19	20	21	22	23	24	25			21	22	23	24	25	26	27			18	19	20	21	22	23	24	

[a]New Year
[b]Spring (6:48)
[c]Summer (0:21)
[d]Autumn (16:11)
[e]Winter (13:06)
● New moon
◐ First quarter moon
○ Full moon
◑ Last quarter moon

‡Leap year
[a]New Year
[b]Yom Kippur
[c]Sukkot
[d]Winter starts
[e]Ḥanukkah
[f]Purim
[g]Passover
[h]Shavuot
[i]Fast of Av
*New solar cycle

‡Leap year
[a]New Year (4735, Snake)
[b]Lantern Festival
[c]Qīngmíng
[d]Dragon Festival
[e]Qīqiǎo
[f]Hungry Ghosts
[g]Mid-Autumn Festival
[h]Double-Ninth Festival
[i]Dōngzhì
*Start of 60-name cycle

[a]New Year
[b]Building of the Cross
[c]Christmas
[d]Jesus's Circumcision
[e]Epiphany
[f]Easter
[g]Mary's Announcement
[h]Jesus's Transfiguration

PERSIAN (ASTRONOMICAL) 1415/1416‡

Month	Sun	Mon	Tue	Wed	Thu	Fri	Sat
DEY 1415	8	9	10	11	12	13	14
	15	16	17	18	19	20	21
	22	23	24	25	26	27	28
	29	30	*1*	2	3	4	5
BAHMAN 1415	6	7	8	9	10	11	12
	13	14	15	16	17	18	19
	20	21	22	23	24	25	26
	27	28	29	30	*1*	2	3
ESFAND 1415	4	5	6	7	8	9	10
	11	12	13	14	15	16	17
	18	19	20	21	22	23	24
	25	26	27	28	29	*1*[a]	2
FARVARDĪN 1416	3	4	5	6	7	8	9
	10	11	12	13[b]	14	15	16
	17	18	19	20	21	22	23
	24	25	26	27	28	29	30
ORDĪBEHEŠT 1416	31	*1*	2	3	4	5	6
	7	8	9	10	11	12	13
	14	15	16	17	18	19	20
	21	22	23	24	25	26	27
XORDĀD 1416	28	29	30	31	*1*	2	3
	4	5	6	7	8	9	10
	11	12	13	14	15	16	17
	18	19	20	21	22	23	24
	25	26	27	28	29	30	31
TĪR 1416	*1*	2	3	4	5	6	7
	8	9	10	11	12	13	14
	15	16	17	18	19	20	21
	22	23	24	25	26	27	28
MORDĀD 1416	29	30	31	*1*	2	3	4
	5	6	7	8	9	10	11
	12	13	14	15	16	17	18
	19	20	21	22	23	24	25
SHAHRĪVAR 1416	26	27	28	29	30	31	*1*
	2	3	4	5	6	7	8
	9	10	11	12	13	14	15
	16	17	18	19	20	21	22
	23	24	25	26	27	28	29
MEHR 1416	30	31	*1*	2	3	4	5
	6	7	8	9	10	11	12
	13	14	15	16	17	18	19
	20	21	22	23	24	25	26
ĀBĀN 1416	27	28	29	30	*1*	2	3
	4	5	6	7	8	9	10
	11	12	13	14	15	16	17
	18	19	20	21	22	23	24
ĀZAR 1416	25	26	27	28	29	30	*1*
	2	3	4	5	6	7	8
	9	10	11	12	13	14	15
	16	17	18	19	20	21	22
	23	24	25	26	27	28	29
DEY 1416	30	*1*	2	3	4	5	6
	7	8	9	10	11	12	13

HINDU LUNAR 2093/2094‡

Month	Sun	Mon	Tue	Wed	Thu	Fri	Sat
PAUSHA 2093	10	11	12	13	14	**15**	17
	18	19	20	21	22	23	24
	25	26	27	28	29	30	1
MĀGHA 2093	2	3	4	5	6	7	8
	9	10	11	12	13	14	15
	16	17	18	19	**20**	22	23
	24	25	26	27	28	29[h]	29
PHĀLGUNA 2093	30	1	2	3	4	5	6
	7	8	9	10	11	12	13
	14[i]	16	17	18	19	20	21
	22	23	24	25	26	27	28
CHAITRA 2094	29	30	1[a]	2	2	3	4
	5	6	7	**8**[b]	10	11	12
	13	14	15	16	17	18	19
	20	21	22	23	24	25	26
VAIŚĀKHA 2094	27	28	29	30	1	2	3
	4	5	6	7	8	9	10
	11	**12**	14	15	16	17	18
	19	20	21	22	23	24	25
LEAP JYAISHTHA 2094	26	26	27	28	29	30	1
	2	3	4	**5**	7	8	9
	10	11	12	13	14	15	16
	17	18	19	20	21	22	23
	24	25	26	27	28	29	30
JYAISHTHA 2094	1	2	3	4	5	6	7
	8	10	11	12	13	14	15
	16	17	18	19	20	21	22
	23	23	24	25	26	27	28
ĀSHĀḌHA 2094	29	30	**1**	3	4	5	6
	7	8	9	10	11	12	13
	14	15	16	17	18	19	20
	21	22	23	24	25	26	27
ŚRĀVAṆA 2094	28	29	30	1	2	3	**4**
	6	7	8	9	10	11	12
	13	14	15	16	17	18	19
	19	20	21	22	23[c]	24	25
BHĀDRAPADA 2094	26	**27**	29	30	1	2	3
	4[d]	5	6	7	8	9	10
	11	12	13	14	15	16	17
	18	19	20	21	22	23	24
ĀŚVINA 2094	25	26	27	28	29	**30**	2
	3	4	5	6	7	8[e]	9[e]
	10[e]	11	12	13	14	*14*	15
	16	17	18	19	20	21	22
	23	**24**	26	27	28	29	30
KĀRTTIKA 2094	1[f]	2	3	4	5	6	7
	8	9	10	11	12	13	14
	15	16	17	18	19	20	21
	22	23	24	25	26	27	28
MĀRGAŚĪRA 2094	**29**	1	2	3	4	5	6
	7	7	8	9	10	11[g]	12
	13	14	15	16	17	18	19
	20	21	**22**	24	25	26	27

HINDU SOLAR 1958‡/1959

Month	Sun	Mon	Tue	Wed	Thu	Fri	Sat
PAUSHA 1958	13	14	15	16	17	18	19
	20	21	22	23	24	25	26
MĀGHA 1958	27	28	29	1[b]	2	3	4
	5	6	7	8	9	10	11
	12	13	14	15	16	17	18
	19	20	21	22	23	24	25
PHĀLGUNA 1958	26	27	28	29	1	2	3
	4	5	6	7	8	9	10
	11	12	13	14	15	16	17
	18	19	20	21	22	23	24
CHAITRA 1958	25	26	27	28	29	30	1
	2	3	4	5	6	7	8
	9	10	11	12	13	14	15
	16	17	18	19	20	21	22
	23	24	25	26	27	28	29
VAIŚĀKHA 1959	30	31	1[a]	2	3	4	5
	6	7	8	9	10	11	12
	13	14	15	16	17	18	19
	20	21	22	23	24	25	26
JYAISHTHA 1959	27	28	29	30	31	1	2
	3	4	5	6	7	8	9
	10	11	12	13	14	15	16
	17	18	19	20	21	22	23
	24	25	26	27	28	29	30
ĀSHĀḌHA 1959	31	1	2	3	4	5	6
	7	8	9	10	11	12	13
	14	15	16	17	18	19	20
	21	22	23	24	25	26	27
ŚRĀVAṆA 1959	28	29	30	31	32	1	2
	3	4	5	6	7	8	9
	10	11	12	13	14	15	16
	17	18	19	20	21	22	23
	24	25	26	27	28	29	30
BHĀDRAPADA 1959	31	1	2	3	4	5	6
	7	8	9	10	11	12	13
	14	15	16	17	18	19	20
	21	22	23	24	25	26	27
ĀŚVINA 1959	28	29	30	31	1	2	3
	4	5	6	7	8	9	10
	11	12	13	14	15	16	17
	18	19	20	21	22	23	24
KĀRTTIKA 1959	25	26	27	28	29	30	1
	2	3	4	5	6	7	8
	9	10	11	12	13	14	15
	16	17	18	19	20	21	22
	23	24	25	26	27	28	29
MĀRGAŚĪRA 1959	30	1	2	3	4	5	6
	7	8	9	10	11	12	13
	14	15	16	17	18	19	20
	21	22	23	24	25	26	27
PAUSHA 1959	28	29	30	1	2	3	4
	5	6	7	8	9	10	11
	12	13	14	15	16	17	18

ISLAMIC (ASTRONOMICAL) 1458/1459

Month	Sun	Mon	Tue	Wed	Thu	Fri	Sat
DHU AL-QA'DA 1458	10	11	12	13	14	15	16
	17	18	19	20	21	22	23
	24	25	26	27	28	29	30
DHU AL-ḤIJJA 1458	*1*	2	3	4	5	6	7
	8	9	10[g]	11	12	13	14
	15	16	17	18	19	20	21
	22	23	24	25	26	27	28
MUḤARRAM 1459	29	30	*1*[a]	2	3	4	5
	6	7	8	9	10[b]	11	12
	13	14	15	16	17	18	19
	20	21	22	23	24	25	26
ṢAFAR 1459	27	28	29	*1*	2	3	4
	5	6	7	8	9	10	11
	12	13	14	15	16	17	18
	19	20	21	22	23	24	25
RABĪ' I 1459	26	27	28	29	30	*1*	2
	3	4	5	6	7	8	9
	10	11	12[c]	13	14	15	16
	17	18	19	20	21	22	23
	24	25	26	27	28	29	30
RABĪ' II 1459	*1*	2	3	4	5	6	7
	8	9	10	11	12	13	14
	15	16	17	18	19	20	21
	22	23	24	25	26	27	28
JUMĀDĀ I 1459	29	*1*	2	3	4	5	6
	7	8	9	10	11	12	13
	14	15	16	17	18	19	20
	21	22	23	24	25	26	27
JUMĀDĀ II 1459	28	29	1	*2*	3	4	5
	6	7	8	9	10	11	12
	13	14	15	16	17	18	19
	20	21	22	23	24	25	26
RAJAB 1459	27	28	29	30	*1*	2	3
	4	5	6	7	8	9	10
	11	12	13	14	15	16	17
	18	19	20	21	22	23	24
SHA'BĀN 1459	25	26	27[d]	28	29	1	2
	3	4	5	6	7	8	9
	10	11	12	13	14	15	16
	17	18	19	20	21	22	23
RAMAḌĀN 1459	24	25	26	27	28	29	1[e]
	2	3	4	5	6	7	8
	9	10	11	12	13	14	15
	16	17	18	19	20	21	22
	23	24	25	26	27	28	29
SHAWWĀL 1459	30	1[f]	2	3	4	5	6
	7	8	9	10	11	12	13
	14	15	16	17	18	19	20
	21	22	23	24	25	26	27
DHU AL-QA'DA 1459	28	29	1	*2*	3	4	5
	6	7	8	9	10	11	12
	13	14	15	16	17	18	19
	20	21	22	23	24	25	26

GREGORIAN 2037

Julian (Sun)	Sun	Mon	Tue	Wed	Thu	Fri	Sat	Month
Dec 15	*28*	29	30	31	1	2	3	JANUARY 2037
	4	5	6	7[a]	8	9	10	
Dec 29	*11*	12	13	14[b]	15	16	17	
	18	19	20	21	22	23	24	
Jan 12	*25*	26	27	28	29	30	31	
	1	2	3	4	5	6	7	FEBRUARY 2037
Jan 26	*8*	9	10	11	12	13	14	
	15	16	17	18[c]	19	20	21	
Feb 9	*22*[d]	23	24	25	26	27	28	
	1	2	3	4	5	6	7	MARCH 2037
Feb 23	*8*	9	10	11	12	13	14	
	15	16	17	18	19	20	21	
Mar 9	*22*	23	24	25	26	27	28	
	29	30	31	1	2	3	4	APRIL 2037
Mar 23	*5*[e]	6	7	8	9	10	11	
	12	13	14	15	16	17	18	
Apr 6	*19*	20	21	22	23	24	25	
	26	27	28	29	30	1	2	MAY 2037
Apr 20	*3*	4	5	6	7	8	9	
	10	11	12	13	14	15	16	
May 4	*17*	18	19	20	21	22	23	
	24	25	26	27	28	29	30	
May 18	*31*	1	2	3	4	5	6	JUNE 2037
	7	8	9	10	11	12	13	
Jun 1	*14*	15	16	17	18	19	20	
	21	22	23	24	25	26	27	
Jun 15	*28*	29	30	1	2	3	4	JULY 2037
	5	6	7	8	9	10	11	
Jun 29	*12*	13	14	15	16	17	18	
	19	20	21	22	23	24	25	
Jul 13	*26*	27	28	29	30	31	1	AUGUST 2037
	2	3	4	5	6	7	8	
Jul 27	*9*	10	11	12	13	14	15	
	16	17	18	19	20	21	22	
Aug 10	*23*	24	25	26	27	28	29	
	30	31	1	2	3	4	5	SEPTEMBER 2037
Aug 24	*6*	7	8	9	10	11	12	
	13	14	15	16	17	18	19	
Sep 7	*20*	21	22	23	24	25	26	
	27	28	29	30	1	2	3	OCTOBER 2037
Sep 21	*4*	5	6	7	8	9	10	
	11	12	13	14	15	16	17	
Oct 5	*18*	19	20	21	22	23	24	
	25	26	27	28	29	30	31	
Oct 19	*1*	2	3	4	5	6	7	NOVEMBER 2037
	8	9	10	11	12	13	14	
Nov 2	*15*	16	17	18	19	20	21	
	22	23	24	25	26	27	28	
Nov 16	*29*[g]	30	1	2	3	4	5	DECEMBER 2037
	6	7	8	9	10	11	12	
Nov 30	*13*	14	15	16	17	18	19	
	20	21	22	23	24	25[h]	26	
Dec 14	*27*	28	29	30	31	1	2	

Persian:
‡Leap year
[a]New Year
[b]Sizdeh Bedar

Hindu Lunar:
‡Leap year
[a]New Year (Piṅgala)
[b]Birthday of Rāma
[c]Birthday of Krishna
[d]Gaṇēśa Chaturthī
[e]Dashara
[f]Diwali
[g]Birthday of Vishnu
[h]Night of Śiva
[i]Holi

Hindu Solar:
‡Leap year
[a]New Year (Prajāpati)
[b]Pongal

Islamic:
[a]New Year
[b]'Ashūrā'
[c]Prophet's Birthday
[d]Ascent of the Prophet
[e]Start of Ramaḍān
[f]'Id al-Fiṭr
[g]'Id al-'Aḍḥā

Gregorian:
[a]Orthodox Christmas
[b]Julian New Year
[c]Ash Wednesday
[d]Feast of Orthodoxy
[e]Easter (also Orthodox)
[g]Advent
[h]Christmas

2038

Month	Sun	Mon	Tue	Wed	Thu	Fri	Sat	Lunar Phases	ISO WEEK (Mon)	JULIAN DAY (Sun noon)	Hebrew month	Sun	Mon	Tue	Wed	Thu	Fri	Sat	Molad	Chinese month	Sun	Mon	Tue	Wed	Thu	Fri	Sat	Solar Term	Coptic month	Sun	Mon	Tue	Wed	Thu	Fri	Sat	Ethiopic month
	GREGORIAN 2038								**ISO**	**JULIAN**	**HEBREW 5798‡/5799**									**CHINESE Dīng-Sì/Wù-Wǔ**									**COPTIC 1754/1755‡**								**ETHIOPIC 2030/2031‡**
JANUARY 2038	27	28	◑	30	31	1[a]	2	14:04	53	2465420	TEVETH 5798	19	20	21	22	23	24	25		MONTH 11 Dīng-Sì	21	22	23	24	25	26	27		KOIAK 1754	18	19	20	21	22	23	24	TĀKHŚĀŚ 2030
	3	4	●	6	7	8	9	13:40	1	2465427		26	27	28	29	1	2	3	Wed 3h 46m 1p		28	29	1	2	3	4	5	Xiǎo hán		25	26	27	28	29[c]	30	1	
	10	11	12	◐	14	15	16	12:33	2	2465434	SHEVAT 5798	4	5	6	7	8	9	10		MONTH 12 Dīng-Sì	6	7	8	9	10	11	12		TŌBE 1754	2	3	4	5	6[d]	7	8	ṬER 2030
	17	18	19	20	○	22	23	3:59	3	2465441		11	12	13	14	15	16	17			13	14	15	16	17	18	19	Dà hán		9	10	11[e]	12	13	14	15	
	24	25	26	◑	28	29	30	21:59	4	2465448		18	19	20	21	22	23	24			20	21	22	23	24	25	26			16	17	18	19	20	21	22	
FEBRUARY 2038	31	1	2	3	●	5	6	5:51	5	2465455		25	26	27	28	29	30	1	Thu 16h 30m 16p		27	28	29	30	1[a]	2	3	Lì chūn		23	24	25	26	27	28	29	
	7	8	9	10	11	◐	13	9:28	6	2465462	ADAR I 5798	2	3	4	5	6	7	8		MONTH 1 Wù-Wǔ	4	5	6	7	8	9	10		MESHIR 1754	30	1	2	3	4	5	6	YAKĀTIT 2030
	14	15	16	17	18	○	20	16:08	7	2465469		9	10	11	12	13	14	15			11	12	13*	14	15[b]	16	17	Yǔ shuǐ		7	8	9	10	11	12	13	
	21	22	23	24	25	◑	27	6:55	8	2465476		16	17	18	19	20	21	22			18	19	20	21	22	23	24			14	15	16	17	18	19	20	
MARCH 2038	28	1	2	3	4	●	6	23:14	9	2465483		23	24	25	26	27	28	29			25	26	27	28	29	30	1	Jīng zhé		21	22	23	24	25	26	27	
	7	8	9	10	11	12	13		10	2465490	ADAR II 5798	30	1	2	3	4	5	6	Sat 5h 14m 17p	MONTH 2 Wù-Wǔ	2	3	4	5	6	7	8		PAREMOTEP 1754	28	29	30	1	2	3	4	MAGĀBIT 2030
	◐	15	16	17	18	19	20[b]	3:40	11	2465497		7	8	9	10	11	12	13			9	10	11	12	13	14	15	Chūn fēn		5	6	7	8	9	10	11	
	○	22	23	24	25	26	◑	2:08 17:35	12	2465504		14[f]	15	16	17	18	19	20			16	17	18	19	20	21	22			12	13	14	15	16	17	18	
APRIL 2038	28	29	30	31	1	2	3		13	2465511		21	22	23	24	25	26	27			23	24	25	26	27	28	29			19	20	21	22	23	24	25	
	●	5	6	7	8	9	10	16:42	14	2465518	NISAN 5798	28	29	1	2	3	4	5	Sun 17h 59m 0p	MONTH 3 Wù-Wǔ	30	1[c]	2	3	4	5	6	Qīng míng	PARMOUTE 1754	26	27	28	29	30	1	2	MIYĀZYĀ 2030
	11	◐	13	14	15	16	17	18:01	15	2465525		6	7	8	9	10	11	12			7	8	9	10	11	12	13*			3	4	5	6	7	8	9	
	18	○	20	21	22	23	24	10:35	16	2465532		13	14	15[g]	16	17	18	19			14	15	16	17	18	19	20	Gǔ yǔ		10	11	12	13	14	15	16	
MAY 2038	25	◑	27	28	29	30	1	6:14	17	2465539		20	21	22	23	24	25	26			21	22	23	24	25	26	27			17[f]	18	19	20	21	22	23	
	2	3	●	5	6	7	8	9:18	18	2465546	IYAR 5798	27	28	29	30	1	2	3	Tue 6h 43m 1p	MONTH 4 Wù-Wǔ	28	29	1	2	3	4	5	Lì xià	PASHONS 1754	24	25	26	27	28	29[g]	30	GENBOT 2030
	9	10	11	◐	13	14	15	4:17	19	2465553		4	5	6	7	8	9	10			6	7	8	9	10	11	12			1	2	3	4	5	6	7	
	16	17	○	19	20	21	22	18:22	20	2465560		11	12	13	14	15	16	17			13	14	15	16	17	18	19	Xiǎo mǎn		8	9	10	11	12	13	14	
	23	24	◑	26	27	28	29	20:42	21	2465567		18	19	20	21	22	23	24			20	21	22	23	24	25	26			15	16	17	18	19	20	21	
JUNE 2038	30	31	1	2	●	4	5	0:23	22	2465574	SIVAN 5798	25	26	27	28	29	1	2	Wed 19h 27m 2p	MONTH 5 Wù-Wǔ	27	28	29	30	1	2	3	Máng zhòng	PAŌNE 1754	22	23	24	25	26	27	28	SANĒ 2030
	6	7	8	9	◐	11	12	11:10	23	2465581		3	4	5	6[h]	7	8	9			4	5[d]	6	7	8	9	10			29	30	1	2	3	4	5	
	13	14	15	16	○	18	19	2:29	24	2465588		10	11	12	13	14	15	16			11	12	13	14*	15	16	17			6	7	8	9	10	11	12	
	20	21[c]	22	23	◑	25	26	12:38	25	2465595		17	18	19	20	21	22	23			18	19	20	21	22	23	24	Xià zhì		13	14	15	16	17	18	19	
JULY 2038	27	28	29	30	1	●	3	13:31	26	2465602		24	25	26	27	28	29	30			25	26	27	28	29	1	2			20	21	22	23	24	25	26	
	4	5	6	7	8	◐	10	15:59	27	2465609	TAMMUZ 5798	1	2	3	4	5	6	7	Fri 8h 11m 3p	MONTH 6 Wù-Wǔ	3	4	5	6	7	8	9	Xiǎo shǔ	EPĒP 1754	27	28	29	30	1	2	3	ḤAMLĒ 2030
	11	12	13	14	15	○	17	11:47	28	2465616		8	9	10	11	12	13	14			10	11	12	13	14	15	16			4	5	6	7	8	9	10	
	18	19	20	21	22	23	◑	5:39	29	2465623		15	16	17	18	19	20	21			17	18	19	20	21	22	23	Dà shǔ		11	12	13	14	15	16	17	
	25	26	27	28	29	30	31		30	2465630		22	23	24	25	26	27	28			24	25	26	27	28	29	30			18	19	20	21	22	23	24	
AUGUST 2038	●	2	3	4	5	6	◐	0:39 20:20	31	2465637	AV 5798	29	1	2	3	4	5	6	Sat 20h 55m 4p	MONTH 7 Wù-Wǔ	1	2	3	4	5	6	7[e]	Lì qiū	MESORĒ 1754	25	26	27	28	29	30	1	NAḤASĒ 2030
	8	9	10	11	12	13	○	22:55	32	2465644		7	8	9[i]	10	11	12	13			8	9	10	11	12	13	14			2	3	4	5	6	7	8	
	15	16	17	18	19	20	21		33	2465651		14	15	16	17	18	19	20			15[f]*	16	17	18	19	20	21			9	10	11	12	13[h]	14	15	
	◑	23	24	25	26	27	28	23:11	34	2465658		21	22	23	24	25	26	27			22	23	24	25	26	27	28	Chǔ shǔ		16	17	18	19	20	21	22	
SEPTEMBER 2038	29	●	31	1	2	3	4	10:11	35	2465665	ELUL 5798	28	29	30	1	2	3	4	Mon 9h 39m 5p	MONTH 8 Wù-Wǔ	29	1	2	3	4	5	6			23	24	25	26	27	28	29	
	5	◐	7	8	9	10	11	1:50	36	2465672		5	6	7	8	9	10	11			7	8	9	10	11	12	13	Bái lù	EPAG. 1754	30	1	2	3	4	5	1[a]	PĀG. 2030
	12	○	14	15	16	17	18	12:23	37	2465679		12	13	14	15	16	17	18			14	15[g]	16	17	18	19	20		THOOUT 1755	2	3	4	5	6	7	8	MASKARAM 2031
	19	20	◑	22[d]	23	24	25	16:26	38	2465686		19	20	21	22	23	24	25			21	22	23	24	25	26	27	Qiū fēn		9	10	11	12	13	14	15	
OCTOBER 2038	26	27	●	29	30	1	2	18:56	39	2465693	TISHRI 5799	26	27	28	29	1[a]	2[a]	3	Tue 22h 23m 6p	MONTH 9 Wù-Wǔ	28	29	30	1	2	3	4			16	17[b]	18	19	20	21	22	
	3	4	◐	6	7	8	9	9:51	40	2465700		4	5	6	7	8	9	10[b]			5	6	7	8	9[h]	10	11	Hán lù	PAOPE 1755	23	24	25	26	27	28	29	ṬEQEMT 2031
	10	11	12	○	14	15	16	4:20	41	2465707		11	12	13	14	15[c]	16	17			12	13	14	15	16*	17	18			30	1	2	3	4	5	6	
	17	18	19	20	◑	22	23	8:22	42	2465714		18	19	20	21	22	23	24			19	20	21	22	23	24	25	Shuāng jiàng		7	8	9	10	11	12	13	
NOVEMBER 2038	24	25	26	27	●	29	30	3:52	43	2465721		25	26	27	28	29	30	1	Thu 11h 7m 7p		26	27	28	29	1	2	3			14	15	16	17	18	19	20	
	31	1	2	◐	4	5	6	21:23	44	2465728	ḤESHVAN 5799	2	3	4	5	6	7	8		MONTH 10 Wù-Wǔ	4	5	6	7	8	9	10		ATHŌR 1755	21	22	23	24	25	26	27	ḪEDĀR 2031
	7	8	9	10	○	12	13	22:26	45	2465735		9	10	11	12	13	14	15			11	12	13	14	15	16	17	Lì dōng		28	29	30	1	2	3	4	
	14	15	16	17	18	◑	20	22:09	46	2465742		16	17	18	19	20	21	22			18	19	20	21	22	23	24			5	6	7	8	9	10	11	
	21	22	23	24	25	●	27	13:45	47	2465749		23	24	25	26	27	28	29			25	26	27	28	29	1	2	Xiǎo xuě		12	13	14	15	16	17	18	
DECEMBER 2038	28	29	30	1	2	◐	4	12:45	48	2465756	KISLEV 5799	1	2	3	4	5	6	7	Fri 23h 51m 8p	MONTH 11* Wù-Wǔ	3	4	5	6	7	8	9			19	20	21	22	23	24	25	
	5	6	7	8	9	10	○	17:29	49	2465763		8[d]	9	10	11	12	13	14			10	11	12	13	14	15	16	Dà xuě	KOIAK 1755	26	27	28	29	30	1	2	TĀKHŚĀŚ 2031
	12	13	14	15	16	17	18		50	2465770		15	16	17	18	19	20	21			17	18*	19	20	21	22	23			3	4	5	6	7	8	9	
	◑	20	21[e]	22	23	24	25	9:28	51	2465777		22	23	24	25[e]	26[e]	27[e]	28[e]	Sun 12h 35m 9p		24	25	26	27[i]	28	29	30	Dōng zhì		10	11	12	13	14	15	16	
	●	27	28	29	30	31	1	1:01	52	2465784		29[e]	30[e]	1[e]	2[e]	3	4	5			1	2	3	4	5	6	7			17	18	19	20	21	22	23	

[a]New Year
[b]Spring (12:39)
[c]Summer (6:08)
[d]Autumn (22:01)
[e]Winter (19:00)
● New moon
◐ First quarter moon
○ Full moon
◑ Last quarter moon

‡Leap year
[a]New Year
[b]Yom Kippur
[c]Sukkot
[d]Winter starts
[e]Ḥanukkah
[f]Purim
[g]Passover
[h]Shavuot
[i]Fast of Av

[a]New Year (4736, Horse)
[b]Lantern Festival
[c]Qīngmíng
[d]Dragon Festival
[e]Qīqiǎo
[f]Hungry Ghosts
[g]Mid-Autumn Festival
[h]Double-Ninth Festival
[i]Dōngzhì
*Start of 60-name cycle

‡Leap year
[a]New Year
[b]Building of the Cross
[c]Christmas
[d]Jesus's Circumcision
[e]Epiphany
[f]Easter
[g]Mary's Announcement
[h]Jesus's Transfiguration

PERSIAN (ASTRONOMICAL) 1416‡/1417

Month	Sun	Mon	Tue	Wed	Thu	Fri	Sat
DEY 1416	7	8	9	10	11	12	13
	14	15	16	17	18	19	20
	21	22	23	24	25	26	27
	28	29	30	1	2	3	4
BAHMAN 1416	5	6	7	8	9	10	11
	12	13	14	15	16	17	18
	19	20	21	22	23	24	25
	26	27	28	29	30	1	2
ESFAND 1416	3	4	5	6	7	8	9
	10	11	12	13	14	15	16
	17	18	19	20	21	22	23
	24	25	26	27	28	29	30
FARVARDĪN 1417	1[a]	2	3	4	5	6	7
	8	9	10	11	12	13[b]	14
	15	16	17	18	19	20	21
	22	23	24	25	26	27	28
	29	30	31	1	2	3	4
ORDĪBEHEŠT 1417	5	6	7	8	9	10	11
	12	13	14	15	16	17	18
	19	20	21	22	23	24	25
	26	27	28	29	30	31	1
XORDĀD 1417	2	3	4	5	6	7	8
	9	10	11	12	13	14	15
	16	17	18	19	20	21	22
	23	24	25	26	27	28	29
	30	31	1	2	3	4	5
TĪR 1417	6	7	8	9	10	11	12
	13	14	15	16	17	18	19
	20	21	22	23	24	25	26
	27	28	29	30	31	1	2
MORDĀD 1417	3	4	5	6	7	8	9
	10	11	12	13	14	15	16
	17	18	19	20	21	22	23
	24	25	26	27	28	29	30
	31	1	2	3	4	5	6
SHAHRĪVAR 1417	7	8	9	10	11	12	13
	14	15	16	17	18	19	20
	21	22	23	24	25	26	27
	28	29	30	31	1	2	3
MEHR 1417	4	5	6	7	8	9	10
	11	12	13	14	15	16	17
	18	19	20	21	22	23	24
	25	26	27	28	29	30	1
ĀBĀN 1417	2	3	4	5	6	7	8
	9	10	11	12	13	14	15
	16	17	18	19	20	21	22
	23	24	25	26	27	28	29
	30	1	2	3	4	5	6
ĀZAR 1417	7	8	9	10	11	12	13
	14	15	16	17	18	19	20
	21	22	23	24	25	26	27
	28	29	30	1	2	3	4
DEY 1417	5	6	7	8	9	10	11

‡Leap year
[a]New Year
[b]Sizdeh Bedar

HINDU LUNAR 2094‡/2095

Month	Sun	Mon	Tue	Wed	Thu	Fri	Sat
MĀRGAŚĪRA 2094	20	21	22	24	25	26	27
	28	29	30	1	2	3	4
PAUSHA 2094	5	6	7	8	9	10	10
	11	12	13	14	15	16	18
	19	20	21	22	23	24	25
	26	27	28	29	30	1	2
MĀGHA 2094	3	4	5	6	7	8	9
	10	11	12	13	14	15	16
	17	18	19	20	21	23	24
	25	26	27	28	29[h]	30	1
PHĀLGUNA 2094	2	2	3	4	5	6	7
	8	9	10	11	12	13	14
	15[i]	17	18	19	20	21	22
	23	24	25	26	27	28	29
	30	1[a]	2	3	4	5	6
CHAITRA 2095	6	7	9[b]	10	11	12	13
	14	15	16	17	18	19	20
	22	23	24	25	26	26	27
	28	29	30	1	2	3	4
VAIŚĀKHA 2095	5	6	7	8	9	10	11
	12	14	15	16	17	18	19
	20	21	22	23	24	25	26
	27	28	29	30	1	1	2
JYAISHTHA 2095	3	4	6	7	8	9	10
	11	12	13	14	15	16	18
	19	20	21	22	22	23	24
	25	26	27	28	29	30	1
ĀSHĀḌHA 2095	2	3	4	5	6	7	8
	10	11	12	13	14	15	16
	17	18	19	20	21	22	23
	24	25	26	27	28	29	29
ŚRĀVANA 2095	1	2	3	4	5	6	7
	8	9	10	11	13	14	15
	16	17	18	19	19	20	21
	22	23[c]	24	25	26	27	28
	29	30	1	2	3[d]	4	6
BHĀDRAPADA 2095	7	8	9	10	11	12	13
	14	15	16	17	18	19	20
	21	22	23	24	24	25	26
	28	29	30	1	2	3	4
ĀŚVINA 2095	5	6	7	8[e]	10[e]	11	12
	13	14	14	15	16	17	18
	19	20	21	22	23	24	25
	26	27	28	29	30	1[f]	3
KĀRTTIKA 2095	4	5	6	7	8	9	10
	11	12	13	14	15	16	17
	17	18	19	20	21	22	23
	24	25	27	28	29	30	1
MĀRGAŚĪRA 2095	2	3	4	5	6	7	8
	9	10	11[g]	12	13	14	15
	16	17	18	19	20	21	22
	23	24	25	26	27	28	29
	1	2	3	4	5	6	7

‡Leap year
[a]New Year (Kālayukta)
[b]Birthday of Rāma
[c]Birthday of Krishna
[d]Ganēśa Chaturthī
[e]Dashara
[f]Diwali
[g]Birthday of Vishnu
[h]Night of Śiva
[i]Holi

HINDU SOLAR 1959/1960

Month	Sun	Mon	Tue	Wed	Thu	Fri	Sat
PAUSHA 1959	12	13	14	15	16	17	18
	19	20	21	22	23	24	25
	26	27	28	29	1[b]	2	3
MĀGHA 1959	4	5	6	7	8	9	10
	11	12	13	14	15	16	17
	18	19	20	21	22	23	24
	25	26	27	28	29	30	1
PHĀLGUNA 1959	2	3	4	5	6	7	8
	9	10	11	12	13	14	15
	16	17	18	19	20	21	22
	23	24	25	26	27	28	29
	1	2	3	4	5	6	7
CHAITRA 1959	8	9	10	11	12	13	14
	15	16	17	18	19	20	21
	22	23	24	25	26	27	28
	29	30	31	1[a]	2	3	4
VAIŚĀKHA 1960	5	6	7	8	9	10	11
	12	13	14	15	16	17	18
	19	20	21	22	23	24	25
	26	27	28	29	30	31	1
JYAISHTHA 1960	2	3	4	5	6	7	8
	9	10	11	12	13	14	15
	16	17	18	19	20	21	22
	23	24	25	26	27	28	29
	30	31	1	2	3	4	5
ĀSHĀḌHA 1960	6	7	8	9	10	11	12
	13	14	15	16	17	18	19
	20	21	22	23	24	25	26
	27	28	29	30	31	32	1
ŚRĀVANA 1960	2	3	4	5	6	7	8
	9	10	11	12	13	14	15
	16	17	18	19	20	21	22
	23	24	25	26	27	28	29
	30	31	1	2	3	4	5
BHĀDRAPADA 1960	6	7	8	9	10	11	12
	13	14	15	16	17	18	19
	20	21	22	23	24	25	26
	27	28	29	30	31	1	2
ĀŚVINA 1960	3	4	5	6	7	8	9
	10	11	12	13	14	15	16
	17	18	19	20	21	22	23
	24	25	26	27	28	29	30
	31	1	2	3	4	5	6
KĀRTTIKA 1960	7	8	9	10	11	12	13
	14	15	16	17	18	19	20
	21	22	23	24	25	26	27
	28	29	30	1	2	3	4
MĀRGAŚĪRA 1960	5	6	7	8	9	10	11
	12	13	14	15	16	17	18
	19	20	21	22	23	24	25
	26	27	28	29	1	2	3
PAUSHA 1960	4	5	6	7	8	9	10
	11	12	13	14	15	16	17

[a]New Year (Aṅgiras)
[b]Pongal

ISLAMIC (ASTRONOMICAL) 1459/1460

Month	Sun	Mon	Tue	Wed	Thu	Fri	Sat
DHU AL-QA'DA 1459	20	21	22	23	24	25	26
	27	28	29	30	1	2	3
DHU AL-HIJJA 1459	4	5	6	7	8	9	10[g]
	11	12	13	14	15	16	17
	18	19	20	21	22	23	24
	25	26	27	28	29	30	1[a]
MUHARRAM 1460	2	3	4	5	6	7	8
	9	10[b]	11	12	13	14	15
	16	17	18	19	20	21	22
	23	24	25	26	27	28	29
	1	2	3	4	5	6	7
SAFAR 1460	8	9	10	11	12	13	14
	15	16	17	18	19	20	21
	22	23	24	25	26	27	28
	29	30	1	2	3	4	5
RABĪ' I 1460	6	7	8	9	10	11	12[c]
	13	14	15	16	17	18	19
	20	21	22	23	24	25	26
	27	28	29	30	1	2	3
RABĪ' II 1460	4	5	6	7	8	9	10
	11	12	13	14	15	16	17
	18	19	20	21	22	23	24
	25	26	27	28	29	1	2
JUMĀDĀ I 1460	3	4	5	6	7	8	9
	10	11	12	13	14	15	16
	17	18	19	20	21	22	23
	24	25	26	27	28	29	30
	1	2	3	4	5	6	7
JUMĀDĀ II 1460	8	9	10	11	12	13	14
	15	16	17	18	19	20	21
	22	23	24	25	26	27	28
	29	1	2	3	4	5	6
RAJAB 1460	7	8	9	10	11	12	13
	14	15	16	17	18	19	20
	21	22	23	24	25	26	27[d]
	28	29	30	1	2	3	4
SHA'BĀN 1460	5	6	7	8	9	10	11
	12	13	14	15	16	17	18
	19	20	21	22	23	24	25
	26	27	28	29	1[e]	2	3
RAMAḌĀN 1460	4	5	6	7	8	9	10
	11	12	13	14	15	16	17
	18	19	20	21	22	23	24
	25	26	27	28	29	1[f]	2
SHAWWĀL 1460	3	4	5	6	7	8	9
	10	11	12	13	14	15	16
	17	18	19	20	21	22	23
	24	25	26	27	28	29	30
	1	2	3	4	5	6	7
DHU AL-QA'DA 1460	8	9	10	11	12	13	14
	15	16	17	18	19	20	21
	22	23	24	25	26	27	28
	29	1	2	3	4	5	6

[a]New Year
[b]'Āshūrā'
[c]Prophet's Birthday
[d]Ascent of the Prophet
[e]Start of Ramaḍān
[f]'Īd al-Fiṭr
[g]'Īd al-'Aḍḥā

GREGORIAN 2038

Julian (Sun)	Sun	Mon	Tue	Wed	Thu	Fri	Sat	Month
Dec 14	27	28	29	30	31	1	2	
	3	4	5	6	7[a]	8	9	JANUARY 2038
Dec 28	10	11	12	13	14[b]	15	16	
	17	18	19	20	21	22	23	
Jan 11	24	25	26	27	28	29	30	
	31	1	2	3	4	5	6	
Jan 25	7	8	9	10	11	12	13	FEBRUARY 2038
	14	15	16	17	18	19	20	
Feb 8	21	22	23	24	25	26	27	
	28	1	2	3	4	5	6	
Feb 22	7	8	9	10[c]	11	12	13	MARCH 2038
	14[d]	15	16	17	18	19	20	
Mar 8	21	22	23	24	25	26	27	
	28	29	30	31	1	2	3	
Mar 22	4	5	6	7	8	9	10	APRIL 2038
	11	12	13	14	15	16	17	
Apr 5	18	19	20	21	22	23	24	
	25[e]	26	27	28	29	30	1	
Apr 19	2	3	4	5	6	7	8	MAY 2038
	9	10	11	12	13	14	15	
May 3	16	17	18	19	20	21	22	
	23	24	25	26	27	28	29	
May 17	30	31	1	2	3	4	5	
	6	7	8	9	10	11	12	JUNE 2038
May 31	13	14	15	16	17	18	19	
	20	21	22	23	24	25	26	
Jun 14	27	28	29	30	1	2	3	
	4	5	6	7	8	9	10	JULY 2038
Jun 28	11	12	13	14	15	16	17	
	18	19	20	21	22	23	24	
Jul 12	25	26	27	28	29	30	31	
	1	2	3	4	5	6	7	AUGUST 2038
Jul 26	8	9	10	11	12	13	14	
	15	16	17	18	19	20	21	
Aug 9	22	23	24	25	26	27	28	
	29	30	31	1	2	3	4	
Aug 23	5	6	7	8	9	10	11	SEPTEMBER 2038
	12	13	14	15	16	17	18	
Sep 6	19	20	21	22	23	24	25	
	26	27	28	29	30	1	2	
Sep 20	3	4	5	6	7	8	9	OCTOBER 2038
	10	11	12	13	14	15	16	
Oct 4	17	18	19	20	21	22	23	
	24	25	26	27	28	29	30	
Oct 18	31	1	2	3	4	5	6	
	7	8	9	10	11	12	13	NOVEMBER 2038
Nov 1	14	15	16	17	18	19	20	
	21	22	23	24	25	26	27	
Nov 15	28[g]	29	30	1	2	3	4	
	5	6	7	8	9	10	11	DECEMBER 2038
Nov 29	12	13	14	15	16	17	18	
	19	20	21	22	23	24	25[h]	
Dec 13	26	27	28	29	30	31	1	

[a]Orthodox Christmas
[b]Julian New Year
[c]Ash Wednesday
[d]Feast of Orthodoxy
[e]Easter (also Orthodox)
[g]Advent
[h]Christmas

Gregorian 2039	Sun	Mon	Tue	Wed	Thu	Fri	Sat	Lunar Phases	ISO Week (Mon)	Julian Day (Sun noon)
JANUARY 2039	●	27	28	29	30	31	1[a]	1:01	52	2465784
	◐	3	4	5	6	7	8	7:35	1	2465791
	9	○	11	12	13	14	15	11:44	2	2465798
	16	◑	18	19	20	21	22	18:40	3	2465805
	23	●	25	26	27	28	29	13:35	4	2465812
FEBRUARY 2039	30	31	◐	2	3	4	5	4:44	5	2465819
	6	7	8	○	10	11	12	3:38	6	2465826
	13	14	15	◑	17	18	19	2:35	7	2465833
	20	21	22	●	24	25	26	3:16	8	2465840
MARCH 2039	27	28	1	2	◐	4	5	2:14	9	2465847
	6	7	8	9	○	11	12	16:34	10	2465854
	13	14	15	16	◑	18	19	10:06	11	2465861
	20[b]	21	22	23	●	25	26	17:58	12	2465868
APRIL 2039	27	28	29	30	31	◐	2	21:53	13	2465875
	3	4	5	6	7	8	○	2:52	14	2465882
	10	11	12	13	14	◑	16	18:06	15	2465889
	17	18	19	20	21	22	●	9:33	16	2465896
	24	25	26	27	28	29	30		17	2465903
MAY 2039	◐	2	3	4	5	6	7	14:06	18	2465910
	○	9	10	11	12	13	14	11:19	19	2465917
	◑	16	17	18	19	20	21	3:16	20	2465924
	22	●	24	25	26	27	28	1:37	21	2465931
JUNE 2039	29	30	◐	1	2	3	4	2:23	22	2465938
	5	○	7	8	9	10	11	18:46	23	2465945
	12	◑	14	15	16	17	18	14:15	24	2465952
	19	20	●[c]	22	23	24	25	17:20	25	2465959
JULY 2039	26	27	28	◐	30	1	2	11:16	26	2465966
	3	4	5	○	7	8	9	2:02	27	2465973
	10	11	12	◑	14	15	16	3:37	28	2465980
	17	18	19	20	●	22	23	7:53	29	2465987
	24	25	26	27	◐	29	30	17:48	30	2465994
AUGUST 2039	31	1	2	3	○	5	6	9:55	31	2466001
	7	8	9	10	◑	12	13	19:34	32	2466008
	14	15	16	17	18	●	20	20:49	33	2466015
	21	22	23	24	25	◐	27	23:15	34	2466022
SEPTEMBER 2039	28	29	30	31	1	○	3	19:22	35	2466029
	4	5	6	7	8	9	◑	13:44	36	2466036
	11	12	13	14	15	16	17		37	2466043
	●	19	20	21	22	23[d]	24	8:22	38	2466050
OCTOBER 2039	◐	26	27	28	29	30	1	4:51	39	2466057
	○	3	4	5	6	7	8	7:22	40	2466064
	9	◑	11	12	13	14	15	8:58	41	2466071
	16	●	18	19	20	21	22	19:08	42	2466078
	23	◐	25	26	27	28	29	11:49	43	2466085
NOVEMBER 2039	30	○	1	2	3	4	5	22:35	44	2466092
	6	7	8	◑	10	11	12	3:45	45	2466099
	13	14	15	●	17	18	19	5:45	46	2466106
	20	21	◐	23	24	25	26	21:15	47	2466113
DECEMBER 2039	27	28	29	○	1	2	3	16:48	48	2466120
	4	5	6	7	◑	9	10	20:43	49	2466127
	11	12	13	14	●	16	17	16:31	50	2466134
	18	19	20	21	◐[e]	23	24	10:00	51	2466141
	25	26	27	28	29	○	31	12:36	52	2466148

ISO Week	Hebrew 5799/5800	Sun	Mon	Tue	Wed	Thu	Fri	Sat	Molad
52	TEVETH 5799	29[e]	30[e]	1[e]	2[e]	3	4	5	Sun 12h35m9p
1		6	7	8	9	10	11	12	
2		13	14	15	16	17	18	19	
3		20	21	22	23	24	25	26	
4	SHEVAT 5799	27	28	29	1	2	3	4	Tue 1h19m10p
5		5	6	7	8	9	10	11	
6		12	13	14	15	16	17	18	
7		19	20	21	22	23	24	25	
8	ADAR 5799	26	27	28	29	30	1	2	Wed 14h3m11p
9		3	4	5	6	7	8	9	
10		10	11	12	13	14[f]	15	16	
11		17	18	19	20	21	22	23	
12	NISAN 5799	24	25	26	27	28	29	1	Fri 2h47m12p
13		2	3	4	5	6	7	8	
14		9	10	11	12	13	14	15[g]	
15		16	17	18	19	20	21	22	
16		23	24	25	26	27	28	29	
17	IYYAR 5799	30	1	2	3	4	5	6	Sat 15h31m13p
18		7	8	9	10	11	12	13	
19		14	15	16	17	18	19	20	
20		21	22	23	24	25	26	27	
21	SIVAN 5799	28	29	1	2	3	4	5	Mon 4h15m14p
22		6[h]	7	8	9	10	11	12	
23		13	14	15	16	17	18	19	
24		20	21	22	23	24	25	26	
25	TAMMUZ 5799	27	28	29	30	1	2	3	Tue 16h59m15p
26		4	5	6	7	8	9	10	
27		11	12	13	14	15	16	17	
28		18	19	20	21	22	23	24	
29	AV 5799	25	26	27	28	29	1	2	Thu 5h43m16p
30		3	4	5	6	7	8	9	
31		10[i]	11	12	13	14	15	16	
32		17	18	19	20	21	22	23	
33		24	25	26	27	28	29	30	
34	ELUL 5799	1	2	3	4	5	6	7	Fri 18h27m17p
35		8	9	10	11	12	13	14	
36		15	16	17	18	19	20	21	
37		22	23	24	25	26	27	28	
38	TISHRI 5800	29	1[a]	2[a]	3	4	5	6	Sun 7h12m0p
39		7	8	9	10[b]	11	12	13	
40		14	15[c]	16	17	18	19	20	
41		21	22	23	24	25	26	27	
42	HESHVAN 5800	28	29	30	1	2	3	4	Mon 19h56m1p
43		5	6	7	8	9	10	11	
44		12	13	14	15	16	17	18	
45		19	20	21	22	23	24	25	
46	KISLEV 5800	26	27	28	29	30	1	2	Wed 8h40m2p
47		3	4	5	6	7	8	9	
48		10	11	12	13	14	15	16	
49		17	18	19[d]	20	21	22	23	
50		24	25[e]	26[e]	27[e]	28[e]	29[e]	30[e]	
51	TEVETH 5800	1[e]	2[e]	3	4	5	6	7	Thu 21h24m3p
52		8	9	10	11	12	13	14	

ISO Week	Chinese Wù-Wǔ/Jǐ-Wèi‡	Sun	Mon	Tue	Wed	Thu	Fri	Sat	Solar Term
52	MONTH 12 Wù-Wǔ	1	2	3	4	5	6	7	
1		8	9	10	*11*	12	13	14	Xiǎo hán
2		15	16	17	18	19	20	21	
3		22	23	24	25	**26**	27	28	Dà hán
4	MONTH 1 Jǐ-Wèi	29	1[a]	2	3	4	5	6	
5		7	8	9	10	11	*12*	13	Lì chūn
6		14	15[b]	16	17	18	19*	20	
7		21	22	23	24	25	26	**27**	Yǔ shuǐ
8	MONTH 2 Jǐ-Wèi	28	29	30	1	2	3	4	
9		5	6	7	8	9	10	11	
10		*12*	13	14	15	16	17	18	Jīng zhé
11		19	20	21	22	23	24	25	
12		26	**27**	28	29	30	1	2	Chūn fēn
13	MONTH 3 Jǐ-Wèi	3	4	5	6	7	8	9	
14		10	11	12[c]	13	14	15	16	Qīng míng
15		17	18	19*	20	21	22	23	
16		24	25	26	**27**	28	29	1	Gǔ yǔ
17	MONTH 4 Jǐ-Wèi	2	3	4	5	6	7	8	
18		9	10	11	12	*13*	14	15	Lì xià
19		16	17	18	19	20	21	22	
20		23	24	25	26	27	28	**29**	Xiǎo mǎn
21	MONTH 5 Jǐ-Wèi	30	1	2	3	4	5[d]	6	
22		7	8	9	10	11	12	13	
23		14	*15*	16	17	18	19	20*	Máng zhòng
24		21	22	23	24	25	26	27	
25	LEAP MONTH 5 Jǐ-Wèi	28	29	**30**	1	2	3	4	Xià zhì
26		5	6	7	8	9	10	11	
27		12	13	14	15	*16*	17	18	Xiǎo shǔ
28		19	20	21	22	23	24	25	
29	MONTH 6 Jǐ-Wèi	26	27	28	29	1	2	**3**	Dà shǔ
30		4	5	6	7	8	9	10	
31		11	12	13	14	15	16	17	
32		*18*	19	20	21*	22	23	24	Lì qiū
33	MONTH 7 Jǐ-Wèi	25	26	27	28	29	30	1	
34		2	3	**4**	5	6	7[e]	8	Chǔ shǔ
35		9	10	11	12	13	14	15[f]	
36		16	17	18	19	*20*	21	22	Bái lù
37		23	24	25	26	27	28	29	
38	MONTH 8 Jǐ-Wèi	1	2	3	4	5	**6**	7	Qiū fēn
39		8	9	10	11	12	13	14	
40		15[g]	16	17	18	19	20	*21*	Hán lù
41		22*	23	24	25	26	27	28	
42	MONTH 9 Jǐ-Wèi	29	30	1	2	3	4	5	
43		**6**	7	8	9[h]	10	11	12	Shuāng jiàng
44		13	14	15	16	17	18	19	
45		20	*21*	22	23	24	25	26	Lì dōng
46	MONTH 10 Jǐ-Wèi	27	28	29	1	2	3	4	
47		5	6	**7**	8	9	10	11	Xiǎo xuě
48		12	13	14	15	16	17	18	
49		19	20	21	*22*	23*	24	25	Dà xuě
50	MONTH 11 Jǐ-Wèi	26	27	28	29	30	1	2	
51		3	4	5	6	7[i]	8	9	Dōng zhì
52		10	11	12	13	14	15	16	

ISO Week	Coptic 1755‡/1756	Sun	Mon	Tue	Wed	Thu	Fri	Sat	Ethiopic 2031‡/2032
52	KOIAK 1755	17	18	19	20	21	22	23	TĀKHŚĀŚ 2031
1		24	25	26	27	28	29[c]	30	
2	TŌBE 1755	1	2	3	4	5	6[d]	7	ṬER 2031
3		8	9	10	11[e]	12	13	14	
4		15	16	17	18	19	20	21	
5		22	23	24	25	26	27	28	
6	MESHIR 1755	29	30	1	2	3	4	5	YAKĀTIT 2031
7		6	7	8	9	10	11	12	
8		13	14	15	16	17	18	19	
9		20	21	22	23	24	25	26	
10	PAREMOTEP 1755	27	28	29	30	1	2	3	MAGĀBIT 2031
11		4	5	6	7	8	9	10	
12		11	12	13	14	15	16	17	
13		18	19	20	21	22	23	24	
14	PARMOUTE 1755	25	26	27	28	29	30	1	MIYĀZYĀ 2031
15		2	3	4	5	6	7	8	
16		9[f]	10	11	12	13	14	15	
17		16	17	18	19	20	21	22	
18		23	24	25	26	27	28	29[g]	
19	PASHONS 1755	30	1	2	3	4	5	6	GENBOT 2031
20		7	8	9	10	11	12	13	
21		14	15	16	17	18	19	20	
22		21	22	23	24	25	26	27	
23	PAŌNE 1755	28	29	30	1	2	3	4	SANĒ 2031
24		5	6	7	8	9	10	11	
25		12	13	14	15	16	17	18	
26		19	20	21	22	23	24	25	
27	EPĒP 1755	26	27	28	29	30	1	2	ḤAMLĒ 2031
28		3	4	5	6	7	8	9	
29		10	11	12	13	14	15	16	
30		17	18	19	20	21	22	23	
31		24	25	26	27	28	29	30	
32	MESORĒ 1755	1	2	3	4	5	6	7	NAHASĒ 2031
33		8	9	10	11	12	13[h]	14	
34		15	16	17	18	19	20	21	
35		22	23	24	25	26	27	28	
36	EPAG. 1755	29	30	1	2	3	4	5	PĀG. 2031
37	THOOUT 1756	6	1[a]	2	3	4	5	6	MASKARAM 2032
38		7	8	9	10	11	12	13	
39		14	15	16	17[b]	18	19	20	
40		21	22	23	24	25	26	27	
41	PAOPE 1756	28	29	30	1	2	3	4	TEQEMT 2032
42		5	6	7	8	9	10	11	
43		12	13	14	15	16	17	18	
44		19	20	21	22	23	24	25	
45	ATHŌR 1756	26	27	28	29	30	1	2	ḤEDĀR 2032
46		3	4	5	6	7	8	9	
47		10	11	12	13	14	15	16	
48		17	18	19	20	21	22	23	
49		24	25	26	27	28	29	30	
50	KOIAK 1756	1	2	3	4	5	6	7	TĀKHŚĀŚ 2032
51		8	9	10	11	12	13	14	
52		15	16	17	18	19	20	21	

Gregorian:
[a]New Year
[b]Spring (18:31)
[c]Summer (11:56)
[d]Autumn (3:48)
[e]Winter (0:39)
● New moon
◐ First quarter moon
○ Full moon
◑ Last quarter moon

Hebrew:
[a]New Year
[b]Yom Kippur
[c]Sukkot
[d]Winter starts
[e]Ḥanukkah
[f]Purim
[g]Passover
[h]Shavuot
[i]Fast of Av

Chinese:
‡Leap year
[a]New Year (4737, Sheep)
[b]Lantern Festival
[c]Qīngmíng
[d]Dragon Festival
[e]Qīqiǎo
[f]Hungry Ghosts
[g]Mid-Autumn Festival
[h]Double-Ninth Festival
[i]Dōngzhì
*Start of 60-name cycle

Coptic/Ethiopic:
‡Leap year
[a]New Year
[b]Building of the Cross
[c]Christmas
[d]Jesus's Circumcision
[e]Epiphany
[f]Easter
[g]Mary's Announcement
[h]Jesus's Transfiguration

PERSIAN (ASTRONOMICAL) 1417/1418

Month	Sun	Mon	Tue	Wed	Thu	Fri	Sat
DEY 1417	5	6	7	8	9	10	11
	12	13	14	15	16	17	18
	19	20	21	22	23	24	25
	26	27	28	29	30	| 1	2
BAHMAN 1417	3	4	5	6	7	8	9
	10	11	12	13	14	15	16
	17	18	19	20	21	22	23
	24	25	26	27	28	29	30
ESFAND 1417	1	2	3	4	5	6	7
	8	9	10	11	12	13	14
	15	16	17	18	19	20	21
	22	23	24	25	26	27	28
	29	| 1[a]	2	3	4	5	6
FARVARDĪN 1418	7	8	9	10	11	12	13[b]
	14	15	16	17	18	19	20
	21	22	23	24	25	26	27
	28	29	30	31	| 1	2	3
ORDĪBEHEŠT 1418	4	5	6	7	8	9	10
	11	12	13	14	15	16	17
	18	19	20	21	22	23	24
	25	26	27	28	29	30	31
XORDĀD 1418	1	2	3	4	5	6	7
	8	9	10	11	12	13	14
	15	16	17	18	19	20	21
	22	23	24	25	26	27	28
	29	30	31	| 1	2	3	4
TĪR 1418	5	6	7	8	9	10	11
	12	13	14	15	16	17	18
	19	20	21	22	23	24	25
	26	27	28	29	30	31	| 1
MORDĀD 1418	2	3	4	5	6	7	8
	9	10	11	12	13	14	15
	16	17	18	19	20	21	22
	23	24	25	26	27	28	29
	30	31	| 1	2	3	4	5
SHAHRĪVAR 1418	6	7	8	9	10	11	12
	13	14	15	16	17	18	19
	20	21	22	23	24	25	26
	27	28	29	30	31	| 1	2
MEHR 1418	3	4	5	6	7	8	9
	10	11	12	13	14	15	16
	17	18	19	20	21	22	23
	24	25	26	27	28	29	30
ĀBĀN 1418	1	2	3	4	5	6	7
	8	9	10	11	12	13	14
	15	16	17	18	19	20	21
	22	23	24	25	26	27	28
	29	30	| 1	2	3	4	5
ĀZAR 1418	6	7	8	9	10	11	12
	13	14	15	16	17	18	19
	20	21	22	23	24	25	26
	27	28	29	30	| 1	2	3
DEY 1418	4	5	6	7	8	9	10

[a]New Year
[b]Sizdeh Bedar

HINDU LUNAR 2095/2096‡

Month	Sun	Mon	Tue	Wed	Thu	Fri	Sat
PAUSHA 2095	1	2	3	4	5	6	7
	8	9	10	*10*	11	12	13
	14	15	16	17	18	19	20
	21	22	**23**	25	26	27	28
	29	30	| 1	2	3	4	5
MĀGHA 2095	6	7	8	9	10	11	12
	12	13	14	15	16	**17**	19
	20	21	22	23	24	25	26
	27	28[h]	29	30	| 1	2	3
PHĀLGUNA 2095	4	5	6	7	8	9	10
	11	12	13	14	15[i]	16	17
	18	19	20	21	**22**	24	25
	26	27	28	29	30	| 1[a]	2
CHAITRA 2096	3	4	5	*5*	6	7	8[b]
	9	10	11	12	13	14	15
	16	18	19	20	21	22	23
	24	25	26	27	28	29	30
VAIŚĀKHA 2096	1	2	3	4	5	6	7
	8	9	10	11	12	13	14
	15	16	17	18	19	**20**	22
	23	24	25	26	27	28	29
	30	*30*	| 1	2	3	4	5
JYAISHTHA 2096	6	7	8	9	10	11	**12**
	14	15	16	17	18	19	20
	21	22	23	24	25	26	27
	28	29	30	| 1	2	3	4
ĀSHĀDHA 2096	5	6	7	8	9	10	11
	12	13	14	**15**	17	18	19
	20	21	22	23	24	25	26
	27	*27*	28	29	30	| 1	2
ŚRĀVAṆA 2096	3	4	5	6	7	**8**	10
	11	12	13	14	15	16	17
	18	19	20	21	22	23[c]	24
	25	26	27	28	29	30	| 1
BHĀDRAPADA 2096	2	3	4[d]	5	6	7	8
	9	10	**11**	13	14	15	16
	17	18	19	20	21	22	23
	23	24	25	26	27	28	29
	30	| 1	2	3	**4**	6	7
LEAP ĀŚVINA 2096	8	9	10	11	12	13	14
	15	16	17	18	19	20	21
	22	23	24	25	26	27	28
	29	30	| 1	2	3	4	5
ĀŚVINA 2096	6	7	**8**[e]	10[e]	11	12	13
	14	15	16	17	18	*18*	19
	20	21	22	23	24	25	26
	27	28	29	30	| 1[f]	**2**	4
KĀRTTIKA 2096	5	6	7	8	9	10	11
	12	13	14	15	16	17	18
	19	20	21	*21*	22	23	24
	25	27	28	29	30	| 1	2
MĀRGAŚĪRA 2096	3	4	5	6	7	8	9
	10	11[g]	12	13	14	15	16

‡Leap year
[a]New Year (Siddhārthin)
[b]Birthday of Rāma
[c]Birthday of Krishna
[d]Ganēśa Chaturthī
[e]Dashara
[f]Diwali
[g]Birthday of Vishnu
[h]Night of Śiva
[i]Holi

HINDU SOLAR 1960/1961

Month	Sun	Mon	Tue	Wed	Thu	Fri	Sat
PAUSHA 1960	11	12	13	14	15	16	17
	18	19	20	21	22	23	24
	25	26	27	28	29	| 1[b]	2
MĀGHA 1960	3	4	5	6	7	8	9
	10	11	12	13	14	15	16
	17	18	19	20	21	22	23
	24	25	26	27	28	29	30
	1	2	3	4	5	6	7
PHĀLGUNA 1960	8	9	10	11	12	13	14
	15	16	17	18	19	20	21
	22	23	24	25	26	27	28
	29	30	| 1	2	3	4	5
CHAITRA 1960	6	7	8	9	10	11	12
	13	14	15	16	17	18	19
	20	21	22	23	24	25	26
	27	28	29	30	| 1[a]	2	3
VAIŚĀKHA 1961	4	5	6	7	8	9	10
	11	12	13	14	15	16	17
	18	19	20	21	22	23	24
	25	26	27	28	29	30	31
JYAISHTHA 1961	1	2	3	4	5	6	7
	8	9	10	11	12	13	14
	15	16	17	18	19	20	21
	22	23	24	25	26	27	28
	29	30	31	| 1	2	3	4
ĀSHĀDHA 1961	5	6	7	8	9	10	11
	12	13	14	15	16	17	18
	19	20	21	22	23	24	25
	26	27	28	29	30	31	32
ŚRĀVAṆA 1961	1	2	3	4	5	6	7
	8	9	10	11	12	13	14
	15	16	17	18	19	20	21
	22	23	24	25	26	27	28
	29	30	31	32	| 1	2	3
BHĀDRAPADA 1961	4	5	6	7	8	9	10
	11	12	13	14	15	16	17
	18	19	20	21	22	23	24
	25	26	27	28	29	30	31
ĀŚVINA 1961	1	2	3	4	5	6	7
	8	9	10	11	12	13	14
	15	16	17	18	19	20	21
	22	23	24	25	26	27	28
	29	30	| 1	2	3	4	5
KĀRTTIKA 1961	6	7	8	9	10	11	12
	13	14	15	16	17	18	19
	20	21	22	23	24	25	26
	27	28	29	30	| 1	2	3
MĀRGAŚĪRA 1961	4	5	6	7	8	9	10
	11	12	13	14	15	16	17
	18	19	20	21	22	23	24
	25	26	27	28	29	| 1	2
PAUSHA 1961	3	4	5	6	7	8	9
	10	11	12	13	14	15	16

[a]New Year (Śrīmukha)
[b]Pongal

ISLAMIC (ASTRONOMICAL) 1460/1461

Month	Sun	Mon	Tue	Wed	Thu	Fri	Sat
DHU AL-ḤIJJA 1460	29	| 1	2	3	4	5	6
	7	8	9	10[g]	11	12	13
	14	15	16	17	18	19	20
	21	22	23	24	25	26	27
	28	29	30	| 1[a]	2	3	4
MUḤARRAM 1461	5	6	7	8	9	10[b]	11
	12	13	14	15	16	17	18
	19	20	21	22	23	24	25
	26	27	28	29	| 1	2	3
ṢAFAR 1461	4	5	6	7	8	9	10
	11	12	13	14	15	16	17
	18	19	20	21	22	23	24
	25	26	27	28	29	30	| 1
RABĪʿ I 1461	2	3	4	5	6	7	8
	9	10	11	12[c]	13	14	15
	16	17	18	19	20	21	22
	23	24	25	26	27	28	29
	30	| 1	2	3	4	5	6
RABĪʿ II 1461	7	8	9	10	11	12	13
	14	15	16	17	18	19	20
	21	22	23	24	25	26	27
	28	29	| 1	2	3	4	5
JUMĀDĀ I 1461	6	7	8	9	10	11	12
	13	14	15	16	17	18	19
	20	21	22	23	24	25	26
	27	28	29	30	| 1	2	3
JUMĀDĀ II 1461	4	5	6	7	8	9	10
	11	12	13	14	15	16	17
	18	19	20	21	22	23	24
	25	26	27	28	29	30	| 1
RAJAB 1461	2	3	4	5	6	7	8
	9	10	11	12	13	14	15
	16	17	18	19	20	21	22
	23	24	25	26	27[d]	28	29
SHAʿBĀN 1461	1	2	3	4	5	6	7
	8	9	10	11	12	13	14
	15	16	17	18	19	20	21
	22	23	24	25	26	27	28
	29	| 1[e]	2	3	4	5	6
RAMAḌĀN 1461	7	8	9	10	11	12	13
	14	15	16	17	18	19	20
	21	22	23	24	25	26	27
	28	29	30	| 1[f]	2	3	4
SHAWWĀL 1461	5	6	7	8	9	10	11
	12	13	14	15	16	17	18
	19	20	21	22	23	24	25
	26	27	28	29	30	| 1	2
DHU AL-QAʿDA 1461	3	4	5	6	7	8	9
	10	11	12	13	14	15	16
	17	18	19	20	21	22	23
	24	25	26	27	28	29	| 1
DHU AL-ḤIJJA 1461	2	3	4	5	6	7	8
	9	10[g]	11	12	13	14	15

[a]New Year
[b]ʿAshūrāʾ
[c]Prophet's Birthday
[d]Ascent of the Prophet
[e]Start of Ramaḍān
[f]ʿĪd al-Fiṭr
[g]ʿĪd al-ʾAḍḥā

GREGORIAN 2039

Julian (Sun)	Sun	Mon	Tue	Wed	Thu	Fri	Sat	Month
Dec 13	26	27	28	29	30	31	| 1	JANUARY 2039
	2	3	4	5	6	7[a]	8	
Dec 27	9	10	11	12	13	14[b]	15	
	16	17	18	19	20	21	22	
Jan 10	23	24	25	26	27	28	29	
	30	31	| 1	2	3	4	5	FEBRUARY 2039
Jan 24	6	7	8	9	10	11	12	
	13	14	15	16	17	18	19	
Feb 7	20	21	22	23[c]	24	25	26	
	27	28	| 1	2	3	4	5	MARCH 2039
Feb 21	6[d]	7	8	9	10	11	12	
	13	14	15	16	17	18	19	
Mar 7	20	21	22	23	24	25	26	
	27	28	29	30	31	| 1	2	APRIL 2039
Mar 21	3	4	5	6	7	8	9	
	10[e]	11	12	13	14	15	16	
Apr 4	17[f]	18	19	20	21	22	23	
	24	25	26	27	28	29	30	
Apr 18	1	2	3	4	5	6	7	MAY 2039
	8	9	10	11	12	13	14	
May 2	15	16	17	18	19	20	21	
	22	23	24	25	26	27	28	
May 16	29	30	31	| 1	2	3	4	JUNE 2039
	5	6	7	8	9	10	11	
May 30	12	13	14	15	16	17	18	
	19	20	21	22	23	24	25	
Jun 13	26	27	28	29	30	| 1	2	JULY 2039
	3	4	5	6	7	8	9	
Jun 27	10	11	12	13	14	15	16	
	17	18	19	20	21	22	23	
Jul 11	24	25	26	27	28	29	30	
	31	| 1	2	3	4	5	6	AUGUST 2039
Jul 25	7	8	9	10	11	12	13	
	14	15	16	17	18	19	20	
Aug 8	21	22	23	24	25	26	27	
	28	29	30	31	| 1	2	3	SEPTEMBER 2039
Aug 22	4	5	6	7	8	9	10	
	11	12	13	14	15	16	17	
Sep 5	18	19	20	21	22	23	24	
	25	26	27	28	29	30	| 1	OCTOBER 2039
Sep 19	2	3	4	5	6	7	8	
	9	10	11	12	13	14	15	
Oct 3	16	17	18	19	20	21	22	
	23	24	25	26	27	28	29	
Oct 17	30	31	| 1	2	3	4	5	NOVEMBER 2039
	6	7	8	9	10	11	12	
Oct 31	13	14	15	16	17	18	19	
	20	21	22	23	24	25	26	
Nov 14	27[g]	28	29	30	| 1	2	3	DECEMBER 2039
	4	5	6	7	8	9	10	
Nov 28	11	12	13	14	15	16	17	
	18	19	20	21	22	23	24	
Dec 12	25[h]	26	27	28	29	30	31	

[a]Orthodox Christmas
[b]Julian New Year
[c]Ash Wednesday
[d]Feast of Orthodoxy
[e]Easter
[f]Orthodox Easter
[g]Advent
[h]Christmas

2040

Gregorian 2040‡

Month	Sun	Mon	Tue	Wed	Thu	Fri	Sat	Lunar Phases	ISO Week (Mon)	Julian Day (Sun noon)
January 2040	1[a]	2	3	4	5	6	◑	11:04	1	2466155
	8	9	10	11	12	13	●	3:24	2	2466162
	15	16	17	18	19	20	◐	2:20	3	2466169
	22	23	24	25	26	27	28		4	2466176
	○	30	31	1	2	3	4	7:53	5	2466183
February 2040	◑	6	7	8	9	10	11	22:31	6	2466190
	●	13	14	15	16	17	18	14:23	7	2466197
	◐	20	21	22	23	24	25	21:32	8	2466204
	26	27	○	29	1	2	3	0:58	9	2466211
March 2040	4	5	◑	7	8	9	10	7:17	10	2466218
	11	12	●	14	15	16	17	1:45	11	2466225
	18	19	◐[b]	21	22	23	24	17:58	12	2466232
	25	26	27	○	29	30	31	15:10	13	2466239
April 2040	1	2	3	◑	5	6	7	14:05	14	2466246
	8	9	10	●	12	13	14	13:59	15	2466253
	15	16	17	18	◐	20	21	13:36	16	2466260
	22	23	24	25	26	○	28	2:37	17	2466267
	29	30	1	2	◑	4	5	19:58	18	2466274
May 2040	6	7	8	9	10	●	12	3:26	19	2466281
	13	14	15	16	17	18	◐	6:59	20	2466288
	20	21	22	23	24	25	○	11:46	21	2466295
	27	28	29	30	31	1	◑	2:16	22	2466302
June 2040	3	4	5	6	7	8	●	18:02	23	2466309
	10	11	12	13	14	15	16		24	2466316
	◐	18	19	20[c]	21	22	23	21:31	25	2466323
	○	25	26	27	28	29	30	19:18	26	2466330
July 2040	◑	2	3	4	5	6	7	10:16	27	2466337
	8	●	10	11	12	13	14	9:13	28	2466344
	15	16	◐	18	19	20	21	9:15	29	2466351
	22	23	○	25	26	27	28	2:04	30	2466358
	29	◑	31	1	2	3	4	21:04	31	2466365
August 2040	5	6	7	●	9	10	11	0:25	32	2466372
	12	13	14	◐	16	17	18	18:35	33	2466379
	19	20	21	○	23	24	25	9:08	34	2466386
	26	27	28	◑	30	31	1	11:15	35	2466393
September 2040	2	3	4	5	●	7	8	15:12	36	2466400
	9	10	11	12	13	◐	15	2:06	37	2466407
	16	17	18	19	○	21	22[d]	17:42	38	2466414
	23	24	25	26	27	◑	29	4:40	39	2466421
	30	1	2	3	4	5	●	5:25	40	2466428
October 2040	7	8	9	10	11	12	◐	8:40	41	2466435
	14	15	16	17	18	19	○	4:49	42	2466442
	21	22	23	24	25	26	27		43	2466449
	◑	29	30	31	1	2	3	0:25	44	2466456
November 2040	●	5	6	7	8	9	10	18:55	45	2466463
	◐	12	13	14	15	16	17	15:22	46	2466470
	○	19	20	21	22	23	24	19:05	47	2466477
	25	◑	27	28	29	30	1	21:06	48	2466484
December 2040	2	3	●	5	6	7	8	7:32	49	2466491
	9	◐	11	12	13	14	15	23:28	50	2466498
	16	17	○	19	20	21[e]	22	12:14	51	2466505
	23	24	25	◑	27	28	29	17:01	52	2466512
	30	31	1	●	3	4	5	19:06	1	2466519

Hebrew 5800/5801‡

Julian Day	Month	Sun	Mon	Tue	Wed	Thu	Fri	Sat	Molad
2466155	Teveth 5800	15	16	17	18	19	20	21	
2466162		22	23	24	25	26	27	28	
2466169	Shevat 5800	29	1	2	3	4	5	6	Sat 10h8m4p
2466176		7	8	9	10	11	12	13	
2466183		14	15	16	17	18	19	20	
2466190		21	22	23	24	25	26	27	
2466197	Adar 5800	28	29	30	1	2	3	4	Sun 22h52m5p
2466204		5	6	7	8	9	10	11	
2466211		12	13	14[f]	15	16	17	18	
2466218		19	20	21	22	23	24	25	
2466225	Nisan 5800	26	27	28	29	1	2	3	Tue 11h36m6p
2466232		4	5	6	7	8	9	10	
2466239		11	12	13	14	15[g]	16	17	
2466246		18	19	20	21	22	23	24	
2466253	Iyyar 5800	25	26	27	28	29	30	1	Thu 0h20m7p
2466260		2	3	4	5	6	7	8	
2466267		9	10	11	12	13	14	15	
2466274		16	17	18	19	20	21	22	
2466281		23	24	25	26	27	28	29	
2466288	Sivan 5800	1	2	3	4	5	6[h]	7	Fri 13h4m8p
2466295		8	9	10	11	12	13	14	
2466302		15	16	17	18	19	20	21	
2466309		22	23	24	25	26	27	28	
2466316	Tammuz 5800	29	30	1	2	3	4	5	Sun 1h48m9p
2466323		6	7	8	9	10	11	12	
2466330		13	14	15	16	17	18	19	
2466337		20	21	22	23	24	25	26	
2466344	Av 5800	27	28	29	1	2	3	4	Mon 14h32m10p
2466351		5	6	7	8	9[i]	10	11	
2466358		12	13	14	15	16	17	18	
2466365		19	20	21	22	23	24	25	
2466372	Elul 5800	26	27	28	29	30	1	2	Wed 3h16m11p
2466379		3	4	5	6	7	8	9	
2466386		10	11	12	13	14	15	16	
2466393		17	18	19	20	21	22	23	
2466400		24	25	26	27	28	29	1[a]	Thu 16h0m12p
2466407	Tishri 5801	2[a]	3	4	5	6	7	8	
2466414		9	10[b]	11	12	13	14	15[c]	
2466421		16	17	18	19	20	21	22	
2466428		23	24	25	26	27	28	29	
2466435	Heshvan 5801	30	1	2	3	4	5	6	Sat 4h44m13p
2466442		7	8	9	10	11	12	13	
2466449		14	15	16	17	18	19	20	
2466456		21	22	23	24	25	26	27	
2466463	Kislev 5801	28	29	1	2	3	4	5	Sun 17h28m14p
2466470		6	7	8	9	10	11	12	
2466477		13	14	15	16	17	18	19	
2466484		20	21	22	23	24	25[e]	26[e]	
2466491	Teveth 5801	27[e]	28[e]	29[e]	1[d][e]	2[e]	3[e]	4	Tue 6h12m15p
2466498		5	6	7	8	9	10	11	
2466505		12	13	14	15	16	17	18	
2466512		19	20	21	22	23	24	25	
2466519		26	27	28	29	1	2	3	Wed 18h56m16p

Chinese Jǐ-Wèi‡/Gēng-Shēn

Julian Day	Month	Sun	Mon	Tue	Wed	Thu	Fri	Sat	Solar Term
2466155	Month 11 Jǐ-Wèi	17	18	19	20	21	22	23	Xiǎo hán
2466162		24	25	26	27	28	29	1	
2466169	Month 12 Jǐ-Wèi	2	3	4	5	6	7	8	Dà hán
2466176		9	10	11	12	13	14	15	
2466183		16	17	18	19	20	21	22	Lì chūn
2466190		23	24*	25	26	27	28	29	
2466197	Month 1 Gēng-Shēn	1[a]	2	3	4	5	6	7	
2466204		8	9	10	11	12	13	14	Yǔ shuǐ
2466211		15[b]	16	17	18	19	20	21	
2466218		22	23	24	25	26	27	28	Jīng zhé
2466225	Month 2 Gēng-Shēn	29	30	1	2	3	4	5	
2466232		6	7	8	9	10	11	12	Chūn fēn
2466239		13	14	15	16	17	18	19	
2466246		20	21	22	23[c]	24	25*	26	Qīng míng
2466253	Month 3 Gēng-Shēn	27	28	29	1	2	3	4	
2466260		5	6	7	8	9	10	11	Gǔ yǔ
2466267		12	13	14	15	16	17	18	
2466274		19	20	21	22	23	24	25	Lì xià
2466281	Month 4 Gēng-Shēn	26	27	28	29	30	1	2	
2466288		3	4	5	6	7	8	9	
2466295		10	11	12	13	14	15	16	Xiǎo mǎn
2466302		17	18	19	20	21	22	23	
2466309		24	25	26*	27	28	29	30	Máng zhǒng
2466316	Month 5 Gēng-Shēn	1	2	3	4	5[d]	6	7	
2466323		8	9	10	11	12	13	14	Xià zhì
2466330		15	16	17	18	19	20	21	
2466337		22	23	24	25	26	27	28	Xiǎo shǔ
2466344	Month 6 Gēng-Shēn	29	1	2	3	4	5	6	
2466351		7	8	9	10	11	12	13	
2466358		14	15	16	17	18	19	20	Dà shǔ
2466365		21	22	23	24	25	26	27*	
2466372	Month 7 Gēng-Shēn	28	29	30	1	2	3	4	Lì qiū
2466379		5	6	7[e]	8	9	10	11	
2466386		12	13	14	15[f]	16	17	18	Chǔ shǔ
2466393		19	20	21	22	23	24	25	
2466400	Month 8 Gēng-Shēn	26	27	28	29	1	2	3	Bái lù
2466407		4	5	6	7	8	9	10	
2466414		11	12	13	14	15[g]	16	17	Qiū fēn
2466421		18	19	20	21	22	23	24	
2466428	Month 9 Gēng-Shēn	25	26	27	28*	29	30	1	
2466435		2	3	4	5	6	7	8	Hán lù
2466442		9[h]	10	11	12	13	14	15	
2466449		16	17	18	19	20	21	22	Shuāng jiàng
2466456		23	24	25	26	27	28	29	
2466463	Month 10 Gēng-Shēn	30	1	2	3	4	5	6	Lì dōng
2466470		7	8	9	10	11	12	13	
2466477		14	15	16	17	18	19	20	Xiǎo xuě
2466484		21	22	23	24	25	26	27	
2466491	Month 11 Gēng-Shēn	28*	29	1	2	3	4	5	Dà xuě
2466498		6	7	8	9	10	11	12	
2466505		13	14	15	16	17	18[i]	19	Dōng zhì
2466512		20	21	22	23	24	25	26	
2466519		27	28	29	30	1	2	3	Xiǎo hán

Coptic 1756/1757 – Ethiopic 2032/2033

Julian Day	Coptic Month	Sun	Mon	Tue	Wed	Thu	Fri	Sat	Ethiopic Month
2466155	Koiak 1756	22	23	24	25	26	27	28	Tāḫśāś 2032
2466162		29[c]	30	1	2	3	4	5	
2466169	Tōbe 1756	6[d]	7	8	9	10	11[e]	12	Ṭer 2032
2466176		13	14	15	16	17	18	19	
2466183		20	21	22	23	24	25	26	
2466190		27	28	29	30	1	2	3	
2466197	Meshir 1756	4	5	6	7	8	9	10	Yakātit 2032
2466204		11	12	13	14	15	16	17	
2466211		18	19	20	21	22	23	24	
2466218		25	26	27	28	29	30	1	
2466225	Paremotep 1756	2	3	4	5	6	7	8	Magābit 2032
2466232		9	10	11	12	13	14	15	
2466239		16	17	18	19	20	21	22	
2466246		23	24	25	26	27	28	29	
2466253	Parmoute 1756	30	1	2	3	4	5	6	Miyāzyā 2032
2466260		7	8	9	10	11	12	13	
2466267		14	15	16	17	18	19	20	
2466274		21	22	23	24	25	26	27	
2466281	Pashons 1756	28[f]	29[g]	30	1	2	3	4	Genbot 2032
2466288		5	6	7	8	9	10	11	
2466295		12	13	14	15	16	17	18	
2466302		19	20	21	22	23	24	25	
2466309	Paōne 1756	26	27	28	29	30	1	2	Sanē 2032
2466316		3	4	5	6	7	8	9	
2466323		10	11	12	13	14	15	16	
2466330		17	18	19	20	21	22	23	
2466337	Epēp 1756	24	25	26	27	28	29	30	Ḥamlē 2032
2466344		1	2	3	4	5	6	7	
2466351		8	9	10	11	12	13	14	
2466358		15	16	17	18	19	20	21	
2466365		22	23	24	25	26	27	28	
2466372	Mesorē 1756	29	30	1	2	3	4	5	Naḥasē 2032
2466379		6	7	8	9	10	11	12	
2466386		13[h]	14	15	16	17	18	19	
2466393		20	21	22	23	24	25	26	
2466400	Epag. 1756	27	28	29	30	1	2	3	Pāg. 2032
2466407	Thoout 1757	4	5	1[a]	2	3	4	5	Maskaram 2033
2466414		6	7	8	9	10	11	12	
2466421		13	14	15	16	17[b]	18	19	
2466428		20	21	22	23	24	25	26	
2466435	Paope 1757	27	28	29	30	1	2	3	Ṭeqemt 2033
2466442		4	5	6	7	8	9	10	
2466449		11	12	13	14	15	16	17	
2466456		18	19	20	21	22	23	24	
2466463	Athōr 1757	25	26	27	28	29	30	1	Ḫedār 2033
2466470		2	3	4	5	6	7	8	
2466477		9	10	11	12	13	14	15	
2466484		16	17	18	19	20	21	22	
2466491	Koiak 1757	23	24	25	26	27	28	29	Tāḫśāś 2033
2466498		30	1	2	3	4	5	6	
2466505		7	8	9	10	11	12	13	
2466512		14	15	16	17	18	19	20	
2466519		21	22	23	24	25	26	27	

‡Leap year
[a]New Year
[b]Spring (0:10)
[c]Summer (17:45)
[d]Autumn (9:43)
[e]Winter (6:31)
● New moon
◐ First quarter moon
○ Full moon
◑ Last quarter moon

‡Leap year
[a]New Year
[b]Yom Kippur
[c]Sukkot
[d]Winter starts
[e]Ḥanukkah
[f]Purim
[g]Passover
[h]Shavuot
[i]Fast of Av

‡Leap year
[a]New Year (4738, Monkey)
[b]Lantern Festival
[c]Qīngmíng
[d]Dragon Festival
[e]Qīqiǎo
[f]Hungry Ghosts
[g]Mid-Autumn Festival
[h]Double-Ninth Festival
[i]Dōngzhì
*Start of 60-name cycle

[a]New Year
[b]Building of the Cross
[c]Christmas
[d]Jesus's Circumcision
[e]Epiphany
[f]Easter
[g]Mary's Announcement
[h]Jesus's Transfiguration

PERSIAN (ASTRONOMICAL) 1418/1419

Month	Sun	Mon	Tue	Wed	Thu	Fri	Sat
DEY 1418	11	12	13	14	15	16	17
	18	19	20	21	22	23	24
	25	26	27	28	29	30	1
BAHMAN 1418	2	3	4	5	6	7	8
	9	10	11	12	13	14	15
	16	17	18	19	20	21	22
	23	24	25	26	27	28	29
	30	1	2	3	4	5	6
ESFAND 1418	7	8	9	10	11	12	13
	14	15	16	17	18	19	20
	21	22	23	24	25	26	27
	28	29	1[a]	2	3	4	5
FARVARDĪN 1419	6	7	8	9	10	11	12
	13[b]	14	15	16	17	18	19
	20	21	22	23	24	25	26
	27	28	29	30	31	1	2
ORDĪBEHEŠT 1419	3	4	5	6	7	8	9
	10	11	12	13	14	15	16
	17	18	19	20	21	22	23
	24	25	26	27	28	29	30
	31	1	2	3	4	5	6
XORDĀD 1419	7	8	9	10	11	12	13
	14	15	16	17	18	19	20
	21	22	23	24	25	26	27
	28	29	30	31	1	2	3
TĪR 1419	4	5	6	7	8	9	10
	11	12	13	14	15	16	17
	18	19	20	21	22	23	24
	25	26	27	28	29	30	31
MORDĀD 1419	1	2	3	4	5	6	7
	8	9	10	11	12	13	14
	15	16	17	18	19	20	21
	22	23	24	25	26	27	28
	29	30	31	1	2	3	4
SHAHRĪVAR 1419	5	6	7	8	9	10	11
	12	13	14	15	16	17	18
	19	20	21	22	23	24	25
	26	27	28	29	30	31	1
MEHR 1419	2	3	4	5	6	7	8
	9	10	11	12	13	14	15
	16	17	18	19	20	21	22
	23	24	25	26	27	28	29
	30	1	2	3	4	5	6
ĀBĀN 1419	7	8	9	10	11	12	13
	14	15	16	17	18	19	20
	21	22	23	24	25	26	27
	28	29	30	1	2	3	4
ĀZAR 1419	5	6	7	8	9	10	11
	12	13	14	15	16	17	18
	19	20	21	22	23	24	25
	26	27	28	29	30	1	2
DEY 1419	3	4	5	6	7	8	9
	10	11	12	13	14	15	16

HINDU LUNAR 2096‡/2097

Month	Sun	Mon	Tue	Wed	Thu	Fri	Sat
MĀRGAŚĪRA 2096	17	18	19	20	21	22	23
	24	25	26	27	28	29	30
PAUSHA 2096	2	3	4	5	6	7	8
	9	10	11	12	13	13	14
	15	16	17	18	19	20	21
	22	23	24	25	27	28	29
MĀGHA 2096	30	1	2	3	4	5	6
	7	8	9	10	11	12	13
	14	15	16	17	18	19	20
	21	22	23	24	25	26	27
PHĀLGUNA 2096	28[h]	29	30	2	3	4	5
	5	6	7	8	9	10	11
	12	13	14	15[i]	16	17	18
	19	20	21	22	23	25	26
CHAITRA 2097	27	28	29	30	1[a]	2	3
	4	5	6	7	8	9[b]	9
	10	11	12	13	14	15	16
	18	19	20	21	22	23	24
VAIŚĀKHA 2097	25	26	27	28	29	30	1
	2	3	4	5	6	7	8
	9	10	11	12	13	14	15
	16	17	18	19	20	22	23
	24	25	26	27	28	29	30
JYAISHTHA 2097	1	2	3	4	4	5	6
	7	8	9	10	11	12	14
	15	16	17	18	19	20	21
	22	23	24	25	26	27	28
ĀSHĀDHA 2097	29	30	1	2	3	4	5
	6	7	8	9	10	11	12
	13	14	15	17	18	19	20
	21	22	23	24	25	26	27
ŚRĀVANA 2097	28	29	30	1	1	2	3
	4	5	6	7	8	10	11
	12	13	14	15	16	17	18
	19	20	21	22	23[c]	24	25
BHĀDRAPADA 2097	26	27	28	29	30	1	2
	3	4[d]	5	6	7	8	9
	10	11	13	14	15	16	17
	18	19	20	21	22	23	24
	25	26	27	27	28	29	30
ĀŚVINA 2097	1	2	3	4	5	7	8[e]
	9[e]	10[e]	11	12	13	14	15
	16	17	18	19	20	21	22
	23	24	25	26	27	28	29
KĀRTTIKA 2097	30	1[f]	2	3	4	5	6
	7	8	9	11	12	13	14
	15	16	17	18	19	20	21
	21	22	23	24	25	26	27
MĀRGAŚĪRA 2097	28	29	30	1	2	3	5
	6	7	8	9	10	11[g]	12
	13	14	15	16	17	18	19
	20	21	22	23	24	25	25
	27	28	29	30	1	2	3

HINDU SOLAR 1961/1962‡

Month	Sun	Mon	Tue	Wed	Thu	Fri	Sat
PAUSHA 1961	17	18	19	20	21	22	23
	24	25	26	27	28	29	30
MĀGHA 1961	1[b]	2	3	4	5	6	7
	8	9	10	11	12	13	14
	15	16	17	18	19	20	21
	22	23	24	25	26	27	28
PHĀLGUNA 1961	29	1	2	3	4	5	6
	7	8	9	10	11	12	13
	14	15	16	17	18	19	20
	21	22	23	24	25	26	27
CHAITRA 1961	28	29	30	1	2	3	4
	5	6	7	8	9	10	11
	12	13	14	15	16	17	18
	19	20	21	22	23	24	25
VAIŚĀKHA 1962	26	27	28	29	30	1[a]	2
	3	4	5	6	7	8	9
	10	11	12	13	14	15	16
	17	18	19	20	21	22	23
	24	25	26	27	28	29	30
JYAISHTHA 1962	31	1	2	3	4	5	6
	7	8	9	10	11	12	13
	14	15	16	17	18	19	20
	21	22	23	24	25	26	27
ĀSHĀDHA 1962	28	29	30	31	32	1	2
	3	4	5	6	7	8	9
	10	11	12	13	14	15	16
	17	18	19	20	21	22	23
	24	25	26	27	28	29	30
ŚRĀVANA 1962	31	1	2	3	4	5	6
	7	8	9	10	11	12	13
	14	15	16	17	18	19	20
	21	22	23	24	25	26	27
BHĀDRAPADA 1962	28	29	30	31	32	1	2
	3	4	5	6	7	8	9
	10	11	12	13	14	15	16
	17	18	19	20	21	22	23
	24	25	26	27	28	29	30
ĀŚVINA 1962	31	1	2	3	4	5	6
	7	8	9	10	11	12	13
	14	15	16	17	18	19	20
	21	22	23	24	25	26	27
KĀRTTIKA 1962	28	29	30	1	2	3	4
	5	6	7	8	9	10	11
	12	13	14	15	16	17	18
	19	20	21	22	23	24	25
MĀRGAŚĪRA 1962	26	27	28	29	30	1	2
	3	4	5	6	7	8	9
	10	11	12	13	14	15	16
	17	18	19	20	21	22	23
	24	25	26	27	28	29	30
PAUSHA 1962	1	2	3	4	5	6	7
	8	9	10	11	12	13	14
	15	16	17	18	19	20	21

ISLAMIC (ASTRONOMICAL) 1461/1462‡/1463‡

Month	Sun	Mon	Tue	Wed	Thu	Fri	Sat
DHU AL-HIJJA 1461	16	17	18	19	20	21	22
	23	24	25	26	27	28	29
MUHARRAM 1462	1[a]	2[A]	3	4	5	6	7
	8	9	10[b]	11	12	13	14
	15	16	17	18	19	20	21
	22	23	24	25	26	27	28
SAFAR 1462	29	30	1	2	3	4	5
	6	7	8	9	10	11	12
	13	14	15	16	17	18	19
	20	21	22	23	24	25	26
RABĪ' I 1462	27	28	29	1	2	3	4
	5	6	7	8	9	10	11
	12[c]	13	14	15	16	17	18
	19	20	21	22	23	24	25
RABĪ' II 1462	26	27	28	29	30	1	2
	3	4	5	6	7	8	9
	10	11	12	13	14	15	16
	17	18	19	20	21	22	23
JUMĀDĀ I 1462	24	25	26	27	28	29	1
	2	3	4	5	6	7	8
	9	10	11	12	13	14	15
	16	17	18	19	20	21	22
	23	24	25	26	27	28	29
JUMĀDĀ II 1462	30	1	2	3	4	5	6
	7	8	9	10	11	12	13
	14	15	16	17	18	19	20
	21	22	23	24	25	26	27
RAJAB 1462	28	29	30	1	2	3	4
	5	6	7	8	9	10	11
	12	13	14	15	16	17	18
	19	20	21	22	23	24	25
SHA'BĀN 1462	26	27[d]	28	29	1	2	3
	4	5	6	7	8	9	10
	11	12	13	14	15	16	17
	18	19	20	21	22	23	24
RAMADĀN 1462	25	26	27	28	29	30	1[e]
	2	3	4	5	6	7	8
	9	10	11	12	13	14	15
	16	17	18	19	20	21	22
	23	24	25	26	27	28	29
SHAWWĀL 1462	30	1[f]	2	3	4	5	6
	7	8	9	10	11	12	13
	14	15	16	17	18	19	20
	21	22	23	24	25	26	27
DHU AL-QA'DA 1462	28	29	1	2	3	4	5
	6	7	8	9	10	11	12
	13	14	15	16	17	18	19
	20	21	22	23	24	25	26
DHU AL-HIJJA 1462	27	28	29	30	1	2	3
	4	5	6	7	8	9	10[g]
	11	12	13	14	15	16	17
	18	19	20	21	22	23	24
	25	26	27	28	29	1	2

GREGORIAN 2040‡

Julian‡ (Sun)	Sun	Mon	Tue	Wed	Thu	Fri	Sat	Month
Dec 19	1	2	3	4	5	6	7[a]	JANUARY 2040
	8	9	10	11	12	13	14[b]	
Jan 2	15	16	17	18	19	20	21	
	22	23	24	25	26	27	28	
Jan 16	29	30	31	1	2	3	4	FEBRUARY 2040
	5	6	7	8	9	10	11	
Jan 30	12	13	14	15[c]	16	17	18	
	19	20	21	22	23	24	25	
Feb 13	26	27	28	29	1	2	3	MARCH 2040
	4	5	6	7	8	9	10	
Feb 27	11	12	13	14	15	16	17	
	18	19	20	21	22	23	24	
Mar 12	25[d]	26	27	28	29	30	31	
	1[e]	2	3	4	5	6	7	APRIL 2040
Mar 26	8	9	10	11	12	13	14	
	15	16	17	18	19	20	21	
Apr 9	22	23	24	25	26	27	28	
	29	30	1	2	3	4	5	MAY 2040
Apr 23	6[f]	7	8	9	10	11	12	
	13	14	15	16	17	18	19	
May 7	20	21	22	23	24	25	26	
	27	28	29	30	31	1	2	JUNE 2040
May 21	3	4	5	6	7	8	9	
	10	11	12	13	14	15	16	
Jun 4	17	18	19	20	21	22	23	
	24	25	26	27	28	29	30	
Jun 18	1	2	3	4	5	6	7	JULY 2040
	8	9	10	11	12	13	14	
Jul 2	15	16	17	18	19	20	21	
	22	23	24	25	26	27	28	
Jul 16	29	30	31	1	2	3	4	AUGUST 2040
	5	6	7	8	9	10	11	
Jul 30	12	13	14	15	16	17	18	
	19	20	21	22	23	24	25	
Aug 13	26	27	28	29	30	31	1	SEPTEMBER 2040
	2	3	4	5	6	7	8	
Aug 27	9	10	11	12	13	14	15	
	16	17	18	19	20	21	22	
Sep 10	23	24	25	26	27	28	29	
	30	1	2	3	4	5	6	OCTOBER 2040
Sep 24	7	8	9	10	11	12	13	
	14	15	16	17	18	19	20	
Oct 8	21	22	23	24	25	26	27	
	28	29	30	31	1	2	3	NOVEMBER 2040
Oct 22	4	5	6	7	8	9	10	
	11	12	13	14	15	16	17	
Nov 5	18	19	20	21	22	23	24	
	25	26	27	28	29	30	1	DECEMBER 2040
Nov 19	2[g]	3	4	5	6	7	8	
	9	10	11	12	13	14	15	
Dec 3	16	17	18	19	20	21	22	
	23	24	25[h]	26	27	28	29	
Dec 17	30	31	1	2	3	4	5	

Persian:
[a]New Year
[b]Sizdeh Bedar

Hindu Lunar:
‡Leap year
[a]New Year (Rāudra)
[b]Birthday of Rāma
[c]Birthday of Krishna
[d]Ganēśa Chaturthī
[e]Dashara
[f]Diwali
[g]Birthday of Vishnu
[h]Night of Śiva
[i]Holi

Hindu Solar:
‡Leap year
[a]New Year (Bhāva)
[b]Pongal

Islamic:
‡Leap year
[a]New Year
[A]New Year (Arithmetic)
[b]'Ashūrā'
[c]Prophet's Birthday
[d]Ascent of the Prophet
[e]Start of Ramaḍān
[f]'Id al-Fiṭr
[g]'Id al-'Aḍḥā

Gregorian:
‡Leap year
[a]Orthodox Christmas
[b]Julian New Year
[c]Ash Wednesday
[d]Feast of Orthodoxy
[e]Easter
[f]Orthodox Easter
[g]Advent
[h]Christmas

2041

GREGORIAN 2041 — Lunar Phases — ISO WEEK — JULIAN DAY

Month	Sun	Mon	Tue	Wed	Thu	Fri	Sat	Lunar Phases	ISO Week (Mon)	Julian Day (Sun noon)
JANUARY 2041	30	31	1[a]	●	3	4	5	19:06	1	2466519
	6	7	8	◐	10	11	12	10:04	2	2466526
	13	14	15	16	○	18	19	7:10	3	2466533
	20	21	22	23	24	◑	26	10:32	4	2466540
FEBRUARY 2041	27	28	29	30	31	●	2	5:41	5	2466547
	3	4	5	6	◐	8	9	23:39	6	2466554
	10	11	12	13	14	15	○	2:20	7	2466561
	17	18	19	20	21	22	23		8	2466568
MARCH 2041	◑	25	26	27	28	1	●	0:28 15:38	9	2466575
	3	4	5	6	7	8	◐	15:50	10	2466582
	10	11	12	13	14	15	16		11	2466589
	○	18	19	20[b]	21	22	23	20:18	12	2466596
	24	◑	26	27	28	29	30	10:31	13	2466603
APRIL 2041	31	●	2	3	4	5	6	1:28	14	2466610
	7	◐	9	10	11	12	13	9:37	15	2466617
	14	15	○	17	18	19	20	11:59	16	2466624
	21	22	◑	24	25	26	27	17:23	17	2466631
MAY 2041	28	29	●	1	2	3	4	11:45	18	2466638
	5	6	7	◐	9	10	11	3:53	19	2466645
	12	13	14	15	○	17	18	0:51	20	2466652
	19	20	21	◑	23	24	25	22:25	21	2466659
JUNE 2041	26	27	28	●	30	31	1	22:54	22	2466666
	2	3	4	5	◐	7	8	21:39	23	2466673
	9	10	11	12	13	○	15	10:57	24	2466680
	16	17	18	19	20[c]	◑	22	3:11	25	2466687
	23	24	25	26	27	●	29	11:15	26	2466694
JULY 2041	30	1	2	3	4	5	◐	14:11	27	2466701
	7	8	9	10	11	12	○	18:59	28	2466708
	14	15	16	17	18	19	◑	9:12	29	2466715
	21	22	23	24	25	26	27		30	2466722
AUGUST 2041	●	29	30	31	1	2	3	1:01	31	2466729
	4	◐	6	7	8	9	10	4:51	32	2466736
	11	○	13	14	15	16	17	2:03	33	2466743
	◑	19	20	21	22	23	24	17:42	34	2466750
	25	●	27	28	29	30	31	16:15	35	2466757
SEPTEMBER 2041	1	2	◐	4	5	6	7	17:17	36	2466764
	8	9	○	11	12	13	14	9:23	37	2466771
	15	16	◑	18	19	20	21	5:32	38	2466778
	22[d]	23	24	●	26	27	28	8:40	39	2466785
OCTOBER 2041	29	30	1	2	◐	4	5	3:31	40	2466792
	6	7	8	○	10	11	12	18:01	41	2466799
	13	14	15	◑	17	18	19	21:04	42	2466806
	20	21	22	23	24	●	26	1:29	43	2466813
NOVEMBER 2041	27	28	29	30	31	◐	2	12:03	44	2466820
	3	4	5	6	7	○	9	4:42	45	2466827
	10	11	12	13	14	◑	16	16:05	46	2466834
	17	18	19	20	21	22	●	17:35	47	2466841
	24	25	26	27	28	29	◐	19:47	48	2466848
DECEMBER 2041	1	2	3	4	5	6	○	17:41	49	2466855
	8	9	10	11	12	13	14		50	2466862
	◑	16	17	18	19	20	21[e]	13:31	51	2466869
	22	●	24	25	26	27	28	8:05	52	2466876
	29	◐	31	1	2	3	4	3:44	1	2466883

HEBREW 5801‡/5802

ISO Week	Month	Sun	Mon	Tue	Wed	Thu	Fri	Sat	Molad
1	SHEVAT 5801	26	27	28	29	1	2	3	Wed 18h56m16p
2		4	5	6	7	8	9	10	
3		11	12	13	14	15	16	17	
4		18	19	20	21	22	23	24	
5	ADAR I 5801	25	26	27	28	29	30	1	Fri 7h40m17p
6		2	3	4	5	6	7	8	
7		9	10	11	12	13	14	15	
8		16	17	18	19	20	21	22	
9		23	24	25	26	27	28	29	
10	ADAR II 5801	30	1	2	3	4	5	6	Sat 20h25m0p
11		7	8	9	10	11	12	13	
12		14[f]	15	16	17	18	19	20	
13		21	22	23	24	25	26	27	
14	NISAN 5801	28	29	1	2	3	4	5	Mon 9h9m1p
15		6	7	8	9	10	11	12	
16		13	14	15[g]	16	17	18	19	
17		20	21	22	23	24	25	26	
18	IYAR 5801	27	28	29	30	1	2	3	Tue 21h53m2p
19		4	5	6	7	8	9	10	
20		11	12	13	14	15	16	17	
21		18	19	20	21	22	23	24	
22	SIVAN 5801	25	26	27	28	29	1	2	Thu 10h37m3p
23		3	4	5	6[h]	7	8	9	
24		10	11	12	13	14	15	16	
25		17	18	19	20	21	22	23	
26		24	25	26	27	28	29	30	
27	TAMMUZ 5801	1	2	3	4	5	6	7	Fri 23h21m4p
28		8	9	10	11	12	13	14	
29		15	16	17	18	19	20	21	
30		22	23	24	25	26	27	28	
31	AV 5801	29	1	2	3	4	5	6	Sun 12h5m5p
32		7	8	9[i]	10	11	12	13	
33		14	15	16	17	18	19	20	
34		21	22	23	24	25	26	27	
35	ELUL 5801	28	29	30	1	2	3	4	Tue 0h49m6p
36		5	6	7	8	9	10	11	
37		12	13	14	15	16	17	18	
38		19	20	21	22	23	24	25	
39	TISHRI 5802	26	27	28	29	1[a]	2[a]	3	Wed 13h33m7p
40		4	5	6	7	8	9	10[b]	
41		11	12	13	14	15[c]	16	17	
42		18	19	20	21	22	23	24	
43	HESHVAN 5802	25	26	27	28	29	30	1	Fri 2h17m8p
44		2	3	4	5	6	7	8	
45		9	10	11	12	13	14	15	
46		16	17	18	19	20	21	22	
47		23	24	25	26	27	28	29	
48	KISLEV 5802	1	2	3	4	5	6	7	Sat 15h1m9p
49		8	9	10	11	12[d]	13	14	
50		15	16	17	18	19	20	21	
51		22	23	24	25[e]	26[e]	27[e]	28[e]	
52	TEVETH 5802	29[e]	30[e]	1[e]	2[e]	3	4	5	Mon 3h45m10p
1		6	7	8	9	10	11	12	

CHINESE Gēng-Shēn/Xīn-Yǒu

ISO Week	Month	Sun	Mon	Tue	Wed	Thu	Fri	Sat	Solar Term
1	MONTH 12 Gēng-Shēn	27	28	29	30	1	2	*3*	Xiǎo hán
2		4	5	6	7	8	9	10	
3		11	12	13	14	15	16	17	
4		***18***	19	20	21	22	23	24	**Dà hán**
5	MONTH 1 Xīn-Yǒu	25	26	27	28	29*	1[a]	2	
6		*3*	4	5	6	7	8	9	Lì chūn
7		10	11	12	13	14	15[b]	16	
8		17	**18**	19	20	21	22	23	**Yǔ shuǐ**
9	MONTH 2 Xīn-Yǒu	24	25	26	27	28	29	1	
10		2	3	*4*	5	6	7	8	Jīng zhé
11		9	10	11	12	13	14	15	
12		16	17	18	**19**	20	21	22	**Chūn fēn**
13		23	24	25	26	27	28	29	
14	MONTH 3 Xīn-Yǒu	30	1*	2	3	*4*[c]	5	6	Qīng míng
15		7	8	9	10	11	12	13	
16		14	15	16	17	18	19	**20**	**Gǔ yǔ**
17		21	22	23	24	25	26	27	
18	MONTH 4 Xīn-Yǒu	28	29	1	2	3	4	5	
19		*6*	7	8	9	10	11	12	Lì xià
20		13	14	15	16	17	18	19	
21		20	**21**	22	23	24	25	26	**Xiǎo mǎn**
22	MONTH 5 Xīn-Yǒu	27	28	29	30	1	2*	3	
23		4	5[d]	6	*7*	8	9	10	Máng zhòng
24		11	12	13	14	15	16	17	
25		18	19	20	21	22	**23**	24	**Xià zhì**
26	MONTH 6 Xīn-Yǒu	25	26	27	28	29	1	2	
27		3	4	5	6	7	8	9	
28		*10*	11	12	13	14	15	16	Xiǎo shǔ
29		17	18	19	20	21	22	23	
30		24	**25**	26	27	28	29	30	**Dà shǔ**
31	MONTH 7 Xīn-Yǒu	1	2	3*	4	5	6	7[e]	
32		8	9	10	*11*	12	13	14	Lì qiū
33		15[f]	16	17	18	19	20	21	
34		22	23	24	25	26	**27**	28	**Chǔ shǔ**
35	MONTH 8 Xīn-Yǒu	29	30	1	2	3	4	5	
36		6	7	8	9	10	11	*12*	Bái lù
37		13	14	15[g]	16	17	18	19	
38		20	21	22	23	24	25	26	
39	MONTH 9 Xīn-Yǒu	**27**	28	29	1	2	3	4*	**Qiū fēn**
40		5	6	7	8	9[h]	10	11	
41		12	13	*14*	15	16	17	18	Hán lù
42		19	20	21	22	23	24	25	
43	MONTH 10 Xīn-Yǒu	26	27	28	**29**	30	1	2	**Shuāng jiàng**
44		3	4	5	6	7	8	9	
45		10	11	12	13	*14*	15	16	Lì dōng
46		17	18	19	20	21	22	23	
47		24	25	26	27	28	**29**	30	**Xiǎo xuě**
48	MONTH 11 Xīn-Yǒu	1	2	3	4*	5	6	7	
49		8	9	10	11	12	13	*14*	Dà xuě
50		15	16	17	18	19	20	21	
51		22	23	24	25	26	27	**28**[i]	**Dōng zhì**
52	MONTH 12 Xīn-Yǒu	29	1	2	3	4	5	6	
1		7	8	9	10	11	12	13	

COPTIC 1757/1758 — ETHIOPIC 2033/2034

ISO Week	Coptic Month	Sun	Mon	Tue	Wed	Thu	Fri	Sat	Ethiopic Month
1	KOIAK 1757	21	22	23	24	25	26	27	TĀKHŚĀŚ 2033
2		28	29[c]	30	1	2	3	4	
3	TÔBE 1757	5	6[d]	7	8	9	10	11[e]	ṬER 2033
4		12	13	14	15	16	17	18	
5		19	20	21	22	23	24	25	
6		26	27	28	29	30	1	2	
7	MESHIR 1757	3	4	5	6	7	8	9	YAKĀTIT 2033
8		10	11	12	13	14	15	16	
9		17	18	19	20	21	22	23	
10		24	25	26	27	28	29	30	
11	PAREMOTEP 1757	1	2	3	4	5	6	7	MAGĀBIT 2033
12		8	9	10	11	12	13	14	
13		15	16	17	18	19	20	21	
14		22	23	24	25	26	27	28	
15		29	30	1	2	3	4	5	
16	PARMOUTE 1757	6	7	8	9	10	11	12	MIYĀZYĀ 2033
17		13[f]	14	15	16	17	18	19	
18		20	21	22	23	24	25	26	
19		27	28	29[g]	30	1	2	3	
20	PASHONS 1757	4	5	6	7	8	9	10	GENBOT 2033
21		11	12	13	14	15	16	17	
22		18	19	20	21	22	23	24	
23		25	26	27	28	29	30	1	
24	PAÔNE 1757	2	3	4	5	6	7	8	SANĒ 2033
25		9	10	11	12	13	14	15	
26		16	17	18	19	20	21	22	
27		23	24	25	26	27	28	29	
28		30	1	2	3	4	5	6	
29	EPÊP 1757	7	8	9	10	11	12	13	ḤAMLĒ 2033
30		14	15	16	17	18	19	20	
31		21	22	23	24	25	26	27	
32		28	29	30	1	2	3	4	
33	MESORÊ 1757	5	6	7	8	9	10	11	NAHASĒ 2033
34		12	13[h]	14	15	16	17	18	
35		19	20	21	22	23	24	25	
36		26	27	28	29	30	1	2	
37	EPAG. 1757 / THOOUT 1758	3	4	5	1[a]	2	3	4	PĀG. 2033 / MASKARAM 2034
38		5	6	7	8	9	10	11	
39		12	13	14	15	16	17[b]	18	
40		19	20	21	22	23	24	25	
41		26	27	28	29	30	1	2	
42	PAOPE 1758	3	4	5	6	7	8	9	ṬEQEMT 2034
43		10	11	12	13	14	15	16	
44		17	18	19	20	21	22	23	
45		24	25	26	27	28	29	30	
46	ATHÔR 1758	1	2	3	4	5	6	7	HEDĀR 2034
47		8	9	10	11	12	13	14	
48		15	16	17	18	19	20	21	
49		22	23	24	25	26	27	28	
50		29	30	1	2	3	4	5	
51	KOIAK 1758	6	7	8	9	10	11	12	TĀKHŚĀŚ 2034
52		13	14	15	16	17	18	19	
1		20	21	22	23	24	25	26	

Gregorian notes:
[a]New Year
[b]Spring (6:05)
[c]Summer (23:35)
[d]Autumn (15:25)
[e]Winter (12:17)
● New moon
◐ First quarter moon
○ Full moon
◑ Last quarter moon

Hebrew notes:
‡Leap year
[a]New Year
[b]Yom Kippur
[c]Sukkot
[d]Winter starts
[e]Ḥanukkah
[f]Purim
[g]Passover
[h]Shavuot
[i]Fast of Av

Chinese notes:
[a]New Year (4739, Fowl)
[b]Lantern Festival
[c]Qīngmíng
[d]Dragon Festival
[e]Qīqiǎo
[f]Hungry Ghosts
[g]Mid-Autumn Festival
[h]Double-Ninth Festival
[i]Dōngzhì
*Start of 60-name cycle

Coptic/Ethiopic notes:
[a]New Year
[b]Building of the Cross
[c]Christmas
[d]Jesus's Circumcision
[e]Epiphany
[f]Easter
[g]Mary's Announcement
[h]Jesus's Transfiguration

PERSIAN (ASTRONOMICAL) 1419/1420‡

Month	Sun	Mon	Tue	Wed	Thu	Fri	Sat
DEY 1419	10	11	12	13	14	15	16
	17	18	19	20	21	22	23
	24	25	26	27	28	29	30
BAHMAN 1419	1	2	3	4	5	6	7
	8	9	10	11	12	13	14
	15	16	17	18	19	20	21
	22	23	24	25	26	27	28
ESFAND 1419	29	30	1	2	3	4	5
	6	7	8	9	10	11	12
	13	14	15	16	17	18	19
	20	21	22	23	24	25	26
FARVARDĪN 1420	27	28	29	1[a]	2	3	4
	5	6	7	8	9	10	11
	12	13[b]	14	15	16	17	18
	19	20	21	22	23	24	25
	26	27	28	29	30	31	1
ORDĪBEHEŠT 1420	2	3	4	5	6	7	8
	9	10	11	12	13	14	15
	16	17	18	19	20	21	22
	23	24	25	26	27	28	29
XORDĀD 1420	30	31	1	2	3	4	5
	6	7	8	9	10	11	12
	13	14	15	16	17	18	19
	20	21	22	23	24	25	26
TĪR 1420	27	28	29	30	31	1	2
	3	4	5	6	7	8	9
	10	11	12	13	14	15	16
	17	18	19	20	21	22	23
	24	25	26	27	28	29	30
MORDĀD 1420	31	1	2	3	4	5	6
	7	8	9	10	11	12	13
	14	15	16	17	18	19	20
	21	22	23	24	25	26	27
SHAHRĪVAR 1420	28	29	30	31	1	2	3
	4	5	6	7	8	9	10
	11	12	13	14	15	16	17
	18	19	20	21	22	23	24
	25	26	27	28	29	30	31
MEHR 1420	1	2	3	4	5	6	7
	8	9	10	11	12	13	14
	15	16	17	18	19	20	21
	22	23	24	25	26	27	28
ĀBĀN 1420	29	30	1	2	3	4	5
	6	7	8	9	10	11	12
	13	14	15	16	17	18	19
	20	21	22	23	24	25	26
ĀZAR 1420	27	28	29	30	1	2	3
	4	5	6	7	8	9	10
	11	12	13	14	15	16	17
	18	19	20	21	22	23	24
DEY 1420	25	26	27	28	29	30	1
	2	3	4	5	6	7	8
	9	10	11	12	13	14	15

HINDU LUNAR 2097/2098

Month	Sun	Mon	Tue	Wed	Thu	Fri	Sat
PAUSHA 2097	27	28	29	30	1	2	3
	4	5	6	7	8	9	11
	12	13	13	14	15	16	17
	18	19	20	21	22	23	24
MĀGHA 2097	25	26	27	28	29	30	1
	3	4	5	6	7	8	9
	10	11	12	13	14	15	15
	16	17	18	19	20	21	22
	23	24	25	26	28	29[h]	30
PHĀLGUNA 2097	1	2	3	4	5	6	7
	8	9	10	11	12	13	14
	15[i]	16	17	18	19	20	21
	22	23	24	25	26	27	28
CHAITRA 2098	29	30[a]	2	3	4	5	6
	7	8	9[b]	9	10	11	12
	13	14	15	16	17	18	19
	20	21	22	23	25	26	27
VAIŚĀKHA 2098	28	29	30	1	2	3	4
	5	6	7	8	9	10	11
	12	13	13	14	15	17	18
	19	20	21	22	23	24	25
JYAISHTHA 2098	26	27	29	30	1	2	3
	4	4	5	6	7	8	9
	10	11	12	13	14	15	16
	17	18	19	20	22	23	24
ĀSHĀDHA 2098	25	26	27	28	29	30	1
	2	3	4	5	6	7	8
	9	10	11	12	13	14	15
	16	17	18	19	20	21	22
	23	25	26	27	28	29	30
ŚRĀVAṆA 2098	1	1	2	3	4	5	6
	7	8	9	10	11	12	13
	14	15	17	18	19	20	21
	22	23[c]	24	25	26	27	28
BHĀDRAPADA 2098	29	30	1	2	3	4[d]	5
	6	7	8	9	10	11	12
	13	14	15	16	17	18	19
	21	22	23	24	25	26	27
ĀŚVINA 2098	27	28	29	30	1	2	3
	4	5	6	7	8[e]	9[e]	10[e]
	11	12	14	15	16	17	18
	19	20	21	22	23	24	25
KĀRTTIKA 2098	26	27	28	29	30	1	1[f]
	2	3	4	5	7	8	9
	10	11	12	13	14	15	16
	17	18	19	20	21	22	23
	24	25	26	27	28	29	30
MĀRGAŚĪRA 2098	1	2	3	4	5	6	7
	8	9	10[g]	12	13	14	15
	16	17	18	19	20	21	22
	23	24	24	25	26	27	28
PAUSHA 2098	29	30	1	2	3	4	6
	7	8	9	10	11	12	13

HINDU SOLAR 1962‡/1963

Month	Sun	Mon	Tue	Wed	Thu	Fri	Sat
PAUSHA 1962	15	16	17	18	19	20	21
	22	23	24	25	26	27	28
MĀGHA 1962	29	1[b]	2	3	4	5	6
	7	8	9	10	11	12	13
	14	15	16	17	18	19	20
	21	22	23	24	25	26	27
PHĀLGUNA 1962	28	29	1	2	3	4	5
	6	7	8	9	10	11	12
	13	14	15	16	17	18	19
	20	21	22	23	24	25	26
CHAITRA 1962	27	28	29	30	1	2	3
	4	5	6	7	8	9	10
	11	12	13	14	15	16	17
	18	19	20	21	22	23	24
	25	26	27	28	29	30	31
VAIŚĀKHA 1963	1[a]	2	3	4	5	6	7
	8	9	10	11	12	13	14
	15	16	17	18	19	20	21
	22	23	24	25	26	27	28
JYAISHTHA 1963	29	30	31	1	2	3	4
	5	6	7	8	9	10	11
	12	13	14	15	16	17	18
	19	20	21	22	23	24	25
ĀSHĀDHA 1963	26	27	28	29	30	31	1
	2	3	4	5	6	7	8
	9	10	11	12	13	14	15
	16	17	18	19	20	21	22
	23	24	25	26	27	28	29
ŚRĀVAṆA 1963	30	31	32	1	2	3	4
	5	6	7	8	9	10	11
	12	13	14	15	16	17	18
	19	20	21	22	23	24	25
BHĀDRAPADA 1963	26	27	28	29	30	31	1
	2	3	4	5	6	7	8
	9	10	11	12	13	14	15
	16	17	18	19	20	21	22
	23	24	25	26	27	28	29
ĀŚVINA 1963	30	31	1	2	3	4	5
	6	7	8	9	10	11	12
	13	14	15	16	17	18	19
	20	21	22	23	24	25	26
KĀRTTIKA 1963	27	28	29	30	31	1	2
	3	4	5	6	7	8	9
	10	11	12	13	14	15	16
	17	18	19	20	21	22	23
MĀRGAŚĪRA 1963	24	25	26	27	28	29	1
	2	3	4	5	6	7	8
	9	10	11	12	13	14	15
	16	17	18	19	20	21	22
	23	24	25	26	27	28	29
PAUSHA 1963	30	1	2	3	4	5	6
	7	8	9	10	11	12	13
	14	15	16	17	18	19	20

ISLAMIC (ASTRONOMICAL) 1462‡/1463‡/1464

Month	Sun	Mon	Tue	Wed	Thu	Fri	Sat
MUHARRAM 1463	25	26	27	28	29	1[a]	2
	3	4	5	6	7	8	9
	10[b]	11	12	13	14	15	16
	17	18	19	20	21	22	23
SAFAR 1463	24	25	26	27	28	29	1
	2	3	4	5	6	7	8
	9	10	11	12	13	14	15
	16	17	18	19	20	21	22
	23	24	25	26	27	28	29
RABĪʿ I 1463	30	1	2	3	4	5	6
	7	8	9	10	11	12[c]	13
	14	15	16	17	18	19	20
	21	22	23	24	25	26	27
RABĪʿ II 1463	28	29	1	2	3	4	5
	6	7	8	9	10	11	12
	13	14	15	16	17	18	19
	20	21	22	23	24	25	26
JUMĀDĀ I 1463	27	28	29	30	1	2	3
	4	5	6	7	8	9	10
	11	12	13	14	15	16	17
	18	19	20	21	22	23	24
JUMĀDĀ II 1463	25	26	27	28	29	1	2
	3	4	5	6	7	8	9
	10	11	12	13	14	15	16
	17	18	19	20	21	22	23
	24	25	26	27	28	29	30
RAJAB 1463	1	2	3	4	5	6	7
	8	9	10	11	12	13	14
	15	16	17	18	19	20	21
	22	23	24	25	26	27[d]	28
SHAʿBĀN 1463	29	1	2	3	4	5	6
	7	8	9	10	11	12	13
	14	15	16	17	18	19	20
	21	22	23	24	25	26	27
RAMAḌĀN 1463	28	29	30	1[e]	2	3	4
	5	6	7	8	9	10	11
	12	13	14	15	16	17	18
	19	20	21	22	23	24	25
SHAWWĀL 1463	26	27	28	29	30	1[f]	2
	3	4	5	6	7	8	9
	10	11	12	13	14	15	16
	17	18	19	20	21	22	23
	24	25	26	27	28	29	30
DHU AL-QAʿDA 1463	1	2	3	4	5	6	7
	8	9	10	11	12	13	14
	15	16	17	18	19	20	21
	22	23	24	25	26	27	28
DHU AL-ḤIJJA 1463	29	30	1	2	3	4	5
	6	7	8	9	10[g]	11	12
	13	14	15	16	17	18	19
	20	21	22	23	24	25	26
MUHARRAM 1464	27	28	29[d]	1[a]	2	3	4
	5	6	7	8	9	10	11

GREGORIAN 2041

Julian (Sun)	Sun	Mon	Tue	Wed	Thu	Fri	Sat	Month
Dec 17	30	31	1	2	3	4	5	JANUARY 2041
	6	7[a]	8	9	10	11	12	
Dec 31	13	14[b]	15	16	17	18	19	
	20	21	22	23	24	25	26	
Jan 14	27	28	29	30	31	1	2	FEBRUARY 2041
	3	4	5	6	7	8	9	
Jan 28	10	11	12	13	14	15	16	
	17	18	19	20	21	22	23	
Feb 11	24	25	26	27	28	1	2	MARCH 2041
	3	4	5	6[c]	7	8	9	
Feb 25	10[d]	11	12	13	14	15	16	
	17	18	19	20	21	22	23	
Mar 11	24	25	26	27	28	29	30	
	31	1	2	3	4	5	6	APRIL 2041
Mar 25	7	8	9	10	11	12	13	
	14	15	16	17	18	19	20	
Apr 8	21[e]	22	23	24	25	26	27	
	28	29	30	1	2	3	4	MAY 2041
Apr 22	5	6	7	8	9	10	11	
	12	13	14	15	16	17	18	
May 6	19	20	21	22	23	24	25	
	26	27	28	29	30	31	1	JUNE 2041
May 20	2	3	4	5	6	7	8	
	9	10	11	12	13	14	15	
Jun 3	16	17	18	19	20	21	22	
	23	24	25	26	27	28	29	
Jun 17	30	1	2	3	4	5	6	JULY 2041
	7	8	9	10	11	12	13	
Jul 1	14	15	16	17	18	19	20	
	21	22	23	24	25	26	27	
Jul 15	28	29	30	31	1	2	3	AUGUST 2041
	4	5	6	7	8	9	10	
Jul 29	11	12	13	14	15	16	17	
	18	19	20	21	22	23	24	
Aug 12	25	26	27	28	29	30	31	
	1	2	3	4	5	6	7	SEPTEMBER 2041
Aug 26	8	9	10	11	12	13	14	
	15	16	17	18	19	20	21	
Sep 9	22	23	24	25	26	27	28	
	29	30	1	2	3	4	5	OCTOBER 2041
Sep 23	6	7	8	9	10	11	12	
	13	14	15	16	17	18	19	
Oct 7	20	21	22	23	24	25	26	
	27	28	29	30	31	1	2	NOVEMBER 2041
Oct 21	3	4	5	6	7	8	9	
	10	11	12	13	14	15	16	
Nov 4	17	18	19	20	21	22	23	
	24	25	26	27	28	29	30	
Nov 18	1[g]	2	3	4	5	6	7	DECEMBER 2041
	8	9	10	11	12	13	14	
Dec 2	15	16	17	18	19	20	21	
	22	23	24	25[h]	26	27	28	
Dec 16	29	30	31	1	2	3	4	

Persian: ‡Leap year; [a]New Year; [b]Sizdeh Bedar

Hindu Lunar: [a]New Year (Durmati); [b]Birthday of Rāma; [c]Birthday of Krishna; [d]Ganēśa Chaturthī; [e]Dashara; [f]Diwali; [g]Birthday of Vishnu; [h]Night of Śiva; [i]Holi

Hindu Solar: ‡Leap year; [a]New Year (Yuvan); [b]Pongal

Islamic: ‡Leap year; [a]New Year; [a]New Year (Arithmetic); [b]ʿAshūrāʾ; [c]Prophet's Birthday; [d]Ascent of the Prophet; [e]Start of Ramaḍān; [f]ʿId al-Fiṭr; [g]ʿId al-ʾAḍḥā

Gregorian: [a]Orthodox Christmas; [b]Julian New Year; [c]Ash Wednesday; [d]Feast of Orthodoxy; [e]Easter (also Orthodox); [g]Advent; [h]Christmas

2042

Gregorian 2042	Sun	Mon	Tue	Wed	Thu	Fri	Sat	Lunar Phases	ISO Week (Mon)	Julian Day (Sun noon)	Hebrew 5802/5803‡	Sun	Mon	Tue	Wed	Thu	Fri	Sat	Molad	Chinese Xīn-Yǒu/Rén-Xū‡	Sun	Mon	Tue	Wed	Thu	Fri	Sat	Solar Term	Coptic 1758/1759‡	Sun	Mon	Tue	Wed	Thu	Fri	Sat	Ethiopic 2034/2035‡
	29	◐	31	1[a]	2	3	4	3:44	1	2466883		6	7	8	9	10	11	12			7	8	9	10	11	12	13			20	21	22	23	24	25	26	Tāḫśāś 2034
	5	○	7	8	9	10	11	8:52	2	2466890	Teveth 5802	13	14	15	16	17	18	19		Month 12 Xīn-Yǒu	14	15	16	17	18	19	20	Xiǎo hán	Koiak 1758	27	28	29[c]	30	1	2	3	
January 2042	12	13	◑	15	16	17	18	11:23	3	2466897		20	21	22	23	24	25	26			21	22	23	24	25	26	27			4	5	6[d]	7	8	9	10	
	19	20	●	22	23	24	25	20:41	4	2466904		27	28	29	1	2	3	4	Tue 16h29m11p		28	29	30	1[a]	2	3	4	Dà hán	Tōbe 1758	11[e]	12	13	14	15	16	17	Ṭer 2034
	26	27	◐	29	30	31	1	12:47	5	2466911		5	6	7	8	9	10	11			5*	6	7	8	9	10	11			18	19	20	21	22	23	24	
	2	3	4	○	6	7	8	1:56	6	2466918	Shevat 5802	12	13	14	15	16	17	18		Month 1 Rén-Xū	12	13	14	15[b]	16	17	18	Lì chūn		25	26	27	28	29	30	1	
February 2042	9	10	11	12	◑	14	15	7:15	7	2466925		19	20	21	22	23	24	25			19	20	21	22	23	24	25			2	3	4	5	6	7	8	
	16	17	18	19	●	21	22	7:38	8	2466932		26	27	28	29	30	1	2	Thu 5h13m12p		26	27	28	29	1	2	3	Yǔ shuǐ	Meshir 1758	9	10	11	12	13	14	15	Yakātit 2034
	23	24	25	◐	27	28	1	23:28	9	2466939		3	4	5	6	7	8	9			4	5	6	7	8	9	10			16	17	18	19	20	21	22	
	2	3	4	5	○	7	8	20:08	10	2466946	Adar 5802	10	11	12	13	14[f]	15	16		Month 2 Rén-Xū	11	12	13	14	15	16	17	Jīng zhé		23	24	25	26	27	28	29	
March 2042	9	10	11	12	13	◑	15	23:20	11	2466953		17	18	19	20	21	22	23			18	19	20	21	22	23	24			30	1	2	3	4	5	6	
	16	17	18	19	20[b]	●	22	17:22	12	2466960		24	25	26	27	28	29	1	Fri 17h57m13p		25	26	27	28	29	30	1	Chūn fēn		7	8	9	10	11	12	13	
	23	24	25	26	27	◐	29	11:58	13	2466967		2	3	4	5	6	7	8			2	3	4	5	6*	7	8		Paremotep 1758	14	15	16	17	18	19	20	Magābit 2034
	30	31	1	2	3	4	○	14:15	14	2466974	Nisan 5802	9	10	11	12	13	14	15[g]		Leap Month 2 Rén-Xū	9	10	11	12	13	14[c]	15	Qīng míng		21	22	23	24	25	26	27	
	6	7	8	9	10	11	12		15	2466981		16	17	18	19	20	21	22			16	17	18	19	20	21	22			28	29	30	1	2	3	4	
April 2042	◑	14	15	16	17	18	19	11:08	16	2466988		23	24	25	26	27	28	29	Sun 6h41m14p		23	24	25	26	27	28	29			5[f]	6	7	8	9	10	11	
	●	21	22	23	24	25	26	2:18	17	2466995		30	1	2	3	4	5	6			1	2	3	4	5	6	7	Gǔ yǔ	Parmoute 1758	12	13	14	15	16	17	18	Miyāzyā 2034
	◐	28	29	30	1	2	3	2:18	18	2467002		7	8	9	10	11	12	13			8	9	10	11	12	13	14			19	20	21	22	23	24	25	
	4	○	6	7	8	9	10	6:47	19	2467009	Iyyar 5802	14	15	16	17	18	19	20		Month 3 Rén-Xū	15	16	17	18	19	20	21	Lì xià		26	27	28	29[g]	30	1	2	
May 2042	11	◑	13	14	15	16	17	19:17	20	2467016		21	22	23	24	25	26	27			22	23	24	25	26	27	28			3	4	5	6	7	8	9	
	18	●	20	21	22	23	24	10:54	21	2467023		28	29	1	2	3	4	5	Mon 19h25m15p		29	1	2	3	4	5	6	Xiǎo mǎn	Pashons 1758	10	11	12	13	14	15	16	Genbot 2034
	25	◐	27	28	29	30	31	18:17	22	2467030		6[h]	7	8	9	10	11	12			7	8*	9	10	11	12	13			17	18	19	20	21	22	23	
	1	2	○	4	5	6	7	20:47	23	2467037	Sivan 5802	13	14	15	16	17	18	19		Month 4 Rén-Xū	14	15	16	17	18	19	20	Máng zhòng		24	25	26	27	28	29	30	
	8	9	10	◑	12	13	14	0:59	24	2467044		20	21	22	23	24	25	26			21	22	23	24	25	26	27			1	2	3	4	5	6	7	
June 2042	15	16	●	18	19	20	21[c]	19:47	25	2467051		27	28	29	30	1	2	3	Wed 8h9m16p		28	29	30	1	2	3	4	Xià zhì		8	9	10	11	12	13	14	Sanē 2034
	22	23	24	◐	26	27	28	11:27	26	2467058		4	5	6	7	8	9	10			5[d]	6	7	8	9	10	11		Paōne 1758	15	16	17	18	19	20	21	
	29	30	1	2	○	4	5	8:08	27	2467065	Tammuz 5802	11	12	13	14	15	16	17		Month 5 Rén-Xū	12	13	14	15	16	17	18	Xiǎo shǔ		22	23	24	25	26	27	28	
	6	7	8	9	◑	11	12	5:37	28	2467072		18	19	20	21	22	23	24			19	20	21	22	23	24	25			29	30	1	2	3	4	5	
July 2042	13	14	15	16	●	18	19	5:50	29	2467079		25	26	27	28	29	1	2	Thu 20h53m17p		26	27	28	29	1	2	3			6	7	8	9	10	11	12	
	20	21	22	23	24	◐	26	5:00	30	2467086		3	4	5	6	7	8	9			4	5	6	7	8	9*	10	Dà shǔ	Epēp 1758	13	14	15	16	17	18	19	Ḥamlē 2034
	27	28	29	30	31	○	2	17:32	31	2467093	Av 5802	10[i]	11	12	13	14	15	16		Month 6 Rén-Xū	11	12	13	14	15	16	17			20	21	22	23	24	25	26	
	3	4	5	6	7	◑	9	10:33	32	2467100		17	18	19	20	21	22	23			18	19	20	21	22	23	24	Lì qiū		27	28	29	30	1	2	3	
August 2042	10	11	12	13	14	●	16	18:00	33	2467107		24	25	26	27	28	29	30			25	26	27	28	29	30	1			4	5	6	7	8	9	10	
	17	18	19	20	21	22	◐	21:54	34	2467114		1	2	3	4	5	6	7	Sat 9h38m0p		2	3	4	5	6	7[e]	8	Chǔ shǔ	Mesorē 1758	11	12	13[h]	14	15	16	17	Naḥasē 2034
	24	25	26	27	28	29	30		35	2467121		8	9	10	11	12	13	14		Month 7 Rén-Xū	9	10	11	12	13	14	15[f]			18	19	20	21	22	23	24	
	○	1	2	3	4	5	◑	2:01 17:08	36	2467128	Elul 5802	15	16	17	18	19	20	21			16	17	18	19	20	21	22	Bái lù		25	26	27	28	29	30	1	
	7	8	9	10	11	12	13		37	2467135		22	23	24	25	26	27	28			23	24	25	26	27	28	29		Epag. 1758	2	3	4	5	1[a]	2	3	Pāg. 2034
September 2042	●	15	16	17	18	19	20	8:49	38	2467142		29	1[a]	2[a]	3	4	5	6	Sun 22h22m1p		1	2	3	4	5	6	7			4	5	6	7	8	9	10	
	21	◐[d]	23	24	25	26	27	13:19	39	2467149		7	8	9	10[b]	11	12	13			8	9	10*	11	12	13	14	Qiū fēn	Thoout 1759	11	12	13	14	15	16	17[b]	Maskaram 2035
	28	○	30	1	2	3	4	10:33	40	2467156	Tishri 5803	14	15[c]	16	17	18	19	20		Month 8 Rén-Xū	15[g]	16	17	18	19	20	21			18	19	20	21	22	23	24	
	5	◑	7	8	9	10	11	2:33	41	2467163		21	22	23	24	25	26	27			22	23	24	25	26	27	28	Hán lù		25	26	27	28	29	30	1	
October 2042	12	13	●	15	16	17	18	2:02	42	2467170		28	29	30	1	2	3	4	Tue 11h6m2p		29	30	1	2	3	4	5			2	3	4	5	6	7	8	
	19	20	21	◐	23	24	25	2:52	43	2467177		5	6	7	8	9	10	11			6	7	8	9[h]	10	11	12	Shuāng jiàng	Paope 1759	9	10	11	12	13	14	15	Ṭeqemt 2035
	26	27	○	29	30	31	1	19:47	44	2467184	Heshvan 5803	12	13	14	15	16	17	18		Month 9 Rén-Xū	13	14	15	16	17	18	19			16	17	18	19	20	21	22	
	2	3	◑	5	6	7	8	15:50	45	2467191		19	20	21	22	23	24	25			20	21	22	23	24	25	26	Lì dōng		23	24	25	26	27	28	29	
November 2042	9	10	11	●	13	14	15	20:27	46	2467198		26	27	28	29	30	1	2	Wed 23h50m3p		27	28	29	30	1	2	3			30	1	2	3	4	5	6	
	16	17	18	19	◐	21	22	14:30	47	2467205		3	4	5	6	7	8	9			4	5	6	7	8	9	10*	Xiǎo xuě	Athōr 1759	7	8	9	10	11	12	13	Ḫedār 2035
	23	24	25	26	○	28	29	6:05	48	2467212	Kislev 5803	10	11	12	13	14	15	16		Month 10 Rén-Xū	11	12	13	14	15	16	17			14	15	16	17	18	19	20	
	30	1	2	3	◑	5	6	9:17	49	2467219		17	18	19	20	21	22[d]	23			18	19	20	21	22	23	24			21	22	23	24	25	26	27	
	7	8	9	10	11	●	13	14:28	50	2467226		24	25[e]	26[e]	27[e]	28[e]	29[e]	30[e]			25	26	27	28	29	1	2	Dà xuě		28	29	30	1	2	3	4	
December 2042	14	15	16	17	18	19	◐	0:26	51	2467233		1[e]	2[e]	3	4	5	6	7	Fri 12h34m4p	Month 11 Rén-Xū	3	4	5	6	7	8	9		Koiak 1759	5	6	7	8	9	10	11	Tāḫśāś 2035
	21[e]	22	23	24	25	○	27	17:41	52	2467240	Teveth 5803	8	9	10	11	12	13	14			10	11[i]	12	13	14	15	16	Dōng zhì		12	13	14	15	16	17	18	
	28	29	30	31	1	2	◑	6:07	1	2467247		15	16	17	18	19	20	21			17	18	19	20	21	22	23			19	20	21	22	23	24	25	

[a]New Year
[b]Spring (11:51)
[c]Summer (5:15)
[d]Autumn (21:10)
[e]Winter (18:03)
● New moon
◐ First quarter moon
○ Full moon
◑ Last quarter moon

‡Leap year
[a]New Year
[b]Yom Kippur
[c]Sukkot
[d]Winter starts
[e]Ḥanukkah
[f]Purim
[g]Passover
[h]Shavuot
[i]Fast of Av

‡Leap year
[a]New Year (4740, Dog)
[b]Lantern Festival
[c]Qīngmíng
[d]Dragon Festival
[e]Qīqiǎo
[f]Hungry Ghosts
[g]Mid-Autumn Festival
[h]Double-Ninth Festival
[i]Dōngzhì
*Start of 60-name cycle

‡Leap year
[a]New Year
[b]Building of the Cross
[c]Christmas
[d]Jesus's Circumcision
[e]Epiphany
[f]Easter
[g]Mary's Announcement
[h]Jesus's Transfiguration

PERSIAN (ASTRONOMICAL) 1420‡/1421

Month	Sun	Mon	Tue	Wed	Thu	Fri	Sat
DEY 1420	9	10	11	12	13	14	15
	16	17	18	19	20	21	22
	23	24	25	26	27	28	29
BAHMAN 1420	30	1	2	3	4	5	6
	7	8	9	10	11	12	13
	14	15	16	17	18	19	20
	21	22	23	24	25	26	27
ESFAND 1420	28	29	30	1	2	3	4
	5	6	7	8	9	10	11
	12	13	14	15	16	17	18
	19	20	21	22	23	24	25
FARVARDĪN 1421	26	27	28	29	30	1[a]	2
	3	4	5	6	7	8	9
	10	11	12	13[b]	14	15	16
	17	18	19	20	21	22	23
	24	25	26	27	28	29	30
ORDĪBEHEŠT 1421	31	1	2	3	4	5	6
	7	8	9	10	11	12	13
	14	15	16	17	18	19	20
	21	22	23	24	25	26	27
XORDĀD 1421	28	29	30	31	1	2	3
	4	5	6	7	8	9	10
	11	12	13	14	15	16	17
	18	19	20	21	22	23	24
	25	26	27	28	29	30	31
TĪR 1421	1	2	3	4	5	6	7
	8	9	10	11	12	13	14
	15	16	17	18	19	20	21
	22	23	24	25	26	27	28
MORDĀD 1421	29	30	31	1	2	3	4
	5	6	7	8	9	10	11
	12	13	14	15	16	17	18
	19	20	21	22	23	24	25
SHAHRĪVAR 1421	26	27	28	29	30	31	1
	2	3	4	5	6	7	8
	9	10	11	12	13	14	15
	16	17	18	19	20	21	22
	23	24	25	26	27	28	29
MEHR 1421	30	31	1	2	3	4	5
	6	7	8	9	10	11	12
	13	14	15	16	17	18	19
	20	21	22	23	24	25	26
ĀBĀN 1421	27	28	29	30	1	2	3
	4	5	6	7	8	9	10
	11	12	13	14	15	16	17
	18	19	20	21	22	23	24
ĀZAR 1421	25	26	27	28	29	30	1
	2	3	4	5	6	7	8
	9	10	11	12	13	14	15
	16	17	18	19	20	21	22
	23	24	25	26	27	28	29
DEY 1421	30	1	2	3	4	5	6
	7	8	9	10	11	12	13

‡Leap year
[a]New Year
[b]Sizdeh Bedar

HINDU LUNAR 2098/2099‡

Month	Sun	Mon	Tue	Wed	Thu	Fri	Sat
PAUSHA 2098	7	8	9	10	11	12	13
	14	15	16	17	18	19	20
	21	22	23	24	25	26	27
MĀGHA 2098	28	29	30	1	2	3	4
	5	6	7	8	**9**	11	12
	13	14	15	16	*16*	17	18
	19	20	21	22	23	24	25
PHĀLGUNA 2098	26	27	28[h]	29	30	1	2
	3	5	6	7	8	9	10
	11	12	13	14	15[i]	16	17
	18	*18*	19	20	21	22	23
CHAITRA 2099	24	25	**26**	28	29	30	1[a]
	2	3	4	5	6	7	8[b]
	9	10	11	12	13	14	15
	16	17	18	19	20	21	22
	23	24	25	26	27	28	29
VAIŚĀKHA 2099	**30**	2	3	4	5	6	7
	8	9	10	11	12	13	*13*
	14	15	16	17	18	19	20
	21	22	23	**24**	26	27	28
JYAISHTHA 2099	29	30	1	2	3	4	5
	6	7	8	9	10	11	12
	13	14	15	16	17	18	19
	20	21	22	23	24	25	26
LEAP ĀSHĀḌHA 2099	**27**	29	30	1	2	3	4
	5	6	7	8	9	9	10
	11	12	13	14	15	16	17
	18	19	**20**	22	23	24	25
ĀSHĀḌHA 2099	26	27	28	29	30	1	2
	3	4	5	6	7	8	9
	10	11	12	13	14	15	16
	17	18	19	20	21	**22**	24
ŚRĀVAṆA 2099	25	26	27	28	29	30	1
	2	3	4	5	5	6	7
	8	9	10	11	12	13	14
	15	17	18	19	20	21	22
	23[c]	24	25	26	27	28	29
BHĀDRAPADA 2099	30	1	2	3	4[d]	5	6
	7	8	9	10	11	12	13
	14	15	16	17	18	**19**	21
	22	23	24	25	26	27	28
ĀŚVINA 2099	29	30	1	*1*	2	3	4
	5	6	7	8[e]	9[e]	10[e]	11
	12	14	15	16	17	18	19
	20	21	22	23	24	25	26
KĀRTTIKA 2099	27	28	29	30	1[f]	2	3
	4	5	6	7	8	9	10
	11	12	13	14	15	16	**17**
	19	20	21	22	23	24	*24*
MĀRGAŚĪRA 2099	25	26	27	28	29	30	1
	2	3	4	5	6	7	8
	9	10	11[g]	13	14	15	16
	17	18	19	20	21	22	23

‡Leap year
[a]New Year (Dundubhi)
[b]Birthday of Rāma
[c]Birthday of Krishna
[d]Gaṇēśa Chaturthī
[e]Dashara
[f]Diwali
[g]Birthday of Vishnu
[h]Night of Śiva
[i]Holi

HINDU SOLAR 1963/1964

Month	Sun	Mon	Tue	Wed	Thu	Fri	Sat
PAUSHA 1963	14	15	16	17	18	19	20
	21	22	23	24	25	26	27
MĀGHA 1963	28	29	1[b]	2	3	4	5
	6	7	8	9	10	11	12
	13	14	15	16	17	18	19
	20	21	22	23	24	25	26
PHĀLGUNA 1963	27	28	29	30	1	2	3
	4	5	6	7	8	9	10
	11	12	13	14	15	16	17
	18	19	20	21	22	23	24
CHAITRA 1963	25	26	27	28	29	1	2
	3	4	5	6	7	8	9
	10	11	12	13	14	15	16
	17	18	19	20	21	22	23
	24	25	26	27	28	29	30
VAIŚĀKHA 1964	31	1[a]	2	3	4	5	6
	7	8	9	10	11	12	13
	14	15	16	17	18	19	20
	21	22	23	24	25	26	27
JYAISHTHA 1964	28	29	30	31	1	2	3
	4	5	6	7	8	9	10
	11	12	13	14	15	16	17
	18	19	20	21	22	23	24
	25	26	27	28	29	30	31
ĀSHĀḌHA 1964	1	2	3	4	5	6	7
	8	9	10	11	12	13	14
	15	16	17	18	19	20	21
	22	23	24	25	26	27	28
ŚRĀVAṆA 1964	29	30	31	32	1	2	3
	4	5	6	7	8	9	10
	11	12	13	14	15	16	17
	18	19	20	21	22	23	24
	25	26	27	28	29	30	31
BHĀDRAPADA 1964	1	2	3	4	5	6	7
	8	9	10	11	12	13	14
	15	16	17	18	19	20	21
	22	23	24	25	26	27	28
ĀŚVINA 1964	29	30	31	1	2	3	4
	5	6	7	8	9	10	11
	12	13	14	15	16	17	18
	19	20	21	22	23	24	25
KĀRTTIKA 1964	26	27	28	29	30	31	1
	2	3	4	5	6	7	8
	9	10	11	12	13	14	15
	16	17	18	19	20	21	22
	23	24	25	26	27	28	29
MĀRGAŚĪRA 1964	30	1	2	3	4	5	6
	7	8	9	10	11	12	13
	14	15	16	17	18	19	20
	21	22	23	24	25	26	27
PAUSHA 1964	28	29	1	2	3	4	5
	6	7	8	9	10	11	12
	13	14	15	16	17	18	19

[a]New Year (Dhātṛi)
[b]Pongal

ISLAMIC (ASTRONOMICAL) 1464/1465‡

Month	Sun	Mon	Tue	Wed	Thu	Fri	Sat
MUḤARRAM 1464	5	6	7	8	9	10[b]	11
	12	13	14	15	16	17	18
	19	20	21	22	23	24	25
ṢAFAR 1464	26	27	28	29	1	2	3
	4	5	6	7	8	9	10
	11	12	13	14	15	16	17
	18	19	20	21	22	23	24
RABĪ' I 1464	25	26	27	28	29	1	2
	3	4	5	6	7	8	9
	10	11	12[c]	13	14	15	16
	17	18	19	20	21	22	23
	24	25	26	27	28	29	30
RABĪ' II 1464	1	2	3	4	5	6	7
	8	9	10	11	12	13	14
	15	16	17	18	19	20	21
	22	23	24	25	26	27	28
JUMĀDĀ I 1464	29	1	2	3	4	5	6
	7	8	9	10	11	12	13
	14	15	16	17	18	19	20
	21	22	23	24	25	26	27
JUMĀDĀ II 1464	28	29	30	1	2	3	4
	5	6	7	8	9	10	11
	12	13	14	15	16	17	18
	19	20	21	22	23	24	25
RAJAB 1464	26	27	28	29	1	2	3
	4	5	6	7	8	9	10
	11	12	13	14	15	16	17
	18	19	20	21	22	23	24
SHA'BĀN 1464	25	26	27[d]	28	29	1	2
	3	4	5	6	7	8	9
	10	11	12	13	14	15	16
	17	18	19	20	21	22	23
	24	25	26	27	28	29	30
RAMAḌĀN 1464	1[e]	2	3	4	5	6	7
	8	9	10	11	12	13	14
	15	16	17	18	19	20	21
	22	23	24	25	26	27	28
SHAWWĀL 1464	29	30	1[f]	2	3	4	5
	6	7	8	9	10	11	12
	13	14	15	16	17	18	19
	20	21	22	23	24	25	26
DHU AL-QA'DA 1464	27	28	29	30	1	2	3
	4	5	6	7	8	9	10
	11	12	13	14	15	16	17
	18	19	20	21	22	23	24
DHU AL-ḤIJJA 1464	25	26	27	28	29	30	1
	2	3	4	5	6	7	8
	9	10[g]	11	12	13	14	15
	16	17	18	19	20	21	22
	23	24	25	26	27	28	29
MUḤARRAM 1465	1[a]	2	3	4	5	6	7
	8	9	10[b]	11	12	13	14
	15	16	17	18	19	20	21

‡Leap year
[a]New Year
[b]'Ashūrā'
[c]Prophet's Birthday
[d]Ascent of the Prophet
[e]Start of Ramaḍān
[f]'Id al-Fiṭr
[g]'Id al-'Aḍḥā

GREGORIAN 2042

Julian (Sun)	Month	Sun	Mon	Tue	Wed	Thu	Fri	Sat
Dec 16	JANUARY 2042	29	30	31	1	2	3	4
		5	6	7[a]	8	9	10	11
Dec 30		12	13	14[b]	15	16	17	18
		19	20	21	22	23	24	25
Jan 13	FEBRUARY 2042	26	27	28	29	30	31	1
		2	3	4	5	6	7	8
Jan 27		9	10	11	12	13	14	15
		16	17	18	19[c]	20	21	22
Feb 10	MARCH 2042	23	24	25	26	27	28	1
		2[d]	3	4	5	6	7	8
Feb 24		9	10	11	12	13	14	15
		16	17	18	19	20	21	22
Mar 10		23	24	25	26	27	28	29
	APRIL 2042	30	31	1	2	3	4	5
Mar 24		6[e]	7	8	9	10	11	12
		13[f]	14	15	16	17	18	19
Apr 7		20	21	22	23	24	25	26
	MAY 2042	27	28	29	30	1	2	3
Apr 21		4	5	6	7	8	9	10
		11	12	13	14	15	16	17
May 5		18	19	20	21	22	23	24
		25	26	27	28	29	30	31
May 19	JUNE 2042	1	2	3	4	5	6	7
		8	9	10	11	12	13	14
Jun 2		15	16	17	18	19	20	21
		22	23	24	25	26	27	28
Jun 16	JULY 2042	29	30	1	2	3	4	5
		6	7	8	9	10	11	12
Jun 30		13	14	15	16	17	18	19
		20	21	22	23	24	25	26
Jul 14	AUGUST 2042	27	28	29	30	31	1	2
		3	4	5	6	7	8	9
Jul 28		10	11	12	13	14	15	16
		17	18	19	20	21	22	23
Aug 11		24	25	26	27	28	29	30
	SEPTEMBER 2042	31	1	2	3	4	5	6
Aug 25		7	8	9	10	11	12	13
		14	15	16	17	18	19	20
Sep 8		21	22	23	24	25	26	27
	OCTOBER 2042	28	29	30	1	2	3	4
Sep 22		5	6	7	8	9	10	11
		12	13	14	15	16	17	18
Oct 6		19	20	21	22	23	24	25
	NOVEMBER 2042	26	27	28	29	30	31	1
Oct 20		2	3	4	5	6	7	8
		9	10	11	12	13	14	15
Nov 3		16	17	18	19	20	21	22
		23	24	25	26	27	28	29
Nov 17	DECEMBER 2042	30[g]	1	2	3	4	5	6
		7	8	9	10	11	12	13
Dec 1		14	15	16	17	18	19	20
		21	22	23	24	25[h]	26	27
Dec 15		28	29	30	31	1	2	3

[a]Orthodox Christmas
[b]Julian New Year
[c]Ash Wednesday
[d]Feast of Orthodoxy
[e]Easter
[f]Orthodox Easter
[g]Advent
[h]Christmas

2043

GREGORIAN 2043 · ISO WEEK · JULIAN DAY

Month	Sun	Mon	Tue	Wed	Thu	Fri	Sat	Lunar Phases	ISO WEEK (Mon)	JULIAN DAY (Sun noon)
	28	29	30	31	1[a]	2	◑	6:07	1	2467247
	4	5	6	7	8	9	10		2	2467254
JANUARY 2043	●	12	13	14	15	16	17	6:52	3	2467261
	◐	19	20	21	22	23	24	9:03	4	2467268
	○	26	27	28	29	30	31	6:55	5	2467275
	1	◑	3	4	5	6	7	4:13	6	2467282
FEBRUARY 2043	8	●	10	11	12	13	14	21:06	7	2467289
	15	◐	17	18	19	20	21	16:59	8	2467296
	22	○	24	25	26	27	28	21:56	9	2467303
	1	2	3	◑	5	6	7	1:06	10	2467310
	8	9	10	●	12	13	14	9:08	11	2467317
MARCH 2043	15	16	17	◐	19	20[b]	21	1:02	12	2467324
	22	23	24	○	26	27	28	14:25	13	2467331
	29	30	31	1	◑	3	4	18:55	14	2467338
	5	6	7	8	●	10	11	19:05	15	2467345
APRIL 2043	12	13	14	15	◐	17	18	10:07	16	2467352
	19	20	21	22	23	○	25	7:22	17	2467359
	26	27	28	29	30	1	◑	8:57	18	2467366
	3	4	5	6	7	8	●	3:20	19	2467373
MAY 2043	10	11	12	13	14	◐	16	21:04	20	2467380
	17	18	19	20	21	22	○	23:36	21	2467387
	24	25	26	27	28	29	30		22	2467394
	◑	1	2	3	4	5	6	19:23	23	2467401
	●	8	9	10	11	12	13	10:34	24	2467408
JUNE 2043	◐	15	16	17	18	19	20	10:17	25	2467415
	21[c]	○	23	24	25	26	27	14:19	26	2467422
	28	29	◑	1	2	3	4	2:52	27	2467429
	5	●	7	8	9	10	11	17:49	28	2467436
JULY 2043	12	13	◐	15	16	17	18	1:45	29	2467443
	19	20	21	○	23	24	25	3:23	30	2467450
	26	27	28	◑	30	31	1	8:21	31	2467457
	2	3	4	●	6	7	8	2:21	32	2467464
AUGUST 2043	9	10	11	◐	13	14	15	18:56	33	2467471
	16	17	18	19	○	21	22	15:03	34	2467478
	23	24	25	26	◑	28	29	13:08	35	2467485
	30	31	1	2	●	4	5	13:16	36	2467492
	6	7	8	9	10	◐	12	13:00	37	2467499
SEPTEMBER 2043	13	14	15	16	17	18	○	1:46	38	2467506
	20	21	22	23[d]	24	◑	26	18:39	39	2467513
	27	28	29	30	1	2	●	3:11	40	2467520
	4	5	6	7	8	9	10		41	2467527
OCTOBER 2043	◐	12	13	14	15	16	17	7:04	42	2467534
	○	19	20	21	22	23	24	11:54	43	2467541
	◑	26	27	28	29	30	31	2:26	44	2467548
	●	2	3	4	5	6	7	19:56	45	2467555
	8	9	◐	11	12	13	14	0:12	46	2467562
NOVEMBER 2043	15	○	17	18	19	20	21	21:51	47	2467569
	22	◑	24	25	26	27	28	13:44	48	2467576
	29	30	●	2	3	4	5	14:36	49	2467583
	6	7	8	◐	10	11	12	15:26	50	2467590
DECEMBER 2043	13	14	15	○	17	18	19	8:01	51	2467597
	20	21[e]	22	◑	24	25	26	5:03	52	2467604
	27	28	29	30	●	1	2	9:47	53	2467611

HEBREW 5803‡/5804

ISO WEEK	Month	Sun	Mon	Tue	Wed	Thu	Fri	Sat	Molad
1	TEVETH 5803	15	16	17	18	19	20	21	
2		22	23	24	25	26	27	28	
3		29	1	2	3	4	5	6	Sun 1h18m5p
4	SHEVAT 5803	7	8	9	10	11	12	13	
5		14	15	16	17	18	19	20	
6		21	22	23	24	25	26	27	
7		28	29	30	1	2	3	4	Mon 14h2m6p
8	ADAR I 5803	5	6	7	8	9	10	11	
9		12	13	14	15	16	17	18	
10		19	20	21	22	23	24	25	
11		26	27	28	29	30	1	2	Wed 2h46m7p
12	ADAR II 5803	3	4	5	6	7	8	9	
13		10	11	12	13	14[f]	15	16	
14		17	18	19	20	21	22	23	
15		24	25	26	27	28	29	1	Thu 15h30m8p
16		2	3	4	5	6	7	8	
17	NISAN 5803	9	10	11	12	13	14	15[g]	
18		16	17	18	19	20	21	22	
19		23	24	25	26	27	28	29	
20		30	1	2	3	4	5	6	Sat 4h14m9p
21		7	8	9	10	11	12	13	
22	IYAR 5803	14	15	16	17	18	19	20	
23		21	22	23	24	25	26	27	
24		28	29	1	2	3	4	5	Sun 16h58m10p
25		6[h]	7	8	9	10	11	12	
26	SIVAN 5803	13	14	15	16	17	18	19	
27		20	21	22	23	24	25	26	
28		27	28	29	30	1	2	3	Tue 5h42m11p
29		4	5	6	7	8	9	10	
30	TAMMUZ 5803	11	12	13	14	15	16	17	
31		18	19	20	21	22	23	24	
32		25	26	27	28	29	1	2	Wed 18h26m12p
33		3	4	5	6	7	8	9	
34	AV 5803	10[i]	11	12	13	14	15	16	
35		17	18	19	20	21	22	23	
36		24	25	26	27	28	29	30	
37		1	2	3	4	5	6	7	Fri 7h10m13p
38	ELUL 5803	8	9	10	11	12	13	14	
39		15	16	17	18	19	20	21	
40		22	23	24	25	26	27	28	
41		29	1[a]	2[a]	3	4	5	6	Sat 19h54m14p
42	TISHRI 5804	7	8	9	10[b]	11	12	13	
43		14	15[c]	16	17	18	19	20	
44		21	22	23	24	25	26	27	
45		28	29	30	1	2	3	4	Mon 8h38m15p
46		5	6	7	8	9	10	11	
47	HESHVAN 5804	12	13	14	15	16	17	18	
48		19	20	21	22	23	24	25	
49		26	27	28	29	1	2	3	Tue 21h22m16p
50		4[d]	5	6	7	8	9	10	
51	KISLEV 5804	11	12	13	14	15	16	17	
52		18	19	20	21	22	23	24	
53		25[e]	26[e]	27[e]	28[e]	29[e]	1[e]	2[e]	Thu 10h6m17p

CHINESE Rén-Xū‡/Guǐ-Hài

ISO WEEK	Month	Sun	Mon	Tue	Wed	Thu	Fri	Sat	Solar Term
1	MONTH 11 Rén-Xū	17	18	19	20	21	22	23	
2		24	25	26	27	28	29	30	Xiǎo hán
3		1	2	3	4	5	6	7	
4	MONTH 12 Rén-Xū	8	9	10	11*	12	13	14	Dà hán
5		15	16	17	18	19	20	21	
6		22	23	24	25	26	27	28	Lì chūn
7		29	30	1[a]	2	3	4	5	
8	MONTH 1 Guǐ-Hài	6	7	8	9	10	11	12	Yǔ shuǐ
9		13	14	15[b]	16	17	18	19	
10		20	21	22	23	24	25	26	Jīng zhé
11		27	28	29	1	2	3	4	
12	MONTH 2 Guǐ-Hài	5	6	7	8	9	10	11	Chūn fēn
13		12*	13	14	15	16	17	18	
14		19	20	21	22	23	24	25	
15		26[c]	27	28	29	30	1	2	Qīng míng
16	MONTH 3 Guǐ-Hài	3	4	5	6	7	8	9	
17		10	11	12	13	14	15	16	Gǔ yǔ
18		17	18	19	20	21	22	23	
19		24	25	26	27	28	29	1	Lì xià
20	MONTH 4 Guǐ-Hài	2	3	4	5	6	7	8	
21		9	10	11	12	13*	14	15	Xiǎo mǎn
22		16	17	18	19	20	21	22	
23		23	24	25	26	27	28	29	Máng zhòng
24		1	2	3	4	5[d]	6	7	
25	MONTH 5 Guǐ-Hài	8	9	10	11	12	13	14	
26		15	16	17	18	19	20	21	Xià zhì
27		22	23	24	25	26	27	28	
28		29	30	1	2	3	4	5	Xiǎo shǔ
29	MONTH 6 Guǐ-Hài	6	7	8	9	10	11	12	
30		13	14*	15	16	17	18	19	Dà shǔ
31		20	21	22	23	24	25	26	
32		27	28	29	1	2	3	4	Lì qiū
33	MONTH 7 Guǐ-Hài	5	6	7[e]	8	9	10	11	
34		12	13	14	15[f]	16	17	18	
35		19	20	21	22	23	24	25	Chǔ shǔ
36		26	27	28	29	1	2	3	
37	MONTH 8 Guǐ-Hài	4	5	6	7	8	9	10	Bái lù
38		11	12	13	14	15[g]	16*	17	
39		18	19	20	21	22	23	24	Qiū fēn
40		25	26	27	28	29	30	1	
41		2	3	4	5	6	7	8	Hán lù
42	MONTH 9 Guǐ-Hài	9[h]	10	11	12	13	14	15	
43		16	17	18	19	20	21	22	Shuāng jiàng
44		23	24	25	26	27	28	29	
45		30	1	2	3	4	5	6	Lì dōng
46		7	8	9	10	11	12	13	
47	MONTH 10 Guǐ-Hài	14	15	16*	17	18	19	20	Xiǎo xuě
48		21	22	23	24	25	26	27	
49		28	29	1	2	3	4	5	
50		6	7	8	9	10	11	12	Dà xuě
51	MONTH 11* Guǐ-Hài	13	14	15	16	17	18	19	
52		20	21	22[i]	23	24	25	26	Dōng zhì
53		27	28	29	30	1	2	3	

COPTIC 1759‡/1760 · ETHIOPIC 2035‡/2036

ISO WEEK	Coptic Month	Sun	Mon	Tue	Wed	Thu	Fri	Sat	Ethiopic Month
1	KOIAK 1759	19	20	21	22	23	24	25	
2		26	27	28	29[c]	30	1	2	TĀKHŚĀŚ 2035
3		3	4	5	6[d]	7	8	9	
4	TŌBE 1759	10	11[e]	12	13	14	15	16	ṬER 2035
5		17	18	19	20	21	22	23	
6		24	25	26	27	28	29	30	
7		1	2	3	4	5	6	7	
8	MESHIR 1759	8	9	10	11	12	13	14	
9		15	16	17	18	19	20	21	YAKĀTIT 2035
10		22	23	24	25	26	27	28	
11		29	30	1	2	3	4	5	
12		6	7	8	9	10	11	12	
13	PAREMOTEP 1759	13	14	15	16	17	18	19	MAGĀBIT 2035
14		20	21	22	23	24	25	26	
15		27	28	29	30	1	2	3	
16		4	5	6	7	8	9	10	
17	PARMOUTE 1759	11	12	13	14	15	16	17	MIYĀZYĀ 2035
18		18	19	20	21	22	23	24	
19		25[f]	26	27	28	29[g]	30	1	
20		2	3	4	5	6	7	8	
21	PASHONS 1759	9	10	11	12	13	14	15	GENBOT 2035
22		16	17	18	19	20	21	22	
23		23	24	25	26	27	28	29	
24		30	1	2	3	4	5	6	
25		7	8	9	10	11	12	13	
26	PAŌNE 1759	14	15	16	17	18	19	20	SANĒ 2035
27		21	22	23	24	25	26	27	
28		28	29	30	1	2	3	4	
29		5	6	7	8	9	10	11	
30	EPĒP 1759	12	13	14	15	16	17	18	HAMLĒ 2035
31		19	20	21	22	23	24	25	
32		26	27	28	29	30	1	2	
33		3	4	5	6	7	8	9	
34	MESORĒ 1759	10	11	12	13[h]	14	15	16	
35		17	18	19	20	21	22	23	NAḤASĒ 2035
36		24	25	26	27	28	29	30	
37	EPAG. 1759	1	2	3	4	5	6	1[a]	PĀG. 2035
38		2	3	4	5	6	7	8	
39	THOOUT 1760	9	10	11	12	13	14	15	MASKARAM 2036
40		16	17[b]	18	19	20	21	22	
41		23	24	25	26	27	28	29	
42		30	1	2	3	4	5	6	
43		7	8	9	10	11	12	13	ṬEQEMT 2036
44	PAOPE 1760	14	15	16	17	18	19	20	
45		21	22	23	24	25	26	27	
46		28	29	30	1	2	3	4	
47		5	6	7	8	9	10	11	
48	ATHŌR 1760	12	13	14	15	16	17	18	HEDĀR 2036
49		19	20	21	22	23	24	25	
50		26	27	28	29	30	1	2	
51		3	4	5	6	7	8	9	
52	KOIAK 1760	10	11	12	13	14	15	16	TĀKHŚĀŚ 2036
53		17	18	19	20	21	22	23	

Gregorian notes

[a]New Year
[b]Spring (17:26)
[c]Summer (10:56)
[d]Autumn (3:05)
[e]Winter (0:00)
● New moon
◐ First quarter moon
○ Full moon
◑ Last quarter moon

Hebrew notes

‡Leap year
[a]New Year
[b]Yom Kippur
[c]Sukkot
[d]Winter starts
[e]Ḥanukkah
[f]Purim
[g]Passover
[h]Shavuot
[i]Fast of Av

Chinese notes

‡Leap year
[a]New Year (4741, Pig)
[b]Lantern Festival
[c]Qīngmíng
[d]Dragon Festival
[e]Qǐqiǎo
[f]Hungry Ghosts
[g]Mid-Autumn Festival
[h]Double-Ninth Festival
[i]Dōngzhì
*Start of 60-name cycle

Coptic/Ethiopic notes

‡Leap year
[a]New Year
[b]Building of the Cross
[c]Christmas
[d]Jesus's Circumcision
[e]Epiphany
[f]Easter
[g]Mary's Announcement
[h]Jesus's Transfiguration

PERSIAN (ASTRONOMICAL) 1421/1422

Month	Sun	Mon	Tue	Wed	Thu	Fri	Sat
	7	8	9	10	11	12	13
DEY 1421	14	15	16	17	18	19	20
	21	22	23	24	25	26	27
	28	29	30	1	2	3	4
	5	6	7	8	9	10	11
BAHMAN 1421	12	13	14	15	16	17	18
	19	20	21	22	23	24	25
	26	27	28	29	30	1	2
	3	4	5	6	7	8	9
ESFAND 1421	10	11	12	13	14	15	16
	17	18	19	20	21	22	23
	24	25	26	27	28	29	1[a]
	2	3	4	5	6	7	8
FARVARDIN 1422	9	10	11	12	13[b]	14	15
	16	17	18	19	20	21	22
	23	24	25	26	27	28	29
	30	31	1	2	3	4	5
ORDIBEHEŠT 1422	6	7	8	9	10	11	12
	13	14	15	16	17	18	19
	20	21	22	23	24	25	26
	27	28	29	30	31	1	2
	3	4	5	6	7	8	9
XORDĀD 1422	10	11	12	13	14	15	16
	17	18	19	20	21	22	23
	24	25	26	27	28	29	30
	31	1	2	3	4	5	6
	7	8	9	10	11	12	13
TĪR 1422	14	15	16	17	18	19	20
	21	22	23	24	25	26	27
	28	29	30	31	1	2	3
	4	5	6	7	8	9	10
MORDĀD 1422	11	12	13	14	15	16	17
	18	19	20	21	22	23	24
	25	26	27	28	29	30	31
	1	2	3	4	5	6	7
SHAHRĪVAR 1422	8	9	10	11	12	13	14
	15	16	17	18	19	20	21
	22	23	24	25	26	27	28
	29	30	31	1	2	3	4
	5	6	7	8	9	10	11
MEHR 1422	12	13	14	15	16	17	18
	19	20	21	22	23	24	25
	26	27	28	29	30	1	2
	3	4	5	6	7	8	9
ĀBĀN 1422	10	11	12	13	14	15	16
	17	18	19	20	21	22	23
	24	25	26	27	28	29	30
	1	2	3	4	5	6	7
	8	9	10	11	12	13	14
ĀZAR 1422	15	16	17	18	19	20	21
	22	23	24	25	26	27	28
	29	30	1	2	3	4	5
DEY 1422	6	7	8	9	10	11	12

[a]New Year
[b]Sizdeh Bedar

HINDU LUNAR 2099‡/2100

Month	Sun	Mon	Tue	Wed	Thu	Fri	Sat
	17	18	19	20	21	22	23
MĀRGAŚĪRA 2099	24	25	26	26	27	28	29
	30	1	2	3	4	5	7
	8	9	10	11	12	13	14
PAUSHA 2099	15	16	17	18	19	20	21
	22	23	24	25	26	27	28
	29	30	1	2	3	4	5
	6	7	8	9	10	12	13
MĀGHA 2099	14	15	16	17	18	19	19
	20	21	22	23	24	25	26
	27	28[h]	29	30	1	2	3
	5	6	7	8	9	10	11
PHĀLGUNA 2099	12	13	14	15[i]	16	17	18
	19	20	21	22	22	23	24
	25	26	27	29	30	1[a]	2
	3	4	5	6	7	8[b]	9
CHAITRA 2100	10	11	12	13	14	15	16
	17	18	19	20	21	22	23
	24	25	26	27	28	29	30
	1	3	4	5	6	7	8
	9	10	11	12	13	14	15
VAIŚĀKHA 2100	16	16	17	18	19	20	21
	22	23	24	26	27	28	29
	30	1	2	3	4	5	6
	7	8	9	10	11	12	13
JYAISHTHA 2100	14	15	16	17	18	19	20
	21	22	23	24	25	26	27
	29	30	1	2	3	4	5
	6	7	8	9	10	11	12
ĀSHĀDHA 2100	13	13	14	15	16	17	18
	19	21	22	23	24	25	26
	27	28	29	30	1	2	4
	4	5	6	7	8	9	10
ŚRĀVANA 2100	11	12	13	14	15	16	17
	18	19	20	21	22[c]	24	25
	26	27	28	29	30	1	2
	3	4[d]	5	6	7	8	9
BHĀDRAPADA 2100	10	10	11	12	13	14	15
	17	18	19	20	21	22	23
	24	25	26	27	28	29	30
	1	2	3	4	5	6	7
	8[e]	9[e]	10[e]	11	12	13	14
ĀŚVINA 2100	15	16	17	18	19	21	22
	23	24	25	26	27	28	29
	30	1[f]	2	3	4	4	5
	6	7	8	9	10	11	12
KĀRTTIKA 2100	13	15	16	17	18	19	20
	21	22	23	24	25	26	27
	28	29	30	1	2	3	4
	5	6	7	8	9	10	11[g]
MĀRGAŚĪRA 2100	12	13	14	15	16	17	18
	20	21	22	23	24	25	26
	27	27	28	29	30	1	2

‡Leap year
[a]New Year (Rudhirodgārin)
[b]Birthday of Rāma
[c]Birthday of Krishna
[d]Ganēśa Chaturthī
[e]Dashara
[f]Diwali
[g]Birthday of Vishnu
[h]Night of Śiva
[i]Holi

HINDU SOLAR 1964/1965

Month	Sun	Mon	Tue	Wed	Thu	Fri	Sat
	13	14	15	16	17	18	19
PAUSHA 1964	20	21	22	23	24	25	26
	27	28	29	1[b]	2	3	4
	5	6	7	8	9	10	11
MĀGHA 1964	12	13	14	15	16	17	18
	19	20	21	22	23	24	25
	26	27	28	29	30	1	2
	3	4	5	6	7	8	9
PHĀLGUNA 1964	10	11	12	13	14	15	16
	17	18	19	20	21	22	23
	24	25	26	27	28	29	30
	1	2	3	4	5	6	7
	8	9	10	11	12	13	14
CHAITRA 1964	15	16	17	18	19	20	21
	22	23	24	25	26	27	28
	29	30	1[a]	2	3	4	5
	6	7	8	9	10	11	12
VAIŚĀKHA 1965	13	14	15	16	17	18	19
	20	21	22	23	24	25	26
	27	28	29	30	31	1	2
	3	4	5	6	7	8	9
JYAISHTHA 1965	10	11	12	13	14	15	16
	17	18	19	20	21	22	23
	24	25	26	27	28	29	30
	31	1	2	3	4	5	6
	7	8	9	10	11	12	13
ĀSHĀDHA 1965	14	15	16	17	18	19	20
	21	22	23	24	25	26	27
	28	29	30	31	32	1	2
	3	4	5	6	7	8	9
ŚRĀVANA 1965	10	11	12	13	14	15	16
	17	18	19	20	21	22	23
	24	25	26	27	28	29	30
	31	32	1	2	3	4	5
	6	7	8	9	10	11	12
BHĀDRAPADA 1965	13	14	15	16	17	18	19
	20	21	22	23	24	25	26
	27	28	29	30	31	1	2
	3	4	5	6	7	8	9
ĀŚVINA 1965	10	11	12	13	14	15	16
	17	18	19	20	21	22	23
	24	25	26	27	28	29	30
	1	2	3	4	5	6	7
	8	9	10	11	12	13	14
KĀRTTIKA 1965	15	16	17	18	19	20	21
	22	23	24	25	26	27	28
	29	30	1	2	3	4	5
	6	7	8	9	10	11	12
MĀRGAŚĪRA 1965	13	14	15	16	17	18	19
	20	21	22	23	24	25	26
	27	28	29	1	2	3	4
PAUSHA 1965	5	6	7	8	9	10	11
	12	13	14	15	16	17	18

[a]New Year (Īśvara)
[b]Pongal

ISLAMIC (ASTRONOMICAL) 1465‡/1466

Month	Sun	Mon	Tue	Wed	Thu	Fri	Sat
	15	16	17	18	19	20	21
MUHARRAM 1465	22	23	24	25	26	27	28
	29	30	1	2	3	4	5
	6	7	8	9	10	11	12
ṢAFAR 1465	13	14	15	16	17	18	19
	20	21	22	23	24	25	26
	27	28	29	1	2	3	4
	5	6	7	8	9	10	11
RABĪ' I 1465	12[c]	13	14	15	16	17	18
	19	20	21	22	23	24	25
	26	27	28	29	30	1	2
	3	4	5	6	7	8	9
RABĪ' II 1465	10	11	12	13	14	15	16
	17	18	19	20	21	22	23
	24	25	26	27	28	29	1
	2	3	4	5	6	7	8
JUMĀDĀ I 1465	9	10	11	12	13	14	15
	16	17	18	19	20	21	22
	23	24	25	26	27	28	29
	1	2	3	4	5	6	7
JUMĀDĀ II 1465	8	9	10	11	12	13	14
	15	16	17	18	19	20	21
	22	23	24	25	26	27	28
	29	1	2	3	4	5	6
	7	8	9	10	11	12	13
RAJAB 1465	14	15	16	17	18	19	20
	21	22	23	24	25	26	27[d]
	28	29	30	1	2	3	4
	5	6	7	8	9	10	11
SHA'BĀN 1465	12	13	14	15	16	17	18
	19	20	21	22	23	24	25
	26	27	28	29	1[e]	2	3
	4	5	6	7	8	9	10
RAMAḌĀN 1465	11	12	13	14	15	16	17
	18	19	20	21	22	23	24
	25	26	27	28	29	30	1[f]
	2	3	4	5	6	7	8
SHAWWĀL 1465	9	10	11	12	13	14	15
	16	17	18	19	20	21	22
	23	24	25	26	27	28	29
	30	1	2	3	4	5	6
DHU AL-QA'DA 1465	7	8	9	10	11	12	13
	14	15	16	17	18	19	20
	21	22	23	24	25	26	27
	28	29	30	1	2	3	4
	5	6	7	8	9	10[g]	11
DHU AL-ḤIJJA 1465	12	13	14	15	16	17	18
	19	20	21	22	23	24	25
	26	27	28	29	30[d]	1[a]	2
	3	4	5	6	7	8	9
MUHARRAM 1466	10[b]	11	12	13	14	15	16
	17	18	19	20	21	22	23
	24	25	26	27	28	29	1

‡Leap year
[a]New Year
[d]New Year (Arithmetic)
[b]'Ashūrā'
[c]Prophet's Birthday
[d]Ascent of the Prophet
[e]Start of Ramaḍān
[f]'Id al-Fiṭr
[g]'Id al-'Aḍḥā

GREGORIAN 2043

Julian (Sun)	Sun	Mon	Tue	Wed	Thu	Fri	Sat	Month
Dec 15	28	29	30	31	1	2	3	
	4	5	6	7[a]	8	9	10	JANUARY 2043
Dec 29	11	12	13	14[b]	15	16	17	
	18	19	20	21	22	23	24	
Jan 12	25	26	27	28	29	30	31	
	1	2	3	4	5	6	7	
Jan 26	8	9	10	11[c]	12	13	14	FEBRUARY 2043
	15	16	17	18	19	20	21	
Feb 9	22	23	24	25	26	27	28	
	1	2	3	4	5	6	7	
Feb 23	8	9	10	11	12	13	14	MARCH 2043
	15	16	17	18	19	20	21	
Mar 9	22[d]	23	24	25	26	27	28	
	29[e]	30	31	1	2	3	4	
Mar 23	5	6	7	8	9	10	11	APRIL 2043
	12	13	14	15	16	17	18	
Apr 6	19	20	21	22	23	24	25	
	26	27	28	29	30	1	2	
Apr 20	3[f]	4	5	6	7	8	9	
	10	11	12	13	14	15	16	MAY 2043
May 4	17	18	19	20	21	22	23	
	24	25	26	27	28	29	30	
May 18	31	1	2	3	4	5	6	
	7	8	9	10	11	12	13	
Jun 1	14	15	16	17	18	19	20	JUNE 2043
	21	22	23	24	25	26	27	
Jun 15	28	29	30	1	2	3	4	
	5	6	7	8	9	10	11	
Jun 29	12	13	14	15	16	17	18	JULY 2043
	19	20	21	22	23	24	25	
Jul 13	26	27	28	29	30	31	1	
	2	3	4	5	6	7	8	
Jul 27	9	10	11	12	13	14	15	AUGUST 2043
	16	17	18	19	20	21	22	
Aug 10	23	24	25	26	27	28	29	
	30	31	1	2	3	4	5	
Aug 24	6	7	8	9	10	11	12	SEPTEMBER 2043
	13	14	15	16	17	18	19	
Sep 7	20	21	22	23	24	25	26	
	27	28	29	30	1	2	3	
Sep 21	4	5	6	7	8	9	10	OCTOBER 2043
	11	12	13	14	15	16	17	
Oct 5	18	19	20	21	22	23	24	
	25	26	27	28	29	30	31	
Oct 19	1	2	3	4	5	6	7	NOVEMBER 2043
	8	9	10	11	12	13	14	
Nov 2	15	16	17	18	19	20	21	
	22	23	24	25	26	27	28	
Nov 16	29[g]	30	1	2	3	4	5	
	6	7	8	9	10	11	12	DECEMBER 2043
Nov 30	13	14	15	16	17	18	19	
	20	21	22	23	24	25[h]	26	
Dec 14	27	28	29	30	31	1	2	

[a]Orthodox Christmas
[b]Julian New Year
[c]Ash Wednesday
[d]Feast of Orthodoxy
[e]Easter
[f]Orthodox Easter
[g]Advent
[h]Christmas

2044

Gregorian 2044‡	Sun	Mon	Tue	Wed	Thu	Fri	Sat	Lunar Phases	ISO Week (Mon)	Julian Day (Sun noon)	Hebrew 5804/5805	Sun	Mon	Tue	Wed	Thu	Fri	Sat	Molad	Chinese Guǐ-Hài/Jiǎ-Zǐ‡	Sun	Mon	Tue	Wed	Thu	Fri	Sat	Solar Term	Coptic 1760/1761	Sun	Mon	Tue	Wed	Thu	Fri	Sat	Ethiopic 2036/2037
January 2044	27	28	29	30	●	1[a]	2	9:47	53	2467611	Teveth 5804	25[e]	26[e]	27[e]	28[e]	29[e]	1[e]	2[e]	Thu 10h6m17p	Month 12 Guǐ-Hài	27	28	29	30	1	2	3		Koiak 1760	17	18	19	20	21	22	23	Tākhśāś 2036
	3	4	5	6	7	◐	9	4:00	1	2467618		3[e]	4	5	6	7	8	9			4	5	6	7	8	9	10	Xiǎo hán		24	25	26	27	28	29[c]	30	
	10	11	12	13	○	15	16	18:50	2	2467625		10	11	12	13	14	15	16			11	12	13	14	15	16	17*		Ṭōbe 1760	1	2	3	4	5	6[d]	7	Ṭer 2036
	17	18	19	20	◑	22	23	23:46	3	2467632		17	18	19	20	21	22	23			18	19	20	21	22	23	24	Dà hán		8	9	10	11[e]	12	13	14	
	24	25	26	27	28	29	●	4:03	4	2467639	Shevat 5804	24	25	26	27	28	29	1	Fri 22h51m0p	Month 1 Jiǎ-Zǐ	25	26	27	28	29	30	1[a]			15	16	17	18	19	20	21	
February 2044	31	1	2	3	4	5	◐	13:45	5	2467646		2	3	4	5	6	7	8			2	3	4	5	6	7	8	Lì chūn		22	23	24	25	26	27	28	
	7	8	9	10	11	12	○	6:40	6	2467653		9	10	11	12	13	14	15			9	10	11	12	13	14	15[b]		Meshir 1760	29	30	1	2	3	4	5	Yakātit 2036
	14	15	16	17	18	19	◑	20:19	7	2467660		16	17	18	19	20	21	22			16	17	18	19	20	21	22	Yǔ shuǐ		6	7	8	9	10	11	12	
	21	22	23	24	25	26	27		8	2467667		23	24	25	26	27	28	29			23	24	25	26	27	28	29			13	14	15	16	17	18	19	
March 2044	●	29	1	2	3	4	5	20:11	9	2467674	Adar 5804	30	1	2	3	4	5	6	Sun 11h35m1p	Month 2 Jiǎ-Zǐ	30	1	2	3	4	5	6	Jīng zhé		20	21	22	23	24	25	26	
	◐	7	8	9	10	11	12	21:16	10	2467681		7	8	9	10	11	12	13			7	8	9	10	11	12	13		Paremotep 1760	27	28	29	30	1	2	3	Magābit 2036
	○	14	15	16	17	18	19[b]	19:40	11	2467688		14[f]	15	16	17	18	19	20			14	15	16	17*	18	19	20			4	5	6	7	8	9	10	
	20	◑	22	23	24	25	26	16:51	12	2467695		21	22	23	24	25	26	27			21	22	23	24	25	26	27	Chūn fēn		11	12	13	14	15	16	17	
April 2044	27	28	●	30	31	1	2	9:25	13	2467702	Nisan 5804	28	29	1	2	3	4	5	Tue 0h19m2p	Month 3 Jiǎ-Zǐ	28	29	1	2	3	4	5			18	19	20	21	22	23	24	
	3	4	◐	6	7	8	9	3:44	14	2467709		6	7	8	9	10	11	12			6	7[c]	8	9	10	11	12	Qīng míng	Parmoute 1760	25	26	27	28	29	30	1	Miyāzyā 2036
	10	11	○	13	14	15	16	9:38	15	2467716		13	14	15[g]	16	17	18	19			13	14	15	16	17	18	19			2	3	4	5	6	7	8	
	17	18	19	◑	21	22	23	11:47	16	2467723		20	21	22	23	24	25	26			20	21	22	23	24	25	26	Gǔ yǔ		9	10	11	12	13	14	15	
	24	25	26	●	28	29	30	19:41	17	2467730	Iyyar 5804	27	28	29	30	1	2	3	Wed 13h3m3p	Month 4 Jiǎ-Zǐ	27	28	29	30	1	2	3			16[f]	17	18	19	20	21	22	
May 2044	1	2	3	◐	5	6	7	10:27	18	2467737		4	5	6	7	8	9	10			4	5	6	7	8	9	10	Lì xià		23	24	25	26	27	28	29[g]	
	8	9	10	11	○	13	14	0:15	19	2467744		11	12	13	14	15	16	17			11	12	13	14	15	16	17		Pashons 1760	30	1	2	3	4	5	6	Genbot 2036
	15	16	17	18	19	◑	21	4:00	20	2467751		18	19	20	21	22	23	24			18*	19	20	21	22	23	24	Xiǎo mǎn		7	8	9	10	11	12	13	
	22	23	24	25	26	●	28	3:38	21	2467758	Sivan 5804	25	26	27	28	29	1	2	Fri 1h47m4p	Month 5 Jiǎ-Zǐ	25	26	27	28	29	1	2			14	15	16	17	18	19	20	
June 2044	29	30	31	1	◐	3	4	18:32	22	2467765		3	4	5	6[h]	7	8	9			3	4	5[d]	6	7	8	9			21	22	23	24	25	26	27	
	5	6	7	8	9	○	11	15:15	23	2467772		10	11	12	13	14	15	16			10	11	12	13	14	15	16	Máng zhòng	Paōne 1760	28	29	30	1	2	3	4	Sanē 2036
	12	13	14	15	16	17	◑	15:58	24	2467779		17	18	19	20	21	22	23			17	18	19	20	21	22	23			5	6	7	8	9	10	11	
	19	20[c]	21	22	23	24	●	10:23	25	2467786		24	25	26	27	28	29	30		Month 6 Jiǎ-Zǐ	24	25	26	27	28	29	1	Xià zhì		12	13	14	15	16	17	18	
July 2044	26	27	28	29	30	1	◐	4:47	26	2467793	Tammuz 5804	1	2	3	4	5	6	7	Sat 14h31m5p		2	3	4	5	6	7	8			19	20	21	22	23	24	25	
	3	4	5	6	7	8	9		27	2467800		8	9	10	11	12	13	14			9	10	11	12	13	14	15	Xiǎo shǔ	Epēp 1760	26	27	28	29	30	1	2	Ḥamlē 2036
	○	11	12	13	14	15	16	6:21	28	2467807		15	16	17	18	19	20	21			16	17	18	19	20*	21	22			3	4	5	6	7	8	9	
	17	◑	19	20	21	22	23	2:45	29	2467814		22	23	24	25	26	27	28			23	24	25	26	27	28	29	Dà shǔ		10	11	12	13	14	15	16	
	●	25	26	27	28	29	30	17:09	30	2467821	Av 5804	29	1	2	3	4	5	6	Mon 3h15m6p	Month 7 Jiǎ-Zǐ	30	1	2	3	4	5	6			17	18	19	20	21	22	23	
August 2044	◐	1	2	3	4	5	6	17:39	31	2467828		7	8	9[i]	10	11	12	13			7[e]	8	9	10	11	12	13			24	25	26	27	28	29	30	
	7	○	9	10	11	12	13	21:12	32	2467835		14	15	16	17	18	19	20			14	15[f]	16	17	18	19	20	Lì qiū	Mesorē 1760	1	2	3	4	5	6	7	Naḥasē 2036
	14	15	◑	17	18	19	20	10:02	33	2467842		21	22	23	24	25	26	27			21	22	23	24	25	26	27			8	9	10	11	12	13[h]	14	
	21	22	●	24	25	26	27	1:04	34	2467849	Elul 5804	28	29	30	1	2	3	4	Tue 15h59m7p	Leap Month 7 Jiǎ-Zǐ	28	29	1	2	3	4	5	Chǔ shǔ		15	16	17	18	19	20	21	
September 2044	28	29	◐	31	1	2	3	9:17	35	2467856		5	6	7	8	9	10	11			6	7	8	9	10	11	12			22	23	24	25	26	27	28	
	4	5	6	○	8	9	10	11:23	36	2467863		12	13	14	15	16	17	18			13	14	15	16	17	18	19	Bái lù	Epag. 1760	29	30	1	2	3	4	5	Pāg. 2036
	11	12	13	◑	15	16	17	15:56	37	2467870		19	20	21	22	23	24	25			20	21*	22	23	24	25	26		Thoout 1761	1[a]	2	3	4	5	6	7	Maskaram 2037
	18	19	20	●	22[d]	23	24	11:02	38	2467877	Tishri 5805	26	27	28	29	1[a]	2[a]	3	Thu 4h43m8p	Month 8 Jiǎ-Zǐ	27	28	29	1	2	3	4	Qiū fēn		8	9	10	11	12	13	14	
October 2044	25	26	27	28	◐	30	1	3:29	39	2467884		4	5	6	7	8	9	10[b]			5	6	7	8	9	10	11			15	16	17[b]	18	19	20	21	
	2	3	4	5	6	○	8	0:29	40	2467891		11	12	13	14	15[c]	16	17			12	13	14	15[g]	16	17	18	Hán lù		22	23	24	25	26	27	28	
	9	10	11	12	◑	14	15	21:51	41	2467898		18	19	20	21	22	23	24			19	20	21	22	23	24	25		Paope 1761	29	30	1	2	3	4	5	Ṭeqemt 2037
	16	17	18	19	●	21	22	23:35	42	2467905	Heshvan 5805	25	26	27	28	29	30	1	Fri 17h27m9p	Month 9 Jiǎ-Zǐ	26	27	28	29	30	1	2			6	7	8	9	10	11	12	
	23	24	25	26	27	◐	29	23:26	43	2467912		2	3	4	5	6	7	8			3	4	5	6	7	8	9[h]	Shuāng jiàng		13	14	15	16	17	18	19	
November 2044	30	31	1	2	3	4	○	12:25	44	2467919		9	10	11	12	13	14	15			10	11	12	13	14	15	16			20	21	22	23	24	25	26	
	6	7	8	9	10	11	◑	5:08	45	2467926		16	17	18	19	20	21	22			17	18	19	20	21	22*	23	Lì dōng	Athōr 1761	27	28	29	30	1	2	3	Hedār 2037
	13	14	15	16	17	18	●	14:56	46	2467933		23	24	25	26	27	28	29		Month 10 Jiǎ-Zǐ	24	25	26	27	28	29	1			4	5	6	7	8	9	10	
	20	21	22	23	24	25	26		47	2467940	Kislev 5805	30	1	2	3	4	5	6	Sun 6h11m10p		2	3	4	5	6	7	8	Xiǎo xuě		11	12	13	14	15	16	17	
December 2044	◐	28	29	30	1	2	3	19:35	48	2467947		7	8	9	10	11	12	13			9	10	11	12	13	14	15			18	19	20	21	22	23	24	
	○	5	6	7	8	9	10	23:33	49	2467954		14	15[d]	16	17	18	19	20			16	17	18	19	20	21	22	Dà xuě	Koiak 1761	25	26	27	28	29	30	1	Tākhśāś 2037
	◑	12	13	14	15	16	17	14:51	50	2467961		21	22	23	24	25[e]	26[e]	27[e]			23	24	25	26	27	28	29			2	3	4	5	6	7	8	
	18	●	20	21[e]	22	23	24	8:52	51	2467968	Teveth 5805	28[e]	29[e]	30[e]	1[e]	2[e]	3	4	Mon 18h55m11p	Month 11 Jiǎ-Zǐ	30	1	2	3[i]	4	5	6	Dōng zhì		9	10	11	12	13	14	15	
	25	26	◐	28	29	30	31	13:59	52	2467975		5	6	7	8	9	10	11			7	8	9	10	11	12	13			16	17	18	19	20	21	22	

‡Leap year
[a]New Year
[b]Spring (23:19)
[c]Summer (16:49)
[d]Autumn (8:46)
[e]Winter (5:42)
● New moon
◐ First quarter moon
○ Full moon
◑ Last quarter moon

[a]New Year
[b]Yom Kippur
[c]Sukkot
[d]Winter starts
[e]Ḥanukkah
[f]Purim
[g]Passover
[h]Shavuot
[i]Fast of Av

‡Leap year
[a]New Year (4742, Rat)
[b]Lantern Festival
[c]Qīngmíng
[d]Dragon Festival
[e]Qīqiǎo
[f]Hungry Ghosts
[g]Mid-Autumn Festival
[h]Double-Ninth Festival
[i]Dōngzhì
*Start of 60-name cycle

[a]New Year
[b]Building of the Cross
[c]Christmas
[d]Jesus's Circumcision
[e]Epiphany
[f]Easter
[g]Mary's Announcement
[h]Jesus's Transfiguration

PERSIAN (ASTRONOMICAL) 1422/1423

Month	Sun	Mon	Tue	Wed	Thu	Fri	Sat
	6	7	8	9	10	11	12
DEY 1422	13	14	15	16	17	18	19
	20	21	22	23	24	25	26
	27	28	29	30	1	2	3
BAHMAN 1422	4	5	6	7	8	9	10
	11	12	13	14	15	16	17
	18	19	20	21	22	23	24
	25	26	27	28	29	30	1
ESFAND 1422	2	3	4	5	6	7	8
	9	10	11	12	13	14	15
	16	17	18	19	20	21	22
	23	24	25	26	27	28	29
FARVARDĪN 1423	1[a]	2	3	4	5	6	7
	8	9	10	11	12	13[b]	14
	15	16	17	18	19	20	21
	22	23	24	25	26	27	28
	29	30	31	1	2	3	4
ORDĪBEHEŠT 1423	5	6	7	8	9	10	11
	12	13	14	15	16	17	18
	19	20	21	22	23	24	25
	26	27	28	29	30	31	1
XORDĀD 1423	2	3	4	5	6	7	8
	9	10	11	12	13	14	15
	16	17	18	19	20	21	22
	23	24	25	26	27	28	29
	30	31	1	2	3	4	5
TĪR 1423	6	7	8	9	10	11	12
	13	14	15	16	17	18	19
	20	21	22	23	24	25	26
	27	28	29	30	31	1	2
MORDĀD 1423	3	4	5	6	7	8	9
	10	11	12	13	14	15	16
	17	18	19	20	21	22	23
	24	25	26	27	28	29	30
	31	1	2	3	4	5	6
SHAHRĪVAR 1423	7	8	9	10	11	12	13
	14	15	16	17	18	19	20
	21	22	23	24	25	26	27
	28	29	30	31	1	2	3
MEHR 1423	4	5	6	7	8	9	10
	11	12	13	14	15	16	17
	18	19	20	21	22	23	24
	25	26	27	28	29	30	1
ĀBĀN 1423	2	3	4	5	6	7	8
	9	10	11	12	13	14	15
	16	17	18	19	20	21	22
	23	24	25	26	27	28	29
	30	1	2	3	4	5	6
ĀZAR 1423	7	8	9	10	11	12	13
	14	15	16	17	18	19	20
	21	22	23	24	25	26	27
DEY 1423	28	29	30	1	2	3	4
	5	6	7	8	9	10	11

[a]New Year
[b]Sizdeh Bedar

HINDU LUNAR 2100/2101

Month	Sun	Mon	Tue	Wed	Thu	Fri	Sat
	27	27	28	29	30	1	2
PAUSHA 2100	3	4	5	6	7	8	9
	10	11	**12**	14	15	16	17
	18	19	20	21	22	23	24
	25	26	27	28	29	29	30
	1	2	3	4	5	**6**	8
MĀGHA 2100	9	10	11	12	13	14	15
	16	17	18	19	20	21	22
	23	24	25	26	27	28	29[h]
	30	1	2	3	4	5	6
PHĀLGUNA 2100	7	8	9	**10**	12	13	14
	15[i]	16	17	18	19	20	21
	22	22	23	24	25	26	27
	28	29	30	1[a]	2	3	**4**
CHAITRA 2101	6	7	8	9[b]	10	11	12
	13	14	15	16	17	18	19
	20	21	22	23	24	25	26
	27	28	29	30	1	2	3
VAIŚĀKHA 2101	4	5	6	7	**8**	10	11
	12	13	14	15	16	16	17
	18	19	20	21	22	23	24
	25	26	27	28	29	30	**1**
JYAISHṬHA 2101	3	4	5	6	7	8	9
	10	11	12	13	14	15	16
	17	18	19	20	21	22	23
	24	25	26	27	28	29	30
ĀSHĀḌHA 2101	1	2	3	**4**	6	7	8
	9	10	11	12	13	13	14
	15	16	17	18	19	20	21
	22	23	24	25	26	**27**	29
	30	1	2	3	4	5	6
ŚRĀVAṆA 2101	7	8	9	10	11	12	13
	14	15	16	17	18	19	20
	21	22	23[c]	24	25	26	27
	28	29	**30**	2	3	4[d]	5
BHĀDRAPADA 2101	6	7	8	9	9	10	11
	12	13	14	15	16	17	18
	19	20	21	22	**23**	25	26
	27	28	29	30	1	2	3
ĀŚVINA 2101	4	5	6	7	8[e]	9[e]	10[e]
	11	12	13	14	15	16	17
	18	19	20	21	22	23	24
	25	26	**27**	29	30	1[f]	2
KĀRTTIKA 2101	3	4	4	5	6	7	8
	9	10	11	12	13	14	15
	16	17	18	19	**20**	22	23
	24	25	26	27	28	29	30
	1	2	3	4	5	6	7
MĀRGAŚĪRA 2101	7	8	9	10	11[g]	12	13
	14	16	17	18	19	20	21
	22	23	24	25	26	27	28
PAUSHA 2101	29	30	1	2	3	4	5
	6	7	8	9	10	11	12

[a]New Year (Raktāksha)
[b]Birthday of Rāma
[c]Birthday of Krishna
[d]Ganēśa Chaturthī
[e]Dashara
[f]Diwali
[g]Birthday of Vishnu
[h]Night of Śiva
[i]Holi

HINDU SOLAR 1965/1966‡

Month	Sun	Mon	Tue	Wed	Thu	Fri	Sat
	12	13	14	15	16	17	18
PAUSHA 1965	19	20	21	22	23	24	25
	26	27	28	29	30	1[b]	2
MĀGHA 1965	3	4	5	6	7	8	9
	10	11	12	13	14	15	16
	17	18	19	20	21	22	23
	24	25	26	27	28	29	1
	2	3	4	5	6	7	8
PHĀLGUNA 1965	9	10	11	12	13	14	15
	16	17	18	19	20	21	22
	23	24	25	26	27	28	29
	30	1	2	3	4	5	6
CHAITRA 1965	7	8	9	10	11	12	13
	14	15	16	17	18	19	20
	21	22	23	24	25	26	27
	28	29	30	1[a]	2	3	4
VAIŚĀKHA 1966	5	6	7	8	9	10	11
	12	13	14	15	16	17	18
	19	20	21	22	23	24	25
	26	27	28	29	30	31	1
JYAISHṬHA 1966	2	3	4	5	6	7	8
	9	10	11	12	13	14	15
	16	17	18	19	20	21	22
	23	24	25	26	27	28	29
	30	31	32	1	2	3	4
ĀSHĀḌHA 1966	5	6	7	8	9	10	11
	12	13	14	15	16	17	18
	19	20	21	22	23	24	25
	26	27	28	29	30	31	1
ŚRĀVAṆA 1966	2	3	4	5	6	7	8
	9	10	11	12	13	14	15
	16	17	18	19	20	21	22
	23	24	25	26	27	28	29
	30	31	32	1	2	3	4
BHĀDRAPADA 1966	5	6	7	8	9	10	11
	12	13	14	15	16	17	18
	19	20	21	22	23	24	25
	26	27	28	29	30	31	1
ĀŚVINA 1966	2	3	4	5	6	7	8
	9	10	11	12	13	14	15
	16	17	18	19	20	21	22
	23	24	25	26	27	28	29
	30	1	2	3	4	5	6
KĀRTTIKA 1966	7	8	9	10	11	12	13
	14	15	16	17	18	19	20
	21	22	23	24	25	26	27
	28	29	30	1	2	3	4
MĀRGAŚĪRA 1966	5	6	7	8	9	10	11
	12	13	14	15	16	17	18
	19	20	21	22	23	24	25
	26	27	28	29	30	1	2
PAUSHA 1966	3	4	5	6	7	8	9
	10	11	12	13	14	15	16

‡Leap year
[a]New Year (Bahudhānya)
[b]Pongal

ISLAMIC (ASTRONOMICAL) 1466/1467

Month	Sun	Mon	Tue	Wed	Thu	Fri	Sat
	24	25	26	27	28	29	1
ṢAFAR 1466	2	3	4	5	6	7	8
	9	10	11	12	13	14	15
	16	17	18	19	20	21	22
	23	24	25	26	27	28	29
RABĪ' I 1466	1	2	3	4	5	6	7
	8	9	10	11	12[c]	13	14
	15	16	17	18	19	20	21
	22	23	24	25	26	27	28
	29	30	1	2	3	4	5
RABĪ' II 1466	6	7	8	9	10	11	12
	13	14	15	16	17	18	19
	20	21	22	23	24	25	26
	27	28	29	30	1	2	3
JUMĀDĀ I 1466	4	5	6	7	8	9	10
	11	12	13	14	15	16	17
	18	19	20	21	22	23	24
	25	26	27	28	29	1	2
JUMĀDĀ II 1466	3	4	5	6	7	8	9
	10	11	12	13	14	15	16
	17	18	19	20	21	22	23
	24	25	26	27	28	29	1
RAJAB 1466	2	3	4	5	6	7	8
	9	10	11	12	13	14	15
	16	17	18	19	20	21	22
	23	24	25	26	27[d]	28	29
SHA'BĀN 1466	1	2	3	4	5	6	7
	8	9	10	11	12	13	14
	15	16	17	18	19	20	21
	22	23	24	25	26	27	28
	29	30	1[e]	2	3	4	5
RAMAḌĀN 1466	6	7	8	9	10	11	12
	13	14	15	16	17	18	19
	20	21	22	23	24	25	26
	27	28	29	30	1[f]	2	3
SHAWWĀL 1466	4	5	6	7	8	9	10
	11	12	13	14	15	16	17
	18	19	20	21	22	23	24
	25	26	27	28	29	30	1
DHŪ AL-QA'DA 1466	2	3	4	5	6	7	8
	9	10	11	12	13	14	15
	16	17	18	19	20	21	22
	23	24	25	26	27	28	29
DHŪ AL-ḤIJJA 1466	1	2	3	4	5	6	7
	8	9	10[g]	11	12	13	14
	15	16	17	18	19	20	21
	22	23	24	25	26	27	28
	29	30	1[a]	2	3	4	5
MUḤARRAM 1467	6	7	8	9	10[b]	11	12
	13	14	15	16	17	18	19
	20	21	22	23	24	25	26
	27	28	29	1	2	3	4
ṢAFAR 1467	5	6	7	8	9	10	11

[a]New Year
[b]'Ashūrā'
[c]Prophet's Birthday
[d]Ascent of the Prophet
[e]Start of Ramaḍān
[f]'Īd al-Fiṭr
[g]'Īd al-'Aḍḥā

GREGORIAN 2044‡

Julian‡ (Sun)	Sun	Mon	Tue	Wed	Thu	Fri	Sat	Month
Dec 14	27	28	29	30	31	1	2	
	3	4	5	6	7[a]	8	9	JANUARY 2044
Dec 28	10	11	12	13	14[b]	15	16	
	17	18	19	20	21	22	23	
Jan 11	24	25	26	27	28	29	30	
	31	1	2	3	4	5	6	
Jan 25	7	8	9	10	11	12	13	FEBRUARY 2044
	14	15	16	17	18	19	20	
Feb 8	21	22	23	24	25	26	27	
	28	29	1	2[c]	3	4	5	
Feb 22	6	7	8	9	10	11	12	MARCH 2044
	13[d]	14	15	16	17	18	19	
Mar 7	20	21	22	23	24	25	26	
	27	28	29	30	31	1	2	
Mar 21	3	4	5	6	7	8	9	APRIL 2044
	10	11	12	13	14	15	16	
Apr 4	17[e]	18	19	20	21	22	23	
	24[f]	25	26	27	28	29	30	
Apr 18	1	2	3	4	5	6	7	
	8	9	10	11	12	13	14	MAY 2044
May 2	15	16	17	18	19	20	21	
	22	23	24	25	26	27	28	
May 16	29	30	31	1	2	3	4	
	5	6	7	8	9	10	11	
May 30	12	13	14	15	16	17	18	JUNE 2044
	19	20	21	22	23	24	25	
Jun 13	26	27	28	29	30	1	2	
	3	4	5	6	7	8	9	
Jun 27	10	11	12	13	14	15	16	JULY 2044
	17	18	19	20	21	22	23	
Jul 11	24	25	26	27	28	29	30	
	31	1	2	3	4	5	6	
Jul 25	7	8	9	10	11	12	13	AUGUST 2044
	14	15	16	17	18	19	20	
Aug 8	21	22	23	24	25	26	27	
	28	29	30	31	1	2	3	
Aug 22	4	5	6	7	8	9	10	SEPTEMBER 2044
	11	12	13	14	15	16	17	
Sep 5	18	19	20	21	22	23	24	
	25	26	27	28	29	30	1	
Sep 19	2	3	4	5	6	7	8	OCTOBER 2044
	9	10	11	12	13	14	15	
Oct 3	16	17	18	19	20	21	22	
	23	24	25	26	27	28	29	
Oct 17	30	31	1	2	3	4	5	
	6	7	8	9	10	11	12	NOVEMBER 2044
Oct 31	13	14	15	16	17	18	19	
	20	21	22	23	24	25	26	
Nov 14	27[g]	28	29	30	1	2	3	
	4	5	6	7	8	9	10	DECEMBER 2044
Nov 28	11	12	13	14	15	16	17	
	18	19	20	21	22	23	24	
Dec 12	25[h]	26	27	28	29	30	31	

‡Leap year
[a]Orthodox Christmas
[b]Julian New Year
[c]Ash Wednesday
[d]Feast of Orthodoxy
[e]Easter
[f]Orthodox Easter
[g]Advent
[h]Christmas

2045

GREGORIAN 2045 · ISO WEEK · JULIAN DAY

Month	Sun	Mon	Tue	Wed	Thu	Fri	Sat	Lunar Phases	ISO WEEK (Mon)	JULIAN DAY (Sun noon)
JANUARY 2045	1[a]	2	○	4	5	6	7	10:19	1	2467982
	8	9	◑	11	12	13	14	3:31	2	2467989
	15	16	17	●	19	20	21	4:24	3	2467996
	22	23	24	25	◐	27	28	5:08	4	2468003
FEBRUARY 2045	29	30	31	○	2	3	4	21:04	5	2468010
	5	6	7	◑	9	10	11	19:02	6	2468017
	12	13	14	15	●	17	18	23:50	7	2468024
	19	20	21	22	23	◐	25	16:35	8	2468031
MARCH 2045	26	27	28	1	2	○	4	7:51	9	2468038
	5	6	7	8	9	◑	11	12:48	10	2468045
	12	13	14	15	16	17	●	17:13	11	2468052
	19	20[b]	21	22	23	24	25		12	2468059
APRIL 2045	◐	27	28	29	30	31	○	0:55 18:42	13	2468066
	2	3	4	5	6	7	8		14	2468073
	◑	10	11	12	13	14	15	7:51	15	2468080
	16	●	18	19	20	21	22	7:25	16	2468087
	23	◐	25	26	27	28	29	7:10	17	2468094
MAY 2045	30	○	2	3	4	5	6	5:51	18	2468101
	7	8	◑	10	11	12	13	2:50	19	2468108
	14	15	●	17	18	19	20	18:25	20	2468115
	21	22	◐	24	25	26	27	12:37	21	2468122
JUNE 2045	28	29	○	31	1	2	3	17:51	22	2468129
	4	5	6	◑	8	9	10	20:22	23	2468136
	11	12	13	14	●	16	17	3:03	24	2468143
	18	19	20[c]	◐	22	23	24	18:27	25	2468150
JULY 2045	25	26	27	28	○	30	1	7:14	26	2468157
	2	3	4	5	6	◑	8	11:29	27	2468164
	9	10	11	12	13	●	15	10:27	28	2468171
	16	17	18	19	20	◐	22	1:51	29	2468178
	23	24	25	26	27	○	29	22:09	30	2468185
AUGUST 2045	30	31	1	2	3	4	◑	23:56	31	2468192
	6	7	8	9	10	11	●	17:38	32	2468199
	13	14	15	16	17	18	◐	11:54	33	2468206
	20	21	22	23	24	25	26		34	2468213
SEPTEMBER 2045	○	28	29	30	31	1	2	14:06	35	2468220
	3	◑	5	6	7	8	9	10:02	36	2468227
	10	●	12	13	14	15	16	1:26	37	2468234
	17	◐	19	20	21	22[d]	23	1:29	38	2468241
	24	25	○	27	28	29	30	6:10	39	2468248
OCTOBER 2045	1	2	◑	4	5	6	7	18:30	40	2468255
	8	9	●	11	12	13	14	10:35	41	2468262
	15	16	◐	18	19	20	21	18:54	42	2468269
	22	23	24	○	26	27	28	21:30	43	2468276
NOVEMBER 2045	29	30	31	1	◑	3	4	2:08	44	2468283
	5	6	7	●	9	10	11	21:48	45	2468290
	12	13	14	15	◐	17	18	15:24	46	2468297
	19	20	21	22	23	○	25	11:42	47	2468304
DECEMBER 2045	26	27	28	29	30	◑	2	9:45	48	2468311
	3	4	5	6	7	●	9	11:40	49	2468318
	10	11	12	13	14	15	◐	13:07	50	2468325
	17	18	19	20	21[e]	22	23		51	2468332
	○	25	26	27	28	29	◑	0:48 18:10	52	2468339
	31	1	2	3	4	5	6		1	2468346

HEBREW 5805/5806‡

ISO WEEK	Month	Sun	Mon	Tue	Wed	Thu	Fri	Sat	Molad
1	TEVETH 5805	12	13	14	15	16	17	18	
2		19	20	21	22	23	24	25	
3	SHEVAT 5805	26	27	28	29	1	2	3	Wed $7^{h}39^{m}12^{p}$
4		4	5	6	7	8	9	10	
5		11	12	13	14	15	16	17	
6		18	19	20	21	22	23	24	
7	ADAR 5805	25	26	27	28	29	30	1	Thu $20^{h}23^{m}13^{p}$
8		2	3	4	5	6	7	8	
9		9	10	11	12	13	14[f]	15	
10		16	17	18	19	20	21	22	
11		23	24	25	26	27	28	29	
12	NISAN 5805	1	2	3	4	5	6	7	Sat $9^{h}7^{m}14^{p}$
13		8	9	10	11	12	13	14	
14		15[g]	16	17	18	19	20	21	
15		22	23	24	25	26	27	28	
16	IYYAR 5805	29	30	1	2	3	4	5	Sun $21^{h}51^{m}15^{p}$
17		6	7	8	9	10	11	12	
18		13	14	15	16	17	18	19	
19		20	21	22	23	24	25	26	
20	SIVAN 5805	27	28	29	1	2	3	4	Tue $10^{h}35^{m}16^{p}$
21		5	6[h]	7	8	9	10	11	
22		12	13	14	15	16	17	18	
23		19	20	21	22	23	24	25	
24	TAMMUZ 5805	26	27	28	29	30	1	2	Wed $23^{h}19^{m}17^{p}$
25		3	4	5	6	7	8	9	
26		10	11	12	13	14	15	16	
27		17	18	19	20	21	22	23	
28	AV 5805	24	25	26	27	28	29	1	Fri $12^{h}4^{m}0^{p}$
29		2	3	4	5	6	7	8	
30		9[i]	10	11	12	13	14	15	
31		16	17	18	19	20	21	22	
32		23	24	25	26	27	28	29	
33	ELUL 5805	30	1	2	3	4	5	6	Sun $0^{h}48^{m}1^{p}$
34		7	8	9	10	11	12	13	
35		14	15	16	17	18	19	20	
36		21	22	23	24	25	26	27	
37	TISHRI 5806	28	29	1[a]	2[a]	3	4	5	Mon $13^{h}32^{m}2^{p}$
38		6	7	8	9	10[b]	11	12	
39		13	14	15[c]	16	17	18	19	
40		20	21	22	23	24	25	26	
41	HESHVAN 5806	27	28	29	30	1	2	3	Wed $2^{h}16^{m}3^{p}$
42		4	5	6	7	8	9	10	
43		11	12	13	14	15	16	17	
44		18	19	20	21	22	23	24	
45	KISLEV 5806	25	26	27	28	29	1	2	Thu $15^{h}0^{m}4^{p}$
46		3	4	5	6	7	8	9	
47		10	11	12	13	14	15	16	
48		17	18	19	20	21	22	23	
49		24	25[e]	26[d,e]	27[e]	28[e]	29[e]	30[e]	
50	TEVETH 5806	1[e]	2[e]	3	4	5	6	7	Sat $3^{h}44^{m}5^{p}$
51		8	9	10	11	12	13	14	
52		15	16	17	18	19	20	21	
1		22	23	24	25	26	27	28	

CHINESE Jiǎ-Zǐ‡/Yǐ-Chǒu

ISO WEEK	Month	Sun	Mon	Tue	Wed	Thu	Fri	Sat	Solar Term
1	MONTH 11 Jiǎ-Zǐ	14	15	16	17	*18*	19	20	Xiǎo hán
2		21	22	23*	24	25	26	27	
3	MONTH 12 Jiǎ-Zǐ	28	29	30	1	2	*3*	4	Dà hán
4		5	6	7	8	9	10	11	
5		12	13	14	15	16	*17*	18	Lì chūn
6		19	20	21	22	23	24	25	
7	MONTH 1 Yǐ-Chǒu	26	27	28	29	30	1[a]	*2*	Yǔ shuǐ
8		3	4	5	6	7	8	9	
9		10	11	12	13	14	15[b]	16	
10		*17*	18	19	20	21	22	23*	Jīng zhé
11		24	25	26	27	28	29	30	
12	MONTH 2 Yǐ-Chǒu	1	*2*	3	4	5	6	7	Chūn fēn
13		8	9	10	11	12	13	14	
14		15	16	*17*[c]	18	19	20	21	Qīng míng
15		22	23	24	25	26	27	28	
16	MONTH 3 Yǐ-Chǒu	29	1	2	*3*	4	5	6	Gǔ yǔ
17		7	8	9	10	11	12	13	
18		14	15	16	17	18	*19*	20	Lì xià
19		21	22	23	24*	25	26	27	
20	MONTH 4 Yǐ-Chǒu	28	29	30	1	2	3	*4*	Xiǎo mǎn
21		5	6	7	8	9	10	11	
22		12	13	14	15	16	17	18	
23		19	*20*	21	22	23	24	25	Máng zhòng
24	MONTH 5 Yǐ-Chǒu	26	27	28	29	1	2	3	
25		4	5[d]	6	*7*	8	9	10	Xià zhì
26		11	12	13	14	15	16	17	
27		18	19	20	21	22	*23*	24	Xiǎo shǔ
28	MONTH 6 Yǐ-Chǒu	25*	26	27	28	29	1	2	
29		3	4	5	6	7	8	*9*	Dà shǔ
30		10	11	12	13	14	15	16	
31		17	18	19	20	21	22	23	
32		24	*25*	26	27	28	29	30	Lì qiū
33	MONTH 7 Yǐ-Chǒu	1	2	3	4	5	6	7[e]	
34		8	9	10	*11*	12	13	14	Chǔ shǔ
35		15[f]	16	17	18	19	20	21	
36		22	23	24	25	26*	27	28	Bái lù
37	MONTH 8 Yǐ-Chǒu	29	1	2	3	4	5	6	
38		7	8	9	10	11	*12*	13	Qiū fēn
39		14	15[g]	16	17	18	19	20	
40		21	22	23	24	25	26	27	
41	MONTH 9 Yǐ-Chǒu	28	29	1	2	3	4	5	Hán lù
42		6	7	8	9[h]	10	11	12	
43		13	*14*	15	16	17	18	19	Shuāng jiàng
44		20	21	22	23	24	25	26	
45	MONTH 10 Yǐ-Chǒu	27	28*	29	30	1	2	3	Lì dōng
46		4	5	6	7	8	9	10	
47		11	12	13	*14*	15	16	17	Xiǎo xuě
48		18	19	20	21	22	23	24	
49	MONTH 11 Yǐ-Chǒu	25	26	27	28	29	1	2	Dà xuě
50		3	4	5	6	7	8	9	
51		10	11	12	13	*14*[i]	15	16	Dōng zhì
52		17	18	19	20	21	22	23	
1		24	25	26	27	28	*29*	30	Xiǎo hán

COPTIC 1761/1762 · ETHIOPIC 2037/2038

ISO WEEK	Coptic Month	Sun	Mon	Tue	Wed	Thu	Fri	Sat	Ethiopic Month
1	KOIAK 1761	23	24	25	26	27	28	29[c]	TĀKHŚĀŚ 2037
2		30	1	2	3	4	5	6[d]	
3	TÔBE 1761	7	8	9	10	11[e]	12	13	ṬER 2037
4		14	15	16	17	18	19	20	
5		21	22	23	24	25	26	27	
6	MESHIR 1761	28	29	30	1	2	3	4	YAKĀTIT 2037
7		5	6	7	8	9	10	11	
8		12	13	14	15	16	17	18	
9		19	20	21	22	23	24	25	
10	PAREMOTEP 1761	26	27	28	29	30	1	2	MAGĀBIT 2037
11		3	4	5	6	7	8	9	
12		10	11	12	13	14	15	16	
13		17	18	19	20	21	22	23	
14		24	25	26	27	28	29	30	
15	PARMOUTE 1761	1[f]	2	3	4	5	6	7	MIYĀZYĀ 2037
16		8	9	10	11	12	13	14	
17		15	16	17	18	19	20	21	
18		22	23	24	25	26	27	28	
19	PASHONS 1761	29[g]	30	1	2	3	4	5	GENBOT 2037
20		6	7	8	9	10	11	12	
21		13	14	15	16	17	18	19	
22		20	21	22	23	24	25	26	
23	PAÔNE 1761	27	28	29	30	1	2	3	SANÉ 2037
24		4	5	6	7	8	9	10	
25		11	12	13	14	15	16	17	
26		18	19	20	21	22	23	24	
27	EPÊP 1761	25	26	27	28	29	30	1	ḤAMLÉ 2037
28		2	3	4	5	6	7	8	
29		9	10	11	12	13	14	15	
30		16	17	18	19	20	21	22	
31		23	24	25	26	27	28	29	
32	MESORÊ 1761	30	1	2	3	4	5	6	NAHASÉ 2037
33		7	8	9	10	11	12	13[h]	
34		14	15	16	17	18	19	20	
35		21	22	23	24	25	26	27	
36	EPAG. 1761	28	29	30	1	2	3	4	PĀG. 2037
37	THOOUT 1762	5	1[a]	2	3	4	5	6	MASKARAM 2038
38		7	8	9	10	11	12	13	
39		14	15	16	17[b]	18	19	20	
40		21	22	23	24	25	26	27	
41	PAOPE 1762	28	29	30	1	2	3	4	ṬEQEMT 2038
42		5	6	7	8	9	10	11	
43		12	13	14	15	16	17	18	
44		19	20	21	22	23	24	25	
45	ATHÔR 1762	26	27	28	29	30	1	2	HEDĀR 2038
46		3	4	5	6	7	8	9	
47		10	11	12	13	14	15	16	
48		17	18	19	20	21	22	23	
49		24	25	26	27	28	29	30	
50	KOIAK 1762	1	2	3	4	5	6	7	TĀKHŚĀŚ 2038
51		8	9	10	11	12	13	14	
52		15	16	17	18	19	20	21	
1		22	23	24	25	26	27	28	

Gregorian notes:
[a]New Year
[b]Spring (5:05)
[c]Summer (22:32)
[d]Autumn (14:31)
[e]Winter (11:33)
● New moon
◐ First quarter moon
○ Full moon
◑ Last quarter moon

Hebrew notes:
‡Leap year
[a]New Year
[b]Yom Kippur
[c]Sukkot
[d]Winter starts
[e]Ḥanukkah
[f]Purim
[g]Passover
[h]Shavuot
[i]Fast of Av

Chinese notes:
‡Leap year
[a]New Year (4743, Ox)
[b]Lantern Festival
[c]Qīngmíng
[d]Dragon Festival
[e]Qīqiǎo
[f]Hungry Ghosts
[g]Mid-Autumn Festival
[h]Double-Ninth Festival
[i]Dōngzhì
*Start of 60-name cycle

Coptic/Ethiopic notes:
[a]New Year
[b]Building of the Cross
[c]Christmas
[d]Jesus's Circumcision
[e]Epiphany
[f]Easter
[g]Mary's Announcement
[h]Jesus's Transfiguration

PERSIAN (ASTRONOMICAL) 1423/1424‡

Month	Sun	Mon	Tue	Wed	Thu	Fri	Sat
DEY 1423	12	13	14	15	16	17	18
	19	20	21	22	23	24	25
	26	27	28	29	30	1	2
BAHMAN 1423	3	4	5	6	7	8	9
	10	11	12	13	14	15	16
	17	18	19	20	21	22	23
	24	25	26	27	28	29	30
ESFAND 1423	1	2	3	4	5	6	7
	8	9	10	11	12	13	14
	15	16	17	18	19	20	21
	22	23	24	25	26	27	28
	29	1[a]	2	3	4	5	6
FARVARDĪN 1424	7	8	9	10	11	12	13[b]
	14	15	16	17	18	19	20
	21	22	23	24	25	26	27
	28	29	30	31	1	2	3
ORDĪBEHEŠT 1424	4	5	6	7	8	9	10
	11	12	13	14	15	16	17
	18	19	20	21	22	23	24
	25	26	27	28	29	30	31
XORDĀD 1424	1	2	3	4	5	6	7
	8	9	10	11	12	13	14
	15	16	17	18	19	20	21
	22	23	24	25	26	27	28
	29	30	31	1	2	3	4
TĪR 1424	5	6	7	8	9	10	11
	12	13	14	15	16	17	18
	19	20	21	22	23	24	25
	26	27	28	29	30	31	1
MORDĀD 1424	2	3	4	5	6	7	8
	9	10	11	12	13	14	15
	16	17	18	19	20	21	22
	23	24	25	26	27	28	29
	30	31	1	2	3	4	5
SHAHRĪVAR 1424	6	7	8	9	10	11	12
	13	14	15	16	17	18	19
	20	21	22	23	24	25	26
	27	28	29	30	31	1	2
MEHR 1424	3	4	5	6	7	8	9
	10	11	12	13	14	15	16
	17	18	19	20	21	22	23
	24	25	26	27	28	29	30
ĀBĀN 1424	1	2	3	4	5	6	7
	8	9	10	11	12	13	14
	15	16	17	18	19	20	21
	22	23	24	25	26	27	28
	29	30	1	2	3	4	5
ĀZAR 1424	6	7	8	9	10	11	12
	13	14	15	16	17	18	19
	20	21	22	23	24	25	26
	27	28	29	30	1	2	3
DEY 1424	4	5	6	7	8	9	10
	11	12	13	14	15	16	17

HINDU LUNAR 2101/2102‡

Month	Sun	Mon	Tue	Wed	Thu	Fri	Sat
PAUSHA 2101	13	14	15	16	17	18	19
	21	22	23	24	25	26	27
	28	29	30	30	1	2	3
MĀGHA 2101	4	5	6	7	8	9	10
	11	12	13	15	16	17	18
	19	20	21	22	23	24	25
	26	27	28	29[h]	30	1	2
PHĀLGUNA 2101	2	3	4	5	6	8	9
	10	11	12	13	14	15[i]	16
	17	18	19	20	21	22	23
	24	25	26	27	28	29	30
	1[a]	2	3	4	5	6	7
CHAITRA 2102	8	9[b]	10	11	13	14	15
	16	17	18	19	20	21	22
	23	24	25	25	26	27	28
	29	30	1	2	3	4	5
VAIŚĀKHA 2102	7	8	9	10	11	12	13
	14	15	16	17	18	19	20
	21	22	23	24	25	26	27
	28	29	30	1	2	3	4
LEAP JYAISHṬHA 2102	5	6	7	8	10	11	12
	13	14	15	16	17	18	19
	20	21	21	22	23	24	25
	26	27	28	29	30	1	3
JYAISHṬHA 2102	4	5	6	7	8	9	10
	11	12	13	14	15	16	17
	18	19	20	21	22	23	24
	25	26	27	28	29	30	1
ĀSHĀḌHA 2102	2	3	4	6	7	8	9
	10	11	12	13	14	15	16
	17	17	18	19	20	21	22
	23	24	25	26	27	29	30
	1	2	3	4	5	6	7
ŚRĀVAṆA 2102	8	9	10	11	12	13	14
	15	16	17	18	19	20	21
	22	23[c]	24	25	26	27	28
	29	30	2	3	4[d]	5	6
BHĀDRAPADA 2102	7	8	9	10	11	12	13
	13	14	15	16	17	18	19
	20	21	22	23	25	26	27
	28	29	30	1	2	3	4
ĀŚVINA 2102	5	6	7	8[e]	9[e]	10[e]	11
	12	13	14	15	16	17	18
	19	20	21	22	23	24	25
	26	27	29	30	1[f]	2	3
KĀRTTIKA 2102	4	5	6	7	7	8	9
	10	11	12	13	14	15	16
	17	18	19	20	21	23	24
	25	26	27	28	29	30	1
MĀRGAŚĪRA 2102	2	3	4	5	6	7	8
	9	10	10	11[g]	12	13	14
	16	17	18	19	20	21	22
	23	24	25	26	27	28	29

HINDU SOLAR 1966‡/1967

Month	Sun	Mon	Tue	Wed	Thu	Fri	Sat
PAUSHA 1966	17	18	19	20	21	22	23
	24	25	26	27	28	29	1[b]
MĀGHA 1966	2	3	4	5	6	7	8
	9	10	11	12	13	14	15
	16	17	18	19	20	21	22
	23	24	25	26	27	28	29
	1	2	3	4	5	6	7
PHĀLGUNA 1966	8	9	10	11	12	13	14
	15	16	17	18	19	20	21
	22	23	24	25	26	27	28
	29	30	1	2	3	4	5
CHAITRA 1966	6	7	8	9	10	11	12
	13	14	15	16	17	18	19
	20	21	22	23	24	25	26
	27	28	29	30	31	1[a]	2
VAIŚĀKHA 1967	3	4	5	6	7	8	9
	10	11	12	13	14	15	16
	17	18	19	20	21	22	23
	24	25	26	27	28	29	30
	31	1	2	3	4	5	6
JYAISHṬHA 1967	7	8	9	10	11	12	13
	14	15	16	17	18	19	20
	21	22	23	24	25	26	27
	28	29	30	31	1	2	3
ĀSHĀḌHA 1967	4	5	6	7	8	9	10
	11	12	13	14	15	16	17
	18	19	20	21	22	23	24
	25	26	27	28	29	30	31
	32	1	2	3	4	5	6
ŚRĀVAṆA 1967	7	8	9	10	11	12	13
	14	15	16	17	18	19	20
	21	22	23	24	25	26	27
	28	29	30	31	1	2	3
BHĀDRAPADA 1967	4	5	6	7	8	9	10
	11	12	13	14	15	16	17
	18	19	20	21	22	23	24
	25	26	27	28	29	30	31
	1	2	3	4	5	6	7
ĀŚVINA 1967	8	9	10	11	12	13	14
	15	16	17	18	19	20	21
	22	23	24	25	26	27	28
	29	30	31	1	2	3	4
KĀRTTIKA 1967	5	6	7	8	9	10	11
	12	13	14	15	16	17	18
	19	20	21	22	23	24	25
	26	27	28	29	1	2	3
MĀRGAŚĪRA 1967	4	5	6	7	8	9	10
	11	12	13	14	15	16	17
	18	19	20	21	22	23	24
	25	26	27	28	29	30	1
PAUSHA 1967	2	3	4	5	6	7	8
	9	10	11	12	13	14	15
	16	17	18	19	20	21	22

ISLAMIC (ASTRONOMICAL) 1467/1468

Month	Sun	Mon	Tue	Wed	Thu	Fri	Sat
ṢAFAR 1467	12	13	14	15	16	17	18
	19	20	21	22	23	24	25
	26	27	28	29	30	1	2
RABĪʿ I 1467	3	4	5	6	7	8	9
	10	11	12[c]	13	14	15	16
	17	18	19	20	21	22	23
	24	25	26	27	28	29	1
RABĪʿ II 1467	2	3	4	5	6	7	8
	9	10	11	12	13	14	15
	16	17	18	19	20	21	22
	23	24	25	26	27	28	29
	30	1	2	3	4	5	6
JUMĀDĀ I 1467	7	8	9	10	11	12	13
	14	15	16	17	18	19	20
	21	22	23	24	25	26	27
	28	29	1	2	3	4	5
JUMĀDĀ II 1467	6	7	8	9	10	11	12
	13	14	15	16	17	18	19
	20	21	22	23	24	25	26
	27	28	29	30	1	2	3
RAJAB 1467	4	5	6	7	8	9	10
	11	12	13	14	15	16	17
	18	19	20	21	22	23	24
	25	26	27[d]	28	29	1	2
SHAʿBĀN 1467	3	4	5	6	7	8	9
	10	11	12	13	14	15	16
	17	18	19	20	21	22	23
	24	25	26	27	28	29	30
RAMAḌĀN 1467	1[e]	2	3	4	5	6	7
	8	9	10	11	12	13	14
	15	16	17	18	19	20	21
	22	23	24	25	26	27	28
	29	1[f]	2	3	4	5	6
SHAWWĀL 1467	7	8	9	10	11	12	13
	14	15	16	17	18	19	20
	21	22	23	24	25	26	27
	28	29	30	1	2	3	4
DHU AL-QAʿDA 1467	5	6	7	8	9	10	11
	12	13	14	15	16	17	18
	19	20	21	22	23	24	25
	26	27	28	29	30	1	2
DHU AL-ḤIJJA 1467	3	4	5	6	7	8	9
	10[g]	11	12	13	14	15	16
	17	18	19	20	21	22	23
	24	25	26	27	28	29	1[a]
MUḤARRAM 1468	2	3	4	5	6	7	8
	9	10[b]	11	12	13	14	15
	16	17	18	19	20	21	22
	23	24	25	26	27	28	29
ṢAFAR 1468	1	2	3	4	5	6	7
	8	9	10	11	12	13	14
	15	16	17	18	19	20	21
	22	23	24	25	26	27	28

GREGORIAN 2045

Julian (Sun)	Sun	Mon	Tue	Wed	Thu	Fri	Sat	Month
Dec 19	1	2	3	4	5	6	7[a]	JANUARY 2045
	8	9	10	11	12	13	14[b]	
Jan 2	15	16	17	18	19	20	21	
	22	23	24	25	26	27	28	
Jan 16	29	30	31	1	2	3	4	FEBRUARY 2045
	5	6	7	8	9	10	11	
Jan 30	12	13	14	15	16	17	18	
	19	20	21	22[c]	23	24	25	
Feb 13	26[d]	27	28	1	2	3	4	MARCH 2045
	5	6	7	8	9	10	11	
Feb 27	12	13	14	15	16	17	18	
	19	20	21	22	23	24	25	
Mar 13	26	27	28	29	30	31	1	APRIL 2045
	2	3	4	5	6	7	8	
Mar 27	9[e]	10	11	12	13	14	15	
	16	17	18	19	20	21	22	
Apr 10	23	24	25	26	27	28	29	
	30	1	2	3	4	5	6	MAY 2045
Apr 24	7	8	9	10	11	12	13	
	14	15	16	17	18	19	20	
May 8	21	22	23	24	25	26	27	
	28	29	30	31	1	2	3	JUNE 2045
May 22	4	5	6	7	8	9	10	
	11	12	13	14	15	16	17	
Jun 5	18	19	20	21	22	23	24	
	25	26	27	28	29	30	1	JULY 2045
Jun 19	2	3	4	5	6	7	8	
	9	10	11	12	13	14	15	
Jul 3	16	17	18	19	20	21	22	
	23	24	25	26	27	28	29	
Jul 17	30	31	1	2	3	4	5	AUGUST 2045
	6	7	8	9	10	11	12	
Jul 31	13	14	15	16	17	18	19	
	20	21	22	23	24	25	26	
Aug 14	27	28	29	30	31	1	2	SEPTEMBER 2045
	3	4	5	6	7	8	9	
Aug 28	10	11	12	13	14	15	16	
	17	18	19	20	21	22	23	
Sep 11	24	25	26	27	28	29	30	
	1	2	3	4	5	6	7	OCTOBER 2045
Sep 25	8	9	10	11	12	13	14	
	15	16	17	18	19	20	21	
Oct 9	22	23	24	25	26	27	28	
	29	30	31	1	2	3	4	NOVEMBER 2045
Oct 23	5	6	7	8	9	10	11	
	12	13	14	15	16	17	18	
Nov 6	19	20	21	22	23	24	25	
	26	27	28	29	30	1	2	DECEMBER 2045
Nov 20	3[g]	4	5	6	7	8	9	
	10	11	12	13	14	15	16	
Dec 4	17	18	19	20	21	22	23	
	24	25[h]	26	27	28	29	30	
Dec 18	31	1	2	3	4	5	6	

Persian: ‡Leap year; [a]New Year; [b]Sizdeh Bedar

Hindu Lunar: ‡Leap year; [a]New Year (Krodhana); [b]Birthday of Rāma; [c]Birthday of Krishna; [d]Ganēśa Chaturthī; [e]Dashara; [f]Diwali; [g]Birthday of Vishnu; [h]Night of Śiva; [i]Holi

Hindu Solar: ‡Leap year; [a]New Year (Pramāthin); [b]Pongal

Islamic: [a]New Year; [b]ʿAshūrāʾ; [c]Prophet's Birthday; [d]Ascent of the Prophet; [e]Start of Ramaḍān; [f]ʿId al-Fiṭr; [g]ʿId al-ʾAḍḥā

Gregorian: [a]Orthodox Christmas; [b]Julian New Year; [c]Ash Wednesday; [d]Feast of Orthodoxy; [e]Easter (also Orthodox); [g]Advent; [h]Christmas

2046

Gregorian 2046	Sun	Mon	Tue	Wed	Thu	Fri	Sat	Lunar Phases	ISO Week (Mon)	Julian Day (Sun noon)	Hebrew 5806‡/5807	Sun	Mon	Tue	Wed	Thu	Fri	Sat	Molad	Chinese Yǐ-Chǒu/Bǐng-Yín	Sun	Mon	Tue	Wed	Thu	Fri	Sat	Solar Term	Coptic 1762/1763‡	Sun	Mon	Tue	Wed	Thu	Fri	Sat	Ethiopic 2038/2039‡
January 2046	31	1[a]	2	3	4	5	6		1	2468346	Teveth 5806	22	23	24	25	26	27	28		Month 12 Yǐ-Chǒu	24	25	26	27	28	29*	30	Xiǎo hán	Koiak 1762	22	23	24	25	26	27	28	Tākhśāś 2038
	●	8	9	10	11	12	13	4:23	2	2468353	Shevat 5806	29	1	2	3	4	5	6	Sun 16h28m6p		1	2	3	4	5	6	7		Tōbe 1762	29[c]	30	1	2	3	4	5	Ṭer 2038
	14	◐	16	17	18	19	20	9:41	3	2468360		7	8	9	10	11	12	13			8	9	10	11	12	13	**14**	Dà hán		6[d]	7	8	9	10	11[e]	12	
	21	○	23	24	25	26	27	12:50	4	2468367		14	15	16	17	18	19	20			15	16	17	18	19	20	21			13	14	15	16	17	18	19	
February 2046	28	◑	30	31	1	2	3	4:10	5	2468374		21	22	23	24	25	26	27			22	23	24	25	26	27	28			20	21	22	23	24	25	26	
	4	●	6	7	8	9	10	23:08	6	2468381	Adar I 5806	28	29	30	1	2	3	4	Tue 5h12m7p	Month 1 Bǐng-Yín	29	30	1[a]	2	3	4	5	Lì chūn	Meshir 1762	27	28	29	30	1	2	3	Yakātit 2038
	11	12	13	◐	15	16	17	3:19	7	2468388		5	6	7	8	9	10	11			6	7	8	9	10	11	12			4	5	6	7	8	9	10	
	18	19	○	21	22	23	24	23:43	8	2468395		12	13	14	15	16	17	18			**13**	14	15[b]	16	17	18	19	Yǔ shuǐ		11	12	13	14	15	16	17	
March 2046	25	26	◑	28	1	2	3	16:22	9	2468402		19	20	21	22	23	24	25			20	21	22	23	24	25	26			18	19	20	21	22	23	24	
	4	5	6	●	8	9	10	18:14	10	2468409	Adar II 5806	26	27	28	29	30	1	2	Wed 17h56m8p	Month 2 Bǐng-Yín	27	28	29*	30	1	2	3	Jīng zhé	Paremotep 1762	25	26	27	28	29	30	1	Magābit 2038
	11	12	13	14	◐	16	17	17:11	11	2468416		3	4	5	6	7	8	9			4	5	6	7	8	9	10			2	3	4	5	6	7	8	
	18	19	20[b]	21	○	23	24	9:25	12	2468423		10	11	12	13	14[f]	15	16			11	12	**13**	14	15	16	17	Chūn fēn		9	10	11	12	13	14	15	
	25	26	27	28	◑	30	31	6:56	13	2468430		17	18	19	20	21	22	23			18	19	20	21	22	23	24			16	17	18	19	20	21	22	
April 2046	1	2	3	4	5	●	7	11:50	14	2468437	Nisan 5806	24	25	26	27	28	29	1	Fri 6h40m9p	Month 3 Bǐng-Yín	25	26	27	28[c]	29	1	2	Qīng míng		23	24	25	26	27	28	29	
	8	9	10	11	12	13	◐	3:20	15	2468444		2	3	4	5	6	7	8			3	4	5	6	7	8	9		Parmoute 1762	30	1	2	3	4	5	6	Miyāzyā 2038
	15	16	17	18	19	○	21	18:19	16	2468451		9	10	11	12	13	14	15[g]			10	11	12	13	14	**15**	16	Gǔ yǔ		7	8	9	10	11	12	13	
	22	23	24	25	26	◑	28	23:29	17	2468458		16	17	18	19	20	21	22			17	18	19	20	21	22	23			14	15	16	17	18	19	20	
May 2046	29	30	1	2	3	4	5		18	2468465		23	24	25	26	27	28	29			24	25	26	27	28	29	30*	Lì xià		21[f]	22	23	24	25	26	27	
	●	7	8	9	10	11	12	2:54	19	2468472	Iyar 5806	30	1	2	3	4	5	6	Sat 19h24m10p	Month 4 Bǐng-Yín	1	2	3	4	5	6	7		Pashons 1762	28	29[g]	30	1	2	3	4	Genbot 2038
	◐	14	15	16	17	18	19	10:23	20	2468479		7	8	9	10	11	12	13			8	9	10	11	12	13	14			5	6	7	8	9	10	11	
	○	21	22	23	24	25	26	3:14	21	2468486		14	15	16	17	18	19	20			15	**16**	17	18	19	20	21	Xiǎo mǎn		12	13	14	15	16	17	18	
June 2046	◑	28	29	30	31	1	2	17:05	22	2468493		21	22	23	24	25	26	27			22	23	24	25	26	27	28			19	20	21	22	23	24	25	
	3	●	5	6	7	8	9	15:21	23	2468500	Sivan 5806	28	29	1	2	3	4	5	Mon 8h8m11p	Month 5 Bǐng-Yín	29	1	2	3	4	5[d]	6	Máng zhòng	Paōne 1762	26	27	28	29	30	1	2	Sanē 2038
	10	◐	12	13	14	15	16	15:26	24	2468507		6[h]	7	8	9	10	11	12			7	8	9	10	11	12	13			3	4	5	6	7	8	9	
	17	○	19	20	21[c]	22	23	13:08	25	2468514		13	14	15	16	17	18	19			14	15	16	17	**18**	19	20	Xià zhì		10	11	12	13	14	15	16	
	24	25	◑	27	28	29	30	10:38	26	2468521		20	21	22	23	24	25	26			21	22	23	24	25	26	27			17	18	19	20	21	22	23	
July 2046	1	2	3	●	5	6	7	1:37	27	2468528	Tammuz 5806	27	28	29	30	1	2	3	Tue 20h52m12p	Month 6 Bǐng-Yín	28	29	30	1*	2	3	4	Xiǎo shǔ		24	25	26	27	28	29	30	
	8	9	◐	11	12	13	14	19:52	28	2468535		4	5	6	7	8	9	10			5	6	7	8	9	10	11		Epēp 1762	1	2	3	4	5	6	7	Ḥamlē 2038
	15	16	17	○	19	20	21	0:53	29	2468542		11	12	13	14	15	16	17			12	13	14	15	16	17	18			8	9	10	11	12	13	14	
	22	23	24	25	◑	27	28	3:18	30	2468549		18	19	20	21	22	23	24			**19**	20	21	22	23	24	25	Dà shǔ		15	16	17	18	19	20	21	
August 2046	29	30	31	1	●	3	4	10:24	31	2468556	Av 5806	25	26	27	28	29	1	2	Thu 9h36m13p	Month 7 Bǐng-Yín	26	27	28	29	1	2	3			22	23	24	25	26	27	28	
	5	6	7	8	◐	10	11	1:14	32	2468563		3	4	5	6	7	8	9			4	5	6	7[e]	8	9	10	Lì qiū	Mesorē 1762	29	30	1	2	3	4	5	Naḥasē 2038
	12	13	14	15	○	17	18	14:49	33	2468570		10[i]	11	12	13	14	15	16			11	12	13	14	15[f]	16	17			6	7	8	9	10	11	12	
	19	20	21	22	23	◑	25	18:35	34	2468577		17	18	19	20	21	22	23			18	19	20	21	**22**	23	24	Chǔ shǔ		13[h]	14	15	16	17	18	19	
September 2046	26	27	28	29	30	●	1	18:24	35	2468584		24	25	26	27	28	29	30		Month 8 Bǐng-Yín	25	26	27	28	29	30	1			20	21	22	23	24	25	26	
	2	3	4	5	6	◐	8	9:05	36	2468591	Elul 5806	1	2	3	4	5	6	7	Fri 22h20m14p		2*	3	4	5	6	7	8	Bái lù	Epag. 1762	27	28	29	30	1	2	3	Pāg. 2038
	9	10	11	12	13	14	○	6:38	37	2468598		8	9	10	11	12	13	14			9	10	11	12	13	14	15[g]		Thoout 1763	4	5	1[a]	2	3	4	5	Maskaram 2039
	16	17	18	19	20	21	22[d]		38	2468605		15	16	17	18	19	20	21			16	17	18	19	20	21	22			6	7	8	9	10	11	12	
	◑	24	25	26	27	28	29	8:14	39	2468612		22	23	24	25	26	27	28			**23**	24	25	26	27	28	29	Qiū fēn		13	14	15	16	17[b]	18	19	
October 2046	●	1	2	3	4	5	◐	2:24 20:40	40	2468619	Tishri 5807	29	1[a]	2[a]	3	4	5	6	Sun 11h4m15p	Month 9 Bǐng-Yín	1	2	3	4	5	6	7			20	21	22	23	24	25	26	
	7	8	9	10	11	12	13		41	2468626		7	8	9	10[b]	11	12	13			8	9[h]	10	11	12	13	14	Hán lù	Paope 1763	27	28	29	30	1	2	3	Ṭeqemt 2039
	○	15	16	17	18	19	20	23:40	42	2468633		14	15[c]	16	17	18	19	20			15	16	17	18	19	20	21			4	5	6	7	8	9	10	
	21	◑	23	24	25	26	27	20:06	43	2468640		21	22	23	24	25	26	27			22	23	**24**	25	26	27	28	Shuāng jiàng		11	12	13	14	15	16	17	
November 2046	28	●	30	31	1	2	3	11:16	44	2468647	Heshvan 5807	28	29	30	1	2	3	4	Mon 23h48m16p	Month 10 Bǐng-Yín	29	1	2	3	4*	5	6			18	19	20	21	22	23	24	
	4	◐	6	7	8	9	10	12:27	45	2468654		5	6	7	8	9	10	11			7	8	9	10	11	12	13	Lì dōng	Athōr 1763	25	26	27	28	29	30	1	Hedār 2039
	11	12	○	14	15	16	17	17:03	46	2468661		12	13	14	15	16	17	18			14	15	16	17	18	19	20			2	3	4	5	6	7	8	
	18	19	20	◑	22	23	24	6:09	47	2468668		19	20	21	22	23	24	25			21	22	23	24	**25**	26	27	Xiǎo xuě		9	10	11	12	13	14	15	
December 2046	25	26	●	28	29	30	1	21:49	48	2468675	Kislev 5807	26	27	28	29	30	1	2		Month 11 Bǐng-Yín	28	29	30	1	2	3	4			16	17	18	19	20	21	22	
	2	3	4	◐	6	7	8	7:55	49	2468682		3	4	5	6[d]	7	8	9	Wed 12h32m17p		5	6	7	8	9	10	11	Dà xuě		23	24	25	26	27	28	29	
	9	10	11	12	○	14	15	9:54	50	2468689		10	11	12	13	14	15	16			12	13	14	15	16	17	18		Koiak 1763	30	1	2	3	4	5	6	Tākhśāś 2039
	16	17	18	19	◑	21[e]	22	14:42	51	2468696		17	18	19	20	21	22	23			19	20	21	22	23	24	25[i]	Dōng zhì		7	8	9	10	11	12	13	
	23	24	25	26	●	28	29	10:37	52	2468703		24	25[e]	26[e]	27[e]	28[e]	29[e]	30[e]	Fri 1h17m0p	Month 12 Bǐng-Yín	26	27	28	29	1	2	3			14	15	16	17	18	19	20	
	30	31	1	2	3	◐	5	5:30	1	2468710		1[e]	2[e]	3	4	5	6	7			4	5*	6	7	8	9	10	Xiǎo hán		21	22	23	24	25	26	27	

[a]New Year
[b]Spring (10:56)
[c]Summer (4:13)
[d]Autumn (20:20)
[e]Winter (17:26)
● New moon
◐ First quarter moon
○ Full moon
◑ Last quarter moon

‡Leap year
[a]New Year
[b]Yom Kippur
[c]Sukkot
[d]Winter starts
[e]Ḥanukkah
[f]Purim
[g]Passover
[h]Shavuot
[i]Fast of Av

[a]New Year (4744, Tiger)
[b]Lantern Festival
[c]Qīngmíng
[d]Dragon Festival
[e]Qīqiǎo
[f]Hungry Ghosts
[g]Mid-Autumn Festival
[h]Double-Ninth Festival
[i]Dōngzhì
*Start of 60-name cycle

‡Leap year
[a]New Year
[b]Building of the Cross
[c]Christmas
[d]Jesus's Circumcision
[e]Epiphany
[f]Easter
[g]Mary's Announcement
[h]Jesus's Transfiguration

PERSIAN (ASTRONOMICAL) 1424‡/1425

Month	Sun	Mon	Tue	Wed	Thu	Fri	Sat
DEY 1424	11	12	13	14	15	16	17
	18	19	20	21	22	23	24
	25	26	27	28	29	30	*1*
BAHMAN 1424	2	3	4	5	6	7	8
	9	10	11	12	13	14	15
	16	17	18	19	20	21	22
	23	24	25	26	27	28	29
	30	*1*	2	3	4	5	6
ESFAND 1424	7	8	9	10	11	12	13
	14	15	16	17	18	19	20
	21	22	23	24	25	26	27
	28	29	30	*1*[a]	2	3	4
FARVARDĪN 1425	5	6	7	8	9	10	11
	12	13[b]	14	15	16	17	18
	19	20	21	22	23	24	25
	26	27	28	29	30	31	*1*
ORDĪBEHEŠT 1425	2	3	4	5	6	7	8
	9	10	11	12	13	14	15
	16	17	18	19	20	21	22
	23	24	25	26	27	28	29
	30	31	*1*	2	3	4	5
XORDĀD 1425	6	7	8	9	10	11	12
	13	14	15	16	17	18	19
	20	21	22	23	24	25	26
	27	28	29	30	31	*1*	2
TĪR 1425	3	4	5	6	7	8	9
	10	11	12	13	14	15	16
	17	18	19	20	21	22	23
	24	25	26	27	28	29	30
	31	*1*	2	3	4	5	6
MORDĀD 1425	7	8	9	10	11	12	13
	14	15	16	17	18	19	20
	21	22	23	24	25	26	27
	28	29	30	31	*1*	2	3
SHAHRĪVAR 1425	4	5	6	7	8	9	10
	11	12	13	14	15	16	17
	18	19	20	21	22	23	24
	25	26	27	28	29	30	31
MEHR 1425	*1*	2	3	4	5	6	7
	8	9	10	11	12	13	14
	15	16	17	18	19	20	21
	22	23	24	25	26	27	28
	29	30	*1*	2	3	4	5
ĀBĀN 1425	6	7	8	9	10	11	12
	13	14	15	16	17	18	19
	20	21	22	23	24	25	26
	27	28	29	30	*1*	2	3
ĀZAR 1425	4	5	6	7	8	9	10
	11	12	13	14	15	16	17
	18	19	20	21	22	23	24
	25	26	27	28	29	30	*1*
DEY 1425	2	3	4	5	6	7	8
	9	10	11	12	13	14	15

‡Leap year
[a]New Year
[b]Sizdeh Bedar

HINDU LUNAR 2102‡/2103

Month	Sun	Mon	Tue	Wed	Thu	Fri	Sat
MĀRGAŚĪRA 2102	23	24	25	26	27	28	29
PAUSHA 2102	30	1	2	3	4	5	6
	7	8	9	10	11	12	13
	14	15	16	17	18	19	**20**
	22	23	24	25	26	27	28
MĀGHA 2102	29	30	1	2	2	3	4
	5	6	7	8	9	10	11
	12	13	**14**	16	17	18	19
	20	21	22	23	24	25	26
	27	28[h]	29	30	1	2	3
PHĀLGUNA 2102	4	5	6	7	8	9	10
	11	12	13	14	15[i]	16	17
	18	**19**	21	22	23	24	25
	25	26	27	28	29	30	1[a]
CHAITRA 2103	2	3	4	5	6	7	8
	9[b]	10	11	**12**	14	15	16
	17	18	19	20	21	22	23
	24	25	26	27	28	29	*29*
	30	1	2	3	4	**5**	7
VAIŚĀKHA 2103	8	9	10	11	12	13	14
	15	16	17	18	19	20	21
	22	23	24	25	26	27	28
	29	30	1	2	3	4	5
JYAISHṬHA 2103	6	7	**8**	10	11	12	13
	14	15	16	17	18	19	20
	21	22	23	24	25	*25*	26
	27	28	29	30	**1**	3	4
ĀSHĀḌHA 2103	5	6	7	8	9	10	11
	12	**13**	15	16	*16*	17	18
	19	20	21	22	23	24	25
	26	27	28	29	30	1	2
ŚRĀVAṆA 2103	3	**4**	6	7	8	9	10
	11	12	13	14	15	16	17
	18	19	20	21	22	*22*	23[c]
	24	25	**26**	28	29	30	1
BHĀDRAPADA 2103	2	3	4[d]	5	6	7	**8**
	10	11	12	13	*13*	14	15
	16	17	18	19	20	21	22
	23	24	25	26	27	28	29
ĀŚVINA 2103	**30**	2	3	4	5	6	7
	8[e]	9[e]	10[e]	11	12	13	14
	15	16	17	*17*	18	19	20
	21	22	**23**	25	26	27	28
KĀRTTIKA 2103	29	30	1[f]	2	3	4	5
	6	7	8	9	10	11	12
	13	14	15	16	17	18	19
	20	21	22	23	24	25	26
	27	**28**	30	1	2	3	4
MĀRGAŚĪRA 2103	5	6	7	8	9	10	*10*
	11[g]	12	13	14	15	16	17
	18	19	20	21	**22**	24	25
PAUSHA 2103	26	27	28	29	30	1	2
	3	4	5	6	7	8	9

‡Leap year
[a]New Year (Kshaya)
[b]Birthday of Rāma
[c]Birthday of Krishna
[d]Ganēśa Chaturthī
[e]Dashara
[f]Diwali
[g]Birthday of Vishnu
[h]Night of Śiva
[i]Holi

HINDU SOLAR 1967/1968

Month	Sun	Mon	Tue	Wed	Thu	Fri	Sat
PAUSHA 1967	16	17	18	19	20	21	22
	23	24	25	26	27	28	29
MĀGHA 1967	1[b]	2	3	4	5	6	7
	8	9	10	11	12	13	14
	15	16	17	18	19	20	21
	22	23	24	25	26	27	28
PHĀLGUNA 1967	29	30	1	2	3	4	5
	6	7	8	9	10	11	12
	13	14	15	16	17	18	19
	20	21	22	23	24	25	26
CHAITRA 1967	27	28	29	30	1	2	3
	4	5	6	7	8	9	10
	11	12	13	14	15	16	17
	18	19	20	21	22	23	24
VAIŚĀKHA 1968	25	26	27	28	29	30	1[a]
	2	3	4	5	6	7	8
	9	10	11	12	13	14	15
	16	17	18	19	20	21	22
	23	24	25	26	27	28	29
JYAISHṬHA 1968	30	31	1	2	3	4	5
	6	7	8	9	10	11	12
	13	14	15	16	17	18	19
	20	21	22	23	24	25	26
ĀSHĀḌHA 1968	27	28	29	30	31	1	2
	3	4	5	6	7	8	9
	10	11	12	13	14	15	16
	17	18	19	20	21	22	23
	24	25	26	27	28	29	30
ŚRĀVAṆA 1968	31	32	1	2	3	4	5
	6	7	8	9	10	11	12
	13	14	15	16	17	18	19
	20	21	22	23	24	25	26
BHĀDRAPADA 1968	27	28	29	30	31	1	2
	3	4	5	6	7	8	9
	10	11	12	13	14	15	16
	17	18	19	20	21	22	23
	24	25	26	27	28	29	30
ĀŚVINA 1968	31	1	2	3	4	5	6
	7	8	9	10	11	12	13
	14	15	16	17	18	19	20
	21	22	23	24	25	26	27
KĀRTTIKA 1968	28	29	30	31	1	2	3
	4	5	6	7	8	9	10
	11	12	13	14	15	16	17
	18	19	20	21	22	23	24
MĀRGAŚĪRA 1968	25	26	27	28	29	30	1
	2	3	4	5	6	7	8
	9	10	11	12	13	14	15
	16	17	18	19	20	21	22
	23	24	25	26	27	28	29
PAUSHA 1968	1	2	3	4	5	6	7
	8	9	10	11	12	13	14
	15	16	17	18	19	20	21

[a]New Year (Vikrama)
[b]Pongal

ISLAMIC (ASTRONOMICAL) 1468/1469‡

Month	Sun	Mon	Tue	Wed	Thu	Fri	Sat
ṢAFAR 1468	22	23	24	25	26	27	28
RABĪ' I 1468	29	30	*1*	2	3	4	5
	6	7	8	9	10	11	12[c]
	13	14	15	16	17	18	19
	20	21	22	23	24	25	26
RABĪ' II 1468	27	28	29	1	2	3	4
	5	6	7	8	9	10	11
	12	13	14	15	16	17	18
	19	20	21	22	23	24	25
JUMĀDĀ I 1468	26	27	28	29	30	*1*	2
	3	4	5	6	7	8	9
	10	11	12	13	14	15	16
	17	18	19	20	21	22	23
	24	25	26	27	28	29	30
JUMĀDĀ II 1468	*1*	2	3	4	5	6	7
	8	9	10	11	12	13	14
	15	16	17	18	19	20	21
	22	23	24	25	26	27	28
RAJAB 1468	29	*1*	2	3	4	5	6
	7	8	9	10	11	12	13
	14	15	16	17	18	19	20
	21	22	23	24	25	26	27[d]
SHA'BĀN 1468	28	29	30	*1*	2	3	4
	5	6	7	8	9	10	11
	12	13	14	15	16	17	18
	19	20	21	22	23	24	25
RAMAḌĀN 1468	26	27	28	29	*1*[e]	2	3
	4	5	6	7	8	9	10
	11	12	13	14	15	16	17
	18	19	20	21	22	23	24
SHAWWĀL 1468	25	26	27	28	29	30	*1*[f]
	2	3	4	5	6	7	8
	9	10	11	12	13	14	15
	16	17	18	19	20	21	22
	23	24	25	26	27	28	29
DHU AL-QA'DA 1468	*30*	1	2	3	4	5	6
	7	8	9	10	11	12	13
	14	15	16	17	18	19	20
	21	22	23	24	25	26	27
DHU AL-ḤIJJA 1468	28	29	*1*	2	3	4	5
	6	7	8	9	10[g]	11	12
	13	14	15	16	17	18	19
	20	21	22	23	24	25	26
MUḤARRAM 1469	27	28	29	*1*[a]	2	3	4
	5	6	7	8	9	10[b]	11
	12	13	14	15	16	17	18
	19	20	21	22	23	24	25
ṢAFAR 1469	26	27	28	29	1	2	3
	4	5	6	7	8	9	10
	11	12	13	14	15	16	17
	18	19	20	21	22	23	24
RABĪ' I 1469	25	26	27	28	29	30	*1*
	2	3	4	5	6	7	8

‡Leap year
[a]New Year
[b]'Ashūrā'
[c]Prophet's Birthday
[d]Ascent of the Prophet
[e]Start of Ramaḍān
[f]'Id al-Fiṭr
[g]'Id al-'Aḍḥā

GREGORIAN 2046

Julian (Sun)	Sun	Mon	Tue	Wed	Thu	Fri	Sat	Month
Dec 18	*31*	1	2	3	4	5	6	JANUARY 2046
	7[a]	8	9	10	11	12	13	
Jan 1	*14*[b]	15	16	17	18	19	20	
	21	22	23	24	25	26	27	
Jan 15	*28*	29	30	31	1	2	3	FEBRUARY 2046
	4	5	6	7[c]	8	9	10	
Jan 29	*11*	12	13	14	15	16	17	
	18	19	20	21	22	23	24	
Feb 12	*25*	26	27	28	1	2	3	MARCH 2046
	4	5	6	7	8	9	10	
Feb 26	*11*	12	13	14	15	16	17	
	18[d]	19	20	21	22	23	24	
Mar 12	*25*[e]	26	27	28	29	30	31	
	1	2	3	4	5	6	7	APRIL 2046
Mar 26	*8*	9	10	11	12	13	14	
	15	16	17	18	19	20	21	
Apr 9	*22*	23	24	25	26	27	28	
	29[f]	30	1	2	3	4	5	MAY 2046
Apr 23	*6*	7	8	9	10	11	12	
	13	14	15	16	17	18	19	
May 7	*20*	21	22	23	24	25	26	
	27	28	29	30	31	1	2	JUNE 2046
May 21	*3*	4	5	6	7	8	9	
	10	11	12	13	14	15	16	
Jun 4	*17*	18	19	20	21	22	23	
	24	25	26	27	28	29	30	
Jun 18	*1*	2	3	4	5	6	7	JULY 2046
	8	9	10	11	12	13	14	
Jul 2	*15*	16	17	18	19	20	21	
	22	23	24	25	26	27	28	
Jul 16	*29*	30	31	1	2	3	4	AUGUST 2046
	5	6	7	8	9	10	11	
Jul 30	*12*	13	14	15	16	17	18	
	19	20	21	22	23	24	25	
Aug 13	*26*	27	28	29	30	31	1	SEPTEMBER 2046
	2	3	4	5	6	7	8	
Aug 27	*9*	10	11	12	13	14	15	
	16	17	18	19	20	21	22	
Sep 10	*23*	24	25	26	27	28	29	
	30	1	2	3	4	5	6	OCTOBER 2046
Sep 24	*7*	8	9	10	11	12	13	
	14	15	16	17	18	19	20	
Oct 8	*21*	22	23	24	25	26	27	
	28	29	30	31	1	2	3	NOVEMBER 2046
Oct 22	*4*	5	6	7	8	9	10	
	11	12	13	14	15	16	17	
Nov 5	*18*	19	20	21	22	23	24	
	25	26	27	28	29	30	1	DECEMBER 2046
Nov 19	*2*[g]	3	4	5	6	7	8	
	9	10	11	12	13	14	15	
Dec 3	*16*	17	18	19	20	21	22	
	23	24	25[h]	26	27	28	29	
Dec 17	*30*	31	1	2	3	4	5	

[a]Orthodox Christmas
[b]Julian New Year
[c]Ash Wednesday
[d]Feast of Orthodoxy
[e]Easter
[f]Orthodox Easter
[g]Advent
[h]Christmas

2047

Gregorian 2047	Sun	Mon	Tue	Wed	Thu	Fri	Sat	Lunar Phases	ISO Week (Mon)	Julian Day (Sun noon)
	30	31	1[a]	2	3	◐	5	5:30	1	2468710
JANUARY 2047	6	7	8	9	10	11	○	1:20	2	2468717
	13	14	15	16	17	◑	19	22:31	3	2468724
	20	21	22	23	24	25	●	1:42	4	2468731
	27	28	29	30	31	1	2		5	2468738
FEBRUARY 2047	◐	4	5	6	7	8	9	3:08	6	2468745
	○	11	12	13	14	15	16	14:38	7	2468752
	◑	18	19	20	21	22	23	6:41	8	2468759
	●	25	26	27	28	1	2	18:25	9	2468766
MARCH 2047	3	◐	5	6	7	8	9	22:50	10	2468773
	10	11	○	13	14	15	16	1:35	11	2468780
	17	◑	19	20[b]	21	22	23	16:09	12	2468787
	24	25	●	27	28	29	30	11:43	13	2468794
APRIL 2047	31	1	2	◐	4	5	6	15:09	14	2468801
	7	8	9	○	11	12	13	10:34	15	2468808
	14	15	16	◑	18	19	20	3:29	16	2468815
	21	22	23	24	●	26	27	4:38	17	2468822
MAY 2047	28	29	30	1	2	◐	4	3:25	18	2468829
	5	6	7	8	○	10	11	18:23	19	2468836
	12	13	14	15	◑	17	18	16:44	20	2468843
	19	20	21	22	23	●	25	20:26	21	2468850
	26	27	28	29	30	31	◐	11:53	22	2468857
JUNE 2047	2	3	4	5	6	7	○	2:03	23	2468864
	9	10	11	12	13	14	◑	7:44	24	2468871
	16	17	18	19	20	21[c]	22		25	2468878
	●	24	25	26	27	28	29	10:34	26	2468885
JULY 2047	◐	1	2	3	4	5	6	17:35	27	2468892
	○	8	9	10	11	12	13	10:32	28	2468899
	14	◑	16	17	18	19	20	0:08	29	2468906
	21	●	23	24	25	26	27	22:48	30	2468913
AUGUST 2047	28	◐	30	31	1	2	3	22:01	31	2468920
	4	○	6	7	8	9	10	20:37	32	2468927
	11	12	◑	14	15	16	17	17:33	33	2468934
	18	19	20	●	22	23	24	9:15	34	2468941
	25	26	27	◐	29	30	31	2:48	35	2468948
SEPTEMBER 2047	1	2	3	○	5	6	7	8:53	36	2468955
	8	9	10	11	◑	13	14	11:17	37	2468962
	15	16	17	18	●	20	21	18:30	38	2468969
	22	23[d]	24	25	◐	27	28	9:27	39	2468976
OCTOBER 2047	29	30	1	2	○	4	5	23:41	40	2468983
	6	7	8	9	10	11	◑	4:20	41	2468990
	13	14	15	16	17	18	●	3:27	42	2468997
	20	21	22	23	24	◐	26	19:11	43	2469004
NOVEMBER 2047	27	28	29	30	31	1	○	16:57	44	2469011
	3	4	5	6	7	8	9		45	2469018
	◑	11	12	13	14	15	16	19:38	46	2469025
	●	18	19	20	21	22	23	12:58	47	2469032
	◐	25	26	27	28	29	30	8:39	48	2469039
DECEMBER 2047	1	○	3	4	5	6	7	11:54	49	2469046
	8	9	◑	11	12	13	14	8:27	50	2469053
	15	●	17	18	19	20	21[e]	23:37	51	2469060
	22	23	◐	25	26	27	28	1:49	52	2469067
	29	30	31	○	2	3	4	6:56	1	2469074

ISO Week	Hebrew 5807/5808	Sun	Mon	Tue	Wed	Thu	Fri	Sat	Molad
1		1[e]	2[e]	3	4	5	6	7	Fri 1h17m0p
2	TEVETH 5807	8	9	10	11	12	13	14	
3		15	16	17	18	19	20	21	
4		22	23	24	25	26	27	28	
5		29	1	2	3	4	5	6	Sat 14h1m1p
6	SHEVAT 5807	7	8	9	10	11	12	13	
7		14	15	16	17	18	19	20	
8		21	22	23	24	25	26	27	
9		28	29	30	1	2	3	4	Mon 2h45m2p
10	ADAR 5807	5	6	7	8	9	10	11	
11		12	13	14[f]	15	16	17	18	
12		19	20	21	22	23	24	25	
13		26	27	28	29	1	2	3	Tue 15h29m3p
14	NISAN 5807	4	5	6	7	8	9	10	
15		11	12	13	14	15[g]	16	17	
16		18	19	20	21	22	23	24	
17		25	26	27	28	29	30	1	Thu 4h13m4p
18	IYYAR 5807	2	3	4	5	6	7	8	
19		9	10	11	12	13	14	15	
20		16	17	18	19	20	21	22	
21		23	24	25	26	27	28	29	
22		1	2	3	4	5	6[h]	7	Fri 16h57m5p
23	SIVAN 5807	8	9	10	11	12	13	14	
24		15	16	17	18	19	20	21	
25		22	23	24	25	26	27	28	
26		29	30	1	2	3	4	5	Sun 5h41m6p
27	TAMMUZ 5807	6	7	8	9	10	11	12	
28		13	14	15	16	17	18	19	
29		20	21	22	23	24	25	26	
30		27	28	29	1	2	3	4	Mon 18h25m7p
31	AV 5807	5	6	7	8	9[i]	10	11	
32		12	13	14	15	16	17	18	
33		19	20	21	22	23	24	25	
34		26	27	28	29	30	1	2	Wed 7h9m8p
35	ELUL 5807	3	4	5	6	7	8	9	
36		10	11	12	13	14	15	16	
37		17	18	19	20	21	22	23	
38		24	25	26	27	28	29	1[a]	Thu 19h53m9p
39	TISHRI 5808	2[a]	3	4	5	6	7	8	
40		9	10[b]	11	12	13	14	15[c]	
41		16	17	18	19	20	21	22	
42		23	24	25	26	27	28	29	
43		30	1	2	3	4	5	6	Sat 8h37m10p
44	ḤESHVAN 5808	7	8	9	10	11	12	13	
45		14	15	16	17	18	19	20	
46		21	22	23	24	25	26	27	
47		28	29	1	2	3	4	5	Sun 21h21m11p
48	KISLEV 5808	6	7	8	9	10	11	12	
49		13	14	15	16	17	18[d]	19	
50		20	21	22	23	24	25[e]	26[e]	
51		27[e]	28[e]	29[e]	1[e]	2[e]	3[e]	4	Tue 10h5m12p
52	TEVETH 5808	5	6	7	8	9	10	11	
1		12	13	14	15	16	17	18	

ISO Week	Chinese Bǐng-Yín/Dīng-Mǎo‡	Sun	Mon	Tue	Wed	Thu	Fri	Sat	Solar Term
1		4	5	6	7	8	9	*10*	Xiǎo hán
2	MONTH 12 Bǐng-Yín	11	12	13	14	15	16	17	
3		18	19	20	21	22	23	24	
4		***25***	26	27	28	29	30	1[a]	**Dà hán**
5		2	3	4	5	6	7	8	
6	MONTH 1 Dīng-Mǎo	9	*10*	11	12	13	14	15[b]	Lì chūn
7		16	17	18	19	20	21	22	
8		23	24	***25***	26	27	28	29	**Yǔ shuǐ**
9		30	1	2	3	4	5*	6	
10	MONTH 2 Dīng-Mǎo	7	8	9	*10*	11	12	13	Jīng zhé
11		14	15	16	17	18	19	20	
12		21	22	23	24	***25***	26	27	**Chūn fēn**
13		28	29	1	2	3	4	5	
14	MONTH 3 Dīng-Mǎo	6	7	8	9	10	*11*[c]	12	Qīng míng
15		13	14	15	16	17	18	19	
16		20	21	22	23	24	25	***26***	**Gǔ yǔ**
17		27	28	29	30	1	2	3	
18	MONTH 4 Dīng-Mǎo	4	5	6*	7	8	9	10	
19		*11*	12	13	14	15	16	17	Lì xià
20		18	19	20	21	22	23	24	
21		25	26	***27***	28	29	30	1	**Xiǎo mǎn**
22	MONTH 5 Dīng-Mǎo	2	3	4	5[d]	6	7	8	
23		9	10	11	12	*13*	14	15	Máng zhòng
24		16	17	18	19	20	21	22	
25		23	24	25	26	27	***28***	29	**Xià zhì**
26		1	2	3	4	5	6	7*	
27	*LEAP MONTH 5* Dīng-Mǎo	8	9	10	11	12	13	14	
28		*15*	16	17	18	19	20	21	Xiǎo shǔ
29		22	23	24	25	26	27	28	
30		29	30	***1***	2	3	4	5	**Dà shǔ**
31	MONTH 6 Dīng-Mǎo	6	7	8	9	10	11	12	
32		13	14	15	*16*	17	18	19	Lì qiū
33		20	21	22	23	24	25	26	
34		27	28	29	1	2	***3***	4	**Chǔ shǔ**
35	MONTH 7 Dīng-Mǎo	5	6	7[e]	8*	9	10	11	
36		12	13	14	15[f]	16	17	18	
37		*19*	20	21	22	23	24	25	Bái lù
38		26	27	28	29	30	1	2	
39	MONTH 8 Dīng-Mǎo	3	***4***	5	6	7	8	9	**Qiū fēn**
40		10	11	12	13	14	15[g]	16	
41		17	18	*19*	20	21	22	23	Hán lù
42		24	25	26	27	28	29	1	
43	MONTH 9 Dīng-Mǎo	2	3	4	***5***	6	7	8	**Shuāng jiàng**
44		9[h]*	10	11	12	13	14	15	
45		16	17	18	19	*20*	21	22	Lì dōng
46		23	24	25	26	27	28	29	
47		1	2	3	4	5	***6***	7	**Xiǎo xuě**
48	MONTH 10 Dīng-Mǎo	8	9	10	11	12	13	14	
49		15	16	17	18	19	20	*21*	Dà xuě
50		22	23	24	25	26	27	28	
51	MONTH 11 Dīng-Mǎo	29	30	1	2	3	4	5	
52		***6***[i]	7	8	9	10*	11	12	**Dōng zhì**
1		13	14	15	16	17	18	19	

ISO Week	Coptic 1763‡/1764	Sun	Mon	Tue	Wed	Thu	Fri	Sat	Ethiopic 2039‡/2040
1	KOIAK 1763	21	22	23	24	25	26	27	TĀKHŚĀŚ 2039
2		28	29[c]	30	1	2	3	4	
3	ṬŌBE 1763	5	6[d]	7	8	9	10	11[e]	ṬER 2039
4		12	13	14	15	16	17	18	
5		19	20	21	22	23	24	25	
6		26	27	28	29	30	1	2	
7	MESHIR 1763	3	4	5	6	7	8	9	YAKĀTIT 2039
8		10	11	12	13	14	15	16	
9		17	18	19	20	21	22	23	
10		24	25	26	27	28	29	30	
11	PAREMOTEP 1763	1	2	3	4	5	6	7	MAGĀBIT 2039
12		8	9	10	11	12	13	14	
13		15	16	17	18	19	20	21	
14		22	23	24	25	26	27	28	
15		29	30	1	2	3	4	5	
16	PARMOUTE 1763	6	7	8	9	10	11	12	MIYĀZYĀ 2039
17		13[f]	14	15	16	17	18	19	
18		20	21	22	23	24	25	26	
19		27	28	29[g]	30	1	2	3	
20	PASHONS 1763	4	5	6	7	8	9	10	GENBOT 2039
21		11	12	13	14	15	16	17	
22		18	19	20	21	22	23	24	
23		25	26	27	28	29	30	1	
24	PAŌNE 1763	2	3	4	5	6	7	8	SANĒ 2039
25		9	10	11	12	13	14	15	
26		16	17	18	19	20	21	22	
27		23	24	25	26	27	28	29	
28		30	1	2	3	4	5	6	
29	EPĒP 1763	7	8	9	10	11	12	13	ḤAMLĒ 2039
30		14	15	16	17	18	19	20	
31		21	22	23	24	25	26	27	
32		28	29	30	1	2	3	4	
33	MESORĒ 1763	5	6	7	8	9	10	11	NAḤASĒ 2039
34		12	13[h]	14	15	16	17	18	
35		19	20	21	22	23	24	25	
36		26	27	28	29	30	1	2	
37	EPAG. 1763	3	4	5	6	1[a]	2	3	PĀG. 2039
38	THOOUT 1764	4	5	6	7	8	9	10	MASKARAM 2040
39		11	12	13	14	15	16	17[b]	
40		18	19	20	21	22	23	24	
41		25	26	27	28	29	30	1	
42	PAOPE 1764	2	3	4	5	6	7	8	ṬEQEMT 2040
43		9	10	11	12	13	14	15	
44		16	17	18	19	20	21	22	
45		23	24	25	26	27	28	29	
46		30	1	2	3	4	5	6	
47	ATHŌR 1764	7	8	9	10	11	12	13	ḪEDĀR 2040
48		14	15	16	17	18	19	20	
49		21	22	23	24	25	26	27	
50		28	29	30	1	2	3	4	
51	KOIAK 1764	5	6	7	8	9	10	11	TĀKHŚĀŚ 2040
52		12	13	14	15	16	17	18	
1		19	20	21	22	23	24	25	

Gregorian:
[a]New Year
[b]Spring (16:51)
[c]Summer (10:01)
[d]Autumn (2:06)
[e]Winter (23:06)
● New moon
◐ First quarter moon
○ Full moon
◑ Last quarter moon

Hebrew:
[a]New Year
[b]Yom Kippur
[c]Sukkot
[d]Winter starts
[e]Ḥanukkah
[f]Purim
[g]Passover
[h]Shavuot
[i]Fast of Av

Chinese:
‡Leap year
[a]New Year (4745, Hare)
[b]Lantern Festival
[c]Qīngmíng
[d]Dragon Festival
[e]Qīqiǎo
[f]Hungry Ghosts
[g]Mid-Autumn Festival
[h]Double-Ninth Festival
[i]Dōngzhì
*Start of 60-name cycle

Coptic/Ethiopic:
‡Leap year
[a]New Year
[b]Building of the Cross
[c]Christmas
[d]Jesus's Circumcision
[e]Epiphany
[f]Easter
[g]Mary's Announcement
[h]Jesus's Transfiguration

PERSIAN (ASTRONOMICAL) 1425/1426

Month	Sun	Mon	Tue	Wed	Thu	Fri	Sat
DEY 1425	9	10	11	12	13	14	15
	16	17	18	19	20	21	22
	23	24	25	26	27	28	29
	30	1	2	3	4	5	6
BAHMAN 1425	7	8	9	10	11	12	13
	14	15	16	17	18	19	20
	21	22	23	24	25	26	27
	28	29	30	1	2	3	4
ESFAND 1425	5	6	7	8	9	10	11
	12	13	14	15	16	17	18
	19	20	21	22	23	24	25
	26	27	28	29	1[a]	2	3
FARVARDĪN 1426	4	5	6	7	8	9	10
	11	12	13[b]	14	15	16	17
	18	19	20	21	22	23	24
	25	26	27	28	29	30	31
ORDĪBEHEŠT 1426	1	2	3	4	5	6	7
	8	9	10	11	12	13	14
	15	16	17	18	19	20	21
	22	23	24	25	26	27	28
	29	30	31	1	2	3	4
XORDĀD 1426	5	6	7	8	9	10	11
	12	13	14	15	16	17	18
	19	20	21	22	23	24	25
	26	27	28	29	30	31	1
TĪR 1426	2	3	4	5	6	7	8
	9	10	11	12	13	14	15
	16	17	18	19	20	21	22
	23	24	25	26	27	28	29
	30	31	1	2	3	4	5
MORDĀD 1426	6	7	8	9	10	11	12
	13	14	15	16	17	18	19
	20	21	22	23	24	25	26
	27	28	29	30	31	1	2
SHAHRĪVAR 1426	3	4	5	6	7	8	9
	10	11	12	13	14	15	16
	17	18	19	20	21	22	23
	24	25	26	27	28	29	30
	31	1	2	3	4	5	6
MEHR 1426	7	8	9	10	11	12	13
	14	15	16	17	18	19	20
	21	22	23	24	25	26	27
	28	29	30	1	2	3	4
ĀBĀN 1426	5	6	7	8	9	10	11
	12	13	14	15	16	17	18
	19	20	21	22	23	24	25
	26	27	28	29	30	1	2
ĀZAR 1426	3	4	5	6	7	8	9
	10	11	12	13	14	15	16
	17	18	19	20	21	22	23
	24	25	26	27	28	29	30
DEY 1426	1	2	3	4	5	6	7
	8	9	10	11	12	13	14

[a]New Year
[b]Sizdeh Bedar

HINDU LUNAR 2103/2104‡

Month	Sun	Mon	Tue	Wed	Thu	Fri	Sat
PAUSHA 2103	3	4	5	6	7	8	9
	10	11	12	13	14	14	16
	17	18	19	20	21	22	23
	24	25	26	27	28	30	1
MĀGHA 2103	2	2	3	4	5	6	7
	8	9	10	11	12	13	14
	15	16	17	18	19	20	21
	23	24	25	26	27	28[h]	29
PHĀLGUNA 2103	30	1	2	3	4	5	5
	6	7	8	9	10	11	12
	13	14	15[i]	17	18	19	20
	21	22	23	24	25	26	27
	28	29	30	1[a]	2	3	4
CHAITRA 2104	5	6	7	8	9[b]	10	11
	12	13	14	15	16	17	18
	19	21	22	23	24	25	26
	27	28	29	29	30	1	2
VAIŚĀKHA 2104	3	4	5	6	7	8	9
	10	11	12	14	15	16	17
	18	19	20	21	22	23	24
	25	26	27	28	29	30	1
JYAISHTHA 2104	2	3	4	5	6	7	8
	9	10	11	12	13	14	15
	16	18	19	20	21	22	23
	24	25	25	26	27	28	29
	30	1	2	3	4	5	6
ĀSHĀDHA 2104	7	8	10	11	12	13	14
	15	16	17	18	19	20	21
	22	23	24	25	26	27	28
	29	30	1	2	3	4	5
ŚRĀVANA 2104	6	7	8	9	10	11	13
	14	15	16	17	18	19	20
	21	22	22	23[c]	24	25	26
	27	28	29	30	1	2	3[d]
BHĀDRAPADA 2104	4	6	7	8	9	10	11
	12	13	14	15	16	17	18
	19	20	21	22	23	24	25
	26	27	28	29	30	1	2
ĀŚVINA 2104	3	4	5	6	7[e]	9[e]	10[e]
	11	12	13	14	15	16	17
	17	18	19	20	21	22	23
	24	25	26	27	28	29	30
	1[f]	3	4	5	6	7	8
KĀRTTIKA 2104	9	10	11	12	13	14	15
	16	17	18	19	20	21	21
	22	23	25	26	27	28	29
	30	1	2	3	4	5	6
LEAP MĀRGAŚĪRA 2104	7	9	10	10	11	12	13
	14	15	16	17	18	19	20
	21	22	23	24	25	26	27
	28	29	1	2	3	4	5
MĀRGAŚĪRA 2104	6	7	8	9	10	11[g]	12
	13	13	14	15	16	17	18

‡Leap year
[a]New Year (Prabhava)
[b]Birthday of Rāma
[c]Birthday of Krishna
[d]Ganēśa Chaturthī
[e]Dashara
[f]Diwali
[g]Birthday of Vishnu
[h]Night of Śiva
[i]Holi

HINDU SOLAR 1968/1969

Month	Sun	Mon	Tue	Wed	Thu	Fri	Sat
PAUSHA 1968	15	16	17	18	19	20	21
	22	23	24	25	26	27	28
	29	1[b]	2	3	4	5	6
MĀGHA 1968	7	8	9	10	11	12	13
	14	15	16	17	18	19	20
	21	22	23	24	25	26	27
	28	29	30	1	2	3	4
PHĀLGUNA 1968	5	6	7	8	9	10	11
	12	13	14	15	16	17	18
	19	20	21	22	23	24	25
	26	27	28	29	30	1	2
CHAITRA 1968	3	4	5	6	7	8	9
	10	11	12	13	14	15	16
	17	18	19	20	21	22	23
	24	25	26	27	28	29	30
VAIŚĀKHA 1969	1[a]	2	3	4	5	6	7
	8	9	10	11	12	13	14
	15	16	17	18	19	20	21
	22	23	24	25	26	27	28
	29	30	31	1	2	3	4
JYAISHTHA 1969	5	6	7	8	9	10	11
	12	13	14	15	16	17	18
	19	20	21	22	23	24	25
	26	27	28	29	30	31	32
ĀSHĀDHA 1969	1	2	3	4	5	6	7
	8	9	10	11	12	13	14
	15	16	17	18	19	20	21
	22	23	24	25	26	27	28
	29	30	31	1	2	3	4
ŚRĀVANA 1969	5	6	7	8	9	10	11
	12	13	14	15	16	17	18
	19	20	21	22	23	24	25
	26	27	28	29	30	31	32
BHĀDRAPADA 1969	1	2	3	4	5	6	7
	8	9	10	11	12	13	14
	15	16	17	18	19	20	21
	22	23	24	25	26	27	28
	29	30	31	1	2	3	4
ĀŚVINA 1969	5	6	7	8	9	10	11
	12	13	14	15	16	17	18
	19	20	21	22	23	24	25
	26	27	28	29	30	1	2
KĀRTTIKA 1969	3	4	5	6	7	8	9
	10	11	12	13	14	15	16
	17	18	19	20	21	22	23
	24	25	26	27	28	29	30
MĀRGAŚĪRA 1969	1	2	3	4	5	6	7
	8	9	10	11	12	13	14
	15	16	17	18	19	20	21
	22	23	24	25	26	27	28
	29	1	2	3	4	5	6
PAUSHA 1969	7	8	9	10	11	12	13
	14	15	16	17	18	19	20

[a]New Year (Vṛisha)
[b]Pongal

ISLAMIC (ASTRONOMICAL) 1469‡/1470‡

Month	Sun	Mon	Tue	Wed	Thu	Fri	Sat
RABĪ' I 1469	2	3	4	5	6	7	8
	9	10	11	12[c]	13	14	15
	16	17	18	19	20	21	22
	23	24	25	26	27	28	29
RABĪ' II 1469	1	2	3	4	5	6	7
	8	9	10	11	12	13	14
	15	16	17	18	19	20	21
	22	23	24	25	26	27	28
	29	30	1	2	3	4	5
JUMĀDĀ I 1469	6	7	8	9	10	11	12
	13	14	15	16	17	18	19
	20	21	22	23	24	25	26
	27	28	29	30	1	2	3
JUMĀDĀ II 1469	4	5	6	7	8	9	10
	11	12	13	14	15	16	17
	18	19	20	21	22	23	24
	25	26	27	28	29	1	2
RAJAB 1469	3	4	5	6	7	8	9
	10	11	12	13	14	15	16
	17	18	19	20	21	22	23
	24	25	26	27[d]	28	29	30
SHA'BĀN 1469	1	2	3	4	5	6	7
	8	9	10	11	12	13	14
	15	16	17	18	19	20	21
	22	23	24	25	26	27	28
	29	30	1[e]	2	3	4	5
RAMAḌĀN 1469	6	7	8	9	10	11	12
	13	14	15	16	17	18	19
	20	21	22	23	24	25	26
	27	28	29	30	1[f]	2	3
SHAWWĀL 1469	4	5	6	7	8	9	10
	11	12	13	14	15	16	17
	18	19	20	21	22	23	24
	25	26	27	28	29	1	2
DHU AL-QA'DA 1469	3	4	5	6	7	8	9
	10	11	12	13	14	15	16
	17	18	19	20	21	22	23
	24	25	26	27	28	29	30
DHU AL-ḤIJJA 1469	1	2	3	4	5	6	7
	8	9	10[g]	11	12	13	14
	15	16	17	18	19	20	21
	22	23	24	25	26	27	28
	29	1[a]	2	3	4	5	6
MUḤARRAM 1470	7	8	9	10[b]	11	12	13
	14	15	16	17	18	19	20
	21	22	23	24	25	26	27
	28	29	1	2	3	4	5
ṢAFAR 1470	6	7	8	9	10	11	12
	13	14	15	16	17	18	19
	20	21	22	23	24	25	26
	27	28	29	1	2	3	4
RABĪ' I 1470	5	6	7	8	9	10	11
	12[c]	13	14	15	16	17	18

‡Leap year
[a]New Year
[b]'Ashūrā'
[c]Prophet's Birthday
[d]Ascent of the Prophet
[e]Start of Ramaḍān
[f]'Id al-Fiṭr
[g]'Id al-'Aḍḥā

GREGORIAN 2047

Julian (Sun)	Sun	Mon	Tue	Wed	Thu	Fri	Sat	Month
Dec 17	30	31	1	2	3	4	5	JANUARY 2047
	6	7[a]	8	9	10	11	12	
Dec 31	13	14[b]	15	16	17	18	19	
	20	21	22	23	24	25	26	
Jan 14	27	28	29	30	31	1	2	FEBRUARY 2047
	3	4	5	6	7	8	9	
Jan 28	10	11	12	13	14	15	16	
	17	18	19	20	21	22	23	
Feb 11	24	25	26	27[c]	28	1	2	MARCH 2047
	3	4	5	6	7	8	9	
Feb 25	10[d]	11	12	13	14	15	16	
	17	18	19	20	21	22	23	
Mar 11	24	25	26	27	28	29	30	
	31	1	2	3	4	5	6	APRIL 2047
Mar 25	7	8	9	10	11	12	13	
	14[e]	15	16	17	18	19	20	
Apr 8	21[f]	22	23	24	25	26	27	
	28	29	30	1	2	3	4	MAY 2047
Apr 22	5	6	7	8	9	10	11	
	12	13	14	15	16	17	18	
May 6	19	20	21	22	23	24	25	
	26	27	28	29	30	31	1	JUNE 2047
May 20	2	3	4	5	6	7	8	
	9	10	11	12	13	14	15	
Jun 3	16	17	18	19	20	21	22	
	23	24	25	26	27	28	29	
Jun 17	30	1	2	3	4	5	6	JULY 2047
	7	8	9	10	11	12	13	
Jul 1	14	15	16	17	18	19	20	
	21	22	23	24	25	26	27	
Jul 15	28	29	30	31	1	2	3	AUGUST 2047
	4	5	6	7	8	9	10	
Jul 29	11	12	13	14	15	16	17	
	18	19	20	21	22	23	24	
Aug 12	25	26	27	28	29	30	31	
	1	2	3	4	5	6	7	SEPTEMBER 2047
Aug 26	8	9	10	11	12	13	14	
	15	16	17	18	19	20	21	
Sep 9	22	23	24	25	26	27	28	
	29	30	1	2	3	4	5	OCTOBER 2047
Sep 23	6	7	8	9	10	11	12	
	13	14	15	16	17	18	19	
Oct 7	20	21	22	23	24	25	26	
	27	28	29	30	31	1	2	NOVEMBER 2047
Oct 21	3	4	5	6	7	8	9	
	10	11	12	13	14	15	16	
Nov 4	17	18	19	20	21	22	23	
	24	25	26	27	28	29	30	
Nov 18	1[g]	2	3	4	5	6	7	DECEMBER 2047
	8	9	10	11	12	13	14	
Dec 2	15	16	17	18	19	20	21	
	22	23	24	25[h]	26	27	28	
Dec 16	29	30	31	1	2	3	4	

[a]Orthodox Christmas
[b]Julian New Year
[c]Ash Wednesday
[d]Feast of Orthodoxy
[e]Easter
[f]Orthodox Easter
[g]Advent
[h]Christmas

2048

GREGORIAN 2048[‡], Lunar Phases, ISO WEEK (Mon), JULIAN DAY (Sun noon)

Month	Sun	Mon	Tue	Wed	Thu	Fri	Sat	Lunar Phases	ISO Week	Julian Day
JANUARY 2048	29	30	31	○[a]	2	3	4	6:56	1	2469074
	5	6	7	◑	9	10	11	18:48	2	2469081
	12	13	14	●	16	17	18	11:31	3	2469088
	19	20	21	◐	23	24	25	21:55	4	2469095
	26	27	28	29	30	○	1	0:13	5	2469102
FEBRUARY 2048	2	3	4	5	6	◑	8	3:15	6	2469109
	9	10	11	12	13	●	15	0:30	7	2469116
	16	17	18	19	20	◐	22	19:21	8	2469123
	23	24	25	26	27	28	○	14:36	9	2469130
MARCH 2048	1	2	3	4	5	6	◑	10:44	10	2469137
	8	9	10	11	12	13	●	14:26	11	2469144
	15	16	17	18	19[b]	20	21		12	2469151
	◐	23	24	25	26	27	28	16:02	13	2469158
APRIL 2048	29	○	31	1	2	3	4	2:03	14	2469165
	◑	6	7	8	9	10	11	18:09	15	2469172
	12	●	14	15	16	17	18	5:18	16	2469179
	19	20	◐	22	23	24	25	10:01	17	2469186
MAY 2048	26	27	○	29	30	1	2	11:12	18	2469193
	3	4	◑	6	7	8	9	2:21	19	2469200
	10	11	●	13	14	15	16	20:57	20	2469207
	17	18	19	20	◐	22	23	0:15	21	2469214
	24	25	26	○	28	29	30	18:56	22	2469221
JUNE 2048	31	1	2	◑	4	5	6	12:03	23	2469228
	7	8	9	10	●	12	13	12:48	24	2469235
	14	15	16	17	18	◐	20[c]	10:48	25	2469242
	21	22	23	24	25	○	27	2:07	26	2469249
JULY 2048	28	29	30	1	◑	3	4	23:56	27	2469256
	5	6	7	8	9	10	●	4:03	28	2469263
	12	13	14	15	16	17	◐	18:30	29	2469270
	19	20	21	22	23	24	○	9:32	30	2469277
AUGUST 2048	26	27	28	29	30	31	◑	14:29	31	2469284
	2	3	4	5	6	7	8		32	2469291
	●	10	11	12	13	14	15	17:57	33	2469298
	16	◐	18	19	20	21	22	0:30	34	2469305
	○	24	25	26	27	28	29	18:06	35	2469312
SEPTEMBER 2048	30	◑	1	2	3	4	5	7:40	36	2469319
	6	7	●	9	10	11	12	6:23	37	2469326
	13	14	◐	16	17	18	19	6:02	38	2469333
	20	21	○[d]	23	24	25	26	4:45	39	2469340
OCTOBER 2048	27	28	29	◑	1	2	3	2:44	40	2469347
	4	5	6	●	8	9	10	17:44	41	2469354
	11	12	13	◐	15	16	17	12:19	42	2469361
	18	19	20	○	22	23	24	18:24	43	2469368
	25	26	27	28	◑	30	31	22:13	44	2469375
NOVEMBER 2048	1	2	3	4	5	●	7	4:37	45	2469382
	8	9	10	11	◐	13	14	20:27	46	2469389
	15	16	17	18	19	○	21	11:18	47	2469396
	22	23	24	25	26	27	◑	16:32	48	2469403
DECEMBER 2048	29	30	1	2	3	4	●	15:29	49	2469410
	6	7	8	9	10	11	◐	7:28	50	2469417
	13	14	15	16	17	18	19		51	2469424
	○	21[e]	22	23	24	25	26	6:38	52	2469431
	27	◑	29	30	31	1	2	8:30	53	2469438

HEBREW 5808/5809[‡], Molad

ISO Week	Month	Sun	Mon	Tue	Wed	Thu	Fri	Sat	Molad
1	TEVETH 5808	12	13	14	15	16	17	18	
2		19	20	21	22	23	24	25	
3	SHEVAT 5808	26	27	28	29	1	2	3	Wed 22h 49m 13p
4		4	5	6	7	8	9	10	
5		11	12	13	14	15	16	17	
6		18	19	20	21	22	23	24	Fri 11h 33m 14p
7	ADAR 5808	25	26	27	28	29	30	1	
8		2	3	4	5	6	7	8	
9		9	10	11	12	13	14[f]	15	
10		16	17	18	19	20	21	22	
11		23	24	25	26	27	28	29	
12	NISAN 5808	1	2	3	4	5	6	7	Sun 0h 17m 15p
13		8	9	10	11	12	13	14	
14		15[g]	16	17	18	19	20	21	
15		22	23	24	25	26	27	28	
16	IYYAR 5808	29	30	1	2	3	4	5	Mon 13h 1m 16p
17		6	7	8	9	10	11	12	
18		13	14	15	16	17	18	19	
19		20	21	22	23	24	25	26	
20	SIVAN 5808	27	28	29	1	2	3	4	Wed 1h 45m 17p
21		5	6[h]	7	8	9	10	11	
22		12	13	14	15	16	17	18	
23		19	20	21	22	23	24	25	
24	TAMMUZ 5808	26	27	28	29	30	1	2	Thu 14h 30m 0p
25		3	4	5	6	7	8	9	
26		10	11	12	13	14	15	16	
27		17	18	19	20	21	22	23	
28	AV 5808	24	25	26	27	28	29	1	Sat 3h 14m 1p
29		2	3	4	5	6	7	8	
30		9[i]	10	11	12	13	14	15	
31		16	17	18	19	20	21	22	
32		23	24	25	26	27	28	29	
33	ELUL 5808	30	1	2	3	4	5	6	Sun 15h 58m 2p
34		7	8	9	10	11	12	13	
35		14	15	16	17	18	19	20	
36		21	22	23	24	25	26	27	
37	TISHRI 5809	28	29	1[a]	2[a]	3	4	5	Tue 4h 42m 3p
38		6	7	8	9	10[b]	11	12	
39		13	14	15[c]	16	17	18	19	
40		20	21	22	23	24	25	26	
41	HESHVAN 5809	27	28	29	30	1	2	3	Wed 17h 26m 4p
42		4	5	6	7	8	9	10	
43		11	12	13	14	15	16	17	
44		18	19	20	21	22	23	24	
45	KISLEV 5809	25	26	27	28	29	1	2	Fri 6h 10m 5p
46		3	4	5	6	7	8	9	
47		10	11	12	13	14	15	16	
48		17	18	19	20	21	22	23	
49		24	25[e]	26[e]	27[e]	28[e]	29[e]	30[d][e]	
50	TEVETH 5809	1[e]	2[e]	3	4	5	6	7	Sat 18h 54m 6p
51		8	9	10	11	12	13	14	
52		15	16	17	18	19	20	21	
53		22	23	24	25	26	27	28	

CHINESE Dīng-Mǎo[‡]/Wù-Chén, Solar Term

ISO Week	Month	Sun	Mon	Tue	Wed	Thu	Fri	Sat	Solar Term
1	MONTH 11 Dīng-Mǎo	13	14	15	16	17	18	19	
2		20	21	22	23	24	25	26	Xiǎo hán
3	MONTH 12 Dīng-Mǎo	27	28	29	1	2	3	4	
4		5	6	7	8	9	10	11	Dà hán
5		12	13	14	15	16	17	18	
6		19	20	21	22	23	24	25	Lì chūn
7	MONTH 1 Wù-Chén	26	27	28	29	30	1[a]	2	
8		3	4	5	6	7	8	9	Yǔ shuǐ
9		10	11*	12	13	14	15[b]	16	
10		17	18	19	20	21	22	23	Jīng zhé
11	MONTH 2 Wù-Chén	24	25	26	27	28	29	1	
12		2	3	4	5	6	7	8	Chūn fēn
13		9	10	11	12	13	14	15	
14		16	17	18	19	20	21	22[c]	Qīng míng
15		23	24	25	26	27	28	29	
16	MONTH 3 Wù-Chén	30	1	2	3	4	5	6	
17		7	8	9	10	11	12*	13	Gǔ yǔ
18		14	15	16	17	18	19	20	
19		21	22	23	24	25	26	27	Lì xià
20	MONTH 4 Wù-Chén	28	29	30	1	2	3	4	
21		5	6	7	8	9	10	11	Xiǎo mǎn
22		12	13	14	15	16	17	18	
23		19	20	21	22	23	24	25	Máng zhòng
24	MONTH 5 Wù-Chén	26	27	28	29	1	2	3	
25		4	5[d]	6	7	8	9	10	Xià zhì
26		11	12	13*	14	15	16	17	
27		18	19	20	21	22	23	24	Xiǎo shǔ
28	MONTH 6 Wù-Chén	25	26	27	28	29	30	1	
29		2	3	4	5	6	7	8	
30		9	10	11	12	13	14	15	Dà shǔ
31		16	17	18	19	20	21	22	
32		23	24	25	26	27	28	29	Lì qiū
33	MONTH 7 Wù-Chén	30	1	2	3	4	5	6	
34		7[e]	8	9	10	11	12	13*	Chǔ shǔ
35		14	15[f]	16	17	18	19	20	
36		21	22	23	24	25	26	27	
37	MONTH 8 Wù-Chén	28	29	1	2	3	4	5	Bái lù
38		6	7	8	9	10	11	12	
39		13	14	15[g]	16	17	18	19	Qiū fēn
40		20	21	22	23	24	25	26	
41	MONTH 9 Wù-Chén	27	28	29	30	1	2	3	Hán lù
42		4	5	6	7	8	9[h]	10	
43		11	12	13	14*	15	16	17	Shuāng jiàng
44		18	19	20	21	22	23	24	
45	MONTH 10 Wù-Chén	25	26	27	28	29	1	2	Lì dōng
46		3	4	5	6	7	8	9	
47		10	11	12	13	14	15	16	Xiǎo xuě
48		17	18	19	20	21	22	23	
49	MONTH 11* Wù-Chén	24	25	26	27	28	29	1	
50		2	3	4	5	6	7	8	Dà xuě
51		9	10	11	12	13	14	15	
52		16*	17[i]	18	19	20	21	22	Dōng zhì
53		23	24	25	26	27	28	29	

COPTIC 1764/1765 and **ETHIOPIC 2040/2041**

ISO Week	Coptic Month	Sun	Mon	Tue	Wed	Thu	Fri	Sat	Ethiopic Month
1	KOIAK 1764	19	20	21	22	23	24	25	TĀKHŚĀŚ 2040
2	TŌBE 1764	26	27	28	29[c]	30	1	2	ṬER 2040
3		3	4	5	6[d]	7	8	9	
4		10	11[e]	12	13	14	15	16	
5		17	18	19	20	21	22	23	
6		24	25	26	27	28	29	30	
7	MESHIR 1764	1	2	3	4	5	6	7	YAKĀTIT 2040
8		8	9	10	11	12	13	14	
9		15	16	17	18	19	20	21	
10		22	23	24	25	26	27	28	
11	PAREMOTEP 1764	29	30	1	2	3	4	5	MAGĀBIT 2040
12		6	7	8	9	10	11	12	
13		13	14	15	16	17	18	19	
14		20	21	22	23	24	25	26	
15	PARMOUTE 1764	27[f]	28	29	30	1	2	3	MIYĀZYĀ 2040
16		4	5	6	7	8	9	10	
17		11	12	13	14	15	16	17	
18		18	19	20	21	22	23	24	
19	PASHONS 1764	25	26	27	28	29[g]	30	1	GENBOT 2040
20		2	3	4	5	6	7	8	
21		9	10	11	12	13	14	15	
22		16	17	18	19	20	21	22	
23		23	24	25	26	27	28	29	
24	PAŌNE 1764	30	1	2	3	4	5	6	SANĒ 2040
25		7	8	9	10	11	12	13	
26		14	15	16	17	18	19	20	
27		21	22	23	24	25	26	27	
28	EPĒP 1764	28	29	30	1	2	3	4	ḤAMLĒ 2040
29		5	6	7	8	9	10	11	
30		12	13	14	15	16	17	18	
31		19	20	21	22	23	24	25	
32	MESORĒ 1764	26	27	28	29	30	1	2	NAḤASĒ 2040
33		3	4	5	6	7	8	9	
34		10	11	12	13[h]	14	15	16	
35		17	18	19	20	21	22	23	
36		24	25	26	27	28	29	30	
37	EPAG. 1764 / THOOUT 1765	1	2	3	4	5	1[a]	2	PĀG. 2040 / MASKARAM 2041
38		3	4	5	6	7	8	9	
39		10	11	12	13	14	15	16	
40		17[b]	18	19	20	21	22	23	
41		24	25	26	27	28	29	30	
42	PAOPE 1765	1	2	3	4	5	6	7	ṬEQEMT 2041
43		8	9	10	11	12	13	14	
44		15	16	17	18	19	20	21	
45		22	23	24	25	26	27	28	
46	ATHŌR 1765	29	30	1	2	3	4	5	ḪEDĀR 2041
47		6	7	8	9	10	11	12	
48		13	14	15	16	17	18	19	
49		20	21	22	23	24	25	26	
50	KOIAK 1765	27	28	29	30	1	2	3	TĀKHŚĀŚ 2041
51		4	5	6	7	8	9	10	
52		11	12	13	14	15	16	17	
53		18	19	20	21	22	23	24	

Gregorian:
[‡]Leap year
[a]New Year
[b]Spring (22:32)
[c]Summer (15:52)
[d]Autumn (7:59)
[e]Winter (5:00)
● New moon
◐ First quarter moon
○ Full moon
◑ Last quarter moon

Hebrew:
[‡]Leap year
[a]New Year
[b]Yom Kippur
[c]Sukkot
[d]Winter starts
[e]Ḥanukkah
[f]Purim
[g]Passover
[h]Shavuot
[i]Fast of Av

Chinese:
[‡]Leap year
[a]New Year (4746, Dragon)
[b]Lantern Festival
[c]Qīngmíng
[d]Dragon Festival
[e]Qīqiǎo
[f]Hungry Ghosts
[g]Mid-Autumn Festival
[h]Double-Ninth Festival
[i]Dōngzhì
*Start of 60-name cycle

Coptic/Ethiopic:
[a]New Year
[b]Building of the Cross
[c]Christmas
[d]Jesus's Circumcision
[e]Epiphany
[f]Easter
[g]Mary's Announcement
[h]Jesus's Transfiguration

PERSIAN (ASTRONOMICAL) 1426/1427	Sun	Mon	Tue	Wed	Thu	Fri	Sat
DEY 1426	8	9	10	11	12	13	14
	15	16	17	18	19	20	21
	22	23	24	25	26	27	28
	29	30	1	2	3	4	5
BAHMAN 1426	6	7	8	9	10	11	12
	13	14	15	16	17	18	19
	20	21	22	23	24	25	26
	27	28	29	30	1	2	3
ESFAND 1426	4	5	6	7	8	9	10
	11	12	13	14	15	16	17
	18	19	20	21	22	23	24
	25	26	27	28	29	1[a]	2
FARVARDĪN 1427	3	4	5	6	7	8	9
	10	11	12	13[b]	14	15	16
	17	18	19	20	21	22	23
	24	25	26	27	28	29	30
	31	1	2	3	4	5	6
ORDĪBEHEŠT 1427	7	8	9	10	11	12	13
	14	15	16	17	18	19	20
	21	22	23	24	25	26	27
	28	29	30	31	1	2	3
XORDĀD 1427	4	5	6	7	8	9	10
	11	12	13	14	15	16	17
	18	19	20	21	22	23	24
	25	26	27	28	29	30	31
TĪR 1427	1	2	3	4	5	6	7
	8	9	10	11	12	13	14
	15	16	17	18	19	20	21
	22	23	24	25	26	27	28
	29	30	31	1	2	3	4
MORDĀD 1427	5	6	7	8	9	10	11
	12	13	14	15	16	17	18
	19	20	21	22	23	24	25
	26	27	28	29	30	31	1
SHAHRĪVAR 1427	2	3	4	5	6	7	8
	9	10	11	12	13	14	15
	16	17	18	19	20	21	22
	23	24	25	26	27	28	29
	30	31	1	2	3	4	5
MEHR 1427	6	7	8	9	10	11	12
	13	14	15	16	17	18	19
	20	21	22	23	24	25	26
	27	28	29	30	1	2	3
ABĀN 1427	4	5	6	7	8	9	10
	11	12	13	14	15	16	17
	18	19	20	21	22	23	24
	25	26	27	28	29	30	1
ĀZAR 1427	2	3	4	5	6	7	8
	9	10	11	12	13	14	15
	16	17	18	19	20	21	22
	23	24	25	26	27	28	29
DEY 1427	30	1	2	3	4	5	6
	7	8	9	10	11	12	13

[a]New Year
[b]Sizdeh Bedar

HINDU LUNAR 2104‡/2105	Sun	Mon	Tue	Wed	Thu	Fri	Sat
MĀRGAŚĪRA 2104	13	13	14	15	16	17	18
	19	20	21	22	23	25	26
	27	28	29	30	1	2	3
MĀGHA 2104	4	5	6	7	8	9	10
	11	12	13	14	15	16	17
	18	19	20	21	22	23	24
	25	26	27	28[h]	30	1	2
LEAP PHĀLGUNA 2104	3	4	5	5	6	7	8
	9	10	11	12	13	14	15
	16	17	18	19	20	21	22
	24	25	26	27	28	29	30
PHĀLGUNA 2104	1	2	3	4	5	6	7
	8	8	9	10	11	12	13
	14	15[i]	17	18	19	20	21
	22	23	24	25	26	27	28
	29	30	1[a]	2	3	4	5
CHAITRA 2105	6	7	8	9[b]	10	11	12
	13	14	15	16	17	18	19
	21	22	23	24	25	26	27
	28	29	30	1	2	3	3
VAIŚĀKHA 2105	4	5	6	7	8	9	10
	11	12	13	15	16	17	18
	19	20	21	22	23	24	25
	26	27	28	29	30	1	2
JYAISHTHA 2105	3	4	5	6	7	8	9
	10	11	12	13	14	15	17
	18	19	20	21	22	23	24
	25	26	27	28	29	29	30
ĀSHĀDHA 2105	1	2	3	4	5	6	7
	8	10	11	12	13	14	15
	16	17	18	19	20	21	22
	23	24	25	26	27	28	29
ŚRĀVAṆA 2105	30	1	2	3	4	5	6
	7	8	9	10	11	13	14
	15	16	17	18	19	20	21
	22	23[c]	24	25	26	26	27
	28	29	30	1	2	3[d]	4
BHĀDRAPADA 2105	6	7	8	9	10	11	12
	13	14	15	16	17	18	19
	20	21	22	23	24	25	26
	27	28	29	30	1	2	3
ĀŚVINA 2105	4	5	6	7	8[e]	10[e]	11
	12	13	14	15	16	17	18
	19	20	20	21	22	23	24
	25	26	27	28	29	30	1[f]
KĀRTTIKA 2105	2	4	5	6	7	8	9
	10	11	12	13	14	15	16
	17	18	19	20	21	22	23
	24	25	26	27	28	29	30
MĀRGAŚĪRA 2105	1	2	3	4	5	6	8
	9	10	11[g]	12	13	13	14
	15	16	17	18	19	20	21
	22	23	24	25	26	27	28

‡Leap year
[a]New Year (Vibhava)
[b]Birthday of Rāma
[c]Birthday of Krishna
[d]Ganēśa Chaturthī
[e]Dashara
[f]Diwali
[g]Birthday of Vishnu
[h]Night of Śiva
[i]Holi

HINDU SOLAR 1969/1970‡	Sun	Mon	Tue	Wed	Thu	Fri	Sat
PAUSHA 1969	14	15	16	17	18	19	20
	21	22	23	24	25	26	27
	28	29	30	1[b]	2	3	4
MĀGHA 1969	5	6	7	8	9	10	11
	12	13	14	15	16	17	18
	19	20	21	22	23	24	25
	26	27	28	29	1	2	3
PHĀLGUNA 1969	4	5	6	7	8	9	10
	11	12	13	14	15	16	17
	18	19	20	21	22	23	24
	25	26	27	28	29	30	1
CHAITRA 1969	2	3	4	5	6	7	8
	9	10	11	12	13	14	15
	16	17	18	19	20	21	22
	23	24	25	26	27	28	29
	30	1[a]	2	3	4	5	6
VAIŚĀKHA 1970	7	8	9	10	11	12	13
	14	15	16	17	18	19	20
	21	22	23	24	25	26	27
	28	29	30	31	1	2	3
JYAISHTHA 1970	4	5	6	7	8	9	10
	11	12	13	14	15	16	17
	18	19	20	21	22	23	24
	25	26	27	28	29	30	31
	32	1	2	3	4	5	6
ĀSHĀDHA 1970	7	8	9	10	11	12	13
	14	15	16	17	18	19	20
	21	22	23	24	25	26	27
	28	29	30	31	1	2	3
ŚRĀVAṆA 1970	4	5	6	7	8	9	10
	11	12	13	14	15	16	17
	18	19	20	21	22	23	24
	25	26	27	28	29	30	31
	32	1	2	3	4	5	6
BHĀDRAPADA 1970	7	8	9	10	11	12	13
	14	15	16	17	18	19	20
	21	22	23	24	25	26	27
	28	29	30	31	1	2	3
ĀŚVINA 1970	4	5	6	7	8	9	10
	11	12	13	14	15	16	17
	18	19	20	21	22	23	24
	25	26	27	28	29	30	1
KĀRTTIKA 1970	2	3	4	5	6	7	8
	9	10	11	12	13	14	15
	16	17	18	19	20	21	22
	23	24	25	26	27	28	29
	30	1	2	3	4	5	6
MĀRGAŚĪRA 1970	7	8	9	10	11	12	13
	14	15	16	17	18	19	20
	21	22	23	24	25	26	27
	28	29	30	1	2	3	4
PAUSHA 1970	5	6	7	8	9	10	11
	12	13	14	15	16	17	18

‡Leap year
[a]New Year (Chitrabhānu)
[b]Pongal

ISLAMIC (ASTRONOMICAL) 1470‡/1471	Sun	Mon	Tue	Wed	Thu	Fri	Sat
RABĪ' I 1470	12	13	14	15	16	17	18
	19	20	21	22	23	24	25
	26	27	28	29	30	1	2
RABĪ' II 1470	3	4	5	6	7	8	9
	10	11	12	13	14	15	16
	17	18	19	20	21	22	23
	24	25	26	27	28	29	1
JUMĀDĀ I 1470	2	3	4	5	6	7	8
	9	10	11	12	13	14	15
	16	17	18	19	20	21	22
	23	24	25	26	27	28	29
	30	1	2	3	4	5	6
JUMĀDĀ II 1470	7	8	9	10	11	12	13
	14	15	16	17	18	19	20
	21	22	23	24	25	26	27
	28	29	1	2	3	4	5
RAJAB 1470	6	7	8	9	10	11	12
	13	14	15	16	17	18	19
	20	21	22	23	24	25	26
	27[d]	28	29	30	1	2	3
SHA'BĀN 1470	4	5	6	7	8	9	10
	11	12	13	14	15	16	17
	18	19	20	21	22	23	24
	25	26	27	28	29	30	1[e]
RAMAḌĀN 1470	2	3	4	5	6	7	8
	9	10	11	12	13	14	15
	16	17	18	19	20	21	22
	23	24	25	26	27	28	29
	30	1[f]	2	3	4	5	6
SHAWWĀL 1470	7	8	9	10	11	12	13
	14	15	16	17	18	19	20
	21	22	23	24	25	26	27
	28	29	30	1	2	3	4
DHU AL-QA'DA 1470	5	6	7	8	9	10	11
	12	13	14	15	16	17	18
	19	20	21	22	23	24	25
	26	27	28	29	30	1	2
DHU AL-ḤIJJA 1470	3	4	5	6	7	8	9
	10[g]	11	12	13	14	15	16
	17	18	19	20	21	22	23
	24	25	26	27	28	29[d]	1[a]
MUḤARRAM 1471	2	3	4	5	6	7	8
	9	10[b]	11	12	13	14	15
	16	17	18	19	20	21	22
	23	24	25	26	27	28	29
ṢAFAR 1471	1	2	3	4	5	6	7
	8	9	10	11	12	13	14
	15	16	17	18	19	20	21
	22	23	24	25	26	27	28
	29	1	2	3	4	5	6
RABĪ' I 1471	7	8	9	10	11	12[c]	13
	14	15	16	17	18	19	20
	21	22	23	24	25	26	27

‡Leap year
[a]New Year
[d]New Year (Arithmetic)
[b]'Ashūrā'
[c]Prophet's Birthday
[d]Ascent of the Prophet
[e]Start of Ramaḍān
[f]'Id al-Fiṭr
[g]'Id al-'Aḍḥā

Julian‡ (Sun)	Sun	Mon	Tue	Wed	Thu	Fri	Sat	GREGORIAN 2048‡
Dec 16	29	30	31	1	2	3	4	JANUARY 2048
	5	6	7[a]	8	9	10	11	
Dec 30	12	13	14[b]	15	16	17	18	
	19	20	21	22	23	24	25	
Jan 13	26	27	28	29	30	31	1	FEBRUARY 2048
	2	3	4	5	6	7	8	
Jan 27	9	10	11	12	13	14	15	
	16	17	18	19[c]	20	21	22	
Feb 10	23[d]	24	25	26	27	28	29	
	1	2	3	4	5	6	7	MARCH 2048
Feb 24	8	9	10	11	12	13	14	
	15	16	17	18	19	20	21	
Mar 9	22	23	24	25	26	27	28	
	29	30	31	1	2	3	4	APRIL 2048
Mar 23	5[e]	6	7	8	9	10	11	
	12	13	14	15	16	17	18	
Apr 6	19	20	21	22	23	24	25	
	26	27	28	29	30	1	2	MAY 2048
Apr 20	3	4	5	6	7	8	9	
	10	11	12	13	14	15	16	
May 4	17	18	19	20	21	22	23	
	24	25	26	27	28	29	30	
May 18	31	1	2	3	4	5	6	JUNE 2048
	7	8	9	10	11	12	13	
Jun 1	14	15	16	17	18	19	20	
	21	22	23	24	25	26	27	
Jun 15	28	29	30	1	2	3	4	JULY 2048
	5	6	7	8	9	10	11	
Jun 29	12	13	14	15	16	17	18	
	19	20	21	22	23	24	25	
Jul 13	26	27	28	29	30	31	1	AUGUST 2048
	2	3	4	5	6	7	8	
Jul 27	9	10	11	12	13	14	15	
	16	17	18	19	20	21	22	
Aug 10	23	24	25	26	27	28	29	
	30	31	1	2	3	4	5	SEPTEMBER 2048
Aug 24	6	7	8	9	10	11	12	
	13	14	15	16	17	18	19	
Sep 7	20	21	22	23	24	25	26	
	27	28	29	30	1	2	3	OCTOBER 2048
Sep 21	4	5	6	7	8	9	10	
	11	12	13	14	15	16	17	
Oct 5	18	19	20	21	22	23	24	
	25	26	27	28	29	30	31	
Oct 19	1	2	3	4	5	6	7	NOVEMBER 2048
	8	9	10	11	12	13	14	
Nov 2	15	16	17	18	19	20	21	
	22	23	24	25	26	27	28	
Nov 16	29[g]	30	1	2	3	4	5	DECEMBER 2048
	6	7	8	9	10	11	12	
Nov 30	13	14	15	16	17	18	19	
	20	21	22	23	24	25[h]	26	
Dec 14	27	28	29	30	31	1	2	

‡Leap year
[a]Orthodox Christmas
[b]Julian New Year
[c]Ash Wednesday
[d]Feast of Orthodoxy
[e]Easter (also Orthodox)
[g]Advent
[h]Christmas

2049

Gregorian 2049 / ISO week / Julian day

Month	Sun	Mon	Tue	Wed	Thu	Fri	Sat	Lunar Phases	ISO WEEK (Mon)	JULIAN DAY (Sun noon)
	27	◑	29	30	31	1[a]	2	8:30	53	2469438
JANUARY 2049	3	●	5	6	7	8	9	2:23	1	2469445
	◐	11	12	13	14	15	16	21:54	2	2469452
	17	18	○	20	21	22	23	2:28	3	2469459
	24	25	◑	27	28	29	30	21:31	4	2469466
	31	1	●	3	4	5	6	13:14	5	2469473
FEBRUARY 2049	7	8	◐	10	11	12	13	15:37	6	2469480
	14	15	16	○	18	19	20	20:46	7	2469487
	21	22	23	24	◑	26	27	7:35	8	2469494
	28	1	2	3	●	5	6	0:10	9	2469501
MARCH 2049	7	8	9	10	◐	12	13	11:25	10	2469508
	14	15	16	17	18	○	20[b]	12:22	11	2469515
	21	22	23	24	25	◑	27	15:09	12	2469522
	28	29	30	31	1	●	3	11:38	13	2469529
APRIL 2049	4	5	6	7	8	9	◐	7:26	14	2469536
	11	12	13	14	15	16	17		15	2469543
	○	19	20	21	22	23	◑	1:03 21:10	16	2469550
	25	26	27	28	29	30	1		17	2469557
MAY 2049	●	3	4	5	6	7	8	0:09	18	2469564
	9	◐	11	12	13	14	15	1:56	19	2469571
	16	○	18	19	20	21	22	11:12	20	2469578
	23	◑	25	26	27	28	29	2:53	21	2469585
	30	●	1	2	3	4	5	13:58	22	2469592
JUNE 2049	6	7	◐	9	10	11	12	17:55	23	2469599
	13	14	○	16	17	18	19	19:25	24	2469606
	20[c]	21	◑	23	24	25	26	9:40	25	2469613
	27	28	29	●	1	2	3	4:49	26	2469620
JULY 2049	4	5	6	7	◐	9	10	7:09	27	2469627
	11	12	13	14	○	16	17	2:28	28	2469634
	18	19	20	◑	22	23	24	18:47	29	2469641
	25	26	27	28	●	30	31	20:06	30	2469648
AUGUST 2049	1	2	3	4	5	◐	7	17:50	31	2469655
	8	9	10	11	12	○	14	9:18	32	2469662
	15	16	17	18	19	◑	21	7:09	33	2469669
	22	23	24	25	26	27	●	11:17	34	2469676
	29	30	31	1	2	3	4		35	2469683
SEPTEMBER 2049	◐	6	7	8	9	10	○	2:27 17:03	36	2469690
	12	13	14	15	16	17	◑	23:02	37	2469697
	19	20	21	22[d]	23	24	25		38	2469704
	26	●	28	29	30	1	2	2:03	39	2469711
OCTOBER 2049	3	◐	5	6	7	8	9	9:37	40	2469718
	10	○	12	13	14	15	16	2:52	41	2469725
	17	◑	19	20	21	22	23	17:54	42	2469732
	24	25	●	27	28	29	30	16:13	43	2469739
	31	1	◐	3	4	5	6	16:18	44	2469746
NOVEMBER 2049	7	8	○	10	11	12	13	15:36	45	2469753
	14	15	16	◑	18	19	20	14:31	46	2469760
	21	22	23	24	●	26	27	5:34	47	2469767
	28	29	30	◐	2	3	4	23:38	48	2469774
DECEMBER 2049	5	6	7	8	○	10	11	7:26	49	2469781
	12	13	14	15	16	◑	18	11:13	50	2469788
	19	20	21[e]	22	23	●	25	17:50	51	2469795
	26	27	28	29	30	◐	1	8:51	52	2469802

Hebrew 5809‡/5810

ISO WEEK	Month	Sun	Mon	Tue	Wed	Thu	Fri	Sat	Molad
53	TEVETH 5809	22	23	24	25	26	27	28	
1		29	1	2	3	4	5	6	Mon 7h38m7p
2	SHEVAT 5809	7	8	9	10	11	12	13	
3		14	15	16	17	18	19	20	
4		21	22	23	24	25	26	27	
5		28	29	30	1	2	3	4	Tue 20h22m8p
6	ADAR I 5809	5	6	7	8	9	10	11	
7		12	13	14	15	16	17	18	
8		19	20	21	22	23	24	25	
9		26	27	28	29	30	1	2	Thu 9h6m9p
10	ADAR II 5809	3	4	5	6	7	8	9	
11		10	11	12	13	14[f]	15	16	
12		17	18	19	20	21	22	23	
13		24	25	26	27	28	29	1	Fri 21h50m10p
14	NISAN 5809	2	3	4	5	6	7	8	
15		9	10	11	12	13	14	15[g]	
16		16	17	18	19	20	21	22	
17		23	24	25	26	27	28	29	
18		30	1	2	3	4	5	6	Sun 10h34m11p
19	IYAR 5809	7	8	9	10	11	12	13	
20		14	15	16	17	18	19	20	
21		21	22	23	24	25	26	27	
22		28	29	1	2	3	4	5	Mon 23h18m12p
23	SIVAN 5809	6[h]	7	8	9	10	11	12	
24		13	14	15	16	17	18	19	
25		20	21	22	23	24	25	26	
26		27	28	29	30	1	2	3	Wed 12h2m13p
27	TAMMUZ 5809	4	5	6	7	8	9	10	
28		11	12	13	14	15	16	17	
29		18	19	20	21	22	23	24	
30		25	26	27	28	29	1	2	Fri 0h46m14p
31	AV 5809	3	4	5	6	7	8	9	
32		10[i]	11	12	13	14	15	16	
33		17	18	19	20	21	22	23	
34		24	25	26	27	28	29	30	
35	ELUL 5809	1	2	3	4	5	6	7	Sat 13h30m15p
36		8	9	10	11	12	13	14	
37		15	16	17	18	19	20	21	
38		22	23	24	25	26	27	28	
39		29	1[a]	2[a]	3	4	5	6	Mon 2h14m16p
40	TISHRI 5810	7	8	9	10[b]	11	12	13	
41		14	15[c]	16	17	18	19	20	
42		21	22	23	24	25	26	27	
43		28	29	30	1	2	3	4	Tue 14h58m17p
44	ḤESHVAN 5810	5	6	7	8	9	10	11	
45		12	13	14	15	16	17	18	
46		19	20	21	22	23	24	25	
47		26	27	28	29	30	1	2	Thu 3h43m0p
48	KISLEV 5810	3	4	5	6	7	8	9	
49		10[d]	11	12	13	14	15	16	
50		17	18	19	20	21	22	23	
51		24	25[e]	26[e]	27[e]	28[e]	29[e]	30[e]	Fri 16h27m1p
52		1[e]	2[e]	3	4	5	6	7	

Chinese Wù-Chén/Jǐ-Sì

ISO WEEK	Month	Sun	Mon	Tue	Wed	Thu	Fri	Sat	Solar Term
53	MONTH 11* Wù-Chén	23	24	25	26	27	28	29	
1	MONTH 12 Wù-Chén	30	1	2	3	4	5	6	Xiǎo hán
2		7	8	9	10	11	12	13	
3		14	15	**16**	17	18	19	20	Dà hán
4		21	22	23	24	25	26	27	
5		28	29	1[a]	2	3	4	5	Lì chūn
6	MONTH 1 Jǐ-Sì	6	7	8	9	10	11	12	
7		13	14	15[b]	16	**17***	18	19	Yǔ shuǐ
8		20	21	22	23	24	25	26	
9		27	28	29	30	1	2	3	Jīng zhé
10	MONTH 2 Jǐ-Sì	4	5	6	7	8	9	10	
11		11	12	13	14	15	16	**17**	Chūn fēn
12		18	19	20	21	22	23	24	
13		25	26	27	28	29	1	2	
14	MONTH 3 Jǐ-Sì	3[c]	4	5	6	7	8	9	Qīng míng
15		10	11	12	13	14	15	16	
16		17	**18***	19	20	21	22	23	Gǔ yǔ
17		24	25	26	27	28	29	30	
18	MONTH 4 Jǐ-Sì	1	2	3	4	5	6	7	Lì xià
19		8	9	10	11	12	13	14	
20		15	16	17	18	**19**	20	21	Xiǎo mǎn
21		22	23	24	25	26	27	28	
22		29	1	2	3	4	5[d]	6	Máng zhòng
23	MONTH 5 Jǐ-Sì	7	8	9	10	11	12	13	
24		14	15	16	17	18	19*	20	
25		21	**22**	23	24	25	26	27	Xià zhì
26		28	29	30	1	2	3	4	
27	MONTH 6 Jǐ-Sì	5	6	7	8	9	10	11	Xiǎo shǔ
28		12	13	14	15	16	17	18	
29		19	20	21	22	**23**	24	25	Dà shǔ
30		26	27	28	29	30	1	2	
31	MONTH 7 Jǐ-Sì	3	4	5	6	7[e]	8	9	Lì qiū
32		10	11	12	13	14	15[f]	16	
33		17	18	19*	20	21	22	23	
34		**24**	25	26	27	28	29	1	Chǔ shǔ
35	MONTH 8 Jǐ-Sì	2	3	4	5	6	7	8	
36		9	10	11	12	13	14	15[g]	Bái lù
37		16	17	18	19	20	21	22	
38		23	24	25	**26**	27	28	29	Qiū fēn
39		30	1	2	3	4	5	6	
40	MONTH 9 Jǐ-Sì	7	8	9[h]	10	11	12	13	Hán lù
41		14	15	16	17	18	19	20*	
42		21	22	23	24	25	26	**27**	Shuāng jiàng
43		28	29	30	1	2	3	4	
44	MONTH 10 Jǐ-Sì	5	6	7	8	9	10	11	
45		12	13	14	15	16	17	18	Lì dōng
46		19	20	21	22	23	24	25	
47		26	**27**	28	29	1	2	3	Xiǎo xuě
48	MONTH 11 Jǐ-Sì	4	5	6	7	8	9	10	
49		11	12	13	14	15	16	17	Dà xuě
50		18	19	20	21*	22	23	24	
51		25	26	27[i]	28	29	30	1	Dōng zhì
52	MONTH 12 Jǐ-Sì	2	3	4	5	6	7	8	

Coptic 1765/1766 – Ethiopic 2041/2042

ISO WEEK	Coptic Month	Sun	Mon	Tue	Wed	Thu	Fri	Sat	Ethiopic Month
53	KOIAK 1765	18	19	20	21	22	23	24	TĀKHŚĀŚ 2041
1		25	26	27	28	29[c]	30	1	
2	TŌBE 1765	2	3	4	5	6[d]	7	8	ṬER 2041
3		9	10	11[e]	12	13	14	15	
4		16	17	18	19	20	21	22	
5		23	24	25	26	27	28	29	
6	MESHIR 1765	30	1	2	3	4	5	6	YAKĀTIT 2041
7		7	8	9	10	11	12	13	
8		14	15	16	17	18	19	20	
9		21	22	23	24	25	26	27	
10	PAREMOTEP 1765	28	29	30	1	2	3	4	MAGĀBIT 2041
11		5	6	7	8	9	10	11	
12		12	13	14	15	16	17	18	
13		19	20	21	22	23	24	25	
14	PARMOUTE 1765	26	27	28	29	30	1	2	MIYĀZYĀ 2041
15		3	4	5	6	7	8	9	
16		10	11	12	13	14	15	16	
17		17[f]	18	19	20	21	22	23	
18		24	25	26	27	28	29[g]	30	
19	PASHONS 1765	1	2	3	4	5	6	7	GENBOT 2041
20		8	9	10	11	12	13	14	
21		15	16	17	18	19	20	21	
22		22	23	24	25	26	27	28	
23	PAŌNE 1765	29	30	1	2	3	4	5	SANĒ 2041
24		6	7	8	9	10	11	12	
25		13	14	15	16	17	18	19	
26		20	21	22	23	24	25	26	
27	EPĒP 1765	27	28	29	30	1	2	3	ḤAMLĒ 2041
28		4	5	6	7	8	9	10	
29		11	12	13	14	15	16	17	
30		18	19	20	21	22	23	24	
31	MESORĒ 1765	25	26	27	28	29	30	1	NAḤASĒ 2041
32		2	3	4	5	6	7	8	
33		9	10	11	12	13[h]	14	15	
34		16	17	18	19	20	21	22	
35		23	24	25	26	27	28	29	
36	EPAG. 1765	30	1	2	3	4	5	1[a]	PĀG. 2041
37	THOOUT 1766	2	3	4	5	6	7	8	MASKARAM 2042
38		9	10	11	12	13	14	15	
39		16	17[b]	18	19	20	21	22	
40		23	24	25	26	27	28	29	
41	PAOPE 1766	30	1	2	3	4	5	6	ṬEQEMT 2042
42		7	8	9	10	11	12	13	
43		14	15	16	17	18	19	20	
44		21	22	23	24	25	26	27	
45	ATHŌR 1766	28	29	30	1	2	3	4	ḪEDĀR 2042
46		5	6	7	8	9	10	11	
47		12	13	14	15	16	17	18	
48		19	20	21	22	23	24	25	
49	KOIAK 1766	26	27	28	29	30	1	2	TĀKHŚĀŚ 2042
50		3	4	5	6	7	8	9	
51		10	11	12	13	14	15	16	
52		17	18	19	20	21	22	23	

Gregorian notes:
[a]New Year
[b]Spring (4:27)
[c]Summer (21:46)
[d]Autumn (13:41)
[e]Winter (10:50)
● New moon
◐ First quarter moon
○ Full moon
◑ Last quarter moon

Hebrew notes:
‡Leap year
[a]New Year
[b]Yom Kippur
[c]Sukkot
[d]Winter starts
[e]Ḥanukkah
[f]Purim
[g]Passover
[h]Shavuot
[i]Fast of Av

Chinese notes:
[a]New Year (4747, Snake)
[b]Lantern Festival
[c]Qīngmíng
[d]Dragon Festival
[e]Qīqiǎo
[f]Hungry Ghosts
[g]Mid-Autumn Festival
[h]Double-Ninth Festival
[i]Dōngzhì
*Start of 60-name cycle

Coptic/Ethiopic notes:
[a]New Year
[b]Building of the Cross
[c]Christmas
[d]Jesus's Circumcision
[e]Epiphany
[f]Easter
[g]Mary's Announcement
[h]Jesus's Transfiguration

PERSIAN (ASTRONOMICAL) 1427/1428‡

Month	Sun	Mon	Tue	Wed	Thu	Fri	Sat
DEY 1427	7	8	9	10	11	12	13
	14	15	16	17	18	19	20
	21	22	23	24	25	26	27
	28	29	30	*1*	2	3	4
BAHMAN 1427	5	6	7	8	9	10	11
	12	13	14	15	16	17	18
	19	20	21	22	23	24	25
	26	27	28	29	30	*1*	2
ESFAND 1427	3	4	5	6	7	8	9
	10	11	12	13	14	15	16
	17	18	19	20	21	22	23
	24	25	26	27	28	29	*1*[a]
FARVARDĪN 1428	2	3	4	5	6	7	8
	9	10	11	12	13[b]	14	15
	16	17	18	19	20	21	22
	23	24	25	26	27	28	29
	30	31	*1*	2	3	4	5
ORDĪBEHEŠT 1428	6	7	8	9	10	11	12
	13	14	15	16	17	18	19
	20	21	22	23	24	25	26
	27	28	29	30	31	*1*	2
XORDĀD 1428	3	4	5	6	7	8	9
	10	11	12	13	14	15	16
	17	18	19	20	21	22	23
	24	25	26	27	28	29	30
	31	*1*	2	3	4	5	6
TĪR 1428	7	8	9	10	11	12	13
	14	15	16	17	18	19	20
	21	22	23	24	25	26	27
	28	29	30	31	*1*	2	3
MORDĀD 1428	4	5	6	7	8	9	10
	11	12	13	14	15	16	17
	18	19	20	21	22	23	24
	25	26	27	28	29	30	31
SHAHRĪVAR 1428	*1*	2	3	4	5	6	7
	8	9	10	11	12	13	14
	15	16	17	18	19	20	21
	22	23	24	25	26	27	28
	29	30	31	*1*	2	3	4
MEHR 1428	5	6	7	8	9	10	11
	12	13	14	15	16	17	18
	19	20	21	22	23	24	25
	26	27	28	29	30	*1*	2
ABĀN 1428	3	4	5	6	7	8	9
	10	11	12	13	14	15	16
	17	18	19	20	21	22	23
	24	25	26	27	28	29	30
ĀZAR 1428	*1*	2	3	4	5	6	7
	8	9	10	11	12	13	14
	15	16	17	18	19	20	21
	22	23	24	25	26	27	28
DEY 1428	29	30	*1*	2	3	4	5
	6	7	8	9	10	11	12

‡Leap year
[a]New Year
[b]Sizdeh Bedar

HINDU LUNAR 2105/2106

Month	Sun	Mon	Tue	Wed	Thu	Fri	Sat
MĀRGAŚĪRA 2105	22	23	24	25	26	27	28
PAUSHA 2105	29	**30**	2	3	4	5	6
	7	8	9	10	11	12	13
	14	15	16	*16*	17	18	19
	20	21	22	23	**24**	26	27
MĀGHA 2105	28	29	30	1	2	3	4
	5	6	7	8	9	10	11
	12	13	14	15	16	17	18
	19	20	21	22	23	24	25
PHĀLGUNA 2105	26	27	28[h]	**29**	1	2	3
	4	5	6	7	8	*8*	9
	10	11	12	13	14	15[i]	16
	17	18	19	20	21	22	**23**
CHAITRA 2106	25	26	27	28	29	30	1[a]
	2	3	4	5	6	7	8
	9[b]	10	11	12	*12*	13	14
	15	17	18	19	20	21	22
	23	24	25	26	27	**28**	30
VAIŚĀKHA 2106	1	2	*2*	3	4	5	6
	7	8	9	10	11	12	13
	14	15	16	17	18	19	**20**
	22	23	24	25	26	27	28
JYAISHṬHA 2106	29	30	1	2	3	4	5
	6	7	*7*	8	9	10	11
	12	14	15	16	17	18	19
	20	21	22	23	**24**	26	27
ĀSHĀḌHA 2106	28	*28*	29	30	1	2	3
	4	5	6	7	8	9	10
	11	12	13	14	**15**	17	18
	19	20	21	22	23	24	25
ŚRĀVAṆA 2106	26	27	28	29	30	1	2
	3	4	*4*	5	6	**7**	9
	10	11	12	13	14	15	16
	17	18	**19**	21	22	23[c]	24
	25	*25*	26	27	28	29	30
BHĀDRAPADA 2106	1	2	3	4[d]	5	6	7
	8	9	10	**11**	13	14	15
	16	17	18	19	20	21	22
	23	24	25	26	27	28	29
ĀŚVINA 2106	30	*30*	1	2	3	**4**	6
	7	8[e]	9[e]	10[e]	11	12	13
	14	15	16	**17**	19	20	*20*
	21	22	23	24	25	26	27
KĀRTTIKA 2106	28	29	30	1[f]	2	3	4
	5	6	7	**8**	10	11	12
	13	14	15	16	17	18	19
	20	21	22	23	*23*	24	25
MĀRGAŚĪRA 2106	26	27	28	29	30	1	**2**
	4	5	6	7	8	9	10
	11[g]	12	13	14	15	16	17
	18	19	20	21	22	23	24
PAUSHA 2106	25	26	27	28	29	30	1
	2	3	4	5	6	**7**	9

[a]New Year (Śukla)
[b]Birthday of Rāma
[c]Birthday of Krishna
[d]Ganēśa Chaturthī
[e]Dashara
[f]Diwali
[g]Birthday of Vishnu
[h]Night of Śiva
[i]Holi

HINDU SOLAR 1970‡/1971

Month	Sun	Mon	Tue	Wed	Thu	Fri	Sat
PAUSHA 1970	12	13	14	15	16	17	18
	19	20	21	22	23	24	25
MĀGHA 1970	26	27	28	29	1[b]	2	3
	4	5	6	7	8	9	10
	11	12	13	14	15	16	17
	18	19	20	21	22	23	24
PHĀLGUNA 1970	25	26	27	28	29	1	2
	3	4	5	6	7	8	9
	10	11	12	13	14	15	16
	17	18	19	20	21	22	23
	24	25	26	27	28	29	30
CHAITRA 1970	1	2	3	4	5	6	7
	8	9	10	11	12	13	14
	15	16	17	18	19	20	21
	22	23	24	25	26	27	28
VAIŚĀKHA 1971	29	30	31	1[a]	2	3	4
	5	6	7	8	9	10	11
	12	13	14	15	16	17	18
	19	20	21	22	23	24	25
JYAISHṬHA 1971	26	27	28	29	30	31	1
	2	3	4	5	6	7	8
	9	10	11	12	13	14	15
	16	17	18	19	20	21	22
	23	24	25	26	27	28	29
ĀSHĀḌHA 1971	30	31	1	2	3	4	5
	6	7	8	9	10	11	12
	13	14	15	16	17	18	19
	20	21	22	23	24	25	26
ŚRĀVAṆA 1971	27	28	29	30	31	32	1
	2	3	4	5	6	7	8
	9	10	11	12	13	14	15
	16	17	18	19	20	21	22
	23	24	25	26	27	28	29
BHĀDRAPADA 1971	30	31	1	2	3	4	5
	6	7	8	9	10	11	12
	13	14	15	16	17	18	19
	20	21	22	23	24	25	26
ĀŚVINA 1971	27	28	29	30	31	1	2
	3	4	5	6	7	8	9
	10	11	12	13	14	15	16
	17	18	19	20	21	22	23
	24	25	26	27	28	29	30
KĀRTTIKA 1971	31	1	2	3	4	5	6
	7	8	9	10	11	12	13
	14	15	16	17	18	19	20
	21	22	23	24	25	26	27
MĀRGAŚĪRA 1971	28	29	1	2	3	4	5
	6	7	8	9	10	11	12
	13	14	15	16	17	18	19
	20	21	22	23	24	25	26
PAUSHA 1971	27	28	29	30	1	2	3
	4	5	6	7	8	9	10
	11	12	13	14	15	16	17

‡Leap year
[a]New Year (Subhānu)
[b]Pongal

ISLAMIC (ASTRONOMICAL) 1471/1472

Month	Sun	Mon	Tue	Wed	Thu	Fri	Sat
RABĪʿ I 1471	21	22	23	24	25	26	27
RABĪʿ II 1471	28	29	1	2	3	4	5
	6	7	8	9	10	11	12
	13	14	15	16	17	18	19
	20	21	22	23	24	25	26
JUMĀDĀ I 1471	27	28	29	30	1	2	3
	4	5	6	7	8	9	10
	11	12	13	14	15	16	17
	18	19	20	21	22	23	24
JUMĀDĀ II 1471	25	26	27	28	29	1	2
	3	4	5	6	7	8	9
	10	11	12	13	14	15	16
	17	18	19	20	21	22	23
	24	25	26	27	28	29	30
RAJAB 1471	1	2	3	4	5	6	7
	8	9	10	11	12	13	14
	15	16	17	18	19	20	21
	22	23	24	25	26	27[d]	28
SHAʿBĀN 1471	29	1	2	3	4	5	6
	7	8	9	10	11	12	13
	14	15	16	17	18	19	20
	21	22	23	24	25	26	27
RAMAḌĀN 1471	28	29	30	1[e]	2	3	4
	5	6	7	8	9	10	11
	12	13	14	15	16	17	18
	19	20	21	22	23	24	25
SHAWWĀL 1471	26	27	28	29	30	1[f]	2
	3	4	5	6	7	8	9
	10	11	12	13	14	15	16
	17	18	19	20	21	22	23
	24	25	26	27	28	29	*30*
DHU AL-QAʿDA 1471	1	2	3	4	5	6	7
	8	9	10	11	12	13	14
	15	16	17	18	19	20	21
	22	23	24	25	26	27	28
DHU AL-ḤIJJA 1471	29	30	1	2	3	4	5
	6	7	8	9	10[g]	11	12
	13	14	15	16	17	18	19
	20	21	22	23	24	25	26
MUḤARRAM 1472	27	28	29[d]	1[a]	2	3	4
	5	6	7	8	9	10[b]	11
	12	13	14	15	16	17	18
	19	20	21	22	23	24	25
ṢAFAR 1472	26	27	28	29	1	2	3
	4	5	6	7	8	9	10
	11	12	13	14	15	16	17
	18	19	20	21	22	23	24
RABĪʿ I 1472	25	26	27	28	29	30	1
	2	3	4	5	6	7	8
	9	10	11	12[c]	13	14	15
	16	17	18	19	20	21	22
	23	24	25	26	27	28	29
	1	2	3	4	5	6	7

[a]New Year
[A]New Year (Arithmetic)
[b]ʿAshūrāʾ
[c]Prophet's Birthday
[d]Ascent of the Prophet
[e]Start of Ramaḍān
[f]ʿĪd al-Fiṭr
[g]ʿĪd al-ʾAḍḥā

GREGORIAN 2049

Julian (Sun)	Sun	Mon	Tue	Wed	Thu	Fri	Sat	Month
Dec 14	27	28	29	30	31	1	2	JANUARY 2049
	3	4	5	6	7[a]	8	9	
Dec 28	10	11	12	13	14[b]	15	16	
	17	18	19	20	21	22	23	
Jan 11	24	25	26	27	28	29	30	
	31	1	2	3	4	5	6	FEBRUARY 2049
Jan 25	7	8	9	10	11	12	13	
	14	15	16	17	18	19	20	
Feb 8	21	22	23	24	25	26	27	
	28	1	2	3[c]	4	5	6	MARCH 2049
Feb 22	7	8	9	10	11	12	13	
	14[d]	15	16	17	18	19	20	
Mar 8	21	22	23	24	25	26	27	
	28	29	30	31	1	2	3	APRIL 2049
Mar 22	4	5	6	7	8	9	10	
	11	12	13	14	15	16	17	
Apr 5	18[e]	19	20	21	22	23	24	
	25[f]	26	27	28	29	30	1	MAY 2049
Apr 19	2	3	4	5	6	7	8	
	9	10	11	12	13	14	15	
May 3	16	17	18	19	20	21	22	
	23	24	25	26	27	28	29	
May 17	30	31	1	2	3	4	5	JUNE 2049
	6	7	8	9	10	11	12	
May 31	13	14	15	16	17	18	19	
	20	21	22	23	24	25	26	
Jun 14	27	28	29	30	1	2	3	JULY 2049
	4	5	6	7	8	9	10	
Jun 28	11	12	13	14	15	16	17	
	18	19	20	21	22	23	24	
Jul 12	25	26	27	28	29	30	31	
	1	2	3	4	5	6	7	AUGUST 2049
Jul 26	8	9	10	11	12	13	14	
	15	16	17	18	19	20	21	
Aug 9	22	23	24	25	26	27	28	
	29	30	31	1	2	3	4	SEPTEMBER 2049
Aug 23	5	6	7	8	9	10	11	
	12	13	14	15	16	17	18	
Sep 6	19	20	21	22	23	24	25	
	26	27	28	29	30	1	2	OCTOBER 2049
Sep 20	3	4	5	6	7	8	9	
	10	11	12	13	14	15	16	
Oct 4	17	18	19	20	21	22	23	
	24	25	26	27	28	29	30	
Oct 18	31	1	2	3	4	5	6	NOVEMBER 2049
	7	8	9	10	11	12	13	
Nov 1	14	15	16	17	18	19	20	
	21	22	23	24	25	26	27	
Nov 15	28[g]	29	30	1	2	3	4	DECEMBER 2049
	5	6	7	8	9	10	11	
Nov 29	12	13	14	15	16	17	18	
	19	20	21	22	23	24	25[h]	
Dec 13	26	27	28	29	30	31	1	

[a]Orthodox Christmas
[b]Julian New Year
[c]Ash Wednesday
[d]Feast of Orthodoxy
[e]Easter
[f]Orthodox Easter
[g]Advent
[h]Christmas

2050

GREGORIAN 2050	Sun Mon Tue Wed Thu Fri Sat	Lunar Phases	ISO WEEK (Mon)	JULIAN DAY (Sun noon)	HEBREW 5810/5811	Sun Mon Tue Wed Thu Fri Sat	Molad	CHINESE Jǐ-Sì/Gēng-Wǔ‡	Sun Mon Tue Wed Thu Fri Sat	Solar Term	COPTIC 1766/1767‡	Sun Mon Tue Wed Thu Fri Sat	ETHIOPIC 2042/2043‡
	26 27 28 29 30 ◐ 1[a]	8:51	52	2469802		1[e] 2[e] 3 4 5 6 7	Fri 16h27m1p	MONTH 12 Jǐ-Sì	2 3 4 5 6 7 8		KOIAK 1766	17 18 19 20 21 22 23	TĀKHŚĀŚ 2042
JANUARY 2050	2 3 4 5 6 7 ○	1:37	1	2469809	TEVETH 5810	8 9 10 11 12 13 14			9 10 11 12 13 14 15	Xiǎo hán		24 25 26 27 28 29[c] 30	
	9 10 11 12 13 14 15		2	2469816		15 16 17 18 19 20 21			16 17 18 19 20 21 22			1 2 3 4 5 6[d] 7	
	◑ 17 18 19 20 21 22	6:16	3	2469823		22 23 24 25 26 27 28			23 24 25 26 27 28 29	Dà hán	TÔBE 1766	8 9 10 11[e] 12 13 14	
	● 24 25 26 27 28 ◐	4:55 20:46	4	2469830		29 1 2 3 4 5 6	Sun 5h11m2p	MONTH 1 Gēng-Wǔ	1[a] 2 3 4 5 6 7			15 16 17 18 19 20 21	ṬER 2042
	30 31 1 2 3 4 5		5	2469837	SHEVAT 5810	7 8 9 10 11 12 13			8 9 10 11 12 13 14	Lì chūn		22 23 24 25 26 27 28	
FEBRUARY 2050	○ 7 8 9 10 11 12	20:46	6	2469844		14 15 16 17 18 19 20			15[b] 16 17 18 19 20 21			29 30 1 2 3 4 5	
	13 ◑ 15 16 17 18 19	22:09	7	2469851		21 22 23 24 25 26 27			22* 23 24 25 26 27 28	Yǔ shuǐ	MESHIR 1766	6 7 8 9 10 11 12	
	20 ● 22 23 24 25 26	15:02	8	2469858		28 29 30 1 2 3 4	Mon 17h55m3p		29 1 2 3 4 5 6			13 14 15 16 17 18 19	YAKĀTIT 2042
	27 ◐ 1 2 3 4 5	11:28	9	2469865	ADAR 5810	5 6 7 8 9 10 11		MONTH 2 Gēng-Wǔ	7 8 9 10 11 12 13	Jīng zhé		20 21 22 23 24 25 26	
MARCH 2050	6 7 ○ 9 10 11 12	15:22	10	2469872		12 13 14[f] 15 16 17 18			14 15 16 17 18 19 20			27 28 29 30 1 2 3	
	13 14 15 ◑ 17 18 19	10:06	11	2469879		19 20 21 22 23 24 25			21 22 23 24 25 26 27		PAREMOTEP 1766	4 5 6 7 8 9 10	
	20[b] 21 22 ● 24 25 26	0:39	12	2469886		26 27 28 29 1 2 3	Wed 6h39m4p		28 29 30 1 2 3 4	Chūn fēn		11 12 13 14 15 16 17	MAGĀBIT 2042
	27 28 29 ◐ 31 1 2	4:16	13	2469893	NISAN 5810	4 5 6 7 8 9 10		MONTH 3 Gēng-Wǔ	5 6 7 8 9 10 11			18 19 20 21 22 23 24	
APRIL 2050	3 4 5 6 ○ 8 9	8:11	14	2469900		11 12 13 14 15[g] 16 17			12 13[c] 14 15 16 17 18	Qīng míng		25 26 27 28 29 30 1	
	10 11 12 13 ◑ 15 16	18:22	15	2469907		18 19 20 21 22 23 24			19 20 21 22 23* 24 25		PARMOUTE 1766	2 3 4 5 6 7 8	
	17 18 19 20 ● 22 23	10:24	16	2469914		25 26 27 28 29 30 1	Thu 19h23m5p		26 27 28 29 1 2 3	Gǔ yǔ		9[f] 10 11 12 13 14 15	MIYĀZYĀ 2042
	24 25 26 27 ◐ 29 30	22:07	17	2469921	IYYAR 5810	2 3 4 5 6 7 8		LEAP MONTH 3 Gēng-Wǔ	4 5 6 7 8 9 10			16 17 18 19 20 21 22	
MAY 2050	1 2 3 4 5 ○ 7	22:25	18	2469928		9 10 11 12 13 14 15			11 12 13 14 15 16 17	Lì xià		23 24 25 26 27 28 29[g]	
	8 9 10 11 12 13 ◑	0:02	19	2469935		16 17 18 19 20 21 22			18 19 20 21 22 23 24			30 1 2 3 4 5 6	
	15 16 17 18 19 ● 21	20:49	20	2469942		23 24 25 26 27 28 29			25 26 27 28 29 30 1	Xiǎo mǎn	PASHONS 1766	7 8 9 10 11 12 13	
	22 23 24 25 26 27 ◐	16:03	21	2469949	SIVAN 5810	1 2 3 4 5 6[h] 7	Sat 8h7m6p	MONTH 4 Gēng-Wǔ	2 3 4 5 6 7 8			14 15 16 17 18 19 20	GENBOT 2042
	29 30 31 1 2 3 4		22	2469956		8 9 10 11 12 13 14			9 10 11 12 13 14 15			21 22 23 24 25 26 27	
JUNE 2050	○ 6 7 8 9 10 11	9:50	23	2469963		15 16 17 18 19 20 21			16 17 18 19 20 21 22	Máng zhòng		28 29 30 1 2 3 4	
	◑ 13 14 15 16 17 18	4:38	24	2469970		22 23 24 25 26 27 28			23 24* 25 26 27 28 29			5 6 7 8 9 10 11	
	● 20 21[c] 22 23 24 25	8:20	25	2469977		29 30 1 2 3 4 5	Sun 20h51m7p		1 2 3 4 5[d] 6 7	Xià zhì	PAÔNE 1766	12 13 14 15 16 17 18	SANĒ 2042
	26 ◐ 28 29 30 1 2	9:15	26	2469984	TAMMUZ 5810	6 7 8 9 10 11 12		MONTH 5 Gēng-Wǔ	8 9 10 11 12 13 14			19 20 21 22 23 24 25	
JULY 2050	3 ○ 5 6 7 8 9	18:49	27	2469991		13 14 15 16 17 18 19			15 16 17 18 19 20 21	Xiǎo shǔ		26 27 28 29 30 1 2	
	10 ◑ 12 13 14 15 16	9:44	28	2469998		20 21 22 23 24 25 26			22 23 24 25 26 27 28		EPÊP 1766	3 4 5 6 7 8 9	ḤAMLĒ 2042
	17 ● 19 20 21 22 23	21:15	29	2470005		27 28 29 1 2 3 4	Tue 9h35m8p		29 30 1 2 3 4 5	Dà shǔ		10 11 12 13 14 15 16	
	24 25 26 ◐ 28 29 30	1:04	30	2470012	AV 5810	5 6 7 8 9[i] 10 11		MONTH 6 Gēng-Wǔ	6 7 8 9 10 11 12			17 18 19 20 21 22 23	
	31 1 2 ○ 4 5 6	2:19	31	2470019		12 13 14 15 16 17 18			13 14 15 16 17 18 19			24 25 26 27 28 29 30	
AUGUST 2050	7 8 ◑ 10 11 12 13	16:47	32	2470026		19 20 21 22 23 24 25			20 21 22 23 24 25* 26	Lì qiū		1 2 3 4 5 6 7	
	14 15 16 ● 18 19 20	11:46	33	2470033		26 27 28 29 30 1 2	Wed 22h19m9p		27 28 29 1 2 3 4			8 9 10 11 12 13[h] 14	NAHASĒ 2042
	21 22 23 24 ◐ 26 27	14:55	34	2470040	ELUL 5810	3 4 5 6 7 8 9		MONTH 7 Gēng-Wǔ	5 6 7[e] 8 9 10 11	Chǔ shǔ	MESORÊ 1766	15 16 17 18 19 20 21	
	28 29 30 31 ○ 2 3	9:29	35	2470047		10 11 12 13 14 15 16			12 13 14 15[f] 16 17 18			22 23 24 25 26 27 28	
SEPTEMBER 2050	4 5 6 7 ◑ 9 10	2:50	36	2470054		17 18 19 20 21 22 23			19 20 21 22 23 24 25	Bái lù	EPAG. 1766	29 30 1 2 3 4 5	PĀG. 2042
	11 12 13 14 15 ● 17	3:47	37	2470061		24 25 26 27 28 29 1[a]	Fri 11h3m10p		26 27 28 29 30 1 2			1[a] 2 3 4 5 6 7	
	18 19 20 21 22[d] 23 ◐	2:32	38	2470068	TISHRI 5811	2[a] 3 4 5 6 7 8		MONTH 8 Gēng-Wǔ	3 4 5 6 7 8 9	Qiū fēn	THOOUT 1767	8 9 10 11 12 13 14	MASKARAM 2043
	25 26 27 28 29 ○ 1	17:30	39	2470075		9 10[b] 11 12 13 14 15[c]			10 11 12 13 14 15[g] 16			15 16 17[b] 18 19 20 21	
OCTOBER 2050	2 3 4 5 6 ◑ 8	16:31	40	2470082		16 17 18 19 20 21 22			17 18 19 20 21 22 23	Hán lù		22 23 24 25 26 27 28	
	9 10 11 12 13 14 ●	20:47	41	2470089		23 24 25 26 27 28 29			24 25 26* 27 28 29 30			29 30 1 2 3 4 5	
	16 17 18 19 20 21 22		42	2470096		30 1 2 3 4 5 6	Sat 23h47m11p		1 2 3 4 5 6 7			6 7 8 9 10 11 12	
	◐ 24 25 26 27 28 29	12:09	43	2470103	HESHVAN 5811	7 8 9 10 11 12 13		MONTH 9 Gēng-Wǔ	8 9[h] 10 11 12 13 14	Shuāng jiàng	PAOPE 1767	13 14 15 16 17 18 19	ṬEQEMT 2043
	○ 31 1 2 3 4 5	3:14	44	2470110		14 15 16 17 18 19 20			15 16 17 18 19 20 21			20 21 22 23 24 25 26	
NOVEMBER 2050	◑ 7 8 9 10 11 12	9:55	45	2470117		21 22 23 24 25 26 27			22 23 24 25 26 27 28	Lì dōng		27 28 29 30 1 2 3	
	13 ● 15 16 17 18 19	13:40	46	2470124		28 29 30 1 2 3 4	Mon 12h31m12p		29 1 2 3 4 5 6			4 5 6 7 8 9 10	
	20 ◐ 22 23 24 25 26	20:24	47	2470131	KISLEV 5811	5 6 7 8 9 10 11		MONTH 10 Gēng-Wǔ	7 8 9 10 11 12 13	Xiǎo xuě	ATHÔR 1767	11 12 13 14 15 16 17	HEDĀR 2043
	27 ○ 29 30 1 2 3	15:08	48	2470138		12 13 14 15 16 17 18			14 15 16 17 18 19 20			18 19 20 21 22 23 24	
DECEMBER 2050	4 5 ◑ 7 8 9 10	6:26	49	2470145		19 20[d] 21 22 23 24 25[e]			21 22 23 24 25 26 27*	Dà xuě		25 26 27 28 29 30 1	
	11 12 13 ● 15 16 17	5:16	50	2470152		26[e] 27[e] 28[e] 29[e] 30[e] 1[e] 2[e]	Wed 1h15m13p		28 29 30 1 2 3 4		KOIAK 1767	2 3 4 5 6 7 8	TĀKHŚĀŚ 2043
	18 19 20 ◐[e] 22 23 24	4:13	51	2470159	TEVETH 5811	3 4 5 6 7 8 9		MONTH 11 Gēng-Wǔ	5 6 7 8 9[i] 10 11	Dōng zhì		9 10 11 12 13 14 15	
	25 26 27 ○ 29 30 31	5:14	52	2470166		10 11 12 13 14 15 16			12 13 14 15 16 17 18			16 17 18 19 20 21 22	

[a]New Year
[b]Spring (10:18)
[c]Summer (3:32)
[d]Autumn (19:27)
[e]Winter (16:37)
● New moon
◐ First quarter moon
○ Full moon
◑ Last quarter moon

[a]New Year
[b]Yom Kippur
[c]Sukkot
[d]Winter starts
[e]Ḥanukkah
[f]Purim
[g]Passover
[h]Shavuot
[i]Fast of Av

‡Leap year
[a]New Year (4748, Horse)
[b]Lantern Festival
[c]Qīngmíng
[d]Dragon Festival
[e]Qīqiǎo
[f]Hungry Ghosts
[g]Mid-Autumn Festival
[h]Double-Ninth Festival
[i]Dōngzhì
*Start of 60-name cycle

‡Leap year
[a]New Year
[b]Building of the Cross
[c]Christmas
[d]Jesus's Circumcision
[e]Epiphany
[f]Easter
[g]Mary's Announcement
[h]Jesus's Transfiguration

PERSIAN (ASTRONOMICAL) 1428†/1429

Month	Sun	Mon	Tue	Wed	Thu	Fri	Sat
DEY 1428	6	7	8	9	10	11	12
	13	14	15	16	17	18	19
	20	21	22	23	24	25	26
	27	28	29	30	1	2	3
BAHMAN 1428	4	5	6	7	8	9	10
	11	12	13	14	15	16	17
	18	19	20	21	22	23	24
	25	26	27	28	29	30	1
ESFAND 1428	2	3	4	5	6	7	8
	9	10	11	12	13	14	15
	16	17	18	19	20	21	22
	23	24	25	26	27	28	29
	30	1[a]	2	3	4	5	6
FARVARDĪN 1429	7	8	9	10	11	12	13[b]
	14	15	16	17	18	19	20
	21	22	23	24	25	26	27
	28	29	30	31	1	2	3
ORDĪBEHEŠT 1429	4	5	6	7	8	9	10
	11	12	13	14	15	16	17
	18	19	20	21	22	23	24
	25	26	27	28	29	30	31
XORDĀD 1429	1	2	3	4	5	6	7
	8	9	10	11	12	13	14
	15	16	17	18	19	20	21
	22	23	24	25	26	27	28
	29	30	31	1	2	3	4
TĪR 1429	5	6	7	8	9	10	11
	12	13	14	15	16	17	18
	19	20	21	22	23	24	25
	26	27	28	29	30	31	1
MORDĀD 1429	2	3	4	5	6	7	8
	9	10	11	12	13	14	15
	16	17	18	19	20	21	22
	23	24	25	26	27	28	29
	30	31	1	2	3	4	5
SHAHRĪVAR 1429	6	7	8	9	10	11	12
	13	14	15	16	17	18	19
	20	21	22	23	24	25	26
	27	28	29	30	31	1	2
MEHR 1429	3	4	5	6	7	8	9
	10	11	12	13	14	15	16
	17	18	19	20	21	22	23
	24	25	26	27	28	29	30
ĀBĀN 1429	1	2	3	4	5	6	7
	8	9	10	11	12	13	14
	15	16	17	18	19	20	21
	22	23	24	25	26	27	28
	29	30	1	2	3	4	5
ĀZAR 1429	6	7	8	9	10	11	12
	13	14	15	16	17	18	19
	20	21	22	23	24	25	26
	27	28	29	30	1	2	3
DEY 1429	4	5	6	7	8	9	10

†Leap year
[a]New Year
[b]Sizdeh Bedar

HINDU LUNAR 2106/2107†

Month	Sun	Mon	Tue	Wed	Thu	Fri	Sat
PAUSHA 2106	2	3	4	5	6	7	9
	10	11	12	13	14	15	16
	16	17	18	19	20	21	22
	23	24	25	26	27	28	29
MĀGHA 2106	30	1	3	4	5	6	7
	8	9	10	11	12	13	14
	15	16	17	18	18	19	20
	21	22	23	24	25	27	28
PHĀLGUNA 2106	29[h]	30	1	2	3	4	5
	6	7	8	9	10	11	12
	13	14	15[i]	16	17	18	19
	20	21	22	23	24	25	26
CHAITRA 2107	27	28	29	30[a]	2	3	4
	5	6	7	8	9[b]	10	11
	12	12	13	14	15	16	17
	18	19	20	21	22	23	25
VAIŚĀKHA 2107	26	27	28	29	30	1	2
	3	4	5	6	7	8	9
	10	11	12	13	14	15	16
	17	18	19	20	21	22	23
JYAISHTHA 2107	24	25	26	27	29	30	1
	2	3	4	5	6	7	7
	8	9	10	11	12	13	14
	15	16	17	18	19	20	22
	23	24	25	26	27	28	29
ĀSHĀDHA 2107	30	1	2	3	4	5	6
	7	8	9	10	11	12	13
	14	15	16	17	18	19	20
	21	22	23	25	26	27	28
LEAP ŚRĀVAṆA 2107	29	30	1	2	3	3	4
	5	6	7	8	9	10	11
	12	13	14	15	17	18	19
	20	21	22	23	24	25	26
ŚRĀVAṆA 2107	27	28	29	30	1	2	3
	4	5	6	7	8	9	10
	11	12	13	14	15	16	17
	18	20	21	22	23[c]	24	25
BHĀDRAPADA 2107	26	27	28	29	30	30	1
	2	3	4[d]	5	6	7	8
	9	10	11	12	14	15	16
	17	18	19	20	21	22	23
	24	25	26	27	28	29	30
ĀŚVINA 2107	1	2	3	4	5	6	7
	8[e]	9[e]	10[e]	11	12	13	14
	15	16	18	19	20	21	22
	23	24	24	25	26	27	28
KĀRTTIKA 2107	29	30	1[f]	2	3	4	5
	6	7	8	9	11	12	13
	14	15	16	17	18	19	20
	21	22	23	24	25	26	26
MĀRGAŚIRA 2107	27	28	29	30	1	2	3
	5	6	7	8	9	10	11[g]
	12	13	14	15	16	17	18

†Leap year
[a]New Year (Pramoda)
[b]Birthday of Rāma
[c]Birthday of Krishna
[d]Ganēśa Chaturthī
[e]Dashara
[f]Diwali
[g]Birthday of Vishnu
[h]Night of Śiva
[i]Holi

HINDU SOLAR 1971/1972

Month	Sun	Mon	Tue	Wed	Thu	Fri	Sat
PAUSHA 1971	11	12	13	14	15	16	17
	18	19	20	21	22	23	24
	25	26	27	28	29	1[b]	2
MĀGHA 1971	3	4	5	6	7	8	9
	10	11	12	13	14	15	16
	17	18	19	20	21	22	23
	24	25	26	27	28	29	30
PHĀLGUNA 1971	1	2	3	4	5	6	7
	8	9	10	11	12	13	14
	15	16	17	18	19	20	21
	22	23	24	25	26	27	28
CHAITRA 1971	29	30	1	2	3	4	5
	6	7	8	9	10	11	12
	13	14	15	16	17	18	19
	20	21	22	23	24	25	26
VAIŚĀKHA 1972	27	28	29	30	1[a]	2	3
	4	5	6	7	8	9	10
	11	12	13	14	15	16	17
	18	19	20	21	22	23	24
	25	26	27	28	29	30	31
JYAISHTHA 1972	1	2	3	4	5	6	7
	8	9	10	11	12	13	14
	15	16	17	18	19	20	21
	22	23	24	25	26	27	28
ĀSHĀDHA 1972	29	30	31	1	2	3	4
	5	6	7	8	9	10	11
	12	13	14	15	16	17	18
	19	20	21	22	23	24	25
	26	27	28	29	30	31	32
ŚRĀVAṆA 1972	1	2	3	4	5	6	7
	8	9	10	11	12	13	14
	15	16	17	18	19	20	21
	22	23	24	25	26	27	28
BHĀDRAPADA 1972	29	30	31	1	2	3	4
	5	6	7	8	9	10	11
	12	13	14	15	16	17	18
	19	20	21	22	23	24	25
ĀŚVINA 1972	26	27	28	29	30	31	1
	2	3	4	5	6	7	8
	9	10	11	12	13	14	15
	16	17	18	19	20	21	22
	23	24	25	26	27	28	29
KĀRTTIKA 1972	30	31	1	2	3	4	5
	6	7	8	9	10	11	12
	13	14	15	16	17	18	19
	20	21	22	23	24	25	26
MĀRGAŚIRA 1972	27	28	29	30	1	2	3
	4	5	6	7	8	9	10
	11	12	13	14	15	16	17
	18	19	20	21	22	23	24
PAUSHA 1972	25	26	27	28	29	1	2
	3	4	5	6	7	8	9
	10	11	12	13	14	15	16

[a]New Year (Tāraṇa)
[b]Pongal

ISLAMIC (ASTRONOMICAL) 1472/1473

Month	Sun	Mon	Tue	Wed	Thu	Fri	Sat
RABĪ' II 1472	1	2	3	4	5	6	7
	8	9	10	11	12	13	14
	15	16	17	18	19	20	21
	22	23	24	25	26	27	28
JUMĀDĀ I 1472	29	1	2	3	4	5	6
	7	8	9	10	11	12	13
	14	15	16	17	18	19	20
	21	22	23	24	25	26	27
JUMĀDĀ II 1472	28	29	30	1	2	3	4
	5	6	7	8	9	10	11
	12	13	14	15	16	17	18
	19	20	21	22	23	24	25
RAJAB 1472	26	27	28	29	1	2	3
	4	5	6	7	8	9	10
	11	12	13	14	15	16	17
	18	19	20	21	22	23	24
SHA'BĀN 1472	25	26	27[d]	28	29	30	1
	2	3	4	5	6	7	8
	9	10	11	12	13	14	15
	16	17	18	19	20	21	22
	23	24	25	26	27	28	29
RAMAḌĀN 1472	1[e]	2	3	4	5	6	7
	8	9	10	11	12	13	14
	15	16	17	18	19	20	21
	22	23	24	25	26	27	28
SHAWWĀL 1472	29	30	1[f]	2	3	4	5
	6	7	8	9	10	11	12
	13	14	15	16	17	18	19
	20	21	22	23	24	25	26
DHU AL-QA'DA 1472	27	28	29	30	1	2	3
	4	5	6	7	8	9	10
	11	12	13	14	15	16	17
	18	19	20	21	22	23	24
DHU AL-ḤIJJA 1472	25	26	27	28	29	30	1
	2	3	4	5	6	7	8
	9	10[g]	11	12	13	14	15
	16	17	18	19	20	21	22
	23	24	25	26	27	28	29
MUḤARRAM 1473	1[a]	2	3	4	5	6	7
	8	9	10[b]	11	12	13	14
	15	16	17	18	19	20	21
	22	23	24	25	26	27	28
ṢAFAR 1473	29	30	1	2	3	4	5
	6	7	8	9	10	11	12
	13	14	15	16	17	18	19
	20	21	22	23	24	25	26
RABĪ' I 1473	27	28	29	1	2	3	4
	5	6	7	8	9	10	11
	12[c]	13	14	15	16	17	18
	19	20	21	22	23	24	25
RABĪ' II 1473	26	27	28	29	1	2	3
	4	5	6	7	8	9	10
	11	12	13	14	15	16	17

[a]New Year
[b]'Ashūrā'
[c]Prophet's Birthday
[d]Ascent of the Prophet
[e]Start of Ramaḍān
[f]'Īd al-Fiṭr
[g]'Īd al-'Aḍḥā

GREGORIAN 2050

Julian (Sun)	Sun	Mon	Tue	Wed	Thu	Fri	Sat	Month
Dec 13	26	27	28	29	30	31	1	JANUARY 2050
	2	3	4	5	6	7[a]	8	
Dec 27	9	10	11	12	13	14[b]	15	
	16	17	18	19	20	21	22	
Jan 10	23	24	25	26	27	28	29	
	30	31	1	2	3	4	5	FEBRUARY 2050
Jan 24	6	7	8	9	10	11	12	
	13	14	15	16	17	18	19	
Feb 7	20	21	22	23[c]	24	25	26	
	27	28	1	2	3	4	5	MARCH 2050
Feb 21	6[d]	7	8	9	10	11	12	
	13	14	15	16	17	18	19	
Mar 7	20	21	22	23	24	25	26	
	27	28	29	30	31	1	2	APRIL 2050
Mar 21	3	4	5	6	7	8	9	
	10[e]	11	12	13	14	15	16	
Apr 4	17[f]	18	19	20	21	22	23	
	24	25	26	27	28	29	30	
Apr 18	1	2	3	4	5	6	7	MAY 2050
	8	9	10	11	12	13	14	
May 2	15	16	17	18	19	20	21	
	22	23	24	25	26	27	28	
May 16	29	30	31	1	2	3	4	JUNE 2050
	5	6	7	8	9	10	11	
May 30	12	13	14	15	16	17	18	
	19	20	21	22	23	24	25	
Jun 13	26	27	28	29	30	1	2	JULY 2050
	3	4	5	6	7	8	9	
Jun 27	10	11	12	13	14	15	16	
	17	18	19	20	21	22	23	
Jul 11	24	25	26	27	28	29	30	
	31	1	2	3	4	5	6	AUGUST 2050
Jul 25	7	8	9	10	11	12	13	
	14	15	16	17	18	19	20	
Aug 8	21	22	23	24	25	26	27	
	28	29	30	31	1	2	3	SEPTEMBER 2050
Aug 22	4	5	6	7	8	9	10	
	11	12	13	14	15	16	17	
Sep 5	18	19	20	21	22	23	24	
	25	26	27	28	29	30	1	OCTOBER 2050
Sep 19	2	3	4	5	6	7	8	
	9	10	11	12	13	14	15	
Oct 3	16	17	18	19	20	21	22	
	23	24	25	26	27	28	29	
Oct 17	30	31	1	2	3	4	5	NOVEMBER 2050
	6	7	8	9	10	11	12	
Oct 31	13	14	15	16	17	18	19	
	20	21	22	23	24	25	26	
Nov 14	27[g]	28	29	30	1	2	3	DECEMBER 2050
	4	5	6	7	8	9	10	
Nov 28	11	12	13	14	15	16	17	
	18	19	20	21	22	23	24	
Dec 12	25[h]	26	27	28	29	30	31	

[a]Orthodox Christmas
[b]Julian New Year
[c]Ash Wednesday
[d]Feast of Orthodoxy
[e]Easter
[f]Orthodox Easter
[g]Advent
[h]Christmas

2051

Month	Sun	Mon	Tue	Wed	Thu	Fri	Sat	Lunar Phases	ISO WEEK (Mon)	JULIAN DAY (Sun noon)	Hebrew Month	Sun	Mon	Tue	Wed	Thu	Fri	Sat	Molad	Chinese Month	Sun	Mon	Tue	Wed	Thu	Fri	Sat	Solar Term	Coptic Month	Sun	Mon	Tue	Wed	Thu	Fri	Sat	Ethiopic Month
	GREGORIAN 2051										HEBREW 5811/5812‡									CHINESE Gēng-Wǔ‡/Xīn-Wèi									COPTIC 1767‡/1768								ETHIOPIC 2043‡/2044
JANUARY 2051	1[a]	2	3	4	◑	6	7	4:27	1	2470173	TEVETH 5811	17	18	19	20	21	22	23		MONTH 11 Gēng-Wǔ	19	20	21	22	23	24	25	Xiǎo hán	KOIAK 1767	23	24	25	26	27	28	29[c]	TĀKHŚĀŚ 2043
	8	9	10	11	●	13	14	18:56	2	2470180		24	25	26	27	28	29	1	Thu 13h59m14p	MONTH 12 Gēng-Wǔ	26	27	28	29	30	1	2		TŌBE 1767	30	1	2	3	4	5	6[d]	ṬER 2043
	15	16	17	18	◐	20	21	12:36	3	2470187	SHEVAT 5811	2	3	4	5	6	7	8			3	4	5	6	7	**8**	9	Dà hán		7	8	9	10	11[e]	12	13	
	22	23	24	25	○	27	28	21:18	4	2470194		9	10	11	12	13	14	15			10	11	12	13	14	15	16			14	15	16	17	18	19	20	
	29	30	31	1	2	3	◑	1:38	5	2470201		16	17	18	19	20	21	22			17	18	19	20	21	22	23	Lì chūn		21	22	23	24	25	26	27	
FEBRUARY 2051	5	6	7	8	9	10	●	6:40	6	2470208		23	24	25	26	27	28	29		MONTH 1 Xīn-Wèi	24	25	26	27*	28	29	1[a]		MESHIR 1767	28	29	30	1	2	3	4	YAKĀTIT 2043
	12	13	14	15	16	◐	18	22:15	7	2470215	ADAR 5811	30	1	2	3	4	5	6	Sat 2h43m15p		2	3	4	5	6	7	8			5	6	7	8	9	10	11	
	19	20	21	22	23	24	○	14:52	8	2470222		7	8	9	10	11	12	13			**9**	10	11	12	13	14	15[b]	Yǔ shuǐ		12	13	14	15	16	17	18	
	26	27	28	1	2	3	4		9	2470229		14[f]	15	16	17	18	19	20			16	17	18	19	20	21	22			19	20	21	22	23	24	25	
MARCH 2051	◑	6	7	8	9	10	11	19:45	10	2470236		21	22	23	24	25	26	27			23	24	25	26	27	28	29	Jīng zhé	PAREMOTEP 1767	26	27	28	29	30	1	2	MAGĀBIT 2043
	●	13	14	15	16	17	18	16:51	11	2470243	NISAN 5811	28	29	1	2	3	4	5	Sun 15h27m16p	MONTH 2 Xīn-Wèi	30	1	2	3	4	5	6			3	4	5	6	7	8	9	
	◐	20[b]	21	22	23	24	25	9:33	12	2470250		6	7	8	9	10	11	12			7	**8**	9	10	11	12	13	Chūn fēn		10	11	12	13	14	15	16	
	26	○	28	29	30	31	1	8:58	13	2470257		13	14	15[g]	16	17	18	19			14	15	16	17	18	19	20			17	18	19	20	21	22	23	
APRIL 2051	2	3	◑	5	6	7	8	9:40	14	2470264		20	21	22	23	24	25	26			21	22	23	24[c]	25	26	27	Qīng míng		24	25	26	27	28	29	30	
	9	10	●	12	13	14	15	1:58	15	2470271	IYYAR 5811	27	28	29	30	1	2	3	Tue 4h11m17p	MONTH 3 Xīn-Wèi	28*	29	1	2	3	4	5		PARMOUTE 1767	1	2	3	4	5	6	7	MIYĀZYĀ 2043
	16	◐	18	19	20	21	22	22:37	16	2470278		4	5	6	7	8	9	10			6	7	8	9	**10**	11	12	Gǔ yǔ		8	9	10	11	12	13	14	
	23	24	25	○	27	28	29	2:18	17	2470285		11	12	13	14	15	16	17			13	14	15	16	17	18	19			15	16	17	18	19	20	21	
	30	1	2	◑	4	5	6	19:29	18	2470292		18	19	20	21	22	23	24			20	21	22	23	24	25	26	Lì xià		22	23	24	25	26	27	28	
MAY 2051	7	8	9	●	11	12	13	10:28	19	2470299	SIVAN 5811	25	26	27	28	29	1	2	Wed 16h55m18p	MONTH 4 Xīn-Wèi	27	28	29	1	2	3	4		PASHONS 1767	29[f][g]	30	1	2	3	4	5	GENBOT 2043
	14	15	16	◐	18	19	20	13:28	20	2470306		3	4	5	6[h]	7	8	9			5	6	7	8	9	10	11			6	7	8	9	10	11	12	
	21	22	23	24	○	26	27	17:33	21	2470313		10	11	12	13	14	15	16			**12**	13	14	15	16	17	18	Xiǎo mǎn		13	14	15	16	17	18	19	
	28	29	30	31	1	◑	3	2:14	22	2470320		17	18	19	20	21	22	23			19	20	21	22	23	24	25			20	21	22	23	24	25	26	
JUNE 2051	4	5	6	7	●	9	10	18:55	23	2470327		24	25	26	27	28	29	30		MONTH 5 Xīn-Wèi	26	27	28	29	30*	1	2	Máng zhòng	PAŌNE 1767	27	28	29	30	1	2	3	SANĒ 2043
	11	12	13	14	15	◐	17	5:54	24	2470334	TAMMUZ 5811	1	2	3	4	5	6	7	Fri 5h40m1p		3	4	5[d]	6	7	8	9			4	5	6	7	8	9	10	
	18	19	20	21[c]	22	23	○	6:13	25	2470341		8	9	10	11	12	13	14			10	11	12	**13**	14	15	16	Xià zhì		11	12	13	14	15	16	17	
	25	26	27	28	29	30	◑	7:13	26	2470348		15	16	17	18	19	20	21			17	18	19	20	21	22	23			18	19	20	21	22	23	24	
JULY 2051	2	3	4	5	6	7	●	4:08	27	2470355		22	23	24	25	26	27	28		MONTH 6 Xīn-Wèi	24	25	26	27	28	29	1	Xiǎo shǔ	EPĒP 1767	25	26	27	28	29	30	1	ḤAMLĒ 2043
	9	10	11	12	13	14	◐	23:19	28	2470362	AV 5811	29	1	2	3	4	5	6	Sat 18h24m2p		2	3	4	5	6	7	8			2	3	4	5	6	7	8	
	16	17	18	19	20	21	22		29	2470369		7	8	9[i]	10	11	12	13			9	10	11	12	13	14	15			9	10	11	12	13	14	15	
	○	24	25	26	27	28	29	16:35	30	2470376		14	15	16	17	18	19	20			**16**	17	18	19	20	21	22	Dà shǔ		16	17	18	19	20	21	22	
	◑	31	1	2	3	4	5	11:51	31	2470383		21	22	23	24	25	26	27			23	24	25	26	27	28	29			23	24	25	26	27	28	29	
AUGUST 2051	●	7	8	9	10	11	12	15:03	32	2470390	ELUL 5811	28	29	30	1	2	3	4	Mon 7h8m3p	MONTH 7 Xīn-Wèi	1	2*	3	4	5	6	7[e]	Lì qiū	MESORĒ 1767	30	1	2	3	4	5	6	NAḤASĒ 2043
	13	◐	15	16	17	18	19	16:48	33	2470397		5	6	7	8	9	10	11			8	9	10	11	12	13	14			7	8	9	10	11	12	13[h]	
	20	21	○	23	24	25	26	1:34	34	2470404		12	13	14	15	16	17	18			15[f]	16	17	**18**	19	20	21	Chǔ shǔ		14	15	16	17	18	19	20	
	27	◑	29	30	31	1	2	17:28	35	2470411		19	20	21	22	23	24	25			22	23	24	25	26	27	28			21	22	23	24	25	26	27	
SEPTEMBER 2051	3	4	●	6	7	8	9	4:32	36	2470418	TISHRI 5812	26	27	28	29	1[a]	2[a]	3	Tue 19h52m4p	MONTH 8 Xīn-Wèi	29	30	1	2	3	4	5	Bái lù	EPAG. 1767	28	29	30	1	2	3	4	PĀG. 2043
	10	11	12	◐	14	15	16	9:19	37	2470425		4	5	6	7	8	9	10[b]			6	7	8	9	10	11	12		THOOUT 1768	5	6	1[a]	2	3	4	5	MASKARAM 2044
	17	18	19	○	21	22	23[d]	10:10	38	2470432		11	12	13	14	15[c]	16	17			13	14	15[g]	16	17	18	**19**	Qiū fēn		6	7	8	9	10	11	12	
	24	25	26	◑	28	29	30	1:20	39	2470439		18	19	20	21	22	23	24			20	21	22	23	24	25	26			13	14	15	16	17[b]	18	19	
OCTOBER 2051	1	2	3	●	5	6	7	20:45	40	2470446	HESHVAN 5812	25	26	27	28	29	30	1	Thu 8h36m5p	MONTH 9 Xīn-Wèi	27	28	29	30	1	2*	3	Hán lù		20	21	22	23	24	25	26	
	8	9	10	11	12	◐	14	0:11	41	2470453		2	3	4	5	6	7	8			4	5	6	7	8	9[h]	10		PAOPE 1768	27	28	29	30	1	2	3	ṬEQEMT 2044
	15	16	17	18	○	20	21	19:12	42	2470460		9	10	11	12	13	14	15			11	12	13	14	15	16	17			4	5	6	7	8	9	10	
	22	23	24	25	◑	27	28	12:37	43	2470467		16	17	18	19	20	21	22			18	**19**	20	21	22	23	24	Shuāng jiàng		11	12	13	14	15	16	17	
	29	30	31	1	2	●	4	14:58	44	2470474		23	24	25	26	27	28	29		MONTH 10 Xīn-Wèi	25	26	27	28	29	1	2			18	19	20	21	22	23	24	
NOVEMBER 2051	5	6	7	8	9	10	◐	13:05	45	2470481	KISLEV 5812	1	2	3	4	5	6	7	Fri 21h20m6p		3	4	5	6	7	8	9	Lì dōng	ATHŌR 1768	25	26	27	28	29	30	1	ḪEDĀR 2044
	12	13	14	15	16	17	○	5:05	46	2470488		8	9	10	11	12	13	14			10	11	12	13	14	15	16			2	3	4	5	6	7	8	
	19	20	21	22	23	24	◑	4:01	47	2470495		15	16	17	18	19	20	21			17	18	19	**20**	21	22	23	Xiǎo xuě		9	10	11	12	13	14	15	
	26	27	28	29	30	1	2		48	2470502		22	23	24	25[e]	26[e]	27[e]	28[e]			24	25	26	27	28	29	30			16	17	18	19	20	21	22	
DECEMBER 2051	●	4	5	6	7	8	9	9:35	49	2470509	TEVETH 5812	29[e]	1[e]	2[e]	3[d][e]	4	5	6	Sun 10h4m7p	MONTH 11 Xīn-Wèi	1	2	3*	4	5	6	7	Dà xuě		23	24	25	26	27	28	29	
	10	◐	12	13	14	15	16	0:05	50	2470516		7	8	9	10	11	12	13			8	9	10	11	12	13	14		KOIAK 1768	30	1	2	3	4	5	6	TĀKHŚĀŚ 2044
	○	18	19	20	21[e]	22	23	16:04	51	2470523		14	15	16	17	18	19	20			15	16	17	18	19	20[i]	21	Dōng zhì		7	8	9	10	11	12	13	
	◑	25	26	27	28	29	30	23:19	52	2470530		21	22	23	24	25	26	27	Mon 22h48m8p		22	23	24	25	26	27	28			14	15	16	17	18	19	20	
	31	1	●	3	4	5	6	3:04	1	2470537		28	29	1	2	3	4	5			29	30	1	2	3	4	5	Xiǎo hán		21	22	23	24	25	26	27	

[a]New Year
[b]Spring (15:57)
[c]Summer (9:17)
[d]Autumn (1:25)
[e]Winter (22:32)
● New moon
◐ First quarter moon
○ Full moon
◑ Last quarter moon

‡Leap year
[a]New Year
[b]Yom Kippur
[c]Sukkot
[d]Winter starts
[e]Ḥanukkah
[f]Purim
[g]Passover
[h]Shavuot
[i]Fast of Av

‡Leap year
[a]New Year (4749, Sheep)
[b]Lantern Festival
[c]Qīngmíng
[d]Dragon Festival
[e]Qīqiǎo
[f]Hungry Ghosts
[g]Mid-Autumn Festival
[h]Double-Ninth Festival
[i]Dōngzhì
*Start of 60-name cycle

‡Leap year
[a]New Year
[b]Building of the Cross
[c]Christmas
[d]Jesus's Circumcision
[e]Epiphany
[f]Easter
[g]Mary's Announcement
[h]Jesus's Transfiguration

PERSIAN (ASTRONOMICAL) 1429/1430

Month	Sun	Mon	Tue	Wed	Thu	Fri	Sat
DEY 1429	11	12	13	14	15	16	17
	18	19	20	21	22	23	24
BAHMAN 1429	25	26	27	28	29	30	1
	2	3	4	5	6	7	8
	9	10	11	12	13	14	15
	16	17	18	19	20	21	22
	23	24	25	26	27	28	29
ESFAND 1429	30	1	2	3	4	5	6
	7	8	9	10	11	12	13
	14	15	16	17	18	19	20
	21	22	23	24	25	26	27
FARVARDĪN 1430	28	29	1[a]	2	3	4	5
	6	7	8	9	10	11	12
	13[b]	14	15	16	17	18	19
	20	21	22	23	24	25	26
ORDĪBEHEŠT 1430	27	28	29	30	31	1	2
	3	4	5	6	7	8	9
	10	11	12	13	14	15	16
	17	18	19	20	21	22	23
	24	25	26	27	28	29	30
XORDĀD 1430	31	1	2	3	4	5	6
	7	8	9	10	11	12	13
	14	15	16	17	18	19	20
	21	22	23	24	25	26	27
TĪR 1430	28	29	30	31	1	2	3
	4	5	6	7	8	9	10
	11	12	13	14	15	16	17
	18	19	20	21	22	23	24
	25	26	27	28	29	30	31
MORDĀD 1430	1	2	3	4	5	6	7
	8	9	10	11	12	13	14
	15	16	17	18	19	20	21
	22	23	24	25	26	27	28
SHAHRĪVAR 1430	29	30	31	1	2	3	4
	5	6	7	8	9	10	11
	12	13	14	15	16	17	18
	19	20	21	22	23	24	25
MEHR 1430	26	27	28	29	30	31	1
	2	3	4	5	6	7	8
	9	10	11	12	13	14	15
	16	17	18	19	20	21	22
	23	24	25	26	27	28	29
ĀBĀN 1430	30	1	2	3	4	5	6
	7	8	9	10	11	12	13
	14	15	16	17	18	19	20
	21	22	23	24	25	26	27
ĀZAR 1430	28	29	30	1	2	3	4
	5	6	7	8	9	10	11
	12	13	14	15	16	17	18
	19	20	21	22	23	24	25
DEY 1430	26	27	28	29	30	1	2
	3	4	5	6	7	8	9
	10	11	12	13	14	15	16

HINDU LUNAR 2107‡/2108

Month	Sun	Mon	Tue	Wed	Thu	Fri	Sat
MĀRGAŚĪRA 2107	19	20	21	22	23	24	25
PAUSHA 2107	26	27	28	29	30	1	2
	3	4	5	6	7	**8**	10
	11	12	13	14	15	16	17
	18	19	19	20	21	22	23
	24	25	26	27	28	29	30
MĀGHA 2107	1	**2**	4	5	6	7	8
	9	10	11	12	13	14	15
	16	17	18	19	20	21	21
	22	23	24	**25**	27	28	29[h]
PHĀLGUNA 2107	30	1	2	3	4	5	6
	7	8	9	10	11	12	13
	14	15[i]	16	17	18	19	20
	21	22	23	24	25	26	27
CHAITRA 2108	28	29	**30**[a]	2	3	4	5
	6	7	8	9[b]	10	11	12
	13	14	15	15	16	17	18
	19	20	21	22	23	**24**	26
VAIŚĀKHA 2108	27	28	29	30	1	2	3
	4	5	6	7	8	9	10
	11	12	13	14	15	16	17
	18	19	20	21	22	23	24
JYAISHṬHA 2108	25	26	**27**	29	30	1	2
	3	4	5	6	7	8	9
	10	11	11	12	13	14	15
	16	17	18	19	**20**	22	23
	24	25	26	27	28	29	30
ĀSHĀḌHA 2108	1	2	3	4	5	6	7
	8	9	10	11	12	13	14
	15	16	17	18	19	20	21
	22	24	25	26	27	28	29
ŚRĀVAṆA 2108	30	1	2	3	4	5	6
	7	8	8	9	10	11	12
	13	14	**15**	17	18	19	20
	21	22	23[c]	24	25	26	27
BHĀDRAPADA 2108	28	29	30	1	2	3	4[d]
	5	6	7	8	9	10	11
	12	13	14	15	16	17	18
	19	21	22	23	24	25	26
ĀŚVINA 2108	27	28	29	30	1	2	3
	3	4	5	6	7	8[e]	9[e]
	10[e]	11	**12**	14	15	16	17
	18	19	20	21	22	23	24
KĀRTTIKA 2108	25	26	27	28	29	30	1[f]
	2	3	4	5	6	7	8
	9	10	11	12	13	14	15
	16	18	19	20	21	22	23
	24	25	26	27	27	28	29
MĀRGAŚĪRA 2108	30	1	2	3	4	5	6
	7	8	9	**10**[g]	12	13	14
	15	16	17	18	19	20	21
	22	23	24	25	26	27	28
	29	29	30	1	2	3	**4**

HINDU SOLAR 1972/1973

Month	Sun	Mon	Tue	Wed	Thu	Fri	Sat
PAUSHA 1972	17	18	19	20	21	22	23
	24	25	26	27	28	29	30
MĀGHA 1972	1[b]	2	3	4	5	6	7
	8	9	10	11	12	13	14
	15	16	17	18	19	20	21
	22	23	24	25	26	27	28
PHĀLGUNA 1972	29	1	2	3	4	5	6
	7	8	9	10	11	12	13
	14	15	16	17	18	19	20
	21	22	23	24	25	26	27
CHAITRA 1972	28	29	30	1	2	3	4
	5	6	7	8	9	10	11
	12	13	14	15	16	17	18
	19	20	21	22	23	24	25
VAIŚĀKHA 1973	26	27	28	29	30	1[a]	2
	3	4	5	6	7	8	9
	10	11	12	13	14	15	16
	17	18	19	20	21	22	23
	24	25	26	27	28	29	30
JYAISHṬHA 1973	31	1	2	3	4	5	6
	7	8	9	10	11	12	13
	14	15	16	17	18	19	20
	21	22	23	24	25	26	27
ĀSHĀḌHA 1973	28	29	30	31	32	1	2
	3	4	5	6	7	8	9
	10	11	12	13	14	15	16
	17	18	19	20	21	22	23
	24	25	26	27	28	29	30
ŚRĀVAṆA 1973	31	1	2	3	4	5	6
	7	8	9	10	11	12	13
	14	15	16	17	18	19	20
	21	22	23	24	25	26	27
BHĀDRAPADA 1973	28	29	30	31	32	1	2
	3	4	5	6	7	8	9
	10	11	12	13	14	15	16
	17	18	19	20	21	22	23
	24	25	26	27	28	29	30
ĀŚVINA 1973	31	1	2	3	4	5	6
	7	8	9	10	11	12	13
	14	15	16	17	18	19	20
	21	22	23	24	25	26	27
KĀRTTIKA 1973	28	29	30	1	2	3	4
	5	6	7	8	9	10	11
	12	13	14	15	16	17	18
	19	20	21	22	23	24	25
MĀRGAŚĪRA 1973	26	27	28	29	30	1	2
	3	4	5	6	7	8	9
	10	11	12	13	14	15	16
	17	18	19	20	21	22	23
PAUSHA 1973	24	25	26	27	28	29	1
	2	3	4	5	6	7	8
	9	10	11	12	13	14	15
	16	17	18	19	20	21	22

ISLAMIC (ASTRONOMICAL) 1473/1474

Month	Sun	Mon	Tue	Wed	Thu	Fri	Sat
RABĪ' II 1473	18	19	20	21	22	23	24
JUMĀDĀ I 1473	25	26	27	28	29	30	1
	2	3	4	5	6	7	8
	9	10	11	12	13	14	15
	16	17	18	19	20	21	22
	23	24	25	26	27	28	29
JUMĀDĀ II 1473	1	2	3	4	5	6	7
	8	9	10	11	12	13	14
	15	16	17	18	19	20	21
	22	23	24	25	26	27	28
RAJAB 1473	29	30	1	2	3	4	5
	6	7	8	9	10	11	12
	13	14	15	16	17	18	19
	20	21	22	23	24	25	26
SHA'BĀN 1473	27[d]	28	29	1	2	3	4
	5	6	7	8	9	10	11
	12	13	14	15	16	17	18
	19	20	21	22	23	24	25
RAMAḌĀN 1473	26	27	28	29	30	1[e]	2
	3	4	5	6	7	8	9
	10	11	12	13	14	15	16
	17	18	19	20	21	22	23
SHAWWĀL 1473	24	25	26	27	28	29	1[f]
	2	3	4	5	6	7	8
	9	10	11	12	13	14	15
	16	17	18	19	20	21	22
	23	24	25	26	27	28	29
DHU AL-QA'DA 1473	30	1	2	3	4	5	6
	7	8	9	10	11	12	13
	14	15	16	17	18	19	20
	21	22	23	24	25	26	27
DHU AL-ḤIJJA 1473	28	29	30	1	2	3	4
	5	6	7	8	9	10[g]	11
	12	13	14	15	16	17	18
	19	20	21	22	23	24	25
MUḤARRAM 1474	26	27	28	29	1[a]	2	3
	4	5	6	7	8	9	10[b]
	11	12	13	14	15	16	17
	18	19	20	21	22	23	24
ṢAFAR 1474	25	26	27	28	29	30	1
	2	3	4	5	6	7	8
	9	10	11	12	13	14	15
	16	17	18	19	20	21	22
	23	24	25	26	27	28	29
RABĪ' I 1474	1	2	3	4	5	6	7
	8	9	10	11	12[c]	13	14
	15	16	17	18	19	20	21
	22	23	24	25	26	27	28
RABĪ' II 1474	29	30	1	2	3	4	5
	6	7	8	9	10	11	12
	13	14	15	16	17	18	19
	20	21	22	23	24	25	26
	27	28	29	1	2	3	4

GREGORIAN 2051

Julian (Sun)	Sun	Mon	Tue	Wed	Thu	Fri	Sat	Month
Dec 19	1	2	3	4	5	6	7[a]	JANUARY 2051
	8	9	10	11	12	13	14[b]	
Jan 2	15	16	17	18	19	20	21	
	22	23	24	25	26	27	28	
Jan 16	29	30	31	1	2	3	4	FEBRUARY 2051
	5	6	7	8	9	10	11	
Jan 30	12	13	14	15[c]	16	17	18	
	19	20	21	22	23	24	25	
Feb 13	26	27	28	1	2	3	4	MARCH 2051
	5	6	7	8	9	10	11	
Feb 27	12	13	14	15	16	17	18	
	19	20	21	22	23	24	25	
Mar 13	26[d]	27	28	29	30	31	1	APRIL 2051
	2[e]	3	4	5	6	7	8	
Mar 27	9	10	11	12	13	14	15	
	16	17	18	19	20	21	22	
Apr 10	23	24	25	26	27	28	29	
	30	1	2	3	4	5	6	MAY 2051
Apr 24	7[f]	8	9	10	11	12	13	
	14	15	16	17	18	19	20	
May 8	21	22	23	24	25	26	27	
	28	29	30	31	1	2	3	JUNE 2051
May 22	4	5	6	7	8	9	10	
	11	12	13	14	15	16	17	
Jun 5	18	19	20	21	22	23	24	
	25	26	27	28	29	30	1	JULY 2051
Jun 19	2	3	4	5	6	7	8	
	9	10	11	12	13	14	15	
Jul 3	16	17	18	19	20	21	22	
	23	24	25	26	27	28	29	
Jul 17	30	31	1	2	3	4	5	AUGUST 2051
	6	7	8	9	10	11	12	
Jul 31	13	14	15	16	17	18	19	
	20	21	22	23	24	25	26	
Aug 14	27	28	29	30	31	1	2	SEPTEMBER 2051
	3	4	5	6	7	8	9	
Aug 28	10	11	12	13	14	15	16	
	17	18	19	20	21	22	23	
Sep 11	24	25	26	27	28	29	30	
	1	2	3	4	5	6	7	OCTOBER 2051
Sep 25	8	9	10	11	12	13	14	
	15	16	17	18	19	20	21	
Oct 9	22	23	24	25	26	27	28	
	29	30	31	1	2	3	4	NOVEMBER 2051
Oct 23	5	6	7	8	9	10	11	
	12	13	14	15	16	17	18	
Nov 6	19	20	21	22	23	24	25	
	26	27	28	29	30	1	2	DECEMBER 2051
Nov 20	3[g]	4	5	6	7	8	9	
	10	11	12	13	14	15	16	
Dec 4	17	18	19	20	21	22	23	
	24	25[h]	26	27	28	29	30	
Dec 18	31	1	2	3	4	5	6	

Persian: [a]New Year; [b]Sizdeh Bedar

Hindu Lunar: ‡Leap year; [a]New Year (Prajāpati); [b]Birthday of Rāma; [c]Birthday of Krishna; [d]Ganēśa Chaturthī; [e]Dashara; [f]Diwali; [g]Birthday of Vishnu; [h]Night of Śiva; [i]Holi

Hindu Solar: [a]New Year (Pārthiva); [b]Pongal

Islamic: [a]New Year; [b]'Ashūrā'; [c]Prophet's Birthday; [d]Ascent of the Prophet; [e]Start of Ramaḍān; [f]'Īd al-Fiṭr; [g]'Īd al-'Aḍḥā

Gregorian: [a]Orthodox Christmas; [b]Julian New Year; [c]Ash Wednesday; [d]Feast of Orthodoxy; [e]Easter; [f]Orthodox Easter; [g]Advent; [h]Christmas

2052

Month	Sun	Mon	Tue	Wed	Thu	Fri	Sat	Lunar Phases	ISO WEEK (Mon)	JULIAN DAY (Sun noon)	Hebrew month	Sun	Mon	Tue	Wed	Thu	Fri	Sat	Molad	Chinese month	Sun	Mon	Tue	Wed	Thu	Fri	Sat	Solar Term	Coptic month	Sun	Mon	Tue	Wed	Thu	Fri	Sat	Ethiopic month
GREGORIAN 2052‡									ISO WEEK	JULIAN DAY	HEBREW 5812‡/5813								Molad	CHINESE Xīn-Wèi/Rén-Shēn‡								Solar Term	COPTIC 1768/1769								ETHIOPIC 2044/2045
	31	1[a]	●	3	4	5	6	3:04	1	2470537		28	29	1	2	3	4	5	Mon 22h 48m 8p		29	30	1	2	3	4	5	Xiǎo hán		21	22	23	24	25	26	27	TĀKHŚĀŚ 2044
JANUARY 2052	7	8	◐	10	11	12	13	9:25	2	2470544	SHEVAT 5812	6	7	8	9	10	11	12		MONTH 12 Xīn-Wèi	6	7	8	9	10	11	12		KOIAK 1768	28	29[c]	30	1	2	3	4	
	14	15	○	17	18	19	20	4:23	3	2470551		13	14	15	16	17	18	19			13	14	15	16	17	18	**19**	Dà hán	TŌBE 1768	5	6[d]	7	8	9	10	11[e]	TER 2044
	21	22	◑	24	25	26	27	21:02	4	2470558		20	21	22	23	24	25	26	Wed 11h 32m 9p		20	21	22	23	24	25	26			12	13	14	15	16	17	18	
	28	29	30	●	1	2	3	18:29	5	2470565		27	28	29	30	1	2	3			27	28	29	30	1[a]	2	3*			19	20	21	22	23	24	25	
FEBRUARY 2052	4	5	6	◐	8	9	10	17:34	6	2470572	ADAR I 5812	4	5	6	7	8	9	10		MONTH 1 Rén-Shēn	4	5	6	7	8	9	10	Lì chūn		26	27	28	29	30	1	2	
	11	12	13	○	15	16	17	18:20	7	2470579		11	12	13	14	15	16	17			11	12	13	14	15[b]	16	17		MESHIR 1768	3	4	5	6	7	8	9	YAKĀTIT 2044
	18	19	20	21	◑	23	24	18:43	8	2470586		18	19	20	21	22	23	24	Fri 0h 16m 10p		18	**19**	20	21	22	23	24	Yǔ shuǐ		10	11	12	13	14	15	16	
	25	26	27	28	29	●	2	7:34	9	2470593		25	26	27	28	29	30	1			25	26	27	28	29	1	2			17	18	19	20	21	22	23	
MARCH 2052	3	4	5	6	7	◐	9	1:16	10	2470600	ADAR II 5812	2	3	4	5	6	7	8		MONTH 2 Rén-Shēn	3	4	5	6	7	8	9	Jīng zhé		24	25	26	27	28	29	30	
	10	11	12	13	14	○	16	9:53	11	2470607		9	10	11	12	13	14[f]	15			10	11	12	13	14	15	16			1	2	3	4	5	6	7	
	17	18	19[b]	20	21	22	◑	14:08	12	2470614		16	17	18	19	20	21	22			17	18	19	**20**	21	22	23	Chūn fēn	PAREMOTEP 1768	8	9	10	11	12	13	14	MAGĀBIT 2044
	24	25	26	27	28	29	●	18:26	13	2470621		23	24	25	26	27	28	29	Sat 13h 0m 1p		24	25	26	27	28	29	30			15	16	17	18	19	20	21	
	31	1	2	3	4	5	◐	9:27	14	2470628		1	2	3	4	5	6	7			1	2	3	4*	5[c]	6	7	Qīng míng		22	23	24	25	26	27	28	
APRIL 2052	7	8	9	10	11	12	13		15	2470635	NISAN 5812	8	9	10	11	12	13	14		MONTH 3 Rén-Shēn	8	9	10	11	12	13	14			29	30	1	2	3	4	5	
	○	15	16	17	18	19	20	2:28	16	2470642		15[g]	16	17	18	19	20	21			15	16	17	18	19	**20**	21	Gǔ yǔ	PARMOUTE 1768	6	7	8	9	10	11	12	MIYĀZYĀ 2044
	21	◑	23	24	25	26	27	6:02	17	2470649		22	23	24	25	26	27	28			22	23	24	25	26	27	28			13[f]	14	15	16	17	18	19	
	28	●	30	1	2	3	4	3:19	18	2470656		29	30	1	2	3	4	5	Mon 1h 44m 12p		29	1	2	3	4	5	6			20	21	22	23	24	25	26	
MAY 2052	◐	6	7	8	9	10	11	19:03	19	2470663	IYAR 5812	6	7	8	9	10	11	12		MONTH 4 Rén-Shēn	7	8	9	10	11	12	13	Lì xià		27	28	29[g]	30	1	2	3	
	12	○	14	15	16	17	18	18:58	20	2470670		13	14	15	16	17	18	19			14	15	16	17	18	19	20		PASHONS 1768	4	5	6	7	8	9	10	GENBOT 2044
	19	20	◑	22	23	24	25	18:13	21	2470677		20	21	22	23	24	25	26			21	**22**	23	24	25	26	27	Xiǎo mǎn		11	12	13	14	15	16	17	
	26	27	●	29	30	31	1	10:49	22	2470684		27	28	29	1	2	3	4	Tue 14h 28m 13p		28	29	1	2	3	4	5[d]			18	19	20	21	22	23	24	
JUNE 2052	2	3	◐	5	6	7	8	6:48	23	2470691	SIVAN 5812	5	6[h]	7	8	9	10	11		MONTH 5 Rén-Shēn	6*	7	8	9	10	11	12	Máng zhòng		25	26	27	28	29	30	1	
	9	10	11	○	13	14	15	10:26	24	2470698		12	13	14	15	16	17	18			13	14	15	16	17	18	19		PAŌNE 1768	2	3	4	5	6	7	8	SANĒ 2044
	16	17	18	19	◑[c]	21	22	3:09	25	2470705		19	20	21	22	23	24	25			20	21	22	23	**24**	25	26	Xià zhì		9	10	11	12	13	14	15	
	23	24	25	●	27	28	29	17:48	26	2470712		26	27	28	29	30	1	2	Thu 3h 12m 14p		27	28	29	30	1	2	3			16	17	18	19	20	21	22	
JULY 2052	30	1	2	◐	4	5	6	20:58	27	2470719	TAMMUZ 5812	3	4	5	6	7	8	9		MONTH 6 Rén-Shēn	4	5	6	7	8	9	*10*	Xiǎo shǔ		23	24	25	26	27	28	29	
	7	8	9	10	11	○	13	0:22	28	2470726		10	11	12	13	14	15	16			11	12	13	14	15	16	17			30	1	2	3	4	5	6	
	14	15	16	17	18	◑	20	9:36	29	2470733		17	18	19	20	21	22	23			18	19	20	21	22	23	24		EPĒP 1768	7	8	9	10	11	12	13	HAMLĒ 2044
	21	22	23	24	25	●	27	1:29	30	2470740		24	25	26	27	28	29	1	Fri 15h 56m 15p		25	**26**	27	28	29	1	2	Dà shǔ		14	15	16	17	18	19	20	
AUGUST 2052	28	29	30	31	1	◐	3	13:18	31	2470747	AV 5812	2	3	4	5	6	7	8		MONTH 7 Rén-Shēn	3	4	5	6	7[e]*	8	9			21	22	23	24	25	26	27	
	4	5	6	7	8	9	○	12:51	32	2470754		9[i]	10	11	12	13	14	15			10	11	12	*13*	14	15[f]	16	Lì qiū		28	29	30	1	2	3	4	
	11	12	13	14	15	◑	17	14:42	33	2470761		16	17	18	19	20	21	22			17	18	19	20	21	22	23		MESORĒ 1768	5	6	7	8	9	10	11	NAHASĒ 2044
	18	19	20	21	22	23	●	11:05	34	2470768		23	24	25	26	27	28	29			24	25	26	27	**28**	29	1	Chǔ shǔ		12	13[h]	14	15	16	17	18	
	25	26	27	28	29	30	31		35	2470775		30	1	2	3	4	5	6	Sun 4h 40m 16p		2	3	4	5	6	7	8			19	20	21	22	23	24	25	
SEPTEMBER 2052	◐	2	3	4	5	6	7	7:08	36	2470782	ELUL 5812	7	8	9	10	11	12	13		MONTH 8 Rén-Shēn	9	10	11	12	13	14	15[g]	Bái lù	EPAG. 1768	26	27	28	29	30	1	2	
	8	○	10	11	12	13	14	0:14	37	2470789		14	15	16	17	18	19	20			16	17	18	19	20	21	22			3	4	5	1[a]	2	3	4	PĀG. 2044
	◑	16	17	18	19	20	21	19:47	38	2470796		21	22	23	24	25	26	27			23	24	25	26	27	28	29		THOOUT 1769	5	6	7	8	9	10	11	MASKARAM 2045
	●[d]	23	24	25	26	27	28	23:31	39	2470803		28	29	1[a]	2[a]	3	4	5	Mon 17h 24m 17p		**30**	1	2	3	4	5	6	Qiū fēn		12	13	14	15	16	17[b]	18	
OCTOBER 2052	29	30	◐	2	3	4	5	1:35	40	2470810	TISHRI 5813	6	7	8	9	10[b]	11	12		LEAP MONTH 8 Rén-Shēn	7	8*	9	10	11	12	13			19	20	21	22	23	24	25	
	6	7	○	9	10	11	12	10:53	41	2470817		13	14	15[c]	16	17	18	19			14	*15*	16	17	18	19	20	Hán lù		26	27	28	29	30	1	2	
	13	14	◑	16	17	18	19	2:21	42	2470824		20	21	22	23	24	25	26			21	22	23	24	25	26	27		PAOPE 1769	3	4	5	6	7	8	9	TEQEMT 2045
	20	21	●	23	24	25	26	15:02	43	2470831		27	28	29	30	1	2	3	Wed 6h 9m 0p		28	29	1	**2**	3	4	5	Shuāng jiàng		10	11	12	13	14	15	16	
NOVEMBER 2052	27	28	29	◐	31	1	2	19:38	44	2470838	ḤESHVAN 5813	4	5	6	7	8	9	10		MONTH 9 Rén-Shēn	6	7	8	9[h]	10	11	12			17	18	19	20	21	22	23	
	3	4	5	○	7	8	9	21:07	45	2470845		11	12	13	14	15	16	17			13	14	15	16	*17*	18	19	Lì dōng		24	25	26	27	28	29	30	
	10	11	12	◑	14	15	16	11:48	46	2470852		18	19	20	21	22	23	24			20	21	22	23	24	25	26		ATHŌR 1769	1	2	3	4	5	6	7	HEDĀR 2045
	17	18	19	20	●	22	23	9:01	47	2470859		25	26	27	28	29	1	2	Thu 18h 53m 1p		27	28	29	30	*1*	2	3	Xiǎo xuě		8	9	10	11	12	13	14	
	24	25	26	27	28	◐	30	12:15	48	2470866	KISLEV 5813	3	4	5	6	7	8	9		MONTH 10 Rén-Shēn	4	5	6	7	8	9*	10			15	16	17	18	19	20	21	
DECEMBER 2052	1	2	3	4	5	○	7	7:16	49	2470873		10	11	12	13	14[d]	15	16			11	12	13	14	15	*16*	17	Dà xuě		22	23	24	25	26	27	28	
	8	9	10	11	12	◑	14	1:06	50	2470880		17	18	19	20	21	22	23			18	19	20	21	22	23	24			29	30	1	2	3	4	5	
	15	16	17	18	19	20	●[e]	4:13	51	2470887		24	25[e]	26[e]	27[e]	28[e]	29[e]	30[e]			25	26	27	28	29	30	1[i]	Dōng zhì	KOIAK 1769	6	7	8	9	10	11	12	TĀKHŚĀŚ 2045
	22	23	24	25	26	27	28		52	2470894	TEVETH 5813	1[e]	2[e]	3	4	5	6	7	Sat 7h 37m 2p	MONTH 11 Rén-Shēn	2	3	4	5	6	7	8			13	14	15	16	17	18	19	
	◐	30	31	1	2	3	○	2:27 17:44	1	2470901		8	9	10	11	12	13	14			9	10	11	12	13	14	15			20	21	22	23	24	25	26	

‡Leap year
[a]New Year
[b]Spring (21:54)
[c]Summer (15:14)
[d]Autumn (7:14)
[e]Winter (4:16)
● New moon
◐ First quarter moon
○ Full moon
◑ Last quarter moon

‡Leap year
[a]New Year
[b]Yom Kippur
[c]Sukkot
[d]Winter starts
[e]Ḥanukkah
[f]Purim
[g]Passover
[h]Shavuot
[i]Fast of Av

‡Leap year
[a]New Year (4750, Monkey)
[b]Lantern Festival
[c]Qīngmíng
[d]Dragon Festival
[e]Qīqiǎo
[f]Hungry Ghosts
[g]Mid-Autumn Festival
[h]Double-Ninth Festival
[i]Dōngzhì
*Start of 60-name cycle

[a]New Year
[b]Building of the Cross
[c]Christmas
[d]Jesus's Circumcision
[e]Epiphany
[f]Easter
[g]Mary's Announcement
[h]Jesus's Transfiguration

2052

PERSIAN (ASTRONOMICAL) 1430/1431

Month	Sun	Mon	Tue	Wed	Thu	Fri	Sat
DEY 1430	10	11	12	13	14	15	16
	17	18	19	20	21	22	23
	24	25	26	27	28	29	30
BAHMAN 1430	1	2	3	4	5	6	7
	8	9	10	11	12	13	14
	15	16	17	18	19	20	21
	22	23	24	25	26	27	28
ESFAND 1430	29	30	1	2	3	4	5
	6	7	8	9	10	11	12
	13	14	15	16	17	18	19
	20	21	22	23	24	25	26
FARVARDĪN 1431	27	28	29	1[a]	2	3	4
	5	6	7	8	9	10	11
	12	13[b]	14	15	16	17	18
	19	20	21	22	23	24	25
ORDĪBEHEŠT 1431	26	27	28	29	30	31	1
	2	3	4	5	6	7	8
	9	10	11	12	13	14	15
	16	17	18	19	20	21	22
	23	24	25	26	27	28	29
XORDĀD 1431	30	31	1	2	3	4	5
	6	7	8	9	10	11	12
	13	14	15	16	17	18	19
	20	21	22	23	24	25	26
TĪR 1431	27	28	29	30	31	1	2
	3	4	5	6	7	8	9
	10	11	12	13	14	15	16
	17	18	19	20	21	22	23
	24	25	26	27	28	29	30
MORDĀD 1431	31	1	2	3	4	5	6
	7	8	9	10	11	12	13
	14	15	16	17	18	19	20
	21	22	23	24	25	26	27
SHAHRĪVAR 1431	28	29	30	31	1	2	3
	4	5	6	7	8	9	10
	11	12	13	14	15	16	17
	18	19	20	21	22	23	24
	25	26	27	28	29	30	31
MEHR 1431	1	2	3	4	5	6	7
	8	9	10	11	12	13	14
	15	16	17	18	19	20	21
	22	23	24	25	26	27	28
ĀBĀN 1431	29	30	1	2	3	4	5
	6	7	8	9	10	11	12
	13	14	15	16	17	18	19
	20	21	22	23	24	25	26
ĀZAR 1431	27	28	29	30	1	2	3
	4	5	6	7	8	9	10
	11	12	13	14	15	16	17
	18	19	20	21	22	23	24
DEY 1431	25	26	27	28	29	30	1
	2	3	4	5	6	7	8
	9	10	11	12	13	14	15

HINDU LUNAR 2108/2109

Month	Sun	Mon	Tue	Wed	Thu	Fri	Sat
PAUSHA 2108	29	29	30	1	2	3	**4**
	6	7	8	9	10	11	12
	13	14	15	16	17	18	19
	20	21	22	23	24	25	26
MĀGHA 2108	27	28	29	30	1	2	3
	4	5	6	7	8	**9**	11
	12	13	14	15	16	17	18
	19	20	21	22	22	23	24
PHĀLGUNA 2108	25	26	27	28[h]	29	30	1
	2	**3**	5	6	7	8	9
	10	11	12	13	14	15[i]	16
	17	18	19	20	21	22	23
	24	25	26	27	28	29	30
CHAITRA 2109	1[a]	2	3	4	5	6	7
	8[b]	10	11	12	13	14	15
	15	16	17	18	19	20	21
	22	23	24	25	26	27	28
VAIŚĀKHA 2109	29	30	**1**	3	4	5	6
	7	8	9	10	11	12	13
	14	15	16	17	18	19	19
	20	21	22	**23**	25	26	27
JYAISHṬHA 2109	28	29	30	1	2	3	4
	5	7	8	9	10	10	11
	12	13	14	15	16	17	18
	19	20	21	22	23	24	25
ĀSHĀḌHA 2109	26	**27**	29	30	1	2	3
	4	5	6	7	8	9	10
	11	12	13	14	15	16	16
	17	**18**	20	21	22	23	24
ŚRĀVAṆA 2109	25	26	27	28	29	**30**	2
	3	4	5	6	7	7	8
	9	10	11	12	13	14	15
	16	17	18	19	20	21	22
	23[c]	25	26	27	28	29	30
BHĀDRAPADA 2109	1	2	3	4[d]	5	6	7
	8	9	10	11	12	13	13
	15	16	17	18	19	20	21
	22	23	24	25	**26**	28	29
ĀŚVINA 2109	30	1	2	3	3	4	5
	6	7	8[e]	9[e]	10[e]	11	12
	13	14	15	16	17	18	**19**
	21	22	23	24	25	26	27
KĀRTTIKA 2109	28	29	30	1[f]	2	3	4
	5	6	7	7	8	9	10
	11	**12**	14	15	16	17	18
	19	20	21	22	23	24	25
MĀRGAŚIRA 2109	26	27	28	29	30	1	2
	3	4	5	6	7	8	9
	10	11[g]	12	13	14	15	16
	17	19	20	21	22	23	24
	25	26	27	28	29	30	30
PAUSHA 2109	1	2	3	4	5	6	7
	8	9	10	**11**	13	14	15

HINDU SOLAR 1973/1974‡

Month	Sun	Mon	Tue	Wed	Thu	Fri	Sat
PAUSHA 1973	16	17	18	19	20	21	22
	23	24	25	26	27	28	29
MĀGHA 1973	30	1[b]	2	3	4	5	6
	7	8	9	10	11	12	13
	14	15	16	17	18	19	20
	21	22	23	24	25	26	27
PHĀLGUNA 1973	28	29	1	2	3	4	5
	6	7	8	9	10	11	12
	13	14	15	16	17	18	19
	20	21	22	23	24	25	26
CHAITRA 1973	27	28	29	30	1	2	3
	4	5	6	7	8	9	10
	11	12	13	14	15	16	17
	18	19	20	21	22	23	24
VAIŚĀKHA 1974	25	26	27	28	29	30	1[a]
	2	3	4	5	6	7	8
	9	10	11	12	13	14	15
	16	17	18	19	20	21	22
	23	24	25	26	27	28	29
JYAISHṬHA 1974	30	31	1	2	3	4	5
	6	7	8	9	10	11	12
	13	14	15	16	17	18	19
	20	21	22	23	24	25	26
ĀSHĀḌHA 1974	27	28	29	30	31	32	1
	2	3	4	5	6	7	8
	9	10	11	12	13	14	15
	16	17	18	19	20	21	22
	23	24	25	26	27	28	29
ŚRĀVAṆA 1974	30	31	1	2	3	4	5
	6	7	8	9	10	11	12
	13	14	15	16	17	18	19
	20	21	22	23	24	25	26
BHĀDRAPADA 1974	27	28	29	30	31	32	1
	2	3	4	5	6	7	8
	9	10	11	12	13	14	15
	16	17	18	19	20	21	22
	23	24	25	26	27	28	29
ĀŚVINA 1974	30	31	1	2	3	4	5
	6	7	8	9	10	11	12
	13	14	15	16	17	18	19
	20	21	22	23	24	25	26
KĀRTTIKA 1974	27	28	29	30	1	2	3
	4	5	6	7	8	9	10
	11	12	13	14	15	16	17
	18	19	20	21	22	23	24
MĀRGAŚIRA 1974	25	26	27	28	29	30	1
	2	3	4	5	6	7	8
	9	10	11	12	13	14	15
	16	17	18	19	20	21	22
	23	24	25	26	27	28	29
PAUSHA 1974	30	1	2	3	4	5	6
	7	8	9	10	11	12	13
	14	15	16	17	18	19	20

ISLAMIC (ASTRONOMICAL) 1474/1475‡

Month	Sun	Mon	Tue	Wed	Thu	Fri	Sat
JUMĀDĀ I 1474	27	28	29	1	2	3	4
	5	6	7	8	9	10	11
	12	13	14	15	16	17	18
	19	20	21	22	23	24	25
JUMĀDĀ II 1474	26	27	28	29	30	1	2
	3	4	5	6	7	8	9
	10	11	12	13	14	15	16
	17	18	19	20	21	22	23
	24	25	26	27	28	29	30
RAJAB 1474	1	2	3	4	5	6	7
	8	9	10	11	12	13	14
	15	16	17	18	19	20	21
	22	23	24	25	26	27[d]	28
SHA'BĀN 1474	29	1	2	3	4	5	6
	7	8	9	10	11	12	13
	14	15	16	17	18	19	20
	21	22	23	24	25	26	27
RAMAḌĀN 1474	28	29	1[e]	2	3	4	5
	6	7	8	9	10	11	12
	13	14	15	16	17	18	19
	20	21	22	23	24	25	26
SHAWWĀL 1474	27	28	29	30	1[f]	2	3
	4	5	6	7	8	9	10
	11	12	13	14	15	16	17
	18	19	20	21	22	23	24
DHU AL-QA'DA 1474	25	26	27	28	29	1	2
	3	4	5	6	7	8	9
	10	11	12	13	14	15	16
	17	18	19	20	21	22	23
	24	25	26	27	28	29	30
DHU AL-ḤIJJA 1474	1	2	3	4	5	6	7
	8	9	10[g]	11	12	13	14
	15	16	17	18	19	20	21
	22	23	24	25	26	27	28
MUḤARRAM 1475	29	1[a]	2	3	4	5	6
	7	8	9	10[b]	11	12	13
	14	15	16	17	18	19	20
	21	22	23	24	25	26	27
ṢAFAR 1475	28	29	30	1	2	3	4
	5	6	7	8	9	10	11
	12	13	14	15	16	17	18
	19	20	21	22	23	24	25
RABĪ' I 1475	26	27	28	29	1	2	3
	4	5	6	7	8	9	10
	11	12[c]	13	14	15	16	17
	18	19	20	21	22	23	24
RABĪ' II 1475	25	26	27	28	29	30	1
	2	3	4	5	6	7	8
	9	10	11	12	13	14	15
	16	17	18	19	20	21	22
	23	24	25	26	27	28	29
JUMĀDĀ I 1475	1	2	3	4	5	6	7
	8	9	10	11	12	13	14

GREGORIAN 2052‡

Julian‡ (Sun)	Sun	Mon	Tue	Wed	Thu	Fri	Sat	Month
Dec 18	31	1	2	3	4	5	6	JANUARY 2052
	7[a]	8	9	10	11	12	13	
Jan 1	14[b]	15	16	17	18	19	20	
	21	22	23	24	25	26	27	
Jan 15	28	29	30	31	1	2	3	FEBRUARY 2052
	4	5	6	7	8	9	10	
Jan 29	11	12	13	14	15	16	17	
	18	19	20	21	22	23	24	
Feb 12	25	26	27	28	29	1	2	MARCH 2052
	3	4	5	6[c]	7	8	9	
Feb 26	10[d]	11	12	13	14	15	16	
	17	18	19	20	21	22	23	
Mar 11	24	25	26	27	28	29	30	
	31	1	2	3	4	5	6	APRIL 2052
Mar 25	7	8	9	10	11	12	13	
	14	15	16	17	18	19	20	
Apr 8	21[e]	22	23	24	25	26	27	
	28	29	30	1	2	3	4	MAY 2052
Apr 22	5	6	7	8	9	10	11	
	12	13	14	15	16	17	18	
May 6	19	20	21	22	23	24	25	
	26	27	28	29	30	31	1	JUNE 2052
May 20	2	3	4	5	6	7	8	
	9	10	11	12	13	14	15	
Jun 3	16	17	18	19	20	21	22	
	23	24	25	26	27	28	29	
Jun 17	30	1	2	3	4	5	6	JULY 2052
	7	8	9	10	11	12	13	
Jul 1	14	15	16	17	18	19	20	
	21	22	23	24	25	26	27	
Jul 15	28	29	30	31	1	2	3	AUGUST 2052
	4	5	6	7	8	9	10	
Jul 29	11	12	13	14	15	16	17	
	18	19	20	21	22	23	24	
Aug 12	25	26	27	28	29	30	31	
	1	2	3	4	5	6	7	SEPTEMBER 2052
Aug 26	8	9	10	11	12	13	14	
	15	16	17	18	19	20	21	
Sep 9	22	23	24	25	26	27	28	
	29	30	1	2	3	4	5	OCTOBER 2052
Sep 23	6	7	8	9	10	11	12	
	13	14	15	16	17	18	19	
Oct 7	20	21	22	23	24	25	26	
	27	28	29	30	31	1	2	NOVEMBER 2052
Oct 21	3	4	5	6	7	8	9	
	10	11	12	13	14	15	16	
Nov 4	17	18	19	20	21	22	23	
	24	25	26	27	28	29	30	
Nov 18	1[g]	2	3	4	5	6	7	DECEMBER 2052
	8	9	10	11	12	13	14	
Dec 2	15	16	17	18	19	20	21	
	22	23	24	25[h]	26	27	28	
Dec 16	29	30	31	1	2	3	4	

Persian: [a] New Year; [b] Sizdeh Bedar

Hindu Lunar: [a] New Year (Aṅgiras); [b] Birthday of Rāma; [c] Birthday of Krishna; [d] Gaṇēśa Chaturthī; [e] Dashara; [f] Diwali; [g] Birthday of Vishnu; [h] Night of Śiva; [i] Holi

Hindu Solar: ‡ Leap year; [a] New Year (Vyaya); [b] Pongal

Islamic: ‡ Leap year; [a] New Year; [b] 'Ashūrā'; [c] Prophet's Birthday; [d] Ascent of the Prophet; [e] Start of Ramaḍān; [f] 'Id al-Fiṭr; [g] 'Id al-'Aḍḥā

Gregorian: ‡ Leap year; [a] Orthodox Christmas; [b] Julian New Year; [c] Ash Wednesday; [d] Feast of Orthodoxy; [e] Easter (also Orthodox); [g] Advent; [h] Christmas

2053

Gregorian 2053	Sun	Mon	Tue	Wed	Thu	Fri	Sat	Lunar Phases	ISO Week (Mon)	Julian Day (Sun noon)
January 2053	◐	30	31	1[a]	2	3	○	17:44 2:27	1	2470901
	5	6	7	8	9	10	◑	18:08	2	2470908
	12	13	14	15	16	17	18		3	2470915
	●	20	21	22	23	24	25	23:11	4	2470922
February 2053	26	◐	28	29	30	31	1	13:40	5	2470929
	2	○	4	5	6	7	8	4:56	6	2470936
	9	◑	11	12	13	14	15	13:48	7	2470943
	16	17	●	19	20	21	22	16:30	8	2470950
March 2053	23	24	◐	26	27	28	1	22:08	9	2470957
	2	3	○	5	6	7	8	17:08	10	2470964
	9	10	11	◑	13	14	15	10:20	11	2470971
	16	17	18	19	●[b]	21	22	7:10	12	2470978
	23	24	25	26	◐	28	29	4:49	13	2470985
April 2053	30	31	1	2	○	4	5	6:21	14	2470992
	6	7	8	9	10	◑	12	6:03	15	2470999
	13	14	15	16	17	●	19	18:47	16	2471006
	20	21	22	23	24	◐	26	11:01	17	2471013
May 2053	27	28	29	30	1	○	3	20:23	18	2471020
	4	5	6	7	8	9	◑	23:39	19	2471027
	11	12	13	14	15	16	17		20	2471034
	●	19	20	21	22	23	◐	18:03 3:42	21	2471041
	25	26	27	28	29	30	31		22	2471048
June 2053	○	2	3	4	5	6	7	11:01	23	2471055
	8	◑	10	11	12	13	14	14:18	24	2471062
	15	●	17	18	19	20[c]	21	10:50	25	2471069
	22	◐	24	25	26	27	28	2:54	26	2471076
July 2053	29	30	○	2	3	4	5	1:59	27	2471083
	6	7	8	◑	10	11	12	1:46	28	2471090
	13	14	●	16	17	18	19	17:25	29	2471097
	20	21	◐	23	24	25	26	14:14	30	2471104
August 2053	27	28	29	○	31	1	2	17:05	31	2471111
	3	4	5	6	◑	8	9	10:24	32	2471118
	10	11	12	13	●	15	16	0:39	33	2471125
	17	18	19	20	◐	22	23	4:25	34	2471132
	24	25	26	27	28	○	30	7:52	35	2471139
September 2053	31	1	2	3	4	◑	6	17:03	36	2471146
	7	8	9	10	11	●	13	9:34	37	2471153
	14	15	16	17	18	◐	20	21:28	38	2471160
	21	22[d]	23	24	25	26	○	21:49	39	2471167
October 2053	28	29	30	1	2	3	◑	23:00	40	2471174
	5	6	7	8	9	10	●	20:52	41	2471181
	12	13	14	15	16	17	18		42	2471188
	◐	20	21	22	23	24	25	16:53	43	2471195
November 2053	26	○	28	29	30	31	1	10:37	44	2471202
	2	◑	4	5	6	7	8	5:36	45	2471209
	9	●	11	12	13	14	15	10:54	46	2471216
	16	17	◐	19	20	21	22	13:25	47	2471223
	23	24	○	26	27	28	29	22:20	48	2471230
December 2053	30	1	◑	3	4	5	6	14:03	49	2471237
	7	8	9	●	11	12	13	3:39	50	2471244
	14	15	16	17	◐	19	20	9:10	51	2471251
	21[e]	22	23	24	○	26	27	9:22	52	2471258
	28	29	30	31	◑	2	3	1:09	1	2471265

ISO Week	Hebrew 5813/5814‡	Sun	Mon	Tue	Wed	Thu	Fri	Sat	Molad
1	Teveth 5813	8	9	10	11	12	13	14	
2		15	16	17	18	19	20	21	
3		22	23	24	25	26	27	28	
4	Shevat 5813	29	1	2	3	4	5	6	Sun $20^h21^m3^p$
5		7	8	9	10	11	12	13	
6		14	15	16	17	18	19	20	
7		21	22	23	24	25	26	27	
8	Adar 5813	28	29	30	1	2	3	4	Tue $9^h5^m4^p$
9		5	6	7	8	9	10	11	
10		12	13	14[f]	15	16	17	18	
11		19	20	21	22	23	24	25	
12	Nisan 5813	26	27	28	29	1	2	3	Wed $21^h49^m5^p$
13		4	5	6	7	8	9	10	
14		11	12	13	14	15[g]	16	17	
15		18	19	20	21	22	23	24	
16	Iyyar 5813	25	26	27	28	29	30	1	Fri $10^h33^m6^p$
17		2	3	4	5	6	7	8	
18		9	10	11	12	13	14	15	
19		16	17	18	19	20	21	22	
20		23	24	25	26	27	28	29	
21	Sivan 5813	1	2	3	4	5	6[h]	7	Sat $23^h17^m7^p$
22		8	9	10	11	12	13	14	
23		15	16	17	18	19	20	21	
24		22	23	24	25	26	27	28	
25	Tammuz 5813	29	30	1	2	3	4	5	Mon $12^h1^m8^p$
26		6	7	8	9	10	11	12	
27		13	14	15	16	17	18	19	
28		20	21	22	23	24	25	26	
29	Av 5813	27	28	29	1	2	3	4	Wed $0^h45^m9^p$
30		5	6	7	8	9[i]	10	11	
31		12	13	14	15	16	17	18	
32		19	20	21	22	23	24	25	
33	Elul 5813	26	27	28	29	30	1	2	Thu $13^h29^m10^p$
34		3	4	5	6	7	8	9	
35		10	11	12	13	14	15	16	
36		17	18	19	20	21	22	23	
37	Tishri 5814	24	25	26	27	28	29	1[a]	Sat $2^h13^m11^p$
38		2[a]	3	4	5	6	7	8	
39		9	10[b]	11	12	13	14	15[c]	
40		16	17	18	19	20	21	22	
41		23	24	25	26	27	28	29	
42	Heshvan 5814	30	1	2	3	4	5	6	Sun $14^h57^m12^p$
43		7	8	9	10	11	12	13	
44		14	15	16	17	18	19	20	
45		21	22	23	24	25	26	27	
46	Kislev 5814	28	29	30	1	2	3	4	Tue $3^h41^m13^p$
47		5	6	7	8	9	10	11	
48		12	13	14	15	16	17	18	
49		19	20	21	22	23	24[d]	25[e]	
50	Teveth 5814	26[e]	27[e]	28[e]	29[e]	30[e]	1[e]	2[e]	Wed $16^h25^m14^p$
51		3	4	5	6	7	8	9	
52		10	11	12	13	14	15	16	
1		17	18	19	20	21	22	23	

ISO Week	Chinese Rén-Shēn‡/Guǐ-Yǒu	Sun	Mon	Tue	Wed	Thu	Fri	Sat	Solar Term
1	Month 11 Rén-Shēn	9	10	11	12	13	14	15	
2		*16*	17	18	19	20	21	22	Xiǎo hán
3		23	24	25	26	27	28	29	
4	Month 12 Rén-Shēn	**30**	1	2	3	4	5	6	**Dà hán**
5		7	8	9*	10	11	12	13	
6		14	*15*	16	17	18	19	20	Lì chūn
7		21	22	23	24	25	26	27	
8	Month 1 Guǐ-Yǒu	28	29	**30**	1[a]	2	3	4	**Yǔ shuǐ**
9		5	6	7	8	9	10	11	
10		12	13	14	*15*[b]	16	17	18	Jīng zhé
11		19	20	21	22	23	24	25	
12	Month 2 Guǐ-Yǒu	26	27	28	29	**1**	2	3	**Chūn fēn**
13		4	5	6	7	8	9	10*	
14		11	12	13	14	15	*16*[c]	17	Qīng míng
15		18	19	20	21	22	23	24	
16	Month 3 Guǐ-Yǒu	25	26	27	28	29	30	**1**	**Gǔ yǔ**
17		2	3	4	5	6	7	8	
18		9	10	11	12	13	14	15	
19		16	*17*	18	19	20	21	22	Lì xià
20		23	24	25	26	27	28	29	
21	Month 4 Guǐ-Yǒu	1	2	**3**	4	5	6	7	**Xiǎo mǎn**
22		8	9	10	11*	12	13	14	
23		15	16	17	18	*19*	20	21	Máng zhòng
24		22	23	24	25	26	27	28	
25	Month 5 Guǐ-Yǒu	29	1	2	3	4	5[d]	**6**	**Xià zhì**
26		7	8	9	10	11	12	13	
27		14	15	16	17	18	19	20	
28		*21*	22	23	24	25	26	27	Xiǎo shǔ
29	Month 6 Guǐ-Yǒu	28	29	30	1	2	3	4	
30		5	6	**7**	8	9	10	11	**Dà shǔ**
31		12*	13	14	15	16	17	18	
32		19	20	21	22	*23*	24	25	Lì qiū
33	Month 7 Guǐ-Yǒu	26	27	28	29	1	2	3	
34		4	5	6	7[e]	8	**9**	10	**Chǔ shǔ**
35		11	12	13	14	15[f]	16	17	
36		18	19	20	21	22	23	24	
37	Month 8 Guǐ-Yǒu	*25*	26	27	28	29	1	2	Bái lù
38		3	4	5	6	7	8	9	
39		10	**11**	12	13	14*	15[g]	16	**Qiū fēn**
40		17	18	19	20	21	22	23	
41		24	25	26	*27*	28	29	30	Hán lù
42	Month 9 Guǐ-Yǒu	1	2	3	4	5	6	7	
43		8	9[h]	10	11	**12**	13	14	**Shuāng jiàng**
44		15	16	17	18	19	20	21	
45		22	23	24	25	26	*27*	28	Lì dōng
46	Month 10 Guǐ-Yǒu	29	1	2	3	4	5	6	
47		7	8	9	10	11	12	**13**	**Xiǎo xuě**
48		14	15*	16	17	18	19	20	
49		21	22	23	24	25	26	27	
50	Month 11* Guǐ-Yǒu	*28*	29	30	1	2	3	4	Dà xuě
51		5	6	7	8	9	10	11	
52		**12**[i]	13	14	15	16	17	18	**Dōng zhì**
1		19	20	21	22	23	24	25	

ISO Week	Coptic 1769/1770	Sun	Mon	Tue	Wed	Thu	Fri	Sat	Ethiopic 2045/2046
1	Koiak 1769	20	21	22	23	24	25	26	Tākhśāś 2045
2		27	28	29[c]	30	1	2	3	
3	Tōbe 1769	4	5	6[d]	7	8	9	10	Ṭer 2045
4		11[e]	12	13	14	15	16	17	
5		18	19	20	21	22	23	24	
6		25	26	27	28	29	30	1	
7	Meshir 1769	2	3	4	5	6	7	8	Yakātit 2045
8		9	10	11	12	13	14	15	
9		16	17	18	19	20	21	22	
10		23	24	25	26	27	28	29	
11	Paremotep 1769	30	1	2	3	4	5	6	Magābit 2045
12		7	8	9	10	11	12	13	
13		14	15	16	17	18	19	20	
14		21	22	23	24	25	26	27	
15	Parmoute 1769	28	29	30	1	2	3	4	Miyāzyā 2045
16		5[f]	6	7	8	9	10	11	
17		12	13	14	15	16	17	18	
18		19	20	21	22	23	24	25	
19	Pashons 1769	26	27	28	29[g]	30	1	2	Genbot 2045
20		3	4	5	6	7	8	9	
21		10	11	12	13	14	15	16	
22		17	18	19	20	21	22	23	
23		24	25	26	27	28	29	30	
24	Paōne 1769	1	2	3	4	5	6	7	Sanē 2045
25		8	9	10	11	12	13	14	
26		15	16	17	18	19	20	21	
27		22	23	24	25	26	27	28	
28	Epēp 1769	29	30	1	2	3	4	5	Ḥamlē 2045
29		6	7	8	9	10	11	12	
30		13	14	15	16	17	18	19	
31		20	21	22	23	24	25	26	
32	Mesorē 1769	27	28	29	30	1	2	3	Naḥasē 2045
33		4	5	6	7	8	9	10	
34		11	12	13[h]	14	15	16	17	
35		18	19	20	21	22	23	24	
36	Epag. 1769	25	26	27	28	29	30	1	Pāg. 2045
37	Thoout 1770	2	3	4	5	1[a]	2	3	Maskaram 2046
38		4	5	6	7	8	9	10	
39		11	12	13	14	15	16	17[b]	
40		18	19	20	21	22	23	24	
41	Paope 1770	25	26	27	28	29	30	1	Teqemt 2046
42		2	3	4	5	6	7	8	
43		9	10	11	12	13	14	15	
44		16	17	18	19	20	21	22	
45		23	24	25	26	27	28	29	
46	Athōr 1770	30	1	2	3	4	5	6	Ḫedār 2046
47		7	8	9	10	11	12	13	
48		14	15	16	17	18	19	20	
49		21	22	23	24	25	26	27	
50	Koiak 1770	28	29	30	1	2	3	4	Tākhśāś 2046
51		5	6	7	8	9	10	11	
52		12	13	14	15	16	17	18	
1		19	20	21	22	23	24	25	

[a]New Year
[b]Spring (3:45)
[c]Summer (21:02)
[d]Autumn (13:04)
[e]Winter (10:08)
● New moon
◐ First quarter moon
○ Full moon
◑ Last quarter moon

‡Leap year
[a]New Year
[b]Yom Kippur
[c]Sukkot
[d]Winter starts
[e]Ḥanukkah
[f]Purim
[g]Passover
[h]Shavuot
[i]Fast of Av

‡Leap year
[a]New Year (4751, Fowl)
[b]Lantern Festival
[c]Qīngmíng
[d]Dragon Festival
[e]Qīqiǎo
[f]Hungry Ghosts
[g]Mid-Autumn Festival
[h]Double-Ninth Festival
[i]Dōngzhì
*Start of 60-name cycle

[a]New Year
[b]Building of the Cross
[c]Christmas
[d]Jesus's Circumcision
[e]Epiphany
[f]Easter
[g]Mary's Announcement
[h]Jesus's Transfiguration

PERSIAN (ASTRONOMICAL) 1431/1432‡

Month	Sun	Mon	Tue	Wed	Thu	Fri	Sat
DEY 1431	9	10	11	12	13	14	15
	16	17	18	19	20	21	22
	23	24	25	26	27	28	29
	30	*1*	2	3	4	5	6
BAHMAN 1431	7	8	9	10	11	12	13
	14	15	16	17	18	19	20
	21	22	23	24	25	26	27
	28	29	30	*1*	2	3	4
ESFAND 1431	5	6	7	8	9	10	11
	12	13	14	15	16	17	18
	19	20	21	22	23	24	25
	26	27	28	29	*1*[a]	2	3
FARVARDIN 1432	4	5	6	7	8	9	10
	11	12	13[b]	14	15	16	17
	18	19	20	21	22	23	24
	25	26	27	28	29	30	31
ORDIBEHEST 1432	*1*	2	3	4	5	6	7
	8	9	10	11	12	13	14
	15	16	17	18	19	20	21
	22	23	24	25	26	27	28
	29	30	31	*1*	2	3	4
XORDAD 1432	5	6	7	8	9	10	11
	12	13	14	15	16	17	18
	19	20	21	22	23	24	25
	26	27	28	29	30	31	*1*
TIR 1432	2	3	4	5	6	7	8
	9	10	11	12	13	14	15
	16	17	18	19	20	21	22
	23	24	25	26	27	28	29
	30	31	*1*	2	3	4	5
MORDAD 1432	6	7	8	9	10	11	12
	13	14	15	16	17	18	19
	20	21	22	23	24	25	26
	27	28	29	30	31	*1*	2
SHAHRIVAR 1432	3	4	5	6	7	8	9
	10	11	12	13	14	15	16
	17	18	19	20	21	22	23
	24	25	26	27	28	29	30
	31	*1*	2	3	4	5	6
MEHR 1432	7	8	9	10	11	12	13
	14	15	16	17	18	19	20
	21	22	23	24	25	26	27
	28	29	30	*1*	2	3	4
ABAN 1432	5	6	7	8	9	10	11
	12	13	14	15	16	17	18
	19	20	21	22	23	24	25
	26	27	28	29	30	*1*	2
AZAR 1432	3	4	5	6	7	8	9
	10	11	12	13	14	15	16
	17	18	19	20	21	22	23
	24	25	26	27	28	29	30
DEY 1432	*1*	2	3	4	5	6	7
	8	9	10	11	12	13	14

‡Leap year
[a]New Year
[b]Sizdeh Bedar

HINDU LUNAR 2109/2110‡

Month	Sun	Mon	Tue	Wed	Thu	Fri	Sat
PAUSHA 2109	8	9	10	**11**	13	14	15
	16	17	18	19	20	21	22
	23	24	25	26	27	28	29
	30	1	2	3	4	5	6
MĀGHA 2109	7	8	9	10	11	12	13
	14	15	16	**17**	19	20	21
	21	22	23	24	25	26	27
	28[h]	29	30	1	2	3	4
PHĀLGUNA 2109	5	6	7	8	9	**10**	12
	13	14	15[i]	16	17	18	19
	20	21	22	23	24	25	*25*
	26	27	28	29	30	1[a]	2
CHAITRA 2110	3	**4**	6	7	8	9[b]	10
	11	12	13	14	15	16	17
	18	19	20	21	22	23	24
	25	26	27	28	29	30	1
VAIŚĀKHA 2110	2	3	4	5	6	7	**8**
	10	11	12	13	14	15	16
	17	18	19	*19*	20	21	22
	23	24	25	26	27	28	29
	30	**1**	3	4	5	6	7
JYAISHṬHA 2110	8	9	10	11	12	13	14
	15	16	17	18	19	20	21
	22	23	24	25	26	27	28
	29	30	1	2	3	**4**	6
LEAP ĀSHĀḌHA 2110	7	8	9	10	11	12	13
	14	15	*15*	16	17	18	19
	20	21	22	23	24	25	26
	27	29	30	1	2	3	4
ĀSHĀḌHA 2110	5	6	7	8	9	10	11
	12	13	14	15	16	17	18
	19	20	21	22	23	24	25
	26	27	28	29	**30**	2	3
ŚRĀVAṆA 2110	4	5	6	7	8	9	10
	11	12	*12*	13	14	15	16
	17	18	19	20	21	22	**23**[c]
	25	26	27	28	29	30	1
BHĀDRAPADA 2110	2	3	4[d]	5	6	7	8
	9	10	11	12	13	14	15
	16	17	18	19	20	21	22
	23	24	25	**26**	28	29	30
	1	2	3	4	5	6	7
ĀŚVINA 2110	*7*	8[e]	9[e]	10[e]	11	12	13
	14	15	16	17	18	19	**20**
	22	23	24	25	26	27	28
	29	30	1[f]	2	3	4	5
KĀRTTIKA 2110	6	7	8	9	10	11	*11*
	12	14	15	16	17	18	19
	20	21	22	23	24	25	**26**
	28	29	*29*	30	1	2	3
MĀRGAŚĪRA 2110	4	5	6	7	8	9	10
	11[g]	12	13	14	15	16	17
	18	20	21	22	23	24	25

‡Leap year
[a]New Year (Śrīmukha)
[b]Birthday of Rāma
[c]Birthday of Krishna
[d]Ganēśa Chaturthī
[e]Dashara
[f]Diwali
[g]Birthday of Vishnu
[h]Night of Śiva
[i]Holi

HINDU SOLAR 1974‡/1975

Month	Sun	Mon	Tue	Wed	Thu	Fri	Sat
PAUSHA 1974	14	15	16	17	18	19	20
	21	22	23	24	25	26	27
	28	29	1[b]	2	3	4	5
MĀGHA 1974	6	7	8	9	10	11	12
	13	14	15	16	17	18	19
	20	21	22	23	24	25	26
	27	28	29	1	2	3	4
PHĀLGUNA 1974	5	6	7	8	9	10	11
	12	13	14	15	16	17	18
	19	20	21	22	23	24	25
	26	27	28	29	30	1	2
CHAITRA 1974	3	4	5	6	7	8	9
	10	11	12	13	14	15	16
	17	18	19	20	21	22	23
	24	25	26	27	28	29	30
	31	1[a]	2	3	4	5	6
VAIŚĀKHA 1975	7	8	9	10	11	12	13
	14	15	16	17	18	19	20
	21	22	23	24	25	26	27
	28	29	30	31	1	2	3
JYAISHṬHA 1975	4	5	6	7	8	9	10
	11	12	13	14	15	16	17
	18	19	20	21	22	23	24
	25	26	27	28	29	30	31
	1	2	3	4	5	6	7
ĀSHĀḌHA 1975	8	9	10	11	12	13	14
	15	16	17	18	19	20	21
	22	23	24	25	26	27	28
	29	30	31	32	1	2	3
ŚRĀVAṆA 1975	4	5	6	7	8	9	10
	11	12	13	14	15	16	17
	18	19	20	21	22	23	24
	25	26	27	28	29	30	31
	1	2	3	4	5	6	7
BHĀDRAPADA 1975	8	9	10	11	12	13	14
	15	16	17	18	19	20	21
	22	23	24	25	26	27	28
	29	30	31	1	2	3	4
ĀŚVINA 1975	5	6	7	8	9	10	11
	12	13	14	15	16	17	18
	19	20	21	22	23	24	25
	26	27	28	29	30	31	1
KĀRTTIKA 1975	2	3	4	5	6	7	8
	9	10	11	12	13	14	15
	16	17	18	19	20	21	22
	23	24	25	26	27	28	29
	30	1	2	3	4	5	6
MĀRGAŚĪRA 1975	7	8	9	10	11	12	13
	14	15	16	17	18	19	20
	21	22	23	24	25	26	27
	28	29	1	2	3	4	5
PAUSHA 1975	6	7	8	9	10	11	12
	13	14	15	16	17	18	19

‡Leap year
[a]New Year (Sarvajit)
[b]Pongal

ISLAMIC (ASTRONOMICAL) 1475‡/1476

Month	Sun	Mon	Tue	Wed	Thu	Fri	Sat
JUMĀDĀ I 1475	8	9	10	11	12	13	14
	15	16	17	18	19	20	21
	22	23	24	25	26	27	28
	29	30	*1*	2	3	4	5
JUMĀDĀ II 1475	6	7	8	9	10	11	12
	13	14	15	16	17	18	19
	20	21	22	23	24	25	26
	27	28	29	*30*	1	2	3
RAJAB 1475	4	5	6	7	8	9	10
	11	12	13	14	15	16	17
	18	19	20	21	22	23	24
	25	26	27[d]	28	29	*30*	1
SHA'BĀN 1475	2	3	4	5	6	7	8
	9	10	11	12	13	14	15
	16	17	18	19	20	21	22
	23	24	25	26	27	28	*29*
RAMAḌĀN 1475	1[e]	2	3	4	5	6	7
	8	9	10	11	12	13	14
	15	16	17	18	19	20	21
	22	23	24	25	26	27	28
	29	1[f]	2	3	4	5	6
SHAWWĀL 1475	7	8	9	10	11	12	13
	14	15	16	17	18	19	20
	21	22	23	24	25	26	27
	28	29	*30*	1	2	3	4
DHU AL-QA'DA 1475	5	6	7	8	9	10	11
	12	13	14	15	16	17	18
	19	20	21	22	23	24	25
	26	27	28	29	*1*	2	3
DHU AL-ḤIJJA 1475	4	5	6	7	8	9	10[g]
	11	12	13	14	15	16	17
	18	19	20	21	22	23	24
	25	26	27	28	29	30	*1*[a]
MUḤARRAM 1476	2	3	4	5	6	7	8
	9	10[b]	11	12	13	14	15
	16	17	18	19	20	21	22
	23	24	25	26	27	28	29
ṢAFAR 1476	1	2	3	4	5	6	7
	8	9	10	11	12	13	14
	15	16	17	18	19	20	21
	22	23	24	25	26	27	28
	29	1	*2*	3	4	5	6
RABĪ' I 1476	7	8	9	10	11	12[c]	13
	14	15	16	17	18	19	20
	21	22	23	24	25	26	27
	28	29	30	1	2	3	4
RABĪ' II 1476	5	6	7	8	9	10	11
	12	13	14	15	16	17	18
	19	20	21	22	23	24	25
	26	27	28	29	1	2	3
JUMĀDĀ I 1476	4	5	6	7	8	9	10
	11	12	13	14	15	16	17
	18	19	20	21	22	23	24

‡Leap year
[a]New Year
[b]'Ashūrā'
[c]Prophet's Birthday
[d]Ascent of the Prophet
[e]Start of Ramaḍān
[f]'Id al-Fiṭr
[g]'Id al-'Aḍḥā

GREGORIAN 2053

Julian (Sun)	Sun	Mon	Tue	Wed	Thu	Fri	Sat	Month
Dec 16	*29*	30	31	1	2	3	4	
	5	6	7[a]	8	9	10	11	JANUARY 2053
Dec 30	*12*	13	14[b]	15	16	17	18	
	19	20	21	22	23	24	25	
Jan 13	*26*	27	28	29	30	31	1	
	2	3	4	5	6	7	8	FEBRUARY 2053
Jan 27	*9*	10	11	12	13	14	15	
	16	17	18	19[c]	20	21	22	
Feb 10	*23*	24	25	26	27	28	1	
	2[d]	3	4	5	6	7	8	MARCH 2053
Feb 24	*9*	10	11	12	13	14	15	
	16	17	18	19	20	21	22	
Mar 10	*23*	24	25	26	27	28	29	
	30	31	1	2	3	4	5	
Mar 24	*6*[e]	7	8	9	10	11	12	APRIL 2053
	13[f]	14	15	16	17	18	19	
Apr 7	*20*	21	22	23	24	25	26	
	27	28	29	30	1	2	3	
Apr 21	*4*	5	6	7	8	9	10	MAY 2053
	11	12	13	14	15	16	17	
May 5	*18*	19	20	21	22	23	24	
	25	26	27	28	29	30	31	
May 19	*1*	2	3	4	5	6	7	JUNE 2053
	8	9	10	11	12	13	14	
Jun 2	*15*	16	17	18	19	20	21	
	22	23	24	25	26	27	28	
Jun 16	*29*	30	1	2	3	4	5	
	6	7	8	9	10	11	12	JULY 2053
Jun 30	*13*	14	15	16	17	18	19	
	20	21	22	23	24	25	26	
Jul 14	*27*	28	29	30	31	1	2	
	3	4	5	6	7	8	9	AUGUST 2053
Jul 28	*10*	11	12	13	14	15	16	
	17	18	19	20	21	22	23	
Aug 11	*24*	25	26	27	28	29	30	
	31	1	2	3	4	5	6	
Aug 25	*7*	8	9	10	11	12	13	SEPTEMBER 2053
	14	15	16	17	18	19	20	
Sep 8	*21*	22	23	24	25	26	27	
	28	29	30	1	2	3	4	
Sep 22	*5*	6	7	8	9	10	11	OCTOBER 2053
	12	13	14	15	16	17	18	
Oct 6	*19*	20	21	22	23	24	25	
	26	27	28	29	30	31	1	
Oct 20	*2*	3	4	5	6	7	8	NOVEMBER 2053
	9	10	11	12	13	14	15	
Nov 3	*16*	17	18	19	20	21	22	
	23	24	25	26	27	28	29	
Nov 17	*30*[g]	1	2	3	4	5	6	
	7	8	9	10	11	12	13	DECEMBER 2053
Dec 1	*14*	15	16	17	18	19	20	
	21	22	23	24	25[h]	26	27	
Dec 15	*28*	29	30	31	1	2	3	

[a]Orthodox Christmas
[b]Julian New Year
[c]Ash Wednesday
[d]Feast of Orthodoxy
[e]Easter
[f]Orthodox Easter
[g]Advent
[h]Christmas

2054

Gregorian 2054 (with lunar phases, ISO week and Julian day)

ISO Week (Mon)	Month	Sun	Mon	Tue	Wed	Thu	Fri	Sat	Lunar Phases	Julian Day (Sun noon)
1	JANUARY 2054	28	29	30	31	◑[a]	2	3	1:09	2471265
2		4	5	6	7	●	9	10	22:32	2471272
3		11	12	13	14	15	16	◐	2:13	2471279
4		18	19	20	21	22	○	24	20:06	2471286
5		25	26	27	28	29	◑	31	15:07	2471293
6	FEBRUARY 2054	1	2	3	4	5	6	●	18:12	2471300
7		8	9	10	11	12	13	14		2471307
8		◐	16	17	18	19	20	21	15:34	2471314
9		○	23	24	25	26	27	28	6:45	2471321
10	MARCH 2054	◑	2	3	4	5	6	7	7:35	2471328
11		8	●	10	11	12	13	14	12:44	2471335
12		15	16	◐	18	19	20[b]	21	1:19	2471342
13		22	○	24	25	26	27	28	17:20	2471349
14		29	30	◑	1	2	3	4	1:49	2471356
15	APRIL 2054	5	6	7	●	9	10	11	4:31	2471363
16		12	13	14	◐	16	17	18	8:22	2471370
17		19	20	21	○	23	24	25	4:00	2471377
18		26	27	28	◑	30	1	2	20:45	2471384
19	MAY 2054	3	4	5	6	●	8	9	16:59	2471391
20		10	11	12	13	◐	15	16	13:56	2471398
21		17	18	19	20	○	22	23	15:15	2471405
22		24	25	26	27	28	◑	30	15:02	2471412
23		31	1	2	3	4	5	●	2:39	2471419
24	JUNE 2054	7	8	9	10	11	◐	13	19:16	2471426
25		14	15	16	17	18	19	○	3:41	2471433
26		21[c]	22	23	24	25	26	27		2471440
27		◑	29	30	1	2	3	4	7:29	2471447
28	JULY 2054	●	6	7	8	9	10	11	10:32	2471454
29		◐	13	14	15	16	17	18	1:35	2471461
30		○	20	21	22	23	24	25	17:46	2471468
31		26	◑	28	29	30	31	1	21:26	2471475
32	AUGUST 2054	2	●	4	5	6	7	8	17:46	2471482
33		9	◐	11	12	13	14	15	10:04	2471489
34		16	17	○	19	20	21	22	9:20	2471496
35		23	24	25	◑	27	28	29	8:55	2471503
36		30	31	1	●	3	4	5	1:17	2471510
37	SEPTEMBER 2054	6	7	◐	9	10	11	12	21:45	2471517
38		13	14	15	16	○	18	19	1:40	2471524
39		20	21	22[d]	23	◑	25	26	18:24	2471531
40		27	28	29	30	●	2	3	9:48	2471538
41	OCTOBER 2054	4	5	6	7	◐	9	10	13:18	2471545
42		11	12	13	14	15	○	17	17:43	2471552
43		18	19	20	21	22	23	◑	2:38	2471559
44		25	26	27	28	29	●	31	20:00	2471566
45	NOVEMBER 2054	1	2	3	4	5	6	◐	8:33	2471573
46		8	9	10	11	12	13	14		2471580
47		○	16	17	18	19	20	21	8:47	2471587
48		◑	23	24	25	26	27	28	10:21	2471594
49		●	30	1	2	3	4	5	8:32	2471601
50	DECEMBER 2054	6	◐	8	9	10	11	12	6:05	2471608
51		13	○	15	16	17	18	19	22:39	2471615
52		20	◑[e]	22	23	24	25	26	18:21	2471622
53		27	●	29	30	31	1	2	23:50	2471629

Hebrew 5814‡/5815

ISO Week	Month	Sun	Mon	Tue	Wed	Thu	Fri	Sat	Molad
1	TEVETH 5814	17	18	19	20	21	22	23	
2		24	25	26	27	28	29	1	Fri $5^h9^m15^p$
3	SHEVAT 5814	2	3	4	5	6	7	8	
4		9	10	11	12	13	14	15	
5		16	17	18	19	20	21	22	
6		23	24	25	26	27	28	29	
7	ADAR I 5814	30	1	2	3	4	5	6	Sat $17^h53^m16^p$
8		7	8	9	10	11	12	13	
9		14	15	16	17	18	19	20	
10		21	22	23	24	25	26	27	
11	ADAR II 5814	28	29	30	1	2	3	4	Mon $6^h37^m17^p$
12		5	6	7	8	9	10	11	
13		12	13	14[f]	15	16	17	18	
14		19	20	21	22	23	24	25	
15	NISAN 5814	26	27	28	29	1	2	3	Tue $19^h22^m0^p$
16		4	5	6	7	8	9	10	
17		11	12	13	14	15[g]	16	17	
18		18	19	20	21	22	23	24	
19	IYAR 5814	25	26	27	28	29	30	1	Thu $8^h6^m1^p$
20		2	3	4	5	6	7	8	
21		9	10	11	12	13	14	15	
22		16	17	18	19	20	21	22	
23		23	24	25	26	27	28	29	
24	SIVAN 5814	1	2	3	4	5	6[h]	7	Fri $20^h50^m2^p$
25		8	9	10	11	12	13	14	
26		15	16	17	18	19	20	21	
27		22	23	24	25	26	27	28	
28	TAMMUZ 5814	29	30	1	2	3	4	5	Sun $9^h34^m3^p$
29		6	7	8	9	10	11	12	
30		13	14	15	16	17	18	19	
31		20	21	22	23	24	25	26	
32	AV 5814	27	28	29	1	2	3	4	Mon $22^h18^m4^p$
33		5	6	7	8	9[i]	10	11	
34		12	13	14	15	16	17	18	
35		19	20	21	22	23	24	25	
36	ELUL 5814	26	27	28	29	30	1	2	Wed $11^h2^m5^p$
37		3	4	5	6	7	8	9	
38		10	11	12	13	14	15	16	
39		17	18	19	20	21	22	23	
40	TISHRI 5815	24	25	26	27	28	29	1[a]	Thu $23^h46^m6^p$
41		2[a]	3	4	5	6	7	8	
42		9	10[b]	11	12	13	14	15[c]	
43		16	17	18	19	20	21	22	
44		23	24	25	26	27	28	29	
45	HESHVAN 5815	30	1	2	3	4	5	6	Sat $12^h30^m7^p$
46		7	8	9	10	11	12	13	
47		14	15	16	17	18	19	20	
48		21	22	23	24	25	26	27	
49	KISLEV 5815	28	29	30	1	2	3	4[d]	Mon $1^h14^m8^p$
50		5	6	7	8	9	10	11	
51		12	13	14	15	16	17	18	
52		19	20	21	22	23	24	25[e]	
53		26[e]	27[e]	28[e]	29[e]	30[e]	1[e]	2[e]	Tue $13^h58^m9^p$

Chinese Guǐ-Yǒu/Jiǎ-Xū

ISO Week	Month	Sun	Mon	Tue	Wed	Thu	Fri	Sat	Solar Term
1	MONTH 11* Guǐ-Yǒu	19	20	21	22	23	24	25	
2		26	*27*	28	29	30	1	2	Xiǎo hán
3	MONTH 12 Guǐ-Yǒu	3	4	5	6	7	8	9	
4		10	11	**12**	13	14	15*	16	Dà hán
5		17	18	19	20	21	22	23	
6		24	25	*26*	27	28	29	30	Lì chūn
7	MONTH 1 Jiǎ-Xū	1[a]	2	3	4	5	6	7	
8		8	9	10	**11**	12	13	14	Yǔ shuǐ
9		15[b]	16	17	18	19	20	21	
10		22	23	24	25	*26*	27	28	Jīng zhé
11		29	1	2	3	4	5	6	
12	MONTH 2 Jiǎ-Xū	7	8	9	10	11	**12**	13	Chūn fēn
13		14	15	16*	17	18	19	20	
14		21	22	23	24	25	26	*27*[c]	Qīng míng
15		28	29	30	1	2	3	4	
16	MONTH 3 Jiǎ-Xū	5	6	7	8	9	10	11	
17		12	**13**	14	15	16	17	18	Gǔ yǔ
18		19	20	21	22	23	24	25	
19		26	27	*28*	29	30	1	2	Lì xià
20	MONTH 4 Jiǎ-Xū	3	4	5	6	7	8	9	
21		10	11	12	13	**14**	15	16*	Xiǎo mǎn
22		17	18	19	20	21	22	23	
23		24	25	26	27	28	*29*	1	Máng zhòng
24	MONTH 5 Jiǎ-Xū	2	3	4	5[d]	6	7	8	
25		9	10	11	12	13	14	15	
26		**16**	17	18	19	20	21	22	Xià zhì
27		23	24	25	26	27	28	29	
28		1	2	*3*	4	5	6	7	Xiǎo shǔ
29	MONTH 6 Jiǎ-Xū	8	9	10	11	12	13	14	
30		15	16	17	**18***	19	20	21	Dà shǔ
31		22	23	24	25	26	27	28	
32		29	30	1	2	3	*4*	5	Lì qiū
33	MONTH 7 Jiǎ-Xū	6	7[e]	8	9	10	11	12	
34		13	14	15[f]	16	17	18	19	
35		**20**	21	22	23	24	25	26	Chǔ shǔ
36		27	28	29	1	2	3	4	
37	MONTH 8 Jiǎ-Xū	5	6	7	8	9	10	11	Bái lù
38		12	13	14	15[g]	16	17	18	
39		19*	20	21	**22**	23	24	25	Qiū fēn
40		26	27	28	29	1	2	3	
41	MONTH 9 Jiǎ-Xū	4	5	6	7	*8*	9[h]	10	Hán lù
42		11	12	13	14	15	16	17	
43		18	19	20	21	22	**23**	24	Shuāng jiàng
44		25	26	27	28	29	30	1	
45	MONTH 10 Jiǎ-Xū	2	3	4	5	6	7	*8*	Lì dōng
46		9	10	11	12	13	14	15	
47		16	17	18	19	20*	21	22	
48		**23**	24	25	26	27	28	29	Xiǎo xuě
49	MONTH 11 Jiǎ-Xū	1	2	3	4	5	6	7	
50		8	*9*	10	11	12	13	14	Dà xuě
51		15	16	17	18	19	20	21	
52		22	23	**24**[i]	25	26	27	28	Dōng zhì
53		29	30	1	2	3	4	5	

Coptic 1770/1771‡ — Ethiopic 2046/2047‡

ISO Week	Coptic Month	Sun	Mon	Tue	Wed	Thu	Fri	Sat	Ethiopic Month
1	KOIAK 1770	19	20	21	22	23	24	25	TĀḪŚĀŚ 2046
2		26	27	28	29[c]	30	1	2	
3	ṬŌBE 1770	3	4	5	6[d]	7	8	9	ṬER 2046
4		10	11[e]	12	13	14	15	16	
5		17	18	19	20	21	22	23	
6		24	25	26	27	28	29	30	
7	MESHIR 1770	1	2	3	4	5	6	7	YAKĀTIT 2046
8		8	9	10	11	12	13	14	
9		15	16	17	18	19	20	21	
10		22	23	24	25	26	27	28	
11	PAREMOTEP 1770	29	30	1	2	3	4	5	MAGĀBIT 2046
12		6	7	8	9	10	11	12	
13		13	14	15	16	17	18	19	
14		20	21	22	23	24	25	26	
15	PARMOUTE 1770	27	28	29	30	1	2	3	MIYĀZYĀ 2046
16		4	5	6	7	8	9	10	
17		11	12	13	14	15	16	17	
18		18	19	20	21	22	23	24	
19	PASHONS 1770	25[f]	26	27	28	29[g]	30	1	GENBOT 2046
20		2	3	4	5	6	7	8	
21		9	10	11	12	13	14	15	
22		16	17	18	19	20	21	22	
23		23	24	25	26	27	28	29	
24	PAŌNE 1770	30	1	2	3	4	5	6	SANĒ 2046
25		7	8	9	10	11	12	13	
26		14	15	16	17	18	19	20	
27		21	22	23	24	25	26	27	
28	EPĒP 1770	28	29	30	1	2	3	4	ḤAMLĒ 2046
29		5	6	7	8	9	10	11	
30		12	13	14	15	16	17	18	
31		19	20	21	22	23	24	25	
32	MESORĒ 1770	26	27	28	29	30	1	2	NAḤASĒ 2046
33		3	4	5	6	7	8	9	
34		10	11	12	13[h]	14	15	16	
35		17	18	19	20	21	22	23	
36		24	25	26	27	28	29	30	
37	EPAG. 1770 / THOOUT 1771	1	2	3	4	5	1[a]	2	PĀG. 2046 / MASKARAM 2047
38		3	4	5	6	7	8	9	
39		10	11	12	13	14	15	16	
40		17[b]	18	19	20	21	22	23	
41		24	25	26	27	28	29	30	
42	PAOPE 1771	1	2	3	4	5	6	7	ṬEQEMT 2047
43		8	9	10	11	12	13	14	
44		15	16	17	18	19	20	21	
45		22	23	24	25	26	27	28	
46	ATHŌR 1771	29	30	1	2	3	4	5	ḪEDĀR 2047
47		6	7	8	9	10	11	12	
48		13	14	15	16	17	18	19	
49		20	21	22	23	24	25	26	
50	KOIAK 1771	27	28	29	30	1	2	3	TĀḪŚĀŚ 2047
51		4	5	6	7	8	9	10	
52		11	12	13	14	15	16	17	
53		18	19	20	21	22	23	24	

Gregorian notes:
[a]New Year
[b]Spring (9:33)
[c]Summer (2:45)
[d]Autumn (18:57)
[e]Winter (16:08)
● New moon
◐ First quarter moon
○ Full moon
◑ Last quarter moon

Hebrew notes:
‡Leap year
[a]New Year
[b]Yom Kippur
[c]Sukkot
[d]Winter starts
[e]Ḥanukkah
[f]Purim
[g]Passover
[h]Shavuot
[i]Fast of Av

Chinese notes:
[a]New Year (4752, Dog)
[b]Lantern Festival
[c]Qīngmíng
[d]Dragon Festival
[e]Qīqiǎo
[f]Hungry Ghosts
[g]Mid-Autumn Festival
[h]Double-Ninth Festival
[i]Dōngzhì
*Start of 60-name cycle

Coptic/Ethiopic notes:
‡Leap year
[a]New Year
[b]Building of the Cross
[c]Christmas
[d]Jesus's Circumcision
[e]Epiphany
[f]Easter
[g]Mary's Announcement
[h]Jesus's Transfiguration

2054

PERSIAN (ASTRONOMICAL) 1432‡/1433

Month	Sun	Mon	Tue	Wed	Thu	Fri	Sat
DEY 1432	8	9	10	11	12	13	14
	15	16	17	18	19	20	21
	22	23	24	25	26	27	28
BAHMAN 1432	29	30	1	2	3	4	5
	6	7	8	9	10	11	12
	13	14	15	16	17	18	19
	20	21	22	23	24	25	26
ESFAND 1432	27	28	29	30	1	2	3
	4	5	6	7	8	9	10
	11	12	13	14	15	16	17
	18	19	20	21	22	23	24
FARVARDĪN 1433	25	26	27	28	29	30	1[a]
	2	3	4	5	6	7	8
	9	10	11	12	13[b]	14	15
	16	17	18	19	20	21	22
	23	24	25	26	27	28	29
ORDĪBEHEŠT 1433	30	31	1	2	3	4	5
	6	7	8	9	10	11	12
	13	14	15	16	17	18	19
	20	21	22	23	24	25	26
XORDĀD 1433	27	28	29	30	31	1	2
	3	4	5	6	7	8	9
	10	11	12	13	14	15	16
	17	18	19	20	21	22	23
	24	25	26	27	28	29	30
TĪR 1433	31	1	2	3	4	5	6
	7	8	9	10	11	12	13
	14	15	16	17	18	19	20
	21	22	23	24	25	26	27
MORDĀD 1433	28	29	30	31	1	2	3
	4	5	6	7	8	9	10
	11	12	13	14	15	16	17
	18	19	20	21	22	23	24
	25	26	27	28	29	30	31
SHAHRĪVAR 1433	1	2	3	4	5	6	7
	8	9	10	11	12	13	14
	15	16	17	18	19	20	21
	22	23	24	25	26	27	28
MEHR 1433	29	30	31	1	2	3	4
	5	6	7	8	9	10	11
	12	13	14	15	16	17	18
	19	20	21	22	23	24	25
ĀBĀN 1433	26	27	28	29	30	1	2
	3	4	5	6	7	8	9
	10	11	12	13	14	15	16
	17	18	19	20	21	22	23
	24	25	26	27	28	29	30
ĀZAR 1433	1	2	3	4	5	6	7
	8	9	10	11	12	13	14
	15	16	17	18	19	20	21
	22	23	24	25	26	27	28
DEY 1433	29	30	1	2	3	4	5
	6	7	8	9	10	11	12

‡Leap year
[a]New Year
[b]Sizdeh Bedar

HINDU LUNAR 2110‡/2111

Month	Sun	Mon	Tue	Wed	Thu	Fri	Sat
MĀRGAŚIRA 2110	18	20	21	22	23	24	25
PAUSHA 2110	26	27	28	29	30	1	2
	2	3	4	5	6	7	8
	9	10	11	12	14	15	16
	17	18	19	20	21	22	23
	24	25	26	27	28	29	30
MĀGHA 2110	1	2	3	4	5	6	7
	8	9	10	11	12	13	14
	15	16	17	18	20	21	22
	23	24	25	25	26	27	28[h]
PHĀLGUNA 2110	29	30	1	2	3	4	5
	6	7	8	9	10	11	13
	14	15[i]	16	17	18	19	20
	21	22	23	24	25	26	27
CHAITRA 2111	28	28	29	30	1[a]	2	3
	4	6	7	8	9[b]	10	11
	12	13	14	15	16	17	18
	19	20	21	22	23	24	25
VAIŚĀKHA 2111	26	27	28	29	30	1	2
	3	4	5	6	7	8	10
	11	12	13	14	15	16	17
	18	19	20	21	22	23	23
	24	25	26	27	28	29	30
JYAISHṬHA 2111	1	3	4	5	6	7	8
	9	10	11	12	13	14	15
	16	17	18	19	20	21	22
	23	24	25	26	27	28	29
ĀSHĀḌHA 2111	30	1	2	3	4	6	7
	8	9	10	11	12	13	14
	15	16	17	18	19	20	20
	21	22	23	24	25	26	27
ŚRĀVAṆA 2111	29	30	1	2	3	4	5
	6	7	8	9	10	11	12
	13	14	15	16	17	18	19
	20	21	22	23[c]	24	25	26
BHĀDRAPADA 2111	27	28	29	30	2	3	4[d]
	5	6	7	8	9	10	11
	12	13	14	15	16	16	17
	18	19	20	21	22	23	25
ĀŚVINA 2111	26	27	28	29	30	1	2
	3	4	5	6	7	8[e]	9[e]
	10[e]	11	12	13	14	15	16
	17	18	19	20	21	22	23
KĀRTTIKA 2111	24	25	26	27	29	30	1[f]
	2	3	4	5	6	7	8
	9	10	10	11	12	13	14
	15	16	17	18	19	20	21
	23	24	25	26	27	28	29
MĀRGAŚIRA 2111	30	1	2	3	4	5	6
	7	8	9	10	11[g]	12	13
	14	15	16	17	18	19	20
	21	22	23	24	25	26	28
	29	30	1	2	3	3	4

‡Leap year
[a]New Year (Bhāva)
[b]Birthday of Rāma
[c]Birthday of Krishna
[d]Ganēśa Chaturthī
[e]Dashara
[f]Diwali
[g]Birthday of Vishnu
[h]Night of Śiva
[i]Holi

HINDU SOLAR 1975/1976

Month	Sun	Mon	Tue	Wed	Thu	Fri	Sat
PAUSHA 1975	13	14	15	16	17	18	19
	20	21	22	23	24	25	26
MĀGHA 1975	27	28	29	1[b]	2	3	4
	5	6	7	8	9	10	11
	12	13	14	15	16	17	18
	19	20	21	22	23	24	25
PHĀLGUNA 1975	26	27	28	29	30	1	2
	3	4	5	6	7	8	9
	10	11	12	13	14	15	16
	17	18	19	20	21	22	23
	24	25	26	27	28	29	30
CHAITRA 1975	1	2	3	4	5	6	7
	8	9	10	11	12	13	14
	15	16	17	18	19	20	21
	22	23	24	25	26	27	28
VAIŚĀKHA 1976	29	30	1[a]	2	3	4	5
	6	7	8	9	10	11	12
	13	14	15	16	17	18	19
	20	21	22	23	24	25	26
JYAISHṬHA 1976	27	28	29	30	31	1	2
	3	4	5	6	7	8	9
	10	11	12	13	14	15	16
	17	18	19	20	21	22	23
	24	25	26	27	28	29	30
ĀSHĀḌHA 1976	31	1	2	3	4	5	6
	7	8	9	10	11	12	13
	14	15	16	17	18	19	20
	21	22	23	24	25	26	27
ŚRĀVAṆA 1976	28	29	30	31	32	1	2
	3	4	5	6	7	8	9
	10	11	12	13	14	15	16
	17	18	19	20	21	22	23
	24	25	26	27	28	29	30
BHĀDRAPADA 1976	31	1	2	3	4	5	6
	7	8	9	10	11	12	13
	14	15	16	17	18	19	20
	21	22	23	24	25	26	27
ĀŚVINA 1976	28	29	30	31	1	2	3
	4	5	6	7	8	9	10
	11	12	13	14	15	16	17
	18	19	20	21	22	23	24
	25	26	27	28	29	30	31
KĀRTTIKA 1976	1	2	3	4	5	6	7
	8	9	10	11	12	13	14
	15	16	17	18	19	20	21
	22	23	24	25	26	27	28
MĀRGAŚIRA 1976	29	30	1	2	3	4	5
	6	7	8	9	10	11	12
	13	14	15	16	17	18	19
	20	21	22	23	24	25	26
PAUSHA 1976	27	28	29	1	2	3	4
	5	6	7	8	9	10	11
	12	13	14	15	16	17	18

[a]New Year (Sarvadhārin)
[b]Pongal

ISLAMIC (ASTRONOMICAL) 1476/1477‡

Month	Sun	Mon	Tue	Wed	Thu	Fri	Sat
JUMĀDĀ I 1476	18	19	20	21	22	23	24
JUMĀDĀ II 1476	25	26	27	28	29	30	1
	2	3	4	5	6	7	8
	9	10	11	12	13	14	15
	16	17	18	19	20	21	22
	23	24	25	26	27	28	29
RAJAB 1476	30	1	2	3	4	5	6
	7	8	9	10	11	12	13
	14	15	16	17	18	19	20
	21	22	23	24	25	26	27[d]
SHA'BĀN 1476	28	29	30	1	2	3	4
	5	6	7	8	9	10	11
	12	13	14	15	16	17	18
	19	20	21	22	23	24	25
RAMAḌĀN 1476	26	27	28	29	1[e]	2	3
	4	5	6	7	8	9	10
	11	12	13	14	15	16	17
	18	19	20	21	22	23	24
SHAWWĀL 1476	25	26	27	28	29	30	1[f]
	2	3	4	5	6	7	8
	9	10	11	12	13	14	15
	16	17	18	19	20	21	22
	23	24	25	26	27	28	29
DHU AL-QA'DA 1476	1	2	3	4	5	6	7
	8	9	10	11	12	13	14
	15	16	17	18	19	20	21
	22	23	24	25	26	27	28
DHU AL-ḤIJJA 1476	29	30	1	2	3	4	5
	6	7	8	9	10[g]	11	12
	13	14	15	16	17	18	19
	20	21	22	23	24	25	26
MUḤARRAM 1477	27	28	29	1[a]	2	3	4
	5	6	7	8	9	10[b]	11
	12	13	14	15	16	17	18
	19	20	21	22	23	24	25
ṢAFAR 1477	26	27	28	29	1	2	3
	4	5	6	7	8	9	10
	11	12	13	14	15	16	17
	18	19	20	21	22	23	24
RABĪ' I 1477	25	26	27	28	29	30	1
	2	3	4	5	6	7	8
	9	10	11	12[c]	13	14	15
	16	17	18	19	20	21	22
	23	24	25	26	27	28	29
RABĪ' II 1477	1	2	3	4	5	6	7
	8	9	10	11	12	13	14
	15	16	17	18	19	20	21
	22	23	24	25	26	27	28
JUMĀDĀ I 1477	29	30	1	2	3	4	5
	6	7	8	9	10	11	12
	13	14	15	16	17	18	19
	20	21	22	23	24	25	26
	27	28	29	1	2	3	4

‡Leap year
[a]New Year
[b]'Ashūrā'
[c]Prophet's Birthday
[d]Ascent of the Prophet
[e]Start of Ramaḍān
[f]'Id al-Fiṭr
[g]'Id al-'Aḍḥā

GREGORIAN 2054

Julian (Sun)	Sun	Mon	Tue	Wed	Thu	Fri	Sat	Month
Dec 15	28	29	30	31	1	2	3	JANUARY 2054
	4	5	6	7[a]	8	9	10	
Dec 29	11	12	13	14[b]	15	16	17	
	18	19	20	21	22	23	24	
Jan 12	25	26	27	28	29	30	31	
	1	2	3	4	5	6	7	FEBRUARY 2054
Jan 26	8	9	10	11[c]	12	13	14	
	15	16	17	18	19	20	21	
Feb 9	22	23	24	25	26	27	28	
	1	2	3	4	5	6	7	MARCH 2054
Feb 23	8	9	10	11	12	13	14	
	15	16	17	18	19	20	21	
Mar 9	22[d]	23	24	25	26	27	28	
	29[e]	30	31	1	2	3	4	APRIL 2054
Mar 23	5	6	7	8	9	10	11	
	12	13	14	15	16	17	18	
Apr 6	19	20	21	22	23	24	25	
	26	27	28	29	30	1	2	MAY 2054
Apr 20	3[f]	4	5	6	7	8	9	
	10	11	12	13	14	15	16	
May 4	17	18	19	20	21	22	23	
	24	25	26	27	28	29	30	
May 18	31	1	2	3	4	5	6	JUNE 2054
	7	8	9	10	11	12	13	
Jun 1	14	15	16	17	18	19	20	
	21	22	23	24	25	26	27	
Jun 15	28	29	30	1	2	3	4	JULY 2054
	5	6	7	8	9	10	11	
Jun 29	12	13	14	15	16	17	18	
	19	20	21	22	23	24	25	
Jul 13	26	27	28	29	30	31	1	AUGUST 2054
	2	3	4	5	6	7	8	
Jul 27	9	10	11	12	13	14	15	
	16	17	18	19	20	21	22	
Aug 10	23	24	25	26	27	28	29	
	30	31	1	2	3	4	5	SEPTEMBER 2054
Aug 24	6	7	8	9	10	11	12	
	13	14	15	16	17	18	19	
Sep 7	20	21	22	23	24	25	26	
	27	28	29	30	1	2	3	OCTOBER 2054
Sep 21	4	5	6	7	8	9	10	
	11	12	13	14	15	16	17	
Oct 5	18	19	20	21	22	23	24	
	25	26	27	28	29	30	31	
Oct 19	1	2	3	4	5	6	7	NOVEMBER 2054
	8	9	10	11	12	13	14	
Nov 2	15	16	17	18	19	20	21	
	22	23	24	25	26	27	28	
Nov 16	29[g]	30	1	2	3	4	5	DECEMBER 2054
	6	7	8	9	10	11	12	
Nov 30	13	14	15	16	17	18	19	
	20	21	22	23	24	25[h]	26	
Dec 14	27	28	29	30	31	1	2	

[a]Orthodox Christmas
[b]Julian New Year
[c]Ash Wednesday
[d]Feast of Orthodoxy
[e]Easter
[f]Orthodox Easter
[g]Advent
[h]Christmas

2055

GREGORIAN 2055 / Lunar Phases / ISO WEEK / JULIAN DAY

Month	Sun	Mon	Tue	Wed	Thu	Fri	Sat	Lunar Phases	ISO WEEK (Mon)	JULIAN DAY (Sun noon)
JANUARY 2055	27	●	29	30	31	1[a]	2	23:50	53	2471629
	3	4	5	◐	7	8	9	3:38	1	2471636
	10	11	12	○	14	15	16	11:20	2	2471643
	17	18	19	◑	21	22	23	3:23	3	2471650
	24	25	26	●	28	29	30	17:38	4	2471657
FEBRUARY 2055	31	1	2	3	◐	5	6	22:58	5	2471664
	7	8	9	10	○	12	13	22:47	6	2471671
	14	15	16	17	◑	19	20	14:13	7	2471678
	21	22	23	24	25	●	27	12:38	8	2471685
MARCH 2055	28	1	2	3	4	5	◐	14:46	9	2471692
	7	8	9	10	11	12	○	8:55	10	2471699
	14	15	16	17	18	19	◑[b]	3:17	11	2471706
	21	22	23	24	25	26	27		12	2471713
APRIL 2055	●	29	30	31	1	2	3	6:59	13	2471720
	4	◐	6	7	8	9	10	2:42	14	2471727
	○	12	13	14	15	16	17	17:57	15	2471734
	◑	19	20	21	22	23	24	18:34	16	2471741
MAY 2055	25	●	27	28	29	30	1	23:16	17	2471748
	2	3	◐	5	6	7	8	11:09	18	2471755
	9	10	○	12	13	14	15	2:30	19	2471762
	16	17	◑	19	20	21	22	11:29	20	2471769
	23	24	25	●	27	28	29	12:56	21	2471776
JUNE 2055	30	31	1	◐	3	4	5	17:00	22	2471783
	6	7	8	○	10	11	12	11:35	23	2471790
	13	14	15	16	◑	18	19	5:01	24	2471797
	20	21[c]	22	23	24	●	26	0:14	25	2471804
JULY 2055	27	28	29	30	◐	2	3	21:30	26	2471811
	4	5	6	7	○	9	10	22:10	27	2471818
	11	12	13	14	15	◑	17	22:13	28	2471825
	18	19	20	21	22	23	●	9:46	29	2471832
	25	26	27	28	29	30	◐	2:10	30	2471839
AUGUST 2055	1	2	3	4	5	6	○	10:56	31	2471846
	8	9	10	11	12	13	14		32	2471853
	◑	16	17	18	19	20	21	14:25	33	2471860
	●	23	24	25	26	27	28	18:13	34	2471867
SEPTEMBER 2055	◐	30	31	1	2	3	4	8:34	35	2471874
	5	○	7	8	9	10	11	1:55	36	2471881
	12	13	◑	15	16	17	18	5:13	37	2471888
	19	20	●	22	23[d]	24	25	2:18	38	2471895
OCTOBER 2055	26	◐	28	29	30	1	2	18:09	39	2471902
	3	4	○	6	7	8	9	18:37	40	2471909
	10	11	12	◑	14	15	16	18:21	41	2471916
	17	18	19	●	21	22	23	10:48	42	2471923
	24	25	26	◐	28	29	30	7:52	43	2471930
NOVEMBER 2055	31	1	2	3	○	5	6	12:10	44	2471937
	7	8	9	10	11	◑	13	5:37	45	2471944
	14	15	16	17	●	19	20	20:33	46	2471951
	21	22	23	24	25	◐	27	1:40	47	2471958
DECEMBER 2055	28	29	30	1	2	3	○	5:39	48	2471965
	5	6	7	8	9	10	◑	15:04	49	2471972
	12	13	14	15	16	17	●	8:14	50	2471979
	19	20	21[e]	22	23	24	◐	22:28	51	2471986
	26	27	28	29	30	31	1		52	2471993

HEBREW 5815/5816

ISO WEEK	Month	Sun	Mon	Tue	Wed	Thu	Fri	Sat	Molad
53	TEVETH 5815	26[e]	27[e]	28[e]	29[e]	30[e]	1[e]	2[e]	Tue 13h58m9p
1		3	4	5	6	7	8	9	
2		10	11	12	13	14	15	16	
3		17	18	19	20	21	22	23	
4	SHEVAT 5815	24	25	26	27	28	29	1	Thu 2h42m10p
5		2	3	4	5	6	7	8	
6		9	10	11	12	13	14	15	
7		16	17	18	19	20	21	22	
8		23	24	25	26	27	28	29	
9	ADAR 5815	30	1	2	3	4	5	6	Fri 15h26m11p
10		7	8	9	10	11	12	13	
11		14[f]	15	16	17	18	19	20	
12		21	22	23	24	25	26	27	
13	NISAN 5815	28	29	1	2	3	4	5	Sun 4h10m12p
14		6	7	8	9	10	11	12	
15		13	14	15[g]	16	17	18	19	
16		20	21	22	23	24	25	26	
17	IYYAR 5815	27	28	29	30	1	2	3	Mon 16h54m13p
18		4	5	6	7	8	9	10	
19		11	12	13	14	15	16	17	
20		18	19	20	21	22	23	24	
21	SIVAN 5815	25	26	27	28	29	1	2	Wed 5h38m14p
22		3	4	5	6[h]	7	8	9	
23		10	11	12	13	14	15	16	
24		17	18	19	20	21	22	23	
25		24	25	26	27	28	29	30	
26	TAMMUZ 5815	1	2	3	4	5	6	7	Thu 18h22m15p
27		8	9	10	11	12	13	14	
28		15	16	17	18	19	20	21	
29		22	23	24	25	26	27	28	
30	AV 5815	29	1	2	3	4	5	6	Sat 7h6m16p
31		7	8	9[i]	10	11	12	13	
32		14	15	16	17	18	19	20	
33		21	22	23	24	25	26	27	
34	ELUL 5815	28	29	30	1	2	3	4	Sun 19h50m17p
35		5	6	7	8	9	10	11	
36		12	13	14	15	16	17	18	
37		19	20	21	22	23	24	25	
38	TISHRI 5816	26	27	28	29	1[a]	2[a]	3	Tue 8h35m0p
39		4	5	6	7	8	9	10[b]	
40		11	12	13	14	15[c]	16	17	
41		18	19	20	21	22	23	24	
42	ḤESHVAN 5816	25	26	27	28	29	30	1	Wed 21h19m1p
43		2	3	4	5	6	7	8	
44		9	10	11	12	13	14	15	
45		16	17	18	19	20	21	22	
46		23	24	25	26	27	28	29	
47	KISLEV 5816	1	2	3	4	5	6	7	Fri 10h3m2p
48		8	9	10	11	12	13	14	
49		15	16[d]	17	18	19	20	21	
50		22	23	24	25[e]	26[e]	27[e]	28[e]	
51	TEVETH 5816	29[e]	30[e]	1[e]	2[e]	3	4	5	Sat 22h47m3p
52		6	7	8	9	10	11	12	

CHINESE Jiǎ-Xū/Yǐ-Hài‡

ISO WEEK	Month	Sun	Mon	Tue	Wed	Thu	Fri	Sat	Solar Term
53	MONTH 12 Jiǎ-Xū	29	30	1	2	3	4	5	
1		6	7	*8*	9	10	11	12	*Xiǎo hán*
2		13	14	15	16	17	18	19	
3		20	21*	22	***23***	24	25	26	***Dà hán***
4	MONTH 1 Yǐ-Hài	27	28	29	30	1[a]	2	3	
5		4	5	6	7	*8*	9	10	*Lì chūn*
6		11	12	13	14	15[b]	16	17	
7		18	19	20	21	22	***23***	24	***Yǔ shuǐ***
8	MONTH 2 Yǐ-Hài	25	26	27	28	29	1	2	
9		3	4	5	6	7	*8*	9	*Jīng zhé*
10		10	11	12	13	14	15	16	
11		17	18	19	20	21	22*	***23***	***Chūn fēn***
12		24	25	26	27	28	29	30	
13	MONTH 3 Yǐ-Hài	1	2	3	4	5	6	7	
14		8	*9*[c]	10	11	12	13	14	*Qīng míng*
15		15	16	17	18	19	20	21	
16		22	23	***24***	25	26	27	28	***Gǔ yǔ***
17	MONTH 4 Yǐ-Hài	29	30	1	2	3	4	5	
18		6	7	8	*9*	10	11	12	*Lì xià*
19		13	14	15	16	17	18	19	
20		20	21	22*	23	24	***25***	26	***Xiǎo mǎn***
21	MONTH 5 Yǐ-Hài	27	28	29	1	2	3	4	
22		5[d]	6	7	8	9	10	*11*	*Máng zhòng*
23		12	13	14	15	16	17	18	
24		19	20	21	22	23	24	25	
25	MONTH 6 Yǐ-Hài	26	***27***	28	29	30	1	2	***Xià zhì***
26		3	4	5	6	7	8	9	
27		10	11	12	*13*	14	15	16	*Xiǎo shǔ*
28		17	18	19	20	21	22	23*	
29	LEAP MONTH 6 Yǐ-Hài	24	25	26	27	28	***29***	1	***Dà shǔ***
30		2	3	4	5	6	7	8	
31		9	10	11	12	13	14	*15*	*Lì qiū*
32		16	17	18	19	20	21	22	
33		23	24	25	26	27	28	29	
34	MONTH 7 Yǐ-Hài	30	***1***	2	3	4	5	6	***Chǔ shǔ***
35		7[e]	8	9	10	11	12	13	
36		14	15[f]	*16*	17	18	19	20	*Bái lù*
37		21	22	23	24*	25	26	27	
38	MONTH 8 Yǐ-Hài	28	29	1	2	***3***	4	5	***Qiū fēn***
39		6	7	8	9	10	11	12	
40		13	14	15[g]	16	17	*18*	19	*Hán lù*
41		20	21	22	23	24	25	26	
42	MONTH 9 Yǐ-Hài	27	28	29	1	2	3	***4***	***Shuāng jiàng***
43		5	6	7	8	9[h]	10	11	
44		12	13	14	15	16	17	18	
45		*19*	20	21	22	23	24	25	*Lì dōng*
46	MONTH 10 Yǐ-Hài	26*	27	28	29	30	1	2	
47		3	***4***	5	6	7	8	9	***Xiǎo xuě***
48		10	11	12	13	14	15	16	
49		17	18	*19*	20	21	22	23	*Dà xuě*
50	MONTH 11 Yǐ-Hài	24	25	26	27	28	29	1	
51		2	3	4	***5***[i]	6	7	8	***Dōng zhì***
52		9	10	11	12	13	14	15	

COPTIC 1771‡/1772 ETHIOPIC 2047‡/2048

ISO WEEK	Coptic Month	Sun	Mon	Tue	Wed	Thu	Fri	Sat	Ethiopic Month
53	KOIAK 1771	18	19	20	21	22	23	24	TĀKHŚĀŚ 2047
1		25	26	27	28	29[c]	30	1	
2	TŌBE 1771	2	3	4	5	6[d]	7	8	ṬER 2047
3		9	10	11[e]	12	13	14	15	
4		16	17	18	19	20	21	22	
5		23	24	25	26	27	28	29	
6	MESHIR 1771	30	1	2	3	4	5	6	YAKĀTIT 2047
7		7	8	9	10	11	12	13	
8		14	15	16	17	18	19	20	
9		21	22	23	24	25	26	27	
10	PAREMOTEP 1771	28	29	30	1	2	3	4	MAGĀBIT 2047
11		5	6	7	8	9	10	11	
12		12	13	14	15	16	17	18	
13		19	20	21	22	23	24	25	
14	PARMOUTE 1771	26	27	28	29	30	1	2	MIYĀZYĀ 2047
15		3	4	5	6	7	8	9	
16		10[f]	11	12	13	14	15	16	
17		17	18	19	20	21	22	23	
18		24	25	26	27	28	29[g]	30	
19	PASHONS 1771	1	2	3	4	5	6	7	GENBOT 2047
20		8	9	10	11	12	13	14	
21		15	16	17	18	19	20	21	
22		22	23	24	25	26	27	28	
23	PAŌNE 1771	29	30	1	2	3	4	5	SANĒ 2047
24		6	7	8	9	10	11	12	
25		13	14	15	16	17	18	19	
26		20	21	22	23	24	25	26	
27	EPĒP 1771	27	28	29	30	1	2	3	ḤAMLĒ 2047
28		4	5	6	7	8	9	10	
29		11	12	13	14	15	16	17	
30		18	19	20	21	22	23	24	
31	MESORĒ 1771	25	26	27	28	29	30	1	NAḤASĒ 2047
32		2	3	4	5	6	7	8	
33		9	10	11	12	13[h]	14	15	
34		16	17	18	19	20	21	22	
35		23	24	25	26	27	28	29	
36	EPAG. 1771	30	1	2	3	4	5	6	PĀG. 2047
37	THOOUT 1772	1[a]	2	3	4	5	6	7	MASKARAM 2048
38		8	9	10	11	12	13	14	
39		15	16	17[b]	18	19	20	21	
40		22	23	24	25	26	27	28	
41	PAOPE 1772	29	30	1	2	3	4	5	ṬEQEMT 2048
42		6	7	8	9	10	11	12	
43		13	14	15	16	17	18	19	
44		20	21	22	23	24	25	26	
45	ATHŌR 1772	27	28	29	30	1	2	3	ḤEDĀR 2048
46		4	5	6	7	8	9	10	
47		11	12	13	14	15	16	17	
48		18	19	20	21	22	23	24	
49	KOIAK 1772	25	26	27	28	29	30	1	TĀKHŚĀŚ 2048
50		2	3	4	5	6	7	8	
51		9	10	11	12	13	14	15	
52		16	17	18	19	20	21	22	

[a]New Year
[b]Spring (15:27)
[c]Summer (8:38)
[d]Autumn (0:47)
[e]Winter (21:54)
● New moon
◐ First quarter moon
○ Full moon
◑ Last quarter moon

[a]New Year
[b]Yom Kippur
[c]Sukkot
[d]Winter starts
[e]Ḥanukkah
[f]Purim
[g]Passover
[h]Shavuot
[i]Fast of Av

‡Leap year
[a]New Year (4753, Pig)
[b]Lantern Festival
[c]Qīngmíng
[d]Dragon Festival
[e]Qīqiǎo
[f]Hungry Ghosts
[g]Mid-Autumn Festival
[h]Double-Ninth Festival
[i]Dōngzhì
*Start of 60-name cycle

‡Leap year
[a]New Year
[b]Building of the Cross
[c]Christmas
[d]Jesus's Circumcision
[e]Epiphany
[f]Easter
[g]Mary's Announcement
[h]Jesus's Transfiguration

PERSIAN (ASTRONOMICAL) 1433/1434

Month	Sun	Mon	Tue	Wed	Thu	Fri	Sat
	6	7	8	9	10	11	12
DEY 1433	13	14	15	16	17	18	19
	20	21	22	23	24	25	26
	27	28	29	30	1	2	3
BAHMAN 1433	4	5	6	7	8	9	10
	11	12	13	14	15	16	17
	18	19	20	21	22	23	24
	25	26	27	28	29	30	1
ESFAND 1433	2	3	4	5	6	7	8
	9	10	11	12	13	14	15
	16	17	18	19	20	21	22
	23	24	25	26	27	28	29
	1[a]	2	3	4	5	6	7
FARVARDĪN 1434	8	9	10	11	12	13[b]	14
	15	16	17	18	19	20	21
	22	23	24	25	26	27	28
	29	30	31	1	2	3	4
ORDĪBEHEŠT 1434	5	6	7	8	9	10	11
	12	13	14	15	16	17	18
	19	20	21	22	23	24	25
	26	27	28	29	30	31	1
XORDĀD 1434	2	3	4	5	6	7	8
	9	10	11	12	13	14	15
	16	17	18	19	20	21	22
	23	24	25	26	27	28	29
	30	31	1	2	3	4	5
TĪR 1434	6	7	8	9	10	11	12
	13	14	15	16	17	18	19
	20	21	22	23	24	25	26
	27	28	29	30	31	1	2
MORDĀD 1434	3	4	5	6	7	8	9
	10	11	12	13	14	15	16
	17	18	19	20	21	22	23
	24	25	26	27	28	29	30
	31	1	2	3	4	5	6
SHAHRĪVAR 1434	7	8	9	10	11	12	13
	14	15	16	17	18	19	20
	21	22	23	24	25	26	27
	28	29	30	31	1	2	3
MEHR 1434	4	5	6	7	8	9	10
	11	12	13	14	15	16	17
	18	19	20	21	22	23	24
	25	26	27	28	29	30	1
ĀBĀN 1434	2	3	4	5	6	7	8
	9	10	11	12	13	14	15
	16	17	18	19	20	21	22
	23	24	25	26	27	28	29
	30	1	2	3	4	5	6
ĀZAR 1434	7	8	9	10	11	12	13
	14	15	16	17	18	19	20
	21	22	23	24	25	26	27
DEY 1434	28	29	30	1	2	3	4
	5	6	7	8	9	10	11

HINDU LUNAR 2111/2112

Month	Sun	Mon	Tue	Wed	Thu	Fri	Sat
	29	30	1	2	3	3	4
PAUSHA 2111	5	6	7	8	9	10	11
	12	13	14	15	16	17	18
	19	21	22	23	24	25	26
	27	28	29	30	1	2	3
MĀGHA 2111	4	5	5	6	7	8	9
	10	11	12	**13**	15	16	17
	18	19	20	21	22	23	24
	25	26	27	28[h]	29	30	1
	2	3	4	5	6	7	8
PHĀLGUNA 2111	9	10	11	12	13	14	15[i]
	16	17	**18**	20	21	22	23
	24	25	26	27	28	28	29
	30	1[a]	2	3	4	5	6
CHAITRA 2112	7	8	9[b]	10	11	**12**	14
	15	16	17	18	19	20	21
	22	23	24	25	26	27	28
	29	30	1	2	2	**3**	5
VAIŚĀKHA 2112	6	7	8	9	10	11	12
	13	14	15	**16**	18	19	20
	21	22	23	23	24	25	26
	27	28	29	30	1	2	3
JYAISHTHA 2112	4	5	6	7	**8**	10	11
	12	13	14	15	16	17	18
	19	20	21	22	23	24	25
	26	27	28	28	**29**	1	2
ĀSHĀDHA 2112	3	4	5	6	7	8	9
	10	11	**12**	14	15	16	17
	18	19	19	20	21	22	23
	24	25	26	27	28	29	30
	1	2	3	**4**	6	7	8
ŚRĀVANA 2112	9	10	11	12	13	14	15
	16	17	18	19	20	21	22
	23[c]	24	25	26	27	28	29
	30	1	2	3	4[d]	5	6
BHĀDRAPADA 2112	**7**	9	10	11	12	13	14
	15	16	16	17	18	19	20
	21	22	23	24	25	26	27
	28	29	**30**	2	3	4	5
	6	7	8[e]	9[e]	10[e]	11	12
ĀŚVINA 2112	13	14	15	16	17	18	19
	20	20	21	**22**	24	25	26
	27	28	29	30	1[f]	2	3
	4	**5**	7	8	9	10	10
KĀRTTIKA 2112	11	12	13	14	15	16	17
	18	19	20	21	22	23	24
	25	26	27	**28**	30	1	2
	3	4	5	6	7	8	9
MĀRGAŚĪRA 2112	10	11[g]	12	13	13	14	15
	16	17	18	19	20	21	**22**
	24	25	26	27	28	29	30
PAUSHA 2112	1	2	3	4	5	6	7
	8	9	10	11	12	13	14

HINDU SOLAR 1976/1977

Month	Sun	Mon	Tue	Wed	Thu	Fri	Sat
	12	13	14	15	16	17	18
PAUSHA 1976	19	20	21	22	23	24	25
	26	27	28	29	30	1[b]	2
MĀGHA 1976	3	4	5	6	7	8	9
	10	11	12	13	14	15	16
	17	18	19	20	21	22	23
	24	25	26	27	28	29	1
PHĀLGUNA 1976	2	3	4	5	6	7	8
	9	10	11	12	13	14	15
	16	17	18	19	20	21	22
	23	24	25	26	27	28	29
	30	1	2	3	4	5	6
CHAITRA 1976	7	8	9	10	11	12	13
	14	15	16	17	18	19	20
	21	22	23	24	25	26	27
	28	29	30	1[a]	2	3	4
VAIŚĀKHA 1977	5	6	7	8	9	10	11
	12	13	14	15	16	17	18
	19	20	21	22	23	24	25
	26	27	28	29	30	31	1
JYAISHTHA 1977	2	3	4	5	6	7	8
	9	10	11	12	13	14	15
	16	17	18	19	20	21	22
	23	24	25	26	27	28	29
	30	31	32	1	2	3	4
ĀSHĀDHA 1977	5	6	7	8	9	10	11
	12	13	14	15	16	17	18
	19	20	21	22	23	24	25
	26	27	28	29	30	31	1
ŚRĀVANA 1977	2	3	4	5	6	7	8
	9	10	11	12	13	14	15
	16	17	18	19	20	21	22
	23	24	25	26	27	28	29
	30	31	32	1	2	3	4
BHĀDRAPADA 1977	5	6	7	8	9	10	11
	12	13	14	15	16	17	18
	19	20	21	22	23	24	25
	26	27	28	29	30	31	1
	2	3	4	5	6	7	8
ĀŚVINA 1977	9	10	11	12	13	14	15
	16	17	18	19	20	21	22
	23	24	25	26	27	28	29
	30	1	2	3	4	5	6
KĀRTTIKA 1977	7	8	9	10	11	12	13
	14	15	16	17	18	19	20
	21	22	23	24	25	26	27
	28	29	30	1	2	3	4
MĀRGAŚĪRA 1977	5	6	7	8	9	10	11
	12	13	14	15	16	17	18
	19	20	21	22	23	24	25
	26	27	28	29	30	1	2
PAUSHA 1977	3	4	5	6	7	8	9
	10	11	12	13	14	15	16

ISLAMIC (ASTRONOMICAL) 1477‡/1478

Month	Sun	Mon	Tue	Wed	Thu	Fri	Sat
	27	28	29	1	2	3	4
JUMĀDĀ II 1477	5	6	7	8	9	10	11
	12	13	14	15	16	17	18
	19	20	21	22	23	24	25
	26	27	28	29	30	1	2
RAJAB 1477	3	4	5	6	7	8	9
	10	11	12	13	14	15	16
	17	18	19	20	21	22	23
	24	25	26	27[d]	28	29	30
	1	2	3	4	5	6	7
SHA'BĀN 1477	8	9	10	11	12	13	14
	15	16	17	18	19	20	21
	22	23	24	25	26	27	28
	29	30	1[e]	2	3	4	5
RAMAḌĀN 1477	6	7	8	9	10	11	12
	13	14	15	16	17	18	19
	20	21	22	23	24	25	26
	27	28	29	1[f]	2	3	4
SHAWWĀL 1477	5	6	7	8	9	10	11
	12	13	14	15	16	17	18
	19	20	21	22	23	24	25
	26	27	28	29	30	1	2
DHU AL-QA'DA 1477	3	4	5	6	7	8	9
	10	11	12	13	14	15	16
	17	18	19	20	21	22	23
	24	25	26	27	28	29	1
DHU AL-ḤIJJA 1477	2	3	4	5	6	7	8
	9	10[g]	11	12	13	14	15
	16	17	18	19	20	21	22
	23	24	25	26	27	28	29
	30	1[a]	2	3	4	5	6
MUḤARRAM 1478	7	8	9	10[b]	11	12	13
	14	15	16	17	18	19	20
	21	22	23	24	25	26	27
	28	29	1	2	3	4	5
ṢAFAR 1478	6	7	8	9	10	11	12
	13	14	15	16	17	18	19
	20	21	22	23	24	25	26
	27	28	29	1	2	3	4
RABĪ' I 1478	5	6	7	8	9	10	11
	12[c]	13	14	15	16	17	18
	19	20	21	22	23	24	25
	26	27	28	29	30	1	2
RABĪ' II 1478	3	4	5	6	7	8	9
	10	11	12	13	14	15	16
	17	18	19	20	21	22	23
	24	25	26	27	28	29	1
JUMĀDĀ I 1478	2	3	4	5	6	7	8
	9	10	11	12	13	14	15
	16	17	18	19	20	21	22
	23	24	25	26	27	28	29
JUMĀDĀ II 1478	30	1	2	3	4	5	6
	7	8	9	10	11	12	13

GREGORIAN 2055

Julian (Sun)	Sun	Mon	Tue	Wed	Thu	Fri	Sat	Month
Dec 14	27	28	29	30	31	1	2	
	3	4	5	6	7[a]	8	9	JANUARY 2055
Dec 28	10	11	12	13	14[b]	15	16	
	17	18	19	20	21	22	23	
Jan 11	24	25	26	27	28	29	30	
	31	1	2	3	4	5	6	
Jan 25	7	8	9	10	11	12	13	FEBRUARY 2055
	14	15	16	17	18	19	20	
Feb 8	21	22	23	24	25	26	27	
	28	1	2	3[c]	4	5	6	
Feb 22	7[d]	8	9	10	11	12	13	
	14	15	16	17	18	19	20	MARCH 2055
Mar 8	21	22	23	24	25	26	27	
	28	29	30	31	1	2	3	
Mar 22	4	5	6	7	8	9	10	
	11	12	13	14	15	16	17	APRIL 2055
Apr 5	18[e]	19	20	21	22	23	24	
	25	26	27	28	29	30	1	
Apr 19	2	3	4	5	6	7	8	
	9	10	11	12	13	14	15	MAY 2055
May 3	16	17	18	19	20	21	22	
	23	24	25	26	27	28	29	
May 17	30	31	1	2	3	4	5	
	6	7	8	9	10	11	12	JUNE 2055
May 31	13	14	15	16	17	18	19	
	20	21	22	23	24	25	26	
Jun 14	27	28	29	30	1	2	3	
	4	5	6	7	8	9	10	JULY 2055
Jun 28	11	12	13	14	15	16	17	
	18	19	20	21	22	23	24	
Jul 12	25	26	27	28	29	30	31	
	1	2	3	4	5	6	7	AUGUST 2055
Jul 26	8	9	10	11	12	13	14	
	15	16	17	18	19	20	21	
Aug 9	22	23	24	25	26	27	28	
	29	30	31	1	2	3	4	
Aug 23	5	6	7	8	9	10	11	SEPTEMBER 2055
	12	13	14	15	16	17	18	
Sep 6	19	20	21	22	23	24	25	
	26	27	28	29	30	1	2	
Sep 20	3	4	5	6	7	8	9	OCTOBER 2055
	10	11	12	13	14	15	16	
Oct 4	17	18	19	20	21	22	23	
	24	25	26	27	28	29	30	
Oct 18	31	1	2	3	4	5	6	
	7	8	9	10	11	12	13	NOVEMBER 2055
Nov 1	14	15	16	17	18	19	20	
	21	22	23	24	25	26	27	
Nov 15	28[g]	29	30	1	2	3	4	
	5	6	7	8	9	10	11	DECEMBER 2055
Nov 29	12	13	14	15	16	17	18	
	19	20	21	22	23	24	25[h]	
Dec 13	26	27	28	29	30	31	1	

Persian: [a]New Year; [b]Sizdeh Bedar

Hindu Lunar: [a]New Year (Yuvan); [b]Birthday of Rāma; [c]Birthday of Krishna; [d]Ganēśa Chaturthī; [e]Dashara; [f]Diwali; [g]Birthday of Vishnu; [h]Night of Śiva; [i]Holi

Hindu Solar: [a]New Year (Virodhin); [b]Pongal

Islamic: ‡Leap year; [a]New Year; [b]'Ashūrā'; [c]Prophet's Birthday; [d]Ascent of the Prophet; [e]Start of Ramaḍān; [f]'Īd al-Fiṭr; [g]'Īd al-'Aḍḥā

Gregorian: [a]Orthodox Christmas; [b]Julian New Year; [c]Ash Wednesday; [d]Feast of Orthodoxy; [e]Easter (also Orthodox); [g]Advent; [h]Christmas

2056

Gregorian 2056‡	Sun	Mon	Tue	Wed	Thu	Fri	Sat	Lunar Phases	ISO Week (Mon)	Julian Day (Sun noon)	Hebrew 5816/5817‡	Sun	Mon	Tue	Wed	Thu	Fri	Sat	Molad	Chinese Yĭ-Hài‡/Bĭng-Zĭ	Sun	Mon	Tue	Wed	Thu	Fri	Sat	Solar Term	Coptic 1772/1773	Sun	Mon	Tue	Wed	Thu	Fri	Sat	Ethiopic 2048/2049
	26	27	28	29	30	31	1[a]		52	2471993		6	7	8	9	10	11	12			9	10	11	12	13	14	15			16	17	18	19	20	21	22	
January 2056	○	3	4	5	6	7	8	22:04	1	2472000	Teveth 5816	13	14	15	16	17	18	19		Month 11 Yĭ-Hài	16	17	18	19	20	21	22	Xiǎo hán	Koiak 1772	23	24	25	26	27	28	29[c]	Tākhśāś 2048
	◑	10	11	12	13	14	15	23:12	2	2472007		20	21	22	23	24	25	26			23	24	25	26	27*	28	29			30	1	2	3	4	5	6[d]	
	●	17	18	19	20	21	22	22:09	3	2472014		27	28	29	1	2	3	4	Mon 11h31m4p		30	1	2	3	4	5	6	Dà hán	Tôbe 1772	7	8	9	10	11[e]	12	13	Ṭer 2048
	23	◐	25	26	27	28	29	20:19	4	2472021	Shevat 5816	5	6	7	8	9	10	11		Month 12 Yĭ-Hài	7	8	9	10	11	12	13			14	15	16	17	18	19	20	
	30	31	○	2	3	4	5	12:34	5	2472028		12	13	14	15	16	17	18			14	15	16	17	18	19	20	Lì chūn		21	22	23	24	25	26	27	
February 2056	6	7	◑	9	10	11	12	7:00	6	2472035		19	20	21	22	23	24	25			21	22	23	24	25	26	27			28	29	30	1	2	3	4	
	13	14	●	16	17	18	19	13:58	7	2472042		26	27	28	29	30	1	2	Wed 0h15m5p		28	29	1[a]	2	3	4	5	Yǔ shuǐ	Meshir 1772	5	6	7	8	9	10	11	Yakātit 2048
	20	21	22	◐	24	25	26	17:10	8	2472049	Adar 5816	3	4	5	6	7	8	9		Month 1 Bĭng-Zĭ	6	7	8	9	10	11	12			12	13	14	15	16	17	18	
	27	28	29	1	○	3	4	0:38	9	2472056		10	11	12	13	14[f]	15	16			13	14	15[b]	16	17	18	19			19	20	21	22	23	24	25	
March 2056	5	6	7	◑	9	10	11	15:30	10	2472063		17	18	19	20	21	22	23			20	21	22	23	24	25	26	Jīng zhé		26	27	28	29	30	1	2	
	12	13	14	15	●	17	18	6:51	11	2472070		24	25	26	27	28	29	1	Thu 12h59m6p		27	28*	29	30	1	2	3		Paremotep 1772	3	4	5	6	7	8	9	Magābit 2048
	19[b]	20	21	22	23	◐	25	11:16	12	2472077	Nisan 5816	2	3	4	5	6	7	8		Month 2 Bĭng-Zĭ	4	5	6	7	8	9	10	Chūn fēn		10	11	12	13	14	15	16	
	26	27	28	29	30	○	1	10:23	13	2472084		9	10	11	12	13	14	15[g]			11	12	13	14	15	16	17			17	18	19	20	21	22	23	
April 2056	2	3	4	5	6	◑	8	1:32	14	2472091		16	17	18	19	20	21	22			18	19	20[c]	21	22	23	24	Qīng míng		24	25	26	27	28	29	30	
	9	10	11	12	13	●	15	23:49	15	2472098		23	24	25	26	27	28	29			25	26	27	28	29	30	1			1[f]	2	3	4	5	6	7	
	16	17	18	19	20	21	22		16	2472105		30	1	2	3	4	5	6	Sat 1h43m7p	Month 3 Bĭng-Zĭ	2	3	4	5	6	7	8	Gǔ yǔ	Parmoute 1772	8	9	10	11	12	13	14	Miyāzyā 2048
	◐	24	25	26	27	28	○	1:32 18:29	17	2472112	Iyyar 5816	7	8	9	10	11	12	13			9	10	11	12	13	14	15			15	16	17	18	19	20	21	
May 2056	30	1	2	3	4	5	◑	13:29	18	2472119		14	15	16	17	18	19	20			16	17	18	19	20	21	22	Lì xià		22	23	24	25	26	27	28	
	7	8	9	10	11	12	13		19	2472126		21	22	23	24	25	26	27			23	24	25	26	27	28*	29			29[g]	30	1	2	3	4	5	
	●	15	16	17	18	19	20	16:05	20	2472133		28	29	1	2	3	4	5	Sun 14h27m8p		30	1	2	3	4	5	6	Xiǎo mǎn	Pashons 1772	6	7	8	9	10	11	12	Genbot 2048
	21	◐	23	24	25	26	27	11:49	21	2472140	Sivan 5816	6[h]	7	8	9	10	11	12		Month 4 Bĭng-Zĭ	7	8	9	10	11	12	13			13	14	15	16	17	18	19	
	28	○	30	31	1	2	3	1:56	22	2472147		13	14	15	16	17	18	19			14	15	16	17	18	19	20			20	21	22	23	24	25	26	
June 2056	4	◑	6	7	8	9	10	3:20	23	2472154		20	21	22	23	24	25	26			21	22	23	24	25	26	27	Máng zhòng		27	28	29	30	1	2	3	
	11	12	●	14	15	16	17	7:02	24	2472161		27	28	29	30	1	2	3	Tue 3h11m9p		28	29	1	2	3	4	5[d]		Paône 1772	4	5	6	7	8	9	10	Sanē 2048
	18	19	◐[c]	21	22	23	24	18:47	25	2472168	Tammuz 5816	4	5	6	7	8	9	10		Month 5 Bĭng-Zĭ	6	7	8	9	10	11	12	Xià zhì		11	12	13	14	15	16	17	
	25	26	○	28	29	30	1	9:46	26	2472175		11	12	13	14	15	16	17			13	14	15	16	17	18	19			18	19	20	21	22	23	24	
July 2056	2	3	◑	5	6	7	8	18:53	27	2472182		18	19	20	21	22	23	24			20	21	22	23	24	25	26	Xiǎo shǔ		25	26	27	28	29	30	1	
	9	10	11	●	13	14	15	20:19	28	2472189		25	26	27	28	29	1	2	Wed 15h55m10p		27	28	29*	30	1	2	3		Epêp 1772	2	3	4	5	6	7	8	Ḥamlē 2048
	16	17	18	◐	20	21	22	23:43	29	2472196	Av 5816	3	4	5	6	7	8	9		Month 6 Bĭng-Zĭ	4	5	6	7	8	9	10	Dà shǔ		9	10	11	12	13	14	15	
	23	24	25	○	27	28	29	18:53	30	2472203		10[i]	11	12	13	14	15	16			11	12	13	14	15	16	17			16	17	18	19	20	21	22	
	30	31	1	2	◑	4	5	11:51	31	2472210		17	18	19	20	21	22	23			18	19	20	21	22	23	24			23	24	25	26	27	28	29	
August 2056	6	7	8	9	10	●	12	7:47	32	2472217		24	25	26	27	28	29	30	Fri 4h39m11p		25	26	27	28	29	1	2	Lì qiū		30	1	2	3	4	5	6	
	13	14	15	16	17	◐	19	4:12	33	2472224	Elul 5816	1	2	3	4	5	6	7		Month 7 Bĭng-Zĭ	3	4	5	6	7[e]	8	9		Mesorê 1772	7	8	9	10	11	12	13[h]	Naḥasē 2048
	20	21	22	23	24	○	26	5:59	34	2472231		8	9	10	11	12	13	14			10	11	12	13	14	15[f]	16	Chǔ shǔ		14	15	16	17	18	19	20	
	27	28	29	30	31	1	◑	5:41	35	2472238		15	16	17	18	19	20	21			17	18	19	20	21	22	23			21	22	23	24	25	26	27	
September 2056	3	4	5	6	7	8	●	17:46	36	2472245		22	23	24	25	26	27	28			24	25	26	27	28	29	30*	Bái lù	Epag. 1772	28	29	30	1	2	3	4	Pāg. 2048
	10	11	12	13	14	15	◐	9:49	37	2472252		29	1[a]	2[a]	3	4	5	6	Sat 17h23m12p		1	2	3	4	5	6	7			5	1[a]	2	3	4	5	6	Maskaram 2049
	17	18	19	20	21	22[d]	○	19:33	38	2472259	Tishri 5817	7	8	9	10[b]	11	12	13		Month 8 Bĭng-Zĭ	8	9	10	11	12	13	14	Qiū fēn	Thoout 1773	7	8	9	10	11	12	13	
	24	25	26	27	28	29	30		39	2472266		14	15[c]	16	17	18	19	20			15[g]	16	17	18	19	20	21			14	15	16	17[b]	18	19	20	
October 2056	◑	2	3	4	5	6	7	23:32	40	2472273		21	22	23	24	25	26	27			22	23	24	25	26	27	28	Hán lù		21	22	23	24	25	26	27	
	8	●	10	11	12	13	14	2:59	41	2472280		28	29	30	1	2	3	4	Mon 6h7m13p		29	1	2	3	4	5	6			28	29	30	1	2	3	4	
	◐	16	17	18	19	20	21	17:57	42	2472287	Ḥeshvan 5817	5	6	7	8	9	10	11		Month 9 Bĭng-Zĭ	7	8	9[h]	10	11	12	13		Paope 1773	5	6	7	8	9	10	11	Ṭeqemt 2049
	22	○	24	25	26	27	28	11:45	43	2472294		12	13	14	15	16	17	18			14	15	16	17	18	19	20	Shuāng jiàng		12	13	14	15	16	17	18	
	29	30	◑	1	2	3	4	16:11	44	2472301		19	20	21	22	23	24	25			21	22	23	24	25	26	27			19	20	21	22	23	24	25	
November 2056	5	6	●	8	9	10	11	12:20	45	2472308		26	27	28	29	1	2	3	Tue 18h51m14p		28	29	1	2*	3	4	5	Lì dōng		26	27	28	29	30	1	2	
	12	13	◐	15	16	17	18	5:32	46	2472315	Kislev 5817	4	5	6	7	8	9	10		Month 10 Bĭng-Zĭ	6	7	8	9	10	11	12		Athôr 1773	3	4	5	6	7	8	9	Ḫedār 2049
	19	20	21	○	23	24	25	6:10	47	2472322		11	12	13	14	15	16	17			13	14	15	16	17	18	19	Xiǎo xuě		10	11	12	13	14	15	16	
	26	27	28	29	◑	1	2	6:36	48	2472329		18	19	20	21	22	23	24			20	21	22	23	24	25	26			17	18	19	20	21	22	23	
December 2056	3	4	5	●	7	8	9	22:30	49	2472336		25[e]	26[e]	27[d,e]	28[e]	29[e]	1[e]	2[e]	Thu 7h35m15p		27	28	29	30	1	2	3	Dà xuě		24	25	26	27	28	29	30	
	10	11	12	◐	14	15	16	20:52	50	2472343	Teveth 5817	3[e]	4	5	6	7	8	9		Month 11 Bĭng-Zĭ	4	5	6	7	8	9	10		Koiak 1773	1	2	3	4	5	6	7	Tākhśāś 2049
	17	18	19	20	21[e]	○	23	1:32	51	2472350		10	11	12	13	14	15	16			11	12	13	14	15[i]	16	17	Dōng zhì		8	9	10	11	12	13	14	
	24	25	26	27	28	◑	30	18:21	52	2472357		17	18	19	20	21	22	23			18	19	20	21	22	23	24			15	16	17	18	19	20	21	
	31	1	2	3	4	●	6	9:48	1	2472364		24	25	26	27	28	29	1	Fri 20h19m16p		25	26	27	28	29	1	2	Xiǎo hán		22	23	24	25	26	27	28	

‡Leap year
[a]New Year
[b]Spring (21:09)
[c]Summer (14:27)
[d]Autumn (6:38)
[e]Winter (3:50)
● New moon
◐ First quarter moon
○ Full moon
◑ Last quarter moon

‡Leap year
[a]New Year
[b]Yom Kippur
[c]Sukkot
[d]Winter starts
[e]Ḥanukkah
[f]Purim
[g]Passover
[h]Shavuot
[i]Fast of Av

‡Leap year
[a]New Year (4754, Rat)
[b]Lantern Festival
[c]Qīngmíng
[d]Dragon Festival
[e]Qīqiǎo
[f]Hungry Ghosts
[g]Mid-Autumn Festival
[h]Double-Ninth Festival
[i]Dōngzhì
*Start of 60-name cycle

[a]New Year
[b]Building of the Cross
[c]Christmas
[d]Jesus's Circumcision
[e]Epiphany
[f]Easter
[g]Mary's Announcement
[h]Jesus's Transfiguration

PERSIAN (ASTRONOMICAL) 1434/1435

Month	Sun	Mon	Tue	Wed	Thu	Fri	Sat
DEY 1434	5	6	7	8	9	10	11
	12	13	14	15	16	17	18
	19	20	21	22	23	24	25
	26	27	28	29	30	1	2
BAHMAN 1434	3	4	5	6	7	8	9
	10	11	12	13	14	15	16
	17	18	19	20	21	22	23
	24	25	26	27	28	29	30
ESFAND 1434	1	2	3	4	5	6	7
	8	9	10	11	12	13	14
	15	16	17	18	19	20	21
	22	23	24	25	26	27	28
	29	1[a]	2	3	4	5	6
FARVARDĪN 1435	7	8	9	10	11	12	13[b]
	14	15	16	17	18	19	20
	21	22	23	24	25	26	27
	28	29	30	31	1	2	3
ORDĪBEHEŠT 1435	4	5	6	7	8	9	10
	11	12	13	14	15	16	17
	18	19	20	21	22	23	24
	25	26	27	28	29	30	31
XORDĀD 1435	1	2	3	4	5	6	7
	8	9	10	11	12	13	14
	15	16	17	18	19	20	21
	22	23	24	25	26	27	28
	29	30	31	1	2	3	4
TĪR 1435	5	6	7	8	9	10	11
	12	13	14	15	16	17	18
	19	20	21	22	23	24	25
	26	27	28	29	30	31	1
MORDĀD 1435	2	3	4	5	6	7	8
	9	10	11	12	13	14	15
	16	17	18	19	20	21	22
	23	24	25	26	27	28	29
	30	31	1	2	3	4	5
SHAHRĪVAR 1435	6	7	8	9	10	11	12
	13	14	15	16	17	18	19
	20	21	22	23	24	25	26
	27	28	29	30	31	1	2
MEHR 1435	3	4	5	6	7	8	9
	10	11	12	13	14	15	16
	17	18	19	20	21	22	23
	24	25	26	27	28	29	30
ĀBĀN 1435	1	2	3	4	5	6	7
	8	9	10	11	12	13	14
	15	16	17	18	19	20	21
	22	23	24	25	26	27	28
	29	30	1	2	3	4	5
ĀZAR 1435	6	7	8	9	10	11	12
	13	14	15	16	17	18	19
	20	21	22	23	24	25	26
	27	28	29	30	1	2	3
DEY 1435	4	5	6	7	8	9	10
	11	12	13	14	15	16	17

[a]New Year
[b]Sizdeh Bedar

HINDU LUNAR 2112/2113‡

Month	Sun	Mon	Tue	Wed	Thu	Fri	Sat
PAUSHA 2112	8	9	10	11	12	13	14
	15	16	17	18	19	20	21
	22	23	24	25	26	28	29
MĀGHA 2112	30	1	2	3	4	5	6
	6	7	8	9	10	11	12
	13	14	15	16	17	18	19
	20	22	23	24	25	26	27
PHĀLGUNA 2112	28[h]	29	30	1	2	3	4
	5	6	7	8	8	9	10
	11	12	13	14[i]	16	17	18
	19	20	21	22	23	24	25
CHAITRA 2113	26	27	28	29	30	1[a]	2
	3	4	5	6	7	8	9[b]
	10	11	12	13	14	15	16
	17	18	19	21	22	23	24
LEAP VAIŚĀKHA 2113	25	26	27	28	29	30	1
	1	2	3	4	5	6	7
	8	9	10	11	12	14	15
	16	17	18	19	20	21	22
	23	24	25	26	27	28	29
VAIŚĀKHA 2113	30	1	2	3	4	5	6
	7	8	9	10	11	12	13
	14	15	16	18	19	20	21
	22	23	24	25	26	27	27
JYAISHṬHA 2113	28	29	30	1	2	3	4
	5	6	7	8	10	11	12
	13	14	15	16	17	18	19
	20	21	22	23	24	25	26
ĀSHĀḌHA 2113	27	28	29	30	1	2	3
	4	5	6	7	8	9	10
	11	13	14	15	16	17	18
	19	20	21	22	23	24	24
ŚRĀVAṆA 2113	25	26	27	28	29	30	1
	2	3	4	6	7	8	9
	10	11	12	13	14	15	16
	17	18	19	20	21	22	23[c]
	24	25	26	27	28	29	30
BHĀDRAPADA 2113	1	2	3	4[d]	5	6	7
	9	10	11	12	13	14	15
	16	17	18	19	20	20	21
	22	23	24	25	26	27	28
ĀŚVINA 2113	29	30	1	3	4	5	6
	7	8[e]	9[e]	10[e]	11	12	13
	14	15	16	17	18	19	20
	21	22	23	24	25	26	27
KĀRTTIKA 2113	28	29	30	1[f]	2	3	4
	5	7	8	9	10	11	12
	13	14	14	15	16	17	18
	19	20	21	22	23	24	25
MĀRGAŚĪRA 2113	26	27	28	29	1	2	3
	4	5	6	7	8	9	10
	11[g]	12	13	14	15	16	16
	17	18	19	20	21	22	24
PAUSHA	25	26	27	28	29	30	1

‡Leap year
[a]New Year (Dhātṛi)
[b]Birthday of Rāma
[c]Birthday of Krishna
[d]Ganēśa Chaturthī
[e]Dashara
[f]Diwali
[g]Birthday of Vishnu
[h]Night of Śiva
[i]Holi

HINDU SOLAR 1977/1978‡

Month	Sun	Mon	Tue	Wed	Thu	Fri	Sat
PAUSHA 1977	10	11	12	13	14	15	16
	17	18	19	20	21	22	23
	24	25	26	27	28	29	1[b]
MĀGHA 1977	2	3	4	5	6	7	8
	9	10	11	12	13	14	15
	16	17	18	19	20	21	22
	23	24	25	26	27	28	29
PHĀLGUNA 1977	1	2	3	4	5	6	7
	8	9	10	11	12	13	14
	15	16	17	18	19	20	21
	22	23	24	25	26	27	28
CHAITRA 1977	29	30	1	2	3	4	5
	6	7	8	9	10	11	12
	13	14	15	16	17	18	19
	20	21	22	23	24	25	26
VAIŚĀKHA 1978	27	28	29	30	1[a]	2	3
	4	5	6	7	8	9	10
	11	12	13	14	15	16	17
	18	19	20	21	22	23	24
	25	26	27	28	29	30	31
JYAISHṬHA 1978	1	2	3	4	5	6	7
	8	9	10	11	12	13	14
	15	16	17	18	19	20	21
	22	23	24	25	26	27	28
ĀSHĀḌHA 1978	29	30	31	32	1	2	3
	4	5	6	7	8	9	10
	11	12	13	14	15	16	17
	18	19	20	21	22	23	24
	25	26	27	28	29	30	31
ŚRĀVAṆA 1978	1	2	3	4	5	6	7
	8	9	10	11	12	13	14
	15	16	17	18	19	20	21
	22	23	24	25	26	27	28
BHĀDRAPADA 1978	29	30	31	32	1	2	3
	4	5	6	7	8	9	10
	11	12	13	14	15	16	17
	18	19	20	21	22	23	24
	25	26	27	28	29	30	31
ĀŚVINA 1978	1	2	3	4	5	6	7
	8	9	10	11	12	13	14
	15	16	17	18	19	20	21
	22	23	24	25	26	27	28
KĀRTTIKA 1978	29	30	1	2	3	4	5
	6	7	8	9	10	11	12
	13	14	15	16	17	18	19
	20	21	22	23	24	25	26
MĀRGAŚĪRA 1978	27	28	29	30	1	2	3
	4	5	6	7	8	9	10
	11	12	13	14	15	16	17
	18	19	20	21	22	23	24
PAUSHA 1978	25	26	27	28	29	30	1
	2	3	4	5	6	7	8
	9	10	11	12	13	14	15
	16	17	18	19	20	21	22

‡Leap year
[a]New Year (Vikṛita)
[b]Pongal

ISLAMIC (ASTRONOMICAL) 1478/1479

Month	Sun	Mon	Tue	Wed	Thu	Fri	Sat
JUMĀDĀ II 1478	7	8	9	10	11	12	13
	14	15	16	17	18	19	20
	21	22	23	24	25	26	27
RAJAB 1478	28	29	1	2	3	4	5
	6	7	8	9	10	11	12
	13	14	15	16	17	18	19
	20	21	22	23	24	25	26
SHA'BĀN 1478	27[d]	28	29	30	1	2	3
	4	5	6	7	8	9	10
	11	12	13	14	15	16	17
	18	19	20	21	22	23	24
RAMAḌĀN 1478	25	26	27	28	29	30	1[e]
	2	3	4	5	6	7	8
	9	10	11	12	13	14	15
	16	17	18	19	20	21	22
	23	24	25	26	27	28	29
SHAWWĀL 1478	1[f]	2	3	4	5	6	7
	8	9	10	11	12	13	14
	15	16	17	18	19	20	21
	22	23	24	25	26	27	28
DHU AL-QA'DA 1478	29	30	1	2	3	4	5
	6	7	8	9	10	11	12
	13	14	15	16	17	18	19
	20	21	22	23	24	25	26
DHU AL-ḤIJJA 1478	27	28	29	30	1	2	3
	4	5	6	7	8	9	10[g]
	11	12	13	14	15	16	17
	18	19	20	21	22	23	24
MUḤARRAM 1479	25	26	27	28	29	1[a]	2
	3	4	5	6	7	8	9
	10[b]	11	12	13	14	15	16
	17	18	19	20	21	22	23
	24	25	26	27	28	29	30
ṢAFAR 1479	1	2	3	4	5	6	7
	8	9	10	11	12	13	14
	15	16	17	18	19	20	21
	22	23	24	25	26	27	28
RABĪ' I 1479	29	1	2	3	4	5	6
	7	8	9	10	11	12[c]	13
	14	15	16	17	18	19	20
	21	22	23	24	25	26	27
RABĪ' II 1479	28	29	1	2	3	4	5
	6	7	8	9	10	11	12
	13	14	15	16	17	18	19
	20	21	22	23	24	25	26
JUMĀDĀ I 1479	27	28	29	30	1	2	3
	4	5	6	7	8	9	10
	11	12	13	14	15	16	17
	18	19	20	21	22	23	24
JUMĀDĀ II 1479	25	26	27	28	29	1	2
	3	4	5	6	7	8	9
	10	11	12	13	14	15	16
	17	18	19	20	21	22	23
	24	25	26	27	28	29	30

[a]New Year
[b]'Ashūrā'
[c]Prophet's Birthday
[d]Ascent of the Prophet
[e]Start of Ramaḍān
[f]'Id al-Fiṭr
[g]'Id al-'Aḍḥā

GREGORIAN 2056‡

Julian† (Sun)	Sun	Mon	Tue	Wed	Thu	Fri	Sat	Month
Dec 13	26	27	28	29	30	31	1	
	2	3	4	5	6	7[a]	8	JANUARY 2056
Dec 27	9	10	11	12	13	14[b]	15	
	16	17	18	19	20	21	22	
Jan 10	23	24	25	26	27	28	29	
	30	31	1	2	3	4	5	
Jan 24	6	7	8	9	10	11	12	FEBRUARY 2056
	13	14	15	16[c]	17	18	19	
Feb 7	20	21	22	23	24	25	26	
	27[d]	28	29	1	2	3	4	
Feb 21	5	6	7	8	9	10	11	MARCH 2056
	12	13	14	15	16	17	18	
Mar 6	19	20	21	22	23	24	25	
	26	27	28	29	30	31	1	
Mar 20	2[e]	3	4	5	6	7	8	APRIL 2056
	9[f]	10	11	12	13	14	15	
Apr 3	16	17	18	19	20	21	22	
	23	24	25	26	27	28	29	
Apr 17	30	1	2	3	4	5	6	
	7	8	9	10	11	12	13	MAY 2056
May 1	14	15	16	17	18	19	20	
	21	22	23	24	25	26	27	
May 15	28	29	30	31	1	2	3	
	4	5	6	7	8	9	10	JUNE 2056
May 29	11	12	13	14	15	16	17	
	18	19	20	21	22	23	24	
Jun 12	25	26	27	28	29	30	1	
	2	3	4	5	6	7	8	JULY 2056
Jun 26	9	10	11	12	13	14	15	
	16	17	18	19	20	21	22	
Jul 10	23	24	25	26	27	28	29	
	30	31	1	2	3	4	5	
Jul 24	6	7	8	9	10	11	12	AUGUST 2056
	13	14	15	16	17	18	19	
Aug 7	20	21	22	23	24	25	26	
	27	28	29	30	31	1	2	
Aug 21	3	4	5	6	7	8	9	SEPTEMBER 2056
	10	11	12	13	14	15	16	
Sep 4	17	18	19	20	21	22	23	
	24	25	26	27	28	29	30	
Sep 18	1	2	3	4	5	6	7	OCTOBER 2056
	8	9	10	11	12	13	14	
Oct 2	15	16	17	18	19	20	21	
	22	23	24	25	26	27	28	
Oct 16	29	30	31	1	2	3	4	
	5	6	7	8	9	10	11	NOVEMBER 2056
Oct 30	12	13	14	15	16	17	18	
	19	20	21	22	23	24	25	
Nov 13	26	27	28	29	30	1	2	
	3[g]	4	5	6	7	8	9	DECEMBER 2056
Nov 27	10	11	12	13	14	15	16	
	17	18	19	20	21	22	23	
Dec 11	24	25[h]	26	27	28	29	30	
	31	1	2	3	4	5	6	

‡Leap year
[a]Orthodox Christmas
[b]Julian New Year
[c]Ash Wednesday
[d]Feast of Orthodoxy
[e]Easter
[f]Orthodox Easter
[g]Advent
[h]Christmas

2057

	GREGORIAN 2057							Lunar Phases	ISO WEEK	JULIAN DAY		HEBREW 5817‡/5818							Molad		CHINESE Bǐng-Zǐ/Dīng-Chǒu							Solar Term		COPTIC 1773/1774							ETHIOPIC 2049/2050
	Sun	Mon	Tue	Wed	Thu	Fri	Sat		(Mon)	(Sun noon)		Sun	Mon	Tue	Wed	Thu	Fri	Sat			Sun	Mon	Tue	Wed	Thu	Fri	Sat			Sun	Mon	Tue	Wed	Thu	Fri	Sat	
	31	1[a]	2	3	4	●	6	9:48	1	2472364		24	25	26	27	28	29	1	Fri 20h19m16p		25	26	27	28	29	*1*	2	Xiǎo hán	KOIAK 1773	22	23	24	25	26	27	28	TĀKHŚĀŚ 2049
	7	8	9	10	11	◐	13	15:33	2	2472371		2	3	4	5	6	7	8			3*	4	5	6	7	8	9			29[c]	30	1	2	3	4	5	
JANUARY 2057	14	15	16	17	18	19	○	20:00	3	2472378	SHEVAT 5817	9	10	11	12	13	14	15		MONTH 12 Bǐng-Zǐ	10	11	12	13	14	**15**	16	Dà hán	TŌBE 1773	6[d]	7	8	9	10	11[e]	12	ṬER 2049
	21	22	23	24	25	26	27		4	2472385		16	17	18	19	20	21	22			17	18	19	20	21	22	23			13	14	15	16	17	18	19	
	◑	29	30	31	1	2	●	3:42 22:09	5	2472392		23	24	25	26	27	28	29	Sun 9h3m17p		24	25	26	27	28	29	*30*	Lì chūn		20	21	22	23	24	25	26	
	4	5	6	7	8	9	10		6	2472399		30	1	2	3	4	5	6			1[a]	2	3	4	5	6	7			27	28	29	30	1	2	3	
FEBRUARY 2057	◐	12	13	14	15	16	17	12:24	7	2472406		7	8	9	10	11	12	13		MONTH 1 Dīng-Chǒu	8	9	10	11	12	13	14			4	5	6	7	8	9	10	
	18	○	20	21	22	23	24	11:55	8	2472413	ADAR I 5817	14	15	16	17	18	19	20			15[b]	16	17	18	19	20	21	Yǔ shuǐ	MESHIR 1773	11	12	13	14	15	16	17	YAKĀTIT 2049
	25	◑	27	28	1	2	3	11:29	9	2472420		21	22	23	24	25	26	27			22	23	24	25	26	27	28			18	19	20	21	22	23	24	
	4	●	6	7	8	9	10	11:23	10	2472427		28	29	30	1	2	3	4	Mon 21h48m0p		29	*1*	2	3	4*	5	6	Jīng zhé		25	26	27	28	29	30	1	
MARCH 2057	11	12	◐	14	15	16	17	9:34	11	2472434		5	6	7	8	9	10	11		MONTH 2 Dīng-Chǒu	7	8	9	10	11	12	13			2	3	4	5	6	7	8	
	18	19	20[b]	○	22	23	24	0:43	12	2472441	ADAR II 5817	12	13	14[f]	15	16	17	18			14	15	**16**	17	18	19	20	Chūn fēn	PAREMOTEP 1773	9	10	11	12	13	14	15	MAGĀBIT 2049
	25	26	◑	28	29	30	31	18:38	13	2472448		19	20	21	22	23	24	25			21	22	23	24	25	26	27			16	17	18	19	20	21	22	
	1	2	3	●	5	6	7	1:30	14	2472455		26	27	28	29	1	2	3	Wed 10h32m1p		28	29	30	1[c]	2	3	4	Qīng míng		23	24	25	26	27	28	29	
	8	9	10	11	◐	13	14	4:58	15	2472462		4	5	6	7	8	9	10		MONTH 3 Dīng-Chǒu	5	6	7	8	9	10	11			30	1	2	3	4	5	6	
APRIL 2057	15	16	17	18	○	20	21	10:48	16	2472469	NISAN 5817	11	12	13	14	15[g]	16	17			12	13	14	15	**16**	17	18	Gǔ yǔ	PARMOUTE 1773	7	8	9	10	11	12	13	MIYĀZYĀ 2049
	22	23	24	25	◑	27	28	2:05	17	2472476		18	19	20	21	22	23	24			19	20	21	22	23	24	25			14	15	16	17	18	19	20	
	29	30	1	2	●	4	5	16:31	18	2472483		25	26	27	28	29	30	1	Thu 23h16m2p		26	27	28	29	30	1	2	Lì xià		21[f]	22	23	24	25	26	27	
	6	7	8	9	10	◐	12	21:05	19	2472490		2	3	4	5	6	7	8		MONTH 4 Dīng-Chǒu	3	4*	5	6	7	8	9			28	29[g]	30	1	2	3	4	
MAY 2057	13	14	15	16	17	○	19	19:01	20	2472497	IYAR 5817	9	10	11	12	13	14	15			10	11	12	13	14	15	16		PASHONS 1773	5	6	7	8	9	10	11	GENBOT 2049
	20	21	22	23	24	◑	26	10:39	21	2472504		16	17	18	19	20	21	22			**17**	18	19	20	21	22	23	Xiǎo mǎn		12	13	14	15	16	17	18	
	27	28	29	30	31	1	●	8:09	22	2472511		23	24	25	26	27	28	29			24	25	26	27	28	29	1			19	20	21	22	23	24	25	
	3	4	5	6	7	8	9		23	2472518		1	2	3	4	5	6[h]	7	Sat 12h0m3p		2	3	*4*	5[d]	6	7	8	Máng zhòng		26	27	28	29	30	1	2	
JUNE 2057	◐	11	12	13	14	15	16	9:28	24	2472525		8	9	10	11	12	13	14		MONTH 5 Dīng-Chǒu	9	10	11	12	13	14	15			3	4	5	6	7	8	9	
	○	18	19	20[c]	21	22	◑	2:17 21:07	25	2472532	SIVAN 5817	15	16	17	18	19	20	21			16	17	18	19	**20**	21	22	Xià zhì	PAŌNE 1773	10	11	12	13	14	15	16	SANĒ 2049
	24	25	26	27	28	29	30		26	2472539		22	23	24	25	26	27	28			23	24	25	26	27	28	29			17	18	19	20	21	22	23	
	●	2	3	4	5	6	7	23:46	27	2472546		29	30	1	2	3	4	5	Mon 0h44m4p		30	1	2	3	4	5*	6	Xiǎo shǔ		24	25	26	27	28	29	30	
	8	◐	10	11	12	13	14	18:36	28	2472553		6	7	8	9	10	11	12		MONTH 6 Dīng-Chǒu	7	8	9	10	11	12	13			1	2	3	4	5	6	7	
JULY 2057	15	○	17	18	19	20	21	9:27	29	2472560	TAMMUZ 5817	13	14	15	16	17	18	19			14	15	16	17	18	19	20		EPĒP 1773	8	9	10	11	12	13	14	ḤAMLĒ 2049
	22	◑	24	25	26	27	28	10:07	30	2472567		20	21	22	23	24	25	26			**21**	22	23	24	25	26	27	Dà shǔ		15	16	17	18	19	20	21	
	29	30	●	1	2	3	4	14:31	31	2472574		27	28	29	1	2	3	4	Tue 13h28m5p		28	29	1	2	3	4	5			22	23	24	25	26	27	28	
	5	6	7	◐	9	10	11	1:20	32	2472581		5	6	7	8	9[i]	10	11		MONTH 7 Dīng-Chǒu	6	7[e]	8	9	10	11	12	Lì qiū		29	30	1	2	3	4	5	
AUGUST 2057	12	13	○	15	16	17	18	17:20	33	2472588	AV 5817	12	13	14	15	16	17	18			13	14	15[f]	16	17	18	19		MESORĒ 1773	6	7	8	9	10	11	12	NAḤASĒ 2049
	19	20	21	◑	23	24	25	2:00	34	2472595		19	20	21	22	23	24	25			20	21	22	**23**	24	25	26	Chǔ shǔ		13[h]	14	15	16	17	18	19	
	26	27	28	29	●	31	1	3:53	35	2472602		26	27	28	29	30	1	2	Thu 2h12m6p		27	28	29	30	1	2	3			20	21	22	23	24	25	26	
	2	3	4	5	◐	7	8	7:17	36	2472609		3	4	5	6	7	8	9		MONTH 8 Dīng-Chǒu	4	5	6*	7	8	9	10	Bái lù	EPAG. 1773	27	28	29	30	1	2	3	PĀG. 2049
SEPTEMBER 2057	9	10	11	12	○	14	15	2:52	37	2472616	ELUL 5817	10	11	12	13	14	15	16			11	12	13	14	15[g]	16	17			4	5	1[a]	2	3	4	5	
	16	17	18	19	◑	21	22[d]	20:24	38	2472623		17	18	19	20	21	22	23			18	19	20	21	22	23	**24**	Qiū fēn	THOOUT 1774	6	7	8	9	10	11	12	MASKARAM 2050
	23	24	25	26	27	●	29	15:59	39	2472630		24	25	26	27	28	29	1[a]	Fri 14h56m7p		25	26	27	28	29	1	2			13	14	15	16	17[b]	18	19	
	30	1	2	3	4	◐	6	13:12	40	2472637		2[a]	3	4	5	6	7	8			3	4	5	6	7	8	9[h]			20	21	22	23	24	25	26	
OCTOBER 2057	7	8	9	10	11	○	13	15:00	41	2472644	TISHRI 5818	9	10[b]	11	12	13	14	15[c]		MONTH 9 Dīng-Chǒu	10	*11*	12	13	14	15	16	Hán lù		27	28	29	30	1	2	3	
	14	15	16	17	18	19	◑	16:08	42	2472651		16	17	18	19	20	21	22			17	18	19	20	21	22	23			4	5	6	7	8	9	10	
	21	22	23	24	25	26	27		43	2472658		23	24	25	26	27	28	29			24	25	**26**	27	28	29	30	Shuāng jiàng	PAOPE 1774	11	12	13	14	15	16	17	ṬEQEMT 2050
	●	29	30	31	1	2	◐	3:18 20:23	44	2472665		30	1	2	3	4	5	6	Sun 3h40m8p		1	2	3	4	5	6	7*			18	19	20	21	22	23	24	
	4	5	6	7	8	9	10		45	2472672		7	8	9	10	11	12	13		MONTH 10 Dīng-Chǒu	8	9	10	*11*	12	13	14	Lì dōng		25	26	27	28	29	30	1	
NOVEMBER 2057	○	12	13	14	15	16	17	6:23	46	2472679	HESHVAN 5818	14	15	16	17	18	19	20			15	16	17	18	19	20	21			2	3	4	5	6	7	8	
	18	◑	20	21	22	23	24	11:30	47	2472686		21	22	23	24	25	26	27			22	23	24	25	**26**	27	28	Xiǎo xuě	ATHŌR 1774	9	10	11	12	13	14	15	ḪEDĀR 2050
	25	●	27	28	29	30	1	14:21	48	2472693		28	29	30	1	2	3	4	Mon 16h24m9p		29	1	2	3	4	5	6			16	17	18	19	20	21	22	
	2	◐	4	5	6	7	8	5:52	49	2472700		5	6	7	8[d]	9	10	11		MONTH 11 Dīng-Chǒu	7	8	9	10	*11*	12	13	Dà xuě		23	24	25	26	27	28	29	
DECEMBER 2057	9	10	○	12	13	14	15	0:45	50	2472707	KISLEV 5818	12	13	14	15	16	17	18			14	15	16	17	18	19	20			30	1	2	3	4	5	6	
	16	17	18	◑	20	21[e]	22	5:01	51	2472714		19	20	21	22	23	24	25[e]			21	22	23	24	25	26[i]	27	Dōng zhì	KOIAK 1774	7	8	9	10	11	12	13	TĀKHŚĀŚ 2050
	23	24	25	●	27	28	29	1:21	52	2472721		26[e]	27[e]	28[e]	29[e]	30[e]	1[e]	2[e]	Wed 5h8m10p		28	29	30	1	2	3	4			14	15	16	17	18	19	20	
	30	31	◐	2	3	4	5	18:29	1	2472728	TEVETH 5818	3	4	5	6	7	8	9		MONTH 12 Dīng-Chǒu	5	6	7	8	9	10	*11*	Xiǎo hán		21	22	23	24	25	26	27	

[a]New Year
[b]Spring (3:06)
[c]Summer (20:17)
[d]Autumn (12:22)
[e]Winter (9:41)
● New moon
◐ First quarter moon
○ Full moon
◑ Last quarter moon

‡Leap year
[a]New Year
[b]Yom Kippur
[c]Sukkot
[d]Winter starts
[e]Ḥanukkah
[f]Purim
[g]Passover
[h]Shavuot
[i]Fast of Av

[a]New Year (4755, Ox)
[b]Lantern Festival
[c]Qīngmíng
[d]Dragon Festival
[e]Qīqiǎo
[f]Hungry Ghosts
[g]Mid-Autumn Festival
[h]Double-Ninth Festival
[i]Dōngzhì
*Start of 60-name cycle

[a]New Year
[b]Building of the Cross
[c]Christmas
[d]Jesus's Circumcision
[e]Epiphany
[f]Easter
[g]Mary's Announcement
[h]Jesus's Transfiguration

PERSIAN (ASTRONOMICAL) 1435/1436‡

Month	Sun	Mon	Tue	Wed	Thu	Fri	Sat
DEY 1435	11	12	13	14	15	16	17
	18	19	20	21	22	23	24
	25	26	27	28	29	30	1
BAHMAN 1435	2	3	4	5	6	7	8
	9	10	11	12	13	14	15
	16	17	18	19	20	21	22
	23	24	25	26	27	28	29
	30	1	2	3	4	5	6
ESFAND 1435	7	8	9	10	11	12	13
	14	15	16	17	18	19	20
	21	22	23	24	25	26	27
	28	29	1[a]	2	3	4	5
FARVARDĪN 1436	6	7	8	9	10	11	12
	13[b]	14	15	16	17	18	19
	20	21	22	23	24	25	26
	27	28	29	30	31	1	2
ORDĪBEHEŠT 1436	3	4	5	6	7	8	9
	10	11	12	13	14	15	16
	17	18	19	20	21	22	23
	24	25	26	27	28	29	30
	31	1	2	3	4	5	6
XORDĀD 1436	7	8	9	10	11	12	13
	14	15	16	17	18	19	20
	21	22	23	24	25	26	27
	28	29	30	31	1	2	3
TĪR 1436	4	5	6	7	8	9	10
	11	12	13	14	15	16	17
	18	19	20	21	22	23	24
	25	26	27	28	29	30	31
MORDĀD 1436	1	2	3	4	5	6	7
	8	9	10	11	12	13	14
	15	16	17	18	19	20	21
	22	23	24	25	26	27	28
	29	30	31	1	2	3	4
SHAHRĪVAR 1436	5	6	7	8	9	10	11
	12	13	14	15	16	17	18
	19	20	21	22	23	24	25
	26	27	28	29	30	31	1
MEHR 1436	2	3	4	5	6	7	8
	9	10	11	12	13	14	15
	16	17	18	19	20	21	22
	23	24	25	26	27	28	29
	30	1	2	3	4	5	6
ĀBĀN 1436	7	8	9	10	11	12	13
	14	15	16	17	18	19	20
	21	22	23	24	25	26	27
	28	29	30	1	2	3	4
ĀZAR 1436	5	6	7	8	9	10	11
	12	13	14	15	16	17	18
	19	20	21	22	23	24	25
	26	27	28	29	30	1	2
DEY 1436	3	4	5	6	7	8	9
	10	11	12	13	14	15	16

‡Leap year
[a]New Year
[b]Sizdeh Bedar

HINDU LUNAR 2113‡/2114

Month	Sun	Mon	Tue	Wed	Thu	Fri	Sat
	25	26	27	28	29	30	1
PAUSHA 2113	2	3	4	5	6	7	8
	9	10	11	12	13	14	15
	16	17	18	19	20	21	22
	23	24	25	26	**27**	29	30
MĀGHA 2113	1	2	3	4	5	6	7
	8	8	9	10	11	12	13
	14	15	16	17	18	19	20
	21	**22**	24	25	26	27	28[h]
	29	30	1	2	3	4	5
PHĀLGUNA 2113	6	7	8	9	10	11	11
	12	13	**14**[i]	16	17	18	19
	20	21	22	23	24	25	26
	27	**28**	30	30	1[a]	2	3
CHAITRA 2114	4	5	6	7	8	9[b]	10
	11	12	13	14	15	16	17
	18	**19**	21	22	23	24	25
	26	27	28	29	30	1	2
VAIŚĀKHA 2114	3	4	5	5	6	7	8
	9	10	11	**12**	14	15	16
	17	18	19	20	21	22	23
	24	25	26	27	28	29	30
JYAISHṬHA 2114	1	2	3	4	5	6	7
	8	9	10	11	12	13	14
	15	**16**	18	19	20	21	22
	23	24	25	26	27	28	29
	30	1	1	2	3	4	5
ĀSHĀḌHA 2114	6	7	**8**	10	11	12	13
	14	15	16	17	18	19	20
	21	22	23	24	25	26	27
	28	29	30	1	2	3	4
ŚRĀVAṆA 2114	5	6	7	8	9	10	**11**
	13	14	15	16	17	18	19
	20	21	22	23[c]	24	25	26
	27	28	28	29	30	1	2
BHĀDRAPADA 2114	3[d]	**4**	6	7	8	9	10
	11	12	13	14	15	16	17
	18	19	20	21	22	23	24
	25	26	27	28	29	30	1
ĀŚVINA 2114	2	3	4	5	6	7	**8**[e]
	10[e]	11	12	13	14	15	16
	17	18	19	20	21	22	23
	23	24	25	26	27	28	29
KĀRTTIKA 2114	30	1[f]	3	4	5	6	7
	8	9	10	11	12	13	14
	15	16	17	18	19	20	21
	22	23	24	25	26	27	28
	29	30	1	2	3	4	5
MĀRGAŚIRA 2114	**6**	8	9	10	11[g]	12	13
	14	15	16	17	17	18	19
	20	21	22	23	24	25	26
PAUSHA 2114	27	28	29	**30**	2	3	4
	5	6	7	8	9	10	11

‡Leap year
[a]New Year (Īśvara)
[b]Birthday of Rāma
[c]Birthday of Krishna
[d]Ganēśa Chaturthī
[e]Dashara
[f]Diwali
[g]Birthday of Vishnu
[h]Night of Śiva
[i]Holi

HINDU SOLAR 1978‡/1979

Month	Sun	Mon	Tue	Wed	Thu	Fri	Sat
PAUSHA 1978	16	17	18	19	20	21	22
	23	24	25	26	27	28	29
MĀGHA 1978	1[b]	2	3	4	5	6	7
	8	9	10	11	12	13	14
	15	16	17	18	19	20	21
	22	23	24	25	26	27	28
	29	30	1	2	3	4	5
PHĀLGUNA 1978	6	7	8	9	10	11	12
	13	14	15	16	17	18	19
	20	21	22	23	24	25	26
	27	28	29	1	2	3	4
CHAITRA 1978	5	6	7	8	9	10	11
	12	13	14	15	16	17	18
	19	20	21	22	23	24	25
	26	27	28	29	30	31	1[a]
VAIŚĀKHA 1979	2	3	4	5	6	7	8
	9	10	11	12	13	14	15
	16	17	18	19	20	21	22
	23	24	25	26	27	28	29
	30	31	1	2	3	4	5
JYAISHṬHA 1979	6	7	8	9	10	11	12
	13	14	15	16	17	18	19
	20	21	22	23	24	25	26
	27	28	29	30	31	1	2
ĀSHĀḌHA 1979	3	4	5	6	7	8	9
	10	11	12	13	14	15	16
	17	18	19	20	21	22	23
	24	25	26	27	28	29	30
	31	32	1	2	3	4	5
ŚRĀVAṆA 1979	6	7	8	9	10	11	12
	13	14	15	16	17	18	19
	20	21	22	23	24	25	26
	27	28	29	30	31	1	2
BHĀDRAPADA 1979	3	4	5	6	7	8	9
	10	11	12	13	14	15	16
	17	18	19	20	21	22	23
	24	25	26	27	28	29	30
	31	1	2	3	4	5	6
ĀŚVINA 1979	7	8	9	10	11	12	13
	14	15	16	17	18	19	20
	21	22	23	24	25	26	27
	28	29	30	31	1	2	3
KĀRTTIKA 1979	4	5	6	7	8	9	10
	11	12	13	14	15	16	17
	18	19	20	21	22	23	24
	25	26	27	28	29	30	1
MĀRGAŚIRA 1979	2	3	4	5	6	7	8
	9	10	11	12	13	14	15
	16	17	18	19	20	21	22
	23	24	25	26	27	28	29
PAUSHA 1979	1	2	3	4	5	6	7
	8	9	10	11	12	13	14
	15	16	17	18	19	20	21

‡Leap year
[a]New Year (Khara)
[b]Pongal

ISLAMIC (ASTRONOMICAL) 1479/1480

Month	Sun	Mon	Tue	Wed	Thu	Fri	Sat
	24	25	26	27	28	29	30
RAJAB 1479	1	2	3	4	5	6	7
	8	9	10	11	12	13	14
	15	16	17	18	19	20	21
	22	23	24	25	26	27[d]	28
SHA'BĀN 1479	29	1	2	3	4	5	6
	7	8	9	10	11	12	13
	14	15	16	17	18	19	20
	21	22	23	24	25	26	27
RAMAḌĀN 1479	28	29	30	1[e]	2	3	4
	5	6	7	8	9	10	11
	12	13	14	15	16	17	18
	19	20	21	22	23	24	25
SHAWWĀL 1479	26	27	28	29	1[f]	2	3
	4	5	6	7	8	9	10
	11	12	13	14	15	16	17
	18	19	20	21	22	23	24
DHU AL-QA'DA 1479	25	26	27	28	29	30	1
	2	3	4	5	6	7	8
	9	10	11	12	13	14	15
	16	17	18	19	20	21	22
	23	24	25	26	27	28	29
DHU AL-ḤIJJA 1479	30	1	2	3	4	5	6
	7	8	9	10[g]	11	12	13
	14	15	16	17	18	19	20
	21	22	23	24	25	26	27
MUḤARRAM 1480	28	29	1[a]	2	3	4	5
	6	7	8	9	10[b]	11	12
	13	14	15	16	17	18	19
	20	21	22	23	24	25	26
ṢAFAR 1480	27	28	29	30	1	2	3
	4	5	6	7	8	9	10
	11	12	13	14	15	16	17
	18	19	20	21	22	23	24
RABĪ' I 1480	25	26	27	28	29	1	2
	3	4	5	6	7	8	9
	10	11	12[c]	13	14	15	16
	17	18	19	20	21	22	23
	24	25	26	27	28	29	30
RABĪ' II 1480	1	2	3	4	5	6	7
	8	9	10	11	12	13	14
	15	16	17	18	19	20	21
	22	23	24	25	26	27	28
JUMĀDĀ I 1480	29	1	2	3	4	5	6
	7	8	9	10	11	12	13
	14	15	16	17	18	19	20
	21	22	23	24	25	26	27
JUMĀDĀ II 1480	28	29	30	1	2	3	4
	5	6	7	8	9	10	11
	12	13	14	15	16	17	18
	19	20	21	22	23	24	25
RAJAB 1480	26	27	28	29	1	2	3
	4	5	6	7	8	9	10

[a]New Year
[b]'Ashūrā'
[c]Prophet's Birthday
[d]Ascent of the Prophet
[e]Start of Ramaḍān
[f]'Īd al-Fiṭr
[g]'Īd al-'Aḍḥā

GREGORIAN 2057

Julian (Sun)	Sun	Mon	Tue	Wed	Thu	Fri	Sat	Month
Dec 18	31	1	2	3	4	5	6	
	7[a]	8	9	10	11	12	13	JANUARY 2057
Jan 1	14[b]	15	16	17	18	19	20	
	21	22	23	24	25	26	27	
Jan 15	28	29	30	31	1	2	3	
	4	5	6	7	8	9	10	FEBRUARY 2057
Jan 29	11	12	13	14	15	16	17	
	18	19	20	21	22	23	24	
Feb 12	25	26	27	28	1	2	3	
	4	5	6	7[c]	8	9	10	MARCH 2057
Feb 26	11	12	13	14	15	16	17	
	18[d]	19	20	21	22	23	24	
Mar 12	25	26	27	28	29	30	31	
	1	2	3	4	5	6	7	APRIL 2057
Mar 26	8	9	10	11	12	13	14	
	15	16	17	18	19	20	21	
Apr 9	22[e]	23	24	25	26	27	28	
	29[f]	30	1	2	3	4	5	
Apr 23	6	7	8	9	10	11	12	MAY 2057
	13	14	15	16	17	18	19	
May 7	20	21	22	23	24	25	26	
	27	28	29	30	31	1	2	
May 21	3	4	5	6	7	8	9	JUNE 2057
	10	11	12	13	14	15	16	
Jun 4	17	18	19	20	21	22	23	
	24	25	26	27	28	29	30	
Jun 18	1	2	3	4	5	6	7	JULY 2057
	8	9	10	11	12	13	14	
Jul 2	15	16	17	18	19	20	21	
	22	23	24	25	26	27	28	
Jul 16	29	30	31	1	2	3	4	
	5	6	7	8	9	10	11	AUGUST 2057
Jul 30	12	13	14	15	16	17	18	
	19	20	21	22	23	24	25	
Aug 13	26	27	28	29	30	31	1	
	2	3	4	5	6	7	8	SEPTEMBER 2057
Aug 27	9	10	11	12	13	14	15	
	16	17	18	19	20	21	22	
Sep 10	23	24	25	26	27	28	29	
	30	1	2	3	4	5	6	
Sep 24	7	8	9	10	11	12	13	OCTOBER 2057
	14	15	16	17	18	19	20	
Oct 8	21	22	23	24	25	26	27	
	28	29	30	31	1	2	3	
Oct 22	4	5	6	7	8	9	10	NOVEMBER 2057
	11	12	13	14	15	16	17	
Nov 5	18	19	20	21	22	23	24	
	25	26	27	28	29	30	1	
Nov 19	2[g]	3	4	5	6	7	8	DECEMBER 2057
	9	10	11	12	13	14	15	
Dec 3	16	17	18	19	20	21	22	
	23	24	25[h]	26	27	28	29	
Dec 17	30	31	1	2	3	4	5	

[a]Orthodox Christmas
[b]Julian New Year
[c]Ash Wednesday
[d]Feast of Orthodoxy
[e]Easter
[f]Orthodox Easter
[g]Advent
[h]Christmas

2058

Gregorian 2058	Sun	Mon	Tue	Wed	Thu	Fri	Sat	Lunar Phases	ISO Week (Mon)	Julian Day (Sun noon)	Hebrew 5818/5819	Sun	Mon	Tue	Wed	Thu	Fri	Sat	Molad	Chinese Dīng-Chǒu/Wù-Yín‡	Sun	Mon	Tue	Wed	Thu	Fri	Sat	Solar Term	Coptic 1774/1775‡	Sun	Mon	Tue	Wed	Thu	Fri	Sat	Ethiopic 2050/2051‡
	30	31	◐[a]	2	3	4	5	18:29	1	2472728		3	4	5	6	7	8	9			5	6	7	8*	9	10	*11*	Xiǎo hán		21	22	23	24	25	26	27	Tākhśāś 2050
January 2058	6	7	8	○	10	11	12	20:37	2	2472735	Teveth 5818	10	11	12	13	14	15	16		Month 12 Dīng-Chǒu	12	13	14	15	16	17	18		Koiak 1774	28	29[c]	30	1	2	3	4	
	13	14	15	16	◑	18	19	19:42	3	2472742		17	18	19	20	21	22	23			19	20	21	22	23	24	25			5	6[d]	7	8	9	10	11[e]	Ṭer 2050
	20	21	22	23	●	25	26	12:13	4	2472749		24	25	26	27	28	29	1			**26**	27	28	29	1[a]	2	3	**Dà hán**	Tōbe 1774	12	13	14	15	16	17	18	
	27	28	29	30	◐	1	2	10:27	5	2472756		2	3	4	5	6	7	8	Thu 17h52m11p	Month 1 Wù-Yín	4	5	6	7	8	9	10			19	20	21	22	23	24	25	
	3	4	5	6	7	○	9	15:53	6	2472763	Shevat 5818	9	10	11	12	13	14	15			*11*	12	13	14	15[b]	16	17	Lì chūn		26	27	28	29	30	1	2	
February 2058	10	11	12	13	14	15	◑	7:15	7	2472770		16	17	18	19	20	21	22			18	19	20	21	22	23	24			3	4	5	6	7	8	9	
	17	18	19	20	21	●	23	22:55	8	2472777		23	24	25	26	27	28	29			25	**26**	27	28	29	30	1	**Yǔ shuǐ**	Meshir 1774	10	11	12	13	14	15	16	Yakātit 2050
	24	25	26	27	28	1	◐	5:09	9	2472784		30	1	2	3	4	5	6	Sat 6h36m12p	Month 2 Wù-Yín	2	3	4	5	6	7	8			17	18	19	20	21	22	23	
	3	4	5	6	7	8	9		10	2472791	Adar 5818	7	8	9	10	11	12	13			9*	10	*11*	12	13	14	15	Jīng zhé		24	25	26	27	28	29	30	
March 2058	○	11	12	13	14	15	16	8:51	11	2472798		14[f]	15	16	17	18	19	20			16	17	18	19	20	21	22			1	2	3	4	5	6	7	
	◑	18	19	20[b]	21	22	23	15:55	12	2472805		21	22	23	24	25	26	27			23	24	25	**26**	27	28	29	**Chūn fēn**		8	9	10	11	12	13	14	
	●	25	26	27	28	29	30	9:48	13	2472812		28	29	1	2	3	4	5	Sun 19h20m13p		1	2	3	4	5	6	7		Paremotep 1774	15	16	17	18	19	20	21	Magābit 2050
	31	◐	2	3	4	5	6	1:02	14	2472819	Nisan 5818	6	7	8	9	10	11	12		Month 3 Wù-Yín	8	9	10	11	*12*[c]	13	14	Qīng míng		22	23	24	25	26	27	28	
April 2058	7	○	9	10	11	12	13	22:54	15	2472826		13	14	15[g]	16	17	18	19			15	16	17	18	19	20	21			29	30	1	2	3	4	5	
	14	◑	16	17	18	19	20	22:26	16	2472833		20	21	22	23	24	25	26			22	23	24	25	26	27	**28**	**Gǔ yǔ**		6[f]	7	8	9	10	11	12	
	21	●	23	24	25	26	27	21:28	17	2472840		27	28	29	30	1	2	3	Tue 8h4m14p		29	30	1	2	3	4	5		Parmoute 1774	13	14	15	16	17	18	19	Miyāzyā 2050
	28	29	◐	1	2	3	4	20:17	18	2472847	Iyyar 5818	4	5	6	7	8	9	10		Month 4 Wù-Yín	6	7	8	9	10*	11	12			20	21	22	23	24	25	26	
May 2058	5	6	7	○	9	10	11	10:11	19	2472854		11	12	13	14	15	16	17			*13*	14	15	16	17	18	19	Lì xià		27	28	29[g]	30	1	2	3	
	12	13	14	◑	16	17	18	3:57	20	2472861		18	19	20	21	22	23	24			20	21	22	23	24	25	26			4	5	6	7	8	9	10	
	19	20	21	●	23	24	25	10:22	21	2472868		25	26	27	28	29	1	2	Wed 20h48m15p		27	28	**29**	1	2	3	4	**Xiǎo mǎn**	Pashons 1774	11	12	13	14	15	16	17	Genbot 2050
	26	27	28	29	◐	31	1	13:32	22	2472875	Sivan 5818	3	4	5	6[h]	7	8	9		Leap Month 4 Wù-Yín	5	6	7	8	9	10	11			18	19	20	21	22	23	24	
June 2058	2	3	4	5	○	7	8	19:14	23	2472882		10	11	12	13	14	15	16			12	13	14	*15*	16	17	18	Máng zhòng		25	26	27	28	29	30	1	
	9	10	11	12	◑	14	15	9:49	24	2472889		17	18	19	20	21	22	23			19	20	21	22	23	24	25			2	3	4	5	6	7	8	
	16	17	18	19	20	●[c]	22	0:34	25	2472896		24	25	26	27	28	29	30			26	27	28	29	30	***1***	2	**Xià zhì**	Paōne 1774	9	10	11	12	13	14	15	Sanē 2050
	23	24	25	26	27	28	◐	4:12	26	2472903		1	2	3	4	5	6	7	Fri 9h32m16p	Month 5 Wù-Yín	3	4	5[d]	6	7	8	9			16	17	18	19	20	21	22	
	30	1	2	3	4	5	○	2:45	27	2472910	Tammuz 5818	8	9	10	11	12	13	14			10	11*	12	13	14	15	16			23	24	25	26	27	28	29	
July 2058	7	8	9	10	11	◑	13	17:27	28	2472917		15	16	17	18	19	20	21			*17*	18	19	20	21	22	23	Xiǎo shǔ		30	1	2	3	4	5	6	
	14	15	16	17	18	19	●	15:38	29	2472924		22	23	24	25	26	27	28			24	25	26	27	28	29	1		Epēp 1774	7	8	9	10	11	12	13	Ḥamlē 2050
	21	22	23	24	25	26	27		30	2472931		29	1	2	3	4	5	6	Sat 22h16m17p	Month 6 Wù-Yín	2	**3**	4	5	6	7	8	**Dà shǔ**		14	15	16	17	18	19	20	
	◐	29	30	31	1	2	3	16:18	31	2472938	Av 5818	7	8	9[i]	10	11	12	13			9	10	11	12	13	14	15			21	22	23	24	25	26	27	
August 2058	○	5	6	7	8	9	10	9:36	32	2472945		14	15	16	17	18	19	20			16	17	18	*19*	20	21	22	Lì qiū		28	29	30	1	2	3	4	
	◑	12	13	14	15	16	17	3:59	33	2472952		21	22	23	24	25	26	27			23	24	25	26	27	28	29			5	6	7	8	9	10	11	
	18	●	20	21	22	23	24	7:02	34	2472959		28	29	30	1	2	3	4	Mon 11h1m0p		30	1	2	3	4	**5**	6	**Chǔ shǔ**	Mesorē 1774	12	13[h]	14	15	16	17	18	Naḥasē 2050
	25	26	◐	28	29	30	31	2:09	35	2472966	Elul 5818	5	6	7	8	9	10	11		Month 7 Wù-Yín	7[e]	8	9	10	11	12*	13			19	20	21	22	23	24	25	
	1	○	3	4	5	6	7	16:50	36	2472973		12	13	14	15	16	17	18			14	15[f]	16	17	18	19	*20*	Bái lù		26	27	28	29	30	1	2	
September 2058	8	◑	10	11	12	13	14	18:06	37	2472980		19	20	21	22	23	24	25			21	22	23	24	25	26	27		Epag. 1774	3	4	5	1[a]	2	3	4	Pāg. 2050
	15	16	●	18	19	20	21	22:16	38	2472987		26	27	28	29	1[a]	2[a]	3	Tue 23h45m1p		28	29	30	1	2	3	4			5	6	7	8	9	10	11	
	22[d]	23	24	◐	26	27	28	10:13	39	2472994	Tishri 5819	4	5	6	7	8	9	10[b]		Month 8 Wù-Yín	5	**6**	7	8	9	10	11	**Qiū fēn**	Thoout 1775	12	13	14	15	16	17[b]	18	Maskaram 2051
	29	30	1	○	3	4	5	1:35	40	2473001		11	12	13	14	15[c]	16	17			12	13	14	15[g]	16	17	18			19	20	21	22	23	24	25	
October 2058	6	7	8	◑	10	11	12	11:40	41	2473008		18	19	20	21	22	23	24			19	20	*21*	22	23	24	25	Hán lù		26	27	28	29	30	1	2	
	13	14	15	16	●	18	19	13:03	42	2473015		25	26	27	28	29	30	1	Thu 12h29m2p		26	27	28	29	1	2	3			3	4	5	6	7	8	9	
	20	21	22	23	◐	25	26	17:15	43	2473022	Heshvan 5819	2	3	4	5	6	7	8		Month 9 Wù-Yín	4	5	6	**7**	8	9[h]	10	**Shuāng jiàng**	Paope 1775	10	11	12	13	14	15	16	Teqemt 2051
	27	28	29	30	○	1	2	12:53	44	2473029		9	10	11	12	13	14	15			11	12	13*	14	15	16	17			17	18	19	20	21	22	23	
November 2058	3	4	5	6	7	◑	9	7:46	45	2473036		16	17	18	19	20	21	22			18	19	20	21	*22*	23	24	Lì dōng		24	25	26	27	28	29	30	
	10	11	12	13	14	15	●	3:08	46	2473043		23	24	25	26	27	28	29			25	26	27	28	29	30	1			1	2	3	4	5	6	7	
	17	18	19	20	21	22	◐	0:15	47	2473050		1	2	3	4	5	6	7	Sat 1h13m3p	Month 10 Wù-Yín	2	3	4	5	6	**7**	8	**Xiǎo xuě**	Athōr 1775	8	9	10	11	12	13	14	Ḫedār 2051
	24	25	26	27	28	29	○	3:16	48	2473057	Kislev 5819	8	9	10	11	12	13	14			9	10	11	12	13	14	15			15	16	17	18	19	20	21	
	1	2	3	4	5	6	7		49	2473064		15	16	17	18	19[d]	20	21			16	17	18	19	20	21	*22*	Dà xuě		22	23	24	25	26	27	28	
December 2058	◑	9	10	11	12	13	14	4:50	50	2473071		22	23	24	25[e]	26[e]	27[e]	28[e]			23	24	25	26	27	28	29			29	30	1	2	3	4	5	
	●	16	17	18	19	20	21[e]	16:10	51	2473078		29[e]	30[e]	1[e]	2[e]	3	4	5	Sun 13h57m4p		30	1	2	3	4	5	**6**[i]	**Dōng zhì**	Koiak 1775	6	7	8	9	10	11	12	Tākhśāś 2051
	◐	23	24	25	26	27	28	8:25	52	2473085	Teveth 5819	6	7	8	9	10	11	12		Month 11* Wù-Yín	7	8	9	10	11	12	13*			13	14	15	16	17	18	19	
	○	30	31	1	2	3	4	20:24	1	2473092		13	14	15	16	17	18	19			14	15	16	17	18	19	20			20	21	22	23	24	25	26	

[a]New Year
[b]Spring (9:03)
[c]Summer (2:02)
[d]Autumn (18:07)
[e]Winter (15:23)
● New moon
◐ First quarter moon
○ Full moon
◑ Last quarter moon

[a]New Year
[b]Yom Kippur
[c]Sukkot
[d]Winter starts
[e]Ḥanukkah
[f]Purim
[g]Passover
[h]Shavuot
[i]Fast of Av

‡Leap year
[a]New Year (4756, Tiger)
[b]Lantern Festival
[c]Qīngmíng
[d]Dragon Festival
[e]Qīqiǎo
[f]Hungry Ghosts
[g]Mid-Autumn Festival
[h]Double-Ninth Festival
[i]Dōngzhì
*Start of 60-name cycle

‡Leap year
[a]New Year
[b]Building of the Cross
[c]Christmas
[d]Jesus's Circumcision
[e]Epiphany
[f]Easter
[g]Mary's Announcement
[h]Jesus's Transfiguration

PERSIAN (ASTRONOMICAL) 1436[‡]/1437

Month	Sun	Mon	Tue	Wed	Thu	Fri	Sat
DEY 1436	10	11	12	13	14	15	16
	17	18	19	20	21	22	23
	24	25	26	27	28	29	30
BAHMAN 1436	1	2	3	4	5	6	7
	8	9	10	11	12	13	14
	15	16	17	18	19	20	21
	22	23	24	25	26	27	28
ESFAND 1436	29	30	1	2	3	4	5
	6	7	8	9	10	11	12
	13	14	15	16	17	18	19
	20	21	22	23	24	25	26
FARVARDĪN 1437	27	28	29	30*[d]	1[a]	2	3
	4	5	6	7	8	9	10
	11	12	13[b]	14	15	16	17
	18	19	20	21	22	23	24
	25	26	27	28	29	30	31
ORDĪBEHEŠT 1437	1	2	3	4	5	6	7
	8	9	10	11	12	13	14
	15	16	17	18	19	20	21
	22	23	24	25	26	27	28
XORDĀD 1437	29	30	31	1	2	3	4
	5	6	7	8	9	10	11
	12	13	14	15	16	17	18
	19	20	21	22	23	24	25
TĪR 1437	26	27	28	29	30	31	1
	2	3	4	5	6	7	8
	9	10	11	12	13	14	15
	16	17	18	19	20	21	22
	23	24	25	26	27	28	29
MORDĀD 1437	30	31	1	2	3	4	5
	6	7	8	9	10	11	12
	13	14	15	16	17	18	19
	20	21	22	23	24	25	26
SHAHRĪVAR 1437	27	28	29	30	31	1	2
	3	4	5	6	7	8	9
	10	11	12	13	14	15	16
	17	18	19	20	21	22	23
	24	25	26	27	28	29	30
MEHR 1437	31	1	2	3	4	5	6
	7	8	9	10	11	12	13
	14	15	16	17	18	19	20
	21	22	23	24	25	26	27
ĀBĀN 1437	28	29	30	1	2	3	4
	5	6	7	8	9	10	11
	12	13	14	15	16	17	18
	19	20	21	22	23	24	25
ĀZAR 1437	26	27	28	29	30	1	2
	3	4	5	6	7	8	9
	10	11	12	13	14	15	16
	17	18	19	20	21	22	23
	24	25	26	27	28	29	30
DEY 1437	1	2	3	4	5	6	7
	8	9	10	11	12	13	14

[‡]Leap year
[a]New Year (or prior day)
*Near New Year: −0′53″
[d]New Year (Arithmetic)
[b]Sizdeh Bedar

HINDU LUNAR 2114/2115[‡]

Month	Sun	Mon	Tue	Wed	Thu	Fri	Sat
PAUSHA 2114	5	6	7	8	9	10	11
	12	13	14	15	16	17	18
	19	19	20	21	22	**23**	25
MĀGHA 2114	26	27	28	29	30	1	2
	3	4	5	6	7	8	9
	10	11	12	13	14	15	16
	17	18	19	20	21	22	23
PHĀLGUNA 2114	24	25	26	27	**28**[h]	30	1
	2	3	4	5	6	7	8
	9	10	11	11	12	13	14
	15[i]	16	17	18	19	20	21
	22	24	25	26	27	28	29
CHAITRA 2115	30	1[a]	2	3	4	5	6
	7	8	9[b]	10	11	12	13
	14	15	16	17	18	19	20
	21	22	23	24	25	26	**27**
VAIŚĀKHA 2115	29	30	1	2	3	4	5
	5	6	7	8	9	10	11
	12	13	14	15	16	17	18
	19	**20**	22	23	24	25	26
JYAISHTHA 2115	27	28	29	30	1	2	3
	4	5	6	7	8	9	10
	11	12	13	14	15	16	17
	18	19	20	21	22	**23**	25
ĀSHĀDHA 2115	26	27	28	29	30	1	1
	2	3	4	5	6	7	8
	9	10	11	12	13	14	15
	16	18	19	20	21	22	23
	24	25	26	27	28	29	30
ŚRĀVANA 2115	1	2	3	4	5	6	7
	8	9	10	11	12	13	14
	15	16	17	18	**19**	21	22
	23[c]	24	25	26	27	28	28
LEAP BHĀDRAPADA 2115	29	30	1	2	3	4	5
	6	7	8	9	10	**11**	13
	14	15	16	17	18	19	20
	21	22	23	24	25	26	27
BHĀDRAPADA 2115	28	29	30	1	2	3	4[d]
	5	6	7	8	9	10	11
	12	13	14	**15**	17	18	19
	20	21	22	23	23	24	25
ĀŚVINA 2115	26	27	28	29	30	1	2
	3	4	5	6	7	**8**[e]	10[e]
	11	12	13	14	15	16	17
	18	19	20	21	22	23	24
	25	26	26	27	28	29	30
KĀRTTIKA 2115	1[f]	**2**	4	5	6	7	8
	9	10	11	12	13	14	15
	16	17	18	19	20	21	22
	23	24	25	26	27	28	29
MĀRGAŚIRA 2115	30	1	2	3	4	5	**6**
	8	9	10	11[g]	12	13	14
	15	16	17	18	19	19	20

[‡]Leap year
[a]New Year (Bahudhānya)
[b]Birthday of Rāma
[c]Birthday of Krishna
[d]Ganēśa Chaturthī
[e]Dashara
[f]Diwali
[g]Birthday of Vishnu
[h]Night of Śiva
[i]Holi

HINDU SOLAR 1979/1980

Month	Sun	Mon	Tue	Wed	Thu	Fri	Sat
PAUSHA 1979	15	16	17	18	19	20	21
	22	23	24	25	26	27	28
MĀGHA 1979	29	1[b]	2	3	4	5	6
	7	8	9	10	11	12	13
	14	15	16	17	18	19	20
	21	22	23	24	25	26	27
PHĀLGUNA 1979	28	29	30	1	2	3	4
	5	6	7	8	9	10	11
	12	13	14	15	16	17	18
	19	20	21	22	23	24	25
CHAITRA 1979	26	27	28	29	30	1	2
	3	4	5	6	7	8	9
	10	11	12	13	14	15	16
	17	18	19	20	21	22	23
	24	25	26	27	28	29	30
VAIŚĀKHA 1980	1[a]	2	3	4	5	6	7
	8	9	10	11	12	13	14
	15	16	17	18	19	20	21
	22	23	24	25	26	27	28
JYAISHTHA 1980	29	30	31	1	2	3	4
	5	6	7	8	9	10	11
	12	13	14	15	16	17	18
	19	20	21	22	23	24	25
ĀSHĀDHA 1980	26	27	28	29	30	31	1
	2	3	4	5	6	7	8
	9	10	11	12	13	14	15
	16	17	18	19	20	21	22
	23	24	25	26	27	28	29
ŚRĀVANA 1980	30	31	32	1	2	3	4
	5	6	7	8	9	10	11
	12	13	14	15	16	17	18
	19	20	21	22	23	24	25
BHĀDRAPADA 1980	26	27	28	29	30	31	1
	2	3	4	5	6	7	8
	9	10	11	12	13	14	15
	16	17	18	19	20	21	22
	23	24	25	26	27	28	29
ĀŚVINA 1980	30	31	1	2	3	4	5
	6	7	8	9	10	11	12
	13	14	15	16	17	18	19
	20	21	22	23	24	25	26
KĀRTTIKA 1980	27	28	29	30	31	1	2
	3	4	5	6	7	8	9
	10	11	12	13	14	15	16
	17	18	19	20	21	22	23
	24	25	26	27	28	29	30
MĀRGAŚIRA 1980	1	2	3	4	5	6	7
	8	9	10	11	12	13	14
	15	16	17	18	19	20	21
	22	23	24	25	26	27	28
PAUSHA 1980	29	1	2	3	4	5	6
	7	8	9	10	11	12	13
	14	15	16	17	18	19	20

[a]New Year (Nandana)
[b]Pongal

ISLAMIC (ASTRONOMICAL) 1480/1481

Month	Sun	Mon	Tue	Wed	Thu	Fri	Sat
RAJAB 1480	4	5	6	7	8	9	10
	11	12	13	14	15	16	17
	18	19	20	21	22	23	24
SHA'BĀN 1480	25	26	27[d]	28	29	30	1
	2	3	4	5	6	7	8
	9	10	11	12	13	14	15
	16	17	18	19	20	21	22
	23	24	25	26	27	28	29
RAMAḌĀN 1480	1[e]	2	3	4	5	6	7
	8	9	10	11	12	13	14
	15	16	17	18	19	20	21
	22	23	24	25	26	27	28
SHAWWĀL 1480	29	30	1[f]	2	3	4	5
	6	7	8	9	10	11	12
	13	14	15	16	17	18	19
	20	21	22	23	24	25	26
DHU AL-QA'DA 1480	27	28	29	1	2	3	4
	5	6	7	8	9	10	11
	12	13	14	15	16	17	18
	19	20	21	22	23	24	25
DHU AL-ḤIJJA 1480	26	27	28	29	30	1	2
	3	4	5	6	7	8	9
	10[g]	11	12	13	14	15	16
	17	18	19	20	21	22	23
MUḤARRAM 1481	24	25	26	27	28	29	1[a]
	2[d]	3	4	5	6	7	8
	9	10[b]	11	12	13	14	15
	16	17	18	19	20	21	22
	23	24	25	26	27	28	29
ṢAFAR 1481	30	1	2	3	4	5	6
	7	8	9	10	11	12	13
	14	15	16	17	18	19	20
	21	22	23	24	25	26	27
RABĪ' I 1481	28	29	30	1	2	3	4
	5	6	7	8	9	10	11
	12[c]	13	14	15	16	17	18
	19	20	21	22	23	24	25
RABĪ' II 1481	26	27	28	29	1	2	3
	4	5	6	7	8	9	10
	11	12	13	14	15	16	17
	18	19	20	21	22	23	24
JUMĀDĀ I 1481	25	26	27	28	29	30	1
	2	3	4	5	6	7	8
	9	10	11	12	13	14	15
	16	17	18	19	20	21	22
	23	24	25	26	27	28	29
JUMĀDĀ II 1481	30	1	2	3	4	5	6
	7	8	9	10	11	12	13
	14	15	16	17	18	19	20
	21	22	23	24	25	26	27
RAJAB 1481	28	29	1	2	3	4	5
	6	7	8	9	10	11	12
	13	14	15	16	17	18	19

[a]New Year
[d]New Year (Arithmetic)
[b]'Ashūrā'
[c]Prophet's Birthday
[d]Ascent of the Prophet
[e]Start of Ramaḍān
[f]'Id al-Fiṭr
[g]'Id al-'Aḍḥā

GREGORIAN 2058

Julian (Sun)	Sun	Mon	Tue	Wed	Thu	Fri	Sat	Month
Dec 17	30	31	1	2	3	4	5	JANUARY 2058
	6	7[a]	8	9	10	11	12	
Dec 31	13	14[b]	15	16	17	18	19	
	20	21	22	23	24	25	26	
Jan 14	27	28	29	30	31	1	2	FEBRUARY 2058
	3	4	5	6	7	8	9	
Jan 28	10	11	12	13	14	15	16	
	17	18	19	20	21	22	23	
Feb 11	24	25	26	27[c]	28	1	2	MARCH 2058
	3[d]	4	5	6	7	8	9	
Feb 25	10	11	12	13	14	15	16	
	17	18	19	20	21	22	23	
Mar 11	24	25	26	27	28	29	30	
	31	1	2	3	4	5	6	APRIL 2058
Mar 25	7	8	9	10	11	12	13	
	14[e]	15	16	17	18	19	20	
Apr 8	21	22	23	24	25	26	27	
	28	29	30	1	2	3	4	MAY 2058
Apr 22	5	6	7	8	9	10	11	
	12	13	14	15	16	17	18	
May 6	19	20	21	22	23	24	25	
	26	27	28	29	30	31	1	JUNE 2058
May 20	2	3	4	5	6	7	8	
	9	10	11	12	13	14	15	
Jun 3	16	17	18	19	20	21	22	
	23	24	25	26	27	28	29	
Jun 17	30	1	2	3	4	5	6	JULY 2058
	7	8	9	10	11	12	13	
Jul 1	14	15	16	17	18	19	20	
	21	22	23	24	25	26	27	
Jul 15	28	29	30	31	1	2	3	AUGUST 2058
	4	5	6	7	8	9	10	
Jul 29	11	12	13	14	15	16	17	
	18	19	20	21	22	23	24	
Aug 12	25	26	27	28	29	30	31	
	1	2	3	4	5	6	7	SEPTEMBER 2058
Aug 26	8	9	10	11	12	13	14	
	15	16	17	18	19	20	21	
Sep 9	22	23	24	25	26	27	28	
	29	30	1	2	3	4	5	OCTOBER 2058
Sep 23	6	7	8	9	10	11	12	
	13	14	15	16	17	18	19	
Oct 7	20	21	22	23	24	25	26	
	27	28	29	30	31	1	2	NOVEMBER 2058
Oct 21	3	4	5	6	7	8	9	
	10	11	12	13	14	15	16	
Nov 4	17	18	19	20	21	22	23	
	24	25	26	27	28	29	30	
Nov 18	1[g]	2	3	4	5	6	7	DECEMBER 2058
	8	9	10	11	12	13	14	
Dec 2	15	16	17	18	19	20	21	
	22	23	24	25[h]	26	27	28	
Dec 16	29	30	31	1	2	3	4	

[a]Orthodox Christmas
[b]Julian New Year
[c]Ash Wednesday
[d]Feast of Orthodoxy
[e]Easter (also Orthodox)
[g]Advent
[h]Christmas

2059

Gregorian 2059

Month	Sun	Mon	Tue	Wed	Thu	Fri	Sat	Lunar Phases	ISO Week (Mon)	Julian Day (Sun noon)
JANUARY 2059	○	30	31	1[a]	2	3	4	20:24	1	2473092
	5	6	◑	8	9	10	11	1:05	2	2473099
	12	13	●	15	16	17	18	3:56	3	2473106
	19	◐	21	22	23	24	25	18:49	4	2473113
	26	27	○	29	30	31	1	15:10	5	2473120
FEBRUARY 2059	2	3	4	◑	6	7	8	18:47	6	2473127
	9	10	11	●	13	14	15	14:26	7	2473134
	16	17	18	◐	20	21	22	7:56	8	2473141
	23	24	25	26	○	28	1	10:04	9	2473148
MARCH 2059	2	3	4	5	6	◑	8	8:46	10	2473155
	9	10	11	12	13	●	15	0:04	11	2473162
	16	17	18	19	◐[b]	21	22	23:28	12,	2473169
	23	24	25	26	27	28	○	3:46	13	2473176
APRIL 2059	30	31	1	2	3	4	◑	18:45	14	2473183
	6	7	8	9	10	11	●	9:27	15	2473190
	13	14	15	16	17	18	◐	16:36	16	2473197
	20	21	22	23	24	25	26		17	2473204
MAY 2059	○	28	29	30	1	2	3	19:16	18	2473211
	4	◑	6	7	8	9	10	1:28	19	2473218
	●	12	13	14	15	16	17	19:14	20	2473225
	18	◐	20	21	22	23	24	10:21	21	2473232
	25	26	○	28	29	30	31	8:02	22	2473239
JUNE 2059	1	2	◑	4	5	6	7	6:18	23	2473246
	8	9	●	11	12	13	14	5:56	24	2473253
	15	16	17	◐	19	20	21[c]	3:54	25	2473260
	22	23	24	○	26	27	28	18:11	26	2473267
JULY 2059	29	30	1	◑	3	4	5	10:52	27	2473274
	6	7	8	●	10	11	12	17:57	28	2473281
	13	14	15	16	◐	18	19	20:33	29	2473288
	20	21	22	23	24	○	26	2:22	30	2473295
AUGUST 2059	27	28	29	30	◑	1	2	16:41	31	2473302
	3	4	5	6	7	●	9	7:36	32	2473309
	10	11	12	13	14	15	◐	11:39	33	2473316
	17	18	19	20	21	22	○	9:41	34	2473323
	24	25	26	27	28	29	◑	1:04	35	2473330
SEPTEMBER 2059	31	1	2	3	4	5	●	22:59	36	2473337
	7	8	9	10	11	12	13		37	2473344
	14	◐	16	17	18	19	20	0:43	38	2473351
	○	22	23[d]	24	25	26	27	17:17	39	2473358
OCTOBER 2059	◑	29	30	1	2	3	4	12:53	40	2473365
	5	●	7	8	9	10	11	15:48	41	2473372
	12	13	◐	15	16	17	18	11:37	42	2473379
	19	20	○	22	23	24	25	2:14	43	2473386
NOVEMBER 2059	26	27	◑	29	30	31	1	4:30	44	2473393
	2	3	4	●	6	7	8	9:10	45	2473400
	9	10	11	◐	13	14	15	20:44	46	2473407
	16	17	18	○	20	21	22	13:08	47	2473414
	23	24	25	◑	27	28	29	23:41	48	2473421
DECEMBER 2059	30	1	2	3	4	●	6	1:48	49	2473428
	7	8	9	10	11	◐	13	4:49	50	2473435
	14	15	16	17	18	○	20	2:10	51	2473442
	21[e]	22	23	24	25	◑	27	21:16	52	2473449
	28	29	30	31	1	2	●	16:39	1	2473456

Hebrew 5819/5820‡

ISO Week	Month	Sun	Mon	Tue	Wed	Thu	Fri	Sat	Molad
1	TEVETH 5819	13	14	15	16	17	18	19	
2		20	21	22	23	24	25	26	
3	SHEVAT 5819	27	28	29	1	2	3	4	Tue 2h41m5p
4		5	6	7	8	9	10	11	
5		12	13	14	15	16	17	18	
6		19	20	21	22	23	24	25	
7	ADAR 5819	26	27	28	29	30	1	2	Wed 15h25m6p
8		3	4	5	6	7	8	9	
9		10	11	12	13	14[f]	15	16	
10		17	18	19	20	21	22	23	
11	NISAN 5819	24	25	26	27	28	29	1	Fri 4h9m7p
12		2	3	4	5	6	7	8	
13		9	10	11	12	13	14	15[g]	
14		16	17	18	19	20	21	22	
15		23	24	25	26	27	28	29	
16	IYYAR 5819	30	1	2	3	4	5	6	Sat 16h53m8p
17		7	8	9	10	11	12	13	
18		14	15	16	17	18	19	20	
19		21	22	23	24	25	26	27	
20	SIVAN 5819	28	29	1	2	3	4	5	Mon 5h37m9p
21		6[h]	7	8	9	10	11	12	
22		13	14	15	16	17	18	19	
23		20	21	22	23	24	25	26	
24	TAMMUZ 5819	27	28	29	30	1	2	3	Tue 18h21m10p
25		4	5	6	7	8	9	10	
26		11	12	13	14	15	16	17	
27		18	19	20	21	22	23	24	
28	AV 5819	25	26	27	28	29	1	2	Thu 7h5m11p
29		3	4	5	6	7	8	9	
30		10[i]	11	12	13	14	15	16	
31		17	18	19	20	21	22	23	
32		24	25	26	27	28	29	30	
33	ELUL 5819	1	2	3	4	5	6	7	Fri 19h49m12p
34		8	9	10	11	12	13	14	
35		15	16	17	18	19	20	21	
36		22	23	24	25	26	27	28	
37	TISHRI 5820	29	1[a]	2[a]	3	4	5	6	Sun 8h33m13p
38		7	8	9	10[b]	11	12	13	
39		14	15[c]	16	17	18	19	20	
40		21	22	23	24	25	26	27	
41	HESHVAN 5820	28	29	30	1	2	3	4	Mon 21h17m14p
42		5	6	7	8	9	10	11	
43		12	13	14	15	16	17	18	
44		19	20	21	22	23	24	25	
45	KISLEV 5820	26	27	28	29	1	2	3	Wed 10h1m15p
46		4	5	6	7	8	9	10	
47		11	12	13	14	15	16	17	
48		18	19	20	21	22	23	24	
49	TEVETH 5820	25[e]	26[e]	27[e]	28[e]	29[e]	1[e]	2[d][e]	Thu 22h45m16p
50		3[e]	4	5	6	7	8	9	
51		10	11	12	13	14	15	16	
52		17	18	19	20	21	22	23	
1		24	25	26	27	28	29	1	Sat 11h29m17p

Chinese Wù-Yín‡/Jǐ-Mǎo

ISO Week	Month	Sun	Mon	Tue	Wed	Thu	Fri	Sat	Solar Term
1	MONTH 11* Wù-Yín	14	15	16	17	18	19	20	
2		*21*	22	23	24	25	26	27	Xiǎo hán
3	MONTH 12 Wù-Yín	28	29	1	2	3	4	5	
4		6	**7**	8	9	10	11	12	Dà hán
5		13	14	15	16	17	18	19	
6		20	21	*22*	23	24	25	26	Lì chūn
7	MONTH 1 Jǐ-Mǎo	27	28	29	1[a]	2	3	4	
8		5	6	7	**8**	9	10	11	Yǔ shuǐ
9		12	13	14	15[b]*	16	17	18	
10		19	20	21	*22*	23	24	25	Jīng zhé
11	MONTH 2 Jǐ-Mǎo	26	27	28	29	30	1	2	
12		3	4	5	6	**7**	8	9	Chūn fēn
13		10	11	12	13	14	15	16	
14		17	18	19	20	21	22	*23*[c]	Qīng míng
15	MONTH 3 Jǐ-Mǎo	24	25	26	27	28	29	1	
16		2	3	4	5	6	7	8	
17		**9**	10	11	12	13	14	15	Gǔ yǔ
18		16*	17	18	19	20	21	22	
19		23	*24*	25	26	27	28	29	Lì xià
20	MONTH 4 Jǐ-Mǎo	30	1	2	3	4	5	6	
21		7	8	9	**10**	11	12	13	Xiǎo mǎn
22		14	15	16	17	18	19	20	
23		21	22	23	24	*25*	26	27	Máng zhòng
24	MONTH 5 Jǐ-Mǎo	28	29	1	2	3	4	5[d]	
25		6	7	8	9	10	11	**12**	Xià zhì
26		13	14	15	16	17*	18	19	
27		20	21	22	23	24	25	26	
28	MONTH 6 Jǐ-Mǎo	27	*28*	29	30	1	2	3	Xiǎo shǔ
29		4	5	6	7	8	9	10	
30		11	12	13	**14**	15	16	17	Dà shǔ
31		18	19	20	21	22	23	24	
32	MONTH 7 Jǐ-Mǎo	25	26	27	28	*29*	1	2	Lì qiū
33		3	4	5	6	7[e]	8	9	
34		10	11	12	13	14	15[f]	**16**	Chǔ shǔ
35		17	18*	19	20	21	22	23	
36		24	25	26	27	28	29	30	
37	MONTH 8 Jǐ-Mǎo	*1*	2	3	4	5	6	7	Bái lù
38		8	9	10	11	12	13	14	
39		15[g]	16	**17**	18	19	20	21	Qiū fēn
40		22	23	24	25	26	27	28	
41	MONTH 9 Jǐ-Mǎo	29	1	2	*3*	4	5	6	Hán lù
42		7	8	9[h]	10	11	12	13	
43		14	15	16	17	**18**	19*	20	Shuāng jiàng
44		21	22	23	24	25	26	27	
45	MONTH 10 Jǐ-Mǎo	28	29	30	1	2	*3*	4	Lì dōng
46		5	6	7	8	9	10	11	
47		12	13	14	15	16	17	**18**	Xiǎo xuě
48		19	20	21	22	23	24	25	
49	MONTH 11 Jǐ-Mǎo	26	27	28	29	30	1	2	
50		*3*	4	5	6	7	8	9	Dà xuě
51		10	11	12	13	14	15	16	
52		17	**18**[i]	19*	20	21	22	23	Dōng zhì
1		24	25	26	27	28	29	30	

Coptic 1775‡/1776 — Ethiopic 2051‡/2052

ISO Week	Coptic Month	Sun	Mon	Tue	Wed	Thu	Fri	Sat	Ethiopic Month
1	KOIAK 1775	20	21	22	23	24	25	26	TĀKHŚĀŚ 2051
2	TÔBE 1775	27	28	29[c]	30	1	2	3	ṬER 2051
3		4	5	6[d]	7	8	9	10	
4		11[e]	12	13	14	15	16	17	
5		18	19	20	21	22	23	24	
6	MESHIR 1775	25	26	27	28	29	30	1	YAKĀTIT 2051
7		2	3	4	5	6	7	8	
8		9	10	11	12	13	14	15	
9		16	17	18	19	20	21	22	
10		23	24	25	26	27	28	29	
11	PAREMOTEP 1775	30	1	2	3	4	5	6	MAGĀBIT 2051
12		7	8	9	10	11	12	13	
13		14	15	16	17	18	19	20	
14		21	22	23	24	25	26	27	
15	PARMOUTE 1775	28	29	30	1	2	3	4	MIYĀZYĀ 2051
16		5	6	7	8	9	10	11	
17		12	13	14	15	16	17	18	
18		19	20	21	22	23	24	25	
19	PASHONS 1775	26[f]	27	28	29[g]	30	1	2	GENBOT 2051
20		3	4	5	6	7	8	9	
21		10	11	12	13	14	15	16	
22		17	18	19	20	21	22	23	
23		24	25	26	27	28	29	30	
24	PAÔNE 1775	1	2	3	4	5	6	7	SANÉ 2051
25		8	9	10	11	12	13	14	
26		15	16	17	18	19	20	21	
27		22	23	24	25	26	27	28	
28	EPÊP 1775	29	30	1	2	3	4	5	ḤAMLĒ 2051
29		6	7	8	9	10	11	12	
30		13	14	15	16	17	18	19	
31		20	21	22	23	24	25	26	
32	MESORÊ 1775	27	28	29	30	1	2	3	NAHASĒ 2051
33		4	5	6	7	8	9	10	
34		11	12	13[h]	14	15	16	17	
35		18	19	20	21	22	23	24	
36	EPAG. 1775	25	26	27	28	29	30	1	PĀG. 2051
37	THOOUT 1776	2	3	4	5	6	1[a]	2	MASKARAM 2052
38		3	4	5	6	7	8	9	
39		10	11	12	13	14	15	16	
40		17[b]	18	19	20	21	22	23	
41		24	25	26	27	28	29	30	
42	PAOPE 1776	1	2	3	4	5	6	7	ṬEQEMT 2052
43		8	9	10	11	12	13	14	
44		15	16	17	18	19	20	21	
45		22	23	24	25	26	27	28	
46	ATHÔR 1776	29	30	1	2	3	4	5	ḤEDĀR 2052
47		6	7	8	9	10	11	12	
48		13	14	15	16	17	18	19	
49		20	21	22	23	24	25	26	
50	KOIAK 1776	27	28	29	30	1	2	3	TĀKHŚĀŚ 2052
51		4	5	6	7	8	9	10	
52		11	12	13	14	15	16	17	
1		18	19	20	21	22	23	24	

Gregorian notes:
[a]New Year
[b]Spring (14:43)
[c]Summer (7:45)
[d]Autumn (0:01)
[e]Winter (21:16)
● New moon
◐ First quarter moon
○ Full moon
◑ Last quarter moon

Hebrew notes:
‡Leap year
[a]New Year
[b]Yom Kippur
[c]Sukkot
[d]Winter starts
[e]Ḥanukkah
[f]Purim
[g]Passover
[h]Shavuot
[i]Fast of Av

Chinese notes:
‡Leap year
[a]New Year (4757, Hare)
[b]Lantern Festival
[c]Qīngmíng
[d]Dragon Festival
[e]Qīqiǎo
[f]Hungry Ghosts
[g]Mid-Autumn Festival
[h]Double-Ninth Festival
[i]Dōngzhì
*Start of 60-name cycle

Coptic/Ethiopic notes:
‡Leap year
[a]New Year
[b]Building of the Cross
[c]Christmas
[d]Jesus's Circumcision
[e]Epiphany
[f]Easter
[g]Mary's Announcement
[h]Jesus's Transfiguration

PERSIAN (ASTRONOMICAL) 1437/1438

Month	Sun	Mon	Tue	Wed	Thu	Fri	Sat
DEY 1437	8	9	10	11	12	13	14
	15	16	17	18	19	20	21
	22	23	24	25	26	27	28
BAHMAN 1437	29	30	1	2	3	4	5
	6	7	8	9	10	11	12
	13	14	15	16	17	18	19
	20	21	22	23	24	25	26
ESFAND 1437	27	28	29	*30*	1	2	3
	4	5	6	7	8	9	10
	11	12	13	14	15	16	17
	18	19	20	21	22	23	24
FARVARDIN 1438	25	26	27	28	29	*1*[a]	2
	3	4	5	6	7	8	9
	10	11	12	13[b]	14	15	16
	17	18	19	20	21	22	23
	24	25	26	27	28	29	30
ORDIBEHEŠT 1438	31	*1*	2	3	4	5	6
	7	8	9	10	11	12	13
	14	15	16	17	18	19	20
	21	22	23	24	25	26	27
XORDĀD 1438	28	29	30	31	*1*	2	3
	4	5	6	7	8	9	10
	11	12	13	14	15	16	17
	18	19	20	21	22	23	24
	25	26	27	28	29	30	31
TĪR 1438	*1*	2	3	4	5	6	7
	8	9	10	11	12	13	14
	15	16	17	18	19	20	21
	22	23	24	25	26	27	28
MORDĀD 1438	29	30	31	*1*	2	3	4
	5	6	7	8	9	10	11
	12	13	14	15	16	17	18
	19	20	21	22	23	24	25
SHAHRĪVAR 1438	26	27	28	29	30	31	*1*
	2	3	4	5	6	7	8
	9	10	11	12	13	14	15
	16	17	18	19	20	21	22
	23	24	25	26	27	28	29
MEHR 1438	30	31	*1*	2	3	4	5
	6	7	8	9	10	11	12
	13	14	15	16	17	18	19
	20	21	22	23	24	25	26
ĀBĀN 1438	27	28	29	30	*1*	2	3
	4	5	6	7	8	9	10
	11	12	13	14	15	16	17
	18	19	20	21	22	23	24
ĀZAR 1438	25	26	27	28	29	30	*1*
	2	3	4	5	6	7	8
	9	10	11	12	13	14	15
	16	17	18	19	20	21	22
	23	24	25	26	27	28	29
DEY 1438	30	*1*	2	3	4	5	6
	7	8	9	10	11	12	13

[a]New Year
[b]Sizdeh Bedar

HINDU LUNAR 2115‡/2116

Month	Sun	Mon	Tue	Wed	Thu	Fri	Sat
MĀRGAŚIRA 2115	15	16	17	18	19	*19*	20
	21	22	23	24	25	26	27
PAUSHA 2115	28	29	30	**1**	3	4	5
	6	7	8	9	10	11	12
	13	14	15	16	17	18	19
	20	21	22	23	24	25	26
MĀGHA 2115	27	28	29	30	1	2	3
	4	5	6	**7**	9	10	11
	11	12	13	14	15	16	17
	18	19	20	21	22	23	24
PHĀLGUNA 2115	25	26	27	28[h]	**29**	1	2
	3	4	5	6	7	8	9
	10	11	12	13	14	*14*	15[i]
	16	17	18	19	20	21	22
	23	25	26	27	28	29	30
CHAITRA 2116	1[a]	2	3	4	5	6	7
	8	9[b]	10	11	12	13	14
	15	16	17	18	19	20	21
	22	23	24	25	26	**27**	29
VAIŚĀKHA 2116	30	1	2	3	4	5	6
	7	8	9	*9*	10	11	12
	13	14	15	16	17	18	19
	20	22	23	24	25	26	27
JYAISHTHA 2116	28	29	30	1	2	3	4
	5	6	7	8	9	10	11
	12	13	14	15	16	17	18
	19	20	21	22	**23**	25	26
ĀSHĀDHA 2116	27	28	29	30	1	2	3
	4	5	6	*6*	7	8	9
	10	11	12	13	14	**15**	17
	18	19	20	21	22	23	24
ŚRĀVAṆA 2116	25	26	27	28	29	30	1
	2	3	4	5	6	7	8
	9	10	11	12	13	14	15
	16	17	**18**	20	21	22	23[c]
	24	25	26	27	28	29	30
BHĀDRAPADA 2116	1	2	*2*	3[d]	4	5	6
	7	8	9	10	11	**12**	14
	15	16	17	18	19	20	21
	22	23	24	25	26	27	28
ĀŚVINA 2116	29	30	1	2	3	4	5
	6	7	8[e]	9[e]	10[e]	11	12
	13	14	**15**	17	18	19	20
	21	22	23	24	25	26	27
KĀRTTIKA 2116	*27*	28	29	30	1[f]	2	3
	4	5	6	7	8	**9**	11
	12	13	14	15	16	17	18
	19	20	21	22	23	24	25
MĀRGAŚIRA 2116	26	27	28	29	30	1	*1*
	3	4	5	6	7	8	9
	10	11[g]	12	13	14	**15**	17
	18	19	*19*	20	21	22	23
	24	25	26	27	28	29	30

‡Leap year
[a]New Year (Pramāthin)
[b]Birthday of Rāma
[c]Birthday of Krishna
[d]Gaṇēśa Chaturthī
[e]Dashara
[f]Diwali
[g]Birthday of Vishnu
[h]Night of Śiva
[i]Holi

HINDU SOLAR 1980/1981‡

Month	Sun	Mon	Tue	Wed	Thu	Fri	Sat
PAUSHA 1980	14	15	16	17	18	19	20
	21	22	23	24	25	26	27
MĀGHA 1980	28	29	30	1[b]	2	3	4
	5	6	7	8	9	10	11
	12	13	14	15	16	17	18
	19	20	21	22	23	24	25
PHĀLGUNA 1980	26	27	28	29	1	2	3
	4	5	6	7	8	9	10
	11	12	13	14	15	16	17
	18	19	20	21	22	23	24
CHAITRA 1980	25	26	27	28	29	30	1
	2	3	4	5	6	7	8
	9	10	11	12	13	14	15
	16	17	18	19	20	21	22
	23	24	25	26	27	28	29
VAIŚĀKHA 1981	30	1[a]	2	3	4	5	6
	7	8	9	10	11	12	13
	14	15	16	17	18	19	20
	21	22	23	24	25	26	27
JYAISHTHA 1981	28	29	30	31	1	2	3
	4	5	6	7	8	9	10
	11	12	13	14	15	16	17
	18	19	20	21	22	23	24
	25	26	27	28	29	30	31
ĀSHĀDHA 1981	32	1	2	3	4	5	6
	7	8	9	10	11	12	13
	14	15	16	17	18	19	20
	21	22	23	24	25	26	27
ŚRĀVAṆA 1981	28	29	30	31	1	2	3
	4	5	6	7	8	9	10
	11	12	13	14	15	16	17
	18	19	20	21	22	23	24
	25	26	27	28	29	30	31
BHĀDRAPADA 1981	32	1	2	3	4	5	6
	7	8	9	10	11	12	13
	14	15	16	17	18	19	20
	21	22	23	24	25	26	27
ĀŚVINA 1981	28	29	30	31	1	2	3
	4	5	6	7	8	9	10
	11	12	13	14	15	16	17
	18	19	20	21	22	23	24
KĀRTTIKA 1981	25	26	27	28	29	30	1
	2	3	4	5	6	7	8
	9	10	11	12	13	14	15
	16	17	18	19	20	21	22
	23	24	25	26	27	28	29
MĀRGAŚIRA 1981	30	1	2	3	4	5	6
	7	8	9	10	11	12	13
	14	15	16	17	18	19	20
	21	22	23	24	25	26	27
PAUSHA 1981	28	29	30	1	2	3	4
	5	6	7	8	9	10	11
	12	13	14	15	16	17	18

‡Leap year
[a]New Year (Vijaya)
[b]Pongal

ISLAMIC (ASTRONOMICAL) 1481/1482‡

Month	Sun	Mon	Tue	Wed	Thu	Fri	Sat
RAJAB 1481	13	14	15	16	17	18	19
	20	21	22	23	24	25	26
SHA'BĀN 1481	27[d]	28	29	1	*2*	*3*	4
	5	6	7	8	9	10	11
	12	13	14	15	16	17	18
	19	20	21	22	23	24	25
RAMAḌĀN 1481	26	27	28	29	30	*1*[e]	2
	3	4	5	6	7	8	9
	10	11	12	13	14	15	16
	17	18	19	20	21	22	23
SHAWWĀL 1481	24	25	26	27	28	29	1[f]
	2	3	4	5	6	7	8
	9	10	11	12	13	14	15
	16	17	18	19	20	21	22
	23	24	25	26	27	28	29
DHU AL-QA'DA 1481	30	*1*	2	3	4	5	6
	7	8	9	10	11	12	13
	14	15	16	17	18	19	20
	21	22	23	24	25	26	27
DHU AL-ḤIJJA 1481	28	29	1	*2*	3	4	5
	6	7	8	9	10[g]	11	12
	13	14	15	16	17	18	19
	20	21	22	23	24	25	26
MUḤARRAM 1482	27	28	29	1[a]	2[d]	3	4
	5	6	7	8	9	10[b]	11
	12	13	14	15	16	17	18
	19	20	21	22	23	24	25
ṢAFAR 1482	26	27	28	29	30	1	2
	3	4	5	6	7	8	9
	10	11	12	13	14	15	16
	17	18	19	20	21	22	23
	24	25	26	27	28	29	30
RABĪ' I 1482	*1*	2	3	4	5	6	7
	8	9	10	11	12[c]	13	14
	15	16	17	18	19	20	21
	22	23	24	25	26	27	28
RABĪ' II 1482	29	1	*2*	3	4	5	6
	7	8	9	10	11	12	13
	14	15	16	17	18	19	20
	21	22	23	24	25	26	27
JUMĀDĀ I 1482	28	29	30	*1*	2	3	4
	5	6	7	8	9	10	11
	12	13	14	15	16	17	18
	19	20	21	22	23	24	25
JUMĀDĀ II 1482	26	27	28	29	30	*1*	2
	3	4	5	6	7	8	9
	10	11	12	13	14	15	16
	17	18	19	20	21	22	23
	24	25	26	27	28	29	*30*
RAJAB 1482	1	2	3	4	5	6	7
	8	9	10	11	12	13	14
	15	16	17	18	19	20	21
	22	23	24	25	26	27	28

‡Leap year
[a]New Year
[d]New Year (Arithmetic)
[b]'Ashūrā'
[c]Prophet's Birthday
[d]Ascent of the Prophet
[e]Start of Ramaḍān
[f]'Īd al-Fiṭr
[g]'Īd al-'Aḍḥā

GREGORIAN 2059

Julian (Sun)	Month	Sun	Mon	Tue	Wed	Thu	Fri	Sat
Dec 16	JANUARY 2059	29	30	31	1	2	3	4
		5	6	7[a]	8	9	10	11
Dec 30		12	13	14[b]	15	16	17	18
		19	20	21	22	23	24	25
Jan 13	FEBRUARY 2059	26	27	28	29	30	31	1
		2	3	4	5	6	7	8
Jan 27		9	10	11	12[c]	13	14	15
		16	17	18	19	20	21	22
Feb 10	MARCH 2059	23	24	25	26	27	28	1
		2	3	4	5	6	7	8
Feb 24		9	10	11	12	13	14	15
		16	17	18	19	20	21	22
Mar 10		23[d]	24	25	26	27	28	29
	APRIL 2059	30[e]	31	1	2	3	4	5
Mar 24		6	7	8	9	10	11	12
		13	14	15	16	17	18	19
Apr 7		20	21	22	23	24	25	26
	MAY 2059	27	28	29	30	1	2	3
Apr 21		4[f]	5	6	7	8	9	10
		11	12	13	14	15	16	17
May 5		18	19	20	21	22	23	24
		25	26	27	28	29	30	31
May 19	JUNE 2059	1	2	3	4	5	6	7
		8	9	10	11	12	13	14
Jun 2		15	16	17	18	19	20	21
		22	23	24	25	26	27	28
Jun 16	JULY 2059	29	30	1	2	3	4	5
		6	7	8	9	10	11	12
Jun 30		13	14	15	16	17	18	19
		20	21	22	23	24	25	26
Jul 14	AUGUST 2059	27	28	29	30	31	1	2
		3	4	5	6	7	8	9
Jul 28		10	11	12	13	14	15	16
		17	18	19	20	21	22	23
Aug 11		24	25	26	27	28	29	30
	SEPTEMBER 2059	31	1	2	3	4	5	6
Aug 25		7	8	9	10	11	12	13
		14	15	16	17	18	19	20
Sep 8		21	22	23	24	25	26	27
	OCTOBER 2059	28	29	30	1	2	3	4
Sep 22		5	6	7	8	9	10	11
		12	13	14	15	16	17	18
Oct 6		19	20	21	22	23	24	25
	NOVEMBER 2059	26	27	28	29	30	31	1
Oct 20		2	3	4	5	6	7	8
		9	10	11	12	13	14	15
Nov 3		16	17	18	19	20	21	22
		23	24	25	26	27	28	29
Nov 17	DECEMBER 2059	30[g]	1	2	3	4	5	6
		7	8	9	10	11	12	13
Dec 1		14	15	16	17	18	19	20
		21	22	23	24	25[h]	26	27
Dec 15		28	29	30	31	1	2	3

[a]Orthodox Christmas
[b]Julian New Year
[c]Ash Wednesday
[d]Feast of Orthodoxy
[e]Easter
[f]Orthodox Easter
[g]Advent
[h]Christmas

2060

GREGORIAN 2060‡ / ISO WEEK / JULIAN DAY

Month	Sun	Mon	Tue	Wed	Thu	Fri	Sat	Lunar Phases	ISO WEEK (Mon)	JULIAN DAY (Sun noon)
	28	29	30	31	1[a]	2	●	16:39	1	2473456
JANUARY 2060	4	5	6	7	8	9	◐	12:51	2	2473463
	11	12	13	14	15	16	○	17:12	3	2473470
	18	19	20	21	22	23	24		4	2473477
	◑	26	27	28	29	30	31	19:13	5	2473484
	1	●	3	4	5	6	7	5:21	6	2473491
FEBRUARY 2060	◐	9	10	11	12	13	14	21:40	7	2473498
	15	○	17	18	19	20	21	9:55	8	2473505
	22	23	◑	25	26	27	28	15:05	9	2473512
	29	1	●	3	4	5	6	16:10	10	2473519
MARCH 2060	7	8	◐	10	11	12	13	7:51	11	2473526
	14	15	16	○	18	19[b]	20	3:40	12	2473533
	21	22	23	24	◑	26	27	7:07	13	2473540
	28	29	30	31	●	2	3	1:36	14	2473547
APRIL 2060	4	5	6	◐	8	9	10	19:41	15	2473554
	11	12	13	14	○	16	17	21:20	16	2473561
	18	19	20	21	22	◑	24	18:52	17	2473568
	25	26	27	28	29	●	1	10:09	18	2473575
MAY 2060	2	3	4	5	6	◐	8	9:18	19	2473582
	9	10	11	12	13	14	○	13:38	20	2473589
	16	17	18	19	20	21	22		21	2473596
	◑	24	25	26	27	28	●	3:00 18:22	22	2473603
	30	31	1	2	3	4	5		23	2473610
JUNE 2060	◐	7	8	9	10	11	12	0:43	24	2473617
	13	○	15	16	17	18	19	3:36	25	2473624
	20[c]	◑	22	23	24	25	26	8:42	26	2473631
	27	●	29	30	1	2	3	2:56	27	2473638
JULY 2060	4	◐	6	7	8	9	10	17:36	28	2473645
	11	12	○	14	15	16	17	15:07	29	2473652
	18	19	◑	21	22	23	24	13:22	30	2473659
	25	26	●	28	29	30	31	12:48	31	2473666
AUGUST 2060	1	2	3	◐	5	6	7	11:15	32	2473673
	8	9	10	11	○	13	14	0:50	33	2473680
	15	16	17	◑	19	20	21	18:21	34	2473687
	22	23	24	25	●	27	28	0:55	35	2473694
	29	30	31	1	2	◐	4	4:35	36	2473701
SEPTEMBER 2060	5	6	7	8	9	○	11	9:43	37	2473708
	12	13	14	15	16	◑	18	0:59	38	2473715
	19	20	21	22[d]	23	●	25	15:52	39	2473722
	26	27	28	29	30	1	◐	20:40	40	2473729
OCTOBER 2060	3	4	5	6	7	8	○	18:40	41	2473736
	10	11	12	13	14	15	◑	10:28	42	2473743
	17	18	19	20	21	22	23		43	2473750
	●	25	26	27	28	29	30	9:24	44	2473757
	31	◐	2	3	4	5	6	10:55	45	2473764
NOVEMBER 2060	7	○	9	10	11	12	13	4:16	46	2473771
	◑	15	16	17	18	19	20	23:47	47	2473778
	21	22	●	24	25	26	27	4:14	48	2473785
	28	29	◐	1	2	3	4	23:09	49	2473792
DECEMBER 2060	5	6	○	8	9	10	11	14:47	50	2473799
	12	13	◑	15	16	17	18	17:14	51	2473806
	19	20	21[e]	●	23	24	25	22:38	52	2473813
	26	27	28	29	◐	31	1	9:27	53	2473820

HEBREW 5820‡/5821

ISO WEEK	Month	Sun	Mon	Tue	Wed	Thu	Fri	Sat	Molad
1		24	25	26	27	28	29	1	Sat 11h29m17p
2	SHEVAT 5820	2	3	4	5	6	7	8	
3		9	10	11	12	13	14	15	
4		16	17	18	19	20	21	22	
5		23	24	25	26	27	28	29	
6		30	1	2	3	4	5	6	Mon 0h14m0p
7	ADAR I 5820	7	8	9	10	11	12	13	
8		14	15	16	17	18	19	20	
9		21	22	23	24	25	26	27	
10		28	29	30	1	2	3	4	Tue 12h58m1p
11	ADAR II 5820	5	6	7	8	9	10	11	
12		12	13	14[f]	15	16	17	18	
13		19	20	21	22	23	24	25	
14		26	27	28	29	1	2	3	Thu 1h42m2p
15	NISAN 5820	4	5	6	7	8	9	10	
16		11	12	13	14	15[g]	16	17	
17		18	19	20	21	22	23	24	
18		25	26	27	28	29	30	1	Fri 14h26m3p
19	IYAR 5820	2	3	4	5	6	7	8	
20		9	10	11	12	13	14	15	
21		16	17	18	19	20	21	22	
22		23	24	25	26	27	28	29	
23		1	2	3	4	5	6[h]	7	Sun 3h10m4p
24	SIVAN 5820	8	9	10	11	12	13	14	
25		15	16	17	18	19	20	21	
26		22	23	24	25	26	27	28	
27		29	30	1	2	3	4	5	Mon 15h54m5p
28	TAMMUZ 5820	6	7	8	9	10	11	12	
29		13	14	15	16	17	18	19	
30		20	21	22	23	24	25	26	
31		27	28	29	1	2	3	4	Wed 4h38m6p
32	AV 5820	5	6	7	8	9[i]	10	11	
33		12	13	14	15	16	17	18	
34		19	20	21	22	23	24	25	
35		26	27	28	29	30	1	2	Thu 17h22m7p
36	ELUL 5820	3	4	5	6	7	8	9	
37		10	11	12	13	14	15	16	
38		17	18	19	20	21	22	23	
39		24	25	26	27	28	29	1[a]	Sat 6h6m8p
40	TISHRI 5821	2[a]	3	4	5	6	7	8	
41		9	10[b]	11	12	13	14	15[c]	
42		16	17	18	19	20	21	22	
43		23	24	25	26	27	28	29	
44		30	1	2	3	4	5	6	Sun 18h50m9p
45	HESHVAN 5821	7	8	9	10	11	12	13	
46		14	15	16	17	18	19	20	
47		21	22	23	24	25	26	27	
48		28	29	30	1	2	3	4	Tue 7h34m10p
49	KISLEV 5821	5	6	7	8	9	10	11	
50		12[d]	13	14	15	16	17	18	
51		19	20	21	22	23	24	25[e]	
52		26[e]	27[e]	28[e]	29[e]	30[e]	1[e]	2[e]	Wed 20h18m11p
53	TEVETH 5821	3	4	5	6	7	8	9	

CHINESE Jǐ-Mǎo/Gēng-Chén

ISO WEEK	Month	Sun	Mon	Tue	Wed	Thu	Fri	Sat	Solar Term
1		24	25	26	27	28	29	30	
2		1	2	3	4	5	6	7	Xiǎo hán
3	MONTH 12 Jǐ-Mǎo	8	9	10	11	12	13	14	
4		15	16	17	18	19	20	21	Dà hán
5		22	23	24	25	26	27	28	
6		29	1[a]	2	3	4	5	6	Lì chūn
7	MONTH 1 Gēng-Chén	7	8	9	10	11	12	13	
8		14	15[b]	16	17	18	19	20*	Yǔ shuǐ
9		21	22	23	24	25	26	27	
10		28	29	30	1	2	3	4	Jīng zhé
11	MONTH 2 Gēng-Chén	5	6	7	8	9	10	11	
12		12	13	14	15	16	17	18	Chūn fēn
13		19	20	21	22	23	24	25	
14		26	27	28	29	1	2	3	
15	MONTH 3 Gēng-Chén	4[c]	5	6	7	8	9	10	Qīng míng
16		11	12	13	14	15	16	17	
17		18	19	20	21*	22	23	24	Gǔ yǔ
18		25	26	27	28	29	1	2	
19	MONTH 4 Gēng-Chén	3	4	5	6	7	8	9	Lì xià
20		10	11	12	13	14	15	16	
21		17	18	19	20	21	22	23	Xiǎo mǎn
22		24	25	26	27	28	29	30	
23		1	2	3	4	5[d]	6	7	Máng zhòng
24	MONTH 5 Gēng-Chén	8	9	10	11	12	13	14	
25		15	16	17	18	19	20	21	
26		22*	23	24	25	26	27	28	Xià zhì
27		29	1	2	3	4	5	6	
28	MONTH 6 Gēng-Chén	7	8	9	10	11	12	13	Xiǎo shǔ
29		14	15	16	17	18	19	20	
30		21	22	23	24	25	26	27	Dà shǔ
31		28	29	1	2	3	4	5	
32	MONTH 7 Gēng-Chén	6	7[e]	8	9	10	11	12	Lì qiū
33		13	14	15[f]	16	17	18	19	
34		20	21	22	23	24*	25	26	
35		27	28	29	30	1	2	3	Chǔ shǔ
36	MONTH 8 Gēng-Chén	4	5	6	7	8	9	10	
37		11	12	13	14	15[g]	16	17	Bái lù
38		18	19	20	21	22	23	24	
39		25	26	27	28	29	1	2	Qiū fēn
40	MONTH 9 Gēng-Chén	3	4	5	6	7	8	9[h]	
41		10	11	12	13	14	15	16	Hán lù
42		17	18	19	20	21	22	23	
43		24	25*	26	27	28	29	30	Shuāng jiàng
44		1	2	3	4	5	6	7	
45	MONTH 10 Gēng-Chén	8	9	10	11	12	13	14	Lì dōng
46		15	16	17	18	19	20	21	
47		22	23	24	25	26	27	28	
48		29	30	1	2	3	4	5	Xiǎo xuě
49	MONTH 11 Gēng-Chén	6	7	8	9	10	11	12	
50		13	14	15	16	17	18	19	Dà xuě
51		20	21	22	23	24	25*	26	
52		27	28	29[i]	30	1	2	3	Dōng zhì
53	MONTH 12 Gēng-Chén	4	5	6	7	8	9	10	

COPTIC 1776/1777 — ETHIOPIC 2052/2053

ISO WEEK	Coptic month	Sun	Mon	Tue	Wed	Thu	Fri	Sat	Ethiopic month
1	KOIAK 1776	18	19	20	21	22	23	24	TĀKHŚĀŚ 2052
2		25	26	27	28	29[c]	30	1	
3	TÔBE 1776	2	3	4	5	6[d]	7	8	ṬER 2052
4		9	10	11[e]	12	13	14	15	
5		16	17	18	19	20	21	22	
6		23	24	25	26	27	28	29	
7		30	1	2	3	4	5	6	
8	MESHIR 1776	7	8	9	10	11	12	13	YAKĀTIT 2052
9		14	15	16	17	18	19	20	
10		21	22	23	24	25	26	27	
11		28	29	30	1	2	3	4	
12	PAREMOTEP 1776	5	6	7	8	9	10	11	MAGĀBIT 2052
13		12	13	14	15	16	17	18	
14		19	20	21	22	23	24	25	
15		26	27	28	29	30	1	2	
16	PARMOUTE 1776	3	4	5	6	7	8	9	MIYĀZYĀ 2052
17		10	11	12	13	14	15	16	
18		17[f]	18	19	20	21	22	23	
19		24	25	26	27	28	29[g]	30	
20		1	2	3	4	5	6	7	
21	PASHONS 1776	8	9	10	11	12	13	14	GENBOT 2052
22		15	16	17	18	19	20	21	
23		22	23	24	25	26	27	28	
24		29	30	1	2	3	4	5	
25	PAÔNE 1776	6	7	8	9	10	11	12	SANĒ 2052
26		13	14	15	16	17	18	19	
27		20	21	22	23	24	25	26	
28		27	28	29	30	1	2	3	
29	EPÊP 1776	4	5	6	7	8	9	10	HAMLĒ 2052
30		11	12	13	14	15	16	17	
31		18	19	20	21	22	23	24	
32		25	26	27	28	29	30	1	
33	MESORÊ 1776	2	3	4	5	6	7	8	NAḤASĒ 2052
34		9	10	11	12	13[h]	14	15	
35		16	17	18	19	20	21	22	
36		23	24	25	26	27	28	29	
37	EPAG. 1776	30	1	2	3	4	5	1[a]	PĀG. 2052
38		2	3	4	5	6	7	8	MASKARAM 2053
39	THOOUT 1777	9	10	11	12	13	14	15	
40		16	17[b]	18	19	20	21	22	
41		23	24	25	26	27	28	29	
42		30	1	2	3	4	5	6	
43	PAOPE 1777	7	8	9	10	11	12	13	ṬEQEMT 2053
44		14	15	16	17	18	19	20	
45		21	22	23	24	25	26	27	
46		28	29	30	1	2	3	4	
47	ATHÔR 1777	5	6	7	8	9	10	11	HEDĀR 2053
48		12	13	14	15	16	17	18	
49		19	20	21	22	23	24	25	
50		26	27	28	29	30	1	2	
51	KOIAK 1777	3	4	5	6	7	8	9	TĀKHŚĀŚ 2053
52		10	11	12	13	14	15	16	
53		17	18	19	20	21	22	23	

‡Leap year
[a]New Year
[b]Spring (20:37)
[c]Summer (13:44)
[d]Autumn (5:47)
[e]Winter (3:00)
● New moon
◐ First quarter moon
○ Full moon
◑ Last quarter moon

‡Leap year
[a]New Year
[b]Yom Kippur
[c]Sukkot
[d]Winter starts
[e]Ḥanukkah
[f]Purim
[g]Passover
[h]Shavuot
[i]Fast of Av

[a]New Year (4758, Dragon)
[b]Lantern Festival
[c]Qīngmíng
[d]Dragon Festival
[e]Qīqiǎo
[f]Hungry Ghosts
[g]Mid-Autumn Festival
[h]Double-Ninth Festival
[i]Dōngzhì
*Start of 60-name cycle

[a]New Year
[b]Building of the Cross
[c]Christmas
[d]Jesus's Circumcision
[e]Epiphany
[f]Easter
[g]Mary's Announcement
[h]Jesus's Transfiguration

PERSIAN (ASTRONOMICAL) 1438/1439

Month	Sun	Mon	Tue	Wed	Thu	Fri	Sat
	7	8	9	10	11	12	13
DEY 1438	14	15	16	17	18	19	20
	21	22	23	24	25	26	27
	28	29	30	1	2	3	4
BAHMAN 1438	5	6	7	8	9	10	11
	12	13	14	15	16	17	18
	19	20	21	22	23	24	25
	26	27	28	29	30	1	2
ESFAND 1438	3	4	5	6	7	8	9
	10	11	12	13	14	15	16
	17	18	19	20	21	22	23
	24	25	26	27	28	29	1[a]
	2	3	4	5	6	7	8
FARVARDĪN 1439	9	10	11	12	13[b]	14	15
	16	17	18	19	20	21	22
	23	24	25	26	27	28	29
	30	31	1	2	3	4	5
ORDĪBEHEŠT 1439	6	7	8	9	10	11	12
	13	14	15	16	17	18	19
	20	21	22	23	24	25	26
	27	28	29	30	31	1	2
	3	4	5	6	7	8	9
XORDĀD 1439	10	11	12	13	14	15	16
	17	18	19	20	21	22	23
	24	25	26	27	28	29	30
	31	1	2	3	4	5	6
TĪR 1439	7	8	9	10	11	12	13
	14	15	16	17	18	19	20
	21	22	23	24	25	26	27
	28	29	30	31	1	2	3
MORDĀD 1439	4	5	6	7	8	9	10
	11	12	13	14	15	16	17
	18	19	20	21	22	23	24
	25	26	27	28	29	30	31
	1	2	3	4	5	6	7
SHAHRĪVAR 1439	8	9	10	11	12	13	14
	15	16	17	18	19	20	21
	22	23	24	25	26	27	28
	29	30	31	1	2	3	4
MEHR 1439	5	6	7	8	9	10	11
	12	13	14	15	16	17	18
	19	20	21	22	23	24	25
	26	27	28	29	30	1	2
ĀBĀN 1439	3	4	5	6	7	8	9
	10	11	12	13	14	15	16
	17	18	19	20	21	22	23
	24	25	26	27	28	29	30
	1	2	3	4	5	6	7
ĀZAR 1439	8	9	10	11	12	13	14
	15	16	17	18	19	20	21
	22	23	24	25	26	27	28
DEY 1439	29	30	1	2	3	4	5
	6	7	8	9	10	11	12

[a]New Year
[b]Sizdeh Bedar

HINDU LUNAR 2116/2117

Month	Sun	Mon	Tue	Wed	Thu	Fri	Sat
	24	25	26	27	28	29	30
	1	2	3	4	5	6	7
PAUSHA 2116	8	10	11	12	13	14	15
	16	17	18	19	20	21	22
	22	23	24	25	26	27	28
	29	30	1	2	4	5	6
MĀGHA 2116	7	8	9	10	11	12	13
	14	15	16	17	18	19	20
	21	22	23	24	25	26	27
	28	29[h]	30	1	2	3	4
PHĀLGUNA 2116	5	6	7	9	10	11	12
	13	14	14	15[i]	16	17	18
	19	20	21	22	23	24	25
	26	27	28	29	30[a]	2	3
	4	5	6	7	8	9[b]	10
CHAITRA 2117	11	12	13	14	15	16	17
	18	18	19	20	21	22	23
	25	26	27	28	29	30	1
VAIŚĀKHA 2117	2	3	4	5	6	7	8
	9	10	11	12	13	14	15
	16	17	18	19	20	21	22
	23	24	25	26	27	29	30
	1	2	3	4	5	6	7
JYAISHTHA 2117	8	9	10	11	12	13	13
	14	15	16	17	18	19	21
	22	23	24	25	26	27	28
	29	30	1	2	3	4	5
ĀSHĀDHA 2117	6	7	8	9	10	11	12
	13	14	15	16	17	18	19
	20	21	22	23	25	26	27
	28	29	30	1	2	3	4
ŚRĀVANA 2117	5	6	7	8	9	10	10
	11	12	13	14	15	17	18
	19	20	21	22	23[c]	24	25
	26	27	29	30	1	1	2
BHĀDRAPADA 2117	3[d]	4	5	6	7	8	9
	10	11	12	13	14	15	16
	17	18	19	21	22	23	24
	25	26	27	28	29	30	1
	2	3	4	5	6	6	7
ĀŚVINA 2117	8[e]	9[e]	10[e]	11	12	14	15
	16	17	18	19	20	21	22
	23	24	25	26	27	28	29
	30	1[f]	2	3	4	5	6
KĀRTTIKA 2117	7	8	9	10	11	12	13
	14	15	16	18	19	20	21
	22	23	24	25	26	27	28
	29	30	30	1	2	3	4
MĀRGAŚIRA 2117	5	6	7	8	9	10[g]	12
	13	14	15	16	17	18	19
	20	21	22	23	24	25	26
PAUSHA 2117	27	28	29	30	1	2	3
	4	5	6	7	8	9	10

[a]New Year (Vikrama)
[b]Birthday of Rāma
[c]Birthday of Krishna
[d]Ganēśa Chaturthī
[e]Dashara
[f]Diwali
[g]Birthday of Vishnu
[h]Night of Śiva
[i]Holi

HINDU SOLAR 1981‡/1982

Month	Sun	Mon	Tue	Wed	Thu	Fri	Sat
	12	13	14	15	16	17	18
PAUSHA 1981	19	20	21	22	23	24	25
	26	27	28	29	1[b]	2	3
MĀGHA 1981	4	5	6	7	8	9	10
	11	12	13	14	15	16	17
	18	19	20	21	22	23	24
	25	26	27	28	29	1	2
PHĀLGUNA 1981	3	4	5	6	7	8	9
	10	11	12	13	14	15	16
	17	18	19	20	21	22	23
	24	25	26	27	28	29	30
	1	2	3	4	5	6	7
CHAITRA 1981	8	9	10	11	12	13	14
	15	16	17	18	19	20	21
	22	23	24	25	26	27	28
	29	30	31	1[a]	2	3	4
VAIŚĀKHA 1982	5	6	7	8	9	10	11
	12	13	14	15	16	17	18
	19	20	21	22	23	24	25
	26	27	28	29	30	1	2
JYAISHTHA 1982	3	4	5	6	7	8	9
	10	11	12	13	14	15	16
	17	18	19	20	21	22	23
	24	25	26	27	28	29	30
	31	32	1	2	3	4	5
ĀSHĀDHA 1982	6	7	8	9	10	11	12
	13	14	15	16	17	18	19
	20	21	22	23	24	25	26
	27	28	29	30	31	32	1
ŚRĀVANA 1982	2	3	4	5	6	7	8
	9	10	11	12	13	14	15
	16	17	18	19	20	21	22
	23	24	25	26	27	28	29
	30	31	1	2	3	4	5
BHĀDRAPADA 1982	6	7	8	9	10	11	12
	13	14	15	16	17	18	19
	20	21	22	23	24	25	26
	27	28	29	30	31	1	2
ĀŚVINA 1982	3	4	5	6	7	8	9
	10	11	12	13	14	15	16
	17	18	19	20	21	22	23
	24	25	26	27	28	29	30
	1	2	3	4	5	6	7
KĀRTTIKA 1982	8	9	10	11	12	13	14
	15	16	17	18	19	20	21
	22	23	24	25	26	27	28
	29	30	1	2	3	4	5
MĀRGAŚIRA 1982	6	7	8	9	10	11	12
	13	14	15	16	17	18	19
	20	21	22	23	24	25	26
	27	28	29	30	1	2	3
PAUSHA 1982	4	5	6	7	8	9	10
	11	12	13	14	15	16	17

‡Leap year
[a]New Year (Jaya)
[b]Pongal

ISLAMIC (ASTRONOMICAL) 1482‡/1483‡

Month	Sun	Mon	Tue	Wed	Thu	Fri	Sat
RAJAB 1482	22	23	24	25	26	27[d]	28
	29	1	2	3	4	5	6
SHA'BĀN 1482	7	8	9	10	11	12	13
	14	15	16	17	18	19	20
	21	22	23	24	25	26	27
	28	29	1[e]	2	3	4	5
RAMAḌĀN 1482	6	7	8	9	10	11	12
	13	14	15	16	17	18	19
	20	21	22	23	24	25	26
	27	28	29	30	1[f]	2	3
SHAWWĀL 1482	4	5	6	7	8	9	10
	11	12	13	14	15	16	17
	18	19	20	21	22	23	24
	25	26	27	28	29	1	2
DHU AL-QA'DA 1482	3	4	5	6	7	8	9
	10	11	12	13	14	15	16
	17	18	19	20	21	22	23
	24	25	26	27	28	29	30
	1	2	3	4	5	6	7
DHU AL-ḤIJJA 1482	8	9	10[g]	11	12	13	14
	15	16	17	18	19	20	21
	22	23	24	25	26	27	28
	29	1[a]	2	3	4	5	6
MUḤARRAM 1483	7	8	9	10[b]	11	12	13
	14	15	16	17	18	19	20
	21	22	23	24	25	26	27
	28	29	1	2	3	4	5
ṢAFAR 1483	6	7	8	9	10	11	12
	13	14	15	16	17	18	19
	20	21	22	23	24	25	26
	27	28	29	30	1	2	3
RABĪ' I 1483	4	5	6	7	8	9	10
	11	12[c]	13	14	15	16	17
	18	19	20	21	22	23	24
	25	26	27	28	29	1	2
RABĪ' II 1483	3	4	5	6	7	8	9
	10	11	12	13	14	15	16
	17	18	19	20	21	22	23
	24	25	26	27	28	29	30
	1	2	3	4	5	6	7
JUMĀDĀ I 1483	8	9	10	11	12	13	14
	15	16	17	18	19	20	21
	22	23	24	25	26	27	28
	29	30	1	2	3	4	5
JUMĀDĀ II 1483	6	7	8	9	10	11	12
	13	14	15	16	17	18	19
	20	21	22	23	24	25	26
	27	28	29	30	1	2	3
RAJAB 1483	4	5	6	7	8	9	10
	11	12	13	14	15	16	17
	18	19	20	21	22	23	24
	25	26	27[d]	28	29	30	1
SHA'BĀN 1483	2	3	4	5	6	7	8

‡Leap year
[a]New Year
[b]'Ashūrā'
[c]Prophet's Birthday
[d]Ascent of the Prophet
[e]Start of Ramaḍān
[f]'Īd al-Fiṭr
[g]'Īd al-'Aḍḥā

GREGORIAN 2060‡

Julian‡ (Sun)	Sun	Mon	Tue	Wed	Thu	Fri	Sat	Month
Dec 15	28	29	30	31	1	2	3	
	4	5	6	7[a]	8	9	10	JANUARY 2060
Dec 29	11	12	13	14[b]	15	16	17	
	18	19	20	21	22	23	24	
Jan 12	25	26	27	28	29	30	31	
	1	2	3	4	5	6	7	
Jan 26	8	9	10	11	12	13	14	FEBRUARY 2060
	15	16	17	18	19	20	21	
Feb 9	22	23	24	25	26	27	28	
	29	1	2	3[c]	4	5	6	
Feb 23	7	8	9	10	11	12	13	MARCH 2060
	14[d]	15	16	17	18	19	20	
Mar 8	21	22	23	24	25	26	27	
	28	29	30	31	1	2	3	
Mar 22	4	5	6	7	8	9	10	APRIL 2060
	11	12	13	14	15	16	17	
Apr 5	18[e]	19	20	21	22	23	24	
	25[f]	26	27	28	29	30	1	
Apr 19	2	3	4	5	6	7	8	MAY 2060
	9	10	11	12	13	14	15	
May 3	16	17	18	19	20	21	22	
	23	24	25	26	27	28	29	
May 17	30	31	1	2	3	4	5	
	6	7	8	9	10	11	12	JUNE 2060
May 31	13	14	15	16	17	18	19	
	20	21	22	23	24	25	26	
Jun 14	27	28	29	30	1	2	3	
	4	5	6	7	8	9	10	JULY 2060
Jun 28	11	12	13	14	15	16	17	
	18	19	20	21	22	23	24	
Jul 12	25	26	27	28	29	30	31	
	1	2	3	4	5	6	7	
Jul 26	8	9	10	11	12	13	14	AUGUST 2060
	15	16	17	18	19	20	21	
Aug 9	22	23	24	25	26	27	28	
	29	30	31	1	2	3	4	
Aug 23	5	6	7	8	9	10	11	SEPTEMBER 2060
	12	13	14	15	16	17	18	
Sep 6	19	20	21	22	23	24	25	
	26	27	28	29	30	1	2	
Sep 20	3	4	5	6	7	8	9	OCTOBER 2060
	10	11	12	13	14	15	16	
Oct 4	17	18	19	20	21	22	23	
	24	25	26	27	28	29	30	
Oct 18	31	1	2	3	4	5	6	
	7	8	9	10	11	12	13	NOVEMBER 2060
Nov 1	14	15	16	17	18	19	20	
	21	22	23	24	25	26	27	
Nov 15	28[g]	29	30	1	2	3	4	
	5	6	7	8	9	10	11	DECEMBER 2060
Nov 29	12	13	14	15	16	17	18	
	19	20	21	22	23	24	25[h]	
Dec 13	26	27	28	29	30	31	1	

‡Leap year
[a]Orthodox Christmas
[b]Julian New Year
[c]Ash Wednesday
[d]Feast of Orthodoxy
[e]Easter
[f]Orthodox Easter
[g]Advent
[h]Christmas

2061

Month	GREGORIAN 2061 Sun Mon Tue Wed Thu Fri Sat	Lunar Phases	ISO WEEK (Mon)	JULIAN DAY (Sun noon)	HEBREW month	HEBREW 5821/5822‡ Sun Mon Tue Wed Thu Fri Sat	Molad	CHINESE month	CHINESE Gēng-Chén/Xīn-Sì‡ Sun Mon Tue Wed Thu Fri Sat	Solar Term	COPTIC month	COPTIC 1777/1778 · ETHIOPIC 2053/2054 Sun Mon Tue Wed Thu Fri Sat	ETHIOPIC month
	26 27 28 29 ◐ 31 1[a]	9:27	53	2473820		3 4 5 6 7 8 9		MONTH 12 Gēng-Chén	4 5 6 7 8 9 10		KOIAK 1777	17 18 19 20 21 22 23	TĀKHŚĀŚ 2053
	2 3 4 5 ○ 7 8	2:23	1	2473827	TEVETH 5821	10 11 12 13 14 15 16			11 12 13 14 15 16 17	Xiǎo hán		24 25 26 27 28 29[c] 30	
JANUARY 2061	9 10 11 12 ◑ 14 15	13:56	2	2473834		17 18 19 20 21 22 23			18 19 20 21 22 23 24			1 2 3 4 5 6[d] 7	
	16 17 18 19 20 ● 22	15:15	3	2473841		24 25 26 27 28 29 1	Fri 9h2m12p		25 26 27 28 29 1[a] 2	Dà hán	TŌBE 1777	8 9 10 11[e] 12 13 14	
	23 24 25 26 27 ◐ 29	18:08	4	2473848		2 3 4 5 6 7 8		MONTH 1 Xīn-Sì	3 4 5 6 7 8 9			15 16 17 18 19 20 21	ṬER 2053
	30 31 1 2 3 ○ 5	15:21	5	2473855	SHEVAT 5821	9 10 11 12 13 14 15			10 11 12 13 14 15[b] 16	Lì chūn		22 23 24 25 26 27 28	
FEBRUARY 2061	6 7 8 9 10 11 ◑	11:50	6	2473862		16 17 18 19 20 21 22			17 18 19 20 21 22 23			29 30 1 2 3 4 5	
	13 14 15 16 17 18 19		7	2473869		23 24 25 26 27 28 29			24 25 26* 27 28 29 30	Yǔ shuǐ	MESHIR 1777	6 7 8 9 10 11 12	
	● 21 22 23 24 25 26	5:30	8	2473876		30 1 2 3 4 5 6	Sat 21h46m13p		1 2 3 4 5 6 7			13 14 15 16 17 18 19	YAKĀTIT 2053
	◐ 28 1 2 3 4 5	1:50	9	2473883		7 8 9 10 11 12 13		MONTH 2 Xīn-Sì	8 9 10 11 12 13 14	Jīng zhé		20 21 22 23 24 25 26	
MARCH 2061	○ 7 8 9 10 11 12	5:53	10	2473890	ADAR 5821	14[f] 15 16 17 18 19 20			15 16 17 18 19 20 21			27 28 29 30 1 2 3	
	13 ◑ 15 16 17 18 19	8:29	11	2473897		21 22 23 24 25 26 27			22 23 24 25 26 27 28		PAREMOTEP 1777	4 5 6 7 8 9 10	MAGĀBIT 2053
	20[b] ● 22 23 24 25 26	17:22	12	2473904		28 29 1 2 3 4 5	Mon 10h30m14p		29 30 1 2 3 4 5	Chūn fēn		11 12 13 14 15 16 17	
	27 ◐ 29 30 31 1 2	9:25	13	2473911		6 7 8 9 10 11 12			6 7 8 9 10 11 12			18 19 20 21 22 23 24	
APRIL 2061	3 ○ 5 6 7 8 9	21:46	14	2473918	NISAN 5821	13 14 15[g] 16 17 18 19		MONTH 3 Xīn-Sì	13 14[c] 15 16 17 18 19	Qīng míng		25 26 27 28 29 30 1	
	10 11 12 ◑ 14 15 16	2:08	15	2473925		20 21 22 23 24 25 26			20 21 22 23 24 25 26*			2[f] 3 4 5 6 7 8	
	17 18 19 ● 21 22 23	3:04	16	2473932		27 28 29 30 1 2 3	Tue 23h14m15p		27 28 29 1 2 3 4	Gǔ yǔ	PARMOUTE 1777	9 10 11 12 13 14 15	MIYĀZYĀ 2053
	24 25 ◐ 27 28 29 30	17:53	17	2473939		4 5 6 7 8 9 10			5 6 7 8 9 10 11			16 17 18 19 20 21 22	
	1 2 3 ○ 5 6 7	14:12	18	2473946	IYYAR 5821	11 12 13 14 15 16 17		LEAP MONTH 3 Xīn-Sì	12 13 14 15 16 17 18	Lì xià		23 24 25 26 27 28 29[g]	
MAY 2061	8 9 10 11 ◑ 13 14	16:09	19	2473953		18 19 20 21 22 23 24			19 20 21 22 23 24 25			30 1 2 3 4 5 6	
	15 16 17 18 ● 20 21	11:02	20	2473960		25 26 27 28 29 1 2	Thu 11h58m16p		26 27 28 29 1 2 3	Xiǎo mǎn	PASHONS 1777	7 8 9 10 11 12 13	GENBOT 2053
	22 23 24 25 ◐ 27 28	4:11	21	2473967		3 4 5 6[h] 7 8 9		MONTH 4 Xīn-Sì	4 5 6 7 8 9 10			14 15 16 17 18 19 20	
	29 30 31 1 2 ○ 4	6:08	22	2473974	SIVAN 5821	10 11 12 13 14 15 16			11 12 13 14 15 16 17			21 22 23 24 25 26 27	
JUNE 2061	5 6 7 8 9 10 ◑	2:41	23	2473981		17 18 19 20 21 22 23			18 19 20 21 22 23 24	Máng zhòng		28 29 30 1 2 3 4	
	12 13 14 15 16 ● 18	18:02	24	2473988		24 25 26 27 28 29 30			25 26 27 28* 29 30 1		PAŌNE 1777	5 6 7 8 9 10 11	
	19 20[c] 21 22 23 ◐ 25	16:52	25	2473995		1 2 3 4 5 6 7	Sat 0h42m17p	MONTH 5 Xīn-Sì	2 3 4 5[d] 6 7 8	Xià zhì		12 13 14 15 16 17 18	SANĒ 2053
	26 27 28 29 30 1 ○	20:51	26	2474002	TAMMUZ 5821	8 9 10 11 12 13 14			9 10 11 12 13 14 15			19 20 21 22 23 24 25	
	3 4 5 6 7 8 9		27	2474009		15 16 17 18 19 20 21			16 17 18 19 20 21 22	Xiǎo shǔ		26 27 28 29 30 1 2	
JULY 2061	◑ 11 12 13 14 15 16	10:22	28	2474016		22 23 24 25 26 27 28			23 24 25 26 27 28 29		EPĒP 1777	3 4 5 6 7 8 9	
	● 18 19 20 21 22 23	1:09	29	2474023		29 1 2 3 4 5 6	Sun 13h27m0p		1 2 3 4 5 6 7	Dà shǔ		10 11 12 13 14 15 16	HAMLĒ 2053
	◐ 25 26 27 28 29 30	8:03	30	2474030	AV 5821	7 8 9[i] 10 11 12 13		MONTH 6 Xīn-Sì	8 9 10 11 12 13 14			17 18 19 20 21 22 23	
	31 ○ 2 3 4 5 6	10:10	31	2474037		14 15 16 17 18 19 20			15 16 17 18 19 20 21			24 25 26 27 28 29 30	
AUGUST 2061	7 ◑ 9 10 11 12 13	16:08	32	2474044		21 22 23 24 25 26 27			22 23 24 25 26 27 28	Lì qiū		1 2 3 4 5 6 7	
	14 ● 16 17 18 19 20	9:38	33	2474051		28 29 30 1 2 3 4	Tue 2h11m1p		29* 1 2 3 4 5 6		MESORĒ 1777	8 9 10 11 12 13[h] 14	
	21 22 ◐ 24 25 26 27	1:17	34	2474058	ELUL 5821	5 6 7 8 9 10 11		MONTH 7 Xīn-Sì	7[e] 8 9 10 11 12 13	Chǔ shǔ		15 16 17 18 19 20 21	NAHASĒ 2053
	28 29 ○ 31 1 2 3	22:17	35	2474065		12 13 14 15 16 17 18			14 15[f] 16 17 18 19 20			22 23 24 25 26 27 28	
SEPTEMBER 2061	4 5 ◑ 7 8 9 10	21:11	36	2474072		19 20 21 22 23 24 25			21 22 23 24 25 26 27	Bái lù	EPAG. 1777	29 30 1 2 3 4 5	PĀG. 2053
	11 12 ● 14 15 16 17	20:36	37	2474079		26 27 28 29 1[a] 2[a] 3	Wed 14h55m2p		28 29 30 1 2 3 4			1[a] 2 3 4 5 6 7	
	18 19 20 ◐ 22[d] 23 24	19:43	38	2474086	TISHRI 5822	4 5 6 7 8 9 10[b]		MONTH 8 Xīn-Sì	5 6 7 8 9 10 11	Qiū fēn	THOOUT 1778	8 9 10 11 12 13 14	MASKARAM 2054
	25 26 27 28 ○ 30 1	9:31	39	2474093		11 12 13 14 15[c] 16 17			12 13 14 15[g] 16 17 18			15 16 17[b] 18 19 20 21	
OCTOBER 2061	2 3 4 5 ◑ 7 8	2:56	40	2474100		18 19 20 21 22 23 24			19 20 21 22 23 24 25	Hán lù		22 23 24 25 26 27 28	
	9 10 11 12 ● 14 15	10:40	41	2474107		25 26 27 28 29 30 1	Fri 3h39m3p		26 27 28 29 1* 2 3			29 30 1 2 3 4 5	
	16 17 18 19 20 ◐ 22	14:23	42	2474114	HESHVAN 5822	2 3 4 5 6 7 8		MONTH 9 Xīn-Sì	4 5 6 7 8 9[h] 10		PAOPE 1778	6 7 8 9 10 11 12	ṬEQEMT 2054
	23 24 25 26 27 ○ 29	20:11	43	2474121		9 10 11 12 13 14 15			11 12 13 14 15 16 17	Shuāng jiàng		13 14 15 16 17 18 19	
	30 31 1 2 3 ◑ 5	10:51	44	2474128		16 17 18 19 20 21 22			18 19 20 21 22 23 24			20 21 22 23 24 25 26	
NOVEMBER 2061	6 7 8 9 10 11 ●	3:39	45	2474135		23 24 25 26 27 28 29			25 26 27 28 29 30 1	Lì dōng		27 28 29 30 1 2 3	
	13 14 15 16 17 18 19		46	2474142		30 1 2 3 4 5 6	Sat 16h23m4p	MONTH 10 Xīn-Sì	2 3 4 5 6 7 8		ATHŌR 1778	4 5 6 7 8 9 10	HEDĀR 2054
	◐ 21 22 23 24 25 26	8:10	47	2474149	KISLEV 5822	7 8 9 10 11 12 13			9 10 11 12 13 14 15	Xiǎo xuě		11 12 13 14 15 16 17	
	○ 28 29 30 1 2 ◑	6:31 22:10	48	2474156		14 15 16 17 18 19 20			16 17 18 19 20 21 22			18 19 20 21 22 23 24	
DECEMBER 2061	4 5 6 7 8 9 10		49	2474163		21 22[d] 23 24 25[e] 26[e] 27[e]			23 24 25 26 27 28 29	Dà xuě		25 26 27 28 29 30 1	
	● 12 13 14 15 16 17	22:31	50	2474170		28[e] 29[e] 30[e] 1[e] 2[e] 3 4	Mon 5h7m5p	MONTH 11 Xīn-Sì	30 1* 2 3 4 5 6		KOIAK 1778	2 3 4 5 6 7 8	TĀKHŚĀŚ 2054
	18 ◐ 20 21[e] 22 23 24	23:57	51	2474177	TEVETH 5822	5 6 7 8 9 10 11			7 8 9 10[i] 11 12 13	Dōng zhì		9 10 11 12 13 14 15	
	25 ○ 27 28 29 30 31	16:5	52	2474184		12 13 14 15 16 17 18			14 15 16 17 18 19 20			16 17 18 19 20 21 22	

[a]New Year
[b]Spring (2:24)
[c]Summer (19:31)
[d]Autumn (11:29)
[e]Winter (8:47)
● New moon
◐ First quarter moon
○ Full moon
◑ Last quarter moon

‡Leap year
[a]New Year
[b]Yom Kippur
[c]Sukkot
[d]Winter starts
[e]Ḥanukkah
[f]Purim
[g]Passover
[h]Shavuot
[i]Fast of Av

‡Leap year
[a]New Year (4759, Snake)
[b]Lantern Festival
[c]Qīngmíng
[d]Dragon Festival
[e]Qīqiǎo
[f]Hungry Ghosts
[g]Mid-Autumn Festival
[h]Double-Ninth Festival
[i]Dōngzhì
*Start of 60-name cycle

[a]New Year
[b]Building of the Cross
[c]Christmas
[d]Jesus's Circumcision
[e]Epiphany
[f]Easter
[g]Mary's Announcement
[h]Jesus's Transfiguration

PERSIAN (ASTRONOMICAL) 1439/1440

Month	Sun	Mon	Tue	Wed	Thu	Fri	Sat
DEY 1439	6	7	8	9	10	11	12
	13	14	15	16	17	18	19
	20	21	22	23	24	25	26
	27	28	29	30	*1*	2	3
BAHMAN 1439	4	5	6	7	8	9	10
	11	12	13	14	15	16	17
	18	19	20	21	22	23	24
	25	26	27	28	29	30	*1*
ESFAND 1439	2	3	4	5	6	7	8
	9	10	11	12	13	14	15
	16	17	18	19	20	21	22
	23	24	25	26	27	28	29
FARVARDĪN 1440	*1*[a]	2	3	4	5	6	7
	8	9	10	11	12	13[b]	14
	15	16	17	18	19	20	21
	22	23	24	25	26	27	28
	29	30	31	*1*	2	3	4
ORDIBEHEŠT 1440	5	6	7	8	9	10	11
	12	13	14	15	16	17	18
	19	20	21	22	23	24	25
	26	27	28	29	30	31	*1*
XORDĀD 1440	2	3	4	5	6	7	8
	9	10	11	12	13	14	15
	16	17	18	19	20	21	22
	23	24	25	26	27	28	29
	30	31	*1*	2	3	4	5
TĪR 1440	6	7	8	9	10	11	12
	13	14	15	16	17	18	19
	20	21	22	23	24	25	26
	27	28	29	30	31	*1*	2
MORDĀD 1440	3	4	5	6	7	8	9
	10	11	12	13	14	15	16
	17	18	19	20	21	22	23
	24	25	26	27	28	29	30
	31	*1*	2	3	4	5	6
SHAHRĪVAR 1440	7	8	9	10	11	12	13
	14	15	16	17	18	19	20
	21	22	23	24	25	26	27
	28	29	30	31	*1*	2	3
MEHR 1440	4	5	6	7	8	9	10
	11	12	13	14	15	16	17
	18	19	20	21	22	23	24
	25	26	27	28	29	30	*1*
ĀBĀN 1440	2	3	4	5	6	7	8
	9	10	11	12	13	14	15
	16	17	18	19	20	21	22
	23	24	25	26	27	28	29
	30	*1*	2	3	4	5	6
ĀZAR 1440	7	8	9	10	11	12	13
	14	15	16	17	18	19	20
	21	22	23	24	25	26	27
	28	29	30	*1*	2	3	4
DEY 1440	5	6	7	8	9	10	11

[a]New Year
[b]Sizdeh Bedar

HINDU LUNAR 2117/2118‡

Month	Sun	Mon	Tue	Wed	Thu	Fri	Sat
PAUSHA 2117	4	5	6	7	8	9	10
	11	12	13	14	**15**	17	18
	19	20	21	22	*22*	23	24
	25	26	27	28	29	30	1
MĀGHA 2117	2	3	4	5	6	7	8
	9	11	12	13	14	15	16
	17	18	19	20	21	22	23
	24	*24*	25	26	27	28[h]	29
PHĀLGUNA 2117	30	1	2	**3**	5	6	7
	8	9	10	11	12	13	14
	15[i]	16	17	18	19	20	21
	22	23	24	25	26	27	28
CHAITRA 2118	29	30	1[a]	2	3	4	5
	6	**7**	9[b]	10	11	12	13
	14	15	16	17	18	*18*	19
	20	21	22	23	24	25	26
	27	28	29	30	**1**	3	4
VAIŚĀKHA 2118	5	6	7	8	9	10	11
	12	13	14	15	16	17	18
	19	20	21	22	23	24	25
	26	27	28	29	30	1	2
JYAISHTHA 2118	3	**4**	6	7	8	9	10
	11	12	13	*13*	14	15	16
	17	18	19	20	21	22	23
	24	25	26	**27**	29	30	1
LEAP ĀSHĀDHA 2118	2	3	4	5	6	7	8
	9	10	11	12	13	14	15
	16	17	18	19	20	21	22
	23	24	25	26	27	28	29
	30	2	3	4	5	6	7
ĀSHĀDHA 2118	8	9	10	*10*	11	12	13
	14	15	16	17	18	19	20
	21	22	**23**	25	26	27	28
	29	30	1	2	3	4	5
ŚRĀVAṆA 2118	6	7	8	9	10	11	12
	13	14	15	16	17	18	19
	20	21	22	23[c]	24	25	**26**
	28	29	30	1	2	3	4[d]
BHĀDRAPADA 2118	5	6	*6*	7	8	9	10
	11	12	13	14	15	16	17
	18	**19**	21	22	23	24	25
	26	27	28	29	30	1	2
ĀŚVINA 2118	3	4	5	6	7	8[e]	9[e]
	10[e]	11	12	13	14	15	16
	17	18	19	20	21	22	23
	24	26	27	28	29	30	*30*
KĀRTTIKA 2118	1[f]	2	3	4	5	6	7
	8	9	10	11	12	13	14
	15	16	**17**	19	20	21	22
	23	24	25	26	27	28	29
MĀRGAŚĪRA 2118	30	1	2	3	*3*	4	5
	6	7	8	9	10	**11**[g]	13
	14	15	16	17	18	19	20

‡Leap year
[a]New Year (Vṛisha)
[b]Birthday of Rāma
[c]Birthday of Krishna
[d]Ganēśa Chaturthī
[e]Dashara
[f]Diwali
[g]Birthday of Vishnu
[h]Night of Śiva
[i]Holi

HINDU SOLAR 1982/1983

Month	Sun	Mon	Tue	Wed	Thu	Fri	Sat
PAUSHA 1982	11	12	13	14	15	16	17
	18	19	20	21	22	23	24
	25	26	27	28	29	1[b]	2
MĀGHA 1982	3	4	5	6	7	8	9
	10	11	12	13	14	15	16
	17	18	19	20	21	22	23
	24	25	26	27	28	29	30
PHĀLGUNA 1982	1	2	3	4	5	6	7
	8	9	10	11	12	13	14
	15	16	17	18	19	20	21
	22	23	24	25	26	27	28
	29	1	2	3	4	5	6
CHAITRA 1982	7	8	9	10	11	12	13
	14	15	16	17	18	19	20
	21	22	23	24	25	26	27
	28	29	30	31	1[a]	2	3
VAIŚĀKHA 1983	4	5	6	7	8	9	10
	11	12	13	14	15	16	17
	18	19	20	21	22	23	24
	25	26	27	28	29	30	31
JYAISHTHA 1983	1	2	3	4	5	6	7
	8	9	10	11	12	13	14
	15	16	17	18	19	20	21
	22	23	24	25	26	27	28
	29	30	31	1	2	3	4
ĀSHĀDHA 1983	5	6	7	8	9	10	11
	12	13	14	15	16	17	18
	19	20	21	22	23	24	25
	26	27	28	29	30	31	32
ŚRĀVAṆA 1983	1	2	3	4	5	6	7
	8	9	10	11	12	13	14
	15	16	17	18	19	20	21
	22	23	24	25	26	27	28
	29	30	31	1	2	3	4
BHĀDRAPADA 1983	5	6	7	8	9	10	11
	12	13	14	15	16	17	18
	19	20	21	22	23	24	25
	26	27	28	29	30	31	1
ĀŚVINA 1983	2	3	4	5	6	7	8
	9	10	11	12	13	14	15
	16	17	18	19	20	21	22
	23	24	25	26	27	28	29
	30	31	1	2	3	4	5
KĀRTTIKA 1983	6	7	8	9	10	11	12
	13	14	15	16	17	18	19
	20	21	22	23	24	25	26
	27	28	29	30	1	2	3
MĀRGAŚĪRA 1983	4	5	6	7	8	9	10
	11	12	13	14	15	16	17
	18	19	20	21	22	23	24
	25	26	27	28	29	1	2
PAUSHA 1983	3	4	5	6	7	8	9
	10	11	12	13	14	15	16

[a]New Year (Manmatha)
[b]Pongal

ISLAMIC (ASTRONOMICAL) 1483‡/1484

Month	Sun	Mon	Tue	Wed	Thu	Fri	Sat
SHA'BĀN 1483	2	3	4	5	6	7	8
	9	10	11	12	13	14	15
	16	17	18	19	20	21	22
	23	24	25	26	27	28	*29*
RAMAḌĀN 1483	1[e]	2	3	4	5	6	7
	8	9	10	11	12	13	14
	15	16	17	18	19	20	21
	22	23	24	25	26	27	28
SHAWWĀL 1483	29	*1*[f]	2	3	4	5	6
	7	8	9	10	11	12	13
	14	15	16	17	18	19	20
	21	22	23	24	25	26	27
DHU AL-QA'DA 1483	28	29	*30*	1	2	3	4
	5	6	7	8	9	10	11
	12	13	14	15	16	17	18
	19	20	21	22	23	24	25
	26	27	28	29	*1*	2	3
DHU AL-ḤIJJA 1483	4	5	6	7	8	9	10[g]
	11	12	13	14	15	16	17
	18	19	20	21	22	23	24
	25	26	27	28	29	30	*1*[a]
MUḤARRAM 1484	2	3	4	5	6	7	8
	9	10[b]	11	12	13	14	15
	16	17	18	19	20	21	22
	23	24	25	26	27	28	29
ṢAFAR 1484	1	2	3	4	5	6	7
	8	9	10	11	12	13	14
	15	16	17	18	19	20	21
	22	23	24	25	26	27	28
RABĪ' I 1484	29	1	2	3	4	5	6
	7	8	9	10	11	12[c]	13
	14	15	16	17	18	19	20
	21	22	23	24	25	26	27
RABĪ' II 1484	28	29	30	1	2	3	4
	5	6	7	8	9	10	11
	12	13	14	15	16	17	18
	19	20	21	22	23	24	25
	26	27	28	29	30	*1*	2
JUMĀDĀ I 1484	3	4	5	6	7	8	9
	10	11	12	13	14	15	16
	17	18	19	20	21	22	23
	24	25	26	27	28	29	30
JUMĀDĀ II 1484	*1*	2	3	4	5	6	7
	8	9	10	11	12	13	14
	15	16	17	18	19	20	21
	22	23	24	25	26	27	28
RAJAB 1484	29	*1*	2	3	4	5	6
	7	8	9	10	11	12	13
	14	15	16	17	18	19	20
	21	22	23	24	25	26	27[d]
SHA'BĀN 1484	28	29	30	*1*	2	3	4
	5	6	7	8	9	10	11
	12	13	14	15	16	17	18

‡Leap year
[a]New Year
[b]'Ashūrā'
[c]Prophet's Birthday
[d]Ascent of the Prophet
[e]Start of Ramaḍān
[f]'Īd al-Fiṭr
[g]'Īd al-'Aḍḥā

GREGORIAN 2061

Julian (Sun)	Sun	Mon	Tue	Wed	Thu	Fri	Sat	Month
Dec 13	*26*	27	28	29	30	31	1	
	2	3	4	5	6	7[a]	8	
Dec 27	*9*	10	11	12	13	14[b]	15	JANUARY 2061
	16	17	18	19	20	21	22	
Jan 10	*23*	24	25	26	27	28	29	
	30	31	1	2	3	4	5	
Jan 24	*6*	7	8	9	10	11	12	FEBRUARY 2061
	13	14	15	16	17	18	19	
Feb 7	*20*	21	22	23[c]	24	25	26	
	27[d]	28	1	2	3	4	5	
Feb 21	*6*	7	8	9	10	11	12	MARCH 2061
	13	14	15	16	17	18	19	
Mar 7	*20*	21	22	23	24	25	26	
	27	28	29	30	31	1	2	
Mar 21	*3*	4	5	6	7	8	9	APRIL 2061
	10[e]	11	12	13	14	15	16	
Apr 4	*17*	18	19	20	21	22	23	
	24	25	26	27	28	29	30	
Apr 18	*1*	2	3	4	5	6	7	
	8	9	10	11	12	13	14	MAY 2061
May 2	*15*	16	17	18	19	20	21	
	22	23	24	25	26	27	28	
May 16	*29*	30	31	1	2	3	4	
	5	6	7	8	9	10	11	JUNE 2061
May 30	*12*	13	14	15	16	17	18	
	19	20	21	22	23	24	25	
Jun 13	*26*	27	28	29	30	1	2	
	3	4	5	6	7	8	9	JULY 2061
Jun 27	*10*	11	12	13	14	15	16	
	17	18	19	20	21	22	23	
Jul 11	*24*	25	26	27	28	29	30	
	31	1	2	3	4	5	6	
Jul 25	*7*	8	9	10	11	12	13	AUGUST 2061
	14	15	16	17	18	19	20	
Aug 8	*21*	22	23	24	25	26	27	
	28	29	30	31	1	2	3	
Aug 22	*4*	5	6	7	8	9	10	SEPTEMBER 2061
	11	12	13	14	15	16	17	
Sep 5	*18*	19	20	21	22	23	24	
	25	26	27	28	29	30	1	
Sep 19	*2*	3	4	5	6	7	8	OCTOBER 2061
	9	10	11	12	13	14	15	
Oct 3	*16*	17	18	19	20	21	22	
	23	24	25	26	27	28	29	
Oct 17	*30*	31	1	2	3	4	5	
	6	7	8	9	10	11	12	NOVEMBER 2061
Oct 31	*13*	14	15	16	17	18	19	
	20	21	22	23	24	25	26	
Nov 14	*27*[g]	28	29	30	1	2	3	
	4	5	6	7	8	9	10	DECEMBER 2061
Nov 28	*11*	12	13	14	15	16	17	
	18	19	20	21	22	23	24	
Dec 12	*25*[h]	26	27	28	29	30	31	

[a]Orthodox Christmas
[b]Julian New Year
[c]Ash Wednesday
[d]Feast of Orthodoxy
[e]Easter (also Orthodox)
[g]Advent
[h]Christmas

2062

GREGORIAN 2062	Sun	Mon	Tue	Wed	Thu	Fri	Sat	Lunar Phases	ISO WEEK (Mon)	JULIAN DAY (Sun noon)
	1[a]	◑	3	4	5	6	7	13:20	1	2474191
JANUARY 2062	8	9	●	11	12	13	14	17:51	2	2474198
	15	16	17	◐	19	20	21	12:50	3	2474205
	22	23	24	○	26	27	28	3:36	4	2474212
	29	30	31	◑	2	3	4	7:42	5	2474219
	5	6	7	8	●	10	11	12:09	6	2474226
FEBRUARY 2062	12	13	14	15	◐	17	18	22:36	7	2474233
	19	20	21	22	○	24	25	15:07	8	2474240
	26	27	28	1	2	◑	4	3:48	9	2474247
	5	6	7	8	9	10	●	4:12	10	2474254
MARCH 2062	12	13	14	15	16	17	◐	5:56	11	2474261
	19	20[b]	21	22	23	24	○	3:34	12	2474268
	26	27	28	29	30	31	◑	23:53	13	2474275
	2	3	4	5	6	7	8		14	2474282
APRIL 2062	●	10	11	12	13	14	15	17:16	15	2474289
	◐	17	18	19	20	21	22	12:02	16	2474296
	○	24	25	26	27	28	29	16:56	17	2474303
	30	◑	2	3	4	5	6	18:32	18	2474310
	7	8	●	10	11	12	13	3:21	19	2474317
MAY 2062	14	◐	16	17	18	19	20	18:16	20	2474324
	21	22	○	24	25	26	27	7:02	21	2474331
	28	29	30	◑	1	2	3	10:43	22	2474338
	4	5	6	●	8	9	10	11:11	23	2474345
JUNE 2062	11	12	13	◐	15	16	17	1:52	24	2474352
	18	19	20	○[c]	22	23	24	21:42	25	2474359
	25	26	27	28	◑	30	1	23:53	26	2474366
	2	3	4	5	●	7	8	17:51	27	2474373
JULY 2062	9	10	11	12	◐	14	15	11:42	28	2474380
	16	17	18	19	20	○	22	12:46	29	2474387
	23	24	25	26	27	28	◑	10:03	30	2474394
	30	31	1	2	3	4	●	0:39	31	2474401
AUGUST 2062	6	7	8	9	10	11	◐	0:20	32	2474408
	13	14	15	16	17	18	19		33	2474415
	○	21	22	23	24	25	26	3:54	34	2474422
	◑	28	29	30	31	1	2	17:47	35	2474429
	●	4	5	6	7	8	9	8:41	36	2474436
SEPTEMBER 2062	◐	11	12	13	14	15	16	15:58	37	2474443
	17	○	19	20	21	22[d]	23	18:35	38	2474450
	24	25	◑	27	28	29	30	0:10	39	2474457
	1	●	3	4	5	6	7	18:48	40	2474464
OCTOBER 2062	8	9	◐	11	12	13	14	10:26	41	2474471
	15	16	17	○	19	20	21	8:17	42	2474478
	22	23	24	◑	26	27	28	6:27	43	2474485
	29	30	31	●	2	3	4	7:31	44	2474492
	5	6	7	8	◐	10	11	6:49	45	2474499
NOVEMBER 2062	12	13	14	15	○	17	18	20:46	46	2474506
	19	20	21	22	◑	24	25	13:57	47	2474513
	26	27	28	29	●	1	2	23:00	48	2474520
	3	4	5	6	7	8	◐	3:27	49	2474527
DECEMBER 2062	10	11	12	13	14	15	○	8:16	50	2474534
	17	18	19	20	21[e]	◑	23	23:39	51	2474541
	24	25	26	27	28	29	●	16:56	52	2474548
	31	1	2	3	4	5	6		1	2474555

ISO WEEK	HEBREW 5822[‡]/5823	Sun	Mon	Tue	Wed	Thu	Fri	Sat	Molad
1	TEVETH 5822	19	20	21	22	23	24	25	
2		26	27	28	29	1	2	3	Tue 17h51m6p
3	SHEVAT 5822	4	5	6	7	8	9	10	
4		11	12	13	14	15	16	17	
5		18	19	20	21	22	23	24	
6		25	26	27	28	29	30	1	Thu 6h35m7p
7	ADAR I 5822	2	3	4	5	6	7	8	
8		9	10	11	12	13	14	15	
9		16	17	18	19	20	21	22	
10		23	24	25	26	27	28	29	
11		30	1	2	3	4	5	6	Fri 19h19m8p
12	ADAR II 5822	7	8	9	10	11	12	13	
13		14[f]	15	16	17	18	19	20	
14		21	22	23	24	25	26	27	
15		28	29	1	2	3	4	5	Sun 8h3m9p
16	NISAN 5822	6	7	8	9	10	11	12	
17		13	14	15[g]	16	17	18	19	
18		20	21	22	23	24	25	26	
19		27	28	29	30	1	2	3	Mon 20h47m10p
20	IYAR 5822	4	5	6	7	8	9	10	
21		11	12	13	14	15	16	17	
22		18	19	20	21	22	23	24	
23		25	26	27	28	29	1	2	Wed 9h31m11p
24	SIVAN 5822	3	4	5	6[h]	7	8	9	
25		10	11	12	13	14	15	16	
26		17	18	19	20	21	22	23	
27		24	25	26	27	28	29	30	
28		1	2	3	4	5	6	7	Thu 22h15m12p
29	TAMMUZ 5822	8	9	10	11	12	13	14	
30		15	16	17	18	19	20	21	
31		22	23	24	25	26	27	28	
32		29	1	2	3	4	5	6	Sat 10h59m13p
33	AV 5822	7	8	9[i]	10	11	12	13	
34		14	15	16	17	18	19	20	
35		21	22	23	24	25	26	27	
36		28	29	30	1	2	3	4	Sun 23h43m14p
37	ELUL 5822	5	6	7	8	9	10	11	
38		12	13	14	15	16	17	18	
39		19	20	21	22	23	24	25	
40		26	27	28	29	1[a]	2[a]	3	Tue 12h27m15p
41	TISHRI 5823	4	5	6	7	8	9	10[b]	
42		11	12	13	14	15[c]	16	17	
43		18	19	20	21	22	23	24	
44		25	26	27	28	29	30	1	Thu 1h11m16p
45	ḤESHVAN 5823	2	3	4	5	6	7	8	
46		9	10	11	12	13	14	15	
47		16	17	18	19	20	21	22	
48		23	24	25	26	27	28	29	
49		1	2	3[d]	4	5	6	7	Fri 13h55m17p
50	KISLEV 5823	8	9	10	11	12	13	14	
51		15	16	17	18	19	20	21	
52		22	23	24	25[e]	26[e]	27[e]	28[e]	
1		29[e]	30[e]	1[e]	2[e]	3	4	5	Sun 2h40m0p

ISO WEEK	CHINESE Xīn-Sì[‡]/Rén-Wǔ	Sun	Mon	Tue	Wed	Thu	Fri	Sat	Solar Term
1	MONTH 11 Xīn-Sì	21	22	23	24	*25*	26	27	*Xiǎo hán*
2		28	29	30	1	2	3	4	
3	MONTH 12 Xīn-Sì	5	6	7	8	9	***10***	11	**Dà hán**
4		12	13	14	15	16	17	18	
5		19	20	21	22	23	*24*	25	*Lì chūn*
6		26	27	28	29	1[a]	2*	3	
7	MONTH 1 Rén-Wǔ	4	5	6	7	8	9	***10***	**Yǔ shuǐ**
8		11	12	13	14	15[b]	16	17	
9		18	19	20	21	22	23	24	
10		*25*	26	27	28	29	30	1	*Jīng zhé*
11	MONTH 2 Rén-Wǔ	2	3	4	5	6	7	8	
12		9	***10***	11	12	13	14	15	**Chūn fēn**
13		16	17	18	19	20	21	22	
14		23	24	*25*[c]	26	27	28	29	*Qīng míng*
15		30	1	2*	3	4	5	6	
16	MONTH 3 Rén-Wǔ	7	8	9	10	***11***	12	13	**Gǔ yǔ**
17		14	15	16	17	18	19	20	
18		21	22	23	24	25	*26*	27	*Lì xià*
19		28	29	1	2	3	4	5	
20	MONTH 4 Rén-Wǔ	6	7	8	9	10	11	12	
21		***13***	14	15	16	17	18	19	**Xiǎo mǎn**
22		20	21	22	23	24	25	26	
23		27	*28*	29	1	2	3	4*	*Máng zhòng*
24	MONTH 5 Rén-Wǔ	5[d]	6	7	8	9	10	11	
25		12	13	14	***15***	16	17	18	**Xià zhì**
26		19	20	21	22	23	24	25	
27		26	27	28	29	30	*1*	2	*Xiǎo shǔ*
28	MONTH 6 Rén-Wǔ	3	4	5	6	7	8	9	
29		10	11	12	13	14	15	***16***	**Dà shǔ**
30		17	18	19	20	21	22	23	
31		24	25	26	27	28	29	1	
32	MONTH 7 Rén-Wǔ	2	*3*	4	5*	6	7[e]	8	*Lì qiū*
33		9	10	11	12	13	14	15[f]	
34		16	17	18	***19***	20	21	22	**Chǔ shǔ**
35		23	24	25	26	27	28	29	
36		1	2	3	4	*5*	6	7	*Bái lù*
37	MONTH 8 Rén-Wǔ	8	9	10	11	12	13	14	
38		15[g]	16	17	18	19	20	***21***	**Qiū fēn**
39		22	23	24	25	26	27	28	
40		29	30	1	2	3	4	5	
41	MONTH 9 Rén-Wǔ	*6**	7	8	9[h]	10	11	12	*Hán lù*
42		13	14	15	16	17	18	19	
43		20	***21***	22	23	24	25	26	**Shuāng jiàng**
44		27	28	29	1	2	3	4	
45	MONTH 10 Rén-Wǔ	5	6	*7*	8	9	10	11	*Lì dōng*
46		12	13	14	15	16	17	18	
47		19	20	21	***22***	23	24	25	**Xiǎo xuě**
48		26	27	28	29	30	1	2	
49	MONTH 11 Rén-Wǔ	3	4	5	6	*7**	8	9	*Dà xuě*
50		10	11	12	13	14	15	16	
51		17	18	19	20	***21***[i]	22	23	**Dōng zhì**
52		24	25	26	27	28	29	30	
1		1	2	3	4	5	*6*	7	*Xiǎo hán*

ISO WEEK	COPTIC 1778/1779[‡]	Sun	Mon	Tue	Wed	Thu	Fri	Sat	ETHIOPIC 2054/2055[‡]
1	KOIAK 1778	23	24	25	26	27	28	29[c]	TĀKHŚĀŚ 2054
2		30	1	2	3	4	5	6[d]	
3	TÔBE 1778	7	8	9	10	11[e]	12	13	ṬER 2054
4		14	15	16	17	18	19	20	
5		21	22	23	24	25	26	27	
6		28	29	30	1	2	3	4	
7	MESHIR 1778	5	6	7	8	9	10	11	
8		12	13	14	15	16	17	18	YAKĀTIT 2054
9		19	20	21	22	23	24	25	
10		26	27	28	29	30	1	2	
11	PAREMOTEP 1778	3	4	5	6	7	8	9	
12		10	11	12	13	14	15	16	MAGĀBIT 2054
13		17	18	19	20	21	22	23	
14		24	25	26	27	28	29	30	
15		1	2	3	4	5	6	7	
16	PARMOUTE 1778	8	9	10	11	12	13	14	MIYĀZYĀ 2054
17		15	16	17	18	19	20	21	
18		22[f]	23	24	25	26	27	28	
19		29[g]	30	1	2	3	4	5	
20	PASHONS 1778	6	7	8	9	10	11	12	GENBOT 2054
21		13	14	15	16	17	18	19	
22		20	21	22	23	24	25	26	
23		27	28	29	30	1	2	3	
24	PAÔNE 1778	4	5	6	7	8	9	10	SANĒ 2054
25		11	12	13	14	15	16	17	
26		18	19	20	21	22	23	24	
27		25	26	27	28	29	30	1	
28	EPÊP 1778	2	3	4	5	6	7	8	
29		9	10	11	12	13	14	15	ḤAMLĒ 2054
30		16	17	18	19	20	21	22	
31		23	24	25	26	27	28	29	
32		30	1	2	3	4	5	6	
33	MESORÊ 1778	7	8	9	10	11	12	13[h]	NAHASĒ 2054
34		14	15	16	17	18	19	20	
35		21	22	23	24	25	26	27	
36	EPAG. 1778	28	29	30	1	2	3	4	PĀG. 2054
37		5	1[a]	2	3	4	5	6	
38	THOOUT 1779	7	8	9	10	11	12	13	MASKARAM 2055
39		14	15	16	17[b]	18	19	20	
40		21	22	23	24	25	26	27	
41		28	29	30	1	2	3	4	
42	PAOPE 1779	5	6	7	8	9	10	11	ṬEQEMT 2055
43		12	13	14	15	16	17	18	
44		19	20	21	22	23	24	25	
45		26	27	28	29	30	1	2	
46	ATHÔR 1779	3	4	5	6	7	8	9	ḪEDĀR 2055
47		10	11	12	13	14	15	16	
48		17	18	19	20	21	22	23	
49		24	25	26	27	28	29	30	
50		1	2	3	4	5	6	7	
51	KOIAK 1779	8	9	10	11	12	13	14	TĀKHŚĀŚ 2055
52		15	16	17	18	19	20	21	
1		22	23	24	25	26	27	28	

[a]New Year
[b]Spring (8:06)
[c]Summer (1:10)
[d]Autumn (17:18)
[e]Winter (14:41)
● New moon
◐ First quarter moon
○ Full moon
◑ Last quarter moon

[‡]Leap year
[a]New Year
[b]Yom Kippur
[c]Sukkot
[d]Winter starts
[e]Ḥanukkah
[f]Purim
[g]Passover
[h]Shavuot
[i]Fast of Av

[‡]Leap year
[a]New Year (4760, Horse)
[b]Lantern Festival
[c]Qīngmíng
[d]Dragon Festival
[e]Qīqiǎo
[f]Hungry Ghosts
[g]Mid-Autumn Festival
[h]Double-Ninth Festival
[i]Dōngzhì
*Start of 60-name cycle

[‡]Leap year
[a]New Year
[b]Building of the Cross
[c]Christmas
[d]Jesus's Circumcision
[e]Epiphany
[f]Easter
[g]Mary's Announcement
[h]Jesus's Transfiguration

	PERSIAN (ASTRONOMICAL) 1440/1441‡							HINDU LUNAR 2118‡/2119								HINDU SOLAR 1983/1984								ISLAMIC (ASTRONOMICAL) 1484/1485‡							Julian (Sun)	GREGORIAN 2062							
	Sun	Mon	Tue	Wed	Thu	Fri	Sat		Sun	Mon	Tue	Wed	Thu	Fri	Sat		Sun	Mon	Tue	Wed	Thu	Fri	Sat		Sun	Mon	Tue	Wed	Thu	Fri	Sat		Sun	Mon	Tue	Wed	Thu	Fri	Sat	
DEY 1440	12	13	14	15	16	17	18	MĀRGAŚIRA 2118	21	22	23	24	25	26	27		17	18	19	20	21	22	23	SHA'BĀN 1484	19	20	21	22	23	24	25	Dec 19	1	2	3	4	5	6	7[a]	
	19	20	21	22	23	24	25		28	29	30	1	2	3	4	PAUSHA 1983	24	25	26	27	28	29	1[b]		26	27	28	29	1[e]	2	3		8	9	10	11	12	13	14[b]	JANUARY 2062
	26	27	28	29	30	1	2	PAUSHA 2118	5	6	7	8	9	10	11		2	3	4	5	6	7	8	RAMAḌĀN 1484	4	5	6	7	8	9	10	Jan 2	15	16	17	18	19	20	21	
BAHMAN 1440	3	4	5	6	7	8	9		12	13	14	15	**16**	18	19	MĀGHA 1983	9	10	11	12	13	14	15		11	12	13	14	15	16	17		22	23	24	25	26	27	28	
	10	11	12	13	14	15	16		20	21	22	23	24	25	25		16	17	18	19	20	21	22		18	19	20	21	22	23	24	Jan 16	29	30	31	1	2	3	4	
	17	18	19	20	21	22	23		26	27	28	29	30	1	2		23	24	25	26	27	28	29		25	26	27	28	29	30	1[f]		5	6	7	8[c]	9	10	11	FEBRUARY 2062
	24	25	26	27	28	29	30	MĀGHA 2118	3	4	5	6	7	8	9		30	1	2	3	4	5	6	SHAWWĀL 1484	2	3	4	5	6	7	8	Jan 30	12	13	14	15	16	17	18	
	1	2	3	4	5	6	7		**10**	12	13	14	15	16	17	PHĀLGUNA 1983	7	8	9	10	11	12	13		9	10	11	12	13	14	15		19	20	21	22	23	24	25	
ESFAND 1440	8	9	10	11	12	13	14		18	19	20	21	22	23	24		14	15	16	17	18	19	20		16	17	18	19	20	21	22	Feb 13	26	27	28	1	2	3	4	
	15	16	17	18	19	20	21		25	26	27	27	28[h]	29	30		21	22	23	24	25	26	27		23	24	25	26	27	28	29		5	6	7	8	9	10	11	MARCH 2062
	22	23	24	25	26	27	28		1	2	**3**	5	6	7	8		28	29	30	1	2	3	4		1	2	3	4	5	6	7	Feb 27	12	13	14	15	16	17	18	
	29	1[a]	2*	3	4	5	6	PHĀLGUNA 2118	9	10	11	12	13	14	15[i]	CHAITRA 1983	5	6	7	8	9	10	11	DHU AL-QA'DA 1484	8	9	10	11	12	13	14		19[d]	20	21	22	23	24	25	
FARVARDĪN 1441	7	8	9	10	11	12	13[b]		16	17	18	19	20	21	22		12	13	14	15	16	17	18		15	16	17	18	19	20	21	Mar 13	26[e]	27	28	29	30	31	1	
	14	15	16	17	18	19	20		23	24	25	26	27	28	29		19	20	21	22	23	24	25		22	23	24	25	26	27	28		2	3	4	5	6	7	8	APRIL 2062
	21	22	23	24	25	26	27		30	1[a]	2	3	4	5	6		26	27	28	29	30	1[a]	2		29	30	1	2	3	4	5	Mar 27	9	10	11	12	13	14	15	
	28	29	30	31	1	2	3	CHAITRA 2119	7	**8**[b]	10	11	12	13	14	VAIŚĀKHA 1984	3	4	5	6	7	8	9	DHU AL-ḤIJJA 1484	6	7	8	9	10[g]	11	12		16	17	18	19	20	21	22	
ORDĪBEHEŠT 1441	4	5	6	7	8	9	10		15	16	17	18	19	20	21		10	11	12	13	14	15	16		13	14	15	16	17	18	19	Apr 10	23	24	25	26	27	28	29	
	11	12	13	14	15	16	17		21	22	23	24	25	26	27		17	18	19	20	21	22	23		20	21	22	23	24	25	26		30[f]	1	2	3	4	5	6	
	18	19	20	21	22	23	24		28	29	30	**1**	3	4	5		24	25	26	27	28	29	30		27	28	29	1[a]	2	3	4	Apr 24	7	8	9	10	11	12	13	MAY 2062
	25	26	27	28	29	30	31	VAIŚĀKHA 2119	6	7	8	9	10	11	12		31	1	2	3	4	5	6	MUḤARRAM 1485	5	6	7	8	9	10[b]	11		14	15	16	17	18	19	20	
	1	2	3	4	5	6	7		13	14	15	16	17	18	19	JYAISHTHA 1984	7	8	9	10	11	12	13		12	13	14	15	16	17	18	May 8	21	22	23	24	25	26	27	
XORDĀD 1441	8	9	10	11	12	13	14		20	21	22	23	24	25	26		14	15	16	17	18	19	20		19	20	21	22	23	24	25		28	29	30	31	1	2	3	
	15	16	17	18	19	20	21		27	28	29	30	1	2	3		21	22	23	24	25	26	27		26	27	28	29	1	2	3	May 22	4	5	6	7	8	9	10	JUNE 2062
	22	23	24	25	26	27	28	JYAISHTHA 2119	**4**	6	7	8	9	10	11		28	29	30	31	1	2	3	ṢAFAR 1485	4	5	6	7	8	9	10		11	12	13	14	15	16	17	
	29	30	31	1	2	3	4		12	13	14	15	16	17	17		4	5	6	7	8	9	10		11	12	13	14	15	16	17	Jun 5	18	19	20	21	22	23	24	
	5	6	7	8	9	10	11		18	19	20	21	22	23	24	ĀSHĀDHA 1984	11	12	13	14	15	16	17		18	19	20	21	22	23	24		25	26	27	28	29	30	1	
TĪR 1441	12	13	14	15	16	17	18		25	26	**27**	29	30	1	2		18	19	20	21	22	23	24		25	26	27	28	29	30	1	Jun 19	2	3	4	5	6	7	8	
	19	20	21	22	23	24	25	ĀSHĀDHA 2119	3	4	5	6	7	8	9		25	26	27	28	29	30	31	RABĪ' I 1485	2	3	4	5	6	7	8		9	10	11	12	13	14	15	JULY 2062
	26	27	28	29	30	31	1		10	11	12	13	14	15	16		32	1	2	3	4	5	6		9	10	11	12[c]	13	14	15	Jul 3	16	17	18	19	20	21	22	
	2	3	4	5	6	7	8		17	18	19	20	21	22	23	ŚRĀVAṆA 1984	7	8	9	10	11	12	13		16	17	18	19	20	21	22		23	24	25	26	27	28	29	
MORDĀD 1441	9	10	11	12	13	14	15		24	25	26	27	28	29	**30**		14	15	16	17	18	19	20		23	24	25	26	27	28	29	Jul 17	30	31	1	2	3	4	5	
	16	17	18	19	20	21	22		2	3	4	5	6	7	8		21	22	23	24	25	26	27		1	2	3	4	5	6	7		6	7	8	9	10	11	12	AUGUST 2062
	23	24	25	26	27	28	29	ŚRĀVAṆA 2119	9	10	11	12	13	14	14		28	29	30	31	32	1	2	RABĪ' II 1485	8	9	10	11	12	13	14	Jul 31	13	14	15	16	17	18	19	
	30	31	1	2	3	4	5		15	16	17	18	19	20	21		3	4	5	6	7	8	9		15	16	17	18	19	20	21		20	21	22	23	24	25	26	
SHAHRĪVAR 1441	6	7	8	9	10	11	12		22	**23**[c]	25	26	27	28	29	BHĀDRAPADA 1984	10	11	12	13	14	15	16		22	23	24	25	26	27	28	Aug 14	27	28	29	30	31	1	2	
	13	14	15	16	17	18	19		30	1	2	3[d]	4	5	6		17	18	19	20	21	22	23		29	30	1	2	3	4	5		3	4	5	6	7	8	9	SEPTEMBER 2062
	20	21	22	23	24	25	26	BHĀDRAPADA 2119	7	8	9	10	11	12	13		24	25	26	27	28	29	30	JUMĀDĀ I 1485	6	7	8	9	10	11	12	Aug 28	10	11	12	13	14	15	16	
	27	28	29	30	31	1	2		14	15	16	17	18	19	20		31	1	2	3	4	5	6		13	14	15	16	17	18	19		17	18	19	20	21	22	23	
	3	4	5	6	7	8	9		21	22	23	24	25	**26**	28	ĀŚVINA 1984	7	8	9	10	11	12	13		20	21	22	23	24	25	26	Sep 11	24	25	26	27	28	29	30	
MEHR 1441	10	11	12	13	14	15	16		29	30	1	2	3	4	5		14	15	16	17	18	19	20		27	28	29	30	1	2	3		1	2	3	4	5	6	7	
	17	18	19	20	21	22	23	ĀŚVINA 2119	6	7	8[e]	9[e]	10[e]	10[e]	11		21	22	23	24	25	26	27	JUMĀDĀ II 1485	4	5	6	7	8	9	10	Sep 25	8	9	10	11	12	13	14	OCTOBER 2062
	24	25	26	27	28	29	30		12	13	14	15	16	17	18		28	29	30	1	2	3	4		11	12	13	14	15	16	17		15	16	17	18	19	20	21	
	1	2	3	4	5	6	7		19	**20**	22	23	24	25	26	KĀRTTIKA 1984	5	6	7	8	9	10	11		18	19	20	21	22	23	24	Oct 9	22	23	24	25	26	27	28	
ĀBĀN 1441	8	9	10	11	12	13	14		27	28	29	30	1[f]	2	3		12	13	14	15	16	17	18		25	26	27	28	29	1	2		29	30	31	1	2	3	4	
	15	16	17	18	19	20	21	KĀRTTIKA 2119	4	5	6	7	8	9	10		19	20	21	22	23	24	25	RAJAB 1485	3	4	5	6	7	8	9	Oct 23	5	6	7	8	9	10	11	NOVEMBER 2062
	22	23	24	25	26	27	28		11	12	13	14	15	16	17		26	27	28	29	30	1	2		10	11	12	13	14	15	16		12	13	14	15	16	17	18	
	29	30	1	2	3	4	5		18	19	20	21	22	23	**24**	MĀRGAŚIRA 1984	3	4	5	6	7	8	9		17	18	19	20	21	22	23	Nov 6	19	20	21	22	23	24	25	
ĀZAR 1441	6	7	8	9	10	11	12		26	27	28	29	30	1	2		10	11	12	13	14	15	16		24	25	26	27[d]	28	29	30		26	27	28	29	30	1	2	
	13	14	15	16	17	18	19	MĀRGAŚIRA 2119	3	3	4	5	6	7	8		17	18	19	20	21	22	23	SHA'BĀN 1485	1	2	3	4	5	6	7	Nov 20	3[g]	4	5	6	7	8	9	DECEMBER 2062
	20	21	22	23	24	25	26		9	10	11[g]	12	13	14	15		24	25	26	27	28	29	1		8	9	10	11	12	13	14		10	11	12	13	14	15	16	
	27	28	29	30	1	2	3		16	17	**18**	20	21	22	23	PAUSHA 1984	2	3	4	5	6	7	8		15	16	17	18	19	20	21	Dec 4	17	18	19	20	21	22	23	
DEY 1441	4	5	6	7	8	9	10		24	25	26	27	28	29	30		9	10	11	12	13	14	15		22	23	24	25	26	27	28		24	25[h]	26	27	28	29	30	
	11	12	13	14	15	16	17		1	2	3	4	5	5	6		16	17	18	19	20	21	22		29	1	2	3	4	5	6	Dec 18	31	1	2	3	4	5	6	

Persian: ‡Leap year; [a]New Year (or next day); *Near New Year: 1′29″; [b]Sizdeh Bedar

Hindu Lunar: ‡Leap year; [a]New Year (Chitrabhānu); [b]Birthday of Rāma; [c]Birthday of Krishna; [d]Ganēśa Chaturthī; [e]Dashara; [f]Diwali; [g]Birthday of Vishnu; [h]Night of Śiva; [i]Holi

Hindu Solar: [a]New Year (Durmukha); [b]Pongal

Islamic: ‡Leap year; [a]New Year; [b]'Ashūrā'; [c]Prophet's Birthday; [d]Ascent of the Prophet; [e]Start of Ramaḍān; [f]'Īd al-Fiṭr; [g]'Īd al-'Aḍḥā

Gregorian: [a]Orthodox Christmas; [b]Julian New Year; [c]Ash Wednesday; [d]Feast of Orthodoxy; [e]Easter; [f]Orthodox Easter; [g]Advent; [h]Christmas

2063

Gregorian 2063

Month	Sun	Mon	Tue	Wed	Thu	Fri	Sat	Lunar Phases	ISO Week (Mon)	Julian Day (Sun noon)
	31	1[a]	2	3	4	5	6		1	2474555
JANUARY 2063	◐	8	9	10	11	12	13	22:14	2	2474562
	○	15	16	17	18	19	20	19:10	3	2474569
	◑	22	23	24	25	26	27	12:04	4	2474576
	28	●	30	31	1	2	3	12:22	5	2474583
FEBRUARY 2063	4	5	◐	7	8	9	10	13:36	6	2474590
	11	12	○	14	15	16	17	5:47	7	2474597
	18	19	◑	21	22	23	24	3:05	8	2474604
	25	26	27	●	1	2	3	7:36	9	2474611
MARCH 2063	4	5	6	7	◐	9	10	1:05	10	2474618
	11	12	13	○	15	16	17	16:13	11	2474625
	18	19	20[b]	◑	22	23	24	20:14	12	2474632
	25	26	27	28	29	●	31	0:48	13	2474639
	1	2	3	4	5	◐	7	9:16	14	2474646
APRIL 2063	8	9	10	11	12	○	14	2:33	15	2474653
	15	16	17	18	19	◑	21	14:41	16	2474660
	22	23	24	25	26	27	●	14:51	17	2474667
	29	30	1	2	3	4	◐	15:18	18	2474674
MAY 2063	6	7	8	9	10	11	○	13:10	19	2474681
	13	14	15	16	17	18	19		20	2474688
	◑	21	22	23	24	25	26	9:15	21	2474695
	27	●	29	30	31	1	2	1:46	22	2474702
JUNE 2063	◐	4	5	6	7	8	9	20:27	23	2474709
	10	○	12	13	14	15	16	0:42	24	2474716
	17	18	◑	20	21[c]	22	23	2:42	25	2474723
	24	25	●	27	28	29	30	10:24	26	2474730
	1	2	◐	4	5	6	7	1:59	27	2474737
JULY 2063	8	9	○	11	12	13	14	13:46	28	2474744
	15	16	17	◑	19	20	21	18:04	29	2474751
	22	23	24	●	26	27	28	17:54	30	2474758
	29	30	31	◐	2	3	4	9:08	31	2474765
AUGUST 2063	5	6	7	8	○	10	11	4:39	32	2474772
	12	13	14	15	16	◑	18	6:59	33	2474779
	19	20	21	22	23	●	25	1:16	34	2474786
	26	27	28	29	◐	31	1	19:03	35	2474793
	2	3	4	5	6	○	8	20:51	36	2474800
SEPTEMBER 2063	9	10	11	12	13	14	◑	17:43	37	2474807
	16	17	18	19	20	21	●[d]	9:20	38	2474814
	23	24	25	26	27	28	◐	8:38	39	2474821
	30	1	2	3	4	5	6		40	2474828
OCTOBER 2063	○	8	9	10	11	12	13	13:25	41	2474835
	14	◑	16	17	18	19	20	2:48	42	2474842
	●	22	23	24	25	26	27	18:45	43	2474849
	28	◐	30	31	1	2	3	2:12	44	2474856
NOVEMBER 2063	4	5	○	7	8	9	10	5:21	45	2474863
	11	12	◑	14	15	16	17	10:55	46	2474870
	18	19	●	21	22	23	24	6:08	47	2474877
	25	26	◐	28	29	30	1	22:58	48	2474884
	2	3	4	○	6	7	8	20:05	49	2474891
DECEMBER 2063	9	10	11	◑	13	14	15	18:48	50	2474898
	16	17	18	●	20	21[e]	22	20:02	51	2474905
	23	24	25	26	◐	28	29	20:56	52	2474912
	30	31	1	2	3	○	5	9:30	1	2474919

Hebrew 5823/5824

ISO Week	Month	Sun	Mon	Tue	Wed	Thu	Fri	Sat	Molad
1		29[e]	30[e]	1[e]	2[e]	3	4	5	Sun 2h40m0p
2	TEVETH 5823	6	7	8	9	10	11	12	
3		13	14	15	16	17	18	19	
4		20	21	22	23	24	25	26	
5		27	28	29	1	2	3	4	Mon 15h24m1p
6	SHEVAT 5823	5	6	7	8	9	10	11	
7		12	13	14	15	16	17	18	
8		19	20	21	22	23	24	25	
9		26	27	28	29	30	1	2	Wed 4h8m2p
10	ADAR 5823	3	4	5	6	7	8	9	
11		10	11	12	13	14[f]	15	16	
12		17	18	19	20	21	22	23	
13		24	25	26	27	28	29	1	Thu 16h52m3p
14	NISAN 5823	2	3	4	5	6	7	8	
15		9	10	11	12	13	14	15[g]	
16		16	17	18	19	20	21	22	
17		23	24	25	26	27	28	29	
18		30	1	2	3	4	5	6	Sat 5h36m4p
19	IYYAR 5823	7	8	9	10	11	12	13	
20		14	15	16	17	18	19	20	
21		21	22	23	24	25	26	27	
22		28	29	1	2	3	4	5	Sun 18h20m5p
23	SIVAN 5823	6[h]	7	8	9	10	11	12	
24		13	14	15	16	17	18	19	
25		20	21	22	23	24	25	26	
26		27	28	29	30	1	2	3	Tue 7h4m6p
27	TAMMUZ 5823	4	5	6	7	8	9	10	
28		11	12	13	14	15	16	17	
29		18	19	20	21	22	23	24	
30		25	26	27	28	29	1	2	Wed 19h48m7p
31	AV 5823	3	4	5	6	7	8	9	
32		10[i]	11	12	13	14	15	16	
33		17	18	19	20	21	22	23	
34		24	25	26	27	28	29	30	
35		1	2	3	4	5	6	7	Fri 8h32m8p
36	ELUL 5823	8	9	10	11	12	13	14	
37		15	16	17	18	19	20	21	
38		22	23	24	25	26	27	28	
39		29	1[a]	2[a]	3	4	5	6	Sat 21h16m9p
40	TISHRI 5824	7	8	9	10[b]	11	12	13	
41		14	15[c]	16	17	18	19	20	
42		21	22	23	24	25	26	27	
43		28	29	30	1	2	3	4	Mon 10h0m10p
44	HESHVAN 5824	5	6	7	8	9	10	11	
45		12	13	14	15	16	17	18	
46		19	20	21	22	23	24	25	
47		26	27	28	29	1	2	3	Tue 22h44m11p
48	KISLEV 5824	4	5	6	7	8	9	10	
49		11	12	13	14	15[d]	16	17	
50		18	19	20	21	22	23	24	
51		25[e]	26[e]	27[e]	28[e]	29[e]	1[e]	2[e]	Thu 11h28m12p
52	TEVETH 5824	3[e]	4	5	6	7	8	9	
1		10	11	12	13	14	15	16	

Chinese Rén-Wǔ/Guǐ-Wèi‡

ISO Week	Month	Sun	Mon	Tue	Wed	Thu	Fri	Sat	Solar Term
1		1	2	3	4	5	6	7	Xiǎo hán
2	MONTH 12 Rén-Wǔ	8	9	10	11	12	13	14	
3		15	16	17	18	19	20	21	Dà hán
4		22	23	24	25	26	27	28	
5		29	1[a]	2	3	4	5	6	
6	MONTH 1 Guǐ-Wèi	7	8*	9	10	11	12	13	Lì chūn
7		14	15[b]	16	17	18	19	20	
8		21	22	23	24	25	26	27	Yǔ shuǐ
9		28	29	30	1	2	3	4	
10	MONTH 2 Guǐ-Wèi	5	6	7	8	9	10	11	Jīng zhé
11		12	13	14	15	16	17	18	
12		19	20	21	22	23	24	25	Chūn fēn
13		26	27	28	29	30	1	2	
14	MONTH 3 Guǐ-Wèi	3	4	5	6	7[c]	8*	9	Qīng míng
15		10	11	12	13	14	15	16	
16		17	18	19	20	21	22	23	Gǔ yǔ
17		24	25	26	27	28	29	1	
18	MONTH 4 Guǐ-Wèi	2	3	4	5	6	7	8	Lì xià
19		9	10	11	12	13	14	15	
20		16	17	18	19	20	21	22	
21		23	24	25	26	27	28	29	Xiǎo mǎn
22		30	1	2	3	4	5[d]	6	
23	MONTH 5 Guǐ-Wèi	7	8	9*	10	11	12	13	Máng zhòng
24		14	15	16	17	18	19	20	
25		21	22	23	24	25	26	27	Xià zhì
26		28	29	1	2	3	4	5	
27	MONTH 6 Guǐ-Wèi	6	7	8	9	10	11	12	Xiǎo shǔ
28		13	14	15	16	17	18	19	
29		20	21	22	23	24	25	26	
30		27	28	29	30	1	2	3	Dà shǔ
31	MONTH 7 Guǐ-Wèi	4	5	6	7[e]	8	9	10*	
32		11	12	13	14	15[f]	16	17	Lì qiū
33		18	19	20	21	22	23	24	
34		25	26	27	28	29	1	2	Chǔ shǔ
35	LEAP MONTH 7 Guǐ-Wèi	3	4	5	6	7	8	9	
36		10	11	12	13	14	15	16	Bái lù
37		17	18	19	20	21	22	23	
38		24	25	26	27	28	29	1	
39	MONTH 8 Guǐ-Wèi	2	3	4	5	6	7	8	Qiū fēn
40		9	10	11	12*	13	14	15[g]	
41		16	17	18	19	20	21	22	Hán lù
42		23	24	25	26	27	28	29	
43		30	1	2	3	4	5	6	Shuāng jiàng
44	MONTH 9 Guǐ-Wèi	7	8	9[h]	10	11	12	13	
45		14	15	16	17	18	19	20	Lì dōng
46		21	22	23	24	25	26	27	
47		28	29	1	2	3	4	5	Xiǎo xuě
48	MONTH 10 Guǐ-Wèi	6	7	8	9	10	11	12	
49		13*	14	15	16	17	18	19	Dà xuě
50		20	21	22	23	24	25	26	
51		27	28	29	30	1	2	3[i]	Dōng zhì
52	MONTH 11* Guǐ-Wèi	4	5	6	7	8	9	10	
1		11	12	13	14	15	16	17	Xiǎo hán

Coptic 1779‡/1780 and Ethiopic 2055‡/2056

ISO Week	Coptic Month	Sun	Mon	Tue	Wed	Thu	Fri	Sat	Ethiopic Month
1	KOIAK 1779	22	23	24	25	26	27	28	TĀKHŚĀŚ 2055
2		29[c]	30	1	2	3	4	5	
3	TŌBE 1779	6[d]	7	8	9	10	11[e]	12	ṬER 2055
4		13	14	15	16	17	18	19	
5		20	21	22	23	24	25	26	
6		27	28	29	30	1	2	3	
7	MESHIR 1779	4	5	6	7	8	9	10	YAKĀTIT 2055
8		11	12	13	14	15	16	17	
9		18	19	20	21	22	23	24	
10		25	26	27	28	29	30	1	
11		2	3	4	5	6	7	8	
12	PAREMOTEP 1779	9	10	11	12	13	14	15	MAGĀBIT 2055
13		16	17	18	19	20	21	22	
14		23	24	25	26	27	28	29	
15		30	1	2	3	4	5	6	
16	PARMOUTE 1779	7	8	9	10	11	12	13	MIYĀZYĀ 2055
17		14[f]	15	16	17	18	19	20	
18		21	22	23	24	25	26	27	
19		28	29[g]	30	1	2	3	4	
20		5	6	7	8	9	10	11	
21	PASHONS 1779	12	13	14	15	16	17	18	GENBOT 2055
22		19	20	21	22	23	24	25	
23		26	27	28	29	30	1	2	
24		3	4	5	6	7	8	9	
25	PAŌNE 1779	10	11	12	13	14	15	16	SANĒ 2055
26		17	18	19	20	21	22	23	
27		24	25	26	27	28	29	30	
28		1	2	3	4	5	6	7	
29	EPĒP 1779	8	9	10	11	12	13	14	ḤAMLĒ 2055
30		15	16	17	18	19	20	21	
31		22	23	24	25	26	27	28	
32		29	30	1	2	3	4	5	
33	MESORĒ 1779	6	7	8	9	10	11	12	NAHASĒ 2055
34		13[h]	14	15	16	17	18	19	
35		20	21	22	23	24	25	26	
36	EPAG. 1779	27	28	29	30	1	2	3	PĀG. 2055
37		4	5	6	1[a]	2	3	4	
38		5	6	7	8	9	10	11	MASKARAM 2056
39	THOOUT 1780	12	13	14	15	16	17[b]	18	
40		19	20	21	22	23	24	25	
41		26	27	28	29	30	1	2	
42	PAOPE 1780	3	4	5	6	7	8	9	ṬEQEMT 2056
43		10	11	12	13	14	15	16	
44		17	18	19	20	21	22	23	
45		24	25	26	27	28	29	30	
46		1	2	3	4	5	6	7	
47	ATHŌR 1780	8	9	10	11	12	13	14	ḪEDĀR 2056
48		15	16	17	18	19	20	21	
49		22	23	24	25	26	27	28	
50		29	30	1	2	3	4	5	
51	KOIAK 1780	6	7	8	9	10	11	12	TĀKHŚĀŚ 2056
52		13	14	15	16	17	18	19	
1		20	21	22	23	24	25	26	

Gregorian notes:
[a]New Year
[b]Spring (13:58)
[c]Summer (7:00)
[d]Autumn (23:07)
[e]Winter (20:19)
● New moon
◐ First quarter moon
○ Full moon
◑ Last quarter moon

Hebrew notes:
[a]New Year
[b]Yom Kippur
[c]Sukkot
[d]Winter starts
[e]Ḥanukkah
[f]Purim
[g]Passover
[h]Shavuot
[i]Fast of Av

Chinese notes:
‡Leap year
[a]New Year (4761, Sheep)
[b]Lantern Festival
[c]Qīngmíng
[d]Dragon Festival
[e]Qǐqiǎo
[f]Hungry Ghosts
[g]Mid-Autumn Festival
[h]Double-Ninth Festival
[i]Dōngzhì
*Start of 60-name cycle

Coptic/Ethiopic notes:
‡Leap year
[a]New Year
[b]Building of the Cross
[c]Christmas
[d]Jesus's Circumcision
[e]Epiphany
[f]Easter
[g]Mary's Announcement
[h]Jesus's Transfiguration

2063

PERSIAN (ASTRONOMICAL) 1441‡/1442

Month	Sun	Mon	Tue	Wed	Thu	Fri	Sat
DEY 1441	11	12	13	14	15	16	17
	18	19	20	21	22	23	24
	25	26	27	28	29	30	1
BAHMAN 1441	2	3	4	5	6	7	8
	9	10	11	12	13	14	15
	16	17	18	19	20	21	22
	23	24	25	26	27	28	29
	30	1	2	3	4	5	6
ESFAND 1441	7	8	9	10	11	12	13
	14	15	16	17	18	19	20
	21	22	23	24	25	26	27
	28	29	30	1[a]	2	3	4
FARVARDĪN 1442	5	6	7	8	9	10	11
	12	13[b]	14	15	16	17	18
	19	20	21	22	23	24	25
	26	27	28	29	30	31	1
ORDĪBEHEŠT 1442	2	3	4	5	6	7	8
	9	10	11	12	13	14	15
	16	17	18	19	20	21	22
	23	24	25	26	27	28	29
	30	31	1	2	3	4	5
XORDĀD 1442	6	7	8	9	10	11	12
	13	14	15	16	17	18	19
	20	21	22	23	24	25	26
	27	28	29	30	31	1	2
TĪR 1442	3	4	5	6	7	8	9
	10	11	12	13	14	15	16
	17	18	19	20	21	22	23
	24	25	26	27	28	29	30
	31	1	2	3	4	5	6
MORDĀD 1442	7	8	9	10	11	12	13
	14	15	16	17	18	19	20
	21	22	23	24	25	26	27
	28	29	30	31	1	2	3
SHAHRĪVAR 1442	4	5	6	7	8	9	10
	11	12	13	14	15	16	17
	18	19	20	21	22	23	24
	25	26	27	28	29	30	31
MEHR 1442	1	2	3	4	5	6	7
	8	9	10	11	12	13	14
	15	16	17	18	19	20	21
	22	23	24	25	26	27	28
	29	30	1	2	3	4	5
ĀBĀN 1442	6	7	8	9	10	11	12
	13	14	15	16	17	18	19
	20	21	22	23	24	25	26
	27	28	29	30	1	2	3
ĀZAR 1442	4	5	6	7	8	9	10
	11	12	13	14	15	16	17
	18	19	20	21	22	23	24
	25	26	27	28	29	30	1
DEY 1442	2	3	4	5	6	7	8
	9	10	11	12	13	14	15

‡Leap year
[a]New Year
[b]Sizdeh Bedar

HINDU LUNAR 2119/2120

Month	Sun	Mon	Tue	Wed	Thu	Fri	Sat
PAUSHA 2119	1	2	3	4	5	5	6
	7	8	9	10	11	12	14
	15	16	17	18	19	20	21
	22	23	24	25	26	27	28
MĀGHA 2119	29	30	1	2	3	4	5
	6	7	8	9	10	11	12
	13	14	15	16	17	19	20
	21	22	23	24	25	26	27
	28	28[h]	29	30	1	2	3
PHĀLGUNA 2119	4	5	6	7	8	9	10
	11	13	14	15[i]	16	17	18
	19	20	21	22	23	24	25
	26	27	28	29	30	1[a]	1
CHAITRA 2120	2	3	5	6	7	8	9[b]
	10	11	12	13	14	15	16
	18	19	20	21	21	22	23
	24	25	26	27	28	29	30
VAIŚĀKHA 2120	1	2	3	4	5	6	7
	8	10	11	12	13	14	15
	16	17	18	19	20	21	22
	23	24	25	25	26	27	28
	29	30	1	3	4	5	6
JYAISHṬHA 2120	7	8	9	10	11	12	13
	15	16	16	17	18	19	20
	21	22	23	24	25	26	27
	28	29	30	1	2	3	4
ĀSHĀḌHA 2120	6	7	8	9	10	11	12
	13	14	15	16	17	18	19
	20	21	22	22	23	24	25
	26	28	29	30	1	2	3
ŚRĀVAṆA 2120	4	5	6	7	8	10	11
	12	13	14	14	15	16	17
	18	19	20	21	22	23[c]	24
	25	26	27	28	29	30	2
BHĀDRAPADA 2120	3	4[d]	5	6	7	8	9
	10	11	12	13	14	15	16
	17	18	19	19	20	21	22
	24	25	26	27	28	29	30
ĀŚVINA 2120	1	2	3	4	6	7	8[e]
	9[e]	9[e]	10[e]	11	12	13	14
	15	16	17	18	19	20	21
	22	23	24	25	26	27	29
	30	1[f]	2	3	4	5	6
KĀRTTIKA 2120	7	8	9	10	11	12	13
	13	14	15	16	17	18	19
	20	22	23	24	25	26	27
	28	29	30	1	2	3	4
MĀRGAŚĪRA 2120	5	6	7	8	9	10	11[g]
	12	13	14	15	16	17	18
	19	20	21	22	23	24	25
	27	28	29	30	1	2	3
PAUSHA 2120	4	5	6	6	7	8	9
	10	11	12	13	14	15	16

[a]New Year (Subhānu)
[b]Birthday of Rāma
[c]Birthday of Krishna
[d]Ganēśa Chaturthī
[e]Dashara
[f]Diwali
[g]Birthday of Vishnu
[h]Night of Śiva
[i]Holi

HINDU SOLAR 1984/1985‡

Month	Sun	Mon	Tue	Wed	Thu	Fri	Sat
PAUSHA 1984	16	17	18	19	20	21	22
	23	24	25	26	27	28	29
	30	1[b]	2	3	4	5	6
MĀGHA 1984	7	8	9	10	11	12	13
	14	15	16	17	18	19	20
	21	22	23	24	25	26	27
	28	29	1	2	3	4	5
PHĀLGUNA 1984	6	7	8	9	10	11	12
	13	14	15	16	17	18	19
	20	21	22	23	24	25	26
	27	28	29	30	1	2	3
CHAITRA 1984	4	5	6	7	8	9	10
	11	12	13	14	15	16	17
	18	19	20	21	22	23	24
	25	26	27	28	29	30	1[a]
VAIŚĀKHA 1985	2	3	4	5	6	7	8
	9	10	11	12	13	14	15
	16	17	18	19	20	21	22
	23	24	25	26	27	28	29
	30	31	1	2	3	4	5
JYAISHṬHA 1985	6	7	8	9	10	11	12
	13	14	15	16	17	18	19
	20	21	22	23	24	25	26
	27	28	29	30	31	32	1
ĀSHĀḌHA 1985	2	3	4	5	6	7	8
	9	10	11	12	13	14	15
	16	17	18	19	20	21	22
	23	24	25	26	27	28	29
	30	31	1	2	3	4	5
ŚRĀVAṆA 1985	6	7	8	9	10	11	12
	13	14	15	16	17	18	19
	20	21	22	23	24	25	26
	27	28	29	30	31	32	1
BHĀDRAPADA 1985	2	3	4	5	6	7	8
	9	10	11	12	13	14	15
	16	17	18	19	20	21	22
	23	24	25	26	27	28	29
	30	31	1	2	3	4	5
ĀŚVINA 1985	6	7	8	9	10	11	12
	13	14	15	16	17	18	19
	20	21	22	23	24	25	26
	27	28	29	30	1	2	3
KĀRTTIKA 1985	4	5	6	7	8	9	10
	11	12	13	14	15	16	17
	18	19	20	21	22	23	24
	25	26	27	28	29	30	1
MĀRGAŚĪRA 1985	2	3	4	5	6	7	8
	9	10	11	12	13	14	15
	16	17	18	19	20	21	22
	23	24	25	26	27	28	29
	30	1	2	3	4	5	6
PAUSHA 1985	7	8	9	10	11	12	13
	14	15	16	17	18	19	20

‡Leap year
[a]New Year (Hemalamba)
[b]Pongal

ISLAMIC (ASTRONOMICAL) 1485‡/1486

Month	Sun	Mon	Tue	Wed	Thu	Fri	Sat
RAMAḌĀN 1485	29	1[e]	2	3	4	5	6
	7	8	9	10	11	12	13
	14	15	16	17	18	19	20
	21	22	23	24	25	26	27
SHAWWĀL 1485	28	29	30	1[f]	2	3	4
	5	6	7	8	9	10	11
	12	13	14	15	16	17	18
	19	20	21	22	23	24	25
DHU AL-QA'DA 1485	26	27	28	29	30	1	2
	3	4	5	6	7	8	9
	10	11	12	13	14	15	16
	17	18	19	20	21	22	23
DHU AL-ḤIJJA 1485	24	25	26	27	28	29	1
	2	3	4	5	6	7	8
	9	10[g]	11	12	13	14	15
	16	17	18	19	20	21	22
	23	24	25	26	27	28	29
MUḤARRAM 1486	30[a]	1[a]	2	3	4	5	6
	7	8	9	10[b]	11	12	13
	14	15	16	17	18	19	20
	21	22	23	24	25	26	27
ṢAFAR 1486	28	29	1	2	3	4	5
	6	7	8	9	10	11	12
	13	14	15	16	17	18	19
	20	21	22	23	24	25	26
RABĪ' I 1486	27	28	29	30	1	2	3
	4	5	6	7	8	9	10
	11	12[c]	13	14	15	16	17
	18	19	20	21	22	23	24
RABĪ' II 1486	25	26	27	28	29	1	2
	3	4	5	6	7	8	9
	10	11	12	13	14	15	16
	17	18	19	20	21	22	23
	24	25	26	27	28	29	30
JUMĀDĀ I 1486	1	2	3	4	5	6	7
	8	9	10	11	12	13	14
	15	16	17	18	19	20	21
	22	23	24	25	26	27	28
JUMĀDĀ II 1486	29	1	2	3	4	5	6
	7	8	9	10	11	12	13
	14	15	16	17	18	19	20
	21	22	23	24	25	26	27
RAJAB 1486	28	29	30	1	2	3	4
	5	6	7	8	9	10	11
	12	13	14	15	16	17	18
	19	20	21	22	23	24	25
SHA'BĀN 1486	26	27[d]	28	29	1	2	3
	4	5	6	7	8	9	10
	11	12	13	14	15	16	17
	18	19	20	21	22	23	24
RAMAḌĀN 1486	25	26	27	28	29	1[e]	2
	3	4	5	6	7	8	9
	10	11	12	13	14	15	16

‡Leap year
[a]New Year
[a]New Year (Arithmetic)
[b]'Ashūrā'
[c]Prophet's Birthday
[d]Ascent of the Prophet
[e]Start of Ramaḍān
[f]'Īd al-Fiṭr
[g]'Īd al-'Aḍḥā

GREGORIAN 2063

Julian (Sun)	Month	Sun	Mon	Tue	Wed	Thu	Fri	Sat
Dec 18		31	1	2	3	4	5	6
	JANUARY 2063	7[a]	8	9	10	11	12	13
Jan 1		14[b]	15	16	17	18	19	20
		21	22	23	24	25	26	27
Jan 15		28	29	30	31	1	2	3
	FEBRUARY 2063	4	5	6	7	8	9	10
Jan 29		11	12	13	14	15	16	17
		18	19	20	21	22	23	24
Feb 12		25	26	27	28[c]	1	2	3
	MARCH 2063	4	5	6	7	8	9	10
Feb 26		11[d]	12	13	14	15	16	17
		18	19	20	21	22	23	24
Mar 12		25	26	27	28	29	30	31
	APRIL 2063	1	2	3	4	5	6	7
Mar 26		8	9	10	11	12	13	14
		15[e]	16	17	18	19	20	21
Apr 9		22[f]	23	24	25	26	27	28
		29	30	1	2	3	4	5
Apr 23	MAY 2063	6	7	8	9	10	11	12
		13	14	15	16	17	18	19
May 7		20	21	22	23	24	25	26
		27	28	29	30	31	1	2
May 21	JUNE 2063	3	4	5	6	7	8	9
		10	11	12	13	14	15	16
Jun 4		17	18	19	20	21	22	23
		24	25	26	27	28	29	30
Jun 18	JULY 2063	1	2	3	4	5	6	7
		8	9	10	11	12	13	14
Jul 2		15	16	17	18	19	20	21
		22	23	24	25	26	27	28
Jul 16		29	30	31	1	2	3	4
	AUGUST 2063	5	6	7	8	9	10	11
Jul 30		12	13	14	15	16	17	18
		19	20	21	22	23	24	25
Aug 13		26	27	28	29	30	31	1
	SEPTEMBER 2063	2	3	4	5	6	7	8
Aug 27		9	10	11	12	13	14	15
		16	17	18	19	20	21	22
Sep 10		23	24	25	26	27	28	29
	OCTOBER 2063	30	1	2	3	4	5	6
Sep 24		7	8	9	10	11	12	13
		14	15	16	17	18	19	20
Oct 8		21	22	23	24	25	26	27
		28	29	30	31	1	2	3
Oct 22	NOVEMBER 2063	4	5	6	7	8	9	10
		11	12	13	14	15	16	17
Nov 5		18	19	20	21	22	23	24
		25	26	27	28	29	30	1
Nov 19	DECEMBER 2063	2[g]	3	4	5	6	7	8
		9	10	11	12	13	14	15
Dec 3		16	17	18	19	20	21	22
		23	24	25[h]	26	27	28	29
Dec 17		30	31	1	2	3	4	5

[a]Orthodox Christmas
[b]Julian New Year
[c]Ash Wednesday
[d]Feast of Orthodoxy
[e]Easter
[f]Orthodox Easter
[g]Advent
[h]Christmas

2064

GREGORIAN 2064‡

Month	Sun	Mon	Tue	Wed	Thu	Fri	Sat	Lunar Phases	ISO WEEK (Mon)	JULIAN DAY (Sun noon)
JANUARY 2064	30	31	1[a]	2	3	○	5	9:30	1	2474919
	6	7	8	9	10	◑	12	3:13	2	2474926
	13	14	15	16	17	●	19	12:35	3	2474933
	20	21	22	23	24	25	◐	17:40	4	2474940
	27	28	29	30	31	1	○	21:35	5	2474947
FEBRUARY 2064	3	4	5	6	7	8	◑	12:54	6	2474954
	10	11	12	13	14	15	16		7	2474961
	●	18	19	20	21	22	23	7:01	8	2474968
	24	◐	26	27	28	29	1	11:21	9	2474975
MARCH 2064	2	○	4	5	6	7	8	8:17	10	2474982
	9	◑	11	12	13	14	15	0:32	11	2474989
	16	17	●	19[b]	20	21	22	1:44	12	2474996
	23	24	25	◐	27	28	29	1:12	13	2475003
	30	31	○	2	3	4	5	17:38	14	2475010
APRIL 2064	6	7	◑	9	10	11	12	14:24	15	2475017
	13	14	15	●	17	18	19	19:00	16	2475024
	20	21	22	23	◐	25	26	11:16	17	2475031
	27	28	29	30	○	2	3	2:06	18	2475038
MAY 2064	4	5	6	7	◑	9	10	6:15	19	2475045
	11	12	13	14	15	●	17	9:54	20	2475052
	18	19	20	21	22	◐	24	18:14	21	2475059
	25	26	27	28	29	○	31	10:35	22	2475066
JUNE 2064	1	2	3	4	5	◑	7	23:22	23	2475073
	8	9	10	11	12	13	●	22:19	24	2475080
	15	16	17	18	19	20[c]	◐	23:12	25	2475087
	22	23	24	25	26	27	○	20:07	26	2475094
	29	30	1	2	3	4	5		27	2475101
JULY 2064	◑	7	8	9	10	11	12	16:47	28	2475108
	13	●	15	16	17	18	19	8:44	29	2475115
	20	◐	22	23	24	25	26	3:34	30	2475122
	27	○	29	30	31	1	2	7:39	31	2475129
AUGUST 2064	3	4	◑	6	7	8	9	9:40	32	2475136
	10	11	●	13	14	15	16	17:48	33	2475143
	17	18	◐	20	21	22	23	8:53	34	2475150
	24	25	○	27	28	29	30	21:34	35	2475157
	31	1	2	3	◑	5	6	1:28	36	2475164
SEPTEMBER 2064	7	8	9	10	●	12	13	2:09	37	2475171
	14	15	16	◐	18	19	20	16:44	38	2475178
	21	22[d]	23	24	○	26	27	13:37	39	2475185
	28	29	30	1	2	◑	4	15:49	40	2475192
OCTOBER 2064	5	6	7	8	9	●	11	10:33	41	2475199
	12	13	14	15	16	◐	18	4:21	42	2475206
	19	20	21	22	23	24	○	7:04	43	2475213
	26	27	28	29	30	31	1		44	2475220
NOVEMBER 2064	◑	3	4	5	6	7	●	4:23 20:13	45	2475227
	9	10	11	12	13	14	◐	19:44	46	2475234
	16	17	18	19	20	21	22		47	2475241
	23	○	25	26	27	28	29	0:57	48	2475248
	30	◑	2	3	4	5	6	14:58	49	2475255
DECEMBER 2064	7	●	9	10	11	12	13	6:27	50	2475262
	14	◐	16	17	18	19	20	15:44	51	2475269
	21[e]	22	○	24	25	26	27	18:13	52	2475276
	28	29	◑	31	1	2	3	23:48	1	2475283

HEBREW 5824/5825‡

ISO WEEK	Month	Sun	Mon	Tue	Wed	Thu	Fri	Sat	Molad
1	TEVETH 5824	10	11	12	13	14	15	16	
2		17	18	19	20	21	22	23	
3	SHEVAT 5824	24	25	26	27	28	29	1	Sat 0h12m13p
4		2	3	4	5	6	7	8	
5		9	10	11	12	13	14	15	
6		16	17	18	19	20	21	22	
7		23	24	25	26	27	28	29	
8	ADAR 5824	30	1	2	3	4	5	6	Sun 12h56m14p
9		7	8	9	10	11	12	13	
10		14[f]	15	16	17	18	19	20	
11		21	22	23	24	25	26	27	
12	NISAN 5824	28	29	1	2	3	4	5	Tue 1h40m15p
13		6	7	8	9	10	11	12	
14		13	14	15[g]	16	17	18	19	
15		20	21	22	23	24	25	26	
16	IYYAR 5824	27	28	29	30	1	2	3	Wed 14h24m16p
17		4	5	6	7	8	9	10	
18		11	12	13	14	15	16	17	
19		18	19	20	21	22	23	24	
20	SIVAN 5824	25	26	27	28	29	1	2	Fri 3h8m17p
21		3	4	5	6[h]	7	8	9	
22		10	11	12	13	14	15	16	
23		17	18	19	20	21	22	23	
24		24	25	26	27	28	29	30	
25	TAMMUZ 5824	1	2	3	4	5	6	7	Sat 15h53m0p
26		8	9	10	11	12	13	14	
27		15	16	17	18	19	20	21	
28		22	23	24	25	26	27	28	
29	AV 5824	29	1	2	3	4	5	6	Mon 4h37m1p
30		7	8	9[i]	10	11	12	13	
31		14	15	16	17	18	19	20	
32		21	22	23	24	25	26	27	
33	ELUL 5824	28	29	30	1	2	3	4	Tue 17h21m2p
34		5	6	7	8	9	10	11	
35		12	13	14	15	16	17	18	
36		19	20	21	22	23	24	25	
37	TISHRI 5825	26	27	28	29	1[a]	2[a]	3	Thu 6h5m3p
38		4	5	6	7	8	9	10[b]	
39		11	12	13	14	15[c]	16	17	
40		18	19	20	21	22	23	24	
41	HESHVAN 5825	25	26	27	28	29	30	1	Fri 18h49m4p
42		2	3	4	5	6	7	8	
43		9	10	11	12	13	14	15	
44		16	17	18	19	20	21	22	
45		23	24	25	26	27	28	29	
46	KISLEV 5825	30	1	2	3	4	5	6	Sun 7h33m5p
47		7	8	9	10	11	12	13	
48		14	15	16	17	18	19	20	
49		21	22	23	24	25[e]	26[d,e]	27[e]	
50	TEVETH 5825	28[e]	29[e]	30[e]	1[e]	2[e]	3	4	Mon 20h17m6p
51		5	6	7	8	9	10	11	
52		12	13	14	15	16	17	18	
1		19	20	21	22	23	24	25	

CHINESE Guǐ-Wèi‡/Jiǎ-Shēn

ISO WEEK	Month	Sun	Mon	Tue	Wed	Thu	Fri	Sat	Solar Term
1	MONTH 11* Guǐ-Wèi	11	12	13	14	15	16	17	Xiǎo hán
2		18	19	20	21	22	23	24	
3	MONTH 12 Guǐ-Wèi	25	26	27	28	29	1	2	
4		3	4	5	6	7	8	9	Dà hán
5		10	11	12	13	14*	15	16	
6		17	18	19	20	21	22	23	Lì chūn
7		24	25	26	27	28	29	30	
8	MONTH 1 Jiǎ-Shēn	1[a]	2	3	4	5	6	7	Yǔ shuǐ
9		8	9	10	11	12	13	14	
10		15[b]	16	17	18	19	20	21	Jīng zhé
11		22	23	24	25	26	27	28	
12	MONTH 2 Jiǎ-Shēn	29	30	1	2	3	4	5	Chūn fēn
13		6	7	8	9	10	11	12	
14		13	14*	15	16	17	18[c]	19	Qīng míng
15		20	21	22	23	24	25	26	
16	MONTH 3 Jiǎ-Shēn	27	28	29	30	1	2	3	Gǔ yǔ
17		4	5	6	7	8	9	10	
18		11	12	13	14	15	16	17	
19		18	19	20	21	22	23	24	Lì xià
20	MONTH 4 Jiǎ-Shēn	25	26	27	28	29	1	2	
21		3	4	5	6	7	8	9	Xiǎo mǎn
22		10	11	12	13	14	15*	16	
23		17	18	19	20	21	22	23	Máng zhòng
24		24	25	26	27	28	29	30	
25	MONTH 5 Jiǎ-Shēn	1	2	3	4	5[d]	6	7	Xià zhì
26		8	9	10	11	12	13	14	
27		15	16	17	18	19	20	21	
28		22	23	24	25	26	27	28	Xiǎo shǔ
29	MONTH 6 Jiǎ-Shēn	29	1	2	3	4	5	6	
30		7	8	9	10	11	12	13	Dà shǔ
31		14	15	16*	17	18	19	20	
32		21	22	23	24	25	26	27	Lì qiū
33	MONTH 7 Jiǎ-Shēn	28	29	30	1	2	3	4	
34		5	6	7[e]	8	9	10	11	Chǔ shǔ
35		12	13	14	15[f]	16	17	18	
36		19	20	21	22	23	24	25	
37	MONTH 8 Jiǎ-Shēn	26	27	28	29	1	2	3	Bái lù
38		4	5	6	7	8	9	10	
39		11	12	13	14	15[g]	16	17*	Qiū fēn
40		18	19	20	21	22	23	24	
41	MONTH 9 Jiǎ-Shēn	25	26	27	28	29	1	2	Hán lù
42		3	4	5	6	7	8	9[h]	
43		10	11	12	13	14	15	16	Shuāng jiàng
44		17	18	19	20	21	22	23	
45		24	25	26	27	28	29	30	Lì dōng
46	MONTH 10 Jiǎ-Shēn	1	2	3	4	5	6	7	
47		8	9	10	11	12	13	14	Xiǎo xuě
48		15	16	17	18*	19	20	21	
49		22	23	24	25	26	27	28	Dà xuě
50	MONTH 11 Jiǎ-Shēn	29	1	2	3	4	5	6	
51		7	8	9	10	11	12	13	
52		14[i]	15	16	17	18	19	20	Dōng zhì
1		21	22	23	24	25	26	27	

COPTIC 1780/1781 — ETHIOPIC 2056/2057

ISO WEEK	Coptic Month	Sun	Mon	Tue	Wed	Thu	Fri	Sat	Ethiopic Month
1	KOIAK 1780	20	21	22	23	24	25	26	TĀKHŚĀŚ 2056
2	TŌBE 1780	27	28	29[c]	30	1	2	3	ṬER 2056
3		4	5	6[d]	7	8	9	10	
4		11[e]	12	13	14	15	16	17	
5		18	19	20	21	22	23	24	
6	MESHIR 1780	25	26	27	28	29	30	1	YAKĀTIT 2056
7		2	3	4	5	6	7	8	
8		9	10	11	12	13	14	15	
9		16	17	18	19	20	21	22	
10		23	24	25	26	27	28	29	
11	PAREMOTEP 1780	30	1	2	3	4	5	6	MAGĀBIT 2056
12		7	8	9	10	11	12	13	
13		14	15	16	17	18	19	20	
14		21	22	23	24	25	26	27	
15	PARMOUTE 1780	28	29	30	1	2	3	4	MIYĀZYĀ 2056
16		5[f]	6	7	8	9	10	11	
17		12	13	14	15	16	17	18	
18		19	20	21	22	23	24	25	
19	PASHONS 1780	26	27	28	29[g]	30	1	2	GENBOT 2056
20		3	4	5	6	7	8	9	
21		10	11	12	13	14	15	16	
22		17	18	19	20	21	22	23	
23		24	25	26	27	28	29	30	
24	PAŌNE 1780	1	2	3	4	5	6	7	SANĒ 2056
25		8	9	10	11	12	13	14	
26		15	16	17	18	19	20	21	
27		22	23	24	25	26	27	28	
28	EPĒP 1780	29	30	1	2	3	4	5	ḤAMLĒ 2056
29		6	7	8	9	10	11	12	
30		13	14	15	16	17	18	19	
31		20	21	22	23	24	25	26	
32	MESORĒ 1780	27	28	29	30	1	2	3	NAḤASĒ 2056
33		4	5	6	7	8	9	10	
34		11	12	13[h]	14	15	16	17	
35		18	19	20	21	22	23	24	
36	EPAG. 1780	25	26	27	28	29	30	1	PĀG. 2056
37	THOOUT 1781	2	3	4	5	1[a]	2	3	MASKARAM 2057
38		4	5	6	7	8	9	10	
39		11	12	13	14	15	16	17[b]	
40		18	19	20	21	22	23	24	
41	PAOPE 1781	25	26	27	28	29	30	1	ṬEQEMT 2057
42		2	3	4	5	6	7	8	
43		9	10	11	12	13	14	15	
44		16	17	18	19	20	21	22	
45		23	24	25	26	27	28	29	
46	ATHŌR 1781	30	1	2	3	4	5	6	HEDĀR 2057
47		7	8	9	10	11	12	13	
48		14	15	16	17	18	19	20	
49		21	22	23	24	25	26	27	
50	KOIAK 1781	28	29	30	1	2	3	4	TĀKHŚĀŚ 2057
51		5	6	7	8	9	10	11	
52		12	13	14	15	16	17	18	
1		19	20	21	22	23	24	25	

Gregorian:
‡Leap year
[a]New Year
[b]Spring (19:37)
[c]Summer (12:44)
[d]Autumn (4:55)
[e]Winter (2:07)
● New moon
◐ First quarter moon
○ Full moon
◑ Last quarter moon

Hebrew:
‡Leap year
[a]New Year
[b]Yom Kippur
[c]Sukkot
[d]Winter starts
[e]Ḥanukkah
[f]Purim
[g]Passover
[h]Shavuot
[i]Fast of Av

Chinese:
‡Leap year
[a]New Year (4762, Monkey)
[b]Lantern Festival
[c]Qīngmíng
[d]Dragon Festival
[e]Qīqiǎo
[f]Hungry Ghosts
[g]Mid-Autumn Festival
[h]Double-Ninth Festival
[i]Dōngzhì
*Start of 60-name cycle

Coptic/Ethiopic:
[a]New Year
[b]Building of the Cross
[c]Christmas
[d]Jesus's Circumcision
[e]Epiphany
[f]Easter
[g]Mary's Announcement
[h]Jesus's Transfiguration

PERSIAN (ASTRONOMICAL) 1442/1443

Month	Sun	Mon	Tue	Wed	Thu	Fri	Sat
	9	10	11	12	13	14	15
DEY 1442	16	17	18	19	20	21	22
	23	24	25	26	27	28	29
	30	1	2	3	4	5	6
BAHMAN 1442	7	8	9	10	11	12	13
	14	15	16	17	18	19	20
	21	22	23	24	25	26	27
	28	29	30	1	2	3	4
ESFAND 1442	5	6	7	8	9	10	11
	12	13	14	15	16	17	18
	19	20	21	22	23	24	25
	26	27	28	29	1[a]	2	3
FARVARDĪN 1443	4	5	6	7	8	9	10
	11	12	13[b]	14	15	16	17
	18	19	20	21	22	23	24
	25	26	27	28	29	30	31
	1	2	3	4	5	6	7
ORDĪBEHEŠT 1443	8	9	10	11	12	13	14
	15	16	17	18	19	20	21
	22	23	24	25	26	27	28
	29	30	31	1	2	3	4
XORDĀD 1443	5	6	7	8	9	10	11
	12	13	14	15	16	17	18
	19	20	21	22	23	24	25
	26	27	28	29	30	31	1
	2	3	4	5	6	7	8
TĪR 1443	9	10	11	12	13	14	15
	16	17	18	19	20	21	22
	23	24	25	26	27	28	29
	30	31	1	2	3	4	5
MORDĀD 1443	6	7	8	9	10	11	12
	13	14	15	16	17	18	19
	20	21	22	23	24	25	26
	27	28	29	30	31	1	2
SHAHRĪVAR 1443	3	4	5	6	7	8	9
	10	11	12	13	14	15	16
	17	18	19	20	21	22	23
	24	25	26	27	28	29	30
	31	1	2	3	4	5	6
MEHR 1443	7	8	9	10	11	12	13
	14	15	16	17	18	19	20
	21	22	23	24	25	26	27
	28	29	30	1	2	3	4
ĀBĀN 1443	5	6	7	8	9	10	11
	12	13	14	15	16	17	18
	19	20	21	22	23	24	25
	26	27	28	29	30	1	2
ĀZAR 1443	3	4	5	6	7	8	9
	10	11	12	13	14	15	16
	17	18	19	20	21	22	23
	24	25	26	27	28	29	30
DEY 1443	1	2	3	4	5	6	7
	8	9	10	11	12	13	14

[a]New Year
[b]Sizdeh Bedar

HINDU LUNAR 2120/2121‡

Month	Sun	Mon	Tue	Wed	Thu	Fri	Sat
	10	11	12	13	14	15	16
PAUSHA 2120	17	18	**19**	21	22	23	24
	25	26	27	28	29	30	1
	2	3	4	5	6	7	8
MĀGHA 2120	8	9	10	11	**12**	14	15
	16	17	18	19	20	21	22
	23	24	25	26	27	28[h]	29
	30	1	2	3	4	5	6
PHĀLGUNA 2120	7	8	9	10	11	12	13
	14	15[i]	16	17	**18**	20	21
	22	23	24	25	26	27	28
	29	30	1[a]	1	2	3	4
CHAITRA 2121	5	6	7	8	9[b]	10	11
	12	14	15	16	17	18	19
	20	21	22	23	24	25	26
	27	28	29	30	1	2	3
VAIŚĀKHA 2121	4	5	6	7	8	9	10
	11	12	13	14	**15**	17	18
	19	20	21	22	23	24	25
	25	26	27	28	29	30	1
LEAP JYAISHṬHA 2121	2	3	4	5	6	7	**8**
	10	11	12	13	14	15	16
	17	18	19	20	21	22	23
	24	25	26	27	28	29	30
	1	2	3	4	5	6	7
JYAISHṬHA 2121	8	9	10	11	**12**	14	15
	16	17	18	19	20	21	22
	22	23	24	25	26	27	28
	29	30	1	2	3	**4**	6
ĀSHĀḌHA 2121	7	8	9	10	11	12	13
	14	15	16	17	18	19	20
	21	22	23	24	25	26	27
	28	29	30	1	2	3	4
ŚRĀVAṆA 2121	5	6	**7**	9	10	11	12
	13	14	15	16	17	18	18
	19	20	21	22	23[c]	24	25
	26	27	28	29	**30**	2	3
BHĀDRAPADA 2121	4[d]	5	6	7	8	9	10
	11	12	13	14	15	16	17
	18	19	20	21	22	23	24
	25	26	27	28	29	30	1
ĀŚVINA 2121	2	3	**4**	6	7	8[e]	9[e]
	10[e]	11	12	13	13	14	15
	16	17	18	19	20	21	22
	23	24	25	26	**27**	29	30
	1[f]	2	3	4	5	6	7
KĀRTTIKA 2121	8	9	10	11	12	13	14
	15	16	16	17	18	19	20
	21	23	24	25	26	27	28
	29	30	1	2	3	4	5
MĀRGAŚĪRA 2121	6	7	8	9	10	11[g]	12
	13	14	15	16	17	18	19
	20	21	22	23	24	25	**26**

‡Leap year
[a]New Year (Tāraṇa)
[b]Birthday of Rāma
[c]Birthday of Krishna
[d]Ganēśa Chaturthī
[e]Dashara
[f]Diwali
[g]Birthday of Vishnu
[h]Night of Śiva
[i]Holi

HINDU SOLAR 1985‡/1986

Month	Sun	Mon	Tue	Wed	Thu	Fri	Sat
	14	15	16	17	18	19	20
PAUSHA 1985	21	22	23	24	25	26	27
	28	29	1[b]	2	3	4	5
	6	7	8	9	10	11	12
MĀGHA 1985	13	14	15	16	17	18	19
	20	21	22	23	24	25	26
	27	28	29	1	2	3	4
	5	6	7	8	9	10	11
PHĀLGUNA 1985	12	13	14	15	16	17	18
	19	20	21	22	23	24	25
	26	27	28	29	30	1	2
	3	4	5	6	7	8	9
CHAITRA 1985	10	11	12	13	14	15	16
	17	18	19	20	21	22	23
	24	25	26	27	28	29	30
	31	1[a]	2	3	4	5	6
VAIŚĀKHA 1986	7	8	9	10	11	12	13
	14	15	16	17	18	19	20
	21	22	23	24	25	26	27
	28	29	30	1	2	3	4
JYAISHṬHA 1986	5	6	7	8	9	10	11
	12	13	14	15	16	17	18
	19	20	21	22	23	24	25
	26	27	28	29	30	31	32
	1	2	3	4	5	6	7
ĀSHĀḌHA 1986	8	9	10	11	12	13	14
	15	16	17	18	19	20	21
	22	23	24	25	26	27	28
	29	30	31	32	1	2	3
ŚRĀVAṆA 1986	4	5	6	7	8	9	10
	11	12	13	14	15	16	17
	18	19	20	21	22	23	24
	25	26	27	28	29	30	31
	1	2	3	4	5	6	7
BHĀDRAPADA 1986	8	9	10	11	12	13	14
	15	16	17	18	19	20	21
	22	23	24	25	26	27	28
	29	30	31	1	2	3	4
ĀŚVINA 1986	5	6	7	8	9	10	11
	12	13	14	15	16	17	18
	19	20	21	22	23	24	25
	26	27	28	29	30	1	2
KĀRTTIKA 1986	3	4	5	6	7	8	9
	10	11	12	13	14	15	16
	17	18	19	20	21	22	23
	24	25	26	27	28	29	30
	1	2	3	4	5	6	7
MĀRGAŚĪRA 1986	8	9	10	11	12	13	14
	15	16	17	18	19	20	21
	22	23	24	25	26	27	28
	29	30	1	2	3	4	5
PAUSHA 1986	6	7	8	9	10	11	12
	13	14	15	16	17	18	19

‡Leap year
[a]New Year (Vilamba)
[b]Pongal

ISLAMIC (ASTRONOMICAL) 1486/1487

Month	Sun	Mon	Tue	Wed	Thu	Fri	Sat
	10	11	12	13	14	15	16
RAMAḌĀN 1486	17	18	19	20	21	22	23
	24	25	26	27	28	29	30
	1[f]	2	3	4	5	6	7
SHAWWĀL 1486	8	9	10	11	12	13	14
	15	16	17	18	19	20	21
	22	23	24	25	26	27	28
	29	30	1	2	3	4	5
DHU AL-QA'DA 1486	6	7	8	9	10	11	12
	13	14	15	16	17	18	19
	20	21	22	23	24	25	26
	27	28	29	1	2	3	4
DHU AL-ḤIJJA 1486	5	6	7	8	9	10[g]	11
	12	13	14	15	16	17	18
	19	20	21	22	23	24	25
	26	27	28	29	30	1[a]	2
MUḤARRAM 1487	3	4	5	6	7	8	9
	10[b]	11	12	13	14	15	16
	17	18	19	20	21	22	23
	24	25	26	27	28	29	30
	1	2	3	4	5	6	7
ṢAFAR 1487	8	9	10	11	12	13	14
	15	16	17	18	19	20	21
	22	23	24	25	26	27	28
	29	1	2	3	4	5	6
RABĪ' I 1487	7	8	9	10	11	12[c]	13
	14	15	16	17	18	19	20
	21	22	23	24	25	26	27
	28	29	30	1	2	3	4
RABĪ' II 1487	5	6	7	8	9	10	11
	12	13	14	15	16	17	18
	19	20	21	22	23	24	25
	26	27	28	29	1	2	3
JUMĀDĀ I 1487	4	5	6	7	8	9	10
	11	12	13	14	15	16	17
	18	19	20	21	22	23	24
	25	26	27	28	29	30	1
JUMĀDĀ II 1487	2	3	4	5	6	7	8
	9	10	11	12	13	14	15
	16	17	18	19	20	21	22
	23	24	25	26	27	28	29
	1	2	3	4	5	6	7
RAJAB 1487	8	9	10	11	12	13	14
	15	16	17	18	19	20	21
	22	23	24	25	26	27[d]	28
	29	30	1	2	3	4	5
SHA'BĀN 1487	6	7	8	9	10	11	12
	13	14	15	16	17	18	19
	20	21	22	23	24	25	26
	27	28	29	1[e]	2	3	4
RAMAḌĀN 1487	5	6	7	8	9	10	11
	12	13	14	15	16	17	18
	19	20	21	22	23	24	25

[a]New Year
[b]'Ashūrā'
[c]Prophet's Birthday
[d]Ascent of the Prophet
[e]Start of Ramaḍān
[f]'Id al-Fiṭr
[g]'Id al-'Aḍḥā

GREGORIAN 2064‡

Julian‡ (Sun)	Sun	Mon	Tue	Wed	Thu	Fri	Sat	Month
Dec 17	30	31	1	2	3	4	5	
	6	7[a]	8	9	10	11	12	JANUARY 2064
Dec 31	13	14[b]	15	16	17	18	19	
	20	21	22	23	24	25	26	
Jan 14	27	28	29	30	31	1	2	
	3	4	5	6	7	8	9	FEBRUARY 2064
Jan 28	10	11	12	13	14	15	16	
	17	18	19	20[c]	21	22	23	
Feb 11	24	25	26	27	28	29	1	
	2[d]	3	4	5	6	7	8	
Feb 25	9	10	11	12	13	14	15	MARCH 2064
	16	17	18	19	20	21	22	
Mar 10	23	24	25	26	27	28	29	
	30	31	1	2	3	4	5	
Mar 24	6[e]	7	8	9	10	11	12	APRIL 2064
	13[f]	14	15	16	17	18	19	
Apr 7	20	21	22	23	24	25	26	
	27	28	29	30	1	2	3	
Apr 21	4	5	6	7	8	9	10	MAY 2064
	11	12	13	14	15	16	17	
May 5	18	19	20	21	22	23	24	
	25	26	27	28	29	30	31	
May 19	1	2	3	4	5	6	7	
	8	9	10	11	12	13	14	JUNE 2064
Jun 2	15	16	17	18	19	20	21	
	22	23	24	25	26	27	28	
Jun 16	29	30	1	2	3	4	5	
	6	7	8	9	10	11	12	JULY 2064
Jun 30	13	14	15	16	17	18	19	
	20	21	22	23	24	25	26	
Jul 14	27	28	29	30	31	1	2	
	3	4	5	6	7	8	9	AUGUST 2064
Jul 28	10	11	12	13	14	15	16	
	17	18	19	20	21	22	23	
Aug 11	24	25	26	27	28	29	30	
	31	1	2	3	4	5	6	
Aug 25	7	8	9	10	11	12	13	SEPTEMBER 2064
	14	15	16	17	18	19	20	
Sep 8	21	22	23	24	25	26	27	
	28	29	30	1	2	3	4	
Sep 22	5	6	7	8	9	10	11	OCTOBER 2064
	12	13	14	15	16	17	18	
Oct 6	19	20	21	22	23	24	25	
	26	27	28	29	30	31	1	
Oct 20	2	3	4	5	6	7	8	NOVEMBER 2064
	9	10	11	12	13	14	15	
Nov 3	16	17	18	19	20	21	22	
	23	24	25	26	27	28	29	
Nov 17	30[g]	1	2	3	4	5	6	
	7	8	9	10	11	12	13	DECEMBER 2064
Dec 1	14	15	16	17	18	19	20	
	21	22	23	24	25[h]	26	27	
Dec 15	28	29	30	31	1	2	3	

‡Leap year
[a]Orthodox Christmas
[b]Julian New Year
[c]Ash Wednesday
[d]Feast of Orthodoxy
[e]Easter
[f]Orthodox Easter
[g]Advent
[h]Christmas

2065

Gregorian 2065 month	Sun	Mon	Tue	Wed	Thu	Fri	Sat	Lunar Phases	ISO WEEK (Mon)	JULIAN DAY (Sun noon)	Hebrew 5825‡/5826 month	Sun	Mon	Tue	Wed	Thu	Fri	Sat	Molad
	28	29	◑	31	1[a]	2	3	23:48	1	2475283	TEVETH 5825	19	20	21	22	23	24	25	
	4	5	●	7	8	9	10	19:13	2	2475290		26	27	28	29	1	2	3	Wed 9h1m7p
JANUARY 2065	11	12	13	◐	15	16	17	13:17	3	2475297		4	5	6	7	8	9	10	
	18	19	20	21	○	23	24	9:52	4	2475304	SHEVAT 5825	11	12	13	14	15	16	17	
	25	26	27	28	◑	30	31	7:37	5	2475311		18	19	20	21	22	23	24	
	1	2	3	4	●	6	7	10:01	6	2475318		25	26	27	28	29	30	1	Thu 21h45m8p
	8	9	10	11	12	◐	14	10:49	7	2475325		2	3	4	5	6	7	8	
FEBRUARY 2065	15	16	17	18	19	○	21	23:10	8	2475332	ADAR I 5825	9	10	11	12	13	14	15	
	22	23	24	25	26	◑	28	15:28	9	2475339		16	17	18	19	20	21	22	
	1	2	3	4	5	6	●	2:14	10	2475346		23	24	25	26	27	28	29	
	8	9	10	11	12	13	14		11	2475353		30	1	2	3	4	5	6	Sat 10h29m9p
MARCH 2065	◐	16	17	18	19	20[b]	21	6:24	12	2475360		7	8	9	10	11	12	13	
	○	23	24	25	26	27	28	9:55	13	2475367	ADAR II 5825	14[f]	15	16	17	18	19	20	
	◑	30	31	1	2	3	4	0:23	14	2475374		21	22	23	24	25	26	27	
	●	6	7	8	9	10	11	19:00	15	2475381		28	29	1	2*	3	4	5	Sun 23h13m10p
APRIL 2065	12	◐	14	15	16	17	18	22:36	16	2475388		6	7	8	9	10	11	12	
	19	○	21	22	23	24	25	18:34	17	2475395	NISAN 5825	13	14	15[g]	16	17	18	19	
	26	◑	28	29	30	1	2	11:01	18	2475402		20	21	22	23	24	25	26	
	3	4	●	6	7	8	9	11:29	19	2475409		27	28	29	30	1	2	3	Tue 11h57m11p
MAY 2065	10	11	12	◐	14	15	16	10:51	20	2475416		4	5	6	7	8	9	10	
	17	18	19	○	21	22	23	2:04	21	2475423	IYAR 5825	11	12	13	14	15	16	17	
	24	25	◑	27	28	29	30	23:37	22	2475430		18	19	20	21	22	23	24	
	31	1	2	3	●	5	6	3:03	23	2475437		25	26	27	28	29	1	2	Thu 0h41m12p
	7	8	9	10	◐	12	13	19:24	24	2475444		3	4	5	6[h]	7	8	9	
JUNE 2065	14	15	16	17	○	19	20[c]	9:27	25	2475451	SIVAN 5825	10	11	12	13	14	15	16	
	21	22	23	24	◑	26	27	14:07	26	2475458		17	18	19	20	21	22	23	
	28	29	30	1	2	●	4	17:14	27	2475465		24	25	26	27	28	29	30	Fri 13h25m13p
	5	6	7	8	9	10	◐	1:15	28	2475472		1	2	3	4	5	6	7	
JULY 2065	12	13	14	15	16	○	18	17:44	29	2475479	TAMMUZ 5825	8	9	10	11	12	13	14	
	19	20	21	22	23	24	◑	6:20	30	2475486		15	16	17	18	19	20	21	
	26	27	28	29	30	31	1		31	2475493		22	23	24	25	26	27	28	
	●	3	4	5	6	7	8	5:45	32	2475500		29	1	2	3	4	5	6	Sun 2h9m14p
	◐	10	11	12	13	14	15	5:51	33	2475507		7	8	9[i]	10	11	12	13	
AUGUST 2065	○	17	18	19	20	21	22	3:44	34	2475514	AV 5825	14	15	16	17	18	19	20	
	◑	24	25	26	27	28	29	23:55	35	2475521		21	22	23	24	25	26	27	
	30	●	1	2	3	4	5	16:38	36	2475528		28	29	30	1	2	3	4	Mon 14h53m15p
	6	◐	8	9	10	11	12	10:48	37	2475535		5	6	7	8	9	10	11	
SEPTEMBER 2065	13	○	15	16	17	18	19	16:04	38	2475542	ELUL 5825	12	13	14	15	16	17	18	
	20	21	◑[d]	23	24	25	26	18:08	39	2475549		19	20	21	22	23	24	25	
	27	28	29	●	1	2	3	2:23	40	2475556		26	27	28	29	1[a]	2[a]	3	Wed 3h37m16p
	4	5	◐	7	8	9	10	17:36	41	2475563		4	5	6	7	8	9	10[b]	
OCTOBER 2065	11	12	13	○	15	16	17	7:03	42	2475570	TISHRI 5826	11	12	13	14	15[c]	16	17	
	18	19	20	21	◑	23	24	11:52	43	2475577		18	19	20	21	22	23	24	
	25	26	27	28	●	30	31	11:47	44	2475584		25	26	27	28	29	30	1	Thu 16h21m17p
	1	2	3	4	◐	6	7	3:25	45	2475591		2	3	4	5	6	7	8	
	8	9	10	11	12	○	14	0:36	46	2475598	HESHVAN 5826	9	10	11	12	13	14	15	
NOVEMBER 2065	15	16	17	18	19	20	◑	3:50	47	2475605		16	17	18	19	20	21	22	
	22	23	24	25	26	●	28	21:38	48	2475612		23	24	25	26	27	28	29	
	29	30	1	2	3	◐	5	16:53	49	2475619		1	2	3	4	5	6	7[d]	Sat 5h6m0p
	6	7	8	9	10	11	○	19:51	50	2475626		8	9	10	11	12	13	14	
DECEMBER 2065	13	14	15	16	17	18	19		51	2475633	KISLEV 5826	15	16	17	18	19	20	21	
	◑	21[e]	22	23	24	25	26	17:11	52	2475640		22	23	24	25[e]	26[e]	27[e]	28[e]	Sun 17h50m1p
	●	28	29	30	31	1	2	8:26	53	2475647		29[e]	30[e]	1[e]	2[e]	3	4	5	

ISO WEEK	Chinese Jiǎ-Shēn/Yǐ-Yǒu month	Sun	Mon	Tue	Wed	Thu	Fri	Sat	Solar Term	Coptic 1781/1782 month	Sun	Mon	Tue	Wed	Thu	Fri	Sat	Ethiopic 2057/2058 month
1	MONTH 11 Jiǎ-Shēn	21	22	23	24	25	26	27		KOIAK 1781	19	20	21	22	23	24	25	TĀKHŚĀŚ 2057
2		28	29	30	1	2	3	4	Xiǎo hán		26	27	28	29[c]	30	1	2	
3	MONTH 12 Jiǎ-Shēn	5	6	7	8	9	10	11			3	4	5	6[d]	7	8	9	
4		12	13	14	15	16	17	18	Dà hán	TŌBE 1781	10	11[e]	12	13	14	15	16	ṬER 2057
5		19*	20	21	22	23	24	25			17	18	19	20	21	22	23	
6		26	27	28	29	1[a]	2	3	Lì chūn		24	25	26	27	28	29	30	
7		4	5	6	7	8	9	10			1	2	3	4	5	6	7	
8	MONTH 1 Yǐ-Yǒu	11	12	13	14	15[b]	16	17	Yǔ shuǐ	MESHIR 1781	8	9	10	11	12	13	14	YAKĀTĪT 2057
9		18	19	20	21	22	23	24			15	16	17	18	19	20	21	
10		25	26	27	28	29	30	1	Jīng zhé		22	23	24	25	26	27	28	
11		2	3	4	5	6	7	8			29	30	1	2	3	4	5	
12	MONTH 2 Yǐ-Yǒu	9	10	11	12	13	14	15	Chūn fēn		6	7	8	9	10	11	12	
13		16	17	18	19	20*	21	22		PAREMOTEP 1781	13	14	15	16	17	18	19	MAGĀBIT 2057
14		23	24	25	26	27	28	29[c]	Qīng míng		20	21	22	23	24	25	26	
15		30	1	2	3	4	5	6			27	28	29	30	1	2	3	
16		7	8	9	10	11	12	13			4	5	6	7	8	9	10	
17	MONTH 3 Yǐ-Yǒu	14	15	16	17	18	19	20	Gǔ yǔ	PARMOUTE 1781	11	12	13	14	15	16	17	MIYĀZYĀ 2057
18		21	22	23	24	25	26	27			18[f]	19	20	21	22	23	24	
19		28	29	1	2	3	4	5	Lì xià		25	26	27	28	29[g]	30	1	
20		6	7	8	9	10	11	12			2	3	4	5	6	7	8	
21	MONTH 4 Yǐ-Yǒu	13	14	15	16	17	18	19	Xiǎo mǎn	PASHONS 1781	9	10	11	12	13	14	15	GENBOT 2057
22		20	21*	22	23	24	25	26			16	17	18	19	20	21	22	
23		27	28	29	30	1	2	3	Máng zhòng		23	24	25	26	27	28	29	
24		4	5[d]	6	7	8	9	10			30	1	2	3	4	5	6	
25	MONTH 5 Yǐ-Yǒu	11	12	13	14	15	16	17			7	8	9	10	11	12	13	SANĒ 2057
26		18	19	20	21	22	23	24	Xià zhì	PAŌNE 1781	14	15	16	17	18	19	20	
27		25	26	27	28	29	30	1			21	22	23	24	25	26	27	
28		2	3	4	5	6	7	8	Xiǎo shǔ		28	29	30	1	2	3	4	
29	MONTH 6 Yǐ-Yǒu	9	10	11	12	13	14	15			5	6	7	8	9	10	11	
30		16	17	18	19	20	21*	22	Dà shǔ	EPĒP 1781	12	13	14	15	16	17	18	ḤAMLĒ 2057
31		23	24	25	26	27	28	29			19	20	21	22	23	24	25	
32		1	2	3	4	5	6	7[e]	Lì qiū		26	27	28	29	30	1	2	
33		8	9	10	11	12	13	14			3	4	5	6	7	8	9	
34	MONTH 7 Yǐ-Yǒu	15[f]	16	17	18	19	20	21	Chǔ shǔ	MESORĒ 1781	10	11	12	13[h]	14	15	16	NAḤASĒ 2057
35		22	23	24	25	26	27	28			17	18	19	20	21	22	23	
36		29	30	1	2	3	4	5			24	25	26	27	28	29	30	
37		6	7	8	9	10	11	12	Bái lù	EPAG. 1781	1	2	3	4	5	1[a]	2	PĀG. 2057
38	MONTH 8 Yǐ-Yǒu	13	14	15[g]	16	17	18	19			3	4	5	6	7	8	9	MASKARAM 2058
39		20	21	22*	23	24	25	26	Qiū fēn	THOOUT 1782	10	11	12	13	14	15	16	
40		27	28	29	1	2	3	4			17[b]	18	19	20	21	22	23	
41		5	6	7	8	9[h]	10	11	Hán lù		24	25	26	27	28	29	30	
42	MONTH 9 Yǐ-Yǒu	12	13	14	15	16	17	18			1	2	3	4	5	6	7	
43		19	20	21	22	23	24	25	Shuāng jiàng	PAOPE 1782	8	9	10	11	12	13	14	ṬEQEMT 2058
44		26	27	28	29	1	2	3			15	16	17	18	19	20	21	
45		4	5	6	7	8	9	10	Lì dōng		22	23	24	25	26	27	28	
46	MONTH 10 Yǐ-Yǒu	11	12	13	14	15	16	17			29	30	1	2	3	4	5	
47		18	19	20	21	22	23	24*	Xiǎo xuě	ATHŌR 1782	6	7	8	9	10	11	12	ḤEDĀR 2058
48		25	26	27	28	29	30	1			13	14	15	16	17	18	19	
49		2	3	4	5	6	7	8			20	21	22	23	24	25	26	
50		9	10	11	12	13	14	15	Dà xuě		27	28	29	30	1	2	3	
51	MONTH 11 Yǐ-Yǒu	16	17	18	19	20	21	22		KOIAK 1782	4	5	6	7	8	9	10	TĀKHŚĀŚ 2058
52		23	24[i]	25	26	27	28	29	Dōng zhì		11	12	13	14	15	16	17	
53		1	2	3	4	5	6	7			18	19	20	21	22	23	24	

[a]New Year
[b]Spring (1:26)
[c]Summer (18:31)
[d]Autumn (10:41)
[e]Winter (7:58)
● New moon
◐ First quarter moon
○ Full moon
◑ Last quarter moon

‡Leap year
[a]New Year
[b]Yom Kippur
[c]Sukkot
[d]Winter starts
[e]Ḥanukkah
[f]Purim
[g]Passover
[h]Shavuot
[i]Fast of Av
*New solar cycle

[a]New Year (4763, Fowl)
[b]Lantern Festival
[c]Qīngmíng
[d]Dragon Festival
[e]Qīqiǎo
[f]Hungry Ghosts
[g]Mid-Autumn Festival
[h]Double-Ninth Festival
[i]Dōngzhì
*Start of 60-name cycle

[a]New Year
[b]Building of the Cross
[c]Christmas
[d]Jesus's Circumcision
[e]Epiphany
[f]Easter
[g]Mary's Announcement
[h]Jesus's Transfiguration

PERSIAN (ASTRONOMICAL) 1443/1444

Month	Sun	Mon	Tue	Wed	Thu	Fri	Sat
	8	9	10	11	12	13	14
DEY 1443	15	16	17	18	19	20	21
	22	23	24	25	26	27	28
	29	30	1	2	3	4	5
BAHMAN 1443	6	7	8	9	10	11	12
	13	14	15	16	17	18	19
	20	21	22	23	24	25	26
	27	28	29	30	1	2	3
ESFAND 1443	4	5	6	7	8	9	10
	11	12	13	14	15	16	17
	18	19	20	21	22	23	24
	25	26	27	28	29	1[a]	2
FARVARDĪN 1444	3	4	5	6	7	8	9
	10	11	12	13[b]	14	15	16
	17	18	19	20	21	22	23
	24	25	26	27	28	29	30
	31	1	2	3	4	5	6
ORDĪBEHEŠT 1444	7	8	9	10	11	12	13
	14	15	16	17	18	19	20
	21	22	23	24	25	26	27
	28	29	30	31	1	2	3
XORDĀD 1444	4	5	6	7	8	9	10
	11	12	13	14	15	16	17
	18	19	20	21	22	23	24
	25	26	27	28	29	30	31
	1	2	3	4	5	6	7
TĪR 1444	8	9	10	11	12	13	14
	15	16	17	18	19	20	21
	22	23	24	25	26	27	28
	29	30	31	1	2	3	4
MORDĀD 1444	5	6	7	8	9	10	11
	12	13	14	15	16	17	18
	19	20	21	22	23	24	25
	26	27	28	29	30	31	1
SHAHRĪVAR 1444	2	3	4	5	6	7	8
	9	10	11	12	13	14	15
	16	17	18	19	20	21	22
	23	24	25	26	27	28	29
	30	31	1	2	3	4	5
MEHR 1444	6	7	8	9	10	11	12
	13	14	15	16	17	18	19
	20	21	22	23	24	25	26
	27	28	29	30	1	2	3
ĀBĀN 1444	4	5	6	7	8	9	10
	11	12	13	14	15	16	17
	18	19	20	21	22	23	24
	25	26	27	28	29	30	1
ĀZAR 1444	2	3	4	5	6	7	8
	9	10	11	12	13	14	15
	16	17	18	19	20	21	22
	23	24	25	26	27	28	29
DEY 1444	30	1	2	3	4	5	6
	7	8	9	10	11	12	13

[a]New Year
[b]Sizdeh Bedar

HINDU LUNAR 2121‡/2122

Month	Sun	Mon	Tue	Wed	Thu	Fri	Sat
MĀRGAŚIRA 2121	20	21	22	23	24	25	**26**
	28	29	30	1	2	3	4
PAUSHA 2121	5	6	7	8	9	9	10
	11	12	13	14	15	16	17
	18	19	**20**	22	23	24	25
	26	27	28	29	30	1	2
MĀGHA 2121	3	4	5	6	7	8	9
	10	11	12	13	14	15	16
	17	18	19	20	21	22	23
	24	25	**26**	28	29[h]	30	1
PHĀLGUNA 2121	1	2	3	4	5	6	7
	8	9	10	11	12	13	14
	15[i]	16	17	18	**19**	21	22
	23	24	25	26	27	28	29
	30	1[a]	2	3	4	4	5
CHAITRA 2122	6	7	8[b]	9	10	11	**12**
	14	15	16	17	18	19	20
	21	22	23	24	25	26	27
	28	29	30	1	2	3	4
VAIŚĀKHA 2122	5	6	7	8	9	10	11
	12	13	14	15	**16**	18	19
	20	21	22	23	24	25	26
	27	28	29	29	30	1	2
JYAISHṬHA 2122	3	4	5	6	7	**8**	10
	11	12	13	14	15	16	17
	18	19	20	21	22	23	24
	25	26	27	28	29	30	1
ĀSHĀḌHA 2122	2	3	4	5	6	7	8
	9	10	**11**	13	14	15	16
	17	18	19	20	21	22	23
	24	25	26	26	27	28	29
	30	1	2	3	**4**	6	7
ŚRĀVAṆA 2122	8	9	10	11	12	13	14
	15	16	17	18	19	20	21
	22	23[c]	24	25	26	27	28
	29	30	1	2	3	4[d]	5
BHĀDRAPADA 2122	6	**7**	9	10	11	12	13
	14	15	16	17	18	19	20
	21	22	22	23	24	25	26
	27	28	29	**30**	2	3	4
ĀŚVINA 2122	5	6	7	8[e]	9[e]	10[e]	11
	12	13	14	15	16	17	18
	19	20	21	22	23	24	25
	26	27	28	29	30	1[f]	2
KĀRTTIKA 2122	3	**4**	6	7	8	9	10
	11	12	13	14	15	16	16
	17	18	19	20	21	22	23
	24	25	26	27	**28**	30	1
MĀRGAŚIRA 2122	2	3	4	5	6	7	8
	9	10	11[g]	12	13	14	15
	16	17	18	19	20	21	22
	23	24	25	26	27	28	29
	30	1	2	3	**4**	6	7

‡Leap year
[a]New Year (Pārthiva)
[b]Birthday of Rāma
[c]Birthday of Krishna
[d]Ganēśa Chaturthī
[e]Dashara
[f]Diwali
[g]Birthday of Vishnu
[h]Night of Śiva
[i]Holi

HINDU SOLAR 1986/1987

Month	Sun	Mon	Tue	Wed	Thu	Fri	Sat
PAUSHA 1986	13	14	15	16	17	18	19
	20	21	22	23	24	25	26
	27	28	29	1[b]	2	3	4
MĀGHA 1986	5	6	7	8	9	10	11
	12	13	14	15	16	17	18
	19	20	21	22	23	24	25
	26	27	28	29	30	1	2
PHĀLGUNA 1986	3	4	5	6	7	8	9
	10	11	12	13	14	15	16
	17	18	19	20	21	22	23
	24	25	26	27	28	29	1
CHAITRA 1986	2	3	4	5	6	7	8
	9	10	11	12	13	14	15
	16	17	18	19	20	21	22
	23	24	25	26	27	28	29
	30	31	1[a]	2	3	4	5
VAIŚĀKHA 1987	6	7	8	9	10	11	12
	13	14	15	16	17	18	19
	20	21	22	23	24	25	26
	27	28	29	30	31	1	2
JYAISHṬHA 1987	3	4	5	6	7	8	9
	10	11	12	13	14	15	16
	17	18	19	20	21	22	23
	24	25	26	27	28	29	30
	31	1	2	3	4	5	6
ĀSHĀḌHA 1987	7	8	9	10	11	12	13
	14	15	16	17	18	19	20
	21	22	23	24	25	26	27
	28	29	30	31	32	1	2
ŚRĀVAṆA 1987	3	4	5	6	7	8	9
	10	11	12	13	14	15	16
	17	18	19	20	21	22	23
	24	25	26	27	28	29	30
	31	1	2	3	4	5	6
BHĀDRAPADA 1987	7	8	9	10	11	12	13
	14	15	16	17	18	19	20
	21	22	23	24	25	26	27
	28	29	30	31	1	2	3
ĀŚVINA 1987	4	5	6	7	8	9	10
	11	12	13	14	15	16	17
	18	19	20	21	22	23	24
	25	26	27	28	29	30	31
	1	2	3	4	5	6	7
KĀRTTIKA 1987	8	9	10	11	12	13	14
	15	16	17	18	19	20	21
	22	23	24	25	26	27	28
	29	30	1	2	3	4	5
MĀRGAŚIRA 1987	6	7	8	9	10	11	12
	13	14	15	16	17	18	19
	20	21	22	23	24	25	26
	27	28	29	1	2	3	4
PAUSHA 1987	5	6	7	8	9	10	11
	12	13	14	15	16	17	18

[a]New Year (Vikārin)
[b]Pongal

ISLAMIC (ASTRONOMICAL) 1487/1488

Month	Sun	Mon	Tue	Wed	Thu	Fri	Sat
RAMAḌĀN 1487	19	20	21	22	23	24	25
	26	27	28	29	1[f]	2	3
SHAWWĀL 1487	4	5	6	7	8	9	10
	11	12	13	14	15	16	17
	18	19	20	21	22	23	24
	25	26	27	28	29	30	1
DHU AL-QAʿDA 1487	2	3	4	5	6	7	8
	9	10	11	12	13	14	15
	16	17	18	19	20	21	22
	23	24	25	26	27	28	29
DHU AL-ḤIJJA 1487	1	2	3	4	5	6	7
	8	9	10[g]	11	12	13	14
	15	16	17	18	19	20	21
	22	23	24	25	26	27	28
	29	30	1[a]	2	3	4	5
MUḤARRAM 1488	6	7	8	9	10[b]	11	12
	13	14	15	16	17	18	19
	20	21	22	23	24	25	26
	27	28	29	30	1	2	3
ṢAFAR 1488	4	5	6	7	8	9	10
	11	12	13	14	15	16	17
	18	19	20	21	22	23	24
	25	26	27	28	29	1	2
RABĪʿ I 1488	3	4	5	6	7	8	9
	10	11	12[c]	13	14	15	16
	17	18	19	20	21	22	23
	24	25	26	27	28	29	30
RABĪʿ II 1488	1	2	3	4	5	6	7
	8	9	10	11	12	13	14
	15	16	17	18	19	20	21
	22	23	24	25	26	27	28
	29	30	1	2	3	4	5
JUMĀDĀ I 1488	6	7	8	9	10	11	12
	13	14	15	16	17	18	19
	20	21	22	23	24	25	26
	27	28	29	30	1	2	3
JUMĀDĀ II 1488	4	5	6	7	8	9	10
	11	12	13	14	15	16	17
	18	19	20	21	22	23	24
	25	26	27	28	29	1	2
RAJAB 1488	3	4	5	6	7	8	9
	10	11	12	13	14	15	16
	17	18	19	20	21	22	23
	24	25	26	27[d]	28	29	1
SHAʿBĀN 1488	2	3	4	5	6	7	8
	9	10	11	12	13	14	15
	16	17	18	19	20	21	22
	23	24	25	26	27	28	29
RAMAḌĀN 1488	1[e]	2	3	4	5	6	7
	8	9	10	11	12	13	14
	15	16	17	18	19	20	21
	22	23	24	25	26	27	28
	29	30	1[f]	2	3	4	5

[a]New Year
[b]ʿAshūrāʾ
[c]Prophet's Birthday
[d]Ascent of the Prophet
[e]Start of Ramaḍān
[f]ʿĪd al-Fiṭr
[g]ʿĪd al-ʾAḍḥā

GREGORIAN 2065

Julian (Sun)	Sun	Mon	Tue	Wed	Thu	Fri	Sat	Month
Dec 15	28	29	30	31	1	2	3	
	4	5	6	7[a]	8	9	10	JANUARY 2065
Dec 29	11	12	13	14[b]	15	16	17	
	18	19	20	21	22	23	24	
Jan 12	25	26	27	28	29	30	31	
	1	2	3	4	5	6	7	
Jan 26	8	9	10	11[c]	12	13	14	FEBRUARY 2065
	15	16	17	18	19	20	21	
Feb 9	22	23	24	25	26	27	28	
	1	2	3	4	5	6	7	
Feb 23	8	9	10	11	12	13	14	
	15[d]	16	17	18	19	20	21	MARCH 2065
Mar 9	22	23	24	25	26	27	28	
	29[e]	30	31	1	2	3	4	
Mar 23	5	6	7	8	9	10	11	
	12	13	14	15	16	17	18	APRIL 2065
Apr 6	19	20	21	22	23	24	25	
	26[f]	27	28	29	30	1	2	
Apr 20	3	4	5	6	7	8	9	
	10	11	12	13	14	15	16	MAY 2065
May 4	17	18	19	20	21	22	23	
	24	25	26	27	28	29	30	
May 18	31	1	2	3	4	5	6	
	7	8	9	10	11	12	13	
Jun 1	14	15	16	17	18	19	20	JUNE 2065
	21	22	23	24	25	26	27	
Jun 15	28	29	30	1	2	3	4	
	5	6	7	8	9	10	11	
Jun 29	12	13	14	15	16	17	18	JULY 2065
	19	20	21	22	23	24	25	
Jul 13	26	27	28	29	30	31	1	
	2	3	4	5	6	7	8	
Jul 27	9	10	11	12	13	14	15	AUGUST 2065
	16	17	18	19	20	21	22	
Aug 10	23	24	25	26	27	28	29	
	30	31	1	2	3	4	5	
Aug 24	6	7	8	9	10	11	12	
	13	14	15	16	17	18	19	SEPTEMBER 2065
Sep 7	20	21	22	23	24	25	26	
	27	28	29	30	1	2	3	
Sep 21	4	5	6	7	8	9	10	
	11	12	13	14	15	16	17	OCTOBER 2065
Oct 5	18	19	20	21	22	23	24	
	25	26	27	28	29	30	31	
Oct 19	1	2	3	4	5	6	7	
	8	9	10	11	12	13	14	
Nov 2	15	16	17	18	19	20	21	NOVEMBER 2065
	22	23	24	25	26	27	28	
Nov 16	29[g]	30	1	2	3	4	5	
	6	7	8	9	10	11	12	
Nov 30	13	14	15	16	17	18	19	DECEMBER 2065
	20	21	22	23	24	25[h]	26	
Dec 14	27	28	29	30	31	1	2	

[a]Orthodox Christmas
[b]Julian New Year
[c]Ash Wednesday
[d]Feast of Orthodoxy
[e]Easter
[f]Orthodox Easter
[g]Advent
[h]Christmas

2066

Gregorian 2066 month	Gregorian 2066 (Sun Mon Tue Wed Thu Fri Sat)	Lunar Phases	ISO Week (Mon)	Julian Day (Sun noon)	Hebrew 5826/5827 month	Hebrew (Sun Mon Tue Wed Thu Fri Sat)	Molad	Chinese Yǐ-Yǒu/Bǐng-Xū‡ month	Chinese (Sun Mon Tue Wed Thu Fri Sat)	Solar Term	Coptic 1782/1783‡ month	Coptic/Ethiopic (Sun Mon Tue Wed Thu Fri Sat)	Ethiopic 2058/2059‡ month
January 2066	● 28 29 30 31 1[a] 2	8:26	53	2475647	Tevet 5826	29[e] 30[e] 1[e] 2[e] 3 4 5	Sun 17h50m1p	Month 12 Yǐ-Yǒu	1 2 3 4 5 6 7		Koiak 1782	18 19 20 21 22 23 24	Tākhśāś 2058
	◐ 4 5 6 7 8 9	9:55	1	2475654		6 7 8 9 10 11 12			8 9 10 11 12 13 14	Xiǎo hán	Tōbe 1782	25 26 27 28 29[c] 30 1	Ṭer 2058
	10 ○ 12 13 14 15 16	15:06	2	2475661		13 14 15 16 17 18 19			15 16 17 18 19 20 21			2 3 4 5 6[d] 7 8	
	17 18 ◑ 20 21 22 23	3:46	3	2475668		20 21 22 23 24 25 26			22 23 24 25* 26 27 28	Dà hán		9 10 11[e] 12 13 14 15	
	24 ● 26 27 28 29 30	20:13	4	2475675	Shevat 5826	27 28 29 1 2 3 4	Tue 6h34m2p	Month 1 Bǐng-Xū	29 30 1[a] 2 3 4 5			16 17 18 19 20 21 22	
February 2066	31 1 ◐ 3 4 5 6	5:43	5	2475682		5 6 7 8 9 10 11			6 7 8 9 10 11 12	Lì chūn		23 24 25 26 27 28 29	
	7 8 9 ○ 11 12 13	8:27	6	2475689		12 13 14 15 16 17 18			13 14 15[b] 16 17 18 19		Meshir 1782	30 1 2 3 4 5 6	Yakātit 2058
	14 15 16 ◑ 18 19 20	12:12	7	2475696		19 20 21 22 23 24 25			20 21 22 23 24 25 26	Yǔ shuǐ		7 8 9 10 11 12 13	
	21 22 23 ● 25 26 27	8:49	8	2475703	Adar 5826	26 27 28 29 30 1 2	Wed 19h18m3p	Month 2 Bǐng-Xū	27 28 29 1 2 3 4			14 15 16 17 18 19 20	
March 2066	28 1 2 3 ◐ 5 6	2:47	9	2475710		3 4 5 6 7 8 9			5 6 7 8 9 10 11	Jīng zhé		21 22 23 24 25 26 27	
	7 8 9 10 ○ 12 13	22:46	10	2475717		10 11 12 13 14[f] 15 16			12 13 14 15 16 17 18		Paremotep 1782	28 29 30 1 2 3 4	Magābit 2058
	14 15 16 17 ◑ 19 20[b]	19:24	11	2475724		17 18 19 20 21 22 23			19 20 21 22 23 24 25	Chūn fēn		5 6 7 8 9 10 11	
	21 22 23 24 ● 26 27	22:12	12	2475731	Nisan 5826	24 25 26 27 28 29 1	Fri 8h2m4p	Month 3 Bǐng-Xū	26* 27 28 29 30 1 2			12 13 14 15 16 17 18	
April 2066	28 29 30 31 1 ◐ 3	23:08	13	2475738		2 3 4 5 6 7 8			3 4 5 6 7 8 9			19 20 21 22 23 24 25	
	4 5 6 7 8 9 ○	10:02	14	2475745		9 10 11 12 13 14 15[g]			10[c] 11 12 13 14 15 16	Qīng míng	Parmoute 1782	26 27 28 29 30 1 2	Miyāzyā 2058
	11 12 13 14 15 16 ◑	2:22	15	2475752		16 17 18 19 20 21 22			17 18 19 20 21 22 23	Gǔ yǔ		3 4 5 6 7 8 9	
	18 19 20 21 22 23 ●	12:28	16	2475759		23 24 25 26 27 28 29		Month 4 Bǐng-Xū	24 25 26 27 28 29 1			10[f] 11 12 13 14 15 16	
May 2066	25 26 27 28 29 30 1		17	2475766	Iyyar 5826	30 1 2 3 4 5 6	Sat 20h46m5p		2 3 4 5 6 7 8			17 18 19 20 21 22 23	
	◐ 3 4 5 6 7 8	16:56	18	2475773		7 8 9 10 11 12 13			9 10 11 12 13 14 15	Lì xià		24 25 26 27 28 29[g] 30	
	○ 10 11 12 13 14 15	18:57	19	2475780		14 15 16 17 18 19 20			16 17 18 19 20 21 22		Pashons 1782	1 2 3 4 5 6 7	Genbot 2058
	◑ 17 18 19 20 21 22	10:00	20	2475787		21 22 23 24 25 26 27			23 24 25 26 27* 28 29	Xiǎo mǎn		8 9 10 11 12 13 14	
	23 ● 25 26 27 28 29	3:37	21	2475794	Sivan 5826	28 29 1 2 3 4 5	Mon 9h30m6p	Month 5 Bǐng-Xū	30 1 2 3 4 5[d] 6			15 16 17 18 19 20 21	
June 2066	30 31 ◐ 2 3 4 5	7:12	22	2475801		6[h] 7 8 9 10 11 12			7 8 9 10 11 12 13	Máng zhòng		22 23 24 25 26 27 28	
	6 7 ○ 9 10 11 12	2:29	23	2475808		13 14 15 16 17 18 19			14 15 16 17 18 19 20		Paōne 1782	29 30 1 2 3 4 5	Sanē 2058
	13 ◑ 15 16 17 18 19	19:09	24	2475815		20 21 22 23 24 25 26			21 22 23 24 25 26 27	Xià zhì		6 7 8 9 10 11 12	
	20 21[c] ● 23 24 25 26	19:14	25	2475822	Tammuz 5826	27 28 29 30 1 2 3	Tue 22h14m7p	Leap Month 5 Bǐng-Xū	28 29 30 1 2 3 4			13 14 15 16 17 18 19	
July 2066	27 28 29 ◐ 1 2 3	17:58	26	2475829		4 5 6 7 8 9 10			5 6 7 8 9 10 11			20 21 22 23 24 25 26	
	4 5 6 ○ 8 9 10	9:33	27	2475836		11 12 13 14 15 16 17			12 13 14 15 16 17 18	Xiǎo shǔ	Epēp 1782	27 28 29 30 1 2 3	Ḥamlē 2058
	11 12 13 ◑ 15 16 17	6:37	28	2475843		18 19 20 21 22 23 24			19 20 21 22 23 24 25			4 5 6 7 8 9 10	
	18 19 20 21 ● 23 24	10:32	29	2475850	Av 5826	25 26 27 28 29 1 2	Thu 10h58m8p	Month 6 Bǐng-Xū	26 27* 28 29 1 2 3	Dà shǔ		11 12 13 14 15 16 17	
August 2066	25 26 27 28 29 ◐ 31	2:00	30	2475857		3 4 5 6 7 8 9			4 5 6 7 8 9 10			18 19 20 21 22 23 24	
	1 2 3 4 ○ 6 7	16:58	31	2475864		10[i] 11 12 13 14 15 16			11 12 13 14 15 16 17	Lì qiū	Mesorē 1782	25 26 27 28 29 30 1	Naḥasē 2058
	8 9 10 11 ◑ 13 14	20:58	32	2475871		17 18 19 20 21 22 23			18 19 20 21 22 23 24			2 3 4 5 6 7 8	
	15 16 17 18 19 20 ●	0:49	33	2475878		24 25 26 27 28 29 30		Month 7 Bǐng-Xū	25 26 27 28 29 30 1			9 10 11 12 13[h] 14 15	
	22 23 24 25 26 27 ◐	8:24	34	2475885	Elul 5826	1 2 3 4 5 6 7	Fri 23h42m9p		2 3 4 5 6 7[e] 8	Chǔ shǔ		16 17 18 19 20 21 22	
September 2066	29 30 31 1 2 3 ○	1:36	35	2475892		8 9 10 11 12 13 14			9 10 11 12 13 14 15[f]			23 24 25 26 27 28 29	
	5 6 7 8 9 10 ◑	14:15	36	2475899		15 16 17 18 19 20 21			16 17 18 19 20 21 22	Bái lù	Epag. 1782	30 1 2 3 4 5 1[a]	Pāg. 2058
	12 13 14 15 16 17 18		37	2475906		22 23 24 25 26 27 28		Month 8 Bǐng-Xū	23 24 25 26 27 28* 29		Thoout 1783	2 3 4 5 6 7 8	Maskaram 2059
	● 20 21 22[d] 23 24 25	13:46	38	2475913	Tishri 5827	29 1[a] 2[a] 3 4 5 6	Sun 12h26m10p		1 2 3 4 5 6 7	Qiū fēn		9 10 11 12 13 14 15	
October 2066	◐ 27 28 29 30 1 2	14:18	39	2475920		7 8 9 10[b] 11 12 13			8 9 10 11 12 13 14			16 17[b] 18 19 20 21 22	
	○ 4 5 6 7 8 9	12:24	40	2475927		14 15[c] 16 17 18 19 20			15[g] 16 17 18 19 20 21	Hán lù		23 24 25 26 27 28 29	
	10 ◑ 12 13 14 15 16	9:42	41	2475934		21 22 23 24 25 26 27		Month 9 Bǐng-Xū	22 23 24 25 26 27 28		Paope 1783	30 1 2 3 4 5 6	Ṭeqemt 2059
	17 18 ● 20 21 22 23	1:41	42	2475941	Ḥeshvan 5827	28 29 30 1 2 3 4	Tue 1h10m11p		29 30 1 2 3 4 5	Shuāng jiàng		7 8 9 10 11 12 13	
	24 ◐ 26 27 28 29 30	20:51	43	2475948		5 6 7 8 9 10 11			6 7 8 9[h] 10 11 12			14 15 16 17 18 19 20	
November 2066	31 1 ○ 3 4 5 6	2:12	44	2475955		12 13 14 15 16 17 18			13 14 15 16 17 18 19			21 22 23 24 25 26 27	
	7 8 9 ◑ 11 12 13	5:44	45	2475962		19 20 21 22 23 24 25		Month 10 Bǐng-Xū	20 21 22 23 24 25 26	Lì dōng	Athōr 1783	28 29 30 1 2 3 4	Ḫedār 2059
	14 15 16 ● 18 19 20	13:05	46	2475969	Kislev 5827	26 27 28 29 30 1 2	Wed 13h54m12p		27 28 29* 1 2 3 4			5 6 7 8 9 10 11	
	21 22 23 ◐ 25 26 27	5:08	47	2475976		3 4 5 6 7 8 9			5 6 7 8 9 10 11	Xiǎo xuě		12 13 14 15 16 17 18	
December 2066	28 29 30 ○ 2 3 4	19:15	48	2475983		10 11 12 13 14 15 16			12 13 14 15 16 17 18			19 20 21 22 23 24 25	
	5 6 7 8 9 ◑ 11	0:37	49	2475990		17[d] 18 19 20 21 22 23		Month 11 Bǐng-Xū	19 20 21 22 23 24 25	Dà xuě	Koiak 1783	26 27 28 29 30 1 2	Tākhśāś 2059
	12 13 14 15 16 ● 18	0:16	50	2475997	Tevet 5827	24 25[e] 26[e] 27[e] 28[e] 29[e] 30[e]	Fri 2h38m13p		26 27 28 29 30 1 2			3 4 5 6 7 8 9	
	19 20 21[e] 22 ◐ 24 25	16:05	51	2476004		1[e] 2[e] 3 4 5 6 7			3 4 5[i] 6 7 8 9	Dōng zhì		10 11 12 13 14 15 16	
	26 27 28 29 30 ○ 1	14:39	52	2476011		8 9 10 11 12 13 14			10 11 12 13 14 15 16			17 18 19 20 21 22 23	

[a]New Year
[b]Spring (7:18)
[c]Summer (0:15)
[d]Autumn (16:25)
[e]Winter (13:44)
● New moon
◐ First quarter moon
○ Full moon
◑ Last quarter moon

[a]New Year
[b]Yom Kippur
[c]Sukkot
[d]Winter starts
[e]Ḥanukkah
[f]Purim
[g]Passover
[h]Shavuot
[i]Fast of Av

‡Leap year
[a]New Year (4764, Dog)
[b]Lantern Festival
[c]Qīngmíng
[d]Dragon Festival
[e]Qīqiǎo
[f]Hungry Ghosts
[g]Mid-Autumn Festival
[h]Double-Ninth Festival
[i]Dōngzhì
*Start of 60-name cycle

‡Leap year
[a]New Year
[b]Building of the Cross
[c]Christmas
[d]Jesus's Circumcision
[e]Epiphany
[f]Easter
[g]Mary's Announcement
[h]Jesus's Transfiguration

PERSIAN (ASTRONOMICAL) 1444/1445‡

Month	Sun	Mon	Tue	Wed	Thu	Fri	Sat
	7	8	9	10	11	12	13
DEY 1444	14	15	16	17	18	19	20
	21	22	23	24	25	26	27
	28	29	30	1	2	3	4
BAHMAN 1444	5	6	7	8	9	10	11
	12	13	14	15	16	17	18
	19	20	21	22	23	24	25
	26	27	28	29	30	1	2
ESFAND 1444	3	4	5	6	7	8	9
	10	11	12	13	14	15	16
	17	18	19	20	21	22	23
	24	25	26	27	28	29	1[a]
FARVARDĪN 1445	2	3	4	5	6	7	8
	9	10	11	12	13[b]	14	15
	16	17	18	19	20	21	22
	23	24	25	26	27	28	29
	30	31	1	2	3	4	5
ORDĪBEHEŠT 1445	6	7	8	9	10	11	12
	13	14	15	16	17	18	19
	20	21	22	23	24	25	26
	27	28	29	30	31	1	2
XORDĀD 1445	3	4	5	6	7	8	9
	10	11	12	13	14	15	16
	17	18	19	20	21	22	23
	24	25	26	27	28	29	30
	31	1	2	3	4	5	6
TĪR 1445	7	8	9	10	11	12	13
	14	15	16	17	18	19	20
	21	22	23	24	25	26	27
	28	29	30	31	1	2	3
MORDĀD 1445	4	5	6	7	8	9	10
	11	12	13	14	15	16	17
	18	19	20	21	22	23	24
	25	26	27	28	29	30	31
SHAHRĪVAR 1445	1	2	3	4	5	6	7
	8	9	10	11	12	13	14
	15	16	17	18	19	20	21
	22	23	24	25	26	27	28
	29	30	31	1	2	3	4
MEHR 1445	5	6	7	8	9	10	11
	12	13	14	15	16	17	18
	19	20	21	22	23	24	25
	26	27	28	29	30	1	2
ĀBĀN 1445	3	4	5	6	7	8	9
	10	11	12	13	14	15	16
	17	18	19	20	21	22	23
	24	25	26	27	28	29	30
ĀZAR 1445	1	2	3	4	5	6	7
	8	9	10	11	12	13	14
	15	16	17	18	19	20	21
	22	23	24	25	26	27	28
DEY 1445	29	30	1	2	3	4	5
	6	7	8	9	10	11	12

‡Leap year
[a]New Year
[b]Sizdeh Bedar

HINDU LUNAR 2122/2123‡

Month	Sun	Mon	Tue	Wed	Thu	Fri	Sat
	30	1	2	3	4	6	7
PAUSHA 2122	8	8	9	10	11	12	13
	14	15	16	17	18	19	20
	21	22	23	24	25	26	27
	29	30	1	2	3	4	5
MĀGHA 2122	6	7	8	9	10	11	11
	12	13	14	15	16	17	18
	19	20	21	23	24	25	26
	27	28[h]	29	30	1	2	3
PHĀLGUNA 2122	4	5	6	7	8	9	10
	11	12	13	14	15[i]	16	17
	18	19	20	21	22	23	24
	25	26	28	29	30	1[a]	2
CHAITRA 2123	3	4	4	5	6	7	8
	9[b]	10	11	12	13	14	15
	16	17	18	19	21	22	23
	24	25	26	27	28	29	30
VAIŚĀKHA 2123	1	2	3	4	5	6	7
	8	8	9	10	11	12	14
	15	16	17	18	19	20	21
	22	23	24	26	27	28	29
	29	30	1	2	3	4	5
JYAISHTHA 2123	6	7	8	9	10	11	12
	13	14	15	16	18	19	20
	21	22	23	24	25	26	27
	28	29	30	1	2	3	4
ĀSHĀḌHA 2123	4	5	6	7	9	10	11
	12	13	14	15	16	17	18
	19	21	22	23	24	25	26
	26	27	28	29	30	1	2
ŚRĀVAṆA 2123	3	4	5	6	7	8	9
	10	11	13	14	15	16	17
	18	19	20	21	22	23[c]	24
	25	26	27	28	29	30	1
BHĀDRAPADA 2123	2	2	4[d]	5	6	7	8
	9	10	11	12	13	14	15
	17	18	19	20	21	22	22
	23	24	25	26	27	28	29
	30	1	2	3	4	5	6
ĀŚVINA 2123	7	8[e]	10[e]	11	12	13	14
	15	16	17	18	19	20	21
	22	23	24	25	26	26	27
	28	29	30[f]	2	3	4	5
KĀRTTIKA 2123	6	7	8	9	10	11	12
	13	14	15	16	17	18	19
	20	21	22	23	24	25	26
	27	28	29	30	1	2	3
MĀRGAŚĪRA 2123	4	5	7	8	9	10	11[g]
	12	13	14	15	16	17	18
	19	19	20	21	22	23	24
	25	26	27	28	29	1	2
PAUSHA 2123	3	4	5	6	7	8	9
	10	11	12	13	14	15	16

‡Leap year
[a]New Year (Vyaya)
[b]Birthday of Rāma
[c]Birthday of Krishna
[d]Ganēśa Chaturthī
[e]Dashara
[f]Diwali
[g]Birthday of Vishnu
[h]Night of Śiva
[i]Holi

HINDU SOLAR 1987/1988

Month	Sun	Mon	Tue	Wed	Thu	Fri	Sat
PAUSHA 1987	12	13	14	15	16	17	18
	19	20	21	22	23	24	25
	26	27	28	29	1[b]	2	3
MĀGHA 1987	4	5	6	7	8	9	10
	11	12	13	14	15	16	17
	18	19	20	21	22	23	24
	25	26	27	28	29	30	1
PHĀLGUNA 1987	2	3	4	5	6	7	8
	9	10	11	12	13	14	15
	16	17	18	19	20	21	22
	23	24	25	26	27	28	29
	30	1	2	3	4	5	6
CHAITRA 1987	7	8	9	10	11	12	13
	14	15	16	17	18	19	20
	21	22	23	24	25	26	27
	28	29	30	1[a]	2	3	4
VAIŚĀKHA 1988	5	6	7	8	9	10	11
	12	13	14	15	16	17	18
	19	20	21	22	23	24	25
	26	27	28	29	30	31	1
JYAISHTHA 1988	2	3	4	5	6	7	8
	9	10	11	12	13	14	15
	16	17	18	19	20	21	22
	23	24	25	26	27	28	29
	30	31	1	2	3	4	5
ĀSHĀḌHA 1988	6	7	8	9	10	11	12
	13	14	15	16	17	18	19
	20	21	22	23	24	25	26
	27	28	29	30	31	32	1
ŚRĀVAṆA 1988	2	3	4	5	6	7	8
	9	10	11	12	13	14	15
	16	17	18	19	20	21	22
	23	24	25	26	27	28	29
	30	31	32	1	2	3	4
BHĀDRAPADA 1988	5	6	7	8	9	10	11
	12	13	14	15	16	17	18
	19	20	21	22	23	24	25
	26	27	28	29	30	31	1
ĀŚVINA 1988	2	3	4	5	6	7	8
	9	10	11	12	13	14	15
	16	17	18	19	20	21	22
	23	24	25	26	27	28	29
	30	1	2	3	4	5	6
KĀRTTIKA 1988	7	8	9	10	11	12	13
	14	15	16	17	18	19	20
	21	22	23	24	25	26	27
	28	29	30	1	2	3	4
MĀRGAŚĪRA 1988	5	6	7	8	9	10	11
	12	13	14	15	16	17	18
	19	20	21	22	23	24	25
	26	27	28	29	1	2	3
PAUSHA 1988	4	5	6	7	8	9	10
	11	12	13	14	15	16	17

[a]New Year (Śārvari)
[b]Pongal

ISLAMIC (ASTRONOMICAL) 1488/1489

Month	Sun	Mon	Tue	Wed	Thu	Fri	Sat
	29	30	1	2	3	4	5
SHAWWĀL 1488	6	7	8	9	10	11	12
	13	14	15	16	17	18	19
	20	21	22	23	24	25	26
	27	28	29	1	2	3	4
DHU AL-QA'DA 1488	5	6	7	8	9	10	11
	12	13	14	15	16	17	18
	19	20	21	22	23	24	25
	26	27	28	29	30	1	2
DHU AL-ḤIJJA 1488	3	4	5	6	7	8	9
	10[g]	11	12	13	14	15	16
	17	18	19	20	21	22	23
	24	25	26	27	28	29	1[a]
MUḤARRAM 1489	2[a]	3	4	5	6	7	8
	9	10[b]	11	12	13	14	15
	16	17	18	19	20	21	22
	23	24	25	26	27	28	29
	30	1	2	3	4	5	6
ṢAFAR 1489	7	8	9	10	11	12	13
	14	15	16	17	18	19	20
	21	22	23	24	25	26	27
	28	29	1	2	3	4	5
RABĪ' I 1489	6	7	8	9	10	11	12[c]
	13	14	15	16	17	18	19
	20	21	22	23	24	25	26
	27	28	29	30	1	2	3
RABĪ' II 1489	4	5	6	7	8	9	10
	11	12	13	14	15	16	17
	18	19	20	21	22	23	24
	25	26	27	28	29	30	1
JUMĀDĀ I 1489	2	3	4	5	6	7	8
	9	10	11	12	13	14	15
	16	17	18	19	20	21	22
	23	24	25	26	27	28	29
	30	1	2	3	4	5	6
JUMĀDĀ II 1489	7	8	9	10	11	12	13
	14	15	16	17	18	19	20
	21	22	23	24	25	26	27
	28	29	30	1	2	3	4
RAJAB 1489	5	6	7	8	9	10	11
	12	13	14	15	16	17	18
	19	20	21	22	23	24	25
	26	27[d]	28	29	1	2	3
SHA'BĀN 1489	4	5	6	7	8	9	10
	11	12	13	14	15	16	17
	18	19	20	21	22	23	24
	25	26	27	28	29	1[e]	2
RAMAḌĀN 1489	3	4	5	6	7	8	9
	10	11	12	13	14	15	16
	17	18	19	20	21	22	23
	24	25	26	27	28	29	1[f]
SHAWWĀL 1489	2	3	4	5	6	7	8
	9	10	11	12	13	14	15

[a]New Year
[a]New Year (Arithmetic)
[b]'Ashūrā'
[c]Prophet's Birthday
[d]Ascent of the Prophet
[e]Start of Ramaḍān
[f]'Īd al-Fiṭr
[g]'Īd al-'Aḍḥā

GREGORIAN 2066

Julian (Sun)	Sun	Mon	Tue	Wed	Thu	Fri	Sat	Month
Dec 14	27	28	29	30	31	1	2	
	3	4	5	6	7[a]	8	9	JANUARY 2066
Dec 28	10	11	12	13	14[b]	15	16	
	17	18	19	20	21	22	23	
Jan 11	24	25	26	27	28	29	30	
	31	1	2	3	4	5	6	
Jan 25	7	8	9	10	11	12	13	FEBRUARY 2066
	14	15	16	17	18	19	20	
Feb 8	21	22	23	24[c]	25	26	27	
	28	1	2	3	4	5	6	
Feb 22	7[d]	8	9	10	11	12	13	MARCH 2066
	14	15	16	17	18	19	20	
Mar 8	21	22	23	24	25	26	27	
	28	29	30	31	1	2	3	
Mar 22	4	5	6	7	8	9	10	APRIL 2066
	11[e]	12	13	14	15	16	17	
Apr 5	18[f]	19	20	21	22	23	24	
	25	26	27	28	29	30	1	
Apr 19	2	3	4	5	6	7	8	MAY 2066
	9	10	11	12	13	14	15	
May 3	16	17	18	19	20	21	22	
	23	24	25	26	27	28	29	
May 17	30	31	1	2	3	4	5	
	6	7	8	9	10	11	12	JUNE 2066
May 31	13	14	15	16	17	18	19	
	20	21	22	23	24	25	26	
Jun 14	27	28	29	30	1	2	3	
	4	5	6	7	8	9	10	JULY 2066
Jun 28	11	12	13	14	15	16	17	
	18	19	20	21	22	23	24	
Jul 12	25	26	27	28	29	30	31	
	1	2	3	4	5	6	7	
Jul 26	8	9	10	11	12	13	14	AUGUST 2066
	15	16	17	18	19	20	21	
Aug 9	22	23	24	25	26	27	28	
	29	30	31	1	2	3	4	
Aug 23	5	6	7	8	9	10	11	SEPTEMBER 2066
	12	13	14	15	16	17	18	
Sep 6	19	20	21	22	23	24	25	
	26	27	28	29	30	1	2	
Sep 20	3	4	5	6	7	8	9	OCTOBER 2066
	10	11	12	13	14	15	16	
Oct 4	17	18	19	20	21	22	23	
	24	25	26	27	28	29	30	
Oct 18	31	1	2	3	4	5	6	
	7	8	9	10	11	12	13	NOVEMBER 2066
Nov 1	14	15	16	17	18	19	20	
	21	22	23	24	25	26	27	
Nov 15	28[g]	29	30	1	2	3	4	
	5	6	7	8	9	10	11	DECEMBER 2066
Nov 29	12	13	14	15	16	17	18	
	19	20	21	22	23	24	25[h]	
Dec 13	26	27	28	29	30	31	1	

[a]Orthodox Christmas
[b]Julian New Year
[c]Ash Wednesday
[d]Feast of Orthodoxy
[e]Easter
[f]Orthodox Easter
[g]Advent
[h]Christmas

2067

Month	GREGORIAN 2067 (Sun Mon Tue Wed Thu Fri Sat)	Lunar Phases	ISO WEEK (Mon)	JULIAN DAY (Sun noon)	Hebrew month	HEBREW 5827/5828‡ (Sun Mon Tue Wed Thu Fri Sat)	Molad	Chinese month	CHINESE Bǐng-Xū‡/Dīng-Hài (Sun Mon Tue Wed Thu Fri Sat)	Solar Term	Coptic month	COPTIC 1783‡/1784 (Sun Mon Tue Wed Thu Fri Sat)	ETHIOPIC 2059‡/2060
	26 27 28 29 30 ○ 1[a]	14:39	52	2476011	TEVETH 5827	8 9 10 11 12 13 14		MONTH 11 Bǐng-Xū	10 11 12 13 14 15 16		KOIAK 1783	17 18 19 20 21 22 23	TĀKHŚĀŚ 2059
	2 3 4 5 6 7 ◑	17:00	1	2476018		15 16 17 18 19 20 21			17 18 19 20 21 22 23	Xiǎo hán		24 25 26 27 28 29[c] 30	
JANUARY 2067	9 10 11 12 13 14 ●	11:15	2	2476025		22 23 24 25 26 27 28			24 25 26 27 28 29 1*		TŌBE 1783	1 2 3 4 5 6[d] 7	
	16 17 18 19 20 21 ◐	6:15	3	2476032		29 1 2 3 4 5 6		MONTH 12 Bǐng-Xū	2 3 4 5 6 7 8	Dà hán		8 9 10 11[e] 12 13 14	ṬER 2059
	23 24 25 26 27 28 29		4	2476039	SHEVAT 5827	7 8 9 10 11 12 13	Sat 15h22m14p		9 10 11 12 13 14 15			15 16 17 18 19 20 21	
	○ 31 1 2 3 4 5	10:28	5	2476046		14 15 16 17 18 19 20			16 17 18 19 20 21 22	Lì chūn		22 23 24 25 26 27 28	
FEBRUARY 2067	6 ◑ 8 9 10 11 12	6:13	6	2476053		21 22 23 24 25 26 27			23 24 25 26 27 28 29		MESHIR 1783	29 30 1 2 3 4 5	
	● 14 15 16 17 18 19	21:56	7	2476060	ADAR 5827	28 29 30 1 2 3 4			30 1[a] 2 3 4 5 6	Yǔ shuǐ		6 7 8 9 10 11 12	YAKĀTIT 2059
	◐ 21 22 23 24 25 26	23:29	8	2476067		5 6 7 8 9 10 11	Mon 4h6m15p	MONTH 1 Dīng-Hài	7 8 9 10 11 12 13			13 14 15 16 17 18 19	
	27 28 ○ 2 3 4 5	4:40	9	2476074		12 13 14[f] 15 16 17 18			14 15[b] 16 17 18 19 20	Jīng zhé		20 21 22 23 24 25 26	
MARCH 2067	6 7 ◑ 9 10 11 12	16:14	10	2476081		19 20 21 22 23 24 25			21 22 23 24 25 26 27		PAREMOTEP 1783	27 28 29 30 1 2 3	
	13 14 ● 16 17 18 19	8:27	11	2476088	NISAN 5827	26 27 28 29 1 2 3			28 29 1 2* 3 4 5			4 5 6 7 8 9 10	MAGĀBIT 2059
	20[b] 21 ◐ 23 24 25 26	18:43	12	2476095		4 5 6 7 8 9 10	Tue 16h50m16p	MONTH 2 Dīng-Hài	6 7 8 9 10 11 12	Chūn fēn		11 12 13 14 15 16 17	
	27 28 29 ○ 31 1 2	20:07	13	2476102		11 12 13 14 15[g] 16 17			13 14 15 16 17 18 19			18 19 20 21 22 23 24	
	3 4 5 ◑ 7 8 9	23:36	14	2476109		18 19 20 21 22 23 24			20 21 22[c] 23 24 25 26	Qīng míng	PARMOUTE 1783	25 26 27 28 29 30 1	
APRIL 2067	10 11 12 ● 14 15 16	19:22	15	2476116	IYYAR 5827	25 26 27 28 29 30 1			27 28 29 30 1 2 3			2[f] 3 4 5 6 7 8	MIYĀZYĀ 2059
	17 18 19 20 ◐ 22 23	14:14	16	2476123		2 3 4 5 6 7 8	Thu 5h34m17p	MONTH 3 Dīng-Hài	4 5 6 7 8 9 10	Gǔ yǔ		9 10 11 12 13 14 15	
	24 25 26 27 28 ○ 30	8:39	17	2476130		9 10 11 12 13 14 15			11 12 13 14 15 16 17			16 17 18 19 20 21 22	
	1 2 3 4 5 ◑ 7	5:18	18	2476137		16 17 18 19 20 21 22			18 19 20 21 22 23 24	Lì xià		23 24 25 26 27 28 29[g]	
MAY 2067	8 9 10 11 12 ● 14	7:19	19	2476144		23 24 25 26 27 28 29			25 26 27 28 29 1 2		PASHONS 1783	30 1 2 3 4 5 6	
	15 16 17 18 19 20 ◐	8:28	20	2476151	SIVAN 5827	1 2 3 4 5 6[h] 7	Fri 18h19m0p	MONTH 4 Dīng-Hài	3* 4 5 6 7 8 9	Xiǎo mǎn		7 8 9 10 11 12 13	GENBOT 2059
	22 23 24 25 26 27 ○	18:40	21	2476158		8 9 10 11 12 13 14			10 11 12 13 14 15 16			14 15 16 17 18 19 20	
	29 30 31 1 2 3 ◑	10:37	22	2476165		15 16 17 18 19 20 21			17 18 19 20 21 22 23			21 22 23 24 25 26 27	
JUNE 2067	5 6 7 8 9 10 ●	20:39	23	2476172		22 23 24 25 26 27 28			24 25 26 27 28 29 30	Máng zhòng	PAŌNE 1783	28 29 30 1 2 3 4	
	12 13 14 15 16 17 18		24	2476179	TAMMUZ 5827	29 30 1 2 3 4 5	Sun 7h3m1p	MONTH 5 Dīng-Hài	1 2 3 4 5[d] 6 7			5 6 7 8 9 10 11	SANĒ 2059
	19 ◐ 21[c] 22 23 24 25	0:27	25	2476186		6 7 8 9 10 11 12			8 9 10 11 12 13 14	Xià zhì		12 13 14 15 16 17 18	
	26 ○ 28 29 30 1 2	2:51	26	2476193		13 14 15 16 17 18 19			15 16 17 18 19 20 21			19 20 21 22 23 24 25	
	◑ 4 5 6 7 8 9	17:01	27	2476200		20 21 22 23 24 25 26			22 23 24 25 26 27 28	Xiǎo shǔ	EPĒP 1783	26 27 28 29 30 1 2	
JULY 2067	10 ● 12 13 14 15 16	11:15	28	2476207	AV 5827	27 28 29 1 2 3 4	Mon 19h47m2p	MONTH 6 Dīng-Hài	29 1 2 3 4* 5 6			3 4 5 6 7 8 9	HAMLĒ 2059
	17 18 ◐ 20 21 22 23	13:58	29	2476214		5 6 7 8 9[i] 10 11			7 8 9 10 11 12 13	Dà shǔ		10 11 12 13 14 15 16	
	24 25 ○ 27 28 29 30	9:57	30	2476221		12 13 14 15 16 17 18			14 15 16 17 18 19 20			17 18 19 20 21 22 23	
	31 1 ◑ 3 4 5 6	1:50	31	2476228		19 20 21 22 23 24 25			21 22 23 24 25 26 27			24 25 26 27 28 29 30	
AUGUST 2067	7 8 9 ● 11 12 13	2:35	32	2476235	ELUL 5827	26 27 28 29 30 1 2	Wed 8h31m3p	MONTH 7 Dīng-Hài	28 29 30 1 2 3 4	Lì qiū	MESORĒ 1783	1 2 3 4 5 6 7	
	14 15 16 17 ◐ 19 20	1:08	33	2476242		3 4 5 6 7 8 9			5 6 7[e] 8 9 10 11			8 9 10 11 12 13[h] 14	NAHASĒ 2059
	21 22 23 ○ 25 26 27	16:56	34	2476249		10 11 12 13 14 15 16			12 13 14 15[f] 16 17 18	Chǔ shǔ		15 16 17 18 19 20 21	
	28 29 30 ◑ 1 2 3	14:03	35	2476256		17 18 19 20 21 22 23			19 20 21 22 23 24 25			22 23 24 25 26 27 28	
SEPTEMBER 2067	4 5 6 7 ● 9 10	18:07	36	2476263		24 25 26 27 28 29 1[a]	Thu 21h15m4p	MONTH 8 Dīng-Hài	26 27 28 29 30 1 2	Bái lù	EPAG. 1783	29 30 1 2 3 4 5	PĀG. 2059
	11 12 13 14 15 ◐ 17	10:18	37	2476270	TISHRI 5828	2[a] 3 4 5 6 7 8			3 4* 5 6 7 8 9		THOOUT 1784	6 1[a] 2 3 4 5 6	
	18 19 20 21 22[d] ○ 24	0:53	38	2476277		9 10[b] 11 12 13 14 15[c]			10 11 12 13 14 15[g] 16	Qiū fēn		7 8 9 10 11 12 13	MASKARAM 2060
	25 26 27 28 29 ◑ 1	6:00	39	2476284		16 17 18 19 20 21 22			17 18 19 20 21 22 23			14 15 16 17[b] 18 19 20	
OCTOBER 2067	2 3 4 5 6 7 ●	9:27	40	2476291		23 24 25 26 27 28 29			24 25 26 27 28 29 1	Hán lù		21 22 23 24 25 26 27	
	9 10 11 12 13 14 ◐	18:01	41	2476298	HESHVAN 5828	30 1 2 3 4 5 6	Sat 9h59m5p	MONTH 9 Dīng-Hài	2 3 4 5 6 7 8		PAOPE 1784	28 29 30 1 2 3 4	
	16 17 18 19 20 21 ○	10:55	42	2476305		7 8 9 10 11 12 13			9[h] 10 11 12 13 14 15			5 6 7 8 9 10 11	TEQEMT 2060
	23 24 25 26 27 28 29		43	2476312		14 15 16 17 18 19 20			16 17 18 19 20 21 22	Shuāng jiàng		12 13 14 15 16 17 18	
	◑ 31 1 2 3 4 5	1:07	44	2476319		21 22 23 24 25 26 27			23 24 25 26 27 28 29			19 20 21 22 23 24 25	
NOVEMBER 2067	6 ● 8 9 10 11 12	0:13	45	2476326	KISLEV 5828	28 29 1 2 3 4 5	Sun 22h43m6p	MONTH 10 Dīng-Hài	30 1 2 3 4 5* 6	Lì dōng	ATHŌR 1784	26 27 28 29 30 1 2	
	13 ◐ 15 16 17 18 19	1:06	46	2476333		6 7 8 9 10 11 12			7 8 9 10 11 12 13			3 4 5 6 7 8 9	HEDĀR 2060
	○ 21 22 23 24 25 26	23:48	47	2476340		13 14 15 16 17 18 19			14 15 16 17 18 19 20	Xiǎo xuě		10 11 12 13 14 15 16	
	27 ◑ 29 30 1 2 3	22:05	48	2476347		20 21 22 23 24 25[e] 26[e]			21 22 23 24 25 26 27			17 18 19 20 21 22 23	
DECEMBER 2067	4 5 ● 7 8 9 10	14:03	49	2476354	TEVETH 5828	27[e] 28[e] 29[d] 1[e] 2[e] 3[e] 4	Tue 11h27m7p	MONTH 11 Dīng-Hài	28 29 1 2 3 4 5	Dà xuě		24 25 26 27 28 29 30	
	11 12 ◐ 14 15 16 17	8:37	50	2476361		5 6 7 8 9 10 11			6 7 8 9 10 11 12		KOIAK 1784	1 2 3 4 5 6 7	TĀKHŚĀŚ 2060
	18 19 ○ 21[e] 22 23 24	15:40	51	2476368		12 13 14 15 16 17 18			13 14 15 16 17[i] 18 19	Dōng zhì		8 9 10 11 12 13 14	
	25 26 27 ◑ 29 30 31	19:09	52	2476375		19 20 21 22 23 24 25			20 21 22 23 24 25 26			15 16 17 18 19 20 21	

[a]New Year
[b]Spring (12:52)
[c]Summer (5:54)
[d]Autumn (22:18)
[e]Winter (19:42)
● New moon
◐ First quarter moon
○ Full moon
◑ Last quarter moon

‡Leap year
[a]New Year
[b]Yom Kippur
[c]Sukkot
[d]Winter starts
[e]Ḥanukkah
[f]Purim
[g]Passover
[h]Shavuot
[i]Fast of Av

‡Leap year
[a]New Year (4765, Pig)
[b]Lantern Festival
[c]Qīngmíng
[d]Dragon Festival
[e]Qīqiǎo
[f]Hungry Ghosts
[g]Mid-Autumn Festival
[h]Double-Ninth Festival
[i]Dōngzhì
*Start of 60-name cycle

‡Leap year
[a]New Year
[b]Building of the Cross
[c]Christmas
[d]Jesus's Circumcision
[e]Epiphany
[f]Easter
[g]Mary's Announcement
[h]Jesus's Transfiguration

PERSIAN (ASTRONOMICAL) 1445‡/1446

Month	Sun	Mon	Tue	Wed	Thu	Fri	Sat
DEY 1445	6	7	8	9	10	11	12
	13	14	15	16	17	18	19
	20	21	22	23	24	25	26
	27	28	29	30	1	2	3
BAHMAN 1445	4	5	6	7	8	9	10
	11	12	13	14	15	16	17
	18	19	20	21	22	23	24
	25	26	27	28	29	30	1
ESFAND 1445	2	3	4	5	6	7	8
	9	10	11	12	13	14	15
	16	17	18	19	20	21	22
	23	24	25	26	27	28	29
	30	1[a]	2	3	4	5	6
FARVARDĪN 1446	7	8	9	10	11	12	13[b]
	14	15	16	17	18	19	20
	21	22	23	24	25	26	27
	28	29	30	31	1	2	3
ORDĪBEHEŠT 1446	4	5	6	7	8	9	10
	11	12	13	14	15	16	17
	18	19	20	21	22	23	24
	25	26	27	28	29	30	31
XORDĀD 1446	1	2	3	4	5	6	7
	8	9	10	11	12	13	14
	15	16	17	18	19	20	21
	22	23	24	25	26	27	28
	29	30	31	1	2	3	4
TĪR 1446	5	6	7	8	9	10	11
	12	13	14	15	16	17	18
	19	20	21	22	23	24	25
	26	27	28	29	30	31	1
MORDĀD 1446	2	3	4	5	6	7	8
	9	10	11	12	13	14	15
	16	17	18	19	20	21	22
	23	24	25	26	27	28	29
	30	31	1	2	3	4	5
SHAHRĪVAR 1446	6	7	8	9	10	11	12
	13	14	15	16	17	18	19
	20	21	22	23	24	25	26
	27	28	29	30	31	1	2
MEHR 1446	3	4	5	6	7	8	9
	10	11	12	13	14	15	16
	17	18	19	20	21	22	23
	24	25	26	27	28	29	30
ĀBĀN 1446	1	2	3	4	5	6	7
	8	9	10	11	12	13	14
	15	16	17	18	19	20	21
	22	23	24	25	26	27	28
	29	30	1	2	3	4	5
ĀZAR 1446	6	7	8	9	10	11	12
	13	14	15	16	17	18	19
	20	21	22	23	24	25	26
	27	28	29	30	1	2	3
DEY 1446	4	5	6	7	8	9	10

HINDU LUNAR 2123‡/2124

Month	Sun	Mon	Tue	Wed	Thu	Fri	Sat
PAUSHA 2123	10	11	12	13	14	15	16
	17	18	19	20	21	22	23
	24	25	26	27	28	29	30
MĀGHA 2123	1	2	3	**4**	6	7	8
	9	10	11	12	12	13	14
	15	16	17	18	19	20	21
	22	23	24	25	26	27	**28**[h]
LEAP PHĀLGUNA 2123	30	1	2	3	4	5	6
	7	8	9	10	11	12	13
	14	14	15	16	17	18	19
	20	21	**22**	24	25	26	27
PHĀLGUNA 2123	28	29	30	1	2	3	4
	5	6	7	8	9	10	11
	12	13	14	15[i]	16	17	18
	19	20	21	22	23	24	25
CHAITRA 2124	**26**	28	29	30	1[a]	2	3
	4	5	6	7	8	8[b]	9
	10	11	12	13	14	15	16
	17	18	19	**20**	22	23	24
VAIŚĀKHA 2124	25	26	27	28	29	30	1
	2	3	4	5	6	7	8
	9	10	11	12	13	14	15
	16	17	18	19	20	21	22
	23	25	26	27	28	29	30
JYAISHTHA 2124	1	2	3	4	4	5	6
	7	8	9	10	11	12	13
	14	15	**16**	18	19	20	21
	22	23	24	25	26	27	28
ĀSHĀḌHA 2124	29	30	1	2	3	4	5
	6	7	8	9	10	11	12
	13	14	15	16	17	**18**	20
	21	22	23	24	25	26	27
ŚRĀVAṆA 2124	28	29	30	30	1	2	3
	4	5	6	7	8	9	10
	11	13	14	15	16	17	18
	19	20	21	22	23[c]	24	25
BHĀDRAPADA 2124	26	27	28	29	30	1	2
	3	4[d]	5	6	7	8	9
	10	11	12	13	14	**15**	17
	18	19	20	21	22	23	24
	25	26	26	27	28	29	30
ĀŚVINA 2124	1	2	3	4	5	6	7
	8[e]	10[e]	11	12	13	14	15
	16	17	18	19	20	21	22
	23	24	25	26	27	28	29
KĀRTTIKA 2124	30	1[f]	2	3	4	5	6
	7	8	9	10	11	12	**13**
	15	16	17	18	19	20	20
	21	22	23	24	25	26	27
MĀRGAŚĪRA 2124	28	29	30	1	2	3	4
	5	**6**	8	9	10	11[g]	12
	13	14	15	16	17	18	19
	20	21	22	22	23	24	25

HINDU SOLAR 1988/1989‡

Month	Sun	Mon	Tue	Wed	Thu	Fri	Sat
PAUSHA 1988	11	12	13	14	15	16	17
	18	19	20	21	22	23	24
	25	26	27	28	29	30	1[b]
MĀGHA 1988	2	3	4	5	6	7	8
	9	10	11	12	13	14	15
	16	17	18	19	20	21	22
	23	24	25	26	27	28	29
PHĀLGUNA 1988	1	2	3	4	5	6	7
	8	9	10	11	12	13	14
	15	16	17	18	19	20	21
	22	23	24	25	26	27	28
CHAITRA 1988	29	30	1	2	3	4	5
	6	7	8	9	10	11	12
	13	14	15	16	17	18	19
	20	21	22	23	24	25	26
VAIŚĀKHA 1989	27	28	29	30	1[a]	2	3
	4	5	6	7	8	9	10
	11	12	13	14	15	16	17
	18	19	20	21	22	23	24
	25	26	27	28	29	30	31
JYAISHTHA 1989	1	2	3	4	5	6	7
	8	9	10	11	12	13	14
	15	16	17	18	19	20	21
	22	23	24	25	26	27	28
ĀSHĀḌHA 1989	29	30	31	32	1	2	3
	4	5	6	7	8	9	10
	11	12	13	14	15	16	17
	18	19	20	21	22	23	24
	25	26	27	28	29	30	31
ŚRĀVAṆA 1989	1	2	3	4	5	6	7
	8	9	10	11	12	13	14
	15	16	17	18	19	20	21
	22	23	24	25	26	27	28
BHĀDRAPADA 1989	29	30	31	32	1	2	3
	4	5	6	7	8	9	10
	11	12	13	14	15	16	17
	18	19	20	21	22	23	24
	25	26	27	28	29	30	31
ĀŚVINA 1989	1	2	3	4	5	6	7
	8	9	10	11	12	13	14
	15	16	17	18	19	20	21
	22	23	24	25	26	27	28
KĀRTTIKA 1989	29	30	1	2	3	4	5
	6	7	8	9	10	11	12
	13	14	15	16	17	18	19
	20	21	22	23	24	25	26
MĀRGAŚĪRA 1989	27	28	29	30	1	2	3
	4	5	6	7	8	9	10
	11	12	13	14	15	16	17
	18	19	20	21	22	23	24
PAUSHA 1989	25	26	27	28	29	30	1
	2	3	4	5	6	7	8
	9	10	11	12	13	14	15

ISLAMIC (ASTRONOMICAL) 1489/1490‡

Month	Sun	Mon	Tue	Wed	Thu	Fri	Sat
SHAWWĀL 1489	9	10	11	12	13	14	15
	16	17	18	19	20	21	22
	23	24	25	26	27	28	29
DHU AL-QA'DA 1489	30	1	2	3	4	5	6
	7	8	9	10	11	12	13
	14	15	16	17	18	19	20
	21	22	23	24	25	26	27
DHU AL-ḤIJJA 1489	28	29	1	2	3	4	5
	6	7	8	9	10[g]	11	12
	13	14	15	16	17	18	19
	20	21	22	23	24	25	26
MUHARRAM 1490	27	28	29	1[a]	2[A]	3	4
	5	6	7	8	9	10[b]	11
	12	13	14	15	16	17	18
	19	20	21	22	23	24	25
ṢAFAR 1490	26	27	28	29	30	1	2
	3	4	5	6	7	8	9
	10	11	12	13	14	15	16
	17	18	19	20	21	22	23
	24	25	26	27	28	29	30
RABĪ' I 1490	1	2	3	4	5	6	7
	8	9	10	11	12[c]	13	14
	15	16	17	18	19	20	21
	22	23	24	25	26	27	28
RABĪ' II 1490	29	1	2	3	4	5	6
	7	8	9	10	11	12	13
	14	15	16	17	18	19	20
	21	22	23	24	25	26	27
JUMĀDĀ I 1490	28	29	30	1	2	3	4
	5	6	7	8	9	10	11
	12	13	14	15	16	17	18
	19	20	21	22	23	24	25
JUMĀDĀ II 1490	26	27	28	29	30	31	1
	2	3	4	5	6	7	8
	9	10	11	12	13	14	15
	16	17	18	19	20	21	22
	23	24	25	26	27	28	29
RAJAB 1490	1	2	3	4	5	6	7
	8	9	10	11	12	13	14
	15	16	17	18	19	20	21
	22	23	24	25	26	27[d]	28
SHA'BĀN 1490	29	30	1	2	3	4	5
	6	7	8	9	10	11	12
	13	14	15	16	17	18	19
	20	21	22	23	24	25	26
RAMAḌĀN 1490	27	28	29	1[e]	2	3	4
	5	6	7	8	9	10	11
	12	13	14	15	16	17	18
	19	20	21	22	23	24	25
SHAWWĀL 1490	26	27	28	29	1[f]	2	3
	4	5	6	7	8	9	10
	11	12	13	14	15	16	17
	18	19	20	21	22	23	24

GREGORIAN 2067

Julian (Sun)	Sun	Mon	Tue	Wed	Thu	Fri	Sat	Month
Dec 13	26	27	28	29	30	31	1	JANUARY 2067
	2	3	4	5	6	7[a]	8	
Dec 27	9	10	11	12	13	14[b]	15	
	16	17	18	19	20	21	22	
Jan 10	23	24	25	26	27	28	29	
	30	31	1	2	3	4	5	FEBRUARY 2067
Jan 24	6	7	8	9	10	11	12	
	13	14	15	16[c]	17	18	19	
Feb 7	20	21	22	23	24	25	26	
	27[d]	28	1	2	3	4	5	MARCH 2067
Feb 21	6	7	8	9	10	11	12	
	13	14	15	16	17	18	19	
Mar 7	20	21	22	23	24	25	26	
	27	28	29	30	31	1	2	APRIL 2067
Mar 21	3[e]	4	5	6	7	8	9	
	10[f]	11	12	13	14	15	16	
Apr 4	17	18	19	20	21	22	23	
	24	25	26	27	28	29	30	
Apr 18	1	2	3	4	5	6	7	MAY 2067
	8	9	10	11	12	13	14	
May 2	15	16	17	18	19	20	21	
	22	23	24	25	26	27	28	
May 16	29	30	31	1	2	3	4	JUNE 2067
	5	6	7	8	9	10	11	
May 30	12	13	14	15	16	17	18	
	19	20	21	22	23	24	25	
Jun 13	26	27	28	29	30	1	2	JULY 2067
	3	4	5	6	7	8	9	
Jun 27	10	11	12	13	14	15	16	
	17	18	19	20	21	22	23	
Jul 11	24	25	26	27	28	29	30	
	31	1	2	3	4	5	6	AUGUST 2067
Jul 25	7	8	9	10	11	12	13	
	14	15	16	17	18	19	20	
Aug 8	21	22	23	24	25	26	27	
	28	29	30	31	1	2	3	SEPTEMBER 2067
Aug 22	4	5	6	7	8	9	10	
	11	12	13	14	15	16	17	
Sep 5	18	19	20	21	22	23	24	
	25	26	27	28	29	30	1	OCTOBER 2067
Sep 19	2	3	4	5	6	7	8	
	9	10	11	12	13	14	15	
Oct 3	16	17	18	19	20	21	22	
	23	24	25	26	27	28	29	
Oct 17	30	31	1	2	3	4	5	NOVEMBER 2067
	6	7	8	9	10	11	12	
Oct 31	13	14	15	16	17	18	19	
	20	21	22	23	24	25	26	
Nov 14	27[g]	28	29	30	1	2	3	DECEMBER 2067
	4	5	6	7	8	9	10	
Nov 28	11	12	13	14	15	16	17	
	18	19	20	21	22	23	24	
Dec 12	25[h]	26	27	28	29	30	31	

Persian:
‡Leap year
[a]New Year
[b]Sizdeh Bedar

Hindu Lunar:
‡Leap year
[a]New Year (Sarvajit)
[b]Birthday of Rāma
[c]Birthday of Krishna
[d]Ganēśa Chaturthī
[e]Dashara
[f]Diwali
[g]Birthday of Vishnu
[h]Night of Śiva
[i]Holi

Hindu Solar:
‡Leap year
[a]New Year (Plava)
[b]Pongal

Islamic:
‡Leap year
[a]New Year
[A]New Year (Arithmetic)
[b]'Ashūrā'
[c]Prophet's Birthday
[d]Ascent of the Prophet
[e]Start of Ramaḍān
[f]'Id al-Fiṭr
[g]'Id al-'Aḍḥā

Gregorian:
[a]Orthodox Christmas
[b]Julian New Year
[c]Ash Wednesday
[d]Feast of Orthodoxy
[e]Easter
[f]Orthodox Easter
[g]Advent
[h]Christmas

2068

Gregorian 2068‡	Sun	Mon	Tue	Wed	Thu	Fri	Sat	Lunar Phases	ISO Week (Mon)	Julian Day (Sun noon)	Hebrew 5828‡/5829	Sun	Mon	Tue	Wed	Thu	Fri	Sat	Molad	Chinese Dīng-Hài/Wù-Zǐ	Sun	Mon	Tue	Wed	Thu	Fri	Sat	Solar Term	Coptic 1784/1785	Sun	Mon	Tue	Wed	Thu	Fri	Sat	Ethiopic 2060/2061
JANUARY 2068	1[a]	2	3	4	●	6	7	2:37	1	2476382	SHEVAT 5828	26	27	28	29	1	2	3	Thu 0h11m8p	MONTH 12 Dīng-Hài	27	28	29	30	1	2	3	Xiǎo hán	KOIAK 1784	22	23	24	25	26	27	28	TĀḪŚĀŚ 2060
	8	9	10	◐	12	13	14	17:45	2	2476389		4	5	6	7	8	9	10			4	5	6*	7	8	9	10		ṬŌBE 1784	29[c]	30	1	2	3	4	5	ṬER 2060
	15	16	17	18	○	20	21	9:44	3	2476396		11	12	13	14	15	16	17			11	12	13	14	15	16	17	Dà hán		6[d]	7	8	9	10	11[e]	12	
	22	23	24	25	26	◑	28	14:26	4	2476403		18	19	20	21	22	23	24			18	19	20	21	22	23	24			13	14	15	16	17	18	19	
FEBRUARY 2068	29	30	31	1	2	●	4	13:43	5	2476410	ADAR I 5828	25	26	27	28	29	30	1	Fri 12h55m9p	MONTH 1 Wù-Zǐ	25	26	27	28	29	1[a]	2	Lì chūn		20	21	22	23	24	25	26	
	5	6	7	8	9	◐	11	5:19	6	2476417		2	3	4	5	6	7	8			3	4	5	6	7	8	9		MESHIR 1784	27	28	29	30	1	2	3	YAKĀTIT 2060
	12	13	14	15	16	17	○	4:37	7	2476424		9	10	11	12	13	14	15			10	11	12	13	14	15[b]	16			4	5	6	7	8	9	10	
	19	20	21	22	23	24	25		8	2476431		16	17	18	19	20	21	22			17	18	19	20	21	22	23	Yǔ shuǐ		11	12	13	14	15	16	17	
MARCH 2068	◑	27	28	29	1	2	●	6:24 19:25	9	2476438		23	24	25	26	27	28	29	Sun 1h39m10p		24	25	26	27	28	29	30			18	19	20	21	22	23	24	
	4	5	6	7	8	9	◐	23:36	10	2476445	ADAR II 5828	30	1	2	3	4	5	6		MONTH 2 Wù-Zǐ	1	2	3	4	5	6	7*	Jīng zhé	PAREMOTEP 1784	25	26	27	28	29	30	1	MAGĀBIT 2060
	11	12	13	14	15	16	17		11	2476452		7	8	9	10	11	12	13			8	9	10	11	12	13	14			2	3	4	5	6	7	8	
	○	19[b]	20	21	22	23	24	22:54	12	2476459		14[f]	15	16	17	18	19	20			15	16	17	18	19	20	21	Chūn fēn		9	10	11	12	13	14	15	
	25	◑	27	28	29	30	31	18:19	13	2476466		21	22	23	24	25	26	27			22	23	24	25	26	27	28			16	17	18	19	20	21	22	
APRIL 2068	1	●	3	4	5	6	7	8:50	14	2476473	NISAN 5828	28	29	1	2	3	4	5	Mon 14h23m11p	MONTH 3 Wù-Zǐ	29	1	2	3[c]	4	5	6	Qīng míng		23	24	25	26	27	28	29	
	8	◐	10	11	12	13	14	11:31	15	2476480		6	7	8	9	10	11	12			7	8	9	10	11	12	13		PARMOUTE 1784	30	1	2	3	4	5	6	MIYĀZYĀ 2060
	15	16	○	18	19	20	21	15:28	16	2476487		13	14	15[g]	16	17	18	19			14	15	16	17	18	19	20	Gǔ yǔ		7	8	9	10	11	12	13	
	22	23	24	◑	26	27	28	2:28	17	2476494		20	21	22	23	24	25	26			21	22	23	24	25	26	27			14	15	16	17	18	19	20	
MAY 2068	29	30	●	2	3	4	5	18:06	18	2476501	IYAR 5828	27	28	29	30	1	2	3	Wed 3h7m12p	MONTH 4 Wù-Zǐ	28	29	30	1	2	3	4	Lì xià		21[f]	22	23	24	25	26	27	
	6	7	8	◐	10	11	12	4:46	19	2476508		4	5	6	7	8	9	10			5	6	7	8*	9	10	11		PASHONS 1784	28	29[g]	30	1	2	3	4	GENBOT 2060
	13	14	15	16	○	18	19	5:33	20	2476515		11	12	13	14	15	16	17			12	13	14	15	16	17	18			5	6	7	8	9	10	11	
	20	21	22	23	◑	25	26	7:59	21	2476522		18	19	20	21	22	23	24			19	20	21	22	23	24	25	Xiǎo mǎn		12	13	14	15	16	17	18	
JUNE 2068	27	28	29	30	●	1	2	4:02	22	2476529	SIVAN 5828	25	26	27	28	29	1	2	Thu 15h51m13p	MONTH 5 Wù-Zǐ	26	27	28	29	1	2	3			19	20	21	22	23	24	25	
	3	4	5	6	◐	8	9	22:19	23	2476536		3	4	5	6[h]	7	8	9			4	5[d]	6	7	8	9	10	Máng zhòng	PAŌNE 1784	26	27	28	29	30	1	2	SANĒ 2060
	10	11	12	13	14	○	16	16:58	24	2476543		10	11	12	13	14	15	16			11	12	13	14	15	16	17			3	4	5	6	7	8	9	
	17	18	19	20[c]	21	◑	23	12:24	25	2476550		17	18	19	20	21	22	23			18	19	20	21	22	23	24	Xià zhì		10	11	12	13	14	15	16	
	24	25	26	27	28	●	30	15:10	26	2476557		24	25	26	27	28	29	30		MONTH 6 Wù-Zǐ	25	26	27	28	29	1	2			17	18	19	20	21	22	23	
JULY 2068	1	2	3	4	5	6	◐	15:30	27	2476564	TAMMUZ 5828	1	2	3	4	5	6	7	Sat 4h35m14p		3	4	5	6	7	8	9	Xiǎo shǔ		24	25	26	27	28	29	30	
	8	9	10	11	12	13	14		28	2476571		8	9	10	11	12	13	14			10*	11	12	13	14	15	16		EPĒP 1784	1	2	3	4	5	6	7	ḤAMLĒ 2060
	○	16	17	18	19	20	◑	2:06 17:20	29	2476578		15	16	17	18	19	20	21			17	18	19	20	21	22	23			8	9	10	11	12	13	14	
	22	23	24	25	26	27	28		30	2476585		22	23	24	25	26	27	28			24	25	26	27	28	29	30	Dà shǔ		15	16	17	18	19	20	21	
AUGUST 2068	●	30	31	1	2	3	4	3:53	31	2476592	AV 5828	29	1	2	3	4	5	6	Sun 17h19m15p	MONTH 7 Wù-Zǐ	1	2	3	4	5	6	7[e]			22	23	24	25	26	27	28	
	5	◐	7	8	9	10	11	7:37	32	2476599		7	8	9[i]	10	11	12	13			8	9	10	11	12	13	14	Lì qiū	MESORĒ 1784	29	30	1	2	3	4	5	NAḤASĒ 2060
	12	○	14	15	16	17	18	9:50	33	2476606		14	15	16	17	18	19	20			15[f]	16	17	18	19	20	21			6	7	8	9	10	11	12	
	19	◑	21	22	23	24	25	0:15	34	2476613		21	22	23	24	25	26	27			22	23	24	25	26	27	28	Chǔ shǔ		13[h]	14	15	16	17	18	19	
SEPTEMBER 2068	26	●	28	29	30	31	1	18:27	35	2476620	ELUL 5828	28	29	30	1	2	3	4	Tue 6h3m16p	MONTH 8 Wù-Zǐ	29	30	1	2	3	4	5			20	21	22	23	24	25	26	
	2	3	◐	5	6	7	8	22:02	36	2476627		5	6	7	8	9	10	11			6	7	8	9	10*	11	12	Bái lù	EPAG. 1784	27	28	29	30	1	2	3	PĀG. 2060
	9	10	○	12	13	14	15	17:18	37	2476634		12	13	14	15	16	17	18			13	14	15[g]	16	17	18	19		THOOUT 1785	4	5	1[a]	2	3	4	5	MASKARAM 2061
	16	17	◑	19	20	21	22[d]	10:15	38	2476641		19	20	21	22	23	24	25			20	21	22	23	24	25	26	Qiū fēn		6	7	8	9	10	11	12	
	23	24	25	●	27	28	29	10:47	39	2476648	TISHRI 5829	26	27	28	29	1[a]	2[a]	3	Wed 18h47m17p	MONTH 9 Wù-Zǐ	27	28	29	1	2	3	4			13	14	15	16	17[b]	18	19	
OCTOBER 2068	30	1	2	3	◐	5	6	10:22	40	2476655		4	5	6	7	8	9	10[b]			5	6	7	8	9[h]	10	11			20	21	22	23	24	25	26	
	7	8	9	10	○	12	13	1:38	41	2476662		11	12	13	14	15[c]	16	17			12	13	14	15	16	17	18	Hán lù	PAOPE 1785	27	28	29	30	1	2	3	ṬEQEMT 2061
	14	15	16	◑	18	19	20	23:59	42	2476669		18	19	20	21	22	23	24			19	20	21	22	23	24	25			4	5	6	7	8	9	10	
	21	22	23	24	25	●	27	4:16	43	2476676	ḤESHVAN 5829	25	26	27	28	29	30	1		MONTH 10 Wù-Zǐ	26	27	28	29	30	1	2	Shuāng jiàng		11	12	13	14	15	16	17	
NOVEMBER 2068	28	29	30	31	1	◐	3	20:37	44	2476683		2	3	4	5	6	7	8	Fri 7h32m0p		3	4	5	6	7	8	9			18	19	20	21	22	23	24	
	4	5	6	7	8	○	10	11:39	45	2476690		9	10	11	12	13	14	15			10	11*	12	13	14	15	16	Lì dōng	ATHŌR 1785	25	26	27	28	29	30	1	ḪEDĀR 2061
	11	12	13	14	15	◑	17	17:31	46	2476697		16	17	18	19	20	21	22			17	18	19	20	21	22	23			2	3	4	5	6	7	8	
	18	19	20	21	22	23	●	21:41	47	2476704		23	24	25	26	27	28	29			24	25	26	27	28	29	30	Xiǎo xuě		9	10	11	12	13	14	15	
DECEMBER 2068	25	26	27	28	29	30	1		48	2476711	KISLEV 5829	1	2	3	4	5	6	7	Sat 20h16m1p	MONTH 11* Wù-Zǐ	1	2	3	4	5	6	7			16	17	18	19	20	21	22	
	◐	3	4	5	6	7	○	5:19 23:41	49	2476718		8	9	10	11[d]	12	13	14			8	9	10	11	12	13	14	Dà xuě		23	24	25	26	27	28	29	
	9	10	11	12	13	14	15		50	2476725		15	16	17	18	19	20	21			15	16	17	18	19	20	21		KOIAK 1785	30	1	2	3	4	5	6	TĀḪŚĀŚ 2061
	◑	17	18	19	20	21[e]	22	14:10	51	2476732		22	23	24	25[e]	26[e]	27[e]	28[e]			22	23	24	25	26	27[i]	28	Dōng zhì		7	8	9	10	11	12	13	
	23	●	25	26	27	28	29	13:43	52	2476739	TEVETH 5829	29[e]	30[e]	1[e]	2[e]	3	4	5	Mon 9h0m2p	MONTH 12 Wù-Zǐ	29	1	2	3	4	5	6			14	15	16	17	18	19	20	
	30	◐	1	2	3	4	5	13:21	1	2476746		6	7	8	9	10	11	12			7	8	9	10	11	12	13	Xiǎo hán		21	22	23	24	25	26	27	

‡Leap year
[a]New Year
[b]Spring (18:47)
[c]Summer (11:52)
[d]Autumn (4:06)
[e]Winter (1:31)
● New moon
◐ First quarter moon
○ Full moon
◑ Last quarter moon

‡Leap year
[a]New Year
[b]Yom Kippur
[c]Sukkot
[d]Winter starts
[e]Ḥanukkah
[f]Purim
[g]Passover
[h]Shavuot
[i]Fast of Av

[a]New Year (4766, Rat)
[b]Lantern Festival
[c]Qīngmíng
[d]Dragon Festival
[e]Qīqiǎo
[f]Hungry Ghosts
[g]Mid-Autumn Festival
[h]Double-Ninth Festival
[i]Dōngzhì
*Start of 60-name cycle

[a]New Year
[b]Building of the Cross
[c]Christmas
[d]Jesus's Circumcision
[e]Epiphany
[f]Easter
[g]Mary's Announcement
[h]Jesus's Transfiguration

PERSIAN (ASTRONOMICAL) 1446/1447

Month	Sun	Mon	Tue	Wed	Thu	Fri	Sat
DEY 1446	11	12	13	14	15	16	17
	18	19	20	21	22	23	24
	25	26	27	28	29	30	*1*
BAHMAN 1446	2	3	4	5	6	7	8
	9	10	11	12	13	14	15
	16	17	18	19	20	21	22
	23	24	25	26	27	28	29
	30	*1*	2	3	4	5	6
ESFAND 1446	7	8	9	10	11	12	13
	14	15	16	17	18	19	20
	21	22	23	24	25	26	27
	28	29	*1*[a]	2	3	4	5
FARVARDĪN 1447	6	7	8	9	10	11	12
	13[b]	14	15	16	17	18	19
	20	21	22	23	24	25	26
	27	28	29	30	31	*1*	2
ORDĪBEHEŠT 1447	3	4	5	6	7	8	9
	10	11	12	13	14	15	16
	17	18	19	20	21	22	23
	24	25	26	27	28	29	30
	31	*1*	2	3	4	5	6
XORDĀD 1447	7	8	9	10	11	12	13
	14	15	16	17	18	19	20
	21	22	23	24	25	26	27
	28	29	30	31	*1*	2	3
TĪR 1447	4	5	6	7	8	9	10
	11	12	13	14	15	16	17
	18	19	20	21	22	23	24
	25	26	27	28	29	30	31
MORDĀD 1447	*1*	2	3	4	5	6	7
	8	9	10	11	12	13	14
	15	16	17	18	19	20	21
	22	23	24	25	26	27	28
	29	30	31	*1*	2	3	4
SHAHRĪVAR 1447	5	6	7	8	9	10	11
	12	13	14	15	16	17	18
	19	20	21	22	23	24	25
	26	27	28	29	30	31	*1*
MEHR 1447	2	3	4	5	6	7	8
	9	10	11	12	13	14	15
	16	17	18	19	20	21	22
	23	24	25	26	27	28	29
	30	*1*	2	3	4	5	6
ĀBĀN 1447	7	8	9	10	11	12	13
	14	15	16	17	18	19	20
	21	22	23	24	25	26	27
	28	29	30	*1*	2	3	4
ĀZAR 1447	5	6	7	8	9	10	11
	12	13	14	15	16	17	18
	19	20	21	22	23	24	25
	26	27	28	29	30	*1*	2
DEY 1447	3	4	5	6	7	8	9
	10	11	12	13	14	15	16

HINDU LUNAR 2124/2125

Month	Sun	Mon	Tue	Wed	Thu	Fri	Sat
PAUSHA 2124	26	27	28	29	**30**	2	3
	4	5	6	7	8	9	10
	11	12	13	14	15	16	17
	18	19	20	21	22	23	24
	25	26	27	28	29	30	1
MĀGHA 2124	2	3	4	**5**	7	8	9
	10	11	12	13	14	15	*15*
	16	17	18	19	20	21	22
	23	24	25	26	27	28[h]	29
PHĀLGUNA 2124	1	2	3	4	5	6	7
	8	9	10	11	12	13	14
	15[i]	16	17	*17*	18	19	20
	21	**22**	24	25	26	27	28
	29	30	1[a]	2	3	4	5
CHAITRA 2125	6	7	8[b]	9	10	11	12
	13	14	15	16	17	18	19
	20	21	22	23	24	25	26
	27	29	30	1	2	3	4
VAIŚĀKHA 2125	5	6	7	8	9	10	11
	11	12	13	14	15	16	17
	18	19	**20**	22	23	24	25
	26	27	28	29	30	1	2
JYAISHTHA 2125	3	4	5	6	7	8	9
	10	11	12	13	14	15	16
	17	18	19	20	21	22	**23**
	25	26	27	28	29	30	1
ĀSHĀDHA 2125	2	3	4	5	6	7	8
	8	9	10	11	12	13	14
	15	17	18	19	20	21	22
	23	24	25	26	27	28	29
	30	1	2	3	4	5	6
ŚRĀVANA 2125	7	8	9	10	11	12	13
	14	15	16	17	**18**	20	21
	22	23[c]	24	25	26	27	28
	29	30	1	2	3	4[d]	5
BHĀDRAPADA 2125	*5*	6	7	8	9	10	**11**
	13	14	15	16	17	18	19
	20	21	22	23	24	25	26
	27	28	29	30	1	2	3
ĀŚVINA 2125	4	5	6	7	8[e]	9[e]	10[e]
	11	12	13	14	**15**	17	18
	19	20	21	22	23	24	25
	26	27	28	29	*29*	30	1[f]
KĀRTTIKA 2125	2	3	4	5	6	7	8
	9	11	12	13	14	15	16
	17	18	19	20	21	22	23
	24	25	26	27	28	29	30
MĀRGAŚIRA 2125	1	2	3	4	5	6	7
	8	9	10	11[g]	12	**13**	15
	16	17	18	19	20	21	22
	23	*23*	24	25	26	27	28
PAUSHA 2125	29	30	1	2	3	4	5
	6	**7**	9	10	11	12	13

HINDU SOLAR 1989‡/1990

Month	Sun	Mon	Tue	Wed	Thu	Fri	Sat
PAUSHA 1989	16	17	18	19	20	21	22
	23	24	25	26	27	28	29
MĀGHA 1989	1[b]	2	3	4	5	6	7
	8	9	10	11	12	13	14
	15	16	17	18	19	20	21
	22	23	24	25	26	27	28
	29	1	2	3	4	5	6
PHĀLGUNA 1989	7	8	9	10	11	12	13
	14	15	16	17	18	19	20
	21	22	23	24	25	26	27
	28	29	30	1	2	3	4
CHAITRA 1989	5	6	7	8	9	10	11
	12	13	14	15	16	17	18
	19	20	21	22	23	24	25
	26	27	28	29	30	31	1[a]
VAIŚĀKHA 1990	2	3	4	5	6	7	8
	9	10	11	12	13	14	15
	16	17	18	19	20	21	22
	23	24	25	26	27	28	29
	30	31	1	2	3	4	5
JYAISHTHA 1990	6	7	8	9	10	11	12
	13	14	15	16	17	18	19
	20	21	22	23	24	25	26
	27	28	29	30	31	1	2
ĀSHĀDHA 1990	3	4	5	6	7	8	9
	10	11	12	13	14	15	16
	17	18	19	20	21	22	23
	24	25	26	27	28	29	30
	31	32	1	2	3	4	5
ŚRĀVANA 1990	6	7	8	9	10	11	12
	13	14	15	16	17	18	19
	20	21	22	23	24	25	26
	27	28	29	30	31	1	2
BHĀDRAPADA 1990	3	4	5	6	7	8	9
	10	11	12	13	14	15	16
	17	18	19	20	21	22	23
	24	25	26	27	28	29	30
	31	1	2	3	4	5	6
ĀŚVINA 1990	7	8	9	10	11	12	13
	14	15	16	17	18	19	20
	21	22	23	24	25	26	27
	28	29	30	31	1	2	3
KĀRTTIKA 1990	4	5	6	7	8	9	10
	11	12	13	14	15	16	17
	18	19	20	21	22	23	24
	25	26	27	28	29	1	2
MĀRGAŚIRA 1990	3	4	5	6	7	8	9
	10	11	12	13	14	15	16
	17	18	19	20	21	22	23
	24	25	26	27	28	29	30
PAUSHA 1990	1	2	3	4	5	6	7
	8	9	10	11	12	13	14
	15	16	17	18	19	20	21

ISLAMIC (ASTRONOMICAL) 1490‡/1491‡

Month	Sun	Mon	Tue	Wed	Thu	Fri	Sat
DHU AL-QA'DA 1490	25	26	27	28	29	*1*	*2*
	3	4	5	6	7	8	9
	10	11	12	13	14	15	16
	17	18	19	20	21	22	23
	24	25	26	27	28	29	30
DHU AL-ḤIJJA 1490	*1*	*2*	*3*	*4*	*5*	*6*	*7*
	8	9	10[g]	11	12	13	14
	15	16	17	18	19	20	21
	22	23	24	25	26	27	28
	29	*1*[a]	2	3	4	5	6
MUḤARRAM 1491	7	8	9	10[b]	11	12	13
	14	15	16	17	18	19	20
	21	22	23	24	25	26	27
	28	29	1	2	3	4	5
ṢAFAR 1491	6	7	8	9	10	11	12
	13	14	15	16	17	18	19
	20	21	22	23	24	25	26
	27	28	29	30	*1*	2	3
RABĪ' I 1491	4	5	6	7	8	9	10
	11	12[c]	13	14	15	16	17
	18	19	20	21	22	23	24
	25	26	27	28	29	1	*2*
RABĪ' II 1491	3	4	5	6	7	8	9
	10	11	12	13	14	15	16
	17	18	19	20	21	22	23
	24	25	26	27	28	29	30
JUMĀDĀ I 1491	*1*	2	3	4	5	6	7
	8	9	10	11	12	13	14
	15	16	17	18	19	20	21
	22	23	24	25	26	27	28
	29	30	*1*	2	3	4	5
JUMĀDĀ II 1491	6	7	8	9	10	11	12
	13	14	15	16	17	18	19
	20	21	22	23	24	25	26
	27	28	29	*30*	1	2	3
RAJAB 1491	4	5	6	7	8	9	10
	11	12	13	14	15	16	17
	18	19	20	21	22	23	24
	25	26	27[d]	28	29	*30*	1
SHA'BĀN 1491	2	3	4	5	6	7	8
	9	10	11	12	13	14	15
	16	17	18	19	20	21	22
	23	24	25	26	27	28	*29*
RAMAḌĀN 1491	1[e]	2	3	4	5	6	7
	8	9	10	11	12	13	14
	15	16	17	18	19	20	21
	22	23	24	25	26	27	28
	29	*1*[f]	2	3	4	5	6
SHAWWĀL 1491	7	8	9	10	11	12	13
	14	15	16	17	18	19	20
	21	22	23	24	25	26	27
	28	29	*30*	1	2	3	4
DHU AL-QA'DA 1491	5	6	7	8	9	10	11

GREGORIAN 2068‡

Julian† (Sun)	Sun	Mon	Tue	Wed	Thu	Fri	Sat	Month
Dec 19	*1*	2	3	4	5	6	*7*[a]	JANUARY 2068
	8	9	10	11	12	13	14[b]	
Jan 2	*15*	16	17	18	19	20	21	
	22	23	24	25	26	27	28	
Jan 16	*29*	30	31	1	2	3	4	
	5	6	7	8	9	10	11	FEBRUARY 2068
Jan 30	*12*	13	14	15	16	17	18	
	19	20	21	22	23	24	25	
Feb 13	*26*	27	28	29	1	2	3	
	4	5	6	7[c]	8	9	10	MARCH 2068
Feb 27	*11*	12	13	14	15	16	17	
	18[d]	19	20	21	22	23	24	
Mar 12	*25*	26	27	28	29	30	31	
	1	2	3	4	5	6	7	APRIL 2068
Mar 26	*8*	9	10	11	12	13	14	
	15	16	17	18	19	20	21	
Apr 9	*22*[e]	23	24	25	26	27	28	
	29[f]	30	1	2	3	4	5	MAY 2068
Apr 23	*6*	7	8	9	10	11	12	
	13	14	15	16	17	18	19	
May 7	*20*	21	22	23	24	25	26	
	27	28	29	30	31	1	2	JUNE 2068
May 21	*3*	4	5	6	7	8	9	
	10	11	12	13	14	15	16	
Jun 4	*17*	18	19	20	21	22	23	
	24	25	26	27	28	29	30	
Jun 18	*1*	2	3	4	5	6	7	JULY 2068
	8	9	10	11	12	13	14	
Jul 2	*15*	16	17	18	19	20	21	
	22	23	24	25	26	27	28	
Jul 16	*29*	30	31	1	2	3	4	AUGUST 2068
	5	6	7	8	9	10	11	
Jul 30	*12*	13	14	15	16	17	18	
	19	20	21	22	23	24	25	
Aug 13	*26*	27	28	29	30	31	1	SEPTEMBER 2068
	2	3	4	5	6	7	8	
Aug 27	*9*	10	11	12	13	14	15	
	16	17	18	19	20	21	22	
Sep 10	*23*	24	25	26	27	28	29	
	30	1	2	3	4	5	6	OCTOBER 2068
Sep 24	*7*	8	9	10	11	12	13	
	14	15	16	17	18	19	20	
Oct 8	*21*	22	23	24	25	26	27	
	28	29	30	31	1	2	3	NOVEMBER 2068
Oct 22	*4*	5	6	7	8	9	10	
	11	12	13	14	15	16	17	
Nov 5	*18*	19	20	21	22	23	24	
	25	26	27	28	29	30	1	DECEMBER 2068
Nov 19	2[g]	3	4	5	6	7	8	
	9	10	11	12	13	14	15	
Dec 3	*16*	17	18	19	20	21	22	
	23	24	25[h]	26	27	28	29	
Dec 17	*30*	31	1	2	3	4	5	

Persian: [a]New Year; [b]Sizdeh Bedar

Hindu Lunar: [a]New Year (Sarvadhārin); [b]Birthday of Rāma; [c]Birthday of Krishna; [d]Ganēśa Chaturthī; [e]Dashara; [f]Diwali; [g]Birthday of Vishnu; [h]Night of Śiva; [i]Holi

Hindu Solar: ‡Leap year; [a]New Year (Śubhakṛit); [b]Pongal

Islamic: ‡Leap year; [a]New Year; [b]'Ashūrā'; [c]Prophet's Birthday; [d]Ascent of the Prophet; [e]Start of Ramaḍān; [f]'Īd al-Fiṭr; [g]'Īd al-'Aḍḥā

Gregorian: ‡Leap year; [a]Orthodox Christmas; [b]Julian New Year; [c]Ash Wednesday; [d]Feast of Orthodoxy; [e]Easter; [f]Orthodox Easter; [g]Advent; [h]Christmas

2069

	GREGORIAN 2069 (Sun Mon Tue Wed Thu Fri Sat)	Lunar Phases	ISO WEEK (Mon)	JULIAN DAY (Sun noon)		HEBREW 5829/5830 (Sun Mon Tue Wed Thu Fri Sat)	Molad		CHINESE Wù-Zǐ/Jǐ-Chǒu[‡] (Sun Mon Tue Wed Thu Fri Sat)	Solar Term		COPTIC 1785/1786 / ETHIOPIC 2061/2062 (Sun Mon Tue Wed Thu Fri Sat)	
JANUARY 2069	30 ◐ 1[a] 2 3 4 5	13:21	1	2476746	TEVETH 5829	6 7 8 9 10 11 12		MONTH 12 Wù-Zǐ	7 8 9 10 11 12* *13*	Xiǎo hán	KOIAK 1785	21 22 23 24 25 26 27	TĀKHŚĀŚ 2061
	6 ○ 8 9 10 11 12	13:42	2	2476753		13 14 15 16 17 18 19			14 15 16 17 18 19 20			28 29[c] 30 1 2 3 4	
	13 14 ◑ 16 17 18 19	12:15	3	2476760		20 21 22 23 24 25 26			21 22 23 24 25 26 **27**	Dà hán	TŌBE 1785	5 6[d] 7 8 9 10 11[e]	
	20 21 22 ● 24 25 26	3:35	4	2476767	SHEVAT 5829	27 28 29 1 2 3 4	Tue 21h44m3p	MONTH 1 Jǐ-Chǒu	28 29 30 1[a] 2 3 4			12 13 14 15 16 17 18	ṬER 2061
FEBRUARY 2069	27 28 ◐ 30 31 1 2	21:38	5	2476774		5 6 7 8 9 10 11			5 6 7 8 9 10 11			19 20 21 22 23 24 25	
	3 4 5 ○ 7 8 9	5:28	6	2476781		12 13 14 15 16 17 18			*12* 13 14 15[b] 16 17 18	Lì chūn		26 27 28 29 30 1 2	YAKĀTĪT 2061
	10 11 12 13 ◑ 15 16	9:26	7	2476788		19 20 21 22 23 24 25			19 20 21 22 23 24 25		MESHIR 1785	3 4 5 6 7 8 9	
	17 18 19 20 ● 22 23	15:16	8	2476795	ADAR 5829	26 27 28 29 30 1 2	Thu 10h28m4p	MONTH 2 Jǐ-Chǒu	26 **27** 28 29 1 2 3	Yǔ shuǐ		10 11 12 13 14 15 16	
MARCH 2069	24 25 26 27 ◐ 1 2	6:53	9	2476802		3 4 5 6 7 8 9			4 5 6 7 8 9 10			17 18 19 20 21 22 23	
	3 4 5 6 ○ 8 9	22:34	10	2476809		10 11 12 13 14[f] 15 16			11 12 *13** 14 15 16 17	Jīng zhé		24 25 26 27 28 29 30	
	10 11 12 13 14 15 ◑	3:29	11	2476816		17 18 19 20 21 22 23			18 19 20 21 22 23 24		PAREMOTEP 1785	1 2 3 4 5 6 7	MAGĀBIT 2061
	17 18 19 20[b] 21 22 ●	1:12	12	2476823	NISAN 5829	24 25 26 27 28 29 1	Fri 23h12m5p	MONTH 3 Jǐ-Chǒu	25 26 27 **28** 29 30 1	Chūn fēn		8 9 10 11 12 13 14	
APRIL 2069	24 25 26 27 28 ◐ 30	17:33	13	2476830		2 3 4 5 6 7 8			2 3 4 5 6 7 8			15 16 17 18 19 20 21	
	31 1 2 3 4 5 ○	16:12	14	2476837		9 10 11 12 13 14 15[g]			9 10 11 12 13[c] 14 15	Qīng míng		22 23 24 25 26 27 28	
	7 8 9 10 11 12 13		15	2476844		16 17 18 19 20 21 22			16 17 18 19 20 21 22		PARMOUTE 1785	29 30 1 2 3 4 5	
	◑ 15 16 17 18 19 20	17:20	16	2476851		23 24 25 26 27 28 29			23 24 25 26 27 **28** 29	Gǔ yǔ		6[f] 7 8 9 10 11 12	MIYĀZYĀ 2061
	● 22 23 24 25 26 27	9:57	17	2476858	IYYAR 5829	30 1 2 3 4 5 6	Sun 11h56m6p	MONTH 4 Jǐ-Chǒu	1 2 3 4 5 6 7			13 14 15 16 17 18 19	
MAY 2069	◐ 29 30 1 2 3 4	5:55	18	2476865		7 8 9 10 11 12 13			8 9 10 11 12 13 14*			20 21 22 23 24 25 26	
	5 ○ 7 8 9 10 11	9:10	19	2476872		14 15 16 17 18 19 20			*15* 16 17 18 19 20 21	Lì xià		27 28 29[g] 30 1 2 3	
	12 13 ◑ 15 16 17 18	3:09	20	2476879		21 22 23 24 25 26 27			22 23 24 25 26 27 28		PASHONS 1785	4 5 6 7 8 9 10	GENBOT 2061
	19 ● 21 22 23 24 25	18:05	21	2476886	SIVAN 5829	28 29 1 2 3 4 5	Tue 0h40m7p	LEAP MONTH 4 Jǐ-Chǒu	29 **30** 1 2 3 4 5	Xiǎo mǎn		11 12 13 14 15 16 17	
JUNE 2069	26 ◐ 28 29 30 31 1	20:08	22	2476893		6[h] 7 8 9 10 11 12			6 7 8 9 10 11 12			18 19 20 21 22 23 24	
	2 3 4 ○ 6 7 8	0:18	23	2476900		13 14 15 16 17 18 19			13 14 15 *16* 17 18 19	Máng zhòng		25 26 27 28 29 30 1	
	9 10 11 ◑ 13 14 15	9:55	24	2476907		20 21 22 23 24 25 26			20 21 22 23 24 25 26		PAŌNĒ 1785	2 3 4 5 6 7 8	SANĒ 2061
	16 17 18 ● 20[c] 21 22	2:13	25	2476914	TAMMUZ 5829	27 28 29 30 1 2 3	Wed 13h24m8p	MONTH 5 Jǐ-Chǒu	27 28 29 1 2 **3** 4	Xià zhì		9 10 11 12 13 14 15	
	23 24 25 ◐ 27 28 29	12:08	26	2476921		4 5 6 7 8 9 10			5[d] 6 7 8 9 10 11			16 17 18 19 20 21 22	
JULY 2069	30 1 2 3 ○ 5 6	13:04	27	2476928		11 12 13 14 15 16 17			12 13 14 15* 16 17 *18*	Xiǎo shǔ		23 24 25 26 27 28 29	
	7 8 9 10 ◑ 12 13	14:58	28	2476935		18 19 20 21 22 23 24			19 20 21 22 23 24 25		EPĒP 1785	30 1 2 3 4 5 6	HAMLĒ 2061
	14 15 16 17 ● 19 20	11:12	29	2476942	AV 5829	25 26 27 28 29 1 2	Fri 2h8m9p	MONTH 6 Jǐ-Chǒu	26 27 28 29 1 2 3			7 8 9 10 11 12 13	
	21 22 23 24 25 ◐ 27	5:29	30	2476949		3 4 5 6 7 8 9			4 **5** 6 7 8 9 10	Dà shǔ		14 15 16 17 18 19 20	
AUGUST 2069	28 29 30 31 1 ○ 3	23:43	31	2476956		10[i] 11 12 13 14 15 16			11 12 13 14 15 16 17			21 22 23 24 25 26 27	
	4 5 6 7 8 ◑ 10	19:40	32	2476963		17 18 19 20 21 22 23			18 19 20 *21* 22 23 24	Lì qiū	MESORĒ 1785	28 29 30 1 2 3 4	
	11 12 13 14 15 ● 17	22:02	33	2476970		24 25 26 27 28 29 30	Sat 14h52m10p	MONTH 7 Jǐ-Chǒu	25 26 27 28 29 30 1			5 6 7 8 9 10 11	NAḤASĒ 2061
	18 19 20 21 22 23 ◐	23:15	34	2476977	ELUL 5829	1 2 3 4 5 6 7			2 3 4 5 **6** 7[e] 8	Chǔ shǔ		12 13[h] 14 15 16 17 18	
	25 26 27 28 29 30 31		35	2476984		8 9 10 11 12 13 14			9 10 11 12 13 14 15[f]			19 20 21 22 23 24 25	
SEPTEMBER 2069	○ 2 3 4 5 6 7	9:05	36	2476991		15 16 17 18 19 20 21			16* 17 18 19 20 21 *22*	Bái lù	EPAG. 1785	26 27 28 29 30 1 2	PĀG. 2061
	◑ 9 10 11 12 13 14	1:21	37	2476998		22 23 24 25 26 27 28			23 24 25 26 27 28 29		THOOUT 1786	3 4 5 1[a] 2 3 4	MASKARAM 2062
	● 16 17 18 19 20 21	11:34	38	2477005	TISHRI 5830	29 1[a] 2[a] 3 4 5 6	Mon 3h36m11p	MONTH 8 Jǐ-Chǒu	1 2 3 4 5 6 7			5 6 7 8 9 10 11	
	22[d] ◐ 24 25 26 27 28	16:22	39	2477012		7 8 9 10[b] 11 12 13			**8** 9 10 11 12 13 14	Qiū fēn		12 13 14 15 16 17[b] 18	
OCTOBER 2069	29 ○ 1 2 3 4 5	18:08	40	2477019		14 15[c] 16 17 18 19 20			15[g] 16 17 18 19 20 21			19 20 21 22 23 24 25	
	6 ◑ 8 9 10 11 12	9:18	41	2477026		21 22 23 24 25 26 27			22 23 *24* 25 26 27 28	Hán lù	PAOPE 1786	26 27 28 29 30 1 2	ṬEQEMT 2062
	13 14 ● 16 17 18 19	4:02	42	2477033	ḤESHVAN 5830	28 29 30 1 2 3 4	Tue 16h20m12p	MONTH 9 Jǐ-Chǒu	29 30 1 2 3 4 5			3 4 5 6 7 8 9	
	20 21 22 ◐ 24 25 26	7:56	43	2477040		5 6 7 8 9 10 11			6 7 8 9[h] 10 11 12	Shuāng jiàng		10 11 12 13 14 15 16	
NOVEMBER 2069	27 28 29 ○ 31 1 2	3:34	44	2477047		12 13 14 15 16 17 18			13 14 15 16 17* 18 19			17 18 19 20 21 22 23	
	3 4 ◑ 6 7 8 9	20:39	45	2477054		19 20 21 22 23 24 25			20 21 22 23 *24* 25 26	Lì dōng		24 25 26 27 28 29 30	
	10 11 12 ● 14 15 16	22:36	46	2477061	KISLEV 5830	26 27 28 29 30 1 2	Thu 5h4m13p	MONTH 10 Jǐ-Chǒu	27 28 29 30 1 2 3		ATHŌR 1786	1 2 3 4 5 6 7	ḪEDĀR 2062
	17 18 19 20 ◐ 22 23	21:30	47	2477068		3 4 5 6 7 8 9			4 5 6 7 8 **9** 10	Xiǎo xuě		8 9 10 11 12 13 14	
	24 25 26 27 ○ 29 30	13:45	48	2477075		10 11 12 13 14 15 16			11 12 13 14 15 16 17			15 16 17 18 19 20 21	
DECEMBER 2069	1 2 3 4 ◑ 6 7	12:02	49	2477082		17 18 19 20 21[d] 22 23			18 19 20 21 22 *23* 24			22 23 24 25 26 27 28	
	8 9 10 11 12 ● 14	17:37	50	2477089		24 25[e] 26[e] 27[e] 28[e] 29[e] 30[e]	Fri 17h48m14p	MONTH 11 Jǐ-Chǒu	25 26 27 28 29 30 1	Dà xuě	KOIAK 1786	29 30 1 2 3 4 5	
	15 16 17 18 19 20 ◐[e]	8:58	51	2477096	TEVETH 5830	1[e] 2[e] 3 4 5 6 7			2 3 4 5 6 7 8[i]	Dōng zhì		6 7 8 9 10 11 12	TĀKHŚĀŚ 2062
	22 23 24 25 26 27 ○	0:49	52	2477103		8 9 10 11 12 13 14			9 10 11 12 13 14 15			13 14 15 16 17 18 19	
	29 30 31 1 2 3 ◑	7:14	1	2477110		15 16 17 18 19 20 21			16 17* 18 19 20 21 22			20 21 22 23 24 25 26	

[a]New Year
[b]Spring (0:43)
[c]Summer (17:40)
[d]Autumn (9:50)
[e]Winter (7:20)
● New moon
◐ First quarter moon
○ Full moon
◑ Last quarter moon

[a]New Year
[b]Yom Kippur
[c]Sukkot
[d]Winter starts
[e]Ḥanukkah
[f]Purim
[g]Passover
[h]Shavuot
[i]Fast of Av

[‡]Leap year
[a]New Year (4767, Ox)
[b]Lantern Festival
[c]Qīngmíng
[d]Dragon Festival
[e]Qīqiǎo
[f]Hungry Ghosts
[g]Mid-Autumn Festival
[h]Double-Ninth Festival
[i]Dōngzhì
*Start of 60-name cycle

[a]New Year
[b]Building of the Cross
[c]Christmas
[d]Jesus's Circumcision
[e]Epiphany
[f]Easter
[g]Mary's Announcement
[h]Jesus's Transfiguration

PERSIAN (ASTRONOMICAL) 1447/1448

Month	Sun	Mon	Tue	Wed	Thu	Fri	Sat
DEY 1447	10	11	12	13	14	15	16
	17	18	19	20	21	22	23
	24	25	26	27	28	29	30
BAHMAN 1447	*1*	2	3	4	5	6	7
	8	9	10	11	12	13	14
	15	16	17	18	19	20	21
	22	23	24	25	26	27	28
ESFAND 1447	29	30	*1*	2	3	4	5
	6	7	8	9	10	11	12
	13	14	15	16	17	18	19
	20	21	22	23	24	25	26
FARVARDĪN 1448	27	28	29	*1*[a]	2	3	4
	5	6	7	8	9	10	11
	12	13[b]	14	15	16	17	18
	19	20	21	22	23	24	25
ORDĪBEHEŠT 1448	26	27	28	29	30	31	*1*
	2	3	4	5	6	7	8
	9	10	11	12	13	14	15
	16	17	18	19	20	21	22
	23	24	25	26	27	28	29
XORDĀD 1448	30	31	*1*	2	3	4	5
	6	7	8	9	10	11	12
	13	14	15	16	17	18	19
	20	21	22	23	24	25	26
TĪR 1448	27	28	29	30	31	*1*	2
	3	4	5	6	7	8	9
	10	11	12	13	14	15	16
	17	18	19	20	21	22	23
	24	25	26	27	28	29	30
MORDĀD 1448	31	*1*	2	3	4	5	6
	7	8	9	10	11	12	13
	14	15	16	17	18	19	20
	21	22	23	24	25	26	27
SHAHRĪVAR 1448	28	29	30	31	*1*	2	3
	4	5	6	7	8	9	10
	11	12	13	14	15	16	17
	18	19	20	21	22	23	24
	25	26	27	28	29	30	31
MEHR 1448	*1*	2	3	4	5	6	7
	8	9	10	11	12	13	14
	15	16	17	18	19	20	21
	22	23	24	25	26	27	28
ĀBĀN 1448	29	30	*1*	2	3	4	5
	6	7	8	9	10	11	12
	13	14	15	16	17	18	19
	20	21	22	23	24	25	26
ĀZAR 1448	27	28	29	30	*1*	2	3
	4	5	6	7	8	9	10
	11	12	13	14	15	16	17
	18	19	20	21	22	23	24
DEY 1448	25	26	27	28	29	30	*1*
	2	3	4	5	6	7	8
	9	10	11	12	13	14	15

[a]New Year
[b]Sizdeh Bedar

HINDU LUNAR 2125/2126‡

Month	Sun	Mon	Tue	Wed	Thu	Fri	Sat
PAUSHA 2125	6	**7**	9	10	11	12	13
	14	15	16	17	18	19	20
	21	22	23	24	25	*25*	26
MĀGHA 2125	27	28	29	30	**1**	3	4
	5	6	7	8	9	10	11
	12	13	14	15	16	17	18
	19	20	21	22	23	24	25
PHĀLGUNA 2125	26	27	28	29[h]	30	1	2
	3	4	5	**6**	8	9	10
	11	12	13	14	15[i]	16	17
	17	18	19	20	21	22	23
	24	25	26	27	28	29	**30**[a]
CHAITRA 2126	2	3	4	5	6	7	8
	9[b]	10	11	12	13	14	15
	16	17	18	19	20	21	22
	23	24	25	26	27	28	29
VAIŚĀKHA 2126	30	1	2	3	**4**	6	7
	8	9	10	11	*11*	12	13
	14	15	16	17	18	19	20
	21	22	23	24	25	26	**27**
JYAISHṬHA 2126	29	30	1	2	3	4	5
	6	7	8	9	10	11	12
	13	14	15	16	*16*	17	18
	19	21	22	23	24	25	26
ĀSHĀḌHA 2126	27	28	29	30	**1**	3	4
	5	6	7	8	*8*	9	10
	11	12	13	14	15	16	17
	18	19	20	21	22	**23**	25
	26	27	28	29	30	1	2
LEAP ŚRĀVAṆA 2126	3	4	5	6	7	8	9
	10	11	12	13	14	15	16
	17	18	19	20	21	22	23
	24	25	**26**	28	29	30	1
ŚRĀVAṆA 2126	2	3	4	*4*	5	6	7
	8	9	10	11	12	13	14
	15	16	17	18	**19**	21	22
	23[c]	24	25	26	27	28	29
BHĀDRAPADA 2126	30	1	2	3	4[d]	5	6
	7	8	9	10	11	12	13
	14	15	16	17	18	19	20
	21	22	**23**	25	26	27	28
	29	*29*	30	1	2	3	4
ĀŚVINA 2126	5	6	7	8[e]	9[e]	10[e]	11
	12	13	14	15	**16**	18	19
	20	21	22	23	24	25	26
	27	28	29	30	1[f]	2	*2*
KĀRTTIKA 2126	3	4	5	6	7	8	**9**
	11	12	13	14	15	16	17
	18	19	20	21	22	23	24
	25	26	27	28	29	30	1
MĀRGAŚĪRA 2126	2	3	4	5	6	7	8
	9	10	11[g]	12	13	**14**	16
	17	18	19	20	21	22	23

‡Leap year
[a]New Year (Virodhin)
[b]Birthday of Rāma
[c]Birthday of Krishna
[d]Ganēśa Chaturthī
[e]Dashara
[f]Diwali
[g]Birthday of Vishnu
[h]Night of Śiva
[i]Holi

HINDU SOLAR 1990/1991

Month	Sun	Mon	Tue	Wed	Thu	Fri	Sat
PAUSHA 1990	15	16	17	18	19	20	21
	22	23	24	25	26	27	28
MĀGHA 1990	29	1[b]	2	3	4	5	6
	7	8	9	10	11	12	13
	14	15	16	17	18	19	20
	21	22	23	24	25	26	27
PHĀLGUNA 1990	28	29	30	1	2	3	4
	5	6	7	8	9	10	11
	12	13	14	15	16	17	18
	19	20	21	22	23	24	25
CHAITRA 1990	26	27	28	29	1	2	3
	4	5	6	7	8	9	10
	11	12	13	14	15	16	17
	18	19	20	21	22	23	24
	25	26	27	28	29	30	31
VAIŚĀKHA 1991	1[a]	2	3	4	5	6	7
	8	9	10	11	12	13	14
	15	16	17	18	19	20	21
	22	23	24	25	26	27	28
JYAISHṬHA 1991	29	30	31	1	2	3	4
	5	6	7	8	9	10	11
	12	13	14	15	16	17	18
	19	20	21	22	23	24	25
ĀSHĀḌHA 1991	26	27	28	29	30	31	1
	2	3	4	5	6	7	8
	9	10	11	12	13	14	15
	16	17	18	19	20	21	22
	23	24	25	26	27	28	29
ŚRĀVAṆA 1991	30	31	32	1	2	3	4
	5	6	7	8	9	10	11
	12	13	14	15	16	17	18
	19	20	21	22	23	24	25
BHĀDRAPADA 1991	26	27	28	29	30	31	1
	2	3	4	5	6	7	8
	9	10	11	12	13	14	15
	16	17	18	19	20	21	22
	23	24	25	26	27	28	29
ĀŚVINA 1991	30	31	1	2	3	4	5
	6	7	8	9	10	11	12
	13	14	15	16	17	18	19
	20	21	22	23	24	25	26
KĀRTTIKA 1991	27	28	29	30	31	1	2
	3	4	5	6	7	8	9
	10	11	12	13	14	15	16
	17	18	19	20	21	22	23
	24	25	26	27	28	29	30
MĀRGAŚĪRA 1991	1	2	3	4	5	6	7
	8	9	10	11	12	13	14
	15	16	17	18	19	20	21
	22	23	24	25	26	27	28
PAUSHA 1991	29	1	2	3	4	5	6
	7	8	9	10	11	12	13
	14	15	16	17	18	19	20

[a]New Year (Śobhana)
[b]Pongal

ISLAMIC (ASTRONOMICAL) 1491‡/1492

Month	Sun	Mon	Tue	Wed	Thu	Fri	Sat
DHU AL-QA'DA 1491	5	6	7	8	9	10	11
	12	13	14	15	16	17	18
	19	20	21	22	23	24	25
DHU AL-ḤIJJA 1491	26	27	28	29	*1*	2	3
	4	5	6	7	8	9	10[g]
	11	12	13	14	15	16	17
	18	19	20	21	22	23	24
MUḤARRAM 1492	25	26	27	28	29	30	*1*[a]
	2	3	4	5	6	7	8
	9	10[b]	11	12	13	14	15
	16	17	18	19	20	21	22
	23	24	25	26	27	28	29
ṢAFAR 1492	*1*	2	3	4	5	6	7
	8	9	10	11	12	13	14
	15	16	17	18	19	20	21
	22	23	24	25	26	27	28
RABĪ' I 1492	29	30	*1*	2	3	4	5
	6	7	8	9	10	11	12[c]
	13	14	15	16	17	18	19
	20	21	22	23	24	25	26
RABĪ' II 1492	27	28	29	1	*2*	3	4
	5	6	7	8	9	10	11
	12	13	14	15	16	17	18
	19	20	21	22	23	24	25
JUMĀDĀ I 1492	26	27	28	29	30	*1*	2
	3	4	5	6	7	8	9
	10	11	12	13	14	15	16
	17	18	19	20	21	22	23
JUMĀDĀ II 1492	24	25	26	27	28	29	1
	2	3	4	5	6	7	8
	9	10	11	12	13	14	15
	16	17	18	19	20	21	22
	23	24	25	26	27	28	29
RAJAB 1492	30	*1*	2	3	4	5	6
	7	8	9	10	11	12	13
	14	15	16	17	18	19	20
	21	22	23	24	25	26	27[d]
SHA'BĀN 1492	28	29	30	*1*	2	3	4
	5	6	7	8	9	10	11
	12	13	14	15	16	17	18
	19	20	21	22	23	24	25
RAMAḌĀN 1492	26	27	28	29	*1*[e]	2	3
	4	5	6	7	8	9	10
	11	12	13	14	15	16	17
	18	19	20	21	22	23	24
SHAWWĀL 1492	25	26	27	28	29	*1*[f]	2
	3	4	5	6	7	8	9
	10	11	12	13	14	15	16
	17	18	19	20	21	22	23
	24	25	26	27	28	29	30
DHU AL-QA'DA 1492	*1*	2	3	4	5	6	7
	8	9	10	11	12	13	14
	15	16	17	18	19	20	21

‡Leap year
[a]New Year
[b]'Ashūrā'
[c]Prophet's Birthday
[d]Ascent of the Prophet
[e]Start of Ramaḍān
[f]'Id al-Fiṭr
[g]'Id al-'Aḍḥā

GREGORIAN 2069

Julian (Sun)	Sun	Mon	Tue	Wed	Thu	Fri	Sat	Month
Dec 17	*30*	31	1	2	3	4	5	
	6	7[a]	8	9	10	11	12	JANUARY 2069
Dec 31	*13*	14[b]	15	16	17	18	19	
	20	21	22	23	24	25	26	
Jan 14	*27*	28	29	30	31	1	2	
	3	4	5	6	7	8	9	FEBRUARY 2069
Jan 28	*10*	11	12	13	14	15	16	
	17	18	19	20	21	22	23	
Feb 11	*24*	25	26	27[c]	28	1	2	
	3[d]	4	5	6	7	8	9	
Feb 25	*10*	11	12	13	14	15	16	MARCH 2069
	17	18	19	20	21	22	23	
Mar 11	*24*	25	26	27	28	29	30	
	31	1	2	3	4	5	6	
Mar 25	*7*	8	9	10	11	12	13	APRIL 2069
	14[e]	15	16	17	18	19	20	
Apr 8	*21*	22	23	24	25	26	27	
	28	29	30	1	2	3	4	
Apr 22	*5*	6	7	8	9	10	11	MAY 2069
	12	13	14	15	16	17	18	
May 6	*19*	20	21	22	23	24	25	
	26	27	28	29	30	31	1	
May 20	*2*	3	4	5	6	7	8	
	9	10	11	12	13	14	15	JUNE 2069
Jun 3	*16*	17	18	19	20	21	22	
	23	24	25	26	27	28	29	
Jun 17	*30*	1	2	3	4	5	6	
	7	8	9	10	11	12	13	JULY 2069
Jul 1	*14*	15	16	17	18	19	20	
	21	22	23	24	25	26	27	
Jul 15	*28*	29	30	31	1	2	3	
	4	5	6	7	8	9	10	AUGUST 2069
Jul 29	*11*	12	13	14	15	16	17	
	18	19	20	21	22	23	24	
Aug 12	*25*	26	27	28	29	30	31	
	1	2	3	4	5	6	7	
Aug 26	*8*	9	10	11	12	13	14	SEPTEMBER 2069
	15	16	17	18	19	20	21	
Sep 9	*22*	23	24	25	26	27	28	
	29	30	1	2	3	4	5	
Sep 23	*6*	7	8	9	10	11	12	OCTOBER 2069
	13	14	15	16	17	18	19	
Oct 7	*20*	21	22	23	24	25	26	
	27	28	29	30	31	1	2	
Oct 21	*3*	4	5	6	7	8	9	
	10	11	12	13	14	15	16	NOVEMBER 2069
Nov 4	*17*	18	19	20	21	22	23	
	24	25	26	27	28	29	30	
Nov 18	*1*[g]	2	3	4	5	6	7	
	8	9	10	11	12	13	14	DECEMBER 2069
Dec 2	*15*	16	17	18	19	20	21	
	22	23	24	25[h]	26	27	28	
Dec 16	*29*	30	31	1	2	3	4	

[a]Orthodox Christmas
[b]Julian New Year
[c]Ash Wednesday
[d]Feast of Orthodoxy
[e]Easter (also Orthodox)
[g]Advent
[h]Christmas

2070

Month	Sun	Mon	Tue	Wed	Thu	Fri	Sat	Lunar Phases	ISO WEEK (Mon)	JULIAN DAY (Sun noon)	HEBREW 5830/5831‡	Sun	Mon	Tue	Wed	Thu	Fri	Sat	Molad	CHINESE Jǐ-Chǒu‡/Gēng-Yín	Sun	Mon	Tue	Wed	Thu	Fri	Sat	Solar Term	COPTIC 1786/1787‡	Sun	Mon	Tue	Wed	Thu	Fri	Sat	ETHIOPIC 2062/2063‡
JANUARY 2070	29	30	31	1[a]	2	3	◑	7:14	1	2477110	TEVETH 5830	15	16	17	18	19	20	21		MONTH 11 Jǐ-Chǒu	16	17	18	19	20	21	22		KOIAK 1786	20	21	22	23	24	25	26	TĀḪŚĀŚ 2062
	5	6	7	8	9	10	11		2	2477117		22	23	24	25	26	27	28			23	24	25	26	27	28	29	Xiǎo hán		27	28	29[c]	30	1	2	3	ṬER 2062
	●	13	14	15	16	17	18	11:21	3	2477124	SHEVAT 5830	29	1	2	3	4	5	6	Sun 6h32m15p	MONTH 12 Jǐ-Chǒu	1	2	3	4	5	6	7		TÔBE 1786	4	5	6[d]	7	8	9	10	
	◐	20	21	22	23	24	25	18:30	4	2477131		7	8	9	10	11	12	13			8	**9**	10	11	12	13	14	Dà hán		11[e]	12	13	14	15	16	17	
FEBRUARY 2070	○	27	28	29	30	31	1	12:58	5	2477138		14	15	16	17	18	19	20			15	16	17	18	19	20	21			18	19	20	21	22	23	24	
	2	◑	4	5	6	7	8	4:44	6	2477145		21	22	23	24	25	26	27			22	23	24	25	26	27	28	Lì chūn	MESHIR 1786	25	26	27	28	29	30	1	YAKĀTIT 2062
	9	10	●	12	13	14	15	2:51	7	2477152	ADAR 5830	28	29	30	1	2	3	4	Mon 19h16m16p	MONTH 1 Gēng-Yín	29	30	1[a]	2	3	4	5			2	3	4	5	6	7	8	
	16	17	◐	19	20	21	22	2:32	8	2477159		5	6	7	8	9	10	11			6	7	**8**	9	10	11	12	Yǔ shuǐ		9	10	11	12	13	14	15	
MARCH 2070	23	24	○	26	27	28	1	2:30	9	2477166		12	13	14[f]	15	16	17	18			13	14	15[b]	16	17	18*	19			16	17	18	19	20	21	22	
	2	3	4	◑	6	7	8	2:10	10	2477173		19	20	21	22	23	24	25			20	21	22	23	24	25	26	Jīng zhé		23	24	25	26	27	28	29	
	9	10	11	●	13	14	15	15:51	11	2477180	NISAN 5830	26	27	28	29	1	2	3	Wed 8h0m17p	MONTH 2 Gēng-Yín	27	28	29	1	2	3	4		PAREMOTEP 1786	30	1	2	3	4	5	6	MAGĀBIT 2062
	16	17	18	◐	20[b]	21	22	9:52	12	2477187		4	5	6	7	8	9	10			5	6	7	8	**9**	10	11	Chūn fēn		7	8	9	10	11	12	13	
	23	24	25	○	27	28	29	17:29	13	2477194		11	12	13	14	15[g]	16	17			12	13	14	15	16	17	18			14	15	16	17	18	19	20	
APRIL 2070	30	31	1	2	◑	4	5	21:21	14	2477201		18	19	20	21	22	23	24			19	20	21	22	23	**24**[c]	25	Qīng míng		21	22	23	24	25	26	27	
	6	7	8	9	10	●	12	2:29	15	2477208	IYYAR 5830	25	26	27	28	29	30	1	Thu 20h45m0p	MONTH 3 Gēng-Yín	26	27	28	29	30	1	2		PARMOUTE 1786	28	29	30	1	2	3	4	MIYĀZYĀ 2062
	13	14	15	16	◐	18	19	17:30	16	2477215		2	3	4	5	6	7	8			3	4	5	6	7	8	9			5	6	7	8	9	10	11	
	20	21	22	23	24	○	26	9:30	17	2477222		9	10	11	12	13	14	15			**10**	11	12	13	14	15	16	Gǔ yǔ		12	13	14	15	16	17	18	
MAY 2070	27	28	29	30	1	2	◑	13:10	18	2477229		16	17	18	19	20	21	22			17	18	19*	20	21	22	23			19	20	21	22	23	24	25	
	4	5	6	7	8	9	●	11:07	19	2477236		23	24	25	26	27	28	29		MONTH 4 Gēng-Yín	24	25	26	27	28	29	1	Lì xià	PASHONS 1786	26[f]	27	28	29[g]	30	1	2	GENBOT 2062
	11	12	13	14	15	16	◐	2:29	20	2477243	SIVAN 5830	1	2	3	4	5	6[h]	7	Sat 9h29m1p		2	3	4	5	6	7	8			3	4	5	6	7	8	9	
	18	19	20	21	22	23	24		21	2477250		8	9	10	11	12	13	14			9	10	**11**	12	13	14	15	Xiǎo mǎn		10	11	12	13	14	15	16	
	○	26	27	28	29	30	31	1:36	22	2477257		15	16	17	18	19	20	21			16	17	18	19	20	21	22			17	18	19	20	21	22	23	
JUNE 2070	1	◑	3	4	5	6	7	1:25	23	2477264		22	23	24	25	26	27	28			23	24	25	26	27	28	29	Máng zhòng		24	25	26	27	28	29	30	
	●	9	10	11	12	13	14	18:23	24	2477271	TAMMUZ 5830	29	30	1	2	3	4	5	Sun 22h13m2p	MONTH 5 Gēng-Yín	30	1	2	3	4	5[d]	6		PAÔNE 1786	1	2	3	4	5	6	7	SANĒ 2062
	◐	16	17	18	19	20[c]	21	13:39	25	2477278		6	7	8	9	10	11	12			7	8	9	10	11	12	**13**	Xià zhì		8	9	10	11	12	13	14	
	22	○	24	25	26	27	28	16:56	26	2477285		13	14	15	16	17	18	19			14	15	16	17	18	19	20*			15	16	17	18	19	20	21	
JULY 2070	29	30	◑	2	3	4	5	10:32	27	2477292		20	21	22	23	24	25	26			21	22	23	24	25	26	27			22	23	24	25	26	27	28	
	6	7	●	9	10	11	12	1:13	28	2477299	AV 5830	27	28	29	1	2	3	4	Tue 10h57m3p	MONTH 6 Gēng-Yín	28	29	1	2	3	4	5	Xiǎo shǔ	EPÊP 1786	29	30	1	2	3	4	5	ḤAMLĒ 2062
	13	14	◐	16	17	18	19	3:25	29	2477306		5	6	7	8	9[i]	10	11			6	7	8	9	10	11	12			6	7	8	9	10	11	12	
	20	21	22	○	24	25	26	7:01	30	2477313		12	13	14	15	16	17	18			13	14	**15**	16	17	18	19	Dà shǔ		13	14	15	16	17	18	19	
AUGUST 2070	27	28	29	◑	31	1	2	17:16	31	2477320		19	20	21	22	23	24	25			20	21	22	23	24	25	26			20	21	22	23	24	25	26	
	3	4	5	●	7	8	9	8:50	32	2477327	ELUL 5830	26	27	28	29	30	1	2	Wed 23h41m4p	MONTH 7 Gēng-Yín	27	28	29	1	2	3	4	Lì qiū	MESORĒ 1786	27	28	29	30	1	2	3	NAḤASĒ 2062
	10	11	12	◐	14	15	16	19:39	33	2477334		3	4	5	6	7	8	9			5	6	7[e]	8	9	10	11			4	5	6	7	8	9	10	
	17	18	19	20	○	22	23	19:53	34	2477341		10	11	12	13	14	15	16			12	13	14	15[f]	16	17	**18**	Chǔ shǔ		11	12	13[h]	14	15	16	17	
	24	25	26	27	◑	29	30	22:40	35	2477348		17	18	19	20	21	22	23			19	20	21	22*	23	24	25			18	19	20	21	22	23	24	
SEPTEMBER 2070	31	1	2	3	●	5	6	18:27	36	2477355	TISHRI 5831	24	25	26	27	28	29	1[a]	Fri 12h25m5p	MONTH 8 Gēng-Yín	26	27	28	29	30	1	2		EPAG. 1786	25	26	27	28	29	30	1	PĀG. 2062
	7	8	9	10	11	◐	13	13:43	37	2477362		2[a]	3	4	5	6	7	8			3	4	5	6	7	8	9	Bái lù	THOOUT 1787	2	3	4	5	1[a]	2	3	MASKARAM 2063
	14	15	16	17	18	19	○	7:46	38	2477369		9	10[b]	11	12	13	14	15[c]			10	11	12	13	14	15[g]	16			4	5	6	7	8	9	10	
	21	22[d]	23	24	25	26	◑	4:01	39	2477376		16	17	18	19	20	21	22			17	**18**	19	20	21	22	23	Qiū fēn		11	12	13	14	15	16	17[b]	
OCTOBER 2070	28	29	30	1	2	3	●	7:00	40	2477383		23	24	25	26	27	28	29		MONTH 9 Gēng-Yín	24	25	26	27	28	29	1			18	19	20	21	22	23	24	
	5	6	7	8	9	10	11		41	2477390	ḤESHVAN 5831	30	1	2	3	4	5	6	Sun 1h9m6p		2	3	4	5	6	7	8	Hán lù	PAOPE 1787	25	26	27	28	29	30	1	TEQEMT 2063
	◐	13	14	15	16	17	18	8:39	42	2477397		7	8	9	10	11	12	13			9[h]	10	11	12	13	14	15			2	3	4	5	6	7	8	
	○	20	21	22	23	24	25	18:57	43	2477404		14	15	16	17	18	19	20			16	17	18	19	**20**	21	22	Shuāng jiàng		9	10	11	12	13	14	15	
NOVEMBER 2070	◑	27	28	29	30	31	1	10:46	44	2477411		21	22	23	24	25	26	27			23*	24	25	26	27	28	29			16	17	18	19	20	21	22	
	●	3	4	5	6	7	8	22:41	45	2477418	KISLEV 5831	28	29	1	2	3	4	5	Mon 13h53m7p	MONTH 10 Gēng-Yín	30	1	2	3	4	5	6	Lì dōng		23	24	25	26	27	28	29	
	9	10	◐	12	13	14	15	3:19	46	2477425		6	7	8	9	10	11	12			7	8	9	10	11	12	13		ATHŌR 1787	30	1	2	3	4	5	6	ḪEDĀR 2063
	16	17	○	19	20	21	22	5:39	47	2477432		13	14	15	16	17	18	19			14	15	16	17	18	19	**20**	Xiǎo xuě		7	8	9	10	11	12	13	
	23	◑	25	26	27	28	29	20:18	48	2477439		20	21	22	23	24	25[e]	26[e]			21	22	23	24	25	26	27			14	15	16	17	18	19	20	
DECEMBER 2070	30	1	●	3	4	5	6	16:52	49	2477446	TEVETH 5831	27[e]	28[e]	29[e]	1[e]	2[e]	3[d,e]	4	Wed 2h37m8p	MONTH 11 Gēng-Yín	28	29	30	1	2	3	4			21	22	23	24	25	26	27	
	7	8	9	◐	11	12	13	20:31	50	2477453		5	6	7	8	9	10	11			5	6	7	8	9	10	11	Dà xuě	KOIAK 1787	28	29	30	1	2	3	4	TĀḪŚĀŚ 2063
	14	15	16	○	18	19	20	16:04	51	2477460		12	13	14	15	16	17	18			12	13	14	15	16	17	18			5	6	7	8	9	10	11	
	21[e]	22	23	◑	25	26	27	9:30	52	2477467		19	20	21	22	23	24	25			**19**[i]	20	21	22	23*	24	25	Dōng zhì		12	13	14	15	16	17	18	
	28	29	30	31	●	2	3	12:14	1	2477474		26	27	28	29	1	2	3	Thu 15h21m9p		26	27	28	29	1	2	3			19	20	21	22	23	24	25	

[a]New Year
[b]Spring (6:33)
[c]Summer (23:21)
[d]Autumn (15:43)
[e]Winter (13:18)
● New moon
◐ First quarter moon
○ Full moon
◑ Last quarter moon

‡Leap year
[a]New Year
[b]Yom Kippur
[c]Sukkot
[d]Winter starts
[e]Ḥanukkah
[f]Purim
[g]Passover
[h]Shavuot
[i]Fast of Av

‡Leap year
[a]New Year (4768, Tiger)
[b]Lantern Festival
[c]Qīngmíng
[d]Dragon Festival
[e]Qīqiǎo
[f]Hungry Ghosts
[g]Mid-Autumn Festival
[h]Double-Ninth Festival
[i]Dōngzhì
*Start of 60-name cycle

‡Leap year
[a]New Year
[b]Building of the Cross
[c]Christmas
[d]Jesus's Circumcision
[e]Epiphany
[f]Easter
[g]Mary's Announcement
[h]Jesus's Transfiguration

PERSIAN (ASTRONOMICAL) 1448/1449‡

Month	Sun	Mon	Tue	Wed	Thu	Fri	Sat
DEY 1448	9	10	11	12	13	14	15
	16	17	18	19	20	21	22
	23	24	25	26	27	28	29
	30	1	2	3	4	5	6
BAHMAN 1448	7	8	9	10	11	12	13
	14	15	16	17	18	19	20
	21	22	23	24	25	26	27
	28	29	30	1	2	3	4
ESFAND 1448	5	6	7	8	9	10	11
	12	13	14	15	16	17	18
	19	20	21	22	23	24	25
	26	27	28	29	1[a]	2	3
FARVARDĪN 1449	4	5	6	7	8	9	10
	11	12	13[b]	14	15	16	17
	18	19	20	21	22	23	24
	25	26	27	28	29	30	31
ORDĪBEHEŠT 1449	1	2	3	4	5	6	7
	8	9	10	11	12	13	14
	15	16	17	18	19	20	21
	22	23	24	25	26	27	28
	29	30	31	1	2	3	4
XORDĀD 1449	5	6	7	8	9	10	11
	12	13	14	15	16	17	18
	19	20	21	22	23	24	25
	26	27	28	29	30	31	1
TĪR 1449	2	3	4	5	6	7	8
	9	10	11	12	13	14	15
	16	17	18	19	20	21	22
	23	24	25	26	27	28	29
	30	31	1	2	3	4	5
MORDĀD 1449	6	7	8	9	10	11	12
	13	14	15	16	17	18	19
	20	21	22	23	24	25	26
	27	28	29	30	31	1	2
SHAHRĪVAR 1449	3	4	5	6	7	8	9
	10	11	12	13	14	15	16
	17	18	19	20	21	22	23
	24	25	26	27	28	29	30
	31	1	2	3	4	5	6
MEHR 1449	7	8	9	10	11	12	13
	14	15	16	17	18	19	20
	21	22	23	24	25	26	27
	28	29	30	1	2	3	4
ĀBĀN 1449	5	6	7	8	9	10	11
	12	13	14	15	16	17	18
	19	20	21	22	23	24	25
	26	27	28	29	30	1	2
ĀZAR 1449	3	4	5	6	7	8	9
	10	11	12	13	14	15	16
	17	18	19	20	21	22	23
	24	25	26	27	28	29	30
DEY 1449	1	2	3	4	5	6	7
	8	9	10	11	12	13	14

HINDU LUNAR 2126‡/2127

Month	Sun	Mon	Tue	Wed	Thu	Fri	Sat
MĀRGAŚĪRA 2126	17	18	19	20	21	22	23
	24	25	25	26	27	28	29
	30	1	2	3	4	5	6
PAUSHA 2126	7	8	10	11	12	13	14
	15	16	17	18	19	20	21
	22	23	24	25	26	27	28
	28	29	30	1	2	4	5
MĀGHA 2126	6	7	8	9	10	11	12
	13	14	15	16	17	18	19
	20	21	22	23	24	25	26
	27	28[h]	29	30	1	2	3
PHĀLGUNA 2126	4	5	6	7	9	10	11
	12	13	14	15[i]	16	17	18
	19	20	20	21	22	23	24
	25	26	27	28	29	30	1[a]
CHAITRA 2127	3	4	5	6	7	8	9[b]
	10	11	12	13	14	15	16
	17	18	19	20	21	22	23
	24	25	26	27	28	29	30
VAIŚĀKHA 2127	1	2	3	4	6	7	8
	9	10	11	12	13	14	15
	15	16	17	18	19	20	21
	22	23	24	25	26	27	29
	30	1	2	3	4	5	6
JYAISHṬHA 2127	7	8	9	10	11	12	13
	14	15	16	17	18	19	20
	21	22	23	24	25	26	27
	28	29	30	2	3	4	5
ĀSHĀḌHA 2127	6	7	8	9	10	11	12
	12	13	14	15	16	17	18
	19	20	21	22	23	25	26
	27	28	29	30	1	2	3
ŚRĀVAṆA 2127	4	5	6	7	8	9	10
	11	12	13	14	15	16	17
	18	19	20	21	22	23[c]	24
	25	26	28	29	30	1	2
BHĀDRAPADA 2127	3	4[d]	5	6	7	8	8
	9	10	11	12	13	14	15
	16	17	18	19	21	22	23
	24	25	26	27	28	29	30
ĀŚVINA 2127	1	2	3	4	5	6	7
	8[e]	9[e]	10[e]	11	12	13	14
	15	16	17	18	19	20	21
	22	23	25	26	27	28	29
KĀRTTIKA 2127	30	1[f]	2	3	3	4	5
	6	7	8	9	10	11	12
	13	14	15	16	17	19	20
	21	22	23	24	25	26	27
MĀRGAŚĪRA 2127	28	29	30	1	2	3	4
	5	6	6	7	8	9	10[g]
	12	13	14	15	16	17	18
	19	20	21	22	23	24	25
	26	27	28	29	30	1	2

HINDU SOLAR 1991/1992

Month	Sun	Mon	Tue	Wed	Thu	Fri	Sat
PAUSHA 1991	14	15	16	17	18	19	20
	21	22	23	24	25	26	27
	28	29	1[b]	2	3	4	5
MĀGHA 1991	6	7	8	9	10	11	12
	13	14	15	16	17	18	19
	20	21	22	23	24	25	26
	27	28	29	30	1	2	3
PHĀLGUNA 1991	4	5	6	7	8	9	10
	11	12	13	14	15	16	17
	18	19	20	21	22	23	24
	25	26	27	28	29	30	1
CHAITRA 1991	2	3	4	5	6	7	8
	9	10	11	12	13	14	15
	16	17	18	19	20	21	22
	23	24	25	26	27	28	29
	30	1[a]	2	3	4	5	6
VAIŚĀKHA 1992	7	8	9	10	11	12	13
	14	15	16	17	18	19	20
	21	22	23	24	25	26	27
	28	29	30	31	1	2	3
JYAISHṬHA 1992	4	5	6	7	8	9	10
	11	12	13	14	15	16	17
	18	19	20	21	22	23	24
	25	26	27	28	29	30	31
ĀSHĀḌHA 1992	1	2	3	4	5	6	7
	8	9	10	11	12	13	14
	15	16	17	18	19	20	21
	22	23	24	25	26	27	28
	29	30	31	32	1	2	3
ŚRĀVAṆA 1992	4	5	6	7	8	9	10
	11	12	13	14	15	16	17
	18	19	20	21	22	23	24
	25	26	27	28	29	30	31
	32	1	2	3	4	5	6
BHĀDRAPADA 1992	7	8	9	10	11	12	13
	14	15	16	17	18	19	20
	21	22	23	24	25	26	27
	28	29	30	31	1	2	3
ĀŚVINA 1992	4	5	6	7	8	9	10
	11	12	13	14	15	16	17
	18	19	20	21	22	23	24
	25	26	27	28	29	30	1
KĀRTTIKA 1992	2	3	4	5	6	7	8
	9	10	11	12	13	14	15
	16	17	18	19	20	21	22
	23	24	25	26	27	28	29
	30	1	2	3	4	5	6
MĀRGAŚĪRA 1992	7	8	9	10	11	12	13
	14	15	16	17	18	19	20
	21	22	23	24	25	26	27
	28	29	1	2	3	4	5
PAUSHA 1992	6	7	8	9	10	11	12
	13	14	15	16	17	18	19

ISLAMIC (ASTRONOMICAL) 1492/1493‡

Month	Sun	Mon	Tue	Wed	Thu	Fri	Sat
DHU AL-QA'DA 1492	15	16	17	18	19	20	21
	22	23	24	25	26	27	28
	29	30	1	2	3	4	5
DHU AL-ḤIJJA 1492	6	7	8	9	10[g]	11	12
	13	14	15	16	17	18	19
	20	21	22	23	24	25	26
	27	28	29	1[a]	2	3	4
MUḤARRAM 1493	5	6	7	8	9	10[b]	11
	12	13	14	15	16	17	18
	19	20	21	22	23	24	25
	26	27	28	29	30	1	2
ṢAFAR 1493	3	4	5	6	7	8	9
	10	11	12	13	14	15	16
	17	18	19	20	21	22	23
	24	25	26	27	28	29	1
RABĪ' I 1493	2	3	4	5	6	7	8
	9	10	11	12[c]	13	14	15
	16	17	18	19	20	21	22
	23	24	25	26	27	28	29
	30	1	2	3	4	5	6
RABĪ' II 1493	7	8	9	10	11	12	13
	14	15	16	17	18	19	20
	21	22	23	24	25	26	27
	28	29	1	2	3	4	5
JUMĀDĀ I 1493	6	7	8	9	10	11	12
	13	14	15	16	17	18	19
	20	21	22	23	24	25	26
	27	28	29	30	1	2	3
JUMĀDĀ II 1493	4	5	6	7	8	9	10
	11	12	13	14	15	16	17
	18	19	20	21	22	23	24
	25	26	27	28	29	1	2
RAJAB 1493	3	4	5	6	7	8	9
	10	11	12	13	14	15	16
	17	18	19	20	21	22	23
	24	25	26	27[d]	28	29	30
SHA'BĀN 1493	1	2	3	4	5	6	7
	8	9	10	11	12	13	14
	15	16	17	18	19	20	21
	22	23	24	25	26	27	28
RAMAḌĀN 1493	29	1[e]	2	3	4	5	6
	7	8	9	10	11	12	13
	14	15	16	17	18	19	20
	21	22	23	24	25	26	27
SHAWWĀL 1493	28	29	1[f]	2	3	4	5
	6	7	8	9	10	11	12
	13	14	15	16	17	18	19
	20	21	22	23	24	25	26
DHU AL-QA'DA 1493	27	28	29	30	1	2	3
	4	5	6	7	8	9	10
	11	12	13	14	15	16	17
	18	19	20	21	22	23	24
	25	26	27	28	29	30	1

GREGORIAN 2070

Julian (Sun)	Sun	Mon	Tue	Wed	Thu	Fri	Sat	Month
Dec 16	29	30	31	1	2	3	4	JANUARY 2070
	5	6	7[a]	8	9	10	11	
Dec 30	12	13	14[b]	15	16	17	18	
	19	20	21	22	23	24	25	
Jan 13	26	27	28	29	30	31	1	FEBRUARY 2070
	2	3	4	5	6	7	8	
Jan 27	9	10	11	12[c]	13	14	15	
	16	17	18	19	20	21	22	
Feb 10	23	24	25	26	27	28	1	MARCH 2070
	2	3	4	5	6	7	8	
Feb 24	9	10	11	12	13	14	15	
	16	17	18	19	20	21	22	
Mar 10	23[d]	24	25	26	27	28	29	
	30[e]	31	1	2	3	4	5	APRIL 2070
Mar 24	6	7	8	9	10	11	12	
	13	14	15	16	17	18	19	
Apr 7	20	21	22	23	24	25	26	
	27	28	29	30	1	2	3	MAY 2070
Apr 21	4[f]	5	6	7	8	9	10	
	11	12	13	14	15	16	17	
May 5	18	19	20	21	22	23	24	
	25	26	27	28	29	30	31	
May 19	1	2	3	4	5	6	7	JUNE 2070
	8	9	10	11	12	13	14	
Jun 2	15	16	17	18	19	20	21	
	22	23	24	25	26	27	28	
Jun 16	29	30	1	2	3	4	5	JULY 2070
	6	7	8	9	10	11	12	
Jun 30	13	14	15	16	17	18	19	
	20	21	22	23	24	25	26	
Jul 14	27	28	29	30	31	1	2	AUGUST 2070
	3	4	5	6	7	8	9	
Jul 28	10	11	12	13	14	15	16	
	17	18	19	20	21	22	23	
Aug 11	24	25	26	27	28	29	30	
	31	1	2	3	4	5	6	SEPTEMBER 2070
Aug 25	7	8	9	10	11	12	13	
	14	15	16	17	18	19	20	
Sep 8	21	22	23	24	25	26	27	
	28	29	30	1	2	3	4	OCTOBER 2070
Sep 22	5	6	7	8	9	10	11	
	12	13	14	15	16	17	18	
Oct 6	19	20	21	22	23	24	25	
	26	27	28	29	30	31	1	NOVEMBER 2070
Oct 20	2	3	4	5	6	7	8	
	9	10	11	12	13	14	15	
Nov 3	16	17	18	19	20	21	22	
	23	24	25	26	27	28	29	
Nov 17	30[g]	1	2	3	4	5	6	DECEMBER 2070
	7	8	9	10	11	12	13	
Dec 1	14	15	16	17	18	19	20	
	21	22	23	24	25[h]	26	27	
Dec 15	28	29	30	31	1	2	3	

Persian: ‡Leap year; [a]New Year; [b]Sizdeh Bedar

Hindu Lunar: ‡Leap year; [a]New Year (Vikṛita); [b]Birthday of Rāma; [c]Birthday of Krishna; [d]Ganēśa Chaturthī; [e]Dashara; [f]Diwali; [g]Birthday of Vishnu; [h]Night of Śiva; [i]Holi

Hindu Solar: [a]New Year (Krodhin); [b]Pongal

Islamic: ‡Leap year; [a]New Year; [b]'Ashūrā'; [c]Prophet's Birthday; [d]Ascent of the Prophet; [e]Start of Ramaḍān; [f]'Īd al-Fiṭr; [g]'Īd al-'Aḍḥā

Gregorian: [a]Orthodox Christmas; [b]Julian New Year; [c]Ash Wednesday; [d]Feast of Orthodoxy; [e]Easter; [f]Orthodox Easter; [g]Advent; [h]Christmas

2071

Gregorian 2071	Sun	Mon	Tue	Wed	Thu	Fri	Sat	Lunar Phases	ISO Week (Mon)	Julian Day (Sun noon)	Hebrew 5831‡/5832	Sun	Mon	Tue	Wed	Thu	Fri	Sat	Molad	Chinese Gēng-Yín/Xīn-Mǎo‡	Sun	Mon	Tue	Wed	Thu	Fri	Sat	Solar Term	Coptic 1787‡/1788	Sun	Mon	Tue	Wed	Thu	Fri	Sat	Ethiopic 2063‡/2064
January 2071	28	29	30	31	●[a]	2	3	12:14	1	2477474	Shevat 5831	26	27	28	29	1	2	3	Thu 15h21m9p	Month 12 Gēng-Yín	26	27	28	29	1	2	3		Koiak 1787	19	20	21	22	23	24	25	Tākhśāś 2063
	4	5	6	7	8	◐	10	11:07	2	2477481		4	5	6	7	8	9	10			4	5	6	7	8	9	10	Xiǎo hán	Tōbe 1787	26	27	28	29[c]	30	1	2	Ṭer 2063
	11	12	13	14	15	○	17	2:34	3	2477488		11	12	13	14	15	16	17			11	12	13	14	15	16	17			3	4	5	6[d]	7	8	9	
	18	19	20	21	22	◑	24	2:15	4	2477495		18	19	20	21	22	23	24			18	19	**20**	21	22	23	24	Dà hán		10	11[e]	12	13	14	15	16	
	25	26	27	28	29	30	●	7:14	5	2477502	Adar I 5831	25	26	27	28	29	30	1	Sat 4h5m10p	Month 1 Xīn-Mǎo	25	26	27	28	29	30	1[a]			17	18	19	20	21	22	23	
February 2071	1	2	3	4	5	6	◐	22:29	6	2477509		2	3	4	5	6	7	8			2	3	4	5	6	7	8	Lì chūn		24	25	26	27	28	29	30	
	8	9	10	11	12	13	○	13:32	7	2477516		9	10	11	12	13	14	15			9	10	11	12	13	14	15[b]		Meshir 1787	1	2	3	4	5	6	7	Yakātit 2063
	15	16	17	18	19	20	◑	21:28	8	2477523		16	17	18	19	20	21	22			16	17	18	***19***	20	21	22	Yǔ shuǐ		8	9	10	11	12	13	14	
	22	23	24	25	26	27	28		9	2477530		23	24	25	26	27	28	29			23	24*	25	26	27	28	29			15	16	17	18	19	20	21	
March 2071	1	●	3	4	5	6	7	0:30	10	2477537	Adar II 5831	30	1	2	3	4	5	6	Sun 16h49m11p	Month 2 Xīn-Mǎo	30	1	2	3	*4*	5	6	Jīng zhé		22	23	24	25	26	27	28	
	8	◐	10	11	12	13	14	6:52	11	2477544		7	8	9	10	11	12	13			7	8	9	10	11	12	13		Paremotep 1787	29	30	1	2	3	4	5	Magābit 2063
	15	○	17	18	19	20[b]	21	1:16	12	2477551		14[f]	15	16	17	18	19	20			14	15	16	17	18	**19**	20	Chūn fēn		6	7	8	9	10	11	12	
	22	◑	24	25	26	27	28	17:31	13	2477558		21	22	23	24	25	26	27			21	22	23	24	25	26	27			13	14	15	16	17	18	19	
April 2071	29	30	●	1	2	3	4	15:02	14	2477565	Nisan 5831	28	29	1	2	3	4	5	Tue 5h33m12p	Month 3 Xīn-Mǎo	28	29	1	2	3	4	5	Qīng míng		20	21	22	23	24	25	26	
	5	6	◐	8	9	10	11	13:16	15	2477572		6	7	8	9	10	11	12			6[c]	7	8	9	10	11	12		Parmoute 1787	27	28	29	30	1	2	3	Miyāzyā 2063
	12	13	○	15	16	17	18	13:55	16	2477579		13	14	15[g]	16	17	18	19			13	14	15	16	17	18	19			4	5	6	7	8	9	10	
	19	20	21	◑	23	24	25	12:51	17	2477586		20	21	22	23	24	25	26			20	**21**	22	23	24	25*	26	Gǔ yǔ		11[f]	12	13	14	15	16	17	
May 2071	26	27	28	29	●	1	2	2:29	18	2477593	Iyar 5831	27	28	29	30	1	2	3	Wed 18h17m13p	Month 4 Xīn-Mǎo	27	28	29	30	1	2	3			18	19	20	21	22	23	24	
	3	4	5	◐	7	8	9	19:04	19	2477600		4	5	6	7	8	9	10			4	5	6	7	8	9	10	Lì xià	Pashons 1787	25	26	27	28	29[g]	30	1	Genbot 2063
	10	11	12	13	○	15	16	3:23	20	2477607		11	12	13	14	15	16	17			11	12	13	14	15	16	17			2	3	4	5	6	7	8	
	17	18	19	20	21	◑	23	6:17	21	2477614		18	19	20	21	22	23	24			18	19	20	21	**22**	23	24	Xiǎo mǎn		9	10	11	12	13	14	15	
	24	25	26	27	28	●	30	11:15	22	2477621	Sivan 5831	25	26	27	28	29	1	2	Fri 7h1m14p	Month 5 Xīn-Mǎo	25	26	27	28	29	1	2			16	17	18	19	20	21	22	
June 2071	31	1	2	3	4	◐	6	1:37	23	2477628		3	4	5	6[h]	7	8	9			3	4	5[d]	6	7	*8*	9	Máng zhòng		23	24	25	26	27	28	29	
	7	8	9	10	11	○	13	17:35	24	2477635		10	11	12	13	14	15	16			10	11	12	13	14	15	16		Paōne 1787	30	1	2	3	4	5	6	Sanē 2063
	14	15	16	17	18	19	◑	21:03	25	2477642		17	18	19	20	21	22	23			17	18	19	20	21	22	23			7	8	9	10	11	12	13	
	21[c]	22	23	24	25	26	●	18:19	26	2477649		24	25	26	27	28	29	30			**24**	25	26*	27	28	29	30	Xià zhì		14	15	16	17	18	19	20	
July 2071	28	29	30	1	2	3	◐	10:01	27	2477656	Tammuz 5831	1	2	3	4	5	6	7	Sat 19h45m15p	Month 6 Xīn-Mǎo	1	2	3	4	5	6	7			21	22	23	24	25	26	27	
	5	6	7	8	9	10	11		28	2477663		8	9	10	11	12	13	14			8	9	*10*	11	12	13	14	Xiǎo shǔ	Epēp 1787	28	29	30	1	2	3	4	Ḥamlē 2063
	○	13	14	15	16	17	18	8:24	29	2477670		15	16	17	18	19	20	21			15	16	17	18	19	20	21			5	6	7	8	9	10	11	
	19	◑	21	22	23	24	25	8:51	30	2477677		22	23	24	25	26	27	28			22	23	24	25	**26**	27	28	Dà shǔ		12	13	14	15	16	17	18	
August 2071	26	●	28	29	30	31	1	0:55	31	2477684	Av 5831	29	1	2	3	4	5	6	Mon 8h29m16p	Month 7 Xīn-Mǎo	29	1	2	3	4	5	6			19	20	21	22	23	24	25	
	◐	3	4	5	6	7	8	21:03	32	2477691		7	8	9[i]	10	11	12	13			7[e]	8	9	10	11	*12*	13	Lì qiū	Mesōrē 1787	26	27	28	29	30	1	2	Naḥasē 2063
	9	○	11	12	13	14	15	23:38	33	2477698		14	15	16	17	18	19	20			14	15[f]	16	17	18	19	20			3	4	5	6	7	8	9	
	16	17	◑	19	20	21	22	17:56	34	2477705		21	22	23	24	25	26	27			21	22	23	24	25	26	27*			10	11	12	13[h]	14	15	16	
	23	24	●	26	27	28	29	8:15	35	2477712	Elul 5831	28	29	30	1	2	3	4	Tue 21h13m17p	Month 8 Xīn-Mǎo	**28**	29	1	2	3	4	5	Chǔ shǔ		17	18	19	20	21	22	23	
September 2071	30	31	◐	2	3	4	5	11:08	36	2477719		5	6	7	8	9	10	11			6	7	8	9	10	11	12			24	25	26	27	28	29	30	
	6	7	8	○	10	11	12	14:50	37	2477726		12	13	14	15	16	17	18			13	*14*	15[g]	16	17	18	19	Bái lù	Epag. 1787 / Thout 1788	1	2	3	4	5	6	1[a]	Pāg. 2063 / Maskaram 2064
	13	14	15	16	◑	18	19	1:06	38	2477733		19	20	21	22	23	24	25			20	21	22	23	24	25	26			2	3	4	5	6	7	8	
	20	21	22[d]	●	24	25	26	17:20	39	2477740	Tishri 5832	26	27	28	29	1[a]	2[a]	3	Thu 9h58m0p	Leap Month 8 Xīn-Mǎo	27	28	29	**30**	1	2	3	Qiū fēn		9	10	11	12	13	14	15	
October 2071	27	28	29	30	◐	2	3	4:19	40	2477747		4	5	6	7	8	9	10[b]			4	5	6	7	8	9	10			16	17[b]	18	19	20	21	22	
	4	5	6	7	8	○	10	5:22	41	2477754		11	12	13	14	15[c]	16	17			11	12	13	14	*15*	16	17	Hán lù		23	24	25	26	27	28	29	
	11	12	13	14	15	◑	17	7:29	42	2477761		18	19	20	21	22	23	24			18	19	20	21	22	23	24		Paope 1788	30	1	2	3	4	5	6	Ṭeqemt 2064
	18	19	20	21	22	●	24	4:48	43	2477768	Ḥeshvan 5832	25	26	27	28	29	30	1	Fri 22h42m1p	Month 9 Xīn-Mǎo	25	26	27	28*	29	***1***	2	Shuāng jiàng		7	8	9	10	11	12	13	
	25	26	27	28	29	30	◐	0:05	44	2477775		2	3	4	5	6	7	8			3	4	5	6	7	8	9[h]			14	15	16	17	18	19	20	
November 2071	1	2	3	4	5	6	○	18:46	45	2477782		9	10	11	12	13	14	15			10	11	12	13	14	15	*16*	Lì dōng		21	22	23	24	25	26	27	
	8	9	10	11	12	13	◑	14:23	46	2477789		16	17	18	19	20	21	22			17	18	19	20	21	22	23		Athōr 1788	28	29	30	1	2	3	4	Ḫedār 2064
	15	16	17	18	19	20	●	18:58	47	2477796		23	24	25	26	27	28	29			24	25	26	27	28	29	30			5	6	7	8	9	10	11	
	22	23	24	25	26	27	28		48	2477803	Kislev 5832	30	1	2	3	4	5	6	Sun 11h26m2p	Month 10 Xīn-Mǎo	***1***	2	3	4	5	6	7	Xiǎo xuě		12	13	14	15	16	17	18	
December 2071	◐	30	1	2	3	4	5	21:05	49	2477810		7	8	9	10	11	12	13			8	9	10	11	12	13	14			19	20	21	22	23	24	25	
	6	○	8	9	10	11	12	6:56	50	2477817		14[d]	15	16	17	18	19	20			15	*16*	17	18	19	20	21	Dà xuě	Koiak 1788	26	27	28	29	30	1	2	Tākhśāś 2064
	◑	14	15	16	17	18	19	22:56	51	2477824		21	22	23	24	25[e]	26[e]	27[e]			22	23	24	25	26	27	28			3	4	5	6	7	8	9	
	20	●[e]	22	23	24	25	26	11:46	52	2477831	Teveth 5832	28[e]	29[e]	30[e]	1[e]	2[e]	3	4	Tue 0h10m3p	Month 11 Xīn-Mǎo	29*	1	**2**[i]	3	4	5	6	Dōng zhì		10	11	12	13	14	15	16	
	27	28	◐	30	31	1	2	17:15	53	2477838		5	6	7	8	9	10	11			7	8	9	10	11	12	13			17	18	19	20	21	22	23	

[a]New Year
[b]Spring (12:33)
[c]Summer (5:19)
[d]Autumn (21:36)
[e]Winter (19:02)
● New moon
◐ First quarter moon
○ Full moon
◑ Last quarter moon

‡Leap year
[a]New Year
[b]Yom Kippur
[c]Sukkot
[d]Winter starts
[e]Ḥanukkah
[f]Purim
[g]Passover
[h]Shavuot
[i]Fast of Av

‡Leap year
[a]New Year (4769, Hare)
[b]Lantern Festival
[c]Qīngmíng
[d]Dragon Festival
[e]Qǐqiǎo
[f]Hungry Ghosts
[g]Mid-Autumn Festival
[h]Double-Ninth Festival
[i]Dōngzhì
*Start of 60-name cycle

‡Leap year
[a]New Year
[b]Building of the Cross
[c]Christmas
[d]Jesus's Circumcision
[e]Epiphany
[f]Easter
[g]Mary's Announcement
[h]Jesus's Transfiguration

PERSIAN (ASTRONOMICAL) 1449‡/1450

Month	Sun	Mon	Tue	Wed	Thu	Fri	Sat
DEY 1449	8	9	10	11	12	13	14
	15	16	17	18	19	20	21
	22	23	24	25	26	27	28
BAHMAN 1449	29	30	1	2	3	4	5
	6	7	8	9	10	11	12
	13	14	15	16	17	18	19
	20	21	22	23	24	25	26
ESFAND 1449	27	28	29	30	1	2	3
	4	5	6	7	8	9	10
	11	12	13	14	15	16	17
	18	19	20	21	22	23	24
FARVARDĪN 1450	25	26	27	28	29	30	1[a]
	2	3	4	5	6	7	8
	9	10	11	12	13[b]	14	15
	16	17	18	19	20	21	22
	23	24	25	26	27	28	29
ORDĪBEHEŠT 1450	30	31	1	2	3	4	5
	6	7	8	9	10	11	12
	13	14	15	16	17	18	19
	20	21	22	23	24	25	26
XORDĀD 1450	27	28	29	30	31	1	2
	3	4	5	6	7	8	9
	10	11	12	13	14	15	16
	17	18	19	20	21	22	23
	24	25	26	27	28	29	30
TĪR 1450	31	1	2	3	4	5	6
	7	8	9	10	11	12	13
	14	15	16	17	18	19	20
	21	22	23	24	25	26	27
MORDĀD 1450	28	29	30	31	1	2	3
	4	5	6	7	8	9	10
	11	12	13	14	15	16	17
	18	19	20	21	22	23	24
	25	26	27	28	29	30	31
SHAHRĪVAR 1450	1	2	3	4	5	6	7
	8	9	10	11	12	13	14
	15	16	17	18	19	20	21
	22	23	24	25	26	27	28
MEHR 1450	29	30	31	1	2	3	4
	5	6	7	8	9	10	11
	12	13	14	15	16	17	18
	19	20	21	22	23	24	25
ĀBĀN 1450	26	27	28	29	30	1	2
	3	4	5	6	7	8	9
	10	11	12	13	14	15	16
	17	18	19	20	21	22	23
	24	25	26	27	28	29	30
ĀZAR 1450	1	2	3	4	5	6	7
	8	9	10	11	12	13	14
	15	16	17	18	19	20	21
	22	23	24	25	26	27	28
DEY 1450	29	30	1	2	3	4	5
	6	7	8	9	10	11	12

‡Leap year
[a]New Year
[b]Sizdeh Bedar

HINDU LUNAR 2127/2128

Month	Sun	Mon	Tue	Wed	Thu	Fri	Sat
PAUSHA 2127	26	27	28	29	30	1	2
	3	4	5	6	7	8	9
	10	11	12	13	14	**15**	17
	18	19	20	21	22	23	24
	25	26	27	28	*28*	29	30
MĀGHA 2127	1	2	3	4	5	6	7
	8	**9**	11	12	13	14	15
	16	17	18	19	20	21	22
	23	24	25	26	27	28	29[h]
PHĀLGUNA 2127	30	1	2	3	4	5	6
	7	8	9	10	11	12	13
	14	**15**[i]	17	18	19	20	*20*
	21	22	23	24	25	26	27
CHAITRA 2128	28	29	30	1[a]	2	3	4
	5	6	7	**8**[b]	10	11	12
	13	14	15	16	17	18	19
	20	21	22	23	24	*24*	25
VAIŚĀKHA 2128	26	27	28	29	30	**1**	3
	4	5	6	7	8	9	10
	11	12	13	14	15	16	17
	18	19	20	21	22	23	24
JYAISHṬHA 2128	25	26	27	28	29	30	1
	2	3	**4**	6	7	8	9
	10	11	12	13	14	15	16
	17	18	19	20	*20*	21	22
	23	24	25	26	**27**	29	30
ĀSHĀḌHA 2128	1	2	3	4	5	6	7
	8	9	10	11	12	13	14
	15	16	17	18	19	20	21
	22	23	24	25	26	27	28
ŚRĀVAṆA 2128	29	**30**	2	3	4	5	6
	7	8	9	10	11	12	13
	14	15	16	17	*17*	18	19
	20	21	**22**[c]	24	25	26	27
BHĀDRAPADA 2128	28	29	30	1	2	3[d]	4
	5	6	7	8	9	10	11
	12	13	14	15	16	17	18
	19	20	21	22	23	24	25
ĀŚVINA 2128	**26**	28	29	30	1	2	3
	4	5	6	7	8[e]	9[e]	10[e]
	11	12	*12*	13	14	15	16
	17	18	**19**	21	22	23	24
KĀRTTIKA 2128	25	26	27	28	29	30	1[f]
	2	3	4	5	6	7	8
	9	10	11	12	13	14	15
	16	17	18	19	20	21	22
	23	**24**	26	27	28	29	30
MĀRGAŚIRA 2128	1	2	3	4	5	6	*6*
	7	8	9	10	11[g]	12	13
	14	15	16	17	**18**	20	21
	22	23	24	25	26	27	28
PAUSHA 2128	29	30	1	2	3	4	5
	6	7	8	9	10	11	12

[a]New Year (Khara)
[b]Birthday of Rāma
[c]Birthday of Krishna
[d]Ganēśa Chaturthī
[e]Dashara
[f]Diwali
[g]Birthday of Vishnu
[h]Night of Śiva
[i]Holi

HINDU SOLAR 1992/1993‡

Month	Sun	Mon	Tue	Wed	Thu	Fri	Sat
PAUSHA 1992	13	14	15	16	17	18	19
	20	21	22	23	24	25	26
MĀGHA 1992	27	28	29	30	1[b]	2	3
	4	5	6	7	8	9	10
	11	12	13	14	15	16	17
	18	19	20	21	22	23	24
PHĀLGUNA 1992	25	26	27	28	29	1	2
	3	4	5	6	7	8	9
	10	11	12	13	14	15	16
	17	18	19	20	21	22	23
	24	25	26	27	28	29	30
CHAITRA 1992	1	2	3	4	5	6	7
	8	9	10	11	12	13	14
	15	16	17	18	19	20	21
	22	23	24	25	26	27	28
VAIŚĀKHA 1993	29	30	1[a]	2	3	4	5
	6	7	8	9	10	11	12
	13	14	15	16	17	18	19
	20	21	22	23	24	25	26
JYAISHṬHA 1993	27	28	29	30	31	1	2
	3	4	5	6	7	8	9
	10	11	12	13	14	15	16
	17	18	19	20	21	22	23
	24	25	26	27	28	29	30
ĀSHĀḌHA 1993	31	32	1	2	3	4	5
	6	7	8	9	10	11	12
	13	14	15	16	17	18	19
	20	21	22	23	24	25	26
ŚRĀVAṆA 1993	27	28	29	30	31	1	2
	3	4	5	6	7	8	9
	10	11	12	13	14	15	16
	17	18	19	20	21	22	23
	24	25	26	27	28	29	30
BHĀDRAPADA 1993	31	32	1	2	3	4	5
	6	7	8	9	10	11	12
	13	14	15	16	17	18	19
	20	21	22	23	24	25	26
ĀŚVINA 1993	27	28	29	30	31	1	2
	3	4	5	6	7	8	9
	10	11	12	13	14	15	16
	17	18	19	20	21	22	23
	24	25	26	27	28	29	30
KĀRTTIKA 1993	1	2	3	4	5	6	7
	8	9	10	11	12	13	14
	15	16	17	18	19	20	21
	22	23	24	25	26	27	28
MĀRGAŚIRA 1993	29	30	1	2	3	4	5
	6	7	8	9	10	11	12
	13	14	15	16	17	18	19
	20	21	22	23	24	25	26
PAUSHA 1993	27	28	29	30	1	2	3
	4	5	6	7	8	9	10
	11	12	13	14	15	16	17

‡Leap year
[a]New Year (Viśvāvasu)
[b]Pongal

ISLAMIC (ASTRONOMICAL) 1493‡/1494

Month	Sun	Mon	Tue	Wed	Thu	Fri	Sat
DHU AL-ḤIJJA 1493	25	26	27	28	29	30	1
	2	3	4	5	6	7	8
	9	10[g]	11	12	13	14	15
	16	17	18	19	20	21	22
	23	24	25	26	27	28	29
MUḤARRAM 1494	30[d]	1[a]	2	3	4	5	6
	7	8	9	10[b]	11	12	13
	14	15	16	17	18	19	20
	21	22	23	24	25	26	27
ṢAFAR 1494	28	29	1	2	3	4	5
	6	7	8	9	10	11	12
	13	14	15	16	17	18	19
	20	21	22	23	24	25	26
RABĪ' I 1494	27	28	29	30	1	2	3
	4	5	6	7	8	9	10
	11	12[c]	13	14	15	16	17
	18	19	20	21	22	23	24
RABĪ' II 1494	25	26	27	28	29	1	2
	3	4	5	6	7	8	9
	10	11	12	13	14	15	16
	17	18	19	20	21	22	23
	24	25	26	27	28	29	30
JUMĀDĀ I 1494	1	2	3	4	5	6	7
	8	9	10	11	12	13	14
	15	16	17	18	19	20	21
	22	23	24	25	26	27	28
JUMĀDĀ II 1494	29	1	2	3	4	5	6
	7	8	9	10	11	12	13
	14	15	16	17	18	19	20
	21	22	23	24	25	26	27
RAJAB 1494	28	29	30	1	2	3	4
	5	6	7	8	9	10	11
	12	13	14	15	16	17	18
	19	20	21	22	23	24	25
SHA'BĀN 1494	26	27[d]	28	29	1	2	3
	4	5	6	7	8	9	10
	11	12	13	14	15	16	17
	18	19	20	21	22	23	24
RAMAḌĀN 1494	25	26	27	28	29	1[e]	2
	3	4	5	6	7	8	9
	10	11	12	13	14	15	16
	17	18	19	20	21	22	23
SHAWWĀL 1494	24	25	26	27	28	29	1[f]
	2	3	4	5	6	7	8
	9	10	11	12	13	14	15
	16	17	18	19	20	21	22
	23	24	25	26	27	28	29
DHU AL-QA'DA 1494	30	1	2	3	4	5	6
	7	8	9	10	11	12	13
	14	15	16	17	18	19	20
	21	22	23	24	25	26	27
DHU AL-ḤIJJA 1494	28	29	30	1	2	3	4
	5	6	7	8	9	10	11

‡Leap year
[a]New Year
[d]New Year (Arithmetic)
[b]'Ashūrā'
[c]Prophet's Birthday
[d]Ascent of the Prophet
[e]Start of Ramaḍān
[f]'Īd al-Fiṭr
[g]'Īd al-'Aḍḥā

GREGORIAN 2071

Julian (Sun)	Sun	Mon	Tue	Wed	Thu	Fri	Sat	Month
Dec 15	28	29	30	31	1	2	3	JANUARY 2071
	4	5	6	7[a]	8	9	10	
Dec 29	11	12	13	14[b]	15	16	17	
	18	19	20	21	22	23	24	
Jan 12	25	26	27	28	29	30	31	
	1	2	3	4	5	6	7	FEBRUARY 2071
Jan 26	8	9	10	11	12	13	14	
	15	16	17	18	19	20	21	
Feb 9	22	23	24	25	26	27	28	
	1	2	3	4[c]	5	6	7	MARCH 2071
Feb 23	8[d]	9	10	11	12	13	14	
	15	16	17	18	19	20	21	
Mar 9	22	23	24	25	26	27	28	
	29	30	31	1	2	3	4	APRIL 2071
Mar 23	5	6	7	8	9	10	11	
	12	13	14	15	16	17	18	
Apr 6	19[e]	20	21	22	23	24	25	
	26	27	28	29	30	1	2	MAY 2071
Apr 20	3	4	5	6	7	8	9	
	10	11	12	13	14	15	16	
May 4	17	18	19	20	21	22	23	
	24	25	26	27	28	29	30	
May 18	31	1	2	3	4	5	6	JUNE 2071
	7	8	9	10	11	12	13	
Jun 1	14	15	16	17	18	19	20	
	21	22	23	24	25	26	27	
Jun 15	28	29	30	1	2	3	4	JULY 2071
	5	6	7	8	9	10	11	
Jun 29	12	13	14	15	16	17	18	
	19	20	21	22	23	24	25	
Jul 13	26	27	28	29	30	31	1	AUGUST 2071
	2	3	4	5	6	7	8	
Jul 27	9	10	11	12	13	14	15	
	16	17	18	19	20	21	22	
Aug 10	23	24	25	26	27	28	29	
	30	31	1	2	3	4	5	SEPTEMBER 2071
Aug 24	6	7	8	9	10	11	12	
	13	14	15	16	17	18	19	
Sep 7	20	21	22	23	24	25	26	
	27	28	29	30	1	2	3	OCTOBER 2071
Sep 21	4	5	6	7	8	9	10	
	11	12	13	14	15	16	17	
Oct 5	18	19	20	21	22	23	24	
	25	26	27	28	29	30	31	
Oct 19	1	2	3	4	5	6	7	NOVEMBER 2071
	8	9	10	11	12	13	14	
Nov 2	15	16	17	18	19	20	21	
	22	23	24	25	26	27	28	
Nov 16	29[g]	30	1	2	3	4	5	DECEMBER 2071
	6	7	8	9	10	11	12	
Nov 30	13	14	15	16	17	18	19	
	20	21	22	23	24	25[h]	26	
Dec 14	27	28	29	30	31	1	2	

[a]Orthodox Christmas
[b]Julian New Year
[c]Ash Wednesday
[d]Feast of Orthodoxy
[e]Easter (also Orthodox)
[g]Advent
[h]Christmas

2072

Gregorian 2072‡	Sun	Mon	Tue	Wed	Thu	Fri	Sat	Lunar Phases	ISO WEEK (Mon)	JULIAN DAY (Sun noon)	Hebrew 5832/5833‡	Sun	Mon	Tue	Wed	Thu	Fri	Sat	Molad	Chinese Xīn-Mǎo‡/Rén-Chén	Sun	Mon	Tue	Wed	Thu	Fri	Sat	Solar Term	Coptic 1788/1789	Sun	Mon	Tue	Wed	Thu	Fri	Sat	Ethiopic 2064/2065
JANUARY 2072	27	28	◐	30	31	1[a]	2	17:15	53	2477838	TEVETH 5832	5	6	7	8	9	10	11		MONTH 11 Xīn-Mǎo	7	8	9	10	11	12	13		KOIAK 1788	17	18	19	20	21	22	23	TĀKHŚĀŚ 2064
	3	4	○	6	7	8	9	18:12	1	2477845		12	13	14	15	16	17	18			14	15	16	17	18	19	20	Xiǎo hán		24	25	26	27	28	29[c]	30	
	10	11	◑	13	14	15	16	9:53	2	2477852		19	20	21	22	23	24	25			21	22	23	24	25	26	27		TŌBE 1788	1	2	3	4	5	6[d]	7	TER 2064
	17	18	19	●	21	22	23	6:34	3	2477859	SHEVAT 5832	26	27	28	29	1	2	3	Wed 12h54m4p	MONTH 12 Xīn-Mǎo	28	29	30	1	2	3	4	Dà hán		8	9	10	11[e]	12	13	14	
	24	25	26	27	◐	29	30	10:35	4	2477866		4	5	6	7	8	9	10			5	6	7	8	9	10	11			15	16	17	18	19	20	21	
FEBRUARY 2072	31	1	2	3	○	5	6	4:54	5	2477873		11	12	13	14	15	16	17			12	13	14	15	16	17	18	Lì chūn		22	23	24	25	26	27	28	
	7	8	9	◑	11	12	13	23:25	6	2477880		18	19	20	21	22	23	24			19	20	21	22	23	24	25		MESHIR 1788	29	30	1	2	3	4	5	YAKĀTIT 2064
	14	15	16	17	18	●	20	2:02	7	2477887	ADAR 5832	25	26	27	28	29	30	1	Fri 1h38m5p	MONTH 1 Rén-Chén	26	27	28	29	30*	1[a]	2	Yǔ shuǐ		6	7	8	9	10	11	12	
	21	22	23	24	25	26	◐	0:01	8	2477894		2	3	4	5	6	7	8			3	4	5	6	7	8	9			13	14	15	16	17	18	19	
MARCH 2072	28	29	1	2	3	○	5	15:16	9	2477901		9	10	11	12	13	14[f]	15			10	11	12	13	14	15[b]	16	Jīng zhé		20	21	22	23	24	25	26	
	6	7	8	9	10	◑	12	15:17	10	2477908		16	17	18	19	20	21	22			17	18	19	20	21	22	23		PAREMOTEP 1788	27	28	29	30	1	2	3	MAGĀBIT 2064
	13	14	15	16	17	18	●[b]	20:20	11	2477915		23	24	25	26	27	28	29			24	25	26	27	28	29	30			4	5	6	7	8	9	10	
	20	21	22	23	24	25	26		12	2477922	NISAN 5832	1	2	3	4	5	6	7	Sat 14h22m6p	MONTH 2 Rén-Chén	1	2	3	4	5	6	7	Chūn fēn		11	12	13	14	15	16	17	
APRIL 2072	◐	28	29	30	31	1	2	9:41	13	2477929		8	9	10	11	12	13	14			8	9	10	11	12	13	14			18	19	20	21	22	23	24	
	○	4	5	6	7	8	9	1:24	14	2477936		15[g]	16	17	18	19	20	21			15	16[c]	17	18	19	20	21	Qīng míng	PARMOUTE 1788	25	26	27	28	29	30	1	MIYĀZYĀ 2064
	◑	11	12	13	14	15	16	8:52	15	2477943		22	23	24	25	26	27	28			22	23	24	25	26	27	28			2[f]	3	4	5	6	7	8	
	17	●	19	20	21	22	23	11:55	16	2477950	IYYAR 5832	29	30	1	2	3	4	5	Mon 3h6m7p	MONTH 3 Rén-Chén	29	1*	2	3	4	5	6	Gǔ yǔ		9	10	11	12	13	14	15	
	24	◐	26	27	28	29	30	16:33	17	2477957		6	7	8	9	10	11	12			7	8	9	10	11	12	13			16	17	18	19	20	21	22	
MAY 2072	1	○	3	4	5	6	7	11:32	18	2477964		13	14	15	16	17	18	19			14	15	16	17	18	19	20	Lì xià		23	24	25	26	27	28	29[g]	
	8	9	◑	11	12	13	14	3:16	19	2477971		20	21	22	23	24	25	26			21	22	23	24	25	26	27		PASHONS 1788	30	1	2	3	4	5	6	GENBOT 2064
	15	16	17	●	19	20	21	0:17	20	2477978	SIVAN 5832	27	28	29	1	2	3	4	Tue 15h50m8p	MONTH 4 Rén-Chén	28	29	30	1	2	3	4	Xiǎo mǎn		7	8	9	10	11	12	13	
	22	23	◐	25	26	27	28	21:52	21	2477985		5	6[h]	7	8	9	10	11			5	6	7	8	9	10	11			14	15	16	17	18	19	20	
JUNE 2072	29	30	○	1	2	3	4	22:17	22	2477992		12	13	14	15	16	17	18			12	13	14	15	16	17	18			21	22	23	24	25	26	27	
	5	6	7	◑	9	10	11	21:19	23	2477999		19	20	21	22	23	24	25			19	20	21	22	23	24	25	Máng zhòng	PAŌNE 1788	28	29	30	1	2	3	4	SANĒ 2064
	12	13	14	15	●	17	18	9:56	24	2478006	TAMMUZ 5832	26	27	28	29	30	1	2	Thu 4h34m9p	MONTH 5 Rén-Chén	26	27	28	29	1	2*	3	Xià zhì		5	6	7	8	9	10	11	
	19	20[c]	21	22	◐	24	25	2:55	25	2478013		3	4	5	6	7	8	9			4	5[d]	6	7	8	9	10			12	13	14	15	16	17	18	
JULY 2072	26	27	28	29	○	1	2	10:20	26	2478020		10	11	12	13	14	15	16			11	12	13	14	15	16	17			19	20	21	22	23	24	25	
	3	4	5	6	7	◑	9	13:52	27	2478027		17	18	19	20	21	22	23			18	19	20	21	22	23	24	Xiǎo shǔ	EPĒP 1788	26	27	28	29	30	1	2	HAMLĒ 2064
	10	11	12	13	14	●	16	17:55	28	2478034	AV 5832	24	25	26	27	28	29	1	Fri 17h18m10p	MONTH 6 Rén-Chén	25	26	27	28	29	30	1			3	4	5	6	7	8	9	
	17	18	19	20	21	◐	23	9:00	29	2478041		2	3	4	5	6	7	8			2	3	4	5	6	7	8	Dà shǔ		10	11	12	13	14	15	16	
	24	25	26	27	28	29	○	0:15	30	2478048		9[i]	10	11	12	13	14	15			9	10	11	12	13	14	15			17	18	19	20	21	22	23	
AUGUST 2072	31	1	2	3	4	5	6		31	2478055		16	17	18	19	20	21	22			16	17	18	19	20	21	22	Lì qiū		24	25	26	27	28	29	30	
	◑	8	9	10	11	12	13	4:14	32	2478062		23	24	25	26	27	28	29			23	24	25	26	27	28	29		MESORĒ 1788	1	2	3	4	5	6	7	NAHASĒ 2064
	●	15	16	17	18	19	◐	1:20 17:19	33	2478069	ELUL 5832	30	1	2	3	4	5	6	Sun 6h2m11p	MONTH 7 Rén-Chén	1	2	3*	4	5	6	7[e]			8	9	10	11	12	13[h]	14	
	21	22	23	24	25	26	27		34	2478076		7	8	9	10	11	12	13			8	9	10	11	12	13	14	Chǔ shǔ		15	16	17	18	19	20	21	
SEPTEMBER 2072	○	29	30	31	1	2	3	15:58	35	2478083		14	15	16	17	18	19	20			15[f]	16	17	18	19	20	21			22	23	24	25	26	27	28	
	4	◑	6	7	8	9	10	16:18	36	2478090		21	22	23	24	25	26	27			22	23	24	25	26	27	28	Bái lù	EPAG. 1788	29	30	1	2	3	4	5	PĀG. 2064
	11	●	13	14	15	16	17	9:05	37	2478097	TISHRI 5833	28	29	1[a]	2[a]	3	4	5	Mon 18h46m12p	MONTH 8 Rén-Chén	29	1	2	3	4	5	6		THOOUT 1789	1[a]	2	3	4	5	6	7	MASKARAM 2065
	18	◐	20	21	22[d]	23	24	4:57	38	2478104		6	7	8	9	10[b]	11	12			7	8	9	10	11	12	13	Qiū fēn		8	9	10	11	12	13	14	
OCTOBER 2072	25	26	○	28	29	30	1	8:42	39	2478111		13	14	15[c]	16	17	18	19			14	15[g]	16	17	18	19	20			15	16	17[b]	18	19	20	21	
	2	3	4	◑	6	7	8	2:27	40	2478118		20	21	22	23	24	25	26			21	22	23	24	25	26	27	Hán lù		22	23	24	25	26	27	28	
	9	10	●	12	13	14	15	17:54	41	2478125	HESHVAN 5833	27	28	29	30	1	2	3	Wed 7h30m13p	MONTH 9 Rén-Chén	28	29	30	1	2	3	4*		PAOPE 1789	29	30	1	2	3	4	5	TEQEMT 2065
	16	17	◐	19	20	21	22	20:36	42	2478132		4	5	6	7	8	9	10			5	6	7	8	9[h]	10	11	Shuāng jiàng		6	7	8	9	10	11	12	
	23	24	25	26	○	28	29	1:20	43	2478139		11	12	13	14	15	16	17			12	13	14	15	16	17	18			13	14	15	16	17	18	19	
NOVEMBER 2072	30	31	1	2	◑	4	5	11:15	44	2478146		18	19	20	21	22	23	24			19	20	21	22	23	24	25			20	21	22	23	24	25	26	
	6	7	8	9	●	11	12	4:20	45	2478153	KISLEV 5833	25	26	27	28	29	1	2	Thu 20h14m14p	MONTH 10 Rén-Chén	26	27	28	29	1	2	3	Lì dōng	ATHŌR 1789	27	28	29	30	1	2	3	HEDĀR 2065
	13	14	15	16	◐	18	19	16:02	46	2478160		3	4	5	6	7	8	9			4	5	6	7	8	9	10			4	5	6	7	8	9	10	
	20	21	22	23	24	○	26	16:58	47	2478167		10	11	12	13	14	15	16			11	12	13	14	15	16	17	Xiǎo xuě		11	12	13	14	15	16	17	
DECEMBER 2072	27	28	29	30	1	◑	3	19:21	48	2478174		17	18	19	20	21	22	23			18	19	20	21	22	23	24			18	19	20	21	22	23	24	
	4	5	6	7	8	●	10	16:58	49	2478181	TEVETH 5833	24	25[d,e]	26[e]	27[e]	28[e]	29[e]	30[e]	Sat 8h58m15p	MONTH 11 Rén-Chén	25	26	27	28	29	30	1	Dà xuě	KOIAK 1789	25	26	27	28	29	30	1	TĀKHŚĀŚ 2065
	11	12	13	14	15	16	◐	13:49	50	2478188		1[e]	2[e]	3	4	5	6	7			2	3	4	5*	6	7	8			2	3	4	5	6	7	8	
	18	19	20	21[e]	22	23	24		51	2478195		8	9	10	11	12	13	14			9	10	11	12[i]	13	14	15	Dōng zhì		9	10	11	12	13	14	15	
	○	26	27	28	29	30	31	7:14	52	2478202		15	16	17	18	19	20	21			16	17	18	19	20	21	22			16	17	18	19	20	21	22	

‡Leap year
[a]New Year
[b]Spring (18:19)
[c]Summer (11:12)
[d]Autumn (3:26)
[e]Winter (0:54)
● New moon
◐ First quarter moon
○ Full moon
◑ Last quarter moon

‡Leap year
[a]New Year
[b]Yom Kippur
[c]Sukkot
[d]Winter starts
[e]Ḥanukkah
[f]Purim
[g]Passover
[h]Shavuot
[i]Fast of Av

‡Leap year
[a]New Year (4770, Dragon)
[b]Lantern Festival
[c]Qīngmíng
[d]Dragon Festival
[e]Qīqiǎo
[f]Hungry Ghosts
[g]Mid-Autumn Festival
[h]Double-Ninth Festival
[i]Dōngzhì
*Start of 60-name cycle

[a]New Year
[b]Building of the Cross
[c]Christmas
[d]Jesus's Circumcision
[e]Epiphany
[f]Easter
[g]Mary's Announcement
[h]Jesus's Transfiguration

PERSIAN (ASTRONOMICAL) 1450/1451

Month	Sun	Mon	Tue	Wed	Thu	Fri	Sat
DEY 1450	6	7	8	9	10	11	12
	13	14	15	16	17	18	19
	20	21	22	23	24	25	26
	27	28	29	30	*1*	2	3
BAHMAN 1450	4	5	6	7	8	9	10
	11	12	13	14	15	16	17
	18	19	20	21	22	23	24
	25	26	27	28	29	30	*1*
ESFAND 1450	2	3	4	5	6	7	8
	9	10	11	12	13	14	15
	16	17	18	19	20	21	22
	23	24	25	26	27	28	29
FARVARDĪN 1451	*1*[a]	2	3	4	5	6	7
	8	9	10	11	12	13[b]	14
	15	16	17	18	19	20	21
	22	23	24	25	26	27	28
	29	30	31	*1*	2	3	4
ORDĪBEHEŠT 1451	5	6	7	8	9	10	11
	12	13	14	15	16	17	18
	19	20	21	22	23	24	25
	26	27	28	29	30	31	*1*
XORDĀD 1451	2	3	4	5	6	7	8
	9	10	11	12	13	14	15
	16	17	18	19	20	21	22
	23	24	25	26	27	28	29
	30	31	*1*	2	3	4	5
TĪR 1451	6	7	8	9	10	11	12
	13	14	15	16	17	18	19
	20	21	22	23	24	25	26
	27	28	29	30	31	*1*	2
MORDĀD 1451	3	4	5	6	7	8	9
	10	11	12	13	14	15	16
	17	18	19	20	21	22	23
	24	25	26	27	28	29	30
	31	*1*	2	3	4	5	6
SHAHRĪVAR 1451	7	8	9	10	11	12	13
	14	15	16	17	18	19	20
	21	22	23	24	25	26	27
	28	29	30	31	*1*	2	3
MEHR 1451	4	5	6	7	8	9	10
	11	12	13	14	15	16	17
	18	19	20	21	22	23	24
	25	26	27	28	29	30	*1*
ĀBĀN 1451	2	3	4	5	6	7	8
	9	10	11	12	13	14	15
	16	17	18	19	20	21	22
	23	24	25	26	27	28	29
	30	*1*	2	3	4	5	6
ĀZAR 1451	7	8	9	10	11	12	13
	14	15	16	17	18	19	20
	21	22	23	24	25	26	27
	28	29	30	*1*	2	3	4
DEY 1451	5	6	7	8	9	10	11

[a]New Year
[b]Sizdeh Bedar

HINDU LUNAR 2128/2129‡

Month	Sun	Mon	Tue	Wed	Thu	Fri	Sat
PAUSHA 2128	6	7	8	9	10	11	12
	13	14	15	16	17	18	19
	20	21	22	**23**	25	26	27
	28	*28*	29	30	1	2	3
MĀGHA 2128	4	5	6	7	8	9	10
	11	12	13	14	15	**16**	18
	19	20	21	22	23	24	25
	26	27	28	29[h]	30	1	*1*
PHĀLGUNA 2128	2	3	4	5	6	7	8
	9	**10**	12	13	14	15[i]	16
	17	18	19	20	21	22	23
	24	25	26	27	28	29	30
CHAITRA 2129	1[a]	2	3	4	5	6	7
	8	9[b]	10	11	12	13	14
	15	17	18	19	20	21	22
	23	24	*24*	25	26	27	28
	29	30	1	2	3	4	5
VAIŚĀKHA 2129	6	7	**8**	10	11	12	13
	14	15	16	17	18	19	20
	21	22	23	24	25	26	27
	28	29	30	1	2	3	4
JYAISHTHA 2129	5	6	7	8	9	10	11
	12	14	15	16	17	18	19
	19	20	21	22	23	24	25
	26	27	28	29	30	1	2
LEAP ĀSHĀDHA 2129	3	**4**	6	7	8	9	10
	11	12	13	14	15	16	17
	18	19	20	21	22	23	24
	25	26	27	28	29	30	1
ĀSHĀDHA 2129	2	3	4	5	6	**7**	9
	10	11	12	13	14	15	16
	16	17	18	19	20	21	22
	23	24	25	26	27	28	29
	30	2	3	4	5	6	7
ŚRĀVAṆA 2129	8	9	10	11	12	13	14
	15	16	17	18	19	20	21
	22	23[c]	24	25	26	27	28
	29	30	1	2	**3**[d]	5	6
BHĀDRAPADA 2129	7	8	9	10	11	12	*12*
	13	14	15	16	17	18	19
	20	21	22	23	24	25	26
	27	29	30	1	2	3	4
ĀŚVINA 2129	5	6	7	8[e]	9[e]	10[e]	11
	12	13	14	15	16	*16*	17
	18	**19**	21	22	23	24	25
	26	27	28	29	30	1[f]	**2**
KĀRTTIKA 2129	4	5	*5*	6	7	8	9
	10	11	12	13	14	15	16
	17	18	19	20	21	22	23
	24	26	27	28	29	30	1
MĀRGAŚĪRA 2129	2	3	4	5	6	7	8
	9	*9*	10	11[g]	12	13	14
	15	16	17	18	**19**	21	22

‡Leap year
[a]New Year (Nandana)
[b]Birthday of Rāma
[c]Birthday of Krishna
[d]Ganēśa Chaturthī
[e]Dashara
[f]Diwali
[g]Birthday of Vishnu
[h]Night of Śiva
[i]Holi

HINDU SOLAR 1993‡/1994

Month	Sun	Mon	Tue	Wed	Thu	Fri	Sat
PAUSHA 1993	11	12	13	14	15	16	17
	18	19	20	21	22	23	24
	25	26	27	28	29	1[b]	2
MĀGHA 1993	3	4	5	6	7	8	9
	10	11	12	13	14	15	16
	17	18	19	20	21	22	23
	24	25	26	27	28	29	1
PHĀLGUNA 1993	2	3	4	5	6	7	8
	9	10	11	12	13	14	15
	16	17	18	19	20	21	22
	23	24	25	26	27	28	29
	30	1	2	3	4	5	6
CHAITRA 1993	7	8	9	10	11	12	13
	14	15	16	17	18	19	20
	21	22	23	24	25	26	27
	28	29	30	31	1[a]	2	3
VAIŚĀKHA 1994	4	5	6	7	8	9	10
	11	12	13	14	15	16	17
	18	19	20	21	22	23	24
	25	26	27	28	29	30	31
	1	2	3	4	5	6	7
JYAISHTHA 1994	8	9	10	11	12	13	14
	15	16	17	18	19	20	21
	22	23	24	25	26	27	28
	29	30	31	1	2	3	4
ĀSHĀDHA 1994	5	6	7	8	9	10	11
	12	13	14	15	16	17	18
	19	20	21	22	23	24	25
	26	27	28	29	30	31	32
	1	2	3	4	5	6	7
ŚRĀVAṆA 1994	8	9	10	11	12	13	14
	15	16	17	18	19	20	21
	22	23	24	25	26	27	28
	29	30	31	1	2	3	4
BHĀDRAPADA 1994	5	6	7	8	9	10	11
	12	13	14	15	16	17	18
	19	20	21	22	23	24	25
	26	27	28	29	30	31	1
ĀŚVINA 1994	2	3	4	5	6	7	8
	9	10	11	12	13	14	15
	16	17	18	19	20	21	22
	23	24	25	26	27	28	29
	30	31	1	2	3	4	5
KĀRTTIKA 1994	6	7	8	9	10	11	12
	13	14	15	16	17	18	19
	20	21	22	23	24	25	26
	27	28	29	1	2	3	4
MĀRGAŚĪRA 1994	5	6	7	8	9	10	11
	12	13	14	15	16	17	18
	19	20	21	22	23	24	25
	26	27	28	29	30	1	2
PAUSHA 1994	3	4	5	6	7	8	9
	10	11	12	13	14	15	16

‡Leap year
[a]New Year (Parābhava)
[b]Pongal

ISLAMIC (ASTRONOMICAL) 1494/1495

Month	Sun	Mon	Tue	Wed	Thu	Fri	Sat
DHU AL-ḤIJJA 1494	5	6	7	8	9	10[g]	11
	12	13	14	15	16	17	18
	19	20	21	22	23	24	25
	26	27	28	29	30	*1*[a]	2
MUHARRAM 1495	3	4	5	6	7	8	9
	10[b]	11	12	13	14	15	16
	17	18	19	20	21	22	23
	24	25	26	27	28	29	1
ṢAFAR 1495	2	3	4	5	6	7	8
	9	10	11	12	13	14	15
	16	17	18	19	20	21	22
	23	24	25	26	27	28	29
	30	*1*	2	3	4	5	6
RABĪʿ I 1495	7	8	9	10	11	12[c]	13
	14	15	16	17	18	19	20
	21	22	23	24	25	26	27
	28	29	30	*1*	2	3	4
RABĪʿ II 1495	5	6	7	8	9	10	11
	12	13	14	15	16	17	18
	19	20	21	22	23	24	25
	26	27	28	29	*1*	2	3
JUMĀDĀ I 1495	4	5	6	7	8	9	10
	11	12	13	14	15	16	17
	18	19	20	21	22	23	24
	25	26	27	28	29	30	*1*
JUMĀDĀ II 1495	2	3	4	5	6	7	8
	9	10	11	12	13	14	15
	16	17	18	19	20	21	22
	23	24	25	26	27	28	29
	1	2	3	4	5	6	7
RAJAB 1495	8	9	10	11	12	13	14
	15	16	17	18	19	20	21
	22	23	24	25	26	27[d]	28
	29	30	*1*	2	3	4	5
SHAʿBĀN 1495	6	7	8	9	10	11	12
	13	14	15	16	17	18	19
	20	21	22	23	24	25	26
	27	28	29	*1*[e]	2	3	4
RAMAḌĀN 1495	5	6	7	8	9	10	11
	12	13	14	15	16	17	18
	19	20	21	22	23	24	25
	26	27	28	29	1[f]	2	3
SHAWWĀL 1495	4	5	6	7	8	9	10
	11	12	13	14	15	16	17
	18	19	20	21	22	23	24
	25	26	27	28	29	1	2
DHU AL-QAʿDA 1495	3	4	5	6	7	8	9
	10	11	12	13	14	15	16
	17	18	19	20	21	22	23
	24	25	26	27	28	29	30
DHU AL-ḤIJJA 1495	1	2	3	4	5	6	7
	8	9	10[g]	11	12	13	14
	15	16	17	18	19	20	21

[a]New Year
[b]ʿAshūrā'
[c]Prophet's Birthday
[d]Ascent of the Prophet
[e]Start of Ramaḍān
[f]ʿId al-Fiṭr
[g]ʿId al-ʾAḍḥā

GREGORIAN 2072‡

Julian† (Sun)	Sun	Mon	Tue	Wed	Thu	Fri	Sat	Month
Dec 14	27	28	29	30	31	1	2	JANUARY 2072
	3	4	5	6	7[a]	8	9	
Dec 28	10	11	12	13	14[b]	15	16	
	17	18	19	20	21	22	23	
Jan 11	24	25	26	27	28	29	30	
	31	1	2	3	4	5	6	FEBRUARY 2072
Jan 25	7	8	9	10	11	12	13	
	14	15	16	17	18	19	20	
Feb 8	21	22	23	24[c]	25	26	27	
	28[d]	29	1	2	3	4	5	MARCH 2072
Feb 22	6	7	8	9	10	11	12	
	13	14	15	16	17	18	19	
Mar 7	20	21	22	23	24	25	26	
	27	28	29	30	31	1	2	APRIL 2072
Mar 21	3	4	5	6	7	8	9	
	10[e]	11	12	13	14	15	16	
Apr 4	17	18	19	20	21	22	23	
	24	25	26	27	28	29	30	
Apr 18	1	2	3	4	5	6	7	MAY 2072
	8	9	10	11	12	13	14	
May 2	15	16	17	18	19	20	21	
	22	23	24	25	26	27	28	
May 16	29	30	31	1	2	3	4	JUNE 2072
	5	6	7	8	9	10	11	
May 30	12	13	14	15	16	17	18	
	19	20	21	22	23	24	25	
Jun 13	26	27	28	29	30	1	2	JULY 2072
	3	4	5	6	7	8	9	
Jun 27	10	11	12	13	14	15	16	
	17	18	19	20	21	22	23	
Jul 11	24	25	26	27	28	29	30	
	31	1	2	3	4	5	6	AUGUST 2072
Jul 25	7	8	9	10	11	12	13	
	14	15	16	17	18	19	20	
Aug 8	21	22	23	24	25	26	27	
	28	29	30	31	1	2	3	SEPTEMBER 2072
Aug 22	4	5	6	7	8	9	10	
	11	12	13	14	15	16	17	
Sep 5	18	19	20	21	22	23	24	
	25	26	27	28	29	30	1	OCTOBER 2072
Sep 19	2	3	4	5	6	7	8	
	9	10	11	12	13	14	15	
Oct 3	16	17	18	19	20	21	22	
	23	24	25	26	27	28	29	
Oct 17	30	31	1	2	3	4	5	NOVEMBER 2072
	6	7	8	9	10	11	12	
Oct 31	13	14	15	16	17	18	19	
	20	21	22	23	24	25	26	
Nov 14	27[g]	28	29	30	1	2	3	DECEMBER 2072
	4	5	6	7	8	9	10	
Nov 28	11	12	13	14	15	16	17	
	18	19	20	21	22	23	24	
Dec 12	25[h]	26	27	28	29	30	31	

‡Leap year
[a]Orthodox Christmas
[b]Julian New Year
[c]Ash Wednesday
[d]Feast of Orthodoxy
[e]Easter (also Orthodox)
[g]Advent
[h]Christmas

2073

GREGORIAN 2073

Month	Sun	Mon	Tue	Wed	Thu	Fri	Sat	Lunar Phases	ISO WEEK (Mon)	JULIAN DAY (Sun noon)
JANUARY 2073	◑[a]	2	3	4	5	6	7	3:26	1	2478209
	●	9	10	11	12	13	14	8:10	2	2478216
	15	◐	17	18	19	20	21	11:32	3	2478223
	22	○	24	25	26	27	28	20:04	4	2478230
	29	◑	31	1	2	3	4	12:17	5	2478237
FEBRUARY 2073	5	6	●	8	9	10	11	1:39	6	2478244
	12	13	14	◐	16	17	18	6:56	7	2478251
	19	20	21	○	23	24	25	7:25	8	2478258
	26	27	◑	1	2	3	4	22:38	9	2478265
MARCH 2073	5	6	7	●	9	10	11	20:14	10	2478272
	12	13	14	15	◐	17	18	22:42	11	2478279
	19	20[b]	21	22	○	24	25	17:16	12	2478286
	26	27	28	29	◑	31	1	11:02	13	2478293
APRIL 2073	2	3	4	5	6	●	8	14:13	14	2478300
	9	10	11	12	13	14	◐	10:35	15	2478307
	16	17	18	19	20	21	○	1:53	16	2478314
	23	24	25	26	27	28	◑	1:36	17	2478321
	30	1	2	3	4	5	6		18	2478328
MAY 2073	●	8	9	10	11	12	13	6:14	19	2478335
	◐	15	16	17	18	19	20	18:58	20	2478342
	○	22	23	24	25	26	27	10:01	21	2478349
	◑	29	30	31	1	2	3	17:56	22	2478356
JUNE 2073	4	●	6	7	8	9	10	19:50	23	2478363
	11	12	◐	14	15	16	17	0:46	24	2478370
	18	○	20[c]	21	22	23	24	18:43	25	2478377
	25	26	◑	28	29	30	1	11:11	26	2478384
JULY 2073	2	3	4	●	6	7	8	7:15	27	2478391
	9	10	11	◐	13	14	15	5:14	28	2478398
	16	17	18	○	20	21	22	5:03	29	2478405
	23	24	25	26	◑	28	29	4:27	30	2478412
	30	31	1	2	●	4	5	17:03	31	2478419
AUGUST 2073	6	7	8	9	◐	11	12	9:53	32	2478426
	13	14	15	16	○	18	19	17:44	33	2478433
	20	21	22	23	24	◑	26	21:04	34	2478440
	27	28	29	30	31	1	●	1:51	35	2478447
SEPTEMBER 2073	3	4	5	6	7	◐	9	16:18	36	2478454
	10	11	12	13	14	15	○	8:51	37	2478461
	17	18	19	20	21	22[d]	23		38	2478468
	◑	25	26	27	28	29	30	12:30	39	2478475
OCTOBER 2073	●	2	3	4	5	6	7	10:20	40	2478482
	◐	9	10	11	12	13	14	1:55	41	2478489
	15	○	17	18	19	20	21	1:53	42	2478496
	22	23	◑	25	26	27	28	2:21	43	2478503
	29	●	31	1	2	3	4	19:12	44	2478510
NOVEMBER 2073	5	◐	7	8	9	10	11	15:41	45	2478517
	12	13	○	15	16	17	18	19:53	46	2478524
	19	20	21	◑	23	24	25	14:14	47	2478531
	26	27	28	●	30	1	2	5:11	48	2478538
DECEMBER 2073	3	4	5	◐	7	8	9	9:31	49	2478545
	10	11	12	13	○	15	16	13:48	50	2478552
	17	18	19	20	21[e]	◑	23	0:05	51	2478559
	24	25	26	27	●	29	30	16:54	52	2478566
	31	1	2	3	4	◐	6	6:17	1	2478573

HEBREW 5833‡/5834

ISO WEEK	Month	Sun	Mon	Tue	Wed	Thu	Fri	Sat	Molad
1	TEVETH 5833	22	23	24	25	26	27	28	
2	SHEVAT 5833	29	1	2	3	4	5	6	Sun 21h42m16p
3		7	8	9	10	11	12	13	
4		14	15	16	17	18	19	20	
5		21	22	23	24	25	26	27	Tue 10h26m17p
6	ADAR I 5833	28	29	30	1	2	3	4	
7		5	6	7	8	9	10	11	
8		12	13	14	15	16	17	18	
9		19	20	21	22	23	24	25	Wed 23h11m0p
10	ADAR II 5833	26	27	28	29	30	1	2	
11		3	4	5	6	7	8	9	
12		10	11	12	13	14[f]	15	16	
13		17	18	19	20	21	22	23	Fri 11h55m1p
14	NISAN 5833	24	25	26	27	28	29	1	
15		2	3	4	5	6	7	8	
16		9	10	11	12	13	14	15[g]	
17		16	17	18	19	20	21	22	
18		23	24	25	26	27	28	29	Sun 0h39m2p
19	IYAR 5833	30	1	2	3	4	5	6	
20		7	8	9	10	11	12	13	
21		14	15	16	17	18	19	20	
22		21	22	23	24	25	26	27	Mon 13h23m3p
23	SIVAN 5833	28	29	1	2	3	4	5	
24		6[h]	7	8	9	10	11	12	
25		13	14	15	16	17	18	19	
26		20	21	22	23	24	25	26	
27	TAMMUZ 5833	27	28	29	30	1	2	3	Wed 2h7m4p
28		4	5	6	7	8	9	10	
29		11	12	13	14	15	16	17	
30		18	19	20	21	22	23	24	
31	AV 5833	25	26	27	28	29	1	2	Thu 14h51m5p
32		3	4	5	6	7	8	9	
33		10[i]	11	12	13	14	15	16	
34		17	18	19	20	21	22	23	
35		24	25	26	27	28	29	30	Sat 3h35m6p
36	ELUL 5833	1	2	3	4	5	6	7	
37		8	9	10	11	12	13	14	
38		15	16	17	18	19	20	21	
39		22	23	24	25	26	27	28	
40	TISHRI 5834	29	1[a]	2[a]	3	4	5	6	Sun 16h19m7p
41		7	8	9	10[b]	11	12	13	
42		14	15[c]	16	17	18	19	20	
43		21	22	23	24	25	26	27	
44	HESHVAN 5834	28	29	30	1	2	3	4	Tue 5h3m8p
45		5	6	7	8	9	10	11	
46		12	13	14	15	16	17	18	
47		19	20	21	22	23	24	25	
48	KISLEV 5834	26	27	28	29	30	1	2	Wed 17h47m9p
49		3	4	5[d]	6	7	8	9	
50		10	11	12	13	14	15	16	
51		17	18	19	20	21	22	23	
52		24	25[e]	26[e]	27[e]	28[e]	29[e]	30[e]	Fri 6h31m10p
1		1[e]	2[e]	3	4	5	6	7	

CHINESE Rén-Chén/Guǐ-Sì

ISO WEEK	Month	Sun	Mon	Tue	Wed	Thu	Fri	Sat	Solar Term
1		23	24	25	26	27	28	29	Xiǎo hán
2	MONTH 12 Rén-Chén	1	2	3	4	5	6	7	
3		8	9	10	11	12	13	14	Dà hán
4		15	16	17	18	19	20	21	
5		22	23	24	25	26	27	28	Lì chūn
6	MONTH 1 Guǐ-Sì	29	30	1[a]	2	3	4	5	
7		6*	7	8	9	10	11	12	Yǔ shuǐ
8		13	14	15[b]	16	17	18	19	
9		20	21	22	23	24	25	26	
10	MONTH 2 Guǐ-Sì	27	28	29	30	1	2	3	Jīng zhé
11		4	5	6	7	8	9	10	
12		11	12	13	14	15	16	17	Chūn fēn
13		18	19	20	21	22	23	24	
14	MONTH 3 Guǐ-Sì	25	26	27[c]	28	29	1	2	Qīng míng
15		3	4	5	6	7*	8	9	
16		10	11	12	13	14	15	16	Gǔ yǔ
17		17	18	19	20	21	22	23	
18		24	25	26	27	28	29	30	Lì xià
19	MONTH 4 Guǐ-Sì	1	2	3	4	5	6	7	
20		8	9	10	11	12	13	14	Xiǎo mǎn
21		15	16	17	18	19	20	21	
22		22	23	24	25	26	27	28	
23	MONTH 5 Guǐ-Sì	29	30	1	2	3	4	5[d]	Máng zhòng
24		6	7*	8	9	10	11	12	
25		13	14	15	16	17	18	19	Xià zhì
26		20	21	22	23	24	25	26	
27	MONTH 6 Guǐ-Sì	27	28	29	1	2	3	4	Xiǎo shǔ
28		5	6	7	8	9	10	11	
29		12	13	14	15	16	17	18	Dà shǔ
30		19	20	21	22	23	24	25	
31	MONTH 7 Guǐ-Sì	26	27	28	29	30	1	2	
32		3	4	5	6	7[e]	8*	9	Lì qiū
33		10	11	12	13	14	15[f]	16	
34		17	18	19	20	21	22	23	Chǔ shǔ
35	MONTH 8 Guǐ-Sì	24	25	26	27	28	29	1	
36		2	3	4	5	6	7	8	Bái lù
37		9	10	11	12	13	14	15[g]	
38		16	17	18	19	20	21	22	Qiū fēn
39		23	24	25	26	27	28	29	
40	MONTH 9 Guǐ-Sì	1	2	3	4	5	6	7	Hán lù
41		8	9[h]	10*	11	12	13	14	
42		15	16	17	18	19	20	21	
43		22	23	24	25	26	27	28	Shuāng jiàng
44	MONTH 10 Guǐ-Sì	29	30	1	2	3	4	5	
45		6	7	8	9	10	11	12	Lì dōng
46		13	14	15	16	17	18	19	
47		20	21	22	23	24	25	26	Xiǎo xuě
48	MONTH 11* Guǐ-Sì	27	28	29	1	2	3	4	
49		5	6	7	8	9	10	11*	Dà xuě
50		12	13	14	15	16	17	18	
51		19	20	21	22	23[i]	24	25	Dōng zhì
52	MONTH 12 Guǐ-Sì	26	27	28	29	30	1	2	
1		3	4	5	6	7	8	9	Xiǎo hán

COPTIC 1789/1790 — ETHIOPIC 2065/2066

ISO WEEK	Coptic Month	Sun	Mon	Tue	Wed	Thu	Fri	Sat	Ethiopic Month
1	KOIAK 1789	23	24	25	26	27	28	29[c]	TĀKHŚĀŚ 2065
2	TŌBE 1789	30	1	2	3	4	5	6[d]	TER 2065
3		7	8	9	10	11[e]	12	13	
4		14	15	16	17	18	19	20	
5		21	22	23	24	25	26	27	
6	MESHIR 1789	28	29	30	1	2	3	4	YAKĀTIT 2065
7		5	6	7	8	9	10	11	
8		12	13	14	15	16	17	18	
9		19	20	21	22	23	24	25	
10	PAREMOTEP 1789	26	27	28	29	30	1	2	MAGĀBIT 2065
11		3	4	5	6	7	8	9	
12		10	11	12	13	14	15	16	
13		17	18	19	20	21	22	23	
14		24	25	26	27	28	29	30	
15	PARMOUTE 1789	1	2	3	4	5	6	7	MIYĀZYĀ 2065
16		8	9	10	11	12	13	14	
17		15	16	17	18	19	20	21	
18		22[f]	23	24	25	26	27	28	
19	PASHONS 1789	29[g]	30	1	2	3	4	5	GENBOT 2065
20		6	7	8	9	10	11	12	
21		13	14	15	16	17	18	19	
22		20	21	22	23	24	25	26	
23	PAÔNE 1789	27	28	29	30	1	2	3	SANÉ 2065
24		4	5	6	7	8	9	10	
25		11	12	13	14	15	16	17	
26		18	19	20	21	22	23	24	
27	EPÊP 1789	25	26	27	28	29	30	1	ḤAMLĒ 2065
28		2	3	4	5	6	7	8	
29		9	10	11	12	13	14	15	
30		16	17	18	19	20	21	22	
31		23	24	25	26	27	28	29	
32	MESORÊ 1789	30	1	2	3	4	5	6	NAḤASĒ 2065
33		7	8	9	10	11	12	13[h]	
34		14	15	16	17	18	19	20	
35		21	22	23	24	25	26	27	
36	EPAG. 1789	28	29	30	1	2	3	4	PĀG. 2065
37	THOOUT 1790	5	1[a]	2	3	4	5	6	MASKARAM 2066
38		7	8	9	10	11	12	13	
39		14	15	16	17[b]	18	19	20	
40		21	22	23	24	25	26	27	
41	PAOPE 1790	28	29	30	1	2	3	4	TEQEMT 2066
42		5	6	7	8	9	10	11	
43		12	13	14	15	16	17	18	
44		19	20	21	22	23	24	25	
45	ATHŌR 1790	26	27	28	29	30	1	2	ḪEDĀR 2066
46		3	4	5	6	7	8	9	
47		10	11	12	13	14	15	16	
48		17	18	19	20	21	22	23	
49		24	25	26	27	28	29	30	
50	KOIAK 1790	1	2	3	4	5	6	7	TĀKHŚĀŚ 2066
51		8	9	10	11	12	13	14	
52		15	16	17	18	19	20	21	
1		22	23	24	25	26	27	28	

[a]New Year
[b]Spring (0:12)
[c]Summer (17:05)
[d]Autumn (9:14)
[e]Winter (6:49)
● New moon
◐ First quarter moon
○ Full moon
◑ Last quarter moon

‡Leap year
[a]New Year
[b]Yom Kippur
[c]Sukkot
[d]Winter starts
[e]Ḥanukkah
[f]Purim
[g]Passover
[h]Shavuot
[i]Fast of Av

[a]New Year (4771, Snake)
[b]Lantern Festival
[c]Qīngmíng
[d]Dragon Festival
[e]Qīqiǎo
[f]Hungry Ghosts
[g]Mid-Autumn Festival
[h]Double-Ninth Festival
[i]Dōngzhì
*Start of 60-name cycle

[a]New Year
[b]Building of the Cross
[c]Christmas
[d]Jesus's Circumcision
[e]Epiphany
[f]Easter
[g]Mary's Announcement
[h]Jesus's Transfiguration

PERSIAN (ASTRONOMICAL) 1451/1452

Month	Sun	Mon	Tue	Wed	Thu	Fri	Sat
DEY 1451	12	13	14	15	16	17	18
	19	20	21	22	23	24	25
	26	27	28	29	30	1	2
BAHMAN 1451	3	4	5	6	7	8	9
	10	11	12	13	14	15	16
	17	18	19	20	21	22	23
	24	25	26	27	28	29	30
ESFAND 1451	1	2	3	4	5	6	7
	8	9	10	11	12	13	14
	15	16	17	18	19	20	21
	22	23	24	25	26	27	28
FARVARDĪN 1452	29	1[a]	2	3	4	5	6
	7	8	9	10	11	12	13[b]
	14	15	16	17	18	19	20
	21	22	23	24	25	26	27
ORDĪBEHEŠT 1452	28	29	30	31	1	2	3
	4	5	6	7	8	9	10
	11	12	13	14	15	16	17
	18	19	20	21	22	23	24
	25	26	27	28	29	30	31
XORDĀD 1452	1	2	3	4	5	6	7
	8	9	10	11	12	13	14
	15	16	17	18	19	20	21
	22	23	24	25	26	27	28
TĪR 1452	29	30	31	1	2	3	4
	5	6	7	8	9	10	11
	12	13	14	15	16	17	18
	19	20	21	22	23	24	25
MORDĀD 1452	26	27	28	29	30	31	1
	2	3	4	5	6	7	8
	9	10	11	12	13	14	15
	16	17	18	19	20	21	22
	23	24	25	26	27	28	29
SHAHRĪVAR 1452	30	31	1	2	3	4	5
	6	7	8	9	10	11	12
	13	14	15	16	17	18	19
	20	21	22	23	24	25	26
MEHR 1452	27	28	29	30	31	1	2
	3	4	5	6	7	8	9
	10	11	12	13	14	15	16
	17	18	19	20	21	22	23
	24	25	26	27	28	29	30
ĀBĀN 1452	1	2	3	4	5	6	7
	8	9	10	11	12	13	14
	15	16	17	18	19	20	21
	22	23	24	25	26	27	28
ĀZAR 1452	29	30	1	2	3	4	5
	6	7	8	9	10	11	12
	13	14	15	16	17	18	19
	20	21	22	23	24	25	26
DEY 1452	27	28	29	30	1	2	3
	4	5	6	7	8	9	10
	11	12	13	14	15	16	17

[a]New Year
[b]Sizdeh Bedar

HINDU LUNAR 2129‡/2130

Month	Sun	Mon	Tue	Wed	Thu	Fri	Sat
MĀRGAŚĪRA 2129	23	24	25	26	27	28	29
PAUSHA 2129	30	1	2	3	4	5	6
	7	8	9	10	11	12	13
	14	15	16	17	18	19	20
	21	22	23	24	26	27	28
MĀGHA 2129	29	30	1	1	2	3	4
	5	6	7	8	9	10	11
	12	13	14	15	16	17	19
	20	21	22	23	24	25	26
PHĀLGUNA 2129	27	28[h]	29	30	1	2	3
	3	4	5	6	7	8	9
	10	11	13	14	15[i]	16	17
	18	19	20	21	22	23	24
CHAITRA 2130	25	26	27	28	29	30	1[a]
	2	3	4	5	6	7	8
	9[b]	10	11	12	13	14	15
	17	18	19	20	21	22	23
	24	25	26	27	28	28	29
VAIŚĀKHA 2130	30	1	2	3	4	5	6
	7	8	9	11	12	13	14
	15	16	17	18	19	20	21
	22	23	24	25	26	27	28
JYAISHṬHA 2130	29	30	1	2	3	4	5
	6	7	8	9	10	11	12
	14	15	16	17	18	19	20
	21	22	23	24	24	25	26
ĀSHĀḌHA 2130	27	28	29	30	1	2	3
	4	6	7	8	9	10	11
	12	13	14	15	16	17	18
	19	20	21	22	23	24	25
ŚRĀVAṆA 2130	26	27	28	29	30	1	2
	3	4	5	6	7	9	10
	11	12	13	14	15	16	17
	18	19	20	21	21	22	23[c]
	24	25	26	27	28	29	30
BHĀDRAPADA 2130	2	3	4[d]	5	6	7	8
	9	10	11	12	13	14	15
	16	17	18	19	20	21	22
	23	24	25	26	27	28	29
ĀŚVINA 2130	30	1	2	3	4	6	7
	8[e]	9[e]	10[e]	11	12	13	14
	15	16	16	17	18	19	20
	21	22	23	24	25	26	27
KĀRTTIKA 2130	29	30	1[f]	2	3	4	5
	6	7	8	9	10	11	12
	13	14	15	16	17	18	19
	20	21	22	23	24	25	26
MĀRGAŚĪRA 2130	27	28	29	30	1	2	4
	5	6	7	8	9	9	10
	11[g]	12	13	14	15	16	17
	18	19	20	21	22	23	24
PAUSHA 2130	25	27	28	29	30	1	2
	3	4	5	6	7	8	9

‡Leap year
[a]New Year (Vijaya)
[b]Birthday of Rāma
[c]Birthday of Krishna
[d]Ganēśa Chaturthī
[e]Dashara
[f]Diwali
[g]Birthday of Vishnu
[h]Night of Śiva
[i]Holi

HINDU SOLAR 1994/1995

Month	Sun	Mon	Tue	Wed	Thu	Fri	Sat
PAUSHA 1994	17	18	19	20	21	22	23
	24	25	26	27	28	29	1[b]
MĀGHA 1994	2	3	4	5	6	7	8
	9	10	11	12	13	14	15
	16	17	18	19	20	21	22
	23	24	25	26	27	28	29
	30	1	2	3	4	5	6
PHĀLGUNA 1994	7	8	9	10	11	12	13
	14	15	16	17	18	19	20
	21	22	23	24	25	26	27
	28	29	30	1	2	3	4
CHAITRA 1994	5	6	7	8	9	10	11
	12	13	14	15	16	17	18
	19	20	21	22	23	24	25
	26	27	28	29	30	1[a]	2
VAIŚĀKHA 1995	3	4	5	6	7	8	9
	10	11	12	13	14	15	16
	17	18	19	20	21	22	23
	24	25	26	27	28	29	30
	31	1	2	3	4	5	6
JYAISHṬHA 1995	7	8	9	10	11	12	13
	14	15	16	17	18	19	20
	21	22	23	24	25	26	27
	28	29	30	31	1	2	3
ĀSHĀḌHA 1995	4	5	6	7	8	9	10
	11	12	13	14	15	16	17
	18	19	20	21	22	23	24
	25	26	27	28	29	30	31
	32	1	2	3	4	5	6
ŚRĀVAṆA 1995	7	8	9	10	11	12	13
	14	15	16	17	18	19	20
	21	22	23	24	25	26	27
	28	29	30	31	1	2	3
BHĀDRAPADA 1995	4	5	6	7	8	9	10
	11	12	13	14	15	16	17
	18	19	20	21	22	23	24
	25	26	27	28	29	30	31
ĀŚVINA 1995	1	2	3	4	5	6	7
	8	9	10	11	12	13	14
	15	16	17	18	19	20	21
	22	23	24	25	26	27	28
	29	30	31	1	2	3	4
KĀRTTIKA 1995	5	6	7	8	9	10	11
	12	13	14	15	16	17	18
	19	20	21	22	23	24	25
	26	27	28	29	30	1	2
MĀRGAŚĪRA 1995	3	4	5	6	7	8	9
	10	11	12	13	14	15	16
	17	18	19	20	21	22	23
	24	25	26	27	28	29	1
PAUSHA 1995	2	3	4	5	6	7	8
	9	10	11	12	13	14	15
	16	17	18	19	20	21	22

[a]New Year (Plavaṅga)
[b]Pongal

ISLAMIC (ASTRONOMICAL) 1495/1496/1497‡

Month	Sun	Mon	Tue	Wed	Thu	Fri	Sat
DHU AL-ḤIJJA 1495	22	23	24	25	26	27	28
	29	30	1[a]	2	3	4	5
MUHARRAM 1496	6	7	8	9	10[b]	11	12
	13	14	15	16	17	18	19
	20	21	22	23	24	25	26
	27	28	29	1	2	3	4
ṢAFAR 1496	5	6	7	8	9	10	11
	12	13	14	15	16	17	18
	19	20	21	22	23	24	25
	26	27	28	29	30	1	2
RABĪ' I 1496	3	4	5	6	7	8	9
	10	11	12[c]	13	14	15	16
	17	18	19	20	21	22	23
	24	25	26	27	28	29	30
	1	2	3	4	5	6	7
RABĪ' II 1496	8	9	10	11	12	13	14
	15	16	17	18	19	20	21
	22	23	24	25	26	27	28
	29	30	1	2	3	4	5
JUMĀDĀ I 1496	6	7	8	9	10	11	12
	13	14	15	16	17	18	19
	20	21	22	23	24	25	26
	27	28	29	1	2	3	4
JUMĀDĀ II 1496	5	6	7	8	9	10	11
	12	13	14	15	16	17	18
	19	20	21	22	23	24	25
	26	27	28	29	30	1	2
RAJAB 1496	3	4	5	6	7	8	9
	10	11	12	13	14	15	16
	17	18	19	20	21	22	23
	24	25	26	27[d]	28	29	1
SHA'BĀN 1496	2	3	4	5	6	7	8
	9	10	11	12	13	14	15
	16	17	18	19	20	21	22
	23	24	25	26	27	28	29
RAMAḌĀN 1496	1[e]	2	3	4	5	6	7
	8	9	10	11	12	13	14
	15	16	17	18	19	20	21
	22	23	24	25	26	27	28
	29	30	1[f]	2	3	4	5
SHAWWĀL 1496	6	7	8	9	10	11	12
	13	14	15	16	17	18	19
	20	21	22	23	24	25	26
	27	28	29	1	2	3	4
DHU AL-QA'DA 1496	5	6	7	8	9	10	11
	12	13	14	15	16	17	18
	19	20	21	22	23	24	25
	26	27	28	29	1	2	3
DHU AL-ḤIJJA 1496	4	5	6	7	8	9	10[g]
	11	12	13	14	15	16	17
	18	19	20	21	22	23	24
	25	26	27	28	29	30	1[a]
MUHARRAM 1497	2[d]	3	4	5	6	7	8

‡Leap year
[a]New Year
[d]New Year (Arithmetic)
[b]'Ashūrā'
[c]Prophet's Birthday
[d]Ascent of the Prophet
[e]Start of Ramaḍān
[f]'Id al-Fiṭr
[g]'Id al-'Aḍḥā

GREGORIAN 2073

Julian (Sun)	Sun	Mon	Tue	Wed	Thu	Fri	Sat	Month
Dec 19	1	2	3	4	5	6	7[a]	JANUARY 2073
	8	9	10	11	12	13	14[b]	
Jan 2	15	16	17	18	19	20	21	
	22	23	24	25	26	27	28	
Jan 16	29	30	31	1	2	3	4	
	5	6	7	8[c]	9	10	11	FEBRUARY 2073
Jan 30	12	13	14	15	16	17	18	
	19	20	21	22	23	24	25	
Feb 13	26	27	28	1	2	3	4	
	5	6	7	8	9	10	11	MARCH 2073
Feb 27	12	13	14	15	16	17	18	
	19[d]	20	21	22	23	24	25	
Mar 13	26[e]	27	28	29	30	31	1	
	2	3	4	5	6	7	8	APRIL 2073
Mar 27	9	10	11	12	13	14	15	
	16	17	18	19	20	21	22	
Apr 10	23	24	25	26	27	28	29	
	30[f]	1	2	3	4	5	6	
Apr 24	7	8	9	10	11	12	13	MAY 2073
	14	15	16	17	18	19	20	
May 8	21	22	23	24	25	26	27	
	28	29	30	31	1	2	3	
May 22	4	5	6	7	8	9	10	JUNE 2073
	11	12	13	14	15	16	17	
Jun 5	18	19	20	21	22	23	24	
	25	26	27	28	29	30	1	
Jun 19	2	3	4	5	6	7	8	JULY 2073
	9	10	11	12	13	14	15	
Jul 3	16	17	18	19	20	21	22	
	23	24	25	26	27	28	29	
Jul 17	30	31	1	2	3	4	5	
	6	7	8	9	10	11	12	AUGUST 2073
Jul 31	13	14	15	16	17	18	19	
	20	21	22	23	24	25	26	
Aug 14	27	28	29	30	31	1	2	
	3	4	5	6	7	8	9	SEPTEMBER 2073
Aug 28	10	11	12	13	14	15	16	
	17	18	19	20	21	22	23	
Sep 11	24	25	26	27	28	29	30	
	1	2	3	4	5	6	7	OCTOBER 2073
Sep 25	8	9	10	11	12	13	14	
	15	16	17	18	19	20	21	
Oct 9	22	23	24	25	26	27	28	
	29	30	31	1	2	3	4	
Oct 23	5	6	7	8	9	10	11	NOVEMBER 2073
	12	13	14	15	16	17	18	
Nov 6	19	20	21	22	23	24	25	
	26	27	28	29	30	1	2	
Nov 20	3[g]	4	5	6	7	8	9	DECEMBER 2073
	10	11	12	13	14	15	16	
Dec 4	17	18	19	20	21	22	23	
	24	25[h]	26	27	28	29	30	
Dec 18	31	1	2	3	4	5	6	

[a]Orthodox Christmas
[b]Julian New Year
[c]Ash Wednesday
[d]Feast of Orthodoxy
[e]Easter
[f]Orthodox Easter
[g]Advent
[h]Christmas

2074

GREGORIAN 2074 / ISO WEEK / JULIAN DAY

Month	Sun	Mon	Tue	Wed	Thu	Fri	Sat	Lunar Phases	ISO WEEK (Mon)	JULIAN DAY (Sun noon)
	31	1[a]	2	3	4	◐	6	6:17	1	2478573
JANUARY 2074	7	8	9	10	11	12	○	6:30	2	2478580
	14	15	16	17	18	19	◑	8:19	3	2478587
	21	22	23	24	25	26	●	6:36	4	2478594
	28	29	30	31	1	2	3		5	2478601
FEBRUARY 2074	◐	5	6	7	8	9	10	4:01	6	2478608
	○	12	13	14	15	16	17	21:04	7	2478615
	◑	19	20	21	22	23	24	15:54	8	2478622
	●	26	27	28	1	2	3	21:59	9	2478629
MARCH 2074	4	5	◐	7	8	9	10	0:42	10	2478636
	11	12	○	14	15	16	17	9:00	11	2478643
	18	◑	20[b]	21	22	23	24	23:57	12	2478650
	25	26	●	28	29	30	31	14:18	13	2478657
APRIL 2074	1	2	3	◐	5	6	7	18:39	14	2478664
	8	9	10	○	12	13	14	18:29	15	2478671
	15	16	17	◑	19	20	21	9:21	16	2478678
	22	23	24	25	●	27	28	6:46	17	2478685
	29	30	1	2	3	◐	5	8:52	18	2478692
MAY 2074	6	7	8	9	10	○	12	2:16	19	2478699
	13	14	15	16	◑	18	19	20:38	20	2478706
	20	21	22	23	24	●	26	22:43	21	2478713
	27	28	29	30	31	1	◐	19:13	22	2478720
JUNE 2074	3	4	5	6	7	8	○	9:26	23	2478727
	10	11	12	13	14	15	◑	9:55	24	2478734
	17	18	19	20[c]	21	22	23		25	2478741
	●	25	26	27	28	29	30	13:37	26	2478748
JULY 2074	1	◐	3	4	5	6	7	2:21	27	2478755
	○	9	10	11	12	13	14	17:04	28	2478762
	15	◑	17	18	19	20	21	1:10	29	2478769
	22	23	●	25	26	27	28	3:06	30	2478776
	29	30	◐	1	2	3	4	7:29	31	2478783
AUGUST 2074	5	6	○	8	9	10	11	2:04	32	2478790
	12	13	◑	15	16	17	18	18:08	33	2478797
	19	20	21	●	23	24	25	14:58	34	2478804
	26	27	28	◐	30	31	1	12:11	35	2478811
SEPTEMBER 2074	2	3	4	○	6	7	8	13:12	36	2478818
	9	10	11	12	◑	14	15	12:20	37	2478825
	16	17	18	19	20	●	22[d]	1:27	38	2478832
	23	24	25	26	◐	28	29	17:58	39	2478839
	30	1	2	3	4	○	6	2:54	40	2478846
OCTOBER 2074	7	8	9	10	11	12	◑	6:46	41	2478853
	14	15	16	17	18	19	●	11:10	42	2478860
	21	22	23	24	25	26	◐	2:14	43	2478867
	28	29	30	31	1	2	○	19:20	44	2478874
NOVEMBER 2074	4	5	6	7	8	9	10		45	2478881
	11	◑	13	14	15	16	17	0:06	46	2478888
	●	19	20	21	22	23	24	20:55	47	2478895
	◐	26	27	28	29	30	1	13:51	48	2478902
DECEMBER 2074	2	○	4	5	6	7	8	14:02	49	2478909
	9	10	◑	12	13	14	15	15:06	50	2478916
	16	17	●	19	20	21[e]	22	7:18	51	2478923
	23	24	◐	26	27	28	29	5:05	52	2478930
	30	31	1	○	3	4	5	9:38	1	2478937

HEBREW 5834/5835

ISO WEEK	Month	Sun	Mon	Tue	Wed	Thu	Fri	Sat	Molad
1	TEVETH 5834	1[e]	2[e]	3	4	5	6	7	Fri 6h31m10p
2		8	9	10	11	12	13	14	
3		15	16	17	18	19	20	21	
4		22	23	24	25	26	27	28	
5	SHEVAT 5834	29	1	2	3	4	5	6	Sat 19h15m11p
6		7	8	9	10	11	12	13	
7		14	15	16	17	18	19	20	
8		21	22	23	24	25	26	27	
9	ADAR 5834	28	29	30	1	2	3	4	Mon 7h59m12p
10		5	6	7	8	9	10	11	
11		12	13	14[f]	15	16	17	18	
12		19	20	21	22	23	24	25	
13	NISAN 5834	26	27	28	29	1	2	3	Tue 20h43m13p
14		4	5	6	7	8	9	10	
15		11	12	13	14	15[g]	16	17	
16		18	19	20	21	22	23	24	
17	IYYAR 5834	25	26	27	28	29	30	1	Thu 9h27m14p
18		2	3	4	5	6	7	8	
19		9	10	11	12	13	14	15	
20		16	17	18	19	20	21	22	
21		23	24	25	26	27	28	29	
22	SIVAN 5834	1	2	3	4	5	6[h]	7	Fri 22h11m15p
23		8	9	10	11	12	13	14	
24		15	16	17	18	19	20	21	
25		22	23	24	25	26	27	28	
26	TAMMUZ 5834	29	30	1	2	3	4	5	Sun 10h55m16p
27		6	7	8	9	10	11	12	
28		13	14	15	16	17	18	19	
29		20	21	22	23	24	25	26	
30	AV 5834	27	28	29	1	2	3	4	Mon 23h39m17p
31		5	6	7	8	9[i]	10	11	
32		12	13	14	15	16	17	18	
33		19	20	21	22	23	24	25	
34	ELUL 5834	26	27	28	29	30	1	2	Wed 12h24m0p
35		3	4	5	6	7	8	9	
36		10	11	12	13	14	15	16	
37		17	18	19	20	21	22	23	
38	TISHRI 5835	24	25	26	27	28	29	1[a]	Fri 1h8m1p
39		2[a]	3	4	5	6	7	8	
40		9	10[b]	11	12	13	14	15[c]	
41		16	17	18	19	20	21	22	
42		23	24	25	26	27	28	29	
43	HESHVAN 5835	30	1	2	3	4	5	6	Sat 13h52m2p
44		7	8	9	10	11	12	13	
45		14	15	16	17	18	19	20	
46		21	22	23	24	25	26	27	
47	KISLEV 5835	28	29	1	2	3	4	5	Mon 2h36m3p
48		6	7	8	9	10	11	12	
49		13	14	15	16[d]	17	18	19	
50		20	21	22	23	24	25[e]	26[e]	
51	TEVETH 5835	27[e]	28[e]	29[e]	1[e]	2[e]	3[e]	4	Tue 15h20m4p
52		5	6	7	8	9	10	11	
1		12	13	14	15	16	17	18	

CHINESE Guǐ-Sì/Jiă-Wǔ‡

ISO WEEK	Month	Sun	Mon	Tue	Wed	Thu	Fri	Sat	Solar Term
1	MONTH 12 Guǐ-Sì	3	4	5	6	7	*8*	9	Xiǎo hán
2		10	11	12	13	14	15	16	
3		17	18	19	20	21	22	**23**	**Dà hán**
4	MONTH 1 Jiă-Wǔ	24	25	26	27	28	29	1[a]	
5		2	3	4	5	6	7	*8*	
6		9	10	11	12*	13	14	15[b]	Lì chūn
7		16	17	18	19	20	21	22	
8		**23**	24	25	26	27	28	29	**Yǔ shuǐ**
9	MONTH 2 Jiă-Wǔ	30	1	2	3	4	5	6	
10		7	*8*	9	10	11	12	13	Jīng zhé
11		14	15	16	17	18	19	20	
12		21	22	**23**	24	25	26	27	**Chūn fēn**
13	MONTH 3 Jiă-Wǔ	28	29	1	2	3	4	5	
14		6	7	8	9[c]	10	11	12	Qīng míng
15		13*	14	15	16	17	18	19	
16		20	21	22	23	24	**25**	26	**Gǔ yǔ**
17	MONTH 4 Jiă-Wǔ	27	28	29	30	1	2	3	
18		4	5	6	7	8	9	*10*	Lì xià
19		11	12	13	14	15	16	17	
20		18	19	20	21	22	23	24	
21	MONTH 5 Jiă-Wǔ	**25**	26	27	28	29	30	1	**Xiǎo mǎn**
22		2	3	4	5[d]	6	7	8	
23		9	10	*11*	12	13*	14	15	Máng zhòng
24		16	17	18	19	20	21	22	
25		23	24	25	26	**27**	28	29	**Xià zhì**
26	MONTH 6 Jiă-Wǔ	1	2	3	4	5	6	7	
27		8	9	10	11	12	13	*14*	Xiǎo shǔ
28		15	16	17	18	19	20	21	
29		22	23	24	25	26	27	28	
30	LEAP MONTH 6 Jiă-Wǔ	**29**	30	1	2	3	4	5	**Dà shǔ**
31		6	7	8	9	10	11	12	
32		13	14*	*15*	16	17	18	19	Lì qiū
33		20	21	22	23	24	25	26	
34	MONTH 7 Jiă-Wǔ	27	28	29	1	**2**	3	4	**Chǔ shǔ**
35		5	6	7[e]	8	9	10	11	
36		12	13	14	15[f]	16	*17*	18	Bái lù
37		19	20	21	22	23	24	25	
38	MONTH 8 Jiă-Wǔ	26	27	28	29	30	1	**2**	**Qiū fēn**
39		3	4	5	6	7	8	9	
40		10	11	12	13	14	15[g]*	16	
41		17	*18*	19	20	21	22	23	Hán lù
42	MONTH 9 Jiă-Wǔ	24	25	26	27	28	29	1	
43		2	3	**4**	5	6	7	8	**Shuāng jiàng**
44		9[h]	10	11	12	13	14	15	
45		16	17	18	*19*	20	21	22	Lì dōng
46		23	24	25	26	27	28	29	
47	MONTH 10 Jiă-Wǔ	30	1	2	3	**4**	5	6	**Xiǎo xuě**
48		7	8	9	10	11	12	13	
49		14	15	16*	17	18	*19*	20	Dà xuě
50		21	22	23	24	25	26	27	
51	MONTH 11 Jiă-Wǔ	28	29	1	2	3	4[i]	5	**Dōng zhì**
52		6	7	8	9	10	11	12	
1		13	14	15	16	17	18	*19*	Xiǎo hán

COPTIC 1790/1791‡ / ETHIOPIC 2066/2067‡

ISO WEEK	Coptic Month	Sun	Mon	Tue	Wed	Thu	Fri	Sat	Ethiopic Month
1	KOIAK 1790	22	23	24	25	26	27	28	TĀKHŚĀŚ 2066
2		29[c]	30	1	2	3	4	5	
3	TŌBE 1790	6[d]	7	8	9	10	11[e]	12	ṬER 2066
4		13	14	15	16	17	18	19	
5		20	21	22	23	24	25	26	
6		27	28	29	30	1	2	3	
7	MESHIR 1790	4	5	6	7	8	9	10	YAKĀTIT 2066
8		11	12	13	14	15	16	17	
9		18	19	20	21	22	23	24	
10		25	26	27	28	29	30	1	
11	PAREMOTEP 1790	2	3	4	5	6	7	8	MAGĀBIT 2066
12		9	10	11	12	13	14	15	
13		16	17	18	19	20	21	22	
14		23	24	25	26	27	28	29	
15	PARMOUTE 1790	30	1	2	3	4	5	6	MIYĀZYĀ 2066
16		7	8	9	10	11	12	13	
17		14[f]	15	16	17	18	19	20	
18		21	22	23	24	25	26	27	
19	PASHONS 1790	28	29[g]	30	1	2	3	4	GENBOT 2066
20		5	6	7	8	9	10	11	
21		12	13	14	15	16	17	18	
22		19	20	21	22	23	24	25	
23		26	27	28	29	30	1	2	
24	PAĆNE 1790	3	4	5	6	7	8	9	SANĒ 2066
25		10	11	12	13	14	15	16	
26		17	18	19	20	21	22	23	
27		24	25	26	27	28	29	30	
28	EPĒP 1790	1	2	3	4	5	6	7	ḤAMLĒ 2066
29		8	9	10	11	12	13	14	
30		15	16	17	18	19	20	21	
31		22	23	24	25	26	27	28	
32	MESORĒ 1790	29	30	1	2	3	4	5	NAḤASĒ 2066
33		6	7	8	9	10	11	12	
34		13[h]	14	15	16	17	18	19	
35		20	21	22	23	24	25	26	
36	EPAG. 1790	27	28	29	30	1	2	3	PĀG. 2066
37	THOOUT 1791	4	5	1[a]	2	3	4	5	MASKARAM 2067
38		6	7	8	9	10	11	12	
39		13	14	15	16	17[b]	18	19	
40		20	21	22	23	24	25	26	
41	PAOPE 1791	27	28	29	30	1	2	3	TEQEMT 2067
42		4	5	6	7	8	9	10	
43		11	12	13	14	15	16	17	
44		18	19	20	21	22	23	24	
45	ATHŌR 1791	25	26	27	28	29	30	1	ḪEDĀR 2067
46		2	3	4	5	6	7	8	
47		9	10	11	12	13	14	15	
48		16	17	18	19	20	21	22	
49		23	24	25	26	27	28	29	
50	KOIAK 1791	30	1	2	3	4	5	6	TĀKHŚĀŚ 2067
51		7	8	9	10	11	12	13	
52		14	15	16	17	18	19	20	
1		21	22	23	24	25	26	27	

[a]New Year
[b]Spring (6:07)
[c]Summer (22:57)
[d]Autumn (15:02)
[e]Winter (12:34)
● New moon
◐ First quarter moon
○ Full moon
◑ Last quarter moon

[a]New Year
[b]Yom Kippur
[c]Sukkot
[d]Winter starts
[e]Ḥanukkah
[f]Purim
[g]Passover
[h]Shavuot
[i]Fast of Av

‡Leap year
[a]New Year (4772, Horse)
[b]Lantern Festival
[c]Qīngmíng
[d]Dragon Festival
[e]Qīqiǎo
[f]Hungry Ghosts
[g]Mid-Autumn Festival
[h]Double-Ninth Festival
[i]Dōngzhì
*Start of 60-name cycle

‡Leap year
[a]New Year
[b]Building of the Cross
[c]Christmas
[d]Jesus's Circumcision
[e]Epiphany
[f]Easter
[g]Mary's Announcement
[h]Jesus's Transfiguration

PERSIAN (ASTRONOMICAL) 1452/1453‡

Month	Sun	Mon	Tue	Wed	Thu	Fri	Sat
DEY 1452	11	12	13	14	15	16	17
	18	19	20	21	22	23	24
	25	26	27	28	29	30	1
BAHMAN 1452	2	3	4	5	6	7	8
	9	10	11	12	13	14	15
	16	17	18	19	20	21	22
	23	24	25	26	27	28	29
	30	1	2	3	4	5	6
ESFAND 1452	7	8	9	10	11	12	13
	14	15	16	17	18	19	20
	21	22	23	24	25	26	27
	28	29	1[a]	2	3	4	5
FARVARDĪN 1453	6	7	8	9	10	11	12
	13[b]	14	15	16	17	18	19
	20	21	22	23	24	25	26
	27	28	29	30	31	1	2
ORDĪBEHEŠT 1453	3	4	5	6	7	8	9
	10	11	12	13	14	15	16
	17	18	19	20	21	22	23
	24	25	26	27	28	29	30
	31	1	2	3	4	5	6
XORDĀD 1453	7	8	9	10	11	12	13
	14	15	16	17	18	19	20
	21	22	23	24	25	26	27
	28	29	30	31	1	2	3
TĪR 1453	4	5	6	7	8	9	10
	11	12	13	14	15	16	17
	18	19	20	21	22	23	24
	25	26	27	28	29	30	31
MORDĀD 1453	1	2	3	4	5	6	7
	8	9	10	11	12	13	14
	15	16	17	18	19	20	21
	22	23	24	25	26	27	28
	29	30	31	1	2	3	4
SHAHRĪVAR 1453	5	6	7	8	9	10	11
	12	13	14	15	16	17	18
	19	20	21	22	23	24	25
	26	27	28	29	30	31	1
MEHR 1453	2	3	4	5	6	7	8
	9	10	11	12	13	14	15
	16	17	18	19	20	21	22
	23	24	25	26	27	28	29
	30	1	2	3	4	5	6
ĀBĀN 1453	7	8	9	10	11	12	13
	14	15	16	17	18	19	20
	21	22	23	24	25	26	27
	28	29	30	1	2	3	4
ĀZAR 1453	5	6	7	8	9	10	11
	12	13	14	15	16	17	18
	19	20	21	22	23	24	25
	26	27	28	29	30	1	2
DEY 1453	3	4	5	6	7	8	9
	10	11	12	13	14	15	16

HINDU LUNAR 2130/2131

Month	Sun	Mon	Tue	Wed	Thu	Fri	Sat
PAUSHA 2130	3	4	5	6	7	8	9
	10	11	11	12	13	14	15
	16	17	18	19	**20**	22	23
	24	25	26	27	28	29	30
MĀGHA 2130	1	2	3	4	5	6	7
	8	9	10	11	12	13	14
	15	16	17	18	19	20	21
	22	23	**24**	26	27	28	29[h]
PHĀLGUNA 2130	30	1	2	3	4	4	5
	6	7	8	9	10	11	12
	13	14	15[i]	16	17	**18**	20
	21	22	23	24	25	26	27
CHAITRA 2131	28	29	30	1[a]	2	3	4
	5	6	7	7	8[b]	9	10
	11	13	14	15	16	17	18
	19	20	21	22	23	24	25
VAIŚĀKHA 2131	26	27	28	29	30	1	2
	3	4	5	6	7	8	9
	10	11	12	13	14	15	**16**
	18	19	20	21	22	23	24
JYAISHṬHA 2131	25	26	27	28	29	30	1
	2	2	3	4	5	6	7
	8	10	11	12	13	14	15
	16	17	18	19	20	21	22
	23	24	25	26	27	28	29
ĀSHĀḌHA 2131	30	1	2	3	4	5	6
	7	8	9	10	**11**	13	14
	15	16	17	18	19	20	21
	22	23	24	25	26	27	28
ŚRĀVAṆA 2131	29	29	30	1	2	3	**4**
	6	7	8	9	10	11	12
	13	14	15	**16**	18	19	20
	20	21	22	23[c]	24	25	26
BHĀDRAPADA 2131	27	28	29	30	1	2	3
	4[d]	5	6	**7**	9	10	11
	12	13	14	15	16	17	18
	19	20	21	22	23	24	25
	25	26	27	28	29	**30**	2
ĀŚVINA 2131	3	4	5	6	7	8[e]	9[e]
	10[e]	11	12	13	14	15	16
	17	18	19	20	21	22	23
	24	25	26	27	28	29	30
KĀRTTIKA 2131	1[f]	2	3	**4**	6	7	8
	9	10	11	12	13	14	15
	16	17	18	19	19	20	21
	22	23	24	25	26	27	**28**
MĀRGAŚĪRA 2131	30	1	2	3	4	5	6
	7	8	9	10	11[g]	12	13
	14	15	16	17	18	19	20
	21	22	23	24	25	26	27
PAUSHA 2131	28	29	30	1	2	**3**	5
	6	7	8	9	10	11	12
	12	13	14	15	16	17	18

HINDU SOLAR 1995/1996

Month	Sun	Mon	Tue	Wed	Thu	Fri	Sat
PAUSHA 1995	16	17	18	19	20	21	22
	23	24	25	26	27	28	29
MĀGHA 1995	1[b]	2	3	4	5	6	7
	8	9	10	11	12	13	14
	15	16	17	18	19	20	21
	22	23	24	25	26	27	28
PHĀLGUNA 1995	29	30	1	2	3	4	5
	6	7	8	9	10	11	12
	13	14	15	16	17	18	19
	20	21	22	23	24	25	26
CHAITRA 1995	27	28	29	30	1	2	3
	4	5	6	7	8	9	10
	11	12	13	14	15	16	17
	18	19	20	21	22	23	24
VAIŚĀKHA 1996	25	26	27	28	29	30	1[a]
	2	3	4	5	6	7	8
	9	10	11	12	13	14	15
	16	17	18	19	20	21	22
	23	24	25	26	27	28	29
JYAISHṬHA 1996	30	31	1	2	3	4	5
	6	7	8	9	10	11	12
	13	14	15	16	17	18	19
	20	21	22	23	24	25	26
ĀSHĀḌHA 1996	27	28	29	30	31	32	1
	2	3	4	5	6	7	8
	9	10	11	12	13	14	15
	16	17	18	19	20	21	22
	23	24	25	26	27	28	29
ŚRĀVAṆA 1996	30	31	1	2	3	4	5
	6	7	8	9	10	11	12
	13	14	15	16	17	18	19
	20	21	22	23	24	25	26
BHĀDRAPADA 1996	27	28	29	30	31	32	1
	2	3	4	5	6	7	8
	9	10	11	12	13	14	15
	16	17	18	19	20	21	22
	23	24	25	26	27	28	29
ĀŚVINA 1996	30	31	1	2	3	4	5
	6	7	8	9	10	11	12
	13	14	15	16	17	18	19
	20	21	22	23	24	25	26
KĀRTTIKA 1996	27	28	29	30	1	2	3
	4	5	6	7	8	9	10
	11	12	13	14	15	16	17
	18	19	20	21	22	23	24
MĀRGAŚĪRA 1996	25	26	27	28	29	30	1
	2	3	4	5	6	7	8
	9	10	11	12	13	14	15
	16	17	18	19	20	21	22
	23	24	25	26	27	28	29
PAUSHA 1996	1	2	3	4	5	6	7
	8	9	10	11	12	13	14
	15	16	17	18	19	20	21

ISLAMIC (ASTRONOMICAL) 1497‡/1498

Month	Sun	Mon	Tue	Wed	Thu	Fri	Sat
MUHARRAM 1497	2	3	4	5	6	7	8
	9	10[b]	11	12	13	14	15
	16	17	18	19	20	21	22
	23	24	25	26	27	28	29
ṢAFAR 1497	30	1	2	3	4	5	6
	7	8	9	10	11	12	13
	14	15	16	17	18	19	20
	21	22	23	24	25	26	27
RABĪʿ I 1497	28	29	1	2	3	4	5
	6	7	8	9	10	11	12[c]
	13	14	15	16	17	18	19
	20	21	22	23	24	25	26
RABĪʿ II 1497	27	28	29	30	1	2	3
	4	5	6	7	8	9	10
	11	12	13	14	15	16	17
	18	19	20	21	22	23	24
JUMĀDĀ I 1497	25	26	27	28	29	30	1
	2	3	4	5	6	7	8
	9	10	11	12	13	14	15
	16	17	18	19	20	21	22
	23	24	25	26	27	28	29
JUMĀDĀ II 1497	1	2	3	4	5	6	7
	8	9	10	11	12	13	14
	15	16	17	18	19	20	21
	22	23	24	25	26	27	28
RAJAB 1497	29	30	1	2	3	4	5
	6	7	8	9	10	11	12
	13	14	15	16	17	18	19
	20	21	22	23	24	25	26
SHAʿBĀN 1497	27[d]	28	29	30	1	2	3
	4	5	6	7	8	9	10
	11	12	13	14	15	16	17
	18	19	20	21	22	23	24
RAMAḌĀN 1497	25	26	27	28	29	1[e]	2
	3	4	5	6	7	8	9
	10	11	12	13	14	15	16
	17	18	19	20	21	22	23
SHAWWĀL 1497	24	25	26	27	28	29	1[f]
	2	3	4	5	6	7	8
	9	10	11	12	13	14	15
	16	17	18	19	20	21	22
	23	24	25	26	27	28	29
DHU AL-QAʿDA 1497	30	1	2	3	4	5	6
	7	8	9	10	11	12	13
	14	15	16	17	18	19	20
	21	22	23	24	25	26	27
DHU AL-ḤIJJA 1497	28	29	1	2	3	4	5
	6	7	8	9	10[g]	11	12
	13	14	15	16	17	18	19
	20	21	22	23	24	25	26
MUHARRAM 1498	27	28	29	30	1[a]	2	3
	4	5	6	7	8	9	10[b]
	11	12	13	14	15	16	17

GREGORIAN 2074

Julian (Sun)	Sun	Mon	Tue	Wed	Thu	Fri	Sat	Month
Dec 18	31	1	2	3	4	5	6	JANUARY 2074
	7[a]	8	9	10	11	12	13	
Jan 1	14[b]	15	16	17	18	19	20	
	21	22	23	24	25	26	27	
Jan 15	28	29	30	31	1	2	3	FEBRUARY 2074
	4	5	6	7	8	9	10	
Jan 29	11	12	13	14	15	16	17	
	18	19	20	21	22	23	24	
Feb 12	25	26	27	28[c]	1	2	3	MARCH 2074
	4	5	6	7	8	9	10	
Feb 26	11[d]	12	13	14	15	16	17	
	18	19	20	21	22	23	24	
Mar 12	25	26	27	28	29	30	31	
	1	2	3	4	5	6	7	APRIL 2074
Mar 26	8	9	10	11	12	13	14	
	15[e]	16	17	18	19	20	21	
Apr 9	22[f]	23	24	25	26	27	28	
	29	30	1	2	3	4	5	MAY 2074
Apr 23	6	7	8	9	10	11	12	
	13	14	15	16	17	18	19	
May 7	20	21	22	23	24	25	26	
	27	28	29	30	31	1	2	JUNE 2074
May 21	3	4	5	6	7	8	9	
	10	11	12	13	14	15	16	
Jun 4	17	18	19	20	21	22	23	
	24	25	26	27	28	29	30	
Jun 18	1	2	3	4	5	6	7	JULY 2074
	8	9	10	11	12	13	14	
Jul 2	15	16	17	18	19	20	21	
	22	23	24	25	26	27	28	
Jul 16	29	30	31	1	2	3	4	AUGUST 2074
	5	6	7	8	9	10	11	
Jul 30	12	13	14	15	16	17	18	
	19	20	21	22	23	24	25	
Aug 13	26	27	28	29	30	31	1	SEPTEMBER 2074
	2	3	4	5	6	7	8	
Aug 27	9	10	11	12	13	14	15	
	16	17	18	19	20	21	22	
Sep 10	23	24	25	26	27	28	29	
	30	1	2	3	4	5	6	OCTOBER 2074
Sep 24	7	8	9	10	11	12	13	
	14	15	16	17	18	19	20	
Oct 8	21	22	23	24	25	26	27	
	28	29	30	31	1	2	3	NOVEMBER 2074
Oct 22	4	5	6	7	8	9	10	
	11	12	13	14	15	16	17	
Nov 5	18	19	20	21	22	23	24	
	25	26	27	28	29	30	1	DECEMBER 2074
Nov 19	2[g]	3	4	5	6	7	8	
	9	10	11	12	13	14	15	
Dec 3	16	17	18	19	20	21	22	
	23	24	25[h]	26	27	28	29	
Dec 17	30	31	1	2	3	4	5	

Persian:
‡Leap year
[a]New Year
[b]Sizdeh Bedar

Hindu Lunar:
[a]New Year (Jaya)
[b]Birthday of Rāma
[c]Birthday of Krishna
[d]Ganēśa Chaturthī
[e]Dashara
[f]Diwali
[g]Birthday of Vishnu
[h]Night of Śiva
[i]Holi

Hindu Solar:
[a]New Year (Kīlaka)
[b]Pongal

Islamic:
‡Leap year
[a]New Year
[b]ʿAshūrāʾ
[c]Prophet's Birthday
[d]Ascent of the Prophet
[e]Start of Ramaḍān
[f]ʿId al-Fiṭr
[g]ʿId al-ʾAḍḥā

Gregorian:
[a]Orthodox Christmas
[b]Julian New Year
[c]Ash Wednesday
[d]Feast of Orthodoxy
[e]Easter
[f]Orthodox Easter
[g]Advent
[h]Christmas

2075

GREGORIAN 2075	Sun	Mon	Tue	Wed	Thu	Fri	Sat	Lunar Phases	ISO WEEK (Mon)	JULIAN DAY (Sun noon)	HEBREW 5835/5836‡	Sun	Mon	Tue	Wed	Thu	Fri	Sat	Molad	CHINESE Jiǎ-Wǔ‡/Yǐ-Wèi	Sun	Mon	Tue	Wed	Thu	Fri	Sat	Solar Term	COPTIC 1791‡/1792	Sun	Mon	Tue	Wed	Thu	Fri	Sat	ETHIOPIC 2067‡/2068
JANUARY 2075	30	31	1[a]	○	3	4	5	9:38	1	2478937	TEVETH 5835	12	13	14	15	16	17	18		MONTH 11 Jiǎ-Wǔ	13	14	15	16	17	18	19	Xiǎo hán	KOIAK 1791	21	22	23	24	25	26	27	TĀKHŚĀŚ 2067
	6	7	8	9	◑	11	12	3:13	2	2478944		19	20	21	22	23	24	25			20	21	22	23	24	25	26		TŌBE 1791	28	29[c]	30	1	2	3	4	TER 2067
	13	14	15	●	17	18	19	18:35	3	2478951	SHEVAT 5835	26	27	28	29	1	2	3	Thu 4h4m5p	MONTH 12 Jiǎ-Wǔ	27	28	29	30	1	2	3			5	6[d]	7	8	9	10	11[e]	
	20	21	22	◐	24	25	26	23:31	4	2478958		4	5	6	7	8	9	10			4	5	6	7	8	9	10	Dà hán		12	13	14	15	16	17	18	
	27	28	29	30	31	○	2	4:12	5	2478965		11	12	13	14	15	16	17			11	12	13	14	15	16	17*			19	20	21	22	23	24	25	
FEBRUARY 2075	3	4	5	6	7	◑	9	12:40	6	2478972		18	19	20	21	22	23	24			18	19	20	21	22	23	24	Lì chūn	MESHIR 1791	26	27	28	29	30	1	2	YAKĀTIT 2067
	10	11	12	13	14	●	16	6:39	7	2478979	ADAR 5835	25	26	27	28	29	30	1	Fri 16h48m6p	MONTH 1 Yǐ-Wèi	25	26	27	28	29	1[a]	2			3	4	5	6	7	8	9	
	17	18	19	20	21	◐	23	19:59	8	2478986		2	3	4	5	6	7	8			3	4	5	6	7	8	9	Yǔ shuǐ		10	11	12	13	14	15	16	
	24	25	26	27	28	1	○	20:05	9	2478993		9	10	11	12	13	14[f]	15			10	11	12	13	14	15[b]	16			17	18	19	20	21	22	23	
MARCH 2075	3	4	5	6	7	8	◑	20:16	10	2479000		16	17	18	19	20	21	22			17	18	19	20	21	22	23	Jīng zhé		24	25	26	27	28	29	30	
	10	11	12	13	14	15	●	19:24	11	2479007		23	24	25	26	27	28	29			24	25	26	27	28	29	30		PAREMOTEP 1791	1	2	3	4	5	6	7	MAGĀBIT 2067
	17	18	19	20[b]	21	22	23		12	2479014	NISAN 5835	1	2	3	4	5	6	7	Sun 5h32m7p	MONTH 2 Yǐ-Wèi	1	2	3	4	5	6	7	Chūn fēn		8	9	10	11	12	13	14	
	◐	25	26	27	28	29	30	16:44	13	2479021		8	9	10	11	12	13	14			8	9	10	11	12	13	14			15	16	17	18	19	20	21	
APRIL 2075	31	○	2	3	4	5	6	8:44	14	2479028		15[g]	16	17	18	19	20	21			15	16	17	18*	19[c]	20	21	Qīng míng		22	23	24	25	26	27	28	
	7	◑	9	10	11	12	13	3:02	15	2479035		22	23	24	25	26	27	28			22	23	24	25	26	27	28		PARMOUTE 1791	29[f]	30	1	2	3	4	5	MIYĀZYĀ 2067
	14	●	16	17	18	19	20	8:54	16	2479042	IYYAR 5835	29	30	1	2	3	4	5	Mon 18h16m8p	MONTH 3 Yǐ-Wèi	29	1	2	3	4	5	6	Gǔ yǔ		6	7	8	9	10	11	12	
	21	22	◐	24	25	26	27	11:52	17	2479049		6	7	8	9	10	11	12			7	8	9	10	11	12	13			13	14	15	16	17	18	19	
MAY 2075	28	29	○	1	2	3	4	18:36	18	2479056		13	14	15	16	17	18	19			14	15	16	17	18	19	20			20	21	22	23	24	25	26	
	5	6	◑	8	9	10	11	9:58	19	2479063		20	21	22	23	24	25	26			21	22	23	24	25	26	27	Lì xià	PASHONS 1791	27	28	29[g]	30	1	2	3	GENBOT 2067
	12	13	●	15	16	17	18	23:21	20	2479070	SIVAN 5835	27	28	29	1	2	3	4	Wed 7h0m9p	MONTH 4 Yǐ-Wèi	28	29	30	1	2	3	4			4	5	6	7	8	9	10	
	19	20	21	22	◐	24	25	3:55	21	2479077		5	6[h]	7	8	9	10	11			5	6	7	8	9	10	11	Xiǎo mǎn		11	12	13	14	15	16	17	
JUNE 2075	26	27	28	29	○	31	1	2:37	22	2479084		12	13	14	15	16	17	18			12	13	14	15	16	17	18			18	19	20	21	22	23	24	
	2	3	4	◑	6	7	8	17:59	23	2479091		19	20	21	22	23	24	25			19*	20	21	22	23	24	25	Máng zhòng	PAŌNE 1791	25	26	27	28	29	30	1	SANĒ 2067
	9	10	11	12	●	14	15	14:38	24	2479098	TAMMUZ 5835	26	27	28	29	30	1	2	Thu 19h44m10p	MONTH 5 Yǐ-Wèi	26	27	28	29	1	2	3			2	3	4	5	6	7	8	
	16	17	18	19	20	◐[c]	22	15:28	25	2479105		3	4	5	6	7	8	9			4	5[d]	6	7	8	9	10	Xià zhì		9	10	11	12	13	14	15	
	23	24	25	26	27	○	29	9:45	26	2479112		10	11	12	13	14	15	16			11	12	13	14	15	16	17			16	17	18	19	20	21	22	
JULY 2075	30	1	2	3	4	◑	6	3:59	27	2479119		17	18	19	20	21	22	23			18	19	20	21	22	23	24			23	24	25	26	27	28	29	
	7	8	9	10	11	12	●	6:10	28	2479126	AV 5835	24	25	26	27	28	29	1	Sat 8h28m11p	MONTH 6 Yǐ-Wèi	25	26	27	28	29	30	1	Xiǎo shǔ	EPĒP 1791	30	1	2	3	4	5	6	HAMLĒ 2067
	14	15	16	17	18	19	20		29	2479133		2	3	4	5	6	7	8			2	3	4	5	6	7	8			7	8	9	10	11	12	13	
	◐	22	23	24	25	26	○	1:54 16:53	30	2479140		9[i]	10	11	12	13	14	15			9	10	11	12	13	14	15	Dà shǔ		14	15	16	17	18	19	20	
AUGUST 2075	28	29	30	31	1	2	◑	16:42	31	2479147		16	17	18	19	20	21	22			16	17	18	19	20*	21	22			21	22	23	24	25	26	27	
	4	5	6	7	8	9	10		32	2479154		23	24	25	26	27	28	29			23	24	25	26	27	28	29	Lì qiū	MESORĒ 1791	28	29	30	1	2	3	4	NAHASĒ 2067
	●	12	13	14	15	16	17	21:09	33	2479161	ELUL 5835	30	1	2	3	4	5	6	Sun 21h12m12p	MONTH 7 Yǐ-Wèi	30	1	2	3	4	5	6			5	6	7	8	9	10	11	
	18	◐	20	21	22	23	24	9:11	34	2479168		7	8	9	10	11	12	13			7[e]	8	9	10	11	12	13	Chǔ shǔ		12	13[h]	14	15	16	17	18	
	25	○	27	28	29	30	31	0:49	35	2479175		14	15	16	17	18	19	20			14	15[f]	16	17	18	19	20			19	20	21	22	23	24	25	
SEPTEMBER 2075	1	◑	3	4	5	6	7	8:33	36	2479182		21	22	23	24	25	26	27			21	22	23	24	25	26	27	Bái lù	EPAG. 1791	26	27	28	29	30	1	2	PĀG. 2067
	8	9	●	11	12	13	14	11:01	37	2479189	TISHRI 5836	28	29	1[a]	2[a]	3	4	5	Tue 9h56m13p	MONTH 8 Yǐ-Wèi	28	29	1	2	3	4	5		THOOUT 1792	3	4	5	6	1[a]	2	3	MASKARAM 2068
	15	16	◐	18	19	20	21	15:24	38	2479196		6	7	8	9	10[b]	11	12			6	7	8	9	10	11	12			4	5	6	7	8	9	10	
	22[d]	23	○	25	26	27	28	10:29	39	2479203		13	14	15[c]	16	17	18	19			13	14	15[g]	16	17	18	19	Qiū fēn		11	12	13	14	15	16	17[b]	
OCTOBER 2075	29	30	1	◑	3	4	5	3:12	40	2479210		20	21	22	23	24	25	26			20	21*	22	23	24	25	26			18	19	20	21	22	23	24	
	6	7	8	●	10	11	12	23:42	41	2479217	HESHVAN 5836	27	28	29	30	1	2	3	Wed 22h40m14p	MONTH 9 Yǐ-Wèi	27	28	29	30	1	2	3	Hán lù	PAOPE 1792	25	26	27	28	29	30	1	TEQEMT 2068
	13	14	15	◐	17	18	19	21:40	42	2479224		4	5	6	7	8	9	10			4	5	6	7	8	9[h]	10			2	3	4	5	6	7	8	
	20	21	22	○	24	25	26	22:48	43	2479231		11	12	13	14	15	16	17			11	12	13	14	15	16	17	Shuāng jiàng		9	10	11	12	13	14	15	
NOVEMBER 2075	27	28	29	30	◑	1	2	23:25	44	2479238		18	19	20	21	22	23	24			18	19	20	21	22	23	24			16	17	18	19	20	21	22	
	3	4	5	6	7	●	9	11:34	45	2479245	KISLEV 5836	25	26	27	28	29	1	2	Fri 11h24m15p	MONTH 10 Yǐ-Wèi	25	26	27	28	29	1	2	Lì dōng		23	24	25	26	27	28	29	
	10	11	12	13	14	◐	16	5:05	46	2479252		3	4	5	6	7	8	9			3	4	5	6	7	8	9		ATHŌR 1792	30	1	2	3	4	5	6	HEDĀR 2068
	17	18	19	20	21	○	23	14:19	47	2479259		10	11	12	13	14	15	16			10	11	12	13	14	15	16	Xiǎo xuě		7	8	9	10	11	12	13	
	24	25	26	27	28	29	◑	19:21	48	2479266		17	18	19	20	21	22	23			17	18	19	20	21	22*	23			14	15	16	17	18	19	20	
DECEMBER 2075	1	2	3	4	5	6	●	23:02	49	2479273		24	25[e]	26[e]	27[e]	28[e]	29[d,e]	30[e]			24	25	26	27	28	29	30	Dà xuě		21	22	23	24	25	26	27	
	8	9	10	11	12	13	◐	14:36	50	2479280	TEVETH 5836	1[e]	2[e]	3	4	5	6	7	Sun 0h8m16p	MONTH 11 Yǐ-Wèi	1	2	3	4	5	6	7		KOIAK 1792	28	29	30	1	2	3	4	TĀKHŚĀŚ 2068
	15	16	17	18	19	20	21[e]		51	2479287		8	9	10	11	12	13	14			8	9	10	11	12	13	14			5	6	7	8	9	10	11	
	○	23	24	25	26	27	28	8:46	52	2479294		15	16	17	18	19	20	21			15[i]	16	17	18	19	20	21	Dōng zhì		12	13	14	15	16	17	18	
	29	◑	31	1	2	3	4	13:19	1	2479301		22	23	24	25	26	27	28			22	23	24	25	26	27	28			19	20	21	22	23	24	25	

[a]New Year
[b]Spring (11:45)
[c]Summer (4:38)
[d]Autumn (20:57)
[e]Winter (18:25)
● New moon
◐ First quarter moon
○ Full moon
◑ Last quarter moon

‡Leap year
[a]New Year
[b]Yom Kippur
[c]Sukkot
[d]Winter starts
[e]Ḥanukkah
[f]Purim
[g]Passover
[h]Shavuot
[i]Fast of Av

‡Leap year
[a]New Year (4773, Sheep)
[b]Lantern Festival
[c]Qīngmíng
[d]Dragon Festival
[e]Qīqiǎo
[f]Hungry Ghosts
[g]Mid-Autumn Festival
[h]Double-Ninth Festival
[i]Dōngzhì
*Start of 60-name cycle

‡Leap year
[a]New Year
[b]Building of the Cross
[c]Christmas
[d]Jesus's Circumcision
[e]Epiphany
[f]Easter
[g]Mary's Announcement
[h]Jesus's Transfiguration

PERSIAN (ASTRONOMICAL) 1453‡/1454

Month	Sun	Mon	Tue	Wed	Thu	Fri	Sat
DEY 1453	10	11	12	13	14	15	16
	17	18	19	20	21	22	23
	24	25	26	27	28	29	30
BAHMAN 1453	1	2	3	4	5	6	7
	8	9	10	11	12	13	14
	15	16	17	18	19	20	21
	22	23	24	25	26	27	28
ESFAND 1453	29	30	1	2	3	4	5
	6	7	8	9	10	11	12
	13	14	15	16	17	18	19
	20	21	22	23	24	25	26
FARVARDĪN 1454	27	28	29	30	1[a]	2	3
	4	5	6	7	8	9	10
	11	12	13[b]	14	15	16	17
	18	19	20	21	22	23	24
	25	26	27	28	29	30	31
ORDĪBEHEŠT 1454	1	2	3	4	5	6	7
	8	9	10	11	12	13	14
	15	16	17	18	19	20	21
	22	23	24	25	26	27	28
XORDĀD 1454	29	30	31	1	2	3	4
	5	6	7	8	9	10	11
	12	13	14	15	16	17	18
	19	20	21	22	23	24	25
TĪR 1454	26	27	28	29	30	31	1
	2	3	4	5	6	7	8
	9	10	11	12	13	14	15
	16	17	18	19	20	21	22
	23	24	25	26	27	28	29
MORDĀD 1454	30	31	1	2	3	4	5
	6	7	8	9	10	11	12
	13	14	15	16	17	18	19
	20	21	22	23	24	25	26
SHAHRĪVAR 1454	27	28	29	30	31	1	2
	3	4	5	6	7	8	9
	10	11	12	13	14	15	16
	17	18	19	20	21	22	23
	24	25	26	27	28	29	30
MEHR 1454	31	1	2	3	4	5	6
	7	8	9	10	11	12	13
	14	15	16	17	18	19	20
	21	22	23	24	25	26	27
ĀBĀN 1454	28	29	30	1	2	3	4
	5	6	7	8	9	10	11
	12	13	14	15	16	17	18
	19	20	21	22	23	24	25
ĀZAR 1454	26	27	28	29	30	1	2
	3	4	5	6	7	8	9
	10	11	12	13	14	15	16
	17	18	19	20	21	22	23
	24	25	26	27	28	29	30
DEY 1454	1	2	3	4	5	6	7
	8	9	10	11	12	13	14

‡Leap year
[a]New Year
[b]Sizdeh Bedar

HINDU LUNAR 2131/2132‡

Month	Sun	Mon	Tue	Wed	Thu	Fri	Sat
PAUSHA 2131	12	13	14	15	16	17	18
	19	20	21	22	23	24	25
MĀGHA 2131	26	27	29	30	1	2	3
	4	5	6	7	8	9	10
	11	12	13	14	14	15	16
	17	18	19	20	22	23	24
PHĀLGUNA 2131	25	26	27	28[h]	29	30	1
	2	3	4	5	6	7	8
	9	10	11	12	13	14	15[i]
	16	17	18	19	20	21	22
	23	24	25	27	28	29	30
CHAITRA 2132	1[a]	2	3	4	5	6	7
	7	8[b]	9	10	11	12	13
	14	15	16	17	18	19	21
	22	23	24	25	26	27	28
LEAP VAIŚĀKHA 2132	29	30	1	2	3	4	5
	6	7	8	9	10	11	12
	13	14	15	16	17	18	19
	20	21	22	23	25	26	27
VAIŚĀKHA 2132	28	29	30	1	2	2	3
	4	5	6	7	8	9	10
	11	12	13	14	15	16	18
	19	20	21	22	23	24	25
JYAISHṬHA 2132	26	27	28	29	30	1	2
	3	4	5	6	7	8	9
	10	11	12	13	14	15	16
	17	18	19	21	22	23	24
	25	26	27	28	28	29	30
ĀSHĀḌHA 2132	1	2	3	4	5	6	7
	8	9	10	11	13	14	15
	16	17	18	19	20	21	22
	23	24	25	26	27	28	29
ŚRĀVAṆA 2132	30	1	2	3	4	5	6
	7	8	9	10	11	12	13
	14	16	17	18	19	20	21
	22	23[c]	24	25	25	26	27
BHĀDRAPADA 2132	28	29	30	1	2	3	4[d]
	5	6	7	8	10	11	12
	13	14	15	16	17	18	19
	20	21	22	23	24	25	26
ĀŚVINA 2132	27	28	29	30	1	2	3
	4	5	6	7	8[e]	9[e]	10[e]
	11	12	14	15	16	17	18
	19	19	20	21	22	23	24
KĀRTTIKA 2132	25	26	27	28	29	30	1[f]
	2	3	4	5	7	8	9
	10	11	12	13	14	15	16
	17	18	19	20	21	22	22
	23	24	25	26	27	28	29
MĀRGAŚIRA 2132	1	2	3	4	5	6	7
	8	9	10	11[g]	12	13	14
	15	16	17	18	19	20	21
	22	23	24	25	26	27	28

‡Leap year
[a]New Year (Manmatha)
[b]Birthday of Rāma
[c]Birthday of Krishna
[d]Ganēśa Chaturthī
[e]Dashara
[f]Diwali
[g]Birthday of Vishnu
[h]Night of Śiva
[i]Holi

HINDU SOLAR 1996/1997‡

Month	Sun	Mon	Tue	Wed	Thu	Fri	Sat
PAUSHA 1996	15	16	17	18	19	20	21
	22	23	24	25	26	27	28
MĀGHA 1996	29	30	1[b]	2	3	4	5
	6	7	8	9	10	11	12
	13	14	15	16	17	18	19
	20	21	22	23	24	25	26
PHĀLGUNA 1996	27	28	29	1	2	3	4
	5	6	7	8	9	10	11
	12	13	14	15	16	17	18
	19	20	21	22	23	24	25
CHAITRA 1996	26	27	28	29	30	1	2
	3	4	5	6	7	8	9
	10	11	12	13	14	15	16
	17	18	19	20	21	22	23
	24	25	26	27	28	29	30
VAIŚĀKHA 1997	1[a]	2	3	4	5	6	7
	8	9	10	11	12	13	14
	15	16	17	18	19	20	21
	22	23	24	25	26	27	28
JYAISHṬHA 1997	29	30	31	1	2	3	4
	5	6	7	8	9	10	11
	12	13	14	15	16	17	18
	19	20	21	22	23	24	25
	26	27	28	29	30	31	32
ĀSHĀḌHA 1997	1	2	3	4	5	6	7
	8	9	10	11	12	13	14
	15	16	17	18	19	20	21
	22	23	24	25	26	27	28
ŚRĀVAṆA 1997	29	30	31	1	2	3	4
	5	6	7	8	9	10	11
	12	13	14	15	16	17	18
	19	20	21	22	23	24	25
	26	27	28	29	30	31	32
BHĀDRAPADA 1997	1	2	3	4	5	6	7
	8	9	10	11	12	13	14
	15	16	17	18	19	20	21
	22	23	24	25	26	27	28
ĀŚVINA 1997	29	30	31	1	2	3	4
	5	6	7	8	9	10	11
	12	13	14	15	16	17	18
	19	20	21	22	23	24	25
KĀRTTIKA 1997	26	27	28	29	30	1	2
	3	4	5	6	7	8	9
	10	11	12	13	14	15	16
	17	18	19	20	21	22	23
	24	25	26	27	28	29	30
MĀRGAŚIRA 1997	1	2	3	4	5	6	7
	8	9	10	11	12	13	14
	15	16	17	18	19	20	21
	22	23	24	25	26	27	28
PAUSHA 1997	29	30	1	2	3	4	5
	6	7	8	9	10	11	12
	13	14	15	16	17	18	19

‡Leap year
[a]New Year (Saumya)
[b]Pongal

ISLAMIC (ASTRONOMICAL) 1498/1499‡

Month	Sun	Mon	Tue	Wed	Thu	Fri	Sat
MUḤARRAM 1498	11	12	13	14	15	16	17
	18	19	20	21	22	23	24
ṢAFAR 1498	25	26	27	28	29	1	2
	3	4	5	6	7	8	9
	10	11	12	13	14	15	16
	17	18	19	20	21	22	23
RABĪ' I 1498	24	25	26	27	28	29	1
	2	3	4	5	6	7	8
	9	10	11	12[c]	13	14	15
	16	17	18	19	20	21	22
	23	24	25	26	27	28	29
RABĪ' II 1498	30	1	2	3	4	5	6
	7	8	9	10	11	12	13
	14	15	16	17	18	19	20
	21	22	23	24	25	26	27
JUMĀDĀ I 1498	28	29	30	1	2	3	4
	5	6	7	8	9	10	11
	12	13	14	15	16	17	18
	19	20	21	22	23	24	25
JUMĀDĀ II 1498	26	27	28	29	1	2	3
	4	5	6	7	8	9	10
	11	12	13	14	15	16	17
	18	19	20	21	22	23	24
RAJAB 1498	25	26	27	28	29	30	1
	2	3	4	5	6	7	8
	9	10	11	12	13	14	15
	16	17	18	19	20	21	22
	23	24	25	26	27[d]	28	29
SHA'BĀN 1498	30	1	2	3	4	5	6
	7	8	9	10	11	12	13
	14	15	16	17	18	19	20
	21	22	23	24	25	26	27
RAMAḌĀN 1498	28	29	1[e]	2	3	4	5
	6	7	8	9	10	11	12
	13	14	15	16	17	18	19
	20	21	22	23	24	25	26
SHAWWĀL 1498	27	28	29	30	1[f]	2	3
	4	5	6	7	8	9	10
	11	12	13	14	15	16	17
	18	19	20	21	22	23	24
DHU AL-QA'DA 1498	25	26	27	28	29	1	2
	3	4	5	6	7	8	9
	10	11	12	13	14	15	16
	17	18	19	20	21	22	23
	24	25	26	27	28	29	30
DHU AL-ḤIJJA 1498	1	2	3	4	5	6	7
	8	9	10[g]	11	12	13	14
	15	16	17	18	19	20	21
	22	23	24	25	26	27	28
MUḤARRAM 1499	29	1[a]	2	3	4	5	6
	7	8	9	10[b]	11	12	13
	14	15	16	17	18	19	20
	21	22	23	24	25	26	27

‡Leap year
[a]New Year
[b]'Ashūrā'
[c]Prophet's Birthday
[d]Ascent of the Prophet
[e]Start of Ramaḍān
[f]'Id al-Fiṭr
[g]'Id al-'Aḍḥā

GREGORIAN 2075

Julian (Sun)	Sun	Mon	Tue	Wed	Thu	Fri	Sat	Month
Dec 17	30	31	1	2	3	4	5	JANUARY 2075
	6	7[a]	8	9	10	11	12	
Dec 31	13	14[b]	15	16	17	18	19	
	20	21	22	23	24	25	26	
Jan 14	27	28	29	30	31	1	2	FEBRUARY 2075
	3	4	5	6	7	8	9	
Jan 28	10	11	12	13	14	15	16	
	17	18	19	20[c]	21	22	23	
Feb 11	24[d]	25	26	27	28	1	2	MARCH 2075
	3	4	5	6	7	8	9	
Feb 25	10	11	12	13	14	15	16	
	17	18	19	20	21	22	23	
Mar 11	24	25	26	27	28	29	30	
	31	1	2	3	4	5	6	APRIL 2075
Mar 25	7[e]	8	9	10	11	12	13	
	14	15	16	17	18	19	20	
Apr 8	21	22	23	24	25	26	27	
	28	29	30	1	2	3	4	MAY 2075
Apr 22	5	6	7	8	9	10	11	
	12	13	14	15	16	17	18	
May 6	19	20	21	22	23	24	25	
	26	27	28	29	30	31	1	JUNE 2075
May 20	2	3	4	5	6	7	8	
	9	10	11	12	13	14	15	
Jun 3	16	17	18	19	20	21	22	
	23	24	25	26	27	28	29	
Jun 17	30	1	2	3	4	5	6	JULY 2075
	7	8	9	10	11	12	13	
Jul 1	14	15	16	17	18	19	20	
	21	22	23	24	25	26	27	
Jul 15	28	29	30	31	1	2	3	AUGUST 2075
	4	5	6	7	8	9	10	
Jul 29	11	12	13	14	15	16	17	
	18	19	20	21	22	23	24	
Aug 12	25	26	27	28	29	30	31	
	1	2	3	4	5	6	7	SEPTEMBER 2075
Aug 26	8	9	10	11	12	13	14	
	15	16	17	18	19	20	21	
Sep 9	22	23	24	25	26	27	28	
	29	30	1	2	3	4	5	OCTOBER 2075
Sep 23	6	7	8	9	10	11	12	
	13	14	15	16	17	18	19	
Oct 7	20	21	22	23	24	25	26	
	27	28	29	30	31	1	2	NOVEMBER 2075
Oct 21	3	4	5	6	7	8	9	
	10	11	12	13	14	15	16	
Nov 4	17	18	19	20	21	22	23	
	24	25	26	27	28	29	30	
Nov 18	1[g]	2	3	4	5	6	7	DECEMBER 2075
	8	9	10	11	12	13	14	
Dec 2	15	16	17	18	19	20	21	
	22	23	24	25[h]	26	27	28	
Dec 16	29	30	31	1	2	3	4	

[a]Orthodox Christmas
[b]Julian New Year
[c]Ash Wednesday
[d]Feast of Orthodoxy
[e]Easter (also Orthodox)
[g]Advent
[h]Christmas

2076

GREGORIAN 2076‡	Sun	Mon	Tue	Wed	Thu	Fri	Sat	Lunar Phases	ISO WEEK (Mon)	JULIAN DAY (Sun noon)	HEBREW 5836‡/5837	Sun	Mon	Tue	Wed	Thu	Fri	Sat	Molad	CHINESE Yǐ-Wèi/Bǐng-Shēn	Sun	Mon	Tue	Wed	Thu	Fri	Sat	Solar Term	COPTIC 1792/1793	Sun	Mon	Tue	Wed	Thu	Fri	Sat	ETHIOPIC 2068/2069
JANUARY 2076	29	◑	31	1[a]	2	3	4	13:19	1	2479301	TEVETH 5836	22	23	24	25	26	27	28		MONTH 11 Yǐ-Wèi	22	23	24	25	26	27	28		KOIAK 1792	19	20	21	22	23	24	25	TĀKHŚĀŚ 2068
	5	●	7	8	9	10	11	10:13	2	2479308	SHEVAT 5836	29	1	2	3	4	5	6	Mon 12h52m17p	MONTH 12 Yǐ-Wèi	29	1	2	3	4	5	6	Xiǎo hán	TŌBE 1792	26	27	28	29[c]	30	1	2	ṬER 2068
	12	◐	14	15	16	17	18	3:01	3	2479315		7	8	9	10	11	12	13			7	8	9	10	11	12	13			3	4	5	6[d]	7	8	9	
	19	20	○	22	23	24	25	4:38	4	2479322		14	15	16	17	18	19	20			14	15	16	17	18	19	20	Dà hán		10	11[e]	12	13	14	15	16	
FEBRUARY 2076	26	27	28	◑	30	31	1	4:16	5	2479329		21	22	23	24	25	26	27			21	22	23*	24	25	26	27			17	18	19	20	21	22	23	
	2	3	●	5	6	7	8	21:00	6	2479336	ADAR I 5836	28	29	30	1	2	3	4	Wed 1h37m0p	MONTH 1 Bǐng-Shēn	28	29	30	1[a]	2	3	4	Lì chūn		24	25	26	27	28	29	30	
	9	10	◐	12	13	14	15	18:34	7	2479343		5	6	7	8	9	10	11			5	6	7	8	9	10	11		MESHIR 1792	1	2	3	4	5	6	7	YAKĀTIT 2068
	16	17	18	○	20	21	22	23:48	8	2479350		12	13	14	15	16	17	18			12	13	14	15[b]	16	17	18	Yǔ shuǐ		8	9	10	11	12	13	14	
	23	24	25	26	◑	28	29	15:53	9	2479357		19	20	21	22	23	24	25			19	20	21	22	23	24	25			15	16	17	18	19	20	21	
MARCH 2076	1	2	3	4	●	6	7	7:23	10	2479364	ADAR II 5836	26	27	28	29	30	1	2	Thu 14h21m1p	MONTH 2 Bǐng-Shēn	26	27	28	29	1	2	3	Jīng zhé		22	23	24	25	26	27	28	
	8	9	10	11	◐	13	14	12:40	11	2479371		3	4	5	6	7	8	9			4	5	6	7	8	9	10		PAREMOTEP 1792	29	30	1	2	3	4	5	MAGĀBIT 2068
	15	16	17	18	19[b]	○	21	16:36	12	2479378		10	11	12	13	14[f]	15	16			11	12	13	14	15	16	17	Chūn fēn		6	7	8	9	10	11	12	
	22	23	24	25	26	27	◑	0:24	13	2479385		17	18	19	20	21	22	23			18	19	20	21	22	23	24*			13	14	15	16	17	18	19	
APRIL 2076	29	30	31	1	2	●	4	17:46	14	2479392	NISAN 5836	24	25	26	27	28	29	1	Sat 3h5m2p	MONTH 3 Bǐng-Shēn	25	26	27	28	29	30	1[c]	Qīng míng		20	21	22	23	24	25	26	
	5	6	7	8	9	10	◐	7:58	15	2479399		2	3	4	5	6	7	8			2	3	4	5	6	7	8		PARMOUTE 1792	27	28	29	30	1	2	3	MIYĀZYĀ 2068
	12	13	14	15	16	17	18		16	2479406		9	10	11	12	13	14	15[g]			9	10	11	12	13	14	15			4	5	6	7	8	9	10	
	○	20	21	22	23	24	25	6:28	17	2479413		16	17	18	19	20	21	22			16	17	18	19	20	21	22	Gǔ yǔ		11	12	13	14	15	16	17	
MAY 2076	◑	27	28	29	30	1	2	6:39	18	2479420		23	24	25	26	27	28	29			23	24	25	26	27	28	29			18[f]	19	20	21	22	23	24	
	●	4	5	6	7	8	9	4:50	19	2479427	IYAR 5836	30	1	2	3	4	5	6	Sun 15h49m3p	MONTH 4 Bǐng-Shēn	1	2	3	4	5	6	7	Lì xià	PASHONS 1792	25	26	27	28	29[g]	30	1	GENBOT 2068
	10	◐	12	13	14	15	16	2:49	20	2479434		7	8	9	10	11	12	13			8	9	10	11	12	13	14			2	3	4	5	6	7	8	
	17	○	19	20	21	22	23	17:37	21	2479441		14	15	16	17	18	19	20			15	16	17	18	19	20	21	Xiǎo mǎn		9	10	11	12	13	14	15	
	24	◑	26	27	28	29	30	11:50	22	2479448		21	22	23	24	25	26	27			22	23	24	25*	26	27	28			16	17	18	19	20	21	22	
JUNE 2076	31	●	2	3	4	5	6	17:12	23	2479455	SIVAN 5836	28	29	1	2	3	4	5	Tue 4h33m4p	MONTH 5 Bǐng-Shēn	29	30	1	2	3	4	5[d]	Máng zhòng		23	24	25	26	27	28	29	
	7	8	◐	10	11	12	13	19:57	24	2479462		6[h]	7	8	9	10	11	12			6	7	8	9	10	11	12		PAŌNE 1792	30	1	2	3	4	5	6	SANĒ 2068
	14	15	16	○	18	19	20[c]	2:37	25	2479469		13	14	15	16	17	18	19			13	14	15	16	17	18	19	Xià zhì		7	8	9	10	11	12	13	
	21	22	◑	24	25	26	27	17:20	26	2479476		20	21	22	23	24	25	26			20	21	22	23	24	25	26			14	15	16	17	18	19	20	
JULY 2076	28	29	30	●	2	3	4	7:03	27	2479483	TAMMUZ 5836	27	28	29	30	1	2	3	Wed 17h17m5p	MONTH 6 Bǐng-Shēn	27	28	29	1	2	3	4			21	22	23	24	25	26	27	
	5	6	7	8	◐	10	11	10:48	28	2479490		4	5	6	7	8	9	10			5	6	7	8	9	10	11	Xiǎo shǔ	EPĒP 1792	28	29	30	1	2	3	4	HAMLĒ 2068
	12	13	14	15	○	17	18	10:11	29	2479497		11	12	13	14	15	16	17			12	13	14	15	16	17	18			5	6	7	8	9	10	11	
	19	20	21	22	◑	24	25	0:38	30	2479504		18	19	20	21	22	23	24			19	20	21	22	23	24	25	Dà shǔ		12	13	14	15	16	17	18	
AUGUST 2076	26	27	28	29	●	31	1	22:04	31	2479511	AV 5836	25	26	27	28	29	1	2	Fri 6h1m6p	MONTH 7 Bǐng-Shēn	26*	27	28	29	30	1	2			19	20	21	22	23	24	25	
	2	3	4	5	6	◐	8	23:20	32	2479518		3	4	5	6	7	8	9			3	4	5	6	7[e]	8	9	Lì qiū	MESORĒ 1792	26	27	28	29	30	1	2	NAHASĒ 2068
	9	10	11	12	13	○	15	17:11	33	2479525		10[i]	11	12	13	14	15	16			10	11	12	13	14	15[f]	16			3	4	5	6	7	8	9	
	16	17	18	19	20	◑	22	10:59	34	2479532		17	18	19	20	21	22	23			17	18	19	20	21	22	23	Chǔ shǔ		10	11	12	13[h]	14	15	16	
	23	24	25	26	27	28	●	13:42	35	2479539		24	25	26	27	28	29	30		MONTH 8 Bǐng-Shēn	24	25	26	27	28	29	1			17	18	19	20	21	22	23	
SEPTEMBER 2076	30	31	1	2	3	4	5		36	2479546	ELUL 5836	1	2	3	4	5	6	7	Sat 18h45m7p		2	3	4	5	6	7	8			24	25	26	27	28	29	30	
	◐	7	8	9	10	11	12	9:45	37	2479553		8	9	10	11	12	13	14			9	10	11	12	13	14	15[g]	Bái lù	EPAG. 1792 / THOOUT 1793	1	2	3	4	5	1[a]	2	PĀG. 2068 / MASKARAM 2069
	○	14	15	16	17	18	19	0:37	38	2479560		15	16	17	18	19	20	21			16	17	18	19	20	21	22			3	4	5	6	7	8	9	
	◑	21	22[d]	23	24	25	26	1:05	39	2479567		22	23	24	25	26	27	28			23	24	25	26	27*	28	29	Qiū fēn		10	11	12	13	14	15	16	
OCTOBER 2076	27	●	29	30	1	2	3	5:26	40	2479574	TISHRI 5837	29	1[a]	2[a]	3	4	5	6	Mon 7h29m8p	MONTH 9 Bǐng-Shēn	30	1	2	3	4	5	6			17[b]	18	19	20	21	22	23	
	4	◐	6	7	8	9	10	18:25	41	2479581		7	8	9	10[b]	11	12	13			7	8	9[h]	10	11	12	13	Hán lù		24	25	26	27	28	29	30	
	11	○	13	14	15	16	17	9:36	42	2479588		14	15[c]	16	17	18	19	20			14	15	16	17	18	19	20		PAOPE 1793	1	2	3	4	5	6	7	ṬEQEMT 2069
	18	◑	20	21	22	23	24	18:49	43	2479595		21	22	23	24	25	26	27			21	22	23	24	25	26	27	Shuāng jiàng		8	9	10	11	12	13	14	
	25	26	●	28	29	30	31	20:49	44	2479602	HESHVAN 5837	28	29	30	1	2	3	4	Tue 20h13m9p	MONTH 10 Bǐng-Shēn	28	29	30	1	2	3	4			15	16	17	18	19	20	21	
NOVEMBER 2076	1	2	3	◐	5	6	7	1:56	45	2479609		5	6	7	8	9	10	11			5	6	7	8	9	10	11	Lì dōng		22	23	24	25	26	27	28	
	8	9	○	11	12	13	14	21:06	46	2479616		12	13	14	15	16	17	18			12	13	14	15	16	17	18		ATHŌR 1793	29	30	1	2	3	4	5	HEDĀR 2069
	15	16	17	◑	19	20	21	15:14	47	2479623		19	20	21	22	23	24	25			19	20	21	22	23	24	25	Xiǎo xuě		6	7	8	9	10	11	12	
	22	23	24	25	●	27	28	11:27	48	2479630	KISLEV 5837	26	27	28	29	30	1	2	Thu 8h57m10p	MONTH 11 Bǐng-Shēn	26	27*	28	29	1	2	3			13	14	15	16	17	18	19	
DECEMBER 2076	29	30	1	2	◐	4	5	9:14	49	2479637		3	4	5	6	7	8	9[d]			4	5	6	7	8	9	10			20	21	22	23	24	25	26	
	6	7	8	9	○	11	12	11:34	50	2479644		10	11	12	13	14	15	16			11	12	13	14	15	16	17	Dà xuě	KOIAK 1793	27	28	29	30	1	2	3	TĀKHŚĀŚ 2069
	13	14	15	16	17	◑	19	12:38	51	2479651		17	18	19	20	21	22	23			18	19	20	21	22	23	24			4	5	6	7	8	9	10	
	20	21[e]	22	23	24	25	●	0:52	52	2479658		24	25[e]	26[e]	27[e]	28[e]	29[e]	30[e]	Fri 21h41m11p	MONTH 12 Bǐng-Shēn	25	26[i]	27	28	29	30	1	Dōng zhì		11	12	13	14	15	16	17	
	27	28	29	30	31	◐	2	17:26	53	2479665		1[e]	2[e]	3	4	5	6	7			2	3	4	5	6	7	8			18	19	20	21	22	23	24	

‡Leap year
[a]New Year
[b]Spring (17:37)
[c]Summer (10:35)
[d]Autumn (2:48)
[e]Winter (0:12)
● New moon
◐ First quarter moon
○ Full moon
◑ Last quarter moon

‡Leap year
[a]New Year
[b]Yom Kippur
[c]Sukkot
[d]Winter starts
[e]Ḥanukkah
[f]Purim
[g]Passover
[h]Shavuot
[i]Fast of Av

[a]New Year (4774, Monkey)
[b]Lantern Festival
[c]Qīngmíng
[d]Dragon Festival
[e]Qǐqiǎo
[f]Hungry Ghosts
[g]Mid-Autumn Festival
[h]Double-Ninth Festival
[i]Dōngzhì
*Start of 60-name cycle

[a]New Year
[b]Building of the Cross
[c]Christmas
[d]Jesus's Circumcision
[e]Epiphany
[f]Easter
[g]Mary's Announcement
[h]Jesus's Transfiguration

2076

PERSIAN (ASTRONOMICAL) 1454/1455

Month	Sun	Mon	Tue	Wed	Thu	Fri	Sat
DEY 1454	8	9	10	11	12	13	14
	15	16	17	18	19	20	21
	22	23	24	25	26	27	28
	29	30	1	2	3	4	5
BAHMAN 1454	6	7	8	9	10	11	12
	13	14	15	16	17	18	19
	20	21	22	23	24	25	26
	27	28	29	30	1	2	3
ESFAND 1454	4	5	6	7	8	9	10
	11	12	13	14	15	16	17
	18	19	20	21	22	23	24
	25	26	27	28	29	1[a]	2
FARVARDĪN 1455	3	4	5	6	7	8	9
	10	11	12	13[b]	14	15	16
	17	18	19	20	21	22	23
	24	25	26	27	28	29	30
	31	1	2	3	4	5	6
ORDĪBEHEŠT 1455	7	8	9	10	11	12	13
	14	15	16	17	18	19	20
	21	22	23	24	25	26	27
	28	29	30	31	1	2	3
XORDĀD 1455	4	5	6	7	8	9	10
	11	12	13	14	15	16	17
	18	19	20	21	22	23	24
	25	26	27	28	29	30	31
TĪR 1455	1	2	3	4	5	6	7
	8	9	10	11	12	13	14
	15	16	17	18	19	20	21
	22	23	24	25	26	27	28
	29	30	31	1	2	3	4
MORDĀD 1455	5	6	7	8	9	10	11
	12	13	14	15	16	17	18
	19	20	21	22	23	24	25
	26	27	28	29	30	31	1
SHAHRĪVAR 1455	2	3	4	5	6	7	8
	9	10	11	12	13	14	15
	16	17	18	19	20	21	22
	23	24	25	26	27	28	29
	30	31	1	2	3	4	5
MEHR 1455	6	7	8	9	10	11	12
	13	14	15	16	17	18	19
	20	21	22	23	24	25	26
	27	28	29	30	1	2	3
ĀBĀN 1455	4	5	6	7	8	9	10
	11	12	13	14	15	16	17
	18	19	20	21	22	23	24
	25	26	27	28	29	30	1
ĀZAR 1455	2	3	4	5	6	7	8
	9	10	11	12	13	14	15
	16	17	18	19	20	21	22
	23	24	25	26	27	28	29
DEY 1455	30	1	2	3	4	5	6
	7	8	9	10	11	12	13

HINDU LUNAR 2132‡/2133

Month	Sun	Mon	Tue	Wed	Thu	Fri	Sat
MĀRGAŚĪRA 2132	22	23	24	25	26	27	28
	29	30	1	2	**3**	5	6
PAUSHA 2132	7	8	9	10	11	12	13
	14	15	*15*	16	17	18	19
	20	21	22	23	24	25	26
	27	**28**	30	1	2	3	4
MĀGHA 2132	5	6	7	8	9	10	11
	12	13	14	15	16	17	*17*
	18	19	20	**21**	23	24	25
	26	27	28[h]	29	30	1	2
PHĀLGUNA 2132	3	4	5	6	7	8	9
	10	11	12	13	14	15[i]	16
	17	18	19	20	21	22	23
	24	25	**26**	28	29	30	1[a]
CHAITRA 2133	2	3	4	5	6	7	8
	9[b]	10	*10*	11	12	13	14
	15	16	17	18	19	**20**	22
	23	24	25	26	27	28	29
	30	1	2	3	4	5	6
VAIŚĀKHA 2133	7	8	9	10	11	12	13
	14	15	16	17	18	19	20
	21	22	**23**	25	26	27	28
	29	30	1	2	3	4	5
JYAISHTHA 2133	6	*6*	7	8	9	10	11
	12	13	14	15	**16**	18	19
	20	21	22	23	24	25	26
	27	28	29	30	1	2	3
ĀSHĀDHA 2133	4	5	6	7	8	9	10
	11	12	13	14	15	16	17
	18	**19**	21	22	23	24	25
	26	27	28	29	30	1	2
ŚRĀVAṆA 2133	3	*3*	4	5	6	7	8
	9	10	**11**	13	14	15	16
	17	18	19	20	21	22	23[c]
	24	25	26	27	28	29	30
BHĀDRAPADA 2133	1	2	3	4[d]	5	6	7
	8	9	10	11	12	13	14
	15	17	18	19	20	21	22
	23	24	25	26	27	28	*28*
	29	30	1	2	3	4	5
ĀŚVINA 2133	6	7	**8**[e]	10[e]	11	12	13
	14	15	16	17	18	19	20
	21	22	23	24	25	26	27
	28	29	30	1[f]	2	3	4
KĀRTTIKA 2133	5	6	7	8	9	10	11
	12	14	15	16	17	18	19
	20	21	22	23	*23*	24	25
	26	27	28	29	30	1	2
MĀRGAŚĪRA 2133	3	4	5	**6**	8	9	10
	11[g]	12	13	14	15	16	17
	18	19	20	21	22	23	24
PAUSHA 2133	25	*25*	26	27	28	**29**	1
	2	3	4	5	6	7	8

HINDU SOLAR 1997‡/1998

Month	Sun	Mon	Tue	Wed	Thu	Fri	Sat
PAUSHA 1997	13	14	15	16	17	18	19
	20	21	22	23	24	25	26
	27	28	29	1[b]	2	3	4
MĀGHA 1997	5	6	7	8	9	10	11
	12	13	14	15	16	17	18
	19	20	21	22	23	24	25
	26	27	28	29	1	2	3
PHĀLGUNA 1997	4	5	6	7	8	9	10
	11	12	13	14	15	16	17
	18	19	20	21	22	23	24
	25	26	27	28	29	30	1
CHAITRA 1997	2	3	4	5	6	7	8
	9	10	11	12	13	14	15
	16	17	18	19	20	21	22
	23	24	25	26	27	28	29
	30	31	1[a]	2	3	4	5
VAIŚĀKHA 1998	6	7	8	9	10	11	12
	13	14	15	16	17	18	19
	20	21	22	23	24	25	26
	27	28	29	30	31	1	2
JYAISHTHA 1998	3	4	5	6	7	8	9
	10	11	12	13	14	15	16
	17	18	19	20	21	22	23
	24	25	26	27	28	29	30
	31	1	2	3	4	5	6
ĀSHĀDHA 1998	7	8	9	10	11	12	13
	14	15	16	17	18	19	20
	21	22	23	24	25	26	27
	28	29	30	31	32	1	2
ŚRĀVAṆA 1998	3	4	5	6	7	8	9
	10	11	12	13	14	15	16
	17	18	19	20	21	22	23
	24	25	26	27	28	29	30
	31	1	2	3	4	5	6
BHĀDRAPADA 1998	7	8	9	10	11	12	13
	14	15	16	17	18	19	20
	21	22	23	24	25	26	27
	28	29	30	31	1	2	3
ĀŚVINA 1998	4	5	6	7	8	9	10
	11	12	13	14	15	16	17
	18	19	20	21	22	23	24
	25	26	27	28	29	30	31
KĀRTTIKA 1998	1	2	3	4	5	6	7
	8	9	10	11	12	13	14
	15	16	17	18	19	20	21
	22	23	24	25	26	27	28
	29	1	2	3	4	5	6
MĀRGAŚĪRA 1998	7	8	9	10	11	12	13
	14	15	16	17	18	19	20
	21	22	23	24	25	26	27
	28	29	30	1	2	3	4
PAUSHA 1998	5	6	7	8	9	10	11
	12	13	14	15	16	17	18

ISLAMIC (ASTRONOMICAL) 1499‡/1500

Month	Sun	Mon	Tue	Wed	Thu	Fri	Sat
MUHARRAM 1499	21	22	23	24	25	26	27
	28	29	30	1	2	3	4
ṢAFAR 1499	5	6	7	8	9	10	11
	12	13	14	15	16	17	18
	19	20	21	22	23	24	25
	26	27	28	29	1	2	3
RABĪ' I 1499	4	5	6	7	8	9	10
	11	12[c]	13	14	15	16	17
	18	19	20	21	22	23	24
	25	26	27	28	29	1	2
RABĪ' II 1499	3	4	5	6	7	8	9
	10	11	12	13	14	15	16
	17	18	19	20	21	22	23
	24	25	26	27	28	29	30
JUMĀDĀ I 1499	1	2	3	4	5	6	7
	8	9	10	11	12	13	14
	15	16	17	18	19	20	21
	22	23	24	25	26	27	28
	29	1	2	3	4	5	6
JUMĀDĀ II 1499	7	8	9	10	11	12	13
	14	15	16	17	18	19	20
	21	22	23	24	25	26	27
	28	29	30	1	2	3	4
RAJAB 1499	5	6	7	8	9	10	11
	12	13	14	15	16	17	18
	19	20	21	22	23	24	25
	26	27[d]	28	29	30	1	2
SHA'BĀN 1499	3	4	5	6	7	8	9
	10	11	12	13	14	15	16
	17	18	19	20	21	22	23
	24	25	26	27	28	29	1[e]
RAMAḌĀN 1499	2	3	4	5	6	7	8
	9	10	11	12	13	14	15
	16	17	18	19	20	21	22
	23	24	25	26	27	28	29
	30	1[f]	2	3	4	5	6
SHAWWĀL 1499	7	8	9	10	11	12	13
	14	15	16	17	18	19	20
	21	22	23	24	25	26	27
	28	29	1	2	3	4	5
DHU AL-QA'DA 1499	6	7	8	9	10	11	12
	13	14	15	16	17	18	19
	20	21	22	23	24	25	26
	27	28	29	30	1	2	3
DHU AL-ḤIJJA 1499	4	5	6	7	8	9	10[g]
	11	12	13	14	15	16	17
	18	19	20	21	22	23	24
	25	26	27	28	29	30	1[a]
MUHARRAM 1500	2	3	4	5	6	7	8
	9	10[b]	11	12	13	14	15
	16	17	18	19	20	21	22
	23	24	25	26	27	28	29
	1	2	3	4	5	6	7

GREGORIAN 2076‡

Julian‡ (Sun)	Sun	Mon	Tue	Wed	Thu	Fri	Sat	Month
Dec 16	29	30	31	1	2	3	4	JANUARY 2076
	5	6	7[a]	8	9	10	11	
Dec 30	12	13	14[b]	15	16	17	18	
	19	20	21	22	23	24	25	
Jan 13	26	27	28	29	30	31	1	FEBRUARY 2076
	2	3	4	5	6	7	8	
Jan 27	9	10	11	12	13	14	15	
	16	17	18	19	20	21	22	
Feb 10	23	24	25	26	27	28	29	
	1	2	3	4[c]	5	6	7	MARCH 2076
Feb 24	8	9	10	11	12	13	14	
	15[d]	16	17	18	19	20	21	
Mar 9	22	23	24	25	26	27	28	
	29	30	31	1	2	3	4	APRIL 2076
Mar 23	5	6	7	8	9	10	11	
	12	13	14	15	16	17	18	
Apr 6	19[e]	20	21	22	23	24	25	
	26[f]	27	28	29	30	1	2	MAY 2076
Apr 20	3	4	5	6	7	8	9	
	10	11	12	13	14	15	16	
May 4	17	18	19	20	21	22	23	
	24	25	26	27	28	29	30	
May 18	31	1	2	3	4	5	6	JUNE 2076
	7	8	9	10	11	12	13	
Jun 1	14	15	16	17	18	19	20	
	21	22	23	24	25	26	27	
Jun 15	28	29	30	1	2	3	4	JULY 2076
	5	6	7	8	9	10	11	
Jun 29	12	13	14	15	16	17	18	
	19	20	21	22	23	24	25	
Jul 13	26	27	28	29	30	31	1	AUGUST 2076
	2	3	4	5	6	7	8	
Jul 27	9	10	11	12	13	14	15	
	16	17	18	19	20	21	22	
Aug 10	23	24	25	26	27	28	29	
	30	31	1	2	3	4	5	SEPTEMBER 2076
Aug 24	6	7	8	9	10	11	12	
	13	14	15	16	17	18	19	
Sep 7	20	21	22	23	24	25	26	
	27	28	29	30	1	2	3	OCTOBER 2076
Sep 21	4	5	6	7	8	9	10	
	11	12	13	14	15	16	17	
Oct 5	18	19	20	21	22	23	24	
	25	26	27	28	29	30	31	
Oct 19	1	2	3	4	5	6	7	NOVEMBER 2076
	8	9	10	11	12	13	14	
Nov 2	15	16	17	18	19	20	21	
	22	23	24	25	26	27	28	
Nov 16	29[g]	30	1	2	3	4	5	DECEMBER 2076
	6	7	8	9	10	11	12	
Nov 30	13	14	15	16	17	18	19	
	20	21	22	23	24	25[h]	26	
Dec 14	27	28	29	30	31	1	2	

Persian:
[a]New Year
[b]Sizdeh Bedar

Hindu Lunar:
‡Leap year
[a]New Year (Durmukha)
[b]Birthday of Rāma
[c]Birthday of Krishna
[d]Ganēśa Chaturthī
[e]Dashara
[f]Diwali
[g]Birthday of Vishnu
[h]Night of Śiva
[i]Holi

Hindu Solar:
‡Leap year
[a]New Year (Sādhāraṇa)
[b]Pongal

Islamic:
‡Leap year
[a]New Year
[b]'Āshūrā'
[c]Prophet's Birthday
[d]Ascent of the Prophet
[e]Start of Ramaḍān
[f]'Id al-Fiṭr
[g]'Id al-'Aḍḥā

Gregorian:
‡Leap year
[a]Orthodox Christmas
[b]Julian New Year
[c]Ash Wednesday
[d]Feast of Orthodoxy
[e]Easter
[f]Orthodox Easter
[g]Advent
[h]Christmas

2077

Gregorian 2077 · ISO week · Julian day

Month	Sun	Mon	Tue	Wed	Thu	Fri	Sat	Lunar Phases	ISO WEEK (Mon)	JULIAN DAY (Sun noon)
	27	28	29	30	31	◐[a]	2	17:26	53	2479665
	3	4	5	6	7	8	○	4:36	1	2479672
JANUARY 2077	10	11	12	13	14	15	16		2	2479679
	◑	18	19	20	21	22	23	9:08	3	2479686
	●	25	26	27	28	29	30	12:44	4	2479693
	◐	1	2	3	4	5	6	3:34	5	2479700
	○	8	9	10	11	12	13	23:07	6	2479707
FEBRUARY 2077	14	15	◑	17	18	19	20	2:57	7	2479714
	21	●	23	24	25	26	27	23:05	8	2479721
	28	◐	2	3	4	5	6	16:09	9	2479728
	7	8	○	10	11	12	13	17:41	10	2479735
MARCH 2077	14	15	16	◑	18	19[b]	20	16:55	11	2479742
	21	22	23	●	25	26	27	8:23	12	2479749
	28	29	30	◐	1	2	3	7:01	13	2479756
	4	5	6	7	○	9	10	11:04	14	2479763
APRIL 2077	11	12	13	14	15	◑	17	2:49	15	2479770
	18	19	20	21	●	23	24	17:19	16	2479777
	25	26	27	28	◐	30	1	23:27	17	2479784
	2	3	4	5	6	7	○	2:22	18	2479791
MAY 2077	9	10	11	12	13	14	◑	9:25	19	2479798
	16	17	18	19	20	21	●	2:37	20	2479805
	23	24	25	26	27	28	◐	16:42	21	2479812
	30	31	1	2	3	4	5		22	2479819
	○	7	8	9	10	11	12	15:06	23	2479826
JUNE 2077	◑	14	15	16	17	18	19	14:07	24	2479833
	●[c]	21	22	23	24	25	26	12:54	25	2479840
	27	◐	29	30	1	2	3	10:04	26	2479847
	4	5	○	7	8	9	10	1:20	27	2479854
JULY 2077	11	◑	13	14	15	16	17	18:32	28	2479861
	18	19	●	21	22	23	24	0:40	29	2479868
	25	26	27	◐	29	30	31	2:54	30	2479875
	1	2	3	○	5	6	7	9:45	31	2479882
	8	9	10	◑	12	13	14	0:15	32	2479889
AUGUST 2077	15	16	17	●	19	20	21	14:16	33	2479896
	22	23	24	25	◐	27	28	18:29	34	2479903
	29	30	31	1	○	3	4	17:22	35	2479910
	5	6	7	8	◑	10	11	8:34	36	2479917
SEPTEMBER 2077	12	13	14	15	16	●	18	5:51	37	2479924
	19	20	21	22[d]	23	24	◐	8:14	38	2479931
	26	27	28	29	30	1	○	1:20	39	2479938
	3	4	5	6	7	◑	9	20:25	40	2479945
OCTOBER 2077	10	11	12	13	14	15	●	23:06	41	2479952
	17	18	19	20	21	22	23		42	2479959
	◐	25	26	27	28	29	30	19:50	43	2479966
	○	1	2	3	4	5	6	10:35	44	2479973
	◑	8	9	10	11	12	13	12:08	45	2479980
NOVEMBER 2077	14	●	16	17	18	19	20	16:59	46	2479987
	21	22	◐	24	25	26	27	5:30	47	2479994
	28	○	30	1	2	3	4	21:42	48	2480001
	5	6	◑	8	9	10	11	7:24	49	2480008
DECEMBER 2077	12	13	14	●	16	17	18	10:05	50	2480015
	19	20	21[e]	◐	23	24	25	13:54	51	2480022
	26	27	28	○	30	31	1	10:44	52	2480029

Hebrew 5837/5838

ISO WEEK	Month	Sun	Mon	Tue	Wed	Thu	Fri	Sat	Molad
53		1[e]	2[e]	3	4	5	6	7	
1		8	9	10	11	12	13	14	Fri 21h41m11p
2	TEVETH 5837	15	16	17	18	19	20	21	
3		22	23	24	25	26	27	28	
4		29	1	2	3	4	5	6	Sun 10h25m12p
5		7	8	9	10	11	12	13	
6	SHEVAT 5837	14	15	16	17	18	19	20	
7		21	22	23	24	25	26	27	
8		28	29	30	1	2	3	4	Mon 23h9m13p
9		5	6	7	8	9	10	11	
10	ADAR 5837	12	13	14[f]	15	16	17	18	
11		19	20	21	22	23	24	25	
12		26	27	28	29	1	2	3	Wed 11h53m14p
13		4	5	6	7	8	9	10	
14	NISAN 5837	11	12	13	14	15[g]	16	17	
15		18	19	20	21	22	23	24	
16		25	26	27	28	29	30	1	Fri 0h37m15p
17		2	3	4	5	6	7	8	
18	IYYAR 5837	9	10	11	12	13	14	15	
19		16	17	18	19	20	21	22	
20		23	24	25	26	27	28	29	
21		1	2	3	4	5	6[h]	7	Sat 13h21m16p
22		8	9	10	11	12	13	14	
23	SIVAN 5837	15	16	17	18	19	20	21	
24		22	23	24	25	26	27	28	
25		29	30	1	2	3	4	5	Mon 2h5m17p
26		6	7	8	9	10	11	12	
27	TAMMUZ 5837	13	14	15	16	17	18	19	
28		20	21	22	23	24	25	26	
29		27	28	29	1	2	3	4	Tue 14h50m0p
30		5	6	7	8	9[i]	10	11	
31	AV 5837	12	13	14	15	16	17	18	
32		19	20	21	22	23	24	25	
33		26	27	28	29	30	1	2	Thu 3h34m1p
34		3	4	5	6	7	8	9	
35	ELUL 5837	10	11	12	13	14	15	16	
36		17	18	19	20	21	22	23	
37		24	25	26	27	28	29	1[a]	Fri 16h18m2p
38		2[a]	3	4	5	6	7	8	
39	TISHRI 5838	9	10[b]	11	12	13	14	15[c]	
40		16	17	18	19	20	21	22	
41		23	24	25	26	27	28	29	
42		30	1	2	3	4	5	6	Sun 5h2m3p
43		7	8	9	10	11	12	13	
44	ḤESHVAN 5838	14	15	16	17	18	19	20	
45		21	22	23	24	25	26	27	
46		28	29	30	1	2	3	4	Mon 17h46m4p
47		5	6	7	8	9	10	11	
48	KISLEV 5838	12	13	14	15	16	17	18	
49		19[d]	20	21	22	23	24	25[e]	
50		26[e]	27[e]	28[e]	29[e]	30[e]	1[e]	2[e]	Wed 6h30m5p
51	TEVETH 5838	3	4	5	6	7	8	9	
52		10	11	12	13	14	15	16	

Chinese Bǐng-Shēn/Dīng-Yǒu‡

ISO WEEK	Month	Sun	Mon	Tue	Wed	Thu	Fri	Sat	Solar Term
53		2	3	4	5	6	7	8	
1	MONTH 12 Bǐng-Shēn	9	10	*11*	12	13	14	15	Xiǎo hán
2		16	17	18	19	20	21	22	
3		23	24	**25**	26	27	28*	29	Dà hán
4		1[a]	2	3	4	5	6	7	
5	MONTH 1 Dīng-Yǒu	8	9	10	*11*	12	13	14	Lì chūn
6		15[b]	16	17	18	19	20	21	
7		22	23	24	25	**26**	27	28	Yǔ shuǐ
8		29	30	1	2	3	4	5	
9	MONTH 2 Dīng-Yǒu	6	7	8	9	10	*11*	12	Jīng zhé
10		13	14	15	16	17	18	19	
11		20	21	22	23	24	25	**26**	Chūn fēn
12		27	28	29*	1	2	3	4	
13	MONTH 3 Dīng-Yǒu	5	6	7	8	9	10	11	
14		12[c]	13	14	15	16	17	18	Qīng míng
15		19	20	21	22	23	24	25	
16		26	**27**	28	29	30	1	2	Gǔ yǔ
17		3	4	5	6	7	8	9	
18	MONTH 4 Dīng-Yǒu	10	11	12	*13*	14	15	16	Lì xià
19		17	18	19	20	21	22	23	
20		24	25	26	27	**28**	29	1*	Xiǎo mǎn
21		2	3	4	5	6	7	8	
22	LEAP MONTH 4 Dīng-Yǒu	9	10	11	12	13	14	*15*	Máng zhòng
23		16	17	18	19	20	21	22	
24		23	24	25	26	27	28	29	
25		1	**2**	3	4	5[d]	6	7	Xià zhì
26		8	9	10	11	12	13	14	
27	MONTH 5 Dīng-Yǒu	15	16	*17*	18	19	20	21	Xiǎo shǔ
28		22	23	24	25	26	27	28	
29		29	30	1	2*	**3**	4	5	Dà shǔ
30		6	7	8	9	10	11	12	
31	MONTH 6 Dīng-Yǒu	13	14	15	16	17	18	*19*	Lì qiū
32		20	21	22	23	24	25	26	
33		27	28	29	1	2	3	4	
34		**5**	6	7[e]	8	9	10	11	Chǔ shǔ
35	MONTH 7 Dīng-Yǒu	12	13	14	15[f]	16	17	18	
36		19	20	*21*	22	23	24	25	Bái lù
37		26	27	28	29	30	1	2	
38		3*	4	5	**6**	7	8	9	Qiū fēn
39	MONTH 8 Dīng-Yǒu	10	11	12	13	14	15[g]	16	
40		17	18	19	20	*21*	22	23	Hán lù
41		24	25	26	27	28	29	30	
42		1	2	3	4	5	6	**7**	Shuāng jiàng
43		8	9[h]	10	11	12	13	14	
44	MONTH 9 Dīng-Yǒu	15	16	17	18	19	20	21	
45		*22*	23	24	25	26	27	28	Lì dōng
46		29	30	1	2	3*	4	5	
47		6	**7**	8	9	10	11	12	Xiǎo xuě
48	MONTH 10 Dīng-Yǒu	13	14	15	16	17	18	19	
49		20	*21*	22	23	24	25	26	Dà xuě
50		27	28	29	1	2	3	4	
51	MONTH 11 Dīng-Yǒu	5	6	7[i]	8	9	10	11	Dōng zhì
52		12	13	14	15	16	17	18	

Coptic 1793/1794 · Ethiopic 2069/2070

ISO WEEK	Coptic month	Sun	Mon	Tue	Wed	Thu	Fri	Sat	Ethiopic month
53	KOIAK 1793	18	19	20	21	22	23	24	TĀKHŚĀŚ 2069
1		25	26	27	28	29[c]	30	1	
2		2	3	4	5	6[d]	7	8	ṬER 2069
3	TÔBE 1793	9	10	11[e]	12	13	14	15	
4		16	17	18	19	20	21	22	
5		23	24	25	26	27	28	29	
6		30	1	2	3	4	5	6	
7	MESHIR 1793	7	8	9	10	11	12	13	YAKĀTIT 2069
8		14	15	16	17	18	19	20	
9		21	22	23	24	25	26	27	
10		28	29	30	1	2	3	4	
11	PAREMOTEP 1793	5	6	7	8	9	10	11	MAGĀBIT 2069
12		12	13	14	15	16	17	18	
13		19	20	21	22	23	24	25	
14		26	27	28	29	30	1	2	
15	PARMOUTE 1793	3	4	5	6	7	8	9	MIYĀZYĀ 2069
16		10[f]	11	12	13	14	15	16	
17		17	18	19	20	21	22	23	
18		24	25	26	27	28	29[g]	30	
19		1	2	3	4	5	6	7	
20	PASHONS 1793	8	9	10	11	12	13	14	GENBOT 2069
21		15	16	17	18	19	20	21	
22		22	23	24	25	26	27	28	
23		29	30	1	2	3	4	5	
24	PAÔNE 1793	6	7	8	9	10	11	12	SANĒ 2069
25		13	14	15	16	17	18	19	
26		20	21	22	23	24	25	26	
27		27	28	29	30	1	2	3	
28	EPÊP 1793	4	5	6	7	8	9	10	ḤAMLĒ 2069
29		11	12	13	14	15	16	17	
30		18	19	20	21	22	23	24	
31		25	26	27	28	29	30	1	
32		2	3	4	5	6	7	8	
33	MESORÊ 1793	9	10	11	12	13[h]	14	15	NAHASĒ 2069
34		16	17	18	19	20	21	22	
35		23	24	25	26	27	28	29	
36	EPAG. 1793	30	1	2	3	4	5	1[a]	PĀG. 2069
37		2	3	4	5	6	7	8	MASKARAM 2070
38	THOOUT 1794	9	10	11	12	13	14	15	
39		16	17[b]	18	19	20	21	22	
40		23	24	25	26	27	28	29	
41		30	1	2	3	4	5	6	
42	PAOPE 1794	7	8	9	10	11	12	13	TEQEMT 2070
43		14	15	16	17	18	19	20	
44		21	22	23	24	25	26	27	
45		28	29	30	1	2	3	4	
46		5	6	7	8	9	10	11	ḪEDĀR 2070
47	ATHÔR 1794	12	13	14	15	16	17	18	
48		19	20	21	22	23	24	25	
49		26	27	28	29	30	1	2	
50	KOIAK 1794	3	4	5	6	7	8	9	TĀKHŚĀŚ 2070
51		10	11	12	13	14	15	16	
52		17	18	19	20	21	22	23	

[a]New Year
[b]Spring (23:29)
[c]Summer (16:22)
[d]Autumn (8:34)
[e]Winter (5:59)
● New moon
◐ First quarter moon
○ Full moon
◑ Last quarter moon

[a]New Year
[b]Yom Kippur
[c]Sukkot
[d]Winter starts
[e]Ḥanukkah
[f]Purim
[g]Passover
[h]Shavuot
[i]Fast of Av

‡Leap year
[a]New Year (4775, Fowl)
[b]Lantern Festival
[c]Qīngmíng
[d]Dragon Festival
[e]Qīqiǎo
[f]Hungry Ghosts
[g]Mid-Autumn Festival
[h]Double-Ninth Festival
[i]Dōngzhì
*Start of 60-name cycle

[a]New Year
[b]Building of the Cross
[c]Christmas
[d]Jesus's Circumcision
[e]Epiphany
[f]Easter
[g]Mary's Announcement
[h]Jesus's Transfiguration

PERSIAN (ASTRONOMICAL) 1455/1456

Month	Sun	Mon	Tue	Wed	Thu	Fri	Sat
DEY 1455	7	8	9	10	11	12	13
	14	15	16	17	18	19	20
	21	22	23	24	25	26	27
	28	29	30	1	2	3	4
BAHMAN 1455	5	6	7	8	9	10	11
	12	13	14	15	16	17	18
	19	20	21	22	23	24	25
	26	27	28	29	30	1	2
ESFAND 1455	3	4	5	6	7	8	9
	10	11	12	13	14	15	16
	17	18	19	20	21	22	23
	24	25	26	27	28	29	1[a]
FARVARDĪN 1456	2	3	4	5	6	7	8
	9	10	11	12	13[b]	14	15
	16	17	18	19	20	21	22
	23	24	25	26	27	28	29
	30	31	1	2	3	4	5
ORDĪBEHEŠT 1456	6	7	8	9	10	11	12
	13	14	15	16	17	18	19
	20	21	22	23	24	25	26
	27	28	29	30	31	1	2
XORDĀD 1456	3	4	5	6	7	8	9
	10	11	12	13	14	15	16
	17	18	19	20	21	22	23
	24	25	26	27	28	29	30
	31	1	2	3	4	5	6
TĪR 1456	7	8	9	10	11	12	13
	14	15	16	17	18	19	20
	21	22	23	24	25	26	27
	28	29	30	31	1	2	3
MORDĀD 1456	4	5	6	7	8	9	10
	11	12	13	14	15	16	17
	18	19	20	21	22	23	24
	25	26	27	28	29	30	31
SHAHRĪVAR 1456	1	2	3	4	5	6	7
	8	9	10	11	12	13	14
	15	16	17	18	19	20	21
	22	23	24	25	26	27	28
	29	30	31	1	2	3	4
MEHR 1456	5	6	7	8	9	10	11
	12	13	14	15	16	17	18
	19	20	21	22	23	24	25
	26	27	28	29	30	1	2
ĀBĀN 1456	3	4	5	6	7	8	9
	10	11	12	13	14	15	16
	17	18	19	20	21	22	23
	24	25	26	27	28	29	30
ĀZAR 1456	1	2	3	4	5	6	7
	8	9	10	11	12	13	14
	15	16	17	18	19	20	21
	22	23	24	25	26	27	28
	29	30	1	2	3	4	5
DEY 1456	6	7	8	9	10	11	12

[a]New Year
[b]Sizdeh Bedar

HINDU LUNAR 2133/2134‡

Month	Sun	Mon	Tue	Wed	Thu	Fri	Sat
	2	3	4	5	6	7	8
PAUSHA 2133	9	10	11	12	13	14	15
	16	17	18	19	20	21	22
	23	24	25	26	27	28	29
	30	1	2	3	4	5	7
MĀGHA 2133	8	9	10	11	12	13	14
	15	16	17	17	18	19	20
	21	22	23	24	25	26	27
	28[h]	29	1	2	3	4	5
PHĀLGUNA 2133	6	7	8	9	10	11	12
	13	14	15[i]	16	17	18	19
	20	21	22	23	24	25	26
	27	28	29	30	1[a]	2	3
CHAITRA 2134	4	6	7	8	9[b]	10	10
	11	12	13	14	15	16	17
	18	19	20	21	22	23	24
	25	26	27	29	30	1	2
VAIŚĀKHA 2134	3	4	5	6	7	8	9
	10	11	12	13	14	14	15
	16	17	18	19	21	22	23
	24	25	26	27	28	29	30
JYAISHTHA 2134	1	2	3	4	5	6	7
	8	9	10	11	12	13	14
	15	16	17	18	19	20	21
	22	23	25	26	27	28	29
	30	1	2	3	4	5	6
ĀSHĀḌHA 2134	7	8	9	10	10	11	12
	13	14	15	17	18	19	20
	21	22	23	24	25	26	27
	29	30	1	2	2	3	4
ŚRĀVAṆA 2134	5	6	7	8	9	10	11
	12	13	14	15	16	17	18
	19	21	22	23[c]	24	25	26
	27	28	29	30	1	2	3
LEAP BHĀDRAPADA 2134	4	5	6	7	7	8	9
	10	12	13	14	15	16	17
	18	19	20	21	22	23	25
	26	27	28	28	29	30	1
BHĀDRAPADA 2134	2	3	4[d]	5	6	7	8
	9	10	11	12	13	14	15
	17	18	19	20	21	22	23
	24	25	26	27	28	29	30
	1	2	2	3	4	5	6
ĀŚVINA 2134	7	8[e]	10[e]	11	12	13	14
	15	16	17	18	19	20	21
	22	23	24	25	26	27	28
	29	30	1[f]	2	3	4	5
KĀRTTIKA 2134	6	7	8	9	10	11	12
	13	15	16	17	18	19	20
	21	22	23	24	25	25	26
	27	28	29	30	1	2	3
MĀRGAŚĪRA 2134	4	5	6	7	9	10	11[g]
	12	13	14	15	16	17	18

‡Leap year
[a]New Year (Hemalamba)
[b]Birthday of Rāma
[c]Birthday of Krishna
[d]Ganēśa Chaturthī
[e]Dashara
[f]Diwali
[g]Birthday of Vishnu
[h]Night of Śiva
[i]Holi

HINDU SOLAR 1998/1999

Month	Sun	Mon	Tue	Wed	Thu	Fri	Sat
PAUSHA 1998	12	13	14	15	16	17	18
	19	20	21	22	23	24	25
	26	27	28	29	1[b]	2	3
MĀGHA 1998	4	5	6	7	8	9	10
	11	12	13	14	15	16	17
	18	19	20	21	22	23	24
	25	26	27	28	29	30	1
PHĀLGUNA 1998	2	3	4	5	6	7	8
	9	10	11	12	13	14	15
	16	17	18	19	20	21	22
	23	24	25	26	27	28	29
	30	1	2	3	4	5	6
CHAITRA 1998	7	8	9	10	11	12	13
	14	15	16	17	18	19	20
	21	22	23	24	25	26	27
	28	29	30	1[a]	2	3	4
VAIŚĀKHA 1999	5	6	7	8	9	10	11
	12	13	14	15	16	17	18
	19	20	21	22	23	24	25
	26	27	28	29	30	31	1
JYAISHTHA 1999	2	3	4	5	6	7	8
	9	10	11	12	13	14	15
	16	17	18	19	20	21	22
	23	24	25	26	27	28	29
	30	31	1	2	3	4	5
ĀSHĀḌHA 1999	6	7	8	9	10	11	12
	13	14	15	16	17	18	19
	20	21	22	23	24	25	26
	27	28	29	30	31	32	1
ŚRĀVAṆA 1999	2	3	4	5	6	7	8
	9	10	11	12	13	14	15
	16	17	18	19	20	21	22
	23	24	25	26	27	28	29
	30	31	1	2	3	4	5
BHĀDRAPADA 1999	6	7	8	9	10	11	12
	13	14	15	16	17	18	19
	20	21	22	23	24	25	26
	27	28	29	30	31	1	2
ĀŚVINA 1999	3	4	5	6	7	8	9
	10	11	12	13	14	15	16
	17	18	19	20	21	22	23
	24	25	26	27	28	29	30
	31	1	2	3	4	5	6
KĀRTTIKA 1999	7	8	9	10	11	12	13
	14	15	16	17	18	19	20
	21	22	23	24	25	26	27
	28	29	30	1	2	3	4
MĀRGAŚĪRA 1999	5	6	7	8	9	10	11
	12	13	14	15	16	17	18
	19	20	21	22	23	24	25
	26	27	28	29	1	2	3
PAUSHA 1999	4	5	6	7	8	9	10
	11	12	13	14	15	16	17

[a]New Year (Virodhakṛit)
[b]Pongal

ISLAMIC (ASTRONOMICAL) 1500/1501‡

Month	Sun	Mon	Tue	Wed	Thu	Fri	Sat
ṢAFAR 1500	1	2	3	4	5	6	7
	8	9	10	11	12	13	14
	15	16	17	18	19	20	21
	22	23	24	25	26	27	28
	29	30	1	2	3	4	5
RABĪʿ I 1500	6	7	8	9	10	11	12[c]
	13	14	15	16	17	18	19
	20	21	22	23	24	25	26
	27	28	29	1	2	3	4
RABĪʿ II 1500	5	6	7	8	9	10	11
	12	13	14	15	16	17	18
	19	20	21	22	23	24	25
	26	27	28	29	1	2	3
JUMĀDĀ I 1500	4	5	6	7	8	9	10
	11	12	13	14	15	16	17
	18	19	20	21	22	23	24
	25	26	27	28	29	30	1
JUMĀDĀ II 1500	2	3	4	5	6	7	8
	9	10	11	12	13	14	15
	16	17	18	19	20	21	22
	23	24	25	26	27	28	29
RAJAB 1500	1	2	3	4	5	6	7
	8	9	10	11	12	13	14
	15	16	17	18	19	20	21
	22	23	24	25	26	27[d]	28
	29	30	1	2	3	4	5
SHAʿBĀN 1500	6	7	8	9	10	11	12
	13	14	15	16	17	18	19
	20	21	22	23	24	25	26
	27	28	29	1[e]	2	3	4
RAMAḌĀN 1500	5	6	7	8	9	10	11
	12	13	14	15	16	17	18
	19	20	21	22	23	24	25
	26	27	28	29	30	1[f]	2
SHAWWĀL 1500	3	4	5	6	7	8	9
	10	11	12	13	14	15	16
	17	18	19	20	21	22	23
	24	25	26	27	28	29	30
DHU AL-QAʿDA 1500	1	2	3	4	5	6	7
	8	9	10	11	12	13	14
	15	16	17	18	19	20	21
	22	23	24	25	26	27	28
	29	30	1	2	3	4	5
DHU AL-ḤIJJA 1500	6	7	8	9	10[g]	11	12
	13	14	15	16	17	18	19
	20	21	22	23	24	25	26
	27	28	29	1[a]	2	3	4
MUḤARRAM 1501	5	6	7	8	9	10[b]	11
	12	13	14	15	16	17	18
	19	20	21	22	23	24	25
	26	27	28	29	30	1	2
ṢAFAR 1501	3	4	5	6	7	8	9
	10	11	12	13	14	15	16

‡Leap year
[a]New Year
[b]ʿAshūrāʾ
[c]Prophet's Birthday
[d]Ascent of the Prophet
[e]Start of Ramaḍān
[f]ʿId al-Fiṭr
[g]ʿId al-ʾAḍḥā

GREGORIAN 2077

Julian (Sun)	Sun	Mon	Tue	Wed	Thu	Fri	Sat	Month
Dec 14	27	28	29	30	31	1	2	
	3	4	5	6	7[a]	8	9	JANUARY 2077
Dec 28	10	11	12	13	14[b]	15	16	
	17	18	19	20	21	22	23	
Jan 11	24	25	26	27	28	29	30	
	31	1	2	3	4	5	6	
Jan 25	7	8	9	10	11	12	13	FEBRUARY 2077
	14	15	16	17	18	19	20	
Feb 8	21	22	23	24[c]	25	26	27	
	28	1	2	3	4	5	6	
Feb 22	7[d]	8	9	10	11	12	13	MARCH 2077
	14	15	16	17	18	19	20	
Mar 8	21	22	23	24	25	26	27	
	28	29	30	31	1	2	3	
Mar 22	4	5	6	7	8	9	10	APRIL 2077
	11[e]	12	13	14	15	16	17	
Apr 5	18[f]	19	20	21	22	23	24	
	25	26	27	28	29	30	1	
Apr 19	2	3	4	5	6	7	8	MAY 2077
	9	10	11	12	13	14	15	
May 3	16	17	18	19	20	21	22	
	23	24	25	26	27	28	29	
May 17	30	31	1	2	3	4	5	
	6	7	8	9	10	11	12	JUNE 2077
May 31	13	14	15	16	17	18	19	
	20	21	22	23	24	25	26	
Jun 14	27	28	29	30	1	2	3	
	4	5	6	7	8	9	10	JULY 2077
Jun 28	11	12	13	14	15	16	17	
	18	19	20	21	22	23	24	
Jul 12	25	26	27	28	29	30	31	
	1	2	3	4	5	6	7	
Jul 26	8	9	10	11	12	13	14	AUGUST 2077
	15	16	17	18	19	20	21	
Aug 9	22	23	24	25	26	27	28	
	29	30	31	1	2	3	4	
Aug 23	5	6	7	8	9	10	11	SEPTEMBER 2077
	12	13	14	15	16	17	18	
Sep 6	19	20	21	22	23	24	25	
	26	27	28	29	30	1	2	
Sep 20	3	4	5	6	7	8	9	OCTOBER 2077
	10	11	12	13	14	15	16	
Oct 4	17	18	19	20	21	22	23	
	24	25	26	27	28	29	30	
Oct 18	31	1	2	3	4	5	6	
	7	8	9	10	11	12	13	NOVEMBER 2077
Nov 1	14	15	16	17	18	19	20	
	21	22	23	24	25	26	27	
Nov 15	28[g]	29	30	1	2	3	4	
	5	6	7	8	9	10	11	DECEMBER 2077
Nov 29	12	13	14	15	16	17	18	
	19	20	21	22	23	24	25[h]	
Dec 13	26	27	28	29	30	31	1	

[a]Orthodox Christmas
[b]Julian New Year
[c]Ash Wednesday
[d]Feast of Orthodoxy
[e]Easter
[f]Orthodox Easter
[g]Advent
[h]Christmas

2078

Month	GREGORIAN 2078 Sun	Mon	Tue	Wed	Thu	Fri	Sat	Lunar Phases	ISO WEEK (Mon)	JULIAN DAY (Sun noon)
	26	27	28	○	30	31	1[a]	10:44	52	2480029
JANUARY 2078	2	3	4	5	◑	7	8	5:03	1	2480036
	9	10	11	12	13	●	15	1:13	2	2480043
	16	17	18	19	◐	21	22	21:58	3	2480050
	23	24	25	26	27	○	29	1:32	4	2480057
	30	31	1	2	3	4	◑	2:59	5	2480064
FEBRUARY 2078	6	7	8	9	10	11	●	13:57	6	2480071
	13	14	15	16	17	18	◐	6:30	7	2480078
	20	21	22	23	24	25	○	17:49	8	2480085
	27	28	1	2	3	4	5		9	2480092
MARCH 2078	◑	7	8	9	10	11	12	22:46	10	2480099
	13	●	15	16	17	18	19	0:36	11	2480106
	◐[b]	21	22	23	24	25	26	16:09	12	2480113
	27	○	29	30	31	1	2	11:03	13	2480120
APRIL 2078	3	4	◑	6	7	8	9	14:44	14	2480127
	10	11	●	13	14	15	16	9:44	15	2480134
	17	18	◐	20	21	22	23	3:18	16	2480141
	24	25	26	○	28	29	30	4:18	17	2480148
MAY 2078	1	2	3	4	◑	6	7	2:28	18	2480155
	8	9	10	●	12	13	14	17:55	19	2480162
	15	16	17	◐	19	20	21	16:14	20	2480169
	22	23	24	25	○	27	28	20:22	21	2480176
	29	30	31	1	2	◑	4	10:37	22	2480183
JUNE 2078	5	6	7	8	9	●	11	1:48	23	2480190
	12	13	14	15	16	◐	18	7:07	24	2480197
	19	20[c]	21	22	23	24	○	10:21	25	2480204
	26	27	28	29	30	1	◑	16:24	26	2480211
JULY 2078	3	4	5	6	7	8	●	10:07	27	2480218
	10	11	12	13	14	15	◐	23:46	28	2480225
	17	18	19	20	21	22	23		29	2480232
	○	25	26	27	28	29	30	22:06	30	2480239
	◑	1	2	3	4	5	6	21:10	31	2480246
AUGUST 2078	●	8	9	10	11	12	13	19:51	32	2480253
	14	◐	16	17	18	19	20	17:32	33	2480260
	21	22	○	24	25	26	27	8:10	34	2480267
	28	29	◑	31	1	2	3	2:15	35	2480274
SEPTEMBER 2078	4	5	●	7	8	9	10	7:58	36	2480281
	11	12	13	◐	15	16	17	11:21	37	2480288
	18	19	20	○	22[d]	23	24	17:30	38	2480295
	25	26	27	◑	29	30	1	8:59	39	2480302
OCTOBER 2078	2	3	4	●	6	7	8	23:04	40	2480309
	9	10	11	12	13	◐	15	4:06	41	2480316
	16	17	18	19	20	○	22	2:54	42	2480323
	23	24	25	26	◑	28	29	18:33	43	2480330
	30	31	1	2	3	●	5	16:55	44	2480337
NOVEMBER 2078	6	7	8	9	10	11	◐	19:03	45	2480344
	13	14	15	16	17	18	○	12:51	46	2480351
	20	21	22	23	24	25	◑	7:53	47	2480358
	27	28	29	30	1	2	3		48	2480365
DECEMBER 2078	●	5	6	7	8	9	10	12:07	49	2480372
	11	◐	13	14	15	16	17	7:51	50	2480379
	○	19	20	21[e]	22	23	24	23:33	51	2480386
	25	◑	27	28	29	30	31	1:15	52	2480393

ISO WEEK	Month	HEBREW 5838/5839‡ Sun	Mon	Tue	Wed	Thu	Fri	Sat	Molad
52		10	11	12	13	14	15	16	
1	TEVETH 5838	17	18	19	20	21	22	23	
2		24	25	26	27	28	29	1	Thu 19h14m8p
3		2	3	4	5	6	7	8	
4	SHEVAT 5838	9	10	11	12	13	14	15	
5		16	17	18	19	20	21	22	
6		23	24	25	26	27	28	29	
7		30	1	2	3	4	5	6	Sat 7h58m7p
8	ADAR 5838	7	8	9	10	11	12	13	
9		14[f]	15	16	17	18	19	20	
10		21	22	23	24	25	26	27	
11		28	29	1	2	3	4	5	Sun 20h42m8p
12	NISAN 5838	6	7	8	9	10	11	12	
13		13	14	15[g]	16	17	18	19	
14		20	21	22	23	24	25	26	
15		27	28	29	30	1	2	3	Tue 9h26m9p
16	IYYAR 5838	4	5	6	7	8	9	10	
17		11	12	13	14	15	16	17	
18		18	19	20	21	22	23	24	
19		25	26	27	28	29	1	2	Wed 22h10m10p
20	SIVAN 5838	3	4	5	6[h]	7	8	9	
21		10	11	12	13	14	15	16	
22		17	18	19	20	21	22	23	
23		24	25	26	27	28	29	30	Fri 10h54m11p
24		1	2	3	4	5	6	7	
25	TAMMUZ 5838	8	9	10	11	12	13	14	
26		15	16	17	18	19	20	21	
27		22	23	24	25	26	27	28	Sat 23h38m12p
28		29	1	2	3	4	5	6	
29	AV 5838	7	8	9[i]	10	11	12	13	
30		14	15	16	17	18	19	20	
31		21	22	23	24	25	26	27	
32		28	29	30	1	2	3	4	Mon 12h22m13p
33	ELUL 5838	5	6	7	8	9	10	11	
34		12	13	14	15	16	17	18	
35		19	20	21	22	23	24	25	
36		26	27	28	29	1[a]	2[a]	3	Wed 1h6m14p
37	TISHRI 5839	4	5	6	7	8	9	10[b]	
38		11	12	13	14	15[c]	16	17	
39		18	19	20	21	22	23	24	
40		25	26	27	28	29	30	1	Thu 13h50m15p
41	HESHVAN 5839	2	3	4	5	6	7	8	
42		9	10	11	12	13	14	15	
43		16	17	18	19	20	21	22	
44		23	24	25	26	27	28	29	
45		1	2	3	4	5	6	7	Sat 2h34m16p
46	KISLEV 5839	8	9	10	11	12	13	14	
47		15	16	17	18	19	20	21	
48		22	23	24	25[e]	26[e]	27[e]	28[e]	
49		29[e]	1[d][e]	2[e]	3[e]	4	5	6	Sun 15h18m17p
50	TEVETH 5839	7	8	9	10	11	12	13	
51		14	15	16	17	18	19	20	
52		21	22	23	24	25	26	27	

ISO WEEK	Month	CHINESE Dīng-Yǒu‡/Wù-Xū Sun	Mon	Tue	Wed	Thu	Fri	Sat	Solar Term
52	MONTH 11 Dīng-Yǒu	12	13	14	15	16	17	18	
1		19	20	21	22	23	24	25	Xiǎo hán
2		26	27	28	29	30	1	2	
3	MONTH 12 Dīng-Yǒu	3	4*	5	6	7	8	9	Dà hán
4		10	11	12	13	14	15	16	
5		17	18	19	20	21	22	23	Lì chūn
6		24	25	26	27	28	29	1[a]	
7	MONTH 1 Wù-Xū	2	3	4	5	6	7	8	Yǔ shuǐ
8		9	10	11	12	13	14	15[b]	
9		16	17	18	19	20	21	22	Jīng zhé
10		23	24	25	26	27	28	29	
11		30	1	2	3	4	5*	6	Chūn fēn
12	MONTH 2 Wù-Xū	7	8	9	10	11	12	13	
13		14	15	16	17	18	19	20	
14		21	22[c]	23	24	25	26	27	Qīng míng
15		28	29	1	2	3	4	5	
16	MONTH 3 Wù-Xū	6	7	8	9	10	11	12	Gǔ yǔ
17		13	14	15	16	17	18	19	
18		20	21	22	23	24	25	26	Lì xià
19		27	28	29	30	1	2	3	
20	MONTH 4 Wù-Xū	4	5	6*	7	8	9	10	Xiǎo mǎn
21		11	12	13	14	15	16	17	
22		18	19	20	21	22	23	24	
23		25	26	27	28	29	1	2	Máng zhòng
24	MONTH 5 Wù-Xū	3	4	5[d]	6	7	8	9	
25		10	11	12	13	14	15	16	Xià zhì
26		17	18	19	20	21	22	23	
27		24	25	26	27	28	29	1	Xiǎo shǔ
28	MONTH 6 Wù-Xū	2	3	4	5	6	7	8*	
29		9	10	11	12	13	14	15	Dà shǔ
30		16	17	18	19	20	21	22	
31		23	24	25	26	27	28	29	
32		30	1	2	3	4	5	6	Lì qiū
33	MONTH 7 Wù-Xū	7[e]	8	9	10	11	12	13	
34		14	15[f]	16	17	18	19	20	Chǔ shǔ
35		21	22	23	24	25	26	27	
36		28	29	1	2	3	4	5	Bái lù
37	MONTH 8 Wù-Xū	6	7	8	9*	10	11	12	
38		13	14	15[g]	16	17	18	19	Qiū fēn
39		20	21	22	23	24	25	26	
40		27	28	29	30	1	2	3	Hán lù
41	MONTH 9 Wù-Xū	4	5	6	7	8	9[h]	10	
42		11	12	13	14	15	16	17	
43		18	19	20	21	22	23	24	Shuāng jiàng
44		25	26	27	28	29	30	1	
45	MONTH 10 Wù-Xū	2	3	4	5	6	7	8	Lì dōng
46		9*	10	11	12	13	14	15	
47		16	17	18	19	20	21	22	Xiǎo xuě
48		23	24	25	26	27	28	29	
49		1	2	3	4	5	6	7	Dà xuě
50	MONTH 11* Wù-Xū	8	9	10	11	12	13	14	
51		15	16	17	18[i]	19	20	21	Dōng zhì
52		22	23	24	25	26	27	28	

ISO WEEK	COPTIC 1794/1795‡ month	Sun	Mon	Tue	Wed	Thu	Fri	Sat	ETHIOPIC 2070/2071‡ month
52		17	18	19	20	21	22	23	TĀKHŚĀŚ 2070
1	KOIAK 1794	24	25	26	27	28	29[c]	30	
2		1	2	3	4	5	6[d]	7	
3		8	9	10	11[e]	12	13	14	
4	TÔBE 1794	15	16	17	18	19	20	21	ṬER 2070
5		22	23	24	25	26	27	28	
6		29	30	1	2	3	4	5	
7		6	7	8	9	10	11	12	
8	MESHIR 1794	13	14	15	16	17	18	19	YAKĀTIT 2070
9		20	21	22	23	24	25	26	
10		27	28	29	30	1	2	3	
11	PAREMOTEP 1794	4	5	6	7	8	9	10	
12		11	12	13	14	15	16	17	MAGĀBIT 2070
13		18	19	20	21	22	23	24	
14		25	26	27	28	29	30	1	
15		2	3	4	5	6	7	8	
16	PARMOUTE 1794	9	10	11	12	13	14	15	MIYĀZYĀ 2070
17		16	17	18	19	20	21	22	
18		23	24	25	26	27	28	29[g]	
19		30[f]	1	2	3	4	5	6	
20	PASHONS 1794	7	8	9	10	11	12	13	GENBOT 2070
21		14	15	16	17	18	19	20	
22		21	22	23	24	25	26	27	
23		28	29	30	1	2	3	4	
24	PAÔNE 1794	5	6	7	8	9	10	11	SANĒ 2070
25		12	13	14	15	16	17	18	
26		19	20	21	22	23	24	25	
27		26	27	28	29	30	1	2	
28	EPÊP 1794	3	4	5	6	7	8	9	ḤAMLĒ 2070
29		10	11	12	13	14	15	16	
30		17	18	19	20	21	22	23	
31		24	25	26	27	28	29	30	
32	MESORÊ 1794	1	2	3	4	5	6	7	NAHASĒ 2070
33		8	9	10	11	12	13[h]	14	
34		15	16	17	18	19	20	21	
35		22	23	24	25	26	27	28	
36	EPAG. 1794	29	30	1	2	3	4	5	PĀG. 2070
37	THOOUT 1795	1[a]	2	3	4	5	6	7	MASKARAM 2071
38		8	9	10	11	12	13	14	
39		15	16	17[b]	18	19	20	21	
40		22	23	24	25	26	27	28	
41	PAOPE 1795	29	30	1	2	3	4	5	ṬEQEMT 2071
42		6	7	8	9	10	11	12	
43		13	14	15	16	17	18	19	
44		20	21	22	23	24	25	26	
45	ATHÔR 1795	27	28	29	30	1	2	3	ḪEDĀR 2071
46		4	5	6	7	8	9	10	
47		11	12	13	14	15	16	17	
48		18	19	20	21	22	23	24	
49	KOIAK 1795	25	26	27	28	29	30	1	TĀKHŚĀŚ 2071
50		2	3	4	5	6	7	8	
51		9	10	11	12	13	14	15	
52		16	17	18	19	20	21	22	

[a]New Year
[b]Spring (5:09)
[c]Summer (21:56)
[d]Autumn (14:23)
[e]Winter (11:56)
● New moon
◐ First quarter moon
○ Full moon
◑ Last quarter moon

‡Leap year
[a]New Year
[b]Yom Kippur
[c]Sukkot
[d]Winter starts
[e]Ḥanukkah
[f]Purim
[g]Passover
[h]Shavuot
[i]Fast of Av

‡Leap year
[a]New Year (4776, Dog)
[b]Lantern Festival
[c]Qīngmíng
[d]Dragon Festival
[e]Qīqiǎo
[f]Hungry Ghosts
[g]Mid-Autumn Festival
[h]Double-Ninth Festival
[i]Dōngzhì
*Start of 60-name cycle

‡Leap year
[a]New Year
[b]Building of the Cross
[c]Christmas
[d]Jesus's Circumcision
[e]Epiphany
[f]Easter
[g]Mary's Announcement
[h]Jesus's Transfiguration

PERSIAN (ASTRONOMICAL) 1456/1457‡

Month	Sun	Mon	Tue	Wed	Thu	Fri	Sat
DEY 1456	6	7	8	9	10	11	12
	13	14	15	16	17	18	19
	20	21	22	23	24	25	26
BAHMAN 1456	27	28	29	30	1	2	3
	4	5	6	7	8	9	10
	11	12	13	14	15	16	17
	18	19	20	21	22	23	24
ESFAND 1456	25	26	27	28	29	30	1
	2	3	4	5	6	7	8
	9	10	11	12	13	14	15
	16	17	18	19	20	21	22
	23	24	25	26	27	28	29
FARVARDĪN 1457	1[a]	2	3	4	5	6	7
	8	9	10	11	12	13[b]	14
	15	16	17	18	19	20	21
	22	23	24	25	26	27	28
ORDĪBEHEŠT 1457	29	30	31	1	2	3	4
	5	6	7	8	9	10	11
	12	13	14	15	16	17	18
	19	20	21	22	23	24	25
XORDĀD 1457	26	27	28	29	30	31	1
	2	3	4	5	6	7	8
	9	10	11	12	13	14	15
	16	17	18	19	20	21	22
	23	24	25	26	27	28	29
TĪR 1457	30	31	1	2	3	4	5
	6	7	8	9	10	11	12
	13	14	15	16	17	18	19
	20	21	22	23	24	25	26
MORDĀD 1457	27	28	29	30	31	1	2
	3	4	5	6	7	8	9
	10	11	12	13	14	15	16
	17	18	19	20	21	22	23
	24	25	26	27	28	29	30
SHAHRĪVAR 1457	31	1	2	3	4	5	6
	7	8	9	10	11	12	13
	14	15	16	17	18	19	20
	21	22	23	24	25	26	27
MEHR 1457	28	29	30	31	1	2	3
	4	5	6	7	8	9	10
	11	12	13	14	15	16	17
	18	19	20	21	22	23	24
ABĀN 1457	25	26	27	28	29	30	1
	2	3	4	5	6	7	8
	9	10	11	12	13	14	15
	16	17	18	19	20	21	22
	23	24	25	26	27	28	29
ĀZAR 1457	30	1	2	3	4	5	6
	7	8	9	10	11	12	13
	14	15	16	17	18	19	20
	21	22	23	24	25	26	27
DEY 1457	28	29	30	1	2	3	4
	5	6	7	8	9	10	11

‡Leap year
[a]New Year
[b]Sizdeh Bedar

HINDU LUNAR 2134‡/2135

Month	Sun	Mon	Tue	Wed	Thu	Fri	Sat
MĀRGAŚĪRA 2134	12	13	14	15	16	17	18
	19	20	21	22	23	24	25
	26	27	28	29	30	1	2
PAUSHA 2134	3	4	5	6	7	8	9
	10	11	12	**13**	15	16	17
	17	18	19	20	21	22	23
	24	25	26	27	28	29	30
MĀGHA 2134	1	2	3	4	5	**6**	8
	9	10	11	12	13	14	15
	16	17	18	19	20	*20*	21
	22	23	24	25	26	27	28[h]
PHĀLGUNA 2134	29	**30**	2	3	4	5	6
	7	8	9	10	11	12	13
	14	15[i]	16	17	18	19	20
	21	22	23	24	25	26	27
CHAITRA 2135	28	29	30	1[a]	2	3	**4**
	6	7	8	9[b]	10	11	12
	13	14	*14*	15	16	17	18
	19	20	21	22	23	24	25
VAIŚĀKHA 2135	26	**27**	29	30	1	2	3
	4	5	6	7	8	9	10
	11	12	13	14	15	16	17
	18	19	20	21	22	23	24
JYAISHTHA 2135	25	26	27	28	29	**30**	2
	3	4	5	6	7	8	9
	10	*10*	11	12	13	14	15
	16	17	18	19	20	21	22
	23	25	26	27	28	29	30
ĀSHĀDHA 2135	1	2	3	4	5	6	7
	8	9	10	11	12	13	14
	15	16	17	18	19	20	21
	22	23	24	25	**26**	28	29
ŚRĀVAṆA 2135	30	1	2	3	4	5	6
	7	*7*	8	9	10	11	12
	13	14	15	16	17	18	**19**
	21	22	23[c]	24	25	26	27
BHĀDRAPADA 2135	28	29	30	1	2	3	4[d]
	5	6	7	8	9	10	11
	12	13	14	15	16	17	18
	19	20	21	**22**	24	25	26
ĀŚVINA 2135	27	28	29	30	1	2	*2*
	3	4	5	6	7	8[e]	9[e]
	10[e]	11	12	13	14	15	**16**
	18	19	20	21	22	23	24
KĀRTTIKA 2135	25	26	27	28	29	30	1[f]
	2	3	4	5	6	*6*	7
	8	10	11	12	13	14	15
	16	17	18	19	20	**21**	23
	24	25	*25*	26	27	28	29
MĀRGAŚĪRA 2135	30	1	2	3	4	5	6
	7	8	9	10	11[g]	12	13
	14	16	17	18	19	20	21
	22	23	24	25	26	27	28

‡Leap year
[a]New Year (Vilamba)
[b]Birthday of Rāma
[c]Birthday of Krishna
[d]Gaṇēśa Chaturthī
[e]Dashara
[f]Diwali
[g]Birthday of Vishnu
[h]Night of Śiva
[i]Holi

HINDU SOLAR 1999/2000

Month	Sun	Mon	Tue	Wed	Thu	Fri	Sat
PAUSHA 1999	11	12	13	14	15	16	17
	18	19	20	21	22	23	24
MĀGHA 1999	25	26	27	28	29	30	1[b]
	2	3	4	5	6	7	8
	9	10	11	12	13	14	15
	16	17	18	19	20	21	22
	23	24	25	26	27	28	29
PHĀLGUNA 1999	1	2	3	4	5	6	7
	8	9	10	11	12	13	14
	15	16	17	18	19	20	21
	22	23	24	25	26	27	28
CHAITRA 1999	29	30	1	2	3	4	5
	6	7	8	9	10	11	12
	13	14	15	16	17	18	19
	20	21	22	23	24	25	26
VAIŚĀKHA 2000	27	28	29	30	1[a]	2	3
	4	5	6	7	8	9	10
	11	12	13	14	15	16	17
	18	19	20	21	22	23	24
	25	26	27	28	29	30	31
JYAISHTHA 2000	1	2	3	4	5	6	7
	8	9	10	11	12	13	14
	15	16	17	18	19	20	21
	22	23	24	25	26	27	28
ĀSHĀDHA 2000	29	30	31	32	1	2	3
	4	5	6	7	8	9	10
	11	12	13	14	15	16	17
	18	19	20	21	22	23	24
	25	26	27	28	29	30	31
ŚRĀVAṆA 2000	1	2	3	4	5	6	7
	8	9	10	11	12	13	14
	15	16	17	18	19	20	21
	22	23	24	25	26	27	28
BHĀDRAPADA 2000	29	30	31	32	1	2	3
	4	5	6	7	8	9	10
	11	12	13	14	15	16	17
	18	19	20	21	22	23	24
	25	26	27	28	29	30	31
ĀŚVINA 2000	1	2	3	4	5	6	7
	8	9	10	11	12	13	14
	15	16	17	18	19	20	21
	22	23	24	25	26	27	28
KĀRTTIKA 2000	29	30	1	2	3	4	5
	6	7	8	9	10	11	12
	13	14	15	16	17	18	19
	20	21	22	23	24	25	26
MĀRGAŚĪRA 2000	27	28	29	30	1	2	3
	4	5	6	7	8	9	10
	11	12	13	14	15	16	17
	18	19	20	21	22	23	24
PAUSHA 2000	25	26	27	28	29	1	2
	3	4	5	6	7	8	9
	10	11	12	13	14	15	16

[a]New Year (Paridhāvin)
[b]Pongal

ISLAMIC (ASTRONOMICAL) 1501‡/1502

Month	Sun	Mon	Tue	Wed	Thu	Fri	Sat
ṢAFAR 1501	10	11	12	13	14	15	16
	17	18	19	20	21	22	23
RABĪʿ I 1501	24	25	26	27	28	29	1
	2	3	4	5	6	7	8
	9	10	11	12[c]	13	14	15
	16	17	18	19	20	21	22
	23	24	25	26	27	28	29
RABĪʿ II 1501	30	1	2	3	4	5	6
	7	8	9	10	11	12	13
	14	15	16	17	18	19	20
	21	22	23	24	25	26	27
JUMĀDĀ I 1501	28	29	1	2	3	4	5
	6	7	8	9	10	11	12
	13	14	15	16	17	18	19
	20	21	22	23	24	25	26
JUMĀDĀ II 1501	27	28	29	30	1	2	3
	4	5	6	7	8	9	10
	11	12	13	14	15	16	17
	18	19	20	21	22	23	24
RAJAB 1501	25	26	27	28	29	1	2
	3	4	5	6	7	8	9
	10	11	12	13	14	15	16
	17	18	19	20	21	22	23
SHAʿBĀN 1501	24	25	26	27[d]	28	29	1
	2	3	4	5	6	7	8
	9	10	11	12	13	14	15
	16	17	18	19	20	21	22
	23	24	25	26	27	28	29
RAMAḌĀN 1501	30	1[e]	2	3	4	5	6
	7	8	9	10	11	12	13
	14	15	16	17	18	19	20
	21	22	23	24	25	26	27
SHAWWĀL 1501	28	29	1[f]	2	3	4	5
	6	7	8	9	10	11	12
	13	14	15	16	17	18	19
	20	21	22	23	24	25	26
DHU AL-QAʿDA 1501	27	28	29	30	1	2	3
	4	5	6	7	8	9	10
	11	12	13	14	15	16	17
	18	19	20	21	22	23	24
DHU AL-ḤIJJA 1501	25	26	27	28	29	30	1
	2	3	4	5	6	7	8
	9	10[g]	11	12	13	14	15
	16	17	18	19	20	21	22
	23	24	25	26	27	28	29
MUHARRAM 1502	30[d]	1[a]	2	3	4	5	6
	7	8	9	10[b]	11	12	13
	14	15	16	17	18	19	20
	21	22	23	24	25	26	27
ṢAFAR 1502	28	29	1	2	3	4	5
	6	7	8	9	10	11	12
	13	14	15	16	17	18	19
	20	21	22	23	24	25	26

‡Leap year
[a]New Year
[d]New Year (Arithmetic)
[b]ʿAshūrāʾ
[c]Prophet's Birthday
[d]Ascent of the Prophet
[e]Start of Ramaḍān
[f]ʿId al-Fiṭr
[g]ʿId al-ʾAḍḥā

GREGORIAN 2078

Julian (Sun)	Sun	Mon	Tue	Wed	Thu	Fri	Sat	Month
Dec 13	26	27	28	29	30	31	1	JANUARY 2078
	2	3	4	5	6	7[a]	8	
Dec 27	9	10	11	12	13	14[b]	15	
	16	17	18	19	20	21	22	
Jan 10	23	24	25	26	27	28	29	
	30	31	1	2	3	4	5	FEBRUARY 2078
Jan 24	6	7	8	9	10	11	12	
	13	14	15	16[c]	17	18	19	
Feb 7	20	21	22	23	24	25	26	
	27	28	1	2	3	4	5	MARCH 2078
Feb 21	6	7	8	9	10	11	12	
	13	14	15	16	17	18	19	
Mar 7	20	21	22	23	24	25	26	
	27[d]	28	29	30	31	1	2	APRIL 2078
Mar 21	3[e]	4	5	6	7	8	9	
	10	11	12	13	14	15	16	
Apr 4	17	18	19	20	21	22	23	
	24	25	26	27	28	29	30	
Apr 18	1	2	3	4	5	6	7	MAY 2078
	8[f]	9	10	11	12	13	14	
May 2	15	16	17	18	19	20	21	
	22	23	24	25	26	27	28	
May 16	29	30	31	1	2	3	4	JUNE 2078
	5	6	7	8	9	10	11	
May 30	12	13	14	15	16	17	18	
	19	20	21	22	23	24	25	
Jun 13	26	27	28	29	30	1	2	JULY 2078
	3	4	5	6	7	8	9	
Jun 27	10	11	12	13	14	15	16	
	17	18	19	20	21	22	23	
Jul 11	24	25	26	27	28	29	30	
	31	1	2	3	4	5	6	AUGUST 2078
Jul 25	7	8	9	10	11	12	13	
	14	15	16	17	18	19	20	
Aug 8	21	22	23	24	25	26	27	
	28	29	30	31	1	2	3	SEPTEMBER 2078
Aug 22	4	5	6	7	8	9	10	
	11	12	13	14	15	16	17	
Sep 5	18	19	20	21	22	23	24	
	25	26	27	28	29	30	1	OCTOBER 2078
Sep 19	2	3	4	5	6	7	8	
	9	10	11	12	13	14	15	
Oct 3	16	17	18	19	20	21	22	
	23	24	25	26	27	28	29	
Oct 17	30	31	1	2	3	4	5	NOVEMBER 2078
	6	7	8	9	10	11	12	
Oct 31	13	14	15	16	17	18	19	
	20	21	22	23	24	25	26	
Nov 14	27[g]	28	29	30	1	2	3	DECEMBER 2078
	4	5	6	7	8	9	10	
Nov 28	11	12	13	14	15	16	17	
	18	19	20	21	22	23	24	
Dec 12	25[h]	26	27	28	29	30	31	

[a]Orthodox Christmas
[b]Julian New Year
[c]Ash Wednesday
[d]Feast of Orthodoxy
[e]Easter
[f]Orthodox Easter
[g]Advent
[h]Christmas

GREGORIAN 2079								Lunar Phases	ISO WEEK	JULIAN DAY	HEBREW 5839‡/5840								Molad	CHINESE Wù-Xū/Jǐ-Hài								Solar Term	COPTIC 1795‡/1796								ETHIOPIC 2071‡/2072
	Sun	Mon	Tue	Wed	Thu	Fri	Sat		(Mon)	(Sun noon)		Sun	Mon	Tue	Wed	Thu	Fri	Sat			Sun	Mon	Tue	Wed	Thu	Fri	Sat			Sun	Mon	Tue	Wed	Thu	Fri	Sat	
	1[a]	2	●	4	5	6	7	6:49	1	2480400		28	29	1	2	3	4	5			29	30	1	2	3	4	5	Xiǎo hán	KOIAK 1795	23	24	25	26	27	28	29[c]	TĀKHŚĀŚ 2071
JANUARY 2079	8	9	◐	11	12	13	14	18:27	2	2480407		6	7	8	9	10	11	12	Tue 4h3m0p		6	7	8	9	10*	11	12			30	1	2	3	4	5	6[d]	
	15	16	○	18	19	20	21	11:05	3	2480414	SHEVAT 5839	13	14	15	16	17	18	19		MONTH 12 Wù-Xū	13	14	15	16	17	18	19	Dà hán	TŌBE 1795	7	8	9	10	11[e]	12	13	
	22	23	◑	25	26	27	28	21:45	4	2480421		20	21	22	23	24	25	26			20	21	22	23	24	25	26			14	15	16	17	18	19	20	ṬER 2071
	29	30	31	●	2	3	4	23:34	5	2480428		27	28	29	30	1	2	3	Wed 16h47m1p		27	28	29	30	1[a]	2	3	Lì chūn		21	22	23	24	25	26	27	
	5	6	7	8	◐	10	11	3:10	6	2480435		4	5	6	7	8	9	10			4	5	6	7	8	9	10			28	29	30	1	2	3	4	
FEBRUARY 2079	12	13	14	○	16	17	18	23:44	7	2480442	ADAR I 5839	11	12	13	14	15	16	17		MONTH 1 Jǐ-Hài	11	12	13	14	15[b]	16	17	Yǔ shuǐ	MESHIR 1795	5	6	7	8	9	10	11	
	19	20	21	22	◑	24	25	19:22	8	2480449		18	19	20	21	22	23	24			18	19	20	21	22	23	24			12	13	14	15	16	17	18	YAKĀTIT 2071
	26	27	28	1	2	●	4	13:47	9	2480456		25	26	27	28	29	30	1	Fri 5h31m2p		25	26	27	28	29	1	2			19	20	21	22	23	24	25	
	5	6	7	8	9	◐	11	10:36	10	2480463		2	3	4	5	6	7	8			3	4	5	6	7	8	9	Jīng zhé		26	27	28	29	30	1	2	
MARCH 2079	12	13	14	15	16	○	18	13:44	11	2480470	ADAR II 5839	9	10	11	12	13	14[f]	15		MONTH 2 Jǐ-Hài	10	11*	12	13	14	15	16		PAREMOTEP 1795	3	4	5	6	7	8	9	
	19	20[b]	21	22	23	24	◑	15:45	12	2480477		16	17	18	19	20	21	22			17	18	19	20	21	22	23	Chūn fēn		10	11	12	13	14	15	16	MAGĀBIT 2071
	26	27	28	29	30	31	1		13	2480484		23	24	25	26	27	28	29	Sat 18h15m3p		24	25	26	27	28	29	30			17	18	19	20	21	22	23	
	●	3	4	5	6	7	◐	1:29 17:43	14	2480491		1	2	3	4	5	6	7			1	2	3[c]	4	5	6	7	Qīng míng		24	25	26	27	28	29	30	
APRIL 2079	9	10	11	12	13	14	15		15	2480498		8	9	10	11	12	13	14		MONTH 3 Jǐ-Hài	8	9	10	11	12	13	14			1	2	3	4	5	6	7	
	○	17	18	19	20	21	22	5:01	16	2480505	NISAN 5839	15[g]	16	17	18	19	20	21			15	16	17	18	19	20	21	Gǔ yǔ	PARMOUTE 1795	8	9	10	11	12	13	14	MIYĀZYĀ 2071
	23	◑	25	26	27	28	29	9:14	17	2480512		22	23	24	25	26	27	28			22	23	24	25	26	27	28			15[f]	16	17	18	19	20	21	
	30	●	2	3	4	5	6	10:56	18	2480519		29	30	1	2	3	4	5	Mon 6h59m4p		29	1	2	3	4	5	6	Lì xià		22	23	24	25	26	27	28	
MAY 2079	7	◐	9	10	11	12	13	1:36	19	2480526		6	7	8	9	10	11	12			7	8	9	10	11	12*	13			29[g]	30	1	2	3	4	5	
	14	○	16	17	18	19	20	20:57	20	2480533	IYAR 5839	13	14	15	16	17	18	19		MONTH 4 Jǐ-Hài	14	15	16	17	18	19	20		PASHONS 1795	6	7	8	9	10	11	12	GENBOT 2071
	21	22	◑	24	25	26	27	23:14	21	2480540		20	21	22	23	24	25	26			21	22	23	24	25	26	27	Xiǎo mǎn		13	14	15	16	17	18	19	
	28	29	●	31	1	2	3	18:40	22	2480547		27	28	29	1	2	3	4	Tue 19h43m5p		28	29	30	1	2	3	4			20	21	22	23	24	25	26	
JUNE 2079	4	5	◐	7	8	9	10	11:17	23	2480554		5	6[h]	7	8	9	10	11			5[d]	6	7	8	9	10	11	Máng zhòng		27	28	29	30	1	2	3	
	11	12	13	○	15	16	17	12:38	24	2480561	SIVAN 5839	12	13	14	15	16	17	18		MONTH 5 Jǐ-Hài	12	13	14	15	16	17	18		PAŌNE 1795	4	5	6	7	8	9	10	
	18	19	20	21[c]	◑	23	24	9:55	25	2480568		19	20	21	22	23	24	25			19	20	21	22	23	24	25	Xià zhì		11	12	13	14	15	16	17	SANĒ 2071
	25	26	27	28	●	30	1	1:30	26	2480575		26	27	28	29	30	1	2	Thu 8h27m6p		26	27	28	29	1	2	3			18	19	20	21	22	23	24	
	2	3	4	◐	6	7	8	23:30	27	2480582		3	4	5	6	7	8	9			4	5	6	7	8	9	10	Xiǎo shǔ		25	26	27	28	29	30	1	
JULY 2079	9	10	11	12	13	○	15	3:22	28	2480589	TAMMUZ 5839	10	11	12	13	14	15	16		MONTH 6 Jǐ-Hài	11	12	13*	14	15	16	17		EPĒP 1795	2	3	4	5	6	7	8	
	16	17	18	19	20	◑	22	17:53	29	2480596		17	18	19	20	21	22	23			18	19	20	21	22	23	24	Dà shǔ		9	10	11	12	13	14	15	ḤAMLĒ 2071
	23	24	25	26	27	●	29	8:32	30	2480603		24	25	26	27	28	29	1	Fri 21h11m7p		25	26	27	28	29	1	2			16	17	18	19	20	21	22	
	30	31	1	2	3	◐	5	14:26	31	2480610		2	3	4	5	6	7	8			3	4	5	6	7[e]	8	9			23	24	25	26	27	28	29	
AUGUST 2079	6	7	8	9	10	11	○	16:59	32	2480617	AV 5839	9[i]	10	11	12	13	14	15		MONTH 7 Jǐ-Hài	10	11	12	13	14	15[f]	16	Lì qiū		30	1	2	3	4	5	6	
	13	14	15	16	17	18	◑	23:58	33	2480624		16	17	18	19	20	21	22			17	18	19	20	21	22	23		MESORĒ 1795	7	8	9	10	11	12	13[h]	
	20	21	22	23	24	25	●	17:01	34	2480631		23	24	25	26	27	28	29			24	25	26	27	28	29	30	Chǔ shǔ		14	15	16	17	18	19	20	NAḤASĒ 2071
	27	28	29	30	31	1	2		35	2480638		30	1	2	3	4	5	6	Sun 9h55m8p		1	2	3	4	5	6	7			21	22	23	24	25	26	27	
SEPTEMBER 2079	◐	4	5	6	7	8	9	7:45	36	2480645		7	8	9	10	11	12	13			8	9	10	11	12	13	14*	Bái lù		28	29	30	1	2	3	4	
	10	○	12	13	14	15	16	5:34	37	2480652	ELUL 5839	14	15	16	17	18	19	20		MONTH 8 Jǐ-Hài	15[g]	16	17	18	19	20	21		EPAG. 1795	5	6	1[a]	2	3	4	5	PĀG. 2071
	17	◑	19	20	21	22[d]	23	5:20	38	2480659		21	22	23	24	25	26	27			22	23	24	25	26	27	28	Qiū fēn		6	7	8	9	10	11	12	
	24	●	26	27	28	29	30	4:04	39	2480666		28	29	1[a]	2[a]	3	4	5	Mon 22h39m9p		29	1	2	3	4	5	6		THOOUT 1796	13	14	15	16	17[b]	18	19	MASKARAM 2072
	1	2	◐	4	5	6	7	2:34	40	2480673		6	7	8	9	10[b]	11	12			7	8	9[h]	10	11	12	13			20	21	22	23	24	25	26	
OCTOBER 2079	8	9	○	11	12	13	14	17:22	41	2480680	TISHRI 5840	13	14	15[c]	16	17	18	19		MONTH 9 Jǐ-Hài	14	15	16	17	18	19	20	Hán lù		27	28	29	30	1	2	3	
	15	16	◑	18	19	20	21	11:21	42	2480687		20	21	22	23	24	25	26			21	22	23	24	25	26	27		PAOPE 1796	4	5	6	7	8	9	10	
	22	23	●	25	26	27	28	18:18	43	2480694		27	28	29	30	1	2	3	Wed 11h23m10p		28	29	30	1	2	3	4	Shuāng jiàng		11	12	13	14	15	16	17	ṬEQEMT 2072
	29	30	31	◐	2	3	4	21:48	44	2480701		4	5	6	7	8	9	10			5	6	7	8	9	10	11			18	19	20	21	22	23	24	
NOVEMBER 2079	5	6	7	8	○	10	11	4:33	45	2480708	ḤESHVAN 5840	11	12	13	14	15	16	17		MONTH 10 Jǐ-Hài	12	13	14	15*	16	17	18	Lì dōng		25	26	27	28	29	30	1	
	12	13	14	◑	16	17	18	19:24	46	2480715		18	19	20	21	22	23	24			19	20	21	22	23	24	25			2	3	4	5	6	7	8	
	19	20	21	22	●	24	25	11:28	47	2480722		25	26	27	28	29	1	2	Fri 0h7m11p		26	27	28	29	1	2	3	Xiǎo xuě	ATHŌR 1796	9	10	11	12	13	14	15	ḪEDĀR 2072
	26	27	28	29	30	◐	2	16:12	48	2480729		3	4	5	6	7	8	9			4	5	6	7	8	9	10			16	17	18	19	20	21	22	
	3	4	5	6	7	○	9	15:15	49	2480736	KISLEV 5840	10	11	12	13[d]	14	15	16		MONTH 11 Jǐ-Hài	11	12	13	14	15	16	17	Dà xuě		23	24	25	26	27	28	29	
DECEMBER 2079	10	11	12	13	14	◑	16	6:42	50	2480743		17	18	19	20	21	22	23			18	19	20	21	22	23	24			30	1	2	3	4	5	6	
	17	18	19	20	21[e]	22	●	6:30	51	2480750		24	25[e]	26[e]	27[e]	28[e]	29[e]	30[e]	Sat 12h51m12p	MONTH 12 Jǐ-Hài	25	26	27	28	29	30[i]	1	Dōng zhì	KOIAK 1796	7	8	9	10	11	12	13	
	24	25	26	27	28	29	30		52	2480757		1[e]	2[e]	3	4	5	6	7			2	3	4	5	6	7	8			14	15	16	17	18	19	20	TĀKHŚĀŚ 2072
	◐	1	2	3	4	5	6	8:27	1	2480764	TEVETH 5840	8	9	10	11	12	13	14			9	10	11	12	13	14	15	Xiǎo hán		21	22	23	24	25	26	27	

[a]New Year
[b]Spring (10:59)
[c]Summer (3:48)
[d]Autumn (20:12)
[e]Winter (17:42)
● New moon
◐ First quarter moon
○ Full moon
◑ Last quarter moon

‡Leap year
[a]New Year
[b]Yom Kippur
[c]Sukkot
[d]Winter starts
[e]Ḥanukkah
[f]Purim
[g]Passover
[h]Shavuot
[i]Fast of Av

[a]New Year (4777, Pig)
[b]Lantern Festival
[c]Qīngmíng
[d]Dragon Festival
[e]Qīqiǎo
[f]Hungry Ghosts
[g]Mid-Autumn Festival
[h]Double-Ninth Festival
[i]Dōngzhì
*Start of 60-name cycle

‡Leap year
[a]New Year
[b]Building of the Cross
[c]Christmas
[d]Jesus's Circumcision
[e]Epiphany
[f]Easter
[g]Mary's Announcement
[h]Jesus's Transfiguration

PERSIAN (ASTRONOMICAL) 1457‡/1458

Month	Sun	Mon	Tue	Wed	Thu	Fri	Sat
	12	13	14	15	16	17	18
DEY 1457	19	20	21	22	23	24	25
	26	27	28	29	30	1	2
	3	4	5	6	7	8	9
BAHMAN 1457	10	11	12	13	14	15	16
	17	18	19	20	21	22	23
	24	25	26	27	28	29	30
	1	2	3	4	5	6	7
ESFAND 1457	8	9	10	11	12	13	14
	15	16	17	18	19	20	21
	22	23	24	25	26	27	28
	29	30	1[a]	2	3	4	5
	6	7	8	9	10	11	12
FARVARDĪN 1458	13[b]	14	15	16	17	18	19
	20	21	22	23	24	25	26
	27	28	29	30	31	1	2
	3	4	5	6	7	8	9
ORDĪBEHEŠT 1458	10	11	12	13	14	15	16
	17	18	19	20	21	22	23
	24	25	26	27	28	29	30
	31	1	2	3	4	5	6
	7	8	9	10	11	12	13
XORDĀD 1458	14	15	16	17	18	19	20
	21	22	23	24	25	26	27
	28	29	30	31	1	2	3
	4	5	6	7	8	9	10
TĪR 1458	11	12	13	14	15	16	17
	18	19	20	21	22	23	24
	25	26	27	28	29	30	31
	1	2	3	4	5	6	7
	8	9	10	11	12	13	14
MORDĀD 1458	15	16	17	18	19	20	21
	22	23	24	25	26	27	28
	29	30	31	1	2	3	4
	5	6	7	8	9	10	11
SHAHRĪVAR 1458	12	13	14	15	16	17	18
	19	20	21	22	23	24	25
	26	27	28	29	30	31	1
	2	3	4	5	6	7	8
MEHR 1458	9	10	11	12	13	14	15
	16	17	18	19	20	21	22
	23	24	25	26	27	28	29
	30	1	2	3	4	5	6
	7	8	9	10	11	12	13
ĀBĀN 1458	14	15	16	17	18	19	20
	21	22	23	24	25	26	27
	28	29	30	1	2	3	4
	5	6	7	8	9	10	11
ĀZAR 1458	12	13	14	15	16	17	18
	19	20	21	22	23	24	25
	26	27	28	29	30	1	2
DEY 1458	3	4	5	6	7	8	9
	10	11	12	13	14	15	16

‡Leap year
[a]New Year
[b]Sizdeh Bedar

HINDU LUNAR 2135/2136

Month	Sun	Mon	Tue	Wed	Thu	Fri	Sat
	28	29	30	1	2	3	4
PAUSHA 2135	5	6	7	**8**	10	11	12
	13	14	15	16	17	18	19
	20	21	22	23	24	25	26
	27	28	29	30	1	2	3
MĀGHA 2135	4	5	6	7	8	9	10
	11	12	**13**	15	16	17	18
	19	20	21	21	22	23	24
	25	26	27	28[h]	29	30	1
PHĀLGUNA 2135	2	3	4	5	6	**7**	9
	10	11	12	13	14	15[i]	16
	17	18	19	20	21	22	23
	23	24	25	26	27	28	29
	30[a]	2	3	4	5	6	7
CHAITRA 2136	8	9[b]	10	11	12	13	14
	15	16	17	18	19	20	21
	22	23	24	25	26	27	28
	29	30	1	2	3	**4**	6
VAIŚĀKHA 2136	7	8	9	10	11	12	13
	14	15	16	17	18	18	19
	20	21	22	23	24	25	26
	27	29	30	1	2	3	4
JYAISHTHA 2136	5	6	7	8	9	10	11
	12	13	14	15	16	17	18
	19	20	21	22	23	24	25
	26	27	28	29	**30**	2	3
ĀSHĀDHA 2136	4	5	6	7	8	9	10
	11	12	13	14	14	15	16
	17	18	19	20	21	22	**23**
	25	26	27	28	29	30	1
ŚRĀVAṆA 2136	2	3	4	5	6	7	8
	9	10	11	12	13	14	15
	16	17	18	19	20	21	22
	23[c]	24	25	**26**	28	29	30
	1	2	3	4[d]	5	6	7
BHĀDRAPADA 2136	8	9	10	11	11	12	13
	14	15	16	17	18	**19**	21
	22	23	24	25	26	27	28
	29	30	1	2	3	4	5
ĀŚVINA 2136	6	7	8[e]	9[e]	10[e]	11	12
	13	14	15	16	17	18	19
	20	21	22	**23**	25	26	27
	28	29	30	1[f]	2	3	4
KĀRTTIKA 2136	5	6	6	7	8	9	10
	11	12	13	14	15	**16**	18
	19	20	21	22	23	24	25
	26	27	28	29	30	1	2
MĀRGAŚĪRA 2136	3	4	5	6	7	8	9
	10	11[g]	12	13	14	15	16
	17	18	19	20	**21**	23	24
	25	26	27	28	29	29	30
PAUSHA 2136	1	2	3	4	5	6	7
	8	9	10	11	12	13	14

[a]New Year (Vikārin)
[b]Birthday of Rāma
[c]Birthday of Krishna
[d]Ganēśa Chaturthī
[e]Dashara
[f]Diwali
[g]Birthday of Vishnu
[h]Night of Śiva
[i]Holi

HINDU SOLAR 2000/2001‡

Month	Sun	Mon	Tue	Wed	Thu	Fri	Sat
PAUSHA 2000	17	18	19	20	21	22	23
	24	25	26	27	28	29	30
	1[b]	2	3	4	5	6	7
MĀGHA 2000	8	9	10	11	12	13	14
	15	16	17	18	19	20	21
	22	23	24	25	26	27	28
	29	1	2	3	4	5	6
PHĀLGUNA 2000	7	8	9	10	11	12	13
	14	15	16	17	18	19	20
	21	22	23	24	25	26	27
	28	29	30	1	2	3	4
CHAITRA 2000	5	6	7	8	9	10	11
	12	13	14	15	16	17	18
	19	20	21	22	23	24	25
	26	27	28	29	30	1[a]	2
	3	4	5	6	7	8	9
VAIŚĀKHA 2001	10	11	12	13	14	15	16
	17	18	19	20	21	22	23
	24	25	26	27	28	29	30
	31	1	2	3	4	5	6
	7	8	9	10	11	12	13
JYAISHTHA 2001	14	15	16	17	18	19	20
	21	22	23	24	25	26	27
	28	29	30	31	32	1	2
	3	4	5	6	7	8	9
ĀSHĀDHA 2001	10	11	12	13	14	15	16
	17	18	19	20	21	22	23
	24	25	26	27	28	29	30
	31	1	2	3	4	5	6
	7	8	9	10	11	12	13
ŚRĀVAṆA 2001	14	15	16	17	18	19	20
	21	22	23	24	25	26	27
	28	29	30	31	32	1	2
	3	4	5	6	7	8	9
BHĀDRAPADA 2001	10	11	12	13	14	15	16
	17	18	19	20	21	22	23
	24	25	26	27	28	29	30
	31	1	2	3	4	5	6
	7	8	9	10	11	12	13
ĀŚVINA 2001	14	15	16	17	18	19	20
	21	22	23	24	25	26	27
	28	29	30	1	2	3	4
	5	6	7	8	9	10	11
KĀRTTIKA 2001	12	13	14	15	16	17	18
	19	20	21	22	23	24	25
	26	27	28	29	30	1	2
	3	4	5	6	7	8	9
MĀRGAŚĪRA 2001	10	11	12	13	14	15	16
	17	18	19	20	21	22	23
	24	25	26	27	28	29	30
	1	2	3	4	5	6	7
PAUSHA 2001	8	9	10	11	12	13	14
	15	16	17	18	19	20	21

‡Leap year
[a]New Year (Pramādin)
[b]Pongal

ISLAMIC (ASTRONOMICAL) 1502/1503

Month	Sun	Mon	Tue	Wed	Thu	Fri	Sat
	27	28	29	30	1	2	3
	4	5	6	7	8	9	10
RABĪ' I 1502	11	12[c]	13	14	15	16	17
	18	19	20	21	22	23	24
	25	26	27	28	29	1	2
	3	4	5	6	7	8	9
RABĪ' II 1502	10	11	12	13	14	15	16
	17	18	19	20	21	22	23
	24	25	26	27	28	29	30
	1	2	3	4	5	6	7
	8	9	10	11	12	13	14
JUMĀDĀ I 1502	15	16	17	18	19	20	21
	22	23	24	25	26	27	28
	29	1	2	3	4	5	6
JUMĀDĀ II 1502	7	8	9	10	11	12	13
	14	15	16	17	18	19	20
	21	22	23	24	25	26	27
	28	29	30	1	2	3	4
	5	6	7	8	9	10	11
RAJAB 1502	12	13	14	15	16	17	18
	19	20	21	22	23	24	25
	26	27[d]	28	29	1	2	3
	4	5	6	7	8	9	10
SHA'BĀN 1502	11	12	13	14	15	16	17
	18	19	20	21	22	23	24
	25	26	27	28	29	1[e]	2
	3	4	5	6	7	8	9
RAMAḌĀN 1502	10	11	12	13	14	15	16
	17	18	19	20	21	22	23
	24	25	26	27	28	29	1[f]
	2	3	4	5	6	7	8
SHAWWĀL 1502	9	10	11	12	13	14	15
	16	17	18	19	20	21	22
	23	24	25	26	27	28	29
	30	1	2	3	4	5	6
	7	8	9	10	11	12	13
DHU AL-QA'DA 1502	14	15	16	17	18	19	20
	21	22	23	24	25	26	27
	28	29	30	1	2	3	4
	5	6	7	8	9	10[g]	11
DHU AL-HIJJA 1502	12	13	14	15	16	17	18
	19	20	21	22	23	24	25
	26	27	28	29	30	1[a]	2
	3	4	5	6	7	8	9
MUHARRAM 1503	10[b]	11	12	13	14	15	16
	17	18	19	20	21	22	23
	24	25	26	27	28	29	1
	2	3	4	5	6	7	8
SAFAR 1503	9	10	11	12	13	14	15
	16	17	18	19	20	21	22
	23	24	25	26	27	28	29
	30	1	2	3	4	5	6
RABĪ' I 1503	7	8	9	10	11	12	13

[a]New Year
[b]'Ashūrā'
[c]Prophet's Birthday
[d]Ascent of the Prophet
[e]Start of Ramaḍān
[f]'Id al-Fiṭr
[g]'Id al-'Aḍḥā

GREGORIAN 2079

Julian (Sun)	Sun	Mon	Tue	Wed	Thu	Fri	Sat	Month
Dec 19	1	2	3	4	5	6	7[a]	
	8	9	10	11	12	13	14[b]	JANUARY 2079
Jan 2	15	16	17	18	19	20	21	
	22	23	24	25	26	27	28	
Jan 16	29	30	31	1	2	3	4	
	5	6	7	8	9	10	11	FEBRUARY 2079
Jan 30	12	13	14	15	16	17	18	
	19	20	21	22	23	24	25	
Feb 13	26	27	28	1	2	3	4	
	5	6	7	8[c]	9	10	11	MARCH 2079
Feb 27	12[d]	13	14	15	16	17	18	
	19	20	21	22	23	24	25	
Mar 13	26	27	28	29	30	31	1	
	2	3	4	5	6	7	8	
Mar 27	9	10	11	12	13	14	15	APRIL 2079
	16	17	18	19	20	21	22	
Apr 10	23[e]	24	25	26	27	28	29	
	30	1	2	3	4	5	6	
Apr 24	7	8	9	10	11	12	13	MAY 2079
	14	15	16	17	18	19	20	
May 8	21	22	23	24	25	26	27	
	28	29	30	31	1	2	3	
May 22	4	5	6	7	8	9	10	JUNE 2079
	11	12	13	14	15	16	17	
Jun 5	18	19	20	21	22	23	24	
	25	26	27	28	29	30	1	
Jun 19	2	3	4	5	6	7	8	
	9	10	11	12	13	14	15	JULY 2079
Jul 3	16	17	18	19	20	21	22	
	23	24	25	26	27	28	29	
Jul 17	30	31	1	2	3	4	5	
	6	7	8	9	10	11	12	AUGUST 2079
Jul 31	13	14	15	16	17	18	19	
	20	21	22	23	24	25	26	
Aug 14	27	28	29	30	31	1	2	
	3	4	5	6	7	8	9	SEPTEMBER 2079
Aug 28	10	11	12	13	14	15	16	
	17	18	19	20	21	22	23	
Sep 11	24	25	26	27	28	29	30	
	1	2	3	4	5	6	7	OCTOBER 2079
Sep 25	8	9	10	11	12	13	14	
	15	16	17	18	19	20	21	
Oct 9	22	23	24	25	26	27	28	
	29	30	31	1	2	3	4	NOVEMBER 2079
Oct 23	5	6	7	8	9	10	11	
	12	13	14	15	16	17	18	
Nov 6	19	20	21	22	23	24	25	
	26	27	28	29	30	1	2	
Nov 20	3[g]	4	5	6	7	8	9	DECEMBER 2079
	10	11	12	13	14	15	16	
Dec 4	17	18	19	20	21	22	23	
	24	25[h]	26	27	28	29	30	
Dec 18	31	1	2	3	4	5	6	

[a]Orthodox Christmas
[b]Julian New Year
[c]Ash Wednesday
[d]Feast of Orthodoxy
[e]Easter (also Orthodox)
[g]Advent
[h]Christmas

2080

GREGORIAN 2080‡	Sun	Mon	Tue	Wed	Thu	Fri	Sat	Lunar Phases	ISO WEEK (Mon)	JULIAN DAY (Sun noon)	HEBREW 5840/5841‡	Sun	Mon	Tue	Wed	Thu	Fri	Sat	Molad	CHINESE Jǐ-Hài/Gēng-Zǐ‡	Sun	Mon	Tue	Wed	Thu	Fri	Sat	Solar Term	COPTIC 1796/1797	Sun	Mon	Tue	Wed	Thu	Fri	Sat	ETHIOPIC 2072/2073
JANUARY 2080	◐	1[a]	2	3	4	5	6	8:27	1	2480764	TEVETH 5840	8	9	10	11	12	13	14		MONTH 12 Jǐ-Hài	9	10	11	12	13	14	15	Xiǎo hán	KOIAK 1796	21	22	23	24	25	26	27	TĀKHŚĀŚ 2072
	○	8	9	10	11	12	◑	1:43 21:39	2	2480771		15	16	17	18	19	20	21			16*	17	18	19	20	21	22			28	29[c]	30	1	2	3	4	
	14	15	16	17	18	19	20		3	2480778		22	23	24	25	26	27	28			23	24	25	26	27	28	29	Dà hán	TŌBE 1796	5	6[d]	7	8	9	10	11[e]	TER 2072
	21	●	23	24	25	26	27	1:54	4	2480785		29	1	2	3	4	5	6	Mon 1h35m13p		30	1[a]	2	3	4	5	6			12	13	14	15	16	17	18	
	28	◐	30	31	1	2	3	21:36	5	2480792	SHEVAT 5840	7	8	9	10	11	12	13		MONTH 1 Gēng-Zǐ	7	8	9	10	11	12	13			19	20	21	22	23	24	25	
FEBRUARY 2080	4	○	6	7	8	9	10	12:20	6	2480799		14	15	16	17	18	19	20			14	15[b]	16	17	18	19	20	Lì chūn		26	27	28	29	30	1	2	
	11	◑	13	14	15	16	17	15:36	7	2480806		21	22	23	24	25	26	27			21	22	23	24	25	26	27		MESHIR 1796	3	4	5	6	7	8	9	YAKĀTIT 2072
	18	19	●	21	22	23	24	20:10	8	2480813		28	29	30	1	2	3	4	Tue 14h19m14p		28	29	30	1	2	3	4	Yǔ shuǐ		10	11	12	13	14	15	16	
	25	26	27	◐	29	1	2	7:23	9	2480820	ADAR 5840	5	6	7	8	9	10	11		MONTH 2 Gēng-Zǐ	5	6	7	8	9	10	11			17	18	19	20	21	22	23	
MARCH 2080	3	4	○	6	7	8	9	23:28	10	2480827		12	13	14[f]	15	16	17	18			12	13	14	15	16*	17	18	Jīng zhé		24	25	26	27	28	29	30	
	10	11	12	◑	14	15	16	11:11	11	2480834		19	20	21	22	23	24	25			19	20	21	22	23	24	25		PAREMOTEP 1796	1	2	3	4	5	6	7	MAGĀBIT 2072
	17	18	19[b]	20	●	22	23	12:05	12	2480841		26	27	28	29	1	2	3	Thu 3h3m15p		26	27	28	29	1	2	3	Chūn fēn		8	9	10	11	12	13	14	
	24	25	26	27	◐	29	30	14:30	13	2480848	NISAN 5840	4	5	6	7	8	9	10		MONTH 3 Gēng-Zǐ	4	5	6	7	8	9	10			15	16	17	18	19	20	21	
	31	1	2	3	○	5	6	11:23	14	2480855		11	12	13	14	15[g]	16	17			11	12	13	14	15[c]	16	17	Qīng míng		22	23	24	25	26	27	28	
APRIL 2080	7	8	9	10	11	◑	13	6:48	15	2480862		18	19	20	21	22	23	24			18	19	20	21	22	23	24			29	30	1	2	3	4	5	
	14	15	16	17	18	19	●	0:59	16	2480869		25	26	27	28	29	30	1	Fri 15h47m16p		25	26	27	28	29	30	1	Gǔ yǔ	PARMOUTE 1796	6[f]	7	8	9	10	11	12	MIYĀZYĀ 2072
	21	22	23	24	25	◐	27	20:15	17	2480876	IYYAR 5840	2	3	4	5	6	7	8		LEAP MONTH 3 Gēng-Zǐ	2	3	4	5	6	7	8			13	14	15	16	17	18	19	
	28	29	30	1	2	3	○	0:09	18	2480883		9	10	11	12	13	14	15			9	10	11	12	13	14	15	Lì xià		20	21	22	23	24	25	26	
MAY 2080	5	6	7	8	9	10	11		19	2480890		16	17	18	19	20	21	22			16	17*	18	19	20	21	22			27	28	29[g]	30	1	2	3	
	◑	13	14	15	16	17	18	1:10	20	2480897		23	24	25	26	27	28	29			23	24	25	26	27	28	29		PASHONS 1796	4	5	6	7	8	9	10	GENBOT 2072
	●	20	21	22	23	24	25	10:55	21	2480904	SIVAN 5840	1	2	3	4	5	6[h]	7	Sun 4h31m17p	MONTH 4 Gēng-Zǐ	1	2	3	4	5	6	7	Xiǎo mǎn		11	12	13	14	15	16	17	
	◐	27	28	29	30	31	1	2:02	22	2480911		8	9	10	11	12	13	14			8	9	10	11	12	13	14			18	19	20	21	22	23	24	
JUNE 2080	○	3	4	5	6	7	8	13:44	23	2480918		15	16	17	18	19	20	21			15	16	17	18	19	20	21	Máng zhòng		25	26	27	28	29	30	1	
	9	◑	11	12	13	14	15	17:19	24	2480925		22	23	24	25	26	27	28			22	23	24	25	26	27	28		PAŌNE 1796	2	3	4	5	6	7	8	SANĒ 2072
	16	●	18	19	20[c]	21	22	13:39	25	2480932		29	30	1	2	3	4	5	Mon 17h16m0p		29	30	1	2	3	4	5[d]	Xià zhì		9	10	11	12	13	14	15	
	23	◐	25	26	27	28	29	9:11	26	2480939	TAMMUZ 5840	6	7	8	9	10	11	12		MONTH 5 Gēng-Zǐ	6	7	8	9	10	11	12			16	17	18	19	20	21	22	
	30	1	○	3	4	5	6	4:08	27	2480946		13	14	15	16	17	18	19			13	14	15	16	17	18*	19	Xiǎo shǔ		23	24	25	26	27	28	29	
JULY 2080	7	8	9	◑	11	12	13	6:44	28	2480953		20	21	22	23	24	25	26			20	21	22	23	24	25	26		EPĒP 1796	30	1	2	3	4	5	6	HAMLĒ 2072
	14	15	16	●	18	19	20	1:20	29	2480960		27	28	29	1	2	3	4	Wed 6h0m1p		27	28	29	1	2	3	4			7	8	9	10	11	12	13	
	21	22	◐	24	25	26	27	18:39	30	2480967	AV 5840	5	6	7	8	9[i]	10	11		MONTH 6 Gēng-Zǐ	5	6	7	8	9	10	11	Dà shǔ		14	15	16	17	18	19	20	
	28	29	30	○	1	2	3	19:12	31	2480974		12	13	14	15	16	17	18			12	13	14	15	16	17	18			21	22	23	24	25	26	27	
AUGUST 2080	4	5	6	7	◑	9	10	17:20	32	2480981		19	20	21	22	23	24	25			19	20	21	22	23	24	25	Lì qiū		28	29	30	1	2	3	4	
	11	12	13	14	●	16	17	8:12	33	2480988		26	27	28	29	30	1	2	Thu 18h44m2p		26	27	28	29	1	2	3		MESORĒ 1796	5	6	7	8	9	10	11	NAHASĒ 2072
	18	19	20	21	◐	23	24	7:06	34	2480995	ELUL 5840	3	4	5	6	7	8	9		MONTH 7 Gēng-Zǐ	4	5	6	7[e]	8	9	10	Chǔ shǔ		12	13[h]	14	15	16	17	18	
	25	26	27	28	29	○	31	10:40	35	2481002		10	11	12	13	14	15	16			11	12	13	14	15[f]	16	17			19	20	21	22	23	24	25	
SEPTEMBER 2080	1	2	3	4	5	6	◑	1:36	36	2481009		17	18	19	20	21	22	23			18	19	20*	21	22	23	24	Bái lù	EPAG. 1796	26	27	28	29	30	1	2	PĀG. 2072
	8	9	10	11	12	●	14	16:23	37	2481016		24	25	26	27	28	29	1[a]	Sat 7h28m3p		25	26	27	28	29	30	1			3	4	5	1[a]	2	3	4	
	15	16	17	18	19	◐	21	22:47	38	2481023	TISHRI 5841	2[a]	3	4	5	6	7	8		MONTH 8 Gēng-Zǐ	2	3	4	5	6	7	8		THOOUT 1797	5	6	7	8	9	10	11	MASKARAM 2073
	22[d]	23	24	25	26	27	28		39	2481030		9	10[b]	11	12	13	14	15[c]			9	10	11	12	13	14	15[g]	Qiū fēn		12	13	14	15	16	17[b]	18	
	○	30	1	2	3	4	5	1:53	40	2481037		16	17	18	19	20	21	22			16	17	18	19	20	21	22			19	20	21	22	23	24	25	
OCTOBER 2080	◑	7	8	9	10	11	12	8:29	41	2481044		23	24	25	26	27	28	29			23	24	25	26	27	28	29	Hán lù		26	27	28	29	30	1	2	
	●	14	15	16	17	18	19	2:43	42	2481051		30	1	2	3	4	5	6	Sun 20h12m4p	MONTH 9 Gēng-Zǐ	1	2	3	4	5	6	7		PAOPE 1797	3	4	5	6	7	8	9	TEQEMT 2073
	◐	21	22	23	24	25	26	17:30	43	2481058	HESHVAN 5841	7	8	9	10	11	12	13			8	9[h]	10	11	12	13	14	Shuāng jiàng		10	11	12	13	14	15	16	
	27	○	29	30	31	1	2	16:11	44	2481065		14	15	16	17	18	19	20			15	16	17	18	19	20	21*			17	18	19	20	21	22	23	
NOVEMBER 2080	3	◑	5	6	7	8	9	15:09	45	2481072		21	22	23	24	25	26	27			22	23	24	25	26	27	28	Lì dōng		24	25	26	27	28	29	30	
	10	●	12	13	14	15	16	15:36	46	2481079		28	29	30	1	2	3	4	Tue 8h56m5p		29	1	2	3	4	5	6		ATHŌR 1797	1	2	3	4	5	6	7	HEDĀR 2073
	17	18	◐	20	21	22	23	14:18	47	2481086	KISLEV 5841	5	6	7	8	9	10	11		MONTH 10 Gēng-Zǐ	7	8	9	10	11	12	13	Xiǎo xuě		8	9	10	11	12	13	14	
	24	25	26	○	28	29	30	5:13	48	2481093		12	13	14	15	16	17	18			14	15	16	17	18	19	20			15	16	17	18	19	20	21	
DECEMBER 2080	1	2	◑	4	5	6	7	22:51	49	2481100		19	20	21	22	23[d]	24	25[e]			21	22	23	24	25	26	27	Dà xuě		22	23	24	25	26	27	28	
	8	9	10	●	12	13	14	7:09	50	2481107		26[e]	27[e]	28[e]	29[e]	30[e]	1[e]	2[e]	Wed 21h40m6p		28	29	30	1	2	3	4		KOIAK 1797	29	30	1	2	3	4	5	TĀKHŚĀŚ 2073
	15	16	17	18	◐	20[e]	21	11:22	51	2481114	TEVETH 5841	3	4	5	6	7	8	9		MONTH 11 Gēng-Zǐ	5	6	7	8	9	10	11[i]	Dōng zhì		6	7	8	9	10	11	12	
	22	23	24	25	○	27	28	17:02	52	2481121		10	11	12	13	14	15	16			12	13	14	15	16	17	18			13	14	15	16	17	18	19	
	29	30	31	1	◑	3	4	8:31	1	2481128		17	18	19	20	21	22	23			19	20	21	22	23	24	25			20	21	22	23	24	25	26	

‡Leap year
[a]New Year
[b]Spring (16:42)
[c]Summer (9:33)
[d]Autumn (1:55)
[e]Winter (23:31)
● New moon
◐ First quarter moon
○ Full moon
◑ Last quarter moon

‡Leap year
[a]New Year
[b]Yom Kippur
[c]Sukkot
[d]Winter starts
[e]Ḥanukkah
[f]Purim
[g]Passover
[h]Shavuot
[i]Fast of Av

‡Leap year
[a]New Year (4778, Rat)
[b]Lantern Festival
[c]Qīngmíng
[d]Dragon Festival
[e]Qīqiǎo
[f]Hungry Ghosts
[g]Mid-Autumn Festival
[h]Double-Ninth Festival
[i]Dōngzhì
*Start of 60-name cycle

[a]New Year
[b]Building of the Cross
[c]Christmas
[d]Jesus's Circumcision
[e]Epiphany
[f]Easter
[g]Mary's Announcement
[h]Jesus's Transfiguration

PERSIAN (ASTRONOMICAL) 1458/1459

Month	Sun	Mon	Tue	Wed	Thu	Fri	Sat
DEY 1458	10	11	12	13	14	15	16
	17	18	19	20	21	22	23
	24	25	26	27	28	29	30
BAHMAN 1458	1	2	3	4	5	6	7
	8	9	10	11	12	13	14
	15	16	17	18	19	20	21
	22	23	24	25	26	27	28
ESFAND 1458	29	30	1	2	3	4	5
	6	7	8	9	10	11	12
	13	14	15	16	17	18	19
	20	21	22	23	24	25	26
FARVARDĪN 1459	27	28	29	1[a]	2	3	4
	5	6	7	8	9	10	11
	12	13[b]	14	15	16	17	18
	19	20	21	22	23	24	25
ORDĪBEHEŠT 1459	26	27	28	29	30	31	1
	2	3	4	5	6	7	8
	9	10	11	12	13	14	15
	16	17	18	19	20	21	22
	23	24	25	26	27	28	29
XORDĀD 1459	30	31	1	2	3	4	5
	6	7	8	9	10	11	12
	13	14	15	16	17	18	19
	20	21	22	23	24	25	26
TĪR 1459	27	28	29	30	31	1	2
	3	4	5	6	7	8	9
	10	11	12	13	14	15	16
	17	18	19	20	21	22	23
	24	25	26	27	28	29	30
MORDĀD 1459	31	1	2	3	4	5	6
	7	8	9	10	11	12	13
	14	15	16	17	18	19	20
	21	22	23	24	25	26	27
SHAHRĪVAR 1459	28	29	30	31	1	2	3
	4	5	6	7	8	9	10
	11	12	13	14	15	16	17
	18	19	20	21	22	23	24
	25	26	27	28	29	30	31
MEHR 1459	1	2	3	4	5	6	7
	8	9	10	11	12	13	14
	15	16	17	18	19	20	21
	22	23	24	25	26	27	28
ĀBĀN 1459	29	30	1	2	3	4	5
	6	7	8	9	10	11	12
	13	14	15	16	17	18	19
	20	21	22	23	24	25	26
ĀZAR 1459	27	28	29	30	1	2	3
	4	5	6	7	8	9	10
	11	12	13	14	15	16	17
	18	19	20	21	22	23	24
DEY 1459	25	26	27	28	29	30	1
	2	3	4	5	6	7	8
	9	10	11	12	13	14	15

[a]New Year
[b]Sizdeh Bedar

HINDU LUNAR 2136/2137‡

Month	Sun	Mon	Tue	Wed	Thu	Fri	Sat
PAUSHA 2136	8	9	10	11	12	13	14
	15	17	18	19	20	21	22
	23	24	25	26	27	28	29
MĀGHA 2136	30	1	1	2	3	4	5
	6	7	8	9	11	12	13
	14	15	16	17	18	19	20
	21	22	23	24	25	26	27
PHĀLGUNA 2136	28[h]	29	30	1	2	3	4
	5	6	7	8	9	10	11
	12	13	14[i]	16	17	18	19
	20	21	22	23	24	24	25
CHAITRA 2137	26	27	28	29	30	1[a]	2
	3	4	5	6	7	9[b]	10
	11	12	13	14	15	16	17
	18	19	20	21	22	23	24
	25	26	27	27	28	29	30
VAIŚĀKHA 2137	2	3	4	5	6	7	8
	9	10	11	12	14	15	16
	17	17	18	19	20	21	22
	23	24	25	26	27	28	29
JYAISHṬHA 2137	30	1	2	3	4	6	7
	8	9	10	11	12	13	14
	15	16	17	18	19	20	21
	22	22	23	24	25	26	27
LEAP ĀSHĀḌHA 2137	29	30	1	2	3	4	5
	6	7	8	10	11	12	13
	14	14	15	16	17	18	19
	20	21	22	23	24	25	26
ĀSHĀḌHA 2137	27	28	29	30	2	3	4
	5	6	7	8	9	10	11
	12	13	14	15	16	17	18
	19	20	20	21	23	24	25
ŚRĀVAṆA 2137	26	27	28	29	30	1	2
	3	4	6	7	8	9	10
	11	11	12	13	14	15	16
	17	18	19	20	21	22	23[c]
BHĀDRAPADA 2137	24	25	26	28	29	30	1
	2	3	4[d]	5	6	7	8
	9	10	11	12	13	14	15
	15	16	17	18	20	21	22
	23	24	25	26	27	28	29
ĀŚVINA 2137	30	1	3	4	5	5	6
	7	8[e]	9[e]	10[e]	11	12	13
	14	15	16	17	18	19	20
	21	22	23	25	26	27	28
KĀRTTIKA 2137	29	30	1[f]	2	3	4	5
	6	7	8	9	9	10	11
	12	13	14	15	16	17	19
	20	21	22	23	24	25	26
MĀRGAŚĪRA 2137	27	28	29	30	1	2	3
	4	5	6	7	8	9	10
	11[g]	12	13	14	15	16	17
	18	19	20	21	22	24	25

‡Leap year
[a]New Year (Śārvari)
[b]Birthday of Rāma
[c]Birthday of Krishna
[d]Ganēśa Chaturthī
[e]Dashara
[f]Diwali
[g]Birthday of Vishnu
[h]Night of Śiva
[i]Holi

HINDU SOLAR 2001‡/2002

Month	Sun	Mon	Tue	Wed	Thu	Fri	Sat
PAUSHA 2001	15	16	17	18	19	20	21
	22	23	24	25	26	27	28
MĀGHA 2001	29	1[b]	2	3	4	5	6
	7	8	9	10	11	12	13
	14	15	16	17	18	19	20
	21	22	23	24	25	26	27
PHĀLGUNA 2001	28	29	1	2	3	4	5
	6	7	8	9	10	11	12
	13	14	15	16	17	18	19
	20	21	22	23	24	25	26
CHAITRA 2001	27	28	29	30	1	2	3
	4	5	6	7	8	9	10
	11	12	13	14	15	16	17
	18	19	20	21	22	23	24
	25	26	27	28	29	30	31
VAIŚĀKHA 2002	1[a]	2	3	4	5	6	7
	8	9	10	11	12	13	14
	15	16	17	18	19	20	21
	22	23	24	25	26	27	28
JYAISHṬHA 2002	29	30	31	1	2	3	4
	5	6	7	8	9	10	11
	12	13	14	15	16	17	18
	19	20	21	22	23	24	25
ĀSHĀḌHA 2002	26	27	28	29	30	31	1
	2	3	4	5	6	7	8
	9	10	11	12	13	14	15
	16	17	18	19	20	21	22
	23	24	25	26	27	28	29
ŚRĀVAṆA 2002	30	31	32	1	2	3	4
	5	6	7	8	9	10	11
	12	13	14	15	16	17	18
	19	20	21	22	23	24	25
BHĀDRAPADA 2002	26	27	28	29	30	31	1
	2	3	4	5	6	7	8
	9	10	11	12	13	14	15
	16	17	18	19	20	21	22
	23	24	25	26	27	28	29
ĀŚVINA 2002	30	31	1	2	3	4	5
	6	7	8	9	10	11	12
	13	14	15	16	17	18	19
	20	21	22	23	24	25	26
KĀRTTIKA 2002	27	28	29	30	31	1	2
	3	4	5	6	7	8	9
	10	11	12	13	14	15	16
	17	18	19	20	21	22	23
MĀRGAŚĪRA 2002	24	25	26	27	28	29	1
	2	3	4	5	6	7	8
	9	10	11	12	13	14	15
	16	17	18	19	20	21	22
	23	24	25	26	27	28	29
PAUSHA 2002	30	1	2	3	4	5	6
	7	8	9	10	11	12	13
	14	15	16	17	18	19	20

‡Leap year
[a]New Year (Ānanda)
[b]Pongal

ISLAMIC (ASTRONOMICAL) 1503/1504‡

Month	Sun	Mon	Tue	Wed	Thu	Fri	Sat
RABĪʿ I 1503	7	8	9	10	11	12[c]	13
	14	15	16	17	18	19	20
	21	22	23	24	25	26	27
RABĪʿ II 1503	28	29	30	1	2	3	4
	5	6	7	8	9	10	11
	12	13	14	15	16	17	18
	19	20	21	22	23	24	25
JUMĀDĀ I 1503	26	27	28	29	1	2	3
	4	5	6	7	8	9	10
	11	12	13	14	15	16	17
	18	19	20	21	22	23	24
JUMĀDĀ II 1503	25	26	27	28	29	30	1
	2	3	4	5	6	7	8
	9	10	11	12	13	14	15
	16	17	18	19	20	21	22
	23	24	25	26	27	28	29
RAJAB 1503	1	2	3	4	5	6	7
	8	9	10	11	12	13	14
	15	16	17	18	19	20	21
	22	23	24	25	26	27[d]	28
SHAʿBĀN 1503	29	30	1	2	3	4	5
	6	7	8	9	10	11	12
	13	14	15	16	17	18	19
	20	21	22	23	24	25	26
RAMAḌĀN 1503	27	28	29	1[e]	2	3	4
	5	6	7	8	9	10	11
	12	13	14	15	16	17	18
	19	20	21	22	23	24	25
SHAWWĀL 1503	26	27	28	29	1[f]	2	3
	4	5	6	7	8	9	10
	11	12	13	14	15	16	17
	18	19	20	21	22	23	24
DHU AL-QAʿDA 1503	25	26	27	28	29	30	1
	2	3	4	5	6	7	8
	9	10	11	12	13	14	15
	16	17	18	19	20	21	22
	23	24	25	26	27	28	29
DHU AL-ḤIJJA 1503	1	2	3	4	5	6	7
	8	9	10[g]	11	12	13	14
	15	16	17	18	19	20	21
	22	23	24	25	26	27	28
MUḤARRAM 1504	29	30	1[a]	2	3	4	5
	6	7	8	9	10[b]	11	12
	13	14	15	16	17	18	19
	20	21	22	23	24	25	26
ṢAFAR 1504	27	28	29	30	1	2	3
	4	5	6	7	8	9	10
	11	12	13	14	15	16	17
	18	19	20	21	22	23	24
RABĪʿ I 1504	25	26	27	28	29	1	2
	3	4	5	6	7	8	9
	10	11	12[c]	13	14	15	16
	17	18	19	20	21	22	23

‡Leap year
[a]New Year
[b]ʿAshūrāʾ
[c]Prophet's Birthday
[d]Ascent of the Prophet
[e]Start of Ramaḍān
[f]ʿId al-Fiṭr
[g]ʿId al-ʾAḍḥā

GREGORIAN 2080‡

Julian† (Sun)	Sun	Mon	Tue	Wed	Thu	Fri	Sat	Month
Dec 18	31	1	2	3	4	5	6	JANUARY 2080
	7[a]	8	9	10	11	12	13	
Jan 1	14[b]	15	16	17	18	19	20	
	21	22	23	24	25	26	27	
Jan 15	28	29	30	31	1	2	3	FEBRUARY 2080
	4	5	6	7	8	9	10	
Jan 29	11	12	13	14	15	16	17	
	18	19	20	21[c]	22	23	24	
Feb 12	25	26	27	28	29	1	2	MARCH 2080
	3[d]	4	5	6	7	8	9	
Feb 26	10	11	12	13	14	15	16	
	17	18	19	20	21	22	23	
Mar 11	24	25	26	27	28	29	30	
	31	1	2	3	4	5	6	APRIL 2080
Mar 25	7[e]	8	9	10	11	12	13	
	14[f]	15	16	17	18	19	20	
Apr 8	21	22	23	24	25	26	27	
	28	29	30	1	2	3	4	MAY 2080
Apr 22	5	6	7	8	9	10	11	
	12	13	14	15	16	17	18	
May 6	19	20	21	22	23	24	25	
	26	27	28	29	30	31	1	JUNE 2080
May 20	2	3	4	5	6	7	8	
	9	10	11	12	13	14	15	
Jun 3	16	17	18	19	20	21	22	
	23	24	25	26	27	28	29	
Jun 17	30	1	2	3	4	5	6	JULY 2080
	7	8	9	10	11	12	13	
Jul 1	14	15	16	17	18	19	20	
	21	22	23	24	25	26	27	
Jul 15	28	29	30	31	1	2	3	AUGUST 2080
	4	5	6	7	8	9	10	
Jul 29	11	12	13	14	15	16	17	
	18	19	20	21	22	23	24	
Aug 12	25	26	27	28	29	30	31	
	1	2	3	4	5	6	7	SEPTEMBER 2080
Aug 26	8	9	10	11	12	13	14	
	15	16	17	18	19	20	21	
Sep 9	22	23	24	25	26	27	28	
	29	30	1	2	3	4	5	OCTOBER 2080
Sep 23	6	7	8	9	10	11	12	
	13	14	15	16	17	18	19	
Oct 7	20	21	22	23	24	25	26	
	27	28	29	30	31	1	2	NOVEMBER 2080
Oct 21	3	4	5	6	7	8	9	
	10	11	12	13	14	15	16	
Nov 4	17	18	19	20	21	22	23	
	24	25	26	27	28	29	30	
Nov 18	1[g]	2	3	4	5	6	7	DECEMBER 2080
	8	9	10	11	12	13	14	
Dec 2	15	16	17	18	19	20	21	
	22	23	24	25[h]	26	27	28	
Dec 16	29	30	31	1	2	3	4	

‡Leap year
[a]Orthodox Christmas
[b]Julian New Year
[c]Ash Wednesday
[d]Feast of Orthodoxy
[e]Easter
[f]Orthodox Easter
[g]Advent
[h]Christmas

2081

GREGORIAN 2081							Lunar Phases	ISO WEEK	JULIAN DAY	HEBREW 5841‡/5842								Molad	CHINESE Gēng-Zǐ‡/Xīn-Chǒu								Solar Term	COPTIC 1797/1798								ETHIOPIC 2073/2074
	Sun	Mon	Tue	Wed	Thu	Fri	Sat		(Mon)	(Sun noon)		Sun	Mon	Tue	Wed	Thu	Fri	Sat			Sun	Mon	Tue	Wed	Thu	Fri	Sat			Sun	Mon	Tue	Wed	Thu	Fri	Sat	
JANUARY 2081	29	30	31	1[a]	◑	3	4	8:31	1	2481128	TEVETH 5841	17	18	19	20	21	22	23	Fri 10h24m7p	MONTH 11 Gēng-Zǐ	19	20	21	22*	23	24	25		KOIAK 1797	20	21	22	23	24	25	26	TĀKHŚĀŚ 2073
	5	6	7	8	9	●	11	1:01	2	2481135		24	25	26	27	28	29	1		MONTH 12 Gēng-Zǐ	26	27	28	29	30	1	2	Xiǎo hán		27	28	29[c]	30	1	2	3	
	12	13	14	15	16	17	◐	6:28	3	2481142	SHEVAT 5841	2	3	4	5	6	7	8			3	4	5	6	7	8	9		TŌBE 1797	4	5	6[d]	7	8	9	10	ṬER 2073
	19	20	21	22	23	24	○	4:00	4	2481149		9	10	11	12	13	14	15			**10**	11	12	13	14	15	16	**Dà hán**		11[e]	12	13	14	15	16	17	
	26	27	28	29	30	◑	1	20:36	5	2481156		16	17	18	19	20	21	22			17	18	19	20	21	22	23			18	19	20	21	22	23	24	
FEBRUARY 2081	2	3	4	5	6	7	●	20:16	6	2481163		23	24	25	26	27	28	29	Sat 23h8m8p		24	*25*	26	27	28	29	30	Lì chūn	MESHIR 1797	25	26	27	28	29	30	1	
	9	10	11	12	13	14	15		7	2481170	ADAR I 5841	30	1	2	3	4	5	6		MONTH 1 Xīn-Chǒu	1[a]	2	3	4	5	6	7			2	3	4	5	6	7	8	YAKĀTIT 2073
	◐	17	18	19	20	21	22	21:58	8	2481177		7	8	9	10	11	12	13			8	9	**10**	11	12	13	14	**Yǔ shuǐ**		9	10	11	12	13	14	15	
	○	24	25	26	27	28	1	14:26	9	2481184		14	15	16	17	18	19	20			15[b]	16	17	18	19	20	21			16	17	18	19	20	21	22	
MARCH 2081	◑	3	4	5	6	7	8	11:05	10	2481191		21	22	23	24	25	26	27			22*	23	24	25	26	27	28	Jīng zhé	PAREMOTEP 1797	23	24	25	26	27	28	29	
	9	●	11	12	13	14	15	15:15	11	2481198	ADAR II 5841	28	29	30	1	2	3	4	Mon 11h52m9p	MONTH 2 Xīn-Chǒu	29	1	2	3	4	5	6			30	1	2	3	4	5	6	MAGĀBIT 2073
	16	17	◐	19[b]	20	21	22	9:26	12	2481205		5	6	7	8	9	10	11			7	8	9	10	**11**	12	13	**Chūn fēn**		7	8	9	10	11	12	13	
	23	24	○	26	27	28	29	0:28	13	2481212		12	13	14[f]	15	16	17	18			14	15	16	17	18	19	20			14	15	16	17	18	19	20	
	30	31	◑	2	3	4	5	3:34	14	2481219		19	20	21	22	23	24	25			21	22	23	24	25	26[c]	27	Qīng míng		21	22	23	24	25	26	27	
APRIL 2081	6	7	8	●	10	11	12	8:14	15	2481226	NISAN 5841	26	27	28	29	1	2	3	Wed 0h36m10p	MONTH 3 Xīn-Chǒu	28	29	30	1	2	3	4		PARMOUTE 1797	28	29	30	1	2	3	4	MIYĀZYĀ 2073
	13	14	15	◐	17	18	19	17:30	16	2481233		4	5	6	7	8	9	10			5	6	7	8	9	10	**11**	**Gǔ yǔ**		5	6	7	8	9	10	11	
	20	21	22	○	24	25	26	10:18	17	2481240		11	12	13	14	15[g]	16	17			12	13	14	15	16	17	18			12	13	14	15	16	17	18	
	27	28	29	◑	1	2	3	21:23	18	2481247		18	19	20	21	22	23	24			19	20	21	22	23*	24	25			19	20	21	22	23	24	25	
MAY 2081	4	5	6	7	●	9	10	22:07	19	2481254	IYAR 5841	25	26	27	28	29	30	1	Thu 13h20m11p	MONTH 4 Xīn-Chǒu	26	*27*	28	29	30	1	2	Lì xià	PASHONS 1797	26[f]	27	28	29[g]	30	1	2	GENBOT 2073
	11	12	13	14	◐	16	17	23:20	20	2481261		2	3	4	5	6	7	8			3	4	5	6	7	8	9			3	4	5	6	7	8	9	
	18	19	20	21	○	23	24	20:25	21	2481268		9	10	11	12	13	14	15			10	11	**12**	13	14	15	16	**Xiǎo mǎn**		10	11	12	13	14	15	16	
	25	26	27	28	29	◑	31	15:34	22	2481275		16	17	18	19	20	21	22			17	18	19	20	21	22	23			17	18	19	20	21	22	23	
JUNE 2081	1	2	3	4	5	6	●	9:00	23	2481282	SIVAN 5841	23	24	25	26	27	28	29			24	25	26	27	*28*	29	1	Máng zhòng	PAŌNE 1797	24	25	26	27	28	29	30	SANĒ 2073
	8	9	10	11	12	13	◐	4:14	24	2481289		1	2	3	4	5	6[h]	7	Sat 2h4m12p	MONTH 5 Xīn-Chǒu	2	3	4	5[d]	6	7	8			1	2	3	4	5	6	7	
	15	16	17	18	19	20[c]	○	7:31	25	2481296		8	9	10	11	12	13	14			9	10	11	12	13	**14**	15	**Xià zhì**		8	9	10	11	12	13	14	
	22	23	24	25	26	27	28		26	2481303		15	16	17	18	19	20	21			16	17	18	19	20	21	22			15	16	17	18	19	20	21	
	◑	30	1	2	3	4	5	8:59	27	2481310		22	23	24	25	26	27	28			23	24*	25	26	27	28	29			22	23	24	25	26	27	28	
JULY 2081	●	7	8	9	10	11	12	17:43	28	2481317	TAMMUZ 5841	29	30	1	2	3	4	5	Sun 14h48m13p	MONTH 6 Xīn-Chǒu	30	1	2	3	4	5	6	Xiǎo shǔ	EPĒP 1797	29	30	1	2	3	4	5	ḤAMLĒ 2073
	◐	14	15	16	17	18	19	9:33	29	2481324		6	7	8	9	10	11	12			7	8	9	10	11	12	13			6	7	8	9	10	11	12	
	○	21	22	23	24	25	26	20:21	30	2481331		13	14	15	16	17	18	19			14	15	**16**	17	18	19	20	**Dà shǔ**		13	14	15	16	17	18	19	
	27	28	◑	30	31	1	2	0:38	31	2481338		20	21	22	23	24	25	26			21	22	23	24	25	26	27			20	21	22	23	24	25	26	
AUGUST 2081	3	4	●	6	7	8	9	1:23	32	2481345	AV 5841	27	28	29	1	2	3	4	Tue 3h32m14p	MONTH 7 Xīn-Chǒu	28	29	1	2	3	4	5	Lì qiū	MESORĒ 1797	27	28	29	30	1	2	3	NAḤASĒ 2073
	10	◐	12	13	14	15	16	16:31	33	2481352		5	6	7	8	9[i]	10	11			6	7[e]	8	9	10	11	12			4	5	6	7	8	9	10	
	17	18	○	20	21	22	23	11:14	34	2481359		12	13	14	15	16	17	18			13	14	15[f]	16	17	**18**	19	**Chǔ shǔ**		11	12	13[h]	14	15	16	17	
	24	25	26	◑	28	29	30	14:07	35	2481366		19	20	21	22	23	24	25			20	21	22	23	24	25*	26			18	19	20	21	22	23	24	
SEPTEMBER 2081	31	1	2	●	4	5	6	9:00	36	2481373	ELUL 5841	26	27	28	29	30	1	2	Wed 16h16m15p	MONTH 8 Xīn-Chǒu	27	28	29	1	2	3	4	Bái lù	EPAG. 1797	25	26	27	28	29	30	1	PĀG. 2073
	7	8	9	◐	11	12	13	2:20	37	2481380		3	4	5	6	7	8	9			5	6	7	8	9	10	11		THOOUT 1798	2	3	4	5	1[a]	2	3	MASKARAM 2074
	14	15	16	17	○	19	20	3:44	38	2481387		10	11	12	13	14	15	16			12	13	14	15[g]	16	17	18			4	5	6	7	8	9	10	
	21	22[d]	23	24	25	◑	27	1:29	39	2481394		17	18	19	20	21	22	23			19	**20**	21	22	23	24	25	**Qiū fēn**		11	12	13	14	15	16	17[b]	
	28	29	30	1	●	3	4	17:22	40	2481401	TISHRI 5842	24	25	26	27	28	29	1[a]	Fri 5h0m16p		26	27	28	29	30	1	2			18	19	20	21	22	23	24	
OCTOBER 2081	5	6	7	8	◐	10	11	15:57	41	2481408		2[a]	3	4	5	6	7	8		MONTH 9 Xīn-Chǒu	3	4	5	6	7	8	9[h]	Hán lù	PAOPE 1798	25	26	27	28	29	30	1	ṬEQEMT 2074
	12	13	14	15	16	○	18	20:49	42	2481415		9	10[b]	11	12	13	14	15[c]			10	11	12	13	14	15	16			2	3	4	5	6	7	8	
	19	20	21	22	23	24	◑	11:11	43	2481422		16	17	18	19	20	21	22			17	18	19	20	**21**	22	23	**Shuāng jiàng**		9	10	11	12	13	14	15	
	26	27	28	29	30	31	●	3:03	44	2481429		23	24	25	26	27	28	29			24	25	26*	27	28	29	1			16	17	18	19	20	21	22	
NOVEMBER 2081	2	3	4	5	6	7	◐	9:39	45	2481436	ḤESHVAN 5842	30	1	2	3	4	5	6	Sat 17h44m17p	MONTH 10 Xīn-Chǒu	2	3	4	5	6	7	8	Lì dōng	ATHŌR 1798	23	24	25	26	27	28	29	HEDĀR 2074
	9	10	11	12	13	14	15		46	2481443		7	8	9	10	11	12	13			9	10	11	12	13	14	15			30	1	2	3	4	5	6	
	○	17	18	19	20	21	22	13:18	47	2481450		14	15	16	17	18	19	20			16	17	18	19	20	**21**	22	**Xiǎo xuě**		7	8	9	10	11	12	13	
	◑	24	25	26	27	28	29	19:47	48	2481457		21	22	23	24	25	26	27			23	24	25	26	27	28	29			14	15	16	17	18	19	20	
	●	1	2	3	4	5	6	14:35	49	2481464	KISLEV 5842	28	29	30	1	2	3[d]	4	Mon 6h29m0p	MONTH 11 Xīn-Chǒu	1	2	3	4	5	6	7	Dà xuě		21	22	23	24	25	26	27	
DECEMBER 2081	7	◐	9	10	11	12	13	6:37	50	2481471		5	6	7	8	9	10	11			8	9	10	11	12	13	14		KOIAK 1798	28	29	30	1	2	3	4	TĀKHŚĀŚ 2074
	14	15	○	17	18	19	20	4:30	51	2481478		12	13	14	15	16	17	18			15	16	17	18	19	20	21	**Dōng zhì**		5	6	7	8	9	10	11	
	21[e]	22	◑	24	25	26	27	3:54	52	2481485		19	20	21	22	23	24	25[e]			22[i]	23	24	25	26	27	28*			12	13	14	15	16	17	18	
	28	29	●	31	1	2	3	4:27	1	2481492		26[e]	27[e]	28[e]	29[e]	30[e]	1[e]	2[e]	Tue 19h13m1p		29	30	1	2	3	4	5			19	20	21	22	23	24	25	

[a]New Year
[b]Spring (22:33)
[c]Summer (15:15)
[d]Autumn (7:36)
[e]Winter (5:21)
● New moon
◐ First quarter moon
○ Full moon
◑ Last quarter moon

‡Leap year
[a]New Year
[b]Yom Kippur
[c]Sukkot
[d]Winter starts
[e]Ḥanukkah
[f]Purim
[g]Passover
[h]Shavuot
[i]Fast of Av

‡Leap year
[a]New Year (4779, Ox)
[b]Lantern Festival
[c]Qīngmíng
[d]Dragon Festival
[e]Qīqiǎo
[f]Hungry Ghosts
[g]Mid-Autumn Festival
[h]Double-Ninth Festival
[i]Dōngzhì
*Start of 60-name cycle

[a]New Year
[b]Building of the Cross
[c]Christmas
[d]Jesus's Circumcision
[e]Epiphany
[f]Easter
[g]Mary's Announcement
[h]Jesus's Transfiguration

PERSIAN (ASTRONOMICAL) 1459/1460

Month	Sun	Mon	Tue	Wed	Thu	Fri	Sat
DEY 1459	9	10	11	12	13	14	15
	16	17	18	19	20	21	22
	23	24	25	26	27	28	29
	30	1	2	3	4	5	6
BAHMAN 1459	7	8	9	10	11	12	13
	14	15	16	17	18	19	20
	21	22	23	24	25	26	27
	28	29	30	1	2	3	4
ESFAND 1459	5	6	7	8	9	10	11
	12	13	14	15	16	17	18
	19	20	21	22	23	24	25
	26	27	28	29	1[a]	2	3
FARVARDĪN 1460	4	5	6	7	8	9	10
	11	12	13[b]	14	15	16	17
	18	19	20	21	22	23	24
	25	26	27	28	29	30	31
ORDĪBEHEŠT 1460	1	2	3	4	5	6	7
	8	9	10	11	12	13	14
	15	16	17	18	19	20	21
	22	23	24	25	26	27	28
	29	30	31	1	2	3	4
XORDĀD 1460	5	6	7	8	9	10	11
	12	13	14	15	16	17	18
	19	20	21	22	23	24	25
	26	27	28	29	30	31	1
TĪR 1460	2	3	4	5	6	7	8
	9	10	11	12	13	14	15
	16	17	18	19	20	21	22
	23	24	25	26	27	28	29
	30	31	1	2	3	4	5
MORDĀD 1460	6	7	8	9	10	11	12
	13	14	15	16	17	18	19
	20	21	22	23	24	25	26
	27	28	29	30	31	1	2
SHAHRĪVAR 1460	3	4	5	6	7	8	9
	10	11	12	13	14	15	16
	17	18	19	20	21	22	23
	24	25	26	27	28	29	30
	31	1	2	3	4	5	6
MEHR 1460	7	8	9	10	11	12	13
	14	15	16	17	18	19	20
	21	22	23	24	25	26	27
	28	29	30	1	2	3	4
ĀBĀN 1460	5	6	7	8	9	10	11
	12	13	14	15	16	17	18
	19	20	21	22	23	24	25
	26	27	28	29	30	1	2
ĀZAR 1460	3	4	5	6	7	8	9
	10	11	12	13	14	15	16
	17	18	19	20	21	22	23
	24	25	26	27	28	29	30
DEY 1460	1	2	3	4	5	6	7
	8	9	10	11	12	13	14

HINDU LUNAR 2137‡/2138

Month	Sun	Mon	Tue	Wed	Thu	Fri	Sat
MĀRGAŚĪRA 2137	18	19	20	21	**22**	24	25
	26	27	28	29	30	1	*1*
PAUSHA 2137	2	3	4	5	6	7	8
	9	10	11	12	13	14	15
	16	18	19	20	21	22	23
	24	25	26	27	28	29	30
	1	2	3	3	4	5	6
MĀGHA 2137	7	8	9	**10**	12	13	14
	15	16	17	18	19	20	21
	22	23	24	25	26	27	28[h]
	29	30	1	2	3	4	5
PHĀLGUNA 2137	6	7	8	9	10	11	12
	13	**14**[i]	16	17	18	19	20
	21	22	23	24	25	26	27
	27	28	29	30	1[a]	2	3
CHAITRA 2138	4	5	6	7	**8**[b]	10	11
	12	13	14	15	16	17	18
	19	20	21	22	23	24	25
	26	27	28	29	30	1	2
VAIŚĀKHA 2138	3	4	5	6	7	8	9
	10	11	**12**	14	15	16	17
	18	19	20	21	22	*22*	23
	24	25	26	27	28	29	30
	1	2	3	4	**5**	7	8
JYAISHṬHA 2138	9	10	11	12	13	14	15
	16	17	18	19	20	21	22
	23	24	25	26	27	28	29
	30	1	2	3	4	5	6
ĀSHĀḌHA 2138	**7**	9	10	11	12	13	14
	15	16	17	18	19	*19*	20
	21	22	23	24	25	26	27
	28	29	**30**	2	3	4	5
ŚRĀVAṆA 2138	6	7	8	9	10	11	12
	13	14	15	16	17	18	19
	20	21	22	23[c]	24	25	26
	27	28	29	30	1	2	3[d]
BHĀDRAPADA 2138	5	6	7	8	9	10	11
	12	13	14	15	*15*	16	17
	18	19	20	21	22	23	24
	25	**26**	28	29	30	1	2
ĀŚVINA 2138	3	4	5	6	7	8[e]	9[e]
	10[e]	11	12	13	14	15	16
	17	18	19	20	21	22	23
	24	25	26	27	28	29	30
KĀRTTIKA 2138	**1**[f]	3	4	5	6	7	8
	9	9	10	11	12	13	14
	15	16	17	18	19	20	21
	22	23	**24**	26	27	28	29
	30	1	2	3	4	5	6
MĀRGAŚĪRA 2138	7	8	9	10	11[g]	12	*12*
	13	14	15	16	17	**18**	20
	21	22	23	24	25	26	27
	28	29	30	1	2	3	4

HINDU SOLAR 2002/2003

Month	Sun	Mon	Tue	Wed	Thu	Fri	Sat
PAUSHA 2002	14	15	16	17	18	19	20
	21	22	23	24	25	26	27
	28	29	1[b]	2	3	4	5
MĀGHA 2002	6	7	8	9	10	11	12
	13	14	15	16	17	18	19
	20	21	22	23	24	25	26
	27	28	29	30	1	2	3
PHĀLGUNA 2002	4	5	6	7	8	9	10
	11	12	13	14	15	16	17
	18	19	20	21	22	23	24
	25	26	27	28	29	30	1
CHAITRA 2002	2	3	4	5	6	7	8
	9	10	11	12	13	14	15
	16	17	18	19	20	21	22
	23	24	25	26	27	28	29
	30	1[a]	2	3	4	5	6
VAIŚĀKHA 2003	7	8	9	10	11	12	13
	14	15	16	17	18	19	20
	21	22	23	24	25	26	27
	28	29	30	31	1	2	3
JYAISHṬHA 2003	4	5	6	7	8	9	10
	11	12	13	14	15	16	17
	18	19	20	21	22	23	24
	25	26	27	28	29	30	31
ĀSHĀḌHA 2003	1	2	3	4	5	6	7
	8	9	10	11	12	13	14
	15	16	17	18	19	20	21
	22	23	24	25	26	27	28
	29	30	31	32	1	2	3
ŚRĀVAṆA 2003	4	5	6	7	8	9	10
	11	12	13	14	15	16	17
	18	19	20	21	22	23	24
	25	26	27	28	29	30	31
BHĀDRAPADA 2003	1	2	3	4	5	6	7
	8	9	10	11	12	13	14
	15	16	17	18	19	20	21
	22	23	24	25	26	27	28
	29	30	31	1	2	3	4
ĀŚVINA 2003	5	6	7	8	9	10	11
	12	13	14	15	16	17	18
	19	20	21	22	23	24	25
	26	27	28	29	30	31	1
KĀRTTIKA 2003	2	3	4	5	6	7	8
	9	10	11	12	13	14	15
	16	17	18	19	20	21	22
	23	24	25	26	27	28	29
	30	1	2	3	4	5	6
MĀRGAŚĪRA 2003	7	8	9	10	11	12	13
	14	15	16	17	18	19	20
	21	22	23	24	25	26	27
	28	29	1	2	3	4	5
PAUSHA 2003	6	7	8	9	10	11	12
	13	14	15	16	17	18	19

ISLAMIC (ASTRONOMICAL) 1504‡/1505

Month	Sun	Mon	Tue	Wed	Thu	Fri	Sat
RABĪ' I 1504	17	18	19	20	21	22	23
	24	25	26	27	28	29	30
	1	2	3	4	5	6	7
RABĪ' II 1504	8	9	10	11	12	13	14
	15	16	17	18	19	20	21
	22	23	24	25	26	27	28
	29	*1*	2	3	4	5	6
JUMĀDĀ I 1504	7	8	9	10	11	12	13
	14	15	16	17	18	19	20
	21	22	23	24	25	26	27
	28	29	30	*1*	2	3	4
JUMĀDĀ II 1504	5	6	7	8	9	10	11
	12	13	14	15	16	17	18
	19	20	21	22	23	24	25
	26	27	28	29	30	1	2
RAJAB 1504	3	4	5	6	7	8	9
	10	11	12	13	14	15	16
	17	18	19	20	21	22	23
	24	25	26	27[d]	28	29	*1*
SHA'BĀN 1504	2	3	4	5	6	7	8
	9	10	11	12	13	14	15
	16	17	18	19	20	21	22
	23	24	25	26	27	28	29
RAMAḌĀN 1504	*1*[e]	2	3	4	5	6	7
	8	9	10	11	12	13	14
	15	16	17	18	19	20	21
	22	23	24	25	26	27	28
	29	30	*1*[f]	2	3	4	5
SHAWWĀL 1504	6	7	8	9	10	11	12
	13	14	15	16	17	18	19
	20	21	22	23	24	25	26
	27	28	29	*1*	2	3	4
DHU AL-QA'DA 1504	5	6	7	8	9	10	11
	12	13	14	15	16	17	18
	19	20	21	22	23	24	25
	26	27	28	29	30	*1*	2
DHU AL-ḤIJJA 1504	3	4	5	6	7	8	9
	10[g]	11	12	13	14	15	16
	17	18	19	20	21	22	23
	24	25	26	27	28	29	*30*[a]
MUHARRAM 1505	1[a]	2	3	4	5	6	7
	8	9	10[b]	11	12	13	14
	15	16	17	18	19	20	21
	22	23	24	25	26	27	28
	29	*1*	2	3	4	5	6
ṢAFAR 1505	7	8	9	10	11	12	13
	14	15	16	17	18	19	20
	21	22	23	24	25	26	27
	28	29	*1*	2	3	4	5
RABĪ' I 1505	6	7	8	9	10	11	*12*[c]
	13	14	15	16	17	18	19
	20	21	22	23	24	25	26
	27	28	29	30	*1*	2	3

GREGORIAN 2081

Julian (Sun)	Sun	Mon	Tue	Wed	Thu	Fri	Sat	Month
Dec 16	29	30	31	1	2	3	4	JANUARY 2081
	5	6	7[a]	8	9	10	11	
Dec 30	*12*	13	14[b]	15	16	17	18	
	19	20	21	22	23	24	25	
Jan 13	*26*	27	28	29	30	31	1	
	2	3	4	5	6	7	8	FEBRUARY 2081
Jan 27	9	10	11	12[c]	13	14	15	
	16	17	18	19	20	21	22	
Feb 10	*23*	24	25	26	27	28	1	
	2	3	4	5	6	7	8	MARCH 2081
Feb 24	9	10	11	12	13	14	15	
	16	17	18	19	20	21	22	
Mar 10	*23*[d]	24	25	26	27	28	29	
	30[e]	31	1	2	3	4	5	
Mar 24	*6*	7	8	9	10	11	12	APRIL 2081
	13	14	15	16	17	18	19	
Apr 7	*20*	21	22	23	24	25	26	
	27	28	29	30	1	2	3	
Apr 21	*4*[f]	5	6	7	8	9	10	MAY 2081
	11	12	13	14	15	16	17	
May 5	*18*	19	20	21	22	23	24	
	25	26	27	28	29	30	31	
May 19	*1*	2	3	4	5	6	7	JUNE 2081
	8	9	10	11	12	13	14	
Jun 2	*15*	16	17	18	19	20	21	
	22	23	24	25	26	27	28	
Jun 16	*29*	30	1	2	3	4	5	
	6	7	8	9	10	11	12	JULY 2081
Jun 30	*13*	14	15	16	17	18	19	
	20	21	22	23	24	25	26	
Jul 14	*27*	28	29	30	31	1	2	
	3	4	5	6	7	8	9	AUGUST 2081
Jul 28	*10*	11	12	13	14	15	16	
	17	18	19	20	21	22	23	
Aug 11	*24*	25	26	27	28	29	30	
	31	1	2	3	4	5	6	
Aug 25	*7*	8	9	10	11	12	13	SEPTEMBER 2081
	14	15	16	17	18	19	20	
Sep 8	*21*	22	23	24	25	26	27	
	28	29	30	1	2	3	4	
Sep 22	*5*	6	7	8	9	10	11	OCTOBER 2081
	12	13	14	15	16	17	18	
Oct 6	*19*	20	21	22	23	24	25	
	26	27	28	29	30	31	1	
Oct 20	*2*	3	4	5	6	7	8	NOVEMBER 2081
	9	10	11	12	13	14	15	
Nov 3	*16*	17	18	19	20	21	22	
	23	24	25	26	27	28	29	
Nov 17	*30*[g]	1	2	3	4	5	6	
	7	8	9	10	11	12	13	DECEMBER 2081
Dec 1	*14*	15	16	17	18	19	20	
	21	22	23	24	25[h]	26	27	
Dec 15	*28*	29	30	31	1	2	3	

Persian:
[a]New Year
[b]Sizdeh Bedar

Hindu Lunar:
‡Leap year
[a]New Year (Plava)
[b]Birthday of Rāma
[c]Birthday of Krishna
[d]Ganēśa Chaturthī
[e]Dashara
[f]Diwali
[g]Birthday of Vishnu
[h]Night of Śiva
[i]Holi

Hindu Solar:
[a]New Year (Rākshasa)
[b]Pongal

Islamic:
‡Leap year
[a]New Year
[a]New Year (Arithmetic)
[b]'Ashūrā'
[c]Prophet's Birthday
[d]Ascent of the Prophet
[e]Start of Ramaḍān
[f]'Id al-Fiṭr
[g]'Id al-'Aḍḥā

Gregorian:
[a]Orthodox Christmas
[b]Julian New Year
[c]Ash Wednesday
[d]Feast of Orthodoxy
[e]Easter
[f]Orthodox Easter
[g]Advent
[h]Christmas

2082

Gregorian 2082	Sun	Mon	Tue	Wed	Thu	Fri	Sat	Lunar Phases	ISO Week (Mon)	Julian Day (Sun noon)	Hebrew 5842/5843	Sun	Mon	Tue	Wed	Thu	Fri	Sat	Molad	Chinese Xīn-Chǒu/Rén-Yín‡	Sun	Mon	Tue	Wed	Thu	Fri	Sat	Solar Term	Coptic 1798/1799‡	Sun	Mon	Tue	Wed	Thu	Fri	Sat	Ethiopic 2074/2075‡
January 2082	28	29	●	31	1[a]	2	3	4:27	1	2481492	Teveth 5842	26[e]	27[e]	28[e]	29[e]	30[e]	1[e]	2[e]	Tue 19h13m1p	Month 12 Xīn-Chǒu	29	30	1	2	3	4	5		Koiak 1798	19	20	21	22	23	24	25	Tākhśāś 2074
	4	5	6	◐	8	9	10	4:44	2	2481499		3	4	5	6	7	8	9			6	7	8	9	10	11	12	Xiǎo hán	Tōbe 1798	26	27	28	29[c]	30	1	2	Ṭer 2074
	11	12	13	○	15	16	17	18:10	3	2481506		10	11	12	13	14	15	16			13	14	15	16	17	18	19			3	4	5	6[d]	7	8	9	
	18	19	20	◑	22	23	24	12:14	4	2481513		17	18	19	20	21	22	23			20	21	22	23	24	25	26	Dà hán		10	11[e]	12	13	14	15	16	
	25	26	27	●	29	30	31	20:45	5	2481520	Shevat 5842	24	25	26	27	28	29	1	Thu 7h57m2p	Month 1 Rén-Yín	27	28	29	30	1[a]	2	3			17	18	19	20	21	22	23	
February 2082	1	2	3	4	5	◐	7	1:33	6	2481527		2	3	4	5	6	7	8			4	5	6	7	8	9	10	Lì chūn		24	25	26	27	28	29	30	
	8	9	10	11	12	○	14	6:15	7	2481534		9	10	11	12	13	14	15			11	12	13	14	15[b]	16	17		Meshir 1798	1	2	3	4	5	6	7	Yakātit 2074
	15	16	17	18	◑	20	21	21:34	8	2481541		16	17	18	19	20	21	22			18	19	20	21	22	23	24	Yǔ shuǐ		8	9	10	11	12	13	14	
	22	23	24	25	26	●	28	14:47	9	2481548		23	24	25	26	27	28	29		Month 2 Rén-Yín	25	26	27	28*	29	1	2			15	16	17	18	19	20	21	
March 2082	1	2	3	4	5	6	◐	19:14	10	2481555	Adar 5842	30	1	2	3	4	5	6	Fri 20h41m3p		3	4	5	6	7	8	9	Jīng zhé		22	23	24	25	26	27	28	
	8	9	10	11	12	13	○	16:44	11	2481562		7	8	9	10	11	12	13			10	11	12	13	14	15	16		Paremotep 1798	29	30	1	2	3	4	5	Magābit 2074
	15	16	17	18	19	20[b]	◑	8:36	12	2481569		14[f]	15	16	17	18	19	20			17	18	19	20	21	22	23	Chūn fēn		6	7	8	9	10	11	12	
	22	23	24	25	26	27	28		13	2481576		21	22	23	24	25	26	27			24	25	26	27	28	29	30			13	14	15	16	17	18	19	
April 2082	●	30	31	1	2	3	4	9:04	14	2481583	Nisan 5842	28	29	1	2	3	4	5	Sun 9h25m4p	Month 3 Rén-Yín	1	2	3	4	5	6	7[c]	Qīng míng		20	21	22	23	24	25	26	
	5	◐	7	8	9	10	11	9:01	15	2481590		6	7	8	9	10	11	12			8	9	10	11	12	13	14		Parmoute 1798	27	28	29	30	1	2	3	Miyāzyā 2074
	12	○	14	15	16	17	18	1:44	16	2481597		13	14	15[g]	16	17	18	19			15	16	17	18	19	20	21			4	5	6	7	8	9	10	
	◑	20	21	22	23	24	25	21:45	17	2481604		20	21	22	23	24	25	26			22	23	24	25	26	27	28	Gǔ yǔ		11[f]	12	13	14	15	16	17	
May 2082	26	27	●	29	30	1	2	2:01	18	2481611	Iyyar 5842	27	28	29	30	1	2	3	Mon 22h9m5p	Month 4 Rén-Yín	29*	30	1	2	3	4	5			18	19	20	21	22	23	24	
	3	4	◐	6	7	8	9	19:03	19	2481618		4	5	6	7	8	9	10			6	7	8	9	10	11	12	Lì xià	Pashons 1798	25	26	27	28	29[g]	30	1	Genbot 2074
	10	11	○	13	14	15	16	9:48	20	2481625		11	12	13	14	15	16	17			13	14	15	16	17	18	19			2	3	4	5	6	7	8	
	17	18	◑	20	21	22	23	12:57	21	2481632		18	19	20	21	22	23	24			20	21	22	23	24	25	26	Xiǎo mǎn		9	10	11	12	13	14	15	
	24	25	26	●	28	29	30	16:46	22	2481639	Sivan 5842	25	26	27	28	29	1	2	Wed 10h53m6p	Month 5 Rén-Yín	27	28	29	30	1	2	3			16	17	18	19	20	21	22	
June 2082	31	1	2	3	◐	5	6	2:00	23	2481646		3	4	5	6[h]	7	8	9			4	5[d]	6	7	8	9	10	Máng zhòng		23	24	25	26	27	28	29	
	7	8	9	○	11	12	13	17:54	24	2481653		10	11	12	13	14	15	16			11	12	13	14	15	16	17		Paōne 1798	30	1	2	3	4	5	6	Sanē 2074
	14	15	16	17	◑	19	20[c]	5:38	25	2481660		17	18	19	20	21	22	23			18	19	20	21	22	23	24	Xià zhì		7	8	9	10	11	12	13	
	21	22	23	24	25	●	27	5:15	26	2481667		24	25	26	27	28	29	30		Month 6 Rén-Yín	25	26	27	28	29*	1	2			14	15	16	17	18	19	20	
July 2082	28	29	30	1	2	◐	4	6:58	27	2481674	Tammuz 5842	1	2	3	4	5	6	7	Thu 23h37m7p		3	4	5	6	7	8	9			21	22	23	24	25	26	27	
	5	6	7	8	9	○	11	3:09	28	2481681		8	9	10	11	12	13	14			10	11	12	13	14	15	16	Xiǎo shǔ	Epēp 1798	28	29	30	1	2	3	4	Ḥamlē 2074
	12	13	14	15	16	◑	18	22:57	29	2481688		15	16	17	18	19	20	21			17	18	19	20	21	22	23			5	6	7	8	9	10	11	
	19	20	21	22	23	24	●	15:53	30	2481695		22	23	24	25	26	27	28		Month 7 Rén-Yín	24	25	26	27	28	29	1	Dà shǔ		12	13	14	15	16	17	18	
August 2082	26	27	28	29	30	31	◐	11:20	31	2481702	Av 5842	29	1	2	3	4	5	6	Sat 12h21m8p		2	3	4	5	6	7[e]	8			19	20	21	22	23	24	25	
	2	3	4	5	6	7	○	14:31	32	2481709		7	8	9[i]	10	11	12	13			9	10	11	12	13	14	15[f]	Lì qiū	Mesorē 1798	26	27	28	29	30	1	2	Naḥasē 2074
	9	10	11	12	13	14	15		33	2481716		14	15	16	17	18	19	20			16	17	18	19	20	21	22			3	4	5	6	7	8	9	
	◑	17	18	19	20	21	22	16:06	34	2481723		21	22	23	24	25	26	27			23	24	25	26	27	28	29	Chǔ shǔ		10	11	12	13[h]	14	15	16	
	23	●	25	26	27	28	29	1:17	35	2481730	Elul 5842	28	29	30	1	2	3	4	Mon 1h5m9p	Leap Month 7 Rén-Yín	30	1*	2	3	4	5	6			17	18	19	20	21	22	23	
September 2082	◐	31	1	2	3	4	5	16:41	36	2481737		5	6	7	8	9	10	11			7	8	9	10	11	12	13			24	25	26	27	28	29	30	
	6	○	8	9	10	11	12	4:29	37	2481744		12	13	14	15	16	17	18			14	15	16	17	18	19	20	Bái lù	Epag. 1798 / Thoout 1799	1	2	3	4	5	1[a]	2	Pāg. 2074 / Maskaram 2075
	13	14	◑	16	17	18	19	8:28	38	2481751		19	20	21	22	23	24	25			21	22	23	24	25	26	27			3	4	5	6	7	8	9	
	20	21	●[d]	23	24	25	26	10:03	39	2481758	Tishri 5843	26	27	28	29	1[a]	2[a]	3	Tue 13h49m10p	Month 8 Rén-Yín	28	29	1	2	3	4	5	Qiū fēn		10	11	12	13	14	15	16	
October 2082	27	28	◐	30	1	2	3	0:33	40	2481765		4	5	6	7	8	9	10[b]			6	7	8	9	10	11	12			17[b]	18	19	20	21	22	23	
	4	5	○	7	8	9	10	20:46	41	2481772		11	12	13	14	15[c]	16	17			13	14	15[g]	16	17	18	19	Hán lù		24	25	26	27	28	29	30	
	11	12	13	◑	15	16	17	23:30	42	2481779		18	19	20	21	22	23	24			20	21	22	23	24	25	26		Paope 1799	1	2	3	4	5	6	7	Ṭeqemt 2075
	18	19	20	●	22	23	24	18:49	43	2481786	Ḥeshvan 5843	25	26	27	28	29	30	1	Thu 2h33m11p	Month 9 Rén-Yín	27	28	29	30	1	2*	3	Shuāng jiàng		8	9	10	11	12	13	14	
	25	26	27	◐	29	30	31	12:12	44	2481793		2	3	4	5	6	7	8			4	5	6	7	8	9[h]	10			15	16	17	18	19	20	21	
November 2082	1	2	3	4	○	6	7	14:37	45	2481800		9	10	11	12	13	14	15			11	12	13	14	15	16	17	Lì dōng		22	23	24	25	26	27	28	
	8	9	10	11	12	◑	14	12:45	46	2481807		16	17	18	19	20	21	22			18	19	20	21	22	23	24		Athōr 1799	29	30	1	2	3	4	5	Ḫedār 2075
	15	16	17	18	19	●	21	4:18	47	2481814		23	24	25	26	27	28	29		Month 10 Rén-Yín	25	26	27	28	29	1	2			6	7	8	9	10	11	12	
	22	23	24	25	26	◐	28	4:06	48	2481821	Kislev 5843	1	2	3	4	5	6	7	Fri 15h17m12p		3	4	5	6	7	8	9	Xiǎo xuě		13	14	15	16	17	18	19	
December 2082	29	30	1	2	3	4	○	8:55	49	2481828		8	9	10	11	12	13	14[d]			10	11	12	13	14	15	16			20	21	22	23	24	25	26	
	6	7	8	9	10	11	◑	23:50	50	2481835		15	16	17	18	19	20	21			17	18	19	20	21	22	23	Dà xuě	Koiak 1799	27	28	29	30	1	2	3	Tākhśāś 2075
	13	14	15	16	17	18	●	15:09	51	2481842		22	23	24	25[e]	26[e]	27[e]	28[e]		Month 11 Rén-Yín	24	25	26	27	28	29	1			4	5	6	7	8	9	10	
	20	21[e]	22	23	24	25	◐	23:36	52	2481849	Teveth 5843	29[e]	30[e]	1[e]	2[e]	3	4	5	Sun 4h1m13p		2	3[i]	4*	5	6	7	8	Dōng zhì		11	12	13	14	15	16	17	
	27	28	29	30	31	1	2		53	2481856		6	7	8	9	10	11	12			9	10	11	12	13	14	15			18	19	20	21	22	23	24	

[a]New Year
[b]Spring (4:29)
[c]Summer (21:02)
[d]Autumn (13:21)
[e]Winter (11:03)
● New moon
◐ First quarter moon
○ Full moon
◑ Last quarter moon

[a]New Year
[b]Yom Kippur
[c]Sukkot
[d]Winter starts
[e]Ḥanukkah
[f]Purim
[g]Passover
[h]Shavuot
[i]Fast of Av

‡Leap year
[a]New Year (4780, Tiger)
[b]Lantern Festival
[c]Qīngmíng
[d]Dragon Festival
[e]Qīqiǎo
[f]Hungry Ghosts
[g]Mid-Autumn Festival
[h]Double-Ninth Festival
[i]Dōngzhì
*Start of 60-name cycle

‡Leap year
[a]New Year
[b]Building of the Cross
[c]Christmas
[d]Jesus's Circumcision
[e]Epiphany
[f]Easter
[g]Mary's Announcement
[h]Jesus's Transfiguration

PERSIAN (ASTRONOMICAL) 1460/1461‡

Month	Sun	Mon	Tue	Wed	Thu	Fri	Sat
	8	9	10	11	12	13	14
DEY 1460	15	16	17	18	19	20	21
	22	23	24	25	26	27	28
	29	30	*1*	2	3	4	5
BAHMAN 1460	6	7	8	9	10	11	12
	13	14	15	16	17	18	19
	20	21	22	23	24	25	26
	27	28	29	30	*1*	2	3
ESFAND 1460	4	5	6	7	8	9	10
	11	12	13	14	15	16	17
	18	19	20	21	22	23	24
	25	26	27	28	29	*1*[a]	2
FARVARDĪN 1461	3	4	5	6	7	8	9
	10	11	12	13[b]	14	15	16
	17	18	19	20	21	22	23
	24	25	26	27	28	29	30
	31	*1*	2	3	4	5	6
ORDĪBEHEŠT 1461	7	8	9	10	11	12	13
	14	15	16	17	18	19	20
	21	22	23	24	25	26	27
	28	29	30	31	*1*	2	3
XORDĀD 1461	4	5	6	7	8	9	10
	11	12	13	14	15	16	17
	18	19	20	21	22	23	24
	25	26	27	28	29	30	31
TĪR 1461	*1*	2	3	4	5	6	7
	8	9	10	11	12	13	14
	15	16	17	18	19	20	21
	22	23	24	25	26	27	28
	29	30	31	*1*	2	3	4
MORDĀD 1461	5	6	7	8	9	10	11
	12	13	14	15	16	17	18
	19	20	21	22	23	24	25
	26	27	28	29	30	31	*1*
SHAHRĪVAR 1461	2	3	4	5	6	7	8
	9	10	11	12	13	14	15
	16	17	18	19	20	21	22
	23	24	25	26	27	28	29
	30	31	*1*	2	3	4	5
MEHR 1461	6	7	8	9	10	11	12
	13	14	15	16	17	18	19
	20	21	22	23	24	25	26
	27	28	29	30	*1*	2	3
ĀBĀN 1461	4	5	6	7	8	9	10
	11	12	13	14	15	16	17
	18	19	20	21	22	23	24
	25	26	27	28	29	30	*1*
ĀZAR 1461	2	3	4	5	6	7	8
	9	10	11	12	13	14	15
	16	17	18	19	20	21	22
	23	24	25	26	27	28	29
DEY 1461	30	*1*	2	3	4	5	6
	7	8	9	10	11	12	13

‡Leap year
[a]New Year
[b]Sizdeh Bedar

HINDU LUNAR 2138/2139

Month	Sun	Mon	Tue	Wed	Thu	Fri	Sat
	28	29	30	*1*	2	3	4
PAUSHA 2138	5	6	7	8	9	10	11
	12	13	14	15	16	17	18
	19	20	21	22	**23**	25	26
	27	28	29	30	*1*	2	3
MĀGHA 2138	4	*4*	5	6	7	8	9
	10	11	12	13	14	15	16
	17	19	20	21	22	23	24
	25	26	27	28[h]	29	30	*1*
PHĀLGUNA 2138	2	3	4	5	6	7	*7*
	8	9	**10**	12	13	14	15[i]
	16	17	18	19	20	21	22
	23	24	25	26	27	28	29
	30	*1*[a]	2	3	4	5	6
CHAITRA 2139	7	8	9[b]	10	11	12	13
	14	**15**	17	18	19	20	21
	22	23	24	25	26	27	28
	29	30	*30*	*1*	2	3	4
VAIŚĀKHA 2139	5	6	7	**8**	10	11	12
	13	14	15	16	17	18	19
	20	21	22	23	24	25	26
	27	28	29	30	*1*	2	3
JYAISHṬHA 2139	4	5	6	7	8	9	10
	11	**12**	14	15	16	17	18
	19	20	21	22	23	24	25
	26	*26*	27	28	29	30	*1*
ĀSHĀḌHA 2139	2	3	**4**	6	7	8	9
	10	11	12	13	14	15	16
	17	18	19	20	21	22	23
	24	25	26	27	28	29	30
	1	2	3	4	5	6	**7**
ŚRĀVAṆA 2139	9	10	11	12	13	14	15
	16	17	18	19	20	21	22
	23	*23*[c]	24	25	26	27	28
	29	**30**	2	3	*4*[d]	5	6
BHĀDRAPADA 2139	7	8	9	10	11	12	13
	14	15	16	17	18	19	20
	21	22	23	24	25	26	27
	28	29	30	*1*	2	**3**	5
ĀŚVINA 2139	6	7	8[e]	9[e]	10[e]	11	12
	13	14	15	16	17	18	*18*
	19	20	21	22	23	24	25
	26	**27**	29	30	*1*[f]	2	3
KĀRTTIKA 2139	4	5	6	7	8	9	10
	11	12	13	14	15	16	17
	18	19	20	21	22	23	24
	25	26	27	28	29	30	**1**
MĀRGAŚIRA 2139	3	4	5	6	7	8	9
	10	11[g]	12	*12*	13	14	15
	16	17	18	19	20	21	22
	23	24	**25**	27	28	29	30
PAUSHA 2139	*1*	2	3	4	5	6	7
	8	9	10	11	12	13	14

[a]New Year (Śubhakṛit)
[b]Birthday of Rāma
[c]Birthday of Krishna
[d]Ganēśa Chaturthī
[e]Dashara
[f]Diwali
[g]Birthday of Vishnu
[h]Night of Śiva
[i]Holi

HINDU SOLAR 2003/2004

Month	Sun	Mon	Tue	Wed	Thu	Fri	Sat
PAUSHA 2003	13	14	15	16	17	18	19
	20	21	22	23	24	25	26
	27	28	29	30	*1*[b]	2	3
MĀGHA 2003	4	5	6	7	8	9	10
	11	12	13	14	15	16	17
	18	19	20	21	22	23	24
	25	26	27	28	29	*1*	2
PHĀLGUNA 2003	3	4	5	6	7	8	9
	10	11	12	13	14	15	16
	17	18	19	20	21	22	23
	24	25	26	27	28	29	30
	1	2	3	4	5	6	7
CHAITRA 2003	8	9	10	11	12	13	14
	15	16	17	18	19	20	21
	22	23	24	25	26	27	28
	29	30	*1*[a]	2	3	4	5
VAIŚĀKHA 2004	6	7	8	9	10	11	12
	13	14	15	16	17	18	19
	20	21	22	23	24	25	26
	27	28	29	30	31	*1*	2
JYAISHṬHA 2004	3	4	5	6	7	8	9
	10	11	12	13	14	15	16
	17	18	19	20	21	22	23
	24	25	26	27	28	29	30
	31	32	*1*	2	3	4	5
ĀSHĀḌHA 2004	6	7	8	9	10	11	12
	13	14	15	16	17	18	19
	20	21	22	23	24	25	26
	27	28	29	30	31	*1*	2
ŚRĀVAṆA 2004	3	4	5	6	7	8	9
	10	11	12	13	14	15	16
	17	18	19	20	21	22	23
	24	25	26	27	28	29	30
	31	32	*1*	2	3	4	5
BHĀDRAPADA 2004	6	7	8	9	10	11	12
	13	14	15	16	17	18	19
	20	21	22	23	24	25	26
	27	28	29	30	31	*1*	2
ĀŚVINA 2004	3	4	5	6	7	8	9
	10	11	12	13	14	15	16
	17	18	19	20	21	22	23
	24	25	26	27	28	29	30
KĀRTTIKA 2004	*1*	2	3	4	5	6	7
	8	9	10	11	12	13	14
	15	16	17	18	19	20	21
	22	23	24	25	26	27	28
	29	30	*1*	2	3	4	5
MĀRGAŚIRA 2004	6	7	8	9	10	11	12
	13	14	15	16	17	18	19
	20	21	22	23	24	25	26
	27	28	29	*1*	2	3	4
PAUSHA 2004	5	6	7	8	9	10	11
	12	13	14	15	16	17	18

[a]New Year (Anala)
[b]Pongal

ISLAMIC (ASTRONOMICAL) 1505/1506‡

Month	Sun	Mon	Tue	Wed	Thu	Fri	Sat
	27	28	29	30	*1*	2	3
RABĪ' II 1505	4	5	6	7	8	9	10
	11	12	13	14	15	16	17
	18	19	20	21	22	23	24
	25	26	27	28	29	*1*	2
JUMĀDĀ I 1505	3	4	5	6	7	8	9
	10	11	12	13	14	15	16
	17	18	19	20	21	22	23
	24	25	26	27	28	29	30
JUMĀDĀ II 1505	*1*	2	3	4	5	6	7
	8	9	10	11	12	13	14
	15	16	17	18	19	20	21
	22	23	24	25	26	27	28
	29	30	*1*	2	3	4	5
RAJAB 1505	6	7	8	9	10	11	12
	13	14	15	16	17	18	19
	20	21	22	23	24	25	26
	27[d]	28	29	*1*	2	3	4
SHA'BĀN 1505	5	6	7	8	9	10	11
	12	13	14	15	16	17	18
	19	20	21	22	23	24	25
	26	27	28	29	*30*	1[e]	2
RAMAḌĀN 1505	3	4	5	6	7	8	9
	10	11	12	13	14	15	16
	17	18	19	20	21	22	23
	24	25	26	27	28	29	*1*[f]
SHAWWĀL 1505	2	3	4	5	6	7	8
	9	10	11	12	13	14	15
	16	17	18	19	20	21	22
	23	24	25	26	27	28	29
	30	1	2	3	4	5	6
DHU AL-QA'DA 1505	7	8	9	10	11	12	13
	14	15	16	17	18	19	20
	21	22	23	24	25	26	27
	28	29	*30*	1	2	3	4
DHU AL-ḤIJJA 1505	5	6	7	8	9	10[g]	11
	12	13	14	15	16	17	18
	19	20	21	22	23	24	25
	26	27	28	29	*1*[a]	2	3
MUḤARRAM 1506	4	5	6	7	8	9	10[b]
	11	12	13	14	15	16	17
	18	19	20	21	22	23	24
	25	26	27	28	29	30	*1*
ṢAFAR 1506	2	3	4	5	6	7	8
	9	10	11	12	13	14	15
	16	17	18	19	20	21	22
	23	24	25	26	27	28	29
RABĪ' I 1506	*1*	2	3	4	5	6	7
	8	9	10	11	12[c]	13	14
	15	16	17	18	19	20	21
	22	23	24	25	26	27	28
RABĪ' II 1506	29	*1*	2	3	4	5	6
	7	8	9	10	11	12	13

‡Leap year
[a]New Year
[b]'Ashūrā'
[c]Prophet's Birthday
[d]Ascent of the Prophet
[e]Start of Ramaḍān
[f]'Īd al-Fiṭr
[g]'Īd al-'Aḍḥā

GREGORIAN 2082

Julian (Sun)	Sun	Mon	Tue	Wed	Thu	Fri	Sat	Month
Dec 15	28	29	30	31	1	2	3	
	4	5	6	7[a]	8	9	10	JANUARY 2082
Dec 29	*11*	12	13	14[b]	15	16	17	
	18	19	20	21	22	23	24	
Jan 12	*25*	26	27	28	29	30	31	
	1	2	3	4	5	6	7	FEBRUARY 2082
Jan 26	*8*	9	10	11	12	13	14	
	15	16	17	18	19	20	21	
Feb 9	*22*	23	24	25	26	27	28	
	1	2	3	4[c]	5	6	7	MARCH 2082
Feb 23	*8*[d]	9	10	11	12	13	14	
	15	16	17	18	19	20	21	
Mar 9	*22*	23	24	25	26	27	28	
	29	30	31	1	2	3	4	
Mar 23	*5*	6	7	8	9	10	11	APRIL 2082
	12	13	14	15	16	17	18	
Apr 6	*19*[e]	20	21	22	23	24	25	
	26	27	28	29	30	1	2	
Apr 20	*3*	4	5	6	7	8	9	MAY 2082
	10	11	12	13	14	15	16	
May 4	*17*	18	19	20	21	22	23	
	24	25	26	27	28	29	30	
May 18	*31*	1	2	3	4	5	6	
	7	8	9	10	11	12	13	JUNE 2082
Jun 1	*14*	15	16	17	18	19	20	
	21	22	23	24	25	26	27	
Jun 15	*28*	29	30	1	2	3	4	
	5	6	7	8	9	10	11	JULY 2082
Jun 29	*12*	13	14	15	16	17	18	
	19	20	21	22	23	24	25	
Jul 13	*26*	27	28	29	30	31	1	
	2	3	4	5	6	7	8	AUGUST 2082
Jul 27	*9*	10	11	12	13	14	15	
	16	17	18	19	20	21	22	
Aug 10	*23*	24	25	26	27	28	29	
	30	31	1	2	3	4	5	
Aug 24	*6*	7	8	9	10	11	12	SEPTEMBER 2082
	13	14	15	16	17	18	19	
Sep 7	*20*	21	22	23	24	25	26	
	27	28	29	30	1	2	3	
Sep 21	*4*	5	6	7	8	9	10	OCTOBER 2082
	11	12	13	14	15	16	17	
Oct 5	*18*	19	20	21	22	23	24	
	25	26	27	28	29	30	31	
Oct 19	*1*	2	3	4	5	6	7	NOVEMBER 2082
	8	9	10	11	12	13	14	
Nov 2	*15*	16	17	18	19	20	21	
	22	23	24	25	26	27	28	
Nov 16	*29*[g]	30	1	2	3	4	5	
	6	7	8	9	10	11	12	DECEMBER 2082
Nov 30	*13*	14	15	16	17	18	19	
	20	21	22	23	24	25[h]	26	
Dec 14	*27*	28	29	30	31	1	2	

[a]Orthodox Christmas
[b]Julian New Year
[c]Ash Wednesday
[d]Feast of Orthodoxy
[e]Easter (also Orthodox)
[g]Advent
[h]Christmas

2083

GREGORIAN 2083

Month	Sun	Mon	Tue	Wed	Thu	Fri	Sat	Lunar Phases	ISO WEEK (Mon)	JULIAN DAY (Sun noon)
	27	28	29	30	31	1[a]	2		53	2481856
JANUARY 2083	3	○	5	6	7	8	9	2:31	1	2481863
	10	◑	12	13	14	15	16	8:54	2	2481870
	17	●	19	20	21	22	23	3:49	3	2481877
	24	◐	26	27	28	29	30	21:02	4	2481884
	31	1	○	3	4	5	6	18:19	5	2481891
FEBRUARY 2083	7	8	◑	10	11	12	13	16:38	6	2481898
	14	15	●	17	18	19	20	18:14	7	2481905
	21	22	23	◐	25	26	27	18:23	8	2481912
	28	1	2	3	○	5	6	7:33	9	2481919
MARCH 2083	7	8	9	10	◑	12	13	0:09	10	2481926
	14	15	16	17	●	19	20[b]	9:55	11	2481933
	21	22	23	24	25	◐	27	13:46	12	2481940
	28	29	30	31	1	○	3	18:05	13	2481947
APRIL 2083	4	5	6	7	8	◑	10	8:30	14	2481954
	11	12	13	14	15	16	●	2:08	15	2481961
	18	19	20	21	22	23	24		16	2481968
	◐	26	27	28	29	30	1	5:53	17	2481975
MAY 2083	○	3	4	5	6	7	◑	2:28 18:29	18	2481982
	9	10	11	12	13	14	15		19	2481989
	●	17	18	19	20	21	22	18:13	20	2481996
	23	◐	25	26	27	28	29	18:10	21	2482003
	30	○	1	2	3	4	5	9:41	22	2482010
JUNE 2083	6	◑	8	9	10	11	12	6:28	23	2482017
	13	14	●	16	17	18	19	9:36	24	2482024
	20	21[c]	22	◐	24	25	26	2:51	25	2482031
	27	28	○	30	1	2	3	16:50	26	2482038
JULY 2083	4	5	◑	7	8	9	10	20:32	27	2482045
	11	12	13	●	15	16	17	23:53	28	2482052
	18	19	20	21	◐	23	24	8:55	29	2482059
	25	26	27	28	○	30	31	0:59	30	2482066
AUGUST 2083	1	2	3	4	◑	6	7	12:37	31	2482073
	8	9	10	11	12	●	14	12:44	32	2482080
	15	16	17	18	19	◐	21	13:45	33	2482087
	22	23	24	25	26	○	28	10:58	34	2482094
	29	30	31	1	2	3	◑	6:23	35	2482101
SEPTEMBER 2083	5	6	7	8	9	10	11		36	2482108
	●	13	14	15	16	17	◐	0:06 18:58	37	2482115
	19	20	21	22[d]	23	24	○	23:24	38	2482122
	26	27	28	29	30	1	2		39	2482129
OCTOBER 2083	3	◑	5	6	7	8	9	1:06	40	2482136
	10	●	12	13	14	15	16	10:22	41	2482143
	17	◐	19	20	21	22	23	1:53	42	2482150
	24	○	26	27	28	29	30	14:35	43	2482157
	31	1	◑	3	4	5	6	19:29	44	2482164
NOVEMBER 2083	7	8	●	10	11	12	13	20:14	45	2482171
	14	15	◐	17	18	19	20	11:47	46	2482178
	21	22	23	○	25	26	27	8:22	47	2482185
	28	29	30	1	◑	3	4	12:05	48	2482192
DECEMBER 2083	5	6	7	8	●	10	11	6:24	49	2482199
	12	13	14	15	◐	17	18	1:12	50	2482206
	19	20	21[e]	22	23	○	25	3:50	51	2482213
	26	27	28	29	30	31	◑	1:53	52	2482220

HEBREW 5843/5844‡

ISO WEEK	Month	Sun	Mon	Tue	Wed	Thu	Fri	Sat	Molad
53		6	7	8	9	10	11	12	
1	TEVETH 5843	13	14	15	16	17	18	19	
2		20	21	22	23	24	25	26	
3		27	28	29	1	2	3	4	Mon 16h45m14p
4	SHEVAT 5843	5	6	7	8	9	10	11	
5		12	13	14	15	16	17	18	
6		19	20	21	22	23	24	25	
7		26	27	28	29	30	1	2	Wed 5h29m15p
8	ADAR 5843	3	4	5	6	7	8	9	
9		10	11	12	13	14[f]	15	16	
10		17	18	19	20	21	22	23	
11		24	25	26	27	28	29	1	Thu 18h13m16p
12		2	3	4	5	6	7	8	
13	NISAN 5843	9	10	11	12	13	14	15[g]	
14		16	17	18	19	20	21	22	
15		23	24	25	26	27	28	29	
16		30	1	2	3	4	5	6	Sat 6h57m17p
17	IYYAR 5843	7	8	9	10	11	12	13	
18		14	15	16	17	18	19	20	
19		21	22	23	24	25	26	27	
20		28	29	1	2	3	4	5	Sun 19h42m0p
21	SIVAN 5843	6[h]	7	8	9	10	11	12	
22		13	14	15	16	17	18	19	
23		20	21	22	23	24	25	26	
24		27	28	29	30	1	2	3	Tue 8h26m1p
25	TAMMUZ 5843	4	5	6	7	8	9	10	
26		11	12	13	14	15	16	17	
27		18	19	20	21	22	23	24	
28		25	26	27	28	29	1	2	Wed 21h10m2p
29	AV 5843	3	4	5	6	7	8	9	
30		10[i]	11	12	13	14	15	16	
31		17	18	19	20	21	22	23	
32		24	25	26	27	28	29	30	
33		1	2	3	4	5	6	7	Fri 9h54m3p
34	ELUL 5843	8	9	10	11	12	13	14	
35		15	16	17	18	19	20	21	
36		22	23	24	25	26	27	28	
37		29	1[a]	2[a]	3	4	5	6	Sat 22h38m4p
38	TISHRI 5844	7	8	9	10[b]	11	12	13	
39		14	15[c]	16	17	18	19	20	
40		21	22	23	24	25	26	27	
41		28	29	30	1	2	3	4	Mon 11h22m5p
42	HESHVAN 5844	5	6	7	8	9	10	11	
43		12	13	14	15	16	17	18	
44		19	20	21	22	23	24	25	
45		26	27	28	29	1	2	3	Wed 0h6m6p
46	KISLEV 5844	4	5	6	7	8	9	10	
47		11	12	13	14	15	16	17	
48		18	19	20	21	22	23	24	
49		25[e]	26[d,e]	27[e]	28[e]	29[e]	1[e]	2[e]	Thu 12h50m7p
50	TEVETH 5844	3[e]	4	5	6	7	8	9	
51		10	11	12	13	14	15	16	
52		17	18	19	20	21	22	23	

CHINESE Rén-Yín‡/Guǐ-Mǎo

ISO WEEK	Month	Sun	Mon	Tue	Wed	Thu	Fri	Sat	Solar Term
53		9	10	11	12	13	14	15	
1	MONTH 11 Rén-Yín	16	17	18	19	20	21	22	Xiǎo hán
2		23	24	25	26	27	28	29	
3		30	1	2	3	4	5	6	Dà hán
4	MONTH 12 Rén-Yín	7	8	9	10	11	12	13	
5		14	15	16	17	18	19	20	Lì chūn
6		21	22	23	24	25	26	27	
7		28	29	30	1[a]	2	3	4*	Yǔ shuǐ
8		5	6	7	8	9	10	11	
9	MONTH 1 Guǐ-Mǎo	12	13	14	15[b]	16	17	18	Jīng zhé
10		19	20	21	22	23	24	25	
11		26	27	28	29	1	2	3	Chūn fēn
12		4	5	6	7	8	9	10	
13	MONTH 2 Guǐ-Mǎo	11	12	13	14	15	16	17	
14		18[c]	19	20	21	22	23	24	Qīng míng
15		25	26	27	28	29	30	1	
16		2	3	4	5*	6	7	8	Gǔ yǔ
17	MONTH 3 Guǐ-Mǎo	9	10	11	12	13	14	15	
18		16	17	18	19	20	21	22	Lì xià
19		23	24	25	26	27	28	29	
20		30	1	2	3	4	5	6	Xiǎo mǎn
21	MONTH 4 Guǐ-Mǎo	7	8	9	10	11	12	13	
22		14	15	16	17	18	19	20	Máng zhòng
23		21	22	23	24	25	26	27	
24		28	29	1	2	3	4	5[d]	
25	MONTH 5 Guǐ-Mǎo	6*	7	8	9	10	11	12	Xià zhì
26		13	14	15	16	17	18	19	
27		20	21	22	23	24	25	26	Xiǎo shǔ
28		27	28	29	30	1	2	3	
29	MONTH 6 Guǐ-Mǎo	4	5	6	7	8	9	10	Dà shǔ
30		11	12	13	14	15	16	17	
31		18	19	20	21	22	23	24	Lì qiū
32		25	26	27	28	29	1	2	
33	MONTH 7 Guǐ-Mǎo	3	4	5	6	7[e]*	8	9	
34		10	11	12	13	14	15[f]	16	Chǔ shǔ
35		17	18	19	20	21	22	23	
36		24	25	26	27	28	29	30	Bái lù
37		1	2	3	4	5	6	7	
38	MONTH 8 Guǐ-Mǎo	8	9	10	11	12	13	14	Qiū fēn
39		15[g]	16	17	18	19	20	21	
40		22	23	24	25	26	27	28	Hán lù
41		29	1	2	3	4	5	6	
42	MONTH 9 Guǐ-Mǎo	7	8*	9[h]	10	11	12	13	Shuāng jiàng
43		14	15	16	17	18	19	20	
44		21	22	23	24	25	26	27	
45		28	29	30	1	2	3	4	Lì dōng
46	MONTH 10 Guǐ-Mǎo	5	6	7	8	9	10	11	
47		12	13	14	15	16	17	18	Xiǎo xuě
48		19	20	21	22	23	24	25	
49		26	27	28	29	1	2	3	Dà xuě
50	MONTH 11* Guǐ-Mǎo	4	5	6	7	8	9*	10	
51		11	12	13	14[i]	15	16	17	Dōng zhì
52		18	19	20	21	22	23	24	

COPTIC 1799‡/1800 — ETHIOPIC 2075‡/2076

ISO WEEK	Coptic month	Sun	Mon	Tue	Wed	Thu	Fri	Sat	Ethiopic month
53	KOIAK 1799	18	19	20	21	22	23	24	TĀKHŚĀŚ 2075
1		25	26	27	28	29[c]	30	1	
2		2	3	4	5	6[d]	7	8	
3	TŌBE 1799	9	10	11[e]	12	13	14	15	ṬER 2075
4		16	17	18	19	20	21	22	
5		23	24	25	26	27	28	29	
6		30	1	2	3	4	5	6	
7	MESHIR 1799	7	8	9	10	11	12	13	YAKĀTIT 2075
8		14	15	16	17	18	19	20	
9		21	22	23	24	25	26	27	
10		28	29	30	1	2	3	4	
11	PAREMOTEP 1799	5	6	7	8	9	10	11	MAGĀBIT 2075
12		12	13	14	15	16	17	18	
13		19	20	21	22	23	24	25	
14		26	27	28	29	30	1	2	
15	PARMOUTE 1799	3[f]	4	5	6	7	8	9	MIYĀZYĀ 2075
16		10	11	12	13	14	15	16	
17		17	18	19	20	21	22	23	
18		24	25	26	27	28	29[g]	30	
19		1	2	3	4	5	6	7	
20	PASHONS 1799	8	9	10	11	12	13	14	GENBOT 2075
21		15	16	17	18	19	20	21	
22		22	23	24	25	26	27	28	
23		29	30	1	2	3	4	5	
24	PAŌNE 1799	6	7	8	9	10	11	12	SANĒ 2075
25		13	14	15	16	17	18	19	
26		20	21	22	23	24	25	26	
27		27	28	29	30	1	2	3	
28	EPĒP 1799	4	5	6	7	8	9	10	ḤAMLĒ 2075
29		11	12	13	14	15	16	17	
30		18	19	20	21	22	23	24	
31		25	26	27	28	29	30	1	
32	MESORĒ 1799	2	3	4	5	6	7	8	NAHASĒ 2075
33		9	10	11	12	13[h]	14	15	
34		16	17	18	19	20	21	22	
35		23	24	25	26	27	28	29	
36	EPAG. 1799	30	1	2	3	4	5	6	PĀG. 2075
37	THOOUT 1800	1[a]	2	3	4	5	6	7	MASKARAM 2076
38		8	9	10	11	12	13	14	
39		15	16	17[b]	18	19	20	21	
40		22	23	24	25	26	27	28	
41		29	30	1	2	3	4	5	
42	PAOPE 1800	6	7	8	9	10	11	12	ṬEQEMT 2076
43		13	14	15	16	17	18	19	
44		20	21	22	23	24	25	26	
45		27	28	29	30	1	2	3	
46	ATHŌR 1800	4	5	6	7	8	9	10	HEDĀR 2076
47		11	12	13	14	15	16	17	
48		18	19	20	21	22	23	24	
49		25	26	27	28	29	30	1	
50	KOIAK 1800	2	3	4	5	6	7	8	TĀKHŚĀŚ 2076
51		9	10	11	12	13	14	15	
52		16	17	18	19	20	21	22	

Gregorian notes:
[a]New Year
[b]Spring (10:08)
[c]Summer (2:42)
[d]Autumn (19:10)
[e]Winter (16:51)
● New moon
◐ First quarter moon
○ Full moon
◑ Last quarter moon

Hebrew notes:
‡Leap year
[a]New Year
[b]Yom Kippur
[c]Sukkot
[d]Winter starts
[e]Ḥanukkah
[f]Purim
[g]Passover
[h]Shavuot
[i]Fast of Av

Chinese notes:
‡Leap year
[a]New Year (4781, Hare)
[b]Lantern Festival
[c]Qīngmíng
[d]Dragon Festival
[e]Qīqiǎo
[f]Hungry Ghosts
[g]Mid-Autumn Festival
[h]Double-Ninth Festival
[i]Dōngzhì
*Start of 60-name cycle

Coptic/Ethiopic notes:
‡Leap year
[a]New Year
[b]Building of the Cross
[c]Christmas
[d]Jesus's Circumcision
[e]Epiphany
[f]Easter
[g]Mary's Announcement
[h]Jesus's Transfiguration

PERSIAN (ASTRONOMICAL) 1461‡/1462

Month	Sun	Mon	Tue	Wed	Thu	Fri	Sat
DEY 1461	7	8	9	10	11	12	13
	14	15	16	17	18	19	20
	21	22	23	24	25	26	27
BAHMAN 1461	28	29	30	*1*	2	3	4
	5	6	7	8	9	10	11
	12	13	14	15	16	17	18
	19	20	21	22	23	24	25
ESFAND 1461	26	27	28	29	30	*1*	2
	3	4	5	6	7	8	9
	10	11	12	13	14	15	16
	17	18	19	20	21	22	23
	24	25	26	27	28	29	30
FARVARDĪN 1462	*1*[a]	2	3	4	5	6	7
	8	9	10	11	12	13[b]	14
	15	16	17	18	19	20	21
	22	23	24	25	26	27	28
ORDĪBEHEŠT 1462	29	30	31	*1*	2	3	4
	5	6	7	8	9	10	11
	12	13	14	15	16	17	18
	19	20	21	22	23	24	25
XORDĀD 1462	26	27	28	29	30	31	*1*
	2	3	4	5	6	7	8
	9	10	11	12	13	14	15
	16	17	18	19	20	21	22
	23	24	25	26	27	28	29
TĪR 1462	30	31	*1*	2	3	4	5
	6	7	8	9	10	11	12
	13	14	15	16	17	18	19
	20	21	22	23	24	25	26
MORDĀD 1462	27	28	29	30	31	*1*	2
	3	4	5	6	7	8	9
	10	11	12	13	14	15	16
	17	18	19	20	21	22	23
	24	25	26	27	28	29	30
SHAHRĪVAR 1462	31	*1*	2	3	4	5	6
	7	8	9	10	11	12	13
	14	15	16	17	18	19	20
	21	22	23	24	25	26	27
MEHR 1462	28	29	30	31	*1*	2	3
	4	5	6	7	8	9	10
	11	12	13	14	15	16	17
	18	19	20	21	22	23	24
ABĀN 1462	25	26	27	28	29	30	*1*
	2	3	4	5	6	7	8
	9	10	11	12	13	14	15
	16	17	18	19	20	21	22
	23	24	25	26	27	28	29
ĀZAR 1462	30	*1*	2	3	4	5	6
	7	8	9	10	11	12	13
	14	15	16	17	18	19	20
	21	22	23	24	25	26	27
DEY 1462	28	29	30	*1*	2	3	4
	5	6	7	8	9	10	11

HINDU LUNAR 2139/2140‡

Month	Sun	Mon	Tue	Wed	Thu	Fri	Sat
PAUSHA 2139	8	9	10	11	12	13	14
	15	*15*	16	17	**18**	20	21
	22	23	24	25	26	27	28
MĀGHA 2139	29	30	1	2	3	4	5
	6	7	8	9	10	11	12
	13	14	15	16	17	18	19
	20	21	22	23	**24**	26	27
PHĀLGUNA 2139	28	29[h]	30	1	2	3	4
	5	6	7	*7*	8	9	10
	11	12	13	14	15[i]	16	17
	18	20	21	22	23	24	25
CHAITRA 2140	26	27	28	29	30	1[a]	2
	3	4	5	6	7	8	9[b]
	10	11	12	13	14	15	16
	17	18	19	20	21	22	**23**
	25	26	27	28	29	30	*30*
VAIŚĀKHA 2140	1	2	3	4	5	6	7
	8	9	10	11	12	13	14
	15	**16**	18	19	20	21	22
	23	24	25	26	27	28	29
LEAP JYAISHTHA 2140	30	1	2	3	4	5	*5*
	6	7	**8**	10	11	12	13
	14	15	16	17	18	19	**20**
	22	23	24	25	26	*26*	27
JYAISHTHA 2140	28	29	30	1	2	3	4
	5	6	7	8	9	10	11
	12	14	15	16	17	18	19
	20	21	22	23	24	25	26
ĀSHĀDHA 2140	27	28	29	30	1	2	3
	4	5	6	7	8	9	10
	11	12	13	14	**15**	17	18
	19	20	21	22	23	*23*	24
ŚRĀVANA 2140	25	26	27	28	29	30	1
	2	3	4	5	6	**7**	9
	10	11	12	13	14	15	16
	17	18	19	20	21	22	23[c]
	24	25	26	27	28	29	30
BHĀDRAPADA 2140	1	2	3	4[d]	5	6	7
	8	9	10	**11**	13	14	15
	16	17	18	19	*19*	20	21
	22	23	24	25	26	27	28
ĀŚVINA 2140	29	30	1	2	3	**4**	6
	7	8[e]	9[e]	10[e]	11	12	13
	14	15	16	17	18	19	20
	21	22	*22*	23	24	25	26
KĀRTTIKA 2140	**27**	29	30	1[f]	2	3	4
	5	6	7	8	9	10	11
	12	13	14	15	16	17	18
	19	20	21	22	23	24	25
MĀRGAŚĪRA 2140	26	27	28	29	30	1	**2**
	4	5	6	7	8	9	10
	11[g]	12	13	14	15	*15*	16
	17	18	19	20	21	22	23

HINDU SOLAR 2004/2005‡

Month	Sun	Mon	Tue	Wed	Thu	Fri	Sat
PAUSHA 2004	12	13	14	15	16	17	18
	19	20	21	22	23	24	25
MĀGHA 2004	26	27	28	29	30	1[b]	2
	3	4	5	6	7	8	9
	10	11	12	13	14	15	16
	17	18	19	20	21	22	23
PHĀLGUNA 2004	24	25	26	27	28	29	1
	2	3	4	5	6	7	8
	9	10	11	12	13	14	15
	16	17	18	19	20	21	22
	23	24	25	26	27	28	29
CHAITRA 2004	30	1	2	3	4	5	6
	7	8	9	10	11	12	13
	14	15	16	17	18	19	20
	21	22	23	24	25	26	27
VAIŚĀKHA 2005	28	29	30	1[a]	2	3	4
	5	6	7	8	9	10	11
	12	13	14	15	16	17	18
	19	20	21	22	23	24	25
JYAISHTHA 2005	26	27	28	29	30	31	1
	2	3	4	5	6	7	8
	9	10	11	12	13	14	15
	16	17	18	19	20	21	22
	23	24	25	26	27	28	29
ĀSHĀDHA 2005	30	31	32	1	2	3	4
	5	6	7	8	9	10	11
	12	13	14	15	16	17	18
	19	20	21	22	23	24	25
ŚRĀVANA 2005	26	27	28	29	30	31	1
	2	3	4	5	6	7	8
	9	10	11	12	13	14	15
	16	17	18	19	20	21	22
	23	24	25	26	27	28	29
BHĀDRAPADA 2005	30	31	32	1	2	3	4
	5	6	7	8	9	10	11
	12	13	14	15	16	17	18
	19	20	21	22	23	24	25
ĀŚVINA 2005	26	27	28	29	30	31	1
	2	3	4	5	6	7	8
	9	10	11	12	13	14	15
	16	17	18	19	20	21	22
	23	24	25	26	27	28	29
KĀRTTIKA 2005	30	1	2	3	4	5	6
	7	8	9	10	11	12	13
	14	15	16	17	18	19	20
	21	22	23	24	25	26	27
MĀRGAŚĪRA 2005	28	29	30	1	2	3	4
	5	6	7	8	9	10	11
	12	13	14	15	16	17	18
	19	20	21	22	23	24	25
PAUSHA 2005	26	27	28	29	30	1	2
	3	4	5	6	7	8	9
	10	11	12	13	14	15	16

ISLAMIC (ASTRONOMICAL) 1506‡/1507‡

Month	Sun	Mon	Tue	Wed	Thu	Fri	Sat
RABĪ' II 1506	7	8	9	10	11	12	13
	14	15	16	17	18	19	20
	21	22	23	24	25	26	27
JUMĀDĀ I 1506	28	29	1	2	3	4	5
	6	7	8	9	10	11	12
	13	14	15	16	17	18	19
	20	21	22	23	24	25	26
JUMĀDĀ II 1506	27	28	29	30	1	2	3
	4	5	6	7	8	9	10
	11	12	13	14	15	16	17
	18	19	20	21	22	23	24
RAJAB 1506	25	26	27	28	29	30	*1*
	2	3	4	5	6	7	8
	9	10	11	12	13	14	15
	16	17	18	19	20	21	22
	23	24	25	26	27[d]	28	29
SHA'BĀN 1506	1	2	3	4	5	6	7
	8	9	10	11	12	13	14
	15	16	17	18	19	20	21
	22	23	24	25	26	27	28
RAMAḌĀN 1506	29	30	1[e]	2	3	4	5
	6	7	8	9	10	11	12
	13	14	15	16	17	18	19
	20	21	22	23	24	25	26
SHAWWĀL 1506	27	28	29	30	1[f]	2	3
	4	5	6	7	8	9	10
	11	12	13	14	15	16	17
	18	19	20	21	22	23	24
DHU AL-QA'DA 1506	25	26	27	28	29	*1*	2
	3	4	5	6	7	8	9
	10	11	12	13	14	15	16
	17	18	19	20	21	22	23
	24	25	26	27	28	29	30
DHU AL-ḤIJJA 1506	*1*	2	3	4	5	6	7
	8	9	10[g]	11	12	13	14
	15	16	17	18	19	20	21
	22	23	24	25	26	27	28
MUḤARRAM 1507	29	30[a]	1[a]	2	3	4	5
	6	7	8	9	10[b]	11	12
	13	14	15	16	17	18	19
	20	21	22	23	24	25	26
ṢAFAR 1507	27	28	29	30	1	2	3
	4	5	6	7	8	9	10
	11	12	13	14	15	16	17
	18	19	20	21	22	23	24
RABĪ' I 1507	25	26	27	28	29	1	2
	3	4	5	6	7	8	9
	10	11	12[c]	13	14	15	16
	17	18	19	20	21	22	23
RABĪ' II 1507	24	25	26	27	28	29	*1*
	2	3	4	5	6	7	8
	9	10	11	12	13	14	15
	16	17	18	19	20	21	22

GREGORIAN 2083

Julian (Sun)	Sun	Mon	Tue	Wed	Thu	Fri	Sat	Month
Dec 14	*27*	28	29	30	31	1	2	
	3	4	5	6	7[a]	8	9	JANUARY 2083
Dec 28	*10*	11	12	13	14[b]	15	16	
	17	18	19	20	21	22	23	
Jan 11	*24*	25	26	27	28	29	30	
	31	1	2	3	4	5	6	FEBRUARY 2083
Jan 25	*7*	8	9	10	11	12	13	
	14	15	16	17[c]	18	19	20	
Feb 8	*21*	22	23	24	25	26	27	
	28[d]	1	2	3	4	5	6	MARCH 2083
Feb 22	*7*	8	9	10	11	12	13	
	14	15	16	17	18	19	20	
Mar 8	*21*	22	23	24	25	26	27	
	28	29	30	31	1	2	3	APRIL 2083
Mar 22	*4*[e]	5	6	7	8	9	10	
	11[f]	12	13	14	15	16	17	
Apr 5	*18*	19	20	21	22	23	24	
	25	26	27	28	29	30	1	MAY 2083
Apr 19	*2*	3	4	5	6	7	8	
	9	10	11	12	13	14	15	
May 3	*16*	17	18	19	20	21	22	
	23	24	25	26	27	28	29	
May 17	*30*	31	1	2	3	4	5	JUNE 2083
	6	7	8	9	10	11	12	
May 31	*13*	14	15	16	17	18	19	
	20	21	22	23	24	25	26	
Jun 14	*27*	28	29	30	1	2	3	JULY 2083
	4	5	6	7	8	9	10	
Jun 28	*11*	12	13	14	15	16	17	
	18	19	20	21	22	23	24	
Jul 12	*25*	26	27	28	29	30	31	
	1	2	3	4	5	6	7	AUGUST 2083
Jul 26	*8*	9	10	11	12	13	14	
	15	16	17	18	19	20	21	
Aug 9	*22*	23	24	25	26	27	28	
	29	30	31	1	2	3	4	SEPTEMBER 2083
Aug 23	*5*	6	7	8	9	10	11	
	12	13	14	15	16	17	18	
Sep 6	*19*	20	21	22	23	24	25	
	26	27	28	29	30	1	2	OCTOBER 2083
Sep 20	*3*	4	5	6	7	8	9	
	10	11	12	13	14	15	16	
Oct 4	*17*	18	19	20	21	22	23	
	24	25	26	27	28	29	30	
Oct 18	*31*	1	2	3	4	5	6	NOVEMBER 2083
	7	8	9	10	11	12	13	
Nov 1	*14*	15	16	17	18	19	20	
	21	22	23	24	25	26	27	
Nov 15	28[g]	29	30	1	2	3	4	DECEMBER 2083
	5	6	7	8	9	10	11	
Nov 29	*12*	13	14	15	16	17	18	
	19	20	21	22	23	24	25[h]	
Dec 13	*26*	27	28	29	30	31	1	

Persian notes:
‡Leap year
[a]New Year
[b]Sizdeh Bedar

Hindu lunar notes:
‡Leap year
[a]New Year (Śobhana)
[b]Birthday of Rāma
[c]Birthday of Krishna
[d]Ganēśa Chaturthī
[e]Dashara
[f]Diwali
[g]Birthday of Vishnu
[h]Night of Śiva
[i]Holi

Hindu solar notes:
‡Leap year
[a]New Year (Piṅgala)
[b]Pongal

Islamic notes:
‡Leap year
[a]New Year
[a]New Year (Arithmetic)
[b]'Ashūrā'
[c]Prophet's Birthday
[d]Ascent of the Prophet
[e]Start of Ramaḍān
[f]'Īd al-Fiṭr
[g]'Īd al-'Aḍḥā

Gregorian notes:
[a]Orthodox Christmas
[b]Julian New Year
[c]Ash Wednesday
[d]Feast of Orthodoxy
[e]Easter
[f]Orthodox Easter
[g]Advent
[h]Christmas

Gregorian 2084[‡]	Sun	Mon	Tue	Wed	Thu	Fri	Sat	Lunar Phases	ISO Week (Mon)	Julian Day (Sun noon)	Hebrew 5844[‡]/5845	Sun	Mon	Tue	Wed	Thu	Fri	Sat	Molad
	26	27	28	29	30	31	◑[a]	1:53	52	2482220	Teveth 5844	17	18	19	20	21	22	23	
January 2084	2	3	4	5	6	●	8	17:16	1	2482227		24	25	26	27	28	29	1	Sat 1h 34m 8p
	9	10	11	12	13	◐	15	18:01	2	2482234	Shevat 5844	2	3	4	5	6	7	8	
	16	17	18	19	20	21	○	23:14	3	2482241		9	10	11	12	13	14	15	
	23	24	25	26	27	28	29		4	2482248		16	17	18	19	20	21	22	
	◑	31	1	2	3	4	5	12:41	5	2482255		23	24	25	26	27	28	29	
February 2084	●	7	8	9	10	11	12	4:52	6	2482262		30	1	2	3	4	5	6	Sun 14h 18m 9p
	◐	14	15	16	17	18	19	13:27	7	2482269	Adar I 5844	7	8	9	10	11	12	13	
	20	○	22	23	24	25	26	16:35	8	2482276		14	15	16	17	18	19	20	
	27	◑	29	1	2	3	4	21:03	9	2482283		21	22	23	24	25	26	27	
March 2084	5	●	7	8	9	10	11	17:03	10	2482290		28	29	30	1	2	3	4	Tue 3h 2m 10p
	12	13	◐	15	16	17	18	10:05	11	2482297	Adar II 5844	5	6	7	8	9	10	11	
	19[b]	20	21	○	23	24	25	6:47	12	2482304		12	13	14[f]	15	16	17	18	
	26	27	28	◑	30	31	1	3:57	13	2482311		19	20	21	22	23	24	25	
April 2084	2	3	4	●	6	7	8	5:51	14	2482318		26	27	28	29	1	2	3	Wed 15h 46m 11p
	9	10	11	12	◐	14	15	6:04	15	2482325	Nisan 5844	4	5	6	7	8	9	10	
	16	17	18	19	○	21	22	17:51	16	2482332		11	12	13	14	15[g]	16	17	
	23	24	25	26	◑	28	29	10:28	17	2482339		18	19	20	21	22	23	24	
	30	1	2	3	●	5	6	19:31	18	2482346		25	26	27	28	29	30	1	Fri 4h 30m 12p
May 2084	7	8	9	10	11	◐	13	23:42	19	2482353	Iyar 5844	2	3	4	5	6	7	8	
	14	15	16	17	18	19	○	2:35	20	2482360		9	10	11	12	13	14	15	
	21	22	23	24	25	◑	27	17:34	21	2482367		16	17	18	19	20	21	22	
	28	29	30	31	1	2	●	10:12	22	2482374		23	24	25	26	27	28	29	Sat 17h 14m 13p
June 2084	4	5	6	7	8	9	10		23	2482381	Sivan 5844	1	2	3	4	5	6[h]	7	
	◐	12	13	14	15	16	17	14:02	24	2482388		8	9	10	11	12	13	14	
	○	19	20[c]	21	22	23	24	9:59	25	2482395		15	16	17	18	19	20	21	
	◑	26	27	28	29	30	1	2:14	26	2482402		22	23	24	25	26	27	28	
July 2084	2	●	4	5	6	7	8	1:37	27	2482409		29	30	1	2	3	4	5	Mon 5h 58m 14p
	9	10	◐	12	13	14	15	1:05	28	2482416	Tammuz 5844	6	7	8	9	10	11	12	
	16	○	18	19	20	21	22	17:00	29	2482423		13	14	15	16	17	18	19	
	23	◑	25	26	27	28	29	13:21	30	2482430		20	21	22	23	24	25	26	
	30	31	●	2	3	4	5	17:03	31	2482437		27	28	29	1	2	3	4	Tue 18h 42m 15p
August 2084	6	7	8	◐	10	11	12	9:31	32	2482444	Av 5844	5	6	7	8	9[i]	10	11	
	13	14	15	○	17	18	19	0:28	33	2482451		12	13	14	15	16	17	18	
	20	21	22	◑	24	25	26	3:33	34	2482458		19	20	21	22	23	24	25	
	27	28	29	30	●	1	2	7:44	35	2482465		26	27	28	29	30	1	2	Thu 7h 26m 16p
September 2084	3	4	5	6	◐	8	9	16:22	36	2482472	Elul 5844	3	4	5	6	7	8	9	
	10	11	12	13	○	15	16	9:14	37	2482479		10	11	12	13	14	15	16	
	17	18	19	20	◑	22[d]	23	20:58	38	2482486		17	18	19	20	21	22	23	
	24	25	26	27	28	●	30	21:15	39	2482493		24	25	26	27	28	29	1[a]	Fri 20h 10m 17p
October 2084	1	2	3	4	5	◐	7	22:41	40	2482500	Tishri 5845	2[a]	3	4	5	6	7	8	
	8	9	10	11	12	○	14	20:12	41	2482507		9	10[b]	11	12	13	14	15[c]	
	15	16	17	18	19	20	◑	16:48	42	2482514		16	17	18	19	20	21	22	
	22	23	24	25	26	27	28		43	2482521		23	24	25	26	27	28	29	
	●	30	31	1	2	3	4	9:46	44	2482528		30	1	2	3	4	5	6	Sun 8h 55m 0p
November 2084	◐	6	7	8	9	10	11	5:32	45	2482535	Heshvan 5845	7	8	9	10	11	12	13	
	○	13	14	15	16	17	18	10:09	46	2482542		14	15	16	17	18	19	20	
	19	◑	21	22	23	24	25	13:22	47	2482549		21	22	23	24	25	26	27	
	26	●	28	29	30	1	2	21:38	48	2482556		28	29	30	1	2	3	4	Mon 21h 39m 1p
December 2084	3	◐	5	6	7	8	9	13:56	49	2482563	Kislev 5845	5	6	7[d]	8	9	10	11	
	10	11	○	13	14	15	16	3:17	50	2482570		12	13	14	15	16	17	18	
	17	18	19	◑[e]	21	22	23	8:43	51	2482577		19	20	21	22	23	24	25[e]	
	24	25	26	●	28	29	30	9:06	52	2482584		26[e]	27[e]	28[e]	29[e]	30[e]	1[e]	2[e]	Wed 10h 23m 2p
	31	1	2	◐	4	5	6	0:46	1	2482591	Teveth 5845	3	4	5	6	7	8	9	

ISO Week	Chinese Guǐ-Mǎo/Jiǎ-Chén	Sun	Mon	Tue	Wed	Thu	Fri	Sat	Solar Term	Coptic 1800/1801	Sun	Mon	Tue	Wed	Thu	Fri	Sat	Ethiopic 2076/2077
52	Month 11* Guǐ-Mǎo	18	19	20	21	22	23	24		Koiak 1800	16	17	18	19	20	21	22	Tākhśāś 2076
1	Month 12 Guǐ-Mǎo	25	26	27	28	29	30	1	Xiǎo hán		23	24	25	26	27	28	29[c]	
2		2	3	4	5	6	7	8			30	1	2	3	4	5	6[d]	
3		9	10	11	12	*13*	14	15	Dà hán	Ṭōbe 1800	7	8	9	10	11[e]	12	13	Ṭer 2076
4		16	17	18	19	20	21	22			14	15	16	17	18	19	20	
5		23	24	25	26	27	*28*	29	Lì chūn		21	22	23	24	25	26	27	
6	Month 1 Jiǎ-Chén	1[a]	2	3	4	5	6	7			28	29	30	1	2	3	4	
7		8	9	10*	11	12	13	*14*	Yǔ shuǐ	Meshir 1800	5	6	7	8	9	10	11	Yakātit 2076
8		15[b]	16	17	18	19	20	21			12	13	14	15	16	17	18	
9		22	23	24	25	26	27	*28*	Jīng zhé		19	20	21	22	23	24	25	
10		29	30	1	2	3	4	5			26	27	28	29	30	1	2	
11	Month 2 Jiǎ-Chén	6	7	8	9	10	11	12		Paremotep 1800	3	4	5	6	7	8	9	Magābit 2076
12		*13*	14	15	16	17	18	19	Chūn fēn		10	11	12	13	14	15	16	
13		20	21	22	23	24	25	26			17	18	19	20	21	22	23	
14		27	28	*29*[c]	1	2	3	4	Qīng míng		24	25	26	27	28	29	30	
15	Month 3 Jiǎ-Chén	5	6	7	8	9	10	11*		Parmoute 1800	1	2	3	4	5	6	7	Miyāzyā 2076
16		12	13	14	*15*	16	17	18	Gǔ yǔ		8	9	10	11	12	13	14	
17		19	20	21	22	23	24	25			15	16	17	18	19	20	21	
18		26	27	28	29	*30*	1	2	Lì xià		22[f]	23	24	25	26	27	28	
19	Month 4 Jiǎ-Chén	3	4	5	6	7	8	9			29[g]	30	1	2	3	4	5	
20		10	11	12	13	14	15	*16*	Xiǎo mǎn	Pashons 1800	6	7	8	9	10	11	12	Genbot 2076
21		17	18	19	20	21	22	23			13	14	15	16	17	18	19	
22		24	25	26	27	28	29	1			20	21	22	23	24	25	26	
23	Month 5 Jiǎ-Chén	2	3	4	*5*[d]	6	7	8	Máng zhòng		27	28	29	30	1	2	3	
24		9	10	11	12*	13	14	15		Paōne 1800	4	5	6	7	8	9	10	Sanē 2076
25		16	17	*18*	19	20	21	22	Xià zhì		11	12	13	14	15	16	17	
26		23	24	25	26	27	28	29			18	19	20	21	22	23	24	
27		30	1	2	3	*4*	5	6	Xiǎo shǔ		25	26	27	28	29	30	1	
28	Month 6 Jiǎ-Chén	7	8	9	10	11	12	13		Epēp 1800	2	3	4	5	6	7	8	Hamlē 2076
29		14	15	16	17	18	19	*20*	Dà shǔ		9	10	11	12	13	14	15	
30		21	22	23	24	25	26	27			16	17	18	19	20	21	22	
31		28	29	30	1	2	3	4			23	24	25	26	27	28	29	
32	Month 7 Jiǎ-Chén	5	6	*7*[e]	8	9	10	11	Lì qiū		30	1	2	3	4	5	6	
33		12*	13	14	15[f]	16	17	18		Mesorē 1800	7	8	9	10	11	12	13[h]	Naḥasē 2076
34		19	20	*21*	22	23	24	25	Chǔ shǔ		14	15	16	17	18	19	20	
35		26	27	28	29	1	2	3			21	22	23	24	25	26	27	
36	Month 8 Jiǎ-Chén	4	5	6	*7*	8	9	10	Bái lù		28	29	30	1	2	3	4	
37		11	12	13	14	15[g]	16	17		Epag. 1800	5	1[a]	2	3	4	5	6	Pāg. 2076
38		18	19	20	21	22	*23*	24	Qiū fēn	Thoout 1801	7	8	9	10	11	12	13	Maskaram 2077
39		25	26	27	28	29	30	1			14	15	16	17[b]	18	19	20	
40	Month 9 Jiǎ-Chén	2	3	4	5	6	7	*8*	Hán lù		21	22	23	24	25	26	27	
41		9[h]	10	11	12	13*	14	15			28	29	30	1	2	3	4	
42		16	17	18	19	20	21	22		Paope 1801	5	6	7	8	9	10	11	Ṭeqemt 2077
43		*23*	24	25	26	27	28	29	Shuāng jiàng		12	13	14	15	16	17	18	
44		1	2	3	4	5	6	7			19	20	21	22	23	24	25	
45	Month 10 Jiǎ-Chén	8	9	10	11	12	13	14	Lì dōng		26	27	28	29	30	1	2	
46		15	16	17	18	19	20	21		Athōr 1801	3	4	5	6	7	8	9	Hedār 2077
47		22	23	*24*	25	26	27	28	Xiǎo xuě		10	11	12	13	14	15	16	
48		29	30	1	2	3	4	5			17	18	19	20	21	22	23	
49	Month 11 Jiǎ-Chén	6	7	8	9	10	11	12	Dà xuě		24	25	26	27	28	29	30	
50		13	14*	15	16	17	18	19		Koiak 1801	1	2	3	4	5	6	7	Tākhśāś 2077
51		20	21	22	23	*24*[i]	25	26	Dōng zhì		8	9	10	11	12	13	14	
52		27	28	29	1	2	3	4			15	16	17	18	19	20	21	
1	Month 12 Jiǎ-Chén	5	6	7	8	9	10	11	Xiǎo hán		22	23	24	25	26	27	28	

‡Leap year
[a]New Year
[b]Spring (15:58)
[c]Summer (8:39)
[d]Autumn (0:58)
[e]Winter (22:40)
● New moon
◐ First quarter moon
○ Full moon
◑ Last quarter moon

‡Leap year
[a]New Year
[b]Yom Kippur
[c]Sukkot
[d]Winter starts
[e]Ḥanukkah
[f]Purim
[g]Passover
[h]Shavuot
[i]Fast of Av

[a]New Year (4782, Dragon)
[b]Lantern Festival
[c]Qīngmíng
[d]Dragon Festival
[e]Qīqiǎo
[f]Hungry Ghosts
[g]Mid-Autumn Festival
[h]Double-Ninth Festival
[i]Dōngzhì
*Start of 60-name cycle

[a]New Year
[b]Building of the Cross
[c]Christmas
[d]Jesus's Circumcision
[e]Epiphany
[f]Easter
[g]Mary's Announcement
[h]Jesus's Transfiguration

PERSIAN (ASTRONOMICAL) 1462/1463

Month	Sun	Mon	Tue	Wed	Thu	Fri	Sat
DEY 1462	5	6	7	8	9	10	11
	12	13	14	15	16	17	18
	19	20	21	22	23	24	25
BAHMAN 1462	26	27	28	29	30	1	2
	3	4	5	6	7	8	9
	10	11	12	13	14	15	16
	17	18	19	20	21	22	23
	24	25	26	27	28	29	30
ESFAND 1462	1	2	3	4	5	6	7
	8	9	10	11	12	13	14
	15	16	17	18	19	20	21
	22	23	24	25	26	27	28
FARVARDĪN 1463	29	1[a]	2	3	4	5	6
	7	8	9	10	11	12	13[b]
	14	15	16	17	18	19	20
	21	22	23	24	25	26	27
ORDĪBEHEŠT 1463	28	29	30	31	1	2	3
	4	5	6	7	8	9	10
	11	12	13	14	15	16	17
	18	19	20	21	22	23	24
	25	26	27	28	29	30	31
XORDĀD 1463	1	2	3	4	5	6	7
	8	9	10	11	12	13	14
	15	16	17	18	19	20	21
	22	23	24	25	26	27	28
TĪR 1463	29	30	31	1	2	3	4
	5	6	7	8	9	10	11
	12	13	14	15	16	17	18
	19	20	21	22	23	24	25
MORDĀD 1463	26	27	28	29	30	31	1
	2	3	4	5	6	7	8
	9	10	11	12	13	14	15
	16	17	18	19	20	21	22
	23	24	25	26	27	28	29
SHAHRĪVAR 1463	30	31	1	2	3	4	5
	6	7	8	9	10	11	12
	13	14	15	16	17	18	19
	20	21	22	23	24	25	26
MEHR 1463	27	28	29	30	31	1	2
	3	4	5	6	7	8	9
	10	11	12	13	14	15	16
	17	18	19	20	21	22	23
	24	25	26	27	28	29	30
ĀBĀN 1463	1	2	3	4	5	6	7
	8	9	10	11	12	13	14
	15	16	17	18	19	20	21
	22	23	24	25	26	27	28
ĀZAR 1463	29	30	1	2	3	4	5
	6	7	8	9	10	11	12
	13	14	15	16	17	18	19
	20	21	22	23	24	25	26
DEY 1463	27	28	29	30	1	2	3
	4	5	6	7	8	9	10
	11	12	13	14	15	16	17

HINDU LUNAR 2140‡/2141

Month	Sun	Mon	Tue	Wed	Thu	Fri	Sat
MĀRGAŚIRA 2140	17	18	19	20	21	22	23
	24	25	**26**	28	29	30	1
PAUSHA 2140	2	3	4	5	6	7	8
	9	10	11	12	13	14	15
	16	17	18	19	20	21	22
	23	24	25	26	27	28	29
MĀGHA 2140	30	1	**2**	4	5	6	7
	7	8	9	10	11	12	13
	14	15	16	17	18	19	20
	21	22	23	24	**25**	27	28
PHĀLGUNA 2140	29[h]	30	1	2	3	4	5
	6	7	8	9	10	10	11
	12	13	14	15[i]	16	17	18
	19	21	22	23	24	25	26
CHAITRA 2141	27	28	29	30	1[a]	2	3
	4	5	6	7	8	9[b]	10
	11	12	13	14	15	16	17
	18	19	20	21	22	**23**	25
VAIŚĀKHA 2141	26	27	28	29	30	1	2
	3	4	4	5	6	7	8
	9	10	11	12	13	14	15
	16	18	19	20	21	22	23
	24	25	26	27	28	29	30
JYAISHṬHA 2141	1	2	3	4	5	6	7
	8	9	10	11	12	13	14
	15	16	17	18	**19**	21	22
	23	24	25	26	27	28	29
ĀSHĀḌHA 2141	30	30	1	2	3	4	5
	6	7	8	9	10	11	**12**
	14	15	16	17	18	19	20
	21	22	23	24	25	26	27
ŚRĀVAṆA 2141	28	29	30	1	2	3	4
	5	6	7	8	9	10	11
	12	13	**14**	16	17	18	19
	20	21	22	23[c]	24	25	26
BHĀDRAPADA 2141	27	27	28	29	30	1	2
	3	4[d]	5	6	**7**	9	10
	11	12	13	14	15	16	17
	18	19	20	21	22	23	24
ĀŚVINA 2141	25	26	27	28	29	30	1
	2	3	4	5	6	7	8[e]
	9[e]	10[e]	**11**	13	14	15	16
	17	18	19	20	21	22	22
	23	24	25	26	27	28	29
KĀRTTIKA 2141	30	1[f]	2	3	4	**5**	7
	8	9	10	11	12	13	14
	15	16	17	18	19	20	21
	22	23	24	25	26	27	28
MĀRGAŚIRA 2141	29	30	1	2	3	4	5
	6	7	8	9	**10**[g]	12	13
	14	15	15	16	17	18	19
	20	21	22	23	24	25	26
PAUSHA 2141	27	28	29	30	1	2	**3**
	5	6	7	8	9	10	11

HINDU SOLAR 2005‡/2006

Month	Sun	Mon	Tue	Wed	Thu	Fri	Sat
PAUSHA 2005	10	11	12	13	14	15	16
	17	18	19	20	21	22	23
MĀGHA 2005	24	25	26	27	28	29	1[b]
	2	3	4	5	6	7	8
	9	10	11	12	13	14	15
	16	17	18	19	20	21	22
	23	24	25	26	27	28	29
PHĀLGUNA 2005	30	1	2	3	4	5	6
	7	8	9	10	11	12	13
	14	15	16	17	18	19	20
	21	22	23	24	25	26	27
CHAITRA 2005	28	29	1	2	3	4	5
	6	7	8	9	10	11	12
	13	14	15	16	17	18	19
	20	21	22	23	24	25	26
VAIŚĀKHA 2006	27	28	29	30	31	1[a]	2
	3	4	5	6	7	8	9
	10	11	12	13	14	15	16
	17	18	19	20	21	22	23
	24	25	26	27	28	29	30
JYAISHṬHA 2006	31	1	2	3	4	5	6
	7	8	9	10	11	12	13
	14	15	16	17	18	19	20
	21	22	23	24	25	26	27
ĀSHĀḌHA 2006	28	29	30	31	1	2	3
	4	5	6	7	8	9	10
	11	12	13	14	15	16	17
	18	19	20	21	22	23	24
	25	26	27	28	29	30	31
ŚRĀVAṆA 2006	32	1	2	3	4	5	6
	7	8	9	10	11	12	13
	14	15	16	17	18	19	20
	21	22	23	24	25	26	27
BHĀDRAPADA 2006	28	29	30	31	1	2	3
	4	5	6	7	8	9	10
	11	12	13	14	15	16	17
	18	19	20	21	22	23	24
	25	26	27	28	29	30	31
ĀŚVINA 2006	1	2	3	4	5	6	7
	8	9	10	11	12	13	14
	15	16	17	18	19	20	21
	22	23	24	25	26	27	28
KĀRTTIKA 2006	29	30	31	1	2	3	4
	5	6	7	8	9	10	11
	12	13	14	15	16	17	18
	19	20	21	22	23	24	25
MĀRGAŚIRA 2006	26	27	28	29	30	1	2
	3	4	5	6	7	8	9
	10	11	12	13	14	15	16
	17	18	19	20	21	22	23
PAUSHA 2006	24	25	26	27	28	29	1
	2	3	4	5	6	7	8
	9	10	11	12	13	14	15
	16	17	18	19	20	21	22

ISLAMIC (ASTRONOMICAL) 1507‡/1508

Month	Sun	Mon	Tue	Wed	Thu	Fri	Sat
RABĪ' II 1507	16	17	18	19	20	21	22
	23	24	25	26	27	28	29
JUMĀDĀ I 1507	1	2	3	4	5	6	7
	8	9	10	11	12	13	14
	15	16	17	18	19	20	21
	22	23	24	25	26	27	28
JUMĀDĀ II 1507	29	1	2	3	4	5	6
	7	8	9	10	11	12	13
	14	15	16	17	18	19	20
	21	22	23	24	25	26	27
RAJAB 1507	28	29	30	1	2	3	4
	5	6	7	8	9	10	11
	12	13	14	15	16	17	18
	19	20	21	22	23	24	25
SHA'BĀN 1507	26	27[d]	28	29	1	2	3
	4	5	6	7	8	9	10
	11	12	13	14	15	16	17
	18	19	20	21	22	23	24
RAMAḌĀN 1507	25	26	27	28	29	30	1[e]
	2	3	4	5	6	7	8
	9	10	11	12	13	14	15
	16	17	18	19	20	21	22
	23	24	25	26	27	28	29
SHAWWĀL 1507	30	1[f]	2	3	4	5	6
	7	8	9	10	11	12	13
	14	15	16	17	18	19	20
	21	22	23	24	25	26	27
DHU AL-QA'DA 1507	28	29	30	1	2	3	4
	5	6	7	8	9	10	11
	12	13	14	15	16	17	18
	19	20	21	22	23	24	25
DHU AL-HIJJA 1507	26	27	28	29	30	1	2
	3	4	5	6	7	8	9
	10[g]	11	12	13	14	15	16
	17	18	19	20	21	22	23
	24	25	26	27	28	29	30[A]
MUHARRAM 1508	1[a]	2	3	4	5	6	7
	8	9	10[b]	11	12	13	14
	15	16	17	18	19	20	21
	22	23	24	25	26	27	28
SAFAR 1508	29	1	2	3	4	5	6
	7	8	9	10	11	12	13
	14	15	16	17	18	19	20
	21	22	23	24	25	26	27
RABĪ' I 1508	28	29	1	2	3	4	5
	6	7	8	9	10	11	12[c]
	13	14	15	16	17	18	19
	20	21	22	23	24	25	26
RABĪ' II 1508	27	28	29	1	2	3	4
	5	6	7	8	9	10	11
	12	13	14	15	16	17	18
	19	20	21	22	23	24	25
JUMĀDĀ I 1508	26	27	28	29	30	1	2
	3	4	5	6	7	8	9

GREGORIAN 2084‡

Julian‡ (Sun)	Sun	Mon	Tue	Wed	Thu	Fri	Sat	Month
Dec 13	26	27	28	29	30	31	1	JANUARY 2084
	2	3	4	5	6	7[a]	8	
Dec 27	9	10	11	12	13	14[b]	15	
	16	17	18	19	20	21	22	
Jan 10	23	24	25	26	27	28	29	
	30	31	1	2	3	4	5	FEBRUARY 2084
Jan 24	6	7	8	9[c]	10	11	12	
	13	14	15	16	17	18	19	
Feb 7	20	21	22	23	24	25	26	
	27	28	29	1	2	3	4	MARCH 2084
Feb 21	5	6	7	8	9	10	11	
	12	13	14	15	16	17	18	
Mar 6	19[d]	20	21	22	23	24	25	
	26[e]	27	28	29	30	31	1	APRIL 2084
Mar 20	2	3	4	5	6	7	8	
	9	10	11	12	13	14	15	
Apr 3	16	17	18	19	20	21	22	
	23	24	25	26	27	28	29	
Apr 17	30[f]	1	2	3	4	5	6	MAY 2084
	7	8	9	10	11	12	13	
May 1	14	15	16	17	18	19	20	
	21	22	23	24	25	26	27	
May 15	28	29	30	31	1	2	3	JUNE 2084
	4	5	6	7	8	9	10	
May 29	11	12	13	14	15	16	17	
	18	19	20	21	22	23	24	
Jun 12	25	26	27	28	29	30	1	JULY 2084
	2	3	4	5	6	7	8	
Jun 26	9	10	11	12	13	14	15	
	16	17	18	19	20	21	22	
Jul 10	23	24	25	26	27	28	29	
	30	31	1	2	3	4	5	AUGUST 2084
Jul 24	6	7	8	9	10	11	12	
	13	14	15	16	17	18	19	
Aug 7	20	21	22	23	24	25	26	
	27	28	29	30	31	1	2	SEPTEMBER 2084
Aug 21	3	4	5	6	7	8	9	
	10	11	12	13	14	15	16	
Sep 4	17	18	19	20	21	22	23	
	24	25	26	27	28	29	30	
Sep 18	1	2	3	4	5	6	7	OCTOBER 2084
	8	9	10	11	12	13	14	
Oct 2	15	16	17	18	19	20	21	
	22	23	24	25	26	27	28	
Oct 16	29	30	31	1	2	3	4	NOVEMBER 2084
	5	6	7	8	9	10	11	
Oct 30	12	13	14	15	16	17	18	
	19	20	21	22	23	24	25	
Nov 13	26	27	28	29	30	1	2	DECEMBER 2084
	3[g]	4	5	6	7	8	9	
Nov 27	10	11	12	13	14	15	16	
	17	18	19	20	21	22	23	
Dec 11	24	25[h]	26	27	28	29	30	
	31	1	2	3	4	5	6	

Persian: [a] New Year; [b] Sizdeh Bedar

Hindu Lunar: ‡ Leap year; [a] New Year (Krodhin); [b] Birthday of Rāma; [c] Birthday of Krishna; [d] Ganēśa Chaturthī; [e] Dashara; [f] Diwali; [g] Birthday of Vishnu; [h] Night of Śiva; [i] Holi

Hindu Solar: ‡ Leap year; [a] New Year (Kālayukta); [b] Pongal

Islamic: ‡ Leap year; [a] New Year; [A] New Year (Arithmetic); [b] 'Ashūrā'; [c] Prophet's Birthday; [d] Ascent of the Prophet; [e] Start of Ramaḍān; [f] 'Id al-Fiṭr; [g] 'Id al-'Aḍḥā

Gregorian: ‡ Leap year; [a] Orthodox Christmas; [b] Julian New Year; [c] Ash Wednesday; [d] Feast of Orthodoxy; [e] Easter; [f] Orthodox Easter; [g] Advent; [h] Christmas

2085

GREGORIAN 2085	Sun	Mon	Tue	Wed	Thu	Fri	Sat	Lunar Phases	ISO WEEK (Mon)	JULIAN DAY (Sun noon)
	31	1[a]	2	◐	4	5	6	0:46	1	2482591
	7	8	9	○	11	12	13	22:41	2	2482598
JANUARY 2085	14	15	16	17	18	◑	20	1:25	3	2482605
	21	22	23	24	●	26	27	20:05	4	2482612
	28	29	30	31	◐	2	3	14:34	5	2482619
	4	5	6	7	8	○	10	18:23	6	2482626
FEBRUARY 2085	11	12	13	14	15	16	◑	14:46	7	2482633
	18	19	20	21	22	23	●	6:31	8	2482640
	25	26	27	28	1	2	◐	7:15	9	2482647
	4	5	6	7	8	9	10		10	2482654
MARCH 2085	○	12	13	14	15	16	17	12:24	11	2482661
	18	◑[b]	20	21	22	23	24	0:43	12	2482668
	●	26	27	28	29	30	31	16:36	13	2482675
	1	◐	3	4	5	6	7	1:50	14	2482682
	8	9	○	11	12	13	14	3:40	15	2482689
APRIL 2085	15	16	◑	18	19	20	21	7:53	16	2482696
	22	23	●	25	26	27	28	2:58	17	2482703
	29	30	◐	2	3	4	5	20:51	18	2482710
	6	7	8	○	10	11	12	16:03	19	2482717
MAY 2085	13	14	15	◑	17	18	19	13:17	20	2482724
	20	21	22	●	24	25	26	14:22	21	2482731
	27	28	29	30	◐	1	2	14:50	22	2482738
	3	4	5	6	7	○	9	2:01	23	2482745
JUNE 2085	10	11	12	13	◑	15	16	18:18	24	2482752
	17	18	19	20[c]	21	●	23	3:17	25	2482759
	24	25	26	27	28	29	◐	6:54	26	2482766
	1	2	3	4	5	6	○	10:13	27	2482773
JULY 2085	8	9	10	11	12	13	◑	0:23	28	2482780
	15	16	17	18	19	20	●	17:42	29	2482787
	22	23	24	25	26	27	28		30	2482794
	◐	30	31	1	2	3	4	20:46	31	2482801
	○	6	7	8	9	10	11	17:28	32	2482808
AUGUST 2085	◑	13	14	15	16	17	18	8:58	33	2482815
	19	●	21	22	23	24	25	9:09	34	2482822
	26	27	◐	29	30	31	1	8:29	35	2482829
	2	3	○	5	6	7	8	0:40	36	2482836
SEPTEMBER 2085	9	◑	11	12	13	14	15	21:07	37	2482843
	16	17	18	●	20	21	22[d]	1:05	38	2482850
	23	24	25	◐	27	28	29	18:17	39	2482857
	30	1	2	○	4	5	6	8:52	40	2482864
OCTOBER 2085	7	8	9	◑	11	12	13	13:08	41	2482871
	14	15	16	17	●	19	20	16:59	42	2482878
	21	22	23	24	25	◐	27	2:33	43	2482885
	28	29	30	31	○	2	3	19:07	44	2482892
	4	5	6	7	8	◑	10	8:30	45	2482899
NOVEMBER 2085	11	12	13	14	15	16	●	8:19	46	2482906
	18	19	20	21	22	23	◐	10:01	47	2482913
	25	26	27	28	29	30	○	8:09	48	2482920
	2	3	4	5	6	7	8		49	2482927
DECEMBER 2085	◑	10	11	12	13	14	15	5:46	50	2482934
	●	17	18	19	20	21[e]	22	22:37	51	2482941
	◐	24	25	26	27	28	29	17:41	52	2482948
	○	31	1	2	3	4	5	23:58	1	2482955

JULIAN DAY	HEBREW 5845/5846	Sun	Mon	Tue	Wed	Thu	Fri	Sat	Molad
2482591		3	4	5	6	7	8	9	
2482598		10	11	12	13	14	15	16	
2482605	TEVETH 5845	17	18	19	20	21	22	23	
2482612		24	25	26	27	28	29	1	Thu 23h7m3p
2482619		2	3	4	5	6	7	8	
2482626		9	10	11	12	13	14	15	
2482633	SHEVAT 5845	16	17	18	19	20	21	22	
2482640		23	24	25	26	27	28	29	
2482647		30	1	2	3	4	5	6	Sat 11h51m4p
2482654		7	8	9	10	11	12	13	
2482661	ADAR 5845	14[f]	15	16	17	18	19	20	
2482668		21	22	23	24	25	26	27	
2482675		28	29	1	2	3	4	5	Mon 0h35m5p
2482682		6	7	8	9	10	11	12	
2482689	NISAN 5845	13	14	15[g]	16	17	18	19	
2482696		20	21	22	23	24	25	26	
2482703		27	28	29	30	1	2	3	Tue 13h19m6p
2482710		4	5	6	7	8	9	10	
2482717	IYYAR 5845	11	12	13	14	15	16	17	
2482724		18	19	20	21	22	23	24	
2482731		25	26	27	28	29	1	2	Thu 2h3m7p
2482738		3	4	5	6[h]	7	8	9	
2482745	SIVAN 5845	10	11	12	13	14	15	16	
2482752		17	18	19	20	21	22	23	
2482759		24	25	26	27	28	29	30	
2482766		1	2	3	4	5	6	7	Fri 14h47m8p
2482773		8	9	10	11	12	13	14	
2482780	TAMMUZ 5845	15	16	17	18	19	20	21	
2482787		22	23	24	25	26	27	28	
2482794		29	1	2	3	4	5	6	Sun 3h31m9p
2482801		7	8	9[i]	10	11	12	13	
2482808	AV 5845	14	15	16	17	18	19	20	
2482815		21	22	23	24	25	26	27	
2482822		28	29	30	1	2	3	4	Mon 16h15m10p
2482829		5	6	7	8	9	10	11	
2482836	ELUL 5845	12	13	14	15	16	17	18	
2482843		19	20	21	22	23	24	25	
2482850		26	27	28	29	1[a]	2[a]	3	Wed 4h59m11p
2482857		4	5	6	7	8	9	10[b]	
2482864	TISHRI 5846	11	12	13	14	15[c]	16	17	
2482871		18	19	20	21	22	23	24	
2482878		25	26	27	28	29	30	1	Thu 17h43m12p
2482885		2	3	4	5	6	7	8	
2482892	HESHVAN 5846	9	10	11	12	13	14	15	
2482899		16	17	18	19	20	21	22	
2482906		23	24	25	26	27	28	29	
2482913		1	2	3	4	5	6	7	Sat 6h27m13p
2482920		8	9	10	11	12	13	14	
2482927	KISLEV 5846	15	16	17	18[d]	19	20	21	
2482934		22	23	24	25[e]	26[e]	27[e]	28[e]	
2482941		29[e]	30[e]	1[e]	2[e]	3	4	5	Sun 19h11m14p
2482948	TEVETH 5846	6	7	8	9	10	11	12	
2482955		13	14	15	16	17	18	19	

JULIAN DAY	CHINESE Jiǎ-Chén/Yǐ-Sì‡	Sun	Mon	Tue	Wed	Thu	Fri	Sat	Solar Term
2482591		5	6	7	8	9	10	11	Xiǎo hán
2482598	MONTH 12 Jiǎ-Chén	12	13	14	15	16	17	18	
2482605		19	20	21	22	23	**24**	25	Dà hán
2482612		26	27	28	29	30	1[a]	2	
2482619		3	4	5	6	7	8	9	Lì chūn
2482626	MONTH 1 Yǐ-Sì	10	11	12	13	14	15[b]*	16	
2482633		17	18	19	20	21	22	23	
2482640		**24**	25	26	27	28	29	1	Yǔ shuǐ
2482647		2	3	4	5	6	7	8	
2482654	MONTH 2 Yǐ-Sì	9	*10*	11	12	13	14	15	Jīng zhé
2482661		16	17	18	19	20	21	22	
2482668		23	24	**25**	26	27	28	29	Chūn fēn
2482675		30	1	2	3	4	5	6	
2482682		7	8	9	10[c]	11	12	13	Qīng míng
2482689	MONTH 3 Yǐ-Sì	14	15	16*	17	18	19	20	
2482696		21	22	23	24	**25**	26	27	Gǔ yǔ
2482703		28	29	1	2	3	4	5	
2482710		6	7	8	9	10	11	*12*	Lì xià
2482717	MONTH 4 Yǐ-Sì	13	14	15	16	17	18	19	
2482724		20	21	22	23	24	25	26	
2482731		*27*	28	29	1	2	3	4	Xiǎo mǎn
2482738		5[d]	6	7	8	9	10	11	
2482745	MONTH 5 Yǐ-Sì	12	13	*14*	15	16	17	18*	Máng zhòng
2482752		19	20	21	22	23	24	25	
2482759		26	27	28	**29**	30	1	2	Xià zhì
2482766		3	4	5	6	7	8	9	
2482773	LEAP MONTH 5 Yǐ-Sì	10	11	12	13	14	*15*	16	Xiǎo shǔ
2482780		17	18	19	20	21	22	23	
2482787		24	25	26	27	28	29	30	
2482794		*1*	2	3	4	5	6	7	Dà shǔ
2482801		8	9	10	11	12	13	14	
2482808	MONTH 6 Yǐ-Sì	15	16	*17*	18*	19	20	21	Lì qiū
2482815		22	23	24	25	26	27	28	
2482822		29	1	2	**3**	4	5	6	Chǔ shǔ
2482829		7[e]	8	9	10	11	12	13	
2482836	MONTH 7 Yǐ-Sì	14	15[f]	16	17	18	*19*	20	Bái lù
2482843		21	22	23	24	25	26	27	
2482850		28	29	30	1	2	3	**4**	Qiū fēn
2482857		5	6	7	8	9	10	11	
2482864	MONTH 8 Yǐ-Sì	12	13	14	15[g]	16	17	18	
2482871		*19**	20	21	22	23	24	25	Hán lù
2482878		26	27	28	29	30	1	2	
2482885		3	4	**5**	6	7	8	9[h]	Shuāng jiàng
2482892	MONTH 9 Yǐ-Sì	10	11	12	13	14	15	16	
2482899		17	18	19	*20*	21	22	23	Lì dōng
2482906		24	25	26	27	28	29	1	
2482913		2	3	4	**5**	6	7	8	Xiǎo xuě
2482920	MONTH 10 Yǐ-Sì	9	10	11	12	13	14	15	
2482927		16	17	18	19	*20**	21	22	Dà xuě
2482934		23	24	25	26	27	28	29	
2482941		30	1	2	3	4	**5**[i]	6	Dōng zhì
2482948	MONTH 11 Yǐ-Sì	7	8	9	10	11	12	13	
2482955		14	15	16	17	18	19	*20*	Xiǎo hán

JULIAN DAY	COPTIC 1801/1802	Sun	Mon	Tue	Wed	Thu	Fri	Sat	ETHIOPIC 2077/2078
2482591	KOIAK 1801	22	23	24	25	26	27	28	TĀKHŚĀŚ 2077
2482598		29[c]	30	1	2	3	4	5	
2482605	TŌBE 1801	6[d]	7	8	9	10	11[e]	12	
2482612		13	14	15	16	17	18	19	ṬER 2077
2482619		20	21	22	23	24	25	26	
2482626		27	28	29	30	1	2	3	
2482633		4	5	6	7	8	9	10	
2482640	MESHIR 1801	11	12	13	14	15	16	17	YAKĀTIT 2077
2482647		18	19	20	21	22	23	24	
2482654		25	26	27	28	29	30	1	
2482661		2	3	4	5	6	7	8	
2482668	PAREMOTEP 1801	9	10	11	12	13	14	15	MAGĀBIT 2077
2482675		16	17	18	19	20	21	22	
2482682		23	24	25	26	27	28	29	
2482689		30	1	2	3	4	5	6	
2482696	PARMOUTE 1801	7[f]	8	9	10	11	12	13	MIYĀZYĀ 2077
2482703		14	15	16	17	18	19	20	
2482710		21	22	23	24	25	26	27	
2482717		28	29[g]	30	1	2	3	4	
2482724		5	6	7	8	9	10	11	
2482731	PASHONS 1801	12	13	14	15	16	17	18	GENBOT 2077
2482738		19	20	21	22	23	24	25	
2482745		26	27	28	29	30	1	2	
2482752		3	4	5	6	7	8	9	
2482759	PAŌNE 1801	10	11	12	13	14	15	16	SANĒ 2077
2482766		17	18	19	20	21	22	23	
2482773		24	25	26	27	28	29	30	
2482780		1	2	3	4	5	6	7	
2482787		8	9	10	11	12	13	14	
2482794	EPĒP 1801	15	16	17	18	19	20	21	ḤAMLĒ 2077
2482801		22	23	24	25	26	27	28	
2482808		29	30	1	2	3	4	5	
2482815		6	7	8	9	10	11	12	
2482822	MESORĒ 1801	13[h]	14	15	16	17	18	19	NAḤASĒ 2077
2482829		20	21	22	23	24	25	26	
2482836		27	28	29	30	1	2	3	
2482843	EPAG. 1801	4	5	1[a]	2	3	4	5	PĀG. 2077
2482850		6	7	8	9	10	11	12	
2482857	THOOUT 1802	13	14	15	16	17[b]	18	19	MASKARAM 2078
2482864		20	21	22	23	24	25	26	
2482871		27	28	29	30	1	2	3	
2482878		4	5	6	7	8	9	10	
2482885	PAOPE 1802	11	12	13	14	15	16	17	ṬEQEMT 2078
2482892		18	19	20	21	22	23	24	
2482899		25	26	27	28	29	30	1	
2482906		2	3	4	5	6	7	8	
2482913	ATHŌR 1802	9	10	11	12	13	14	15	ḪEDĀR 2078
2482920		16	17	18	19	20	21	22	
2482927		23	24	25	26	27	28	29	
2482934		30	1	2	3	4	5	6	
2482941	KOIAK 1802	7	8	9	10	11	12	13	TĀKHŚĀŚ 2078
2482948		14	15	16	17	18	19	20	
2482955		21	22	23	24	25	26	27	

Gregorian:
[a] New Year
[b] Spring (21:51)
[c] Summer (14:31)
[d] Autumn (6:42)
[e] Winter (4:27)
● New moon
◐ First quarter moon
○ Full moon
◑ Last quarter moon

Hebrew:
[a] New Year
[b] Yom Kippur
[c] Sukkot
[d] Winter starts
[e] Ḥanukkah
[f] Purim
[g] Passover
[h] Shavuot
[i] Fast of Av

Chinese:
‡ Leap year
[a] New Year (4783, Snake)
[b] Lantern Festival
[c] Qīngmíng
[d] Dragon Festival
[e] Qīqiǎo
[f] Hungry Ghosts
[g] Mid-Autumn Festival
[h] Double-Ninth Festival
[i] Dōngzhì
* Start of 60-name cycle

Coptic/Ethiopic:
[a] New Year
[b] Building of the Cross
[c] Christmas
[d] Jesus's Circumcision
[e] Epiphany
[f] Easter
[g] Mary's Announcement
[h] Jesus's Transfiguration

PERSIAN (ASTRONOMICAL) 1463/1464

Month	Sun	Mon	Tue	Wed	Thu	Fri	Sat
DEY 1463	11	12	13	14	15	16	17
	18	19	20	21	22	23	24
	25	26	27	28	29	30	1
BAHMAN 1463	2	3	4	5	6	7	8
	9	10	11	12	13	14	15
	16	17	18	19	20	21	22
	23	24	25	26	27	28	29
	30	1	2	3	4	5	6
ESFAND 1463	7	8	9	10	11	12	13
	14	15	16	17	18	19	20
	21	22	23	24	25	26	27
	28	29	1[a]	2	3	4	5
FARVARDĪN 1464	6	7	8	9	10	11	12
	13[b]	14	15	16	17	18	19
	20	21	22	23	24	25	26
	27	28	29	30	31	1	2
ORDĪBEHEŠT 1464	3	4	5	6	7	8	9
	10	11	12	13	14	15	16
	17	18	19	20	21	22	23
	24	25	26	27	28	29	30
	31	1	2	3	4	5	6
XORDĀD 1464	7	8	9	10	11	12	13
	14	15	16	17	18	19	20
	21	22	23	24	25	26	27
	28	29	30	31	1	2	3
TĪR 1464	4	5	6	7	8	9	10
	11	12	13	14	15	16	17
	18	19	20	21	22	23	24
	25	26	27	28	29	30	31
MORDĀD 1464	1	2	3	4	5	6	7
	8	9	10	11	12	13	14
	15	16	17	18	19	20	21
	22	23	24	25	26	27	28
	29	30	31	1	2	3	4
SHAHRĪVAR 1464	5	6	7	8	9	10	11
	12	13	14	15	16	17	18
	19	20	21	22	23	24	25
	26	27	28	29	30	31	1
MEHR 1464	2	3	4	5	6	7	8
	9	10	11	12	13	14	15
	16	17	18	19	20	21	22
	23	24	25	26	27	28	29
	30	1	2	3	4	5	6
ĀBĀN 1464	7	8	9	10	11	12	13
	14	15	16	17	18	19	20
	21	22	23	24	25	26	27
	28	29	30	1	2	3	4
ĀZAR 1464	5	6	7	8	9	10	11
	12	13	14	15	16	17	18
	19	20	21	22	23	24	25
	26	27	28	29	30	1	2
DEY 1464	3	4	5	6	7	8	9
	10	11	12	13	14	15	16

HINDU LUNAR 2141/2142‡

Month	Sun	Mon	Tue	Wed	Thu	Fri	Sat
PAUSHA 2141	5	6	7	8	9	10	11
	12	13	14	15	16	17	17
	18	19	20	21	22	23	24
	25	26	27	29	30	1	2
MĀGHA 2141	3	4	5	6	7	8	9
	10	11	12	13	14	15	16
	17	18	19	20	21	22	23
	24	25	26	27	28[h]	29	30
PHĀLGUNA 2141	1	2	4	5	6	7	8
	9	10	10	11	12	13	14
	15[i]	16	17	18	19	20	21
	22	23	24	25	26	28	29
CHAITRA 2142	30	1[a]	2	3	4	5	6
	7	8	9[b]	10	11	12	13
	13	14	15	16	17	18	19
	21	22	23	24	25	26	27
	28	29	30	1	2	3	4
VAIŚĀKHA 2142	5	6	7	8	9	10	11
	12	13	14	15	16	17	18
	19	20	21	22	23	25	26
	27	28	29	30	1	2	3
JYAISHṬHA 2142	4	5	6	7	8	8	9
	10	11	12	13	14	15	16
	18	19	20	21	22	23	24
	25	26	27	28	29	30	1
ĀSHĀḌHA 2142	2	3	4	5	6	7	8
	9	10	11	12	13	14	15
	16	17	18	19	21	22	23
	24	25	26	27	28	29	30
ŚRĀVAṆA 2142	1	2	3	4	5	5	6
	7	8	9	10	11	13	14
	15	16	17	18	19	20	21
	22	23[c]	24	25	26	27	28
BHĀDRAPADA 2142	29	30	1	2	3	4[d]	5
	6	7	8	9	10	11	12
	13	14	15	17	18	19	20
	21	22	23	24	25	26	27
ĀŚVINA 2142	28	29	30	1	1	2	3
	4	5	6	7	8[e]	10[e]	11
	12	13	14	15	16	17	18
	19	20	21	22	23	24	25
LEAP KĀRTTIKA 2142	26	27	28	29	30	1	2
	3	4	5	6	7	8	9
	10	11	12	14	15	16	17
	18	19	20	21	22	23	24
	25	25	26	27	28	29	30
KĀRTTIKA 2142	1[f]	2	3	4	5	7	8
	9	10	11	12	13	14	15
	16	17	18	19	20	21	22
	23	24	25	26	27	28	29
PAUSHA 2142	30	1	2	3	4	5	6
	7	8	9	10[g]	12	13	14
	15	16	17	18	18	19	20

HINDU SOLAR 2006/2007

Month	Sun	Mon	Tue	Wed	Thu	Fri	Sat
PAUSHA 2006	16	17	18	19	20	21	22
	23	24	25	26	27	28	29
MĀGHA 2006	1[b]	2	3	4	5	6	7
	8	9	10	11	12	13	14
	15	16	17	18	19	20	21
	22	23	24	25	26	27	28
PHĀLGUNA 2006	29	30	1	2	3	4	5
	6	7	8	9	10	11	12
	13	14	15	16	17	18	19
	20	21	22	23	24	25	26
CHAITRA 2006	27	28	29	30	1	2	3
	4	5	6	7	8	9	10
	11	12	13	14	15	16	17
	18	19	20	21	22	23	24
VAIŚĀKHA 2007	25	26	27	28	29	30	1[a]
	2	3	4	5	6	7	8
	9	10	11	12	13	14	15
	16	17	18	19	20	21	22
	23	24	25	26	27	28	29
JYAISHṬHA 2007	30	31	1	2	3	4	5
	6	7	8	9	10	11	12
	13	14	15	16	17	18	19
	20	21	22	23	24	25	26
ĀSHĀḌHA 2007	27	28	29	30	31	1	2
	3	4	5	6	7	8	9
	10	11	12	13	14	15	16
	17	18	19	20	21	22	23
	24	25	26	27	28	29	30
ŚRĀVAṆA 2007	31	32	1	2	3	4	5
	6	7	8	9	10	11	12
	13	14	15	16	17	18	19
	20	21	22	23	24	25	26
BHĀDRAPADA 2007	27	28	29	30	31	1	2
	3	4	5	6	7	8	9
	10	11	12	13	14	15	16
	17	18	19	20	21	22	23
	24	25	26	27	28	29	30
ĀŚVINA 2007	31	1	2	3	4	5	6
	7	8	9	10	11	12	13
	14	15	16	17	18	19	20
	21	22	23	24	25	26	27
KĀRTTIKA 2007	28	29	30	31	1	2	3
	4	5	6	7	8	9	10
	11	12	13	14	15	16	17
	18	19	20	21	22	23	24
MĀRGAŚIRA 2007	25	26	27	28	29	30	1
	2	3	4	5	6	7	8
	9	10	11	12	13	14	15
	16	17	18	19	20	21	22
	23	24	25	26	27	28	29
PAUSHA 2007	1	2	3	4	5	6	7
	8	9	10	11	12	13	14
	15	16	17	18	19	20	21

ISLAMIC (ASTRONOMICAL) 1508/1509

Month	Sun	Mon	Tue	Wed	Thu	Fri	Sat
JUMĀDĀ I 1508	3	4	5	6	7	8	9
	10	11	12	13	14	15	16
	17	18	19	20	21	22	23
	24	25	26	27	28	29	1
JUMĀDĀ II 1508	2	3	4	5	6	7	8
	9	10	11	12	13	14	15
	16	17	18	19	20	21	22
	23	24	25	26	27	28	29
RAJAB 1508	1	2	3	4	5	6	7
	8	9	10	11	12	13	14
	15	16	17	18	19	20	21
	22	23	24	25	26	27[d]	28
SHA'BĀN 1508	29	30	1	2	3	4	5
	6	7	8	9	10	11	12
	13	14	15	16	17	18	19
	20	21	22	23	24	25	26
RAMAḌĀN 1508	27	28	29	1[e]	2	3	4
	5	6	7	8	9	10	11
	12	13	14	15	16	17	18
	19	20	21	22	23	24	25
SHAWWĀL 1508	26	27	28	29	30	1[f]	2
	3	4	5	6	7	8	9
	10	11	12	13	14	15	16
	17	18	19	20	21	22	23
	24	25	26	27	28	29	30
DHU AL-QA'DA 1508	1	2	3	4	5	6	7
	8	9	10	11	12	13	14
	15	16	17	18	19	20	21
	22	23	24	25	26	27	28
DHU AL-ḤIJJA 1508	29	30	1	2	3	4	5
	6	7	8	9	10[g]	11	12
	13	14	15	16	17	18	19
	20	21	22	23	24	25	26
	27	28	29	30[A]	1[a]	2	3
MUḤARRAM 1509	4	5	6	7	8	9	10[b]
	11	12	13	14	15	16	17
	18	19	20	21	22	23	24
	25	26	27	28	29	30	1
ṢAFAR 1509	2	3	4	5	6	7	8
	9	10	11	12	13	14	15
	16	17	18	19	20	21	22
	23	24	25	26	27	28	29
RABĪ' I 1509	1	2	3	4	5	6	7
	8	9	10	11	12[c]	13	14
	15	16	17	18	19	20	21
	22	23	24	25	26	27	28
RABĪ' II 1509	29	1	2	3	4	5	6
	7	8	9	10	11	12	13
	14	15	16	17	18	19	20
	21	22	23	24	25	26	27
JUMĀDĀ I 1509	28	29	1	2	3	4	5
	6	7	8	9	10	11	12
	13	14	15	16	17	18	19

GREGORIAN 2085

Julian (Sun)	Sun	Mon	Tue	Wed	Thu	Fri	Sat	Month
Dec 18	31	1	2	3	4	5	6	JANUARY 2085
	7[a]	8	9	10	11	12	13	
Jan 1	14[b]	15	16	17	18	19	20	
	21	22	23	24	25	26	27	
Jan 15	28	29	30	31	1	2	3	FEBRUARY 2085
	4	5	6	7	8	9	10	
Jan 29	11	12	13	14	15	16	17	
	18	19	20	21	22	23	24	
Feb 12	25	26	27	28[c]	1	2	3	MARCH 2085
	4[d]	5	6	7	8	9	10	
Feb 26	11	12	13	14	15	16	17	
	18	19	20	21	22	23	24	
Mar 12	25	26	27	28	29	30	31	
	1	2	3	4	5	6	7	APRIL 2085
Mar 26	8	9	10	11	12	13	14	
	15[e]	16	17	18	19	20	21	
Apr 9	22	23	24	25	26	27	28	
	29	30	1	2	3	4	5	MAY 2085
Apr 23	6	7	8	9	10	11	12	
	13	14	15	16	17	18	19	
May 7	20	21	22	23	24	25	26	
	27	28	29	30	31	1	2	JUNE 2085
May 21	3	4	5	6	7	8	9	
	10	11	12	13	14	15	16	
Jun 4	17	18	19	20	21	22	23	
	24	25	26	27	28	29	30	
Jun 18	1	2	3	4	5	6	7	JULY 2085
	8	9	10	11	12	13	14	
Jul 2	15	16	17	18	19	20	21	
	22	23	24	25	26	27	28	
Jul 16	29	30	31	1	2	3	4	AUGUST 2085
	5	6	7	8	9	10	11	
Jul 30	12	13	14	15	16	17	18	
	19	20	21	22	23	24	25	
Aug 13	26	27	28	29	30	31	1	SEPTEMBER 2085
	2	3	4	5	6	7	8	
Aug 27	9	10	11	12	13	14	15	
	16	17	18	19	20	21	22	
Sep 10	23	24	25	26	27	28	29	
	30	1	2	3	4	5	6	OCTOBER 2085
Sep 24	7	8	9	10	11	12	13	
	14	15	16	17	18	19	20	
Oct 8	21	22	23	24	25	26	27	
	28	29	30	31	1	2	3	NOVEMBER 2085
Oct 22	4	5	6	7	8	9	10	
	11	12	13	14	15	16	17	
Nov 5	18	19	20	21	22	23	24	
	25	26	27	28	29	30	1	DECEMBER 2085
Nov 19	2[g]	3	4	5	6	7	8	
	9	10	11	12	13	14	15	
Dec 3	16	17	18	19	20	21	22	
	23	24	25[h]	26	27	28	29	
Dec 17	30	31	1	2	3	4	5	

Persian: [a]New Year; [b]Sizdeh Bedar

Hindu lunar: ‡Leap year; [a]New Year (Viśvāvasu); [b]Birthday of Rāma; [c]Birthday of Krishna; [d]Ganēśa Chaturthī; [e]Dashara; [f]Diwali; [g]Birthday of Vishnu; [h]Night of Śiva; [i]Holi

Hindu solar: [a]New Year (Siddhārthin); [b]Pongal

Islamic: [a]New Year; [A]New Year (Arithmetic); [b]'Ashūrā'; [c]Prophet's Birthday; [d]Ascent of the Prophet; [e]Start of Ramaḍān; [f]'Īd al-Fiṭr; [g]'Īd al-'Aḍḥā

Gregorian: [a]Orthodox Christmas; [b]Julian New Year; [c]Ash Wednesday; [d]Feast of Orthodoxy; [e]Easter (also Orthodox); [g]Advent; [h]Christmas

2086

Gregorian 2086	Sun	Mon	Tue	Wed	Thu	Fri	Sat	Lunar Phases	ISO Week (Mon)	Julian Day (Sun noon)	Hebrew 5846/5847‡	Sun	Mon	Tue	Wed	Thu	Fri	Sat	Molad	Chinese Yǐ-Sì‡/Bǐng-Wǔ	Sun	Mon	Tue	Wed	Thu	Fri	Sat	Solar Term	Coptic 1802/1803‡	Sun	Mon	Tue	Wed	Thu	Fri	Sat	Ethiopic 2078/2079‡
JANUARY 2086	○	31	1[a]	2	3	4	5	23:58	1	2482955	TEVETH 5846	13	14	15	16	17	18	19		MONTH 11 Yǐ-Sì	14	15	16	17	18	19	20	Xiǎo hán	KOIAK 1802	21	22	23	24	25	26	27	TĀKHŚĀŚ 2078
	6	7	◑	9	10	11	12	3:04	2	2482962		20	21	22	23	24	25	26			21	22	23	24	25	26	27		TŌBE 1802	28	29[c]	30	1	2	3	4	ṬER 2078
	13	14	●	16	17	18	19	11:23	3	2482969	SHEVAT 5846	27	28	29	1	2	3	4	Tue 7h55m15p	MONTH 12 Yǐ-Sì	28	29	1	2	3	4	5	Dà hán		5	6[d]	7	8	9	10	11[e]	
	20	21	◐	23	24	25	26	2:40	4	2482976		5	6	7	8	9	10	11			6	7	8	9	10	11	12			12	13	14	15	16	17	18	
FEBRUARY 2086	27	28	○	30	31	1	2	17:47	5	2482983		12	13	14	15	16	17	18			13	14	15	16	17	18	19			19	20	21	22	23	24	25	
	3	4	5	◑	7	8	9	22:29	6	2482990		19	20	21	22	23	24	25			20	21*	22	23	24	25	26	Lì chūn	MESHIR 1802	26	27	28	29	30	1	2	YAKĀTIT 2078
	10	11	12	●	14	15	16	22:26	7	2482997	ADAR 5846	26	27	28	29	30	1	2	Wed 20h39m16p	MONTH 1 Bǐng-Wǔ	27	28	29	30	1[a]	2	3			3	4	5	6	7	8	9	
	17	18	19	◐	21	22	23	13:47	8	2483004		3	4	5	6	7	8	9			4	5	6	7	8	9	10	Yǔ shuǐ		10	11	12	13	14	15	16	
MARCH 2086	24	25	26	27	○	1	2	12:20	9	2483011		10	11	12	13	14[f]	15	16			11	12	13	14	15[b]	16	17			17	18	19	20	21	22	23	
	3	4	5	6	7	◑	9	14:29	10	2483018		17	18	19	20	21	22	23			18	19	20	21	22	23	24	Jīng zhé		24	25	26	27	28	29	30	
	10	11	12	13	14	●	16	8:03	11	2483025	NISAN 5846	24	25	26	27	28	29	1	Fri 9h23m17p	MONTH 2 Bǐng-Wǔ	25	26	27	28	29	1	2		PAREMOTEP 1802	1	2	3	4	5	6	7	MAGĀBIT 2078
	17	18	19	20[b]	21	◐	23	3:15	12	2483032		2	3	4	5	6	7	8			3	4	5	6	7	8	9	Chūn fēn		8	9	10	11	12	13	14	
	24	25	26	27	28	29	○	6:16	13	2483039		9	10	11	12	13	14	15[g]			10	11	12	13	14	15	16			15	16	17	18	19	20	21	
APRIL 2086	31	1	2	3	4	5	6		14	2483046		16	17	18	19	20	21	22			17	18	19	20	21[c]	22*	23	Qīng míng		22	23	24	25	26	27	28	
	◑	8	9	10	11	12	●	2:21 16:52	15	2483053		23	24	25	26	27	28	29			24	25	26	27	28	29	30		PARMOUTE 1802	29[f]	30	1	2	3	4	5	MIYĀZYĀ 2078
	14	15	16	17	18	19	◐	18:39	16	2483060	IYYAR 5846	30	1	2	3	4	5	6	Sat 22h8m0p	MONTH 3 Bǐng-Wǔ	1	2	3	4	5	6	7	Gǔ yǔ		6	7	8	9	10	11	12	
	21	22	23	24	25	26	27		17	2483067		7	8	9	10	11	12	13			8	9	10	11	12	13	14			13	14	15	16	17	18	19	
MAY 2086	○	29	30	1	2	3	4	22:34	18	2483074		14	15	16	17	18	19	20			15	16	17	18	19	20	21			20	21	22	23	24	25	26	
	5	◑	7	8	9	10	11	10:25	19	2483081		21	22	23	24	25	26	27			22	23	24	25	26	27	28	Lì xià	PASHONS 1802	27	28	29[g]	30	1	2	3	GENBOT 2078
	12	●	14	15	16	17	18	1:40	20	2483088	SIVAN 5846	28	29	1	2	3	4	5	Mon 10h52m1p	MONTH 4 Bǐng-Wǔ	29	1	2	3	4	5	6			4	5	6	7	8	9	10	
	19	◐	21	22	23	24	25	11:18	21	2483095		6[h]	7	8	9	10	11	12			7	8	9	10	11	12	13	Xiǎo mǎn		11	12	13	14	15	16	17	
JUNE 2086	26	27	○	29	30	31	1	12:34	22	2483102		13	14	15	16	17	18	19			14	15	16	17	18	19	20			18	19	20	21	22	23	24	
	2	3	◑	5	6	7	8	15:50	23	2483109		20	21	22	23	24	25	26			21	22	23*	24	25	26	27	Máng zhòng	PAŌNE 1802	25	26	27	28	29	30	1	SANĒ 2078
	9	10	●	12	13	14	15	11:11	24	2483116	TAMMUZ 5846	27	28	29	30	1	2	3	Tue 23h36m2p	MONTH 5 Bǐng-Wǔ	28	29	1	2	3	4	5[d]			2	3	4	5	6	7	8	
	16	17	18	◐	20[c]	21	22	4:32	25	2483123		4	5	6	7	8	9	10			6	7	8	9	10	11	12	Xià zhì		9	10	11	12	13	14	15	
	23	24	25	26	○	28	29	0:03	26	2483130		11	12	13	14	15	16	17			13	14	15	16	17	18	19			16	17	18	19	20	21	22	
JULY 2086	30	1	2	◑	4	5	6	20:09	27	2483137		18	19	20	21	22	23	24			20	21	22	23	24	25	26	Xiǎo shǔ		23	24	25	26	27	28	29	
	7	8	9	●	11	12	13	22:01	28	2483144	AV 5846	25	26	27	28	29	1	2	Thu 12h20m3p	MONTH 6 Bǐng-Wǔ	27	28	29	30	1	2	3		EPĒP 1802	30	1	2	3	4	5	6	ḤAMLĒ 2078
	14	15	16	17	◐	19	20	21:44	29	2483151		3	4	5	6	7	8	9			4	5	6	7	8	9	10			7	8	9	10	11	12	13	
	21	22	23	24	25	○	27	9:23	30	2483158		10[i]	11	12	13	14	15	16			11	12	13	14	15	16	17	Dà shǔ		14	15	16	17	18	19	20	
AUGUST 2086	28	29	30	31	1	◑	3	1:00	31	2483165		17	18	19	20	21	22	23			18	19	20	21	22	23	24*			21	22	23	24	25	26	27	
	4	5	6	7	8	●	10	10:37	32	2483172		24	25	26	27	28	29	30		MONTH 7 Bǐng-Wǔ	25	26	27	28	29	1	2	Lì qiū	MESORĒ 1802	28	29	30	1	2	3	4	NAHASĒ 2078
	11	12	13	14	15	16	◐	14:13	33	2483179	ELUL 5846	1	2	3	4	5	6	7	Sat 1h4m4p		3	4	5	6	7[e]	8	9			5	6	7	8	9	10	11	
	18	19	20	21	22	23	○	17:24	34	2483186		8	9	10	11	12	13	14			10	11	12	13	14	15[f]	16	Chǔ shǔ		12	13[h]	14	15	16	17	18	
	25	26	27	28	29	30	◑	7:51	35	2483193		15	16	17	18	19	20	21			17	18	19	20	21	22	23			19	20	21	22	23	24	25	
SEPTEMBER 2086	1	2	3	4	5	6	7		36	2483200		22	23	24	25	26	27	28			24	25	26	27	28	29	30	Bái lù	EPAG. 1802	26	27	28	29	30	1	2	PĀG. 2078
	●	9	10	11	12	13	14	1:16	37	2483207	TISHRI 5847	29	1[a]	2[a]	3	4	5	6	Sun 13h48m5p	MONTH 8 Bǐng-Wǔ	1	2	3	4	5	6	7		THOOUT 1803	3	4	5	1[a]	2	3	4	MASKARAM 2079
	15	◐	17	18	19	20	21	5:15	38	2483214		7	8	9	10[b]	11	12	13			8	9	10	11	12	13	14			5	6	7	8	9	10	11	
	22[d]	○	24	25	26	27	28	1:14	39	2483221		14	15[c]	16	17	18	19	20			15[g]	16	17	18	19	20	21	Qiū fēn		12	13	14	15	16	17[b]	18	
OCTOBER 2086	◑	30	1	2	3	4	5	17:51	40	2483228		21	22	23	24	25	26	27			22	23	24	25*	26	27	28			19	20	21	22	23	24	25	
	6	●	8	9	10	11	12	17:55	41	2483235	HESHVAN 5847	28	29	30	1	2	3	4	Tue 2h32m6p	MONTH 9 Bǐng-Wǔ	29	30	1	2	3	4	5	Hán lù	PAOPE 1803	26	27	28	29	30	1	2	ṬEQEMT 2079
	13	14	◐	16	17	18	19	18:17	42	2483242		5	6	7	8	9	10	11			6	7	8	9[h]	10	11	12			3	4	5	6	7	8	9	
	20	21	○	23	24	25	26	9:55	43	2483249		12	13	14	15	16	17	18			13	14	15	16	17	18	19	Shuāng jiàng		10	11	12	13	14	15	16	
NOVEMBER 2086	27	28	◑	30	31	1	2	7:39	44	2483256		19	20	21	22	23	24	25			20	21	22	23	24	25	26			17	18	19	20	21	22	23	
	3	4	5	●	7	8	9	11:52	45	2483263	KISLEV 5847	26	27	28	29	1	2	3	Wed 15h16m7p	MONTH 10 Bǐng-Wǔ	27	28	29	1	2	3	4	Lì dōng		24	25	26	27	28	29	30	
	10	11	12	13	◐	15	16	5:10	46	2483270		4	5	6	7	8	9	10			5	6	7	8	9	10	11		ATHŌR 1803	1	2	3	4	5	6	7	HEDĀR 2079
	17	18	19	○	21	22	23	20:11	47	2483277		11	12	13	14	15	16	17			12	13	14	15	16	17	18	Xiǎo xuě		8	9	10	11	12	13	14	
	24	25	26	27	◑	29	30	1:16	48	2483284		18	19	20	21	22	23	24			19	20	21	22	23	24	25			15	16	17	18	19	20	21	
DECEMBER 2086	1	2	3	4	5	●	7	5:47	49	2483291	TEVETH 5847	25[e]	26[e]	27[e]	28[e]	29[d,e]	1[e]	2[e]	Fri 4h0m8p	MONTH 11 Bǐng-Wǔ	26*	27	28	29	30	1	2	Dà xuě		22	23	24	25	26	27	28	
	8	9	10	11	12	◐	14	14:18	50	2483298		3[e]	4	5	6	7	8	9			3	4	5	6	7	8	9		KOIAK 1803	29	30	1	2	3	4	5	TĀKHŚĀŚ 2079
	15	16	17	18	19	○	21[e]	8:18	51	2483305		10	11	12	13	14	15	16			10	11	12	13	14	15	16[i]	Dōng zhì		6	7	8	9	10	11	12	
	22	23	24	25	26	◑	28	21:57	52	2483312		17	18	19	20	21	22	23			17	18	19	20	21	22	23			13	14	15	16	17	18	19	
	29	30	31	1	2	3	●	22:10	1	2483319		24	25	26	27	28	29	1	Sat 16h44m9p		24	25	26	27	28	29	30			20	21	22	23	24	25	26	

[a]New Year
[b]Spring (3:34)
[c]Summer (20:08)
[d]Autumn (12:31)
[e]Winter (10:21)
● New moon
◐ First quarter moon
○ Full moon
◑ Last quarter moon

‡Leap year
[a]New Year
[b]Yom Kippur
[c]Sukkot
[d]Winter starts
[e]Ḥanukkah
[f]Purim
[g]Passover
[h]Shavuot
[i]Fast of Av

‡Leap year
[a]New Year (4784, Horse)
[b]Lantern Festival
[c]Qīngmíng
[d]Dragon Festival
[e]Qǐqiǎo
[f]Hungry Ghosts
[g]Mid-Autumn Festival
[h]Double-Ninth Festival
[i]Dōngzhì
*Start of 60-name cycle

‡Leap year
[a]New Year
[b]Building of the Cross
[c]Christmas
[d]Jesus's Circumcision
[e]Epiphany
[f]Easter
[g]Mary's Announcement
[h]Jesus's Transfiguration

PERSIAN (ASTRONOMICAL) 1464/1465‡

Month	Sun	Mon	Tue	Wed	Thu	Fri	Sat
	10	11	12	13	14	15	16
DEY 1464	17	18	19	20	21	22	23
	24	25	26	27	28	29	30
	1	2	3	4	5	6	7
	8	9	10	11	12	13	14
BAHMAN 1464	15	16	17	18	19	20	21
	22	23	24	25	26	27	28
	29	30	1	2	3	4	5
ESFAND 1464	6	7	8	9	10	11	12
	13	14	15	16	17	18	19
	20	21	22	23	24	25	26
	27	28	29	1[a]	2	3	4
	5	6	7	8	9	10	11
FARVARDĪN 1465	12	13[b]	14	15	16	17	18
	19	20	21	22	23	24	25
	26	27	28	29	30	31	1
	2	3	4	5	6	7	8
ORDĪBEHEŠT 1465	9	10	11	12	13	14	15
	16	17	18	19	20	21	22
	23	24	25	26	27	28	29
	30	31	1	2	3	4	5
	6	7	8	9	10	11	12
XORDĀD 1465	13	14	15	16	17	18	19
	20	21	22	23	24	25	26
	27	28	29	30	31	1	2
	3	4	5	6	7	8	9
TĪR 1465	10	11	12	13	14	15	16
	17	18	19	20	21	22	23
	24	25	26	27	28	29	30
	31	1	2	3	4	5	6
	7	8	9	10	11	12	13
MORDĀD 1465	14	15	16	17	18	19	20
	21	22	23	24	25	26	27
	28	29	30	31	1	2	3
	4	5	6	7	8	9	10
SHAHRĪVAR 1465	11	12	13	14	15	16	17
	18	19	20	21	22	23	24
	25	26	27	28	29	30	31
	1	2	3	4	5	6	7
MEHR 1465	8	9	10	11	12	13	14
	15	16	17	18	19	20	21
	22	23	24	25	26	27	28
	29	30	1	2	3	4	5
ĀBĀN 1465	6	7	8	9	10	11	12
	13	14	15	16	17	18	19
	20	21	22	23	24	25	26
	27	28	29	30	1	2	3
ĀZAR 1465	4	5	6	7	8	9	10
	11	12	13	14	15	16	17
	18	19	20	21	22	23	24
	25	26	27	28	29	30	1
DEY 1465	2	3	4	5	6	7	8
	9	10	11	12	13	14	15

HINDU LUNAR 2142‡/2143

Month	Sun	Mon	Tue	Wed	Thu	Fri	Sat
PAUSHA 2142	15	16	17	18	18	19	20
	21	22	23	24	25	26	27
	28	29	30	1	2	3	4
MĀGHA 2142	6	7	8	9	10	11	12
	13	14	15	16	17	18	19
	20	20	21	22	23	24	25
	26	27	28[h]	30	1	2	3
LEAP PHĀLGUNA 2142	4	5	6	7	8	9	10
	11	12	13	14	15	16	17
	18	19	20	21	22	23	24
	25	26	27	28	29	30	1
PHĀLGUNA 2142	2	3	5	6	7	8	9
	10	11	12	13	13	14	15[i]
	16	17	18	19	20	21	22
	23	24	25	26	27	29	30
CHAITRA 2143	1[a]	2	3	4	5	6	7
	8	9[b]	10	11	12	13	14
	15	16	17	18	19	20	21
	22	23	24	25	26	27	28
	29	30	1	3	4	5	6
VAIŚĀKHA 2143	7	8	8	9	10	11	12
	13	14	15	16	17	18	19
	20	21	22	23	25	26	27
	28	29	30	1	2	3	4
JYAISHṬHA 2143	5	6	7	8	9	10	11
	12	13	14	15	16	17	18
	19	20	21	22	23	24	25
	26	28	29	30	1	2	3
ĀSHĀḌHA 2143	4	5	5	6	7	8	9
	10	11	12	13	14	15	16
	17	18	19	21	22	23	24
	25	26	27	28	29	30	1
ŚRĀVAṆA 2143	2	3	4	5	6	7	8
	9	10	11	12	13	14	15
	16	17	18	19	20	21	22[c]
	24	25	26	27	28	29	30
BHĀDRAPADA 2143	1	1	2	3[d]	4	5	6
	7	8	9	10	11	12	13
	14	15	17	18	19	20	21
	22	23	24	25	26	27	28
	29	30	1	2	3	4	5
ĀŚVINA 2143	6	6	8[e]	9[e]	10[e]	11	12
	13	14	15	16	17	18	19
	20	22	23	24	25	25	26
	27	28	29	30	1[f]	2	3
KĀRTTIKA 2143	4	5	6	7	8	9	10
	11	12	14	15	16	17	18
	19	20	21	22	23	24	25
	26	27	28	28	29	30	1
MĀRGAŚIRA 2143	2	3	4	5	6	8	9
	10	11[g]	12	13	14	15	16
	17	18	19	20	21	22	23
	24	25	26	27	28	29	30

HINDU SOLAR 2007/2008

Month	Sun	Mon	Tue	Wed	Thu	Fri	Sat
PAUSHA 2007	15	16	17	18	19	20	21
	22	23	24	25	26	27	28
	29	30	1[b]	2	3	4	5
MĀGHA 2007	6	7	8	9	10	11	12
	13	14	15	16	17	18	19
	20	21	22	23	24	25	26
	27	28	29	1	2	3	4
PHĀLGUNA 2007	5	6	7	8	9	10	11
	12	13	14	15	16	17	18
	19	20	21	22	23	24	25
	26	27	28	29	30	1	2
CHAITRA 2007	3	4	5	6	7	8	9
	10	11	12	13	14	15	16
	17	18	19	20	21	22	23
	24	25	26	27	28	29	30
VAIŚĀKHA 2008	1[a]	2	3	4	5	6	7
	8	9	10	11	12	13	14
	15	16	17	18	19	20	21
	22	23	24	25	26	27	28
	29	30	31	1	2	3	4
JYAISHṬHA 2008	5	6	7	8	9	10	11
	12	13	14	15	16	17	18
	19	20	21	22	23	24	25
	26	27	28	29	30	31	32
ĀSHĀḌHA 2008	1	2	3	4	5	6	7
	8	9	10	11	12	13	14
	15	16	17	18	19	20	21
	22	23	24	25	26	27	28
	29	30	31	1	2	3	4
ŚRĀVAṆA 2008	5	6	7	8	9	10	11
	12	13	14	15	16	17	18
	19	20	21	22	23	24	25
	26	27	28	29	30	31	32
BHĀDRAPADA 2008	1	2	3	4	5	6	7
	8	9	10	11	12	13	14
	15	16	17	18	19	20	21
	22	23	24	25	26	27	28
	29	30	31	1	2	3	4
ĀŚVINA 2008	5	6	7	8	9	10	11
	12	13	14	15	16	17	18
	19	20	21	22	23	24	25
	26	27	28	29	30	1	2
KĀRTTIKA 2008	3	4	5	6	7	8	9
	10	11	12	13	14	15	16
	17	18	19	20	21	22	23
	24	25	26	27	28	29	30
MĀRGAŚIRA 2008	1	2	3	4	5	6	7
	8	9	10	11	12	13	14
	15	16	17	18	19	20	21
	22	23	24	25	26	27	28
PAUSHA 2008	29	30	1	2	3	4	5
	6	7	8	9	10	11	12
	13	14	15	16	17	18	19

ISLAMIC (ASTRONOMICAL) 1509/1510

Month	Sun	Mon	Tue	Wed	Thu	Fri	Sat
JUMĀDĀ I 1509	13	14	15	16	17	18	19
	20	21	22	23	24	25	26
	27	28	29	30	1	2	3
JUMĀDĀ II 1509	4	5	6	7	8	9	10
	11	12	13	14	15	16	17
	18	19	20	21	22	23	24
	25	26	27	28	29	1	2
RAJAB 1509	3	4	5	6	7	8	9
	10	11	12	13	14	15	16
	17	18	19	20	21	22	23
	24	25	26	27[d]	28	29	1
SHA'BĀN 1509	2	3	4	5	6	7	8
	9	10	11	12	13	14	15
	16	17	18	19	20	21	22
	23	24	25	26	27	28	29
RAMAḌĀN 1509	30	1[e]	2	3	4	5	6
	7	8	9	10	11	12	13
	14	15	16	17	18	19	20
	21	22	23	24	25	26	27
	28	29	1[f]	2	3	4	5
SHAWWĀL 1509	6	7	8	9	10	11	12
	13	14	15	16	17	18	19
	20	21	22	23	24	25	26
	27	28	29	30	1	2	3
DHU AL-QA'DA 1509	4	5	6	7	8	9	10
	11	12	13	14	15	16	17
	18	19	20	21	22	23	24
	25	26	27	28	29	30	1
DHU AL-ḤIJJA 1509	2	3	4	5	6	7	8
	9	10[g]	11	12	13	14	15
	16	17	18	19	20	21	22
	23	24	25	26	27	28	29
	30[d]	1[a]	2	3	4	5	6
MUḤARRAM 1510	7	8	9	10[b]	11	12	13
	14	15	16	17	18	19	20
	21	22	23	24	25	26	27
	28	29	30	1	2	3	4
ṢAFAR 1510	5	6	7	8	9	10	11
	12	13	14	15	16	17	18
	19	20	21	22	23	24	25
	26	27	28	29	1	2	3
RABĪ' I 1510	4	5	6	7	8	9	10
	11	12[c]	13	14	15	16	17
	18	19	20	21	22	23	24
	25	26	27	28	29	1	2
RABĪ' II 1510	3	4	5	6	7	8	9
	10	11	12	13	14	15	16
	17	18	19	20	21	22	23
	24	25	26	27	28	29	30
	1	2	3	4	5	6	7
JUMĀDĀ I 1510	8	9	10	11	12	13	14
	15	16	17	18	19	20	21
	22	23	24	25	26	27	28

GREGORIAN 2086

Julian (Sun)	Sun	Mon	Tue	Wed	Thu	Fri	Sat	Month
Dec 17	30	31	1	2	3	4	5	
	6	7[a]	8	9	10	11	12	JANUARY 2086
Dec 31	13	14[b]	15	16	17	18	19	
	20	21	22	23	24	25	26	
Jan 14	27	28	29	30	31	1	2	
	3	4	5	6	7	8	9	FEBRUARY 2086
Jan 28	10	11	12	13[c]	14	15	16	
	17	18	19	20	21	22	23	
Feb 11	24[d]	25	26	27	28	1	2	
	3	4	5	6	7	8	9	
Feb 25	10	11	12	13	14	15	16	MARCH 2086
	17	18	19	20	21	22	23	
Mar 11	24	25	26	27	28	29	30	
	31[e]	1	2	3	4	5	6	
Mar 25	7[f]	8	9	10	11	12	13	
	14	15	16	17	18	19	20	APRIL 2086
Apr 8	21	22	23	24	25	26	27	
	28	29	30	1	2	3	4	
Apr 22	5	6	7	8	9	10	11	
	12	13	14	15	16	17	18	MAY 2086
May 6	19	20	21	22	23	24	25	
	26	27	28	29	30	31	1	
May 20	2	3	4	5	6	7	8	
	9	10	11	12	13	14	15	JUNE 2086
Jun 3	16	17	18	19	20	21	22	
	23	24	25	26	27	28	29	
Jun 17	30	1	2	3	4	5	6	
	7	8	9	10	11	12	13	
Jul 1	14	15	16	17	18	19	20	JULY 2086
	21	22	23	24	25	26	27	
Jul 15	28	29	30	31	1	2	3	
	4	5	6	7	8	9	10	
Jul 29	11	12	13	14	15	16	17	AUGUST 2086
	18	19	20	21	22	23	24	
Aug 12	25	26	27	28	29	30	31	
	1	2	3	4	5	6	7	
Aug 26	8	9	10	11	12	13	14	SEPTEMBER 2086
	15	16	17	18	19	20	21	
Sep 9	22	23	24	25	26	27	28	
	29	30	1	2	3	4	5	
Sep 23	6	7	8	9	10	11	12	OCTOBER 2086
	13	14	15	16	17	18	19	
Oct 7	20	21	22	23	24	25	26	
	27	28	29	30	31	1	2	
Oct 21	3	4	5	6	7	8	9	NOVEMBER 2086
	10	11	12	13	14	15	16	
Nov 4	17	18	19	20	21	22	23	
	24	25	26	27	28	29	30	
Nov 18	1[g]	2	3	4	5	6	7	
	8	9	10	11	12	13	14	DECEMBER 2086
Dec 2	15	16	17	18	19	20	21	
	22	23	24	25[h]	26	27	28	
Dec 16	29	30	31	1	2	3	4	

Persian: ‡Leap year; [a]New Year; [b]Sizdeh Bedar

Hindu Lunar: ‡Leap year; [a]New Year (Parābhava); [b]Birthday of Rāma; [c]Birthday of Krishna; [d]Ganēśa Chaturthī; [e]Dashara; [f]Diwali; [g]Birthday of Vishnu; [h]Night of Śiva; [i]Holi

Hindu Solar: [a]New Year (Rāudra); [b]Pongal

Islamic: [a]New Year; [d]New Year (Arithmetic); [b]'Ashūrā'; [c]Prophet's Birthday; [d]Ascent of the Prophet; [e]Start of Ramaḍān; [f]'Id al-Fiṭr; [g]'Id al-'Aḍḥā

Gregorian: [a]Orthodox Christmas; [b]Julian New Year; [c]Ash Wednesday; [d]Feast of Orthodoxy; [e]Easter; [f]Orthodox Easter; [g]Advent; [h]Christmas

2087

	GREGORIAN 2087							Lunar Phases	ISO WEEK	JULIAN DAY		HEBREW 5847‡/5848							Molad		CHINESE Bǐng-Wǔ/Dīng-Wèi							Solar Term		COPTIC 1803‡/1804							ETHIOPIC 2079‡/2080
	Sun	Mon	Tue	Wed	Thu	Fri	Sat		(Mon)	(Sun noon)		Sun	Mon	Tue	Wed	Thu	Fri	Sat			Sun	Mon	Tue	Wed	Thu	Fri	Sat			Sun	Mon	Tue	Wed	Thu	Fri	Sat	
	29	30	31	1[a]	2	3	●	22:10	1	2483319		24	25	26	27	28	29	1	Sat 16h44m9p		24	25	26	27	28	29	30		KOIAK 1803	20	21	22	23	24	25	26	TĀKHŚĀŚ 2079
	5	6	7	8	9	10	◐	22:29	2	2483326		2	3	4	5	6	7	8			1	2	3	4	5	6	7	Xiǎo hán		27	28	29[c]	30	1	2	3	
JANUARY 2087	12	13	14	15	16	17	○	22:10	3	2483333	SHEVAT 5847	9	10	11	12	13	14	15		MONTH 12 Bǐng-Wǔ	8	9	10	11	12	13	14		TŌBE 1803	4	5	6[d]	7	8	9	10	
	19	20	21	22	23	24	25		4	2483340		16	17	18	19	20	21	22			15	16	17	18	19	20	21	Dà hán		11[e]	12	13	14	15	16	17	ṬER 2079
	◑	27	28	29	30	31	1	20:00	5	2483347		23	24	25	26	27	28	29			22	23	24	25	26*	27	28			18	19	20	21	22	23	24	
	2	●	4	5	6	7	8	12:09	6	2483354		30	1	2	3	4	5	6	Mon 5h28m10p		29	1[a]	2	3	4	5	6	Lì chūn		25	26	27	28	29	30	1	
FEBRUARY 2087	9	◐	11	12	13	14	15	6:36	7	2483361		7	8	9	10	11	12	13			7	8	9	10	11	12	13			2	3	4	5	6	7	8	
	16	○	18	19	20	21	22	13:33	8	2483368	ADAR I 5847	14	15	16	17	18	19	20		MONTH 1 Dīng-Wèi	14	15[b]	16	17	18	19	20	Yǔ shuǐ	MESHIR 1803	9	10	11	12	13	14	15	YAKĀTIT 2079
	23	24	◑	26	27	28	1	17:05	9	2483375		21	22	23	24	25	26	27			21	22	23	24	25	26	27			16	17	18	19	20	21	22	
	2	3	●	5	6	7	8	23:44	10	2483382		28	29	30	1	2	3	4	Tue 18h12m11p		28	29	30	1	2	3	4	Jīng zhé		23	24	25	26	27	28	29	
MARCH 2087	9	10	◐	12	13	14	15	15:25	11	2483389		5	6	7	8	9	10	11			5	6	7	8	9	10	11			30	1	2	3	4	5	6	
	16	17	18	○	20[b]	21	22	6:08	12	2483396	ADAR II 5847	12	13	14[f]	15	16	17	18		MONTH 2 Dīng-Wèi	12	13	14	15	16	17	18	Chūn fēn		7	8	9	10	11	12	13	
	23	24	25	26	◑	28	29	11:02	13	2483403		19	20	21	22	23	24	25			19	20	21	22	23	24	25		PAREMOTEP 1803	14	15	16	17	18	19	20	MAGĀBIT 2079
	30	31	1	2	●	4	5	9:25	14	2483410		26	27	28	29	1	2	3	Thu 6h56m12p		26	27*	28	29	1	2[c]	3	Qīng míng		21	22	23	24	25	26	27	
	6	7	8	9	◐	11	12	1:28	15	2483417		4	5	6	7	8	9	10			4	5	6	7	8	9	10			28	29	30	1	2	3	4	
APRIL 2087	13	14	15	16	○	18	19	23:16	16	2483424	NISAN 5847	11	12	13	14	15[g]	16	17		MONTH 3 Dīng-Wèi	11	12	13	14	15	16	17			5	6	7	8	9	10	11	
	20	21	22	23	24	25	◑	0:50	17	2483431		18	19	20	21	22	23	24			18	19	20	21	22	23	24	Gǔ yǔ	PARMOUTE 1803	12	13	14	15	16	17	18	MIYĀZYĀ 2079
	27	28	29	30	1	●	3	17:50	18	2483438		25	26	27	28	29	30	1	Fri 19h40m13p		25	26	27	28	29	30	1			19[f]	20	21	22	23	24	25	
	4	5	6	7	8	◐	10	13:08	19	2483445		2	3	4	5	6	7	8			2	3	4	5	6	7	8	Lì xià		26	27	28	29[g]	30	1	2	
MAY 2087	11	12	13	14	15	16	○	15:54	20	2483452	IYAR 5847	9	10	11	12	13	14	15		MONTH 4 Dīng-Wèi	9	10	11	12	13	14	15			3	4	5	6	7	8	9	
	18	19	20	21	22	23	24		21	2483459		16	17	18	19	20	21	22			16	17	18	19	20	21	22	Xiǎo mǎn	PASHONS 1803	10	11	12	13	14	15	16	GENBOT 2079
	◑	26	27	28	29	30	31	10:40	22	2483466		23	24	25	26	27	28	29			23	24	25	26	27	28*	29			17	18	19	20	21	22	23	
	●	2	3	4	5	6	7	1:37	23	2483473		1	2	3	4	5	6[h]	7	Sun 8h24m14p		1	2	3	4	5[d]	6	7	Máng zhòng		24	25	26	27	28	29	30	
	◐	9	10	11	12	13	14	2:44	24	2483480		8	9	10	11	12	13	14			8	9	10	11	12	13	14			1	2	3	4	5	6	7	
JUNE 2087	15	○	17	18	19	20	21[c]	6:57	25	2483487	SIVAN 5847	15	16	17	18	19	20	21		MONTH 5 Dīng-Wèi	15	16	17	18	19	20	21	Xià zhì	PAŌNE 1803	8	9	10	11	12	13	14	
	22	◑	24	25	26	27	28	17:32	26	2483494		22	23	24	25	26	27	28			22	23	24	25	26	27	28			15	16	17	18	19	20	21	SANĒ 2079
	29	●	1	2	3	4	5	9:30	27	2483501		29	30	1	2	3	4	5	Mon 21h8m15p		29	1	2	3	4	5	6			22	23	24	25	26	27	28	
	6	◐	8	9	10	11	12	18:23	28	2483508		6	7	8	9	10	11	12			7	8	9	10	11	12	13	Xiǎo shǔ		29	30	1	2	3	4	5	
JULY 2087	13	14	○	16	17	18	19	19:53	29	2483515	TAMMUZ 5847	13	14	15	16	17	18	19		MONTH 6 Dīng-Wèi	14	15	16	17	18	19	20			6	7	8	9	10	11	12	
	20	21	◑	23	24	25	26	22:42	30	2483522		20	21	22	23	24	25	26			21	22	23	24	25	26	27	Dà shǔ	EPĒP 1803	13	14	15	16	17	18	19	HAMLĒ 2079
	27	28	●	30	31	1	2	18:19	31	2483529		27	28	29	1	2	3	4	Wed 9h52m16p		28	29	30*	1	2	3	4			20	21	22	23	24	25	26	
	3	4	5	◐	7	8	9	11:42	32	2483536		5	6	7	8	9[i]	10	11			5	6	7[e]	8	9	10	11	Lì qiū		27	28	29	30	1	2	3	
AUGUST 2087	10	11	12	13	○	15	16	6:53	33	2483543	AV 5847	12	13	14	15	16	17	18		MONTH 7 Dīng-Wèi	12	13	14	15[f]	16	17	18			4	5	6	7	8	9	10	
	17	18	19	20	◑	22	23	3:33	34	2483550		19	20	21	22	23	24	25			19	20	21	22	23	24	25	Chǔ shǔ	MESORĒ 1803	11	12	13[h]	14	15	16	17	NAḤASĒ 2079
	24	25	26	27	●	29	30	5:07	35	2483557		26	27	28	29	30	1	2	Thu 22h36m17p		26	27	28	29	1	2	3			18	19	20	21	22	23	24	
	31	1	2	3	4	◐	6	5:48	36	2483564		3	4	5	6	7	8	9			4	5	6	7	8	9	10		EPAG. 1803	25	26	27	28	29	30	1	PĀG. 2079
SEPTEMBER 2087	7	8	9	10	11	○	13	16:42	37	2483571	ELUL 5847	10	11	12	13	14	15	16		MONTH 8 Dīng-Wèi	11	12	13	14	15[g]	16	17	Bái lù		2	3	4	5	6	1[a]	2	
	14	15	16	17	18	◑	20	9:22	38	2483578		17	18	19	20	21	22	23			18	19	20	21	22	23	24			3	4	5	6	7	8	9	MASKARAM 2080
	21	22[d]	23	24	25	●	27	18:45	39	2483585		24	25	26	27	28	29	1[a]	Sat 11h21m0p		25	26	27	28	29	30	1*	Qiū fēn	THOOUT 1804	10	11	12	13	14	15	16	
	28	29	30	1	2	3	◐	23:31	40	2483592		2[a]	3	4	5	6	7	8			2	3	4	5	6	7	8			17[b]	18	19	20	21	22	23	
	5	6	7	8	9	10	11	2:13	41	2483599	TISHRI 5848	9	10[b]	11	12	13	14	15[c]		MONTH 9 Dīng-Wèi	9[h]	10	11	12	13	14	15	Hán lù		24	25	26	27	28	29	30	
OCTOBER 2087	○	13	14	15	16	17	◑	17:26	42	2483606		16	17	18	19	20	21	22			16	17	18	19	20	21	22			1	2	3	4	5	6	7	
	19	20	21	22	23	24	25		43	2483613		23	24	25	26	27	28	29			23	24	25	26	27	28	29	Shuāng jiàng		8	9	10	11	12	13	14	
	●	27	28	29	30	31	1	11:28	44	2483620		30	1	2	3	4	5	6	Mon 0h5m1p		1	2	3	4	5	6	7		PAOPE 1804	15	16	17	18	19	20	21	ṬEQEMT 2080
	2	◐	4	5	6	7	8	15:47	45	2483627		7	8	9	10	11	12	13			8	9	10	11	12	13	14	Lì dōng		22	23	24	25	26	27	28	
NOVEMBER 2087	9	○	11	12	13	14	15	12:04	46	2483634	HESHVAN 5848	14	15	16	17	18	19	20		MONTH 10 Dīng-Wèi	15	16	17	18	19	20	21			29	30	1	2	3	4	5	
	16	◑	18	19	20	21	22	4:49	47	2483641		21	22	23	24	25	26	27			22	23	24	25	26	27	28	Xiǎo xuě		6	7	8	9	10	11	12	
	23	24	●	26	27	28	29	6:22	48	2483648		28	29	30	1	2	3	4	Tue 12h49m2p		29	30	1	2*	3	4	5		ATHŌR 1804	13	14	15	16	17	18	19	ḪEDĀR 2080
	30	1	2	◐	4	5	6	5:59	49	2483655		5	6	7	8	9	10	11[d]			6	7	8	9	10	11	12			20	21	22	23	24	25	26	
	7	8	○	10	11	12	13	22:30	50	2483662	KISLEV 5848	12	13	14	15	16	17	18		MONTH 11 Dīng-Wèi	13	14	15	16	17	18	19	Dà xuě		27	28	29	30	1	2	3	
DECEMBER 2087	14	15	◑	17	18	19	20	20:10	51	2483669		19	20	21	22	23	24	25[e]			20	21	22	23	24	25	26			4	5	6	7	8	9	10	
	21[e]	22	23	24	●	26	27	1:41	52	2483676		26[e]	27[e]	28[e]	29[e]	30[e]	1[e]	2[e]	Thu 1h33m3p		27	28[i]	29	30	1	2	3	Dōng zhì	KOIAK 1804	11	12	13	14	15	16	17	TĀKHŚĀŚ 2080
	28	29	30	31	◐	2	3	17:52	1	2483683	TEVETH 5848	3	4	5	6	7	8	9		MONTH 12 Dīng-Wèi	4	5	6	7	8	9	10			18	19	20	21	22	23	24	

[a]New Year
[b]Spring (9:27)
[c]Summer (2:05)
[d]Autumn (18:27)
[e]Winter (16:07)
● New moon
◐ First quarter moon
○ Full moon
◑ Last quarter moon

‡Leap year
[a]New Year
[b]Yom Kippur
[c]Sukkot
[d]Winter starts
[e]Ḥanukkah
[f]Purim
[g]Passover
[h]Shavuot
[i]Fast of Av

[a]New Year (4785, Sheep)
[b]Lantern Festival
[c]Qīngmíng
[d]Dragon Festival
[e]Qīqiǎo
[f]Hungry Ghosts
[g]Mid-Autumn Festival
[h]Double-Ninth Festival
[i]Dōngzhì
*Start of 60-name cycle

‡Leap year
[a]New Year
[b]Building of the Cross
[c]Christmas
[d]Jesus's Circumcision
[e]Epiphany
[f]Easter
[g]Mary's Announcement
[h]Jesus's Transfiguration

PERSIAN (ASTRONOMICAL) 1465‡/1466

Month	Sun	Mon	Tue	Wed	Thu	Fri	Sat
	9	10	11	12	13	14	15
DEY 1465	16	17	18	19	20	21	22
	23	24	25	26	27	28	29
	30	*1*	2	3	4	5	6
BAHMAN 1465	7	8	9	10	11	12	13
	14	15	16	17	18	19	20
	21	22	23	24	25	26	27
	28	29	30	*1*	2	3	4
ESFAND 1465	5	6	7	8	9	10	11
	12	13	14	15	16	17	18
	19	20	21	22	23	24	25
	26	27	28	29	30*	*1*[a]	2
FARVARDĪN 1466	3	4	5	6	7	8	9
	10	11	12	13[b]	14	15	16
	17	18	19	20	21	22	23
	24	25	26	27	28	29	30
	31	*1*	2	3	4	5	6
ORDĪBEHEŠT 1466	7	8	9	10	11	12	13
	14	15	16	17	18	19	20
	21	22	23	24	25	26	27
	28	29	30	31	*1*	2	3
XORDĀD 1466	4	5	6	7	8	9	10
	11	12	13	14	15	16	17
	18	19	20	21	22	23	24
	25	26	27	28	29	30	31
	1	2	3	4	5	6	7
TĪR 1466	8	9	10	11	12	13	14
	15	16	17	18	19	20	21
	22	23	24	25	26	27	28
	29	30	31	*1*	2	3	4
MORDĀD 1466	5	6	7	8	9	10	11
	12	13	14	15	16	17	18
	19	20	21	22	23	24	25
	26	27	28	29	30	31	*1*
SHAHRĪVAR 1466	2	3	4	5	6	7	8
	9	10	11	12	13	14	15
	16	17	18	19	20	21	22
	23	24	25	26	27	28	29
	30	31	*1*	2	3	4	5
MEHR 1466	6	7	8	9	10	11	12
	13	14	15	16	17	18	19
	20	21	22	23	24	25	26
	27	28	29	30	*1*	2	3
ABĀN 1466	4	5	6	7	8	9	10
	11	12	13	14	15	16	17
	18	19	20	21	22	23	24
	25	26	27	28	29	30	*1*
ĀZAR 1466	2	3	4	5	6	7	8
	9	10	11	12	13	14	15
	16	17	18	19	20	21	22
	23	24	25	26	27	28	29
DEY 1466	30	*1*	2	3	4	5	6
	7	8	9	10	11	12	13

‡Leap year
[a]New Year (or prior day)
*Near New Year: −1′53″
[b]Sizdeh Bedar

HINDU LUNAR 2143/2144

Month	Sun	Mon	Tue	Wed	Thu	Fri	Sat
	24	25	26	27	28	29	30
	1	2	3	4	5	6	7
PAUSHA 2143	8	9	10	**11**	13	14	15
	16	17	18	19	20	21	*21*
	22	23	24	25	26	27	28
	29	30	1	2	3	4	**5**
MĀGHA 2143	7	8	9	10	11	12	13
	14	15	16	17	18	19	20
	21	22	23	*23*	24	25	26
	27	28[h]	**29**	1	2	3	4
PHĀLGUNA 2143	5	6	7	8	9	10	11
	12	13	14	15[i]	16	17	18
	19	20	21	22	23	24	25
	26	27	28	29	30	1[a]	2
	3	**4**	6	7	8	9[b]	10
CHAITRA 2144	11	12	13	14	15	16	17
	17	18	19	20	21	22	23
	24	25	26	**27**	29	30	1
	2	3	4	5	6	7	8
VAIŚĀKHA 2144	9	10	11	12	13	14	15
	16	17	18	19	20	21	22
	23	24	25	26	27	28	29
	30	2	3	4	5	6	7
	8	9	10	11	12	*12*	13
JYAISHṬHA 2144	14	15	16	17	18	19	20
	21	22	**23**	25	26	27	28
	29	30	1	2	3	4	5
	6	7	8	9	10	11	12
ĀSHĀḌHA 2144	13	14	15	16	17	18	19
	20	21	22	23	24	25	**26**
	28	29	30	1	2	3	4
	5	6	7	8	9	*9*	10
ŚRĀVAṆA 2144	11	12	13	14	15	16	17
	18	**19**	21	22	23[c]	24	25
	26	27	28	29	30	1	2
	3	4[d]	5	6	7	8	9
BHĀDRAPADA 2144	10	11	12	13	14	15	16
	17	18	19	20	21	**22**	24
	25	26	27	28	29	30	1
	2	3	4	5	*5*	6	7
ĀŚVINA 2144	8[e]	9[e]	10[e]	11	12	13	14
	15	17	18	19	20	21	22
	23	24	25	26	27	28	29
	30	1[f]	2	3	4	5	6
KĀRTTIKA 2144	7	8	9	10	11	12	13
	14	15	16	17	18	19	**20**
	22	23	24	25	26	27	28
	29	*29*	30	1	2	3	4
MĀRGAŚIRA 2144	5	6	7	8	9	10	11[g]
	12	**13**	15	16	17	18	19
	20	21	22	23	24	25	26
PAUSHA 2144	27	28	29	30	1	*1*	2
	3	4	5	6	**7**	9	10

[a]New Year (Plavaṅga)
[b]Birthday of Rāma
[c]Birthday of Krishna
[d]Ganēśa Chaturthī
[e]Dashara
[f]Diwali
[g]Birthday of Vishnu
[h]Night of Śiva
[i]Holi

HINDU SOLAR 2008/2009‡

Month	Sun	Mon	Tue	Wed	Thu	Fri	Sat
	13	14	15	16	17	18	19
PAUSHA 2008	20	21	22	23	24	25	26
	27	28	29	1[b]	2	3	4
	5	6	7	8	9	10	11
MĀGHA 2008	12	13	14	15	16	17	18
	19	20	21	22	23	24	25
	26	27	28	29	1	2	3
	4	5	6	7	8	9	10
PHĀLGUNA 2008	11	12	13	14	15	16	17
	18	19	20	21	22	23	24
	25	26	27	28	29	30	1
	2	3	4	5	6	7	8
CHAITRA 2008	9	10	11	12	13	14	15
	16	17	18	19	20	21	22
	23	24	25	26	27	28	29
	30	1[a]	2	3	4	5	6
VAIŚĀKHA 2009	7	8	9	10	11	12	13
	14	15	16	17	18	19	20
	21	22	23	24	25	26	27
	28	29	30	31	1	2	3
JYAISHṬHA 2009	4	5	6	7	8	9	10
	11	12	13	14	15	16	17
	18	19	20	21	22	23	24
	25	26	27	28	29	30	31
	32	1	2	3	4	5	6
ĀSHĀḌHA 2009	7	8	9	10	11	12	13
	14	15	16	17	18	19	20
	21	22	23	24	25	26	27
	28	29	30	31	32	1	2
	3	4	5	6	7	8	9
ŚRĀVAṆA 2009	10	11	12	13	14	15	16
	17	18	19	20	21	22	23
	24	25	26	27	28	29	30
	31	1	2	3	4	5	6
BHĀDRAPADA 2009	7	8	9	10	11	12	13
	14	15	16	17	18	19	20
	21	22	23	24	25	26	27
	28	29	30	31	1	2	3
	4	5	6	7	8	9	10
ĀŚVINA 2009	11	12	13	14	15	16	17
	18	19	20	21	22	23	24
	25	26	27	28	29	30	1
	2	3	4	5	6	7	8
KĀRTTIKA 2009	9	10	11	12	13	14	15
	16	17	18	19	20	21	22
	23	24	25	26	27	28	29
	30	1	2	3	4	5	6
	7	8	9	10	11	12	13
MĀRGAŚIRA 2009	14	15	16	17	18	19	20
	21	22	23	24	25	26	27
	28	29	30	1	2	3	4
PAUSHA 2009	5	6	7	8	9	10	11
	12	13	14	15	16	17	18

‡Leap year
[a]New Year (Durmati)
[b]Pongal

ISLAMIC (ASTRONOMICAL) 1510/1511

Month	Sun	Mon	Tue	Wed	Thu	Fri	Sat
	22	23	24	25	26	27	28
JUMĀDĀ I 1510	29	*1*	2	3	4	5	6
JUMĀDĀ II 1510	7	8	9	10	11	12	13
	14	15	16	17	18	19	20
	21	22	23	24	25	26	27
	28	29	*30*	1	2	3	4
RAJAB 1510	5	6	7	8	9	10	11
	12	13	14	15	16	17	18
	19	20	21	22	23	24	25
	26	27[d]	28	29	*1*	2	3
SHA'BĀN 1510	4	5	6	7	8	9	10
	11	12	13	14	15	16	17
	18	19	20	21	22	23	24
	25	26	27	28	29	*30*	1[e]
RAMAḌĀN 1510	2	3	4	5	6	7	8
	9	10	11	12	13	14	15
	16	17	18	19	20	21	22
	23	24	25	26	27	28	29
	1[f]	2	3	4	5	6	7
SHAWWĀL 1510	8	9	10	11	12	13	14
	15	16	17	18	19	20	21
	22	23	24	25	26	27	28
	29	*1*	2	3	4	5	6
DHU AL-QA'DA 1510	7	8	9	10	11	12	13
	14	15	16	17	18	19	20
	21	22	23	24	25	26	27
	28	29	30	*1*	2	3	4
DHU AL-ḤIJJA 1510	5	6	7	8	9	10[g]	11
	12	13	14	15	16	17	18
	19	20	21	22	23	24	25
	26	27	28	29	30	*1*[a]	2
MUḤARRAM 1511	3	4	5	6	7	8	9
	10[b]	11	12	13	14	15	16
	17	18	19	20	21	22	23
	24	25	26	27	28	29	1
ṢAFAR 1511	*2*	3	4	5	6	7	8
	9	10	11	12	13	14	15
	16	17	18	19	20	21	22
	23	24	25	26	27	28	29
	30	*1*	2	3	4	5	6
RABĪ' I 151	7	8	9	10	11	12[c]	13
	14	15	16	17	18	19	20
	21	22	23	24	25	26	27
	28	29	1	2	3	4	5
RABĪ' II 1511	6	7	8	9	10	11	12
	13	14	15	16	17	18	19
	20	21	22	23	24	25	26
	27	28	29	30	*1*	2	3
JUMĀDĀ I 1511	4	5	6	7	8	9	10
	11	12	13	14	15	16	17
	18	19	20	21	22	23	24
JUMĀDĀ II 1511	25	26	27	28	29	1	2
	3	4	5	6	7	8	9

[a]New Year
[b]'Ashūrā'
[c]Prophet's Birthday
[d]Ascent of the Prophet
[e]Start of Ramaḍān
[f]'Īd al-Fiṭr
[g]'Īd al-'Aḍḥā

GREGORIAN 2087

Julian (Sun)	Sun	Mon	Tue	Wed	Thu	Fri	Sat	Month
Dec 16	*29*	30	31	1	2	3	4	
	5	6	7[a]	8	9	10	11	JANUARY 2087
Dec 30	*12*	13	14[b]	15	16	17	18	
	19	20	21	22	23	24	25	
Jan 13	*26*	27	28	29	30	31	1	
	2	3	4	5	6	7	8	FEBRUARY 2087
Jan 27	9	10	11	12	13	14	15	
	16	17	18	19	20	21	22	
Feb 10	*23*	24	25	26	27	28	1	
	2	3	4	5[c]	6	7	8	MARCH 2087
Feb 24	9	10	11	12	13	14	15	
	16[d]	17	18	19	20	21	22	
Mar 10	*23*	24	25	26	27	28	29	
	30	31	1	2	3	4	5	
Mar 24	6	7	8	9	10	11	12	APRIL 2087
	13	14	15	16	17	18	19	
Apr 7	*20*[e]	21	22	23	24	25	26	
	27[f]	28	29	30	1	2	3	
Apr 21	*4*	5	6	7	8	9	10	MAY 2087
	11	12	13	14	15	16	17	
May 5	*18*	19	20	21	22	23	24	
	25	26	27	28	29	30	31	
May 19	*1*	2	3	4	5	6	7	
	8	9	10	11	12	13	14	JUNE 2087
Jun 2	*15*	16	17	18	19	20	21	
	22	23	24	25	26	27	28	
Jun 16	*29*	30	1	2	3	4	5	
	6	7	8	9	10	11	12	JULY 2087
Jun 30	*13*	14	15	16	17	18	19	
	20	21	22	23	24	25	26	
Jul 14	*27*	28	29	30	31	1	2	
	3	4	5	6	7	8	9	AUGUST 2087
Jul 28	*10*	11	12	13	14	15	16	
	17	18	19	20	21	22	23	
Aug 11	*24*	25	26	27	28	29	30	
	31	1	2	3	4	5	6	
Aug 25	7	8	9	10	11	12	13	SEPTEMBER 2087
	14	15	16	17	18	19	20	
Sep 8	*21*	22	23	24	25	26	27	
	28	29	30	1	2	3	4	
Sep 22	5	6	7	8	9	10	11	OCTOBER 2087
	12	13	14	15	16	17	18	
Oct 6	*19*	20	21	22	23	24	25	
	26	27	28	29	30	31	1	
Oct 20	2	3	4	5	6	7	8	NOVEMBER 2087
	9	10	11	12	13	14	15	
Nov 3	*16*	17	18	19	20	21	22	
	23	24	25	26	27	28	29	
Nov 17	*30*[g]	1	2	3	4	5	6	
	7	8	9	10	11	12	13	DECEMBER 2087
Dec 1	*14*	15	16	17	18	19	20	
	21	22	23	24	25[h]	26	27	
Dec 15	*28*	29	30	31	1	2	3	

[a]Orthodox Christmas
[b]Julian New Year
[c]Ash Wednesday
[d]Feast of Orthodoxy
[e]Easter
[f]Orthodox Easter
[g]Advent
[h]Christmas

2088

Gregorian 2088‡

Month	Sun	Mon	Tue	Wed	Thu	Fri	Sat	Lunar Phases	ISO Week (Mon)	Julian Day (Sun noon)
January 2088	28	29	30	31	◐[a]	2	3	17:52	1	2483683
	4	5	6	7	○	9	10	9:36	2	2483690
	11	12	13	14	◑	16	17	15:12	3	2483697
	18	19	20	21	22	●	24	19:37	4	2483704
	25	26	27	28	29	30	◐	3:32	5	2483711
February 2088	1	2	3	4	5	○	7	21:31	6	2483718
	8	9	10	11	12	13	◑	12:23	7	2483725
	15	16	17	18	19	20	21		8	2483732
	●	23	24	25	26	27	28	11:08	9	2483739
March 2088	◐	1	2	3	4	5	6	11:25	10	2483746
	○	8	9	10	11	12	13	10:35	11	2483753
	14	◑	16	17	18	19[b]	20	9:28	12	2483760
	21	●	23	24	25	26	27	23:59	13	2483767
	28	◐	30	31	1	2	3	18:22	14	2483774
April 2088	4	5	○	7	8	9	10	0:58	15	2483781
	11	12	13	◑	15	16	17	4:25	16	2483788
	18	19	20	●	22	23	24	10:24	17	2483795
	25	26	27	◐	29	30	1	1:27	18	2483802
May 2088	2	3	4	○	6	7	8	16:24	19	2483809
	9	10	11	12	◑	14	15	20:08	20	2483816
	16	17	18	19	●	21	22	18:48	21	2483823
	23	24	25	26	◐	28	29	9:50	22	2483830
	30	31	1	2	3	○	5	8:07	23	2483837
June 2088	6	7	8	9	10	11	◑	8:26	24	2483844
	13	14	15	16	17	18	●	1:53	25	2483851
	20[c]	21	22	23	24	◐	26	20:28	26	2483858
	27	28	29	30	1	2	○	23:21	27	2483865
July 2088	4	5	6	7	8	9	10		28	2483872
	◑	12	13	14	15	16	17	17:51	29	2483879
	●	19	20	21	22	23	24	8:37	30	2483886
	◐	26	27	28	29	30	31	9:53	31	2483893
August 2088	1	○	3	4	5	6	7	13:38	32	2483900
	8	9	◑	11	12	13	14	0:56	33	2483907
	15	●	17	18	19	20	21	16:14	34	2483914
	22	23	◐	25	26	27	28	2:04	35	2483921
	29	30	31	○	2	3	4	2:57	36	2483928
September 2088	5	6	7	◑	9	10	11	6:42	37	2483935
	12	13	14	●	16	17	18	1:56	38	2483942
	19	20	21	◐[d]	23	24	25	20:24	39	2483949
	26	27	28	29	○	1	2	15:24	40	2483956
October 2088	3	4	5	6	◑	8	9	12:23	41	2483963
	10	11	12	13	●	15	16	14:38	42	2483970
	17	18	19	20	21	◐	23	15:50	43	2483977
	24	25	26	27	28	29	○	3:09	44	2483984
	31	1	2	3	4	◑	6	19:21	45	2483991
November 2088	7	8	9	10	11	12	●	6:30	46	2483998
	14	15	16	17	18	19	20		47	2484005
	◐	22	23	24	25	26	27	11:07	48	2484012
	○	29	30	1	2	3	4	14:17	49	2484019
December 2088	◑	6	7	8	9	10	11	4:57	50	2484026
	12	●	14	15	16	17	18	0:51	51	2484033
	19	20[e]	◐	22	23	24	25	4:50	52	2484040
	26	27	○	29	30	31	1	0:56	53	2484047

Hebrew 5848/5849

ISO Week	Month	Sun	Mon	Tue	Wed	Thu	Fri	Sat	Molad
1	Tevet 5848	3	4	5	6	7	8	9	
2		10	11	12	13	14	15	16	
3		17	18	19	20	21	22	23	Fri 14h17m4p
4		24	25	26	27	28	29	1	
5	Shevat 5848	2	3	4	5	6	7	8	
6		9	10	11	12	13	14	15	
7		16	17	18	19	20	21	22	
8		23	24	25	26	27	28	29	Sun 3h1m5p
9		30	1	2	3	4	5	6	
10	Adar 5848	7	8	9	10	11	12	13	
11		14[f]	15	16	17	18	19	20	
12		21	22	23	24	25	26	27	Mon 15h45m6p
13		28	29	1	2	3	4	5	
14	Nisan 5848	6	7	8	9	10	11	12	
15		13	14	15[g]	16	17	18	19	
16		20	21	22	23	24	25	26	
17		27	28	29	30	1	2	3	Wed 4h29m7p
18	Iyyar 5848	4	5	6	7	8	9	10	
19		11	12	13	14	15	16	17	
20		18	19	20	21	22	23	24	
21		25	26	27	28	29	1	2	Thu 17h13m8p
22	Sivan 5848	3	4	5	6[h]	7	8	9	
23		10	11	12	13	14	15	16	
24		17	18	19	20	21	22	23	
25		24	25	26	27	28	29	30	Sat 5h57m9p
26	Tammuz 5848	1	2	3	4	5	6	7	
27		8	9	10	11	12	13	14	
28		15	16	17	18	19	20	21	
29		22	23	24	25	26	27	28	Sun 18h41m10p
30		29	1	2	3	4	5	6	
31	Av 5848	7	8	9[i]	10	11	12	13	
32		14	15	16	17	18	19	20	
33		21	22	23	24	25	26	27	Tue 7h25m11p
34		28	29	30	1	2	3	4	
35	Elul 5848	5	6	7	8	9	10	11	
36		12	13	14	15	16	17	18	
37		19	20	21	22	23	24	25	Wed 20h9m12p
38		26	27	28	29	1[a]	2[a]	3	
39	Tishri 5849	4	5	6	7	8	9	10[b]	
40		11	12	13	14	15[c]	16	17	
41		18	19	20	21	22	23	24	Fri 8h53m13p
42		25	26	27	28	29	30	1	
43	Ḥeshvan 5849	2	3	4	5	6	7	8	
44		9	10	11	12	13	14	15	
45		16	17	18	19	20	21	22	
46		23	24	25	26	27	28	29	Sat 21h37m14p
47	Kislev 5849	1	2	3	4	5	6	7	
48		8	9	10	11	12	13	14	
49		15	16	17	18	19	20	21	
50		22[d]	23	24	25[e]	26[e]	27[e]	28[e]	Mon 10h21m15p
51		29[e]	30[e]	1[e]	2[e]	3	4	5	
52	Tevet 5849	6	7	8	9	10	11	12	
53		13	14	15	16	17	18	19	

Chinese Dīng-Wèi/Wù-Shēn‡

ISO Week	Month	Sun	Mon	Tue	Wed	Thu	Fri	Sat	Solar Term
1	Month 12 Dīng-Wèi	4	5	6	7	8	9	10	
2		11	12	13	14	15	16	17	Xiǎohán
3		18	19	20	21	22	23	24	
4		25	26	27	28	29	30	1[a]	Dàhán
5	Month 1 Wù-Shēn	2*	3	4	5	6	7	8	
6		9	10	11	12	13	14	15[b]	Lìchūn
7		16	17	18	19	20	21	22	
8		23	24	25	26	27	28	29	Yǔshuǐ
9		1	2	3	4	5	6	7	
10	Month 2 Wù-Shēn	8	9	10	11	12	13	14	Jīngzhé
11		15	16	17	18	19	20	21	
12		22	23	24	25	26	27	28	Chūnfēn
13		29	30	1	2	3*	4	5	
14	Month 3 Wù-Shēn	6	7	8	9	10	11	12	
15		13[c]	14	15	16	17	18	19	Qīngmíng
16		20	21	22	23	24	25	26	
17		27	28	29	1	2	3	4	Gǔyǔ
18	Month 4 Wù-Shēn	5	6	7	8	9	10	11	
19		12	13	14	15	16	17	18	Lìxià
20		19	20	21	22	23	24	25	
21		26	27	28	29	30	1	2	Xiǎomǎn
22	Leap Month 4 Wù-Shēn	3	4*	5	6	7	8	9	
23		10	11	12	13	14	15	16	Mángzhòng
24		17	18	19	20	21	22	23	
25		24	25	26	27	28	29	1	
26	Month 5 Wù-Shēn	2	3	4	5[d]	6	7	8	Xiàzhì
27		9	10	11	12	13	14	15	
28		16	17	18	19	20	21	22	Xiǎoshǔ
29		23	24	25	26	27	28	29	
30	Month 6 Wù-Shēn	1	2	3	4	5	6*	7	Dàshǔ
31		8	9	10	11	12	13	14	
32		15	16	17	18	19	20	21	Lìqiū
33		22	23	24	25	26	27	28	
34		29	30	1	2	3	4	5	
35	Month 7 Wù-Shēn	6	7[e]	8	9	10	11	12	Chǔshǔ
36		13	14	15[f]	16	17	18	19	
37		20	21	22	23	24	25	26	Báilù
38		27	28	29	1	2	3	4	
39	Month 8 Wù-Shēn	5	6	7*	8	9	10	11	Qiūfēn
40		12	13	14	15[g]	16	17	18	
41		19	20	21	22	23	24	25	Hánlù
42		26	27	28	29	1	2	3	
43	Month 9 Wù-Shēn	4	5	6	7	8	9[h]	10	Shuāngjiàng
44		11	12	13	14	15	16	17	
45		18	19	20	21	22	23	24	Lìdōng
46		25	26	27	28	29	30	1	
47	Month 10 Wù-Shēn	2	3	4	5	6	7	8*	Xiǎoxuě
48		9	10	11	12	13	14	15	
49		16	17	18	19	20	21	22	
50		23	24	25	26	27	28	29	Dàxuě
51	Month 11* Wù-Shēn	30	1	2	3	4	5	6	
52		7	8	9[i]	10	11	12	13	Dōngzhì
53		14	15	16	17	18	19	20	

Coptic 1804/1805 — Ethiopic 2080/2081

ISO Week	Coptic Month	Sun	Mon	Tue	Wed	Thu	Fri	Sat	Ethiopic Month
1	Koiak 1804	18	19	20	21	22	23	24	Tākhśāś 2080
2		25	26	27	28	29[c]	30	1	
3	Ṭōbe 1804	2	3	4	5	6[d]	7	8	Ṭer 2080
4		9	10	11[e]	12	13	14	15	
5		16	17	18	19	20	21	22	
6		23	24	25	26	27	28	29	
7	Meshir 1804	30	1	2	3	4	5	6	Yakātīt 2080
8		7	8	9	10	11	12	13	
9		14	15	16	17	18	19	20	
10		21	22	23	24	25	26	27	
11	Paremotep 1804	28	29	30	1	2	3	4	Magābit 2080
12		5	6	7	8	9	10	11	
13		12	13	14	15	16	17	18	
14		19	20	21	22	23	24	25	
15	Parmoute 1804	26	27	28	29	30	1	2	Miyāzyā 2080
16		3	4	5	6	7	8	9	
17		10[f]	11	12	13	14	15	16	
18		17	18	19	20	21	22	23	
19	Pashons 1804	24	25	26	27	28	29[g]	30	Genbot 2080
20		1	2	3	4	5	6	7	
21		8	9	10	11	12	13	14	
22		15	16	17	18	19	20	21	
23	Paōne 1804	22	23	24	25	26	27	28	Sanē 2080
24		29	30	1	2	3	4	5	
25		6	7	8	9	10	11	12	
26		13	14	15	16	17	18	19	
27		20	21	22	23	24	25	26	
28	Epēp 1804	27	28	29	30	1	2	3	Ḥamlē 2080
29		4	5	6	7	8	9	10	
30		11	12	13	14	15	16	17	
31		18	19	20	21	22	23	24	
32	Mesorē 1804	25	26	27	28	29	30	1	Naḥasē 2080
33		2	3	4	5	6	7	8	
34		9	10	11	12	13[h]	14	15	
35		16	17	18	19	20	21	22	
36		23	24	25	26	27	28	29	
37	Epag. 1804	30	1	2	3	4	5	1[a]	Pāg. 2080
38	Thoout 1805	2	3	4	5	6	7	8	Maskaram 2081
39		9	10	11	12	13	14	15	
40		16	17[b]	18	19	20	21	22	
41	Paope 1805	23	24	25	26	27	28	29	Ṭeqemt 2081
42		30	1	2	3	4	5	6	
43		7	8	9	10	11	12	13	
44		14	15	16	17	18	19	20	
45	Athōr 1805	21	22	23	24	25	26	27	Ḫedār 2081
46		28	29	30	1	2	3	4	
47		5	6	7	8	9	10	11	
48		12	13	14	15	16	17	18	
49		19	20	21	22	23	24	25	
50	Koiak 1805	26	27	28	29	30	1	2	Tākhśāś 2081
51		3	4	5	6	7	8	9	
52		10	11	12	13	14	15	16	
53		17	18	19	20	21	22	23	

Gregorian notes:
‡Leap year
[a]New Year
[b]Spring (15:15)
[c]Summer (7:56)
[d]Autumn (0:17)
[e]Winter (21:55)
● New moon
◐ First quarter moon
○ Full moon
◑ Last quarter moon

Hebrew notes:
[a]New Year
[b]Yom Kippur
[c]Sukkot
[d]Winter starts
[e]Ḥanukkah
[f]Purim
[g]Passover
[h]Shavuot
[i]Fast of Av

Chinese notes:
‡Leap year
[a]New Year (4786, Monkey)
[b]Lantern Festival
[c]Qīngmíng
[d]Dragon Festival
[e]Qīqiǎo
[f]Hungry Ghosts
[g]Mid-Autumn Festival
[h]Double-Ninth Festival
[i]Dōngzhì
*Start of 60-name cycle

Coptic/Ethiopic notes:
[a]New Year
[b]Building of the Cross
[c]Christmas
[d]Jesus's Circumcision
[e]Epiphany
[f]Easter
[g]Mary's Announcement
[h]Jesus's Transfiguration

PERSIAN (ASTRONOMICAL) 1466/1467	Sun	Mon	Tue	Wed	Thu	Fri	Sat
DEY 1466	7	8	9	10	11	12	13
	14	15	16	17	18	19	20
	21	22	23	24	25	26	27
	28	29	30	1	2	3	4
BAHMAN 1466	5	6	7	8	9	10	11
	12	13	14	15	16	17	18
	19	20	21	22	23	24	25
	26	27	28	29	30	1	2
ESFAND 1466	3	4	5	6	7	8	9
	10	11	12	13	14	15	16
	17	18	19	20	21	22	23
	24	25	26	27	28	29	1[a]
FARVARDĪN 1467	2	3	4	5	6	7	8
	9	10	11	12	13[b]	14	15
	16	17	18	19	20	21	22
	23	24	25	26	27	28	29
	30	31	1	2	3	4	5
ORDĪBEHEŠT 1467	6	7	8	9	10	11	12
	13	14	15	16	17	18	19
	20	21	22	23	24	25	26
	27	28	29	30	31	1	2
XORDĀD 1467	3	4	5	6	7	8	9
	10	11	12	13	14	15	16
	17	18	19	20	21	22	23
	24	25	26	27	28	29	30
	31	1	2	3	4	5	6
TĪR 1467	7	8	9	10	11	12	13
	14	15	16	17	18	19	20
	21	22	23	24	25	26	27
	28	29	30	31	1	2	3
MORDĀD 1467	4	5	6	7	8	9	10
	11	12	13	14	15	16	17
	18	19	20	21	22	23	24
	25	26	27	28	29	30	31
SHAHRĪVAR 1467	1	2	3	4	5	6	7
	8	9	10	11	12	13	14
	15	16	17	18	19	20	21
	22	23	24	25	26	27	28
	29	30	31	1	2	3	4
MEHR 1467	5	6	7	8	9	10	11
	12	13	14	15	16	17	18
	19	20	21	22	23	24	25
	26	27	28	29	30	1	2
ĀBĀN 1467	3	4	5	6	7	8	9
	10	11	12	13	14	15	16
	17	18	19	20	21	22	23
	24	25	26	27	28	29	30
ĀZAR 1467	1	2	3	4	5	6	7
	8	9	10	11	12	13	14
	15	16	17	18	19	20	21
	22	23	24	25	26	27	28
	29	30	1	2	3	4	5
DEY 1467	6	7	8	9	10	11	12

[a]New Year
[b]Sizdeh Bedar

HINDU LUNAR 2144/2145‡	Sun	Mon	Tue	Wed	Thu	Fri	Sat
PAUSHA 2144	3	4	5	6	7	9	10
	11	12	13	14	15	16	17
	18	19	20	21	22	23	24
	25	26	27	28	29	30	1
MĀGHA 2144	2	3	4	5	6	7	8
	9	10	11	12	14	15	16
	17	18	19	20	21	22	23
	23	24	25	26	27	28[h]	29
PHĀLGUNA 2144	30	1	2	3	4	5	6
	8	9	10	11	12	13	14
	15[i]	16	17	18	19	20	21
	22	23	24	25	26	27	27
	28	29	1[a]	2	3	4	5
CHAITRA 2145	6	7	8	9[b]	10	11	12
	14	15	16	16	17	18	19
	20	21	22	23	24	25	26
	27	28	29	30	1	2	3
VAIŚĀKHA 2145	4	6	7	8	9	10	11
	12	13	14	15	16	17	18
	19	20	20	21	22	23	24
	25	26	27	29	30	1	2
JYAISHṬHA 2145	3	4	5	6	7	8	9
	10	11	12	13	14	15	16
	17	18	19	20	21	22	23
	24	25	26	27	28	29	30
ĀSHĀḌHA 2145	2	3	4	5	6	7	8
	9	10	11	12	13	14	15
	16	17	17	18	19	20	21
	22	23	25	26	27	28	29
	30	1	2	3	4	5	7
LEAP ŚRĀVAṆA 2145	8	8	9	10	11	12	13
	14	15	16	17	18	19	20
	21	22	23	24	25	26	28
	29	30	1	2	3	4	5
ŚRĀVAṆA 2145	6	7	8	9	10	11	12
	13	14	14	15	16	17	18
	20	21	22	23[c]	24	25	26
	27	28	29	30	1	3	4[d]
BHĀDRAPADA 2145	4	5	6	7	8	9	10
	11	12	13	14	15	16	17
	18	19	20	21	22	24	25
	26	27	28	29	30	1	2
ĀŚVINA 2145	3	4	5	6	7	8	8[e]
	9[e]	10[e]	11	12	13	14	15
	16	18	19	20	21	22	23
	24	25	26	27	28	29	30
	1[f]	2	3	4	5	6	7
KĀRTTIKA 2145	8	9	10	11	12	13	14
	15	16	17	18	19	20	22
	23	24	25	26	27	28	29
MĀRGAŚĪRA 2145	30	1	2	2	3	4	5
	6	7	8	9	10	11[g]	12
	13	14	16	17	18	19	20

‡Leap year
[a]New Year (Kīlaka)
[b]Birthday of Rāma
[c]Birthday of Krishna
[d]Ganēśa Chaturthī
[e]Dashara
[f]Diwali
[g]Birthday of Vishnu
[h]Night of Śiva
[i]Holi

HINDU SOLAR 2009‡/2010	Sun	Mon	Tue	Wed	Thu	Fri	Sat
PAUSHA 2009	12	13	14	15	16	17	18
	19	20	21	22	23	24	25
	26	27	28	29	1[b]	2	3
MĀGHA 2009	4	5	6	7	8	9	10
	11	12	13	14	15	16	17
	18	19	20	21	22	23	24
	25	26	27	28	29	30	1
PHĀLGUNA 2009	2	3	4	5	6	7	8
	9	10	11	12	13	14	15
	16	17	18	19	20	21	22
	23	24	25	26	27	28	29
	1	2	3	4	5	6	7
CHAITRA 2009	8	9	10	11	12	13	14
	15	16	17	18	19	20	21
	22	23	24	25	26	27	28
	29	30	31	1[a]	2	3	4
VAIŚĀKHA 2010	5	6	7	8	9	10	11
	12	13	14	15	16	17	18
	19	20	21	22	23	24	25
	26	27	28	29	30	31	1
JYAISHṬHA 2010	2	3	4	5	6	7	8
	9	10	11	12	13	14	15
	16	17	18	19	20	21	22
	23	24	25	26	27	28	29
	30	31	1	2	3	4	5
ĀSHĀḌHA 2010	6	7	8	9	10	11	12
	13	14	15	16	17	18	19
	20	21	22	23	24	25	26
	27	28	29	30	31	32	1
ŚRĀVAṆA 2010	2	3	4	5	6	7	8
	9	10	11	12	13	14	15
	16	17	18	19	20	21	22
	23	24	25	26	27	28	29
	30	31	1	2	3	4	5
BHĀDRAPADA 2010	6	7	8	9	10	11	12
	13	14	15	16	17	18	19
	20	21	22	23	24	25	26
	27	28	29	30	31	1	2
ĀŚVINA 2010	3	4	5	6	7	8	9
	10	11	12	13	14	15	16
	17	18	19	20	21	22	23
	24	25	26	27	28	29	30
	31	1	2	3	4	5	6
KĀRTTIKA 2010	7	8	9	10	11	12	13
	14	15	16	17	18	19	20
	21	22	23	24	25	26	27
	28	29	30	1	2	3	4
MĀRGAŚĪRA 2010	5	6	7	8	9	10	11
	12	13	14	15	16	17	18
	19	20	21	22	23	24	25
	26	27	28	29	1	2	3
PAUSHA 2010	4	5	6	7	8	9	10
	11	12	13	14	15	16	17

‡Leap year
[a]New Year (Dundubhi)
[b]Pongal

ISLAMIC (ASTRONOMICAL) 1511/1512‡	Sun	Mon	Tue	Wed	Thu	Fri	Sat
JUMĀDĀ II 1511	3	4	5	6	7	8	9
	10	11	12	13	14	15	16
	17	18	19	20	21	22	23
	24	25	26	27	28	29	30
RAJAB 1511	1	2	3	4	5	6	7
	8	9	10	11	12	13	14
	15	16	17	18	19	20	21
	22	23	24	25	26	27[d]	28
	29	30	1	2	3	4	5
SHA'BĀN 1511	6	7	8	9	10	11	12
	13	14	15	16	17	18	19
	20	21	22	23	24	25	26
	27	28	29	1[e]	2	3	4
RAMAḌĀN 1511	5	6	7	8	9	10	11
	12	13	14	15	16	17	18
	19	20	21	22	23	24	25
	26	27	28	29	30	1[f]	2
SHAWWĀL 1511	3	4	5	6	7	8	9
	10	11	12	13	14	15	16
	17	18	19	20	21	22	23
	24	25	26	27	28	29	1
DHU AL-QA'DA 1511	2	3	4	5	6	7	8
	9	10	11	12	13	14	15
	16	17	18	19	20	21	22
	23	24	25	26	27	28	29
	30	1	2	3	4	5	6
DHU AL-ḤIJJA 1511	7	8	9	10[g]	11	12	13
	14	15	16	17	18	19	20
	21	22	23	24	25	26	27
	28	29	1[a]	2	3	4	5
MUḤARRAM 1512	6	7	8	9	10[b]	11	12
	13	14	15	16	17	18	19
	20	21	22	23	24	25	26
	27	28	29	30	1	2	3
ṢAFAR 1512	4	5	6	7	8	9	10
	11	12	13	14	15	16	17
	18	19	20	21	22	23	24
	25	26	27	28	29	1	2
RABĪ' I 1512	3	4	5	6	7	8	9
	10	11	12[c]	13	14	15	16
	17	18	19	20	21	22	23
	24	25	26	27	28	29	1
RABĪ' II 1512	2	3	4	5	6	7	8
	9	10	11	12	13	14	15
	16	17	18	19	20	21	22
	23	24	25	26	27	28	29
	30	1	2	3	4	5	6
JUMĀDĀ I 1512	7	8	9	10	11	12	13
	14	15	16	17	18	19	20
	21	22	23	24	25	26	27
	28	29	1	2	3	4	5
JUMĀDĀ II 1512	6	7	8	9	10	11	12
	13	14	15	16	17	18	19

‡Leap year
[a]New Year
[b]'Ashūrā'
[c]Prophet's Birthday
[d]Ascent of the Prophet
[e]Start of Ramaḍān
[f]'Īd al-Fiṭr
[g]'Īd al-'Aḍḥā

Julian‡ (Sun)	Sun	Mon	Tue	Wed	Thu	Fri	Sat	GREGORIAN 2088‡
Dec 15	28	29	30	31	1	2	3	
	4	5	6	7[a]	8	9	10	JANUARY 2088
Dec 29	11	12	13	14[b]	15	16	17	
	18	19	20	21	22	23	24	
Jan 12	25	26	27	28	29	30	31	
	1	2	3	4	5	6	7	FEBRUARY 2088
Jan 26	8	9	10	11	12	13	14	
	15	16	17	18	19	20	21	
Feb 9	22	23	24	25[c]	26	27	28	
	29	1	2	3	4	5	6	
Feb 23	7[d]	8	9	10	11	12	13	MARCH 2088
	14	15	16	17	18	19	20	
Mar 8	21	22	23	24	25	26	27	
	28	29	30	31	1	2	3	
Mar 22	4	5	6	7	8	9	10	APRIL 2088
	11[e]	12	13	14	15	16	17	
Apr 5	18[f]	19	20	21	22	23	24	
	25	26	27	28	29	30	1	
Apr 19	2	3	4	5	6	7	8	MAY 2088
	9	10	11	12	13	14	15	
May 3	16	17	18	19	20	21	22	
	23	24	25	26	27	28	29	
May 17	30	31	1	2	3	4	5	
	6	7	8	9	10	11	12	JUNE 2088
May 31	13	14	15	16	17	18	19	
	20	21	22	23	24	25	26	
Jun 14	27	28	29	30	1	2	3	
	4	5	6	7	8	9	10	JULY 2088
Jun 28	11	12	13	14	15	16	17	
	18	19	20	21	22	23	24	
Jul 12	25	26	27	28	29	30	31	
	1	2	3	4	5	6	7	AUGUST 2088
Jul 26	8	9	10	11	12	13	14	
	15	16	17	18	19	20	21	
Aug 9	22	23	24	25	26	27	28	
	29	30	31	1	2	3	4	
Aug 23	5	6	7	8	9	10	11	SEPTEMBER 2088
	12	13	14	15	16	17	18	
Sep 6	19	20	21	22	23	24	25	
	26	27	28	29	30	1	2	
Sep 20	3	4	5	6	7	8	9	OCTOBER 2088
	10	11	12	13	14	15	16	
Oct 4	17	18	19	20	21	22	23	
	24	25	26	27	28	29	30	
Oct 18	31	1	2	3	4	5	6	
	7	8	9	10	11	12	13	NOVEMBER 2088
Nov 1	14	15	16	17	18	19	20	
	21	22	23	24	25	26	27	
Nov 15	28[g]	29	30	1	2	3	4	
	5	6	7	8	9	10	11	DECEMBER 2088
Nov 29	12	13	14	15	16	17	18	
	19	20	21	22	23	24	25[h]	
Dec 13	26	27	28	29	30	31	1	

‡Leap year
[a]Orthodox Christmas
[b]Julian New Year
[c]Ash Wednesday
[d]Feast of Orthodoxy
[e]Easter
[f]Orthodox Easter
[g]Advent
[h]Christmas

2089

Gregorian 2089, Lunar Phases, ISO Week (Mon), Julian Day (Sun noon)

Month	Sun	Mon	Tue	Wed	Thu	Fri	Sat	Lunar Phases	ISO Week	Julian Day
	26	27	○	29	30	31	1[a]	0:56	53	2484047
JANUARY 2089	2	◑	4	5	6	7	8	17:59	1	2484054
	9	10	●	12	13	14	15	20:16	2	2484061
	16	17	18	◐	20	21	22	19:46	3	2484068
	23	24	25	○	27	28	29	11:23	4	2484075
	30	31	1	◑	3	4	5	10:22	5	2484082
FEBRUARY 2089	6	7	8	9	●	11	12	15:15	6	2484089
	13	14	15	16	17	◐	19	7:14	7	2484096
	20	21	22	23	○	25	26	22:04	8	2484103
	27	28	1	2	3	◑	5	5:04	9	2484110
MARCH 2089	6	7	8	9	10	11	●	8:23	10	2484117
	13	14	15	16	17	18	◐[b]	15:29	11	2484124
	20	21	22	23	24	25	○	9:19	12	2484131
	27	28	29	30	31	1	2		13	2484138
APRIL 2089	◑	4	5	6	7	8	9	0:34	14	2484145
	●	11	12	13	14	15	16	22:45	15	2484152
	◐	18	19	20	21	22	23	21:36	16	2484159
	○	25	26	27	28	29	30	21:21	17	2484166
	1	◑	3	4	5	6	7	19:31	18	2484173
MAY 2089	8	9	●	11	12	13	14	10:03	19	2484180
	15	16	◐	18	19	20	21	3:00	20	2484187
	22	23	○	25	26	27	28	10:16	21	2484194
	29	30	31	◑	2	3	4	12:48	22	2484201
JUNE 2089	5	6	7	●	9	10	11	18:43	23	2484208
	12	13	14	◐	16	17	18	9:08	24	2484215
	19	20[c]	21	22	○	24	25	0:06	25	2484222
	26	27	28	29	30	◑	2	3:42	26	2484229
JULY 2089	3	4	5	6	7	●	9	1:46	27	2484236
	10	11	12	13	◐	15	16	17:10	28	2484243
	17	18	19	20	21	○	23	14:49	29	2484250
	24	25	26	27	28	29	◑	15:54	30	2484257
	31	1	2	3	4	5	●	8:27	31	2484264
AUGUST 2089	7	8	9	10	11	12	◐	3:57	32	2484271
	14	15	16	17	18	19	20		33	2484278
	○	22	23	24	25	26	27	6:14	34	2484285
	28	◑	30	31	1	2	3	1:31	35	2484292
SEPTEMBER 2089	●	5	6	7	8	9	10	15:56	36	2484299
	◐	12	13	14	15	16	17	18:00	37	2484306
	18	○	20	21	22[d]	23	24	21:54	38	2484313
	25	26	◑	28	29	30	1	9:14	39	2484320
OCTOBER 2089	2	3	●	5	6	7	8	1:13	40	2484327
	9	10	◐	12	13	14	15	11:21	41	2484334
	16	17	18	○	20	21	22	13:03	42	2484341
	23	24	25	◑	27	28	29	16:05	43	2484348
	30	31	1	●	3	4	5	12:54	44	2484355
NOVEMBER 2089	6	7	8	9	◐	11	12	7:27	45	2484362
	13	14	15	16	17	○	19	3:01	46	2484369
	20	21	22	23	◑	25	26	23:17	47	2484376
	27	28	29	30	1	●	3	3:10	48	2484383
DECEMBER 2089	4	5	6	7	8	9	◐	4:51	49	2484390
	11	12	13	14	15	16	○	15:36	50	2484397
	18	19	20	21[e]	22	23	◑	7:54	51	2484404
	25	26	27	28	29	30	●	19:56	52	2484411

Hebrew 5849/5850‡

ISO Week	Month	Sun	Mon	Tue	Wed	Thu	Fri	Sat	Molad
53		13	14	15	16	17	18	19	
1	TEVETH 5849	20	21	22	23	24	25	26	Tue 23h5m16p
2		27	28	29	1	2	3	4	
3		5	6	7	8	9	10	11	
4	SHEVAT 5849	12	13	14	15	16	17	18	
5		19	20	21	22	23	24	25	Thu 11h49m17p
6		26	27	28	29	30	1	2	
7		3	4	5	6	7	8	9	
8	ADAR 5849	10	11	12	13	14[f]	15	16	
9		17	18	19	20	21	22	23	
10		24	25	26	27	28	29	1	Sat 0h34m0p
11		2	3	4	5	6	7	8	
12	NISAN 5849	9	10	11	12	13	14	15[g]	
13		16	17	18	19	20	21	22	
14		23	24	25	26	27	28	29	
15		30	1	2	3	4	5	6	Sun 13h18m1p
16	IYYAR 5849	7	8	9	10	11	12	13	
17		14	15	16	17	18	19	20	
18		21	22	23	24	25	26	27	
19		28	29	1	2	3	4	5	Tue 2h2m2p
20	SIVAN 5849	6[h]	7	8	9	10	11	12	
21		13	14	15	16	17	18	19	
22		20	21	22	23	24	25	26	
23		27	28	29	30	1	2	3	Wed 14h45m3p
24	TAMMUZ 5849	4	5	6	7	8	9	10	
25		11	12	13	14	15	16	17	
26		18	19	20	21	22	23	24	
27		25	26	27	28	29	1	2	Fri 3h30m4p
28	AV 5849	3	4	5	6	7	8	9	
29		10[i]	11	12	13	14	15	16	
30		17	18	19	20	21	22	23	
31		24	25	26	27	28	29	30	
32		1	2	3	4	5	6	7	Sat 16h14m5p
33	ELUL 5849	8	9	10	11	12	13	14	
34		15	16	17	18	19	20	21	
35		22	23	24	25	26	27	28	
36		29	1[a]	2[a]	3	4	5	6	Mon 4h58m6p
37	TISHRI 5850	7	8	9	10[b]	11	12	13	
38		14	15[c]	16	17	18	19	20	
39		21	22	23	24	25	26	27	
40		28	29	30	1	2	3	4	Tue 17h42m7p
41	HESHVAN 5850	5	6	7	8	9	10	11	
42		12	13	14	15	16	17	18	
43		19	20	21	22	23	24	25	
44		26	27	28	29	30	1	2	Thu 6h26m8p
45	KISLEV 5850	3	4	5	6	7	8	9	
46		10	11	12	13	14	15	16	
47		17	18	19	20	21	22	23	
48		24	25[e]	26[e]	27[e]	28[e]	29[e]	30[e]	
49		1[e]	2[d,e]	3	4	5	6	7	Fri 19h10m9p
50	TEVETH 5850	8	9	10	11	12	13	14	
51		15	16	17	18	19	20	21	
52		22	23	24	25	26	27	28	

Chinese Wù-Shēn‡/Jǐ-Yǒu

ISO Week	Month	Sun	Mon	Tue	Wed	Thu	Fri	Sat	Solar Term
53		14	15	16	17	18	19	20	
1	MONTH 11* Wù-Shēn	21	22	23	24	25	26	27	Xiǎo hán
2		28	29	30	1	2	3	4	
3		5	6	7	8*	9	10	11	Dà hán
4	MONTH 12 Wù-Shēn	12	13	14	15	16	17	18	
5		19	20	21	22	23	24	25	Lì chūn
6		26	27	28	29	1[a]	2	3	
7	MONTH 1 Jǐ-Yǒu	4	5	6	7	8	9	10	Yǔ shuǐ
8		11	12	13	14	15[b]	16	17	
9		18	19	20	21	22	23	24	Jīng zhé
10		25	26	27	28	29	30	1	
11		2	3	4	5	6	7	8	Chūn fēn
12	MONTH 2 Jǐ-Yǒu	9*	10	11	12	13	14	15	
13		16	17	18	19	20	21	22	
14		23	24[c]	25	26	27	28	29	Qīng míng
15		30	1	2	3	4	5	6	
16	MONTH 3 Jǐ-Yǒu	7	8	9	10	11	12	13	Gǔ yǔ
17		14	15	16	17	18	19	20	
18		21	22	23	24	25	26	27	Lì xià
19		28	29	1	2	3	4	5	
20	MONTH 4 Jǐ-Yǒu	6	7	8	9	10*	11	12	Xiǎo mǎn
21		13	14	15	16	17	18	19	
22		20	21	22	23	24	25	26	
23		27	28	29	30	1	2	3	Máng zhòng
24	MONTH 5 Jǐ-Yǒu	4	5[d]	6	7	8	9	10	
25		11	12	13	14	15	16	17	Xià zhì
26		18	19	20	21	22	23	24	
27		25	26	27	28	29	1	2	Xiǎo shǔ
28	MONTH 6 Jǐ-Yǒu	3	4	5	6	7	8	9	
29		10	11*	12	13	14	15	16	Dà shǔ
30		17	18	19	20	21	22	23	
31		24	25	26	27	28	29	1	
32	MONTH 7 Jǐ-Yǒu	2	3	4	5	6	7[e]	8	Lì qiū
33		9	10	11	12	13	14	15[f]	
34		16	17	18	19	20	21	22	Chǔ shǔ
35		23	24	25	26	27	28	29	
36		1	2	3	4	5	6	7	Bái lù
37	MONTH 8 Jǐ-Yǒu	8	9	10	11	12	13*	14	
38		15[g]	16	17	18	19	20	21	Qiū fēn
39		22	23	24	25	26	27	28	
40		29	30	1	2	3	4	5	Hán lù
41	MONTH 9 Jǐ-Yǒu	6	7	8	9[h]	10	11	12	
42		13	14	15	16	17	18	19	Shuāng jiàng
43		20	21	22	23	24	25	26	
44		27	28	29	1	2	3	4	
45	MONTH 10 Jǐ-Yǒu	5	6	7	8	9	10	11	Lì dōng
46		12	13	14*	15	16	17	18	
47		19	20	21	22	23	24	25	Xiǎo xuě
48		26	27	28	29	30	1	2	
49	MONTH 11 Jǐ-Yǒu	3	4	5	6	7	8	9	Dà xuě
50		10	11	12	13	14	15	16	
51		17	18	19	20[i]	21	22	23	Dōng zhì
52		24	25	26	27	28	29	30	

Coptic 1805/1806, Ethiopic 2081/2082

ISO Week	Coptic Month	Sun	Mon	Tue	Wed	Thu	Fri	Sat	Ethiopic Month
53	KOIAK 1805	17	18	19	20	21	22	23	TĀKHŚĀŚ 2081
1		24	25	26	27	28	29[c]	30	
2		1	2	3	4	5	6[d]	7	
3	TŌBE 1805	8	9	10	11[e]	12	13	14	ṬER 2081
4		15	16	17	18	19	20	21	
5		22	23	24	25	26	27	28	
6		29	30	1	2	3	4	5	
7	MESHIR 1805	6	7	8	9	10	11	12	YAKĀTIT 2081
8		13	14	15	16	17	18	19	
9		20	21	22	23	24	25	26	
10		27	28	29	30	1	2	3	
11	PAREMOTEP 1805	4	5	6	7	8	9	10	MAGĀBIT 2081
12		11	12	13	14	15	16	17	
13		18	19	20	21	22	23	24	
14		25	26	27	28	29	30	1	
15	PARMOUTE 1805	2	3	4	5	6	7	8	MIYĀZYĀ 2081
16		9	10	11	12	13	14	15	
17		16	17	18	19	20	21	22	
18		23[f]	24	25	26	27	28	29[g]	
19		30	1	2	3	4	5	6	
20	PASHONS 1805	7	8	9	10	11	12	13	GENBOT 2081
21		14	15	16	17	18	19	20	
22		21	22	23	24	25	26	27	
23		28	29	30	1	2	3	4	
24	PAŌNE 1805	5	6	7	8	9	10	11	SANĒ 2081
25		12	13	14	15	16	17	18	
26		19	20	21	22	23	24	25	
27		26	27	28	29	30	1	2	
28	EPĒP 1805	3	4	5	6	7	8	9	ḤAMLĒ 2081
29		10	11	12	13	14	15	16	
30		17	18	19	20	21	22	23	
31		24	25	26	27	28	29	30	
32	MESORĒ 1805	1	2	3	4	5	6	7	NAHASĒ 2081
33		8	9	10	11	12	13[h]	14	
34		15	16	17	18	19	20	21	
35		22	23	24	25	26	27	28	
36	EPAG. 1805	29	30	1	2	3	4	5	PĀG. 2081
37	THOOUT 1806	1[a]	2	3	4	5	6	7	MASKARAM 2082
38		8	9	10	11	12	13	14	
39		15	16	17[b]	18	19	20	21	
40		22	23	24	25	26	27	28	
41	PAOPE 1806	29	30	1	2	3	4	5	TEQEMT 2082
42		6	7	8	9	10	11	12	
43		13	14	15	16	17	18	19	
44		20	21	22	23	24	25	26	
45	ATHŌR 1806	27	28	29	30	1	2	3	HEDĀR 2082
46		4	5	6	7	8	9	10	
47		11	12	13	14	15	16	17	
48		18	19	20	21	22	23	24	
49	KOIAK 1806	25	26	27	28	29	30	1	TĀKHŚĀŚ 2082
50		2	3	4	5	6	7	8	
51		9	10	11	12	13	14	15	
52		16	17	18	19	20	21	22	

[a]New Year
[b]Spring (21:05)
[c]Summer (13:41)
[d]Autumn (6:05)
[e]Winter (3:51)
● New moon
◐ First quarter moon
○ Full moon
◑ Last quarter moon

‡Leap year
[a]New Year
[b]Yom Kippur
[c]Sukkot
[d]Winter starts
[e]Ḥanukkah
[f]Purim
[g]Passover
[h]Shavuot
[i]Fast of Av

‡Leap year
[a]New Year (4787, Fowl)
[b]Lantern Festival
[c]Qīngmíng
[d]Dragon Festival
[e]Qīqiǎo
[f]Hungry Ghosts
[g]Mid-Autumn Festival
[h]Double-Ninth Festival
[i]Dōngzhì
*Start of 60-name cycle

[a]New Year
[b]Building of the Cross
[c]Christmas
[d]Jesus's Circumcision
[e]Epiphany
[f]Easter
[g]Mary's Announcement
[h]Jesus's Transfiguration

PERSIAN (ASTRONOMICAL) 1467/1468

Month	Sun	Mon	Tue	Wed	Thu	Fri	Sat
DEY 1467	6	7	8	9	10	11	12
	13	14	15	16	17	18	19
	20	21	22	23	24	25	26
BAHMAN 1467	27	28	29	30	1	2	3
	4	5	6	7	8	9	10
	11	12	13	14	15	16	17
	18	19	20	21	22	23	24
ESFAND 1467	25	26	27	28	29	30	1
	2	3	4	5	6	7	8
	9	10	11	12	13	14	15
	16	17	18	19	20	21	22
	23	24	25	26	27	28	29
FARVARDĪN 1468	1[a]	2	3	4	5	6	7
	8	9	10	11	12	13[b]	14
	15	16	17	18	19	20	21
	22	23	24	25	26	27	28
ORDĪBEHEŠT 1468	29	30	31	1	2	3	4
	5	6	7	8	9	10	11
	12	13	14	15	16	17	18
	19	20	21	22	23	24	25
XORDĀD 1468	26	27	28	29	30	31	1
	2	3	4	5	6	7	8
	9	10	11	12	13	14	15
	16	17	18	19	20	21	22
	23	24	25	26	27	28	29
TĪR 1468	30	31	1	2	3	4	5
	6	7	8	9	10	11	12
	13	14	15	16	17	18	19
	20	21	22	23	24	25	26
MORDĀD 1468	27	28	29	30	31	1	2
	3	4	5	6	7	8	9
	10	11	12	13	14	15	16
	17	18	19	20	21	22	23
	24	25	26	27	28	29	30
SHAHRĪVAR 1468	31	1	2	3	4	5	6
	7	8	9	10	11	12	13
	14	15	16	17	18	19	20
	21	22	23	24	25	26	27
MEHR 1468	28	29	30	31	1	2	3
	4	5	6	7	8	9	10
	11	12	13	14	15	16	17
	18	19	20	21	22	23	24
ĀBĀN 1468	25	26	27	28	29	30	1
	2	3	4	5	6	7	8
	9	10	11	12	13	14	15
	16	17	18	19	20	21	22
	23	24	25	26	27	28	29
ĀZAR 1468	30	1	2	3	4	5	6
	7	8	9	10	11	12	13
	14	15	16	17	18	19	20
	21	22	23	24	25	26	27
DEY 1468	28	29	30	1	2	3	4
	5	6	7	8	9	10	11

[a]New Year
[b]Sizdeh Bedar

HINDU LUNAR 2145‡/2146

Month	Sun	Mon	Tue	Wed	Thu	Fri	Sat
MĀRGAŚIRA 2145	13	**14**	16	17	18	19	20
	21	22	23	24	25	26	27
PAUSHA 2145	28	29	30	1	2	3	4
	4	5	6	7	**8**	10	11
	12	13	14	15	16	17	18
	19	20	21	22	23	24	25
MĀGHA 2145	26	27	28	29	30	1	2
	3	4	5	6	7	8	9
	10	11	12	**13**	15	16	17
	18	19	20	21	22	23	24
	25	26	*26*	27	28[h]	29	30
PHĀLGUNA 2145	1	2	3	4	5	6	**7**
	9	10	11	12	13	14	15[i]
	16	17	18	19	20	21	22
	23	24	25	26	27	28	29
CHAITRA 2146	30	1[a]	2	3	4	5	6
	7	8	9[b]	10	**11**	13	14
	15	16	17	18	19	20	*20*
	21	22	23	24	25	26	27
VAIŚĀKHA 2146	28	29	30	1	2	3	**4**
	6	7	8	9	10	11	12
	13	14	15	16	17	18	19
	20	21	22	23	24	25	26
JYAISHṬHA 2146	27	28	29	30	1	2	3
	4	5	6	7	**8**	10	11
	12	13	14	15	16	*16*	17
	18	19	20	21	22	23	24
ĀSHĀḌHA 2146	25	26	27	28	29	**30**	2
	3	4	5	6	7	8	9
	10	11	12	13	14	15	16
	17	18	19	20	21	22	23
	24	25	26	27	28	29	30
ŚRĀVAṆA 2146	1	2	**3**	5	6	7	8
	9	10	11	12	13	*13*	14
	15	16	17	18	19	20	21
	22	23[c]	24	25	**26**	28	29
BHĀDRAPADA 2146	30	1	2	3	4[d]	5	6
	7	8	9	10	11	12	13
	14	15	16	17	18	19	20
	21	22	23	24	25	26	27
ĀŚVINA 2146	28	29	**30**	2	3	4	5
	6	7	8[e]	9[e]	*9*[e]	10[e]	11
	12	13	14	15	16	17	18
	19	20	21	22	**23**	25	26
KĀRTTIKA 2146	27	28	29	30	1[f]	2	3
	4	5	6	7	8	9	10
	11	12	*12*	13	14	15	**16**
	18	19	20	21	22	23	24
MĀRGAŚIRA 2146	25	26	27	28	29	30	1
	2	3	4	5	6	7	8
	9	10	11[g]	12	13	14	15
	16	17	18	19	20	**21**	23
	24	25	26	27	28	29	30

‡Leap year
[a]New Year (Saumya)
[b]Birthday of Rāma
[c]Birthday of Krishna
[d]Ganēśa Chaturthī
[e]Dashara
[f]Diwali
[g]Birthday of Vishnu
[h]Night of Śiva
[i]Holi

HINDU SOLAR 2010/2011

Month	Sun	Mon	Tue	Wed	Thu	Fri	Sat
PAUSHA 2010	11	12	13	14	15	16	17
	18	19	20	21	22	23	24
MĀGHA 2010	25	26	27	28	29	1[b]	2
	3	4	5	6	7	8	9
	10	11	12	13	14	15	16
	17	18	19	20	21	22	23
	24	25	26	27	28	29	30
PHĀLGUNA 2010	1	2	3	4	5	6	7
	8	9	10	11	12	13	14
	15	16	17	18	19	20	21
	22	23	24	25	26	27	28
CHAITRA 2010	29	30	1	2	3	4	5
	6	7	8	9	10	11	12
	13	14	15	16	17	18	19
	20	21	22	23	24	25	26
VAIŚĀKHA 2011	27	28	29	30	1[a]	2	3
	4	5	6	7	8	9	10
	11	12	13	14	15	16	17
	18	19	20	21	22	23	24
	25	26	27	28	29	30	31
JYAISHṬHA 2011	1	2	3	4	5	6	7
	8	9	10	11	12	13	14
	15	16	17	18	19	20	21
	22	23	24	25	26	27	28
ĀSHĀḌHA 2011	29	30	31	1	2	3	4
	5	6	7	8	9	10	11
	12	13	14	15	16	17	18
	19	20	21	22	23	24	25
	26	27	28	29	30	31	32
ŚRĀVAṆA 2011	1	2	3	4	5	6	7
	8	9	10	11	12	13	14
	15	16	17	18	19	20	21
	22	23	24	25	26	27	28
BHĀDRAPADA 2011	29	30	31	1	2	3	4
	5	6	7	8	9	10	11
	12	13	14	15	16	17	18
	19	20	21	22	23	24	25
	26	27	28	29	30	31	32
ĀŚVINA 2011	1	2	3	4	5	6	7
	8	9	10	11	12	13	14
	15	16	17	18	19	20	21
	22	23	24	25	26	27	28
KĀRTTIKA 2011	29	30	1	2	3	4	5
	6	7	8	9	10	11	12
	13	14	15	16	17	18	19
	20	21	22	23	24	25	26
MĀRGAŚIRA 2011	27	28	29	30	1	2	3
	4	5	6	7	8	9	10
	11	12	13	14	15	16	17
	18	19	20	21	22	23	24
PAUSHA 2011	25	26	27	28	29	1	2
	3	4	5	6	7	8	9
	10	11	12	13	14	15	16

[a]New Year (Rudhirodgārin)
[b]Pongal

ISLAMIC (ASTRONOMICAL) 1512‡/1513

Month	Sun	Mon	Tue	Wed	Thu	Fri	Sat
JUMĀDĀ II 1512	13	14	15	16	17	18	19
	20	21	22	23	24	25	26
RAJAB 1512	27	28	29	30	1	2	3
	4	5	6	7	8	9	10
	11	12	13	14	15	16	17
	18	19	20	21	22	23	24
SHA'BĀN 1512	25	26	27[d]	28	29	30	1
	2	3	4	5	6	7	8
	9	10	11	12	13	14	15
	16	17	18	19	20	21	22
	23	24	25	26	27	28	29
RAMAḌĀN 1512	30	1[e]	2	3	4	5	6
	7	8	9	10	11	12	13
	14	15	16	17	18	19	20
	21	22	23	24	25	26	27
SHAWWĀL 1512	28	29	1[f]	2	3	4	5
	6	7	8	9	10	11	12
	13	14	15	16	17	18	19
	20	21	22	23	24	25	26
DHU AL-QA'DA 1512	27	28	29	30	1	2	3
	4	5	6	7	8	9	10
	11	12	13	14	15	16	17
	18	19	20	21	22	23	24
DHU AL-ḤIJJA 1512	25	26	27	28	29	1	2
	3	4	5	6	7	8	9
	10[g]	11	12	13	14	15	16
	17	18	19	20	21	22	23
	24	25	26	27	28	29	30[A]
MUḤARRAM 1513	1[a]	2	3	4	5	6	7
	8	9	10[b]	11	12	13	14
	15	16	17	18	19	20	21
	22	23	24	25	26	27	28
ṢAFAR 1513	29	1	2	3	4	5	6
	7	8	9	10	11	12	13
	14	15	16	17	18	19	20
	21	22	23	24	25	26	27
RABĪ' I 1513	28	29	1	2	3	4	5
	6	7	8	9	10	11	12[c]
	13	14	15	16	17	18	19
	20	21	22	23	24	25	26
RABĪ' II 1513	27	28	29	1	2	3	4
	5	6	7	8	9	10	11
	12	13	14	15	16	17	18
	19	20	21	22	23	24	25
JUMĀDĀ I 1513	26	27	28	29	30	1	2
	3	4	5	6	7	8	9
	10	11	12	13	14	15	16
	17	18	19	20	21	22	23
JUMĀDĀ II 1513	24	25	26	27	28	29	1
	2	3	4	5	6	7	8
	9	10	11	12	13	14	15
	16	17	18	19	20	21	22
	23	24	25	26	27	28	29

‡Leap year
[a]New Year
[A]New Year (Arithmetic)
[b]'Ashūrā'
[c]Prophet's Birthday
[d]Ascent of the Prophet
[e]Start of Ramaḍān
[f]'Id al-Fiṭr
[g]'Id al-'Aḍḥā

GREGORIAN 2089

Julian (Sun)	Month	Sun	Mon	Tue	Wed	Thu	Fri	Sat
Dec 13		26	27	28	29	30	31	1
	JANUARY 2089	2	3	4	5	6	7[a]	8
Dec 27		9	10	11	12	13	14[b]	15
		16	17	18	19	20	21	22
Jan 10		23	24	25	26	27	28	29
	FEBRUARY 2089	30	31	1	2	3	4	5
Jan 24		6	7	8	9	10	11	12
		13	14	15	16[c]	17	18	19
Feb 7		20	21	22	23	24	25	26
	MARCH 2089	27	28	1	2	3	4	5
Feb 21		6	7	8	9	10	11	12
		13	14	15	16	17	18	19
Mar 7		20[d]	21	22	23	24	25	26
	APRIL 2089	27	28	29	30	31	1	2
Mar 21		3[e]	4	5	6	7	8	9
		10	11	12	13	14	15	16
Apr 4		17	18	19	20	21	22	23
		24	25	26	27	28	29	30
Apr 18	MAY 2089	1[f]	2	3	4	5	6	7
		8	9	10	11	12	13	14
May 2		15	16	17	18	19	20	21
		22	23	24	25	26	27	28
May 16	JUNE 2089	29	30	31	1	2	3	4
		5	6	7	8	9	10	11
May 30		12	13	14	15	16	17	18
		19	20	21	22	23	24	25
Jun 13	JULY 2089	26	27	28	29	30	1	2
		3	4	5	6	7	8	9
Jun 27		10	11	12	13	14	15	16
		17	18	19	20	21	22	23
Jul 11		24	25	26	27	28	29	30
	AUGUST 2089	31	1	2	3	4	5	6
Jul 25		7	8	9	10	11	12	13
		14	15	16	17	18	19	20
Aug 8		21	22	23	24	25	26	27
	SEPTEMBER 2089	28	29	30	31	1	2	3
Aug 22		4	5	6	7	8	9	10
		11	12	13	14	15	16	17
Sep 5		18	19	20	21	22	23	24
	OCTOBER 2089	25	26	27	28	29	30	1
Sep 19		2	3	4	5	6	7	8
		9	10	11	12	13	14	15
Oct 3		16	17	18	19	20	21	22
		23	24	25	26	27	28	29
Oct 17	NOVEMBER 2089	30	31	1	2	3	4	5
		6	7	8	9	10	11	12
Oct 31		13	14	15	16	17	18	19
		20	21	22	23	24	25	26
Nov 14	DECEMBER 2089	27[g]	28	29	30	1	2	3
		4	5	6	7	8	9	10
Nov 28		11	12	13	14	15	16	17
		18	19	20	21	22	23	24
Dec 12		25[h]	26	27	28	29	30	31

[a]Orthodox Christmas
[b]Julian New Year
[c]Ash Wednesday
[d]Feast of Orthodoxy
[e]Easter
[f]Orthodox Easter
[g]Advent
[h]Christmas

2090

Gregorian 2090 (month)	Gregorian Sun Mon Tue Wed Thu Fri Sat	Lunar Phases	ISO Week (Mon)	Julian Day (Sun noon)	Hebrew 5850‡/5851 (month)	Hebrew Sun Mon Tue Wed Thu Fri Sat	Molad	Chinese Jǐ-Yǒu/Gēng-Xū‡ (month)	Chinese Sun Mon Tue Wed Thu Fri Sat	Solar Term	Coptic 1806/1807‡ (month)	Coptic/Ethiopic Sun Mon Tue Wed Thu Fri Sat	Ethiopic 2082/2083‡ (month)
January 2090	1[a] 2 3 4 5 6 7		1	2484418		29 1 2 3 4 5 6	Sun 7h54m10p	Month 12 Jǐ-Yǒu	1 2 3 4 5 6 7	Xiǎo hán	Koiak 1806	23 24 25 26 27 28 29[c]	Tākhśāś 2082
	8 ◐ 10 11 12 13 14	1:20	2	2484425	Shevat 5850	7 8 9 10 11 12 13			8 9 10 11 12 13 14*		Tōbe 1806	30 1 2 3 4 5 6[d]	Ter 2082
	15 ○ 17 18 19 20 21	3:01	3	2484432		14 15 16 17 18 19 20			15 16 17 18 19 20 21	Dà hán		7 8 9 10 11[e] 12 13	
	◑ 23 24 25 26 27 28	18:37	4	2484439		21 22 23 24 25 26 27			22 23 24 25 26 27 28			14 15 16 17 18 19 20	
February 2090	29 ● 31 1 2 3 4	14:33	5	2484446	Adar I 5850	28 29 30 1 2 3 4	Mon 20h38m11p	Month 1 Gēng-Xū	29 1[a] 2 3 4 5 6	Lì chūn		21 22 23 24 25 26 27	
	5 6 ◐ 8 9 10 11	18:51	6	2484453		5 6 7 8 9 10 11			7 8 9 10 11 12 13		Meshir 1806	28 29 30 1 2 3 4	Yakātit 2082
	12 13 ○ 15 16 17 18	13:38	7	2484460		12 13 14 15 16 17 18			14 15[b] 16 17 18 19 20	Yǔ shuǐ		5 6 7 8 9 10 11	
	19 20 ◑ 22 23 24 25	7:41	8	2484467		19 20 21 22 23 24 25			21 22 23 24 25 26 27			12 13 14 15 16 17 18	
March 2090	26 27 28 ● 2 3 4	9:45	9	2484474	Adar II 5850	26 27 28 29 30 1 2	Wed 9h22m12p	Month 2 Gēng-Xū	28 29 30 1 2 3 4			19 20 21 22 23 24 25	
	5 6 7 8 ◐ 10 11	8:19	10	2484481		3 4 5 6 7 8 9			5 6 7 8 9 10 11	Jīng zhé	Paremotep 1806	26 27 28 29 30 1 2	Magābit 2082
	12 13 14 ○ 16 17 18	23:41	11	2484488		10 11 12 13 14[f] 15 16			12 13 14 15* 16 17 18			3 4 5 6 7 8 9	
	19 20[b] 21 ◑ 23 24 25	22:54	12	2484495		17 18 19 20 21 22 23			19 20 21 22 23 24 25	Chūn fēn		10 11 12 13 14 15 16	
April 2090	26 27 28 29 30 ● 1	3:47	13	2484502	Nisan 5850	24 25 26 27 28 29 1	Thu 22h6m13p	Month 3 Gēng-Xū	26 27 28 29 30 1 2			17 18 19 20 21 22 23	
	2 3 4 5 6 ◐ 8	17:55	14	2484509		2 3 4 5 6 7 8			3 4 5[c] 6 7 8 9	Qīng míng		24 25 26 27 28 29 30	
	9 10 11 12 13 ○ 15	9:21	15	2484516		9 10 11 12 13 14 15[g]			10 11 12 13 14 15 16		Parmoute 1806	1 2 3 4 5 6 7	Miyāzyā 2082
	16 17 18 19 20 ◑ 22	15:49	16	2484523		16 17 18 19 20 21 22			17 18 19 20 21 22 23	Gǔ yǔ		8 9 10 11 12 13 14	
	23 24 25 26 27 28 ●	19:11	17	2484530		23 24 25 26 27 28 29			24 25 26 27 28 29 30			15[f] 16 17 18 19 20 21	
May 2090	30 1 2 3 4 5 6		18	2484537	Iyar 5850	30 1 2 3 4 5 6	Sat 10h50m14p	Month 4 Gēng-Xū	1 2 3 4 5 6 7	Lì xià		22 23 24 25 26 27 28	
	◐ 8 9 10 11 12 ○	0:37 19:00	19	2484544		7 8 9 10 11 12 13			8 9 10 11 12 13 14		Pashons 1806	29[g] 30 1 2 3 4 5	Genbot 2082
	14 15 16 17 18 19 20		20	2484551		14 15 16 17 18 19 20			15* 16 17 18 19 20 21	Xiǎo mǎn		6 7 8 9 10 11 12	
	◑ 22 23 24 25 26 27	9:42	21	2484558		21 22 23 24 25 26 27			22 23 24 25 26 27 28			13 14 15 16 17 18 19	
June 2090	28 ● 30 31 1 2 3	7:28	22	2484565	Sivan 5850	28 29 1 2 3 4 5	Sun 23h34m15p	Month 5 Gēng-Xū	29 1 2 3 4 5[d] 6			20 21 22 23 24 25 26	
	4 ◐ 6 7 8 9 10	5:44	23	2484572		6[h] 7 8 9 10 11 12			7 8 9 10 11 12 13	Máng zhòng	Paōne 1806	27 28 29 30 1 2 3	Sanē 2082
	11 ○ 13 14 15 16 17	5:17	24	2484579		13 14 15 16 17 18 19			14 15 16 17 18 19 20			4 5 6 7 8 9 10	
	18 19 ◑[c] 21 22 23 24	3:32	25	2484586		20 21 22 23 24 25 26			21 22 23 24 25 26 27	Xià zhì		11 12 13 14 15 16 17	
July 2090	25 26 ● 28 29 30 1	17:10	26	2484593	Tammuz 5850	27 28 29 30 1 2 3	Tue 12h18m16p	Month 6 Gēng-Xū	28 29 30 1 2 3 4			18 19 20 21 22 23 24	
	2 3 ◐ 5 6 7 8	10:36	27	2484600		4 5 6 7 8 9 10			5 6 7 8 9 10 11	Xiǎo shǔ	Epēp 1806	25 26 27 28 29 30 1	Ḥamlē 2082
	9 10 ○ 12 13 14 15	17:01	28	2484607		11 12 13 14 15 16 17			12 13 14 15 16* 17 18			2 3 4 5 6 7 8	
	16 17 18 ◑ 20 21 22	20:15	29	2484614		18 19 20 21 22 23 24			19 20 21 22 23 24 25	Dà shǔ		9 10 11 12 13 14 15	
	23 24 25 26 ● 28 29	1:18	30	2484621	Av 5850	25 26 27 28 29 1 2	Thu 1h2m17p	Month 7 Gēng-Xū	26 27 28 29 1 2 3			16 17 18 19 20 21 22	
August 2090	30 31 1 ◐ 3 4 5	16:30	31	2484628		3 4 5 6 7 8 9			4 5 6 7[e] 8 9 10			23 24 25 26 27 28 29	
	6 7 8 9 ○ 11 12	6:50	32	2484635		10[i] 11 12 13 14 15 16			11 12 13 14 15[f] 16 17	Lì qiū	Mesorē 1806	30 1 2 3 4 5 6	Naḥasē 2082
	13 14 15 16 17 ◑ 19	11:04	33	2484642		17 18 19 20 21 22 23			18 19 20 21 22 23 24			7 8 9 10 11 12 13[h]	
	20 21 22 23 24 ● 26	8:58	34	2484649		24 25 26 27 28 29 30			25 26 27 28 29 1 2	Chǔ shǔ		14 15 16 17 18 19 20	
September 2090	27 28 29 30 31 ◐ 2	0:43	35	2484656	Elul 5850	1 2 3 4 5 6 7	Fri 13h47m0p	Month 8 Gēng-Xū	3 4 5 6 7 8 9			21 22 23 24 25 26 27	
	3 4 5 6 7 ○ 9	22:43	36	2484663		8 9 10 11 12 13 14			10 11 12 13 14 15[g] 16	Bái lù	Epag. 1806	28 29 30 1 2 3 4	Pāg. 2082
	10 11 12 13 14 15 ◑	23:47	37	2484670		15 16 17 18 19 20 21			17 18* 19 20 21 22 23		Thoout 1807	5 1[a] 2 3 4 5 6	Maskaram 2083
	17 18 19 20 21 22[d] ●	17:02	38	2484677		22 23 24 25 26 27 28			24 25 26 27 28 29 30	Qiū fēn		7 8 9 10 11 12 13	
	24 25 26 27 28 29 ◐	12:20	39	2484684	Tishri 5851	29 1[a] 2[a] 3 4 5 6	Sun 2h31m1p	Leap Month 8 Gēng-Xū	1 2 3 4 5 6 7			14 15 16 17[b] 18 19 20	
October 2090	1 2 3 4 5 6 7		40	2484691		7 8 9 10[b] 11 12 13			8 9 10 11 12 13 14			21 22 23 24 25 26 27	
	○ 9 10 11 12 13 14	15:53	41	2484698		14 15[c] 16 17 18 19 20			15 16 17 18 19 20 21	Hán lù	Paope 1807	28 29 30 1 2 3 4	Teqemt 2083
	15 ◑ 17 18 19 20 21	10:35	42	2484705		21 22 23 24 25 26 27			22 23 24 25 26 27 28			5 6 7 8 9 10 11	
	22 ● 24 25 26 27 28	2:08	43	2484712	Heshvan 5851	28 29 30 1 2 3 4	Mon 15h15m2p	Month 9 Gēng-Xū	29 1 2 3 4 5 6	Shuāng jiàng		12 13 14 15 16 17 18	
November 2090	29 ◐ 31 1 2 3 4	4:03	44	2484719		5 6 7 8 9 10 11			7 8 9[h] 10 11 12 13			19 20 21 22 23 24 25	
	5 6 ○ 8 9 10 11	9:04	45	2484726		12 13 14 15 16 17 18			14 15 16 17 18 19* 20	Lì dōng	Athōr 1807	26 27 28 29 30 1 2	Ḫedār 2083
	12 13 ◑ 15 16 17 18	19:57	46	2484733		19 20 21 22 23 24 25			21 22 23 24 25 26 27			3 4 5 6 7 8 9	
	19 20 ● 22 23 24 25	12:47	47	2484740	Kislev 5851	26 27 28 29 1 2 3	Wed 3h59m3p	Month 10 Gēng-Xū	28 29 1 2 3 4 5	Xiǎo xuě		10 11 12 13 14 15 16	
December 2090	26 27 ◐ 29 30 1 2	23:39	48	2484747		4 5 6 7 8 9 10			6 7 8 9 10 11 12			17 18 19 20 21 22 23	
	3 4 5 6 ○ 8 9	1:13	49	2484754		11 12 13[d] 14 15 16 17			13 14 15 16 17 18 19	Dà xuě		24 25 26 27 28 29 30	
	10 11 12 13 ◑ 15 16	4:24	50	2484761		18 19 20 21 22 23 24			20 21 22 23 24 25 26		Koiak 1807	1 2 3 4 5 6 7	Tākhśāś 2083
	17 18 19 20 ●[e] 22 23	1:28	51	2484768	Tevet 5851	25[e] 26[e] 27[e] 28[e] 29[e] 1[e] 2[e]	Thu 16h43m4p	Month 11 Gēng-Xū	27 28 29 30 1[i] 2 3	Dōng zhì		8 9 10 11 12 13 14	
	24 25 26 27 ◐ 29 30	21:35	52	2484775		3[e] 4 5 6 7 8 9			4 5 6 7 8 9 10			15 16 17 18 19 20 21	
	31 1 2 3 4 ○ 6	15:49	1	2484782		10 11 12 13 14 15 16			11 12 13 14 15 16 17	Xiǎo hán		22 23 24 25 26 27 28	

[a]New Year
[b]Spring (3:00)
[c]Summer (19:34)
[d]Autumn (11:58)
[e]Winter (9:42)
● New moon
◐ First quarter moon
○ Full moon
◑ Last quarter moon

‡Leap year
[a]New Year
[b]Yom Kippur
[c]Sukkot
[d]Winter starts
[e]Ḥanukkah
[f]Purim
[g]Passover
[h]Shavuot
[i]Fast of Av

‡Leap year
[a]New Year (4788, Dog)
[b]Lantern Festival
[c]Qīngmíng
[d]Dragon Festival
[e]Qīqiǎo
[f]Hungry Ghosts
[g]Mid-Autumn Festival
[h]Double-Ninth Festival
[i]Dōngzhì
*Start of 60-name cycle

‡Leap year
[a]New Year
[b]Building of the Cross
[c]Christmas
[d]Jesus's Circumcision
[e]Epiphany
[f]Easter
[g]Mary's Announcement
[h]Jesus's Transfiguration

PERSIAN (ASTRONOMICAL) 1468/1469	Sun	Mon	Tue	Wed	Thu	Fri	Sat
	12	13	14	15	16	17	18
DEY 1468	19	20	21	22	23	24	25
	26	27	28	29	30	1	2
	3	4	5	6	7	8	9
BAHMAN 1468	10	11	12	13	14	15	16
	17	18	19	20	21	22	23
	24	25	26	27	28	29	30
	1	2	3	4	5	6	7
ESFAND 1468	8	9	10	11	12	13	14
	15	16	17	18	19	20	21
	22	23	24	25	26	27	28
	29	1[a]	2	3	4	5	6
	7	8	9	10	11	12	13[b]
FARVARDĪN 1469	14	15	16	17	18	19	20
	21	22	23	24	25	26	27
	28	29	30	31	1	2	3
	4	5	6	7	8	9	10
ORDĪBEHEŠT 1469	11	12	13	14	15	16	17
	18	19	20	21	22	23	24
	25	26	27	28	29	30	31
	1	2	3	4	5	6	7
XORDĀD 1469	8	9	10	11	12	13	14
	15	16	17	18	19	20	21
	22	23	24	25	26	27	28
	29	30	31	1	2	3	4
	5	6	7	8	9	10	11
TĪR 1469	12	13	14	15	16	17	18
	19	20	21	22	23	24	25
	26	27	28	29	30	31	1
	2	3	4	5	6	7	8
MORDĀD 1469	9	10	11	12	13	14	15
	16	17	18	19	20	21	22
	23	24	25	26	27	28	29
	30	31	1	2	3	4	5
SHAHRĪVAR 1469	6	7	8	9	10	11	12
	13	14	15	16	17	18	19
	20	21	22	23	24	25	26
	27	28	29	30	31	1	2
	3	4	5	6	7	8	9
MEHR 1469	10	11	12	13	14	15	16
	17	18	19	20	21	22	23
	24	25	26	27	28	29	30
	1	2	3	4	5	6	7
ĀBĀN 1469	8	9	10	11	12	13	14
	15	16	17	18	19	20	21
	22	23	24	25	26	27	28
	29	30	1	2	3	4	5
ĀZAR 1469	6	7	8	9	10	11	12
	13	14	15	16	17	18	19
	20	21	22	23	24	25	26
	27	28	29	30	1	2	3
DEY 1469	4	5	6	7	8	9	10
	11	12	13	14	15	16	17

HINDU LUNAR 2146/2147	Sun	Mon	Tue	Wed	Thu	Fri	Sat
	1	2	3	4	4	5	6
PAUSHA 2146	7	8	9	10	11	12	13
	14	15	16	18	19	20	21
	22	23	24	25	26	27	28
	29	30	1	2	3	4	5
MĀGHA 2146	6	7	8	9	10	11	12
	13	14	15	16	17	18	19
	20	21	23	24	25	26	26
	27	28[h]	29	30	1	2	3
PHĀLGUNA 2146	4	5	6	7	8	9	10
	11	12	13	14[i]	16	17	18
	19	20	21	22	23	24	25
	26	27	28	29	29	30	1[a]
CHAITRA 2147	2	3	4	5	6	7	8[b]
	10	11	12	13	14	15	16
	17	18	19	20	21	22	23
	24	25	26	27	28	29	30
	1	2	3	4	5	6	7
VAIŚĀKHA 2147	8	9	10	11	12	14	15
	16	17	18	19	20	21	22
	23	24	24	25	26	27	28
	29	30	1	2	3	4	5
JYAISHṬHA 2147	7	8	9	10	11	12	13
	14	15	16	17	18	19	20
	21	22	23	24	25	26	27
	28	29	30	1	2	3	4
ĀSHĀḌHA 2147	5	6	7	9	10	11	12
	13	14	15	16	17	18	19
	20	21	21	22	23	24	25
	26	27	28	29	30	2	3
ŚRĀVAṆA 2147	4	5	6	7	8	9	10
	11	12	13	14	15	16	17
	18	19	20	21	22	23[c]	24
	25	26	27	28	29	30	1
	2	3[d]	5	6	7	8	9
BHĀDRAPADA 2147	10	11	12	13	14	15	16
	17	17	18	19	20	21	22
	23	24	25	26	28	29	30
	1	2	3	4	5	6	7
ĀŚVINA 2147	8[e]	9[e]	10[e]	11	12	13	14
	15	16	17	18	19	20	21
	22	23	24	25	26	27	28
	29	30[f]	2	3	4	5	6
KĀRTTIKA 2147	7	8	9	10	11	12	12
	13	14	15	16	17	18	19
	20	21	22	23	24	26	27
	28	29	30	1	2	3	4
MĀRGAŚĪRA 2147	5	6	7	8	9	10	11[g]
	12	13	14	15	16	17	18
	19	20	21	22	23	24	25
	26	27	28	29	1	2	3
PAUSHA 2147	4	4	5	6	7	8	9
	10	11	12	13	14	15	16

HINDU SOLAR 2011/2012‡	Sun	Mon	Tue	Wed	Thu	Fri	Sat
PAUSHA 2011	17	18	19	20	21	22	23
	24	25	26	27	28	29	30
	1[b]	2	3	4	5	6	7
MĀGHA 2011	8	9	10	11	12	13	14
	15	16	17	18	19	20	21
	22	23	24	25	26	27	28
	29	1	2	3	4	5	6
PHĀLGUNA 2011	7	8	9	10	11	12	13
	14	15	16	17	18	19	20
	21	22	23	24	25	26	27
	28	29	30	1	2	3	4
CHAITRA 2011	5	6	7	8	9	10	11
	12	13	14	15	16	17	18
	19	20	21	22	23	24	25
	26	27	28	29	30	1[a]	2
	3	4	5	6	7	8	9
VAIŚĀKHA 2012	10	11	12	13	14	15	16
	17	18	19	20	21	22	23
	24	25	26	27	28	29	30
	31	1	2	3	4	5	6
JYAISHṬHA 2012	7	8	9	10	11	12	13
	14	15	16	17	18	19	20
	21	22	23	24	25	26	27
	28	29	30	31	32	1	2
	3	4	5	6	7	8	9
ĀSHĀḌHA 2012	10	11	12	13	14	15	16
	17	18	19	20	21	22	23
	24	25	26	27	28	29	30
	31	1	2	3	4	5	6
ŚRĀVAṆA 2012	7	8	9	10	11	12	13
	14	15	16	17	18	19	20
	21	22	23	24	25	26	27
	28	29	30	31	32	1	2
	3	4	5	6	7	8	9
BHĀDRAPADA 2012	10	11	12	13	14	15	16
	17	18	19	20	21	22	23
	24	25	26	27	28	29	30
	31	1	2	3	4	5	6
ĀŚVINA 2012	7	8	9	10	11	12	13
	14	15	16	17	18	19	20
	21	22	23	24	25	26	27
	28	29	30	1	2	3	4
KĀRTTIKA 2012	5	6	7	8	9	10	11
	12	13	14	15	16	17	18
	19	20	21	22	23	24	25
	26	27	28	29	30	1	2
MĀRGAŚĪRA 2012	3	4	5	6	7	8	9
	10	11	12	13	14	15	16
	17	18	19	20	21	22	23
	24	25	26	27	28	29	30
	1	2	3	4	5	6	7
PAUSHA 2012	8	9	10	11	12	13	14
	15	16	17	18	19	20	21

ISLAMIC (ASTRONOMICAL) 1513/1514‡	Sun	Mon	Tue	Wed	Thu	Fri	Sat
	30	1	2	3	4	5	6
RAJAB 1513	7	8	9	10	11	12	13
	14	15	16	17	18	19	20
	21	22	23	24	25	26	27[d]
	28	29	30	1	2	3	4
SHA'BĀN 1513	5	6	7	8	9	10	11
	12	13	14	15	16	17	18
	19	20	21	22	23	24	25
	26	27	28	29	30	1[e]	2
RAMAḌĀN 1513	3	4	5	6	7	8	9
	10	11	12	13	14	15	16
	17	18	19	20	21	22	23
	24	25	26	27	28	29	1[f]
SHAWWĀL 1513	2	3	4	5	6	7	8
	9	10	11	12	13	14	15
	16	17	18	19	20	21	22
	23	24	25	26	27	28	29
	30	1	2	3	4	5	6
DHU AL-QA'DA 1513	7	8	9	10	11	12	13
	14	15	16	17	18	19	20
	21	22	23	24	25	26	27
	28	29	30	1	2	3	4
DHU AL-ḤIJJA 1513	5	6	7	8	9	10[g]	11
	12	13	14	15	16	17	18
	19	20	21	22	23	24	25
	26	27	28	29	1[a]	2	3
MUḤARRAM 1514	4	5	6	7	8	9	10[b]
	11	12	13	14	15	16	17
	18	19	20	21	22	23	24
	25	26	27	28	29	30	1
ṢAFAR 1514	2	3	4	5	6	7	8
	9	10	11	12	13	14	15
	16	17	18	19	20	21	22
	23	24	25	26	27	28	29
	1	2	3	4	5	6	7
RABĪ' I 1514	8	9	10	11	12[c]	13	14
	15	16	17	18	19	20	21
	22	23	24	25	26	27	28
	29	1	2	3	4	5	6
RABĪ' II 1514	7	8	9	10	11	12	13
	14	15	16	17	18	19	20
	21	22	23	24	25	26	27
	28	29	1	2	3	4	5
JUMĀDĀ I 1514	6	7	8	9	10	11	12
	13	14	15	16	17	18	19
	20	21	22	23	24	25	26
	27	28	29	30	1	2	3
JUMĀDĀ II 1514	4	5	6	7	8	9	10
	11	12	13	14	15	16	17
	18	19	20	21	22	23	24
	25	26	27	28	29	1	2
RAJAB 1514	3	4	5	6	7	8	9
	10	11	12	13	14	15	16

Julian (Sun)	Sun	Mon	Tue	Wed	Thu	Fri	Sat	GREGORIAN 2090
Dec 19	1	2	3	4	5	6	7[a]	
	8	9	10	11	12	13	14[b]	JANUARY 2090
Jan 2	15	16	17	18	19	20	21	
	22	23	24	25	26	27	28	
Jan 16	29	30	31	1	2	3	4	
	5	6	7	8	9	10	11	
Jan 30	12	13	14	15	16	17	18	FEBRUARY 2090
	19	20	21	22	23	24	25	
Feb 13	26	27	28	1[c]	2	3	4	
	5	6	7	8	9	10	11	
Feb 27	12[d]	13	14	15	16	17	18	MARCH 2090
	19	20	21	22	23	24	25	
Mar 13	26	27	28	29	30	31	1	
	2	3	4	5	6	7	8	
Mar 27	9	10	11	12	13	14	15	APRIL 2090
	16[e]	17	18	19	20	21	22	
Apr 10	23[f]	24	25	26	27	28	29	
	30	1	2	3	4	5	6	
Apr 24	7	8	9	10	11	12	13	MAY 2090
	14	15	16	17	18	19	20	
May 8	21	22	23	24	25	26	27	
	28	29	30	31	1	2	3	
May 22	4	5	6	7	8	9	10	
	11	12	13	14	15	16	17	JUNE 2090
Jun 5	18	19	20	21	22	23	24	
	25	26	27	28	29	30	1	
Jun 19	2	3	4	5	6	7	8	
	9	10	11	12	13	14	15	JULY 2090
Jul 3	16	17	18	19	20	21	22	
	23	24	25	26	27	28	29	
Jul 17	30	31	1	2	3	4	5	
	6	7	8	9	10	11	12	
Jul 31	13	14	15	16	17	18	19	AUGUST 2090
	20	21	22	23	24	25	26	
Aug 14	27	28	29	30	31	1	2	
	3	4	5	6	7	8	9	
Aug 28	10	11	12	13	14	15	16	SEPTEMBER 2090
	17	18	19	20	21	22	23	
Sep 11	24	25	26	27	28	29	30	
	1	2	3	4	5	6	7	
Sep 25	8	9	10	11	12	13	14	OCTOBER 2090
	15	16	17	18	19	20	21	
Oct 9	22	23	24	25	26	27	28	
	29	30	31	1	2	3	4	
Oct 23	5	6	7	8	9	10	11	
	12	13	14	15	16	17	18	NOVEMBER 2090
Nov 6	19	20	21	22	23	24	25	
	26	27	28	29	30	1	2	
Nov 20	3[g]	4	5	6	7	8	9	
	10	11	12	13	14	15	16	DECEMBER 2090
Dec 4	17	18	19	20	21	22	23	
	24	25[h]	26	27	28	29	30	
Dec 18	31	1	2	3	4	5	6	

Persian: [a]New Year; [b]Sizdeh Bedar

Hindu lunar: [a]New Year (Sādhāraṇa); [b]Birthday of Rāma; [c]Birthday of Krishna; [d]Ganēśa Chaturthī; [e]Dashara; [f]Diwali; [g]Birthday of Vishnu; [h]Night of Śiva; [i]Holi

Hindu solar: ‡Leap year; [a]New Year (Raktāksha); [b]Pongal

Islamic: ‡Leap year; [a]New Year; [b]'Ashūrā'; [c]Prophet's Birthday; [d]Ascent of the Prophet; [e]Start of Ramaḍān; [f]'Īd al-Fiṭr; [g]'Īd al-'Aḍḥā

Gregorian: [a]Orthodox Christmas; [b]Julian New Year; [c]Ash Wednesday; [d]Feast of Orthodoxy; [e]Easter; [f]Orthodox Easter; [g]Advent; [h]Christmas

2091

Gregorian 2091	Sun Mon Tue Wed Thu Fri Sat	Lunar Phases	ISO WEEK (Mon)	JULIAN DAY (Sun noon)	Hebrew 5851/5852‡	Sun Mon Tue Wed Thu Fri Sat	Molad	Chinese Gēng-Xū‡/Xīn-Hài	Sun Mon Tue Wed Thu Fri Sat	Solar Term	Coptic 1807‡/1808	Sun Mon Tue Wed Thu Fri Sat	Ethiopic 2083‡/2084
JANUARY 2091	31 1[a] 2 3 4 ○ 6	15:49	1	2484782	TEVETH 5851	10 11 12 13 14 15 16		MONTH 11 Gēng-Xū	11 12 13 14 15 16 17	Xiǎo hán	KOIAK 1807	22 23 24 25 26 27 28	TĀKHŚĀŚ 2083
	7 8 9 10 11 ◑ 13	12:33	2	2484789		17 18 19 20 21 22 23			18 19 20* 21 22 23 24		TŌBE 1807	29[c] 30 1 2 3 4 5	ṬER 2083
	14 15 16 17 18 ● 20	16:30	3	2484796	SHEVAT 5851	24 25 26 27 28 29 1	Sat 5h27m5p	MONTH 12 Gēng-Xū	25 26 27 28 29 30 1	Dà hán		6[d] 7 8 9 10 11[e] 12	
	21 22 23 24 25 26 ◐	19:22	4	2484803		2 3 4 5 6 7 8			2 3 4 5 6 7 8			13 14 15 16 17 18 19	
FEBRUARY 2091	28 29 30 31 1 2 3		5	2484810		9 10 11 12 13 14 15			9 10 11 12 13 14 15	Lì chūn		20 21 22 23 24 25 26	
	○ 5 6 7 8 9 ◑	4:45 21:10	6	2484817		16 17 18 19 20 21 22			16 17 18 19 20 21 22		MESHIR 1807	27 28 29 30 1 2 3	YAKĀTIT 2083
	11 12 13 14 15 16 17		7	2484824		23 24 25 26 27 28 29			23 24 25 26 27 28 29			4 5 6 7 8 9 10	
	● 19 20 21 22 23 24	9:37	8	2484831	ADAR 5851	30 1 2 3 4 5 6	Sun 18h11m8p	MONTH 1 Xīn-Hài	1[a] 2 3 4 5 6 7	Yǔ shuǐ		11 12 13 14 15 16 17	
MARCH 2091	25 ◐ 27 28 1 2 3	14:46	9	2484838		7 8 9 10 11 12 13			8 9 10 11 12 13 14			18 19 20 21 22 23 24	
	4 ○ 6 7 8 9 10	15:57	10	2484845		14[f] 15 16 17 18 19 20			15[b] 16 17 18 19 20 21*	Jīng zhé	PAREMOTEP 1807	25 26 27 28 29 30 1	MAGĀBIT 2083
	11 ◑ 13 14 15 16 17	7:01	11	2484852		21 22 23 24 25 26 27			22 23 24 25 26 27 28			2 3 4 5 6 7 8	
	18 19 ●[b] 21 22 23 24	3:45	12	2484859	NISAN 5851	28 29 1 2 3 4 5	Tue 6h55m7p	MONTH 2 Xīn-Hài	29 30 1 2 3 4 5	Chūn fēn		9 10 11 12 13 14 15	
APRIL 2091	25 26 27 ◐ 29 30 31	6:30	13	2484866		6 7 8 9 10 11 12			6 7 8 9 10 11 12			16 17 18 19 20 21 22	
	1 2 3 ○ 5 6 7	1:30	14	2484873		13 14 15[g] 16 17 18 19			13 14 15 16[c] 17 18 19	Qīng míng		23 24 25 26 27 28 29	
	8 9 ◑ 11 12 13 14	18:44	15	2484880		20 21 22 23 24 25 26			20 21 22 23 24 25 26		PARMOUTE 1807	30[f] 1 2 3 4 5 6	MIYĀZYĀ 2083
	15 16 17 ● 19 20 21	21:19	16	2484887	IYYAR 5851	27 28 29 30 1 2 3	Wed 19h39m8p	MONTH 3 Xīn-Hài	27 28 29 30 1 2 3	Gǔ yǔ		7 8 9 10 11 12 13	
	22 23 24 25 ◐ 27 28	18:19	17	2484894		4 5 6 7 8 9 10			4 5 6 7 8 9 10			14 15 16 17 18 19 20	
MAY 2091	29 30 1 2 ○ 4 5	9:44	18	2484901		11 12 13 14 15 16 17			11 12 13 14 15 16 17	Lì xià		21 22 23 24 25 26 27	
	6 7 8 9 ◑ 11 12	8:35	19	2484908		18 19 20 21 22 23 24			18 19 20 21* 22 23 24		PASHONS 1807	28 29[g] 30 1 2 3 4	GENBOT 2083
	13 14 15 16 17 ● 19	13:06	20	2484915	SIVAN 5851	25 26 27 28 29 1 2	Fri 8h23m9p	MONTH 4 Xīn-Hài	25 26 27 28 29 1 2			5 6 7 8 9 10 11	
	20 21 22 23 24 25 ◐	2:41	21	2484922		3 4 5 6[h] 7 8 9			3 4 5 6 7 8 9	Xiǎo mǎn		12 13 14 15 16 17 18	
JUNE 2091	27 28 29 30 31 ○ 2	17:30	22	2484929		10 11 12 13 14 15 16			10 11 12 13 14 15 16			19 20 21 22 23 24 25	
	3 4 5 6 7 8 ◑	0:21	23	2484936		17 18 19 20 21 22 23			17 18 19 20 21 22 23	Máng zhòng	PAŌNE 1807	26 27 28 29 30 1 2	SANĒ 2083
	10 11 12 13 14 15 16		24	2484943		24 25 26 27 28 29 30			24 25 26 27 28 29 30			3 4 5 6 7 8 9	
	● 18 19 20 21[c] 22 23	2:40	25	2484950	TAMMUZ 5851	1 2 3 4 5 6 7	Sat 21h7m10p	MONTH 5 Xīn-Hài	1 2 3 4 5[d] 6 7	Xià zhì		10 11 12 13 14 15 16	
	◐ 25 26 27 28 29 30	8:30	26	2484957		8 9 10 11 12 13 14			8 9 10 11 12 13 14			17 18 19 20 21 22 23	
JULY 2091	○ 2 3 4 5 6 7	1:53	27	2484964		15 16 17 18 19 20 21			15 16 17 18 19 20 21	Xiǎo shǔ		24 25 26 27 28 29 30	
	◑ 9 10 11 12 13 14	17:20	28	2484971		22 23 24 25 26 27 28			22* 23 24 25 26 27 28		EPĒP 1807	1 2 3 4 5 6 7	ḤAMLĒ 2083
	15 ● 17 18 19 20 21	14:14	29	2484978	AV 5851	29 1 2 3 4 5 6	Mon 9h51m11p	MONTH 6 Xīn-Hài	29 1 2 3 4 5 6			8 9 10 11 12 13 14	
	22 ◐ 24 25 26 27 28	13:01	30	2484985		7 8 9[i] 10 11 12 13			7 8 9 10 11 12 13	Dà shǔ		15 16 17 18 19 20 21	
AUGUST 2091	29 ○ 31 1 2 3 4	12:00	31	2484992		14 15 16 17 18 19 20			14 15 16 17 18 19 20			22 23 24 25 26 27 28	
	5 6 ◑ 8 9 10 11	10:44	32	2484999		21 22 23 24 25 26 27			21 22 23 24 25 26 27	Lì qiū	MESORĒ 1807	29 30 1 2 3 4 5	NAḤASĒ 2083
	12 13 14 ● 16 17 18	0:21	33	2485006	ELUL 5851	28 29 30 1 2 3 4	Tue 22h35m12p	MONTH 7 Xīn-Hài	28 29 30 1 2 3 4			6 7 8 9 10 11 12	
	19 20 ◐ 22 23 24 25	17:42	34	2485013		5 6 7 8 9 10 11			5 6 7[e] 8 9 10 11	Chǔ shǔ		13[h] 14 15 16 17 18 19	
SEPTEMBER 2091	26 27 28 ○ 30 31 1	0:38	35	2485020		12 13 14 15 16 17 18			12 13 14 15[f] 16 17 18			20 21 22 23 24 25 26	
	2 3 4 5 ◑ 7 8	3:46	36	2485027		19 20 21 22 23 24 25			19 20 21 22 23* 24 25	Bái lù	EPAG. 1807	27 28 29 30 1 2 3	PĀG. 2083
	9 10 11 12 ● 14 15	9:33	37	2485034	TISHRI 5852	26 27 28 29 1[a] 2[a] 3	Thu 11h19m13p	MONTH 8 Xīn-Hài	26 27 28 29 1 2 3		THOOUT 1808	4 5 6 1[a] 2 3 4	MASKARAM 2084
	16 17 18 19 ◐ 21 22[d]	0:09	38	2485041		4 5 6 7 8 9 10[b]			4 5 6 7 8 9 10			5 6 7 8 9 10 11	
	23 24 25 26 ○ 28 29	15:55	39	2485048		11 12 13 14 15[c] 16 17			11 12 13 14 15[g] 16 17	Qiū fēn		12 13 14 15 16 17[b] 18	
OCTOBER 2091	30 1 2 3 4 ◑ 6	19:52	40	2485055		18 19 20 21 22 23 24			18 19 20 21 22 23 24			19 20 21 22 23 24 25	
	7 8 9 10 11 ● 13	18:28	41	2485062	ḤESHVAN 5852	25 26 27 28 29 30 1	Sat 0h3m14p	MONTH 9 Xīn-Hài	25 26 27 28 29 30 1	Hán lù	PAOPE 1808	26 27 28 29 30 1 2	ṬEQEMT 2084
	14 15 16 17 18 ◐ 20	9:49	42	2485069		2 3 4 5 6 7 8			2 3 4 5 6 7 8			3 4 5 6 7 8 9	
	21 22 23 24 25 26 ○	9:17	43	2485076		9 10 11 12 13 14 15			9[h] 10 11 12 13 14 15	Shuāng jiàng		10 11 12 13 14 15 16	
NOVEMBER 2091	28 29 30 31 1 2 3		44	2485083		16 17 18 19 20 21 22			16 17 18 19 20 21 22			17 18 19 20 21 22 23	
	◑ 5 6 7 8 9 10	10:26 3:41	45	2485090		23 24 25 26 27 28 29			23 24* 25 26 27 28 29	Lì dōng		24 25 26 27 28 29 30	
	● 12 13 14 15 16 ◐	23:37	46	2485097	KISLEV 5852	30 1 2 3 4 5 6	Sun 12h47m15p	MONTH 10 Xīn-Hài	1 2 3 4 5 6 7		ATHŌR 1808	1 2 3 4 5 6 7	HEDĀR 2084
	18 19 20 21 22 23 24		47	2485104		7 8 9 10 11 12 13			8 9 10 11 12 13 14	Xiǎo xuě		8 9 10 11 12 13 14	
DECEMBER 2091	25 ○ 27 28 29 30 1	3:42	48	2485111		14 15 16 17 18 19 20			15 16 17 18 19 20 21			15 16 17 18 19 20 21	
	2 ◑ 4 5 6 7 8	22:54	49	2485118		21 22 23 24 25[d,e] 26e 27[e]			22 23 24 25 26 27 28	Dà xuě		22 23 24 25 26 27 28	
	9 ● 11 12 13 14 15	13:53	50	2485125	TEVETH 5852	28e 29e 30e 1e 2e 3 4	Tue 1h31m16p	MONTH 11 Xīn-Hài	29 1 2 3 4 5 6		KOIAK 1808	29 30 1 2 3 4 5	TĀKHŚĀŚ 2084
	16 ◐ 18 19 20 21e 22	17:28	51	2485132		5 6 7 8 9 10 11			7 8 9 10 11 12[i] 13	Dōng zhì		6 7 8 9 10 11 12	
	23 24 ○ 26 27 28 29	21:58	52	2485139		12 13 14 15 16 17 18			14 15 16 17 18 19 20			13 14 15 16 17 18 19	
	30 31 1 ◑ 3 4 5	9:06	1	2485146		19 20 21 22 23 24 25			21 22 23 24 25 26 27	Xiǎo hán		20 21 22 23 24 25 26	

Gregorian:
[a]New Year
[b]Spring (8:40)
[c]Summer (1:17)
[d]Autumn (17:49)
[e]Winter (15:37)
● New moon
◐ First quarter moon
○ Full moon
◑ Last quarter moon

Hebrew:
‡Leap year
[a]New Year
[b]Yom Kippur
[c]Sukkot
[d]Winter starts
[e]Ḥanukkah
[f]Purim
[g]Passover
[h]Shavuot
[i]Fast of Av

Chinese:
‡Leap year
[a]New Year (4789, Pig)
[b]Lantern Festival
[c]Qīngmíng
[d]Dragon Festival
[e]Qīqiǎo
[f]Hungry Ghosts
[g]Mid-Autumn Festival
[h]Double-Ninth Festival
[i]Dōngzhì
*Start of 60-name cycle

Coptic/Ethiopic:
‡Leap year
[a]New Year
[b]Building of the Cross
[c]Christmas
[d]Jesus's Circumcision
[e]Epiphany
[f]Easter
[g]Mary's Announcement
[h]Jesus's Transfiguration

PERSIAN (ASTRONOMICAL) 1469/1470‡

Month	Sun	Mon	Tue	Wed	Thu	Fri	Sat
DEY 1469	11	12	13	14	15	16	17
	18	19	20	21	22	23	24
	25	26	27	28	29	30	1
BAHMAN 1469	2	3	4	5	6	7	8
	9	10	11	12	13	14	15
	16	17	18	19	20	21	22
	23	24	25	26	27	28	29
	30	1	2	3	4	5	6
ESFAND 1469	7	8	9	10	11	12	13
	14	15	16	17	18	19	20
	21	22	23	24	25	26	27
	28	29	1[a]	2*	3	4	5
FARVARDĪN 1470	6	7	8	9	10	11	12
	13[b]	14	15	16	17	18	19
	20	21	22	23	24	25	26
	27	28	29	30	31	1	2
ORDĪBEHEŠT 1470	3	4	5	6	7	8	9
	10	11	12	13	14	15	16
	17	18	19	20	21	22	23
	24	25	26	27	28	29	30
	31	1	2	3	4	5	6
XORDĀD 1470	7	8	9	10	11	12	13
	14	15	16	17	18	19	20
	21	22	23	24	25	26	27
	28	29	30	31	1	2	3
TĪR 1470	4	5	6	7	8	9	10
	11	12	13	14	15	16	17
	18	19	20	21	22	23	24
	25	26	27	28	29	30	31
MORDĀD 1470	1	2	3	4	5	6	7
	8	9	10	11	12	13	14
	15	16	17	18	19	20	21
	22	23	24	25	26	27	28
	29	30	31	1	2	3	4
SHAHRĪVAR 1470	5	6	7	8	9	10	11
	12	13	14	15	16	17	18
	19	20	21	22	23	24	25
	26	27	28	29	30	31	1
MEHR 1470	2	3	4	5	6	7	8
	9	10	11	12	13	14	15
	16	17	18	19	20	21	22
	23	24	25	26	27	28	29
	30	1	2	3	4	5	6
ĀBĀN 1470	7	8	9	10	11	12	13
	14	15	16	17	18	19	20
	21	22	23	24	25	26	27
	28	29	30	1	2	3	4
ĀZAR 1470	5	6	7	8	9	10	11
	12	13	14	15	16	17	18
	19	20	21	22	23	24	25
	26	27	28	29	30	1	2
DEY 1470	3	4	5	6	7	8	9
	10	11	12	13	14	15	16

HINDU LUNAR 2147/2148‡

Month	Sun	Mon	Tue	Wed	Thu	Fri	Sat
PAUSHA 2147	10	11	12	13	14	15	16
	17	18	19	20	21	22	24
	25	26	27	28	29	30	1
MĀGHA 2147	2	3	4	5	6	7	7
	8	9	10	11	12	13	14
	15	16	17	19	20	21	22
	23	24	25	26	27	28[h]	29
	30	1	2	3	4	5	6
PHĀLGUNA 2147	7	8	9	10	11	12	13
	14	15[i]	16	17	18	19	20
	21	23	24	25	26	27	28
	29	30	30	1[a]	2	3	4
CHAITRA 2148	5	6	7	8	9[b]	10	11
	12	13	14	15	17	18	19
	20	21	22	23	24	25	26
	27	28	29	30	1	2	3
VAIŚĀKHA 2148	3	4	5	6	7	8	10
	11	12	13	14	15	16	17
	18	19	20	21	22	23	24
	25	26	27	28	29	30	1
JYAISHṬHA 2148	2	3	4	5	6	7	8
	9	10	11	12	14	15	16
	17	18	19	20	21	22	23
	24	25	26	27	28	29	29
	30	1	2	3	4	6	7
LEAP ĀSHĀḌHA 2148	8	9	10	11	12	13	14
	15	16	18	19	20	20	21
	22	23	24	25	26	27	28
	29	30	1	2	3	4	5
ĀSHĀḌHA 2148	6	7	9	10	11	12	13
	14	15	16	17	18	19	20
	21	22	23	24	25	26	26
	27	28	29	1	2	3	4
ŚRĀVAṆA 2148	5	6	7	8	9	10	11
	13	14	15	16	17	17	18
	19	20	21	22	23[c]	24	25
	26	27	28	29	30	1	2
BHĀDRAPADA 2148	3[d]	5	6	7	8	9	10
	11	12	13	14	15	16	17
	18	19	20	21	21	22	23
	24	25	26	28	29	30	1
ĀŚVINA 2148	2	3	4	5	6	7	8[e]
	9[e]	10[e]	11	12	13	14	15
	16	17	18	19	20	21	22
	23	24	25	26	27	28	29
	30	1[f]	3	4	5	6	7
KĀRTTIKA 2148	8	9	10	11	12	13	14
	15	15	16	17	18	19	20
	21	22	23	24	25	27	28
	29	30	1	2	3	4	5
MĀRGAŚIRA 2148	6	7	8	9	10	11[g]	12
	13	14	15	16	17	18	19
	20	21	22	23	24	25	26

HINDU SOLAR 2012‡/2013

Month	Sun	Mon	Tue	Wed	Thu	Fri	Sat
PAUSHA 2012	15	16	17	18	19	20	21
	22	23	24	25	26	27	28
	29	1[b]	2	3	4	5	6
MĀGHA 2012	7	8	9	10	11	12	13
	14	15	16	17	18	19	20
	21	22	23	24	25	26	27
	28	29	1	2	3	4	5
PHĀLGUNA 2012	6	7	8	9	10	11	12
	13	14	15	16	17	18	19
	20	21	22	23	24	25	26
	27	28	29	30	1	2	3
CHAITRA 2012	4	5	6	7	8	9	10
	11	12	13	14	15	16	17
	18	19	20	21	22	23	24
	25	26	27	28	29	30	31
VAIŚĀKHA 2013	1[a]	2	3	4	5	6	7
	8	9	10	11	12	13	14
	15	16	17	18	19	20	21
	22	23	24	25	26	27	28
	29	30	1	2	3	4	5
JYAISHṬHA 2013	6	7	8	9	10	11	12
	13	14	15	16	17	18	19
	20	21	22	23	24	25	26
	27	28	29	30	31	32	1
ĀSHĀḌHA 2013	2	3	4	5	6	7	8
	9	10	11	12	13	14	15
	16	17	18	19	20	21	22
	23	24	25	26	27	28	29
	30	31	32	1	2	3	4
ŚRĀVAṆA 2013	5	6	7	8	9	10	11
	12	13	14	15	16	17	18
	19	20	21	22	23	24	25
	26	27	28	29	30	31	1
BHĀDRAPADA 2013	2	3	4	5	6	7	8
	9	10	11	12	13	14	15
	16	17	18	19	20	21	22
	23	24	25	26	27	28	29
	30	31	1	2	3	4	5
ĀŚVINA 2013	6	7	8	9	10	11	12
	13	14	15	16	17	18	19
	20	21	22	23	24	25	26
	27	28	29	30	1	2	3
KĀRTTIKA 2013	4	5	6	7	8	9	10
	11	12	13	14	15	16	17
	18	19	20	21	22	23	24
	25	26	27	28	29	30	1
MĀRGAŚIRA 2013	2	3	4	5	6	7	8
	9	10	11	12	13	14	15
	16	17	18	19	20	21	22
	23	24	25	26	27	28	29
	30	1	2	3	4	5	6
PAUSHA 2013	7	8	9	10	11	12	13
	14	15	16	17	18	19	20

ISLAMIC (ASTRONOMICAL) 1514‡/1515

Month	Sun	Mon	Tue	Wed	Thu	Fri	Sat
RAJAB 1514	10	11	12	13	14	15	16
	17	18	19	20	21	22	23
	24	25	26	27[d]	28	29	30
SHA'BĀN 1514	1	2	3	4	5	6	7
	8	9	10	11	12	13	14
	15	16	17	18	19	20	21
	22	23	24	25	26	27	28
	29	30	1[e]	2	3	4	5
RAMAḌĀN 1514	6	7	8	9	10	11	12
	13	14	15	16	17	18	19
	20	21	22	23	24	25	26
	27	28	29	30	1[f]	2	3
SHAWWĀL 1514	4	5	6	7	8	9	10
	11	12	13	14	15	16	17
	18	19	20	21	22	23	24
	25	26	27	28	29	1	2
DHU AL-QA'DA 1514	3	4	5	6	7	8	9
	10	11	12	13	14	15	16
	17	18	19	20	21	22	23
	24	25	26	27	28	29	30
DHU AL-ḤIJJA 1514	1	2	3	4	5	6	7
	8	9	10[g]	11	12	13	14
	15	16	17	18	19	20	21
	22	23	24	25	26	27	28
	29	30[d]	1[a]	2	3	4	5
MUḤARRAM 1515	6	7	8	9	10[b]	11	12
	13	14	15	16	17	18	19
	20	21	22	23	24	25	26
	27	28	29	1	2	3	4
ṢAFAR 1515	5	6	7	8	9	10	11
	12	13	14	15	16	17	18
	19	20	21	22	23	24	25
	26	27	28	29	1	2	3
RABĪ' I 1515	4	5	6	7	8	9	10
	11	12[c]	13	14	15	16	17
	18	19	20	21	22	23	24
	25	26	27	28	29	30	1
RABĪ' II 1515	2	3	4	5	6	7	8
	9	10	11	12	13	14	15
	16	17	18	19	20	21	22
	23	24	25	26	27	28	29
JUMĀDĀ I 1515	1	2	3	4	5	6	7
	8	9	10	11	12	13	14
	15	16	17	18	19	20	21
	22	23	24	25	26	27	28
	29	1	2	3	4	5	6
JUMĀDĀ II 1515	7	8	9	10	11	12	13
	14	15	16	17	18	19	20
	21	22	23	24	25	26	27
	28	29	30	1	2	3	4
RAJAB 1515	5	6	7	8	9	10	11
	12	13	14	15	16	17	18
	19	20	21	22	23	24	25

GREGORIAN 2091

Julian (Sun)	Sun	Mon	Tue	Wed	Thu	Fri	Sat	Month
Dec 18	31	1	2	3	4	5	6	JANUARY 2091
	7[a]	8	9	10	11	12	13	
Jan 1	14[b]	15	16	17	18	19	20	
	21	22	23	24	25	26	27	
Jan 15	28	29	30	31	1	2	3	FEBRUARY 2091
	4	5	6	7	8	9	10	
Jan 29	11	12	13	14	15	16	17	
	18	19	20	21[c]	22	23	24	
Feb 12	25[d]	26	27	28	1	2	3	MARCH 2091
	4	5	6	7	8	9	10	
Feb 26	11	12	13	14	15	16	17	
	18	19	20	21	22	23	24	
Mar 12	25	26	27	28	29	30	31	
	1	2	3	4	5	6	7	APRIL 2091
Mar 26	8[e]	9	10	11	12	13	14	
	15	16	17	18	19	20	21	
Apr 9	22	23	24	25	26	27	28	
	29	30	1	2	3	4	5	MAY 2091
Apr 23	6	7	8	9	10	11	12	
	13	14	15	16	17	18	19	
May 7	20	21	22	23	24	25	26	
	27	28	29	30	31	1	2	JUNE 2091
May 21	3	4	5	6	7	8	9	
	10	11	12	13	14	15	16	
Jun 4	17	18	19	20	21	22	23	
	24	25	26	27	28	29	30	
Jun 18	1	2	3	4	5	6	7	JULY 2091
	8	9	10	11	12	13	14	
Jul 2	15	16	17	18	19	20	21	
	22	23	24	25	26	27	28	
Jul 16	29	30	31	1	2	3	4	AUGUST 2091
	5	6	7	8	9	10	11	
Jul 30	12	13	14	15	16	17	18	
	19	20	21	22	23	24	25	
Aug 13	26	27	28	29	30	31	1	SEPTEMBER 2091
	2	3	4	5	6	7	8	
Aug 27	9	10	11	12	13	14	15	
	16	17	18	19	20	21	22	
Sep 10	23	24	25	26	27	28	29	
	30	1	2	3	4	5	6	OCTOBER 2091
Sep 24	7	8	9	10	11	12	13	
	14	15	16	17	18	19	20	
Oct 8	21	22	23	24	25	26	27	
	28	29	30	31	1	2	3	NOVEMBER 2091
Oct 22	4	5	6	7	8	9	10	
	11	12	13	14	15	16	17	
Nov 5	18	19	20	21	22	23	24	
	25	26	27	28	29	30	1	DECEMBER 2091
Nov 19	2[g]	3	4	5	6	7	8	
	9	10	11	12	13	14	15	
Dec 3	16	17	18	19	20	21	22	
	23	24	25[h]	26	27	28	29	
Dec 17	30	31	1	2	3	4	5	

Persian: ‡Leap year; [a]New Year (or next day); *Near New Year: 0′4″; [b]Sizdeh Bedar

Hindu Lunar: ‡Leap year; [a]New Year (Virodhakṛit); [b]Birthday of Rāma; [c]Birthday of Krishna; [d]Gaṇēśa Chaturthī; [e]Dashara; [f]Diwali; [g]Birthday of Vishnu; [h]Night of Śiva; [i]Holi

Hindu Solar: ‡Leap year; [a]New Year (Krodhana); [b]Pongal

Islamic: ‡Leap year; [a]New Year; [d]New Year (Arithmetic); [b]'Ashūrā'; [c]Prophet's Birthday; [d]Ascent of the Prophet; [e]Start of Ramaḍān; [f]'Id al-Fiṭr; [g]'Id al-'Aḍḥā

Gregorian: [a]Orthodox Christmas; [b]Julian New Year; [c]Ash Wednesday; [d]Feast of Orthodoxy; [e]Easter (also Orthodox); [g]Advent; [h]Christmas

2092

Gregorian 2092‡ / ISO Week / Julian Day

Month	Sun	Mon	Tue	Wed	Thu	Fri	Sat	Lunar Phases	ISO Week (Mon)	Julian Day (Sun noon)
January 2092	30	31	1[a]	◑	3	4	5	9:06	1	2485146
	6	7	8	●	10	11	12	1:36	2	2485153
	13	14	15	◐	17	18	19	14:07	3	2485160
	20	21	22	23	○	25	26	14:54	4	2485167
	27	28	29	30	◑	1	2	17:24	5	2485174
February 2092	3	4	5	6	●	8	9	15:02	6	2485181
	10	11	12	13	14	◐	16	11:39	7	2485188
	17	18	19	20	21	22	○	5:28	8	2485195
	24	25	26	27	28	29	◑	0:45	9	2485202
March 2092	2	3	4	5	6	7	●	5:55	10	2485209
	9	10	11	12	13	14	15		11	2485216
	◐	17	18	19[b]	20	21	22	8:06	12	2485223
	○	24	25	26	27	28	29	17:14	13	2485230
	◑	31	1	2	3	4	5	8:20	14	2485237
April 2092	●	7	8	9	10	11	12	21:40	15	2485244
	13	14	◐	16	17	18	19	1:53	16	2485251
	20	21	○	23	24	25	26	2:28	17	2485258
	27	◑	29	30	1	2	3	17:07	18	2485265
May 2092	4	5	●	7	8	9	10	13:38	19	2485272
	11	12	13	◐	15	16	17	16:05	20	2485279
	18	19	20	○	22	23	24	9:59	21	2485286
	25	26	27	◑	29	30	31	3:45	22	2485293
June 2092	1	2	3	4	●	6	7	5:16	23	2485300
	8	9	10	11	12	◐	14	2:32	24	2485307
	15	16	17	18	○	20[c]	21	16:55	25	2485314
	22	23	24	25	◑	27	28	16:31	26	2485321
	29	30	1	2	3	●	5	20:09	27	2485328
July 2092	6	7	8	9	10	11	◐	9:53	28	2485335
	13	14	15	16	17	18	○	0:23	29	2485342
	20	21	22	23	24	25	◑	7:29	30	2485349
	27	28	29	30	31	1	2		31	2485356
August 2092	●	4	5	6	7	8	9	9:53	32	2485363
	◐	11	12	13	14	15	16	15:17	33	2485370
	○	18	19	20	21	22	23	9:21	34	2485377
	24	◑	26	27	28	29	30	0:31	35	2485384
September 2092	31	●	2	3	4	5	6	22:13	36	2485391
	7	◐	9	10	11	12	13	20:14	37	2485398
	14	○	16	17	18	19	20	20:32	38	2485405
	21[d]	22	◑	24	25	26	27	19:04	39	2485412
	28	29	30	●	2	3	4	9:14	40	2485419
October 2092	5	6	7	◐	9	10	11	2:15	41	2485426
	12	13	14	○	16	17	18	10:24	42	2485433
	19	20	21	22	◑	24	25	14:06	43	2485440
	26	27	28	29	●	31	1	19:28	44	2485447
November 2092	2	3	4	5	◐	7	8	10:39	45	2485454
	9	10	11	12	13	○	15	3:04	46	2485461
	16	17	18	19	20	21	◑	8:06	47	2485468
	23	24	25	26	27	28	●	5:35	48	2485475
December 2092	30	1	2	3	4	◐	6	22:17	49	2485482
	7	8	9	10	11	12	○	21:58	50	2485489
	14	15	16	17	18	19	20[e]		51	2485496
	◑	22	23	24	25	26	27	23:38	52	2485503
	●	29	30	31	1	2	3	16:09	1	2485510

Hebrew 5852‡/5853

Julian Day	Month	Sun	Mon	Tue	Wed	Thu	Fri	Sat	Molad
2485146	TEVETH 5852	19	20	21	22	23	24	25	
2485153		26	27	28	29	1	2	3	Wed 14h15m17p
2485160	SHEVAT 5852	4	5	6	7	8	9	10	
2485167		11	12	13	14	15	16	17	
2485174		18	19	20	21	22	23	24	
2485181		25	26	27	28	29	30	1	Fri 3h0m0p
2485188	ADAR I 5852	2	3	4	5	6	7	8	
2485195		9	10	11	12	13	14	15	
2485202		16	17	18	19	20	21	22	
2485209		23	24	25	26	27	28	29	
2485216		30	1	2	3	4	5	6	Sat 15h44m1p
2485223	ADAR II 5852	7	8	9	10	11	12	13	
2485230		14[f]	15	16	17	18	19	20	
2485237		21	22	23	24	25	26	27	
2485244		28	29	1	2	3	4	5	Mon 4h28m2p
2485251	NISAN 5852	6	7	8	9	10	11	12	
2485258		13	14	15[g]	16	17	18	19	
2485265		20	21	22	23	24	25	26	
2485272		27	28	29	30	1	2	3	Tue 17h12m3p
2485279	IYAR 5852	4	5	6	7	8	9	10	
2485286		11	12	13	14	15	16	17	
2485293		18	19	20	21	22	23	24	
2485300		25	26	27	28	29	1	2	Thu 5h56m4p
2485307	SIVAN 5852	3	4	5	6[h]	7	8	9	
2485314		10	11	12	13	14	15	16	
2485321		17	18	19	20	21	22	23	
2485328		24	25	26	27	28	29	30	
2485335	TAMMUZ 5852	1	2	3	4	5	6	7	Fri 18h40m5p
2485342		8	9	10	11	12	13	14	
2485349		15	16	17	18	19	20	21	
2485356		22	23	24	25	26	27	28	
2485363		29	1	2	3	4	5	6	Sun 7h24m6p
2485370	AV 5852	7	8	9[i]	10	11	12	13	
2485377		14	15	16	17	18	19	20	
2485384		21	22	23	24	25	26	27	
2485391		28	29	30	1	2	3	4	Mon 20h8m7p
2485398	ELUL 5852	5	6	7	8	9	10	11	
2485405		12	13	14	15	16	17	18	
2485412		19	20	21	22	23	24	25	
2485419		26	27	28	29	1[a]	2[a]	3	Wed 8h52m8p
2485426	TISHRI 5853	4	5	6	7	8	9	10[b]	
2485433		11	12	13	14	15[c]	16	17	
2485440		18	19	20	21	22	23	24	
2485447		25	26	27	28	29	30	1	Thu 21h36m9p
2485454	HESHVAN 5853	2	3	4	5	6	7	8	
2485461		9	10	11	12	13	14	15	
2485468		16	17	18	19	20	21	22	
2485475		23	24	25	26	27	28	29	
2485482		1	2	3	4	5	6[d]	7	Sat 10h20m10p
2485489	KISLEV 5853	8	9	10	11	12	13	14	
2485496		15	16	17	18	19	20	21	
2485503		22	23	24	25[e]	26[e]	27[e]	28[e]	
2485510		29[e]	30[e]	1[e]	2[e]	3	4	5	Sun 23h4m11p

Chinese Xīn-Hài/Rén-Zǐ

Julian Day	Month	Sun	Mon	Tue	Wed	Thu	Fri	Sat	Solar Term
2485146	MONTH 11 Xīn-Hài	21	22	23	24	25	26*	27	Xiǎo hán
2485153	MONTH 12 Xīn-Hài	28	29	30	1	2	3	4	
2485160		5	6	7	8	9	10	11	
2485167		12	13	14	15	16	17	18	Dà hán
2485174		19	20	21	22	23	24	25	
2485181		26	27	28	29	1[a]	2	3	Lì chūn
2485188	MONTH 1 Rén-Zǐ	4	5	6	7	8	9	10	
2485195		11	12	13	14	15[b]	16	17	Yǔ shuǐ
2485202		18	19	20	21	22	23	24	
2485209		25	26	27*	28	29	30	1	Jīng zhé
2485216		2	3	4	5	6	7	8	
2485223	MONTH 2 Rén-Zǐ	9	10	11	12	13	14	15	Chūn fēn
2485230		16	17	18	19	20	21	22	
2485237		23	24	25	26	27	28[c]	29	Qīng míng
2485244		30	1	2	3	4	5	6	
2485251	MONTH 3 Rén-Zǐ	7	8	9	10	11	12	13	Gǔ yǔ
2485258		14	15	16	17	18	19	20	
2485265		21	22	23	24	25	26	27*	
2485272		28	29	1	2	3	4	5	Lì xià
2485279	MONTH 4 Rén-Zǐ	6	7	8	9	10	11	12	
2485286		13	14	15	16	17	18	19	Xiǎo mǎn
2485293		20	21	22	23	24	25	26	
2485300		27	28	29	30	1	2	3	Máng zhòng
2485307	MONTH 5 Rén-Zǐ	4	5[d]	6	7	8	9	10	
2485314		11	12	13	14	15	16	17	Xià zhì
2485321		18	19	20	21	22	23	24	
2485328		25	26	27	28*	29	30	1	
2485335	MONTH 6 Rén-Zǐ	2	3	4	5	6	7	8	Xiǎo shǔ
2485342		9	10	11	12	13	14	15	
2485349		16	17	18	19	20	21	22	Dà shǔ
2485356		23	24	25	26	27	28	29	
2485363		1	2	3	4	5	6	7[e]	Lì qiū
2485370	MONTH 7 Rén-Zǐ	8	9	10	11	12	13	14	
2485377		15[f]	16	17	18	19	20	21	Chǔ shǔ
2485384		22	23	24	25	26	27	28	
2485391		29*	30	1	2	3	4	5	Bái lù
2485398	MONTH 8 Rén-Zǐ	6	7	8	9	10	11	12	
2485405		13	14	15[g]	16	17	18	19	
2485412		20	21	22	23	24	25	26	Qiū fēn
2485419		27	28	29	1	2	3	4	
2485426	MONTH 9 Rén-Zǐ	5	6	7	8	9[h]	10	11	Hán lù
2485433		12	13	14	15	16	17	18	
2485440		19	20	21	22	23	24	25	Shuāng jiàng
2485447		26	27	28	29	30*	1	2	
2485454	MONTH 10 Rén-Zǐ	3	4	5	6	7	8	9	Lì dōng
2485461		10	11	12	13	14	15	16	
2485468		17	18	19	20	21	22	23	Xiǎo xuě
2485475		24	25	26	27	28	29	1	
2485482		2	3	4	5	6	7	8	Dà xuě
2485489	MONTH 11 Rén-Zǐ	9	10	11	12	13	14	15	
2485496		16	17	18	19	20	21	22	
2485503		23[i]	24	25	26	27	28	29	Dōng zhì
2485510		30	1*	2	3	4	5	6	

Coptic 1808/1809 — Ethiopic 2084/2085

Julian Day	Coptic Month	Sun	Mon	Tue	Wed	Thu	Fri	Sat	Ethiopic Month
2485146	KOIAK 1808	20	21	22	23	24	25	26	TĀKHŚĀŚ 2084
2485153		27	28	29[c]	30	1	2	3	
2485160	TŌBE 1808	4	5	6[d]	7	8	9	10	ṬER 2084
2485167		11[e]	12	13	14	15	16	17	
2485174		18	19	20	21	22	23	24	
2485181		25	26	27	28	29	30	1	
2485188	MESHIR 1808	2	3	4	5	6	7	8	YAKĀTIT 2084
2485195		9	10	11	12	13	14	15	
2485202		16	17	18	19	20	21	22	
2485209		23	24	25	26	27	28	29	
2485216		30	1	2	3	4	5	6	
2485223	PAREMOTEP 1808	7	8	9	10	11	12	13	MAGĀBIT 2084
2485230		14	15	16	17	18	19	20	
2485237		21	22	23	24	25	26	27	
2485244		28	29	30	1	2	3	4	
2485251	PARMOUTE 1808	5	6	7	8	9	10	11	MIYĀZYĀ 2084
2485258		12	13	14	15	16	17	18	
2485265		19[f]	20	21	22	23	24	25	
2485272		26	27	28	29[g]	30	1	2	
2485279	PASHONS 1808	3	4	5	6	7	8	9	GENBOT 2084
2485286		10	11	12	13	14	15	16	
2485293		17	18	19	20	21	22	23	
2485300		24	25	26	27	28	29	30	
2485307	PAŌNE 1808	1	2	3	4	5	6	7	SANĒ 2084
2485314		8	9	10	11	12	13	14	
2485321		15	16	17	18	19	20	21	
2485328		22	23	24	25	26	27	28	
2485335		29	30	1	2	3	4	5	
2485342	EPĒP 1808	6	7	8	9	10	11	12	ḤAMLĒ 2084
2485349		13	14	15	16	17	18	19	
2485356		20	21	22	23	24	25	26	
2485363		27	28	29	30	1	2	3	
2485370	MESORĒ 1808	4	5	6	7	8	9	10	NAHASĒ 2084
2485377		11	12	13[h]	14	15	16	17	
2485384		18	19	20	21	22	23	24	
2485391		25	26	27	28	29	30	1	
2485398	EPAG. 1808	2	3	4	5	1[a]	2	3	PĀG. 2084
2485405	THOOUT 1809	4	5	6	7	8	9	10	MASKARAM 2085
2485412		11	12	13	14	15	16	17[b]	
2485419		18	19	20	21	22	23	24	
2485426		25	26	27	28	29	30	1	
2485433	PAOPE 1809	2	3	4	5	6	7	8	ṬEQEMT 2085
2485440		9	10	11	12	13	14	15	
2485447		16	17	18	19	20	21	22	
2485454		23	24	25	26	27	28	29	
2485461		30	1	2	3	4	5	6	
2485468	ATHŌR 1809	7	8	9	10	11	12	13	ḤEDĀR 2085
2485475		14	15	16	17	18	19	20	
2485482		21	22	23	24	25	26	27	
2485489		28	29	30	1	2	3	4	
2485496	KOIAK 1809	5	6	7	8	9	10	11	TĀKHŚĀŚ 2085
2485503		12	13	14	15	16	17	18	
2485510		19	20	21	22	23	24	25	

‡Leap year
[a]New Year
[b]Spring (14:32)
[c]Summer (7:13)
[d]Autumn (23:40)
[e]Winter (21:30)
● New moon
◐ First quarter moon
○ Full moon
◑ Last quarter moon

‡Leap year
[a]New Year
[b]Yom Kippur
[c]Sukkot
[d]Winter starts
[e]Ḥanukkah
[f]Purim
[g]Passover
[h]Shavuot
[i]Fast of Av

[a]New Year (4790, Rat)
[b]Lantern Festival
[c]Qīngmíng
[d]Dragon Festival
[e]Qīqiǎo
[f]Hungry Ghosts
[g]Mid-Autumn Festival
[h]Double-Ninth Festival
[i]Dōngzhì
*Start of 60-name cycle

[a]New Year
[b]Building of the Cross
[c]Christmas
[d]Jesus's Circumcision
[e]Epiphany
[f]Easter
[g]Mary's Announcement
[h]Jesus's Transfiguration

PERSIAN (ASTRONOMICAL) 1470‡/1471

Month	Sun	Mon	Tue	Wed	Thu	Fri	Sat
DEY 1470	10	11	12	13	14	15	16
	17	18	19	20	21	22	23
	24	25	26	27	28	29	30
BAHMAN 1470	1	2	3	4	5	6	7
	8	9	10	11	12	13	14
	15	16	17	18	19	20	21
	22	23	24	25	26	27	28
ESFAND 1470	29	30	1	2	3	4	5
	6	7	8	9	10	11	12
	13	14	15	16	17	18	19
	20	21	22	23	24	25	26
FARVARDĪN 1471	27	28	29	30	1[a]	2	3
	4	5	6	7	8	9	10
	11	12	13[b]	14	15	16	17
	18	19	20	21	22	23	24
	25	26	27	28	29	30	31
ORDĪBEHEŠT 1471	1	2	3	4	5	6	7
	8	9	10	11	12	13	14
	15	16	17	18	19	20	21
	22	23	24	25	26	27	28
XORDĀD 1471	29	30	31	1	2	3	4
	5	6	7	8	9	10	11
	12	13	14	15	16	17	18
	19	20	21	22	23	24	25
TĪR 1471	26	27	28	29	30	31	1
	2	3	4	5	6	7	8
	9	10	11	12	13	14	15
	16	17	18	19	20	21	22
	23	24	25	26	27	28	29
MORDĀD 1471	30	31	1	2	3	4	5
	6	7	8	9	10	11	12
	13	14	15	16	17	18	19
	20	21	22	23	24	25	26
SHAHRĪVAR 1471	27	28	29	30	31	1	2
	3	4	5	6	7	8	9
	10	11	12	13	14	15	16
	17	18	19	20	21	22	23
	24	25	26	27	28	29	30
MEHR 1471	31	1	2	3	4	5	6
	7	8	9	10	11	12	13
	14	15	16	17	18	19	20
	21	22	23	24	25	26	27
ĀBĀN 1471	28	29	30	1	2	3	4
	5	6	7	8	9	10	11
	12	13	14	15	16	17	18
	19	20	21	22	23	24	25
ĀZAR 1471	26	27	28	29	30	1	2
	3	4	5	6	7	8	9
	10	11	12	13	14	15	16
	17	18	19	20	21	22	23
	24	25	26	27	28	29	30
DEY 1471	1	2	3	4	5	6	7
	8	9	10	11	12	13	14

‡Leap year
[a]New Year
[b]Sizdeh Bedar

HINDU LUNAR 2148‡/2149

Month	Sun	Mon	Tue	Wed	Thu	Fri	Sat
MĀRGAŚĪRA 2148	20	21	22	23	24	25	26
PAUSHA 2148	27	28	29	**30**	2	3	4
	5	6	7	7	8	9	10
	11	12	13	14	15	16	17
	18	19	20	21	22	**23**	25
MĀGHA 2148	26	27	28	29	30	1	2
	3	4	5	6	7	8	9
	10	10	11	12	13	14	15
	16	17	**18**	20	21	22	23
	24	25	26	27	28[h]	29	30
PHĀLGUNA 2148	1	2	3	4	5	6	7
	8	9	10	11	12	13	14
	15[i]	16	17	18	19	20	21
	22	24	25	26	27	28	29
CHAITRA 2149	30	1[a]	2	3	3	4	5
	6	7	8	9[b]	10	11	12
	13	14	15	**16**	18	19	20
	21	22	23	24	25	26	27
VAIŚĀKHA 2149	28	29	30	1	2	3	4
	5	6	7	8	9	10	11
	12	13	14	15	16	17	18
	19	21	22	23	24	25	26
JYAISHTHA 2149	27	28	28	29	30	1	2
	3	4	5	6	7	8	9
	10	11	**12**	14	15	16	17
	18	19	20	21	22	23	24
ĀSHĀḌHA 2149	25	26	27	28	29	30	1
	2	3	4	5	6	7	8
	9	10	11	12	13	14	**15**
	17	18	19	20	21	22	23
	24	25	25	26	27	28	29
ŚRĀVAṆA 2149	30	1	2	3	4	5	6
	7	9	10	11	12	13	14
	15	16	17	18	19	20	21
	22	23[c]	24	25	26	27	28
BHĀDRAPADA 2149	29	30	1	2	3	4[d]	5
	6	7	8	9	10	**11**	13
	14	15	16	17	18	19	20
	21	21	22	23	24	25	26
ĀŚVINA 2149	27	28	29	30	1	2	3
	4	6	7	8[e]	9[e]	10[e]	11
	12	13	14	15	16	17	18
	19	20	21	22	23	24	25
KĀRTTIKA 2149	26	27	28	29	30	1[f]	2
	3	4	5	6	7	**8**	10
	11	12	13	14	15	15	16
	17	18	19	20	21	22	23
	24	25	26	27	28	29	30
MĀRGAŚĪRA 2149	1	**2**	4	5	6	7	8
	9	10	11[g]	12	13	14	15
	16	17	18	18	19	20	21
	22	23	24	25	**26**	28	29
	30	1	2	3	4	5	6

‡Leap year
[a]New Year (Paridhāvin)
[b]Birthday of Rāma
[c]Birthday of Krishna
[d]Ganēśa Chaturthī
[e]Dashara
[f]Diwali
[g]Birthday of Vishnu
[h]Night of Śiva
[i]Holi

HINDU SOLAR 2013/2014

Month	Sun	Mon	Tue	Wed	Thu	Fri	Sat
PAUSHA 2013	14	15	16	17	18	19	20
	21	22	23	24	25	26	27
MĀGHA 2013	28	29	1[b]	2	3	4	5
	6	7	8	9	10	11	12
	13	14	15	16	17	18	19
	20	21	22	23	24	25	26
PHĀLGUNA 2013	27	28	29	30	1	2	3
	4	5	6	7	8	9	10
	11	12	13	14	15	16	17
	18	19	20	21	22	23	24
CHAITRA 2013	25	26	27	28	29	1	2
	3	4	5	6	7	8	9
	10	11	12	13	14	15	16
	17	18	19	20	21	22	23
	24	25	26	27	28	29	30
VAIŚĀKHA 2014	31	1[a]	2	3	4	5	6
	7	8	9	10	11	12	13
	14	15	16	17	18	19	20
	21	22	23	24	25	26	27
JYAISHTHA 2014	28	29	30	31	1	2	3
	4	5	6	7	8	9	10
	11	12	13	14	15	16	17
	18	19	20	21	22	23	24
	25	26	27	28	29	30	31
ĀSHĀḌHA 2014	1	2	3	4	5	6	7
	8	9	10	11	12	13	14
	15	16	17	18	19	20	21
	22	23	24	25	26	27	28
ŚRĀVAṆA 2014	29	30	31	32	1	2	3
	4	5	6	7	8	9	10
	11	12	13	14	15	16	17
	18	19	20	21	22	23	24
	25	26	27	28	29	30	31
BHĀDRAPADA 2014	1	2	3	4	5	6	7
	8	9	10	11	12	13	14
	15	16	17	18	19	20	21
	22	23	24	25	26	27	28
ĀŚVINA 2014	29	30	31	1	2	3	4
	5	6	7	8	9	10	11
	12	13	14	15	16	17	18
	19	20	21	22	23	24	25
KĀRTTIKA 2014	26	27	28	29	30	31	1
	2	3	4	5	6	7	8
	9	10	11	12	13	14	15
	16	17	18	19	20	21	22
	23	24	25	26	27	28	29
MĀRGAŚĪRA 2014	30	1	2	3	4	5	6
	7	8	9	10	11	12	13
	14	15	16	17	18	19	20
	21	22	23	24	25	26	27
PAUSHA 2014	28	29	1	2	3	4	5
	6	7	8	9	10	11	12
	13	14	15	16	17	18	19

[a]New Year (Kshaya)
[b]Pongal

ISLAMIC (ASTRONOMICAL) 1515/1516

Month	Sun	Mon	Tue	Wed	Thu	Fri	Sat
RAJAB 1515	19	20	21	22	23	24	25
SHA'BĀN 1515	26	27[d]	28	29	1	2	3
	4	5	6	7	8	9	10
	11	12	13	14	15	16	17
	18	19	20	21	22	23	24
RAMAḌĀN 1515	25	26	27	28	29	30	1[e]
	2	3	4	5	6	7	8
	9	10	11	12	13	14	15
	16	17	18	19	20	21	22
	23	24	25	26	27	28	29
SHAWWĀL 1515	30	1[f]	2	3	4	5	6
	7	8	9	10	11	12	13
	14	15	16	17	18	19	20
	21	22	23	24	25	26	27
DHU AL-QA'DA 1515	28	29	1	2	3	4	5
	6	7	8	9	10	11	12
	13	14	15	16	17	18	19
	20	21	22	23	24	25	26
DHU AL-ḤIJJA 1515	27	28	29	30	1	2	3
	4	5	6	7	8	9	10[g]
	11	12	13	14	15	16	17
	18	19	20	21	22	23	24
	25	26	27	28	29	30[d]	1[a]
MUḤARRAM 1516	2	3	4	5	6	7	8
	9	10[b]	11	12	13	14	15
	16	17	18	19	20	21	22
	23	24	25	26	27	28	29
ṢAFAR 1516	1	2	3	4	5	6	7
	8	9	10	11	12	13	14
	15	16	17	18	19	20	21
	22	23	24	25	26	27	28
RABĪ' I 1516	29	30	1	2	3	4	5
	6	7	8	9	10	11	12[c]
	13	14	15	16	17	18	19
	20	21	22	23	24	25	26
RABĪ' II 1516	27	28	29	1	2	3	4
	5	6	7	8	9	10	11
	12	13	14	15	16	17	18
	19	20	21	22	23	24	25
JUMĀDĀ I 1516	26	27	28	29	30	1	2
	3	4	5	6	7	8	9
	10	11	12	13	14	15	16
	17	18	19	20	21	22	23
JUMĀDĀ II 1516	24	25	26	27	28	29	1
	2	3	4	5	6	7	8
	9	10	11	12	13	14	15
	16	17	18	19	20	21	22
	23	24	25	26	27	28	29
RAJAB 1516	1	2	3	4	5	6	7
	8	9	10	11	12	13	14
	15	16	17	18	19	20	21
	22	23	24	25	26	27[d]	28
	29	30	1	2	3	4	5

[a]New Year
[b]New Year (Arithmetic)
[b]'Ashūrā'
[c]Prophet's Birthday
[d]Ascent of the Prophet
[e]Start of Ramaḍān
[f]'Id al-Fiṭr
[g]'Id al-'Aḍḥā

GREGORIAN 2092‡

Julian‡ (Sun)	Sun	Mon	Tue	Wed	Thu	Fri	Sat	Month
Dec 17	30	31	1	2	3	4	5	JANUARY 2092
	6	7[a]	8	9	10	11	12	
Dec 31	13	14[b]	15	16	17	18	19	
	20	21	22	23	24	25	26	
Jan 14	27	28	29	30	31	1	2	FEBRUARY 2092
	3	4	5	6	7	8	9	
Jan 28	10	11	12	13[c]	14	15	16	
	17	18	19	20	21	22	23	
Feb 11	24	25	26	27	28	29	1	MARCH 2092
	2	3	4	5	6	7	8	
Feb 25	9	10	11	12	13	14	15	
	16[d]	17	18	19	20	21	22	
Mar 10	23	24	25	26	27	28	29	
	30[e]	31	1	2	3	4	5	APRIL 2092
Mar 24	6	7	8	9	10	11	12	
	13	14	15	16	17	18	19	
Apr 7	20	21	22	23	24	25	26	
	27[f]	28	29	30	1	2	3	MAY 2092
Apr 21	4	5	6	7	8	9	10	
	11	12	13	14	15	16	17	
May 5	18	19	20	21	22	23	24	
	25	26	27	28	29	30	31	
May 19	1	2	3	4	5	6	7	JUNE 2092
	8	9	10	11	12	13	14	
Jun 2	15	16	17	18	19	20	21	
	22	23	24	25	26	27	28	
Jun 16	29	30	1	2	3	4	5	JULY 2092
	6	7	8	9	10	11	12	
Jun 30	13	14	15	16	17	18	19	
	20	21	22	23	24	25	26	
Jul 14	27	28	29	30	31	1	2	AUGUST 2092
	3	4	5	6	7	8	9	
Jul 28	10	11	12	13	14	15	16	
	17	18	19	20	21	22	23	
Aug 11	24	25	26	27	28	29	30	
	31	1	2	3	4	5	6	SEPTEMBER 2092
Aug 25	7	8	9	10	11	12	13	
	14	15	16	17	18	19	20	
Sep 8	21	22	23	24	25	26	27	
	28	29	30	1	2	3	4	OCTOBER 2092
Sep 22	5	6	7	8	9	10	11	
	12	13	14	15	16	17	18	
Oct 6	19	20	21	22	23	24	25	
	26	27	28	29	30	31	1	NOVEMBER 2092
Oct 20	2	3	4	5	6	7	8	
	9	10	11	12	13	14	15	
Nov 3	16	17	18	19	20	21	22	
	23	24	25	26	27	28	29	
Nov 17	30[g]	1	2	3	4	5	6	DECEMBER 2092
	7	8	9	10	11	12	13	
Dec 1	14	15	16	17	18	19	20	
	21	22	23	24	25[h]	26	27	
Dec 15	28	29	30	31	1	2	3	

‡Leap year
[a]Orthodox Christmas
[b]Julian New Year
[c]Ash Wednesday
[d]Feast of Orthodoxy
[e]Easter
[f]Orthodox Easter
[g]Advent
[h]Christmas

2093

Month	Sun	Mon	Tue	Wed	Thu	Fri	Sat	Lunar Phases	ISO Week	Julian Day	Hebrew month	Sun	Mon	Tue	Wed	Thu	Fri	Sat	Molad	Chinese month	Sun	Mon	Tue	Wed	Thu	Fri	Sat	Solar Term	Coptic month	Sun	Mon	Tue	Wed	Thu	Fri	Sat	Ethiopic month
GREGORIAN 2093									ISO WEEK (Mon)	JULIAN DAY (Sun noon)	HEBREW 5853/5854								Molad	CHINESE Rén-Zǐ/Guǐ-Chǒu‡								Solar Term	COPTIC 1809/1810								ETHIOPIC 2085/2086
JANUARY 2093	●	29	30	31	1[a]	2	3	16:09	1	2485510	TEVETH 5853	29[e]	30[e]	1[e]	2[e]	3	4	5	Sun 23h4m1p	MONTH 12 Rén-Zǐ	30	1	2	3	4	5	6		KOIAK 1809	19	20	21	22	23	24	25	TĀKHŚĀŚ 2085
	◐	5	6	7	8	9	10	13:21	2	2485517		6	7	8	9	10	11	12			*7*	8	9	10	11	12	13	Xiǎo hán	TÔBE 1809	26	27	28	29[c]	30	1	2	ṬER 2085
	11	○	13	14	15	16	17	17:42	3	2485524		13	14	15	16	17	18	19			14	15	16	17	18	19	20			3	4	5	6[d]	7	8	9	
	18	19	◑	21	22	23	24	12:02	4	2485531		20	21	22	23	24	25	26			21	**22**	23	24	25	26	27	Dà hán		10	11[e]	12	13	14	15	16	
	25	26	●	28	29	30	31	3:21	5	2485538	SHEVAT 5853	27	28	29	1	2	3	4	Tue 11h48m12p	MONTH 1 Guǐ-Chǒu	28	29	1[a]	2	3	4	5			17	18	19	20	21	22	23	
FEBRUARY 2093	1	2	◐	4	5	6	7	7:26	6	2485545		5	6	7	8	9	10	11			6	7	*8*	9	10	11	12	Lì chūn		24	25	26	27	28	29	30	
	8	9	10	○	12	13	14	12:17	7	2485552		12	13	14	15	16	17	18			13	14	15[b]	16	17	18	19		MESHIR 1809	1	2	3	4	5	6	7	YAKĀTIT 2085
	15	16	17	◑	19	20	21	21:31	8	2485559		19	20	21	22	23	24	25			20	21	22	**23**	24	25	26	Yǔ shuǐ		8	9	10	11	12	13	14	
	22	23	24	●	26	27	28	15:04	9	2485566	ADAR 5853	26	27	28	29	30	1	2	Thu 0h32m13p	MONTH 2 Guǐ-Chǒu	27	28	29	1	2	3*	4			15	16	17	18	19	20	21	
MARCH 2093	1	2	3	4	◐	6	7	3:26	10	2485573		3	4	5	6	7	8	9			5	6	7	8	*9*	10	11	Jīng zhé		22	23	24	25	26	27	28	
	8	9	10	11	12	○	14	4:05	11	2485580		10	11	12	13	14[f]	15	16			12	13	14	15	16	17	18		PAREMOTEP 1809	29	30	1	2	3	4	5	MAGĀBIT 2085
	15	16	17	18	19[b]	◑	21	4:55	12	2485587		17	18	19	20	21	22	23			19	20	21	22	23	**24**	25	Chūn fēn		6	7	8	9	10	11	12	
	22	23	24	25	26	●	28	3:17	13	2485594	NISAN 5853	24	25	26	27	28	29	1	Fri 13h16m14p	MONTH 3 Guǐ-Chǒu	26	27	28	29	30	1	2			13	14	15	16	17	18	19	
APRIL 2093	29	30	31	1	2	◐	4	23:46	14	2485601		2	3	4	5	6	7	8			3	4	5	6	7	8	*9*[c]	Qīng míng		20	21	22	23	24	25	26	
	5	6	7	8	9	10	○	16:34	15	2485608		9	10	11	12*	13	14	15[g]			10	11	12	13	14	15	16		PARMOUTE 1809	27	28	29	30	1	2	3	MIYĀZYĀ 2085
	12	13	14	15	16	17	◑	11:19	16	2485615		16	17	18	19	20	21	22			17	18	19	20	21	22	23			4	5	6	7	8	9	10	
	19	20	21	22	23	24	●	16:11	17	2485622		23	24	25	26	27	28	29			**24**	25	26	27	28	29	30	Gǔ yǔ		11[f]	12	13	14	15	16	17	
MAY 2093	26	27	28	29	30	1	2		18	2485629	IYYAR 5853	30	1	2	3	4	5	6	Sun 2h0m15p	MONTH 4 Guǐ-Chǒu	1	2	3*	4	5	6	7			18	19	20	21	22	23	24	
	◐	4	5	6	7	8	9	18:36	19	2485636		7	8	9	10	11	12	13			8	9	*10*	11	12	13	14	Lì xià	PASHONS 1809	25	26	27	28	29[g]	30	1	GENBOT 2085
	10	○	12	13	14	15	16	2:16	20	2485643		14	15	16	17	18	19	20			15	16	17	18	19	20	21			2	3	4	5	6	7	8	
	◑	18	19	20	21	22	23	17:46	21	2485650		21	22	23	24	25	26	27			22	23	24	**25**	26	27	28	Xiǎo mǎn		9	10	11	12	13	14	15	
	24	●	26	27	28	29	30	6:06	22	2485657	SIVAN 5853	28	29	1	2	3	4	5	Mon 14h44m16p	MONTH 5 Guǐ-Chǒu	29	1	2	3	4	5[d]	6			16	17	18	19	20	21	22	
JUNE 2093	31	1	◐	3	4	5	6	10:38	23	2485664		6[h]	7	8	9	10	11	12			7	8	9	10	11	*12*	13	Máng zhòng		23	24	25	26	27	28	29	
	7	8	○	10	11	12	13	10:08	24	2485671		13	14	15	16	17	18	19			14	15	16	17	18	19	20		PAÔNE 1809	30	1	2	3	4	5	6	SANĒ 2085
	14	15	◑	17	18	19	20[c]	1:18	25	2485678		20	21	22	23	24	25	26			21	22	23	24	25	26	**27**	Xià zhì		7	8	9	10	11	12	13	
	21	22	●	24	25	26	27	21:03	26	2485685	TAMMUZ 5853	27	28	29	30	1	2	3	Wed 3h28m17p	MONTH 6 Guǐ-Chǒu	28	29	30	1	2	3	4*			14	15	16	17	18	19	20	
JULY 2093	28	29	30	◐	2	3	4	23:23	27	2485692		4	5	6	7	8	9	10			5	6	7	8	9	10	11			21	22	23	24	25	26	27	
	5	6	7	○	9	10	11	17:13	28	2485699		11	12	13	14	15	16	17			12	*13*	14	15	16	17	18	Xiǎo shǔ	EPÊP 1809	28	29	30	1	2	3	4	ḤAMLĒ 2085
	12	13	14	◑	16	17	18	10:53	29	2485706		18	19	20	21	22	23	24			19	20	21	22	23	24	25			5	6	7	8	9	10	11	
	19	20	21	22	●	24	25	12:35	30	2485713	AV 5853	25	26	27	28	29	1	2	Thu 16h13m0p	LEAP MONTH 6 Guǐ-Chǒu	26	27	28	**29**	1	2	3	Dà shǔ		12	13	14	15	16	17	18	
AUGUST 2093	26	27	28	29	30	◐	1	9:12	31	2485720		3	4	5	6	7	8	9			4	5	6	7	8	9	10			19	20	21	22	23	24	25	
	2	3	4	5	6	○	8	0:22	32	2485727		10[i]	11	12	13	14	15	16			11	12	13	14	15	*16*	17	Lì qiū	MESORÊ 1809	26	27	28	29	30	1	2	NAḤASĒ 2085
	9	10	11	12	◑	14	15	23:22	33	2485734		17	18	19	20	21	22	23			18	19	20	21	22	23	24			3	4	5	6	7	8	9	
	16	17	18	19	20	21	●	3:52	34	2485741		24	25	26	27	28	29	30		MONTH 7 Guǐ-Chǒu	25	26	27	28	29	30	**1**	Chǔ shǔ		10	11	12	13[h]	14	15	16	
	23	24	25	26	27	28	◐	16:57	35	2485748	ELUL 5853	1	2	3	4	5	6	7	Sat 4h57m1p		2	3	4	5*	6	7[e]	8			17	18	19	20	21	22	23	
SEPTEMBER 2093	30	31	1	2	3	4	○	8:27	36	2485755		8	9	10	11	12	13	14			9	10	11	12	13	14	15[f]			24	25	26	27	28	29	30	
	6	7	8	9	10	11	◑	15:14	37	2485762		15	16	17	18	19	20	21			16	*17*	18	19	20	21	22	Bái lù	EPAG. 1809 / THOOUT 1810	1	2	3	4	5	1[a]	2	PĀG. 2085 / MASKARAM 2086
	13	14	15	16	17	18	19		38	2485769		22	23	24	25	26	27	28			23	24	25	26	27	28	29			3	4	5	6	7	8	9	
	●	21	22[d]	23	24	25	26	18:15	39	2485776	TISHRI 5854	29	1[a]	2[a]	3	4	5	6	Sun 17h41m2p	MONTH 8 Guǐ-Chǒu	30	1	**2**	3	4	5	6	Qiū fēn		10	11	12	13	14	15	16	
OCTOBER 2093	◐	28	29	30	1	2	3	23:38	40	2485783		7	8	9	10[b]	11	12	13			7	8	9	10	11	12	13			17[b]	18	19	20	21	22	23	
	○	5	6	7	8	9	10	18:17	41	2485790		14	15[c]	16	17	18	19	20			14	15[g]	16	*17*	18	19	20	Hán lù		24	25	26	27	28	29	30	
	11	◑	13	14	15	16	17	10:09	42	2485797		21	22	23	24	25	26	27			21	22	23	24	25	26	27		PAOPE 1810	1	2	3	4	5	6	7	ṬEQEMT 2086
	18	19	●	21	22	23	24	7:32	43	2485804	HESHVAN 5854	28	29	30	1	2	3	4	Tue 6h25m3p	MONTH 9 Guǐ-Chǒu	28	29	1	2	**3**	4	5	Shuāng jiàng		8	9	10	11	12	13	14	
	25	26	◐	28	29	30	31	6:17	44	2485811		5	6	7	8	9	10	11			6*	7	8	9[h]	10	11	12			15	16	17	18	19	20	21	
NOVEMBER 2093	1	2	○	4	5	6	7	6:45	45	2485818		12	13	14	15	16	17	18			13	14	15	16	17	*18*	19	Lì dōng		22	23	24	25	26	27	28	
	8	9	10	◑	12	13	14	6:49	46	2485825		19	20	21	22	23	24	25			20	21	22	23	24	25	26		ATHÔR 1810	29	30	1	2	3	4	5	ḪEDĀR 2086
	15	16	17	●	19	20	21	19:56	47	2485832	KISLEV 5854	26	27	28	29	30	1	2	Wed 19h9m4p	MONTH 10 Guǐ-Chǒu	27	28	29	30	1	2	**3**	Xiǎo xuě		6	7	8	9	10	11	12	
	22	23	24	◐	26	27	28	13:53	48	2485839		3	4	5	6	7	8	9			4	5	6	7	8	9	10			13	14	15	16	17	18	19	
DECEMBER 2093	29	30	1	○	3	4	5	22:23	49	2485846		10	11	12	13	14	15	16[d]			11	12	13	14	15	16	17			20	21	22	23	24	25	26	
	6	7	8	9	10	◑	12	3:14	50	2485853		17	18	19	20	21	22	23			*18*	19	20	21	22	23	24	Dà xuě	KOIAK 1810	27	28	29	30	1	2	3	TĀKHŚĀŚ 2086
	13	14	15	16	17	●	19	7:47	51	2485860		24	25[e]	26[e]	27[e]	28[e]	29[e]	30[e]		MONTH 11* Guǐ-Chǒu	25	26	27	28	29	1	2			4	5	6	7	8	9	10	
	20	21[e]	22	23	◐	25	26	23:24	52	2485867	TEVETH 5854	1[e]	2[e]	3	4	5	6	7	Fri 7h53m5p		3	**4**[i]	5	6	7*	8	9	Dōng zhì		11	12	13	14	15	16	17	
	27	28	29	30	31	○	2	16:50	53	2485874		8	9	10	11	12	13	14			10	11	12	13	14	15	16			18	19	20	21	22	23	24	

[a]New Year
[b]Spring (20:33)
[c]Summer (13:05)
[d]Autumn (5:27)
[e]Winter (3:19)
● New moon
◐ First quarter moon
○ Full moon
◑ Last quarter moon

[a]New Year
[b]Yom Kippur
[c]Sukkot
[d]Winter starts
[e]Ḥanukkah
[f]Purim
[g]Passover
[h]Shavuot
[i]Fast of Av
*New solar cycle

‡Leap year
[a]New Year (4791, Ox)
[b]Lantern Festival
[c]Qīngmíng
[d]Dragon Festival
[e]Qǐqiǎo
[f]Hungry Ghosts
[g]Mid-Autumn Festival
[h]Double-Ninth Festival
[i]Dōngzhì
*Start of 60-name cycle

[a]New Year
[b]Building of the Cross
[c]Christmas
[d]Jesus's Circumcision
[e]Epiphany
[f]Easter
[g]Mary's Announcement
[h]Jesus's Transfiguration

PERSIAN (ASTRONOMICAL) 1471/1472

Month	Sun	Mon	Tue	Wed	Thu	Fri	Sat
DEY 1471	8	9	10	11	12	13	14
	15	16	17	18	19	20	21
	22	23	24	25	26	27	28
	29	30	1	2	3	4	5
BAHMAN 1471	6	7	8	9	10	11	12
	13	14	15	16	17	18	19
	20	21	22	23	24	25	26
	27	28	29	30	1	2	3
ESFAND 1471	4	5	6	7	8	9	10
	11	12	13	14	15	16	17
	18	19	20	21	22	23	24
	25	26	27	28	29	1[a]	2
FARVARDĪN 1472	3	4	5	6	7	8	9
	10	11	12	13[b]	14	15	16
	17	18	19	20	21	22	23
	24	25	26	27	28	29	30
	31	1	2	3	4	5	6
ORDĪBEHEŠT 1472	7	8	9	10	11	12	13
	14	15	16	17	18	19	20
	21	22	23	24	25	26	27
	28	29	30	31	1	2	3
XORDĀD 1472	4	5	6	7	8	9	10
	11	12	13	14	15	16	17
	18	19	20	21	22	23	24
	25	26	27	28	29	30	31
TĪR 1472	1	2	3	4	5	6	7
	8	9	10	11	12	13	14
	15	16	17	18	19	20	21
	22	23	24	25	26	27	28
	29	30	31	1	2	3	4
MORDĀD 1472	5	6	7	8	9	10	11
	12	13	14	15	16	17	18
	19	20	21	22	23	24	25
	26	27	28	29	30	31	1
SHAHRĪVAR 1472	2	3	4	5	6	7	8
	9	10	11	12	13	14	15
	16	17	18	19	20	21	22
	23	24	25	26	27	28	29
	30	31	1	2	3	4	5
MEHR 1472	6	7	8	9	10	11	12
	13	14	15	16	17	18	19
	20	21	22	23	24	25	26
	27	28	29	30	1	2	3
ĀBĀN 1472	4	5	6	7	8	9	10
	11	12	13	14	15	16	17
	18	19	20	21	22	23	24
	25	26	27	28	29	30	1
ĀZAR 1472	2	3	4	5	6	7	8
	9	10	11	12	13	14	15
	16	17	18	19	20	21	22
	23	24	25	26	27	28	29
DEY 1472	30	1	2	3	4	5	6
	7	8	9	10	11	12	13

HINDU LUNAR 2149/2150

Month	Sun	Mon	Tue	Wed	Thu	Fri	Sat
	30	1	2	3	4	5	6
PAUSHA 2149	7	8	9	10	11	12	13
	14	15	16	17	18	19	20
	21	22	23	24	25	26	27
	28	29	30	**1**	3	4	5
MĀGHA 2149	6	7	8	9	10	10	11
	12	13	14	15	16	17	18
	19	20	21	22	23	24	**25**
	27	28[h]	29	30	1	2	3
PHĀLGUNA 2149	4	5	6	7	8	9	10
	11	12	13	13	14	15[i]	16
	17	**18**	20	21	22	23	24
	25	26	27	28	29	30	1[a]
CHAITRA 2150	2	3	4	5	6	7	8
	9[b]	10	11	12	13	14	15
	16	17	18	19	20	21	22
	23	25	26	27	28	29	30
	1	2	3	4	5	6	7
VAIŚĀKHA 2150	7	8	9	10	11	12	13
	14	15	**16**	18	19	20	21
	22	23	24	25	26	27	28
	29	30	1	2	3	4	5
JYAISHTHA 2150	6	7	8	9	10	11	12
	13	14	15	16	17	18	**19**
	21	22	23	24	25	26	27
	28	29	30	1	2	3	3
ĀSHĀDHA 2150	4	5	6	7	8	9	10
	11	**12**	14	15	16	17	18
	19	20	21	22	23	24	25
	26	27	28	29	30	1	2
ŚRĀVAṆA 2150	3	4	5	6	7	8	9
	10	11	12	13	**14**	16	17
	18	19	20	21	22	23[c]	24
	25	26	27	28	29	29	30
	1	2	3[d]	4	5	6	**7**
BHĀDRAPADA 2150	9	10	11	12	13	14	15
	16	17	18	19	20	21	22
	23	24	25	26	27	28	29
	30	1	2	3	4	5	6
ĀŚVINA 2150	7	8[e]	9[e]	10[e]	**11**	13	14
	15	16	17	18	19	20	21
	22	23	24	25	25	26	27
	28	29	30	1[f]	2	3	**4**
KĀRTTIKA 2150	6	7	8	9	10	11	12
	13	14	15	16	17	18	19
	20	21	22	23	24	25	26
	27	28	29	30	1	2	3
MĀRGAŚIRA 2150	4	5	6	7	8	**9**	11[g]
	12	13	14	15	16	17	18
	18	19	20	21	22	23	24
	25	26	27	28	29	30	1
PAUSHA 2150	2	**3**	5	6	7	8	9
	10	11	12	13	14	15	16

HINDU SOLAR 2014/2015

Month	Sun	Mon	Tue	Wed	Thu	Fri	Sat
PAUSHA 2014	13	14	15	16	17	18	19
	20	21	22	23	24	25	26
	27	28	29	1[b]	2	3	4
MĀGHA 2014	5	6	7	8	9	10	11
	12	13	14	15	16	17	18
	19	20	21	22	23	24	25
	26	27	28	29	30	1	2
PHĀLGUNA 2014	3	4	5	6	7	8	9
	10	11	12	13	14	15	16
	17	18	19	20	21	22	23
	24	25	26	27	28	29	30
	1	2	3	4	5	6	7
CHAITRA 2014	8	9	10	11	12	13	14
	15	16	17	18	19	20	21
	22	23	24	25	26	27	28
	29	30	1[a]	2	3	4	5
VAIŚĀKHA 2015	6	7	8	9	10	11	12
	13	14	15	16	17	18	19
	20	21	22	23	24	25	26
	27	28	29	30	31	1	2
JYAISHTHA 2015	3	4	5	6	7	8	9
	10	11	12	13	14	15	16
	17	18	19	20	21	22	23
	24	25	26	27	28	29	30
	31	1	2	3	4	5	6
ĀSHĀDHA 2015	7	8	9	10	11	12	13
	14	15	16	17	18	19	20
	21	22	23	24	25	26	27
	28	29	30	31	32	1	2
ŚRĀVAṆA 2015	3	4	5	6	7	8	9
	10	11	12	13	14	15	16
	17	18	19	20	21	22	23
	24	25	26	27	28	29	30
	31	32	1	2	3	4	5
BHĀDRAPADA 2015	6	7	8	9	10	11	12
	13	14	15	16	17	18	19
	20	21	22	23	24	25	26
	27	28	29	30	31	1	2
ĀŚVINA 2015	3	4	5	6	7	8	9
	10	11	12	13	14	15	16
	17	18	19	20	21	22	23
	24	25	26	27	28	29	30
	1	2	3	4	5	6	7
KĀRTTIKA 2015	8	9	10	11	12	13	14
	15	16	17	18	19	20	21
	22	23	24	25	26	27	28
	29	30	1	2	3	4	5
MĀRGAŚIRA 2015	6	7	8	9	10	11	12
	13	14	15	16	17	18	19
	20	21	22	23	24	25	26
	27	28	29	1	2	3	4
PAUSHA 2015	5	6	7	8	9	10	11
	12	13	14	15	16	17	18

ISLAMIC (ASTRONOMICAL) 1516/1517

Month	Sun	Mon	Tue	Wed	Thu	Fri	Sat
	29	30	1	2	3	4	5
SHA'BĀN 1516	6	7	8	9	10	11	12
	13	14	15	16	17	18	19
	20	21	22	23	24	25	26
	27	28	29	1[e]	2	3	4
RAMAḌĀN 1516	5	6	7	8	9	10	11
	12	13	14	15	16	17	18
	19	20	21	22	23	24	25
	26	27	28	29	30	1[f]	2
SHAWWĀL 1516	3	4	5	6	7	8	9
	10	11	12	13	14	15	16
	17	18	19	20	21	22	23
	24	25	26	27	28	29	1
DHU AL-QA'DA 1516	2	3	4	5	6	7	8
	9	10	11	12	13	14	15
	16	17	18	19	20	21	22
	23	24	25	26	27	28	29
	30	1	2	3	4	5	6
DHU AL-HIJJA 1516	7	8	9	10[g]	11	12	13
	14	15	16	17	18	19	20
	21	22	23	24	25	26	27
	28	29	30	1[a]	2	3	4
MUHARRAM 1517	5	6	7	8	9	10[b]	11
	12	13	14	15	16	17	18
	19	20	21	22	23	24	25
	26	27	28	29	1	2	3
ṢAFAR 1517	4	5	6	7	8	9	10
	11	12	13	14	15	16	17
	18	19	20	21	22	23	24
	25	26	27	28	29	30	1
RABĪ' I 1517	2	3	4	5	6	7	8
	9	10	11	12[c]	13	14	15
	16	17	18	19	20	21	22
	23	24	25	26	27	28	29
	1	2	3	4	5	6	7
RABĪ' II 1517	8	9	10	11	12	13	14
	15	16	17	18	19	20	21
	22	23	24	25	26	27	28
	29	30	1	2	3	4	5
JUMĀDĀ I 1517	6	7	8	9	10	11	12
	13	14	15	16	17	18	19
	20	21	22	23	24	25	26
	27	28	29	30	1	2	3
JUMĀDĀ II 1517	4	5	6	7	8	9	10
	11	12	13	14	15	16	17
	18	19	20	21	22	23	24
	25	26	27	28	29	1	2
RAJAB 1517	3	4	5	6	7	8	9
	10	11	12	13	14	15	16
	17	18	19	20	21	22	23
	24	25	26	27[d]	28	29	30
	1	2	3	4	5	6	7
SHA'BĀN 1517	8	9	10	11	12	13	14

GREGORIAN 2093

Julian (Sun)	Sun	Mon	Tue	Wed	Thu	Fri	Sat	Month
Dec 15	28	29	30	31	1	2	3	
	4	5	6	7[a]	8	9	10	JANUARY 2093
Dec 29	11	12	13	14[b]	15	16	17	
	18	19	20	21	22	23	24	
Jan 12	25	26	27	28	29	30	31	
	1	2	3	4	5	6	7	
Jan 26	8	9	10	11	12	13	14	FEBRUARY 2093
	15	16	17	18	19	20	21	
Feb 9	22	23	24	25[c]	26	27	28	
	1	2	3	4	5	6	7	
Feb 23	8[d]	9	10	11	12	13	14	MARCH 2093
	15	16	17	18	19	20	21	
Mar 9	22	23	24	25	26	27	28	
	29	30	31	1	2	3	4	
Mar 23	5	6	7	8	9	10	11	APRIL 2093
	12[e]	13	14	15	16	17	18	
Apr 6	19[f]	20	21	22	23	24	25	
	26	27	28	29	30	1	2	
Apr 20	3	4	5	6	7	8	9	MAY 2093
	10	11	12	13	14	15	16	
May 4	17	18	19	20	21	22	23	
	24	25	26	27	28	29	30	
May 18	31	1	2	3	4	5	6	
	7	8	9	10	11	12	13	JUNE 2093
Jun 1	14	15	16	17	18	19	20	
	21	22	23	24	25	26	27	
Jun 15	28	29	30	1	2	3	4	
	5	6	7	8	9	10	11	JULY 2093
Jun 29	12	13	14	15	16	17	18	
	19	20	21	22	23	24	25	
Jul 13	26	27	28	29	30	31	1	
	2	3	4	5	6	7	8	
Jul 27	9	10	11	12	13	14	15	AUGUST 2093
	16	17	18	19	20	21	22	
Aug 10	23	24	25	26	27	28	29	
	30	31	1	2	3	4	5	
Aug 24	6	7	8	9	10	11	12	SEPTEMBER 2093
	13	14	15	16	17	18	19	
Sep 7	20	21	22	23	24	25	26	
	27	28	29	30	1	2	3	
Sep 21	4	5	6	7	8	9	10	OCTOBER 2093
	11	12	13	14	15	16	17	
Oct 5	18	19	20	21	22	23	24	
	25	26	27	28	29	30	31	
Oct 19	1	2	3	4	5	6	7	
	8	9	10	11	12	13	14	NOVEMBER 2093
Nov 2	15	16	17	18	19	20	21	
	22	23	24	25	26	27	28	
Nov 16	29[g]	30	1	2	3	4	5	
	6	7	8	9	10	11	12	DECEMBER 2093
Nov 30	13	14	15	16	17	18	19	
	20	21	22	23	24	25[h]	26	
Dec 14	27	28	29	30	31	1	2	

Persian: [a]New Year; [b]Sizdeh Bedar

Hindu Lunar: [a]New Year (Pramādin); [b]Birthday of Rāma; [c]Birthday of Krishna; [d]Ganēśa Chaturthī; [e]Dashara; [f]Diwali; [g]Birthday of Vishnu; [h]Night of Śiva; [i]Holi

Hindu Solar: [a]New Year (Prabhava); [b]Pongal

Islamic: [a]New Year; [b]'Ashūrā'; [c]Prophet's Birthday; [d]Ascent of the Prophet; [e]Start of Ramaḍān; [f]'Īd al-Fiṭr; [g]'Īd al-'Aḍḥā

Gregorian: [a]Orthodox Christmas; [b]Julian New Year; [c]Ash Wednesday; [d]Feast of Orthodoxy; [e]Easter; [f]Orthodox Easter; [g]Advent; [h]Christmas

2094

Gregorian month	Sun	Mon	Tue	Wed	Thu	Fri	Sat	Lunar Phases	ISO WEEK (Mon)	JULIAN DAY (Sun noon)	Hebrew month	Sun	Mon	Tue	Wed	Thu	Fri	Sat	Molad	Chinese month	Sun	Mon	Tue	Wed	Thu	Fri	Sat	Solar Term	Coptic month	Sun	Mon	Tue	Wed	Thu	Fri	Sat	Ethiopic month
GREGORIAN 2094											HEBREW 5854/5855‡									CHINESE Guǐ-Chǒu‡/Jiǎ-Yín									COPTIC 1810/1811‡								ETHIOPIC 2086/2087‡
JANUARY 2094	27	28	29	30	31	○[a]	2	16:50	53	2485874	TEVETH 5854	8	9	10	11	12	13	14		MONTH 11* Guǐ-Chǒu	10	11	12	13	14	15	16		KOIAK 1810	18	19	20	21	22	23	24	TĀKHŚĀŚ 2086
	3	4	5	6	7	8	◑	21:35	1	2485881		15	16	17	18	19	20	21			17	18	19	20	21	22	23	Xiǎo hán	TŌBE 1810	25	26	27	28	29[c]	30	1	TER 2086
	10	11	12	13	14	15	●	19:04	2	2485888		22	23	24	25	26	27	28			24	25	26	27	28	29	30			2	3	4	5	6[d]	7	8	
	17	18	19	20	21	22	◐	11:32	3	2485895	SHEVAT 5854	29	1	2	3	4	5	6	Sat 20h37m6p	MONTH 12 Guǐ-Chǒu	1	2	3	4	5	6	7	Dà hán		9	10	11[e]	12	13	14	15	
	24	25	26	27	28	29	30		4	2485902		7	8	9	10	11	12	13			8	9	10	11	12	13	14			16	17	18	19	20	21	22	
FEBRUARY 2094	○	1	2	3	4	5	6	12:36	5	2485909		14	15	16	17	18	19	20			15	16	17	18	19	20	21	Lì chūn		23	24	25	26	27	28	29	
	7	◑	9	10	11	12	13	12:44	6	2485916		21	22	23	24	25	26	27			22	23	24	25	26	27	28		MESHIR 1810	30	1	2	3	4	5	6	YAKĀTIT 2086
	14	●	16	17	18	19	20	5:42	7	2485923	ADAR 5854	28	29	30	1	2	3	4	Mon 9h21m7p	MONTH 1 Jiǎ-Yín	29	1[a]	2	3	4	5	6	Yǔ shuǐ		7	8	9	10	11	12	13	
	21	◐	23	24	25	26	27	2:35	8	2485930		5	6	7	8	9	10	11			7	8*	9	10	11	12	13			14	15	16	17	18	19	20	
MARCH 2094	28	1	○	3	4	5	6	7:34	9	2485937		12	13	14[f]	15	16	17	18			14	15[b]	16	17	18	19	20	Jīng zhé		21	22	23	24	25	26	27	
	7	8	9	◑	11	12	13	0:21	10	2485944		19	20	21	22	23	24	25			21	22	23	24	25	26	27		PAREMOTEP 1810	28	29	30	1	2	3	4	MAGĀBIT 2086
	14	15	●	17	18	19	20[b]	15:43	11	2485951	NISAN 5854	26	27	28	29	1	2	3	Tue 22h5m8p	MONTH 2 Jiǎ-Yín	28	29	1	2	3	4	5	Chūn fēn		5	6	7	8	9	10	11	
	21	22	◐	24	25	26	27	20:04	12	2485958		4	5	6	7	8	9	10			6	7	8	9	10	11	12			12	13	14	15	16	17	18	
APRIL 2094	28	29	30	31	○	2	3	0:10	13	2485965		11	12	13	14	15[g]	16	17			13	14	15	16	17	18	19			19	20	21	22	23	24	25	
	4	5	6	7	◑	9	10	8:45	14	2485972		18	19	20	21	22	23	24			20[c]	21	22	23	24	25	26	Qīng míng	PARMOUTE 1810	26	27	28	29	30	1	2	MIYĀZYĀ 2086
	11	12	13	14	●	16	17	1:36	15	2485979	IYYAR 5854	25	26	27	28	29	30	1	Thu 10h49m9p	MONTH 3 Jiǎ-Yín	27	28	29	30	1	2	3			3[f]	4	5	6	7	8	9	
	18	19	20	21	◐	23	24	14:47	16	2485986		2	3	4	5	6	7	8			4	5	6	7	8	9*	10	Gǔ yǔ		10	11	12	13	14	15	16	
MAY 2094	25	26	27	28	29	○	1	13:53	17	2485993		9	10	11	12	13	14	15			11	12	13	14	15	16	17			17	18	19	20	21	22	23	
	2	3	4	5	6	◑	8	14:46	18	2486000		16	17	18	19	20	21	22			18	19	20	21	22	23	24	Lì xià		24	25	26	27	28	29[g]	30	
	9	10	11	12	13	●	15	12:08	19	2486007		23	24	25	26	27	28	29		MONTH 4 Jiǎ-Yín	25	26	27	28	29	1	2		PASHONS 1810	1	2	3	4	5	6	7	GENBOT 2086
	16	17	18	19	20	21	◐	9:15	20	2486014	SIVAN 5854	1	2	3	4	5	6[h]	7	Fri 23h33m10p		3	4	5	6	7	8	9	Xiǎo mǎn		8	9	10	11	12	13	14	
	23	24	25	26	27	28	29		21	2486021		8	9	10	11	12	13	14			10	11	12	13	14	15	16			15	16	17	18	19	20	21	
JUNE 2094	○	31	1	2	3	4	◑	0:57 19:40	22	2486028		15	16	17	18	19	20	21			17	18	19	20	21	22	23	Máng zhòng		22	23	24	25	26	27	28	
	6	7	8	9	10	11	12		23	2486035		22	23	24	25	26	27	28			24	25	26	27	28	29	30		PAŌNE 1810	29	30	1	2	3	4	5	SANĒ 2086
	●	14	15	16	17	18	19	0:02	24	2486042	TAMMUZ 5854	29	30	1	2	3	4	5	Sun -2h17m11p	MONTH 5 Jiǎ-Yín	1	2	3	4	5[d]	6	7			6	7	8	9	10	11	12	
	20[c]	◐	22	23	24	25	26	2:18	25	2486049		6	7	8	9	10	11	12			8	9	10*	11	12	13	14	Xià zhì		13	14	15	16	17	18	19	
JULY 2094	27	○	29	30	1	2	3	9:57	26	2486056		13	14	15	16	17	18	19			15	16	17	18	19	20	21			20	21	22	23	24	25	26	
	4	◑	6	7	8	9	10	0:53	27	2486063		20	21	22	23	24	25	26			22	23	24	25	26	27	28	Xiǎo shǔ	EPĒP 1810	27	28	29	30	1	2	3	HAMLĒ 2086
	11	●	13	14	15	16	17	13:36	28	2486070	AV 5854	27	28	29	1	2	3	4	Tue 1h1m12p	MONTH 6 Jiǎ-Yín	29	1	2	3	4	5	6			4	5	6	7	8	9	10	
	18	19	◐	21	22	23	24	17:24	29	2486077		5	6	7	8	9[i]	10	11			7	8	9	10	11	12	13	Dà shǔ		11	12	13	14	15	16	17	
	25	26	○	28	29	30	31	17:38	30	2486084		12	13	14	15	16	17	18			14	15	16	17	18	19	20			18	19	20	21	22	23	24	
AUGUST 2094	1	2	◑	4	5	6	7	7:56	31	2486091		19	20	21	22	23	24	25			21	22	23	24	25	26	27	Lì qiū	MESORĒ 1810	25	26	27	28	29	30	1	NAHASĒ 2086
	8	9	10	●	12	13	14	4:36	32	2486098	ELUL 5854	26	27	28	29	30	1	2	Wed 13h45m13p	MONTH 7 Jiǎ-Yín	28	29	30	1	2	3	4			2	3	4	5	6	7	8	
	15	16	17	18	◐	20	21	6:25	33	2486105		3	4	5	6	7	8	9			5	6	7[e]	8	9	10	11*			9	10	11	12	13[h]	14	15	
	22	23	24	25	○	27	28	0:50	34	2486112		10	11	12	13	14	15	16			12	13	14	15[f]	16	17	18	Chǔ shǔ		16	17	18	19	20	21	22	
SEPTEMBER 2094	29	30	31	◑	2	3	4	18:08	35	2486119		17	18	19	20	21	22	23			19	20	21	22	23	24	25			23	24	25	26	27	28	29	
	5	6	7	8	●	10	11	20:30	36	2486126		24	25	26	27	28	29	1[a]	Fri 2h29m14p	MONTH 8 Jiǎ-Yín	26	27	28	29	30	1	2	Bái lù	EPAG. 1810	30	1	2	3	4	5	1[a]	PĀG. 2086
	12	13	14	15	16	◐	18	17:27	37	2486133	TISHRI 5855	2[a]	3	4	5	6	7	8			3	4	5	6	7	8	9		THOOUT 1811	2	3	4	5	6	7	8	MASKARAM 2087
	19	20	21	22[d]	23	○	25	8:32	38	2486140		9	10[b]	11	12	13	14	15[c]			10	11	12	13	14	15[g]	16	Qiū fēn		9	10	11	12	13	14	15	
OCTOBER 2094	26	27	28	29	30	◑	2	8:14	39	2486147		16	17	18	19	20	21	22			17	18	19	20	21	22	23			16	17[b]	18	19	20	21	22	
	3	4	5	6	7	8	●	12:43	40	2486154		23	24	25	26	27	28	29		MONTH 9 Jiǎ-Yín	24	25	26	27	28	29	1	Hán lù		23	24	25	26	27	28	29	
	10	11	12	13	14	15	16		41	2486161	ḤESHVAN 5855	30	1	2	3	4	5	6	Sat 15h13m15p		2	3	4	5	6	7	8		PAOPE 1811	30	1	2	3	4	5	6	TEQEMT 2087
	◐	18	19	20	21	22	○	2:44 17:47	42	2486168		7	8	9	10	11	12	13			9[h]	10	11	12*	13	14	15	Shuāng jiàng		7	8	9	10	11	12	13	
	24	25	26	27	28	29	30		43	2486175		14	15	16	17	18	19	20			16	17	18	19	20	21	22			14	15	16	17	18	19	20	
NOVEMBER 2094	◑	1	2	3	4	5	6	2:08	44	2486182		21	22	23	24	25	26	27			23	24	25	26	27	28	29			21	22	23	24	25	26	27	
	7	●	9	10	11	12	13	4:41	45	2486189	KISLEV 5855	28	29	1	2	3	4	5	Mon 3h57m16p	MONTH 10 Jiǎ-Yín	30	1	2	3	4	5	6	Lì dōng	ATHŌR 1811	28	29	30	1	2	3	4	HEDĀR 2087
	14	◐	16	17	18	19	20	10:43	46	2486196		6	7	8	9	10	11	12			7	8	9	10	11	12	13			5	6	7	8	9	10	11	
	21	○	23	24	25	26	27	5:26	47	2486203		13	14	15	16	17	18	19			14	15	16	17	18	19	20	Xiǎo xuě		12	13	14	15	16	17	18	
DECEMBER 2094	28	◑	30	1	2	3	4	22:47	48	2486210		20	21	22	23	24	25[e]	26[e]			21	22	23	24	25	26	27			19	20	21	22	23	24	25	
	5	6	●	8	9	10	11	19:49	49	2486217	TEVETH 5855	27[d,e]	28[e]	29[e]	1[e]	2[e]	3[e]	4	Tue 16h41m17p	MONTH 11 Jiǎ-Yín	28	29	30	1	2	3	4	Dà xuě	KOIAK 1811	26	27	28	29	30	1	2	TĀKHŚĀŚ 2087
	12	13	◐	15	16	17	18	18:16	50	2486224		5	6	7	8	9	10	11			5	6	7	8	9	10	11			3	4	5	6	7	8	9	
	19	20	○[e]	22	23	24	25	19:55	51	2486231		12	13	14	15	16	17	18			12*	13	14[i]	15	16	17	18	Dōng zhì		10	11	12	13	14	15	16	
	26	27	28	◑	30	31	1	20:26	52	2486238		19	20	21	22	23	24	25			19	20	21	22	23	24	25			17	18	19	20	21	22	23	

[a]New Year
[b]Spring (2:20)
[c]Summer (18:41)
[d]Autumn (11:15)
[e]Winter (9:12)
● New moon
◐ First quarter moon
○ Full moon
◑ Last quarter moon

‡Leap year
[a]New Year
[b]Yom Kippur
[c]Sukkot
[d]Winter starts
[e]Ḥanukkah
[f]Purim
[g]Passover
[h]Shavuot
[i]Fast of Av

‡Leap year
[a]New Year (4792, Tiger)
[b]Lantern Festival
[c]Qīngmíng
[d]Dragon Festival
[e]Qīqiǎo
[f]Hungry Ghosts
[g]Mid-Autumn Festival
[h]Double-Ninth Festival
[i]Dōngzhì
*Start of 60-name cycle

‡Leap year
[a]New Year
[b]Building of the Cross
[c]Christmas
[d]Jesus's Circumcision
[e]Epiphany
[f]Easter
[g]Mary's Announcement
[h]Jesus's Transfiguration

2094

PERSIAN (ASTRONOMICAL) 1472/1473

Month	Sun	Mon	Tue	Wed	Thu	Fri	Sat
DEY 1472	7	8	9	10	11	12	13
	14	15	16	17	18	19	20
	21	22	23	24	25	26	27
	28	29	30	1	2	3	4
BAHMAN 1472	5	6	7	8	9	10	11
	12	13	14	15	16	17	18
	19	20	21	22	23	24	25
	26	27	28	29	30	1	2
ESFAND 1472	3	4	5	6	7	8	9
	10	11	12	13	14	15	16
	17	18	19	20	21	22	23
	24	25	26	27	28	29	1[a]
FARVARDĪN 1473	2	3	4	5	6	7	8
	9	10	11	12	13[b]	14	15
	16	17	18	19	20	21	22
	23	24	25	26	27	28	29
	30	31	1	2	3	4	5
ORDĪBEHEŠT 1473	6	7	8	9	10	11	12
	13	14	15	16	17	18	19
	20	21	22	23	24	25	26
	27	28	29	30	31	1	2
XORDĀD 1473	3	4	5	6	7	8	9
	10	11	12	13	14	15	16
	17	18	19	20	21	22	23
	24	25	26	27	28	29	30
	31	1	2	3	4	5	6
TĪR 1473	7	8	9	10	11	12	13
	14	15	16	17	18	19	20
	21	22	23	24	25	26	27
	28	29	30	31	1	2	3
MORDĀD 1473	4	5	6	7	8	9	10
	11	12	13	14	15	16	17
	18	19	20	21	22	23	24
	25	26	27	28	29	30	31
SHAHRĪVAR 1473	1	2	3	4	5	6	7
	8	9	10	11	12	13	14
	15	16	17	18	19	20	21
	22	23	24	25	26	27	28
	29	30	31	1	2	3	4
MEHR 1473	5	6	7	8	9	10	11
	12	13	14	15	16	17	18
	19	20	21	22	23	24	25
	26	27	28	29	30	1	2
ĀBĀN 1473	3	4	5	6	7	8	9
	10	11	12	13	14	15	16
	17	18	19	20	21	22	23
	24	25	26	27	28	29	30
ĀZAR 1473	1	2	3	4	5	6	7
	8	9	10	11	12	13	14
	15	16	17	18	19	20	21
	22	23	24	25	26	27	28
	29	30	1	2	3	4	5
DEY 1473	6	7	8	9	10	11	12

[a]New Year
[b]Sizdeh Bedar

HINDU LUNAR 2150/2151‡

Month	Sun	Mon	Tue	Wed	Thu	Fri	Sat
PAUSHA 2150	10	11	12	13	14	15	16
	17	18	19	20	20	21	22
	23	24	25	**26**	28	29	30
MĀGHA 2150	1	2	3	4	5	6	7
	8	9	10	11	12	13	14
	15	16	17	18	19	20	21
	22	23	24	25	26	27	28[h]
	29	30	1	**2**	4	5	6
PHĀLGUNA 2150	7	8	9	10	11	12	13
	13	14	15[i]	16	17	18	19
	20	21	22	23	24	25	**26**
	28	29	30	1[a]	2	3	4
CHAITRA 2151	5	6	7	8	9[b]	10	11
	12	13	14	15	16	17	17
	19	20	21	22	23	24	25
	26	27	28	29	**30**	2	3
LEAP VAIŚĀKHA 2151	4	5	6	6	7	8	9
	10	11	12	13	14	15	16
	17	18	19	20	21	22	**23**
	25	26	27	28	29	30	1
VAIŚĀKHA 2151	2	3	4	5	6	7	8
	9	10	11	11	12	13	14
	15	17	18	19	20	21	22
	23	24	25	26	**27**	29	30
	1	2	2	3	4	5	6
JYAISHṬHA 2151	7	8	9	10	11	12	13
	14	15	16	17	18	**19**	21
	22	23	24	25	26	27	28
	29	30	1	2	3	4	5
ĀSHĀḌHA 2151	6	7	8	8	9	**10**	12
	13	14	15	16	17	18	19
	20	21	**22**	24	25	26	27
	28	29	29	30	1	2	3
ŚRĀVAṆA 2151	4	5	6	7	8	9	10
	11	12	13	14	**15**	17	18
	19	20	21	22	23[c]	24	25
	26	27	28	29	30	1	2
BHĀDRAPADA 2151	3	4[d]	4	5	**6**	8	9
	10	11	12	13	14	15	16
	17	18	**19**	21	22	23	24
	25	25	26	27	28	29	30
ĀŚVINA 2151	1	2	3	4	5	6	7
	8[e]	9[e]	10[e]	**11**	13	14	15
	16	17	18	19	20	21	22
	23	24	25	26	27	28	28
	29	30	1[f]	2	3	4	**5**
KĀRTTIKA 2151	7	8	9	10	11	12	13
	14	15	16	17	18	19	20
	21	22	23	24	25	26	27
	28	29	30	1	2	3	4
MĀRGAŚĪRA 2151	5	6	7	8	9	**10**[g]	12
	13	14	15	16	17	18	19
	20	21	21	22	23	24	25

‡Leap year
[a]New Year (Ānanda)
[b]Birthday of Rāma
[c]Birthday of Krishna
[d]Ganēśa Chaturthī
[e]Dashara
[f]Diwali
[g]Birthday of Vishnu
[h]Night of Śiva
[i]Holi

HINDU SOLAR 2015/2016‡

Month	Sun	Mon	Tue	Wed	Thu	Fri	Sat
PAUSHA 2015	12	13	14	15	16	17	18
	19	20	21	22	23	24	25
	26	27	28	29	30	1[b]	2
MĀGHA 2015	3	4	5	6	7	8	9
	10	11	12	13	14	15	16
	17	18	19	20	21	22	23
	24	25	26	27	28	29	1
PHĀLGUNA 2015	2	3	4	5	6	7	8
	9	10	11	12	13	14	15
	16	17	18	19	20	21	22
	23	24	25	26	27	28	29
	30	1	2	3	4	5	6
CHAITRA 2015	7	8	9	10	11	12	13
	14	15	16	17	18	19	20
	21	22	23	24	25	26	27
	28	29	30	1[a]	2	3	4
VAIŚĀKHA 2016	5	6	7	8	9	10	11
	12	13	14	15	16	17	18
	19	20	21	22	23	24	25
	26	27	28	29	30	31	1
JYAISHṬHA 2016	2	3	4	5	6	7	8
	9	10	11	12	13	14	15
	16	17	18	19	20	21	22
	23	24	25	26	27	28	29
	30	31	32	1	2	3	4
ĀSHĀḌHA 2016	5	6	7	8	9	10	11
	12	13	14	15	16	17	18
	19	20	21	22	23	24	25
	26	27	28	29	30	31	1
ŚRĀVAṆA 2016	2	3	4	5	6	7	8
	9	10	11	12	13	14	15
	16	17	18	19	20	21	22
	23	24	25	26	27	28	29
	30	31	32	1	2	3	4
BHĀDRAPADA 2016	5	6	7	8	9	10	11
	12	13	14	15	16	17	18
	19	20	21	22	23	24	25
	26	27	28	29	30	31	1
ĀŚVINA 2016	2	3	4	5	6	7	8
	9	10	11	12	13	14	15
	16	17	18	19	20	21	22
	23	24	25	26	27	28	29
	30	1	2	3	4	5	6
KĀRTTIKA 2016	7	8	9	10	11	12	13
	14	15	16	17	18	19	20
	21	22	23	24	25	26	27
	28	29	30	1	2	3	4
MĀRGAŚĪRA 2016	5	6	7	8	9	10	11
	12	13	14	15	16	17	18
	19	20	21	22	23	24	25
	26	27	28	29	30	1	2
PAUSHA 2016	3	4	5	6	7	8	9
	10	11	12	13	14	15	16

‡Leap year
[a]New Year (Vibhava)
[b]Pongal

ISLAMIC (ASTRONOMICAL) 1517/1518

Month	Sun	Mon	Tue	Wed	Thu	Fri	Sat
SHA'BĀN 1517	8	9	10	11	12	13	14
	15	16	17	18	19	20	21
	22	23	24	25	26	27	28
	29	1[e]	2	3	4	5	6
RAMAḌĀN 1517	7	8	9	10	11	12	13
	14	15	16	17	18	19	20
	21	22	23	24	25	26	27
	28	29	1[f]	2	3	4	5
SHAWWĀL 1517	6	7	8	9	10	11	12
	13	14	15	16	17	18	19
	20	21	22	23	24	25	26
	27	28	29	30	1	2	3
DHU AL-QA'DA 1517	4	5	6	7	8	9	10
	11	12	13	14	15	16	17
	18	19	20	21	22	23	24
	25	26	27	28	29	1	2
DHU AL-HIJJA 1517	3	4	5	6	7	8	9
	10[g]	11	12	13	14	15	16
	17	18	19	20	21	22	23
	24	25	26	27	28	29	30
MUHARRAM 1518	1[a]	2	3	4	5	6	7
	8	9	10[b]	11	12	13	14
	15	16	17	18	19	20	21
	22	23	24	25	26	27	28
	29	1	2	3	4	5	6
SAFAR 1518	7	8	9	10	11	12	13
	14	15	16	17	18	19	20
	21	22	23	24	25	26	27
	28	29	30	1	2	3	4
RABĪ' I 1518	5	6	7	8	9	10	11
	12[c]	13	14	15	16	17	18
	19	20	21	22	23	24	25
	26	27	28	29	1	2	3
RABĪ' II 1518	4	5	6	7	8	9	10
	11	12	13	14	15	16	17
	18	19	20	21	22	23	24
	25	26	27	28	29	30	1
JUMĀDĀ I 1518	2	3	4	5	6	7	8
	9	10	11	12	13	14	15
	16	17	18	19	20	21	22
	23	24	25	26	27	28	29
	30	1	2	3	4	5	6
JUMĀDĀ II 1518	7	8	9	10	11	12	13
	14	15	16	17	18	19	20
	21	22	23	24	25	26	27
	28	29	30	1	2	3	4
RAJAB 1518	5	6	7	8	9	10	11
	12	13	14	15	16	17	18
	19	20	21	22	23	24	25
	26	27[d]	28	29	1	2	3
SHA'BĀN 1518	4	5	6	7	8	9	10
	11	12	13	14	15	16	17
	18	19	20	21	22	23	24

[a]New Year
[b]'Ashūrā'
[c]Prophet's Birthday
[d]Ascent of the Prophet
[e]Start of Ramaḍān
[f]'Id al-Fiṭr
[g]'Id al-'Aḍḥā

GREGORIAN 2094

Julian (Sun)	Sun	Mon	Tue	Wed	Thu	Fri	Sat	Month
Dec 14	27	28	29	30	31	1	2	JANUARY 2094
	3	4	5	6	7[a]	8	9	
Dec 28	10	11	12	13	14[b]	15	16	
	17	18	19	20	21	22	23	
Jan 11	24	25	26	27	28	29	30	
	31	1	2	3	4	5	6	FEBRUARY 2094
Jan 25	7	8	9	10	11	12	13	
	14	15	16	17[c]	18	19	20	
Feb 8	21	22	23	24	25	26	27	
	28[d]	1	2	3	4	5	6	MARCH 2094
Feb 22	7	8	9	10	11	12	13	
	14	15	16	17	18	19	20	
Mar 8	21	22	23	24	25	26	27	
	28	29	30	31	1	2	3	APRIL 2094
Mar 22	4[e]	5	6	7	8	9	10	
	11[f]	12	13	14	15	16	17	
Apr 5	18	19	20	21	22	23	24	
	25	26	27	28	29	30	1	MAY 2094
Apr 19	2	3	4	5	6	7	8	
	9	10	11	12	13	14	15	
May 3	16	17	18	19	20	21	22	
	23	24	25	26	27	28	29	
May 17	30	31	1	2	3	4	5	JUNE 2094
	6	7	8	9	10	11	12	
May 31	13	14	15	16	17	18	19	
	20	21	22	23	24	25	26	
Jun 14	27	28	29	30	1	2	3	JULY 2094
	4	5	6	7	8	9	10	
Jun 28	11	12	13	14	15	16	17	
	18	19	20	21	22	23	24	
Jul 12	25	26	27	28	29	30	31	
	1	2	3	4	5	6	7	AUGUST 2094
Jul 26	8	9	10	11	12	13	14	
	15	16	17	18	19	20	21	
Aug 9	22	23	24	25	26	27	28	
	29	30	31	1	2	3	4	SEPTEMBER 2094
Aug 23	5	6	7	8	9	10	11	
	12	13	14	15	16	17	18	
Sep 6	19	20	21	22	23	24	25	
	26	27	28	29	30	1	2	OCTOBER 2094
Sep 20	3	4	5	6	7	8	9	
	10	11	12	13	14	15	16	
Oct 4	17	18	19	20	21	22	23	
	24	25	26	27	28	29	30	
Oct 18	31	1	2	3	4	5	6	NOVEMBER 2094
	7	8	9	10	11	12	13	
Nov 1	14	15	16	17	18	19	20	
	21	22	23	24	25	26	27	
Nov 15	28[g]	29	30	1	2	3	4	DECEMBER 2094
	5	6	7	8	9	10	11	
Nov 29	12	13	14	15	16	17	18	
	19	20	21	22	23	24	25[h]	
Dec 13	26	27	28	29	30	31	1	

[a]Orthodox Christmas
[b]Julian New Year
[c]Ash Wednesday
[d]Feast of Orthodoxy
[e]Easter
[f]Orthodox Easter
[g]Advent
[h]Christmas

2095

Gregorian 2095	Sun	Mon	Tue	Wed	Thu	Fri	Sat	Lunar Phases	ISO Week (Mon)	Julian Day (Sun noon)	Hebrew 5855‡/5856	Sun	Mon	Tue	Wed	Thu	Fri	Sat	Molad	Chinese Jiă-Yín/Yĭ-Măo	Sun	Mon	Tue	Wed	Thu	Fri	Sat	Solar Term	Coptic 1811‡/1812	Sun	Mon	Tue	Wed	Thu	Fri	Sat	Ethiopic 2087‡/2088
	26	27	28	◑	30	31	1[a]	20:26	52	2486238	Tevet 5855	19	20	21	22	23	24	25		Month 11 Jiă-Yín	19	20	21	22	23	24	25		Koiak 1811	17	18	19	20	21	22	23	Tākhśāś 2087
	2	3	4	5	●	7	8	9:32	1	2486245		26	27	28	29	1	2	3	Thu 5h26m0p	Month 12 Jiă-Yín	26	27	28	29	1	2	3	Xiǎo hán		24	25	26	27	28	29[c]	30	
January 2095	9	10	11	12	◐	14	15	2:27	2	2486252		4	5	6	7	8	9	10			4	5	6	7	8	9	10			1	2	3	4	5	6[d]	7	
	16	17	18	19	○	21	22	12:47	3	2486259	Shevat 5855	11	12	13	14	15	16	17			11	12	13	14	15	16	17	Dà hán	Tōbe 1811	8	9	10	11[e]	12	13	14	Ṭer 2087
	23	24	25	26	27	◑	29	17:06	4	2486266		18	19	20	21	22	23	24			18	19	20	21	22	23	24			15	16	17	18	19	20	21	
	30	31	1	2	3	●	5	21:27	5	2486273		25	26	27	28	29	30	1	Fri 18h10m1p		25	26	27	28	29	30	1[a]	Lì chūn		22	23	24	25	26	27	28	
February 2095	6	7	8	9	10	◐	12	12:16	6	2486280	Adar I 5855	2	3	4	5	6	7	8		Month 1 Yĭ-Măo	2	3	4	5	6	7	8			29	30	1	2	3	4	5	
	13	14	15	16	17	18	○	6:58	7	2486287		9	10	11	12	13	14	15			9	10	11	12	13*	14	15[b]	Yǔ shuǐ	Meshir 1811	6	7	8	9	10	11	12	
	20	21	22	23	24	25	26		8	2486294		16	17	18	19	20	21	22			16	17	18	19	20	21	22			13	14	15	16	17	18	19	Yakātit 2087
	◑	28	1	2	3	4	5	10:57	9	2486301		23	24	25	26	27	28	29			23	24	25	26	27	28	29	Jīng zhé		20	21	22	23	24	25	26	
March 2095	●	7	8	9	10	11	12	7:38	10	2486308		30	1	2	3	4	5	6	Sun 6h54m2p		1	2	3	4	5	6	7			27	28	29	30	1	2	3	
	◐	14	15	16	17	18	19	0:17	11	2486315	Adar II 5855	7	8	9	10	11	12	13		Month 2 Yĭ-Măo	8	9	10	11	12	13	14		Paremotep 1811	4	5	6	7	8	9	10	
	20[b]	○	22	23	24	25	26	1:09	12	2486322		14[f]	15	16	17	18	19	20			15	16	17	18	19	20	21	Chūn fēn		11	12	13	14	15	16	17	Magābit 2087
	27	28	◑	30	31	1	2	0:53	13	2486329		21	22	23	24	25	26	27			22	23	24	25	26	27	28			18	19	20	21	22	23	24	
April 2095	3	●	5	6	7	8	9	16:35	14	2486336		28	29	1	2	3	4	5	Mon 19h38m3p		29	30[c]	1	2	3	4	5	Qīng míng		25	26	27	28	29	30	1	
	10	◐	12	13	14	15	16	14:26	15	2486343		6	7	8	9	10	11	12		Month 3 Yĭ-Măo	6	7	8	9	10	11	12		Parmoute 1811	2	3	4	5	6	7	8	
	17	18	○	20	21	22	23	18:13	16	2486350	Nisan 5855	13	14	15[g]	16	17	18	19			13	14*	15	16	17	18	19	Gǔ yǔ		9	10	11	12	13	14	15	Miyāzyā 2087
	24	25	26	◑	28	29	30	10:44	17	2486357		20	21	22	23	24	25	26			20	21	22	23	24	25	26			16[f]	17	18	19	20	21	22	
	1	2	3	●	5	6	7	1:05	18	2486364		27	28	29	30	1	2	3	Wed 8h22m4p		27	28	29	1	2	3	4	Lì xià		23	24	25	26	27	28	29[g]	
May 2095	8	9	10	◐	12	13	14	6:13	19	2486371		4	5	6	7	8	9	10		Month 4 Yĭ-Măo	5	6	7	8	9	10	11			30	1	2	3	4	5	6	
	15	16	17	18	○	20	21	9:20	20	2486378	Iyar 5855	11	12	13	14	15	16	17			12	13	14	15	16	17	18	Xiǎo mǎn	Pashons 1811	7	8	9	10	11	12	13	
	22	23	24	25	◑	27	28	17:16	21	2486385		18	19	20	21	22	23	24			19	20	21	22	23	24	25			14	15	16	17	18	19	20	Genbot 2087
	29	30	31	1	●	3	4	9:57	22	2486392		25	26	27	28	29	1	2	Thu 21h6m5p		26	27	28	29	1	2	3			21	22	23	24	25	26	27	
June 2095	5	6	7	8	◐	10	11	23:01	23	2486399		3	4	5	6[h]	7	8	9		Month 5 Yĭ-Măo	4	5[d]	6	7	8	9	10	Máng zhǒng		28	29	30	1	2	3	4	
	12	13	14	15	16	○	18	22:05	24	2486406	Sivan 5855	10	11	12	13	14	15	16			11	12	13	14	15	16*	17		Paōne 1811	5	6	7	8	9	10	11	
	19	20	21[c]	22	23	◑	25	21:54	25	2486413		17	18	19	20	21	22	23			18	19	20	21	22	23	24	Xià zhì		12	13	14	15	16	17	18	Sanē 2087
	26	27	28	29	30	●	2	19:53	26	2486420		24	25	26	27	28	29	30			25	26	27	28	29	30	1			19	20	21	22	23	24	25	
July 2095	3	4	5	6	7	8	◐	16:15	27	2486427		1	2	3	4	5	6	7	Sat 9h50m6p	Month 6 Yĭ-Măo	2	3	4	5	6	7	8	Xiǎo shǔ		26	27	28	29	30	1	2	
	10	11	12	13	14	15	16		28	2486434		8	9	10	11	12	13	14			9	10	11	12	13	14	15		Epēp 1811	3	4	5	6	7	8	9	
	○	18	19	20	21	22	23	8:30	29	2486441	Tammuz 5855	15	16	17	18	19	20	21			16	17	18	19	20	21	22	Dà shǔ		10	11	12	13	14	15	16	Ḥamlē 2087
	◑	25	26	27	28	29	30	2:16	30	2486448		22	23	24	25	26	27	28			23	24	25	26	27	28	29			17	18	19	20	21	22	23	
	●	1	2	3	4	5	6	7:28	31	2486455		29	1	2	3	4	5	6	Sun 22h34m7p		1	2	3	4	5	6	7[e]			24	25	26	27	28	29	30	
August 2095	7	◐	9	10	11	12	13	9:18	32	2486462		7	8	9[i]	10	11	12	13		Month 7 Yĭ-Măo	8	9	10	11	12	13	14	Lì qiū		1	2	3	4	5	6	7	
	14	○	16	17	18	19	20	17:12	33	2486469	Av 5855	14	15	16	17	18	19	20			15[f]	16	17*	18	19	20	21		Mesorē 1811	8	9	10	11	12	13[h]	14	Naḥasē 2087
	21	◑	23	24	25	26	27	7:55	34	2486476		21	22	23	24	25	26	27			22	23	24	25	26	27	28	Chǔ shǔ		15	16	17	18	19	20	21	
	28	●	30	31	1	2	3	21:04	35	2486483		28	29	30	1	2	3	4	Tue 11h18m8p		29	30	1	2	3	4	5			22	23	24	25	26	27	28	
September 2095	4	5	6	◐	8	9	10	1:25	36	2486490		5	6	7	8	9	10	11		Month 8 Yĭ-Măo	6	7	8	9	10	11	12	Bái lù	Epag. 1811	29	30	1	2	3	4	5	Pāg. 2087
	11	12	13	○	15	16	17	1:10	37	2486497	Elul 5855	12	13	14	15	16	17	18			13	14	15[g]	16	17	18	19			6	1[a]	2	3	4	5	6	
	18	19	◑	21	22[d]	23	24	16:14	38	2486504		19	20	21	22	23	24	25			20	21	22	23	24	25	26	Qiū fēn	Thoout 1812	7	8	9	10	11	12	13	Maskaram 2088
	25	26	27	●	29	30	1	12:53	39	2486511		26	27	28	29	1[a]	2[a]	3	Thu 0h2m9p		27	28	29	1	2	3	4			14	15	16	17[b]	18	19	20	
October 2095	2	3	4	5	◐	7	8	15:51	40	2486518		4	5	6	7	8	9	10[b]		Month 9 Yĭ-Măo	5	6	7	8	9[h]	10	11	Hán lù		21	22	23	24	25	26	27	
	9	10	11	12	○	14	15	9:30	41	2486525	Tishri 5856	11	12	13	14	15[c]	16	17			12	13	14	15	16	17	18*			28	29	30	1	2	3	4	
	16	17	18	19	◑	21	22	4:07	42	2486532		18	19	20	21	22	23	24			19	20	21	22	23	24	25		Paope 1812	5	6	7	8	9	10	11	Ṭeqemt 2088
	23	24	25	26	27	●	29	6:31	43	2486539		25	26	27	28	29	30	1	Fri 12h46m10p		26	27	28	29	30	1	2	Shuāng jiàng		12	13	14	15	16	17	18	
	30	31	1	2	3	4	◐	4:08	44	2486546		2	3	4	5	6	7	8		Month 10 Yĭ-Măo	3	4	5	6	7	8	9			19	20	21	22	23	24	25	
November 2095	6	7	8	9	10	○	12	19:04	45	2486553	Heshvan 5856	9	10	11	12	13	14	15			10	11	12	13	14	15	16	Lì dōng		26	27	28	29	30	1	2	
	13	14	15	16	17	◑	19	19:54	46	2486560		16	17	18	19	20	21	22			17	18	19	20	21	22	23		Athōr 1812	3	4	5	6	7	8	9	Ḫedār 2088
	20	21	22	23	24	25	26		47	2486567		23	24	25	26	27	28	29			24	25	26	27	28	29	30	Xiǎo xuě		10	11	12	13	14	15	16	
	●	28	29	30	1	2	3	0:53	48	2486574		1	2	3	4	5	6	7	Sun 1h30m11p		1	2	3	4	5	6	7			17	18	19	20	21	22	23	
December 2095	◐	5	6	7	8	9	10	14:20	49	2486581		8	9	10[d]	11	12	13	14		Month 11 Yĭ-Măo	8	9	10	11	12	13	14	Dà xuě		24	25	26	27	28	29	30	
	○	12	13	14	15	16	17	6:20	50	2486588	Kislev 5856	15	16	17	18	19	20	21			15	16	17	18*	19	20	21		Koiak 1812	1	2	3	4	5	6	7	
	◑	19	20	21[e]	22	23	24	15:13	51	2486595		22	23	24	25[e]	26[e]	27[e]	28[e]			22	23	24	25[i]	26	27	28	Dōng zhì		8	9	10	11	12	13	14	Tākhśāś 2088
	25	●	27	28	29	30	31	18:22	52	2486602		29[e]	30[e]	1[e]	2[e]	3	4	5	Mon 14h14m12p		29	30	1	2	3	4	5			15	16	17	18	19	20	21	

[a]New Year
[b]Spring (8:14)
[c]Summer (0:37)
[d]Autumn (17:10)
[e]Winter (14:59)
● New moon
◐ First quarter moon
○ Full moon
◑ Last quarter moon

‡Leap year
[a]New Year
[b]Yom Kippur
[c]Sukkot
[d]Winter starts
[e]Ḥanukkah
[f]Purim
[g]Passover
[h]Shavuot
[i]Fast of Av

[a]New Year (4793, Hare)
[b]Lantern Festival
[c]Qīngmíng
[d]Dragon Festival
[e]Qǐqiǎo
[f]Hungry Ghosts
[g]Mid-Autumn Festival
[h]Double-Ninth Festival
[i]Dōngzhì
*Start of 60-name cycle

‡Leap year
[a]New Year
[b]Building of the Cross
[c]Christmas
[d]Jesus's Circumcision
[e]Epiphany
[f]Easter
[g]Mary's Announcement
[h]Jesus's Transfiguration

PERSIAN (ASTRONOMICAL) 1473/1474‡

Month	Sun	Mon	Tue	Wed	Thu	Fri	Sat
DEY 1473	6	7	8	9	10	11	12
	13	14	15	16	17	18	19
	20	21	22	23	24	25	26
BAHMAN 1473	27	28	29	30	1	2	3
	4	5	6	7	8	9	10
	11	12	13	14	15	16	17
	18	19	20	21	22	23	24
ESFAND 1473	25	26	27	28	29	30	1
	2	3	4	5	6	7	8
	9	10	11	12	13	14	15
	16	17	18	19	20	21	22
	23	24	25	26	27	28	29
FARVARDĪN 1474	1[a]	2*	3	4	5	6	7
	8	9	10	11	12	13[b]	14
	15	16	17	18	19	20	21
	22	23	24	25	26	27	28
ORDĪBEHEŠT 1474	29	30	31	1	2	3	4
	5	6	7	8	9	10	11
	12	13	14	15	16	17	18
	19	20	21	22	23	24	25
XORDĀD 1474	26	27	28	29	30	31	1
	2	3	4	5	6	7	8
	9	10	11	12	13	14	15
	16	17	18	19	20	21	22
	23	24	25	26	27	28	29
TĪR 1474	30	31	1	2	3	4	5
	6	7	8	9	10	11	12
	13	14	15	16	17	18	19
	20	21	22	23	24	25	26
MORDĀD 1474	27	28	29	30	31	1	2
	3	4	5	6	7	8	9
	10	11	12	13	14	15	16
	17	18	19	20	21	22	23
	24	25	26	27	28	29	30
SHAHRĪVAR 1474	31	1	2	3	4	5	6
	7	8	9	10	11	12	13
	14	15	16	17	18	19	20
	21	22	23	24	25	26	27
MEHR 1474	28	29	30	31	1	2	3
	4	5	6	7	8	9	10
	11	12	13	14	15	16	17
	18	19	20	21	22	23	24
ĀBĀN 1474	25	26	27	28	29	30	1
	2	3	4	5	6	7	8
	9	10	11	12	13	14	15
	16	17	18	19	20	21	22
	23	24	25	26	27	28	29
ĀZAR 1474	30	1	2	3	4	5	6
	7	8	9	10	11	12	13
	14	15	16	17	18	19	20
	21	22	23	24	25	26	27
DEY 1474	28	29	30	1	2	3	4
	5	6	7	8	9	10	11

‡Leap year
[a]New Year (or next day)
*Near New Year: 1′10″
[b]Sizdeh Bedar

HINDU LUNAR 2151‡/2152

Month	Sun	Mon	Tue	Wed	Thu	Fri	Sat
MĀRGAŚĪRA 2151	20	21	21	22	23	24	25
PAUSHA 2151	26	27	28	29	30	1	2
	3	**4**	6	7	8	9	10
	11	12	13	14	15	16	17
	18	19	20	21	22	23	23
MĀGHA 2151	24	25	26	**27**	29	30	1
	2	3	4	5	6	7	8
	9	10	11	12	13	14	15
	16	17	18	19	20	21	22
	23	24	25	26	27	28[h]	29
PHĀLGUNA 2151	30	1	**2**	4	5	6	7
	8	9	10	11	12	13	14
	15[i]	16	16	17	18	19	20
	21	22	23	24	25	**26**	28
CHAITRA 2152	29	30	1[a]	2	3	4	5
	6	7	8[b]	9	10	11	12
	13	14	15	16	17	18	19
	20	21	22	23	24	25	26
VAIŚĀKHA 2152	27	28	29	**30**	2	3	4
	5	6	7	8	9	10	11
	11	12	13	14	15	16	17
	18	19	20	21	22	**23**	25
JYAISHTHA 2152	26	27	28	29	30	1	2
	3	4	5	6	7	8	9
	10	11	12	13	14	15	16
	17	18	19	20	21	22	23
ĀSHĀḌHA 2152	24	25	**26**	28	29	30	1
	2	3	4	5	6	7	7
	8	9	10	11	12	13	14
	15	16	17	18	**19**	21	22
	23	24	25	26	27	28	29
ŚRĀVAṆA 2152	30	1	2	3	4	5	6
	7	8	9	10	11	12	13
	14	15	16	17	18	19	20
	21	22[c]	24	25	26	27	28
BHĀDRAPADA 2152	29	30	1	2	3	4[d]	4
	5	6	7	8	9	10	11
	12	13	14	**15**	17	18	19
	20	21	22	23	24	25	26
ĀŚVINA 2152	27	28	29	30	1	2	3
	4	5	6	7	8[e]	9[e]	10[e]
	11	12	13	14	15	16	17
	18	**19**	21	22	23	24	25
KĀRTTIKA 2152	26	27	28	28	29	30	1[f]
	2	3	4	5	6	7	8
	9	10	11	**12**	14	15	16
	17	18	19	20	21	22	23
	24	25	26	27	28	29	30
MĀRGAŚĪRA 2152	1	1	2	3	4	**5**	7
	8	9	10	11[g]	12	13	14
	15	16	17	18	19	20	21
	22	23	24	25	26	27	28
PAUSHA 2152	29	30	1	2	3	4	5

‡Leap year
[a]New Year (Rākshasa)
[b]Birthday of Rāma
[c]Birthday of Krishna
[d]Ganēśa Chaturthī
[e]Dashara
[f]Diwali
[g]Birthday of Vishnu
[h]Night of Śiva
[i]Holi

HINDU SOLAR 2016‡/2017

Month	Sun	Mon	Tue	Wed	Thu	Fri	Sat
PAUSHA 2016	10	11	12	13	14	15	16
	17	18	19	20	21	22	23
MĀGHA 2016	24	25	26	27	28	29	1[b]
	2	3	4	5	6	7	8
	9	10	11	12	13	14	15
	16	17	18	19	20	21	22
	23	24	25	26	27	28	29
PHĀLGUNA 2016	1	2	3	4	5	6	7
	8	9	10	11	12	13	14
	15	16	17	18	19	20	21
	22	23	24	25	26	27	28
CHAITRA 2016	29	30	1	2	3	4	5
	6	7	8	9	10	11	12
	13	14	15	16	17	18	19
	20	21	22	23	24	25	26
VAIŚĀKHA 2017	27	28	29	30	31	1[a]	2
	3	4	5	6	7	8	9
	10	11	12	13	14	15	16
	17	18	19	20	21	22	23
	24	25	26	27	28	29	30
JYAISHTHA 2017	31	1	2	3	4	5	6
	7	8	9	10	11	12	13
	14	15	16	17	18	19	20
	21	22	23	24	25	26	27
ĀSHĀḌHA 2017	28	29	30	31	1	2	3
	4	5	6	7	8	9	10
	11	12	13	14	15	16	17
	18	19	20	21	22	23	24
	25	26	27	28	29	30	31
ŚRĀVAṆA 2017	32	1	2	3	4	5	6
	7	8	9	10	11	12	13
	14	15	16	17	18	19	20
	21	22	23	24	25	26	27
BHĀDRAPADA 2017	28	29	30	31	1	2	3
	4	5	6	7	8	9	10
	11	12	13	14	15	16	17
	18	19	20	21	22	23	24
	25	26	27	28	29	30	31
ĀŚVINA 2017	1	2	3	4	5	6	7
	8	9	10	11	12	13	14
	15	16	17	18	19	20	21
	22	23	24	25	26	27	28
KĀRTTIKA 2017	29	30	1	2	3	4	5
	6	7	8	9	10	11	12
	13	14	15	16	17	18	19
	20	21	22	23	24	25	26
MĀRGAŚĪRA 2017	27	28	29	30	1	2	3
	4	5	6	7	8	9	10
	11	12	13	14	15	16	17
	18	19	20	21	22	23	24
PAUSHA 2017	25	26	27	28	29	30	1
	2	3	4	5	6	7	8
	9	10	11	12	13	14	15

‡Leap year
[a]New Year (Śukla)
[b]Pongal

ISLAMIC (ASTRONOMICAL) 1518/1519‡

Month	Sun	Mon	Tue	Wed	Thu	Fri	Sat
SHA'BĀN 1518	18	19	20	21	22	23	24
RAMAḌĀN 1518	25	26	27	28	29	30	1[e]
	2	3	4	5	6	7	8
	9	10	11	12	13	14	15
	16	17	18	19	20	21	22
	23	24	25	26	27	28	29
SHAWWĀL 1518	1[f]	2	3	4	5	6	7
	8	9	10	11	12	13	14
	15	16	17	18	19	20	21
	22	23	24	25	26	27	28
DHU AL-QA'DA 1518	29	1	2	3	4	5	6
	7	8	9	10	11	12	13
	14	15	16	17	18	19	20
	21	22	23	24	25	26	27
DHU AL-ḤIJJA 1518	28	29	30	1	2	3	4
	5	6	7	8	9	10[g]	11
	12	13	14	15	16	17	18
	19	20	21	22	23	24	25
MUHARRAM 1519	26	27	28	29	1[a]	2[A]	3
	4	5	6	7	8	9	10[b]
	11	12	13	14	15	16	17
	18	19	20	21	22	23	24
ṢAFAR 1519	25	26	27	28	29	30	1
	2	3	4	5	6	7	8
	9	10	11	12	13	14	15
	16	17	18	19	20	21	22
	23	24	25	26	27	28	29
RABĪ' I 1519	1	2	3	4	5	6	7
	8	9	10	11	12[c]	13	14
	15	16	17	18	19	20	21
	22	23	24	25	26	27	28
RABĪ' II 1519	29	30	1	2	3	4	5
	6	7	8	9	10	11	12
	13	14	15	16	17	18	19
	20	21	22	23	24	25	26
JUMĀDĀ I 1519	27	28	29	1	2	3	4
	5	6	7	8	9	10	11
	12	13	14	15	16	17	18
	19	20	21	22	23	24	25
JUMĀDĀ II 1519	26	27	28	29	30	1	2
	3	4	5	6	7	8	9
	10	11	12	13	14	15	16
	17	18	19	20	21	22	23
	24	25	26	27	28	29	30
RAJAB 1519	1	2	3	4	5	6	7
	8	9	10	11	12	13	14
	15	16	17	18	19	20	21
	22	23	24	25	26	27[d]	28
SHA'BĀN 1519	29	30	1	2	3	4	5
	6	7	8	9	10	11	12
	13	14	15	16	17	18	19
	20	21	22	23	24	25	26
	27	28	29	1[e]	2	3	4

‡Leap year
[a]New Year
[A]New Year (Arithmetic)
[b]'Ashūrā'
[c]Prophet's Birthday
[d]Ascent of the Prophet
[e]Start of Ramaḍān
[f]'Id al-Fiṭr
[g]'Id al-'Aḍḥā

GREGORIAN 2095

Julian (Sun)	Sun	Mon	Tue	Wed	Thu	Fri	Sat	Month
Dec 13	26	27	28	29	30	31	1	JANUARY 2095
	2	3	4	5	6	7[a]	8	
Dec 27	9	10	11	12	13	14[b]	15	
	16	17	18	19	20	21	22	
Jan 10	23	24	25	26	27	28	29	
	30	31	1	2	3	4	5	FEBRUARY 2095
Jan 24	6	7	8	9	10	11	12	
	13	14	15	16	17	18	19	
Feb 7	20	21	22	23	24	25	26	
	27	28	1	2	3	4	5	MARCH 2095
Feb 21	6	7	8	9[c]	10	11	12	
	13[d]	14	15	16	17	18	19	
Mar 7	20	21	22	23	24	25	26	
	27	28	29	30	31	1	2	APRIL 2095
Mar 21	3	4	5	6	7	8	9	
	10	11	12	13	14	15	16	
Apr 4	17	18	19	20	21	22	23	
	24[e]	25	26	27	28	29	30	
Apr 18	1	2	3	4	5	6	7	MAY 2095
	8	9	10	11	12	13	14	
May 2	15	16	17	18	19	20	21	
	22	23	24	25	26	27	28	
May 16	29	30	31	1	2	3	4	JUNE 2095
	5	6	7	8	9	10	11	
May 30	12	13	14	15	16	17	18	
	19	20	21	22	23	24	25	
Jun 13	26	27	28	29	30	1	2	JULY 2095
	3	4	5	6	7	8	9	
Jun 27	10	11	12	13	14	15	16	
	17	18	19	20	21	22	23	
Jul 11	24	25	26	27	28	29	30	
	31	1	2	3	4	5	6	AUGUST 2095
Jul 25	7	8	9	10	11	12	13	
	14	15	16	17	18	19	20	
Aug 8	21	22	23	24	25	26	27	
	28	29	30	31	1	2	3	SEPTEMBER 2095
Aug 22	4	5	6	7	8	9	10	
	11	12	13	14	15	16	17	
Sep 5	18	19	20	21	22	23	24	
	25	26	27	28	29	30	1	OCTOBER 2095
Sep 19	2	3	4	5	6	7	8	
	9	10	11	12	13	14	15	
Oct 3	16	17	18	19	20	21	22	
	23	24	25	26	27	28	29	
Oct 17	30	31	1	2	3	4	5	NOVEMBER 2095
	6	7	8	9	10	11	12	
Oct 31	13	14	15	16	17	18	19	
	20	21	22	23	24	25	26	
Nov 14	27[g]	28	29	30	1	2	3	DECEMBER 2095
	4	5	6	7	8	9	10	
Nov 28	11	12	13	14	15	16	17	
	18	19	20	21	22	23	24	
Dec 12	25[h]	26	27	28	29	30	31	

[a]Orthodox Christmas
[b]Julian New Year
[c]Ash Wednesday
[d]Feast of Orthodoxy
[e]Easter (also Orthodox)
[g]Advent
[h]Christmas

2096

Gregorian 2096[‡] / ISO week / Julian day

Month	Sun	Mon	Tue	Wed	Thu	Fri	Sat	Lunar Phases	ISO WEEK (Mon)	JULIAN DAY (Sun noon)
JANUARY 2096	1[a]	◐	3	4	5	6	7	23:01	1	2486609
	8	○	10	11	12	13	14	19:19	2	2486616
	15	16	◑	18	19	20	21	12:50	3	2486623
	22	23	24	●	26	27	28	9:44	4	2486630
	29	30	31	◐	2	3	4	7:02	5	2486637
FEBRUARY 2096	5	6	7	○	9	10	11	9:49	6	2486644
	12	13	14	15	◑	17	18	10:38	7	2486651
	19	20	21	22	●	24	25	22:27	8	2486658
	26	27	28	29	◐	2	3	15:15	9	2486665
MARCH 2096	4	5	6	7	8	○	10	1:36	10	2486672
	11	12	13	14	15	16	◑	6:17	11	2486679
	18	19[b]	20	21	22	23	●	8:54	12	2486686
	25	26	27	28	29	30	◐	0:20	13	2486693
APRIL 2096	1	2	3	4	5	6	○	18:17	14	2486700
	8	9	10	11	12	13	14		15	2486707
	◑	16	17	18	19	20	21	22:09	16	2486714
	●	23	24	25	26	27	28	17:42	17	2486721
	◐	30	1	2	3	4	5	10:48	18	2486728
MAY 2096	6	○	8	9	10	11	12	11:05	19	2486735
	13	14	◑	16	17	18	19	9:53	20	2486742
	20	21	●	23	24	25	26	1:34	21	2486749
	27	◐	29	30	31	1	2	23:06	22	2486756
JUNE 2096	3	4	5	○	7	8	9	2:57	23	2486763
	10	11	12	◑	14	15	16	18:08	24	2486770
	17	18	19	●[c]	21	22	23	9:11	25	2486777
	24	25	26	◐	28	29	30	13:30	26	2486784
JULY 2096	1	2	3	4	○	6	7	17:01	27	2486791
	8	9	10	11	12	◑	14	0:04	28	2486798
	15	16	17	18	●	20	21	17:19	29	2486805
	22	23	24	25	26	◐	28	5:58	30	2486812
	29	30	31	1	2	3	○	5:04	31	2486819
AUGUST 2096	5	6	7	8	9	10	◑	5:00	32	2486826
	12	13	14	15	16	17	●	2:59	33	2486833
	19	20	21	22	23	24	◐	23:55	34	2486840
	26	27	28	29	30	31	1		35	2486847
SEPTEMBER 2096	○	3	4	5	6	7	8	15:35	36	2486854
	◑	10	11	12	13	14	15	10:16	37	2486861
	●	17	18	19	20	21[d]	22	15:09	38	2486868
	23	◐	25	26	27	28	29	18:13	39	2486875
	30	1	○	3	4	5	6	1:24	40	2486882
OCTOBER 2096	7	◑	9	10	11	12	13	17:08	41	2486889
	14	15	●	17	18	19	20	6:27	42	2486896
	21	22	23	◐	25	26	27	11:39	43	2486903
	28	29	30	○	1	2	3	11:15	44	2486910
NOVEMBER 2096	4	5	6	◑	8	9	10	2:47	45	2486917
	11	12	13	14	●	16	17	0:35	46	2486924
	18	19	20	21	22	◐	24	3:17	47	2486931
	25	26	27	28	○	30	1	21:33	48	2486938
DECEMBER 2096	2	3	4	5	◑	7	8	16:06	49	2486945
	9	10	11	12	13	●	15	20:05	50	2486952
	16	17	18	19	20[e]	21	◐	16:34	51	2486959
	23	24	25	26	27	28	○	8:22	52	2486966
	30	31	1	2	3	4	◑	9:19	1	2486973

Hebrew 5856/5857

ISO WEEK	Month	Sun	Mon	Tue	Wed	Thu	Fri	Sat	Molad
1	TEVETH 5856	6	7	8	9	10	11	12	
2		13	14	15	16	17	18	19	
3		20	21	22	23	24	25	26	
4		27	28	29	1	2	3	4	Wed $2^h58^m13^p$
5	SHEVAT 5856	5	6	7	8	9	10	11	
6		12	13	14	15	16	17	18	
7		19	20	21	22	23	24	25	
8		26	27	28	29	30	1	2	Thu $15^h42^m14^p$
9	ADAR 5856	3	4	5	6	7	8	9	
10		10	11	12	13	14[f]	15	16	
11		17	18	19	20	21	22	23	
12		24	25	26	27	28	29	1	Sat $4^h26^m15^p$
13	NISAN 5856	2	3	4	5	6	7	8	
14		9	10	11	12	13	14	15[g]	
15		16	17	18	19	20	21	22	
16		23	24	25	26	27	28	29	
17		30	1	2	3	4	5	6	Sun $17^h10^m16^p$
18	IYYAR 5856	7	8	9	10	11	12	13	
19		14	15	16	17	18	19	20	
20		21	22	23	24	25	26	27	
21		28	29	1	2	3	4	5	Tue $5^h54^m17^p$
22	SIVAN 5856	6[h]	7	8	9	10	11	12	
23		13	14	15	16	17	18	19	
24		20	21	22	23	24	25	26	
25		27	28	29	30	1	2	3	Wed $18^h39^m0^p$
26	TAMMUZ 5856	4	5	6	7	8	9	10	
27		11	12	13	14	15	16	17	
28		18	19	20	21	22	23	24	
29		25	26	27	28	29	1	2	Fri $7^h23^m1^p$
30	AV 5856	3	4	5	6	7	8	9	
31		10[i]	11	12	13	14	15	16	
32		17	18	19	20	21	22	23	
33		24	25	26	27	28	29	30	
34	ELUL 5856	1	2	3	4	5	6	7	Sat $20^h7^m2^p$
35		8	9	10	11	12	13	14	
36		15	16	17	18	19	20	21	
37		22	23	24	25	26	27	28	
38		29	1[a]	2[a]	3	4	5	6	Mon $8^h51^m3^p$
39	TISHRI 5857	7	8	9	10[b]	11	12	13	
40		14	15[c]	16	17	18	19	20	
41		21	22	23	24	25	26	27	
42		28	29	30	1	2	3	4	Tue $21^h35^m4^p$
43	ḤESHVAN 5857	5	6	7	8	9	10	11	
44		12	13	14	15	16	17	18	
45		19	20	21	22	23	24	25	
46		26	27	28	29	30	1	2	Thu $10^h19^m5^p$
47	KISLEV 5857	3	4	5	6	7	8	9	
48		10	11	12	13	14	15	16	
49		17	18	19	20[d]	21	22	23	
50		24	25[e]	26[e]	27[e]	28[e]	29[e]	30[e]	
51	TEVETH 5857	1[e]	2[e]	3	4	5	6	7	Fri $23^h3^m6^p$
52		8	9	10	11	12	13	14	
1		15	16	17	18	19	20	21	

Chinese Yǐ-Mǎo/Bǐng-Chén[‡]

ISO WEEK	Month	Sun	Mon	Tue	Wed	Thu	Fri	Sat	Solar Term
1	MONTH 12 Yǐ-Mǎo	6	7	8	9	10	11	12	Xiǎo hán
2		13	14	15	16	17	18	19	
3		20	21	22	23	24	25	26	Dà hán
4		27	28	29	1[a]	2	3	4	
5	MONTH 1 Bǐng-Chén	5	6	7	8	9	10	11	Lì chūn
6		12	13	14	15[b]	16	17	18	
7		19*	20	21	22	23	24	25	Yǔ shuǐ
8		26	27	28	29	30	1	2	
9	MONTH 2 Bǐng-Chén	3	4	5	6	7	8	9	
10		10	11	12	13	14	15	16	Jīng zhé
11		17	18	19	20	21	22	23	
12		24	25	26	27	28	29	1	Chūn fēn
13	MONTH 3 Bǐng-Chén	2	3	4	5	6	7	8	
14		9	10	11	12[c]	13	14	15	Qīng míng
15		16	17	18	19	20*	21	22	
16		23	24	25	26	27	28	29	Gǔ yǔ
17		30	1	2	3	4	5	6	
18	MONTH 4 Bǐng-Chén	7	8	9	10	11	12	13	Lì xià
19		14	15	16	17	18	19	20	
20		21	22	23	24	25	26	27	
21		28	29	1	2	3	4	5	Xiǎo mǎn
22	LEAP MONTH 4 Bǐng-Chén	6	7	8	9	10	11	12	
23		13	14	15	16	17	18	19	Máng zhòng
24		20	21*	22	23	24	25	26	
25		27	28	29	1	2	3	4	Xià zhì
26	MONTH 5 Bǐng-Chén	5[d]	6	7	8	9	10	11	
27		12	13	14	15	16	17	18	Xiǎo shǔ
28		19	20	21	22	23	24	25	
29		26	27	28	29	30	1	2	
30	MONTH 6 Bǐng-Chén	3	4	5	6	7	8	9	Dà shǔ
31		10	11	12	13	14	15	16	
32		17	18	19	20	21	22*	23	Lì qiū
33		24	25	26	27	28	29	1	
34	MONTH 7 Bǐng-Chén	2	3	4	5	6	7[e]	8	Chǔ shǔ
35		9	10	11	12	13	14	15[f]	
36		16	17	18	19	20	21	22	Bái lù
37		23	24	25	26	27	28	29	
38	MONTH 8 Bǐng-Chén	1	2	3	4	5	6	7	Qiū fēn
39		8	9	10	11	12	13	14	
40		15[g]	16	17	18	19	20	21	
41		22	23	24*	25	26	27	28	Hán lù
42		29	30	1	2	3	4	5	
43	MONTH 9 Bǐng-Chén	6	7	8	9[h]	10	11	12	Shuāng jiàng
44		13	14	15	16	17	18	19	
45		20	21	22	23	24	25	26	Lì dōng
46		27	28	29	30	1	2	3	
47	MONTH 10 Bǐng-Chén	4	5	6	7	8	9	10	Xiǎo xuě
48		11	12	13	14	15	16	17	
49		18	19	20	21	22	23	24*	Dà xuě
50		25	26	27	28	29	30	1	
51	MONTH 11 Bǐng-Chén	2	3	4	5	6	7[i]	8	Dōng zhì
52		9	10	11	12	13	14	15	
1		16	17	18	19	20	21	22	Xiǎo hán

Coptic 1812/1813 / Ethiopic 2088/2089

ISO WEEK	Coptic month	Sun	Mon	Tue	Wed	Thu	Fri	Sat	Ethiopic month
1	KOIAK 1812	22	23	24	25	26	27	28	TĀKHŚĀŚ 2088
2		29[c]	30	1	2	3	4	5	
3	TŌBE 1812	6[d]	7	8	9	10	11[e]	12	ṬER 2088
4		13	14	15	16	17	18	19	
5		20	21	22	23	24	25	26	
6		27	28	29	30	1	2	3	
7	MESHIR 1812	4	5	6	7	8	9	10	YAKĀTIT 2088
8		11	12	13	14	15	16	17	
9		18	19	20	21	22	23	24	
10		25	26	27	28	29	30	1	
11	PAREMOTEP 1812	2	3	4	5	6	7	8	MAGĀBIT 2088
12		9	10	11	12	13	14	15	
13		16	17	18	19	20	21	22	
14		23	24	25	26	27	28	29	
15		30	1	2	3	4	5	6	
16	PARMOUTE 1812	7[f]	8	9	10	11	12	13	MIYĀZYĀ 2088
17		14	15	16	17	18	19	20	
18		21	22	23	24	25	26	27	
19		28	29[g]	30	1	2	3	4	
20	PASHONS 1812	5	6	7	8	9	10	11	GENBOT 2088
21		12	13	14	15	16	17	18	
22		19	20	21	22	23	24	25	
23		26	27	28	29	30	1	2	
24	PAŌNE 1812	3	4	5	6	7	8	9	SANĒ 2088
25		10	11	12	13	14	15	16	
26		17	18	19	20	21	22	23	
27		24	25	26	27	28	29	30	
28	EPĒP 1812	1	2	3	4	5	6	7	ḤAMLĒ 2088
29		8	9	10	11	12	13	14	
30		15	16	17	18	19	20	21	
31		22	23	24	25	26	27	28	
32		29	30	1	2	3	4	5	
33	MESORĒ 1812	6	7	8	9	10	11	12	NAḤASĒ 2088
34		13[h]	14	15	16	17	18	19	
35		20	21	22	23	24	25	26	
36		27	28	29	30	1	2	3	
37	EPAG. 1812	4	5	1[a]	2	3	4	5	PĀG. 2088
38	THOOUT 1813	6	7	8	9	10	11	12	MASKARAM 2089
39		13	14	15	16	17[b]	18	19	
40		20	21	22	23	24	25	26	
41		27	28	29	30	1	2	3	
42	PAOPE 1813	4	5	6	7	8	9	10	TEQEMT 2089
43		11	12	13	14	15	16	17	
44		18	19	20	21	22	23	24	
45		25	26	27	28	29	30	1	
46	ATHŌR 1813	2	3	4	5	6	7	8	HEDĀR 2089
47		9	10	11	12	13	14	15	
48		16	17	18	19	20	21	22	
49		23	24	25	26	27	28	29	
50		30	1	2	3	4	5	6	
51	KOIAK 1813	7	8	9	10	11	12	13	TĀKHŚĀŚ 2089
52		14	15	16	17	18	19	20	
1		21	22	23	24	25	26	27	

[‡]Leap year
[a]New Year
[b]Spring (14:01)
[c]Summer (6:29)
[d]Autumn (22:53)
[e]Winter (20:45)
● New moon
◐ First quarter moon
○ Full moon
◑ Last quarter moon

[a]New Year
[b]Yom Kippur
[c]Sukkot
[d]Winter starts
[e]Ḥanukkah
[f]Purim
[g]Passover
[h]Shavuot
[i]Fast of Av

[‡]Leap year
[a]New Year (4794, Dragon)
[b]Lantern Festival
[c]Qīngmíng
[d]Dragon Festival
[e]Qīqiǎo
[f]Hungry Ghosts
[g]Mid-Autumn Festival
[h]Double-Ninth Festival
[i]Dōngzhì
*Start of 60-name cycle

[a]New Year
[b]Building of the Cross
[c]Christmas
[d]Jesus's Circumcision
[e]Epiphany
[f]Easter
[g]Mary's Announcement
[h]Jesus's Transfiguration

PERSIAN (ASTRONOMICAL) 1474‡/1475

Month	Sun	Mon	Tue	Wed	Thu	Fri	Sat
	12	13	14	15	16	17	18
DEY 1474	19	20	21	22	23	24	25
	26	27	28	29	30	1	2
	3	4	5	6	7	8	9
BAHMAN 1474	10	11	12	13	14	15	16
	17	18	19	20	21	22	23
	24	25	26	27	28	29	30
	1	2	3	4	5	6	7
	8	9	10	11	12	13	14
ESFAND 1474	15	16	17	18	19	20	21
	22	23	24	25	26	27	28
	29	30	1[a]	2	3	4	5
	6	7	8	9	10	11	12
FARVARDĪN 1475	13[b]	14	15	16	17	18	19
	20	21	22	23	24	25	26
	27	28	29	30	31	1	2
	3	4	5	6	7	8	9
ORDĪBEHEŠT 1475	10	11	12	13	14	15	16
	17	18	19	20	21	22	23
	24	25	26	27	28	29	30
	31	1	2	3	4	5	6
	7	8	9	10	11	12	13
XORDĀD 1475	14	15	16	17	18	19	20
	21	22	23	24	25	26	27
	28	29	30	31	1	2	3
	4	5	6	7	8	9	10
TĪR 1475	11	12	13	14	15	16	17
	18	19	20	21	22	23	24
	25	26	27	28	29	30	31
	1	2	3	4	5	6	7
	8	9	10	11	12	13	14
MORDĀD 1475	15	16	17	18	19	20	21
	22	23	24	25	26	27	28
	29	30	31	1	2	3	4
	5	6	7	8	9	10	11
SHAHRĪVAR 1475	12	13	14	15	16	17	18
	19	20	21	22	23	24	25
	26	27	28	29	30	31	1
	2	3	4	5	6	7	8
MEHR 1475	9	10	11	12	13	14	15
	16	17	18	19	20	21	22
	23	24	25	26	27	28	29
	30	1	2	3	4	5	6
	7	8	9	10	11	12	13
ĀBĀN 1475	14	15	16	17	18	19	20
	21	22	23	24	25	26	27
	28	29	30	1	2	3	4
	5	6	7	8	9	10	11
ĀZAR 1475	12	13	14	15	16	17	18
	19	20	21	22	23	24	25
	26	27	28	29	30	1	2
DEY 1475	3	4	5	6	7	8	9
	10	11	12	13	14	15	16

HINDU LUNAR 2152/2153‡

Month	Sun	Mon	Tue	Wed	Thu	Fri	Sat
	6	7	8	9	10	11	13
PAUSHA 2152	14	15	16	17	18	19	20
	21	22	23	24	24	25	26
	27	28	29	30	1	2	3
	4	5	7	8	9	10	11
MĀGHA 2152	12	13	14	15	16	17	18
	19	20	21	22	23	24	25
	26	27	28	29[h]	30	1	2
	3	4	5	6	7	8	9
PHĀLGUNA 2152	10	12	13	14	15[i]	16	16
	17	18	19	20	21	22	23
	24	25	26	27	28	29	30
	1[a]	2	3	5	6	7	8
CHAITRA 2153	9[b]	10	11	12	13	14	15
	16	17	18	19	19	20	21
	22	23	24	25	26	27	29
	30	1	2	3	4	5	6
VAIŚĀKHA 2153	7	8	9	10	11	12	13
	14	15	16	17	18	19	20
	21	22	23	24	25	26	27
	28	29	30	2	3	4	5
JYAISHTHA 2153	6	7	8	9	10	11	12
	13	14	15	15	16	17	18
	19	20	21	22	23	25	26
	27	28	29	30	1	2	3
	4	5	6	7	8	9	10
ĀSHĀDHA 2153	11	12	13	14	15	16	17
	18	19	20	21	22	23	24
	25	26	28	29	30	1	2
ŚRĀVANA 2153	3	4	5	6	7	8	9
	10	11	11	12	13	14	15
	16	17	18	19	21	22	23[c]
	24	25	26	27	28	29	30
	1	2	3	4	5	6	7
LEAP BHĀDRAPADA 2153	8	9	10	11	12	13	14
	15	16	17	18	19	20	21
	22	24	25	26	27	28	29
	30	1	2	3	4[d]	5	6
BHĀDRAPADA 2153	7	7	8	9	10	11	12
	13	14	15	17	18	19	20
	21	22	23	24	25	26	27
	28	29	30	1	2	3	4
ĀŚVINA 2153	5	6	7	8[e]	9[e]	10[e]	11
	12	13	14	15	16	17	18
	19	21	22	23	24	25	26
	27	28	29	30	1	1[f]	2
	3	4	5	6	7	8	9
KĀRTTIKA 2153	10	11	12	13	15	16	17
	18	19	20	21	22	23	24
	25	26	27	28	29	30	1
MĀRGAŚIRA 2153	2	3	4	5	6	7	8
	9	10	11[g]	12	13	14	15
	16	17	18	19	21	22	23

HINDU SOLAR 2017/2018

Month	Sun	Mon	Tue	Wed	Thu	Fri	Sat
PAUSHA 2017	16	17	18	19	20	21	22
	23	24	25	26	27	28	29
	1[b]	2	3	4	5	6	7
MĀGHA 2017	8	9	10	11	12	13	14
	15	16	17	18	19	20	21
	22	23	24	25	26	27	28
	29	30	1	2	3	4	5
PHĀLGUNA 2017	6	7	8	9	10	11	12
	13	14	15	16	17	18	19
	20	21	22	23	24	25	26
	27	28	29	1	2	3	4
CHAITRA 2017	5	6	7	8	9	10	11
	12	13	14	15	16	17	18
	19	20	21	22	23	24	25
	26	27	28	29	30	31	1[a]
	2	3	4	5	6	7	8
VAIŚĀKHA 2018	9	10	11	12	13	14	15
	16	17	18	19	20	21	22
	23	24	25	26	27	28	29
	30	31	1	2	3	4	5
JYAISHTHA 2018	6	7	8	9	10	11	12
	13	14	15	16	17	18	19
	20	21	22	23	24	25	26
	27	28	29	30	31	1	2
ĀSHĀDHA 2018	3	4	5	6	7	8	9
	10	11	12	13	14	15	16
	17	18	19	20	21	22	23
	24	25	26	27	28	29	30
	31	32	1	2	3	4	5
ŚRĀVANA 2018	6	7	8	9	10	11	12
	13	14	15	16	17	18	19
	20	21	22	23	24	25	26
	27	28	29	30	31	1	2
BHĀDRAPADA 2018	3	4	5	6	7	8	9
	10	11	12	13	14	15	16
	17	18	19	20	21	22	23
	24	25	26	27	28	29	30
	31	1	2	3	4	5	6
ĀŚVINA 2018	7	8	9	10	11	12	13
	14	15	16	17	18	19	20
	21	22	23	24	25	26	27
	28	29	30	31	1	2	3
KĀRTTIKA 2018	4	5	6	7	8	9	10
	11	12	13	14	15	16	17
	18	19	20	21	22	23	24
	25	26	27	28	29	30	1
MĀRGAŚĪRA 2018	2	3	4	5	6	7	8
	9	10	11	12	13	14	15
	16	17	18	19	20	21	22
	23	24	25	26	27	28	29
	1	2	3	4	5	6	7
PAUSHA 2018	8	9	10	11	12	13	14
	15	16	17	18	19	20	21

ISLAMIC (ASTRONOMICAL) 1519‡/1520‡

Month	Sun	Mon	Tue	Wed	Thu	Fri	Sat
	5	6	7	8	9	10	11
RAMAḌĀN 1519	12	13	14	15	16	17	18
	19	20	21	22	23	24	25
	26	27	28	29	30	1[f]	2
	3	4	5	6	7	8	9
SHAWWĀL 1519	10	11	12	13	14	15	16
	17	18	19	20	21	22	23
	24	25	26	27	28	29	1
	2	3	4	5	6	7	8
DHU AL-QA'DA 1519	9	10	11	12	13	14	15
	16	17	18	19	20	21	22
	23	24	25	26	27	28	29
	1	2	3	4	5	6	7
DHU AL-ḤIJJA 1519	8	9	10[g]	11	12	13	14
	15	16	17	18	19	20	21
	22	23	24	25	26	27	28
	29	30	1[a]	2	3	4	5
MUḤARRAM 1520	6	7	8	9	10[b]	11	12
	13	14	15	16	17	18	19
	20	21	22	23	24	25	26
	27	28	29	1	2	3	4
ṢAFAR 1520	5	6	7	8	9	10	11
	12	13	14	15	16	17	18
	19	20	21	22	23	24	25
	26	27	28	29	1	2	3
	4	5	6	7	8	9	10
RABĪ' I 1520	11	12[c]	13	14	15	16	17
	18	19	20	21	22	23	24
	25	26	27	28	29	30	1
	2	3	4	5	6	7	8
RABĪ' II 1520	9	10	11	12	13	14	15
	16	17	18	19	20	21	22
	23	24	25	26	27	28	29
	1	2	3	4	5	6	7
JUMĀDĀ I 1520	8	9	10	11	12	13	14
	15	16	17	18	19	20	21
	22	23	24	25	26	27	28
	29	30	1	2	3	4	5
	6	7	8	9	10	11	12
JUMĀDĀ II 1520	13	14	15	16	17	18	19
	20	21	22	23	24	25	26
	27	28	29	30	1	2	3
	4	5	6	7	8	9	10
RAJAB 1520	11	12	13	14	15	16	17
	18	19	20	21	22	23	24
	25	26	27[d]	28	29	30	1
	2	3	4	5	6	7	8
SHA'BĀN 1520	9	10	11	12	13	14	15
	16	17	18	19	20	21	22
	23	24	25	26	27	28	29
	30	1[e]	2	3	4	5	6
RAMAḌĀN 1520	7	8	9	10	11	12	13
	14	15	16	17	18	19	20

GREGORIAN 2096‡

Julian† (Sun)	Sun	Mon	Tue	Wed	Thu	Fri	Sat	Month
Dec 19	1	2	3	4	5	6	7[a]	
	8	9	10	11	12	13	14[b]	JANUARY 2096
Jan 2	15	16	17	18	19	20	21	
	22	23	24	25	26	27	28	
Jan 16	29	30	31	1	2	3	4	
	5	6	7	8	9	10	11	FEBRUARY 2096
Jan 30	12	13	14	15	16	17	18	
	19	20	21	22	23	24	25	
Feb 13	26	27	28	29[c]	1	2	3	
	4[d]	5	6	7	8	9	10	MARCH 2096
Feb 27	11	12	13	14	15	16	17	
	18	19	20	21	22	23	24	
Mar 12	25	26	27	28	29	30	31	
	1	2	3	4	5	6	7	
Mar 26	8	9	10	11	12	13	14	APRIL 2096
	15[e]	16	17	18	19	20	21	
Apr 9	22	23	24	25	26	27	28	
	29	30	1	2	3	4	5	
Apr 23	6	7	8	9	10	11	12	MAY 2096
	13	14	15	16	17	18	19	
May 7	20	21	22	23	24	25	26	
	27	28	29	30	31	1	2	
May 21	3	4	5	6	7	8	9	JUNE 2096
	10	11	12	13	14	15	16	
Jun 4	17	18	19	20	21	22	23	
	24	25	26	27	28	29	30	
Jun 18	1	2	3	4	5	6	7	
	8	9	10	11	12	13	14	JULY 2096
Jul 2	15	16	17	18	19	20	21	
	22	23	24	25	26	27	28	
Jul 16	29	30	31	1	2	3	4	
	5	6	7	8	9	10	11	AUGUST 2096
Jul 30	12	13	14	15	16	17	18	
	19	20	21	22	23	24	25	
Aug 13	26	27	28	29	30	31	1	
	2	3	4	5	6	7	8	SEPTEMBER 2096
Aug 27	9	10	11	12	13	14	15	
	16	17	18	19	20	21	22	
Sep 10	23	24	25	26	27	28	29	
	30	1	2	3	4	5	6	
Sep 24	7	8	9	10	11	12	13	OCTOBER 2096
	14	15	16	17	18	19	20	
Oct 8	21	22	23	24	25	26	27	
	28	29	30	31	1	2	3	
Oct 22	4	5	6	7	8	9	10	NOVEMBER 2096
	11	12	13	14	15	16	17	
Nov 5	18	19	20	21	22	23	24	
	25	26	27	28	29	30	1	
Nov 19	2[g]	3	4	5	6	7	8	
	9	10	11	12	13	14	15	DECEMBER 2096
Dec 3	16	17	18	19	20	21	22	
	23	24	25[h]	26	27	28	29	
Dec 17	30	31	1	2	3	4	5	

Persian: ‡Leap year; [a]New Year; [b]Sizdeh Bedar

Hindu Lunar: ‡Leap year; [a]New Year (Anala); [b]Birthday of Rāma; [c]Birthday of Krishna; [d]Ganēśa Chaturthī; [e]Dashara; [f]Diwali; [g]Birthday of Vishnu; [h]Night of Śiva; [i]Holi

Hindu Solar: [a]New Year (Pramoda); [b]Pongal

Islamic: ‡Leap year; [a]New Year; [b]'Ashūrā'; [c]Prophet's Birthday; [d]Ascent of the Prophet; [e]Start of Ramaḍān; [f]'Īd al-Fiṭr; [g]'Īd al-'Aḍḥā

Gregorian: ‡Leap year; [a]Orthodox Christmas; [b]Julian New Year; [c]Ash Wednesday; [d]Feast of Orthodoxy; [e]Easter (also Orthodox); [g]Advent; [h]Christmas

2097

Gregorian 2097	Sun	Mon	Tue	Wed	Thu	Fri	Sat	Lunar Phases	ISO Week (Mon)	Julian Day (Sun noon)	Hebrew 5857/5858‡	Sun	Mon	Tue	Wed	Thu	Fri	Sat	Molad	Chinese Bǐng-Chén‡/Dīng-Sì	Sun	Mon	Tue	Wed	Thu	Fri	Sat	Solar Term	Coptic 1813/1814	Sun	Mon	Tue	Wed	Thu	Fri	Sat	Ethiopic 2089/2090
January 2097	30	31	1[a]	2	3	4	◑	9:19	1	2486973	Teveth 5857	15	16	17	18	19	20	21		Month 11 Bǐng-Chén	16	17	18	19	20	21	22	Xiǎo hán	Koiak 1813	21	22	23	24	25	26	27	Tākhśāś 2089
	6	7	8	9	10	11	12		2	2486980		22	23	24	25	26	27	28			23	24	25	26	27	28	29		Ṭōbe 1813	28	29[c]	30	1	2	3	4	Ṭer 2089
	●	14	15	16	17	18	19	14:59	3	2486987	Shevat 5857	29	1	2	3	4	5	6	Sun 11h47m7p	Month 12 Bǐng-Chén	1	2	3	4	5	6	7	Dà hán		5	6[d]	7	8	9	10	11[e]	
	20	◐	22	23	24	25	26	3:26	4	2486994		7	8	9	10	11	12	13			8	9	10	11	12	13	14			12	13	14	15	16	17	18	
February 2097	○	28	29	30	31	1	2	19:46	5	2487001		14	15	16	17	18	19	20			15	16	17	18	19	20	21			19	20	21	22	23	24	25	
	3	◑	5	6	7	8	9	5:31	6	2487008		21	22	23	24	25	26	27			22	23	24	25*	26	27	28	Lì chūn	Meshir 1813	26	27	28	29	30	1	2	Yakātit 2089
	10	11	●	13	14	15	16	7:48	7	2487015	Adar 5857	28	29	30	1	2	3	4	Tue 0h31m8p	Month 1 Dīng-Sì	29	30	1[a]	2	3	4	5			3	4	5	6	7	8	9	
	17	18	◐	20	21	22	23	12:06	8	2487022		5	6	7	8	9	10	11			6	7	8	9	10	11	12	Yǔ shuǐ		10	11	12	13	14	15	16	
March 2097	24	25	○	27	28	1	2	8:01	9	2487029		12	13	14[f]	15	16	17	18			13	14	15[b]	16	17	18	19			17	18	19	20	21	22	23	
	3	4	5	◑	7	8	9	2:46	10	2487036		19	20	21	22	23	24	25			20	21	22	23	24	25	26	Jīng zhé		24	25	26	27	28	29	30	
	10	11	12	●	14	15	16	21:56	11	2487043	Nisan 5857	26	27	28	29	1	2	3	Wed 13h15m9p	Month 2 Dīng-Sì	27	28	29	30	1	2	3		Paremotep 1813	1	2	3	4	5	6	7	Magābit 2089
	17	18	19[b]	◐	21	22	23	19:15	12	2487050		4	5	6	7	8	9	10			4	5	6	7	8	9	10	Chūn fēn		8	9	10	11	12	13	14	
	24	25	26	○	28	29	30	21:27	13	2487057		11	12	13	14	15[g]	16	17			11	12	13	14	15	16	17			15	16	17	18	19	20	21	
April 2097	31	1	2	3	◑	5	6	22:49	14	2487064		18	19	20	21	22	23	24			18	19	20	21	22[c]	23	24	Qīng míng		22	23	24	25	26	27	28	
	7	8	9	10	11	●	13	9:25	15	2487071	Iyyar 5857	25	26	27	28	29	30	1	Fri 1h59m10p	Month 3 Dīng-Sì	25*	26	27	28	29	1	2		Parmoute 1813	29	30	1	2	3	4	5	Miyāzyā 2089
	14	15	16	17	18	◐	20	1:53	16	2487078		2	3	4	5	6	7	8			3	4	5	6	7	8	9	Gǔ yǔ		6	7	8	9	10	11	12	
	21	22	23	24	25	○	27	12:08	17	2487085		9	10	11	12	13	14	15			10	11	12	13	14	15	16			13	14	15	16	17	18	19	
May 2097	28	29	30	1	2	3	◑	16:07	18	2487092		16	17	18	19	20	21	22			17	18	19	20	21	22	23			20	21	22	23	24	25	26	
	5	6	7	8	9	10	●	18:39	19	2487099		23	24	25	26	27	28	29			24	25	26	27	28	29	30	Lì xià	Pashons 1813	27[f]	28	29[g]	30	1	2	3	Genbot 2089
	12	13	14	15	16	17	◐	9:13	20	2487106	Sivan 5857	1	2	3	4	5	6[h]	7	Sat 14h43m11p	Month 4 Dīng-Sì	1	2	3	4	5	6	7			4	5	6	7	8	9	10	
	19	20	21	22	23	24	25		21	2487113		8	9	10	11	12	13	14			8	9	10	11	12	13	14	Xiǎo mǎn		11	12	13	14	15	16	17	
June 2097	○	27	28	29	30	31	1	3:35	22	2487120		15	16	17	18	19	20	21			15	16	17	18	19	20	21			18	19	20	21	22	23	24	
	2	◑	4	5	6	7	8	6:10	23	2487127		22	23	24	25	26	27	28			22	23	24	25	26*	27	28	Máng zhòng	Paōne 1813	25	26	27	28	29	30	1	Sanē 2089
	9	●	11	12	13	14	15	2:12	24	2487134	Tammuz 5857	29	30	1	2	3	4	5	Mon 3h27m12p	Month 5 Dīng-Sì	29	1	2	3	4	5[d]	6			2	3	4	5	6	7	8	
	◐	17	18	19	20[c]	21	22	18:21	25	2487141		6	7	8	9	10	11	12			7	8	9	10	11	12	13	Xià zhì		9	10	11	12	13	14	15	
	23	○	25	26	27	28	29	19:02	26	2487148		13	14	15	16	17	18	19			14	15	16	17	18	19	20			16	17	18	19	20	21	22	
July 2097	30	1	◑	3	4	5	6	17:04	27	2487155		20	21	22	23	24	25	26			21	22	23	24	25	26	27	Xiǎo shǔ		23	24	25	26	27	28	29	
	7	8	●	10	11	12	13	8:57	28	2487162	Av 5857	27	28	29	1	2	3	4	Tue 16h11m13p	Month 6 Dīng-Sì	28	29	1	2	3	4	5		Epēp 1813	30	1	2	3	4	5	6	Ḥamlē 2089
	14	15	◐	17	18	19	20	6:09	29	2487169		5	6	7	8	9[i]	10	11			6	7	8	9	10	11	12			7	8	9	10	11	12	13	
	21	22	23	○	25	26	27	9:53	30	2487176		12	13	14	15	16	17	18			13	14	15	16	17	18	19	Dà shǔ		14	15	16	17	18	19	20	
August 2097	28	29	30	31	◑	2	3	1:23	31	2487183		19	20	21	22	23	24	25			20	21	22	23	24	25	26			21	22	23	24	25	26	27	
	4	5	6	●	8	9	10	15:59	32	2487190	Elul 5857	26	27	28	29	30	1	2	Thu 4h55m14p	Month 7 Dīng-Sì	27	28*	29	1	2	3	4	Lì qiū	Mesorē 1813	28	29	30	1	2	3	4	Naḥasē 2089
	11	12	13	◐	15	16	17	20:55	33	2487197		3	4	5	6	7	8	9			5	6	7[e]	8	9	10	11			5	6	7	8	9	10	11	
	18	19	20	21	○	23	24	23:52	34	2487204		10	11	12	13	14	15	16			12	13	14	15[f]	16	17	18	Chǔ shǔ		12	13[h]	14	15	16	17	18	
	25	26	27	28	29	◑	31	7:53	35	2487211		17	18	19	20	21	22	23			19	20	21	22	23	24	25			19	20	21	22	23	24	25	
September 2097	1	2	3	4	5	●	7	0:32	36	2487218	Tishri 5858	24	25	26	27	28	29	1[a]	Fri 17h39m15p	Month 8 Dīng-Sì	26	27	28	29	30	1	2	Bái lù	Epag. 1813	26	27	28	29	30	1	2	Pāg. 2089
	8	9	10	11	12	◐	14	14:21	37	2487225		2[a]	3	4	5	6	7	8			3	4	5	6	7	8	9		Thoout 1814	3	4	5	1[a]	2	3	4	Maskaram 2090
	15	16	17	18	19	20	○	12:59	38	2487232		9	10[b]	11	12	13	14	15[c]			10	11	12	13	14	15[g]	16	Qiū fēn		5	6	7	8	9	10	11	
	22[d]	23	24	25	26	27	◑	13:38	39	2487239		16	17	18	19	20	21	22			17	18	19	20	21	22	23			12	13	14	15	16	17[b]	18	
October 2097	29	30	1	2	3	4	●	11:44	40	2487246		23	24	25	26	27	28	29		Month 9 Dīng-Sì	24	25	26	27	28	29*	1			19	20	21	22	23	24	25	
	6	7	8	9	10	11	12		41	2487253	Heshvan 5858	30	1	2	3	4	5	6	Sun 6h23m16p		2	3	4	5	6	7	8	Hán lù	Paope 1814	26	27	28	29	30	1	2	Ṭeqemt 2090
	◐	14	15	16	17	18	19	9:34	42	2487260		7	8	9	10	11	12	13			9[h]	10	11	12	13	14	15			3	4	5	6	7	8	9	
	20	○	22	23	24	25	26	1:22	43	2487267		14	15	16	17	18	19	20			16	17	18	19	20	21	22	Shuāng jiàng		10	11	12	13	14	15	16	
November 2097	◑	28	29	30	31	1	2	19:55	44	2487274		21	22	23	24	25	26	27			23	24	25	26	27	28	29			17	18	19	20	21	22	23	
	3	●	5	6	7	8	9	2:07	45	2487281	Kislev 5858	28	29	30	1	2	3	4	Mon 19h7m17p	Month 10 Dīng-Sì	30	1	2	3	4	5	6	Lì dōng		24	25	26	27	28	29	30	
	10	11	◐	13	14	15	16	5:22	46	2487288		5	6	7	8	9	10	11			7	8	9	10	11	12	13		Athōr 1814	1	2	3	4	5	6	7	Ḫedār 2090
	17	18	○	20	21	22	23	13:02	47	2487295		12	13	14	15	16	17	18			14	15	16	17	18	19	20	Xiǎo xuě		8	9	10	11	12	13	14	
	24	25	◑	27	28	29	30	4:06	48	2487302		19	20	21	22	23	24	25[e]			21	22	23	24	25	26	27			15	16	17	18	19	20	21	
December 2097	1	2	●	4	5	6	7	19:25	49	2487309	Teveth 5858	26[e]	27[e]	28[e]	29[e]	30[d,e]	1[e]	2[e]	Wed 7h52m0p	Month 11 Dīng-Sì	28	29	30*	1	2	3	4	Dà xuě		22	23	24	25	26	27	28	
	8	9	10	11	◐	13	14	0:18	50	2487316		3	4	5	6	7	8	9			5	6	7	8	9	10	11		Koiak 1814	29	30	1	2	3	4	5	Tākhśāś 2090
	15	16	17	18	○	20	21[e]	0:03	51	2487323		10	11	12	13	14	15	16			12	13	14	15	16	17	18[i]	Dōng zhì		6	7	8	9	10	11	12	
	22	23	24	◑	26	27	28	15:19	52	2487330		17	18	19	20	21	22	23			19	20	21	22	23	24	25			13	14	15	16	17	18	19	
	29	30	31	1	●	3	4	14:3	1	2487337		24	25	26	27	28	29	1	Thu 20h36m1p		26	27	28	29	1	2	3			20	21	22	23	24	25	26	

[a]New Year
[b]Spring (19:47)
[c]Summer (12:12)
[d]Autumn (4:34)
[e]Winter (2:36)
● New moon
◐ First quarter moon
○ Full moon
◑ Last quarter moon

‡Leap year
[a]New Year
[b]Yom Kippur
[c]Sukkot
[d]Winter starts
[e]Ḥanukkah
[f]Purim
[g]Passover
[h]Shavuot
[i]Fast of Av

‡Leap year
[a]New Year (4795, Snake)
[b]Lantern Festival
[c]Qīngmíng
[d]Dragon Festival
[e]Qīqiǎo
[f]Hungry Ghosts
[g]Mid-Autumn Festival
[h]Double-Ninth Festival
[i]Dōngzhì
*Start of 60-name cycle

[a]New Year
[b]Building of the Cross
[c]Christmas
[d]Jesus's Circumcision
[e]Epiphany
[f]Easter
[g]Mary's Announcement
[h]Jesus's Transfiguration

PERSIAN (ASTRONOMICAL) 1475/1476

Month	Sun	Mon	Tue	Wed	Thu	Fri	Sat
DEY 1475	10	11	12	13	14	15	16
	17	18	19	20	21	22	23
	24	25	26	27	28	29	30
BAHMAN 1475	1	2	3	4	5	6	7
	8	9	10	11	12	13	14
	15	16	17	18	19	20	21
	22	23	24	25	26	27	28
ESFAND 1475	29	30	1	2	3	4	5
	6	7	8	9	10	11	12
	13	14	15	16	17	18	19
	20	21	22	23	24	25	26
FARVARDĪN 1476	27	28	29	1[a]	2	3	4
	5	6	7	8	9	10	11
	12	13[b]	14	15	16	17	18
	19	20	21	22	23	24	25
ORDĪBEHEŠT 1476	26	27	28	29	30	31	1
	2	3	4	5	6	7	8
	9	10	11	12	13	14	15
	16	17	18	19	20	21	22
	23	24	25	26	27	28	29
XORDĀD 1476	30	31	1	2	3	4	5
	6	7	8	9	10	11	12
	13	14	15	16	17	18	19
	20	21	22	23	24	25	26
TĪR 1476	27	28	29	30	31	1	2
	3	4	5	6	7	8	9
	10	11	12	13	14	15	16
	17	18	19	20	21	22	23
	24	25	26	27	28	29	30
MORDĀD 1476	31	1	2	3	4	5	6
	7	8	9	10	11	12	13
	14	15	16	17	18	19	20
	21	22	23	24	25	26	27
SHAHRĪVAR 1476	28	29	30	31	1	2	3
	4	5	6	7	8	9	10
	11	12	13	14	15	16	17
	18	19	20	21	22	23	24
	25	26	27	28	29	30	31
MEHR 1476	1	2	3	4	5	6	7
	8	9	10	11	12	13	14
	15	16	17	18	19	20	21
	22	23	24	25	26	27	28
ĀBĀN 1476	29	30	1	2	3	4	5
	6	7	8	9	10	11	12
	13	14	15	16	17	18	19
	20	21	22	23	24	25	26
ĀZAR 1476	27	28	29	30	1	2	3
	4	5	6	7	8	9	10
	11	12	13	14	15	16	17
	18	19	20	21	22	23	24
DEY 1476	25	26	27	28	29	30	1
	2	3	4	5	6	7	8
	9	10	11	12	13	14	15

HINDU LUNAR 2153‡/2154

Month	Sun	Mon	Tue	Wed	Thu	Fri	Sat
MĀRGAŚIRA 2153	16	17	18	**19**	21	22	23
	24	24	25	26	27	28	29
PAUSHA 2153	30	1	2	3	4	5	6
	7	8	9	10	11	**12**	14
	15	16	17	18	19	20	21
	22	23	24	25	26	26	27
MĀGHA 2153	28	29	30	1	2	3	4
	5	**6**	8	9	10	11	12
	13	14	15	16	17	18	19
	20	21	22	23	24	25	26
PHĀLGUNA 2153	27	28	29[h]	30	1	2	3
	4	5	6	7	8	9	10
	11	13	14	15[i]	16	17	18
	19	19	20	21	22	23	24
CHAITRA 2154	25	26	27	28	29	30	1[a]
	2	3	**4**	6	7	8	9[b]
	10	11	12	13	14	15	16
	17	18	19	20	21	22	23
	23	24	25	**26**	28	29	30
VAIŚĀKHA 2154	1	2	3	4	5	6	7
	8	10	11	12	13	14	14
	15	16	17	18	19	20	21
	22	23	24	25	26	27	28
JYAISHṬHA 2154	29	**30**	2	3	4	5	6
	7	8	9	10	11	12	13
	14	15	16	17	18	19	20
	20	21	**22**	24	25	26	27
ĀSHĀḌHA 2154	28	29	30	1	2	3	**4**
	6	7	8	9	10	11	11
	12	13	14	15	16	17	18
	19	20	21	22	23	24	25
ŚRĀVAṆA 2154	**26**	28	29	30	1	2	3
	4	5	6	7	8	9	10
	11	12	13	14	15	16	17
	18	19	20	21	22	23[c]	24
BHĀDRAPADA 2154	25	26	27	28	**29**	1	2
	3	4[d]	5	6	7	7	8
	9	10	11	12	13	14	15
	16	17	18	19	20	21	**22**
	24	25	26	27	28	29	30
ĀŚVINA 2154	1	2	3	4	5	6	7
	8[e]	9[e]	10[e]	11	11	12	13
	14	**15**	17	18	19	20	21
	22	23	24	25	26	27	**28**
KĀRTTIKA 2154	30	30	1[f]	2	3	4	5
	6	7	8	9	10	11	12
	13	14	15	16	17	18	19
	20	22	23	24	25	26	27
MĀRGAŚIRA 2154	28	29	30	1	2	3	4
	4	5	6	7	8	9	10
	11[g]	12	13	**14**	16	17	18
	19	20	21	22	23	24	25
	26	27	28	29	30	1	2

HINDU SOLAR 2018/2019

Month	Sun	Mon	Tue	Wed	Thu	Fri	Sat
PAUSHA 2018	15	16	17	18	19	20	21
	22	23	24	25	26	27	28
MĀGHA 2018	29	1[b]	2	3	4	5	6
	7	8	9	10	11	12	13
	14	15	16	17	18	19	20
	21	22	23	24	25	26	27
PHĀLGUNA 2018	28	29	30	1	2	3	4
	5	6	7	8	9	10	11
	12	13	14	15	16	17	18
	19	20	21	22	23	24	25
CHAITRA 2018	26	27	28	29	30	1	2
	3	4	5	6	7	8	9
	10	11	12	13	14	15	16
	17	18	19	20	21	22	23
	24	25	26	27	28	29	30
VAIŚĀKHA 2019	1[a]	2	3	4	5	6	7
	8	9	10	11	12	13	14
	15	16	17	18	19	20	21
	22	23	24	25	26	27	28
JYAISHṬHA 2019	29	30	31	1	2	3	4
	5	6	7	8	9	10	11
	12	13	14	15	16	17	18
	19	20	21	22	23	24	25
ĀSHĀḌHA 2019	26	27	28	29	30	31	1
	2	3	4	5	6	7	8
	9	10	11	12	13	14	15
	16	17	18	19	20	21	22
	23	24	25	26	27	28	29
ŚRĀVAṆA 2019	30	31	32	1	2	3	4
	5	6	7	8	9	10	11
	12	13	14	15	16	17	18
	19	20	21	22	23	24	25
	26	27	28	29	30	31	32
BHĀDRAPADA 2019	1	2	3	4	5	6	7
	8	9	10	11	12	13	14
	15	16	17	18	19	20	21
	22	23	24	25	26	27	28
ĀŚVINA 2019	29	30	31	1	2	3	4
	5	6	7	8	9	10	11
	12	13	14	15	16	17	18
	19	20	21	22	23	24	25
KĀRTTIKA 2019	26	27	28	29	30	1	2
	3	4	5	6	7	8	9
	10	11	12	13	14	15	16
	17	18	19	20	21	22	23
	24	25	26	27	28	29	30
MĀRGAŚIRA 2019	1	2	3	4	5	6	7
	8	9	10	11	12	13	14
	15	16	17	18	19	20	21
	22	23	24	25	26	27	28
PAUSHA 2019	29	1	2	3	4	5	6
	7	8	9	10	11	12	13
	14	15	16	17	18	19	20

ISLAMIC (ASTRONOMICAL) 1520‡/1521

Month	Sun	Mon	Tue	Wed	Thu	Fri	Sat
RAMAḌĀN 1520	14	15	16	17	18	19	20
	21	22	23	24	25	26	27
SHAWWĀL 1520	28	29	1[f]	2	3	4	5
	6	7	8	9	10	11	12
	13	14	15	16	17	18	19
	20	21	22	23	24	25	26
DHU AL-QA'DA 1520	27	28	29	30	1	2	3
	4	5	6	7	8	9	10
	11	12	13	14	15	16	17
	18	19	20	21	22	23	24
DHU AL-ḤIJJA 1520	25	26	27	28	29	1	2
	3	4	5	6	7	8	9
	10[g]	11	12	13	14	15	16
	17	18	19	20	21	22	23
	24	25	26	27	28	29	30[d]
MUḤARRAM 1521	1[a]	2	3	4	5	6	7
	8	9	10[b]	11	12	13	14
	15	16	17	18	19	20	21
	22	23	24	25	26	27	28
ṢAFAR 1521	29	1	2	3	4	5	6
	7	8	9	10	11	12	13
	14	15	16	17	18	19	20
	21	22	23	24	25	26	27
RABĪ' I 1521	28	29	1	2	3	4	5
	6	7	8	9	10	11	12[c]
	13	14	15	16	17	18	19
	20	21	22	23	24	25	26
RABĪ' II 1521	27	28	29	1	2	3	4
	5	6	7	8	9	10	11
	12	13	14	15	16	17	18
	19	20	21	22	23	24	25
JUMĀDĀ I 1521	26	27	28	29	30	1	2
	3	4	5	6	7	8	9
	10	11	12	13	14	15	16
	17	18	19	20	21	22	23
JUMĀDĀ II 1521	24	25	26	27	28	29	1
	2	3	4	5	6	7	8
	9	10	11	12	13	14	15
	16	17	18	19	20	21	22
	23	24	25	26	27	28	29
RAJAB 1521	30	1	2	3	4	5	6
	7	8	9	10	11	12	13
	14	15	16	17	18	19	20
	21	22	23	24	25	26	27[d]
SHA'BĀN 1521	28	29	30	1	2	3	4
	5	6	7	8	9	10	11
	12	13	14	15	16	17	18
	19	20	21	22	23	24	25
RAMAḌĀN 1521	26	27	28	29	30	1[e]	2
	3	4	5	6	7	8	9
	10	11	12	13	14	15	16
	17	18	19	20	21	22	23
	24	25	26	27	28	29	1

GREGORIAN 2097

Julian (Sun)	Sun	Mon	Tue	Wed	Thu	Fri	Sat	Month
Dec 17	30	31	1	2	3	4	5	JANUARY 2097
	6	7[a]	8	9	10	11	12	
Dec 31	13	14[b]	15	16	17	18	19	
	20	21	22	23	24	25	26	
Jan 14	27	28	29	30	31	1	2	
	3	4	5	6	7	8	9	FEBRUARY 2097
Jan 28	10	11	12	13[c]	14	15	16	
	17	18	19	20	21	22	23	
Feb 11	24	25	26	27	28	1	2	
	3	4	5	6	7	8	9	MARCH 2097
Feb 25	10	11	12	13	14	15	16	
	17	18	19	20	21	22	23	
Mar 11	24[d]	25	26	27	28	29	30	
	31[e]	1	2	3	4	5	6	
Mar 25	7	8	9	10	11	12	13	APRIL 2097
	14	15	16	17	18	19	20	
Apr 8	21	22	23	24	25	26	27	
	28	29	30	1	2	3	4	
Apr 22	5[f]	6	7	8	9	10	11	MAY 2097
	12	13	14	15	16	17	18	
May 6	19	20	21	22	23	24	25	
	26	27	28	29	30	31	1	
May 20	2	3	4	5	6	7	8	JUNE 2097
	9	10	11	12	13	14	15	
Jun 3	16	17	18	19	20	21	22	
	23	24	25	26	27	28	29	
Jun 17	30	1	2	3	4	5	6	
	7	8	9	10	11	12	13	JULY 2097
Jul 1	14	15	16	17	18	19	20	
	21	22	23	24	25	26	27	
Jul 15	28	29	30	31	1	2	3	
	4	5	6	7	8	9	10	AUGUST 2097
Jul 29	11	12	13	14	15	16	17	
	18	19	20	21	22	23	24	
Aug 12	25	26	27	28	29	30	31	
	1	2	3	4	5	6	7	SEPTEMBER 2097
Aug 26	8	9	10	11	12	13	14	
	15	16	17	18	19	20	21	
Sep 9	22	23	24	25	26	27	28	
	29	30	1	2	3	4	5	
Sep 23	6	7	8	9	10	11	12	OCTOBER 2097
	13	14	15	16	17	18	19	
Oct 7	20	21	22	23	24	25	26	
	27	28	29	30	31	1	2	
Oct 21	3	4	5	6	7	8	9	NOVEMBER 2097
	10	11	12	13	14	15	16	
Nov 4	17	18	19	20	21	22	23	
	24	25	26	27	28	29	30	
Nov 18	1[g]	2	3	4	5	6	7	DECEMBER 2097
	8	9	10	11	12	13	14	
Dec 2	15	16	17	18	19	20	21	
	22	23	24	25[h]	26	27	28	
Dec 16	29	30	31	1	2	3	4	

Persian: [a]New Year; [b]Sizdeh Bedar

Hindu Lunar: ‡Leap year; [a]New Year (Piṅgala); [b]Birthday of Rāma; [c]Birthday of Krishna; [d]Ganēśa Chaturthī; [e]Dashara; [f]Diwali; [g]Birthday of Vishnu; [h]Night of Śiva; [i]Holi

Hindu Solar: [a]New Year (Prajāpati); [b]Pongal

Islamic: ‡Leap year; [a]New Year; [d]New Year (Arithmetic); [b]'Ashūrā'; [c]Prophet's Birthday; [d]Ascent of the Prophet; [e]Start of Ramaḍān; [f]'Id al-Fiṭr; [g]'Id al-'Aḍḥā

Gregorian: [a]Orthodox Christmas; [b]Julian New Year; [c]Ash Wednesday; [d]Feast of Orthodoxy; [e]Easter; [f]Orthodox Easter; [g]Advent; [h]Christmas

2098

	GREGORIAN 2098							Lunar Phases	ISO WEEK	JULIAN DAY		HEBREW 5858‡/5859							Molad		CHINESE Dīng-Sì/Wù-Wǔ							Solar Term		COPTIC 1814/1815‡				ETHIOPIC 2090/2091‡			
	Sun	Mon	Tue	Wed	Thu	Fri	Sat		(Mon)	(Sun noon)		Sun	Mon	Tue	Wed	Thu	Fri	Sat			Sun	Mon	Tue	Wed	Thu	Fri	Sat			Sun	Mon	Tue	Wed	Thu	Fri	Sat	
	29	30	31	1[a]	●	3	4	14:31	1	2487337		24	25	26	27	28	29	1	Thu 20h36m1p		26	27	28	29	1	2	3			20	21	22	23	24	25	26	
	5	6	7	8	9	◐	11	16:56	2	2487344		2	3	4	5	6	7	8			*4*	5	6	7	8	9	10	Xiǎo hán	KOIAK 1814	27	28	29[c]	30	1	2	3	TĀKHŚĀŚ 2090
JANUARY 2098	12	13	14	15	16	○	18	10:35	3	2487351	SHEVAT 5858	9	10	11	12	13	14	15		MONTH 12 Dīng-Sì	11	12	13	14	15	16	17			4	5	6[d]	7	8	9	10	
	19	20	21	22	23	◑	25	5:57	4	2487358		16	17	18	19	20	21	22			**18**	19	20	21	22	23	24	**Dà hán**	TŌBE 1814	11[e]	12	13	14	15	16	17	ṬER 2090
	26	27	28	29	30	31	●	9:53	5	2487365		23	24	25	26	27	28	29			25	26	27	28	29	30	1[a]*			18	19	20	21	22	23	24	
	2	3	4	5	6	7	8		6	2487372		30	1	2	3	4	5	6	Sat 9h20m2p		2	*3*	4	5	6	7	8	Lì chūn		25	26	27	28	29	30	1	
FEBRUARY 2098	◐	10	11	12	13	14	○	6:15 20:59	7	2487379		7	8	9	10	11	12	13		MONTH 1 Wù-Wǔ	9	10	11	12	13	14	15[b]			2	3	4	5	6	7	8	
	16	17	18	19	20	21	◑	23:25	8	2487386	ADAR I 5858	14	15	16	17	18	19	20			16	17	**18**	19	20	21	22	**Yǔ shuǐ**	MESHIR 1814	9	10	11	12	13	14	15	YAKĀTIT 2090
	23	24	25	26	27	28	1		9	2487393		21	22	23	24	25	26	27			23	24	25	26	27	28	29			16	17	18	19	20	21	22	
	2	●	4	5	6	7	8	4:01	10	2487400		28	29	30	1	2	3	4	Sun 22h4m3p		30	1	2	*3*	4	5	6	Jīng zhé		23	24	25	26	27	28	29	
MARCH 2098	9	◐	11	12	13	14	15	16:00	11	2487407		5	6	7	8	9	10	11			7	8	9	10	11	12	13			30	1	2	3	4	5	6	
	16	○	18	19	20[b]	21	22	7:42	12	2487414	ADAR II 5858	12	13	14[f]	15	16	17	18		MONTH 2 Wù-Wǔ	14	15	16	17	**18**	19	20	**Chūn fēn**	PAREMOTEP 1814	7	8	9	10	11	12	13	MAGĀBIT 2090
	23	◑	25	26	27	28	29	18:25	13	2487421		19	20	21	22	23	24	25			21	22	23	24	25	26	27			14	15	16	17	18	19	20	
	30	31	●	2	3	4	5	19:46	14	2487428		26	27	28	29	1	2	3	Tue 10h48m4p		28	29	30	1*	2	*3*[c]	4	Qīng míng		21	22	23	24	25	26	27	
	6	7	◐	9	10	11	12	22:55	15	2487435		4	5	6	7	8	9	10			5	6	7	8	9	10	11			28	29	30	1	2	3	4	
APRIL 2098	13	14	○	16	17	18	19	19:03	16	2487442	NISAN 5858	11	12	13	14	15[g]	16	17		MONTH 3 Wù-Wǔ	12	13	14	15	16	17	**18**	**Gǔ yǔ**	PARMOUTE 1814	5	6	7	8	9	10	11	MIYĀZYĀ 2090
	20	21	22	◑	24	25	26	13:33	17	2487449		18	19	20	21	22	23	24			19	20	21	22	23	24	25			12	13	14	15	16	17	18	
	27	28	29	30	●	2	3	8:31	18	2487456		25	26	27	28	29	30	1	Wed 23h32m5p		26	27	28	29	1	2	3			19[f]	20	21	22	23	24	25	
	4	5	6	7	◐	9	10	4:20	19	2487463		2	3	4	5	6	7	8			4	*5*	6	7	8	9	10	Lì xià		26	27	28	29[g]	30	1	2	
MAY 2098	11	12	13	14	○	16	17	7:15	20	2487470	IYAR 5858	9	10	11	12	13	14	15		MONTH 4 Wù-Wǔ	11	12	13	14	15	16	17		PASHONS 1814	3	4	5	6	7	8	9	GENBOT 2090
	18	19	20	21	22	◑	24	7:38	21	2487477		16	17	18	19	20	21	22			18	19	**20**	21	22	23	24	**Xiǎo mǎn**		10	11	12	13	14	15	16	
	25	26	27	28	29	●	31	18:22	22	2487484		23	24	25	26	27	28	29			25	26	27	28	29	30	1			17	18	19	20	21	22	23	
	1	2	3	4	5	◐	7	9:44	23	2487491		1	2	3	4	5	6[h]	7	Fri 12h16m6p		2*	3	4	5[d]	*6*	7	8	Máng zhòng		24	25	26	27	28	29	30	
	8	9	10	11	12	○	14	20:24	24	2487498		8	9	10	11	12	13	14		MONTH 5 Wù-Wǔ	9	10	11	12	13	14	15			1	2	3	4	5	6	7	
JUNE 2098	15	16	17	18	19	20[c]	◑	23:49	25	2487505	SIVAN 5858	15	16	17	18	19	20	21			16	17	18	19	20	21	**22**	**Xià zhì**	PAŌNE 1814	8	9	10	11	12	13	14	SANĒ 2090
	22	23	24	25	26	27	28		26	2487512		22	23	24	25	26	27	28			23	24	25	26	27	28	29			15	16	17	18	19	20	21	
	●	30	1	2	3	4	◐	2:05 16:30	27	2487519		29	30	1	2	3	4	5	Sun 1h0m7p		1	2	3	4	5	6	7			22	23	24	25	26	27	28	
	6	7	8	9	10	11	12		28	2487526		6	7	8	9	10	11	12			*8*	9	10	11	12	13	14	Xiǎo shǔ		29	30	1	2	3	4	5	
JULY 2098	○	14	15	16	17	18	19	10:34	29	2487533	TAMMUZ 5858	13	14	15	16	17	18	19		MONTH 6 Wù-Wǔ	15	16	17	18	19	20	21		EPĒP 1814	6	7	8	9	10	11	12	ḤAMLĒ 2090
	20	◑	22	23	24	25	26	13:33	30	2487540		20	21	22	23	24	25	26			22	23	**24**	25	26	27	28	**Dà shǔ**		13	14	15	16	17	18	19	
	27	●	29	30	31	1	2	8:50	31	2487547		27	28	29	1	2	3	4	Mon 13h44m8p		29	1	2	3	4*	5	6			20	21	22	23	24	25	26	
	3	◐	5	6	7	8	9	1:42	32	2487554		5	6	7	8	9[i]	10	11			7[e]	8	9	10	*11*	12	13	Lì qiū		27	28	29	30	1	2	3	
AUGUST 2098	10	11	○	13	14	15	16	1:43	33	2487561	AV 5858	12	13	14	15	16	17	18		MONTH 7 Wù-Wǔ	14	15[f]	16	17	18	19	20		MESORĒ 1814	4	5	6	7	8	9	10	NAḤASĒ 2090
	17	18	19	◑	21	22	23	0:40	34	2487568		19	20	21	22	23	24	25			21	22	23	24	25	**26**	27	**Chǔ shǔ**		11	12	13[h]	14	15	16	17	
	24	25	●	27	28	29	30	15:51	35	2487575		26	27	28	29	30	1	2	Wed 2h28m9p		28	29	1	2	3	4	5			18	19	20	21	22	23	24	
	31	1	◐	3	4	5	6	14:02	36	2487582		3	4	5	6	7	8	9			6	7	8	9	10	11	12			25	26	27	28	29	30	1	
	7	8	9	○	11	12	13	17:32	37	2487589	ELUL 5858	10	11	12	13	14	15	16		MONTH 8 Wù-Wǔ	*13*	14	15[g]	16	17	18	19	Bái lù	EPAG. 1814	2	3	4	5	1[a]	2	3	PĀG. 2090
SEPTEMBER 2098	14	15	16	17	◑	19	20	9:31	38	2487596		17	18	19	20	21	22	23			20	21	22	23	24	25	26		THOOUT 1815	4	5	6	7	8	9	10	MASKARAM 2091
	21	22[d]	23	24	●	26	27	0:15	39	2487603		24	25	26	27	28	29	1[a]	Thu 15h12m10p		27	**28**	29	30	1	2	3	**Qiū fēn**		11	12	13	14	15	16	17[b]	
	28	29	30	1	◐	3	4	5:47	40	2487610		2[a]	3	4	5	6	7	8			4	5*	6	7	8	9[h]	10			18	19	20	21	22	23	24	
	5	6	7	8	9	○	11	9:19	41	2487617	TISHRI 5859	9	10[b]	11	12	13	14	15[c]		MONTH 9 Wù-Wǔ	11	12	13	*14*	15	16	17	Hán lù		25	26	27	28	29	30	1	
OCTOBER 2098	12	13	14	15	16	◑	18	16:56	42	2487624		16	17	18	19	20	21	22			18	19	20	21	22	23	24			2	3	4	5	6	7	8	
	19	20	21	22	23	●	25	10:48	43	2487631		23	24	25	26	27	28	29			25	26	27	28	**29**	1	2	**Shuāng jiàng**	PAOPE 1815	9	10	11	12	13	14	15	ṬEQEMT 2091
	26	27	28	29	30	31	◐	0:46	44	2487638		30	1	2	3	4	5	6	Sat 3h56m11p		3	4	5	6	7	8	9			16	17	18	19	20	21	22	
	2	3	4	5	6	7	8		45	2487645		7	8	9	10	11	12	13		MONTH 10 Wù-Wǔ	10	11	12	13	14	*15*	16	Lì dōng		23	24	25	26	27	28	29	
	○	10	11	12	13	14	◑	0:14 0:00	46	2487652	ḤESHVAN 5859	14	15	16	17	18	19	20			17	18	19	20	21	22	23			30	1	2	3	4	5	6	
NOVEMBER 2098	16	17	18	19	20	21	●	23:50	47	2487659		21	22	23	24	25	26	27			24	25	26	27	28	29	**30**	**Xiǎo xuě**	ATHŌR 1815	7	8	9	10	11	12	13	ḪEDĀR 2091
	23	24	25	26	27	28	29		48	2487666		28	29	1	2	3	4	5	Sun 16h40m12p		1	2	3	4	5	6*	7			14	15	16	17	18	19	20	
	◐	1	2	3	4	5	6	21:55	49	2487673		6	7	8	9	10	11[d]	12			8	9	10	11	12	13	*14*	Dà xuě		21	22	23	24	25	26	27	
	7	○	9	10	11	12	13	13:44	50	2487680	KISLEV 5859	13	14	15	16	17	18	19		MONTH 11* Wù-Wǔ	15	16	17	18	19	20	21			28	29	30	1	2	3	4	
DECEMBER 2098	14	◑	16	17	18	19	20	7:52	51	2487687		20	21	22	23	24	25[e]	26[e]			22	23	24	25	26	27	28		KOIAK 1815	5	6	7	8	9	10	11	TĀKHŚĀŚ 2091
	21[e]	●	23	24	25	26	27	15:23	52	2487694		27[e]	28[e]	29[e]	1[e]	2[e]	3[e]	4	Tue 5h24m13p		**29**[i]	1	2	3	4	5	6	**Dōng zhì**		12	13	14	15	16	17	18	
	28	29	◐	31	1	2	3	19:19	1	2487701	TEVETH 5859	5	6	7	8	9	10	11		MONTH 12 Wù-Wǔ	7	8	9	10	11	12	13			19	20	21	22	23	24	25	

[a]New Year
[b]Spring (1:39)
[c]Summer (18:02)
[d]Autumn (10:23)
[e]Winter (8:19)
● New moon
◐ First quarter moon
○ Full moon
◑ Last quarter moon

‡Leap year
[a]New Year
[b]Yom Kippur
[c]Sukkot
[d]Winter starts
[e]Ḥanukkah
[f]Purim
[g]Passover
[h]Shavuot
[i]Fast of Av

[a]New Year (4796, Horse)
[b]Lantern Festival
[c]Qīngmíng
[d]Dragon Festival
[e]Qīqiǎo
[f]Hungry Ghosts
[g]Mid-Autumn Festival
[h]Double-Ninth Festival
[i]Dōngzhì
*Start of 60-name cycle

‡Leap year
[a]New Year
[b]Building of the Cross
[c]Christmas
[d]Jesus's Circumcision
[e]Epiphany
[f]Easter
[g]Mary's Announcement
[h]Jesus's Transfiguration

PERSIAN (ASTRONOMICAL) 1476/1477

Month	Sun	Mon	Tue	Wed	Thu	Fri	Sat
DEY 1476	9	10	11	12	13	14	15
	16	17	18	19	20	21	22
	23	24	25	26	27	28	29
BAHMAN 1476	30	1	2	3	4	5	6
	7	8	9	10	11	12	13
	14	15	16	17	18	19	20
	21	22	23	24	25	26	27
ESFAND 1476	28	29	30	1	2	3	4
	5	6	7	8	9	10	11
	12	13	14	15	16	17	18
	19	20	21	22	23	24	25
FARVARDĪN 1477	26	27	28	29	1[a]	2	3
	4	5	6	7	8	9	10
	11	12	13[b]	14	15	16	17
	18	19	20	21	22	23	24
	25	26	27	28	29	30	31
ORDĪBEHEŠT 1477	1	2	3	4	5	6	7
	8	9	10	11	12	13	14
	15	16	17	18	19	20	21
	22	23	24	25	26	27	28
XORDĀD 1477	29	30	31	1	2	3	4
	5	6	7	8	9	10	11
	12	13	14	15	16	17	18
	19	20	21	22	23	24	25
TĪR 1477	26	27	28	29	30	31	1
	2	3	4	5	6	7	8
	9	10	11	12	13	14	15
	16	17	18	19	20	21	22
	23	24	25	26	27	28	29
MORDĀD 1477	30	31	1	2	3	4	5
	6	7	8	9	10	11	12
	13	14	15	16	17	18	19
	20	21	22	23	24	25	26
SHAHRĪVAR 1477	27	28	29	30	31	1	2
	3	4	5	6	7	8	9
	10	11	12	13	14	15	16
	17	18	19	20	21	22	23
	24	25	26	27	28	29	30
MEHR 1477	31	1	2	3	4	5	6
	7	8	9	10	11	12	13
	14	15	16	17	18	19	20
	21	22	23	24	25	26	27
ABĀN 1477	28	29	30	1	2	3	4
	5	6	7	8	9	10	11
	12	13	14	15	16	17	18
	19	20	21	22	23	24	25
ĀZAR 1477	26	27	28	29	30	1	2
	3	4	5	6	7	8	9
	10	11	12	13	14	15	16
	17	18	19	20	21	22	23
	24	25	26	27	28	29	30
DEY 1477	1	2	3	4	5	6	7
	8	9	10	11	12	13	14

HINDU LUNAR 2154/2155

Month	Sun	Mon	Tue	Wed	Thu	Fri	Sat
PAUSHA 2154	26	27	28	29	30	1	2
	3	4	5	6	7	8	9
	10	11	12	13	14	15	16
MĀGHA 2154	17	18	**19**	21	22	23	24
	25	26	27	27	28	29	30
	1	2	3	4	5	6	7
	8	9	10	11	12	**13**	15
	16	17	18	19	20	21	22
	23	24	25	26	27	28	29[h]
PHĀLGUNA 2154	29	30	1	2	3	4	5
	6	**7**	9	10	11	12	13
	14	15[i]	16	17	18	19	20
	21	22	23	24	25	26	27
CHAITRA 2155	28	29	30	1[a]	2	3	4
	5	6	7	8	9[b]	10	**11**
	13	14	15	16	17	18	19
	20	21	22	23	23	24	25
VAIŚĀKHA 2155	26	27	28	29	30	1	2
	3	**4**	6	7	8	9	10
	11	12	13	14	15	16	17
	18	19	20	21	22	23	24
JYAISHṬHA 2155	25	26	27	28	29	30	1
	2	3	4	5	6	7	**8**
	10	11	12	13	14	15	16
	17	18	19	19	20	21	22
	23	24	25	26	27	28	29
ĀSHĀḌHA 2155	**30**	2	3	4	5	6	7
	8	9	10	11	12	13	14
	15	16	17	18	19	20	21
	22	23	24	25	26	27	28
ŚRĀVAṆA 2155	29	30	1	2	**3**	5	6
	7	8	9	10	11	12	13
	14	15	16	16	17	18	19
	20	21	22	23[c]	24	25	**26**
BHĀDRAPADA 2155	28	29	30	1	2	3	4[d]
	5	6	7	8	9	10	11
	12	13	14	15	16	17	18
	19	20	21	22	23	24	25
ĀŚVINA 2155	26	27	28	**29**	1	2	3
	4	5	6	7	8[e]	9[e]	10[e]
	11	11	12	13	14	15	16
	17	18	19	20	21	22	**23**
KĀRTTIKA 2155	25	26	27	28	29	30	1[f]
	2	3	4	5	6	7	8
	9	10	11	12	13	14	15
	16	17	18	19	20	21	22
	23	24	25	26	**27**	29	30
MĀRGAŚĪRA 2155	1	2	3	4	5	5	6
	7	8	9	10	11[g]	12	13
	14	15	16	17	18	19	20
	21	23	24	25	26	27	28
PAUSHA 2155	29	30	1	2	3	4	5
	6	7	7	8	9	10	11

HINDU SOLAR 2019/2020‡

Month	Sun	Mon	Tue	Wed	Thu	Fri	Sat
PAUSHA 2019	14	15	16	17	18	19	20
	21	22	23	24	25	26	27
MĀGHA 2019	28	29	30	1[b]	2	3	4
	5	6	7	8	9	10	11
	12	13	14	15	16	17	18
	19	20	21	22	23	24	25
PHĀLGUNA 2019	26	27	28	29	1	2	3
	4	5	6	7	8	9	10
	11	12	13	14	15	16	17
	18	19	20	21	22	23	24
CHAITRA 2019	25	26	27	28	29	30	1
	2	3	4	5	6	7	8
	9	10	11	12	13	14	15
	16	17	18	19	20	21	22
	23	24	25	26	27	28	29
VAIŚĀKHA 2020	30	1[a]	2	3	4	5	6
	7	8	9	10	11	12	13
	14	15	16	17	18	19	20
	21	22	23	24	25	26	27
JYAISHṬHA 2020	28	29	30	31	1	2	3
	4	5	6	7	8	9	10
	11	12	13	14	15	16	17
	18	19	20	21	22	23	24
	25	26	27	28	29	30	31
ĀSHĀḌHA 2020	32	1	2	3	4	5	6
	7	8	9	10	11	12	13
	14	15	16	17	18	19	20
	21	22	23	24	25	26	27
ŚRĀVAṆA 2020	28	29	30	31	1	2	3
	4	5	6	7	8	9	10
	11	12	13	14	15	16	17
	18	19	20	21	22	23	24
	25	26	27	28	29	30	31
BHĀDRAPADA 2020	32	1	2	3	4	5	6
	7	8	9	10	11	12	13
	14	15	16	17	18	19	20
	21	22	23	24	25	26	27
ĀŚVINA 2020	28	29	30	31	1	2	3
	4	5	6	7	8	9	10
	11	12	13	14	15	16	17
	18	19	20	21	22	23	24
KĀRTTIKA 2020	25	26	27	28	29	30	1
	2	3	4	5	6	7	8
	9	10	11	12	13	14	15
	16	17	18	19	20	21	22
	23	24	25	26	27	28	29
MĀRGAŚĪRA 2020	30	1	2	3	4	5	6
	7	8	9	10	11	12	13
	14	15	16	17	18	19	20
	21	22	23	24	25	26	27
PAUSHA 2020	28	29	30	1	2	3	4
	5	6	7	8	9	10	11
	12	13	14	15	16	17	18

ISLAMIC (ASTRONOMICAL) 1521/1522

Month	Sun	Mon	Tue	Wed	Thu	Fri	Sat
SHAWWĀL 1521	24	25	26	27	28	29	1[f]
	2	3	4	5	6	7	8
	9	10	11	12	13	14	15
	16	17	18	19	20	21	22
	23	24	25	26	27	28	29
DHU AL-QA'DA 1521	30	1	2	3	4	5	6
	7	8	9	10	11	12	13
	14	15	16	17	18	19	20
	21	22	23	24	25	26	27
DHU AL-ḤIJJA 1521	28	29	1	2	3	4	5
	6	7	8	9	10[g]	11	12
	13	14	15	16	17	18	19
	20	21	22	23	24	25	26
MUḤARRAM 1522	27	28	29	30	1[a]	2	3
	4	5	6	7	8	9	10[b]
	11	12	13	14	15	16	17
	18	19	20	21	22	23	24
ṢAFAR 1522	25	26	27	28	29	30	1
	2	3	4	5	6	7	8
	9	10	11	12	13	14	15
	16	17	18	19	20	21	22
	23	24	25	26	27	28	29
RABĪ' I 1522	1	2	3	4	5	6	7
	8	9	10	11	12[c]	13	14
	15	16	17	18	19	20	21
	22	23	24	25	26	27	28
RABĪ' II 1522	29	1	2	3	4	5	6
	7	8	9	10	11	12	13
	14	15	16	17	18	19	20
	21	22	23	24	25	26	27
JUMĀDĀ I 1522	28	29	1	2	3	4	5
	6	7	8	9	10	11	12
	13	14	15	16	17	18	19
	20	21	22	23	24	25	26
JUMĀDĀ II 1522	27	28	29	30	1	2	3
	4	5	6	7	8	9	10
	11	12	13	14	15	16	17
	18	19	20	21	22	23	24
RAJAB 1522	25	26	27	28	29	30	1
	2	3	4	5	6	7	8
	9	10	11	12	13	14	15
	16	17	18	19	20	21	22
	23	24	25	26	27[d]	28	29
SHA'BĀN 1522	1	2	3	4	5	6	7
	8	9	10	11	12	13	14
	15	16	17	18	19	20	21
	22	23	24	25	26	27	28
RAMAḌĀN 1522	29	30	1[e]	2	3	4	5
	6	7	8	9	10	11	12
	13	14	15	16	17	18	19
	20	21	22	23	24	25	26
SHAWWĀL 1522	27	28	29	1[f]	2	3	4
	5	6	7	8	9	10	11

GREGORIAN 2098

Julian (Sun)	Sun	Mon	Tue	Wed	Thu	Fri	Sat	Month
Dec 16	29	30	31	1	2	3	4	JANUARY 2098
	5	6	7[a]	8	9	10	11	
Dec 30	12	13	14[b]	15	16	17	18	
	19	20	21	22	23	24	25	
Jan 13	26	27	28	29	30	31	1	FEBRUARY 2098
	2	3	4	5	6	7	8	
Jan 27	9	10	11	12	13	14	15	
	16	17	18	19	20	21	22	
Feb 10	23	24	25	26	27	28	1	MARCH 2098
	2	3	4	5[c]	6	7	8	
Feb 24	9	10	11	12	13	14	15	
	16[d]	17	18	19	20	21	22	
Mar 10	23	24	25	26	27	28	29	
	30	31	1	2	3	4	5	APRIL 2098
Mar 24	6	7	8	9	10	11	12	
	13	14	15	16	17	18	19	
Apr 7	20[e]	21	22	23	24	25	26	
	27[f]	28	29	30	1	2	3	MAY 2098
Apr 21	4	5	6	7	8	9	10	
	11	12	13	14	15	16	17	
May 5	18	19	20	21	22	23	24	
	25	26	27	28	29	30	31	
May 19	1	2	3	4	5	6	7	JUNE 2098
	8	9	10	11	12	13	14	
Jun 2	15	16	17	18	19	20	21	
	22	23	24	25	26	27	28	
Jun 16	29	30	1	2	3	4	5	JULY 2098
	6	7	8	9	10	11	12	
Jun 30	13	14	15	16	17	18	19	
	20	21	22	23	24	25	26	
Jul 14	27	28	29	30	31	1	2	AUGUST 2098
	3	4	5	6	7	8	9	
Jul 28	10	11	12	13	14	15	16	
	17	18	19	20	21	22	23	
Aug 11	24	25	26	27	28	29	30	
	31	1	2	3	4	5	6	SEPTEMBER 2098
Aug 25	7	8	9	10	11	12	13	
	14	15	16	17	18	19	20	
Sep 8	21	22	23	24	25	26	27	
	28	29	30	1	2	3	4	OCTOBER 2098
Sep 22	5	6	7	8	9	10	11	
	12	13	14	15	16	17	18	
Oct 6	19	20	21	22	23	24	25	
	26	27	28	29	30	31	1	NOVEMBER 2098
Oct 20	2	3	4	5	6	7	8	
	9	10	11	12	13	14	15	
Nov 3	16	17	18	19	20	21	22	
	23	24	25	26	27	28	29	
Nov 17	30[g]	1	2	3	4	5	6	DECEMBER 2098
	7	8	9	10	11	12	13	
Dec 1	14	15	16	17	18	19	20	
	21	22	23	24	25[h]	26	27	
Dec 15	28	29	30	31	1	2	3	

Persian: [a]New Year; [b]Sizdeh Bedar

Hindu Lunar: [a]New Year (Kālayukta); [b]Birthday of Rāma; [c]Birthday of Krishna; [d]Ganēśa Chaturthī; [e]Dashara; [f]Diwali; [g]Birthday of Vishnu; [h]Night of Śiva; [i]Holi

Hindu Solar: ‡Leap year; [a]New Year (Aṅgiras); [b]Pongal

Islamic: [a]New Year; [b]'Ashūrā'; [c]Prophet's Birthday; [d]Ascent of the Prophet; [e]Start of Ramaḍān; [f]'Īd al-Fiṭr; [g]'Īd al-'Aḍḥā

Gregorian: [a]Orthodox Christmas; [b]Julian New Year; [c]Ash Wednesday; [d]Feast of Orthodoxy; [e]Easter; [f]Orthodox Easter; [g]Advent; [h]Christmas

2099

Gregorian 2099	Sun	Mon	Tue	Wed	Thu	Fri	Sat	Lunar Phases	ISO Week (Mon)	Julian Day (Sun noon)
JANUARY 2099	28	29	◐	31	1[a]	2	3	19:19	1	2487701
	4	5	6	○	8	9	10	1:49	2	2487708
	11	12	◑	14	15	16	17	17:25	3	2487715
	18	19	20	●	22	23	24	9:06	4	2487722
	25	26	27	28	◐	30	31	14:37	5	2487729
FEBRUARY 2099	1	2	3	4	○	6	7	12:47	6	2487736
	8	9	10	11	◑	13	14	5:07	7	2487743
	15	16	17	18	19	●	21	4:05	8	2487750
	22	23	24	25	26	27	◐	6:12	9	2487757
MARCH 2099	1	2	3	4	5	○	7	22:58	10	2487764
	8	9	10	11	12	◑	14	18:59	11	2487771
	15	16	17	18	19	20[b]	●	22:45	12	2487778
	22	23	24	25	26	27	28		13	2487785
APRIL 2099	◐	30	31	1	2	3	4	17:37	14	2487792
	○	6	7	8	9	10	11	8:36	15	2487799
	◑	13	14	15	16	17	18	10:46	16	2487806
	19	●	21	22	23	24	25	15:29	17	2487813
	26	27	◐	29	30	1	2	1:34	18	2487820
MAY 2099	3	○	5	6	7	8	9	17:57	19	2487827
	10	11	◑	13	14	15	16	3:59	20	2487834
	17	18	19	●	21	22	23	5:15	21	2487841
	24	25	26	◐	28	29	30	7:15	22	2487848
JUNE 2099	31	1	2	○	4	5	6	3:36	23	2487855
	7	8	9	◑	11	12	13	21:48	24	2487862
	14	15	16	17	●	19	20[c]	16:09	25	2487869
	21	22	23	24	◐	26	27	11:59	26	2487876
JULY 2099	28	29	30	1	○	3	4	14:20	27	2487883
	5	6	7	8	9	◑	11	15:13	28	2487890
	12	13	14	15	16	17	●	1:00	29	2487897
	19	20	21	22	23	◐	25	17:08	30	2487904
	26	27	28	29	30	31	○	2:59	31	2487911
AUGUST 2099	2	3	4	5	6	7	8		32	2487918
	◑	10	11	12	13	14	15	7:13	33	2487925
	●	17	18	19	20	21	◐	8:53 0:00	34	2487932
	23	24	25	26	27	28	29		35	2487939
SEPTEMBER 2099	○	31	1	2	3	4	5	17:55	36	2487946
	6	◑	8	9	10	11	12	21:17	37	2487953
	13	●	15	16	17	18	19	16:49	38	2487960
	20	◐	22[d]	23	24	25	26	9:47	39	2487967
OCTOBER 2099	27	28	○	30	1	2	3	10:44	40	2487974
	4	5	6	◑	8	9	10	9:20	41	2487981
	11	12	13	●	15	16	17	1:31	42	2487988
	18	19	◐	21	22	23	24	23:26	43	2487995
	25	26	27	28	○	30	31	4:19	44	2488002
NOVEMBER 2099	1	2	3	4	◑	6	7	19:41	45	2488009
	8	9	10	11	●	13	14	11:28	46	2488016
	15	16	17	18	◐	20	21	17:16	47	2488023
	22	23	24	25	26	○	28	21:21	48	2488030
DECEMBER 2099	29	30	1	2	3	4	◑	4:44	49	2488037
	6	7	8	9	10	●	12	23:08	50	2488044
	13	14	15	16	17	18	◐	14:21	51	2488051
	20	21[e]	22	23	24	25	26		52	2488058
	○	28	29	30	31	1	2	12:57	53	2488065

ISO Week	Hebrew 5859/5860‡	Sun	Mon	Tue	Wed	Thu	Fri	Sat	Molad
1	TEVETH 5859	5	6	7	8	9	10	11	
2		12	13	14	15	16	17	18	
3		19	20	21	22	23	24	25	
4		26	27	28	29	1	2	3	Wed 18h8m14p
5	SHEVAT 5859	4	5	6	7	8	9	10	
6		11	12	13	14	15	16	17	
7		18	19	20	21	22	23	24	
8		25	26	27	28	29	30	1	Fri 6h52m15p
9	ADAR 5859	2	3	4	5	6	7	8	
10		9	10	11	12	13	14[f]	15	
11		16	17	18	19	20	21	22	
12		23	24	25	26	27	28	29	
13		1	2	3	4	5	6	7	Sat 19h36m16p
14	NISAN 5859	8	9	10	11	12	13	14	
15		15[g]	16	17	18	19	20	21	
16		22	23	24	25	26	27	28	
17		29	30	1	2	3	4	5	Mon 8h20m17p
18	IYYAR 5859	6	7	8	9	10	11	12	
19		13	14	15	16	17	18	19	
20		20	21	22	23	24	25	26	
21		27	28	29	1	2	3	4	Tue 21h5m0p
22	SIVAN 5859	5	6[h]	7	8	9	10	11	
23		12	13	14	15	16	17	18	
24		19	20	21	22	23	24	25	
25		26	27	28	29	30	1	2	Thu 9h49m1p
26	TAMMUZ 5859	3	4	5	6	7	8	9	
27		10	11	12	13	14	15	16	
28		17	18	19	20	21	22	23	
29		24	25	26	27	28	29	1	Fri 22h33m2p
30	AV 5859	2	3	4	5	6	7	8	
31		9[i]	10	11	12	13	14	15	
32		16	17	18	19	20	21	22	
33		23	24	25	26	27	28	29	
34		30	1	2	3	4	5	6	Sun 11h17m3p
35	ELUL 5859	7	8	9	10	11	12	13	
36		14	15	16	17	18	19	20	
37		21	22	23	24	25	26	27	
38		28	29	1[a]	2[a]	3	4	5	Tue 0h1m4p
39	TISHRI 5860	6	7	8	9	10[b]	11	12	
40		13	14	15[c]	16	17	18	19	
41		20	21	22	23	24	25	26	
42		27	28	29	30	1	2	3	Wed 12h45m5p
43	ḤESHVAN 5860	4	5	6	7	8	9	10	
44		11	12	13	14	15	16	17	
45		18	19	20	21	22	23	24	
46		25	26	27	28	29	1	2	Fri 1h29m6p
47	KISLEV 5860	3	4	5	6	7	8	9	
48		10	11	12	13	14	15	16	
49		17	18	19	20	21	22	23	
50		24[d]	25[e]	26[e]	27[e]	28[e]	29[e]	30[e]	
51	TEVETH 5860	1[e]	2[e]	3	4	5	6	7	Sat 14h13m7p
52		8	9	10	11	12	13	14	
53		15	16	17	18	19	20	21	

ISO Week	Chinese Wù-Wŭ/Jĭ-Wèi‡	Sun	Mon	Tue	Wed	Thu	Fri	Sat	Solar Term
1	MONTH 12 Wù-Wŭ	7	8	9	10	11	12	13	
2		14	15	16	17	18	19	20	Xiǎo hán
3		21	22	23	24	25	26	27	
4		28	29	30	1[a]	2	3	4	Dà hán
5	MONTH 1 Jĭ-Wèi	5	6	7*	8	9	10	11	
6		12	13	14	15[b]	16	17	18	Lì chūn
7		19	20	21	22	23	24	25	
8		26	27	28	29	30	1	2	Yŭ shuĭ
9	MONTH 2 Jĭ-Wèi	3	4	5	6	7	8	9	
10		10	11	12	13	14	15	16	Jīng zhé
11		17	18	19	20	21	22	23	
12		24	25	26	27	28	29	30	Chūn fēn
13	LEAP MONTH 2 Jĭ-Wèi	1	2	3	4	5	6	7*	
14		8	9	10	11	12	13	14[c]	Qīng míng
15		15	16	17	18	19	20	21	
16		22	23	24	25	26	27	28	
17		29	1	2	3	4	5	6	Gŭ yŭ
18	MONTH 3 Jĭ-Wèi	7	8	9	10	11	12	13	
19		14	15	16	17	18	19	20	Lì xià
20		21	22	23	24	25	26	27	
21		28	29	30	1	2	3	4	Xiǎo mǎn
22	MONTH 4 Jĭ-Wèi	5	6	7	8*	9	10	11	
23		12	13	14	15	16	17	18	Máng zhòng
24		19	20	21	22	23	24	25	
25		26	27	28	29	30	1	2	Xià zhì
26	MONTH 5 Jĭ-Wèi	3	4	5[d]	6	7	8	9	
27		10	11	12	13	14	15	16	
28		17	18	19	20	21	22	23	Xiǎo shŭ
29		24	25	26	27	28	29	1	
30	MONTH 6 Jĭ-Wèi	2	3	4	5	6	7	8	Dà shŭ
31		9*	10	11	12	13	14	15	
32		16	17	18	19	20	21	22	Lì qiū
33		23	24	25	26	27	28	29	
34		1	2	3	4	5	6	7[e]	
35	MONTH 7 Jĭ-Wèi	8	9	10	11	12	13	14	Chŭ shŭ
36		15[f]	16	17	18	19	20	21	
37		22	23	24	25	26	27	28	Bái lù
38		29	30	1	2	3	4	5	
39	MONTH 8 Jĭ-Wèi	6	7	8	9	10*	11	12	Qiū fēn
40		13	14	15[g]	16	17	18	19	
41		20	21	22	23	24	25	26	Hán lù
42		27	28	29	1	2	3	4	
43	MONTH 9 Jĭ-Wèi	5	6	7	8	9[h]	10	11	Shuāng jiàng
44		12	13	14	15	16	17	18	
45		19	20	21	22	23	24	25	Lì dōng
46		26	27	28	29	1	2	3	
47	MONTH 10 Jĭ-Wèi	4	5	6	7	8	9	10	
48		11	12*	13	14	15	16	17	Xiǎo xuě
49		18	19	20	21	22	23	24	
50		25	26	27	28	29	30	1	Dà xuě
51	MONTH 11 Jĭ-Wèi	2	3	4	5	6	7	8	
52		9	10[i]	11	12	13	14	15	Dōng zhì
53		16	17	18	19	20	21	22	

ISO Week	Coptic 1815‡/1816	Sun	Mon	Tue	Wed	Thu	Fri	Sat	Ethiopic 2091‡/2092
1	KOIAK 1815	19	20	21	22	23	24	25	TĀKHŚĀŚ 2091
2		26	27	28	29[c]	30	1	2	
3	TŌBE 1815	3	4	5	6[d]	7	8	9	ṬER 2091
4		10	11[e]	12	13	14	15	16	
5		17	18	19	20	21	22	23	
6		24	25	26	27	28	29	30	
7	MESHIR 1815	1	2	3	4	5	6	7	YAKĀTIT 2091
8		8	9	10	11	12	13	14	
9		15	16	17	18	19	20	21	
10		22	23	24	25	26	27	28	
11		29	30	1	2	3	4	5	
12	PAREMOTEP 1815	6	7	8	9	10	11	12	MAGĀBIT 2091
13		13	14	15	16	17	18	19	
14		20	21	22	23	24	25	26	
15		27	28	29	30	1	2	3	
16	PARMOUTE 1815	4[f]	5	6	7	8	9	10	MIYĀZYĀ 2091
17		11	12	13	14	15	16	17	
18		18	19	20	21	22	23	24	
19		25	26	27	28	29[g]	30	1	
20	PASHONS 1815	2	3	4	5	6	7	8	GENBOT 2091
21		9	10	11	12	13	14	15	
22		16	17	18	19	20	21	22	
23		23	24	25	26	27	28	29	
24		30	1	2	3	4	5	6	
25	PAŌNE 1815	7	8	9	10	11	12	13	SANĒ 2091
26		14	15	16	17	18	19	20	
27		21	22	23	24	25	26	27	
28		28	29	30	1	2	3	4	
29	EPĒP 1815	5	6	7	8	9	10	11	HAMLĒ 2091
30		12	13	14	15	16	17	18	
31		19	20	21	22	23	24	25	
32		26	27	28	29	30	1	2	
33	MESORĒ 1815	3	4	5	6	7	8	9	NAHASĒ 2091
34		10	11	12	13[h]	14	15	16	
35		17	18	19	20	21	22	23	
36		24	25	26	27	28	29	30	
37	EPAG. 1815	1	2	3	4	5	6	1[a]	PĀG. 2091
38	THOOUT 1816	2	3	4	5	6	7	8	MASKARAM 2092
39		9	10	11	12	13	14	15	
40		16	17[b]	18	19	20	21	22	
41		23	24	25	26	27	28	29	
42		30	1	2	3	4	5	6	
43	PAOPE 1816	7	8	9	10	11	12	13	ṬEQEMT 2092
44		14	15	16	17	18	19	20	
45		21	22	23	24	25	26	27	
46		28	29	30	1	2	3	4	
47	ATHŌR 1816	5	6	7	8	9	10	11	HEDĀR 2092
48		12	13	14	15	16	17	18	
49		19	20	21	22	23	24	25	
50		26	27	28	29	30	1	2	
51	KOIAK 1816	3	4	5	6	7	8	9	TĀKHŚĀŚ 2092
52		10	11	12	13	14	15	16	
53		17	18	19	20	21	22	23	

[a]New Year
[b]Spring (7:16)
[c]Summer (23:40)
[d]Autumn (16:09)
[e]Winter (14:03)
● New moon
◐ First quarter moon
○ Full moon
◑ Last quarter moon

‡Leap year
[a]New Year
[b]Yom Kippur
[c]Sukkot
[d]Winter starts
[e]Ḥanukkah
[f]Purim
[g]Passover
[h]Shavuot
[i]Fast of Av

‡Leap year
[a]New Year (4797, Sheep)
[b]Lantern Festival
[c]Qīngmíng
[d]Dragon Festival
[e]Qīqiǎo
[f]Hungry Ghosts
[g]Mid-Autumn Festival
[h]Double-Ninth Festival
[i]Dōngzhì
*Start of 60-name cycle

‡Leap year
[a]New Year
[b]Building of the Cross
[c]Christmas
[d]Jesus's Circumcision
[e]Epiphany
[f]Easter
[g]Mary's Announcement
[h]Jesus's Transfiguration

PERSIAN (ASTRONOMICAL) 1477/1478‡

Month	Sun	Mon	Tue	Wed	Thu	Fri	Sat
DEY 1477	8	9	10	11	12	13	14
	15	16	17	18	19	20	21
	22	23	24	25	26	27	28
	29	30	1	2	3	4	5
BAHMAN 1477	6	7	8	9	10	11	12
	13	14	15	16	17	18	19
	20	21	22	23	24	25	26
	27	28	29	30	1	2	3
ESFAND 1477	4	5	6	7	8	9	10
	11	12	13	14	15	16	17
	18	19	20	21	22	23	24
	25	26	27	28	29	1[a]	2
FARVARDĪN 1478	3	4	5	6	7	8	9
	10	11	12	13[b]	14	15	16
	17	18	19	20	21	22	23
	24	25	26	27	28	29	30
	31	1	2	3	4	5	6
ORDĪBEHEŠT 1478	7	8	9	10	11	12	13
	14	15	16	17	18	19	20
	21	22	23	24	25	26	27
	28	29	30	31	1	2	3
XORDĀD 1478	4	5	6	7	8	9	10
	11	12	13	14	15	16	17
	18	19	20	21	22	23	24
	25	26	27	28	29	30	31
TĪR 1478	1	2	3	4	5	6	7
	8	9	10	11	12	13	14
	15	16	17	18	19	20	21
	22	23	24	25	26	27	28
	29	30	31	1	2	3	4
MORDĀD 1478	5	6	7	8	9	10	11
	12	13	14	15	16	17	18
	19	20	21	22	23	24	25
	26	27	28	29	30	31	1
SHAHRĪVAR 1478	2	3	4	5	6	7	8
	9	10	11	12	13	14	15
	16	17	18	19	20	21	22
	23	24	25	26	27	28	29
	30	31	1	2	3	4	5
MEHR 1478	6	7	8	9	10	11	12
	13	14	15	16	17	18	19
	20	21	22	23	24	25	26
	27	28	29	30	1	2	3
ĀBĀN 1478	4	5	6	7	8	9	10
	11	12	13	14	15	16	17
	18	19	20	21	22	23	24
	25	26	27	28	29	30	1
ĀZAR 1478	2	3	4	5	6	7	8
	9	10	11	12	13	14	15
	16	17	18	19	20	21	22
	23	24	25	26	27	28	29
DEY 1478	30	1	2	3	4	5	6
	7	8	9	10	11	12	13

‡Leap year
[a]New Year
[b]Sizdeh Bedar

HINDU LUNAR 2155/2156‡

Month	Sun	Mon	Tue	Wed	Thu	Fri	Sat
PAUSHA 2155	6	7	7	8	9	10	11
	12	13	14	**15**	17	18	19
	20	21	22	23	24	25	26
	27	28	29	30	1	2	3
MĀGHA 2155	4	5	6	7	8	9	10
	11	12	13	14	15	16	17
	18	19	**20**	22	23	24	25
	26	27	28	29[h]	30	30	1
PHĀLGUNA 2155	2	3	4	5	6	7	8
	9	10	11	12	13	14[i]	16
	17	18	19	20	21	22	23
	24	25	26	27	28	29	30
CHAITRA 2156	1[a]	2	2	3	4	5	6
	7	9[b]	10	11	12	13	14
	15	16	17	18	19	20	21
	22	23	24	25	26	27	28
	29	30	1	2	3	4	5
VAIŚĀKHA 2156	6	7	8	9	10	**11**	13
	14	15	16	17	18	19	20
	21	22	23	24	25	26	27
	27	28	29	30	1	2	3
JYAISHTHA 2156	**4**	6	7	8	9	10	11
	12	13	14	15	16	17	18
	19	20	21	22	23	24	25
	26	27	28	29	30	1	2
LEAP ĀSHĀDHA 2156	3	4	5	6	7	**8**	10
	11	12	13	14	15	16	17
	18	19	20	21	22	23	23
	24	25	26	27	28	29	**30**
ĀSHĀDHA 2156	2	3	4	5	6	7	8
	9	10	11	12	13	14	15
	16	17	18	19	20	21	22
	23	24	25	26	27	28	29
	30	1	2	**3**	5	6	7
ŚRĀVAṆA 2156	8	9	10	11	12	13	14
	15	16	17	18	19	20	20
	21	22	23[c]	24	25	**26**	28
	29	30	1	2	3	4[d]	5
BHĀDRAPADA 2156	6	7	8	9	10	11	12
	13	14	15	16	17	18	19
	20	21	22	23	24	25	26
	27	28	29	**30**	2	3	4
ĀŚVINA 2156	5	6	7	8[e]	9[e]	10[e]	11
	12	13	14	14	15	16	17
	18	19	20	21	22	**23**	25
	26	27	28	29	30	1[f]	2
KĀRTTIKA 2156	3	4	5	6	7	8	9
	10	11	12	13	14	15	16
	17	18	19	20	21	22	23
	24	25	26	27	**28**	30	1
MĀRGAŚĪRA 2156	2	3	4	5	6	7	8
	8	9	10	11[g]	12	13	14
	15	16	17	18	19	20	21

‡Leap year
[a]New Year (Siddhārthin)
[b]Birthday of Rāma
[c]Birthday of Krishna
[d]Ganēśa Chaturthī
[e]Dashara
[f]Diwali
[g]Birthday of Vishnu
[h]Night of Śiva
[i]Holi

HINDU SOLAR 2020‡/2021

Month	Sun	Mon	Tue	Wed	Thu	Fri	Sat
PAUSHA 2020	12	13	14	15	16	17	18
	19	20	21	22	23	24	25
	26	27	28	29	1[b]	2	3
MĀGHA 2020	4	5	6	7	8	9	10
	11	12	13	14	15	16	17
	18	19	20	21	22	23	24
	25	26	27	28	29	1	2
PHĀLGUNA 2020	3	4	5	6	7	8	9
	10	11	12	13	14	15	16
	17	18	19	20	21	22	23
	24	25	26	27	28	29	30
	1	2	3	4	5	6	7
CHAITRA 2020	8	9	10	11	12	13	14
	15	16	17	18	19	20	21
	22	23	24	25	26	27	28
	29	30	31	1[a]	2	3	4
VAIŚĀKHA 2021	5	6	7	8	9	10	11
	12	13	14	15	16	17	18
	19	20	21	22	23	24	25
	26	27	28	29	30	31	1
JYAISHTHA 2021	2	3	4	5	6	7	8
	9	10	11	12	13	14	15
	16	17	18	19	20	21	22
	23	24	25	26	27	28	29
	30	31	1	2	3	4	5
ĀSHĀDHA 2021	6	7	8	9	10	11	12
	13	14	15	16	17	18	19
	20	21	22	23	24	25	26
	27	28	29	30	31	32	1
ŚRĀVAṆA 2021	2	3	4	5	6	7	8
	9	10	11	12	13	14	15
	16	17	18	19	20	21	22
	23	24	25	26	27	28	29
	30	31	1	2	3	4	5
BHĀDRAPADA 2021	6	7	8	9	10	11	12
	13	14	15	16	17	18	19
	20	21	22	23	24	25	26
	27	28	29	30	31	1	2
ĀŚVINA 2021	3	4	5	6	7	8	9
	10	11	12	13	14	15	16
	17	18	19	20	21	22	23
	24	25	26	27	28	29	30
	31	1	2	3	4	5	6
KĀRTTIKA 2021	7	8	9	10	11	12	13
	14	15	16	17	18	19	20
	21	22	23	24	25	26	27
	28	29	1	2	3	4	5
MĀRGAŚĪRA 2021	6	7	8	9	10	11	12
	13	14	15	16	17	18	19
	20	21	22	23	24	25	26
	27	28	29	30	1	2	3
PAUSHA 2021	4	5	6	7	8	9	10
	11	12	13	14	15	16	17

‡Leap year
[a]New Year (Śrīmukha)
[b]Pongal

ISLAMIC (ASTRONOMICAL) 1522/1523

Month	Sun	Mon	Tue	Wed	Thu	Fri	Sat
SHAWWĀL 1522	5	6	7	8	9	10	11
	12	13	14	15	16	17	18
	19	20	21	22	23	24	25
	26	27	28	29	30	1	2
DHU AL-QA'DA 1522	3	4	5	6	7	8	9
	10	11	12	13	14	15	16
	17	18	19	20	21	22	23
	24	25	26	27	28	29	30
DHU AL-ḤIJJA 1522	1	2	3	4	5	6	7
	8	9	10[g]	11	12	13	14
	15	16	17	18	19	20	21
	22	23	24	25	26	27	28
MUḤARRAM 1523	29	1[a]	2	3	4	5	6
	7	8	9	10[b]	11	12	13
	14	15	16	17	18	19	20
	21	22	23	24	25	26	27
	28	29	30	1	2	3	4
ṢAFAR 1523	5	6	7	8	9	10	11
	12	13	14	15	16	17	18
	19	20	21	22	23	24	25
	26	27	28	29	1	2	3
RABĪ' I 1523	4	5	6	7	8	9	10
	11	12[c]	13	14	15	16	17
	18	19	20	21	22	23	24
	25	26	27	28	29	30	1
RABĪ' II 1523	2	3	4	5	6	7	8
	9	10	11	12	13	14	15
	16	17	18	19	20	21	22
	23	24	25	26	27	28	29
JUMĀDĀ I 1523	1	2	3	4	5	6	7
	8	9	10	11	12	13	14
	15	16	17	18	19	20	21
	22	23	24	25	26	27	28
	29	30	1	2	3	4	5
JUMĀDĀ II 1523	6	7	8	9	10	11	12
	13	14	15	16	17	18	19
	20	21	22	23	24	25	26
	27	28	29	1	2	3	4
RAJAB 1523	5	6	7	8	9	10	11
	12	13	14	15	16	17	18
	19	20	21	22	23	24	25
	26	27[d]	28	29	30	1	2
SHA'BĀN 1523	3	4	5	6	7	8	9
	10	11	12	13	14	15	16
	17	18	19	20	21	22	23
	24	25	26	27	28	29	1[e]
RAMAḌĀN 1523	2	3	4	5	6	7	8
	9	10	11	12	13	14	15
	16	17	18	19	20	21	22
	23	24	25	26	27	28	29
SHAWWĀL 1523	30	1[f]	2	3	4	5	6
	7	8	9	10	11	12	13
	14	15	16	17	18	19	20

[a]New Year
[b]'Ashūrā'
[c]Prophet's Birthday
[d]Ascent of the Prophet
[e]Start of Ramaḍān
[f]'Id al-Fiṭr
[g]'Id al-'Aḍḥā

GREGORIAN 2099

Julian (Sun)	Sun	Mon	Tue	Wed	Thu	Fri	Sat	Month
Dec 15	28	29	30	31	1	2	3	
	4	5	6	7[a]	8	9	10	JANUARY 2099
Dec 29	11	12	13	14[b]	15	16	17	
	18	19	20	21	22	23	24	
Jan 12	25	26	27	28	29	30	31	
	1	2	3	4	5	6	7	FEBRUARY 2099
Jan 26	8	9	10	11	12	13	14	
	15	16	17	18	19	20	21	
Feb 9	22	23	24	25[c]	26	27	28	
	1[d]	2	3	4	5	6	7	MARCH 2099
Feb 23	8	9	10	11	12	13	14	
	15	16	17	18	19	20	21	
Mar 9	22	23	24	25	26	27	28	
	29	30	31	1	2	3	4	APRIL 2099
Mar 23	5	6	7	8	9	10	11	
	12[e]	13	14	15	16	17	18	
Apr 6	19	20	21	22	23	24	25	
	26	27	28	29	30	1	2	MAY 2099
Apr 20	3	4	5	6	7	8	9	
	10	11	12	13	14	15	16	
May 4	17	18	19	20	21	22	23	
	24	25	26	27	28	29	30	
May 18	31	1	2	3	4	5	6	JUNE 2099
	7	8	9	10	11	12	13	
Jun 1	14	15	16	17	18	19	20	
	21	22	23	24	25	26	27	
Jun 15	28	29	30	1	2	3	4	JULY 2099
	5	6	7	8	9	10	11	
Jun 29	12	13	14	15	16	17	18	
	19	20	21	22	23	24	25	
Jul 13	26	27	28	29	30	31	1	AUGUST 2099
	2	3	4	5	6	7	8	
Jul 27	9	10	11	12	13	14	15	
	16	17	18	19	20	21	22	
Aug 10	23	24	25	26	27	28	29	
	30	31	1	2	3	4	5	SEPTEMBER 2099
Aug 24	6	7	8	9	10	11	12	
	13	14	15	16	17	18	19	
Sep 7	20	21	22	23	24	25	26	
	27	28	29	30	1	2	3	OCTOBER 2099
Sep 21	4	5	6	7	8	9	10	
	11	12	13	14	15	16	17	
Oct 5	18	19	20	21	22	23	24	
	25	26	27	28	29	30	31	
Oct 19	1	2	3	4	5	6	7	NOVEMBER 2099
	8	9	10	11	12	13	14	
Nov 2	15	16	17	18	19	20	21	
	22	23	24	25	26	27	28	
Nov 16	29[g]	30	1	2	3	4	5	DECEMBER 2099
	6	7	8	9	10	11	12	
Nov 30	13	14	15	16	17	18	19	
	20	21	22	23	24	25[h]	26	
Dec 14	27	28	29	30	31	1	2	

[a]Orthodox Christmas
[b]Julian New Year
[c]Ash Wednesday
[d]Feast of Orthodoxy
[e]Easter (also Orthodox)
[g]Advent
[h]Christmas

2100

Gregorian 2100	Sun Mon Tue Wed Thu Fri Sat	Lunar Phases	ISO Week (Mon)	Julian Day (Sun noon)	Hebrew 5860‡/5861	Sun Mon Tue Wed Thu Fri Sat	Molad	Chinese Jǐ-Wèi‡/Gēng-Shēn	Sun Mon Tue Wed Thu Fri Sat	Solar Term	Coptic 1816/1817	Sun Mon Tue Wed Thu Fri Sat	Ethiopic 2092/2093
JANUARY 2100	○ 28 29 30 31 1[a] 2	12:57	53	2488065	TEVETH 5860	15 16 17 18 19 20 21		MONTH 11 Jǐ-Wèi	16 17 18 19 20 21 22		KOIAK 1816	17 18 19 20 21 22 23	TĀKHŚĀŚ 2092
	◑ 4 5 6 7 8 9	13:02	1	2488072		22 23 24 25 26 27 28			23 24 25 26 27 28 29	Xiǎo hán		24 25 26 27 28 29[c] 30	
	● 11 12 13 14 15 16	12:55	2	2488079	SHEVAT 5860	29 1 2 3 4 5 6	Mon 2h57m8p	MONTH 12 Jǐ-Wèi	1 2 3 4 5 6 7		TÔBE 1816	1 2 3 4 5 6[d] 7	ṬER 2092
	17 ◐ 19 20 21 22 23	12:33	3	2488086		7 8 9 10 11 12 13			8 9 10 11 12 13* 14	Dà hán		8 9 10 11[e] 12 13 14	
	24 25 ○ 27 28 29 30	2:48	4	2488093		14 15 16 17 18 19 20			15 16 17 18 19 20 21			15 16 17 18 19 20 21	
FEBRUARY 2100	31 ◑ 2 3 4 5 6	21:15	5	2488100		21 22 23 24 25 26 27			22 23 24 25 26 27 28	Lì chūn		22 23 24 25 26 27 28	
	7 8 ● 10 11 12 13	4:54	6	2488107	ADAR I 5860	28 29 30 1 2 3 4	Tue 15h41m9p	MONTH 1 Gēng-Shēn	29 30 1[a] 2 3 4 5		MESHIR 1816	29 30 1 2 3 4 5	YAKĀTIT 2092
	14 15 16 ◐ 18 19 20	9:21	7	2488114		5 6 7 8 9 10 11			6 7 8 9 10 11 12	Yǔ shuǐ		6 7 8 9 10 11 12	
	21 22 23 ○ 25 26 27	14:50	8	2488121		12 13 14 15 16 17 18			13 14 15[b] 16 17 18 19			13 14 15 16 17 18 19	
MARCH 2100	28 1 2 ◑ 4 5 6	6:10	9	2488128		19 20 21 22 23 24 25			20 21 22 23 24 25 26	Jīng zhé		20 21 22 23 24 25 26	
	7 8 9 ● 11 12 13	22:28	10	2488135	ADAR II 5860	26 27 28 29 30 1 2	Thu 4h25m10p	MONTH 2 Gēng-Shēn	27 28 29 30 1 2 3		PAREMOTEP 1816	27 28 29 30 1 2 3	MAGĀBIT 2092
	14 15 16 17 18 ◐ 20[b]	2:57	11	2488142		3 4 5 6 7 8 9			4 5 6 7 8 9 10	Chūn fēn		4 5 6 7 8 9 10	
	21 22 23 24 25 ○ 27	1:04	12	2488149		10 11 12 13 14[f] 15 16			11 12 13* 14 15 16 17			11 12 13 14 15 16 17	
APRIL 2100	28 29 30 31 ◑ 2 3	16:34	13	2488156		17 18 19 20 21 22 23			18 19 20 21 22 23 24			18 19 20 21 22 23 24	
	4 5 6 7 8 ● 10	16:16	14	2488163	NISAN 5860	24 25 26 27 28 29 1	Fri 17h9m11p	MONTH 3 Gēng-Shēn	25 26[c] 27 28 29 30 1	Qīng míng	PARMOUTE 1816	25 26 27 28 29 30 1	MIYĀZYĀ 2092
	11 12 13 14 15 16 ◐	16:41	15	2488170		2 3 4 5 6 7 8			2 3 4 5 6 7 8			2 3 4 5 6 7 8	
	18 19 20 21 22 23 ○	9:42	16	2488177		9 10 11 12 13 14 15[g]			9 10 11 12 13 14 15	Gǔ yǔ		9 10 11 12 13 14 15	
MAY 2100	25 26 27 28 29 30 ◑	5:00	17	2488184		16 17 18 19 20 21 22			16 17 18 19 20 21 22			16 17 18 19 20 21 22	
	2 3 4 5 6 7 8		18	2488191		23 24 25 26 27 28 29			23 24 25 26 27 28 29	Lì xià		23[f] 24 25 26 27 28 29[g]	
	● 10 11 12 13 14 15	8:53	19	2488198	IYAR 5860	30 1 2 3 4 5 6	Sun 5h53m12p	MONTH 4 Gēng-Shēn	1 2 3 4 5 6 7		PASHONS 1816	30 1 2 3 4 5 6	GENBOT 2092
	16 ◐ 18 19 20 21 22	2:41	20	2488205		7 8 9 10 11 12 13			8 9 10 11 12 13 14*	Xiǎo mǎn		7 8 9 10 11 12 13	
	○ 24 25 26 27 28 29	17:24	21	2488212		14 15 16 17 18 19 20			15 16 17 18 19 20 21			14 15 16 17 18 19 20	
JUNE 2100	◑ 31 1 2 3 4 5	19:34	22	2488219		21 22 23 24 25 26 27			22 23 24 25 26 27 28	Máng zhòng		21 22 23 24 25 26 27	
	6 ● 8 9 10 11 12	23:30	23	2488226	SIVAN 5860	28 29 1 2 3 4 5	Mon 18h37m13p	MONTH 5 Gēng-Shēn	29 30 1 2 3 4 5[d]		PAÔNE 1816	28 29 30 1 2 3 4	SANĒ 2092
	13 14 ◐ 16 17 18 19	9:40	24	2488233		6[h] 7 8 9 10 11 12			6 7 8 9 10 11 12			5 6 7 8 9 10 11	
	20 21[c] ○ 23 24 25 26	1:10	25	2488240		13 14 15 16 17 18 19			13 14 15 16 17 18 19	Xià zhì		12 13 14 15 16 17 18	
JULY 2100	27 28 ◑ 30 1 2 3	11:51	26	2488247		20 21 22 23 24 25 26			20 21 22 23 24 25 26			19 20 21 22 23 24 25	
	4 5 6 ● 8 9 10	12:05	27	2488254	TAMMUZ 5860	27 28 29 30 1 2 3	Wed 7h21m14p	MONTH 6 Gēng-Shēn	27 28 29 1 2 3 4	Xiǎo shǔ	EPÊP 1816	26 27 28 29 30 1 2	ḤAMLĒ 2092
	11 12 13 ◐ 15 16 17	14:42	28	2488261		4 5 6 7 8 9 10			5 6 7 8 9 10 11			3 4 5 6 7 8 9	
	18 19 20 ○ 22 23 24	10:11	29	2488268		11 12 13 14 15 16 17			12 13 14 15* 16 17 18	Dà shǔ		10 11 12 13 14 15 16	
AUGUST 2100	25 26 27 28 ◑ 30 31	5:07	30	2488275		18 19 20 21 22 23 24			19 20 21 22 23 24 25			17 18 19 20 21 22 23	
	1 2 3 4 ● 6 7	23:01	31	2488282	AV 5860	25 26 27 28 29 1 2	Thu 20h5m15p	MONTH 7 Gēng-Shēn	26 27 28 29 30 1 2	Lì qiū		24 25 26 27 28 29 30	
	8 9 10 11 ◐ 13 14	19:09	32	2488289		3 4 5 6 7 8 9			3 4 5 6 7[e] 8 9		MESORÊ 1816	1 2 3 4 5 6 7	NAHASĒ 2092
	15 16 17 18 ○ 20 21	21:29	33	2488296		10[i] 11 12 13 14 15 16			10 11 12 13 14 15[f] 16			8 9 10 11 12 13[h] 14	
	22 23 24 25 26 ◑ 28	22:36	34	2488303		17 18 19 20 21 22 23			17 18 19 20 21 22 23	Chǔ shǔ		15 16 17 18 19 20 21	
SEPTEMBER 2100	29 30 31 1 2 3 ●	8:48	35	2488310		24 25 26 27 28 29 30		MONTH 8 Gēng-Shēn	24 25 26 27 28 29 1			22 23 24 25 26 27 28	
	5 6 7 8 9 10 ◐	0:34	36	2488317	ELUL 5860	1 2 3 4 5 6 7	Sat 8h49m16p		2 3 4 5 6 7 8	Bái lù	EPAG. 1816	29 30 1 2 3 4 5	PĀG. 2092
	12 13 14 15 16 17 ○	11:31	37	2488324		8 9 10 11 12 13 14			9 10 11 12 13 14 15[g]		THOOUT 1817	1[a] 2 3 4 5 6 7	MASKARAM 2093
	19 20 21 22[d] 23 24 25		38	2488331		15 16 17 18 19 20 21			16* 17 18 19 20 21 22	Qiū fēn		8 9 10 11 12 13 14	
OCTOBER 2100	◑ 27 28 29 30 1 2	15:32	39	2488338		22 23 24 25 26 27 28			23 24 25 26 27 28 29			15 16 17[b] 18 19 20 21	
	● 4 5 6 7 8 9	18:02	40	2488345	TISHRI 5861	29 1[a] 2[a] 3 4 5 6	Sun 21h33m17p	MONTH 9 Gēng-Shēn	30 1 2 3 4 5 6	Hán lù		22 23 24 25 26 27 28	
	◐ 11 12 13 14 15 16	8:32	41	2488352		7 8 9 10[b] 11 12 13			7 8 9[h] 10 11 12 13		PAOPE 1817	29 30 1 2 3 4 5	ṬEQEMT 2093
	17 ○ 19 20 21 22 23	4:05	42	2488359		14 15[c] 16 17 18 19 20			14 15 16 17 18 19 20	Shuāng jiàng		6 7 8 9 10 11 12	
NOVEMBER 2100	24 25 ◑ 27 28 29 30	7:18	43	2488366		21 22 23 24 25 26 27			21 22 23 24 25 26 27			13 14 15 16 17 18 19	
	31 1 ● 3 4 5 6	3:13	44	2488373	ḤESHVAN 5861	28 29 30 1 2 3 4	Tue 10h18m0p	MONTH 10 Gēng-Shēn	28 29 1 2 3 4 5			20 21 22 23 24 25 26	
	7 ◐ 9 10 11 12 13	20:14	45	2488380		5 6 7 8 9 10 11			6 7 8 9 10 11 12	Lì dōng	ATHÔR 1817	27 28 29 30 1 2 3	ḪEDĀR 2093
	14 15 ○ 17 18 19 20	22:18	46	2488387		12 13 14 15 16 17 18			13 14 15 16 17* 18 19			4 5 6 7 8 9 10	
DECEMBER 2100	21 22 23 ◑ 25 26 27	21:12	47	2488394		19 20 21 22 23 24 25			20 21 22 23 24 25 26	Xiǎo xuě		11 12 13 14 15 16 17	
	28 29 30 ● 2 3 4	12:59	48	2488401	KISLEV 5861	26 27 28 29 30 1 2	Wed 23h2m1p	MONTH 11 Gēng-Shēn	27 28 29 1 2 3 4			18 19 20 21 22 23 24	
	5 6 7 ◐ 9 10 11	12:08	49	2488408		3 4[d] 5 6 7 8 9			5 6 7 8 9 10 11	Dà xuě	KOIAK 1817	25 26 27 28 29 30 1	TĀKHŚĀŚ 2093
	12 13 14 15 ○ 17 18	16:59	50	2488415		10 11 12 13 14 15 16			12 13 14 15 16 17 18			2 3 4 5 6 7 8	
	19 20 21[e] 22 23 ◑ 25	8:45	51	2488422		17 18 19 20 21 22 23			19 20 21 22[i] 23 24 25	Dōng zhì		9 10 11 12 13 14 15	
	26 27 28 29 ● 31 1	23:55	52	2488429		24 25[e] 26[e] 27[e] 28[e] 29[e] 30[e]			26 27 28 29 30 1 2			16 17 18 19 20 21 22	

[a]New Year
[b]Spring (13:02)
[c]Summer (5:31)
[d]Autumn (21:59)
[e]Winter (19:49)
● New moon
◐ First quarter moon
○ Full moon
◑ Last quarter moon

‡Leap year
[a]New Year
[b]Yom Kippur
[c]Sukkot
[d]Winter starts
[e]Ḥanukkah
[f]Purim
[g]Passover
[h]Shavuot
[i]Fast of Av

‡Leap year
[a]New Year (4798, Monkey)
[b]Lantern Festival
[c]Qīngmíng
[d]Dragon Festival
[e]Qīqiǎo
[f]Hungry Ghosts
[g]Mid-Autumn Festival
[h]Double-Ninth Festival
[i]Dōngzhì
*Start of 60-name cycle

[a]New Year
[b]Building of the Cross
[c]Christmas
[d]Jesus's Circumcision
[e]Epiphany
[f]Easter
[g]Mary's Announcement
[h]Jesus's Transfiguration

PERSIAN (ASTRONOMICAL) 1478‡/1479

Month	Sun	Mon	Tue	Wed	Thu	Fri	Sat
DEY 1478	7	8	9	10	11	12	13
	14	15	16	17	18	19	20
	21	22	23	24	25	26	27
BAHMAN 1478	28	29	30	1	2	3	4
	5	6	7	8	9	10	11
	12	13	14	15	16	17	18
	19	20	21	22	23	24	25
ESFAND 1478	26	27	28	29	30	1	2
	3	4	5	6	7	8	9
	10	11	12	13	14	15	16
	17	18	19	20	21	22	23
	24	25	26	27	28	29	30
FARVARDĪN 1479	1[a]	2	3	4	5	6	7
	8	9	10	11	12	13[b]	14
	15	16	17	18	19	20	21
	22	23	24	25	26	27	28
ORDĪBEHEŠT 1479	29	30	31	1	2	3	4
	5	6	7	8	9	10	11
	12	13	14	15	16	17	18
	19	20	21	22	23	24	25
XORDĀD 1479	26	27	28	29	30	31	1
	2	3	4	5	6	7	8
	9	10	11	12	13	14	15
	16	17	18	19	20	21	22
	23	24	25	26	27	28	29
TĪR 1479	30	31	1	2	3	4	5
	6	7	8	9	10	11	12
	13	14	15	16	17	18	19
	20	21	22	23	24	25	26
MORDĀD 1479	27	28	29	30	31	1	2
	3	4	5	6	7	8	9
	10	11	12	13	14	15	16
	17	18	19	20	21	22	23
	24	25	26	27	28	29	30
SHAHRĪVAR 1479	31	1	2	3	4	5	6
	7	8	9	10	11	12	13
	14	15	16	17	18	19	20
	21	22	23	24	25	26	27
MEHR 1479	28	29	30	31	1	2	3
	4	5	6	7	8	9	10
	11	12	13	14	15	16	17
	18	19	20	21	22	23	24
ĀBĀN 1479	25	26	27	28	29	30	1
	2	3	4	5	6	7	8
	9	10	11	12	13	14	15
	16	17	18	19	20	21	22
	23	24	25	26	27	28	29
ĀZAR 1479	30	1	2	3	4	5	6
	7	8	9	10	11	12	13
	14	15	16	17	18	19	20
	21	22	23	24	25	26	27
DEY 1479	28	29	30	1	2	3	4
	5	6	7	8	9	10	11

‡Leap year
[a]New Year
[b]Sizdeh Bedar

HINDU LUNAR 2156‡/2157

Month	Sun	Mon	Tue	Wed	Thu	Fri	Sat
MĀRGAŚIRA 2156	15	16	17	18	19	20	21
	22	24	25	26	27	28	29
PAUSHA 2156	30	1	2	3	4	5	6
	7	8	9	10	*10*	11	12
	13	14	15	**16**	18	19	20
	21	22	23	24	25	26	27
MĀGHA 2156	28	29	30	1	2	3	4
	5	6	7	8	9	10	11
	12	13	14	15	16	17	18
	19	20	**21**	23	24	25	26
PHĀLGUNA 2156	27	28	29[h]	30	1	2	3
	3	4	5	6	7	8	9
	10	11	12	13	14	**15**[i]	17
	18	19	20	21	22	23	24
CHAITRA 2157	25	26	27	28	29	30	1[a]
	2	3	4	5	6	7	8
	9[b]	10	11	12	13	14	15
	16	17	18	**19**	21	22	23
	24	25	26	27	*27*	28	29
VAIŚĀKHA 2157	30	1	2	3	4	5	6
	7	8	9	10	11	**12**	14
	15	16	17	18	19	20	21
	22	23	24	25	26	27	28
JYAISHTHA 2157	29	30	1	2	*2*	**3**	5
	6	7	8	9	10	11	12
	13	14	**15**	17	18	19	20
	21	22	23	*23*	24	25	26
ĀSHĀDHA 2157	27	28	29	30	1	2	3
	4	5	6	7	**8**	10	11
	12	13	14	15	16	17	18
	19	20	21	22	23	24	25
ŚRĀVANA 2157	26	27	28	29	30	1	2
	3	4	5	6	7	8	9
	10	**11**	13	14	15	16	17
	18	19	20	*20*	21	22	23[c]
	24	25	26	27	28	29	30
BHĀDRAPADA 2157	1	2	**3**[d]	5	6	7	8
	9	10	11	12	13	14	15
	16	17	18	19	20	21	22
	23	24	25	26	27	28	29
ĀŚVINA 2157	30	1	2	3	4	5	6
	7[e]	9[e]	10[e]	11	12	13	14
	15	*15*	16	17	18	19	20
	21	22	23	24	25	26	27
KĀRTTIKA 2157	28	29	30	**1**[f]	3	4	5
	6	7	8	9	10	11	12
	13	14	15	16	17	18	*18*
	19	20	21	22	23	**24**	26
MĀRGAŚIRA 2157	27	28	29	30	1	2	3
	4	5	6	7	8	9	10
	11[g]	12	13	14	15	16	17
	18	19	20	21	22	23	24
	25	26	27	28	**29**	1	2

‡Leap year
[a]New Year (Rāudra)
[b]Birthday of Rāma
[c]Birthday of Krishna
[d]Ganēśa Chaturthī
[e]Dashara
[f]Diwali
[g]Birthday of Vishnu
[h]Night of Śiva
[i]Holi

HINDU SOLAR 2021/2022

Month	Sun	Mon	Tue	Wed	Thu	Fri	Sat
PAUSHA 2021	11	12	13	14	15	16	17
	18	19	20	21	22	23	24
MĀGHA 2021	25	26	27	28	29	1[b]	2
	3	4	5	6	7	8	9
	10	11	12	13	14	15	16
	17	18	19	20	21	22	23
	24	25	26	27	28	29	30
PHĀLGUNA 2021	1	2	3	4	5	6	7
	8	9	10	11	12	13	14
	15	16	17	18	19	20	21
	22	23	24	25	26	27	28
CHAITRA 2021	29	1	2	3	4	5	6
	7	8	9	10	11	12	13
	14	15	16	17	18	19	20
	21	22	23	24	25	26	27
VAIŚĀKHA 2022	28	29	30	31	1[a]	2	3
	4	5	6	7	8	9	10
	11	12	13	14	15	16	17
	18	19	20	21	22	23	24
	25	26	27	28	29	30	31
JYAISHTHA 2022	1	2	3	4	5	6	7
	8	9	10	11	12	13	14
	15	16	17	18	19	20	21
	22	23	24	25	26	27	28
ĀSHĀDHA 2022	29	30	31	1	2	3	4
	5	6	7	8	9	10	11
	12	13	14	15	16	17	18
	19	20	21	22	23	24	25
	26	27	28	29	30	31	32
ŚRĀVANA 2022	1	2	3	4	5	6	7
	8	9	10	11	12	13	14
	15	16	17	18	19	20	21
	22	23	24	25	26	27	28
BHĀDRAPADA 2022	29	30	31	1	2	3	4
	5	6	7	8	9	10	11
	12	13	14	15	16	17	18
	19	20	21	22	23	24	25
ĀŚVINA 2022	26	27	28	29	30	31	1
	2	3	4	5	6	7	8
	9	10	11	12	13	14	15
	16	17	18	19	20	21	22
	23	24	25	26	27	28	29
KĀRTTIKA 2022	30	31	1	2	3	4	5
	6	7	8	9	10	11	12
	13	14	15	16	17	18	19
	20	21	22	23	24	25	26
MĀRGAŚIRA 2022	27	28	29	30	1	2	3
	4	5	6	7	8	9	10
	11	12	13	14	15	16	17
	18	19	20	21	22	23	24
PAUSHA 2022	25	26	27	28	29	1	2
	3	4	5	6	7	8	9
	10	11	12	13	14	15	16

[a]New Year (Bhāva)
[b]Pongal

ISLAMIC (ASTRONOMICAL) 1523/1524

Month	Sun	Mon	Tue	Wed	Thu	Fri	Sat
SHAWWĀL 1523	14	15	16	17	18	19	20
	21	22	23	24	25	26	27
DHU AL-QA'DA 1523	28	29	1	2	3	4	5
	6	7	8	9	10	11	12
	13	14	15	16	17	18	19
	20	21	22	23	24	25	26
DHU AL-ḤIJJA 1523	27	28	29	30	1	2	3
	4	5	6	7	8	9	10[g]
	11	12	13	14	15	16	17
	18	19	20	21	22	23	24
MUḤARRAM 1524	25	26	27	28	29	1[a]	2
	3	4	5	6	7	8	9
	10[b]	11	12	13	14	15	16
	17	18	19	20	21	22	23
	24	25	26	27	28	29	30
ṢAFAR 1524	1	2	3	4	5	6	7
	8	9	10	11	12	13	14
	15	16	17	18	19	20	21
	22	23	24	25	26	27	28
RABĪ' I 1524	29	30	1	2	3	4	5
	6	7	8	9	10	11	12[c]
	13	14	15	16	17	18	19
	20	21	22	23	24	25	26
RABĪ' II 1524	27	28	29	1	2	3	4
	5	6	7	8	9	10	11
	12	13	14	15	16	17	18
	19	20	21	22	23	24	25
JUMĀDĀ I 1524	26	27	28	29	30	1	2
	3	4	5	6	7	8	9
	10	11	12	13	14	15	16
	17	18	19	20	21	22	23
JUMĀDĀ II 1524	24	25	26	27	28	29	1
	2	3	4	5	6	7	8
	9	10	11	12	13	14	15
	16	17	18	19	20	21	22
	23	24	25	26	27	28	29
RAJAB 1524	30	1	2	3	4	5	6
	7	8	9	10	11	12	13
	14	15	16	17	18	19	20
	21	22	23	24	25	26	27[d]
SHA'BĀN 1524	28	29	30	1	2	3	4
	5	6	7	8	9	10	11
	12	13	14	15	16	17	18
	19	20	21	22	23	24	25
RAMAḌĀN 1524	26	27	28	29	1[e]	2	3
	4	5	6	7	8	9	10
	11	12	13	14	15	16	17
	18	19	20	21	22	23	24
SHAWWĀL 1524	25	26	27	28	29	1[f]	2
	3	4	5	6	7	8	9
	10	11	12	13	14	15	16
	17	18	19	20	21	22	23
	24	25	26	27	28	29	1

[a]New Year
[b]'Ashūrā'
[c]Prophet's Birthday
[d]Ascent of the Prophet
[e]Start of Ramaḍān
[f]'Id al-Fiṭr
[g]'Id al-'Aḍḥā

GREGORIAN 2100

Julian‡ (Sun)	Sun	Mon	Tue	Wed	Thu	Fri	Sat	Month
Dec 14	27	28	29	30	31	1	2	JANUARY 2100
	3	4	5	6	7[a]	8	9	
Dec 28	10	11	12	13	14[b]	15	16	
	17	18	19	20	21	22	23	
Jan 11	24	25	26	27	28	29	30	
	31	1	2	3	4	5	6	FEBRUARY 2100
Jan 25	7	8	9	10[c]	11	12	13	
	14	15	16	17	18	19	20	
Feb 8	21	22	23	24	25	26	27	
	28	1	2	3	4	5	6	MARCH 2100
Feb 22	7	8	9	10	11	12	13	
	14	15	16	17	18	19	20	
Mar 7	21[d]	22	23	24	25	26	27	
	28[e]	29	30	31	1	2	3	APRIL 2100
Mar 21	4	5	6	7	8	9	10	
	11	12	13	14	15	16	17	
Apr 4	18	19	20	21	22	23	24	
	25	26	27	28	29	30	1	MAY 2100
Apr 18	2[f]	3	4	5	6	7	8	
	9	10	11	12	13	14	15	
May 2	16	17	18	19	20	21	22	
	23	24	25	26	27	28	29	
May 16	30	31	1	2	3	4	5	JUNE 2100
	6	7	8	9	10	11	12	
May 30	13	14	15	16	17	18	19	
	20	21	22	23	24	25	26	
Jun 13	27	28	29	30	1	2	3	JULY 2100
	4	5	6	7	8	9	10	
Jun 27	11	12	13	14	15	16	17	
	18	19	20	21	22	23	24	
Jul 11	25	26	27	28	29	30	31	
	1	2	3	4	5	6	7	AUGUST 2100
Jul 25	8	9	10	11	12	13	14	
	15	16	17	18	19	20	21	
Aug 8	22	23	24	25	26	27	28	
	29	30	31	1	2	3	4	SEPTEMBER 2100
Aug 22	5	6	7	8	9	10	11	
	12	13	14	15	16	17	18	
Sep 5	19	20	21	22	23	24	25	
	26	27	28	29	30	1	2	OCTOBER 2100
Sep 19	3	4	5	6	7	8	9	
	10	11	12	13	14	15	16	
Oct 3	17	18	19	20	21	22	23	
	24	25	26	27	28	29	30	
Oct 17	31	1	2	3	4	5	6	NOVEMBER 2100
	7	8	9	10	11	12	13	
Oct 31	14	15	16	17	18	19	20	
	21	22	23	24	25	26	27	
Nov 14	28[g]	29	30	1	2	3	4	DECEMBER 2100
	5	6	7	8	9	10	11	
Nov 28	12	13	14	15	16	17	18	
	19	20	21	22	23	24	25[h]	
Dec 12	26	27	28	29	30	31	1	

‡Julian leap year
[a]Orthodox Christmas
[b]Julian New Year
[c]Ash Wednesday
[d]Feast of Orthodoxy
[e]Easter
[f]Orthodox Easter
[g]Advent
[h]Christmas

2101

Gregorian 2101 (month)	Sun	Mon	Tue	Wed	Thu	Fri	Sat	Lunar Phases	ISO Week (Mon)	Julian Day (Sun noon)	Hebrew 5861/5862 (month)	Sun	Mon	Tue	Wed	Thu	Fri	Sat	Molad	Chinese Gēng-Shēn/Xīn-Yǒu‡ (month)	Sun	Mon	Tue	Wed	Thu	Fri	Sat	Solar Term	Coptic 1817/1818 (month)	Sun	Mon	Tue	Wed	Thu	Fri	Sat	Ethiopic 2093/2094 (month)
	26	27	28	29	●	31	1[a]	23:55	52	2488429		24	25[e]	26[e]	27[e]	28[e]	29[e]	30[e]			26	27	28	29	30	1	2		Koiak 1817	16	17	18	19	20	21	22	Tākhśāś 2093
January 2101	2	3	4	5	6	◐	8	7:32	1	2488436	Teveth 5861	1[e]	2[e]	3	4	5	6	7	Fri 11h 46m 2p	Month 12 Gēng-Shēn	3	4	5	6	7	8	9	Xiǎo hán		23	24	25	26	27	28	29[c]	
	9	10	11	12	13	14	○	10:50	2	2488443		8	9	10	11	12	13	14			10	11	12	13	14	15	16			30	1	2	3	4	5	6[d]	
	16	17	18	19	20	21	◑	17:59	3	2488450		15	16	17	18	19	20	21			17	18*	19	20	**21**	22	23	Dà hán	Tōbe 1817	7	8	9	10	11[e]	12	13	Ṭer 2093
	23	24	25	26	27	28	●	12:23	4	2488457		22	23	24	25	26	27	28			24	25	26	27	28	29	1[a]			14	15	16	17	18	19	20	
	30	31	1	2	3	4	5		5	2488464		29	1	2	3	4	5	6	Sun 0h 30m 3p		2	3	4	5	6	7	8	Lì chūn		21	22	23	24	25	26	27	
February 2101	◐	7	8	9	10	11	12	4:45	6	2488471	Shevat 5861	7	8	9	10	11	12	13		Month 1 Xīn-Yǒu	9	10	11	12	13	14	15[b]			28	29	30	1	2	3	4	
	13	○	15	16	17	18	19	2:42	7	2488478		14	15	16	17	18	19	20			16	17	18	19	20	21	**22**	Yǔ shuǐ	Meshir 1817	5	6	7	8	9	10	11	Yakātit 2093
	20	◑	22	23	24	25	26	1:35	8	2488485		21	22	23	24	25	26	27			23	24	25	26	27	28	29			12	13	14	15	16	17	18	
	27	●	1	2	3	4	5	2:23	9	2488492		28	29	30	1	2	3	4	Mon 13h 14m 4p		30	1	2	3	4	5	6			19	20	21	22	23	24	25	
March 2101	6	7	◐	9	10	11	12	1:49	10	2488499	Adar 5861	5	6	7	8	9	10	11		Month 2 Xīn-Yǒu	7	8	9	10	11	12	13	Jīng zhé		26	27	28	29	30	1	2	
	13	14	○	16	17	18	19	15:49	11	2488506		12	13	14[f]	15	16	17	18			14	15	16	17	18	19*	20		Paremotep 1817	3	4	5	6	7	8	9	Magābit 2093
	20[b]	21	◑	23	24	25	26	8:43	12	2488513		19	20	21	22	23	24	25			21	**22**	23	24	25	26	27	Chūn fēn		10	11	12	13	14	15	16	
	27	28	●	30	31	1	2	17:30	13	2488520		26	27	28	29	1	2	3	Wed 1h 58m 5p		28	29	30	1	2	3	4			17	18	19	20	21	22	23	
April 2101	3	4	5	◐	7	8	9	20:58	14	2488527	Nisan 5861	4	5	6	7	8	9	10		Month 3 Xīn-Yǒu	5	6	7[c]	8	9	10	11	Qīng míng		24	25	26	27	28	29	30	
	10	11	12	13	○	15	16	2:07	15	2488534		11	12	13	14	15[g]	16	17			12	13	14	15	16	17	18		Parmoute 1817	1	2	3	4	5	6	7	Miyāzyā 2093
	17	18	19	◑	21	22	23	16:30	16	2488541		18	19	20	21	22	23	24			19	20	21	**22**	23	24	25	Gǔ yǔ		8	9	10	11	12	13	14	
	24	25	26	27	●	29	30	9:09	17	2488548		25	26	27	28	29	30	1	Thu 14h 42m 6p		26	27	28	29	1	2	3			15[f]	16	17	18	19	20	21	
May 2101	1	2	3	4	5	◐	7	12:59	18	2488555	Iyyar 5861	2	3	4	5	6	7	8		Month 4 Xīn-Yǒu	4	5	6	7	8	9	10	Lì xià		22	23	24	25	26	27	28	
	8	9	10	11	12	○	14	10:14	19	2488562		9	10	11	12	13	14	15			11	12	13	14	15	16	17			29[g]	30	1	2	3	4	5	
	15	16	17	18	19	◑	21	1:51	20	2488569		16	17	18	19	20	21	22			18	19	20*	21	22	23	**24**	Xiǎo mǎn	Pashons 1817	6	7	8	9	10	11	12	Genbot 2093
	22	23	24	25	26	27	●	0:49	21	2488576		23	24	25	26	27	28	29			25	26	27	28	29	30	1			13	14	15	16	17	18	19	
	29	30	31	1	2	3	4		22	2488583		1	2	3	4	5	6[h]	7	Sat 3h 26m 7p		2	3	4	5[d]	6	7	8			20	21	22	23	24	25	26	
June 2101	◐	6	7	8	9	10	○	1:20 13:16	23	2488590	Sivan 5861	8	9	10	11	12	13	14		Month 5 Xīn-Yǒu	9	*10*	11	12	13	14	15	Máng zhòng		27	28	29	30	1	2	3	
	12	13	14	15	16	17	◑	17:13	24	2488597		15	16	17	18	19	20	21			16	17	18	19	20	21	22		Paōne 1817	4	5	6	7	8	9	10	Sanē 2093
	19	20	21[c]	22	23	24	25		25	2488604		22	23	24	25	26	27	28			23	24	**25**	26	27	28	29	Xià zhì		11	12	13	14	15	16	17	
	●	27	28	29	30	1	2	16:04	26	2488611		29	30	1	2	3	4	5	Sun 16h 10m 8p		30	1	2	3	4	5	6			18	19	20	21	22	23	24	
July 2101	3	◐	5	6	7	8	9	10:13	27	2488618	Tammuz 5861	6	7	8	9	10	11	12		Month 6 Xīn-Yǒu	7	8	9	10	*11*	12	13	Xiǎo shǔ		25	26	27	28	29	30	1	
	10	○	12	13	14	15	16	0:13	28	2488625		13	14	15	16	17	18	19			14	15	16	17	18	19	20*		Epēp 1817	2	3	4	5	6	7	8	Ḥamlē 2093
	17	◑	19	20	21	22	23	2:58	29	2488632		20	21	22	23	24	25	26			21	22	23	24	25	26	**27**	Dà shǔ		9	10	11	12	13	14	15	
	24	25	●	27	28	29	30	6:30	30	2488639		27	28	29	1	2	3	4	Tue 4h 54m 9p		28	29	1	2	3	4	5			16	17	18	19	20	21	22	
	31	1	◐	3	4	5	6	16:35	31	2488646	Av 5861	5	6	7	8	9[i]	10	11		Month 7 Xīn-Yǒu	6	7[e]	8	9	10	11	12			23	24	25	26	27	28	29	
August 2101	7	8	○	10	11	12	13	8:18	32	2488653		12	13	14	15	16	17	18			*13*	14	15[f]	16	17	18	19	Lì qiū		30	1	2	3	4	5	6	
	14	15	◑	17	18	19	20	18:58	33	2488660		19	20	21	22	23	24	25			20	21	22	23	24	25	26		Mesorē 1817	7	8	9	10	11	12	13[h]	Naḥasē 2093
	21	22	23	●	25	26	27	19:45	34	2488667		26	27	28	29	30	1	2	Wed 17h 38m 10p		27	28	**29**	30	1	2	3	Chǔ shǔ		14	15	16	17	18	19	20	
	28	29	30	◐	1	2	3	21:44	35	2488674	Elul 5861	3	4	5	6	7	8	9		Leap Month 7 Xīn-Yǒu	4	5	6	7	8	9	10			21	22	23	24	25	26	27	
September 2101	4	5	6	○	8	9	10	18:20	36	2488681		10	11	12	13	14	15	16			11	12	13	14	*15*	16	17	Bái lù	Epag. 1817	28	29	30	1	2	3	4	Pāg. 2093
	11	12	13	14	◑	16	17	12:58	37	2488688		17	18	19	20	21	22	23			18	19	20	21*	22	23	24			5	1[a]	2	3	4	5	6	Maskaram 2094
	18	19	20	21	22	●[d]	24	7:40	38	2488695		24	25	26	27	28	29	1[a]	Fri 6h 22m 11p		25	26	27	28	29	*1*	2	Qiū fēn	Thoout 1818	7	8	9	10	11	12	13	
	25	26	27	28	29	◐	1	3:10	39	2488702		2[a]	3	4	5	6	7	8			3	4	5	6	7	8	9			14	15	16	17[b]	18	19	20	
October 2101	2	3	4	5	6	○	8	6:54	40	2488709	Tishri 5862	9	10[b]	11	12	13	14	15[c]		Month 8 Xīn-Yǒu	10	11	12	13	14	15[g]	*16*	Hán lù		21	22	23	24	25	26	27	
	9	10	11	12	13	14	◑	8:11	41	2488716		16	17	18	19	20	21	22			17	18	19	20	21	22	23			28	29	30	1	2	3	4	
	16	17	18	19	20	21	●	18:29	42	2488723		23	24	25	26	27	28	29			24	25	26	27	28	29	30		Paope 1818	5	6	7	8	9	10	11	Ṭeqemt 2094
	23	24	25	26	27	28	◐	10:20	43	2488730		30	1	2	3	4	5	6	Sat 19h 6m 12p		*1*	2	3	4	5	6	7	Shuāng jiàng		12	13	14	15	16	17	18	
	30	31	1	2	3	4	○	22:16	44	2488737	Heshvan 5862	7	8	9	10	11	12	13		Month 9 Xīn-Yǒu	8	9[h]	10	11	12	13	14			19	20	21	22	23	24	25	
November 2101	6	7	8	9	10	11	12		45	2488744		14	15	16	17	18	19	20			15	*16*	17	18	19	20	21	Lì dōng		26	27	28	29	30	1	2	
	13	◑	15	16	17	18	19	3:13	46	2488751		21	22	23	24	25	26	27			22*	23	24	25	26	27	28		Athōr 1818	3	4	5	6	7	8	9	Ḫedār 2094
	20	●	22	23	24	25	26	4:47	47	2488758		28	29	30	1	2	3	4	Mon 7h 50m 13p		29	1	**2**	3	4	5	6	Xiǎo xuě		10	11	12	13	14	15	16	
	◐	28	29	30	1	2	3	20:19	48	2488765	Kislev 5862	5	6	7	8	9	10	11		Month 10 Xīn-Yǒu	7	8	9	10	11	12	13			17	18	19	20	21	22	23	
December 2101	4	○	6	7	8	9	10	16:16	49	2488772		12	13	14[d]	15	16	17	18			14	15	16	*17*	18	19	20	Dà xuě		24	25	26	27	28	29	30	
	11	12	◑	14	15	16	17	20:24	50	2488779		19	20	21	22	23	24	25[e]			21	22	23	24	25	26	27		Koiak 1818	1	2	3	4	5	6	7	Tākhśāś 2094
	18	19	●	21	22[e]	23	24	15:13	51	2488786	Teveth 5862	26[e]	27[e]	28[e]	29[e]	30[e]	1[e]	2[e]	Tue 20h 34m 14p	Month 11 Xīn-Yǒu	28	29	1	2	3[i]	4	5	Dōng zhì		8	9	10	11	12	13	14	
	25	26	◐	28	29	30	31	9:38	52	2488793		3	4	5	6	7	8	9			6	7	8	9	10	11	12			15	16	17	18	19	20	21	

Gregorian:
[a]New Year
[b]Spring (18:54)
[c]Summer (11:20)
[d]Autumn (3:45)
[e]Winter (1:37)
● New moon
◐ First quarter moon
○ Full moon
◑ Last quarter moon

Hebrew:
[a]New Year
[b]Yom Kippur
[c]Sukkot
[d]Winter starts
[e]Ḥanukkah
[f]Purim
[g]Passover
[h]Shavuot
[i]Fast of Av

Chinese:
‡Leap year
[a]New Year (4799, Fowl)
[b]Lantern Festival
[c]Qīngmíng
[d]Dragon Festival
[e]Qǐqiǎo
[f]Hungry Ghosts
[g]Mid-Autumn Festival
[h]Double-Ninth Festival
[i]Dōngzhì
*Start of 60-name cycle

Coptic/Ethiopic:
[a]New Year
[b]Building of the Cross
[c]Christmas
[d]Jesus's Circumcision
[e]Epiphany
[f]Easter
[g]Mary's Announcement
[h]Jesus's Transfiguration

PERSIAN (ASTRONOMICAL) 1479/1480

Month	Sun	Mon	Tue	Wed	Thu	Fri	Sat
	5	6	7	8	9	10	11
DEY 1479	12	13	14	15	16	17	18
	19	20	21	22	23	24	25
	26	27	28	29	30	1	2
	3	4	5	6	7	8	9
BAHMAN 1479	10	11	12	13	14	15	16
	17	18	19	20	21	22	23
	24	25	26	27	28	29	30
	1	2	3	4	5	6	7
ESFAND 1479	8	9	10	11	12	13	14
	15	16	17	18	19	20	21
	22	23	24	25	26	27	28
	29	1[a]	2	3	4	5	6
FARVARDĪN 1480	7	8	9	10	11	12	13[b]
	14	15	16	17	18	19	20
	21	22	23	24	25	26	27
	28	29	30	31	1	2	3
ORDĪBEHEŠT 1480	4	5	6	7	8	9	10
	11	12	13	14	15	16	17
	18	19	20	21	22	23	24
	25	26	27	28	29	30	31
	1	2	3	4	5	6	7
XORDĀD 1480	8	9	10	11	12	13	14
	15	16	17	18	19	20	21
	22	23	24	25	26	27	28
	29	30	31	1	2	3	4
TĪR 1480	5	6	7	8	9	10	11
	12	13	14	15	16	17	18
	19	20	21	22	23	24	25
	26	27	28	29	30	31	1
	2	3	4	5	6	7	8
MORDĀD 1480	9	10	11	12	13	14	15
	16	17	18	19	20	21	22
	23	24	25	26	27	28	29
	30	31	1	2	3	4	5
SHAHRĪVAR 1480	6	7	8	9	10	11	12
	13	14	15	16	17	18	19
	20	21	22	23	24	25	26
	27	28	29	30	31	1	2
MEHR 1480	3	4	5	6	7	8	9
	10	11	12	13	14	15	16
	17	18	19	20	21	22	23
	24	25	26	27	28	29	30
	1	2	3	4	5	6	7
ĀBĀN 1480	8	9	10	11	12	13	14
	15	16	17	18	19	20	21
	22	23	24	25	26	27	28
	29	30	1	2	3	4	5
ĀZAR 1480	6	7	8	9	10	11	12
	13	14	15	16	17	18	19
	20	21	22	23	24	25	26
	27	28	29	30	1	2	3
DEY 1480	4	5	6	7	8	9	10

[a] New Year
[b] Sizdeh Bedar

HINDU LUNAR 2157/2158

Month	Sun	Mon	Tue	Wed	Thu	Fri	Sat
	25	26	27	28	29	1	2
PAUSHA 2157	3	4	5	6	7	8	9
	10	10	11	12	13	14	15
	16	17	18	19	20	21	22
	23	25	26	27	28	29	30
	1	2	3	4	5	6	7
MĀGHA 2157	8	9	10	11	12	13	13
	14	15	16	18	19	20	21
	22	23	24	25	26	27	28[h]
	29	30	1	2	3	4	5
PHĀLGUNA 2157	6	7	8	9	10	11	12
	13	14	15[i]	16	17	18	19
	20	21	22	24	25	26	27
	28	29	30	1[a]	2	3	4
CHAITRA 2158	5	6	6	7	8[b]	9	10
	11	12	13	14	15	17	18
	19	20	21	22	23	24	25
	26	27	28	29	30	1	2
VAIŚĀKHA 2158	3	4	5	6	7	8	9
	10	11	12	13	14	15	16
	17	18	19	21	22	23	24
	25	26	27	28	29	30	1
JYAISHTHA 2158	1	2	3	4	5	6	7
	8	9	10	11	12	14	15
	16	17	18	19	20	21	22
	23	24	25	26	27	28	29
	30	1	2	3	4	5	6
ĀSHĀḌHA 2158	7	8	9	10	11	12	13
	14	15	17	18	19	20	21
	22	23	24	25	26	27	27
	28	29	30	1	2	3	4
ŚRĀVAṆA 2158	5	6	7	9	10	11	12
	13	14	15	16	17	18	19
	20	21	22	23[c]	24	25	26
	27	28	29	30	1	2	3
BHĀDRAPADA 2158	4[d]	5	6	7	8	9	10
	12	13	14	15	16	17	18
	19	20	21	22	23	24	24
	25	26	27	28	29	30	1
ĀŚVINA 2158	2	3	4	6	7	8[e]	9[e]
	10[e]	11	12	13	14	15	16
	17	18	19	20	21	22	23
	24	25	26	27	28	29	30
	1[f]	2	3	4	5	6	7
KĀRTTIKA 2158	8	10	11	12	13	14	15
	16	17	18	18	19	20	21
	22	23	24	25	26	27	28
	29	30	1	3	4	5	6
MĀRGAŚĪRA 2158	7	8	9	10	11[g]	12	13
	14	15	16	17	18	19	20
	21	21	22	23	24	26	27
PAUSHA 2158	28	29	30	1	2	3	4
	5	6	7	8	9	10	11

[a] New Year (Durmati)
[b] Birthday of Rāma
[c] Birthday of Krishna
[d] Ganēśa Chaturthī
[e] Dashara
[f] Diwali
[g] Birthday of Vishnu
[h] Night of Śiva
[i] Holi

HINDU SOLAR 2022/2023

Month	Sun	Mon	Tue	Wed	Thu	Fri	Sat
	10	11	12	13	14	15	16
PAUSHA 2022	17	18	19	20	21	22	23
	24	25	26	27	28	29	1[b]
	2	3	4	5	6	7	8
MĀGHA 2022	9	10	11	12	13	14	15
	16	17	18	19	20	21	22
	23	24	25	26	27	28	29
	30	1	2	3	4	5	6
PHĀLGUNA 2022	7	8	9	10	11	12	13
	14	15	16	17	18	19	20
	21	22	23	24	25	26	27
	28	29	30	1	2	3	4
CHAITRA 2022	5	6	7	8	9	10	11
	12	13	14	15	16	17	18
	19	20	21	22	23	24	25
	26	27	28	29	30	1[a]	2
VAIŚĀKHA 2023	3	4	5	6	7	8	9
	10	11	12	13	14	15	16
	17	18	19	20	21	22	23
	24	25	26	27	28	29	30
	31	1	2	3	4	5	6
JYAISHTHA 2023	7	8	9	10	11	12	13
	14	15	16	17	18	19	20
	21	22	23	24	25	26	27
	28	29	30	31	1	2	3
ĀSHĀḌHA 2023	4	5	6	7	8	9	10
	11	12	13	14	15	16	17
	18	19	20	21	22	23	24
	25	26	27	28	29	30	31
	32	1	2	3	4	5	6
ŚRĀVAṆA 2023	7	8	9	10	11	12	13
	14	15	16	17	18	19	20
	21	22	23	24	25	26	27
	28	29	30	31	32	1	2
BHĀDRAPADA 2023	3	4	5	6	7	8	9
	10	11	12	13	14	15	16
	17	18	19	20	21	22	23
	24	25	26	27	28	29	30
	31	1	2	3	4	5	6
ĀŚVINA 2023	7	8	9	10	11	12	13
	14	15	16	17	18	19	20
	21	22	23	24	25	26	27
	28	29	30	1	2	3	4
KĀRTTIKA 2023	5	6	7	8	9	10	11
	12	13	14	15	16	17	18
	19	20	21	22	23	24	25
	26	27	28	29	30	1	2
MĀRGAŚĪRA 2023	3	4	5	6	7	8	9
	10	11	12	13	14	15	16
	17	18	19	20	21	22	23
	24	25	26	27	28	29	1
PAUSHA 2023	2	3	4	5	6	7	8
	9	10	11	12	13	14	15

[a] New Year (Yuvan)
[b] Pongal

ISLAMIC (ASTRONOMICAL) 1524/1525‡

Month	Sun	Mon	Tue	Wed	Thu	Fri	Sat
	24	25	26	27	28	29	1
DHU AL-QA'DA 1524	2	3	4	5	6	7	8
	9	10	11	12	13	14	15
	16	17	18	19	20	21	22
	23	24	25	26	27	28	29
	30	1	2	3	4	5	6
DHU AL-HIJJA 1524	7	8	9	10[g]	11	12	13
	14	15	16	17	18	19	20
	21	22	23	24	25	26	27
	28	29	1[a]	2[d]	3	4	5
MUHARRAM 1525	6	7	8	9	10[b]	11	12
	13	14	15	16	17	18	19
	20	21	22	23	24	25	26
	27	28	29	30	1	2	3
SAFAR 1525	4	5	6	7	8	9	10
	11	12	13	14	15	16	17
	18	19	20	21	22	23	24
	25	26	27	28	29	30	1
RABĪ' I 1525	2	3	4	5	6	7	8
	9	10	11	12[c]	13	14	15
	16	17	18	19	20	21	22
	23	24	25	26	27	28	29
	1	2	3	4	5	6	7
RABĪ' II 1525	8	9	10	11	12	13	14
	15	16	17	18	19	20	21
	22	23	24	25	26	27	28
	29	30	1	2	3	4	5
JUMĀDĀ I 1525	6	7	8	9	10	11	12
	13	14	15	16	17	18	19
	20	21	22	23	24	25	26
	27	28	29	30	1	2	3
JUMĀDĀ II 1525	4	5	6	7	8	9	10
	11	12	13	14	15	16	17
	18	19	20	21	22	23	24
	25	26	27	28	29	30	1
RAJAB 1525	2	3	4	5	6	7	8
	9	10	11	12	13	14	15
	16	17	18	19	20	21	22
	23	24	25	26	27[d]	28	29
	30	1	2	3	4	5	6
SHA'BĀN 1525	7	8	9	10	11	12	13
	14	15	16	17	18	19	20
	21	22	23	24	25	26	27
	28	29	1[e]	2	3	4	5
RAMAḌĀN 1525	6	7	8	9	10	11	12
	13	14	15	16	17	18	19
	20	21	22	23	24	25	26
	27	28	29	1[f]	2	3	4
SHAWWĀL 1525	5	6	7	8	9	10	11
	12	13	14	15	16	17	18
	19	20	21	22	23	24	25
DHU AL-QA'DA 1525	26	27	28	29	1	2	3
	4	5	6	7	8	9	10

‡ Leap year
[a] New Year
[d] New Year (Arithmetic)
[b] 'Ashūrā'
[c] Prophet's Birthday
[d] Ascent of the Prophet
[e] Start of Ramaḍān
[f] 'Īd al-Fiṭr
[g] 'Īd al-'Aḍḥā

GREGORIAN 2101

Julian (Sun)	Sun	Mon	Tue	Wed	Thu	Fri	Sat	Month
Dec 12	26	27	28	29	30	31	1	
	2	3	4	5	6	7	8[a]	JANUARY 2101
Dec 26	9	10	11	12	13	14	15[b]	
	16	17	18	19	20	21	22	
Jan 9	23	24	25	26	27	28	29	
	30	31	1	2	3	4	5	
Jan 23	6	7	8	9	10	11	12	FEBRUARY 2101
	13	14	15	16	17	18	19	
Feb 6	20	21	22	23	24	25	26	
	27	28	1	2[c]	3	4	5	
Feb 20	6	7	8	9	10	11	12	MARCH 2101
	13[d]	14	15	16	17	18	19	
Mar 6	20	21	22	23	24	25	26	
	27	28	29	30	31	1	2	
Mar 20	3	4	5	6	7	8	9	APRIL 2101
	10	11	12	13	14	15	16	
Apr 3	17[e]	18	19	20	21	22	23	
	24[f]	25	26	27	28	29	30	
Apr 17	1	2	3	4	5	6	7	
	8	9	10	11	12	13	14	MAY 2101
May 1	15	16	17	18	19	20	21	
	22	23	24	25	26	27	28	
May 15	29	30	31	1	2	3	4	
	5	6	7	8	9	10	11	JUNE 2101
May 29	12	13	14	15	16	17	18	
	19	20	21	22	23	24	25	
Jun 12	26	27	28	29	30	1	2	
	3	4	5	6	7	8	9	
Jun 26	10	11	12	13	14	15	16	JULY 2101
	17	18	19	20	21	22	23	
Jul 10	24	25	26	27	28	29	30	
	31	1	2	3	4	5	6	
Jul 24	7	8	9	10	11	12	13	AUGUST 2101
	14	15	16	17	18	19	20	
Aug 7	21	22	23	24	25	26	27	
	28	29	30	31	1	2	3	
Aug 21	4	5	6	7	8	9	10	SEPTEMBER 2101
	11	12	13	14	15	16	17	
Sep 4	18	19	20	21	22	23	24	
	25	26	27	28	29	30	1	
Sep 18	2	3	4	5	6	7	8	OCTOBER 2101
	9	10	11	12	13	14	15	
Oct 2	16	17	18	19	20	21	22	
	23	24	25	26	27	28	29	
Oct 16	30	31	1	2	3	4	5	
	6	7	8	9	10	11	12	NOVEMBER 2101
Oct 30	13	14	15	16	17	18	19	
	20	21	22	23	24	25	26	
Nov 13	27[g]	28	29	30	1	2	3	
	4	5	6	7	8	9	10	DECEMBER 2101
Nov 27	11	12	13	14	15	16	17	
	18	19	20	21	22	23	24	
Dec 11	25[h]	26	27	28	29	30	31	

[a] Orthodox Christmas
[b] Julian New Year
[c] Ash Wednesday
[d] Feast of Orthodoxy
[e] Easter
[f] Orthodox Easter
[g] Advent
[h] Christmas

2102

GREGORIAN 2102 / ISO WEEK / JULIAN DAY

Month	Sun	Mon	Tue	Wed	Thu	Fri	Sat	Lunar Phases	ISO WEEK (Mon)	JULIAN DAY (Sun noon)
JANUARY 2102	1[a]	2	3	○	5	6	7	11:52	1	2488800
	8	9	10	11	◑	13	14	10:35	2	2488807
	15	16	17	18	●	20	21	2:06	3	2488814
	22	23	24	25	◐	27	28	2:09	4	2488821
	29	30	31	1	2	○	4	7:18	5	2488828
FEBRUARY 2102	5	6	7	8	9	◑	11	21:31	6	2488835
	12	13	14	15	16	●	18	13:27	7	2488842
	19	20	21	22	23	◐	25	21:07	8	2488849
	26	27	28	1	2	3	4		9	2488856
MARCH 2102	○	6	7	8	9	10	11	0:36	10	2488863
	◑	13	14	15	16	17	18	5:47	11	2488870
	●	20	21[b]	22	23	24	25	1:10	12	2488877
	◐	27	28	29	30	31	1	17:15	13	2488884
APRIL 2102	2	○	4	5	6	7	8	14:39	14	2488891
	9	◑	11	12	13	14	15	12:23	15	2488898
	16	●	18	19	20	21	22	13:23	16	2488905
	23	24	◐	26	27	28	29	12:51	17	2488912
	30	1	2	○	4	5	6	1:33	18	2488919
MAY 2102	7	8	◑	10	11	12	13	18:28	19	2488926
	14	15	16	●	18	19	20	2:29	20	2488933
	21	22	23	24	◐	26	27	6:20	21	2488940
	28	29	30	31	○	2	3	10:08	22	2488947
JUNE 2102	4	5	6	7	◑	9	10	1:07	23	2488954
	11	12	13	14	●	16	17	1E:45	24	2488961
	18	19	20	21[c]	22	◐	24	20:47	25	2488968
	25	26	27	28	29	○	1	17:27	26	2488975
JULY 2102	2	3	4	5	6	◑	8	9:21	27	2488982
	9	10	11	12	13	14	●	8:00	28	2488989
	16	17	18	19	20	21	22		29	2488996
	◐	24	25	26	27	28	29	8:10	30	2489003
	○	31	1	2	3	4	◑	0:29 20:09	31	2489010
AUGUST 2102	6	7	8	9	10	11	12		32	2489017
	●	14	15	16	17	18	19	23:36	33	2489024
	20	◐	22	23	24	25	26	17:04	34	2489031
	27	○	29	30	31	1	2	8:04	35	2489038
SEPTEMBER 2102	3	◑	5	6	7	8	9	10:16	36	2489045
	10	11	●	13	14	15	16	14:44	37	2489052
	17	18	19	◐	21	22	23[d]	0:25	38	2489059
	24	25	○	27	28	29	30	17:00	39	2489066
OCTOBER 2102	1	2	3	◑	5	6	7	3:50	40	2489073
	8	9	10	11	●	13	14	4:50	41	2489080
	15	16	17	18	◐	20	21	7:10	42	2489087
	22	23	24	25	○	27	28	4:08	43	2489094
	29	30	31	1	2	◑	4	0:02	44	2489101
NOVEMBER 2102	5	6	7	8	9	●	11	17:56	45	2489108
	12	13	14	15	16	◐	18	14:19	46	2489115
	19	20	21	22	23	○	25	18:13	47	2489122
	26	27	28	29	30	1	◑	21:03	48	2489129
DECEMBER 2102	3	4	5	6	7	8	9		49	2489136
	●	11	12	13	14	15	◐	6:15 22:49	50	2489143
	17	18	19	20	21	22[e]	23		51	2489150
	○	25	26	27	28	29	30	11:24	52	2489157
	31	◑	2	3	4	5	6	16:50	1	2489164

HEBREW 5862/5863‡

ISO WEEK	Month	Sun	Mon	Tue	Wed	Thu	Fri	Sat	Molad
1	TEVETH 5862	10	11	12	13	14	15	16	
2		17	18	19	20	21	22	23	
3		24	25	26	27	28	29	1	Thu $9^{h}18^{m}15^{p}$
4	SHEVAT 5862	2	3	4	5	6	7	8	
5		9	10	11	12	13	14	15	
6		16	17	18	19	20	21	22	
7		23	24	25	26	27	28	29	
8		30	1	2	3	4	5	6	Fri $22^{h}2^{m}16^{p}$
9	ADAR 5862	7	8	9	10	11	12	13	
10		14[f]	15	16	17	18	19	20	
11		21	22	23	24	25	26	27	
12		28	29	1	2	3	4	5	Sun $10^{h}46^{m}17^{p}$
13	NISAN 5862	6	7	8	9	10	11	12	
14		13	14	15[g]	16	17	18	19	
15		20	21	22	23	24	25	26	
16		27	28	29	30	1	2	3	Mon $23^{h}31^{m}0^{p}$
17	IYYAR 5862	4	5	6	7	8	9	10	
18		11	12	13	14	15	16	17	
19		18	19	20	21	22	23	24	
20		25	26	27	28	29	1	2	Wed $12^{h}15^{m}1^{p}$
21	SIVAN 5862	3	4	5	6[h]	7	8	9	
22		10	11	12	13	14	15	16	
23		17	18	19	20	21	22	23	
24		24	25	26	27	28	29	30	
25		1	2	3	4	5	6	7	Fri $0^{h}59^{m}2^{p}$
26	TAMMUZ 5862	8	9	10	11	12	13	14	
27		15	16	17	18	19	20	21	
28		22	23	24	25	26	27	28	
29		29	1	2	3	4	5	6	Sat $13^{h}43^{m}3^{p}$
30	AV 5862	7	8	9[i]	10	11	12	13	
31		14	15	16	17	18	19	20	
32		21	22	23	24	25	26	27	
33		28	29	30	1	2	3	4	Mon $2^{h}27^{m}4^{p}$
34	ELUL 5862	5	6	7	8	9	10	11	
35		12	13	14	15	16	17	18	
36		19	20	21	22	23	24	25	
37		26	27	28	29	1[a]	2[a]	3	Tue $15^{h}11^{m}5^{p}$
38	TISHRI 5863	4	5	6	7	8	9	10[b]	
39		11	12	13	14	15[c]	16	17	
40		18	19	20	21	22	23	24	
41		25	26	27	28	29	30	1	Thu $3^{h}55^{m}6^{p}$
42	ḤESHVAN 5863	2	3	4	5	6	7	8	
43		9	10	11	12	13	14	15	
44		16	17	18	19	20	21	22	
45		23	24	25	26	27	28	29	
46	KISLEV 5863	1	2	3	4	5	6	7	Fri $16^{h}39^{m}7^{p}$
47		8	9	10	11	12	13	14	
48		15	16	17	18	19	20	21	
49		22	23	24	25[d,e]	26[e]	27[e]	28[e]	
50		29[e]	1[e]	2[e]	3[e]	4	5	6	Sun $5^{h}23^{m}8^{p}$
51	TEVETH 5863	7	8	9	10	11	12	13	
52		14	15	16	17	18	19	20	
1		21	22	23	24	25	26	27	

CHINESE Xīn-Yǒu‡/Rén-Xū

ISO WEEK	Month	Sun	Mon	Tue	Wed	Thu	Fri	Sat	Solar Term
1	MONTH 11 Xīn-Yǒu	13	14	15	16	17	18	19	Xiǎo hán
2		20	21	22	23	24*	25	26	
3		27	28	29	30	1	2	3	Dà hán
4	MONTH 12 Xīn-Yǒu	4	5	6	7	8	9	10	
5		11	12	13	14	15	16	17	Lì chūn
6		18	19	20	21	22	23	24	
7		25	26	27	28	29	1[a]	2	
8	MONTH 1 Rén-Xū	3	4	5	6	7	8	9	Yǔ shuǐ
9		10	11	12	13	14	15[b]	16	
10		17	18	19	20	21	22	23	Jīng zhé
11		24	25*	26	27	28	29	30	
12	MONTH 2 Rén-Xū	1	2	3	4	5	6	7	Chūn fēn
13		8	9	10	11	12	13	14	
14		15	16	17	18[c]	19	20	21	Qīng míng
15		22	23	24	25	26	27	28	
16		29	1	2	3	4	5	6	Gǔ yǔ
17	MONTH 3 Rén-Xū	7	8	9	10	11	12	13	
18		14	15	16	17	18	19	20	Lì xià
19		21	22	23	24	25	26*	27	
20		28	29	30	1	2	3	4	
21	MONTH 4 Rén-Xū	5	6	7	8	9	10	11	Xiǎo mǎn
22		12	13	14	15	16	17	18	
23		19	20	21	22	23	24	25	Máng zhòng
24		26	27	28	29	30	1	2	
25	MONTH 5 Rén-Xū	3	4	5[d]	6	7	8	9	Xià zhì
26		10	11	12	13	14	15	16	
27		17	18	19	20	21	22	23	Xiǎo shǔ
28		24	25	26*	27	28	29	1	
29	MONTH 6 Rén-Xū	2	3	4	5	6	7	8	
30		9	10	11	12	13	14	15	Dà shǔ
31		16	17	18	19	20	21	22	
32		23	24	25	26	27	28	29	Lì qiū
33		30	1	2	3	4	5	6	
34	MONTH 7 Rén-Xū	7[e]	8	9	10	11	12	13	Chǔ shǔ
35		14	15[f]	16	17	18	19	20	
36		21	22	23	24	25	26	27*	Bái lù
37		28	29	1	2	3	4	5	
38	MONTH 8 Rén-Xū	6	7	8	9	10	11	12	Qiū fēn
39		13	14	15[g]	16	17	18	19	
40		20	21	22	23	24	25	26	
41		27	28	29	30	1	2	3	Hán lù
42	MONTH 9 Rén-Xū	4	5	6	7	8	9[h]	10	
43		11	12	13	14	15	16	17	Shuāng jiàng
44		18	19	20	21	22	23	24	
45		25	26	27	28*	29	30	1	Lì dōng
46	MONTH 10 Rén-Xū	2	3	4	5	6	7	8	
47		9	10	11	12	13	14	15	Xiǎo xuě
48		16	17	18	19	20	21	22	
49		23	24	25	26	27	28	29	Dà xuě
50	MONTH 11 Rén-Xū	1	2	3	4	5	6	7	
51		8	9	10	11	12	13[i]	14	Dōng zhì
52		15	16	17	18	19	20	21	
1		22	23	24	25	26	27	28	Xiǎo hán

COPTIC 1818/1819‡ — ETHIOPIC 2094/2095‡

ISO WEEK	Coptic Month	Sun	Mon	Tue	Wed	Thu	Fri	Sat	Ethiopic Month
1	KOIAK 1818	22	23	24	25	26	27	28	TĀKHŚĀŚ 2094
2		29[c]	30	1	2	3	4	5	
3	TŌBE 1818	6[d]	7	8	9	10	11[e]	12	ṬER 2094
4		13	14	15	16	17	18	19	
5		20	21	22	23	24	25	26	
6		27	28	29	30	1	2	3	
7	MESHIR 1818	4	5	6	7	8	9	10	
8		11	12	13	14	15	16	17	YAKĀTIT 2094
9		18	19	20	21	22	23	24	
10		25	26	27	28	29	30	1	
11	PAREMOTEP 1818	2	3	4	5	6	7	8	
12		9	10	11	12	13	14	15	MAGĀBIT 2094
13		16	17	18	19	20	21	22	
14		23	24	25	26	27	28	29	
15		30[f]	1	2	3	4	5	6	
16	PARMOUTE 1818	7	8	9	10	11	12	13	MIYĀZYĀ 2094
17		14	15	16	17	18	19	20	
18		21	22	23	24	25	26	27	
19		28	29[g]	30	1	2	3	4	
20	PASHONS 1818	5	6	7	8	9	10	11	GENBOT 2094
21		12	13	14	15	16	17	18	
22		19	20	21	22	23	24	25	
23		26	27	28	29	30	1	2	
24	PAŌNE 1818	3	4	5	6	7	8	9	SANĒ 2094
25		10	11	12	13	14	15	16	
26		17	18	19	20	21	22	23	
27		24	25	26	27	28	29	30	
28	EPĒP 1818	1	2	3	4	5	6	7	ḤAMLĒ 2094
29		8	9	10	11	12	13	14	
30		15	16	17	18	19	20	21	
31		22	23	24	25	26	27	28	
32		29	30	1	2	3	4	5	
33	MESORĒ 1818	6	7	8	9	10	11	12	NAḤASĒ 2094
34		13[h]	14	15	16	17	18	19	
35		20	21	22	23	24	25	26	
36		27	28	29	30	1	2	3	PĀG. 2094
37	EPAG. 1818	4	5	1[a]	2	3	4	5	MASKARAM 2095
38	THOOUT 1819	6	7	8	9	10	11	12	
39		13	14	15	16	17[b]	18	19	
40		20	21	22	23	24	25	26	
41		27	28	29	30	1	2	3	
42	PAOPE 1819	4	5	6	7	8	9	10	TEQEMT 2095
43		11	12	13	14	15	16	17	
44		18	19	20	21	22	23	24	
45		25	26	27	28	29	30	1	
46	ATHŌR 1819	2	3	4	5	6	7	8	ḪEDĀR 2095
47		9	10	11	12	13	14	15	
48		16	17	18	19	20	21	22	
49		23	24	25	26	27	28	29	
50		30	1	2	3	4	5	6	
51	KOIAK 1819	7	8	9	10	11	12	13	TĀKHŚĀŚ 2095
52		14	15	16	17	18	19	20	
1		21	22	23	24	25	26	27	

[a]New Year
[b]Spring (0:34)
[c]Summer (16:52)
[d]Autumn (9:30)
[e]Winter (7:31)
● New moon
◐ First quarter moon
○ Full moon
◑ Last quarter moon

‡Leap year
[a]New Year
[b]Yom Kippur
[c]Sukkot
[d]Winter starts
[e]Ḥanukkah
[f]Purim
[g]Passover
[h]Shavuot
[i]Fast of Av

‡Leap year
[a]New Year (4800, Dog)
[b]Lantern Festival
[c]Qīngmíng
[d]Dragon Festival
[e]Qīqiǎo
[f]Hungry Ghosts
[g]Mid-Autumn Festival
[h]Double-Ninth Festival
[i]Dōngzhì
*Start of 60-name cycle

‡Leap year
[a]New Year
[b]Building of the Cross
[c]Christmas
[d]Jesus's Circumcision
[e]Epiphany
[f]Easter
[g]Mary's Announcement
[h]Jesus's Transfiguration

PERSIAN (ASTRONOMICAL) 1480/1481

Month	Sun	Mon	Tue	Wed	Thu	Fri	Sat
DEY 1480	11	12	13	14	15	16	17
	18	19	20	21	22	23	24
	25	26	27	28	29	30	1
BAHMAN 1480	2	3	4	5	6	7	8
	9	10	11	12	13	14	15
	16	17	18	19	20	21	22
	23	24	25	26	27	28	29
	30	1	2	3	4	5	6
ESFAND 1480	7	8	9	10	11	12	13
	14	15	16	17	18	19	20
	21	22	23	24	25	26	27
	28	29	1[a]	2	3	4	5
FARVARDĪN 1481	6	7	8	9	10	11	12
	13[b]	14	15	16	17	18	19
	20	21	22	23	24	25	26
	27	28	29	30	31	1	2
ORDĪBEHEŠT 1481	3	4	5	6	7	8	9
	10	11	12	13	14	15	16
	17	18	19	20	21	22	23
	24	25	26	27	28	29	30
	31	1	2	3	4	5	6
XORDĀD 1481	7	8	9	10	11	12	13
	14	15	16	17	18	19	20
	21	22	23	24	25	26	27
	28	29	30	31	1	2	3
TĪR 1481	4	5	6	7	8	9	10
	11	12	13	14	15	16	17
	18	19	20	21	22	23	24
	25	26	27	28	29	30	31
MORDĀD 1481	1	2	3	4	5	6	7
	8	9	10	11	12	13	14
	15	16	17	18	19	20	21
	22	23	24	25	26	27	28
	29	30	31	1	2	3	4
SHAHRĪVAR 1481	5	6	7	8	9	10	11
	12	13	14	15	16	17	18
	19	20	21	22	23	24	25
	26	27	28	29	30	31	1
MEHR 1481	2	3	4	5	6	7	8
	9	10	11	12	13	14	15
	16	17	18	19	20	21	22
	23	24	25	26	27	28	29
	30	1	2	3	4	5	6
ĀBĀN 1481	7	8	9	10	11	12	13
	14	15	16	17	18	19	20
	21	22	23	24	25	26	27
	28	29	30	1	2	3	4
ĀZAR 1481	5	6	7	8	9	10	11
	12	13	14	15	16	17	18
	19	20	21	22	23	24	25
	26	27	28	29	30	1	2
DEY 1481	3	4	5	6	7	8	9
	10	11	12	13	14	15	16

[a]New Year
[b]Sizdeh Bedar

HINDU LUNAR 2158/2159‡

Month	Sun	Mon	Tue	Wed	Thu	Fri	Sat
PAUSHA 2158	12	13	14	15	16	17	18
	19	20	21	22	23	24	25
	26	27	28	29	**30**	2	3
MĀGHA 2158	4	5	6	7	8	9	10
	11	12	13	*13*	14	15	16
	17	18	19	20	21	22	23
	24	26	27	28[h]	29	30	1
PHĀLGUNA 2158	2	3	4	5	6	7	8
	9	10	11	12	13	14	15[i]
	16	17	18	19	20	21	22
	23	24	25	26	27	28	**29**
CHAITRA 2159	1[a]	2	3	4	5	6	6
	7	8[b]	9	10	11	12	13
	14	15	16	17	18	19	20
	21	**22**	24	25	26	27	28
	29	30	1	2	3	4	5
VAIŚĀKHA 2159	6	7	8	9	9	10	11
	12	13	14	**15**	17	18	19
	20	21	22	23	24	25	26
	27	28	29	30	1	2	3
LEAP JYAISHṬHA 2159	4	5	6	7	8	9	10
	11	12	13	14	15	16	17
	18	**19**	21	22	23	24	25
	26	27	28	29	30	1	2
JYAISHṬHA 2159	3	4	5	5	6	7	8
	9	10	11	**12**	14	15	16
	17	18	19	20	21	22	23
	24	25	26	27	28	29	30
ĀSHĀḌHA 2159	1	2	3	4	5	6	7
	8	9	10	11	12	13	14
	15	17	18	19	20	21	22
	23	24	25	26	27	28	29
	30	1	2	2	3	4	5
ŚRĀVAṆA 2159	6	**7**	9	10	11	12	13
	14	15	16	17	18	**19**	21
	22	23	23[c]	24	25	26	27
	28	29	30	1	2	3	4[d]
BHĀDRAPADA 2159	5	6	7	8	9	10	**11**
	13	14	15	16	17	18	19
	20	21	22	23	24	25	26
	27	27	28	29	30	1	2
ĀŚVINA 2159	3	**4**	6	7	8[e]	9[e]	10[e]
	11	12	13	14	15	16	17
	18	19	20	21	22	23	24
	25	26	27	28	29	30	1[f]
KĀRTTIKA 2159	2	3	4	5	6	7	**8**
	10	11	12	13	14	15	16
	17	18	19	20	21	*21*	22
	23	24	25	26	27	28	29
MĀRGAŚĪRA 2159	30	1	**2**	4	5	6	7
	8	9	10	11[g]	12	13	14
	15	16	17	18	19	20	21
	22	23	24	25	26	27	28

‡Leap year
[a]New Year (Dundubhi)
[b]Birthday of Rāma
[c]Birthday of Krishna
[d]Ganēśa Chaturthī
[e]Dashara
[f]Diwali
[g]Birthday of Vishnu
[h]Night of Śiva
[i]Holi

HINDU SOLAR 2023/2024‡

Month	Sun	Mon	Tue	Wed	Thu	Fri	Sat
PAUSHA 2023	16	17	18	19	20	21	22
	23	24	25	26	27	28	29
	30	1[b]	2	3	4	5	6
MĀGHA 2023	7	8	9	10	11	12	13
	14	15	16	17	18	19	20
	21	22	23	24	25	26	27
	28	29	1	2	3	4	5
PHĀLGUNA 2023	6	7	8	9	10	11	12
	13	14	15	16	17	18	19
	20	21	22	23	24	25	26
	27	28	29	30	1	2	3
CHAITRA 2023	4	5	6	7	8	9	10
	11	12	13	14	15	16	17
	18	19	20	21	22	23	24
	25	26	27	28	29	30	1[a]
VAIŚĀKHA 2024	2	3	4	5	6	7	8
	9	10	11	12	13	14	15
	16	17	18	19	20	21	22
	23	24	25	26	27	28	29
	30	31	1	2	3	4	5
JYAISHṬHA 2024	6	7	8	9	10	11	12
	13	14	15	16	17	18	19
	20	21	22	23	24	25	26
	27	28	29	30	31	32	1
ĀSHĀḌHA 2024	2	3	4	5	6	7	8
	9	10	11	12	13	14	15
	16	17	18	19	20	21	22
	23	24	25	26	27	28	29
	30	31	1	2	3	4	5
ŚRĀVAṆA 2024	6	7	8	9	10	11	12
	13	14	15	16	17	18	19
	20	21	22	23	24	25	26
	27	28	29	30	31	32	1
BHĀDRAPADA 2024	2	3	4	5	6	7	8
	9	10	11	12	13	14	15
	16	17	18	19	20	21	22
	23	24	25	26	27	28	29
	30	31	1	2	3	4	5
ĀŚVINA 2024	6	7	8	9	10	11	12
	13	14	15	16	17	18	19
	20	21	22	23	24	25	26
	27	28	29	30	1	2	3
KĀRTTIKA 2024	4	5	6	7	8	9	10
	11	12	13	14	15	16	17
	18	19	20	21	22	23	24
	25	26	27	28	29	30	1
MĀRGAŚĪRA 2024	2	3	4	5	6	7	8
	9	10	11	12	13	14	15
	16	17	18	19	20	21	22
	23	24	25	26	27	28	29
	30	1	2	3	4	5	6
PAUSHA 2024	7	8	9	10	11	12	13
	14	15	16	17	18	19	20

‡Leap year
[a]New Year (Dhātṛi)
[b]Pongal

ISLAMIC (ASTRONOMICAL) 1525‡/1526

Month	Sun	Mon	Tue	Wed	Thu	Fri	Sat
DHU AL-QA'DA 1525	11	12	13	14	15	16	17
	18	19	20	21	22	23	24
	25	26	27	28	29	1	2
DHU AL-ḤIJJA 1525	3	4	5	6	7	8	9
	10[g]	11	12	13	14	15	16
	17	18	19	20	21	22	23
	24	25	26	27	28	29	30
MUḤARRAM 1526	1[a]	2	3	4	5	6	7
	8	9	10[b]	11	12	13	14
	15	16	17	18	19	20	21
	22	23	24	25	26	27	28
	29	1	2	3	4	5	6
ṢAFAR 1526	7	8	9	10	11	12	13
	14	15	16	17	18	19	20
	21	22	23	24	25	26	27
	28	29	30	1	2	3	4
RABĪ' I 1526	5	6	7	8	9	10	11
	12[c]	13	14	15	16	17	18
	19	20	21	22	23	24	25
	26	27	28	29	1	2	3
RABĪ' II 1526	4	5	6	7	8	9	10
	11	12	13	14	15	16	17
	18	19	20	21	22	23	24
	25	26	27	28	29	30	1
JUMĀDĀ I 1526	2	3	4	5	6	7	8
	9	10	11	12	13	14	15
	16	17	18	19	20	21	22
	23	24	25	26	27	28	29
	30	1	2	3	4	5	6
JUMĀDĀ II 1526	7	8	9	10	11	12	13
	14	15	16	17	18	19	20
	21	22	23	24	25	26	27
	28	29	30	1	2	3	4
RAJAB 1526	5	6	7	8	9	10	11
	12	13	14	15	16	17	18
	19	20	21	22	23	24	25
	26	27[d]	28	29	30	1	2
SHA'BĀN 1526	3	4	5	6	7	8	9
	10	11	12	13	14	15	16
	17	18	19	20	21	22	23
	24	25	26	27	28	29	1[e]
RAMAḌĀN 1526	2	3	4	5	6	7	8
	9	10	11	12	13	14	15
	16	17	18	19	20	21	22
	23	24	25	26	27	28	29
	30	1[f]	2	3	4	5	6
SHAWWĀL 1526	7	8	9	10	11	12	13
	14	15	16	17	18	19	20
	21	22	23	24	25	26	27
	28	29	1	2	3	4	5
DHU AL-QA'DA 1526	6	7	8	9	10	11	12
	13	14	15	16	17	18	19
	20	21	22	23	24	25	26

‡Leap year
[a]New Year
[b]'Ashūrā'
[c]Prophet's Birthday
[d]Ascent of the Prophet
[e]Start of Ramaḍān
[f]'Īd al-Fiṭr
[g]'Īd al-'Aḍḥā

GREGORIAN 2102

Julian (Sun)	Sun	Mon	Tue	Wed	Thu	Fri	Sat	Month
Dec 18	1	2	3	4	5	6	7	JANUARY 2102
	8[a]	9	10	11	12	13	14	
Jan 1	15[b]	16	17	18	19	20	21	
	22	23	24	25	26	27	28	
Jan 15	29	30	31	1	2	3	4	FEBRUARY 2102
	5	6	7	8	9	10	11	
Jan 29	12	13	14	15	16	17	18	
	19	20	21	22[c]	23	24	25	
Feb 12	26[d]	27	28	1	2	3	4	MARCH 2102
	5	6	7	8	9	10	11	
Feb 26	12	13	14	15	16	17	18	
	19	20	21	22	23	24	25	
Mar 12	26	27	28	29	30	31	1	APRIL 2102
	2	3	4	5	6	7	8	
Mar 26	9[e]	10	11	12	13	14	15	
	16	17	18	19	20	21	22	
Apr 9	23	24	25	26	27	28	29	
	30	1	2	3	4	5	6	MAY 2102
Apr 23	7	8	9	10	11	12	13	
	14	15	16	17	18	19	20	
May 7	21	22	23	24	25	26	27	
	28	29	30	31	1	2	3	JUNE 2102
May 21	4	5	6	7	8	9	10	
	11	12	13	14	15	16	17	
Jun 4	18	19	20	21	22	23	24	
	25	26	27	28	29	30	1	JULY 2102
Jun 18	2	3	4	5	6	7	8	
	9	10	11	12	13	14	15	
Jul 2	16	17	18	19	20	21	22	
	23	24	25	26	27	28	29	
Jul 16	30	31	1	2	3	4	5	AUGUST 2102
	6	7	8	9	10	11	12	
Jul 30	13	14	15	16	17	18	19	
	20	21	22	23	24	25	26	
Aug 13	27	28	29	30	31	1	2	SEPTEMBER 2102
	3	4	5	6	7	8	9	
Aug 27	10	11	12	13	14	15	16	
	17	18	19	20	21	22	23	
Sep 10	24	25	26	27	28	29	30	
	1	2	3	4	5	6	7	OCTOBER 2102
Sep 24	8	9	10	11	12	13	14	
	15	16	17	18	19	20	21	
Oct 8	22	23	24	25	26	27	28	
	29	30	31	1	2	3	4	NOVEMBER 2102
Oct 22	5	6	7	8	9	10	11	
	12	13	14	15	16	17	18	
Nov 5	19	20	21	22	23	24	25	
	26	27	28	29	30	1	2	DECEMBER 2102
Nov 19	3[g]	4	5	6	7	8	9	
	10	11	12	13	14	15	16	
Dec 3	17	18	19	20	21	22	23	
	24	25[h]	26	27	28	29	30	
Dec 17	31	1	2	3	4	5	6	

[a]Orthodox Christmas
[b]Julian New Year
[c]Ash Wednesday
[d]Feast of Orthodoxy
[e]Easter (also Orthodox)
[g]Advent
[h]Christmas

Gregorian 2103	Sun	Mon	Tue	Wed	Thu	Fri	Sat	Lunar Phases	ISO WEEK (Mon)	JULIAN DAY (Sun noon)
JANUARY 2103	31	◑[a]	2	3	4	5	6	16:50	1	2489164
	7	●	9	10	11	12	13	17:56	2	2489171
	14	◐	16	17	18	19	20	9:29	3	2489178
	21	22	○	24	25	26	27	6:42	4	2489185
	28	29	30	◑	1	2	3	9:47	5	2489192
FEBRUARY 2103	4	5	6	●	8	9	10	4:53	6	2489199
	11	12	◐	14	15	16	17	22:52	7	2489206
	18	19	20	21	○	23	24	2:13	8	2489213
	25	26	27	28	◑	2	3	23:12	9	2489220
MARCH 2103	4	5	6	7	●	9	10	15:01	10	2489227
	11	12	13	14	◐	16	17	14:56	11	2489234
	18	19	20	21[b]	22	○	24	20:01	12	2489241
	25	26	27	28	29	30	◑	9:05	13	2489248
APRIL 2103	1	2	3	4	5	6	●	0:39	14	2489255
	8	9	10	11	12	13	◐	8:52	15	2489262
	15	16	17	18	19	20	21		16	2489269
	○	23	24	25	26	27	28	11:05	17	2489276
	◑	30	1	2	3	4	5	16:04	18	2489283
MAY 2103	●	7	8	9	10	11	12	10:30	19	2489290
	13	◐	15	16	17	18	19	3:23	20	2489297
	20	○	22	23	24	25	26	23:21	21	2489304
	27	◑	29	30	31	1	2	21:14	22	2489311
JUNE 2103	3	●	5	6	7	8	9	21:23	23	2489318
	10	11	◐	13	14	15	16	21:38	24	2489325
	17	18	19	○	21[c]	22	23	9:18	25	2489332
	24	25	26	◑	28	29	30	1:58	26	2489339
JULY 2103	1	2	3	●	5	6	7	9:56	27	2489346
	8	9	10	11	◐	13	14	13:19	28	2489353
	15	16	17	18	○	20	21	17:36	29	2489360
	22	23	24	25	◑	27	28	7:49	30	2489367
	29	30	31	1	2	●	4	0:12	31	2489374
AUGUST 2103	5	6	7	8	9	10	◐	3:35	32	2489381
	12	13	14	15	16	17	○	1:02	33	2489388
	19	20	21	22	23	◑	25	16:14	34	2489395
	26	27	28	29	30	31	●	15:49	35	2489402
SEPTEMBER 2103	2	3	4	5	6	7	8		36	2489409
	◐	10	11	12	13	14	15	15:54	37	2489416
	○	17	18	19	20	21	22	8:30	38	2489423
	◑[d]	24	25	26	27	28	29	4:19	39	2489430
	30	●	2	3	4	5	6	8:10	40	2489437
OCTOBER 2103	7	8	◐	10	11	12	13	2:20	41	2489444
	14	○	16	17	18	19	20	16:59	42	2489451
	21	◑	23	24	25	26	27	20:26	43	2489458
	28	29	30	●	1	2	3	0:36	44	2489465
NOVEMBER 2103	4	5	6	◐	8	9	10	11:11	45	2489472
	11	12	13	○	15	16	17	3:28	46	2489479
	18	19	20	◑	22	23	24	16:00	47	2489486
	25	26	27	28	●	30	1	16:30	48	2489493
DECEMBER 2103	2	3	4	5	◐	7	8	19:00	49	2489500
	9	10	11	12	○	14	15	16:34	50	2489507
	16	17	18	19	20	◑	22[e]	13:30	51	2489514
	23	24	25	26	27	28	●	7:12	52	2489521
	30	31	1	2	3	4	◐	2:46	1	2489528

ISO WEEK	HEBREW 5863‡/5864	Sun	Mon	Tue	Wed	Thu	Fri	Sat	Molad
1	TEVETH 5863	21	22	23	24	25	26	27	Mon 18h7m9p
2		28	29	1	2	3	4	5	
3	SHEVAT 5863	6	7	8	9	10	11	12	
4		13	14	15	16	17	18	19	
5		20	21	22	23	24	25	26	
6		27	28	29	30	1	2	3	Wed 6h51m10p
7		4	5	6	7	8	9	10	
8	ADAR I 5863	11	12	13	14	15	16	17	
9		18	19	20	21	22	23	24	
10		25	26	27	28	29	30	1	Thu 19h35m11p
11	ADAR II 5863	2	3	4	5	6	7	8	
12		9	10	11	12	13	14[f]	15	
13		16	17	18	19	20	21	22	
14		23	24	25	26	27	28	29	
15		1	2	3	4	5	6	7	Sat 8h19m12p
16		8	9	10	11	12	13	14	
17	NISAN 5863	15[g]	16	17	18	19	20	21	
18		22	23	24	25	26	27	28	
19		29	30	1	2	3	4	5	Sun 21h3m13p
20	IYAR 5863	6	7	8	9	10	11	12	
21		13	14	15	16	17	18	19	
22		20	21	22	23	24	25	26	
23		27	28	29	1	2	3	4	Tue 9h47m14p
24	SIVAN 5863	5	6[h]	7	8	9	10	11	
25		12	13	14	15	16	17	18	
26		19	20	21	22	23	24	25	
27		26	27	28	29	30	1	2	Wed 22h31m15p
28	TAMMUZ 5863	3	4	5	6	7	8	9	
29		10	11	12	13	14	15	16	
30		17	18	19	20	21	22	23	
31		24	25	26	27	28	29	1	Fri 11h15m16p
32		2	3	4	5	6	7	8	
33	AV 5863	9[i]	10	11	12	13	14	15	
34		16	17	18	19	20	21	22	
35		23	24	25	26	27	28	29	
36		30	1	2	3	4	5	6	Sat 23h59m17p
37	ELUL 5863	7	8	9	10	11	12	13	
38		14	15	16	17	18	19	20	
39		21	22	23	24	25	26	27	
40		28	29	1[a]	2[a]	3	4	5	Mon 12h44m0p
41	TISHRI 5864	6	7	8	9	10[b]	11	12	
42		13	14	15[c]	16	17	18	19	
43		20	21	22	23	24	25	26	
44		27	28	29	30	1	2	3	Wed 1h28m1p
45	HESHVAN 5864	4	5	6	7	8	9	10	
46		11	12	13	14	15	16	17	
47		18	19	20	21	22	23	24	
48		25	26	27	28	29	1	2	Thu 14h12m2p
49	KISLEV 5864	3	4	5	6	7	8[d]	9	
50		10	11	12	13	14	15	16	
51		17	18	19	20	21	22	23	
52		24	25[e]	26[e]	27[e]	28[e]	29[e]	30[e]	Sat 2h56m3p
1		1[e]	2[e]	3	4	5	6	7	

ISO WEEK	CHINESE Rén-Xū/Guǐ-Hài	Sun	Mon	Tue	Wed	Thu	Fri	Sat	Solar Term
1	MONTH 11 Rén-Xū	22	23	24	25	26	27	*28*	Xiǎo hán
2		29*	30	1	2	3	4	5	
3	MONTH 12 Rén-Xū	6	7	8	9	10	11	12	
4		***13***	14	15	16	17	18	19	Dà hán
5		20	21	22	23	24	25	26	
6		*27*	28	29	1[a]	2	3	4	Lì chūn
7	MONTH 1 Guǐ-Hài	5	6	7	8	9	10	11	
8		12	***13***	14	15[b]	16	17	18	Yǔ shuǐ
9		19	20	21	22	23	24	25	
10		26	27	*28*	29	1*	2	3	Jīng zhé
11	MONTH 2 Guǐ-Hài	4	5	6	7	8	9	10	
12		11	12	13	***14***	15	16	17	Chūn fēn
13		18	19	20	21	22	23	24	
14		25	26	27	28	29[c]	30	1	Qīng míng
15	MONTH 3 Guǐ-Hài	2	3	4	5	6	7	8	
16		9	10	11	12	13	14	***15***	Gǔ yǔ
17		16	17	18	19	20	21	22	
18		23	24	25	26	27	28	29	
19		*1*	2*	3	4	5	6	7	Lì xià
20	MONTH 4 Guǐ-Hài	8	9	10	11	12	13	14	
21		15	***16***	17	18	19	20	21	Xiǎo mǎn
22		22	23	24	25	26	27	28	
23		29	30	1	*2*	3	4	5[d]	Máng zhòng
24	MONTH 5 Guǐ-Hài	6	7	8	9	10	11	12	
25		13	14	15	16	17	***18***	19	Xià zhì
26		20	21	22	23	24	25	26	
27		27	28	29	1	2	3*	4	
28	MONTH 6 Guǐ-Hài	5	6	7	8	9	10	11	Xiǎo shǔ
29		12	13	14	15	16	17	18	
30		19	***20***	21	22	23	24	25	Dà shǔ
31		26	27	28	29	30	1	2	
32	MONTH 7 Guǐ-Hài	3	4	5	6	7[e]	8	9	Lì qiū
33		10	11	12	13	14	15[f]	16	
34		17	18	19	20	21	***22***	23	Chǔ shǔ
35		24	25	26	27	28	29	1	
36		2	3	4*	5	6	7	*8*	Bái lù
37	MONTH 8 Guǐ-Hài	9	10	11	12	13	14	15[g]	
38		16	17	18	19	20	21	22	
39		***23***	24	25	26	27	28	29	Qiū fēn
40		30	1	2	3	4	5	6	
41	MONTH 9 Guǐ-Hài	7	8	*9*[h]	10	11	12	13	Hán lù
42		14	15	16	17	18	19	20	
43		21	22	23	***24***	25	26	27	Shuāng jiàng
44		28	29	30	1	2	3	4*	
45	MONTH 10 Guǐ-Hài	5	6	7	8	9	10	11	Lì dōng
46		12	13	14	15	16	17	18	
47		19	20	21	22	23	***24***	25	Xiǎo xuě
48		26	27	28	29	30	1	2	
49	MONTH 11* Guǐ-Hài	3	4	5	6	7	8	9	Dà xuě
50		10	11	12	13	14	15	16	
51		17	18	19	20	21	22	***23***[i]	Dōng zhì
52		24	25	26	27	28	29	1	
1	MONTH 12 Guǐ-Hài	2	3	4	5	6	7	8	

ISO WEEK	COPTIC 1819‡/1820	Sun	Mon	Tue	Wed	Thu	Fri	Sat	ETHIOPIC 2095‡/2096
1	KOIAK 1819	21	22	23	24	25	26	27	TĀKHŚĀŚ 2095
2		28	29[c]	30	1	2	3	4	
3	TŌBE 1819	5	6[d]	7	8	9	10	11[e]	
4		12	13	14	15	16	17	18	TER 2095
5		19	20	21	22	23	24	25	
6		26	27	28	29	30	1	2	
7		3	4	5	6	7	8	9	
8	MESHIR 1819	10	11	12	13	14	15	16	YAKĀTIT 2095
9		17	18	19	20	21	22	23	
10		24	25	26	27	28	29	30	
11		1	2	3	4	5	6	7	
12	PAREMOTEP 1819	8	9	10	11	12	13	14	MAGĀBIT 2095
13		15	16	17	18	19	20	21	
14		22	23	24	25	26	27	28	
15		29	30	1	2	3	4	5	
16	PARMOUTE 1819	6	7	8	9	10	11	12	MIYĀZYĀ 2095
17		13	14	15	16	17	18	19	
18		20[f]	21	22	23	24	25	26	
19		27	28	29[g]	30	1	2	3	
20	PASHONS 1819	4	5	6	7	8	9	10	GENBOT 2095
21		11	12	13	14	15	16	17	
22		18	19	20	21	22	23	24	
23		25	26	27	28	29	30	1	
24		2	3	4	5	6	7	8	
25	PAŌNE 1819	9	10	11	12	13	14	15	SANĒ 2095
26		16	17	18	19	20	21	22	
27		23	24	25	26	27	28	29	
28		30	1	2	3	4	5	6	
29	EPĒP 1819	7	8	9	10	11	12	13	HAMLĒ 2095
30		14	15	16	17	18	19	20	
31		21	22	23	24	25	26	27	
32		28	29	30	1	2	3	4	
33	MESORĒ 1819	5	6	7	8	9	10	11	NAHASĒ 2095
34		12	13[h]	14	15	16	17	18	
35		19	20	21	22	23	24	25	
36		26	27	28	29	30	1	2	
37	EPAG. 1819	3	4	5	6	1[a]	2	3	PĀG. 2095
38		4	5	6	7	8	9	10	
39	THOOUT 1820	11	12	13	14	15	16	17[b]	MASKARAM 2096
40		18	19	20	21	22	23	24	
41		25	26	27	28	29	30	1	
42		2	3	4	5	6	7	8	
43	PAOPE 1820	9	10	11	12	13	14	15	TEQEMT 2096
44		16	17	18	19	20	21	22	
45		23	24	25	26	27	28	29	
46		30	1	2	3	4	5	6	
47	ATHŌR 1820	7	8	9	10	11	12	13	HEDĀR 2096
48		14	15	16	17	18	19	20	
49		21	22	23	24	25	26	27	
50		28	29	30	1	2	3	4	
51	KOIAK 1820	5	6	7	8	9	10	11	TĀKHŚĀŚ 2096
52		12	13	14	15	16	17	18	
1		19	20	21	22	23	24	25	

Gregorian notes:
[a]New Year
[b]Spring (6:22)
[c]Summer (22:44)
[d]Autumn (15:23)
[e]Winter (13:23)
● New moon
◐ First quarter moon
○ Full moon
◑ Last quarter moon

Hebrew notes:
‡Leap year
[a]New Year
[b]Yom Kippur
[c]Sukkot
[d]Winter starts
[e]Ḥanukkah
[f]Purim
[g]Passover
[h]Shavuot
[i]Fast of Av

Chinese notes:
[a]New Year (4801, Pig)
[b]Lantern Festival
[c]Qīngmíng
[d]Dragon Festival
[e]Qīqiǎo
[f]Hungry Ghosts
[g]Mid-Autumn Festival
[h]Double-Ninth Festival
[i]Dōngzhì
*Start of 60-name cycle

Coptic/Ethiopic notes:
‡Leap year
[a]New Year
[b]Building of the Cross
[c]Christmas
[d]Jesus's Circumcision
[e]Epiphany
[f]Easter
[g]Mary's Announcement
[h]Jesus's Transfiguration

PERSIAN (ASTRONOMICAL) 1481/1482‡

Month	Sun	Mon	Tue	Wed	Thu	Fri	Sat
DEY 1481	10	11	12	13	14	15	16
	17	18	19	20	21	22	23
	24	25	26	27	28	29	30
BAHMAN 1481	1	2	3	4	5	6	7
	8	9	10	11	12	13	14
	15	16	17	18	19	20	21
	22	23	24	25	26	27	28
ESFAND 1481	29	30	1	2	3	4	5
	6	7	8	9	10	11	12
	13	14	15	16	17	18	19
	20	21	22	23	24	25	26
FARVARDĪN 1482	27	28	29	1[a]	2	3	4
	5	6	7	8	9	10	11
	12	13[b]	14	15	16	17	18
	19	20	21	22	23	24	25
ORDĪBEHEŠT 1482	26	27	28	29	30	31	1
	2	3	4	5	6	7	8
	9	10	11	12	13	14	15
	16	17	18	19	20	21	22
	23	24	25	26	27	28	29
XORDĀD 1482	30	31	1	2	3	4	5
	6	7	8	9	10	11	12
	13	14	15	16	17	18	19
	20	21	22	23	24	25	26
TĪR 1482	27	28	29	30	31	1	2
	3	4	5	6	7	8	9
	10	11	12	13	14	15	16
	17	18	19	20	21	22	23
	24	25	26	27	28	29	30
MORDĀD 1482	31	1	2	3	4	5	6
	7	8	9	10	11	12	13
	14	15	16	17	18	19	20
	21	22	23	24	25	26	27
SHAHRĪVAR 1482	28	29	30	31	1	2	3
	4	5	6	7	8	9	10
	11	12	13	14	15	16	17
	18	19	20	21	22	23	24
	25	26	27	28	29	30	31
MEHR 1482	1	2	3	4	5	6	7
	8	9	10	11	12	13	14
	15	16	17	18	19	20	21
	22	23	24	25	26	27	28
ĀBĀN 1482	29	30	1	2	3	4	5
	6	7	8	9	10	11	12
	13	14	15	16	17	18	19
	20	21	22	23	24	25	26
ĀZAR 1482	27	28	29	30	1	2	3
	4	5	6	7	8	9	10
	11	12	13	14	15	16	17
	18	19	20	21	22	23	24
DEY 1482	25	26	27	28	29	30	1
	2	3	4	5	6	7	8
	9	10	11	12	13	14	15

‡Leap year
[a]New Year
[b]Sizdeh Bedar

HINDU LUNAR 2159‡/2160

Month	Sun	Mon	Tue	Wed	Thu	Fri	Sat
MĀRGAŚĪRA 2159	22	23	24	25	26	27	28
PAUSHA 2159	29	30	1	2	3	4	5
	6	7	**8**	10	11	12	13
	13	14	15	16	17	18	19
	20	21	22	23	24	25	26
MĀGHA 2159	27	28	29	30	**1**	3	4
	5	6	7	8	9	10	11
	12	13	14	15	16	16	17
	18	19	20	21	22	23	24
PHĀLGUNA 2159	**25**	27	28	29[h]	30	1	2
	3	4	5	6	7	8	9
	10	11	12	13	14	15[i]	16
	17	18	19	20	21	22	23
	24	25	26	27	28	29	**30**[a]
CHAITRA 2160	2	3	4	5	6	7	8
	9[b]	9	10	11	12	13	14
	15	16	17	18	19	20	21
	22	**23**	25	26	27	28	29
VAIŚĀKHA 2160	30	1	2	3	4	5	6
	7	8	9	10	11	12	13
	14	15	16	17	18	19	20
	21	22	23	24	25	26	**27**
JYAISHṬHA 2160	29	30	1	2	3	4	5
	5	6	7	8	9	10	11
	12	13	14	15	16	17	18
	19	21	22	23	24	25	26
ĀSHĀḌHA 2160	27	28	29	30	1	2	3
	4	5	6	7	8	9	10
	11	12	13	14	15	16	17
	18	19	20	21	**22**	24	25
ŚRĀVAṆA 2160	26	27	28	29	30	1	2
	2	3	4	5	6	7	8
	9	10	11	12	13	14	**15**
	17	18	19	20	21	22	23[c]
	24	25	26	27	28	29	30
BHĀDRAPADA 2160	1	2	3	4[d]	5	6	7
	8	9	10	11	12	13	14
	15	16	17	**18**	20	21	22
	23	24	25	26	27	28	28
ĀŚVINA 2160	29	30	1	2	3	4	5
	6	7	8[e]	9[e]	10[e]	**11**	13
	14	15	16	17	18	19	20
	21	22	23	24	25	26	27
KĀRTTIKA 2160	28	29	30	1	1[f]	2	3
	4	6	7	8	9	10	11
	12	13	14	15	16	**17**	19
	20	21	21	22	23	24	25
MĀRGAŚĪRA 2160	26	27	28	29	30	1	2
	3	4	5	6	7	8	**9**
	11[g]	12	13	14	15	16	17
	18	19	20	21	22	23	24
	24	25	26	27	28	29	30
	1	2	**3**	5	6	7	8

‡Leap year
[a]New Year (Rudhirodgārin)
[b]Birthday of Rāma
[c]Birthday of Krishna
[d]Ganēśa Chaturthī
[e]Dashara
[f]Diwali
[g]Birthday of Vishnu
[h]Night of Śiva
[i]Holi

HINDU SOLAR 2024‡/2025

Month	Sun	Mon	Tue	Wed	Thu	Fri	Sat
PAUSHA 2024	14	15	16	17	18	19	20
	21	22	23	24	25	26	27
MĀGHA 2024	28	29	1[b]	2	3	4	5
	6	7	8	9	10	11	12
	13	14	15	16	17	18	19
	20	21	22	23	24	25	26
PHĀLGUNA 2024	27	28	29	1	2	3	4
	5	6	7	8	9	10	11
	12	13	14	15	16	17	18
	19	20	21	22	23	24	25
CHAITRA 2024	26	27	28	29	30	1	2
	3	4	5	6	7	8	9
	10	11	12	13	14	15	16
	17	18	19	20	21	22	23
	24	25	26	27	28	29	30
VAIŚĀKHA 2025	31	1[a]	2	3	4	5	6
	7	8	9	10	11	12	13
	14	15	16	17	18	19	20
	21	22	23	24	25	26	27
JYAISHṬHA 2025	28	29	30	31	1	2	3
	4	5	6	7	8	9	10
	11	12	13	14	15	16	17
	18	19	20	21	22	23	24
	25	26	27	28	29	30	31
ĀSHĀḌHA 2025	1	2	3	4	5	6	7
	8	9	10	11	12	13	14
	15	16	17	18	19	20	21
	22	23	24	25	26	27	28
ŚRĀVAṆA 2025	29	30	31	32	1	2	3
	4	5	6	7	8	9	10
	11	12	13	14	15	16	17
	18	19	20	21	22	23	24
	25	26	27	28	29	30	31
BHĀDRAPADA 2025	1	2	3	4	5	6	7
	8	9	10	11	12	13	14
	15	16	17	18	19	20	21
	22	23	24	25	26	27	28
ĀŚVINA 2025	29	30	31	1	2	3	4
	5	6	7	8	9	10	11
	12	13	14	15	16	17	18
	19	20	21	22	23	24	25
KĀRTTIKA 2025	26	27	28	29	30	31	1
	2	3	4	5	6	7	8
	9	10	11	12	13	14	15
	16	17	18	19	20	21	22
	23	24	25	26	27	28	29
MĀRGAŚĪRA 2025	1	2	3	4	5	6	7
	8	9	10	11	12	13	14
	15	16	17	18	19	20	21
	22	23	24	25	26	27	28
PAUSHA 2025	29	30	1	2	3	4	5
	6	7	8	9	10	11	12
	13	14	15	16	17	18	19

‡Leap year
[a]New Year (Īśvara)
[b]Pongal

ISLAMIC (ASTRONOMICAL) 1526/1527‡

Month	Sun	Mon	Tue	Wed	Thu	Fri	Sat
DHU AL-QAʿDA 1526	20	21	22	23	24	25	26
DHU AL-ḤIJJA 1526	27	28	29	1	2	3	4
	5	6	7	8	9	10[g]	11
	12	13	14	15	16	17	18
	19	20	21	22	23	24	25
MUḤARRAM 1527	26	27	28	29	1[a]	2[a]	3
	4	5	6	7	8	9	10[b]
	11	12	13	14	15	16	17
	18	19	20	21	22	23	24
ṢAFAR 1527	25	26	27	28	29	30	1
	2	3	4	5	6	7	8
	9	10	11	12	13	14	15
	16	17	18	19	20	21	22
	23	24	25	26	27	28	29
RABĪʿ I 1527	1	2	3	4	5	6	7
	8	9	10	11	12[c]	13	14
	15	16	17	18	19	20	21
	22	23	24	25	26	27	28
RABĪʿ II 1527	29	30	1	2	3	4	5
	6	7	8	9	10	11	12
	13	14	15	16	17	18	19
	20	21	22	23	24	25	26
JUMĀDĀ I 1527	27	28	29	1	2	3	4
	5	6	7	8	9	10	11
	12	13	14	15	16	17	18
	19	20	21	22	23	24	25
JUMĀDĀ II 1527	26	27	28	29	30	1	2
	3	4	5	6	7	8	9
	10	11	12	13	14	15	16
	17	18	19	20	21	22	23
	24	25	26	27	28	29	30
RAJAB 1527	1	2	3	4	5	6	7
	8	9	10	11	12	13	14
	15	16	17	18	19	20	21
	22	23	24	25	26	27[d]	28
SHAʿBĀN 1527	29	30	1	2	3	4	5
	6	7	8	9	10	11	12
	13	14	15	16	17	18	19
	20	21	22	23	24	25	26
RAMAḌĀN 1527	27	28	29	30	1[e]	2	3
	4	5	6	7	8	9	10
	11	12	13	14	15	16	17
	18	19	20	21	22	23	24
SHAWWĀL 1527	25	26	27	28	29	1[f]	2
	3	4	5	6	7	8	9
	10	11	12	13	14	15	16
	17	18	19	20	21	22	23
DHU AL-QAʿDA 1527	24	25	26	27	28	29	1
	2	3	4	5	6	7	8
	9	10	11	12	13	14	15
	16	17	18	19	20	21	22
	23	24	25	26	27	28	29
	30	1	2	3	4	5	6

‡Leap year
[a]New Year
[a]New Year (Arithmetic)
[b]ʿAshūrāʾ
[c]Prophet's Birthday
[d]Ascent of the Prophet
[e]Start of Ramaḍān
[f]ʿId al-Fiṭr
[g]ʿId al-ʾAḍḥā

GREGORIAN 2103

Julian (Sun)	Sun	Mon	Tue	Wed	Thu	Fri	Sat	Month
Dec 17	31	1	2	3	4	5	6	JANUARY 2103
	7	8[a]	9	10	11	12	13	
Dec 31	14	15[b]	16	17	18	19	20	
	21	22	23	24	25	26	27	
Jan 14	28	29	30	31	1	2	3	FEBRUARY 2103
	4	5	6	7[c]	8	9	10	
Jan 28	11	12	13	14	15	16	17	
	18	19	20	21	22	23	24	
Feb 11	25	26	27	28	1	2	3	MARCH 2103
	4	5	6	7	8	9	10	
Feb 25	11	12	13	14	15	16	17	
	18[d]	19	20	21	22	23	24	
Mar 11	25[e]	26	27	28	29	30	31	
	1	2	3	4	5	6	7	APRIL 2103
Mar 25	8	9	10	11	12	13	14	
	15	16	17	18	19	20	21	
Apr 8	22	23	24	25	26	27	28	
	29[f]	30	1	2	3	4	5	MAY 2103
Apr 22	6	7	8	9	10	11	12	
	13	14	15	16	17	18	19	
May 6	20	21	22	23	24	25	26	
	27	28	29	30	31	1	2	JUNE 2103
May 20	3	4	5	6	7	8	9	
	10	11	12	13	14	15	16	
Jun 3	17	18	19	20	21	22	23	
	24	25	26	27	28	29	30	
Jun 17	1	2	3	4	5	6	7	JULY 2103
	8	9	10	11	12	13	14	
Jul 1	15	16	17	18	19	20	21	
	22	23	24	25	26	27	28	
Jul 15	29	30	31	1	2	3	4	AUGUST 2103
	5	6	7	8	9	10	11	
Jul 29	12	13	14	15	16	17	18	
	19	20	21	22	23	24	25	
Aug 12	26	27	28	29	30	31	1	SEPTEMBER 2103
	2	3	4	5	6	7	8	
Aug 26	9	10	11	12	13	14	15	
	16	17	18	19	20	21	22	
Sep 9	23	24	25	26	27	28	29	
	30	1	2	3	4	5	6	OCTOBER 2103
Sep 23	7	8	9	10	11	12	13	
	14	15	16	17	18	19	20	
Oct 7	21	22	23	24	25	26	27	
	28	29	30	31	1	2	3	NOVEMBER 2103
Oct 21	4	5	6	7	8	9	10	
	11	12	13	14	15	16	17	
Nov 4	18	19	20	21	22	23	24	
	25	26	27	28	29	30	1	DECEMBER 2103
Nov 18	2[g]	3	4	5	6	7	8	
	9	10	11	12	13	14	15	
Dec 2	16	17	18	19	20	21	22	
	23	24	25[h]	26	27	28	29	
Dec 16	30	31	1	2	3	4	5	

[a]Orthodox Christmas
[b]Julian New Year
[c]Ash Wednesday
[d]Feast of Orthodoxy
[e]Easter
[f]Orthodox Easter
[g]Advent
[h]Christmas

2104

Gregorian 2104‡	Sun	Mon	Tue	Wed	Thu	Fri	Sat	Lunar Phases	ISO Week (Mon)	Julian Day (Sun noon)	Hebrew 5864/5865	Sun	Mon	Tue	Wed	Thu	Fri	Sat	Molad	Chinese Guǐ-Hài/Jiǎ-Zǐ‡	Sun	Mon	Tue	Wed	Thu	Fri	Sat	Solar Term	Coptic 1820/1821	Sun	Mon	Tue	Wed	Thu	Fri	Sat	Ethiopic 2096/2097
JANUARY 2104	30	31	1[a]	2	3	4	◐	2:46	1	2489528	TEVETH 5864	1[e]	2[e]	3	4	5	6	7	Sat $2^h56^m3^p$	MONTH 12 Guǐ-Hài	2	3	4	5*	6	7	8		KOIAK 1820	19	20	21	22	23	24	25	TĀḪŚĀŚ 2096
	6	7	8	9	10	11	○	8:17	2	2489535		8	9	10	11	12	13	14			9	10	11	12	13	14	15	Xiǎo hán	TŌBE 1820	26	27	28	29[c]	30	1	2	ṬER 2096
	13	14	15	16	17	18	19		3	2489542		15	16	17	18	19	20	21			16	17	18	19	20	21	22			3	4	5	6[d]	7	8	9	
	◑	21	22	23	24	25	26	10:58	4	2489549		22	23	24	25	26	27	28			23	**24**	25	26	27	28	29	Dà hán		10	11[e]	12	13	14	15	16	
FEBRUARY 2104	●	28	29	30	31	1	2	20:07	5	2489556	SHEVAT 5864	29	1	2	3	4	5	6	Sun $15^h40^m4^p$	MONTH 1 Jiǎ-Zǐ	30	1[a]	2	3	4	5	6			17	18	19	20	21	22	23	
	◐	4	5	6	7	8	9	11:33	6	2489563		7	8	9	10	11	12	13			7	8	*9*	10	11	12	13	Lì chūn		24	25	26	27	28	29	30	
	10	○	12	13	14	15	16	1:49	7	2489570		14	15	16	17	18	19	20			14	15[b]	16	17	18	19	20		MESHIR 1820	1	2	3	4	5	6	7	YAKĀTIT 2096
	17	18	◑	20	21	22	23	6:27	8	2489577		21	22	23	24	25	26	27			21	22	**23**	24	25	26	27	Yǔ shuǐ		8	9	10	11	12	13	14	
MARCH 2104	24	25	●	27	28	29	1	7:03	9	2489584	ADAR 5864	28	29	30	1	2	3	4	Tue $4^h24^m5^p$	MONTH 2 Jiǎ-Zǐ	28	29	1	2	3	4	5			15	16	17	18	19	20	21	
	2	◐	4	5	6	7	8	22:12	10	2489591		5	6	7	8	9	10	11			6*	7	8	9	10	11	12	Jīng zhé		22	23	24	25	26	27	28	
	9	10	○	12	13	14	15	19:57	11	2489598		12	13	14[f]	15	16	17	18			13	14	15	16	17	18	19		PAREMOTEP 1820	29	30	1	2	3	4	5	MAGĀBIT 2096
	16	17	18	◑	20[b]	21	22	22:25	12	2489605		19	20	21	22	23	24	25			20	21	22	23	**24**	25	26	Chūn fēn		6	7	8	9	10	11	12	
	23	24	25	●	27	28	29	16:23	13	2489612	NISAN 5864	26	27	28	29	1	2	3	Wed $17^h8^m6^p$	MONTH 3 Jiǎ-Zǐ	27	28	29	30	1	2	3			13	14	15	16	17	18	19	
APRIL 2104	30	31	1	◐	3	4	5	11:00	14	2489619		4	5	6	7	8	9	10			4	5	6	7	8	9[c]	10	Qīng míng		20	21	22	23	24	25	26	
	6	7	8	9	○	11	12	13:30	15	2489626		11	12	13	14	15[g]	16	17			11	12	13	14	15	16	17		PARMOUTE 1820	27	28	29	30	1	2	3	MIYĀZYĀ 2096
	13	14	15	16	17	◑	19	10:13	16	2489633		18	19	20	21	22	23	24			18	19	20	21	22	23	24			4	5	6	7	8	9	10	
	20	21	22	23	24	●	26	0:48	17	2489640	IYYAR 5864	25	26	27	28	29	30	1	Fri $5^h52^m7^p$	MONTH 4 Jiǎ-Zǐ	**25**	26	27	28	29	1	2	Gǔ yǔ		11[f]	12	13	14	15	16	17	
MAY 2104	27	28	29	30	1	◐	3	1:41	18	2489647		2	3	4	5	6	7	8			3	4	5	6	7*	8	9			18	19	20	21	22	23	24	
	4	5	6	7	8	9	○	5:32	19	2489654		9	10	11	12	13	14	15			10	*11*	12	13	14	15	16	Lì xià	PASHONS 1820	25	26	27	28	29[g]	30	1	GENBOT 2096
	11	12	13	14	15	16	◑	18:14	20	2489661		16	17	18	19	20	21	22			17	18	19	20	21	22	23			2	3	4	5	6	7	8	
	18	19	20	21	22	23	●	9:10	21	2489668		23	24	25	26	27	28	29		MONTH 5 Jiǎ-Zǐ	24	25	26	**27**	28	29	1	Xiǎo mǎn		9	10	11	12	13	14	15	
	25	26	27	28	29	30	◐	17:45	22	2489675	SIVAN 5864	1	2	3	4	5	6[h]	7	Sat $18^h36^m8^p$		2	3	4	5[d]	6	7	8			16	17	18	19	20	21	22	
JUNE 2104	1	2	3	4	5	6	7		23	2489682		8	9	10	11	12	13	14			9	10	11	12	*13*	14	15	Máng zhòng		23	24	25	26	27	28	29	
	○	9	10	11	12	13	14	19:27	24	2489689		15	16	17	18	19	20	21			16	17	18	19	20	21	22		PAŌNE 1820	30	1	2	3	4	5	6	SANĒ 2096
	◑	16	17	18	19	20	21[c]	23:37	25	2489696		22	23	24	25	26	27	28			23	24	25	26	27	28	**29**	Xià zhì		7	8	9	10	11	12	13	
	●	23	24	25	26	27	28	18:19	26	2489703	TAMMUZ 5864	29	30	1	2	3	4	5	Mon $7^h20^m9^p$	LEAP MONTH 5 Jiǎ-Zǐ	30	1	2	3	4	5	6			14	15	16	17	18	19	20	
JULY 2104	29	◐	1	2	3	4	5	10:41	27	2489710		6	7	8	9	10	11	12			7	8*	9	10	11	12	13			21	22	23	24	25	26	27	
	6	7	○	9	10	11	12	7:03	28	2489717		13	14	15	16	17	18	19			14	*15*	16	17	18	19	20	Xiǎo shǔ	EPĒP 1820	28	29	30	1	2	3	4	ḤAMLĒ 2096
	13	14	◑	16	17	18	19	3:53	29	2489724		20	21	22	23	24	25	26			21	22	23	24	25	26	27			5	6	7	8	9	10	11	
	20	21	●	23	24	25	26	4:53	30	2489731	AV 5864	27	28	29	1	2	3	4	Tue $20^h4^m10^p$	MONTH 6 Jiǎ-Zǐ	28	29	**1**	2	3	4	5	Dà shǔ		12	13	14	15	16	17	18	
AUGUST 2104	27	28	29	◐	31	1	2	3:57	31	2489738		5	6	7	8	9[i]	10	11			6	7	8	9	10	11	12			19	20	21	22	23	24	25	
	3	4	5	○	7	8	9	16:39	32	2489745		12	13	14	15	16	17	18			13	14	15	16	*17*	18	19	Lì qiū	MESORĒ 1820	26	27	28	29	30	1	2	NAḤASĒ 2096
	10	11	12	◑	14	15	16	8:43	33	2489752		19	20	21	22	23	24	25			20	21	22	23	24	25	26			3	4	5	6	7	8	9	
	17	18	19	●	21	22	23	17:25	34	2489759	ELUL 5864	26	27	28	29	30	1	2	Thu $8^h48^m11^p$	MONTH 7 Jiǎ-Zǐ	27	28	29	30	1	2	**3**	Chǔ shǔ		10	11	12	13[h]	14	15	16	
	24	25	26	27	◐	29	30	20:51	35	2489766		3	4	5	6	7	8	9			4	5	6	7[e]	8	9*	10			17	18	19	20	21	22	23	
SEPTEMBER 2104	31	1	2	3	4	○	6	1:03	36	2489773		10	11	12	13	14	15	16			11	12	13	14	15[f]	16	17			24	25	26	27	28	29	30	
	7	8	9	10	◑	12	13	15:34	37	2489780		17	18	19	20	21	22	23			*18*	19	20	21	22	23	24	Bái lù	EPAG. 1820 / THOOUT 1821	1	2	3	4	5	1[a]	2	PĀG. 2096 / MASKARAM 2097
	14	15	16	17	18	●	20	8:13	38	2489787	TISHRI 5865	24	25	26	27	28	29	1[a]	Fri $21^h32^m12^p$	MONTH 8 Jiǎ-Zǐ	25	26	27	28	29	1	2			3	4	5	6	7	8	9	
	21	22[d]	23	24	25	26	◐	12:33	39	2489794		2[a]	3	4	5	6	7	8			3	4	**5**	6	7	8	9	Qiū fēn		10	11	12	13	14	15	16	
OCTOBER 2104	28	29	30	1	2	3	○	9:16	40	2489801		9	10[b]	11	12	13	14	15[c]			10	11	12	13	14	15[g]	16			17[b]	18	19	20	21	22	23	
	5	6	7	8	9	10	◑	1:36	41	2489808		16	17	18	19	20	21	22			17	18	19	*20*	21	22	23	Hán lù		24	25	26	27	28	29	30	
	12	13	14	15	16	17	18		42	2489815		23	24	25	26	27	28	29			24	25	26	27	28	29	30		PAOPE 1821	1	2	3	4	5	6	7	ṬEQEMT 2097
	●	20	21	22	23	24	25	1:11	43	2489822	HESHVAN 5865	30	1	2	3	4	5	6	Sun $10^h16^m13^p$	MONTH 9 Jiǎ-Zǐ	1	2	3	4	**5**	6	7	Shuāng jiàng		8	9	10	11	12	13	14	
NOVEMBER 2104	26	◐	28	29	30	31	1	2:18	44	2489829		7	8	9	10	11	12	13			8	9[h]	10*	11	12	13	14			15	16	17	18	19	20	21	
	○	3	4	5	6	7	8	18:18	45	2489836		14	15	16	17	18	19	20			15	16	17	18	19	*20*	21	Lì dōng		22	23	24	25	26	27	28	
	◑	10	11	12	13	14	15	15:28	46	2489843		21	22	23	24	25	26	27			22	23	24	25	26	27	28		ATHŌR 1821	29	30	1	2	3	4	5	ḪEDĀR 2097
	16	●	18	19	20	21	22	19:35	47	2489850	KISLEV 5865	28	29	30	1	2	3	4	Mon $23^h0^m14^p$	MONTH 10 Jiǎ-Zǐ	29	30	1	2	3	4	**5**	Xiǎo xuě		6	7	8	9	10	11	12	
	23	24	◐	26	27	28	29	13:48	48	2489857		5	6	7	8	9	10	11			6	7	8	9	10	11	12			13	14	15	16	17	18	19	
DECEMBER 2104	30	1	○	3	4	5	6	4:49	49	2489864		12	13	14	15	16	17	18[d]			13	14	15	16	17	18	19			20	21	22	23	24	25	26	
	7	8	◑	10	11	12	13	9:07	50	2489871		19	20	21	22	23	24	25[e]			*20*	21	22	23	24	25	26	Dà xuě	KOIAK 1821	27	28	29	30	1	2	3	TĀḪŚĀŚ 2097
	14	15	16	●	18	19	20	13:56	51	2489878	TEVETH 5865	26[e]	27[e]	28[e]	29[e]	30[e]	1[e]	2[e]	Wed $11^h44^m15^p$	MONTH 11 Jiǎ-Zǐ	27	28	29	1	2	3	4			4	5	6	7	8	9	10	
	21[e]	22	23	◐	25	26	27	23:19	52	2489885		3	4	5	6	7	8	9			5	6[i]	7	8	9	10	11*	Dōng zhì		11	12	13	14	15	16	17	
	28	29	30	○	1	2	3	16:58	1	2489892		10	11	12	13	14	15	16			12	13	14	15	16	17	18			18	19	20	21	22	23	24	

‡Leap year
[a]New Year
[b]Spring (12:13)
[c]Summer (4:36)
[d]Autumn (21:08)
[e]Winter (19:11)
● New moon
◐ First quarter moon
○ Full moon
◑ Last quarter moon

[a]New Year
[b]Yom Kippur
[c]Sukkot
[d]Winter starts
[e]Ḥanukkah
[f]Purim
[g]Passover
[h]Shavuot
[i]Fast of Av

‡Leap year
[a]New Year (4802, Rat)
[b]Lantern Festival
[c]Qīngmíng
[d]Dragon Festival
[e]Qīqiǎo
[f]Hungry Ghosts
[g]Mid-Autumn Festival
[h]Double-Ninth Festival
[i]Dōngzhì
*Start of 60-name cycle

[a]New Year
[b]Building of the Cross
[c]Christmas
[d]Jesus's Circumcision
[e]Epiphany
[f]Easter
[g]Mary's Announcement
[h]Jesus's Transfiguration

PERSIAN (ASTRONOMICAL) 1482‡/1483

Month	Sun	Mon	Tue	Wed	Thu	Fri	Sat
	9	10	11	12	13	14	15
DEY 1482	16	17	18	19	20	21	22
	23	24	25	26	27	28	29
	30	1	2	3	4	5	6
BAHMAN 1482	7	8	9	10	11	12	13
	14	15	16	17	18	19	20
	21	22	23	24	25	26	27
	28	29	30	1	2	3	4
ESFAND 1482	5	6	7	8	9	10	11
	12	13	14	15	16	17	18
	19	20	21	22	23	24	25
	26	27	28	29	30	1[a]	2
FARVARDĪN 1483	3	4	5	6	7	8	9
	10	11	12	13[b]	14	15	16
	17	18	19	20	21	22	23
	24	25	26	27	28	29	30
	31	1	2	3	4	5	6
ORDĪBEHEŠT 1483	7	8	9	10	11	12	13
	14	15	16	17	18	19	20
	21	22	23	24	25	26	27
	28	29	30	31	1	2	3
XORDĀD 1483	4	5	6	7	8	9	10
	11	12	13	14	15	16	17
	18	19	20	21	22	23	24
	25	26	27	28	29	30	31
	1	2	3	4	5	6	7
TĪR 1483	8	9	10	11	12	13	14
	15	16	17	18	19	20	21
	22	23	24	25	26	27	28
	29	30	31	1	2	3	4
MORDĀD 1483	5	6	7	8	9	10	11
	12	13	14	15	16	17	18
	19	20	21	22	23	24	25
	26	27	28	29	30	31	1
SHAHRĪVAR 1483	2	3	4	5	6	7	8
	9	10	11	12	13	14	15
	16	17	18	19	20	21	22
	23	24	25	26	27	28	29
	30	31	1	2	3	4	5
MEHR 1483	6	7	8	9	10	11	12
	13	14	15	16	17	18	19
	20	21	22	23	24	25	26
	27	28	29	30	1	2	3
ĀBĀN 1483	4	5	6	7	8	9	10
	11	12	13	14	15	16	17
	18	19	20	21	22	23	24
	25	26	27	28	29	30	1
ĀZAR 1483	2	3	4	5	6	7	8
	9	10	11	12	13	14	15
	16	17	18	19	20	21	22
	23	24	25	26	27	28	29
DEY 1483	30	1	2	3	4	5	6
	7	8	9	10	11	12	13

‡Leap year
[a]New Year
[b]Sizdeh Bedar

HINDU LUNAR 2160/2161

Month	Sun	Mon	Tue	Wed	Thu	Fri	Sat
	1	2	**3**	5	6	7	8
PAUSHA 2160	9	10	11	12	13	14	15
	16	17	18	19	20	21	22
	23	24	25	26	27	28	29
	30	1	2	3	4	5	6
MĀGHA 2160	7	**8**	10	11	12	13	14
	15	16	*16*	17	18	19	20
	21	22	23	24	25	26	27
	28[h]	29	30	1	**2**	4	5
PHĀLGUNA 2160	6	7	8	9	10	11	12
	13	14	15[i]	16	17	18	19
	19	20	21	22	23	24	25
	26	28	29	30	1[a]	2	3
CHAITRA 2161	4	5	6	7	8[b]	9	10
	11	12	13	14	15	16	17
	18	19	20	21	22	23	24
	25	26	27	28	29	**30**	2
VAIŚĀKHA 2161	3	4	5	6	7	8	9
	10	11	12	13	*13*	14	15
	16	17	18	19	20	21	22
	23	25	26	27	28	29	30
	1	2	3	4	5	6	7
JYAISHTHA 2161	8	9	10	11	12	13	14
	15	16	17	18	19	20	21
	22	23	24	25	**26**	28	29
	30	1	2	3	4	5	6
ĀSHĀḌHA 2161	7	8	9	*9*	10	11	12
	13	14	15	16	17	18	**19**
	21	22	23	24	25	26	27
	28	29	30	1	2	3	4
ŚRĀVAṆA 2161	5	6	7	8	9	10	11
	12	13	14	15	16	17	18
	19	20	21	**22**[c]	24	25	26
	27	28	29	30	1	2	3
BHĀDRAPADA 2161	4[d]	5	6	*6*	7	8	9
	10	11	12	13	14	**15**	17
	18	19	20	21	22	23	24
	25	26	27	28	29	30	1
LEAP ĀŚVINA 2161	2	3	4	5	6	7	8
	9	10	11	12	13	14	15
	16	17	**18**	20	21	22	23
	24	25	26	27	28	29	30
	1	*1*	2	3	4	5	6
ĀŚVINA 2161	7	8[e]	9[e]	10[e]	11	**12**	14
	15	16	17	18	19	20	21
	22	23	24	25	26	27	28
	29	30	1[f]	2	3	4	5
KĀRTTIKA 2161	6	7	8	9	10	11	12
	13	14	15	16	**17**	19	20
	21	22	23	24	*24*	25	26
	27	28	29	30	1	2	3
MĀRGAŚĪRA 2161	4	5	6	7	8	9	**10**[g]
	12	13	14	15	16	17	18

[a]New Year (Raktāksha)
[b]Birthday of Rāma
[c]Birthday of Krishna
[d]Gaṇēśa Chaturthī
[e]Dashara
[f]Diwali
[g]Birthday of Vishnu
[h]Night of Śiva
[i]Holi

HINDU SOLAR 2025/2026

Month	Sun	Mon	Tue	Wed	Thu	Fri	Sat
PAUSHA 2025	13	14	15	16	17	18	19
	20	21	22	23	24	25	26
	27	28	29	1[b]	2	3	4
MĀGHA 2025	5	6	7	8	9	10	11
	12	13	14	15	16	17	18
	19	20	21	22	23	24	25
	26	27	28	29	30	1	2
PHĀLGUNA 2025	3	4	5	6	7	8	9
	10	11	12	13	14	15	16
	17	18	19	20	21	22	23
	24	25	26	27	28	29	30
	1	2	3	4	5	6	7
CHAITRA 2025	8	9	10	11	12	13	14
	15	16	17	18	19	20	21
	22	23	24	25	26	27	28
	29	30	1[a]	2	3	4	5
VAIŚĀKHA 2026	6	7	8	9	10	11	12
	13	14	15	16	17	18	19
	20	21	22	23	24	25	26
	27	28	29	30	31	1	2
JYAISHTHA 2026	3	4	5	6	7	8	9
	10	11	12	13	14	15	16
	17	18	19	20	21	22	23
	24	25	26	27	28	29	30
	31	1	2	3	4	5	6
ĀSHĀḌHA 2026	7	8	9	10	11	12	13
	14	15	16	17	18	19	20
	21	22	23	24	25	26	27
	28	29	30	31	32	1	2
ŚRĀVAṆA 2026	3	4	5	6	7	8	9
	10	11	12	13	14	15	16
	17	18	19	20	21	22	23
	24	25	26	27	28	29	30
	31	1	2	3	4	5	6
BHĀDRAPADA 2026	7	8	9	10	11	12	13
	14	15	16	17	18	19	20
	21	22	23	24	25	26	27
	28	29	30	31	1	2	3
ĀŚVINA 2026	4	5	6	7	8	9	10
	11	12	13	14	15	16	17
	18	19	20	21	22	23	24
	25	26	27	28	29	30	31
	1	2	3	4	5	6	7
KĀRTTIKA 2026	8	9	10	11	12	13	14
	15	16	17	18	19	20	21
	22	23	24	25	26	27	28
	29	30	1	2	3	4	5
MĀRGAŚĪRA 2026	6	7	8	9	10	11	12
	13	14	15	16	17	18	19
	20	21	22	23	24	25	26
	27	28	29	1	2	3	4
PAUSHA 2026	5	6	7	8	9	10	11
	12	13	14	15	16	17	18

[a]New Year (Bahudhānya)
[b]Pongal

ISLAMIC (ASTRONOMICAL) 1527‡/1528‡

Month	Sun	Mon	Tue	Wed	Thu	Fri	Sat
	30	1	2	3	4	5	6
DHU AL-ḤIJJA 1527	7	8	9	10[g]	11	12	13
	14	15	16	17	18	19	20
	21	22	23	24	25	26	27
	28	29	1[a]	2	3	4	5
MUḤARRAM 1528	6	7	8	9	10[b]	11	12
	13	14	15	16	17	18	19
	20	21	22	23	24	25	26
	27	28	29	1	2	3	4
ṢAFAR 1528	5	6	7	8	9	10	11
	12	13	14	15	16	17	18
	19	20	21	22	23	24	25
	26	27	28	29	30	1	2
RABĪ' I 1528	3	4	5	6	7	8	9
	10	11	12[c]	13	14	15	16
	17	18	19	20	21	22	23
	24	25	26	27	28	29	1
RABĪ' II 1528	2	3	4	5	6	7	8
	9	10	11	12	13	14	15
	16	17	18	19	20	21	22
	23	24	25	26	27	28	29
	30	1	2	3	4	5	6
JUMĀDĀ I 1528	7	8	9	10	11	12	13
	14	15	16	17	18	19	20
	21	22	23	24	25	26	27
	28	29	1	2	3	4	5
JUMĀDĀ II 1528	6	7	8	9	10	11	12
	13	14	15	16	17	18	19
	20	21	22	23	24	25	26
	27	28	29	30	1	2	3
RAJAB 1528	4	5	6	7	8	9	10
	11	12	13	14	15	16	17
	18	19	20	21	22	23	24
	25	26	27[d]	28	29	30	1
SHA'BĀN 1528	2	3	4	5	6	7	8
	9	10	11	12	13	14	15
	16	17	18	19	20	21	22
	23	24	25	26	27	28	29
	30	1[e]	2	3	4	5	6
RAMAḌĀN 1528	7	8	9	10	11	12	13
	14	15	16	17	18	19	20
	21	22	23	24	25	26	27
	28	29	1[f]	2	3	4	5
SHAWWĀL 1528	6	7	8	9	10	11	12
	13	14	15	16	17	18	19
	20	21	22	23	24	25	26
	27	28	29	1	2	3	4
DHU AL-QA'DA 1528	5	6	7	8	9	10	11
	12	13	14	15	16	17	18
	19	20	21	22	23	24	25
	26	27	28	29	30	1	2
DHU AL-ḤIJJA 1528	3	4	5	6	7	8	9
	10[g]	11	12	13	14	15	16

‡Leap year
[a]New Year
[b]'Ashūrā'
[c]Prophet's Birthday
[d]Ascent of the Prophet
[e]Start of Ramaḍān
[f]'Id al-Fiṭr
[g]'Id al-'Aḍḥā

GREGORIAN 2104‡

Julian‡ (Sun)	Sun	Mon	Tue	Wed	Thu	Fri	Sat	Month
Dec 16	30	31	1	2	3	4	5	
	6	7	8[a]	9	10	11	12	JANUARY 2104
Dec 30	13	14	15[b]	16	17	18	19	
	20	21	22	23	24	25	26	
Jan 13	27	28	29	30	31	1	2	
	3	4	5	6	7	8	9	FEBRUARY 2104
Jan 27	10	11	12	13	14	15	16	
	17	18	19	20	21	22	23	
Feb 10	24	25	26	27[c]	28	29	1	
	2	3	4	5	6	7	8	MARCH 2104
Feb 24	9[d]	10	11	12	13	14	15	
	16	17	18	19	20	21	22	
Mar 9	23	24	25	26	27	28	29	
	30	31	1	2	3	4	5	
Mar 23	6	7	8	9	10	11	12	APRIL 2104
	13[e]	14	15	16	17	18	19	
Apr 6	20[f]	21	22	23	24	25	26	
	27	28	29	30	1	2	3	
Apr 20	4	5	6	7	8	9	10	MAY 2104
	11	12	13	14	15	16	17	
May 4	18	19	20	21	22	23	24	
	25	26	27	28	29	30	31	
May 18	1	2	3	4	5	6	7	
	8	9	10	11	12	13	14	JUNE 2104
Jun 1	15	16	17	18	19	20	21	
	22	23	24	25	26	27	28	
Jun 15	29	30	1	2	3	4	5	
	6	7	8	9	10	11	12	JULY 2104
Jun 29	13	14	15	16	17	18	19	
	20	21	22	23	24	25	26	
Jul 13	27	28	29	30	31	1	2	
	3	4	5	6	7	8	9	
Jul 27	10	11	12	13	14	15	16	AUGUST 2104
	17	18	19	20	21	22	23	
Aug 10	24	25	26	27	28	29	30	
	31	1	2	3	4	5	6	
Aug 24	7	8	9	10	11	12	13	SEPTEMBER 2104
	14	15	16	17	18	19	20	
Sep 7	21	22	23	24	25	26	27	
	28	29	30	1	2	3	4	
Sep 21	5	6	7	8	9	10	11	OCTOBER 2104
	12	13	14	15	16	17	18	
Oct 5	19	20	21	22	23	24	25	
	26	27	28	29	30	31	1	
Oct 19	2	3	4	5	6	7	8	NOVEMBER 2104
	9	10	11	12	13	14	15	
Nov 2	16	17	18	19	20	21	22	
	23	24	25	26	27	28	29	
Nov 16	30[g]	1	2	3	4	5	6	
	7	8	9	10	11	12	13	DECEMBER 2104
Nov 30	14	15	16	17	18	19	20	
	21	22	23	24	25[h]	26	27	
Dec 14	28	29	30	31	1	2	3	

‡Leap year
[a]Orthodox Christmas
[b]Julian New Year
[c]Ash Wednesday
[d]Feast of Orthodoxy
[e]Easter
[f]Orthodox Easter
[g]Advent
[h]Christmas

2105

Gregorian 2105	Gregorian Sun Mon Tue Wed Thu Fri Sat	Lunar Phases	ISO Week (Mon)	Julian Day (Sun noon)	Hebrew 5865/5866‡	Hebrew Sun Mon Tue Wed Thu Fri Sat	Molad	Chinese Jiǎ-Zǐ‡/Yǐ-Chǒu	Chinese Sun Mon Tue Wed Thu Fri Sat	Solar Term	Coptic 1821/1822	Coptic Sun Mon Tue Wed Thu Fri Sat	Ethiopic 2097/2098
January 2105	28 29 30 ○ 1[a] 2 3	16:58	1	2489892	Teveth 5865	10 11 12 13 14 15 16		Month 11 Jiǎ-Zǐ	12 13 14 15 16 17 18		Koiak 1821	18 19 20 21 22 23 24	Tākhśāś 2097
	4 5 6 7 ◑ 9 10	5:45	2	2489899		17 18 19 20 21 22 23			19 20 21 22 23 24 25	Xiǎo hán		25 26 27 28 29[c] 30 1	
	11 12 13 14 15 ● 17	6:35	3	2489906	Shevat 5865	24 25 26 27 28 29 1	Fri 0h28m16p	Month 12 Jiǎ-Zǐ	26 27 28 29 30 1 2		Tôbe 1821	2 3 4 5 6[d] 7 8	Ṭer 2097
	18 19 20 21 22 ◐ 24	7:36	4	2489913		2 3 4 5 6 7 8			3 4 5 6 7 8 9	Dà hán		9 10 11[e] 12 13 14 15	
	25 26 27 28 29 ○ 31	6:36	5	2489920		9 10 11 12 13 14 15			10 11 12 13 14 15 16			16 17 18 19 20 21 22	
February 2105	1 2 3 4 5 6 ◑	3:42	6	2489927		16 17 18 19 20 21 22			17 18 19 20 21 22 23	Lì chūn		23 24 25 26 27 28 29	
	8 9 10 11 12 13 ●	20:39	7	2489934		23 24 25 26 27 28 29			24 25 26 27 28 29 30		Meshir 1821	30 1 2 3 4 5 6	Yakātit 2097
	15 16 17 18 19 20 ◐	15:31	8	2489941	Adar 5865	30 1 2 3 4 5 6	Sat 13h12m17p	Month 1 Yǐ-Chǒu	1[a] 2 3 4 5 6 7	Yǔ shuǐ		7 8 9 10 11 12 13	
	22 23 24 25 26 27 ○	21:33	9	2489948		7 8 9 10 11 12 13			8 9 10 11* 12 13 14			14 15 16 17 18 19 20	
March 2105	1 2 3 4 5 6 7		10	2489955		14[f] 15 16 17 18 19 20			15[b] 16 17 18 19 20 21	Jīng zhé		21 22 23 24 25 26 27	
	8 ◑ 10 11 12 13 14	0:36	11	2489962		21 22 23 24 25 26 27			22 23 24 25 26 27 28		Paremotep 1821	28 29 30 1 2 3 4	Magābit 2097
	15 ● 17 18 19 20[b] 21	8:05	12	2489969	Nisan 5865	28 29 1 2 3 4 5	Mon 1h57m0p	Month 2 Yǐ-Chǒu	29 1 2 3 4 5 6	Chūn fēn		5 6 7 8 9 10 11	
	◐ 23 24 25 26 27 28	23:52	13	2489976		6 7 8 9 10 11 12			7 8 9 10 11 12 13			12 13 14 15 16 17 18	
April 2105	29 ○ 31 1 2 3 4	13:35	14	2489983		13 14 15[g] 16 17 18 19			14 15 16 17 18 19 20			19 20 21 22 23 24 25	
	5 6 ◑ 8 9 10 11	18:25	15	2489990		20 21 22 23 24 25 26			21[c] 22 23 24 25 26 27	Qīng míng	Parmoute 1821	26[f] 27 28 29 30 1 2	Miyāzyā 2097
	12 13 ● 15 16 17 18	17:30	16	2489997	Iyyar 5865	27 28 29 30 1 2 3	Tue 14h41m1p	Month 3 Yǐ-Chǒu	28 29 30 1 2 3 4			3 4 5 6 7 8 9	
	19 20 ◐ 22 23 24 25	9:16	17	2490004		4 5 6 7 8 9 10			5 6 7 8 9 10 11	Gǔ yǔ		10 11 12 13 14 15 16	
May 2105	26 27 28 ○ 30 1 2	6:12	18	2490011		11 12 13 14 15 16 17			12* 13 14 15 16 17 18			17 18 19 20 21 22 23	
	3 4 5 6 ◑ 8 9	8:11	19	2490018		18 19 20 21 22 23 24			19 20 21 22 23 24 25	Lì xià		24 25 26 27 28 29[g] 30	
	10 11 12 13 ● 15 16	1:36	20	2490025	Sivan 5865	25 26 27 28 29 1 2	Thu 3h25m2p	Month 4 Yǐ-Chǒu	26 27 28 29 1 2 3		Pashons 1821	1 2 3 4 5 6 7	Genbot 2097
	17 18 19 ◐ 21 22 23	20:17	21	2490032		3 4 5 6[h] 7 8 9			4 5 6 7 8 9 10	Xiǎo mǎn		8 9 10 11 12 13 14	
	24 25 26 27 ○ 29 30	22:31	22	2490039		10 11 12 13 14 15 16			11 12 13 14 15 16 17			15 16 17 18 19 20 21	
June 2105	31 1 2 3 4 ◑ 6	18:05	23	2490046		17 18 19 20 21 22 23			18 19 20 21 22 23 24	Máng zhòng		22 23 24 25 26 27 28	
	7 8 9 10 11 ● 13	9:07	24	2490053		24 25 26 27 28 29 30		Month 5 Yǐ-Chǒu	25 26 27 28 29 1 2		Paône 1821	29 30 1 2 3 4 5	Sanē 2097
	14 15 16 17 18 ◐ 20	9:20	25	2490060	Tammuz 5865	1 2 3 4 5 6 7	Fri 16h9m3p		3 4 5[d] 6 7 8 9			6 7 8 9 10 11 12	
	21[c] 22 23 24 25 26 ○	13:33	26	2490067		8 9 10 11 12 13 14			10 11 12 13 14* 15 16	Xià zhì		13 14 15 16 17 18 19	
July 2105	28 29 30 1 2 3 4		27	2490074		15 16 17 18 19 20 21			17 18 19 20 21 22 23			20 21 22 23 24 25 26	
	◑ 6 7 8 9 10 ●	1:06 16:48	28	2490081		22 23 24 25 26 27 28			24 25 26 27 28 29 30	Xiǎo shǔ	Epêp 1821	27 28 29 30 1 2 3	Ḥamlē 2097
	12 13 14 15 16 17 18		29	2490088	Av 5865	29 1 2 3 4 5 6	Sun 4h53m4p	Month 6 Yǐ-Chǒu	1 2 3 4 5 6 7			4 5 6 7 8 9 10	
	◐ 20 21 22 23 24 25	0:39	30	2490095		7 8 9[i] 10 11 12 13			8 9 10 11 12 13 14	Dà shǔ		11 12 13 14 15 16 17	
August 2105	26 ○ 28 29 30 31 1	2:42	31	2490102		14 15 16 17 18 19 20			15 16 17 18 19 20 21			18 19 20 21 22 23 24	
	2 ◑ 4 5 6 7 8	6:28	32	2490109		21 22 23 24 25 26 27			22 23 24 25 26 27 28	Lì qiū	Mesorê 1821	25 26 27 28 29 30 1	Naḥasē 2097
	9 ● 11 12 13 14 15	1:32	33	2490116	Elul 5865	28 29 30 1 2 3 4	Mon 17h37m5p	Month 7 Yǐ-Chǒu	29 1 2 3 4 5 6			2 3 4 5 6 7 8	
	16 ◐ 18 19 20 21 22	17:59	34	2490123		5 6 7 8 9 10 11			7[e] 8 9 10 11 12 13			9 10 11 12 13[h] 14 15	
	23 24 ○ 26 27 28 29	14:06	35	2490130		12 13 14 15 16 17 18			14 15[f]* 16 17 18 19 20	Chǔ shǔ		16 17 18 19 20 21 22	
September 2105	30 31 ◑ 2 3 4 5	11:32	36	2490137		19 20 21 22 23 24 25			21 22 23 24 25 26 27			23 24 25 26 27 28 29	
	6 7 ● 9 10 11 12	12:21	37	2490144	Tishri 5866	26 27 28 29 1[a] 2[a] 3	Wed 6h21m6p	Month 8 Yǐ-Chǒu	28 29 1 2 3 4 5	Bái lù	Epag. 1821 / Thoout 1822	30 1 2 3 4 5 1[a]	Pāg. 2097 / Maskaram 2098
	13 14 15 ◐ 17 18 19	12:27	38	2490151		4 5 6 7 8 9 10[b]			6 7 8 9 10 11 12			2 3 4 5 6 7 8	
	20 21 22 23[d] ○ 25 26	0:24	39	2490158		11 12 13 14 15[c] 16 17			13 14 15[g] 16 17 18 19	Qiū fēn		9 10 11 12 13 14 15	
October 2105	27 28 29 ◑ 1 2 3	17:32	40	2490165		18 19 20 21 22 23 24			20 21 22 23 24 25 26			16 17[b] 18 19 20 21 22	
	4 5 6 7 ● 9 10	2:07	41	2490172	Heshvan 5866	25 26 27 28 29 30 1	Thu 19h5m7p	Month 9 Yǐ-Chǒu	27 28 29 30 1 2 3	Hán lù		23 24 25 26 27 28 29	
	11 12 13 14 15 ◐ 17	6:47	42	2490179		2 3 4 5 6 7 8			4 5 6 7 8 9[h] 10		Paope 1822	30 1 2 3 4 5 6	Ṭeqemt 2098
	18 19 20 21 22 ○ 24	10:25	43	2490186		9 10 11 12 13 14 15			11 12 13 14 15 16* 17	Shuāng jiàng		7 8 9 10 11 12 13	
	25 26 27 28 29 ◑ 31	1:43	44	2490193		16 17 18 19 20 21 22			18 19 20 21 22 23 24			14 15 16 17 18 19 20	
November 2105	1 2 3 4 5 ● 7	19:03	45	2490200		23 24 25 26 27 28 29		Month 10 Yǐ-Chǒu	25 26 27 28 29 30 1	Lì dōng		21 22 23 24 25 26 27	
	8 9 10 11 12 13 ◐	23:44	46	2490207	Kislev 5866	30 1 2 3 4 5 6	Sat 7h49m8p		2 3 4 5 6 7 8		Athôr 1822	28 29 30 1 2 3 4	Ḫedār 2098
	15 16 17 18 19 20 ○	20:40	47	2490214		7 8 9 10 11 12 13			9 10 11 12 13 14 15			5 6 7 8 9 10 11	
	22 23 24 25 26 27 ◑	13:08	48	2490221		14 15 16 17 18 19 20			16 17 18 19 20 21 22	Xiǎo xuě		12 13 14 15 16 17 18	
December 2105	29 30 1 2 3 4 5		49	2490228		21 22 23 24 25[e] 26[e] 27[e]			23 24 25 26 27 28 29			19 20 21 22 23 24 25	
	● 7 8 9 10 11 12	14:14	50	2490235	Teveth 5866	28[d][e] 29[e] 30[e] 1[e] 2[e] 3 4	Sun 20h33m9p	Month 11 Yǐ-Chǒu	1 2 3 4 5 6 7	Dà xuě	Koiak 1822	26 27 28 29 30 1 2	Tākhśāś 2098
	13 ◐ 15 16 17 18 19	14:30	51	2490242		5 6 7 8 9 10 11			8 9 10 11 12 13 14			3 4 5 6 7 8 9	
	20 ○ 22[e] 23 24 25 26	7:19	52	2490249		12 13 14 15 16 17 18			15 16 17[i]* 18 19 20 21	Dōng zhì		10 11 12 13 14 15 16	
	27 ◑ 29 30 31 1 2	4:22	53	2490256		19 20 21 22 23 24 25			22 23 24 25 26 27 28			17 18 19 20 21 22 23	

[a]New Year
[b]Spring (18:05)
[c]Summer (10:17)
[d]Autumn (2:51)
[e]Winter (1:02)
● New moon
◐ First quarter moon
○ Full moon
◑ Last quarter moon

‡Leap year
[a]New Year
[b]Yom Kippur
[c]Sukkot
[d]Winter starts
[e]Ḥanukkah
[f]Purim
[g]Passover
[h]Shavuot
[i]Fast of Av

‡Leap year
[a]New Year (4803, Ox)
[b]Lantern Festival
[c]Qīngmíng
[d]Dragon Festival
[e]Qīqiǎo
[f]Hungry Ghosts
[g]Mid-Autumn Festival
[h]Double-Ninth Festival
[i]Dōngzhì
*Start of 60-name cycle

[a]New Year
[b]Building of the Cross
[c]Christmas
[d]Jesus's Circumcision
[e]Epiphany
[f]Easter
[g]Mary's Announcement
[h]Jesus's Transfiguration

2105

PERSIAN (ASTRONOMICAL) 1483/1484

Month	Sun	Mon	Tue	Wed	Thu	Fri	Sat
DEY 1483	7	8	9	10	11	12	13
	14	15	16	17	18	19	20
	21	22	23	24	25	26	27
BAHMAN 1483	28	29	30	1	2	3	4
	5	6	7	8	9	10	11
	12	13	14	15	16	17	18
	19	20	21	22	23	24	25
ESFAND 1483	26	27	28	29	30	1	2
	3	4	5	6	7	8	9
	10	11	12	13	14	15	16
	17	18	19	20	21	22	23
FARVARDĪN 1484	24	25	26	27	28	29	1[a]
	2	3	4	5	6	7	8
	9	10	11	12	13[b]	14	15
	16	17	18	19	20	21	22
	23	24	25	26	27	28	29
ORDĪBEHEŠT 1484	30	31	1	2	3	4	5
	6	7	8	9	10	11	12
	13	14	15	16	17	18	19
	20	21	22	23	24	25	26
XORDĀD 1484	27	28	29	30	31	1	2
	3	4	5	6	7	8	9
	10	11	12	13	14	15	16
	17	18	19	20	21	22	23
	24	25	26	27	28	29	30
TĪR 1484	31	1	2	3	4	5	6
	7	8	9	10	11	12	13
	14	15	16	17	18	19	20
	21	22	23	24	25	26	27
MORDĀD 1484	28	29	30	31	1	2	3
	4	5	6	7	8	9	10
	11	12	13	14	15	16	17
	18	19	20	21	22	23	24
	25	26	27	28	29	30	31
SHAHRĪVAR 1484	1	2	3	4	5	6	7
	8	9	10	11	12	13	14
	15	16	17	18	19	20	21
	22	23	24	25	26	27	28
MEHR 1484	29	30	31	1	2	3	4
	5	6	7	8	9	10	11
	12	13	14	15	16	17	18
	19	20	21	22	23	24	25
ĀBĀN 1484	26	27	28	29	30	1	2
	3	4	5	6	7	8	9
	10	11	12	13	14	15	16
	17	18	19	20	21	22	23
	24	25	26	27	28	29	30
ĀZAR 1484	1	2	3	4	5	6	7
	8	9	10	11	12	13	14
	15	16	17	18	19	20	21
	22	23	24	25	26	27	28
DEY 1484	29	30	1	2	3	4	5
	6	7	8	9	10	11	12

HINDU LUNAR 2161/2162‡

Month	Sun	Mon	Tue	Wed	Thu	Fri	Sat
MĀRGAŚĪRA 2161	12	13	14	15	16	17	18
	19	20	21	22	23	24	25
MĀGHA 2161	26	26	27	28	29	30	1
	2	3	**4**	6	7	8	9
	10	11	12	13	14	15	16
	17	18	19	20	21	22	23
	24	25	26	27	28	29[h]	30
PHĀLGUNA 2161	1	2	3	4	5	6	7
	8	**9**	11	12	13	14	15[i]
	16	17	18	19	19	20	21
	22	23	24	25	26	27	28
LEAP CHAITRA 2162	29	30	1[a]	2	**3**	5	6
	7	8	9	10	11	12	13
	14	15	16	17	18	19	20
	21	22	22	23	24	25	**26**
CHAITRA 2162	28	29	30	1	2	3	4
	5	6	7	8[b]	**9**	11	12
	12	13	14	15	16	17	18
	19	20	21	22	23	24	25
VAIŚĀKHA 2162	26	27	28	29	**30**	2	3
	4	5	6	7	8	9	10
	11	12	13	14	15	16	17
	17	18	19	20	21	22	**23**
JYAIṢṬHA 2162	25	26	27	28	29	30	1
	2	3	4	5	6	7	8
	9	10	11	12	13	14	15
	16	17	18	19	20	21	22
	23	24	25	**26**	28	29	30
ĀSHĀḌHA 2162	1	2	3	4	5	6	7
	8	9	10	11	12	13	14
	14	15	16	17	**18**	20	21
	22	23	24	25	26	27	28
ŚRĀVAṆA 2162	29	**30**	2	3	4	5	5
	6	7	8	9	10	11	12
	13	14	15	16	17	18	19
	20	21	**22**[c]	24	25	26	27
BHĀDRAPADA 2162	28	29	30	1	2	3	4[d]
	5	6	7	8	9	10	10
	11	12	13	**14**	16	17	18
	19	20	21	22	23	24	25
ĀŚVINA 2162	26	**27**	29	30	30	1	2
	3	4	5	6	7	8[e]	9[e]
	10[e]	11	12	13	14	15	16
	17	18	**19**	21	22	23	24
KĀRTTIKA 2162	25	26	27	28	29	30	1[f]
	2	3	4	4	5	6	7
	8	9	10	11	12	**13**	15
	16	17	18	19	20	21	22
	23	24	25	26	27	28	29
MĀRGAŚĪRA 2162	30	1	2	3	4	5	6
	7	8	9	10	11[g]	12	13
	14	15	16	**17**	19	20	21
	22	23	24	25	26	27	27

HINDU SOLAR 2026/2027

Month	Sun	Mon	Tue	Wed	Thu	Fri	Sat
PAUSHA 2026	12	13	14	15	16	17	18
	19	20	21	22	23	24	25
MĀGHA 2026	26	27	28	29	1[b]	2	3
	4	5	6	7	8	9	10
	11	12	13	14	15	16	17
	18	19	20	21	22	23	24
PHĀLGUNA 2026	25	26	27	28	29	30	1
	2	3	4	5	6	7	8
	9	10	11	12	13	14	15
	16	17	18	19	20	21	22
	23	24	25	26	27	28	29
CHAITRA 2026	30	1	2	3	4	5	6
	7	8	9	10	11	12	13
	14	15	16	17	18	19	20
	21	22	23	24	25	26	27
VAIŚĀKHA 2027	28	29	30	1[a]	2	3	4
	5	6	7	8	9	10	11
	12	13	14	15	16	17	18
	19	20	21	22	23	24	25
JYAISHTHA 2027	26	27	28	29	30	31	1
	2	3	4	5	6	7	8
	9	10	11	12	13	14	15
	16	17	18	19	20	21	22
	23	24	25	26	27	28	29
ĀSHĀḌHA 2027	30	31	32	1	2	3	4
	5	6	7	8	9	10	11
	12	13	14	15	16	17	18
	19	20	21	22	23	24	25
ŚRĀVAṆA 2027	26	27	28	29	30	31	1
	2	3	4	5	6	7	8
	9	10	11	12	13	14	15
	16	17	18	19	20	21	22
	23	24	25	26	27	28	29
BHĀDRAPADA 2027	30	31	32	1	2	3	4
	5	6	7	8	9	10	11
	12	13	14	15	16	17	18
	19	20	21	22	23	24	25
ĀŚVINA 2027	26	27	28	29	30	31	1
	2	3	4	5	6	7	8
	9	10	11	12	13	14	15
	16	17	18	19	20	21	22
	23	24	25	26	27	28	29
KĀRTTIKA 2027	30	1	2	3	4	5	6
	7	8	9	10	11	12	13
	14	15	16	17	18	19	20
	21	22	23	24	25	26	27
MĀRGAŚĪRA 2027	28	29	30	1	2	3	4
	5	6	7	8	9	10	11
	12	13	14	15	16	17	18
	19	20	21	22	23	24	25
PAUSHA 2027	26	27	28	29	1	2	3
	4	5	6	7	8	9	10
	11	12	13	14	15	16	17

ISLAMIC (ASTRONOMICAL) 1528‡/1529

Month	Sun	Mon	Tue	Wed	Thu	Fri	Sat
DHU AL-ḤIJJA 1528	10	11	12	13	14	15	16
	17	18	19	20	21	22	23
	24	25	26	27	28	29	30[a]
MUḤARRAM 1529	1[a]	2	3	4	5	6	7
	8	9	10[b]	11	12	13	14
	15	16	17	18	19	20	21
	22	23	24	25	26	27	28
ṢAFAR 1529	29	1	2	3	4	5	6
	7	8	9	10	11	12	13
	14	15	16	17	18	19	20
	21	22	23	24	25	26	27
RABĪʿ I 1529	28	29	1	2	3	4	5
	6	7	8	9	10	11	12[c]
	13	14	15	16	17	18	19
	20	21	22	23	24	25	26
RABĪʿ II 1529	27	28	29	30	1	2	3
	4	5	6	7	8	9	10
	11	12	13	14	15	16	17
	18	19	20	21	22	23	24
JUMĀDĀ I 1529	25	26	27	28	29	1	2
	3	4	5	6	7	8	9
	10	11	12	13	14	15	16
	17	18	19	20	21	22	23
	24	25	26	27	28	29	30
JUMĀDĀ II 1529	1	2	3	4	5	6	7
	8	9	10	11	12	13	14
	15	16	17	18	19	20	21
	22	23	24	25	26	27	28
RAJAB 1529	29	1	2	3	4	5	6
	7	8	9	10	11	12	13
	14	15	16	17	18	19	20
	21	22	23	24	25	26	27[d]
SHAʿBĀN 1529	28	29	30	1	2	3	4
	5	6	7	8	9	10	11
	12	13	14	15	16	17	18
	19	20	21	22	23	24	25
RAMAḌĀN 1529	26	27	28	29	30	1[e]	2
	3	4	5	6	7	8	9
	10	11	12	13	14	15	16
	17	18	19	20	21	22	23
SHAWWĀL 1529	24	25	26	27	28	29	1[f]
	2	3	4	5	6	7	8
	9	10	11	12	13	14	15
	16	17	18	19	20	21	22
	23	24	25	26	27	28	29
DHU AL-QAʿDA 1529	1	2	3	4	5	6	7
	8	9	10	11	12	13	14
	15	16	17	18	19	20	21
	22	23	24	25	26	27	28
DHU AL-ḤIJJA 1529	29	30	1	2	3	4	5
	6	7	8	9	10[g]	11	12
	13	14	15	16	17	18	19
	20	21	22	23	24	25	26

GREGORIAN 2105

Julian (Sun)	Sun	Mon	Tue	Wed	Thu	Fri	Sat	Month
Dec 14	28	29	30	31	1	2	3	JANUARY 2105
	4	5	6	7	8[a]	9	10	
Dec 28	11	12	13	14	15[b]	16	17	
	18	19	20	21	22	23	24	
Jan 11	25	26	27	28	29	30	31	
	1	2	3	4	5	6	7	FEBRUARY 2105
Jan 25	8	9	10	11	12	13	14	
	15	16	17	18[c]	19	20	21	
Feb 8	22[d]	23	24	25	26	27	28	
	1	2	3	4	5	6	7	MARCH 2105
Feb 22	8	9	10	11	12	13	14	
	15	16	17	18	19	20	21	
Mar 8	22	23	24	25	26	27	28	
	29	30	31	1	2	3	4	APRIL 2105
Mar 22	5[e]	6	7	8	9	10	11	
	12	13	14	15	16	17	18	
Apr 5	19	20	21	22	23	24	25	
	26	27	28	29	30	1	2	MAY 2105
Apr 19	3	4	5	6	7	8	9	
	10	11	12	13	14	15	16	
May 3	17	18	19	20	21	22	23	
	24	25	26	27	28	29	30	
May 17	31	1	2	3	4	5	6	JUNE 2105
	7	8	9	10	11	12	13	
May 31	14	15	16	17	18	19	20	
	21	22	23	24	25	26	27	
Jun 14	28	29	30	1	2	3	4	JULY 2105
	5	6	7	8	9	10	11	
Jun 28	12	13	14	15	16	17	18	
	19	20	21	22	23	24	25	
Jul 12	26	27	28	29	30	31	1	AUGUST 2105
	2	3	4	5	6	7	8	
Jul 26	9	10	11	12	13	14	15	
	16	17	18	19	20	21	22	
Aug 9	23	24	25	26	27	28	29	
	30	31	1	2	3	4	5	SEPTEMBER 2105
Aug 23	6	7	8	9	10	11	12	
	13	14	15	16	17	18	19	
Sep 6	20	21	22	23	24	25	26	
	27	28	29	30	1	2	3	OCTOBER 2105
Sep 20	4	5	6	7	8	9	10	
	11	12	13	14	15	16	17	
Oct 4	18	19	20	21	22	23	24	
	25	26	27	28	29	30	31	
Oct 18	1	2	3	4	5	6	7	NOVEMBER 2105
	8	9	10	11	12	13	14	
Nov 1	15	16	17	18	19	20	21	
	22	23	24	25	26	27	28	
Nov 15	29[g]	30	1	2	3	4	5	DECEMBER 2105
	6	7	8	9	10	11	12	
Nov 29	13	14	15	16	17	18	19	
	20	21	22	23	24	25[h]	26	
Dec 13	27	28	29	30	31	1	2	

Persian: [a]New Year; [b]Sizdeh Bedar

Hindu Lunar: ‡Leap year; [a]New Year (Krodhana); [b]Birthday of Rāma; [c]Birthday of Krishna; [d]Ganēśa Chaturthī; [e]Dashara; [f]Diwali; [g]Birthday of Vishnu; [h]Night of Śiva; [i]Holi

Hindu Solar: [a]New Year (Pramāthin); [b]Pongal

Islamic: ‡Leap year; [a]New Year; [A]New Year (Arithmetic); [b]ʿĀshūrāʾ; [c]Prophet's Birthday; [d]Ascent of the Prophet; [e]Start of Ramaḍān; [f]ʿĪd al-Fiṭr; [g]ʿĪd al-ʾAḍḥā

Gregorian: [a]Orthodox Christmas; [b]Julian New Year; [c]Ash Wednesday; [d]Feast of Orthodoxy; [e]Easter (also Orthodox); [g]Advent; [h]Christmas

2106

GREGORIAN 2106	Sun Mon Tue Wed Thu Fri Sat	Lunar Phases	ISO WEEK (Mon)	JULIAN DAY (Sun noon)	HEBREW 5866‡/5867	Sun Mon Tue Wed Thu Fri Sat	Molad	CHINESE Yǐ-Chǒu/Bǐng-Yín	Sun Mon Tue Wed Thu Fri Sat	Solar Term	COPTIC 1822/1823‡	Sun Mon Tue Wed Thu Fri Sat	ETHIOPIC 2098/2099‡
JANUARY 2106	27 ◑ 29 30 31 1[a] 2	4:22	53	2490256	TEVETH 5866	19 20 21 22 23 24 25		MONTH 11 Yǐ-Chǒu	22 23 24 25 26 27 28		KOIAK 1822	17 18 19 20 21 22 23	TĀKHŚĀŚ 2098
	3 4 ● 6 7 8 9	9:46	1	2490263	SHEVAT 5866	26 27 28 29 1 2 3	Tue 9h17m10p	MONTH 12 Yǐ-Chǒu	29 30 1 2 3 4 5	Xiǎo hán		24 25 26 27 28 29[c] 30	
	10 11 12 ◐ 14 15 16	2:44	2	2490270		4 5 6 7 8 9 10			6 7 8 9 10 11 12		TŌBE 1822	1 2 3 4 5 6[d] 7	ṬER 2098
	17 18 ○ 20 21 22 23	18:22	3	2490277		11 12 13 14 15 16 17			13 14 15 16 17 18 19	Dà hán		8 9 10 11[e] 12 13 14	
	24 25 ◑ 27 28 29 30	23:07	4	2490284		18 19 20 21 22 23 24			20 21 22 23 24 25 26			15 16 17 18 19 20 21	
FEBRUARY 2106	31 1 2 3 ● 5 6	3:47	5	2490291	ADAR I 5866	25 26 27 28 29 30 1	Wed 22h1m11p	MONTH 1 Bǐng-Yín	27 28 29 30 1[a] 2 3	Lì chūn		22 23 24 25 26 27 28	
	7 8 9 10 ◐ 12 13	12:28	6	2490298		2 3 4 5 6 7 8			4 5 6 7 8 9 10		MESHIR 1822	29 30 1 2 3 4 5	YAKĀTIT 2098
	14 15 16 17 ○ 19 20	6:00	7	2490305		9 10 11 12 13 14 15			11 12 13 14 15[b] 16 17*	Yǔ shuǐ		6 7 8 9 10 11 12	
	21 22 23 24 ◑ 26 27	19:55	8	2490312		16 17 18 19 20 21 22			18 19 20 21 22 23 24			13 14 15 16 17 18 19	
MARCH 2106	28 1 2 3 4 ● 6	19:15	9	2490319		23 24 25 26 27 28 29	Fri 10h45m12p	MONTH 2 Bǐng-Yín	25 26 27 28 29 30 1	Jīng zhé		20 21 22 23 24 25 26	
	7 8 9 10 11 ◐ 13	20:10	10	2490326	ADAR II 5866	30 1 2 3 4 5 6			2 3 4 5 6 7 8		PAREMOTEP 1822	27 28 29 30 1 2 3	MAGĀBIT 2098
	14 15 16 17 18 ○ 20	18:33	11	2490333		7 8 9 10 11 12 13			9 10 11 12 13 14 15			4 5 6 7 8 9 10	
	21[b] 22 23 24 25 26 ◑	16:37	12	2490340		14[f] 15 16 17 18 19 20			16 17 18 19 20 21 22	Chūn fēn		11 12 13 14 15 16 17	
APRIL 2106	28 29 30 31 1 2 3		13	2490347		21 22 23 24 25 26 27			23 24 25 26 27 28 29			18 19 20 21 22 23 24	
	● 5 6 7 8 9 10	7:58	14	2490354	NISAN 5866	28 29 1 2 3 4 5	Sat 23h29m13p	MONTH 3 Bǐng-Yín	1 2[c] 3 4 5 6 7	Qīng míng	PARMOUTE 1822	25 26 27 28 29 30 1	MIYĀZYĀ 2098
	◐ 12 13 14 15 16 17	2:44	15	2490361		6 7 8 9 10 11 12			8 9 10 11 12 13 14			2 3 4 5 6 7 8	
	○ 19 20 21 22 23 24	8:20	16	2490368		13 14 15[g] 16 17 18 19			15 16 17 18* 19 20 21	Gǔ yǔ		9 10 11 12 13 14 15	
MAY 2106	25 ◑ 27 28 29 30 1	11:18	17	2490375		20 21 22 23 24 25 26			22 23 24 25 26 27 28			16[f] 17 18 19 20 21 22	
	2 ● 4 5 6 7 8	18:10	18	2490382	IYAR 5866	27 28 29 30 1 2 3	Mon 12h13m14p	MONTH 4 Bǐng-Yín	29 30 1 2 3 4 5	Lì xià		23 24 25 26 27 28 29[g]	
	9 ◐ 11 12 13 14 15	9:19	19	2490389		4 5 6 7 8 9 10			6 7 8 9 10 11 12		PASHONS 1822	30 1 2 3 4 5 6	GENBOT 2098
	16 ○ 18 19 20 21 22	23:12	20	2490396		11 12 13 14 15 16 17			13 14 15 16 17 18 19	Xiǎo mǎn		7 8 9 10 11 12 13	
	23 24 25 ◑ 27 28 29	2:58	21	2490403		18 19 20 21 22 23 24			20 21 22 23 24 25 26			14 15 16 17 18 19 20	
JUNE 2106	30 31 1 ● 3 4 5	2:23	22	2490410	SIVAN 5866	25 26 27 28 29 1 2	Wed 0h57m15p	MONTH 5 Bǐng-Yín	27 28 29 1 2 3 4			21 22 23 24 25 26 27	
	6 7 ◐ 9 10 11 12	17:10	23	2490417		3 4 5 6[h] 7 8 9			5[d] 6 7 8 9 10 11	Máng zhòng	PAŌNE 1822	28 29 30 1 2 3 4	SANĒ 2098
	13 14 15 ○ 17 18 19	14:36	24	2490424		10 11 12 13 14 15 16			12 13 14 15 16 17 18			5 6 7 8 9 10 11	
	20 21[c] 22 23 ◑ 25 26	15:29	25	2490431		17 18 19 20 21 22 23			19* 20 21 22 23 24 25	Xià zhì		12 13 14 15 16 17 18	
JULY 2106	27 28 29 30 ● 2 3	9:22	26	2490438		24 25 26 27 28 29 30	Thu 13h41m16p	MONTH 6 Bǐng-Yín	26 27 28 29 1 2 3			19 20 21 22 23 24 25	
	4 5 6 7 ◐ 9 10	3:19	27	2490445	TAMMUZ 5866	1 2 3 4 5 6 7			4 5 6 7 8 9 10	Xiǎo shǔ	EPĒP 1822	26 27 28 29 30 1 2	ḤAMLĒ 2098
	11 12 13 14 15 ○ 17	5:47	28	2490452		8 9 10 11 12 13 14			11 12 13 14 15 16 17			3 4 5 6 7 8 9	
	18 19 20 21 22 23 ◑	1:10	29	2490459		15 16 17 18 19 20 21			18 19 20 21 22 23 24	Dà shǔ		10 11 12 13 14 15 16	
	25 26 27 28 29 ● 31	16:05	30	2490466		22 23 24 25 26 27 28	Sat 2h25m17p	MONTH 7 Bǐng-Yín	25 26 27 28 29 30 1			17 18 19 20 21 22 23	
AUGUST 2106	1 2 3 4 5 ◐ 7	16:28	31	2490473	AV 5866	29 1 2 3 4 5 6			2 3 4 5 6 7[e] 8			24 25 26 27 28 29 30	
	8 9 10 11 12 13 ○	20:20	32	2490480		7 8 9[i] 10 11 12 13			9 10 11 12 13 14 15[f]	Lì qiū	MESORĒ 1822	1 2 3 4 5 6 7	NAHASĒ 2098
	15 16 17 18 19 20 21		33	2490487		14 15 16 17 18 19 20			16 17 18 19 20* 21 22			8 9 10 11 12 13[h] 14	
	◑ 23 24 25 26 27 ●	8:41 23:46	34	2490494		21 22 23 24 25 26 27			23 24 25 26 27 28 29	Chǔ shǔ		15 16 17 18 19 20 21	
SEPTEMBER 2106	29 30 31 1 2 3 4		35	2490501	ELUL 5866	28 29 30 1 2 3 4	Sun 15h10m0p	MONTH 8 Bǐng-Yín	1 2 3 4 5 6 7			22 23 24 25 26 27 28	
	◐ 6 7 8 9 10 11	8:39	36	2490508		5 6 7 8 9 10 11			8 9 10 11 12 13 14	Bái lù	EPAG. 1822	29 30 1 2 3 4 5	PĀG. 2098
	12 ○ 14 15 16 17 18	10:07	37	2490515		12 13 14 15 16 17 18			15[g] 16 17 18 19 20 21		THOOUT 1823	1[a] 2 3 4 5 6 7	MASKARAM 2099
	19 ◑ 21 22 23[d] 24 25	14:52	38	2490522		19 20 21 22 23 24 25			22 23 24 25 26 27 28	Qiū fēn		8 9 10 11 12 13 14	
OCTOBER 2106	26 ● 28 29 30 1 2	9:36	39	2490529	TISHRI 5867	26 27 28 29 1[a] 2[a] 3	Tue 3h54m1p	MONTH 9 Bǐng-Yín	29 1 2 3 4 5 6			15 16 17[b] 18 19 20 21	
	3 4 ◐ 6 7 8 9	3:14	40	2490536		4 5 6 7 8 9 10[b]			7 8 9[h] 10 11 12 13	Hán lù		22 23 24 25 26 27 28	
	10 11 ○ 13 14 15 16	23:09	41	2490543		11 12 13 14 15[c] 16 17			14 15 16 17 18 19 20		PAOPE 1823	29 30 1 2 3 4 5	ṬEQEMT 2099
	17 18 ◑ 20 21 22 23	20:53	42	2490550		18 19 20 21 22 23 24			21 22* 23 24 25 26 27			6 7 8 9 10 11 12	
	24 25 ● 27 28 29 30	22:27	43	2490557	HESHVAN 5867	25 26 27 28 29 30 1	Wed 16h38m2p	MONTH 10 Bǐng-Yín	28 29 30 1 2 3 4	Shuāng jiàng		13 14 15 16 17 18 19	
NOVEMBER 2106	31 1 2 ◐ 4 5 6	23:09	44	2490564		2 3 4 5 6 7 8			5 6 7 8 9 10 11			20 21 22 23 24 25 26	
	7 8 9 10 ○ 12 13	11:27	45	2490571		9 10 11 12 13 14 15			12 13 14 15 16 17 18	Lì dōng	ATHŌR 1823	27 28 29 30 1 2 3	HEDĀR 2099
	14 15 16 17 ◑ 19 20	4:04	46	2490578		16 17 18 19 20 21 22			19 20 21 22 23 24 25			4 5 6 7 8 9 10	
	21 22 23 24 ● 26 27	14:27	47	2490585		23 24 25 26 27 28 29		MONTH 11 Bǐng-Yín	26 27 28 29 1 2 3	Xiǎo xuě		11 12 13 14 15 16 17	
DECEMBER 2106	28 29 30 1 2 ◐ 4	18:58	48	2490592	KISLEV 5867	1 2 3 4 5 6 7	Fri 5h22m3p		4 5 6 7 8 9 10			18 19 20 21 22 23 24	
	5 6 7 8 9 ○ 11	22:59	49	2490599		8 9[d] 10 11 12 13 14			11 12 13 14 15 16 17	Dà xuě	KOIAK 1823	25 26 27 28 29 30 1	TĀKHŚĀŚ 2099
	12 13 14 15 16 ◑ 18	13:40	50	2490606		15 16 17 18 19 20 21			18 19 20 21 22 23* 24			2 3 4 5 6 7 8	
	19 20 21 22[e] 23 24 ●	8:52	51	2490613		22 23 24 25[e] 26[e] 27[e] 28[e]	Sat 18h6m4p	MONTH 12 Bǐng-Yín	25 26 27 28[i] 29 30 1	Dōng zhì		9 10 11 12 13 14 15	
	26 27 28 29 30 31 1		52	2490620		29[e] 30[e] 1[e] 2[e] 3 4 5			2 3 4 5 6 7 8			16 17 18 19 20 21 22	

[a]New Year
[b]Spring (0:03)
[c]Summer (16:12)
[d]Autumn (8:45)
[e]Winter (6:52)
● New moon
◐ First quarter moon
○ Full moon
◑ Last quarter moon

‡Leap year
[a]New Year
[b]Yom Kippur
[c]Sukkot
[d]Winter starts
[e]Ḥanukkah
[f]Purim
[g]Passover
[h]Shavuot
[i]Fast of Av

[a]New Year (4804, Tiger)
[b]Lantern Festival
[c]Qīngmíng
[d]Dragon Festival
[e]Qīqiǎo
[f]Hungry Ghosts
[g]Mid-Autumn Festival
[h]Double-Ninth Festival
[i]Dōngzhì
*Start of 60-name cycle

‡Leap year
[a]New Year
[b]Building of the Cross
[c]Christmas
[d]Jesus's Circumcision
[e]Epiphany
[f]Easter
[g]Mary's Announcement
[h]Jesus's Transfiguration

PERSIAN (ASTRONOMICAL) 1484/1485

Month	Sun	Mon	Tue	Wed	Thu	Fri	Sat
DEY 1484	6	7	8	9	10	11	12
	13	14	15	16	17	18	19
	20	21	22	23	24	25	26
	27	28	29	30	1	2	3
BAHMAN 1484	4	5	6	7	8	9	10
	11	12	13	14	15	16	17
	18	19	20	21	22	23	24
	25	26	27	28	29	30	1
ESFAND 1484	2	3	4	5	6	7	8
	9	10	11	12	13	14	15
	16	17	18	19	20	21	22
	23	24	25	26	27	28	29
FARVARDĪN 1485	1[a]	2	3	4	5	6	7
	8	9	10	11	12	13[b]	14
	15	16	17	18	19	20	21
	22	23	24	25	26	27	28
	29	30	31	1	2	3	4
ORDĪBEHEŠT 1485	5	6	7	8	9	10	11
	12	13	14	15	16	17	18
	19	20	21	22	23	24	25
	26	27	28	29	30	31	1
XORDĀD 1485	2	3	4	5	6	7	8
	9	10	11	12	13	14	15
	16	17	18	19	20	21	22
	23	24	25	26	27	28	29
	30	31	1	2	3	4	5
TĪR 1485	6	7	8	9	10	11	12
	13	14	15	16	17	18	19
	20	21	22	23	24	25	26
	27	28	29	30	31	1	2
MORDĀD 1485	3	4	5	6	7	8	9
	10	11	12	13	14	15	16
	17	18	19	20	21	22	23
	24	25	26	27	28	29	30
	31	1	2	3	4	5	6
SHAHRĪVAR 1485	7	8	9	10	11	12	13
	14	15	16	17	18	19	20
	21	22	23	24	25	26	27
	28	29	30	31	1	2	3
MEHR 1485	4	5	6	7	8	9	10
	11	12	13	14	15	16	17
	18	19	20	21	22	23	24
	25	26	27	28	29	30	1
ĀBĀN 1485	2	3	4	5	6	7	8
	9	10	11	12	13	14	15
	16	17	18	19	20	21	22
	23	24	25	26	27	28	29
	30	1	2	3	4	5	6
ĀZAR 1485	7	8	9	10	11	12	13
	14	15	16	17	18	19	20
	21	22	23	24	25	26	27
	28	29	30	1	2	3	4
DEY 1485	5	6	7	8	9	10	11

[a]New Year
[b]Sizdeh Bedar

HINDU LUNAR 2162‡/2163

Month	Sun	Mon	Tue	Wed	Thu	Fri	Sat
MĀRGAŚĪRA 2162	22	23	24	25	26	27	27
PAUSHA 2162	28	29	30	1	2	3	4
	5	6	7	8	9	10	**11**
	13	14	15	16	17	18	19
	20	21	22	23	24	25	26
MĀGHA 2162	27	28	29	29	30	1	2
	3	4	**5**	7	8	9	10
	11	12	13	14	15	16	17
	18	19	20	21	22	23	24
PHĀLGUNA 2162	25	26	27	28[h]	29	30	1
	2	3	4	5	6	7	8
	9	**10**	12	13	14	15[i]	16
	17	18	19	20	21	22	22
	23	24	25	26	27	28	29
CHAITRA 2163	30	1[a]	2	3	**4**	6	7
	8	9[b]	10	11	12	13	14
	15	16	17	18	19	20	21
	22	23	24	25	26	27	28
VAIŚĀKHA 2163	29	30	1	2	3	4	5
	6	7	**8**	10	11	12	13
	14	15	16	17	17	18	19
	20	21	22	23	24	25	26
JYAISHTHA 2163	27	28	29	30	**1**	3	4
	5	6	7	8	9	10	11
	12	13	14	15	16	17	18
	19	20	21	22	23	24	25
ĀSHĀDHA 2163	26	27	28	29	30	1	2
	3	**4**	6	7	8	9	10
	11	12	13	14	14	15	16
	17	18	19	20	21	22	23
ŚRĀVAṆA 2163	24	25	**26**	28	29	30	1
	2	3	4	5	6	7	8
	9	10	11	12	13	14	15
	16	17	18	19	20	21	22
	23[c]	24	25	26	27	28	**29**
BHĀDRAPADA 2163	1	2	3	4[d]	5	6	7
	8	9	10	10	11	12	13
	14	15	16	17	18	19	20
	21	**22**	24	25	26	27	28
ĀŚVINA 2163	29	30	1	2	3	4	5
	6	7	8[e]	9[e]	10[e]	11	12
	13	14	15	16	17	18	19
	20	21	22	23	24	25	**26**
KĀRTTIKA 2163	28	29	30	1[f]	2	3	4
	5	5	6	7	8	9	10
	11	12	13	14	15	16	17
	18	19	**20**	22	23	24	25
MĀRGAŚĪRA 2163	26	27	28	29	30	1	2
	3	4	5	6	7	7	8
	9	10	11[g]	12	**13**	15	16
	17	18	19	20	21	22	23
	24	25	26	27	28	29	30
	1	2	3	4	5	6	7

‡Leap year
[a]New Year (Kshaya)
[b]Birthday of Rāma
[c]Birthday of Krishna
[d]Ganēśa Chaturthī
[e]Dashara
[f]Diwali
[g]Birthday of Vishnu
[h]Night of Śiva
[i]Holi

HINDU SOLAR 2027/2028‡

Month	Sun	Mon	Tue	Wed	Thu	Fri	Sat
PAUSHA 2027	11	12	13	14	15	16	17
	18	19	20	21	22	23	24
	25	26	27	28	29	30	1[b]
MĀGHA 2027	2	3	4	5	6	7	8
	9	10	11	12	13	14	15
	16	17	18	19	20	21	22
	23	24	25	26	27	28	29
PHĀLGUNA 2027	1	2	3	4	5	6	7
	8	9	10	11	12	13	14
	15	16	17	18	19	20	21
	22	23	24	25	26	27	28
CHAITRA 2027	29	30	1	2	3	4	5
	6	7	8	9	10	11	12
	13	14	15	16	17	18	19
	20	21	22	23	24	25	26
VAIŚĀKHA 2028	27	28	29	30	1[a]	2	3
	4	5	6	7	8	9	10
	11	12	13	14	15	16	17
	18	19	20	21	22	23	24
	25	26	27	28	29	30	31
JYAISHTHA 2028	1	2	3	4	5	6	7
	8	9	10	11	12	13	14
	15	16	17	18	19	20	21
	22	23	24	25	26	27	28
ĀSHĀDHA 2028	29	30	31	32	1	2	3
	4	5	6	7	8	9	10
	11	12	13	14	15	16	17
	18	19	20	21	22	23	24
	25	26	27	28	29	30	31
ŚRĀVAṆA 2028	1	2	3	4	5	6	7
	8	9	10	11	12	13	14
	15	16	17	18	19	20	21
	22	23	24	25	26	27	28
BHĀDRAPADA 2028	29	30	31	32	1	2	3
	4	5	6	7	8	9	10
	11	12	13	14	15	16	17
	18	19	20	21	22	23	24
	25	26	27	28	29	30	31
ĀŚVINA 2028	1	2	3	4	5	6	7
	8	9	10	11	12	13	14
	15	16	17	18	19	20	21
	22	23	24	25	26	27	28
KĀRTTIKA 2028	29	30	1	2	3	4	5
	6	7	8	9	10	11	12
	13	14	15	16	17	18	19
	20	21	22	23	24	25	26
MĀRGAŚĪRA 2028	27	28	29	30	1	2	3
	4	5	6	7	8	9	10
	11	12	13	14	15	16	17
	18	19	20	21	22	23	24
PAUSHA 2028	25	26	27	28	29	30	1
	2	3	4	5	6	7	8
	9	10	11	12	13	14	15

‡Leap year
[a]New Year (Vikrama)
[b]Pongal

ISLAMIC (ASTRONOMICAL) 1529/1530/1531

Month	Sun	Mon	Tue	Wed	Thu	Fri	Sat
DHU AL-ḤIJJA 1529	20	21	22	23	24	25	26
MUḤARRAM 1530	27	28	29	30	1[a]	2	3
	4	5	6	7	8	9	10[b]
	11	12	13	14	15	16	17
	18	19	20	21	22	23	24
ṢAFAR 1530	25	26	27	28	29	1	2
	3	4	5	6	7	8	9
	10	11	12	13	14	15	16
	17	18	19	20	21	22	23
	24	25	26	27	28	29	30
RABĪ' I 1530	1	2	3	4	5	6	7
	8	9	10	11	12[c]	13	14
	15	16	17	18	19	20	21
	22	23	24	25	26	27	28
RABĪ' II 1530	29	30	1	2	3	4	5
	6	7	8	9	10	11	12
	13	14	15	16	17	18	19
	20	21	22	23	24	25	26
JUMĀDĀ I 1530	27	28	29	1	2	3	4
	5	6	7	8	9	10	11
	12	13	14	15	16	17	18
	19	20	21	22	23	24	25
JUMĀDĀ II 1530	26	27	28	29	1	2	3
	4	5	6	7	8	9	10
	11	12	13	14	15	16	17
	18	19	20	21	22	23	24
RAJAB 1530	25	26	27	28	29	30	1
	2	3	4	5	6	7	8
	9	10	11	12	13	14	15
	16	17	18	19	20	21	22
	23	24	25	26	27[d]	28	29
SHA'BĀN 1530	30	1	2	3	4	5	6
	7	8	9	10	11	12	13
	14	15	16	17	18	19	20
	21	22	23	24	25	26	27
RAMAḌĀN 1530	28	29	1[e]	2	3	4	5
	6	7	8	9	10	11	12
	13	14	15	16	17	18	19
	20	21	22	23	24	25	26
SHAWWĀL 1530	27	28	29	1[f]	2	3	4
	5	6	7	8	9	10	11
	12	13	14	15	16	17	18
	19	20	21	22	23	24	25
DHU AL-QA'DA 1530	26	27	28	29	30	1	2
	3	4	5	6	7	8	9
	10	11	12	13	14	15	16
	17	18	19	20	21	22	23
DHU AL-ḤIJJA 1530	24	25	26	27	28	29	1
	2	3	4	5	6	7	8
	9	10[g]	11	12	13	14	15
	16	17	18	19	20	21	22
	23	24	25	26	27	28	29
	30	1[a]	2	3	4	5	6

[a]New Year
[b]'Ashūrā'
[c]Prophet's Birthday
[d]Ascent of the Prophet
[e]Start of Ramaḍān
[f]'Id al-Fiṭr
[g]'Id al-'Aḍḥā

GREGORIAN 2106

Julian (Sun)	Sun	Mon	Tue	Wed	Thu	Fri	Sat	Month
Dec 13	27	28	29	30	31	1	2	JANUARY 2106
	3	4	5	6	7	8[a]	9	
Dec 27	10	11	12	13	14	15[b]	16	
	17	18	19	20	21	22	23	
Jan 10	24	25	26	27	28	29	30	
	31	1	2	3	4	5	6	FEBRUARY 2106
Jan 24	7	8	9	10	11	12	13	
	14	15	16	17	18	19	20	
Feb 7	21	22	23	24	25	26	27	
	28	1	2	3[c]	4	5	6	MARCH 2106
Feb 21	7	8	9	10	11	12	13	
	14[d]	15	16	17	18	19	20	
Mar 7	21	22	23	24	25	26	27	
	28	29	30	31	1	2	3	APRIL 2106
Mar 21	4	5	6	7	8	9	10	
	11	12	13	14	15	16	17	
Apr 4	18[e]	19	20	21	22	23	24	
	25[f]	26	27	28	29	30	1	MAY 2106
Apr 18	2	3	4	5	6	7	8	
	9	10	11	12	13	14	15	
May 2	16	17	18	19	20	21	22	
	23	24	25	26	27	28	29	
May 16	30	31	1	2	3	4	5	JUNE 2106
	6	7	8	9	10	11	12	
May 30	13	14	15	16	17	18	19	
	20	21	22	23	24	25	26	
Jun 13	27	28	29	30	1	2	3	JULY 2106
	4	5	6	7	8	9	10	
Jun 27	11	12	13	14	15	16	17	
	18	19	20	21	22	23	24	
Jul 11	25	26	27	28	29	30	31	
	1	2	3	4	5	6	7	AUGUST 2106
Jul 25	8	9	10	11	12	13	14	
	15	16	17	18	19	20	21	
Aug 8	22	23	24	25	26	27	28	
	29	30	31	1	2	3	4	SEPTEMBER 2106
Aug 22	5	6	7	8	9	10	11	
	12	13	14	15	16	17	18	
Sep 5	19	20	21	22	23	24	25	
	26	27	28	29	30	1	2	OCTOBER 2106
Sep 19	3	4	5	6	7	8	9	
	10	11	12	13	14	15	16	
Oct 3	17	18	19	20	21	22	23	
	24	25	26	27	28	29	30	
Oct 17	31	1	2	3	4	5	6	NOVEMBER 2106
	7	8	9	10	11	12	13	
Oct 31	14	15	16	17	18	19	20	
	21	22	23	24	25	26	27	
Nov 14	28[g]	29	30	1	2	3	4	DECEMBER 2106
	5	6	7	8	9	10	11	
Nov 28	12	13	14	15	16	17	18	
	19	20	21	22	23	24	25[h]	
Dec 12	26	27	28	29	30	31	1	

[a]Orthodox Christmas
[b]Julian New Year
[c]Ash Wednesday
[d]Feast of Orthodoxy
[e]Easter
[f]Orthodox Easter
[g]Advent
[h]Christmas

2107

GREGORIAN 2107	Sun	Mon	Tue	Wed	Thu	Fri	Sat	Lunar Phases	ISO WEEK (Mon)	JULIAN DAY (Sun noon)	HEBREW 5867/5868	Sun	Mon	Tue	Wed	Thu	Fri	Sat	Molad	CHINESE Bǐng-Yín/Dīng-Mǎo‡	Sun	Mon	Tue	Wed	Thu	Fri	Sat	Solar Term	COPTIC 1823‡/1824	Sun	Mon	Tue	Wed	Thu	Fri	Sat	ETHIOPIC 2099‡/2100
JANUARY 2107	26	27	28	29	30	31	1[a]		52	2490620	TEVETH 5867	29[e]	30[e]	1[e]	2[e]	3	4	5	Sat 18h 6m 4p	MONTH 12 Bǐng-Yín	2	3	4	5	6	7	8		KOIAK 1823	16	17	18	19	20	21	22	TĀKHŚĀŚ 2099
	◐	3	4	5	6	7	8	13:09	1	2490627		6	7	8	9	10	11	12			9	10	11	12	13	14	15	Xiǎo hán		23	24	25	26	27	28	29[c]	
	○	10	11	12	13	14	15	9:47	2	2490634		13	14	15	16	17	18	19			16	17	18	19	20	21	22		TŌBE 1823	30	1	2	3	4	5	6[d]	ṬER 2099
	◑	17	18	19	20	21	22	2:29	3	2490641		20	21	22	23	24	25	26			23	24	25	26	27	28	29			7	8	9	10	11[e]	12	13	
	23	●	25	26	27	28	29	4:16	4	2490648	SHEVAT 5867	27	28	29	1	2	3	4	Mon 6h 50m 5p	MONTH 1 Dīng-Mǎo	30	1[a]	2	3	4	5	6	Dà hán		14	15	16	17	18	19	20	
FEBRUARY 2107	30	31	◐	2	3	4	5	4:20	5	2490655		5	6	7	8	9	10	11			7	8	9	10	11	12	13	Lì chūn		21	22	23	24	25	26	27	
	6	○	8	9	10	11	12	20:09	6	2490662		12	13	14	15	16	17	18			14	15[b]	16	17	18	19	20		MESHIR 1823	28	29	30	1	2	3	4	YAKĀTIT 2099
	13	◑	15	16	17	18	19	18:26	7	2490669		19	20	21	22	23	24	25			21	22	23*	24	25	26	27	Yǔ shuǐ		5	6	7	8	9	10	11	
	20	21	●	23	24	25	26	23:07	8	2490676	ADAR 5867	26	27	28	29	30	1	2	Tue 19h 34m 6p	MONTH 2 Dīng-Mǎo	28	29	30	1	2	3	4			12	13	14	15	16	17	18	
MARCH 2107	27	28	1	◐	3	4	5	15:50	9	2490683		3	4	5	6	7	8	9			5	6	7	8	9	10	11			19	20	21	22	23	24	25	
	6	7	8	○	10	11	12	6:29	10	2490690		10	11	12	13	14[f]	15	16			12	13	14	15	16	17	18	Jīng zhé	PAREMOTEP 1823	26	27	28	29	30	1	2	MAGĀBIT 2099
	13	14	15	◑	17	18	19	12:33	11	2490697		17	18	19	20	21	22	23			19	20	21	22	23	24	25			3	4	5	6	7	8	9	
	20	21[b]	22	23	●	25	26	16:05	12	2490704	NISAN 5867	24	25	26	27	28	29	1	Thu 8h 18m 7p	MONTH 3 Dīng-Mǎo	26	27	28	29	30	1	2	Chūn fēn		10	11	12	13	14	15	16	
APRIL 2107	27	28	29	30	◐	1	2	23:58	13	2490711		2	3	4	5	6	7	8			3	4	5	6	7	8	9			17	18	19	20	21	22	23	
	3	4	5	6	○	8	9	17:14	14	2490718		9	10	11	12	13	14	15[g]			10	11	12[c]	13	14	15	16	Qīng míng		24	25	26	27	28	29	30	
	10	11	12	13	14	◑	16	7:29	15	2490725		16	17	18	19	20	21	22			17	18	19	20	21	22	23*		PARMOUTE 1823	1	2	3	4	5	6	7	MIYĀZYĀ 2099
	17	18	19	20	21	22	●	6:17	16	2490732	IYYAR 5867	23	24	25	26	27	28	29	Fri 21h 2m 8p	MONTH 4 Dīng-Mǎo	24	25	26	27	28	29	1	Gǔ yǔ		8[f]	9	10	11	12	13	14	
	24	25	26	27	28	29	◐	5:49	17	2490739		30	1	2	3	4	5	6			2	3	4	5	6	7	8			15	16	17	18	19	20	21	
MAY 2107	1	2	3	4	5	6	○	4:42	18	2490746		7	8	9	10	11	12	13			9	10	11	12	13	14	15	Lì xià		22	23	24	25	26	27	28	
	8	9	10	11	12	13	14		19	2490753		14	15	16	17	18	19	20			16	17	18	19	20	21	22		PASHONS 1823	29[g]	30	1	2	3	4	5	GENBOT 2099
	◑	16	17	18	19	20	21	2:02	20	2490760		21	22	23	24	25	26	27			23	24	25	26	27	28	29	Xiǎo mǎn		6	7	8	9	10	11	12	
	●	23	24	25	26	27	28	17:29	21	2490767	SIVAN 5867	28	29	1	2	3	4	5	Sun 9h 46m 9p	LEAP MONTH 4 Dīng-Mǎo	30	1	2	3	4	5	6			13	14	15	16	17	18	19	
JUNE 2107	◐	30	31	1	2	3	4	10:53	22	2490774		6[h]	7	8	9	10	11	12			7	8	9	10	11	12	13			20	21	22	23	24	25	26	
	○	6	7	8	9	10	11	17:07	23	2490781		13	14	15	16	17	18	19			14	15	16	17	18	19	20	Máng zhòng	PAŌNE 1823	27	28	29	30	1	2	3	SANĒ 2099
	12	◑	14	15	16	17	18	19:13	24	2490788		20	21	22	23	24	25	26			21	22	23	24*	25	26	27			4	5	6	7	8	9	10	
	19	20	●[c]	22	23	24	25	2:07	25	2490795	TAMMUZ 5867	27	28	29	30	1	2	3	Mon 22h 30m 10p	MONTH 5 Dīng-Mǎo	28	29	1	2	3	4	5[d]	Xià zhì		11	12	13	14	15	16	17	
JULY 2107	26	◐	28	29	30	1	2	16:38	26	2490802		4	5	6	7	8	9	10			6	7	8	9	10	11	12			18	19	20	21	22	23	24	
	3	4	○	6	7	8	9	6:37	27	2490809		11	12	13	14	15	16	17			13	14	15	16	17	18	19	Xiǎo shǔ	EPĒP 1823	25	26	27	28	29	30	1	ḤAMLĒ 2099
	10	11	12	◑	14	15	16	10:20	28	2490816		18	19	20	21	22	23	24			20	21	22	23	24	25	26			2	3	4	5	6	7	8	
	17	18	19	●	21	22	23	9:14	29	2490823	AV 5867	25	26	27	28	29	1	2	Wed 11h 14m 11p	MONTH 6 Dīng-Mǎo	27	28	29	1	2	3	4	Dà shǔ		9	10	11	12	13	14	15	
	24	25	26	◐	28	29	30	0:22	30	2490830		3	4	5	6	7	8	9			5	6	7	8	9	10	11			16	17	18	19	20	21	22	
AUGUST 2107	31	1	2	○	4	5	6	21:16	31	2490837		10[i]	11	12	13	14	15	16			12	13	14	15	16	17	18			23	24	25	26	27	28	29	
	7	8	9	10	◑	12	13	22:58	32	2490844		17	18	19	20	21	22	23			19	20	21	22	23	24	25	Lì qiū	MESORĒ 1823	30	1	2	3	4	5	6	NAHASĒ 2099
	14	15	16	17	●	19	20	16:02	33	2490851		24	25	26	27	28	29	30	Thu 23h 58m 12p	MONTH 7 Dīng-Mǎo	26*	27	28	29	30	1	2			7	8	9	10	11	12	13[h]	
	21	22	23	24	◐	26	27	10:58	34	2490858	ELUL 5867	1	2	3	4	5	6	7			3	4	5	6	7[e]	8	9	Chǔ shǔ		14	15	16	17	18	19	20	
SEPTEMBER 2107	28	29	30	31	1	○	3	12:56	35	2490865		8	9	10	11	12	13	14			10	11	12	13	14	15[f]	16			21	22	23	24	25	26	27	
	4	5	6	7	8	9	◑	9:10	36	2490872		15	16	17	18	19	20	21			17	18	19	20	21	22	23	Bái lù	EPAG. 1823	28	29	30	1	2	3	4	PĀG. 2099
	11	12	13	14	15	●	17	23:45	37	2490879		22	23	24	25	26	27	28		MONTH 8 Dīng-Mǎo	24	25	26	27	28	29	1		THOOUT 1824	5	6	1[a]	2	3	4	5	MASKARAM 2100
	18	19	20	21	22	23[d]	◐	1:00	38	2490886	TISHRI 5868	29	1[a]	2[a]	3	4	5	6	Sat 12h 42m 13p		2	3	4	5	6	7	8	Qiū fēn		6	7	8	9	10	11	12	
OCTOBER 2107	25	26	27	28	29	30	1		39	2490893		7	8	9	10[b]	11	12	13			9	10	11	12	13	14	15[g]			13	14	15	16	17[b]	18	19	
	○	3	4	5	6	7	8	5:05	40	2490900		14	15[c]	16	17	18	19	20			16	17	18	19	20	21	22			20	21	22	23	24	25	26	
	◑	10	11	12	13	14	15	17:28	41	2490907		21	22	23	24	25	26	27			23	24	25	26	27*	28	29	Hán lù	PAOPE 1824	27	28	29	30	1	2	3	ṬEQEMT 2100
	●	17	18	19	20	21	22	9:16	42	2490914	HESHVAN 5868	28	29	30	1	2	3	4	Mon 1h 26m 14p	MONTH 9 Dīng-Mǎo	1	2	3	4	5	6	7			4	5	6	7	8	9	10	
	◐	24	25	26	27	28	29	18:31	43	2490921		5	6	7	8	9	10	11			8	9[h]	10	11	12	13	14	Shuāng jiàng		11	12	13	14	15	16	17	
NOVEMBER 2107	30	○	1	2	3	4	5	20:50	44	2490928		12	13	14	15	16	17	18			15	16	17	18	19	20	21			18	19	20	21	22	23	24	
	6	7	◑	9	10	11	12	0:48	45	2490935		19	20	21	22	23	24	25			22	23	24	25	26	27	28	Lì dōng	ATHŌR 1824	25	26	27	28	29	30	1	ḤEDĀR 2100
	13	●	15	16	17	18	19	21:07	46	2490942	KISLEV 5868	26	27	28	29	1	2	3	Tue 14h 10m 15p	MONTH 10 Dīng-Mǎo	29	30	1	2	3	4	5			2	3	4	5	6	7	8	
	20	21	◐	23	24	25	26	14:55	47	2490949		4	5	6	7	8	9	10			6	7	8	9	10	11	12	Xiǎo xuě		9	10	11	12	13	14	15	
DECEMBER 2107	27	28	29	○	1	2	3	11:21	48	2490956		11	12	13	14	15	16	17			13	14	15	16	17	18	19			16	17	18	19	20	21	22	
	4	5	6	◑	8	9	10	8:16	49	2490963		18	19	20	21[d]	22	23	24			20	21	22	23	24	25	26	Dà xuě		23	24	25	26	27	28	29	
	11	12	13	●	15	16	17	11:27	50	2490970	TEVETH 5868	25[e]	26[e]	27[e]	28[e]	29[e]	1[e]	2[e]	Thu 2h 54m 16p	MONTH 11 Dīng-Mǎo	27	28*	29	1	2	3	4		KOIAK 1824	30	1	2	3	4	5	6	TĀKHŚĀŚ 2100
	18	19	20	21	◐[e]	23	24	12:38	51	2490977		3[e]	4	5	6	7	8	9			5	6	7	8	9[i]	10	11	Dōng zhì		7	8	9	10	11	12	13	
	25	26	27	28	29	○	31	0:17	52	2490984		10	11	12	13	14	15	16			12	13	14	15	16	17	18			14	15	16	17	18	19	20	

[a]New Year
[b]Spring (5:49)
[c]Summer (21:59)
[d]Autumn (14:36)
[e]Winter (12:41)
● New moon
◐ First quarter moon
○ Full moon
◑ Last quarter moon

[a]New Year
[b]Yom Kippur
[c]Sukkot
[d]Winter starts
[e]Ḥanukkah
[f]Purim
[g]Passover
[h]Shavuot
[i]Fast of Av

‡Leap year
[a]New Year (4805, Hare)
[b]Lantern Festival
[c]Qīngmíng
[d]Dragon Festival
[e]Qīqiǎo
[f]Hungry Ghosts
[g]Mid-Autumn Festival
[h]Double-Ninth Festival
[i]Dōngzhì
*Start of 60-name cycle

‡Leap year
[a]New Year
[b]Building of the Cross
[c]Christmas
[d]Jesus's Circumcision
[e]Epiphany
[f]Easter
[g]Mary's Announcement
[h]Jesus's Transfiguration

PERSIAN (ASTRONOMICAL) 1485/1486‡

Month	Sun	Mon	Tue	Wed	Thu	Fri	Sat
DEY 1485	5	6	7	8	9	10	11
	12	13	14	15	16	17	18
	19	20	21	22	23	24	25
	26	27	28	29	30	1	2
BAHMAN 1485	3	4	5	6	7	8	9
	10	11	12	13	14	15	16
	17	18	19	20	21	22	23
	24	25	26	27	28	29	30
ESFAND 1485	1	2	3	4	5	6	7
	8	9	10	11	12	13	14
	15	16	17	18	19	20	21
	22	23	24	25	26	27	28
FARVARDĪN 1486	29	1[a]	2	3	4	5	6
	7	8	9	10	11	12	13[b]
	14	15	16	17	18	19	20
	21	22	23	24	25	26	27
	28	29	30	31	1	2	3
ORDĪBEHEŠT 1486	4	5	6	7	8	9	10
	11	12	13	14	15	16	17
	18	19	20	21	22	23	24
	25	26	27	28	29	30	31
XORDĀD 1486	1	2	3	4	5	6	7
	8	9	10	11	12	13	14
	15	16	17	18	19	20	21
	22	23	24	25	26	27	28
TĪR 1486	29	30	31	1	2	3	4
	5	6	7	8	9	10	11
	12	13	14	15	16	17	18
	19	20	21	22	23	24	25
MORDĀD 1486	26	27	28	29	30	31	1
	2	3	4	5	6	7	8
	9	10	11	12	13	14	15
	16	17	18	19	20	21	22
	23	24	25	26	27	28	29
SHAHRĪVAR 1486	30	31	1	2	3	4	5
	6	7	8	9	10	11	12
	13	14	15	16	17	18	19
	20	21	22	23	24	25	26
MEHR 1486	27	28	29	30	31	1	2
	3	4	5	6	7	8	9
	10	11	12	13	14	15	16
	17	18	19	20	21	22	23
	24	25	26	27	28	29	30
ABĀN 1486	1	2	3	4	5	6	7
	8	9	10	11	12	13	14
	15	16	17	18	19	20	21
	22	23	24	25	26	27	28
ĀZAR 1486	29	30	1	2	3	4	5
	6	7	8	9	10	11	12
	13	14	15	16	17	18	19
	20	21	22	23	24	25	26
DEY 1486	27	28	29	30	1	2	3
	4	5	6	7	8	9	10

HINDU LUNAR 2163/2164‡

Month	Sun	Mon	Tue	Wed	Thu	Fri	Sat
PAUSHA 2163	1	2	3	4	5	6	7
	8	9	10	11	12	13	14
	15	16	17	**18**	20	21	22
	23	24	25	26	27	28	29
MĀGHA 2163	30	*30*	1	2	3	4	5
	6	7	8	9	10	11	**12**
	14	15	16	17	18	19	20
	21	22	23	24	25	26	27
PHĀLGUNA 2163	28[h]	29	30	1	2	*2*	3
	4	5	**6**	8	9	10	11
	12	13	14	15[i]	16	17	18
	19	20	21	22	23	24	25
CHAITRA 2164	26	27	28	29	30	1[a]	2
	3	4	5	6	7	8	9[b]
	10	**11**	13	14	15	16	17
	18	19	20	21	22	23	24
	25	*25*	26	27	28	29	30
VAIŚĀKHA 2164	1	2	3	**4**	6	7	8
	9	10	11	12	13	14	15
	16	17	18	19	20	21	22
	23	24	25	26	27	28	29
JYAISHTHA 2164	30	1	2	3	4	5	6
	7	**8**	10	11	12	13	14
	15	16	17	18	19	20	21
	21	22	23	24	25	26	27
ĀSHĀḌHA 2164	28	29	**30**	2	3	4	5
	6	7	8	9	10	11	12
	13	14	15	16	17	18	19
	20	21	22	23	24	25	26
LEAP ŚRĀVAṆA 2164	27	28	29	30	1	2	**3**
	5	6	7	8	9	10	11
	12	13	14	15	16	17	18
	18	19	20	21	22	23	24
ŚRĀVAṆA 2164	25	**26**	28	29	30	1	2
	3	4	5	6	7	8	9
	10	11	12	13	14	15	16
	17	18	19	20	21	22	23[c]
BHĀDRAPADA 2164	24	25	26	27	28	**29**	1
	2	3	4[d]	5	6	7	8
	9	10	11	12	13	14	*14*
	15	16	17	18	19	20	21
	22	**23**	25	26	27	28	29
ĀŚVINA 2164	30	1	2	3	4	5	6
	7	8[e]	9[e]	10[e]	11	12	13
	14	15	16	17	18	19	20
	21	22	23	24	25	26	**27**
KĀRTTIKA 2164	29	30	1[f]	2	3	4	5
	6	7	8	*8*	9	10	11
	12	13	14	15	16	17	18
	19	20	**21**	23	24	25	26
MĀRGAŚĪRA 2164	27	28	29	30	1	2	3
	4	5	6	7	8	9	10
	10	11[g]	12	13	**14**	16	17

HINDU SOLAR 2028‡/2029

Month	Sun	Mon	Tue	Wed	Thu	Fri	Sat
PAUSHA 2028	9	10	11	12	13	14	15
	16	17	18	19	20	21	22
	23	24	25	26	27	28	29
MĀGHA 2028	1[b]	2	3	4	5	6	7
	8	9	10	11	12	13	14
	15	16	17	18	19	20	21
	22	23	24	25	26	27	28
PHĀLGUNA 2028	29	1	2	3	4	5	6
	7	8	9	10	11	12	13
	14	15	16	17	18	19	20
	21	22	23	24	25	26	27
CHAITRA 2028	28	29	30	1	2	3	4
	5	6	7	8	9	10	11
	12	13	14	15	16	17	18
	19	20	21	22	23	24	25
VAIŚĀKHA 2029	26	27	28	29	30	31	1[a]
	2	3	4	5	6	7	8
	9	10	11	12	13	14	15
	16	17	18	19	20	21	22
	23	24	25	26	27	28	29
JYAISHTHA 2029	30	31	1	2	3	4	5
	6	7	8	9	10	11	12
	13	14	15	16	17	18	19
	20	21	22	23	24	25	26
ĀSHĀḌHA 2029	27	28	29	30	31	1	2
	3	4	5	6	7	8	9
	10	11	12	13	14	15	16
	17	18	19	20	21	22	23
	24	25	26	27	28	29	30
ŚRĀVAṆA 2029	31	32	1	2	3	4	5
	6	7	8	9	10	11	12
	13	14	15	16	17	18	19
	20	21	22	23	24	25	26
BHĀDRAPADA 2029	27	28	29	30	31	1	2
	3	4	5	6	7	8	9
	10	11	12	13	14	15	16
	17	18	19	20	21	22	23
	24	25	26	27	28	29	30
ĀŚVINA 2029	31	1	2	3	4	5	6
	7	8	9	10	11	12	13
	14	15	16	17	18	19	20
	21	22	23	24	25	26	27
KĀRTTIKA 2029	28	29	30	31	1	2	3
	4	5	6	7	8	9	10
	11	12	13	14	15	16	17
	18	19	20	21	22	23	24
MĀRGAŚĪRA 2029	25	26	27	28	29	1	2
	3	4	5	6	7	8	9
	10	11	12	13	14	15	16
	17	18	19	20	21	22	23
	24	25	26	27	28	29	30
PAUSHA 2029	1	2	3	4	5	6	7
	8	9	10	11	12	13	14

ISLAMIC (ASTRONOMICAL) 1530/1531/1532

Month	Sun	Mon	Tue	Wed	Thu	Fri	Sat
MUḤARRAM 1531	30	1	2	3	4	5	6
	7	8	9	10[b]	11	12	13
	14	15	16	17	18	19	20
	21	22	23	24	25	26	27
ṢAFAR 1531	28	29	1	2	3	4	5
	6	7	8	9	10	11	12
	13	14	15	16	17	18	19
	20	21	22	23	24	25	26
RABĪ' I 1531	27	28	29	30	1	2	3
	4	5	6	7	8	9	10
	11	12[c]	13	14	15	16	17
	18	19	20	21	22	23	24
RABĪ' II 1531	25	26	27	28	29	30	1
	2	3	4	5	6	7	8
	9	10	11	12	13	14	15
	16	17	18	19	20	21	22
	23	24	25	26	27	28	29
JUMĀDĀ I 1531	1	2	3	4	5	6	7
	8	9	10	11	12	13	14
	15	16	17	18	19	20	21
	22	23	24	25	26	27	28
JUMĀDĀ II 1531	29	30	1	2	3	4	5
	6	7	8	9	10	11	12
	13	14	15	16	17	18	19
	20	21	22	23	24	25	26
RAJAB 1531	27	28	29	30	1	2	3
	4	5	6	7	8	9	10
	11	12	13	14	15	16	17
	18	19	20	21	22	23	24
SHA'BĀN 1531	25	26	27[d]	28	29	1	2
	3	4	5	6	7	8	9
	10	11	12	13	14	15	16
	17	18	19	20	21	22	23
RAMAḌĀN 1531	24	25	26	27	28	29	1[e]
	2	3	4	5	6	7	8
	9	10	11	12	13	14	15
	16	17	18	19	20	21	22
	23	24	25	26	27	28	29
SHAWWĀL 1531	30	1[f]	2	3	4	5	6
	7	8	9	10	11	12	13
	14	15	16	17	18	19	20
	21	22	23	24	25	26	27
DHU AL-QA'DA 1531	28	29	1	2	3	4	5
	6	7	8	9	10	11	12
	13	14	15	16	17	18	19
	20	21	22	23	24	25	26
DHU AL-ḤIJJA 1531	27	28	29	1	2	3	4
	5	6	7	8	9	10[g]	11
	12	13	14	15	16	17	18
	19	20	21	22	23	24	25
MUḤARRAM 1532	26	27	28	29	30	1[a]	2
	3	4	5	6	7	8	9
	10[b]	11	12	13	14	15	16

GREGORIAN 2107

Julian (Sun)	Sun	Mon	Tue	Wed	Thu	Fri	Sat	Month
Dec 12	26	27	28	29	30	31	1	JANUARY 2107
	2	3	4	5	6	7	8[a]	
Dec 26	9	10	11	12	13	14	15[b]	
	16	17	18	19	20	21	22	
Jan 9	23	24	25	26	27	28	29	
	30	31	1	2	3	4	5	FEBRUARY 2107
Jan 23	6	7	8	9	10	11	12	
	13	14	15	16	17	18	19	
Feb 6	20	21	22	23[c]	24	25	26	
	27	28	1	2	3	4	5	MARCH 2107
Feb 20	6[d]	7	8	9	10	11	12	
	13	14	15	16	17	18	19	
Mar 6	20	21	22	23	24	25	26	
	27	28	29	30	31	1	2	APRIL 2107
Mar 20	3	4	5	6	7	8	9	
	10[e]	11	12	13	14	15	16	
Apr 3	17[f]	18	19	20	21	22	23	
	24	25	26	27	28	29	30	
Apr 17	1	2	3	4	5	6	7	MAY 2107
	8	9	10	11	12	13	14	
May 1	15	16	17	18	19	20	21	
	22	23	24	25	26	27	28	
May 15	29	30	31	1	2	3	4	JUNE 2107
	5	6	7	8	9	10	11	
May 29	12	13	14	15	16	17	18	
	19	20	21	22	23	24	25	
Jun 12	26	27	28	29	30	1	2	JULY 2107
	3	4	5	6	7	8	9	
Jun 26	10	11	12	13	14	15	16	
	17	18	19	20	21	22	23	
Jul 10	24	25	26	27	28	29	30	
	31	1	2	3	4	5	6	AUGUST 2107
Jul 24	7	8	9	10	11	12	13	
	14	15	16	17	18	19	20	
Aug 7	21	22	23	24	25	26	27	
	28	29	30	31	1	2	3	SEPTEMBER 2107
Aug 21	4	5	6	7	8	9	10	
	11	12	13	14	15	16	17	
Sep 4	18	19	20	21	22	23	24	
	25	26	27	28	29	30	1	OCTOBER 2107
Sep 18	2	3	4	5	6	7	8	
	9	10	11	12	13	14	15	
Oct 2	16	17	18	19	20	21	22	
	23	24	25	26	27	28	29	
Oct 16	30	31	1	2	3	4	5	NOVEMBER 2107
	6	7	8	9	10	11	12	
Oct 30	13	14	15	16	17	18	19	
	20	21	22	23	24	25	26	
Nov 13	27[g]	28	29	30	1	2	3	DECEMBER 2107
	4	5	6	7	8	9	10	
Nov 27	11	12	13	14	15	16	17	
	18	19	20	21	22	23	24	
Dec 11	25[h]	26	27	28	29	30	31	

Persian:
‡Leap year
[a]New Year
[b]Sizdeh Bedar

Hindu Lunar:
‡Leap year
[a]New Year (Prabhava)
[b]Birthday of Rāma
[c]Birthday of Krishna
[d]Ganēśa Chaturthī
[e]Dashara
[f]Diwali
[g]Birthday of Vishnu
[h]Night of Śiva
[i]Holi

Hindu Solar:
‡Leap year
[a]New Year (Vṛisha)
[b]Pongal

Islamic:
[a]New Year
[b]'Ashūrā'
[c]Prophet's Birthday
[d]Ascent of the Prophet
[e]Start of Ramaḍān
[f]'Id al-Fiṭr
[g]'Id al-'Aḍḥā

Gregorian:
[a]Orthodox Christmas
[b]Julian New Year
[c]Ash Wednesday
[d]Feast of Orthodoxy
[e]Easter
[f]Orthodox Easter
[g]Advent
[h]Christmas

2108

GREGORIAN 2108‡	Sun	Mon	Tue	Wed	Thu	Fri	Sat	Lunar Phases	ISO WEEK (Mon)	JULIAN DAY (Sun noon)
JANUARY 2108	1[a]	2	3	4	◑	6	7	16:53	1	2490991
	8	9	10	11	12	●	14	4:06	2	2490998
	15	16	17	18	19	20	◐	9:22	3	2491005
	22	23	24	25	26	27	○	11:49	4	2491012
	29	30	31	1	2	3	◑	3:21	5	2491019
FEBRUARY 2108	5	6	7	8	9	10	●	22:28	6	2491026
	12	13	14	15	16	17	18		7	2491033
	19	◐	21	22	23	24	25	2:59	8	2491040
	○	27	28	29	1	2	3	22:16	9	2491047
MARCH 2108	◑	5	6	7	8	9	10	15:52	10	2491054
	11	●	13	14	15	16	17	17:20	11	2491061
	18	19	◐[b]	21	22	23	24	16:27	12	2491068
	25	26	○	28	29	30	31	7:58	13	2491075
APRIL 2108	1	2	◑	4	5	6	7	6:24	14	2491082
	8	9	10	●	12	13	14	11:03	15	2491089
	15	16	17	18	◐	20	21	1:58	16	2491096
	22	23	24	○	26	27	28	17:11	17	2491103
	29	30	1	◑	3	4	5	22:38	18	2491110
MAY 2108	6	7	8	9	10	●	12	2:17	19	2491117
	13	14	15	16	17	◐	19	8:34	20	2491124
	20	21	22	23	24	○	26	2:22	21	2491131
	27	28	29	30	31	◑	2	16:01	22	2491138
JUNE 2108	3	4	5	6	7	8	●	14:32	23	2491145
	10	11	12	13	14	15	◐	13:32	24	2491152
	17	18	19	20	21[c]	22	○	12:15	25	2491159
	24	25	26	27	28	29	30		26	2491166
JULY 2108	◑	2	3	4	5	6	7	9:42	27	2491173
	8	●	10	11	12	13	14	0:21	28	2491180
	◐	16	17	18	19	20	21	18:16	29	2491187
	○	23	24	25	26	27	28	23:45	30	2491194
	29	30	◑	1	2	3	4	2:37	31	2491201
AUGUST 2108	5	6	●	8	9	10	11	8:42	32	2491208
	12	13	◐	15	16	17	18	0:05	33	2491215
	19	20	○	22	23	24	25	13:31	34	2491222
	26	27	28	◑	30	31	1	17:58	35	2491229
SEPTEMBER 2108	2	3	4	●	6	7	8	16:40	36	2491236
	9	10	11	◐	13	14	15	8:14	37	2491243
	16	17	18	19	○	21	22[d]	5:37	38	2491250
	23	24	25	26	27	◑	29	7:21	39	2491257
	30	1	2	3	4	●	6	1:05	40	2491264
OCTOBER 2108	7	8	9	10	◐	12	13	19:53	41	2491271
	14	15	16	17	18	○	20	23:12	42	2491278
	21	22	23	24	25	26	◑	18:50	43	2491285
	28	29	30	31	1	2	●	10:31	44	2491292
NOVEMBER 2108	4	5	6	7	8	9	◐	11:41	45	2491299
	11	12	13	14	15	16	17		46	2491306
	○	19	20	21	22	23	24	16:55	47	2491313
	25	◑	27	28	29	30	1	4:45	48	2491320
DECEMBER 2108	●	3	4	5	6	7	8	21:21	49	2491327
	9	◐	11	12	13	14	15	7:23	50	2491334
	16	17	○	19	20	21[e]	22	9:31	51	2491341
	23	24	◑	26	27	28	29	13:30	52	2491348
	30	31	●	2	3	4	5	10:01	1	2491355

ISO WEEK	HEBREW 5868/5869‡	Sun	Mon	Tue	Wed	Thu	Fri	Sat	Molad
1	TEVETH 5868	17	18	19	20	21	22	23	
2		24	25	26	27	28	29	1	Fri 15h38m17p
3	SHEVAT 5868	2	3	4	5	6	7	8	
4		9	10	11	12	13	14	15	
5		16	17	18	19	20	21	22	
6		23	24	25	26	27	28	29	
7		30	1	2	3	4	5	6	Sun 4h23m0p
8	ADAR 5868	7	8	9	10	11	12	13	
9		14[f]	15	16	17	18	19	20	
10		21	22	23	24	25	26	27	
11		28	29	1	2	3	4	5	Mon 17h7m1p
12	NISAN 5868	6	7	8	9	10	11	12	
13		13	14	15[g]	16	17	18	19	
14		20	21	22	23	24	25	26	
15		27	28	29	30	1	2	3	Wed 5h51m2p
16	IYYAR 5868	4	5	6	7	8	9	10	
17		11	12	13	14	15	16	17	
18		18	19	20	21	22	23	24	
19		25	26	27	28	29	1	2	Thu 18h35m3p
20	SIVAN 5868	3	4	5	6[h]	7	8	9	
21		10	11	12	13	14	15	16	
22		17	18	19	20	21	22	23	
23		24	25	26	27	28	29	30	
24	TAMMUZ 5868	1	2	3	4	5	6	7	Sat 7h19m4p
25		8	9	10	11	12	13	14	
26		15	16	17	18	19	20	21	
27		22	23	24	25	26	27	28	
28		29	1	2	3	4	5	6	Sun 20h3m5p
29	AV 5868	7	8	9[i]	10	11	12	13	
30		14	15	16	17	18	19	20	
31		21	22	23	24	25	26	27	
32		28	29	30	1	2	3	4	Tue 8h47m6p
33	ELUL 5868	5	6	7	8	9	10	11	
34		12	13	14	15	16	17	18	
35		19	20	21	22	23	24	25	
36		26	27	28	29	1[a]	2[a]	3	Wed 21h31m7p
37	TISHRI 5869	4	5	6	7	8	9	10[b]	
38		11	12	13	14	15[c]	16	17	
39		18	19	20	21	22	23	24	
40		25	26	27	28	29	30	1	Fri 10h15m8p
41	HESHVAN 5869	2	3	4	5	6	7	8	
42		9	10	11	12	13	14	15	
43		16	17	18	19	20	21	22	
44		23	24	25	26	27	28	29	
45		30	1	2	3	4	5	6	Sat 22h59m9p
46	KISLEV 5869	7	8	9	10	11	12	13	
47		14	15	16	17	18	19	20	
48		21	22	23	24	25[e]	26[e]	27[e]	
49		28[e]	29[e]	30[e]	1[e]	2[d,e]	3	4	Mon 11h43m10p
50	TEVETH 5869	5	6	7	8	9	10	11	
51		12	13	14	15	16	17	18	
52		19	20	21	22	23	24	25	
53		26	27	28	29	1	2	3	Wed 0h27m11p

ISO WEEK	CHINESE Dīng-Mǎo‡/Wù-Chén	Sun	Mon	Tue	Wed	Thu	Fri	Sat	Solar Term
1	MONTH 11 Dīng-Mǎo	19	20	21	22	23	*24*	25	*Xiǎo hán*
2		26	27	28	29	30	1	2	
3	MONTH 12 Dīng-Mǎo	3	4	5	6	7	8	***9***	**Dà hán**
4		10	11	12	13	14	15	16	
5		17	18	19	20	21	22	23	
6		*24*	25	26	27	28	29*	30	*Lì chūn*
7	MONTH 1 Wù-Chén	1[a]	2	3	4	5	6	7	
8		***8***	9	10	11	12	13	14	**Yǔ shuǐ**
9		15[b]	16	17	18	19	20	21	
10		22	*23*	24	25	26	27	28	*Jīng zhé*
11		29	30	1	2	3	4	5	
12	MONTH 2 Wù-Chén	6	7	***8***	9	10	11	12	**Chūn fēn**
13		13	14	15	16	17	18	19	
14		20	21	22	23[c]	24	25	26	*Qīng míng*
15		27	28	29*	1	2	3	4	
16	MONTH 3 Wù-Chén	5	6	7	8	9	***10***	11	**Gǔ yǔ**
17		12	13	14	15	16	17	18	
18		19	20	21	22	23	24	*25*	*Lì xià*
19		26	27	28	29	30	1	2	
20	MONTH 4 Wù-Chén	3	4	5	6	7	8	9	
21		10	***11***	12	13	14	15	16	**Xiǎo mǎn**
22		17	18	19	20	21	22	23	
23		24	25	*26*	27	28	29	1*	*Máng zhòng*
24	MONTH 5 Wù-Chén	2	3	4	5[d]	6	7	8	
25		9	10	11	12	***13***	14	15	**Xià zhì**
26		16	17	18	19	20	21	22	
27		23	24	25	26	27	28	*29*	*Xiǎo shǔ*
28		30	1	2	3	4	5	6	
29	MONTH 6 Wù-Chén	7	8	9	10	11	12	13	
30		***14***	15	16	17	18	19	20	**Dà shǔ**
31		21	22	23	24	25	26	27	
32		28	29	*1*	2*	3	4	5	*Lì qiū*
33	MONTH 7 Wù-Chén	6	7[e]	8	9	10	11	12	
34		13	14	15[f]	16	***17***	18	19	**Chǔ shǔ**
35		20	21	22	23	24	25	26	
36		27	28	29	30	1	*2*	3	*Bái lù*
37	MONTH 8 Wù-Chén	4	5	6	7	8	9	10	
38		11	12	13	14	15[g]	16	17	
39		***18***	19	20	21	22	23	24	**Qiū fēn**
40		25	26	27	28	29	1	2	
41	MONTH 9 Wù-Chén	3*	*4*	5	6	7	8	9[h]	*Hán lù*
42		10	11	12	13	14	15	16	
43		17	18	***19***	20	21	22	23	**Shuāng jiàng**
44		24	25	26	27	28	29	1	
45	MONTH 10 Wù-Chén	2	3	4	*5*	6	7	8	*Lì dōng*
46		9	10	11	12	13	14	15	
47		16	17	18	19	***20***	21	22	**Xiǎo xuě**
48		23	24	25	26	27	28	29	
49		30	1	2	3	4*	*5*	6	*Dà xuě*
50	MONTH 11* Wù-Chén	7	8	9	10	11	12	13	
51		14	15	16	17	18	19	***20***[i]	**Dōng zhì**
52		21	22	23	24	25	26	27	
53		28	29	1	2	3	4	5	*Xiǎo hán*

ISO WEEK	COPTIC 1824/1825	Sun	Mon	Tue	Wed	Thu	Fri	Sat	ETHIOPIC 2100/2101
1	KOIAK 1824	21	22	23	24	25	26	27	TĀḪŚĀŚ 2100
2		28	29[c]	30	1	2	3	4	
3	TŌBE 1824	5	6[d]	7	8	9	10	11[e]	ṬER 2100
4		12	13	14	15	16	17	18	
5		19	20	21	22	23	24	25	
6		26	27	28	29	30	1	2	
7	MESHIR 1824	3	4	5	6	7	8	9	YAKĀTIT 2100
8		10	11	12	13	14	15	16	
9		17	18	19	20	21	22	23	
10		24	25	26	27	28	29	30	
11	PAREMOTEP 1824	1	2	3	4	5	6	7	MAGĀBIT 2100
12		8	9	10	11	12	13	14	
13		15	16	17	18	19	20	21	
14		22	23	24	25	26	27	28	
15		29	30	1	2	3	4	5	
16	PARMOUTE 1824	6	7	8	9	10	11	12	MIYĀZYĀ 2100
17		13	14	15	16	17	18	19	
18		20	21	22	23	24	25	26	
19		27[f]	28	29[g]	30	1	2	3	
20	PASHONS 1824	4	5	6	7	8	9	10	GENBOT 2100
21		11	12	13	14	15	16	17	
22		18	19	20	21	22	23	24	
23		25	26	27	28	29	30	1	
24	PAŌNE 1824	2	3	4	5	6	7	8	SANĒ 2100
25		9	10	11	12	13	14	15	
26		16	17	18	19	20	21	22	
27		23	24	25	26	27	28	29	
28		30	1	2	3	4	5	6	
29	EPĒP 1824	7	8	9	10	11	12	13	ḤAMLĒ 2100
30		14	15	16	17	18	19	20	
31		21	22	23	24	25	26	27	
32		28	29	30	1	2	3	4	
33	MESORĒ 1824	5	6	7	8	9	10	11	NAḤASĒ 2100
34		12	13[h]	14	15	16	17	18	
35		19	20	21	22	23	24	25	
36		26	27	28	29	30	1	2	PĀG. 2100
37	EPAG. 1824	3	4	5	1[a]	2	3	4	
38	THOOUT 1825	5	6	7	8	9	10	11	MASKARAM 2101
39		12	13	14	15	16	17[b]	18	
40		19	20	21	22	23	24	25	
41		26	27	28	29	30	1	2	
42	PAOPE 1825	3	4	5	6	7	8	9	TEQEMT 2101
43		10	11	12	13	14	15	16	
44		17	18	19	20	21	22	23	
45		24	25	26	27	28	29	30	
46	ATHŌR 1825	1	2	3	4	5	6	7	ḪEDĀR 2101
47		8	9	10	11	12	13	14	
48		15	16	17	18	19	20	21	
49		22	23	24	25	26	27	28	
50		29	30	1	2	3	4	5	
51	KOIAK 1825	6	7	8	9	10	11	12	TĀḪŚĀŚ 2101
52		13	14	15	16	17	18	19	
53		20	21	22	23	24	25	26	

‡Leap year
[a]New Year
[b]Spring (11:38)
[c]Summer (3:56)
[d]Autumn (20:27)
[e]Winter (18:33)
● New moon
◐ First quarter moon
○ Full moon
◑ Last quarter moon

‡Leap year
[a]New Year
[b]Yom Kippur
[c]Sukkot
[d]Winter starts
[e]Ḥanukkah
[f]Purim
[g]Passover
[h]Shavuot
[i]Fast of Av

‡Leap year
[a]New Year (4806, Dragon)
[b]Lantern Festival
[c]Qīngmíng
[d]Dragon Festival
[e]Qīqiǎo
[f]Hungry Ghosts
[g]Mid-Autumn Festival
[h]Double-Ninth Festival
[i]Dōngzhì
*Start of 60-name cycle

[a]New Year
[b]Building of the Cross
[c]Christmas
[d]Jesus's Circumcision
[e]Epiphany
[f]Easter
[g]Mary's Announcement
[h]Jesus's Transfiguration

PERSIAN (ASTRONOMICAL) 1486‡/1487

Month	Sun	Mon	Tue	Wed	Thu	Fri	Sat
DEY 1486	11	12	13	14	15	16	17
	18	19	20	21	22	23	24
	25	26	27	28	29	30	1
BAHMAN 1486	2	3	4	5	6	7	8
	9	10	11	12	13	14	15
	16	17	18	19	20	21	22
	23	24	25	26	27	28	29
	30	1	2	3	4	5	6
ESFAND 1486	7	8	9	10	11	12	13
	14	15	16	17	18	19	20
	21	22	23	24	25	26	27
	28	29	30‡	1[a]	2	3	4
FARVARDĪN 1487	5	6	7	8	9	10	11
	12	13[b]	14	15	16	17	18
	19	20	21	22	23	24	25
	26	27	28	29	30	31	1
ORDĪBEHEŠT 1487	2	3	4	5	6	7	8
	9	10	11	12	13	14	15
	16	17	18	19	20	21	22
	23	24	25	26	27	28	29
	30	31	1	2	3	4	5
XORDĀD 1487	6	7	8	9	10	11	12
	13	14	15	16	17	18	19
	20	21	22	23	24	25	26
	27	28	29	30	31	1	2
TĪR 1487	3	4	5	6	7	8	9
	10	11	12	13	14	15	16
	17	18	19	20	21	22	23
	24	25	26	27	28	29	30
	31	1	2	3	4	5	6
MORDĀD 1487	7	8	9	10	11	12	13
	14	15	16	17	18	19	20
	21	22	23	24	25	26	27
	28	29	30	31	1	2	3
SHAHRĪVAR 1487	4	5	6	7	8	9	10
	11	12	13	14	15	16	17
	18	19	20	21	22	23	24
	25	26	27	28	29	30	31
MEHR 1487	1	2	3	4	5	6	7
	8	9	10	11	12	13	14
	15	16	17	18	19	20	21
	22	23	24	25	26	27	28
	29	30	1	2	3	4	5
ĀBĀN 1487	6	7	8	9	10	11	12
	13	14	15	16	17	18	19
	20	21	22	23	24	25	26
	27	28	29	30	1	2	3
ĀZAR 1487	4	5	6	7	8	9	10
	11	12	13	14	15	16	17
	18	19	20	21	22	23	24
	25	26	27	28	29	30	1
DEY 1487	2	3	4	5	6	7	8
	9	10	11	12	13	14	15

‡Leap year
[a]New Year
[b]Sizdeh Bedar

HINDU LUNAR 2164‡/2165

Month	Sun	Mon	Tue	Wed	Thu	Fri	Sat
MĀRGAŚĪRA 2164	18	19	20	21	22	23	24
	25	26	27	28	29	30	1
PAUSHA 2164	2	3	4	5	6	7	8
	9	10	11	12	13	14	15
	16	17	18	**19**	21	22	23
	24	25	26	27	28	29	30
MĀGHA 2164	1	2	2	3	4	5	6
	7	8	9	10	11	12	13
	14	16	17	18	19	20	21
	22	23	24	25	26	27	28[h]
PHĀLGUNA 2164	29	30	1	2	3	4	5
	6	7	8	9	10	11	12
	13	14	15[i]	16	17	**18**	20
	21	22	23	24	25	26	26
CHAITRA 2165	27	28	29	30	1[a]	2	3
	4	5	6	7	8	9[b]	10
	11	13	14	15	16	17	18
	19	20	21	22	23	24	25
VAIŚĀKHA 2165	26	27	28	29	29	30	1
	2	3	**4**	6	7	8	9
	10	11	12	13	14	15	**16**
	18	19	20	*20*	21	22	23
	24	25	26	27	28	29	30
JYAISHṬHA 2165	1	2	3	4	5	6	7
	8	10	11	12	13	14	15
	16	17	18	19	20	21	22
	23	24	25	26	*26*	27	28
ĀSHĀḌHA 2165	29	**30**	2	3	4	5	6
	7	8	9	10	**11**	13	14
	15	16	17	*17*	18	19	20
	21	22	23	24	25	26	27
ŚRĀVAṆA 2165	28	29	30	1	2	**3**	5
	6	7	8	9	10	11	12
	13	14	15	16	17	18	19
	20	21	22	23	23[c]	24	**25**
BHĀDRAPADA 2165	27	28	29	30	1	2	3
	4[d]	5	6	**7**	9	10	11
	12	13	14	*14*	15	16	17
	18	19	20	21	22	23	24
ĀŚVINA 2165	25	26	27	28	29	**30**	2
	3	4	5	6	7	8[e]	9[e]
	10[e]	11	12	13	14	15	16
	17	*17*	18	19	20	21	22
	23	25	26	27	28	29	30
KĀRTTIKA 2165	1[f]	2	3	4	5	6	7
	8	9	10	11	12	13	14
	15	16	17	18	19	20	21
	22	23	24	25	26	27	**28**
MĀRGAŚĪRA 2165	30	1	2	3	4	5	6
	7	8	9	10	11	11[g]	12
	13	14	15	16	17	18	19
	20	21	**22**	24	25	26	27
	28	29	30	1	2	3	4

‡Leap year
[a]New Year (Vibhava)
[b]Birthday of Rāma
[c]Birthday of Krishna
[d]Gaṇēśa Chaturthī
[e]Dashara
[f]Diwali
[g]Birthday of Vishnu
[h]Night of Śiva
[i]Holi

HINDU SOLAR 2029/2030

Month	Sun	Mon	Tue	Wed	Thu	Fri	Sat
PAUSHA 2029	15	16	17	18	19	20	21
	22	23	24	25	26	27	28
MĀGHA 2029	29	1[b]	2	3	4	5	6
	7	8	9	10	11	12	13
	14	15	16	17	18	19	20
	21	22	23	24	25	26	27
PHĀLGUNA 2029	28	29	30	1	2	3	4
	5	6	7	8	9	10	11
	12	13	14	15	16	17	18
	19	20	21	22	23	24	25
CHAITRA 2029	26	27	28	29	30	1	2
	3	4	5	6	7	8	9
	10	11	12	13	14	15	16
	17	18	19	20	21	22	23
	24	25	26	27	28	29	30
VAIŚĀKHA 2030	1[a]	2	3	4	5	6	7
	8	9	10	11	12	13	14
	15	16	17	18	19	20	21
	22	23	24	25	26	27	28
JYAISHṬHA 2030	29	30	31	1	2	3	4
	5	6	7	8	9	10	11
	12	13	14	15	16	17	18
	19	20	21	22	23	24	25
ĀSHĀḌHA 2030	26	27	28	29	30	31	1
	2	3	4	5	6	7	8
	9	10	11	12	13	14	15
	16	17	18	19	20	21	22
	23	24	25	26	27	28	29
ŚRĀVAṆA 2030	30	31	32	1	2	3	4
	5	6	7	8	9	10	11
	12	13	14	15	16	17	18
	19	20	21	22	23	24	25
BHĀDRAPADA 2030	26	27	28	29	30	31	1
	2	3	4	5	6	7	8
	9	10	11	12	13	14	15
	16	17	18	19	20	21	22
	23	24	25	26	27	28	29
ĀŚVINA 2030	30	31	1	2	3	4	5
	6	7	8	9	10	11	12
	13	14	15	16	17	18	19
	20	21	22	23	24	25	26
KĀRTTIKA 2030	27	28	29	30	31	1	2
	3	4	5	6	7	8	9
	10	11	12	13	14	15	16
	17	18	19	20	21	22	23
	24	25	26	27	28	29	30
MĀRGAŚĪRA 2030	1	2	3	4	5	6	7
	8	9	10	11	12	13	14
	15	16	17	18	19	20	21
	22	23	24	25	26	27	28
PAUSHA 2030	29	1	2	3	4	5	6
	7	8	9	10	11	12	13
	14	15	16	17	18	19	20

[a]New Year (Chitrabhānu)
[b]Pongal

ISLAMIC (ASTRONOMICAL) 1532/1533‡

Month	Sun	Mon	Tue	Wed	Thu	Fri	Sat
MUḤARRAM 1532	17	18	19	20	21	22	23
ṢAFAR 1532	24	25	26	27	28	29	1
	2	3	4	5	6	7	8
	9	10	11	12	13	14	15
	16	17	18	19	20	21	22
	23	24	25	26	27	28	29
RABĪʿ I 1532	30	1	2	3	4	5	6
	7	8	9	10	11	12[c]	13
	14	15	16	17	18	19	20
	21	22	23	24	25	26	27
RABĪʿ II 1532	28	29	30	1	2	3	4
	5	6	7	8	9	10	11
	12	13	14	15	16	17	18
	19	20	21	22	23	24	25
JUMĀDĀ I 1532	26	27	28	29	30	1	2
	3	4	5	6	7	8	9
	10	11	12	13	14	15	16
	17	18	19	20	21	22	23
JUMĀDĀ II 1532	24	25	26	27	28	29	1
	2	3	4	5	6	7	8
	9	10	11	12	13	14	15
	16	17	18	19	20	21	22
	23	24	25	26	27	28	29
RAJAB 1532	30	1	2	3	4	5	6
	7	8	9	10	11	12	13
	14	15	16	17	18	19	20
	21	22	23	24	25	26	27[d]
SHAʿBĀN 1532	28	29	30	1	2	3	4
	5	6	7	8	9	10	11
	12	13	14	15	16	17	18
	19	20	21	22	23	24	25
RAMAḌĀN 1532	26	27	28	29	1[e]	2	3
	4	5	6	7	8	9	10
	11	12	13	14	15	16	17
	18	19	20	21	22	23	24
SHAWWĀL 1532	25	26	27	28	29	1[f]	2
	3	4	5	6	7	8	9
	10	11	12	13	14	15	16
	17	18	19	20	21	22	23
DHU AL-QAʿDA 1532	24	25	26	27	28	29	1
	2	3	4	5	6	7	8
	9	10	11	12	13	14	15
	16	17	18	19	20	21	22
	23	24	25	26	27	28	29
DHU AL-ḤIJJA 1532	30	1	2	3	4	5	6
	7	8	9	10[g]	11	12	13
	14	15	16	17	18	19	20
	21	22	23	24	25	26	27
MUḤARRAM 1533	28	29	1[a]	2[d]	3	4	5
	6	7	8	9	10[b]	11	12
	13	14	15	16	17	18	19
	20	21	22	23	24	25	26
	27	28	29	30	1	2	3

‡Leap year
[a]New Year
[d]New Year (Arithmetic)
[b]ʿAshūrāʾ
[c]Prophet's Birthday
[d]Ascent of the Prophet
[e]Start of Ramaḍān
[f]ʿĪd al-Fiṭr
[g]ʿĪd al-ʾAḍḥā

GREGORIAN 2108‡

Julian‡ (Sun)	Sun	Mon	Tue	Wed	Thu	Fri	Sat	Month
Dec 18	1	2	3	4	5	6	7	JANUARY 2108
	8[a]	9	10	11	12	13	14	
Jan 1	15[b]	16	17	18	19	20	21	
	22	23	24	25	26	27	28	
Jan 15	29	30	31	1	2	3	4	FEBRUARY 2108
	5	6	7	8	9	10	11	
Jan 29	12	13	14	15[c]	16	17	18	
	19	20	21	22	23	24	25	
Feb 12	26	27	28	29	1	2	3	MARCH 2108
	4	5	6	7	8	9	10	
Feb 26	11	12	13	14	15	16	17	
	18	19	20	21	22	23	24	
Mar 11	25[d]	26	27	28	29	30	31	
	1[e]	2	3	4	5	6	7	APRIL 2108
Mar 25	8	9	10	11	12	13	14	
	15	16	17	18	19	20	21	
Apr 8	22	23	24	25	26	27	28	
	29	30	1	2	3	4	5	MAY 2108
Apr 22	6[f]	7	8	9	10	11	12	
	13	14	15	16	17	18	19	
May 6	20	21	22	23	24	25	26	
	27	28	29	30	31	1	2	JUNE 2108
May 20	3	4	5	6	7	8	9	
	10	11	12	13	14	15	16	
Jun 3	17	18	19	20	21	22	23	
	24	25	26	27	28	29	30	
Jun 17	1	2	3	4	5	6	7	JULY 2108
	8	9	10	11	12	13	14	
Jul 1	15	16	17	18	19	20	21	
	22	23	24	25	26	27	28	
Jul 15	29	30	31	1	2	3	4	AUGUST 2108
	5	6	7	8	9	10	11	
Jul 29	12	13	14	15	16	17	18	
	19	20	21	22	23	24	25	
Aug 12	26	27	28	29	30	31	1	SEPTEMBER 2108
	2	3	4	5	6	7	8	
Aug 26	9	10	11	12	13	14	15	
	16	17	18	19	20	21	22	
Sep 9	23	24	25	26	27	28	29	
	30	1	2	3	4	5	6	OCTOBER 2108
Sep 23	7	8	9	10	11	12	13	
	14	15	16	17	18	19	20	
Oct 7	21	22	23	24	25	26	27	
	28	29	30	31	1	2	3	NOVEMBER 2108
Oct 21	4	5	6	7	8	9	10	
	11	12	13	14	15	16	17	
Nov 4	18	19	20	21	22	23	24	
	25	26	27	28	29	30	1	DECEMBER 2108
Nov 18	2[g]	3	4	5	6	7	8	
	9	10	11	12	13	14	15	
Dec 2	16	17	18	19	20	21	22	
	23	24	25[h]	26	27	28	29	
Dec 16	30	31	1	2	3	4	5	

‡Leap year
[a]Orthodox Christmas
[b]Julian New Year
[c]Ash Wednesday
[d]Feast of Orthodoxy
[e]Easter
[f]Orthodox Easter
[g]Advent
[h]Christmas

2109

GREGORIAN 2109 · Lunar Phases · ISO WEEK (Mon) · JULIAN DAY (Sun noon)

Month	Sun	Mon	Tue	Wed	Thu	Fri	Sat	Lunar Phases	ISO Week	Julian Day
JANUARY 2109	30	31	●[a]	2	3	4	5	10:01	1	2491355
	6	7	8	◐	10	11	12	5:21	2	2491362
	13	14	15	16	○	18	19	0:23	3	2491369
	20	21	22	◑	24	25	26	21:39	4	2491376
FEBRUARY 2109	27	28	29	30	●	1	2	0:47	5	2491383
	3	4	5	6	7	◐	9	3:07	6	2491390
	10	11	12	13	14	○	16	13:20	7	2491397
	17	18	19	20	21	◑	23	5:57	8	2491404
MARCH 2109	24	25	26	27	28	●	2	17:28	9	2491411
	3	4	5	6	7	8	◐	22:26	10	2491418
	10	11	12	13	14	15	16		11	2491425
	○	18	19	20[b]	21	22	◑	0:21 15:15	12	2491432
	24	25	26	27	28	29	30		13	2491439
APRIL 2109	●	1	2	3	4	5	6	11:04	14	2491446
	7	◐	9	10	11	12	13	14:05	15	2491453
	14	○	16	17	18	19	20	9:34	16	2491460
	21	◑	23	24	25	26	27	2:17	17	2491467
MAY 2109	28	29	●	1	2	3	4	4:13	18	2491474
	5	6	7	◐	9	10	11	1:52	19	2491481
	12	13	○	15	16	17	18	17:28	20	2491488
	19	20	◑	22	23	24	25	15:27	21	2491495
JUNE 2109	26	27	28	●	30	31	1	19:47	22	2491502
	2	3	4	5	◐	7	8	10:16	23	2491509
	9	10	11	12	○	14	15	0:54	24	2491516
	16	17	18	19	◑	21[c]	22	6:42	25	2491523
	23	24	25	26	27	●	29	9:24	26	2491530
JULY 2109	30	1	2	3	4	◐	6	16:11	27	2491537
	7	8	9	10	11	○	13	9:02	28	2491544
	14	15	16	17	18	◑	20	23:30	29	2491551
	21	22	23	24	25	26	●	21:13	30	2491558
AUGUST 2109	28	29	30	31	1	2	◐	20:48	31	2491565
	4	5	6	7	8	9	○	19:02	32	2491572
	11	12	13	14	15	16	17		33	2491579
	◑	19	20	21	22	23	24	17:03	34	2491586
	25	●	27	28	29	30	31	7:42	35	2491593
SEPTEMBER 2109	1	◐	3	4	5	6	7	1:37	36	2491600
	8	○	10	11	12	13	14	7:41	37	2491607
	15	16	◑	18	19	20	21	10:35	38	2491614
	22	23[d]	●	25	26	27	28	17:23	39	2491621
OCTOBER 2109	29	30	◐	2	3	4	5	8:10	40	2491628
	6	7	○	9	10	11	12	23:10	41	2491635
	13	14	15	16	◑	18	19	3:22	42	2491642
	20	21	22	23	●	25	26	2:44	43	2491649
NOVEMBER 2109	27	28	29	◐	31	1	2	17:55	44	2491656
	3	4	5	6	○	8	9	16:50	45	2491663
	10	11	12	13	14	◑	16	18:37	46	2491670
	17	18	19	20	21	●	23	12:18	47	2491677
	24	25	26	27	28	◐	30	7:44	48	2491684
DECEMBER 2109	1	2	3	4	5	6	○	11:37	49	2491691
	8	9	10	11	12	13	14		50	2491698
	◑	16	17	18	19	20	●	7:38 22:40	51	2491705
	22[e]	23	24	25	26	27	28		52	2491712
	◐	30	31	1	2	3	4	1:29	1	2491719

HEBREW 5869‡/5870 · Molad

ISO Week	Month	Sun	Mon	Tue	Wed	Thu	Fri	Sat	Molad
1	SHEVAT 5869	26	27	28	29	1	2	3	Wed $0^h27^m1^p$
2		4	5	6	7	8	9	10	
3		11	12	13	14	15	16	17	
4		18	19	20	21	22	23	24	
5	ADAR I 5869	25	26	27	28	29	30	1	Thu $13^h11^m12^p$
6		2	3	4	5	6	7	8	
7		9	10	11	12	13	14	15	
8		16	17	18	19	20	21	22	
9		23	24	25	26	27	28	29	
10	ADAR II 5869	30	1	2	3	4	5	6	Sat $1^h55^m13^p$
11		7	8	9	10	11	12	13	
12		14[f]	15	16	17	18	19	20	
13		21	22	23	24	25	26	27	
14	NISAN 5869	28	29	1	2	3	4	5	Sun $14^h39^m14^p$
15		6	7	8	9	10	11	12	
16		13	14	15[g]	16	17	18	19	
17		20	21	22	23	24	25	26	
18	IYAR 5869	27	28	29	30	1	2	3	Tue $3^h23^m15^p$
19		4	5	6	7	8	9	10	
20		11	12	13	14	15	16	17	
21		18	19	20	21	22	23	24	
22	SIVAN 5869	25	26	27	28	29	1	2	Wed $16^h7^m16^p$
23		3	4	5	6[h]	7	8	9	
24		10	11	12	13	14	15	16	
25		17	18	19	20	21	22	23	
26		24	25	26	27	28	29	30	
27	TAMMUZ 5869	1	2	3	4	5	6	7	Fri $4^h51^m17^p$
28		8	9	10	11	12	13	14	
29		15	16	17	18	19	20	21	
30		22	23	24	25	26	27	28	
31	AV 5869	29	1	2	3	4	5	6	Sat $17^h36^m0^p$
32		7	8	9[i]	10	11	12	13	
33		14	15	16	17	18	19	20	
34		21	22	23	24	25	26	27	
35	ELUL 5869	28	29	30	1	2	3	4	Mon $6^h20^m1^p$
36		5	6	7	8	9	10	11	
37		12	13	14	15	16	17	18	
38		19	20	21	22	23	24	25	
39	TISHRI 5870	26	27	28	29	1[a]	2[a]	3	Tue $19^h4^m2^p$
40		4	5	6	7	8	9	10[b]	
41		11	12	13	14	15[c]	16	17	
42		18	19	20	21	22	23	24	
43	HESHVAN 5870	25	26	27	28	29	30	1	Thu $7^h48^m3^p$
44		2	3	4	5	6	7	8	
45		9	10	11	12	13	14	15	
46		16	17	18	19	20	21	22	
47		23	24	25	26	27	28	29	
48	KISLEV 5870	1	2	3	4	5	6	7	Fri $20^h32^m4^p$
49		8	9	10	11	12	13[d]	14	
50		15	16	17	18	19	20	21	
51		22	23	24	25[e]	26[e]	27[e]	28[e]	
52	TEVETH 5870	29[e]	30[e]	1[e]	2[e]	3	4	5	Sun $9^h16^m5^p$
1		6	7	8	9	10	11	12	

CHINESE Wù-Chén/Jǐ-Sì‡ · Solar Term

ISO Week	Month	Sun	Mon	Tue	Wed	Thu	Fri	Sat	Solar Term
1	MONTH 12 Wù-Chén	28	29	1	2	3	4	*5*	Xiǎo hán
2		6	7	8	9	10	11	12	
3		13	14	15	16	17	18	19	
4		***20***	21	22	23	24	25	26	Dà hán
5	MONTH 1 Jǐ-Sì	27	28	29	30	1[a]	2	3	
6		4	5*	6	7	8	9	10	Lì chūn
7		11	12	13	14	15[b]	16	17	
8		18	19	***20***	21	22	23	24	Yǔ shuǐ
9	MONTH 2 Jǐ-Sì	25	26	27	28	29	30	1	
10		2	3	4	*5*	6	7	8	Jīng zhé
11		9	10	11	12	13	14	15	
12		16	17	18	19	***20***	21	22	Chūn fēn
13		23	24	25	26	27	28	29	
14	MONTH 3 Jǐ-Sì	1	2	3	4	5	6[c]*	7	Qīng míng
15		8	9	10	11	12	13	14	
16		15	16	17	18	19	20	***21***	Gǔ yǔ
17		22	23	24	25	26	27	28	
18	MONTH 4 Jǐ-Sì	29	30	1	2	3	4	5	
19		6	7	8	9	10	11	12	Lì xià
20		13	14	15	16	17	18	19	
21		20	21	***22***	23	24	25	26	Xiǎo mǎn
22	MONTH 5 Jǐ-Sì	27	28	29	30	1	2	3	
23		4	5[d]	6*	7	*8*	9	10	Máng zhòng
24		11	12	13	14	15	16	17	
25		18	19	20	21	22	***23***	24	Xià zhì
26	MONTH 6 Jǐ-Sì	25	26	27	28	29	1	2	
27		3	4	5	6	7	8	9	
28		*10*	11	12	13	14	15	16	Xiǎo shǔ
29		17	18	19	20	21	22	23	
30		24	25	***26***	27	28	29	30	Dà shǔ
31	MONTH 7 Jǐ-Sì	1	2	3	4	5	6	7[e]*	
32		8	9	10	*11*	12	13	14	Lì qiū
33		15[f]	16	17	18	19	20	21	
34		22	23	24	25	26	***27***	28	Chǔ shǔ
35	MONTH 8 Jǐ-Sì	29	1	2	3	4	5	6	
36		7	8	9	10	11	12	13	
37		*14*	15[g]	16	17	18	19	20	Bái lù
38		21	22	23	24	25	26	27	
39	MONTH 9 Jǐ-Sì	28	***29***	30	1	2	3	4	Qiū fēn
40		5	6	7	8*	9[h]	10	11	
41		12	13	*14*	15	16	17	18	Hán lù
42		19	20	21	22	23	24	25	
43	LEAP MONTH 9 Jǐ-Sì	26	27	28	***29***	1	2	3	Shuāng jiàng
44		4	5	6	7	8	9	10	
45		11	12	13	14	*15*	16	17	Lì dōng
46		18	19	20	21	22	23	24	
47	MONTH 10 Jǐ-Sì	25	26	27	28	29	***1***	2	Xiǎo xuě
48		3	4	5	6	7	8	9	
49		10*	11	12	13	14	15	*16*	Dà xuě
50		17	18	19	20	21	22	23	
51		24	25	26	27	28	29	30	
52	MONTH 11 Jǐ-Sì	***1***[i]	2	3	4	5	6	7	Dōng zhì
1		8	9	10	11	12	13	14	

COPTIC 1825/1826 · ETHIOPIC 2101/2102

ISO Week	Coptic Month	Sun	Mon	Tue	Wed	Thu	Fri	Sat	Ethiopic Month
1	KOIAK 1825	20	21	22	23	24	25	26	TĀKHŚĀŚ 2101
2	TÔBE 1825	27	28	29[c]	30	1	2	3	ṬER 2101
3		4	5	6[d]	7	8	9	10	
4		11[e]	12	13	14	15	16	17	
5		18	19	20	21	22	23	24	
6	MESHIR 1825	25	26	27	28	29	30	1	YAKĀTIT 2101
7		2	3	4	5	6	7	8	
8		9	10	11	12	13	14	15	
9		16	17	18	19	20	21	22	
10		23	24	25	26	27	28	29	
11	PAREMOTEP 1825	30	1	2	3	4	5	6	MAGĀBIT 2101
12		7	8	9	10	11	12	13	
13		14	15	16	17	18	19	20	
14		21	22	23	24	25	26	27	
15	PARMOUTE 1825	28	29	30	1	2	3	4	MIYĀZYĀ 2101
16		5	6	7	8	9	10	11	
17		12[f]	13	14	15	16	17	18	
18		19	20	21	22	23	24	25	
19	PASHONS 1825	26	27	28	29[g]	30	1	2	GENBOT 2101
20		3	4	5	6	7	8	9	
21		10	11	12	13	14	15	16	
22		17	18	19	20	21	22	23	
23		24	25	26	27	28	29	30	
24	PAÔNE 1825	1	2	3	4	5	6	7	SANĒ 2101
25		8	9	10	11	12	13	14	
26		15	16	17	18	19	20	21	
27		22	23	24	25	26	27	28	
28	EPÊP 1825	29	30	1	2	3	4	5	ḤAMLĒ 2101
29		6	7	8	9	10	11	12	
30		13	14	15	16	17	18	19	
31		20	21	22	23	24	25	26	
32	MESORÊ 1825	27	28	29	30	1	2	3	NAḤASĒ 2101
33		4	5	6	7	8	9	10	
34		11	12	13[h]	14	15	16	17	
35		18	19	20	21	22	23	24	
36	EPAG. 1825	25	26	27	28	29	30	1	PĀG. 2101
37	THOOUT 1826	2	3	4	5	1[a]	2	3	MASKARAM 2102
38		4	5	6	7	8	9	10	
39		11	12	13	14	15	16	17[b]	
40		18	19	20	21	22	23	24	
41	PAOPE 1826	25	26	27	28	29	30	1	ṬEQEMT 2102
42		2	3	4	5	6	7	8	
43		9	10	11	12	13	14	15	
44		16	17	18	19	20	21	22	
45		23	24	25	26	27	28	29	
46	ATHÔR 1826	30	1	2	3	4	5	6	HEDĀR 2102
47		7	8	9	10	11	12	13	
48		14	15	16	17	18	19	20	
49		21	22	23	24	25	26	27	
50	KOIAK 1826	28	29	30	1	2	3	4	TĀKHŚĀŚ 2102
51		5	6	7	8	9	10	11	
52		12	13	14	15	16	17	18	
1		19	20	21	22	23	24	25	

Gregorian notes:
[a]New Year
[b]Spring (17:34)
[c]Summer (9:54)
[d]Autumn (2:18)
[e]Winter (0:26)
● New moon
◐ First quarter moon
○ Full moon
◑ Last quarter moon

Hebrew notes:
‡Leap year
[a]New Year
[b]Yom Kippur
[c]Sukkot
[d]Winter starts
[e]Ḥanukkah
[f]Purim
[g]Passover
[h]Shavuot
[i]Fast of Av

Chinese notes:
‡Leap year
[a]New Year (4807, Snake)
[b]Lantern Festival
[c]Qīngmíng
[d]Dragon Festival
[e]Qīqiǎo
[f]Hungry Ghosts
[g]Mid-Autumn Festival
[h]Double-Ninth Festival
[i]Dōngzhì
*Start of 60-name cycle

Coptic/Ethiopic notes:
[a]New Year
[b]Building of the Cross
[c]Christmas
[d]Jesus's Circumcision
[e]Epiphany
[f]Easter
[g]Mary's Announcement
[h]Jesus's Transfiguration

2109

Persian (Astronomical) 1487/1488

Month	Sun	Mon	Tue	Wed	Thu	Fri	Sat
DEY 1487	9	10	11	12	13	14	15
	16	17	18	19	20	21	22
	23	24	25	26	27	28	29
BAHMAN 1487	30	1	2	3	4	5	6
	7	8	9	10	11	12	13
	14	15	16	17	18	19	20
	21	22	23	24	25	26	27
ESFAND 1487	28	29	30	1	2	3	4
	5	6	7	8	9	10	11
	12	13	14	15	16	17	18
	19	20	21	22	23	24	25
FARVARDĪN 1488	26	27	28	29	1[a]	2	3
	4	5	6	7	8	9	10
	11	12	13[b]	14	15	16	17
	18	19	20	21	22	23	24
	25	26	27	28	29	30	31
ORDĪBEHEŠT 1488	1	2	3	4	5	6	7
	8	9	10	11	12	13	14
	15	16	17	18	19	20	21
	22	23	24	25	26	27	28
XORDĀD 1488	29	30	31	1	2	3	4
	5	6	7	8	9	10	11
	12	13	14	15	16	17	18
	19	20	21	22	23	24	25
TĪR 1488	26	27	28	29	30	31	1
	2	3	4	5	6	7	8
	9	10	11	12	13	14	15
	16	17	18	19	20	21	22
	23	24	25	26	27	28	29
MORDĀD 1488	30	31	1	2	3	4	5
	6	7	8	9	10	11	12
	13	14	15	16	17	18	19
	20	21	22	23	24	25	26
SHAHRĪVAR 1488	27	28	29	30	31	1	2
	3	4	5	6	7	8	9
	10	11	12	13	14	15	16
	17	18	19	20	21	22	23
	24	25	26	27	28	29	30
MEHR 1488	31	1	2	3	4	5	6
	7	8	9	10	11	12	13
	14	15	16	17	18	19	20
	21	22	23	24	25	26	27
ĀBĀN 1488	28	29	30	1	2	3	4
	5	6	7	8	9	10	11
	12	13	14	15	16	17	18
	19	20	21	22	23	24	25
ĀZAR 1488	26	27	28	29	30	1	2
	3	4	5	6	7	8	9
	10	11	12	13	14	15	16
	17	18	19	20	21	22	23
	24	25	26	27	28	29	30
DEY 1488	1	2	3	4	5	6	7
	8	9	10	11	12	13	14

[a]New Year
[b]Sizdeh Bedar

Hindu Lunar 2165/2166

Month	Sun	Mon	Tue	Wed	Thu	Fri	Sat
PAUSHA 2165	28	29	30	1	2	3	4
	5	6	7	8	9	10	11
	12	13	14	15	16	17	18
	19	20	21	22	23	24	25
MĀGHA 2165	26	**27**	29	30	1	2	3
	3	4	5	6	7	8	9
	10	11	12	13	14	15	16
	17	18	19	**20**	22	23	24
PHĀLGUNA 2165	25	26	27	28[h]	29	30	1
	2	3	4	5	5	6	7
	8	9	10	11	12	13	**14**[i]
	16	17	18	19	20	21	22
	23	24	25	26	27	28	29
CHAITRA 2166	30	1[a]	2	3	4	5	6
	7	8	9[b]	10	11	12	13
	14	15	16	17	18	**19**	21
	22	23	24	25	26	27	28
VAIŚĀKHA 2166	29	29	30	1	2	3	4
	5	6	7	8	9	10	11
	12	14	15	16	17	18	19
	20	21	22	23	24	25	26
JYAISHṬHA 2166	27	28	29	30	1	2	3
	4	5	6	7	8	9	10
	11	12	13	14	**15**	17	18
	19	20	21	22	23	24	25
ĀSHĀḌHA 2166	25	26	27	28	29	30	1
	2	3	4	5	6	7	**8**
	10	11	12	13	14	15	16
	17	18	19	20	21	22	23
	24	25	26	27	28	29	30
ŚRĀVAṆA 2166	1	2	3	4	5	6	7
	8	9	10	**11**	13	14	15
	16	17	18	19	20	21	22
	22	23[c]	24	25	26	27	28
BHĀDRAPADA 2166	29	30	1	2	**3**[d]	5	6
	7	8	9	10	11	12	13
	14	15	16	17	18	19	20
	21	22	23	24	25	26	27
ĀŚVINA 2166	28	29	30	1	2	3	4
	5	6	**7**[e]	9[e]	10[e]	11	12
	13	14	15	16	17	17	18
	19	20	21	22	23	24	25
KĀRTTIKA 2166	26	27	28	29	**30**[f]	2	3
	4	5	6	7	8	9	10
	11	12	13	14	15	16	17
	18	19	20	21	22	22	24
MĀRGAŚĪRA 2166	25	26	27	28	29	30	1
	2	3	4	5	**6**	8	9
	10	11	11[g]	12	13	14	15
	16	17	18	19	20	21	22
	23	24	25	26	27	**28**	30
PAUSHA 2166	1	2	3	4	5	6	7
	8	9	10	11	12	13	13

[a]New Year (Śukla)
[b]Birthday of Rāma
[c]Birthday of Krishna
[d]Ganēśa Chaturthī
[e]Dashara
[f]Diwali
[g]Birthday of Vishnu
[h]Night of Śiva
[i]Holi

Hindu Solar 2030/2031

Month	Sun	Mon	Tue	Wed	Thu	Fri	Sat
PAUSHA 2030	14	15	16	17	18	19	20
	21	22	23	24	25	26	27
MĀGHA 2030	28	29	30	1[b]	2	3	4
	5	6	7	8	9	10	11
	12	13	14	15	16	17	18
	19	20	21	22	23	24	25
PHĀLGUNA 2030	26	27	28	29	1	2	3
	4	5	6	7	8	9	10
	11	12	13	14	15	16	17
	18	19	20	21	22	23	24
CHAITRA 2030	25	26	27	28	29	30	1
	2	3	4	5	6	7	8
	9	10	11	12	13	14	15
	16	17	18	19	20	21	22
	23	24	25	26	27	28	29
VAIŚĀKHA 2031	30	1[a]	2	3	4	5	6
	7	8	9	10	11	12	13
	14	15	16	17	18	19	20
	21	22	23	24	25	26	27
JYAISHṬHA 2031	28	29	30	31	1	2	3
	4	5	6	7	8	9	10
	11	12	13	14	15	16	17
	18	19	20	21	22	23	24
	25	26	27	28	29	30	31
ĀSHĀḌHA 2031	32	1	2	3	4	5	6
	7	8	9	10	11	12	13
	14	15	16	17	18	19	20
	21	22	23	24	25	26	27
ŚRĀVAṆA 2031	28	29	30	31	1	2	3
	4	5	6	7	8	9	10
	11	12	13	14	15	16	17
	18	19	20	21	22	23	24
	25	26	27	28	29	30	31
BHĀDRAPADA 2031	32	1	2	3	4	5	6
	7	8	9	10	11	12	13
	14	15	16	17	18	19	20
	21	22	23	24	25	26	27
ĀŚVINA 2031	28	29	30	31	1	2	3
	4	5	6	7	8	9	10
	11	12	13	14	15	16	17
	18	19	20	21	22	23	24
KĀRTTIKA 2031	25	26	27	28	29	30	1
	2	3	4	5	6	7	8
	9	10	11	12	13	14	15
	16	17	18	19	20	21	22
	23	24	25	26	27	28	29
MĀRGAŚĪRA 2031	30	1	2	3	4	5	6
	7	8	9	10	11	12	13
	14	15	16	17	18	19	20
	21	22	23	24	25	26	27
PAUSHA 2031	28	29	1	2	3	4	5
	6	7	8	9	10	11	12
	13	14	15	16	17	18	19

[a]New Year (Subhānu)
[b]Pongal

Islamic (Astronomical) 1533‡/1534

Month	Sun	Mon	Tue	Wed	Thu	Fri	Sat
ṢAFAR 1533	27	28	29	30	1	2	3
	4	5	6	7	8	9	10
	11	12	13	14	15	16	17
	18	19	20	21	22	23	24
RABĪ' I 1533	25	26	27	28	29	1	2
	3	4	5	6	7	8	9
	10	11	12[c]	13	14	15	16
	17	18	19	20	21	22	23
	24	25	26	27	28	29	30
RABĪ' II 1533	1	2	3	4	5	6	7
	8	9	10	11	12	13	14
	15	16	17	18	19	20	21
	22	23	24	25	26	27	28
JUMĀDĀ I 1533	29	30	1	2	3	4	5
	6	7	8	9	10	11	12
	13	14	15	16	17	18	19
	20	21	22	23	24	25	26
JUMĀDĀ II 1533	27	28	29	30	1	2	3
	4	5	6	7	8	9	10
	11	12	13	14	15	16	17
	18	19	20	21	22	23	24
RAJAB 1533	25	26	27	28	29	1	2
	3	4	5	6	7	8	9
	10	11	12	13	14	15	16
	17	18	19	20	21	22	23
	24	25	26	27[d]	28	29	30
SHA'BĀN 1533	1	2	3	4	5	6	7
	8	9	10	11	12	13	14
	15	16	17	18	19	20	21
	22	23	24	25	26	27	28
RAMAḌĀN 1533	29	30	1[e]	2	3	4	5
	6	7	8	9	10	11	12
	13	14	15	16	17	18	19
	20	21	22	23	24	25	26
SHAWWĀL 1533	27	28	29	1[f]	2	3	4
	5	6	7	8	9	10	11
	12	13	14	15	16	17	18
	19	20	21	22	23	24	25
DHU AL-QA'DA 1533	26	27	28	29	1	2	3
	4	5	6	7	8	9	10
	11	12	13	14	15	16	17
	18	19	20	21	22	23	24
DHU AL-ḤIJJA 1533	25	26	27	28	29	1	2
	3	4	5	6	7	8	9
	10[g]	11	12	13	14	15	16
	17	18	19	20	21	22	23
	24	25	26	27	28	29	30
MUḤARRAM 1534	1[a]	2	3	4	5	6	7
	8	9	10[b]	11	12	13	14
	15	16	17	18	19	20	21
	22	23	24	25	26	27	28
ṢAFAR 1534	29	1	2	3	4	5	6
	7	8	9	10	11	12	13

‡Leap year
[a]New Year
[b]'Ashūrā'
[c]Prophet's Birthday
[d]Ascent of the Prophet
[e]Start of Ramaḍān
[f]'Id al-Fiṭr
[g]'Id al-'Aḍḥā

Gregorian 2109

Julian (Sun)	Sun	Mon	Tue	Wed	Thu	Fri	Sat	Month
Dec 16	30	31	1	2	3	4	5	JANUARY 2109
	6	7	8[a]	9	10	11	12	
Dec 30	13	14	15[b]	16	17	18	19	
	20	21	22	23	24	25	26	
Jan 13	27	28	29	30	31	1	2	FEBRUARY 2109
	3	4	5	6	7	8	9	
Jan 27	10	11	12	13	14	15	16	
	17	18	19	20	21	22	23	
Feb 10	24	25	26	27	28	1	2	MARCH 2109
	3	4	5	6[c]	7	8	9	
Feb 24	10[d]	11	12	13	14	15	16	
	17	18	19	20	21	22	23	
Mar 10	24	25	26	27	28	29	30	
	31	1	2	3	4	5	6	APRIL 2109
Mar 24	7	8	9	10	11	12	13	
	14	15	16	17	18	19	20	
Apr 7	21[e]	22	23	24	25	26	27	
	28	29	30	1	2	3	4	MAY 2109
Apr 21	5	6	7	8	9	10	11	
	12	13	14	15	16	17	18	
May 5	19	20	21	22	23	24	25	
	26	27	28	29	30	31	1	JUNE 2109
May 19	2	3	4	5	6	7	8	
	9	10	11	12	13	14	15	
Jun 2	16	17	18	19	20	21	22	
	23	24	25	26	27	28	29	
Jun 16	30	1	2	3	4	5	6	JULY 2109
	7	8	9	10	11	12	13	
Jun 30	14	15	16	17	18	19	20	
	21	22	23	24	25	26	27	
Jul 14	28	29	30	31	1	2	3	AUGUST 2109
	4	5	6	7	8	9	10	
Jul 28	11	12	13	14	15	16	17	
	18	19	20	21	22	23	24	
Aug 11	25	26	27	28	29	30	31	
	1	2	3	4	5	6	7	SEPTEMBER 2109
Aug 25	8	9	10	11	12	13	14	
	15	16	17	18	19	20	21	
Sep 8	22	23	24	25	26	27	28	
	29	30	1	2	3	4	5	OCTOBER 2109
Sep 22	6	7	8	9	10	11	12	
	13	14	15	16	17	18	19	
Oct 6	20	21	22	23	24	25	26	
	27	28	29	30	31	1	2	NOVEMBER 2109
Oct 20	3	4	5	6	7	8	9	
	10	11	12	13	14	15	16	
Nov 3	17	18	19	20	21	22	23	
	24	25	26	27	28	29	30	
Nov 17	1[g]	2	3	4	5	6	7	DECEMBER 2109
	8	9	10	11	12	13	14	
Dec 1	15	16	17	18	19	20	21	
	22	23	24	25[h]	26	27	28	
Dec 15	29	30	31	1	2	3	4	

[a]Orthodox Christmas
[b]Julian New Year
[c]Ash Wednesday
[d]Feast of Orthodoxy
[e]Easter (also Orthodox)
[g]Advent
[h]Christmas

2110

GREGORIAN 2110	Sun	Mon	Tue	Wed	Thu	Fri	Sat	Lunar Phases	ISO WEEK (Mon)	JULIAN DAY (Sun noon)
JANUARY 2110	◐	30	31	1[a]	2	3	4	1:29	1	2491719
	5	○	7	8	9	10	11	6:10	2	2491726
	12	◑	14	15	16	17	18	18:07	3	2491733
	19	●	21	22	23	24	25	10:17	4	2491740
FEBRUARY 2110	26	◐	28	29	30	31	1	21:55	5	2491747
	2	3	○	5	6	7	8	23:13	6	2491754
	9	10	11	◑	13	14	15	2:24	7	2491761
	16	17	●	19	20	21	22	23:22	8	2491768
MARCH 2110	23	24	25	◐	27	28	1	19:09	9	2491775
	2	3	4	5	○	7	8	13:44	10	2491782
	9	10	11	12	◑	14	15	9:29	11	2491789
	16	17	18	19	●[b]	21	22	13:43	12	2491796
	23	24	25	26	27	◐	29	15:19	13	2491803
APRIL 2110	30	31	1	2	3	4	○	1:19	14	2491810
	6	7	8	9	10	◑	12	16:35	15	2491817
	13	14	15	16	17	18	●	4:53	16	2491824
	20	21	22	23	24	25	26		17	2491831
MAY 2110	◐	28	29	30	1	2	3	8:56	18	2491838
	○	5	6	7	8	9	10	10:18	19	2491845
	◑	12	13	14	15	16	17	0:46	20	2491852
	●	19	20	21	22	23	24	20:21	21	2491859
	25	◐	27	28	29	30	31	23:08	22	2491866
JUNE 2110	1	○	3	4	5	6	7	17:35	23	2491873
	8	◑	10	11	12	13	14	10:48	24	2491880
	15	16	●	18	19	20	21[c]	11:44	25	2491887
	22	23	24	◐	26	27	28	9:46	26	2491894
JULY 2110	29	30	1	○	3	4	5	0:21	27	2491901
	6	7	◑	9	10	11	12	23:08	28	2491908
	13	14	15	16	●	18	19	2:40	29	2491915
	20	21	22	23	◐	25	26	17:24	30	2491922
AUGUST 2110	27	28	29	30	○	1	2	7:45	31	2491929
	3	4	5	6	◑	8	9	13:53	32	2491936
	10	11	12	13	14	●	16	16:43	33	2491943
	17	18	19	20	21	◐	23	23:09	34	2491950
	24	25	26	27	28	○	30	16:44	35	2491957
SEPTEMBER 2110	31	1	2	3	4	5	◑	7:00	36	2491964
	7	8	9	10	11	12	13		37	2491971
	●	15	16	17	18	19	20	5:33	38	2491978
	◐	22	23[d]	24	25	26	27	4:25	39	2491985
OCTOBER 2110	○	29	30	1	2	3	4	4:02	40	2491992
	5	◑	7	8	9	10	11	1:57	41	2491999
	12	●	14	15	16	17	18	17:08	42	2492006
	19	◐	21	22	23	24	25	10:41	43	2492013
NOVEMBER 2110	26	○	28	29	30	31	1	18:05	44	2492020
	2	3	◑	5	6	7	8	21:34	45	2492027
	9	10	11	●	13	14	15	3:52	46	2492034
	16	17	◐	19	20	21	22	19:13	47	2492041
	23	24	25	○	27	28	29	10:55	48	2492048
DECEMBER 2110	30	1	2	3	◑	5	6	16:09	49	2492055
	7	8	9	10	●	12	13	14:20	50	2492062
	14	15	16	17	◐	19	20	6:49	51	2492069
	21	22[e]	23	24	25	○	27	5:57	52	2492076
	28	29	30	31	1	2	◑	8:09	1	2492083

ISO WEEK	HEBREW 5870/5871‡	Sun	Mon	Tue	Wed	Thu	Fri	Sat	Molad
1	TEVETH 5870	6	7	8	9	10	11	12	
2		13	14	15	16	17	18	19	
3		20	21	22	23	24	25	26	
4	SHEVAT 5870	27	28	29	1	2	3	4	Mon 22h0m6p
5		5	6	7	8	9	10	11	
6		12	13	14	15	16	17	18	
7		19	20	21	22	23	24	25	
8	ADAR 5870	26	27	28	29	30	1	2	Wed 10h44m7p
9		3	4	5	6	7	8	9	
10		10	11	12	13	14[f]	15	16	
11		17	18	19	20	21	22	23	
12	NISAN 5870	24	25	26	27	28	29	1	Thu 23h28m8p
13		2	3	4	5	6	7	8	
14		9	10	11	12	13	14	15[g]	
15		16	17	18	19	20	21	22	
16		23	24	25	26	27	28	29	
17	IYYAR 5870	30	1	2	3	4	5	6	Sat 12h12m9p
18		7	8	9	10	11	12	13	
19		14	15	16	17	18	19	20	
20		21	22	23	24	25	26	27	
21	SIVAN 5870	28	29	1	2	3	4	5	Mon 0h56m10p
22		6[h]	7	8	9	10	11	12	
23		13	14	15	16	17	18	19	
24		20	21	22	23	24	25	26	
25	TAMMUZ 5870	27	28	29	30	1	2	3	Tue 13h40m11p
26		4	5	6	7	8	9	10	
27		11	12	13	14	15	16	17	
28		18	19	20	21	22	23	24	
29	AV 5870	25	26	27	28	29	1	2	Thu 2h24m12p
30		3	4	5	6	7	8	9	
31		10[i]	11	12	13	14	15	16	
32		17	18	19	20	21	22	23	
33		24	25	26	27	28	29	30	
34	ELUL 5870	1	2	3	4	5	6	7	Fri 15h8m13p
35		8	9	10	11	12	13	14	
36		15	16	17	18	19	20	21	
37		22	23	24	25	26	27	28	
38	TISHRI 5871	29	1[a]	2[a]	3	4	5	6	Sun 3h52m14p
39		7	8	9	10[b]	11	12	13	
40		14	15[c]	16	17	18	19	20	
41		21	22	23	24	25	26	27	
42	ḤESHVAN 5871	28	29	30	1	2	3	4	Mon 16h36m15p
43		5	6	7	8	9	10	11	
44		12	13	14	15	16	17	18	
45		19	20	21	22	23	24	25	
46	KISLEV 5871	26	27	28	29	1	2	3	Wed 5h20m16p
47		4	5	6	7	8	9	10	
48		11	12	13	14	15	16	17	
49		18	19	20	21	22	23	24[d]	
50	TEVETH 5871	25[e]	26[e]	27[e]	28[e]	29[e]	1[e]	2[e]	Thu 18h4m17p
51		3[e]	4	5	6	7	8	9	
52		10	11	12	13	14	15	16	
1		17	18	19	20	21	22	23	

ISO WEEK	CHINESE Jǐ-Sì‡/Gēng-Wǔ	Sun	Mon	Tue	Wed	Thu	Fri	Sat	Solar Term
1	MONTH 11 Jǐ-Sì	8	9	10	11	12	13	14	
2		15	16	17	18	19	20	21	Xiǎo hán
3		22	23	24	25	26	27	28	
4	MONTH 12 Jǐ-Sì	29	1	2	3	4	5	6	Dà hán
5		7	8	9	10	11*	12	13	
6		14	15	16	17	18	19	20	Lì chūn
7		21	22	23	24	25	26	27	
8	MONTH 1 Gēng-Wǔ	28	29	30	1[a]	2	3	4	Yǔ shuǐ
9		5	6	7	8	9	10	11	
10		12	13	14	15[b]	16	17	18	Jīng zhé
11		19	20	21	22	23	24	25	
12	MONTH 2 Gēng-Wǔ	26	27	28	29	1	2	3	Chūn fēn
13		4	5	6	7	8	9	10	
14		11	12*	13	14	15	16	17[c]	Qīng míng
15		18	19	20	21	22	23	24	
16	MONTH 3 Gēng-Wǔ	25	26	27	28	29	30	1	
17		2	3	4	5	6	7	8	Gǔ yǔ
18		9	10	11	12	13	14	15	
19		16	17	18	19	20	21	22	Lì xià
20		23	24	25	26	27	28	29	
21	MONTH 4 Gēng-Wǔ	30	1	2	3	4	5	6	Xiǎo mǎn
22		7	8	9	10	11	12*	13	
23		14	15	16	17	18	19	20	Máng zhòng
24		21	22	23	24	25	26	27	
25	MONTH 5 Gēng-Wǔ	28	29	1	2	3	4	5[d]	Xià zhì
26		6	7	8	9	10	11	12	
27		13	14	15	16	17	18	19	
28		20	21	22	23	24	25	26	Xiǎo shǔ
29	MONTH 6 Gēng-Wǔ	27	28	29	30	1	2	3	
30		4	5	6	7	8	9	10	Dà shǔ
31		11	12	13*	14	15	16	17	
32		18	19	20	21	22	23	24	Lì qiū
33	MONTH 7 Gēng-Wǔ	25	26	27	28	29	30	1	
34		2	3	4	5	6	7[e]	8	Chǔ shǔ
35		9	10	11	12	13	14	15[f]	
36		16	17	18	19	20	21	22	
37		23	24	25	26	27	28	29	Bái lù
38	MONTH 8 Gēng-Wǔ	1	2	3	4	5	6	7	
39		8	9	10	11	12	13	14*	Qiū fēn
40		15[g]	16	17	18	19	20	21	
41		22	23	24	25	26	27	28	Hán lù
42	MONTH 9 Gēng-Wǔ	29	30	1	2	3	4	5	
43		6	7	8	9[h]	10	11	12	Shuāng jiàng
44		13	14	15	16	17	18	19	
45		20	21	22	23	24	25	26	Lì dōng
46	MONTH 10 Gēng-Wǔ	27	28	29	1	2	3	4	
47		5	6	7	8	9	10	11	
48		12	13	14	15*	16	17	18	Xiǎo xuě
49		19	20	21	22	23	24	25	
50	MONTH 11 Gēng-Wǔ	26	27	28	29	1	2	3	Dà xuě
51		4	5	6	7	8	9	10	
52		11	12[i]	13	14	15	16	17	Dōng zhì
1		18	19	20	21	22	23	24	

ISO WEEK	COPTIC 1826/1827‡	Sun	Mon	Tue	Wed	Thu	Fri	Sat	ETHIOPIC 2102/2103‡
1	KOIAK 1826	19	20	21	22	23	24	25	TĀKHŚĀŚ 2102
2		26	27	28	29[c]	30	1	2	
3	TÔBE 1826	3	4	5	6[d]	7	8	9	ṬER 2102
4		10	11[e]	12	13	14	15	16	
5		17	18	19	20	21	22	23	
6		24	25	26	27	28	29	30	
7	MESHIR 1826	1	2	3	4	5	6	7	YAKĀTIT 2102
8		8	9	10	11	12	13	14	
9		15	16	17	18	19	20	21	
10		22	23	24	25	26	27	28	
11	PAREMOTEP 1826	29	30	1	2	3	4	5	MAGĀBIT 2102
12		6	7	8	9	10	11	12	
13		13	14	15	16	17	18	19	
14		20	21	22	23	24	25	26	
15	PARMOUTE 1826	27	28	29	30	1	2	3	MIYĀZYĀ 2102
16		4[f]	5	6	7	8	9	10	
17		11	12	13	14	15	16	17	
18		18	19	20	21	22	23	24	
19	PASHONS 1826	25	26	27	28	29[g]	30	1	GENBOT 2102
20		2	3	4	5	6	7	8	
21		9	10	11	12	13	14	15	
22		16	17	18	19	20	21	22	
23		23	24	25	26	27	28	29	
24	PAÔNE 1826	30	1	2	3	4	5	6	SANĒ 2102
25		7	8	9	10	11	12	13	
26		14	15	16	17	18	19	20	
27		21	22	23	24	25	26	27	
28	EPÊP 1826	28	29	30	1	2	3	4	ḤAMLĒ 2102
29		5	6	7	8	9	10	11	
30		12	13	14	15	16	17	18	
31		19	20	21	22	23	24	25	
32	MESORĒ 1826	26	27	28	29	30	1	2	NAHASĒ 2102
33		3	4	5	6	7	8	9	
34		10	11	12	13[h]	14	15	16	
35		17	18	19	20	21	22	23	
36		24	25	26	27	28	29	30	
37	EPAG. 1826 / THOOUT 1827	1	2	3	4	5	1[a]	2	PĀG. 2102 / MASKARAM 2103
38		3	4	5	6	7	8	9	
39		10	11	12	13	14	15	16	
40		17[b]	18	19	20	21	22	23	
41		24	25	26	27	28	29	30	
42	PAOPE 1827	1	2	3	4	5	6	7	TEQEMT 2103
43		8	9	10	11	12	13	14	
44		15	16	17	18	19	20	21	
45		22	23	24	25	26	27	28	
46	ATHÔR 1827	29	30	1	2	3	4	5	ḤEDĀR 2103
47		6	7	8	9	10	11	12	
48		13	14	15	16	17	18	19	
49		20	21	22	23	24	25	26	
50	KOIAK 1827	27	28	29	30	1	2	3	TĀKHŚĀŚ 2103
51		4	5	6	7	8	9	10	
52		11	12	13	14	15	16	17	
1		18	19	20	21	22	23	24	

[a]New Year
[b]Spring (23:20)
[c]Summer (15:31)
[d]Autumn (8:06)
[e]Winter (6:17)
● New moon
◐ First quarter moon
○ Full moon
◑ Last quarter moon

‡Leap year
[a]New Year
[b]Yom Kippur
[c]Sukkot
[d]Winter starts
[e]Ḥanukkah
[f]Purim
[g]Passover
[h]Shavuot
[i]Fast of Av

‡Leap year
[a]New Year (4808, Horse)
[b]Lantern Festival
[c]Qīngmíng
[d]Dragon Festival
[e]Qīqiǎo
[f]Hungry Ghosts
[g]Mid-Autumn Festival
[h]Double-Ninth Festival
[i]Dōngzhì
*Start of 60-name cycle

‡Leap year
[a]New Year
[b]Building of the Cross
[c]Christmas
[d]Jesus's Circumcision
[e]Epiphany
[f]Easter
[g]Mary's Announcement
[h]Jesus's Transfiguration

PERSIAN (ASTRONOMICAL) 1488/1489

Month	Sun	Mon	Tue	Wed	Thu	Fri	Sat
DEY 1488	8	9	10	11	12	13	14
	15	16	17	18	19	20	21
	22	23	24	25	26	27	28
	29	30	1	2	3	4	5
BAHMAN 1488	6	7	8	9	10	11	12
	13	14	15	16	17	18	19
	20	21	22	23	24	25	26
	27	28	29	30	1	2	3
ESFAND 1488	4	5	6	7	8	9	10
	11	12	13	14	15	16	17
	18	19	20	21	22	23	24
	25	26	27	28	29	1[a]	2
FARVARDIN 1489	3	4	5	6	7	8	9
	10	11	12	13[b]	14	15	16
	17	18	19	20	21	22	23
	24	25	26	27	28	29	30
	31	1	2	3	4	5	6
ORDIBEHEST 1489	7	8	9	10	11	12	13
	14	15	16	17	18	19	20
	21	22	23	24	25	26	27
	28	29	30	31	1	2	3
XORDAD 1489	4	5	6	7	8	9	10
	11	12	13	14	15	16	17
	18	19	20	21	22	23	24
	25	26	27	28	29	30	31
TIR 1489	1	2	3	4	5	6	7
	8	9	10	11	12	13	14
	15	16	17	18	19	20	21
	22	23	24	25	26	27	28
	29	30	31	1	2	3	4
MORDAD 1489	5	6	7	8	9	10	11
	12	13	14	15	16	17	18
	19	20	21	22	23	24	25
	26	27	28	29	30	31	1
SHAHRIVAR 1489	2	3	4	5	6	7	8
	9	10	11	12	13	14	15
	16	17	18	19	20	21	22
	23	24	25	26	27	28	29
	30	31	1	2	3	4	5
MEHR 1489	6	7	8	9	10	11	12
	13	14	15	16	17	18	19
	20	21	22	23	24	25	26
	27	28	29	30	1	2	3
ABAN 1489	4	5	6	7	8	9	10
	11	12	13	14	15	16	17
	18	19	20	21	22	23	24
	25	26	27	28	29	30	1
AZAR 1489	2	3	4	5	6	7	8
	9	10	11	12	13	14	15
	16	17	18	19	20	21	22
	23	24	25	26	27	28	29
	30	1	2	3	4	5	6
DEY 1489	7	8	9	10	11	12	13

[a]New Year
[b]Sizdeh Bedar

HINDU LUNAR 2166/2167‡

Month	Sun	Mon	Tue	Wed	Thu	Fri	Sat
PAUSHA 2166	8	9	10	11	12	13	13
	14	15	16	17	18	19	20
	21	22	**23**	25	26	27	28
	29	30	1	2	3	4	5
MĀGHA 2166	6	7	8	9	10	11	12
	13	14	15	16	17	18	19
	20	21	22	23	24	25	26
	27	**28**[h]	30	1	2	3	4
PHĀLGUNA 2166	5	6	6	7	8	9	10
	11	12	13	14	15[i]	16	17
	18	19	20	**21**	23	24	25
	26	27	28	29	30	1[a]	2
CHAITRA 2167	3	4	5	6	7	8	8[b]
	9	10	11	12	13	14	**15**
	17	18	19	20	21	22	23
	24	25	26	27	28	29	30
VAIŚĀKHA 2167	1	2	3	4	5	6	7
	8	9	10	11	12	13	14
	15	16	17	18	**19**	21	22
	23	24	25	26	27	28	29
	30	1	2	3	3	4	5
JYAISHṬHA 2167	6	7	8	9	10	11	**12**
	14	15	16	17	18	19	20
	21	22	23	24	25	26	27
	28	29	30	1	2	3	4
LEAP ĀSHĀḌHA 2167	5	6	7	8	9	10	11
	12	13	14	**15**	17	18	19
	20	21	22	23	24	25	26
	27	28	29	30	30	1	2
ĀSHĀḌHA 2167	3	4	5	6	**7**	9	10
	11	12	13	14	15	16	17
	18	19	20	21	22	23	24
	25	26	27	28	29	30	1
ŚRĀVAṆA 2167	2	3	4	5	6	7	8
	9	10	**11**	13	14	15	16
	17	18	19	20	21	22	23[c]
	24	25	26	26	27	28	29
	30	1	2	3[d]	5	6	7
BHĀDRAPADA 2167	8	9	10	11	12	13	14
	15	16	17	18	19	20	21
	22	23	24	25	26	27	28
	29	30	1	2	3	4	5
ĀŚVINA 2167	6	7[e]	9[e]	10[e]	11	12	13
	14	15	16	17	18	19	20
	21	21	22	23	24	25	26
	27	28	29	30	1[f]	3	4
KĀRTTIKA 2167	5	6	7	8	9	10	11
	12	13	14	15	16	17	18
	19	20	21	22	23	24	25
	26	27	28	29	30	1	2
MĀRGAŚĪRA 2167	3	4	5	**6**	8	9	10
	11[g]	12	13	14	14	15	16
	17	18	19	20	21	22	23

‡Leap year
[a]New Year (Pramoda)
[b]Birthday of Rāma
[c]Birthday of Krishna
[d]Ganēśa Chaturthī
[e]Dashara
[f]Diwali
[g]Birthday of Vishnu
[h]Night of Śiva
[i]Holi

HINDU SOLAR 2031/2032‡

Month	Sun	Mon	Tue	Wed	Thu	Fri	Sat
PAUSHA 2031	13	14	15	16	17	18	19
	20	21	22	23	24	25	26
	27	28	29	30	1[b]	2	3
MĀGHA 2031	4	5	6	7	8	9	10
	11	12	13	14	15	16	17
	18	19	20	21	22	23	24
	25	26	27	28	29	1	2
PHĀLGUNA 2031	3	4	5	6	7	8	9
	10	11	12	13	14	15	16
	17	18	19	20	21	22	23
	24	25	26	27	28	29	30
CHAITRA 2031	1	2	3	4	5	6	7
	8	9	10	11	12	13	14
	15	16	17	18	19	20	21
	22	23	24	25	26	27	28
	29	30	1[a]	2	3	4	5
VAIŚĀKHA 2032	6	7	8	9	10	11	12
	13	14	15	16	17	18	19
	20	21	22	23	24	25	26
	27	28	29	30	31	1	2
JYAISHṬHA 2032	3	4	5	6	7	8	9
	10	11	12	13	14	15	16
	17	18	19	20	21	22	23
	24	25	26	27	28	29	30
	31	32	1	2	3	4	5
ĀSHĀḌHA 2032	6	7	8	9	10	11	12
	13	14	15	16	17	18	19
	20	21	22	23	24	25	26
	27	28	29	30	31	1	2
ŚRĀVAṆA 2032	3	4	5	6	7	8	9
	10	11	12	13	14	15	16
	17	18	19	20	21	22	23
	24	25	26	27	28	29	30
	31	32	1	2	3	4	5
BHĀDRAPADA 2032	6	7	8	9	10	11	12
	13	14	15	16	17	18	19
	20	21	22	23	24	25	26
	27	28	29	30	31	1	2
ĀŚVINA 2032	3	4	5	6	7	8	9
	10	11	12	13	14	15	16
	17	18	19	20	21	22	23
	24	25	26	27	28	29	30
KĀRTTIKA 2032	1	2	3	4	5	6	7
	8	9	10	11	12	13	14
	15	16	17	18	19	20	21
	22	23	24	25	26	27	28
MĀRGAŚĪRA 2032	29	30	1	2	3	4	5
	6	7	8	9	10	11	12
	13	14	15	16	17	18	19
	20	21	22	23	24	25	26
	27	28	29	30	1	2	3
PAUSHA 2032	4	5	6	7	8	9	10
	11	12	13	14	15	16	17

‡Leap year
[a]New Year (Tāraṇa)
[b]Pongal

ISLAMIC (ASTRONOMICAL) 1534/1535‡

Month	Sun	Mon	Tue	Wed	Thu	Fri	Sat
ṢAFAR 1534	7	8	9	10	11	12	13
	14	15	16	17	18	19	20
	21	22	23	24	25	26	27
	28	29	30	1	2	3	4
RABĪ' I 1534	5	6	7	8	9	10	11
	12[c]	13	14	15	16	17	18
	19	20	21	22	23	24	25
	26	27	28	29	1	2	3
RABĪ' II 1534	4	5	6	7	8	9	10
	11	12	13	14	15	16	17
	18	19	20	21	22	23	24
	25	26	27	28	29	30	1
JUMĀDĀ I 1534	2	3	4	5	6	7	8
	9	10	11	12	13	14	15
	16	17	18	19	20	21	22
	23	24	25	26	27	28	29
	30	1	2	3	4	5	6
JUMĀDĀ II 1534	7	8	9	10	11	12	13
	14	15	16	17	18	19	20
	21	22	23	24	25	26	27
	28	29	1	2	3	4	5
RAJAB 1534	6	7	8	9	10	11	12
	13	14	15	16	17	18	19
	20	21	22	23	24	25	26
	27[d]	28	29	30	1	2	3
SHA'BĀN 1534	4	5	6	7	8	9	10
	11	12	13	14	15	16	17
	18	19	20	21	22	23	24
	25	26	27	28	29	30	1[e]
RAMAḌĀN 1534	2	3	4	5	6	7	8
	9	10	11	12	13	14	15
	16	17	18	19	20	21	22
	23	24	25	26	27	28	29
SHAWWĀL 1534	1[f]	2	3	4	5	6	7
	8	9	10	11	12	13	14
	15	16	17	18	19	20	21
	22	23	24	25	26	27	28
	29	30	1	2	3	4	5
DHU AL-QA'DA 1534	6	7	8	9	10	11	12
	13	14	15	16	17	18	19
	20	21	22	23	24	25	26
	27	28	29	1	2	3	4
DHU AL-ḤIJJA 1534	5	6	7	8	9	10[g]	11
	12	13	14	15	16	17	18
	19	20	21	22	23	24	25
	26	27	28	29	1[a]	2	3
MUḤARRAM 1535	4	5	6	7	8	9	10[b]
	11	12	13	14	15	16	17
	18	19	20	21	22	23	24
	25	26	27	28	29	30	1
ṢAFAR 1535	2	3	4	5	6	7	8
	9	10	11	12	13	14	15
	16	17	18	19	20	21	22

‡Leap year
[a]New Year
[b]'Ashūrā'
[c]Prophet's Birthday
[d]Ascent of the Prophet
[e]Start of Ramaḍān
[f]'Īd al-Fiṭr
[g]'Īd al-'Aḍḥā

GREGORIAN 2110

Julian (Sun)	Sun	Mon	Tue	Wed	Thu	Fri	Sat	Month
Dec 15	29	30	31	1	2	3	4	JANUARY 2110
	5	6	7	8[a]	9	10	11	
Dec 29	12	13	14	15[b]	16	17	18	
	19	20	21	22	23	24	25	
Jan 12	26	27	28	29	30	31	1	FEBRUARY 2110
	2	3	4	5	6	7	8	
Jan 26	9	10	11	12	13	14	15	
	16	17	18	19[c]	20	21	22	
Feb 9	23	24	25	26	27	28	1	MARCH 2110
	2[d]	3	4	5	6	7	8	
Feb 23	9	10	11	12	13	14	15	
	16	17	18	19	20	21	22	
Mar 9	23	24	25	26	27	28	29	
	30	31	1	2	3	4	5	APRIL 2110
Mar 23	6[e]	7	8	9	10	11	12	
	13[f]	14	15	16	17	18	19	
Apr 6	20	21	22	23	24	25	26	
	27	28	29	30	1	2	3	MAY 2110
Apr 20	4	5	6	7	8	9	10	
	11	12	13	14	15	16	17	
May 4	18	19	20	21	22	23	24	
	25	26	27	28	29	30	31	
May 18	1	2	3	4	5	6	7	JUNE 2110
	8	9	10	11	12	13	14	
Jun 1	15	16	17	18	19	20	21	
	22	23	24	25	26	27	28	
Jun 15	29	30	1	2	3	4	5	JULY 2110
	6	7	8	9	10	11	12	
Jun 29	13	14	15	16	17	18	19	
	20	21	22	23	24	25	26	
Jul 13	27	28	29	30	31	1	2	AUGUST 2110
	3	4	5	6	7	8	9	
Jul 27	10	11	12	13	14	15	16	
	17	18	19	20	21	22	23	
Aug 10	24	25	26	27	28	29	30	
	31	1	2	3	4	5	6	SEPTEMBER 2110
Aug 24	7	8	9	10	11	12	13	
	14	15	16	17	18	19	20	
Sep 7	21	22	23	24	25	26	27	
	28	29	30	1	2	3	4	OCTOBER 2110
Sep 21	5	6	7	8	9	10	11	
	12	13	14	15	16	17	18	
Oct 5	19	20	21	22	23	24	25	
	26	27	28	29	30	31	1	NOVEMBER 2110
Oct 19	2	3	4	5	6	7	8	
	9	10	11	12	13	14	15	
Nov 2	16	17	18	19	20	21	22	
	23	24	25	26	27	28	29	
Nov 16	30[g]	1	2	3	4	5	6	DECEMBER 2110
	7	8	9	10	11	12	13	
Nov 30	14	15	16	17	18	19	20	
	21	22	23	24	25[h]	26	27	
Dec 14	28	29	30	31	1	2	3	

[a]Orthodox Christmas
[b]Julian New Year
[c]Ash Wednesday
[d]Feast of Orthodoxy
[e]Easter
[f]Orthodox Easter
[g]Advent
[h]Christmas

2111

Gregorian 2111	Sun	Mon	Tue	Wed	Thu	Fri	Sat	Lunar Phases	ISO Week (Mon)	Julian Day (Sun noon)	Hebrew 5871‡/5872	Sun	Mon	Tue	Wed	Thu	Fri	Sat	Molad	Chinese Gēng-Wǔ/Xīn-Wèi	Sun	Mon	Tue	Wed	Thu	Fri	Sat	Solar Term	Coptic 1827‡/1828	Sun	Mon	Tue	Wed	Thu	Fri	Sat	Ethiopic 2103‡/2104
January 2111	28	29	30	31	1[a]	2	◑	8:09	1	2492083	Teveth 5871	17	18	19	20	21	22	23		Month 11 Gēng-Wǔ	18	19	20	21	22	23	24		Koiak 1827	18	19	20	21	22	23	24	Tāḫśāś 2103
	4	5	6	7	8	9	●	1:01	2	2492090	Shevat 5871	24	25	26	27	28	29	1	Sat 6h49m0p	Month 12 Gēng-Wǔ	25	26	27	28	29	30	1	Xiǎo hán	Tōbe 1827	25	26	27	28	29[c]	30	1	Ṭer 2103
	11	12	13	14	15	◐	17	21:39	3	2492097		2	3	4	5	6	7	8			2	3	4	5	6	7	8			2	3	4	5	6[d]	7	8	
	18	19	20	21	22	23	24		4	2492104		9	10	11	12	13	14	15			9	10	11	12	13	14	15	Dà hán		9	10	11[e]	12	13	14	15	
	○	26	27	28	29	30	31	1:45	5	2492111		16	17	18	19	20	21	22			16*	17	18	19	20	21	22			16	17	18	19	20	21	22	
February 2111	◑	2	3	4	5	6	7	20:47	6	2492118		23	24	25	26	27	28	29			23	24	25	26	27	28	29	Lì chūn		23	24	25	26	27	28	29	
	●	9	10	11	12	13	14	12:04	7	2492125	Adar I 5871	30	1	2	3	4	5	6	Sun 19h33m1p	Month 1 Xīn-Wèi	1[a]	2	3	4	5	6	7		Meshir 1827	30	1	2	3	4	5	6	Yakātit 2103
	◐	16	17	18	19	20	21	15:18	8	2492132		7	8	9	10	11	12	13			8	9	10	11	12	13	14	Yǔ shuǐ		7	8	9	10	11	12	13	
	22	○	24	25	26	27	28	20:17	9	2492139		14	15	16	17	18	19	20			15[b]	16	17	18	19	20	21			14	15	16	17	18	19	20	
March 2111	1	2	◑	4	5	6	7	6:16	10	2492146		21	22	23	24	25	26	27			22	23	24	25	26	27	28	Jīng zhé		21	22	23	24	25	26	27	
	8	●	10	11	12	13	14	23:24	11	2492153	Adar II 5871	28	29	30	1	2	3	4	Tue 8h17m2p	Month 2 Xīn-Wèi	29	30	1	2	3	4	5		Paremotep 1827	28	29	30	1	2	3	4	Magābit 2103
	15	16	◐	18	19	20	21[b]	10:47	12	2492160		5	6	7	8	9	10	11			6	7	8	9	10	11	12	Chūn fēn		5	6	7	8	9	10	11	
	22	23	24	○	26	27	28	11:57	13	2492167		12	13	14[f]	15	16	17	18			13	14	15	16	17*	18	19			12	13	14	15	16	17	18	
April 2111	29	30	31	◑	2	3	4	13:27	14	2492174		19	20	21	22	23	24	25			20	21	22	23	24	25	26			19	20	21	22	23	24	25	
	5	6	7	●	9	10	11	11:03	15	2492181	Nisan 5871	26	27	28	29	1	2	3	Wed 21h1m3p	Month 3 Xīn-Wèi	27[c]	28	29	1	2	3	4	Qīng míng	Parmoute 1827	26	27	28	29	30	1	2	Miyāzyā 2103
	12	13	14	15	◐	17	18	6:38	16	2492188		4	5	6	7	8	9	10			5	6	7	8	9	10	11			3	4	5	6	7	8	9	
	19	20	21	22	23	○	25	0:16	17	2492195		11	12	13	14	15[g]	16	17			12	13	14	15	16	17	18	Gǔ yǔ		10	11	12	13	14	15	16	
May 2111	26	27	28	29	◑	1	2	19:29	18	2492202		18	19	20	21	22	23	24			19	20	21	22	23	24	25			17	18	19	20	21	22	23	
	3	4	5	6	●	8	9	23:22	19	2492209	Iyar 5871	25	26	27	28	29	30	1	Fri 9h45m4p	Month 4 Xīn-Wèi	26	27	28	29	30	1	2	Lì xià	Pashons 1827	24[f]	25	26	27	28	29[g]	30	Genbot 2103
	10	11	12	13	14	15	◐	1:12	20	2492216		2	3	4	5	6	7	8			3	4	5	6	7	8	9			1	2	3	4	5	6	7	
	17	18	19	20	21	22	○	9:49	21	2492223		9	10	11	12	13	14	15			10	11	12	13	14	15	16	Xiǎo mǎn		8	9	10	11	12	13	14	
	24	25	26	27	28	29	◑	1:30	22	2492230		16	17	18	19	20	21	22			17	18*	19	20	21	22	23			15	16	17	18	19	20	21	
June 2111	31	1	2	3	4	5	●	12:47	23	2492237		23	24	25	26	27	28	29		Month 5 Xīn-Wèi	24	25	26	27	28	29	1	Máng zhòng		22	23	24	25	26	27	28	
	7	8	9	10	11	12	13		24	2492244	Sivan 5871	1	2	3	4	5	6[h]	7	Sat 22h29m5p		2	3	4	5[d]	6	7	8		Paōne 1827	29	30	1	2	3	4	5	Sanē 2103
	◐	15	16	17	18	19	20	17:14	25	2492251		8	9	10	11	12	13	14			9	10	11	12	13	14	15			6	7	8	9	10	11	12	
	○[c]	22	23	24	25	26	27	17:36	26	2492258		15	16	17	18	19	20	21			16	17	18	19	20	21	22	Xià zhì		13	14	15	16	17	18	19	
July 2111	◑	29	30	1	2	3	4	8:36	27	2492265		22	23	24	25	26	27	28			23	24	25	26	27	28	29			20	21	22	23	24	25	26	
	5	●	7	8	9	10	11	3:28	28	2492272	Tammuz 5871	29	30	1	2	3	4	5	Mon 11h13m6p	Month 6 Xīn-Wèi	30	1	2	3	4	5	6	Xiǎo shǔ	Epēp 1827	27	28	29	30	1	2	3	Ḥamlē 2103
	12	13	◐	15	16	17	18	6:15	29	2492279		6	7	8	9	10	11	12			7	8	9	10	11	12	13			4	5	6	7	8	9	10	
	19	20	○	22	23	24	25	0:40	30	2492286		13	14	15	16	17	18	19			14	15	16	17	18	19*	20	Dà shǔ		11	12	13	14	15	16	17	
August 2111	26	◑	28	29	30	31	1	17:51	31	2492293		20	21	22	23	24	25	26			21	22	23	24	25	26	27			18	19	20	21	22	23	24	
	2	3	●	5	6	7	8	19:01	32	2492300	Av 5871	27	28	29	1	2	3	4	Tue 23h57m7p	Month 7 Xīn-Wèi	28	29	30	1	2	3	4	Lì qiū	Mesorē 1827	25	26	27	28	29	30	1	Naḥasē 2103
	9	10	11	◐	13	14	15	16:31	33	2492307		5	6	7	8	9[i]	10	11			5	6	7[e]	8	9	10	11			2	3	4	5	6	7	8	
	16	17	18	○	20	21	22	7:56	34	2492314		12	13	14	15	16	17	18			12	13	14	15[f]	16	17	18			9	10	11	12	13[h]	14	15	
	23	24	25	◑	27	28	29	6:10	35	2492321		19	20	21	22	23	24	25			19	20	21	22	23	24	25	Chǔ shǔ		16	17	18	19	20	21	22	
September 2111	30	31	1	2	●	4	5	10:40	36	2492328	Elul 5871	26	27	28	29	30	1	2	Thu 12h41m8p	Month 8 Xīn-Wèi	26	27	28	29	1	2	3			23	24	25	26	27	28	29	
	6	7	8	9	10	◐	12	0:48	37	2492335		3	4	5	6	7	8	9			4	5	6	7	8	9	10	Bái lù	Epag. 1827	30	1	2	3	4	5	6	Pāg. 2103
	13	14	15	16	○	18	19	16:11	38	2492342		10	11	12	13	14	15	16			11	12	13	14	15[g]	16	17		Thoout 1828	1[a]	2	3	4	5	6	7	Maskaram 2104
	20	21	22	23[d]	◑	25	26	22:04	39	2492349		17	18	19	20	21	22	23			18	19	20*	21	22	23	24	Qiū fēn		8	9	10	11	12	13	14	
October 2111	27	28	29	30	1	2	●	1:36	40	2492356	Tishri 5872	24	25	26	27	28	29	1[a]	Sat 1h25m9p	Month 9 Xīn-Wèi	25	26	27	28	29	30	1			15	16	17[b]	18	19	20	21	
	4	5	6	7	8	9	◐	7:59	41	2492363		2[a]	3	4	5	6	7	8			2	3	4	5	6	7	8	Hán lù		22	23	24	25	26	27	28	
	11	12	13	14	15	16	○	2:13	42	2492370		9	10[b]	11	12	13	14	15[c]			9[h]	10	11	12	13	14	15		Paope 1828	29	30	1	2	3	4	5	Ṭeqemt 2104
	18	19	20	21	22	23	◑	17:16	43	2492377		16	17	18	19	20	21	22			16	17	18	19	20	21	22	Shuāng jiàng		6	7	8	9	10	11	12	
	25	26	27	28	29	30	31		44	2492384		23	24	25	26	27	28	29			23	24	25	26	27	28	29			13	14	15	16	17	18	19	
November 2111	●	2	3	4	5	6	7	15:29	45	2492391	Ḥeshvan 5872	30	1	2	3	4	5	6	Sun 14h9m10p	Month 10 Xīn-Wèi	1	2	3	4	5	6	7			20	21	22	23	24	25	26	
	◐	9	10	11	12	13	14	15:01	46	2492398		7	8	9	10	11	12	13			8	9	10	11	12	13	14	Lì dōng	Athōr 1828	27	28	29	30	1	2	3	Ḫedār 2104
	○	16	17	18	19	20	21	14:51	47	2492405		14	15	16	17	18	19	20			15	16	17	18	19	20	21*			4	5	6	7	8	9	10	
	22	◑	24	25	26	27	28	14:21	48	2492412		21	22	23	24	25	26	27			22	23	24	25	26	27	28	Xiǎo xuě		11	12	13	14	15	16	17	
December 2111	29	30	●	2	3	4	5	4:25	49	2492419	Kislev 5872	28	29	30	1	2	3	4	Tue 2h53m11p	Month 11 Xīn-Wèi	29	30	1	2	3	4	5			18	19	20	21	22	23	24	
	6	◐	8	9	10	11	12	22:49	50	2492426		5	6[d]	7	8	9	10	11			6	7	8	9	10	11	12	Dà xuě	Koiak 1828	25	26	27	28	29	30	1	Tāḫśāś 2104
	13	14	○	16	17	18	19	6:33	51	2492433		12	13	14	15	16	17	18			13	14	15	16	17	18	19			2	3	4	5	6	7	8	
	20	21	22[e]	◑	24	25	26	11:11	52	2492440		19	20	21	22	23	24	25[e]			20	21	22[i]	23	24	25	26	Dōng zhì		9	10	11	12	13	14	15	
	27	28	29	●	31	1	2	16:33	53	2492447		26[e]	27[e]	28[e]	29[e]	30[e]	1[e]	2[e]	Wed 15h37m12p		27	28	29	30	1	2	3			16	17	18	19	20	21	22	

[a]New Year
[b]Spring (5:09)
[c]Summer (21:24)
[d]Autumn (14:04)
[e]Winter (12:06)
● New moon
◐ First quarter moon
○ Full moon
◑ Last quarter moon

‡Leap year
[a]New Year
[b]Yom Kippur
[c]Sukkot
[d]Winter starts
[e]Ḥanukkah
[f]Purim
[g]Passover
[h]Shavuot
[i]Fast of Av

[a]New Year (4809, Sheep)
[b]Lantern Festival
[c]Qīngmíng
[d]Dragon Festival
[e]Qīqiǎo
[f]Hungry Ghosts
[g]Mid-Autumn Festival
[h]Double-Ninth Festival
[i]Dōngzhì
*Start of 60-name cycle

‡Leap year
[a]New Year
[b]Building of the Cross
[c]Christmas
[d]Jesus's Circumcision
[e]Epiphany
[f]Easter
[g]Mary's Announcement
[h]Jesus's Transfiguration

PERSIAN (ASTRONOMICAL) 1489/1490‡

Month	Sun	Mon	Tue	Wed	Thu	Fri	Sat
	7	8	9	10	11	12	13
DEY 1489	14	15	16	17	18	19	20
	21	22	23	24	25	26	27
	28	29	30	1	2	3	4
BAHMAN 1489	5	6	7	8	9	10	11
	12	13	14	15	16	17	18
	19	20	21	22	23	24	25
	26	27	28	29	30	*1*	2
ESFAND 1489	3	4	5	6	7	8	9
	10	11	12	13	14	15	16
	17	18	19	20	21	22	23
	24	25	26	27	28	29	*1*[a]
FARVARDĪN 1490	2	3	4	5	6	7	8
	9	10	11	12	13[b]	14	15
	16	17	18	19	20	21	22
	23	24	25	26	27	28	29
	30	31	*1*	2	3	4	5
ORDĪBEHEŠT 1490	6	7	8	9	10	11	12
	13	14	15	16	17	18	19
	20	21	22	23	24	25	26
	27	28	29	30	31	*1*	2
XORDĀD 1490	3	4	5	6	7	8	9
	10	11	12	13	14	15	16
	17	18	19	20	21	22	23
	24	25	26	27	28	29	30
	31	*1*	2	3	4	5	6
TĪR 1490	7	8	9	10	11	12	13
	14	15	16	17	18	19	20
	21	22	23	24	25	26	27
	28	29	30	31	*1*	2	3
MORDĀD 1490	4	5	6	7	8	9	10
	11	12	13	14	15	16	17
	18	19	20	21	22	23	24
	25	26	27	28	29	30	31
SHAHRĪVAR 1490	*1*	2	3	4	5	6	7
	8	9	10	11	12	13	14
	15	16	17	18	19	20	21
	22	23	24	25	26	27	28
	29	30	31	*1*	2	3	4
MEHR 1490	5	6	7	8	9	10	11
	12	13	14	15	16	17	18
	19	20	21	22	23	24	25
	26	27	28	29	30	*1*	2
ABĀN 1490	3	4	5	6	7	8	9
	10	11	12	13	14	15	16
	17	18	19	20	21	22	23
	24	25	26	27	28	29	30
ĀZAR 1490	*1*	2	3	4	5	6	7
	8	9	10	11	12	13	14
	15	16	17	18	19	20	21
	22	23	24	25	26	27	28
DEY 1490	29	30	*1*	2	3	4	5
	6	7	8	9	10	11	12

HINDU LUNAR 2167‡/2168

Month	Sun	Mon	Tue	Wed	Thu	Fri	Sat
MĀRGAŚĪRA 2167	17	18	19	20	21	22	23
	24	25	26	27	28	29	**30**
	2	3	4	5	6	7	8
PAUSHA 2167	9	10	11	12	13	14	15
	16	*16*	17	18	19	20	21
	22	23	**24**	26	27	28	29
	30	1	2	3	4	5	6
MĀGHA 2167	7	8	9	10	11	12	13
	14	15	16	17	18	19	20
	21	22	23	24	25	26	27
	28[h]	30	1	2	3	4	5
PHĀLGUNA 2167	6	7	8	9	*9*	10	11
	12	13	14	15[i]	16	17	18
	19	20	21	**22**	24	25	26
	27	28	29	30	1[a]	2	3
CHAITRA 2168	4	5	6	7	8	9[b]	10
	11	12	13	*13*	**14**	16	17
	18	19	20	21	22	23	24
	25	26	**27**	29	30	1	2
VAIŚĀKHA 2168	3	*3*	4	5	6	7	8
	9	10	11	12	13	14	15
	16	17	18	**19**	21	22	23
	24	25	26	27	28	29	30
JYAISHTHA 2168	1	2	3	4	5	6	7
	8	*8*	9	10	**11**	13	14
	15	16	17	18	19	20	21
	22	**23**	25	26	27	28	29
	29	30	1	2	3	4	5
ĀSHĀḌHA 2168	6	7	8	9	10	11	12
	13	14	**15**	17	18	19	20
	21	22	23	24	25	26	27
	28	29	30	1	2	3	4
ŚRĀVAṆA 2168	5	6	7	8	9	10	11
	12	13	14	15	16	17	**18**
	20	21	22	23[c]	24	25	26
	26	27	28	29	30	1	2
BHĀDRAPADA 2168	3	4[d]	5	6	7	8	9
	10	**11**	13	14	15	16	17
	18	19	20	21	22	23	24
	25	26	27	28	29	30	1
ĀŚVINA 2168	*1*	2	**3**	5	6	7	**8**[e]
	9[e]	10[e]	11	12	13	14	**15**
	17	18	19	20	21	*21*	22
	23	24	25	26	27	28	29
	30	1[f]	2	3	4	5	6
KĀRTTIKA 2168	7	**8**	10	11	12	13	14
	15	16	17	18	19	20	21
	22	23	24	*24*	25	26	27
	28	29	30	1	**2**	4	5
MĀRGAŚĪRA 2168	6	7	8	9	10	11[g]	12
	13	14	15	16	17	18	19
	20	21	22	23	24	25	26
	27	28	29	30	1	2	3

HINDU SOLAR 2032‡/2033

Month	Sun	Mon	Tue	Wed	Thu	Fri	Sat
PAUSHA 2032	11	12	13	14	15	16	17
	18	19	20	21	22	23	24
	25	26	27	28	29	1[b]	2
MĀGHA 2032	3	4	5	6	7	8	9
	10	11	12	13	14	15	16
	17	18	19	20	21	22	23
	24	25	26	27	28	29	1
PHĀLGUNA 2032	2	3	4	5	6	7	8
	9	10	11	12	13	14	15
	16	17	18	19	20	21	22
	23	24	25	26	27	28	29
	30	1	2	3	4	5	6
CHAITRA 2032	7	8	9	10	11	12	13
	14	15	16	17	18	19	20
	21	22	23	24	25	26	27
	28	29	30	31	1[a]	2	3
VAIŚĀKHA 2033	4	5	6	7	8	9	10
	11	12	13	14	15	16	17
	18	19	20	21	22	23	24
	25	26	27	28	29	30	31
JYAISHTHA 2033	1	2	3	4	5	6	7
	8	9	10	11	12	13	14
	15	16	17	18	19	20	21
	22	23	24	25	26	27	28
	29	30	31	1	2	3	4
ĀSHĀḌHA 2033	5	6	7	8	9	10	11
	12	13	14	15	16	17	18
	19	20	21	22	23	24	25
	26	27	28	29	30	31	32
ŚRĀVAṆA 2033	1	2	3	4	5	6	7
	8	9	10	11	12	13	14
	15	16	17	18	19	20	21
	22	23	24	25	26	27	28
	29	30	31	1	2	3	4
BHĀDRAPADA 2033	5	6	7	8	9	10	11
	12	13	14	15	16	17	18
	19	20	21	22	23	24	25
	26	27	28	29	30	31	1
ĀŚVINA 2033	2	3	4	5	6	7	8
	9	10	11	12	13	14	15
	16	17	18	19	20	21	22
	23	24	25	26	27	28	29
	30	31	1	2	3	4	5
KĀRTTIKA 2033	6	7	8	9	10	11	12
	13	14	15	16	17	18	19
	20	21	22	23	24	25	26
	27	28	29	30	1	2	3
MĀRGAŚĪRA 2033	4	5	6	7	8	9	10
	11	12	13	14	15	16	17
	18	19	20	21	22	23	24
	25	26	27	28	29	1	2
PAUSHA 2033	3	4	5	6	7	8	9
	10	11	12	13	14	15	16

ISLAMIC (ASTRONOMICAL) 1535‡/1536

Month	Sun	Mon	Tue	Wed	Thu	Fri	Sat
SAFAR 1535	16	17	18	19	20	21	22
	23	24	25	26	27	28	29
	1	2	3	4	5	6	7
RABĪʿ I 1535	8	9	10	11	12[c]	13	14
	15	16	17	18	19	20	21
	22	23	24	25	26	27	28
	29	30	*1*	2	3	4	5
RABĪʿ II 1535	6	7	8	9	10	11	12
	13	14	15	16	17	18	19
	20	21	22	23	24	25	26
	27	28	29	*1*	2	3	4
JUMĀDĀ I 1535	5	6	7	8	9	10	11
	12	13	14	15	16	17	18
	19	20	21	22	23	24	25
	26	27	28	29	30	*1*	2
JUMĀDĀ II 1535	3	4	5	6	7	8	9
	10	11	12	13	14	15	16
	17	18	19	20	21	22	23
	24	25	26	27	28	29	*1*
RAJAB 1535	2	3	4	5	6	7	8
	9	10	11	12	13	14	15
	16	17	18	19	20	21	22
	23	24	25	26	27[d]	28	29
	30	*1*	2	3	4	5	6
SHAʿBĀN 1535	7	8	9	10	11	12	13
	14	15	16	17	18	19	20
	21	22	23	24	25	26	27
	28	29	*30*	1[e]	2	3	4
RAMAḌĀN 1535	5	6	7	8	9	10	11
	12	13	14	15	16	17	18
	19	20	21	22	23	24	25
	26	27	28	29	*1*[f]	2	3
SHAWWĀL 1535	4	5	6	7	8	9	10
	11	12	13	14	15	16	17
	18	19	20	21	22	23	24
	25	26	27	28	29	*30*	1
DHU AL-QAʿDA 1535	2	3	4	5	6	7	8
	9	10	11	12	13	14	15
	16	17	18	19	20	21	22
	23	24	25	26	27	28	29
DHU AL-ḤIJJA 1535	*1*	2	3	4	5	6	7
	8	9	10[g]	11	12	13	14
	15	16	17	18	19	20	21
	22	23	24	25	26	27	28
	29	30	*1*[a]	2	3	4	5
MUHARRAM 1536	6	7	8	9	10[b]	11	12
	13	14	15	16	17	18	19
	20	21	22	23	24	25	26
	27	28	29	1	2	3	4
SAFAR 1536	5	6	7	8	9	10	11
	12	13	14	15	16	17	18
	19	20	21	22	23	24	25
	26	27	28	29	30	*1*	2

GREGORIAN 2111

Julian (Sun)	Sun	Mon	Tue	Wed	Thu	Fri	Sat	Month
Dec 14	*28*	29	30	31	1	2	3	
	4	5	6	7	8[a]	9	10	JANUARY 2111
Dec 28	*11*	12	13	14	15[b]	16	17	
	18	19	20	21	22	23	24	
Jan 11	*25*	26	27	28	29	30	31	
	1	2	3	4	5	6	7	FEBRUARY 2111
Jan 25	*8*	9	10	11[c]	12	13	14	
	15	16	17	18	19	20	21	
Feb 8	*22*	23	24	25	26	27	28	
	1	2	3	4	5	6	7	MARCH 2111
Feb 22	*8*	9	10	11	12	13	14	
	15	16	17	18	19	20	21	
Mar 8	*22*[d]	23	24	25	26	27	28	
	29[e]	30	31	1	2	3	4	
Mar 22	*5*	6	7	8	9	10	11	APRIL 2111
	12	13	14	15	16	17	18	
Apr 5	*19*	20	21	22	23	24	25	
	26	27	28	29	30	1	2	
Apr 19	*3*[f]	4	5	6	7	8	9	MAY 2111
	10	11	12	13	14	15	16	
May 3	*17*	18	19	20	21	22	23	
	24	25	26	27	28	29	30	
May 17	*31*	1	2	3	4	5	6	
	7	8	9	10	11	12	13	JUNE 2111
May 31	*14*	15	16	17	18	19	20	
	21	22	23	24	25	26	27	
Jun 14	*28*	29	30	1	2	3	4	
	5	6	7	8	9	10	11	JULY 2111
Jun 28	*12*	13	14	15	16	17	18	
	19	20	21	22	23	24	25	
Jul 12	*26*	27	28	29	30	31	1	
	2	3	4	5	6	7	8	AUGUST 2111
Jul 26	*9*	10	11	12	13	14	15	
	16	17	18	19	20	21	22	
Aug 9	*23*	24	25	26	27	28	29	
	30	31	1	2	3	4	5	
Aug 23	*6*	7	8	9	10	11	12	SEPTEMBER 2111
	13	14	15	16	17	18	19	
Sep 6	*20*	21	22	23	24	25	26	
	27	28	29	30	1	2	3	
Sep 20	*4*	5	6	7	8	9	10	OCTOBER 2111
	11	12	13	14	15	16	17	
Oct 4	*18*	19	20	21	22	23	24	
	25	26	27	28	29	30	31	
Oct 18	*1*	2	3	4	5	6	7	NOVEMBER 2111
	8	9	10	11	12	13	14	
Nov 1	*15*	16	17	18	19	20	21	
	22	23	24	25	26	27	28	
Nov 15	*29*[g]	30	1	2	3	4	5	
	6	7	8	9	10	11	12	DECEMBER 2111
Nov 29	*13*	14	15	16	17	18	19	
	20	21	22	23	24	25[h]	26	
Dec 13	*27*	28	29	30	31	1	2	

Persian:
‡Leap year
[a]New Year
[b]Sizdeh Bedar

Hindu Lunar:
‡Leap year
[a]New Year (Prajāpati)
[b]Birthday of Rāma
[c]Birthday of Krishna
[d]Ganēśa Chaturthī
[e]Dashara
[f]Diwali
[g]Birthday of Vishnu
[h]Night of Śiva
[i]Holi

Hindu Solar:
‡Leap year
[a]New Year (Pārthiva)
[b]Pongal

Islamic:
‡Leap year
[a]New Year
[b]ʿAshūrāʾ
[c]Prophet's Birthday
[d]Ascent of the Prophet
[e]Start of Ramaḍān
[f]ʿId al-Fiṭr
[g]ʿId al-ʾAḍḥā

Gregorian:
[a]Orthodox Christmas
[b]Julian New Year
[c]Ash Wednesday
[d]Feast of Orthodoxy
[e]Easter
[f]Orthodox Easter
[g]Advent
[h]Christmas

2112

GREGORIAN 2112‡	Sun	Mon	Tue	Wed	Thu	Fri	Sat	Lunar Phases	ISO WEEK (Mon)	JULIAN DAY (Sun noon)	HEBREW 5872/5873	Sun	Mon	Tue	Wed	Thu	Fri	Sat	Molad	CHINESE Xīn-Wèi/Rén-Shēn‡	Sun	Mon	Tue	Wed	Thu	Fri	Sat	Solar Term	COPTIC 1828/1829	Sun	Mon	Tue	Wed	Thu	Fri	Sat	ETHIOPIC 2104/2105
	27	28	29	●	31	1[a]	2	16:33	53	2492447		26[e]	27[e]	28[e]	29[e]	30[e]	1[e]	2[e]	Wed 15h37m12p		27	28	29	30	1	2	3		KOIAK 1828	16	17	18	19	20	21	22	TĀKHŚĀŚ 2104
JANUARY 2112	3	4	5	◐	7	8	9	8:16	1	2492454	TEVETH 5872	3	4	5	6	7	8	9		MONTH 12 Xīn-Wèi	4	5	6	7	8	9	10	Xiǎo hán		23	24	25	26	27	28	29[c]	
	10	11	12	13	○	15	16	0:56	2	2492461		10	11	12	13	14	15	16			11	12	13	14	15	16	17			30	1	2	3	4	5	6[d]	
	17	18	19	20	21	◑	23	5:50	3	2492468		17	18	19	20	21	22	23			18	19	20	21*	**22**	23	24	Dà hán	TŌBE 1828	7	8	9	10	11[e]	12	13	ṬER 2104
	24	25	26	27	28	●	30	3:54	4	2492475		24	25	26	27	28	29	1	Fri 4h21m13p		25	26	27	28	29	1[a]	2			14	15	16	17	18	19	20	
	31	1	2	3	◐	5	6	20:04	5	2492482		2	3	4	5	6	7	8		MONTH 1 Rén-Shēn	3	4	5	6	7	*8*	9	Lì chūn		21	22	23	24	25	26	27	
FEBRUARY 2112	7	8	9	10	11	○	13	20:29	6	2492489	SHEVAT 5872	9	10	11	12	13	14	15			10	11	12	13	14	15[b]	16			28	29	30	1	2	3	4	
	14	15	16	17	18	19	◑	21:06	7	2492496		16	17	18	19	20	21	22			17	18	19	20	21	**22**	23	Yǔ shuǐ	MESHIR 1828	5	6	7	8	9	10	11	YAKĀTIT 2104
	21	22	23	24	25	26	●	14:20	8	2492503		23	24	25	26	27	28	29			24	25	26	27	28	29	1			12	13	14	15	16	17	18	
	28	29	1	2	3	4	◐	10:33	9	2492510		30	1	2	3	4	5	6	Sat 17h5m14p		2	3	4	5	6	7	*8*	Jīng zhé		19	20	21	22	23	24	25	
MARCH 2112	6	7	8	9	10	11	12		10	2492517	ADAR 5872	7	8	9	10	11	12	13		MONTH 2 Rén-Shēn	9	10	11	12	13	14	15			26	27	28	29	30	1	2	
	○	14	15	16	17	18	19	15:12	11	2492524		14[f]	15	16	17	18	19	20			16	17	18	19	20	21	22		PAREMOTEP 1828	3	4	5	6	7	8	9	MAGĀBIT 2104
	20[b]	◑	22	23	24	25	26	8:41	12	2492531		21	22	23	24	25	26	27			**23***	24	25	26	27	28	29	Chūn fēn		10	11	12	13	14	15	16	
	●	28	29	30	31	1	2	23:57	13	2492538		28	29	1	2	3	4	5	Mon 5h49m15p		30	1	2	3	4	5	6			17	18	19	20	21	22	23	
APRIL 2112	3	◐	5	6	7	8	9	3:21	14	2492545	NISAN 5872	6	7	8	9	10	11	12		MONTH 3 Rén-Shēn	7	8[c]	9	10	11	12	13	Qīng míng		24	25	26	27	28	29	30	
	10	11	○	13	14	15	16	7:35	15	2492552		13	14	15[g]	16	17	18	19			14	15	16	17	18	19	20			1	2	3	4	5	6	7	
	17	18	◑	20	21	22	23	16:57	16	2492559		20	21	22	23	24	25	26			21	22	23	**24**	25	26	27	Gǔ yǔ	PARMOUTE 1828	8[f]	9	10	11	12	13	14	MIYĀZYĀ 2104
	24	25	●	27	28	29	30	9:20	17	2492566		27	28	29	30	1	2	3	Tue 18h33m16p		28	29	1	2	3	4	5			15	16	17	18	19	20	21	
MAY 2112	1	2	◐	4	5	6	7	21:27	18	2492573	IYYAR 5872	4	5	6	7	8	9	10		MONTH 4 Rén-Shēn	6	7	8	9	*10*	11	12	Lì xià		22	23	24	25	26	27	28	
	8	9	10	○	12	13	14	21:08	19	2492580		11	12	13	14	15	16	17			13	14	15	16	17	18	19			29[g]	30	1	2	3	4	5	
	15	16	17	◑	19	20	21	22:46	20	2492587		18	19	20	21	22	23	24			20	21	22	23	24*	25	**26**	Xiǎo mǎn	PASHONS 1828	6	7	8	9	10	11	12	GENBOT 2104
	22	23	24	●	26	27	28	19:21	21	2492594		25	26	27	28	29	1	2	Thu 7h17m17p		27	28	29	30	1	2	3			13	14	15	16	17	18	19	
	29	30	31	1	◐	3	4	15:33	22	2492601	SIVAN 5872	3	4	5	6[h]	7	8	9		MONTH 5 Rén-Shēn	4	5[d]	6	7	8	9	10			20	21	22	23	24	25	26	
JUNE 2112	5	6	7	8	9	○	11	8:09	23	2492608		10	11	12	13	14	15	16			*11*	12	13	14	15	16	17	Máng zhòng		27	28	29	30	1	2	3	
	12	13	14	15	16	◑	18	3:25	24	2492615		17	18	19	20	21	22	23			18	19	20	21	22	23	24		PAŌNE 1828	4	5	6	7	8	9	10	SANĒ 2104
	19	20	21[c]	22	23	●	25	6:49	25	2492622		24	25	26	27	28	29	30			25	26	**27**	28	29	1	2	Xià zhì		11	12	13	14	15	16	17	
	26	27	28	29	30	1	◐	8:35	26	2492629	TAMMUZ 5872	1	2	3	4	5	6	7	Fri 20h2m0p	MONTH 6 Rén-Shēn	3	4	5	6	7	8	9			18	19	20	21	22	23	24	
JULY 2112	3	4	5	6	7	8	○	17:14	27	2492636		8	9	10	11	12	13	14			10	11	12	13	*14*	15	16	Xiǎo shǔ		25	26	27	28	29	30	1	
	10	11	12	13	14	15	◑	8:25	28	2492643		15	16	17	18	19	20	21			17	18	19	20	21	22	23		EPĒP 1828	2	3	4	5	6	7	8	ḤAMLĒ 2104
	17	18	19	20	21	22	●	20:08	29	2492650		22	23	24	25	26	27	28			24	25*	26	27	28	**29**	30	Dà shǔ		9	10	11	12	13	14	15	
	24	25	26	27	28	29	30		30	2492657		29	1	2	3	4	5	6	Sun 8h46m1p	LEAP MONTH 6 Rén-Shēn	1	2	3	4	5	6	7			16	17	18	19	20	21	22	
	◐	1	2	3	4	5	6	23:58	31	2492664	AV 5872	7	8	9[i]	10	11	12	13			8	9	10	11	12	13	14			23	24	25	26	27	28	29	
AUGUST 2112	7	○	9	10	11	12	13	1:06	32	2492671		14	15	16	17	18	19	20			*15*	16	17	18	19	20	21	Lì qiū		30	1	2	3	4	5	6	
	◑	15	16	17	18	19	20	15:18	33	2492678		21	22	23	24	25	26	27			22	23	24	25	26	27	28		MESORĒ 1828	7	8	9	10	11	12	13[h]	NAḤASĒ 2104
	21	●	23	24	25	26	27	11:10	34	2492685		28	29	30	1	2	3	4	Mon 21h30m2p		29	1	**2**	3	4	5	6	Chǔ shǔ		14	15	16	17	18	19	20	
	28	29	◐	31	1	2	3	13:32	35	2492692	ELUL 5872	5	6	7	8	9	10	11		MONTH 7 Rén-Shēn	7[e]	8	9	10	11	12	13			21	22	23	24	25	26	27	
SEPTEMBER 2112	4	5	○	7	8	9	10	8:35	36	2492699		12	13	14	15	16	17	18			14	15[f]	16	*17*	18	19	20	Bái lù	EPAG. 1828	28	29	30	1	2	3	4	PĀG. 2104
	11	12	◑	14	15	16	17	1:25	37	2492706		19	20	21	22	23	24	25			21	22	23	24	25	26*	27			5	1[a]	2	3	4	5	6	
	18	19	20	●	22[d]	23	24	3:24	38	2492713		26	27	28	29	1[a]	2[a]	3	Wed 10h14m3p		28	29	30	1	2	**3**	4	Qiū fēn	THOOUT 1829	7	8	9	10	11	12	13	MASKARAM 2105
	25	26	27	28	◐	30	1	1:14	39	2492720	TISHRI 5873	4	5	6	7	8	9	10[b]		MONTH 8 Rén-Shēn	5	6	7	8	9	10	11			14	15	16	17[b]	18	19	20	
OCTOBER 2112	2	3	4	○	6	7	8	16:35	40	2492727		11	12	13	14	15[c]	16	17			12	13	14	15[g]	16	17	*18*	Hán lù		21	22	23	24	25	26	27	
	9	10	11	◑	13	14	15	15:34	41	2492734		18	19	20	21	22	23	24			19	20	21	22	23	24	25			28	29	30	1	2	3	4	
	16	17	18	19	●	21	22	20:08	42	2492741		25	26	27	28	29	30	1	Thu 22h58m4p		26	27	28	29	30	1	2		PAOPE 1829	5	6	7	8	9	10	11	ṬEQEMT 2105
	23	24	25	26	27	◐	29	11:09	43	2492748	ḤESHVAN 5873	2	3	4	5	6	7	8		MONTH 9 Rén-Shēn	**3**	4	5	6	7	8	9[h]	Shuāng jiàng		12	13	14	15	16	17	18	
	30	31	1	2	3	○	5	2:05	44	2492755		9	10	11	12	13	14	15			10	11	12	13	14	15	16			19	20	21	22	23	24	25	
NOVEMBER 2112	6	7	8	9	10	11	◑	9:37	45	2492762		16	17	18	19	20	21	22			17	*18*	19	20	21	22	23	Lì dōng		26	27	28	29	30	1	2	
	13	14	15	16	17	18	●	12:40	46	2492769		23	24	25	26	27	28	29			24	25	26*	27	28	29	1		ATHŌR 1829	3	4	5	6	7	8	9	ḪEDĀR 2105
	20	21	22	23	24	25	◐	19:37	47	2492776		1	2	3	4	5	6	7	Sat 11h42m5p	MONTH 10 Rén-Shēn	2	3	**4**	5	6	7	8	Xiǎo xuě		10	11	12	13	14	15	16	
	27	28	29	30	1	2	○	13:54	48	2492783	KISLEV 5873	8	9	10	11	12	13	14			9	10	11	12	13	14	15			17	18	19	20	21	22	23	
DECEMBER 2112	4	5	6	7	8	9	10		49	2492790		15	16	17[d]	18	19	20	21			16	17	18	*19*	20	21	22	Dà xuě		24	25	26	27	28	29	30	
	◑	12	13	14	15	16	17	6:28	50	2492797		22	23	24	25[e]	26[e]	27[e]	28[e]			23	24	25	26	27	28	29		KOIAK 1829	1	2	3	4	5	6	7	TĀKHŚĀŚ 2105
	18	●	20	21[e]	22	23	24	4:16	51	2492804	TEVETH 5873	29[e]	30[e]	1[e]	2[e]	3	4	5	Mon 0h26m6p	MONTH 11 Rén-Shēn	30	1	2	3	4[i]	5	6	Dōng zhì		8	9	10	11	12	13	14	
	25	◐	27	28	29	30	31	3:23	52	2492811		6	7	8	9	10	11	12			7	8	9	10	11	12	13			15	16	17	18	19	20	21	

‡Leap year
[a]New Year
[b]Spring (11:01)
[c]Summer (3:18)
[d]Autumn (19:54)
[e]Winter (17:55)
● New moon
◐ First quarter moon
○ Full moon
◑ Last quarter moon

[a]New Year
[b]Yom Kippur
[c]Sukkot
[d]Winter starts
[e]Ḥanukkah
[f]Purim
[g]Passover
[h]Shavuot
[i]Fast of Av

‡Leap year
[a]New Year (4810, Monkey)
[b]Lantern Festival
[c]Qīngmíng
[d]Dragon Festival
[e]Qīqiǎo
[f]Hungry Ghosts
[g]Mid-Autumn Festival
[h]Double-Ninth Festival
[i]Dōngzhì
*Start of 60-name cycle

[a]New Year
[b]Building of the Cross
[c]Christmas
[d]Jesus's Circumcision
[e]Epiphany
[f]Easter
[g]Mary's Announcement
[h]Jesus's Transfiguration

PERSIAN (ASTRONOMICAL) 1490‡/1491

Month	Sun	Mon	Tue	Wed	Thu	Fri	Sat
DEY 1490	6	7	8	9	10	11	12
	13	14	15	16	17	18	19
	20	21	22	23	24	25	26
	27	28	29	30	1	2	3
BAHMAN 1490	4	5	6	7	8	9	10
	11	12	13	14	15	16	17
	18	19	20	21	22	23	24
	25	26	27	28	29	30	1
ESFAND 1490	2	3	4	5	6	7	8
	9	10	11	12	13	14	15
	16	17	18	19	20	21	22
	23	24	25	26	27	28	29
	30	1[a]	2	3	4	5	6
FARVARDIN 1491	7	8	9	10	11	12	13[b]
	14	15	16	17	18	19	20
	21	22	23	24	25	26	27
	28	29	30	31	1	2	3
ORDIBEHEŠT 1491	4	5	6	7	8	9	10
	11	12	13	14	15	16	17
	18	19	20	21	22	23	24
	25	26	27	28	29	30	31
XORDĀD 1491	1	2	3	4	5	6	7
	8	9	10	11	12	13	14
	15	16	17	18	19	20	21
	22	23	24	25	26	27	28
	29	30	31	1	2	3	4
TĪR 1491	5	6	7	8	9	10	11
	12	13	14	15	16	17	18
	19	20	21	22	23	24	25
	26	27	28	29	30	31	1
MORDĀD 1491	2	3	4	5	6	7	8
	9	10	11	12	13	14	15
	16	17	18	19	20	21	22
	23	24	25	26	27	28	29
	30	31	1	2	3	4	5
SHAHRĪVAR 1491	6	7	8	9	10	11	12
	13	14	15	16	17	18	19
	20	21	22	23	24	25	26
	27	28	29	30	31	1	2
MEHR 1491	3	4	5	6	7	8	9
	10	11	12	13	14	15	16
	17	18	19	20	21	22	23
	24	25	26	27	28	29	30
ĀBĀN 1491	1	2	3	4	5	6	7
	8	9	10	11	12	13	14
	15	16	17	18	19	20	21
	22	23	24	25	26	27	28
	29	30	1	2	3	4	5
ĀZAR 1491	6	7	8	9	10	11	12
	13	14	15	16	17	18	19
	20	21	22	23	24	25	26
	27	28	29	30	1	2	3
DEY 1491	4	5	6	7	8	9	10

‡Leap year
[a]New Year
[b]Sizdeh Bedar

HINDU LUNAR 2168/2169

Month	Sun	Mon	Tue	Wed	Thu	Fri	Sat
	27	28	29	30	1	2	3
PAUSHA 2168	4	5	6	**7**	9	10	11
	12	13	14	15	16	17	17
	18	19	20	21	22	23	24
	25	26	27	28	29	30	**1**
MĀGHA 2168	3	4	5	6	7	8	9
	10	11	12	13	14	15	16
	17	18	19	19	20	21	22
	23	**24**	26	27	28	29[h]	30
PHĀLGUNA 2168	1	2	3	4	5	6	7
	8	9	10	11	12	13	14
	15[i]	16	17	18	19	20	21
	22	23	24	25	26	27	28
	29	1[a]	2	3	4	5	6
CHAITRA 2169	7	8	9[b]	10	11	12	12
	13	14	15	16	17	18	19
	20	21	22	**23**	25	26	27
	28	29	30	1	2	3	4
VAIŚĀKHA 2169	5	6	7	8	9	10	11
	12	13	14	15	16	17	18
	19	20	21	22	23	24	25
	26	28	29	30	1	2	3
JYAISHTHA 2169	4	5	6	7	7	8	9
	10	11	12	13	14	15	16
	17	18	**19**	21	22	23	24
	25	26	27	28	29	30	1
ĀSHĀDHA 2169	2	3	4	5	6	7	8
	9	10	11	12	13	14	15
	16	17	18	19	20	21	**22**
	24	25	26	27	28	29	30
ŚRĀVAṆA 2169	1	2	3	4	4	5	6
	7	8	9	10	11	12	13
	14	**15**	17	18	19	20	21
	22	23[c]	24	25	26	27	28
BHĀDRAPADA 2169	29	30	1	2	3	4[d]	5
	6	7	8	9	10	11	12
	13	14	15	16	17	**18**	20
	21	22	23	24	25	26	27
	28	29	30	30	1	2	3
ĀŚVINA 2169	4	5	6	7	8[e]	9[e]	10[e]
	11	13	14	15	16	17	18
	19	20	21	22	23	24	25
	26	27	28	29	30	1[f]	2
KĀRTTIKA 2169	3	4	5	6	7	8	9
	10	11	12	13	14	**15**	17
	18	19	20	21	22	23	24
	24	25	26	27	28	29	30
MĀRGAŚIRA 2169	1	2	3	4	5	6	7
	8	**9**	11[g]	12	13	14	15
	16	17	18	19	20	21	22
	23	24	25	26	27	27	28
PAUSHA 2169	29	30	1	2	**3**	5	6
	7	8	9	10	11	12	13

[a]New Year (Aṅgiras)
[b]Birthday of Rāma
[c]Birthday of Krishna
[d]Ganēśa Chaturthī
[e]Dashara
[f]Diwali
[g]Birthday of Vishnu
[h]Night of Śiva
[i]Holi

HINDU SOLAR 2033/2034

Month	Sun	Mon	Tue	Wed	Thu	Fri	Sat
	10	11	12	13	14	15	16
PAUSHA 2033	17	18	19	20	21	22	23
	24	25	26	27	28	29	1[b]
MĀGHA 2033	2	3	4	5	6	7	8
	9	10	11	12	13	14	15
	16	17	18	19	20	21	22
	23	24	25	26	27	28	29
	30	1	2	3	4	5	6
PHĀLGUNA 2033	7	8	9	10	11	12	13
	14	15	16	17	18	19	20
	21	22	23	24	25	26	27
	28	29	30	1	2	3	4
CHAITRA 2033	5	6	7	8	9	10	11
	12	13	14	15	16	17	18
	19	20	21	22	23	24	25
	26	27	28	29	30	1[a]	2
VAIŚĀKHA 2034	3	4	5	6	7	8	9
	10	11	12	13	14	15	16
	17	18	19	20	21	22	23
	24	25	26	27	28	29	30
	31	1	2	3	4	5	6
JYAISHTHA 2034	7	8	9	10	11	12	13
	14	15	16	17	18	19	20
	21	22	23	24	25	26	27
	28	29	30	31	1	2	3
ĀSHĀDHA 2034	4	5	6	7	8	9	10
	11	12	13	14	15	16	17
	18	19	20	21	22	23	24
	25	26	27	28	29	30	31
	32	1	2	3	4	5	6
ŚRĀVAṆA 2034	7	8	9	10	11	12	13
	14	15	16	17	18	19	20
	21	22	23	24	25	26	27
	28	29	30	31	1	2	3
BHĀDRAPADA 2034	4	5	6	7	8	9	10
	11	12	13	14	15	16	17
	18	19	20	21	22	23	24
	25	26	27	28	29	30	31
ĀŚVINA 2034	1	2	3	4	5	6	7
	8	9	10	11	12	13	14
	15	16	17	18	19	20	21
	22	23	24	25	26	27	28
	29	30	31	1	2	3	4
KĀRTTIKA 2034	5	6	7	8	9	10	11
	12	13	14	15	16	17	18
	19	20	21	22	23	24	25
	26	27	28	29	30	1	2
MĀRGAŚIRA 2034	3	4	5	6	7	8	9
	10	11	12	13	14	15	16
	17	18	19	20	21	22	23
	24	25	26	27	28	29	1
PAUSHA 2034	2	3	4	5	6	7	8
	9	10	11	12	13	14	15

[a]New Year (Vyaya)
[b]Pongal

ISLAMIC (ASTRONOMICAL) 1536/1537

Month	Sun	Mon	Tue	Wed	Thu	Fri	Sat
	26	27	28	29	30	1	2
RABĪʻ I 1536	3	4	5	6	7	8	9
	10	11	12[c]	13	14	15	16
	17	18	19	20	21	22	23
	24	25	26	27	28	29	1
RABĪʻ II 1536	2	3	4	5	6	7	8
	9	10	11	12	13	14	15
	16	17	18	19	20	21	22
	23	24	25	26	27	28	29
	30	1	2	3	4	5	6
JUMĀDĀ I 1536	7	8	9	10	11	12	13
	14	15	16	17	18	19	20
	21	22	23	24	25	26	27
	28	29	1	2	3	4	5
JUMĀDĀ II 1536	6	7	8	9	10	11	12
	13	14	15	16	17	18	19
	20	21	22	23	24	25	26
	27	28	29	30	1	2	3
RAJAB 1536	4	5	6	7	8	9	10
	11	12	13	14	15	16	17
	18	19	20	21	22	23	24
	25	26	27[d]	28	29	1	2
SHAʻBĀN 1536	3	4	5	6	7	8	9
	10	11	12	13	14	15	16
	17	18	19	20	21	22	23
	24	25	26	27	28	29	30
RAMAḌĀN 1536	1[e]	2	3	4	5	6	7
	8	9	10	11	12	13	14
	15	16	17	18	19	20	21
	22	23	24	25	26	27	28
SHAWWĀL 1536	29	1[f]	2	3	4	5	6
	7	8	9	10	11	12	13
	14	15	16	17	18	19	20
	21	22	23	24	25	26	27
	28	29	30	1	2	3	4
DHU AL-QAʻDA 1536	5	6	7	8	9	10	11
	12	13	14	15	16	17	18
	19	20	21	22	23	24	25
	26	27	28	29	1	2	3
DHU AL-ḤIJJA 1536	4	5	6	7	8	9	10[g]
	11	12	13	14	15	16	17
	18	19	20	21	22	23	24
	25	26	27	28	29	30	1[a]
MUḤARRAM 1537	2	3	4	5	6	7	8
	9	10[b]	11	12	13	14	15
	16	17	18	19	20	21	22
	23	24	25	26	27	28	29
	30	1	2	3	4	5	6
ṢAFAR 1537	7	8	9	10	11	12	13
	14	15	16	17	18	19	20
	21	22	23	24	25	26	27
RABĪʻ I 1537	28	29	1	2	3	4	5
	6	7	8	9	10	11	12[c]

[a]New Year
[b]ʻAshūrāʼ
[c]Prophet's Birthday
[d]Ascent of the Prophet
[e]Start of Ramaḍān
[f]ʻId al-Fiṭr
[g]ʻId al-ʼAḍḥā

GREGORIAN 2112‡

Julian† (Sun)	Sun	Mon	Tue	Wed	Thu	Fri	Sat	Month
Dec 13	27	28	29	30	31	1	2	
	3	4	5	6	7	8[a]	9	JANUARY 2112
Dec 27	10	11	12	13	14	15[b]	16	
	17	18	19	20	21	22	23	
Jan 10	24	25	26	27	28	29	30	
	31	1	2	3	4	5	6	
Jan 24	7	8	9	10	11	12	13	FEBRUARY 2112
	14	15	16	17	18	19	20	
Feb 7	21	22	23	24	25	26	27	
	28	29	1	2[c]	3	4	5	
Feb 21	6[d]	7	8	9	10	11	12	MARCH 2112
	13	14	15	16	17	18	19	
Mar 6	20	21	22	23	24	25	26	
	27	28	29	30	31	1	2	
Mar 20	3	4	5	6	7	8	9	APRIL 2112
	10	11	12	13	14	15	16	
Apr 3	17[e]	18	19	20	21	22	23	
	24	25	26	27	28	29	30	
Apr 17	1	2	3	4	5	6	7	MAY 2112
	8	9	10	11	12	13	14	
May 1	15	16	17	18	19	20	21	
	22	23	24	25	26	27	28	
May 15	29	30	31	1	2	3	4	
	5	6	7	8	9	10	11	JUNE 2112
May 29	12	13	14	15	16	17	18	
	19	20	21	22	23	24	25	
Jun 12	26	27	28	29	30	1	2	
	3	4	5	6	7	8	9	JULY 2112
Jun 26	10	11	12	13	14	15	16	
	17	18	19	20	21	22	23	
Jul 10	24	25	26	27	28	29	30	
	31	1	2	3	4	5	6	
Jul 24	7	8	9	10	11	12	13	AUGUST 2112
	14	15	16	17	18	19	20	
Aug 7	21	22	23	24	25	26	27	
	28	29	30	31	1	2	3	
Aug 21	4	5	6	7	8	9	10	SEPTEMBER 2112
	11	12	13	14	15	16	17	
Sep 4	18	19	20	21	22	23	24	
	25	26	27	28	29	30	1	
Sep 18	2	3	4	5	6	7	8	OCTOBER 2112
	9	10	11	12	13	14	15	
Oct 2	16	17	18	19	20	21	22	
	23	24	25	26	27	28	29	
Oct 16	30	31	1	2	3	4	5	
	6	7	8	9	10	11	12	NOVEMBER 2112
Oct 30	13	14	15	16	17	18	19	
	20	21	22	23	24	25	26	
Nov 13	27[g]	28	29	30	1	2	3	
	4	5	6	7	8	9	10	DECEMBER 2112
Nov 27	11	12	13	14	15	16	17	
	18	19	20	21	22	23	24	
Dec 11	25[h]	26	27	28	29	30	31	

‡Leap year
[a]Orthodox Christmas
[b]Julian New Year
[c]Ash Wednesday
[d]Feast of Orthodoxy
[e]Easter (also Orthodox)
[g]Advent
[h]Christmas

2113

GREGORIAN 2113								Lunar Phases	ISO WEEK	JULIAN DAY	HEBREW 5873/5874‡								Molad	CHINESE Rén-Shēn‡/Guǐ-Yǒu								Solar Term	COPTIC 1829/1830								ETHIOPIC 2105/2106
	Sun	Mon	Tue	Wed	Thu	Fri	Sat		(Mon)	(Sun noon)		Sun	Mon	Tue	Wed	Thu	Fri	Sat			Sun	Mon	Tue	Wed	Thu	Fri	Sat			Sun	Mon	Tue	Wed	Thu	Fri	Sat	
JANUARY 2113	1[a]	○	3	4	5	6	7	4:20	1	2492818	TEVETH 5873	13	14	15	16	17	18	19		MONTH 11 Rén-Shēn	14	15	16	17	18	19	20	Xiǎo hán	KOIAK 1829	22	23	24	25	26	27	28	TĀKHŚĀŚ 2105
	8	9	◑	11	12	13	14	4:16	2	2492825		20	21	22	23	24	25	26	Tue 13h10m7p		21	22	23	24	25	26	27*		ṬŌBE 1829	29[c]	30	1	2	3	4	5	ṬER 2105
	15	16	●	18	19	20	21	18:14	3	2492832	SHEVAT 5873	27	28	29	1	2	3	4		MONTH 12 Rén-Shēn	28	29	30	1	2	3	4	Dà hán		6[d]	7	8	9	10	11[e]	12	
	22	23	◐	25	26	27	28	11:28	4	2492839		5	6	7	8	9	10	11			5	6	7	8	9	10	11			13	14	15	16	17	18	19	
FEBRUARY 2113	29	30	○	1	2	3	4	20:57	5	2492846		12	13	14	15	16	17	18			12	13	14	15	16	17	18			20	21	22	23	24	25	26	
	5	6	7	8	◑	10	11	0:59	6	2492853		19	20	21	22	23	24	25			19	20	21	22	23	24	25	Lì chūn	MESHIR 1829	27	28	29	30	1	2	3	YAKĀTIT 2105
	12	13	14	15	●	17	18	6:08	7	2492860	ADAR 5873	26	27	28	29	30	1	2	Thu 1h54m8p	MONTH 1 Guǐ-Yǒu	26	27	28	29	1[a]	2	3			4	5	6	7	8	9	10	
	19	20	21	◐	23	24	25	20:55	8	2492867		3	4	5	6	7	8	9			4	5	6	7	8	9	10	Yǔ shuǐ		11	12	13	14	15	16	17	
MARCH 2113	26	27	28	1	○	3	4	14:44	9	2492874		10	11	12	13	14[f]	15	16			11	12	13	14	15[b]	16	17			18	19	20	21	22	23	24	
	5	6	7	8	9	◑	11	18:49	10	2492881		17	18	19	20	21	22	23			18	19	20	21	22	23	24	Jīng zhé	PAREMOTEP 1829	25	26	27	28	29	30	1	MAGĀBIT 2105
	12	13	14	15	16	●	18	16:04	11	2492888	NISAN 5873	24	25	26	27	28	29	1	Fri 14h38m9p	MONTH 2 Guǐ-Yǒu	25	26	27	28*	29	30	1			2	3	4	5	6	7	8	
	19	20[b]	21	22	23	◐	25	8:20	12	2492895		2	3	4	5	6	7	8			2	3	4	5	6	7	8	Chūn fēn		9	10	11	12	13	14	15	
APRIL 2113	26	27	28	29	30	31	○	8:29	13	2492902		9	10	11	12	13	14	15[g]			9	10	11	12	13	14	15			16	17	18	19	20	21	22	
	2	3	4	5	6	7	8		14	2492909		16	17	18	19	20	21	22			16	17	18	19[c]	20	21	22	Qīng míng		23	24	25	26	27	28	29	
	◑	10	11	12	13	14	15	8:42	15	2492916		23	24	25	26	27	28	29	Sun 3h22m10p		23	24	25	26	27	28	29		PARMOUTE 1829	30[f]	1	2	3	4	5	6	MIYĀZYĀ 2105
	●	17	18	19	20	21	◐	0:39 21:46	16	2492923	IYYAR 5873	30	1	2	3	4	5	6		MONTH 3 Guǐ-Yǒu	1	2	3	4	5	6	7	Gǔ yǔ		7	8	9	10	11	12	13	
	23	24	25	26	27	28	29		17	2492930		7	8	9	10	11	12	13			8	9	10	11	12	13	14			14	15	16	17	18	19	20	
MAY 2113	30	○	2	3	4	5	6	1:12	18	2492937		14	15	16	17	18	19	20			15	16	17	18	19	20	21	Lì xià		21	22	23	24	25	26	27	
	7	◑	9	10	11	12	13	18:30	19	2492944		21	22	23	24	25	26	27	Mon 16h6m11p		22	23	24	25	26	27	28		PASHONS 1829	28	29[g]	30	1	2	3	4	GENBOT 2105
	14	●	16	17	18	19	20	8:44	20	2492951	SIVAN 5873	28	29	1	2	3	4	5		MONTH 4 Guǐ-Yǒu	29*	1	2	3	4	5	6			5	6	7	8	9	10	11	
	21	◐	23	24	25	26	27	12:53	21	2492958		6[h]	7	8	9	10	11	12			7	8	9	10	11	12	13	Xiǎo mǎn		12	13	14	15	16	17	18	
JUNE 2113	28	29	○	31	1	2	3	16:10	22	2492965		13	14	15	16	17	18	19			14	15	16	17	18	19	20			19	20	21	22	23	24	25	
	4	5	6	◑	8	9	10	1:01	23	2492972		20	21	22	23	24	25	26			21	22	23	24	25	26	27	Máng zhòng	PAŌNE 1829	26	27	28	29	30	1	2	SANĒ 2105
	11	12	●	14	15	16	17	17:14	24	2492979	TAMMUZ 5873	27	28	29	30	1	2	3	Wed 4h50m12p	MONTH 5 Guǐ-Yǒu	28	29	30	1	2	3	4			3	4	5	6	7	8	9	
	18	19	20	◐[c]	22	23	24	5:16	25	2492986		4	5	6	7	8	9	10			5[d]	6	7	8	9	10	11	Xià zhì		10	11	12	13	14	15	16	
JULY 2113	25	26	27	28	○	30	1	4:58	26	2492993		11	12	13	14	15	16	17			12	13	14	15	16	17	18			17	18	19	20	21	22	23	
	2	3	4	5	◑	7	8	5:39	27	2493000		18	19	20	21	22	23	24			19	20	21	22	23	24	25	Xiǎo shǔ		24	25	26	27	28	29	30	
	9	10	11	12	●	14	15	2:53	28	2493007	AV 5873	25	26	27	28	29	1	2	Thu 17h34m13p	MONTH 6 Guǐ-Yǒu	26	27	28	29	1*	2	3		EPĒP 1829	1	2	3	4	5	6	7	HAMLĒ 2105
	16	17	18	19	◐	21	22	22:24	29	2493014		3	4	5	6	7	8	9			4	5	6	7	8	9	10			8	9	10	11	12	13	14	
	23	24	25	26	27	○	29	15:38	30	2493021		10[i]	11	12	13	14	15	16			11	12	13	14	15	16	17	Dà shǔ		15	16	17	18	19	20	21	
AUGUST 2113	30	31	1	2	3	◑	5	10:01	31	2493028		17	18	19	20	21	22	23			18	19	20	21	22	23	24			22	23	24	25	26	27	28	
	6	7	8	9	10	●	12	14:20	32	2493035	ELUL 5873	24	25	26	27	28	29	30	Sat 6h18m14p	MONTH 7 Guǐ-Yǒu	25	26	27	28	29	1	2	Lì qiū	MESORĒ 1829	29	30	1	2	3	4	5	NAḤASĒ 2105
	13	14	15	16	17	18	◐	15:44	33	2493042		1	2	3	4	5	6	7			3	4	5	6	7[e]	8	9			6	7	8	9	10	11	12	
	20	21	22	23	24	25	26		34	2493049		8	9	10	11	12	13	14			10	11	12	13	14	15[f]	16	Chǔ shǔ		13[h]	14	15	16	17	18	19	
SEPTEMBER 2113	○	28	29	30	31	1	◑	0:41 15:42	35	2493056		15	16	17	18	19	20	21			17	18	19	20	21	22	23			20	21	22	23	24	25	26	
	3	4	5	6	7	8	9		36	2493063		22	23	24	25	26	27	28			24	25	26	27	28	29	30	Bái lù	EPAG. 1829	27	28	29	30	1	2	3	PĀG. 2105
	●	11	12	13	14	15	16	4:00	37	2493070	TISHRI 5874	29	1[a]	2[a]	3	4	5	6	Sun 19h2m15p	MONTH 8 Guǐ-Yǒu	1	2*	3	4	5	6	7		THOOUT 1830	4	5	1[a]	2	3	4	5	MASKARAM 2106
	17	◐	19	20	21	22	23[d]	8:25	38	2493077		7	8	9	10[b]	11	12	13			8	9	10	11	12	13	14	Qiū fēn		6	7	8	9	10	11	12	
	24	○	26	27	28	29	30	9:04	39	2493084		14	15[c]	16	17	18	19	20			15[g]	16	17	18	19	20	21			13	14	15	16	17[b]	18	19	
OCTOBER 2113	1	◑	3	4	5	6	7	0:04	40	2493091		21	22	23	24	25	26	27			22	23	24	25	26	27	28			20	21	22	23	24	25	26	
	8	●	10	11	12	13	14	20:04	41	2493098	ḤESHVAN 5874	28	29	30	1	2	3	4	Tue 7h46m16p	MONTH 9 Guǐ-Yǒu	29	30	1	2	3	4	5	Hán lù	PAOPE 1830	27	28	29	30	1	2	3	ṬEQEMT 2106
	15	16	◐	18	19	20	21	23:34	42	2493105		5	6	7	8	9	10	11			6	7	8	9[h]	10	11	12			4	5	6	7	8	9	10	
	22	23	○	25	26	27	28	17:47	43	2493112		12	13	14	15	16	17	18			13	14	15	16	17	18	19	Shuāng jiàng		11	12	13	14	15	16	17	
NOVEMBER 2113	29	30	◑	1	2	3	4	12:00	44	2493119		19	20	21	22	23	24	25			20	21	22	23	24	25	26			18	19	20	21	22	23	24	
	5	6	7	●	9	10	11	14:05	45	2493126	KISLEV 5874	26	27	28	29	30	1	2	Wed 20h30m17p	MONTH 10 Guǐ-Yǒu	27	28	29	1	2	3*	4	Lì dōng	ATHŌR 1830	25	26	27	28	29	30	1	ḪEDĀR 2106
	12	13	14	15	◐	17	18	12:32	46	2493133		3	4	5	6	7	8	9			5	6	7	8	9	10	11			2	3	4	5	6	7	8	
	19	20	21	22	○	24	25	3:40	47	2493140		10	11	12	13	14	15	16			12	13	14	15	16	17	18	Xiǎo xuě		9	10	11	12	13	14	15	
DECEMBER 2113	26	27	28	29	◑	1	2	3:49	48	2493147		17	18	19	20	21	22	23			19	20	21	22	23	24	25			16	17	18	19	20	21	22	
	3	4	5	6	7	●	9	8:53	49	2493154		24	25[e]	26[e]	27[d][e]	28[e]	29[e]	30[e]		MONTH 11* Guǐ-Yǒu	26	27	28	29	30	1	2	Dà xuě		23	24	25	26	27	28	29	
	10	11	12	13	14	◐	16	23:13	50	2493161	TEVETH 5874	1[e]	2[e]	3	4	5	6	7	Fri 9h15m0p		3	4	5	6	7	8	9		KOIAK 1830	30	1	2	3	4	5	6	TĀKHŚĀŚ 2106
	17	18	19	20	21[e]	○	23	15:03	51	2493168		8	9	10	11	12	13	14			10	11	12	13	14	15[i]	16	Dōng zhì		7	8	9	10	11	12	13	
	24	25	26	27	28	◑	30	23:05	52	2493175		15	16	17	18	19	20	21			17	18	19	20	21	22	23			14	15	16	17	18	19	20	
	31	1	2	3	4	5	6		1	2493182		22	23	24	25	26	27	28			24	25	26	27	28	29	30	Xiǎo hán		21	22	23	24	25	26	27	

[a]New Year
[b]Spring (16:49)
[c]Summer (8:56)
[d]Autumn (1:34)
[e]Winter (23:45)
● New moon
◐ First quarter moon
○ Full moon
◑ Last quarter moon

‡Leap year
[a]New Year
[b]Yom Kippur
[c]Sukkot
[d]Winter starts
[e]Ḥanukkah
[f]Purim
[g]Passover
[h]Shavuot
[i]Fast of Av

‡Leap year
[a]New Year (4811, Fowl)
[b]Lantern Festival
[c]Qīngmíng
[d]Dragon Festival
[e]Qīqiǎo
[f]Hungry Ghosts
[g]Mid-Autumn Festival
[h]Double-Ninth Festival
[i]Dōngzhì
*Start of 60-name cycle

[a]New Year
[b]Building of the Cross
[c]Christmas
[d]Jesus's Circumcision
[e]Epiphany
[f]Easter
[g]Mary's Announcement
[h]Jesus's Transfiguration

PERSIAN (ASTRONOMICAL) 1491/1492

Month	Sun	Mon	Tue	Wed	Thu	Fri	Sat
DEY 1491	11	12	13	14	15	16	17
	18	19	20	21	22	23	24
	25	26	27	28	29	30	*1*
BAHMAN 1491	2	3	4	5	6	7	8
	9	10	11	12	13	14	15
	16	17	18	19	20	21	22
	23	24	25	26	27	28	29
ESFAND 1491	30	*1*	2	3	4	5	6
	7	8	9	10	11	12	13
	14	15	16	17	18	19	20
	21	22	23	24	25	26	27
FARVARDĪN 1492	28	29	*1*[a]	2	3	4	5
	6	7	8	9	10	11	12
	13[b]	14	15	16	17	18	19
	20	21	22	23	24	25	26
	27	28	29	30	31	*1*	2
ORDĪBEHEŠT 1492	3	4	5	6	7	8	9
	10	11	12	13	14	15	16
	17	18	19	20	21	22	23
	24	25	26	27	28	29	30
XORDĀD 1492	31	*1*	2	3	4	5	6
	7	8	9	10	11	12	13
	14	15	16	17	18	19	20
	21	22	23	24	25	26	27
TĪR 1492	28	29	30	31	*1*	2	3
	4	5	6	7	8	9	10
	11	12	13	14	15	16	17
	18	19	20	21	22	23	24
	25	26	27	28	29	30	31
MORDĀD 1492	*1*	2	3	4	5	6	7
	8	9	10	11	12	13	14
	15	16	17	18	19	20	21
	22	23	24	25	26	27	28
SHAHRĪVAR 1492	29	30	31	*1*	2	3	4
	5	6	7	8	9	10	11
	12	13	14	15	16	17	18
	19	20	21	22	23	24	25
MEHR 1492	26	27	28	29	30	31	*1*
	2	3	4	5	6	7	8
	9	10	11	12	13	14	15
	16	17	18	19	20	21	22
	23	24	25	26	27	28	29
ĀBĀN 1492	30	*1*	2	3	4	5	6
	7	8	9	10	11	12	13
	14	15	16	17	18	19	20
	21	22	23	24	25	26	27
ĀZAR 1492	28	29	30	*1*	2	3	4
	5	6	7	8	9	10	11
	12	13	14	15	16	17	18
	19	20	21	22	23	24	25
DEY 1492	26	27	28	29	30	*1*	2
	3	4	5	6	7	8	9
	10	11	12	13	14	15	16

HINDU LUNAR 2169/2170‡

Month	Sun	Mon	Tue	Wed	Thu	Fri	Sat
PAUSHA 2169	14	15	16	17	18	19	20
	21	22	23	24	25	26	27
MĀGHA 2169	28	29	30	1	2	3	4
	5	6	7	**8**	10	11	12
	13	14	15	16	17	18	19
	19	20	21	22	23	24	25
PHĀLGUNA 2169	26	27	28[h]	29	30	1	**2**
	4	5	6	7	8	9	10
	11	12	13	14	15[i]	16	17
	18	19	20	21	22	*22*	23
CHAITRA 2170	24	**25**	27	28	29	30	1[a]
	2	3	4	5	6	7	**8**[b]
	10	11	*11*	12	13	14	15
	16	17	18	19	20	21	22
	23	24	25	26	27	28	29
LEAP VAIŚĀKHA 2170	**30**	2	3	4	5	6	7
	8	9	10	11	12	13	14
	15	*15*	16	17	18	19	20
	21	22	**23**	25	26	27	28
VAIŚĀKHA 2170	29	30	1	2	3	4	5
	6	7	8	9	10	11	12
	13	14	15	16	17	18	19
	20	21	22	23	24	25	**26**
JYAISHṬHA 2170	28	29	30	1	2	3	4
	5	6	7	8	9	10	11
	12	*12*	13	14	15	16	17
	18	**19**	21	22	23	24	25
ĀSHĀḌHA 2170	26	27	28	29	30	1	2
	3	4	5	6	7	8	9
	10	11	12	13	14	15	16
	17	18	19	20	21	**22**	24
ŚRĀVAṆA 2170	25	26	27	28	29	30	1
	2	3	4	5	6	7	8
	8	9	10	11	12	13	**14**
	16	17	18	19	20	21	22
	23[c]	24	25	26	27	28	29
BHĀDRAPADA 2170	30	1	2	3	4[d]	5	6
	7	8	9	10	11	12	13
	14	15	16	17	**18**	20	21
	22	23	24	25	26	27	28
ĀŚVINA 2170	29	30	1	2	3	4	*4*
	5	6	7	8[e]	9[e]	10[e]	11
	12	14	15	16	17	18	19
	20	21	22	23	24	25	26
KĀRTTIKA 2170	27	28	29	30	1[f]	2	3
	4	5	6	7	8	9	10
	11	12	13	14	15	**16**	18
	19	20	21	22	23	24	25
MĀRGAŚĪRA 2170	26	27	*27*	28	29	30	1
	2	3	4	5	6	7	8
	9	**10**[g]	12	13	14	15	16
	17	18	19	20	21	22	23
	24	25	26	27	28	29	30

HINDU SOLAR 2034/2035

Month	Sun	Mon	Tue	Wed	Thu	Fri	Sat
PAUSHA 2034	16	17	18	19	20	21	22
	23	24	25	26	27	28	29
MĀGHA 2034	30	1[b]	2	3	4	5	6
	7	8	9	10	11	12	13
	14	15	16	17	18	19	20
	21	22	23	24	25	26	27
PHĀLGUNA 2034	28	29	1	2	3	4	5
	6	7	8	9	10	11	12
	13	14	15	16	17	18	19
	20	21	22	23	24	25	26
CHAITRA 2034	27	28	29	30	1	2	3
	4	5	6	7	8	9	10
	11	12	13	14	15	16	17
	18	19	20	21	22	23	24
VAIŚĀKHA 2035	25	26	27	28	29	30	1[a]
	2	3	4	5	6	7	8
	9	10	11	12	13	14	15
	16	17	18	19	20	21	22
	23	24	25	26	27	28	29
JYAISHṬHA 2035	30	31	1	2	3	4	5
	6	7	8	9	10	11	12
	13	14	15	16	17	18	19
	20	21	22	23	24	25	26
ĀSHĀḌHA 2035	27	28	29	30	31	32	1
	2	3	4	5	6	7	8
	9	10	11	12	13	14	15
	16	17	18	19	20	21	22
	23	24	25	26	27	28	29
ŚRĀVAṆA 2035	30	31	1	2	3	4	5
	6	7	8	9	10	11	12
	13	14	15	16	17	18	19
	20	21	22	23	24	25	26
BHĀDRAPADA 2035	27	28	29	30	31	32	1
	2	3	4	5	6	7	8
	9	10	11	12	13	14	15
	16	17	18	19	20	21	22
	23	24	25	26	27	28	29
ĀŚVINA 2035	30	31	1	2	3	4	5
	6	7	8	9	10	11	12
	13	14	15	16	17	18	19
	20	21	22	23	24	25	26
KĀRTTIKA 2035	27	28	29	30	1	2	3
	4	5	6	7	8	9	10
	11	12	13	14	15	16	17
	18	19	20	21	22	23	24
MĀRGAŚĪRA 2035	25	26	27	28	29	30	1
	2	3	4	5	6	7	8
	9	10	11	12	13	14	15
	16	17	18	19	20	21	22
	23	24	25	26	27	28	29
PAUSHA 2035	30	1	2	3	4	5	6
	7	8	9	10	11	12	13
	14	15	16	17	18	19	20

ISLAMIC (ASTRONOMICAL) 1537/1538

Month	Sun	Mon	Tue	Wed	Thu	Fri	Sat
RABĪ' I 1537	13	14	15	16	17	18	19
	20	21	22	23	24	25	26
RABĪ' II 1537	27	28	29	30	*1*	2	3
	4	5	6	7	8	9	10
	11	12	13	14	15	16	17
	18	19	20	21	22	23	24
JUMĀDĀ I 1537	25	26	27	28	29	*1*	2
	3	4	5	6	7	8	9
	10	11	12	13	14	15	16
	17	18	19	20	21	22	23
	24	25	26	27	28	29	30
JUMĀDĀ II 1537	*1*	2	3	4	5	6	7
	8	9	10	11	12	13	14
	15	16	17	18	19	20	21
	22	23	24	25	26	27	28
RAJAB 1537	29	*1*	2	3	4	5	6
	7	8	9	10	11	12	13
	14	15	16	17	18	19	20
	21	22	23	24	25	26	27[d]
SHA'BĀN 1537	28	29	1	2	3	4	5
	6	7	8	9	10	11	12
	13	14	15	16	17	18	19
	20	21	22	23	24	25	26
RAMAḌĀN 1537	27	28	29	30	*1*[e]	2	3
	4	5	6	7	8	9	10
	11	12	13	14	15	16	17
	18	19	20	21	22	23	24
SHAWWĀL 1537	25	26	27	28	29	*1*[f]	2
	3	4	5	6	7	8	9
	10	11	12	13	14	15	16
	17	18	19	20	21	22	23
	24	25	26	27	28	29	30
DHU AL-QA'DA 1537	*1*	2	3	4	5	6	7
	8	9	10	11	12	13	14
	15	16	17	18	19	20	21
	22	23	24	25	26	27	28
DHU AL-ḤIJJA 1537	29	1	*2*	3	4	5	6
	7	8	9	10[g]	11	12	13
	14	15	16	17	18	19	20
	21	22	23	24	25	26	27
MUḤARRAM 1538	28	29	30	1[a]	2[A]	3	4
	5	6	7	8	9	10[b]	11
	12	13	14	15	16	17	18
	19	20	21	22	23	24	25
ṢAFAR 1538	26	27	28	29	30	1	2
	3	4	5	6	7	8	9
	10	11	12	13	14	15	16
	17	18	19	20	21	22	23
	24	25	26	27	28	29	30
RABĪ' I 1538	*1*	2	3	4	5	6	7
	8	9	10	11	12[c]	13	14
	15	16	17	18	19	20	21
	22	23	24	25	26	27	28

GREGORIAN 2113

Julian (Sun)	Sun	Mon	Tue	Wed	Thu	Fri	Sat	Month
Dec 18	*1*	2	3	4	5	6	7	JANUARY 2113
	8[a]	9	10	11	12	13	14	
Jan 1	15[b]	16	17	18	19	20	21	
	22	23	24	25	26	27	28	
Jan 15	29	30	31	1	2	3	4	FEBRUARY 2113
	5	6	7	8	9	10	11	
Jan 29	12	13	14	15[c]	16	17	18	
	19	20	21	22	23	24	25	
Feb 12	26[d]	27	28	1	2	3	4	MARCH 2113
	5	6	7	8	9	10	11	
Feb 26	12	13	14	15	16	17	18	
	19	20	21	22	23	24	25	
Mar 12	26	27	28	29	30	31	1	APRIL 2113
	2[e]	3	4	5	6	7	8	
Mar 26	9[f]	10	11	12	13	14	15	
	16	17	18	19	20	21	22	
Apr 9	23	24	25	26	27	28	29	
	30	1	2	3	4	5	6	MAY 2113
Apr 23	7	8	9	10	11	12	13	
	14	15	16	17	18	19	20	
May 7	21	22	23	24	25	26	27	
	28	29	30	31	1	2	3	JUNE 2113
May 21	4	5	6	7	8	9	10	
	11	12	13	14	15	16	17	
Jun 4	18	19	20	21	22	23	24	
	25	26	27	28	29	30	1	JULY 2113
Jun 18	2	3	4	5	6	7	8	
	9	10	11	12	13	14	15	
Jul 2	16	17	18	19	20	21	22	
	23	24	25	26	27	28	29	
Jul 16	30	31	1	2	3	4	5	AUGUST 2113
	6	7	8	9	10	11	12	
Jul 30	13	14	15	16	17	18	19	
	20	21	22	23	24	25	26	
Aug 13	27	28	29	30	31	1	2	SEPTEMBER 2113
	3	4	5	6	7	8	9	
Aug 27	10	11	12	13	14	15	16	
	17	18	19	20	21	22	23	
Sep 10	24	25	26	27	28	29	30	
	1	2	3	4	5	6	7	OCTOBER 2113
Sep 24	8	9	10	11	12	13	14	
	15	16	17	18	19	20	21	
Oct 8	22	23	24	25	26	27	28	
	29	30	31	1	2	3	4	NOVEMBER 2113
Oct 22	5	6	7	8	9	10	11	
	12	13	14	15	16	17	18	
Nov 5	19	20	21	22	23	24	25	
	26	27	28	29	30	1	2	DECEMBER 2113
Nov 19	3[g]	4	5	6	7	8	9	
	10	11	12	13	14	15	16	
Dec 3	17	18	19	20	21	22	23	
	24	25[h]	26	27	28	29	30	
Dec 17	31	1	2	3	4	5	6	

Persian: [a]New Year; [b]Sizdeh Bedar

Hindu Lunar: ‡Leap year; [a]New Year (Śrīmukha); [b]Birthday of Rāma; [c]Birthday of Krishna; [d]Ganēśa Chaturthī; [e]Dashara; [f]Diwali; [g]Birthday of Vishnu; [h]Night of Śiva; [i]Holi

Hindu Solar: [a]New Year (Sarvajit); [b]Pongal

Islamic: [a]New Year; [A]New Year (Arithmetic); [b]'Ashūrā'; [c]Prophet's Birthday; [d]Ascent of the Prophet; [e]Start of Ramaḍān; [f]'Id al-Fiṭr; [g]'Id al-'Aḍḥā

Gregorian: [a]Orthodox Christmas; [b]Julian New Year; [c]Ash Wednesday; [d]Feast of Orthodoxy; [e]Easter; [f]Orthodox Easter; [g]Advent; [h]Christmas

2114

GREGORIAN 2114	Sun	Mon	Tue	Wed	Thu	Fri	Sat	Lunar Phases	ISO WEEK (Mon)	JULIAN DAY (Sun noon)	HEBREW 5874[‡]/5875	Sun	Mon	Tue	Wed	Thu	Fri	Sat	Molad	CHINESE Guǐ-Yǒu/Jiǎ-Xū	Sun	Mon	Tue	Wed	Thu	Fri	Sat	Solar Term	COPTIC 1830/1831[‡]	Sun	Mon	Tue	Wed	Thu	Fri	Sat	ETHIOPIC 2106/2107[‡]
JANUARY 2114	31	1[a]	2	3	4	5	6		1	2493182	TEVETH 5874	22	23	24	25	26	27	28		MONTH 12 Guǐ-Yǒu	24	25	26	27	28	29	30	Xiǎo hán	KOIAK 1830	21	22	23	24	25	26	27	TĀKHŠĀŠ 2106
	●	8	9	10	11	12	13	2:43	2	2493189		29	1	2	3	4	5	6	Sat $21^h59^m1^p$		1	2	3*	4	5	6	7			28	29[c]	30	1	2	3	4	
	◐	15	16	17	18	19	20	8:07	3	2493196	SHEVAT 5874	7	8	9	10	11	12	13			8	9	10	11	12	13	**14**	Dà hán	TŌBE 1830	5	6[d]	7	8	9	10	11[e]	ṬER 2106
	○	22	23	24	25	26	27	3:54	4	2493203		14	15	16	17	18	19	20			15	16	17	18	19	20	21			12	13	14	15	16	17	18	
	◑	29	30	31	1	2	3	20:34	5	2493210		21	22	23	24	25	26	27			22	23	24	25	26	27	28			19	20	21	22	23	24	25	
FEBRUARY 2114	4	●	6	7	8	9	10	18:11	6	2493217		28	29	30	1	2	3	4	Mon $10^h43^m2^p$	MONTH 1 Jiǎ-Xū	29	30	1[a]	2	3	4	5	Lì chūn		26	27	28	29	30	1	2	
	11	◐	13	14	15	16	17	16:03	7	2493224	ADAR I 5874	5	6	7	8	9	10	11			6	7	8	9	10	11	12		MESHIR 1830	3	4	5	6	7	8	9	YAKĀTIT 2106
	18	○	20	21	22	23	24	18:01	8	2493231		12	13	14	15	16	17	18			13	**14**	15[b]	16	17	18	19	Yǔ shuǐ		10	11	12	13	14	15	16	
	25	26	◑	28	1	2	3	18:10	9	2493238		19	20	21	22	23	24	25			20	21	22	23	24	25	26			17	18	19	20	21	22	23	
MARCH 2114	4	5	6	●	8	9	10	6:50	10	2493245		26	27	28	29	30	1	2	Tue $23^h27^m3^p$		27	28	29	1	2	3	4*	Jīng zhé		24	25	26	27	28	29	30	
	11	12	◐	14	15	16	17	23:54	11	2493252	ADAR II 5874	3	4	5	6	7	8	9		MONTH 2 Jiǎ-Xū	5	6	7	8	9	10	11		PAREMOTEP 1830	1	2	3	4	5	6	7	MAGĀBIT 2106
	18	19	20[b]	○	22	23	24	9:16	12	2493259		10	11	12	13	14[f]	15	16			12	13	14	**15**	16	17	18	Chūn fēn		8	9	10	11	12	13	14	
	25	26	27	28	◑	30	31	13:38	13	2493266		17	18	19	20	21	22	23			19	20	21	22	23	24	25			15	16	17	18	19	20	21	
APRIL 2114	1	2	3	4	●	6	7	17:03	14	2493273		24	25	26	27	28	29	1	Thu $12^h11^m4^p$		26	27	28	29	30[c]	1	2	Qīng míng		22	23	24	25	26	27	28	
	8	9	10	11	◐	13	14	8:26	15	2493280	NISAN 5874	2	3	4	5	6	7	8		MONTH 3 Jiǎ-Xū	3	4	5	6	7	8	9		PARMOUTE 1830	29	30	1	2	3	4	5	MIYĀZYĀ 2106
	15	16	17	18	19	○	21	1:24	16	2493287		9	10	11	12	13	14	15[g]			10	11	12	13	14	**15**	16	Gǔ yǔ		6	7	8	9	10	11	12	
	22	23	24	25	26	27	◑	5:25	17	2493294		16	17	18	19	20	21	22			17	18	19	20	21	22	23			13	14	15	16	17	18	19	
	29	30	1	2	3	4	●	1:35	18	2493301		23	24	25	26	27	28	29			24	25	26	27	28	29	1			20[f]	21	22	23	24	25	26	
MAY 2114	6	7	8	9	10	◐	12	18:15	19	2493308	IYAR 5874	30	1	2	3	4	5	6	Sat $0^h55^m5^p$	MONTH 4 Jiǎ-Xū	2	3	4	5*	6	7	8	Lì xià	PASHONS 1830	27	28	29[g]	30	1	2	3	GENBOT 2106
	13	14	15	16	17	18	○	17:47	20	2493315		7	8	9	10	11	12	13			9	10	11	12	13	14	15			4	5	6	7	8	9	10	
	20	21	22	23	24	25	26		21	2493322		14	15	16	17	18	19	20			16	**17**	18	19	20	21	22	Xiǎo mǎn		11	12	13	14	15	16	17	
	◑	28	29	30	31	1	2	17:11	22	2493329		21	22	23	24	25	26	27			23	24	25	26	27	28	29			18	19	20	21	22	23	24	
JUNE 2114	●	4	5	6	7	8	9	9:10	23	2493336		28	29	1	2	3	4	5	Sun $13^h39^m6^p$	MONTH 5 Jiǎ-Xū	1	2	3	4	5[d]	6	7	Máng zhòng	PAŌNE 1830	25	26	27	28	29	30	1	SANĒ 2106
	◐	11	12	13	14	15	16	5:56	24	2493343	SIVAN 5874	6[h]	7	8	9	10	11	12			8	9	10	11	12	13	14			2	3	4	5	6	7	8	
	17	○	19	20	21[c]	22	23	9:29	25	2493350		13	14	15	16	17	18	19			15	16	17	18	**19**	20	21	Xià zhì		9	10	11	12	13	14	15	
	24	25	◑	27	28	29	30	1:35	26	2493357		20	21	22	23	24	25	26			22	23	24	25	26	27	28			16	17	18	19	20	21	22	
JULY 2114	1	●	3	4	5	6	7	16:34	27	2493364	TAMMUZ 5874	27	28	29	30	1	2	3	Tue $2^h23^m7^p$	MONTH 6 Jiǎ-Xū	29	30	1	2	3	4	5	Xiǎo shǔ	EPĒP 1830	23	24	25	26	27	28	29	ḤAMLĒ 2106
	8	◐	10	11	12	13	14	19:54	28	2493371		4	5	6	7	8	9	10			6*	7	8	9	10	11	12			30	1	2	3	4	5	6	
	15	16	○	18	19	20	21	23:41	29	2493378		11	12	13	14	15	16	17			13	14	15	16	17	18	19			7	8	9	10	11	12	13	
	22	23	24	◑	26	27	28	7:44	30	2493385		18	19	20	21	22	23	24			20	**21**	22	23	24	25	26	Dà shǔ		14	15	16	17	18	19	20	
	29	30	31	●	2	3	4	0:36	31	2493392		25	26	27	28	29	1	2	Wed $15^h7^m8^p$		27	28	29	1	2	3	4			21	22	23	24	25	26	27	
AUGUST 2114	5	6	7	◐	9	10	11	12:14	32	2493399	AV 5874	3	4	5	6	7	8	9		MONTH 7 Jiǎ-Xū	5	6	7[e]	8	9	10	11	Lì qiū	MESORĒ 1830	28	29	30	1	2	3	4	NAHASĒ 2106
	12	13	14	15	○	17	18	12:05	33	2493406		10[i]	11	12	13	14	15	16			12	13	14	15[f]	16	17	18			5	6	7	8	9	10	11	
	19	20	21	22	◑	24	25	12:55	34	2493413		17	18	19	20	21	22	23			19	20	21	22	**23**	24	25	Chǔ shǔ		12	13[h]	14	15	16	17	18	
	26	27	28	29	●	31	1	10:15	35	2493420		24	25	26	27	28	29	30			26	27	28	29	1	2	3			19	20	21	22	23	24	25	
SEPTEMBER 2114	2	3	4	5	6	◐	8	6:24	36	2493427	ELUL 5874	1	2	3	4	5	6	7	Fri $3^h51^m9^p$	MONTH 8 Jiǎ-Xū	4	5	6	7	8*	9	*10*	Bái lù	EPAG. 1830	26	27	28	29	30	1	2	PĀG. 2106
	9	10	11	12	13	○	15	23:05	37	2493434		8	9	10	11	12	13	14			11	12	13	14	15[g]	16	17		THOOUT 1831	3	4	5	1[a]	2	3	4	MASKARAM 2107
	16	17	18	19	20	◑	22	18:24	38	2493441		15	16	17	18	19	20	21			18	19	20	21	22	23	24			5	6	7	8	9	10	11	
	23[d]	24	25	26	27	●	29	22:31	39	2493448		22	23	24	25	26	27	28			**25**	26	27	28	29	30	1	Qiū fēn		12	13	14	15	16	17[b]	18	
OCTOBER 2114	30	1	2	3	4	5	6		40	2493455	TISHRI 5875	29	1[a]	2[a]	3	4	5	6	Sat $16^h35^m10^p$	MONTH 9 Jiǎ-Xū	2	3	4	5	6	7	8			19	20	21	22	23	24	25	
	◐	8	9	10	11	12	13	1:13	41	2493462		7	8	9	10[b]	11	12	13			9[h]	*10*	11	12	13	14	15	Hán lù	PAOPE 1831	26	27	28	29	30	1	2	ṬEQEMT 2107
	○	15	16	17	18	19	20	9:24	42	2493469		14	15[c]	16	17	18	19	20			16	17	18	19	20	21	22			3	4	5	6	7	8	9	
	◑	22	23	24	25	26	27	1:27	43	2493476		21	22	23	24	25	26	27			23	24	25	**26**	27	28	29	Shuāng jiàng		10	11	12	13	14	15	16	
	●	29	30	31	1	2	3	14:00	44	2493483		28	29	30	1	2	3	4	Mon $5^h19^m11^p$	MONTH 10 Jiǎ-Xū	1	2	3	4	5	6	7			17	18	19	20	21	22	23	
NOVEMBER 2114	4	◐	6	7	8	9	10	19:19	45	2493490	HESHVAN 5875	5	6	7	8	9	10	11			8	9*	10	11	*12*	13	14	Lì dōng	ATHŌR 1831	24	25	26	27	28	29	30	ḪEDĀR 2107
	11	○	13	14	15	16	17	19:43	46	2493497		12	13	14	15	16	17	18			15	16	17	18	19	20	21			1	2	3	4	5	6	7	
	18	◑	20	21	22	23	24	11:10	47	2493504		19	20	21	22	23	24	25			22	23	24	25	**26**	27	28	Xiǎo xuě		8	9	10	11	12	13	14	
	25	26	●	28	29	30	1	8:22	48	2493511		26	27	28	29	1	2	3	Tue $18^h3^m12^p$		29	30	1	2	3	4	5			15	16	17	18	19	20	21	
DECEMBER 2114	2	3	4	◐	6	7	8	11:34	49	2493518	KISLEV 5875	4	5	6	7	8[d]	9	10		MONTH 11 Jiǎ-Xū	6	7	8	9	10	*11*	12	Dà xuě	KOIAK 1831	22	23	24	25	26	27	28	TĀKHŠĀŠ 2107
	9	10	11	○	13	14	15	6:19	50	2493525		11	12	13	14	15	16	17			13	14	15	16	17	18	19			29	30	1	2	3	4	5	
	16	17	18	◑	20	21	22[e]	0:26	51	2493532		18	19	20	21	22	23	24			20	21	22	23	24	25	26[i]	Dōng zhì		6	7	8	9	10	11	12	
	23	24	25	26	●	28	29	4:05	52	2493539	TEVETH 5875	25[e]	26[e]	27[e]	28[e]	29[e]	1[e]	2[e]	Thu $6^h47^m13^p$	MONTH 12 Jiǎ-Xū	27	28	29	30	1	2	3			13	14	15	16	17	18	19	
	30	31	1	2	3	◐	5	1:18	1	2493546		3[e]	4	5	6	7	8	9			4	5	6	7	8	9	10			20	21	22	23	24	25	26	

[a]New Year
[b]Spring (22:38)
[c]Summer (14:46)
[d]Autumn (7:27)
[e]Winter (5:38)
● New moon
◐ First quarter moon
○ Full moon
◑ Last quarter moon

[‡]Leap year
[a]New Year
[b]Yom Kippur
[c]Sukkot
[d]Winter starts
[e]Ḥanukkah
[f]Purim
[g]Passover
[h]Shavuot
[i]Fast of Av

[a]New Year (4812, Dog)
[b]Lantern Festival
[c]Qīngmíng
[d]Dragon Festival
[e]Qīqiǎo
[f]Hungry Ghosts
[g]Mid-Autumn Festival
[h]Double-Ninth Festival
[i]Dōngzhì
*Start of 60-name cycle

[‡]Leap year
[a]New Year
[b]Building of the Cross
[c]Christmas
[d]Jesus's Circumcision
[e]Epiphany
[f]Easter
[g]Mary's Announcement
[h]Jesus's Transfiguration

PERSIAN (ASTRONOMICAL) 1492/1493	Sun	Mon	Tue	Wed	Thu	Fri	Sat
DEY 1492	10	11	12	13	14	15	16
	17	18	19	20	21	22	23
	24	25	26	27	28	29	30
BAHMAN 1492	1	2	3	4	5	6	7
	8	9	10	11	12	13	14
	15	16	17	18	19	20	21
	22	23	24	25	26	27	28
	29	30	1	2	3	4	5
ESFAND 1492	6	7	8	9	10	11	12
	13	14	15	16	17	18	19
	20	21	22	23	24	25	26
	27	28	29	1[a]	2	3	4
FARVARDĪN 1493	5	6	7	8	9	10	11
	12	13[b]	14	15	16	17	18
	19	20	21	22	23	24	25
	26	27	28	29	30	31	1
ORDĪBEHEŠT 1493	2	3	4	5	6	7	8
	9	10	11	12	13	14	15
	16	17	18	19	20	21	22
	23	24	25	26	27	28	29
	30	31	1	2	3	4	5
XORDĀD 1493	6	7	8	9	10	11	12
	13	14	15	16	17	18	19
	20	21	22	23	24	25	26
	27	28	29	30	31	1	2
TĪR 1493	3	4	5	6	7	8	9
	10	11	12	13	14	15	16
	17	18	19	20	21	22	23
	24	25	26	27	28	29	30
	31	1	2	3	4	5	6
MORDĀD 1493	7	8	9	10	11	12	13
	14	15	16	17	18	19	20
	21	22	23	24	25	26	27
	28	29	30	31	1	2	3
SHAHRĪVAR 1493	4	5	6	7	8	9	10
	11	12	13	14	15	16	17
	18	19	20	21	22	23	24
	25	26	27	28	29	30	31
MEHR 1493	1	2	3	4	5	6	7
	8	9	10	11	12	13	14
	15	16	17	18	19	20	21
	22	23	24	25	26	27	28
	29	30	1	2	3	4	5
ĀBĀN 1493	6	7	8	9	10	11	12
	13	14	15	16	17	18	19
	20	21	22	23	24	25	26
	27	28	29	30	1	2	3
ĀZAR 1493	4	5	6	7	8	9	10
	11	12	13	14	15	16	17
	18	19	20	21	22	23	24
	25	26	27	28	29	30	1
DEY 1493	2	3	4	5	6	7	8
	9	10	11	12	13	14	15

HINDU LUNAR 2170‡/2171	Sun	Mon	Tue	Wed	Thu	Fri	Sat
MĀRGAŚIRA 2170	24	25	26	27	28	29	30
PAUSHA 2170	30	1	2	**3**	5	6	7
	8	9	10	11	12	13	14
	15	16	17	18	19	20	21
	22	23	24	25	26	27	28
	29	30	1	2	3	4	5
MĀGHA 2170	6	7	8	**9**	11	12	13
	14	15	16	17	18	19	20
	21	22	22	23	24	25	26
	27	28[h]	29	30	1	2	**3**
PHĀLGUNA 2170	5	6	7	8	9	10	11
	12	13	14	15[i]	16	17	18
	19	20	21	22	23	24	25
	26	27	28	29	30	1[a]	2
CHAITRA 2171	3	4	5	6	**7**	9[b]	10
	11	12	13	14	15	16	16
	17	18	19	20	21	22	23
	24	25	26	27	28	29	**30**
VAIŚĀKHA 2171	2	3	4	5	6	7	8
	9	10	11	12	13	14	15
	16	17	18	19	20	20	21
	22	24	25	26	27	28	29
	30	1	2	3	**4**	6	7
JYAISHṬHA 2171	8	9	10	11	11	12	13
	14	15	16	17	18	19	20
	21	22	23	24	25	**26**	28
	29	30	1	2	3	4	5
ĀSHĀḌHA 2171	6	7	8	9	10	11	12
	13	14	15	16	17	18	19
	20	21	22	23	24	25	26
	27	28	**29**	1	2	3	4
ŚRĀVAṆA 2171	5	6	7	8	8	9	10
	11	12	13	14	15	16	17
	18	19	20	21	**22**[c]	24	25
	26	27	28	29	30	1	2
BHĀDRAPADA 2171	3	4[d]	5	6	7	8	9
	10	11	12	13	14	15	16
	17	18	19	20	21	22	23
	24	25	**26**	28	29	30	1
ĀŚVINA 2171	2	3	4	4	5	6	7
	8[e]	9[e]	10[e]	11	12	13	14
	15	16	17	18	**19**	21	22
	23	24	25	26	27	28	29
	30	1[f]	2	3	4	5	6
KĀRTTIKA 2171	7	7	8	9	10	11	**12**
	14	15	16	17	18	19	20
	21	22	23	24	25	26	27
	28	29	30	1	2	3	4
MĀRGAŚIRA 2171	5	6	7	8	9	10	11[g]
	12	13	14	15	16	**17**	19
	20	21	22	23	24	25	26
PAUSHA 2171	27	28	29	30	30	1	2
	3	4	5	6	7	8	9

HINDU SOLAR 2035/2036‡	Sun	Mon	Tue	Wed	Thu	Fri	Sat
PAUSHA 2035	14	15	16	17	18	19	20
	21	22	23	24	25	26	27
	28	29	1[b]	2	3	4	5
MĀGHA 2035	6	7	8	9	10	11	12
	13	14	15	16	17	18	19
	20	21	22	23	24	25	26
	27	28	29	1	2	3	4
PHĀLGUNA 2035	5	6	7	8	9	10	11
	12	13	14	15	16	17	18
	19	20	21	22	23	24	25
	26	27	28	29	30	1	2
CHAITRA 2035	3	4	5	6	7	8	9
	10	11	12	13	14	15	16
	17	18	19	20	21	22	23
	24	25	26	27	28	29	30
VAIŚĀKHA 2036	1[a]	2	3	4	5	6	7
	8	9	10	11	12	13	14
	15	16	17	18	19	20	21
	22	23	24	25	26	27	28
	29	30	31	1	2	3	4
JYAISHṬHA 2036	5	6	7	8	9	10	11
	12	13	14	15	16	17	18
	19	20	21	22	23	24	25
	26	27	28	29	30	31	32
ĀSHĀḌHA 2036	1	2	3	4	5	6	7
	8	9	10	11	12	13	14
	15	16	17	18	19	20	21
	22	23	24	25	26	27	28
	29	30	31	1	2	3	4
ŚRĀVAṆA 2036	5	6	7	8	9	10	11
	12	13	14	15	16	17	18
	19	20	21	22	23	24	25
	26	27	28	29	30	31	32
BHĀDRAPADA 2036	1	2	3	4	5	6	7
	8	9	10	11	12	13	14
	15	16	17	18	19	20	21
	22	23	24	25	26	27	28
	29	30	31	1	2	3	4
ĀŚVINA 2036	5	6	7	8	9	10	11
	12	13	14	15	16	17	18
	19	20	21	22	23	24	25
	26	27	28	29	30	1	2
KĀRTTIKA 2036	3	4	5	6	7	8	9
	10	11	12	13	14	15	16
	17	18	19	20	21	22	23
	24	25	26	27	28	29	30
MĀRGAŚIRA 2036	1	2	3	4	5	6	7
	8	9	10	11	12	13	14
	15	16	17	18	19	20	21
	22	23	24	25	26	27	28
PAUSHA 2036	29	30	1	2	3	4	5
	6	7	8	9	10	11	12
	13	14	15	16	17	18	19

ISLAMIC (ASTRONOMICAL) 1538/1539‡	Sun	Mon	Tue	Wed	Thu	Fri	Sat
RABĪ' I 1538	22	23	24	25	26	27	28
RABĪ' II 1538	29	30	1	2	3	4	5
	6	7	8	9	10	11	12
	13	14	15	16	17	18	19
	20	21	22	23	24	25	26
JUMĀDĀ I 1538	27	28	29	1	2	3	4
	5	6	7	8	9	10	11
	12	13	14	15	16	17	18
	19	20	21	22	23	24	25
JUMĀDĀ II 1538	26	27	28	29	1	2	3
	4	5	6	7	8	9	10
	11	12	13	14	15	16	17
	18	19	20	21	22	23	24
RAJAB 1538	25	26	27	28	29	30	1
	2	3	4	5	6	7	8
	9	10	11	12	13	14	15
	16	17	18	19	20	21	22
	23	24	25	26	27[d]	28	29
SHA'BĀN 1538	1	2	3	4	5	6	7
	8	9	10	11	12	13	14
	15	16	17	18	19	20	21
	22	23	24	25	26	27	28
RAMAḌĀN 1538	29	1[e]	2	3	4	5	6
	7	8	9	10	11	12	13
	14	15	16	17	18	19	20
	21	22	23	24	25	26	27
SHAWWĀL 1538	28	29	30	1[f]	2	3	4
	5	6	7	8	9	10	11
	12	13	14	15	16	17	18
	19	20	21	22	23	24	25
DHU AL-QA'DA 1538	26	27	28	29	1	2	3
	4	5	6	7	8	9	10
	11	12	13	14	15	16	17
	18	19	20	21	22	23	24
DHU AL-ḤIJJA 1538	25	26	27	28	29	30	1
	2	3	4	5	6	7	8
	9	10[g]	11	12	13	14	15
	16	17	18	19	20	21	22
	23	24	25	26	27	28	29
MUḤARRAM 1539	1[a]	2[d]	3	4	5	6	7
	8	9	10[h]	11	12	13	14
	15	16	17	18	19	20	21
	22	23	24	25	26	27	28
ṢAFAR 1539	29	30	1	2	3	4	5
	6	7	8	9	10	11	12
	13	14	15	16	17	18	19
	20	21	22	23	24	25	26
RABĪ' I 1539	27	28	29	30	1	2	3
	4	5	6	7	8	9	10
	11	12[c]	13	14	15	16	17
	18	19	20	21	22	23	24
RABĪ' II 1539	25	26	27	28	29	30	1
	2	3	4	5	6	7	8

Julian (Sun)	Sun	Mon	Tue	Wed	Thu	Fri	Sat	GREGORIAN 2114
Dec 17	31	1	2	3	4	5	6	JANUARY 2114
	7	8[a]	9	10	11	12	13	
Dec 31	14	15[b]	16	17	18	19	20	
	21	22	23	24	25	26	27	
Jan 14	28	29	30	31	1	2	3	FEBRUARY 2114
	4	5	6	7	8	9	10	
Jan 28	11	12	13	14	15	16	17	
	18	19	20	21	22	23	24	
Feb 11	25	26	27	28	1	2	3	MARCH 2114
	4	5	6	7[c]	8	9	10	
Feb 25	11	12	13	14	15	16	17	
	18[d]	19	20	21	22	23	24	
Mar 11	25	26	27	28	29	30	31	
	1	2	3	4	5	6	7	APRIL 2114
Mar 25	8	9	10	11	12	13	14	
	15	16	17	18	19	20	21	
Apr 8	22[e]	23	24	25	26	27	28	
	29[f]	30	1	2	3	4	5	MAY 2114
Apr 22	6	7	8	9	10	11	12	
	13	14	15	16	17	18	19	
May 6	20	21	22	23	24	25	26	
	27	28	29	30	31	1	2	JUNE 2114
May 20	3	4	5	6	7	8	9	
	10	11	12	13	14	15	16	
Jun 3	17	18	19	20	21	22	23	
	24	25	26	27	28	29	30	
Jun 17	1	2	3	4	5	6	7	JULY 2114
	8	9	10	11	12	13	14	
Jul 1	15	16	17	18	19	20	21	
	22	23	24	25	26	27	28	
Jul 15	29	30	31	1	2	3	4	AUGUST 2114
	5	6	7	8	9	10	11	
Jul 29	12	13	14	15	16	17	18	
	19	20	21	22	23	24	25	
Aug 12	26	27	28	29	30	31	1	SEPTEMBER 2114
	2	3	4	5	6	7	8	
Aug 26	9	10	11	12	13	14	15	
	16	17	18	19	20	21	22	
Sep 9	23	24	25	26	27	28	29	
	30	1	2	3	4	5	6	OCTOBER 2114
Sep 23	7	8	9	10	11	12	13	
	14	15	16	17	18	19	20	
Oct 7	21	22	23	24	25	26	27	
	28	29	30	31	1	2	3	NOVEMBER 2114
Oct 21	4	5	6	7	8	9	10	
	11	12	13	14	15	16	17	
Nov 4	18	19	20	21	22	23	24	
	25	26	27	28	29	30	1	DECEMBER 2114
Nov 18	2[g]	3	4	5	6	7	8	
	9	10	11	12	13	14	15	
Dec 2	16	17	18	19	20	21	22	
	23	24	25[h]	26	27	28	29	
Dec 16	30	31	1	2	3	4	5	

Persian:
[a]New Year
[b]Sizdeh Bedar

Hindu Lunar:
‡Leap year
[a]New Year (Bhāva)
[b]Birthday of Rāma
[c]Birthday of Krishna
[d]Ganēśa Chaturthī
[e]Dashara
[f]Diwali
[g]Birthday of Vishnu
[h]Night of Śiva
[i]Holi

Hindu Solar:
‡Leap year
[a]New Year (Virodhin)
[b]Pongal

Islamic:
‡Leap year
[a]New Year
[d]New Year (Arithmetic)
[h]‘Ashūrā’
[c]Prophet's Birthday
[d]Ascent of the Prophet
[e]Start of Ramaḍān
[f]‘Id al-Fiṭr
[g]‘Id al-'Aḍḥā

Gregorian:
[a]Orthodox Christmas
[b]Julian New Year
[c]Ash Wednesday
[d]Feast of Orthodoxy
[e]Easter
[f]Orthodox Easter
[g]Advent
[h]Christmas

2115

Gregorian 2115

ISO Week (Mon)	Month	Sun	Mon	Tue	Wed	Thu	Fri	Sat	Lunar Phases	Julian Day (Sun noon)
1	January 2115	30	31	1[a]	2	3	◐	5	1:18	2493546
2		6	7	8	9	○	11	12	17:12	2493553
3		13	14	15	16	◑	18	19	17:25	2493560
4		20	21	22	23	24	●	26	23:07	2493567
5		27	28	29	30	31	1	◐	12:21	2493574
6	February 2115	3	4	5	6	7	8	○	4:25	2493581
7		10	11	12	13	14	15	◑	13:15	2493588
8		17	18	19	20	21	22	23		2493595
9		●	25	26	27	28	1	2	15:56	2493602
10	March 2115	◐	4	5	6	7	8	9	20:56	2493609
11		○	11	12	13	14	15	16	16:14	2493616
12		17	◑	19	20	21[b]	22	23	10:03	2493623
13		24	25	●	27	28	29	30	5:56	2493630
14		31	1	◐	3	4	5	6	3:48	2493637
15	April 2115	7	8	○	10	11	12	13	5:05	2493644
16		14	15	16	◑	18	19	20	5:45	2493651
17		21	22	23	●	25	26	27	17:14	2493658
18		28	29	30	◐	2	3	4	9:59	2493665
19	May 2115	5	6	7	○	9	10	11	19:09	2493672
20		12	13	14	15	◑	17	18	22:54	2493679
21		19	20	21	22	23	●	25	2:17	2493686
22		26	27	28	29	◐	31	1	16:47	2493693
23	June 2115	2	3	4	5	6	○	8	10:09	2493700
24		9	10	11	12	13	14	◑	13:00	2493707
25		16	17	18	19	20	21[c]	●	9:43	2493714
26		23	24	25	26	27	28	◐	1:26	2493721
27		30	1	2	3	4	5	6		2493728
28	July 2115	○	8	9	10	11	12	13	1:27	2493735
29		14	◑	16	17	18	19	20	0:11	2493742
30		●	22	23	24	25	26	27	16:25	2493749
31		◐	29	30	31	1	2	3	12:52	2493756
32	August 2115	4	○	6	7	8	9	10	16:25	2493763
33		11	12	◑	14	15	16	17	8:55	2493770
34		18	●	20	21	22	23	24	23:30	2493777
35		25	26	◐	28	29	30	31	3:30	2493784
36	September 2115	1	2	3	○	5	6	7	6:48	2493791
37		8	9	10	◑	12	13	14	15:52	2493798
38		15	16	17	●	19	20	21	8:10	2493805
39		22	23[d]	24	◐	26	27	28	21:04	2493812
40		29	30	1	2	○	4	5	20:29	2493819
41	October 2115	6	7	8	9	◑	11	12	22:01	2493826
42		13	14	15	16	●	18	19	19:31	2493833
43		20	21	22	23	24	◐	26	16:41	2493840
44		27	28	29	30	31	1	○	9:26	2493847
45	November 2115	3	4	5	6	7	8	◑	4:35	2493854
46		10	11	12	13	14	15	●	10:04	2493861
47		17	18	19	20	21	22	23		2493868
48		◐	25	26	27	28	29	30	12:59	2493875
49	December 2115	○	2	3	4	5	6	7	21:36	2493882
50		◑	9	10	11	12	13	14	12:53	2493889
51		15	●	17	18	19	20	21	3:28	2493896
52		22[e]	23	◐	25	26	27	28	8:24	2493903
1		29	30	○	1	2	3	4	8:52	2493910

Hebrew 5875/5876

ISO Week	Month	Sun	Mon	Tue	Wed	Thu	Fri	Sat	Molad
1	Teveth 5875	3[e]	4	5	6	7	8	9	
2		10	11	12	13	14	15	16	
3		17	18	19	20	21	22	23	
4		24	25	26	27	28	29	1	Fri 19h31m14p
5	Shevat 5875	2	3	4	5	6	7	8	
6		9	10	11	12	13	14	15	
7		16	17	18	19	20	21	22	
8		23	24	25	26	27	28	29	
9		30	1	2	3	4	5	6	Sun 8h15m15p
10	Adar 5875	7	8	9	10	11	12	13	
11		14[f]	15	16	17	18	19	20	
12		21	22	23	24	25	26	27	
13		28	29	1	2	3	4	5	Mon 20h59m16p
14	Nisan 5875	6	7	8	9	10	11	12	
15		13	14	15[g]	16	17	18	19	
16		20	21	22	23	24	25	26	
17		27	28	29	30	1	2	3	Wed 9h43m17p
18	Iyyar 5875	4	5	6	7	8	9	10	
19		11	12	13	14	15	16	17	
20		18	19	20	21	22	23	24	
21		25	26	27	28	29	1	2	Thu 22h28m0p
22	Sivan 5875	3	4	5	6[h]	7	8	9	
23		10	11	12	13	14	15	16	
24		17	18	19	20	21	22	23	
25		24	25	26	27	28	29	30	
26	Tammuz 5875	1	2	3	4	5	6	7	Sat 11h12m1p
27		8	9	10	11	12	13	14	
28		15	16	17	18	19	20	21	
29		22	23	24	25	26	27	28	
30		29	1	2	3	4	5	6	Sun 23h56m2p
31	Av 5875	7	8	9[i]	10	11	12	13	
32		14	15	16	17	18	19	20	
33		21	22	23	24	25	26	27	
34		28	29	30	1	2	3	4	Tue 12h40m3p
35	Elul 5875	5	6	7	8	9	10	11	
36		12	13	14	15	16	17	18	
37		19	20	21	22	23	24	25	
38		26	27	28	29	1[a]	2[a]	3	Thu 1h24m4p
39	Tishri 5876	4	5	6	7	8	9	10[b]	
40		11	12	13	14	15[c]	16	17	
41		18	19	20	21	22	23	24	
42		25	26	27	28	29	30	1	Fri 14h8m5p
43	Heshvan 5876	2	3	4	5	6	7	8	
44		9	10	11	12	13	14	15	
45		16	17	18	19	20	21	22	
46		23	24	25	26	27	28	29	
47	Kislev 5876	1	2	3	4	5	6	7	Sun 2h52m6p
48		8	9	10	11	12	13	14	
49		15	16	17	18	19	20	21[d]	
50		22	23	24	25[e]	26[e]	27[e]	28[e]	
51		29[e]	30[e]	1[e]	2[e]	3	4	5	Mon 15h36m7p
52	Teveth 5876	6	7	8	9	10	11	12	
1		13	14	15	16	17	18	19	

Chinese Jiă-Xū/Yĭ-Hài‡

ISO Week	Month	Sun	Mon	Tue	Wed	Thu	Fri	Sat	Solar Term
1	Month 12 Jiă-Xū	4	5	6	7	8	9*	10	
2		11	12	13	14	15	16	17	Xiǎo hán
3		18	19	20	21	22	23	24	
4		25	26	27	28	29	30	1[a]	Dà hán
5	Month 1 Yĭ-Hài	2	3	4	5	6	7	8	
6		9	10	11	12	13	14	15[b]	Lì chūn
7		16	17	18	19	20	21	22	
8		23	24	25	26	27	28	29	Yǔ shuǐ
9	Month 2 Yĭ-Hài	1	2	3	4	5	6	7	
10		8	9	10*	11	12	13	14	Jīng zhé
11		15	16	17	18	19	20	21	
12		22	23	24	25	26	27	28	Chūn fēn
13		29	30	1	2	3	4	5	
14	Month 3 Yĭ-Hài	6	7	8	9	10	11[c]	12	Qīng míng
15		13	14	15	16	17	18	19	
16		20	21	22	23	24	25	26	Gǔ yǔ
17		27	28	29	30	1	2	3	
18	Month 4 Yĭ-Hài	4	5	6	7	8	9	10*	
19		11	12	13	14	15	16	17	Lì xià
20		18	19	20	21	22	23	24	
21		25	26	27	28	29	1	2	Xiǎo mǎn
22	Leap Month 4 Yĭ-Hài	3	4	5	6	7	8	9	
23		10	11	12	13	14	15	16	Máng zhòng
24		17	18	19	20	21	22	23	
25		24	25	26	27	28	29	1	Xià zhì
26	Month 5 Yĭ-Hài	2	3	4	5[d]	6	7	8	
27		9	10	11	12*	13	14	15	
28		16	17	18	19	20	21	22	Xiǎo shǔ
29		23	24	25	26	27	28	29	
30		30	1	2	3	4	5	6	Dà shǔ
31	Month 6 Yĭ-Hài	7	8	9	10	11	12	13	
32		14	15	16	17	18	19	20	Lì qiū
33		21	22	23	24	25	26	27	
34		28	29	1	2	3	4	5	Chǔ shǔ
35	Month 7 Yĭ-Hài	6	7[e]	8	9	10	11	12	
36		13*	14	15[f]	16	17	18	19	
37		20	21	22	23	24	25	26	Bái lù
38		27	28	29	1	2	3	4	
39	Month 8 Yĭ-Hài	5	6	7	8	9	10	11	Qiū fēn
40		12	13	14	15[g]	16	17	18	
41		19	20	21	22	23	24	25	Hán lù
42		26	27	28	29	30	1	2	
43	Month 9 Yĭ-Hài	3	4	5	6	7	8	9[h]	Shuāng jiàng
44		10	11	12	13	14*	15	16	
45		17	18	19	20	21	22	23	
46		24	25	26	27	28	29	1	Lì dōng
47	Month 10 Yĭ-Hài	2	3	4	5	6	7	8	Xiǎo xuě
48		9	10	11	12	13	14	15	
49		16	17	18	19	20	21	22	
50		23	24	25	26	27	28	29	Dà xuě
51		30	1	2	3	4	5	6	
52	Month 11 Yĭ-Hài	7[i]	8	9	10	11	12	13	Dōng zhì
1		14	15*	16	17	18	19	20	

Coptic 1831‡/1832 — Ethiopic 2107‡/2108

ISO Week	Coptic Month	Sun	Mon	Tue	Wed	Thu	Fri	Sat	Ethiopic Month
1	Koiak 1831	20	21	22	23	24	25	26	Tākhśāś 2107
2		27	28	29[c]	30	1	2	3	
3	Tōbe 1831	4	5	6[d]	7	8	9	10	Ṭer 2107
4		11[e]	12	13	14	15	16	17	
5		18	19	20	21	22	23	24	
6		25	26	27	28	29	30	1	
7	Meshir 1831	2	3	4	5	6	7	8	Yakātit 2107
8		9	10	11	12	13	14	15	
9		16	17	18	19	20	21	22	
10		23	24	25	26	27	28	29	
11		30	1	2	3	4	5	6	
12	Paremotep 1831	7	8	9	10	11	12	13	Magābit 2107
13		14	15	16	17	18	19	20	
14		21	22	23	24	25	26	27	
15		28	29	30	1	2	3	4	
16	Parmoute 1831	5[f]	6	7	8	9	10	11	Miyāzyā 2107
17		12	13	14	15	16	17	18	
18		19	20	21	22	23	24	25	
19		26	27	28	29[g]	30	1	2	
20	Pashons 1831	3	4	5	6	7	8	9	Genbot 2107
21		10	11	12	13	14	15	16	
22		17	18	19	20	21	22	23	
23		24	25	26	27	28	29	30	
24	Paōne 1831	1	2	3	4	5	6	7	Sanē 2107
25		8	9	10	11	12	13	14	
26		15	16	17	18	19	20	21	
27		22	23	24	25	26	27	28	
28		29	30	1	2	3	4	5	
29	Epēp 1831	6	7	8	9	10	11	12	Ḥamlē 2107
30		13	14	15	16	17	18	19	
31		20	21	22	23	24	25	26	
32		27	28	29	30	1	2	3	
33	Mesorē 1831	4	5	6	7	8	9	10	Naḥasē 2107
34		11	12	13[h]	14	15	16	17	
35		18	19	20	21	22	23	24	
36		25	26	27	28	29	30	1	
37	Epag. 1831 / Thoout 1832	2	3	4	5	6	1[a]	2	Pāg. 2107 / Maskaram 2108
38		3	4	5	6	7	8	9	
39		10	11	12	13	14	15	16	
40		17[b]	18	19	20	21	22	23	
41		24	25	26	27	28	29	30	
42	Paope 1832	1	2	3	4	5	6	7	Ṭeqemt 2108
43		8	9	10	11	12	13	14	
44		15	16	17	18	19	20	21	
45		22	23	24	25	26	27	28	
46		29	30	1	2	3	4	5	
47	Athōr 1832	6	7	8	9	10	11	12	Hedār 2108
48		13	14	15	16	17	18	19	
49		20	21	22	23	24	25	26	
50		27	28	29	30	1	2	3	
51	Koiak 1832	4	5	6	7	8	9	10	Tākhśāś 2108
52		11	12	13	14	15	16	17	
1		18	19	20	21	22	23	24	

[a]New Year
[b]Spring (4:21)
[c]Summer (20:29)
[d]Autumn (13:11)
[e]Winter (11:26)
● New moon
◐ First quarter moon
○ Full moon
◑ Last quarter moon

[a]New Year
[b]Yom Kippur
[c]Sukkot
[d]Winter starts
[e]Ḥanukkah
[f]Purim
[g]Passover
[h]Shavuot
[i]Fast of Av

‡Leap year
[a]New Year (4813, Pig)
[b]Lantern Festival
[c]Qīngmíng
[d]Dragon Festival
[e]Qīqiǎo
[f]Hungry Ghosts
[g]Mid-Autumn Festival
[h]Double-Ninth Festival
[i]Dōngzhì
*Start of 60-name cycle

‡Leap year
[a]New Year
[b]Building of the Cross
[c]Christmas
[d]Jesus's Circumcision
[e]Epiphany
[f]Easter
[g]Mary's Announcement
[h]Jesus's Transfiguration

PERSIAN (ASTRONOMICAL) 1493/1494‡

Month	Sun	Mon	Tue	Wed	Thu	Fri	Sat
	9	10	11	12	13	14	15
DEY 1493	16	17	18	19	20	21	22
	23	24	25	26	27	28	29
	30	1	2	3	4	5	6
BAHMAN 1493	7	8	9	10	11	12	13
	14	15	16	17	18	19	20
	21	22	23	24	25	26	27
	28	29	30	1	2	3	4
ESFAND 1493	5	6	7	8	9	10	11
	12	13	14	15	16	17	18
	19	20	21	22	23	24	25
	26	27	28	29	1[a]	2	3
FARVARDĪN 1494	4	5	6	7	8	9	10
	11	12	13[b]	14	15	16	17
	18	19	20	21	22	23	24
	25	26	27	28	29	30	31
ORDĪBEHEŠT 1494	1	2	3	4	5	6	7
	8	9	10	11	12	13	14
	15	16	17	18	19	20	21
	22	23	24	25	26	27	28
	29	30	31	1	2	3	4
XORDĀD 1494	5	6	7	8	9	10	11
	12	13	14	15	16	17	18
	19	20	21	22	23	24	25
	26	27	28	29	30	31	1
TĪR 1494	2	3	4	5	6	7	8
	9	10	11	12	13	14	15
	16	17	18	19	20	21	22
	23	24	25	26	27	28	29
	30	31	1	2	3	4	5
MORDĀD 1494	6	7	8	9	10	11	12
	13	14	15	16	17	18	19
	20	21	22	23	24	25	26
	27	28	29	30	31	1	2
SHAHRĪVAR 1494	3	4	5	6	7	8	9
	10	11	12	13	14	15	16
	17	18	19	20	21	22	23
	24	25	26	27	28	29	30
	31	1	2	3	4	5	6
MEHR 1494	7	8	9	10	11	12	13
	14	15	16	17	18	19	20
	21	22	23	24	25	26	27
	28	29	30	1	2	3	4
ABĀN 1494	5	6	7	8	9	10	11
	12	13	14	15	16	17	18
	19	20	21	22	23	24	25
	26	27	28	29	30	1	2
ĀZAR 1494	3	4	5	6	7	8	9
	10	11	12	13	14	15	16
	17	18	19	20	21	22	23
	24	25	26	27	28	29	30
DEY 1494	1	2	3	4	5	6	7
	8	9	10	11	12	13	14

‡Leap year
[a]New Year
[b]Sizdeh Bedar

HINDU LUNAR 2171/2172‡

Month	Sun	Mon	Tue	Wed	Thu	Fri	Sat
	3	4	5	6	7	8	9
PAUSHA 2171	10	**11**	13	14	15	16	17
	18	19	20	21	22	23	24
	25	26	27	28	29	30	1
MĀGHA 2171	2	3	4	5	6	7	8
	9	10	11	12	13	14	15
	16	**17**	19	20	21	22	22
	23	24	25	26	27	28[h]	29
PHĀLGUNA 2171	30	1	2	3	4	5	6
	7	8	9	**10**	12	13	14
	15[i]	16	17	18	19	20	21
	22	23	24	25	25	26	27
CHAITRA 2172	28	29	30	1[a]	2	3	**4**
	6	7	8	9[b]	10	11	12
	13	14	15	16	17	18	19
	20	21	22	23	24	25	26
VAIŚĀKHA 2172	27	28	29	30	1	2	3
	4	5	6	**7**	9	10	11
	12	13	14	15	16	17	18
	19	19	20	21	22	23	24
JYAISHṬHA 2172	25	26	27	28	29	30	**1**
	3	4	5	6	7	8	9
	10	11	12	13	14	15	16
	17	18	19	20	21	22	23
	24	25	26	27	28	29	30
ĀSHĀḌHA 2172	1	2	3	**4**	6	7	8
	9	10	11	12	13	14	15
	16	16	17	18	19	20	21
	22	23	24	25	**26**	28	29
ŚRĀVAṆA 2172	30	1	2	3	4	5	6
	7	8	9	10	11	12	13
	14	15	16	17	18	19	20
	21	22	23[c]	24	25	26	27
LEAP BHĀDRAPADA 2172	28	**29**	1	2	3	4	5
	6	7	8	9	10	11	12
	12	13	14	15	16	17	18
	19	20	21	**22**	24	25	26
	27	28	29	30	1	2	3[d]
BHĀDRAPADA 2172	4	5	6	7	8	9	10
	11	12	13	14	15	16	17
	18	19	20	21	22	23	24
	25	**26**	28	29	30	1	2
ĀŚVINA 2172	3	4	5	6	7	7	8[e]
	9[e]	10[e]	11	12	13	14	15
	16	17	18	**19**	21	22	23
	24	25	26	27	28	29	30
KĀRTTIKA 2172	1[f]	2	3	4	5	6	7
	8	9	10	11	12	13	14
	15	16	17	18	19	20	21
	22	23	24	**25**	27	28	29
MĀRGAŚIRA 2172	30	30	1	2	3	4	5
	6	7	8	9	10	11[g]	12
	13	14	15	16	17	**18**	20

‡Leap year
[a]New Year (Yuvan)
[b]Birthday of Rāma
[c]Birthday of Krishna
[d]Ganēśa Chaturthī
[e]Dashara
[f]Diwali
[g]Birthday of Vishnu
[h]Night of Śiva
[i]Holi

HINDU SOLAR 2036‡/2037

Month	Sun	Mon	Tue	Wed	Thu	Fri	Sat
PAUSHA 2036	13	14	15	16	17	18	19
	20	21	22	23	24	25	26
	27	28	29	1[b]	2	3	4
MĀGHA 2036	5	6	7	8	9	10	11
	12	13	14	15	16	17	18
	19	20	21	22	23	24	25
	26	27	28	29	30	1	2
PHĀLGUNA 2036	3	4	5	6	7	8	9
	10	11	12	13	14	15	16
	17	18	19	20	21	22	23
	24	25	26	27	28	29	1
CHAITRA 2036	2	3	4	5	6	7	8
	9	10	11	12	13	14	15
	16	17	18	19	20	21	22
	23	24	25	26	27	28	29
	30	31	1[a]	2	3	4	5
VAIŚĀKHA 2037	6	7	8	9	10	11	12
	13	14	15	16	17	18	19
	20	21	22	23	24	25	26
	27	28	29	30	31	1	2
JYAISHṬHA 2037	3	4	5	6	7	8	9
	10	11	12	13	14	15	16
	17	18	19	20	21	22	23
	24	25	26	27	28	29	30
	31	1	2	3	4	5	6
ĀSHĀḌHA 2037	7	8	9	10	11	12	13
	14	15	16	17	18	19	20
	21	22	23	24	25	26	27
	28	29	30	31	32	1	2
ŚRĀVAṆA 2037	3	4	5	6	7	8	9
	10	11	12	13	14	15	16
	17	18	19	20	21	22	23
	24	25	26	27	28	29	30
	31	1	2	3	4	5	6
BHĀDRAPADA 2037	7	8	9	10	11	12	13
	14	15	16	17	18	19	20
	21	22	23	24	25	26	27
	28	29	30	31	1	2	3
ĀŚVINA 2037	4	5	6	7	8	9	10
	11	12	13	14	15	16	17
	18	19	20	21	22	23	24
	25	26	27	28	29	30	31
KĀRTTIKA 2037	1	2	3	4	5	6	7
	8	9	10	11	12	13	14
	15	16	17	18	19	20	21
	22	23	24	25	26	27	28
	29	30	1	2	3	4	5
MĀRGAŚIRA 2037	6	7	8	9	10	11	12
	13	14	15	16	17	18	19
	20	21	22	23	24	25	26
	27	28	29	1	2	3	4
PAUSHA 2037	5	6	7	8	9	10	11
	12	13	14	15	16	17	18

‡Leap year
[a]New Year (Vikṛita)
[b]Pongal

ISLAMIC (ASTRONOMICAL) 1539‡/1540

Month	Sun	Mon	Tue	Wed	Thu	Fri	Sat
	2	3	4	5	6	7	8
RABĪʿ II 1539	9	10	11	12	13	14	15
	16	17	18	19	20	21	22
	23	24	25	26	27	28	29
JUMĀDĀ I 1539	1	2	3	4	5	6	7
	8	9	10	11	12	13	14
	15	16	17	18	19	20	21
	22	23	24	25	26	27	28
JUMĀDĀ II 1539	29	30	1	2	3	4	5
	6	7	8	9	10	11	12
	13	14	15	16	17	18	19
	20	21	22	23	24	25	26
RAJAB 1539	27	28	29	1	2	3	4
	5	6	7	8	9	10	11
	12	13	14	15	16	17	18
	19	20	21	22	23	24	25
SHAʿBĀN 1539	26	27[d]	28	29	30	1	2
	3	4	5	6	7	8	9
	10	11	12	13	14	15	16
	17	18	19	20	21	22	23
RAMAḌĀN 1539	24	25	26	27	28	29	1[e]
	2	3	4	5	6	7	8
	9	10	11	12	13	14	15
	16	17	18	19	20	21	22
	23	24	25	26	27	28	29
SHAWWĀL 1539	1[f]	2	3	4	5	6	7
	8	9	10	11	12	13	14
	15	16	17	18	19	20	21
	22	23	24	25	26	27	28
DHU AL-QAʿDA 1539	29	30	1	2	3	4	5
	6	7	8	9	10	11	12
	13	14	15	16	17	18	19
	20	21	22	23	24	25	26
DHU AL-ḤIJJA 1539	27	28	29	1	2	3	4
	5	6	7	8	9	10[g]	11
	12	13	14	15	16	17	18
	19	20	21	22	23	24	25
MUḤARRAM 1540	26	27	28	29	30	1[a]	2
	3	4	5	6	7	8	9
	10[b]	11	12	13	14	15	16
	17	18	19	20	21	22	23
ṢAFAR 1540	24	25	26	27	28	29	1
	2	3	4	5	6	7	8
	9	10	11	12	13	14	15
	16	17	18	19	20	21	22
	23	24	25	26	27	28	29
RABĪʿ I 1540	30	1	2	3	4	5	6
	7	8	9	10	11	12[c]	13
	14	15	16	17	18	19	20
	21	22	23	24	25	26	27
RABĪʿ II 1540	28	29	30	1	2	3	4
	5	6	7	8	9	10	11
	12	13	14	15	16	17	18

‡Leap year
[a]New Year
[b]ʿAshūrāʾ
[c]Prophet's Birthday
[d]Ascent of the Prophet
[e]Start of Ramaḍān
[f]ʿId al-Fiṭr
[g]ʿId al-ʾAḍḥā

GREGORIAN 2115

Julian (Sun)	Sun	Mon	Tue	Wed	Thu	Fri	Sat	Month
Dec 16	30	31	1	2	3	4	5	
	6	7	8[a]	9	10	11	12	JANUARY 2115
Dec 30	13	14	15[b]	16	17	18	19	
	20	21	22	23	24	25	26	
Jan 13	27	28	29	30	31	1	2	
	3	4	5	6	7	8	9	FEBRUARY 2115
Jan 27	10	11	12	13	14	15	16	
	17	18	19	20	21	22	23	
Feb 10	24	25	26	27[c]	28	1	2	
	3[d]	4	5	6	7	8	9	MARCH 2115
Feb 24	10	11	12	13	14	15	16	
	17	18	19	20	21	22	23	
Mar 10	24	25	26	27	28	29	30	
	31	1	2	3	4	5	6	
Mar 24	7	8	9	10	11	12	13	APRIL 2115
	14[e]	15	16	17	18	19	20	
Apr 7	21	22	23	24	25	26	27	
	28	29	30	1	2	3	4	
Apr 21	5	6	7	8	9	10	11	MAY 2115
	12	13	14	15	16	17	18	
May 5	19	20	21	22	23	24	25	
	26	27	28	29	30	31	1	
May 19	2	3	4	5	6	7	8	JUNE 2115
	9	10	11	12	13	14	15	
Jun 2	16	17	18	19	20	21	22	
	23	24	25	26	27	28	29	
Jun 16	30	1	2	3	4	5	6	
	7	8	9	10	11	12	13	JULY 2115
Jun 30	14	15	16	17	18	19	20	
	21	22	23	24	25	26	27	
Jul 14	28	29	30	31	1	2	3	
	4	5	6	7	8	9	10	AUGUST 2115
Jul 28	11	12	13	14	15	16	17	
	18	19	20	21	22	23	24	
Aug 11	25	26	27	28	29	30	31	
	1	2	3	4	5	6	7	
Aug 25	8–	9	10	11	12	13	14	SEPTEMBER 2115
	15	16	17	18	19	20	21	
Sep 8	22	23	24	25	26	27	28	
	29	30	1	2	3	4	5	
Sep 22	6	7	8	9	10	11	12	OCTOBER 2115
	13	14	15	16	17	18	19	
Oct 6	20	21	22	23	24	25	26	
	27	28	29	30	31	1	2	
Oct 20	3	4	5	6	7	8	9	NOVEMBER 2115
	10	11	12	13	14	15	16	
Nov 3	17	18	19	20	21	22	23	
	24	25	26	27	28	29	30	
Nov 17	1[g]	2	3	4	5	6	7	
	8	9	10	11	12	13	14	DECEMBER 2115
Dec 1	15	16	17	18	19	20	21	
	22	23	24	25[h]	26	27	28	
Dec 15	29	30	31	1	2	3	4	

[a]Orthodox Christmas
[b]Julian New Year
[c]Ash Wednesday
[d]Feast of Orthodoxy
[e]Easter (also Orthodox)
[g]Advent
[h]Christmas

2116

GREGORIAN 2116‡

Month	Sun	Mon	Tue	Wed	Thu	Fri	Sat	Lunar Phases	ISO WEEK (Mon)	JULIAN DAY (Sun noon)
	29	30	○	1[a]	2	3	4	8:52	1	2493910
JANUARY 2116	5	◑	7	8	9	10	11	0:00	2	2493917
	12	13	●	15	16	17	18	22:33	3	2493924
	19	20	21	22	◐	24	25	1:23	4	2493931
	26	27	28	○	30	31	1	19:24	5	2493938
	2	3	4	◑	6	7	8	14:16	6	2493945
FEBRUARY 2116	9	10	11	12	●	14	15	17:48	7	2493952
	16	17	18	19	20	◐	22	14:48	8	2493959
	23	24	25	26	27	○	29	5:34	9	2493966
	1	2	3	4	5	◑	7	7:10	10	2493973
	8	9	10	11	12	13	●	11:45	11	2493980
MARCH 2116	15	16	17	18	19	20[b]	21		12	2493987
	◐	23	24	25	26	27	○	0:30 15:50	13	2493994
	29	30	31	1	2	3	4		14	2494001
	◑	6	7	8	9	10	11	1:33	15	2494008
APRIL 2116	12	●	14	15	16	17	18	3:19	16	2494015
	19	◐	21	22	23	24	25	7:13	17	2494022
	26	○	28	29	30	1	2	2:38	18	2494029
	3	◑	5	6	7	8	9	20:10	19	2494036
MAY 2116	10	11	●	13	14	15	16	15:56	20	2494043
	17	18	◐	20	21	22	23	12:20	21	2494050
	24	25	○	27	28	29	30	14:18	22	2494057
	31	1	2	◑	4	5	6	14:01	23	2494064
	7	8	9	10	●	12	13	1:44	24	2494071
JUNE 2116	14	15	16	◐	18	19	20	17:25	25	2494078
	21[c]	22	23	24	○	26	27	3:02	26	2494085
	28	29	30	1	2	◑	4	6:17	27	2494092
	5	6	7	8	9	●	11	9:29	28	2494099
JULY 2116	12	13	14	15	◐	17	18	23:52	29	2494106
	19	20	21	22	23	○	25	17:02	30	2494113
	26	27	28	29	30	31	◑	20:22	31	2494120
	2	3	4	5	6	7	●	16:22	32	2494127
AUGUST 2116	9	10	11	12	13	14	◐	8:51	33	2494134
	16	17	18	19	20	21	22		34	2494141
	○	24	25	26	27	28	29	8:18	35	2494148
	30	◑	1	2	3	4	5	8:03	36	2494155
	●	7	8	9	10	11	12	23:36	37	2494162
SEPTEMBER 2116	◐	14	15	16	17	18	19	21:06	38	2494169
	20	21	○[d]	23	24	25	26	0:30	39	2494176
	27	28	◑	30	1	2	3	17:31	40	2494183
	4	5	●	7	8	9	10	8:15	41	2494190
OCTOBER 2116	11	12	◐	14	15	16	17	12:57	42	2494197
	18	19	20	○	22	23	24	16:52	43	2494204
	25	26	27	28	◑	30	31	1:29	44	2494211
	1	2	3	●	5	6	7	19:01	45	2494218
	8	9	10	11	◐	13	14	8:09	46	2494225
NOVEMBER 2116	15	16	17	18	19	○	21	8:21	47	2494232
	22	23	24	25	26	◑	28	8:55	48	2494239
	29	30	1	2	3	●	5	8:10	49	2494246
	6	7	8	9	10	11	◐	5:36	50	2494253
DECEMBER 2116	13	14	15	16	17	18	○	22:18	51	2494260
	20	21[e]	22	23	24	25	◑	16:55	52	2494267
	27	28	29	30	31	1	●	23:40	53	2494274

HEBREW 5876/5877‡

ISO WEEK	Month	Sun	Mon	Tue	Wed	Thu	Fri	Sat	Molad
1	TEVETH 5876	13	14	15	16	17	18	19	
2		20	21	22	23	24	25	26	
3		27	28	29	1	2	3	4	Wed $4^h20^m8^p$
4	SHEVAT 5876	5	6	7	8	9	10	11	
5		12	13	14	15	16	17	18	
6		19	20	21	22	23	24	25	
7		26	27	28	29	30	1	2	Thu $17^h4^m9^p$
8	ADAR 5876	3	4	5	6	7	8	9	
9		10	11	12	13	14[f]	15	16	
10		17	18	19	20	21	22	23	
11		24	25	26	27	28	29	1	Sat $5^h48^m10^p$
12	NISAN 5876	2	3	4	5	6	7	8	
13		9	10	11	12	13	14	15[g]	
14		16	17	18	19	20	21	22	
15		23	24	25	26	27	28	29	Sun $18^h32^m11^p$
16		30	1	2	3	4	5	6	
17	IYYAR 5876	7	8	9	10	11	12	13	
18		14	15	16	17	18	19	20	
19		21	22	23	24	25	26	27	
20		28	29	1	2	3	4	5	Tue $7^h16^m12^p$
21	SIVAN 5876	6[h]	7	8	9	10	11	12	
22		13	14	15	16	17	18	19	
23		20	21	22	23	24	25	26	
24		27	28	29	30	1	2	3	Wed $20^h0^m13^p$
25	TAMMUZ 5876	4	5	6	7	8	9	10	
26		11	12	13	14	15	16	17	
27		18	19	20	21	22	23	24	
28		25	26	27	28	29	1	2	Fri $8^h44^m14^p$
29	AV 5876	3	4	5	6	7	8	9	
30		10[i]	11	12	13	14	15	16	
31		17	18	19	20	21	22	23	
32		24	25	26	27	28	29	30	Sat $21^h28^m15^p$
33	ELUL 5876	1	2	3	4	5	6	7	
34		8	9	10	11	12	13	14	
35		15	16	17	18	19	20	21	
36		22	23	24	25	26	27	28	
37		29	1[a]	2[a]	3	4	5	6	Mon $10^h12^m16^p$
38	TISHRI 5877	7	8	9	10[b]	11	12	13	
39		14	15[c]	16	17	18	19	20	
40		21	22	23	24	25	26	27	
41		28	29	30	1	2	3	4	Tue $22^h56^m17^p$
42	HESHVAN 5877	5	6	7	8	9	10	11	
43		12	13	14	15	16	17	18	
44		19	20	21	22	23	24	25	
45		26	27	28	29	30	1	2	Thu $11^h41^m0^p$
46	KISLEV 5877	3	4	5	6	7	8	9	
47		10	11	12	13	14	15	16	
48		17	18	19	20	21	22	23	
49		24	25[e]	26[e]	27[e]	28[e]	29[e]	30[e]	
50		1[d,e]	2[e]	3	4	5	6	7	Sat $0^h25^m1^p$
51	TEVETH 5877	8	9	10	11	12	13	14	
52		15	16	17	18	19	20	21	
53		22	23	24	25	26	27	28	

CHINESE Yǐ-Hài‡/Bǐng-Zǐ

ISO WEEK	Month	Sun	Mon	Tue	Wed	Thu	Fri	Sat	Solar Term
1	MONTH 11 Yǐ-Hài	14	15	16	17	18	19	20	
2		21	22	23	24	25	26	27	Xiǎo hán
3		28	29	30	1	2	3	4	
4	MONTH 12 Yǐ-Hài	5	6	7	8	9	10	11	Dà hán
5		12	13	14	15	16	17	18	
6		19	20	21	22	23	24	25	Lì chūn
7		26	27	28	29	30	1[a]	2	
8	MONTH 1 Bǐng-Zǐ	3	4	5	6	7	8	9	Yǔ shuǐ
9		10	11	12	13	14	15[b]*	16	
10		17	18	19	20	21	22	23	Jīng zhé
11		24	25	26	27	28	29	1	
12	MONTH 2 Bǐng-Zǐ	2	3	4	5	6	7	8	Chūn fēn
13		9	10	11	12	13	14	15	
14		16	17	18	19	20	21	22[c]	Qīng míng
15		23	24	25	26	27	28	29	
16		30	1	2	3	4	5	6	
17	MONTH 3 Bǐng-Zǐ	7	8	9	10	11	12	13	Gǔ yǔ
18		14	15	16*	17	18	19	20	
19		21	22	23	24	25	26	27	Lì xià
20		28	29	1	2	3	4	5	
21	MONTH 4 Bǐng-Zǐ	6	7	8	9	10	11	12	Xiǎo mǎn
22		13	14	15	16	17	18	19	
23		20	21	22	23	24	25	26	Máng zhòng
24		27	28	29	30	1	2	3	
25	MONTH 5 Bǐng-Zǐ	4	5[d]	6	7	8	9	10	Xià zhì
26		11	12	13	14	15	16	17*	
27		18	19	20	21	22	23	24	
28		25	26	27	28	29	1	2	Xiǎo shǔ
29	MONTH 6 Bǐng-Zǐ	3	4	5	6	7	8	9	
30		10	11	12	13	14	15	16	Dà shǔ
31		17	18	19	20	21	22	23	
32		24	25	26	27	28	29	30	Lì qiū
33	MONTH 7 Bǐng-Zǐ	1	2	3	4	5	6	7[e]	
34		8	9	10	11	12	13	14	
35		15[f]	16	17	18*	19	20	21	Chǔ shǔ
36		22	23	24	25	26	27	28	
37		29	1	2	3	4	5	6	Bái lù
38	MONTH 8 Bǐng-Zǐ	7	8	9	10	11	12	13	
39		14	15[g]	16	17	18	19	20	Qiū fēn
40		21	22	23	24	25	26	27	
41		28	29	1	2	3	4	5	Hán lù
42	MONTH 9 Bǐng-Zǐ	6	7	8	9[h]	10	11	12	
43		13	14	15	16	17	18	19	Shuāng jiàng
44		20*	21	22	23	24	25	26	
45		27	28	29	30	1	2	3	Lì dōng
46	MONTH 10 Bǐng-Zǐ	4	5	6	7	8	9	10	
47		11	12	13	14	15	16	17	
48		18	19	20	21	22	23	24	Xiǎo xuě
49		25	26	27	28	29	1	2	
50	MONTH 11 Bǐng-Zǐ	3	4	5	6	7	8	9	Dà xuě
51		10	11	12	13	14	15	16	
52		17	18	19[i]	20	21*	22	23	Dōng zhì
53		24	25	26	27	28	29	30	

COPTIC 1832/1833 — ETHIOPIC 2108/2109

ISO WEEK	Coptic Month	Sun	Mon	Tue	Wed	Thu	Fri	Sat	Ethiopic Month
1	KOIAK 1832	18	19	20	21	22	23	24	TĀKHŚĀŚ 2108
2		25	26	27	28	29[c]	30	1	
3	TŌBE 1832	2	3	4	5	6[d]	7	8	
4		9	10	11[e]	12	13	14	15	ṬER 2108
5		16	17	18	19	20	21	22	
6		23	24	25	26	27	28	29	
7		30	1	2	3	4	5	6	
8	MESHIR 1832	7	8	9	10	11	12	13	YAKĀTIT 2108
9		14	15	16	17	18	19	20	
10		21	22	23	24	25	26	27	
11		28	29	30	1	2	3	4	
12	PAREMOTEP 1832	5	6	7	8	9	10	11	MAGĀBIT 2108
13		12	13	14	15	16	17	18	
14		19	20	21	22	23	24	25	
15		26	27	28	29	30	1	2	
16	PARMOUTE 1832	3	4	5	6	7	8	9	MIYĀZYĀ 2108
17		10	11	12	13	14	15	16	
18		17	18	19	20	21	22	23	
19		24[f]	25	26	27	28	29[g]	30	
20	PASHONS 1832	1	2	3	4	5	6	7	GENBOT 2108
21		8	9	10	11	12	13	14	
22		15	16	17	18	19	20	21	
23		22	23	24	25	26	27	28	
24		29	30	1	2	3	4	5	
25	PAŌNE 1832	6	7	8	9	10	11	12	SANĒ 2108
26		13	14	15	16	17	18	19	
27		20	21	22	23	24	25	26	
28		27	28	29	30	1	2	3	
29	EPĒP 1832	4	5	6	7	8	9	10	ḤAMLĒ 2108
30		11	12	13	14	15	16	17	
31		18	19	20	21	22	23	24	
32		25	26	27	28	29	30	1	
33	MESORĒ 1832	2	3	4	5	6	7	8	NAHASĒ 2108
34		9	10	11	12	13[h]	14	15	
35		16	17	18	19	20	21	22	
36		23	24	25	26	27	28	29	
37	EPAG. 1832	30	1	2	3	4	5	1[a]	PĀG. 2108
38	THOOUT 1833	2	3	4	5	6	7	8	MASKARAM 2109
39		9	10	11	12	13	14	15	
40		16	17[b]	18	19	20	21	22	
41		23	24	25	26	27	28	29	
42	PAOPE 1833	30	1	2	3	4	5	6	ṬEQEMT 2109
43		7	8	9	10	11	12	13	
44		14	15	16	17	18	19	20	
45		21	22	23	24	25	26	27	
46	ATHŌR 1833	28	29	30	1	2	3	4	ḪEDĀR 2109
47		5	6	7	8	9	10	11	
48		12	13	14	15	16	17	18	
49		19	20	21	22	23	24	25	
50	KOIAK 1833	26	27	28	29	30	1	2	TĀKHŚĀŚ 2109
51		3	4	5	6	7	8	9	
52		10	11	12	13	14	15	16	
53		17	18	19	20	21	22	23	

‡Leap year
[a]New Year
[b]Spring (10:07)
[c]Summer (2:16)
[d]Autumn (18:55)
[e]Winter (17:13)
● New moon
◐ First quarter moon
○ Full moon
◑ Last quarter moon

‡Leap year
[a]New Year
[b]Yom Kippur
[c]Sukkot
[d]Winter starts
[e]Ḥanukkah
[f]Purim
[g]Passover
[h]Shavuot
[i]Fast of Av

‡Leap year
[a]New Year (4814, Rat)
[b]Lantern Festival
[c]Qīngmíng
[d]Dragon Festival
[e]Qīqiǎo
[f]Hungry Ghosts
[g]Mid-Autumn Festival
[h]Double-Ninth Festival
[i]Dōngzhì
*Start of 60-name cycle

[a]New Year
[b]Building of the Cross
[c]Christmas
[d]Jesus's Circumcision
[e]Epiphany
[f]Easter
[g]Mary's Announcement
[h]Jesus's Transfiguration

PERSIAN (ASTRONOMICAL) 1494‡/1495

Month	Sun	Mon	Tue	Wed	Thu	Fri	Sat
DEY 1494	8	9	10	11	12	13	14
	15	16	17	18	19	20	21
	22	23	24	25	26	27	28
BAHMAN 1494	29	30	1	2	3	4	5
	6	7	8	9	10	11	12
	13	14	15	16	17	18	19
	20	21	22	23	24	25	26
ESFAND 1494	27	28	29	30	1	2	3
	4	5	6	7	8	9	10
	11	12	13	14	15	16	17
	18	19	20	21	22	23	24
FARVARDĪN 1495	25	26	27	28	29	30	1[a]
	2	3	4	5	6	7	8
	9	10	11	12	13[b]	14	15
	16	17	18	19	20	21	22
	23	24	25	26	27	28	29
ORDĪBEHEŠT 1495	30	31	1	2	3	4	5
	6	7	8	9	10	11	12
	13	14	15	16	17	18	19
	20	21	22	23	24	25	26
XORDĀD 1495	27	28	29	30	31	1	2
	3	4	5	6	7	8	9
	10	11	12	13	14	15	16
	17	18	19	20	21	22	23
	24	25	26	27	28	29	30
TĪR 1495	31	1	2	3	4	5	6
	7	8	9	10	11	12	13
	14	15	16	17	18	19	20
	21	22	23	24	25	26	27
MORDĀD 1495	28	29	30	31	1	2	3
	4	5	6	7	8	9	10
	11	12	13	14	15	16	17
	18	19	20	21	22	23	24
	25	26	27	28	29	30	31
SHAHRĪVAR 1495	1	2	3	4	5	6	7
	8	9	10	11	12	13	14
	15	16	17	18	19	20	21
	22	23	24	25	26	27	28
MEHR 1495	29	30	31	1	2	3	4
	5	6	7	8	9	10	11
	12	13	14	15	16	17	18
	19	20	21	22	23	24	25
ĀBĀN 1495	26	27	28	29	30	1	2
	3	4	5	6	7	8	9
	10	11	12	13	14	15	16
	17	18	19	20	21	22	23
	24	25	26	27	28	29	30
ĀZAR 1495	1	2	3	4	5	6	7
	8	9	10	11	12	13	14
	15	16	17	18	19	20	21
	22	23	24	25	26	27	28
DEY 1495	29	30	1	2	3	4	5
	6	7	8	9	10	11	12

‡Leap year
[a]New Year
[b]Sizdeh Bedar

HINDU LUNAR 2172‡/2173

Month	Sun	Mon	Tue	Wed	Thu	Fri	Sat
MĀRGAŚĪRA 2172	13	14	15	16	17	**18**	20
	21	22	23	24	25	26	27
PAUSHA 2172	28	29	30	1	2	3	3
	4	5	6	7	8	9	10
	11	**12**	14	15	16	17	18
	19	20	21	22	23	24	25
MĀGHA 2172	26	27	28	29	30	1	2
	3	4	5	6	7	8	9
	10	11	12	13	14	15	16
	17	19	20	21	22	23	24
	25	*25*	26	27	28[h]	29	30
PHĀLGUNA 2172	1	2	3	4	5	6	7
	8	9	10	**11**	13	14	15[i]
	16	17	18	19	20	21	22
	23	24	25	26	27	28	*28*
CHAITRA 2173	29	30	1[a]	2	3	**4**	6
	7	8	9[b]	10	11	12	13
	14	15	16	17	18	19	20
	21	22	23	24	25	26	27
VAIŚĀKHA 2173	28	29	30	1	2	3	4
	5	6	7	**8**	10	11	12
	13	14	15	16	17	18	19
	20	21	22	23	*23*	24	25
JYAISHṬHA 2173	26	27	28	29	**30**	2	3
	4	5	6	7	8	9	10
	11	12	13	14	15	16	17
	18	19	20	21	22	23	24
ĀSHĀḌHA 2173	25	26	27	28	29	30	1
	2	**3**	5	6	7	8	9
	10	11	12	13	14	15	16
	17	18	19	20	*20*	21	22
	23	24	25	**26**	28	29	30
ŚRĀVAṆA 2173	1	2	3	4	5	6	7
	8	10	11	*11*	12	13	14
	15	16	17	18	19	20	21
	22	23[c]	24	25	26	27	28
BHĀDRAPADA 2173	**29**	1	2	3	4[d]	5	6
	7	8	9	10	11	12	13
	14	15	16	*16*	17	18	19
	20	21	**22**	24	25	26	27
ĀŚVINA 2173	28	29	30	1	2	3	4
	5	6	7	8[e]	9[e]	10[e]	11
	12	13	14	15	16	17	18
	19	20	21	22	23	24	25
KĀRTTIKA 2173	**26**	28	29	30	1[f]	2	3
	4	5	6	7	8	9	10
	10	11	12	13	14	15	16
	17	18	19	**20**	22	23	24
MĀRGAŚĪRA 2173	25	26	27	28	29	30	1
	2	3	4	5	6	7	8
	9	10	11[g]	12	13	14	15
	16	17	18	19	20	21	22
	23	24	**25**	27	28	29	30

‡Leap year
[a]New Year (Dhātṛi)
[b]Birthday of Rāma
[c]Birthday of Krishna
[d]Ganēśa Chaturthī
[e]Dashara
[f]Diwali
[g]Birthday of Vishnu
[h]Night of Śiva
[i]Holi

HINDU SOLAR 2037/2038

Month	Sun	Mon	Tue	Wed	Thu	Fri	Sat
PAUSHA 2037	12	13	14	15	16	17	18
	19	20	21	22	23	24	25
MĀGHA 2037	26	27	28	29	1[b]	2	3
	4	5	6	7	8	9	10
	11	12	13	14	15	16	17
	18	19	20	21	22	23	24
PHĀLGUNA 2037	25	26	27	28	29	30	1
	2	3	4	5	6	7	8
	9	10	11	12	13	14	15
	16	17	18	19	20	21	22
	23	24	25	26	27	28	29
CHAITRA 2037	30	1	2	3	4	5	6
	7	8	9	10	11	12	13
	14	15	16	17	18	19	20
	21	22	23	24	25	26	27
VAIŚĀKHA 2038	28	29	30	1[a]	2	3	4
	5	6	7	8	9	10	11
	12	13	14	15	16	17	18
	19	20	21	22	23	24	25
JYAISHṬHA 2038	26	27	28	29	30	31	1
	2	3	4	5	6	7	8
	9	10	11	12	13	14	15
	16	17	18	19	20	21	22
	23	24	25	26	27	28	29
ĀSHĀḌHA 2038	30	31	1	2	3	4	5
	6	7	8	9	10	11	12
	13	14	15	16	17	18	19
	20	21	22	23	24	25	26
ŚRĀVAṆA 2038	27	28	29	30	31	32	1
	2	3	4	5	6	7	8
	9	10	11	12	13	14	15
	16	17	18	19	20	21	22
	23	24	25	26	27	28	29
BHĀDRAPADA 2038	30	31	1	2	3	4	5
	6	7	8	9	10	11	12
	13	14	15	16	17	18	19
	20	21	22	23	24	25	26
ĀŚVINA 2038	27	28	29	30	31	1	2
	3	4	5	6	7	8	9
	10	11	12	13	14	15	16
	17	18	19	20	21	22	23
	24	25	26	27	28	29	30
KĀRTTIKA 2038	31	1	2	3	4	5	6
	7	8	9	10	11	12	13
	14	15	16	17	18	19	20
	21	22	23	24	25	26	27
MĀRGAŚĪRA 2038	28	29	30	1	2	3	4
	5	6	7	8	9	10	11
	12	13	14	15	16	17	18
	19	20	21	22	23	24	25
PAUSHA 2038	26	27	28	29	1	2	3
	4	5	6	7	8	9	10
	11	12	13	14	15	16	17

[a]New Year (Khara)
[b]Pongal

ISLAMIC (ASTRONOMICAL) 1540/1541‡

Month	Sun	Mon	Tue	Wed	Thu	Fri	Sat
RABĪ' II 1540	12	13	14	15	16	17	18
	19	20	21	22	23	24	25
JUMĀDĀ I 1540	26	27	28	29	1	2	3
	4	5	6	7	8	9	10
	11	12	13	14	15	16	17
	18	19	20	21	22	23	24
JUMĀDĀ II 1540	25	26	27	28	29	30	1
	2	3	4	5	6	7	8
	9	10	11	12	13	14	15
	16	17	18	19	20	21	22
	23	24	25	26	27	28	29
RAJAB 1540	30	1	2	3	4	5	6
	7	8	9	10	11	12	13
	14	15	16	17	18	19	20
	21	22	23	24	25	26	27[d]
SHA'BĀN 1540	28	29	1	2	3	4	5
	6	7	8	9	10	11	12
	13	14	15	16	17	18	19
	20	21	22	23	24	25	26
RAMAḌĀN 1540	27	28	29	30	1[e]	2	3
	4	5	6	7	8	9	10
	11	12	13	14	15	16	17
	18	19	20	21	22	23	24
SHAWWĀL 1540	25	26	27	28	29	1[f]	2
	3	4	5	6	7	8	9
	10	11	12	13	14	15	16
	17	18	19	20	21	22	23
DHU AL-QA'DA 1540	24	25	26	27	28	29	1
	2	3	4	5	6	7	8
	9	10	11	12	13	14	15
	16	17	18	19	20	21	22
	23	24	25	26	27	28	29
DHU AL-ḤIJJA 1540	30	1	2	3	4	5	6
	7	8	9	10[g]	11	12	13
	14	15	16	17	18	19	20
	21	22	23	24	25	26	27
MUḤARRAM 1541	28	29	1[a]	2[A]	3	4	5
	6	7	8	9	10[b]	11	12
	13	14	15	16	17	18	19
	20	21	22	23	24	25	26
ṢAFAR 1541	27	28	29	30	1	2	3
	4	5	6	7	8	9	10
	11	12	13	14	15	16	17
	18	19	20	21	22	23	24
RABĪ' I 1541	25	26	27	28	29	30	1
	2	3	4	5	6	7	8
	9	10	11	12[c]	13	14	15
	16	17	18	19	20	21	22
	23	24	25	26	27	28	29
RABĪ' II 1541	1	2	3	4	5	6	7
	8	9	10	11	12	13	14
	15	16	17	18	19	20	21
	22	23	24	25	26	27	28

‡Leap year
[a]New Year
[A]New Year (Arithmetic)
[b]'Ashūrā'
[c]Prophet's Birthday
[d]Ascent of the Prophet
[e]Start of Ramaḍān
[f]'Īd al-Fiṭr
[g]'Īd al-'Aḍḥā

GREGORIAN 2116‡

Julian† (Sun)	Sun	Mon	Tue	Wed	Thu	Fri	Sat	Month
Dec 15	29	30	31	1	2	3	4	JANUARY 2116
	5	6	7	8[a]	9	10	11	
Dec 29	12	13	14	15[b]	16	17	18	
	19	20	21	22	23	24	25	
Jan 12	26	27	28	29	30	31	1	FEBRUARY 2116
	2	3	4	5	6	7	8	
Jan 26	9	10	11	12[c]	13	14	15	
	16	17	18	19	20	21	22	
Feb 9	23	24	25	26	27	28	29	
	1	2	3	4	5	6	7	MARCH 2116
Feb 23	8	9	10	11	12	13	14	
	15	16	17	18	19	20	21	
Mar 8	22[d]	23	24	25	26	27	28	
	29[e]	30	31	1	2	3	4	APRIL 2116
Mar 22	5	6	7	8	9	10	11	
	12	13	14	15	16	17	18	
Apr 5	19	20	21	22	23	24	25	
	26	27	28	29	30	1	2	MAY 2116
Apr 19	3[f]	4	5	6	7	8	9	
	10	11	12	13	14	15	16	
May 3	17	18	19	20	21	22	23	
	24	25	26	27	28	29	30	
May 17	31	1	2	3	4	5	6	JUNE 2116
	7	8	9	10	11	12	13	
May 31	14	15	16	17	18	19	20	
	21	22	23	24	25	26	27	
Jun 14	28	29	30	1	2	3	4	JULY 2116
	5	6	7	8	9	10	11	
Jun 28	12	13	14	15	16	17	18	
	19	20	21	22	23	24	25	
Jul 12	26	27	28	29	30	31	1	AUGUST 2116
	2	3	4	5	6	7	8	
Jul 26	9	10	11	12	13	14	15	
	16	17	18	19	20	21	22	
Aug 9	23	24	25	26	27	28	29	
	30	31	1	2	3	4	5	SEPTEMBER 2116
Aug 23	6	7	8	9	10	11	12	
	13	14	15	16	17	18	19	
Sep 6	20	21	22	23	24	25	26	
	27	28	29	30	1	2	3	OCTOBER 2116
Sep 20	4	5	6	7	8	9	10	
	11	12	13	14	15	16	17	
Oct 4	18	19	20	21	22	23	24	
	25	26	27	28	29	30	31	
Oct 18	1	2	3	4	5	6	7	NOVEMBER 2116
	8	9	10	11	12	13	14	
Nov 1	15	16	17	18	19	20	21	
	22	23	24	25	26	27	28	
Nov 15	29[g]	30	1	2	3	4	5	DECEMBER 2116
	6	7	8	9	10	11	12	
Nov 29	13	14	15	16	17	18	19	
	20	21	22	23	24	25[h]	26	
Dec 13	27	28	29	30	31	1	2	

‡Leap year
[a]Orthodox Christmas
[b]Julian New Year
[c]Ash Wednesday
[d]Feast of Orthodoxy
[e]Easter
[f]Orthodox Easter
[g]Advent
[h]Christmas

2117

Gregorian month	GREGORIAN 2117 (Sun Mon Tue Wed Thu Fri Sat)	Lunar Phases	ISO WEEK (Mon)	JULIAN DAY (Sun noon)	Hebrew month	HEBREW 5877‡/5878 (Sun Mon Tue Wed Thu Fri Sat)	Molad	Chinese month	CHINESE Bǐng-Zǐ/Dīng-Chǒu (Sun Mon Tue Wed Thu Fri Sat)	Solar Term	Coptic month	COPTIC 1833/1834 · ETHIOPIC 2109/2110 (Sun Mon Tue Wed Thu Fri Sat)	Ethiopic month
	27 28 29 30 31 1[a] ●	23:40	53	2494274	TEVETH 5877	22 23 24 25 26 27 28			24 25 26 27 28 29 30		KOIAK 1833	17 18 19 20 21 22 23	TĀKHŚĀŚ 2109
JANUARY 2117	3 4 5 6 7 8 9		1	2494281		29 1 2 3 4 5 6	Sun 13h9m2p		1 2 3 4 5 6 7	Xiǎo hán		24 25 26 27 28 29[c] 30	
	10 ◐ 12 13 14 15 16	3:14	2	2494288	SHEVAT 5877	7 8 9 10 11 12 13		MONTH 12 Bǐng-Zǐ	8 9 10 11 12 13 14			1 2 3 4 5 6[d] 7	
	17 ○ 19 20 21 22 23	10:35	3	2494295		14 15 16 17 18 19 20			15 16 17 **18** 19 20 21	Dà hán	TŌBE 1833	8 9 10 11[e] 12 13 14	TER 2109
	24 ◑ 26 27 28 29 30	2:18	4	2494302		21 22 23 24 25 26 27			22 23 24 25 26 27 28			15 16 17 18 19 20 21	
	31 ● 2 3 4 5 6	17:09	5	2494309		28 29 30 1 2 3 4	Tue 1h53m3p		29 30 1[a] 2 3 4 5	Lì chūn		22 23 24 25 26 27 28	
FEBRUARY 2117	7 8 ◐ 10 11 12 13	22:40	6	2494316	ADAR I 5877	5 6 7 8 9 10 11		MONTH 1 Dīng-Chǒu	6 7 8 9 10 11 12			29 30 1 2 3 4 5	
	14 15 ○ 17 18 19 20	21:29	7	2494323		12 13 14 15 16 17 18			13 14 15[b] 16 17 **18** 19	Yǔ shuǐ	MESHIR 1833	6 7 8 9 10 11 12	YAKĀTIT 2109
	21 22 ◑ 24 25 26 27	13:34	8	2494330		19 20 21 22 23 24 25			20 21* 22 23 24 25 26			13 14 15 16 17 18 19	
	28 1 2 ● 4 5 6	11:46	9	2494337		26 27 28 29 30 1 2	Wed 14h37m4p		27 28 29 1 2 3 4	Jīng zhé		20 21 22 23 24 25 26	
MARCH 2117	7 8 9 10 ◐ 12 13	14:16	10	2494344	ADAR II 5877	3 4 5 6 7 8 9		MONTH 2 Dīng-Chǒu	5 6 7 8 9 10 11			27 28 29 30 1 2 3	
	14 15 16 17 ○ 19 20[b]	7:23	11	2494351		10 11 12 13 14[f] 15 16			12 13 14 15 16 17 18		PAREMOTEP 1833	4 5 6 7 8 9 10	
	21 22 23 24 ◑ 26 27	2:47	12	2494358		17 18 19 20 21 22 23			**19** 20 21 22 23 24 25	Chūn fēn		11 12 13 14 15 16 17	MAGABIT 2109
	28 29 30 31 1 ● 3	6:05	13	2494365		24 25 26 27 28 29 1	Fri 3h21m5p		26 27 28 29 30 1 2			18 19 20 21 22 23 24	
APRIL 2117	4 5 6 7 8 9 ◐	1:39	14	2494372		2 3 4 5 6 7 8		MONTH 3 Dīng-Chǒu	3 4[c] 5 6 7 8 9	Qīng míng		25 26 27 28 29 30 1	
	11 12 13 14 15 ○ 17	16:36	15	2494379	NISAN 5877	9 10 11 12 13 14 15[g]			10 11 12 13 14 15 16			2 3 4 5 6 7 8	
	18 19 20 21 22 ◑ 24	17:52	16	2494386		16 17 18 19 20 21 22			17 18 **19** 20 21 22* 23	Gǔ yǔ	PARMOUTE 1833	9 10 11 12 13 14 15	MIYĀZYĀ 2109
	25 26 27 28 29 30 ●	22:34	17	2494393		23 24 25 26 27 28 29			24 25 26 27 28 29 30			16[f] 17 18 19 20 21 22	
	2 3 4 5 6 7 8		18	2494400		30 1 2 3 4 5 6	Sat 16h5m6p		1 2 3 4 5 6 7	Lì xià		23 24 25 26 27 28 29[g]	
MAY 2117	◐ 10 11 12 13 14 15	9:30	19	2494407	IYAR 5877	7 8 9 10 11 12 13		MONTH 4 Dīng-Chǒu	8 9 10 11 12 13 14			30 1 2 3 4 5 6	
	○ 17 18 19 20 21 22	1:30	20	2494414		14 15 16 17 18 19 20			15 16 17 18 19 **20** 21	Xiǎo mǎn	PASHONS 1833	7 8 9 10 11 12 13	GENBOT 2109
	◑ 24 25 26 27 28 29	10:28	21	2494421		21 22 23 24 25 26 27			22 23 24 25 26 27 28			14 15 16 17 18 19 20	
	30 ● 1 2 3 4 5	12:15	22	2494428		28 29 1 2 3 4 5	Mon 4h49m7p		29 1 2 3 4 5[d] 6	Máng zhòng		21 22 23 24 25 26 27	
JUNE 2117	6 ◐ 8 9 10 11 12	15:05	23	2494435	SIVAN 5877	6[h] 7 8 9 10 11 12		MONTH 5 Dīng-Chǒu	7 8 9 10 11 12 13			28 29 30 1 2 3 4	
	13 ○ 15 16 17 18 19	10:44	24	2494442		13 14 15 16 17 18 19			14 15 16 17 18 19 20		PAŌNE 1833	5 6 7 8 9 10 11	
	20 21[c] ◑ 23 24 25 26	3:59	25	2494449		20 21 22 23 24 25 26			21 **22** 23* 24 25 26 27	Xià zhì		12 13 14 15 16 17 18	SANĒ 2109
	27 28 ● 30 1 2 3	23:14	26	2494456		27 28 29 30 1 2 3	Tue 17h33m8p		28 29 30 1 2 3 4			19 20 21 22 23 24 25	
JULY 2117	4 5 ◐ 7 8 9 10	19:43	27	2494463	TAMMUZ 5877	4 5 6 7 8 9 10		MONTH 6 Dīng-Chǒu	5 6 7 *8* 9 10 11	Xiǎo shǔ		26 27 28 29 30 1 2	
	11 12 ○ 14 15 16 17	21:11	28	2494470		11 12 13 14 15 16 17			12 13 14 15 16 17 18		EPĒP 1833	3 4 5 6 7 8 9	
	18 19 20 ◑ 22 23 24	21:26	29	2494477		18 19 20 21 22 23 24			19 20 21 22 23 **24** 25	Dà shǔ		10 11 12 13 14 15 16	HAMLĒ 2109
	25 26 27 28 ● 30 31	8:17	30	2494484		25 26 27 28 29 1 2	Thu 6h17m9p		26 27 28 29 1 2 3			17 18 19 20 21 22 23	
AUGUST 2117	1 2 3 4 ◐ 6 7	0:48	31	2494491	AV 5877	3 4 5 6 7 8 9		MONTH 7 Dīng-Chǒu	4 5 6 7[e] 8 9 *10*	Lì qiū		24 25 26 27 28 29 30	
	8 9 10 11 ○ 13 14	9:42	32	2494498		10[i] 11 12 13 14 15 16			11 12 13 14 15[f] 16 17			1 2 3 4 5 6 7	
	15 16 17 18 19 ◑ 21	13:51	33	2494505		17 18 19 20 21 22 23			18 19 20 21 22 23 24*	Chǔ shǔ	MESORĒ 1833	8 9 10 11 12 13[h] 14	NAHASĒ 2109
	22 23 24 25 26 ● 28	16:29	34	2494512		24 25 26 27 28 29 30			25 **26** 27 28 29 30 1			15 16 17 18 19 20 21	
	29 30 31 1 2 ◐ 4	7:36	35	2494519		1 2 3 4 5 6 7	Fri 19h1m10p		2 3 4 5 6 7 8			22 23 24 25 26 27 28	
SEPTEMBER 2117	5 6 7 8 9 10 ○	0:44	36	2494526	ELUL 5877	8 9 10 11 12 13 14		MONTH 8 Dīng-Chǒu	9 10 *11* 12 13 14 15[g]	Bái lù	EPAG. 1833	29 30 1 2 3 4 5	PĀG. 2109
	12 13 14 15 16 17 18		37	2494533		15 16 17 18 19 20 21			16 17 18 19 20 21 22			1[a] 2 3 4 5 6 7	
	◑ 20 21 22 23[d] 24 25	4:32	38	2494540		22 23 24 25 26 27 28			23 24 25 26 **27** 28 29	Qiū fēn	THOOUT 1834	8 9 10 11 12 13 14	MASKARAM 2110
	● 27 28 29 30 1 ◐	0:46 17:23	39	2494547		29 1[a] 2[a] 3 4 5 6	Sun 7h45m11p		1 2 3 4 5 6 7			15 16 17[b] 18 19 20 21	
OCTOBER 2117	3 4 5 6 7 8 9		40	2494554	TISHRI 5878	7 8 9 10[b] 11 12 13		MONTH 9 Dīng-Chǒu	8 9[h] 10 11 12 *13* 14	Hán lù		22 23 24 25 26 27 28	
	○ 11 12 13 14 15 16	17:54	41	2494561		14 15[c] 16 17 18 19 20			15 16 17 18 19 20 21			29 30 1 2 3 4 5	
	17 ◑ 19 20 21 22 23	17:18	42	2494568		21 22 23 24 25 26 27			22 23 24 25* 26 27 **28**	Shuāng jiàng	PAOPE 1834	6 7 8 9 10 11 12	TEQEMT 2110
	24 ● 26 27 28 29 30	9:49	43	2494575		28 29 30 1 2 3 4	Mon 20h29m12p		29 1 2 3 4 5 6			13 14 15 16 17 18 19	
	31 ◐ 2 3 4 5 6	7:06	44	2494582	ḤESHVAN 5878	5 6 7 8 9 10 11		MONTH 10 Dīng-Chǒu	7 8 9 10 11 12 13			20 21 22 23 24 25 26	
NOVEMBER 2117	7 8 ○ 10 11 12 13	11:58	45	2494589		12 13 14 15 16 17 18			*14* 15 16 17 18 19 20	Lì dōng		27 28 29 30 1 2 3	
	14 15 16 ◑ 18 19 20	4:16	46	2494596		19 20 21 22 23 24 25			21 22 23 24 25 26 27		ATHŌR 1834	4 5 6 7 8 9 10	
	21 22 ● 24 25 26 27	20:01	47	2494603		26 27 28 29 30 1 2	Wed 9h13m13p		28 **29** 30 1 2 3 4	Xiǎo xuě		11 12 13 14 15 16 17	HEDAR 2110
	28 29 30 ◐ 2 3 4	1:00	48	2494610	KISLEV 5878	3 4 5 6 7 8 9		MONTH 11 Dīng-Chǒu	5 6 7 8 9 10 11			18 19 20 21 22 23 24	
DECEMBER 2117	5 6 7 8 ○ 10 11	5:28	49	2494617		10 11[d] 12 13 14 15 16			12 13 *14* 15 16 17 18	Dà xuě		25 26 27 28 29 30 1	
	12 13 14 15 ◑ 17 18	13:44	50	2494624		17 18 19 20 21 22 23			19 20 21 22 23 24 25		KOIAK 1834	2 3 4 5 6 7 8	
	19 20 21[e] 22 ● 24 25	7:45	51	2494631		24 25[e] 26[e] 27[e] 28[e] 29[e] 30[e]	Thu 21h57m14p		26* 27 28 29[i] 1 2 3	Dōng zhì		9 10 11 12 13 14 15	TĀKHŚĀŚ 2110
	26 27 28 29 ◐ 31 1	22:07	52	2494638		1[e] 2[e] 3 4 5 6 7		MONTH 12 Dīng-Chǒu	4 5 6 7 8 9 10			16 17 18 19 20 21 22	

[a]New Year
[b]Spring (16:04)
[c]Summer (8:08)
[d]Autumn (0:43)
[e]Winter (23:02)
● New moon
◐ First quarter moon
○ Full moon
◑ Last quarter moon

‡Leap year
[a]New Year
[b]Yom Kippur
[c]Sukkot
[d]Winter starts
[e]Ḥanukkah
[f]Purim
[g]Passover
[h]Shavuot
[i]Fast of Av

[a]New Year (4815, Ox)
[b]Lantern Festival
[c]Qīngmíng
[d]Dragon Festival
[e]Qīqiǎo
[f]Hungry Ghosts
[g]Mid-Autumn Festival
[h]Double-Ninth Festival
[i]Dōngzhì
*Start of 60-name cycle

[a]New Year
[b]Building of the Cross
[c]Christmas
[d]Jesus's Circumcision
[e]Epiphany
[f]Easter
[g]Mary's Announcement
[h]Jesus's Transfiguration

PERSIAN (ASTRONOMICAL) 1495/1496

Month	Sun	Mon	Tue	Wed	Thu	Fri	Sat
DEY 1495	6	7	8	9	10	11	12
	13	14	15	16	17	18	19
	20	21	22	23	24	25	26
	27	28	29	30	1	2	3
BAHMAN 1495	4	5	6	7	8	9	10
	11	12	13	14	15	16	17
	18	19	20	21	22	23	24
	25	26	27	28	29	30	1
ESFAND 1495	2	3	4	5	6	7	8
	9	10	11	12	13	14	15
	16	17	18	19	20	21	22
	23	24	25	26	27	28	29
FARVARDIN 1496	1[a]	2	3	4	5	6	7
	8	9	10	11	12	13[b]	14
	15	16	17	18	19	20	21
	22	23	24	25	26	27	28
	29	30	31	1	2	3	4
ORDIBEHEŠT 1496	5	6	7	8	9	10	11
	12	13	14	15	16	17	18
	19	20	21	22	23	24	25
	26	27	28	29	30	31	1
XORDĀD 1496	2	3	4	5	6	7	8
	9	10	11	12	13	14	15
	16	17	18	19	20	21	22
	23	24	25	26	27	28	29
	30	31	1	2	3	4	5
TĪR 1496	6	7	8	9	10	11	12
	13	14	15	16	17	18	19
	20	21	22	23	24	25	26
	27	28	29	30	31	1	2
MORDĀD 1496	3	4	5	6	7	8	9
	10	11	12	13	14	15	16
	17	18	19	20	21	22	23
	24	25	26	27	28	29	30
	31	1	2	3	4	5	6
SHAHRĪVAR 1496	7	8	9	10	11	12	13
	14	15	16	17	18	19	20
	21	22	23	24	25	26	27
	28	29	30	31	1	2	3
MEHR 1496	4	5	6	7	8	9	10
	11	12	13	14	15	16	17
	18	19	20	21	22	23	24
	25	26	27	28	29	30	1
ĀBĀN 1496	2	3	4	5	6	7	8
	9	10	11	12	13	14	15
	16	17	18	19	20	21	22
	23	24	25	26	27	28	29
	30	1	2	3	4	5	6
ĀZAR 1496	7	8	9	10	11	12	13
	14	15	16	17	18	19	20
	21	22	23	24	25	26	27
	28	29	30	1	2	3	4
DEY 1496	5	6	7	8	9	10	11

[a]New Year
[b]Sizdeh Bedar

HINDU LUNAR 2173/2174

Month	Sun	Mon	Tue	Wed	Thu	Fri	Sat
PAUSHA 2173	23	24	25	27	28	29	30
	1	2	3	3	4	5	6
	7	8	9	10	11	12	13
	14	15	16	17	18	19	21
	22	23	24	25	26	27	28
MĀGHA 2173	29	30	1	2	3	4	5
	5	6	7	8	9	10	11
	12	13	15	16	17	18	19
	20	21	22	23	24	25	26
	27	28[h]	29	30	1	2	3
PHĀLGUNA 2173	4	5	6	7	8	9	10
	11	12	13	14	15[i]	16	17
	18	20	21	22	23	24	25
	26	27	28	28	29	30	1[a]
CHAITRA 2174	2	3	4	5	6	7	8
	9[b]	10	11	13	14	15	16
	17	18	19	20	21	22	23
	24	25	26	27	28	29	30
VAIŚĀKHA 2174	1	2	3	4	5	6	7
	8	9	10	11	12	13	14
	15	17	18	19	20	21	22
	23	23	24	25	26	27	28
	29	30	1	2	3	4	5
JYAISHTHA 2174	6	7	8	10	11	12	13
	14	15	16	17	18	19	20
	21	22	23	24	25	26	27
	28	29	30	1	2	3	4
ĀSHĀDHA 2174	5	6	7	8	9	10	11
	13	14	15	16	17	18	19
	20	20	21	22	23	24	25
	26	27	28	29	30	1	2
ŚRĀVAṆA 2174	3	5	6	7	8	9	10
	11	12	13	14	15	16	17
	18	19	20	21	22	23[c]	24
	25	26	27	28	29	30	1
BHĀDRAPADA 2174	2	3	4[d]	5	6	7	9
	10	11	12	13	14	15	16
	16	17	18	19	20	21	22
	23	24	25	26	27	28	29
ĀŚVINA 2174	30	2	3	4	5	6	7
	8[e]	9[e]	10[e]	11	12	13	14
	15	16	17	18	19	20	21
	22	23	24	25	26	27	28
	29	30	1[f]	2	3	4	6
KĀRTTIKA 2174	7	8	9	10	11	11	12
	13	14	15	16	17	18	19
	20	21	22	23	24	25	26
	27	29	30	1	2	3	4
MĀRGAŚĪRA 2174	5	6	7	8	9	10	11[g]
	12	13	13	14	15	16	17
	18	19	20	21	23	24	25
PAUSHA 2174	26	27	28	29	30	1	2
	3	4	5	6	7	8	9

[a]New Year (Īśvara)
[b]Birthday of Rāma
[c]Birthday of Krishna
[d]Ganēśa Chaturthī
[e]Dashara
[f]Diwali
[g]Birthday of Vishnu
[h]Night of Śiva
[i]Holi

HINDU SOLAR 2038/2039‡

Month	Sun	Mon	Tue	Wed	Thu	Fri	Sat
PAUSHA 2038	11	12	13	14	15	16	17
	18	19	20	21	22	23	24
	25	26	27	28	29	30	1[b]
MĀGHA 2038	2	3	4	5	6	7	8
	9	10	11	12	13	14	15
	16	17	18	19	20	21	22
	23	24	25	26	27	28	29
PHĀLGUNA 2038	1	2	3	4	5	6	7
	8	9	10	11	12	13	14
	15	16	17	18	19	20	21
	22	23	24	25	26	27	28
	29	30	1	2	3	4	5
CHAITRA 2038	6	7	8	9	10	11	12
	13	14	15	16	17	18	19
	20	21	22	23	24	25	26
	27	28	29	30	1[a]	2	3
VAIŚĀKHA 2039	4	5	6	7	8	9	10
	11	12	13	14	15	16	17
	18	19	20	21	22	23	24
	25	26	27	28	29	30	31
JYAISHTHA 2039	1	2	3	4	5	6	7
	8	9	10	11	12	13	14
	15	16	17	18	19	20	21
	22	23	24	25	26	27	28
	29	30	31	32	1	2	3
ĀSHĀDHA 2039	4	5	6	7	8	9	10
	11	12	13	14	15	16	17
	18	19	20	21	22	23	24
	25	26	27	28	29	30	31
ŚRĀVAṆA 2039	1	2	3	4	5	6	7
	8	9	10	11	12	13	14
	15	16	17	18	19	20	21
	22	23	24	25	26	27	28
	29	30	31	32	1	2	3
BHĀDRAPADA 2039	4	5	6	7	8	9	10
	11	12	13	14	15	16	17
	18	19	20	21	22	23	24
	25	26	27	28	29	30	31
ĀŚVINA 2039	1	2	3	4	5	6	7
	8	9	10	11	12	13	14
	15	16	17	18	19	20	21
	22	23	24	25	26	27	28
	29	30	1	2	3	4	5
KĀRTTIKA 2039	6	7	8	9	10	11	12
	13	14	15	16	17	18	19
	20	21	22	23	24	25	26
	27	28	29	30	1	2	3
MĀRGAŚĪRA 2039	4	5	6	7	8	9	10
	11	12	13	14	15	16	17
	18	19	20	21	22	23	24
	25	26	27	28	29	30	1
PAUSHA 2039	2	3	4	5	6	7	8
	9	10	11	12	13	14	15

‡Leap year
[a]New Year (Nandana)
[b]Pongal

ISLAMIC (ASTRONOMICAL) 1541‡/1542‡

Month	Sun	Mon	Tue	Wed	Thu	Fri	Sat
RABĪ' II 1541	22	23	24	25	26	27	28
	29	30	1	2	3	4	5
JUMĀDĀ I 1541	6	7	8	9	10	11	12
	13	14	15	16	17	18	19
	20	21	22	23	24	25	26
	27	28	29	1	2	3	4
JUMĀDĀ II 1541	5	6	7	8	9	10	11
	12	13	14	15	16	17	18
	19	20	21	22	23	24	25
	26	27	28	29	30	1	2
RAJAB 1541	3	4	5	6	7	8	9
	10	11	12	13	14	15	16
	17	18	19	20	21	22	23
	24	25	26	27[d]	28	29	30
SHA'BĀN 1541	1	2	3	4	5	6	7
	8	9	10	11	12	13	14
	15	16	17	18	19	20	21
	22	23	24	25	26	27	28
	29	1[e]	2	3	4	5	6
RAMAḌĀN 1541	7	8	9	10	11	12	13
	14	15	16	17	18	19	20
	21	22	23	24	25	26	27
	28	29	30	1[f]	2	3	4
SHAWWĀL 1541	5	6	7	8	9	10	11
	12	13	14	15	16	17	18
	19	20	21	22	23	24	25
	26	27	28	29	1	2	3
DHU AL-QA'DA 1541	4	5	6	7	8	9	10
	11	12	13	14	15	16	17
	18	19	20	21	22	23	24
	25	26	27	28	29	1	2
DHU AL-ḤIJJA 1541	3	4	5	6	7	8	9
	10[g]	11	12	13	14	15	16
	17	18	19	20	21	22	23
	24	25	26	27	28	29	30
MUḤARRAM 1542	1[a]	2	3	4	5	6	7
	8	9	10[b]	11	12	13	14
	15	16	17	18	19	20	21
	22	23	24	25	26	27	28
ṢAFAR 1542	29	30	1	2	3	4	5
	6	7	8	9	10	11	12
	13	14	15	16	17	18	19
	20	21	22	23	24	25	26
	27	28	29	1	2	3	4
RABĪ' I 1542	5	6	7	8	9	10	11
	12[c]	13	14	15	16	17	18
	19	20	21	22	23	24	25
	26	27	28	29	30	1	2
RABĪ' II 1542	3	4	5	6	7	8	9
	10	11	12	13	14	15	16
	17	18	19	20	21	22	23
	24	25	26	27	28	29	1
JUMĀDĀ I 1542	2	3	4	5	6	7	8

‡Leap year
[a]New Year
[b]'Ashūrā'
[c]Prophet's Birthday
[d]Ascent of the Prophet
[e]Start of Ramaḍān
[f]'Īd al-Fiṭr
[g]'Īd al-'Aḍḥā

GREGORIAN 2117

Julian (Sun)	Sun	Mon	Tue	Wed	Thu	Fri	Sat	Month
Dec 13	27	28	29	30	31	1	2	JANUARY 2117
	3	4	5	6	7	8[a]	9	
Dec 27	10	11	12	13	14	15[b]	16	
	17	18	19	20	21	22	23	
Jan 10	24	25	26	27	28	29	30	
	31	1	2	3	4	5	6	FEBRUARY 2117
Jan 24	7	8	9	10	11	12	13	
	14	15	16	17	18	19	20	
Feb 7	21	22	23	24	25	26	27	
	28	1	2	3[c]	4	5	6	MARCH 2117
Feb 21	7	8	9	10	11	12	13	
	14[d]	15	16	17	18	19	20	
Mar 7	21	22	23	24	25	26	27	
	28	29	30	31	1	2	3	APRIL 2117
Mar 21	4	5	6	7	8	9	10	
	11	12	13	14	15	16	17	
Apr 4	18[e]	19	20	21	22	23	24	
	25[f]	26	27	28	29	30	1	MAY 2117
Apr 18	2	3	4	5	6	7	8	
	9	10	11	12	13	14	15	
May 2	16	17	18	19	20	21	22	
	23	24	25	26	27	28	29	
May 16	30	31	1	2	3	4	5	JUNE 2117
	6	7	8	9	10	11	12	
May 30	13	14	15	16	17	18	19	
	20	21	22	23	24	25	26	
Jun 13	27	28	29	30	1	2	3	JULY 2117
	4	5	6	7	8	9	10	
Jun 27	11	12	13	14	15	16	17	
	18	19	20	21	22	23	24	
Jul 11	25	26	27	28	29	30	31	
	1	2	3	4	5	6	7	AUGUST 2117
Jul 25	8	9	10	11	12	13	14	
	15	16	17	18	19	20	21	
Aug 8	22	23	24	25	26	27	28	
	29	30	31	1	2	3	4	SEPTEMBER 2117
Aug 22	5	6	7	8	9	10	11	
	12	13	14	15	16	17	18	
Sep 5	19	20	21	22	23	24	25	
	26	27	28	29	30	1	2	OCTOBER 2117
Sep 19	3	4	5	6	7	8	9	
	10	11	12	13	14	15	16	
Oct 3	17	18	19	20	21	22	23	
	24	25	26	27	28	29	30	
Oct 17	31	1	2	3	4	5	6	NOVEMBER 2117
	7	8	9	10	11	12	13	
Oct 31	14	15	16	17	18	19	20	
	21	22	23	24	25	26	27	
Nov 14	28[g]	29	30	1	2	3	4	DECEMBER 2117
	5	6	7	8	9	10	11	
Nov 28	12	13	14	15	16	17	18	
	19	20	21	22	23	24	25[h]	
Dec 12	26	27	28	29	30	31	1	

[a]Orthodox Christmas
[b]Julian New Year
[c]Ash Wednesday
[d]Feast of Orthodoxy
[e]Easter
[f]Orthodox Easter
[g]Advent
[h]Christmas

2118

Month	GREGORIAN 2118 (Sun Mon Tue Wed Thu Fri Sat)	Lunar Phases	ISO WEEK (Mon)	JULIAN DAY (Sun noon)	Month	HEBREW 5878/5879‡ (Sun Mon Tue Wed Thu Fri Sat)	Molad	Month	CHINESE Dīng-Chǒu/Wù-Yín‡ (Sun Mon Tue Wed Thu Fri Sat)	Solar Term	Month	COPTIC 1834/1835‡ (Sun Mon Tue Wed Thu Fri Sat)	ETHIOPIC 2110/2111‡
	26 27 28 29 ◐ 31 1[a]	22:07	52	2494638	TEVETH 5878	1[e] 2[e] 3 4 5 6 7	Thu 21h57m14p	MONTH 12 Dīng-Chǒu	4 5 6 7 8 9 10		KOIAK 1834	16 17 18 19 20 21 22	TĀKHŚĀŚ 2110
JANUARY 2118	2 3 4 5 6 ○ 8	21:24	1	2494645		8 9 10 11 12 13 14			11 12 13 14 15 16 17	Xiǎo hán		23 24 25 26 27 28 29[c]	
	9 10 11 12 13 ◑ 15	22:10	2	2494652		15 16 17 18 19 20 21			18 19 20 21 22 23 24		TÔBE 1834	30 1 2 3 4 5 6[d]	ṬER 2110
	16 17 18 19 20 ● 22	21:21	3	2494659		22 23 24 25 26 27 28		MONTH 1 Wù-Yín	25 26 27 28 29 30 1[a]	Dà hán		7 8 9 10 11[e] 12 13	
	23 24 25 26 27 28 ◐	20:17	4	2494666		29 1 2 3 4 5 6	Sat 10h41m15p		2 3 4 5 6 7 8			14 15 16 17 18 19 20	
	30 31 1 2 3 4 5		5	2494673	SHEVAT 5878	7 8 9 10 11 12 13			9 10 11 12 13 14 15[b]	Lì chūn		21 22 23 24 25 26 27	
FEBRUARY 2118	○ 7 8 9 10 11 12	11:22	6	2494680		14 15 16 17 18 19 20			16 17 18 19 20 21 22		MESHIR 1834	28 29 30 1 2 3 4	YAKĀTIT 2110
	◑ 14 15 16 17 18 19	6:12	7	2494687		21 22 23 24 25 26 27			23 24 25 26 27* 28 29	Yǔ shuǐ		5 6 7 8 9 10 11	
	● 21 22 23 24 25 26	12:56	8	2494694		28 29 30 1 2 3 4	Sun 23h25m16p	MONTH 2 Wù-Yín	1 2 3 4 5 6 7			12 13 14 15 16 17 18	
	27 ◐ 1 2 3 4 5	16:59	9	2494701	ADAR 5878	5 6 7 8 9 10 11			8 9 10 11 12 13 14			19 20 21 22 23 24 25	
MARCH 2118	6 ○ 8 9 10 11 12	23:17	10	2494708		12 13 14[f] 15 16 17 18			15 16 17 18 19 20 21	Jīng zhé	PAREMOTEP 1834	26 27 28 29 30 1 2	MAGĀBIT 2110
	13 ◑ 15 16 17 18 19	14:40	11	2494715		19 20 21 22 23 24 25			22 23 24 25 26 27 28			3 4 5 6 7 8 9	
	20[b] 21 ● 23 24 25 26	5:59	12	2494722		26 27 28 29 1 2 3	Tue 12h9m17p	MONTH 3 Wù-Yín	29 30 1 2 3 4 5	Chūn fēn		10 11 12 13 14 15 16	
	27 28 29 ◐ 31 1 2	10:30	13	2494729	NISAN 5878	4 5 6 7 8 9 10			6 7 8 9 10 11 12			17 18 19 20 21 22 23	
APRIL 2118	3 4 5 ○ 7 8 9	9:15	14	2494736		11 12 13 14 15[g] 16 17			13 14 15[c] 16 17 18 19	Qīng míng		24 25 26 27 28 29 30	
	10 11 12 ◑ 14 15 16	0:27	15	2494743		18 19 20 21 22 23 24			20 21 22 23 24 25 26		PARMOUTE 1834	1 2 3 4 5 6 7	MIYĀZYĀ 2110
	17 18 19 ● 21 22 23	23:18	16	2494750		25 26 27 28 29 30 1	Thu 0h54m0p	LEAP MONTH 3 Wù-Yín	27 28* 29 30 1 2 3	Gǔ yǔ		8[f] 9 10 11 12 13 14	
	24 25 26 27 28 ◐ 30	0:10	17	2494757	IYYAR 5878	2 3 4 5 6 7 8			4 5 6 7 8 9 10			15 16 17 18 19 20 21	
MAY 2118	1 2 3 4 ○ 6 7	17:34	18	2494764		9 10 11 12 13 14 15			11 12 13 14 15 16 17	Lì xià		22 23 24 25 26 27 28	
	8 9 10 11 ◑ 13 14	12:11	19	2494771		16 17 18 19 20 21 22			18 19 20 21 22 23 24		PASHONS 1834	29[g] 30 1 2 3 4 5	GENBOT 2110
	15 16 17 18 19 ● 21	15:37	20	2494778		23 24 25 26 27 28 29			25 26 27 28 29 1 2	Xiǎo mǎn		6 7 8 9 10 11 12	
	22 23 24 25 26 27 ◐	10:12	21	2494785	SIVAN 5878	1 2 3 4 5 6[h] 7	Fri 13h38m1p	MONTH 4 Wù-Yín	3 4 5 6 7 8 9			13 14 15 16 17 18 19	
JUNE 2118	29 30 31 1 2 3 ○	0:57	22	2494792		8 9 10 11 12 13 14			10 11 12 13 14 15 16			20 21 22 23 24 25 26	
	5 6 7 8 9 10 ◑	2:09	23	2494799		15 16 17 18 19 20 21			17 18 19 20 21 22 23	Máng zhòng	PAÔNE 1834	27 28 29 30 1 2 3	SANÉ 2110
	12 13 14 15 16 17 18		24	2494806		22 23 24 25 26 27 28			24 25 26 27 28 29* 30			4 5 6 7 8 9 10	
	● 20 21[c] 22 23 24 25	6:11	25	2494813		29 30 1 2 3 4 5	Sun 2h22m2p	MONTH 5 Wù-Yín	1 2 3 4 5[d] 6 7	Xià zhì		11 12 13 14 15 16 17	
	◐ 27 28 29 30 1 2	17:17	26	2494820	TAMMUZ 5878	6 7 8 9 10 11 12			8 9 10 11 12 13 14			18 19 20 21 22 23 24	
JULY 2118	○ 4 5 6 7 8 9	8:28	27	2494827		13 14 15 16 17 18 19			15 16 17 18 19 20 21	Xiǎo shǔ		25 26 27 28 29 30 1	
	◑ 11 12 13 14 15 16	18:05	28	2494834		20 21 22 23 24 25 26			22 23 24 25 26 27 28		EPÊP 1834	2 3 4 5 6 7 8	ḤAMLÉ 2110
	17 ● 19 20 21 22 23	18:56	29	2494841		27 28 29 1 2 3 4	Mon 15h6m3p	MONTH 6 Wù-Yín	29 30 1 2 3 4 5	Dà shǔ		9 10 11 12 13 14 15	
	24 ◐ 26 27 28 29 30	22:27	30	2494848	AV 5878	5 6 7 8 9[i] 10 11			6 7 8 9 10 11 12			16 17 18 19 20 21 22	
AUGUST 2118	31 ○ 2 3 4 5 6	17:19	31	2494855		12 13 14 15 16 17 18			13 14 15 16 17 18 19			23 24 25 26 27 28 29	
	7 8 ◑ 10 11 12 13	11:22	32	2494862		19 20 21 22 23 24 25			20 21 22 23 24 25 26	Lì qiū	MESORÊ 1834	30 1 2 3 4 5 6	NAHASÉ 2110
	14 15 16 ● 18 19 20	6:12	33	2494869		26 27 28 29 30 1 2	Wed 3h50m4p	MONTH 7 Wù-Yín	27 28 29* 1 2 3 4			7 8 9 10 11 12 13[h]	
	21 22 23 ◐ 25 26 27	3:03	34	2494876	ELUL 5878	3 4 5 6 7 8 9			5 6 7[e] 8 9 10 11	Chǔ shǔ		14 15 16 17 18 19 20	
	28 29 30 ○ 1 2 3	4:34	35	2494883		10 11 12 13 14 15 16			12 13 14 15[f] 16 17 18			21 22 23 24 25 26 27	
SEPTEMBER 2118	4 5 6 7 ◑ 9 10	5:11	36	2494890		17 18 19 20 21 22 23			19 20 21 22 23 24 25	Bái lù	EPAG. 1834	28 29 30 1 2 3 4	PĀG. 2110
	11 12 13 14 ● 16 17	16:26	37	2494897		24 25 26 27 28 29 1[a]	Thu 16h34m5p		26 27 28 29 30 1 2		THOOUT 1835	5 1[a] 2 3 4 5 6	MASKARAM 2111
	18 19 20 21 ◐ 23[d] 24	8:37	38	2494904	TISHRI 5879	2[a] 3 4 5 6 7 8		MONTH 8 Wù-Yín	3 4 5 6 7 8 9	Qiū fēn		7 8 9 10 11 12 13	
	25 26 27 28 ○ 30 1	18:43	39	2494911		9 10[b] 11 12 13 14 15[c]			10 11 12 13 14 15[g] 16			14 15 16 17[b] 18 19 20	
OCTOBER 2118	2 3 4 5 6 ◑ 8	22:44	40	2494918		16 17 18 19 20 21 22			17 18 19 20 21 22 23	Hán lù		21 22 23 24 25 26 27	
	9 10 11 12 13 14 ●	2:08	41	2494925		23 24 25 26 27 28 29			24 25 26 27 28 29 1*		PAOPE 1835	28 29 30 1 2 3 4	ṬEQEMT 2111
	16 17 18 19 20 ◐ 22	16:39	42	2494932		30 1 2 3 4 5 6	Sat 5h18m6p	MONTH 9 Wù-Yín	2 3 4 5 6 7 8			5 6 7 8 9 10 11	
	23 24 25 26 27 28 ○	11:32	43	2494939	ḤESHVAN 5879	7 8 9 10 11 12 13			9[h] 10 11 12 13 14 15	Shuāng jiàng		12 13 14 15 16 17 18	
	30 31 1 2 3 4 5		44	2494946		14 15 16 17 18 19 20			16 17 18 19 20 21 22			19 20 21 22 23 24 25	
NOVEMBER 2118	◑ 7 8 9 10 11 12	15:11	45	2494953		21 22 23 24 25 26 27			23 24 25 26 27 28 29	Lì dōng	ATHÔR 1835	26 27 28 29 30 1 2	HEDĀR 2111
	● 14 15 16 17 18 19	11:43	46	2494960		28 29 1 2 3 4 5	Sun 18h2m7p	MONTH 10 Wù-Yín	1 2 3 4 5 6 7			3 4 5 6 7 8 9	
	◐ 21 22 23 24 25 26	4:24	47	2494967	KISLEV 5879	6 7 8 9 10 11 12			8 9 10 11 12 13 14	Xiǎo xuě		10 11 12 13 14 15 16	
	27 ○ 29 30 1 2 3	6:05	48	2494974		13 14 15 16 17 18 19			15 16 17 18 19 20 21			17 18 19 20 21 22 23	
DECEMBER 2118	4 5 ◑ 7 8 9 10	5:41	49	2494981		20 21 22[d] 23 24 25[e] 26[e]			22 23 24 25 26 27 28	Dà xuě		24 25 26 27 28 29 30	
	11 ● 13 14 15 16 17	21:44	50	2494988		27[e] 28[e] 29[e] 1[e] 2[e] 3[e] 4	Tue 6h46m8p	MONTH 11* Wù-Yín	29 30 1 2* 3 4 5		KOIAK 1835	1 2 3 4 5 6 7	TĀKHŚĀŚ 2111
	18 ◐ 20 21 22[e] 23 24	20:15	51	2494995	TEVETH 5879	5 6 7 8 9 10 11			6 7 8 9 10[i] 11 12	Dōng zhì		8 9 10 11 12 13 14	
	25 26 27 ○ 29 30 31	1:03	52	2495002		12 13 14 15 16 17 18			13 14 15 16 17 18 19			15 16 17 18 19 20 21	

Gregorian notes:
[a]New Year
[b]Spring (21:52)
[c]Summer (13:42)
[d]Autumn (6:25)
[e]Winter (4:47)
● New moon
◐ First quarter moon
○ Full moon
◑ Last quarter moon

Hebrew notes:
‡Leap year
[a]New Year
[b]Yom Kippur
[c]Sukkot
[d]Winter starts
[e]Ḥanukkah
[f]Purim
[g]Passover
[h]Shavuot
[i]Fast of Av

Chinese notes:
‡Leap year
[a]New Year (4816, Tiger)
[b]Lantern Festival
[c]Qīngmíng
[d]Dragon Festival
[e]Qīqiǎo
[f]Hungry Ghosts
[g]Mid-Autumn Festival
[h]Double-Ninth Festival
[i]Dōngzhì
*Start of 60-name cycle

Coptic/Ethiopic notes:
‡Leap year
[a]New Year
[b]Building of the Cross
[c]Christmas
[d]Jesus's Circumcision
[e]Epiphany
[f]Easter
[g]Mary's Announcement
[h]Jesus's Transfiguration

PERSIAN (ASTRONOMICAL) 1496/1497

Month	Sun	Mon	Tue	Wed	Thu	Fri	Sat
DEY 1496	5	6	7	8	9	10	11
	12	13	14	15	16	17	18
	19	20	21	22	23	24	25
	26	27	28	29	30	1	2
BAHMAN 1496	3	4	5	6	7	8	9
	10	11	12	13	14	15	16
	17	18	19	20	21	22	23
	24	25	26	27	28	29	30
ESFAND 1496	1	2	3	4	5	6	7
	8	9	10	11	12	13	14
	15	16	17	18	19	20	21
	22	23	24	25	26	27	28
	29	1[a]	2	3	4	5	6
FARVARDĪN 1497	7	8	9	10	11	12	13[b]
	14	15	16	17	18	19	20
	21	22	23	24	25	26	27
	28	29	30	31	1	2	3
ORDĪBEHEŠT 1497	4	5	6	7	8	9	10
	11	12	13	14	15	16	17
	18	19	20	21	22	23	24
	25	26	27	28	29	30	31
XORDĀD 1497	1	2	3	4	5	6	7
	8	9	10	11	12	13	14
	15	16	17	18	19	20	21
	22	23	24	25	26	27	28
	29	30	31	1	2	3	4
TĪR 1497	5	6	7	8	9	10	11
	12	13	14	15	16	17	18
	19	20	21	22	23	24	25
	26	27	28	29	30	31	1
MORDĀD 1497	2	3	4	5	6	7	8
	9	10	11	12	13	14	15
	16	17	18	19	20	21	22
	23	24	25	26	27	28	29
	30	31	1	2	3	4	5
SHAHRĪVAR 1497	6	7	8	9	10	11	12
	13	14	15	16	17	18	19
	20	21	22	23	24	25	26
	27	28	29	30	31	1	2
MEHR 1497	3	4	5	6	7	8	9
	10	11	12	13	14	15	16
	17	18	19	20	21	22	23
	24	25	26	27	28	29	30
ĀBĀN 1497	1	2	3	4	5	6	7
	8	9	10	11	12	13	14
	15	16	17	18	19	20	21
	22	23	24	25	26	27	28
	29	30	1	2	3	4	5
ĀZAR 1497	6	7	8	9	10	11	12
	13	14	15	16	17	18	19
	20	21	22	23	24	25	26
	27	28	29	30	1	2	3
DEY 1497	4	5	6	7	8	9	10

[a]New Year
[b]Sizdeh Bedar

HINDU LUNAR 2174/2175‡

Month	Sun	Mon	Tue	Wed	Thu	Fri	Sat
PAUSHA 2174	3	4	5	6	7	8	9
	10	11	12	13	14	15	16
	17	18	19	20	21	22	23
	24	25	**26**	28	29	30	1
MĀGHA 2174	2	3	4	5	6	6	7
	8	9	10	11	12	13	14
	15	16	17	18	19	**20**	22
	23	24	25	26	27	28[h]	29
	30	1	2	3	4	5	6
PHĀLGUNA 2174	7	8	8	9	10	11	12
	13	**14**[i]	16	17	18	19	20
	21	22	23	24	25	26	27
	28	29	30	1[a]	2	3	4
CHAITRA 2175	5	6	7	8	9[b]	10	11
	12	13	14	15	16	17	**18**
	20	21	22	23	24	25	26
	27	28	29	30	1	2	2
VAIŚĀKHA 2175	3	4	5	6	7	8	9
	10	11	**12**	14	15	16	17
	18	19	20	21	22	23	24
	25	26	27	28	29	30	1
JYAISHTHA 2175	2	3	4	5	6	7	8
	9	10	11	12	13	14	**15**
	17	18	19	20	21	22	23
	24	25	26	27	28	28	29
	30	1	2	3	4	5	6
LEAP ĀSHĀDHA 2175	7	**8**	10	11	12	13	14
	15	16	17	18	19	20	21
	22	23	24	25	26	27	28
	29	30	1	2	3	4	5
ĀSHĀDHA 2175	6	7	8	9	10	**11**	13
	14	15	16	17	18	19	20
	21	22	23	24	24	25	26
	27	28	29	30	1	2	**3**
ŚRĀVAṆA 2175	5	6	7	8	9	10	11
	12	13	14	15	16	17	18
	19	20	21	22	23[c]	24	25
	26	27	28	29	30	1	2
BHĀDRAPADA 2175	3	4[d]	5	6	**7**	9	10
	11	12	13	14	15	16	17
	18	19	20	20	21	22	23
	24	25	26	27	28	29	**30**
	2	3	4	5	6	7	8[e]
ĀŚVINA 2175	9[e]	10[e]	11	12	13	14	15
	16	17	18	19	20	21	22
	23	24	25	26	27	28	29
	30	1[f]	2	3	**4**	6	7
KĀRTTIKA 2175	8	9	10	11	12	13	14
	14	15	16	17	18	19	20
	21	22	23	24	25	26	27
	28	30	1	2	3	4	5
MĀRGAŚĪRA 2175	6	7	8	9	10	11[g]	12
	13	14	15	16	16	17	18

‡Leap year
[a]New Year (Bahudhānya)
[b]Birthday of Rāma
[c]Birthday of Krishna
[d]Ganēśa Chaturthī
[e]Dashara
[f]Diwali
[g]Birthday of Vishnu
[h]Night of Śiva
[i]Holi

HINDU SOLAR 2039‡/2040

Month	Sun	Mon	Tue	Wed	Thu	Fri	Sat
PAUSHA 2039	9	10	11	12	13	14	15
	16	17	18	19	20	21	22
	23	24	25	26	27	28	29
	1[b]	2	3	4	5	6	7
MĀGHA 2039	8	9	10	11	12	13	14
	15	16	17	18	19	20	21
	22	23	24	25	26	27	28
	29	1	2	3	4	5	6
PHĀLGUNA 2039	7	8	9	10	11	12	13
	14	15	16	17	18	19	20
	21	22	23	24	25	26	27
	28	29	30	1	2	3	4
CHAITRA 2039	5	6	7	8	9	10	11
	12	13	14	15	16	17	18
	19	20	21	22	23	24	25
	26	27	28	29	30	31	1[a]
VAIŚĀKHA 2040	2	3	4	5	6	7	8
	9	10	11	12	13	14	15
	16	17	18	19	20	21	22
	23	24	25	26	27	28	29
	30	1	2	3	4	5	6
JYAISHTHA 2040	7	8	9	10	11	12	13
	14	15	16	17	18	19	20
	21	22	23	24	25	26	27
	28	29	30	31	32	1	2
ĀSHĀDHA 2040	3	4	5	6	7	8	9
	10	11	12	13	14	15	16
	17	18	19	20	21	22	23
	24	25	26	27	28	29	30
	31	32	1	2	3	4	5
ŚRĀVAṆA 2040	6	7	8	9	10	11	12
	13	14	15	16	17	18	19
	20	21	22	23	24	25	26
	27	28	29	30	31	1	2
BHĀDRAPADA 2040	3	4	5	6	7	8	9
	10	11	12	13	14	15	16
	17	18	19	20	21	22	23
	24	25	26	27	28	29	30
	31	1	2	3	4	5	6
ĀŚVINA 2040	7	8	9	10	11	12	13
	14	15	16	17	18	19	20
	21	22	23	24	25	26	27
	28	29	30	1	2	3	4
KĀRTTIKA 2040	5	6	7	8	9	10	11
	12	13	14	15	16	17	18
	19	20	21	22	23	24	25
	26	27	28	29	30	1	2
MĀRGAŚĪRA 2040	3	4	5	6	7	8	9
	10	11	12	13	14	15	16
	17	18	19	20	21	22	23
	24	25	26	27	28	29	30
PAUSHA 2040	1	2	3	4	5	6	7
	8	9	10	11	12	13	14

‡Leap year
[a]New Year (Vijaya)
[b]Pongal

ISLAMIC (ASTRONOMICAL) 1542‡/1543

Month	Sun	Mon	Tue	Wed	Thu	Fri	Sat
JUMĀDĀ I 1542	2	3	4	5	6	7	8
	9	10	11	12	13	14	15
	16	17	18	19	20	21	22
	23	24	25	26	27	28	29
JUMĀDĀ II 1542	1	2	3	4	5	6	7
	8	9	10	11	12	13	14
	15	16	17	18	19	20	21
	22	23	24	25	26	27	28
	29	30	1	2	3	4	5
RAJAB 1542	6	7	8	9	10	11	12
	13	14	15	16	17	18	19
	20	21	22	23	24	25	26
	27[d]	28	29	30	1	2	3
SHA'BĀN 1542	4	5	6	7	8	9	10
	11	12	13	14	15	16	17
	18	19	20	21	22	23	24
	25	26	27	28	29	1[e]	2
RAMAḌĀN 1542	3	4	5	6	7	8	9
	10	11	12	13	14	15	16
	17	18	19	20	21	22	23
	24	25	26	27	28	29	30
SHAWWĀL 1542	1[f]	2	3	4	5	6	7
	8	9	10	11	12	13	14
	15	16	17	18	19	20	21
	22	23	24	25	26	27	28
	29	1	2	3	4	5	6
DHU AL-QA'DA 1542	7	8	9	10	11	12	13
	14	15	16	17	18	19	20
	21	22	23	24	25	26	27
	28	29	30	1	2	3	4
DHU AL-ḤIJJA 1542	5	6	7	8	9	10[g]	11
	12	13	14	15	16	17	18
	19	20	21	22	23	24	25
	26	27	28	29	30[d]	1[a]	2
MUḤARRAM 1543	3	4	5	6	7	8	9
	10[b]	11	12	13	14	15	16
	17	18	19	20	21	22	23
	24	25	26	27	28	29	30
ṢAFAR 1543	1	2	3	4	5	6	7
	8	9	10	11	12	13	14
	15	16	17	18	19	20	21
	22	23	24	25	26	27	28
	29	1	2	3	4	5	6
RABĪ' I 1543	7	8	9	10	11	12[c]	13
	14	15	16	17	18	19	20
	21	22	23	24	25	26	27
	28	29	1	2	3	4	5
RABĪ' II 1543	6	7	8	9	10	11	12
	13	14	15	16	17	18	19
	20	21	22	23	24	25	26
	27	28	29	1	2	3	4
JUMĀDĀ I 1543	5	6	7	8	9	10	11
	12	13	14	15	16	17	18

‡Leap year
[a]New Year
[A]New Year (Arithmetic)
[b]'Ashūrā'
[c]Prophet's Birthday
[d]Ascent of the Prophet
[e]Start of Ramaḍān
[f]'Id al-Fiṭr
[g]'Id al-'Aḍḥā

GREGORIAN 2118

Julian (Sun)	Sun	Mon	Tue	Wed	Thu	Fri	Sat	Month
Dec 12	26	27	28	29	30	31	1	
	2	3	4	5	6	7	8[a]	JANUARY 2118
Dec 26	9	10	11	12	13	14	15[b]	
	16	17	18	19	20	21	22	
Jan 9	23	24	25	26	27	28	29	
	30	31	1	2	3	4	5	
Jan 23	6	7	8	9	10	11	12	FEBRUARY 2118
	13	14	15	16	17	18	19	
Feb 6	20	21	22	23[c]	24	25	26	
	27	28	1	2	3	4	5	
Feb 20	6[d]	7	8	9	10	11	12	MARCH 2118
	13	14	15	16	17	18	19	
Mar 6	20	21	22	23	24	25	26	
	27	28	29	30	31	1	2	
Mar 20	3	4	5	6	7	8	9	APRIL 2118
	10[e]	11	12	13	14	15	16	
Apr 3	17[f]	18	19	20	21	22	23	
	24	25	26	27	28	29	30	
Apr 17	1	2	3	4	5	6	7	MAY 2118
	8	9	10	11	12	13	14	
May 1	15	16	17	18	19	20	21	
	22	23	24	25	26	27	28	
May 15	29	30	31	1	2	3	4	
	5	6	7	8	9	10	11	JUNE 2118
May 29	12	13	14	15	16	17	18	
	19	20	21	22	23	24	25	
Jun 12	26	27	28	29	30	1	2	
	3	4	5	6	7	8	9	JULY 2118
Jun 26	10	11	12	13	14	15	16	
	17	18	19	20	21	22	23	
Jul 10	24	25	26	27	28	29	30	
	31	1	2	3	4	5	6	
Jul 24	7	8	9	10	11	12	13	AUGUST 2118
	14	15	16	17	18	19	20	
Aug 7	21	22	23	24	25	26	27	
	28	29	30	31	1	2	3	
Aug 21	4	5	6	7	8	9	10	SEPTEMBER 2118
	11	12	13	14	15	16	17	
Sep 4	18	19	20	21	22	23	24	
	25	26	27	28	29	30	1	
Sep 18	2	3	4	5	6	7	8	OCTOBER 2118
	9	10	11	12	13	14	15	
Oct 2	16	17	18	19	20	21	22	
	23	24	25	26	27	28	29	
Oct 16	30	31	1	2	3	4	5	
	6	7	8	9	10	11	12	NOVEMBER 2118
Oct 30	13	14	15	16	17	18	19	
	20	21	22	23	24	25	26	
Nov 13	27[g]	28	29	30	1	2	3	
	4	5	6	7	8	9	10	DECEMBER 2118
Nov 27	11	12	13	14	15	16	17	
	18	19	20	21	22	23	24	
Dec 11	25[h]	26	27	28	29	30	31	

[a]Orthodox Christmas
[b]Julian New Year
[c]Ash Wednesday
[d]Feast of Orthodoxy
[e]Easter
[f]Orthodox Easter
[g]Advent
[h]Christmas

2119

GREGORIAN 2119

Month	Sun	Mon	Tue	Wed	Thu	Fri	Sat	Lunar Phases	ISO WEEK (Mon)	JULIAN DAY (Sun noon)
JANUARY 2119	1[a]	2	3	◑	5	6	7	17:38	1	2495009
	8	9	10	●	12	13	14	8:41	2	2495016
	15	16	17	◐	19	20	21	15:26	3	2495023
	22	23	24	25	○	27	28	19:04	4	2495030
FEBRUARY 2119	29	30	31	1	2	◑	4	2:58	5	2495037
	5	6	7	8	●	10	11	20:54	6	2495044
	12	13	14	15	16	◐	18	12:21	7	2495051
	19	20	21	22	23	24	○	10:56	8	2495058
MARCH 2119	26	27	28	1	2	3	◑	10:26	9	2495065
	5	6	7	8	9	10	●	10:25	10	2495072
	12	13	14	15	16	17	18		11	2495079
	◐	20	21[b]	22	23	24	25	9:06	12	2495086
APRIL 2119	○	27	28	29	30	31	1	23:55	13	2495093
	◑	3	4	5	6	7	8	17:10	14	2495100
	9	●	11	12	13	14	15	0:56	15	2495107
	16	17	◐	19	20	21	22	4:00	16	2495114
	23	24	○	26	27	28	29	10:01	17	2495121
MAY 2119	30	1	◑	3	4	5	6	0:25	18	2495128
	7	8	●	10	11	12	13	16:02	19	2495135
	14	15	16	◐	18	19	20	19:57	20	2495142
	21	22	23	○	25	26	27	17:55	21	2495149
JUNE 2119	28	29	30	◑	1	2	3	9:11	22	2495156
	4	5	6	7	●	9	10	7:20	23	2495163
	11	12	13	14	15	◐	17	8:24	24	2495170
	18	19	20	21[c]	22	○	24	0:43	25	2495177
JULY 2119	25	26	27	28	◑	30	1	20:05	26	2495184
	2	3	4	5	6	●	8	22:31	27	2495191
	9	10	11	12	13	14	◐	17:35	28	2495198
	16	17	18	19	20	21	○	7:37	29	2495205
	23	24	25	26	27	28	◑	9:28	30	2495212
AUGUST 2119	30	31	1	2	3	4	5		31	2495219
	●	7	8	9	10	11	12	13:10	32	2495226
	13	◐	15	16	17	18	19	0:17	33	2495233
	○	21	22	23	24	25	26	15:43	34	2495240
SEPTEMBER 2119	27	◑	29	30	31	1	2	1:25	35	2495247
	3	4	●	6	7	8	9	2:51	36	2495254
	10	11	◐	13	14	15	16	5:48	37	2495261
	17	18	○	20	21	22	23[d]	1:51	38	2495268
	24	25	◑	27	28	29	30	19:41	39	2495275
OCTOBER 2119	1	2	3	●	5	6	7	15:20	40	2495282
	8	9	10	◐	12	13	14	11:33	41	2495289
	15	16	17	○	19	20	21	14:34	42	2495296
	22	23	24	25	◑	27	28	15:24	43	2495303
NOVEMBER 2119	29	30	31	1	2	●	4	2:42	44	2495310
	5	6	7	8	◐	10	11	18:55	45	2495317
	12	13	14	15	16	○	18	6:06	46	2495324
	19	20	21	22	23	24	◑	11:01	47	2495331
DECEMBER 2119	26	27	28	29	30	1	●	13:26	48	2495338
	3	4	5	6	7	8	◐	4:56	49	2495345
	10	11	12	13	14	15	16		50	2495352
	○	18	19	20	21	22[e]	23	0:14	51	2495359
	24	◑	26	27	28	29	30	4:43	52	2495366
	31	●	2	3	4	5	6	0:04	1	2495373

HEBREW 5879‡/5880

ISO WEEK	Month	Sun	Mon	Tue	Wed	Thu	Fri	Sat	Molad
1	TEVETH 5879	19	20	21	22	23	24	25	
2	SHEVAT 5879	26	27	28	29	1	2	3	Wed 19h30m9p
3		4	5	6	7	8	9	10	
4		11	12	13	14	15	16	17	
5		18	19	20	21	22	23	24	
6	ADAR I 5879	25	26	27	28	29	30	1	Fri 8h14m10p
7		2	3	4	5	6	7	8	
8		9	10	11	12	13	14	15	
9		16	17	18	19	20	21	22	
10		23	24	25	26	27	28	29	
11	ADAR II 5879	30	1	2	3	4	5	6	Sat 20h58m11p
12		7	8	9	10	11	12	13	
13		14[f]	15	16	17	18	19	20	
14		21	22	23	24	25	26	27	
15	NISAN 5879	28	29	1	2	3	4	5	Mon 9h42m12p
16		6	7	8	9	10	11	12	
17		13	14	15[g]	16	17	18	19	
18		20	21	22	23	24	25	26	
19	IYAR 5879	27	28	29	30	1	2	3	Tue 22h26m13p
20		4	5	6	7	8	9	10	
21		11	12	13	14	15	16	17	
22		18	19	20	21	22	23	24	
23	SIVAN 5879	25	26	27	28	29	1	2	Thu 11h10m14p
24		3	4	5	6[h]	7	8	9	
25		10	11	12	13	14	15	16	
26		17	18	19	20	21	22	23	
27		24	25	26	27	28	29	30	
28	TAMMUZ 5879	1	2	3	4	5	6	7	Fri 23h54m15p
29		8	9	10	11	12	13	14	
30		15	16	17	18	19	20	21	
31		22	23	24	25	26	27	28	
32	AV 5879	29	1	2	3	4	5	6	Sun 12h38m16p
33		7	8	9[i]	10	11	12	13	
34		14	15	16	17	18	19	20	
35		21	22	23	24	25	26	27	
36	ELUL 5879	28	29	30	1	2	3	4	Tue 1h22m17p
37		5	6	7	8	9	10	11	
38		12	13	14	15	16	17	18	
39		19	20	21	22	23	24	25	
40	TISHRI 5880	26	27	28	29	1[a]	2[a]	3	Wed 14h7m0p
41		4	5	6	7	8	9	10[b]	
42		11	12	13	14	15[c]	16	17	
43		18	19	20	21	22	23	24	
44	HESHVAN 5880	25	26	27	28	29	30	1	Fri 2h51m1p
45		2	3	4	5	6	7	8	
46		9	10	11	12	13	14	15	
47		16	17	18	19	20	21	22	
48		23	24	25	26	27	28	29	
49	KISLEV 5880	1	2	3	4	5[d]	6	7	Sat 15h35m2p
50		8	9	10	11	12	13	14	
51		15	16	17	18	19	20	21	
52		22	23	24	25[e]	26[e]	27[e]	28[e]	
1		29[e]	30[e]	1[e]	2[e]	3	4	5	Mon 4h19m3p

CHINESE Wù-Yín‡/Jǐ-Mǎo

ISO WEEK	Month	Sun	Mon	Tue	Wed	Thu	Fri	Sat	Solar Term
1	MONTH 11* Wù-Yín	20	21	22	23	24	25	26	Xiǎo hán
2	MONTH 12 Wù-Yín	27	28	29	1	2	3	4	
3		5	6	7	8	9	10	11	Dà hán
4		12	13	14	15	16	17	18	
5		19	20	21	22	23	24	25	Lì chūn
6	MONTH 1 Jǐ-Mǎo	26	27	28	29	30	1[a]	2	
7		3*	4	5	6	7	8	9	
8		10	11	12	13	14	15[b]	16	Yǔ shuǐ
9		17	18	19	20	21	22	23	
10	MONTH 2 Jǐ-Mǎo	24	25	26	27	28	29	1	Jīng zhé
11		2	3	4	5	6	7	8	
12		9	10	11	12	13	14	15	Chūn fēn
13		16	17	18	19	20	21	22	
14		23	24	25	26[c]	27	28	29	Qīng míng
15	MONTH 3 Jǐ-Mǎo	30	1	2	3	4*	5	6	
16		7	8	9	10	11	12	13	Gǔ yǔ
17		14	15	16	17	18	19	20	
18		21	22	23	24	25	26	27	Lì xià
19	MONTH 4 Jǐ-Mǎo	28	29	30	1	2	3	4	
20		5	6	7	8	9	10	11	
21		12	13	14	15	16	17	18	Xiǎo mǎn
22		19	20	21	22	23	24	25	
23	MONTH 5 Jǐ-Mǎo	26	27	28	29	1	2	3	Máng zhòng
24		4	5[d]*	6	7	8	9	10	
25		11	12	13	14	15	16	17	Xià zhì
26		18	19	20	21	22	23	24	
27	MONTH 6 Jǐ-Mǎo	25	26	27	28	29	30	1	Xiǎo shǔ
28		2	3	4	5	6	7	8	
29		9	10	11	12	13	14	15	
30		16	17	18	19	20	21	22	Dà shǔ
31		23	24	25	26	27	28	29	
32	MONTH 7 Jǐ-Mǎo	1	2	3	4	5	6*	7[e]	Lì qiū
33		8	9	10	11	12	13	14	
34		15[f]	16	17	18	19	20	21	Chǔ shǔ
35		22	23	24	25	26	27	28	
36	MONTH 8 Jǐ-Mǎo	29	30	1	2	3	4	5	Bái lù
37		6	7	8	9	10	11	12	
38		13	14	15[g]	16	17	18	19	Qiū fēn
39		20	21	22	23	24	25	26	
40	MONTH 9 Jǐ-Mǎo	27	28	29	1	2	3	4	
41		5	6	7*	8	9[h]	10	11	Hán lù
42		12	13	14	15	16	17	18	
43		19	20	21	22	23	24	25	Shuāng jiàng
44	MONTH 10 Jǐ-Mǎo	26	27	28	29	30	1	2	
45		3	4	5	6	7	8	9	Lì dōng
46		10	11	12	13	14	15	16	
47		17	18	19	20	21	22	23	Xiǎo xuě
48	MONTH 11 Jǐ-Mǎo	24	25	26	27	28	29	1	
49		2	3	4	5	6	7	8*	Dà xuě
50		9	10	11	12	13	14	15	
51		16	17	18	19	20	21[i]	22	Dōng zhì
52		23	24	25	26	27	28	29	
1		30	1	2	3	4	5	6	Xiǎo hán

COPTIC 1835‡/1836 — ETHIOPIC 2111‡/2112

ISO WEEK	Coptic Month	Sun	Mon	Tue	Wed	Thu	Fri	Sat	Ethiopic Month
1	KOIAK 1835	22	23	24	25	26	27	28	TĀKHŚĀŚ 2111
2	TŌBE 1835	29[c]	30	1	2	3	4	5	ṬER 2111
3		6[d]	7	8	9	10	11[e]	12	
4		13	14	15	16	17	18	19	
5		20	21	22	23	24	25	26	
6	MESHIR 1835	27	28	29	30	1	2	3	YAKĀTIT 2111
7		4	5	6	7	8	9	10	
8		11	12	13	14	15	16	17	
9		18	19	20	21	22	23	24	
10	PAREMOTEP 1835	25	26	27	28	29	30	1	MAGĀBIT 2111
11		2	3	4	5	6	7	8	
12		9	10	11	12	13	14	15	
13		16	17	18	19	20	21	22	
14		23	24	25	26	27	28	29	
15	PARMOUTE 1835	30	1	2	3	4	5	6	MIYĀZYĀ 2111
16		7	8	9	10	11	12	13	
17		14	15	16	17	18	19	20	
18		21[f]	22	23	24	25	26	27	
19	PASHONS 1835	28	29[g]	30	1	2	3	4	GENBOT 2111
20		5	6	7	8	9	10	11	
21		12	13	14	15	16	17	18	
22		19	20	21	22	23	24	25	
23	PAŌNE 1835	26	27	28	29	30	1	2	SANĒ 2111
24		3	4	5	6	7	8	9	
25		10	11	12	13	14	15	16	
26		17	18	19	20	21	22	23	
27		24	25	26	27	28	29	30	
28	EPĒP 1835	1	2	3	4	5	6	7	ḤAMLĒ 2111
29		8	9	10	11	12	13	14	
30		15	16	17	18	19	20	21	
31		22	23	24	25	26	27	28	
32	MESORĒ 1835	29	30	1	2	3	4	5	NAḤASĒ 2111
33		6	7	8	9	10	11	12	
34		13[h]	14	15	16	17	18	19	
35		20	21	22	23	24	25	26	
36	EPAG. 1835	27	28	29	30	1	2	3	PĀG. 2111
37	THOOUT 1836	4	5	6	1[a]	2	3	4	MASKARAM 2112
38		5	6	7	8	9	10	11	
39		12	13	14	15	16	17[b]	18	
40		19	20	21	22	23	24	25	
41	PAOPE 1836	26	27	28	29	30	1	2	TEQEMT 2112
42		3	4	5	6	7	8	9	
43		10	11	12	13	14	15	16	
44		17	18	19	20	21	22	23	
45		24	25	26	27	28	29	30	
46	ATHŌR 1836	1	2	3	4	5	6	7	ḪEDĀR 2112
47		8	9	10	11	12	13	14	
48		15	16	17	18	19	20	21	
49		22	23	24	25	26	27	28	
50	KOIAK 1836	29	30	1	2	3	4	5	TĀKHŚĀŚ 2112
51		6	7	8	9	10	11	12	
52		13	14	15	16	17	18	19	
1		20	21	22	23	24	25	26	

Gregorian notes

[a]New Year
[b]Spring (3:37)
[c]Summer (19:34)
[d]Autumn (12:18)
[e]Winter (10:35)
● New moon
◐ First quarter moon
○ Full moon
◑ Last quarter moon

Hebrew notes

‡Leap year
[a]New Year
[b]Yom Kippur
[c]Sukkot
[d]Winter starts
[e]Ḥanukkah
[f]Purim
[g]Passover
[h]Shavuot
[i]Fast of Av

Chinese notes

‡Leap year
[a]New Year (4817, Hare)
[b]Lantern Festival
[c]Qīngmíng
[d]Dragon Festival
[e]Qīqiǎo
[f]Hungry Ghosts
[g]Mid-Autumn Festival
[h]Double-Ninth Festival
[i]Dōngzhì
*Start of 60-name cycle

Coptic/Ethiopic notes

‡Leap year
[a]New Year
[b]Building of the Cross
[c]Christmas
[d]Jesus's Circumcision
[e]Epiphany
[f]Easter
[g]Mary's Announcement
[h]Jesus's Transfiguration

PERSIAN (ASTRONOMICAL) 1497/1498‡

Month	Sun	Mon	Tue	Wed	Thu	Fri	Sat
DEY 1497	11	12	13	14	15	16	17
	18	19	20	21	22	23	24
	25	26	27	28	29	30	1
BAHMAN 1497	2	3	4	5	6	7	8
	9	10	11	12	13	14	15
	16	17	18	19	20	21	22
	23	24	25	26	27	28	29
	30	1	2	3	4	5	6
ESFAND 1497	7	8	9	10	11	12	13
	14	15	16	17	18	19	20
	21	22	23	24	25	26	27
	28	29	1[a]	2	3	4	5
FARVARDĪN 1498	6	7	8	9	10	11	12
	13[b]	14	15	16	17	18	19
	20	21	22	23	24	25	26
	27	28	29	30	31	1	2
ORDĪBEHEŠT 1498	3	4	5	6	7	8	9
	10	11	12	13	14	15	16
	17	18	19	20	21	22	23
	24	25	26	27	28	29	30
	31	1	2	3	4	5	6
XORDĀD 1498	7	8	9	10	11	12	13
	14	15	16	17	18	19	20
	21	22	23	24	25	26	27
	28	29	30	31	1	2	3
TĪR 1498	4	5	6	7	8	9	10
	11	12	13	14	15	16	17
	18	19	20	21	22	23	24
	25	26	27	28	29	30	31
MORDĀD 1498	1	2	3	4	5	6	7
	8	9	10	11	12	13	14
	15	16	17	18	19	20	21
	22	23	24	25	26	27	28
	29	30	31	1	2	3	4
SHAHRĪVAR 1498	5	6	7	8	9	10	11
	12	13	14	15	16	17	18
	19	20	21	22	23	24	25
	26	27	28	29	30	31	1
MEHR 1498	2	3	4	5	6	7	8
	9	10	11	12	13	14	15
	16	17	18	19	20	21	22
	23	24	25	26	27	28	29
	30	1	2	3	4	5	6
ABĀN 1498	7	8	9	10	11	12	13
	14	15	16	17	18	19	20
	21	22	23	24	25	26	27
	28	29	30	1	2	3	4
ĀZAR 1498	5	6	7	8	9	10	11
	12	13	14	15	16	17	18
	19	20	21	22	23	24	25
	26	27	28	29	30	1	2
DEY 1498	3	4	5	6	7	8	9
	10	11	12	13	14	15	16

‡Leap year
[a]New Year
[b]Sizdeh Bedar

HINDU LUNAR 2175‡/2176

Month	Sun	Mon	Tue	Wed	Thu	Fri	Sat
MĀRGAŚĪRA 2175	19	20	21	22	24	25	26
	27	28	29	30	1	2	3
PAUSHA 2175	4	5	6	7	8	9	10
	11	12	13	14	15	16	17
	18	19	20	21	22	23	24
	25	26	27	29	30	1	2
MĀGHA 2175	3	4	5	6	7	8	9
	9	10	11	12	13	14	15
	16	17	18	19	20	21	23
	24	25	26	27	28[h]	29	30
	1	2	3	4	5	6	7
PHĀLGUNA 2175	8	9	10	11	12	12	13
	15[i]	16	17	18	19	20	21
	22	23	24	25	26	28	29
	30	1[a]	1	2	3	4	5
CHAITRA 2176	6	7	8	9[b]	10	11	12
	13	14	15	16	17	18	19
	21	22	23	24	25	26	27
	28	29	30	1	2	3	4
VAIŚĀKHA 2176	5	6	6	7	8	9	10
	11	12	14	15	16	17	18
	19	20	21	22	23	24	25
	26	27	28	29	30	1	2
JYAISHṬHA 2176	3	4	5	6	7	8	9
	10	11	12	13	14	15	17
	18	19	20	21	22	23	24
	25	26	27	28	29	30	1
ĀSHĀḌHA 2176	2	2	3	4	5	6	7
	9	10	11	12	13	14	15
	16	17	18	19	21	22	23
	24	24	25	26	27	28	29
	30	1	2	3	4	5	6
ŚRĀVAṆA 2176	7	8	9	10	11	13	14
	15	16	17	18	19	20	21
	22	23[c]	24	25	26	27	28
	29	29	30	1	2	3[d]	5
BHĀDRAPADA 2176	6	7	8	9	10	11	12
	13	14	15	17	18	19	19
	20	21	22	23	24	25	26
	27	28	29	30	1	2	3
ĀŚVINA 2176	4	5	6	7[e]	9[e]	10[e]	11
	12	13	14	15	16	17	18
	19	20	21	22	23	23	24
	25	26	27	28	29	30	1[f]
KĀRTTIKA 2176	3	4	5	6	7	8	9
	10	11	12	13	14	15	16
	17	18	19	20	21	22	23
	24	25	26	27	28	29	30
MĀRGAŚĪRA 2176	1	2	3	4	5	7	8
	9	10	11[g]	12	13	14	15
	16	17	17	18	19	20	21
	22	23	24	25	26	27	28
	29	1	2	3	4	5	6

‡Leap year
[a]New Year (Pramāthin)
[b]Birthday of Rāma
[c]Birthday of Krishna
[d]Ganēśa Chaturthī
[e]Dashara
[f]Diwali
[g]Birthday of Vishnu
[h]Night of Śiva
[i]Holi

HINDU SOLAR 2040/2041

Month	Sun	Mon	Tue	Wed	Thu	Fri	Sat
PAUSHA 2040	15	16	17	18	19	20	21
	22	23	24	25	26	27	28
	29	1[b]	2	3	4	5	6
MĀGHA 2040	7	8	9	10	11	12	13
	14	15	16	17	18	19	20
	21	22	23	24	25	26	27
	28	29	30	1	2	3	4
PHĀLGUNA 2040	5	6	7	8	9	10	11
	12	13	14	15	16	17	18
	19	20	21	22	23	24	25
	26	27	28	29	1	2	3
CHAITRA 2040	4	5	6	7	8	9	10
	11	12	13	14	15	16	17
	18	19	20	21	22	23	24
	25	26	27	28	29	30	31
VAIŚĀKHA 2041	1[a]	2	3	4	5	6	7
	8	9	10	11	12	13	14
	15	16	17	18	19	20	21
	22	23	24	25	26	27	28
	29	30	31	1	2	3	4
JYAISHṬHA 2041	5	6	7	8	9	10	11
	12	13	14	15	16	17	18
	19	20	21	22	23	24	25
	26	27	28	29	30	31	1
ĀSHĀḌHA 2041	2	3	4	5	6	7	8
	9	10	11	12	13	14	15
	16	17	18	19	20	21	22
	23	24	25	26	27	28	29
	30	31	32	1	2	3	4
ŚRĀVAṆA 2041	5	6	7	8	9	10	11
	12	13	14	15	16	17	18
	19	20	21	22	23	24	25
	26	27	28	29	30	31	1
BHĀDRAPADA 2041	2	3	4	5	6	7	8
	9	10	11	12	13	14	15
	16	17	18	19	20	21	22
	23	24	25	26	27	28	29
	30	31	1	2	3	4	5
ĀŚVINA 2041	6	7	8	9	10	11	12
	13	14	15	16	17	18	19
	20	21	22	23	24	25	26
	27	28	29	30	31	1	2
KĀRTTIKA 2041	3	4	5	6	7	8	9
	10	11	12	13	14	15	16
	17	18	19	20	21	22	23
	24	25	26	27	28	29	30
MĀRGAŚĪRA 2041	1	2	3	4	5	6	7
	8	9	10	11	12	13	14
	15	16	17	18	19	20	21
	22	23	24	25	26	27	28
	29	1	2	3	4	5	6
PAUSHA 2041	7	8	9	10	11	12	13
	14	15	16	17	18	19	20

[a]New Year (Jaya)
[b]Pongal

ISLAMIC (ASTRONOMICAL) 1543/1544

Month	Sun	Mon	Tue	Wed	Thu	Fri	Sat
JUMĀDĀ I 1543	19	20	21	22	23	24	25
	26	27	28	29	30	1	2
JUMĀDĀ II 1543	3	4	5	6	7	8	9
	10	11	12	13	14	15	16
	17	18	19	20	21	22	23
	24	25	26	27	28	29	1
RAJAB 1543	2	3	4	5	6	7	8
	9	10	11	12	13	14	15
	16	17	18	19	20	21	22
	23	24	25	26	27[d]	28	29
	30	1	2	3	4	5	6
SHA'BĀN 1543	7	8	9	10	11	12	13
	14	15	16	17	18	19	20
	21	22	23	24	25	26	27
	28	29	1[e]	2	3	4	5
RAMAḌĀN 1543	6	7	8	9	10	11	12
	13	14	15	16	17	18	19
	20	21	22	23	24	25	26
	27	28	29	30	1[f]	2	3
SHAWWĀL 1543	4	5	6	7	8	9	10
	11	12	13	14	15	16	17
	18	19	20	21	22	23	24
	25	26	27	28	29	30	1
DHU AL-QA'DA 1543	2	3	4	5	6	7	8
	9	10	11	12	13	14	15
	16	17	18	19	20	21	22
	23	24	25	26	27	28	29
DHU AL-ḤIJJA 1543	1	2	3	4	5	6	7
	8	9	10[g]	11	12	13	14
	15	16	17	18	19	20	21
	22	23	24	25	26	27	28
	29	30	1[a]	2	3	4	5
MUḤARRAM 1544	6	7	8	9	10[b]	11	12
	13	14	15	16	17	18	19
	20	21	22	23	24	25	26
	27	28	29	30	1	2	3
ṢAFAR 1544	4	5	6	7	8	9	10
	11	12	13	14	15	16	17
	18	19	20	21	22	23	24
	25	26	27	28	29	30	1
RABĪ' I 1544	2	3	4	5	6	7	8
	9	10	11	12[c]	13	14	15
	16	17	18	19	20	21	22
	23	24	25	26	27	28	29
RABĪ' II 1544	1	2	3	4	5	6	7
	8	9	10	11	12	13	14
	15	16	17	18	19	20	21
	22	23	24	25	26	27	28
	29	1	2	3	4	5	6
JUMĀDĀ I 1544	7	8	9	10	11	12	13
	14	15	16	17	18	19	20
	21	22	23	24	25	26	27
	28	29	1	2	3	4	5

[a]New Year
[b]'Ashūrā'
[c]Prophet's Birthday
[d]Ascent of the Prophet
[e]Start of Ramaḍān
[f]'Īd al-Fiṭr
[g]'Īd al-'Aḍḥā

GREGORIAN 2119

Julian (Sun)	Sun	Mon	Tue	Wed	Thu	Fri	Sat	Month
Dec 18	1	2	3	4	5	6	7	JANUARY 2119
	8[a]	9	10	11	12	13	14	
Jan 1	15[b]	16	17	18	19	20	21	
	22	23	24	25	26	27	28	
Jan 15	29	30	31	1	2	3	4	FEBRUARY 2119
	5	6	7	8[c]	9	10	11	
Jan 29	12	13	14	15	16	17	18	
	19	20	21	22	23	24	25	
Feb 12	26	27	28	1	2	3	4	MARCH 2119
	5	6	7	8	9	10	11	
Feb 26	12	13	14	15	16	17	18	
	19[d]	20	21	22	23	24	25	
Mar 12	26[e]	27	28	29	30	31	1	APRIL 2119
	2	3	4	5	6	7	8	
Mar 26	9	10	11	12	13	14	15	
	16	17	18	19	20	21	22	
Apr 9	23	24	25	26	27	28	29	
	30[f]	1	2	3	4	5	6	MAY 2119
Apr 23	7	8	9	10	11	12	13	
	14	15	16	17	18	19	20	
May 7	21	22	23	24	25	26	27	
	28	29	30	31	1	2	3	JUNE 2119
May 21	4	5	6	7	8	9	10	
	11	12	13	14	15	16	17	
Jun 4	18	19	20	21	22	23	24	
	25	26	27	28	29	30	1	JULY 2119
Jun 18	2	3	4	5	6	7	8	
	9	10	11	12	13	14	15	
Jul 2	16	17	18	19	20	21	22	
	23	24	25	26	27	28	29	
Jul 16	30	31	1	2	3	4	5	AUGUST 2119
	6	7	8	9	10	11	12	
Jul 30	13	14	15	16	17	18	19	
	20	21	22	23	24	25	26	
Aug 13	27	28	29	30	31	1	2	SEPTEMBER 2119
	3	4	5	6	7	8	9	
Aug 27	10	11	12	13	14	15	16	
	17	18	19	20	21	22	23	
Sep 10	24	25	26	27	28	29	30	
	1	2	3	4	5	6	7	OCTOBER 2119
Sep 24	8	9	10	11	12	13	14	
	15	16	17	18	19	20	21	
Oct 8	22	23	24	25	26	27	28	
	29	30	31	1	2	3	4	NOVEMBER 2119
Oct 22	5	6	7	8	9	10	11	
	12	13	14	15	16	17	18	
Nov 5	19	20	21	22	23	24	25	
	26	27	28	29	30	1	2	DECEMBER 2119
Nov 19	3[g]	4	5	6	7	8	9	
	10	11	12	13	14	15	16	
Dec 3	17	18	19	20	21	22	23	
	24	25[h]	26	27	28	29	30	
Dec 17	31	1	2	3	4	5	6	

[a]Orthodox Christmas
[b]Julian New Year
[c]Ash Wednesday
[d]Feast of Orthodoxy
[e]Easter
[f]Orthodox Easter
[g]Advent
[h]Christmas

2120

GREGORIAN 2120‡ · Lunar Phases · ISO WEEK · JULIAN DAY

Month	Sun	Mon	Tue	Wed	Thu	Fri	Sat	Lunar Phases	ISO WEEK (Mon)	JULIAN DAY (Sun noon)
JANUARY 2120	31	●[a]	2	3	4	5	6	0:04	1	2495373
	◐	8	9	10	11	12	13	18:05	2	2495380
	14	○	16	17	18	19	20	19:54	3	2495387
	21	22	◑	24	25	26	27	19:13	4	2495394
FEBRUARY 2120	28	29	●	31	1	2	3	10:54	5	2495401
	4	5	◐	7	8	9	10	10:14	6	2495408
	11	12	13	○	15	16	17	15:16	7	2495415
	18	19	20	21	◑	23	24	6:13	8	2495422
MARCH 2120	25	26	27	●	29	1	2	21:56	9	2495429
	3	4	5	6	◐	8	9	4:40	10	2495436
	10	11	12	13	14	○	16	8:26	11	2495443
	17	18	19	20[b]	21	◑	23	14:21	12	2495450
	24	25	26	27	28	●	30	9:10	13	2495457
APRIL 2120	31	1	2	3	4	5	◐	0:15	14	2495464
	7	8	9	10	11	12	○	22:20	15	2495471
	14	15	16	17	18	19	◑	20:41	16	2495478
	21	22	23	24	25	26	●	20:48	17	2495485
MAY 2120	28	29	30	1	2	3	4		18	2495492
	◐	6	7	8	9	10	11	19:27	19	2495499
	12	○	14	15	16	17	18	9:05	20	2495506
	19	◑	21	22	23	24	25	2:22	21	2495513
JUNE 2120	26	●	28	29	30	31	1	9:21	22	2495520
	2	3	◐	5	6	7	8	12:49	23	2495527
	9	10	○	12	13	14	15	17:34	24	2495534
	16	17	◑	19	20	21[c]	22	8:36	25	2495541
	23	24	●	26	27	28	29	23:14	26	2495548
JULY 2120	30	1	2	3	◐	5	6	3:27	27	2495555
	7	8	9	10	○	12	13	0:53	28	2495562
	14	15	16	◑	18	19	20	16:29	29	2495569
	21	22	23	24	●	26	27	14:23	30	2495576
AUGUST 2120	28	29	30	31	1	◐	3	15:14	31	2495583
	4	5	6	7	8	○	10	8:00	32	2495590
	11	12	13	14	15	◑	17	3:03	33	2495597
	18	19	20	21	22	23	●	6:13	34	2495604
	25	26	27	28	29	30	31		35	2495611
SEPTEMBER 2120	◐	2	3	4	5	6	○	0:40 17:07	36	2495618
	8	9	10	11	12	13	◑	15:46	37	2495625
	15	16	17	18	19	20	21		38	2495632
	●[d]	23	24	25	26	27	28	21:50	39	2495639
OCTOBER 2120	29	◐	1	2	3	4	5	8:34	40	2495646
	6	○	8	9	10	11	12	0:55	41	2495653
	13	◑	15	16	17	18	19	10:52	42	2495660
	20	21	●	23	24	25	26	12:33	43	2495667
NOVEMBER 2120	27	28	◐	30	31	1	2	15:47	44	2495674
	3	4	○	6	7	8	9	12:15	45	2495681
	10	11	12	◑	14	15	16	7:24	46	2495688
	17	18	19	20	●	22	23	2:12	47	2495695
	24	25	26	◐	28	29	30	23:14	48	2495702
DECEMBER 2120	1	2	3	4	○	6	7	2:26	49	2495709
	8	9	10	11	12	◑	14	4:49	50	2495716
	15	16	17	18	19	●	21[e]	14:55	51	2495723
	22	23	24	25	26	◐	28	7:46	52	2495730
	29	30	31	1	2	○	4	19:33	1	2495737

HEBREW 5880/5881 · Molad

ISO WEEK	Month	Sun	Mon	Tue	Wed	Thu	Fri	Sat	Molad
1	TEVETH 5880	29[e]	30[e]	1[e]	2[e]	3	4	5	Mon 4h 19m 3p
2		6	7	8	9	10	11	12	
3		13	14	15	16	17	18	19	
4		20	21	22	23	24	25	26	
5	SHEVAT 5880	27	28	29	1	2	3	4	Tue 17h 3m 4p
6		5	6	7	8	9	10	11	
7		12	13	14	15	16	17	18	
8		19	20	21	22	23	24	25	
9	ADAR 5880	26	27	28	29	30	1	2	Thu 5h 47m 5p
10		3	4	5	6	7	8	9	
11		10	11	12	13	14[f]	15	16	
12		17	18	19	20	21	22	23	
13	NISAN 5880	24	25	26	27	28	29	1	Fri 18h 31m 6p
14		2	3	4	5	6	7	8	
15		9	10	11	12	13	14	15[g]	
16		16	17	18	19	20	21	22	
17		23	24	25	26	27	28	29	
18	IYYAR 5880	30	1	2	3	4	5	6	Sun 7h 15m 7p
19		7	8	9	10	11	12	13	
20		14	15	16	17	18	19	20	
21		21	22	23	24	25	26	27	
22	SIVAN 5880	28	29	1	2	3	4	5	Mon 19h 59m 8p
23		6[h]	7	8	9	10	11	12	
24		13	14	15	16	17	18	19	
25		20	21	22	23	24	25	26	
26	TAMMUZ 5880	27	28	29	30	1	2	3	Wed 8h 43m 9p
27		4	5	6	7	8	9	10	
28		11	12	13	14	15	16	17	
29		18	19	20	21	22	23	24	
30	AV 5880	25	26	27	28	29	1	2	Thu 21h 27m 10p
31		3	4	5	6	7	8	9	
32		10[i]	11	12	13	14	15	16	
33		17	18	19	20	21	22	23	
34		24	25	26	27	28	29	30	Sat 10h 11m 11p
35	ELUL 5880	1	2	3	4	5	6	7	
36		8	9	10	11	12	13	14	
37		15	16	17	18	19	20	21	
38		22	23	24	25	26	27	28	
39	TISHRI 5881	29	1[a]	2[a]	3	4	5	6	Sun 22h 55m 12p
40		7	8	9	10[b]	11	12	13	
41		14	15[c]	16	17	18	19	20	
42		21	22	23	24	25	26	27	
43	ḤESHVAN 5881	28	29	30	1	2	3	4	Tue 11h 39m 13p
44		5	6	7	8	9	10	11	
45		12	13	14	15	16	17	18	
46		19	20	21	22	23	24	25	
47	KISLEV 5881	26	27	28	29	30	1	2	Thu 0h 23m 14p
48		3	4	5	6	7	8	9	
49		10	11	12	13	14	15[d]	16	
50		17	18	19	20	21	22	23	
51		24	25[e]	26[e]	27[e]	28[e]	29[e]	30[e]	
52	TEVETH 5881	1[e]	2[e]	3	4	5	6	7	Fri 13h 7m 15p
1		8	9	10	11	12	13	14	

CHINESE Jǐ-Mǎo/Gēng-Chén‡ · Solar Term

ISO WEEK	Month	Sun	Mon	Tue	Wed	Thu	Fri	Sat	Solar Term
1	MONTH 12 Jǐ-Mǎo	30	1	2	3	4	5	6	Xiǎo hán
2		7	8	9	10	11	12	13	
3		14	15	16	17	18	19	20	
4		**21**	22	23	24	25	26	27	Dà hán
5	MONTH 1 Gēng-Chén	28	29	1[a]	2	3	4	5	
6		6	7	8	9*	10	11	12	Lì chūn
7		13	14	15[b]	16	17	18	19	
8		20	**21**	22	23	24	25	26	Yǔ shuǐ
9	MONTH 2 Gēng-Chén	27	28	29	30	1	2	3	
10		4	5	6	7	8	9	10	Jīng zhé
11		11	12	13	14	15	16	17	
12		18	19	20	**21**	22	23	24	Chūn fēn
13	MONTH 3 Gēng-Chén	25	26	27	28	29	1	2	
14		3	4	5	6	7[c]	8	9	Qīng míng
15		10*	11	12	13	14	15	16	
16		17	18	19	20	21	22	**23**	Gǔ yǔ
17		24	25	26	27	28	29	30	
18	MONTH 4 Gēng-Chén	1	2	3	4	5	6	7	
19		*8*	9	10	11	12	13	14	Lì xià
20		15	16	17	18	19	20	21	
21		22	23	**24**	25	26	27	28	Xiǎo mǎn
22	MONTH 5 Gēng-Chén	29	1	2	3	4	5[d]	6	
23		7	8	9	*10*	11*	12	13	Máng zhòng
24		14	15	16	17	18	19	20	
25		21	22	23	24	25	**26**	27	Xià zhì
26	MONTH 6 Gēng-Chén	28	29	30	1	2	3	4	
27		5	6	7	8	9	10	11	
28		*12*	13	14	15	16	17	18	Xiǎo shǔ
29		19	20	21	22	23	24	25	
30	MONTH 7 Gēng-Chén	26	**27**	28	29	1	2	3	Dà shǔ
31		4	5	6	7[e]	8	9	10	
32		11	12*	13	*14*	15[f]	16	17	Lì qiū
33		18	19	20	21	22	23	24	
34	LEAP MONTH 7 Gēng-Chén	25	26	27	28	29	**30**	1	Chǔ shǔ
35		2	3	4	5	6	7	8	
36		9	10	11	12	13	14	*15*	Bái lù
37		16	17	18	19	20	21	22	
38		23	24	25	26	27	28	29	
39	MONTH 8 Gēng-Chén	30	*1*	2	3	4	5	6	Qiū fēn
40		7	8	9	10	11	12*	13	
41		14	15[g]	16	17	18	19	20	Hán lù
42		21	22	23	24	25	26	27	
43	MONTH 9 Gēng-Chén	28	29	1	**2**	3	4	5	Shuāng jiàng
44		6	7	8	9[h]	10	11	12	
45		13	14	15	16	*17*	18	19	Lì dōng
46		20	21	22	23	24	25	26	
47	MONTH 10 Gēng-Chén	27	28	29	30	1	**2**	3	Xiǎo xuě
48		4	5	6	7	8	9	10	
49		11	12	13*	14	15	16	*17*	Dà xuě
50		18	19	20	21	22	23	24	
51	MONTH 11 Gēng-Chén	25	26	27	28	29	1	2	
52		3[i]	4	5	6	7	8	9	Dōng zhì
1		10	11	12	13	14	15	16	

COPTIC 1836/1837 · ETHIOPIC 2112/2113

ISO WEEK	Coptic Month	Sun	Mon	Tue	Wed	Thu	Fri	Sat	Ethiopic Month
1	KOIAK 1836	20	21	22	23	24	25	26	TĀḪŚĀŚ 2112
2	TŌBE 1836	27	28	29[c]	30	1	2	3	ṬER 2112
3		4	5	6[d]	7	8	9	10	
4		11[e]	12	13	14	15	16	17	
5		18	19	20	21	22	23	24	
6	MESHIR 1836	25	26	27	28	29	30	1	YAKĀTIT 2112
7		2	3	4	5	6	7	8	
8		9	10	11	12	13	14	15	
9		16	17	18	19	20	21	22	
10		23	24	25	26	27	28	29	
11	PAREMOTEP 1836	30	1	2	3	4	5	6	MAGĀBIT 2112
12		7	8	9	10	11	12	13	
13		14	15	16	17	18	19	20	
14		21	22	23	24	25	26	27	
15	PARMOUTE 1836	28	29	30	1	2	3	4	MIYĀZYĀ 2112
16		5	6	7	8	9	10	11	
17		12[f]	13	14	15	16	17	18	
18		19	20	21	22	23	24	25	
19	PASHONS 1836	26	27	28	29[g]	30	1	2	GENBOT 2112
20		3	4	5	6	7	8	9	
21		10	11	12	13	14	15	16	
22		17	18	19	20	21	22	23	
23		24	25	26	27	28	29	30	
24	PAŌNE 1836	1	2	3	4	5	6	7	SANĒ 2112
25		8	9	10	11	12	13	14	
26		15	16	17	18	19	20	21	
27		22	23	24	25	26	27	28	
28	EPĒP 1836	29	30	1	2	3	4	5	ḤAMLĒ 2112
29		6	7	8	9	10	11	12	
30		13	14	15	16	17	18	19	
31		20	21	22	23	24	25	26	
32	MESORĒ 1836	27	28	29	30	1	2	3	NAḤASĒ 2112
33		4	5	6	7	8	9	10	
34		11	12	13[h]	14	15	16	17	
35		18	19	20	21	22	23	24	
36	EPAG. 1836	25	26	27	28	29	30	1	ṖĀG. 2112
37	THOOUT 1837	2	3	4	5	1[a]	2	3	MASKARAM 2113
38		4	5	6	7	8	9	10	
39		11	12	13	14	15	16	17[b]	
40		18	19	20	21	22	23	24	
41	PAOPE 1837	25	26	27	28	29	30	1	ṬEQEMT 2113
42		2	3	4	5	6	7	8	
43		9	10	11	12	13	14	15	
44		16	17	18	19	20	21	22	
45		23	24	25	26	27	28	29	
46	ATHŌR 1837	30	1	2	3	4	5	6	ḪEDĀR 2113
47		7	8	9	10	11	12	13	
48		14	15	16	17	18	19	20	
49		21	22	23	24	25	26	27	
50	KOIAK 1837	28	29	30	1	2	3	4	TĀḪŚĀŚ 2113
51		5	6	7	8	9	10	11	
52		12	13	14	15	16	17	18	
1		19	20	21	22	23	24	25	

‡Leap year
[a]New Year
[b]Spring (9:27)
[c]Summer (1:31)
[d]Autumn (18:04)
[e]Winter (16:22)
● New moon
◐ First quarter moon
○ Full moon
◑ Last quarter moon

[a]New Year
[b]Yom Kippur
[c]Sukkot
[d]Winter starts
[e]Ḥanukkah
[f]Purim
[g]Passover
[h]Shavuot
[i]Fast of Av

‡Leap year
[a]New Year (4818, Dragon)
[b]Lantern Festival
[c]Qīngmíng
[d]Dragon Festival
[e]Qīqiǎo
[f]Hungry Ghosts
[g]Mid-Autumn Festival
[h]Double-Ninth Festival
[i]Dōngzhì
*Start of 60-name cycle

[a]New Year
[b]Building of the Cross
[c]Christmas
[d]Jesus's Circumcision
[e]Epiphany
[f]Easter
[g]Mary's Announcement
[h]Jesus's Transfiguration

PERSIAN (ASTRONOMICAL) 1498‡/1499

Month	Sun	Mon	Tue	Wed	Thu	Fri	Sat
DEY 1498	10	11	12	13	14	15	16
	17	18	19	20	21	22	23
	24	25	26	27	28	29	30
BAHMAN 1498	1	2	3	4	5	6	7
	8	9	10	11	12	13	14
	15	16	17	18	19	20	21
	22	23	24	25	26	27	28
ESFAND 1498	29	30	1	2	3	4	5
	6	7	8	9	10	11	12
	13	14	15	16	17	18	19
	20	21	22	23	24	25	26
FARVARDĪN 1499	27	28	29	30*	1[a]	2	3
	4	5	6	7	8	9	10
	11	12	13[b]	14	15	16	17
	18	19	20	21	22	23	24
	25	26	27	28	29	30	31
ORDĪBEHEŠT 1499	1	2	3	4	5	6	7
	8	9	10	11	12	13	14
	15	16	17	18	19	20	21
	22	23	24	25	26	27	28
XORDĀD 1499	29	30	31	1	2	3	4
	5	6	7	8	9	10	11
	12	13	14	15	16	17	18
	19	20	21	22	23	24	25
TĪR 1499	26	27	28	29	30	31	1
	2	3	4	5	6	7	8
	9	10	11	12	13	14	15
	16	17	18	19	20	21	22
	23	24	25	26	27	28	29
MORDĀD 1499	30	31	1	2	3	4	5
	6	7	8	9	10	11	12
	13	14	15	16	17	18	19
	20	21	22	23	24	25	26
SHAHRĪVAR 1499	27	28	29	30	31	1	2
	3	4	5	6	7	8	9
	10	11	12	13	14	15	16
	17	18	19	20	21	22	23
	24	25	26	27	28	29	30
MEHR 1499	31	1	2	3	4	5	6
	7	8	9	10	11	12	13
	14	15	16	17	18	19	20
	21	22	23	24	25	26	27
ĀBĀN 1499	28	29	30	1	2	3	4
	5	6	7	8	9	10	11
	12	13	14	15	16	17	18
	19	20	21	22	23	24	25
ĀZAR 1499	26	27	28	29	30	1	2
	3	4	5	6	7	8	9
	10	11	12	13	14	15	16
	17	18	19	20	21	22	23
	24	25	26	27	28	29	30
DEY 1499	1	2	3	4	5	6	7
	8	9	10	11	12	13	14

HINDU LUNAR 2176/2177

Month	Sun	Mon	Tue	Wed	Thu	Fri	Sat
PAUSHA 2176	**29**	1	2	3	4	5	6
	7	8	9	10	11	12	13
	14	15	16	17	18	19	19
	20	21	**22**	24	25	26	27
MĀGHA 2176	28	29	30	1	2	3	4
	5	6	7	8	9	10	11
	12	13	14	15	16	17	18
	19	20	21	22	23	24	25
PHĀLGUNA 2176	26	27	**28**[h]	30	1	2	3
	4	5	6	7	8	9	10
	11	11	12	13	14	15[i]	16
	17	18	19	20	21	**22**	24
CHAITRA 2177	25	26	27	28	29	30	1[a]
	2	3	4	5	6	7	8
	9[b]	10	11	12	13	14	15
	16	17	18	19	20	21	22
	23	24	25	**26**	28	29	30
VAIŚĀKHA 2177	1	2	3	4	5	6	6
	7	8	9	10	11	12	13
	14	15	16	17	18	**19**	21
	22	23	24	25	26	27	28
JYAISHṬHA 2177	29	30	1	2	3	4	5
	6	7	8	9	10	11	12
	13	14	15	16	17	18	19
	20	21	**22**	24	25	26	27
ĀSHĀḌHA 2177	28	29	30	1	2	2	3
	4	5	6	7	8	9	10
	11	12	13	14	**15**	17	18
	19	20	21	22	23	24	25
ŚRĀVAṆA 2177	26	27	28	29	30	1	2
	3	4	5	6	7	8	9
	10	11	12	13	14	15	16
	17	**18**	20	21	22	23[c]	24
	25	26	27	28	29	29	30
BHĀDRAPADA 2177	1	2	3	4[d]	5	6	7
	8	9	10	**11**	13	14	15
	16	17	18	19	20	21	22
	23	24	25	26	27	28	29
ĀŚVINA 2177	30	1	2	3	4	5	6
	7	8[e]	9[e]	10[e]	11	12	13
	14	16	17	18	19	20	21
	22	23	24	24	25	26	27
KĀRTTIKA 2177	28	29	30	1[f]	2	3	4
	5	6	7	**8**	10	11	12
	13	14	15	16	17	18	19
	20	21	22	23	24	25	26
MĀRGAŚĪRA 2177	27	27	28	29	30	**1**	3
	4	5	6	7	8	9	10
	11[g]	12	13	14	15	16	17
	18	19	20	21	22	23	24
PAUSHA 2177	25	26	27	28	29	30	1
	2	3	4	5	**6**	8	9
	10	11	12	13	14	15	16

HINDU SOLAR 2041/2042

Month	Sun	Mon	Tue	Wed	Thu	Fri	Sat
PAUSHA 2041	14	15	16	17	18	19	20
	21	22	23	24	25	26	27
MĀGHA 2041	28	29	1[b]	2	3	4	5
	6	7	8	9	10	11	12
	13	14	15	16	17	18	19
	20	21	22	23	24	25	26
PHĀLGUNA 2041	27	28	29	30	1	2	3
	4	5	6	7	8	9	10
	11	12	13	14	15	16	17
	18	19	20	21	22	23	24
CHAITRA 2041	25	26	27	28	29	30	1
	2	3	4	5	6	7	8
	9	10	11	12	13	14	15
	16	17	18	19	20	21	22
	23	24	25	26	27	28	29
VAIŚĀKHA 2042	30	1[a]	2	3	4	5	6
	7	8	9	10	11	12	13
	14	15	16	17	18	19	20
	21	22	23	24	25	26	27
JYAISHṬHA 2042	28	29	30	31	1	2	3
	4	5	6	7	8	9	10
	11	12	13	14	15	16	17
	18	19	20	21	22	23	24
	25	26	27	28	29	30	31
ĀSHĀḌHA 2042	1	2	3	4	5	6	7
	8	9	10	11	12	13	14
	15	16	17	18	19	20	21
	22	23	24	25	26	27	28
ŚRĀVAṆA 2042	29	30	31	32	1	2	3
	4	5	6	7	8	9	10
	11	12	13	14	15	16	17
	18	19	20	21	22	23	24
	25	26	27	28	29	30	31
BHĀDRAPADA 2042	32	1	2	3	4	5	6
	7	8	9	10	11	12	13
	14	15	16	17	18	19	20
	21	22	23	24	25	26	27
ĀŚVINA 2042	28	29	30	31	1	2	3
	4	5	6	7	8	9	10
	11	12	13	14	15	16	17
	18	19	20	21	22	23	24
KĀRTTIKA 2042	25	26	27	28	29	30	1
	2	3	4	5	6	7	8
	9	10	11	12	13	14	15
	16	17	18	19	20	21	22
	23	24	25	26	27	28	29
MĀRGAŚĪRA 2042	30	1	2	3	4	5	6
	7	8	9	10	11	12	13
	14	15	16	17	18	19	20
	21	22	23	24	25	26	27
PAUSHA 2042	28	29	1	2	3	4	5
	6	7	8	9	10	11	12
	13	14	15	16	17	18	19

ISLAMIC (ASTRONOMICAL) 1544/1545

Month	Sun	Mon	Tue	Wed	Thu	Fri	Sat
JUMĀDĀ II 1544	28	29	1	2	3	4	5
	6	7	8	9	10	11	12
	13	14	15	16	17	18	19
	20	21	22	23	24	25	26
RAJAB 1544	27	28	29	30	1	2	3
	4	5	6	7	8	9	10
	11	12	13	14	15	16	17
	18	19	20	21	22	23	24
SHA'BĀN 1544	25	26	27[d]	28	29	1	2
	3	4	5	6	7	8	9
	10	11	12	13	14	15	16
	17	18	19	20	21	22	23
	24	25	26	27	28	29	30
RAMAḌĀN 1544	1[e]	2	3	4	5	6	7
	8	9	10	11	12	13	14
	15	16	17	18	19	20	21
	22	23	24	25	26	27	28
SHAWWĀL 1544	29	1[f]	2	3	4	5	6
	7	8	9	10	11	12	13
	14	15	16	17	18	19	20
	21	22	23	24	25	26	27
DHU AL-QA'DA 1544	28	29	30	1	2	3	4
	5	6	7	8	9	10	11
	12	13	14	15	16	17	18
	19	20	21	22	23	24	25
DHU AL-ḤIJJA 1544	26	27	28	29	1	2	3
	4	5	6	7	8	9	10[g]
	11	12	13	14	15	16	17
	18	19	20	21	22	23	24
MUḤARRAM 1545	25	26	27	28	29	30	1[a]
	2	3	4	5	6	7	8
	9	10[b]	11	12	13	14	15
	16	17	18	19	20	21	22
	23	24	25	26	27	28	29
ṢAFAR 1545	30	31	1	2	3	4	5
	6	7	8	9	10	11	12
	13	14	15	16	17	18	19
	20	21	22	23	24	25	26
RABĪ' I 1545	27	28	29	1	2	3	4
	5	6	7	8	9	10	11
	12[c]	13	14	15	16	17	18
	19	20	21	22	23	24	25
RABĪ' II 1545	26	27	28	29	30	1	2
	3	4	5	6	7	8	9
	10	11	12	13	14	15	16
	17	18	19	20	21	22	23
JUMĀDĀ I 1545	24	25	26	27	28	29	1
	2	3	4	5	6	7	8
	9	10	11	12	13	14	15
	16	17	18	19	20	21	22
	23	24	25	26	27	28	29
JUMĀDĀ II 1545	1	2	3	4	5	6	7
	8	9	10	11	12	13	14

GREGORIAN 2120‡

Julian† (Sun)	Sun	Mon	Tue	Wed	Thu	Fri	Sat	Month
Dec 17	31	1	2	3	4	5	6	JANUARY 2120
	7	8[a]	9	10	11	12	13	
Dec 31	14	15[b]	16	17	18	19	20	
	21	22	23	24	25	26	27	
Jan 14	28	29	30	31	1	2	3	FEBRUARY 2120
	4	5	6	7	8	9	10	
Jan 28	11	12	13	14	15	16	17	
	18	19	20	21	22	23	24	
Feb 11	25	26	27	28[c]	29	1	2	MARCH 2120
	3	4	5	6	7	8	9	
Feb 25	10[d]	11	12	13	14	15	16	
	17	18	19	20	21	22	23	
Mar 10	24	25	26	27	28	29	30	
	31	1	2	3	4	5	6	APRIL 2120
Mar 24	7	8	9	10	11	12	13	
	14[e]	15	16	17	18	19	20	
Apr 7	21[f]	22	23	24	25	26	27	
	28	29	30	1	2	3	4	MAY 2120
Apr 21	5	6	7	8	9	10	11	
	12	13	14	15	16	17	18	
May 5	19	20	21	22	23	24	25	
	26	27	28	29	30	31	1	JUNE 2120
May 19	2	3	4	5	6	7	8	
	9	10	11	12	13	14	15	
Jun 2	16	17	18	19	20	21	22	
	23	24	25	26	27	28	29	
Jun 16	30	1	2	3	4	5	6	JULY 2120
	7	8	9	10	11	12	13	
Jun 30	14	15	16	17	18	19	20	
	21	22	23	24	25	26	27	
Jul 14	28	29	30	31	1	2	3	AUGUST 2120
	4	5	6	7	8	9	10	
Jul 28	11	12	13	14	15	16	17	
	18	19	20	21	22	23	24	
Aug 11	25	26	27	28	29	30	31	
	1	2	3	4	5	6	7	SEPTEMBER 2120
Aug 25	8	9	10	11	12	13	14	
	15	16	17	18	19	20	21	
Sep 8	22	23	24	25	26	27	28	
	29	30	1	2	3	4	5	OCTOBER 2120
Sep 22	6	7	8	9	10	11	12	
	13	14	15	16	17	18	19	
Oct 6	20	21	22	23	24	25	26	
	27	28	29	30	31	1	2	NOVEMBER 2120
Oct 20	3	4	5	6	7	8	9	
	10	11	12	13	14	15	16	
Nov 3	17	18	19	20	21	22	23	
	24	25	26	27	28	29	30	
Nov 17	1[g]	2	3	4	5	6	7	DECEMBER 2120
	8	9	10	11	12	13	14	
Dec 1	15	16	17	18	19	20	21	
	22	23	24	25[h]	26	27	28	
Dec 15	29	30	31	1	2	3	4	

Persian: ‡Leap year; [a]New Year (or prior day); *Near New Year: −1′52″; [b]Sizdeh Bedar

Hindu Lunar: [a]New Year (Vikrama); [b]Birthday of Rāma; [c]Birthday of Krishna; [d]Ganēśa Chaturthī; [e]Dashara; [f]Diwali; [g]Birthday of Vishnu; [h]Night of Śiva; [i]Holi

Hindu Solar: [a]New Year (Manmatha); [b]Pongal

Islamic: [a]New Year; [b]'Ashūrā'; [c]Prophet's Birthday; [d]Ascent of the Prophet; [e]Start of Ramaḍān; [f]'Īd al-Fiṭr; [g]'Īd al-'Aḍḥā

Gregorian: ‡Leap year; [a]Orthodox Christmas; [b]Julian New Year; [c]Ash Wednesday; [d]Feast of Orthodoxy; [e]Easter; [f]Orthodox Easter; [g]Advent; [h]Christmas

Gregorian 2121	Sun	Mon	Tue	Wed	Thu	Fri	Sat	Lunar Phases	ISO Week (Mon)	Julian Day (Sun noon)
January 2121	29	30	31	1[a]	2	○	4	19:33	1	2495737
	5	6	7	8	9	10	11		2	2495744
	◑	13	14	15	16	17	18	0:55	3	2495751
	●	20	21	22	23	24	◐	2:45 18:12	4	2495758
	26	27	28	29	30	31	1		5	2495765
February 2121	○	3	4	5	6	7	8	14:40	6	2495772
	9	◑	11	12	13	14	15	18:02	7	2495779
	16	●	18	19	20	21	22	13:35	8	2495786
	23	◐	25	26	27	28	1	7:05	9	2495793
March 2121	2	3	○	5	6	7	8	9:54	10	2495800
	9	10	11	◑	13	14	15	7:28	11	2495807
	16	17	●	19	20[b]	21	22	23:23	12	2495814
	23	24	◐	26	27	28	29	22:29	13	2495821
	30	31	1	2	○	4	5	3:25	14	2495828
April 2121	6	7	8	9	◑	11	12	17:16	15	2495835
	13	14	15	16	●	18	19	8:34	16	2495842
	20	21	22	23	◐	25	26	15:45	17	2495849
	27	28	29	30	1	○	3	18:18	18	2495856
May 2121	4	5	6	7	8	9	◑	0:06	19	2495863
	11	12	13	14	15	●	17	17:54	20	2495870
	18	19	20	21	22	23	◐	9:46	21	2495877
	25	26	27	28	29	30	31		22	2495884
June 2121	○	2	3	4	5	6	7	6:30	23	2495891
	◑	9	10	11	12	13	14	5:04	24	2495898
	●	16	17	18	19	20	21[c]	4:21	25	2495905
	22	◐	24	25	26	27	28	3:21	26	2495912
	29	○	1	2	3	4	5	16:30	27	2495919
July 2121	6	◑	8	9	10	11	12	9:38	28	2495926
	13	●	15	16	17	18	19	16:35	29	2495933
	20	21	◐	23	24	25	26	19:43	30	2495940
	27	28	29	○	31	1	2	0:59	31	2495947
August 2121	3	4	◑	6	7	8	9	15:19	32	2495954
	10	11	12	●	14	15	16	6:48	33	2495961
	17	18	19	20	◐	22	23	10:27	34	2495968
	24	25	26	27	○	29	30	8:41	35	2495975
	31	1	2	◑	4	5	6	23:37	36	2495982
September 2121	7	8	9	10	●	12	13	22:37	37	2495989
	14	15	16	17	18	◐	20	23:24	38	2495996
	21	22[d]	23	24	25	○	27	16:28	39	2496003
	28	29	30	1	2	◑	4	11:42	40	2496010
October 2121	5	6	7	8	9	10	●	15:24	41	2496017
	12	13	14	15	16	17	18		42	2496024
	◐	20	21	22	23	24	25	10:31	43	2496031
	○	27	28	29	30	31	1	1:15	44	2496038
November 2121	◑	3	4	5	6	7	8	3:56	45	2496045
	9	●	11	12	13	14	15	8:22	46	2496052
	16	◐	18	19	20	21	22	19:55	47	2496059
	23	○	25	26	27	28	29	11:56	48	2496066
	30	◑	2	3	4	5	6	23:38	49	2496073
December 2121	7	8	9	●	11	12	13	0:46	50	2496080
	14	15	16	◐	18	19	20	4:04	51	2496087
	21[e]	22	23	○	25	26	27	1:04	52	2496094
	28	29	30	◑	1	2	3	21:16	1	2496101

ISO Week	Hebrew 5881/5882‡	Sun	Mon	Tue	Wed	Thu	Fri	Sat	Molad
1	Teveth 5881	8	9	10	11	12	13	14	
2		15	16	17	18	19	20	21	
3		22	23	24	25	26	27	28	
4	Shevat 5881	29	1	2	3	4	5	6	Sun 1h51m16p
5		7	8	9	10	11	12	13	
6		14	15	16	17	18	19	20	
7		21	22	23	24	25	26	27	
8	Adar 5881	28	29	30	1	2	3	4	Mon 14h35m17p
9		5	6	7	8	9	10	11	
10		12	13	14[f]	15	16	17	18	
11		19	20	21	22	23	24	25	
12	Nisan 5881	26	27	28	29	1	2	3	Wed 3h20m0p
13		4	5	6	7	8	9	10	
14		11	12	13	14	15[g]	16	17	
15		18	19	20	21*	22	23	24	
16	Iyyar 5881	25	26	27	28	29	30	1	Thu 16h4m1p
17		2	3	4	5	6	7	8	
18		9	10	11	12	13	14	15	
19		16	17	18	19	20	21	22	
20		23	24	25	26	27	28	29	
21	Sivan 5881	1	2	3	4	5	6[h]	7	Sat 4h48m2p
22		8	9	10	11	12	13	14	
23		15	16	17	18	19	20	21	
24		22	23	24	25	26	27	28	
25	Tammuz 5881	29	30	1	2	3	4	5	Sun 17h32m3p
26		6	7	8	9	10	11	12	
27		13	14	15	16	17	18	19	
28		20	21	22	23	24	25	26	
29	Av 5881	27	28	29	1	2	3	4	Tue 6h16m4p
30		5	6	7	8	9[i]	10	11	
31		12	13	14	15	16	17	18	
32		19	20	21	22	23	24	25	
33	Elul 5881	26	27	28	29	30	1	2	Wed 19h0m5p
34		3	4	5	6	7	8	9	
35		10	11	12	13	14	15	16	
36		17	18	19	20	21	22	23	
37	Tishri 5882	24	25	26	27	28	29	1[a]	Fri 7h44m6p
38		2[a]	3	4	5	6	7	8	
39		9	10[b]	11	12	13	14	15[c]	
40		16	17	18	19	20	21	22	
41		23	24	25	26	27	28	29	
42	Heshvan 5882	30	1	2	3	4	5	6	Sat 20h28m7p
43		7	8	9	10	11	12	13	
44		14	15	16	17	18	19	20	
45		21	22	23	24	25	26	27	
46	Kislev 5882	28	29	1	2	3	4	5	Mon 9h12m8p
47		6	7	8	9	10	11	12	
48		13	14	15	16	17	18	19	
49		20	21	22	23	24	25[e]	26[d,e]	
50	Teveth 5882	27[e]	28[e]	29[e]	1[e]	2[e]	3[e]	4	Tue 21h56m9p
51		5	6	7	8	9	10	11	
52		12	13	14	15	16	17	18	
1		19	20	21	22	23	24	25	

ISO Week	Chinese Gēng-Chén‡/Xīn-Sì	Sun	Mon	Tue	Wed	Thu	Fri	Sat	Solar Term
1	Month 11 Gēng-Chén	10	11	12	13	14	15	16	
2		17	18	19	20	21	22	23	Xiǎo hán
3		24	25	26	27	28	29	30	
4	Month 12 Gēng-Chén	1	2	3	4	5	6	7	Dà hán
5		8	9	10	11	12	13	14*	
6		15	16	17	18	19	20	21	Lì chūn
7		22	23	24	25	26	27	28	
8	Month 1 Xīn-Sì	29	1[a]	2	3	4	5	6	Yǔ shuǐ
9		7	8	9	10	11	12	13	
10		14	15[b]	16	17	18	19	20	Jīng zhé
11		21	22	23	24	25	26	27	
12	Month 2 Xīn-Sì	28	29	30	1	2	3	4	Chūn fēn
13		5	6	7	8	9	10	11	
14		12	13	14	15*	16	17	18[c]	Qīng míng
15		19	20	21	22	23	24	25	
16	Month 3 Xīn-Sì	26	27	28	29	1	2	3	
17		4	5	6	7	8	9	10	Gǔ yǔ
18		11	12	13	14	15	16	17	
19		18	19	20	21	22	23	24	Lì xià
20	Month 4 Xīn-Sì	25	26	27	28	29	30	1	
21		2	3	4	5	6	7	8	Xiǎo mǎn
22		9	10	11	12	13	14	15	
23		16*	17	18	19	20	21	22	Máng zhòng
24		23	24	25	26	27	28	29	
25	Month 5 Xīn-Sì	1	2	3	4	5[d]	6	7	Xià zhì
26		8	9	10	11	12	13	14	
27		15	16	17	18	19	20	21	
28		22	23	24	25	26	27	28	Xiǎo shǔ
29	Month 6 Xīn-Sì	29	30	1	2	3	4	5	
30		6	7	8	9	10	11	12	Dà shǔ
31		13	14	15	16	17*	18	19	
32		20	21	22	23	24	25	26	Lì qiū
33	Month 7 Xīn-Sì	27	28	29	1	2	3	4	
34		5	6	7[e]	8	9	10	11	Chǔ shǔ
35		12	13	14	15[f]	16	17	18	
36		19	20	21	22	23	24	25	
37	Month 8 Xīn-Sì	26	27	28	29	30	1	2	Bái lù
38		3	4	5	6	7	8	9	
39		10	11	12	13	14	15[g]	16	Qiū fēn
40		17	18*	19	20	21	22	23	
41	Month 9 Xīn-Sì	24	25	26	27	28	29	1	Hán lù
42		2	3	4	5	6	7	8	
43		9[h]	10	11	12	13	14	15	Shuāng jiàng
44		16	17	18	19	20	21	22	
45		23	24	25	26	27	28	29	Lì dōng
46	Month 10 Xīn-Sì	30	1	2	3	4	5	6	
47		7	8	9	10	11	12	13	Xiǎo xuě
48		14	15	16	17	18	19*	20	
49		21	22	23	24	25	26	27	
50	Month 11 Xīn-Sì	28	29	30	1	2	3	4	Dà xuě
51		5	6	7	8	9	10	11	
52		12	13[i]	14	15	16	17	18	Dōng zhì
1		19	20	21	22	23	24	25	

ISO Week	Coptic 1837/1838	Sun	Mon	Tue	Wed	Thu	Fri	Sat	Ethiopic 2113/2114
1	Koiak 1837	19	20	21	22	23	24	25	Tāḫśāś 2113
2	Tōbe 1837	26	27	28	29[c]	30	1	2	Ṭer 2113
3		3	4	5	6[d]	7	8	9	
4		10	11[e]	12	13	14	15	16	
5		17	18	19	20	21	22	23	
6		24	25	26	27	28	29	30	
7	Meshir 1837	1	2	3	4	5	6	7	Yakātit 2113
8		8	9	10	11	12	13	14	
9		15	16	17	18	19	20	21	
10		22	23	24	25	26	27	28	
11	Paremotep 1837	29	30	1	2	3	4	5	Magābit 2113
12		6	7	8	9	10	11	12	
13		13	14	15	16	17	18	19	
14		20	21	22	23	24	25	26	
15	Parmoute 1837	27	28	29	30	1	2	3	Miyāzyā 2113
16		4[f]	5	6	7	8	9	10	
17		11	12	13	14	15	16	17	
18		18	19	20	21	22	23	24	
19	Pashons 1837	25	26	27	28	29[g]	30	1	Genbot 2113
20		2	3	4	5	6	7	8	
21		9	10	11	12	13	14	15	
22		16	17	18	19	20	21	22	
23		23	24	25	26	27	28	29	
24	Paōne 1837	30	1	2	3	4	5	6	Sanē 2113
25		7	8	9	10	11	12	13	
26		14	15	16	17	18	19	20	
27		21	22	23	24	25	26	27	
28	Epēp 1837	28	29	30	1	2	3	4	Ḥamlē 2113
29		5	6	7	8	9	10	11	
30		12	13	14	15	16	17	18	
31		19	20	21	22	23	24	25	
32	Mesorē 1837	26	27	28	29	30	1	2	Naḥasē 2113
33		3	4	5	6	7	8	9	
34		10	11	12	13[h]	14	15	16	
35		17	18	19	20	21	22	23	
36		24	25	26	27	28	29	30	
37	Epag. 1837	1	2	3	4	5	1[a]	2	Pāg. 2113
38	Thout 1838	3	4	5	6	7	8	9	Maskaram 2114
39		10	11	12	13	14	15	16	
40		17[b]	18	19	20	21	22	23	
41		24	25	26	27	28	29	30	
42	Paope 1838	1	2	3	4	5	6	7	Ṭeqemt 2114
43		8	9	10	11	12	13	14	
44		15	16	17	18	19	20	21	
45		22	23	24	25	26	27	28	
46	Athōr 1838	29	30	1	2	3	4	5	Ḫedār 2114
47		6	7	8	9	10	11	12	
48		13	14	15	16	17	18	19	
49		20	21	22	23	24	25	26	
50	Koiak 1838	27	28	29	30	1	2	3	Tāḫśāś 2114
51		4	5	6	7	8	9	10	
52		11	12	13	14	15	16	17	
1		18	19	20	21	22	23	24	

[a]New Year
[b]Spring (15:14)
[c]Summer (7:10)
[d]Autumn (23:42)
[e]Winter (22:09)
● New moon
◐ First quarter moon
○ Full moon
◑ Last quarter moon

‡Leap year
[a]New Year
[b]Yom Kippur
[c]Sukkot
[d]Winter starts
[e]Ḥanukkah
[f]Purim
[g]Passover
[h]Shavuot
[i]Fast of Av
*New solar cycle

‡Leap year
[a]New Year (4819, Snake)
[b]Lantern Festival
[c]Qīngmíng
[d]Dragon Festival
[e]Qīqiǎo
[f]Hungry Ghosts
[g]Mid-Autumn Festival
[h]Double-Ninth Festival
[i]Dōngzhì
*Start of 60-name cycle

[a]New Year
[b]Building of the Cross
[c]Christmas
[d]Jesus's Circumcision
[e]Epiphany
[f]Easter
[g]Mary's Announcement
[h]Jesus's Transfiguration

PERSIAN (ASTRONOMICAL) 1499/1500

Month	Sun	Mon	Tue	Wed	Thu	Fri	Sat
	8	9	10	11	12	13	14
DEY 1499	15	16	17	18	19	20	21
	22	23	24	25	26	27	28
	29	30	1	2	3	4	5
	6	7	8	9	10	11	12
BAHMAN 1499	13	14	15	16	17	18	19
	20	21	22	23	24	25	26
	27	28	29	30	1	2	3
	4	5	6	7	8	9	10
ESFAND 1499	11	12	13	14	15	16	17
	18	19	20	21	22	23	24
	25	26	27	28	29	1[a]	2
	3	4	5	6	7	8	9
FARVARDĪN 1500	10	11	12	13[b]	14	15	16
	17	18	19	20	21	22	23
	24	25	26	27	28	29	30
	31	1	2	3	4	5	6
ORDĪBEHEŠT 1500	7	8	9	10	11	12	13
	14	15	16	17	18	19	20
	21	22	23	24	25	26	27
	28	29	30	31	1	2	3
XORDĀD 1500	4	5	6	7	8	9	10
	11	12	13	14	15	16	17
	18	19	20	21	22	23	24
	25	26	27	28	29	30	31
	1	2	3	4	5	6	7
TĪR 1500	8	9	10	11	12	13	14
	15	16	17	18	19	20	21
	22	23	24	25	26	27	28
	29	30	31	1	2	3	4
MORDĀD 1500	5	6	7	8	9	10	11
	12	13	14	15	16	17	18
	19	20	21	22	23	24	25
	26	27	28	29	30	31	1
SHAHRĪVAR 1500	2	3	4	5	6	7	8
	9	10	11	12	13	14	15
	16	17	18	19	20	21	22
	23	24	25	26	27	28	29
	30	31	1	2	3	4	5
MEHR 1500	6	7	8	9	10	11	12
	13	14	15	16	17	18	19
	20	21	22	23	24	25	26
	27	28	29	30	1	2	3
ĀBĀN 1500	4	5	6	7	8	9	10
	11	12	13	14	15	16	17
	18	19	20	21	22	23	24
	25	26	27	28	29	30	1
ĀZAR 1500	2	3	4	5	6	7	8
	9	10	11	12	13	14	15
	16	17	18	19	20	21	22
	23	24	25	26	27	28	29
DEY 1500	30	1	2	3	4	5	6
	7	8	9	10	11	12	13

HINDU LUNAR 2177/2178‡

Month	Sun	Mon	Tue	Wed	Thu	Fri	Sat
	10	11	12	13	14	15	16
PAUSHA 2177	17	18	19	19	20	21	22
	23	24	25	26	27	28	29
	30	2	3	4	5	6	7
MĀGHA 2177	8	9	10	11	12	13	14
	15	16	17	18	19	20	21
	22	23	24	25	26	27	28[h]
	29	30	1	2	3	4	5
PHĀLGUNA 2177	**6**	8	9	10	11	11	12
	13	14	15[i]	16	17	18	19
	20	21	22	23	24	25	26
	27	28	**29**	1[a]	2	3	4
CHAITRA 2178	5	6	7	8	9[b]	10	11
	12	13	14	14	15	16	17
	18	19	20	21	22	**23**	25
	26	27	28	29	30	1	2
LEAP VAIŚĀKHA 2178	3	4	5	6	7	8	9
	10	11	12	13	14	15	16
	17	18	19	20	21	22	23
	24	25	**26**	28	29	30	1
VAIŚĀKHA 2178	2	3	4	5	6	7	8
	9	10	10	11	12	13	14
	15	16	17	18	**19**	21	22
	23	24	25	26	27	28	29
	30	1	2	3	4	5	6
JYAISHTHA 2178	7	8	9	10	11	12	13
	14	15	16	17	18	19	20
	21	**22**	24	25	26	27	28
	29	30	1	2	3	4	5
ĀSHĀDHA 2178	6	6	7	8	9	10	11
	12	13	14	**15**	17	18	19
	20	21	22	23	24	25	26
	27	28	29	30	1	2	3
ŚRĀVANA 2178	4	5	6	7	8	9	10
	11	12	13	14	15	16	17
	18	20	21	22	23[c]	24	25
	26	27	28	29	30	1	2
BHĀDRAPADA 2178	2	3[d]	4	5	6	7	8
	9	10	**11**	13	14	15	16
	17	18	19	20	21	22	23
	24	25	26	27	28	29	30
	1	2	3	4	5	6	7
ĀŚVINA 2178	8[e]	9[e]	10[e]	11	12	13	14
	15	17	18	19	20	21	22
	23	24	25	26	27	27	28
	29	30	1[f]	2	3	4	5
KĀRTTIKA 2178	6	7	8	**9**	11	12	13
	14	15	16	17	18	19	20
	21	22	23	24	25	26	27
	28	29	30	1	2	3	4
MĀRGAŚIRA 2178	5	6	7	8	9	10	11[g]
	12	13	**14**	16	17	18	19
	20	20	21	22	23	24	25

HINDU SOLAR 2042/2043‡

Month	Sun	Mon	Tue	Wed	Thu	Fri	Sat
	13	14	15	16	17	18	19
PAUSHA 2042	20	21	22	23	24	25	26
	27	28	29	30	1[b]	2	3
	4	5	6	7	8	9	10
MĀGHA 2042	11	12	13	14	15	16	17
	18	19	20	21	22	23	24
	25	26	27	28	29	1	2
	3	4	5	6	7	8	9
PHĀLGUNA 2042	10	11	12	13	14	15	16
	17	18	19	20	21	22	23
	24	25	26	27	28	29	30
	1	2	3	4	5	6	7
CHAITRA 2042	8	9	10	11	12	13	14
	15	16	17	18	19	20	21
	22	23	24	25	26	27	28
	29	30	1[a]	2	3	4	5
VAIŚĀKHA 2043	6	7	8	9	10	11	12
	13	14	15	16	17	18	19
	20	21	22	23	24	25	26
	27	28	29	30	31	1	2
JYAISHTHA 2043	3	4	5	6	7	8	9
	10	11	12	13	14	15	16
	17	18	19	20	21	22	23
	24	25	26	27	28	29	30
	31	32	1	2	3	4	5
ĀSHĀDHA 2043	6	7	8	9	10	11	12
	13	14	15	16	17	18	19
	20	21	22	23	24	25	26
	27	28	29	30	31	1	2
ŚRĀVANA 2043	3	4	5	6	7	8	9
	10	11	12	13	14	15	16
	17	18	19	20	21	22	23
	24	25	26	27	28	29	30
	31	32	1	2	3	4	5
BHĀDRAPADA 2043	6	7	8	9	10	11	12
	13	14	15	16	17	18	19
	20	21	22	23	24	25	26
	27	28	29	30	31	1	2
ĀŚVINA 2043	3	4	5	6	7	8	9
	10	11	12	13	14	15	16
	17	18	19	20	21	22	23
	24	25	26	27	28	29	30
KĀRTTIKA 2043	1	2	3	4	5	6	7
	8	9	10	11	12	13	14
	15	16	17	18	19	20	21
	22	23	24	25	26	27	28
	29	30	1	2	3	4	5
MĀRGAŚIRA 2043	6	7	8	9	10	11	12
	13	14	15	16	17	18	19
	20	21	22	23	24	25	26
	27	28	29	30	1	2	3
PAUSHA 2043	4	5	6	7	8	9	10
	11	12	13	14	15	16	17

ISLAMIC (ASTRONOMICAL) 1545/1546‡

Month	Sun	Mon	Tue	Wed	Thu	Fri	Sat
	8	9	10	11	12	13	14
JUMĀDĀ II 1545	15	16	17	18	19	20	21
	22	23	24	25	26	27	28
	29	1	2	3	4	5	6
RAJAB 1545	7	8	9	10	11	12	13
	14	15	16	17	18	19	20
	21	22	23	24	25	26	27[d]
	28	29	30	1	2	3	4
SHA'BĀN 1545	5	6	7	8	9	10	11
	12	13	14	15	16	17	18
	19	20	21	22	23	24	25
	26	27	28	29	1[e]	2	3
RAMAḌĀN 1545	4	5	6	7	8	9	10
	11	12	13	14	15	16	17
	18	19	20	21	22	23	24
	25	26	27	28	29	1[f]	2
SHAWWĀL 1545	3	4	5	6	7	8	9
	10	11	12	13	14	15	16
	17	18	19	20	21	22	23
	24	25	26	27	28	29	30
DHU AL-QA'DA 1545	1	2	3	4	5	6	7
	8	9	10	11	12	13	14
	15	16	17	18	19	20	21
	22	23	24	25	26	27	28
	29	1	2	3	4	5	6
DHU AL-ḤIJJA 1545	7	8	9	10[g]	11	12	13
	14	15	16	17	18	19	20
	21	22	23	24	25	26	27
	28	29	30	1[a]	2	3	4
MUḤARRAM 1546	5	6	7	8	9	10[b]	11
	12	13	14	15	16	17	18
	19	20	21	22	23	24	25
	26	27	28	29	30	31	1
ṢAFAR 1546	2	3	4	5	6	7	8
	9	10	11	12	13	14	15
	16	17	18	19	20	21	22
	23	24	25	26	27	28	29
	30	1	2	3	4	5	6
RABĪ' I 1546	7	8	9	10	11	12[c]	13
	14	15	16	17	18	19	20
	21	22	23	24	25	26	27
	28	29	1	2	3	4	5
RABĪ' II 1546	6	7	8	9	10	11	12
	13	14	15	16	17	18	19
	20	21	22	23	24	25	26
	27	28	29	1	2	3	4
JUMĀDĀ I 1546	5	6	7	8	9	10	11
	12	13	14	15	16	17	18
	19	20	21	22	23	24	25
	26	27	28	29	30	1	2
JUMĀDĀ II 1546	3	4	5	6	7	8	9
	10	11	12	13	14	15	16
	17	18	19	20	21	22	23

GREGORIAN 2121

Julian (Sun)	Sun	Mon	Tue	Wed	Thu	Fri	Sat	Month
Dec 15	29	30	31	1	2	3	4	
	5	6	7	8[a]	9	10	11	JANUARY 2121
Dec 29	12	13	14	15[b]	16	17	18	
	19	20	21	22	23	24	25	
Jan 12	26	27	28	29	30	31	1	
	2	3	4	5	6	7	8	FEBRUARY 2121
Jan 26	9	10	11	12	13	14	15	
	16	17	18	19[c]	20	21	22	
Feb 9	23	24	25	26	27	28	1	
	2[d]	3	4	5	6	7	8	MARCH 2121
Feb 23	9	10	11	12	13	14	15	
	16	17	18	19	20	21	22	
Mar 9	23	24	25	26	27	28	29	
	30	31	1	2	3	4	5	
Mar 23	6[e]	7	8	9	10	11	12	APRIL 2121
	13[f]	14	15	16	17	18	19	
Apr 6	20	21	22	23	24	25	26	
	27	28	29	30	1	2	3	
Apr 20	4	5	6	7	8	9	10	MAY 2121
	11	12	13	14	15	16	17	
May 4	18	19	20	21	22	23	24	
	25	26	27	28	29	30	31	
May 18	1	2	3	4	5	6	7	JUNE 2121
	8	9	10	11	12	13	14	
Jun 1	15	16	17	18	19	20	21	
	22	23	24	25	26	27	28	
Jun 15	29	30	1	2	3	4	5	
	6	7	8	9	10	11	12	JULY 2121
Jun 29	13	14	15	16	17	18	19	
	20	21	22	23	24	25	26	
Jul 13	27	28	29	30	31	1	2	
	3	4	5	6	7	8	9	AUGUST 2121
Jul 27	10	11	12	13	14	15	16	
	17	18	19	20	21	22	23	
Aug 10	24	25	26	27	28	29	30	
	31	1	2	3	4	5	6	
Aug 24	7	8	9	10	11	12	13	SEPTEMBER 2121
	14	15	16	17	18	19	20	
Sep 7	21	22	23	24	25	26	27	
	28	29	30	1	2	3	4	
Sep 21	5	6	7	8	9	10	11	OCTOBER 2121
	12	13	14	15	16	17	18	
Oct 5	19	20	21	22	23	24	25	
	26	27	28	29	30	31	1	
Oct 19	2	3	4	5	6	7	8	NOVEMBER 2121
	9	10	11	12	13	14	15	
Nov 2	16	17	18	19	20	21	22	
	23	24	25	26	27	28	29	
Nov 16	30[g]	1	2	3	4	5	6	
	7	8	9	10	11	12	13	DECEMBER 2121
Nov 30	14	15	16	17	18	19	20	
	21	22	23	24	25[h]	26	27	
Dec 14	28	29	30	31	1	2	3	

Persian: [a]New Year; [b]Sizdeh Bedar

Hindu Lunar: ‡Leap year; [a]New Year (Vṛisha); [b]Birthday of Rāma; [c]Birthday of Krishna; [d]Ganēśa Chaturthī; [e]Dashara; [f]Diwali; [g]Birthday of Vishnu; [h]Night of Śiva; [i]Holi

Hindu Solar: ‡Leap year; [a]New Year (Durmukha); [b]Pongal

Islamic: ‡Leap year; [a]New Year; [b]'Ashūrā'; [c]Prophet's Birthday; [d]Ascent of the Prophet; [e]Start of Ramaḍān; [f]'Id al-Fiṭr; [g]'Id al-'Aḍḥā

Gregorian: [a]Orthodox Christmas; [b]Julian New Year; [c]Ash Wednesday; [d]Feast of Orthodoxy; [e]Easter; [f]Orthodox Easter; [g]Advent; [h]Christmas

2122

Month	Sun	Mon	Tue	Wed	Thu	Fri	Sat	Lunar Phases	ISO WEEK (Mon)	JULIAN DAY (Sun noon)
	28	29	30	◑	1[a]	2	3	21:16	1	2496101
JANUARY 2122	4	5	6	7	●	9	10	15:47	2	2496108
	11	12	13	14	◐	16	17	11:52	3	2496115
	18	19	20	21	○	23	24	16:35	4	2496122
	25	26	27	28	29	◑	31	18:48	5	2496129
FEBRUARY 2122	1	2	3	4	5	6	●	4:46	6	2496136
	8	9	10	11	12	◐	14	20:23	7	2496143
	15	16	17	18	19	20	○	9:44	8	2496150
	22	23	24	25	26	27	28		9	2496157
MARCH 2122	◑	2	3	4	5	6	7	14:14	10	2496164
	●	9	10	11	12	13	14	15:33	11	2496171
	◐	16	17	18	19	20[b]	21	6:30	12	2496178
	22	○	24	25	26	27	28	3:24	13	2496185
	29	30	◑	1	2	3	4	6:08	14	2496192
APRIL 2122	5	6	●	8	9	10	11	0:34	15	2496199
	12	◐	14	15	16	17	18	18:37	16	2496206
	19	20	○	22	23	24	25	20:32	17	2496213
	26	27	28	◑	30	1	2	17:55	18	2496220
MAY 2122	3	4	5	●	7	8	9	8:36	19	2496227
	10	11	12	◐	14	15	16	8:36	20	2496234
	17	18	19	20	○	22	23	12:20	21	2496241
	24	25	26	27	28	◑	30	1:56	22	2496248
	31	1	2	3	●	5	6	16:36	23	2496255
JUNE 2122	7	8	9	10	11	◐	13	0:08	24	2496262
	14	15	16	17	18	19	○	2:15	25	2496269
	21[c]	22	23	24	25	26	◑	7:20	26	2496276
	28	29	30	1	2	3	●	1:26	27	2496283
JULY 2122	5	6	7	8	9	10	◐	16:51	28	2496290
	12	13	14	15	16	17	18		29	2496297
	○	20	21	22	23	24	25	14:03	30	2496304
	◑	27	28	29	30	31	1	11:40	31	2496311
AUGUST 2122	●	3	4	5	6	7	8	11:51	32	2496318
	9	◐	11	12	13	14	15	10:14	33	2496325
	16	○	18	19	20	21	22	23:59	34	2496332
	23	◑	25	26	27	28	29	16:32	35	2496339
	30	31	●	2	3	4	5	0:22	36	2496346
SEPTEMBER 2122	6	7	8	◐	10	11	12	3:36	37	2496353
	13	14	15	○	17	18	19	8:47	38	2496360
	20	21	◑	23[d]	24	25	26	23:27	39	2496367
	27	28	29	●	1	2	3	15:19	40	2496374
OCTOBER 2122	4	5	6	7	◐	9	10	19:58	41	2496381
	11	12	13	14	○	16	17	17:26	42	2496388
	18	19	20	21	◑	23	24	9:33	43	2496395
	25	26	27	28	29	●	31	8:38	44	2496402
NOVEMBER 2122	1	2	3	4	5	6	◐	10:25	45	2496409
	8	9	10	11	12	13	○	2:50	46	2496416
	15	16	17	18	19	◑	21	23:27	47	2496423
	22	23	24	25	26	27	28		48	2496430
	●	30	1	2	3	4	5	3:26	49	2496437
DECEMBER 2122	◐	7	8	9	10	11	12	22:30	50	2496444
	○	14	15	16	17	18	19	13:32	51	2496451
	◑	21	22[e]	23	24	25	26	17:04	52	2496458
	27	●	29	30	31	1	2	22:08	53	2496465

HEBREW 5882‡/5883

ISO WEEK	Month	Sun	Mon	Tue	Wed	Thu	Fri	Sat	Molad
1	TEVETH 5882	19	20	21	22	23	24	25	
2		26	27	28	29	1	2	3	Thu 10h40m10p
3	SHEVAT 5882	4	5	6	7	8	9	10	
4		11	12	13	14	15	16	17	
5		18	19	20	21	22	23	24	
6		25	26	27	28	29	30	1	Fri 23h24m11p
7	ADAR I 5882	2	3	4	5	6	7	8	
8		9	10	11	12	13	14	15	
9		16	17	18	19	20	21	22	
10		23	24	25	26	27	28	29	
11		30	1	2	3	4	5	6	Sun 12h8m12p
12	ADAR II 5882	7	8	9	10	11	12	13	
13		14[f]	15	16	17	18	19	20	
14		21	22	23	24	25	26	27	
15		28	29	1	2	3	4	5	Tue 0h52m13p
16	NISAN 5882	6	7	8	9	10	11	12	
17		13	14	15[g]	16	17	18	19	
18		20	21	22	23	24	25	26	
19		27	28	29	30	1	2	3	Wed 13h36m14p
20	IYAR 5882	4	5	6	7	8	9	10	
21		11	12	13	14	15	16	17	
22		18	19	20	21	22	23	24	
23		25	26	27	28	29	1	2	Fri 2h20m15p
24	SIVAN 5882	3	4	5	6[h]	7	8	9	
25		10	11	12	13	14	15	16	
26		17	18	19	20	21	22	23	
27		24	25	26	27	28	29	30	
28	TAMMUZ 5882	1	2	3	4	5	6	7	Sat 15h4m16p
29		8	9	10	11	12	13	14	
30		15	16	17	18	19	20	21	
31		22	23	24	25	26	27	28	
32	AV 5882	29	1	2	3	4	5	6	Mon 3h48m17p
33		7	8	9[i]	10	11	12	13	
34		14	15	16	17	18	19	20	
35		21	22	23	24	25	26	27	
36		28	29	30	1	2	3	4	Tue 16h33m0p
37	ELUL 5882	5	6	7	8	9	10	11	
38		12	13	14	15	16	17	18	
39		19	20	21	22	23	24	25	
40		26	27	28	29	1[a]	2[a]	3	Thu 5h17m1p
41	TISHRI 5883	4	5	6	7	8	9	10[b]	
42		11	12	13	14	15[c]	16	17	
43		18	19	20	21	22	23	24	
44		25	26	27	28	29	30	1	Fri 18h1m2p
45	ḤESHVAN 5883	2	3	4	5	6	7	8	
46		9	10	11	12	13	14	15	
47		16	17	18	19	20	21	22	
48		23	24	25	26	27	28	29	
49		30	1	2	3	4	5	6	Sun 6h45m3p
50	KISLEV 5883	7[d]	8	9	10	11	12	13	
51		14	15	16	17	18	19	20	
52		21	22	23	24	25[e]	26[e]	27[e]	
53		28[e]	29[e]	30[e]	1[e]	2[e]	3	4	Mon 19h29m4p

CHINESE Xīn-Sì/Rén-Wǔ

ISO WEEK	Month	Sun	Mon	Tue	Wed	Thu	Fri	Sat	Solar Term
1	MONTH 11 Xīn-Sì	19	20	21	22	23	24	25	
2	MONTH 12 Xīn-Sì	26	27	28	29	1	2	3	Xiǎo hán
3		4	5	6	7	8	9	10	
4		11	12	13	14	15	16	17	Dà hán
5		18	19	20*	21	22	23	24	
6		25	26	27	28	29	30	1[a]	Lì chūn
7	MONTH 1 Rén-Wǔ	2	3	4	5	6	7	8	
8		9	10	11	12	13	14	15[b]	Yǔ shuǐ
9		16	17	18	19	20	21	22	
10		23	24	25	26	27	28	29	Jīng zhé
11	MONTH 2 Rén-Wǔ	1	2	3	4	5	6	7	
12		8	9	10	11	12	13	14	Chūn fēn
13		15	16	17	18	19	20	21*	
14		22	23	24	25	26	27	28	
15		29[c]	30	1	2	3	4	5	Qīng míng
16	MONTH 3 Rén-Wǔ	6	7	8	9	10	11	12	
17		13	14	15	16	17	18	19	Gǔ yǔ
18		20	21	22	23	24	25	26	
19		27	28	29	1	2	3	4	Lì xià
20	MONTH 4 Rén-Wǔ	5	6	7	8	9	10	11	
21		12	13	14	15	16	17	18	Xiǎo mǎn
22		19	20	21	22*	23	24	25	
23		26	27	28	29	30	1	2	Máng zhòng
24	MONTH 5 Rén-Wǔ	3	4	5[d]	6	7	8	9	
25		10	11	12	13	14	15	16	
26		17	18	19	20	21	22	23	Xià zhì
27		24	25	26	27	28	29	1	
28	MONTH 6 Rén-Wǔ	2	3	4	5	6	7	8	Xiǎo shǔ
29		9	10	11	12	13	14	15	
30		16	17	18	19	20	21	22	Dà shǔ
31		23*	24	25	26	27	28	29	
32	MONTH 7 Rén-Wǔ	1	2	3	4	5	6	7[e]	Lì qiū
33		8	9	10	11	12	13	14	
34		15[f]	16	17	18	19	20	21	Chǔ shǔ
35		22	23	24	25	26	27	28	
36		29	30	1	2	3	4	5	
37	MONTH 8 Rén-Wǔ	6	7	8	9	10	11	12	Bái lù
38		13	14	15[g]	16	17	18	19	
39		20	21	22	23	24*	25	26	Qiū fēn
40		27	28	29	1	2	3	4	
41	MONTH 9 Rén-Wǔ	5	6	7	8	9[h]	10	11	Hán lù
42		12	13	14	15	16	17	18	
43		19	20	21	22	23	24	25	Shuāng jiàng
44		26	27	28	29	30	1	2	
45	MONTH 10 Rén-Wǔ	3	4	5	6	7	8	9	
46		10	11	12	13	14	15	16	Lì dōng
47		17	18	19	20	21	22	23	
48		24	25*	26	27	28	29	30	Xiǎo xuě
49	MONTH 11 Rén-Wǔ	1	2	3	4	5	6	7	
50		8	9	10	11	12	13	14	Dà xuě
51		15	16	17	18	19	20	21	
52		22	23	24[i]	25	26	27	28	Dōng zhì
53		29	30	1	2	3	4	5	

COPTIC 1838/1839‡ — ETHIOPIC 2114/2115‡

ISO WEEK	Coptic Month	Sun	Mon	Tue	Wed	Thu	Fri	Sat	Ethiopic Month
1	KOIAK 1838	18	19	20	21	22	23	24	TĀKHŚĀŚ 2114
2		25	26	27	28	29[c]	30	1	
3	ṬÔBE 1838	2	3	4	5	6[d]	7	8	ṬER 2114
4		9	10	11[e]	12	13	14	15	
5		16	17	18	19	20	21	22	
6		23	24	25	26	27	28	29	
7	MESHIR 1838	30	1	2	3	4	5	6	YAKĀTIT 2114
8		7	8	9	10	11	12	13	
9		14	15	16	17	18	19	20	
10		21	22	23	24	25	26	27	
11	PAREMOTEP 1838	28	29	30	1	2	3	4	MAGĀBIT 2114
12		5	6	7	8	9	10	11	
13		12	13	14	15	16	17	18	
14		19	20	21	22	23	24	25	
15	PARMOUTE 1838	26	27	28	29	30	1	2	MIYĀZYĀ 2114
16		3	4	5	6	7	8	9	
17		10	11	12	13	14	15	16	
18		17	18	19	20	21	22	23	
19		24[f]	25	26	27	28	29[g]	30	
20	PASHONS 1838	1	2	3	4	5	6	7	GENBOT 2114
21		8	9	10	11	12	13	14	
22		15	16	17	18	19	20	21	
23		22	23	24	25	26	27	28	
24	PAÔNE 1838	29	30	1	2	3	4	5	SANĒ 2114
25		6	7	8	9	10	11	12	
26		13	14	15	16	17	18	19	
27		20	21	22	23	24	25	26	
28	EPÊP 1838	27	28	29	30	1	2	3	ḤAMLĒ 2114
29		4	5	6	7	8	9	10	
30		11	12	13	14	15	16	17	
31		18	19	20	21	22	23	24	
32	MESORÊ 1838	25	26	27	28	29	30	1	NAḤASĒ 2114
33		2	3	4	5	6	7	8	
34		9	10	11	12	13[h]	14	15	
35		16	17	18	19	20	21	22	
36		23	24	25	26	27	28	29	
37	EPAG. 1838	30	1	2	3	4	5	1[a]	PĀG. 2114
38	THOOUT 1839	2	3	4	5	6	7	8	MASKARAM 2115
39		9	10	11	12	13	14	15	
40		16	17[b]	18	19	20	21	22	
41		23	24	25	26	27	28	29	
42	PAOPE 1839	30	1	2	3	4	5	6	ṬEQEMT 2115
43		7	8	9	10	11	12	13	
44		14	15	16	17	18	19	20	
45		21	22	23	24	25	26	27	
46	ATHÔR 1839	28	29	30	1	2	3	4	ḪEDĀR 2115
47		5	6	7	8	9	10	11	
48		12	13	14	15	16	17	18	
49		19	20	21	22	23	24	25	
50	KOIAK 1839	26	27	28	29	30	1	2	TĀKHŚĀŚ 2115
51		3	4	5	6	7	8	9	
52		10	11	12	13	14	15	16	
53		17	18	19	20	21	22	23	

Gregorian notes:
[a]New Year
[b]Spring (21:02)
[c]Summer (13:01)
[d]Autumn (5:37)
[e]Winter (3:59)
● New moon
◐ First quarter moon
○ Full moon
◑ Last quarter moon

Hebrew notes:
‡Leap year
[a]New Year
[b]Yom Kippur
[c]Sukkot
[d]Winter starts
[e]Ḥanukkah
[f]Purim
[g]Passover
[h]Shavuot
[i]Fast of Av

Chinese notes:
[a]New Year (4820, Horse)
[b]Lantern Festival
[c]Qīngmíng
[d]Dragon Festival
[e]Qīqiǎo
[f]Hungry Ghosts
[g]Mid-Autumn Festival
[h]Double-Ninth Festival
[i]Dōngzhì
*Start of 60-name cycle

Coptic/Ethiopic notes:
‡Leap year
[a]New Year
[b]Building of the Cross
[c]Christmas
[d]Jesus's Circumcision
[e]Epiphany
[f]Easter
[g]Mary's Announcement
[h]Jesus's Transfiguration

PERSIAN (ASTRONOMICAL) 1500/1501

Month	Sun	Mon	Tue	Wed	Thu	Fri	Sat
	7	8	9	10	11	12	13
DEY 1500	14	15	16	17	18	19	20
	21	22	23	24	25	26	27
	28	29	30	1	2	3	4
BAHMAN 1500	5	6	7	8	9	10	11
	12	13	14	15	16	17	18
	19	20	21	22	23	24	25
	26	27	28	29	30	1	2
ESFAND 1500	3	4	5	6	7	8	9
	10	11	12	13	14	15	16
	17	18	19	20	21	22	23
	24	25	26	27	28	29	1[a]
FARVARDĪN 1501	2	3	4	5	6	7	8
	9	10	11	12	13[b]	14	15
	16	17	18	19	20	21	22
	23	24	25	26	27	28	29
	30	31	1	2	3	4	5
ORDĪBEHEŠT 1501	6	7	8	9	10	11	12
	13	14	15	16	17	18	19
	20	21	22	23	24	25	26
	27	28	29	30	31	1	2
XORDĀD 1501	3	4	5	6	7	8	9
	10	11	12	13	14	15	16
	17	18	19	20	21	22	23
	24	25	26	27	28	29	30
	31	1	2	3	4	5	6
TĪR 1501	7	8	9	10	11	12	13
	14	15	16	17	18	19	20
	21	22	23	24	25	26	27
	28	29	30	31	1	2	3
MORDĀD 1501	4	5	6	7	8	9	10
	11	12	13	14	15	16	17
	18	19	20	21	22	23	24
	25	26	27	28	29	30	31
SHAHRĪVAR 1501	1	2	3	4	5	6	7
	8	9	10	11	12	13	14
	15	16	17	18	19	20	21
	22	23	24	25	26	27	28
	29	30	31	1	2	3	4
MEHR 1501	5	6	7	8	9	10	11
	12	13	14	15	16	17	18
	19	20	21	22	23	24	25
	26	27	28	29	30	1	2
ĀBĀN 1501	3	4	5	6	7	8	9
	10	11	12	13	14	15	16
	17	18	19	20	21	22	23
	24	25	26	27	28	29	30
ĀZAR 1501	1	2	3	4	5	6	7
	8	9	10	11	12	13	14
	15	16	17	18	19	20	21
	22	23	24	25	26	27	28
DEY 1501	29	30	1	2	3	4	5
	6	7	8	9	10	11	12

[a]New Year
[b]Sizdeh Bedar

HINDU LUNAR 2178‡/2179

Month	Sun	Mon	Tue	Wed	Thu	Fri	Sat
MĀRGAŚĪRA 2178	20	20	21	22	23	24	25
	26	27	28	29	30	1	2
PAUSHA 2178	3	4	5	6	7	9	10
	11	12	13	14	15	16	17
	18	19	20	21	22	22	23
	24	25	26	27	28	29	30
	1	3	4	5	6	7	8
MĀGHA 2178	9	10	11	12	13	14	15
	16	17	18	19	20	21	22
	23	24	25	26	27	28	29[h]
	30	1	2	3	4	5	6
PHĀLGUNA 2178	8	9	10	11	12	13	14
	15	15[i]	16	17	18	19	20
	21	22	23	24	25	26	27
	28	29	30[a]	2	3	4	5
CHAITRA 2179	6	7	8	9[b]	10	11	12
	13	14	15	16	17	18	18
	19	20	21	22	24	25	26
	27	28	29	30	1	2	3
VAIŚĀKHA 2179	4	5	7	8	9	9	10
	11	12	13	14	15	16	17
	18	19	20	21	22	23	24
	25	26	28	29	30	1	2
JYAISHTHA 2179	3	4	5	6	7	8	9
	10	11	12	13	14	14	15
	16	17	18	19	21	22	23
	24	25	26	27	28	29	30
	2	3	4	5	6	6	7
ĀSHĀDHA 2179	8	9	10	11	12	13	14
	15	16	17	18	19	20	21
	22	24	25	26	27	28	29
	30	1	2	3	4	5	6
ŚRĀVAṆA 2179	7	8	9	10	11	11	12
	13	14	16	17	18	19	20
	21	22	23[c]	24	25	26	28
	29	30	1	2	2	3[d]	4
BHĀDRAPADA 2179	5	6	7	8	9	10	11
	12	13	14	15	16	17	18
	20	21	22	23	24	25	26
	27	28	29	30	1	2	3
ĀŚVINA 2179	4	5	6	6	7	8[e]	9[e]
	10[e]	11	13	14	15	16	17
	18	19	20	21	22	23	24
	25	26	27	28	29	30	1[f]
KĀRTTIKA 2179	2	3	4	5	6	7	8
	9	10	11	12	13	14	15
	16	18	19	20	21	22	23
	24	25	26	27	28	29	30
	30	1	2	3	4	5	6
MĀRGAŚĪRA 2179	7	8	9	11[g]	12	13	14
	15	16	17	18	19	20	21
	22	23	24	25	26	27	28
	29	30	1	2	3	4	5

‡Leap year
[a]New Year (Chitrabhānu)
[b]Birthday of Rāma
[c]Birthday of Krishna
[d]Ganēśa Chaturthī
[e]Dashara
[f]Diwali
[g]Birthday of Vishnu
[h]Night of Śiva
[i]Holi

HINDU SOLAR 2043‡/2044

Month	Sun	Mon	Tue	Wed	Thu	Fri	Sat
PAUSHA 2043	11	12	13	14	15	16	17
	18	19	20	21	22	23	24
	25	26	27	28	29	1[b]	2
MĀGHA 2043	3	4	5	6	7	8	9
	10	11	12	13	14	15	16
	17	18	19	20	21	22	23
	24	25	26	27	28	29	1
PHĀLGUNA 2043	2	3	4	5	6	7	8
	9	10	11	12	13	14	15
	16	17	18	19	20	21	22
	23	24	25	26	27	28	29
	30	1	2	3	4	5	6
CHAITRA 2043	7	8	9	10	11	12	13
	14	15	16	17	18	19	20
	21	22	23	24	25	26	27
	28	29	30	31	1[a]	2	3
VAIŚĀKHA 2044	4	5	6	7	8	9	10
	11	12	13	14	15	16	17
	18	19	20	21	22	23	24
	25	26	27	28	29	30	31
JYAISHTHA 2044	1	2	3	4	5	6	7
	8	9	10	11	12	13	14
	15	16	17	18	19	20	21
	22	23	24	25	26	27	28
	29	30	31	1	2	3	4
ĀSHĀDHA 2044	5	6	7	8	9	10	11
	12	13	14	15	16	17	18
	19	20	21	22	23	24	25
	26	27	28	29	30	31	32
ŚRĀVAṆA 2044	1	2	3	4	5	6	7
	8	9	10	11	12	13	14
	15	16	17	18	19	20	21
	22	23	24	25	26	27	28
	29	30	31	1	2	3	4
BHĀDRAPADA 2044	5	6	7	8	9	10	11
	12	13	14	15	16	17	18
	19	20	21	22	23	24	25
	26	27	28	29	30	31	1
ĀŚVINA 2044	2	3	4	5	6	7	8
	9	10	11	12	13	14	15
	16	17	18	19	20	21	22
	23	24	25	26	27	28	29
	30	1	2	3	4	5	6
KĀRTTIKA 2044	7	8	9	10	11	12	13
	14	15	16	17	18	19	20
	21	22	23	24	25	26	27
	28	29	30	1	2	3	4
MĀRGAŚĪRA 2044	5	6	7	8	9	10	11
	12	13	14	15	16	17	18
	19	20	21	22	23	24	25
	26	27	28	29	30	1	2
PAUSHA 2044	3	4	5	6	7	8	9
	10	11	12	13	14	15	16

‡Leap year
[a]New Year (Hemalamba)
[b]Pongal

ISLAMIC (ASTRONOMICAL) 1546‡/1547

Month	Sun	Mon	Tue	Wed	Thu	Fri	Sat
JUMĀDĀ II 1546	17	18	19	20	21	22	23
	24	25	26	27	28	29	1
RAJAB 1546	2	3	4	5	6	7	8
	9	10	11	12	13	14	15
	16	17	18	19	20	21	22
	23	24	25	26	27[d]	28	29
	1	2	3	4	5	6	7
SHA'BĀN 1546	8	9	10	11	12	13	14
	15	16	17	18	19	20	21
	22	23	24	25	26	27	28
	29	30	1[e]	2	3	4	5
RAMAḌĀN 1546	6	7	8	9	10	11	12
	13	14	15	16	17	18	19
	20	21	22	23	24	25	26
	27	28	29	1[f]	2	3	4
SHAWWĀL 1546	5	6	7	8	9	10	11
	12	13	14	15	16	17	18
	19	20	21	22	23	24	25
	26	27	28	29	1	2	3
DHU AL-QA'DA 1546	4	5	6	7	8	9	10
	11	12	13	14	15	16	17
	18	19	20	21	22	23	24
	25	26	27	28	29	30	1
DHU AL-ḤIJJA 1546	2	3	4	5	6	7	8
	9	10[g]	11	12	13	14	15
	16	17	18	19	20	21	22
	23	24	25	26	27	28	29
	30	1[a]	2	3	4	5	6
MUḤARRAM 1547	7	8	9	10[b]	11	12	13
	14	15	16	17	18	19	20
	21	22	23	24	25	26	27
	28	29	30	1	2	3	4
ṢAFAR 1547	5	6	7	8	9	10	11
	12	13	14	15	16	17	18
	19	20	21	22	23	24	25
	26	27	28	29	30	1	2
RABĪ' I 1547	3	4	5	6	7	8	9
	10	11	12[c]	13	14	15	16
	17	18	19	20	21	22	23
	24	25	26	27	28	29	1
RABĪ' II 1547	2	3	4	5	6	7	8
	9	10	11	12	13	14	15
	16	17	18	19	20	21	22
	23	24	25	26	27	28	29
	1	2	3	4	5	6	7
JUMĀDĀ I 1547	8	9	10	11	12	13	14
	15	16	17	18	19	20	21
	22	23	24	25	26	27	28
	29	30	1	2	3	4	5
JUMĀDĀ II 1547	6	7	8	9	10	11	12
	13	14	15	16	17	18	19
	20	21	22	23	24	25	26
	27	28	29	1	2	3	4

‡Leap year
[a]New Year
[b]'Ashūrā'
[c]Prophet's Birthday
[d]Ascent of the Prophet
[e]Start of Ramaḍān
[f]'Id al-Fiṭr
[g]'Id al-'Aḍḥā

GREGORIAN 2122

Julian (Sun)	Sun	Mon	Tue	Wed	Thu	Fri	Sat	Month
Dec 14	28	29	30	31	1	2	3	
	4	5	6	7	8[a]	9	10	JANUARY 2122
Dec 28	11	12	13	14	15[b]	16	17	
	18	19	20	21	22	23	24	
Jan 11	25	26	27	28	29	30	31	
	1	2	3	4	5	6	7	
Jan 25	8	9	10	11[c]	12	13	14	FEBRUARY 2122
	15	16	17	18	19	20	21	
Feb 8	22	23	24	25	26	27	28	
	1	2	3	4	5	6	7	
Feb 22	8	9	10	11	12	13	14	MARCH 2122
	15	16	17	18	19	20	21	
Mar 8	22[d]	23	24	25	26	27	28	
	29[e]	30	31	1	2	3	4	
Mar 22	5	6	7	8	9	10	11	
	12	13	14	15	16	17	18	APRIL 2122
Apr 5	19	20	21	22	23	24	25	
	26	27	28	29	30	1	2	
Apr 19	3[f]	4	5	6	7	8	9	
	10	11	12	13	14	15	16	MAY 2122
May 3	17	18	19	20	21	22	23	
	24	25	26	27	28	29	30	
May 17	31	1	2	3	4	5	6	
	7	8	9	10	11	12	13	
May 31	14	15	16	17	18	19	20	JUNE 2122
	21	22	23	24	25	26	27	
Jun 14	28	29	30	1	2	3	4	
	5	6	7	8	9	10	11	
Jun 28	12	13	14	15	16	17	18	JULY 2122
	19	20	21	22	23	24	25	
Jul 12	26	27	28	29	30	31	1	
	2	3	4	5	6	7	8	
Jul 26	9	10	11	12	13	14	15	AUGUST 2122
	16	17	18	19	20	21	22	
Aug 9	23	24	25	26	27	28	29	
	30	31	1	2	3	4	5	
Aug 23	6	7	8	9	10	11	12	SEPTEMBER 2122
	13	14	15	16	17	18	19	
Sep 6	20	21	22	23	24	25	26	
	27	28	29	30	1	2	3	
Sep 20	4	5	6	7	8	9	10	OCTOBER 2122
	11	12	13	14	15	16	17	
Oct 4	18	19	20	21	22	23	24	
	25	26	27	28	29	30	31	
Oct 18	1	2	3	4	5	6	7	
	8	9	10	11	12	13	14	NOVEMBER 2122
Nov 1	15	16	17	18	19	20	21	
	22	23	24	25	26	27	28	
Nov 15	29[g]	30	1	2	3	4	5	
	6	7	8	9	10	11	12	DECEMBER 2122
Nov 29	13	14	15	16	17	18	19	
	20	21	22	23	24	25[h]	26	
Dec 13	27	28	29	30	31	1	2	

[a]Orthodox Christmas
[b]Julian New Year
[c]Ash Wednesday
[d]Feast of Orthodoxy
[e]Easter
[f]Orthodox Easter
[g]Advent
[h]Christmas

2123

GREGORIAN 2123								Lunar Phases	ISO WEEK	JULIAN DAY	HEBREW 5883/5884								Molad	CHINESE Rén-Wǔ/Guǐ-Wèi‡								Solar Term	COPTIC 1839‡/1840								ETHIOPIC 2115‡/2116
	Sun	Mon	Tue	Wed	Thu	Fri	Sat		(Mon)	(Sun noon)		Sun	Mon	Tue	Wed	Thu	Fri	Sat			Sun	Mon	Tue	Wed	Thu	Fri	Sat			Sun	Mon	Tue	Wed	Thu	Fri	Sat	
JANUARY 2123	27	●	29	30	31	1[a]	2	22:08	53	2496465	TEVETH 5883	28[e]	29[e]	30[e]	1[e]	2[e]	3	4	Mon 19h29m4p	MONTH 12 Rén-Wǔ	29	30	1	2	3	4	5		KOIAK 1839	17	18	19	20	21	22	23	TĀKHŚĀŚ 2115
	3	4	◐	6	7	8	9	8:22	1	2496472		5	6	7	8	9	10	11			6	7	8	*9*	10	11	12	Xiǎo hán		24	25	26	27	28	29[c]	30	
	10	11	○	13	14	15	16	1:39	2	2496479		12	13	14	15	16	17	18			13	14	15	16	17	18	19		TŌBE 1839	1	2	3	4	5	6[d]	7	ṬER 2115
	17	18	◑	20	21	22	23	13:35	3	2496486		19	20	21	22	23	24	25			20	21	22	**23**	24	25*	26	Dà hán		8	9	10	11[e]	12	13	14	
	24	25	26	●	28	29	30	14:59	4	2496493	SHEVAT 5883	26	27	28	29	1	2	3	Wed 8h13m5p	MONTH 1 Guǐ-Wèi	27	28	29	1[a]	2	3	4			15	16	17	18	19	20	21	
FEBRUARY 2123	31	1	2	◐	4	5	6	16:41	5	2496500		4	5	6	7	8	9	10			5	6	7	8	*9*	10	11	Lì chūn		22	23	24	25	26	27	28	
	7	8	9	○	11	12	13	15:01	6	2496507		11	12	13	14	15	16	17			12	13	14	15[b]	16	17	18		MESHIR 1839	29	30	1	2	3	4	5	YAKĀTIT 2115
	14	15	16	17	◑	19	20	11:18	7	2496514		18	19	20	21	22	23	24			19	20	21	22	23	**24**	25	Yǔ shuǐ		6	7	8	9	10	11	12	
	21	22	23	24	25	●	27	5:02	8	2496521	ADAR 5883	25	26	27	28	29	30	1	Thu 20h57m6p	MONTH 2 Guǐ-Wèi	26	27	28	29	30	1	2			13	14	15	16	17	18	19	
MARCH 2123	28	1	2	3	4	◐	6	0:20	9	2496528		2	3	4	5	6	7	8			3	4	5	6	7	8	*9*	Jīng zhé		20	21	22	23	24	25	26	
	7	8	9	10	11	○	13	5:27	10	2496535		9	10	11	12	13	14[f]	15			10	11	12	13	14	15	16		PAREMOTEP 1839	27	28	29	30	1	2	3	MAGĀBIT 2115
	14	15	16	17	18	19	◑	7:58	11	2496542		16	17	18	19	20	21	22			17	18	19	20	21	22	23			4	5	6	7	8	9	10	
	21[b]	22	23	24	25	26	●	16:18	12	2496549		23	24	25	26	27	28	29			**24**	25	26*	27	28	29	30	Chūn fēn		11	12	13	14	15	16	17	
APRIL 2123	28	29	30	31	1	2	◐	8:12	13	2496556	NISAN 5883	1	2	3	4	5	6	7	Sat 9h41m7p	MONTH 3 Guǐ-Wèi	1	2	3	4	5	6	7			18	19	20	21	22	23	24	
	4	5	6	7	8	9	○	20:54	14	2496563		8	9	10	11	12	13	14			8	9[c]	10	11	12	13	14	Qīng míng	PARMOUTE 1839	25	26	27	28	29	30	1	MIYĀZYĀ 2115
	11	12	13	14	15	16	17		15	2496570		15[g]	16	17	18	19	20	21			15	16	17	18	19	20	21			2	3	4	5	6	7	8	
	18	◑	20	21	22	23	24	1:38	16	2496577		22	23	24	25	26	27	28			22	23	**24**	25	26	27	28	Gǔ yǔ		9[f]	10	11	12	13	14	15	
	25	●	27	28	29	30	1	1:27	17	2496584	IYYAR 5883	29	30	1	2	3	4	5	Sun 22h25m8p	MONTH 4 Guǐ-Wèi	29	1	2	3	4	5	6			16	17	18	19	20	21	22	
MAY 2123	◐	3	4	5	6	7	8	17:00	18	2496591		6	7	8	9	10	11	12			7	8	9	10	*11*	12	13	Lì xià		23	24	25	26	27	28	29[g]	
	9	○	11	12	13	14	15	13:00	19	2496598		13	14	15	16	17	18	19			14	15	16	17	18	19	20		PASHONS 1839	30	1	2	3	4	5	6	GENBOT 2115
	16	17	◑	19	20	21	22	15:22	20	2496605		20	21	22	23	24	25	26			21	22	23	24	25	**26**	27*	Xiǎo mǎn		7	8	9	10	11	12	13	
	23	24	●	26	27	28	29	9:16	21	2496612	SIVAN 5883	27	28	29	1	2	3	4	Tue 11h9m9p	MONTH 5 Guǐ-Wèi	28	29	1	2	3	4	5[d]			14	15	16	17	18	19	20	
JUNE 2123	30	31	◐	2	3	4	5	3:22	22	2496619		5	6[h]	7	8	9	10	11			6	7	8	9	10	11	12			21	22	23	24	25	26	27	
	6	7	8	○	10	11	12	5:02	23	2496626		12	13	14	15	16	17	18			*13*	14	15	16	17	18	19	Máng zhòng	PAŌNE 1839	28	29	30	1	2	3	4	SANĒ 2115
	13	14	15	16	◑	18	19	1:24	24	2496633		19	20	21	22	23	24	25			20	21	22	23	24	25	26			5	6	7	8	9	10	11	
	20	21[c]	22	●	24	25	26	16:34	25	2496640	TAMMUZ 5883	26	27	28	29	30	1	2	Wed 23h53m10p	LEAP MONTH 5 Guǐ-Wèi	27	28	**29**	30	1	2	3	Xià zhì		12	13	14	15	16	17	18	
JULY 2123	27	28	29	◐	1	2	3	15:54	26	2496647		3	4	5	6	7	8	9			4	5	6	7	8	9	10			19	20	21	22	23	24	25	
	4	5	6	7	○	9	10	20:04	27	2496654		10	11	12	13	14	15	16			11	12	13	*14*	15	16	17	Xiǎo shǔ	EPĒP 1839	26	27	28	29	30	1	2	ḤAMLĒ 2115
	11	12	13	14	15	◑	17	8:37	28	2496661		17	18	19	20	21	22	23			18	19	20	21	22	23	24			3	4	5	6	7	8	9	
	18	19	20	21	22	●	24	0:06	29	2496668	AV 5883	24	25	26	27	28	29	1	Fri 12h37m11p	MONTH 6 Guǐ-Wèi	25	26	27	28*	29	**1**	2	Dà shǔ		10	11	12	13	14	15	16	
	25	26	27	28	29	◐	31	6:57	30	2496675		2	3	4	5	6	7	8			3	4	5	6	7	8	9			17	18	19	20	21	22	23	
AUGUST 2123	1	2	3	4	5	6	○	9:30	31	2496682		9[i]	10	11	12	13	14	15			10	11	12	13	14	15	16			24	25	26	27	28	29	30	
	8	9	10	11	12	13	◑	14:16	32	2496689		16	17	18	19	20	21	22			*17*	18	19	20	21	22	23	Lì qiū	MESORĒ 1839	1	2	3	4	5	6	7	NAḤASĒ 2115
	15	16	17	18	19	20	●	8:49	33	2496696		23	24	25	26	27	28	29			24	25	26	27	28	29	1			8	9	10	11	12	13[h]	14	
	22	23	24	25	26	27	28		34	2496703	ELUL 5883	30	1	2	3	4	5	6	Sun 1h21m12p	MONTH 7 Guǐ-Wèi	2	**3**	4	5	6	7[e]	8	Chǔ shǔ		15	16	17	18	19	20	21	
SEPTEMBER 2123	◐	30	31	1	2	3	4	0:21	35	2496710		7	8	9	10	11	12	13			9	10	11	12	13	14	15[f]			22	23	24	25	26	27	28	
	○	6	7	8	9	10	11	21:22	36	2496717		14	15	16	17	18	19	20			16	17	18	*19*	20	21	22	Bái lù	EPAG. 1839	29	30	1	2	3	4	5	PĀG. 2115
	◑	13	14	15	16	17	18	19:36	37	2496724		21	22	23	24	25	26	27			23	24	25	26	27	28	29		THOOUT 1840	6	1[a]	2	3	4	5	6	MASKARAM 2116
	●	20	21	22	23[d]	24	25	19:42	38	2496731	TISHRI 5884	28	29	1[a]	2[a]	3	4	5	Mon 14h5m13p	MONTH 8 Guǐ-Wèi	30*	1	2	3	**4**	5	6	Qiū fēn		7	8	9	10	11	12	13	
OCTOBER 2123	26	◐	28	29	30	1	2	19:13	39	2496738		6	7	8	9	10[b]	11	12			7	8	9	10	11	12	13			14	15	16	17[b]	18	19	20	
	3	4	○	6	7	8	9	8:12	40	2496745		13	14	15[c]	16	17	18	19			14	15[g]	16	17	18	19	*20*	Hán lù		21	22	23	24	25	26	27	
	10	11	◑	13	14	15	16	1:50	41	2496752		20	21	22	23	24	25	26			21	22	23	24	25	26	27		PAOPE 1840	28	29	30	1	2	3	4	TEQEMT 2116
	17	18	●	20	21	22	23	9:38	42	2496759	HESHVAN 5884	27	28	29	30	1	2	3	Wed 2h49m14p	MONTH 9 Guǐ-Wèi	28	29	1	2	3	4	5			5	6	7	8	9	10	11	
	24	25	26	◐	28	29	30	14:09	43	2496766		4	5	6	7	8	9	10			**6**	7	8	9[h]	10	11	12	Shuāng jiàng		12	13	14	15	16	17	18	
NOVEMBER 2123	31	1	2	○	4	5	6	18:43	44	2496773		11	12	13	14	15	16	17			13	14	15	16	17	18	19			19	20	21	22	23	24	25	
	7	8	9	◑	11	12	13	10:10	45	2496780		18	19	20	21	22	23	24			20	*21*	22	23	24	25	26	Lì dōng	ATHŌR 1840	26	27	28	29	30	1	2	ḤEDĀR 2116
	14	15	16	17	●	19	20	2:47	46	2496787	KISLEV 5884	25	26	27	28	29	1	2	Thu 15h33m15p	MONTH 10 Guǐ-Wèi	27	28	29	30	1*	2	3			3	4	5	6	7	8	9	
	21	22	23	24	25	◐	27	7:46	47	2496794		3	4	5	6	7	8	9			4	5	**6**	7	8	9	10	Xiǎo xuě		10	11	12	13	14	15	16	
DECEMBER 2123	28	29	30	1	2	○	4	5:21	48	2496801		10	11	12	13	14	15	16			11	12	13	14	15	16	17			17	18	19	20	21	22	23	
	5	6	7	8	◑	10	11	21:34	49	2496808		17	18	19[d]	20	21	22	23			18	19	*20*	21	22	23	24	Dà xuě		24	25	26	27	28	29	30	
	12	13	14	15	16	●	18	22:10	50	2496815		24	25[e]	26[e]	27[e]	28[e]	29[e]	30[e]		MONTH 11* Guǐ-Wèi	25	26	27	28	29	30	1		KOIAK 1840	1	2	3	4	5	6	7	TĀKHŚĀŚ 2116
	19	20	21	22[e]	23	24	◐	23:03	51	2496822	TEVETH 5884	1[e]	2[e]	3	4	5	6	7	Sat 4h17m16p		2	3	4	**5**[i]	6	7	8	Dōng zhì		8	9	10	11	12	13	14	
	26	27	28	29	30	31	○	16:10	52	2496829		8	9	10	11	12	13	14			9	10	11	12	13	14	15			15	16	17	18	19	20	21	

[a]New Year
[b]Spring (2:47)
[c]Summer (18:48)
[d]Autumn (11:28)
[e]Winter (9:44)
● New moon
◐ First quarter moon
○ Full moon
◑ Last quarter moon

[a]New Year
[b]Yom Kippur
[c]Sukkot
[d]Winter starts
[e]Ḥanukkah
[f]Purim
[g]Passover
[h]Shavuot
[i]Fast of Av

‡Leap year
[a]New Year (4821, Sheep)
[b]Lantern Festival
[c]Qīngmíng
[d]Dragon Festival
[e]Qīqiǎo
[f]Hungry Ghosts
[g]Mid-Autumn Festival
[h]Double-Ninth Festival
[i]Dōngzhì
*Start of 60-name cycle

‡Leap year
[a]New Year
[b]Building of the Cross
[c]Christmas
[d]Jesus's Circumcision
[e]Epiphany
[f]Easter
[g]Mary's Announcement
[h]Jesus's Transfiguration

PERSIAN (ASTRONOMICAL) 1501/1502	Sun	Mon	Tue	Wed	Thu	Fri	Sat
	6	7	8	9	10	11	12
DEY 1501	13	14	15	16	17	18	19
	20	21	22	23	24	25	26
	27	28	29	30	*1*	2	3
	4	5	6	7	8	9	10
BAHMAN 1501	11	12	13	14	15	16	17
	18	19	20	21	22	23	24
	25	26	27	28	29	30	*1*
	2	3	4	5	6	7	8
ESFAND 1501	9	10	11	12	13	14	15
	16	17	18	19	20	21	22
	23	24	25	26	27	28	29
	1[a]	2	3	4	5	6	7
FARVARDĪN 1502	8	9	10	11	12	13[b]	14
	15	16	17	18	19	20	21
	22	23	24	25	26	27	28
	29	30	31	*1*	2	3	4
ORDĪBEHEŠT 1502	5	6	7	8	9	10	11
	12	13	14	15	16	17	18
	19	20	21	22	23	24	25
	26	27	28	29	30	31	*1*
	2	3	4	5	6	7	8
XORDĀD 1502	9	10	11	12	13	14	15
	16	17	18	19	20	21	22
	23	24	25	26	27	28	29
	30	31	*1*	2	3	4	5
TĪR 1502	6	7	8	9	10	11	12
	13	14	15	16	17	18	19
	20	21	22	23	24	25	26
	27	28	29	30	31	*1*	2
MORDĀD 1502	3	4	5	6	7	8	9
	10	11	12	13	14	15	16
	17	18	19	20	21	22	23
	24	25	26	27	28	29	30
	31	*1*	2	3	4	5	6
SHAHRĪVAR 1502	7	8	9	10	11	12	13
	14	15	16	17	18	19	20
	21	22	23	24	25	26	27
	28	29	30	31	*1*	2	3
MEHR 1502	4	5	6	7	8	9	10
	11	12	13	14	15	16	17
	18	19	20	21	22	23	24
	25	26	27	28	29	30	*1*
	2	3	4	5	6	7	8
ABĀN 1502	9	10	11	12	13	14	15
	16	17	18	19	20	21	22
	23	24	25	26	27	28	29
	30	*1*	2	3	4	5	6
ĀZAR 1502	7	8	9	10	11	12	13
	14	15	16	17	18	19	20
	21	22	23	24	25	26	27
	28	29	30	*1*	2	3	4
DEY 1502	5	6	7	8	9	10	11

HINDU LUNAR 2179/2180‡	Sun	Mon	Tue	Wed	Thu	Fri	Sat
	29	30	1	2	3	4	5
PAUSHA 2179	6	7	8	9	10	11	12
	13	**14**	16	17	18	19	20
	21	22	23	*23*	24	25	26
	27	28	29	30	1	2	3
MĀGHA 2179	4	5	6	7	**8**	10	11
	12	13	14	15	16	17	18
	19	20	21	22	23	24	25
	25	26	27	28[h]	29	30	1
PHĀLGUNA 2179	**2**	4	5	6	7	8	9
	10	11	12	13	14	15[i]	16
	17	18	19	20	21	22	23
	24	25	26	27	28	29	30
	1[a]	2	3	4	5	6	**7**
CHAITRA 2180	9[b]	10	11	12	13	14	15
	16	17	18	*18*	19	20	21
	22	23	24	25	26	27	28
	29	**30**	2	3	4	5	6
VAIŚĀKHA 2180	7	8	9	10	11	12	13
	14	15	16	17	18	19	20
	21	22	23	24	25	26	27
	28	29	30	1	2	3	**4**
JYAISHṬHA 2180	6	7	8	9	10	11	12
	13	14	*14*	15	16	17	18
	19	20	21	22	23	24	25
	26	**27**	29	30	1	2	3
ĀSHĀḌHA 2180	4	5	6	7	8	9	10
	11	12	13	14	15	16	17
	18	19	20	21	22	23	24
	25	26	27	28	**29**	1	2
ŚRĀVAṆA 2180	3	4	5	6	7	8	9
	10	*10*	11	12	13	14	15
	16	17	18	19	20	21	22[c]
	24	25	26	27	28	29	30
LEAP BHĀDRAPADA 2180	1	2	3	4	5	6	7
	8	9	10	11	12	13	14
	15	16	17	18	19	20	21
	22	23	24	**25**	27	28	29
	30	1	2	3	4[d]	5	6
BHĀDRAPADA 2180	6	7	8	9	10	11	12
	13	14	15	16	17	18	**19**
	21	22	23	24	25	26	27
	28	29	30	1	2	3	4
ĀŚVINA 2180	5	6	7	8[e]	9[e]	10[e]	11
	12	13	14	15	16	17	18
	19	20	21	22	**23**	25	26
	27	28	29	30	*30*	1[f]	2
KĀRTTIKA 2180	3	4	5	6	7	8	9
	10	11	12	13	14	15	**16**
	18	19	20	21	22	23	24
	25	26	27	28	29	30	1
MĀRGAŚĪRA 2180	2	3	*3*	4	5	6	7
	8	9	**10**[g]	12	13	14	15

HINDU SOLAR 2044/2045	Sun	Mon	Tue	Wed	Thu	Fri	Sat
PAUSHA 2044	10	11	12	13	14	15	16
	17	18	19	20	21	22	23
	24	25	26	27	28	29	1[b]
MĀGHA 2044	2	3	4	5	6	7	8
	9	10	11	12	13	14	15
	16	17	18	19	20	21	22
	23	24	25	26	27	28	29
	30	1	2	3	4	5	6
PHĀLGUNA 2044	7	8	9	10	11	12	13
	14	15	16	17	18	19	20
	21	22	23	24	25	26	27
	28	29	1	2	3	4	5
CHAITRA 2044	6	7	8	9	10	11	12
	13	14	15	16	17	18	19
	20	21	22	23	24	25	26
	27	28	29	30	31	1[a]	2
VAIŚĀKHA 2045	3	4	5	6	7	8	9
	10	11	12	13	14	15	16
	17	18	19	20	21	22	23
	24	25	26	27	28	29	30
	31	1	2	3	4	5	6
JYAISHṬHA 2045	7	8	9	10	11	12	13
	14	15	16	17	18	19	20
	21	22	23	24	25	26	27
	28	29	30	31	1	2	3
ĀSHĀḌHA 2045	4	5	6	7	8	9	10
	11	12	13	14	15	16	17
	18	19	20	21	22	23	24
	25	26	27	28	29	30	31
	32	1	2	3	4	5	6
ŚRĀVAṆA 2045	7	8	9	10	11	12	13
	14	15	16	17	18	19	20
	21	22	23	24	25	26	27
	28	29	30	31	1	2	3
BHĀDRAPADA 2045	4	5	6	7	8	9	10
	11	12	13	14	15	16	17
	18	19	20	21	22	23	24
	25	26	27	28	29	30	31
	1	2	3	4	5	6	7
ĀŚVINA 2045	8	9	10	11	12	13	14
	15	16	17	18	19	20	21
	22	23	24	25	26	27	28
	29	30	31	1	2	3	4
KĀRTTIKA 2045	5	6	7	8	9	10	11
	12	13	14	15	16	17	18
	19	20	21	22	23	24	25
	26	27	28	29	30	1	2
MĀRGAŚĪRA 2045	3	4	5	6	7	8	9
	10	11	12	13	14	15	16
	17	18	19	20	21	22	23
	24	25	26	27	28	29	1
PAUSHA 2045	2	3	4	5	6	7	8
	9	10	11	12	13	14	15

ISLAMIC (ASTRONOMICAL) 1547/1548‡	Sun	Mon	Tue	Wed	Thu	Fri	Sat
	27	28	29	*1*	2	3	4
RAJAB 1547	5	6	7	8	9	10	11
	12	13	14	15	16	17	18
	19	20	21	22	23	24	25
	26	27[d]	28	29	30	*1*	2
SHA'BĀN 1547	3	4	5	6	7	8	9
	10	11	12	13	14	15	16
	17	18	19	20	21	22	23
	24	25	26	27	28	29	*1*[e]
RAMAḌĀN 1547	2	3	4	5	6	7	8
	9	10	11	12	13	14	15
	16	17	18	19	20	21	22
	23	24	25	26	27	28	29
	30	*1*[f]	2	3	4	5	6
SHAWWĀL 1547	7	8	9	10	11	12	13
	14	15	16	17	18	19	20
	21	22	23	24	25	26	27
	28	29	*1*	2	3	4	5
DHU AL-QA'DA 1547	6	7	8	9	10	11	12
	13	14	15	16	17	18	19
	20	21	22	23	24	25	26
	27	28	29	*1*	2	3	4
DHU AL-HIJJA 1547	5	6	7	8	9	10[g]	11
	12	13	14	15	16	17	18
	19	20	21	22	23	24	25
	26	27	28	29	30	*1*[a]	2
MUḤARRAM 1548	3	4	5	6	7	8	9
	10[b]	11	12	13	14	15	16
	17	18	19	20	21	22	23
	24	25	26	27	28	29	30
	1	2	3	4	5	6	7
ṢAFAR 1548	8	9	10	11	12	13	14
	15	16	17	18	19	20	21
	22	23	24	25	26	27	28
	29	*30*	1	2	3	4	5
RABĪ' I 1548	6	7	8	9	10	11	12[c]
	13	14	15	16	17	18	19
	20	21	22	23	24	25	26
	27	28	29	*1*	2	3	4
RABĪ' II 1548	5	6	7	8	9	10	11
	12	13	14	15	16	17	18
	19	20	21	22	23	24	25
	26	27	28	29	*1*	2	3
JUMĀDĀ I 1548	4	5	6	7	8	9	10
	11	12	13	14	15	16	17
	18	19	20	21	22	23	24
	25	26	27	28	29	30	*1*
JUMĀDĀ II 1548	2	3	4	5	6	7	8
	9	10	11	12	13	14	15
	16	17	18	19	20	21	22
	23	24	25	26	27	28	29
RAJAB 1548	*1*	2	3	4	5	6	7
	8	9	10	11	12	13	14

Julian (Sun)	Sun	Mon	Tue	Wed	Thu	Fri	Sat	GREGORIAN 2123
Dec 13	*27*	28	29	30	31	1	2	
	3	4	5	6	7	8[a]	9	JANUARY 2123
Dec 27	*10*	11	12	13	14	15[b]	16	
	17	18	19	20	21	22	23	
Jan 10	*24*	25	26	27	28	29	30	
	31	1	2	3	4	5	6	
Jan 24	*7*	8	9	10	11	12	13	FEBRUARY 2123
	14	15	16	17	18	19	20	
Feb 7	*21*	22	23	24[c]	25	26	27	
	28	1	2	3	4	5	6	
Feb 21	*7*[d]	8	9	10	11	12	13	MARCH 2123
	14	15	16	17	18	19	20	
Mar 7	*21*	22	23	24	25	26	27	
	28	29	30	31	1	2	3	
Mar 21	*4*	5	6	7	8	9	10	
	11[e]	12	13	14	15	16	17	APRIL 2123
Apr 4	*18*[f]	19	20	21	22	23	24	
	25	26	27	28	29	30	1	
Apr 18	2	3	4	5	6	7	8	
	9	10	11	12	13	14	15	MAY 2123
May 2	*16*	17	18	19	20	21	22	
	23	24	25	26	27	28	29	
May 16	*30*	31	1	2	3	4	5	
	6	7	8	9	10	11	12	JUNE 2123
May 30	*13*	14	15	16	17	18	19	
	20	21	22	23	24	25	26	
Jun 13	*27*	28	29	30	1	2	3	
	4	5	6	7	8	9	10	JULY 2123
Jun 27	*11*	12	13	14	15	16	17	
	18	19	20	21	22	23	24	
Jul 11	*25*	26	27	28	29	30	31	
	1	2	3	4	5	6	7	
Jul 25	*8*	9	10	11	12	13	14	AUGUST 2123
	15	16	17	18	19	20	21	
Aug 8	*22*	23	24	25	26	27	28	
	29	30	31	1	2	3	4	
Aug 22	*5*	6	7	8	9	10	11	SEPTEMBER 2123
	12	13	14	15	16	17	18	
Sep 5	*19*	20	21	22	23	24	25	
	26	27	28	29	30	1	2	
Sep 19	*3*	4	5	6	7	8	9	
	10	11	12	13	14	15	16	OCTOBER 2123
Oct 3	*17*	18	19	20	21	22	23	
	24	25	26	27	28	29	30	
Oct 17	*31*	1	2	3	4	5	6	
	7	8	9	10	11	12	13	NOVEMBER 2123
Oct 31	*14*	15	16	17	18	19	20	
	21	22	23	24	25	26	27	
Nov 14	*28*[g]	29	30	1	2	3	4	
	5	6	7	8	9	10	11	DECEMBER 2123
Nov 28	*12*	13	14	15	16	17	18	
	19	20	21	22	23	24	25[h]	
Dec 12	*26*	27	28	29	30	31	1	

Persian: [a]New Year; [b]Sizdeh Bedar

Hindu Lunar: ‡Leap year; [a]New Year (Subhānu); [b]Birthday of Rāma; [c]Birthday of Krishna; [d]Ganēśa Chaturthī; [e]Dashara; [f]Diwali; [g]Birthday of Vishnu; [h]Night of Śiva; [i]Holi

Hindu Solar: [a]New Year (Vilamba); [b]Pongal

Islamic: ‡Leap year; [a]New Year; [b]'Ashūrā'; [c]Prophet's Birthday; [d]Ascent of the Prophet; [e]Start of Ramaḍān; [f]'Id al-Fiṭr; [g]'Id al-'Aḍḥā

Gregorian: [a]Orthodox Christmas; [b]Julian New Year; [c]Ash Wednesday; [d]Feast of Orthodoxy; [e]Easter; [f]Orthodox Easter; [g]Advent; [h]Christmas

2124

Gregorian month	GREGORIAN 2124‡ (Sun Mon Tue Wed Thu Fri Sat)	Lunar Phases	ISO WEEK (Mon)	JULIAN DAY (Sun noon)	Hebrew month	HEBREW 5884/5885‡ (Sun Mon Tue Wed Thu Fri Sat)	Molad	Chinese month	CHINESE Guǐ-Wèi‡/Jiă-Shēn (Sun Mon Tue Wed Thu Fri Sat)	Solar Term	Coptic month	COPTIC 1840/1841 (Sun Mon Tue Wed Thu Fri Sat)	Ethiopic month (ETHIOPIC 2116/2117)
	26 27 28 29 30 31 ○[a]	16:10	52	2496829		8 9 10 11 12 13 14		MONTH 11* Guǐ-Wèi	9 10 11 12 13 14 15		KOIAK 1840	15 16 17 18 19 20 21	TĀKHŚĀŚ 2116
JANUARY 2124	2 3 4 5 6 7 ◑	12:38	1	2496836	TEVETH 5884	15 16 17 18 19 20 21			16 17 18 19 20 21 22	Xiǎo hán		22 23 24 25 26 27 28	
	9 10 11 12 13 14 15		2	2496843		22 23 24 25 26 27 28			23 24 25 26 27 28 29			29[c] 30 1 2 3 4 5	
	● 17 18 19 20 21 22	17:51	3	2496850		29 1 2 3 4 5 6	Sun 17h 1m 17p		30 1* 2 3 4 5 6	Dà hán	TŌBE 1840	6[d] 7 8 9 10 11[e] 12	ṬER 2116
	23 ◐ 25 26 27 28 29	11:34	4	2496857	SHEVAT 5884	7 8 9 10 11 12 13		MONTH 12 Guǐ-Wèi	7 8 9 10 11 12 13			13 14 15 16 17 18 19	
	30 ○ 1 2 3 4 5	3:08	5	2496864		14 15 16 17 18 19 20			14 15 16 17 18 19 20	Lì chūn		20 21 22 23 24 25 26	
FEBRUARY 2124	6 ◑ 8 9 10 11 12	7:01	6	2496871		21 22 23 24 25 26 27			21 22 23 24 25 26 27			27 28 29 30 1 2 3	
	13 14 ● 16 17 18 19	11:54	7	2496878		28 29 30 1 2 3 4	Tue 5h 46m 0p		28 29 1[a] 2 3 4 5	Yǔ shuǐ	MESHIR 1840	4 5 6 7 8 9 10	YAKĀTIT 2116
	20 21 ◐ 23 24 25 26	21:20	8	2496885	ADAR 5884	5 6 7 8 9 10 11		MONTH 1 Jiă-Shēn	6 7 8 9 10 11 12			11 12 13 14 15 16 17	
	27 28 ○ 1 2 3 4	14:24	9	2496892		12 13 14[f] 15 16 17 18			13 14 15[b] 16 17 18 19			18 19 20 21 22 23 24	
MARCH 2124	5 6 7 ◑ 9 10 11	3:22	10	2496899		19 20 21 22 23 24 25			20 21 22 23 24 25 26	Jīng zhé		25 26 27 28 29 30 1	
	12 13 14 15 ● 17 18	3:16	11	2496906		26 27 28 29 1 2 3	Wed 18h 30m 1p		27 28 29 30 1 2* 3		PAREMOTEP 1840	2 3 4 5 6 7 8	MAGĀBIT 2116
	19 20[b] 21 22 ◐ 24 25	4:49	12	2496913	NISAN 5884	4 5 6 7 8 9 10		MONTH 2 Jiă-Shēn	4 5 6 7 8 9 10	Chūn fēn		9 10 11 12 13 14 15	
	26 27 28 29 ○ 31 1	2:25	13	2496920		11 12 13 14 15[g] 16 17			11 12 13 14 15 16 17			16 17 18 19 20 21 22	
APRIL 2124	2 3 4 5 ◑ 7 8	23:37	14	2496927		18 19 20 21 22 23 24			18 19 20[c] 21 22 23 24	Qīng míng		23 24 25 26 27 28 29	
	9 10 11 12 13 ● 15	15:47	15	2496934		25 26 27 28 29 30 1	Fri 7h 14m 2p		25 26 27 28 29 1 2		PARMOUTE 1840	30[f] 1 2 3 4 5 6	MIYĀZYĀ 2116
	16 17 18 19 20 ◐ 22	11:00	16	2496941	IYYAR 5884	2 3 4 5 6 7 8		MONTH 3 Jiă-Shēn	3 4 5 6 7 8 9	Gǔ yǔ		7 8 9 10 11 12 13	
	23 24 25 26 27 ○ 29	15:34	17	2496948		9 10 11 12 13 14 15			10 11 12 13 14 15 16			14 15 16 17 18 19 20	
	30 1 2 3 4 5 ◑	18:02	18	2496955		16 17 18 19 20 21 22			17 18 19 20 21 22 23	Lì xià		21 22 23 24 25 26 27	
MAY 2124	7 8 9 10 11 12 13		19	2496962		23 24 25 26 27 28 29			24 25 26 27 28 29 30			28 29[g] 30 1 2 3 4	
	● 15 16 17 18 19 ◐	1:49 17:06	20	2496969		1 2 3 4 5 6[h] 7	Sat 19h 58m 3p		1 2 3* 4 5 6 7		PASHONS 1840	5 6 7 8 9 10 11	GENBOT 2116
	21 22 23 24 25 26 27		21	2496976	SIVAN 5884	8 9 10 11 12 13 14		MONTH 4 Jiă-Shēn	8 9 10 11 12 13 14	Xiǎo mǎn		12 13 14 15 16 17 18	
	○ 29 30 31 1 2 3	5:55	22	2496983		15 16 17 18 19 20 21			15 16 17 18 19 20 21			19 20 21 22 23 24 25	
JUNE 2124	4 ◑ 6 7 8 9 10	9:40	23	2496990		22 23 24 25 26 27 28			22 23 24 25 26 27 28	Máng zhòng		26 27 28 29 30 1 2	
	11 ● 13 14 15 16 17	9:54	24	2496997		29 30 1 2 3 4 5	Mon 8h 42m 4p		29 1 2 3 4 5[d] 6		PAŌNE 1840	3 4 5 6 7 8 9	SANĒ 2116
	18 ◐ 20 21[c] 22 23 24	0:27	25	2497004	TAMMUZ 5884	6 7 8 9 10 11 12		MONTH 5 Jiă-Shēn	7 8 9 10 11 12 13	Xià zhì		10 11 12 13 14 15 16	
	25 ○ 27 28 29 30 1	21:00	26	2497011		13 14 15 16 17 18 19			14 15 16 17 18 19 20			17 18 19 20 21 22 23	
JULY 2124	2 3 ◑ 5 6 7 8	22:23	27	2497018		20 21 22 23 24 25 26			21 22 23 24 25 26 27	Xiǎo shǔ		24 25 26 27 28 29 30	
	9 10 ● 12 13 14 15	16:49	28	2497025		27 28 29 1 2 3 4	Tue 21h 26m 5p		28 29 30 1 2 3 4*		EPĒP 1840	1 2 3 4 5 6 7	ḤAMLĒ 2116
	16 17 ◐ 19 20 21 22	10:12	29	2497032	AV 5884	5 6 7 8 9[i] 10 11		MONTH 6 Jiă-Shēn	5 6 7 8 9 10 11	Dà shǔ		8 9 10 11 12 13 14	
	23 24 25 ○ 27 28 29	12:13	30	2497039		12 13 14 15 16 17 18			12 13 14 15 16 17 18			15 16 17 18 19 20 21	
	30 31 1 2 ◑ 4 5	8:28	31	2497046		19 20 21 22 23 24 25			19 20 21 22 23 24 25			22 23 24 25 26 27 28	
AUGUST 2124	6 7 8 ● 10 11 12	23:36	32	2497053		26 27 28 29 30 1 2	Thu 10h 10m 6p		26 27 28 29 1 2 3	Lì qiū	MESORĒ 1840	29 30 1 2 3 4 5	NAḤASĒ 2116
	13 14 15 ◐ 17 18 19	23:07	33	2497060	ELUL 5884	3 4 5 6 7 8 9		MONTH 7 Jiă-Shēn	4 5 6 7[e] 8 9 10			6 7 8 9 10 11 12	
	20 21 22 23 24 ○ 26	3:04	34	2497067		10 11 12 13 14 15 16			11 12 13 14 15[f] 16 17	Chǔ shǔ		13[h] 14 15 16 17 18 19	
	27 28 29 30 31 ◑ 2	16:28	35	2497074		17 18 19 20 21 22 23			18 19 20 21 22 23 24			20 21 22 23 24 25 26	
SEPTEMBER 2124	3 4 5 6 7 ● 9	7:24	36	2497081		24 25 26 27 28 29 1[a]	Fri 22h 54m 7p		25 26 27 28 29 1 2	Bái lù	EPAG. 1840	27 28 29 30 1 2 3	PĀG. 2116
	10 11 12 13 14 ◐ 16	15:20	37	2497088	TISHRI 5885	2[a] 3 4 5 6 7 8		MONTH 8 Jiă-Shēn	3 4 5 6* 7 8 9		THOOUT 1841	4 5 1[a] 2 3 4 5	MASKARAM 2117
	17 18 19 20 21 22[d] ○	17:22	38	2497095		9 10[b] 11 12 13 14 15[c]			10 11 12 13 14 15[g] 16	Qiū fēn		6 7 8 9 10 11 12	
	24 25 26 27 28 29 ◑	23:08	39	2497102		16 17 18 19 20 21 22			17 18 19 20 21 22 23			13 14 15 16 17[b] 18 19	
OCTOBER 2124	1 2 3 4 5 6 ●	17:24	40	2497109		23 24 25 26 27 28 29			24 25 26 27 28 29 30			20 21 22 23 24 25 26	
	8 9 10 11 12 13 14		41	2497116		30 1 2 3 4 5 6	Sun 11h 38m 8p		1 2 3 4 5 6 7	Hán lù		27 28 29 30 1 2 3	
	◐ 16 17 18 19 20 21	10:14	42	2497123	ḤESHVAN 5885	7 8 9 10 11 12 13		MONTH 9 Jiă-Shēn	8 9[h] 10 11 12 13 14		PAOPE 1841	4 5 6 7 8 9 10	ṬEQEMT 2117
	22 ○ 24 25 26 27 28	7:01	43	2497130		14 15 16 17 18 19 20			15 16 17 18 19 20 21	Shuāng jiàng		11 12 13 14 15 16 17	
	29 ◑ 31 1 2 3 4	5:31	44	2497137		21 22 23 24 25 26 27			22 23 24 25 26 27 28			18 19 20 21 22 23 24	
NOVEMBER 2124	5 ● 7 8 9 10 11	6:25	45	2497144		28 29 30 1 2 3 4	Tue 0h 22m 9p		29 1 2 3 4 5 6	Lì dōng		25 26 27 28 29 30 1	
	12 13 ◐ 15 16 17 18	6:36	46	2497151	KISLEV 5885	5 6 7 8 9 10 11		MONTH 10 Jiă-Shēn	7* 8 9 10 11 12 13		ATHŌR 1841	2 3 4 5 6 7 8	ḪEDĀR 2117
	19 20 ○ 22 23 24 25	19:51	47	2497158		12 13 14 15 16 17 18			14 15 16 17 18 19 20	Xiǎo xuě		9 10 11 12 13 14 15	
	26 27 ◑ 29 30 1 2	12:54	48	2497165		19 20 21 22 23 24 25[e]			21 22 23 24 25 26 27			16 17 18 19 20 21 22	
DECEMBER 2124	3 4 ● 6 7 8 9	22:32	49	2497172		26[e] 27[e] 28[e] 29[d][e] 30[e] 1[e] 2[e]	Wed 13h 6m 10p		28 29 30 1 2 3 4	Dà xuě		23 24 25 26 27 28 29	
	10 11 12 13 ◐ 15 16	2:54	50	2497179	TEVETH 5885	3 4 5 6 7 8 9		MONTH 11 Jiă-Shēn	5 6 7 8 9 10 11		KOIAK 1841	30 1 2 3 4 5 6	TĀKHŚĀŚ 2117
	17 18 19 20 ○[e] 22 23	7:44	51	2497186		10 11 12 13 14 15 16			12 13 14 15 16[i] 17 18	Dōng zhì		7 8 9 10 11 12 13	
	24 25 26 ◑ 28 29 30	22:28	52	2497193		17 18 19 20 21 22 23			19 20 21 22 23 24 25			14 15 16 17 18 19 20	
	31 1 2 3 ● 5 6	16:56	1	2497200		24 25 26 27 28 29 1	Fri 1h 50m 11p		26 27 28 29 30 1 2	Xiǎo hán		21 22 23 24 25 26 27	

‡Leap year
[a]New Year
[b]Spring (8:34)
[c]Summer (0:36)
[d]Autumn (17:17)
[e]Winter (15:33)
● New moon
◐ First quarter moon
○ Full moon
◑ Last quarter moon

‡Leap year
[a]New Year
[b]Yom Kippur
[c]Sukkot
[d]Winter starts
[e]Ḥanukkah
[f]Purim
[g]Passover
[h]Shavuot
[i]Fast of Av

‡Leap year
[a]New Year (4822, Monkey)
[b]Lantern Festival
[c]Qīngmíng
[d]Dragon Festival
[e]Qīqiǎo
[f]Hungry Ghosts
[g]Mid-Autumn Festival
[h]Double-Ninth Festival
[i]Dōngzhì
*Start of 60-name cycle

[a]New Year
[b]Building of the Cross
[c]Christmas
[d]Jesus's Circumcision
[e]Epiphany
[f]Easter
[g]Mary's Announcement
[h]Jesus's Transfiguration

PERSIAN (ASTRONOMICAL) 1502/1503‡

Month	Sun	Mon	Tue	Wed	Thu	Fri	Sat
DEY 1502	5	6	7	8	9	10	11
	12	13	14	15	16	17	18
	19	20	21	22	23	24	25
	26	27	28	29	30	1	2
BAHMAN 1502	3	4	5	6	7	8	9
	10	11	12	13	14	15	16
	17	18	19	20	21	22	23
	24	25	26	27	28	29	30
ESFAND 1502	1	2	3	4	5	6	7
	8	9	10	11	12	13	14
	15	16	17	18	19	20	21
	22	23	24	25	26	27	28
FARVARDĪN 1503	29	1[a]	2*	3	4	5	6
	7	8	9	10	11	12	13[b]
	14	15	16	17	18	19	20
	21	22	23	24	25	26	27
ORDĪBEHEŠT 1503	28	29	30	31	1	2	3
	4	5	6	7	8	9	10
	11	12	13	14	15	16	17
	18	19	20	21	22	23	24
	25	26	27	28	29	30	31
XORDĀD 1503	1	2	3	4	5	6	7
	8	9	10	11	12	13	14
	15	16	17	18	19	20	21
	22	23	24	25	26	27	28
TĪR 1503	29	30	31	1	2	3	4
	5	6	7	8	9	10	11
	12	13	14	15	16	17	18
	19	20	21	22	23	24	25
MORDĀD 1503	26	27	28	29	30	31	1
	2	3	4	5	6	7	8
	9	10	11	12	13	14	15
	16	17	18	19	20	21	22
	23	24	25	26	27	28	29
SHAHRĪVAR 1503	30	31	1	2	3	4	5
	6	7	8	9	10	11	12
	13	14	15	16	17	18	19
	20	21	22	23	24	25	26
MEHR 1503	27	28	29	30	31	1	2
	3	4	5	6	7	8	9
	10	11	12	13	14	15	16
	17	18	19	20	21	22	23
	24	25	26	27	28	29	30
ĀBĀN 1503	1	2	3	4	5	6	7
	8	9	10	11	12	13	14
	15	16	17	18	19	20	21
	22	23	24	25	26	27	28
ĀZAR 1503	29	30	1	2	3	4	5
	6	7	8	9	10	11	12
	13	14	15	16	17	18	19
	20	21	22	23	24	25	26
DEY 1503	27	28	29	30	1	2	3
	4	5	6	7	8	9	10
	11	12	13	14	15	16	17

‡Leap year
[a]New Year (or next day)
*Near New Year: 0′20″
[b]Sizdeh Bedar

HINDU LUNAR 2180‡/2181

Month	Sun	Mon	Tue	Wed	Thu	Fri	Sat
MĀRGAŚIRA 2180	8	9	**10**	12	13	14	15
	16	17	18	19	20	21	22
	23	24	25	26	27	28	29
PAUSHA 2180	30	1	2	3	4	5	6
	7	8	9	10	11	12	13
	14	**15**	17	18	19	20	21
	22	23	24	25	25	26	27
LEAP PHĀLGUNA 2180	28	29	30	1	2	3	4
	5	6	7	8	**9**	11	12
	13	14	15	16	17	18	19
	20	21	22	23	24	25	26
PHĀLGUNA 2180	27	28	28[h]	29	30	1	2
	3	5	6	7	8	9	10
	11	12	13	14	15[i]	16	17
	18	19	20	21	22	23	24
CHAITRA 2181	25	26	27	28	29	30	1[a]
	2	3	4	5	6	**7**	9[b]
	10	11	12	13	14	15	16
	17	18	19	20	21	22	22
	23	24	25	26	27	28	29
VAIŚĀKHA 2181	30	**1**	3	4	5	6	7
	8	9	10	11	12	13	14
	15	16	17	18	19	20	21
	22	23	24	25	26	27	28
JYAISHṬHA 2181	29	30	1	2	3	**4**	6
	7	8	9	10	11	12	13
	14	15	16	17	18	18	19
	20	21	22	23	24	25	**26**
ĀSHĀḌHA 2181	28	29	30	1	2	3	4
	5	6	7	8	9	10	11
	12	13	14	15	16	17	18
	19	20	21	22	23	24	25
ŚRĀVAṆA 2181	26	27	28	**29**	1	2	3
	4	5	6	7	8	9	10
	11	12	13	14	15	15	16
	17	18	19	20	21	22[c]	24
BHĀDRAPADA 2181	25	26	27	28	29	30	1
	2	3[d]	4	5	6	7	8
	9	10	11	12	13	14	15
	16	17	18	19	20	21	22
	23	24	25	**26**	28	29	30
ĀŚVINA 2181	1	2	3	4	5	6	7
	8[e]	9[e]	10[e]	10[e]	11	12	13
	14	15	16	17	18	**19**	21
	22	23	24	25	26	27	28
KĀRTTIKA 2181	29	30	1[f]	2	3	4	5
	6	7	8	9	10	11	12
	13	14	15	16	17	18	19
	20	21	22	23	**24**	26	27
MĀRGAŚIRA 2181	28	29	30	1	2	3	3
	4	5	6	7	8	9	10
	11[g]	12	13	14	15	16	**17**
	19	20	21	22	23	24	25
	26	27	28	29	30	1	2

‡Leap year
[a]New Year (Tāraṇa)
[b]Birthday of Rāma
[c]Birthday of Krishna
[d]Ganēśa Chaturthī
[e]Dashara
[f]Diwali
[g]Birthday of Vishnu
[h]Night of Śiva
[i]Holi

HINDU SOLAR 2045/2046

Month	Sun	Mon	Tue	Wed	Thu	Fri	Sat
PAUSHA 2045	9	10	11	12	13	14	15
	16	17	18	19	20	21	22
	23	24	25	26	27	28	29
MĀGHA 2045	1[b]	2	3	4	5	6	7
	8	9	10	11	12	13	14
	15	16	17	18	19	20	21
	22	23	24	25	26	27	28
PHĀLGUNA 2045	29	30	1	2	3	4	5
	6	7	8	9	10	11	12
	13	14	15	16	17	18	19
	20	21	22	23	24	25	26
CHAITRA 2045	27	28	29	30	1	2	3
	4	5	6	7	8	9	10
	11	12	13	14	15	16	17
	18	19	20	21	22	23	24
VAIŚĀKHA 2046	25	26	27	28	29	30	1[a]
	2	3	4	5	6	7	8
	9	10	11	12	13	14	15
	16	17	18	19	20	21	22
	23	24	25	26	27	28	29
JYAISHṬHA 2046	30	31	1	2	3	4	5
	6	7	8	9	10	11	12
	13	14	15	16	17	18	19
	20	21	22	23	24	25	26
ĀSHĀḌHA 2046	27	28	29	30	31	1	2
	3	4	5	6	7	8	9
	10	11	12	13	14	15	16
	17	18	19	20	21	22	23
	24	25	26	27	28	29	30
ŚRĀVAṆA 2046	31	32	1	2	3	4	5
	6	7	8	9	10	11	12
	13	14	15	16	17	18	19
	20	21	22	23	24	25	26
BHĀDRAPADA 2046	27	28	29	30	31	32	1
	2	3	4	5	6	7	8
	9	10	11	12	13	14	15
	16	17	18	19	20	21	22
	23	24	25	26	27	28	29
ĀŚVINA 2046	30	31	1	2	3	4	5
	6	7	8	9	10	11	12
	13	14	15	16	17	18	19
	20	21	22	23	24	25	26
KĀRTTIKA 2046	27	28	29	30	1	2	3
	4	5	6	7	8	9	10
	11	12	13	14	15	16	17
	18	19	20	21	22	23	24
MĀRGAŚIRA 2046	25	26	27	28	29	30	1
	2	3	4	5	6	7	8
	9	10	11	12	13	14	15
	16	17	18	19	20	21	22
	23	24	25	26	27	28	29
PAUSHA 2046	1	2	3	4	5	6	7
	8	9	10	11	12	13	14
	15	16	17	18	19	20	21

[a]New Year (Vikārin)
[b]Pongal

ISLAMIC (ASTRONOMICAL) 1548‡/1549

Month	Sun	Mon	Tue	Wed	Thu	Fri	Sat
RAJAB 1548	8	9	10	11	12	13	14
	15	16	17	18	19	20	21
	22	23	24	25	26	27[d]	28
SHA'BĀN 1548	29	30	1	2	3	4	5
	6	7	8	9	10	11	12
	13	14	15	16	17	18	19
	20	21	22	23	24	25	26
RAMAḌĀN 1548	27	28	29	30	1[e]	2	3
	4	5	6	7	8	9	10
	11	12	13	14	15	16	17
	18	19	20	21	22	23	24
SHAWWĀL 1548	25	26	27	28	29	1[f]	2
	3	4	5	6	7	8	9
	10	11	12	13	14	15	16
	17	18	19	20	21	22	23
	24	25	26	27	28	29	30
DHU AL-QA'DA 1548	1	2	3	4	5	6	7
	8	9	10	11	12	13	14
	15	16	17	18	19	20	21
	22	23	24	25	26	27	28
DHU AL-ḤIJJA 1548	29	1	2	3	4	5	6
	7	8	9	10[g]	11	12	13
	14	15	16	17	18	19	20
	21	22	23	24	25	26	27
MUḤARRAM 1549	28	29	30	1[a]	2	3	4
	5	6	7	8	9	10[b]	11
	12	13	14	15	16	17	18
	19	20	21	22	23	24	25
ṢAFAR 1549	26	27	28	29	1	2	3
	4	5	6	7	8	9	10
	11	12	13	14	15	16	17
	18	19	20	21	22	23	24
RABĪ' I 1549	25	26	27	28	29	30	1
	2	3	4	5	6	7	8
	9	10	11	12[c]	13	14	15
	16	17	18	19	20	21	22
	23	24	25	26	27	28	29
RABĪ' II 1549	1	2	3	4	5	6	7
	8	9	10	11	12	13	14
	15	16	17	18	19	20	21
	22	23	24	25	26	27	28
JUMĀDĀ I 1549	29	30	1	2	3	4	5
	6	7	8	9	10	11	12
	13	14	15	16	17	18	19
	20	21	22	23	24	25	26
JUMĀDĀ II 1549	27	28	29	1	2	3	4
	5	6	7	8	9	10	11
	12	13	14	15	16	17	18
	19	20	21	22	23	24	25
RAJAB 1549	26	27	28	29	1	2	3
	4	5	6	7	8	9	10
	11	12	13	14	15	16	17
	18	19	20	21	22	23	24
	25	26	27	28	29	30	1

‡Leap year
[a]New Year
[b]'Ashūrā'
[c]Prophet's Birthday
[d]Ascent of the Prophet
[e]Start of Ramaḍān
[f]'Īd al-Fiṭr
[g]'Īd al-'Aḍḥā

GREGORIAN 2124‡

Julian† (Sun)	Sun	Mon	Tue	Wed	Thu	Fri	Sat	Month
Dec 12	26	27	28	29	30	31	1	
	2	3	4	5	6	7	8[a]	JANUARY 2124
Dec 26	9	10	11	12	13	14	15[b]	
	16	17	18	19	20	21	22	
Jan 9	23	24	25	26	27	28	29	
	30	31	1	2	3	4	5	
Jan 23	6	7	8	9	10	11	12	FEBRUARY 2124
	13	14	15	16[c]	17	18	19	
Feb 6	20	21	22	23	24	25	26	
	27[d]	28	29	1	2	3	4	
Feb 20	5	6	7	8	9	10	11	MARCH 2124
	12	13	14	15	16	17	18	
Mar 5	19	20	21	22	23	24	25	
	26	27	28	29	30	31	1	
Mar 19	2[e]	3	4	5	6	7	8	APRIL 2124
	9[f]	10	11	12	13	14	15	
Apr 2	16	17	18	19	20	21	22	
	23	24	25	26	27	28	29	
Apr 16	30	1	2	3	4	5	6	
	7	8	9	10	11	12	13	MAY 2124
Apr 30	14	15	16	17	18	19	20	
	21	22	23	24	25	26	27	
May 14	28	29	30	31	1	2	3	
	4	5	6	7	8	9	10	JUNE 2124
May 28	11	12	13	14	15	16	17	
	18	19	20	21	22	23	24	
Jun 11	25	26	27	28	29	30	1	
	2	3	4	5	6	7	8	JULY 2124
Jun 25	9	10	11	12	13	14	15	
	16	17	18	19	20	21	22	
Jul 9	23	24	25	26	27	28	29	
	30	31	1	2	3	4	5	
Jul 23	6	7	8	9	10	11	12	AUGUST 2124
	13	14	15	16	17	18	19	
Aug 6	20	21	22	23	24	25	26	
	27	28	29	30	31	1	2	
Aug 20	3	4	5	6	7	8	9	SEPTEMBER 2124
	10	11	12	13	14	15	16	
Sep 3	17	18	19	20	21	22	23	
	24	25	26	27	28	29	30	
Sep 17	1	2	3	4	5	6	7	OCTOBER 2124
	8	9	10	11	12	13	14	
Oct 1	15	16	17	18	19	20	21	
	22	23	24	25	26	27	28	
Oct 15	29	30	31	1	2	3	4	
	5	6	7	8	9	10	11	NOVEMBER 2124
Oct 29	12	13	14	15	16	17	18	
	19	20	21	22	23	24	25	
Nov 12	26	27	28	29	30	1	2	
	3[g]	4	5	6	7	8	9	DECEMBER 2124
Nov 26	10	11	12	13	14	15	16	
	17	18	19	20	21	22	23	
Dec 10	24	25[h]	26	27	28	29	30	
	31	1	2	3	4	5	6	

‡Leap year
[a]Orthodox Christmas
[b]Julian New Year
[c]Ash Wednesday
[d]Feast of Orthodoxy
[e]Easter
[f]Orthodox Easter
[g]Advent
[h]Christmas

2125

GREGORIAN 2125

Month	ISO Week (Mon)	Sun	Mon	Tue	Wed	Thu	Fri	Sat	Lunar Phases	Julian Day (Sun noon)
JANUARY 2125	1	31	1[a]	2	3	●	5	6	16:56	2497200
	2	7	8	9	10	11	◐	13	21:26	2497207
	3	14	15	16	17	18	○	20	18:39	2497214
	4	21	22	23	24	25	◑	27	11:01	2497221
	5	28	29	30	31	1	2	●	12:14	2497228
FEBRUARY 2125	6	4	5	6	7	8	9	10		2497235
	7	◐	12	13	14	15	16	17	12:48	2497242
	8	○	19	20	21	22	23	24	4:51	2497249
	9	◑	26	27	28	1	2	3	2:27	2497256
MARCH 2125	10	4	●	6	7	8	9	10	6:53	2497263
	11	11	12	◐	14	15	16	17	0:18	2497270
	12	18	○	20[b]	21	22	23	24	14:48	2497277
	13	25	◑	27	28	29	30	31	19:55	2497284
APRIL 2125	14	1	2	●	4	5	6	7	23:38	2497291
	15	8	9	10	◐	12	13	14	8:17	2497298
	16	15	16	17	○	19	20	21	1:02	2497305
	17	22	23	24	◑	26	27	28	14:16	2497312
	18	29	30	1	2	●	4	5	13:40	2497319
MAY 2125	19	6	7	8	9	◐	11	12	13:54	2497326
	20	13	14	15	16	○	18	19	11:57	2497333
	21	20	21	22	23	24	◑	26	8:25	2497340
	22	27	28	29	30	31	1	●	0:47	2497347
JUNE 2125	23	3	4	5	6	7	◐	9	18:41	2497354
	24	10	11	12	13	14	○	16	23:54	2497361
	25	17	18	19	20	21[c]	22	23		2497368
	26	◑	25	26	27	28	29	30	1:32	2497375
JULY 2125	27	●	2	3	4	5	6	7	9:27	2497382
	28	◐	9	10	11	12	13	14	0:08	2497389
	29	○	16	17	18	19	20	21	13:08	2497396
	30	22	◑	24	25	26	27	28	16:55	2497403
	31	29	●	31	1	2	3	4	16:41	2497410
AUGUST 2125	32	5	◐	7	8	9	10	11	7:38	2497417
	33	12	13	○	15	16	17	18	3:47	2497424
	34	19	20	21	◑	23	24	25	6:04	2497431
	35	26	27	●	29	30	31	1	23:43	2497438
SEPTEMBER 2125	36	2	3	◐	5	6	7	8	18:07	2497445
	37	9	10	11	○	13	14	15	19:44	2497452
	38	16	17	18	19	◑	21	22[d]	16:54	2497459
	39	23	24	25	26	●	28	29	7:40	2497466
OCTOBER 2125	40	30	1	2	3	◐	5	6	8:10	2497473
	41	7	8	9	10	11	○	13	12:24	2497480
	42	14	15	16	17	18	19	◑	1:49	2497487
	43	21	22	23	24	25	●	27	17:27	2497494
	44	28	29	30	31	1	2	◐	1:52	2497501
NOVEMBER 2125	45	4	5	6	7	8	9	10		2497508
	46	○	12	13	14	15	16	17	4:44	2497515
	47	◑	19	20	21	22	23	24	9:37	2497522
	48	●	26	27	28	29	30	1	5:29	2497529
DECEMBER 2125	49	◐	3	4	5	6	7	8	22:31	2497536
	50	9	○	11	12	13	14	15	19:46	2497543
	51	16	◑	18	19	20	21[e]	22	17:20	2497550
	52	23	●	25	26	27	28	29	19:50	2497557
	1	30	31	◐	2	3	4	5	20:28	2497564

HEBREW 5885‡/5886

ISO Week	Month	Sun	Mon	Tue	Wed	Thu	Fri	Sat	Molad
1		24	25	26	27	28	29	1	Fri 1h50m11p
2	SHEVAT 5885	2	3	4	5	6	7	8	
3		9	10	11	12	13	14	15	
4		16	17	18	19	20	21	22	
5		23	24	25	26	27	28	29	
6	ADAR I 5885	30	1	2	3	4	5	6	Sat 14h34m12p
7		7	8	9	10	11	12	13	
8		14	15	16	17	18	19	20	
9		21	22	23	24	25	26	27	
10		28	29	30	1	2	3	4	Mon 3h18m13p
11	ADAR II 5885	5	6	7	8	9	10	11	
12		12	13	14[f]	15	16	17	18	
13		19	20	21	22	23	24	25	
14		26	27	28	29	1	2	3	Tue 16h2m14p
15	NISAN 5885	4	5	6	7	8	9	10	
16		11	12	13	14	15[g]	16	17	
17		18	19	20	21	22	23	24	
18		25	26	27	28	29	30	1	Thu 4h46m15p
19	IYAR 5885	2	3	4	5	6	7	8	
20		9	10	11	12	13	14	15	
21		16	17	18	19	20	21	22	
22		23	24	25	26	27	28	29	
23		1	2	3	4	5	6[h]	7	Fri 17h30m16p
24	SIVAN 5885	8	9	10	11	12	13	14	
25		15	16	17	18	19	20	21	
26		22	23	24	25	26	27	28	
27		29	30	1	2	3	4	5	Sun 6h14m17p
28	TAMMUZ 5885	6	7	8	9	10	11	12	
29		13	14	15	16	17	18	19	
30		20	21	22	23	24	25	26	
31		27	28	29	1	2	3	4	Mon 18h59m0p
32	AV 5885	5	6	7	8	9[i]	10	11	
33		12	13	14	15	16	17	18	
34		19	20	21	22	23	24	25	
35		26	27	28	29	30	1	2	Wed 7h43m1p
36	ELUL 5885	3	4	5	6	7	8	9	
37		10	11	12	13	14	15	16	
38		17	18	19	20	21	22	23	
39		24	25	26	27	28	29	1[a]	Thu 20h27m2p
40	TISHRI 5886	2[a]	3	4	5	6	7	8	
41		9	10[b]	11	12	13	14	15[c]	
42		16	17	18	19	20	21	22	
43		23	24	25	26	27	28	29	
44		30	1	2	3	4	5	6	Sat 9h11m3p
45	HESHVAN 5886	7	8	9	10	11	12	13	
46		14	15	16	17	18	19	20	
47		21	22	23	24	25	26	27	
48		28	29	30	1	2	3	4	Sun 21h55m4p
49	KISLEV 5886	5	6	7	8	9[d]	10	11	
50		12	13	14	15	16	17	18	
51		19	20	21	22	23	24	25[e]	
52		26[e]	27[e]	28[e]	29[e]	30[e]	1[e]	2[e]	Tue 10h39m5p
1	TEVETH 5886	3	4	5	6	7	8	9	

CHINESE Jiă-Shēn/Yĭ-Yŏu

ISO Week	Month	Sun	Mon	Tue	Wed	Thu	Fri	Sat	Solar Term
1		26	27	28	29	30	*1*	2	Xiǎo hán
2	MONTH 12 Jiă-Shēn	3	4	5	6	7*	8	9	
3		10	11	12	13	14	15	**16**	Dà hán
4		17	18	19	20	21	22	23	
5		24	25	26	27	28	29	1[a]	
6	MONTH 1 Yĭ-Yŏu	*2*	3	4	5	6	7	8	Lì chūn
7		9	10	11	12	13	14	15[b]	
8		16	**17**	18	19	20	21	22	Yǔ shuǐ
9		23	24	25	26	27	28	29	
10		30	*1*	2	3	4	5	6	Jīng zhé
11	MONTH 2 Yĭ-Yŏu	7	8*	9	10	11	12	13	
12		14	15	**16**	17	18	19	20	Chūn fēn
13		21	22	23	24	25	26	27	
14		28	29	30	1	2[c]	3	4	Qīng míng
15	MONTH 3 Yĭ-Yŏu	5	6	7	8	9	10	11	
16		12	13	14	15	16	**17**	18	Gǔ yǔ
17		19	20	21	22	23	24	25	
18		26	27	28	29	1	2	*3*	Lì xià
19	MONTH 4 Yĭ-Yŏu	4	5	6	7	8	9*	10	
20		11	12	13	14	15	16	17	
21		18	**19**	20	21	22	23	24	Xiǎo mǎn
22		25	26	27	28	29	30	1	
23	MONTH 5 Yĭ-Yŏu	2	3	*4*	5[d]	6	7	8	Máng zhòng
24		9	10	11	12	13	14	15	
25		16	17	18	19	**20**	21	22	Xià zhì
26		23	24	25	26	27	28	29	
27	MONTH 6 Yĭ-Yŏu	1	2	3	4	5	6	*7*	Xiǎo shǔ
28		8	9	10*	11	12	13	14	
29		15	16	17	18	19	20	21	
30		22	**23**	24	25	26	27	28	Dà shǔ
31		29	30	1	2	3	4	5	
32	MONTH 7 Yĭ-Yŏu	6	7[e]	*8*	9	10	11	12	Lì qiū
33		13	14	15[f]	16	17	18	19	
34		20	21	22	23	**24**	25	26	Chǔ shǔ
35		27	28	29	1	2	3	4	
36	MONTH 8 Yĭ-Yŏu	5	6	7	8	9	*10*	11*	Bái lù
37		12	13	14	15[g]	16	17	18	
38		19	20	21	22	23	24	25	
39		**26**	27	28	29	1	2	3	Qiū fēn
40	MONTH 9 Yĭ-Yŏu	4	5	6	7	8	9[h]	10	
41		11	*12*	13	14	15	16	17	Hán lù
42		18	19	20	21	22	23	24	
43		25	26	**27**	28	29	30	1	Shuāng jiàng
44	MONTH 10 Yĭ-Yŏu	2	3	4	5	6	7	8	
45		9	10	11	*12**	13	14	15	Lì dōng
46		16	17	18	19	20	21	22	
47		23	24	25	26	**27**	28	29	Xiǎo xuě
48	MONTH 11 Yĭ-Yŏu	1	2	3	4	5	6	7	
49		8	9	10	11	12	*13*	14	Dà xuě
50		15	16	17	18	19	20	21	
51		22	23	24	25	26	27	**28**[i]	Dōng zhì
52	MONTH 12 Yĭ-Yŏu	29	30	1	2	3	4	5	
1		6	7	8	9	10	11	*12*	Xiǎo hán

COPTIC 1841/1842 — ETHIOPIC 2117/2118

ISO Week	Coptic Month	Sun	Mon	Tue	Wed	Thu	Fri	Sat	Ethiopic Month
1	KOIAK 1841	21	22	23	24	25	26	27	TĀKHŚĀŚ 2117
2		28	29[c]	30	1	2	3	4	
3	TÔBE 1841	5	6[d]	7	8	9	10	11[e]	ṬER 2117
4		12	13	14	15	16	17	18	
5		19	20	21	22	23	24	25	
6		26	27	28	29	30	1	2	
7	MESHIR 1841	3	4	5	6	7	8	9	YAKĀTIT 2117
8		10	11	12	13	14	15	16	
9		17	18	19	20	21	22	23	
10		24	25	26	27	28	29	30	
11	PAREMOTEP 1841	1	2	3	4	5	6	7	MAGĀBIT 2117
12		8	9	10	11	12	13	14	
13		15	16	17	18	19	20	21	
14		22	23	24	25	26	27	28	
15		29	30	1	2	3	4	5	
16	PARMOUTE 1841	6	7	8	9	10	11	12	MIYĀZYĀ 2117
17		13	14	15	16	17	18	19	
18		20[f]	21	22	23	24	25	26	
19		27	28	29[g]	30	1	2	3	
20	PASHONS 1841	4	5	6	7	8	9	10	GENBOT 2117
21		11	12	13	14	15	16	17	
22		18	19	20	21	22	23	24	
23		25	26	27	28	29	30	1	
24	PAÔNE 1841	2	3	4	5	6	7	8	SANĒ 2117
25		9	10	11	12	13	14	15	
26		16	17	18	19	20	21	22	
27		23	24	25	26	27	28	29	
28		30	1	2	3	4	5	6	
29	EPÊP 1841	7	8	9	10	11	12	13	ḤAMLĒ 2117
30		14	15	16	17	18	19	20	
31		21	22	23	24	25	26	27	
32		28	29	30	1	2	3	4	
33	MESORÊ 1841	5	6	7	8	9	10	11	NAḤASĒ 2117
34		12	13[h]	14	15	16	17	18	
35		19	20	21	22	23	24	25	
36		26	27	28	29	30	1	2	
37	EPAG. 1841	3	4	5	1[a]	2	3	4	PĀG. 2117
38	THOOUT 1842	5	6	7	8	9	10	11	MASKARAM 2118
39		12	13	14	15	16	17[b]	18	
40		19	20	21	22	23	24	25	
41		26	27	28	29	30	1	2	
42	PAOPE 1842	3	4	5	6	7	8	9	ṬEQEMT 2118
43		10	11	12	13	14	15	16	
44		17	18	19	20	21	22	23	
45		24	25	26	27	28	29	30	
46	ATHÔR 1842	1	2	3	4	5	6	7	ḪEDĀR 2118
47		8	9	10	11	12	13	14	
48		15	16	17	18	19	20	21	
49		22	23	24	25	26	27	28	
50		29	30	1	2	3	4	5	
51	KOIAK 1842	6	7	8	9	10	11	12	TĀKHŚĀŚ 2118
52		13	14	15	16	17	18	19	
1		20	21	22	23	24	25	26	

Gregorian notes:
- [a] New Year
- [b] Spring (14:28)
- [c] Summer (6:31)
- [d] Autumn (23:12)
- [e] Winter (21:30)
- ● New moon
- ◐ First quarter moon
- ○ Full moon
- ◑ Last quarter moon

Hebrew notes:
- ‡ Leap year
- [a] New Year
- [b] Yom Kippur
- [c] Sukkot
- [d] Winter starts
- [e] Ḥanukkah
- [f] Purim
- [g] Passover
- [h] Shavuot
- [i] Fast of Av

Chinese notes:
- [a] New Year (4823, Fowl)
- [b] Lantern Festival
- [c] Qīngmíng
- [d] Dragon Festival
- [e] Qīqiǎo
- [f] Hungry Ghosts
- [g] Mid-Autumn Festival
- [h] Double-Ninth Festival
- [i] Dōngzhì
- * Start of 60-name cycle

Coptic/Ethiopic notes:
- [a] New Year
- [b] Building of the Cross
- [c] Christmas
- [d] Jesus's Circumcision
- [e] Epiphany
- [f] Easter
- [g] Mary's Announcement
- [h] Jesus's Transfiguration

PERSIAN (ASTRONOMICAL) 1503‡/1504

Month	Sun	Mon	Tue	Wed	Thu	Fri	Sat
DEY 1503	11	12	13	14	15	16	17
	18	19	20	21	22	23	24
	25	26	27	28	29	30	1
BAHMAN 1503	2	3	4	5	6	7	8
	9	10	11	12	13	14	15
	16	17	18	19	20	21	22
	23	24	25	26	27	28	29
	30	1	2	3	4	5	6
ESFAND 1503	7	8	9	10	11	12	13
	14	15	16	17	18	19	20
	21	22	23	24	25	26	27
	28	29	30	1[a]	2	3	4
FARVARDĪN 1504	5	6	7	8	9	10	11
	12	13[b]	14	15	16	17	18
	19	20	21	22	23	24	25
	26	27	28	29	30	31	1
ORDĪBEHEŠT 1504	2	3	4	5	6	7	8
	9	10	11	12	13	14	15
	16	17	18	19	20	21	22
	23	24	25	26	27	28	29
	30	31	1	2	3	4	5
XORDĀD 1504	6	7	8	9	10	11	12
	13	14	15	16	17	18	19
	20	21	22	23	24	25	26
	27	28	29	30	31	1	2
TĪR 1504	3	4	5	6	7	8	9
	10	11	12	13	14	15	16
	17	18	19	20	21	22	23
	24	25	26	27	28	29	30
	31	1	2	3	4	5	6
MORDĀD 1504	7	8	9	10	11	12	13
	14	15	16	17	18	19	20
	21	22	23	24	25	26	27
	28	29	30	31	1	2	3
SHAHRĪVAR 1504	4	5	6	7	8	9	10
	11	12	13	14	15	16	17
	18	19	20	21	22	23	24
	25	26	27	28	29	30	31
MEHR 1504	1	2	3	4	5	6	7
	8	9	10	11	12	13	14
	15	16	17	18	19	20	21
	22	23	24	25	26	27	28
	29	30	1	2	3	4	5
ĀBĀN 1504	6	7	8	9	10	11	12
	13	14	15	16	17	18	19
	20	21	22	23	24	25	26
	27	28	29	30	1	2	3
ĀZAR 1504	4	5	6	7	8	9	10
	11	12	13	14	15	16	17
	18	19	20	21	22	23	24
	25	26	27	28	29	30	1
DEY 1504	2	3	4	5	6	7	8
	9	10	11	12	13	14	15

‡Leap year
[a]New Year
[b]Sizdeh Bedar

HINDU LUNAR 2181/2182

Month	Sun	Mon	Tue	Wed	Thu	Fri	Sat
	26	27	28	29	30	1	2
PAUSHA 2181	3	4	5	6	6	7	8
	9	10	**11**	13	14	15	16
	17	18	19	20	21	22	23
	24	25	26	27	28	29	30
MĀGHA 2181	1	2	3	4	5	6	7
	8	9	10	11	12	13	14
	15	**16**	18	19	20	21	22
	23	24	25	26	27	28	28[h]
PHĀLGUNA 2181	29	30	1	2	3	4	5
	6	7	8	9	**10**	12	13
	14	15[i]	16	17	18	19	20
	21	22	23	24	25	26	27
CHAITRA 2182	28	29	30	1[a]	2	3	4
	5	6	7	8	9[b]	10	11
	12	13	14	**15**	17	18	19
	20	21	22	*22*	23	24	25
VAIŚĀKHA 2182	26	27	28	29	30	1	2
	3	4	5	6	7	**8**	10
	11	12	13	14	15	16	17
	18	19	20	21	22	23	24
	25	26	*26*	27	28	29	**30**
JYAISHṬHA 2182	2	3	4	5	6	7	8
	9	10	11	**12**	14	15	16
	17	*17*	18	19	20	21	22
	23	24	25	26	27	28	29
ĀSHĀḌHA 2182	30	1	2	3	**4**	6	7
	8	9	10	11	12	13	14
	15	16	17	18	19	20	21
	22	23	24	*24*	26	27	28
ŚRĀVAṆA 2182	29	30	1	2	3	4	5
	6	**7**	9	10	11	12	13
	14	15	*15*	16	17	18	19
	20	21	22	23[c]	24	25	26
BHĀDRAPADA 2182	27	28	**29**	1	2	3	4[d]
	5	6	7	8	9	10	11
	12	13	14	15	16	17	18
	19	20	*20*	22	23	24	25
ĀŚVINA 2182	26	27	28	29	30	1	2
	3	5	6	7	8[e]	9[e]	10[e]
	10[e]	11	12	13	14	15	16
	17	18	19	20	21	22	23
KĀRTTIKA 2182	24	25	**26**	28	29	30	1[f]
	2	3	4	5	6	7	8
	9	10	11	12	13	*13*	14
	15	16	17	18	19	**20**	22
	23	24	25	26	27	28	29
MĀRGAŚĪRA 2182	30	1	2	3	4	5	6
	7	8	9	10	11[g]	12	13
	14	15	16	17	18	19	20
	21	22	23	**24**	26	27	28
PAUSHA 2182	29	30	1	2	3	4	5
	6	*6*	7	8	9	10	11

[a]New Year (Pārthiva)
[b]Birthday of Rāma
[c]Birthday of Krishna
[d]Ganēśa Chaturthī
[e]Dashara
[f]Diwali
[g]Birthday of Vishnu
[h]Night of Śiva
[i]Holi

HINDU SOLAR 2046/2047‡

Month	Sun	Mon	Tue	Wed	Thu	Fri	Sat
	15	16	17	18	19	20	21
PAUSHA 2046	22	23	24	25	26	27	28
	29	30	1[b]	2	3	4	5
MĀGHA 2046	6	7	8	9	10	11	12
	13	14	15	16	17	18	19
	20	21	22	23	24	25	26
	27	28	29	1	2	3	4
PHĀLGUNA 2046	5	6	7	8	9	10	11
	12	13	14	15	16	17	18
	19	20	21	22	23	24	25
	26	27	28	29	30	1	2
CHAITRA 2046	3	4	5	6	7	8	9
	10	11	12	13	14	15	16
	17	18	19	20	21	22	23
	24	25	26	27	28	29	30
VAIŚĀKHA 2047	1[a]	2	3	4	5	6	7
	8	9	10	11	12	13	14
	15	16	17	18	19	20	21
	22	23	24	25	26	27	28
	29	30	31	1	2	3	4
JYAISHṬHA 2047	5	6	7	8	9	10	11
	12	13	14	15	16	17	18
	19	20	21	22	23	24	25
	26	27	28	29	30	31	32
ĀSHĀḌHA 2047	1	2	3	4	5	6	7
	8	9	10	11	12	13	14
	15	16	17	18	19	20	21
	22	23	24	25	26	27	28
	29	30	31	1	2	3	4
ŚRĀVAṆA 2047	5	6	7	8	9	10	11
	12	13	14	15	16	17	18
	19	20	21	22	23	24	25
	26	27	28	29	30	31	32
BHĀDRAPADA 2047	1	2	3	4	5	6	7
	8	9	10	11	12	13	14
	15	16	17	18	19	20	21
	22	23	24	25	26	27	28
	29	30	31	1	2	3	4
ĀŚVINA 2047	5	6	7	8	9	10	11
	12	13	14	15	16	17	18
	19	20	21	22	23	24	25
	26	27	28	29	30	1	2
KĀRTTIKA 2047	3	4	5	6	7	8	9
	10	11	12	13	14	15	16
	17	18	19	20	21	22	23
	24	25	26	27	28	29	30
MĀRGAŚĪRA 2047	1	2	3	4	5	6	7
	8	9	10	11	12	13	14
	15	16	17	18	19	20	21
	22	23	24	25	26	27	28
	29	30	1	2	3	4	5
PAUSHA 2047	6	7	8	9	10	11	12
	13	14	15	16	17	18	19

‡Leap year
[a]New Year (Śārvari)
[b]Pongal

ISLAMIC (ASTRONOMICAL) 1549/1550‡

Month	Sun	Mon	Tue	Wed	Thu	Fri	Sat
	25	26	27[d]	28	29	30	1
SHA'BĀN 1549	2	3	4	5	6	7	8
	9	10	11	12	13	14	15
	16	17	18	19	20	21	22
	23	24	25	26	27	28	29
	30	1[e]	2	3	4	5	6
RAMAḌĀN 1549	7	8	9	10	11	12	13
	14	15	16	17	18	19	20
	21	22	23	24	25	26	27
	28	29	30	1[f]	2	3	4
SHAWWĀL 1549	5	6	7	8	9	10	11
	12	13	14	15	16	17	18
	19	20	21	22	23	24	25
	26	27	28	29	1	2	3
DHU AL-QA'DA 1549	4	5	6	7	8	9	10
	11	12	13	14	15	16	17
	18	19	20	21	22	23	24
	25	26	27	28	29	30	1
DHU AL-ḤIJJA 1549	2	3	4	5	6	7	8
	9	10[g]	11	12	13	14	15
	16	17	18	19	20	21	22
	23	24	25	26	27	28	29
MUḤARRAM 1550	1[a]	2	3	4	5	6	7
	8	9	10[b]	11	12	13	14
	15	16	17	18	19	20	21
	22	23	24	25	26	27	28
	29	30	1	2	3	4	5
ṢAFAR 1550	6	7	8	9	10	11	12
	13	14	15	16	17	18	19
	20	21	22	23	24	25	26
	27	28	29	30	1	2	3
RABĪ' I 1550	4	5	6	7	8	9	10
	11	12[c]	13	14	15	16	17
	18	19	20	21	22	23	24
	25	26	27	28	29	1	2
RABĪ' II 1550	3	4	5	6	7	8	9
	10	11	12	13	14	15	16
	17	18	19	20	21	22	23
	24	25	26	27	28	29	1
JUMĀDĀ I 1550	2	3	4	5	6	7	8
	9	10	11	12	13	14	15
	16	17	18	19	20	21	22
	23	24	25	26	27	28	29
JUMĀDĀ II 1550	1	2	3	4	5	6	7
	8	9	10	11	12	13	14
	15	16	17	18	19	20	21
	22	23	24	25	26	27	28
	29	1	2	3	4	5	6
RAJAB 1550	7	8	9	10	11	12	13
	14	15	16	17	18	19	20
	21	22	23	24	25	26	27[d]
SHA'BĀN 1550	28	29	30	1	2	3	4
	5	6	7	8	9	10	11

‡Leap year
[a]New Year
[b]'Ashūrā'
[c]Prophet's Birthday
[d]Ascent of the Prophet
[e]Start of Ramaḍān
[f]'Id al-Fiṭr
[g]'Id al-'Aḍḥā

GREGORIAN 2125

Julian (Sun)	Sun	Mon	Tue	Wed	Thu	Fri	Sat	Month
Dec 17	31	1	2	3	4	5	6	
	7	8[a]	9	10	11	12	13	JANUARY 2125
Dec 31	*14*	15[b]	16	17	18	19	20	
	21	22	23	24	25	26	27	
Jan 14	*28*	29	30	31	1	2	3	
	4	5	6	7	8	9	10	FEBRUARY 2125
Jan 28	*11*	12	13	14	15	16	17	
	18	19	20	21	22	23	24	
Feb 11	*25*	26	27	28	1	2	3	
	4	5	6	7[c]	8	9	10	MARCH 2125
Feb 25	*11*	12	13	14	15	16	17	
	18[d]	19	20	21	22	23	24	
Mar 11	*25*	26	27	28	29	30	31	
	1	2	3	4	5	6	7	APRIL 2125
Mar 25	*8*	9	10	11	12	13	14	
	15	16	17	18	19	20	21	
Apr 8	22[e]	23	24	25	26	27	28	
	29[f]	30	1	2	3	4	5	
Apr 22	*6*	7	8	9	10	11	12	MAY 2125
	13	14	15	16	17	18	19	
May 6	*20*	21	22	23	24	25	26	
	27	28	29	30	31	1	2	
May 20	*3*	4	5	6	7	8	9	JUNE 2125
	10	11	12	13	14	15	16	
Jun 3	*17*	18	19	20	21	22	23	
	24	25	26	27	28	29	30	
Jun 17	*1*	2	3	4	5	6	7	JULY 2125
	8	9	10	11	12	13	14	
Jul 1	*15*	16	17	18	19	20	21	
	22	23	24	25	26	27	28	
Jul 15	*29*	30	31	1	2	3	4	
	5	6	7	8	9	10	11	AUGUST 2125
Jul 29	*12*	13	14	15	16	17	18	
	19	20	21	22	23	24	25	
Aug 12	*26*	27	28	29	30	31	1	
	2	3	4	5	6	7	8	SEPTEMBER 2125
Aug 26	*9*	10	11	12	13	14	15	
	16	17	18	19	20	21	22	
Sep 9	*23*	24	25	26	27	28	29	
	30	1	2	3	4	5	6	OCTOBER 2125
Sep 23	*7*	8	9	10	11	12	13	
	14	15	16	17	18	19	20	
Oct 7	*21*	22	23	24	25	26	27	
	28	29	30	31	1	2	3	
Oct 21	*4*	5	6	7	8	9	10	NOVEMBER 2125
	11	12	13	14	15	16	17	
Nov 4	*18*	19	20	21	22	23	24	
	25	26	27	28	29	30	1	
Nov 18	2[g]	3	4	5	6	7	8	DECEMBER 2125
	9	10	11	12	13	14	15	
Dec 2	*16*	17	18	19	20	21	22	
	23	24	25[h]	26	27	28	29	
Dec 16	*30*	31	1	2	3	4	5	

[a]Orthodox Christmas
[b]Julian New Year
[c]Ash Wednesday
[d]Feast of Orthodoxy
[e]Easter
[f]Orthodox Easter
[g]Advent
[h]Christmas

2126

GREGORIAN 2126 · ISO WEEK (Mon) · JULIAN DAY (Sun noon)

Month	Sun	Mon	Tue	Wed	Thu	Fri	Sat	Lunar Phases	ISO Week (Mon)	Julian Day (Sun noon)
	30	31	◐[a]	2	3	4	5	20:28	1	2497564
JANUARY 2126	6	7	8	○	10	11	12	9:00	2	2497571
	13	14	15	◑	17	18	19	1:55	3	2497578
	20	21	22	●	24	25	26	12:18	4	2497585
	27	28	29	30	◐	1	2	17:21	5	2497592
FEBRUARY 2126	3	4	5	6	○	8	9	20:33	6	2497599
	10	11	12	13	◑	15	16	12:02	7	2497606
	17	18	19	20	21	●	23	6:18	8	2497613
	24	25	26	27	28	1	◐	11:00	9	2497620
	3	4	5	6	7	8	○	6:48	10	2497627
MARCH 2126	10	11	12	13	14	◑	16	23:59	11	2497634
	17	18	19	20[b]	21	22	23		12	2497641
	●	25	26	27	28	29	30	0:47	13	2497648
	31	◐	2	3	4	5	6	0:26	14	2497655
APRIL 2126	○	8	9	10	11	12	13	16:08	15	2497662
	◑	15	16	17	18	19	20	13:48	16	2497669
	21	●	23	24	25	26	27	18:11	17	2497676
	28	29	◐	1	2	3	4	9:53	18	2497683
MAY 2126	5	6	○	8	9	10	11	0:55	19	2497690
	12	13	◑	15	16	17	18	5:22	20	2497697
	19	20	21	●	23	24	25	9:15	21	2497704
	26	27	28	◐	30	31	1	16:24	22	2497711
	2	3	4	○	6	7	8	9:41	23	2497718
JUNE 2126	9	10	11	◑	13	14	15	22:18	24	2497725
	16	17	18	19	●	21[c]	22	21:32	25	2497732
	23	24	25	26	◐	28	29	21:19	26	2497739
	30	1	2	3	○	5	6	19:15	27	2497746
JULY 2126	7	8	9	10	11	◑	13	15:52	28	2497753
	14	15	16	17	18	19	●	7:31	29	2497760
	21	22	23	24	25	26	◐	1:59	30	2497767
	28	29	30	31	1	2	○	6:32	31	2497774
AUGUST 2126	4	5	6	7	8	9	10		32	2497781
	◑	12	13	14	15	16	17	9:02	33	2497788
	●	19	20	21	22	23	24	16:09	34	2497795
	◐	26	27	28	29	30	31	7:45	35	2497802
	○	2	3	4	5	6	7	20:19	36	2497809
SEPTEMBER 2126	8	9	◑	11	12	13	14	0:55	37	2497816
	15	16	●	18	19	20	21	0:29	38	2497823
	22	◐[d]	24	25	26	27	28	15:54	39	2497830
	29	30	○	2	3	4	5	12:38	40	2497837
OCTOBER 2126	6	7	8	◑	10	11	12	14:59	41	2497844
	13	14	15	●	17	18	19	9:16	42	2497851
	20	21	22	◐	24	25	26	3:35	43	2497858
	27	28	29	30	○	1	2	6:39	44	2497865
NOVEMBER 2126	3	4	5	6	7	◑	9	3:10	45	2497872
	10	11	12	13	●	15	16	19:00	46	2497879
	17	18	19	20	◐	22	23	19:27	47	2497886
	24	25	26	27	28	29	○	0:50	48	2497893
	1	2	3	4	5	6	◑	13:36	49	2497900
DECEMBER 2126	8	9	10	11	12	13	●	6:00	50	2497907
	15	16	17	18	19	20	◐	15:11	51	2497914
	22[e]	23	24	25	26	27	28		52	2497921
	○	30	31	1	2	3	4	17:5	1	2497928

HEBREW 5886/5887

Julian Day	Month	Sun	Mon	Tue	Wed	Thu	Fri	Sat	Molad
2497564		3	4	5	6	7	8	9	
2497571	TEVETH 5886	10	11	12	13	14	15	16	
2497578		17	18	19	20	21	22	23	Wed 23h23m6p
2497585		24	25	26	27	28	29	1	
2497592		2	3	4	5	6	7	8	
2497599	SHEVAT 5886	9	10	11	12	13	14	15	
2497606		16	17	18	19	20	21	22	
2497613		23	24	25	26	27	28	29	Fri 12h7m7p
2497620		30	1	2	3	4	5	6	
2497627		7	8	9	10	11	12	13	
2497634	ADAR 5886	14[f]	15	16	17	18	19	20	
2497641		21	22	23	24	25	26	27	Sun 0h51m8p
2497648		28	29	1	2	3	4	5	
2497655		6	7	8	9	10	11	12	
2497662	NISAN 5886	13	14	15[g]	16	17	18	19	
2497669		20	21	22	23	24	25	26	Mon 13h35m9p
2497676		27	28	29	30	1	2	3	
2497683		4	5	6	7	8	9	10	
2497690	IYYAR 5886	11	12	13	14	15	16	17	
2497697		18	19	20	21	22	23	24	Wed 2h19m10p
2497704		25	26	27	28	29	1	2	
2497711		3	4	5	6[h]	7	8	9	
2497718	SIVAN 5886	10	11	12	13	14	15	16	
2497725		17	18	19	20	21	22	23	
2497732		24	25	26	27	28	29	30	Thu 15h3m11p
2497739		1	2	3	4	5	6	7	
2497746	TAMMUZ 5886	8	9	10	11	12	13	14	
2497753		15	16	17	18	19	20	21	
2497760		22	23	24	25	26	27	28	Sat 3h47m12p
2497767		29	1	2	3	4	5	6	
2497774		7	8	9[i]	10	11	12	13	
2497781	AV 5886	14	15	16	17	18	19	20	
2497788		21	22	23	24	25	26	27	Sun 16h31m13p
2497795		28	29	30	1	2	3	4	
2497802	ELUL 5886	5	6	7	8	9	10	11	
2497809		12	13	14	15	16	17	18	
2497816		19	20	21	22	23	24	25	
2497823		26	27	28	29	1[a]	2[a]	3	Tue 5h15m14p
2497830		4	5	6	7	8	9	10[b]	
2497837	TISHRI 5887	11	12	13	14	15[c]	16	17	
2497844		18	19	20	21	22	23	24	
2497851		25	26	27	28	29	30	1	Wed 17h59m15p
2497858		2	3	4	5	6	7	8	
2497865	HESHVAN 5887	9	10	11	12	13	14	15	
2497872		16	17	18	19	20	21	22	
2497879		23	24	25	26	27	28	29	Fri 6h43m16p
2497886		1	2	3	4	5	6	7	
2497893	KISLEV 5887	8	9	10	11	12	13	14	
2497900		15	16	17	18	19	20[d]	21	
2497907		22	23	24	25[e]	26[e]	27[e]	28[e]	
2497914		29[e]	30[e]	1[e]	2[e]	3	4	5	Sat 19h27m17p
2497921	TEVETH 5887	6	7	8	9	10	11	12	
2497928		13	14	15	16	17	18	19	

CHINESE Yǐ-Yǒu/Bǐng-Xū‡

Julian Day	Month	Sun	Mon	Tue	Wed	Thu	Fri	Sat	Solar Term
2497564		6	7	8	9	10	11	*12*	Xiǎo hán
2497571	MONTH 12 Yǐ-Yǒu	13*	14	15	16	17	18	19	
2497578		20	21	22	23	24	25	26	
2497585		***27***	28	29	1[a]	2	3	4	Dà hán
2497592		5	6	7	8	9	10	11	
2497599	MONTH 1 Bǐng-Xū	12	*13*	14	15[b]	16	17	18	Lì chūn
2497606		19	20	21	22	23	24	25	
2497613		26	27	***28***	29	30	1	2	Yǔ shuǐ
2497620		3	4	5	6	7	8	9	
2497627	MONTH 2 Bǐng-Xū	10	11	12	*13*	14*	15	16	Jīng zhé
2497634		17	18	19	20	21	22	23	
2497641		24	25	26	27	***28***	29	30	Chūn fēn
2497648		1	2	3	4	5	6	7	
2497655		8	9	10	11	12	*13*[c]	14	Qīng míng
2497662	MONTH 3 Bǐng-Xū	15	16	17	18	19	20	21	
2497669		22	23	24	25	26	27	***28***	Gǔ yǔ
2497676		29	30	1	2	3	4	5	
2497683		6	7	8	9	10	11	12	
2497690	MONTH 4 Bǐng-Xū	13	*14**	15	16	17	18	19	Lì xià
2497697		20	21	22	23	24	25	26	
2497704		27	28	***29***	1	2	3	4	Xiǎo mǎn
2497711		5	6	7	8	9	10	11	
2497718	LEAP MONTH 4 Bǐng-Xū	12	13	14	15	*16*	17	18	Máng zhòng
2497725		19	20	21	22	23	24	25	
2497732		26	27	28	29	30	***1***	2	Xià zhì
2497739		3	4	5[d]	6	7	8	9	
2497746	MONTH 5 Bǐng-Xū	10	11	12	13	14	15*	16	
2497753		*17*	18	19	20	21	22	23	Xiǎo shǔ
2497760		24	25	26	27	28	29	1	
2497767		2	3	***4***	5	6	7	8	Dà shǔ
2497774	MONTH 6 Bǐng-Xū	9	10	11	12	13	14	15	
2497781		16	17	18	*19*	20	21	22	Lì qiū
2497788		23	24	25	26	27	28	29	
2497795		30	1	2	3	4	***5***	6	Chǔ shǔ
2497802	MONTH 7 Bǐng-Xū	7[e]	8	9	10	11	12	13	
2497809		14	15[f]	16*	17	18	19	20	
2497816		*21*	22	23	24	25	26	27	Bái lù
2497823		28	29	1	2	3	4	5	
2497830	MONTH 8 Bǐng-Xū	6	***7***	8	9	10	11	12	Qiū fēn
2497837		13	14	15[g]	16	17	18	19	
2497844		20	21	*22*	23	24	25	26	Hán lù
2497851		27	28	29	1	2	3	4	
2497858	MONTH 9 Bǐng-Xū	5	6	7	***8***	9[h]	10	11	Shuāng jiàng
2497865		12	13	14	15	16	17	18*	
2497872		19	20	21	22	*23*	24	25	Lì dōng
2497879		26	27	28	29	30	1	2	
2497886	MONTH 10 Bǐng-Xū	3	4	5	6	7	***8***	9	Xiǎo xuě
2497893		10	11	12	13	14	15	16	
2497900		17	18	19	20	21	22	*23*	Dà xuě
2497907		24	25	26	27	28	29	1	
2497914	MONTH 11 Bǐng-Xū	2	3	4	5	6	7	8	
2497921		***9***[i]	10	11	12	13	14	15	Dōng zhì
2497928		16	17	18	19	20	21	22	

COPTIC 1842/1843‡ · ETHIOPIC 2118/2119‡

Julian Day	Coptic Month	Sun	Mon	Tue	Wed	Thu	Fri	Sat	Ethiopic Month
2497564		20	21	22	23	24	25	26	TĀKHŚĀŚ 2118
2497571	KOIAK 1842	27	28	29[c]	30	1	2	3	
2497578		4	5	6[d]	7	8	9	10	
2497585	TŌBE 1842	11[e]	12	13	14	15	16	17	ṬER 2118
2497592		18	19	20	21	22	23	24	
2497599		25	26	27	28	29	30	1	
2497606		2	3	4	5	6	7	8	
2497613	MESHIR 1842	9	10	11	12	13	14	15	YAKĀTIT 2118
2497620		16	17	18	19	20	21	22	
2497627		23	24	25	26	27	28	29	
2497634		30	1	2	3	4	5	6	
2497641	PAREMOTEP 1842	7	8	9	10	11	12	13	MAGĀBIT 2118
2497648		14	15	16	17	18	19	20	
2497655		21	22	23	24	25	26	27	
2497662		28	29	30	1	2	3	4	
2497669	PARMOUTE 1842	5[f]	6	7	8	9	10	11	MIYĀZYĀ 2118
2497676		12	13	14	15	16	17	18	
2497683		19	20	21	22	23	24	25	
2497690		26	27	28	29[g]	30	1	2	
2497697		3	4	5	6	7	8	9	GENBOT 2118
2497704	PASHONS 1842	10	11	12	13	14	15	16	
2497711		17	18	19	20	21	22	23	
2497718		24	25	26	27	28	29	30	
2497725		1	2	3	4	5	6	7	
2497732	PAŌNE 1842	8	9	10	11	12	13	14	SANĒ 2118
2497739		15	16	17	18	19	20	21	
2497746		22	23	24	25	26	27	28	
2497753		29	30	1	2	3	4	5	
2497760		6	7	8	9	10	11	12	HAMLĒ 2118
2497767	EPĒP 1842	13	14	15	16	17	18	19	
2497774		20	21	22	23	24	25	26	
2497781		27	28	29	30	1	2	3	
2497788		4	5	6	7	8	9	10	
2497795	MESORĒ 1842	11	12	13[h]	14	15	16	17	NAḤASĒ 2118
2497802		18	19	20	21	22	23	24	
2497809	EPAG. 1842	25	26	27	28	29	30	1	
2497816		2	3	4	5	1[a]	2	3	PĀG. 2118
2497823		4	5	6	7	8	9	10	
2497830	THOOUT 1843	11	12	13	14	15	16	17[b]	MASKARAM 2119
2497837		18	19	20	21	22	23	24	
2497844		25	26	27	28	29	30	1	
2497851		2	3	4	5	6	7	8	
2497858	PAOPE 1843	9	10	11	12	13	14	15	ṬEQEMT 2119
2497865		16	17	18	19	20	21	22	
2497872		23	24	25	26	27	28	29	
2497879		30	1	2	3	4	5	6	
2497886	ATHŌR 1843	7	8	9	10	11	12	13	HEDĀR 2119
2497893		14	15	16	17	18	19	20	
2497900		21	22	23	24	25	26	27	
2497907		28	29	30	1	2	3	4	
2497914	KOIAK 1843	5	6	7	8	9	10	11	TĀKHŚĀŚ 2119
2497921		12	13	14	15	16	17	18	
2497928		19	20	21	22	23	24	25	

Gregorian:
[a]New Year
[b]Spring (20:14)
[c]Summer (12:08)
[d]Autumn (4:58)
[e]Winter (3:24)
● New moon
◐ First quarter moon
○ Full moon
◑ Last quarter moon

Hebrew:
[a]New Year
[b]Yom Kippur
[c]Sukkot
[d]Winter starts
[e]Ḥanukkah
[f]Purim
[g]Passover
[h]Shavuot
[i]Fast of Av

Chinese:
‡Leap year
[a]New Year (4824, Dog)
[b]Lantern Festival
[c]Qīngmíng
[d]Dragon Festival
[e]Qīqiǎo
[f]Hungry Ghosts
[g]Mid-Autumn Festival
[h]Double-Ninth Festival
[i]Dōngzhì
*Start of 60-name cycle

Coptic/Ethiopic:
‡Leap year
[a]New Year
[b]Building of the Cross
[c]Christmas
[d]Jesus's Circumcision
[e]Epiphany
[f]Easter
[g]Mary's Announcement
[h]Jesus's Transfiguration

PERSIAN (ASTRONOMICAL) 1504/1505

Month	Sun	Mon	Tue	Wed	Thu	Fri	Sat
DEY 1504	9	10	11	12	13	14	15
	16	17	18	19	20	21	22
	23	24	25	26	27	28	29
	30	1	2	3	4	5	6
BAHMAN 1504	7	8	9	10	11	12	13
	14	15	16	17	18	19	20
	21	22	23	24	25	26	27
	28	29	30	1	2	3	4
ESFAND 1504	5	6	7	8	9	10	11
	12	13	14	15	16	17	18
	19	20	21	22	23	24	25
	26	27	28	29	1[a]	2	3
FARVARDĪN 1505	4	5	6	7	8	9	10
	11	12	13[b]	14	15	16	17
	18	19	20	21	22	23	24
	25	26	27	28	29	30	31
ORDĪBEHEŠT 1505	1	2	3	4	5	6	7
	8	9	10	11	12	13	14
	15	16	17	18	19	20	21
	22	23	24	25	26	27	28
	29	30	31	1	2	3	4
XORDĀD 1505	5	6	7	8	9	10	11
	12	13	14	15	16	17	18
	19	20	21	22	23	24	25
	26	27	28	29	30	31	1
TĪR 1505	2	3	4	5	6	7	8
	9	10	11	12	13	14	15
	16	17	18	19	20	21	22
	23	24	25	26	27	28	29
	30	31	1	2	3	4	5
MORDĀD 1505	6	7	8	9	10	11	12
	13	14	15	16	17	18	19
	20	21	22	23	24	25	26
	27	28	29	30	31	1	2
SHAHRĪVAR 1505	3	4	5	6	7	8	9
	10	11	12	13	14	15	16
	17	18	19	20	21	22	23
	24	25	26	27	28	29	30
	31	1	2	3	4	5	6
MEHR 1505	7	8	9	10	11	12	13
	14	15	16	17	18	19	20
	21	22	23	24	25	26	27
	28	29	30	1	2	3	4
ABĀN 1505	5	6	7	8	9	10	11
	12	13	14	15	16	17	18
	19	20	21	22	23	24	25
	26	27	28	29	30	1	2
ĀZAR 1505	3	4	5	6	7	8	9
	10	11	12	13	14	15	16
	17	18	19	20	21	22	23
	24	25	26	27	28	29	30
DEY 1505	1	2	3	4	5	6	7
	8	9	10	11	12	13	14

[a]New Year
[b]Sizdeh Bedar

HINDU LUNAR 2182/2183‡

Month	Sun	Mon	Tue	Wed	Thu	Fri	Sat
PAUSHA 2182	6	6	7	8	9	10	11
	12	13	14	15	16	17	18
	19	21	22	23	24	25	26
	27	28	29	30	1	2	3
MĀGHA 2182	4	5	6	7	8	9	9
	10	11	**12**	14	15	16	17
	18	19	20	21	22	23	24
	25	26	27	28[h]	29	30	1
PHĀLGUNA 2182	2	3	4	5	6	7	8
	9	10	11	12	13	14	15[i]
	16	**17**	19	20	21	22	23
	24	25	26	27	28	29	30
CHAITRA 2183	1[a]	1	2	3	4	5	6
	7	8[b]	9	10	**11**	13	14
	15	16	17	18	19	20	21
	22	23	24	25	26	27	28
VAIŚĀKHA 2183	29	30	1	2	3	4	5
	6	7	8	9	10	11	12
	13	14	**15**	17	18	19	20
	21	22	23	24	25	26	26
	27	28	29	30	1	2	3
JYAISHṬHA 2183	4	5	6	7	**8**	10	11
	12	13	14	15	16	17	18
	19	20	21	22	23	24	25
	26	27	28	29	30	1	2
ĀSHĀḌHA 2183	3	4	5	6	7	8	9
	10	**11**	13	14	15	16	17
	18	19	20	21	22	22	23
	24	25	26	27	28	29	30
LEAP ŚRĀVAṆA 2183	1	2	3	**4**	6	7	8
	9	10	11	12	13	14	15
	16	17	18	19	20	21	22
	23	24	25	26	27	28	29
	30	1	2	3	4	5	**6**
ŚRĀVAṆA 2183	8	9	10	11	12	13	14
	15	16	17	18	19	19	20
	21	22	23[c]	24	25	26	27
	28	29	**30**	2	3	4[d]	5
BHĀDRAPADA 2183	6	7	8	9	10	11	12
	13	14	15	16	17	18	19
	20	21	22	23	24	25	26
	27	28	29	30	1	2	**3**
ĀŚVINA 2183	5	6	7	8[e]	9[e]	10[e]	11
	12	13	14	14	15	16	17
	18	19	20	21	22	23	24
	25	26	**27**	29	30	1[f]	2
KĀRTTIKA 2183	3	4	5	6	7	8	9
	10	11	12	13	14	15	16
	17	17	18	19	**20**	22	23
	24	25	26	27	28	29	30
MĀRGAŚĪRA 2183	1	2	3	4	5	6	7
	8	9	10	11[g]	12	13	14
	15	16	17	18	19	20	21

‡Leap year
[a]New Year (Vyaya)
[b]Birthday of Rāma
[c]Birthday of Krishna
[d]Ganēśa Chaturthī
[e]Dashara
[f]Diwali
[g]Birthday of Vishnu
[h]Night of Śiva
[i]Holi

HINDU SOLAR 2047‡/2048

Month	Sun	Mon	Tue	Wed	Thu	Fri	Sat
PAUSHA 2047	13	14	15	16	17	18	19
	20	21	22	23	24	25	26
	27	28	29	1[b]	2	3	4
MĀGHA 2047	5	6	7	8	9	10	11
	12	13	14	15	16	17	18
	19	20	21	22	23	24	25
	26	27	28	29	1	2	3
PHĀLGUNA 2047	4	5	6	7	8	9	10
	11	12	13	14	15	16	17
	18	19	20	21	22	23	24
	25	26	27	28	29	30	1
CHAITRA 2047	2	3	4	5	6	7	8
	9	10	11	12	13	14	15
	16	17	18	19	20	21	22
	23	24	25	26	27	28	29
	30	31	1[a]	2	3	4	5
VAIŚĀKHA 2048	6	7	8	9	10	11	12
	13	14	15	16	17	18	19
	20	21	22	23	24	25	26
	27	28	29	30	31	1	2
JYAISHṬHA 2048	3	4	5	6	7	8	9
	10	11	12	13	14	15	16
	17	18	19	20	21	22	23
	24	25	26	27	28	29	30
	31	1	2	3	4	5	6
ĀSHĀḌHA 2048	7	8	9	10	11	12	13
	14	15	16	17	18	19	20
	21	22	23	24	25	26	27
	28	29	30	31	32	1	2
ŚRĀVAṆA 2048	3	4	5	6	7	8	9
	10	11	12	13	14	15	16
	17	18	19	20	21	22	23
	24	25	26	27	28	29	30
	31	1	2	3	4	5	6
BHĀDRAPADA 2048	7	8	9	10	11	12	13
	14	15	16	17	18	19	20
	21	22	23	24	25	26	27
	28	29	30	31	1	2	3
ĀŚVINA 2048	4	5	6	7	8	9	10
	11	12	13	14	15	16	17
	18	19	20	21	22	23	24
	25	26	27	28	29	30	31
KĀRTTIKA 2048	1	2	3	4	5	6	7
	8	9	10	11	12	13	14
	15	16	17	18	19	20	21
	22	23	24	25	26	27	28
	29	1	2	3	4	5	6
MĀRGAŚĪRA 2048	7	8	9	10	11	12	13
	14	15	16	17	18	19	20
	21	22	23	24	25	26	27
	28	29	30	1	2	3	4
PAUSHA 2048	5	6	7	8	9	10	11
	12	13	14	15	16	17	18

‡Leap year
[a]New Year (Plava)
[b]Pongal

ISLAMIC (ASTRONOMICAL) 1550‡/1551

Month	Sun	Mon	Tue	Wed	Thu	Fri	Sat
SHA'BĀN 1550	5	6	7	8	9	10	11
	12	13	14	15	16	17	18
	19	20	21	22	23	24	25
	26	27	28	29	30	1[e]	2
RAMAḌĀN 1550	3	4	5	6	7	8	9
	10	11	12	13	14	15	16
	17	18	19	20	21	22	23
	24	25	26	27	28	29	30
SHAWWĀL 1550	1[f]	2	3	4	5	6	7
	8	9	10	11	12	13	14
	15	16	17	18	19	20	21
	22	23	24	25	26	27	28
	29	1	2	3	4	5	6
DHU AL-QA'DA 1550	7	8	9	10	11	12	13
	14	15	16	17	18	19	20
	21	22	23	24	25	26	27
	28	29	30	1	2	3	4
DHU AL-ḤIJJA 1550	5	6	7	8	9	10[g]	11
	12	13	14	15	16	17	18
	19	20	21	22	23	24	25
	26	27	28	29	30[d]	1[a]	2
MUḤARRAM 1551	3	4	5	6	7	8	9
	10[b]	11	12	13	14	15	16
	17	18	19	20	21	22	23
	24	25	26	27	28	29	30
ṢAFAR 1551	1	2	3	4	5	6	7
	8	9	10	11	12	13	14
	15	16	17	18	19	20	21
	22	23	24	25	26	27	28
	29	1	2	3	4	5	6
RABĪ' I 1551	7	8	9	10	11	12[c]	13
	14	15	16	17	18	19	20
	21	22	23	24	25	26	27
	28	29	1	2	3	4	5
RABĪ' II 1551	6	7	8	9	10	11	12
	13	14	15	16	17	18	19
	20	21	22	23	24	25	26
	27	28	29	30	1	2	3
JUMĀDĀ I 1551	4	5	6	7	8	9	10
	11	12	13	14	15	16	17
	18	19	20	21	22	23	24
	25	26	27	28	29	1	2
JUMĀDĀ II 1551	3	4	5	6	7	8	9
	10	11	12	13	14	15	16
	17	18	19	20	21	22	23
	24	25	26	27	28	29	1
RAJAB 1551	2	3	4	5	6	7	8
	9	10	11	12	13	14	15
	16	17	18	19	20	21	22
	23	24	25	26	27[d]	28	29
SHA'BĀN 1551	1	2	3	4	5	6	7
	8	9	10	11	12	13	14
	15	16	17	18	19	20	21

‡Leap year
[a]New Year
[d]New Year (Arithmetic)
[b]'Ashūrā'
[c]Prophet's Birthday
[d]Ascent of the Prophet
[e]Start of Ramaḍān
[f]'Īd al-Fiṭr
[g]'Īd al-'Aḍḥā

GREGORIAN 2126

Julian (Sun)	Sun	Mon	Tue	Wed	Thu	Fri	Sat	Month
Dec 16	30	31	1	2	3	4	5	
	6	7	8[a]	9	10	11	12	JANUARY 2126
Dec 30	13	14	15[b]	16	17	18	19	
	20	21	22	23	24	25	26	
Jan 13	27	28	29	30	31	1	2	
	3	4	5	6	7	8	9	FEBRUARY 2126
Jan 27	10	11	12	13	14	15	16	
	17	18	19	20	21	22	23	
Feb 10	24	25	26	27[c]	28	1	2	
	3[d]	4	5	6	7	8	9	MARCH 2126
Feb 24	10	11	12	13	14	15	16	
	17	18	19	20	21	22	23	
Mar 10	24	25	26	27	28	29	30	
	31	1	2	3	4	5	6	
Mar 24	7	8	9	10	11	12	13	APRIL 2126
	14[e]	15	16	17	18	19	20	
Apr 7	21	22	23	24	25	26	27	
	28	29	30	1	2	3	4	
Apr 21	5	6	7	8	9	10	11	MAY 2126
	12	13	14	15	16	17	18	
May 5	19	20	21	22	23	24	25	
	26	27	28	29	30	31	1	
May 19	2	3	4	5	6	7	8	JUNE 2126
	9	10	11	12	13	14	15	
Jun 2	16	17	18	19	20	21	22	
	23	24	25	26	27	28	29	
Jun 16	30	1	2	3	4	5	6	
	7	8	9	10	11	12	13	JULY 2126
Jun 30	14	15	16	17	18	19	20	
	21	22	23	24	25	26	27	
Jul 14	28	29	30	31	1	2	3	
	4	5	6	7	8	9	10	AUGUST 2126
Jul 28	11	12	13	14	15	16	17	
	18	19	20	21	22	23	24	
Aug 11	25	26	27	28	29	30	31	
	1	2	3	4	5	6	7	SEPTEMBER 2126
Aug 25	8	9	10	11	12	13	14	
	15	16	17	18	19	20	21	
Sep 8	22	23	24	25	26	27	28	
	29	30	1	2	3	4	5	
Sep 22	6	7	8	9	10	11	12	OCTOBER 2126
	13	14	15	16	17	18	19	
Oct 6	20	21	22	23	24	25	26	
	27	28	29	30	31	1	2	
Oct 20	3	4	5	6	7	8	9	NOVEMBER 2126
	10	11	12	13	14	15	16	
Nov 3	17	18	19	20	21	22	23	
	24	25	26	27	28	29	30	
Nov 17	1[g]	2	3	4	5	6	7	DECEMBER 2126
	8	9	10	11	12	13	14	
Dec 1	15	16	17	18	19	20	21	
	22	23	24	25[h]	26	27	28	
Dec 15	29	30	31	1	2	3	4	

[a]Orthodox Christmas
[b]Julian New Year
[c]Ash Wednesday
[d]Feast of Orthodoxy
[e]Easter (also Orthodox)
[g]Advent
[h]Christmas

2127

Gregorian 2127	Sun	Mon	Tue	Wed	Thu	Fri	Sat	Lunar Phases	ISO Week (Mon)	Julian Day (Sun noon)	Hebrew 5887/5888‡	Sun	Mon	Tue	Wed	Thu	Fri	Sat	Molad	Chinese Bǐng-Xū‡/Dīng-Hài	Sun	Mon	Tue	Wed	Thu	Fri	Sat	Solar Term	Coptic 1843‡/1844	Sun	Mon	Tue	Wed	Thu	Fri	Sat	Ethiopic 2119‡/2120
	○	30	31	1[a]	2	3	4	17:50	1	2497928		13	14	15	16	17	18	19		Month 11 Bǐng-Xū	16	17	18	19*	20	21	22			19	20	21	22	23	24	25	Tākhśāś 2119
	◑	6	7	8	9	10	11	22:36	2	2497935	Teveth 5887	20	21	22	23	24	25	26			23	24	25	26	27	28	29	Xiǎo hán	Koiak 1843	26	27	28	29[c]	30	1	2	
January 2127	●	13	14	15	16	17	18	18:35	3	2497942		27	28	29	1	2	3	4	Mon 8h12m0p		30	1	2	3	4	5	6			3	4	5	6[d]	7	8	9	
	19	◐	21	22	23	24	25	13:07	4	2497949		5	6	7	8	9	10	11			7	8	9	10	11	12	13	Dà hán		10	11[e]	12	13	14	15	16	Ṭer 2119
	26	27	○	29	30	31	1	8:54	5	2497956	Shevat 5887	12	13	14	15	16	17	18		Month 12 Bǐng-Xū	14	15	16	17	18	19	20		Tōbe 1843	17	18	19	20	21	22	23	
	2	3	◑	5	6	7	8	6:43	6	2497963		19	20	21	22	23	24	25			21	22	23	24	25	26	27	Lì chūn		24	25	26	27	28	29	30	
February 2127	9	10	●	12	13	14	15	9:02	7	2497970		26	27	28	29	30	1	2	Tue 20h56m1p		28	29	1[a]	2	3	4	5			1	2	3	4	5	6	7	
	16	17	18	◐	20	21	22	10:47	8	2497977		3	4	5	6	7	8	9			6	7	8	9	10	11	12	Yǔ shuǐ		8	9	10	11	12	13	14	
	23	24	25	○	27	28	1	21:49	9	2497984	Adar 5887	10	11	12	13	14[f]	15	16		Month 1 Dīng-Hài	13	14	15[b]	16	17	18	19		Meshir 1843	15	16	17	18	19	20	21	Yakātit 2119
	2	3	4	◑	6	7	8	14:41	10	2497991		17	18	19	20	21	22	23			20*	21	22	23	24	25	26	Jīng zhé		22	23	24	25	26	27	28	
March 2127	9	10	11	12	●	14	15	1:13	11	2497998		24	25	26	27	28	29	1	Thu 9h40m2p		27	28	29	30	1	2	3			29	30	1	2	3	4	5	
	16	17	18	19	20	◐[b]	22	5:57	12	2498005		2	3	4	5	6	7	8			4	5	6	7	8	9	10	Chūn fēn		6	7	8	9	10	11	12	
	23	24	25	26	27	○	29	8:38	13	2498012	Nisan 5887	9	10	11	12	13	14	15[g]		Month 2 Dīng-Hài	11	12	13	14	15	16	17		Paremotep 1843	13	14	15	16	17	18	19	Magābit 2119
	30	31	1	2	◑	4	5	23:25	14	2498019		16	17	18	19	20	21	22			18	19	20	21	22	23	24[c]	Qīng míng		20	21	22	23	24	25	26	
	6	7	8	9	10	●	12	18:18	15	2498026		23	24	25	26	27	28	29			25	26	27	28	29	30	1			27	28	29	30	1	2	3	
April 2127	13	14	15	16	17	18	◐	21:31	16	2498033		30	1	2	3	4	5	6	Fri 22h24m3p	Month 3 Dīng-Hài	2	3	4	5	6	7	8			4	5	6	7	8	9	10	
	20	21	22	23	24	25	○	17:33	17	2498040		7	8	9	10	11	12	13			9	10	11	12	13	14	15	Gǔ yǔ	Parmoute 1843	11	12	13	14	15	16	17	Miyāzyā 2119
	27	28	29	30	1	2	◑	9:46	18	2498047	Iyyar 5887	14	15	16	17	18	19	20			16	17	18	19	20*	21	22			18	19	20	21	22	23	24	
	4	5	6	7	8	9	10		19	2498054		21	22	23	24	25	26	27			23	24	25	26	27	28	29	Lì xià		25[f]	26	27	28	29[g]	30	1	
May 2127	●	12	13	14	15	16	17	11:02	20	2498061		28	29	1	2	3	4	5	Sun 11h8m4p		1	2	3	4	5	6	7			2	3	4	5	6	7	8	
	18	◐	20	21	22	23	24	9:18	21	2498068		6[h]	7	8	9	10	11	12		Month 4 Dīng-Hài	8	9	10	11	12	13	14	Xiǎo mǎn		9	10	11	12	13	14	15	
	25	○	27	28	29	30	31	1:07	22	2498075	Sivan 5887	13	14	15	16	17	18	19			15	16	17	18	19	20	21		Pashons 1843	16	17	18	19	20	21	22	Genbot 2119
	◑	2	3	4	5	6	7	22:17	23	2498082		20	21	22	23	24	25	26			22	23	24	25	26	27	28	Máng zhòng		23	24	25	26	27	28	29	
	8	9	●	11	12	13	14	2:25	24	2498089		27	28	29	30	1	2	3	Mon 23h52m5p		29	30	1	2	3	4	5[d]			30	1	2	3	4	5	6	
June 2127	15	16	◐	18	19	20	21[c]	17:48	25	2498096		4	5	6	7	8	9	10		Month 5 Dīng-Hài	6	7	8	9	10	11	12			7	8	9	10	11	12	13	
	22	23	○	25	26	27	28	8:17	26	2498103	Tammuz 5887	11	12	13	14	15	16	17			13	14	15	16	17	18	19	Xià zhì	Paōne 1843	14	15	16	17	18	19	20	Sanē 2119
	29	30	◑	2	3	4	5	13:04	27	2498110		18	19	20	21	22	23	24			20	21*	22	23	24	25	26			21	22	23	24	25	26	27	
	6	7	8	●	10	11	12	16:06	28	2498117		25	26	27	28	29	1	2	Wed 12h36m6p		27	28	29	30	1	2	3	Xiǎo shǔ		28	29	30	1	2	3	4	
July 2127	13	14	15	◐	17	18	19	23:51	29	2498124		3	4	5	6	7	8	9		Month 6 Dīng-Hài	4	5	6	7	8	9	10			5	6	7	8	9	10	11	
	20	21	22	○	24	25	26	16:15	30	2498131	Av 5887	10[i]	11	12	13	14	15	16			11	12	13	14	15	16	17	Dà shǔ	Epēp 1843	12	13	14	15	16	17	18	Hamlē 2119
	27	28	29	30	◑	1	2	5:43	31	2498138		17	18	19	20	21	22	23			18	19	20	21	22	23	24			19	20	21	22	23	24	25	
	3	4	5	6	7	●	9	4:12	32	2498145		24	25	26	27	28	29	30			25	26	27	28	29	1	2	Lì qiū		26	27	28	29	30	1	2	
August 2127	10	11	12	13	14	◐	16	4:39	33	2498152		1	2	3	4	5	6	7	Fri 1h20m7p	Month 7 Dīng-Hài	3	4	5	6	7[e]	8	9			3	4	5	6	7	8	9	
	17	18	19	20	21	○	23	2:10	34	2498159		8	9	10	11	12	13	14			10	11	12	13	14	15[f]	16	Chǔ shǔ		10	11	12	13[h]	14	15	16	
	24	25	26	27	28	◑	30	23:28	35	2498166	Elul 5887	15	16	17	18	19	20	21			17	18	19	20	21	22*	23		Mesorē 1843	17	18	19	20	21	22	23	Naḥasē 2119
	31	1	2	3	4	5	●	15:08	36	2498173		22	23	24	25	26	27	28			24	25	26	27	28	29	1	Bái lù		24	25	26	27	28	29	30	
	7	8	9	10	11	12	◐	9:38	37	2498180		29	1[a]	2[a]	3	4	5	6	Sat 14h4m8p	Month 8 Dīng-Hài	2	3	4	5	6	7	8		Epag. 1843	1	2	3	4	5	6	1[a]	Pāg. 2119
September 2127	14	15	16	17	18	19	○	14:53	38	2498187		7	8	9	10[b]	11	12	13			9	10	11	12	13	14	15[g]			2	3	4	5	6	7	8	
	21	22	23[d]	24	25	26	27		39	2498194	Tishri 5888	14	15[c]	16	17	18	19	20			16	17	18	19	20	21	22	Qiū fēn	Thoout 1844	9	10	11	12	13	14	15	Maskaram 2120
	◑	29	30	1	2	3	4	17:30	40	2498201		21	22	23	24	25	26	27			23	24	25	26	27	28	29			16	17[b]	18	19	20	21	22	
	5	●	7	8	9	10	11	1:17	41	2498208		28	29	30	1	2	3	4	Mon 2h48m9p		30	1	2	3	4	5	6	Hán lù		23	24	25	26	27	28	29	
October 2127	◐	13	14	15	16	17	18	16:20	42	2498215		5	6	7	8	9	10	11		Month 9 Dīng-Hài	7	8	9[h]	10	11	12	13			30	1	2	3	4	5	6	
	19	○	21	22	23	24	25	6:33	43	2498222	Heshvan 5888	12	13	14	15	16	17	18			14	15	16	17	18	19	20	Shuāng jiàng	Paope 1844	7	8	9	10	11	12	13	Ṭeqemt 2120
	26	27	◑	29	30	31	1	10:57	44	2498229		19	20	21	22	23	24	25			21	22	23*	24	25	26	27			14	15	16	17	18	19	20	
	2	3	●	5	6	7	8	11:06	45	2498236		26	27	28	29	1	2	3			28	29	1	2	3	4	5	Lì dōng		21	22	23	24	25	26	27	
November 2127	9	10	◐	12	13	14	15	2:09	46	2498243		4	5	6	7	8	9	10	Tue 15h32m10p	Month 10 Dīng-Hài	6	7	8	9	10	11	12			28	29	30	1	2	3	4	
	16	17	18	○	20	21	22	0:31	47	2498250	Kislev 5888	11	12	13	14	15	16	17			13	14	15	16	17	18	19	Xiǎo xuě		5	6	7	8	9	10	11	
	23	24	25	26	◑	28	29	2:51	48	2498257		18	19	20	21	22	23	24			20	21	22	23	24	25	26		Athōr 1844	12	13	14	15	16	17	18	Hedār 2120
	30	1	2	●	4	5	6	21:00	49	2498264		25[e]	26[e]	27[e]	28[e]	29[e]	1[e]	2[e]			27	28	29	30	1	2	3			19	20	21	22	23	24	25	
	7	8	9	◐	11	12	13	15:57	50	2498271		3[d]	4	5	6	7	8	9	Thu 4h16m11p	Month 11 Dīng-Hài	4	5	6	7	8	9	10	Dà xuě		26	27	28	29	30	1	2	
December 2127	14	15	16	17	○	19	20	19:35	51	2498278	Teveth 5888	10	11	12	13	14	15	16			11	12	13	14	15	16	17			3	4	5	6	7	8	9	
	21	22[e]	23	24	25	◑	27	16:22	52	2498285		17	18	19	20	21	22	23			18	19[i]	20	21	22	23	24*	Dōng zhì	Koiak 1844	10	11	12	13	14	15	16	Tākhśāś 2120
	28	29	30	31	1	●	3	7:28	1	2498292		24	25	26	27	28	29	1	Fri 17h0m12p		25	26	27	28	29	1	2			17	18	19	20	21	22	23	

[a]New Year
[b]Spring (2:01)
[c]Summer (18:00)
[d]Autumn (10:54)
[e]Winter (9:19)
● New moon
◐ First quarter moon
○ Full moon
◑ Last quarter moon

‡Leap year
[a]New Year
[b]Yom Kippur
[c]Sukkot
[d]Winter starts
[e]Ḥanukkah
[f]Purim
[g]Passover
[h]Shavuot
[i]Fast of Av

‡Leap year
[a]New Year (4825, Pig)
[b]Lantern Festival
[c]Qīngmíng
[d]Dragon Festival
[e]Qīqiǎo
[f]Hungry Ghosts
[g]Mid-Autumn Festival
[h]Double-Ninth Festival
[i]Dōngzhì
*Start of 60-name cycle

‡Leap year
[a]New Year
[b]Building of the Cross
[c]Christmas
[d]Jesus's Circumcision
[e]Epiphany
[f]Easter
[g]Mary's Announcement
[h]Jesus's Transfiguration

PERSIAN (ASTRONOMICAL) 1505/1506

Month	Sun	Mon	Tue	Wed	Thu	Fri	Sat
DEY 1505	8	9	10	11	12	13	14
	15	16	17	18	19	20	21
	22	23	24	25	26	27	28
BAHMAN 1505	29	30	1	2	3	4	5
	6	7	8	9	10	11	12
	13	14	15	16	17	18	19
	20	21	22	23	24	25	26
ESFAND 1505	27	28	29	30	1	2	3
	4	5	6	7	8	9	10
	11	12	13	14	15	16	17
	18	19	20	21	22	23	24
FARVARDĪN 1506	25	26	27	28	29	1[a]	2
	3	4	5	6	7	8	9
	10	11	12	13[b]	14	15	16
	17	18	19	20	21	22	23
	24	25	26	27	28	29	30
ORDĪBEHEŠT 1506	31	1	2	3	4	5	6
	7	8	9	10	11	12	13
	14	15	16	17	18	19	20
	21	22	23	24	25	26	27
XORDĀD 1506	28	29	30	31	1	2	3
	4	5	6	7	8	9	10
	11	12	13	14	15	16	17
	18	19	20	21	22	23	24
	25	26	27	28	29	30	31
TĪR 1506	1	2	3	4	5	6	7
	8	9	10	11	12	13	14
	15	16	17	18	19	20	21
	22	23	24	25	26	27	28
MORDĀD 1506	29	30	31	1	2	3	4
	5	6	7	8	9	10	11
	12	13	14	15	16	17	18
	19	20	21	22	23	24	25
SHAHRĪVAR 1506	26	27	28	29	30	31	1
	2	3	4	5	6	7	8
	9	10	11	12	13	14	15
	16	17	18	19	20	21	22
	23	24	25	26	27	28	29
MEHR 1506	30	31	1	2	3	4	5
	6	7	8	9	10	11	12
	13	14	15	16	17	18	19
	20	21	22	23	24	25	26
ĀBĀN 1506	27	28	29	30	1	2	3
	4	5	6	7	8	9	10
	11	12	13	14	15	16	17
	18	19	20	21	22	23	24
ĀZAR 1506	25	26	27	28	29	30	1
	2	3	4	5	6	7	8
	9	10	11	12	13	14	15
	16	17	18	19	20	21	22
	23	24	25	26	27	28	29
DEY 1506	30	1	2	3	4	5	6
	7	8	9	10	11	12	13

HINDU LUNAR 2183‡/2184

Month	Sun	Mon	Tue	Wed	Thu	Fri	Sat
MĀRGAŚĪRA 2183	15	16	17	18	19	20	21
	22	23	24	**25**	27	28	29
PAUSHA 2183	30	1	2	3	4	5	6
	7	8	9	9	10	11	12
	13	14	15	16	17	18	19
	20	22	23	24	25	26	27
MĀGHA 2183	28	29	30	1	2	3	4
	5	6	7	8	9	10	11
	12	13	14	15	16	17	18
	19	20	21	22	23	24	**25**
PHĀLGUNA 2183	27	28	29[h]	30	1	1	2
	3	4	5	6	7	8	9
	10	11	12	13	14	15[i]	16
	17	**18**	20	21	22	23	24
CHAITRA 2184	25	26	27	28	29	30	1[a]
	2	3	4	4	5	6	7
	8[b]	9	10	**11**	13	14	15
	16	17	18	19	20	21	22
	23	24	25	26	27	28	29
VAIŚĀKHA 2184	30	1	2	3	4	5	6
	7	8	9	10	11	12	13
	14	**15**	17	18	19	20	21
	22	23	24	25	26	27	28
JYAISHTHA 2184	29	30	30	1	2	3	4
	5	6	7	**8**	10	11	12
	13	14	15	16	17	18	19
	20	21	22	23	24	25	26
ĀSHĀḌHA 2184	27	28	29	30	1	2	3
	4	5	6	7	8	9	10
	11	13	14	15	16	17	18
	19	20	21	22	23	24	25
ŚRĀVAṆA 2184	26	27	27	28	29	30	1
	2	**3**	5	6	7	8	9
	10	11	12	13	14	15	16
	17	18	19	20	21	22	23[c]
	24	25	26	27	28	29	30
BHĀDRAPADA 2184	1	2	3	4[d]	5	6	**7**
	9	10	11	12	13	14	15
	16	17	18	19	20	21	22
	23	23	24	25	26	27	28
ĀŚVINA 2184	29	**30**	2	3	4	5	6
	7	8[e]	9[e]	10[e]	11	12	13
	14	15	16	17	18	19	20
	21	22	23	24	25	26	27
KĀRTTIKA 2184	28	29	30	1[f]	2	3	**4**
	6	7	8	9	10	11	12
	13	14	15	16	17	17	18
	19	20	21	22	23	24	25
MĀRGAŚĪRA 2184	26	27	**28**	30	1	2	3
	4	5	6	7	8	9	10
	11[g]	12	13	14	15	16	17
	18	19	20	21	22	23	24
PAUSHA 2184	25	26	27	28	29	30	1

HINDU SOLAR 2048/2049

Month	Sun	Mon	Tue	Wed	Thu	Fri	Sat
PAUSHA 2048	12	13	14	15	16	17	18
	19	20	21	22	23	24	25
MĀGHA 2048	26	27	28	29	1[b]	2	3
	4	5	6	7	8	9	10
	11	12	13	14	15	16	17
	18	19	20	21	22	23	24
PHĀLGUNA 2048	25	26	27	28	29	30	1
	2	3	4	5	6	7	8
	9	10	11	12	13	14	15
	16	17	18	19	20	21	22
	23	24	25	26	27	28	29
CHAITRA 2048	1	2	3	4	5	6	7
	8	9	10	11	12	13	14
	15	16	17	18	19	20	21
	22	23	24	25	26	27	28
VAIŚĀKHA 2049	29	30	31	1[a]	2	3	4
	5	6	7	8	9	10	11
	12	13	14	15	16	17	18
	19	20	21	22	23	24	25
JYAISHTHA 2049	26	27	28	29	30	31	1
	2	3	4	5	6	7	8
	9	10	11	12	13	14	15
	16	17	18	19	20	21	22
	23	24	25	26	27	28	29
ĀSHĀḌHA 2049	30	31	1	2	3	4	5
	6	7	8	9	10	11	12
	13	14	15	16	17	18	19
	20	21	22	23	24	25	26
ŚRĀVAṆA 2049	27	28	29	30	31	32	1
	2	3	4	5	6	7	8
	9	10	11	12	13	14	15
	16	17	18	19	20	21	22
	23	24	25	26	27	28	29
BHĀDRAPADA 2049	30	31	1	2	3	4	5
	6	7	8	9	10	11	12
	13	14	15	16	17	18	19
	20	21	22	23	24	25	26
ĀŚVINA 2049	27	28	29	30	31	1	2
	3	4	5	6	7	8	9
	10	11	12	13	14	15	16
	17	18	19	20	21	22	23
	24	25	26	27	28	29	30
KĀRTTIKA 2049	31	1	2	3	4	5	6
	7	8	9	10	11	12	13
	14	15	16	17	18	19	20
	21	22	23	24	25	26	27
MĀRGAŚĪRA 2049	28	29	30	1	2	3	4
	5	6	7	8	9	10	11
	12	13	14	15	16	17	18
	19	20	21	22	23	24	25
PAUSHA 2049	26	27	28	29	1	2	3
	4	5	6	7	8	9	10
	11	12	13	14	15	16	17

ISLAMIC (ASTRONOMICAL) 1551/1552

Month	Sun	Mon	Tue	Wed	Thu	Fri	Sat
SHA'BĀN 1551	15	16	17	18	19	20	21
	22	23	24	25	26	27	28
RAMAḌĀN 1551	29	30	1[e]	2	3	4	5
	6	7	8	9	10	11	12
	13	14	15	16	17	18	19
	20	21	22	23	24	25	26
SHAWWĀL 1551	27	28	29	30	1[f]	2	3
	4	5	6	7	8	9	10
	11	12	13	14	15	16	17
	18	19	20	21	22	23	24
DHU AL-QA'DA 1551	25	26	27	28	29	1	2
	3	4	5	6	7	8	9
	10	11	12	13	14	15	16
	17	18	19	20	21	22	23
	24	25	26	27	28	29	30
DHU AL-ḤIJJA 1551	1	2	3	4	5	6	7
	8	9	10[g]	11	12	13	14
	15	16	17	18	19	20	21
	22	23	24	25	26	27	28
MUḤARRAM 1552	29	30	1[a]	2	3	4	5
	6	7	8	9	10[b]	11	12
	13	14	15	16	17	18	19
	20	21	22	23	24	25	26
ṢAFAR 1552	27	28	29	30	1	2	3
	4	5	6	7	8	9	10
	11	12	13	14	15	16	17
	18	19	20	21	22	23	24
RABĪ' I 1552	25	26	27	28	29	1	2
	3	4	5	6	7	8	9
	10	11	12[c]	13	14	15	16
	17	18	19	20	21	22	23
	24	25	26	27	28	29	30
RABĪ' II 1552	1	2	3	4	5	6	7
	8	9	10	11	12	13	14
	15	16	17	18	19	20	21
	22	23	24	25	26	27	28
JUMĀDĀ I 1552	29	1	2	3	4	5	6
	7	8	9	10	11	12	13
	14	15	16	17	18	19	20
	21	22	23	24	25	26	27
JUMĀDĀ II 1552	28	29	1	2	3	4	5
	6	7	8	9	10	11	12
	13	14	15	16	17	18	19
	20	21	22	23	24	25	26
RAJAB 1552	27	28	29	30	1	2	3
	4	5	6	7	8	9	10
	11	12	13	14	15	16	17
	18	19	20	21	22	23	24
SHA'BĀN 1552	25	26	27[d]	28	29	1	2
	3	4	5	6	7	8	9
	10	11	12	13	14	15	16
	17	18	19	20	21	22	23
	24	25	26	27	28	29	1

GREGORIAN 2127

Julian (Sun)	Sun	Mon	Tue	Wed	Thu	Fri	Sat	Month
Dec 15	29	30	31	1	2	3	4	JANUARY 2127
	5	6	7	8[a]	9	10	11	
Dec 29	12	13	14	15[b]	16	17	18	
	19	20	21	22	23	24	25	
Jan 12	26	27	28	29	30	31	1	FEBRUARY 2127
	2	3	4	5	6	7	8	
Jan 26	9	10	11	12[c]	13	14	15	
	16	17	18	19	20	21	22	
Feb 9	23	24	25	26	27	28	1	MARCH 2127
	2	3	4	5	6	7	8	
Feb 23	9	10	11	12	13	14	15	
	16	17	18	19	20	21	22	
Mar 9	23[d]	24	25	26	27	28	29	
	30[e]	31	1	2	3	4	5	APRIL 2127
Mar 23	6	7	8	9	10	11	12	
	13	14	15	16	17	18	19	
Apr 6	20	21	22	23	24	25	26	
	27	28	29	30	1	2	3	MAY 2127
Apr 20	4[f]	5	6	7	8	9	10	
	11	12	13	14	15	16	17	
May 4	18	19	20	21	22	23	24	
	25	26	27	28	29	30	31	
May 18	1	2	3	4	5	6	7	JUNE 2127
	8	9	10	11	12	13	14	
Jun 1	15	16	17	18	19	20	21	
	22	23	24	25	26	27	28	
Jun 15	29	30	1	2	3	4	5	JULY 2127
	6	7	8	9	10	11	12	
Jun 29	13	14	15	16	17	18	19	
	20	21	22	23	24	25	26	
Jul 13	27	28	29	30	31	1	2	AUGUST 2127
	3	4	5	6	7	8	9	
Jul 27	10	11	12	13	14	15	16	
	17	18	19	20	21	22	23	
Aug 10	24	25	26	27	28	29	30	
	31	1	2	3	4	5	6	SEPTEMBER 2127
Aug 24	7	8	9	10	11	12	13	
	14	15	16	17	18	19	20	
Sep 7	21	22	23	24	25	26	27	
	28	29	30	1	2	3	4	OCTOBER 2127
Sep 21	5	6	7	8	9	10	11	
	12	13	14	15	16	17	18	
Oct 5	19	20	21	22	23	24	25	
	26	27	28	29	30	31	1	NOVEMBER 2127
Oct 19	2	3	4	5	6	7	8	
	9	10	11	12	13	14	15	
Nov 2	16	17	18	19	20	21	22	
	23	24	25	26	27	28	29	
Nov 16	30[g]	1	2	3	4	5	6	DECEMBER 2127
	7	8	9	10	11	12	13	
Nov 30	14	15	16	17	18	19	20	
	21	22	23	24	25[h]	26	27	
Dec 14	28	29	30	31	1	2	3	

Persian: [a]New Year; [b]Sizdeh Bedar

Hindu Lunar: ‡Leap year; [a]New Year (Sarvajit); [b]Birthday of Rāma; [c]Birthday of Krishna; [d]Ganēśa Chaturthī; [e]Dashara; [f]Diwali; [g]Birthday of Vishnu; [h]Night of Śiva; [i]Holi

Hindu Solar: [a]New Year (Śubhakṛit); [b]Pongal

Islamic: [a]New Year; [b]'Ashūrā'; [c]Prophet's Birthday; [d]Ascent of the Prophet; [e]Start of Ramaḍān; [f]'Id al-Fiṭr; [g]'Id al-'Aḍḥā

Gregorian: [a]Orthodox Christmas; [b]Julian New Year; [c]Ash Wednesday; [d]Feast of Orthodoxy; [e]Easter; [f]Orthodox Easter; [g]Advent; [h]Christmas

2128

GREGORIAN 2128‡	Sun	Mon	Tue	Wed	Thu	Fri	Sat	Lunar Phases	ISO WEEK (Mon)	JULIAN DAY (Sun noon)	HEBREW 5888‡/5889	Sun	Mon	Tue	Wed	Thu	Fri	Sat	Molad	CHINESE Dīng-Hài/Wù-Zǐ‡	Sun	Mon	Tue	Wed	Thu	Fri	Sat	Solar Term	COPTIC 1844/1845	Sun	Mon	Tue	Wed	Thu	Fri	Sat	ETHIOPIC 2120/2121
JANUARY 2128	28	29	30	31	1[a]	●	3	7:28	1	2498292		24	25	26	27	28	29	1	Fri 17h0m12p		25	26	27	28	29	1	2		KOIAK 1844	17	18	19	20	21	22	23	TĀKHŚĀŚ 2120
	4	5	6	7	8	◐	10	9:33	2	2498299	SHEVAT 5888	2	3	4	5	6	7	8		MONTH 12 Dīng-Hài	3	4	5	6	7	8	9	Xiǎo hán		24	25	26	27	28	29[c]	30	
	11	12	13	14	15	16	○	14:21	3	2498306		9	10	11	12	13	14	15			10	11	12	13	14	15	16		TŌBE 1844	1	2	3	4	5	6[d]	7	
	18	19	20	21	22	23	24		4	2498313		16	17	18	19	20	21	22			17	18	19	20	21	22	23	Dà hán		8	9	10	11[e]	12	13	14	ṬER 2120
	◑	26	27	28	29	30	●	3:05 18:57	5	2498320		23	24	25	26	27	28	29			24	25	26	27	28	29	30			15	16	17	18	19	20	21	
FEBRUARY 2128	1	2	3	4	5	6	7		6	2498327		30	1	2	3	4	5	6	Sun 5h44m13p		1[a]	2	3	4	5	6	7	Lì chūn		22	23	24	25	26	27	28	
	◐	9	10	11	12	13	14	5:41	7	2498334	ADAR I 5888	7	8	9	10	11	12	13		MONTH 1 Wù-Zǐ	8	9	10	11	12	13	14		MESHIR 1844	29	30	1	2	3	4	5	
	15	○	17	18	19	20	21	7:26	8	2498341		14	15	16	17	18	19	20			15[b]	16	17	18	19	20	21	Yǔ shuǐ		6	7	8	9	10	11	12	YAKĀTIT 2120
	22	◑	24	25	26	27	28	11:19	9	2498348		21	22	23	24	25	26	27			22	23	24	25*	26	27	28			13	14	15	16	17	18	19	
MARCH 2128	29	●	2	3	4	5	6	7:38	10	2498355		28	29	30	1	2	3	4	Mon 18h28m14p		29	1	2	3	4	5	6	Jīng zhé		20	21	22	23	24	25	26	
	7	8	◐	10	11	12	13	2:33	11	2498362	ADAR II 5888	5	6	7	8	9	10	11		MONTH 2 Wù-Zǐ	7	8	9	10	11	12	13		PAREMOTEP 1844	27	28	29	30	1	2	3	
	14	15	○	17	18	19	20[b]	21:52	12	2498369		12	13	14[f]	15	16	17	18			14	15	16	17	18	19	20	Chūn fēn		4	5	6	7	8	9	10	MAGĀBIT 2120
	21	22	◑	24	25	26	27	18:07	13	2498376		19	20	21	22	23	24	25			21	22	23	24	25	26	27			11	12	13	14	15	16	17	
	28	29	●	31	1	2	3	21:25	14	2498383		26	27	28	29	1	2	3	Wed 7h12m15p		28	29	30	1	2	3	4			18	19	20	21	22	23	24	
APRIL 2128	4	5	6	◐	8	9	10	22:23	15	2498390	NISAN 5888	4	5	6	7	8	9	10		MONTH 3 Wù-Zǐ	5[c]	6	7	8	9	10	11	Qīng míng	PARMOUTE 1844	25	26	27	28	29	30	1	
	11	12	13	14	○	16	17	9:15	16	2498397		11	12	13	14	15[g]	16	17			12	13	14	15	16	17	18			2	3	4	5	6	7	8	MIYĀZYĀ 2120
	18	19	20	21	◑	23	24	0:44	17	2498404		18	19	20	21	22	23	24			19	20	21	22	23	24	25	Gǔ yǔ		9	10	11	12	13	14	15	
	25	26	27	28	●	30	1	11:59	18	2498411		25	26	27	28	29	30	1	Thu 19h56m16p		26*	27	28	29	1	2	3			16[f]	17	18	19	20	21	22	
MAY 2128	2	3	4	5	6	◐	8	15:49	19	2498418	IYAR 5888	2	3	4	5	6	7	8		MONTH 4 Wù-Zǐ	4	5	6	7	8	9	10	Lì xià		23	24	25	26	27	28	29[g]	
	9	10	11	12	13	○	15	18:01	20	2498425		9	10	11	12	13	14	15			11	12	13	14	15	16	17		PASHONS 1844	30	1	2	3	4	5	6	
	16	17	18	19	20	◑	22	8:21	21	2498432		16	17	18	19	20	21	22			18	19	20	21	22	23	24	Xiǎo mǎn		7	8	9	10	11	12	13	GENBOT 2120
	23	24	25	26	27	28	●	2:59	22	2498439		23	24	25	26	27	28	29			25	26	27	28	29	30	1			14	15	16	17	18	19	20	
JUNE 2128	30	31	1	2	3	4	5		23	2498446		1	2	3	4	5	6[h]	7	Sat 8h40m17p		2	3	4	5[d]	6	7	8	Máng zhòng		21	22	23	24	25	26	27	
	◐	7	8	9	10	11	12	6:04	24	2498453	SIVAN 5888	8	9	10	11	12	13	14		MONTH 5 Wù-Zǐ	9	10	11	12	13	14	15		PAŌNE 1844	28	29	30	1	2	3	4	
	○	14	15	16	17	18	◑	1:08 17:51	25	2498460		15	16	17	18	19	20	21			16	17	18	19	20	21	22			5	6	7	8	9	10	11	SANĒ 2120
	20[c]	21	22	23	24	25	26		26	2498467		22	23	24	25	26	27	28			23	24	25	26	27*	28	29	Xià zhì		12	13	14	15	16	17	18	
JULY 2128	●	28	29	30	1	2	3	18:10	27	2498474		29	30	1	2	3	4	5	Sun 21h25m0p		30	1	2	3	4	5	6			19	20	21	22	23	24	25	
	4	◐	6	7	8	9	10	16:56	28	2498481	TAMMUZ 5888	6	7	8	9	10	11	12		MONTH 6 Wù-Zǐ	7	8	9	10	11	12	13	Xiǎo shǔ	EPĒP 1844	26	27	28	29	30	1	2	
	11	○	13	14	15	16	17	7:48	29	2498488		13	14	15	16	17	18	19			14	15	16	17	18	19	20			3	4	5	6	7	8	9	ḤAMLĒ 2120
	18	◑	20	21	22	23	24	5:46	30	2498495		20	21	22	23	24	25	26			21	22	23	24	25	26	27	Dà shǔ		10	11	12	13	14	15	16	
	25	26	●	28	29	30	31	9:10	31	2498502		27	28	29	1	2	3	4	Tue 10h9m1p		28	29	1	2	3	4	5			17	18	19	20	21	22	23	
AUGUST 2128	1	2	3	◐	5	6	7	0:55	32	2498509	AV 5888	5	6	7	8	9[i]	10	11		MONTH 7 Wù-Zǐ	6	7[e]	8	9	10	11	12	Lì qiū		24	25	26	27	28	29	30	
	8	9	○	11	12	13	14	15:11	33	2498516		12	13	14	15	16	17	18			13	14	15[f]	16	17	18	19		MESORĒ 1844	1	2	3	4	5	6	7	
	15	16	◑	18	19	20	21	20:22	34	2498523		19	20	21	22	23	24	25			20	21	22	23	24	25	26	Chǔ shǔ		8	9	10	11	12	13[h]	14	NAHASĒ 2120
	22	23	24	●	26	27	28	23:35	35	2498530		26	27	28	29	30	1	2	Wed 22h53m2p		27	28	29	30	1	2	3			15	16	17	18	19	20	21	
SEPTEMBER 2128	29	30	31	1	◐	3	4	7:04	36	2498537	ELUL 5888	3	4	5	6	7	8	9		MONTH 8 Wù-Zǐ	4	5	6	7	8	9	10			22	23	24	25	26	27	28	
	5	6	7	8	○	10	11	0:15	37	2498544		10	11	12	13	14	15	16			11	12	13	14	15[g]	16	17	Bái lù	EPAG. 1844	29	30	1	2	3	4	5	PĀG. 2120
	12	13	14	15	◑	17	18	13:37	38	2498551		17	18	19	20	21	22	23			18	19	20	21	22	23	24		THOOUT 1845	1[a]	2	3	4	5	6	7	
	19	20	21	22[d]	23	●	25	12:58	39	2498558		24	25	26	27	28	29	1[a]	Fri 11h37m3p		25	26	27	28	29	1	2	Qiū fēn		8	9	10	11	12	13	14	MASKARAM 2121
OCTOBER 2128	26	27	28	29	30	◐	2	12:42	40	2498565	TISHRI 5889	2[a]	3	4	5	6	7	8		MONTH 9 Wù-Zǐ	3	4	5	6	7	8	9[h]			15	16	17[b]	18	19	20	21	
	3	4	5	6	7	○	9	11:42	41	2498572		9	10[b]	11	12	13	14	15[c]			10	11	12	13	14	15	16	Hán lù		22	23	24	25	26	27	28	
	10	11	12	13	14	15	◑	8:58	42	2498579		16	17	18	19	20	21	22			17	18	19	20	21	22	23		PAOPE 1845	29	30	1	2	3	4	5	
	17	18	19	20	21	22	23		43	2498586		23	24	25	26	27	28	29			24	25	26	27	28	29*	30	Shuāng jiàng		6	7	8	9	10	11	12	ṬEQEMT 2121
	●	25	26	27	28	29	◐	1:08 19:15	44	2498593		30	1	2	3	4	5	6	Sun 0h21m4p		1	2	3	4	5	6	7			13	14	15	16	17	18	19	
NOVEMBER 2128	31	1	2	3	4	5	6		45	2498600	HESHVAN 5889	7	8	9	10	11	12	13		MONTH 10 Wù-Zǐ	8	9	10	11	12	13	14			20	21	22	23	24	25	26	
	○	8	9	10	11	12	13	1:54	46	2498607		14	15	16	17	18	19	20			15	16	17	18	19	20	21	Lì dōng	ATHŌR 1845	27	28	29	30	1	2	3	
	14	◑	16	17	18	19	20	5:08	47	2498614		21	22	23	24	25	26	27			22	23	24	25	26	27	28			4	5	6	7	8	9	10	ḪEDĀR 2121
	21	●	23	24	25	26	27	12:21	48	2498621		28	29	30	1	2	3	4	Mon 13h5m5p		29	1	2	3	4	5	6	Xiǎo xuě		11	12	13	14	15	16	17	
DECEMBER 2128	28	◐	30	1	2	3	4	3:54	49	2498628	KISLEV 5889	5	6	7	8	9	10	11		MONTH 11* Wù-Zǐ	7	8	9	10	11	12	13			18	19	20	21	22	23	24	
	5	○	7	8	9	10	11	18:52	50	2498635		12	13[d]	14	15	16	17	18			14	15	16	17	18	19	20	Dà xuě	KOIAK 1845	25	26	27	28	29	30	1	
	12	13	14	◑	16	17	18	0:16	51	2498642		19	20	21	22	23	24	25[e]			21	22	23	24	25	26	27			2	3	4	5	6	7	8	TĀKHŚĀŚ 2121
	19	20	●[e]	22	23	24	25	23:08	52	2498649	TEVETH 5889	26[e]	27[e]	28[e]	29[e]	30[e]	1[e]	2[e]	Wed 1h49m6p	LEAP MONTH 11 Wù-Zǐ	28	29	30[i]*	1	2	3	4	Dōng zhì		9	10	11	12	13	14	15	
	26	27	◐	29	30	31	1	15:25	53	2498656		3	4	5	6	7	8	9			5	6	7	8	9	10	11			16	17	18	19	20	21	22	

‡Leap year
[a]New Year
[b]Spring (7:57)
[c]Summer (23:57)
[d]Autumn (16:44)
[e]Winter (15:11)
● New moon
◐ First quarter moon
○ Full moon
◑ Last quarter moon

‡Leap year
[a]New Year
[b]Yom Kippur
[c]Sukkot
[d]Winter starts
[e]Ḥanukkah
[f]Purim
[g]Passover
[h]Shavuot
[i]Fast of Av

‡Leap year
[a]New Year (4826, Rat)
[b]Lantern Festival
[c]Qīngmíng
[d]Dragon Festival
[e]Qīqiǎo
[f]Hungry Ghosts
[g]Mid-Autumn Festival
[h]Double-Ninth Festival
[i]Dōngzhì
*Start of 60-name cycle

[a]New Year
[b]Building of the Cross
[c]Christmas
[d]Jesus's Circumcision
[e]Epiphany
[f]Easter
[g]Mary's Announcement
[h]Jesus's Transfiguration

PERSIAN (ASTRONOMICAL) 1506/1507‡

Month	Sun	Mon	Tue	Wed	Thu	Fri	Sat
	7	8	9	10	11	12	13
DEY 1506	14	15	16	17	18	19	20
	21	22	23	24	25	26	27
	28	29	30	*1*	2	3	4
	5	6	7	8	9	10	11
BAHMAN 1506	12	13	14	15	16	17	18
	19	20	21	22	23	24	25
	26	27	28	29	30	*1*	2
	3	4	5	6	7	8	9
ESFAND 1506	10	11	12	13	14	15	16
	17	18	19	20	21	22	23
	24	25	26	27	28	29	1[a]
	2*	3	4	5	6	7	8
FARVARDIN 1507	9	10	11	12	13[b]	14	15
	16	17	18	19	20	21	22
	23	24	25	26	27	28	29
	30	31	*1*	2	3	4	5
ORDIBEHESHT 1507	6	7	8	9	10	11	12
	13	14	15	16	17	18	19
	20	21	22	23	24	25	26
	27	28	29	30	31	*1*	2
	3	4	5	6	7	8	9
XORDAD 1507	10	11	12	13	14	15	16
	17	18	19	20	21	22	23
	24	25	26	27	28	29	30
	31	*1*	2	3	4	5	6
	7	8	9	10	11	12	13
TĪR 1507	14	15	16	17	18	19	20
	21	22	23	24	25	26	27
	28	29	30	31	*1*	2	3
	4	5	6	7	8	9	10
MORDĀD 1507	11	12	13	14	15	16	17
	18	19	20	21	22	23	24
	25	26	27	28	29	30	31
	1	2	3	4	5	6	7
	8	9	10	11	12	13	14
SHAHRĪVAR 1507	15	16	17	18	19	20	21
	22	23	24	25	26	27	28
	29	30	31	*1*	2	3	4
	5	6	7	8	9	10	11
MEHR 1507	12	13	14	15	16	17	18
	19	20	21	22	23	24	25
	26	27	28	29	30	*1*	2
	3	4	5	6	7	8	9
ĀBĀN 1507	10	11	12	13	14	15	16
	17	18	19	20	21	22	23
	24	25	26	27	28	29	30
	1	2	3	4	5	6	7
ĀZAR 1507	8	9	10	11	12	13	14
	15	16	17	18	19	20	21
	22	23	24	25	26	27	28
	29	30	*1*	2	3	4	5
DEY 1507	6	7	8	9	10	11	12

‡Leap year
[a]New Year (or next day)
*Near New Year: 1′51″
[b]Sizdeh Bedar

HINDU LUNAR 2184/2185

Month	Sun	Mon	Tue	Wed	Thu	Fri	Sat
	25	26	27	28	29	30	1
PAUSHA 2184	2	**3**	5	6	7	8	9
	9	10	11	12	13	14	15
	16	17	18	19	20	21	22
	23	24	25	26	**27**	29	30
	1	2	3	4	5	6	7
MĀGHA 2184	8	9	10	11	*11*	12	13
	14	15	16	17	18	19	20
	21	23	24	25	26	27	28[h]
	29	30	1	2	3	4	5
PHĀLGUNA 2184	6	7	8	9	10	11	12
	13	14	15[i]	16	17	18	19
	20	21	22	23	24	**25**	27
	28	29	30	1[a]	2	3	4
	5	*5*	6	7	8	9[b]	10
CHAITRA 2185	11	12	13	14	15	16	17
	18	**19**	21	22	23	24	25
	26	27	28	29	30	1	2
	3	4	5	6	7	8	9
VAIŚĀKHA 2185	*9*	**10**	12	13	14	15	16
	17	18	19	20	21	22	**23**
	25	26	27	28	29	30	*30*
	1	2	3	4	5	6	7
JYAISHTHA 2185	8	9	10	11	12	13	14
	15	17	18	19	20	21	22
	23	24	25	26	27	28	29
	30	1	2	3	4	5	6
ĀSHĀḌHA 2185	7	8	9	10	11	12	13
	14	15	16	17	**18**	20	21
	22	23	24	25	26	*26*	27
	28	29	30	1	2	3	4
ŚRĀVAṆA 2185	5	6	7	8	9	10	**11**
	13	14	15	16	17	18	19
	20	21	22	23[c]	24	25	26
	27	28	29	30	1	2	3
BHĀDRAPADA 2185	4[d]	5	6	7	8	9	10
	11	12	13	**14**	16	17	18
	19	20	21	22	23	*23*	24
	25	26	27	28	29	30	1
ĀŚVINA 2185	2	3	4	5	6	**7**[e]	9[e]
	10[e]	11	12	13	14	15	16
	17	18	19	20	21	22	23
	24	25	26	27	*27*	28	**29**
	1[f]	2	3	4	5	6	7
KĀRTTIKA 2185	8	9	10	11	**12**	14	15
	16	*16*	17	18	19	20	21
	22	23	24	25	26	27	28
	29	30	1	2	3	4	**5**
MĀRGAŚĪRA 2185	7	8	9	10	11[g]	12	13
	14	15	16	17	18	19	*19*
	20	21	22	23	24	25	26
	27	28	**29**	1	2	3	4
PAUSHA 2185	5	6	7	8	9	10	11

[a]New Year (Sarvadhārin)
[b]Birthday of Rāma
[c]Birthday of Krishna
[d]Ganēśa Chaturthī
[e]Dashara
[f]Diwali
[g]Birthday of Vishnu
[h]Night of Śiva
[i]Holi

HINDU SOLAR 2049/2050

Month	Sun	Mon	Tue	Wed	Thu	Fri	Sat
	11	12	13	14	15	16	17
PAUSHA 2049	18	19	20	21	22	23	24
	25	26	27	28	29	1[b]	2
	3	4	5	6	7	8	9
MĀGHA 2049	10	11	12	13	14	15	16
	17	18	19	20	21	22	23
	24	25	26	27	28	29	30
	1	2	3	4	5	6	7
PHĀLGUNA 2049	8	9	10	11	12	13	14
	15	16	17	18	19	20	21
	22	23	24	25	26	27	28
	29	30	1	2	3	4	5
	6	7	8	9	10	11	12
CHAITRA 2049	13	14	15	16	17	18	19
	20	21	22	23	24	25	26
	27	28	29	30	1[a]	2	3
	4	5	6	7	8	9	10
VAIŚĀKHA 2050	11	12	13	14	15	16	17
	18	19	20	21	22	23	24
	25	26	27	28	29	30	31
	1	2	3	4	5	6	7
JYAISHTHA 2050	8	9	10	11	12	13	14
	15	16	17	18	19	20	21
	22	23	24	25	26	27	28
	29	30	31	1	2	3	4
	5	6	7	8	9	10	11
ĀSHĀḌHA 2050	12	13	14	15	16	17	18
	19	20	21	22	23	24	25
	26	27	28	29	30	31	32
	1	2	3	4	5	6	7
	8	9	10	11	12	13	14
ŚRĀVAṆA 2050	15	16	17	18	19	20	21
	22	23	24	25	26	27	28
	29	30	31	32	1	2	3
	4	5	6	7	8	9	10
BHĀDRAPADA 2050	11	12	13	14	15	16	17
	18	19	20	21	22	23	24
	25	26	27	28	29	30	31
	1	2	3	4	5	6	7
ĀŚVINA 2050	8	9	10	11	12	13	14
	15	16	17	18	19	20	21
	22	23	24	25	26	27	28
	29	30	1	2	3	4	5
KĀRTTIKA 2050	6	7	8	9	10	11	12
	13	14	15	16	17	18	19
	20	21	22	23	24	25	26
	27	28	29	30	1	2	3
MĀRGAŚĪRA 2050	4	5	6	7	8	9	10
	11	12	13	14	15	16	17
	18	19	20	21	22	23	24
	25	26	27	28	29	1	2
PAUSHA 2050	3	4	5	6	7	8	9
	10	11	12	13	14	15	16

[a]New Year (Śobhana)
[b]Pongal

ISLAMIC (ASTRONOMICAL) 1552/1553

Month	Sun	Mon	Tue	Wed	Thu	Fri	Sat
	24	25	26	27	28	29	1[e]
	2	3	4	5	6	7	8
RAMAḌĀN 1552	9	10	11	12	13	14	15
	16	17	18	19	20	21	22
	23	24	25	26	27	28	29
	30	1[f]	2	3	4	5	6
	7	8	9	10	11	12	13
SHAWWĀL 1552	14	15	16	17	18	19	20
	21	22	23	24	25	26	27
	28	29	30	*1*	2	3	4
	5	6	7	8	9	10	11
DHU AL-QA'DA 1552	12	13	14	15	16	17	18
	19	20	21	22	23	24	25
	26	27	28	29	1	2	3
	4	5	6	7	8	9	10[g]
DHU AL-ḤIJJA 1552	11	12	13	14	15	16	17
	18	19	20	21	22	23	24
	25	26	27	28	29	30	*1*[a]
	2	3	4	5	6	7	8
MUḤARRAM 1553	9	10[b]	11	12	13	14	15
	16	17	18	19	20	21	22
	23	24	25	26	27	28	29
	30	*1*	2	3	4	5	6
	7	8	9	10	11	12	13
ṢAFAR 1553	14	15	16	17	18	19	20
	21	22	23	24	25	26	27
	28	29	*30*	1	2	3	4
	5	6	7	8	9	10	11
RABĪ' I 1553	12[c]	13	14	15	16	17	18
	19	20	21	22	23	24	25
	26	27	28	29	*1*	2	3
	4	5	6	7	8	9	10
RABĪ' II 1553	11	12	13	14	15	16	17
	18	19	20	21	22	23	24
	25	26	27	28	29	*30*	1
	2	3	4	5	6	7	8
JUMĀDĀ I 1553	9	10	11	12	13	14	15
	16	17	18	19	20	21	22
	23	24	25	26	27	28	29
	1	2	3	4	5	6	7
	8	9	10	11	12	13	14
JUMĀDĀ II 1553	15	16	17	18	19	20	21
	22	23	24	25	26	27	28
	29	*1*	2	3	4	5	6
	7	8	9	10	11	12	13
RAJAB 1553	14	15	16	17	18	19	20
	21	22	23	24	25	26	27[d]
	28	29	30	*1*	2	3	4
	5	6	7	8	9	10	11
SHA'BĀN 1553	12	13	14	15	16	17	18
	19	20	21	22	23	24	25
	26	27	28	29	*1*[e]	2	3
RAMAḌĀN 1553	4	5	6	7	8	9	10

[a]New Year
[b]'Ashūrā'
[c]Prophet's Birthday
[d]Ascent of the Prophet
[e]Start of Ramaḍān
[f]'Id al-Fiṭr
[g]'Id al-'Aḍḥā

GREGORIAN 2128‡

Julian‡ (Sun)	Month	Sun	Mon	Tue	Wed	Thu	Fri	Sat
Dec 14		*28*	29	30	31	1	2	3
		4	5	6	7	8[a]	9	10
Dec 28	JANUARY 2128	*11*	12	13	14	15[b]	16	17
		18	19	20	21	22	23	24
Jan 11		*25*	26	27	28	29	30	31
		1	2	3	4	5	6	7
Jan 25	FEBRUARY 2128	*8*	9	10	11	12	13	14
		15	16	17	18	19	20	21
Feb 8		*22*	23	24	25	26	27	28
		29	1	2	3[c]	4	5	6
Feb 22	MARCH 2128	7	8	9	10	11	12	13
		14[d]	15	16	17	18	19	20
Mar 7		*21*	22	23	24	25	26	27
		28	29	30	31	1	2	3
Mar 21		*4*	5	6	7	8	9	10
	APRIL 2128	11	12	13	14	15	16	17
Apr 4		*18*[e]	19	20	21	22	23	24
		25[f]	26	27	28	29	30	1
Apr 18		2	3	4	5	6	7	8
	MAY 2128	9	10	11	12	13	14	15
May 2		*16*	17	18	19	20	21	22
		23	24	25	26	27	28	29
May 16		*30*	31	1	2	3	4	5
		6	7	8	9	10	11	12
May 30	JUNE 2128	*13*	14	15	16	17	18	19
		20	21	22	23	24	25	26
Jun 13		*27*	28	29	30	1	2	3
		4	5	6	7	8	9	10
Jun 27	JULY 2128	*11*	12	13	14	15	16	17
		18	19	20	21	22	23	24
Jul 11		*25*	26	27	28	29	30	31
		1	2	3	4	5	6	7
Jul 25	AUGUST 2128	*8*	9	10	11	12	13	14
		15	16	17	18	19	20	21
Aug 8		*22*	23	24	25	26	27	28
		29	30	31	1	2	3	4
Aug 22		*5*	6	7	8	9	10	11
	SEPTEMBER 2128	12	13	14	15	16	17	18
Sep 5		*19*	20	21	22	23	24	25
		26	27	28	29	30	1	2
Sep 19		*3*	4	5	6	7	8	9
	OCTOBER 2128	10	11	12	13	14	15	16
Oct 3		*17*	18	19	20	21	22	23
		24	25	26	27	28	29	30
Oct 17		*31*	1	2	3	4	5	6
	NOVEMBER 2128	7	8	9	10	11	12	13
Oct 31		*14*	15	16	17	18	19	20
		21	22	23	24	25	26	27
Nov 14		*28*[g]	29	30	1	2	3	4
		5	6	7	8	9	10	11
Nov 28	DECEMBER 2128	*12*	13	14	15	16	17	18
		19	20	21	22	23	24	25[h]
Dec 12		*26*	27	28	29	30	31	1

‡Leap year
[a]Orthodox Christmas
[b]Julian New Year
[c]Ash Wednesday
[d]Feast of Orthodoxy
[e]Easter
[f]Orthodox Easter
[g]Advent
[h]Christmas

2129

Month	GREGORIAN 2129 Sun	Mon	Tue	Wed	Thu	Fri	Sat	Lunar Phases	ISO WEEK (Mon)	JULIAN DAY (Sun noon)	Month	HEBREW 5889/5890‡ Sun	Mon	Tue	Wed	Thu	Fri	Sat	Molad	Month	CHINESE Wù-Zǐ‡/Jǐ-Chǒu Sun	Mon	Tue	Wed	Thu	Fri	Sat	Solar Term	Month	COPTIC 1845/1846 / ETHIOPIC 2121/2122 Sun	Mon	Tue	Wed	Thu	Fri	Sat	Month
JANUARY 2129	26	27	◐	29	30	31	1[a]	15:25	53	2498656	TEVETH 5889	3	4	5	6	7	8	9		LEAP MONTH 11 Wù-Zǐ	5	6	7	8	9	10	11		KOIAK 1845	16	17	18	19	20	21	22	TĀHŚĀŚ 2121
	2	3	4	○	6	7	8	13:58	1	2498663		10	11	12	13	14	15	16			12	13	14	15	16	17	18	Xiǎo hán		23	24	25	26	27	28	29[c]	
	9	10	11	12	◑	14	15	16:38	2	2498670		17	18	19	20	21	22	23			19	20	21	22	23	24	25			30	1	2	3	4	5	6[d]	
	16	17	18	19	●	21	22	9:52	3	2498677	SHEVAT 5889	24	25	26	27	28	29	1	Thu 14h33m7p		26	27	28	29	1	2	3	Dà hán	TŌBE 1845	7	8	9	10	11[e]	12	13	ṬER 2121
	23	24	25	26	◐	28	29	5:57	4	2498684		2	3	4	5	6	7	8		MONTH 12 Wù-Zǐ	4	5	6	7	8	9	10			14	15	16	17	18	19	20	
FEBRUARY 2129	30	31	1	2	3	○	5	9:43	5	2498691		9	10	11	12	13	14	15			11	12	13	14	15	16	17	Lì chūn		21	22	23	24	25	26	27	
	6	7	8	9	10	11	◑	5:26	6	2498698		16	17	18	19	20	21	22			18	19	20	21	22	23	24		MESHIR 1845	28	29	30	1	2	3	4	YAKĀTIT 2121
	13	14	15	16	17	●	19	20:42	7	2498705		23	24	25	26	27	28	29			25	26	27	28	29	30	1[a]*	Yǔ shuǐ		5	6	7	8	9	10	11	
	20	21	22	23	24	◐	26	23:06	8	2498712	ADAR 5889	30	1	2	3	4	5	6	Sat 3h17m8p	MONTH 1 Jǐ-Chǒu	2	3	4	5	6	7	8			12	13	14	15	16	17	18	
MARCH 2129	27	28	1	2	3	4	5		9	2498719		7	8	9	10	11	12	13			9	10	11	12	13	14	15[b]	Jīng zhé		19	20	21	22	23	24	25	
	○	7	8	9	10	11	12	4:08	10	2498726		14[f]	15	16	17	18	19	20			16	17	18	19	20	21	22			26	27	28	29	30	1	2	
	◑	14	15	16	17	18	19	14:52	11	2498733		21	22	23	24	25	26	27			23	24	25	26	27	28	29		PAREMOTEP 1845	3	4	5	6	7	8	9	MAGĀBIT 2121
	●[b]	21	22	23	24	25	26	7:36	12	2498740	NISAN 5889	28	29	1	2	3	4	5	Sun 16h1m9p	MONTH 2 Jǐ-Chǒu	1	2	3	4	5	6	7	Chūn fēn		10	11	12	13	14	15	16	
APRIL 2129	◐	28	29	30	31	1	2	18:00	13	2498747		6	7	8	9	10	11	12			8	9	10	11	12	13	14			17	18	19	20	21	22	23	
	3	○	5	6	7	8	9	19:38	14	2498754		13	14	15[g]	16	17	18	19			15	16	17[c]	18	19	20	21	Qīng míng		24	25	26	27	28	29	30	
	10	◑	12	13	14	15	16	21:51	15	2498761		20	21	22	23	24	25	26			22	23	24	25	26	27	28		PARMOUTE 1845	1[f]	2	3	4	5	6	7	MIYĀZYĀ 2121
	17	●	19	20	21	22	23	18:43	16	2498768	IYYAR 5889	27	28	29	30	1	2	3	Tue 4h45m10p	MONTH 3 Jǐ-Chǒu	29	30	1	2*	3	4	5	Gǔ yǔ		8	9	10	11	12	13	14	
	24	25	◐	27	28	29	30	13:21	17	2498775		4	5	6	7	8	9	10			6	7	8	9	10	11	12			15	16	17	18	19	20	21	
MAY 2129	1	2	3	○	5	6	7	7:49	18	2498782		11	12	13	14	15	16	17			13	14	15	16	17	18	19	Lì xià		22	23	24	25	26	27	28	
	8	9	10	◑	12	13	14	3:33	19	2498789		18	19	20	21	22	23	24			20	21	22	23	24	25	26		PASHONS 1845	29[g]	30	1	2	3	4	5	GENBOT 2121
	15	16	17	●	19	20	21	6:29	20	2498796	SIVAN 5889	25	26	27	28	29	1	2	Wed 17h29m11p		27	28	29	1	2	3	4	Xiǎo mǎn		6	7	8	9	10	11	12	
	22	23	24	25	◐	27	28	7:40	21	2498803		3	4	5	6[h]	7	8	9		MONTH 4 Jǐ-Chǒu	5	6	7	8	9	10	11			13	14	15	16	17	18	19	
JUNE 2129	29	30	31	1	○	3	4	17:15	22	2498810		10	11	12	13	14	15	16			12	13	14	15	16	17	18			20	21	22	23	24	25	26	
	5	6	7	8	◑	10	11	9:12	23	2498817		17	18	19	20	21	22	23			19	20	21	22	23	24	25	Máng zhòng	PAŌNE 1845	27	28	29	30	1	2	3	SANĒ 2121
	12	13	14	15	●	17	18	19:27	24	2498824		24	25	26	27	28	29	30			26	27	28	29	30	1	2	Xià zhì		4	5	6	7	8	9	10	
	19	20	21[c]	22	23	◐	25	23:46	25	2498831	TAMMUZ 5889	1	2	3	4	5	6	7	Fri 6h13m12p	MONTH 5 Jǐ-Chǒu	3*	4	5[d]	6	7	8	9			11	12	13	14	15	16	17	
JULY 2129	26	27	28	29	30	1	○	1:01	26	2498838		8	9	10	11	12	13	14			10	11	12	13	14	15	16			18	19	20	21	22	23	24	
	3	4	5	6	7	◑	9	15:56	27	2498845		15	16	17	18	19	20	21			17	18	19	20	21	22	23	Xiǎo shǔ		25	26	27	28	29	30	1	
	10	11	12	13	14	15	●	9:54	28	2498852		22	23	24	25	26	27	28			24	25	26	27	28	29	1		EPĒP 1845	2	3	4	5	6	7	8	HAMLĒ 2121
	17	18	19	20	21	22	23		29	2498859	AV 5889	29	1	2	3	4	5	6	Sat 18h57m13p	MONTH 6 Jǐ-Chǒu	2	3	4	5	6	7	8	Dà shǔ		9	10	11	12	13	14	15	
	◐	25	26	27	28	29	30	13:07	30	2498866		7	8	9[i]	10	11	12	13			9	10	11	12	13	14	15			16	17	18	19	20	21	22	
AUGUST 2129	○	1	2	3	4	5	6	8:10	31	2498873		14	15	16	17	18	19	20			16	17	18	19	20	21	22			23	24	25	26	27	28	29	
	◑	8	9	10	11	12	13	0:55	32	2498880		21	22	23	24	25	26	27			23	24	25	26	27	28	29	Lì qiū	MESORĒ 1845	30	1	2	3	4	5	6	NAḤASĒ 2121
	14	●	16	17	18	19	20	1:33	33	2498887	ELUL 5889	28	29	30	1	2	3	4	Mon 7h41m14p	MONTH 7 Jǐ-Chǒu	30	1	2	3	4*	5	6			7	8	9	10	11	12	13[h]	
	21	◐	23	24	25	26	27	23:53	34	2498894		5	6	7	8	9	10	11			7[e]	8	9	10	11	12	13	Chǔ shǔ		14	15	16	17	18	19	20	
SEPTEMBER 2129	28	○	30	31	1	2	3	15:36	35	2498901		12	13	14	15	16	17	18			14	15[f]	16	17	18	19	20			21	22	23	24	25	26	27	
	4	◑	6	7	8	9	10	13:06	36	2498908		19	20	21	22	23	24	25			21	22	23	24	25	26	27	Bái lù	EPAG. 1845	28	29	30	1	2	3	4	PĀG. 2121
	11	12	●	14	15	16	17	17:34	37	2498915	TISHRI 5890	26	27	28	29	1[a]	2[a]	3	Tue 20h25m15p	MONTH 8 Jǐ-Chǒu	28	29	30	1	2	3	4		THOOUT 1846	5	1[a]	2	3	4	5	6	MASKARAM 2122
	18	19	20	◐	22[d]	23	24	8:44	38	2498922		4	5	6	7	8	9	10[b]			5	6	7	8	9	10	11	Qiū fēn		7	8	9	10	11	12	13	
OCTOBER 2129	25	26	27	○	29	30	1	0:04	39	2498929		11	12	13	14	15[c]	16	17			12	13	14	15[g]	16	17	18			14	15	16	17[b]	18	19	20	
	2	3	4	◑	6	7	8	5:05	40	2498936		18	19	20	21	22	23	24			19	20	21	22	23	24	25	Hán lù		21	22	23	24	25	26	27	
	9	10	11	12	●	14	15	9:04	41	2498943	HESHVAN 5890	25	26	27	28	29	30	1	Thu 9h9m16p	MONTH 9 Jǐ-Chǒu	26	27	28	29	1	2	3		PAOPE 1846	28	29	30	1	2	3	4	ṬEQEMT 2122
	16	17	18	19	◐	21	22	16:27	42	2498950		2	3	4	5	6	7	8			4	5*	6	7	8	9[h]	10			5	6	7	8	9	10	11	
	23	24	25	26	○	28	29	10:19	43	2498957		9	10	11	12	13	14	15			11	12	13	14	15	16	17	Shuāng jiàng		12	13	14	15	16	17	18	
NOVEMBER 2129	30	31	1	2	3	◑	5	0:32	44	2498964		16	17	18	19	20	21	22			18	19	20	21	22	23	24			19	20	21	22	23	24	25	
	6	7	8	9	10	●	12	23:32	45	2498971		23	24	25	26	27	28	29			25	26	27	28	29	30	1	Lì dōng	ATHŌR 1846	26	27	28	29	30	1	2	ḪEDĀR 2122
	13	14	15	16	17	◐	19	23:52	46	2498978	KISLEV 5890	1	2	3	4	5	6	7	Fri 21h53m17p	MONTH 10 Jǐ-Chǒu	2	3	4	5	6	7	8			3	4	5	6	7	8	9	
	20	21	22	23	24	○	26	23:05	47	2498985		8	9	10	11	12	13	14			9	10	11	12	13	14	15	Xiǎo xuě		10	11	12	13	14	15	16	
DECEMBER 2129	27	28	29	30	1	2	◑	21:58	48	2498992		15	16	17	18	19	20	21			16	17	18	19	20	21	22			17	18	19	20	21	22	23	
	4	5	6	7	8	9	10		49	2498999		22	23	24[d]	25[e]	26[e]	27[e]	28[e]			23	24	25	26	27	28	29	Dà xuě		24	25	26	27	28	29	30	
	●	12	13	14	15	16	17	12:56	50	2499006	TEVETH 5890	29[e]	1[e]	2[e]	3[e]	4	5	6	Sun 10h38m0p	MONTH 11 Jǐ-Chǒu	1	2	3	4	5	6*	7		KOIAK 1846	1	2	3	4	5	6	7	TĀHŚĀŚ 2122
	◐	19	20	21[e]	22	23	24	7:48	51	2499013		7	8	9	10	11	12	13			8	9	10	11	12[i]	13	14	Dōng zhì		8	9	10	11	12	13	14	
	○	26	27	28	29	30	31	14:46	52	2499020		14	15	16	17	18	19	20			15	16	17	18	19	20	21			15	16	17	18	19	20	21	

Gregorian notes:
[a]New Year
[b]Spring (13:53)
[c]Summer (5:36)
[d]Autumn (22:23)
[e]Winter (20:59)
● New moon
◐ First quarter moon
○ Full moon
◑ Last quarter moon

Hebrew notes:
‡Leap year
[a]New Year
[b]Yom Kippur
[c]Sukkot
[d]Winter starts
[e]Ḥanukkah
[f]Purim
[g]Passover
[h]Shavuot
[i]Fast of Av

Chinese notes:
‡Leap year
[a]New Year (4827, Ox)
[b]Lantern Festival
[c]Qīngmíng
[d]Dragon Festival
[e]Qīqiǎo
[f]Hungry Ghosts
[g]Mid-Autumn Festival
[h]Double-Ninth Festival
[i]Dōngzhì
*Start of 60-name cycle

Coptic/Ethiopic notes:
[a]New Year
[b]Building of the Cross
[c]Christmas
[d]Jesus's Circumcision
[e]Epiphany
[f]Easter
[g]Mary's Announcement
[h]Jesus's Transfiguration

PERSIAN (ASTRONOMICAL) 1507‡/1508

Month	Sun	Mon	Tue	Wed	Thu	Fri	Sat
DEY 1507	6	7	8	9	10	11	12
	13	14	15	16	17	18	19
	20	21	22	23	24	25	26
	27	28	29	30	1	2	3
BAHMAN 1507	4	5	6	7	8	9	10
	11	12	13	14	15	16	17
	18	19	20	21	22	23	24
	25	26	27	28	29	30	1
ESFAND 1507	2	3	4	5	6	7	8
	9	10	11	12	13	14	15
	16	17	18	19	20	21	22
	23	24	25	26	27	28	29
	30	1[a]	2	3	4	5	6
FARVARDĪN 1508	7	8	9	10	11	12	13[b]
	14	15	16	17	18	19	20
	21	22	23	24	25	26	27
	28	29	30	31	1	2	3
ORDĪBEHEŠT 1508	4	5	6	7	8	9	10
	11	12	13	14	15	16	17
	18	19	20	21	22	23	24
	25	26	27	28	29	30	31
XORDĀD 1508	1	2	3	4	5	6	7
	8	9	10	11	12	13	14
	15	16	17	18	19	20	21
	22	23	24	25	26	27	28
	29	30	31	1	2	3	4
TĪR 1508	5	6	7	8	9	10	11
	12	13	14	15	16	17	18
	19	20	21	22	23	24	25
	26	27	28	29	30	31	1
MORDĀD 1508	2	3	4	5	6	7	8
	9	10	11	12	13	14	15
	16	17	18	19	20	21	22
	23	24	25	26	27	28	29
	30	31	1	2	3	4	5
SHAHRĪVAR 1508	6	7	8	9	10	11	12
	13	14	15	16	17	18	19
	20	21	22	23	24	25	26
	27	28	29	30	31	1	2
MEHR 1508	3	4	5	6	7	8	9
	10	11	12	13	14	15	16
	17	18	19	20	21	22	23
	24	25	26	27	28	29	30
ĀBĀN 1508	1	2	3	4	5	6	7
	8	9	10	11	12	13	14
	15	16	17	18	19	20	21
	22	23	24	25	26	27	28
	29	30	1	2	3	4	5
ĀZAR 1508	6	7	8	9	10	11	12
	13	14	15	16	17	18	19
	20	21	22	23	24	25	26
	27	28	29	30	1	2	3
DEY 1508	4	5	6	7	8	9	10

‡Leap year
[a]New Year
[b]Sizdeh Bedar

HINDU LUNAR 2185/2186‡

Month	Sun	Mon	Tue	Wed	Thu	Fri	Sat
PAUSHA 2185	5	6	7	8	9	10	11
	12	13	14	15	16	17	18
	19	20	21	22	23	24	25
	26	27	28	29	30	1	2
MĀGHA 2185	3	**4**	6	7	8	9	10
	11	12	*12*	13	14	15	16
	17	18	19	20	21	22	23
	24	25	26	27	**28**[h]	30	1
PHĀLGUNA 2185	2	3	4	5	6	7	8
	9	10	11	12	13	14	*14*
	15[i]	16	17	18	19	20	21
	22	24	25	26	27	28	29
	30	1[a]	2	3	4	5	6
CHAITRA 2186	7	8	9[b]	10	11	12	13
	14	15	16	17	18	19	20
	21	22	23	24	25	**26**	28
	29	30	1	2	3	4	5
VAIŚĀKHA 2186	6	7	8	*8*	9	10	11
	12	13	14	15	16	17	18
	19	21	22	23	24	25	26
	27	28	29	30	1	2	3
LEAP JYAISHṬHA 2186	4	5	6	7	8	9	10
	11	12	13	14	15	16	17
	18	19	20	21	**22**	24	25
	26	27	28	29	30	1	2
JYAISHṬHA 2186	3	4	*4*	5	6	7	8
	9	10	11	12	13	14	**15**
	17	18	19	20	21	22	23
	24	25	26	27	28	29	30
ĀSHĀḌHA 2186	1	2	3	4	5	6	7
	8	9	10	11	12	13	14
	15	16	17	**18**	20	21	22
	23	24	25	26	27	28	29
	30	1	*1*	2	3	4	5
ŚRĀVAṆA 2186	6	7	8	9	10	**11**	13
	14	15	16	17	18	19	20
	21	22	23[c]	24	25	26	27
	28	29	30	1	2	3	4[d]
BHĀDRAPADA 2186	5	6	7	8	9	10	11
	12	13	**14**	16	17	18	19
	20	21	22	23	24	25	26
	26	27	28	29	30	1	2
ĀŚVINA 2186	3	4	5	6	7	**8**[e]	10[e]
	11	12	13	14	15	16	17
	18	19	20	21	22	23	24
	25	26	27	28	29	30	1[f]
KĀRTTIKA 2186	2	3	4	5	6	7	8
	9	10	11	**12**	14	15	16
	17	18	19	20	*20*	21	22
	23	24	25	26	27	28	29
	30	1	2	3	4	5	**6**
MĀRGAŚĪRA 2186	8	9	10	**11**[g]	12	13	14
	15	16	17	18	19	20	21

‡Leap year
[a]New Year (Virodhin)
[b]Birthday of Rāma
[c]Birthday of Krishna
[d]Ganēśa Chaturthī
[e]Dashara
[f]Diwali
[g]Birthday of Vishnu
[h]Night of Śiva
[i]Holi

HINDU SOLAR 2050/2051‡

Month	Sun	Mon	Tue	Wed	Thu	Fri	Sat
PAUSHA 2050	10	11	12	13	14	15	16
	17	18	19	20	21	22	23
	24	25	26	27	28	29	30
	1[b]	2	3	4	5	6	7
MĀGHA 2050	8	9	10	11	12	13	14
	15	16	17	18	19	20	21
	22	23	24	25	26	27	28
	29	1	2	3	4	5	6
PHĀLGUNA 2050	7	8	9	10	11	12	13
	14	15	16	17	18	19	20
	21	22	23	24	25	26	27
	28	29	30	1	2	3	4
CHAITRA 2050	5	6	7	8	9	10	11
	12	13	14	15	16	17	18
	19	20	21	22	23	24	25
	26	27	28	29	30	1[a]	2
VAIŚĀKHA 2051	3	4	5	6	7	8	9
	10	11	12	13	14	15	16
	17	18	19	20	21	22	23
	24	25	26	27	28	29	30
	31	1	2	3	4	5	6
JYAISHṬHA 2051	7	8	9	10	11	12	13
	14	15	16	17	18	19	20
	21	22	23	24	25	26	27
	28	29	30	31	32	1	2
ĀSHĀḌHA 2051	3	4	5	6	7	8	9
	10	11	12	13	14	15	16
	17	18	19	20	21	22	23
	24	25	26	27	28	29	30
	31	1	2	3	4	5	6
ŚRĀVAṆA 2051	7	8	9	10	11	12	13
	14	15	16	17	18	19	20
	21	22	23	24	25	26	27
	28	29	30	31	32	1	2
BHĀDRAPADA 2051	3	4	5	6	7	8	9
	10	11	12	13	14	15	16
	17	18	19	20	21	22	23
	24	25	26	27	28	29	30
	31	1	2	3	4	5	6
ĀŚVINA 2051	7	8	9	10	11	12	13
	14	15	16	17	18	19	20
	21	22	23	24	25	26	27
	28	29	30	1	2	3	4
KĀRTTIKA 2051	5	6	7	8	9	10	11
	12	13	14	15	16	17	18
	19	20	21	22	23	24	25
	26	27	28	29	30	1	2
MĀRGAŚĪRA 2051	3	4	5	6	7	8	9
	10	11	12	13	14	15	16
	17	18	19	20	21	22	23
	24	25	26	27	28	29	30
PAUSHA 2051	1	2	3	4	5	6	7
	8	9	10	11	12	13	14

‡Leap year
[a]New Year (Krodhin)
[b]Pongal

ISLAMIC (ASTRONOMICAL) 1553/1554

Month	Sun	Mon	Tue	Wed	Thu	Fri	Sat
RAMAḌĀN 1553	4	5	6	7	8	9	10
	11	12	13	14	15	16	17
	18	19	20	21	22	23	24
	25	26	27	28	29	30	1[f]
SHAWWĀL 1553	2	3	4	5	6	7	8
	9	10	11	12	13	14	15
	16	17	18	19	20	21	22
	23	24	25	26	27	28	29
DHU AL-QA'DA 1553	1	2	3	4	5	6	7
	8	9	10	11	12	13	14
	15	16	17	18	19	20	21
	22	23	24	25	26	27	28
	29	1	2	3	4	5	6
DHU AL-HIJJA 1553	7	8	9	10[g]	11	12	13
	14	15	16	17	18	19	20
	21	22	23	24	25	26	27
	28	29	30	1[a]	2	3	4
MUHARRAM 1554	5	6	7	8	9	10[b]	11
	12	13	14	15	16	17	18
	19	20	21	22	23	24	25
	26	27	28	29	30	1	2
SAFAR 1554	3	4	5	6	7	8	9
	10	11	12	13	14	15	16
	17	18	19	20	21	22	23
	24	25	26	27	28	29	1
RABĪ' I 1554	2	3	4	5	6	7	8
	9	10	11	12[c]	13	14	15
	16	17	18	19	20	21	22
	23	24	25	26	27	28	29
	30	1	2	3	4	5	6
RABĪ' II 1554	7	8	9	10	11	12	13
	14	15	16	17	18	19	20
	21	22	23	24	25	26	27
	28	29	30	1	2	3	4
JUMĀDĀ I 1554	5	6	7	8	9	10	11
	12	13	14	15	16	17	18
	19	20	21	22	23	24	25
	26	27	28	29	1	2	3
JUMĀDĀ II 1554	4	5	6	7	8	9	10
	11	12	13	14	15	16	17
	18	19	20	21	22	23	24
	25	26	27	28	29	30	1
RAJAB 1554	2	3	4	5	6	7	8
	9	10	11	12	13	14	15
	16	17	18	19	20	21	22
	23	24	25	26	27[d]	28	29
SHA'BĀN 1554	1	2	3	4	5	6	7
	8	9	10	11	12	13	14
	15	16	17	18	19	20	21
	22	23	24	25	26	27	28
	29	30	1[e]	2	3	4	5
RAMAḌĀN 1554	6	7	8	9	10	11	12
	13	14	15	16	17	18	19

[a]New Year
[b]'Ashūrā'
[c]Prophet's Birthday
[d]Ascent of the Prophet
[e]Start of Ramaḍān
[f]'Id al-Fiṭr
[g]'Id al-'Aḍḥā

GREGORIAN 2129

Julian (Sun)	Sun	Mon	Tue	Wed	Thu	Fri	Sat	Month
Dec 12	26	27	28	29	30	31	1	
	2	3	4	5	6	7	8[a]	JANUARY 2129
Dec 26	9	10	11	12	13	14	15[b]	
	16	17	18	19	20	21	22	
Jan 9	23	24	25	26	27	28	29	
	30	31	1	2	3	4	5	
Jan 23	6	7	8	9	10	11	12	FEBRUARY 2129
	13	14	15	16	17	18	19	
Feb 6	20	21	22	23[c]	24	25	26	
	27[d]	28	1	2	3	4	5	
Feb 20	6	7	8	9	10	11	12	MARCH 2129
	13	14	15	16	17	18	19	
Mar 6	20	21	22	23	24	25	26	
	27	28	29	30	31	1	2	
Mar 20	3	4	5	6	7	8	9	APRIL 2129
	10[e]	11	12	13	14	15	16	
Apr 3	17	18	19	20	21	22	23	
	24	25	26	27	28	29	30	
Apr 17	1	2	3	4	5	6	7	
	8	9	10	11	12	13	14	MAY 2129
May 1	15	16	17	18	19	20	21	
	22	23	24	25	26	27	28	
May 15	29	30	31	1	2	3	4	
	5	6	7	8	9	10	11	JUNE 2129
May 29	12	13	14	15	16	17	18	
	19	20	21	22	23	24	25	
Jun 12	26	27	28	29	30	1	2	
	3	4	5	6	7	8	9	JULY 2129
Jun 26	10	11	12	13	14	15	16	
	17	18	19	20	21	22	23	
Jul 10	24	25	26	27	28	29	30	
	31	1	2	3	4	5	6	
Jul 24	7	8	9	10	11	12	13	AUGUST 2129
	14	15	16	17	18	19	20	
Aug 7	21	22	23	24	25	26	27	
	28	29	30	31	1	2	3	
Aug 21	4	5	6	7	8	9	10	SEPTEMBER 2129
	11	12	13	14	15	16	17	
Sep 4	18	19	20	21	22	23	24	
	25	26	27	28	29	30	1	
Sep 18	2	3	4	5	6	7	8	OCTOBER 2129
	9	10	11	12	13	14	15	
Oct 2	16	17	18	19	20	21	22	
	23	24	25	26	27	28	29	
Oct 16	30	31	1	2	3	4	5	
	6	7	8	9	10	11	12	NOVEMBER 2129
Oct 30	13	14	15	16	17	18	19	
	20	21	22	23	24	25	26	
Nov 13	27[g]	28	29	30	1	2	3	
	4	5	6	7	8	9	10	DECEMBER 2129
Nov 27	11	12	13	14	15	16	17	
	18	19	20	21	22	23	24	
Dec 11	25[h]	26	27	28	29	30	31	

[a]Orthodox Christmas
[b]Julian New Year
[c]Ash Wednesday
[d]Feast of Orthodoxy
[e]Easter (also Orthodox)
[g]Advent
[h]Christmas

2130

Gregorian 2130	Sun Mon Tue Wed Thu Fri Sat	Lunar Phases	ISO Week (Mon)	Julian Day (Sun noon)	Hebrew 5890‡/5891	Sun Mon Tue Wed Thu Fri Sat	Molad	Chinese Jǐ-Chǒu/Gēng-Yín	Sun Mon Tue Wed Thu Fri Sat	Solar Term	Coptic 1846/1847‡	Sun Mon Tue Wed Thu Fri Sat	Ethiopic 2122/2123‡
JANUARY 2130	1[a] ◑ 3 4 5 6 7	19:07	1	2499027	TEVETH 5890	21 22 23 24 25 26 27		MONTH 11 Jǐ-Chǒu	22 23 24 25 26 27 28	Xiǎo hán	KOIAK 1846	22 23 24 25 26 27 28	TĀKHŚĀŚ 2122
	8 9 ● 11 12 13 14	1:20	2	2499034		28 29 1 2 3 4 5	Mon $23^h22^m1^p$		29 30 1 2 3 4 5			29[c] 30 1 2 3 4 5	
	15 ◐ 17 18 19 20 21	17:08	3	2499041	SHEVAT 5890	6 7 8 9 10 11 12		MONTH 12 Jǐ-Chǒu	6 7 8 9 10 11 12	Dà hán	TÔBE 1846	6[d] 7 8 9 10 11[e] 12	ṬER 2122
	22 23 ○ 25 26 27 28	8:59	4	2499048		13 14 15 16 17 18 19			13 14 15 16 17 18 19			13 14 15 16 17 18 19	
	29 30 31 ◑ 2 3 4	13:58	5	2499055		20 21 22 23 24 25 26			20 21 22 23 24 25 26	Lì chūn		20 21 22 23 24 25 26	
FEBRUARY 2130	5 6 7 ● 9 10 11	12:39	6	2499062		27 28 29 30 1 2 3	Wed $12^h6^m2^p$		27 28 29 1[a] 2 3 4			27 28 29 30 1 2 3	
	12 13 14 ◐ 16 17 18	4:32	7	2499069	ADAR I 5890	4 5 6 7 8 9 10		MONTH 1 Gēng-Yín	5 6 7* 8 9 10 11		MESHIR 1846	4 5 6 7 8 9 10	YAKĀTIT 2122
	19 20 21 22 ○ 24 25	4:16	8	2499076		11 12 13 14 15 16 17			12 13 14 15[b] 16 17 18	Yǔ shuǐ		11 12 13 14 15 16 17	
	26 27 28 1 2 ◑ 4	5:18	9	2499083		18 19 20 21 22 23 24			19 20 21 22 23 24 25			18 19 20 21 22 23 24	
MARCH 2130	5 6 7 8 ● 10 11	22:50	10	2499090		25 26 27 28 29 30 1	Fri $0^h50^m3^p$		26 27 28 29 30 1 2	Jīng zhé		25 26 27 28 29 30 1	
	12 13 14 15 ◐ 17 18	18:24	11	2499097	ADAR II 5890	2 3 4 5 6 7 8		MONTH 2 Gēng-Yín	3 4 5 6 7 8 9		PAREMOTEP 1846	2 3 4 5 6 7 8	MAGĀBIT 2122
	19 20[b] 21 22 23 ○ 25	22:40	12	2499104		9 10 11 12 13 14[f] 15			10 11 12 13 14 15 16	Chūn fēn		9 10 11 12 13 14 15	
	26 27 28 29 30 31 ◑	16:50	13	2499111		16 17 18 19 20 21 22			17 18 19 20 21 22 23			16 17 18 19 20 21 22	
APRIL 2130	2 3 4 5 6 7 ●	8:03	14	2499118		23 24 25 26 27 28 29			24 25 26 27[c] 28 29 1	Qīng míng		23 24 25 26 27 28 29	
	9 10 11 12 13 14 ◐	10:31	15	2499125		1 2 3 4 5 6 7	Sat $13^h34^m4^p$	MONTH 3 Gēng-Yín	2 3 4 5 6 7 8*			30 1 2 3 4 5 6	
	16 17 18 19 20 21 22		16	2499132	NISAN 5890	8 9 10 11 12 13 14			9 10 11 12 13 14 15	Gǔ yǔ	PARMOUTE 1846	7 8 9 10 11 12 13	MIYĀZYĀ 2122
	○ 24 25 26 27 28 29	14:49	17	2499139		15[g] 16 17 18 19 20 21			16 17 18 19 20 21 22			14 15 16 17 18 19 20	
	30 ◑ 2 3 4 5 6	1:00	18	2499146		22 23 24 25 26 27 28			23 24 25 26 27 28 29	Lì xià		21[f] 22 23 24 25 26 27	
MAY 2130	● 8 9 10 11 12 13	16:57	19	2499153		29 30 1 2 3 4 5	Mon $2^h18^m5^p$		30 1 2 3 4 5 6			28 29[g] 30 1 2 3 4	
	14 ◐ 16 17 18 19 20	4:01	20	2499160	IYAR 5890	6 7 8 9 10 11 12		MONTH 4 Gēng-Yín	7 8 9 10 11 12 13		PASHONS 1846	5 6 7 8 9 10 11	GENBOT 2122
	21 22 ○ 24 25 26 27	4:16	21	2499167		13 14 15 16 17 18 19			14 15 16 17 18 19 20	Xiǎo mǎn		12 13 14 15 16 17 18	
	28 29 ◑ 31 1 2 3	6:41	22	2499174		20 21 22 23 24 25 26			21 22 23 24 25 26 27			19 20 21 22 23 24 25	
JUNE 2130	4 5 ● 7 8 9 10	2:31	23	2499181		27 28 29 1 2 3 4	Tue $15^h2^m6^p$		28 29 1 2 3 4 5[d]	Máng zhòng		26 27 28 29 30 1 2	
	11 12 ◐ 14 15 16 17	21:47	24	2499188	SIVAN 5890	5 6[h] 7 8 9 10 11		MONTH 5 Gēng-Yín	6 7 8 9* 10 11 12		PAÔNE 1846	3 4 5 6 7 8 9	SANĒ 2122
	18 19 20 ○[c] 22 23 24	15:18	25	2499195		12 13 14 15 16 17 18			13 14 15 16 17 18 19	Xià zhì		10 11 12 13 14 15 16	
	25 26 27 ◑ 29 30 1	11:11	26	2499202		19 20 21 22 23 24 25			20 21 22 23 24 25 26			17 18 19 20 21 22. 23	
JULY 2130	2 3 4 ● 6 7 8	13:37	27	2499209		26 27 28 29 30 1 2	Thu $3^h46^m7^p$		27 28 29 1 2 3 4	Xiǎo shǔ		24 25 26 27 28 29 30	
	9 10 11 12 ◐ 14 15	14:51	28	2499216	TAMMUZ 5890	3 4 5 6 7 8 9		MONTH 6 Gēng-Yín	5 6 7 8 9 10 11			1 2 3 4 5 6 7	
	16 17 18 19 20 ○ 22	0:32	29	2499223		10 11 12 13 14 15 16			12 13 14 15 16 17 18		EPÊP 1846	8 9 10 11 12 13 14	ḤAMLĒ 2122
	23 24 25 26 ◑ 28 29	16:02	30	2499230		17 18 19 20 21 22 23			19 20 21 22 23 24 25	Dà shǔ		15 16 17 18 19 20 21	
	30 31 1 2 3 ● 5	2:47	31	2499237		24 25 26 27 28 29 1	Fri $16^h30^m8^p$		26 27 28 29 30 1 2			22 23 24 25 26 27 28	
AUGUST 2130	6 7 8 9 10 11 ◐	6:36	32	2499244	AV 5890	2 3 4 5 6 7 8		MONTH 7 Gēng-Yín	3 4 5 6 7[e] 8 9	Lì qiū		29 30 1 2 3 4 5	
	13 14 15 16 17 18 ○	8:39	33	2499251		9[i] 10 11 12 13 14 15			10* 11 12 13 14 15[f] 16		MESORÊ 1846	6 7 8 9 10 11 12	NAḤASĒ 2122
	20 21 22 23 24 ◑ 26	22:48	34	2499258		16 17 18 19 20 21 22			17 18 19 20 21 22 23	Chǔ shǔ		13[h] 14 15 16 17 18 19	
	27 28 29 30 31 1 ●	17:54	35	2499265		23 24 25 26 27 28 29			24 25 26 27 28 29 30			20 21 22 23 24 25 26	
SEPTEMBER 2130	3 4 5 6 7 8 9		36	2499272		30 1 2 3 4 5 6	Sun $5^h14^m9^p$		1 2 3 4 5 6 7	Bái lù	EPAG. 1846	27 28 29 30 1 2 3	PĀG. 2122
	◐ 11 12 13 14 15 16	20:45	37	2499279	ELUL 5890	7 8 9 10 11 12 13		MONTH 8 Gēng-Yín	8 9 10 11 12 13 14			4 5 1[a] 2 3 4 5	
	○ 18 19 20 21 22 23[d]	16:26	38	2499286		14 15 16 17 18 19 20			15[g] 16 17 18 19 20 21	Qiū fēn	THOOUT 1847	6 7 8 9 10 11 12	MASKARAM 2123
	◑ 25 26 27 28 29 30	8:53	39	2499293		21 22 23 24 25 26 27			22 23 24 25 26 27 28			13 14 15 16 17[b] 18 19	
OCTOBER 2130	1 ● 3 4 5 6 7	10:27	40	2499300		28 29 1[a] 2[a] 3 4 5	Mon $17^h58^m10^p$		29 1 2 3 4 5 6			20 21 22 23 24 25 26	
	8 9 ◐ 11 12 13 14	9:07	41	2499307	TISHRI 5891	6 7 8 9 10[b] 11 12		MONTH 9 Gēng-Yín	7 8 9[h] 10 11* 12 13	Hán lù		27 28 29 30 1 2 3	
	15 16 ○ 18 19 20 21	0:46	42	2499314		13 14 15[c] 16 17 18 19			14 15 16 17 18 19 20		PAOPE 1847	4 5 6 7 8 9 10	TEQEMT 2123
	22 ◑ 24 25 26 27 28	23:04	43	2499321		20 21 22 23 24 25 26			21 22 23 24 25 26 27	Shuāng jiàng		11 12 13 14 15 16 17	
	29 30 31 ● 2 3 4	3:41	44	2499328		27 28 29 30 1 2 3	Wed $6^h42^m11^p$		28 29 30 1 2 3 4			18 19 20 21 22 23 24	
NOVEMBER 2130	5 6 7 ◐ 9 10 11	19:40	45	2499335	ḤESHVAN 5891	4 5 6 7 8 9 10		MONTH 10 Gēng-Yín	5 6 7 8 9 10 11	Lì dōng		25 26 27 28 29 30 1	
	12 13 14 ○ 16 17 18	10:32	46	2499342		11 12 13 14 15 16 17			12 13 14 15 16 17 18		ATHÔR 1847	2 3 4 5 6 7 8	ḤEDĀR 2123
	19 20 21 ◑ 23 24 25	17:15	47	2499349		18 19 20 21 22 23 24			19 20 21 22 23 24 25	Xiǎo xuě		9 10 11 12 13 14 15	
	26 27 28 29 ● 1 2	20:44	48	2499356		25 26 27 28 29 1 2	Thu $19^h26^m12^p$		26 27 28 29 30 1 2			16 17 18 19 20 21 22	
DECEMBER 2130	3 4 5 6 7 ◐ 9	4:34	49	2499363	KISLEV 5891	3 4 5 6[d] 7 8 9		MONTH 11 Gēng-Yín	3 4 5 6 7 8 9	Dà xuě		23 24 25 26 27 28 29	
	10 11 12 13 ○ 15 16	22:28	50	2499370		10 11 12 13 14 15 16			10 11* 12 13 14 15 16			30 1 2 3 4 5 6	
	17 18 19 20 21 ◑[e] 23	14:12	51	2499377		17 18 19 20 21 22 23			17 18 19 20 21 22[i] 23	Dōng zhì	KOIAK 1847	7 8 9 10 11 12 13	TĀKHŚĀŚ 2123
	24 25 26 27 28 29 ●	12:43	52	2499384		24 25[e] 26[e] 27[e] 28[e] 29[e] 30[e]		MONTH 12 Gēng-Yín	24 25 26 27 28 29 1			14 15 16 17 18 19 20	
	31 1 2 3 4 5 ◐	12:30	1	2499391		1[e] 2[e] 3 4 5 6 7	Sat $8^h10^m13^p$		2 3 4 5 6 7 8	Xiǎo hán		21 22 23 24 25 26 27	

[a]New Year
[b]Spring (19:47)
[c]Summer (11:28)
[d]Autumn (4:19)
[e]Winter (2:51)
● New moon
◐ First quarter moon
○ Full moon
◑ Last quarter moon

‡Leap year
[a]New Year
[b]Yom Kippur
[c]Sukkot
[d]Winter starts
[e]Ḥanukkah
[f]Purim
[g]Passover
[h]Shavuot
[i]Fast of Av

[a]New Year (4828, Tiger)
[b]Lantern Festival
[c]Qīngmíng
[d]Dragon Festival
[e]Qīqiǎo
[f]Hungry Ghosts
[g]Mid-Autumn Festival
[h]Double-Ninth Festival
[i]Dōngzhì
*Start of 60-name cycle

‡Leap year
[a]New Year
[b]Building of the Cross
[c]Christmas
[d]Jesus's Circumcision
[e]Epiphany
[f]Easter
[g]Mary's Announcement
[h]Jesus's Transfiguration

2130

PERSIAN (ASTRONOMICAL) 1508/1509

Month	Sun	Mon	Tue	Wed	Thu	Fri	Sat
DEY 1508	11	12	13	14	15	16	17
	18	19	20	21	22	23	24
	25	26	27	28	29	30	1
BAHMAN 1508	2	3	4	5	6	7	8
	9	10	11	12	13	14	15
	16	17	18	19	20	21	22
	23	24	25	26	27	28	29
ESFAND 1508	30	1	2	3	4	5	6
	7	8	9	10	11	12	13
	14	15	16	17	18	19	20
	21	22	23	24	25	26	27
FARVARDĪN 1509	28	29	1[a]	2	3	4	5
	6	7	8	9	10	11	12
	13[b]	14	15	16	17	18	19
	20	21	22	23	24	25	26
ORDĪBEHEŠT 1509	27	28	29	30	31	1	2
	3	4	5	6	7	8	9
	10	11	12	13	14	15	16
	17	18	19	20	21	22	23
	24	25	26	27	28	29	30
XORDĀD 1509	31	1	2	3	4	5	6
	7	8	9	10	11	12	13
	14	15	16	17	18	19	20
	21	22	23	24	25	26	27
TĪR 1509	28	29	30	31	1	2	3
	4	5	6	7	8	9	10
	11	12	13	14	15	16	17
	18	19	20	21	22	23	24
	25	26	27	28	29	30	31
MORDĀD 1509	1	2	3	4	5	6	7
	8	9	10	11	12	13	14
	15	16	17	18	19	20	21
	22	23	24	25	26	27	28
SHAHRĪVAR 1509	29	30	31	1	2	3	4
	5	6	7	8	9	10	11
	12	13	14	15	16	17	18
	19	20	21	22	23	24	25
MEHR 1509	26	27	28	29	30	31	1
	2	3	4	5	6	7	8
	9	10	11	12	13	14	15
	16	17	18	19	20	21	22
	23	24	25	26	27	28	29
ĀBĀN 1509	30	1	2	3	4	5	6
	7	8	9	10	11	12	13
	14	15	16	17	18	19	20
	21	22	23	24	25	26	27
ĀZAR 1509	28	29	30	1	2	3	4
	5	6	7	8	9	10	11
	12	13	14	15	16	17	18
	19	20	21	22	23	24	25
DEY 1509	26	27	28	29	30	1	2
	3	4	5	6	7	8	9
	10	11	12	13	14	15	16

[a] New Year
[b] Sizdeh Bedar

HINDU LUNAR 2186‡/2187

Month	Sun	Mon	Tue	Wed	Thu	Fri	Sat
MĀRGAŚĪRA 2186	22	22	23	24	25	26	27
PAUSHA 2186	28	29	**30**	2	3	4	5
	6	7	8	9	10	11	12
	13	14	15	16	17	18	19
	20	21	22	23	24	25	26
MĀGHA 2186	27	28	29	30	1	2	3
	4	5	7	8	9	10	11
	12	13	14	15	15	16	17
	18	19	20	21	22	23	24
PHĀLGUNA 2186	25	26	27	28[h]	**29**	1	2
	3	4	5	6	7	8	9
	10	11	12	13	14	15[i]	16
	17	17	18	19	20	21	**22**
	24	25	26	27	28	29	30
CHAITRA 2187	1[a]	2	3	4	5	6	7
	8[b]	9	10	11	12	13	14
	15	16	17	18	19	20	21
	22	23	24	25	**26**	28	29
VAIŚĀKHA 2187	30	1	2	3	4	5	6
	7	8	9	10	11	12	12
	13	14	15	16	17	18	**19**
	21	22	23	24	25	26	27
JYAISHṬHA 2187	28	29	30	1	2	3	4
	5	6	7	8	9	10	11
	12	13	14	15	16	17	18
	19	20	21	**22**	24	25	26
ĀSHĀḌHA 2187	27	28	29	30	1	2	3
	4	5	6	7	8	9	9
	10	11	12	13	14	**15**	17
	18	19	20	21	22	23	24
ŚRĀVAṆA 2187	25	26	27	28	29	30	1
	2	3	4	5	6	7	8
	9	10	11	12	13	14	15
	16	17	**18**	20	21	22	23[c]
	24	25	26	27	28	29	30
BHĀDRAPADA 2187	1	2	3	4[d]	5	5	6
	7	8	9	10	**11**	13	14
	15	16	17	18	19	20	21
	22	23	24	25	26	27	28
ĀŚVINA 2187	29	30	1	2	3	4	5
	6	7	8[e]	9[e]	10[e]	11	12
	13	14	**15**	17	18	19	20
	21	22	23	24	25	26	27
KĀRTTIKA 2187	28	29	30	30	1[f]	2	3
	4	5	6	7	**8**	10	11
	12	13	14	15	16	17	18
	19	20	21	22	23	24	25
MĀRGAŚĪRA 2187	26	27	28	29	30	1	2
	3	4	5	6	7	8	9
	10	11[g]	12	**13**	15	16	17
	18	19	20	21	22	23	23
	24	25	26	27	28	29	30
	1	2	3	4	5	6	**7**

‡ Leap year
[a] New Year (Vikṛita)
[b] Birthday of Rāma
[c] Birthday of Krishna
[d] Ganēśa Chaturthī
[e] Dashara
[f] Diwali
[g] Birthday of Vishnu
[h] Night of Śiva
[i] Holi

HINDU SOLAR 2051‡/2052

Month	Sun	Mon	Tue	Wed	Thu	Fri	Sat
PAUSHA 2051	15	16	17	18	19	20	21
	22	23	24	25	26	27	28
MĀGHA 2051	29	1[b]	2	3	4	5	6
	7	8	9	10	11	12	13
	14	15	16	17	18	19	20
	21	22	23	24	25	26	27
PHĀLGUNA 2051	28	29	1	2	3	4	5
	6	7	8	9	10	11	12
	13	14	15	16	17	18	19
	20	21	22	23	24	25	26
CHAITRA 2051	27	28	29	30	1	2	3
	4	5	6	7	8	9	10
	11	12	13	14	15	16	17
	18	19	20	21	22	23	24
	25	26	27	28	29	30	31
VAIŚĀKHA 2052	1[a]	2	3	4	5	6	7
	8	9	10	11	12	13	14
	15	16	17	18	19	20	21
	22	23	24	25	26	27	28
JYAISHṬHA 2052	29	30	31	1	2	3	4
	5	6	7	8	9	10	11
	12	13	14	15	16	17	18
	19	20	21	22	23	24	25
ĀSHĀḌHA 2052	26	27	28	29	30	31	1
	2	3	4	5	6	7	8
	9	10	11	12	13	14	15
	16	17	18	19	20	21	22
	23	24	25	26	27	28	29
ŚRĀVAṆA 2052	30	31	32	1	2	3	4
	5	6	7	8	9	10	11
	12	13	14	15	16	17	18
	19	20	21	22	23	24	25
BHĀDRAPADA 2052	26	27	28	29	30	31	1
	2	3	4	5	6	7	8
	9	10	11	12	13	14	15
	16	17	18	19	20	21	22
	23	24	25	26	27	28	29
ĀŚVINA 2052	30	31	1	2	3	4	5
	6	7	8	9	10	11	12
	13	14	15	16	17	18	19
	20	21	22	23	24	25	26
KĀRTTIKA 2052	27	28	29	30	31	1	2
	3	4	5	6	7	8	9
	10	11	12	13	14	15	16
	17	18	19	20	21	22	23
MĀRGAŚĪRA 2052	24	25	26	27	28	29	1
	2	3	4	5	6	7	8
	9	10	11	12	13	14	15
	16	17	18	19	20	21	22
	23	24	25	26	27	28	29
PAUSHA 2052	30	1	2	3	4	5	6
	7	8	9	10	11	12	13
	14	15	16	17	18	19	20

‡ Leap year
[a] New Year (Viśvāvasu)
[b] Pongal

ISLAMIC (ASTRONOMICAL) 1554/1555‡

Month	Sun	Mon	Tue	Wed	Thu	Fri	Sat
RAMAḌĀN 1554	20	21	22	23	24	25	26
SHAWWĀL 1554	27	28	29	1[f]	2	3	4
	5	6	7	8	9	10	11
	12	13	14	15	16	17	18
	19	20	21	22	23	24	25
DHU AL-QA'DA 1554	26	27	28	29	30	1	2
	3	4	5	6	7	8	9
	10	11	12	13	14	15	16
	17	18	19	20	21	22	23
DHU AL-ḤIJJA 1554	24	25	26	27	28	29	1
	2	3	4	5	6	7	8
	9	10[g]	11	12	13	14	15
	16	17	18	19	20	21	22
	23	24	25	26	27	28	29
MUḤARRAM 1555	1[a]	2[A]	3	4	5	6	7
	8	9	10[b]	11	12	13	14
	15	16	17	18	19	20	21
	22	23	24	25	26	27	28
ṢAFAR 1555	29	30	1	2	3	4	5
	6	7	8	9	10	11	12
	13	14	15	16	17	18	19
	20	21	22	23	24	25	26
RABĪ' I 1555	27	28	29	1	2	3	4
	5	6	7	8	9	10	11
	12[c]	13	14	15	16	17	18
	19	20	21	22	23	24	25
RABĪ' II 1555	26	27	28	29	30	1	2
	3	4	5	6	7	8	9
	10	11	12	13	14	15	16
	17	18	19	20	21	22	23
	24	25	26	27	28	29	30
JUMĀDĀ I 1555	1	2	3	4	5	6	7
	8	9	10	11	12	13	14
	15	16	17	18	19	20	21
	22	23	24	25	26	27	28
JUMĀDĀ II 1555	29	1	2	3	4	5	6
	7	8	9	10	11	12	13
	14	15	16	17	18	19	20
	21	22	23	24	25	26	27
RAJAB 1555	28	29	30	1	2	3	4
	5	6	7	8	9	10	11
	12	13	14	15	16	17	18
	19	20	21	22	23	24	25
SHA'BĀN 1555	26	27[d]	28	29	1	2	3
	4	5	6	7	8	9	10
	11	12	13	14	15	16	17
	18	19	20	21	22	23	24
RAMAḌĀN 1555	25	26	27	28	29	30	1[e]
	2	3	4	5	6	7	8
	9	10	11	12	13	14	15
	16	17	18	19	20	21	22
	23	24	25	26	27	28	29
	30	1	2	3	4	5	6

‡ Leap year
[a] New Year
[A] New Year (Arithmetic)
[b] 'Ashūrā'
[c] Prophet's Birthday
[d] Ascent of the Prophet
[e] Start of Ramaḍān
[f] 'Id al-Fiṭr
[g] 'Id al-'Aḍḥā

GREGORIAN 2130

Julian (Sun)	Sun	Mon	Tue	Wed	Thu	Fri	Sat	Month
Dec 18	1	2	3	4	5	6	7	JANUARY 2130
	8[a]	9	10	11	12	13	14	
Jan 1	15[b]	16	17	18	19	20	21	
	22	23	24	25	26	27	28	
Jan 15	29	30	31	1	2	3	4	FEBRUARY 2130
	5	6	7	8[c]	9	10	11	
Jan 29	12	13	14	15	16	17	18	
	19	20	21	22	23	24	25	
Feb 12	26	27	28	1	2	3	4	MARCH 2130
	5	6	7	8	9	10	11	
Feb 26	12	13	14	15	16	17	18	
	19[d]	20	21	22	23	24	25	
Mar 12	26[e]	27	28	29	30	31	1	APRIL 2130
	2	3	4	5	6	7	8	
Mar 26	9	10	11	12	13	14	15	
	16	17	18	19	20	21	22	
Apr 9	23	24	25	26	27	28	29	
	30[f]	1	2	3	4	5	6	MAY 2130
Apr 23	7	8	9	10	11	12	13	
	14	15	16	17	18	19	20	
May 7	21	22	23	24	25	26	27	
	28	29	30	31	1	2	3	JUNE 2130
May 21	4	5	6	7	8	9	10	
	11	12	13	14	15	16	17	
Jun 4	18	19	20	21	22	23	24	
	25	26	27	28	29	30	1	JULY 2130
Jun 18	2	3	4	5	6	7	8	
	9	10	11	12	13	14	15	
Jul 2	16	17	18	19	20	21	22	
	23	24	25	26	27	28	29	
Jul 16	30	31	1	2	3	4	5	AUGUST 2130
	6	7	8	9	10	11	12	
Jul 30	13	14	15	16	17	18	19	
	20	21	22	23	24	25	26	
Aug 13	27	28	29	30	31	1	2	SEPTEMBER 2130
	3	4	5	6	7	8	9	
Aug 27	10	11	12	13	14	15	16	
	17	18	19	20	21	22	23	
Sep 10	24	25	26	27	28	29	30	
	1	2	3	4	5	6	7	OCTOBER 2130
Sep 24	8	9	10	11	12	13	14	
	15	16	17	18	19	20	21	
Oct 8	22	23	24	25	26	27	28	
	29	30	31	1	2	3	4	NOVEMBER 2130
Oct 22	5	6	7	8	9	10	11	
	12	13	14	15	16	17	18	
Nov 5	19	20	21	22	23	24	25	
	26	27	28	29	30	1	2	DECEMBER 2130
Nov 19	3[g]	4	5	6	7	8	9	
	10	11	12	13	14	15	16	
Dec 3	17	18	19	20	21	22	23	
	24	25[h]	26	27	28	29	30	
Dec 17	31	1	2	3	4	5	6	

[a] Orthodox Christmas
[b] Julian New Year
[c] Ash Wednesday
[d] Feast of Orthodoxy
[e] Easter
[f] Orthodox Easter
[g] Advent
[h] Christmas

2131

GREGORIAN 2131 · ISO WEEK (Mon) · JULIAN DAY (Sun noon)

Month	Sun	Mon	Tue	Wed	Thu	Fri	Sat	Lunar Phases	ISO Week	Julian Day
	31	1[a]	2	3	4	5	◐	12:30	1	2499391
January 2131	7	8	9	10	11	12	○	12:47	2	2499398
	14	15	16	17	18	19	20		3	2499405
	◑	22	23	24	25	26	27	12:04	4	2499412
	28	●	30	31	1	2	3	2:51	5	2499419
	◐	5	6	7	8	9	10	20:28	6	2499426
February 2131	11	○	13	14	15	16	17	5:04	7	2499433
	18	19	◑	21	22	23	24	8:45	8	2499440
	25	26	●	28	1	2	3	14:41	9	2499447
	4	5	◐	7	8	9	10	5:29	10	2499454
March 2131	11	12	○	14	15	16	17	22:22	11	2499461
	18	19	20	21[b]	◑	23	24	2:31	12	2499468
	25	26	27	28	●	30	31	0:22	13	2499475
	1	2	3	◐	5	6	7	16:16	14	2499482
	8	9	10	11	○	13	14	15:39	15	2499489
April 2131	15	16	17	18	19	◑	21	16:20	16	2499496
	22	23	24	25	26	●	28	8:36	17	2499503
	29	30	1	2	3	◐	5	4:59	18	2499510
	6	7	8	9	10	11	○	8:03	19	2499517
May 2131	13	14	15	16	17	18	19		20	2499524
	◑	21	22	23	24	25	●	2:08 19:30	21	2499531
	27	28	29	30	31	1	◐	16:20	22	2499538
	3	4	5	6	7	8	9		23	2499545
June 2131	○	11	12	13	14	15	16	22:54	24	2499552
	17	◑	19	20	21[c]	22	23	8:42	25	2499559
	24	●	26	27	28	29	30	0:30	26	2499566
	1	◐	3	4	5	6	7	11:30	27	2499573
July 2131	8	9	○	11	12	13	14	11:49	28	2499580
	15	16	◑	18	19	20	21	13:24	29	2499587
	22	23	●	25	26	27	28	9:56	30	2499594
	29	30	31	◐	2	3	4	4:36	31	2499601
	5	6	7	○	9	10	11	22:47	32	2499608
August 2131	12	13	14	◑	16	17	18	17:51	33	2499615
	19	20	21	●	23	24	25	21:19	34	2499622
	26	27	28	29	◐	31	1	22:14	35	2499629
	2	3	4	5	6	○	8	8:15	36	2499636
September 2131	9	10	11	12	◑	14	15	23:37	37	2499643
	16	17	18	19	20	●	22	11:05	38	2499650
	23[d]	24	25	26	27	28	◐	15:31	39	2499657
	30	1	2	3	4	5	○	17:05	40	2499664
October 2131	7	8	9	10	11	12	◑	8:03	41	2499671
	14	15	16	17	18	19	20		42	2499678
	●	22	23	24	25	26	27	3:23	43	2499685
	28	◐	30	31	1	2	3	7:23	44	2499692
	4	○	6	7	8	9	10	2:12	45	2499699
November 2131	◑	12	13	14	15	16	17	20:02	46	2499706
	18	●	20	21	22	23	24	21:46	47	2499713
	25	26	◐	28	29	30	1	20:59	48	2499720
	2	3	○	5	6	7	8	12:21	49	2499727
December 2131	9	10	◑	12	13	14	15	11:50	50	2499734
	16	17	18	●	20	21	22[e]	16:55	51	2499741
	23	24	25	26	◐	28	29	8:07	52	2499748
	30	31	1	○	3	4	5	23:48	1	2499755

HEBREW 5891/5892

ISO Week	Month	Sun	Mon	Tue	Wed	Thu	Fri	Sat	Molad
1		1[e]	2[e]	3	4	5	6	7	Sat 8h10m13p
2	Teveth 5891	8	9	10	11	12	13	14	
3		15	16	17	18	19	20	21	
4		22	23	24	25	26	27	28	Sun 20h54m14p
5		29	1	2	3	4	5	6	
6	Shevat 5891	7	8	9	10	11	12	13	
7		14	15	16	17	18	19	20	
8		21	22	23	24	25	26	27	Tue 9h38m15p
9		28	29	30	1	2	3	4	
10	Adar 5891	5	6	7	8	9	10	11	
11		12	13	14[f]	15	16	17	18	
12		19	20	21	22	23	24	25	Wed 22h22m16p
13		26	27	28	29	1	2	3	
14	Nisan 5891	4	5	6	7	8	9	10	
15		11	12	13	14	15[g]	16	17	
16		18	19	20	21	22	23	24	Fri 11h6m17p
17		25	26	27	28	29	30	1	
18	Iyyar 5891	2	3	4	5	6	7	8	
19		9	10	11	12	13	14	15	
20		16	17	18	19	20	21	22	
21		23	24	25	26	27	28	29	Sat 23h51m0p
22		1	2	3	4	5	6[h]	7	
23	Sivan 5891	8	9	10	11	12	13	14	
24		15	16	17	18	19	20	21	
25		22	23	24	25	26	27	28	Mon 12h35m1p
26		29	30	1	2	3	4	5	
27	Tammuz 5891	6	7	8	9	10	11	12	
28		13	14	15	16	17	18	19	
29		20	21	22	23	24	25	26	Wed 1h19m2p
30		27	28	29	1	2	3	4	
31	Av 5891	5	6	7	8	9[i]	10	11	
32		12	13	14	15	16	17	18	
33		19	20	21	22	23	24	25	Thu 14h3m3p
34		26	27	28	29	30	1	2	
35	Elul 5891	3	4	5	6	7	8	9	
36		10	11	12	13	14	15	16	
37		17	18	19	20	21	22	23	Sat 2h47m4p
38		24	25	26	27	28	29	1[a]	
39	Tishri 5892	2[a]	3	4	5	6	7	8	
40		9	10[b]	11	12	13	14	15[c]	
41		16	17	18	19	20	21	22	
42		23	24	25	26	27	28	29	Sun 15h31m5p
43		30	1	2	3	4	5	6	
44	Heshvan 5892	7	8	9	10	11	12	13	
45		14	15	16	17	18	19	20	
46		21	22	23	24	25	26	27	Tue 4h15m6p
47		28	29	30	1	2	3	4	
48	Kislev 5892	5	6	7	8	9	10	11	
49		12	13	14	15	16	17[d]	18	
50		19	20	21	22	23	24	25[e]	Wed 16h59m7p
51		26[e]	27[e]	28[e]	29[e]	30[e]	1[e]	2[e]	
52	Teveth 5892	3	4	5	6	7	8	9	
1		10	11	12	13	14	15	16	

CHINESE Gēng-Yín/Xīn-Mǎo‡

ISO Week	Month	Sun	Mon	Tue	Wed	Thu	Fri	Sat	Solar Term
1		2	3	4	5	6	7	8	Xiǎo hán
2	Month 12 Gēng-Yín	9	10	11	12	13	14	15	
3		16	17	18	19	20	21	22	Dà hán
4		23	24	25	26	27	28	29	
5		30	1[a]	2	3	4	5	6	
6	Month 1 Xīn-Mǎo	7	8	9	10	11	12*	13	Lì chūn
7		14	15[b]	16	17	18	19	20	
8		21	22	23	24	25	26	27	Yǔ shuǐ
9		28	29	1	2	3	4	5	
10	Month 2 Xīn-Mǎo	6	7	8	9	10	11	12	Jīng zhé
11		13	14	15	16	17	18	19	
12		20	21	22	23	24	25	26	Chūn fēn
13		27	28	29	30	1	2	3	
14	Month 3 Xīn-Mǎo	4	5	6	7	8[c]	9	10	Qīng míng
15		11	12	13*	14	15	16	17	
16		18	19	20	21	22	23	24	Gǔ yǔ
17		25	26	27	28	29	1	2	
18	Month 4 Xīn-Mǎo	3	4	5	6	7	8	9	
19		10	11	12	13	14	15	16	Lì xià
20		17	18	19	20	21	22	23	
21		24	25	26	27	28	29	30	Xiǎo mǎn
22		1	2	3	4	5[d]	6	7	
23	Month 5 Xīn-Mǎo	8	9	10	11	12	13	14*	Máng zhòng
24		15	16	17	18	19	20	21	
25		22	23	24	25	26	27	28	Xià zhì
26		29	1	2	3	4	5	6	
27	Month 6 Xīn-Mǎo	7	8	9	10	11	12	13	Xiǎo shǔ
28		14	15	16	17	18	19	20	
29		21	22	23	24	25	26	27	
30		28	29	1	2	3	4	5	Dà shǔ
31	Leap Month 6 Xīn-Mǎo	6	7	8	9	10	11	12	
32		13	14	15	16*	17	18	19	Lì qiū
33		20	21	22	23	24	25	26	
34		27	28	29	30	1	2	3	Chǔ shǔ
35	Month 7 Xīn-Mǎo	4	5	6	7[e]	8	9	10	
36		11	12	13	14	15[f]	16	17	Bái lù
37		18	19	20	21	22	23	24	
38		25	26	27	28	29	1	2	
39	Month 8 Xīn-Mǎo	3	4	5	6	7	8	9	Qiū fēn
40		10	11	12	13	14	15[g]	16	
41		17*	18	19	20	21	22	23	Hán lù
42		24	25	26	27	28	29	30	
43		1	2	3	4	5	6	7	Shuāng jiàng
44	Month 9 Xīn-Mǎo	8	9[h]	10	11	12	13	14	
45		15	16	17	18	19	20	21	Lì dōng
46		22	23	24	25	26	27	28	
47		29	30	1	2	3	4	5	Xiǎo xuě
48	Month 10 Xīn-Mǎo	6	7	8	9	10	11	12	
49		13	14	15	16	17*	18	19	Dà xuě
50		20	21	22	23	24	25	26	
51		27	28	29	30	1	2	3[i]	Dōng zhì
52	Month 11 Xīn-Mǎo	4	5	6	7	8	9	10	
1		11	12	13	14	15	16	17	

COPTIC 1847‡/1848 · ETHIOPIC 2123‡/2124

ISO Week	Coptic Month	Sun	Mon	Tue	Wed	Thu	Fri	Sat	Ethiopic Month
1	Koiak 1847	21	22	23	24	25	26	27	Tākhśāś 2123
2		28	29[c]	30	1	2	3	4	
3	Tōbe 1847	5	6[d]	7	8	9	10	11[e]	Ṭer 2123
4		12	13	14	15	16	17	18	
5		19	20	21	22	23	24	25	
6		26	27	28	29	30	1	2	
7	Meshir 1847	3	4	5	6	7	8	9	Yakātit 2123
8		10	11	12	13	14	15	16	
9		17	18	19	20	21	22	23	
10		24	25	26	27	28	29	30	
11	Paremotep 1847	1	2	3	4	5	6	7	
12		8	9	10	11	12	13	14	Magābit 2123
13		15	16	17	18	19	20	21	
14		22	23	24	25	26	27	28	
15		29	30	1	2	3	4	5	
16	Parmoute 1847	6	7	8	9	10	11	12	Miyāzyā 2123
17		13[f]	14	15	16	17	18	19	
18		20	21	22	23	24	25	26	
19		27	28	29[g]	30	1	2	3	
20	Pashons 1847	4	5	6	7	8	9	10	
21		11	12	13	14	15	16	17	Genbot 2123
22		18	19	20	21	22	23	24	
23		25	26	27	28	29	30	1	
24	Paōne 1847	2	3	4	5	6	7	8	
25		9	10	11	12	13	14	15	Sanē 2123
26		16	17	18	19	20	21	22	
27		23	24	25	26	27	28	29	
28		30	1	2	3	4	5	6	
29	Epēp 1847	7	8	9	10	11	12	13	Hamlē 2123
30		14	15	16	17	18	19	20	
31		21	22	23	24	25	26	27	
32		28	29	30	1	2	3	4	
33	Mesorē 1847	5	6	7	8	9	10	11	Nahasē 2123
34		12	13[h]	14	15	16	17	18	
35		19	20	21	22	23	24	25	
36	Epag. 1847	26	27	28	29	30	1	2	Pāg. 2123
37		3	4	5	6	1[a]	2	3	
38	Thout 1848	4	5	6	7	8	9	10	Maskaram 2124
39		11	12	13	14	15	16	17[b]	
40		18	19	20	21	22	23	24	
41		25	26	27	28	29	30	1	
42	Paope 1848	2	3	4	5	6	7	8	
43		9	10	11	12	13	14	15	Teqemt 2124
44		16	17	18	19	20	21	22	
45		23	24	25	26	27	28	29	
46		30	1	2	3	4	5	6	
47	Athōr 1848	7	8	9	10	11	12	13	Hedār 2124
48		14	15	16	17	18	19	20	
49		21	22	23	24	25	26	27	
50		28	29	30	1	2	3	4	
51	Koiak 1848	5	6	7	8	9	10	11	Tākhśāś 2124
52		12	13	14	15	16	17	18	
1		19	20	21	22	23	24	25	

[a]New Year
[b]Spring (1:35)
[c]Summer (17:19)
[d]Autumn (10:07)
[e]Winter (8:38)
● New moon
◐ First quarter moon
○ Full moon
◑ Last quarter moon

[a]New Year
[b]Yom Kippur
[c]Sukkot
[d]Winter starts
[e]Ḥanukkah
[f]Purim
[g]Passover
[h]Shavuot
[i]Fast of Av

‡Leap year
[a]New Year (4829, Hare)
[b]Lantern Festival
[c]Qīngmíng
[d]Dragon Festival
[e]Qīqiǎo
[f]Hungry Ghosts
[g]Mid-Autumn Festival
[h]Double-Ninth Festival
[i]Dōngzhì
*Start of 60-name cycle

‡Leap year
[a]New Year
[b]Building of the Cross
[c]Christmas
[d]Jesus's Circumcision
[e]Epiphany
[f]Easter
[g]Mary's Announcement
[h]Jesus's Transfiguration

2131

PERSIAN (ASTRONOMICAL) 1509/1510

Month	Sun	Mon	Tue	Wed	Thu	Fri	Sat
DEY 1509	10	11	12	13	14	15	16
	17	18	19	20	21	22	23
	24	25	26	27	28	29	30
BAHMAN 1509	1	2	3	4	5	6	7
	8	9	10	11	12	13	14
	15	16	17	18	19	20	21
	22	23	24	25	26	27	28
	29	30	1	2	3	4	5
ESFAND 1509	6	7	8	9	10	11	12
	13	14	15	16	17	18	19
	20	21	22	23	24	25	26
	27	28	29	1[a]	2	3	4
FARVARDĪN 1510	5	6	7	8	9	10	11
	12	13[b]	14	15	16	17	18
	19	20	21	22	23	24	25
	26	27	28	29	30	31	1
ORDĪBEHEŠT 1510	2	3	4	5	6	7	8
	9	10	11	12	13	14	15
	16	17	18	19	20	21	22
	23	24	25	26	27	28	29
	30	31	1	2	3	4	5
XORDĀD 1510	6	7	8	9	10	11	12
	13	14	15	16	17	18	19
	20	21	22	23	24	25	26
	27	28	29	30	31	1	2
TĪR 1510	3	4	5	6	7	8	9
	10	11	12	13	14	15	16
	17	18	19	20	21	22	23
	24	25	26	27	28	29	30
	31	1	2	3	4	5	6
MORDĀD 1510	7	8	9	10	11	12	13
	14	15	16	17	18	19	20
	21	22	23	24	25	26	27
	28	29	30	31	1	2	3
SHAHRĪVAR 1510	4	5	6	7	8	9	10
	11	12	13	14	15	16	17
	18	19	20	21	22	23	24
	25	26	27	28	29	30	31
MEHR 1510	1	2	3	4	5	6	7
	8	9	10	11	12	13	14
	15	16	17	18	19	20	21
	22	23	24	25	26	27	28
	29	30	1	2	3	4	5
ĀBĀN 1510	6	7	8	9	10	11	12
	13	14	15	16	17	18	19
	20	21	22	23	24	25	26
	27	28	29	30	1	2	3
ĀZAR 1510	4	5	6	7	8	9	10
	11	12	13	14	15	16	17
	18	19	20	21	22	23	24
	25	26	27	28	29	30	1
DEY 1510	2	3	4	5	6	7	8
	9	10	11	12	13	14	15

[a]New Year
[b]Sizdeh Bedar

HINDU LUNAR 2187/2188

Month	Sun	Mon	Tue	Wed	Thu	Fri	Sat
	1	2	3	4	5	6	**7**
PAUSHA 2187	9	10	11	12	13	14	15
	16	17	18	19	20	21	22
	23	24	25	25	26	27	28
	29	30	**1**	3	4	5	6
MĀGHA 2187	7	8	9	10	11	12	13
	14	15	16	17	18	19	20
	21	22	23	24	25	26	27
	28[h]	29	30	1	2	3	4
PHĀLGUNA 2187	5	**6**	8	9	10	11	12
	13	14	15[i]	16	17	18	18
	19	20	21	22	23	24	25
	26	27	28	29	**30**[a]	2	3
CHAITRA 2188	4	5	6	7	8	9[b]	10
	11	12	13	14	15	16	17
	18	19	20	21	22	23	24
	25	26	27	28	29	30	1
VAIŚĀKHA 2188	2	3	**4**	6	7	8	9
	10	11	12	12	13	14	15
	16	17	18	19	20	21	22
	23	24	25	26	**27**	29	30
JYAISHṬHA 2188	1	2	3	4	5	6	7
	8	9	10	11	12	13	14
	15	16	17	18	19	20	21
	22	23	24	25	26	27	28
	29	**30**	2	3	4	5	6
ĀSHĀḌHA 2188	7	8	8	9	10	11	12
	13	14	15	16	17	18	19
	20	21	**22**	24	25	26	27
	28	29	30	1	2	3	4
ŚRĀVAṆA 2188	5	6	7	8	9	10	11
	12	13	14	15	16	17	18
	19	20	21	22	23[c]	24	**25**
	27	28	29	30	1	2	3
BHĀDRAPADA 2188	4[d]	5	5	6	7	8	9
	10	11	12	13	14	15	16
	17	**18**	20	21	22	23	24
	25	26	27	28	29	30	1
ĀŚVINA 2188	2	3	4	5	6	7	8[e]
	9[e]	10[e]	11	12	13	14	15
	16	17	18	19	20	21	22
	24	25	26	27	28	29	30
	30	1[f]	2	3	4	5	6
KĀRTTIKA 2188	7	8	9	10	11	12	13
	14	**15**	17	18	19	20	21
	22	23	24	25	26	27	28
	29	30	1	2	3	3	4
MĀRGAŚĪRA 2188	5	6	7	8	**9**	11[g]	12
	13	14	15	16	17	18	19
	20	21	22	23	24	25	26
	27	28	29	30	1	2	3
PAUSHA 2188	4	5	6	7	8	9	10
	11	12	13	**14**	16	17	18

[a]New Year (Khara)
[b]Birthday of Rāma
[c]Birthday of Krishna
[d]Ganēśa Chaturthī
[e]Dashara
[f]Diwali
[g]Birthday of Vishnu
[h]Night of Śiva
[i]Holi

HINDU SOLAR 2052/2053

Month	Sun	Mon	Tue	Wed	Thu	Fri	Sat
	14	15	16	17	18	19	20
PAUSHA 2052	21	22	23	24	25	26	27
	28	29	1[b]	2	3	4	5
MĀGHA 2052	6	7	8	9	10	11	12
	13	14	15	16	17	18	19
	20	21	22	23	24	25	26
	27	28	29	30	1	2	3
PHĀLGUNA 2052	4	5	6	7	8	9	10
	11	12	13	14	15	16	17
	18	19	20	21	22	23	24
	25	26	27	28	29	30	1
	2	3	4	5	6	7	8
CHAITRA 2052	9	10	11	12	13	14	15
	16	17	18	19	20	21	22
	23	24	25	26	27	28	29
	30	1[a]	2	3	4	5	6
VAIŚĀKHA 2053	7	8	9	10	11	12	13
	14	15	16	17	18	19	20
	21	22	23	24	25	26	27
	28	29	30	31	1	2	3
JYAISHṬHA 2053	4	5	6	7	8	9	10
	11	12	13	14	15	16	17
	18	19	20	21	22	23	24
	25	26	27	28	29	30	31
	1	2	3	4	5	6	7
ĀSHĀḌHA 2053	8	9	10	11	12	13	14
	15	16	17	18	19	20	21
	22	23	24	25	26	27	28
	29	30	31	32	1	2	3
ŚRĀVAṆA 2053	4	5	6	7	8	9	10
	11	12	13	14	15	16	17
	18	19	20	21	22	23	24
	25	26	27	28	29	30	31
	1	2	3	4	5	6	7
BHĀDRAPADA 2053	8	9	10	11	12	13	14
	15	16	17	18	19	20	21
	22	23	24	25	26	27	28
	29	30	31	1	2	3	4
ĀŚVINA 2053	5	6	7	8	9	10	11
	12	13	14	15	16	17	18
	19	20	21	22	23	24	25
	26	27	28	29	30	31	1
	2	3	4	5	6	7	8
KĀRTTIKA 2053	9	10	11	12	13	14	15
	16	17	18	19	20	21	22
	23	24	25	26	27	28	29
	30	1	2	3	4	5	6
MĀRGAŚĪRA 2053	7	8	9	10	11	12	13
	14	15	16	17	18	19	20
	21	22	23	24	25	26	27
	28	29	1	2	3	4	5
PAUSHA 2053	6	7	8	9	10	11	12
	13	14	15	16	17	18	19

[a]New Year (Parābhava)
[b]Pongal

ISLAMIC (ASTRONOMICAL) 1555‡/1556‡

Month	Sun	Mon	Tue	Wed	Thu	Fri	Sat
	30	1[f]	2	3	4	5	6
SHAWWĀL 1555	7	8	9	10	11	12	13
	14	15	16	17	18	19	20
	21	22	23	24	25	26	27
	28	29	1	2	3	4	5
DHU AL-QA'DA 1555	6	7	8	9	10	11	12
	13	14	15	16	17	18	19
	20	21	22	23	24	25	26
	27	28	29	30	1	2	3
DHU AL-HIJJA 1555	4	5	6	7	8	9	10[g]
	11	12	13	14	15	16	17
	18	19	20	21	22	23	24
	25	26	27	28	29	1[a]	2
MUHARRAM 1556	3	4	5	6	7	8	9
	10[b]	11	12	13	14	15	16
	17	18	19	20	21	22	23
	24	25	26	27	28	29	1
ṢAFAR 1556	2	3	4	5	6	7	8
	9	10	11	12	13	14	15
	16	17	18	19	20	21	22
	23	24	25	26	27	28	29
	30	1	2	3	4	5	6
RABĪ' I 1556	7	8	9	10	11	12[c]	13
	14	15	16	17	18	19	20
	21	22	23	24	25	26	27
	28	29	1	2	3	4	5
RABĪ' II 1556	6	7	8	9	10	11	12
	13	14	15	16	17	18	19
	20	21	22	23	24	25	26
	27	28	29	30	1	2	3
JUMĀDĀ I 1556	4	5	6	7	8	9	10
	11	12	13	14	15	16	17
	18	19	20	21	22	23	24
	25	26	27	28	29	1	2
JUMĀDĀ II 1556	3	4	5	6	7	8	9
	10	11	12	13	14	15	16
	17	18	19	20	21	22	23
	24	25	26	27	28	29	30
RAJAB 1556	1	2	3	4	5	6	7
	8	9	10	11	12	13	14
	15	16	17	18	19	20	21
	22	23	24	25	26	27[d]	28
	29	1	2	3	4	5	6
SHA'BĀN 1556	7	8	9	10	11	12	13
	14	15	16	17	18	19	20
	21	22	23	24	25	26	27
	28	29	30	1[e]	2	3	4
RAMAḌĀN 1556	5	6	7	8	9	10	11
	12	13	14	15	16	17	18
	19	20	21	22	23	24	25
	26	27	28	29	30	1[f]	2
SHAWWĀL 1556	3	4	5	6	7	8	9
	10	11	12	13	14	15	16

‡Leap year
[a]New Year
[b]'Ashūrā'
[c]Prophet's Birthday
[d]Ascent of the Prophet
[e]Start of Ramaḍān
[f]'Id al-Fiṭr
[g]'Id al-'Aḍḥā

GREGORIAN 2131

Julian (Sun)	Sun	Mon	Tue	Wed	Thu	Fri	Sat	Month
Dec 17	31	1	2	3	4	5	6	
	7	8[a]	9	10	11	12	13	JANUARY 2131
Dec 31	14	15[b]	16	17	18	19	20	
	21	22	23	24	25	26	27	
Jan 14	28	29	30	31	1	2	3	
	4	5	6	7	8	9	10	FEBRUARY 2131
Jan 28	11	12	13	14	15	16	17	
	18	19	20	21	22	23	24	
Feb 11	25	26	27	28[c]	1	2	3	
	4	5	6	7	8	9	10	MARCH 2131
Feb 25	11[d]	12	13	14	15	16	17	
	18	19	20	21	22	23	24	
Mar 11	25	26	27	28	29	30	31	
	1	2	3	4	5	6	7	
Mar 25	8	9	10	11	12	13	14	APRIL 2131
	15[e]	16	17	18	19	20	21	
Apr 8	22[f]	23	24	25	26	27	28	
	29	30	1	2	3	4	5	
Apr 22	6	7	8	9	10	11	12	
	13	14	15	16	17	18	19	MAY 2131
May 6	20	21	22	23	24	25	26	
	27	28	29	30	31	1	2	
May 20	3	4	5	6	7	8	9	JUNE 2131
	10	11	12	13	14	15	16	
Jun 3	17	18	19	20	21	22	23	
	24	25	26	27	28	29	30	
Jun 17	1	2	3	4	5	6	7	
	8	9	10	11	12	13	14	JULY 2131
Jul 1	15	16	17	18	19	20	21	
	22	23	24	25	26	27	28	
Jul 15	29	30	31	1	2	3	4	
	5	6	7	8	9	10	11	
Jul 29	12	13	14	15	16	17	18	AUGUST 2131
	19	20	21	22	23	24	25	
Aug 12	26	27	28	29	30	31	1	
	2	3	4	5	6	7	8	
Aug 26	9	10	11	12	13	14	15	SEPTEMBER 2131
	16	17	18	19	20	21	22	
Sep 9	23	24	25	26	27	28	29	
	30	1	2	3	4	5	6	
Sep 23	7	8	9	10	11	12	13	OCTOBER 2131
	14	15	16	17	18	19	20	
Oct 7	21	22	23	24	25	26	27	
	28	29	30	31	1	2	3	
Oct 21	4	5	6	7	8	9	10	NOVEMBER 2131
	11	12	13	14	15	16	17	
Nov 4	18	19	20	21	22	23	24	
	25	26	27	28	29	30	1	
Nov 18	2[g]	3	4	5	6	7	8	DECEMBER 2131
	9	10	11	12	13	14	15	
Dec 2	16	17	18	19	20	21	22	
	23	24	25[h]	26	27	28	29	
Dec 16	30	31	1	2	3	4	5	

[a]Orthodox Christmas
[b]Julian New Year
[c]Ash Wednesday
[d]Feast of Orthodoxy
[e]Easter
[f]Orthodox Easter
[g]Advent
[h]Christmas

2132

GREGORIAN 2132‡ (with Lunar Phases, ISO WEEK, JULIAN DAY)

Month	Sun	Mon	Tue	Wed	Thu	Fri	Sat	Lunar Phases	ISO WEEK (Mon)	JULIAN DAY (Sun noon)
	30	31	1[a]	○	3	4	5	23:48	1	2499755
JANUARY 2132	6	7	8	9	◑	11	12	7:00	2	2499762
	13	14	15	16	17	●	19	11:00	3	2499769
	20	21	22	23	24	◐	26	17:10	4	2499776
	27	28	29	30	31	○	2	12:27	5	2499783
FEBRUARY 2132	3	4	5	6	7	8	◑	4:14	6	2499790
	10	11	12	13	14	15	16		7	2499797
	●	18	19	20	21	22	23	2:32	8	2499804
	◐	25	26	27	28	29	1	0:59	9	2499811
	○	3	4	5	6	7	8	2:08	10	2499818
MARCH 2132	9	◑	11	12	13	14	15	1:34	11	2499825
	16	●	18	19	20[b]	21	22	15:04	12	2499832
	23	◐	25	26	27	28	29	8:27	13	2499839
	30	○	1	2	3	4	5	16:48	14	2499846
APRIL 2132	6	7	◑	9	10	11	12	20:49	15	2499853
	13	14	15	●	17	18	19	1:04	16	2499860
	20	21	◐	23	24	25	26	16:24	17	2499867
	27	28	29	○	1	2	3	8:22	18	2499874
MAY 2132	4	5	6	7	◑	9	10	12:31	19	2499881
	11	12	13	14	●	16	17	9:19	20	2499888
	18	19	20	21	◐	23	24	1:36	21	2499895
	25	26	27	28	29	○	31	0:21	22	2499902
	1	2	3	4	5	6	◑	0:22	23	2499909
JUNE 2132	8	9	10	11	12	●	14	16:41	24	2499916
	15	16	17	18	19	◐[c]	21	12:43	25	2499923
	22	23	24	25	26	27	○	15:56	26	2499930
	29	30	1	2	3	4	5		27	2499937
JULY 2132	◑	7	8	9	10	11	●	8:58 23:56	28	2499944
	13	14	15	16	17	18	19		29	2499951
	◐	21	22	23	24	25	26	2:19	30	2499958
	27	○	29	30	31	1	2	6:19	31	2499965
AUGUST 2132	3	◑	5	6	7	8	9	15:25	32	2499972
	10	●	12	13	14	15	16	7:56	33	2499979
	17	◐	19	20	21	22	23	18:35	34	2499986
	24	25	○	27	28	29	30	19:09	35	2499993
	31	1	◑	3	4	5	6	20:54	36	2500000
SEPTEMBER 2132	7	8	●	10	11	12	13	17:38	37	2500007
	14	15	16	◐	18	19	20	13:00	38	2500014
	21	22[d]	23	24	○	26	27	6:41	39	2500021
	28	29	30	1	◑	3	4	2:41	40	2500028
OCTOBER 2132	5	6	7	8	●	10	11	6:02	41	2500035
	12	13	14	15	16	◐	18	8:21	42	2500042
	19	20	21	22	23	○	25	17:33	43	2500049
	26	27	28	29	30	◑	1	9:55	44	2500056
NOVEMBER 2132	2	3	4	5	6	●	8	21:42	45	2500063
	9	10	11	12	13	14	15		46	2500070
	◐	17	18	19	20	21	22	3:05	47	2500077
	○	24	25	26	27	28	◑	4:18 19:42	48	2500084
	30	1	2	3	4	5	6		49	2500091
DECEMBER 2132	●	8	9	10	11	12	13	16:15	50	2500098
	14	◐	16	17	18	19	20	19:54	51	2500105
	21[e]	○	23	24	25	26	27	15:09	52	2500112
	28	◑	30	31	1	2	3	8:51	1	2500119

HEBREW 5892/5893‡ (with Molad)

ISO WEEK	Month	Sun	Mon	Tue	Wed	Thu	Fri	Sat	Molad
1	TEVETH 5892	10	11	12	13	14	15	16	
2		17	18	19	20	21	22	23	
3		24	25	26	27	28	29	1	Fri 5h43m8p
4	SHEVAT 5892	2	3	4	5	6	7	8	
5		9	10	11	12	13	14	15	
6		16	17	18	19	20	21	22	
7		23	24	25	26	27	28	29	
8		30	1	2	3	4	5	6	Sat 18h27m9p
9	ADAR 5892	7	8	9	10	11	12	13	
10		14[f]	15	16	17	18	19	20	
11		21	22	23	24	25	26	27	
12		28	29	1	2	3	4	5	Mon 7h11m10p
13	NISAN 5892	6	7	8	9	10	11	12	
14		13	14	15[g]	16	17	18	19	
15		20	21	22	23	24	25	26	
16		27	28	29	30	1	2	3	Tue 19h55m11p
17	IYYAR 5892	4	5	6	7	8	9	10	
18		11	12	13	14	15	16	17	
19		18	19	20	21	22	23	24	
20		25	26	27	28	29	1	2	Thu 8h39m12p
21	SIVAN 5892	3	4	5	6[h]	7	8	9	
22		10	11	12	13	14	15	16	
23		17	18	19	20	21	22	23	
24		24	25	26	27	28	29	30	
25	TAMMUZ 5892	1	2	3	4	5	6	7	Fri 21h23m13p
26		8	9	10	11	12	13	14	
27		15	16	17	18	19	20	21	
28		22	23	24	25	26	27	28	
29		29	1	2	3	4	5	6	Sun 10h7m14p
30	AV 5892	7	8	9[i]	10	11	12	13	
31		14	15	16	17	18	19	20	
32		21	22	23	24	25	26	27	
33		28	29	30	1	2	3	4	Mon 22h51m15p
34	ELUL 5892	5	6	7	8	9	10	11	
35		12	13	14	15	16	17	18	
36		19	20	21	22	23	24	25	
37		26	27	28	29	1[a]	2[a]	3	Wed 11h35m16p
38	TISHRI 5893	4	5	6	7	8	9	10[b]	
39		11	12	13	14	15[c]	16	17	
40		18	19	20	21	22	23	24	
41		25	26	27	28	29	30	1	Fri 0h19m17p
42	ḤESHVAN 5893	2	3	4	5	6	7	8	
43		9	10	11	12	13	14	15	
44		16	17	18	19	20	21	22	
45		23	24	25	26	27	28	29	
46		30	1	2	3	4	5	6	Sat 13h4m0p
47	KISLEV 5893	7	8	9	10	11	12	13	
48		14	15	16	17	18	19	20	
49		21	22	23	24	25[e]	26[e]	27[d,e]	
50		28[e]	29[e]	30[e]	1[e]	2[e]	3	4	Mon 1h48m1p
51	TEVETH 5893	5	6	7	8	9	10	11	
52		12	13	14	15	16	17	18	
53		19	20	21	22	23	24	25	

CHINESE Xīn-Mǎo‡/Rén-Chén (with Solar Term)

ISO WEEK	Month	Sun	Mon	Tue	Wed	Thu	Fri	Sat	Solar Term
1	MONTH 11 Xīn-Mǎo	11	12	13	14	15	16	17	
2		*18*	19	20	21	22	23	24	Xiǎo hán
3		25	26	27	28	29	1	2	
4	MONTH 12 Xīn-Mǎo	3	**4**	5	6	7	8	9	Dà hán
5		10	11	12	13	14	15	16	
6		17	*18**	19	20	21	22	23	Lì chūn
7		24	25	26	27	28	29	30	
8	MONTH 1 Rén-Chén	1[a]	2	**3**	4	5	6	7	Yǔ shuǐ
9		8	9	10	11	12	13	14	
10		15[b]	16	17	*18*	19	20	21	Jīng zhé
11		22	23	24	25	26	27	28	
12		29	1	2	3	**4**	5	6	Chūn fēn
13	MONTH 2 Rén-Chén	7	8	9	10	11	12	13	
14		14	15	16	17	18	*19*[c]*	20	Qīng míng
15		21	22	23	24	25	26	27	
16		28	29	30	1	2	3	4	
17	MONTH 3 Rén-Chén	**5**	6	7	8	9	10	11	Gǔ yǔ
18		12	13	14	15	16	17	18	
19		19	*20*	21	22	23	24	25	Lì xià
20		26	27	28	29	1	2	3	
21	MONTH 4 Rén-Chén	4	5	**6**	7	8	9	10	Xiǎo mǎn
22		11	12	13	14	15	16	17	
23		18	19	20*	21	*22*	23	24	Máng zhòng
24		25	26	27	28	29	30	1	
25	MONTH 5 Rén-Chén	2	3	4	5[d]	6	7	***8***	Xià zhì
26		9	10	11	12	13	14	15	
27		16	17	18	19	20	21	22	
28		23	*24*	25	26	27	28	29	Xiǎo shǔ
29	MONTH 6 Rén-Chén	1	2	3	4	5	6	7	
30		8	9	**10**	11	12	13	14	Dà shǔ
31		15	16	17	18	19	20	21*	
32		22	23	24	25	*26*	27	28	Lì qiū
33		29	1	2	3	4	5	6	
34	MONTH 7 Rén-Chén	7[e]	8	9	10	11	12	***13***	Chǔ shǔ
35		14	15[f]	16	17	18	19	20	
36		21	22	23	24	25	26	27	
37		28	29	30	1	2	3	4	Bái lù
38	MONTH 8 Rén-Chén	5	6	7	8	9	10	11	
39		12	**13**	14	15[g]	16	17	18	Qiū fēn
40		19	20	21	22*	23	24	25	
41		26	27	28	*29*	1	2	3	Hán lù
42	MONTH 9 Rén-Chén	4	5	6	7	8	9[h]	10	
43		11	12	13	14	**15**	16	17	Shuāng jiàng
44		18	19	20	21	22	23	24	
45		25	26	27	28	29	*30*	1	Lì dōng
46	MONTH 10 Rén-Chén	2	3	4	5	6	7	8	
47		9	10	11	12	13	14	***15***	Xiǎo xuě
48		16	17	18	19	20	21	22	
49		23*	24	25	26	27	28	29	
50		*30*	1	2	3	4	5	6	Dà xuě
51	MONTH 11 Rén-Chén	7	8	9	10	11	12	13	
52		14[i]	15	16	17	18	19	20	Dōng zhì
53		21	22	23	24	25	26	27	

COPTIC 1848/1849 — ETHIOPIC 2124/2125

ISO WEEK	Coptic Month	Sun	Mon	Tue	Wed	Thu	Fri	Sat	Ethiopic Month
1	KOIAK 1848	19	20	21	22	23	24	25	TĀKHŚĀŚ 2124
2		26	27	28	29[c]	30	1	2	
3	TŌBE 1848	3	4	5	6[d]	7	8	9	
4		10	11[e]	12	13	14	15	16	ṬER 2124
5		17	18	19	20	21	22	23	
6		24	25	26	27	28	29	30	
7		1	2	3	4	5	6	7	
8	MESHIR 1848	8	9	10	11	12	13	14	YAKĀTīT 2124
9		15	16	17	18	19	20	21	
10		22	23	24	25	26	27	28	
11		29	30	1	2	3	4	5	
12	PAREMOTEP 1848	6	7	8	9	10	11	12	MAGĀBīT 2124
13		13	14	15	16	17	18	19	
14		20	21	22	23	24	25	26	
15		27[f]	28	29	30	1	2	3	
16	PARMOUTE 1848	4	5	6	7	8	9	10	MIYĀZYĀ 2124
17		11	12	13	14	15	16	17	
18		18	19	20	21	22	23	24	
19		25	26	27	28	29[g]	30	1	
20	PASHONS 1848	2	3	4	5	6	7	8	GENBOT 2124
21		9	10	11	12	13	14	15	
22		16	17	18	19	20	21	22	
23		23	24	25	26	27	28	29	
24		30	1	2	3	4	5	6	
25	PAŌNE 1848	7	8	9	10	11	12	13	SANĒ 2124
26		14	15	16	17	18	19	20	
27		21	22	23	24	25	26	27	
28		28	29	30	1	2	3	4	
29	EPĒP 1848	5	6	7	8	9	10	11	HAMLĒ 2124
30		12	13	14	15	16	17	18	
31		19	20	21	22	23	24	25	
32		26	27	28	29	30	1	2	
33	MESORĒ 1848	3	4	5	6	7	8	9	NAHASĒ 2124
34		10	11	12	13[h]	14	15	16	
35		17	18	19	20	21	22	23	
36		24	25	26	27	28	29	30	
37	EPAG. 1848 / THOUT 1849	1	2	3	4	5	1[a]	2	PĀG. 2124 / MASKARAM 2125
38		3	4	5	6	7	8	9	
39		10	11	12	13	14	15	16	
40		17[b]	18	19	20	21	22	23	
41		24	25	26	27	28	29	30	
42	PAOPE 1849	1	2	3	4	5	6	7	ṬEQEMT 2125
43		8	9	10	11	12	13	14	
44		15	16	17	18	19	20	21	
45		22	23	24	25	26	27	28	
46		29	30	1	2	3	4	5	
47	ATHŌR 1849	6	7	8	9	10	11	12	HEDĀR 2125
48		13	14	15	16	17	18	19	
49		20	21	22	23	24	25	26	
50		27	28	29	30	1	2	3	
51	KOIAK 1849	4	5	6	7	8	9	10	TĀKHŚĀŚ 2125
52		11	12	13	14	15	16	17	
53		18	19	20	21	22	23	24	

‡Leap year
[a]New Year
[b]Spring (7:22)
[c]Summer (23:11)
[d]Autumn (15:50)
[e]Winter (14:24)
● New moon
◐ First quarter moon
○ Full moon
◑ Last quarter moon

‡Leap year
[a]New Year
[b]Yom Kippur
[c]Sukkot
[d]Winter starts
[e]Ḥanukkah
[f]Purim
[g]Passover
[h]Shavuot
[i]Fast of Av

‡Leap year
[a]New Year (4830, Dragon)
[b]Lantern Festival
[c]Qīngmíng
[d]Dragon Festival
[e]Qīqiǎo
[f]Hungry Ghosts
[g]Mid-Autumn Festival
[h]Double-Ninth Festival
[i]Dōngzhì
*Start of 60-name cycle

[a]New Year
[b]Building of the Cross
[c]Christmas
[d]Jesus's Circumcision
[e]Epiphany
[f]Easter
[g]Mary's Announcement
[h]Jesus's Transfiguration

PERSIAN (ASTRONOMICAL) 1510/1511‡

Month	Sun	Mon	Tue	Wed	Thu	Fri	Sat
DEY 1510	9	10	11	12	13	14	15
	16	17	18	19	20	21	22
	23	24	25	26	27	28	29
BAHMAN 1510	30	1	2	3	4	5	6
	7	8	9	10	11	12	13
	14	15	16	17	18	19	20
	21	22	23	24	25	26	27
ESFAND 1510	28	29	30	1	2	3	4
	5	6	7	8	9	10	11
	12	13	14	15	16	17	18
	19	20	21	22	23	24	25
FARVARDIN 1511	26	27	28	29	1[a]	2	3
	4	5	6	7	8	9	10
	11	12	13[b]	14	15	16	17
	18	19	20	21	22	23	24
	25	26	27	28	29	30	31
ORDIBEHEST 1511	1	2	3	4	5	6	7
	8	9	10	11	12	13	14
	15	16	17	18	19	20	21
	22	23	24	25	26	27	28
XORDAD 1511	29	30	31	1	2	3	4
	5	6	7	8	9	10	11
	12	13	14	15	16	17	18
	19	20	21	22	23	24	25
TIR 1511	26	27	28	29	30	31	1
	2	3	4	5	6	7	8
	9	10	11	12	13	14	15
	16	17	18	19	20	21	22
	23	24	25	26	27	28	29
MORDAD 1511	30	31	1	2	3	4	5
	6	7	8	9	10	11	12
	13	14	15	16	17	18	19
	20	21	22	23	24	25	26
SHAHRIVAR 1511	27	28	29	30	31	1	2
	3	4	5	6	7	8	9
	10	11	12	13	14	15	16
	17	18	19	20	21	22	23
	24	25	26	27	28	29	30
MEHR 1511	31	1	2	3	4	5	6
	7	8	9	10	11	12	13
	14	15	16	17	18	19	20
	21	22	23	24	25	26	27
ABAN 1511	28	29	30	1	2	3	4
	5	6	7	8	9	10	11
	12	13	14	15	16	17	18
	19	20	21	22	23	24	25
AZAR 1511	26	27	28	29	30	1	2
	3	4	5	6	7	8	9
	10	11	12	13	14	15	16
	17	18	19	20	21	22	23
	24	25	26	27	28	29	30
DEY 1511	1	2	3	4	5	6	7
	8	9	10	11	12	13	14

‡Leap year
[a]New Year
[b]Sizdeh Bedar

HINDU LUNAR 2188/2189‡

Month	Sun	Mon	Tue	Wed	Thu	Fri	Sat
PAUSHA 2188	11	12	13	**14**	16	17	18
	19	20	21	22	23	24	25
MAGHA 2188	26	26	27	28	29	30	1
	2	3	4	5	6	7	**8**
	10	11	12	13	14	15	16
	17	18	19	20	21	22	23
	24	25	26	27	28	28[h]	29
PHALGUNA 2188	30	**1**	3	4	5	6	7
	8	9	10	11	12	13	14
	15[i]	16	17	18	19	20	21
	22	23	24	25	26	27	28
CHAITRA 2189	29	30	1[a]	2	3	4	5
	6	8	9[b]	10	11	12	13
	14	15	16	17	18	19	20
	21	21	22	23	24	25	26
LEAP VAISAKHA 2189	27	28	29	**30**	2	3	4
	5	6	7	8	9	10	11
	12	13	14	15	16	17	18
	19	20	21	22	23	24	25
VAISAKHA 2189	26	27	28	29	30	1	2
	3	**4**	6	7	8	9	10
	11	12	13	14	15	16	16
	17	18	19	20	21	22	23
JYAISHTHA 2189	24	25	26	**27**	29	30	1
	2	3	4	5	6	7	8
	9	10	11	12	13	14	15
	16	17	18	19	20	21	22
	23	24	25	26	27	28	**29**
ASHADHA 2189	1	2	3	4	5	6	7
	8	9	10	11	12	13	13
	14	15	16	17	18	19	20
	21	**22**	24	25	26	27	28
SRAVANA 2189	29	30	1	2	3	4	5
	6	7	8	9	10	11	12
	13	14	15	16	17	18	19
	20	21	22	23[c]	24	**25**	27
BHADRAPADA 2189	28	29	30	1	2	3	4[d]
	5	6	7	8	9	9	10
	11	12	13	14	15	16	17
	18	20	21	22	23	24	25
ASVINA 2189	26	27	28	29	30	1	2
	3	4	5	6	7	8[e]	9[e]
	10[e]	11	12	13	14	15	16
	17	18	19	20	21	**22**	24
KARTTIKA 2189	25	26	27	28	29	30	1[f]
	2	3	3	4	5	6	7
	8	9	10	11	12	13	14
	15	**16**	18	19	20	21	22
	23	24	25	26	27	28	29
MARGASIRA 2189	30	1	2	3	4	5	6
	6	7	8	**9**	11[g]	12	13
	14	15	16	17	18	19	20
	21	22	23	24	25	26	27

‡Leap year
[a]New Year (Nandana)
[b]Birthday of Rāma
[c]Birthday of Krishna
[d]Ganēśa Chaturthī
[e]Dashara
[f]Diwali
[g]Birthday of Vishnu
[h]Night of Śiva
[i]Holi

HINDU SOLAR 2053/2054

Month	Sun	Mon	Tue	Wed	Thu	Fri	Sat
PAUSHA 2053	13	14	15	16	17	18	19
	20	21	22	23	24	25	26
MAGHA 2053	27	28	29	1[b]	2	3	4
	5	6	7	8	9	10	11
	12	13	14	15	16	17	18
	19	20	21	22	23	24	25
PHALGUNA 2053	26	27	28	29	30	1	2
	3	4	5	6	7	8	9
	10	11	12	13	14	15	16
	17	18	19	20	21	22	23
	24	25	26	27	28	29	30
CHAITRA 2053	1	2	3	4	5	6	7
	8	9	10	11	12	13	14
	15	16	17	18	19	20	21
	22	23	24	25	26	27	28
VAISAKHA 2054	29	30	1[a]	2	3	4	5
	6	7	8	9	10	11	12
	13	14	15	16	17	18	19
	20	21	22	23	24	25	26
JYAISHTHA 2054	27	28	29	30	31	1	2
	3	4	5	6	7	8	9
	10	11	12	13	14	15	16
	17	18	19	20	21	22	23
	24	25	26	27	28	29	30
ASHADHA 2054	31	32	1	2	3	4	5
	6	7	8	9	10	11	12
	13	14	15	16	17	18	19
	20	21	22	23	24	25	26
SRAVANA 2054	27	28	29	30	31	1	2
	3	4	5	6	7	8	9
	10	11	12	13	14	15	16
	17	18	19	20	21	22	23
	24	25	26	27	28	29	30
BHADRAPADA 2054	31	32	1	2	3	4	5
	6	7	8	9	10	11	12
	13	14	15	16	17	18	19
	20	21	22	23	24	25	26
ASVINA 2054	27	28	29	30	31	1	2
	3	4	5	6	7	8	9
	10	11	12	13	14	15	16
	17	18	19	20	21	22	23
	24	25	26	27	28	29	30
KARTTIKA 2054	1	2	3	4	5	6	7
	8	9	10	11	12	13	14
	15	16	17	18	19	20	21
	22	23	24	25	26	27	28
MARGASIRA 2054	29	30	1	2	3	4	5
	6	7	8	9	10	11	12
	13	14	15	16	17	18	19
	20	21	22	23	24	25	26
PAUSHA 2054	27	28	29	1	2	3	4
	5	6	7	8	9	10	11
	12	13	14	15	16	17	18

[a]New Year (Plavaṅga)
[b]Pongal

ISLAMIC (ASTRONOMICAL) 1556‡/1557

Month	Sun	Mon	Tue	Wed	Thu	Fri	Sat
SHAWWAL 1556	10	11	12	13	14	15	16
	17	18	19	20	21	22	23
	24	25	26	27	28	29	30
DHU AL-QA'DA 1556	1	2	3	4	5	6	7
	8	9	10	11	12	13	14
	15	16	17	18	19	20	21
	22	23	24	25	26	27	28
DHU AL-HIJJA 1556	29	1	2	3	4	5	6
	7	8	9	10[g]	11	12	13
	14	15	16	17	18	19	20
	21	22	23	24	25	26	27
MUHARRAM 1557	28	29	30	1[a]	2	3	4
	5	6	7	8	9	10[b]	11
	12	13	14	15	16	17	18
	19	20	21	22	23	24	25
SAFAR 1557	26	27	28	29	1	2	3
	4	5	6	7	8	9	10
	11	12	13	14	15	16	17
	18	19	20	21	22	23	24
RABI' I 1557	25	26	27	28	29	1	2
	3	4	5	6	7	8	9
	10	11	12[c]	13	14	15	16
	17	18	19	20	21	22	23
	24	25	26	27	28	29	30
RABI' II 1557	1	2	3	4	5	6	7
	8	9	10	11	12	13	14
	15	16	17	18	19	20	21
	22	23	24	25	26	27	28
JUMADA I 1557	29	1	2	3	4	5	6
	7	8	9	10	11	12	13
	14	15	16	17	18	19	20
	21	22	23	24	25	26	27
JUMADA II 1557	28	29	1	2	3	4	5
	6	7	8	9	10	11	12
	13	14	15	16	17	18	19
	20	21	22	23	24	25	26
RAJAB 1557	27	28	29	30	1	2	3
	4	5	6	7	8	9	10
	11	12	13	14	15	16	17
	18	19	20	21	22	23	24
SHA'BAN 1557	25	26	27[d]	28	29	30	1
	2	3	4	5	6	7	8
	9	10	11	12	13	14	15
	16	17	18	19	20	21	22
	23	24	25	26	27	28	29
RAMADAN 1557	1[e]	2	3	4	5	6	7
	8	9	10	11	12	13	14
	15	16	17	18	19	20	21
	22	23	24	25	26	27	28
SHAWWAL 1557	29	30	1[f]	2	3	4	5
	6	7	8	9	10	11	12
	13	14	15	16	17	18	19
	20	21	22	23	24	25	26

‡Leap year
[a]New Year
[b]'Ashūrā'
[c]Prophet's Birthday
[d]Ascent of the Prophet
[e]Start of Ramaḍān
[f]'Id al-Fiṭr
[g]'Id al-'Aḍḥā

GREGORIAN 2132‡

Julian† (Sun)	Sun	Mon	Tue	Wed	Thu	Fri	Sat	Month
Dec 16	30	31	1	2	3	4	5	JANUARY 2132
	6	7	8[a]	9	10	11	12	
Dec 30	13	14	15[b]	16	17	18	19	
	20	21	22	23	24	25	26	
Jan 13	27	28	29	30	31	1	2	FEBRUARY 2132
	3	4	5	6	7	8	9	
Jan 27	10	11	12	13	14	15	16	
	17	18	19	20[c]	21	22	23	
Feb 10	24[d]	25	26	27	28	29	1	MARCH 2132
	2	3	4	5	6	7	8	
Feb 24	9	10	11	12	13	14	15	
	16	17	18	19	20	21	22	
Mar 9	23	24	25	26	27	28	29	
	30	31	1	2	3	4	5	APRIL 2132
Mar 23	6[e]	7	8	9	10	11	12	
	13	14	15	16	17	18	19	
Apr 6	20	21	22	23	24	25	26	
	27	28	29	30	1	2	3	MAY 2132
Apr 20	4	5	6	7	8	9	10	
	11	12	13	14	15	16	17	
May 4	18	19	20	21	22	23	24	
	25	26	27	28	29	30	31	
May 18	1	2	3	4	5	6	7	JUNE 2132
	8	9	10	11	12	13	14	
Jun 1	15	16	17	18	19	20	21	
	22	23	24	25	26	27	28	
Jun 15	29	30	1	2	3	4	5	JULY 2132
	6	7	8	9	10	11	12	
Jun 29	13	14	15	16	17	18	19	
	20	21	22	23	24	25	26	
Jul 13	27	28	29	30	31	1	2	AUGUST 2132
	3	4	5	6	7	8	9	
Jul 27	10	11	12	13	14	15	16	
	17	18	19	20	21	22	23	
Aug 10	24	25	26	27	28	29	30	
	31	1	2	3	4	5	6	SEPTEMBER 2132
Aug 24	7	8	9	10	11	12	13	
	14	15	16	17	18	19	20	
Sep 7	21	22	23	24	25	26	27	
	28	29	30	1	2	3	4	OCTOBER 2132
Sep 21	5	6	7	8	9	10	11	
	12	13	14	15	16	17	18	
Oct 5	19	20	21	22	23	24	25	
	26	27	28	29	30	31	1	NOVEMBER 2132
Oct 19	2	3	4	5	6	7	8	
	9	10	11	12	13	14	15	
Nov 2	16	17	18	19	20	21	22	
	23	24	25	26	27	28	29	
Nov 16	30[g]	1	2	3	4	5	6	DECEMBER 2132
	7	8	9	10	11	12	13	
Nov 30	14	15	16	17	18	19	20	
	21	22	23	24	25[h]	26	27	
Dec 14	28	29	30	31	1	2	3	

‡Leap year
[a]Orthodox Christmas
[b]Julian New Year
[c]Ash Wednesday
[d]Feast of Orthodoxy
[e]Easter (also Orthodox)
[g]Advent
[h]Christmas

2133

Gregorian 2133	Sun	Mon	Tue	Wed	Thu	Fri	Sat	Lunar Phases	ISO Week (Mon)	Julian Day (Sun noon)	Hebrew 5893[‡]/5894	Sun	Mon	Tue	Wed	Thu	Fri	Sat	Molad	Chinese Rén-Chén/Guǐ-Sì	Sun	Mon	Tue	Wed	Thu	Fri	Sat	Solar Term	Coptic 1849/1850	Sun	Mon	Tue	Wed	Thu	Fri	Sat	Ethiopic 2125/2126
January 2133	28	◑	30	31	1[a]	2	3	8:51	1	2500119	Teveth 5893	19	20	21	22	23	24	25		Month 11 Rén-Chén	21	22	23	24	25	26	27		Koiak 1849	18	19	20	21	22	23	24	Tāḫśāś 2125
	4	5	●	7	8	9	10	12:07	2	2500126	Shevat 5893	26	27	28	29	1	2	3	Tue 14h32m2p	Month 12 Rén-Chén	28	*29*	1	2	3	4	5	Xiǎo hán	Tōbe 1849	25	26	27	28	29[c]	30	1	Ṭer 2125
	11	12	13	◐	15	16	17	10:00	3	2500133		4	5	6	7	8	9	10			6	7	8	9	10	11	12			2	3	4	5	6[d]	7	8	
	18	19	20	○	22	23	24	2:01	4	2500140		11	12	13	14	15	16	17			13	14	***15***	16	17	18	19	Dà hán		9	10	11[e]	12	13	14	15	
	25	26	27	◑	29	30	31	1:30	5	2500147		18	19	20	21	22	23	24			20	21	22	23	24*	25	26			16	17	18	19	20	21	22	
February 2133	1	2	3	4	●	6	7	7:10	6	2500154	Adar I 5893	25	26	27	28	29	30	1	Thu 3h16m3p	Month 1 Guǐ-Sì	27	28	29	*30*	1[a]	2	3	Lì chūn		23	24	25	26	27	28	29	
	8	9	10	11	◐	13	14	21:09	7	2500161		2	3	4	5	6	7	8			4	5	6	7	8	9	10		Meshir 1849	30	1	2	3	4	5	6	Yakātit 2125
	15	16	17	18	○	20	21	12:58	8	2500168		9	10	11	12	13	14	15			11	12	13	***14***	15[b]	16	17	Yǔ shuǐ		7	8	9	10	11	12	13	
	22	23	24	25	◑	27	28	20:51	9	2500175		16	17	18	19	20	21	22			18	19	20	21	22	23	24			14	15	16	17	18	19	20	
March 2133	1	2	3	4	5	●	7	23:54	10	2500182		23	24	25	26	27	28	29		Month 2 Guǐ-Sì	25	26	27	28	29	30	1	Jīng zhé		21	22	23	24	25	26	27	
	8	9	10	11	12	13	◐	5:38	11	2500189	Adar II 5893	30	1	2	3	4	5	6	Fri 16h0m4p		2	3	4	5	6	7	8		Paremotep 1849	28	29	30	1	2	3	4	Magābit 2125
	15	16	17	18	19	20[b]	○	0:18	12	2500196		7	8	9	10	11	12	13			9	10	11	12	13	***14***	15	Chūn fēn		5	6	7	8	9	10	11	
	22	23	24	25	26	27	◑	17:09	13	2500203		14[f]	15	16	17	18	19	20			16	17	18	19	20	21	22			12	13	14	15	16	17	18	
April 2133	29	30	31	1	2	3	4		14	2500210		21	22	23	24	25	26	27			23	24*	25	26	27	28	29			19	20	21	22	23	24	25	
	●	6	7	8	9	10	11	13:45	15	2500217	Nisan 5893	28	29	1	2	3	4	5	Sun 4h44m5p	Month 3 Guǐ-Sì	*1*[c]	2	3	4	5	6	7	Qīng míng	Parmoute 1849	26	27	28	29	30	1	2	Miyāzyā 2125
	◐	13	14	15	16	17	18	12:11	16	2500224		6	7	8	9	10	11	12			8	9	10	11	12	13	14			3	4	5	6	7	8	9	
	○	20	21	22	23	24	25	12:33	17	2500231		13	14	15[g]	16	17	18	19			15	***16***	17	18	19	20	21	Gǔ yǔ		10	11	12	13	14	15	16	
	26	◑	28	29	30	1	2	12:29	18	2500238		20	21	22	23	24	25	26			22	23	24	25	26	27	28			17[f]	18	19	20	21	22	23	
May 2133	3	4	●	6	7	8	9	0:53	19	2500245	Iyar 5893	27	28	29	30	1	2	3	Mon 17h28m6p	Month 4 Guǐ-Sì	29	30	*1*	2	3	4	5	Lì xià		24	25	26	27	28	29[g]	30	
	10	◐	12	13	14	15	16	17:57	20	2500252		4	5	6	7	8	9	10			6	7	8	9	10	11	12		Pashons 1849	1	2	3	4	5	6	7	Genbot 2125
	17	18	○	20	21	22	23	2:03	21	2500259		11	12	13	14	15	16	17			13	14	15	16	***17***	18	19	Xiǎo mǎn		8	9	10	11	12	13	14	
	24	25	26	◑	28	29	30	5:30	22	2500266		18	19	20	21	22	23	24			20	21	22	23	24	25*	26			15	16	17	18	19	20	21	
June 2133	31	1	2	●	4	5	6	9:47	23	2500273	Sivan 5893	25	26	27	28	29	1	2	Wed 6h12m7p	Month 5 Guǐ-Sì	27	28	29	1	2	3	4	Máng zhòng		22	23	24	25	26	27	28	
	7	8	9	◐	11	12	13	0:17	24	2500280		3	4	5	6[h]	7	8	9			5[d]	6	7	8	9	10	11		Paōne 1849	29	30	1	2	3	4	5	Sanē 2125
	14	15	16	○	18	19	20	16:39	25	2500287		10	11	12	13	14	15	16			12	13	14	15	16	17	18			6	7	8	9	10	11	12	
	21[c]	22	23	24	◑	26	27	19:44	26	2500294		17	18	19	20	21	22	23			***19***	20	21	22	23	24	25	Xià zhì		13	14	15	16	17	18	19	
	28	29	30	1	●	3	4	17:10	27	2500301		24	25	26	27	28	29	30		Month 6 Guǐ-Sì	26	27	28	29	30	1	2			20	21	22	23	24	25	26	
July 2133	5	6	7	8	◐	10	11	8:30	28	2500308	Tammuz 5893	1	2	3	4	5	6	7	Thu 18h56m8p		3	4	5	6	7	8	9	Xiǎo shǔ	Epēp 1849	27	28	29	30	1	2	3	Ḥamlē 2125
	12	13	14	15	16	○	18	7:49	29	2500315		8	9	10	11	12	13	14			10	11	12	13	14	15	16			4	5	6	7	8	9	10	
	19	20	21	22	23	24	◑	7:16	30	2500322		15	16	17	18	19	20	21			17	18	19	***20***	21	22	23	Dà shǔ		11	12	13	14	15	16	17	
	26	27	28	29	30	●	1	23:54	31	2500329		22	23	24	25	26	27	28		Month 7 Guǐ-Sì	24	25	26*	27	28	29	1			18	19	20	21	22	23	24	
August 2133	2	3	4	5	6	◐	8	19:39	32	2500336	Av 5893	29	1	2	3	4	5	6	Sat 7h40m9p		2	3	4	5	6	7[e]	8	Lì qiū	Mesorē 1849	25	26	27	28	29	30	1	Nahasē 2125
	9	10	11	12	13	14	○	23:00	33	2500343		7	8	9[i]	10	11	12	13			9	10	11	12	13	14	15[f]			2	3	4	5	6	7	8	
	16	17	18	19	20	21	22		34	2500350		14	15	16	17	18	19	20			16	17	18	19	20	21	22			9	10	11	12	13[h]	14	15	
	◑	24	25	26	27	28	29	16:29	35	2500357		21	22	23	24	25	26	27			***23***	24	25	26	27	28	29	Chǔ shǔ		16	17	18	19	20	21	22	
September 2133	●	31	1	2	3	4	5	7:07	36	2500364	Elul 5893	28	29	30	1	2	3	4	Sun 20h24m10p	Month 8 Guǐ-Sì	1	2	3	4	5	6	7			23	24	25	26	27	28	29	
	◐	7	8	9	10	11	12	10:13	37	2500371		5	6	7	8	9	10	11			8	9	10	11	12	13	14	Bái lù	Epag. 1849	30	1	2	3	4	5	1[a]	Pāg. 2125
	13	○	15	16	17	18	19	13:50	38	2500378		12	13	14	15	16	17	18			15[g]	16	17	18	19	20	21		Thoout 1850	2	3	4	5	6	7	8	Maskaram 2126
	20	◑	22[d]	23	24	25	26	23:57	39	2500385		19	20	21	22	23	24	25			22	23	24	***25***	26	27	28*	Qiū fēn		9	10	11	12	13	14	15	
October 2133	27	●	29	30	1	2	3	15:58	40	2500392	Tishri 5894	26	27	28	29	1[a]	2[a]	3	Tue 9h8m11p	Month 9 Guǐ-Sì	29	1	2	3	4	5	6			16	17[b]	18	19	20	21	22	
	4	5	◐	7	8	9	10	3:59	41	2500399		4	5	6	7	8	9	10[b]			7	8	9[h]	10	*11*	12	13	Hán lù		23	24	25	26	27	28	29	
	11	12	13	○	15	16	17	4:06	42	2500406		11	12	13	14	15[c]	16	17			14	15	16	17	18	19	20		Paope 1850	30	1	2	3	4	5	6	Ṭeqemt 2126
	18	19	20	◑	22	23	24	6:33	43	2500413		18	19	20	21	22	23	24			21	22	23	24	25	***26***	27	Shuāng jiàng		7	8	9	10	11	12	13	
	25	26	27	●	29	30	31	3:30	44	2500420	Ḥeshvan 5894	25	26	27	28	29	30	1	Wed 21h52m12p	Month 10 Guǐ-Sì	28	29	30	1	2	3	4			14	15	16	17	18	19	20	
November 2133	1	2	3	◐	5	6	7	23:58	45	2500427		2	3	4	5	6	7	8			5	6	7	8	9	10	*11*	Lì dōng		21	22	23	24	25	26	27	
	8	9	10	11	○	13	14	17:39	46	2500434		9	10	11	12	13	14	15			12	13	14	15	16	17	18		Athōr 1850	28	29	30	1	2	3	4	Ḫedār 2126
	15	16	17	18	◑	20	21	13:25	47	2500441		16	17	18	19	20	21	22			19	20	21	22	23	24	25	Xiǎo xuě		5	6	7	8	9	10	11	
	22	23	24	25	●	27	28	18:10	48	2500448		23	24	25	26	27	28	29		Month 11* Guǐ-Sì	***26***	27	28	29*	30	1	2			12	13	14	15	16	17	18	
December 2133	29	30	1	2	3	◐	5	20:43	49	2500455	Kislev 5894	1	2	3	4	5	6	7	Fri 10h36m13p		3	4	5	6	7	8	9			19	20	21	22	23	24	25	
	6	7	8	9	10	11	○	6:14	50	2500462		8[d]	9	10	11	12	13	14			10	*11*	12	13	14	15	16	Dà xuě	Koiak 1850	26	27	28	29	30	1	2	Tāḫśāś 2126
	13	14	15	16	17	◑	19	21:47	51	2500469		15	16	17	18	19	20	21			17	18	19	20	21	22	23			3	4	5	6	7	8	9	
	20	21[e]	22	23	24	25	●	11:35	52	2500476		22	23	24	25[e]	26[e]	27[e]	28[e]		Month 12 Guǐ-Sì	24	25	***26***[i]	27	28	29	1	Dōng zhì		10	11	12	13	14	15	16	
	27	28	29	30	31	1	2		53	2500483	Ṭeveth 5894	29[e]	30[e]	1[e]	2[e]	3	4	5	Sat 23h20m14p		2	3	4	5	6	7	8			17	18	19	20	21	22	23	

[a]New Year
[b]Spring (13:14)
[c]Summer (5:05)
[d]Autumn (21:42)
[e]Winter (20:17)
● New moon
◐ First quarter moon
○ Full moon
◑ Last quarter moon

[‡]Leap year
[a]New Year
[b]Yom Kippur
[c]Sukkot
[d]Winter starts
[e]Ḥanukkah
[f]Purim
[g]Passover
[h]Shavuot
[i]Fast of Av

[a]New Year (4831, Snake)
[b]Lantern Festival
[c]Qīngmíng
[d]Dragon Festival
[e]Qīqiǎo
[f]Hungry Ghosts
[g]Mid-Autumn Festival
[h]Double-Ninth Festival
[i]Dōngzhì
*Start of 60-name cycle

[a]New Year
[b]Building of the Cross
[c]Christmas
[d]Jesus's Circumcision
[e]Epiphany
[f]Easter
[g]Mary's Announcement
[h]Jesus's Transfiguration

PERSIAN (ASTRONOMICAL) 1511‡/1512

Month	Sun	Mon	Tue	Wed	Thu	Fri	Sat
DEY 1511	8	9	10	11	12	13	14
	15	16	17	18	19	20	21
	22	23	24	25	26	27	28
BAHMAN 1511	29	30	1	2	3	4	5
	6	7	8	9	10	11	12
	13	14	15	16	17	18	19
	20	21	22	23	24	25	26
ESFAND 1511	27	28	29	30	1	2	3
	4	5	6	7	8	9	10
	11	12	13	14	15	16	17
	18	19	20	21	22	23	24
FARVARDĪN 1512	25	26	27	28	29	30	1[a]
	2	3	4	5	6	7	8
	9	10	11	12	13[b]	14	15
	16	17	18	19	20	21	22
	23	24	25	26	27	28	29
ORDĪBEHEŠT 1512	30	31	1	2	3	4	5
	6	7	8	9	10	11	12
	13	14	15	16	17	18	19
	20	21	22	23	24	25	26
XORDĀD 1512	27	28	29	30	31	1	2
	3	4	5	6	7	8	9
	10	11	12	13	14	15	16
	17	18	19	20	21	22	23
	24	25	26	27	28	29	30
TĪR 1512	31	1	2	3	4	5	6
	7	8	9	10	11	12	13
	14	15	16	17	18	19	20
	21	22	23	24	25	26	27
MORDĀD 1512	28	29	30	31	1	2	3
	4	5	6	7	8	9	10
	11	12	13	14	15	16	17
	18	19	20	21	22	23	24
	25	26	27	28	29	30	31
SHAHRĪVAR 1512	1	2	3	4	5	6	7
	8	9	10	11	12	13	14
	15	16	17	18	19	20	21
	22	23	24	25	26	27	28
MEHR 1512	29	30	31	1	2	3	4
	5	6	7	8	9	10	11
	12	13	14	15	16	17	18
	19	20	21	22	23	24	25
ĀBĀN 1512	26	27	28	29	30	1	2
	3	4	5	6	7	8	9
	10	11	12	13	14	15	16
	17	18	19	20	21	22	23
	24	25	26	27	28	29	30
ĀZAR 1512	1	2	3	4	5	6	7
	8	9	10	11	12	13	14
	15	16	17	18	19	20	21
	22	23	24	25	26	27	28
DEY 1512	29	30	1	2	3	4	5
	6	7	8	9	10	11	12

HINDU LUNAR 2189‡/2190

Month	Sun	Mon	Tue	Wed	Thu	Fri	Sat
MĀRGAŚĪRA 2189	21	22	23	24	25	26	27
PAUSHA 2189	28	29	30	1	2	3	4
	5	6	7	8	9	10	11
	12	13	14	**15**	17	18	19
	20	21	22	23	24	25	26
MĀGHA 2189	27	28	*28*	29	30	1	2
	3	4	5	6	7	8	**9**
	11	12	13	14	15	16	17
	18	19	20	21	22	23	24
PHĀLGUNA 2189	25	26	27	28	29[h]	30	1
	2	3	4	5	6	7	8
	9	10	11	12	13	**14**[i]	16
	17	18	19	20	21	*21*	22
	23	24	25	26	27	28	29
CHAITRA 2190	30	1[a]	2	3	4	5	6
	7	9[b]	10	11	12	13	14
	15	16	17	18	19	20	21
	22	23	24	*24*	25	26	27
VAIŚĀKHA 2190	28	29	**30**	2	3	4	5
	6	7	8	9	10	11	12
	13	14	15	16	17	18	19
	20	21	22	23	24	25	26
JYAISHTHA 2190	27	28	29	30	1	2	3
	4	6	7	8	9	10	11
	12	13	14	15	16	17	18
	19	20	*20*	21	22	23	24
ĀSHĀḌHA 2190	25	**26**	28	29	30	1	2
	3	4	5	6	7	**8**	10
	11	*11*	12	13	14	15	16
	17	18	19	20	21	22	23
ŚRĀVAṆA 2190	24	25	26	27	28	**29**	1
	2	3	4	5	6	7	8
	9	10	11	12	13	14	15
	16	17	*17*	18	19	20	**21**
	23[c]	24	25	26	27	28	29
BHĀDRAPADA 2190	30	1	2	3[d]	**4**	6	7
	8	*8*	9	10	11	12	13
	14	15	16	17	18	19	20
	21	22	23	24	25	**26**	28
ĀŚVINA 2190	29	30	1	2	3	4	5
	6	7	8[e]	9[e]	10[e]	11	12
	13	*13*	14	15	16	17	18
	19	21	22	23	24	25	26
KĀRTTIKA 2190	27	28	29	30	1[f]	2	3
	4	5	6	7	8	9	10
	11	12	13	14	15	16	17
	18	19	20	21	22	**23**	25
MĀRGAŚĪRA 2190	26	27	28	29	30	1	2
	3	4	5	6	*6*	7	8
	9	10	11[g]	12	13	14	15
	16	**17**	19	20	21	22	23
	24	25	26	27	28	29	30
PAUSHA 2190	1	2	3	4	5	6	7

HINDU SOLAR 2054/2055‡

Month	Sun	Mon	Tue	Wed	Thu	Fri	Sat
PAUSHA 2054	12	13	14	15	16	17	18
	19	20	21	22	23	24	25
MĀGHA 2054	26	27	28	29	30	1[b]	2
	3	4	5	6	7	8	9
	10	11	12	13	14	15	16
	17	18	19	20	21	22	23
PHĀLGUNA 2054	24	25	26	27	28	29	1
	2	3	4	5	6	7	8
	9	10	11	12	13	14	15
	16	17	18	19	20	21	22
	23	24	25	26	27	28	29
CHAITRA 2054	30	1	2	3	4	5	6
	7	8	9	10	11	12	13
	14	15	16	17	18	19	20
	21	22	23	24	25	26	27
VAIŚĀKHA 2055	28	29	30	1[a]	2	3	4
	5	6	7	8	9	10	11
	12	13	14	15	16	17	18
	19	20	21	22	23	24	25
JYAISHTHA 2055	26	27	28	29	30	31	1
	2	3	4	5	6	7	8
	9	10	11	12	13	14	15
	16	17	18	19	20	21	22
	23	24	25	26	27	28	29
ĀSHĀḌHA 2055	30	31	32	1	2	3	4
	5	6	7	8	9	10	11
	12	13	14	15	16	17	18
	19	20	21	22	23	24	25
ŚRĀVAṆA 2055	26	27	28	29	30	31	1
	2	3	4	5	6	7	8
	9	10	11	12	13	14	15
	16	17	18	19	20	21	22
	23	24	25	26	27	28	29
BHĀDRAPADA 2055	30	31	32	1	2	3	4
	5	6	7	8	9	10	11
	12	13	14	15	16	17	18
	19	20	21	22	23	24	25
ĀŚVINA 2055	26	27	28	29	30	31	1
	2	3	4	5	6	7	8
	9	10	11	12	13	14	15
	16	17	18	19	20	21	22
	23	24	25	26	27	28	29
KĀRTTIKA 2055	30	1	2	3	4	5	6
	7	8	9	10	11	12	13
	14	15	16	17	18	19	20
	21	22	23	24	25	26	27
MĀRGAŚĪRA 2055	28	29	30	1	2	3	4
	5	6	7	8	9	10	11
	12	13	14	15	16	17	18
	19	20	21	22	23	24	25
PAUSHA 2055	26	27	28	29	30	1	2
	3	4	5	6	7	8	9
	10	11	12	13	14	15	16

ISLAMIC (ASTRONOMICAL) 1557/1558

Month	Sun	Mon	Tue	Wed	Thu	Fri	Sat
SHAWWĀL 1557	20	21	22	23	24	25	26
DHU AL-QA'DA 1557	27	28	29	30	1	2	3
	4	5	6	7	8	9	10
	11	12	13	14	15	16	17
	18	19	20	21	22	23	24
DHU AL-ḤIJJA 1557	25	26	27	28	29	30	1
	2	3	4	5	6	7	8
	9	10[g]	11	12	13	14	15
	16	17	18	19	20	21	22
	23	24	25	26	27	28	29
MUḤARRAM 1558	1[a]	2	3	4	5	6	7
	8	9	10[b]	11	12	13	14
	15	16	17	18	19	20	21
	22	23	24	25	26	27	28
ṢAFAR 1558	29	30	1	2	3	4	5
	6	7	8	9	10	11	12
	13	14	15	16	17	18	19
	20	21	22	23	24	25	26
RABĪ' I 1558	27	28	29	1	2	3	4
	5	6	7	8	9	10	11
	12[c]	13	14	15	16	17	18
	19	20	21	22	23	24	25
RABĪ' II 1558	26	27	28	29	30	1	2
	3	4	5	6	7	8	9
	10	11	12	13	14	15	16
	17	18	19	20	21	22	23
JUMĀDĀ I 1558	24	25	26	27	28	29	1
	2	3	4	5	6	7	8
	9	10	11	12	13	14	15
	16	17	18	19	20	21	22
	23	24	25	26	27	28	29
JUMĀDĀ II 1558	1	2	3	4	5	6	7
	8	9	10	11	12	13	14
	15	16	17	18	19	20	21
	22	23	24	25	26	27	28
RAJAB 1558	29	1	2	3	4	5	6
	7	8	9	10	11	12	13
	14	15	16	17	18	19	20
	21	22	23	24	25	26	27[d]
SHA'BĀN 1558	28	29	30	1	2	3	4
	5	6	7	8	9	10	11
	12	13	14	15	16	17	18
	19	20	21	22	23	24	25
RAMAḌĀN 1558	26	27	28	29	30	1[e]	2
	3	4	5	6	7	8	9
	10	11	12	13	14	15	16
	17	18	19	20	21	22	23
SHAWWĀL 1558	24	25	26	27	28	29	1[f]
	2	3	4	5	6	7	8
	9	10	11	12	13	14	15
	16	17	18	19	20	21	22
	23	24	25	26	27	28	29
	30	1	2	3	4	5	6

GREGORIAN 2133

Julian (Sun)	Sun	Mon	Tue	Wed	Thu	Fri	Sat	Month
Dec 14	28	29	30	31	1	2	3	JANUARY 2133
	4	5	6	7	8[a]	9	10	
Dec 28	11	12	13	14	15[b]	16	17	
	18	19	20	21	22	23	24	
Jan 11	25	26	27	28	29	30	31	
	1	2	3	4	5	6	7	FEBRUARY 2133
Jan 25	8	9	10	11	12	13	14	
	15	16	17	18	19	20	21	
Feb 8	22	23	24	25	26	27	28	
	1	2	3	4[c]	5	6	7	MARCH 2133
Feb 22	8	9	10	11	12	13	14	
	15[d]	16	17	18	19	20	21	
Mar 8	22	23	24	25	26	27	28	
	29	30	31	1	2	3	4	APRIL 2133
Mar 22	5	6	7	8	9	10	11	
	12	13	14	15	16	17	18	
Apr 5	19[e]	20	21	22	23	24	25	
	26[f]	27	28	29	30	1	2	MAY 2133
Apr 19	3	4	5	6	7	8	9	
	10	11	12	13	14	15	16	
May 3	17	18	19	20	21	22	23	
	24	25	26	27	28	29	30	
May 17	31	1	2	3	4	5	6	JUNE 2133
	7	8	9	10	11	12	13	
May 31	14	15	16	17	18	19	20	
	21	22	23	24	25	26	27	
Jun 14	28	29	30	1	2	3	4	JULY 2133
	5	6	7	8	9	10	11	
Jun 28	12	13	14	15	16	17	18	
	19	20	21	22	23	24	25	
Jul 12	26	27	28	29	30	31	1	AUGUST 2133
	2	3	4	5	6	7	8	
Jul 26	9	10	11	12	13	14	15	
	16	17	18	19	20	21	22	
Aug 9	23	24	25	26	27	28	29	
	30	31	1	2	3	4	5	SEPTEMBER 2133
Aug 23	6	7	8	9	10	11	12	
	13	14	15	16	17	18	19	
Sep 6	20	21	22	23	24	25	26	
	27	28	29	30	1	2	3	OCTOBER 2133
Sep 20	4	5	6	7	8	9	10	
	11	12	13	14	15	16	17	
Oct 4	18	19	20	21	22	23	24	
	25	26	27	28	29	30	31	
Oct 18	1	2	3	4	5	6	7	NOVEMBER 2133
	8	9	10	11	12	13	14	
Nov 1	15	16	17	18	19	20	21	
	22	23	24	25	26	27	28	
Nov 15	29[g]	30	1	2	3	4	5	DECEMBER 2133
	6	7	8	9	10	11	12	
Nov 29	13	14	15	16	17	18	19	
	20	21	22	23	24	25[h]	26	
Dec 13	27	28	29	30	31	1	2	

Persian:
‡Leap year
[a]New Year
[b]Sizdeh Bedar

Hindu Lunar:
‡Leap year
[a]New Year (Vijaya)
[b]Birthday of Rāma
[c]Birthday of Krishna
[d]Ganēśa Chaturthī
[e]Dashara
[f]Diwali
[g]Birthday of Vishnu
[h]Night of Śiva
[i]Holi

Hindu Solar:
‡Leap year
[a]New Year (Kīlaka)
[b]Pongal

Islamic:
[a]New Year
[b]'Ashūrā'
[c]Prophet's Birthday
[d]Ascent of the Prophet
[e]Start of Ramaḍān
[f]'Id al-Fiṭr
[g]'Id al-'Aḍḥā

Gregorian:
[a]Orthodox Christmas
[b]Julian New Year
[c]Ash Wednesday
[d]Feast of Orthodoxy
[e]Easter
[f]Orthodox Easter
[g]Advent
[h]Christmas

2134

Gregorian 2134 / ISO week / Julian day

Month	Sun	Mon	Tue	Wed	Thu	Fri	Sat	ISO Week (Mon)	Julian Day (Sun noon)
	27	28	29	30	31	1[a]	2	53	2500483
January 2134	◐	4	5	6	7	8	9	1	2500490
	○	11	12	13	14	15	16	2	2500497
	◑	18	19	20	21	22	23	3	2500504
	24	●	26	27	28	29	30	4	2500511
	31	1	◐	3	4	5	6	5	2500518
February 2134	7	8	○	10	11	12	13	6	2500525
	14	◑	16	17	18	19	20	7	2500532
	21	22	23	●	25	26	27	8	2500539
	28	1	2	◐	4	5	6	9	2500546
March 2134	7	8	9	○	11	12	13	10	2500553
	14	15	16	◑	18	19	20[b]	11	2500560
	21	22	23	24	●	26	27	12	2500567
	28	29	30	31	1	◐	3	13	2500574
April 2134	4	5	6	7	○	9	10	14	2500581
	11	12	13	14	15	◑	17	15	2500588
	18	19	20	21	22	23	●	16	2500595
	25	26	27	28	29	30	◐	17	2500602
May 2134	2	3	4	5	6	7	○	18	2500609
	9	10	11	12	13	14	15	19	2500616
	◑	17	18	19	20	21	22	20	2500623
	●	24	25	26	27	28	29	21	2500630
	◐	31	1	2	3	4	5	22	2500637
June 2134	○	7	8	9	10	11	12	23	2500644
	13	◑	15	16	17	18	19	24	2500651
	20	21[c]	●	23	24	25	26	25	2500658
	27	28	◐	30	1	2	3	26	2500665
July 2134	4	5	○	7	8	9	10	27	2500672
	11	12	13	◑	15	16	17	28	2500679
	18	19	20	●	22	23	24	29	2500686
	25	26	27	◐	29	30	31	30	2500693
August 2134	1	2	3	○	5	6	7	31	2500700
	8	9	10	11	12	◑	14	32	2500707
	15	16	17	18	●	20	21	33	2500714
	22	23	24	25	◐	27	28	34	2500721
	29	30	31	1	2	○	4	35	2500728
September 2134	5	6	7	8	9	10	◑	36	2500735
	12	13	14	15	16	17	●	37	2500742
	19	20	21	22	23[d]	24	◐	38	2500749
	26	27	28	29	30	1	2	39	2500756
October 2134	○	4	5	6	7	8	9	40	2500763
	10	◑	12	13	14	15	16	41	2500770
	●	18	19	20	21	22	23	42	2500777
	◐	25	26	27	28	29	30	43	2500784
	31	1	○	3	4	5	6	44	2500791
November 2134	7	8	◑	10	11	12	13	45	2500798
	14	15	●	17	18	19	20	46	2500805
	21	22	◐	24	25	26	27	47	2500812
	28	29	30	○	2	3	4	48	2500819
December 2134	5	6	7	◑	9	10	11	49	2500826
	12	13	14	●	16	17	18	50	2500833
	19	20	21	22[e]	◐	24	25	51	2500840
	26	27	28	29	30	○	1	52	2500847

Lunar Phases: 16:32, 17:43, 8:42, 6:33, 9:44, 4:11, 22:31, 1:35, 23:13, 14:02, 14:48, 19:19, 8:49, 23:50, 8:32, 10:41, 15:21, 10:06, 2:40, 23:12, 20:15, 21:16, 20:18, 9:00, 1:04, 9:40, 12:41, 16:53, 7:17, 23:33, 3:12, 23:57, 16:06, 14:59, 15:30, 7:27, 4:19, 7:36, 1:37, 16:23, 20:16, 0:31, 10:08, 3:22, 15:40, 16:34, 17:56, 16:35, 13:20, 6:54

Hebrew 5894/5895

ISO Week	Month	Sun	Mon	Tue	Wed	Thu	Fri	Sat	Molad
53		29[e]	30[e]	1[e]	2[e]	3	4	5	Sat 23h20m14p
1	Teveth 5894	6	7	8	9	10	11	12	
2		13	14	15	16	17	18	19	
3		20	21	22	23	24	25	26	
4		27	28	29	1	2	3	4	Mon 12h4m15p
5	Shevat 5894	5	6	7	8	9	10	11	
6		12	13	14	15	16	17	18	
7		19	20	21	22	23	24	25	
8		26	27	28	29	30	1	2	Wed 0h48m16p
9	Adar 5894	3	4	5	6	7	8	9	
10		10	11	12	13	14[f]	15	16	
11		17	18	19	20	21	22	23	
12		24	25	26	27	28	29	1	Thu 13h32m17p
13	Nisan 5894	2	3	4	5	6	7	8	
14		9	10	11	12	13	14	15[g]	
15		16	17	18	19	20	21	22	
16		23	24	25	26	27	28	29	
17		30	1	2	3	4	5	6	Sat 2h17m0p
18	Iyyar 5894	7	8	9	10	11	12	13	
19		14	15	16	17	18	19	20	
20		21	22	23	24	25	26	27	
21		28	29	1	2	3	4	5	Sun 15h1m1p
22	Sivan 5894	6[h]	7	8	9	10	11	12	
23		13	14	15	16	17	18	19	
24		20	21	22	23	24	25	26	
25		27	28	29	30	1	2	3	Tue 3h45m2p
26	Tammuz 5894	4	5	6	7	8	9	10	
27		11	12	13	14	15	16	17	
28		18	19	20	21	22	23	24	
29		25	26	27	28	29	1	2	Wed 16h29m3p
30	Av 5894	3	4	5	6	7	8	9	
31		10[i]	11	12	13	14	15	16	
32		17	18	19	20	21	22	23	
33		24	25	26	27	28	29	30	
34		1	2	3	4	5	6	7	Fri 5h13m4p
35	Elul 5894	8	9	10	11	12	13	14	
36		15	16	17	18	19	20	21	
37		22	23	24	25	26	27	28	
38		29	1[a]	2[a]	3	4	5	6	Sat 17h57m5p
39	Tishri 5895	7	8	9	10[b]	11	12	13	
40		14	15[c]	16	17	18	19	20	
41		21	22	23	24	25	26	27	
42		28	29	30	1	2	3	4	Mon 6h41m6p
43	Heshvan 5895	5	6	7	8	9	10	11	
44		12	13	14	15	16	17	18	
45		19	20	21	22	23	24	25	
46		26	27	28	29	1	2	3	Tue 19h25m7p
47	Kislev 5895	4	5	6	7	8	9	10	
48		11	12	13	14	15	16	17	
49		18	19[d]	20	21	22	23	24	
50		25[e]	26[e]	27[e]	28[e]	29[e]	1[e]	2[e]	Thu 8h9m8p
51	Teveth 5895	3[e]	4	5	6	7	8	9	
52		10	11	12	13	14	15	16	

Chinese Guǐ-Sì/Jiǎ-Wǔ‡

ISO Week	Month	Sun	Mon	Tue	Wed	Thu	Fri	Sat	Solar Term
53		2	3	4	5	6	7	8	
1	Month 12 Guǐ-Sì	9	10	*11*	12	13	14	15	Xiǎo hán
2		16	17	18	19	20	21	22	
3		23	24	25	**26**	27	28	29	Dà hán
4		30*	1[a]	2	3	4	5	6	
5	Month 1 Jiǎ-Wǔ	7	8	9	10	*11*	12	13	Lì chūn
6		14	15[b]	16	17	18	19	20	
7		21	22	23	24	25	**26**	27	Yǔ shuǐ
8		28	29	30	1	2	3	4	
9	Month 2 Jiǎ-Wǔ	5	6	7	8	9	10	*11*	Jīng zhé
10		12	13	14	15	16	17	18	
11		19	20	21	22	23	24	25	
12		**26**	27	28	29	30*	1	2	Chūn fēn
13	Month 3 Jiǎ-Wǔ	3	4	5	6	7	8	9	
14		10	*11*[c]	12	13	14	15	16	Qīng míng
15		17	18	19	20	21	22	23	
16		24	25	**26**	27	28	29	1	Gǔ yǔ
17	Month 4 Jiǎ-Wǔ	2	3	4	5	6	7	8	
18		9	10	11	*12*	13	14	15	Lì xià
19		16	17	18	19	20	21	22	
20		23	24	25	26	27	**28**	29	Xiǎo mǎn
21		30	1*	2	3	4	5[d]	6	
22	Month 5 Jiǎ-Wǔ	7	8	9	10	11	12	13	
23		*14*	15	16	17	18	19	20	Máng zhòng
24		21	22	23	24	25	26	27	
25		28	**29**	1	2	3	4	5	Xià zhì
26	Leap Month 5 Jiǎ-Wǔ	6	7	8	9	10	11	12	
27		13	14	15	*16*	17	18	19	Xiǎo shǔ
28		20	21	22	23	24	25	26	
29		27	28	29	30	1	2*	3	Dà shǔ
30	Month 6 Jiǎ-Wǔ	4	5	6	7	8	9	10	
31		11	12	13	14	15	16	*17*	Lì qiū
32		18	19	20	21	22	23	24	
33		25	26	27	28	29	1	2	
34	Month 7 Jiǎ-Wǔ	3	**4**	5	6	7[e]	8	9	Chǔ shǔ
35		10	11	12	13	14	15[f]	16	
36		17	18	19	*20*	21	22	23	Bái lù
37		24	25	26	27	28	29	1	
38	Month 8 Jiǎ-Wǔ	2	3	4*	5	**6**	7	8	Qiū fēn
39		9	10	11	12	13	14	15[g]	
40		16	17	18	19	20	*21*	22	Hán lù
41		23	24	25	26	27	28	29	
42		30	1	2	3	4	5	**6**	Shuāng jiàng
43	Month 9 Jiǎ-Wǔ	7	8	9[h]	10	11	12	13	
44		14	15	16	17	18	19	20	
45		*21*	22	23	24	25	26	27	Lì dōng
46		28	29	1	2	3	4	5*	
47	Month 10 Jiǎ-Wǔ	6	**7**	8	9	10	11	12	Xiǎo xuě
48		13	14	15	16	17	18	19	
49		20	21	*22*	23	24	25	26	Dà xuě
50		27	28	29	30	1	2	3	
51	Month 11 Jiǎ-Wǔ	4	5	6	7[i]	8	9	10	Dōng zhì
52		11	12	13	14	15	16	17	

Coptic 1850/1851‡ — Ethiopic 2126/2127‡

ISO Week	Coptic Month	Sun	Mon	Tue	Wed	Thu	Fri	Sat	Ethiopic Month
53	Koiak 1850	17	18	19	20	21	22	23	Tākhśāś 2126
1		24	25	26	27	28	29[c]	30	
2		1	2	3	4	5	6[d]	7	
3	Tôbe 1850	8	9	10	11[e]	12	13	14	Ṭer 2126
4		15	16	17	18	19	20	21	
5		22	23	24	25	26	27	28	
6		29	30	1	2	3	4	5	
7	Meshir 1850	6	7	8	9	10	11	12	Yakātit 2126
8		13	14	15	16	17	18	19	
9		20	21	22	23	24	25	26	
10		27	28	29	30	1	2	3	
11	Paremotep 1850	4	5	6	7	8	9	10	Magābit 2126
12		11	12	13	14	15	16	17	
13		18	19	20	21	22	23	24	
14		25	26	27	28	29	30	1	
15	Parmoute 1850	2	3	4	5	6	7	8	Miyāzyā 2126
16		9[f]	10	11	12	13	14	15	
17		16	17	18	19	20	21	22	
18		23	24	25	26	27	28	29[g]	
19		30	1	2	3	4	5	6	
20	Pashons 1850	7	8	9	10	11	12	13	Genbot 2126
21		14	15	16	17	18	19	20	
22		21	22	23	24	25	26	27	
23		28	29	30	1	2	3	4	
24	Paône 1850	5	6	7	8	9	10	11	Sané 2126
25		12	13	14	15	16	17	18	
26		19	20	21	22	23	24	25	
27		26	27	28	29	30	1	2	
28	Epêp 1850	3	4	5	6	7	8	9	Ḥamlē 2126
29		10	11	12	13	14	15	16	
30		17	18	19	20	21	22	23	
31		24	25	26	27	28	29	30	
32	Mesorê 1850	1	2	3	4	5	6	7	Naḥasé 2126
33		8	9	10	11	12	13[h]	14	
34		15	16	17	18	19	20	21	
35		22	23	24	25	26	27	28	
36	Epag. 1850	29	30	1	2	3	4	5	Pāg. 2126
37	Thoout 1851	1[a]	2	3	4	5	6	7	Maskaram 2127
38		8	9	10	11	12	13	14	
39		15	16	17[b]	18	19	20	21	
40		22	23	24	25	26	27	28	
41		29	30	1	2	3	4	5	
42	Paope 1851	6	7	8	9	10	11	12	Ṭeqemt 2127
43		13	14	15	16	17	18	19	
44		20	21	22	23	24	25	26	
45		27	28	29	30	1	2	3	
46	Athôr 1851	4	5	6	7	8	9	10	Ḫedār 2127
47		11	12	13	14	15	16	17	
48		18	19	20	21	22	23	24	
49		25	26	27	28	29	30	1	
50	Koiak 1851	2	3	4	5	6	7	8	Tākhśāś 2127
51		9	10	11	12	13	14	15	
52		16	17	18	19	20	21	22	

Gregorian notes:
[a]New Year
[b]Spring (19:00)
[c]Summer (10:42)
[d]Autumn (3:26)
[e]Winter (2:01)
● New moon
◐ First quarter moon
○ Full moon
◑ Last quarter moon

Hebrew notes:
[a]New Year
[b]Yom Kippur
[c]Sukkot
[d]Winter starts
[e]Ḥanukkah
[f]Purim
[g]Passover
[h]Shavuot
[i]Fast of Av

Chinese notes:
‡Leap year
[a]New Year (4832, Horse)
[b]Lantern Festival
[c]Qīngmíng
[d]Dragon Festival
[e]Qīqiǎo
[f]Hungry Ghosts
[g]Mid-Autumn Festival
[h]Double-Ninth Festival
[i]Dōngzhì
*Start of 60-name cycle

Coptic/Ethiopic notes:
‡Leap year
[a]New Year
[b]Building of the Cross
[c]Christmas
[d]Jesus's Circumcision
[e]Epiphany
[f]Easter
[g]Mary's Announcement
[h]Jesus's Transfiguration

PERSIAN (ASTRONOMICAL) 1512/1513

Month	Sun	Mon	Tue	Wed	Thu	Fri	Sat
	6	7	8	9	10	11	12
DEY 1512	13	14	15	16	17	18	19
	20	21	22	23	24	25	26
	27	28	29	30	1	2	3
	4	5	6	7	8	9	10
BAHMAN 1512	11	12	13	14	15	16	17
	18	19	20	21	22	23	24
	25	26	27	28	29	30	1
	2	3	4	5	6	7	8
ESFAND 1512	9	10	11	12	13	14	15
	16	17	18	19	20	21	22
	23	24	25	26	27	28	29
	1[a]	2	3	4	5	6	7
FARVARDĪN 1513	8	9	10	11	12	13[b]	14
	15	16	17	18	19	20	21
	22	23	24	25	26	27	28
	29	30	31	1	2	3	4
	5	6	7	8	9	10	11
ORDĪBEHEŠT 1513	12	13	14	15	16	17	18
	19	20	21	22	23	24	25
	26	27	28	29	30	31	1
	2	3	4	5	6	7	8
XORDĀD 1513	9	10	11	12	13	14	15
	16	17	18	19	20	21	22
	23	24	25	26	27	28	29
	30	31	1	2	3	4	5
	6	7	8	9	10	11	12
TĪR 1513	13	14	15	16	17	18	19
	20	21	22	23	24	25	26
	27	28	29	30	31	1	2
	3	4	5	6	7	8	9
MORDĀD 1513	10	11	12	13	14	15	16
	17	18	19	20	21	22	23
	24	25	26	27	28	29	30
	31	1	2	3	4	5	6
	7	8	9	10	11	12	13
SHAHRĪVAR 1513	14	15	16	17	18	19	20
	21	22	23	24	25	26	27
	28	29	30	31	1	2	3
	4	5	6	7	8	9	10
MEHR 1513	11	12	13	14	15	16	17
	18	19	20	21	22	23	24
	25	26	27	28	29	30	1
	2	3	4	5	6	7	8
ĀBĀN 1513	9	10	11	12	13	14	15
	16	17	18	19	20	21	22
	23	24	25	26	27	28	29
	30	1	2	3	4	5	6
	7	8	9	10	11	12	13
ĀZAR 1513	14	15	16	17	18	19	20
	21	22	23	24	25	26	27
	28	29	30	1	2	3	4
DEY 1513	5	6	7	8	9	10	11

[a]New Year
[b]Sizdeh Bedar

HINDU LUNAR 2190/2191‡

Month	Sun	Mon	Tue	Wed	Thu	Fri	Sat
	1	2	3	4	5	6	7
PAUSHA 2190	8	9	10	11	12	13	14
	15	16	17	18	19	20	21
	22	**23**	25	26	27	28	*28*
	29	30	1	2	3	4	5
MĀGHA 2190	6	7	8	9	10	11	12
	13	14	15	**16**	18	19	20
	21	22	23	24	25	26	27
	28	29[h]	30	1	*1*	2	3
PHĀLGUNA 2190	4	5	6	7	8	9	**10**
	12	13	14	15[i]	16	17	18
	19	20	21	22	23	24	25
	26	27	28	29	30	1[a]	2
CHAITRA 2191	3	4	5	6	7	8	9[b]
	10	11	12	13	**14**	16	17
	18	19	20	21	22	23	24
	24	25	26	27	28	29	30
	1	2	3	4	5	6	7
VAIŚĀKHA 2191	**8**	10	11	12	13	14	15
	16	17	18	19	20	21	22
	23	24	25	26	27	28	29
	30	1	2	3	4	5	6
JYAISHṬHA 2191	7	8	9	10	**11**	13	14
	15	16	17	18	19	20	*20*
	21	22	23	24	25	26	27
	28	29	30	1	2	3	**4**
ĀSHĀḌHA 2191	6	7	8	9	10	11	12
	13	14	15	16	17	18	19
	20	21	22	23	24	25	26
	27	28	29	30	1	2	3
ŚRĀVAṆA 2191	4	5	6	**7**	9	10	11
	12	13	14	15	16	17	*17*
	18	19	20	21	22	23[c]	24
	25	26	27	28	**29**	1	2
	3	4	5	6	7	8	9
LEAP BHĀDRAPADA 2191	10	11	12	13	14	15	16
	17	18	19	20	21	22	23
	24	25	26	27	28	29	30
	1	2	**3**[d]	5	6	7	8
BHĀDRAPADA 2191	9	10	11	12	13	*13*	14
	15	16	17	18	19	20	21
	22	23	24	25	**26**	28	29
	30	1	2	3	4	5	6
ĀŚVINA 2191	7	8[e]	9[e]	10[e]	11	12	13
	14	15	16	17	*17*	**18**	20
	21	22	23	24	25	26	27
	28	29	30	1[f]	3	4	5
	6	*6*	7	8	9	10	11
KĀRTTIKA 2191	12	13	14	15	16	17	18
	19	20	21	22	23	**24**	26
	27	28	29	30	1	2	3
MĀRGAŚĪRA 2191	4	5	6	7	8	9	*9*
	10	11[g]	12	13	14	15	16

‡Leap year
[a]New Year (Jaya)
[b]Birthday of Rāma
[c]Birthday of Krishna
[d]Ganēśa Chaturthī
[e]Dashara
[f]Diwali
[g]Birthday of Vishnu
[h]Night of Śiva
[i]Holi

HINDU SOLAR 2055‡/2056

Month	Sun	Mon	Tue	Wed	Thu	Fri	Sat
	10	11	12	13	14	15	16
PAUSHA 2055	17	18	19	20	21	22	23
	24	25	26	27	28	29	1[b]
MĀGHA 2055	2	3	4	5	6	7	8
	9	10	11	12	13	14	15
	16	17	18	19	20	21	22
	23	24	25	26	27	28	29
	1	2	3	4	5	6	7
PHĀLGUNA 2055	8	9	10	11	12	13	14
	15	16	17	18	19	20	21
	22	23	24	25	26	27	28
	29	30	1	2	3	4	5
CHAITRA 2055	6	7	8	9	10	11	12
	13	14	15	16	17	18	19
	20	21	22	23	24	25	26
	27	28	29	30	31	1[a]	2
VAIŚĀKHA 2056	3	4	5	6	7	8	9
	10	11	12	13	14	15	16
	17	18	19	20	21	22	23
	24	25	26	27	28	29	30
	31	1	2	3	4	5	6
JYAISHṬHA 2056	7	8	9	10	11	12	13
	14	15	16	17	18	19	20
	21	22	23	24	25	26	27
	28	29	30	31	1	2	3
ĀSHĀḌHA 2056	4	5	6	7	8	9	10
	11	12	13	14	15	16	17
	18	19	20	21	22	23	24
	25	26	27	28	29	30	31
	32	1	2	3	4	5	6
ŚRĀVAṆA 2056	7	8	9	10	11	12	13
	14	15	16	17	18	19	20
	21	22	23	24	25	26	27
	28	29	30	31	1	2	3
BHĀDRAPADA 2056	4	5	6	7	8	9	10
	11	12	13	14	15	16	17
	18	19	20	21	22	23	24
	25	26	27	28	29	30	31
	1	2	3	4	5	6	7
ĀŚVINA 2056	8	9	10	11	12	13	14
	15	16	17	18	19	20	21
	22	23	24	25	26	27	28
	29	30	31	1	2	3	4
KĀRTTIKA 2056	5	6	7	8	9	10	11
	12	13	14	15	16	17	18
	19	20	21	22	23	24	25
	26	27	28	29	1	2	3
MĀRGAŚĪRA 2056	4	5	6	7	8	9	10
	11	12	13	14	15	16	17
	18	19	20	21	22	23	24
	25	26	27	28	29	30	1
PAUSHA 2056	2	3	4	5	6	7	8
	9	10	11	12	13	14	15

‡Leap year
[a]New Year (Saumya)
[b]Pongal

ISLAMIC (ASTRONOMICAL) 1558/1559

Month	Sun	Mon	Tue	Wed	Thu	Fri	Sat
	30	1	2	3	4	5	6
DHU AL-QA'DA 1558	7	8	9	10	11	12	13
	14	15	16	17	18	19	20
	21	22	23	24	25	26	27
	28	29	30	1	2	3	4
DHU AL-ḤIJJA 1558	5	6	7	8	9	10[g]	11
	12	13	14	15	16	17	18
	19	20	21	22	23	24	25
	26	27	28	29	1[a]	2	3
MUḤARRAM 1559	4	5	6	7	8	9	10[b]
	11	12	13	14	15	16	17
	18	19	20	21	22	23	24
	25	26	27	28	29	30	1
ṢAFAR 1559	2	3	4	5	6	7	8
	9	10	11	12	13	14	15
	16	17	18	19	20	21	22
	23	24	25	26	27	28	29
	30	1	2	3	4	5	6
RABĪ' I 1559	7	8	9	10	11	12[c]	13
	14	15	16	17	18	19	20
	21	22	23	24	25	26	27
	28	29	1	2	3	4	5
RABĪ' II 1559	6	7	8	9	10	11	12
	13	14	15	16	17	18	19
	20	21	22	23	24	25	26
	27	28	29	1	2	3	4
JUMĀDĀ I 1559	5	6	7	8	9	10	11
	12	13	14	15	16	17	18
	19	20	21	22	23	24	25
	26	27	28	29	30	1	2
JUMĀDĀ II 1559	3	4	5	6	7	8	9
	10	11	12	13	14	15	16
	17	18	19	20	21	22	23
	24	25	26	27	28	29	1
RAJAB 1559	2	3	4	5	6	7	8
	9	10	11	12	13	14	15
	16	17	18	19	20	21	22
	23	24	25	26	27[d]	28	29
	30	1	2	3	4	5	6
SHA'BĀN 1559	7	8	9	10	11	12	13
	14	15	16	17	18	19	20
	21	22	23	24	25	26	27
	28	29	1[e]	2	3	4	5
RAMAḌĀN 1559	6	7	8	9	10	11	12
	13	14	15	16	17	18	19
	20	21	22	23	24	25	26
	27	28	29	30	1[f]	2	3
SHAWWĀL 1559	4	5	6	7	8	9	10
	11	12	13	14	15	16	17
	18	19	20	21	22	23	24
	25	26	27	28	29	1	2
DHU AL-QA'DA 1559	3	4	5	6	7	8	9
	10	11	12	13	14	15	16

[a]New Year
[b]'Ashūrā'
[c]Prophet's Birthday
[d]Ascent of the Prophet
[e]Start of Ramaḍān
[f]'Id al-Fiṭr
[g]'Id al-'Aḍḥā

GREGORIAN 2134

Julian (Sun)	Sun	Mon	Tue	Wed	Thu	Fri	Sat	Month
Dec 13	27	28	29	30	31	1	2	
	3	4	5	6	7	8[a]	9	JANUARY 2134
Dec 27	10	11	12	13	14	15[b]	16	
	17	18	19	20	21	22	23	
Jan 10	24	25	26	27	28	29	30	
	31	1	2	3	4	5	6	
Jan 24	7	8	9	10	11	12	13	FEBRUARY 2134
	14	15	16	17	18	19	20	
Feb 7	21	22	23	24[c]	25	26	27	
	28	1	2	3	4	5	6	
Feb 21	7[d]	8	9	10	11	12	13	MARCH 2134
	14	15	16	17	18	19	20	
Mar 7	21	22	23	24	25	26	27	
	28	29	30	31	1	2	3	
Mar 21	4	5	6	7	8	9	10	APRIL 2134
	11[e]	12	13	14	15	16	17	
Apr 4	18[f]	19	20	21	22	23	24	
	25	26	27	28	29	30	1	
Apr 18	2	3	4	5	6	7	8	
	9	10	11	12	13	14	15	MAY 2134
May 2	16	17	18	19	20	21	22	
	23	24	25	26	27	28	29	
May 16	30	31	1	2	3	4	5	
	6	7	8	9	10	11	12	JUNE 2134
May 30	13	14	15	16	17	18	19	
	20	21	22	23	24	25	26	
Jun 13	27	28	29	30	1	2	3	
	4	5	6	7	8	9	10	JULY 2134
Jun 27	11	12	13	14	15	16	17	
	18	19	20	21	22	23	24	
Jul 11	25	26	27	28	29	30	31	
	1	2	3	4	5	6	7	
Jul 25	8	9	10	11	12	13	14	AUGUST 2134
	15	16	17	18	19	20	21	
Aug 8	22	23	24	25	26	27	28	
	29	30	31	1	2	3	4	
Aug 22	5	6	7	8	9	10	11	SEPTEMBER 2134
	12	13	14	15	16	17	18	
Sep 5	19	20	21	22	23	24	25	
	26	27	28	29	30	1	2	
Sep 19	3	4	5	6	7	8	9	OCTOBER 2134
	10	11	12	13	14	15	16	
Oct 3	17	18	19	20	21	22	23	
	24	25	26	27	28	29	30	
Oct 17	31	1	2	3	4	5	6	
	7	8	9	10	11	12	13	NOVEMBER 2134
Oct 31	14	15	16	17	18	19	20	
	21	22	23	24	25	26	27	
Nov 14	28[g]	29	30	1	2	3	4	
	5	6	7	8	9	10	11	DECEMBER 2134
Nov 28	12	13	14	15	16	17	18	
	19	20	21	22	23	24	25[h]	
Dec 12	26	27	28	29	30	31	1	

[a]Orthodox Christmas
[b]Julian New Year
[c]Ash Wednesday
[d]Feast of Orthodoxy
[e]Easter
[f]Orthodox Easter
[g]Advent
[h]Christmas

2135

Gregorian 2135	Sun	Mon	Tue	Wed	Thu	Fri	Sat	Lunar Phases	ISO Week (Mon)	Julian Day (Sun noon)	Hebrew 5895/5896‡	Sun	Mon	Tue	Wed	Thu	Fri	Sat	Molad	Chinese Jiǎ-Wǔ‡/Yǐ-Wèi	Sun	Mon	Tue	Wed	Thu	Fri	Sat	Solar Term	Coptic 1851‡/1852	Sun	Mon	Tue	Wed	Thu	Fri	Sat	Ethiopic 2127‡/2128
	26	27	28	29	30	○	1[a]	6:54	52	2500847		10	11	12	13	14	15	16			11	12	13	14	15	16	17			16	17	18	19	20	21	22	TĀKHŚĀŚ 2127
	2	3	4	5	6	◑	8	2:00	1	2500854	TEVETH 5895	17	18	19	20	21	22	23		MONTH 11 Jiǎ-Wǔ	18	19	20	21	22	23	24	Xiǎo hán	KOIAK 1851	23	24	25	26	27	28	29[c]	
JANUARY 2135	9	10	11	12	13	●	15	7:58	2	2500861		24	25	26	27	28	29	1			25	26	27	28	29	1	2			30	1	2	3	4	5	6[d]	
	16	17	18	19	20	21	◐	11:07	3	2500868		2	3	4	5	6	7	8	Fri 20h53m9p		3	4	5	6*	7	8	9	Dà hán		7	8	9	10	11[e]	12	13	
	23	24	25	26	27	28	○	19:18	4	2500875	SHEVAT 5895	9	10	11	12	13	14	15		MONTH 12 Jiǎ-Wǔ	10	11	12	13	14	15	16		TŌBE 1851	14	15	16	17	18	19	20	ṬER 2127
	30	31	1	2	3	4	◑	11:10	5	2500882		16	17	18	19	20	21	22			17	18	19	20	21	22	23	Lì chūn		21	22	23	24	25	26	27	
	6	7	8	9	10	11	12		6	2500889		23	24	25	26	27	28	29			24	25	26	27	28	29	30			28	29	30	1	2	3	4	
FEBRUARY 2135	●	14	15	16	17	18	19	1:08	7	2500896		30	1	2	3	4	5	6	Sun 9h37m10p		1[a]	2	3	4	5	6	7	Yǔ shuǐ		5	6	7	8	9	10	11	
	20	◐	22	23	24	25	26	6:36	8	2500903		7	8	9	10	11	12	13			8	9	10	11	12	13	14		MESHIR 1851	12	13	14	15	16	17	18	YAKĀTIT 2127
	27	○	1	2	3	4	5	6:05	9	2500910	ADAR 5895	14[f]	15	16	17	18	19	20		MONTH 1 Yǐ-Wèi	15[b]	16	17	18	19	20	21			19	20	21	22	23	24	25	
	◑	7	8	9	10	11	12	21:56	10	2500917		21	22	23	24	25	26	27			22	23	24	25	26	27	28	Jīng zhé		26	27	28	29	30	1	2	
MARCH 2135	13	●	15	16	17	18	19	19:20	11	2500924		28	29	1	2	3	4	5	Mon 22h21m11p		29	30	1	2	3	4	5			3	4	5	6	7	8	9	
	20	21[b]	◐	23	24	25	26	22:11	12	2500931		6	7	8	9	10	11	12			6*	7	8	9	10	11	12	Chūn fēn	PAREMOTEP 1851	10	11	12	13	14	15	16	MAGĀBIT 2127
	27	28	○	30	31	1	2	15:41	13	2500938	NISAN 5895	13	14	15[g]	16	17	18	19		MONTH 2 Yǐ-Wèi	13	14	15	16	17	18	19			17	18	19	20	21	22	23	
	3	4	◑	6	7	8	9	10:29	14	2500945		20	21	22	23	24	25	26			20	21	22[c]	23	24	25	26	Qīng míng		24	25	26	27	28	29	30	
APRIL 2135	10	11	12	●	14	15	16	13:16	15	2500952		27	28	29	30	1	2	3	Wed 11h5m12p		27	28	29	1	2	3	4			1	2	3	4	5	6	7	
	17	18	19	20	◐	22	23	9:30	16	2500959	IYYAR 5895	4	5	6	7	8	9	10			5	6	7	8	9	10	11	Gǔ yǔ		8	9	10	11	12	13	14	
	24	25	26	27	○	29	30	0:29	17	2500966		11	12	13	14	15	16	17		MONTH 3 Yǐ-Wèi	12	13	14	15	16	17	18		PARMOUTE 1851	15	16	17	18	19	20	21	MIYĀZYĀ 2127
	1	2	3	4	◑	6	7	0:51	18	2500973		18	19	20	21	22	23	24			19	20	21	22	23	24	25	Lì xià		22	23	24	25	26	27	28	
	8	9	10	11	12	●	14	5:30	19	2500980		25	26	27	28	29	1	2	Thu 23h49m13p		26	27	28	29	30	1	2			29[f,g]	30	1	2	3	4	5	
MAY 2135	15	16	17	18	19	◐	21	17:19	20	2500987		3	4	5	6[h]	7	8	9			3	4	5	6	7*	8	9	Xiǎo mǎn		6	7	8	9	10	11	12	
	22	23	24	25	26	○	28	8:59	21	2500994	SIVAN 5895	10	11	12	13	14	15	16		MONTH 4 Yǐ-Wèi	10	11	12	13	14	15	16		PASHONS 1851	13	14	15	16	17	18	19	GENBOT 2127
	29	30	31	1	2	◑	4	16:54	22	2501001		17	18	19	20	21	22	23			17	18	19	20	21	22	23			20	21	22	23	24	25	26	
	5	6	7	8	9	10	●	19:09	23	2501008		24	25	26	27	28	29	30			24	25	26	27	28	29	30	Máng zhòng		27	28	29	30	1	2	3	
JUNE 2135	12	13	14	15	16	17	◐	22:51	24	2501015		1	2	3	4	5	6	7	Sat 12h33m14p		1	2	3	4	5[d]	6	7			4	5	6	7	8	9	10	
	19	20	21[c]	22	23	24	○	17:52	25	2501022		8	9	10	11	12	13	14		MONTH 5 Yǐ-Wèi	8	9	10	11	12	13	14	Xià zhì	PAŌNE 1851	11	12	13	14	15	16	17	SANĒ 2127
	26	27	28	29	30	1	2		26	2501029	TAMMUZ 5895	15	16	17	18	19	20	21			15	16	17	18	19	20	21			18	19	20	21	22	23	24	
	◑	4	5	6	7	8	9	10:07	27	2501036		22	23	24	25	26	27	28			22	23	24	25	26	27	28	Xiǎo shǔ		25	26	27	28	29	30	1	
JULY 2135	10	●	12	13	14	15	16	6:16	28	2501043		29	1	2	3	4	5	6	Mon 1h17m15p		29	1	2	3	4	5	6			2	3	4	5	6	7	8	
	17	◐	19	20	21	22	23	3:27	29	2501050		7	8	9[i]	10	11	12	13			7	8*	9	10	11	12	13	Dà shǔ	EPĒP 1851	9	10	11	12	13	14	15	ḤAMLĒ 2127
	24	○	26	27	28	29	30	4:04	30	2501057	AV 5895	14	15	16	17	18	19	20		MONTH 6 Yǐ-Wèi	14	15	16	17	18	19	20			16	17	18	19	20	21	22	
	31	1	◑	3	4	5	6	3:40	31	2501064		21	22	23	24	25	26	27			21	22	23	24	25	26	27			23	24	25	26	27	28	29	
	7	8	●	10	11	12	13	15:35	32	2501071		28	29	30	1	2	3	4	Tue 14h1m16p		28	29	1	2	3	4	5	Lì qiū		30	1	2	3	4	5	6	
AUGUST 2135	14	15	◐	17	18	19	20	8:31	33	2501078		5	6	7	8	9	10	11			6	7[e]	8	9	10	11	12			7	8	9	10	11	12	13[h]	
	21	22	○	24	25	26	27	16:30	34	2501085	ELUL 5895	12	13	14	15	16	17	18		MONTH 7 Yǐ-Wèi	13	14	15[f]	16	17	18	19	Chǔ shǔ	MESORĒ 1851	14	15	16	17	18	19	20	NAHASĒ 2127
	28	29	30	◑	1	2	3	20:31	35	2501092		19	20	21	22	23	24	25			20	21	22	23	24	25	26			21	22	23	24	25	26	27	
	4	5	6	7	●	9	10	0:08	36	2501099		26	27	28	29	1[a]	2[a]	3	Thu 2h45m17p		27	28	29	30	1	2	3	Bái lù		28	29	30	1	2	3	4	
SEPTEMBER 2135	11	12	13	◐	15	16	17	15:20	37	2501106		4	5	6	7	8	9	10[b]			4	5	6	7	8	9*	10		EPAG. 1851	5	6	1[a]	2	3	4	5	PĀG. 2127
	18	19	20	21	○	23[d]	24	7:41	38	2501113	TISHRI 5896	11	12	13	14	15[c]	16	17		MONTH 8 Yǐ-Wèi	11	12	13	14	15[g]	16	17	Qiū fēn		6	7	8	9	10	11	12	
	25	26	27	28	29	◑	1	11:53	39	2501120		18	19	20	21	22	23	24			18	19	20	21	22	23	24		THOOUT 1852	13	14	15	16	17[b]	18	19	MASKARAM 2128
	2	3	4	5	6	●	8	8:50	40	2501127		25	26	27	28	29	30	1	Fri 15h30m0p		25	26	27	28	29	1	2			20	21	22	23	24	25	26	
OCTOBER 2135	9	10	11	12	13	◐	15	1:10	41	2501134		2	3	4	5	6	7	8			3	4	5	6	7	8	9[h]	Hán lù		27	28	29	30	1	2	3	
	16	17	18	19	20	21	○	1:12	42	2501141	HESHVAN 5896	9	10	11	12	13	14	15		MONTH 9 Yǐ-Wèi	10	11	12	13	14	15	16			4	5	6	7	8	9	10	
	23	24	25	26	27	28	29		43	2501148		16	17	18	19	20	21	22			17	18	19	20	21	22	23	Shuāng jiàng	PAOPE 1852	11	12	13	14	15	16	17	ṬEQEMT 2128
	◑	31	1	2	3	4	●	1:22 18:14	44	2501155		23	24	25	26	27	28	29			24	25	26	27	28	29	30			18	19	20	21	22	23	24	
	6	7	8	9	10	11	◐	14:56	45	2501162		30	1	2	3	4	5	6	Sun 4h14m1p		1	2	3	4	5	6	7	Lì dōng		25	26	27	28	29	30	1	
NOVEMBER 2135	13	14	15	16	17	18	19		46	2501169		7	8	9	10	11	12	13			8	9	10*	11	12	13	14			2	3	4	5	6	7	8	
	○	21	22	23	24	25	26	19:43	47	2501176	KISLEV 5896	14	15	16	17	18	19	20		MONTH 10 Yǐ-Wèi	15	16	17	18	19	20	21	Xiǎo xuě	ATHŌR 1852	9	10	11	12	13	14	15	ḪEDĀR 2128
	27	◑	29	30	1	2	3	12:56	48	2501183		21	22	23	24	25[e]	26[e]	27[e]			22	23	24	25	26	27	28			16	17	18	19	20	21	22	
	4	●	6	7	8	9	10	4:40	49	2501190		28[e]	29[e]	30[e]	1[d,e]	2[e]	3	4	Mon 16h58m2p		29	1	2	3	4	5	6	Dà xuě		23	24	25	26	27	28	29	
DECEMBER 2135	11	◐	13	14	15	16	17	8:51	50	2501197		5	6	7	8	9	10	11			7	8	9	10	11	12	13			30	1	2	3	4	5	6	
	18	19	○	21	22[e]	23	24	13:39	51	2501204	TEVETH 5896	12	13	14	15	16	17	18		MONTH 11 Yǐ-Wèi	14	15	16	17	18[i]	19	20	Dōng zhì	KOIAK 1852	7	8	9	10	11	12	13	TĀKHŚĀŚ 2128
	25	26	◑	28	29	30	31	22:47	52	2501211		19	20	21	22	23	24	25			21	22	23	24	25	26	27			14	15	16	17	18	19	20	

[a]New Year
[b]Spring (0:43)
[c]Summer (16:29)
[d]Autumn (9:19)
[e]Winter (7:46)
● New moon
◐ First quarter moon
○ Full moon
◑ Last quarter moon

‡Leap year
[a]New Year
[b]Yom Kippur
[c]Sukkot
[d]Winter starts
[e]Ḥanukkah
[f]Purim
[g]Passover
[h]Shavuot
[i]Fast of Av

‡Leap year
[a]New Year (4833, Sheep)
[b]Lantern Festival
[c]Qīngmíng
[d]Dragon Festival
[e]Qīqiǎo
[f]Hungry Ghosts
[g]Mid-Autumn Festival
[h]Double-Ninth Festival
[i]Dōngzhì
*Start of 60-name cycle

‡Leap year
[a]New Year
[b]Building of the Cross
[c]Christmas
[d]Jesus's Circumcision
[e]Epiphany
[f]Easter
[g]Mary's Announcement
[h]Jesus's Transfiguration

PERSIAN (ASTRONOMICAL) 1513/1514

Month	Sun	Mon	Tue	Wed	Thu	Fri	Sat
DEY 1513	5	6	7	8	9	10	11
	12	13	14	15	16	17	18
	19	20	21	22	23	24	25
	26	27	28	29	30	1	2
BAHMAN 1513	3	4	5	6	7	8	9
	10	11	12	13	14	15	16
	17	18	19	20	21	22	23
	24	25	26	27	28	29	30
ESFAND 1513	1	2	3	4	5	6	7
	8	9	10	11	12	13	14
	15	16	17	18	19	20	21
	22	23	24	25	26	27	28
	29	1[a]	2	3	4	5	6
FARVARDĪN 1514	7	8	9	10	11	12	13[b]
	14	15	16	17	18	19	20
	21	22	23	24	25	26	27
	28	29	30	31	1	2	3
ORDĪBEHEŠT 1514	4	5	6	7	8	9	10
	11	12	13	14	15	16	17
	18	19	20	21	22	23	24
	25	26	27	28	29	30	31
XORDĀD 1514	1	2	3	4	5	6	7
	8	9	10	11	12	13	14
	15	16	17	18	19	20	21
	22	23	24	25	26	27	28
	29	30	31	1	2	3	4
TĪR 1514	5	6	7	8	9	10	11
	12	13	14	15	16	17	18
	19	20	21	22	23	24	25
	26	27	28	29	30	31	1
MORDĀD 1514	2	3	4	5	6	7	8
	9	10	11	12	13	14	15
	16	17	18	19	20	21	22
	23	24	25	26	27	28	29
	30	31	1	2	3	4	5
SHAHRĪVAR 1514	6	7	8	9	10	11	12
	13	14	15	16	17	18	19
	20	21	22	23	24	25	26
	27	28	29	30	31	1	2
MEHR 1514	3	4	5	6	7	8	9
	10	11	12	13	14	15	16
	17	18	19	20	21	22	23
	24	25	26	27	28	29	30
ABĀN 1514	1	2	3	4	5	6	7
	8	9	10	11	12	13	14
	15	16	17	18	19	20	21
	22	23	24	25	26	27	28
	29	30	1	2	3	4	5
ĀZAR 1514	6	7	8	9	10	11	12
	13	14	15	16	17	18	19
	20	21	22	23	24	25	26
DEY 1514	27	28	29	30	1	2	3
	4	5	6	7	8	9	10

[a]New Year
[b]Sizdeh Bedar

HINDU LUNAR 2191‡/2192

Month	Sun	Mon	Tue	Wed	Thu	Fri	Sat
MĀRGAŚIRA 2191	10	11	12	13	14	15	16
	17	**18**	20	21	22	23	24
	25	26	27	28	29	30	1
PAUSHA 2191	2	3	4	5	6	7	8
	9	10	11	12	13	14	15
	16	17	18	19	20	21	22
	23	25	26	27	28	29	30
MĀGHA 2191	1	1	2	3	4	5	6
	7	8	9	10	11	12	13
	14	15	16	**17**	19	20	21
	22	23	24	25	26	27	28[h]
PHĀLGUNA 2191	29	30	1	2	3	4	4
	5	6	7	8	9	10	**11**
	13	14	15[i]	16	17	18	19
	20	21	22	23	24	25	26
	27	28	29	30	1[a]	2	3
CHAITRA 2192	4	5	6	7	8	9[b]	10
	11	12	13	14	**15**	17	18
	19	20	21	22	23	24	25
	26	27	28	28	29	30	1
VAIŚĀKHA 2192	2	3	4	5	6	7	**8**
	10	11	12	13	14	15	16
	17	18	19	20	21	22	23
	24	25	26	27	28	29	30
JYAISHTHA 2192	1	2	3	4	5	6	7
	8	9	10	**11**	13	14	15
	16	17	18	19	20	21	22
	23	24	25	25	26	27	28
	29	30	1	2	3	**4**	6
ĀSHĀḌHA 2192	7	8	9	10	11	12	13
	14	15	16	17	18	19	20
	21	22	23	24	25	26	27
	28	29	30	1	2	3	4
ŚRĀVAṆA 2192	5	6	**7**	9	10	11	12
	13	14	15	16	17	18	19
	20	21	21	22	23[c]	24	25
	26	27	28	**29**	1	2	3
BHĀDRAPADA 2192	4[d]	5	6	7	8	9	10
	11	12	13	14	15	16	17
	18	19	20	21	22	23	24
	25	26	27	28	29	30	1
ĀŚVINA 2192	2	**3**	5	6	7	8[e]	9[e]
	10[e]	11	12	13	14	15	16
	16	17	18	19	20	21	22
	23	24	25	26	**27**	29	30
KĀRTTIKA 2192	1[f]	2	3	4	5	6	7
	8	9	10	11	12	13	14
	15	16	17	18	19	20	21
	22	23	24	25	26	27	28
	29	30	**1**	3	4	5	6
MĀRGAŚIRA 2192	7	8	9	9	10	11[g]	12
	13	14	15	16	17	18	19
	20	21	22	23	24	**25**	27

‡Leap year
[a]New Year (Manmatha)
[b]Birthday of Rāma
[c]Birthday of Krishna
[d]Ganēśa Chaturthī
[e]Dashara
[f]Diwali
[g]Birthday of Vishnu
[h]Night of Śiva
[i]Holi

HINDU SOLAR 2056/2057

Month	Sun	Mon	Tue	Wed	Thu	Fri	Sat
PAUSHA 2056	9	10	11	12	13	14	15
	16	17	18	19	20	21	22
	23	24	25	26	27	28	29
MĀGHA 2056	1[b]	2	3	4	5	6	7
	8	9	10	11	12	13	14
	15	16	17	18	19	20	21
	22	23	24	25	26	27	28
	29	30	1	2	3	4	5
PHĀLGUNA 2056	6	7	8	9	10	11	12
	13	14	15	16	17	18	19
	20	21	22	23	24	25	26
	27	28	29	30	1	2	3
CHAITRA 2056	4	5	6	7	8	9	10
	11	12	13	14	15	16	17
	18	19	20	21	22	23	24
	25	26	27	28	29	30	1[a]
VAIŚĀKHA 2057	2	3	4	5	6	7	8
	9	10	11	12	13	14	15
	16	17	18	19	20	21	22
	23	24	25	26	27	28	29
	30	31	1	2	3	4	5
JYAISHTHA 2057	6	7	8	9	10	11	12
	13	14	15	16	17	18	19
	20	21	22	23	24	25	26
	27	28	29	30	31	1	2
ĀSHĀḌHA 2057	3	4	5	6	7	8	9
	10	11	12	13	14	15	16
	17	18	19	20	21	22	23
	24	25	26	27	28	29	30
	31	32	1	2	3	4	5
ŚRĀVAṆA 2057	6	7	8	9	10	11	12
	13	14	15	16	17	18	19
	20	21	22	23	24	25	26
	27	28	29	30	31	1	2
BHĀDRAPADA 2057	3	4	5	6	7	8	9
	10	11	12	13	14	15	16
	17	18	19	20	21	22	23
	24	25	26	27	28	29	30
	31	1	2	3	4	5	6
ĀŚVINA 2057	7	8	9	10	11	12	13
	14	15	16	17	18	19	20
	21	22	23	24	25	26	27
	28	29	30	31	1	2	3
KĀRTTIKA 2057	4	5	6	7	8	9	10
	11	12	13	14	15	16	17
	18	19	20	21	22	23	24
	25	26	27	28	29	30	1
MĀRGAŚIRA 2057	2	3	4	5	6	7	8
	9	10	11	12	13	14	15
	16	17	18	19	20	21	22
	23	24	25	26	27	28	29
PAUSHA 2057	1	2	3	4	5	6	7
	8	9	10	11	12	13	14

[a]New Year (Sādhāraṇa)
[b]Pongal

ISLAMIC (ASTRONOMICAL) 1559/1560‡

Month	Sun	Mon	Tue	Wed	Thu	Fri	Sat
DHU AL-QA'DA 1559	10	11	12	13	14	15	16
	17	18	19	20	21	22	23
	24	25	26	27	28	29	30
DHU AL-ḤIJJA 1559	1	2	3	4	5	6	7
	8	9	10[g]	11	12	13	14
	15	16	17	18	19	20	21
	22	23	24	25	26	27	28
	29	1[a]	2[d]	3	4	5	6
MUḤARRAM 1560	7	8	9	10[b]	11	12	13
	14	15	16	17	18	19	20
	21	22	23	24	25	26	27
	28	29	30	1	2	3	4
ṢAFAR 1560	5	6	7	8	9	10	11
	12	13	14	15	16	17	18
	19	20	21	22	23	24	25
	26	27	28	29	30	1	2
RABĪ' I 1560	3	4	5	6	7	8	9
	10	11	12[c]	13	14	15	16
	17	18	19	20	21	22	23
	24	25	26	27	28	29	30
RABĪ' II 1560	1	2	3	4	5	6	7
	8	9	10	11	12	13	14
	15	16	17	18	19	20	21
	22	23	24	25	26	27	28
	29	1	2	3	4	5	6
JUMĀDĀ I 1560	7	8	9	10	11	12	13
	14	15	16	17	18	19	20
	21	22	23	24	25	26	27
	28	29	1	2	3	4	5
JUMĀDĀ II 1560	6	7	8	9	10	11	12
	13	14	15	16	17	18	19
	20	21	22	23	24	25	26
	27	28	29	30	1	2	3
RAJAB 1560	4	5	6	7	8	9	10
	11	12	13	14	15	16	17
	18	19	20	21	22	23	24
	25	26	27[d]	28	29	1	2
SHA'BĀN 1560	3	4	5	6	7	8	9
	10	11	12	13	14	15	16
	17	18	19	20	21	22	23
	24	25	26	27	28	29	30
RAMAḌĀN 1560	1[e]	2	3	4	5	6	7
	8	9	10	11	12	13	14
	15	16	17	18	19	20	21
	22	23	24	25	26	27	28
	29	30	1[f]	2	3	4	5
SHAWWĀL 1560	6	7	8	9	10	11	12
	13	14	15	16	17	18	19
	20	21	22	23	24	25	26
	27	28	29	1	2	3	4
DHU AL-QA'DA 1560	5	6	7	8	9	10	11
	12	13	14	15	16	17	18
	19	20	21	22	23	24	25

‡Leap year
[a]New Year
[d]New Year (Arithmetic)
[b]'Ashūrā'
[c]Prophet's Birthday
[d]Ascent of the Prophet
[e]Start of Ramaḍān
[f]'Id al-Fiṭr
[g]'Id al-'Aḍḥā

GREGORIAN 2135

Julian (Sun)	Sun	Mon	Tue	Wed	Thu	Fri	Sat	Month
Dec 12	26	27	28	29	30	31	1	
	2	3	4	5	6	7	8[a]	JANUARY 2135
Dec 26	9	10	11	12	13	14	15[b]	
	16	17	18	19	20	21	22	
Jan 9	23	24	25	26	27	28	29	
	30	31	1	2	3	4	5	
Jan 23	6	7	8	9	10	11	12	FEBRUARY 2135
	13	14	15	16[c]	17	18	19	
Feb 6	20	21	22	23	24	25	26	
	27	28	1	2	3	4	5	
Feb 20	6	7	8	9	10	11	12	MARCH 2135
	13	14	15	16	17	18	19	
Mar 6	20	21	22	23	24	25	26	
	27[d]	28	29	30	31	1	2	
Mar 20	3[e]	4	5	6	7	8	9	APRIL 2135
	10	11	12	13	14	15	16	
Apr 3	17	18	19	20	21	22	23	
	24	25	26	27	28	29	30	
Apr 17	1	2	3	4	5	6	7	
	8[f]	9	10	11	12	13	14	MAY 2135
May 1	15	16	17	18	19	20	21	
	22	23	24	25	26	27	28	
May 15	29	30	31	1	2	3	4	
	5	6	7	8	9	10	11	JUNE 2135
May 29	12	13	14	15	16	17	18	
	19	20	21	22	23	24	25	
Jun 12	26	27	28	29	30	1	2	
	3	4	5	6	7	8	9	
Jun 26	10	11	12	13	14	15	16	JULY 2135
	17	18	19	20	21	22	23	
Jul 10	24	25	26	27	28	29	30	
	31	1	2	3	4	5	6	
Jul 24	7	8	9	10	11	12	13	AUGUST 2135
	14	15	16	17	18	19	20	
Aug 7	21	22	23	24	25	26	27	
	28	29	30	31	1	2	3	
Aug 21	4	5	6	7	8	9	10	SEPTEMBER 2135
	11	12	13	14	15	16	17	
Sep 4	18	19	20	21	22	23	24	
	25	26	27	28	29	30	1	
Sep 18	2	3	4	5	6	7	8	
	9	10	11	12	13	14	15	OCTOBER 2135
Oct 2	16	17	18	19	20	21	22	
	23	24	25	26	27	28	29	
Oct 16	30	31	1	2	3	4	5	
	6	7	8	9	10	11	12	NOVEMBER 2135
Oct 30	13	14	15	16	17	18	19	
	20	21	22	23	24	25	26	
Nov 13	27[g]	28	29	30	1	2	3	
	4	5	6	7	8	9	10	DECEMBER 2135
Nov 27	11	12	13	14	15	16	17	
	18	19	20	21	22	23	24	
Dec 11	25[h]	26	27	28	29	30	31	

[a]Orthodox Christmas
[b]Julian New Year
[c]Ash Wednesday
[d]Feast of Orthodoxy
[e]Easter
[f]Orthodox Easter
[g]Advent
[h]Christmas

2136

Gregorian 2136‡	Sun	Mon	Tue	Wed	Thu	Fri	Sat	Lunar Phases	ISO Week (Mon)	Julian Day (Sun noon)	Hebrew 5896‡/5897	Sun	Mon	Tue	Wed	Thu	Fri	Sat	Molad	Chinese Yǐ-Wèi/Bǐng-Shēn	Sun	Mon	Tue	Wed	Thu	Fri	Sat	Solar Term	Coptic 1852/1853	Sun	Mon	Tue	Wed	Thu	Fri	Sat	Ethiopic 2128/2129
JANUARY 2136	1[a]	2	●	4	5	6	7	16:25	1	2501218		26	27	28	29	1	2	3	Wed 5h 42m 3p		28	29	30	1	2	3	4	Xiǎo hán		21	22	23	24	25	26	27	TĀKHŚĀŚ 2128
	8	9	10	◐	12	13	14	5:56	2	2501225	SHEVAT 5896	4	5	6	7	8	9	10		MONTH 12 Yǐ-Wèi	5	6	7	8	9	10	11*		KOIAK 1852	28	29[c]	30	1	2	3	4	
	15	16	17	18	○	20	21	5:51	3	2501232		11	12	13	14	15	16	17			12	13	14	15	16	17	**18**	Dà hán		5	6[d]	7	8	9	10	11[e]	ṬER 2128
	22	23	24	25	◑	27	28	7:17	4	2501239		18	19	20	21	22	23	24			19	20	21	22	23	24	25		TÔBE 1852	12	13	14	15	16	17	18	
	29	30	31	1	●	3	4	5:47	5	2501246		25	26	27	28	29	30	1	Thu 18h 26m 4p		26	27	28	29	1[a]	2	3	Lì chūn		19	20	21	22	23	24	25	
FEBRUARY 2136	5	6	7	8	9	◐	11	3:58	6	2501253	ADAR I 5896	2	3	4	5	6	7	8		MONTH 1 Bǐng-Shēn	4	5	6	7	8	9	10			26	27	28	29	30	1	2	
	12	13	14	15	16	○	18	19:52	7	2501260		9	10	11	12	13	14	15			11	12	13	14	15[b]	16	17		MESHIR 1852	3	4	5	6	7	8	9	YAKĀTIT 2128
	19	20	21	22	23	◑	25	15:05	8	2501267		16	17	18	19	20	21	22			**18**	19	20	21	22	23	24	Yǔ shuǐ		10	11	12	13	14	15	16	
	26	27	28	29	1	●	3	20:55	9	2501274		23	24	25	26	27	28	29			25	26	27	28	29	30	1			17	18	19	20	21	22	23	
MARCH 2136	4	5	6	7	8	9	10		10	2501281		30	1	2	3	4	5	6	Sat 7h 10m 5p	MONTH 2 Bǐng-Shēn	2	3	4	5	6	7	8	Jīng zhé		24	25	26	27	28	29	30	
	◐	12	13	14	15	16	17	0:30	11	2501288	ADAR II 5896	7	8	9	10	11	12	13			9	10	11	12*	13	14	15			1	2	3	4	5	6	7	
	○	19	20[b]	21	22	23	◑	7:37 23:05	12	2501295		14[f]	15	16	17	18	19	20			16	17	**18**	19	20	21	22	Chūn fēn	PAREMOTEP 1852	8	9	10	11	12	13	14	MAGĀBIT 2128
	25	26	27	28	29	30	31		13	2501302		21	22	23	24	25	26	27			23	24	25	26	27	28	29			15	16	17	18	19	20	21	
APRIL 2136	●	2	3	4	5	6	7	13:23	14	2501309		28	29	1	2	3	4	5	Sun 19h 54m 6p		1	2	3	4[c]	5	6	7	Qīng míng		22	23	24	25	26	27	28	
	8	◐	10	11	12	13	14	17:52	15	2501316	NISAN 5896	6	7	8	9	10	11	12		MONTH 3 Bǐng-Shēn	8	9	10	11	12	13	14			29	30	1	2	3	4	5	
	15	○	17	18	19	20	21	17:18	16	2501323		13	14	15[g]	16	17	18	19			15	16	17	18	19	**20**	21	Gǔ yǔ	PARMOUTE 1852	6	7	8	9	10	11	12	MIYĀZYĀ 2128
	22	◑	24	25	26	27	28	8:13	17	2501330		20	21	22	23	24	25	26			22	23	24	25	26	27	28			13[f]	14	15	16	17	18	19	
	29	30	●	2	3	4	5	6:12	18	2501337		27	28	29	30	1	2	3	Tue 8h 38m 7p		29	30	1	2	3	4	5	Lì xià		20	21	22	23	24	25	26	
MAY 2136	6	7	8	◐	10	11	12	7:30	19	2501344	IYAR 5896	4	5	6	7	8	9	10		MONTH 4 Bǐng-Shēn	6	7	8	9	10	11	12			27	28	29[g]	30	1	2	3	
	13	14	15	○	17	18	19	1:18	20	2501351		11	12	13	14	15	16	17			13*	14	15	16	17	18	19		PASHONS 1852	4	5	6	7	8	9	10	GENBOT 2128
	20	21	◑	23	24	25	26	19:16	21	2501358		18	19	20	21	22	23	24			**20**	21	22	23	24	25	26	Xiǎo mǎn		11	12	13	14	15	16	17	
	27	28	29	●	31	1	2	22:13	22	2501365		25	26	27	28	29	1	2	Wed 21h 22m 8p		27	28	29	30	1	2	3			18	19	20	21	22	23	24	
JUNE 2136	3	4	5	6	◐	8	9	17:36	23	2501372	SIVAN 5896	3	4	5	6[h]	7	8	9		MONTH 5 Bǐng-Shēn	4	5[d]	6	7	8	9	10	Máng zhòng		25	26	27	28	29	30	1	
	10	11	12	13	○	15	16	8:25	24	2501379		10	11	12	13	14	15	16			11	12	13	14	15	16	17			2	3	4	5	6	7	8	
	17	18	19	20[c]	◑	22	23	8:41	25	2501386		17	18	19	20	21	22	23			18	19	20	21	**22**	23	24	Xià zhì	PAÔNE 1852	9	10	11	12	13	14	15	SANĒ 2128
	24	25	26	27	28	●	30	12:45	26	2501393		24	25	26	27	28	29	30			25	26	27	28	29	1	2			16	17	18	19	20	21	22	
JULY 2136	1	2	3	4	5	6	◐	0:50	27	2501400		1	2	3	4	5	6	7	Fri 10h 6m 9p	MONTH 6 Bǐng-Shēn	3	4	5	6	7	*8*	9	Xiǎo shǔ		23	24	25	26	27	28	29	
	8	9	10	11	12	○	14	15:44	28	2501407	TAMMUZ 5896	8	9	10	11	12	13	14			10	11	12	13	14*	15	16			30	1	2	3	4	5	6	
	15	16	17	18	19	20	◑	0:19	29	2501414		15	16	17	18	19	20	21			17	18	19	20	21	22	23		EPÊP 1852	7	8	9	10	11	12	13	ḤAMLĒ 2128
	22	23	24	25	26	27	28		30	2501421		22	23	24	25	26	27	28			**24**	25	26	27	28	29	30	Dà shǔ		14	15	16	17	18	19	20	
	●	30	31	1	2	3	4	1:43	31	2501428		29	1	2	3	4	5	6	Sat 22h 50m 10p		1	2	3	4	5	6	7[e]			21	22	23	24	25	26	27	
AUGUST 2136	◐	6	7	8	9	10	11	6:13	32	2501435	AV 5896	7	8	9[i]	10	11	12	13		MONTH 7 Bǐng-Shēn	8	9	*10*	11	12	13	14	Lì qiū		28	29	30	1	2	3	4	
	○	13	14	15	16	17	18	0:30	33	2501442		14	15	16	17	18	19	20			15[f]	16	17	18	19	20	21			5	6	7	8	9	10	11	
	◑	20	21	22	23	24	25	17:39	34	2501449		21	22	23	24	25	26	27			22	23	24	25	**26**	27	28	Chǔ shǔ	MESORÊ 1852	12	13[h]	14	15	16	17	18	NAHASĒ 2128
	26	●	28	29	30	31	1	13:24	35	2501456		28	29	30	1	2	3	4	Mon 11h 34m 11p		29	1	2	3	4	5	6			19	20	21	22	23	24	25	
SEPTEMBER 2136	2	◐	4	5	6	7	8	11:02	36	2501463	ELUL 5896	5	6	7	8	9	10	11		MONTH 8 Bǐng-Shēn	7	8	9	10	11	*12*	13	Bái lù		26	27	28	29	30	1	2	
	9	○	11	12	13	14	15	11:46	37	2501470		12	13	14	15	16	17	18			14	15[g]	16	17	18	19	20		EPAG. 1852	3	4	5	1[a]	2	3	4	PĀG. 2128
	16	17	◑	19	20	21	22[d]	11:51	38	2501477		19	20	21	22	23	24	25			21	22	23	24	25	26	**27**	Qiū fēn	THOOUT 1853	5	6	7	8	9	10	11	MASKARAM 2129
	23	24	25	●	27	28	29	0:09	39	2501484		26	27	28	29	1[a]	2[a]	3	Wed 0h 18m 12p		28	29	30	1	2	3	4			12	13	14	15	16	17[b]	18	
OCTOBER 2136	30	1	◐	3	4	5	6	16:47	40	2501491	TISHRI 5897	4	5	6	7	8	9	10[b]		MONTH 9 Bǐng-Shēn	5	6	7	8	9[h]	10	11			19	20	21	22	23	24	25	
	7	8	9	○	11	12	13	2:05	41	2501498		11	12	13	14	15[c]	16	17			12	*13*	14	15	16	17	18	Hán lù		26	27	28	29	30	1	2	
	14	15	16	17	◑	19	20	6:01	42	2501505		18	19	20	21	22	23	24			19	20	21	22	23	24	25			3	4	5	6	7	8	9	ṬEQEMT 2129
	21	22	23	24	●	26	27	10:21	43	2501512		25	26	27	28	29	30	1	Thu 13h 2m 13p		26	27	**28**	29	1	2	3	Shuāng jiàng	PAOPE 1853	10	11	12	13	14	15	16	
	28	29	30	31	◐	2	3	0:57	44	2501519	HESHVAN 5897	2	3	4	5	6	7	8		MONTH 10 Bǐng-Shēn	4	5	6	7	8	9	10			17	18	19	20	21	22	23	
NOVEMBER 2136	4	5	6	7	○	9	10	19:09	45	2501526		9	10	11	12	13	14	15			11	12	13	*14*	15	16*	17	Lì dōng		24	25	26	27	28	29	30	
	11	12	13	14	15	◑	17	23:09	46	2501533		16	17	18	19	20	21	22			18	19	20	21	22	23	24			1	2	3	4	5	6	7	
	18	19	20	21	22	●	24	20:20	47	2501540		23	24	25	26	27	28	29			25	26	27	28	**29**	30	1	Xiǎo xuě	ATHÔR 1853	8	9	10	11	12	13	14	HEDĀR 2129
	25	26	27	28	29	◐	1	12:44	48	2501547		1	2	3	4	5	6	7	Sat 1h 46m 14p	MONTH 11 Bǐng-Shēn	2	3	4	5	6	7	8			15	16	17	18	19	20	21	
DECEMBER 2136	2	3	4	5	6	7	○	13:58	49	2501554	KISLEV 5897	8	9	10	11	12[d]	13	14			9	10	11	12	13	*14*	15	Dà xuě		22	23	24	25	26	27	28	
	9	10	11	12	13	14	15		50	2501561		15	16	17	18	19	20	21			16	17	18	19	20	21	22			29	30	1	2	3	4	5	
	◑	17	18	19	20	21[e]	22	14:14	51	2501568		22	23	24	25[e]	26[e]	27[e]	28[e]			23	24	25	26	27	**28**[i]	29	Dōng zhì	KOIAK 1853	6	7	8	9	10	11	12	TĀKHŚĀŚ 2129
	●	24	25	26	27	28	29	6:33	52	2501575		29[e]	30[e]	1[e]	2[e]	3	4	5	Sun 14h 30m 15p	MONTH 12 Bǐng-Shēn	1	2	3	4	5	6	7			13	14	15	16	17	18	19	
	◐	31	1	2	3	4	5	4:27	1	2501582	TEVETH 5897	6	7	8	9	10	11	12			8	9	10	11	12	13	*14*	Xiǎo hán		20	21	22	23	24	25	26	

‡Leap year
[a]New Year
[b]Spring (6:31)
[c]Summer (22:23)
[d]Autumn (15:10)
[e]Winter (13:35)
● New moon
◐ First quarter moon
○ Full moon
◑ Last quarter moon

‡Leap year
[a]New Year
[b]Yom Kippur
[c]Sukkot
[d]Winter starts
[e]Ḥanukkah
[f]Purim
[g]Passover
[h]Shavuot
[i]Fast of Av

[a]New Year (4834, Monkey)
[b]Lantern Festival
[c]Qīngmíng
[d]Dragon Festival
[e]Qīqiǎo
[f]Hungry Ghosts
[g]Mid-Autumn Festival
[h]Double-Ninth Festival
[i]Dōngzhì
*Start of 60-name cycle

[a]New Year
[b]Building of the Cross
[c]Christmas
[d]Jesus's Circumcision
[e]Epiphany
[f]Easter
[g]Mary's Announcement
[h]Jesus's Transfiguration

PERSIAN (ASTRONOMICAL) 1514/1515‡

Month	Sun	Mon	Tue	Wed	Thu	Fri	Sat
DEY 1514	11	12	13	14	15	16	17
	18	19	20	21	22	23	24
	25	26	27	28	29	30	1
BAHMAN 1514	2	3	4	5	6	7	8
	9	10	11	12	13	14	15
	16	17	18	19	20	21	22
	23	24	25	26	27	28	29
	30	1	2	3	4	5	6
ESFAND 1514	7	8	9	10	11	12	13
	14	15	16	17	18	19	20
	21	22	23	24	25	26	27
	28	29	1[a]	2	3	4	5
FARVARDĪN 1515	6	7	8	9	10	11	12
	13[b]	14	15	16	17	18	19
	20	21	22	23	24	25	26
	27	28	29	30	31	1	2
ORDĪBEHEŠT 1515	3	4	5	6	7	8	9
	10	11	12	13	14	15	16
	17	18	19	20	21	22	23
	24	25	26	27	28	29	30
	31	1	2	3	4	5	6
XORDĀD 1515	7	8	9	10	11	12	13
	14	15	16	17	18	19	20
	21	22	23	24	25	26	27
	28	29	30	31	1	2	3
TĪR 1515	4	5	6	7	8	9	10
	11	12	13	14	15	16	17
	18	19	20	21	22	23	24
	25	26	27	28	29	30	31
MORDĀD 1515	1	2	3	4	5	6	7
	8	9	10	11	12	13	14
	15	16	17	18	19	20	21
	22	23	24	25	26	27	28
	29	30	31	1	2	3	4
SHAHRĪVAR 1515	5	6	7	8	9	10	11
	12	13	14	15	16	17	18
	19	20	21	22	23	24	25
	26	27	28	29	30	31	1
MEHR 1515	2	3	4	5	6	7	8
	9	10	11	12	13	14	15
	16	17	18	19	20	21	22
	23	24	25	26	27	28	29
	30	1	2	3	4	5	6
ĀBĀN 1515	7	8	9	10	11	12	13
	14	15	16	17	18	19	20
	21	22	23	24	25	26	27
	28	29	30	1	2	3	4
ĀZAR 1515	5	6	7	8	9	10	11
	12	13	14	15	16	17	18
	19	20	21	22	23	24	25
	26	27	28	29	30	1	2
DEY 1515	3	4	5	6	7	8	9
	10	11	12	13	14	15	16

‡Leap year
[a]New Year
[b]Sizdeh Bedar

HINDU LUNAR 2192/2193

Month	Sun	Mon	Tue	Wed	Thu	Fri	Sat
	28	29	30	1	2	3	4
PAUSHA 2192	5	6	7	8	9	10	11
	12	12	13	14	15	16	17
	18	**19**	21	22	23	24	25
	26	27	28	29	30	1	2
MĀGHA 2192	3	4	5	6	7	8	9
	10	11	12	13	14	15	16
	17	18	19	20	21	22	23
	24	26	27	28	29[h]	30	1
PHĀLGUNA 2192	2	3	4	4	5	6	7
	8	9	10	11	12	13	14
	15[i]	16	17	**18**	20	21	22
	23	24	25	26	27	28	29
	30	1[a]	2	3	4	5	6
CHAITRA 2193	7	8	8[b]	9	**10**	12	13
	14	15	16	17	18	19	20
	21	22	**23**	25	26	27	28
	28	29	30	1	2	3	4
VAIŚĀKHA 2193	5	6	7	8	9	10	11
	12	13	14	**15**	17	18	19
	20	21	22	23	24	25	26
	27	28	29	30	1	2	2
JYAISHṬHA 2193	3	4	5	6	**7**	9	10
	11	12	13	14	15	16	17
	18	19	**20**	22	23	23	24
	25	26	27	28	29	30	1
ĀSHĀḌHA 2193	2	3	4	5	6	7	8
	9	10	**11**	13	14	15	16
	17	18	19	20	21	22	23
	24	25	26	27	28	29	30
	30	1	2	**3**	5	6	7
ŚRĀVAṆA 2193	8	9	10	11	12	13	**14**
	16	17	18	19	20	21	21
	22	23[c]	24	25	26	27	28
	29	30	1	2	3	4[d]	5
BHĀDRAPADA 2193	6	**7**	9	10	11	12	13
	14	15	16	17	18	19	20
	21	22	23	24	25	26	26
	27	28	**29**	1	2	3	4
ĀŚVINA 2193	5	6	7	8[e]	9[e]	10[e]	**11**
	13	14	15	16	16	17	18
	19	20	21	22	23	24	25
	26	27	28	29	30	1[f]	2
KĀRTTIKA 2193	3	**4**	6	7	8	9	10
	11	12	13	14	15	16	17
	18	19	19	20	21	22	23
	24	25	26	**27**	29	30	1
MĀRGAŚIRA 2193	2	3	4	5	6	7	8
	9	10	11[g]	12	13	14	15
	16	17	18	19	20	21	22
	23	24	25	26	27	28	29
PAUSHA 2193	30	1	**2**	4	5	6	7
	8	9	10	11	12	12	13

[a]New Year (Durmukha)
[b]Birthday of Rāma
[c]Birthday of Krishna
[d]Ganēśa Chaturthī
[e]Dashara
[f]Diwali
[g]Birthday of Vishnu
[h]Night of Śiva
[i]Holi

HINDU SOLAR 2057/2058

Month	Sun	Mon	Tue	Wed	Thu	Fri	Sat
	15	16	17	18	19	20	21
PAUSHA 2057	22	23	24	25	26	27	28
	29	30	1[b]	2	3	4	5
MĀGHA 2057	6	7	8	9	10	11	12
	13	14	15	16	17	18	19
	20	21	22	23	24	25	26
	27	28	29	1	2	3	4
PHĀLGUNA 2057	5	6	7	8	9	10	11
	12	13	14	15	16	17	18
	19	20	21	22	23	24	25
	26	27	28	29	30	1	2
CHAITRA 2057	3	4	5	6	7	8	9
	10	11	12	13	14	15	16
	17	18	19	20	21	22	23
	24	25	26	27	28	29	30
VAIŚĀKHA 2058	1[a]	2	3	4	5	6	7
	8	9	10	11	12	13	14
	15	16	17	18	19	20	21
	22	23	24	25	26	27	28
	29	30	31	1	2	3	4
JYAISHṬHA 2058	5	6	7	8	9	10	11
	12	13	14	15	16	17	18
	19	20	21	22	23	24	25
	26	27	28	29	30	31	32
ĀSHĀḌHA 2058	1	2	3	4	5	6	7
	8	9	10	11	12	13	14
	15	16	17	18	19	20	21
	22	23	24	25	26	27	28
	29	30	31	1	2	3	4
ŚRĀVAṆA 2058	5	6	7	8	9	10	11
	12	13	14	15	16	17	18
	19	20	21	22	23	24	25
	26	27	28	29	30	31	32
BHĀDRAPADA 2058	1	2	3	4	5	6	7
	8	9	10	11	12	13	14
	15	16	17	18	19	20	21
	22	23	24	25	26	27	28
	29	30	31	1	2	3	4
ĀŚVINA 2058	5	6	7	8	9	10	11
	12	13	14	15	16	17	18
	19	20	21	22	23	24	25
	26	27	28	29	30	1	2
KĀRTTIKA 2058	3	4	5	6	7	8	9
	10	11	12	13	14	15	16
	17	18	19	20	21	22	23
	24	25	26	27	28	29	30
MĀRGAŚIRA 2058	1	2	3	4	5	6	7
	8	9	10	11	12	13	14
	15	16	17	18	19	20	21
	22	23	24	25	26	27	28
	29	1	2	3	4	5	6
PAUSHA 2058	7	8	9	10	11	12	13
	14	15	16	17	18	19	20

[a]New Year (Virodhakṛit)
[b]Pongal

ISLAMIC (ASTRONOMICAL) 1560‡/1561

Month	Sun	Mon	Tue	Wed	Thu	Fri	Sat
	26	27	28	29	1	2	3
DHU AL-ḤIJJA 1560	4	5	6	7	8	9	10[g]
	11	12	13	14	15	16	17
	18	19	20	21	22	23	24
	25	26	27	28	29	30	1[a]
MUHARRAM 1561	2	3	4	5	6	7	8
	9	10[b]	11	12	13	14	15
	16	17	18	19	20	21	22
	23	24	25	26	27	28	29
ṢAFAR 1561	1	2	3	4	5	6	7
	8	9	10	11	12	13	14
	15	16	17	18	19	20	21
	22	23	24	25	26	27	28
	29	30	1	2	3	4	5
RABĪʿ I 1561	6	7	8	9	10	11	12[c]
	13	14	15	16	17	18	19
	20	21	22	23	24	25	26
	27	28	29	30	1	2	3
RABĪʿ II 1561	4	5	6	7	8	9	10
	11	12	13	14	15	16	17
	18	19	20	21	22	23	24
	25	26	27	28	29	1	2
JUMĀDĀ I 1561	3	4	5	6	7	8	9
	10	11	12	13	14	15	16
	17	18	19	20	21	22	23
	24	25	26	27	28	29	30
JUMĀDĀ II 1561	1	2	3	4	5	6	7
	8	9	10	11	12	13	14
	15	16	17	18	19	20	21
	22	23	24	25	26	27	28
	29	1	2	3	4	5	6
RAJAB 1561	7	8	9	10	11	12	13
	14	15	16	17	18	19	20
	21	22	23	24	25	26	27[d]
	28	29	30	1	2	3	4
SHAʿBĀN 1561	5	6	7	8	9	10	11
	12	13	14	15	16	17	18
	19	20	21	22	23	24	25
	26	27	28	29	30	1[e]	2
RAMAḌĀN 1561	3	4	5	6	7	8	9
	10	11	12	13	14	15	16
	17	18	19	20	21	22	23
	24	25	26	27	28	29	1[f]
SHAWWĀL 1561	2	3	4	5	6	7	8
	9	10	11	12	13	14	15
	16	17	18	19	20	21	22
	23	24	25	26	27	28	29
	30	1	2	3	4	5	6
DHU AL-QAʿDA 1561	7	8	9	10	11	12	13
	14	15	16	17	18	19	20
	21	22	23	24	25	26	27
	28	29	1	2	3	4	5
DHU AL-ḤIJJA 1561	6	7	8	9	10	11	12

‡Leap year
[a]New Year
[b]ʿAshūrāʾ
[c]Prophet's Birthday
[d]Ascent of the Prophet
[e]Start of Ramaḍān
[f]ʿId al-Fiṭr
[g]ʿId al-ʾAḍḥā

GREGORIAN 2136‡

Julian† (Sun)	Sun	Mon	Tue	Wed	Thu	Fri	Sat	Month
Dec 18	1	2	3	4	5	6	7	
	8[a]	9	10	11	12	13	14	JANUARY 2136
Jan 1	15[b]	16	17	18	19	20	21	
	22	23	24	25	26	27	28	
Jan 15	29	30	31	1	2	3	4	
	5	6	7	8	9	10	11	FEBRUARY 2136
Jan 29	12	13	14	15	16	17	18	
	19	20	21	22	23	24	25	
Feb 12	26	27	28	29	1	2	3	
	4	5	6	7[c]	8	9	10	MARCH 2136
Feb 26	11[d]	12	13	14	15	16	17	
	18	19	20	21	22	23	24	
Mar 11	25	26	27	28	29	30	31	
	1	2	3	4	5	6	7	APRIL 2136
Mar 25	8	9	10	11	12	13	14	
	15	16	17	18	19	20	21	
Apr 8	22[e]	23	24	25	26	27	28	
	29	30	1	2	3	4	5	
Apr 22	6	7	8	9	10	11	12	MAY 2136
	13	14	15	16	17	18	19	
May 6	20	21	22	23	24	25	26	
	27	28	29	30	31	1	2	
May 20	3	4	5	6	7	8	9	JUNE 2136
	10	11	12	13	14	15	16	
Jun 3	17	18	19	20	21	22	23	
	24	25	26	27	28	29	30	
Jun 17	1	2	3	4	5	6	7	JULY 2136
	8	9	10	11	12	13	14	
Jul 1	15	16	17	18	19	20	21	
	22	23	24	25	26	27	28	
Jul 15	29	30	31	1	2	3	4	
	5	6	7	8	9	10	11	AUGUST 2136
Jul 29	12	13	14	15	16	17	18	
	19	20	21	22	23	24	25	
Aug 12	26	27	28	29	30	31	1	
	2	3	4	5	6	7	8	SEPTEMBER 2136
Aug 26	9	10	11	12	13	14	15	
	16	17	18	19	20	21	22	
Sep 9	23	24	25	26	27	28	29	
	30	1	2	3	4	5	6	
Sep 23	7	8	9	10	11	12	13	OCTOBER 2136
	14	15	16	17	18	19	20	
Oct 7	21	22	23	24	25	26	27	
	28	29	30	31	1	2	3	
Oct 21	4	5	6	7	8	9	10	NOVEMBER 2136
	11	12	13	14	15	16	17	
Nov 4	18	19	20	21	22	23	24	
	25	26	27	28	29	30	1	
Nov 18	2[g]	3	4	5	6	7	8	DECEMBER 2136
	9	10	11	12	13	14	15	
Dec 2	16	17	18	19	20	21	22	
	23	24	25[h]	26	27	28	29	
Dec 16	30	31	1	2	3	4	5	

‡Leap year
[a]Orthodox Christmas
[b]Julian New Year
[c]Ash Wednesday
[d]Feast of Orthodoxy
[e]Easter (also Orthodox)
[g]Advent
[h]Christmas

2137

GREGORIAN 2137 / Lunar Phases / ISO WEEK / JULIAN DAY

Month	Sun	Mon	Tue	Wed	Thu	Fri	Sat	Lunar Phases	ISO WEEK (Mon)	JULIAN DAY (Sun noon)
JANUARY 2137	◐	31	1[a]	2	3	4	5	4:27	1	2501582
	6	○	8	9	10	11	12	9:09	2	2501589
	13	14	◑	16	17	18	19	2:31	3	2501596
	20	●	22	23	24	25	26	17:27	4	2501603
FEBRUARY 2137	27	◐	29	30	31	1	2	23:22	5	2501610
	3	4	5	○	7	8	9	3:15	6	2501617
	10	11	12	◑	14	15	16	11:55	7	2501624
	17	18	19	●	21	22	23	5:22	8	2501631
MARCH 2137	24	25	26	◐	28	1	2	19:53	9	2501638
	3	4	5	6	○	8	9	19:04	10	2501645
	10	11	12	13	◑	15	16	19:10	11	2501652
	17	18	19	20[b]	●	22	23	18:21	12	2501659
	24	25	26	27	28	◐	30	16:14	13	2501666
APRIL 2137	31	1	2	3	4	5	○	7:53	14	2501673
	7	8	9	10	11	12	◑	1:31	15	2501680
	14	15	16	17	18	19	●	8:16	16	2501687
	21	22	23	24	25	26	27		17	2501694
MAY 2137	◐	29	30	1	2	3	4	10:52	18	2501701
	○	6	7	8	9	10	11	17:46	19	2501708
	◑	13	14	15	16	17	18	8:15	20	2501715
	●	20	21	22	23	24	25	22:50	21	2501722
JUNE 2137	26	27	◐	29	30	31	1	2:45	22	2501729
	2	3	○	5	6	7	8	1:29	23	2501736
	9	◑	11	12	13	14	15	16:28	24	2501743
	16	17	●	19	20	21[c]	22	13:48	25	2501750
	23	24	25	◐	27	28	29	15:23	26	2501757
JULY 2137	30	1	2	○	4	5	6	8:11	27	2501764
	7	8	9	◑	11	12	13	2:55	28	2501771
	14	15	16	17	●	19	20	4:56	29	2501778
	21	22	23	24	25	◐	27	0:54	30	2501785
AUGUST 2137	28	29	30	31	○	2	3	15:04	31	2501792
	4	5	6	7	◑	9	10	16:02	32	2501799
	11	12	13	14	15	●	17	19:51	33	2501806
	18	19	20	21	22	23	◐	8:02	34	2501813
	25	26	27	28	29	○	31	23:14	35	2501820
SEPTEMBER 2137	1	2	3	4	5	6	◑	8:00	36	2501827
	8	9	10	11	12	13	14		37	2501834
	●	16	17	18	19	20	21	10:02	38	2501841
	◐[d]	23	24	25	26	27	28	13:58	39	2501848
OCTOBER 2137	○	30	1	2	3	4	5	9:30	40	2501855
	6	◑	8	9	10	11	12	2:33	41	2501862
	13	●	15	16	17	18	19	23:06	42	2501869
	20	◐	22	23	24	25	26	20:04	43	2501876
NOVEMBER 2137	27	○	29	30	31	1	2	22:23	44	2501883
	3	4	◑	6	7	8	9	22:45	45	2501890
	10	11	12	●	14	15	16	11:01	46	2501897
	17	18	19	◐	21	22	23	3:38	47	2501904
	24	25	26	○	28	29	30	14:04	48	2501911
DECEMBER 2137	1	2	3	4	◑	6	7	18:54	49	2501918
	8	9	10	11	●	13	14	22:08	50	2501925
	15	16	17	18	◐	20	21[e]	13:40	51	2501932
	22	23	24	25	26	○	28	8:15	52	2501939
	29	30	31	1	2	3	◑	13:03	1	2501946

HEBREW 5897/5898‡

ISO WEEK	Month	Sun	Mon	Tue	Wed	Thu	Fri	Sat	Molad
1	TEVETH 5897	6	7	8	9	10	11	12	
2		13	14	15	16	17	18	19	
3		20	21	22	23	24	25	26	Tue 3h14m16p
4		27	28	29	1	2	3	4	
5	SHEVAT 5897	5	6	7	8	9	10	11	
6		12	13	14	15	16	17	18	
7		19	20	21	22	23	24	25	Wed 15h58m17p
8		26	27	28	29	30	1	2	
9	ADAR 5897	3	4	5	6	7	8	9	
10		10	11	12	13	14[f]	15	16	
11		17	18	19	20	21	22	23	
12		24	25	26	27	28	29	1	Fri 4h43m0p
13	NISAN 5897	2	3	4	5	6	7	8	
14		9	10	11	12	13	14	15[g]	
15		16	17	18	19	20	21	22	
16		23	24	25	26	27	28	29	Sat 17h27m1p
17		30	1	2	3	4	5	6	
18	IYYAR 5897	7	8	9	10	11	12	13	
19		14	15	16	17	18	19	20	
20		21	22	23	24	25	26	27	
21		28	29	1	2	3	4	5	Mon 6h11m2p
22	SIVAN 5897	6[h]	7	8	9	10	11	12	
23		13	14	15	16	17	18	19	
24		20	21	22	23	24	25	26	
25		27	28	29	30	1	2	3	Tue 18h55m3p
26	TAMMUZ 5897	4	5	6	7	8	9	10	
27		11	12	13	14	15	16	17	
28		18	19	20	21	22	23	24	
29		25	26	27	28	29	1	2	Thu 7h39m4p
30	AV 5897	3	4	5	6	7	8	9	
31		10[i]	11	12	13	14	15	16	
32		17	18	19	20	21	22	23	
33		24	25	26	27	28	29	30	Fri 20h23m5p
34	ELUL 5897	1	2	3	4	5	6	7	
35		8	9	10	11	12	13	14	
36		15	16	17	18	19	20	21	
37		22	23	24	25	26	27	28	
38		29	1[a]	2[a]	3	4	5	6	Sun 9h7m6p
39	TISHRI 5898	7	8	9	10[b]	11	12	13	
40		14	15[c]	16	17	18	19	20	
41		21	22	23	24	25	26	27	
42		28	29	30	1	2	3	4	Mon 21h51m7p
43	HESHVAN 5898	5	6	7	8	9	10	11	
44		12	13	14	15	16	17	18	
45		19	20	21	22	23	24	25	
46		26	27	28	29	1	2	3	Wed 10h35m8p
47	KISLEV 5898	4	5	6	7	8	9	10	
48		11	12	13	14	15	16	17	
49		18	19	20	21	22	23[d]	24	
50		25[e]	26[e]	27[e]	28[e]	29[e]	1[e]	2[e]	Thu 23h19m9p
51	TEVETH 5898	3[e]	4	5	6	7	8	9	
52		10	11	12	13	14	15	16	
1		17	18	19	20	21	22	23	

CHINESE Bǐng-Shēn/Dīng-Yǒu‡

ISO WEEK	Month	Sun	Mon	Tue	Wed	Thu	Fri	Sat	Solar Term
1	MONTH 12 Bǐng-Shēn	8	9	10	11	12	13	14	Xiǎo hán
2		15	16	17*	18	19	20	21	
3		22	23	24	25	26	27	28	
4	MONTH 1 Dīng-Yǒu	29	30	1[a]	2	3	4	5	Dà hán
5		6	7	8	9	10	11	12	
6		13	14	15[b]	16	17	18	19	Lì chūn
7		20	21	22	23	24	25	26	
8	MONTH 2 Dīng-Yǒu	27	28	29	1	2	3	4	Yǔ shuǐ
9		5	6	7	8	9	10	11	
10		12	13	14	15	16	17	18*	Jīng zhé
11		19	20	21	22	23	24	25	
12	LEAP MONTH 2 Dīng-Yǒu	26	27	28	29	30	1	2	Chūn fēn
13		3	4	5	6	7	8	9	
14		10	11	12	13	14[c]	15	16	Qīng míng
15		17	18	19	20	21	22	23	
16	MONTH 3 Dīng-Yǒu	24	25	26	27	28	29	1	Gǔ yǔ
17		2	3	4	5	6	7	8	
18		9	10	11	12	13	14	15	
19		16	17	18	19*	20	21	22	Lì xià
20		23	24	25	26	27	28	29	
21	MONTH 4 Dīng-Yǒu	30	1	2	3	4	5	6	Xiǎo mǎn
22		7	8	9	10	11	12	13	
23		14	15	16	17	18	19	20	Máng zhòng
24		21	22	23	24	25	26	27	
25	MONTH 5 Dīng-Yǒu	28	29	1	2	3	4	5[d]	Xià zhì
26		6	7	8	9	10	11	12	
27		13	14	15	16	17	18	19	
28		20*	21	22	23	24	25	26	Xiǎo shǔ
29	MONTH 6 Dīng-Yǒu	27	28	29	30	1	2	3	
30		4	5	6	7	8	9	10	Dà shǔ
31		11	12	13	14	15	16	17	
32		18	19	20	21	22	23	24	Lì qiū
33	MONTH 7 Dīng-Yǒu	25	26	27	28	29	30	1	
34		2	3	4	5	6	7[e]	8	Chǔ shǔ
35		9	10	11	12	13	14	15[f]	
36		16	17	18	19	20*	21	22	Bái lù
37		23	24	25	26	27	28	29	
38	MONTH 8 Dīng-Yǒu	1	2	3	4	5	6	7	
39		8	9	10	11	12	13	14	Qiū fēn
40		15[g]	16	17	18	19	20	21	
41		22	23	24	25	26	27	28	Hán lù
42	MONTH 9 Dīng-Yǒu	29	30	1	2	3	4	5	
43		6	7	8	9[h]	10	11	12	Shuāng jiàng
44		13	14	15	16	17	18	19	
45		20	21*	22	23	24	25	26	Lì dōng
46	MONTH 10 Dīng-Yǒu	27	28	29	1	2	3	4	
47		5	6	7	8	9	10	11	Xiǎo xuě
48		12	13	14	15	16	17	18	
49		19	20	21	22	23	24	25	Dà xuě
50	MONTH 11 Dīng-Yǒu	26	27	28	29	30	1	2	
51		3	4	5	6	7	8	9	
52		10[i]	11	12	13	14	15	16	Dōng zhì
1		17	18	19	20	21	22	23	

COPTIC 1853/1854 — ETHIOPIC 2129/2130

ISO WEEK	Coptic Month	Sun	Mon	Tue	Wed	Thu	Fri	Sat	Ethiopic Month
1	KOIAK 1853	20	21	22	23	24	25	26	TĀKHŚĀŚ 2129
2	TŌBE 1853	27	28	29[c]	30	1	2	3	ṬER 2129
3		4	5	6[d]	7	8	9	10	
4		11[e]	12	13	14	15	16	17	
5		18	19	20	21	22	23	24	
6	MESHIR 1853	25	26	27	28	29	30	1	YAKĀTIT 2129
7		2	3	4	5	6	7	8	
8		9	10	11	12	13	14	15	
9		16	17	18	19	20	21	22	
10		23	24	25	26	27	28	29	
11	PAREMOTEP 1853	30	1	2	3	4	5	6	MAGĀBIT 2129
12		7	8	9	10	11	12	13	
13		14	15	16	17	18	19	20	
14		21	22	23	24	25	26	27	
15	PARMOUTE 1853	28	29	30	1	2	3	4	MIYĀZYĀ 2129
16		5[f]	6	7	8	9	10	11	
17		12	13	14	15	16	17	18	
18		19	20	21	22	23	24	25	
19	PASHONS 1853	26	27	28	29[g]	30	1	2	GENBOT 2129
20		3	4	5	6	7	8	9	
21		10	11	12	13	14	15	16	
22		17	18	19	20	21	22	23	
23		24	25	26	27	28	29	30	
24	PAŌNE 1853	1	2	3	4	5	6	7	SANĒ 2129
25		8	9	10	11	12	13	14	
26		15	16	17	18	19	20	21	
27		22	23	24	25	26	27	28	
28	EPĒP 1853	29	30	1	2	3	4	5	ḤAMLĒ 2129
29		6	7	8	9	10	11	12	
30		13	14	15	16	17	18	19	
31		20	21	22	23	24	25	26	
32	MESORĒ 1853	27	28	29	30	1	2	3	NAḤASĒ 2129
33		4	5	6	7	8	9	10	
34		11	12	13[h]	14	15	16	17	
35		18	19	20	21	22	23	24	
36	EPAG. 1853	25	26	27	28	29	30	1	PĀG. 2129
37	THOOUT 1854	2	3	4	5	1[a]	2	3	MASKARAM 2130
38		4	5	6	7	8	9	10	
39		11	12	13	14	15	16	17[b]	
40		18	19	20	21	22	23	24	
41	PAOPE 1854	25	26	27	28	29	30	1	ṬEQEMT 2130
42		2	3	4	5	6	7	8	
43		9	10	11	12	13	14	15	
44		16	17	18	19	20	21	22	
45		23	24	25	26	27	28	29	
46	ATHŌR 1854	30	1	2	3	4	5	6	ḪEDĀR 2130
47		7	8	9	10	11	12	13	
48		14	15	16	17	18	19	20	
49		21	22	23	24	25	26	27	
50	KOIAK 1854	28	29	30	1	2	3	4	TĀKHŚĀŚ 2130
51		5	6	7	8	9	10	11	
52		12	13	14	15	16	17	18	
1		19	20	21	22	23	24	25	

Gregorian notes:
[a]New Year
[b]Spring (12:19)
[c]Summer (3:59)
[d]Autumn (20:46)
[e]Winter (19:21)
● New moon
◐ First quarter moon
○ Full moon
◑ Last quarter moon

Hebrew notes:
‡Leap year
[a]New Year
[b]Yom Kippur
[c]Sukkot
[d]Winter starts
[e]Ḥanukkah
[f]Purim
[g]Passover
[h]Shavuot
[i]Fast of Av

Chinese notes:
‡Leap year
[a]New Year (4835, Fowl)
[b]Lantern Festival
[c]Qīngmíng
[d]Dragon Festival
[e]Qīqiǎo
[f]Hungry Ghosts
[g]Mid-Autumn Festival
[h]Double-Ninth Festival
[i]Dōngzhì
*Start of 60-name cycle

Coptic/Ethiopic notes:
[a]New Year
[b]Building of the Cross
[c]Christmas
[d]Jesus's Circumcision
[e]Epiphany
[f]Easter
[g]Mary's Announcement
[h]Jesus's Transfiguration

PERSIAN (ASTRONOMICAL) 1515‡/1516

Month	Sun	Mon	Tue	Wed	Thu	Fri	Sat
DEY 1515	10	11	12	13	14	15	16
	17	18	19	20	21	22	23
	24	25	26	27	28	29	30
BAHMAN 1515	1	2	3	4	5	6	7
	8	9	10	11	12	13	14
	15	16	17	18	19	20	21
	22	23	24	25	26	27	28
	29	30	1	2	3	4	5
ESFAND 1515	6	7	8	9	10	11	12
	13	14	15	16	17	18	19
	20	21	22	23	24	25	26
	27	28	29	30	1[a]	2	3
FARVARDĪN 1516	4	5	6	7	8	9	10
	11	12	13[b]	14	15	16	17
	18	19	20	21	22	23	24
	25	26	27	28	29	30	31
ORDĪBEHEŠT 1516	1	2	3	4	5	6	7
	8	9	10	11	12	13	14
	15	16	17	18	19	20	21
	22	23	24	25	26	27	28
	29	30	31	1	2	3	4
XORDĀD 1516	5	6	7	8	9	10	11
	12	13	14	15	16	17	18
	19	20	21	22	23	24	25
	26	27	28	29	30	31	1
TĪR 1516	2	3	4	5	6	7	8
	9	10	11	12	13	14	15
	16	17	18	19	20	21	22
	23	24	25	26	27	28	29
	30	31	1	2	3	4	5
MORDĀD 1516	6	7	8	9	10	11	12
	13	14	15	16	17	18	19
	20	21	22	23	24	25	26
	27	28	29	30	31	1	2
SHAHRĪVAR 1516	3	4	5	6	7	8	9
	10	11	12	13	14	15	16
	17	18	19	20	21	22	23
	24	25	26	27	28	29	30
	31	1	2	3	4	5	6
MEHR 1516	7	8	9	10	11	12	13
	14	15	16	17	18	19	20
	21	22	23	24	25	26	27
	28	29	30	1	2	3	4
ĀBĀN 1516	5	6	7	8	9	10	11
	12	13	14	15	16	17	18
	19	20	21	22	23	24	25
	26	27	28	29	30	1	2
ĀZAR 1516	3	4	5	6	7	8	9
	10	11	12	13	14	15	16
	17	18	19	20	21	22	23
	24	25	26	27	28	29	30
DEY 1516	1	2	3	4	5	6	7
	8	9	10	11	12	13	14

‡Leap year
[a]New Year
[b]Sizdeh Bedar

HINDU LUNAR 2193/2194‡

Month	Sun	Mon	Tue	Wed	Thu	Fri	Sat
PAUSHA 2193	8	9	10	11	12	12	13
	14	15	16	17	18	19	20
	21	22	23	24	25	**26**	28
	29	30	1	2	3	4	5
MĀGHA 2193	6	7	8	9	10	11	12
	13	14	14	15	16	17	18
	19	**20**	22	23	24	25	26
	27	28[h]	29	30	1	2	3
PHĀLGUNA 2193	4	5	6	7	8	9	10
	11	12	13	14	15[i]	16	17
	18	19	20	21	22	23	24
	25	27	28	29	30	1[a]	2
CHAITRA 2194	3	4	5	6	7	7	8[b]
	9	10	11	12	13	14	15
	16	17	18	**19**	21	22	23
	24	25	26	27	28	29	30
VAIŚĀKHA 2194	1	2	3	4	5	6	7
	8	9	10	11	12	13	14
	15	16	17	18	19	20	21
	22	24	25	26	27	28	29
	30	1	2	2	3	4	5
JYAISHTHA 2194	6	7	8	9	10	11	12
	13	14	**15**	17	18	19	20
	21	22	23	24	25	26	27
	28	29	30	1	2	3	4
LEAP ĀSHĀDHA 2194	5	6	7	8	9	10	11
	12	13	14	15	16	17	**18**
	20	21	22	23	24	25	26
	27	28	29	29	30	1	2
ĀSHĀDHA 2194	3	4	5	6	7	8	9
	10	**11**	13	14	15	16	17
	18	19	20	21	22	23	24
	25	26	27	28	29	30	1
ŚRĀVAṆA 2194	2	3	4	5	6	7	8
	9	10	11	12	13	**14**	16
	17	18	19	20	21	22	23[c]
	24	25	25	26	27	28	29
	30	1	2	3	4[d]	5	6
BHĀDRAPADA 2194	7	9	10	11	12	13	14
	15	16	17	18	19	20	21
	22	23	24	25	26	27	28
	29	30	1	2	3	4	5
ĀŚVINA 2194	6	7	8[e]	9[e]	10[e]	**11**	13
	14	15	16	17	18	19	20
	20	21	22	23	24	25	26
	27	28	29	30	1[f]	2	3
KĀRTTIKA 2194	4	**5**	7	8	9	10	11
	12	13	14	15	16	17	18
	19	20	21	22	22	23	24
	25	26	27	**28**	30	1	2
MĀRGAŚIRA 2194	3	4	5	6	7	8	9
	10	11[g]	12	13	14	15	16
	17	18	19	20	21	22	23

‡Leap year
[a]New Year (Hemalamba)
[b]Birthday of Rāma
[c]Birthday of Krishna
[d]Ganēśa Chaturthī
[e]Dashara
[f]Diwali
[g]Birthday of Vishnu
[h]Night of Śiva
[i]Holi

HINDU SOLAR 2058/2059‡

Month	Sun	Mon	Tue	Wed	Thu	Fri	Sat
PAUSHA 2058	14	15	16	17	18	19	20
	21	22	23	24	25	26	27
	28	29	30	1[b]	2	3	4
MĀGHA 2058	5	6	7	8	9	10	11
	12	13	14	15	16	17	18
	19	20	21	22	23	24	25
	26	27	28	29	1	2	3
PHĀLGUNA 2058	4	5	6	7	8	9	10
	11	12	13	14	15	16	17
	18	19	20	21	22	23	24
	25	26	27	28	29	30	1
CHAITRA 2058	2	3	4	5	6	7	8
	9	10	11	12	13	14	15
	16	17	18	19	20	21	22
	23	24	25	26	27	28	29
	30	1[a]	2	3	4	5	6
VAIŚĀKHA 2059	7	8	9	10	11	12	13
	14	15	16	17	18	19	20
	21	22	23	24	25	26	27
	28	29	30	31	1	2	3
JYAISHTHA 2059	4	5	6	7	8	9	10
	11	12	13	14	15	16	17
	18	19	20	21	22	23	24
	25	26	27	28	29	30	31
	32	1	2	3	4	5	6
ĀSHĀDHA 2059	7	8	9	10	11	12	13
	14	15	16	17	18	19	20
	21	22	23	24	25	26	27
	28	29	30	31	1	2	3
ŚRĀVAṆA 2059	4	5	6	7	8	9	10
	11	12	13	14	15	16	17
	18	19	20	21	22	23	24
	25	26	27	28	29	30	31
	32	1	2	3	4	5	6
BHĀDRAPADA 2059	7	8	9	10	11	12	13
	14	15	16	17	18	19	20
	21	22	23	24	25	26	27
	28	29	30	31	1	2	3
ĀŚVINA 2059	4	5	6	7	8	9	10
	11	12	13	14	15	16	17
	18	19	20	21	22	23	24
	25	26	27	28	29	30	1
KĀRTTIKA 2059	2	3	4	5	6	7	8
	9	10	11	12	13	14	15
	16	17	18	19	20	21	22
	23	24	25	26	27	28	29
	30	1	2	3	4	5	6
MĀRGAŚĪRA 2059	7	8	9	10	11	12	13
	14	15	16	17	18	19	20
	21	22	23	24	25	26	27
	28	29	30	1	2	3	4
PAUSHA 2059	5	6	7	8	9	10	11
	12	13	14	15	16	17	18

‡Leap year
[a]New Year (Paridhāvin)
[b]Pongal

ISLAMIC (ASTRONOMICAL) 1561/1562‡

Month	Sun	Mon	Tue	Wed	Thu	Fri	Sat
DHU AL-HIJJA 1561	6	7	8	9	10[g]	11	12
	13	14	15	16	17	18	19
	20	21	22	23	24	25	26
	27	28	29	1[a]	2	3	4
MUHARRAM 1562	5	6	7	8	9	10[b]	11
	12	13	14	15	16	17	18
	19	20	21	22	23	24	25
	26	27	28	29	1	2	3
ṢAFAR 1562	4	5	6	7	8	9	10
	11	12	13	14	15	16	17
	18	19	20	21	22	23	24
	25	26	27	28	29	30	1
RABĪʿ I 1562	2	3	4	5	6	7	8
	9	10	11	12[c]	13	14	15
	16	17	18	19	20	21	22
	23	24	25	26	27	28	29
	30	1	2	3	4	5	6
RABĪʿ II 1562	7	8	9	10	11	12	13
	14	15	16	17	18	19	20
	21	22	23	24	25	26	27
	28	29	1	2	3	4	5
JUMĀDĀ I 1562	6	7	8	9	10	11	12
	13	14	15	16	17	18	19
	20	21	22	23	24	25	26
	27	28	29	30	1	2	3
JUMĀDĀ II 1562	4	5	6	7	8	9	10
	11	12	13	14	15	16	17
	18	19	20	21	22	23	24
	25	26	27	28	29	1	2
RAJAB 1562	3	4	5	6	7	8	9
	10	11	12	13	14	15	16
	17	18	19	20	21	22	23
	24	25	26	27[d]	28	29	30
	31	1	2	3	4	5	6
SHAʿBĀN 1562	7	8	9	10	11	12	13
	14	15	16	17	18	19	20
	21	22	23	24	25	26	27
	28	29	30	1[e]	2	3	4
RAMAḌĀN 1562	5	6	7	8	9	10	11
	12	13	14	15	16	17	18
	19	20	21	22	23	24	25
	26	27	28	29	1[f]	2	3
SHAWWĀL 1562	4	5	6	7	8	9	10
	11	12	13	14	15	16	17
	18	19	20	21	22	23	24
	25	26	27	28	29	1	2
DHU AL-QAʿDA 1562	3	4	5	6	7	8	9
	10	11	12	13	14	15	16
	17	18	19	20	21	22	23
	24	25	26	27	28	29	1
DHU AL-HIJJA 1562	2	3	4	5	6	7	8
	9	10[g]	11	12	13	14	15
	16	17	18	19	20	21	22

‡Leap year
[a]New Year
[b]ʿAshūrāʾ
[c]Prophet's Birthday
[d]Ascent of the Prophet
[e]Start of Ramaḍān
[f]ʿĪd al-Fiṭr
[g]ʿĪd al-ʾAḍḥā

GREGORIAN 2137

Julian (Sun)	Sun	Mon	Tue	Wed	Thu	Fri	Sat	Month
Dec 16	30	31	1	2	3	4	5	JANUARY 2137
	6	7	8[a]	9	10	11	12	
Dec 30	13	14	15[b]	16	17	18	19	
	20	21	22	23	24	25	26	
Jan 13	27	28	29	30	31	1	2	FEBRUARY 2137
	3	4	5	6	7	8	9	
Jan 27	10	11	12	13	14	15	16	
	17	18	19	20[c]	21	22	23	
Feb 10	24	25	26	27	28	1	2	MARCH 2137
	3[d]	4	5	6	7	8	9	
Feb 24	10	11	12	13	14	15	16	
	17	18	19	20	21	22	23	
Mar 10	24	25	26	27	28	29	30	
	31	1	2	3	4	5	6	APRIL 2137
Mar 24	7[e]	8	9	10	11	12	13	
	14[f]	15	16	17	18	19	20	
Apr 7	21	22	23	24	25	26	27	
	28	29	30	1	2	3	4	MAY 2137
Apr 21	5	6	7	8	9	10	11	
	12	13	14	15	16	17	18	
May 5	19	20	21	22	23	24	25	
	26	27	28	29	30	31	1	JUNE 2137
May 19	2	3	4	5	6	7	8	
	9	10	11	12	13	14	15	
Jun 2	16	17	18	19	20	21	22	
	23	24	25	26	27	28	29	
Jun 16	30	1	2	3	4	5	6	JULY 2137
	7	8	9	10	11	12	13	
Jun 30	14	15	16	17	18	19	20	
	21	22	23	24	25	26	27	
Jul 14	28	29	30	31	1	2	3	AUGUST 2137
	4	5	6	7	8	9	10	
Jul 28	11	12	13	14	15	16	17	
	18	19	20	21	22	23	24	
Aug 11	25	26	27	28	29	30	31	
	1	2	3	4	5	6	7	SEPTEMBER 2137
Aug 25	8	9	10	11	12	13	14	
	15	16	17	18	19	20	21	
Sep 8	22	23	24	25	26	27	28	
	29	30	1	2	3	4	5	OCTOBER 2137
Sep 22	6	7	8	9	10	11	12	
	13	14	15	16	17	18	19	
Oct 6	20	21	22	23	24	25	26	
	27	28	29	30	31	1	2	NOVEMBER 2137
Oct 20	3	4	5	6	7	8	9	
	10	11	12	13	14	15	16	
Nov 3	17	18	19	20	21	22	23	
	24	25	26	27	28	29	30	
Nov 17	1[g]	2	3	4	5	6	7	DECEMBER 2137
	8	9	10	11	12	13	14	
Dec 1	15	16	17	18	19	20	21	
	22	23	24	25[h]	26	27	28	
Dec 15	29	30	31	1	2	3	4	

[a]Orthodox Christmas
[b]Julian New Year
[c]Ash Wednesday
[d]Feast of Orthodoxy
[e]Easter
[f]Orthodox Easter
[g]Advent
[h]Christmas

2138

	GREGORIAN 2138							Lunar Phases	ISO WEEK	JULIAN DAY		HEBREW 5898‡/5899							Molad		CHINESE Dīng-Yǒu‡/Wù-Xū							Solar Term		COPTIC 1854/1855‡ ETHIOPIC 2130/2131‡							
	Sun	Mon	Tue	Wed	Thu	Fri	Sat		(Mon)	(Sun noon)		Sun	Mon	Tue	Wed	Thu	Fri	Sat			Sun	Mon	Tue	Wed	Thu	Fri	Sat			Sun	Mon	Tue	Wed	Thu	Fri	Sat	
JANUARY 2138	29	30	31	1[a]	2	3	◑	13:03	1	2501946	TEVETH 5898	17	18	19	20	21	22	23		MONTH 11 Dīng-Yǒu	17	18	19	20	21	22*	23		KOIAK 1854	19	20	21	22	23	24	25	TĀKHŚĀŚ 2130
	5	6	7	8	9	10	●	8:56	2	2501953		24	25	26	27	28	29	1	Sat 12h 3m 10p		24	25	26	27	28	29	1	Xiǎo hán		26	27	28	29[c]	30	1	2	
	12	13	14	15	16	17	◐	2:35	3	2501960	SHEVAT 5898	2	3	4	5	6	7	8		MONTH 12 Dīng-Yǒu	2	3	4	5	6	7	8		TŌBE 1854	3	4	5	6[d]	7	8	9	ṬER 2130
	19	20	21	22	23	24	25		4	2501967		9	10	11	12	13	14	15			9	**10**	11	12	13	14	15	Dà hán		10	11[e]	12	13	14	15	16	
	○	27	28	29	30	31	1	3:53	5	2501974		16	17	18	19	20	21	22			16	17	18	19	20	21	22			17	18	19	20	21	22	23	
FEBRUARY 2138	2	◑	4	5	6	7	8	3:47	6	2501981		23	24	25	26	27	28	29			23	24	25	26	27	28	29			24	25	26	27	28	29	30	
	●	10	11	12	13	14	15	19:39	7	2501988	ADAR I 5898	30	1	2	3	4	5	6	Mon 0h 47m 11p		30	1[a]	2	3	4	5	6	Lì chūn	MESHIR 1854	1	2	3	4	5	6	7	YAKĀTIT 2130
	◐	17	18	19	20	21	22	18:17	8	2501995		7	8	9	10	11	12	13		MONTH 1 Wù-Xū	7	8	9	**10**	11	12	13	Yǔ shuǐ		8	9	10	11	12	13	14	
	23	○	25	26	27	28	1	23:08	9	2502002		14	15	16	17	18	19	20			14	15[b]	16	17	18	19	20			15	16	17	18	19	20	21	
MARCH 2138	2	3	◑	5	6	7	8	14:49	10	2502009		21	22	23	24	25	26	27			21	22	23*	24	25	26	27	Jīng zhé		22	23	24	25	26	27	28	
	9	10	●	12	13	14	15	6:20	11	2502016		28	29	30	1	2	3	4	Tue 13h 31m 12p		28	29	1	2	3	4	5		PAREMOTEP 1854	29	30	1	2	3	4	5	MAGĀBIT 2130
	16	17	◐	19	20[b]	21	22	12:08	12	2502023	ADAR II 5898	5	6	7	8	9	10	11		MONTH 2 Wù-Xū	6	7	8	9	10	***11***	12	Chūn fēn		6	7	8	9	10	11	12	
	23	24	25	○	27	28	29	16:08	13	2502030		12	13	14[f]	15	16	17	18			13	14	15	16	17	18	19			13	14	15	16	17	18	19	
	30	31	1	◑	3	4	5	22:48	14	2502037		19	20	21	22	23	24	25			20	21	22	23	24	25	26[c]	Qīng míng		20	21	22	23	24	25	26	
APRIL 2138	6	7	8	●	10	11	12	17:03	15	2502044		26	27	28	29	1	2	3	Thu 2h 15m 13p		27	28	29	30	1	2	3			27	28	29	30	1	2	3	
	13	14	15	16	◐	18	19	7:08	16	2502051	NISAN 5898	4	5	6	7	8	9	10		MONTH 3 Wù-Xū	4	5	6	7	8	9	10		PARMOUTE 1854	4	5	6	7	8	9	10	MIYĀZYĀ 2130
	20	21	22	23	24	○	26	5:52	17	2502058		11	12	13	14	15[g]	16	17			***11***	12	13	14	15	16	17	Gǔ yǔ		11	12	13	14	15	16	17	
	27	28	29	30	1	◑	3	4:52	18	2502065		18	19	20	21	22	23	24			18	19	20	21	22	23	24*			18	19	20	21	22	23	24	
MAY 2138	4	5	6	7	8	●	10	4:08	19	2502072		25	26	27	28	29	30	1	Fri 14h 59m 14p		25	26	27	28	29	1	2	Lì xià		25[f]	26	27	28	29[g]	30	1	
	11	12	13	14	15	16	◐	1:57	20	2502079	IYAR 5898	2	3	4	5	6	7	8		MONTH 4 Wù-Xū	3	4	5	6	7	8	9		PASHONS 1854	2	3	4	5	6	7	8	GENBOT 2130
	18	19	20	21	22	23	○	16:31	21	2502086		9	10	11	12	13	14	15			10	11	12	**13**	14	15	16	Xiǎo mǎn		9	10	11	12	13	14	15	
	25	26	27	28	29	30	◑	10:13	22	2502093		16	17	18	19	20	21	22			17	18	19	20	21	22	23			16	17	18	19	20	21	22	
	1	2	3	4	5	6	●	16:11	23	2502100		23	24	25	26	27	28	29			24	25	26	27	28	29	30	Máng zhòng		23	24	25	26	27	28	29	
JUNE 2138	8	9	10	11	12	13	14		24	2502107		1	2	3	4	5	6[h]	7	Sun 3h 43m 15p		1	2	3	4	5[d]	6	7			30	1	2	3	4	5	6	
	◐	16	17	18	19	20	21[c]	19:14	25	2502114	SIVAN 5898	8	9	10	11	12	13	14		MONTH 5 Wù-Xū	8	9	10	11	12	13	**14**	Xià zhì	PAŌNE 1854	7	8	9	10	11	12	13	SANĒ 2130
	22	○	24	25	26	27	28	0:58	26	2502121		15	16	17	18	19	20	21			15	16	17	18	19	20	21			14	15	16	17	18	19	20	
	◑	30	1	2	3	4	5	16:06	27	2502128		22	23	24	25	26	27	28			22	23	24	25*	26	27	28			21	22	23	24	25	26	27	
JULY 2138	6	●	8	9	10	11	12	5:44	28	2502135		29	30	1	2	3	4	5	Mon 16h 27m 16p		29	*1*	2	3	4	5	6	Xiǎo shǔ		28	29	30	1	2	3	4	
	13	14	◐	16	17	18	19	10:06	29	2502142	TAMMUZ 5898	6	7	8	9	10	11	12		MONTH 6 Wù-Xū	7	8	9	10	11	12	13		EPĒP 1854	5	6	7	8	9	10	11	ḤAMLĒ 2130
	20	21	○	23	24	25	26	8:20	30	2502149		13	14	15	16	17	18	19			14	15	16	**17**	18	19	20	Dà shǔ		12	13	14	15	16	17	18	
	27	◑	29	30	31	1	2	23:41	31	2502156		20	21	22	23	24	25	26			21	22	23	24	25	26	27			19	20	21	22	23	24	25	
AUGUST 2138	3	4	●	6	7	8	9	20:51	32	2502163		27	28	29	1	2	3	4	Wed 5h 11m 17p		28	29	30	1	2	3	4	Lì qiū		26	27	28	29	30	1	2	
	10	11	12	◐	14	15	16	22:20	33	2502170	AV 5898	5	6	7	8	9[i]	10	11		MONTH 7 Wù-Xū	5	6	7[e]	8	9	10	11		MESORĒ 1854	3	4	5	6	7	8	9	NAHASĒ 2130
	17	18	19	○	21	22	23	15:36	34	2502177		12	13	14	15	16	17	18			12	13	14	15[f]	16	17	**18**	Chǔ shǔ		10	11	12	13[h]	14	15	16	
	24	25	26	◑	28	29	30	10:05	35	2502184		19	20	21	22	23	24	25			19	20	21	22	23	24	25			17	18	19	20	21	22	23	
	31	1	2	3	●	5	6	12:56	36	2502191		26	27	28	29	30	1	2	Thu 17h 56m 0p		26*	27	28	29	1	2	3			24	25	26	27	28	29	30	
SEPTEMBER 2138	7	8	9	10	11	◐	13	8:21	37	2502198	ELUL 5898	3	4	5	6	7	8	9		MONTH 8 Wù-Xū	4	5	6	7	8	9	10	Bái lù	EPAG. 1854 / THOOUT 1855	1	2	3	4	5	1[a]	2	PĀG. 2130 / MASKARAM 2131
	14	15	16	17	○	19	20	23:35	38	2502205		10	11	12	13	14	15	16			11	12	13	14	15[g]	16	17			3	4	5	6	7	8	9	
	21	22	23[d]	24	25	◑	27	0:08	39	2502212		17	18	19	20	21	22	23			18	19	**20**	21	22	23	24	Qiū fēn		10	11	12	13	14	15	16	
	28	29	30	1	2	3	●	5:03	40	2502219		24	25	26	27	28	29	1[a]	Sat 6h 40m 1p		25	26	27	28	29	30	1			17[b]	18	19	20	21	22	23	
OCTOBER 2138	5	6	7	8	9	10	◐	16:49	41	2502226	TISHRI 5899	2[a]	3	4	5	6	7	8		MONTH 9 Wù-Xū	2	3	4	5	6	7	8	Hán lù		24	25	26	27	28	29	30	
	12	13	14	15	16	17	○	8:58	42	2502233		9	10[b]	11	12	13	14	15[c]			9[h]	10	11	12	13	14	15		PAOPE 1855	1	2	3	4	5	6	7	ṬEQEMT 2131
	19	20	21	22	23	24	◑	18:03	43	2502240		16	17	18	19	20	21	22			16	17	18	19	**20**	21	22	Shuāng jiàng		8	9	10	11	12	13	14	
	26	27	28	29	30	31	1		44	2502247		23	24	25	26	27	28	29			23	24	25	26	27*	28	29			15	16	17	18	19	20	21	
NOVEMBER 2138	●	3	4	5	6	7	8	20:22	45	2502254		30	1	2	3	4	5	6	Sun 19h 24m 2p		30	1	2	3	4	5	6	Lì dōng		22	23	24	25	26	27	28	
	9	◐	11	12	13	14	15	0:31	46	2502261	HESHVAN 5899	7	8	9	10	11	12	13		MONTH 10 Wù-Xū	7	8	9	10	11	12	13		ATHŌR 1855	29	30	1	2	3	4	5	HEDĀR 2131
	○	17	18	19	20	21	22	20:29	47	2502268		14	15	16	17	18	19	20			14	15	16	17	18	19	**20**	Xiǎo xuě		6	7	8	9	10	11	12	
	23	◑	25	26	27	28	29	14:54	48	2502275		21	22	23	24	25	26	27			21	22	23	24	25	26	27			13	14	15	16	17	18	19	
DECEMBER 2138	30	1	●	3	4	5	6	10:33	49	2502282		28	29	30	1	2	3	4[d]	Tue 8h 8m 3p		28	29	1	2	3	4	5			20	21	22	23	24	25	26	
	7	8	◐	10	11	12	13	8:14	50	2502289	KISLEV 5899	5	6	7	8	9	10	11		MONTH 11* Wù-Xū	6	7	8	9	10	11	12	Dà xuě		27	28	29	30	1	2	3	
	14	15	○	17	18	19	20	10:44	51	2502296		12	13	14	15	16	17	18			13	14	15	16	17	18	19		KOIAK 1855	4	5	6	7	8	9	10	TĀKHŚĀŚ 2131
	21	22[e]	23	◑	25	26	27	12:38	52	2502303		19	20	21	22	23	24	25[e]			20	21[i]	22	23	24	25	26	Dōng zhì		11	12	13	14	15	16	17	
	28	29	30	●	1	2	3	23:37	1	2502310		26[e]	27[e]	28[e]	29[e]	30[e]	1[e]	2[e]	Wed 20h 52m 4p		27	28*	29	30	1	2	3			18	19	20	21	22	23	24	

[a]New Year
[b]Spring (18:02)
[c]Summer (9:43)
[d]Autumn (2:38)
[e]Winter (1:15)
● New moon
◐ First quarter moon
○ Full moon
◑ Last quarter moon

‡Leap year
[a]New Year
[b]Yom Kippur
[c]Sukkot
[d]Winter starts
[e]Ḥanukkah
[f]Purim
[g]Passover
[h]Shavuot
[i]Fast of Av

‡Leap year
[a]New Year (4836, Dog)
[b]Lantern Festival
[c]Qīngmíng
[d]Dragon Festival
[e]Qīqiǎo
[f]Hungry Ghosts
[g]Mid-Autumn Festival
[h]Double-Ninth Festival
[i]Dōngzhì
*Start of 60-name cycle

‡Leap year
[a]New Year
[b]Building of the Cross
[c]Christmas
[d]Jesus's Circumcision
[e]Epiphany
[f]Easter
[g]Mary's Announcement
[h]Jesus's Transfiguration

PERSIAN (ASTRONOMICAL) 1516/1517

Month	Sun	Mon	Tue	Wed	Thu	Fri	Sat
DEY 1516	8	9	10	11	12	13	14
	15	16	17	18	19	20	21
	22	23	24	25	26	27	28
BAHMAN 1516	29	30	1	2	3	4	5
	6	7	8	9	10	11	12
	13	14	15	16	17	18	19
	20	21	22	23	24	25	26
ESFAND 1516	27	28	29	30	1	2	3
	4	5	6	7	8	9	10
	11	12	13	14	15	16	17
	18	19	20	21	22	23	24
FARVARDĪN 1517	25	26	27	28	29	1[a]	2
	3	4	5	6	7	8	9
	10	11	12	13[b]	14	15	16
	17	18	19	20	21	22	23
	24	25	26	27	28	29	30
ORDĪBEHEŠT 1517	31	1	2	3	4	5	6
	7	8	9	10	11	12	13
	14	15	16	17	18	19	20
	21	22	23	24	25	26	27
XORDĀD 1517	28	29	30	31	1	2	3
	4	5	6	7	8	9	10
	11	12	13	14	15	16	17
	18	19	20	21	22	23	24
	25	26	27	28	29	30	31
TĪR 1517	1	2	3	4	5	6	7
	8	9	10	11	12	13	14
	15	16	17	18	19	20	21
	22	23	24	25	26	27	28
MORDĀD 1517	29	30	31	1	2	3	4
	5	6	7	8	9	10	11
	12	13	14	15	16	17	18
	19	20	21	22	23	24	25
SHAHRĪVAR 1517	26	27	28	29	30	31	1
	2	3	4	5	6	7	8
	9	10	11	12	13	14	15
	16	17	18	19	20	21	22
	23	24	25	26	27	28	29
MEHR 1517	30	31	1	2	3	4	5
	6	7	8	9	10	11	12
	13	14	15	16	17	18	19
	20	21	22	23	24	25	26
ĀBĀN 1517	27	28	29	30	1	2	3
	4	5	6	7	8	9	10
	11	12	13	14	15	16	17
	18	19	20	21	22	23	24
ĀZAR 1517	25	26	27	28	29	30	1
	2	3	4	5	6	7	8
	9	10	11	12	13	14	15
	16	17	18	19	20	21	22
	23	24	25	26	27	28	29
DEY 1517	30	1	2	3	4	5	6
	7	8	9	10	11	12	13

[a]New Year
[b]Sizdeh Bedar

HINDU LUNAR 2194‡/2195

Month	Sun	Mon	Tue	Wed	Thu	Fri	Sat
MĀRGAŚĪRA 2194	17	18	19	20	21	22	23
	24	25	26	27	28	29	30
	1	2	3	5	6	7	8
PAUSHA 2194	9	10	11	12	13	14	15
	15	16	17	18	19	20	21
	22	23	24	25	26	27	29
	30	1	2	3	4	5	6
MĀGHA 2194	7	8	9	10	11	12	13
	14	15	16	17	18	18	19
	20	22	23	24	25	26	27
	28[h]	29	30	1	2	3	4
PHĀLGUNA 2194	6	6	7	8	9	10	11
	12	13	14	15[i]	16	17	18
	19	20	21	22	23	24	25
	26	28	29	30	1[a]	2	3
CHAITRA 2195	4	5	6	7	8	9[b]	10
	11	11	12	13	14	15	16
	17	18	19	21	22	23	24
	25	26	27	28	29	30	1
VAIŚĀKHA 2195	2	3	4	5	6	7	8
	9	10	11	12	13	14	15
	16	17	18	19	20	21	22
	24	25	26	27	28	29	30
	1	2	3	4	5	6	6
JYAISHTHA 2195	7	8	9	10	11	12	13
	14	15	17	18	19	20	21
	22	23	24	25	26	27	28
	29	30	1	2	3	4	5
ĀSHĀDHA 2195	6	7	8	9	10	11	12
	13	14	15	16	17	18	20
	21	22	23	24	25	26	27
	28	29	30	1	2	3	3
ŚRĀVAṆA 2195	4	5	6	7	8	9	10
	11	13	14	15	16	17	18
	19	20	21	22	23[c]	24	25
	26	27	28	29	30	1	2
BHĀDRAPADA 2195	3	4[d]	5	6	7	8	9
	10	11	12	13	14	16	17
	18	19	20	21	22	23	24
	25	26	27	28	29	29	30
	1	2	3	4	5	6	7[e]
ĀŚVINA 2195	9[e]	10[e]	11	12	13	14	15
	16	17	18	19	20	21	22
	23	24	25	26	27	28	29
	30	1[f]	2	3	4	5	6
KĀRTTIKA 2195	7	8	9	10	11	13	14
	15	16	17	18	19	20	21
	22	23	23	24	25	26	27
	28	29	30	1	2	3	4
MĀRGAŚĪRA 2195	5	7	8	9	10	11[g]	12
	13	14	15	16	17	18	19
	20	21	22	23	24	25	26
	26	27	28	30	1	2	3

‡Leap year
[a]New Year (Vilamba)
[b]Birthday of Rāma
[c]Birthday of Krishna
[d]Ganēśa Chaturthī
[e]Dashara
[f]Diwali
[g]Birthday of Vishnu
[h]Night of Śiva
[i]Holi

HINDU SOLAR 2059‡/2060

Month	Sun	Mon	Tue	Wed	Thu	Fri	Sat
PAUSHA 2059	12	13	14	15	16	17	18
	19	20	21	22	23	24	25
	26	27	28	29	1[b]	2	3
MĀGHA 2059	4	5	6	7	8	9	10
	11	12	13	14	15	16	17
	18	19	20	21	22	23	24
	25	26	27	28	29	1	2
PHĀLGUNA 2059	3	4	5	6	7	8	9
	10	11	12	13	14	15	16
	17	18	19	20	21	22	23
	24	25	26	27	28	29	30
CHAITRA 2059	1	2	3	4	5	6	7
	8	9	10	11	12	13	14
	15	16	17	18	19	20	21
	22	23	24	25	26	27	28
VAIŚĀKHA 2060	29	30	31	1[a]	2	3	4
	5	6	7	8	9	10	11
	12	13	14	15	16	17	18
	19	20	21	22	23	24	25
JYAISHTHA 2060	26	27	28	29	30	31	1
	2	3	4	5	6	7	8
	9	10	11	12	13	14	15
	16	17	18	19	20	21	22
	23	24	25	26	27	28	29
ĀSHĀDHA 2060	30	31	1	2	3	4	5
	6	7	8	9	10	11	12
	13	14	15	16	17	18	19
	20	21	22	23	24	25	26
ŚRĀVAṆA 2060	27	28	29	30	31	32	1
	2	3	4	5	6	7	8
	9	10	11	12	13	14	15
	16	17	18	19	20	21	22
	23	24	25	26	27	28	29
BHĀDRAPADA 2060	30	31	1	2	3	4	5
	6	7	8	9	10	11	12
	13	14	15	16	17	18	19
	20	21	22	23	24	25	26
	27	28	29	30	31	1	2
ĀŚVINA 2060	3	4	5	6	7	8	9
	10	11	12	13	14	15	16
	17	18	19	20	21	22	23
	24	25	26	27	28	29	30
KĀRTTIKA 2060	31	1	2	3	4	5	6
	7	8	9	10	11	12	13
	14	15	16	17	18	19	20
	21	22	23	24	25	26	27
MĀRGAŚĪRA 2060	28	29	30	1	2	3	4
	5	6	7	8	9	10	11
	12	13	14	15	16	17	18
	19	20	21	22	23	24	25
PAUSHA 2060	26	27	28	29	1	2	3
	4	5	6	7	8	9	10
	11	12	13	14	15	16	17

‡Leap year
[a]New Year (Pramādin)
[b]Pongal

ISLAMIC (ASTRONOMICAL) 1562‡/1563/1564‡

Month	Sun	Mon	Tue	Wed	Thu	Fri	Sat
DHU AL-HIJJA 1562	16	17	18	19	20	21	22
	23	24	25	26	27	28	29
	30	1[a]	2	3	4	5	6
MUHARRAM 1563	7	8	9	10[b]	11	12	13
	14	15	16	17	18	19	20
	21	22	23	24	25	26	27
	28	29	1	2	3	4	5
ṢAFAR 1563	6	7	8	9	10	11	12
	13	14	15	16	17	18	19
	20	21	22	23	24	25	26
	27	28	29	1	2	3	4
RABĪ' I 1563	5	6	7	8	9	10	11
	12[c]	13	14	15	16	17	18
	19	20	21	22	23	24	25
	26	27	28	29	30	1	2
RABĪ' II 1563	3	4	5	6	7	8	9
	10	11	12	13	14	15	16
	17	18	19	20	21	22	23
	24	25	26	27	28	29	1
JUMĀDĀ I 1563	2	3	4	5	6	7	8
	9	10	11	12	13	14	15
	16	17	18	19	20	21	22
	23	24	25	26	27	28	29
	30	1	2	3	4	5	6
JUMĀDĀ II 1563	7	8	9	10	11	12	13
	14	15	16	17	18	19	20
	21	22	23	24	25	26	27
	28	29	30	1	2	3	4
RAJAB 1563	5	6	7	8	9	10	11
	12	13	14	15	16	17	18
	19	20	21	22	23	24	25
	26	27[d]	28	29	30	1	2
SHA'BĀN 1563	3	4	5	6	7	8	9
	10	11	12	13	14	15	16
	17	18	19	20	21	22	23
	24	25	26	27	28	29	30
RAMAḌĀN 1563	1[e]	2	3	4	5	6	7
	8	9	10	11	12	13	14
	15	16	17	18	19	20	21
	22	23	24	25	26	27	28
	29	30	1[f]	2	3	4	5
SHAWWĀL 1563	6	7	8	9	10	11	12
	13	14	15	16	17	18	19
	20	21	22	23	24	25	26
	27	28	29	1	2	3	4
DHU AL-QA'DA 1563	5	6	7	8	9	10	11
	12	13	14	15	16	17	18
	19	20	21	22	23	24	25
	26	27	28	29	1	2	3
DHU AL-HIJJA 1563	4	5	6	7	8	9	10[g]
	11	12	13	14	15	16	17
	18	19	20	21	22	23	24
	25	26	27	28	29	1	2

‡Leap year
[a]New Year
[b]'Ashūrā'
[c]Prophet's Birthday
[d]Ascent of the Prophet
[e]Start of Ramaḍān
[f]'Īd al-Fiṭr
[g]'Īd al-'Aḍḥā

GREGORIAN 2138

Julian (Sun)	Sun	Mon	Tue	Wed	Thu	Fri	Sat	Month
Dec 15	29	30	31	1	2	3	4	JANUARY 2138
	5	6	7	8[a]	9	10	11	
Dec 29	12	13	14	15[b]	16	17	18	
	19	20	21	22	23	24	25	
Jan 12	26	27	28	29	30	31	1	FEBRUARY 2138
	2	3	4	5	6	7	8	
Jan 26	9	10	11	12[c]	13	14	15	
	16	17	18	19	20	21	22	
Feb 9	23	24	25	26	27	28	1	MARCH 2138
	2	3	4	5	6	7	8	
Feb 23	9	10	11	12	13	14	15	
	16	17	18	19	20	21	22	
Mar 9	23[d]	24	25	26	27	28	29	
	30[e]	31	1	2	3	4	5	APRIL 2138
Mar 23	6	7	8	9	10	11	12	
	13	14	15	16	17	18	19	
Apr 6	20	21	22	23	24	25	26	
	27	28	29	30	1	2	3	MAY 2138
Apr 20	4[f]	5	6	7	8	9	10	
	11	12	13	14	15	16	17	
May 4	18	19	20	21	22	23	24	
	25	26	27	28	29	30	31	
May 18	1	2	3	4	5	6	7	JUNE 2138
	8	9	10	11	12	13	14	
Jun 1	15	16	17	18	19	20	21	
	22	23	24	25	26	27	28	
Jun 15	29	30	1	2	3	4	5	JULY 2138
	6	7	8	9	10	11	12	
Jun 29	13	14	15	16	17	18	19	
	20	21	22	23	24	25	26	
Jul 13	27	28	29	30	31	1	2	AUGUST 2138
	3	4	5	6	7	8	9	
Jul 27	10	11	12	13	14	15	16	
	17	18	19	20	21	22	23	
Aug 10	24	25	26	27	28	29	30	
	31	1	2	3	4	5	6	SEPTEMBER 2138
Aug 24	7	8	9	10	11	12	13	
	14	15	16	17	18	19	20	
Sep 7	21	22	23	24	25	26	27	
	28	29	30	1	2	3	4	OCTOBER 2138
Sep 21	5	6	7	8	9	10	11	
	12	13	14	15	16	17	18	
Oct 5	19	20	21	22	23	24	25	
	26	27	28	29	30	31	1	NOVEMBER 2138
Oct 19	2	3	4	5	6	7	8	
	9	10	11	12	13	14	15	
Nov 2	16	17	18	19	20	21	22	
	23	24	25	26	27	28	29	
Nov 16	30[g]	1	2	3	4	5	6	DECEMBER 2138
	7	8	9	10	11	12	13	
Nov 30	14	15	16	17	18	19	20	
	21	22	23	24	25[h]	26	27	
Dec 14	28	29	30	31	1	2	3	

[a]Orthodox Christmas
[b]Julian New Year
[c]Ash Wednesday
[d]Feast of Orthodoxy
[e]Easter
[f]Orthodox Easter
[g]Advent
[h]Christmas

2139

Gregorian 2139	Sun	Mon	Tue	Wed	Thu	Fri	Sat	Lunar Phases	ISO Week (Mon)	Julian Day (Sun noon)
January 2139	28	29	30	●	1[a]	2	3	23:37	1	2502310
	4	5	6	◐	8	9	10	16:46	2	2502317
	11	12	13	14	○	16	17	3:44	3	2502324
	18	19	20	21	22	◑	24	8:58	4	2502331
	25	26	27	28	29	●	31	11:32	5	2502338
February 2139	1	2	3	4	5	◐	7	2:54	6	2502345
	8	9	10	11	12	○	14	22:35	7	2502352
	15	16	17	18	19	20	21		8	2502359
	◑	23	24	25	26	27	●	2:11 22:12	9	2502366
March 2139	1	2	3	4	5	6	◐	15:16	10	2502373
	8	9	10	11	12	13	14		11	2502380
	○	16	17	18	19	20[b]	21	17:28	12	2502387
	22	◑	24	25	26	27	28	15:36	13	2502394
	29	●	31	1	2	3	4	7:40	14	2502401
April 2139	5	◐	7	8	9	10	11	5:58	15	2502408
	12	13	○	15	16	17	18	10:42	16	2502415
	19	20	21	◑	23	24	25	1:19	17	2502422
	26	27	●	29	30	1	2	16:24	18	2502429
May 2139	3	4	◐	6	7	8	9	22:33	19	2502436
	10	11	12	13	○	15	16	1:24	20	2502443
	17	18	19	20	◑	22	23	8:02	21	2502450
	24	25	26	27	●	29	30	1:16	22	2502457
June 2139	31	1	2	3	◐	5	6	16:06	23	2502464
	7	8	9	10	11	○	13	13:34	24	2502471
	14	15	16	17	18	◑	20	12:53	25	2502478
	21[c]	22	23	24	25	●	27	11:19	26	2502485
July 2139	28	29	30	1	2	3	◐	9:33	27	2502492
	5	6	7	8	9	10	○	23:41	28	2502499
	12	13	14	15	16	17	◑	17:18	29	2502506
	19	20	21	22	23	24	●	23:17	30	2502513
	26	27	28	29	30	31	1		31	2502520
August 2139	2	◐	4	5	6	7	8	2:07	32	2502527
	9	○	11	12	13	14	15	8:23	33	2502534
	◑	17	18	19	20	21	22	22:53	34	2502541
	23	●	25	26	27	28	29	13:28	35	2502548
September 2139	30	31	◐	2	3	4	5	17:21	36	2502555
	6	7	○	9	10	11	12	16:25	37	2502562
	13	14	◑	16	17	18	19	7:09	38	2502569
	20	21	22	●[d]	24	25	26	5:31	39	2502576
October 2139	27	28	29	30	◐	2	3	6:58	40	2502583
	4	5	6	7	○	9	10	0:32	41	2502590
	11	12	13	◑	15	16	17	19:14	42	2502597
	18	19	20	21	●	23	24	22:44	43	2502604
	25	26	27	28	29	◐	31	18:46	44	2502611
November 2139	1	2	3	4	5	○	7	9:38	45	2502618
	8	9	10	11	12	◑	14	11:33	46	2502625
	15	16	17	18	19	20	●	16:13	47	2502632
	22	23	24	25	26	27	28		48	2502639
December 2139	◐	30	1	2	3	4	○	4:42 20:30	49	2502646
	6	7	8	9	10	11	12		50	2502653
	◑	14	15	16	17	18	19	7:22	51	2502660
	20	●	22[e]	23	24	25	26	9:04	52	2502667
	27	◐	29	30	31	1	2	13:09	53	2502674

ISO Week	Hebrew 5899/5900	Sun	Mon	Tue	Wed	Thu	Fri	Sat	Molad
1	Teveth 5899	26[e]	27[e]	28[e]	29[e]	30[e]	1[e]	2[e]	Wed 20h52m4p
2		3	4	5	6	7	8	9	
3		10	11	12	13	14	15	16	
4		17	18	19	20	21	22	23	
5		24	25	26	27	28	29	1	Fri 9h36m5p
6	Shevat 5899	2	3	4	5	6	7	8	
7		9	10	11	12	13	14	15	
8		16	17	18	19	20	21	22	
9		23	24	25	26	27	28	29	
10		30	1	2	3	4	5	6	Sat 22h20m6p
11	Adar 5899	7	8	9	10	11	12	13	
12		14[f]	15	16	17	18	19	20	
13		21	22	23	24	25	26	27	
14		28	29	1	2	3	4	5	Mon 11h4m7p
15	Nisan 5899	6	7	8	9	10	11	12	
16		13	14	15[g]	16	17	18	19	
17		20	21	22	23	24	25	26	
18		27	28	29	30	1	2	3	Tue 23h48m8p
19	Iyyar 5899	4	5	6	7	8	9	10	
20		11	12	13	14	15	16	17	
21		18	19	20	21	22	23	24	
22		25	26	27	28	29	1	2	Thu 12h32m9p
23	Sivan 5899	3	4	5	6[h]	7	8	9	
24		10	11	12	13	14	15	16	
25		17	18	19	20	21	22	23	
26		24	25	26	27	28	29	30	
27	Tammuz 5899	1	2	3	4	5	6	7	Sat 1h16m10p
28		8	9	10	11	12	13	14	
29		15	16	17	18	19	20	21	
30		22	23	24	25	26	27	28	
31		29	1	2	3	4	5	6	Sun 14h0m11p
32	Av 5899	7	8	9[i]	10	11	12	13	
33		14	15	16	17	18	19	20	
34		21	22	23	24	25	26	27	
35		28	29	30	1	2	3	4	Tue 2h44m12p
36	Elul 5899	5	6	7	8	9	10	11	
37		12	13	14	15	16	17	18	
38		19	20	21	22	23	24	25	
39		26	27	28	29	1[a]	2[a]	3	Wed 15h28m13p
40	Tishri 5900	4	5	6	7	8	9	10[b]	
41		11	12	13	14	15[c]	16	17	
42		18	19	20	21	22	23	24	
43		25	26	27	28	29	30	1	Fri 4h12m14p
44	Heshvan 5900	2	3	4	5	6	7	8	
45		9	10	11	12	13	14	15	
46		16	17	18	19	20	21	22	
47		23	24	25	26	27	28	29	
48	Kislev 5900	1	2	3	4	5	6	7	Sat 16h56m15p
49		8	9	10	11	12	13	14	
50		15	16[d]	17	18	19	20	21	
51		22	23	24	25[e]	26[e]	27[e]	28[e]	
52		29[e]	30[e]	1[e]	2[e]	3	4	5	Mon 5h40m16p
53	Teveth 5900	6	7	8	9	10	11	12	

ISO Week	Chinese Wù-Xū/Jǐ-Hài‡	Sun	Mon	Tue	Wed	Thu	Fri	Sat	Solar Term
1	Month 12 Wù-Xū	27	28	29	30	1	2	3	
2		4	5	6	7	8	9	10	Xiǎo hán
3		11	12	13	14	15	16	17	
4		18	19	20	21	22	23	24	Dà hán
5		25	26	27	28	29	1[a]	2	
6	Month 1 Jǐ-Hài	3	4	5	6	7	8	9	Lì chūn
7		10	11	12	13	14	15[b]	16	
8		17	18	19	20	21	22	23	Yǔ shuǐ
9		24	25	26	27	28	29*	30	
10		1	2	3	4	5	6	7	Jīng zhé
11	Month 2 Jǐ-Hài	8	9	10	11	12	13	14	
12		15	16	17	18	19	20	21	Chūn fēn
13		22	23	24	25	26	27	28	
14		29	1	2	3	4	5	6	
15	Month 3 Jǐ-Hài	7[c]	8	9	10	11	12	13	Qīng míng
16		14	15	16	17	18	19	20	
17		21	22	23	24	25	26	27	Gǔ yǔ
18		28	29	30*	1	2	3	4	
19	Month 4 Jǐ-Hài	5	6	7	8	9	10	11	Lì xià
20		12	13	14	15	16	17	18	
21		19	20	21	22	23	24	25	Xiǎo mǎn
22		26	27	28	29	1	2	3	
23	Month 5 Jǐ-Hài	4	5[d]	6	7	8	9	10	Máng zhòng
24		11	12	13	14	15	16	17	
25		18	19	20	21	22	23	24	
26		25	26	27	28	29	1	2*	Xià zhì
27	Month 6 Jǐ-Hài	3	4	5	6	7	8	9	
28		10	11	12	13	14	15	16	Xiǎo shǔ
29		17	18	19	20	21	22	23	
30		24	25	26	27	28	29	30	Dà shǔ
31		1	2	3	4	5	6	7[e]	
32	Month 7 Jǐ-Hài	8	9	10	11	12	13	14	Lì qiū
33		15[f]	16	17	18	19	20	21	
34		22	23	24	25	26	27	28	
35		29	1	2	3*	4	5	6	Chǔ shǔ
36	Leap Month 7 Jǐ-Hài	7	8	9	10	11	12	13	
37		14	15	16	17	18	19	20	Bái lù
38		21	22	23	24	25	26	27	
39		28	29	30	1	2	3	4	Qiū fēn
40	Month 8 Jǐ-Hài	5	6	7	8	9	10	11	
41		12	13	14	15[g]	16	17	18	Hán lù
42		19	20	21	22	23	24	25	
43		26	27	28	29	30	1	2	Shuāng jiàng
44	Month 9 Jǐ-Hài	3*	4	5	6	7	8	9[h]	
45		10	11	12	13	14	15	16	
46		17	18	19	20	21	22	23	Lì dōng
47		24	25	26	27	28	29	30	
48		1	2	3	4	5	6	7	Xiǎo xuě
49	Month 10 Jǐ-Hài	8	9	10	11	12	13	14	
50		15	16	17	18	19	20	21	Dà xuě
51		22	23	24	25	26	27	28	
52	Month 11 Jǐ-Hài	29	1	2[i]	3	4*	5	6	Dōng zhì
53		7	8	9	10	11	12	13	

ISO Week	Coptic 1855‡/1856	Sun	Mon	Tue	Wed	Thu	Fri	Sat	Ethiopic 2131‡/2132
1	Koiak 1855	18	19	20	21	22	23	24	Tākhśāś 2131
2		25	26	27	28	29[c]	30	1	
3	Tōbe 1855	2	3	4	5	6[d]	7	8	Ṭer 2131
4		9	10	11[e]	12	13	14	15	
5		16	17	18	19	20	21	22	
6		23	24	25	26	27	28	29	
7	Meshir 1855	30	1	2	3	4	5	6	Yakātīt 2131
8		7	8	9	10	11	12	13	
9		14	15	16	17	18	19	20	
10		21	22	23	24	25	26	27	
11	Paremotep 1855	28	29	30	1	2	3	4	Magābīt 2131
12		5	6	7	8	9	10	11	
13		12	13	14	15	16	17	18	
14		19	20	21	22	23	24	25	
15	Parmoute 1855	26	27	28	29	30	1	2	Miyāzyā 2131
16		3	4	5	6	7	8	9	
17		10[f]	11	12	13	14	15	16	
18		17	18	19	20	21	22	23	
19		24	25	26	27	28	29[g]	30	
20	Pashons 1855	1	2	3	4	5	6	7	Genbot 2131
21		8	9	10	11	12	13	14	
22		15	16	17	18	19	20	21	
23		22	23	24	25	26	27	28	
24	Paōne 1855	29	30	1	2	3	4	5	Sanē 2131
25		6	7	8	9	10	11	12	
26		13	14	15	16	17	18	19	
27		20	21	22	23	24	25	26	
28	Epēp 1855	27	28	29	30	1	2	3	Ḥamlē 2131
29		4	5	6	7	8	9	10	
30		11	12	13	14	15	16	17	
31		18	19	20	21	22	23	24	
32	Mesorē 1855	25	26	27	28	29	30	1	Naḥasē 2131
33		2	3	4	5	6	7	8	
34		9	10	11	12	13[h]	14	15	
35		16	17	18	19	20	21	22	
36		23	24	25	26	27	28	29	
37	Epag. 1855	30	1	2	3	4	5	6	Pāg. 2131
38	Thoout 1856	1[a]	2	3	4	5	6	7	Maskaram 2132
39		8	9	10	11	12	13	14	
40		15	16	17[b]	18	19	20	21	
41		22	23	24	25	26	27	28	
42	Paope 1856	29	30	1	2	3	4	5	Ṭeqemt 2132
43		6	7	8	9	10	11	12	
44		13	14	15	16	17	18	19	
45		20	21	22	23	24	25	26	
46	Athōr 1856	27	28	29	30	1	2	3	Ḫedār 2132
47		4	5	6	7	8	9	10	
48		11	12	13	14	15	16	17	
49		18	19	20	21	22	23	24	
50	Koiak 1856	25	26	27	28	29	30	1	Tākhśāś 2132
51		2	3	4	5	6	7	8	
52		9	10	11	12	13	14	15	
53		16	17	18	19	20	21	22	

[a]New Year
[b]Spring (23:46)
[c]Summer (15:32)
[d]Autumn (8:26)
[e]Winter (7:05)
● New moon
◐ First quarter moon
○ Full moon
◑ Last quarter moon

[a]New Year
[b]Yom Kippur
[c]Sukkot
[d]Winter starts
[e]Ḥanukkah
[f]Purim
[g]Passover
[h]Shavuot
[i]Fast of Av

‡Leap year
[a]New Year (4837, Pig)
[b]Lantern Festival
[c]Qīngmíng
[d]Dragon Festival
[e]Qīqiǎo
[f]Hungry Ghosts
[g]Mid-Autumn Festival
[h]Double-Ninth Festival
[i]Dōngzhì
*Start of 60-name cycle

‡Leap year
[a]New Year
[b]Building of the Cross
[c]Christmas
[d]Jesus's Circumcision
[e]Epiphany
[f]Easter
[g]Mary's Announcement
[h]Jesus's Transfiguration

PERSIAN (ASTRONOMICAL) 1517/1518

Month	Sun	Mon	Tue	Wed	Thu	Fri	Sat
DEY 1517	7	8	9	10	11	12	13
	14	15	16	17	18	19	20
	21	22	23	24	25	26	27
	28	29	30	1	2	3	4
BAHMAN 1517	5	6	7	8	9	10	11
	12	13	14	15	16	17	18
	19	20	21	22	23	24	25
	26	27	28	29	30	1	2
ESFAND 1517	3	4	5	6	7	8	9
	10	11	12	13	14	15	16
	17	18	19	20	21	22	23
	24	25	26	27	28	29	1[a]
FARVARDĪN 1518	2	3	4	5	6	7	8
	9	10	11	12	13[b]	14	15
	16	17	18	19	20	21	22
	23	24	25	26	27	28	29
	30	31	1	2	3	4	5
ORDĪBEHEŠT 1518	6	7	8	9	10	11	12
	13	14	15	16	17	18	19
	20	21	22	23	24	25	26
	27	28	29	30	31	1	2
XORDĀD 1518	3	4	5	6	7	8	9
	10	11	12	13	14	15	16
	17	18	19	20	21	22	23
	24	25	26	27	28	29	30
	31	1	2	3	4	5	6
TĪR 1518	7	8	9	10	11	12	13
	14	15	16	17	18	19	20
	21	22	23	24	25	26	27
	28	29	30	31	1	2	3
MORDĀD 1518	4	5	6	7	8	9	10
	11	12	13	14	15	16	17
	18	19	20	21	22	23	24
	25	26	27	28	29	30	31
SHAHRĪVAR 1518	1	2	3	4	5	6	7
	8	9	10	11	12	13	14
	15	16	17	18	19	20	21
	22	23	24	25	26	27	28
	29	30	31	1	2	3	4
MEHR 1518	5	6	7	8	9	10	11
	12	13	14	15	16	17	18
	19	20	21	22	23	24	25
	26	27	28	29	30	1	2
ĀBĀN 1518	3	4	5	6	7	8	9
	10	11	12	13	14	15	16
	17	18	19	20	21	22	23
	24	25	26	27	28	29	30
ĀZAR 1518	1	2	3	4	5	6	7
	8	9	10	11	12	13	14
	15	16	17	18	19	20	21
	22	23	24	25	26	27	28
DEY 1518	29	30	1	2	3	4	5
	6	7	8	9	10	11	12

HINDU LUNAR 2195/2196

Month	Sun	Mon	Tue	Wed	Thu	Fri	Sat
PAUSHA 2195	26	27	28	30	1	2	3
	4	5	6	7	8	9	10
	11	12	13	14	15	16	17
	18	19	20	21	22	23	24
MĀGHA 2195	25	26	27	28	29	30	1
	2	3	4	6	7	8	9
	10	11	12	13	14	15	16
	17	18	18	19	20	21	22
	23	24	25	26	27	28[h]	30
PHĀLGUNA 2195	1	2	3	4	5	6	7
	8	9	10	11	12	13	14
	15[i]	16	17	18	19	20	21
	22	23	24	25	26	27	28
CHAITRA 2196	29	30	1[a]	2	3	5	6
	7	8	9[b]	10	11	11	12
	13	14	15	16	17	18	19
	20	21	22	23	24	25	26
VAIŚĀKHA 2196	28	29	30	1	2	3	4
	5	6	7	8	9	10	11
	12	13	14	15	15	16	17
	18	19	21	22	23	24	25
JYAISHTHA 2196	26	27	28	29	30	1	3
	4	5	6	6	7	8	9
	10	11	12	13	14	15	16
	17	18	19	20	21	22	24
ĀSHĀḌHA 2196	25	26	27	28	29	30	1
	2	3	4	5	6	7	8
	9	10	11	11	12	13	14
	16	17	18	19	20	21	22
	23	24	25	26	28	29	30
ŚRĀVAṆA 2196	1	2	3	3	4	5	6
	7	8	9	10	11	12	13
	14	15	16	17	18	20	21
	22	23[c]	24	25	26	27	28
BHĀDRAPADA 2196	29	30	1	2	3	4[d]	5
	6	7	8	9	10	11	12
	13	14	15	16	17	18	19
	20	21	22	24	25	26	27
ĀŚVINA 2196	28	29	29	30	1	2	3
	4	5	6	7	8[e]	9[e]	10[e]
	11	12	13	14	15	17	18
	19	20	21	22	23	24	25
KĀRTTIKA 2196	26	27	28	29	30	1[f]	2
	3	3	4	5	6	7	8
	10	11	12	13	14	15	16
	17	18	19	20	21	22	23
	24	25	26	27	28	29	30
MĀRGAŚĪRA 2196	1	2	3	4	5	6	7
	8	9	10	11[g]	12	14	15
	16	17	18	19	20	21	22
	23	24	25	26	26	27	28
PAUSHA 2196	29	30	1	2	3	4	5
	6	8	9	10	11	12	13

HINDU SOLAR 2060/2061

Month	Sun	Mon	Tue	Wed	Thu	Fri	Sat
PAUSHA 2060	11	12	13	14	15	16	17
	18	19	20	21	22	23	24
MĀGHA 2060	25	26	27	28	29	1[b]	2
	3	4	5	6	7	8	9
	10	11	12	13	14	15	16
	17	18	19	20	21	22	23
	24	25	26	27	28	29	30
PHĀLGUNA 2060	1	2	3	4	5	6	7
	8	9	10	11	12	13	14
	15	16	17	18	19	20	21
	22	23	24	25	26	27	28
CHAITRA 2060	29	30	1	2	3	4	5
	6	7	8	9	10	11	12
	13	14	15	16	17	18	19
	20	21	22	23	24	25	26
VAIŚĀKHA 2061	27	28	29	30	1[a]	2	3
	4	5	6	7	8	9	10
	11	12	13	14	15	16	17
	18	19	20	21	22	23	24
	25	26	27	28	29	30	31
JYAISHTHA 2061	1	2	3	4	5	6	7
	8	9	10	11	12	13	14
	15	16	17	18	19	20	21
	22	23	24	25	26	27	28
ĀSHĀḌHA 2061	29	30	31	1	2	3	4
	5	6	7	8	9	10	11
	12	13	14	15	16	17	18
	19	20	21	22	23	24	25
	26	27	28	29	30	31	32
ŚRĀVAṆA 2061	1	2	3	4	5	6	7
	8	9	10	11	12	13	14
	15	16	17	18	19	20	21
	22	23	24	25	26	27	28
BHĀDRAPADA 2061	29	30	31	1	2	3	4
	5	6	7	8	9	10	11
	12	13	14	15	16	17	18
	19	20	21	22	23	24	25
ĀŚVINA 2061	26	27	28	29	30	31	1
	2	3	4	5	6	7	8
	9	10	11	12	13	14	15
	16	17	18	19	20	21	22
	23	24	25	26	27	28	29
KĀRTTIKA 2061	30	31	1	2	3	4	5
	6	7	8	9	10	11	12
	13	14	15	16	17	18	19
	20	21	22	23	24	25	26
MĀRGAŚĪRA 2061	27	28	29	30	1	2	3
	4	5	6	7	8	9	10
	11	12	13	14	15	16	17
	18	19	20	21	22	23	24
PAUSHA 2061	25	26	27	28	29	1	2
	3	4	5	6	7	8	9
	10	11	12	13	14	15	16

ISLAMIC (ASTRONOMICAL) 1563/1564‡/1565

Month	Sun	Mon	Tue	Wed	Thu	Fri	Sat
MUHARRAM 1564	25	26	27	28	29	1[a]	2
	3	4	5	6	7	8	9
	10[b]	11	12	13	14	15	16
	17	18	19	20	21	22	23
	24	25	26	27	28	29	30
SAFAR 1564	1	2	3	4	5	6	7
	8	9	10	11	12	13	14
	15	16	17	18	19	20	21
	22	23	24	25	26	27	28
RABĪʿ I 1564	29	1	2	3	4	5	6
	7	8	9	10	11	12[c]	13
	14	15	16	17	18	19	20
	21	22	23	24	25	26	27
RABĪʿ II 1564	28	29	1	2	3	4	5
	6	7	8	9	10	11	12
	13	14	15	16	17	18	19
	20	21	22	23	24	25	26
JUMĀDĀ I 1564	27	28	29	30	1	2	3
	4	5	6	7	8	9	10
	11	12	13	14	15	16	17
	18	19	20	21	22	23	24
JUMĀDĀ II 1564	25	26	27	28	29	1	2
	3	4	5	6	7	8	9
	10	11	12	13	14	15	16
	17	18	19	20	21	22	23
	24	25	26	27	28	29	30
RAJAB 1564	1	2	3	4	5	6	7
	8	9	10	11	12	13	14
	15	16	17	18	19	20	21
	22	23	24	25	26	27[d]	28
SHAʿBĀN 1564	29	30	1	2	3	4	5
	6	7	8	9	10	11	12
	13	14	15	16	17	18	19
	20	21	22	23	24	25	26
RAMAḌĀN 1564	27	28	29	30	1[e]	2	3
	4	5	6	7	8	9	10
	11	12	13	14	15	16	17
	18	19	20	21	22	23	24
SHAWWĀL 1564	25	26	27	28	29	30	1[f]
	2	3	4	5	6	7	8
	9	10	11	12	13	14	15
	16	17	18	19	20	21	22
	23	24	25	26	27	28	29
DHU AL-QAʿDA 1564	1	2	3	4	5	6	7
	8	9	10	11	12	13	14
	15	16	17	18	19	20	21
	22	23	24	25	26	27	28
DHU AL-ḤIJJA 1564	29	30	1	2	3	4	5
	6	7	8	9	10[g]	11	12
	13	14	15	16	17	18	19
	20	21	22	23	24	25	26
MUHARRAM 1565	27	28	29[d]	1[a]	2	3	4
	5	6	7	8	9	10	11

GREGORIAN 2139

Julian (Sun)	Sun	Mon	Tue	Wed	Thu	Fri	Sat	Month
Dec 14	28	29	30	31	1	2	3	JANUARY 2139
	4	5	6	7	8[a]	9	10	
Dec 28	11	12	13	14	15[b]	16	17	
	18	19	20	21	22	23	24	
Jan 11	25	26	27	28	29	30	31	
	1	2	3	4	5	6	7	FEBRUARY 2139
Jan 25	8	9	10	11	12	13	14	
	15	16	17	18	19	20	21	
Feb 8	22	23	24	25	26	27	28	
	1	2	3	4[c]	5	6	7	MARCH 2139
Feb 22	8[d]	9	10	11	12	13	14	
	15	16	17	18	19	20	21	
Mar 8	22	23	24	25	26	27	28	
	29	30	31	1	2	3	4	APRIL 2139
Mar 22	5	6	7	8	9	10	11	
	12	13	14	15	16	17	18	
Apr 5	19[e]	20	21	22	23	24	25	
	26	27	28	29	30	1	2	MAY 2139
Apr 19	3	4	5	6	7	8	9	
	10	11	12	13	14	15	16	
May 3	17	18	19	20	21	22	23	
	24	25	26	27	28	29	30	
May 17	31	1	2	3	4	5	6	JUNE 2139
	7	8	9	10	11	12	13	
May 31	14	15	16	17	18	19	20	
	21	22	23	24	25	26	27	
Jun 14	28	29	30	1	2	3	4	JULY 2139
	5	6	7	8	9	10	11	
Jun 28	12	13	14	15	16	17	18	
	19	20	21	22	23	24	25	
Jul 12	26	27	28	29	30	31	1	AUGUST 2139
	2	3	4	5	6	7	8	
Jul 26	9	10	11	12	13	14	15	
	16	17	18	19	20	21	22	
Aug 9	23	24	25	26	27	28	29	
	30	31	1	2	3	4	5	SEPTEMBER 2139
Aug 23	6	7	8	9	10	11	12	
	13	14	15	16	17	18	19	
Sep 6	20	21	22	23	24	25	26	
	27	28	29	30	1	2	3	OCTOBER 2139
Sep 20	4	5	6	7	8	9	10	
	11	12	13	14	15	16	17	
Oct 4	18	19	20	21	22	23	24	
	25	26	27	28	29	30	31	
Oct 18	1	2	3	4	5	6	7	NOVEMBER 2139
	8	9	10	11	12	13	14	
Nov 1	15	16	17	18	19	20	21	
	22	23	24	25	26	27	28	
Nov 15	29[g]	30	1	2	3	4	5	DECEMBER 2139
	6	7	8	9	10	11	12	
Nov 29	13	14	15	16	17	18	19	
	20	21	22	23	24	25[h]	26	
Dec 13	27	28	29	30	31	1	2	

Persian: [a] New Year; [b] Sizdeh Bedar

Hindu Lunar: [a] New Year (Vikārin); [b] Birthday of Rāma; [c] Birthday of Krishna; [d] Ganēśa Chaturthī; [e] Dashara; [f] Diwali; [g] Birthday of Vishnu; [h] Night of Śiva; [i] Holi

Hindu Solar: [a] New Year (Ānanda); [b] Pongal

Islamic: ‡ Leap year; [a] New Year; [d] New Year (Arithmetic); [b] ʿĀshūrā'; [c] Prophet's Birthday; [d] Ascent of the Prophet; [e] Start of Ramaḍān; [f] ʿĪd al-Fiṭr; [g] ʿĪd al-'Aḍḥā

Gregorian: [a] Orthodox Christmas; [b] Julian New Year; [c] Ash Wednesday; [d] Feast of Orthodoxy; [e] Easter (also Orthodox); [g] Advent; [h] Christmas

2140

Gregorian 2140‡ / ISO Week / Julian Day

Month	Sun	Mon	Tue	Wed	Thu	Fri	Sat	Lunar Phases	ISO Week (Mon)	Julian Day (Sun noon)
January 2140	27	◐	29	30	31	1[a]	2	13:09	53	2502674
	3	○	5	6	7	8	9	9:37	1	2502681
	10	11	◑	13	14	15	16	5:03	2	2502688
	17	18	19	●	21	22	23	0:20	3	2502695
	24	25	◐	27	28	29	30	20:57	4	2502702
February 2140	31	1	2	○	4	5	6	0:52	5	2502709
	7	8	9	10	◑	12	13	2:32	6	2502716
	14	15	16	17	●	19	20	13:21	7	2502723
	21	22	23	24	◐	26	27	5:11	8	2502730
March 2140	28	29	1	2	○	4	5	17:34	9	2502737
	6	7	8	9	10	◑	12	21:54	10	2502744
	13	14	15	16	17	●	19	23:57	11	2502751
	20[b]	21	22	23	24	◐	26	14:44	12	2502758
April 2140	27	28	29	30	31	1	○	10:44	13	2502765
	3	4	5	6	7	8	9		14	2502772
	◑	11	12	13	14	15	16	13:44	15	2502779
	●	18	19	20	21	22	23	8:38	16	2502786
	◐	25	26	27	28	29	30	2:09	17	2502793
May 2140	1	○	3	4	5	6	7	3:27	18	2502800
	8	9	◑	11	12	13	14	1:29	19	2502807
	15	●	17	18	19	20	21	16:19	20	2502814
	22	◐	24	25	26	27	28	15:28	21	2502821
June 2140	29	30	○	1	2	3	4	19:02	22	2502828
	5	6	7	◑	9	10	11	9:32	23	2502835
	12	13	●	15	16	17	18	23:59	24	2502842
	19	20[c]	21	◐	23	24	25	6:31	25	2502849
July 2140	26	27	28	29	○	1	2	8:59	26	2502856
	3	4	5	6	◑	8	9	15:02	27	2502863
	10	11	12	13	●	15	16	8:36	28	2502870
	17	18	19	20	◐	22	23	23:01	29	2502877
	24	25	26	27	28	○	30	21:02	30	2502884
August 2140	31	1	2	3	4	◑	6	19:28	31	2502891
	7	8	9	10	11	●	13	18:53	32	2502898
	14	15	16	17	18	19	◐	16:35	33	2502905
	21	22	23	24	25	26	27		34	2502912
September 2140	○	29	30	31	1	2	3	7:22	35	2502919
	◑	5	6	7	8	9	10	0:27	36	2502926
	●	12	13	14	15	16	17	7:26	37	2502933
	18	◐	20	21	22[d]	23	24	10:25	38	2502940
October 2140	25	○	27	28	29	30	1	16:38	39	2502947
	2	◑	4	5	6	7	8	7:28	40	2502954
	9	●	11	12	13	14	15	22:35	41	2502961
	16	17	18	◐	20	21	22	3:28	42	2502968
	23	24	25	○	27	28	29	1:43	43	2502975
November 2140	30	31	◑	2	3	4	5	17:39	44	2502982
	6	7	8	●	10	11	12	16:12	45	2502989
	13	14	15	16	◐	18	19	18:37	46	2502996
	20	21	22	23	○	25	26	11:27	47	2503003
December 2140	27	28	29	30	◑	2	3	7:33	48	2503010
	4	5	6	7	8	●	10	11:20	49	2503017
	11	12	13	14	15	16	◐	7:14	50	2503024
	18	19	20	21[e]	22	○	24	22:19	51	2503031
	25	26	27	28	29	30	◑	1:05	52	2503038

Hebrew 5900/5901‡

ISO Week	Month	Sun	Mon	Tue	Wed	Thu	Fri	Sat	Molad
53	Tevet 5900	6	7	8	9	10	11	12	
1		13	14	15	16	17	18	19	
2		20	21	22	23	24	25	26	
3	Shevat 5900	27	28	29	1	2	3	4	Tue 18h24m17p
4		5	6	7	8	9	10	11	
5		12	13	14	15	16	17	18	
6		19	20	21	22	23	24	25	
7	Adar 5900	26	27	28	29	30	1	2	Thu 7h9m0p
8		3	4	5	6	7	8	9	
9		10	11	12	13	14[f]	15	16	
10		17	18	19	20	21	22	23	
11	Nisan 5900	24	25	26	27	28	29	1	Fri 19h53m1p
12		2	3	4	5	6	7	8	
13		9	10	11	12	13	14	15[g]	
14		16	17	18	19	20	21	22	
15		23	24	25	26	27	28	29	
16	Iyyar 5900	30	1	2	3	4	5	6	Sun 8h37m2p
17		7	8	9	10	11	12	13	
18		14	15	16	17	18	19	20	
19		21	22	23	24	25	26	27	
20	Sivan 5900	28	29	1	2	3	4	5	Mon 21h21m3p
21		6[h]	7	8	9	10	11	12	
22		13	14	15	16	17	18	19	
23		20	21	22	23	24	25	26	
24	Tammuz 5900	27	28	29	30	1	2	3	Wed 10h5m4p
25		4	5	6	7	8	9	10	
26		11	12	13	14	15	16	17	
27		18	19	20	21	22	23	24	
28	Av 5900	25	26	27	28	29	1	2	Thu 22h49m5p
29		3	4	5	6	7	8	9	
30		10[i]	11	12	13	14	15	16	
31		17	18	19	20	21	22	23	
32		24	25	26	27	28	29	30	
33	Elul 5900	1	2	3	4	5	6	7	Sat 11h33m6p
34		8	9	10	11	12	13	14	
35		15	16	17	18	19	20	21	
36		22	23	24	25	26	27	28	
37	Tishri 5901	29	1[a]	2[a]	3	4	5	6	Mon 0h17m7p
38		7	8	9	10[b]	11	12	13	
39		14	15[c]	16	17	18	19	20	
40		21	22	23	24	25	26	27	
41	Heshvan 5901	28	29	30	1	2	3	4	Tue 13h1m8p
42		5	6	7	8	9	10	11	
43		12	13	14	15	16	17	18	
44		19	20	21	22	23	24	25	
45	Kislev 5901	26	27	28	29	30	1	2	Thu 1h45m9p
46		3	4	5	6	7	8	9	
47		10	11	12	13	14	15	16	
48		17	18	19	20	21	22	23	
49		24	25[e]	26[d,e]	27[e]	28[e]	29[e]	30[e]	
50	Tevet 5901	1[e]	2[e]	3	4	5	6	7	Fri 14h29m10p
51		8	9	10	11	12	13	14	
52		15	16	17	18	19	20	21	

Chinese Jǐ-Hài‡/Gēng-Zǐ

ISO Week	Month	Sun	Mon	Tue	Wed	Thu	Fri	Sat	Solar Term
53	Month 11 Jǐ-Hài	7	8	9	10	11	12	13	
1		14	15	16	17	18	19	20	Xiǎo hán
2		21	22	23	24	25	26	27	
3	Month 12 Jǐ-Hài	28	29	30	1	2	3	4	Dà hán
4		5	6	7	8	9	10	11	
5		12	13	14	15	16	17	18	Lì chūn
6		19	20	21	22	23	24	25	
7	Month 1 Gēng-Zǐ	26	27	28	29	1[a]	2	3	Yǔ shuǐ
8		4	5*	6	7	8	9	10	
9		11	12	13	14	15[b]	16	17	Jīng zhé
10		18	19	20	21	22	23	24	
11	Month 2 Gēng-Zǐ	25	26	27	28	29	30	1	
12		2	3	4	5	6	7	8	Chūn fēn
13		9	10	11	12	13	14	15	
14		16	17[c]	18	19	20	21	22	Qīng míng
15		23	24	25	26	27	28	29	
16	Month 3 Gēng-Zǐ	1	2	3	4	5	6*	7	Gǔ yǔ
17		8	9	10	11	12	13	14	
18		15	16	17	18	19	20	21	Lì xià
19		22	23	24	25	26	27	28	
20	Month 4 Gēng-Zǐ	29	30	1	2	3	4	5	Xiǎo mǎn
21		6	7	8	9	10	11	12	
22		13	14	15	16	17	18	19	
23		20	21	22	23	24	25	26	Máng zhòng
24	Month 5 Gēng-Zǐ	27	28	29	1	2	3	4	
25		5[d]	6	7*	8	9	10	11	Xià zhì
26		12	13	14	15	16	17	18	
27		19	20	21	22	23	24	25	Xiǎo shǔ
28	Month 6 Gēng-Zǐ	26	27	28	29	1	2	3	
29		4	5	6	7	8	9	10	Dà shǔ
30		11	12	13	14	15	16	17	
31		18	19	20	21	22	23	24	
32	Month 7 Gēng-Zǐ	25	26	27	28	29	30	1	Lì qiū
33		2	3	4	5	6	7[e]	8*	
34		9	10	11	12	13	14	15[f]	Chǔ shǔ
35		16	17	18	19	20	21	22	
36		23	24	25	26	27	28	29	Bái lù
37	Month 8 Gēng-Zǐ	1	2	3	4	5	6	7	
38		8	9	10	11	12	13	14	Qiū fēn
39		15[g]	16	17	18	19	20	21	
40		22	23	24	25	26	27	28	Hán lù
41	Month 9 Gēng-Zǐ	29	30	1	2	3	4	5	
42		6	7	8	9[h]*	10	11	12	
43		13	14	15	16	17	18	19	Shuāng jiàng
44		20	21	22	23	24	25	26	
45	Month 10 Gēng-Zǐ	27	28	29	30	1	2	3	Lì dōng
46		4	5	6	7	8	9	10	
47		11	12	13	14	15	16	17	Xiǎo xuě
48		18	19	20	21	22	23	24	
49	Month 11 Gēng-Zǐ	25	26	27	28	29	1	2	Dà xuě
50		3	4	5	6	7	8	9	
51		10*	11	12	13[i]	14	15	16	Dōng zhì
52		17	18	19	20	21	22	23	

Coptic 1856/1857 / Ethiopic 2132/2133

ISO Week	Coptic Month	Sun	Mon	Tue	Wed	Thu	Fri	Sat	Ethiopic Month
53	Kouak 1856	16	17	18	19	20	21	22	Tākhśāś 2132
1		23	24	25	26	27	28	29[c]	
2	Tōbe 1856	30	1	2	3	4	5	6[d]	Ṭer 2132
3		7	8	9	10	11[e]	12	13	
4		14	15	16	17	18	19	20	
5		21	22	23	24	25	26	27	
6	Meshir 1856	28	29	30	1	2	3	4	Yakātit 2132
7		5	6	7	8	9	10	11	
8		12	13	14	15	16	17	18	
9		19	20	21	22	23	24	25	
10	Paremotep 1856	26	27	28	29	30	1	2	Magābit 2132
11		3	4	5	6	7	8	9	
12		10	11	12	13	14	15	16	
13		17	18	19	20	21	22	23	
14		24	25	26	27	28	29	30	
15	Parmoute 1856	1[f]	2	3	4	5	6	7	Miyāzyā 2132
16		8	9	10	11	12	13	14	
17		15	16	17	18	19	20	21	
18		22	23	24	25	26	27	28	
19	Pashons 1856	29[g]	30	1	2	3	4	5	Genbot 2132
20		6	7	8	9	10	11	12	
21		13	14	15	16	17	18	19	
22		20	21	22	23	24	25	26	
23	Paōne 1856	27	28	29	30	1	2	3	Sanē 2132
24		4	5	6	7	8	9	10	
25		11	12	13	14	15	16	17	
26		18	19	20	21	22	23	24	
27	Epēp 1856	25	26	27	28	29	30	1	Ḥamlē 2132
28		2	3	4	5	6	7	8	
29		9	10	11	12	13	14	15	
30		16	17	18	19	20	21	22	
31		23	24	25	26	27	28	29	
32	Mesorē 1856	30	1	2	3	4	5	6	Naḥasē 2132
33		7	8	9	10	11	12	13[h]	
34		14	15	16	17	18	19	20	
35		21	22	23	24	25	26	27	
36	Epag. 1856	28	29	30	1	2	3	4	Pāg. 2132
37	Thoout 1857	5	1[a]	2	3	4	5	6	Maskaram 2133
38		7	8	9	10	11	12	13	
39		14	15	16	17[b]	18	19	20	
40		21	22	23	24	25	26	27	
41	Paope 1857	28	29	30	1	2	3	4	Ṭeqemt 2133
42		5	6	7	8	9	10	11	
43		12	13	14	15	16	17	18	
44		19	20	21	22	23	24	25	
45	Athōr 1857	26	27	28	29	30	1	2	Ḫedār 2133
46		3	4	5	6	7	8	9	
47		10	11	12	13	14	15	16	
48		17	18	19	20	21	22	23	
49		24	25	26	27	28	29	30	
50	Kouak 1857	1	2	3	4	5	6	7	Tākhśāś 2133
51		8	9	10	11	12	13	14	
52		15	16	17	18	19	20	21	

‡Leap year
[a]New Year
[b]Spring (5:36)
[c]Summer (21:17)
[d]Autumn (14:06)
[e]Winter (12:49)
● New moon
◐ First quarter moon
○ Full moon
◑ Last quarter moon

‡Leap year
[a]New Year
[b]Yom Kippur
[c]Sukkot
[d]Winter starts
[e]Ḥanukkah
[f]Purim
[g]Passover
[h]Shavuot
[i]Fast of Av

‡Leap year
[a]New Year (4838, Rat)
[b]Lantern Festival
[c]Qīngmíng
[d]Dragon Festival
[e]Qīqiǎo
[f]Hungry Ghosts
[g]Mid-Autumn Festival
[h]Double-Ninth Festival
[i]Dōngzhì
*Start of 60-name cycle

[a]New Year
[b]Building of the Cross
[c]Christmas
[d]Jesus's Circumcision
[e]Epiphany
[f]Easter
[g]Mary's Announcement
[h]Jesus's Transfiguration

2140

PERSIAN (ASTRONOMICAL) 1518/1519‡

Month	Sun	Mon	Tue	Wed	Thu	Fri	Sat
DEY 1518	6	7	8	9	10	11	12
	13	14	15	16	17	18	19
	20	21	22	23	24	25	26
	27	28	29	30	1	2	3
BAHMAN 1518	4	5	6	7	8	9	10
	11	12	13	14	15	16	17
	18	19	20	21	22	23	24
	25	26	27	28	29	30	1
ESFAND 1518	2	3	4	5	6	7	8
	9	10	11	12	13	14	15
	16	17	18	19	20	21	22
	23	24	25	26	27	28	29
FARVARDĪN 1519	1[a]	2	3	4	5	6	7
	8	9	10	11	12	13[b]	14
	15	16	17	18	19	20	21
	22	23	24	25	26	27	28
	29	30	31	1	2	3	4
ORDĪBEHEŠT 1519	5	6	7	8	9	10	11
	12	13	14	15	16	17	18
	19	20	21	22	23	24	25
	26	27	28	29	30	31	1
XORDĀD 1519	2	3	4	5	6	7	8
	9	10	11	12	13	14	15
	16	17	18	19	20	21	22
	23	24	25	26	27	28	29
	30	31	1	2	3	4	5
TĪR 1519	6	7	8	9	10	11	12
	13	14	15	16	17	18	19
	20	21	22	23	24	25	26
	27	28	29	30	31	1	2
MORDĀD 1519	3	4	5	6	7	8	9
	10	11	12	13	14	15	16
	17	18	19	20	21	22	23
	24	25	26	27	28	29	30
	31	1	2	3	4	5	6
SHAHRĪVAR 1519	7	8	9	10	11	12	13
	14	15	16	17	18	19	20
	21	22	23	24	25	26	27
	28	29	30	31	1	2	3
MEHR 1519	4	5	6	7	8	9	10
	11	12	13	14	15	16	17
	18	19	20	21	22	23	24
	25	26	27	28	29	30	1
ĀBĀN 1519	2	3	4	5	6	7	8
	9	10	11	12	13	14	15
	16	17	18	19	20	21	22
	23	24	25	26	27	28	29
	30	1	2	3	4	5	6
ĀZAR 1519	7	8	9	10	11	12	13
	14	15	16	17	18	19	20
	21	22	23	24	25	26	27
	28	29	30	1	2	3	4
DEY 1519	5	6	7	8	9	10	11

‡Leap year
[a]New Year
[b]Sizdeh Bedar

HINDU LUNAR 2196/2197‡

Month	Sun	Mon	Tue	Wed	Thu	Fri	Sat
PAUSHA 2196	**6**	8	9	10	11	12	13
	14	15	16	17	18	19	20
	21	22	23	24	25	26	27
MĀGHA 2196	28	29	30	1	2	3	4
	5	6	7	8	9	10	11
	12	14	15	16	17	18	*18*
	19	20	21	22	23	24	25
PHĀLGUNA 2196	26	27	28[h]	29	30	1	2
	3	4	**5**	7	8	9	10
	11	12	13	14	15[i]	16	17
	18	19	20	*20*	21	22	23
CHAITRA 2197	24	25	26	27	28	**29**	1[a]
	2	3	4	5	6	7	8
	9[b]	10	11	12	13	14	15
	16	17	18	19	20	21	22
	23	24	25	26	27	28	29
VAIŚĀKHA 2197	30	1	2	**3**	5	6	7
	8	9	10	11	12	13	14
	14	15	16	17	18	19	20
	21	22	23	24	25	26	**27**
LEAP JYAISHTHA 2197	29	30	1	2	3	4	5
	6	7	8	9	10	11	12
	13	14	15	16	17	18	19
	20	21	22	23	24	25	26
JYAISHTHA 2197	27	28	29	**30**	2	3	4
	5	6	7	8	9	10	11
	11	12	13	14	15	16	17
	18	19	20	21	**22**	24	25
ĀSHĀḌHA 2197	26	27	28	29	30	1	2
	3	4	5	6	7	8	9
	10	11	12	13	14	15	16
	17	18	19	20	21	22	23
ŚRĀVAṆA 2197	24	**25**	27	28	29	30	1
	2	3	4	5	6	7	*7*
	8	9	10	11	12	13	14
	15	16	17	**18**	20	21	22
	23[c]	24	25	26	27	28	29
BHĀDRAPADA 2197	30	1	2	3	4[d]	5	6
	7	8	9	10	11	12	13
	14	15	16	17	18	19	20
	21	**22**	24	25	26	27	28
ĀŚVINA 2197	29	30	1	2	3	*3*	4
	5	6	7	8[e]	9[e]	10[e]	11
	12	13	14	**15**	17	18	19
	20	21	22	23	24	25	26
KĀRTTIKA 2197	27	28	29	30	1[f]	2	3
	4	5	6	7	8	9	10
	11	12	13	14	15	16	17
	18	19	**20**	22	23	24	25
MĀRGAŚĪRA 2197	26	*26*	27	28	29	30	1
	2	3	4	5	6	7	8
	9	10	11[g]	12	**13**	15	16
	17	18	19	20	21	22	23

‡Leap year
[a]New Year (Śārvari)
[b]Birthday of Rāma
[c]Birthday of Krishna
[d]Ganēśa Chaturthī
[e]Dashara
[f]Diwali
[g]Birthday of Vishnu
[h]Night of Śiva
[i]Holi

HINDU SOLAR 2061/2062

Month	Sun	Mon	Tue	Wed	Thu	Fri	Sat
PAUSHA 2061	10	11	12	13	14	15	16
	17	18	19	20	21	22	23
	24	25	26	27	28	29	30
MĀGHA 2061	1[b]	2	3	4	5	6	7
	8	9	10	11	12	13	14
	15	16	17	18	19	20	21
	22	23	24	25	26	27	28
PHĀLGUNA 2061	29	1	2	3	4	5	6
	7	8	9	10	11	12	13
	14	15	16	17	18	19	20
	21	22	23	24	25	26	27
CHAITRA 2061	28	29	30	1	2	3	4
	5	6	7	8	9	10	11
	12	13	14	15	16	17	18
	19	20	21	22	23	24	25
VAIŚĀKHA 2062	26	27	28	29	30	1[a]	2
	3	4	5	6	7	8	9
	10	11	12	13	14	15	16
	17	18	19	20	21	22	23
	24	25	26	27	28	29	30
JYAISHTHA 2062	31	1	2	3	4	5	6
	7	8	9	10	11	12	13
	14	15	16	17	18	19	20
	21	22	23	24	25	26	27
ĀSHĀḌHA 2062	28	29	30	31	32	1	2
	3	4	5	6	7	8	9
	10	11	12	13	14	15	16
	17	18	19	20	21	22	23
	24	25	26	27	28	29	30
ŚRĀVAṆA 2062	31	1	2	3	4	5	6
	7	8	9	10	11	12	13
	14	15	16	17	18	19	20
	21	22	23	24	25	26	27
BHĀDRAPADA 2062	28	29	30	31	32	1	2
	3	4	5	6	7	8	9
	10	11	12	13	14	15	16
	17	18	19	20	21	22	23
	24	25	26	27	28	29	30
ĀŚVINA 2062	31	1	2	3	4	5	6
	7	8	9	10	11	12	13
	14	15	16	17	18	19	20
	21	22	23	24	25	26	27
KĀRTTIKA 2062	28	29	30	1	2	3	4
	5	6	7	8	9	10	11
	12	13	14	15	16	17	18
	19	20	21	22	23	24	25
MĀRGAŚĪRA 2062	26	27	28	29	30	1	2
	3	4	5	6	7	8	9
	10	11	12	13	14	15	16
	17	18	19	20	21	22	23
PAUSHA 2062	24	25	26	27	28	29	1
	2	3	4	5	6	7	8
	9	10	11	12	13	14	15

[a]New Year (Rākshasa)
[b]Pongal

ISLAMIC (ASTRONOMICAL) 1565/1566

Month	Sun	Mon	Tue	Wed	Thu	Fri	Sat
MUHARRAM 1565	5	6	7	8	9	10[b]	11
	12	13	14	15	16	17	18
	19	20	21	22	23	24	25
SAFAR 1565	26	27	28	29	1	2	3
	4	5	6	7	8	9	10
	11	12	13	14	15	16	17
	18	19	20	21	22	23	24
RABĪ' I 1565	25	26	27	28	29	30	1
	2	3	4	5	6	7	8
	9	10	11	12[c]	13	14	15
	16	17	18	19	20	21	22
	23	24	25	26	27	28	29
RABĪ' II 1565	*1*	2	3	4	5	6	7
	8	9	10	11	12	13	14
	15	16	17	18	19	20	21
	22	23	24	25	26	27	28
JUMĀDĀ I 1565	29	1	2	3	4	5	6
	7	8	9	10	11	12	13
	14	15	16	17	18	19	20
	21	22	23	24	25	26	27
JUMĀDĀ II 1565	28	29	30	1	2	3	4
	5	6	7	8	9	10	11
	12	13	14	15	16	17	18
	19	20	21	22	23	24	25
RAJAB 1565	26	27	28	29	1	2	3
	4	5	6	7	8	9	10
	11	12	13	14	15	16	17
	18	19	20	21	22	23	24
SHA'BĀN 1565	25	26	27[d]	28	29	30	1
	2	3	4	5	6	7	8
	9	10	11	12	13	14	15
	16	17	18	19	20	21	22
	23	24	25	26	27	28	29
RAMAḌĀN 1565	30	1[e]	2	3	4	5	6
	7	8	9	10	11	12	13
	14	15	16	17	18	19	20
	21	22	23	24	25	26	27
SHAWWĀL 1565	28	29	30	1[f]	2	3	4
	5	6	7	8	9	10	11
	12	13	14	15	16	17	18
	19	20	21	22	23	24	25
DHU AL-QA'DA 1565	26	27	28	29	1	2	3
	4	5	6	7	8	9	10
	11	12	13	14	15	16	17
	18	19	20	21	22	23	24
DHU AL-ḤIJJA 1565	25	26	27	28	29	30	1
	2	3	4	5	6	7	8
	9	10[g]	11	12	13	14	15
	16	17	18	19	20	21	22
	23	24	25	26	27	28	29
MUHARRAM 1566	1[a]	2	3	4	5	6	7
	8	9	10[b]	11	12	13	14
	15	16	17	18	19	20	21

[a]New Year
[b]'Ashūrā'
[c]Prophet's Birthday
[d]Ascent of the Prophet
[e]Start of Ramaḍān
[f]'Id al-Fiṭr
[g]'Id al-'Aḍḥā

GREGORIAN 2140‡

Julian† (Sun)	Sun	Mon	Tue	Wed	Thu	Fri	Sat	Month
Dec 13	27	28	29	30	31	1	2	JANUARY 2140
	3	4	5	6	7	8[a]	9	
Dec 27	10	11	12	13	14	15[b]	16	
	17	18	19	20	21	22	23	
Jan 10	24	25	26	27	28	29	30	
	31	1	2	3	4	5	6	FEBRUARY 2140
Jan 24	7	8	9	10	11	12	13	
	14	15	16	17[c]	18	19	20	
Feb 7	21	22	23	24	25	26	27	
	28[d]	29	1	2	3	4	5	MARCH 2140
Feb 21	6	7	8	9	10	11	12	
	13	14	15	16	17	18	19	
Mar 6	20	21	22	23	24	25	26	
	27	28	29	30	31	1	2	APRIL 2140
Mar 20	3[e]	4	5	6	7	8	9	
	10[f]	11	12	13	14	15	16	
Apr 3	17	18	19	20	21	22	23	
	24	25	26	27	28	29	30	
Apr 17	1	2	3	4	5	6	7	MAY 2140
	8	9	10	11	12	13	14	
May 1	15	16	17	18	19	20	21	
	22	23	24	25	26	27	28	
May 15	29	30	31	1	2	3	4	JUNE 2140
	5	6	7	8	9	10	11	
May 29	12	13	14	15	16	17	18	
	19	20	21	22	23	24	25	
Jun 12	26	27	28	29	30	1	2	JULY 2140
	3	4	5	6	7	8	9	
Jun 26	10	11	12	13	14	15	16	
	17	18	19	20	21	22	23	
Jul 10	24	25	26	27	28	29	30	
	31	1	2	3	4	5	6	AUGUST 2140
Jul 24	7	8	9	10	11	12	13	
	14	15	16	17	18	19	20	
Aug 7	21	22	23	24	25	26	27	
	28	29	30	31	1	2	3	SEPTEMBER 2140
Aug 21	4	5	6	7	8	9	10	
	11	12	13	14	15	16	17	
Sep 4	18	19	20	21	22	23	24	
	25	26	27	28	29	30	1	OCTOBER 2140
Sep 18	2	3	4	5	6	7	8	
	9	10	11	12	13	14	15	
Oct 2	16	17	18	19	20	21	22	
	23	24	25	26	27	28	29	
Oct 16	30	31	1	2	3	4	5	NOVEMBER 2140
	6	7	8	9	10	11	12	
Oct 30	13	14	15	16	17	18	19	
	20	21	22	23	24	25	26	
Nov 13	27[g]	28	29	30	1	2	3	DECEMBER 2140
	4	5	6	7	8	9	10	
Nov 27	11	12	13	14	15	16	17	
	18	19	20	21	22	23	24	
Dec 11	25[h]	26	27	28	29	30	31	

‡Leap year
[a]Orthodox Christmas
[b]Julian New Year
[c]Ash Wednesday
[d]Feast of Orthodoxy
[e]Easter
[f]Orthodox Easter
[g]Advent
[h]Christmas

2141

Gregorian 2141	Sun	Mon	Tue	Wed	Thu	Fri	Sat	Lunar Phases	ISO Week (Mon)	Julian Day (Sun noon)	Hebrew 5901‡/5902	Sun	Mon	Tue	Wed	Thu	Fri	Sat	Molad	Chinese Gēng-Zǐ/Xīn-Chǒu	Sun	Mon	Tue	Wed	Thu	Fri	Sat	Solar Term	Coptic 1857/1858	Sun	Mon	Tue	Wed	Thu	Fri	Sat	Ethiopic 2133/2134
January 2141	1[a]	2	3	4	5	6	7		1	2503045	Teveth 5901	22	23	24	25	26	27	28		Month 12 Gēng-Zǐ	24	25	26	27	*28*	29	30	Xiǎo hán	Koiak 1857	22	23	24	25	26	27	28	Tākhśāś 2133
	●	9	10	11	12	13	14	6:19	2	2503052	Shevat 5901	29	1	2	3	4	5	6	Sun 3h13m1p		1	2	3	4	5	6	7		Tōbe 1857	29[c]	30	1	2	3	4	5	Ṭer 2133
	◐	16	17	18	19	20	21	17:22	3	2503059		7	8	9	10	11	12	13			8	9	10	11	12	***13***	14	Dà hán		6[d]	7	8	9	10	11[e]	12	
	○	23	24	25	26	27	28	10:20	4	2503066		14	15	16	17	18	19	20			15	16	17	18	19	20	21			13	14	15	16	17	18	19	
February 2141	◑	30	31	1	2	3	4	21:22	5	2503073		21	22	23	24	25	26	27			22	23	24	25	26	27	*28*	Lì chūn		20	21	22	23	24	25	26	
	5	●	7	8	9	10	11	23:17	6	2503080	Adar I 5901	28	29	30	1	2	3	4	Mon 15h57m12p	Month 1 Xīn-Chǒu	29	30	1[a]	2	3	4	5		Meshir 1857	27	28	29	30	1	2	3	Yakātit 2133
	12	13	◐	15	16	17	18	1:40	7	2503087		5	6	7	8	9	10	11			6	7	8	9	10*	11	***12***	Yǔ shuǐ		4	5	6	7	8	9	10	
	19	○	21	22	23	24	25	23:20	8	2503094		12	13	14	15	16	17	18			13	14	15[b]	16	17	18	19			11	12	13	14	15	16	17	
March 2141	26	27	◑	1	2	3	4	18:46	9	2503101		19	20	21	22	23	24	25			20	21	22	23	24	25	26			18	19	20	21	22	23	24	
	5	6	7	●	9	10	11	13:16	10	2503108	Adar II 5901	26	27	28	29	30	1	2	Wed 4h41m13p	Month 2 Xīn-Chǒu	*27*	28	29	1	2	3	4	Jīng zhé	Paremotep 1857	25	26	27	28	29	30	1	Maggābit 2133
	12	13	14	◐	16	17	18	9:03	11	2503115		3	4	5	6	7	8	9			5	6	7	8	9	10	11			2	3	4	5	6	7	8	
	19	20[b]	21	○	23	24	25	13:14	12	2503122		10	11	12	13	14[f]	15	16			12	***13***	14	15	16	17	18	Chūn fēn		9	10	11	12	13	14	15	
April 2141	26	27	28	29	◑	31	1	15:09	13	2503129		17	18	19	20	21	22	23			19	20	21	22	23	24	25			16	17	18	19	20	21	22	
	2	3	4	5	6	●	8	0:21	14	2503136	Nisan 5901	24	25	26	27	28	29	1	Thu 17h25m14p	Month 3 Xīn-Chǒu	26	27	*28*[c]	29	30	1	2	Qīng míng		23	24	25	26	27	28	29	
	9	10	11	12	◐	14	15	16:25	15	2503143		2	3	4	5	6	7	8			3	4	5	6	7	8	9		Parmoute 1857	30	1	2	3	4	5	6	Miyāzyā 2133
	16	17	18	19	20	○	22	4:05	16	2503150		9	10	11	12	13	14	15[g]			10	11*	12	13	***14***	15	16	Gǔ yǔ		7	8	9	10	11	12	13	
	23	24	25	26	27	28	◑	8:39	17	2503157		16	17	18	19	20	21	22			17	18	19	20	21	22	23			14	15	16	17	18	19	20	
May 2141	30	1	2	3	4	5	●	9:15	18	2503164		23	24	25	26	27	28	29		Month 4 Xīn-Chǒu	24	25	26	27	28	29	1	Lì xià		21[f]	22	23	24	25	26	27	
	7	8	9	10	11	12	◐	0:37	19	2503171	Iyar 5901	30	1	2	3	4	5	6	Sat 6h9m15p		2	3	4	5	6	7	8		Pashons 1857	28	29[g]	30	1	2	3	4	Genbot 2133
	14	15	16	17	18	19	○	19:41	20	2503178		7	8	9	10	11	12	13			9	10	11	12	13	14	15			5	6	7	8	9	10	11	
	21	22	23	24	25	26	27		21	2503185		14	15	16	17	18	19	20			***16***	17	18	19	20	21	22	Xiǎo mǎn		12	13	14	15	16	17	18	
June 2141	◑	29	30	31	1	2	3	22:25	22	2503192		21	22	23	24	25	26	27			23	24	25	26	27	28	29			19	20	21	22	23	24	25	
	●	5	6	7	8	9	10	16:52	23	2503199	Sivan 5901	28	29	1	2	3	4	5	Sun 18h53m16p	Month 5 Xīn-Chǒu	30	*1*	2	3	4	5[d]	6	Máng zhòng	Paōne 1857	26	27	28	29	30	1	2	Sanē 2133
	◐	12	13	14	15	16	17	10:25	24	2503206		6[h]	7	8	9	10	11	12			7	8	9	10	11	12*	13			3	4	5	6	7	8	9	
	18	○	20	21[c]	22	23	24	11:29	25	2503213		13	14	15	16	17	18	19			14	15	16	***17***	18	19	20	Xià zhì		10	11	12	13	14	15	16	
July 2141	25	26	◑	28	29	30	1	8:38	26	2503220		20	21	22	23	24	25	26			21	22	23	24	25	26	27			17	18	19	20	21	22	23	
	2	●	4	5	6	7	8	0:00	27	2503227	Tammuz 5901	27	28	29	30	1	2	3	Tue 7h37m17p	Month 6 Xīn-Chǒu	28	29	1	2	3	*4*	5	Xiǎo shǔ		24	25	26	27	28	29	30	
	9	◐	11	12	13	14	15	22:30	28	2503234		4	5	6	7	8	9	10			6	7	8	9	10	11	12		Epēp 1857	1	2	3	4	5	6	7	Ḥamlē 2133
	16	17	18	○	20	21	22	2:35	29	2503241		11	12	13	14	15	16	17			13	14	15	16	17	18	***19***	Dà shǔ		8	9	10	11	12	13	14	
	23	24	25	◑	27	28	29	16:09	30	2503248		18	19	20	21	22	23	24			20	21	22	23	24	25	26			15	16	17	18	19	20	21	
August 2141	30	31	1	●	3	4	5	7:29	31	2503255	Av 5901	25	26	27	28	29	1	2	Wed 20h22m0p	Month 7 Xīn-Chǒu	27	28	29	1	2	3	4			22	23	24	25	26	27	28	
	6	7	8	◐	10	11	12	13:20	32	2503262		3	4	5	6	7	8	9			5	6	7[e]	8	9	10	11	Lì qiū	Mesorē 1857	29	30	1	2	3	4	5	Naḥasē 2133
	13	14	15	16	○	18	19	16:22	33	2503269		10[i]	11	12	13	14	15	16			12	13	14*	15[f]	16	17	18			6	7	8	9	10	11	12	
	20	21	22	23	◑	25	26	22:09	34	2503276		17	18	19	20	21	22	23			19	20	21	***22***	23	24	25	Chǔ shǔ		13[h]	14	15	16	17	18	19	
September 2141	27	28	29	30	●	1	2	16:14	35	2503283		24	25	26	27	28	29	30		Month 8 Xīn-Chǒu	26	27	28	29	30	1	2			20	21	22	23	24	25	26	
	3	4	5	6	7	◐	9	6:51	36	2503290	Elul 5901	1	2	3	4	5	6	7	Fri 9h6m1p		3	4	5	6	*7*	8	9	Bái lù	Epag. 1857	27	28	29	30	1	2	3	Pāg. 2133
	10	11	12	13	14	15	○	4:44	37	2503297		8	9	10	11	12	13	14			10	11	12	13	14	15[g]	16		Thoout 1858	4	5	1[a]	2	3	4	5	Maskaram 2134
	17	18	19	20	21	22[d]	◑	3:48	38	2503304		15	16	17	18	19	20	21			17	18	19	20	21	22	***23***	Qiū fēn		6	7	8	9	10	11	12	
	24	25	26	27	28	29	●	3:14	39	2503311		22	23	24	25	26	27	28		Month 9 Xīn-Chǒu	24	25	26	27	28	29	1			13	14	15	16	17[b]	18	19	
October 2141	1	2	3	4	5	6	7		40	2503318	Tishri 5902	29	1[a]	2[a]	3	4	5	6	Sat 21h50m2p		2	3	4	5	6	7	8			20	21	22	23	24	25	26	
	◐	9	10	11	12	13	14	2:07	41	2503325		7	8	9	10[b]	11	12	13			9[h]	10	11	12	13	14	15*	Hán lù	Paope 1858	27	28	29	30	1	2	3	Ṭeqemt 2134
	○	16	17	18	19	20	21	16:08	42	2503332		14	15[c]	16	17	18	19	20			16	17	18	19	20	21	22			4	5	6	7	8	9	10	
	◑	23	24	25	26	27	28	10:17	43	2503339		21	22	23	24	25	26	27			23	***24***	25	26	27	28	29	Shuāng jiàng		11	12	13	14	15	16	17	
November 2141	●	30	31	1	2	3	4	17:19	44	2503346	Heshvan 5902	28	29	30	1	2	3	4	Mon 10h34m3p	Month 10 Xīn-Chǒu	30	*1*	2	3	4	5	6			18	19	20	21	22	23	24	
	5	◐	7	8	9	10	11	21:39	45	2503353		5	6	7	8	9	10	11			7	8	9	10	11	12	13	Lì dōng	Athōr 1858	25	26	27	28	29	30	1	Ḫedār 2134
	12	13	○	15	16	17	18	3:09	46	2503360		12	13	14	15	16	17	18			14	15	16	17	18	19	20			2	3	4	5	6	7	8	
	19	◑	21	22	23	24	25	18:44	47	2503367		19	20	21	22	23	24	25			21	22	23	***24***	25	26	27	Xiǎo xuě		9	10	11	12	13	14	15	
December 2141	26	27	●	29	30	1	2	10:38	48	2503374	Kislev 5902	26	27	28	29	1	2	3	Tue 23h18m4p	Month 11 Xīn-Chǒu	28	29	1	2	3	4	5			16	17	18	19	20	21	22	
	3	4	5	◐	7	8	9	15:51	49	2503381		4	5	6	7[d]	8	9	10			6	7	8	9	*10*	11	12	Dà xuě		23	24	25	26	27	28	29	
	10	11	12	○	14	15	16	14:06	50	2503388		11	12	13	14	15	16	17			13	14	15	16*	17	18	19		Koiak 1858	30	1	2	3	4	5	6	Tākhśāś 2134
	17	18	19	◑	21[e]	22	23	6:06	51	2503395		18	19	20	21	22	23	24			20	21	22	23	24	25[i]	26	Dōng zhì		7	8	9	10	11	12	13	
	24	25	26	27	●	29	30	6:09	52	2503402	Teveth 5902	25[e]	26[e]	27[e]	28[e]	29[e]	1[e]	2[e]	Thu 12h2m5p	Month 12 Xīn-Chǒu	27	28	29	30	1	2	3			14	15	16	17	18	19	20	
	31	1	2	3	4	◐	6	7:35	1	2503409		3[e]	4	5	6	7	8	9			4	5	6	7	8	9	10	Xiǎo hán		21	22	23	24	25	26	27	

[a]New Year
[b]Spring (11:30)
[c]Summer (3:08)
[d]Autumn (20:00)
[e]Winter (18:44)
● New moon
◐ First quarter moon
○ Full moon
◑ Last quarter moon

‡Leap year
[a]New Year
[b]Yom Kippur
[c]Sukkot
[d]Winter starts
[e]Ḥanukkah
[f]Purim
[g]Passover
[h]Shavuot
[i]Fast of Av

[a]New Year (4839, Ox)
[b]Lantern Festival
[c]Qīngmíng
[d]Dragon Festival
[e]Qīqiǎo
[f]Hungry Ghosts
[g]Mid-Autumn Festival
[h]Double-Ninth Festival
[i]Dōngzhì
*Start of 60-name cycle

[a]New Year
[b]Building of the Cross
[c]Christmas
[d]Jesus's Circumcision
[e]Epiphany
[f]Easter
[g]Mary's Announcement
[h]Jesus's Transfiguration

PERSIAN (ASTRONOMICAL) 1519‡/1520

Month	Sun	Mon	Tue	Wed	Thu	Fri	Sat
DEY 1519	12	13	14	15	16	17	18
	19	20	21	22	23	24	25
	26	27	28	29	30	1	2
BAHMAN 1519	3	4	5	6	7	8	9
	10	11	12	13	14	15	16
	17	18	19	20	21	22	23
	24	25	26	27	28	29	30
ESFAND 1519	1	2	3	4	5	6	7
	8	9	10	11	12	13	14
	15	16	17	18	19	20	21
	22	23	24	25	26	27	28
FARVARDĪN 1520	29	30	1[a]	2	3	4	5
	6	7	8	9	10	11	12
	13[b]	14	15	16	17	18	19
	20	21	22	23	24	25	26
ORDĪBEHEŠT 1520	27	28	29	30	31	1	2
	3	4	5	6	7	8	9
	10	11	12	13	14	15	16
	17	18	19	20	21	22	23
	24	25	26	27	28	29	30
XORDĀD 1520	31	1	2	3	4	5	6
	7	8	9	10	11	12	13
	14	15	16	17	18	19	20
	21	22	23	24	25	26	27
TĪR 1520	28	29	30	31	1	2	3
	4	5	6	7	8	9	10
	11	12	13	14	15	16	17
	18	19	20	21	22	23	24
	25	26	27	28	29	30	31
MORDĀD 1520	1	2	3	4	5	6	7
	8	9	10	11	12	13	14
	15	16	17	18	19	20	21
	22	23	24	25	26	27	28
SHAHRĪVAR 1520	29	30	31	1	2	3	4
	5	6	7	8	9	10	11
	12	13	14	15	16	17	18
	19	20	21	22	23	24	25
MEHR 1520	26	27	28	29	30	31	1
	2	3	4	5	6	7	8
	9	10	11	12	13	14	15
	16	17	18	19	20	21	22
	23	24	25	26	27	28	29
ĀBĀN 1520	30	1	2	3	4	5	6
	7	8	9	10	11	12	13
	14	15	16	17	18	19	20
	21	22	23	24	25	26	27
ĀZAR 1520	28	29	30	1	2	3	4
	5	6	7	8	9	10	11
	12	13	14	15	16	17	18
	19	20	21	22	23	24	25
DEY 1520	26	27	28	29	30	1	2
	3	4	5	6	7	8	9
	10	11	12	13	14	15	16

HINDU LUNAR 2197‡/2198

Month	Sun	Mon	Tue	Wed	Thu	Fri	Sat
MĀRGAŚĪRA 2197	24	25	26	27	28	28	29
PAUSHA 2197	30	1	2	3	4	5	6
	7	9	10	11	12	13	14
	15	16	17	18	19	20	21
	22	23	24	25	26	27	28
MĀGHA 2197	29	30	1	2	3	4	5
	6	7	8	9	10	11	12
	13	15	16	17	18	19	20
	21	21	22	23	24	25	26
PHĀLGUNA 2197	27	28[h]	29	30	1	2	3
	4	5	**6**	8	9	10	11
	12	13	14	15[i]	16	17	18
	19	20	21	22	23	23	24
CHAITRA 2198	25	26	27	28	29	**30**[a]	2
	3	4	5	6	7	8	9[b]
	10	11	12	13	14	15	16
	17	18	19	20	21	22	23
	24	25	26	27	28	29	30
VAIŚĀKHA 2198	1	2	3	**4**	6	7	8
	9	10	11	12	13	14	15
	16	17	18	18	19	20	21
	22	23	24	25	26	**27**	29
JYAISHTHA 2198	30	1	2	3	4	5	6
	7	8	9	10	11	12	13
	14	15	16	17	18	19	20
	21	22	23	24	25	26	27
ĀSHĀḌHA 2198	28	29	**30**	2	3	4	5
	6	7	8	9	10	11	12
	13	14	15	15	16	17	18
	19	20	21	**22**	24	25	26
ŚRĀVAṆA 2198	27	28	29	30	1	2	3
	4	5	6	7	8	9	10
	11	12	13	14	15	16	17
	18	19	20	21	22	23[c]	24
BHĀDRAPADA 2198	**25**	27	28	29	30	1	2
	3	4[d]	5	6	7	8	9
	10	11	11	12	13	14	15
	16	17	**18**	20	21	22	23
	24	25	26	27	28	29	30
ĀŚVINA 2198	1	2	3	4	5	6	7
	8[e]	9[e]	10[e]	11	12	13	14
	15	16	17	18	19	20	21
	22	24	25	26	27	28	29
KĀRTTIKA 2198	30	1[f]	2	3	4	5	6
	6	7	8	9	10	11	12
	13	14	15	**16**	18	19	20
	21	22	23	24	25	26	27
MĀRGAŚĪRA 2198	28	29	30	1	2	3	4
	5	6	7	8	9	10	11[g]
	12	13	14	15	16	17	18
	19	20	**21**	23	24	25	26
PAUSHA 2198	27	28	29	29	30	1	2
	3	4	5	6	7	8	9

HINDU SOLAR 2062/2063‡

Month	Sun	Mon	Tue	Wed	Thu	Fri	Sat
PAUSHA 2062	16	17	18	19	20	21	22
	23	24	25	26	27	28	29
MĀGHA 2062	30	1[b]	2	3	4	5	6
	7	8	9	10	11	12	13
	14	15	16	17	18	19	20
	21	22	23	24	25	26	27
PHĀLGUNA 2062	28	29	1	2	3	4	5
	6	7	8	9	10	11	12
	13	14	15	16	17	18	19
	20	21	22	23	24	25	26
CHAITRA 2062	27	28	29	30	1	2	3
	4	5	6	7	8	9	10
	11	12	13	14	15	16	17
	18	19	20	21	22	23	24
VAIŚĀKHA 2063	25	26	27	28	29	30	1[a]
	2	3	4	5	6	7	8
	9	10	11	12	13	14	15
	16	17	18	19	20	21	22
	23	24	25	26	27	28	29
JYAISHTHA 2063	30	31	1	2	3	4	5
	6	7	8	9	10	11	12
	13	14	15	16	17	18	19
	20	21	22	23	24	25	26
ĀSHĀḌHA 2063	27	28	29	30	31	32	1
	2	3	4	5	6	7	8
	9	10	11	12	13	14	15
	16	17	18	19	20	21	22
	23	24	25	26	27	28	29
ŚRĀVAṆA 2063	30	31	1	2	3	4	5
	6	7	8	9	10	11	12
	13	14	15	16	17	18	19
	20	21	22	23	24	25	26
BHĀDRAPADA 2063	27	28	29	30	31	32	1
	2	3	4	5	6	7	8
	9	10	11	12	13	14	15
	16	17	18	19	20	21	22
	23	24	25	26	27	28	29
ĀŚVINA 2063	30	31	1	2	3	4	5
	6	7	8	9	10	11	12
	13	14	15	16	17	18	19
	20	21	22	23	24	25	26
KĀRTTIKA 2063	27	28	29	30	1	2	3
	4	5	6	7	8	9	10
	11	12	13	14	15	16	17
	18	19	20	21	22	23	24
MĀRGAŚĪRA 2063	25	26	27	28	29	30	1
	2	3	4	5	6	7	8
	9	10	11	12	13	14	15
	16	17	18	19	20	21	22
	23	24	25	26	27	28	29
PAUSHA 2063	30	1	2	3	4	5	6
	7	8	9	10	11	12	13
	14	15	16	17	18	19	20

ISLAMIC (ASTRONOMICAL) 1566/1567

Month	Sun	Mon	Tue	Wed	Thu	Fri	Sat
MUHARRAM 1566	22	23	24	25	26	27	28
ṢAFAR 1566	29	30	1	2	3	4	5
	6	7	8	9	10	11	12
	13	14	15	16	17	18	19
	20	21	22	23	24	25	26
RABĪ' I 1566	27	28	29	1	2	3	4
	5	6	7	8	9	10	11
	12[c]	13	14	15	16	17	18
	19	20	21	22	23	24	25
RABĪ' II 1566	26	27	28	29	30	1	2
	3	4	5	6	7	8	9
	10	11	12	13	14	15	16
	17	18	19	20	21	22	23
JUMĀDĀ I 1566	24	25	26	27	28	29	1
	2	3	4	5	6	7	8
	9	10	11	12	13	14	15
	16	17	18	19	20	21	22
	23	24	25	26	27	28	29
JUMĀDĀ II 1566	1	2	3	4	5	6	7
	8	9	10	11	12	13	14
	15	16	17	18	19	20	21
	22	23	24	25	26	27	28
RAJAB 1566	29	30	1	2	3	4	5
	6	7	8	9	10	11	12
	13	14	15	16	17	18	19
	20	21	22	23	24	25	26
SHA'BĀN 1566	27[d]	28	29	1	2	3	4
	5	6	7	8	9	10	11
	12	13	14	15	16	17	18
	19	20	21	22	23	24	25
RAMAḌĀN 1566	26	27	28	29	30	1[e]	2
	3	4	5	6	7	8	9
	10	11	12	13	14	15	16
	17	18	19	20	21	22	23
	24	25	26	27	28	29	30
SHAWWĀL 1566	1[f]	2	3	4	5	6	7
	8	9	10	11	12	13	14
	15	16	17	18	19	20	21
	22	23	24	25	26	27	28
DHU AL-QA'DA 1566	29	1	2	3	4	5	6
	7	8	9	10	11	12	13
	14	15	16	17	18	19	20
	21	22	23	24	25	26	27
DHU AL-ḤIJJA 1566	28	29	30	1	2	3	4
	5	6	7	8	9	10[g]	11
	12	13	14	15	16	17	18
	19	20	21	22	23	24	25
MUHARRAM 1567	26	27	28	29	1[a]	2	3
	4	5	6	7	8	9	10[b]
	11	12	13	14	15	16	17
	18	19	20	21	22	23	24
ṢAFAR 1567	25	26	27	28	29	30	1
	2	3	4	5	6	7	8

GREGORIAN 2141

Julian (Sun)	Sun	Mon	Tue	Wed	Thu	Fri	Sat	Month
Dec 18	1	2	3	4	5	6	7	JANUARY 2141
	8[a]	9	10	11	12	13	14	
Jan 1	15[b]	16	17	18	19	20	21	
	22	23	24	25	26	27	28	
Jan 15	29	30	31	1	2	3	4	FEBRUARY 2141
	5	6	7	8[c]	9	10	11	
Jan 29	12	13	14	15	16	17	18	
	19	20	21	22	23	24	25	
Feb 12	26	27	28	1	2	3	4	MARCH 2141
	5	6	7	8	9	10	11	
Feb 26	12	13	14	15	16	17	18	
	19[d]	20	21	22	23	24	25	
Mar 12	26[e]	27	28	29	30	31	1	APRIL 2141
	2	3	4	5	6	7	8	
Mar 26	9	10	11	12	13	14	15	
	16	17	18	19	20	21	22	
Apr 9	23	24	25	26	27	28	29	
	30[f]	1	2	3	4	5	6	MAY 2141
Apr 23	7	8	9	10	11	12	13	
	14	15	16	17	18	19	20	
May 7	21	22	23	24	25	26	27	
	28	29	30	31	1	2	3	JUNE 2141
May 21	4	5	6	7	8	9	10	
	11	12	13	14	15	16	17	
Jun 4	18	19	20	21	22	23	24	
	25	26	27	28	29	30	1	JULY 2141
Jun 18	2	3	4	5	6	7	8	
	9	10	11	12	13	14	15	
Jul 2	16	17	18	19	20	21	22	
	23	24	25	26	27	28	29	
Jul 16	30	31	1	2	3	4	5	AUGUST 2141
	6	7	8	9	10	11	12	
Jul 30	13	14	15	16	17	18	19	
	20	21	22	23	24	25	26	
Aug 13	27	28	29	30	31	1	2	SEPTEMBER 2141
	3	4	5	6	7	8	9	
Aug 27	10	11	12	13	14	15	16	
	17	18	19	20	21	22	23	
Sep 10	24	25	26	27	28	29	30	
	1	2	3	4	5	6	7	OCTOBER 2141
Sep 24	8	9	10	11	12	13	14	
	15	16	17	18	19	20	21	
Oct 8	22	23	24	25	26	27	28	
	29	30	31	1	2	3	4	NOVEMBER 2141
Oct 22	5	6	7	8	9	10	11	
	12	13	14	15	16	17	18	
Nov 5	19	20	21	22	23	24	25	
	26	27	28	29	30	1	2	DECEMBER 2141
Nov 19	3[g]	4	5	6	7	8	9	
	10	11	12	13	14	15	16	
Dec 3	17	18	19	20	21	22	23	
	24	25[h]	26	27	28	29	30	
Dec 17	31	1	2	3	4	5	6	

Persian: ‡Leap year; [a]New Year; [b]Sizdeh Bedar

Hindu Lunar: ‡Leap year; [a]New Year (Plava); [b]Birthday of Rāma; [c]Birthday of Krishna; [d]Ganēśa Chaturthī; [e]Dashara; [f]Diwali; [g]Birthday of Vishnu; [h]Night of Śiva; [i]Holi

Hindu Solar: ‡Leap year; [a]New Year (Anala); [b]Pongal

Islamic: [a]New Year; [b]'Ashūrā'; [c]Prophet's Birthday; [d]Ascent of the Prophet; [e]Start of Ramaḍān; [f]'Id al-Fiṭr; [g]'Id al-'Aḍḥā

Gregorian: [a]Orthodox Christmas; [b]Julian New Year; [c]Ash Wednesday; [d]Feast of Orthodoxy; [e]Easter; [f]Orthodox Easter; [g]Advent; [h]Christmas

2142

Gregorian 2142							Lunar Phases	ISO Week	Julian Day	Hebrew 5902/5903							Molad	Chinese Xīn-Chǒu/Rén-Yín‡							Solar Term	Coptic 1858/1859‡							Ethiopic 2134/2135‡
	Sun	Mon	Tue	Wed	Thu	Fri	Sat		(Mon)	(Sun noon)		Sun	Mon	Tue	Wed	Thu	Fri	Sat			Sun	Mon	Tue	Wed	Thu	Fri	Sat			Sun	Mon	Tue	Wed	Thu	Fri	Sat	
	31	1[a]	2	3	4	◐	6	7:35	1	2503409		3[e]	4	5	6	7	8	9			4	5	6	7	8	9	10	Xiǎo hán	Koiak 1858	21	22	23	24	25	26	27	Tākhśāś 2134
January 2142	7	8	9	10	11	○	13	1:01	2	2503416	Tevet 5902	10	11	12	13	14	15	16		Month 12 Xīn-Chǒu	11	12	13	14	15	16	17			28	29[c]	30	1	2	3	4	
	14	15	16	17	◑	19	20	20:54	3	2503423		17	18	19	20	21	22	23			18	19	20	21	22	23	24	Dà hán	Tōbe 1858	5	6[d]	7	8	9	10	11[e]	Ṭer 2134
	21	22	23	24	25	26	●	1:52	4	2503430		24	25	26	27	28	29	1	Sat 0h46m6p		25	26	27	28	29	30	1[a]			12	13	14	15	16	17	18	
	28	29	30	31	1	2	◐	20:19	5	2503437		2	3	4	5	6	7	8			2	3	4	5	6	7	8			19	20	21	22	23	24	25	
February 2142	4	5	6	7	8	9	○	11:49	6	2503444	Shevat 5902	9	10	11	12	13	14	15		Month 1 Rén-Yín	9	10	11	12	13	14	15[b]	Lì chūn		26	27	28	29	30	1	2	
	11	12	13	14	15	16	◑	14:51	7	2503451		16	17	18	19	20	21	22			16*	17	18	19	20	21	22		Meshir 1858	3	4	5	6	7	8	9	Yakātit 2134
	18	19	20	21	22	23	24		8	2503458		23	24	25	26	27	28	29			23	24	25	26	27	28	29	Yǔ shuǐ		10	11	12	13	14	15	16	
	●	26	27	28	1	2	3	19:51	9	2503465		30	1	2	3	4	5	6	Sun 13h30m7p		30	1	2	3	4	5	6			17	18	19	20	21	22	23	
March 2142	4	◐	6	7	8	9	10	6:03	10	2503472	Adar 5902	7	8	9	10	11	12	13		Month 2 Rén-Yín	7	8	9	10	11	12	13	Jīng zhé		24	25	26	27	28	29	30	
	○	12	13	14	15	16	17	22:41	11	2503479		14[f]	15	16	17	18	19	20			14	15	16	17	18	19	20			1	2	3	4	5	6	7	
	18	◑	20[b]	21	22	23	24	10:40	12	2503486		21	22	23	24	25	26	27			21	22	23	24	25	26	27	Chūn fēn	Paremotep 1858	8	9	10	11	12	13	14	Magābit 2134
	25	26	●	28	29	30	31	11:06	13	2503493		28	29	1	2	3	4	5	Tue 2h14m8p		28	29	1	2	3	4	5			15	16	17	18	19	20	21	
	1	2	◐	4	5	6	7	13:20	14	2503500	Nisan 5902	6	7	8	9	10	11	12		Month 3 Rén-Yín	6	7	8	9	10[c]	11	12	Qīng míng		22	23	24	25	26	27	28	
April 2142	8	9	○	11	12	13	14	10:09	15	2503507		13	14	15[g]	16	17	18	19			13	14	15	16	17*	18	19			29	30	1	2	3	4	5	
	15	16	17	◑	19	20	21	6:28	16	2503514		20	21	22	23	24	25	26			20	21	22	23	24	25	26	Gǔ yǔ	Parmoute 1858	6	7	8	9	10	11	12	Miyāzyā 2134
	22	23	24	●	26	27	28	23:28	17	2503521		27	28	29	30	1	2	3	Wed 14h58m9p		27	28	29	30	1	2	3			13[f]	14	15	16	17	18	19	
	29	30	1	◐	3	4	5	19:10	18	2503528	Iyyar 5902	4	5	6	7	8	9	10		Month 4 Rén-Yín	4	5	6	7	8	9	10	Lì xià		20	21	22	23	24	25	26	
May 2142	6	7	8	○	10	11	12	22:43	19	2503535		11	12	13	14	15	16	17			11	12	13	14	15	16	17			27	28	29[g]	30	1	2	3	
	13	14	15	16	17	◑	19	0:38	20	2503542		18	19	20	21	22	23	24			18	19	20	21	22	23	24		Pashons 1858	4	5	6	7	8	9	10	Genbot 2134
	20	21	22	23	24	●	26	9:21	21	2503549		25	26	27	28	29	1	2	Fri 3h42m10p		25	26	27	28	29	1	2	Xiǎo mǎn		11	12	13	14	15	16	17	
	27	28	29	30	31	◐	2	0:50	22	2503556	Sivan 5902	3	4	5	6[h]	7	8	9		Month 5 Rén-Yín	3	4	5[d]	6	7	8	9			18	19	20	21	22	23	24	
June 2142	3	4	5	6	7	○	9	12:35	23	2503563		10	11	12	13	14	15	16			10	11	12	13	14	15	16	Máng zhòng		25	26	27	28	29	30	1	
	10	11	12	13	14	15	◑	16:18	24	2503570		17	18	19	20	21	22	23			17	18*	19	20	21	22	23		Paōne 1858	2	3	4	5	6	7	8	Sanē 2134
	17	18	19	20	21[c]	22	●	17:22	25	2503577		24	25	26	27	28	29	30	Sat 16h26m11p		24	25	26	27	28	29	30	Xià zhì		9	10	11	12	13	14	15	
	24	25	26	27	28	29	◐	7:45	26	2503584		1	2	3	4	5	6	7			1	2	3	4	5	6	7			16	17	18	19	20	21	22	
	1	2	3	4	5	6	7		27	2503591	Tammuz 5902	8	9	10	11	12	13	14		Leap Month 5 Rén-Yín	8	9	10	11	12	13	14	Xiǎo shǔ		23	24	25	26	27	28	29	
July 2142	○	9	10	11	12	13	14	3:26	28	2503598		15	16	17	18	19	20	21			15	16	17	18	19	20	21			30	1	2	3	4	5	6	
	15	◑	17	18	19	20	21	5:17	29	2503605		22	23	24	25	26	27	28			22	23	24	25	26	27	28		Epēp 1858	7	8	9	10	11	12	13	Ḥamlē 2134
	22	●	24	25	26	27	28	0:18	30	2503612		29	1	2	3	4	5	6	Mon 5h10m12p		29	1	2	3	4	5	6	Dà shǔ		14	15	16	17	18	19	20	
	◐	30	31	1	2	3	4	17:10	31	2503619	Av 5902	7	8	9[i]	10	11	12	13		Month 6 Rén-Yín	7	8	9	10	11	12	13			21	22	23	24	25	26	27	
August 2142	5	○	7	8	9	10	11	18:42	32	2503626		14	15	16	17	18	19	20			14	15	16	17	18	19*	20	Lì qiū		28	29	30	1	2	3	4	
	12	13	◑	15	16	17	18	15:49	33	2503633		21	22	23	24	25	26	27			21	22	23	24	25	26	27		Mesorē 1858	5	6	7	8	9	10	11	Naḥasē 2134
	19	20	●	22	23	24	25	7:11	34	2503640		28	29	30	1	2	3	4	Tue 17h54m13p		28	29	1	2	3	4	5	Chǔ shǔ		12	13[h]	14	15	16	17	18	
	26	27	◐	29	30	31	1	5:55	35	2503647	Elul 5902	5	6	7	8	9	10	11		Month 7 Rén-Yín	6	7[e]	8	9	10	11	12			19	20	21	22	23	24	25	
September 2142	2	3	4	○	6	7	8	9:54	36	2503654		12	13	14	15	16	17	18			13	14	15[f]	16	17	18	19	Bái lù	Epag. 1858	26	27	28	29	30	1	2	Ṗāg. 2134
	9	10	11	12	◑	14	15	0:20	37	2503661		19	20	21	22	23	24	25			20	21	22	23	24	25	26			3	4	5	1[a]	2	3	4	
	16	17	18	●	20	21	22	15:09	38	2503668		26	27	28	29	1[a]	2[a]	3	Thu 6h38m14p		27	28	29	1	2	3	4		Thoout 1859	5	6	7	8	9	10	11	Maskaram 2135
	23[d]	24	25	◐	27	28	29	22:11	39	2503675	Tishri 5903	4	5	6	7	8	9	10[b]		Month 8 Rén-Yín	5	6	7	8	9	10	11	Qiū fēn		12	13	14	15	16	17[b]	18	
	30	1	2	3	4	○	6	0:45	40	2503682		11	12	13	14	15[c]	16	17			12	13	14	15[g]	16	17	18			19	20	21	22	23	24	25	
October 2142	7	8	9	10	11	◑	13	7:30	41	2503689		18	19	20	21	22	23	24			19	20	21*	22	23	24	25	Hán lù		26	27	28	29	30	1	2	
	14	15	16	17	18	●	20	1:21	42	2503696		25	26	27	28	29	30	1	Fri 19h22m15p		26	27	28	29	30	1	2		Paope 1859	3	4	5	6	7	8	9	Ṭeqemt 2135
	21	22	23	24	25	◐	27	17:21	43	2503703	Heshvan 5903	2	3	4	5	6	7	8		Month 9 Rén-Yín	3	4	5	6	7	8	9[h]	Shuāng jiàng		10	11	12	13	14	15	16	
	28	29	30	31	1	2	○	14:59	44	2503710		9	10	11	12	13	14	15			10	11	12	13	14	15	16			17	18	19	20	21	22	23	
November 2142	4	5	6	7	8	9	◑	14:16	45	2503717		16	17	18	19	20	21	22			17	18	19	20	21	22	23	Lì dōng		24	25	26	27	28	29	30	
	11	12	13	14	15	16	●	14:31	46	2503724		23	24	25	26	27	28	29			24	25	26	27	28	29	1			1	2	3	4	5	6	7	
	18	19	20	21	22	23	24		47	2503731		30	1	2	3	4	5	6	Sun 8h6m16p	Month 10 Rén-Yín	2	3	4	5	6	7	8	Xiǎo xuě	Athōr 1859	8	9	10	11	12	13	14	Ḫedār 2135
	◐	26	27	28	29	30	1	14:08	48	2503738	Kislev 5903	7	8	9	10	11	12	13			9	10	11	12	13	14	15			15	16	17	18	19	20	21	
	2	○	4	5	6	7	8	4:20	49	2503745		14	15	16	17	18[d]	19	20			16	17	18	19	20	21	22*	Dà xuě		22	23	24	25	26	27	28	
December 2142	◑	10	11	12	13	14	15	21:48	50	2503752		21	22	23	24	25[e]	26[e]	27[e]			23	24	25	26	27	28	29			29	30	1	2	3	4	5	
	16	●	18	19	20	21	22[e]	6:41	51	2503759		28[e]	29[e]	30[e]	1[e]	2[e]	3	4	Mon 20h50m17p	Month 11 Rén-Yín	30	1	2	3	4	5	6[i]	Dōng zhì	Koiak 1859	6	7	8	9	10	11	12	Tākhśāś 2135
	23	24	◐	26	27	28	29	10:50	52	2503766	Tevet 5903	5	6	7	8	9	10	11			7	8	9	10	11	12	13			13	14	15	16	17	18	19	
	30	31	1	2	3	4	5	16:30	1	2503773		12	13	14	15	16	17	18			14	15	16	17	18	19	20			20	21	22	23	24	25	26	

[a]New Year
[b]Spring (17:23)
[c]Summer (8:50)
[d]Autumn (1:46)
[e]Winter (0:32)
● New moon
◐ First quarter moon
○ Full moon
◑ Last quarter moon

[a]New Year
[b]Yom Kippur
[c]Sukkot
[d]Winter starts
[e]Ḥanukkah
[f]Purim
[g]Passover
[h]Shavuot
[i]Fast of Av

‡Leap year
[a]New Year (4840, Tiger)
[b]Lantern Festival
[c]Qīngmíng
[d]Dragon Festival
[e]Qīqiǎo
[f]Hungry Ghosts
[g]Mid-Autumn Festival
[h]Double-Ninth Festival
[i]Dōngzhì
*Start of 60-name cycle

‡Leap year
[a]New Year
[b]Building of the Cross
[c]Christmas
[d]Jesus's Circumcision
[e]Epiphany
[f]Easter
[g]Mary's Announcement
[h]Jesus's Transfiguration

PERSIAN (ASTRONOMICAL) 1520/1521

Month	Sun	Mon	Tue	Wed	Thu	Fri	Sat
DEY 1520	10	11	12	13	14	15	16
	17	18	19	20	21	22	23
	24	25	26	27	28	29	30
BAHMAN 1520	1	2	3	4	5	6	7
	8	9	10	11	12	13	14
	15	16	17	18	19	20	21
	22	23	24	25	26	27	28
ESFAND 1520	29	30	1	2	3	4	5
	6	7	8	9	10	11	12
	13	14	15	16	17	18	19
	20	21	22	23	24	25	26
FARVARDĪN 1521	27	28	29	1[a]	2	3	4
	5	6	7	8	9	10	11
	12	13[b]	14	15	16	17	18
	19	20	21	22	23	24	25
ORDĪBEHEŠT 1521	26	27	28	29	30	31	1
	2	3	4	5	6	7	8
	9	10	11	12	13	14	15
	16	17	18	19	20	21	22
	23	24	25	26	27	28	29
XORDĀD 1521	30	31	1	2	3	4	5
	6	7	8	9	10	11	12
	13	14	15	16	17	18	19
	20	21	22	23	24	25	26
TĪR 1521	27	28	29	30	31	1	2
	3	4	5	6	7	8	9
	10	11	12	13	14	15	16
	17	18	19	20	21	22	23
	24	25	26	27	28	29	30
MORDĀD 1521	31	1	2	3	4	5	6
	7	8	9	10	11	12	13
	14	15	16	17	18	19	20
	21	22	23	24	25	26	27
SHAHRĪVAR 1521	28	29	30	31	1	2	3
	4	5	6	7	8	9	10
	11	12	13	14	15	16	17
	18	19	20	21	22	23	24
	25	26	27	28	29	30	31
MEHR 1521	1	2	3	4	5	6	7
	8	9	10	11	12	13	14
	15	16	17	18	19	20	21
	22	23	24	25	26	27	28
ĀBĀN 1521	29	30	1	2	3	4	5
	6	7	8	9	10	11	12
	13	14	15	16	17	18	19
	20	21	22	23	24	25	26
ĀZAR 1521	27	28	29	30	1	2	3
	4	5	6	7	8	9	10
	11	12	13	14	15	16	17
	18	19	20	21	22	23	24
DEY 1521	25	26	27	28	29	30	1
	2	3	4	5	6	7	8
	9	10	11	12	13	14	15

HINDU LUNAR 2198/2199‡

Month	Sun	Mon	Tue	Wed	Thu	Fri	Sat
PAUSHA 2198	3	4	5	6	7	8	9
	10	11	12	13	**14**	16	17
	18	19	20	21	22	23	24
MĀGHA 2198	25	26	27	28	29	30	1
	1	2	3	4	5	6	7
	8	10	11	12	13	14	15
	16	17	18	19	20	21	22
	23	24	25	26	27	28[h]	29
PHĀLGUNA 2198	30	1	2	3	4	5	6
	7	8	9	10	11	12	**13**
	15[i]	16	17	18	19	20	21
	22	23	24	*24*	25	26	27
CHAITRA 2199	28	29	30	1[a]	2	3	4
	5	6	**7**	**9**[b]	10	11	12
	13	14	15	16	17	18	19
	20	21	22	23	24	25	26
VAIŚĀKHA 2199	27	28	29	30	1	2	3
	4	5	6	7	8	9	10
	11	13	14	15	16	17	18
	18	19	20	21	22	23	24
JYAISHTHA 2199	25	26	27	28	29	30	1
	2	3	**4**	6	7	8	9
	10	11	12	13	14	15	16
	17	18	19	20	21	22	23
	23	24	**25**	27	28	29	30
ĀSHĀDHA 2199	1	2	3	4	5	6	**7**
	9	10	11	12	13	14	15
	15	16	17	18	19	20	21
	22	23	24	25	26	27	28
ŚRĀVAṆA 2199	29	**30**	2	3	4	5	6
	7	8	9	10	11	12	13
	14	15	16	17	18	19	20
	21	22	23[c]	24	25	26	27
LEAP BHĀDRAPADA 2199	28	29	30	1	2	**3**	5
	6	7	8	9	10	11	*11*
	12	13	14	15	16	17	18
	19	20	21	22	23	24	25
BHĀDRAPADA 2199	**26**	28	29	30	1	2	3
	4[d]	5	6	7	8	9	10
	11	12	13	14	15	16	17
	17	19	20	21	22	23	24
ĀŚVINA 2199	25	26	27	28	29	**30**	2
	3	4	5	6	*6*	7	8[e]
	9[e]	10[e]	11	12	13	14	15
	16	17	18	19	20	21	22
	23	25	26	27	28	29	30
KĀRTTIKA 2199	1[f]	2	3	4	5	6	7
	8	9	*9*	10	11	12	13
	14	15	16	**17**	19	20	21
	22	23	24	25	26	27	28
MĀRGAŚIRA 2199	29	30	1	2	3	4	5
	6	7	8	9	10	11[g]	12
	13	14	15	16	17	18	19

HINDU SOLAR 2063‡/2064

Month	Sun	Mon	Tue	Wed	Thu	Fri	Sat
PAUSHA 2063	14	15	16	17	18	19	20
	21	22	23	24	25	26	27
MĀGHA 2063	28	29	1[b]	2	3	4	5
	6	7	8	9	10	11	12
	13	14	15	16	17	18	19
	20	21	22	23	24	25	26
PHĀLGUNA 2063	27	28	29	30	1	2	3
	4	5	6	7	8	9	10
	11	12	13	14	15	16	17
	18	19	20	21	22	23	24
CHAITRA 2063	25	26	27	28	29	1	2
	3	4	5	6	7	8	9
	10	11	12	13	14	15	16
	17	18	19	20	21	22	23
	24	25	26	27	28	29	30
VAIŚĀKHA 2064	31	1[a]	2	3	4	5	6
	7	8	9	10	11	12	13
	14	15	16	17	18	19	20
	21	22	23	24	25	26	27
JYAISHTHA 2064	28	29	30	31	1	2	3
	4	5	6	7	8	9	10
	11	12	13	14	15	16	17
	18	19	20	21	22	23	24
	25	26	27	28	29	30	31
ĀSHĀDHA 2064	1	2	3	4	5	6	7
	8	9	10	11	12	13	14
	15	16	17	18	19	20	21
	22	23	24	25	26	27	28
ŚRĀVAṆA 2064	29	30	31	32	1	2	3
	4	5	6	7	8	9	10
	11	12	13	14	15	16	17
	18	19	20	21	22	23	24
	25	26	27	28	29	30	31
BHĀDRAPADA 2064	1	2	3	4	5	6	7
	8	9	10	11	12	13	14
	15	16	17	18	19	20	21
	22	23	24	25	26	27	28
ĀŚVINA 2064	29	30	31	1	2	3	4
	5	6	7	8	9	10	11
	12	13	14	15	16	17	18
	19	20	21	22	23	24	25
KĀRTTIKA 2064	26	27	28	29	30	31	1
	2	3	4	5	6	7	8
	9	10	11	12	13	14	15
	16	17	18	19	20	21	22
	23	24	25	26	27	28	29
MĀRGAŚIRA 2064	30	1	2	3	4	5	6
	7	8	9	10	11	12	13
	14	15	16	17	18	19	20
	21	22	23	24	25	26	27
PAUSHA 2064	28	29	1	2	3	4	5
	6	7	8	9	10	11	12
	13	14	15	16	17	18	19

ISLAMIC (ASTRONOMICAL) 1567/1568

Month	Sun	Mon	Tue	Wed	Thu	Fri	Sat
ṢAFAR 1567	2	3	4	5	6	7	8
	9	10	11	12	13	14	15
	16	17	18	19	20	21	22
	23	24	25	26	27	28	29
RABĪʿ I 1567	1	2	3	4	5	6	7
	8	9	10	11	12[c]	13	14
	15	16	17	18	19	20	21
	22	23	24	25	26	27	28
RABĪʿ II 1567	29	30	1	2	3	4	5
	6	7	8	9	10	11	12
	13	14	15	16	17	18	19
	20	21	22	23	24	25	26
JUMĀDĀ I 1567	27	28	29	30	1	2	3
	4	5	6	7	8	9	10
	11	12	13	14	15	16	17
	18	19	20	21	22	23	24
JUMĀDĀ II 1567	25	26	27	28	29	1	2
	3	4	5	6	7	8	9
	10	11	12	13	14	15	16
	17	18	19	20	21	22	23
	24	25	26	27	28	29	30
RAJAB 1567	1	2	3	4	5	6	7
	8	9	10	11	12	13	14
	15	16	17	18	19	20	21
	22	23	24	25	26	27[d]	28
SHAʿBĀN 1567	29	1	2	3	4	5	6
	7	8	9	10	11	12	13
	14	15	16	17	18	19	20
	21	22	23	24	25	26	27
RAMAḌĀN 1567	28	29	30	1[e]	2	3	4
	5	6	7	8	9	10	11
	12	13	14	15	16	17	18
	19	20	21	22	23	24	25
SHAWWĀL 1567	26	27	28	29	1[f]	2	3
	4	5	6	7	8	9	10
	11	12	13	14	15	16	17
	18	19	20	21	22	23	24
DHU AL-QAʿDA 1567	25	26	27	28	29	30	1
	2	3	4	5	6	7	8
	9	10	11	12	13	14	15
	16	17	18	19	20	21	22
	23	24	25	26	27	28	29
DHU AL-ḤIJJA 1567	1	2	3	4	5	6	7
	8	9	10[g]	11	12	13	14
	15	16	17	18	19	20	21
	22	23	24	25	26	27	28
MUḤARRAM 1568	29	1[a]	2[d]	3	4	5	6
	7	8	9	10[b]	11	12	13
	14	15	16	17	18	19	20
	21	22	23	24	25	26	27
ṢAFAR 1568	28	29	30	1	2	3	4
	5	6	7	8	9	10	11
	12	13	14	15	16	17	18

GREGORIAN 2142

Julian (Sun)	Sun	Mon	Tue	Wed	Thu	Fri	Sat	Month
Dec 17	31	1	2	3	4	5	6	JANUARY 2142
	7	8[a]	9	10	11	12	13	
Dec 31	14	15[b]	16	17	18	19	20	
	21	22	23	24	25	26	27	
Jan 14	28	29	30	31	1	2	3	FEBRUARY 2142
	4	5	6	7	8	9	10	
Jan 28	11	12	13	14	15	16	17	
	18	19	20	21	22	23	24	
Feb 11	25	26	27	28[c]	1	2	3	MARCH 2142
	4	5	6	7	8	9	10	
Feb 25	11[d]	12	13	14	15	16	17	
	18	19	20	21	22	23	24	
Mar 11	25	26	27	28	29	30	31	
	1	2	3	4	5	6	7	APRIL 2142
Mar 25	8	9	10	11	12	13	14	
	15[e]	16	17	18	19	20	21	
Apr 8	22[f]	23	24	25	26	27	28	
	29	30	1	2	3	4	5	MAY 2142
Apr 22	6	7	8	9	10	11	12	
	13	14	15	16	17	18	19	
May 6	20	21	22	23	24	25	26	
	27	28	29	30	31	1	2	JUNE 2142
May 20	3	4	5	6	7	8	9	
	10	11	12	13	14	15	16	
Jun 3	17	18	19	20	21	22	23	
	24	25	26	27	28	29	30	
Jun 17	1	2	3	4	5	6	7	JULY 2142
	8	9	10	11	12	13	14	
Jul 1	15	16	17	18	19	20	21	
	22	23	24	25	26	27	28	
Jul 15	29	30	31	1	2	3	4	AUGUST 2142
	5	6	7	8	9	10	11	
Jul 29	12	13	14	15	16	17	18	
	19	20	21	22	23	24	25	
Aug 12	26	27	28	29	30	31	1	SEPTEMBER 2142
	2	3	4	5	6	7	8	
Aug 26	9	10	11	12	13	14	15	
	16	17	18	19	20	21	22	
Sep 9	23	24	25	26	27	28	29	
	30	1	2	3	4	5	6	OCTOBER 2142
Sep 23	7	8	9	10	11	12	13	
	14	15	16	17	18	19	20	
Oct 7	21	22	23	24	25	26	27	
	28	29	30	31	1	2	3	NOVEMBER 2142
Oct 21	4	5	6	7	8	9	10	
	11	12	13	14	15	16	17	
Nov 4	18	19	20	21	22	23	24	
	25	26	27	28	29	30	1	DECEMBER 2142
Nov 18	2[g]	3	4	5	6	7	8	
	9	10	11	12	13	14	15	
Dec 2	16	17	18	19	20	21	22	
	23	24	25[h]	26	27	28	29	
Dec 16	30	31	1	2	3	4	5	

Persian: [a]New Year; [b]Sizdeh Bedar

Hindu Lunar: ‡Leap year; [a]New Year (Śubhakṛit); [b]Birthday of Rāma; [c]Birthday of Krishna; [d]Ganēśa Chaturthī; [e]Dashara; [f]Diwali; [g]Birthday of Vishnu; [h]Night of Śiva; [i]Holi

Hindu Solar: ‡Leap year; [a]New Year (Piṅgala); [b]Pongal

Islamic: [a]New Year; [d]New Year (Arithmetic); [b]ʿAshūrāʾ; [c]Prophet's Birthday; [d]Ascent of the Prophet; [e]Start of Ramaḍān; [f]ʿĪd al-Fiṭr; [g]ʿĪd al-ʾAḍḥā

Gregorian: [a]Orthodox Christmas; [b]Julian New Year; [c]Ash Wednesday; [d]Feast of Orthodoxy; [e]Easter; [f]Orthodox Easter; [g]Advent; [h]Christmas

2143

Gregorian 2143	Sun	Mon	Tue	Wed	Thu	Fri	Sat	Lunar Phases	ISO Week (Mon)	Julian Day (Sun noon)
	30	31	○[a]	2	3	4	5	16:30	1	2503773
JANUARY 2143	6	7	◑	9	10	11	12	7:18	2	2503780
	13	14	15	●	17	18	19	1:00	3	2503787
	20	21	22	23	◐	25	26	5:39	4	2503794
	27	28	29	30	○	1	2	3:27	5	2503801
FEBRUARY 2143	3	4	5	◑	7	8	9	19:30	6	2503808
	10	11	12	13	●	15	16	20:05	7	2503815
	17	18	19	20	21	◐	23	21:08	8	2503822
	24	25	26	27	28	○	2	13:26	9	2503829
	3	4	5	6	7	◑	9	10:21	10	2503836
MARCH 2143	10	11	12	13	14	15	●	14:29	11	2503843
	17	18	19	20[b]	21	22	23		12	2503850
	◐	25	26	27	28	29	○	8:37 22:59	13	2503857
	31	1	2	3	4	5	6		14	2503864
	◑	8	9	10	11	12	13	3:10	15	2503871
APRIL 2143	14	●	16	17	18	19	20	7:00	16	2503878
	21	◐	23	24	25	26	27	16:28	17	2503885
	28	○	30	1	2	3	4	8:43	18	2503892
	5	◑	7	8	9	10	11	20:55	19	2503899
MAY 2143	12	13	●	15	16	17	18	20:54	20	2503906
	19	20	◐	22	23	24	25	21:54	21	2503913
	26	27	○	29	30	31	1	19:09	22	2503920
	2	3	4	◑	6	7	8	14:44	23	2503927
JUNE 2143	9	10	11	12	●	14	15	8:00	24	2503934
	16	17	18	19	◐	21[c]	22	2:27	25	2503941
	23	24	25	26	○	28	29	6:42	26	2503948
	30	1	2	3	4	◑	6	7:50	27	2503955
JULY 2143	7	8	9	10	11	●	13	16:46	28	2503962
	14	15	16	17	18	◐	20	7:41	29	2503969
	21	22	23	24	25	○	27	19:43	30	2503976
	28	29	30	31	1	2	◑	23:31	31	2503983
	4	5	6	7	8	9	10		32	2503990
AUGUST 2143	●	12	13	14	15	16	◐	0:12 15:00	33	2503997
	18	19	20	21	22	23	24		34	2504004
	○	26	27	28	29	30	31	10:25	35	2504011
	1	◑	3	4	5	6	7	13:13	36	2504018
SEPTEMBER 2143	8	●	10	11	12	13	14	7:29	37	2504025
	15	◐	17	18	19	20	21	1:25	38	2504032
	22	23[d]	○	25	26	27	28	2:40	39	2504039
	29	30	1	◑	3	4	5	0:44	40	2504046
OCTOBER 2143	6	7	●	9	10	11	12	15:44	41	2504053
	13	14	◐	16	17	18	19	15:31	42	2504060
	20	21	22	○	24	25	26	19:50	43	2504067
	27	28	29	30	◑	1	2	10:16	44	2504074
NOVEMBER 2143	3	4	5	6	●	8	9	1:47	45	2504081
	10	11	12	13	◐	15	16	9:22	46	2504088
	17	18	19	20	21	○	23	12:44	47	2504095
	24	25	26	27	28	◑	30	18:31	48	2504102
	1	2	3	4	5	●	7	13:57	49	2504109
DECEMBER 2143	8	9	10	11	12	13	◐	6:11	50	2504116
	15	16	17	18	19	20	21		51	2504123
	○[e]	23	24	25	26	27	28	4:13	52	2504130
	◑	30	31	1	2	3	4	2:26	1	2504137

ISO Week	Hebrew 5903/5904‡	Sun	Mon	Tue	Wed	Thu	Fri	Sat	Molad
1	TEVETH 5903	12	13	14	15	16	17	18	
2		19	20	21	22	23	24	25	
3		26	27	28	29	1	2	3	Wed 9h35m0p
4	SHEVAT 5903	4	5	6	7	8	9	10	
5		11	12	13	14	15	16	17	
6		18	19	20	21	22	23	24	
7		25	26	27	28	29	30	1	Thu 22h19m1p
8	ADAR 5903	2	3	4	5	6	7	8	
9		9	10	11	12	13	14[f]	15	
10		16	17	18	19	20	21	22	
11		23	24	25	26	27	28	29	
12	NISAN 5903	1	2	3	4	5	6	7	Sat 11h3m2p
13		8	9	10	11	12	13	14	
14		15[g]	16	17	18	19	20	21	
15		22	23	24	25	26	27	28	
16		29	30	1	2	3	4	5	Sun 23h47m3p
17	IYYAR 5903	6	7	8	9	10	11	12	
18		13	14	15	16	17	18	19	
19		20	21	22	23	24	25	26	
20		27	28	29	1	2	3	4	Tue 12h31m4p
21	SIVAN 5903	5	6[h]	7	8	9	10	11	
22		12	13	14	15	16	17	18	
23		19	20	21	22	23	24	25	
24		26	27	28	29	30	1	2	Thu 1h15m5p
25	TAMMUZ 5903	3	4	5	6	7	8	9	
26		10	11	12	13	14	15	16	
27		17	18	19	20	21	22	23	
28		24	25	26	27	28	29	1	Fri 13h59m6p
29	AV 5903	2	3	4	5	6	7	8	
30		9[i]	10	11	12	13	14	15	
31		16	17	18	19	20	21	22	
32		23	24	25	26	27	28	29	
33	ELUL 5903	30	1	2	3	4	5	6	Sun 2h43m7p
34		7	8	9	10	11	12	13	
35		14	15	16	17	18	19	20	
36		21	22	23	24	25	26	27	
37	TISHRI 5904	28	29	1[a]	2[a]	3	4	5	Mon 15h27m8p
38		6	7	8	9	10[b]	11	12	
39		13	14	15[c]	16	17	18	19	
40		20	21	22	23	24	25	26	
41	HESHVAN 5904	27	28	29	30	1	2	3	Wed 4h11m9p
42		4	5	6	7	8	9	10	
43		11	12	13	14	15	16	17	
44		18	19	20	21	22	23	24	
45	KISLEV 5904	25	26	27	28	29	1	2	Thu 16h55m10p
46		3	4	5	6	7	8	9	
47		10	11	12	13	14	15	16	
48		17	18	19	20	21	22	23	
49		24	25[e]	26[e]	27[e]	28[e]	29[e]	30[d,e]	
50	TEVETH 5904	1[e]	2[e]	3	4	5	6	7	Sat 5h39m11p
51		8	9	10	11	12	13	14	
52		15	16	17	18	19	20	21	
1		22	23	24	25	26	27	28	

ISO Week	Chinese Rén-Yín‡/Guǐ-Mǎo	Sun	Mon	Tue	Wed	Thu	Fri	Sat	Solar Term
1	MONTH 11 Rén-Yín	14	15	16	17	18	19	20	
2		21	22	23	24	25	26	27	Xiǎo hán
3		28	29	30	1	2	3	4	
4	MONTH 12 Rén-Yín	5	6	7	8	9	10	11	Dà hán
5		12	13	14	15	16	17	18	
6		19	20	21	22*	23	24	25	
7		26	27	28	29	30	1[a]	2	Lì chūn
8	MONTH 1 Guǐ-Mǎo	3	4	5	6	7	8	9	Yǔ shuǐ
9		10	11	12	13	14	15[b]	16	
10		17	18	19	20	21	22	23	Jīng zhé
11		24	25	26	27	28	29	1	
12	MONTH 2 Guǐ-Mǎo	2	3	4	5	6	7	8	Chūn fēn
13		9	10	11	12	13	14	15	
14		16	17	18	19	20	21[c]	22	Qīng míng
15		23*	24	25	26	27	28	29	
16		30	1	2	3	4	5	6	Gǔ yǔ
17	MONTH 3 Guǐ-Mǎo	7	8	9	10	11	12	13	
18		14	15	16	17	18	19	20	
19		21	22	23	24	25	26	27	Lì xià
20		28	29	30	1	2	3	4	
21	MONTH 4 Guǐ-Mǎo	5	6	7	8	9	10	11	Xiǎo mǎn
22		12	13	14	15	16	17	18	
23		19	20	21	22	23*	24	25	Máng zhòng
24		26	27	28	29	1	2	3	
25	MONTH 5 Guǐ-Mǎo	4	5[d]	6	7	8	9	10	Xià zhì
26		11	12	13	14	15	16	17	
27		18	19	20	21	22	23	24	
28		25	26	27	28	29	30	1	Xiǎo shǔ
29	MONTH 6 Guǐ-Mǎo	2	3	4	5	6	7	8	
30		9	10	11	12	13	14	15	Dà shǔ
31		16	17	18	19	20	21	22	
32		23	24*	25	26	27	28	29	Lì qiū
33	MONTH 7 Guǐ-Mǎo	1	2	3	4	5	6	7[e]	
34		8	9	10	11	12	13	14	Chǔ shǔ
35		15[f]	16	17	18	19	20	21	
36		22	23	24	25	26	27	28	
37		29	1	2	3	4	5	6	Bái lù
38	MONTH 8 Guǐ-Mǎo	7	8	9	10	11	12	13	
39		14	15[g]	16	17	18	19	20	Qiū fēn
40		21	22	23	24	25	26*	27	
41		28	29	1	2	3	4	5	Hán lù
42	MONTH 9 Guǐ-Mǎo	6	7	8	9[h]	10	11	12	
43		13	14	15	16	17	18	19	Shuāng jiàng
44		20	21	22	23	24	25	26	
45		27	28	29	30	1	2	3	Lì dōng
46	MONTH 10 Guǐ-Mǎo	4	5	6	7	8	9	10	
47		11	12	13	14	15	16	17	Xiǎo xuě
48		18	19	20	21	22	23	24	
49		25	26	27*	28	29	1	2	Dà xuě
50	MONTH 11* Guǐ-Mǎo	3	4	5	6	7	8	9	
51		10	11	12	13	14	15	16	
52		17[i]	18	19	20	21	22	23	Dōng zhì
1		24	25	26	27	28	29	30	

ISO Week	Coptic 1859‡/1860	Sun	Mon	Tue	Wed	Thu	Fri	Sat	Ethiopic 2135‡/2136
1	KOIAK 1859	20	21	22	23	24	25	26	TĀKHŚĀŚ 2135
2		27	28	29[c]	30	1	2	3	
3		4	5	6[d]	7	8	9	10	
4	TÔBE 1859	11[e]	12	13	14	15	16	17	ṬER 2135
5		18	19	20	21	22	23	24	
6		25	26	27	28	29	30	1	
7		2	3	4	5	6	7	8	
8	MESHIR 1859	9	10	11	12	13	14	15	YAKĀTIT 2135
9		16	17	18	19	20	21	22	
10		23	24	25	26	27	28	29	
11		30	1	2	3	4	5	6	
12	PAREMOTEP 1859	7	8	9	10	11	12	13	MAGĀBIT 2135
13		14	15	16	17	18	19	20	
14		21	22	23	24	25	26	27	
15		28[f]	29	30	1	2	3	4	
16	PARMOUTE 1859	5	6	7	8	9	10	11	MIYĀZYĀ 2135
17		12	13	14	15	16	17	18	
18		19	20	21	22	23	24	25	
19		26	27	28	29[g]	30	1	2	
20	PASHONS 1859	3	4	5	6	7	8	9	GENBOT 2135
21		10	11	12	13	14	15	16	
22		17	18	19	20	21	22	23	
23		24	25	26	27	28	29	30	
24	PAÔNE 1859	1	2	3	4	5	6	7	SANÉ 2135
25		8	9	10	11	12	13	14	
26		15	16	17	18	19	20	21	
27		22	23	24	25	26	27	28	
28	EPÊP 1859	29	30	1	2	3	4	5	ḤAMLÉ 2135
29		6	7	8	9	10	11	12	
30		13	14	15	16	17	18	19	
31		20	21	22	23	24	25	26	
32	MESORÊ 1859	27	28	29	30	1	2	3	NAHASÉ 2135
33		4	5	6	7	8	9	10	
34		11	12	13[h]	14	15	16	17	
35		18	19	20	21	22	23	24	
36	EPAG. 1859	25	26	27	28	29	30	1	PĀG. 2135
37	THOOUT 1860	2	3	4	5	6	1[a]	2	MASKARAM 2136
38		3	4	5	6	7	8	9	
39		10	11	12	13	14	15	16	
40		17[b]	18	19	20	21	22	23	
41		24	25	26	27	28	29	30	
42	PAOPE 1860	1	2	3	4	5	6	7	ṬEQEMT 2136
43		8	9	10	11	12	13	14	
44		15	16	17	18	19	20	21	
45		22	23	24	25	26	27	28	
46	ATHÔR 1860	29	30	1	2	3	4	5	ḪEDĀR 2136
47		6	7	8	9	10	11	12	
48		13	14	15	16	17	18	19	
49		20	21	22	23	24	25	26	
50	KOIAK 1860	27	28	29	30	1	2	3	TĀKHŚĀŚ 2136
51		4	5	6	7	8	9	10	
52		11	12	13	14	15	16	17	
1		18	19	20	21	22	23	24	

[a]New Year
[b]Spring (23:09)
[c]Summer (14:40)
[d]Autumn (7:38)
[e]Winter (6:21)
● New moon
◐ First quarter moon
○ Full moon
◑ Last quarter moon

‡Leap year
[a]New Year
[b]Yom Kippur
[c]Sukkot
[d]Winter starts
[e]Ḥanukkah
[f]Purim
[g]Passover
[h]Shavuot
[i]Fast of Av

‡Leap year
[a]New Year (4841, Hare)
[b]Lantern Festival
[c]Qīngmíng
[d]Dragon Festival
[e]Qīqiǎo
[f]Hungry Ghosts
[g]Mid-Autumn Festival
[h]Double-Ninth Festival
[i]Dōngzhì
*Start of 60-name cycle

‡Leap year
[a]New Year
[b]Building of the Cross
[c]Christmas
[d]Jesus's Circumcision
[e]Epiphany
[f]Easter
[g]Mary's Announcement
[h]Jesus's Transfiguration

PERSIAN (ASTRONOMICAL) 1521/1522

Month	Sun	Mon	Tue	Wed	Thu	Fri	Sat
DEY 1521	9	10	11	12	13	14	15
	16	17	18	19	20	21	22
	23	24	25	26	27	28	29
	30	1	2	3	4	5	6
BAHMAN 1521	7	8	9	10	11	12	13
	14	15	16	17	18	19	20
	21	22	23	24	25	26	27
	28	29	30	1	2	3	4
ESFAND 1521	5	6	7	8	9	10	11
	12	13	14	15	16	17	18
	19	20	21	22	23	24	25
	26	27	28	29	1[a]	2	3
FARVARDĪN 1522	4	5	6	7	8	9	10
	11	12	13[b]	14	15	16	17
	18	19	20	21	22	23	24
	25	26	27	28	29	30	31
ORDĪBEHEŠT 1522	1	2	3	4	5	6	7
	8	9	10	11	12	13	14
	15	16	17	18	19	20	21
	22	23	24	25	26	27	28
	29	30	31	1	2	3	4
XORDĀD 1522	5	6	7	8	9	10	11
	12	13	14	15	16	17	18
	19	20	21	22	23	24	25
	26	27	28	29	30	31	1
TĪR 1522	2	3	4	5	6	7	8
	9	10	11	12	13	14	15
	16	17	18	19	20	21	22
	23	24	25	26	27	28	29
	30	31	1	2	3	4	5
MORDĀD 1522	6	7	8	9	10	11	12
	13	14	15	16	17	18	19
	20	21	22	23	24	25	26
	27	28	29	30	31	1	2
SHAHRĪVAR 1522	3	4	5	6	7	8	9
	10	11	12	13	14	15	16
	17	18	19	20	21	22	23
	24	25	26	27	28	29	30
	31	1	2	3	4	5	6
MEHR 1522	7	8	9	10	11	12	13
	14	15	16	17	18	19	20
	21	22	23	24	25	26	27
	28	29	30	1	2	3	4
ĀBĀN 1522	5	6	7	8	9	10	11
	12	13	14	15	16	17	18
	19	20	21	22	23	24	25
	26	27	28	29	30	1	2
ĀZAR 1522	3	4	5	6	7	8	9
	10	11	12	13	14	15	16
	17	18	19	20	21	22	23
	24	25	26	27	28	29	30
DEY 1522	1	2	3	4	5	6	7
	8	9	10	11	12	13	14

[a]New Year
[b]Sizdeh Bedar

HINDU LUNAR 2199‡/2200

Month	Sun	Mon	Tue	Wed	Thu	Fri	Sat
MĀRGAŚIRA 2199	13	14	15	16	17	18	19
	20	**21**	23	24	25	26	27
	28	29	30	1	2	2	3
PAUSHA 2199	4	5	6	7	8	9	10
	11	12	13	14	15	**16**	18
	19	20	21	22	23	24	25
	26	27	28	29	30	1	2
MĀGHA 2199	3	4	4	5	6	7	8
	9	11	12	13	14	15	16
	17	18	19	20	21	22	23
	24	25	26	27	28[h]	29	30
PHĀLGUNA 2199	1	2	3	4	5	6	7
	8	9	10	11	12	13	**14**[i]
	16	17	18	19	20	21	22
	23	24	25	26	27	27	28
	29	30	1[a]	2	3	4	5
CHAITRA 2200	6	7	**8**[b]	10	11	12	13
	14	15	16	17	18	19	20
	21	22	23	24	25	26	27
	28	29	30	1	2	3	4
VAIŚĀKHA 2200	5	6	7	8	9	10	**11**
	13	14	15	16	17	18	19
	20	21	22	22	23	24	25
	26	27	28	29	30	1	2
JYAISHTHA 2200	3	**4**	6	7	8	9	10
	11	12	13	14	15	16	17
	18	19	20	21	22	23	24
	25	26	27	28	29	30	1
ĀSHĀDHA 2200	2	3	4	5	6	**7**	9
	10	11	12	13	14	15	16
	17	18	19	19	20	21	22
	23	24	25	26	27	28	**29**
ŚRĀVAṆA 2200	1	2	3	4	5	6	7
	8	9	10	11	12	13	14
	15	16	17	18	19	20	21
	22	23[c]	24	25	26	27	28
BHĀDRAPADA 2200	29	30	1	2	**3**[d]	5	6
	7	8	9	10	11	12	13
	14	15	15	16	17	18	19
	20	21	22	23	24	25	**26**
ĀŚVINA 2200	28	29	30	1	2	3	4
	5	6	7	8[e]	9[e]	10[e]	11
	12	13	14	15	16	17	18
	19	20	21	22	23	24	25
	26	27	28	29	30[f]	2	3
KĀRTTIKA 2200	4	5	6	7	8	9	9
	10	11	12	13	14	15	16
	17	18	19	20	21	22	23
	24	26	27	28	29	30	1
MĀRGAŚIRA 2200	2	3	4	5	6	7	8
	9	10	11[g]	12	12	13	14
	15	16	**17**	19	20	21	22
	23	24	25	26	27	28	29

‡Leap year
[a]New Year (Śobhana)
[b]Birthday of Rāma
[c]Birthday of Krishna
[d]Ganēśa Chaturthī
[e]Dashara
[f]Diwali
[g]Birthday of Vishnu
[h]Night of Śiva
[i]Holi

HINDU SOLAR 2064/2065

Month	Sun	Mon	Tue	Wed	Thu	Fri	Sat
PAUSHA 2064	13	14	15	16	17	18	19
	20	21	22	23	24	25	26
	27	28	29	1[b]	2	3	4
MĀGHA 2064	5	6	7	8	9	10	11
	12	13	14	15	16	17	18
	19	20	21	22	23	24	25
	26	27	28	29	30	1	2
PHĀLGUNA 2064	3	4	5	6	7	8	9
	10	11	12	13	14	15	16
	17	18	19	20	21	22	23
	24	25	26	27	28	29	30
CHAITRA 2064	1	2	3	4	5	6	7
	8	9	10	11	12	13	14
	15	16	17	18	19	20	21
	22	23	24	25	26	27	28
VAIŚĀKHA 2065	29	30	1[a]	2	3	4	5
	6	7	8	9	10	11	12
	13	14	15	16	17	18	19
	20	21	22	23	24	25	26
	27	28	29	30	31	1	2
JYAISHTHA 2065	3	4	5	6	7	8	9
	10	11	12	13	14	15	16
	17	18	19	20	21	22	23
	24	25	26	27	28	29	30
ĀSHĀDHA 2065	31	1	2	3	4	5	6
	7	8	9	10	11	12	13
	14	15	16	17	18	19	20
	21	22	23	24	25	26	27
ŚRĀVAṆA 2065	28	29	30	31	32	1	2
	3	4	5	6	7	8	9
	10	11	12	13	14	15	16
	17	18	19	20	21	22	23
	24	25	26	27	28	29	30
BHĀDRAPADA 2065	31	1	2	3	4	5	6
	7	8	9	10	11	12	13
	14	15	16	17	18	19	20
	21	22	23	24	25	26	27
ĀŚVINA 2065	28	29	30	31	1	2	3
	4	5	6	7	8	9	10
	11	12	13	14	15	16	17
	18	19	20	21	22	23	24
	25	26	27	28	29	30	31
KĀRTTIKA 2065	1	2	3	4	5	6	7
	8	9	10	11	12	13	14
	15	16	17	18	19	20	21
	22	23	24	25	26	27	28
MĀRGAŚIRA 2065	29	30	1	2	3	4	5
	6	7	8	9	10	11	12
	13	14	15	16	17	18	19
	20	21	22	23	24	25	26
PAUSHA 2065	27	28	29	1	2	3	4
	5	6	7	8	9	10	11
	12	13	14	15	16	17	18

[a]New Year (Kālayukta)
[b]Pongal

ISLAMIC (ASTRONOMICAL) 1568/1569‡

Month	Sun	Mon	Tue	Wed	Thu	Fri	Sat
ṢAFAR 1568	12	13	14	15	16	17	18
	19	20	21	22	23	24	25
RABĪ' I 1568	26	27	28	29	1	2	3
	4	5	6	7	8	9	10
	11	12[c]	13	14	15	16	17
	18	19	20	21	22	23	24
RABĪ' II 1568	25	26	27	28	29	30	1
	2	3	4	5	6	7	8
	9	10	11	12	13	14	15
	16	17	18	19	20	21	22
	23	24	25	26	27	28	29
JUMĀDĀ I 1568	30	1	2	3	4	5	6
	7	8	9	10	11	12	13
	14	15	16	17	18	19	20
	21	22	23	24	25	26	27
JUMĀDĀ II 1568	28	29	30	1	2	3	4
	5	6	7	8	9	10	11
	12	13	14	15	16	17	18
	19	20	21	22	23	24	25
RAJAB 1568	26	27	28	29	1	2	3
	4	5	6	7	8	9	10
	11	12	13	14	15	16	17
	18	19	20	21	22	23	24
SHA'BĀN 1568	25	26	27[d]	28	29	30	1
	2	3	4	5	6	7	8
	9	10	11	12	13	14	15
	16	17	18	19	20	21	22
	23	24	25	26	27	28	29
RAMAḌĀN 1568	1[e]	2	3	4	5	6	7
	8	9	10	11	12	13	14
	15	16	17	18	19	20	21
	22	23	24	25	26	27	28
SHAWWĀL 1568	29	30	1[f]	2	3	4	5
	6	7	8	9	10	11	12
	13	14	15	16	17	18	19
	20	21	22	23	24	25	26
DHU AL-QA'DA 1568	27	28	29	1	2	3	4
	5	6	7	8	9	10	11
	12	13	14	15	16	17	18
	19	20	21	22	23	24	25
DHU AL-ḤIJJA 1568	26	27	28	29	1	2	3
	4	5	6	7	8	9	10[g]
	11	12	13	14	15	16	17
	18	19	20	21	22	23	24
MUḤARRAM 1569	25	26	27	28	29	1[a]	2[d]
	3	4	5	6	7	8	9
	10[b]	11	12	13	14	15	16
	17	18	19	20	21	22	23
	24	25	26	27	28	29	30
ṢAFAR 1569	1	2	3	4	5	6	7
	8	9	10	11	12	13	14
	15	16	17	18	19	20	21
	22	23	24	25	26	27	28

‡Leap year
[a]New Year
[d]New Year (Arithmetic)
[b]'Ashūrā'
[c]Prophet's Birthday
[d]Ascent of the Prophet
[e]Start of Ramaḍān
[f]'Id al-Fiṭr
[g]'Id al-'Aḍḥā

GREGORIAN 2143

Julian (Sun)	Sun	Mon	Tue	Wed	Thu	Fri	Sat	Month
Dec 16	30	31	1	2	3	4	5	JANUARY 2143
	6	7	8[a]	9	10	11	12	
Dec 30	13	14	15[b]	16	17	18	19	
	20	21	22	23	24	25	26	
Jan 13	27	28	29	30	31	1	2	FEBRUARY 2143
	3	4	5	6	7	8	9	
Jan 27	10	11	12	13[c]	14	15	16	
	17	18	19	20	21	22	23	
Feb 10	24[d]	25	26	27	28	1	2	MARCH 2143
	3	4	5	6	7	8	9	
Feb 24	10	11	12	13	14	15	16	
	17	18	19	20	21	22	23	
Mar 10	24	25	26	27	28	29	30	
	31[e]	1	2	3	4	5	6	APRIL 2143
Mar 24	7[f]	8	9	10	11	12	13	
	14	15	16	17	18	19	20	
Apr 7	21	22	23	24	25	26	27	
	28	29	30	1	2	3	4	MAY 2143
Apr 21	5	6	7	8	9	10	11	
	12	13	14	15	16	17	18	
May 5	19	20	21	22	23	24	25	
	26	27	28	29	30	31	1	JUNE 2143
May 19	2	3	4	5	6	7	8	
	9	10	11	12	13	14	15	
Jun 2	16	17	18	19	20	21	22	
	23	24	25	26	27	28	29	
Jun 16	30	1	2	3	4	5	6	JULY 2143
	7	8	9	10	11	12	13	
Jun 30	14	15	16	17	18	19	20	
	21	22	23	24	25	26	27	
Jul 14	28	29	30	31	1	2	3	AUGUST 2143
	4	5	6	7	8	9	10	
Jul 28	11	12	13	14	15	16	17	
	18	19	20	21	22	23	24	
Aug 11	25	26	27	28	29	30	31	
	1	2	3	4	5	6	7	SEPTEMBER 2143
Aug 25	8	9	10	11	12	13	14	
	15	16	17	18	19	20	21	
Sep 8	22	23	24	25	26	27	28	
	29	30	1	2	3	4	5	OCTOBER 2143
Sep 22	6	7	8	9	10	11	12	
	13	14	15	16	17	18	19	
Oct 6	20	21	22	23	24	25	26	
	27	28	29	30	31	1	2	NOVEMBER 2143
Oct 20	3	4	5	6	7	8	9	
	10	11	12	13	14	15	16	
Nov 3	17	18	19	20	21	22	23	
	24	25	26	27	28	29	30	
Nov 17	1[g]	2	3	4	5	6	7	DECEMBER 2143
	8	9	10	11	12	13	14	
Dec 1	15	16	17	18	19	20	21	
	22	23	24	25[h]	26	27	28	
Dec 15	29	30	31	1	2	3	4	

[a]Orthodox Christmas
[b]Julian New Year
[c]Ash Wednesday
[d]Feast of Orthodoxy
[e]Easter
[f]Orthodox Easter
[g]Advent
[h]Christmas

2144

Gregorian 2144‡	Sun	Mon	Tue	Wed	Thu	Fri	Sat	Lunar Phases	ISO WEEK (Mon)	JULIAN DAY (Sun noon)	Hebrew 5904‡/5905	Sun	Mon	Tue	Wed	Thu	Fri	Sat	Molad	Chinese Guǐ-Mǎo/Jiă-Chén	Sun	Mon	Tue	Wed	Thu	Fri	Sat	Solar Term	Coptic 1860/1861	Sun	Mon	Tue	Wed	Thu	Fri	Sat	Ethiopic 2136/2137
January 2144	◑	30	31	1[a]	2	3	4	2:26	1	2504137	Teveth 5904	22	23	24	25	26	27	28			24	25	26	27	28	29	30			18	19	20	21	22	23	24	Tākhśāś 2136
	●	6	7	8	9	10	11	4:14	2	2504144		29	1	2	3	4	5	6	Sun 18h23m12p		1	2	3	4	5	6	7		Koiak 1860	25	26	27	28	29[c]	30	1	
	12	◐	14	15	16	17	18	4:17	3	2504151	Shevat 5904	7	8	9	10	11	12	13		Month 12 Guǐ-Mǎo	8	9	10	11	12	13	14	Xiǎo hán		2	3	4	5	6[d]	7	8	
	19	○	21	22	23	24	25	17:40	4	2504158		14	15	16	17	18	19	20			15	16	**17**	18	19	20	21	Dà hán	Tōbe 1860	9	10	11[e]	12	13	14	15	Ṭer 2136
	26	◑	28	29	30	31	1	10:55	5	2504165		21	22	23	24	25	26	27			22	23	24	25	26	27	28*			16	17	18	19	20	21	22	
February 2144	2	●	4	5	6	7	8	20:26	6	2504172		28	29	30	1	2	3	4	Tue 7h7m13p		29	30	1[a]	2	3	4	5	Lì chūn		23	24	25	26	27	28	29	
	9	10	11	◐	13	14	15	1:13	7	2504179	Adar I 5904	5	6	7	8	9	10	11		Month 1 Jiă-Chén	6	7	8	9	10	11	12			30	1	2	3	4	5	6	
	16	17	18	○	20	21	22	5:11	8	2504186		12	13	14	15	16	17	18			13	14	15[b]	**16**	17	18	19	Yǔ shuǐ	Meshir 1860	7	8	9	10	11	12	13	Yakātit 2136
	23	24	◑	26	27	28	29	20:38	9	2504193		19	20	21	22	23	24	25			20	21	22	23	24	25	26			14	15	16	17	18	19	20	
March 2144	1	2	3	●	5	6	7	14:02	10	2504200		26	27	28	29	30	1	2	Wed 19h51m14p		27	28	29	1	2	3	4	Jīng zhé		21	22	23	24	25	26	27	
	8	9	10	11	◐	13	14	18:51	11	2504207	Adar II 5904	3	4	5	6	7	8	9		Month 2 Jiă-Chén	5	6	7	8	9	10	11			28	29	30	1	2	3	4	
	15	16	17	18	○	20[b]	21	15:12	12	2504214		10	11	12	13	14[f]	15	16			12	13	14	15	16	**17**	18	Chūn fēn		5	6	7	8	9	10	11	
	22	23	24	25	◑	27	28	7:58	13	2504221		17	18	19	20	21	22	23			19	20	21	22	23	24	25		Paremotep 1860	12	13	14	15	16	17	18	Magābit 2136
	29	30	31	1	2	●	4	8:03	14	2504228		24	25	26	27	28	29	1	Fri 8h35m15p		26	27	28	29*	30	1	2[c]	Qīng míng		19	20	21	22	23	24	25	
April 2144	5	6	7	8	9	10	◐	8:13	15	2504235		2	3	4	5	6	7	8		Month 3 Jiă-Chén	3	4	5	6	7	8	9			26	27	28	29	30	1	2	
	12	13	14	15	16	17	○	0:10	16	2504242	Nisan 5904	9	10	11	12	13	14	15[g]			10	11	12	13	14	15	16		Parmoute 1860	3	4	5	6	7	8	9	Miyāzyā 2136
	19	20	21	22	23	◑	25	21:04	17	2504249		16	17	18	19	20	21	22			**17**	18	19	20	21	22	23	Gǔ yǔ		10	11	12	13	14	15	16	
	26	27	28	29	30	1	2		18	2504256		23	24	25	26	27	28	29			24	25	26	27	28	29	30			17[f]	18	19	20	21	22	23	
May 2144	●	4	5	6	7	8	9	1:07	19	2504263		30	1	2	3	4	5	6	Sat 21h19m16p		1	2	3	4	5	6	7	Lì xià		24	25	26	27	28	29[g]	30	
	◐	11	12	13	14	15	16	17:38	20	2504270	Iyar 5904	7	8	9	10	11	12	13		Month 4 Jiă-Chén	8	9	10	11	12	13	14			1	2	3	4	5	6	7	
	○	18	19	20	21	22	23	8:32	21	2504277		14	15	16	17	18	19	20			15	16	17	**18**	19	20	21	Xiǎo mǎn	Pashons 1860	8	9	10	11	12	13	14	
	◑	25	26	27	28	29	30	11:59	22	2504284		21	22	23	24	25	26	27			22	23	24	25	26	27	28			15	16	17	18	19	20	21	Genbot 2136
	31	●	2	3	4	5	6	16:04	23	2504291		28	29	1	2	3	4	5	Mon 10h3m17p		29*	30	1	2	3	*4*	5[d]	Máng zhòng		22	23	24	25	26	27	28	
June 2144	7	8	◐	10	11	12	13	0:08	24	2504298	Sivan 5904	6[h]	7	8	9	10	11	12		Month 5 Jiă-Chén	6	7	8	9	10	11	12			29	30	1	2	3	4	5	
	14	○	16	17	18	19	20[c]	16:57	25	2504305		13	14	15	16	17	18	19			13	14	15	16	17	18	19		Paōne 1860	6	7	8	9	10	11	12	Sanē 2136
	21	22	◑	24	25	26	27	4:31	26	2504312		20	21	22	23	24	25	26			**20**	21	22	23	24	25	26	Xià zhì		13	14	15	16	17	18	19	
	28	29	30	●	2	3	4	4:26	27	2504319		27	28	29	30	1	2	3	Tue 22h48m0p		27	28	29	1	2	3	4			20	21	22	23	24	25	26	
July 2144	5	6	7	◐	9	10	11	5:03	28	2504326	Tammuz 5904	4	5	6	7	8	9	10		Month 6 Jiă-Chén	5	6	7	8	9	10	11	Xiǎo shǔ		27	28	29	30	1	2	3	
	12	13	14	○	16	17	18	2:14	29	2504333		11	12	13	14	15	16	17			12	13	14	15	16	17	18		Epēp 1860	4	5	6	7	8	9	10	Hamlē 2136
	19	20	21	◑	23	24	25	22:00	30	2504340		18	19	20	21	22	23	24			19	20	21	**22**	23	24	25	Dà shǔ		11	12	13	14	15	16	17	
	26	27	28	29	●	31	1	14:40	31	2504347		25	26	27	28	29	1	2	Thu 11h32m1p		26	27	28	29	1*	2	3			18	19	20	21	22	23	24	
August 2144	2	3	4	5	◐	7	8	9:44	32	2504354	Av 5904	3	4	5	6	7	8	9		Month 7 Jiă-Chén	4	5	6	7[e]	8	9	10	Lì qiū		25	26	27	28	29	30	1	
	9	10	11	12	○	14	15	13:25	33	2504361		10[i]	11	12	13	14	15	16			11	12	13	14	15[f]	16	17			2	3	4	5	6	7	8	
	16	17	18	19	20	◑	22	15:29	34	2504368		17	18	19	20	21	22	23			18	19	20	21	22	23	**24**	Chǔ shǔ	Mesorē 1860	9	10	11	12	13[h]	14	15	Naḥasē 2136
	23	24	25	26	27	●	29	23:39	35	2504375		24	25	26	27	28	29	30			25	26	27	28	29	30	1			16	17	18	19	20	21	22	
	30	31	1	2	3	◐	5	15:32	36	2504382		1	2	3	4	5	6	7	Sat 0h16m2p	Month 8 Jiă-Chén	2	3	4	5	6	7	8			23	24	25	26	27	28	29	
September 2144	6	7	8	9	10	11	○	3:14	37	2504389	Elul 5904	8	9	10	11	12	13	14			9	*10*	11	12	13	14	15[g]	Bái lù	Epag. 1860	30	1	2	3	4	5	1[a]	Pāg. 2136
	13	14	15	16	17	18	19		38	2504396		15	16	17	18	19	20	21			16	17	18	19	20	21	22			2	3	4	5	6	7	8	Maskaram 2137
	◑	21	22[d]	23	24	25	26	7:57	39	2504403		22	23	24	25	26	27	28			23	24	**25**	26	27	28	29	Qiū fēn	Thoout 1861	9	10	11	12	13	14	15	
	●	28	29	30	1	2	◐	8:24 23:45	40	2504410		29	1[a]	2[a]	3	4	5	6	Sun 13h0m3p		1	2*	3	4	5	6	7			16	17[b]	18	19	20	21	22	
October 2144	4	5	6	7	8	9	10		41	2504417	Tishri 5905	7	8	9	10[b]	11	12	13		Month 9 Jiă-Chén	8	9[h]	10	11	*12*	13	14	Hán lù		23	24	25	26	27	28	29	
	○	12	13	14	15	16	17	19:49	42	2504424		14	15[c]	16	17	18	19	20			15	16	17	18	19	20	21			30	1	2	3	4	5	6	
	18	◑	20	21	22	23	24	22:45	43	2504431		21	22	23	24	25	26	27			22	23	24	25	26	**27**	28	Shuāng jiàng	Paope 1861	7	8	9	10	11	12	13	Ṭeqemt 2137
	25	●	27	28	29	30	31	17:35	44	2504438		28	29	30	1	2	3	4	Tue 1h44m4p		29	30	1	2	3	4	5			14	15	16	17	18	19	20	
November 2144	1	◐	3	4	5	6	7	11:29	45	2504445	Ḥeshvan 5905	5	6	7	8	9	10	11		Month 10 Jiă-Chén	6	7	8	9	10	11	*12*	Lì dōng		21	22	23	24	25	26	27	
	8	9	○	11	12	13	14	14:14	46	2504452		12	13	14	15	16	17	18			13	14	15	16	17	18	19			28	29	30	1	2	3	4	
	15	16	17	◑	19	20	21	11:36	47	2504459		19	20	21	22	23	24	25			20	21	22	23	24	25	26			5	6	7	8	9	10	11	
	22	23	24	●	26	27	28	3:37	48	2504466		26	27	28	29	30	1	2	Wed 14h28m5p		**27**	28	29	1	2	3*	4	Xiǎo xuě	Athōr 1861	12	13	14	15	16	17	18	Ḫedār 2137
	29	30	1	◐	3	4	5	3:22	49	2504473	Kislev 5905	3	4	5	6	7	8	9		Month 11 Jiă-Chén	5	6	7	8	9	10	11			19	20	21	22	23	24	25	
December 2144	6	7	8	9	○	11	12	8:51	50	2504480		10[d]	11	12	13	14	15	16			12	*13*	14	15	16	17	18	Dà xuě		26	27	28	29	30	1	2	
	13	14	15	16	◑	18	19	22:30	51	2504487		17	18	19	20	21	22	23			19	20	21	22	23	24	25		Koiak 1861	3	4	5	6	7	8	9	
	20	21[e]	22	23	●	25	26	14:42	52	2504494		24	25[e]	26[e]	27[e]	28[e]	29[e]	30[e]	Fri 3h12m6p		26	**27**[i]	28	29	1	2	3	Dōng zhì		10	11	12	13	14	15	16	Tākhśāś 2137
	27	28	29	30	◐	1	2	23:03	53	2504501		1[e]	2[e]	3	4	5	6	7		Month 12 Jiă-Chén	4	5	6	7	8	9	10			17	18	19	20	21	22	23	

‡Leap year
[a]New Year
[b]Spring (5:00)
[c]Summer (20:42)
[d]Autumn (13:32)
[e]Winter (12:16)
● New moon
◐ First quarter moon
○ Full moon
◑ Last quarter moon

‡Leap year
[a]New Year
[b]Yom Kippur
[c]Sukkot
[d]Winter starts
[e]Ḥanukkah
[f]Purim
[g]Passover
[h]Shavuot
[i]Fast of Av

[a]New Year (4842, Dragon)
[b]Lantern Festival
[c]Qīngmíng
[d]Dragon Festival
[e]Qīqiǎo
[f]Hungry Ghosts
[g]Mid-Autumn Festival
[h]Double-Ninth Festival
[i]Dōngzhì
*Start of 60-name cycle

[a]New Year
[b]Building of the Cross
[c]Christmas
[d]Jesus's Circumcision
[e]Epiphany
[f]Easter
[g]Mary's Announcement
[h]Jesus's Transfiguration

PERSIAN (ASTRONOMICAL) 1522/1523‡

Month	Sun	Mon	Tue	Wed	Thu	Fri	Sat
	8	9	10	11	12	13	14
DEY 1522	15	16	17	18	19	20	21
	22	23	24	25	26	27	28
	29	30	1	2	3	4	5
	6	7	8	9	10	11	12
BAHMAN 1522	13	14	15	16	17	18	19
	20	21	22	23	24	25	26
	27	28	29	30	1	2	3
	4	5	6	7	8	9	10
ESFAND 1522	11	12	13	14	15	16	17
	18	19	20	21	22	23	24
	25	26	27	28	29	1[a]	2
	3	4	5	6	7	8	9
FARVARDĪN 1523	10	11	12	13[b]	14	15	16
	17	18	19	20	21	22	23
	24	25	26	27	28	29	30
	31	1	2	3	4	5	6
ORDĪBEHEŠT 1523	7	8	9	10	11	12	13
	14	15	16	17	18	19	20
	21	22	23	24	25	26	27
	28	29	30	31	1	2	3
XORDĀD 1523	4	5	6	7	8	9	10
	11	12	13	14	15	16	17
	18	19	20	21	22	23	24
	25	26	27	28	29	30	31
	1	2	3	4	5	6	7
TĪR 1523	8	9	10	11	12	13	14
	15	16	17	18	19	20	21
	22	23	24	25	26	27	28
	29	30	31	1	2	3	4
MORDĀD 1523	5	6	7	8	9	10	11
	12	13	14	15	16	17	18
	19	20	21	22	23	24	25
	26	27	28	29	30	31	1
SHAHRĪVAR 1523	2	3	4	5	6	7	8
	9	10	11	12	13	14	15
	16	17	18	19	20	21	22
	23	24	25	26	27	28	29
	30	31	1	2	3	4	5
MEHR 523	6	7	8	9	10	11	12
	13	14	15	16	17	18	19
	20	21	22	23	24	25	26
	27	28	29	30	1	2	3
ĀBĀN 1523	4	5	6	7	8	9	10
	11	12	13	14	15	16	17
	18	19	20	21	22	23	24
	25	26	27	28	29	30	1
	2	3	4	5	6	7	8
ĀZAR 1523	9	10	11	12	13	14	15
	16	17	18	19	20	21	22
	23	24	25	26	27	28	29
DEY 1523	30	1	2	3	4	5	6
	7	8	9	10	11	12	13

‡Leap year
[a]New Year
[b]Sizdeh Bedar

HINDU LUNAR 2200/2201

Month	Sun	Mon	Tue	Wed	Thu	Fri	Sat
MĀRGAŚĪRA 2200	23	24	25	26	27	28	29
PAUSHA 2200	30	1	2	3	4	5	6
	7	8	9	10	11	12	13
	14	15	16	17	18	19	20
	21	**22**	24	25	26	27	28
	29	30	1	2	3	4	4
MĀGHA 2200	5	6	7	8	9	10	11
	12	13	14	15	16	**17**	19
	20	21	22	23	24	25	26
	27	28[h]	29	30	1	2	3
	4	5	6	7	7	8	**9**
PHĀLGUNA 2200	11	12	13	14	15[i]	16	17
	18	19	20	21	**22**	24	25
	26	27	27	28	29	30	1[a]
CHAITRA 2201	2	3	4	5	6	7	8
	9[b]	10	11	12	13	14	**15**
	17	18	19	20	21	22	23
	24	25	26	27	28	29	30
	1	1	2	3	4	5	6
VAIŚĀKHA 2201	7	**8**	10	11	12	13	14
	15	16	17	18	19	20	21
	22	23	24	25	26	27	28
	29	30	1	2	3	4	5
JYAISHTHA 2201	6	7	8	9	10	**11**	13
	14	15	16	17	18	19	20
	21	22	23	24	25	26	27
	27	28	29	30	1	2	3
ĀSHĀDHA 2201	**4**	6	7	8	9	10	11
	12	13	14	15	16	17	18
	19	20	21	22	23	24	25
	26	27	28	29	30	1	2
ŚRĀVANA 2201	3	4	5	6	**7**	9	10
	11	12	13	14	15	16	17
	18	19	20	21	22	23[c]	24
	24	25	26	27	28	**29**	1
BHĀDRAPADA 2201	2	3	4[d]	5	6	7	8
	9	10	11	12	13	14	15
	16	17	18	19	20	21	22
	23	24	25	26	27	28	29
	30	1	2	**3**	5	6	7
ĀŚVINA 2201	8[e]	9[e]	10[e]	11	12	13	14
	15	16	17	18	19	19	20
	21	22	23	24	25	**26**	28
	29	30	1[f]	2	3	4	5
KĀRTTIKA 2201	6	7	8	9	10	11	12
	13	14	15	16	17	18	19
	20	21	22	23	24	25	26
	27	28	29	30	**1**	3	4
MĀRGAŚĪRA 2201	5	6	7	8	9	10	11[g]
	12	12	13	14	15	16	17
	18	19	20	21	22	23	24
PAUSHA 2201	**25**	27	28	29	30	1	2
	3	4	5	6	7	8	9

[a]New Year (Krodhin)
[b]Birthday of Rāma
[c]Birthday of Krishna
[d]Ganēśa Chaturthī
[e]Dashara
[f]Diwali
[g]Birthday of Vishnu
[h]Night of Śiva
[i]Holi

HINDU SOLAR 2065/2066‡

Month	Sun	Mon	Tue	Wed	Thu	Fri	Sat
	12	13	14	15	16	17	18
PAUSHA 2065	19	20	21	22	23	24	25
	26	27	28	29	30	1[b]	2
	3	4	5	6	7	8	9
MĀGHA 2065	10	11	12	13	14	15	16
	17	18	19	20	21	22	23
	24	25	26	27	28	29	1
	2	3	4	5	6	7	8
PHĀLGUNA 2065	9	10	11	12	13	14	15
	16	17	18	19	20	21	22
	23	24	25	26	27	28	29
	30	1	2	3	4	5	6
CHAITRA 2065	7	8	9	10	11	12	13
	14	15	16	17	18	19	20
	21	22	23	24	25	26	27
	28	29	30	1[a]	2	3	4
VAIŚĀKHA 2066	5	6	7	8	9	10	11
	12	13	14	15	16	17	18
	19	20	21	22	23	24	25
	26	27	28	29	30	31	1
JYAISHTHA 2066	2	3	4	5	6	7	8
	9	10	11	12	13	14	15
	16	17	18	19	20	21	22
	23	24	25	26	27	28	29
	30	31	32	1	2	3	4
ĀSHĀDHA 2066	5	6	7	8	9	10	11
	12	13	14	15	16	17	18
	19	20	21	22	23	24	25
	26	27	28	29	30	31	1
	2	3	4	5	6	7	8
ŚRĀVANA 2066	9	10	11	12	13	14	15
	16	17	18	19	20	21	22
	23	24	25	26	27	28	29
	30	31	32	1	2	3	4
BHĀDRAPADA 2066	5	6	7	8	9	10	11
	12	13	14	15	16	17	18
	19	20	21	22	23	24	25
	26	27	28	29	30	31	1
	2	3	4	5	6	7	8
ĀŚVINA 2066	9	10	11	12	13	14	15
	16	17	18	19	20	21	22
	23	24	25	26	27	28	29
	30	1	2	3	4	5	6
	7	8	9	10	11	12	13
KĀRTTIKA 2066	14	15	16	17	18	19	20
	21	22	23	24	25	26	27
	28	29	30	1	2	3	4
	5	6	7	8	9	10	11
MĀRGAŚĪRA 2066	12	13	14	15	16	17	18
	19	20	21	22	23	24	25
	26	27	28	29	30	1	2
PAUSHA 2066	3	4	5	6	7	8	9
	10	11	12	13	14	15	16

‡Leap year
[a]New Year (Siddhārthin)
[b]Pongal

ISLAMIC (ASTRONOMICAL) 1569‡/1570‡

Month	Sun	Mon	Tue	Wed	Thu	Fri	Sat
SAFAR 1569	22	23	24	25	26	27	28
	29	1	2	3	4	5	6
RABĪ' I 1569	7	8	9	10	11	12[c]	13
	14	15	16	17	18	19	20
	21	22	23	24	25	26	27
	28	29	30	1	2	3	4
RABĪ' II 1569	5	6	7	8	9	10	11
	12	13	14	15	16	17	18
	19	20	21	22	23	24	25
	26	27	28	29	30	1	2
JUMĀDĀ I 1569	3	4	5	6	7	8	9
	10	11	12	13	14	15	16
	17	18	19	20	21	22	23
	24	25	26	27	28	29	30
	1	2	3	4	5	6	7
JUMĀDĀ II 1569	8	9	10	11	12	13	14
	15	16	17	18	19	20	21
	22	23	24	25	26	27	28
	29	1	2	3	4	5	6
RAJAB 1569	7	8	9	10	11	12	13
	14	15	16	17	18	19	20
	21	22	23	24	25	26	27[d]
	28	29	30	1	2	3	4
SHA'BĀN 1569	5	6	7	8	9	10	11
	12	13	14	15	16	17	18
	19	20	21	22	23	24	25
	26	27	28	29	30	1[e]	2
RAMADĀN 1569	3	4	5	6	7	8	9
	10	11	12	13	14	15	16
	17	18	19	20	21	22	23
	24	25	26	27	28	29	30
	1[f]	2	3	4	5	6	7
SHAWWĀL 1569	8	9	10	11	12	13	14
	15	16	17	18	19	20	21
	22	23	24	25	26	27	28
	29	1	2	3	4	5	6
DHU AL-QA'DA 1569	7	8	9	10	11	12	13
	14	15	16	17	18	19	20
	21	22	23	24	25	26	27
	28	29	1	2	3	4	5
DHU AL-HIJJA 1569	6	7	8	9	10[g]	11	12
	13	14	15	16	17	18	19
	20	21	22	23	24	25	26
	27	28	29	1[a]	2	3	4
MUHARRAM 1570	5	6	7	8	9	10[b]	11
	12	13	14	15	16	17	18
	19	20	21	22	23	24	25
	26	27	28	29	1	2	3
SAFAR 1570	4	5	6	7	8	9	10
	11	12	13	14	15	16	17
	18	19	20	21	22	23	24
	25	26	27	28	29	30	1
RABĪ' I 1570	2	3	4	5	6	7	8

‡Leap year
[a]New Year
[b]'Ashūrā'
[c]Prophet's Birthday
[d]Ascent of the Prophet
[e]Start of Ramaḍān
[f]'Id al-Fiṭr
[g]'Id al-'Aḍḥā

GREGORIAN 2144‡

Julian‡ (Sun)	Sun	Mon	Tue	Wed	Thu	Fri	Sat	Month
Dec 15	29	30	31	1	2	3	4	
	5	6	7	8[a]	9	10	11	JANUARY 2144
Dec 29	12	13	14	15[b]	16	17	18	
	19	20	21	22	23	24	25	
Jan 12	26	27	28	29	30	31	1	
	2	3	4	5	6	7	8	FEBRUARY 2144
Jan 26	9	10	11	12	13	14	15	
	16	17	18	19	20	21	22	
Feb 9	23	24	25	26	27	28	29	
	1	2	3	4[c]	5	6	7	
Feb 23	8	9	10	11	12	13	14	MARCH 2144
	15[d]	16	17	18	19	20	21	
Mar 8	22	23	24	25	26	27	28	
	29	30	31	1	2	3	4	
Mar 22	5	6	7	8	9	10	11	APRIL 2144
	12	13	14	15	16	17	18	
Apr 5	19[e]	20	21	22	23	24	25	
	26[f]	27	28	29	30	1	2	
Apr 19	3	4	5	6	7	8	9	MAY 2144
	10	11	12	13	14	15	16	
May 3	17	18	19	20	21	22	23	
	24	25	26	27	28	29	30	
May 17	31	1	2	3	4	5	6	
	7	8	9	10	11	12	13	JUNE 2144
May 31	14	15	16	17	18	19	20	
	21	22	23	24	25	26	27	
Jun 14	28	29	30	1	2	3	4	
	5	6	7	8	9	10	11	JULY 2144
Jun 28	12	13	14	15	16	17	18	
	19	20	21	22	23	24	25	
Jul 12	26	27	28	29	30	31	1	
	2	3	4	5	6	7	8	AUGUST 2144
Jul 26	9	10	11	12	13	14	15	
	16	17	18	19	20	21	22	
Aug 9	23	24	25	26	27	28	29	
	30	31	1	2	3	4	5	
Aug 23	6	7	8	9	10	11	12	SEPTEMBER 2144
	13	14	15	16	17	18	19	
Sep 6	20	21	22	23	24	25	26	
	27	28	29	30	1	2	3	
Sep 20	4	5	6	7	8	9	10	OCTOBER 2144
	11	12	13	14	15	16	17	
Oct 4	18	19	20	21	22	23	24	
	25	26	27	28	29	30	31	
Oct 18	1	2	3	4	5	6	7	NOVEMBER 2144
	8	9	10	11	12	13	14	
Nov 1	15	16	17	18	19	20	21	
	22	23	24	25	26	27	28	
Nov 15	29[g]	30	1	2	3	4	5	
	6	7	8	9	10	11	12	DECEMBER 2144
Nov 29	13	14	15	16	17	18	19	
	20	21	22	23	24	25[h]	26	
Dec 13	27	28	29	30	31	1	2	

‡Leap year
[a]Orthodox Christmas
[b]Julian New Year
[c]Ash Wednesday
[d]Feast of Orthodoxy
[e]Easter
[f]Orthodox Easter
[g]Advent
[h]Christmas

2145

GREGORIAN 2145								Lunar Phases	ISO WEEK	JULIAN DAY	HEBREW 5905/5906								Molad	CHINESE Jiă-Chén/Yĭ-Sì‡								Solar Term	COPTIC 1861/1862								ETHIOPIC 2137/2138
	Sun	Mon	Tue	Wed	Thu	Fri	Sat		(Mon)	(Sun noon)		Sun	Mon	Tue	Wed	Thu	Fri	Sat			Sun	Mon	Tue	Wed	Thu	Fri	Sat			Sun	Mon	Tue	Wed	Thu	Fri	Sat	
JANUARY 2145	27	28	29	30	◐	1[a]	2	23:03	53	2504501	TEVETH 5905	1[e]	2[e]	3	4	5	6	7	Fri $3^{h}12^{m}6^{p}$	MONTH 12 Jiă-Chén	4	5	6	7	8	9	10		KOIAK 1861	17	18	19	20	21	22	23	TĀKHŚĀŚ 2137
	3	4	5	6	7	8	○	2:10	1	2504508		8	9	10	11	12	13	14			11	12	13	14	15	16	17	Xiăo hán		24	25	26	27	28	29[c]	30	
	10	11	12	13	14	15	◑	7:42	2	2504515		15	16	17	18	19	20	21			18	19	20	21	22	23	24		TŌBE 1861	1	2	3	4	5	6[d]	7	ṬER 2137
	17	18	19	20	21	22	●	3:09	3	2504522		22	23	24	25	26	27	28		MONTH 1 Yĭ-Sì	25	26	27	28	29	30	1[a]	Dà hán		8	9	10	11[e]	12	13	14	
	24	25	26	27	28	29	◐	20:50	4	2504529	SHEVAT 5905	29	1	2	3	4	5	6	Sat $15^{h}56^{m}7^{p}$		2	3	4*	5	6	7	8			15	16	17	18	19	20	21	
FEBRUARY 2145	31	1	2	3	4	5	6		5	2504536		7	8	9	10	11	12	13			9	10	11	12	13	14	15[b]	Lì chūn		22	23	24	25	26	27	28	
	○	8	9	10	11	12	13	17:21	6	2504543		14	15	16	17	18	19	20			16	17	18	19	20	21	22		MESHIR 1861	29	30	1	2	3	4	5	YAKĀTIT 2137
	◑	15	16	17	18	19	20	15:42	7	2504550		21	22	23	24	25	26	27			23	24	25	26	27	28	29	Yŭ shuĭ		6	7	8	9	10	11	12	
	●	22	23	24	25	26	27	17:12	8	2504557	ADAR 5905	28	29	30	1	2	3	4	Mon $4^{h}40^{m}8^{p}$	MONTH 2 Yĭ-Sì	30	1	2	3	4	5	6			13	14	15	16	17	18	19	
MARCH 2145	28	◐	2	3	4	5	6	18:17	9	2504564		5	6	7	8	9	10	11			7	8	9	10	11	12	13	Jīng zhé		20	21	22	23	24	25	26	
	7	8	○	10	11	12	13	6:10	10	2504571		12	13	14[f]	15	16	17	18			14	15	16	17	18	19	20		PAREMOTEP 1861	27	28	29	30	1	2	3	MAGĀBIT 2137
	14	◑	16	17	18	19	20[b]	23:17	11	2504578		19	20	21	22	23	24	25			21	22	23	24	25	26	27	Chūn fēn		4	5	6	7	8	9	10	
	21	22	●	24	25	26	27	8:50	12	2504585	NISAN 5905	26	27	28	29	1	2	3	Tue $17^{h}24^{m}9^{p}$	MONTH 3 Yĭ-Sì	28	29	1	2	3	4	5*			11	12	13	14	15	16	17	
APRIL 2145	28	29	30	◐	1	2	3	13:17	13	2504592		4	5	6	7	8	9	10			6	7	8	9	10	11	12			18	19	20	21	22	23	24	
	4	5	6	○	8	9	10	16:45	14	2504599		11	12	13	14	15[g]	16	17			13[c]	14	15	16	17	18	19	Qīng míng	PARMOUTE 1861	25	26	27	28	29	30	1	MIYĀZYĀ 2137
	11	12	13	◑	15	16	17	7:27	15	2504606		18	19	20	21	22	23	24			20	21	22	23	24	25	26			2	3	4	5	6	7	8	
	18	19	20	21	●	23	24	1:21	16	2504613	IYYAR 5905	25	26	27	28	29	30	1	Thu $6^{h}8^{m}10^{p}$	MONTH 4 Yĭ-Sì	27	28	29	30	1	2	3	Gŭ yŭ		9[f]	10	11	12	13	14	15	
MAY 2145	25	26	27	28	29	◐	1	4:45	17	2504620		2	3	4	5	6	7	8			4	5	6	7	8	9	10			16	17	18	19	20	21	22	
	2	3	4	5	6	○	8	1:22	18	2504627		9	10	11	12	13	14	15			11	12	13	14	15	16	17	Lì xià		23	24	25	26	27	28	29[g]	
	9	10	11	12	◑	14	15	17:09	19	2504634		16	17	18	19	20	21	22			18	19	20	21	22	23	24		PASHONS 1861	30	1	2	3	4	5	6	GENBOT 2137
	16	17	18	19	20	●	22	17:41	20	2504641	SIVAN 5905	23	24	25	26	27	28	29	Fri $18^{h}52^{m}11^{p}$	LEAP MONTH 4 Yĭ-Sì	25	26	27	28	29	30	1	Xiăo măn		7	8	9	10	11	12	13	
	23	24	25	26	27	28	◐	16:35	21	2504648		1	2	3	4	5	6[h]	7			2	3	4	5*	6	7	8			14	15	16	17	18	19	20	
JUNE 2145	30	31	1	2	3	4	○	8:41	22	2504655		8	9	10	11	12	13	14			9	10	11	12	13	14	15	Máng zhòng		21	22	23	24	25	26	27	
	6	7	8	9	10	11	◑	5:04	23	2504662		15	16	17	18	19	20	21			16	17	18	19	20	21	22		PAŌNE 1861	28	29	30	1	2	3	4	SANĒ 2137
	13	14	15	16	17	18	19		24	2504669	TAMMUZ 5905	22	23	24	25	26	27	28	Sun $7^{h}36^{m}12^{p}$	MONTH 5 Yĭ-Sì	23	24	25	26	27	28	29			5	6	7	8	9	10	11	
	●	21[c]	22	23	24	25	26	8:57	25	2504676		29	30	1	2	3	4	5			1	2	3	4	5[d]	6	7	Xià zhì		12	13	14	15	16	17	18	
JULY 2145	27	◐	29	30	1	2	3	1:14	26	2504683		6	7	8	9	10	11	12			8	9	10	11	12	13	14			19	20	21	22	23	24	25	
	○	5	6	7	8	9	10	15:40	27	2504690		13	14	15	16	17	18	19			15	16	17	18	19	20	21	Xiăo shŭ	EPĒP 1861	26	27	28	29	30	1	2	ḤAMLĒ 2137
	◑	12	13	14	15	16	17	19:27	28	2504697		20	21	22	23	24	25	26			22	23	24	25	26	27	28			3	4	5	6	7	8	9	
	18	●	20	21	22	23	24	22:46	29	2504704	AV 5905	27	28	29	1	2	3	4	Mon $20^{h}20^{m}13^{p}$	MONTH 6 Yĭ-Sì	29	30	1	2	3	4	5	Dà shŭ		10	11	12	13	14	15	16	
	25	26	◐	28	29	30	31	7:32	30	2504711		5	6	7	8	9[i]	10	11			6*	7	8	9	10	11	12			17	18	19	20	21	22	23	
AUGUST 2145	1	○	3	4	5	6	7	23:31	31	2504718		12	13	14	15	16	17	18			13	14	15	16	17	18	19	Lì qiū		24	25	26	27	28	29	30	
	8	9	◑	11	12	13	14	11:59	32	2504725		19	20	21	22	23	24	25			20	21	22	23	24	25	26		MESORĒ 1861	1	2	3	4	5	6	7	NAḤASĒ 2137
	15	16	17	●	19	20	21	11:14	33	2504732	ELUL 5905	26	27	28	29	30	1	2	Wed $9^{h}4^{m}14^{p}$	MONTH 7 Yĭ-Sì	27	28	29	1	2	3	4			8	9	10	11	12	13[h]	14	
	22	23	24	◐	26	27	28	12:35	34	2504739		3	4	5	6	7	8	9			5	6	7[e]	8	9	10	11	Chŭ shŭ		15	16	17	18	19	20	21	
SEPTEMBER 2145	29	30	31	○	2	3	4	9:26	35	2504746		10	11	12	13	14	15	16			12	13	14	15[f]	16	17	18			22	23	24	25	26	27	28	
	5	6	7	8	◑	10	11	6:00	36	2504753		17	18	19	20	21	22	23			19	20	21	22	23	24	25	Bái lù	EPAG. 1861	29	30	1	2	3	4	5	PĀG. 2137
	12	13	14	15	●	17	18	22:39	37	2504760	TISHRI 5906	24	25	26	27	28	29	1[a]	Thu $21^{h}48^{m}15^{p}$	MONTH 8 Yĭ-Sì	26	27	28	29	30	1	2		THOOUT 1862	1[a]	2	3	4	5	6	7	MASKARAM 2138
	19	20	21	22[d]	◐	24	25	17:48	38	2504767		2[a]	3	4	5	6	7	8			3	4	5	6	7*	8	9	Qiū fēn		8	9	10	11	12	13	14	
OCTOBER 2145	26	27	28	29	○	1	2	22:16	39	2504774		9	10[b]	11	12	13	14	15[c]			10	11	12	13	14	15[g]	16			15	16	17[b]	18	19	20	21	
	3	4	5	6	7	8	◑	0:33	40	2504781		16	17	18	19	20	21	22			17	18	19	20	21	22	23	Hán lù		22	23	24	25	26	27	28	
	10	11	12	13	14	15	●	9:20	41	2504788	HESHVAN 5906	23	24	25	26	27	28	29	Sat $10^{h}32^{m}16^{p}$	MONTH 9 Yĭ-Sì	24	25	26	27	28	29	1		PAOPE 1862	29	30	1	2	3	4	5	ṬEQEMT 2138
	17	18	19	20	21	22	◐	0:40	42	2504795		30	1	2	3	4	5	6			2	3	4	5	6	7	8	Shuāng jiàng		6	7	8	9	10	11	12	
	24	25	26	27	28	29	○	14:08	43	2504802		7	8	9	10	11	12	13			9[h]	10	11	12	13	14	15			13	14	15	16	17	18	19	
NOVEMBER 2145	31	1	2	3	4	5	6		44	2504809		14	15	16	17	18	19	20			16	17	18	19	20	21	22			20	21	22	23	24	25	26	
	◑	8	9	10	11	12	13	18:39	45	2504816	KISLEV 5906	21	22	23	24	25	26	27	Sun $23^{h}16^{m}17^{p}$		23	24	25	26	27	28	29	Lì dōng	ATHŌR 1862	27	28	29	30	1	2	3	ḪEDĀR 2138
	●	15	16	17	18	19	20	19:36	46	2504823		28	29	1	2	3	4	5		MONTH 10 Yĭ-Sì	30	1	2	3	4	5	6			4	5	6	7	8	9	10	
	◐	22	23	24	25	26	27	10:33	47	2504830		6	7	8	9	10	11	12			7	8*	9	10	11	12	13	Xiăo xuě		11	12	13	14	15	16	17	
DECEMBER 2145	28	○	30	1	2	3	4	8:20	48	2504837		13	14	15	16	17	18	19			14	15	16	17	18	19	20			18	19	20	21	22	23	24	
	5	6	◑	8	9	10	11	11:10	49	2504844	TEVETH 5906	20	21[d]	22	23	24	25[e]	26[e]	Tue $12^{h}1^{m}0^{p}$	MONTH 11 Yĭ-Sì	21	22	23	24	25	26	27	Dà xuě	KOIAK 1862	25	26	27	28	29	30	1	TĀKHŚĀŚ 2138
	12	13	●	15	16	17	18	5:47	50	2504851		27[e]	28[e]	29[e]	1[e]	2[e]	3[e]	4			28	29	1	2	3	4	5			2	3	4	5	6	7	8	
	19	20	◐[e]	22	23	24	25	0:17	51	2504858		5	6	7	8	9	10	11			6	7	8	9[i]	10	11	12	Dōng zhì		9	10	11	12	13	14	15	
	26	27	28	○	30	31	1	3:36	52	2504865		12	13	14	15	16	17	18			13	14	15	16	17	18	19			16	17	18	19	20	21	22	

[a]New Year
[b]Spring (10:55)
[c]Summer (2:25)
[d]Autumn (19:10)
[e]Winter (18:03)
● New moon
◐ First quarter moon
○ Full moon
◑ Last quarter moon

[a]New Year
[b]Yom Kippur
[c]Sukkot
[d]Winter starts
[e]Ḥanukkah
[f]Purim
[g]Passover
[h]Shavuot
[i]Fast of Av

‡Leap year
[a]New Year (4843, Snake)
[b]Lantern Festival
[c]Qīngmíng
[d]Dragon Festival
[e]Qĭqiăo
[f]Hungry Ghosts
[g]Mid-Autumn Festival
[h]Double-Ninth Festival
[i]Dōngzhì
*Start of 60-name cycle

[a]New Year
[b]Building of the Cross
[c]Christmas
[d]Jesus's Circumcision
[e]Epiphany
[f]Easter
[g]Mary's Announcement
[h]Jesus's Transfiguration

PERSIAN (ASTRONOMICAL) 1523‡/1524

Month	Sun	Mon	Tue	Wed	Thu	Fri	Sat
	7	8	9	10	11	12	13
DEY 1523	14	15	16	17	18	19	20
	21	22	23	24	25	26	27
	28	29	30	1	2	3	4
	5	6	7	8	9	10	11
BAHMAN 1523	12	13	14	15	16	17	18
	19	20	21	22	23	24	25
	26	27	28	29	30	1	2
	3	4	5	6	7	8	9
ESFAND 1523	10	11	12	13	14	15	16
	17	18	19	20	21	22	23
	24	25	26	27	28	29	30
	1[a]	2	3	4	5	6	7
FARVARDĪN 1524	8	9	10	11	12	13[b]	14
	15	16	17	18	19	20	21
	22	23	24	25	26	27	28
	29	30	31	1	2	3	4
ORDĪBEHEŠT 1524	5	6	7	8	9	10	11
	12	13	14	15	16	17	18
	19	20	21	22	23	24	25
	26	27	28	29	30	31	1
XORDĀD 1524	2	3	4	5	6	7	8
	9	10	11	12	13	14	15
	16	17	18	19	20	21	22
	23	24	25	26	27	28	29
	30	31	1	2	3	4	5
TĪR 1524	6	7	8	9	10	11	12
	13	14	15	16	17	18	19
	20	21	22	23	24	25	26
	27	28	29	30	31	1	2
MORDĀD 1524	3	4	5	6	7	8	9
	10	11	12	13	14	15	16
	17	18	19	20	21	22	23
	24	25	26	27	28	29	30
	31	1	2	3	4	5	6
SHAHRĪVAR 1524	7	8	9	10	11	12	13
	14	15	16	17	18	19	20
	21	22	23	24	25	26	27
	28	29	30	31	1	2	3
MEHR 1524	4	5	6	7	8	9	10
	11	12	13	14	15	16	17
	18	19	20	21	22	23	24
	25	26	27	28	29	30	1
ĀBĀN 1524	2	3	4	5	6	7	8
	9	10	11	12	13	14	15
	16	17	18	19	20	21	22
	23	24	25	26	27	28	29
	30	1	2	3	4	5	6
ĀZAR 1524	7	8	9	10	11	12	13
	14	15	16	17	18	19	20
	21	22	23	24	25	26	27
DEY 1524	28	29	30	1	2	3	4
	5	6	7	8	9	10	11

HINDU LUNAR 2201/2202‡

Month	Sun	Mon	Tue	Wed	Thu	Fri	Sat
	3	4	5	6	7	8	9
PAUSHA 2201	10	11	12	13	14	15	15
	16	17	18	20	21	22	23
	24	25	26	27	28	29	30
	1	2	3	4	5	6	7
MĀGHA 2201	8	9	10	11	12	13	14
	15	16	17	18	19	20	21
	22	23	25	26	27	28[h]	29
	30	1	2	3	4	5	6
PHĀLGUNA 2201	7	7	8	9	10	11	12
	13	14	15[i]	16	17	18	20
	21	22	23	24	25	26	27
	28	29	30	1[a]	2	3	4
CHAITRA 2202	5	6	7	8	9[b]	10	11
	12	13	14	15	16	17	18
	19	20	21	22	24	25	26
	27	28	29	30	1	1	2
VAIŚĀKHA 2202	3	4	5	6	7	8	9
	10	11	12	13	14	15	17
	18	19	20	21	22	23	24
	25	26	27	28	29	30	1
	2	3	4	5	6	7	8
JYAISHṬHA 2202	9	10	11	12	13	14	15
	16	17	18	19	21	22	23
	24	25	26	27	27	28	29
	30	1	2	3	4	5	6
ĀSHĀḌHA 2202	7	8	9	10	11	13	14
	15	16	17	18	19	20	21
	22	23	24	25	26	27	28
	29	30	1	2	3	4	5
LEAP ŚRĀVAṆA 2202	6	7	8	9	10	11	12
	13	14	16	17	18	19	20
	21	22	23	23	24	25	26
	27	28	29	30	1	2	3
ŚRĀVAṆA 2202	4	5	6	7	9	10	11
	12	13	14	15	16	17	18
	19	20	21	22	23[c]	24	25
	26	27	28	29	30	1	2
BHĀDRAPADA 2202	3	4[d]	5	6	7	8	9
	10	12	13	14	15	16	17
	18	19	19	20	21	22	23
	24	25	26	27	28	29	30
	1	2	3	4	6	7	8[e]
ĀŚVINA 2202	9[e]	10[e]	11	12	13	14	15
	16	17	18	19	20	21	22
	22	23	24	25	26	28	29
	30	1[f]	2	3	4	5	6
KĀRTTIKA 2202	7	8	9	10	11	12	13
	14	15	16	17	18	19	20
	21	22	23	24	25	26	27
	28	29	30	1	2	4	5
MĀRGAŚĪRA 2202	6	7	8	9	10	11[g]	12
	13	14	15	15	16	17	18

HINDU SOLAR 2066‡/2067

Month	Sun	Mon	Tue	Wed	Thu	Fri	Sat
	10	11	12	13	14	15	16
PAUSHA 2066	17	18	19	20	21	22	23
	24	25	26	27	28	29	1[b]
	2	3	4	5	6	7	8
MĀGHA 2066	9	10	11	12	13	14	15
	16	17	18	19	20	21	22
	23	24	25	26	27	28	29
	1	2	3	4	5	6	7
PHĀLGUNA 2066	8	9	10	11	12	13	14
	15	16	17	18	19	20	21
	22	23	24	25	26	27	28
	29	30	1	2	3	4	5
CHAITRA 2066	6	7	8	9	10	11	12
	13	14	15	16	17	18	19
	20	21	22	23	24	25	26
	27	28	29	30	31	1[a]	2
VAIŚĀKHA 2067	3	4	5	6	7	8	9
	10	11	12	13	14	15	16
	17	18	19	20	21	22	23
	24	25	26	27	28	29	30
	1	2	3	4	5	6	7
JYAISHṬHA 2067	8	9	10	11	12	13	14
	15	16	17	18	19	20	21
	22	23	24	25	26	27	28
	29	30	31	32	1	2	3
ĀSHĀḌHA 2067	4	5	6	7	8	9	10
	11	12	13	14	15	16	17
	18	19	20	21	22	23	24
	25	26	27	28	29	30	31
	32	1	2	3	4	5	6
ŚRĀVAṆA 2067	7	8	9	10	11	12	13
	14	15	16	17	18	19	20
	21	22	23	24	25	26	27
	28	29	30	31	1	2	3
BHĀDRAPADA 2067	4	5	6	7	8	9	10
	11	12	13	14	15	16	17
	18	19	20	21	22	23	24
	25	26	27	28	29	30	31
	1	2	3	4	5	6	7
ĀŚVINA 2067	8	9	10	11	12	13	14
	15	16	17	18	19	20	21
	22	23	24	25	26	27	28
	29	30	1	2	3	4	5
KĀRTTIKA 2067	6	7	8	9	10	11	12
	13	14	15	16	17	18	19
	20	21	22	23	24	25	26
	27	28	29	30	1	2	3
MĀRGAŚĪRA 2067	4	5	6	7	8	9	10
	11	12	13	14	15	16	17
	18	19	20	21	22	23	24
	25	26	27	28	29	30	1
PAUSHA 2067	2	3	4	5	6	7	8
	9	10	11	12	13	14	15

ISLAMIC (ASTRONOMICAL) 1570‡/1571

Month	Sun	Mon	Tue	Wed	Thu	Fri	Sat
	2	3	4	5	6	7	8
RABĪ' I 1570	9	10	11	12[c]	13	14	15
	16	17	18	19	20	21	22
	23	24	25	26	27	28	29
	1	2	3	4	5	6	7
RABĪ' II 1570	8	9	10	11	12	13	14
	15	16	17	18	19	20	21
	22	23	24	25	26	27	28
	29	30	1	2	3	4	5
JUMĀDĀ I 1570	6	7	8	9	10	11	12
	13	14	15	16	17	18	19
	20	21	22	23	24	25	26
	27	28	29	30	1	2	3
JUMĀDĀ II 1570	4	5	6	7	8	9	10
	11	12	13	14	15	16	17
	18	19	20	21	22	23	24
	25	26	27	28	29	1	2
RAJAB 1570	3	4	5	6	7	8	9
	10	11	12	13	14	15	16
	17	18	19	20	21	22	23
	24	25	26	27[d]	28	29	30
	1	2	3	4	5	6	7
SHA'BĀN 1570	8	9	10	11	12	13	14
	15	16	17	18	19	20	21
	22	23	24	25	26	27	28
	29	30	1[e]	2	3	4	5
RAMAḌĀN 1570	6	7	8	9	10	11	12
	13	14	15	16	17	18	19
	20	21	22	23	24	25	26
	27	28	29	30	1[f]	2	3
SHAWWĀL 1570	4	5	6	7	8	9	10
	11	12	13	14	15	16	17
	18	19	20	21	22	23	24
	25	26	27	28	29	1	2
DHU AL-QA'DA 1570	3	4	5	6	7	8	9
	10	11	12	13	14	15	16
	17	18	19	20	21	22	23
	24	25	26	27	28	29	30
	1	2	3	4	5	6	7
DHU AL-ḤIJJA 1570	8	9	10[g]	11	12	13	14
	15	16	17	18	19	20	21
	22	23	24	25	26	27	28
	29	1[a]	2	3	4	5	6
MUḤARRAM 1571	7	8	9	10[b]	11	12	13
	14	15	16	17	18	19	20
	21	22	23	24	25	26	27
	28	29	1	2	3	4	5
ṢAFAR 1571	6	7	8	9	10	11	12
	13	14	15	16	17	18	19
	20	21	22	23	24	25	26
	27	28	29	1	2	3	4
RABĪ' I 1571	5	6	7	8	9	10	11
	12[c]	13	14	15	16	17	18

GREGORIAN 2145

Julian (Sun)	Sun	Mon	Tue	Wed	Thu	Fri	Sat	Month
Dec 13	27	28	29	30	31	1	2	
	3	4	5	6	7	8[a]	9	JANUARY 2145
Dec 27	10	11	12	13	14	15[b]	16	
	17	18	19	20	21	22	23	
Jan 10	24	25	26	27	28	29	30	
	31	1	2	3	4	5	6	
Jan 24	7	8	9	10	11	12	13	FEBRUARY 2145
	14	15	16	17	18	19	20	
Feb 7	21	22	23	24[c]	25	26	27	
	28	1	2	3	4	5	6	
Feb 21	7[d]	8	9	10	11	12	13	MARCH 2145
	14	15	16	17	18	19	20	
Mar 7	21	22	23	24	25	26	27	
	28	29	30	31	1	2	3	
Mar 21	4	5	6	7	8	9	10	APRIL 2145
	11[e]	12	13	14	15	16	17	
Apr 4	18[f]	19	20	21	22	23	24	
	25	26	27	28	29	30	1	
Apr 18	2	3	4	5	6	7	8	
	9	10	11	12	13	14	15	MAY 2145
May 2	16	17	18	19	20	21	22	
	23	24	25	26	27	28	29	
May 16	30	31	1	2	3	4	5	
	6	7	8	9	10	11	12	JUNE 2145
May 30	13	14	15	16	17	18	19	
	20	21	22	23	24	25	26	
Jun 13	27	28	29	30	1	2	3	
	4	5	6	7	8	9	10	JULY 2145
Jun 27	11	12	13	14	15	16	17	
	18	19	20	21	22	23	24	
Jul 11	25	26	27	28	29	30	31	
	1	2	3	4	5	6	7	
Jul 25	8	9	10	11	12	13	14	AUGUST 2145
	15	16	17	18	19	20	21	
Aug 8	22	23	24	25	26	27	28	
	29	30	31	1	2	3	4	
Aug 22	5	6	7	8	9	10	11	SEPTEMBER 2145
	12	13	14	15	16	17	18	
Sep 5	19	20	21	22	23	24	25	
	26	27	28	29	30	1	2	
Sep 19	3	4	5	6	7	8	9	OCTOBER 2145
	10	11	12	13	14	15	16	
Oct 3	17	18	19	20	21	22	23	
	24	25	26	27	28	29	30	
Oct 17	31	1	2	3	4	5	6	
	7	8	9	10	11	12	13	NOVEMBER 2145
Oct 31	14	15	16	17	18	19	20	
	21	22	23	24	25	26	27	
Nov 14	28[g]	29	30	1	2	3	4	
	5	6	7	8	9	10	11	DECEMBER 2145
Nov 28	12	13	14	15	16	17	18	
	19	20	21	22	23	24	25[h]	
Dec 12	26	27	28	29	30	31	1	

Persian: ‡Leap year; [a]New Year; [b]Sizdeh Bedar

Hindu Lunar: ‡Leap year; [a]New Year (Viśvāvasu); [b]Birthday of Rāma; [c]Birthday of Krishna; [d]Ganēśa Chaturthī; [e]Dashara; [f]Diwali; [g]Birthday of Vishnu; [h]Night of Śiva; [i]Holi

Hindu Solar: ‡Leap year; [a]New Year (Rāudra); [b]Pongal

Islamic: ‡Leap year; [a]New Year; [b]'Ashūrā'; [c]Prophet's Birthday; [d]Ascent of the Prophet; [e]Start of Ramaḍān; [f]'Id al-Fiṭr; [g]'Id al-'Aḍḥā

Gregorian: [a]Orthodox Christmas; [b]Julian New Year; [c]Ash Wednesday; [d]Feast of Orthodoxy; [e]Easter; [f]Orthodox Easter; [g]Advent; [h]Christmas

2146

Gregorian 2146

Month	Sun	Mon	Tue	Wed	Thu	Fri	Sat	Lunar Phases	ISO Week (Mon)	Julian Day (Sun noon)
	26	27	28	○	30	31	1[a]	3:36	52	2504865
JANUARY 2146	2	3	4	5	◑	7	8	1:06	1	2504872
	9	10	11	●	13	14	15	16:18	2	2504879
	16	17	18	◐	20	21	22	17:38	3	2504886
	23	24	25	26	○	28	29	22:28	4	2504893
FEBRUARY 2146	30	31	1	2	3	◑	5	11:58	5	2504900
	6	7	8	9	10	●	12	3:33	6	2504907
	13	14	15	16	17	◐	19	13:22	7	2504914
	20	21	22	23	24	25	○	15:32	8	2504921
MARCH 2146	27	28	1	2	3	4	◑	20:07	9	2504928
	6	7	8	9	10	11	●	15:47	10	2504935
	13	14	15	16	17	18	19		11	2504942
	◐[b]	21	22	23	24	25	26	9:47	12	2504949
APRIL 2146	27	○	29	30	31	1	2	5:49	13	2504956
	3	◑	5	6	7	8	9	2:36	14	2504963
	10	●	12	13	14	15	16	4:59	15	2504970
	17	18	◐	20	21	22	23	5:16	16	2504977
	24	25	○	27	28	29	30	17:02	17	2504984
MAY 2146	1	2	◑	4	5	6	7	8:46	18	2504991
	8	9	●	11	12	13	14	18:58	19	2504998
	15	16	17	◐	19	20	21	22:33	20	2505005
	22	23	24	25	○	27	28	1:38	21	2505012
JUNE 2146	29	30	31	◑	2	3	4	15:52	22	2505019
	5	6	7	8	●	10	11	9:33	23	2505026
	12	13	14	15	16	◐	18	12:53	24	2505033
	19	20	21[c]	22	23	○	25	8:38	25	2505040
JULY 2146	26	27	28	29	30	◑	2	0:54	26	2505047
	3	4	5	6	7	8	●	0:33	27	2505054
	10	11	12	13	14	15	16		28	2505061
	◐	18	19	20	21	22	○	0:04 15:15	29	2505068
	24	25	26	27	28	29	◑	12:29	30	2505075
AUGUST 2146	31	1	2	3	4	5	6		31	2505082
	●	8	9	10	11	12	13	15:43	32	2505089
	14	◐	16	17	18	19	20	8:29	33	2505096
	○	22	23	24	25	26	27	22:42	34	2505103
SEPTEMBER 2146	28	◑	30	31	1	2	3	2:59	35	2505110
	4	5	●	7	8	9	10	6:33	36	2505117
	11	12	◐	14	15	16	17	15:05	37	2505124
	18	19	○	21	22	23[d]	24	7:55	38	2505131
OCTOBER 2146	25	26	◑	28	29	30	1	20:24	39	2505138
	2	3	4	●	6	7	8	20:30	40	2505145
	9	10	11	◐	13	14	15	21:08	41	2505152
	16	17	18	○	20	21	22	19:32	42	2505159
	23	24	25	26	◑	28	29	16:08	43	2505166
NOVEMBER 2146	30	31	1	2	3	●	5	9:16	44	2505173
	6	7	8	9	10	◐	12	3:57	45	2505180
	13	14	15	16	17	○	19	9:53	46	2505187
	20	21	22	23	24	25	◑	12:48	47	2505194
DECEMBER 2146	27	28	29	30	1	2	●	20:57	48	2505201
	4	5	6	7	8	9	◐	12:43	49	2505208
	11	12	13	14	15	16	17		50	2505215
	○	19	20	21[e]	22	23	24	2:56	51	2505222
	25	◑	27	28	29	30	31	8:24	52	2505229

Hebrew 5906/5907‡

ISO Week	Month	Sun	Mon	Tue	Wed	Thu	Fri	Sat	Molad
52	TEVETH 5906	12	13	14	15	16	17	18	
1		19	20	21	22	23	24	25	
2		26	27	28	29	1	2	3	Thu $0^h45^m1^p$
3	SHEVAT 5906	4	5	6	7	8	9	10	
4		11	12	13	14	15	16	17	
5		18	19	20	21	22	23	24	
6		25	26	27	28	29	30	1	Fri $13^h29^m2^p$
7	ADAR 5906	2	3	4	5	6	7	8	
8		9	10	11	12	13	14[f]	15	
9		16	17	18	19	20	21	22	
10		23	24	25	26	27	28	29	
11		1	2	3	4	5	6	7	Sun $2^h13^m3^p$
12	NISAN 5906	8	9	10	11	12	13	14	
13		15[g]	16	17	18	19	20	21	
14		22	23	24	25	26	27	28	
15		29	30	1	2	3	4	5	Mon $14^h57^m4^p$
16	IYYAR 5906	6	7	8	9	10	11	12	
17		13	14	15	16	17	18	19	
18		20	21	22	23	24	25	26	
19		27	28	29	1	2	3	4	Wed $3^h41^m5^p$
20	SIVAN 5906	5	6[h]	7	8	9	10	11	
21		12	13	14	15	16	17	18	
22		19	20	21	22	23	24	25	
23		26	27	28	29	30	1	2	Thu $16^h25^m6^p$
24	TAMMUZ 5906	3	4	5	6	7	8	9	
25		10	11	12	13	14	15	16	
26		17	18	19	20	21	22	23	
27		24	25	26	27	28	29	1	Sat $5^h9^m7^p$
28	AV 5906	2	3	4	5	6	7	8	
29		9[i]	10	11	12	13	14	15	
30		16	17	18	19	20	21	22	
31		23	24	25	26	27	28	29	
32		30	1	2	3	4	5	6	Sun $17^h53^m8^p$
33	ELUL 5906	7	8	9	10	11	12	13	
34		14	15	16	17	18	19	20	
35		21	22	23	24	25	26	27	
36		28	29	1[a]	2[a]	3	4	5	Tue $6^h37^m9^p$
37	TISHRI 5907	6	7	8	9	10[b]	11	12	
38		13	14	15[c]	16	17	18	19	
39		20	21	22	23	24	25	26	
40		27	28	29	30	1	2	3	Wed $19^h21^m10^p$
41	HESHVAN 5907	4	5	6	7	8	9	10	
42		11	12	13	14	15	16	17	
43		18	19	20	21	22	23	24	
44		25	26	27	28	29	1	2	Fri $8^h5^m11^p$
45	KISLEV 5907	3	4	5	6	7	8	9	
46		10	11	12	13	14	15	16	
47		17	18	19	20	21	22	23	
48		24	25[e]	26[e]	27[e]	28[e]	29[e]	30[e]	
49	TEVETH 5907	1[e]	2[e]	3[d]	4	5	6	7	Sat $20^h49^m12^p$
50		8	9	10	11	12	13	14	
51		15	16	17	18	19	20	21	
52		22	23	24	25	26	27	28	

Chinese Yǐ-Sì‡/Bǐng-Wǔ

ISO Week	Month	Sun	Mon	Tue	Wed	Thu	Fri	Sat	Solar Term
52	MONTH 11 Yǐ-Sì	13	14	15	16	17	18	19	
1		20	21	22	23	24	25	26	Xiǎo hán
2		27	28	29	30	1	2	3	
3	MONTH 12 Yǐ-Sì	4	5	6	7	**8**	9*	10	**Dà hán**
4		11	12	13	14	15	16	17	
5		18	19	20	21	22	23	24	Lì chūn
6		25	26	27	28	29	1[a]	2	
7	MONTH 1 Bǐng-Wǔ	3	4	5	6	7	8	**9**	**Yǔ shuǐ**
8		10	11	12	13	14	15[b]	16	
9		17	18	19	20	21	22	23	
10		24	25	26	27	28	29	1	Jīng zhé
11		2	3	4	5	6	7	8	
12	MONTH 2 Bǐng-Wǔ	9	**10**	11*	12	13	14	15	**Chūn fēn**
13		16	17	18	19	20	21	22	
14		23	24	25[c]	26	27	28	29	Qīng míng
15		30	1	2	3	4	5	6	
16	MONTH 3 Bǐng-Wǔ	7	8	9	**10**	11	12	13	**Gǔ yǔ**
17		14	15	16	17	18	19	20	
18		21	22	23	24	25	26	27	Lì xià
19		28	29	30	1	2	3	4	
20	MONTH 4 Bǐng-Wǔ	5	6	7	8	9	10	**11***	**Xiǎo mǎn**
21		12	13	14	15	16	17	18	
22		19	20	21	22	23	24	25	
23		26	27	28	29	1	2	3	Máng zhòng
24	MONTH 5 Bǐng-Wǔ	4	5[d]	6	7	8	9	10	
25		11	12	**13**	14	15	16	17	**Xià zhì**
26		18	19	20	21	22	23	24	
27		25	26	27	28	29	30	1	Xiǎo shǔ
28	MONTH 6 Bǐng-Wǔ	2	3	4	5	6	7	8	
29		9	10	11	12*	13	14	**15**	**Dà shǔ**
30		16	17	18	19	20	21	22	
31		23	24	25	26	27	28	29	
32	MONTH 7 Bǐng-Wǔ	1	2	3	4	5	6	7[e]	Lì qiū
33		8	9	10	11	12	13	14	
34		15[f]	16	**17**	18	19	20	21	**Chǔ shǔ**
35		22	23	24	25	26	27	28	
36		29	30	1	2	3	4	5	Bái lù
37	MONTH 8 Bǐng-Wǔ	6	7	8	9	10	11	12	
38		13*	14	15[g]	16	17	**18**	19	**Qiū fēn**
39		20	21	22	23	24	25	26	
40		27	28	29	30	1	2	3	Hán lù
41	MONTH 9 Bǐng-Wǔ	4	5	6	7	8	9[h]	10	
42		11	12	13	14	15	16	17	
43		**18**	19	20	21	22	23	24	**Shuāng jiàng**
44		25	26	27	28	29	1	2	
45	MONTH 10 Bǐng-Wǔ	3	4	5	6	7	8	9	Lì dōng
46		10	11	12	13	14*	15	16	
47		17	18	**19**	20	21	22	23	**Xiǎo xuě**
48		24	25	26	27	28	29	30	
49	MONTH 11 Bǐng-Wǔ	1	2	3	4	5	6	7	Dà xuě
50		8	9	10	11	12	13	14	
51		15	16	17	18	19[i]	20	21	**Dōng zhì**
52		22	23	24	25	26	27	28	

Coptic 1862/1863‡ — Ethiopic 2138/2139‡

ISO Week	Coptic Month	Sun	Mon	Tue	Wed	Thu	Fri	Sat	Ethiopic Month
52	KOIAK 1862	16	17	18	19	20	21	22	TĀKHŚĀŚ 2138
1		23	24	25	26	27	28	29[c]	
2	TŌBE 1862	30	1	2	3	4	5	6[d]	ṬER 2138
3		7	8	9	10	11[e]	12	13	
4		14	15	16	17	18	19	20	
5		21	22	23	24	25	26	27	
6	MESHIR 1862	28	29	30	1	2	3	4	YAKĀTIT 2138
7		5	6	7	8	9	10	11	
8		12	13	14	15	16	17	18	
9		19	20	21	22	23	24	25	
10	PAREMOTEP 1862	26	27	28	29	30	1	2	MAGĀBIT 2138
11		3	4	5	6	7	8	9	
12		10	11	12	13	14	15	16	
13		17	18	19	20	21	22	23	
14		24	25	26	27	28	29	30	
15	PARMOUTE 1862	1	2	3	4	5	6	7	MIYĀZYĀ 2138
16		8	9	10	11	12	13	14	
17		15	16	17	18	19	20	21	
18		22	23	24	25	26	27	28	
19		29[f][g]	30	1	2	3	4	5	
20	PASHONS 1862	6	7	8	9	10	11	12	GENBOT 2138
21		13	14	15	16	17	18	19	
22		20	21	22	23	24	25	26	
23		27	28	29	30	1	2	3	
24	PAŌNE 1862	4	5	6	7	8	9	10	SANĒ 2138
25		11	12	13	14	15	16	17	
26		18	19	20	21	22	23	24	
27		25	26	27	28	29	30	1	
28	EPĒP 1862	2	3	4	5	6	7	8	ḤAMLĒ 2138
29		9	10	11	12	13	14	15	
30		16	17	18	19	20	21	22	
31		23	24	25	26	27	28	29	
32		30	1	2	3	4	5	6	
33	MESORĒ 1862	7	8	9	10	11	12	13[h]	NAḤASĒ 2138
34		14	15	16	17	18	19	20	
35		21	22	23	24	25	26	27	
36		28	29	30	1	2	3	4	
37	EPAG. 1862 / THOOUT 1863	5	1[a]	2	3	4	5	6	PĀG. 2138 / MASKARAM 2139
38		7	8	9	10	11	12	13	
39		14	15	16	17[b]	18	19	20	
40		21	22	23	24	25	26	27	
41		28	29	30	1	2	3	4	
42	PAOPE 1863	5	6	7	8	9	10	11	ṬEQEMT 2139
43		12	13	14	15	16	17	18	
44		19	20	21	22	23	24	25	
45		26	27	28	29	30	1	2	
46	ATHŌR 1863	3	4	5	6	7	8	9	ḪEDĀR 2139
47		10	11	12	13	14	15	16	
48		17	18	19	20	21	22	23	
49		24	25	26	27	28	29	30	
50	KOIAK 1863	1	2	3	4	5	6	7	TĀKHŚĀŚ 2139
51		8	9	10	11	12	13	14	
52		15	16	17	18	19	20	21	

Gregorian:
[a]New Year
[b]Spring (16:42)
[c]Summer (8:12)
[d]Autumn (1:06)
[e]Winter (23:55)
● New moon
◐ First quarter moon
○ Full moon
◑ Last quarter moon

Hebrew:
‡Leap year
[a]New Year
[b]Yom Kippur
[c]Sukkot
[d]Winter starts
[e]Ḥanukkah
[f]Purim
[g]Passover
[h]Shavuot
[i]Fast of Av

Chinese:
‡Leap year
[a]New Year (4844, Horse)
[b]Lantern Festival
[c]Qīngmíng
[d]Dragon Festival
[e]Qīqiǎo
[f]Hungry Ghosts
[g]Mid-Autumn Festival
[h]Double-Ninth Festival
[i]Dōngzhì
*Start of 60-name cycle

Coptic/Ethiopic:
‡Leap year
[a]New Year
[b]Building of the Cross
[c]Christmas
[d]Jesus's Circumcision
[e]Epiphany
[f]Easter
[g]Mary's Announcement
[h]Jesus's Transfiguration

PERSIAN (ASTRONOMICAL) 1524/1525

Month	Sun	Mon	Tue	Wed	Thu	Fri	Sat
DEY 1524	5	6	7	8	9	10	11
	12	13	14	15	16	17	18
	19	20	21	22	23	24	25
	26	27	28	29	30	1	2
BAHMAN 1524	3	4	5	6	7	8	9
	10	11	12	13	14	15	16
	17	18	19	20	21	22	23
	24	25	26	27	28	29	30
ESFAND 1524	1	2	3	4	5	6	7
	8	9	10	11	12	13	14
	15	16	17	18	19	20	21
	22	23	24	25	26	27	28
FARVARDĪN 1525	29	1[a]	2	3	4	5	6
	7	8	9	10	11	12	13[b]
	14	15	16	17	18	19	20
	21	22	23	24	25	26	27
ORDĪBEHEŠT 1525	28	29	30	31	1	2	3
	4	5	6	7	8	9	10
	11	12	13	14	15	16	17
	18	19	20	21	22	23	24
	25	26	27	28	29	30	31
XORDĀD 1525	1	2	3	4	5	6	7
	8	9	10	11	12	13	14
	15	16	17	18	19	20	21
	22	23	24	25	26	27	28
TĪR 1525	29	30	31	1	2	3	4
	5	6	7	8	9	10	11
	12	13	14	15	16	17	18
	19	20	21	22	23	24	25
MORDĀD 1525	26	27	28	29	30	31	1
	2	3	4	5	6	7	8
	9	10	11	12	13	14	15
	16	17	18	19	20	21	22
	23	24	25	26	27	28	29
SHAHRĪVAR 1525	30	31	1	2	3	4	5
	6	7	8	9	10	11	12
	13	14	15	16	17	18	19
	20	21	22	23	24	25	26
MEHR 1525	27	28	29	30	31	1	2
	3	4	5	6	7	8	9
	10	11	12	13	14	15	16
	17	18	19	20	21	22	23
	24	25	26	27	28	29	30
ĀBĀN 1525	1	2	3	4	5	6	7
	8	9	10	11	12	13	14
	15	16	17	18	19	20	21
	22	23	24	25	26	27	28
ĀZAR 1525	29	30	1	2	3	4	5
	6	7	8	9	10	11	12
	13	14	15	16	17	18	19
	20	21	22	23	24	25	26
DEY 1525	27	28	29	30	1	2	3
	4	5	6	7	8	9	10

[a]New Year
[b]Sizdeh Bedar

HINDU LUNAR 2202‡/2203

Month	Sun	Mon	Tue	Wed	Thu	Fri	Sat
MĀRGAŚĪRA 2202	13	14	15	*15*	16	17	18
	19	20	21	22	23	24	25
PAUSHA 2202	**26**	28	29	30	1	2	3
	4	5	6	7	8	9	10
	11	12	13	14	15	16	17
	18	19	20	21	22	23	24
MĀGHA 2202	25	26	27	28	29	30	**1**
	3	4	5	6	7	*7*	8
	9	10	11	12	13	14	15
	16	17	18	19	20	21	22
	23	24	**25**	27	28	29[h]	30
PHĀLGUNA 2202	1	2	3	4	5	6	7
	8	9	10	*10*	11	12	13
	14	15[i]	16	17	**18**	20	21
	22	23	24	25	26	27	28
CHAITRA 2203	29	30	1[a]	2	3	4	5
	6	7	8	9[b]	10	11	12
	13	14	15	16	17	18	19
	20	21	**22**	24	25	26	27
VAIŚĀKHA 2203	28	29	30	1	2	3	4
	5	*5*	6	7	8	9	10
	11	12	13	14	**15**	17	18
	19	20	21	22	23	24	25
JYAISHTHA 2203	26	27	28	29	30	1	2
	3	4	5	6	7	8	9
	10	11	12	13	14	15	16
	17	**18**	20	21	22	23	24
ĀSHĀḌHA 2203	25	26	27	28	29	30	1
	1	2	3	4	5	6	7
	8	9	10	**11**	13	14	15
	16	17	18	19	20	21	22
	23	24	25	26	27	28	29
ŚRĀVAṆA 2203	30	1	2	3	4	5	6
	7	8	9	10	11	12	13
	14	16	17	18	19	20	21
	22	23[c]	24	25	26	27	28
BHĀDRAPADA 2203	*28*	29	30	1	2	3	4[d]
	5	6	**7**	9	10	11	12
	13	14	15	16	17	18	19
	20	21	22	23	24	25	26
ĀŚVINA 2203	27	28	29	30	1	2	3
	4	5	6	7	8[e]	9[e]	10[e]
	11	13	14	15	16	17	18
	19	20	21	22	*22*	23	24
KĀRTTIKA 2203	25	26	27	28	29	30	1[f]
	2	3	**4**	6	7	8	9
	10	11	12	13	14	15	16
	17	18	19	20	21	22	23
	24	25	26	27	28	29	30
MĀRGAŚĪRA 2203	1	2	3	4	5	6	7
	8	**9**	11[g]	12	13	14	15
	15	16	17	18	19	20	21
	22	23	24	25	26	27	28

‡Leap year
[a]New Year (Parābhava)
[b]Birthday of Rāma
[c]Birthday of Krishna
[d]Ganēśa Chaturthī
[e]Dashara
[f]Diwali
[g]Birthday of Vishnu
[h]Night of Śiva
[i]Holi

HINDU SOLAR 2067/2068

Month	Sun	Mon	Tue	Wed	Thu	Fri	Sat
PAUSHA 2067	9	10	11	12	13	14	15
	16	17	18	19	20	21	22
	23	24	25	26	27	28	29
MĀGHA 2067	1[b]	2	3	4	5	6	7
	8	9	10	11	12	13	14
	15	16	17	18	19	20	21
	22	23	24	25	26	27	28
PHĀLGUNA 2067	29	30	1	2	3	4	5
	6	7	8	9	10	11	12
	13	14	15	16	17	18	19
	20	21	22	23	24	25	26
CHAITRA 2067	27	28	29	1	2	3	4
	5	6	7	8	9	10	11
	12	13	14	15	16	17	18
	19	20	21	22	23	24	25
VAIŚĀKHA 2068	26	27	28	29	30	31	1[a]
	2	3	4	5	6	7	8
	9	10	11	12	13	14	15
	16	17	18	19	20	21	22
	23	24	25	26	27	28	29
JYAISHTHA 2068	30	31	1	2	3	4	5
	6	7	8	9	10	11	12
	13	14	15	16	17	18	19
	20	21	22	23	24	25	26
ĀSHĀḌHA 2068	27	28	29	30	31	1	2
	3	4	5	6	7	8	9
	10	11	12	13	14	15	16
	17	18	19	20	21	22	23
	24	25	26	27	28	29	30
ŚRĀVAṆA 2068	31	32	1	2	3	4	5
	6	7	8	9	10	11	12
	13	14	15	16	17	18	19
	20	21	22	23	24	25	26
BHĀDRAPADA 2068	27	28	29	30	31	1	2
	3	4	5	6	7	8	9
	10	11	12	13	14	15	16
	17	18	19	20	21	22	23
	24	25	26	27	28	29	30
ĀŚVINA 2068	31	1	2	3	4	5	6
	7	8	9	10	11	12	13
	14	15	16	17	18	19	20
	21	22	23	24	25	26	27
KĀRTTIKA 2068	28	29	30	31	1	2	3
	4	5	6	7	8	9	10
	11	12	13	14	15	16	17
	18	19	20	21	22	23	24
MĀRGAŚĪRA 2068	25	26	27	28	29	30	1
	2	3	4	5	6	7	8
	9	10	11	12	13	14	15
	16	17	18	19	20	21	22
	23	24	25	26	27	28	29
PAUSHA 2068	1	2	3	4	5	6	7
	8	9	10	11	12	13	14

[a]New Year (Durmati)
[b]Pongal

ISLAMIC (ASTRONOMICAL) 1571/1572

Month	Sun	Mon	Tue	Wed	Thu	Fri	Sat
RABĪ' I 1571	12	13	14	15	16	17	18
	19	20	21	22	23	24	25
RABĪ' II 1571	26	27	28	29	30	1	2
	3	4	5	6	7	8	9
	10	11	12	13	14	15	16
	17	18	19	20	21	22	23
JUMĀDĀ I 1571	24	25	26	27	28	29	1
	2	3	4	5	6	7	8
	9	10	11	12	13	14	15
	16	17	18	19	20	21	22
	23	24	25	26	27	28	29
JUMĀDĀ II 1571	30	1	2	3	4	5	6
	7	8	9	10	11	12	13
	14	15	16	17	18	19	20
	21	22	23	24	25	26	27
RAJAB 1571	28	29	1	2	3	4	5
	6	7	8	9	10	11	12
	13	14	15	16	17	18	19
	20	21	22	23	24	25	26
SHA'BĀN 1571	27[d]	28	29	30	1	2	3
	4	5	6	7	8	9	10
	11	12	13	14	15	16	17
	18	19	20	21	22	23	24
RAMAḌĀN 1571	25	26	27	28	29	30	1[e]
	2	3	4	5	6	7	8
	9	10	11	12	13	14	15
	16	17	18	19	20	21	22
	23	24	25	26	27	28	29
SHAWWĀL 1571	30	1[f]	2	3	4	5	6
	7	8	9	10	11	12	13
	14	15	16	17	18	19	20
	21	22	23	24	25	26	27
DHU AL-QA'DA 1571	28	29	30	1	2	3	4
	5	6	7	8	9	10	11
	12	13	14	15	16	17	18
	19	20	21	22	23	24	25
DHU AL-ḤIJJA 1571	26	27	28	29	1	2	3
	4	5	6	7	8	9	10[g]
	11	12	13	14	15	16	17
	18	19	20	21	22	23	24
MUḤARRAM 1572	25	26	27	28	29	1[a]	2
	3	4	5	6	7	8	9
	10[b]	11	12	13	14	15	16
	17	18	19	20	21	22	23
	24	25	26	27	28	29	30
ṢAFAR 1572	1	2	3	4	5	6	7
	8	9	10	11	12	13	14
	15	16	17	18	19	20	21
	22	23	24	25	26	27	28
RABĪ' I 1572	29	1	2	3	4	5	6
	7	8	9	10	11	12[c]	13
	14	15	16	17	18	19	20
	21	22	23	24	25	26	27

[a]New Year
[b]'Ashūrā'
[c]Prophet's Birthday
[d]Ascent of the Prophet
[e]Start of Ramaḍān
[f]'Id al-Fiṭr
[g]'Id al-'Aḍḥā

GREGORIAN 2146

Julian (Sun)	Sun	Mon	Tue	Wed	Thu	Fri	Sat	Month
Dec 12	26	27	28	29	30	31	1	JANUARY 2146
	2	3	4	5	6	7	8[a]	
Dec 26	9	10	11	12	13	14	15[b]	
	16	17	18	19	20	21	22	
Jan 9	23	24	25	26	27	28	29	
	30	31	1	2	3	4	5	FEBRUARY 2146
Jan 23	6	7	8	9	10	11	12	
	13	14	15	16[c]	17	18	19	
Feb 6	20	21	22	23	24	25	26	
	27	28	1	2	3	4	5	MARCH 2146
Feb 20	6	7	8	9	10	11	12	
	13	14	15	16	17	18	19	
Mar 6	20	21	22	23	24	25	26	
	27[d]	28	29	30	31	1	2	APRIL 2146
Mar 20	3[e]	4	5	6	7	8	9	
	10	11	12	13	14	15	16	
Apr 3	17	18	19	20	21	22	23	
	24	25	26	27	28	29	30	
Apr 17	1	2	3	4	5	6	7	MAY 2146
	8[f]	9	10	11	12	13	14	
May 1	15	16	17	18	19	20	21	
	22	23	24	25	26	27	28	
May 15	29	30	31	1	2	3	4	JUNE 2146
	5	6	7	8	9	10	11	
May 29	12	13	14	15	16	17	18	
	19	20	21	22	23	24	25	
Jun 12	26	27	28	29	30	1	2	JULY 2146
	3	4	5	6	7	8	9	
Jun 26	10	11	12	13	14	15	16	
	17	18	19	20	21	22	23	
Jul 10	24	25	26	27	28	29	30	
	31	1	2	3	4	5	6	AUGUST 2146
Jul 24	7	8	9	10	11	12	13	
	14	15	16	17	18	19	20	
Aug 7	21	22	23	24	25	26	27	
	28	29	30	31	1	2	3	SEPTEMBER 2146
Aug 21	4	5	6	7	8	9	10	
	11	12	13	14	15	16	17	
Sep 4	18	19	20	21	22	23	24	
	25	26	27	28	29	30	1	OCTOBER 2146
Sep 18	2	3	4	5	6	7	8	
	9	10	11	12	13	14	15	
Oct 2	16	17	18	19	20	21	22	
	23	24	25	26	27	28	29	
Oct 16	30	31	1	2	3	4	5	NOVEMBER 2146
	6	7	8	9	10	11	12	
Oct 30	13	14	15	16	17	18	19	
	20	21	22	23	24	25	26	
Nov 13	27[g]	28	29	30	1	2	3	DECEMBER 2146
	4	5	6	7	8	9	10	
Nov 27	11	12	13	14	15	16	17	
	18	19	20	21	22	23	24	
Dec 11	25[h]	26	27	28	29	30	31	

[a]Orthodox Christmas
[b]Julian New Year
[c]Ash Wednesday
[d]Feast of Orthodoxy
[e]Easter
[f]Orthodox Easter
[g]Advent
[h]Christmas

2147

Gregorian 2147	Sun	Mon	Tue	Wed	Thu	Fri	Sat	Lunar Phases	ISO Week (Mon)	Julian Day (Sun noon)	Hebrew 5907‡/5908	Sun	Mon	Tue	Wed	Thu	Fri	Sat	Molad	Chinese Bǐng-Wǔ/Dīng-Wèi‡	Sun	Mon	Tue	Wed	Thu	Fri	Sat	Solar Term	Coptic 1863‡/1864	Sun	Mon	Tue	Wed	Thu	Fri	Sat	Ethiopic 2139‡/2140
JANUARY 2147	1[a]	●	3	4	5	6	7	7:58	1	2505236	SHEVAT 5907	29	1	2	3	4	5	6	Mon 9h33m13p	MONTH 12 Bǐng-Wǔ	29	1	2	3	4	*5*	6	Xiǎo hán	KOIAK 1863	22	23	24	25	26	27	28	TĀKHŚĀŚ 2139
	8	◐	10	11	12	13	14	0:06	2	2505243		7	8	9	10	11	12	13			7	8	9	10	11	12	13		ṬŌBE 1863	29[c]	30	1	2	3	4	5	ṬER 2139
	15	○	17	18	19	20	21	22:00	3	2505250		14	15	16	17	18	19	20			14	15*	16	17	18	**19**	20	Dà hán		6[d]	7	8	9	10	11[e]	12	
	22	23	24	◑	26	27	28	1:05	4	2505257		21	22	23	24	25	26	27			21	22	23	24	25	26	27			13	14	15	16	17	18	19	
FEBRUARY 2147	29	30	●	1	2	3	4	18:41	5	2505264	ADAR I 5907	28	29	30	1	2	3	4	Tue 22h17m14p	MONTH 1 Dīng-Wèi	28	29	30	1[a]	2	3	*4*	Lì chūn		20	21	22	23	24	25	26	
	5	6	◐	8	9	10	11	14:15	6	2505271		5	6	7	8	9	10	11			5	6	7	8	9	10	11		MESHIR 1863	27	28	29	30	1	2	3	YAKĀTIT 2139
	12	13	14	○	16	17	18	17:37	7	2505278		12	13	14	15	16	17	18			12	13	14	15[b]	16	17	18			4	5	6	7	8	9	10	
	19	20	21	22	◑	24	25	13:59	8	2505285		19	20	21	22	23	24	25			**19**	20	21	22	23	24	25	Yǔ shuǐ		11	12	13	14	15	16	17	
MARCH 2147	26	27	28	1	●	3	4	5:15	9	2505292	ADAR II 5907	26	27	28	29	30	1	2	Thu 11h1m15p	MONTH 2 Dīng-Wèi	26	27	28	29	1	2	3			18	19	20	21	22	23	24	
	5	6	7	8	◐	10	11	6:50	10	2505299		3	4	5	6	7	8	9			4	5	6	7	8	9	10	Jīng zhé	PAREMOTEP 1863	25	26	27	28	29	30	1	MAGĀBIT 2139
	12	13	14	15	16	○	18	11:50	11	2505306		10	11	12	13	14[f]	15	16			11	12	13	14	15	16*	17			2	3	4	5	6	7	8	
	19	20[b]	21	22	23	◑	25	23:20	12	2505313		17	18	19	20	21	22	23			18	19	**20**	21	22	23	24	Chūn fēn		9	10	11	12	13	14	15	
APRIL 2147	26	27	28	29	30	●	1	15:42	13	2505320	NISAN 5907	24	25	26	27	28	29	1	Fri 23h45m16p	MONTH 3 Dīng-Wèi	25	26	27	28	29	1	2			16	17	18	19	20	21	22	
	2	3	4	5	6	7	◐	1:05	14	2505327		2	3	4	5	6	7	8			3	4	5	6[c]	7	8	9	Qīng míng		23	24	25	26	27	28	29	
	9	10	11	12	13	14	15		15	2505334		9	10	11	12	13	14	15[g]			10	11	12	13	14	15	16		PARMOUTE 1863	30	1	2	3	4	5	6	MIYĀZYĀ 2139
	○	17	18	19	20	21	22	3:10	16	2505341		16	17	18	19	20	21	22			17	18	19	20	**21**	22	23	Gǔ yǔ		7	8	9	10	11	12	13	
	◑	24	25	26	27	28	29	6:07	17	2505348		23	24	25	26	27	28	29			24	25	26	27	28	29	30			14[f]	15	16	17	18	19	20	
MAY 2147	●	1	2	3	4	5	6	2:16	18	2505355	IYAR 5907	30	1	2	3	4	5	6	Sun 12h29m17p	MONTH 4 Dīng-Wèi	1	2	3	4	5	6	*7*	Lì xià		21	22	23	24	25	26	27	
	◐	8	9	10	11	12	13	19:56	19	2505362		7	8	9	10	11	12	13			8	9	10	11	12	13	14		PASHONS 1863	28	29[g]	30	1	2	3	4	GENBOT 2139
	14	○	16	17	18	19	20	15:12	20	2505369		14	15	16	17	18	19	20			15	16	17*	18	19	20	21			5	6	7	8	9	10	11	
	21	◑	23	24	25	26	27	11:31	21	2505376		21	22	23	24	25	26	27			**22**	23	24	25	26	27	28	Xiǎo mǎn		12	13	14	15	16	17	18	
JUNE 2147	28	●	30	31	1	2	3	13:30	22	2505383	SIVAN 5907	28	29	1	2	3	4	5	Tue 1h14m0p	MONTH 5 Dīng-Wèi	29	1	2	3	4	5[d]	6			19	20	21	22	23	24	25	
	4	5	◐	7	8	9	10	14:01	23	2505390		6[h]	7	8	9	10	11	12			7	8	9	10	11	12	13	Máng zhòng	PAŌNE 1863	26	27	28	29	30	1	2	SANĒ 2139
	11	12	13	○	15	16	17	0:36	24	2505397		13	14	15	16	17	18	19			14	15	16	17	18	19	20			3	4	5	6	7	8	9	
	18	19	◑	21[c]	22	23	24	16:50	25	2505404		20	21	22	23	24	25	26			21	22	23	**24**	25	26	27	Xià zhì		10	11	12	13	14	15	16	
JULY 2147	25	26	27	●	29	30	1	2:04	26	2505411	TAMMUZ 5907	27	28	29	30	1	2	3	Wed 13h58m1p	MONTH 6 Dīng-Wèi	28	29	30	1	2	3	4			17	18	19	20	21	22	23	
	2	3	4	5	◐	7	8	6:13	27	2505418		4	5	6	7	8	9	10			5	6	7	8	9	*10*	11	Xiǎo shǔ		24	25	26	27	28	29	30	
	9	10	11	12	○	14	15	8:24	28	2505425		11	12	13	14	15	16	17			12	13	14	15	16	17	18*		EPĒP 1863	1	2	3	4	5	6	7	HAMLĒ 2139
	16	17	18	◑	20	21	22	23:17	29	2505432		18	19	20	21	22	23	24			19	20	21	22	23	24	25			8	9	10	11	12	13	14	
	23	24	25	26	●	28	29	16:20	30	2505439	AV 5907	25	26	27	28	29	1	2	Fri 2h42m2p	MONTH 7 Dīng-Wèi	**26**	27	28	29	30	1	2	Dà shǔ		15	16	17	18	19	20	21	
AUGUST 2147	30	31	1	2	3	◐	5	19:57	31	2505446		3	4	5	6	7	8	9			3	4	5	6	7[e]	8	9			22	23	24	25	26	27	28	
	6	7	8	9	10	○	12	15:41	32	2505453		10[i]	11	12	13	14	15	16			10	11	*12*	13	14	15[f]	16	Lì qiū	MESORĒ 1863	29	30	1	2	3	4	5	NAḤASĒ 2139
	13	14	15	16	17	◑	19	8:03	33	2505460		17	18	19	20	21	22	23			17	18	19	20	21	22	23			6	7	8	9	10	11	12	
	20	21	22	23	24	25	●	8:07	34	2505467		24	25	26	27	28	29	30		MONTH 8 Dīng-Wèi	24	25	26	**27**	28	29	1	Chǔ shǔ		13[h]	14	15	16	17	18	19	
SEPTEMBER 2147	27	28	29	30	31	1	2		35	2505474	ELUL 5907	1	2	3	4	5	6	7	Sat 15h26m3p		2	3	4	5	6	7	8			20	21	22	23	24	25	26	
	◐	4	5	6	7	8	○	7:17 20:10	36	2505481		8	9	10	11	12	13	14			9	10	11	12	13	*14*	15[g]	Bái lù	EPAG. 1863	27	28	29	30	1	2	3	PĀG. 2139
	10	11	12	13	14	15	◑	23:21	37	2505488		15	16	17	18	19	20	21			16	17	18	19*	20	21	22		THOOUT 1864	4	5	6	1[a]	2	3	4	MASKARAM 2140
	17	18	19	20	21	22	23[d]		38	2505495		22	23	24	25	26	27	28			23	24	25	26	27	28	**29**	Qiū fēn		5	6	7	8	9	10	11	
	24	●	26	27	28	29	30	0:34	39	2505502	TISHRI 5908	29	1[a]	2[a]	3	4	5	6	Mon 4h10m4p	MONTH 9 Dīng-Wèi	30	1	2	3	4	5	6			12	13	14	15	16	17[b]	18	
OCTOBER 2147	1	◐	3	4	5	6	7	16:45	40	2505509		7	8	9	10[b]	11	12	13			7	8	9[h]	10	11	12	13			19	20	21	22	23	24	25	
	8	○	10	11	12	13	14	8:04	41	2505516		14	15[c]	16	17	18	19	20			*14*	15	16	17	18	19	20	Hán lù	PAOPE 1864	26	27	28	29	30	1	2	ṬEQEMT 2140
	15	◑	17	18	19	20	21	12:15	42	2505523		21	22	23	24	25	26	27			21	22	23	24	25	26	27			3	4	5	6	7	8	9	
	22	23	●	25	26	27	28	16:39	43	2505530	HESHVAN 5908	28	29	30	1	2	3	4	Tue 16h54m5p	MONTH 10 Dīng-Wèi	28	29	**30**	1	2	3	4	Shuāng jiàng		10	11	12	13	14	15	16	
NOVEMBER 2147	29	30	31	◐	2	3	4	1:01	44	2505537		5	6	7	8	9	10	11			5	6	7	8	9	10	11			17	18	19	20	21	22	23	
	5	6	○	8	9	10	11	18:33	45	2505544		12	13	14	15	16	17	18			12	13	14	*15*	16	17	18	Lì dōng		24	25	26	27	28	29	30	
	12	13	14	◑	16	17	18	7:56	46	2505551		19	20	21	22	23	24	25			19*	20	21	22	23	24	25		ATHŌR 1864	1	2	3	4	5	6	7	HEDĀR 2140
	19	20	21	22	●	24	25	7:42	47	2505558	KISLEV 5908	26	27	28	29	30	1	2	Thu 5h38m6p	MONTH 11 Dīng-Wèi	26	27	28	**29**	1	2	3	Xiǎo xuě		8	9	10	11	12	13	14	
DECEMBER 2147	26	27	28	29	◐	1	2	8:48	48	2505565		3	4	5	6	7	8	9			4	5	6	7	8	9	10			15	16	17	18	19	20	21	
	3	4	5	6	○	8	9	7:26	49	2505572		10	11	12	13	14[d]	15	16			11	12	13	14	*15*	16	17	Dà xuě		22	23	24	25	26	27	28	
	10	11	12	13	14	◑	16	5:40	50	2505579		17	18	19	20	21	22	23			18	19	20	21	22	23	24		KOIAK 1864	29	30	1	2	3	4	5	TĀKHŚĀŚ 2140
	17	18	19	20	21	●[e]	23	21:31	51	2505586		24	25[e]	26[e]	27[e]	28[e]	29[e]	30[e]		LEAP MONTH 11 Dīng-Wèi	25	26	27	28	29	**30**[i]	1	Dōng zhì		6	7	8	9	10	11	12	
	24	25	26	27	28	◐	30	16:52	52	2505593	TEVETH 5908	1[e]	2[e]	3	4	5	6	7	Fri 18h22m7p		2	3	4	5	6	7	8			13	14	15	16	17	18	19	
	31	1	2	3	4	○	6	23:03	1	2505600		8	9	10	11	12	13	14			9	10	11	12	13	14	*15*	Xiǎo hán		20	21	22	23	24	25	26	

[a]New Year
[b]Spring (22:31)
[c]Summer (14:06)
[d]Autumn (7:02)
[e]Winter (5:44)
● New moon
◐ First quarter moon
○ Full moon
◑ Last quarter moon

‡Leap year
[a]New Year
[b]Yom Kippur
[c]Sukkot
[d]Winter starts
[e]Ḥanukkah
[f]Purim
[g]Passover
[h]Shavuot
[i]Fast of Av

‡Leap year
[a]New Year (4845, Sheep)
[b]Lantern Festival
[c]Qīngmíng
[d]Dragon Festival
[e]Qīqiǎo
[f]Hungry Ghosts
[g]Mid-Autumn Festival
[h]Double-Ninth Festival
[i]Dōngzhì
*Start of 60-name cycle

‡Leap year
[a]New Year
[b]Building of the Cross
[c]Christmas
[d]Jesus's Circumcision
[e]Epiphany
[f]Easter
[g]Mary's Announcement
[h]Jesus's Transfiguration

PERSIAN (ASTRONOMICAL) 1525/1526

Month	Sun	Mon	Tue	Wed	Thu	Fri	Sat
DEY 1525	11	12	13	14	15	16	17
	18	19	20	21	22	23	24
	25	26	27	28	29	30	1
BAHMAN 1525	2	3	4	5	6	7	8
	9	10	11	12	13	14	15
	16	17	18	19	20	21	22
	23	24	25	26	27	28	29
	30	1	2	3	4	5	6
ESFAND 1525	7	8	9	10	11	12	13
	14	15	16	17	18	19	20
	21	22	23	24	25	26	27
	28	29	1[a]	2	3	4	5
FARVARDĪN 1526	6	7	8	9	10	11	12
	13[b]	14	15	16	17	18	19
	20	21	22	23	24	25	26
	27	28	29	30	31	1	2
ORDĪBEHEŠT 1526	3	4	5	6	7	8	9
	10	11	12	13	14	15	16
	17	18	19	20	21	22	23
	24	25	26	27	28	29	30
	31	1	2	3	4	5	6
XORDĀD 1526	7	8	9	10	11	12	13
	14	15	16	17	18	19	20
	21	22	23	24	25	26	27
	28	29	30	31	1	2	3
TĪR 1526	4	5	6	7	8	9	10
	11	12	13	14	15	16	17
	18	19	20	21	22	23	24
	25	26	27	28	29	30	31
MORDĀD 1526	1	2	3	4	5	6	7
	8	9	10	11	12	13	14
	15	16	17	18	19	20	21
	22	23	24	25	26	27	28
	29	30	31	1	2	3	4
SHAHRĪVAR 1526	5	6	7	8	9	10	11
	12	13	14	15	16	17	18
	19	20	21	22	23	24	25
	26	27	28	29	30	31	1
MEHR 1526	2	3	4	5	6	7	8
	9	10	11	12	13	14	15
	16	17	18	19	20	21	22
	23	24	25	26	27	28	29
	30	1	2	3	4	5	6
ĀBĀN 1526	7	8	9	10	11	12	13
	14	15	16	17	18	19	20
	21	22	23	24	25	26	27
	28	29	30	1	2	3	4
ĀZAR 1526	5	6	7	8	9	10	11
	12	13	14	15	16	17	18
	19	20	21	22	23	24	25
	26	27	28	29	30	1	2
DEY 1526	3	4	5	6	7	8	9
	10	11	12	13	14	15	16

[a]New Year
[b]Sizdeh Bedar

HINDU LUNAR 2203/2204

Month	Sun	Mon	Tue	Wed	Thu	Fri	Sat
PAUSHA 2203	29	30	1	2	3	5	6
	7	8	9	10	11	12	13
	14	15	16	17	18	18	19
	20	21	22	23	24	25	26
MĀGHA 2203	27	29	30	1	2	3	4
	5	6	7	8	9	10	11
	12	13	14	15	16	17	18
	19	20	21	22	23	24	25
PHĀLGUNA 2203	26	27	28[h]	29	30	1	2
	4	5	6	7	8	9	10
	10	11	12	13	14	15[i]	16
	17	18	19	20	21	22	23
CHAITRA 2204	24	25	27	28	29	30	1[a]
	2	3	4	5	6	7	8
	9[b]	10	11	12	13	13	14
	15	16	17	18	20	21	22
VAIŚĀKHA 2204	23	24	25	26	27	28	29
	30	1	2	3	4	5	6
	7	8	9	10	11	12	13
	14	15	16	17	18	19	20
	21	22	24	25	26	27	28
JYAISHTHA 2204	29	30	1	2	3	4	5
	6	7	8	9	9	10	11
	12	13	14	15	17	18	19
	20	21	22	23	24	25	26
ĀSHĀDHA 2204	27	28	29	30	1	2	3
	4	5	6	7	8	9	10
	11	12	13	14	15	16	17
	18	20	21	22	23	24	25
ŚRĀVANA 2204	26	27	28	29	30	1	2
	3	4	5	6	6	7	8
	9	10	12	13	14	15	16
	17	18	19	20	21	22[c]	24
	25	26	27	27	28	29	30
BHĀDRAPADA 2204	1	2	3	4[d]	5	6	7
	8	9	10	11	12	13	14
	16	17	18	19	20	21	22
	23	24	25	26	27	28	29
ĀŚVINA 2204	30	1	2	2	3	4	5
	6	7[e]	9[e]	10[e]	11	12	13
	14	15	16	17	18	19	20
	21	22	23	24	25	26	27
KĀRTTIKA 2204	28	29	30	1[f]	2	3	4
	5	6	7	8	9	10	11
	13	14	15	16	17	18	19
	20	21	22	23	24	25	26
MĀRGAŚĪRA 2204	26	27	28	29	30	1	2
	3	4	5	7	8	9	10
	11[g]	12	13	14	15	16	17
	18	19	20	21	22	23	24
	25	26	27	28	29	30	1
PAUSHA 2204	2	3	4	5	6	7	8
	9	10	12	13	14	15	16

[a]New Year (Plavaṅga)
[b]Birthday of Rāma
[c]Birthday of Krishna
[d]Ganēśa Chaturthī
[e]Dashara
[f]Diwali
[g]Birthday of Vishnu
[h]Night of Śiva
[i]Holi

HINDU SOLAR 2068/2069

Month	Sun	Mon	Tue	Wed	Thu	Fri	Sat
PAUSHA 2068	15	16	17	18	19	20	21
	22	23	24	25	26	27	28
	29	1[b]	2	3	4	5	6
MĀGHA 2068	7	8	9	10	11	12	13
	14	15	16	17	18	19	20
	21	22	23	24	25	26	27
	28	29	30	1	2	3	4
PHĀLGUNA 2068	5	6	7	8	9	10	11
	12	13	14	15	16	17	18
	19	20	21	22	23	24	25
	26	27	28	29	30	1	2
CHAITRA 2068	3	4	5	6	7	8	9
	10	11	12	13	14	15	16
	17	18	19	20	21	22	23
	24	25	26	27	28	29	30
VAIŚĀKHA 2069	1[a]	2	3	4	5	6	7
	8	9	10	11	12	13	14
	15	16	17	18	19	20	21
	22	23	24	25	26	27	28
	29	30	31	1	2	3	4
JYAISHTHA 2069	5	6	7	8	9	10	11
	12	13	14	15	16	17	18
	19	20	21	22	23	24	25
	26	27	28	29	30	31	1
ĀSHĀDHA 2069	2	3	4	5	6	7	8
	9	10	11	12	13	14	15
	16	17	18	19	20	21	22
	23	24	25	26	27	28	29
	30	31	32	1	2	3	4
ŚRĀVANA 2069	5	6	7	8	9	10	11
	12	13	14	15	16	17	18
	19	20	21	22	23	24	25
	26	27	28	29	30	31	1
BHĀDRAPADA 2069	2	3	4	5	6	7	8
	9	10	11	12	13	14	15
	16	17	18	19	20	21	22
	23	24	25	26	27	28	29
	30	31	32	1	2	3	4
ĀŚVINA 2069	5	6	7	8	9	10	11
	12	13	14	15	16	17	18
	19	20	21	22	23	24	25
	26	27	28	29	30	1	2
KĀRTTIKA 2069	3	4	5	6	7	8	9
	10	11	12	13	14	15	16
	17	18	19	20	21	22	23
	24	25	26	27	28	29	30
MĀRGAŚĪRA 2069	1	2	3	4	5	6	7
	8	9	10	11	12	13	14
	15	16	17	18	19	20	21
	22	23	24	25	26	27	28
PAUSHA 2069	29	1	2	3	4	5	6
	7	8	9	10	11	12	13
	14	15	16	17	18	19	20

[a]New Year (Dundubhi)
[b]Pongal

ISLAMIC (ASTRONOMICAL) 1572/1573

Month	Sun	Mon	Tue	Wed	Thu	Fri	Sat
RABĪʿ II 1572	28	29	1	2	3	4	5
	6	7	8	9	10	11	12
	13	14	15	16	17	18	19
	20	21	22	23	24	25	26
JUMĀDĀ I 1572	27	28	29	30	1	2	3
	4	5	6	7	8	9	10
	11	12	13	14	15	16	17
	18	19	20	21	22	23	24
JUMĀDĀ II 1572	25	26	27	28	29	1	2
	3	4	5	6	7	8	9
	10	11	12	13	14	15	16
	17	18	19	20	21	22	23
	24	25	26	27	28	29	30
RAJAB 1572	1	2	3	4	5	6	7
	8	9	10	11	12	13	14
	15	16	17	18	19	20	21
	22	23	24	25	26	27[d]	28
SHAʿBĀN 1572	29	1	2	3	4	5	6
	7	8	9	10	11	12	13
	14	15	16	17	18	19	20
	21	22	23	24	25	26	27
RAMAḌĀN 1572	28	29	30	1[e]	2	3	4
	5	6	7	8	9	10	11
	12	13	14	15	16	17	18
	19	20	21	22	23	24	25
SHAWWĀL 1572	26	27	28	29	30	1[f]	2
	3	4	5	6	7	8	9
	10	11	12	13	14	15	16
	17	18	19	20	21	22	23
DHU AL-QAʿDA 1572	24	25	26	27	28	29	1
	2	3	4	5	6	7	8
	9	10	11	12	13	14	15
	16	17	18	19	20	21	22
	23	24	25	26	27	28	29
DHU AL-ḤIJJA 1572	30	1	2	3	4	5	6
	7	8	9	10[g]	11	12	13
	14	15	16	17	18	19	20
	21	22	23	24	25	26	27
MUḤARRAM 1573	28	29	1[a]	2	3	4	5
	6	7	8	9	10[b]	11	12
	13	14	15	16	17	18	19
	20	21	22	23	24	25	26
ṢAFAR 1573	27	28	29	30	1	2	3
	4	5	6	7	8	9	10
	11	12	13	14	15	16	17
	18	19	20	21	22	23	24
RABĪʿ I 1573	25	26	27	28	29	30	1
	2	3	4	5	6	7	8
	9	10	11	12[c]	13	14	15
	16	17	18	19	20	21	22
	23	24	25	26	27	28	29
RABĪʿ II 1573	1	2	3	4	5	6	7
	8	9	10	11	12	13	14

[a]New Year
[b]ʿAshūrāʾ
[c]Prophet's Birthday
[d]Ascent of the Prophet
[e]Start of Ramaḍān
[f]ʿĪd al-Fiṭr
[g]ʿĪd al-ʾAḍḥā

GREGORIAN 2147

Julian (Sun)	Sun	Mon	Tue	Wed	Thu	Fri	Sat	Month
Dec 18	1	2	3	4	5	6	7	JANUARY 2147
	8[a]	9	10	11	12	13	14	
Jan 1	15[b]	16	17	18	19	20	21	
	22	23	24	25	26	27	28	
Jan 15	29	30	31	1	2	3	4	
	5	6	7	8	9	10	11	FEBRUARY 2147
Jan 29	12	13	14	15	16	17	18	
	19	20	21	22	23	24	25	
Feb 12	26	27	28	1[c]	2	3	4	
	5	6	7	8	9	10	11	MARCH 2147
Feb 26	12[d]	13	14	15	16	17	18	
	19	20	21	22	23	24	25	
Mar 12	26	27	28	29	30	31	1	
	2	3	4	5	6	7	8	APRIL 2147
Mar 26	9	10	11	12	13	14	15	
	16[e]	17	18	19	20	21	22	
Apr 9	23[f]	24	25	26	27	28	29	
	30	1	2	3	4	5	6	
Apr 23	7	8	9	10	11	12	13	MAY 2147
	14	15	16	17	18	19	20	
May 7	21	22	23	24	25	26	27	
	28	29	30	31	1	2	3	
May 21	4	5	6	7	8	9	10	JUNE 2147
	11	12	13	14	15	16	17	
Jun 4	18	19	20	21	22	23	24	
	25	26	27	28	29	30	1	
Jun 18	2	3	4	5	6	7	8	JULY 2147
	9	10	11	12	13	14	15	
Jul 2	16	17	18	19	20	21	22	
	23	24	25	26	27	28	29	
Jul 16	30	31	1	2	3	4	5	
	6	7	8	9	10	11	12	AUGUST 2147
Jul 30	13	14	15	16	17	18	19	
	20	21	22	23	24	25	26	
Aug 13	27	28	29	30	31	1	2	
	3	4	5	6	7	8	9	SEPTEMBER 2147
Aug 27	10	11	12	13	14	15	16	
	17	18	19	20	21	22	23	
Sep 10	24	25	26	27	28	29	30	
	1	2	3	4	5	6	7	OCTOBER 2147
Sep 24	8	9	10	11	12	13	14	
	15	16	17	18	19	20	21	
Oct 8	22	23	24	25	26	27	28	
	29	30	31	1	2	3	4	
Oct 22	5	6	7	8	9	10	11	NOVEMBER 2147
	12	13	14	15	16	17	18	
Nov 5	19	20	21	22	23	24	25	
	26	27	28	29	30	1	2	
Nov 19	3[g]	4	5	6	7	8	9	DECEMBER 2147
	10	11	12	13	14	15	16	
Dec 3	17	18	19	20	21	22	23	
	24	25[h]	26	27	28	29	30	
Dec 17	31	1	2	3	4	5	6	

[a]Orthodox Christmas
[b]Julian New Year
[c]Ash Wednesday
[d]Feast of Orthodoxy
[e]Easter
[f]Orthodox Easter
[g]Advent
[h]Christmas

2148

Gregorian 2148‡

Month	Sun	Mon	Tue	Wed	Thu	Fri	Sat	Lunar Phases	ISO Week (Mon)	Julian Day (Sun noon)
January 2148	31	1[a]	2	3	4	○	6	23:03	1	2505600
	7	8	9	10	11	12	13		2	2505607
	◑	15	16	17	18	19	20	3:04	3	2505614
	●	22	23	24	25	26	27	10:06	4	2505621
February 2148	◐	29	30	31	1	2	3	2:01	5	2505628
	○	5	6	7	8	9	10	17:01	6	2505635
	11	◑	13	14	15	16	17	22:02	7	2505642
	18	●	20	21	22	23	24	21:21	8	2505649
March 2148	25	◐	27	28	29	1	2	12:58	9	2505656
	3	4	○	6	7	8	9	11:57	10	2505663
	10	11	12	◑	14	15	16	13:22	11	2505670
	17	18	19	●[b]	21	22	23	7:14	12	2505677
	24	25	26	◐	28	29	30	2:11	13	2505684
April 2148	31	1	2	3	○	5	6	6:00	14	2505691
	7	8	9	10	11	◑	13	0:51	15	2505698
	14	15	16	17	●	19	20	16:02	16	2505705
	21	22	23	24	◐	26	27	17:34	17	2505712
May 2148	28	29	30	1	2	○	4	21:54	18	2505719
	5	6	7	8	9	10	◑	8:55	19	2505726
	12	13	14	15	16	17	●	0:30	20	2505733
	19	20	21	22	23	24	◐	10:29	21	2505740
June 2148	26	27	28	29	30	31	1		22	2505747
	○	3	4	5	6	7	8	11:15	23	2505754
	◑	10	11	12	13	14	15	14:30	24	2505761
	●	17	18	19	20[c]	21	22	9:38	25	2505768
	23	◐	25	26	27	28	29	3:58	26	2505775
July 2148	30	○	2	3	4	5	6	22:21	27	2505782
	7	◑	9	10	11	12	13	18:54	28	2505789
	14	●	16	17	18	19	20	20:26	29	2505796
	21	22	◐	24	25	26	27	21:05	30	2505803
August 2148	28	29	30	○	1	2	3	7:48	31	2505810
	4	5	◑	7	8	9	10	23:41	32	2505817
	11	12	13	●	15	16	17	9:29	33	2505824
	18	19	20	21	◐	23	24	13:14	34	2505831
	25	26	27	28	○	30	31	16:14	35	2505838
September 2148	1	2	3	4	◑	6	7	6:25	36	2505845
	8	9	10	11	12	●	14	0:44	37	2505852
	15	16	17	18	19	20	◐	4:01	38	2505859
	22[d]	23	24	25	26	27	○	0:24	39	2505866
October 2148	29	30	1	2	3	◑	5	16:30	40	2505873
	6	7	8	9	10	11	●	17:39	41	2505880
	13	14	15	16	17	18	19		42	2505887
	◐	21	22	23	24	25	26	17:07	43	2505894
November 2148	○	28	29	30	31	1	2	9:05	44	2505901
	◑	4	5	6	7	8	9	6:45	45	2505908
	10	●	12	13	14	15	16	11:21	46	2505915
	17	18	◐	20	21	22	23	4:17	47	2505922
	24	○	26	27	28	29	30	19:06	48	2505929
December 2148	1	2	◑	4	5	6	7	1:00	49	2505936
	8	9	10	●	12	13	14	4:53	50	2505943
	15	16	17	◐	19	20	21[e]	13:35	51	2505950
	22	23	24	○	26	27	28	7:05	52	2505957
	29	30	31	◑	2	3	4	22:00	1	2505964

Hebrew 5908/5909‡

ISO Week	Month	Sun	Mon	Tue	Wed	Thu	Fri	Sat	Molad
1	Teveth 5908	8	9	10	11	12	13	14	
2		15	16	17	18	19	20	21	
3		22	23	24	25	26	27	28	
4		29	1	2	3	4	5	6	Sun 7h6m8p
5	Shevat 5908	7	8	9	10	11	12	13	
6		14	15	16	17	18	19	20	
7		21	22	23	24	25	26	27	
8		28	29	30	1	2	3	4	Mon 19h50m9p
9	Adar 5908	5	6	7	8	9	10	11	
10		12	13	14[f]	15	16	17	18	
11		19	20	21	22	23	24	25	
12		26	27	28	29	1	2	3	Wed 8h34m10p
13	Nisan 5908	4	5	6	7	8	9	10	
14		11	12	13	14	15[g]	16	17	
15		18	19	20	21	22	23	24	
16		25	26	27	28	29	30	1	Thu 21h18m11p
17	Iyyar 5908	2	3	4	5	6	7	8	
18		9	10	11	12	13	14	15	
19		16	17	18	19	20	21	22	
20		23	24	25	26	27	28	29	
21	Sivan 5908	1	2	3	4	5	6[h]	7	Sat 10h2m12p
22		8	9	10	11	12	13	14	
23		15	16	17	18	19	20	21	
24		22	23	24	25	26	27	28	
25		29	30	1	2	3	4	5	Sun 22h46m13p
26	Tammuz 5908	6	7	8	9	10	11	12	
27		13	14	15	16	17	18	19	
28		20	21	22	23	24	25	26	
29		27	28	29	1	2	3	4	Tue 11h30m14p
30	Av 5908	5	6	7	8	9[i]	10	11	
31		12	13	14	15	16	17	18	
32		19	20	21	22	23	24	25	
33		26	27	28	29	30	1	2	Thu 0h14m15p
34	Elul 5908	3	4	5	6	7	8	9	
35		10	11	12	13	14	15	16	
36		17	18	19	20	21	22	23	
37		24	25	26	27	28	29	1[a]	Fri 12h58m16p
38	Tishri 5909	2[a]	3	4	5	6	7	8	
39		9	10[b]	11	12	13	14	15[c]	
40		16	17	18	19	20	21	22	
41		23	24	25	26	27	28	29	
42		30	1	2	3	4	5	6	Sun 1h42m17p
43	Heshvan 5909	7	8	9	10	11	12	13	
44		14	15	16	17	18	19	20	
45		21	22	23	24	25	26	27	
46		28	29	1	2	3	4	5	Mon 14h27m0p
47	Kislev 5909	6	7	8	9	10	11	12	
48		13	14	15	16	17	18	19	
49		20	21	22	23	24	25[d,e]	26[e]	
50		27[e]	28[e]	29[e]	1[e]	2[e]	3[e]	4	Wed 3h11m1p
51	Teveth 5909	5	6	7	8	9	10	11	
52		12	13	14	15	16	17	18	
53		19	20	21	22	23	24	25	

Chinese Dīng-Wèi‡/Wù-Shēn

ISO Week	Month	Sun	Mon	Tue	Wed	Thu	Fri	Sat	Solar Term
1	Leap Month 11 Dīng-Wèi	9	10	11	12	13	14	15	Xiǎo hán
2		16	17	18	19	20*	21	22	
3		23	24	25	26	27	28	29	
4		1	2	3	4	5	6	7	Dà hán
5	Month 12 Dīng-Wèi	8	9	10	11	12	13	14	
6		15	16	17	18	19	20	21	Lì chūn
7		22	23	24	25	26	27	28	
8		29	30	1[a]	2	3	4	5	Yǔ shuǐ
9	Month 1 Wù-Shēn	6	7	8	9	10	11	12	
10		13	14	15[b]	16	17	18	19	Jīng zhé
11		20	21*	22	23	24	25	26	
12		27	28	29	1	2	3	4	Chūn fēn
13	Month 2 Wù-Shēn	5	6	7	8	9	10	11	
14		12	13	14	15	16[c]	17	18	Qīng míng
15		19	20	21	22	23	24	25	
16		26	27	28	29	30	1	2	Gǔ yǔ
17	Month 3 Wù-Shēn	3	4	5	6	7	8	9	
18		10	11	12	13	14	15	16	
19		17	18	19	20	21	22*	23	Lì xià
20		24	25	26	27	28	29	1	
21	Month 4 Wù-Shēn	2	3	4	5	6	7	8	Xiǎo mǎn
22		9	10	11	12	13	14	15	
23		16	17	18	19	20	21	22	Máng zhòng
24		23	24	25	26	27	28	29	
25	Month 5 Wù-Shēn	1	2	3	4	5[d]	6	7	Xià zhì
26		8	9	10	11	12	13	14	
27		15	16	17	18	19	20	21	Xiǎo shǔ
28		22	23	24*	25	26	27	28	
29	Month 6 Wù-Shēn	29	30	1	2	3	4	5	
30		6	7	8	9	10	11	12	Dà shǔ
31		13	14	15	16	17	18	19	
32		20	21	22	23	24	25	26	Lì qiū
33	Month 7 Wù-Shēn	27	28	29	1	2	3	4	
34		5	6	7[e]	8	9	10	11	Chǔ shǔ
35		12	13	14	15[f]	16	17	18	
36		19	20	21	22	23	24	25*	Bái lù
37	Month 8 Wù-Shēn	26	27	28	29	30	1	2	
38		3	4	5	6	7	8	9	
39		10	11	12	13	14	15[g]	16	Qiū fēn
40		17	18	19	20	21	22	23	
41		24	25	26	27	28	29	30	Hán lù
42	Month 9 Wù-Shēn	1	2	3	4	5	6	7	
43		8	9[h]	10	11	12	13	14	
44		15	16	17	18	19	20	21	Shuāng jiàng
45		22	23	24	25*	26	27	28	
46	Month 10 Wù-Shēn	29	1	2	3	4	5	6	Lì dōng
47		7	8	9	10	11	12	13	
48		14	15	16	17	18	19	20	Xiǎo xuě
49		21	22	23	24	25	26	27	Dà xuě
50	Month 11* Wù-Shēn	28	29	30	1	2	3	4	
51		5	6	7	8	9	10	11[i]	Dōng zhì
52		12	13	14	15	16	17	18	
53		19	20	21	22	23	24	25	

Coptic 1864/1865 — Ethiopic 2140/2141

ISO Week	Coptic Month	Sun	Mon	Tue	Wed	Thu	Fri	Sat	Ethiopic Month
1	Koiak 1864	20	21	22	23	24	25	26	Tāḫśāś 2140
2		27	28	29[c]	30	1	2	3	
3	Tōbe 1864	4	5	6[d]	7	8	9	10	Ṭer 2140
4		11[e]	12	13	14	15	16	17	
5		18	19	20	21	22	23	24	
6		25	26	27	28	29	30	1	
7	Meshir 1864	2	3	4	5	6	7	8	Yakātit 2140
8		9	10	11	12	13	14	15	
9		16	17	18	19	20	21	22	
10		23	24	25	26	27	28	29	
11	Paremotep 1864	30	1	2	3	4	5	6	Magābit 2140
12		7	8	9	10	11	12	13	
13		14	15	16	17	18	19	20	
14		21	22	23	24	25	26	27	
15	Parmoute 1864	28	29	30	1	2	3	4	Miyāzyā 2140
16		5[f]	6	7	8	9	10	11	
17		12	13	14	15	16	17	18	
18		19	20	21	22	23	24	25	
19	Pashons 1864	26	27	28	29[g]	30	1	2	Genbot 2140
20		3	4	5	6	7	8	9	
21		10	11	12	13	14	15	16	
22		17	18	19	20	21	22	23	
23		24	25	26	27	28	29	30	
24	Paōne 1864	1	2	3	4	5	6	7	Sanē 2140
25		8	9	10	11	12	13	14	
26		15	16	17	18	19	20	21	
27		22	23	24	25	26	27	28	
28	Epēp 1864	29	30	1	2	3	4	5	Ḥamlē 2140
29		6	7	8	9	10	11	12	
30		13	14	15	16	17	18	19	
31		20	21	22	23	24	25	26	
32	Mesorē 1864	27	28	29	30	1	2	3	Naḥasē 2140
33		4	5	6	7	8	9	10	
34		11	12	13[h]	14	15	16	17	
35		18	19	20	21	22	23	24	
36	Epag. 1864	25	26	27	28	29	30	1	Ṗāg. 2140
37	Thoout 1865	2	3	4	5	1[a]	2	3	Maskaram 2141
38		4	5	6	7	8	9	10	
39		11	12	13	14	15	16	17[b]	
40		18	19	20	21	22	23	24	
41	Paope 1865	25	26	27	28	29	30	1	Ṭeqemt 2141
42		2	3	4	5	6	7	8	
43		9	10	11	12	13	14	15	
44		16	17	18	19	20	21	22	
45	Athōr 1865	23	24	25	26	27	28	29	Ḫedār 2141
46		30	1	2	3	4	5	6	
47		7	8	9	10	11	12	13	
48		14	15	16	17	18	19	20	
49	Koiak 1865	21	22	23	24	25	26	27	Tāḫśāś 2141
50		28	29	30	1	2	3	4	
51		5	6	7	8	9	10	11	
52		12	13	14	15	16	17	18	
53		19	20	21	22	23	24	25	

Gregorian notes:
‡Leap year
[a]New Year
[b]Spring (4:21)
[c]Summer (19:54)
[d]Autumn (12:45)
[e]Winter (11:29)
● New moon
◐ First quarter moon
○ Full moon
◑ Last quarter moon

Hebrew notes:
‡Leap year
[a]New Year
[b]Yom Kippur
[c]Sukkot
[d]Winter starts
[e]Ḥanukkah
[f]Purim
[g]Passover
[h]Shavuot
[i]Fast of Av

Chinese notes:
‡Leap year
[a]New Year (4846, Monkey)
[b]Lantern Festival
[c]Qīngmíng
[d]Dragon Festival
[e]Qīqiǎo
[f]Hungry Ghosts
[g]Mid-Autumn Festival
[h]Double-Ninth Festival
[i]Dōngzhì
*Start of 60-name cycle

Coptic/Ethiopic notes:
[a]New Year
[b]Building of the Cross
[c]Christmas
[d]Jesus's Circumcision
[e]Epiphany
[f]Easter
[g]Mary's Announcement
[h]Jesus's Transfiguration

PERSIAN (ASTRONOMICAL) 1526/1527‡

Month	Sun	Mon	Tue	Wed	Thu	Fri	Sat
	10	11	12	13	14	15	16
DEY 1526	17	18	19	20	21	22	23
	24	25	26	27	28	29	30
	1	2	3	4	5	6	7
BAHMAN 1526	8	9	10	11	12	13	14
	15	16	17	18	19	20	21
	22	23	24	25	26	27	28
	29	30	1	2	3	4	5
ESFAND 1526	6	7	8	9	10	11	12
	13	14	15	16	17	18	19
	20	21	22	23	24	25	26
	27	28	29	1[a]	2	3	4
FARVARDĪN 1527	5	6	7	8	9	10	11
	12	13[b]	14	15	16	17	18
	19	20	21	22	23	24	25
	26	27	28	29	30	31	1
ORDĪBEHEŠT 1527	2	3	4	5	6	7	8
	9	10	11	12	13	14	15
	16	17	18	19	20	21	22
	23	24	25	26	27	28	29
	30	31	1	2	3	4	5
XORDĀD 1527	6	7	8	9	10	11	12
	13	14	15	16	17	18	19
	20	21	22	23	24	25	26
	27	28	29	30	31	1	2
TĪR 1527	3	4	5	6	7	8	9
	10	11	12	13	14	15	16
	17	18	19	20	21	22	23
	24	25	26	27	28	29	30
	31	1	2	3	4	5	6
MORDĀD 1527	7	8	9	10	11	12	13
	14	15	16	17	18	19	20
	21	22	23	24	25	26	27
	28	29	30	31	1	2	3
SHAHRĪVAR 1527	4	5	6	7	8	9	10
	11	12	13	14	15	16	17
	18	19	20	21	22	23	24
	25	26	27	28	29	30	31
	1	2	3	4	5	6	7
MEHR 1527	8	9	10	11	12	13	14
	15	16	17	18	19	20	21
	22	23	24	25	26	27	28
	29	30	1	2	3	4	5
ĀBĀN 1527	6	7	8	9	10	11	12
	13	14	15	16	17	18	19
	20	21	22	23	24	25	26
	27	28	29	30	1	2	3
ĀZAR 1527	4	5	6	7	8	9	10
	11	12	13	14	15	16	17
	18	19	20	21	22	23	24
	25	26	27	28	29	30	1
DEY 1527	2	3	4	5	6	7	8
	9	10	11	12	13	14	15

‡Leap year
[a]New Year
[b]Sizdeh Bedar

HINDU LUNAR 2204/2205‡

Month	Sun	Mon	Tue	Wed	Thu	Fri	Sat
	9	**10**	12	13	14	15	16
PAUSHA 2204	17	18	*18*	19	20	21	22
	23	24	25	26	27	28	29
	30	1	2	3	**4**	6	7
MĀGHA 2204	8	9	10	11	12	13	14
	15	16	17	18	19	20	*20*
	21	22	23	24	25	26	27
	28[h]	30	1	2	3	4	5
PHĀLGUNA 2204	6	7	8	9	10	11	12
	13	14	15[i]	16	17	18	19
	20	21	22	23	24	25	26
	27	28	29	30	1[a]	**2**	4
CHAITRA 2205	5	6	7	8	9[b]	10	11
	12	13	14	*14*	15	16	17
	18	19	20	21	22	23	24
	25	**26**	28	29	30	1	2
VAIŚĀKHA 2205	3	4	5	6	7	8	9
	10	11	12	13	14	15	16
	17	18	19	20	21	22	23
	24	25	26	27	28	29	**30**
LEAP JYAISHṬHA 2205	2	3	4	5	6	7	8
	9	*9*	10	11	12	13	14
	15	16	17	18	19	20	21
	22	**23**	25	26	27	28	29
	30	1	2	3	4	5	6
JYAISHṬHA 2205	7	8	9	10	11	12	13
	14	15	16	17	18	19	20
	21	22	23	24	25	**26**	28
	29	30	1	2	3	4	5
ĀSHĀḌHA 2205	5	6	7	8	9	10	11
	12	13	14	15	16	17	**18**
	20	21	22	23	24	25	26
	27	28	29	30	1	2	3
ŚRĀVAṆA 2205	4	5	6	7	8	9	10
	11	12	13	14	15	16	17
	18	19	20	**21**	23[c]	24	25
	26	27	28	29	30	1	2
BHĀDRAPADA 2205	2	3[d]	4	5	6	7	8
	9	10	11	12	13	**14**	16
	17	18	19	20	21	22	23
	24	25	26	27	28	29	30
	1	2	3	4	5	6	7
ĀŚVINA 2205	8[e]	9[e]	10[e]	11	12	13	14
	15	16	17	18	**19**	21	22
	23	24	25	26	*26*	27	28
	29	30	1[f]	2	3	4	5
KĀRTTIKA 2205	6	7	8	9	10	11	**12**
	14	15	16	17	18	19	20
	21	22	23	24	25	26	27
	28	*28*	29	30	1	2	3
MĀRGAŚĪRA 2205	4	5	**6**	8	9	10	11[g]
	12	13	14	15	16	17	18
	19	20	21	22	23	24	25

‡Leap year
[a]New Year (Kīlaka)
[b]Birthday of Rāma
[c]Birthday of Krishna
[d]Ganēśa Chaturthī
[e]Dashara
[f]Diwali
[g]Birthday of Vishnu
[h]Night of Śiva
[i]Holi

HINDU SOLAR 2069/2070‡

Month	Sun	Mon	Tue	Wed	Thu	Fri	Sat
PAUSHA 2069	14	15	16	17	18	19	20
	21	22	23	24	25	26	27
	28	29	30	1[b]	2	3	4
MĀGHA 2069	5	6	7	8	9	10	11
	12	13	14	15	16	17	18
	19	20	21	22	23	24	25
	26	27	28	29	1	2	3
PHĀLGUNA 2069	4	5	6	7	8	9	10
	11	12	13	14	15	16	17
	18	19	20	21	22	23	24
	25	26	27	28	29	30	1
CHAITRA 2069	2	3	4	5	6	7	8
	9	10	11	12	13	14	15
	16	17	18	19	20	21	22
	23	24	25	26	27	28	29
	30	1[a]	2	3	4	5	6
VAIŚĀKHA 2070	7	8	9	10	11	12	13
	14	15	16	17	18	19	20
	21	22	23	24	25	26	27
	28	29	30	31	1	2	3
JYAISHṬHA 2070	4	5	6	7	8	9	10
	11	12	13	14	15	16	17
	18	19	20	21	22	23	24
	25	26	27	28	29	30	31
	32	1	2	3	4	5	6
ĀSHĀḌHA 2070	7	8	9	10	11	12	13
	14	15	16	17	18	19	20
	21	22	23	24	25	26	27
	28	29	30	31	1	2	3
ŚRĀVAṆA 2070	4	5	6	7	8	9	10
	11	12	13	14	15	16	17
	18	19	20	21	22	23	24
	25	26	27	28	29	30	31
	32	1	2	3	4	5	6
BHĀDRAPADA 2070	7	8	9	10	11	12	13
	14	15	16	17	18	19	20
	21	22	23	24	25	26	27
	28	29	30	31	1	2	3
ĀŚVINA 2070	4	5	6	7	8	9	10
	11	12	13	14	15	16	17
	18	19	20	21	22	23	24
	25	26	27	28	29	30	1
KĀRTTIKA 2070	2	3	4	5	6	7	8
	9	10	11	12	13	14	15
	16	17	18	19	20	21	22
	23	24	25	26	27	28	29
	30	1	2	3	4	5	6
MĀRGAŚĪRA 2070	7	8	9	10	11	12	13
	14	15	16	17	18	19	20
	21	22	23	24	25	26	27
	28	29	30	1	2	3	4
PAUSHA 2070	5	6	7	8	9	10	11
	12	13	14	15	16	17	18

‡Leap year
[a]New Year (Rudhirodgārin)
[b]Pongal

ISLAMIC (ASTRONOMICAL) 1573/1574

Month	Sun	Mon	Tue	Wed	Thu	Fri	Sat
RABĪʿ II 1573	8	9	10	11	12	13	14
	15	16	17	18	19	20	21
	22	23	24	25	26	27	28
	29	30	1	2	3	4	5
JUMĀDĀ I 1573	6	7	8	9	10	11	12
	13	14	15	16	17	18	19
	20	21	22	23	24	25	26
	27	28	29	1	2	3	4
JUMĀDĀ II 1573	5	6	7	8	9	10	11
	12	13	14	15	16	17	18
	19	20	21	22	23	24	25
	26	27	28	29	1	2	3
RAJAB 1573	4	5	6	7	8	9	10
	11	12	13	14	15	16	17
	18	19	20	21	22	23	24
	25	26	27[d]	28	29	30	1
SHAʿBĀN 1573	2	3	4	5	6	7	8
	9	10	11	12	13	14	15
	16	17	18	19	20	21	22
	23	24	25	26	27	28	29
	1[e]	2	3	4	5	6	7
RAMAḌĀN 1573	8	9	10	11	12	13	14
	15	16	17	18	19	20	21
	22	23	24	25	26	27	28
	29	30	1[f]	2	3	4	5
SHAWWĀL 1573	6	7	8	9	10	11	12
	13	14	15	16	17	18	19
	20	21	22	23	24	25	26
	27	28	29	1	2	3	4
DHU AL-QAʿDA 1573	5	6	7	8	9	10	11
	12	13	14	15	16	17	18
	19	20	21	22	23	24	25
	26	27	28	29	30	1	2
DHU AL-ḤIJJA 1573	3	4	5	6	7	8	9
	10[g]	11	12	13	14	15	16
	17	18	19	20	21	22	23
	24	25	26	27	28	29	1[a]
MUḤARRAM 1574	2[d]	3	4	5	6	7	8
	9	10[b]	11	12	13	14	15
	16	17	18	19	20	21	22
	23	24	25	26	27	28	29
	30	1	2	3	4	5	6
ṢAFAR 1574	7	8	9	10	11	12	13
	14	15	16	17	18	19	20
	21	22	23	24	25	26	27
	28	29	30	1	2	3	4
RABĪʿ I 1574	5	6	7	8	9	10	11
	12[c]	13	14	15	16	17	18
	19	20	21	22	23	24	25
	26	27	28	29	30	1	2
RABĪʿ II 1574	3	4	5	6	7	8	9
	10	11	12	13	14	15	16
	17	18	19	20	21	22	23

[a]New Year
[d]New Year (Arithmetic)
[b]ʿAshūrāʾ
[c]Prophet's Birthday
[d]Ascent of the Prophet
[e]Start of Ramaḍān
[f]ʿId al-Fiṭr
[g]ʿId al-ʾAḍḥā

GREGORIAN 2148‡

Julian‡ (Sun)	Sun	Mon	Tue	Wed	Thu	Fri	Sat	Month
Dec 17	31	1	2	3	4	5	6	
	7	8[a]	9	10	11	12	13	JANUARY 2148
Dec 31	14	15[b]	16	17	18	19	20	
	21	22	23	24	25	26	27	
Jan 14	28	29	30	31	1	2	3	
	4	5	6	7	8	9	10	FEBRUARY 2148
Jan 28	11	12	13	14	15	16	17	
	18	19	20	21[c]	22	23	24	
Feb 11	25	26	27	28	29	1	2	
	3[d]	4	5	6	7	8	9	MARCH 2148
Feb 25	10	11	12	13	14	15	16	
	17	18	19	20	21	22	23	
Mar 10	24	25	26	27	28	29	30	
	31	1	2	3	4	5	6	
Mar 24	7[e]	8	9	10	11	12	13	APRIL 2148
	14[f]	15	16	17	18	19	20	
Apr 7	21	22	23	24	25	26	27	
	28	29	30	1	2	3	4	
Apr 21	5	6	7	8	9	10	11	MAY 2148
	12	13	14	15	16	17	18	
May 5	19	20	21	22	23	24	25	
	26	27	28	29	30	31	1	
May 19	2	3	4	5	6	7	8	JUNE 2148
	9	10	11	12	13	14	15	
Jun 2	16	17	18	19	20	21	22	
	23	24	25	26	27	28	29	
Jun 16	30	1	2	3	4	5	6	
	7	8	9	10	11	12	13	JULY 2148
Jun 30	14	15	16	17	18	19	20	
	21	22	23	24	25	26	27	
Jul 14	28	29	30	31	1	2	3	
	4	5	6	7	8	9	10	AUGUST 2148
Jul 28	11	12	13	14	15	16	17	
	18	19	20	21	22	23	24	
Aug 11	25	26	27	28	29	30	31	
	1	2	3	4	5	6	7	
Aug 25	8	9	10	11	12	13	14	SEPTEMBER 2148
	15	16	17	18	19	20	21	
Sep 8	22	23	24	25	26	27	28	
	29	30	1	2	3	4	5	
Sep 22	6	7	8	9	10	11	12	OCTOBER 2148
	13	14	15	16	17	18	19	
Oct 6	20	21	22	23	24	25	26	
	27	28	29	30	31	1	2	
Oct 20	3	4	5	6	7	8	9	NOVEMBER 2148
	10	11	12	13	14	15	16	
Nov 3	17	18	19	20	21	22	23	
	24	25	26	27	28	29	30	
Nov 17	1[g]	2	3	4	5	6	7	
	8	9	10	11	12	13	14	DECEMBER 2148
Dec 1	15	16	17	18	19	20	21	
	22	23	24	25[h]	26	27	28	
Dec 15	29	30	31	1	2	3	4	

‡Leap year
[a]Orthodox Christmas
[b]Julian New Year
[c]Ash Wednesday
[d]Feast of Orthodoxy
[e]Easter
[f]Orthodox Easter
[g]Advent
[h]Christmas

2149

Gregorian month	GREGORIAN 2149 (Sun Mon Tue Wed Thu Fri Sat)	Lunar Phases	ISO WEEK (Mon)	JULIAN DAY (Sun noon)	Hebrew month	HEBREW 5909‡/5910 (Sun Mon Tue Wed Thu Fri Sat)	Molad	Chinese month	CHINESE Wù-Shēn/Jǐ-Yǒu (Sun Mon Tue Wed Thu Fri Sat)	Solar Term	Coptic month	COPTIC 1865/1866 · ETHIOPIC 2141/2142 (Sun Mon Tue Wed Thu Fri Sat)	Ethiopic month
JANUARY 2149	29 30 31 ◑[a] 2 3 4	22:00 21:12 21:38 21:13	1	2505964	TEVETH 5909	19 20 21 22 23 24 25	Thu 15^{h}55^{m}2^p	MONTH 11* Wù-Shēn	19 20 21 22 23 24 25		KOIAK 1865	19 20 21 22 23 24 25	TĀKHŚĀŚ 2141
	5 6 7 8 ● 10 11		2	2505971		26 27 28 29 | 1 2 3			26* 27 28 29 30 | 1 2	Xiǎo hán		26 27 28 29[c] 30 | 1 2	
	12 13 14 15 ◐ 17 18		3	2505978	SHEVAT 5909	4 5 6 7 8 9 10		MONTH 12 Wù-Shēn	3 4 5 6 7 8 9		TŌBE 1865	3 4 5 6[d] 7 8 9	ṬER 2141
	19 20 21 22 ○ 24 25		4	2505985		11 12 13 14 15 16 17			10 11 12 13 14 15 16	Dà hán		10 11[e] 12 13 14 15 16	
	26 27 28 29 30 ◑ | 1		5	2505992		18 19 20 21 22 23 24			17 18 19 20 21 22 23			17 18 19 20 21 22 23	
FEBRUARY 2149	2 3 4 5 6 7 ●	19:49 11:25 5:24 13:06	6	2505999		25 26 27 28 29 30 | 1	Sat 4^{h}39^{m}3^p		24 25 26 27 28 29 | 1[a]	Lì chūn		24 25 26 27 28 29 30	
	9 10 11 12 13 14 ◐		7	2506006	ADAR I 5909	2 3 4 5 6 7 8		MONTH 1 Jǐ-Yǒu	2 3 4 5 6 7 8		MESHIR 1865	1 2 3 4 5 6 7	YAKĀTIT 2141
	16 17 18 19 20 21 ○		8	2506013		9 10 11 12 13 14 15			9 10 11 12 13 14 15[b]	Yǔ shuǐ		8 9 10 11 12 13 14	
	23 24 25 26 27 28 | 1		9	2506020		16 17 18 19 20 21 22			16 17 18 19 20 21 22			15 16 17 18 19 20 21	
MARCH 2149	◑ 3 4 5 6 7 8	16:23 23:07 13:58 5:53	10	2506027		23 24 25 26 27 28 29			23 24 25 26 27* 28 29	Jīng zhé		22 23 24 25 26 27 28	
	● 10 11 12 13 14 15		11	2506034		30 | 1 2 3 4 5 6	Sun 17^{h}23^{m}4^p	MONTH 2 Jǐ-Yǒu	30 | 1 2 3 4 5 6		PAREMOTEP 1865	29 30 | 1 2 3 4 5	MAGĀBIT 2141
	◐ 17 18 19 20[b] 21 22		12	2506041	ADAR II 5909	7 8 9 10 11 12 13			7 8 9 10 11 12 13	Chūn fēn		6 7 8 9 10 11 12	
	23 ○ 25 26 27 28 29		13	2506048		14[f] 15 16 17 18 19 20			14 15 16 17 18 19 20			13 14 15 16 17 18 19	
	30 31 | ◑ 2 3 4 5		14	2506055		21 22 23 24 25 26 27			21 22 23 24 25 26[c] 27	Qīng míng		20 21 22 23 24 25 26	
APRIL 2149	6 7 ● 9 10 11 12	10:02 8:32 0:06 22:40	15	2506062		28 29 | 1 2* 3 4 5	Tue 6^{h}7^{m}5^p	MONTH 3 Jǐ-Yǒu	28 29 | 1 2 3 4 5		PARMOUTE 1865	27 28 29 30 | 1 2 3	MIYĀZYĀ 2141
	13 14 ◐ 16 17 18 19		16	2506069	NISAN 5909	6 7 8 9 10 11 12			6 7 8 9 10 11 12			4 5 6 7 8 9 10	
	20 21 ○ 23 24 25 26		17	2506076		13 14 15[g] 16 17 18 19			13 14 15 16 17 18 19	Gǔ yǔ		11 12 13 14 15 16 17	
	27 28 29 ◑ | 1 2 3		18	2506083		20 21 22 23 24 25 26			20 21 22 23 24 25 26			18 19 20 21 22 23 24	
MAY 2149	4 5 6 ● 8 9 10	23:48 16:26 12:07 14:45 9:38	19	2506090		27 28 29 30 | 1 2 3	Wed 18^{h}51^{m}6^p		27 28* 29 30 | 1 2 3	Lì xià		25[f] 26 27 28 29[g] 30 | 1	
	11 12 13 ◐ 15 16 17		20	2506097	IYAR 5909	4 5 6 7 8 9 10		MONTH 4 Jǐ-Yǒu	4 5 6 7 8 9 10		PASHONS 1865	2 3 4 5 6 7 8	GENBOT 2141
	18 19 20 21 ○ 23 24		21	2506104		11 12 13 14 15 16 17			11 12 13 14 15 16 17	Xiǎo mǎn		9 10 11 12 13 14 15	
	25 26 27 28 29 ◑ 31		22	2506111		18 19 20 21 22 23 24			18 19 20 21 22 23 24			16 17 18 19 20 21 22	
JUNE 2149	1 2 3 4 ● 6 7	23:50 2:03 5:32 16:18	23	2506118		25 26 27 28 29 | 1 2	Fri 7^{h}35^{m}7^p		25 26 27 28 29 | 1 2	Máng zhòng		23 24 25 26 27 28 29	
	8 9 10 11 12 ◐ 14		24	2506125	SIVAN 5909	3 4 5 6[h] 7 8 9		MONTH 5 Jǐ-Yǒu	3 4 5[d] 6 7 8 9		PAŌNE 1865	30 | 1 2 3 4 5 6	SANĒ 2141
	15 16 17 18 19 20 ○[c]		25	2506132		10 11 12 13 14 15 16			10 11 12 13 14 15 16	Xià zhì		7 8 9 10 11 12 13	
	22 23 24 25 26 27 ◑		26	2506139		17 18 19 20 21 22 23			17 18 19 20 21 22 23			14 15 16 17 18 19 20	
	29 30 | 1 2 3 4 ●		27	2506146		24 25 26 27 28 29 30	Sat 20^{h}19^{m}8^p		24 25 26 27 28 29* | 1			21 22 23 24 25 26 27	
JULY 2149	6 7 8 9 10 11 ◐	7:45 17:43 18:38 21:09	28	2506153	TAMMUZ 5909	1 2 3 4 5 6 7		MONTH 6 Jǐ-Yǒu	2 3 4 5 6 7 8	Xiǎo shǔ	EPĒP 1865	28 29 30 | 1 2 3 4	HAMLĒ 2141
	13 14 15 16 17 18 19		29	2506160		8 9 10 11 12 13 14			9 10 11 12 13 14 15			5 6 7 8 9 10 11	
	○ 21 22 23 24 25 26		30	2506167		15 16 17 18 19 20 21			16 17 18 19 20 21 22	Dà shǔ		12 13 14 15 16 17 18	
	◑ 28 29 30 31 | 1 2		31	2506174		22 23 24 25 26 27 28			23 24 25 26 27 28 29			19 20 21 22 23 24 25	
AUGUST 2149	● 4 5 6 7 8 9	17:03 10:50 5:58 1:45	32	2506181		29 | 1 2 3 4 5 6	Mon 9^{h}3^{m}9^p		30 | 1 2 3 4 5 6	Lì qiū		26 27 28 29 30 | 1 2	
	10 ◐ 12 13 14 15 16		33	2506188	AV 5909	7 8 9[i] 10 11 12 13		MONTH 7 Jǐ-Yǒu	7[e] 8 9 10 11 12 13		MESORĒ 1865	3 4 5 6 7 8 9	NAḤASĒ 2141
	17 18 ○ 20 21 22 23		34	2506195		14 15 16 17 18 19 20			14 15[f] 16 17 18 19 20	Chǔ shǔ		10 11 12 13[h] 14 15 16	
	24 25 ◑ 27 28 29 30		35	2506202		21 22 23 24 25 26 27			21 22 23 24 25 26 27			17 18 19 20 21 22 23	
SEPTEMBER 2149	31 | 1 ● 3 4 5 6	4:24 4:49 15:55 7:40 18:18	36	2506209		28 29 30 | 1 2 3 4	Tue 21^{h}47^{m}10^p		28 29 | 1* 2 3 4 5			24 25 26 27 28 29 30	
	7 8 9 ◐ 11 12 13		37	2506216	ELUL 5909	5 6 7 8 9 10 11		MONTH 8 Jǐ-Yǒu	6 7 8 9 10 11 12	Bái lù	EPAG. 1865 / THOOUT 1866	1 2 3 4 5 | 1[a] 2	ṖĀG. 2141 / MASKARAM 2142
	14 15 16 ○ 18 19 20		38	2506223		12 13 14 15 16 17 18			13 14 15[g] 16 17 18 19			3 4 5 6 7 8 9	
	21 22[d] 23 ◑ 25 26 27		39	2506230		19 20 21 22 23 24 25			20 21 22 23 24 25 26	Qiū fēn		10 11 12 13 14 15 16	
	28 29 30 | ● 2 3 4		40	2506237		26 27 28 29 | 1[a] 2[a] 3	Thu 10^{h}31^{m}11^p		27 28 29 30 | 1 2 3			17[b] 18 19 20 21 22 23	
OCTOBER 2149	5 6 7 8 ◐ 10 11	22:43 1:13 16:12 10:52	41	2506244	TISHRI 5910	4 5 6 7 8 9 10[b]		MONTH 9 Jǐ-Yǒu	4 5 6 7 8 9[h] 10	Hán lù		24 25 26 27 28 29 30	
	12 13 14 15 16 ○ 18		42	2506251		11 12 13 14 15[c] 16 17			11 12 13 14 15 16 17		PAOPE 1866	1 2 3 4 5 6 7	ṬEQEMT 2142
	19 20 21 22 ◑ 24 25		43	2506258		18 19 20 21 22 23 24			18 19 20 21 22 23 24	Shuāng jiàng		8 9 10 11 12 13 14	
	26 27 28 29 30 ● | 1		44	2506265		25 26 27 28 29 30 | 1	Fri 23^{h}15^{m}12^p		25 26 27 28 29 | 1 2*			15 16 17 18 19 20 21	
NOVEMBER 2149	2 3 4 5 6 7 ◐	15:18 10:44 4:14	45	2506272	HESHVAN 5910	2 3 4 5 6 7 8		MONTH 10 Jǐ-Yǒu	3 4 5 6 7 8 9	Lì dōng		22 23 24 25 26 27 28	
	9 10 11 12 13 14 ○		46	2506279		9 10 11 12 13 14 15			10 11 12 13 14 15 16		ATHŌR 1866	29 30 | 1 2 3 4 5	HEDĀR 2142
	16 17 18 19 20 21 ◑		47	2506286		16 17 18 19 20 21 22			17 18 19 20 21 22 23	Xiǎo xuě		6 7 8 9 10 11 12	
	23 24 25 26 27 28 29		48	2506293		23 24 25 26 27 28 29			24 25 26 27 28 29 30			13 14 15 16 17 18 19	
DECEMBER 2149	● | 1 2 3 4 5 6	5:34 5:31 21:07 19:58 1:01	49	2506300		30 | 1 2 3 4 5 6[d]	Sun 11^{h}59^{m}13^p	MONTH 11 Jǐ-Yǒu	1 2 3 4 5 6 7			20 21 22 23 24 25 26	
	7 ◐ 9 10 11 12 13		50	2506307	KISLEV 5910	7 8 9 10 11 12 13			8 9 10 11 12 13 14	Dà xuě	KOIAK 1866	27 28 29 30 | 1 2 3	TĀKHŚĀŚ 2142
	○ 15 16 17 18 19 20		51	2506314		14 15 16 17 18 19 20			15 16 17 18 19 20 21			4 5 6 7 8 9 10	
	◑[e] 22 23 24 25 26 27		52	2506321		21 22 23 24 25[e] 26[e] 27[e]			22 23[i] 24 25 26 27 28	Dōng zhì		11 12 13 14 15 16 17	
	28 29 ● 31 | 1 2 3		1	2506328		28[e] 29[e] 30[e] | 1[e] 2[e] 3 4	Tue 0^{h}43^{m}14^p		29 30 | 1 2* 3 4 5			18 19 20 21 22 23 24	

[a]New Year
[b]Spring (10:11)
[c]Summer (1:46)
[d]Autumn (18:41)
[e]Winter (17:28)
● New moon
◐ First quarter moon
○ Full moon
◑ Last quarter moon

‡Leap year
[a]New Year
[b]Yom Kippur
[c]Sukkot
[d]Winter starts
[e]Ḥanukkah
[f]Purim
[g]Passover
[h]Shavuot
[i]Fast of Av
*New solar cycle

[a]New Year (4847, Fowl)
[b]Lantern Festival
[c]Qīngmíng
[d]Dragon Festival
[e]Qīqiǎo
[f]Hungry Ghosts
[g]Mid-Autumn Festival
[h]Double-Ninth Festival
[i]Dōngzhì
*Start of 60-name cycle

[a]New Year
[b]Building of the Cross
[c]Christmas
[d]Jesus's Circumcision
[e]Epiphany
[f]Easter
[g]Mary's Announcement
[h]Jesus's Transfiguration

PERSIAN (ASTRONOMICAL) 1527‡/1528

Month	Sun	Mon	Tue	Wed	Thu	Fri	Sat
DEY 1527	9	10	11	12	13	14	15
	16	17	18	19	20	21	22
	23	24	25	26	27	28	29
BAHMAN 1527	30	*1*	2	3	4	5	6
	7	8	9	10	11	12	13
	14	15	16	17	18	19	20
	21	22	23	24	25	26	27
ESFAND 1527	28	29	30	*1*	2	3	4
	5	6	7	8	9	10	11
	12	13	14	15	16	17	18
	19	20	21	22	23	24	25
FARVARDĪN 1528	26	27	28	29	30	*1*[a]	2
	3	4	5	6	7	8	9
	10	11	12	13[b]	14	15	16
	17	18	19	20	21	22	23
	24	25	26	27	28	29	30
ORDĪBEHEŠT 1528	31	*1*	2	3	4	5	6
	7	8	9	10	11	12	13
	14	15	16	17	18	19	20
	21	22	23	24	25	26	27
XORDĀD 1528	28	29	30	31	*1*	2	3
	4	5	6	7	8	9	10
	11	12	13	14	15	16	17
	18	19	20	21	22	23	24
	25	26	27	28	29	30	31
TĪR 1528	*1*	2	3	4	5	6	7
	8	9	10	11	12	13	14
	15	16	17	18	19	20	21
	22	23	24	25	26	27	28
MORDĀD 1528	29	30	31	*1*	2	3	4
	5	6	7	8	9	10	11
	12	13	14	15	16	17	18
	19	20	21	22	23	24	25
SHAHRĪVAR 1528	26	27	28	29	30	31	*1*
	2	3	4	5	6	7	8
	9	10	11	12	13	14	15
	16	17	18	19	20	21	22
	23	24	25	26	27	28	29
MEHR 1528	30	31	*1*	2	3	4	5
	6	7	8	9	10	11	12
	13	14	15	16	17	18	19
	20	21	22	23	24	25	26
ĀBĀN 1528	27	28	29	30	*1*	2	3
	4	5	6	7	8	9	10
	11	12	13	14	15	16	17
	18	19	20	21	22	23	24
ĀZAR 1528	25	26	27	28	29	30	*1*
	2	3	4	5	6	7	8
	9	10	11	12	13	14	15
	16	17	18	19	20	21	22
	23	24	25	26	27	28	29
DEY 1528	30	*1*	2	3	4	5	6
	7	8	9	10	11	12	13

‡Leap year
[a]New Year
[b]Sizdeh Bedar

HINDU LUNAR 2205‡/2206

Month	Sun	Mon	Tue	Wed	Thu	Fri	Sat
PAUSHA MĀRGAŚĪRA 2205	19	20	21	22	23	24	25
	26	27	28	29	30	1	2
	3	4	5	6	7	8	9
	10	**11**	13	14	15	16	17
	18	19	20	21	*21*	22	23
	24	25	26	27	28	29	30
MĀGHA 2205	1	2	3	4	**5**	7	8
	9	10	11	12	13	14	15
	16	17	18	19	20	21	22
	23	*23*	24	25	26	27	**28**[h]
PHĀLGUNA 2205	30	1	2	3	4	5	6
	7	8	9	10	11	12	13
	14	15[i]	16	17	18	19	20
	21	22	23	24	25	26	27
CHAITRA 2206	28	29	30	1[a]	2	**3**	5
	6	7	8	9[b]	10	11	12
	13	14	15	16	17	*17*	18
	19	20	21	22	23	24	25
VAIŚĀKHA 2206	**26**	28	29	30	1	2	3
	4	5	6	7	8	9	10
	11	12	13	14	15	16	17
	18	19	20	21	22	23	24
JYAISHTHA 2206	25	26	27	28	29	**30**	2
	3	4	5	6	7	8	9
	10	11	12	13	*13*	14	15
	16	17	18	19	20	21	**22**
	24	25	26	27	28	29	30
ĀSHĀḌHA 2206	1	2	3	4	5	6	7
	8	9	10	11	12	13	14
	15	16	17	18	19	20	21
	22	23	24	**25**	27	28	29
ŚRĀVAṆA 2206	30	1	2	3	4	5	6
	7	8	9	10	*10*	11	12
	13	14	15	16	17	**18**	20
	21	22	23[c]	24	25	26	27
BHĀDRAPADA 2206	28	29	30	1	2	3[d]	4
	5	6	7	8	9	10	11
	12	13	14	15	16	17	18
	19	20	**21**	23	24	25	26
ĀŚVINA 2206	27	28	29	30	1	2	3
	4	5	*5*	6	7	8[e]	9[e]
	10[e]	11	12	13	14	**15**	17
	18	19	20	21	22	23	24
KĀRTTIKA 2206	25	26	27	28	29	30	1[f]
	2	3	4	5	6	7	8
	9	10	11	12	13	14	15
	16	17	18	**19**	21	22	23
	24	25	26	27	28	29	*29*
MĀRGAŚĪRA 2206	30	1	2	3	4	5	6
	7	8	9	10	11[g]	12	**13**
	15	16	17	18	19	20	21
	22	23	24	25	26	27	28
	29	30	1	*1*	2	3	4

‡Leap year
[a]New Year (Saumya)
[b]Birthday of Rāma
[c]Birthday of Krishna
[d]Ganēśa Chaturthī
[e]Dashara
[f]Diwali
[g]Birthday of Vishnu
[h]Night of Śiva
[i]Holi

HINDU SOLAR 2070‡/2071

Month	Sun	Mon	Tue	Wed	Thu	Fri	Sat
PAUSHA 2070	12	13	14	15	16	17	18
	19	20	21	22	23	24	25
	26	27	28	29	1[b]	2	3
MĀGHA 2070	4	5	6	7	8	9	10
	11	12	13	14	15	16	17
	18	19	20	21	22	23	24
	25	26	27	28	29	1	2
PHĀLGUNA 2070	3	4	5	6	7	8	9
	10	11	12	13	14	15	16
	17	18	19	20	21	22	23
	24	25	26	27	28	29	30
CHAITRA 2070	1	2	3	4	5	6	7
	8	9	10	11	12	13	14
	15	16	17	18	19	20	21
	22	23	24	25	26	27	28
	29	30	31	1[a]	2	3	4
VAIŚĀKHA 2071	5	6	7	8	9	10	11
	12	13	14	15	16	17	18
	19	20	21	22	23	24	25
	26	27	28	29	30	1	2
JYAISHTHA 2071	3	4	5	6	7	8	9
	10	11	12	13	14	15	16
	17	18	19	20	21	22	23
	24	25	26	27	28	29	30
	31	32	1	2	3	4	5
ĀSHĀḌHA 2071	6	7	8	9	10	11	12
	13	14	15	16	17	18	19
	20	21	22	23	24	25	26
	27	28	29	30	31	32	1
ŚRĀVAṆA 2071	2	3	4	5	6	7	8
	9	10	11	12	13	14	15
	16	17	18	19	20	21	22
	23	24	25	26	27	28	29
	30	31	1	2	3	4	5
BHĀDRAPADA 2071	6	7	8	9	10	11	12
	13	14	15	16	17	18	19
	20	21	22	23	24	25	26
	27	28	29	30	31	1	2
ĀŚVINA 2071	3	4	5	6	7	8	9
	10	11	12	13	14	15	16
	17	18	19	20	21	22	23
	24	25	26	27	28	29	30
KĀRTTIKA 2071	1	2	3	4	5	6	7
	8	9	10	11	12	13	14
	15	16	17	18	19	20	21
	22	23	24	25	26	27	28
	29	30	1	2	3	4	5
MĀRGAŚĪRA 2071	6	7	8	9	10	11	12
	13	14	15	16	17	18	19
	20	21	22	23	24	25	26
	27	28	29	30	1	2	3
PAUSHA 2071	4	5	6	7	8	9	10
	11	12	13	14	15	16	17

‡Leap year
[a]New Year (Raktāksha)
[b]Pongal

ISLAMIC (ASTRONOMICAL) 1574/1575‡

Month	Sun	Mon	Tue	Wed	Thu	Fri	Sat
RABĪʿ II 1574	17	18	19	20	21	22	23
	24	25	26	27	28	29	*1*
JUMĀDĀ I 1574	2	3	4	5	6	7	8
	9	10	11	12	13	14	15
	16	17	18	19	20	21	22
	23	24	25	26	27	28	29
JUMĀDĀ II 1574	30	*1*	2	3	4	5	6
	7	8	9	10	11	12	13
	14	15	16	17	18	19	20
	21	22	23	24	25	26	27
RAJAB 1574	28	29	*1*	2	3	4	5
	6	7	8	9	10	11	12
	13	14	15	16	17	18	19
	20	21	22	23	24	25	26
SHAʿBĀN 1574	27[d]	28	29	*1*	2	3	4
	5	6	7	8	9	10	11
	12	13	14	15	16	17	18
	19	20	21	22	23	24	25
RAMAḌĀN 1574	26	27	28	29	30	*1*[e]	2
	3	4	5	6	7	8	9
	10	11	12	13	14	15	16
	17	18	19	20	21	22	23
SHAWWĀL 1574	24	25	26	27	28	29	*1*[f]
	2	3	4	5	6	7	8
	9	10	11	12	13	14	15
	16	17	18	19	20	21	22
	23	24	25	26	27	28	29
DHU AL-QAʿDA 1574	30	*1*	2	3	4	5	6
	7	8	9	10	11	12	13
	14	15	16	17	18	19	20
	21	22	23	24	25	26	27
DHU AL-ḤIJJA 1574	28	29	*1*	2	3	4	5
	6	7	8	9	10[g]	11	12
	13	14	15	16	17	18	19
	20	21	22	23	24	25	26
MUḤARRAM 1575	27	28	29	*1*[a]	2[a]	3	4
	5	6	7	8	9	10[b]	11
	12	13	14	15	16	17	18
	19	20	21	22	23	24	25
ṢAFAR 1575	26	27	28	29	30	*1*	2
	3	4	5	6	7	8	9
	10	11	12	13	14	15	16
	17	18	19	20	21	22	23
	24	25	26	27	28	29	30
RABĪʿ I 1575	*1*	2	3	4	5	6	7
	8	9	10	11	12[c]	13	14
	15	16	17	18	19	20	21
	22	23	24	25	26	27	28
RABĪʿ II 1575	29	30	*1*	2	3	4	5
	6	7	8	9	10	11	12
	13	14	15	16	17	18	19
	20	21	22	23	24	25	26
	27	28	29	*1*	2	3	4

‡Leap year
[a]New Year
[a]New Year (Arithmetic)
[b]ʿAshūrāʾ
[c]Prophet's Birthday
[d]Ascent of the Prophet
[e]Start of Ramaḍān
[f]ʿId al-Fiṭr
[g]ʿId al-ʾAḍḥā

GREGORIAN 2149

Julian (Sun)	Sun	Mon	Tue	Wed	Thu	Fri	Sat	Month
Dec 15	*29*	*30*	*31*	1	2	3	4	
	5	6	7	8[a]	9	10	11	JANUARY 2149
Dec 29	*12*	13	14	15[b]	16	17	18	
	19	20	21	22	23	24	25	
Jan 12	*26*	27	28	29	30	31	1	
	2	3	4	5	6	7	8	FEBRUARY 2149
Jan 26	*9*	10	11	12[c]	13	14	15	
	16	17	18	19	20	21	22	
Feb 9	*23*	24	25	26	27	28	1	
	2	3	4	5	6	7	8	MARCH 2149
Feb 23	9	10	11	12	13	14	15	
	16	17	18	19	20	21	22	
Mar 9	*23*[d]	24	25	26	27	28	29	
	30[e]	31	1	2	3	4	5	
Mar 23	*6*	7	8	9	10	11	12	APRIL 2149
	13	14	15	16	17	18	19	
Apr 6	*20*	21	22	23	24	25	26	
	27	28	29	30	1	2	3	
Apr 20	*4*[f]	5	6	7	8	9	10	MAY 2149
	11	12	13	14	15	16	17	
May 4	*18*	19	20	21	22	23	24	
	25	26	27	28	29	30	31	
May 18	*1*	2	3	4	5	6	7	JUNE 2149
	8	9	10	11	12	13	14	
Jun 1	*15*	16	17	18	19	20	21	
	22	23	24	25	26	27	28	
Jun 15	*29*	30	1	2	3	4	5	
	6	7	8	9	10	11	12	JULY 2149
Jun 29	*13*	14	15	16	17	18	19	
	20	21	22	23	24	25	26	
Jul 13	*27*	28	29	30	31	1	2	
	3	4	5	6	7	8	9	AUGUST 2149
Jul 27	*10*	11	12	13	14	15	16	
	17	18	19	20	21	22	23	
Aug 10	*24*	25	26	27	28	29	30	
	31	1	2	3	4	5	6	
Aug 24	*7*	8	9	10	11	12	13	SEPTEMBER 2149
	14	15	16	17	18	19	20	
Sep 7	*21*	22	23	24	25	26	27	
	28	29	30	1	2	3	4	
Sep 21	*5*	6	7	8	9	10	11	OCTOBER 2149
	12	13	14	15	16	17	18	
Oct 5	*19*	20	21	22	23	24	25	
	26	27	28	29	30	31	1	
Oct 19	*2*	3	4	5	6	7	8	NOVEMBER 2149
	9	10	11	12	13	14	15	
Nov 2	*16*	17	18	19	20	21	22	
	23	24	25	26	27	28	29	
Nov 16	*30*[g]	1	2	3	4	5	6	
	7	8	9	10	11	12	13	DECEMBER 2149
Nov 30	*14*	15	16	17	18	19	20	
	21	22	23	24	25[h]	26	27	
Dec 14	*28*	29	30	31	1	2	3	

[a]Orthodox Christmas
[b]Julian New Year
[c]Ash Wednesday
[d]Feast of Orthodoxy
[e]Easter
[f]Orthodox Easter
[g]Advent
[h]Christmas

2150

Gregorian 2150	Sun	Mon	Tue	Wed	Thu	Fri	Sat	Lunar Phases	ISO WEEK (Mon)	JULIAN DAY (Sun noon)	Hebrew 5910/5911	Sun	Mon	Tue	Wed	Thu	Fri	Sat	Molad	Chinese Jǐ-Yǒu/Gēng-Xū‡	Sun	Mon	Tue	Wed	Thu	Fri	Sat	Solar Term	Coptic 1866/1867‡	Sun	Mon	Tue	Wed	Thu	Fri	Sat	Ethiopic 2142/2143‡
January 2150	28	29	●	31	1[a]	2	3	1:01	1	2506328		28[e]	29[e]	30[e]	1[e]	2[e]	3	4	Tue 0h43m14p		29	30	1	2	3	4	5			18	19	20	21	22	23	24	Tākhśāś 2142
	4	5	◐	7	8	9	10	17:01	2	2506335	Teveth 5910	5	6	7	8	9	10	11		Month 12 Jǐ-Yǒu	6	*7*	8	9	10	11	12	Xiǎo hán	Koiak 1866	25	26	27	28	29[c]	30	1	
	11	12	○	14	15	16	17	8:34	3	2506342		12	13	14	15	16	17	18			13	14	15	16	17	18	19			2	3	4	5	6[d]	7	8	
	18	19	◑	21	22	23	24	14:55	4	2506349		19	20	21	22	23	24	25			20	21	**22**	23	24	25	26	Dà hán	Tōbe 1866	9	10	11[e]	12	13	14	15	Ṭer 2142
	25	26	27	●	29	30	31	19:15	5	2506356		26	27	28	29	1	2	3	Wed 13h27m15p		27	28	29	30	1[a]	2	3			16	17	18	19	20	21	22	
February 2150	1	2	3	4	◐	6	7	2:11	6	2506363	Shevat 5910	4	5	6	7	8	9	10		Month 1 Gēng-Xū	4	5	6	*7*	8	9	10	Lì chūn		23	24	25	26	27	28	29	
	8	9	10	○	12	13	14	20:58	7	2506370		11	12	13	14	15	16	17			11	12	13	14	15[b]	16	17			30	1	2	3	4	5	6	
	15	16	17	18	◑	20	21	11:51	8	2506377		18	19	20	21	22	23	24			18	19	20	21	**22**	23	24	Yǔ shuǐ	Meshir 1866	7	8	9	10	11	12	13	Yakātit 2142
	22	23	24	25	26	●	28	10:47	9	2506384		25	26	27	28	29	30	1	Fri 2h11m16p		25	26	27	28	29	1	2			14	15	16	17	18	19	20	
March 2150	1	2	3	4	5	◐	7	9:49	10	2506391	Adar 5910	2	3	4	5	6	7	8		Month 2 Gēng-Xū	3*	4	5	6	*7*	8	9	Jīng zhé		21	22	23	24	25	26	27	
	8	9	10	11	12	○	14	10:10	11	2506398		9	10	11	12	13	14[f]	15			10	11	12	13	14	15	16			28	29	30	1	2	3	4	
	15	16	17	18	19	20[b]	◑	8:50	12	2506405		16	17	18	19	20	21	22			17	18	19	20	21	22	**23**	Chūn fēn	Paremotep 1866	5	6	7	8	9	10	11	Magābit 2142
	22	23	24	25	26	27	●	23:10	13	2506412		23	24	25	26	27	28	29			24	25	26	27	28	29	30			12	13	14	15	16	17	18	
	29	30	31	1	2	3	◐	16:53	14	2506419	Nisan 5910	1	2	3	4	5	6	7	Sat 14h55m17p		1	2	3	4	5	6	7			19	20	21	22	23	24	25	
April 2150	5	6	7	8	9	10	11		15	2506426		8	9	10	11	12	13	14		Month 3 Gēng-Xū	8[c]	9	10	11	12	13	14	Qīng míng		26	27	28	29	30	1	2	
	○	13	14	15	16	17	18	0:14	16	2506433		15[g]	16	17	18	19	20	21			15	16	17	18	19	20	21		Parmoute 1866	3	4	5	6	7	8	9	Miyāzyā 2142
	19	◑	21	22	23	24	25	3:50	17	2506440		22	23	24	25	26	27	28			22	**23**	24	25	26	27	28	Gǔ yǔ		10[f]	11	12	13	14	15	16	
	26	●	28	29	30	1	2	8:57	18	2506447		29	30	1	2	3	4	5	Mon 3h40m0p		29	1	2	3	4*	5	6			17	18	19	20	21	22	23	
May 2150	3	◐	5	6	7	8	9	0:18	19	2506454	Iyyar 5910	6	7	8	9	10	11	12		Month 4 Gēng-Xū	7	8	9	10	11	12	13	Lì xià		24	25	26	27	28	29[g]	30	
	10	○	12	13	14	15	16	15:14	20	2506461		13	14	15	16	17	18	19			14	15	16	17	18	19	20			1	2	3	4	5	6	7	
	17	18	◑	20	21	22	23	19:28	21	2506468		20	21	22	23	24	25	26			21	22	23	24	**25**	26	27	Xiǎo mǎn	Pashons 1866	8	9	10	11	12	13	14	Genbot 2142
	24	25	●	27	28	29	30	16:59	22	2506475		27	28	29	1	2	3	4	Tue 16h24m1p		28	29	30	1	2	3	4			15	16	17	18	19	20	21	
	31	1	◐	3	4	5	6	8:55	23	2506482	Sivan 5910	5	6[h]	7	8	9	10	11		Month 5 Gēng-Xū	5[d]	6	7	8	9	*10*	11	Máng zhòng		22	23	24	25	26	27	28	
June 2150	7	8	9	○	11	12	13	6:51	24	2506489		12	13	14	15	16	17	18			12	13	14	15	16	17	18			29	30	1	2	3	4	5	
	14	15	16	17	◑	19	20	7:27	25	2506496		19	20	21	22	23	24	25			19	20	21	22	23	24	25			6	7	8	9	10	11	12	
	21[c]	22	23	24	●	26	27	0:10	26	2506503		26	27	28	29	30	1	2	Thu 5h8m2p		**26**	27	28	29	1	2	3	Xià zhì	Paōne 1866	13	14	15	16	17	18	19	Sanē 2142
	28	29	30	◐	2	3	4	19:32	27	2506510	Tammuz 5910	3	4	5	6	7	8	9		Month 6 Gēng-Xū	4	5*	6	7	8	9	10			20	21	22	23	24	25	26	
July 2150	5	6	7	8	○	10	11	22:23	28	2506517		10	11	12	13	14	15	16			11	12	*13*	14	15	16	17	Xiǎo shǔ		27	28	29	30	1	2	3	
	12	13	14	15	16	◑	18	16:20	29	2506524		17	18	19	20	21	22	23			18	19	20	21	22	23	24		Epēp 1866	4	5	6	7	8	9	10	Ḥamlē 2142
	19	20	21	22	23	●	25	7:21	30	2506531		24	25	26	27	28	29	1	Fri 17h52m3p		25	26	27	28	**29**	1	2	Dà shǔ		11	12	13	14	15	16	17	
	26	27	28	29	30	◐	1	8:49	31	2506538		2	3	4	5	6	7	8		Leap Month 6 Gēng-Xū	3	4	5	6	7	8	9			18	19	20	21	22	23	24	
August 2150	2	3	4	5	6	7	○	13:00	32	2506545	Av 5910	9[i]	10	11	12	13	14	15			10	11	12	13	14	*15*	16	Lì qiū		25	26	27	28	29	30	1	
	9	10	11	12	13	14	◑	23:08	33	2506552		16	17	18	19	20	21	22			17	18	19	20	21	22	23			2	3	4	5	6	7	8	
	16	17	18	19	20	21	●	15:22	34	2506559		23	24	25	26	27	28	29			24	25	26	27	28	29	1		Mesōrē 1866	9	10	11	12	13[h]	14	15	Naḥasē 2142
	23	24	25	26	27	28	29		35	2506566		30	1	2	3	4	5	6	Sun 6h36m4p	Month 7 Gēng-Xū	**2**	3	4	5	6	7[e]*	8	Chǔ shǔ		16	17	18	19	20	21	22	
	◐	31	1	2	3	4	5	1:02	36	2506573	Elul 5910	7	8	9	10	11	12	13			9	10	11	12	13	14	15[f]			23	24	25	26	27	28	29	
September 2150	6	○	8	9	10	11	12	2:17	37	2506580		14	15	16	17	18	19	20			16	*17*	18	19	20	21	22	Bái lù	Epag. 1866	30	1	2	3	4	5	1[a]	Ṗāg. 2142
	13	◑	15	16	17	18	19	4:59	38	2506587		21	22	23	24	25	26	27			23	24	25	26	27	28	29			2	3	4	5	6	7	8	
	20	●	22	23[d]	24	25	26	1:10	39	2506594		28	29	1[a]	2[a]	3	4	5	Mon 19h20m5p		30	1	2	**3**	4	5	6	Qiū fēn	Thoout 1867	9	10	11	12	13	14	15	Maskaram 2143
	27	◐	29	30	1	2	3	19:43	40	2506601	Tishri 5911	6	7	8	9	10[b]	11	12		Month 8 Gēng-Xū	7	8	9	10	11	12	13			16	17[b]	18	19	20	21	22	
October 2150	4	5	○	7	8	9	10	14:22	41	2506608		13	14	15[c]	16	17	18	19			14	15[g]	16	17	*18*	19	20	Hán lù		23	24	25	26	27	28	29	
	11	12	◑	14	15	16	17	11:04	42	2506615		20	21	22	23	24	25	26			21	22	23	24	25	26	27			30	1	2	3	4	5	6	
	18	19	●	21	22	23	24	13:42	43	2506622		27	28	29	30	1	2	3	Wed 8h4m6p		28	29	1	2	3	**4**	5	Shuāng jiàng	Paope 1867	7	8	9	10	11	12	13	Ṭeqemt 2143
	25	26	27	◐	29	30	31	15:35	44	2506629	Heshvan 5911	4	5	6	7	8	9	10		Month 9 Gēng-Xū	6	7	8*	9[h]	10	11	12			14	15	16	17	18	19	20	
November 2150	1	2	3	4	○	6	7	1:47	45	2506636		11	12	13	14	15	16	17			13	14	15	16	17	18	*19*	Lì dōng		21	22	23	24	25	26	27	
	8	9	10	◑	12	13	14	18:30	46	2506643		18	19	20	21	22	23	24			20	21	22	23	24	25	26			28	29	30	1	2	3	4	
	15	16	17	18	●	20	21	5:32	47	2506650		25	26	27	28	29	1	2	Thu 20h48m7p		27	28	29	30	1	2	3		Athōr 1867	5	6	7	8	9	10	11	
	22	23	24	25	26	◐	28	10:54	48	2506657	Kislev 5911	3	4	5	6	7	8	9		Month 10 Gēng-Xū	**4**	5	6	7	8	9	10	Xiǎo xuě		12	13	14	15	16	17	18	Ḫedār 2143
	29	30	1	2	3	○	5	12:57	49	2506664		10	11	12	13	14	15	16			11	12	13	14	15	16	17			19	20	21	22	23	24	25	
December 2150	6	7	8	9	10	◑	12	4:20	50	2506671		17[d]	18	19	20	21	22	23			18	*19*	20	21	22	23	24	Dà xuě		26	27	28	29	30	1	2	
	13	14	15	16	17	18	●	0:13	51	2506678		24	25[e]	26[e]	27[e]	28[e]	29[e]	30[e]	Sat 9h32m8p		25	26	27	28	29	30	1		Koiak 1867	3	4	5	6	7	8	9	Tākhśāś 2143
	20	21[e]	22	23	24	25	26		52	2506685	Teveth 5911	1[e]	2[e]	3	4	5	6	7		Month 11 Gēng-Xū	2	3	**4**[i]	5	6	7	8*	Dōng zhì		10	11	12	13	14	15	16	
	◐	28	29	30	31	1	○	4:13 0:00	53	2506692		8	9	10	11	12	13	14			9	10	11	12	13	14	15			17	18	19	20	21	22	23	

[a]New Year
[b]Spring (16:00)
[c]Summer (7:28)
[d]Autumn (0:27)
[e]Winter (23:20)
● New moon
◐ First quarter moon
○ Full moon
◑ Last quarter moon

[a]New Year
[b]Yom Kippur
[c]Sukkot
[d]Winter starts
[e]Ḥanukkah
[f]Purim
[g]Passover
[h]Shavuot
[i]Fast of Av

‡Leap year
[a]New Year (4848, Dog)
[b]Lantern Festival
[c]Qīngmíng
[d]Dragon Festival
[e]Qīqiǎo
[f]Hungry Ghosts
[g]Mid-Autumn Festival
[h]Double-Ninth Festival
[i]Dōngzhì
*Start of 60-name cycle

‡Leap year
[a]New Year
[b]Building of the Cross
[c]Christmas
[d]Jesus's Circumcision
[e]Epiphany
[f]Easter
[g]Mary's Announcement
[h]Jesus's Transfiguration

PERSIAN (ASTRONOMICAL) 1528/1529

Month	Sun	Mon	Tue	Wed	Thu	Fri	Sat
	7	8	9	10	11	12	13
DEY 1528	14	15	16	17	18	19	20
	21	22	23	24	25	26	27
	28	29	30	1	2	3	4
BAHMAN 1528	5	6	7	8	9	10	11
	12	13	14	15	16	17	18
	19	20	21	22	23	24	25
	26	27	28	29	30	1	2
ESFAND 1528	3	4	5	6	7	8	9
	10	11	12	13	14	15	16
	17	18	19	20	21	22	23
	24	25	26	27	28	29	1[a]
FARVARDĪN 1529	2	3	4	5	6	7	8
	9	10	11	12	13[b]	14	15
	16	17	18	19	20	21	22
	23	24	25	26	27	28	29
	30	31	1	2	3	4	5
ORDĪBEHEŠT 1529	6	7	8	9	10	11	12
	13	14	15	16	17	18	19
	20	21	22	23	24	25	26
	27	28	29	30	31	1	2
XORDĀD 1529	3	4	5	6	7	8	9
	10	11	12	13	14	15	16
	17	18	19	20	21	22	23
	24	25	26	27	28	29	30
	31	1	2	3	4	5	6
TĪR 1529	7	8	9	10	11	12	13
	14	15	16	17	18	19	20
	21	22	23	24	25	26	27
	28	29	30	31	1	2	3
MORDĀD 1529	4	5	6	7	8	9	10
	11	12	13	14	15	16	17
	18	19	20	21	22	23	24
	25	26	27	28	29	30	31
SHAHRĪVAR 1529	1	2	3	4	5	6	7
	8	9	10	11	12	13	14
	15	16	17	18	19	20	21
	22	23	24	25	26	27	28
	29	30	31	1	2	3	4
MEHR 1529	5	6	7	8	9	10	11
	12	13	14	15	16	17	18
	19	20	21	22	23	24	25
	26	27	28	29	30	1	2
ĀBĀN 1529	3	4	5	6	7	8	9
	10	11	12	13	14	15	16
	17	18	19	20	21	22	23
	24	25	26	27	28	29	30
ĀZAR 1529	1	2	3	4	5	6	7
	8	9	10	11	12	13	14
	15	16	17	18	19	20	21
	22	23	24	25	26	27	28
DEY 1529	29	30	1	2	3	4	5
	6	7	8	9	10	11	12

HINDU LUNAR 2206/2207

Month	Sun	Mon	Tue	Wed	Thu	Fri	Sat
PAUSHA 2206	29	30	1	1	2	3	4
	5	6	7	9	10	11	12
	13	14	15	16	17	18	19
	20	21	22	23	24	25	26
MĀGHA 2206	27	28	29	30	1	2	3
	4	5	6	7	8	9	10
	11	12	14	15	16	17	18
	19	20	21	22	23	24	24
PHĀLGUNA 2206	25	26	27	28[h]	29	30	1
	2	3	4	5	6	8	9
	10	11	12	13	14	15[i]	16
	17	18	19	20	21	22	23
	24	25	26	27	28	29	30
CHAITRA 2207	1[a]	2	3	4	5	6	7
	8[b]	9	10	11	13	14	15
	16	17	17	18	19	20	21
	22	23	24	25	26	27	28
VAIŚĀKHA 2207	29	30	1	2	3	4	6
	7	8	9	10	11	12	13
	14	15	16	17	18	19	20
	21	21	22	23	24	25	26
JYAISHTHA 2207	28	29	30	1	2	3	4
	5	6	7	8	9	11	11
	12	13	14	15	16	17	18
	19	20	21	22	23	24	25
ĀSHĀDHA 2207	26	27	28	29	30	2	3
	4	5	6	7	8	9	10
	11	12	13	14	15	16	17
	18	18	19	20	21	22	24
ŚRĀVAṆA 2207	25	26	27	28	29	30	1
	2	3	5	6	7	8	9
	9	10	11	12	13	14	15
	16	17	18	19	20	21	22
	23[c]	24	25	27	28	29	30
BHĀDRAPADA 2207	1	2	3	4[d]	5	6	7
	8	9	10	11	12	13	14
	14	15	16	17	19	20	21
	22	23	24	25	26	27	28
ĀŚVINA 2207	29	30	2	3	4	5	5
	6	7	8[e]	9[e]	10[e]	11	12
	13	14	15	16	17	18	19
	20	21	22	24	25	26	27
KĀRTTIKA 2207	28	29	30	1[f]	2	3	4
	5	6	7	8	9	9	10
	11	12	13	14	15	17	18
	19	20	21	22	23	24	25
MĀRGAŚĪRA 2207	26	27	28	29	30	1	2
	3	4	5	6	7	8	9
	10	11[g]	12	13	14	15	16
	17	18	19	20	22	23	24
PAUSHA 2207	25	26	27	28	29	30	1
	2	2	3	4	5	6	7
	8	9	10	11	12	13	14

HINDU SOLAR 2071/2072

Month	Sun	Mon	Tue	Wed	Thu	Fri	Sat
PAUSHA 2071	11	12	13	14	15	16	17
	18	19	20	21	22	23	24
	25	26	27	28	29	1[b]	2
MĀGHA 2071	3	4	5	6	7	8	9
	10	11	12	13	14	15	16
	17	18	19	20	21	22	23
	24	25	26	27	28	29	30
PHĀLGUNA 2071	1	2	3	4	5	6	7
	8	9	10	11	12	13	14
	15	16	17	18	19	20	21
	22	23	24	25	26	27	28
	29	1	2	3	4	5	6
CHAITRA 2071	7	8	9	10	11	12	13
	14	15	16	17	18	19	20
	21	22	23	24	25	26	27
	28	29	30	31	1[a]	2	3
VAIŚĀKHA 2072	4	5	6	7	8	9	10
	11	12	13	14	15	16	17
	18	19	20	21	22	23	24
	25	26	27	28	29	30	31
JYAISHTHA 2072	1	2	3	4	5	6	7
	8	9	10	11	12	13	14
	15	16	17	18	19	20	21
	22	23	24	25	26	27	28
	29	30	31	1	2	3	4
ĀSHĀDHA 2072	5	6	7	8	9	10	11
	12	13	14	15	16	17	18
	19	20	21	22	23	24	25
	26	27	28	29	30	31	32
ŚRĀVAṆA 2072	1	2	3	4	5	6	7
	8	9	10	11	12	13	14
	15	16	17	18	19	20	21
	22	23	24	25	26	27	28
	29	30	31	1	2	3	4
BHĀDRAPADA 2072	5	6	7	8	9	10	11
	12	13	14	15	16	17	18
	19	20	21	22	23	24	25
	26	27	28	29	30	31	1
ĀŚVINA 2072	2	3	4	5	6	7	8
	9	10	11	12	13	14	15
	16	17	18	19	20	21	22
	23	24	25	26	27	28	29
	30	31	1	2	3	4	5
KĀRTTIKA 2072	6	7	8	9	10	11	12
	13	14	15	16	17	18	19
	20	21	22	23	24	25	26
	27	28	29	30	1	2	3
MĀRGAŚĪRA 2072	4	5	6	7	8	9	10
	11	12	13	14	15	16	17
	18	19	20	21	22	23	24
	25	26	27	28	29	1	2
PAUSHA 2072	3	4	5	6	7	8	9
	10	11	12	13	14	15	16

ISLAMIC (ASTRONOMICAL) 1575‡/1576

Month	Sun	Mon	Tue	Wed	Thu	Fri	Sat
	27	28	29	1	2	3	4
JUMĀDĀ I 1575	5	6	7	8	9	10	11
	12	13	14	15	16	17	18
	19	20	21	22	23	24	25
	26	27	28	29	30	1	2
JUMĀDĀ II 1575	3	4	5	6	7	8	9
	10	11	12	13	14	15	16
	17	18	19	20	21	22	23
	24	25	26	27	28	29	30
RAJAB 1575	1	2	3	4	5	6	7
	8	9	10	11	12	13	14
	15	16	17	18	19	20	21
	22	23	24	25	26	27[d]	28
SHA'BĀN 1575	29	1	2	3	4	5	6
	7	8	9	10	11	12	13
	14	15	16	17	18	19	20
	21	22	23	24	25	26	27
RAMAḌĀN 1575	28	29	1[e]	2	3	4	5
	6	7	8	9	10	11	12
	13	14	15	16	17	18	19
	20	21	22	23	24	25	26
SHAWWĀL 1575	27	28	29	30	1[f]	2	3
	4	5	6	7	8	9	10
	11	12	13	14	15	16	17
	18	19	20	21	22	23	24
DHU AL-QA'DA 1575	25	26	27	28	29	1	2
	3	4	5	6	7	8	9
	10	11	12	13	14	15	16
	17	18	19	20	21	22	23
DHU AL-ḤIJJA 1575	24	25	26	27	28	29	1
	2	3	4	5	6	7	8
	9	10[g]	11	12	13	14	15
	16	17	18	19	20	21	22
	23	24	25	26	27	28	29
MUḤARRAM 1576	30	1[a]	2	3	4	5	6
	7	8	9	10[b]	11	12	13
	14	15	16	17	18	19	20
	21	22	23	24	25	26	27
ṢAFAR 1576	28	29	1	2	3	4	5
	6	7	8	9	10	11	12
	13	14	15	16	17	18	19
	20	21	22	23	24	25	26
RABĪ' I 1576	27	28	29	30	1	2	3
	4	5	6	7	8	9	10
	11	12[c]	13	14	15	16	17
	18	19	20	21	22	23	24
RABĪ' II 1576	25	26	27	28	29	30	1
	2	3	4	5	6	7	8
	9	10	11	12	13	14	15
	16	17	18	19	20	21	22
	23	24	25	26	27	28	29
JUMĀDĀ I 1576	30	1	2	3	4	5	6
	7	8	9	10	11	12	13

GREGORIAN 2150

Julian (Sun)	Sun	Mon	Tue	Wed	Thu	Fri	Sat	Month
Dec 14	28	29	30	31	1	2	3	
	4	5	6	7	8[a]	9	10	JANUARY 2150
Dec 28	11	12	13	14	15[b]	16	17	
	18	19	20	21	22	23	24	
Jan 11	25	26	27	28	29	30	31	
	1	2	3	4	5	6	7	FEBRUARY 2150
Jan 25	8	9	10	11	12	13	14	
	15	16	17	18	19	20	21	
Feb 8	22	23	24	25[c]	26	27	28	
	1	2	3	4	5	6	7	MARCH 2150
Feb 22	8[d]	9	10	11	12	13	14	
	15	16	17	18	19	20	21	
Mar 8	22	23	24	25	26	27	28	
	29	30	31	1	2	3	4	
Mar 22	5	6	7	8	9	10	11	APRIL 2150
	12[e]	13	14	15	16	17	18	
Apr 5	19[f]	20	21	22	23	24	25	
	26	27	28	29	30	1	2	
Apr 19	3	4	5	6	7	8	9	MAY 2150
	10	11	12	13	14	15	16	
May 3	17	18	19	20	21	22	23	
	24	25	26	27	28	29	30	
May 17	31	1	2	3	4	5	6	
	7	8	9	10	11	12	13	JUNE 2150
May 31	14	15	16	17	18	19	20	
	21	22	23	24	25	26	27	
Jun 14	28	29	30	1	2	3	4	
	5	6	7	8	9	10	11	JULY 2150
Jun 28	12	13	14	15	16	17	18	
	19	20	21	22	23	24	25	
Jul 12	26	27	28	29	30	31	1	
	2	3	4	5	6	7	8	AUGUST 2150
Jul 26	9	10	11	12	13	14	15	
	16	17	18	19	20	21	22	
Aug 9	23	24	25	26	27	28	29	
	30	31	1	2	3	4	5	
Aug 23	6	7	8	9	10	11	12	SEPTEMBER 2150
	13	14	15	16	17	18	19	
Sep 6	20	21	22	23	24	25	26	
	27	28	29	30	1	2	3	
Sep 20	4	5	6	7	8	9	10	OCTOBER 2150
	11	12	13	14	15	16	17	
Oct 4	18	19	20	21	22	23	24	
	25	26	27	28	29	30	31	
Oct 18	1	2	3	4	5	6	7	NOVEMBER 2150
	8	9	10	11	12	13	14	
Nov 1	15	16	17	18	19	20	21	
	22	23	24	25	26	27	28	
Nov 15	29[g]	30	1	2	3	4	5	
	6	7	8	9	10	11	12	DECEMBER 2150
Nov 29	13	14	15	16	17	18	19	
	20	21	22	23	24	25[h]	26	
Dec 13	27	28	29	30	31	1	2	

Persian: [a]New Year; [b]Sizdeh Bedar

Hindu Lunar: [a]New Year (Sādhāraṇa); [b]Birthday of Rāma; [c]Birthday of Krishna; [d]Ganēśa Chaturthī; [e]Dashara; [f]Diwali; [g]Birthday of Vishnu; [h]Night of Śiva; [i]Holi

Hindu Solar: [a]New Year (Krodhana); [b]Pongal

Islamic: ‡Leap year; [a]New Year; [b]'Ashūrā'; [c]Prophet's Birthday; [d]Ascent of the Prophet; [e]Start of Ramaḍān; [f]'Id al-Fiṭr; [g]'Id al-'Aḍḥā

Gregorian: [a]Orthodox Christmas; [b]Julian New Year; [c]Ash Wednesday; [d]Feast of Orthodoxy; [e]Easter; [f]Orthodox Easter; [g]Advent; [h]Christmas

2151

GREGORIAN 2151	Sun	Mon	Tue	Wed	Thu	Fri	Sat	Lunar Phases	ISO WEEK (Mon)	JULIAN DAY (Sun noon)	HEBREW 5911/5912‡	Sun	Mon	Tue	Wed	Thu	Fri	Sat	Molad	CHINESE Gēng-Xū‡/Xīn-Hài	Sun	Mon	Tue	Wed	Thu	Fri	Sat	Solar Term	COPTIC 1867‡/1868	Sun	Mon	Tue	Wed	Thu	Fri	Sat	ETHIOPIC 2143‡/2144
JANUARY 2151	◐	28	29	30	31	1[a]	○	4:13 0:00	53	2506692	TEVETH 5911	8	9	10	11	12	13	14		MONTH 11 Gēng-Xū	9	10	11	12	13	14	15		KOIAK 1867	17	18	19	20	21	22	23	TĀKHŚĀŚ 2143
	3	4	5	6	7	8	◑	17:18	1	2506699		15	16	17	18	19	20	21			16	17	18	19	20	21	22	Xiǎo hán		24	25	26	27	28	29[c]	30	
	10	11	12	13	14	15	16		2	2506706		22	23	24	25	26	27	28			23	24	25	26	27	28	29		TÔBE 1867	1	2	3	4	5	6[d]	7	ṬER 2143
	●	18	19	20	21	22	23	20:07	3	2506713	SHEVAT 5911	29	1	2	3	4	5	6	Sun $22^h16^m9^p$	MONTH 12 Gēng-Xū	30	1	2	3	4	5	6	Dà hán		8	9	10	11[e]	12	13	14	
	24	◐	26	27	28	29	30	18:38	4	2506720		7	8	9	10	11	12	13			7	8	9	10	11	12	13			15	16	17	18	19	20	21	
FEBRUARY 2151	31	○	2	3	4	5	6	10:49	5	2506727		14	15	16	17	18	19	20			14	15	16	17	18	19	20	Lì chūn		22	23	24	25	26	27	28	
	7	◑	9	10	11	12	13	9:34	6	2506734		21	22	23	24	25	26	27			21	22	23	24	25	26	27		MESHIR 1867	29	30	1	2	3	4	5	YAKĀTIT 2143
	14	15	●	17	18	19	20	15:08	7	2506741	ADAR 5911	28	29	30	1	2	3	4	Tue $11^h0^m10^p$	MONTH 1 Xīn-Hài	28	29	1[a]	2	3	4	5	Yǔ shuǐ		6	7	8	9	10	11	12	
	21	22	23	◐	25	26	27	5:52	8	2506748		5	6	7	8	9	10	11			6	7	8	9*	10	11	12			13	14	15	16	17	18	19	
MARCH 2151	28	1	○	3	4	5	6	21:26	9	2506755		12	13	14[f]	15	16	17	18			13	14	15[b]	16	17	18	19	Jīng zhé		20	21	22	23	24	25	26	
	7	8	9	◑	11	12	13	4:23	10	2506762		19	20	21	22	23	24	25			20	21	22	23	24	25	26		PAREMOTEP 1867	27	28	29	30	1	2	3	MAGĀBIT 2143
	14	15	16	17	●	19	20[b]	7:45	11	2506769	NISAN 5911	26	27	28	29	1	2	3	Wed $23^h44^m11^p$	MONTH 2 Xīn-Hài	27	28	29	30	1	2	3			4	5	6	7	8	9	10	
	21	22	23	24	◐	26	27	14:13	12	2506776		4	5	6	7	8	9	10			4	5	6	7	8	9	10	Chūn fēn		11	12	13	14	15	16	17	
APRIL 2151	28	29	30	31	○	2	3	8:17	13	2506783		11	12	13	14	15[g]	16	17			11	12	13	14	15	16	17			18	19	20	21	22	23	24	
	4	5	6	7	8	◑	10	0:09	14	2506790		18	19	20	21	22	23	24			18	19[c]	20	21	22	23	24	Qīng míng	PARMOUTE 1867	25	26	27	28	29	30	1	MIYĀZYĀ 2143
	11	12	13	14	15	●	17	21:26	15	2506797	IYYAR 5911	25	26	27	28	29	30	1	Fri $12^h28^m12^p$	MONTH 3 Xīn-Hài	25	26	27	28	29	30	1			2[f]	3	4	5	6	7	8	
	18	19	20	21	22	◐	24	20:28	16	2506804		2	3	4	5	6	7	8			2	3	4	5	6	7	8	Gǔ yǔ		9	10	11	12	13	14	15	
	25	26	27	28	29	○	1	19:57	17	2506811		9	10	11	12	13	14	15			9*	10	11	12	13	14	15			16	17	18	19	20	21	22	
MAY 2151	2	3	4	5	6	7	◑	19:06	18	2506818		16	17	18	19	20	21	22			16	17	18	19	20	21	22	Lì xià		23	24	25	26	27	28	29[g]	
	9	10	11	12	13	14	15		19	2506825		23	24	25	26	27	28	29			23	24	25	26	27	28	29		PASHONS 1867	30	1	2	3	4	5	6	GENBOT 2143
	●	17	18	19	20	21	22	8:25	20	2506832	SIVAN 5911	1	2	3	4	5	6[h]	7	Sun $1^h12^m13^p$	MONTH 4 Xīn-Hài	1	2	3	4	5	6	7	Xiǎo mǎn		7	8	9	10	11	12	13	
	◐	24	25	26	27	28	29	1:52	21	2506839		8	9	10	11	12	13	14			8	9	10	11	12	13	14			14	15	16	17	18	19	20	
JUNE 2151	○	31	1	2	3	4	5	8:54	22	2506846		15	16	17	18	19	20	21			15	16	17	18	19	20	21			21	22	23	24	25	26	27	
	6	◑	8	9	10	11	12	12:02	23	2506853		22	23	24	25	26	27	28			22	23	24	25	26	27	28	Máng zhòng	PAÔNE 1867	28	29	30	1	2	3	4	SANĒ 2143
	13	●	15	16	17	18	19	17:14	24	2506860	TAMMUZ 5911	29	30	1	2	3	4	5	Mon $13^h56^m14^p$	MONTH 5 Xīn-Hài	29	30	1	2	3	4	5[d]			5	6	7	8	9	10	11	
	20	◐[c]	22	23	24	25	26	7:47	25	2506867		6	7	8	9	10	11	12			6	7	8	9	10*	11	12	Xià zhì		12	13	14	15	16	17	18	
JULY 2151	27	○	29	30	1	2	3	23:09	26	2506874		13	14	15	16	17	18	19			13	14	15	16	17	18	19			19	20	21	22	23	24	25	
	4	5	6	◑	8	9	10	2:26	27	2506881		20	21	22	23	24	25	26			20	21	22	23	24	25	26	Xiǎo shǔ	EPÊP 1867	26	27	28	29	30	1	2	ḤAMLĒ 2143
	11	12	13	●	15	16	17	0:37	28	2506888	AV 5911	27	28	29	1	2	3	4	Wed $2^h40^m15^p$	MONTH 6 Xīn-Hài	27	28	29	1	2	3	4			3	4	5	6	7	8	9	
	18	19	◐	21	22	23	24	15:38	29	2506895		5	6	7	8	9[i]	10	11			5	6	7	8	9	10	11	Dà shǔ		10	11	12	13	14	15	16	
	25	26	27	○	29	30	31	14:14	30	2506902		12	13	14	15	16	17	18			12	13	14	15	16	17	18			17	18	19	20	21	22	23	
AUGUST 2151	1	2	3	4	◑	6	7	14:22	31	2506909		19	20	21	22	23	24	25			19	20	21	22	23	24	25			24	25	26	27	28	29	30	
	8	9	10	11	●	13	14	7:27	32	2506916	ELUL 5911	26	27	28	29	30	1	2	Thu $15^h24^m16^p$	MONTH 7 Xīn-Hài	26	27	28	29	1	2	3	Lì qiū	MESORÊ 1867	1	2	3	4	5	6	7	NAḤASĒ 2143
	15	16	17	18	◐	20	21	2:33	33	2506923		3	4	5	6	7	8	9			4	5	6	7[e]	8	9	10			8	9	10	11	12	13[h]	14	
	22	23	24	25	26	○	28	5:39	34	2506930		10	11	12	13	14	15	16			11	12*	13	14	15[f]	16	17	Chǔ shǔ		15	16	17	18	19	20	21	
SEPTEMBER 2151	29	30	31	1	2	3	◑	0:06	35	2506937		17	18	19	20	21	22	23			18	19	20	21	22	23	24			22	23	24	25	26	27	28	
	5	6	7	8	9	●	11	14:50	36	2506944	TISHRI 5912	24	25	26	27	28	29	1[a]	Sat $4^h8^m17^p$	MONTH 8 Xīn-Hài	25	26	27	28	29	1	2	Bái lù	EPAG. 1867	29	30	1	2	3	4	5	PĀG. 2143
	12	13	14	15	16	◐	18	17:05	37	2506951		2[a]	3	4	5	6	7	8			3	4	5	6	7	8	9		THOOUT 1868	6	1[a]	2	3	4	5	6	MASKARAM 2144
	19	20	21	22	23[d]	24	○	20:57	38	2506958		9	10[b]	11	12	13	14	15[c]			10	11	12	13	14	15[g]	16	Qiū fēn		7	8	9	10	11	12	13	
OCTOBER 2151	26	27	28	29	30	1	2		39	2506965		16	17	18	19	20	21	22			17	18	19	20	21	22	23			14	15	16	17[b]	18	19	20	
	◑	4	5	6	7	8	●	8:08 23:53	40	2506972		23	24	25	26	27	28	29			24	25	26	27	28	29	30	Hán lù		21	22	23	24	25	26	27	
	10	11	12	13	14	15	16		41	2506979	ḤESHVAN 5912	30	1	2	3	4	5	6	Sun $16^h53^m0^p$	MONTH 9 Xīn-Hài	1	2	3	4	5	6	7		PAOPE 1868	28	29	30	1	2	3	4	ṬEQEMT 2144
	◐	18	19	20	21	22	23	11:01	42	2506986		7	8	9	10	11	12	13			8	9[h]	10	11	12	13*	14			5	6	7	8	9	10	11	
	24	○	26	27	28	29	30	11:50	43	2506993		14	15	16	17	18	19	20			15	16	17	18	19	20	21	Shuāng jiàng		12	13	14	15	16	17	18	
NOVEMBER 2151	31	◑	2	3	4	5	6	15:11	44	2507000		21	22	23	24	25	26	27			22	23	24	25	26	27	28			19	20	21	22	23	24	25	
	7	●	9	10	11	12	13	11:36	45	2507007	KISLEV 5912	28	29	30	1	2	3	4	Tue $5^h37^m1^p$	MONTH 10 Xīn-Hài	29	1	2	3	4	5	6	Lì dōng	ATHÔR 1868	26	27	28	29	30	1	2	HEDĀR 2144
	14	15	◐	17	18	19	20	7:21	46	2507014		5	6	7	8	9	10	11			7	8	9	10	11	12	13			3	4	5	6	7	8	9	
	21	22	23	○	25	26	27	1:56	47	2507021		12	13	14	15	16	17	18			14	15	16	17	18	19	20	Xiǎo xuě		10	11	12	13	14	15	16	
DECEMBER 2151	28	29	◑	1	2	3	4	22:19	48	2507028		19	20	21	22	23	24	25[e]			21	22	23	24	25	26	27			17	18	19	20	21	22	23	
	5	6	7	●	9	10	11	2:22	49	2507035	TEVETH 5912	26[e]	27[e]	28[d,e]	29[e]	30[e]	1[e]	2[e]	Wed $18^h21^m2^p$	MONTH 11 Xīn-Hài	28	29	30	1	2	3	4	Dà xuě		24	25	26	27	28	29	30	
	12	13	14	15	◐	17	18	4:30	50	2507042		3	4	5	6	7	8	9			5	6	7	8	9	10	11		KOIAK 1868	1	2	3	4	5	6	7	TĀKHŚĀŚ 2144
	19	20	21	22[e]	○	24	25	14:55	51	2507049		10	11	12	13	14	15	16			12	13	14*	15[i]	16	17	18	Dōng zhì		8	9	10	11	12	13	14	
	26	27	28	29	◑	31	1	6:44	52	2507056		17	18	19	20	21	22	23			19	20	21	22	23	24	25			15	16	17	18	19	20	21	

[a]New Year
[b]Spring (21:46)
[c]Summer (13:14)
[d]Autumn (6:16)
[e]Winter (5:07)
● New moon
◐ First quarter moon
○ Full moon
◑ Last quarter moon

‡Leap year
[a]New Year
[b]Yom Kippur
[c]Sukkot
[d]Winter starts
[e]Ḥanukkah
[f]Purim
[g]Passover
[h]Shavuot
[i]Fast of Av

‡Leap year
[a]New Year (4849, Pig)
[b]Lantern Festival
[c]Qīngmíng
[d]Dragon Festival
[e]Qīqiǎo
[f]Hungry Ghosts
[g]Mid-Autumn Festival
[h]Double-Ninth Festival
[i]Dōngzhì
*Start of 60-name cycle

‡Leap year
[a]New Year
[b]Building of the Cross
[c]Christmas
[d]Jesus's Circumcision
[e]Epiphany
[f]Easter
[g]Mary's Announcement
[h]Jesus's Transfiguration

PERSIAN (ASTRONOMICAL) 1529/1530

Month	Sun	Mon	Tue	Wed	Thu	Fri	Sat
DEY 1529	6	7	8	9	10	11	12
	13	14	15	16	17	18	19
	20	21	22	23	24	25	26
	27	28	29	30	1	2	3
BAHMAN 1529	4	5	6	7	8	9	10
	11	12	13	14	15	16	17
	18	19	20	21	22	23	24
	25	26	27	28	29	30	1
ESFAND 1529	2	3	4	5	6	7	8
	9	10	11	12	13	14	15
	16	17	18	19	20	21	22
	23	24	25	26	27	28	29
FARVARDĪN 1530	1[a]	2	3	4	5	6	7
	8	9	10	11	12	13[b]	14
	15	16	17	18	19	20	21
	22	23	24	25	26	27	28
	29	30	31	1	2	3	4
ORDĪBEHEŠT 1530	5	6	7	8	9	10	11
	12	13	14	15	16	17	18
	19	20	21	22	23	24	25
	26	27	28	29	30	31	1
XORDĀD 1530	2	3	4	5	6	7	8
	9	10	11	12	13	14	15
	16	17	18	19	20	21	22
	23	24	25	26	27	28	29
	30	31	1	2	3	4	5
TĪR 1530	6	7	8	9	10	11	12
	13	14	15	16	17	18	19
	20	21	22	23	24	25	26
	27	28	29	30	31	1	2
MORDĀD 1530	3	4	5	6	7	8	9
	10	11	12	13	14	15	16
	17	18	19	20	21	22	23
	24	25	26	27	28	29	30
	31	1	2	3	4	5	6
SHAHRĪVAR 1530	7	8	9	10	11	12	13
	14	15	16	17	18	19	20
	21	22	23	24	25	26	27
	28	29	30	31	1	2	3
MEHR 1530	4	5	6	7	8	9	10
	11	12	13	14	15	16	17
	18	19	20	21	22	23	24
	25	26	27	28	29	30	1
ĀBĀN 1530	2	3	4	5	6	7	8
	9	10	11	12	13	14	15
	16	17	18	19	20	21	22
	23	24	25	26	27	28	29
	30	1	2	3	4	5	6
ĀZAR 1530	7	8	9	10	11	12	13
	14	15	16	17	18	19	20
	21	22	23	24	25	26	27
	28	29	30	1	2	3	4
DEY 1530	5	6	7	8	9	10	11

[a]New Year
[b]Sizdeh Bedar

HINDU LUNAR 2207/2208‡

Month	Sun	Mon	Tue	Wed	Thu	Fri	Sat
PAUSHA 2207	8	9	10	11	12	13	**14**
	16	17	18	19	20	21	22
	23	24	25	26	27	28	29
MĀGHA 2207	30	1	2	3	4	5	5
	6	**7**	9	10	11	12	13
	14	15	16	17	18	19	20
	21	22	23	24	25	26	27
PHĀLGUNA 2207	28[h]	29	30	1	2	3	4
	5	6	7	8	9	10	11
	12	**13**	15[i]	16	17	18	19
	20	21	22	23	24	25	26
CHAITRA 2208	27	*27*	28	29	30	1[a]	2
	3	4	5	6	**7**	9[b]	10
	11	12	13	14	15	16	17
	18	19	20	21	22	23	24
LEAP VAIŚĀKHA 2208	25	26	27	28	29	30	1
	2	3	4	5	6	7	8
	9	10	**11**	13	14	15	16
	17	18	19	20	21	*21*	22
	23	24	25	26	27	28	29
VAIŚĀKHA 2208	30	1	2	3	**4**	6	7
	8	9	10	11	12	13	14
	15	16	17	18	19	20	21
	22	23	24	25	26	27	28
JYAISHTHA 2208	29	30	1	2	3	4	5
	6	**7**	9	10	11	12	13
	14	15	16	17	*17*	18	19
	20	21	22	23	24	25	26
ĀSHĀDHA 2208	27	28	29	**30**	2	3	4
	5	6	7	8	9	10	11
	12	13	14	15	16	17	18
	19	20	21	22	23	24	25
ŚRĀVANA 2208	26	27	28	29	30	1	2
	3	5	6	7	8	9	10
	11	12	13	14	*14*	15	16
	17	18	19	20	21	22	23[c]
BHĀDRAPADA 2208	24	25	**26**	28	29	30	1
	2	3	4[d]	5	6	7	8
	9	10	11	12	13	14	15
	16	17	18	19	20	21	22
	23	24	25	26	27	28	**29**
ĀŚVINA 2208	1	2	3	4	5	6	7
	8[e]	9[e]	*9*[e]	10[e]	11	12	13
	14	15	16	17	18	19	20
	21	22	**23**	25	26	27	28
KĀRTTIKA 2208	29	30	1[f]	2	3	4	5
	6	7	8	9	10	11	12
	12	13	14	**15**	17	18	19
	20	21	22	23	24	25	26
MĀRGAŚĪRA 2208	27	28	29	30	1	2	3
	4	5	6	7	8	9	10
	11[g]	12	13	14	15	16	17
	18	19	20	**21**	23	24	25

‡Leap year
[a]New Year (Virodhakṛit)
[b]Birthday of Rāma
[c]Birthday of Krishna
[d]Ganēśa Chaturthī
[e]Dashara
[f]Diwali
[g]Birthday of Vishnu
[h]Night of Śiva
[i]Holi

HINDU SOLAR 2072/2073

Month	Sun	Mon	Tue	Wed	Thu	Fri	Sat
PAUSHA 2072	10	11	12	13	14	15	16
	17	18	19	20	21	22	23
	24	25	26	27	28	29	1[b]
MĀGHA 2072	2	3	4	5	6	7	8
	9	10	11	12	13	14	15
	16	17	18	19	20	21	22
	23	24	25	26	27	28	29
PHĀLGUNA 2072	30	1	2	3	4	5	6
	7	8	9	10	11	12	13
	14	15	16	17	18	19	20
	21	22	23	24	25	26	27
CHAITRA 2072	28	29	30	1	2	3	4
	5	6	7	8	9	10	11
	12	13	14	15	16	17	18
	19	20	21	22	23	24	25
VAIŚĀKHA 2073	26	27	28	29	30	1[a]	2
	3	4	5	6	7	8	9
	10	11	12	13	14	15	16
	17	18	19	20	21	22	23
	24	25	26	27	28	29	30
JYAISHTHA 2073	31	1	2	3	4	5	6
	7	8	9	10	11	12	13
	14	15	16	17	18	19	20
	21	22	23	24	25	26	27
ĀSHĀDHA 2073	28	29	30	31	1	2	3
	4	5	6	7	8	9	10
	11	12	13	14	15	16	17
	18	19	20	21	22	23	24
	25	26	27	28	29	30	31
ŚRĀVANA 2073	32	1	2	3	4	5	6
	7	8	9	10	11	12	13
	14	15	16	17	18	19	20
	21	22	23	24	25	26	27
BHĀDRAPADA 2073	28	29	30	31	32	1	2
	3	4	5	6	7	8	9
	10	11	12	13	14	15	16
	17	18	19	20	21	22	23
	24	25	26	27	28	29	30
ĀŚVINA 2073	31	1	2	3	4	5	6
	7	8	9	10	11	12	13
	14	15	16	17	18	19	20
	21	22	23	24	25	26	27
KĀRTTIKA 2073	28	29	30	1	2	3	4
	5	6	7	8	9	10	11
	12	13	14	15	16	17	18
	19	20	21	22	23	24	25
MĀRGAŚĪRA 2073	26	27	28	29	30	1	2
	3	4	5	6	7	8	9
	10	11	12	13	14	15	16
	17	18	19	20	21	22	23
PAUSHA 2073	24	25	26	27	28	29	1
	2	3	4	5	6	7	8
	9	10	11	12	13	14	15

[a]New Year (Kshaya)
[b]Pongal

ISLAMIC (ASTRONOMICAL) 1576/1577‡

Month	Sun	Mon	Tue	Wed	Thu	Fri	Sat
JUMĀDĀ I 1576	7	8	9	10	11	12	13
	14	15	16	17	18	19	20
	21	22	23	24	25	26	27
JUMĀDĀ II 1576	28	29	1	2	3	4	5
	6	7	8	9	10	11	12
	13	14	15	16	17	18	19
	20	21	22	23	24	25	26
RAJAB 1576	27	28	29	30	1	2	3
	4	5	6	7	8	9	10
	11	12	13	14	15	16	17
	18	19	20	21	22	23	24
SHA'BĀN 1576	25	26	27[d]	28	29	30	1
	2	3	4	5	6	7	8
	9	10	11	12	13	14	15
	16	17	18	19	20	21	22
	23	24	25	26	27	28	29
RAMAḌĀN 1576	1[e]	2	3	4	5	6	7
	8	9	10	11	12	13	14
	15	16	17	18	19	20	21
	22	23	24	25	26	27	28
SHAWWĀL 1576	29	30	1[f]	2	3	4	5
	6	7	8	9	10	11	12
	13	14	15	16	17	18	19
	20	21	22	23	24	25	26
DHU AL-QA'DA 1576	27	28	29	1	2	3	4
	5	6	7	8	9	10	11
	12	13	14	15	16	17	18
	19	20	21	22	23	24	25
DHU AL-ḤIJJA 1576	26	27	28	29	1	2	3
	4	5	6	7	8	9	10[g]
	11	12	13	14	15	16	17
	18	19	20	21	22	23	24
MUḤARRAM 1577	25	26	27	28	29	1[a]	2[d]
	3	4	5	6	7	8	9
	10[b]	11	12	13	14	15	16
	17	18	19	20	21	22	23
	24	25	26	27	28	29	30
ṢAFAR 1577	1	2	3	4	5	6	7
	8	9	10	11	12	13	14
	15	16	17	18	19	20	21
	22	23	24	25	26	27	28
RABĪ' I 1577	29	1	2	3	4	5	6
	7	8	9	10	11	12[c]	13
	14	15	16	17	18	19	20
	21	22	23	24	25	26	27
RABĪ' II 1577	28	29	30	1	2	3	4
	5	6	7	8	9	10	11
	12	13	14	15	16	17	18
	19	20	21	22	23	24	25
JUMĀDĀ I 1577	26	27	28	29	30	1	2
	3	4	5	6	7	8	9
	10	11	12	13	14	15	16
	17	18	19	20	21	22	23

‡Leap year
[a]New Year
[A]New Year (Arithmetic)
[b]'Ashūrā'
[c]Prophet's Birthday
[d]Ascent of the Prophet
[e]Start of Ramaḍān
[f]'Īd al-Fiṭr
[g]'Īd al-'Aḍḥā

GREGORIAN 2151

Julian (Sun)	Sun	Mon	Tue	Wed	Thu	Fri	Sat	Month
Dec 13	27	28	29	30	31	1	2	
	3	4	5	6	7	8[a]	9	JANUARY 2151
Dec 27	10	11	12	13	14	15[b]	16	
	17	18	19	20	21	22	23	
Jan 10	24	25	26	27	28	29	30	
	31	1	2	3	4	5	6	FEBRUARY 2151
Jan 24	7	8	9	10	11	12	13	
	14	15	16	17[c]	18	19	20	
Feb 7	21	22	23	24	25	26	27	
	28[d]	1	2	3	4	5	6	MARCH 2151
Feb 21	7	8	9	10	11	12	13	
	14	15	16	17	18	19	20	
Mar 7	21	22	23	24	25	26	27	
	28	29	30	31	1	2	3	APRIL 2151
Mar 21	4[e]	5	6	7	8	9	10	
	11[f]	12	13	14	15	16	17	
Apr 4	18	19	20	21	22	23	24	
	25	26	27	28	29	30	1	MAY 2151
Apr 18	2	3	4	5	6	7	8	
	9	10	11	12	13	14	15	
May 2	16	17	18	19	20	21	22	
	23	24	25	26	27	28	29	
May 16	30	31	1	2	3	4	5	JUNE 2151
	6	7	8	9	10	11	12	
May 30	13	14	15	16	17	18	19	
	20	21	22	23	24	25	26	
Jun 13	27	28	29	30	1	2	3	JULY 2151
	4	5	6	7	8	9	10	
Jun 27	11	12	13	14	15	16	17	
	18	19	20	21	22	23	24	
Jul 11	25	26	27	28	29	30	31	
	1	2	3	4	5	6	7	AUGUST 2151
Jul 25	8	9	10	11	12	13	14	
	15	16	17	18	19	20	21	
Aug 8	22	23	24	25	26	27	28	
	29	30	31	1	2	3	4	SEPTEMBER 2151
Aug 22	5	6	7	8	9	10	11	
	12	13	14	15	16	17	18	
Sep 5	19	20	21	22	23	24	25	
	26	27	28	29	30	1	2	OCTOBER 2151
Sep 19	3	4	5	6	7	8	9	
	10	11	12	13	14	15	16	
Oct 3	17	18	19	20	21	22	23	
	24	25	26	27	28	29	30	
Oct 17	31	1	2	3	4	5	6	NOVEMBER 2151
	7	8	9	10	11	12	13	
Oct 31	14	15	16	17	18	19	20	
	21	22	23	24	25	26	27	
Nov 14	28[g]	29	30	1	2	3	4	DECEMBER 2151
	5	6	7	8	9	10	11	
Nov 28	12	13	14	15	16	17	18	
	19	20	21	22	23	24	25[h]	
Dec 12	26	27	28	29	30	31	1	

[a]Orthodox Christmas
[b]Julian New Year
[c]Ash Wednesday
[d]Feast of Orthodoxy
[e]Easter
[f]Orthodox Easter
[g]Advent
[h]Christmas

Month	Sun	Mon	Tue	Wed	Thu	Fri	Sat	Lunar Phases	ISO WEEK (Mon)	JULIAN DAY (Sun noon)
	26	27	28	29	◑	31	1[a]	6:44	52	2507056
JANUARY 2152	2	3	4	5	●	7	8	19:43	1	2507063
	9	10	11	12	13	14	◐	0:37	2	2507070
	16	17	18	19	20	21	○	2:32	3	2507077
	23	24	25	26	27	◑	29	17:24	4	2507084
	30	31	1	2	3	4	●	14:30	5	2507091
FEBRUARY 2152	6	7	8	9	10	11	12		6	2507098
	◐	14	15	16	17	18	19	17:59	7	2507105
	○	21	22	23	24	25	26	12:52	8	2507112
	◑	28	29	1	2	3	4	6:43	9	2507119
MARCH 2152	5	●	7	8	9	10	11	9:16	10	2507126
	12	13	◐	15	16	17	18	7:29	11	2507133
	19	○[b]	21	22	23	24	25	22:24	12	2507140
	26	◑	28	29	30	31	1	22:20	13	2507147
APRIL 2152	2	3	4	●	6	7	8	2:43	14	2507154
	9	10	11	◐	13	14	15	17:00	15	2507161
	16	17	18	○	20	21	22	7:44	16	2507168
	23	24	25	◑	27	28	29	15:24	17	2507175
	30	1	2	3	●	5	6	17:54	18	2507182
MAY 2152	7	8	9	10	◐	12	13	23:23	19	2507189
	14	15	16	17	○	19	20	17:30	20	2507196
	21	22	23	24	25	◑	27	9:03	21	2507203
	28	29	30	31	1	2	●	6:21	22	2507210
JUNE 2152	4	5	6	7	8	9	◐	4:05	23	2507217
	11	12	13	14	15	16	○	4:13	24	2507224
	18	19	20[c]	21	22	23	24		25	2507231
	◑	26	27	28	29	30	1	2:30	26	2507238
JULY 2152	●	3	4	5	6	7	8	16:13	27	2507245
	◐	10	11	12	13	14	15	8:42	28	2507252
	○	17	18	19	20	21	22	16:20	29	2507259
	23	◑	25	26	27	28	29	19:04	30	2507266
	30	31	●	2	3	4	5	0:16	31	2507273
AUGUST 2152	6	◐	8	9	10	11	12	14:45	32	2507280
	13	14	○	16	17	18	19	6:09	33	2507287
	20	21	22	◑	24	25	26	10:04	34	2507294
	27	28	29	●	31	1	2	7:37	35	2507301
SEPTEMBER 2152	3	4	◐	6	7	8	9	23:29	36	2507308
	10	11	12	○	14	15	16	21:47	37	2507315
	17	18	19	20	◑	22[d]	23	23:01	38	2507322
	24	25	26	27	●	29	30	15:26	39	2507329
OCTOBER 2152	1	2	3	4	◐	6	7	11:42	40	2507336
	8	9	10	11	12	○	14	14:50	41	2507343
	15	16	17	18	19	20	◑	9:49	42	2507350
	22	23	24	25	26	27	●	0:39	43	2507357
	29	30	31	1	2	3	◐	3:46	44	2507364
NOVEMBER 2152	5	6	7	8	9	10	11		45	2507371
	○	13	14	15	16	17	18	8:18	46	2507378
	◑	20	21	22	23	24	25	18:53	47	2507385
	●	27	28	29	30	1	2	11:50	48	2507392
DECEMBER 2152	◐	4	5	6	7	8	9	23:19	49	2507399
	10	11	○	13	14	15	16	0:51	50	2507406
	17	18	◑	20	21[e]	22	23	3:00	51	2507413
	24	25	●	27	28	29	30	1:05	52	2507420
	31	1	◐	3	4	5	6	21:05	1	2507427

GREGORIAN 2152‡

HEBREW 5912‡/5913

ISO WEEK	Month	Sun	Mon	Tue	Wed	Thu	Fri	Sat	Molad
52	TEVETH 5912	17	18	19	20	21	22	23	
1		24	25	26	27	28	29	1	Fri 7h 5m 3p
2		2	3	4	5	6	7	8	
3	SHEVAT 5912	9	10	11	12	13	14	15	
4		16	17	18	19	20	21	22	
5		23	24	25	26	27	28	29	
6		30	1	2	3	4	5	6	Sat 19h 49m 4p
7	ADAR I 5912	7	8	9	10	11	12	13	
8		14	15	16	17	18	19	20	
9		21	22	23	24	25	26	27	
10		28	29	30	1	2	3	4	Mon 8h 33m 5p
11	ADAR II 5912	5	6	7	8	9	10	11	
12		12	13	14[f]	15	16	17	18	
13		19	20	21	22	23	24	25	
14		26	27	28	29	1	2	3	Tue 21h 17m 6p
15	NISAN 5912	4	5	6	7	8	9	10	
16		11	12	13	14	15[g]	16	17	
17		18	19	20	21	22	23	24	
18		25	26	27	28	29	30	1	Thu 10h 1m 7p
19	IYAR 5912	2	3	4	5	6	7	8	
20		9	10	11	12	13	14	15	
21		16	17	18	19	20	21	22	
22		23	24	25	26	27	28	29	
23		1	2	3	4	5	6[h]	7	Fri 22h 45m 8p
24	SIVAN 5912	8	9	10	11	12	13	14	
25		15	16	17	18	19	20	21	
26		22	23	24	25	26	27	28	
27		29	30	1	2	3	4	5	Sun 11h 29m 9p
28	TAMMUZ 5912	6	7	8	9	10	11	12	
29		13	14	15	16	17	18	19	
30		20	21	22	23	24	25	26	
31		27	28	29	1	2	3	4	Tue 0h 13m 10p
32	AV 5912	5	6	7	8	9[i]	10	11	
33		12	13	14	15	16	17	18	
34		19	20	21	22	23	24	25	
35		26	27	28	29	30	1	2	Wed 12h 57m 11p
36	ELUL 5912	3	4	5	6	7	8	9	
37		10	11	12	13	14	15	16	
38		17	18	19	20	21	22	23	
39		24	25	26	27	28	29	1[a]	Fri 1h 41m 12p
40		2[a]	3	4	5	6	7	8	
41	TISHRI 5913	9	10[b]	11	12	13	14	15[c]	
42		16	17	18	19	20	21	22	
43		23	24	25	26	27	28	29	
44		30	1	2	3	4	5	6	Sat 14h 25m 13p
45	HESHVAN 5913	7	8	9	10	11	12	13	
46		14	15	16	17	18	19	20	
47		21	22	23	24	25	26	27	
48		28	29	30	1	2	3	4	Mon 3h 9m 14p
49	KISLEV 5913	5	6	7	8[d]	9	10	11	
50		12	13	14	15	16	17	18	
51		19	20	21	22	23	24	25[e]	
52	TEVETH 5913	26[e]	27[e]	28[e]	29[e]	30[e]	1[e]	2[e]	Tue 15h 53m 15p
1		3	4	5	6	7	8	9	

CHINESE Xīn-Hài/Rén-Zǐ

ISO WEEK	Month	Sun	Mon	Tue	Wed	Thu	Fri	Sat	Solar Term
52	MONTH 11 Xīn-Hài	19	20	21	22	23	24	25	
1		26	27	28	29	*30*	1	2	Xiǎo hán
2	MONTH 12 Xīn-Hài	3	4	5	6	7	8	9	
3		10	11	12	13	***14***	15	16	Dà hán
4		17	18	19	20	21	22	23	
5		24	25	26	27	28	*29*	1[a]	Lì chūn
6		2	3	4	5	6	7	8	
7	MONTH 1 Rén-Zǐ	9	10	11	12	13	14	***15***[b]*	Yǔ shuǐ
8		16	17	18	19	20	21	22	
9		23	24	25	26	27	28	29	
10		*30*	1	2	3	4	5	6	Jīng zhé
11	MONTH 2 Rén-Zǐ	7	8	9	10	11	12	13	
12		14	***15***	16	17	18	19	20	Chūn fēn
13		21	22	23	24	25	26	27	
14		28	29	*30*[c]	1	2	3	4	Qīng míng
15	MONTH 3 Rén-Zǐ	5	6	7	8	9	10	11	
16		12	13	14	***15****	16	17	18	Gǔ yǔ
17		19	20	21	22	23	24	25	
18		26	27	28	29	30	*1*	2	Lì xià
19	MONTH 4 Rén-Zǐ	3	4	5	6	7	8	9	
20		10	11	12	13	14	15	***16***	Xiǎo mǎn
21		17	18	19	20	21	22	23	
22		24	25	26	27	28	29	1	
23		2	*3*	4	5[d]	6	7	8	Máng zhòng
24	MONTH 5 Rén-Zǐ	9	10	11	12	13	14	15	
25		16*	17	18	***19***	20	21	22	Xià zhì
26		23	24	25	26	27	28	29	
27		30	1	2	3	*4*	5	6	Xiǎo shǔ
28	MONTH 6 Rén-Zǐ	7	8	9	10	11	12	13	
29		14	15	16	17	18	19	***20***	Dà shǔ
30		21	22	23	24	25	26	27	
31		28	29	1	2	3	4	5	
32	MONTH 7 Rén-Zǐ	6	*7*[e]	8	9	10	11	12	Lì qiū
33		13	14	15[f]	16	17*	18	19	
34		20	21	***22***	23	24	25	26	Chǔ shǔ
35		27	28	29	1	2	3	4	
36	MONTH 8 Rén-Zǐ	5	6	7	8	*9*	10	11	Bái lù
37		12	13	14	15[g]	16	17	18	
38		19	20	21	22	23	***24***	25	Qiū fēn
39		26	27	28	29	1	2	3	
40	MONTH 9 Rén-Zǐ	4	5	6	7	8	9[h]	10	
41		*11*	12	13	14	15	16	17	Hán lù
42		18	19*	20	21	22	23	24	
43		25	***26***	27	28	29	30	1	Shuāng jiàng
44	MONTH 10 Rén-Zǐ	2	3	4	5	6	7	8	
45		9	10	*11*	12	13	14	15	Lì dōng
46		16	17	18	19	20	21	22	
47		23	24	25	***26***	27	28	29	Xiǎo xuě
48		1	2	3	4	5	6	7	
49	MONTH 11 Rén-Zǐ	8	9	10	11	*12*	13	14	Dà xuě
50		15	16	17	18	19	20*	21	
51		22	23	24	25	***26***[i]	27	28	Dōng zhì
52	MONTH 12 Rén-Zǐ	29	30	1	2	3	4	5	
1		6	7	8	9	10	*11*	12	Xiǎo hán

COPTIC 1868/1869 — ETHIOPIC 2144/2145

ISO WEEK	Coptic Month	Sun	Mon	Tue	Wed	Thu	Fri	Sat	Ethiopic Month
52	KOIAK 1868	15	16	17	18	19	20	21	TĀKHŚĀŚ 2144
1		22	23	24	25	26	27	28	
2		29[c]	30	1	2	3	4	5	
3	TÔBE 1868	6[d]	7	8	9	10	11[e]	12	ṬER 2144
4		13	14	15	16	17	18	19	
5		20	21	22	23	24	25	26	
6		27	28	29	30	1	2	3	
7	MESHIR 1868	4	5	6	7	8	9	10	YAKĀTIT 2144
8		11	12	13	14	15	16	17	
9		18	19	20	21	22	23	24	
10		25	26	27	28	29	30	1	
11	PAREMOTEP 1868	2	3	4	5	6	7	8	MAGĀBIT 2144
12		9	10	11	12	13	14	15	
13		16	17	18	19	20	21	22	
14		23	24	25	26	27	28	29	
15		30	1	2	3	4	5	6	
16	PARMOUTE 1868	7	8	9	10	11	12	13	MIYĀZYĀ 2144
17		14	15	16	17	18	19	20	
18		21[f]	22	23	24	25	26	27	
19		28	29[g]	30	1	2	3	4	
20	PASHONS 1868	5	6	7	8	9	10	11	GENBOT 2144
21		12	13	14	15	16	17	18	
22		19	20	21	22	23	24	25	
23		26	27	28	29	30	1	2	
24	PAÔNE 1868	3	4	5	6	7	8	9	SANĒ 2144
25		10	11	12	13	14	15	16	
26		17	18	19	20	21	22	23	
27		24	25	26	27	28	29	30	
28	EPÊP 1868	1	2	3	4	5	6	7	ḤAMLĒ 2144
29		8	9	10	11	12	13	14	
30		15	16	17	18	19	20	21	
31		22	23	24	25	26	27	28	
32		29	30	1	2	3	4	5	
33	MESORÊ 1868	6	7	8	9	10	11	12	NAḤASĒ 2144
34		13[h]	14	15	16	17	18	19	
35		20	21	22	23	24	25	26	
36	EPAG. 1868	27	28	29	30	1	2	3	PĀG. 2144
37		4	5	1[a]	2	3	4	5	
38	THOOUT 1869	6	7	8	9	10	11	12	MASKARAM 2145
39		13	14	15	16	17[b]	18	19	
40		20	21	22	23	24	25	26	
41		27	28	29	30	1	2	3	
42	PAOPE 1869	4	5	6	7	8	9	10	ṬEQEMT 2145
43		11	12	13	14	15	16	17	
44		18	19	20	21	22	23	24	
45		25	26	27	28	29	30	1	
46	ATHÔR 1869	2	3	4	5	6	7	8	ḪEDĀR 2145
47		9	10	11	12	13	14	15	
48		16	17	18	19	20	21	22	
49		23	24	25	26	27	28	29	
50		30	1	2	3	4	5	6	
51	KOIAK 1869	7	8	9	10	11	12	13	TĀKHŚĀŚ 2145
52		14	15	16	17	18	19	20	
1		21	22	23	24	25	26	27	

‡Leap year
[a]New Year
[b]Spring (3:37)
[c]Summer (19:10)
[d]Autumn (12:08)
[e]Winter (11:00)
● New moon
◐ First quarter moon
○ Full moon
◑ Last quarter moon

‡Leap year
[a]New Year
[b]Yom Kippur
[c]Sukkot
[d]Winter starts
[e]Ḥanukkah
[f]Purim
[g]Passover
[h]Shavuot
[i]Fast of Av

[a]New Year (4850, Rat)
[b]Lantern Festival
[c]Qīngmíng
[d]Dragon Festival
[e]Qīqiǎo
[f]Hungry Ghosts
[g]Mid-Autumn Festival
[h]Double-Ninth Festival
[i]Dōngzhì
*Start of 60-name cycle

[a]New Year
[b]Building of the Cross
[c]Christmas
[d]Jesus's Circumcision
[e]Epiphany
[f]Easter
[g]Mary's Announcement
[h]Jesus's Transfiguration

PERSIAN (ASTRONOMICAL) 1530/1531‡

Month	Sun	Mon	Tue	Wed	Thu	Fri	Sat
DEY 1530	5	6	7	8	9	10	11
	12	13	14	15	16	17	18
	19	20	21	22	23	24	25
	26	27	28	29	30	1	2
BAHMAN 1530	3	4	5	6	7	8	9
	10	11	12	13	14	15	16
	17	18	19	20	21	22	23
	24	25	26	27	28	29	30
ESFAND 1530	1	2	3	4	5	6	7
	8	9	10	11	12	13	14
	15	16	17	18	19	20	21
	22	23	24	25	26	27	28
	29	1[a]	2	3	4	5	6
FARVARDĪN 1531	7	8	9	10	11	12	13[b]
	14	15	16	17	18	19	20
	21	22	23	24	25	26	27
	28	29	30	31	1	2	3
ORDĪBEHEŠT 1531	4	5	6	7	8	9	10
	11	12	13	14	15	16	17
	18	19	20	21	22	23	24
	25	26	27	28	29	30	31
XORDĀD 1531	1	2	3	4	5	6	7
	8	9	10	11	12	13	14
	15	16	17	18	19	20	21
	22	23	24	25	26	27	28
	29	30	31	1	2	3	4
TĪR 1531	5	6	7	8	9	10	11
	12	13	14	15	16	17	18
	19	20	21	22	23	24	25
	26	27	28	29	30	31	1
MORDĀD 1531	2	3	4	5	6	7	8
	9	10	11	12	13	14	15
	16	17	18	19	20	21	22
	23	24	25	26	27	28	29
	30	31	1	2	3	4	5
SHAHRĪVAR 1531	6	7	8	9	10	11	12
	13	14	15	16	17	18	19
	20	21	22	23	24	25	26
	27	28	29	30	31	1	2
MEHR 1531	3	4	5	6	7	8	9
	10	11	12	13	14	15	16
	17	18	19	20	21	22	23
	24	25	26	27	28	29	30
ABĀN 1531	1	2	3	4	5	6	7
	8	9	10	11	12	13	14
	15	16	17	18	19	20	21
	22	23	24	25	26	27	28
	29	30	1	2	3	4	5
ĀZAR 1531	6	7	8	9	10	11	12
	13	14	15	16	17	18	19
	20	21	22	23	24	25	26
	27	28	29	30	1	2	3
DEY 1531	4	5	6	7	8	9	10
	11	12	13	14	15	16	17

‡Leap year
[a]New Year
[b]Sizdeh Bedar

HINDU LUNAR 2208‡/2209

Month	Sun	Mon	Tue	Wed	Thu	Fri	Sat
PAUSHA / MĀRGAŚĪRA 2208	18	19	20	21	23	24	25
	26	27	28	29	30	1	2
	3	4	4	5	6	7	8
	9	10	11	12	13	14	15
	17	18	19	20	21	22	23
	24	25	26	27	28	29	30
MĀGHA 2208	1	2	3	4	5	6	7
	8	9	10	11	12	13	14
	15	16	17	18	19	20	22
	23	24	25	26	27	27	28[h]
	29	30	1	2	3	4	5
PHĀLGUNA 2208	6	7	8	9	10	11	12
	13	14[i]	16	17	18	19	20
	21	22	23	24	25	26	27
	28	29	30	30	1[a]	2	3
CHAITRA 2209	4	5	6	7	9[b]	10	11
	12	13	14	15	16	17	18
	19	20	21	22	23	24	25
	26	27	28	29	30	1	2
VAIŚĀKHA 2209	3	4	5	6	7	8	9
	10	11	13	14	15	16	17
	18	19	20	21	22	23	24
	25	25	26	27	28	29	30
JYAISHTHA 2209	1	2	3	4	6	7	8
	9	10	11	12	13	14	15
	16	17	18	19	20	21	22
	23	24	25	26	27	28	29
	30	1	2	3	4	5	6
ĀSHĀDHA 2209	7	9	10	11	12	13	14
	15	16	17	18	19	20	21
	22	22	23	24	25	26	27
	28	29	1	2	3	4	5
ŚRĀVANA 2209	6	7	8	9	10	11	12
	13	14	15	16	17	18	19
	20	21	22	23[c]	24	25	26
	27	28	29	30	1	2	3[d]
BHĀDRAPADA 2209	5	6	7	8	9	10	11
	12	13	14	15	16	17	18
	18	19	20	21	22	23	24
	25	26	28	29	30	1	2
ĀŚVINA 2209	3	4	5	6	7	8[e]	9[e]
	10[e]	11	12	13	14	15	16
	17	18	19	20	21	22	23
	24	25	26	27	28	29	30[f]
KĀRTTIKA 2209	2	3	4	5	6	7	8
	9	10	11	12	12	13	14
	15	16	17	18	19	20	21
	22	23	25	26	27	28	29
	30	1	2	3	4	5	6
MĀRGAŚĪRA 2209	7	8	9	10	11[g]	12	13
	14	15	16	17	18	19	20
	21	22	23	24	25	26	27
	28	29	1	2	3	4	5
PAUSHA 2209	5	6	7	8	9	10	11

‡Leap year
[a]New Year (Paridhāvin)
[b]Birthday of Rāma
[c]Birthday of Krishna
[d]Ganēśa Chaturthī
[e]Dashara
[f]Diwali
[g]Birthday of Vishnu
[h]Night of Śiva
[i]Holi

HINDU SOLAR 2073/2074‡

Month	Sun	Mon	Tue	Wed	Thu	Fri	Sat
PAUSHA 2073	9	10	11	12	13	14	15
	16	17	18	19	20	21	22
	23	24	25	26	27	28	29
	30	1[b]	2	3	4	5	6
MĀGHA 2073	7	8	9	10	11	12	13
	14	15	16	17	18	19	20
	21	22	23	24	25	26	27
	28	29	1	2	3	4	5
PHĀLGUNA 2073	6	7	8	9	10	11	12
	13	14	15	16	17	18	19
	20	21	22	23	24	25	26
	27	28	29	30	1	2	3
CHAITRA 2073	4	5	6	7	8	9	10
	11	12	13	14	15	16	17
	18	19	20	21	22	23	24
	25	26	27	28	29	30	1[a]
VAIŚĀKHA 2074	2	3	4	5	6	7	8
	9	10	11	12	13	14	15
	16	17	18	19	20	21	22
	23	24	25	26	27	28	29
	30	31	1	2	3	4	5
JYAISHTHA 2074	6	7	8	9	10	11	12
	13	14	15	16	17	18	19
	20	21	22	23	24	25	26
	27	28	29	30	31	32	1
ĀSHĀDHA 2074	2	3	4	5	6	7	8
	9	10	11	12	13	14	15
	16	17	18	19	20	21	22
	23	24	25	26	27	28	29
	30	31	1	2	3	4	5
ŚRĀVANA 2074	6	7	8	9	10	11	12
	13	14	15	16	17	18	19
	20	21	22	23	24	25	26
	27	28	29	30	31	32	1
BHĀDRAPADA 2074	2	3	4	5	6	7	8
	9	10	11	12	13	14	15
	16	17	18	19	20	21	22
	23	24	25	26	27	28	29
	30	31	1	2	3	4	5
ĀŚVINA 2074	6	7	8	9	10	11	12
	13	14	15	16	17	18	19
	20	21	22	23	24	25	26
	27	28	29	30	1	2	3
KĀRTTIKA 2074	4	5	6	7	8	9	10
	11	12	13	14	15	16	17
	18	19	20	21	22	23	24
	25	26	27	28	29	30	1
MĀRGAŚĪRA 2074	2	3	4	5	6	7	8
	9	10	11	12	13	14	15
	16	17	18	19	20	21	22
	23	24	25	26	27	28	29
	30	1	2	3	4	5	6
PAUSHA 2074	7	8	9	10	11	12	13
	14	15	16	17	18	19	20

‡Leap year
[a]New Year (Prabhava)
[b]Pongal

ISLAMIC (ASTRONOMICAL) 1577‡/1578‡

Month	Sun	Mon	Tue	Wed	Thu	Fri	Sat
JUMĀDĀ I 1577	17	18	19	20	21	22	23
	24	25	26	27	28	29	1
JUMĀDĀ II 1577	2	3	4	5	6	7	8
	9	10	11	12	13	14	15
	16	17	18	19	20	21	22
	23	24	25	26	27	28	29
	30	1	2	3	4	5	6
RAJAB 1577	7	8	9	10	11	12	13
	14	15	16	17	18	19	20
	21	22	23	24	25	26	27[d]
	28	29	30	1	2	3	4
SHA'BĀN 1577	5	6	7	8	9	10	11
	12	13	14	15	16	17	18
	19	20	21	22	23	24	25
	26	27	28	29	1[e]	2	3
RAMADĀN 1577	4	5	6	7	8	9	10
	11	12	13	14	15	16	17
	18	19	20	21	22	23	24
	25	26	27	28	29	30	1[f]
SHAWWĀL 1577	2	3	4	5	6	7	8
	9	10	11	12	13	14	15
	16	17	18	19	20	21	22
	23	24	25	26	27	28	29
DHU AL-QA'DA 1577	1	2	3	4	5	6	7
	8	9	10	11	12	13	14
	15	16	17	18	19	20	21
	22	23	24	25	26	27	28
DHU AL-HIJJA 1577	29	30	1	2	3	4	5
	6	7	8	9	10[g]	11	12
	13	14	15	16	17	18	19
	20	21	22	23	24	25	26
MUHARRAM 1578	27	28	29	1[a]	2	3	4
	5	6	7	8	9	10[b]	11
	12	13	14	15	16	17	18
	19	20	21	22	23	24	25
ṢAFAR 1578	26	27	28	29	1	2	3
	4	5	6	7	8	9	10
	11	12	13	14	15	16	17
	18	19	20	21	22	23	24
RABĪ' I 1578	25	26	27	28	29	30	1
	2	3	4	5	6	7	8
	9	10	11	12[c]	13	14	15
	16	17	18	19	20	21	22
	23	24	25	26	27	28	29
RABĪ' II 1578	30	1	2	3	4	5	6
	7	8	9	10	11	12	13
	14	15	16	17	18	19	20
	21	22	23	24	25	26	27
JUMĀDĀ I 1578	28	29	1	2	3	4	5
	6	7	8	9	10	11	12
	13	14	15	16	17	18	19
	20	21	22	23	24	25	26
JUMĀDĀ II 1578	27	28	29	30	1	2	3
	4	5	6	7	8	9	10

‡Leap year
[a]New Year
[b]'Ashūrā'
[c]Prophet's Birthday
[d]Ascent of the Prophet
[e]Start of Ramaḍān
[f]'Īd al-Fiṭr
[g]'Īd al-'Aḍḥā

GREGORIAN 2152‡

Julian† (Sun)	Sun	Mon	Tue	Wed	Thu	Fri	Sat	Month
Dec 12	26	27	28	29	30	31	1	
	2	3	4	5	6	7	8[a]	JANUARY 2152
Dec 26	9	10	11	12	13	14	15[b]	
	16	17	18	19	20	21	22	
Jan 9	23	24	25	26	27	28	29	
	30	31	1	2	3	4	5	
Jan 23	6	7	8	9	10	11	12	FEBRUARY 2152
	13	14	15	16	17	18	19	
Feb 6	20	21	22	23	24	25	26	
	27	28	29	1	2	3	4	
Feb 20	5	6	7	8[c]	9	10	11	MARCH 2152
	12	13	14	15	16	17	18	
Mar 5	19[d]	20	21	22	23	24	25	
	26	27	28	29	30	31	1	
Mar 19	2	3	4	5	6	7	8	APRIL 2152
	9	10	11	12	13	14	15	
Apr 2	16	17	18	19	20	21	22	
	23[e]	24	25	26	27	28	29	
Apr 16	30[f]	1	2	3	4	5	6	
	7	8	9	10	11	12	13	MAY 2152
Apr 30	14	15	16	17	18	19	20	
	21	22	23	24	25	26	27	
May 14	28	29	30	31	1	2	3	
	4	5	6	7	8	9	10	JUNE 2152
May 28	11	12	13	14	15	16	17	
	18	19	20	21	22	23	24	
Jun 11	25	26	27	28	29	30	1	
	2	3	4	5	6	7	8	JULY 2152
Jun 25	9	10	11	12	13	14	15	
	16	17	18	19	20	21	22	
Jul 9	23	24	25	26	27	28	29	
	30	31	1	2	3	4	5	
Jul 23	6	7	8	9	10	11	12	AUGUST 2152
	13	14	15	16	17	18	19	
Aug 6	20	21	22	23	24	25	26	
	27	28	29	30	31	1	2	
Aug 20	3	4	5	6	7	8	9	SEPTEMBER 2152
	10	11	12	13	14	15	16	
Sep 3	17	18	19	20	21	22	23	
	24	25	26	27	28	29	30	
Sep 17	1	2	3	4	5	6	7	OCTOBER 2152
	8	9	10	11	12	13	14	
Oct 1	15	16	17	18	19	20	21	
	22	23	24	25	26	27	28	
Oct 15	29	30	31	1	2	3	4	
	5	6	7	8	9	10	11	NOVEMBER 2152
Oct 29	12	13	14	15	16	17	18	
	19	20	21	22	23	24	25	
Nov 12	26	27	28	29	30	1	2	
	3[g]	4	5	6	7	8	9	DECEMBER 2152
Nov 26	10	11	12	13	14	15	16	
	17	18	19	20	21	22	23	
Dec 10	24	25[h]	26	27	28	29	30	
	31	1	2	3	4	5	6	

‡Leap year
[a]Orthodox Christmas
[b]Julian New Year
[c]Ash Wednesday
[d]Feast of Orthodoxy
[e]Easter
[f]Orthodox Easter
[g]Advent
[h]Christmas

2153

Gregorian 2153, Lunar Phases, ISO Week, Julian Day

Month	Sun	Mon	Tue	Wed	Thu	Fri	Sat	Lunar Phases	ISO WEEK (Mon)	JULIAN DAY (Sun noon)
	31	1[a]	◐	3	4	5	6	21:05	1	2507427
	7	8	9	○	11	12	13	15:29	2	2507434
JANUARY 2153	14	15	16	◑	18	19	20	11:06	3	2507441
	21	22	23	●	25	26	27	16:15	4	2507448
	28	29	30	31	◐	2	3	18:55	5	2507455
	4	5	6	7	8	○	10	3:57	6	2507462
FEBRUARY 2153	11	12	13	14	◑	16	17	19:59	7	2507469
	18	19	20	21	22	●	24	9:02	8	2507476
	25	26	27	28	1	2	◐	14:24	9	2507483
	4	5	6	7	8	9	○	14:34	10	2507490
MARCH 2153	11	12	13	14	15	16	◑	6:13	11	2507497
	18	19	20[b]	21	22	23	24		12	2507504
	●	26	27	28	29	30	31	2:45	13	2507511
	1	◐	3	4	5	6	7	5:54	14	2507518
	○	9	10	11	12	13	14	23:51	15	2507525
APRIL 2153	◑	16	17	18	19	20	21	18:04	16	2507532
	22	●	24	25	26	27	28	20:17	17	2507539
	29	30	◐	2	3	4	5	17:12	18	2507546
	6	7	○	9	10	11	12	8:16	19	2507553
MAY 2153	13	14	◑	16	17	18	19	7:45	20	2507560
	20	21	22	●	24	25	26	12:18	21	2507567
	27	28	29	30	◐	1	2	1:01	22	2507574
	3	4	5	○	7	8	9	16:24	23	2507581
JUNE 2153	10	11	12	◑	14	15	16	23:16	24	2507588
	17	18	19	20	21[c]	●	23	1:58	25	2507595
	24	25	26	27	28	◐	30	6:34	26	2507602
	1	2	3	4	5	○	7	1:00	27	2507609
	8	9	10	11	12	◑	14	16:16	28	2507616
JULY 2153	15	16	17	18	19	20	●	13:17	29	2507623
	22	23	24	25	26	27	◐	11:14	30	2507630
	29	30	31	1	2	3	○	11:02	31	2507637
	5	6	7	8	9	10	11		32	2507644
AUGUST 2153	◑	13	14	15	16	17	18	9:58	33	2507651
	●	20	21	22	23	24	25	22:56	34	2507658
	◐	27	28	29	30	31	1	16:21	35	2507665
	○	3	4	5	6	7	8	23:28	36	2507672
SEPTEMBER 2153	9	10	◑	12	13	14	15	3:18	37	2507679
	16	17	●	19	20	21	22[d]	7:54	38	2507686
	23	◐	25	26	27	28	29	23:14	39	2507693
	30	1	○	3	4	5	6	14:48	40	2507700
	7	8	9	◑	11	12	13	19:20	41	2507707
OCTOBER 2153	14	15	16	●	18	19	20	17:01	42	2507714
	21	22	23	◐	25	26	27	9:07	43	2507721
	28	29	30	31	○	2	3	8:38	44	2507728
	4	5	6	7	8	◑	10	9:30	45	2507735
NOVEMBER 2153	11	12	13	14	15	●	17	2:46	46	2507742
	18	19	20	21	◐	23	24	22:54	47	2507749
	25	26	27	28	29	30	○	3:34	48	2507756
	2	3	4	5	6	7	◑	21:38	49	2507763
DECEMBER 2153	9	10	11	12	13	14	●	13:23	50	2507770
	16	17	18	19	20	21[e]	◐	16:47	51	2507777
	23	24	25	26	27	28	29		52	2507784
	○	31	1	2	3	4	5	21:50	1	2507791

Hebrew 5913/5914

ISO WEEK	Month	Sun	Mon	Tue	Wed	Thu	Fri	Sat	Molad
1		3	4	5	6	7	8	9	
2	TEVETH 5913	10	11	12	13	14	15	16	
3		17	18	19	20	21	22	23	
4		24	25	26	27	28	29	1	Thu $4^{h}37^{m}16^{p}$
5		2	3	4	5	6	7	8	
6	SHEVAT 5913	9	10	11	12	13	14	15	
7		16	17	18	19	20	21	22	
8		23	24	25	26	27	28	29	Fri $17^{h}21^{m}17^{p}$
9		30	1	2	3	4	5	6	
10	ADAR 5913	7	8	9	10	11	12	13	
11		14[f]	15	16	17	18	19	20	
12		21	22	23	24	25	26	27	
13		28	29	1	2	3	4	5	Sun $6^{h}6^{m}0^{p}$
14		6	7	8	9	10	11	12	
15	NISAN 5913	13	14	15[g]	16	17	18	19	
16		20	21	22	23	24	25	26	
17		27	28	29	30	1	2	3	Mon $18^{h}50^{m}1^{p}$
18		4	5	6	7	8	9	10	
19	IYYAR 5913	11	12	13	14	15	16	17	
20		18	19	20	21	22	23	24	
21		25	26	27	28	29	1	2	Wed $7^{h}34^{m}2^{p}$
22		3	4	5	6[h]	7	8	9	
23	SIVAN 5913	10	11	12	13	14	15	16	
24		17	18	19	20	21	22	23	
25		24	25	26	27	28	29	30	Thu $20^{h}18^{m}3^{p}$
26		1	2	3	4	5	6	7	
27		8	9	10	11	12	13	14	
28	TAMMUZ 5913	15	16	17	18	19	20	21	
29		22	23	24	25	26	27	28	
30		29	1	2	3	4	5	6	Sat $9^{h}2^{m}4^{p}$
31		7	8	9[i]	10	11	12	13	
32	AV 5913	14	15	16	17	18	19	20	
33		21	22	23	24	25	26	27	
34		28	29	30	1	2	3	4	Sun $21^{h}46^{m}5^{p}$
35		5	6	7	8	9	10	11	
36	ELUL 5913	12	13	14	15	16	17	18	
37		19	20	21	22	23	24	25	
38		26	27	28	29	1[a]	2[a]	3	Tue $10^{h}30^{m}6^{p}$
39		4	5	6	7	8	9	10[b]	
40	TISHRI 5914	11	12	13	14	15[c]	16	17	
41		18	19	20	21	22	23	24	
42		25	26	27	28	29	30	1	Wed $23^{h}14^{m}7^{p}$
43		2	3	4	5	6	7	8	
44	HESHVAN 5914	9	10	11	12	13	14	15	
45		16	17	18	19	20	21	22	
46		23	24	25	26	27	28	29	Fri $11^{h}58^{m}8^{p}$
47		1	2	3	4	5	6	7	
48		8	9	10	11	12	13	14	
49	KISLEV 5914	15	16	17	18	19[d]	20	21	
50		22	23	24	25[e]	26[e]	27[e]	28[e]	
51		29[e]	30[e]	1[e]	2[e]	3	4	5	Sun $0^{h}42^{m}9^{p}$
52	TEVETH 5914	6	7	8	9	10	11	12	
1		13	14	15	16	17	18	19	

Chinese Rén-Zǐ/Guǐ-Chǒu‡

ISO WEEK	Month	Sun	Mon	Tue	Wed	Thu	Fri	Sat	Solar Term
1		6	7	8	9	10	*11*	12	Xiǎo hán
2	MONTH 12 Rén-Zǐ	13	14	15	16	17	18	19	
3		20	21	22	23	24	25	**26**	Dà hán
4		27	28	29	30	1[a]	2	3	
5		4	5	6	7	8	9	*10*	Lì chūn
6	MONTH 1 Guǐ-Chǒu	11	12	13	14	15[b]	16	17	
7		18	19	20*	21	22	23	24	
8		**25**	26	27	28	29	1	2	Yǔ shuǐ
9		3	4	5	6	7	8	9	
10	MONTH 2 Guǐ-Chǒu	10	*11*	12	13	14	15	16	Jīng zhé
11		17	18	19	20	21	22	23	
12		24	25	**26**	27	28	29	30	Chūn fēn
13		1	2	3	4	5	6	7	
14		8	9	10	*11*[c]	12	13	14	Qīng míng
15	MONTH 3 Guǐ-Chǒu	15	16	17	18	19	20	21*	
16		22	23	24	25	26	**27**	28	Gǔ yǔ
17		29	30	1	2	3	4	5	
18		6	7	8	9	10	11	*12*	Lì xià
19	MONTH 4 Guǐ-Chǒu	13	14	15	16	17	18	19	
20		20	21	22	23	24	25	26	
21		27	**28**	29	1	2	3	4	Xiǎo mǎn
22		5[d]	6	7	8	9	10	11	
23	MONTH 5 Guǐ-Chǒu	12	13	*14*	15	16	17	18	Máng zhòng
24		19	20	21	22*	23	24	25	
25		26	27	28	29	**30**	1	2	Xià zhì
26		3	4	5	6	7	8	9	
27	LEAP MONTH 5 Guǐ-Chǒu	10	11	12	13	14	15	*16*	Xiǎo shǔ
28		17	18	19	20	21	22	23	
29		24	25	26	27	28	29	1	
30		**2**	3	4	5	6	7	8	Dà shǔ
31	MONTH 6 Guǐ-Chǒu	9	10	11	12	13	14	15	
32		16	17	*18*	19	20	21	22	Lì qiū
33		23*	24	25	26	27	28	29	
34		30	1	2	3	**4**	5	6	Chǔ shǔ
35		7[e]	8	9	10	11	12	13	
36	MONTH 7 Guǐ-Chǒu	14	15[f]	16	17	18	*19*	20	Bái lù
37		21	22	23	24	25	26	27	
38		28	29	1	2	3	4	5	
39		**6**	7	8	9	10	11	12	Qiū fēn
40	MONTH 8 Guǐ-Chǒu	13	14	15[g]	16	17	18	19	
41		20	*21*	22	23	24*	25	26	Hán lù
42		27	28	29	30	1	2	3	
43		4	5	**6**	7	8	9[h]	10	Shuāng jiàng
44	MONTH 9 Guǐ-Chǒu	11	12	13	14	15	16	17	
45		18	19	20	*21*	22	23	24	Lì dōng
46		25	26	27	28	29	1	2	
47		3	4	5	6	**7**	8	9	Xiǎo xuě
48	MONTH 10 Guǐ-Chǒu	10	11	12	13	14	15	16	
49		17	18	19	20	21	*22*	23	Dà xuě
50		24	25*	26	27	28	29	1	
51		2	3	4	5	6	7	**8**[i]	Dōng zhì
52	MONTH 11* Guǐ-Chǒu	9	10	11	12	13	14	15	
1		16	17	18	19	20	21	*22*	Xiǎo hán

Coptic 1869/1870, Ethiopic 2145/2146

ISO WEEK	Coptic Month	Sun	Mon	Tue	Wed	Thu	Fri	Sat	Ethiopic Month
1	KOIAK 1869	21	22	23	24	25	26	27	TĀKHŚĀŚ 2145
2		28	29[c]	30	1	2	3	4	
3	ṬOBE 1869	5	6[d]	7	8	9	10	11[e]	ṬER 2145
4		12	13	14	15	16	17	18	
5		19	20	21	22	23	24	25	
6		26	27	28	29	30	1	2	
7		3	4	5	6	7	8	9	
8	MESHIR 1869	10	11	12	13	14	15	16	YAKĀTIT 2145
9		17	18	19	20	21	22	23	
10		24	25	26	27	28	29	30	
11		1	2	3	4	5	6	7	
12	PAREMOTEP 1869	8	9	10	11	12	13	14	MAGĀBIT 2145
13		15	16	17	18	19	20	21	
14		22	23	24	25	26	27	28	
15		29	30	1	2	3	4	5	
16	PARMOUTE 1869	6[f]	7	8	9	10	11	12	
17		13	14	15	16	17	18	19	MIYĀZYĀ 2145
18		20	21	22	23	24	25	26	
19		27	28	29[g]	30	1	2	3	
20		4	5	6	7	8	9	10	
21	PASHONS 1869	11	12	13	14	15	16	17	GENBOT 2145
22		18	19	20	21	22	23	24	
23		25	26	27	28	29	30	1	
24		2	3	4	5	6	7	8	
25	PAÔNE 1869	9	10	11	12	13	14	15	SANĒ 2145
26		16	17	18	19	20	21	22	
27		23	24	25	26	27	28	29	
28		30	1	2	3	4	5	6	
29		7	8	9	10	11	12	13	
30	EPĒP 1869	14	15	16	17	18	19	20	HAMLĒ 2145
31		21	22	23	24	25	26	27	
32		28	29	30	1	2	3	4	
33		5	6	7	8	9	10	11	
34	MESORĒ 1869	12	13[h]	14	15	16	17	18	NAHASĒ 2145
35		19	20	21	22	23	24	25	
36		26	27	28	29	30	1	2	
37	EPAG. 1869	3	4	5	1[a]	2	3	4	PĀG. 2145
38		5	6	7	8	9	10	11	
39	THOOUT 1870	12	13	14	15	16	17[b]	18	MASKARAM 2146
40		19	20	21	22	23	24	25	
41		26	27	28	29	30	1	2	
42		3	4	5	6	7	8	9	
43	PAOPE 1870	10	11	12	13	14	15	16	TEQEMT 2146
44		17	18	19	20	21	22	23	
45		24	25	26	27	28	29	30	
46		1	2	3	4	5	6	7	
47	ATHŌR 1870	8	9	10	11	12	13	14	HEDĀR 2146
48		15	16	17	18	19	20	21	
49		22	23	24	25	26	27	28	
50		29	30	1	2	3	4	5	
51	KOIAK 1870	6	7	8	9	10	11	12	TĀKHŚĀŚ 2146
52		13	14	15	16	17	18	19	
1		20	21	22	23	24	25	26	

[a]New Year
[b]Spring (9:34)
[c]Summer (0:49)
[d]Autumn (17:43)
[e]Winter (16:43)
● New moon
◐ First quarter moon
○ Full moon
◑ Last quarter moon

[a]New Year
[b]Yom Kippur
[c]Sukkot
[d]Winter starts
[e]Ḥanukkah
[f]Purim
[g]Passover
[h]Shavuot
[i]Fast of Av

‡Leap year
[a]New Year (4851, Ox)
[b]Lantern Festival
[c]Qīngmíng
[d]Dragon Festival
[e]Qīqiǎo
[f]Hungry Ghosts
[g]Mid-Autumn Festival
[h]Double-Ninth Festival
[i]Dōngzhì
*Start of 60-name cycle

[a]New Year
[b]Building of the Cross
[c]Christmas
[d]Jesus's Circumcision
[e]Epiphany
[f]Easter
[g]Mary's Announcement
[h]Jesus's Transfiguration

PERSIAN (ASTRONOMICAL) 1531‡/1532

Month	Sun	Mon	Tue	Wed	Thu	Fri	Sat
Dey 1531	11	12	13	14	15	16	17
	18	19	20	21	22	23	24
Bahman 1531	25	26	27	28	29	30	1
	2	3	4	5	6	7	8
	9	10	11	12	13	14	15
	16	17	18	19	20	21	22
	23	24	25	26	27	28	29
Esfand 1531	30	1	2	3	4	5	6
	7	8	9	10	11	12	13
	14	15	16	17	18	19	20
	21	22	23	24	25	26	27
Farvardin 1532	28	29	30[a]	1[a]	2	3	4
	5	6	7	8	9	10	11
	12	13[b]	14	15	16	17	18
	19	20	21	22	23	24	25
Ordībehešt 1532	26	27	28	29	30	31	1
	2	3	4	5	6	7	8
	9	10	11	12	13	14	15
	16	17	18	19	20	21	22
	23	24	25	26	27	28	29
Xordād 1532	30	31	1	2	3	4	5
	6	7	8	9	10	11	12
	13	14	15	16	17	18	19
	20	21	22	23	24	25	26
Tīr 1532	27	28	29	30	31	1	2
	3	4	5	6	7	8	9
	10	11	12	13	14	15	16
	17	18	19	20	21	22	23
	24	25	26	27	28	29	30
Mordād 1532	31	1	2	3	4	5	6
	7	8	9	10	11	12	13
	14	15	16	17	18	19	20
	21	22	23	24	25	26	27
Shahrīvar 1532	28	29	30	31	1	2	3
	4	5	6	7	8	9	10
	11	12	13	14	15	16	17
	18	19	20	21	22	23	24
	25	26	27	28	29	30	31
Mehr 1532	1	2	3	4	5	6	7
	8	9	10	11	12	13	14
	15	16	17	18	19	20	21
	22	23	24	25	26	27	28
Ābān 1532	29	30	1	2	3	4	5
	6	7	8	9	10	11	12
	13	14	15	16	17	18	19
	20	21	22	23	24	25	26
Āzar 1532	27	28	29	30	1	2	3
	4	5	6	7	8	9	10
	11	12	13	14	15	16	17
	18	19	20	21	22	23	24
Dey 1532	25	26	27	28	29	30	1
	2	3	4	5	6	7	8
	9	10	11	12	13	14	15

‡Leap year
[a]New Year
[a]New Year (Arithmetic)
[b]Sizdeh Bedar

HINDU LUNAR 2209/2210‡

Month	Sun	Mon	Tue	Wed	Thu	Fri	Sat
Pausha 2209	5	6	7	8	9	10	11
	12	13	14	15	16	17	18
	19	20	21	**22**	24	25	26
Māgha 2209	27	28	29	30	1	2	3
	4	5	6	7	*7*	8	9
	10	11	12	13	14	15	**16**
	18	19	20	21	22	23	24
Phālguna 2209	25	26	27	28[h]	29	30	1
	2	3	4	5	6	7	8
	9	10	11	12	13	14	15[i]
	16	17	18	19	20	**21**	23
	24	25	26	27	28	29	30
Chaitra 2210	30	1[a]	2	3	4	5	6
	7	8	9[b]	10	11	12	13
	14	16	17	18	19	20	21
	22	23	24	25	26	27	28
Vaiśākha 2210	29	30	1	2	3	4	*4*
	5	6	**7**	9	10	11	12
	13	14	15	16	17	18	**19**
	21	22	23	24	*24*	25	26
Jyaishṭha 2210	27	28	29	30	1	2	3
	4	5	6	7	8	9	10
	11	13	14	15	16	17	18
	19	20	21	22	23	24	25
Āshāḍha 2210	26	27	28	29	*29*	30	1
	2	**3**	5	6	7	8	9
	10	11	12	13	14	**15**	17
	18	19	20	21	*21*	22	23
	24	25	26	27	28	29	30
Śrāvaṇa 2210	1	2	3	4	5	6	**7**
	9	10	11	12	13	14	15
	16	17	18	19	20	21	22
	23[c]	24	25	26	27	28	29
Leap Bhādrapada 2210	30	1	2	3	4	5	6
	7	8	9	**10**	12	13	14
	15	16	17	18	*18*	19	20
	21	22	23	24	25	26	27
Bhādrapada 2210	28	29	30	1	2	3[d]	5
	6	7	8	9	10	11	12
	13	14	15	16	17	18	19
	20	21	22	*22*	23	24	**25**
Āśvina 2210	27	28	29	30	1	2	3
	4	5	6	7	8[e]	10[e]	11
	11	12	13	14	15	16	17
	18	19	20	21	22	23	24
Kārttika 2210	25	26	27	28	29	30[f]	2
	3	4	5	6	7	8	9
	10	11	12	13	14	15	*15*
	16	17	18	19	20	21	22
	23	**24**	26	27	28	29	30
Mārgaśīra 2210	1	2	3	4	5	6	7
	8	9	10	11[g]	12	13	14
	15	16	17	18	19	20	21

‡Leap year
[a]New Year (Pramādin)
[b]Birthday of Rāma
[c]Birthday of Krishna
[d]Ganēśa Chaturthī
[e]Dashara
[f]Diwali
[g]Birthday of Vishnu
[h]Night of Śiva
[i]Holi

HINDU SOLAR 2074‡/2075

Month	Sun	Mon	Tue	Wed	Thu	Fri	Sat
Pausha 2074	14	15	16	17	18	19	20
	21	22	23	24	25	26	27
Māgha 2074	28	29	1[b]	2	3	4	5
	6	7	8	9	10	11	12
	13	14	15	16	17	18	19
	20	21	22	23	24	25	26
Phālguna 2074	27	28	29	1	2	3	4
	5	6	7	8	9	10	11
	12	13	14	15	16	17	18
	19	20	21	22	23	24	25
Chaitra 2074	26	27	28	29	30	1	2
	3	4	5	6	7	8	9
	10	11	12	13	14	15	16
	17	18	19	20	21	22	23
	24	25	26	27	28	29	30
Vaiśākha 2075	31	1[a]	2	3	4	5	6
	7	8	9	10	11	12	13
	14	15	16	17	18	19	20
	21	22	23	24	25	26	27
Jyaishṭha 2075	28	29	30	31	1	2	3
	4	5	6	7	8	9	10
	11	12	13	14	15	16	17
	18	19	20	21	22	23	24
	25	26	27	28	29	30	31
Āshāḍha 2075	1	2	3	4	5	6	7
	8	9	10	11	12	13	14
	15	16	17	18	19	20	21
	22	23	24	25	26	27	28
Śrāvaṇa 2075	29	30	31	32	1	2	3
	4	5	6	7	8	9	10
	11	12	13	14	15	16	17
	18	19	20	21	22	23	24
	25	26	27	28	29	30	31
Bhādrapada 2075	1	2	3	4	5	6	7
	8	9	10	11	12	13	14
	15	16	17	18	19	20	21
	22	23	24	25	26	27	28
Āśvina 2075	29	30	31	1	2	3	4
	5	6	7	8	9	10	11
	12	13	14	15	16	17	18
	19	20	21	22	23	24	25
Kārttika 2075	26	27	28	29	30	1	2
	3	4	5	6	7	8	9
	10	11	12	13	14	15	16
	17	18	19	20	21	22	23
	24	25	26	27	28	29	30
Mārgaśīra 2075	1	2	3	4	5	6	7
	8	9	10	11	12	13	14
	15	16	17	18	19	20	21
	22	23	24	25	26	27	28
Pausha 2075	29	30	1	2	3	4	5
	6	7	8	9	10	11	12
	13	14	15	16	17	18	19

‡Leap year
[a]New Year (Vibhava)
[b]Pongal

ISLAMIC (ASTRONOMICAL) 1578‡/1579

Month	Sun	Mon	Tue	Wed	Thu	Fri	Sat
Jumādā II 1578	4	5	6	7	8	9	10
	11	12	13	14	15	16	17
	18	19	20	21	22	23	24
Rajab 1578	25	26	27	28	29	1	2
	3	4	5	6	7	8	9
	10	11	12	13	14	15	16
	17	18	19	20	21	22	23
	24	25	26	27[d]	28	29	30
Sha'bān 1578	1	2	3	4	5	6	7
	8	9	10	11	12	13	14
	15	16	17	18	19	20	21
	22	23	24	25	26	27	28
Ramaḍān 1578	29	1[e]	2	3	4	5	6
	7	8	9	10	11	12	13
	14	15	16	17	18	19	20
	21	22	23	24	25	26	27
Shawwāl 1578	28	29	30	1[f]	2	3	4
	5	6	7	8	9	10	11
	12	13	14	15	16	17	18
	19	20	21	22	23	24	25
Dhu al-Qa'da 1578	26	27	28	29	30	1	2
	3	4	5	6	7	8	9
	10	11	12	13	14	15	16
	17	18	19	20	21	22	23
Dhu al-Ḥijja 1578	24	25	26	27	28	29	1
	2	3	4	5	6	7	8
	9	10[g]	11	12	13	14	15
	16	17	18	19	20	21	22
	23	24	25	26	27	28	29
Muḥarram 1579	30	1[a]	2	3	4	5	6
	7	8	9	10[b]	11	12	13
	14	15	16	17	18	19	20
	21	22	23	24	25	26	27
Ṣafar 1579	28	29	1	2	3	4	5
	6	7	8	9	10	11	12
	13	14	15	16	17	18	19
	20	21	22	23	24	25	26
Rabī' I 1579	27	28	29	30	1	2	3
	4	5	6	7	8	9	10
	11	12[c]	13	14	15	16	17
	18	19	20	21	22	23	24
Rabī' II 1579	25	26	27	28	29	1	2
	3	4	5	6	7	8	9
	10	11	12	13	14	15	16
	17	18	19	20	21	22	23
	24	25	26	27	28	29	30
Jumādā I 1579	1	2	3	4	5	6	7
	8	9	10	11	12	13	14
	15	16	17	18	19	20	21
	22	23	24	25	26	27	28
Jumādā II 1579	29	1	2	3	4	5	6
	7	8	9	10	11	12	13
	14	15	16	17	18	19	20

‡Leap year
[a]New Year
[b]'Ashūrā'
[c]Prophet's Birthday
[d]Ascent of the Prophet
[e]Start of Ramaḍān
[f]'Id al-Fiṭr
[g]'Id al-'Aḍḥā

GREGORIAN 2153

Julian (Sun)	Month	Sun	Mon	Tue	Wed	Thu	Fri	Sat
Dec 17	January 2153	31	1	2	3	4	5	6
		7	8[a]	9	10	11	12	13
Dec 31		14	15[b]	16	17	18	19	20
		21	22	23	24	25	26	27
Jan 14	February 2153	28	29	30	31	1	2	3
		4	5	6	7	8	9	10
Jan 28		11	12	13	14	15	16	17
		18	19	20	21	22	23	24
Feb 11	March 2153	25	26	27	28[c]	1	2	3
		4[d]	5	6	7	8	9	10
Feb 25		11	12	13	14	15	16	17
		18	19	20	21	22	23	24
Mar 11		25	26	27	28	29	30	31
	April 2153	1	2	3	4	5	6	7
Mar 25		8	9	10	11	12	13	14
		15[e]	16	17	18	19	20	21
Apr 8		22	23	24	25	26	27	28
	May 2153	29	30	1	2	3	4	5
Apr 22		6	7	8	9	10	11	12
		13	14	15	16	17	18	19
May 6		20	21	22	23	24	25	26
	June 2153	27	28	29	30	31	1	2
May 20		3	4	5	6	7	8	9
		10	11	12	13	14	15	16
Jun 3		17	18	19	20	21	22	23
		24	25	26	27	28	29	30
Jun 17	July 2153	1	2	3	4	5	6	7
		8	9	10	11	12	13	14
Jul 1		15	16	17	18	19	20	21
		22	23	24	25	26	27	28
Jul 15	August 2153	29	30	31	1	2	3	4
		5	6	7	8	9	10	11
Jul 29		12	13	14	15	16	17	18
		19	20	21	22	23	24	25
Aug 12	September 2153	26	27	28	29	30	31	1
		2	3	4	5	6	7	8
Aug 26		9	10	11	12	13	14	15
		16	17	18	19	20	21	22
Sep 9		23	24	25	26	27	28	29
	October 2153	30	1	2	3	4	5	6
Sep 23		7	8	9	10	11	12	13
		14	15	16	17	18	19	20
Oct 7		21	22	23	24	25	26	27
	November 2153	28	29	30	31	1	2	3
Oct 21		4	5	6	7	8	9	10
		11	12	13	14	15	16	17
Nov 4		18	19	20	21	22	23	24
	December 2153	25	26	27	28	29	30	1
Nov 18		2[g]	3	4	5	6	7	8
		9	10	11	12	13	14	15
Dec 2		16	17	18	19	20	21	22
		23	24	25[h]	26	27	28	29
Dec 16		30	31	1	2	3	4	5

[a]Orthodox Christmas
[b]Julian New Year
[c]Ash Wednesday
[d]Feast of Orthodoxy
[e]Easter (also Orthodox)
[g]Advent
[h]Christmas

2154

Gregorian 2154	Sun	Mon	Tue	Wed	Thu	Fri	Sat	Lunar Phases	ISO Week (Mon)	Julian Day (Sun noon)	Hebrew 5914/5915‡	Sun	Mon	Tue	Wed	Thu	Fri	Sat	Molad	Chinese Guǐ-Chǒu‡/Jiǎ-Yín	Sun	Mon	Tue	Wed	Thu	Fri	Sat	Solar Term	Coptic 1870/1871‡	Sun	Mon	Tue	Wed	Thu	Fri	Sat	Ethiopic 2146/2147‡
	○	31	1[a]	2	3	4	5	21:50	1	2507791	TEVETH 5914	13	14	15	16	17	18	19		MONTH 11* Guǐ-Chǒu	16	17	18	19	20	21	22	Xiǎo hán	KOIAK 1870	20	21	22	23	24	25	26	TĀKHŚĀŚ 2146
JANUARY 2154	6	◑	8	9	10	11	12	7:48	2	2507798		20	21	22	23	24	25	26			23	24	25	26	27	28	29			27	28	29[c]	30	1	2	3	
	13	●	15	16	17	18	19	1:04	3	2507805		27	28	29	1	2	3	4	Mon 13h26m10p		30	1	2	3	4	5	6			4	5	6[d]	7	8	9	10	
	20	◐	22	23	24	25	26	13:43	4	2507812	SHEVAT 5914	5	6	7	8	9	10	11		MONTH 12 Guǐ-Chǒu	7	8	9	10	11	12	13	Dà hán	TÔBE 1870	11[e]	12	13	14	15	16	17	TER 2146
	27	28	○	30	31	1	2	14:13	5	2507819		12	13	14	15	16	17	18			14	15	16	17	18	19	20			18	19	20	21	22	23	24	
	3	4	◑	6	7	8	9	16:19	6	2507826		19	20	21	22	23	24	25			21	22	23	24	25	26*	27	Lì chūn		25	26	27	28	29	30	1	
FEBRUARY 2154	10	11	●	13	14	15	16	14:08	7	2507833		26	27	28	29	30	1	2	Wed 2h10m11p		28	29	1[a]	2	3	4	5			2	3	4	5	6	7	8	
	17	18	19	◐	21	22	23	11:31	8	2507840	ADAR 5914	3	4	5	6	7	8	9			6	7	8	9	10	11	12	Yǔ shuǐ		9	10	11	12	13	14	15	YAKĀTIT 2146
	24	25	26	27	○	1	2	4:12	9	2507847		10	11	12	13	14[f]	15	16		MONTH 1 Jiǎ-Yín	13	14	15[b]	16	17	18	19		MESHIR 1870	16	17	18	19	20	21	22	
	3	4	5	◑	7	8	9	23:52	10	2507854		17	18	19	20	21	22	23			20	21	22	23	24	25	26	Jīng zhé		23	24	25	26	27	28	29	
MARCH 2154	10	11	12	13	●	15	16	4:45	11	2507861		24	25	26	27	28	29	1	Thu 14h54m12p		27	28	29	30	1	2	3			30	1	2	3	4	5	6	
	17	18	19	20[b]	21	◐	23	7:50	12	2507868		2	3	4	5	6	7	8			4	5	6	7	8	9	10	Chūn fēn		7	8	9	10	11	12	13	
	24	25	26	27	28	○	30	15:48	13	2507875	NISAN 5914	9	10	11	12	13	14	15[g]		MONTH 2 Jiǎ-Yín	11	12	13	14	15	16	17		PAREMOTEP 1870	14	15	16	17	18	19	20	MAGĀBIT 2146
	31	1	2	3	4	◑	6	7:22	14	2507882		16	17	18	19	20	21	22			18	19	20	21	22	23[c]	24	Qīng míng		21	22	23	24	25	26	27	
	7	8	9	10	11	●	13	20:39	15	2507889		23	24	25	26	27	28	29	Sat 3h38m13p		25	26	27*	28	29	30	1			28	29	30	1	2	3	4	
APRIL 2154	14	15	16	17	18	19	20		16	2507896		30	1	2	3	4	5	6			2	3	4	5	6	7	8	Gǔ yǔ		5	6	7	8	9	10	11	
	◐	22	23	24	25	26	27	1:03	17	2507903	IYYAR 5914	7	8	9	10	11	12	13		MONTH 3 Jiǎ-Yín	9	10	11	12	13	14	15		PARMOUTE 1870	12	13	14	15	16	17	18	MIYĀZYĀ 2146
	○	29	30	1	2	3	◑	15:53 1:13	18	2507910		14	15	16	17	18	19	20			16	17	18	19	20	21	22			19	20	21	22	23	24	25	
	5	6	7	8	9	10	11		19	2507917		21	22	23	24	25	26	27			23	24	25	26	27	28	29	Lì xià		26[f]	27	28	29[g]	30	1	2	
MAY 2154	●	13	14	15	16	17	18	12:59	20	2507924		28	29	1	2	3	4	5	Sun 16h22m14p		1	2	3	4	5	6	7			3	4	5	6	7	8	9	
	19	◐	21	22	23	24	25	14:41	21	2507931	SIVAN 5914	6[h]	7	8	9	10	11	12		MONTH 4 Jiǎ-Yín	8	9	10	11	12	13	14	Xiǎo mǎn	PASHONS 1870	10	11	12	13	14	15	16	GENBOT 2146
	26	○	28	29	30	31	1	8:58	22	2507938		13	14	15	16	17	18	19			15	16	17	18	19	20	21			17	18	19	20	21	22	23	
	2	◑	4	5	6	7	8	2:19	23	2507945		20	21	22	23	24	25	26			22	23	24	25	26	27	28*	Máng zhòng		24	25	26	27	28	29	30	
JUNE 2154	9	10	●	12	13	14	15	4:45	24	2507952		27	28	29	30	1	2	3	Tue 5h6m15p		29	30	1	2	3	4	5[d]			1	2	3	4	5	6	7	
	16	17	18	◐	20	21[c]	22	0:54	25	2507959	TAMMUZ 5914	4	5	6	7	8	9	10		MONTH 5 Jiǎ-Yín	6	7	8	9	10	11	12	Xià zhì	PAÔNE 1870	8	9	10	11	12	13	14	SANĒ 2146
	23	24	○	26	27	28	29	15:52	26	2507966		11	12	13	14	15	16	17			13	14	15	16	17	18	19			15	16	17	18	19	20	21	
	30	1	◑	3	4	5	6	15:14	27	2507973		18	19	20	21	22	23	24			20	21	22	23	24	25	26			22	23	24	25	26	27	28	
	7	8	9	●	11	12	13	19:19	28	2507980		25	26	27	28	29	1	2	Wed 17h50m16p		27	28	29	30	1	2	3	Xiǎo shǔ		29	30	1	2	3	4	5	
JULY 2154	14	15	16	17	◐	19	20	8:23	29	2507987		3	4	5	6	7	8	9			4	5	6	7	8	9	10			6	7	8	9	10	11	12	
	21	22	23	○	25	26	27	23:04	30	2507994	AV 5914	10[i]	11	12	13	14	15	16		MONTH 6 Jiǎ-Yín	11	12	13	14	15	16	17	Dà shǔ	EPÊP 1870	13	14	15	16	17	18	19	HAMLĒ 2146
	28	29	30	31	◑	2	3	6:39	31	2508001		17	18	19	20	21	22	23			18	19	20	21	22	23	24			20	21	22	23	24	25	26	
	4	5	6	7	8	●	10	8:34	32	2508008		24	25	26	27	28	29	30			25	26	27	28*	29	1	2	Lì qiū		27	28	29	30	1	2	3	
AUGUST 2154	11	12	13	14	15	◐	17	14:03	33	2508015		1	2	3	4	5	6	7	Fri 6h34m17p		3	4	5	6	7[e]	8	9			4	5	6	7	8	9	10	
	18	19	20	21	22	○	24	7:48	34	2508022	ELUL 5914	8	9	10	11	12	13	14		MONTH 7 Jiǎ-Yín	10	11	12	13	14	15[f]	16	Chǔ shǔ	MESORÊ 1870	11	12	13[h]	14	15	16	17	NAḤASĒ 2146
	25	26	27	28	29	30	◑	0:04	35	2508029		15	16	17	18	19	20	21			17	18	19	20	21	22	23			18	19	20	21	22	23	24	
	1	2	3	4	5	6	●	20:42	36	2508036		22	23	24	25	26	27	28			24	25	26	27	28	29	30	Bái lù	EPAG. 1870	25	26	27	28	29	30	1	PĀG. 2146
SEPTEMBER 2154	8	9	10	11	12	13	◐	19:08	37	2508043		29	1[a]	2[a]	3	4	5	6	Sat 19h19m0p		1	2	3	4	5	6	7			2	3	4	5	1[a]	2	3	
	15	16	17	18	19	20	○	19:09	38	2508050	TISHRI 5915	7	8	9	10[b]	11	12	13		MONTH 8 Jiǎ-Yín	8	9	10	11	12	13	14		THOOUT 1871	4	5	6	7	8	9	10	MASKARAM 2147
	22[d]	23	24	25	26	27	28		39	2508057		14	15[c]	16	17	18	19	20			15[g]	16	17	18	19	20	21	Qiū fēn		11	12	13	14	15	16	17[b]	
	◑	30	1	2	3	4	5	18:41	40	2508064		21	22	23	24	25	26	27			22	23	24	25	26	27	28			18	19	20	21	22	23	24	
	6	●	8	9	10	11	12	7:59	41	2508071		28	29	30	1	2	3	4	Mon 8h3m1p		29*	1	2	3	4	5	6	Hán lù		25	26	27	28	29	30	1	
OCTOBER 2154	13	◐	15	16	17	18	19	1:06	42	2508078	ḤESHVAN 5915	5	6	7	8	9	10	11		MONTH 9 Jiǎ-Yín	7	8	9[h]	10	11	12	13			2	3	4	5	6	7	8	
	20	○	22	23	24	25	26	9:37	43	2508085		12	13	14	15	16	17	18			14	15	16	17	18	19	20	Shuāng jiàng	PAOPE 1871	9	10	11	12	13	14	15	ṬEQEMT 2147
	27	28	◑	30	31	1	2	13:26	44	2508092		19	20	21	22	23	24	25			21	22	23	24	25	26	27			16	17	18	19	20	21	22	
	3	4	●	6	7	8	9	18:41	45	2508099		26	27	28	29	1	2	3			28	29	30	1	2	3	4	Lì dōng		23	24	25	26	27	28	29	
NOVEMBER 2154	10	11	◐	13	14	15	16	9:24	46	2508106	KISLEV 5915	4	5	6	7	8	9	10	Tue 20h47m2p	MONTH 10 Jiǎ-Yín	5	6	7	8	9	10	11			30	1	2	3	4	5	6	
	17	18	19	○	21	22	23	2:54	47	2508113		11	12	13	14	15	16	17			12	13	14	15	16	17	18	Xiǎo xuě	ATHÔR 1871	7	8	9	10	11	12	13	ḪEDĀR 2147
	24	25	26	27	◑	29	30	7:12	48	2508120		18	19	20	21	22	23	24			19	20	21	22	23	24	25			14	15	16	17	18	19	20	
	1	2	3	4	●	6	7	5:02	49	2508127		25[e]	26[e]	27[e]	28[e]	29[e]	1[d,e]	2[e]			26	27	28	29	1*	2	3	Dà xuě		21	22	23	24	25	26	27	
DECEMBER 2154	8	9	10	◐	12	13	14	21:09	50	2508134	TEVETH 5915	3[e]	4	5	6	7	8	9	Thu 9h31m3p	MONTH 11 Jiǎ-Yín	4	5	6	7	8	9	10			28	29	30	1	2	3	4	
	15	16	17	18	○	20	21[e]	21:55	51	2508141		10	11	12	13	14	15	16			11	12	13	14	15	16	17		KOIAK 1871	5	6	7	8	9	10	11	TĀKHŚĀŚ 2147
	22	23	24	25	26	◑	28	22:47	52	2508148		17	18	19	20	21	22	23	Fri 22h15m4p		18[i]	19	20	21	22	23	24	Dōng zhì		12	13	14	15	16	17	18	
	29	30	31	1	2	●	4	15:24	1	2508155		24	25	26	27	28	29	1			25	26	27	28	29	1	2			19	20	21	22	23	24	25	

[a]New Year
[b]Spring (15:20)
[c]Summer (6:33)
[d]Autumn (23:34)
[e]Winter (22:31)
● New moon
◐ First quarter moon
○ Full moon
◑ Last quarter moon

‡Leap year
[a]New Year
[b]Yom Kippur
[c]Sukkot
[d]Winter starts
[e]Ḥanukkah
[f]Purim
[g]Passover
[h]Shavuot
[i]Fast of Av

‡Leap year
[a]New Year (4852, Tiger)
[b]Lantern Festival
[c]Qīngmíng
[d]Dragon Festival
[e]Qīqiǎo
[f]Hungry Ghosts
[g]Mid-Autumn Festival
[h]Double-Ninth Festival
[i]Dōngzhì
*Start of 60-name cycle

‡Leap year
[a]New Year
[b]Building of the Cross
[c]Christmas
[d]Jesus's Circumcision
[e]Epiphany
[f]Easter
[g]Mary's Announcement
[h]Jesus's Transfiguration

PERSIAN (ASTRONOMICAL) 1532/1533

Month	Sun	Mon	Tue	Wed	Thu	Fri	Sat
	9	10	11	12	13	14	15
DEY 1532	16	17	18	19	20	21	22
	23	24	25	26	27	28	29
	30	1	2	3	4	5	6
	7	8	9	10	11	12	13
BAHMAN 1532	14	15	16	17	18	19	20
	21	22	23	24	25	26	27
	28	29	30	1	2	3	4
	5	6	7	8	9	10	11
ESFAND 1532	12	13	14	15	16	17	18
	19	20	21	22	23	24	25
	26	27	28	29	1[a]	2	3
	4	5	6	7	8	9	10
FARVARDĪN 1533	11	12	13[b]	14	15	16	17
	18	19	20	21	22	23	24
	25	26	27	28	29	30	31
	1	2	3	4	5	6	7
ORDĪBEHEŠT 1533	8	9	10	11	12	13	14
	15	16	17	18	19	20	21
	22	23	24	25	26	27	28
	29	30	31	1	2	3	4
XORDĀD 1533	5	6	7	8	9	10	11
	12	13	14	15	16	17	18
	19	20	21	22	23	24	25
	26	27	28	29	30	31	1
	2	3	4	5	6	7	8
TĪR 1533	9	10	11	12	13	14	15
	16	17	18	19	20	21	22
	23	24	25	26	27	28	29
	30	31	1	2	3	4	5
MORDĀD 1533	6	7	8	9	10	11	12
	13	14	15	16	17	18	19
	20	21	22	23	24	25	26
	27	28	29	30	31	1	2
	3	4	5	6	7	8	9
SHAHRĪVAR 1533	10	11	12	13	14	15	16
	17	18	19	20	21	22	23
	24	25	26	27	28	29	30
	31	1	2	3	4	5	6
MEHR 1533	7	8	9	10	11	12	13
	14	15	16	17	18	19	20
	21	22	23	24	25	26	27
	28	29	30	1	2	3	4
	5	6	7	8	9	10	11
ĀBĀN 1533	12	13	14	15	16	17	18
	19	20	21	22	23	24	25
	26	27	28	29	30	1	2
	3	4	5	6	7	8	9
ĀZAR 1533	10	11	12	13	14	15	16
	17	18	19	20	21	22	23
	24	25	26	27	28	29	30
DEY 1533	1	2	3	4	5	6	7
	8	9	10	11	12	13	14

[a]New Year
[b]Sizdeh Bedar

HINDU LUNAR 2210‡/2211

Month	Sun	Mon	Tue	Wed	Thu	Fri	Sat
MĀRGAŚIRA 2210	15	16	17	18	19	20	21
	22	23	24	25	26	27	28
	29	1	2	3	4	5	6
PAUSHA 2210	7	8	8	9	10	11	12
	13	14	15	16	17	18	19
	20	21	22	**23**	25	26	27
	28	29	30	1	2	3	4
MĀGHA 2210	5	6	7	8	9	10	10
	11	12	13	14	15	16	**17**
	19	20	21	22	23	24	25
	26	27	28[h]	29	30	1	2
PHĀLGUNA 2210	3	4	5	6	7	8	9
	10	11	12	13	14	15[i]	16
	17	18	19	20	21	**22**	24
	25	26	27	28	29	30	1[a]
CHAITRA 2211	2	3	3	4	5	6	7
	8	9[b]	10	11	12	13	14
	15	17	18	19	20	21	22
	23	24	25	26	27	28	29
	30	1	2	3	4	5	6
VAIŚĀKHA 2211	7	8	9	10	11	12	13
	14	15	16	17	**18**	20	21
	22	23	24	25	26	27	28
	29	29	30	1	2	3	4
JYAISHTHA 2211	5	6	7	8	9	10	**11**
	13	14	15	16	17	18	19
	20	21	22	23	24	25	26
	27	28	29	30	1	2	3
ĀSHĀḌHA 2211	4	5	6	7	8	9	10
	11	12	13	**14**	16	17	18
	19	20	21	22	23	24	25
	26	26	27	28	29	30	1
ŚRĀVAṆA 2211	2	3	4	5	6	**7**	9
	10	11	12	13	14	15	16
	17	18	19	20	21	22	23[c]
	24	25	26	27	28	29	30
	1	2	3	4[d]	5	6	7
BHĀDRAPADA 2211	8	9	**10**	12	13	14	15
	16	17	18	19	20	21	22
	22	23	24	25	26	27	28
	29	30	1	2	**3**	5	6
ĀŚVINA 2211	7	8[e]	9[e]	10[e]	11	12	13
	14	15	16	17	18	19	20
	21	22	23	24	25	26	27
	28	29	30	1[f]	2	3	4
KĀRTTIKA 2211	5	6	7	**8**	10	11	12
	13	14	15	16	16	17	18
	19	20	21	22	23	24	25
	26	27	28	29	30	**1**	3
MĀRGAŚIRA 2211	4	5	6	7	8	9	10
	11[g]	12	13	14	15	16	17
	18	18	19	20	21	22	23
	24	**25**	27	28	29	30	1

‡Leap year
[a]New Year (Ānanda)
[b]Birthday of Rāma
[c]Birthday of Krishna
[d]Ganēśa Chaturthī
[e]Dashara
[f]Diwali
[g]Birthday of Vishnu
[h]Night of Śiva
[i]Holi

HINDU SOLAR 2075/2076

Month	Sun	Mon	Tue	Wed	Thu	Fri	Sat
PAUSHA 2075	13	14	15	16	17	18	19
	20	21	22	23	24	25	26
	27	28	29	1[b]	2	3	4
MĀGHA 2075	5	6	7	8	9	10	11
	12	13	14	15	16	17	18
	19	20	21	22	23	24	25
	26	27	28	29	30	1	2
PHĀLGUNA 2075	3	4	5	6	7	8	9
	10	11	12	13	14	15	16
	17	18	19	20	21	22	23
	24	25	26	27	28	29	1
CHAITRA 2075	2	3	4	5	6	7	8
	9	10	11	12	13	14	15
	16	17	18	19	20	21	22
	23	24	25	26	27	28	29
	30	31	1[a]	2	3	4	5
VAIŚĀKHA 2076	6	7	8	9	10	11	12
	13	14	15	16	17	18	19
	20	21	22	23	24	25	26
	27	28	29	30	31	1	2
JYAISHTHA 2076	3	4	5	6	7	8	9
	10	11	12	13	14	15	16
	17	18	19	20	21	22	23
	24	25	26	27	28	29	30
	31	1	2	3	4	5	6
ĀSHĀḌHA 2076	7	8	9	10	11	12	13
	14	15	16	17	18	19	20
	21	22	23	24	25	26	27
	28	29	30	31	32	1	2
ŚRĀVAṆA 2076	3	4	5	6	7	8	9
	10	11	12	13	14	15	16
	17	18	19	20	21	22	23
	24	25	26	27	28	29	30
	31	1	2	3	4	5	6
BHĀDRAPADA 2076	7	8	9	10	11	12	13
	14	15	16	17	18	19	20
	21	22	23	24	25	26	27
	28	29	30	31	1	2	3
ĀŚVINA 2076	4	5	6	7	8	9	10
	11	12	13	14	15	16	17
	18	19	20	21	22	23	24
	25	26	27	28	29	30	31
	1	2	3	4	5	6	7
KĀRTTIKA 2076	8	9	10	11	12	13	14
	15	16	17	18	19	20	21
	22	23	24	25	26	27	28
	29	30	1	2	3	4	5
MĀRGAŚIRA 2076	6	7	8	9	10	11	12
	13	14	15	16	17	18	19
	20	21	22	23	24	25	26
	27	28	29	1	2	3	4
PAUSHA 2076	5	6	7	8	9	10	11
	12	13	14	15	16	17	18

[a]New Year (Śukla)
[b]Pongal

ISLAMIC (ASTRONOMICAL) 1579/1580

Month	Sun	Mon	Tue	Wed	Thu	Fri	Sat
JUMĀDĀ II 1579	14	15	16	17	18	19	20
	21	22	23	24	25	26	27
	28	29	1	2	3	4	5
RAJAB 1579	6	7	8	9	10	11	12
	13	14	15	16	17	18	19
	20	21	22	23	24	25	26
	27[d]	28	29	30	1	2	3
SHA'BĀN 1579	4	5	6	7	8	9	10
	11	12	13	14	15	16	17
	18	19	20	21	22	23	24
	25	26	27	28	29	30	1[e]
RAMAḌĀN 1579	2	3	4	5	6	7	8
	9	10	11	12	13	14	15
	16	17	18	19	20	21	22
	23	24	25	26	27	28	29
SHAWWĀL 1579	1[f]	2	3	4	5	6	7
	8	9	10	11	12	13	14
	15	16	17	18	19	20	21
	22	23	24	25	26	27	28
	29	30	1	2	3	4	5
DHU AL-QA'DA 1579	6	7	8	9	10	11	12
	13	14	15	16	17	18	19
	20	21	22	23	24	25	26
	27	28	29	1	2	3	4
DHU AL-ḤIJJA 1579	5	6	7	8	9	10[g]	11
	12	13	14	15	16	17	18
	19	20	21	22	23	24	25
	26	27	28	29	30	1[a]	2
MUḤARRAM 1580	3	4	5	6	7	8	9
	10[b]	11	12	13	14	15	16
	17	18	19	20	21	22	23
	24	25	26	27	28	29	30
ṢAFAR 1580	1	2	3	4	5	6	7
	8	9	10	11	12	13	14
	15	16	17	18	19	20	21
	22	23	24	25	26	27	28
	29	1	2	3	4	5	6
RABĪ' I 1580	7	8	9	10	11	12[c]	13
	14	15	16	17	18	19	20
	21	22	23	24	25	26	27
	28	29	30	1	2	3	4
RABĪ' II 1580	5	6	7	8	9	10	11
	12	13	14	15	16	17	18
	19	20	21	22	23	24	25
	26	27	28	29	30	1	2
JUMĀDĀ I 1580	3	4	5	6	7	8	9
	10	11	12	13	14	15	16
	17	18	19	20	21	22	23
	24	25	26	27	28	29	1
JUMĀDĀ II 1580	2	3	4	5	6	7	8
	9	10	11	12	13	14	15
	16	17	18	19	20	21	22
	23	24	25	26	27	28	29

[a]New Year
[b]'Ashūrā'
[c]Prophet's Birthday
[d]Ascent of the Prophet
[e]Start of Ramaḍān
[f]'Id al-Fiṭr
[g]'Id al-'Aḍḥā

GREGORIAN 2154

Julian (Sun)	Sun	Mon	Tue	Wed	Thu	Fri	Sat	Month
Dec 16	30	31	1	2	3	4	5	
	6	7	8[a]	9	10	11	12	JANUARY 2154
Dec 30	13	14	15[b]	16	17	18	19	
	20	21	22	23	24	25	26	
Jan 13	27	28	29	30	31	1	2	
	3	4	5	6	7	8	9	FEBRUARY 2154
Jan 27	10	11	12	13[c]	14	15	16	
	17	18	19	20	21	22	23	
Feb 10	24	25	26	27	28	1	2	
	3	4	5	6	7	8	9	
Feb 24	10	11	12	13	14	15	16	MARCH 2154
	17	18	19	20	21	22	23	
Mar 10	24[d]	25	26	27	28	29	30	
	31[e]	1	2	3	4	5	6	
Mar 24	7	8	9	10	11	12	13	
	14	15	16	17	18	19	20	APRIL 2154
Apr 7	21	22	23	24	25	26	27	
	28	29	30	1	2	3	4	
Apr 21	5[f]	6	7	8	9	10	11	
	12	13	14	15	16	17	18	MAY 2154
May 5	19	20	21	22	23	24	25	
	26	27	28	29	30	31	1	
May 19	2	3	4	5	6	7	8	
	9	10	11	12	13	14	15	JUNE 2154
Jun 2	16	17	18	19	20	21	22	
	23	24	25	26	27	28	29	
Jun 16	30	1	2	3	4	5	6	
	7	8	9	10	11	12	13	
Jun 30	14	15	16	17	18	19	20	JULY 2154
	21	22	23	24	25	26	27	
Jul 14	28	29	30	31	1	2	3	
	4	5	6	7	8	9	10	
Jul 28	11	12	13	14	15	16	17	AUGUST 2154
	18	19	20	21	22	23	24	
Aug 11	25	26	27	28	29	30	31	
	1	2	3	4	5	6	7	
Aug 25	8	9	10	11	12	13	14	SEPTEMBER 2154
	15	16	17	18	19	20	21	
Sep 8	22	23	24	25	26	27	28	
	29	30	1	2	3	4	5	
Sep 22	6	7	8	9	10	11	12	OCTOBER 2154
	13	14	15	16	17	18	19	
Oct 6	20	21	22	23	24	25	26	
	27	28	29	30	31	1	2	
Oct 20	3	4	5	6	7	8	9	NOVEMBER 2154
	10	11	12	13	14	15	16	
Nov 3	17	18	19	20	21	22	23	
	24	25	26	27	28	29	30	
Nov 17	1[g]	2	3	4	5	6	7	
	8	9	10	11	12	13	14	DECEMBER 2154
Dec 1	15	16	17	18	19	20	21	
	22	23	24	25[h]	26	27	28	
Dec 15	29	30	31	1	2	3	4	

[a]Orthodox Christmas
[b]Julian New Year
[c]Ash Wednesday
[d]Feast of Orthodoxy
[e]Easter
[f]Orthodox Easter
[g]Advent
[h]Christmas

2155

GREGORIAN 2155 · ISO WEEK (Mon) · JULIAN DAY (Sun noon)

Month	Sun	Mon	Tue	Wed	Thu	Fri	Sat	Lunar Phases	ISO Week	Julian Day
	29	30	31	1[a]	2	●	4	15:24	1	2508155
JANUARY 2155	5	6	7	8	9	◐	11	12:42	2	2508162
	12	13	14	15	16	17	○	17:13	3	2508169
	19	20	21	22	23	24	25		4	2508176
	◑	27	28	29	30	31	1	11:20	5	2508183
FEBRUARY 2155	●	3	4	5	6	7	8	2:11	6	2508190
	◐	10	11	12	13	14	15	7:14	7	2508197
	16	○	18	19	20	21	22	11:20	8	2508204
	23	◑	25	26	27	28	1	20:44	9	2508211
MARCH 2155	2	●	4	5	6	7	8	13:43	10	2508218
	9	10	◐	12	13	14	15	3:18	11	2508225
	16	17	18	○	20[b]	21	22	3:02	12	2508232
	23	24	25	◑	27	28	29	3:47	13	2508239
	30	31	1	●	3	4	5	2:10	14	2508246
APRIL 2155	6	7	8	◐	10	11	12	23:12	15	2508253
	13	14	15	16	○	18	19	15:41	16	2508260
	20	21	22	23	◑	25	26	9:45	17	2508267
	27	28	29	30	●	2	3	15:29	18	2508274
MAY 2155	4	5	6	7	8	◐	10	17:35	19	2508281
	11	12	13	14	15	16	○	1:24	20	2508288
	18	19	20	21	22	◑	24	16:00	21	2508295
	25	26	27	28	29	30	●	5:32	22	2508302
JUNE 2155	1	2	3	4	5	6	7		23	2508309
	◐	9	10	11	12	13	14	9:27	24	2508316
	○	16	17	18	19	20	◑[c]	9:00 23:43	25	2508323
	22	23	24	25	26	27	28		26	2508330
	●	30	1	2	3	4	5	20:13	27	2508337
JULY 2155	6	◐	8	9	10	11	12	22:19	28	2508344
	13	○	15	16	17	18	19	15:38	29	2508351
	20	◑	22	23	24	25	26	9:47	30	2508358
	27	28	●	30	31	1	2	11:22	31	2508365
AUGUST 2155	3	4	5	◐	7	8	9	8:14	32	2508372
	10	11	○	13	14	15	16	22:34	33	2508379
	17	18	◑	20	21	22	23	22:43	34	2508386
	24	25	26	27	●	29	30	2:35	35	2508393
	31	1	2	3	◐	5	6	15:51	36	2508400
SEPTEMBER 2155	7	8	9	10	○	12	13	6:52	37	2508407
	14	15	16	17	◑	19	20	14:43	38	2508414
	21	22	23[d]	24	25	●	27	17:19	39	2508421
	28	29	30	1	2	◐	4	22:15	40	2508428
OCTOBER 2155	5	6	7	8	9	○	11	17:19	41	2508435
	12	13	14	15	16	17	◑	9:33	42	2508442
	19	20	21	22	23	24	25		43	2508449
	●	27	28	29	30	31	1	6:59	44	2508456
NOVEMBER 2155	◐	3	4	5	6	7	8	4:42	45	2508463
	○	10	11	12	13	14	15	6:22	46	2508470
	16	◑	18	19	20	21	22	6:12	47	2508477
	23	●	25	26	27	28	29	19:26	48	2508484
	30	◐	2	3	4	5	6	12:28	49	2508491
DECEMBER 2155	7	○	9	10	11	12	13	22:09	50	2508498
	14	15	16	◑	18	19	20	2:50	51	2508505
	21	22[e]	23	●	25	26	27	6:54	52	2508512
	28	29	◐	31	1	2	3	22:27	1	2508519

HEBREW 5915‡/5916

ISO Week	Month	Sun	Mon	Tue	Wed	Thu	Fri	Sat	Molad
1		24	25	26	27	28	29	1	Fri 22h15m4p
2	SHEVAT 5915	2	3	4	5	6	7	8	
3		9	10	11	12	13	14	15	
4		16	17	18	19	20	21	22	
5		23	24	25	26	27	28	29	
6		30	1	2	3	4	5	6	Sun 10h59m5p
7	ADAR I 5915	7	8	9	10	11	12	13	
8		14	15	16	17	18	19	20	
9		21	22	23	24	25	26	27	
10		28	29	30	1	2	3	4	Mon 23h43m6p
11	ADAR II 5915	5	6	7	8	9	10	11	
12		12	13	14[f]	15	16	17	18	
13		19	20	21	22	23	24	25	
14		26	27	28	29	1	2	3	Wed 12h27m7p
15	NISAN 5915	4	5	6	7	8	9	10	
16		11	12	13	14	15[g]	16	17	
17		18	19	20	21	22	23	24	
18		25	26	27	28	29	30	1	Fri 1h11m8p
19	IYAR 5915	2	3	4	5	6	7	8	
20		9	10	11	12	13	14	15	
21		16	17	18	19	20	21	22	
22		23	24	25	26	27	28	29	
23		1	2	3	4	5	6[h]	7	Sat 13h55m9p
24	SIVAN 5915	8	9	10	11	12	13	14	
25		15	16	17	18	19	20	21	
26		22	23	24	25	26	27	28	
27		29	30	1	2	3	4	5	Mon 2h39m10p
28	TAMMUZ 5915	6	7	8	9	10	11	12	
29		13	14	15	16	17	18	19	
30		20	21	22	23	24	25	26	
31		27	28	29	1	2	3	4	Tue 15h23m11p
32		5	6	7	8	9[i]	10	11	
33	AV 5915	12	13	14	15	16	17	18	
34		19	20	21	22	23	24	25	
35		26	27	28	29	30	1	2	Thu 4h7m12p
36	ELUL 5915	3	4	5	6	7	8	9	
37		10	11	12	13	14	15	16	
38		17	18	19	20	21	22	23	
39		24	25	26	27	28	29	1[a]	Fri 16h51m13p
40		2[a]	3	4	5	6	7	8	
41	TISHRI 5916	9	10[b]	11	12	13	14	15[c]	
42		16	17	18	19	20	21	22	
43		23	24	25	26	27	28	29	
44		30	1	2	3	4	5	6	Sun 5h35m14p
45	HESHVAN 5916	7	8	9	10	11	12	13	
46		14	15	16	17	18	19	20	
47		21	22	23	24	25	26	27	
48		28	29	30	1	2	3	4	Mon 18h19m15p
49	KISLEV 5916	5	6	7	8	9	10	11	
50		12[d]	13	14	15	16	17	18	
51		19	20	21	22	23	24	25[e]	
52		26[e]	27[e]	28[e]	29[e]	30[e]	1[e]	2[e]	
1	TEVETH 5916	3	4	5	6	7	8	9	Wed 7h3m16p

CHINESE Jiǎ-Yín/Yǐ-Mǎo

ISO Week	Month	Sun	Mon	Tue	Wed	Thu	Fri	Sat	Solar Term
1		25	26	27	28	29	1	2	
2	MONTH 12 Jiǎ-Yín	3	4	5	6	7	8	9	Xiǎo hán
3		10	11	12	13	14	15	16	
4		17	**18**	19	20	21	22	23	Dà hán
5		24	25	26	27	28	29	30	
6		1[a]	2*	3	4	5	6	7	Lì chūn
7	MONTH 1 Yǐ-Mǎo	8	9	10	11	12	13	14	
8		15[b]	16	17	**18**	19	20	21	Yǔ shuǐ
9		22	23	24	25	26	27	28	
10		29	1	2	3	4	5	6	Jīng zhé
11	MONTH 2 Yǐ-Mǎo	7	8	9	10	11	12	13	
12		14	15	16	17	18	**19**	20	Chūn fēn
13		21	22	23	24	25	26	27	
14		28	29	30	1	2	3*	4[c]	Qīng míng
15	MONTH 3 Yǐ-Mǎo	5	6	7	8	9	10	11	
16		12	13	14	15	16	17	18	
17		**19**	20	21	22	23	24	25	Gǔ yǔ
18		26	27	28	29	1	2	3	
19	MONTH 4 Yǐ-Mǎo	4	5	6	7	8	9	10	Lì xià
20		11	12	13	14	15	16	17	
21		18	19	20	**21**	22	23	24	Xiǎo mǎn
22		25	26	27	28	29	30	1	
23		2	3	4*	5[d]	6	7	8	Máng zhòng
24	MONTH 5 Yǐ-Mǎo	9	10	11	12	13	14	15	
25		16	17	18	19	20	21	**22**	Xià zhì
26		23	24	25	26	27	28	29	
27		30	1	2	3	4	5	6	
28	MONTH 6 Yǐ-Mǎo	7	8	9	10	11	12	13	Xiǎo shǔ
29		14	15	16	17	18	19	20	
30		21	22	23	**24**	25	26	27	Dà shǔ
31		28	29	1	2	3	4	5*	
32	MONTH 7 Yǐ-Mǎo	6	7[e]	8	9	10	11	12	Lì qiū
33		13	14	15[f]	16	17	18	19	
34		20	21	22	23	24	25	**26**	Chǔ shǔ
35		27	28	29	30	1	2	3	
36	MONTH 8 Yǐ-Mǎo	4	5	6	7	8	9	10	
37		11	12	13	14	15[g]	16	17	Bái lù
38		18	19	20	21	22	23	24	
39		25	26	**27**	28	29	30	1	Qiū fēn
40		2	3	4	5*	6	7	8	
41	MONTH 9 Yǐ-Mǎo	9[h]	10	11	12	13	14	15	Hán lù
42		16	17	18	19	20	21	22	
43		23	24	25	26	**27**	28	29	Shuāng jiàng
44		1	2	3	4	5	6	7	
45	MONTH 10 Yǐ-Mǎo	8	9	10	11	12	13	14	Lì dōng
46		15	16	17	18	19	20	21	
47		22	23	24	25	26	27	**28**	Xiǎo xuě
48		29	30	1	2	3	4	5	
49	MONTH 11 Yǐ-Mǎo	6*	7	8	9	10	11	12	
50		13	14	15	16	17	18	19	Dà xuě
51		20	21	22	23	24	25	26	
52		27	**28**[i]	29	1	2	3	4	Dōng zhì
1	MONTH 12 Yǐ-Mǎo	5	6	7	8	9	10	11	

COPTIC 1871‡/1872 · ETHIOPIC 2147‡/2148

ISO Week	Coptic Month	Sun	Mon	Tue	Wed	Thu	Fri	Sat	Ethiopic Month
1	KOIAK 1871	19	20	21	22	23	24	25	TĀKHŚĀŚ 2147
2		26	27	28	29[c]	30	1	2	
3	TŌBE 1871	3	4	5	6[d]	7	8	9	TER 2147
4		10	11[e]	12	13	14	15	16	
5		17	18	19	20	21	22	23	
6		24	25	26	27	28	29	30	
7	MESHIR 1871	1	2	3	4	5	6	7	YAKĀTĪT 2147
8		8	9	10	11	12	13	14	
9		15	16	17	18	19	20	21	
10		22	23	24	25	26	27	28	
11	PAREMOTEP 1871	29	30	1	2	3	4	5	MAGĀBIT 2147
12		6	7	8	9	10	11	12	
13		13	14	15	16	17	18	19	
14		20	21	22	23	24	25	26	
15	PARMOUTE 1871	27	28	29	30	1	2	3	MIYĀZYĀ 2147
16		4	5	6	7	8	9	10	
17		11	12	13	14	15	16	17	
18		18[f]	19	20	21	22	23	24	
19	PASHONS 1871	25	26	27	28	29[g]	30	1	GENBOT 2147
20		2	3	4	5	6	7	8	
21		9	10	11	12	13	14	15	
22		16	17	18	19	20	21	22	
23		23	24	25	26	27	28	29	
24	PAŌNE 1871	30	1	2	3	4	5	6	SANĒ 2147
25		7	8	9	10	11	12	13	
26		14	15	16	17	18	19	20	
27		21	22	23	24	25	26	27	
28	EPĒP 1871	28	29	30	1	2	3	4	HAMLĒ 2147
29		5	6	7	8	9	10	11	
30		12	13	14	15	16	17	18	
31		19	20	21	22	23	24	25	
32	MESORĒ 1871	26	27	28	29	30	1	2	NAHASĒ 2147
33		3	4	5	6	7	8	9	
34		10	11	12	13[h]	14	15	16	
35		17	18	19	20	21	22	23	
36		24	25	26	27	28	29	30	
37	EPAG. 1871	1	2	3	4	5	6	1[a]	PĀG. 2147
38	THOOUT 1872	2	3	4	5	6	7	8	MASKARAM 2148
39		9	10	11	12	13	14	15	
40		16	17[b]	18	19	20	21	22	
41		23	24	25	26	27	28	29	
42	PAOPE 1872	30	1	2	3	4	5	6	TEQEMT 2148
43		7	8	9	10	11	12	13	
44		14	15	16	17	18	19	20	
45		21	22	23	24	25	26	27	
46	ATHŌR 1872	28	29	30	1	2	3	4	HEDĀR 2148
47		5	6	7	8	9	10	11	
48		12	13	14	15	16	17	18	
49		19	20	21	22	23	24	25	
50	KOIAK 1872	26	27	28	29	30	1	2	TĀKHŚĀŚ 2148
51		3	4	5	6	7	8	9	
52		10	11	12	13	14	15	16	
1		17	18	19	20	21	22	23	

[a]New Year
[b]Spring (21:04)
[c]Summer (12:27)
[d]Autumn (5:26)
[e]Winter (4:20)
● New moon
◐ First quarter moon
○ Full moon
◑ Last quarter moon

‡Leap year
[a]New Year
[b]Yom Kippur
[c]Sukkot
[d]Winter starts
[e]Hanukkah
[f]Purim
[g]Passover
[h]Shavuot
[i]Fast of Av

[a]New Year (4853, Hare)
[b]Lantern Festival
[c]Qīngmíng
[d]Dragon Festival
[e]Qǐqiǎo
[f]Hungry Ghosts
[g]Mid-Autumn Festival
[h]Double-Ninth Festival
[i]Dōngzhì
*Start of 60-name cycle

‡Leap year
[a]New Year
[b]Building of the Cross
[c]Christmas
[d]Jesus's Circumcision
[e]Epiphany
[f]Easter
[g]Mary's Announcement
[h]Jesus's Transfiguration

PERSIAN (ASTRONOMICAL) 1533/1534	Sun	Mon	Tue	Wed	Thu	Fri	Sat
	8	9	10	11	12	13	14
DEY 1533	15	16	17	18	19	20	21
	22	23	24	25	26	27	28
	29	30	1	2	3	4	5
BAHMAN 1533	6	7	8	9	10	11	12
	13	14	15	16	17	18	19
	20	21	22	23	24	25	26
	27	28	29	30	1	2	3
ESFAND 1533	4	5	6	7	8	9	10
	11	12	13	14	15	16	17
	18	19	20	21	22	23	24
	25	26	27	28	29	1[a]	2
FARVARDĪN 1534	3	4	5	6	7	8	9
	10	11	12	13[b]	14	15	16
	17	18	19	20	21	22	23
	24	25	26	27	28	29	30
	31	1	2	3	4	5	6
ORDĪBEHEŠT 1534	7	8	9	10	11	12	13
	14	15	16	17	18	19	20
	21	22	23	24	25	26	27
	28	29	30	31	1	2	3
XORDĀD 1534	4	5	6	7	8	9	10
	11	12	13	14	15	16	17
	18	19	20	21	22	23	24
	25	26	27	28	29	30	31
	1	2	3	4	5	6	7
TĪR 1534	8	9	10	11	12	13	14
	15	16	17	18	19	20	21
	22	23	24	25	26	27	28
	29	30	31	1	2	3	4
MORDĀD 1534	5	6	7	8	9	10	11
	12	13	14	15	16	17	18
	19	20	21	22	23	24	25
	26	27	28	29	30	31	1
SHAHRĪVAR 1534	2	3	4	5	6	7	8
	9	10	11	12	13	14	15
	16	17	18	19	20	21	22
	23	24	25	26	27	28	29
	30	31	1	2	3	4	5
MEHR 1534	6	7	8	9	10	11	12
	13	14	15	16	17	18	19
	20	21	22	23	24	25	26
	27	28	29	30	1	2	3
ĀBĀN 1534	4	5	6	7	8	9	10
	11	12	13	14	15	16	17
	18	19	20	21	22	23	24
	25	26	27	28	29	30	1
ĀZAR 1534	2	3	4	5	6	7	8
	9	10	11	12	13	14	15
	16	17	18	19	20	21	22
	23	24	25	26	27	28	29
DEY 1534	30	1	2	3	4	5	6
	7	8	9	10	11	12	13

HINDU LUNAR 2211/2212	Sun	Mon	Tue	Wed	Thu	Fri	Sat
	24	25	27	28	29	30	1
PAUSHA 2211	2	3	4	5	6	7	8
	9	10	11	12	13	14	15
	16	17	18	19	20	21	22
	23	24	25	26	27	28	29
	30	2	3	4	5	6	7
MĀGHA 2211	8	9	10	10	11	12	13
	14	15	16	17	18	19	20
	21	22	23	24	26	27	28[h]
	29	30	1	2	3	4	5
PHĀLGUNA 2211	6	7	8	9	10	11	12
	13	13	14	15[i]	16	17	19
	20	21	22	23	24	25	26
	27	28	29	30	1[a]	2	3
CHAITRA 2212	4	5	6	7	8	9[b]	10
	11	12	13	14	15	16	17
	18	19	20	21	22	24	25
	26	27	28	29	30	1	2
VAIŚĀKHA 2212	3	4	5	6	7	7	8
	9	10	11	12	13	14	15
	17	18	19	20	21	22	23
	24	25	26	27	28	29	30
JYAISHTHA 2212	1	2	3	4	5	6	7
	8	9	10	11	12	13	14
	15	16	17	18	20	21	22
	23	24	25	26	27	28	29
	30	1	2	3	3	4	5
ĀSHĀḌHA 2212	6	7	8	9	10	11	13
	14	15	16	17	18	19	20
	21	22	23	24	25	26	27
	28	29	30	1	2	3	4
ŚRĀVAṆA 2212	5	6	7	8	9	10	11
	12	13	14	16	17	18	19
	20	21	22	23[c]	24	25	26
	27	28	29	30	30	1	2
BHĀDRAPADA 2212	3[d]	4	5	6	7	9	10
	11	12	13	14	15	16	17
	18	19	20	21	22	23	24
	25	26	27	28	29	30	1
ĀŚVINA 2212	2	3	4	5	6	7	8[e]
	9[e]	10[e]	12	13	14	15	16
	17	18	19	20	21	22	23
	24	25	25	26	27	28	29
KĀRTTIKA 2212	30	1[f]	2	3	4	6	7
	8	9	10	11	12	13	14
	15	16	17	18	19	20	21
	22	23	24	25	26	27	28
MĀRGAŚĪRA 2212	29	30	1	2	3	4	5
	6	7	8	10	11[g]	12	13
	14	15	16	17	18	19	19
	20	21	22	23	24	25	26
PAUSHA 2212	27	28	29	30	1	2	4
	5	6	7	8	9	10	11

HINDU SOLAR 2076/2077	Sun	Mon	Tue	Wed	Thu	Fri	Sat
PAUSHA 2076	12	13	14	15	16	17	18
	19	20	21	22	23	24	25
	26	27	28	29	1[b]	2	3
MĀGHA 2076	4	5	6	7	8	9	10
	11	12	13	14	15	16	17
	18	19	20	21	22	23	24
	25	26	27	28	29	30	1
PHĀLGUNA 2076	2	3	4	5	6	7	8
	9	10	11	12	13	14	15
	16	17	18	19	20	21	22
	23	24	25	26	27	28	29
	30	1	2	3	4	5	6
CHAITRA 2076	7	8	9	10	11	12	13
	14	15	16	17	18	19	20
	21	22	23	24	25	26	27
	28	29	30	1[a]	2	3	4
VAIŚĀKHA 2077	5	6	7	8	9	10	11
	12	13	14	15	16	17	18
	19	20	21	22	23	24	25
	26	27	28	29	30	31	1
JYAISHTHA 2077	2	3	4	5	6	7	8
	9	10	11	12	13	14	15
	16	17	18	19	20	21	22
	23	24	25	26	27	28	29
	30	31	1	2	3	4	5
ĀSHĀḌHA 2077	6	7	8	9	10	11	12
	13	14	15	16	17	18	19
	20	21	22	23	24	25	26
	27	28	29	30	31	32	1
ŚRĀVAṆA 2077	2	3	4	5	6	7	8
	9	10	11	12	13	14	15
	16	17	18	19	20	21	22
	23	24	25	26	27	28	29
	30	31	32	1	2	3	4
BHĀDRAPADA 2077	5	6	7	8	9	10	11
	12	13	14	15	16	17	18
	19	20	21	22	23	24	25
	26	27	28	29	30	31	1
ĀŚVINA 2077	2	3	4	5	6	7	8
	9	10	11	12	13	14	15
	16	17	18	19	20	21	22
	23	24	25	26	27	28	29
	30	1	2	3	4	5	6
KĀRTTIKA 2077	7	8	9	10	11	12	13
	14	15	16	17	18	19	20
	21	22	23	24	25	26	27
	28	29	30	1	2	3	4
MĀRGAŚĪRA 2077	5	6	7	8	9	10	11
	12	13	14	15	16	17	18
	19	20	21	22	23	24	25
	26	27	28	29	1	2	3
PAUSHA 2077	4	5	6	7	8	9	10
	11	12	13	14	15	16	17

ISLAMIC (ASTRONOMICAL) 1580/1581	Sun	Mon	Tue	Wed	Thu	Fri	Sat
	23	24	25	26	27	28	29
	1	2	3	4	5	6	7
RAJAB 1580	8	9	10	11	12	13	14
	15	16	17	18	19	20	21
	22	23	24	25	26	27[d]	28
	29	1	2	3	4	5	6
SHA'BĀN 1580	7	8	9	10	11	12	13
	14	15	16	17	18	19	20
	21	22	23	24	25	26	27
	28	29	30	1[e]	2	3	4
RAMAḌĀN 1580	5	6	7	8	9	10	11
	12	13	14	15	16	17	18
	19	20	21	22	23	24	25
	26	27	28	29	1[f]	2	3
SHAWWĀL 1580	4	5	6	7	8	9	10
	11	12	13	14	15	16	17
	18	19	20	21	22	23	24
	25	26	27	28	29	30	1
DHU AL-QA'DA 1580	2	3	4	5	6	7	8
	9	10	11	12	13	14	15
	16	17	18	19	20	21	22
	23	24	25	26	27	28	29
DHU AL-ḤIJJA 1580	1	2	3	4	5	6	7
	8	9	10[g]	11	12	13	14
	15	16	17	18	19	20	21
	22	23	24	25	26	27	28
	29	30	1[a]	2	3	4	5
MUḤARRAM 1581	6	7	8	9	10[b]	11	12
	13	14	15	16	17	18	19
	20	21	22	23	24	25	26
	27	28	29	30	1	2	3
ṢAFAR 1581	4	5	6	7	8	9	10
	11	12	13	14	15	16	17
	18	19	20	21	22	23	24
	25	26	27	28	29	30	1
RABĪ' I 1581	2	3	4	5	6	7	8
	9	10	11	12[c]	13	14	15
	16	17	18	19	20	21	22
	23	24	25	26	27	28	29
	30	1	2	3	4	5	6
RABĪ' II 158	7	8	9	10	11	12	13
	14	15	16	17	18	19	20
	21	22	23	24	25	26	27
	28	29	1	2	3	4	5
JUMĀDĀ I 1581	6	7	8	9	10	11	12
	13	14	15	16	17	18	19
	20	21	22	23	24	25	26
	27	28	29	30	1	2	3
JUMĀDĀ II 1581	4	5	6	7	8	9	10
	11	12	13	14	15	16	17
	18	19	20	21	22	23	24
	25	26	27	28	29	1	2
RAJAB 1581	3	4	5	6	7	8	9

Julian (Sun)	GREGORIAN 2155	Sun	Mon	Tue	Wed	Thu	Fri	Sat
Dec 15		29	30	31	1	2	3	4
	JANUARY 2155	5	6	7	8[a]	9	10	11
Dec 29		12	13	14	15[b]	16	17	18
		19	20	21	22	23	24	25
Jan 12		26	27	28	29	30	31	1
	FEBRUARY 2155	2	3	4	5	6	7	8
Jan 26		9	10	11	12	13	14	15
		16	17	18	19	20	21	22
Feb 9		23	24	25	26	27	28	1
	MARCH 2155	2	3	4	5[c]	6	7	8
Feb 23		9	10	11	12	13	14	15
		16[d]	17	18	19	20	21	22
Mar 9		23	24	25	26	27	28	29
		30	31	1	2	3	4	5
Mar 23	APRIL 2155	6	7	8	9	10	11	12
		13	14	15	16	17	18	19
Apr 6		20[e]	21	22	23	24	25	26
		27[f]	28	29	30	1	2	3
Apr 20	MAY 2155	4	5	6	7	8	9	10
		11	12	13	14	15	16	17
May 4		18	19	20	21	22	23	24
		25	26	27	28	29	30	31
May 18	JUNE 2155	1	2	3	4	5	6	7
		8	9	10	11	12	13	14
Jun 1		15	16	17	18	19	20	21
		22	23	24	25	26	27	28
Jun 15		29	30	1	2	3	4	5
	JULY 2155	6	7	8	9	10	11	12
Jun 29		13	14	15	16	17	18	19
		20	21	22	23	24	25	26
Jul 13		27	28	29	30	31	1	2
	AUGUST 2155	3	4	5	6	7	8	9
Jul 27		10	11	12	13	14	15	16
		17	18	19	20	21	22	23
Aug 10		24	25	26	27	28	29	30
		31	1	2	3	4	5	6
Aug 24	SEPTEMBER 2155	7	8	9	10	11	12	13
		14	15	16	17	18	19	20
Sep 7		21	22	23	24	25	26	27
		28	29	30	1	2	3	4
Sep 21	OCTOBER 2155	5	6	7	8	9	10	11
		12	13	14	15	16	17	18
Oct 5		19	20	21	22	23	24	25
		26	27	28	29	30	31	1
Oct 19	NOVEMBER 2155	2	3	4	5	6	7	8
		9	10	11	12	13	14	15
Nov 2		16	17	18	19	20	21	22
		23	24	25	26	27	28	29
Nov 16		30[g]	1	2	3	4	5	6
	DECEMBER 2155	7	8	9	10	11	12	13
Nov 30		14	15	16	17	18	19	20
		21	22	23	24	25[h]	26	27
Dec 14		28	29	30	31	1	2	3

Persian: [a]New Year; [b]Sizdeh Bedar

Hindu Lunar: [a]New Year (Rākshasa); [b]Birthday of Rāma; [c]Birthday of Krishna; [d]Ganēśa Chaturthī; [e]Dashara; [f]Diwali; [g]Birthday of Vishnu; [h]Night of Śiva; [i]Holi

Hindu Solar: [a]New Year (Pramoda); [b]Pongal

Islamic: [a]New Year; [b]'Ashūrā'; [c]Prophet's Birthday; [d]Ascent of the Prophet; [e]Start of Ramaḍān; [f]'Id al-Fiṭr; [g]'Id al-'Aḍḥā

Gregorian: [a]Orthodox Christmas; [b]Julian New Year; [c]Ash Wednesday; [d]Feast of Orthodoxy; [e]Easter; [f]Orthodox Easter; [g]Advent; [h]Christmas

GREGORIAN 2156‡	Sun	Mon	Tue	Wed	Thu	Fri	Sat	Lunar Phases	ISO WEEK (Mon)	JULIAN DAY (Sun noon)	HEBREW 5916/5917‡	Sun	Mon	Tue	Wed	Thu	Fri	Sat	Molad	CHINESE Yǐ-Mǎo/Bǐng-Chén‡	Sun	Mon	Tue	Wed	Thu	Fri	Sat	Solar Term	COPTIC 1872/1873	Sun	Mon	Tue	Wed	Thu	Fri	Sat	ETHIOPIC 2148/2149
	28	29	◐	31	1[a]	2	3	22:27	1	2508519		3	4	5	6	7	8	9			5	6	7	8	9	10	11			17	18	19	20	21	22	23	
	4	5	6	○	8	9	10	16:19	2	2508526	TEVETH 5916	10	11	12	13	14	15	16		MONTH 12 Yǐ-Mǎo	12	13	14	15	16	17	18	Xiǎo hán	KOIAK 1872	24	25	26	27	28	29[c]	30	TĀKHŚĀŚ 2148
JANUARY 2156	11	12	13	14	◑	16	17	21:20	3	2508533		17	18	19	20	21	22	23			19	20	21	22	23	24	25			1	2	3	4	5	6[d]	7	
	18	19	20	21	●	23	24	17:46	4	2508540		24	25	26	27	28	29	1	Thu 19h47m17p		26	27	28	29	30	1[a]	2	Dà hán		8	9	10	11[e]	12	13	14	
	25	26	27	28	◐	30	31	11:05	5	2508547		2	3	4	5	6	7	8			3	4	5	6	7*	8	9		TŌBE 1872	15	16	17	18	19	20	21	ṬER 2148
	1	2	3	4	5	○	7	11:49	6	2508554	SHEVAT 5916	9	10	11	12	13	14	15		MONTH 1 Bǐng-Chén	10	11	12	13	14	15[b]	16	Lì chūn		22	23	24	25	26	27	28	
	8	9	10	11	12	13	◑	12:14	7	2508561		16	17	18	19	20	21	22			17	18	19	20	21	22	23			29	30	1	2	3	4	5	
FEBRUARY 2156	15	16	17	18	19	20	●	4:19	8	2508568		23	24	25	26	27	28	29			24	25	26	27	28	29	1	Yǔ shuǐ		6	7	8	9	10	11	12	
	22	23	24	25	26	27	◐	2:15	9	2508575		30	1	2	3	4	5	6	Sat 8h32m0p		2	3	4	5	6	7	8		MESHIR 1872	13	14	15	16	17	18	19	YAKĀTĪT 2148
	29	1	2	3	4	5	6		10	2508582		7	8	9	10	11	12	13		MONTH 2 Bǐng-Chén	9	10	11	12	13	14	15	Jīng zhé		20	21	22	23	24	25	26	
	○	8	9	10	11	12	13	6:51	11	2508589	ADAR 5916	14[f]	15	16	17	18	19	20			16	17	18	19	20	21	22			27	28	29	30	1	2	3	
MARCH 2156	◑	15	16	17	18	19	20[b]	23:15	12	2508596		21	22	23	24	25	26	27			23	24	25	26	27	28	29	Chūn fēn		4	5	6	7	8	9	10	
	●	22	23	24	25	26	27	14:37	13	2508603		28	29	1	2	3	4	5	Sun 21h16m1p		1	2	3	4	5	6	7		PAREMOTEP 1872	11	12	13	14	15	16	17	MAGĀBĪT 2148
	◐	29	30	31	1	2	3	19:27	14	2508610		6	7	8	9	10	11	12			8	9*	10	11	12	13	14			18	19	20	21	22	23	24	
	4	○	6	7	8	9	10	23:39	15	2508617	NISAN 5916	13	14	15[g]	16	17	18	19		MONTH 3 Bǐng-Chén	15[c]	16	17	18	19	20	21	Qīng míng		25	26	27	28	29	30	1	
APRIL 2156	11	12	◑	14	15	16	17	7:06	16	2508624		20	21	22	23	24	25	26			22	23	24	25	26	27	28			2[f]	3	4	5	6	7	8	
	18	19	●	21	22	23	24	0:49	17	2508631		27	28	29	30	1	2	3	Tue 10h0m2p		29	30	1	2	3	4	5	Gǔ yǔ	PARMOUTE 1872	9	10	11	12	13	14	15	MIYĀZYĀ 2148
	25	26	◐	28	29	30	1	13:52	18	2508638		4	5	6	7	8	9	10			6	7	8	9	10	11	12			16	17	18	19	20	21	22	
	2	3	4	○	6	7	8	13:14	19	2508645	IYYAR 5916	11	12	13	14	15	16	17		LEAP MONTH 3 Bǐng-Chén	13	14	15	16	17	18	19	Lì xià		23	24	25	26	27	28	29[g]	
MAY 2156	9	10	11	◑	13	14	15	12:55	20	2508652		18	19	20	21	22	23	24			20	21	22	23	24	25	26			30	1	2	3	4	5	6	
	16	17	18	●	20	21	22	11:21	21	2508659		25	26	27	28	29	1	2	Wed 22h44m3p		27	28	29	1	2	3	4	Xiǎo mǎn		7	8	9	10	11	12	13	
	23	24	25	26	◐	28	29	8:19	22	2508666		3	4	5	6[h]	7	8	9			5	6	7	8	9	10*	11		PASHONS 1872	14	15	16	17	18	19	20	GENBOT 2148
	30	31	1	2	○	4	5	23:48	23	2508673	SIVAN 5916	10	11	12	13	14	15	16		MONTH 4 Bǐng-Chén	12	13	14	15	16	17	18	Máng zhòng		21	22	23	24	25	26	27	
	6	7	8	9	◑	11	12	18:00	24	2508680		17	18	19	20	21	22	23			19	20	21	22	23	24	25			28	29	30	1	2	3	4	
JUNE 2156	13	14	15	16	●	18	19	22:58	25	2508687		24	25	26	27	28	29	30			26	27	28	29	30	1	2			5	6	7	8	9	10	11	
	20[c]	21	22	23	24	25	◐	1:33	26	2508694		1	2	3	4	5	6	7	Fri 11h28m4p		3	4	5[d]	6	7	8	9	Xià zhì	PAŌNE 1872	12	13	14	15	16	17	18	SANĒ 2148
	27	28	29	30	1	2	○	8:17	27	2508701	TAMMUZ 5916	8	9	10	11	12	13	14		MONTH 5 Bǐng-Chén	10	11	12	13	14	15	16			19	20	21	22	23	24	25	
JULY 2156	4	5	6	7	8	◑	10	23:36	28	2508708		15	16	17	18	19	20	21			17	18	19	20	21	22	23	Xiǎo shǔ		26	27	28	29	30	1	2	
	11	12	13	14	15	16	●	12:15	29	2508715		22	23	24	25	26	27	28			24	25	26	27	28	29	1			3	4	5	6	7	8	9	
	18	19	20	21	22	23	24		30	2508722		29	1	2	3	4	5	6	Sun 0h12m5p		2	3	4	5	6	7	8	Dà shǔ	EPĒP 1872	10	11	12	13	14	15	16	ḤAMLĒ 2148
	◐	26	27	28	29	30	31	16:42	31	2508729		7	8	9[i]	10	11	12	13		MONTH 6 Bǐng-Chén	9	10	11*	12	13	14	15			17	18	19	20	21	22	23	
	○	2	3	4	5	6	7	15:47	32	2508736	AV 5916	14	15	16	17	18	19	20			16	17	18	19	20	21	22	Lì qiū		24	25	26	27	28	29	30	
	◑	9	10	11	12	13	14	6:58	33	2508743		21	22	23	24	25	26	27			23	24	25	26	27	28	29			1	2	3	4	5	6	7	
AUGUST 2156	15	●	17	18	19	20	21	3:22	34	2508750		28	29	30	1	2	3	4	Mon 12h56m6p		30	1	2	3	4	5	6			8	9	10	11	12	13[h]	14	
	22	23	◐	25	26	27	28	5:28	35	2508757		5	6	7	8	9	10	11			7[e]	8	9	10	11	12	13	Chǔ shǔ	MESORĒ 1872	15	16	17	18	19	20	21	NAḤASĒ 2148
	29	○	31	1	2	3	4	23:17	36	2508764	ELUL 5916	12	13	14	15	16	17	18		MONTH 7 Bǐng-Chén	14	15[f]	16	17	18	19	20			22	23	24	25	26	27	28	
	5	◑	7	8	9	10	11	17:15	37	2508771		19	20	21	22	23	24	25			21	22	23	24	25	26	27	Bái lù	EPAG. 1872	29	30	1	2	3	4	5	ṖĀG. 2148
SEPTEMBER 2156	12	13	●	15	16	17	18	19:46	38	2508778		26	27	28	29	1[a]	2[a]	3	Wed 1h40m7p		28	29	30	1	2	3	4			1[a]	2	3	4	5	6	7	
	19	20	21	◐[d]	23	24	25	16:07	39	2508785		4	5	6	7	8	9	10[b]			5	6	7	8	9	10	11*	Qiū fēn		8	9	10	11	12	13	14	
	26	27	28	○	30	1	2	7:32	40	2508792	TISHRI 5917	11	12	13	14	15[c]	16	17		MONTH 8 Bǐng-Chén	12	13	14	15[g]	16	17	18		THOOUT 1873	15	16	17[b]	18	19	20	21	MASKARAM 2149
	3	4	5	◑	7	8	9	7:20	41	2508799		18	19	20	21	22	23	24			19	20	21	22	23	24	25	Hán lù		22	23	24	25	26	27	28	
OCTOBER 2156	10	11	12	13	●	15	16	12:24	42	2508806		25	26	27	28	29	30	1	Thu 14h24m8p		26	27	28	29	1	2	3			29	30	1	2	3	4	5	
	17	18	19	20	21	◐	23	1:12	43	2508813		2	3	4	5	6	7	8			4	5	6	7	8	9[h]	10	Shuāng jiàng		6	7	8	9	10	11	12	
	24	25	26	27	○	29	30	17:11	44	2508820	HESHVAN 5917	9	10	11	12	13	14	15		MONTH 9 Bǐng-Chén	11	12	13	14	15	16	17		PAOPE 1873	13	14	15	16	17	18	19	ṬEQEMT 2149
	31	1	2	3	4	◑	6	1:25	45	2508827		16	17	18	19	20	21	22			18	19	20	21	22	23	24			20	21	22	23	24	25	26	
	7	8	9	10	11	12	●	4:18	46	2508834		23	24	25	26	27	28	29			25	26	27	28	29	30	1	Lì dōng		27	28	29	30	1	2	3	
NOVEMBER 2156	14	15	16	17	18	19	◐	9:22	47	2508841		1	2	3	4	5	6	7	Sat 3h8m9p		2	3	4	5	6	7	8			4	5	6	7	8	9	10	
	21	22	23	24	25	26	○	4:52	48	2508848	KISLEV 5917	8	9	10	11	12	13	14		MONTH 10 Bǐng-Chén	9	10	11	12*	13	14	15	Xiǎo xuě	ATHŌR 1873	11	12	13	14	15	16	17	HEDĀR 2149
	28	29	30	1	2	3	◑	22:30	49	2508855		15	16	17	18	19	20	21			16	17	18	19	20	21	22			18	19	20	21	22	23	24	
	5	6	7	8	9	10	11		50	2508862		22	23[d]	24	25[e]	26[e]	27[e]	28[e]			23	24	25	26	27	28	29	Dà xuě		25	26	27	28	29	30	1	
DECEMBER 2156	●	13	14	15	16	17	18	18:59	51	2508869		29[e]	1[e]	2[e]	3[e]	4	5	6	Sun 15h52m10p		30	1	2	3	4	5	6			2	3	4	5	6	7	8	
	◐	20	21[e]	22	23	24	25	17:18	52	2508876	TEVETH 5917	7	8	9	10	11	12	13		MONTH 11 Bǐng-Chén	7	8	9[i]	10	11	12	13	Dōng zhì	KOIAK 1873	9	10	11	12	13	14	15	TĀKHŚĀŚ 2149
	○	27	28	29	30	31	1	19:06	53	2508883		14	15	16	17	18	19	20			14	15	16	17	18	19	20			16	17	18	19	20	21	22	

‡Leap year
[a]New Year
[b]Spring (2:52)
[c]Summer (18:15)
[d]Autumn (11:02)
[e]Winter (10:00)
● New moon
◐ First quarter moon
○ Full moon
◑ Last quarter moon

‡Leap year
[a]New Year
[b]Yom Kippur
[c]Sukkot
[d]Winter starts
[e]Ḥanukkah
[f]Purim
[g]Passover
[h]Shavuot
[i]Fast of Av

‡Leap year
[a]New Year (4854, Dragon)
[b]Lantern Festival
[c]Qīngmíng
[d]Dragon Festival
[e]Qīqiǎo
[f]Hungry Ghosts
[g]Mid-Autumn Festival
[h]Double-Ninth Festival
[i]Dōngzhì
*Start of 60-name cycle

[a]New Year
[b]Building of the Cross
[c]Christmas
[d]Jesus's Circumcision
[e]Epiphany
[f]Easter
[g]Mary's Announcement
[h]Jesus's Transfiguration

PERSIAN (ASTRONOMICAL) 1534/1535

Month	Sun	Mon	Tue	Wed	Thu	Fri	Sat
DEY 1534	7	8	9	10	11	12	13
	14	15	16	17	18	19	20
	21	22	23	24	25	26	27
	28	29	30	1	2	3	4
BAHMAN 1534	5	6	7	8	9	10	11
	12	13	14	15	16	17	18
	19	20	21	22	23	24	25
	26	27	28	29	30	1	2
ESFAND 1534	3	4	5	6	7	8	9
	10	11	12	13	14	15	16
	17	18	19	20	21	22	23
	24	25	26	27	28	29	1[a]
FARVARDĪN 1535	2	3	4	5	6	7	8
	9	10	11	12	13[b]	14	15
	16	17	18	19	20	21	22
	23	24	25	26	27	28	29
	30	31	1	2	3	4	5
ORDĪBEHEŠT 1535	6	7	8	9	10	11	12
	13	14	15	16	17	18	19
	20	21	22	23	24	25	26
	27	28	29	30	31	1	2
XORDĀD 1535	3	4	5	6	7	8	9
	10	11	12	13	14	15	16
	17	18	19	20	21	22	23
	24	25	26	27	28	29	30
	31	1	2	3	4	5	6
TĪR 1535	7	8	9	10	11	12	13
	14	15	16	17	18	19	20
	21	22	23	24	25	26	27
	28	29	30	31	1	2	3
MORDĀD 1535	4	5	6	7	8	9	10
	11	12	13	14	15	16	17
	18	19	20	21	22	23	24
	25	26	27	28	29	30	31
SHAHRĪVAR 1535	1	2	3	4	5	6	7
	8	9	10	11	12	13	14
	15	16	17	18	19	20	21
	22	23	24	25	26	27	28
	29	30	31	1	2	3	4
MEHR 1535	5	6	7	8	9	10	11
	12	13	14	15	16	17	18
	19	20	21	22	23	24	25
	26	27	28	29	30	1	2
ĀBĀN 1535	3	4	5	6	7	8	9
	10	11	12	13	14	15	16
	17	18	19	20	21	22	23
	24	25	26	27	28	29	30
ĀZAR 1535	1	2	3	4	5	6	7
	8	9	10	11	12	13	14
	15	16	17	18	19	20	21
	22	23	24	25	26	27	28
	29	30	1	2	3	4	5
DEY 1535	6	7	8	9	10	11	12

HINDU LUNAR 2212/2213‡

Month	Sun	Mon	Tue	Wed	Thu	Fri	Sat
PAUSHA 2212	5	6	7	8	9	10	11
	12	13	14	15	16	17	18
	19	20	21	*21*	22	23	24
	25	**26**	28	29	30	1	2
MĀGHA 2212	3	4	5	6	7	8	9
	10	11	12	13	14	15	16
	17	18	19	20	21	22	23
	24	25	26	27	28[h]	29	30
PHĀLGUNA 2212	**1**	3	4	5	6	7	8
	9	10	11	12	13	*13*	14
	15[i]	16	17	18	19	20	21
	22	23	24	**25**	27	28	29
CHAITRA 2213	30	1[a]	2	3	4	5	6
	7	8	9[b]	10	11	12	13
	14	15	16	17	18	19	20
	21	22	23	24	25	26	27
	28	29	**30**	2	3	4	5
VAIŚĀKHA 2213	6	7	*7*	8	9	10	11
	12	13	14	15	16	17	18
	19	20	21	**22**	24	25	26
	27	28	29	30	1	2	3
JYAISHṬHA 2213	4	5	6	7	8	9	10
	11	12	*12*	13	**14**	16	17
	18	19	20	21	22	23	24
	25	**26**	28	29	30	1	2
LEAP ĀSHĀḌHA 2213	3	*3*	4	5	6	7	8
	9	10	11	12	13	14	15
	16	17	**18**	20	21	22	23
	24	25	26	27	28	29	30
ĀSHĀḌHA 2213	1	2	3	4	5	6	7
	8	9	10	11	12	13	14
	15	16	17	18	19	20	**21**
	23	24	25	26	27	28	29
	30	*30*	1	2	3	4	5
ŚRĀVAṆA 2213	6	7	8	9	10	11	12
	13	**14**	16	17	18	19	20
	21	22	23[c]	24	25	26	27
	28	29	30	1	2	3	4[d]
BHĀDRAPADA 2213	5	6	7	8	9	10	11
	12	13	14	15	16	17	**18**
	20	21	22	23	24	25	*25*
	26	27	28	29	30	1	2
ĀŚVINA 2213	3	4	5	6	7	8[e]	9[e]
	10[e]	**11**	13	14	15	16	17
	18	19	20	21	22	23	24
	25	26	27	28	*28*	29	30
KĀRTTIKA 2213	1[f]	2	3	**4**	6	7	8
	9	10	11	12	13	14	15
	16	17	18	19	20	21	22
	23	24	25	26	27	28	29
MĀRGAŚĪRA 2213	30	1	2	3	4	5	6
	7	8	**9**	11[g]	12	13	14
	15	16	17	18	19	20	21

HINDU SOLAR 2077/2078‡

Month	Sun	Mon	Tue	Wed	Thu	Fri	Sat
PAUSHA 2077	11	12	13	14	15	16	17
	18	19	20	21	22	23	24
	25	26	27	28	29	30	1[b]
MĀGHA 2077	2	3	4	5	6	7	8
	9	10	11	12	13	14	15
	16	17	18	19	20	21	22
	23	24	25	26	27	28	29
PHĀLGUNA 2077	1	2	3	4	5	6	7
	8	9	10	11	12	13	14
	15	16	17	18	19	20	21
	22	23	24	25	26	27	28
	29	30	1	2	3	4	5
CHAITRA 2077	6	7	8	9	10	11	12
	13	14	15	16	17	18	19
	20	21	22	23	24	25	26
	27	28	29	30	1[a]	2	3
VAIŚĀKHA 2078	4	5	6	7	8	9	10
	11	12	13	14	15	16	17
	18	19	20	21	22	23	24
	25	26	27	28	29	30	31
JYAISHṬHA 2078	1	2	3	4	5	6	7
	8	9	10	11	12	13	14
	15	16	17	18	19	20	21
	22	23	24	25	26	27	28
	29	30	31	32	1	2	3
ĀSHĀḌHA 2078	4	5	6	7	8	9	10
	11	12	13	14	15	16	17
	18	19	20	21	22	23	24
	25	26	27	28	29	30	31
ŚRĀVAṆA 2078	1	2	3	4	5	6	7
	8	9	10	11	12	13	14
	15	16	17	18	19	20	21
	22	23	24	25	26	27	28
	29	30	31	32	1	2	3
BHĀDRAPADA 2078	4	5	6	7	8	9	10
	11	12	13	14	15	16	17
	18	19	20	21	22	23	24
	25	26	27	28	29	30	31
ĀŚVINA 2078	1	2	3	4	5	6	7
	8	9	10	11	12	13	14
	15	16	17	18	19	20	21
	22	23	24	25	26	27	28
	29	30	1	2	3	4	5
KĀRTTIKA 2078	6	7	8	9	10	11	12
	13	14	15	16	17	18	19
	20	21	22	23	24	25	26
	27	28	29	30	1	2	3
MĀRGAŚĪRA 2078	4	5	6	7	8	9	10
	11	12	13	14	15	16	17
	18	19	20	21	22	23	24
	25	26	27	28	29	30	1
PAUSHA 2078	2	3	4	5	6	7	8
	9	10	11	12	13	14	15

ISLAMIC (ASTRONOMICAL) 1581/1582

Month	Sun	Mon	Tue	Wed	Thu	Fri	Sat
RAJAB 1581	3	4	5	6	7	8	9
	10	11	12	13	14	15	16
	17	18	19	20	21	22	23
	24	25	26	27[d]	28	29	1
SHA'BĀN 1581	2	3	4	5	6	7	8
	9	10	11	12	13	14	15
	16	17	18	19	20	21	22
	23	24	25	26	27	28	29
RAMAḌĀN 1581	1[e]	2	3	4	5	6	7
	8	9	10	11	12	13	14
	15	16	17	18	19	20	21
	22	23	24	25	26	27	28
	29	30	1[f]	2	3	4	5
SHAWWĀL 1581	6	7	8	9	10	11	12
	13	14	15	16	17	18	19
	20	21	22	23	24	25	26
	27	28	29	1	2	3	4
DHU AL-QA'DA 1581	5	6	7	8	9	10	11
	12	13	14	15	16	17	18
	19	20	21	22	23	24	25
	26	27	28	29	30	1	2
DHU AL-ḤIJJA 1581	3	4	5	6	7	8	9
	10[g]	11	12	13	14	15	16
	17	18	19	20	21	22	23
	24	25	26	27	28	29	1[a]
MUḤARRAM 1582	2[d]	3	4	5	6	7	8
	9	10[b]	11	12	13	14	15
	16	17	18	19	20	21	22
	23	24	25	26	27	28	29
	30	1	2	3	4	5	6
ṢAFAR 1582	7	8	9	10	11	12	13
	14	15	16	17	18	19	20
	21	22	23	24	25	26	27
	28	29	30	1	2	3	4
RABĪ' I 1582	5	6	7	8	9	10	11
	12[c]	13	14	15	16	17	18
	19	20	21	22	23	24	25
	26	27	28	29	30	1	2
RABĪ' II 1582	3	4	5	6	7	8	9
	10	11	12	13	14	15	16
	17	18	19	20	21	22	23
	24	25	26	27	28	29	30
JUMĀDĀ I 1582	1	2	3	4	5	6	7
	8	9	10	11	12	13	14
	15	16	17	18	19	20	21
	22	23	24	25	26	27	28
	29	1	2	3	4	5	6
JUMĀDĀ II 1582	7	8	9	10	11	12	13
	14	15	16	17	18	19	20
	21	22	23	24	25	26	27
	28	29	1	2	3	4	5
RAJAB 1582	6	7	8	9	10	11	12
	13	14	15	16	17	18	19

GREGORIAN 2156‡

Julian† (Sun)	Sun	Mon	Tue	Wed	Thu	Fri	Sat	Month
Dec 14	28	29	30	31	1	2	3	
	4	5	6	7	8[a]	9	10	JANUARY 2156
Dec 28	11	12	13	14	15[b]	16	17	
	18	19	20	21	22	23	24	
Jan 11	25	26	27	28	29	30	31	
	1	2	3	4	5	6	7	FEBRUARY 2156
Jan 25	8	9	10	11	12	13	14	
	15	16	17	18	19	20	21	
Feb 8	22	23	24	25[c]	26	27	28	
	29[d]	1	2	3	4	5	6	MARCH 2156
Feb 22	7	8	9	10	11	12	13	
	14	15	16	17	18	19	20	
Mar 7	21	22	23	24	25	26	27	
	28	29	30	31	1	2	3	APRIL 2156
Mar 21	4	5	6	7	8	9	10	
	11[e]	12	13	14	15	16	17	
Apr 4	18	19	20	21	22	23	24	
	25	26	27	28	29	30	1	MAY 2156
Apr 18	2	3	4	5	6	7	8	
	9	10	11	12	13	14	15	
May 2	16	17	18	19	20	21	22	
	23	24	25	26	27	28	29	
May 16	30	31	1	2	3	4	5	JUNE 2156
	6	7	8	9	10	11	12	
May 30	13	14	15	16	17	18	19	
	20	21	22	23	24	25	26	
Jun 13	27	28	29	30	1	2	3	JULY 2156
	4	5	6	7	8	9	10	
Jun 27	11	12	13	14	15	16	17	
	18	19	20	21	22	23	24	
Jul 11	25	26	27	28	29	30	31	
	1	2	3	4	5	6	7	AUGUST 2156
Jul 25	8	9	10	11	12	13	14	
	15	16	17	18	19	20	21	
Aug 8	22	23	24	25	26	27	28	
	29	30	31	1	2	3	4	SEPTEMBER 2156
Aug 22	5	6	7	8	9	10	11	
	12	13	14	15	16	17	18	
Sep 5	19	20	21	22	23	24	25	
	26	27	28	29	30	1	2	OCTOBER 2156
Sep 19	3	4	5	6	7	8	9	
	10	11	12	13	14	15	16	
Oct 3	17	18	19	20	21	22	23	
	24	25	26	27	28	29	30	
Oct 17	31	1	2	3	4	5	6	NOVEMBER 2156
	7	8	9	10	11	12	13	
Oct 31	14	15	16	17	18	19	20	
	21	22	23	24	25	26	27	
Nov 14	28[g]	29	30	1	2	3	4	DECEMBER 2156
	5	6	7	8	9	10	11	
Nov 28	12	13	14	15	16	17	18	
	19	20	21	22	23	24	25[h]	
Dec 12	26	27	28	29	30	31	1	

Persian: [a]New Year; [b]Sizdeh Bedar

Hindu Lunar: ‡Leap year; [a]New Year (Anala); [b]Birthday of Rāma; [c]Birthday of Krishna; [d]Ganēśa Chaturthī; [e]Dashara; [f]Diwali; [g]Birthday of Vishnu; [h]Night of Śiva; [i]Holi

Hindu Solar: ‡Leap year; [a]New Year (Prajāpati); [b]Pongal

Islamic: [a]New Year; [d]New Year (Arithmetic); [b]'Ashūrā'; [c]Prophet's Birthday; [d]Ascent of the Prophet; [e]Start of Ramaḍān; [f]'Id al-Fiṭr; [g]'Id al-'Aḍḥā

Gregorian: ‡Leap year; [a]Orthodox Christmas; [b]Julian New Year; [c]Ash Wednesday; [d]Feast of Orthodoxy; [e]Easter (also Orthodox); [g]Advent; [h]Christmas

2157

GREGORIAN 2157 — Lunar Phases — ISO WEEK (Mon) — JULIAN DAY (Sun noon)

Month	Sun	Mon	Tue	Wed	Thu	Fri	Sat	Lunar Phases	ISO Week	Julian Day
	○	27	28	29	30	31	1[a]	19:06	53	2508883
	2	◑	4	5	6	7	8	20:28	1	2508890
JANUARY 2157	9	10	●	12	13	14	15	8:19	2	2508897
	16	17	◐	19	20	21	22	1:46	3	2508904
	23	24	○	26	27	28	29	11:53	4	2508911
	30	31	1	◑	3	4	5	16:55	5	2508918
	6	7	8	●	10	11	12	20:15	6	2508925
FEBRUARY 2157	13	14	15	◐	17	18	19	11:33	7	2508932
	20	21	22	23	○	25	26	6:22	8	2508939
	27	28	1	2	3	◑	5	10:09	9	2508946
	6	7	8	9	10	●	12	6:42	10	2508953
MARCH 2157	13	14	15	16	◐	18	19	23:18	11	2508960
	20[b]	21	22	23	24	25	○	0:52	12	2508967
	27	28	29	30	31	1	◑	23:32	13	2508974
	3	4	5	6	7	8	●	15:47	14	2508981
APRIL 2157	10	11	12	13	14	15	◐	13:17	15	2508988
	17	18	19	20	21	22	23		16	2508995
	○	25	26	27	28	29	30	17:47	17	2509002
	1	◑	3	4	5	6	7	9:11	18	2509009
	8	●	10	11	12	13	14	0:05	19	2509016
MAY 2157	15	◐	17	18	19	20	21	5:13	20	2509023
	22	23	○	25	26	27	28	8:20	21	2509030
	29	30	◑	1	2	3	4	15:50	22	2509037
	5	6	●	8	9	10	11	8:33	23	2509044
JUNE 2157	12	13	◐	15	16	17	18	22:20	24	2509051
	19	20	21[c]	○	23	24	25	20:32	25	2509058
	26	27	28	◑	30	1	2	20:38	26	2509065
	3	4	5	●	7	8	9	18:15	27	2509072
JULY 2157	10	11	12	13	◐	15	16	15:41	28	2509079
	17	18	19	20	21	○	23	6:49	29	2509086
	24	25	26	27	28	◑	30	1:01	30	2509093
	31	1	2	3	4	●	6	6:04	31	2509100
	7	8	9	10	11	12	◐	8:32	32	2509107
AUGUST 2157	14	15	16	17	18	19	○	15:50	33	2509114
	21	22	23	24	25	26	◑	6:34	34	2509121
	28	29	30	31	1	2	●	20:17	35	2509128
	4	5	6	7	8	9	10		36	2509135
SEPTEMBER 2157	11	◐	13	14	15	16	17	0:20	37	2509142
	18	○	20	21	22[d]	23	24	0:15	38	2509149
	◑	26	27	28	29	30	1	14:50	39	2509156
	2	●	4	5	6	7	8	12:35	40	2509163
OCTOBER 2157	9	10	◐	12	13	14	15	14:39	41	2509170
	16	17	○	19	20	21	22	8:45	42	2509177
	23	24	◑	26	27	28	29	2:59	43	2509184
	30	31	1	●	3	4	5	6:13	44	2509191
	6	7	8	9	◐	11	12	3:08	45	2509198
NOVEMBER 2157	13	14	15	○	17	18	19	18:09	46	2509205
	20	21	22	◑	24	25	26	19:21	47	2509212
	27	28	29	30	1	●	3	0:11	48	2509219
	4	5	6	7	8	◐	10	13:35	49	2509226
DECEMBER 2157	11	12	13	14	15	○	17	5:09	50	2509233
	18	19	20	21[e]	22	◑	24	15:11	51	2509240
	25	26	27	28	29	30	●	17:25	52	2509247

HEBREW 5917‡/5918

ISO Week	Month	Sun	Mon	Tue	Wed	Thu	Fri	Sat	Molad
53	TEVETH 5917	14	15	16	17	18	19	20	
1		21	22	23	24	25	26	27	
2		28	29	1	2	3	4	5	Tue 4h36m1p
3	SHEVAT 5917	6	7	8	9	10	11	12	
4		13	14	15	16	17	18	19	
5		20	21	22	23	24	25	26	
6		27	28	29	30	1	2	3	Wed 17h20m12p
7	ADAR I 5917	4	5	6	7	8	9	10	
8		11	12	13	14	15	16	17	
9		18	19	20	21	22	23	24	
10		25	26	27	28	29	30	1	Fri 6h4m13p
11	ADAR II 5917	2	3	4	5	6	7	8	
12		9	10	11	12	13	14[f]	15	
13		16	17	18	19	20	21	22	
14		23	24	25	26	27	28	29	Sat 18h48m14p
15	NISAN 5917	1	2	3	4	5	6	7	
16		8	9	10	11	12	13	14	
17		15[g]	16	17	18	19	20	21	
18		22	23	24	25	26	27	28	
19		29	30	1	2	3	4	5	Mon 7h32m15p
20	IYAR 5917	6	7	8	9	10	11	12	
21		13	14	15	16	17	18	19	
22		20	21	22	23	24	25	26	
23		27	28	29	1	2	3	4	Tue 20h16m16p
24	SIVAN 5917	5	6[h]	7	8	9	10	11	
25		12	13	14	15	16	17	18	
26		19	20	21	22	23	24	25	
27		26	27	28	29	30	1	2	Thu 9h0m17p
28	TAMMUZ 5917	3	4	5	6	7	8	9	
29		10	11	12	13	14	15	16	
30		17	18	19	20	21	22	23	
31		24	25	26	27	28	29	1	Fri 21h45m0p
32	AV 5917	2	3	4	5	6	7	8	
33		9[i]	10	11	12	13	14	15	
34		16	17	18	19	20	21	22	
35		23	24	25	26	27	28	29	
36		30	1	2	3	4	5	6	Sun 10h29m1p
37	ELUL 5917	7	8	9	10	11	12	13	
38		14	15	16	17	18	19	20	
39		21	22	23	24	25	26	27	
40		28	29	1[a]	2[a]	3	4	5	Mon 23h13m2p
41	TISHRI 5918	6	7	8	9	10[b]	11	12	
42		13	14	15[c]	16	17	18	19	
43		20	21	22	23	24	25	26	
44		27	28	29	30	1	2	3	Wed 11h57m3p
45	HESHVAN 5918	4	5	6	7	8	9	10	
46		11	12	13	14	15	16	17	
47		18	19	20	21	22	23	24	
48		25	26	27	28	29	1	2	Fri 0h41m4p
49	KISLEV 5918	3	4	5[d]	6	7	8	9	
50		10	11	12	13	14	15	16	
51		17	18	19	20	21	22	23	
52		24	25[e]	26[e]	27[e]	28[e]	29[e]	30[e]	

CHINESE Bǐng-Chén‡/Dīng-Sì

ISO Week	Month	Sun	Mon	Tue	Wed	Thu	Fri	Sat	Solar Term
53	MONTH 11 Bǐng-Chén	14	15	16	17	18	19	20	
1		21	22	23	24	25	26	27	Xiǎo hán
2		28	29	1	2	3	4	5	
3	MONTH 12 Bǐng-Chén	6	7	8	9	10	11	12	Dà hán
4		13*	14	15	16	17	18	19	
5		20	21	22	23	24	25	26	Lì chūn
6		27	28	29	30	1[a]	2	3	
7	MONTH 1 Dīng-Sì	4	5	6	7	8	9	10	Yǔ shuǐ
8		11	12	13	14	15[b]	16	17	
9		18	19	20	21	22	23	24	Jīng zhé
10		25	26	27	28	29	1	2	
11	MONTH 2 Dīng-Sì	3	4	5	6	7	8	9	
12		10	11	12	13	14*	15	16	Chūn fēn
13		17	18	19	20	21	22	23	
14		24	25[c]	26	27	28	29	1	Qīng míng
15	MONTH 3 Dīng-Sì	2	3	4	5	6	7	8	
16		9	10	11	12	13	14	15	Gǔ yǔ
17		16	17	18	19	20	21	22	
18		23	24	25	26	27	28	29	Lì xià
19		30	1	2	3	4	5	6	
20	MONTH 4 Dīng-Sì	7	8	9	10	11	12	13	Xiǎo mǎn
21		14	15*	16	17	18	19	20	
22		21	22	23	24	25	26	27	
23		28	29	1	2	3	4	5[d]	Máng zhòng
24	MONTH 5 Dīng-Sì	6	7	8	9	10	11	12	
25		13	14	15	16	17	18	19	Xià zhì
26		20	21	22	23	24	25	26	
27		27	28	29	30	1	2	3	Xiǎo shǔ
28	MONTH 6 Dīng-Sì	4	5	6	7	8	9	10	
29		11	12	13	14	15	16*	17	Dà shǔ
30		18	19	20	21	22	23	24	
31		25	26	27	28	29	1	2	
32	MONTH 7 Dīng-Sì	3	4	5	6	7[e]	8	9	Lì qiū
33		10	11	12	13	14	15[f]	16	
34		17	18	19	20	21	22	23	Chǔ shǔ
35		24	25	26	27	28	29	30	
36		1	2	3	4	5	6	7	Bái lù
37	MONTH 8 Dīng-Sì	8	9	10	11	12	13	14	
38		15[g]	16	17*	18	19	20	21	Qiū fēn
39		22	23	24	25	26	27	28	
40		29	1	2	3	4	5	6	Hán lù
41	MONTH 9 Dīng-Sì	7	8	9[h]	10	11	12	13	
42		14	15	16	17	18	19	20	
43		21	22	23	24	25	26	27	Shuāng jiàng
44		28	29	30	1	2	3	4	
45	MONTH 10 Dīng-Sì	5	6	7	8	9	10	11	Lì dōng
46		12	13	14	15	16	17	18*	
47		19	20	21	22	23	24	25	Xiǎo xuě
48		26	27	28	29	30	1	2	
49	MONTH 11 Dīng-Sì	3	4	5	6	7	8	9	Dà xuě
50		10	11	12	13	14	15	16	
51		17	18	19	20[i]	21	22	23	Dōng zhì
52		24	25	26	27	28	29	30	

COPTIC 1873/1874 — ETHIOPIC 2149/2150

ISO Week	Coptic Month	Sun	Mon	Tue	Wed	Thu	Fri	Sat	Ethiopic Month
53	KOIAK 1873	16	17	18	19	20	21	22	TĀKHŚĀŚ 2149
1		23	24	25	26	27	28	29[c]	
2		30	1	2	3	4	5	6[d]	
3	TŌBE 1873	7	8	9	10	11[e]	12	13	ṬER 2149
4		14	15	16	17	18	19	20	
5		21	22	23	24	25	26	27	
6		28	29	30	1	2	3	4	
7	MESHIR 1873	5	6	7	8	9	10	11	YAKĀTIT 2149
8		12	13	14	15	16	17	18	
9		19	20	21	22	23	24	25	
10		26	27	28	29	30	1	2	
11	PAREMOTEP 1873	3	4	5	6	7	8	9	MAGĀBIT 2149
12		10	11	12	13	14	15	16	
13		17	18	19	20	21	22	23	
14		24	25	26	27	28	29	30	
15	PARMOUTE 1873	1	2	3	4	5	6	7	MIYĀZYĀ 2149
16		8	9	10	11	12	13	14	
17		15	16	17	18	19	20	21	
18		22[f]	23	24	25	26	27	28	
19		29[g]	30	1	2	3	4	5	
20	PASHONS 1873	6	7	8	9	10	11	12	GENBOT 2149
21		13	14	15	16	17	18	19	
22		20	21	22	23	24	25	26	
23		27	28	29	30	1	2	3	
24	PAŌNE 1873	4	5	6	7	8	9	10	SANĒ 2149
25		11	12	13	14	15	16	17	
26		18	19	20	21	22	23	24	
27		25	26	27	28	29	30	1	
28	EPĒP 1873	2	3	4	5	6	7	8	ḤAMLĒ 2149
29		9	10	11	12	13	14	15	
30		16	17	18	19	20	21	22	
31		23	24	25	26	27	28	29	
32		30	1	2	3	4	5	6	
33	MESORĒ 1873	7	8	9	10	11	12	13[h]	NAHASĒ 2149
34		14	15	16	17	18	19	20	
35		21	22	23	24	25	26	27	
36		28	29	30	1	2	3	4	
37	EPAG. 1873	5	1[a]	2	3	4	5	6	PĀG. 2149
38	THOOUT 1874	7	8	9	10	11	12	13	MASKARAM 2150
39		14	15	16	17[b]	18	19	20	
40		21	22	23	24	25	26	27	
41		28	29	30	1	2	3	4	
42	PAOPE 1874	5	6	7	8	9	10	11	ṬEQEMT 2150
43		12	13	14	15	16	17	18	
44		19	20	21	22	23	24	25	
45		26	27	28	29	30	1	2	
46	ATHŌR 1874	3	4	5	6	7	8	9	HEDĀR 2150
47		10	11	12	13	14	15	16	
48		17	18	19	20	21	22	23	
49		24	25	26	27	28	29	30	
50	KOIAK 1874	1	2	3	4	5	6	7	TĀKHŚĀŚ 2150
51		8	9	10	11	12	13	14	
52		15	16	17	18	19	20	21	

[a]New Year
[b]Spring (8:37)
[c]Summer (0:03)
[d]Autumn (16:55)
[e]Winter (15:54)
● New moon
◐ First quarter moon
○ Full moon
◑ Last quarter moon

‡Leap year
[a]New Year
[b]Yom Kippur
[c]Sukkot
[d]Winter starts
[e]Ḥanukkah
[f]Purim
[g]Passover
[h]Shavuot
[i]Fast of Av

‡Leap year
[a]New Year (4855, Snake)
[b]Lantern Festival
[c]Qīngmíng
[d]Dragon Festival
[e]Qīqiǎo
[f]Hungry Ghosts
[g]Mid-Autumn Festival
[h]Double-Ninth Festival
[i]Dōngzhì
*Start of 60-name cycle

[a]New Year
[b]Building of the Cross
[c]Christmas
[d]Jesus's Circumcision
[e]Epiphany
[f]Easter
[g]Mary's Announcement
[h]Jesus's Transfiguration

PERSIAN (ASTRONOMICAL) 1535/1536‡

Month	Sun	Mon	Tue	Wed	Thu	Fri	Sat
	6	7	8	9	10	11	12
DEY 1535	13	14	15	16	17	18	19
	20	21	22	23	24	25	26
	27	28	29	30	*1*	2	3
BAHMAN 1535	4	5	6	7	8	9	10
	11	12	13	14	15	16	17
	18	19	20	21	22	23	24
	25	26	27	28	29	30	*1*
ESFAND 1535	2	3	4	5	6	7	8
	9	10	11	12	13	14	15
	16	17	18	19	20	21	22
	23	24	25	26	27	28	29
	1[a]	2*	3	4	5	6	7
FARVARDIN 1536	8	9	10	11	12	13[b]	14
	15	16	17	18	19	20	21
	22	23	24	25	26	27	28
	29	30	31	*1*	2	3	4
ORDIBEHEST 1536	5	6	7	8	9	10	11
	12	13	14	15	16	17	18
	19	20	21	22	23	24	25
	26	27	28	29	30	31	*1*
	2	3	4	5	6	7	8
XORDĀD 1536	9	10	11	12	13	14	15
	16	17	18	19	20	21	22
	23	24	25	26	27	28	29
	30	31	*1*	2	3	4	5
	6	7	8	9	10	11	12
TĪR 1536	13	14	15	16	17	18	19
	20	21	22	23	24	25	26
	27	28	29	30	31	*1*	2
	3	4	5	6	7	8	9
MORDĀD 1536	10	11	12	13	14	15	16
	17	18	19	20	21	22	23
	24	25	26	27	28	29	30
	31	*1*	2	3	4	5	6
SHAHRĪVAR 1536	7	8	9	10	11	12	13
	14	15	16	17	18	19	20
	21	22	23	24	25	26	27
	28	29	30	31	*1*	2	3
MEHR 1536	4	5	6	7	8	9	10
	11	12	13	14	15	16	17
	18	19	20	21	22	23	24
	25	26	27	28	29	30	*1*
	2	3	4	5	6	7	8
ĀBĀN 1536	9	10	11	12	13	14	15
	16	17	18	19	20	21	22
	23	24	25	26	27	28	29
	30	*1*	2	3	4	5	6
ĀZAR 1536	7	8	9	10	11	12	13
	14	15	16	17	18	19	20
	21	22	23	24	25	26	27
DEY 1536	28	29	30	*1*	2	3	4
	5	6	7	8	9	10	11

HINDU LUNAR 2213‡/2214

Month	Sun	Mon	Tue	Wed	Thu	Fri	Sat
MĀRGAŚĪRA 2213	15	16	17	18	19	20	21
	21	22	23	24	25	26	27
	28	29	30	1	2	**3**	5
PAUSHA 2213	6	7	8	9	10	11	12
	13	14	15	16	17	18	19
	20	21	22	23	24	*24*	25
	26	28	29	30	1	2	3
MĀGHA 2213	4	5	6	7	8	9	10
	11	12	13	14	15	16	17
	18	19	20	21	22	23	24
	25	26	27	28[h]	29	30	1
PHĀLGUNA 2213	**2**	4	5	6	7	8	9
	10	11	12	13	14	15[i]	16
	16	17	18	19	20	21	22
	23	24	25	**26**	28	29	30
	1[a]	2	3	4	5	6	7
CHAITRA 2214	8[b]	9	10	11	12	13	14
	15	16	17	18	19	20	21
	22	23	24	25	26	27	28
	29	**30**	2	3	4	5	6
VAIŚĀKHA 2214	7	8	9	10	11	*11*	12
	13	14	15	16	17	18	19
	20	21	22	**23**	25	26	27
	28	29	30	1	2	3	4
JYAISHTHA 2214	5	6	7	8	9	10	11
	12	13	14	15	16	17	18
	19	20	21	22	23	24	25
	26	28	29	30	1	2	3
ĀSHĀDHA 2214	4	5	6	7	8	*8*	9
	10	11	12	13	14	15	16
	17	**18**	20	21	22	23	24
	25	26	27	28	29	30	1
ŚRĀVAṆA 2214	2	3	4	5	6	7	8
	9	10	11	12	13	14	15
	16	17	18	19	20	**21**	23[c]
	24	25	26	27	28	29	30
	1	2	3	4[d]	4	5	6
BHĀDRAPADA 2214	7	8	9	10	11	12	13
	14	16	17	18	19	20	21
	22	23	24	25	26	27	28
	29	30	1	2	3	4	5
ĀŚVINA 2214	6	7	8[e]	9[e]	10[e]	11	12
	13	14	15	16	17	**18**	20
	21	22	23	24	25	26	27
	28	29	*29*	30	1[f]	2	3
KĀRTTIKA 2214	4	5	6	7	8	9	10
	11	**12**	14	15	16	17	18
	19	20	21	22	23	24	25
	26	27	28	29	30	1	2
MĀRGAŚĪRA 2214	2	3	**4**	6	7	8	9
	10	11[g]	12	13	14	15	16
	17	**18**	20	*20*	21	22	23
	24	25	26	27	28	29	30

HINDU SOLAR 2078‡/2079

Month	Sun	Mon	Tue	Wed	Thu	Fri	Sat
PAUSHA 2078	9	10	11	12	13	14	15
	16	17	18	19	20	21	22
	23	24	25	26	27	28	29
MĀGHA 2078	1[b]	2	3	4	5	6	7
	8	9	10	11	12	13	14
	15	16	17	18	19	20	21
	22	23	24	25	26	27	28
PHĀLGUNA 2078	29	1	2	3	4	5	6
	7	8	9	10	11	12	13
	14	15	16	17	18	19	20
	21	22	23	24	25	26	27
CHAITRA 2078	28	29	30	1	2	3	4
	5	6	7	8	9	10	11
	12	13	14	15	16	17	18
	19	20	21	22	23	24	25
	26	27	28	29	30	31	1[a]
VAIŚĀKHA 2079	2	3	4	5	6	7	8
	9	10	11	12	13	14	15
	16	17	18	19	20	21	22
	23	24	25	26	27	28	29
	30	31	1	2	3	4	5
JYAISHTHA 2079	6	7	8	9	10	11	12
	13	14	15	16	17	18	19
	20	21	22	23	24	25	26
	27	28	29	30	31	1	2
ĀSHĀDHA 2079	3	4	5	6	7	8	9
	10	11	12	13	14	15	16
	17	18	19	20	21	22	23
	24	25	26	27	28	29	30
	31	32	1	2	3	4	5
ŚRĀVAṆA 2079	6	7	8	9	10	11	12
	13	14	15	16	17	18	19
	20	21	22	23	24	25	26
	27	28	29	30	31	1	2
BHĀDRAPADA 2079	3	4	5	6	7	8	9
	10	11	12	13	14	15	16
	17	18	19	20	21	22	23
	24	25	26	27	28	29	30
	31	1	2	3	4	5	6
ĀŚVINA 2079	7	8	9	10	11	12	13
	14	15	16	17	18	19	20
	21	22	23	24	25	26	27
	28	29	30	31	1	2	3
KĀRTTIKA 2079	4	5	6	7	8	9	10
	11	12	13	14	15	16	17
	18	19	20	21	22	23	24
	25	26	27	28	29	1	2
MĀRGAŚĪRA 2079	3	4	5	6	7	8	9
	10	11	12	13	14	15	16
	17	18	19	20	21	22	23
	24	25	26	27	28	29	30
PAUSHA 2079	1	2	3	4	5	6	7
	8	9	10	11	12	13	14

ISLAMIC (ASTRONOMICAL) 1582/1583‡

Month	Sun	Mon	Tue	Wed	Thu	Fri	Sat
RAJAB 1582	13	14	15	16	17	18	19
	20	21	22	23	24	25	26
	27[d]	28	29	30	*1*	2	3
SHA'BĀN 1582	4	5	6	7	8	9	10
	11	12	13	14	15	16	17
	18	19	20	21	22	23	24
	25	26	27	28	29	*1*[e]	2
RAMAḌĀN 1582	3	4	5	6	7	8	9
	10	11	12	13	14	15	16
	17	18	19	20	21	22	23
	24	25	26	27	28	29	*1*[f]
SHAWWĀL 1582	*2*	3	4	5	6	7	8
	9	10	11	12	13	14	15
	16	17	18	19	20	21	22
	23	24	25	26	27	28	29
	30	*1*	2	3	4	5	6
DHU AL-QA'DA 1582	7	8	9	10	11	12	13
	14	15	16	17	18	19	20
	21	22	23	24	25	26	27
	28	29	1	2	3	4	5
DHU AL-ḤIJJA 1582	6	7	8	9	10[g]	11	12
	13	14	15	16	17	18	19
	20	21	22	23	24	25	26
	27	28	29	1[a]	2[d]	3	4
MUḤARRAM 1583	5	6	7	8	9	10[b]	11
	12	13	14	15	16	17	18
	19	20	21	22	23	24	25
	26	27	28	29	30	1	*2*
ṢAFAR 1583	3	4	5	6	7	8	9
	10	11	12	13	14	15	16
	17	18	19	20	21	22	23
	24	25	26	27	28	29	30
	1	2	3	4	5	6	7
RABĪ' I 1583	8	9	10	11	12[c]	13	14
	15	16	17	18	19	20	21
	22	23	24	25	26	27	28
	29	30	*1*	2	3	4	5
RABĪ' II 1583	6	7	8	9	10	11	12
	13	14	15	16	17	18	19
	20	21	22	23	24	25	26
	27	28	29	30	1	2	3
JUMĀDĀ I 1583	4	5	6	7	8	9	10
	11	12	13	14	15	16	17
	18	19	20	21	22	23	24
	25	26	27	28	29	*30*	1
JUMĀDĀ II 1583	2	3	4	5	6	7	8
	9	10	11	12	13	14	15
	16	17	18	19	20	21	22
	23	24	25	26	27	28	29
	1	2	3	4	5	6	7
RAJAB 1583	8	9	10	11	12	13	14
	15	16	17	18	19	20	21
	22	23	24	25	26	27[d]	28

GREGORIAN 2157

Julian (Sun)	Sun	Mon	Tue	Wed	Thu	Fri	Sat	Month
Dec 12	*26*	27	28	29	30	31	1	
	2	3	4	5	6	7	8[a]	JANUARY 2157
Dec 26	*9*	10	11	12	13	14	15[b]	
	16	17	18	19	20	21	22	
Jan 9	*23*	24	25	26	27	28	29	
	30	31	1	2	3	4	5	
Jan 23	*6*	7	8	9[c]	10	11	12	FEBRUARY 2157
	13	14	15	16	17	18	19	
Feb 6	*20*	21	22	23	24	25	26	
	27	28	1	2	3	4	5	
Feb 20	*6*	7	8	9	10	11	12	MARCH 2157
	13	14	15	16	17	18	19	
Mar 6	*20*[d]	21	22	23	24	25	26	
	27[e]	28	29	30	31	1	2	
Mar 20	*3*	4	5	6	7	8	9	APRIL 2157
	10	11	12	13	14	15	16	
Apr 3	*17*	18	19	20	21	22	23	
	24	25	26	27	28	29	30	
Apr 17	*1*[f]	2	3	4	5	6	7	
	8	9	10	11	12	13	14	MAY 2157
May 1	*15*	16	17	18	19	20	21	
	22	23	24	25	26	27	28	
May 15	*29*	30	31	1	2	3	4	
	5	6	7	8	9	10	11	JUNE 2157
May 29	*12*	13	14	15	16	17	18	
	19	20	21	22	23	24	25	
Jun 12	*26*	27	28	29	30	1	2	
	3	4	5	6	7	8	9	JULY 2157
Jun 26	*10*	11	12	13	14	15	16	
	17	18	19	20	21	22	23	
Jul 10	*24*	25	26	27	28	29	30	
	31	1	2	3	4	5	6	
Jul 24	*7*	8	9	10	11	12	13	AUGUST 2157
	14	15	16	17	18	19	20	
Aug 7	*21*	22	23	24	25	26	27	
	28	29	30	31	1	2	3	
Aug 21	*4*	5	6	7	8	9	10	SEPTEMBER 2157
	11	12	13	14	15	16	17	
Sep 4	*18*	19	20	21	22	23	24	
	25	26	27	28	29	30	1	
Sep 18	*2*	3	4	5	6	7	8	OCTOBER 2157
	9	10	11	12	13	14	15	
Oct 2	*16*	17	18	19	20	21	22	
	23	24	25	26	27	28	29	
Oct 16	*30*	31	1	2	3	4	5	
	6	7	8	9	10	11	12	NOVEMBER 2157
Oct 30	*13*	14	15	16	17	18	19	
	20	21	22	23	24	25	26	
Nov 13	*27*[g]	28	29	30	1	2	3	
	4	5	6	7	8	9	10	DECEMBER 2157
Nov 27	*11*	12	13	14	15	16	17	
	18	19	20	21	22	23	24	
Dec 11	*25*[h]	26	27	28	29	30	31	

Persian: ‡Leap year; [a]New Year (or next day); *Near New Year: 0′11″; [b]Sizdeh Bedar

Hindu Lunar: ‡Leap year; [a]New Year (Piṅgala); [b]Birthday of Rāma; [c]Birthday of Krishna; [d]Ganēśa Chaturthī; [e]Dashara; [f]Diwali; [g]Birthday of Vishnu; [h]Night of Śiva; [i]Holi

Hindu Solar: ‡Leap year; [a]New Year (Aṅgiras); [b]Pongal

Islamic: ‡Leap year; [a]New Year; [d]New Year (Arithmetic); [b]'Āshūrā'; [c]Prophet's Birthday; [d]Ascent of the Prophet; [e]Start of Ramaḍān; [f]'Īd al-Fiṭr; [g]'Īd al-'Aḍḥā

Gregorian: [a]Orthodox Christmas; [b]Julian New Year; [c]Ash Wednesday; [d]Feast of Orthodoxy; [e]Easter; [f]Orthodox Easter; [g]Advent; [h]Christmas

2158

GREGORIAN 2158 / ISO WEEK / JULIAN DAY

Month	Sun	Mon	Tue	Wed	Thu	Fri	Sat	Lunar Phases	ISO Week (Mon)	Julian Day (Sun noon)
	1[a]	2	3	4	5	6	◐	22:16	1	2509254
JANUARY 2158	8	9	10	11	12	13	○	18:11	2	2509261
	15	16	17	18	19	20	21		3	2509268
	◑	23	24	25	26	27	28	12:49	4	2509275
	29	●	31	1	2	3	4	8:51	5	2509282
FEBRUARY 2158	5	◐	7	8	9	10	11	6:00	6	2509289
	12	○	14	15	16	17	18	9:06	7	2509296
	19	20	◑	22	23	24	25	10:10	8	2509303
	26	27	●	1	2	3	4	21:48	9	2509310
MARCH 2158	5	6	◐	8	9	10	11	13:52	10	2509317
	12	13	14	○	16	17	18	1:17	11	2509324
	19	20[b]	21	22	◑	24	25	5:23	12	2509331
	26	27	28	29	●	31	1	8:12	13	2509338
APRIL 2158	2	3	4	◐	6	7	8	22:51	14	2509345
	9	10	11	12	○	14	15	17:55	15	2509352
	16	17	18	19	20	◑	22	21:07	16	2509359
	23	24	25	26	27	●	29	16:35	17	2509366
	30	1	2	3	4	◐	6	9:35	18	2509373
MAY 2158	7	8	9	10	11	12	○	10:13	19	2509380
	14	15	16	17	18	19	20		20	2509387
	◑	22	23	24	25	26	●	8:53 23:57	21	2509394
	28	29	30	31	1	2	◐	22:16	22	2509401
JUNE 2158	4	5	6	7	8	9	10		23	2509408
	11	○	13	14	15	16	17	1:38	24	2509415
	18	◑	20	21[c]	22	23	24	17:03	25	2509422
	25	●	27	28	29	30	1	7:21	26	2509429
JULY 2158	2	◐	4	5	6	7	8	12:52	27	2509436
	9	10	○	12	13	14	15	15:40	28	2509443
	16	17	◑	19	20	21	22	22:43	29	2509450
	23	24	●	26	27	28	29	15:47	30	2509457
	30	31	1	◐	3	4	5	5:14	31	2509464
AUGUST 2158	6	7	8	9	○	11	12	4:01	32	2509471
	13	14	15	16	◑	18	19	3:20	33	2509478
	20	21	22	23	●	25	26	2:02	34	2509485
	27	28	29	30	◐	1	2	23:00	35	2509492
SEPTEMBER 2158	3	4	5	6	7	○	9	14:49	36	2509499
	10	11	12	13	14	◑	16	8:29	37	2509506
	17	18	19	20	21	●[d]	23	14:40	38	2509513
	24	25	26	27	28	29	◐	17:21	39	2509520
OCTOBER 2158	1	2	3	4	5	6	7		40	2509527
	○	9	10	11	12	13	◑	0:35 15:39	41	2509534
	15	16	17	18	19	20	21		42	2509541
	●	23	24	25	26	27	28	6:00	43	2509548
	29	◐	31	1	2	3	4	11:05	44	2509555
NOVEMBER 2158	5	○	7	8	9	10	11	10:07	45	2509562
	12	◑	14	15	16	17	18	1:54	46	2509569
	19	●	21	22	23	24	25	23:53	47	2509576
	26	27	28	◐	30	1	2	2:53	48	2509583
DECEMBER 2158	3	4	○	6	7	8	9	20:10	49	2509590
	10	11	◑	13	14	15	16	15:47	50	2509597
	17	18	19	●	21[e]	22	23	19:19	51	2509604
	24	25	26	27	◐	29	30	15:59	52	2509611
	31	1	2	3	○	5	6	7:08	1	2509618

HEBREW 5918/5919

ISO Week	Month	Sun	Mon	Tue	Wed	Thu	Fri	Sat	Molad
1		1[e]	2[e]	3	4	5	6	7	Sat 13h25m15p
2	TEVETH 5918	8	9	10	11	12	13	14	
3		15	16	17	18	19	20	21	
4		22	23	24	25	26	27	28	
5		29	1	2	3	4	5	6	Mon 2h9m6p
6	SHEVAT 5918	7	8	9	10	11	12	13	
7		14	15	16	17	18	19	20	
8		21	22	23	24	25	26	27	
9		28	29	30	1	2	3	4	Tue 14h53m7p
10	ADAR 5918	5	6	7	8	9	10	11	
11		12	13	14[f]	15	16	17	18	
12		19	20	21	22	23	24	25	
13		26	27	28	29	1	2	3	Thu 3h37m8p
14	NISAN 5918	4	5	6	7	8	9	10	
15		11	12	13	14	15[g]	16	17	
16		18	19	20	21	22	23	24	
17		25	26	27	28	29	30	1	Fri 16h21m9p
18	IYYAR 5918	2	3	4	5	6	7	8	
19		9	10	11	12	13	14	15	
20		16	17	18	19	20	21	22	
21		23	24	25	26	27	28	29	
22		1	2	3	4	5	6[h]	7	Sun 5h5m10p
23	SIVAN 5918	8	9	10	11	12	13	14	
24		15	16	17	18	19	20	21	
25		22	23	24	25	26	27	28	
26		29	30	1	2	3	4	5	Mon 17h49m11p
27	TAMMUZ 5918	6	7	8	9	10	11	12	
28		13	14	15	16	17	18	19	
29		20	21	22	23	24	25	26	
30		27	28	29	1	2	3	4	Wed 6h33m12p
31	AV 5918	5	6	7	8	9[i]	10	11	
32		12	13	14	15	16	17	18	
33		19	20	21	22	23	24	25	
34		26	27	28	29	30	1	2	Thu 19h17m13p
35	ELUL 5918	3	4	5	6	7	8	9	
36		10	11	12	13	14	15	16	
37		17	18	19	20	21	22	23	
38		24	25	26	27	28	29	1[a]	Sat 8h1m14p
39	TISHRI 5919	2[a]	3	4	5	6	7	8	
40		9	10[b]	11	12	13	14	15[c]	
41		16	17	18	19	20	21	22	
42		23	24	25	26	27	28	29	
43		30	1	2	3	4	5	6	Sun 20h45m15p
44	ḤESHVAN 5919	7	8	9	10	11	12	13	
45		14	15	16	17	18	19	20	
46		21	22	23	24	25	26	27	
47		28	29	30	1	2	3	4	Tue 9h29m16p
48	KISLEV 5919	5	6	7	8	9	10	11	
49		12	13	14	15[d]	16	17	18	
50		19	20	21	22	23	24	25[e]	
51		26[e]	27[e]	28[e]	29[e]	30[e]	1[e]	2[e]	Wed 22h13m17p
52	TEVETH 5919	3	4	5	6	7	8	9	
53		10	11	12	13	14	15	16	

CHINESE Dīng-Sì/Wù-Wǔ‡

ISO Week	Month	Sun	Mon	Tue	Wed	Thu	Fri	Sat	Solar Term
1		1	2	3	4	5	6	7	Xiǎo hán
2	MONTH 12 Dīng-Sì	8	9	10	11	12	13	14	
3		15	16	17	18*	19	**20**	21	Dà hán
4		22	23	24	25	26	27	28	
5		29	1[a]	2	3	4	5	6	Lì chūn
6	MONTH 1 Wù-Wǔ	7	8	9	10	11	12	13	
7		14	15[b]	16	17	18	19	20	
8		**21**	22	23	24	25	26	27	Yǔ shuǐ
9		28	29	30	1	2	3	4	
10		5	6	7	8	9	10	11	Jīng zhé
11	MONTH 2 Wù-Wǔ	12	13	14	15	16	17	18	
12		19*	**20**	21	22	23	24	25	Chūn fēn
13		26	27	28	29	1	2	3	
14		4	5	6	7[c]	8	9	10	Qīng míng
15	MONTH 3 Wù-Wǔ	11	12	13	14	15	16	17	
16		18	19	20	21	**22**	23	24	Gǔ yǔ
17		25	26	27	28	29	30	1	
18		2	3	4	5	6	*7*	8	Lì xià
19	MONTH 4 Wù-Wǔ	9	10	11	12	13	14	15	
20		16	17	18	19	20*	21	22	
21		**23**	24	25	26	27	28	29	Xiǎo mǎn
22		1	2	3	4	5[d]	6	7	
23	MONTH 5 Wù-Wǔ	8	9	10	11	12	13	14	Máng zhòng
24		15	16	17	18	19	20	21	
25		22	23	24	**25**	26	27	28	Xià zhì
26		29	1	2	3	4	5	6	
27	MONTH 6 Wù-Wǔ	7	8	9	10	11	*12*	13	Xiǎo shǔ
28		14	15	16	17	18	19	20	
29		21	22*	23	24	25	26	27	
30		**28**	29	1	2	3	4	5	Dà shǔ
31	MONTH 7 Wù-Wǔ	6	7[e]	8	9	10	11	12	
32		13	*14*	15[f]	16	17	18	19	Lì qiū
33		20	21	22	23	24	25	26	
34		27	28	29	**30**	1	2	3	Chǔ shǔ
35	LEAP MONTH 7 Wù-Wǔ	4	5	6	7	8	9	10	
36		11	12	13	14	*15*	16	17	Bái lù
37		18	19	20	21	22*	23*	24	
38		25	26	27	28	29	1	**2**	Qiū fēn
39		3	4	5	6	7	8	9	
40	MONTH 8 Wù-Wǔ	10	11	12	13	14	15[g]	16	
41		*17*	18	19	20	21	22	23	Hán lù
42		24	25	26	27	28	29	30	
43		1	**2**	3	4	5	6	7	Shuāng jiàng
44	MONTH 9 Wù-Wǔ	8	9[h]	10	11	12	13	14	
45		15	16	*17*	18	19	20	21	Lì dōng
46		22	23	24*	25	26	27	28	
47		29	30	1	**2**	3	4	5	Xiǎo xuě
48	MONTH 10 Wù-Wǔ	6	7	8	9	10	11	12	
49		13	14	15	16	*17*	18	19	Dà xuě
50		20	21	22	23	24	25	26	
51		27	28	29	30	1	**2**[i]	3	Dōng zhì
52	MONTH 11* Wù-Wǔ	4	5	6	7	8	9	10	
53		11	12	13	14	15	*16*	17	Xiǎo hán

COPTIC 1874/1875‡ / ETHIOPIC 2150/2151‡

ISO Week	Coptic Month	Sun	Mon	Tue	Wed	Thu	Fri	Sat	Ethiopic Month
1	KOIAK 1874	22	23	24	25	26	27	28	TĀKHŚĀŚ 2150
2		29[c]	30	1	2	3	4	5	
3	TŌBE 1874	6[d]	7	8	9	10	11[e]	12	ṬER 2150
4		13	14	15	16	17	18	19	
5		20	21	22	23	24	25	26	
6		27	28	29	30	1	2	3	
7	MESHIR 1874	4	5	6	7	8	9	10	YAKĀTIT 2150
8		11	12	13	14	15	16	17	
9		18	19	20	21	22	23	24	
10		25	26	27	28	29	30	1	
11	PAREMOTEP 1874	2	3	4	5	6	7	8	MAGĀBIT 2150
12		9	10	11	12	13	14	15	
13		16	17	18	19	20	21	22	
14		23	24	25	26	27	28	29	
15		30	1	2	3	4	5	6	
16	PARMOUTE 1874	7	8	9	10	11	12	13	MIYĀZYĀ 2150
17		14[f]	15	16	17	18	19	20	
18		21	22	23	24	25	26	27	
19		28	29[g]	30	1	2	3	4	
20	PASHONS 1874	5	6	7	8	9	10	11	GENBOT 2150
21		12	13	14	15	16	17	18	
22		19	20	21	22	23	24	25	
23		26	27	28	29	30	1	2	
24	PAŌNE 1874	3	4	5	6	7	8	9	SANĒ 2150
25		10	11	12	13	14	15	16	
26		17	18	19	20	21	22	23	
27		24	25	26	27	28	29	30	
28		1	2	3	4	5	6	7	
29	EPĒP 1874	8	9	10	11	12	13	14	ḤAMLĒ 2150
30		15	16	17	18	19	20	21	
31		22	23	24	25	26	27	28	
32		29	30	1	2	3	4	5	
33	MESORĒ 1874	6	7	8	9	10	11	12	NAḤASĒ 2150
34		13[h]	14	15	16	17	18	19	
35		20	21	22	23	24	25	26	
36		27	28	29	30	1	2	3	
37	EPAG. 1874	4	5	1[a]	2	3	4	5	PĀG. 2150
38	THOOUT 1875	6	7	8	9	10	11	12	MASKARAM 2151
39		13	14	15	16	17[b]	18	19	
40		20	21	22	23	24	25	26	
41		27	28	29	30	1	2	3	
42	PAOPE 1875	4	5	6	7	8	9	10	ṬEQEMT 2151
43		11	12	13	14	15	16	17	
44		18	19	20	21	22	23	24	
45		25	26	27	28	29	30	1	
46	ATHŌR 1875	2	3	4	5	6	7	8	ḪEDĀR 2151
47		9	10	11	12	13	14	15	
48		16	17	18	19	20	21	22	
49		23	24	25	26	27	28	29	
50		30	1	2	3	4	5	6	
51	KOIAK 1875	7	8	9	10	11	12	13	TĀKHŚĀŚ 2151
52		14	15	16	17	18	19	20	
53		21	22	23	24	25	26	27	

[a]New Year
[b]Spring (14:24)
[c]Summer (5:44)
[d]Autumn (22:42)
[e]Winter (21:41)
● New moon
◐ First quarter moon
○ Full moon
◑ Last quarter moon

[a]New Year
[b]Yom Kippur
[c]Sukkot
[d]Winter starts
[e]Ḥanukkah
[f]Purim
[g]Passover
[h]Shavuot
[i]Fast of Av

‡Leap year
[a]New Year (4856, Horse)
[b]Lantern Festival
[c]Qīngmíng
[d]Dragon Festival
[e]Qīqiǎo
[f]Hungry Ghosts
[g]Mid-Autumn Festival
[h]Double-Ninth Festival
[i]Dōngzhì
*Start of 60-name cycle

‡Leap year
[a]New Year
[b]Building of the Cross
[c]Christmas
[d]Jesus's Circumcision
[e]Epiphany
[f]Easter
[g]Mary's Announcement
[h]Jesus's Transfiguration

PERSIAN (ASTRONOMICAL) 1536‡/1537

Month	Sun	Mon	Tue	Wed	Thu	Fri	Sat
DEY 1536	12	13	14	15	16	17	18
	19	20	21	22	23	24	25
	26	27	28	29	30	1	2
BAHMAN 1536	3	4	5	6	7	8	9
	10	11	12	13	14	15	16
	17	18	19	20	21	22	23
	24	25	26	27	28	29	30
ESFAND 1536	1	2	3	4	5	6	7
	8	9	10	11	12	13	14
	15	16	17	18	19	20	21
	22	23	24	25	26	27	28
	29	30	1[a]	2	3	4	5
FARVARDĪN 1537	6	7	8	9	10	11	12
	13[b]	14	15	16	17	18	19
	20	21	22	23	24	25	26
	27	28	29	30	31	1	2
ORDĪBEHEŠT 1537	3	4	5	6	7	8	9
	10	11	12	13	14	15	16
	17	18	19	20	21	22	23
	24	25	26	27	28	29	30
	31	1	2	3	4	5	6
XORDĀD 1537	7	8	9	10	11	12	13
	14	15	16	17	18	19	20
	21	22	23	24	25	26	27
	28	29	30	31	1	2	3
TĪR 1537	4	5	6	7	8	9	10
	11	12	13	14	15	16	17
	18	19	20	21	22	23	24
	25	26	27	28	29	30	31
MORDĀD 1537	1	2	3	4	5	6	7
	8	9	10	11	12	13	14
	15	16	17	18	19	20	21
	22	23	24	25	26	27	28
	29	30	31	1	2	3	4
SHAHRĪVAR 1537	5	6	7	8	9	10	11
	12	13	14	15	16	17	18
	19	20	21	22	23	24	25
	26	27	28	29	30	31	1
MEHR 1537	2	3	4	5	6	7	8
	9	10	11	12	13	14	15
	16	17	18	19	20	21	22
	23	24	25	26	27	28	29
	30	1	2	3	4	5	6
ĀBĀN 1537	7	8	9	10	11	12	13
	14	15	16	17	18	19	20
	21	22	23	24	25	26	27
	28	29	30	1	2	3	4
ĀZAR 1537	5	6	7	8	9	10	11
	12	13	14	15	16	17	18
	19	20	21	22	23	24	25
	26	27	28	29	30	1	2
DEY 1537	3	4	5	6	7	8	9
	10	11	12	13	14	15	16

‡Leap year
[a]New Year
[b]Sizdeh Bedar

HINDU LUNAR 2214/2215

Month	Sun	Mon	Tue	Wed	Thu	Fri	Sat
PAUSHA 2214	1	2	3	4	5	6	7
	8	9	**10**	12	13	14	15
	16	17	18	19	20	21	22
	23	24	24	25	26	27	28
MĀGHA 2214	29	30	1	2	3	4	**5**
	7	8	9	10	11	12	13
	14	15	16	17	18	19	20
	21	22	23	24	25	26	27
PHĀLGUNA 2214	28	29[h]	30	1	2	3	4
	5	6	7	8	9	**10**	12
	13	14	15[i]	16	16	17	18
	19	20	21	22	23	24	25
CHAITRA 2215	26	27	28	29	30	1[a]	2
	3	5	6	7	8	9[b]	10
	11	12	13	14	15	16	17
	18	19	20	20	21	22	23
VAIŚĀKHA 2215	24	25	**26**	28	29	30	1
	2	3	4	5	6	7	8
	9	10	11	12	13	14	15
	16	17	18	19	20	21	22
	23	24	25	26	27	28	29
JYAISHṬHA 2215	**30**	2	3	4	5	6	7
	8	9	10	11	12	13	14
	15	15	16	17	18	19	20
	21	**22**	24	25	26	27	28
ĀSHĀḌHA 2215	29	30	1	2	3	4	5
	6	7	8	9	10	11	12
	13	14	15	16	17	18	19
	20	21	22	23	24	**25**	27
ŚRĀVAṆA 2215	28	29	30	1	2	3	4
	5	6	7	8	9	10	11
	12	12	13	14	15	16	17
	18	20	21	22	23[c]	24	25
BHĀDRAPADA 2215	26	27	28	29	30	1	2
	3[d]	4	5	6	7	8	9
	10	11	12	13	14	15	16
	17	18	19	20	**21**	23	24
ĀŚVINA 2215	25	26	27	28	29	30	1
	2	3	4	5	6	7	8
	8[e]	9[e]	10[e]	11	12	13	**14**
	16	17	18	19	20	21	22
	23	24	25	26	27	28	29
KĀRTTIKA 2215	30	1[f]	2	3	4	5	6
	7	8	9	10	11	12	13
	14	15	16	17	18	**19**	21
	22	23	24	25	26	27	28
MĀRGAŚĪRA 2215	29	30	1	2	2	3	4
	5	6	7	8	9	10	11[g]
	12	**13**	15	16	17	18	19
	20	21	22	23	24	25	26
PAUSHA 2215	27	28	29	30	1	2	3
	4	5	6	7	8	9	10
	11	12	13	14	15	16	17

[a]New Year (Kālayukta)
[b]Birthday of Rāma
[c]Birthday of Krishna
[d]Ganēśa Chaturthī
[e]Dashara
[f]Diwali
[g]Birthday of Vishnu
[h]Night of Śiva
[i]Holi

HINDU SOLAR 2079/2080

Month	Sun	Mon	Tue	Wed	Thu	Fri	Sat
PAUSHA 2079	15	16	17	18	19	20	21
	22	23	24	25	26	27	28
MĀGHA 2079	29	1[b]	2	3	4	5	6
	7	8	9	10	11	12	13
	14	15	16	17	18	19	20
	21	22	23	24	25	26	27
PHĀLGUNA 2079	28	29	30	1	2	3	4
	5	6	7	8	9	10	11
	12	13	14	15	16	17	18
	19	20	21	22	23	24	25
CHAITRA 2079	26	27	28	29	1	2	3
	4	5	6	7	8	9	10
	11	12	13	14	15	16	17
	18	19	20	21	22	23	24
	25	26	27	28	29	30	31
VAIŚĀKHA 2080	1[a]	2	3	4	5	6	7
	8	9	10	11	12	13	14
	15	16	17	18	19	20	21
	22	23	24	25	26	27	28
JYAISHṬHA 2080	29	30	31	1	2	3	4
	5	6	7	8	9	10	11
	12	13	14	15	16	17	18
	19	20	21	22	23	24	25
ĀSHĀḌHA 2080	26	27	28	29	30	31	1
	2	3	4	5	6	7	8
	9	10	11	12	13	14	15
	16	17	18	19	20	21	22
	23	24	25	26	27	28	29
ŚRĀVAṆA 2080	30	31	32	1	2	3	4
	5	6	7	8	9	10	11
	12	13	14	15	16	17	18
	19	20	21	22	23	24	25
BHĀDRAPADA 2080	26	27	28	29	30	31	1
	2	3	4	5	6	7	8
	9	10	11	12	13	14	15
	16	17	18	19	20	21	22
	23	24	25	26	27	28	29
ĀŚVINA 2080	30	31	1	2	3	4	5
	6	7	8	9	10	11	12
	13	14	15	16	17	18	19
	20	21	22	23	24	25	26
KĀRTTIKA 2080	27	28	29	30	31	1	2
	3	4	5	6	7	8	9
	10	11	12	13	14	15	16
	17	18	19	20	21	22	23
	24	25	26	27	28	29	30
MĀRGAŚĪRA 2080	1	2	3	4	5	6	7
	8	9	10	11	12	13	14
	15	16	17	18	19	20	21
	22	23	24	25	26	27	28
PAUSHA 2080	29	1	2	3	4	5	6
	7	8	9	10	11	12	13
	14	15	16	17	18	19	20

[a]New Year (Śrīmukha)
[b]Pongal

ISLAMIC (ASTRONOMICAL) 1583‡/1584‡

Month	Sun	Mon	Tue	Wed	Thu	Fri	Sat
SHA'BĀN 1583	29	1	2	3	4	5	6
	7	8	9	10	11	12	13
	14	15	16	17	18	19	20
	21	22	23	24	25	26	27
RAMAḌĀN 1583	28	29	30	1[e]	2	3	4
	5	6	7	8	9	10	11
	12	13	14	15	16	17	18
	19	20	21	22	23	24	25
SHAWWĀL 1583	26	27	28	29	1[f]	2	3
	4	5	6	7	8	9	10
	11	12	13	14	15	16	17
	18	19	20	21	22	23	24
DHU AL-QA'DA 1583	25	26	27	28	29	1	2
	3	4	5	6	7	8	9
	10	11	12	13	14	15	16
	17	18	19	20	21	22	23
	24	25	26	27	28	29	30
DHU AL-ḤIJJA 1583	1	2	3	4	5	6	7
	8	9	10[g]	11	12	13	14
	15	16	17	18	19	20	21
	22	23	24	25	26	27	28
MUḤARRAM 1584	29	1[a]	2	3	4	5	6
	7	8	9	10[b]	11	12	13
	14	15	16	17	18	19	20
	21	22	23	24	25	26	27
ṢAFAR 1584	28	29	1	2	3	4	5
	6	7	8	9	10	11	12
	13	14	15	16	17	18	19
	20	21	22	23	24	25	26
RABĪ' I 1584	27	28	29	30	1	2	3
	4	5	6	7	8	9	10
	11	12[c]	13	14	15	16	17
	18	19	20	21	22	23	24
RABĪ' II 1584	25	26	27	28	29	30	1
	2	3	4	5	6	7	8
	9	10	11	12	13	14	15
	16	17	18	19	20	21	22
	23	24	25	26	27	28	29
JUMĀDĀ I 1584	30	1	2	3	4	5	6
	7	8	9	10	11	12	13
	14	15	16	17	18	19	20
	21	22	23	24	25	26	27
JUMĀDĀ II 1584	28	29	30	1	2	3	4
	5	6	7	8	9	10	11
	12	13	14	15	16	17	18
	19	20	21	22	23	24	25
RAJAB 1584	26	27	28	29	1	2	3
	4	5	6	7	8	9	10
	11	12	13	14	15	16	17
	18	19	20	21	22	23	24
SHA'BĀN 1584	25	26	27[d]	28	29	1	2
	3	4	5	6	7	8	9
	10	11	12	13	14	15	16

‡Leap year
[a]New Year
[b]'Ashūrā'
[c]Prophet's Birthday
[d]Ascent of the Prophet
[e]Start of Ramaḍān
[f]'Id al-Fiṭr
[g]'Id al-'Aḍḥā

GREGORIAN 2158

Julian (Sun)	Sun	Mon	Tue	Wed	Thu	Fri	Sat	Month
Dec 18	1	2	3	4	5	6	7	JANUARY 2158
	8[a]	9	10	11	12	13	14	
Jan 1	15[b]	16	17	18	19	20	21	
	22	23	24	25	26	27	28	
Jan 15	29	30	31	1	2	3	4	FEBRUARY 2158
	5	6	7	8	9	10	11	
Jan 29	12	13	14	15	16	17	18	
	19	20	21	22	23	24	25	
Feb 12	26	27	28	1[c]	2	3	4	MARCH 2158
	5	6	7	8	9	10	11	
Feb 26	12[d]	13	14	15	16	17	18	
	19	20	21	22	23	24	25	
Mar 12	26	27	28	29	30	31	1	APRIL 2158
	2	3	4	5	6	7	8	
Mar 26	9	10	11	12	13	14	15	
	16[e]	17	18	19	20	21	22	
Apr 9	23[f]	24	25	26	27	28	29	
	30	1	2	3	4	5	6	MAY 2158
Apr 23	7	8	9	10	11	12	13	
	14	15	16	17	18	19	20	
May 7	21	22	23	24	25	26	27	
	28	29	30	31	1	2	3	JUNE 2158
May 21	4	5	6	7	8	9	10	
	11	12	13	14	15	16	17	
Jun 4	18	19	20	21	22	23	24	
	25	26	27	28	29	30	1	JULY 2158
Jun 18	2	3	4	5	6	7	8	
	9	10	11	12	13	14	15	
Jul 2	16	17	18	19	20	21	22	
	23	24	25	26	27	28	29	
Jul 16	30	31	1	2	3	4	5	AUGUST 2158
	6	7	8	9	10	11	12	
Jul 30	13	14	15	16	17	18	19	
	20	21	22	23	24	25	26	
Aug 13	27	28	29	30	31	1	2	SEPTEMBER 2158
	3	4	5	6	7	8	9	
Aug 27	10	11	12	13	14	15	16	
	17	18	19	20	21	22	23	
Sep 10	24	25	26	27	28	29	30	
	1	2	3	4	5	6	7	OCTOBER 2158
Sep 24	8	9	10	11	12	13	14	
	15	16	17	18	19	20	21	
Oct 8	22	23	24	25	26	27	28	
	29	30	31	1	2	3	4	NOVEMBER 2158
Oct 22	5	6	7	8	9	10	11	
	12	13	14	15	16	17	18	
Nov 5	19	20	21	22	23	24	25	
	26	27	28	29	30	1	2	DECEMBER 2158
Nov 19	3[g]	4	5	6	7	8	9	
	10	11	12	13	14	15	16	
Dec 3	17	18	19	20	21	22	23	
	24	25[h]	26	27	28	29	30	
Dec 17	31	1	2	3	4	5	6	

[a]Orthodox Christmas
[b]Julian New Year
[c]Ash Wednesday
[d]Feast of Orthodoxy
[e]Easter
[f]Orthodox Easter
[g]Advent
[h]Christmas

2159

Gregorian month	GREGORIAN 2159 (Sun Mon Tue Wed Thu Fri Sat)	Lunar Phases	ISO WEEK (Mon)	JULIAN DAY (Sun noon)	Hebrew month	HEBREW 5919/5920‡ (Sun Mon Tue Wed Thu Fri Sat)	Molad	Chinese month	CHINESE Wù-Wǔ‡/Jǐ-Wèi (Sun Mon Tue Wed Thu Fri Sat)	Solar Term	Coptic month	COPTIC 1875‡/1876 (Sun Mon Tue Wed Thu Fri Sat)	ETHIOPIC 2151‡/2152
January 2159	31 1[a] 2 3 ○ 5 6	7:08	1	2509618	Teveth 5919	10 11 12 13 14 15 16		Month 11* Wù-Wǔ	11 12 13 14 15 16 17	Xiǎo hán	Koiak 1875	21 22 23 24 25 26 27	Tākhśāś 2151
	7 8 9 10 ◑ 12 13	9:08	2	2509625		17 18 19 20 21 22 23			18 19 20 21 22 23 24*		Tōbe 1875	28 29[c] 30 1 2 3 4	Ṭer 2151
	14 15 16 17 18 ● 20	14:29	3	2509632	Shevat 5919	24 25 26 27 28 29 1	Fri 10h58m9p	Month 12 Wù-Wǔ	25 26 27 28 29 1 2	Dà hán		5 6[d] 7 8 9 10 11[e]	
	21 22 23 24 25 26 ◐	2:20	4	2509639		2 3 4 5 6 7 8			3 4 5 6 7 8 9			12 13 14 15 16 17 18	
February 2159	28 29 30 31 1 ○ 3	18:59	5	2509646		9 10 11 12 13 14 15			10 11 12 13 14 15 16			19 20 21 22 23 24 25	
	4 5 6 7 8 9 ◑	5:06	6	2509653		16 17 18 19 20 21 22			17 18 19 20 21 22 23	Lì chūn	Meshir 1875	26 27 28 29 30 1 2	Yakātit 2151
	11 12 13 14 15 16 17		7	2509660		23 24 25 26 27 28 29			24 25 26 27 28 29 30			3 4 5 6 7 8 9	
	● 19 20 21 22 23 24	7:30	8	2509667	Adar 5919	30 1 2 3 4 5 6	Sat 23h42m1p	Month 1 Jǐ-Wèi	1[a] 2 3 4 5 6 7	Yǔ shuǐ		10 11 12 13 14 15 16	
March 2159	◐ 26 27 28 1 2 3	10:34	9	2509674		7 8 9 10 11 12 13			8 9 10 11 12 13 14			17 18 19 20 21 22 23	
	○ 5 6 7 8 9 10	7:34	10	2509681		14[f] 15 16 17 18 19 20			15[b] 16 17 18 19 20 21	Jīng zhé		24 25 26 27 28 29 30	
	11 ◑ 13 14 15 16 17	2:07	11	2509688		21 22 23 24 25 26 27			22 23 24 25* 26 27 28		Paremotep 1875	1 2 3 4 5 6 7	Magābit 2151
	18 ● 20[b] 21 22 23 24	21:23	12	2509695	Nisan 5919	28 29 1 2 3 4 5	Mon 12h26m2p	Month 2 Jǐ-Wèi	29 30 1 2 3 4 5	Chūn fēn		8 9 10 11 12 13 14	
	25 ◐ 27 28 29 30 31	17:39	13	2509702		6 7 8 9 10 11 12			6 7 8 9 10 11 12			15 16 17 18 19 20 21	
April 2159	1 ○ 3 4 5 6 7	20:54	14	2509709		13 14 15[g] 16 17 18 19			13 14 15 16 17[c] 18 19	Qīng míng		22 23 24 25 26 27 28	
	8 9 ◑ 11 12 13 14	22:10	15	2509716		20 21 22 23 24 25 26			20 21 22 23 24 25 26		Parmoute 1875	29[f] 30 1 2 3 4 5	Miyāzyā 2151
	15 16 17 ● 19 20 21	8:17	16	2509723	Iyyar 5919	27 28 29 30 1 2 3	Wed 1h10m3p	Month 3 Jǐ-Wèi	27 28 29 1 2 3 4	Gǔ yǔ		6 7 8 9 10 11 12	
	22 23 24 ◐ 26 27 28	0:33	17	2509730		4 5 6 7 8 9 10			5 6 7 8 9 10 11			13 14 15 16 17 18 19	
May 2159	29 30 1 ○ 3 4 5	11:09	18	2509737		11 12 13 14 15 16 17			12 13 14 15 16 17 18	Lì xià		20 21 22 23 24 25 26	
	6 7 8 9 ◑ 11 12	15:32	19	2509744		18 19 20 21 22 23 24			19 20 21 22 23 24 25		Pashons 1875	27 28 29[g] 30 1 2 3	Genbot 2151
	13 14 15 16 ● 18 19	16:58	20	2509751	Sivan 5919	25 26 27 28 29 1 2	Thu 13h54m4p	Month 4 Jǐ-Wèi	26* 27 28 29 30 1 2			4 5 6 7 8 9 10	
	20 21 22 23 ◐ 25 26	8:11	21	2509758		3 4 5 6[h] 7 8 9			3 4 5 6 7 8 9	Xiǎo mǎn		11 12 13 14 15 16 17	
June 2159	27 28 29 30 31 ○ 2	2:17	22	2509765		10 11 12 13 14 15 16			10 11 12 13 14 15 16			18 19 20 21 22 23 24	
	3 4 5 6 7 8 ◑	5:21	23	2509772		17 18 19 20 21 22 23			17 18 19 20 21 22 23	Máng zhòng	Paōne 1875	25 26 27 28 29 30 1	Sanē 2151
	10 11 12 13 14 15 ●	0:23	24	2509779		24 25 26 27 28 29 30		Month 5 Jǐ-Wèi	24 25 26 27 28 29 1			2 3 4 5 6 7 8	
	17 18 19 20 21[c] ◐ 23	17:26	25	2509786	Tammuz 5919	1 2 3 4 5 6 7	Sat 2h38m5p		2 3 4 5[d] 6 7 8	Xià zhì		9 10 11 12 13 14 15	
	24 25 26 27 28 29 ○	17:52	26	2509793		8 9 10 11 12 13 14			9 10 11 12 13 14 15			16 17 18 19 20 21 22	
July 2159	1 2 3 4 5 6 7		27	2509800		15 16 17 18 19 20 21			16 17 18 19 20 21 22	Xiǎo shǔ		23 24 25 26 27 28 29	
	◑ 9 10 11 12 13 14	15:48	28	2509807		22 23 24 25 26 27 28			23 24 25 26 27* 28 29		Epēp 1875	30 1 2 3 4 5 6	Hamlē 2151
	● 16 17 18 19 20 21	7:26	29	2509814	Av 5919	29 1 2 3 4 5 6	Sun 15h22m6p	Month 6 Jǐ-Wèi	1 2 3 4 5 6 7			7 8 9 10 11 12 13	
	◐ 23 24 25 26 27 28	5:08	30	2509821		7 8 9[i] 10 11 12 13			8 9 10 11 12 13 14	Dà shǔ		14 15 16 17 18 19 20	
August 2159	29 ○ 31 1 2 3 4	9:06	31	2509828		14 15 16 17 18 19 20			15 16 17 18 19 20 21			21 22 23 24 25 26 27	
	5 ◑ 7 8 9 10 11	23:41	32	2509835		21 22 23 24 25 26 27			22 23 24 25 26 27 28	Lì qiū	Mesorē 1875	28 29 30 1 2 3 4	Naḥasē 2151
	12 ● 14 15 16 17 18	14:55	33	2509842	Elul 5919	28 29 30 1 2 3 4	Tue 4h6m7p	Month 7 Jǐ-Wèi	29 1 2 3 4 5 6			5 6 7 8 9 10 11	
	19 ◐ 21 22 23 24 25	19:49	34	2509849		5 6 7 8 9 10 11			7[e] 8 9 10 11 12 13	Chǔ shǔ		12 13[h] 14 15 16 17 18	
September 2159	26 27 ○ 29 30 31 1	23:16	35	2509856		12 13 14 15 16 17 18			14 15[f] 16 17 18 19 20			19 20 21 22 23 24 25	
	2 3 4 ◑ 6 7 8	6:05	36	2509863		19 20 21 22 23 24 25			21 22 23 24 25 26 27	Bái lù	Epag. 1875	26 27 28 29 30 1 2	Pāg. 2151
	9 10 ● 12 13 14 15	23:46	37	2509870	Tishri 5920	26 27 28 29 1[a] 2[a] 3	Wed 16h50m8p	Month 8 Jǐ-Wèi	28 29* 30 1 2 3 4		Thoout 1876	3 4 5 6 1[a] 2 3	Maskaram 2152
	16 17 18 ◐ 20 21 22	13:28	38	2509877		4 5 6 7 8 9 10[b]			5 6 7 8 9 10 11			4 5 6 7 8 9 10	
	23[d] 24 25 26 ○ 28 29	12:11	39	2509884		11 12 13 14 15[c] 16 17			12 13 14 15[g] 16 17 18	Qiū fēn		11 12 13 14 15 16 17[b]	
October 2159	30 1 2 3 ◑ 5 6	12:07	40	2509891		18 19 20 21 22 23 24			19 20 21 22 23 24 25			18 19 20 21 22 23 24	
	7 8 9 10 ● 12 13	10:54	41	2509898	Heshvan 5920	25 26 27 28 29 30 1	Fri 5h34m9p	Month 9 Jǐ-Wèi	26 27 28 29 1 2 3	Hán lù	Paope 1876	25 26 27 28 29 30 1	Ṭeqemt 2152
	14 15 16 17 18 ◐ 20	9:09	42	2509905		2 3 4 5 6 7 8			4 5 6 7 8 9[h] 10			2 3 4 5 6 7 8	
	21 22 23 24 25 26 ○	0:10	43	2509912		9 10 11 12 13 14 15			11 12 13 14 15 16 17	Shuāng jiàng		9 10 11 12 13 14 15	
November 2159	28 29 30 31 1 ◑ 3	18:53	44	2509919		16 17 18 19 20 21 22			18 19 20 21 22 23 24			16 17 18 19 20 21 22	
	4 5 6 7 8 9 ●	1:09	45	2509926		23 24 25 26 27 28 29		Month 10 Jǐ-Wèi	25 26 27 28 29 30* 1	Lì dōng		23 24 25 26 27 28 29	
	11 12 13 14 15 16 17		46	2509933	Kislev 5920	30 1 2 3 4 5 6	Sat 18h18m10p		2 3 4 5 6 7 8		Athōr 1876	30 1 2 3 4 5 6	Hedār 2152
	◐ 19 20 21 22 23 24	5:14	47	2509940		7 8 9 10 11 12 13			9 10 11 12 13 14 15	Xiǎo xuě		7 8 9 10 11 12 13	
December 2159	○ 26 27 28 29 30 1	11:40	48	2509947		14 15 16 17 18 19 20			16 17 18 19 20 21 22			14 15 16 17 18 19 20	
	◑ 3 4 5 6 7 8	3:27	49	2509954		21 22 23 24 25[e] 26[d] 27[e]			23 24 25 26 27 28 29	Dà xuě		21 22 23 24 25 26 27	
	● 10 11 12 13 14 15	18:36	50	2509961	Teveth 5920	28[e] 29[e] 30[e] 1[e] 2[e] 3 4	Mon 7h2m11p	Month 11 Jǐ-Wèi	30 1 2 3 4 5 6		Koiak 1876	28 29 30 1 2 3 4	Tākhśāś 2152
	16 ◐ 18 19 20 21 22[e]	23:59	51	2509968		5 6 7 8 9 10 11			7 8 9 10 11 12 13[i]	Dōng zhì		5 6 7 8 9 10 11	
	23 ○ 25 26 27 28 29	22:55	52	2509975		12 13 14 15 16 17 18			14 15 16 17 18 19 20			12 13 14 15 16 17 18	
	30 ◑ 1 2 3 4 5	14:43	1	2509982		19 20 21 22 23 24 25			21 22 23 24 25 26 27			19 20 21 22 23 24 25	

[a]New Year
[b]Spring (20:09)
[c]Summer (11:29)
[d]Autumn (4:32)
[e]Winter (3:24)
● New moon
◐ First quarter moon
○ Full moon
◑ Last quarter moon

‡Leap year
[a]New Year
[b]Yom Kippur
[c]Sukkot
[d]Winter starts
[e]Hanukkah
[f]Purim
[g]Passover
[h]Shavuot
[i]Fast of Av

‡Leap year
[a]New Year (4857, Sheep)
[b]Lantern Festival
[c]Qīngmíng
[d]Dragon Festival
[e]Qīqiǎo
[f]Hungry Ghosts
[g]Mid-Autumn Festival
[h]Double-Ninth Festival
[i]Dōngzhì
*Start of 60-name cycle

‡Leap year
[a]New Year
[b]Building of the Cross
[c]Christmas
[d]Jesus's Circumcision
[e]Epiphany
[f]Easter
[g]Mary's Announcement
[h]Jesus's Transfiguration

PERSIAN (ASTRONOMICAL) 1537/1538

Month	Sun	Mon	Tue	Wed	Thu	Fri	Sat
DEY 1537	10	11	12	13	14	15	16
	17	18	19	20	21	22	23
	24	25	26	27	28	29	30
BAHMAN 1537	1	2	3	4	5	6	7
	8	9	10	11	12	13	14
	15	16	17	18	19	20	21
	22	23	24	25	26	27	28
ESFAND 1537	29	30	1	2	3	4	5
	6	7	8	9	10	11	12
	13	14	15	16	17	18	19
	20	21	22	23	24	25	26
FARVARDĪN 1538	27	28	29	1[a]	2	3	4
	5	6	7	8	9	10	11
	12	13[b]	14	15	16	17	18
	19	20	21	22	23	24	25
ORDĪBEHEŠT 1538	26	27	28	29	30	31	1
	2	3	4	5	6	7	8
	9	10	11	12	13	14	15
	16	17	18	19	20	21	22
	23	24	25	26	27	28	29
XORDĀD 1538	30	31	1	2	3	4	5
	6	7	8	9	10	11	12
	13	14	15	16	17	18	19
	20	21	22	23	24	25	26
TĪR 1538	27	28	29	30	31	1	2
	3	4	5	6	7	8	9
	10	11	12	13	14	15	16
	17	18	19	20	21	22	23
	24	25	26	27	28	29	30
MORDĀD 1538	31	1	2	3	4	5	6
	7	8	9	10	11	12	13
	14	15	16	17	18	19	20
	21	22	23	24	25	26	27
SHAHRĪVAR 1538	28	29	30	31	1	2	3
	4	5	6	7	8	9	10
	11	12	13	14	15	16	17
	18	19	20	21	22	23	24
	25	26	27	28	29	30	31
MEHR 1538	1	2	3	4	5	6	7
	8	9	10	11	12	13	14
	15	16	17	18	19	20	21
	22	23	24	25	26	27	28
ĀBĀN 1538	29	30	1	2	3	4	5
	6	7	8	9	10	11	12
	13	14	15	16	17	18	19
	20	21	22	23	24	25	26
ĀZAR 1538	27	28	29	30	1	2	3
	4	5	6	7	8	9	10
	11	12	13	14	15	16	17
	18	19	20	21	22	23	24
DEY 1538	25	26	27	28	29	30	1
	2	3	4	5	6	7	8
	9	10	11	12	13	14	15

HINDU LUNAR 2215/2216‡

Month	Sun	Mon	Tue	Wed	Thu	Fri	Sat
PAUSHA 2215	11	12	13	14	15	16	17
	18	20	21	22	23	24	*24*
MĀGHA 2215	25	26	27	28	29	30	1
	2	3	4	5	6	7	8
	9	10	**11**	13	14	15	16
	17	18	19	20	21	22	23
	24	25	26	*26*	27	28[h]	29
PHĀLGUNA 2215	30	1	2	3	4	**5**	7
	8	9	10	11	12	13	14
	15[i]	16	17	18	19	20	21
	22	23	24	25	26	27	28
CHAITRA 2216	29	30	1[a]	2	3	4	5
	6	7	8[b]	9	**10**	12	13
	14	15	16	17	18	19	20
	20	21	22	23	24	25	26
VAIŚĀKHA 2216	27	28	29	30	1	2	3
	4	6	7	8	9	10	11
	12	13	14	15	16	17	18
	19	20	21	22	23	24	25
LEAP JYAISHṬHA 2216	26	27	28	29	30	1	2
	3	4	5	6	**7**	9	10
	11	12	13	14	15	*15*	16
	17	18	19	20	21	22	23
	24	25	26	27	28	29	**30**
JYAISHṬHA 2216	2	3	4	5	6	7	8
	9	10	11	12	13	14	15
	16	17	18	19	20	21	22
	23	24	25	26	27	28	29
ĀSHĀḌHA 2216	30	1	2	**3**	5	6	7
	8	9	10	11	12	*12*	13
	14	15	16	17	18	19	20
	21	22	23	24	**25**	27	28
ŚRĀVAṆA 2216	29	30	1	2	3	4	5
	6	7	8	9	10	11	12
	13	14	15	16	17	18	19
	20	21	22	23[c]	24	25	26
BHĀDRAPADA 2216	27	28	**29**	1	2	3	4[d]
	5	6	7	8	*8*	9	10
	11	12	13	14	15	16	17
	18	19	20	21	**22**	24	25
ĀŚVINA 2216	26	27	28	29	30	1	2
	3	4	5	6	7	8[e]	9[e]
	10[e]	11	12	*12*	13	**14**	16
	17	18	19	20	21	22	23
KĀRTTIKA 2216	24	25	26	**27**	29	30	1[f]
	2	*2*	3	4	5	6	7
	8	9	10	11	12	13	14
	15	16	17	18	19	**20**	22
	23	24	25	26	27	28	29
MĀRGAŚĪRA 2216	30	1	2	3	4	5	*5*
	6	7	8	9	10	11[g]	12
	13	**14**	16	17	18	19	20
	21	22	23	24	25	26	27

HINDU SOLAR 2080/2081

Month	Sun	Mon	Tue	Wed	Thu	Fri	Sat
PAUSHA 2080	14	15	16	17	18	19	20
	21	22	23	24	25	26	27
MĀGHA 2080	28	29	1[b]	2	3	4	5
	6	7	8	9	10	11	12
	13	14	15	16	17	18	19
	20	21	22	23	24	25	26
PHĀLGUNA 2080	27	28	29	30	1	2	3
	4	5	6	7	8	9	10
	11	12	13	14	15	16	17
	18	19	20	21	22	23	24
CHAITRA 2080	25	26	27	28	29	30	1
	2	3	4	5	6	7	8
	9	10	11	12	13	14	15
	16	17	18	19	20	21	22
	23	24	25	26	27	28	29
VAIŚĀKHA 2081	30	1[a]	2	3	4	5	6
	7	8	9	10	11	12	13
	14	15	16	17	18	19	20
	21	22	23	24	25	26	27
JYAISHṬHA 2081	28	29	30	31	1	2	3
	4	5	6	7	8	9	10
	11	12	13	14	15	16	17
	18	19	20	21	22	23	24
	25	26	27	28	29	30	31
ĀSHĀḌHA 2081	32	1	2	3	4	5	6
	7	8	9	10	11	12	13
	14	15	16	17	18	19	20
	21	22	23	24	25	26	27
ŚRĀVAṆA 2081	28	29	30	31	1	2	3
	4	5	6	7	8	9	10
	11	12	13	14	15	16	17
	18	19	20	21	22	23	24
	25	26	27	28	29	30	31
BHĀDRAPADA 2081	32	1	2	3	4	5	6
	7	8	9	10	11	12	13
	14	15	16	17	18	19	20
	21	22	23	24	25	26	27
ĀŚVINA 2081	28	29	30	31	1	2	3
	4	5	6	7	8	9	10
	11	12	13	14	15	16	17
	18	19	20	21	22	23	24
KĀRTTIKA 2081	25	26	27	28	29	30	1
	2	3	4	5	6	7	8
	9	10	11	12	13	14	15
	16	17	18	19	20	21	22
	23	24	25	26	27	28	29
MĀRGAŚĪRA 2081	30	1	2	3	4	5	6
	7	8	9	10	11	12	13
	14	15	16	17	18	19	20
	21	22	23	24	25	26	27
PAUSHA 2081	28	29	1	2	3	4	5
	6	7	8	9	10	11	12
	13	14	15	16	17	18	19

ISLAMIC (ASTRONOMICAL) 1584‡/1585

Month	Sun	Mon	Tue	Wed	Thu	Fri	Sat
SHA'BĀN 1584	10	11	12	13	14	15	16
	17	18	19	20	21	22	23
	24	25	26	27	28	29	30
RAMAḌĀN 1584	1[e]	2	3	4	5	6	7
	8	9	10	11	12	13	14
	15	16	17	18	19	20	21
	22	23	24	25	26	27	28
SHAWWĀL 1584	29	30	1[f]	2	3	4	5
	6	7	8	9	10	11	12
	13	14	15	16	17	18	19
	20	21	22	23	24	25	26
DHU AL-QA'DA 1584	27	28	29	1	2	3	4
	5	6	7	8	9	10	11
	12	13	14	15	16	17	18
	19	20	21	22	23	24	25
DHU AL-ḤIJJA 1584	26	27	28	29	1	2	3
	4	5	6	7	8	9	10[g]
	11	12	13	14	15	16	17
	18	19	20	21	22	23	24
MUḤARRAM 1585	25	26	27	28	29	30	1[a]
	2	3	4	5	6	7	8
	9	10[b]	11	12	13	14	15
	16	17	18	19	20	21	22
	23	24	25	26	27	28	29
ṢAFAR 1585	1	2	3	4	5	6	7
	8	9	10	11	12	13	14
	15	16	17	18	19	20	21
	22	23	24	25	26	27	28
RABĪ' I 1585	29	30	1	2	3	4	5
	6	7	8	9	10	11	12[c]
	13	14	15	16	17	18	19
	20	21	22	23	24	25	26
RABĪ' II 1585	27	28	29	30	1	2	3
	4	5	6	7	8	9	10
	11	12	13	14	15	16	17
	18	19	20	21	22	23	24
JUMĀDĀ I 1585	25	26	27	28	29	1	2
	3	4	5	6	7	8	9
	10	11	12	13	14	15	16
	17	18	19	20	21	22	23
	24	25	26	27	28	29	30
JUMĀDĀ II 1585	1	2	3	4	5	6	7
	8	9	10	11	12	13	14
	15	16	17	18	19	20	21
	22	23	24	25	26	27	28
RAJAB 1585	29	1	2	3	4	5	6
	7	8	9	10	11	12	13
	14	15	16	17	18	19	20
	21	22	23	24	25	26	27[d]
SHA'BĀN 1585	28	29	1	2	3	4	5
	6	7	8	9	10	11	12
	13	14	15	16	17	18	19
	20	21	22	23	24	25	26

GREGORIAN 2159

Julian (Sun)	Sun	Mon	Tue	Wed	Thu	Fri	Sat	Month
Dec 17	31	1	2	3	4	5	6	JANUARY 2159
	7	8[a]	9	10	11	12	13	
Dec 31	14	15[b]	16	17	18	19	20	
	21	22	23	24	25	26	27	
Jan 14	28	29	30	31	1	2	3	FEBRUARY 2159
	4	5	6	7	8	9	10	
Jan 28	11	12	13	14	15	16	17	
	18	19	20	21[c]	22	23	24	
Feb 11	25[d]	26	27	28	1	2	3	MARCH 2159
	4	5	6	7	8	9	10	
Feb 25	11	12	13	14	15	16	17	
	18	19	20	21	22	23	24	
Mar 11	25	26	27	28	29	30	31	
	1	2	3	4	5	6	7	APRIL 2159
Mar 25	8[e]	9	10	11	12	13	14	
	15	16	17	18	19	20	21	
Apr 8	22	23	24	25	26	27	28	
	29	30	1	2	3	4	5	MAY 2159
Apr 22	6	7	8	9	10	11	12	
	13	14	15	16	17	18	19	
May 6	20	21	22	23	24	25	26	
	27	28	29	30	31	1	2	JUNE 2159
May 20	3	4	5	6	7	8	9	
	10	11	12	13	14	15	16	
Jun 3	17	18	19	20	21	22	23	
	24	25	26	27	28	29	30	
Jun 17	1	2	3	4	5	6	7	JULY 2159
	8	9	10	11	12	13	14	
Jul 1	15	16	17	18	19	20	21	
	22	23	24	25	26	27	28	
Jul 15	29	30	31	1	2	3	4	AUGUST 2159
	5	6	7	8	9	10	11	
Jul 29	12	13	14	15	16	17	18	
	19	20	21	22	23	24	25	
Aug 12	26	27	28	29	30	31	1	SEPTEMBER 2159
	2	3	4	5	6	7	8	
Aug 26	9	10	11	12	13	14	15	
	16	17	18	19	20	21	22	
Sep 9	23	24	25	26	27	28	29	
	30	1	2	3	4	5	6	OCTOBER 2159
Sep 23	7	8	9	10	11	12	13	
	14	15	16	17	18	19	20	
Oct 7	21	22	23	24	25	26	27	
	28	29	30	31	1	2	3	NOVEMBER 2159
Oct 21	4	5	6	7	8	9	10	
	11	12	13	14	15	16	17	
Nov 4	18	19	20	21	22	23	24	
	25	26	27	28	29	30	1	DECEMBER 2159
Nov 18	2[g]	3	4	5	6	7	8	
	9	10	11	12	13	14	15	
Dec 2	16	17	18	19	20	21	22	
	23	24	25[h]	26	27	28	29	
Dec 16	30	31	1	2	3	4	5	

Persian: [a]New Year; [b]Sizdeh Bedar

Hindu lunar: ‡Leap year; [a]New Year (Siddhārthin); [b]Birthday of Rāma; [c]Birthday of Krishna; [d]Ganēśa Chaturthī; [e]Dashara; [f]Diwali; [g]Birthday of Vishnu; [h]Night of Śiva; [i]Holi

Hindu solar: [a]New Year (Bhāva); [b]Pongal

Islamic: ‡Leap year; [a]New Year; [b]'Ashūrā'; [c]Prophet's Birthday; [d]Ascent of the Prophet; [e]Start of Ramaḍān; [f]'Id al-Fiṭr; [g]'Id al-'Aḍḥā

Gregorian: [a]Orthodox Christmas; [b]Julian New Year; [c]Ash Wednesday; [d]Feast of Orthodoxy; [e]Easter (also Orthodox); [g]Advent; [h]Christmas

2160

GREGORIAN 2160‡ · ISO WEEK · JULIAN DAY

Month	Sun	Mon	Tue	Wed	Thu	Fri	Sat	Lunar Phases	ISO Week (Mon)	Julian Day (Sun noon)
JANUARY 2160	30	◑	1[a]	2	3	4	5	14:43	1	2509982
	6	7	●	9	10	11	12	14:11	2	2509989
	13	14	15	◐	17	18	19	16:05	3	2509996
	20	21	22	○	24	25	26	9:52	4	2510003
	27	28	29	◑	31	1	2	5:12	5	2510010
FEBRUARY 2160	3	4	5	6	●	8	9	9:51	6	2510017
	10	11	12	13	14	◐	16	4:58	7	2510024
	17	18	19	20	○	22	23	20:26	8	2510031
	24	25	26	27	◑	29	1	22:38	9	2510038
MARCH 2160	2	3	4	5	6	7	●	3:42	10	2510045
	9	10	11	12	13	14	◐	14:39	11	2510052
	16	17	18	19	20[b]	21	○	6:53	12	2510059
	23	24	25	26	27	28	◑	17:50	13	2510066
	30	31	1	2	3	4	5		14	2510073
APRIL 2160	●	7	8	9	10	11	12	18:46	15	2510080
	◐	14	15	16	17	18	19	21:42	16	2510087
	○	21	22	23	24	25	26	17:46	17	2510094
	27	◑	29	30	1	2	3	13:09	18	2510101
MAY 2160	4	5	●	7	8	9	10	6:58	19	2510108
	11	12	◐	14	15	16	17	3:12	20	2510115
	18	19	○	21	22	23	24	5:46	21	2510122
	25	26	27	◑	29	30	31	7:05	22	2510129
JUNE 2160	1	2	3	●	5	6	7	16:45	23	2510136
	8	9	10	◐	12	13	14	8:30	24	2510143
	15	16	17	○	19	20[c]	21	19:11	25	2510150
	22	23	24	25	◑	27	28	22:48	26	2510157
JULY 2160	29	30	1	2	3	●	5	0:46	27	2510164
	6	7	8	9	◐	11	12	15:03	28	2510171
	13	14	15	16	17	○	19	9:50	29	2510178
	20	21	22	23	24	25	◑	12:07	30	2510185
	27	28	29	30	31	1	●	7:48	31	2510192
AUGUST 2160	3	4	5	6	7	8	◐	0:11	32	2510199
	10	11	12	13	14	15	16		33	2510206
	○	18	19	20	21	22	23	1:13	34	2510213
	◑	25	26	27	28	29	30	23:11	35	2510220
SEPTEMBER 2160	●	1	2	3	4	5	6	14:51	36	2510227
	◐	8	9	10	11	12	13	12:50	37	2510234
	14	○	16	17	18	19	20	16:49	38	2510241
	21	22[d]	◑	24	25	26	27	8:17	39	2510248
	28	●	30	1	2	3	4	23:03	40	2510255
OCTOBER 2160	5	6	◐	8	9	10	11	5:12	41	2510262
	12	13	14	○	16	17	18	8:14	42	2510269
	19	20	21	◑	23	24	25	15:59	43	2510276
	26	27	28	●	30	31	1	9:27	44	2510283
NOVEMBER 2160	2	3	4	5	◐	7	8	0:39	45	2510290
	9	10	11	12	○	14	15	23:04	46	2510297
	16	17	18	19	◑	21	22	23:08	47	2510304
	23	24	25	26	●	28	29	22:45	48	2510311
DECEMBER 2160	30	1	2	3	4	◐	6	21:47	49	2510318
	7	8	9	10	11	12	○	12:53	50	2510325
	14	15	16	17	18	19	◑	6:49	51	2510332
	21[e]	22	23	24	25	26	●	14:55	52	2510339
	28	29	30	31	1	2	3		1	2510346

HEBREW 5920‡/5921

ISO Week	Month	Sun	Mon	Tue	Wed	Thu	Fri	Sat	Molad
1	TEVETH 5920	19	20	21	22	23	24	25	
2		26	27	28	29	1	2	3	Tue 19h 46m 12p
3	SHEVAT 5920	4	5	6	7	8	9	10	
4		11	12	13	14	15	16	17	
5		18	19	20	21	22	23	24	
6		25	26	27	28	29	30	1	Thu 8h 30m 13p
7	ADAR I 5920	2	3	4	5	6	7	8	
8		9	10	11	12	13	14	15	
9		16	17	18	19	20	21	22	
10		23	24	25	26	27	28	29	
11		30	1	2	3	4	5	6	Fri 21h 14m 14p
12	ADAR II 5920	7	8	9	10	11	12	13	
13		14[f]	15	16	17	18	19	20	
14		21	22	23	24	25	26	27	
15		28	29	1	2	3	4	5	Sun 9h 58m 15p
16	NISAN 5920	6	7	8	9	10	11	12	
17		13	14	15[g]	16	17	18	19	
18		20	21	22	23	24	25	26	
19		27	28	29	30	1	2	3	Mon 22h 42m 16p
20	IYAR 5920	4	5	6	7	8	9	10	
21		11	12	13	14	15	16	17	
22		18	19	20	21	22	23	24	
23		25	26	27	28	29	1	2	Wed 11h 26m 17p
24	SIVAN 5920	3	4	5	6[h]	7	8	9	
25		10	11	12	13	14	15	16	
26		17	18	19	20	21	22	23	
27		24	25	26	27	28	29	30	
28	TAMMUZ 5920	1	2	3	4	5	6	7	Fri 0h 11m 0p
29		8	9	10	11	12	13	14	
30		15	16	17	18	19	20	21	
31		22	23	24	25	26	27	28	
32		29	1	2	3	4	5	6	Sat 12h 55m 1p
33	AV 5920	7	8	9[i]	10	11	12	13	
34		14	15	16	17	18	19	20	
35		21	22	23	24	25	26	27	
36		28	29	30	1	2	3	4	Mon 1h 39m 2p
37	ELUL 5920	5	6	7	8	9	10	11	
38		12	13	14	15	16	17	18	
39		19	20	21	22	23	24	25	
40		26	27	28	29	1[a]	2[a]	3	Tue 14h 23m 3p
41	TISHRI 5921	4	5	6	7	8	9	10[b]	
42		11	12	13	14	15[c]	16	17	
43		18	19	20	21	22	23	24	
44		25	26	27	28	29	30	1	Thu 3h 7m 4p
45	HESHVAN 5921	2	3	4	5	6	7	8	
46		9	10	11	12	13	14	15	
47		16	17	18	19	20	21	22	
48		23	24	25	26	27	28	29	
49		1	2	3	4	5	6	7[d]	Fri 15h 51m 5p
50	KISLEV 5921	8	9	10	11	12	13	14	
51		15	16	17	18	19	20	21	
52		22	23	24	25[e]	26[e]	27[e]	28[e]	Sun 4h 35m 6p
1		29[e]	30[e]	1[e]	2[e]	3	4	5	

CHINESE Jǐ-Wèi/Gēng-Shēn

ISO Week	Month	Sun	Mon	Tue	Wed	Thu	Fri	Sat	Solar Term
1	MONTH 11 Jǐ-Wèi	21	22	23	24	25	26	27	
2	MONTH 12 Jǐ-Wèi	*28*	29	1*	2	3	4	5	*Xiǎo hán*
3		6	7	8	9	10	11	12	
4		***13***	14	15	16	17	18	19	***Dà hán***
5		20	21	22	23	24	25	26	
6		27	*28*	29	30	1[a]	2	3	*Lì chūn*
7	MONTH 1 Gēng-Shēn	4	5	6	7	8	9	10	
8		11	12	***13***	14	15[b]	16	17	***Yǔ shuǐ***
9		18	19	20	21	22	23	24	
10		25	26	27	*28*	29	30	1*	*Jīng zhé*
11	MONTH 2 Gēng-Shēn	2	3	4	5	6	7	8	
12		9	10	11	12	***13***	14	15	***Chūn fēn***
13		16	17	18	19	20	21	22	
14		23	24	25	26	27	*28*[c]	29	*Qīng míng*
15		30	1	2	3	4	5	6	
16	MONTH 3 Gēng-Shēn	7	8	9	10	11	12	***13***	***Gǔ yǔ***
17		14	15	16	17	18	19	20	
18		21	22	23	24	25	26	27	
19		28	*29*	1	2*	3	4	5	*Lì xià*
20	MONTH 4 Gēng-Shēn	6	7	8	9	10	11	12	
21		13	14	***15***	16	17	18	19	***Xiǎo mǎn***
22		20	21	22	23	24	25	26	
23		27	28	29	30	*1*	2	3	*Máng zhòng*
24	MONTH 5 Gēng-Shēn	4	5[d]	6	7	8	9	10	
25		11	12	13	14	15	16	***17***	***Xià zhì***
26		18	19	20	21	22	23	24	
27		25	26	27	28	29	1	2	
28	MONTH 6 Gēng-Shēn	*3**	4	5	6	7	8	9	*Xiǎo shǔ*
29		10	11	12	13	14	15	16	
30		17	18	***19***	20	21	22	23	***Dà shǔ***
31		24	25	26	27	28	29	1	
32	MONTH 7 Gēng-Shēn	2	3	4	5	*6*	7[e]	8	*Lì qiū*
33		9	10	11	12	13	14	15[f]	
34		16	17	18	19	20	***21***	22	***Chǔ shǔ***
35		23	24	25	26	27	28	29	
36	MONTH 8 Gēng-Shēn	1	2	3	4	5*	6	7	
37		*8*	9	10	11	12	13	14	*Bái lù*
38		15[g]	16	17	18	19	20	21	
39		22	***23***	24	25	26	27	28	***Qiū fēn***
40		29	30	1	2	3	4	5	
41	MONTH 9 Gēng-Shēn	6	7	8	9[h]	10	11	12	*Hán lù*
42		13	14	15	16	17	18	19	
43		20	21	22	23	***24***	25	26	***Shuāng jiàng***
44		27	28	29	1	2	3	4	
45	MONTH 10 Gēng-Shēn	5	6*	7	8	9	*10*	11	*Lì dōng*
46		12	13	14	15	16	17	18	
47		19	20	21	22	23	24	***25***	***Xiǎo xuě***
48		26	27	28	29	30	1	2	
49	MONTH 11 Gēng-Shēn	3	4	5	6	7	8	*9*	*Dà xuě*
50		10	11	12	13	14	15	16	
51		17	18	19	20	21	22	23	
52		***24***[i]	25	26	27	28	29	1	***Dōng zhì***
1	MONTH 12 Gēng-Shēn	2	3	4	5	6	7	8	

COPTIC 1876/1877 · ETHIOPIC 2152/2153

ISO Week	Coptic Month	Sun	Mon	Tue	Wed	Thu	Fri	Sat	Ethiopic Month
1	KOIAK 1876	19	20	21	22	23	24	25	TĀKHŚĀŚ 2152
2		26	27	28	29[c]	30	1	2	
3	TŌBE 1876	3	4	5	6[d]	7	8	9	ṬER 2152
4		10	11[e]	12	13	14	15	16	
5		17	18	19	20	21	22	23	
6		24	25	26	27	28	29	30	
7	MESHIR 1876	1	2	3	4	5	6	7	YAKĀTIT 2152
8		8	9	10	11	12	13	14	
9		15	16	17	18	19	20	21	
10		22	23	24	25	26	27	28	
11		29	30	1	2	3	4	5	
12	PAREMOTEP 1876	6	7	8	9	10	11	12	MAGĀBIT 2152
13		13	14	15	16	17	18	19	
14		20	21	22	23	24	25	26	
15		27	28	29	30	1	2	3	
16	PARMOUTE 1876	4	5	6	7	8	9	10	MIYĀZYĀ 2152
17		11	12	13	14	15	16	17	
18		18[f]	19	20	21	22	23	24	
19		25	26	27	28	29[g]	30	1	
20	PASHONS 1876	2	3	4	5	6	7	8	GENBOT 2152
21		9	10	11	12	13	14	15	
22		16	17	18	19	20	21	22	
23		23	24	25	26	27	28	29	
24		30	1	2	3	4	5	6	
25	PAŌNE 1876	7	8	9	10	11	12	13	SANÉ 2152
26		14	15	16	17	18	19	20	
27		21	22	23	24	25	26	27	
28		28	29	30	1	2	3	4	
29	EPĒP 1876	5	6	7	8	9	10	11	ḤAMLĒ 2152
30		12	13	14	15	16	17	18	
31		19	20	21	22	23	24	25	
32		26	27	28	29	30	1	2	
33	MESORĒ 1876	3	4	5	6	7	8	9	NAHASĒ 2152
34		10	11	12	13[h]	14	15	16	
35		17	18	19	20	21	22	23	
36		24	25	26	27	28	29	30	
37	EPAG. 1876	1	2	3	4	5	1[a]	2	PĀG. 2152
38	THOOUT 1877	3	4	5	6	7	8	9	MASKARAM 2153
39		10	11	12	13	14	15	16	
40		17[b]	18	19	20	21	22	23	
41		24	25	26	27	28	29	30	
42	PAOPE 1877	1	2	3	4	5	6	7	ṬEQEMT 2153
43		8	9	10	11	12	13	14	
44		15	16	17	18	19	20	21	
45		22	23	24	25	26	27	28	
46		29	30	1	2	3	4	5	
47	ATHŌR 1877	6	7	8	9	10	11	12	HEDĀR 2153
48		13	14	15	16	17	18	19	
49		20	21	22	23	24	25	26	
50		27	28	29	30	1	2	3	
51	KOIAK 1877	4	5	6	7	8	9	10	TĀKHŚĀŚ 2153
52		11	12	13	14	15	16	17	
1		18	19	20	21	22	23	24	

‡Leap year
[a]New Year
[b]Spring (1:56)
[c]Summer (17:23)
[d]Autumn (10:27)
[e]Winter (9:19)
● New moon
◐ First quarter moon
○ Full moon
◑ Last quarter moon

‡Leap year
[a]New Year
[b]Yom Kippur
[c]Sukkot
[d]Winter starts
[e]Hanukkah
[f]Purim
[g]Passover
[h]Shavuot
[i]Fast of Av

[a]New Year (4858, Monkey)
[b]Lantern Festival
[c]Qīngmíng
[d]Dragon Festival
[e]Qīqiǎo
[f]Hungry Ghosts
[g]Mid-Autumn Festival
[h]Double-Ninth Festival
[i]Dōngzhì
*Start of 60-name cycle

[a]New Year
[b]Building of the Cross
[c]Christmas
[d]Jesus's Circumcision
[e]Epiphany
[f]Easter
[g]Mary's Announcement
[h]Jesus's Transfiguration

PERSIAN (ASTRONOMICAL) 1538/1539

Month	Sun	Mon	Tue	Wed	Thu	Fri	Sat
DEY 1538	9	10	11	12	13	14	15
	16	17	18	19	20	21	22
	23	24	25	26	27	28	29
BAHMAN 1538	30	*1*	2	3	4	5	6
	7	8	9	10	11	12	13
	14	15	16	17	18	19	20
	21	22	23	24	25	26	27
ESFAND 1538	28	29	30	*1*	2	3	4
	5	6	7	8	9	10	11
	12	13	14	15	16	17	18
	19	20	21	22	23	24	25
FARVARDĪN 1539	26	27	28	29	*1*[a]	2	3
	4	5	6	7	8	9	10
	11	12	13[b]	14	15	16	17
	18	19	20	21	22	23	24
	25	26	27	28	29	30	31
ORDĪBEHEŠT 1539	*1*	2	3	4	5	6	7
	8	9	10	11	12	13	14
	15	16	17	18	19	20	21
	22	23	24	25	26	27	28
XORDĀD 1539	29	30	31	*1*	2	3	4
	5	6	7	8	9	10	11
	12	13	14	15	16	17	18
	19	20	21	22	23	24	25
TĪR 1539	26	27	28	29	30	31	*1*
	2	3	4	5	6	7	8
	9	10	11	12	13	14	15
	16	17	18	19	20	21	22
	23	24	25	26	27	28	29
MORDĀD 1539	30	31	*1*	2	3	4	5
	6	7	8	9	10	11	12
	13	14	15	16	17	18	19
	20	21	22	23	24	25	26
SHAHRĪVAR 1539	27	28	29	30	31	*1*	2
	3	4	5	6	7	8	9
	10	11	12	13	14	15	16
	17	18	19	20	21	22	23
	24	25	26	27	28	29	30
MEHR 1539	31	*1*	2	3	4	5	6
	7	8	9	10	11	12	13
	14	15	16	17	18	19	20
	21	22	23	24	25	26	27
ĀBĀN 1539	28	29	30	*1*	2	3	4
	5	6	7	8	9	10	11
	12	13	14	15	16	17	18
	19	20	21	22	23	24	25
ĀZAR 1539	26	27	28	29	30	*1*	2
	3	4	5	6	7	8	9
	10	11	12	13	14	15	16
	17	18	19	20	21	22	23
	24	25	26	27	28	29	30
DEY 1539	*1*	2	3	4	5	6	7
	8	9	10	11	12	13	14

HINDU LUNAR 2216‡/2217

Month	Sun	Mon	Tue	Wed	Thu	Fri	Sat
MĀRGAŚĪRA 2216	21	22	23	24	25	26	27
PAUSHA 2216	28	29	30	1	2	3	4
	5	6	7	8	9	10	11
	12	13	14	15	16	17	18
	19	21	22	23	24	25	26
MĀGHA 2216	27	*27*	28	29	30	1	2
	3	4	5	6	7	8	9
	10	11	**12**	14	15	16	17
	18	19	20	21	22	23	24
	25	26	27	28	29[h]	*29*	30
PHĀLGUNA 2216	1	2	3	4	5	**6**	8
	9	10	11	12	13	14	15[i]
	16	17	18	19	20	21	22
	23	24	25	26	27	28	29
CHAITRA 2217	30	1[a]	2	3	4	5	6
	7	8	9[b]	10	**11**	13	14
	15	16	17	18	19	20	21
	22	23	*23*	24	25	26	27
VAIŚĀKHA 2217	28	29	30	1	2	3	**4**
	6	7	8	9	10	11	12
	13	14	15	16	17	18	19
	20	21	22	23	24	25	26
JYAISHTHA 2217	27	28	29	30	1	2	3
	4	5	6	**7**	9	10	11
	12	13	14	15	16	17	18
	19	*19*	20	21	22	23	24
ĀSHĀDHA 2217	25	26	27	28	29	**30**	2
	3	4	5	6	7	8	9
	10	11	12	13	14	15	16
	17	18	19	20	21	22	23
	24	25	26	27	28	29	30
ŚRĀVAṆA 2217	1	2	**3**	5	6	7	8
	9	10	11	12	13	14	15
	16	*16*	17	18	19	20	21
	22	23[c]	24	**25**	27	28	29
BHĀDRAPADA 2217	30	1	2	3	4[d]	5	6
	7	8	9	10	11	12	13
	14	15	16	17	18	19	20
	21	22	23	24	25	26	27
ĀŚVINA 2217	28	**29**	1	2	3	4	5
	6	7	8[e]	9[e]	10[e]	11	12
	12	13	14	15	16	17	18
	19	20	21	**22**	24	25	26
KĀRTTIKA 2217	27	28	29	30	1[f]	2	3
	4	5	6	7	8	9	10
	11	12	13	14	15	16	17
	18	19	20	21	22	23	24
MĀRGAŚĪRA 2217	25	26	**27**	29	30	1	2
	3	4	5	*5*	6	7	8
	9	10	11[g]	12	13	14	15
	16	17	18	19	20	**21**	23
	24	25	26	27	28	29	30
	1	2	3	4	5	6	7

HINDU SOLAR 2081/2082‡

Month	Sun	Mon	Tue	Wed	Thu	Fri	Sat
PAUSHA 2081	13	14	15	16	17	18	19
	20	21	22	23	24	25	26
MĀGHA 2081	27	28	29	30	1[b]	2	3
	4	5	6	7	8	9	10
	11	12	13	14	15	16	17
	18	19	20	21	22	23	24
PHĀLGUNA 2081	25	26	27	28	29	1	2
	3	4	5	6	7	8	9
	10	11	12	13	14	15	16
	17	18	19	20	21	22	23
	24	25	26	27	28	29	30
CHAITRA 2081	1	2	3	4	5	6	7
	8	9	10	11	12	13	14
	15	16	17	18	19	20	21
	22	23	24	25	26	27	28
VAIŚĀKHA 2082	29	30	1[a]	2	3	4	5
	6	7	8	9	10	11	12
	13	14	15	16	17	18	19
	20	21	22	23	24	25	26
JYAISHTHA 2082	27	28	29	30	31	1	2
	3	4	5	6	7	8	9
	10	11	12	13	14	15	16
	17	18	19	20	21	22	23
	24	25	26	27	28	29	30
ĀSHĀDHA 2082	31	32	1	2	3	4	5
	6	7	8	9	10	11	12
	13	14	15	16	17	18	19
	20	21	22	23	24	25	26
ŚRĀVAṆA 2082	27	28	29	30	31	1	2
	3	4	5	6	7	8	9
	10	11	12	13	14	15	16
	17	18	19	20	21	22	23
	24	25	26	27	28	29	30
BHĀDRAPADA 2082	31	32	1	2	3	4	5
	6	7	8	9	10	11	12
	13	14	15	16	17	18	19
	20	21	22	23	24	25	26
ĀŚVINA 2082	27	28	29	30	31	1	2
	3	4	5	6	7	8	9
	10	11	12	13	14	15	16
	17	18	19	20	21	22	23
	24	25	26	27	28	29	30
KĀRTTIKA 2082	1	2	3	4	5	6	7
	8	9	10	11	12	13	14
	15	16	17	18	19	20	21
	22	23	24	25	26	27	28
MĀRGAŚĪRA 2082	29	30	1	2	3	4	5
	6	7	8	9	10	11	12
	13	14	15	16	17	18	19
	20	21	22	23	24	25	26
PAUSHA 2082	27	28	29	30	1	2	3
	4	5	6	7	8	9	10
	11	12	13	14	15	16	17

ISLAMIC (ASTRONOMICAL) 1585/1586‡

Month	Sun	Mon	Tue	Wed	Thu	Fri	Sat
SHA'BĀN 1585	20	21	22	23	24	25	26
RAMAḌĀN 1585	27	28	29	30	*1*[e]	2	3
	4	5	6	7	8	9	10
	11	12	13	14	15	16	17
	18	19	20	21	22	23	24
SHAWWĀL 1585	25	26	27	28	29	30	*1*[f]
	2	3	4	5	6	7	8
	9	10	11	12	13	14	15
	16	17	18	19	20	21	22
	23	24	25	26	27	28	29
DHU AL-QA'DA 1585	*1*	2	3	4	5	6	7
	8	9	10	11	12	13	14
	15	16	17	18	19	20	21
	22	23	24	25	26	27	28
DHU AL-ḤIJJA 1585	29	30	*1*	2	3	4	5
	6	7	8	9	10[g]	11	12
	13	14	15	16	17	18	19
	20	21	22	23	24	25	26
MUḤARRAM 1586	27	28	29	*1*[a]	2	3	4
	5	6	7	8	9	10[b]	11
	12	13	14	15	16	17	18
	19	20	21	22	23	24	25
ṢAFAR 1586	26	27	28	29	30	*1*	2
	3	4	5	6	7	8	9
	10	11	12	13	14	15	16
	17	18	19	20	21	22	23
RABĪ' I 1586	24	25	26	27	28	29	*1*
	2	3	4	5	6	7	8
	9	10	11	12[c]	13	14	15
	16	17	18	19	20	21	22
	23	24	25	26	27	28	29
RABĪ' II 1586	30	*1*	2	3	4	5	6
	7	8	9	10	11	12	13
	14	15	16	17	18	19	20
	21	22	23	24	25	26	27
JUMĀDĀ I 1586	28	29	30	*1*	2	3	4
	5	6	7	8	9	10	11
	12	13	14	15	16	17	18
	19	20	21	22	23	24	25
JUMĀDĀ II 1586	26	27	28	29	*1*	2	3
	4	5	6	7	8	9	10
	11	12	13	14	15	16	17
	18	19	20	21	22	23	24
RAJAB 1586	25	26	27	28	29	*1*	2
	3	4	5	6	7	8	9
	10	11	12	13	14	15	16
	17	18	19	20	21	22	23
SHA'BĀN 1586	24	25	26	27[d]	28	29	*1*
	2	3	4	5	6	7	8
	9	10	11	12	13	14	15
	16	17	18	19	20	21	22
	23	24	25	26	27	28	29
	30	*1*[e]	2	3	4	5	6

GREGORIAN 2160‡

Julian† (Sun)	Sun	Mon	Tue	Wed	Thu	Fri	Sat	Month
Dec 16	*30*	31	1	2	3	4	5	JANUARY 2160
	6	7	8[a]	9	10	11	12	
Dec 30	*13*	14	15[b]	16	17	18	19	
	20	21	22	23	24	25	26	
Jan 13	*27*	28	29	30	31	1	2	FEBRUARY 2160
	3	4	5	6[c]	7	8	9	
Jan 27	*10*	11	12	13	14	15	16	
	17	18	19	20	21	22	23	
Feb 10	*24*	25	26	27	28	29	1	MARCH 2160
	2	3	4	5	6	7	8	
Feb 24	*9*	10	11	12	13	14	15	
	16[d]	17	18	19	20	21	22	
Mar 9	*23*[e]	24	25	26	27	28	29	
	30	31	1	2	3	4	5	APRIL 2160
Mar 23	*6*	7	8	9	10	11	12	
	13	14	15	16	17	18	19	
Apr 6	*20*	21	22	23	24	25	26	
	27[f]	28	29	30	1	2	3	MAY 2160
Apr 20	*4*	5	6	7	8	9	10	
	11	12	13	14	15	16	17	
May 4	*18*	19	20	21	22	23	24	
	25	26	27	28	29	30	31	
May 18	*1*	2	3	4	5	6	7	JUNE 2160
	8	9	10	11	12	13	14	
Jun 1	*15*	16	17	18	19	20	21	
	22	23	24	25	26	27	28	
Jun 15	*29*	30	1	2	3	4	5	JULY 2160
	6	7	8	9	10	11	12	
Jun 29	*13*	14	15	16	17	18	19	
	20	21	22	23	24	25	26	
Jul 13	*27*	28	29	30	31	1	2	AUGUST 2160
	3	4	5	6	7	8	9	
Jul 27	*10*	11	12	13	14	15	16	
	17	18	19	20	21	22	23	
Aug 10	*24*	25	26	27	28	29	30	
	31	1	2	3	4	5	6	SEPTEMBER 2160
Aug 24	*7*	8	9	10	11	12	13	
	14	15	16	17	18	19	20	
Sep 7	*21*	22	23	24	25	26	27	
	28	29	30	1	2	3	4	OCTOBER 2160
Sep 21	*5*	6	7	8	9	10	11	
	12	13	14	15	16	17	18	
Oct 5	*19*	20	21	22	23	24	25	
	26	27	28	29	30	31	1	NOVEMBER 2160
Oct 19	*2*	3	4	5	6	7	8	
	9	10	11	12	13	14	15	
Nov 2	*16*	17	18	19	20	21	22	
	23	24	25	26	27	28	29	
Nov 16	*30*[g]	1	2	3	4	5	6	DECEMBER 2160
	7	8	9	10	11	12	13	
Nov 30	*14*	15	16	17	18	19	20	
	21	22	23	24	25[h]	26	27	
Dec 14	*28*	29	30	31	1	2	3	

Persian notes:
[a]New Year
[b]Sizdeh Bedar

Hindu Lunar notes:
‡Leap year
[a]New Year (Raudra)
[b]Birthday of Rāma
[c]Birthday of Krishna
[d]Ganēśa Chaturthī
[e]Dashara
[f]Diwali
[g]Birthday of Vishnu
[h]Night of Śiva
[i]Holi

Hindu Solar notes:
‡Leap year
[a]New Year (Yuvan)
[b]Pongal

Islamic notes:
‡Leap year
[a]New Year
[b]'Ashūrā'
[c]Prophet's Birthday
[d]Ascent of the Prophet
[e]Start of Ramaḍān
[f]'Īd al-Fiṭr
[g]'Īd al-'Aḍḥā

Gregorian notes:
‡Leap year
[a]Orthodox Christmas
[b]Julian New Year
[c]Ash Wednesday
[d]Feast of Orthodoxy
[e]Easter
[f]Orthodox Easter
[g]Advent
[h]Christmas

2161

GREGORIAN 2161	Sun	Mon	Tue	Wed	Thu	Fri	Sat	Lunar Phases	ISO WEEK (Mon)	JULIAN DAY (Sun noon)
JANUARY 2161	28	29	30	31	1[a]	2	3		1	2510346
	◐	5	6	7	8	9	10	18:48	2	2510353
	11	○	13	14	15	16	17	1:18	3	2510360
	◑	19	20	21	22	23	24	16:11	4	2510367
	25	●	27	28	29	30	31	9:04	5	2510374
FEBRUARY 2161	1	2	◐	4	5	6	7	13:49	6	2510381
	8	9	○	11	12	13	14	12:13	7	2510388
	15	16	◑	18	19	20	21	3:58	8	2510395
	22	23	24	●	26	27	28	3:51	9	2510402
MARCH 2161	1	2	3	4	◐	6	7	5:20	10	2510409
	8	9	10	○	12	13	14	21:56	11	2510416
	15	16	17	◑	19	20[b]	21	18:11	12	2510423
	22	23	24	25	●	27	28	21:56	13	2510430
APRIL 2161	29	30	31	1	2	◐	4	16:46	14	2510437
	5	6	7	8	9	○	11	7:04	15	2510444
	12	13	14	15	16	◑	18	10:18	16	2510451
	19	20	21	22	23	24	●	14:13	17	2510458
MAY 2161	26	27	28	29	30	1	2		18	2510465
	◐	4	5	6	7	8	○	0:31 16:18	19	2510472
	10	11	12	13	14	15	16		20	2510479
	◑	18	19	20	21	22	23	3:28	21	2510486
	24	●	26	27	28	29	30	4:00	22	2510493
JUNE 2161	31	◐	2	3	4	5	6	5:48	23	2510500
	7	○	9	10	11	12	13	2:17	24	2510507
	14	◑	16	17	18	19	20[c]	20:58	25	2510514
	21	22	●	24	25	26	27	15:08	26	2510521
JULY 2161	28	29	◐	1	2	3	4	10:11	27	2510528
	5	6	○	8	9	10	11	13:29	28	2510535
	12	13	14	◑	16	17	18	14:05	29	2510542
	19	20	21	22	●	24	25	0:04	30	2510549
AUGUST 2161	26	27	28	◐	30	31	1	15:17	31	2510556
	2	3	4	5	○	7	8	2:22	32	2510563
	9	10	11	12	13	◑	15	6:08	33	2510570
	16	17	18	19	20	●	22	7:45	34	2510577
	23	24	25	26	◐	28	29	22:29	35	2510584
SEPTEMBER 2161	30	31	1	2	3	○	5	17:09	36	2510591
	6	7	8	9	10	11	◑	20:27	37	2510598
	13	14	15	16	17	18	●	15:21	38	2510605
	20	21	22[d]	23	24	25	◐	8:53	39	2510612
OCTOBER 2161	27	28	29	30	1	2	3		40	2510619
	○	5	6	7	8	9	10	9:44	41	2510626
	11	◑	13	14	15	16	17	8:39	42	2510633
	●	19	20	21	22	23	24	23:56	43	2510640
	◐	26	27	28	29	30	31	23:03	44	2510647
NOVEMBER 2161	1	2	○	4	5	6	7	3:24	45	2510654
	8	9	◑	11	12	13	14	18:49	46	2510661
	15	16	●	18	19	20	21	10:14	47	2510668
	22	23	◐	25	26	27	28	17:00	48	2510675
DECEMBER 2161	29	30	1	○	3	4	5	20:50	49	2510682
	6	7	8	9	◑	11	12	3:30	50	2510689
	13	14	15	●	17	18	19	22:30	51	2510696
	20	21[e]	22	23	◐	25	26	13:56	52	2510703
	27	28	29	30	31	○	2	12:41	53	2510710

ISO WEEK	HEBREW 5921/5922	Sun	Mon	Tue	Wed	Thu	Fri	Sat	Molad
1	TEVETH 5921	29[e]	30[e]	1[e]	2[e]	3	4	5	Sun $4^{h}35^{m}6^{p}$
2		6	7	8	9	10	11	12	
3		13	14	15	16	17	18	19	
4		20	21	22	23	24	25	26	
5	SHEVAT 5921	27	28	29	1	2	3	4	Mon $17^{h}19^{m}7^{p}$
6		5	6	7	8	9	10	11	
7		12	13	14	15	16	17	18	
8		19	20	21	22	23	24	25	
9	ADAR 5921	26	27	28	29	30	1	2	Wed $6^{h}3^{m}8^{p}$
10		3	4	5	6	7	8	9	
11		10	11	12	13	14[f]	15	16	
12		17	18	19	20	21	22	23	
13	NISAN 5921	24	25	26	27	28	29	1	Thu $18^{h}47^{m}9^{p}$
14		2	3	4	5	6	7	8	
15		9	10	11	12	13	14	15[g]	
16		16	17	18	19	20	21	22	
17		23	24	25	26	27	28	29	
18	IYYAR 5921	30	1	2	3	4	5	6	Sat $7^{h}31^{m}10^{p}$
19		7	8	9	10	11	12	13	
20		14	15	16	17	18	19	20	
21		21	22	23	24	25	26	27	
22	SIVAN 5921	28	29	1	2	3	4	5	Sun $20^{h}15^{m}11^{p}$
23		6[h]	7	8	9	10	11	12	
24		13	14	15	16	17	18	19	
25		20	21	22	23	24	25	26	
26	TAMMUZ 5921	27	28	29	30	1	2	3	Tue $8^{h}59^{m}12^{p}$
27		4	5	6	7	8	9	10	
28		11	12	13	14	15	16	17	
29		18	19	20	21	22	23	24	
30	AV 5921	25	26	27	28	29	1	2	Wed $21^{h}43^{m}13^{p}$
31		3	4	5	6	7	8	9	
32		10[i]	11	12	13	14	15	16	
33		17	18	19	20	21	22	23	
34		24	25	26	27	28	29	30	Fri $10^{h}27^{m}14^{p}$
35	ELUL 5921	1	2	3	4	5	6	7	
36		8	9	10	11	12	13	14	
37		15	16	17	18	19	20	21	
38		22	23	24	25	26	27	28	
39	TISHRI 5922	29	1[a]	2[a]	3	4	5	6	Sat $23^{h}11^{m}15^{p}$
40		7	8	9	10[b]	11	12	13	
41		14	15[c]	16	17	18	19	20	
42		21	22	23	24	25	26	27	
43	HESHVAN 5922	28	29	30	1	2	3	4	Mon $11^{h}55^{m}16^{p}$
44		5	6	7	8	9	10	11	
45		12	13	14	15	16	17	18	
46		19	20	21	22	23	24	25	
47	KISLEV 5922	26	27	28	29	1	2	3	Wed $0^{h}39^{m}17^{p}$
48		4	5	6	7	8	9	10	
49		11	12	13	14	15	16	17	
50		18[d]	19	20	21	22	23	24	
51	TEVETH 5922	25[e]	26[e]	27[e]	28[e]	29[e]	1[e]	2[e]	Thu $13^{h}24^{m}0^{p}$
52		3[e]	4	5	6	7	8	9	
53		10	11	12	13	14	15	16	

ISO WEEK	CHINESE Gēng-Shēn/Xīn-Yǒu‡	Sun	Mon	Tue	Wed	Thu	Fri	Sat	Solar Term
1	MONTH 12 Gēng-Shēn	2	3	4	5	6	7*	8	
2		9	*10*	11	12	13	14	15	Xiǎo hán
3		16	17	18	19	20	21	22	
4		23	24	**25**	26	27	28	29	**Dà hán**
5	MONTH 1 Xīn-Yǒu	30	1[a]	2	3	4	5	6	
6		7	8	*9*	10	11	12	13	Lì chūn
7		14	15[b]	16	17	18	19	20	
8		21	22	23	**24**	25	26	27	**Yǔ shuǐ**
9	MONTH 2 Xīn-Yǒu	28	29	30	1	2	3	4	
10		5	6	7*	8	*9*	10	11	Jīng zhé
11		12	13	14	15	16	17	18	
12		19	20	21	22	23	**24**	25	**Chūn fēn**
13	MONTH 3 Xīn-Yǒu	26	27	28	29	30	1	2	
14		3	4	5	6	7	8	9[c]	Qīng míng
15		10	11	12	13	14	15	16	
16		17	18	19	20	21	22	23	
17	MONTH 4 Xīn-Yǒu	24	**25**	26	27	28	29	1	**Gǔ yǔ**
18		2	3	4	5	6	7	8*	
19		9	10	*11*	12	13	14	15	Lì xià
20		16	17	18	19	20	21	22	
21		23	24	25	**26**	27	28	29	**Xiǎo mǎn**
22	MONTH 5 Xīn-Yǒu	30	1	2	3	4	5[d]	6	
23		7	8	9	10	11	*12*	13	Máng zhòng
24		14	15	16	17	18	19	20	
25		21	22	23	24	25	26	27	
26	MONTH 6 Xīn-Yǒu	**28**	29	1	2	3	4	5	**Xià zhì**
27		6	7	8	9*	10	11	12	
28		13	14	*15*	16	17	18	19	Xiǎo shǔ
29		20	21	22	23	24	25	26	
30	LEAP MONTH 6 Xīn-Yǒu	27	28	29	**30**	1	2	3	**Dà shǔ**
31		4	5	6	7	8	9	10	
32		11	12	13	14	15	*16*	17	Lì qiū
33		18	19	20	21	22	23	24	
34	MONTH 7 Xīn-Yǒu	25	26	27	28	29	1	2	
35		**3**	4	5	6	7[e]	8	9	**Chǔ shǔ**
36		10*	11	12	13	14	15[f]	16	
37		17	*18*	19	20	21	22	23	Bái lù
38	MONTH 8 Xīn-Yǒu	24	25	26	27	28	29	1	
39		2	3	4	**5**	6	7	8	**Qiū fēn**
40		9	10	11	12	13	14	15[g]	
41		16	17	18	19	*20*	21	22	Hán lù
42		23	24	25	26	27	28	29	
43	MONTH 9 Xīn-Yǒu	30	1	2	3	4	**5**	6	**Shuāng jiàng**
44		7	8	9[h]	10	11*	12	13	
45		14	15	16	17	18	19	*20*	Lì dōng
46		21	22	23	24	25	26	27	
47	MONTH 10 Xīn-Yǒu	28	29	1	2	3	4	5	
48		**6**	7	8	9	10	11	12	**Xiǎo xuě**
49		13	14	15	16	17	18	19	
50		20	*21*	22	23	24	25	26	Dà xuě
51	MONTH 11 Xīn-Yǒu	27	28	29	30	1	2	3	
52		4	**5**[i]	6	7	8	9	10	**Dōng zhì**
53		11	12*	13	14	15	16	17	

ISO WEEK	COPTIC 1877/1878	Sun	Mon	Tue	Wed	Thu	Fri	Sat	ETHIOPIC 2153/2154
1	KOIAK 1877	18	19	20	21	22	23	24	TĀKHŚĀŚ 2153
2	TÔBE 1877	25	26	27	28	29[c]	30	1	ṬER 2153
3		2	3	4	5	6[d]	7	8	
4		9	10	11[e]	12	13	14	15	
5		16	17	18	19	20	21	22	
6		23	24	25	26	27	28	29	
7	MESHIR 1877	30	1	2	3	4	5	6	YAKĀTIT 2153
8		7	8	9	10	11	12	13	
9		14	15	16	17	18	19	20	
10		21	22	23	24	25	26	27	
11	PAREMOTEP 1877	28	29	30	1	2	3	4	MAGĀBIT 2153
12		5	6	7	8	9	10	11	
13		12	13	14	15	16	17	18	
14		19	20	21	22	23	24	25	
15	PARMOUTE 1877	26	27	28	29	30	1	2	MIYĀZYĀ 2153
16		3	4	5	6	7	8	9	
17		10[f]	11	12	13	14	15	16	
18		17	18	19	20	21	22	23	
19		24	25	26	27	28	29[g]	30	
20	PASHONS 1877	1	2	3	4	5	6	7	GENBOT 2153
21		8	9	10	11	12	13	14	
22		15	16	17	18	19	20	21	
23		22	23	24	25	26	27	28	
24	PAÔNE 1877	29	30	1	2	3	4	5	SANÉ 2153
25		6	7	8	9	10	11	12	
26		13	14	15	16	17	18	19	
27		20	21	22	23	24	25	26	
28	EPÊP 1877	27	28	29	30	1	2	3	ḤAMLÉ 2153
29		4	5	6	7	8	9	10	
30		11	12	13	14	15	16	17	
31		18	19	20	21	22	23	24	
32	MESORÊ 1877	25	26	27	28	29	30	1	NAḤASÉ 2153
33		2	3	4	5	6	7	8	
34		9	10	11	12	13[h]	14	15	
35		16	17	18	19	20	21	22	
36		23	24	25	26	27	28	29	
37	EPAG. 1877	30	1	2	3	4	5	1[a]	PĀG. 2153
38	THOOUT 1878	2	3	4	5	6	7	8	MASKARAM 2154
39		9	10	11	12	13	14	15	
40		16	17[b]	18	19	20	21	22	
41		23	24	25	26	27	28	29	
42	PAOPE 1878	30	1	2	3	4	5	6	ṬEQEMT 2154
43		7	8	9	10	11	12	13	
44		14	15	16	17	18	19	20	
45		21	22	23	24	25	26	27	
46	ATHÔR 1878	28	29	30	1	2	3	4	ḪEDĀR 2154
47		5	6	7	8	9	10	11	
48		12	13	14	15	16	17	18	
49		19	20	21	22	23	24	25	
50	KOIAK 1878	26	27	28	29	30	1	2	TĀKHŚĀŚ 2154
51		3	4	5	6	7	8	9	
52		10	11	12	13	14	15	16	
53		17	18	19	20	21	22	23	

[a]New Year
[b]Spring (7:50)
[c]Summer (23:04)
[d]Autumn (16:05)
[e]Winter (15:09)
● New moon
◐ First quarter moon
○ Full moon
◑ Last quarter moon

[a]New Year
[b]Yom Kippur
[c]Sukkot
[d]Winter starts
[e]Ḥanukkah
[f]Purim
[g]Passover
[h]Shavuot
[i]Fast of Av

‡Leap year
[a]New Year (4859, Fowl)
[b]Lantern Festival
[c]Qīngmíng
[d]Dragon Festival
[e]Qīqiǎo
[f]Hungry Ghosts
[g]Mid-Autumn Festival
[h]Double-Ninth Festival
[i]Dōngzhì
*Start of 60-name cycle

[a]New Year
[b]Building of the Cross
[c]Christmas
[d]Jesus's Circumcision
[e]Epiphany
[f]Easter
[g]Mary's Announcement
[h]Jesus's Transfiguration

PERSIAN (ASTRONOMICAL) 1539/1540‡

Month	Sun	Mon	Tue	Wed	Thu	Fri	Sat
DEY 1539	8	9	10	11	12	13	14
	15	16	17	18	19	20	21
	22	23	24	25	26	27	28
	29	30	1	2	3	4	5
BAHMAN 1539	6	7	8	9	10	11	12
	13	14	15	16	17	18	19
	20	21	22	23	24	25	26
	27	28	29	30	1	2	3
ESFAND 1539	4	5	6	7	8	9	10
	11	12	13	14	15	16	17
	18	19	20	21	22	23	24
	25	26	27	28	29	1[a]	2
FARVARDĪN 1540	3	4	5	6	7	8	9
	10	11	12	13[b]	14	15	16
	17	18	19	20	21	22	23
	24	25	26	27	28	29	30
	31	1	2	3	4	5	6
ORDĪBEHEŠT 1540	7	8	9	10	11	12	13
	14	15	16	17	18	19	20
	21	22	23	24	25	26	27
	28	29	30	31	1	2	3
XORDĀD 1540	4	5	6	7	8	9	10
	11	12	13	14	15	16	17
	18	19	20	21	22	23	24
	25	26	27	28	29	30	31
TĪR 1540	1	2	3	4	5	6	7
	8	9	10	11	12	13	14
	15	16	17	18	19	20	21
	22	23	24	25	26	27	28
	29	30	31	1	2	3	4
MORDĀD 1540	5	6	7	8	9	10	11
	12	13	14	15	16	17	18
	19	20	21	22	23	24	25
	26	27	28	29	30	31	1
SHAHRĪVAR 1540	2	3	4	5	6	7	8
	9	10	11	12	13	14	15
	16	17	18	19	20	21	22
	23	24	25	26	27	28	29
	30	31	1	2	3	4	5
MEHR 1540	6	7	8	9	10	11	12
	13	14	15	16	17	18	19
	20	21	22	23	24	25	26
	27	28	29	30	1	2	3
ĀBĀN 1540	4	5	6	7	8	9	10
	11	12	13	14	15	16	17
	18	19	20	21	22	23	24
	25	26	27	28	29	30	1
ĀZAR 1540	2	3	4	5	6	7	8
	9	10	11	12	13	14	15
	16	17	18	19	20	21	22
	23	24	25	26	27	28	29
	30	1	2	3	4	5	6
DEY 1540	7	8	9	10	11	12	13

‡Leap year
[a]New Year
[b]Sizdeh Bedar

HINDU LUNAR 2217/2218‡

Month	Sun	Mon	Tue	Wed	Thu	Fri	Sat
PAUSHA 2217	1	2	3	4	5	6	7
	7	8	9	10	11	12	13
	14	**15**	17	18	19	20	21
	22	23	24	25	26	27	28
MĀGHA 2217	29	30	1	2	3	4	5
	6	7	8	9	10	11	12
	13	14	15	16	17	18	**19**
	21	22	23	24	25	26	27
PHĀLGUNA 2217	28	29[h]	30	30	1	2	3
	4	5	6	7	8	9	10
	11	12	**13**	15[i]	16	17	18
	19	20	21	22	23	24	25
CHAITRA 2218	26	27	28	29	30	1[a]	2
	3	3	4	5	**6**	8	9[b]
	10	11	12	13	14	15	16
	17	18	**19**	21	22	22	23
	24	25	26	27	28	29	30
VAIŚĀKHA 2218	1	2	3	4	5	6	7
	8	9	10	**11**	13	14	15
	16	17	18	19	20	21	22
	23	24	25	26	27	27	28
JYAIṢHTHA 2218	29	30	1	2	3	**4**	6
	7	8	9	10	11	12	13
	14	15	16	17	18	19	20
	21	22	23	24	25	26	27
ĀSHĀḌHA 2218	28	29	30	1	2	3	4
	5	6	**7**	9	10	11	12
	13	14	15	16	17	18	19
	20	21	22	23	24	24	25
ŚRĀVAṆA 2218	26	27	28	**29**	1	2	3
	4	5	6	7	8	9	10
	11	13	14	15	15	16	17
	18	19	20	21	22	23[c]	24
LEAP BHĀDRAPADA 2218	25	26	27	28	29	30	1
	2	**3**	5	6	7	8	9
	10	11	12	13	14	15	16
	17	18	19	20	20	21	22
	23	24	**25**	27	28	29	30
BHĀDRAPADA 2218	1	2	3	4[d]	5	6	7
	8	10	10	11	12	13	14
	15	16	17	18	19	20	21
	22	23	24	25	26	27	28
ĀŚVINA 2218	**29**	1	2	3	4	5	6
	7	8[e]	9[e]	10[e]	11	12	13
	14	15	15	16	17	18	19
	20	21	22	**23**	25	26	27
KĀRTTIKA 2218	28	29	30	1[f]	2	3	4
	5	6	7	8	9	10	11
	12	13	14	15	16	17	18
	19	20	21	22	23	24	25
MĀRGAŚĪRA 2218	26	27	**28**	30	1	2	3
	4	5	6	7	8	8	9
	10	11[g]	12	13	14	15	16

‡Leap year
[a]New Year (Durmati)
[b]Birthday of Rāma
[c]Birthday of Krishna
[d]Ganēśa Chaturthī
[e]Dashara
[f]Diwali
[g]Birthday of Vishnu
[h]Night of Śiva
[i]Holi

HINDU SOLAR 2082‡/2083

Month	Sun	Mon	Tue	Wed	Thu	Fri	Sat
PAUSHA 2082	11	12	13	14	15	16	17
	18	19	20	21	22	23	24
	25	26	27	28	29	1[b]	2
MĀGHA 2082	3	4	5	6	7	8	9
	10	11	12	13	14	15	16
	17	18	19	20	21	22	23
	24	25	26	27	28	29	1
PHĀLGUNA 2082	2	3	4	5	6	7	8
	9	10	11	12	13	14	15
	16	17	18	19	20	21	22
	23	24	25	26	27	28	29
	30	1	2	3	4	5	6
CHAITRA 2082	7	8	9	10	11	12	13
	14	15	16	17	18	19	20
	21	22	23	24	25	26	27
	28	29	30	31	1[a]	2	3
VAIŚĀKHA 2083	4	5	6	7	8	9	10
	11	12	13	14	15	16	17
	18	19	20	21	22	23	24
	25	26	27	28	29	30	31
JYAISHTHA 2083	1	2	3	4	5	6	7
	8	9	10	11	12	13	14
	15	16	17	18	19	20	21
	22	23	24	25	26	27	28
	29	30	31	1	2	3	4
ĀSHĀḌHA 2083	5	6	7	8	9	10	11
	12	13	14	15	16	17	18
	19	20	21	22	23	24	25
	26	27	28	29	30	31	32
ŚRĀVAṆA 2083	1	2	3	4	5	6	7
	8	9	10	11	12	13	14
	15	16	17	18	19	20	21
	22	23	24	25	26	27	28
	29	30	31	1	2	3	4
BHĀDRAPADA 2083	5	6	7	8	9	10	11
	12	13	14	15	16	17	18
	19	20	21	22	23	24	25
	26	27	28	29	30	31	1
ĀŚVINA 2083	2	3	4	5	6	7	8
	9	10	11	12	13	14	15
	16	17	18	19	20	21	22
	23	24	25	26	27	28	29
	30	31	1	2	3	4	5
KĀRTTIKA 2083	6	7	8	9	10	11	12
	13	14	15	16	17	18	19
	20	21	22	23	24	25	26
	27	28	29	1	2	3	4
MĀRGAŚĪRA 2083	5	6	7	8	9	10	11
	12	13	14	15	16	17	18
	19	20	21	22	23	24	25
	26	27	28	29	30	1	2
PAUSHA 2083	3	4	5	6	7	8	9
	10	11	12	13	14	15	16

‡Leap year
[a]New Year (Dhātṛi)
[b]Pongal

ISLAMIC (ASTRONOMICAL) 1586‡/1587

Month	Sun	Mon	Tue	Wed	Thu	Fri	Sat
RAMAḌĀN 1586	30	1	2	3	4	5	6
	7	8	9	10	11	12	13
	14	15	16	17	18	19	20
	21	22	23	24	25	26	27
SHAWWĀL 1586	28	29	30	1[f]	2	3	4
	5	6	7	8	9	10	11
	12	13	14	15	16	17	18
	19	20	21	22	23	24	25
DHU AL-QA'DA 1586	26	27	28	29	1	2	3
	4	5	6	7	8	9	10
	11	12	13	14	15	16	17
	18	19	20	21	22	23	24
DHU AL-ḤIJJA 1586	25	26	27	28	29	30	1
	2	3	4	5	6	7	8
	9	10[g]	11	12	13	14	15
	16	17	18	19	20	21	22
	23	24	25	26	27	28	29
MUḤARRAM 1587	30	1[a]	2	3	4	5	6
	7	8	9	10[b]	11	12	13
	14	15	16	17	18	19	20
	21	22	23	24	25	26	27
ṢAFAR 1587	28	29	1	2	3	4	5
	6	7	8	9	10	11	12
	13	14	15	16	17	18	19
	20	21	22	23	24	25	26
RABĪ' I 1587	27	28	29	30	1	2	3
	4	5	6	7	8	9	10
	11	12[c]	13	14	15	16	17
	18	19	20	21	22	23	24
RABĪ' II 1587	25	26	27	28	29	30	1
	2	3	4	5	6	7	8
	9	10	11	12	13	14	15
	16	17	18	19	20	21	22
	23	24	25	26	27	28	29
JUMĀDĀ I 1587	1	2	3	4	5	6	7
	8	9	10	11	12	13	14
	15	16	17	18	19	20	21
	22	23	24	25	26	27	28
JUMĀDĀ II 1587	29	30	1	2	3	4	5
	6	7	8	9	10	11	12
	13	14	15	16	17	18	19
	20	21	22	23	24	25	26
RAJAB 1587	27	28	29	1	2	3	4
	5	6	7	8	9	10	11
	12	13	14	15	16	17	18
	19	20	21	22	23	24	25
SHA'BĀN 1587	26	27[d]	28	29	1	2	3
	4	5	6	7	8	9	10
	11	12	13	14	15	16	17
	18	19	20	21	22	23	24
RAMAḌĀN 1587	25	26	27	28	29	1[e]	2
	3	4	5	6	7	8	9
	10	11	12	13	14	15	16

‡Leap year
[a]New Year
[b]'Ashūrā'
[c]Prophet's Birthday
[d]Ascent of the Prophet
[e]Start of Ramaḍān
[f]'Id al-Fiṭr
[g]'Id al-'Aḍḥā

GREGORIAN 2161

Julian (Sun)	Sun	Mon	Tue	Wed	Thu	Fri	Sat	Month
Dec 14	28	29	30	31	1	2	3	JANUARY 2161
	4	5	6	7	8[a]	9	10	
Dec 28	11	12	13	14	15[b]	16	17	
	18	19	20	21	22	23	24	
Jan 11	25	26	27	28	29	30	31	
	1	2	3	4	5	6	7	FEBRUARY 2161
Jan 25	8	9	10	11	12	13	14	
	15	16	17	18	19	20	21	
Feb 8	22	23	24	25[c]	26	27	28	
	1	2	3	4	5	6	7	MARCH 2161
Feb 22	8[d]	9	10	11	12	13	14	
	15	16	17	18	19	20	21	
Mar 8	22	23	24	25	26	27	28	
	29	30	31	1	2	3	4	APRIL 2161
Mar 22	5	6	7	8	9	10	11	
	12[e]	13	14	15	16	17	18	
Apr 5	19[f]	20	21	22	23	24	25	
	26	27	28	29	30	1	2	MAY 2161
Apr 19	3	4	5	6	7	8	9	
	10	11	12	13	14	15	16	
May 3	17	18	19	20	21	22	23	
	24	25	26	27	28	29	30	
May 17	31	1	2	3	4	5	6	JUNE 2161
	7	8	9	10	11	12	13	
May 31	14	15	16	17	18	19	20	
	21	22	23	24	25	26	27	
Jun 14	28	29	30	1	2	3	4	JULY 2161
	5	6	7	8	9	10	11	
Jun 28	12	13	14	15	16	17	18	
	19	20	21	22	23	24	25	
Jul 12	26	27	28	29	30	31	1	AUGUST 2161
	2	3	4	5	6	7	8	
Jul 26	9	10	11	12	13	14	15	
	16	17	18	19	20	21	22	
Aug 9	23	24	25	26	27	28	29	
	30	31	1	2	3	4	5	SEPTEMBER 2161
Aug 23	6	7	8	9	10	11	12	
	13	14	15	16	17	18	19	
Sep 6	20	21	22	23	24	25	26	
	27	28	29	30	1	2	3	OCTOBER 2161
Sep 20	4	5	6	7	8	9	10	
	11	12	13	14	15	16	17	
Oct 4	18	19	20	21	22	23	24	
	25	26	27	28	29	30	31	
Oct 18	1	2	3	4	5	6	7	NOVEMBER 2161
	8	9	10	11	12	13	14	
Nov 1	15	16	17	18	19	20	21	
	22	23	24	25	26	27	28	
Nov 15	29[g]	30	1	2	3	4	5	DECEMBER 2161
	6	7	8	9	10	11	12	
Nov 29	13	14	15	16	17	18	19	
	20	21	22	23	24	25[h]	26	
Dec 13	27	28	29	30	31	1	2	

[a]Orthodox Christmas
[b]Julian New Year
[c]Ash Wednesday
[d]Feast of Orthodoxy
[e]Easter
[f]Orthodox Easter
[g]Advent
[h]Christmas

2162

GREGORIAN 2162	Sun	Mon	Tue	Wed	Thu	Fri	Sat	Lunar Phases	ISO WEEK (Mon)	JULIAN DAY (Sun noon)	HEBREW 5922/5923‡	Sun	Mon	Tue	Wed	Thu	Fri	Sat	Molad	CHINESE Xīn-Yǒu‡/Rén-Xū	Sun	Mon	Tue	Wed	Thu	Fri	Sat	Solar Term	COPTIC 1878/1879‡	Sun	Mon	Tue	Wed	Thu	Fri	Sat	ETHIOPIC 2154/2155‡
JANUARY 2162	27	28	29	30	31	○[a]	2	12:41	53	2510710	TEVETH 5922	10	11	12	13	14	15	16		MONTH 11 Xīn-Yǒu	11	12	13	14	15	16	17		KOIAK 1878	17	18	19	20	21	22	23	TĀKHŚĀŚ 2154
	3	4	5	6	7	◑	9	11:34	1	2510717		17	18	19	20	21	22	23			18	19	*20*	21	22	23	24	Xiǎo hán		24	25	26	27	28	29[c]	30	
	10	11	12	13	14	●	16	12:40	2	2510724		24	25	26	27	28	29	1	Sat 2h8m1p		25	26	27	28	29	1	2		TŌBE 1878	1	2	3	4	5	6[d]	7	ṬER 2154
	17	18	19	20	21	22	◐	12:04	3	2510731	SHEVAT 5922	2	3	4	5	6	7	8		MONTH 12 Xīn-Yǒu	3	4	5	**6**	7	8	9	Dà hán		8	9	10	11[e]	12	13	14	
	24	25	26	27	28	29	30		4	2510738		9	10	11	12	13	14	15			10	11	12	13	14	15	16			15	16	17	18	19	20	21	
FEBRUARY 2162	○	1	2	3	4	5	◑	2:17 19:54	5	2510745		16	17	18	19	20	21	22			17	18	19	20	*21*	22	23	Lì chūn		22	23	24	25	26	27	28	
	7	8	9	10	11	12	13		6	2510752		23	24	25	26	27	28	29			24	25	26	27	28	29	30			29	30	1	2	3	4	5	
	●	15	16	17	18	19	20	4:31	7	2510759		30	1	2	3	4	5	6	Sun 14h52m2p	MONTH 1 Rén-Xū	1[a]	2	3	4	**5**	6	7	Yǔ shuǐ	MESHIR 1878	6	7	8	9	10	11	12	YAKĀTIT 2154
	21	◐	23	24	25	26	27	8:58	8	2510766	ADAR 5922	7	8	9	10	11	12	13			8	9	10	11	12	13*	14			13	14	15	16	17	18	19	
	28	○	2	3	4	5	6	13:44	9	2510773		14[f]	15	16	17	18	19	20			15[b]	16	17	18	19	*20*	21	Jīng zhé		20	21	22	23	24	25	26	
MARCH 2162	7	◑	9	10	11	12	13	5:11	10	2510780		21	22	23	24	25	26	27			22	23	24	25	26	27	28			27	28	29	30	1	2	3	
	14	●	16	17	18	19	20[b]	21:38	11	2510787		28	29	1	2	3	4	5	Tue 3h36m3p		29	30	1	2	3	4	**5**	Chūn fēn	PAREMOTEP 1878	4	5	6	7	8	9	10	MAGĀBIT 2154
	21	22	23	◐	25	26	27	2:32	12	2510794	NISAN 5922	6	7	8	9	10	11	12		MONTH 2 Rén-Xū	6	7	8	9	10	11	12			11	12	13	14	15	16	17	
APRIL 2162	28	29	○	31	1	2	3	23:29	13	2510801		13	14	15[g]	16	17	18	19			13	14	15	16	17	18	19			18	19	20	21	22	23	24	
	4	5	◑	7	8	9	10	15:52	14	2510808		20	21	22	23	24	25	26			20	*21*[c]	22	23	24	25	26	Qīng míng		25	26	27	28	29	30	1	
	11	12	13	●	15	16	17	15:11	15	2510815		27	28	29	30	1	2	3	Wed 16h20m4p		27	28	29	1	2	3	4		PARMOUTE 1878	2[f]	3	4	5	6	7	8	MIYĀZYĀ 2154
	18	19	20	21	◐	23	24	15:51	16	2510822	IYYAR 5922	4	5	6	7	8	9	10		MONTH 3 Rén-Xū	5	6	**7**	8	9	10	11	Gǔ yǔ		9	10	11	12	13	14	15	
MAY 2162	25	26	27	28	○	30	1	8:05	17	2510829		11	12	13	14	15	16	17			12	13	14*	15	16	17	18			16	17	18	19	20	21	22	
	2	3	4	5	◑	7	8	4:16	18	2510836		18	19	20	21	22	23	24			19	20	21	*22*	23	24	25	Lì xià		23	24	25	26	27	28	29[g]	
	9	10	11	12	13	●	15	7:57	19	2510843		25	26	27	28	29	1	2	Fri 5h4m5p		26	27	28	29	30	1	2			30	1	2	3	4	5	6	
	16	17	18	19	20	21	◐	1:16	20	2510850	SIVAN 5922	3	4	5	6[h]	7	8	9		MONTH 4 Rén-Xū	3	4	5	6	7	**8**	9	Xiǎo mǎn	PASHONS 1878	7	8	9	10	11	12	13	GENBOT 2154
	23	24	25	26	27	○	29	16:06	21	2510857		10	11	12	13	14	15	16			10	11	12	13	14	15	16			14	15	16	17	18	19	20	
JUNE 2162	30	31	1	2	3	◑	5	18:35	22	2510864		17	18	19	20	21	22	23			17	18	19	20	21	22	*23*	Máng zhòng		21	22	23	24	25	26	27	
	6	7	8	9	10	11	●	22:48	23	2510871		24	25	26	27	28	29	30			24	25	26	27	28	29	30			28	29	30	1	2	3	4	
	13	14	15	16	17	18	19		24	2510878		1	2	3	4	5	6	7	Sat 17h48m6p	MONTH 5 Rén-Xū	1	2	3	4	5[d]	6	7		PAŌNE 1878	5	6	7	8	9	10	11	SANĒ 2154
	◐	21[c]	22	23	24	25	26	7:49	25	2510885	TAMMUZ 5922	8	9	10	11	12	13	14			8	**9**	10	11	12	13	14*	Xià zhì		12	13	14	15	16	17	18	
JULY 2162	○	28	29	30	1	2	3	0:13	26	2510892		15	16	17	18	19	20	21			15	16	17	18	19	20	21			19	20	21	22	23	24	25	
	◑	5	6	7	8	9	10	10:44	27	2510899		22	23	24	25	26	27	28			22	23	24	*25*	26	27	28	Xiǎo shǔ		26	27	28	29	30	1	2	
	11	●	13	14	15	16	17	11:19	28	2510906		29	1	2	3	4	5	6	Mon 6h32m7p		29	1	2	3	4	5	6		EPĒP 1878	3	4	5	6	7	8	9	ḤAMLĒ 2154
	18	◐	20	21	22	23	24	12:48	29	2510913	AV 5922	7	8	9[i]	10	11	12	13		MONTH 6 Rén-Xū	7	8	9	10	**11**	12	13	Dà shǔ		10	11	12	13	14	15	16	
	25	○	27	28	29	30	31	9:18	30	2510920		14	15	16	17	18	19	20			14	15	16	17	18	19	20			17	18	19	20	21	22	23	
AUGUST 2162	1	2	◑	4	5	6	7	4:12	31	2510927		21	22	23	24	25	26	27			21	22	23	24	25	26	*27*	Lì qiū		24	25	26	27	28	29	30	
	8	9	●	11	12	13	14	21:51	32	2510934		28	29	30	1	2	3	4	Tue 19h16m8p		28	29	30	1	2	3	4		MESORĒ 1878	1	2	3	4	5	6	7	NAHASĒ 2154
	15	16	◐	18	19	20	21	17:34	33	2510941	ELUL 5922	5	6	7	8	9	10	11		MONTH 7 Rén-Xū	5	6	7[e]	8	9	10	11			8	9	10	11	12	13[h]	14	
	22	23	○	25	26	27	28	20:24	34	2510948		12	13	14	15	16	17	18			12	**13**	14	15[f]*	16	17	18	Chǔ shǔ		15	16	17	18	19	20	21	
SEPTEMBER 2162	29	30	31	◑	2	3	4	22:01	35	2510955		19	20	21	22	23	24	25			19	20	21	22	23	24	25			22	23	24	25	26	27	28	
	5	6	7	8	●	10	11	7:15	36	2510962		26	27	28	29	1[a]	2[a]	3	Thu 8h0m9p		26	27	*28*	29	1	2	3	Bái lù	EPAG. 1878	29	30	1	2	3	4	5	PĀG. 2154
	12	13	14	◐	16	17	18	23:28	37	2510969	TISHRI 5923	4	5	6	7	8	9	10[b]		MONTH 8 Rén-Xū	4	5	6	7	8	9	10		THOOUT 1879	1[a]	2	3	4	5	6	7	MASKARAM 2155
	19	20	21	22[d]	○	24	25	10:19	38	2510976		11	12	13	14	15[c]	16	17			11	12	13	14	**15**[g]	16	17	Qiū fēn		8	9	10	11	12	13	14	
OCTOBER 2162	26	27	28	29	30	◑	2	15:06	39	2510983		18	19	20	21	22	23	24			18	19	20	21	22	23	24			15	16	17[b]	18	19	20	21	
	3	4	5	6	7	●	9	16:26	40	2510990		25	26	27	28	29	30	1	Fri 20h44m10p		25	26	27	28	29	*30*	1	Hán lù		22	23	24	25	26	27	28	
	10	11	12	13	14	◐	16	7:45	41	2510997	HESHVAN 5923	2	3	4	5	6	7	8		MONTH 9 Rén-Xū	2	3	4	5	6	7	8			29	30	1	2	3	4	5	
	17	18	19	20	21	22	○	3:10	42	2511004		9	10	11	12	13	14	15			9[h]	10	11	12	13	14	**15**	Shuāng jiàng	PAOPE 1879	6	7	8	9	10	11	12	ṬEQEMT 2155
	24	25	26	27	28	29	30		43	2511011		16	17	18	19	20	21	22			16*	17	18	19	20	21	22			13	14	15	16	17	18	19	
NOVEMBER 2162	◑	1	2	3	4	5	6	6:36	44	2511018		23	24	25	26	27	28	29			23	24	25	26	27	28	29			20	21	22	23	24	25	26	
	●	8	9	10	11	12	◐	2:01 19:31	45	2511025		30	1	2	3	4	5	6	Sun 9h28m11p	MONTH 10 Rén-Xū	*1*	2	3	4	5	6	7	Lì dōng		27	28	29	30	1	2	3	
	14	15	16	17	18	19	20		46	2511032	KISLEV 5923	7	8	9	10	11	12	13			8	9	10	11	12	13	14		ATHŌR 1879	4	5	6	7	8	9	10	ḪEDĀR 2155
	○	22	23	24	25	26	27	21:57	47	2511039		14	15	16	17	18	19	20			15	**16**	17	18	19	20	21	Xiǎo xuě		11	12	13	14	15	16	17	
DECEMBER 2162	28	◑	30	1	2	3	4	20:05	48	2511046		21	22	23	24	25[e]	26[e]	27[e]			22	23	24	25	26	27	28			18	19	20	21	22	23	24	
	5	●	7	8	9	10	11	12:19	49	2511053		28[e]	29[d][e]	30[e]	1[e]	2[e]	3	4	Mon 22h12m12p		29	1	*2*	3	4	5	6	Dà xuě		25	26	27	28	29	30	1	
	12	◐	14	15	16	17	18	11:24	50	2511060	TEVETH 5923	5	6	7	8	9	10	11		MONTH 11 Rén-Xū	7	8	9	10	11	12	13		KOIAK 1879	2	3	4	5	6	7	8	TĀKHŚĀŚ 2155
	19	20	○[e]	22	23	24	25	16:56	51	2511067		12	13	14	15	16	17	18			14	15	16	**17**[i]	18*	19	20	Dōng zhì		9	10	11	12	13	14	15	
	26	27	28	◑	30	31	1	7:25	52	2511074		19	20	21	22	23	24	25			21	22	23	24	25	26	27			16	17	18	19	20	21	22	

[a]New Year
[b]Spring (13:35)
[c]Summer (4:48)
[d]Autumn (21:57)
[e]Winter (21:02)
● New moon
◐ First quarter moon
○ Full moon
◑ Last quarter moon

‡Leap year
[a]New Year
[b]Yom Kippur
[c]Sukkot
[d]Winter starts
[e]Hanukkah
[f]Purim
[g]Passover
[h]Shavuot
[i]Fast of Av

‡Leap year
[a]New Year (4860, Dog)
[b]Lantern Festival
[c]Qīngmíng
[d]Dragon Festival
[e]Qīqiǎo
[f]Hungry Ghosts
[g]Mid-Autumn Festival
[h]Double-Ninth Festival
[i]Dōngzhì
*Start of 60-name cycle

‡Leap year
[a]New Year
[b]Building of the Cross
[c]Christmas
[d]Jesus's Circumcision
[e]Epiphany
[f]Easter
[g]Mary's Announcement
[h]Jesus's Transfiguration

PERSIAN (ASTRONOMICAL) 1540‡/1541

Month	Sun	Mon	Tue	Wed	Thu	Fri	Sat
DEY 1540	7	8	9	10	11	12	13
	14	15	16	17	18	19	20
	21	22	23	24	25	26	27
	28	29	30	1	2	3	4
BAHMAN 1540	5	6	7	8	9	10	11
	12	13	14	15	16	17	18
	19	20	21	22	23	24	25
	26	27	28	29	30	1	2
ESFAND 1540	3	4	5	6	7	8	9
	10	11	12	13	14	15	16
	17	18	19	20	21	22	23
	24	25	26	27	28	29	30
FARVARDĪN 1541	1[a]	2	3	4	5	6	7
	8	9	10	11	12	13[b]	14
	15	16	17	18	19	20	21
	22	23	24	25	26	27	28
ORDĪBEHEŠT 1541	29	30	31	1	2	3	4
	5	6	7	8	9	10	11
	12	13	14	15	16	17	18
	19	20	21	22	23	24	25
XORDĀD 1541	26	27	28	29	30	31	1
	2	3	4	5	6	7	8
	9	10	11	12	13	14	15
	16	17	18	19	20	21	22
	23	24	25	26	27	28	29
TĪR 1541	30	31	1	2	3	4	5
	6	7	8	9	10	11	12
	13	14	15	16	17	18	19
	20	21	22	23	24	25	26
MORDĀD 1541	27	28	29	30	31	1	2
	3	4	5	6	7	8	9
	10	11	12	13	14	15	16
	17	18	19	20	21	22	23
	24	25	26	27	28	29	30
SHAHRĪVAR 1541	31	1	2	3	4	5	6
	7	8	9	10	11	12	13
	14	15	16	17	18	19	20
	21	22	23	24	25	26	27
MEHR 1541	28	29	30	31	1	2	3
	4	5	6	7	8	9	10
	11	12	13	14	15	16	17
	18	19	20	21	22	23	24
	25	26	27	28	29	30	1
ĀBĀN 1541	2	3	4	5	6	7	8
	9	10	11	12	13	14	15
	16	17	18	19	20	21	22
	23	24	25	26	27	28	29
ĀZAR 1541	30	1	2	3	4	5	6
	7	8	9	10	11	12	13
	14	15	16	17	18	19	20
	21	22	23	24	25	26	27
DEY 1541	28	29	30	1	2	3	4
	5	6	7	8	9	10	11

HINDU LUNAR 2218‡/2219

Month	Sun	Mon	Tue	Wed	Thu	Fri	Sat
MĀRGAŚĪRA 2218	10	11	12	13	14	15	16
	17	18	19	20	21	22	24
	25	26	27	28	29	30	1
PAUSHA 2218	2	3	4	5	6	7	8
	9	10	10	11	12	13	14
	15	17	18	19	20	21	22
	23	24	25	26	27	28	29
	30	1	2	3	4	5	6
MĀGHA 2218	7	8	9	10	11	12	13
	14	15	16	17	18	19	20
	22	23	24	25	26	27	28[h]
	29	30	1	2	3	3	4
PHĀLGUNA 2218	5	6	7	8	9	10	11
	12	13	14[i]	16	17	18	19
	20	21	22	23	24	25	26
	27	28	29	30	1[a]	2	3
CHAITRA 2219	4	5	6	7	8	9[b]	10
	11	12	13	14	15	16	17
	18	20	21	22	23	24	25
	26	27	27	28	29	30	1
VAIŚĀKHA 2219	2	3	4	5	6	7	8
	9	10	11	13	14	15	16
	17	18	19	20	21	22	23
	24	25	26	27	28	29	30
JYAISHTHA 2219	1	2	3	4	5	6	7
	8	9	10	11	12	13	14
	16	17	18	19	20	21	22
	23	24	24	25	26	27	28
	29	30	1	2	3	4	5
ĀSHĀḌHA 2219	6	7	9	10	11	12	13
	14	15	16	17	18	19	20
	21	22	23	24	25	26	27
	28	29	30	1	2	3	4
ŚRĀVAṆA 2219	5	6	7	8	9	10	12
	13	14	15	16	17	18	19
	20	20	21	22	23[c]	24	25
	26	27	28	29	30	1	2
BHĀDRAPADA 2219	3[d]	5	6	7	8	9	10
	11	12	13	14	15	16	17
	18	19	20	21	22	23	24
	25	26	27	28	29	30	1
ĀŚVINA 2219	2	3	4	5	6	7[e]	9[e]
	10[e]	11	12	13	14	15	15
	16	17	18	19	20	21	22
	23	24	25	26	27	28	29
	30[f]	2	3	4	5	6	7
KĀRTTIKA 2219	8	9	10	11	12	13	14
	15	16	17	18	18	19	20
	21	22	23	24	26	27	28
	29	30	1	2	3	4	5
MĀRGAŚĪRA 2219	6	7	8	9	10	11[g]	12
	13	14	15	16	17	18	19
	20	21	22	23	24	25	26

HINDU SOLAR 2083/2084

Month	Sun	Mon	Tue	Wed	Thu	Fri	Sat
PAUSHA 2083	10	11	12	13	14	15	16
	17	18	19	20	21	22	23
	24	25	26	27	28	29	1[b]
MĀGHA 2083	2	3	4	5	6	7	8
	9	10	11	12	13	14	15
	16	17	18	19	20	21	22
	23	24	25	26	27	28	29
	30	1	2	3	4	5	6
PHĀLGUNA 2083	7	8	9	10	11	12	13
	14	15	16	17	18	19	20
	21	22	23	24	25	26	27
	28	29	30	1	2	3	4
CHAITRA 2083	5	6	7	8	9	10	11
	12	13	14	15	16	17	18
	19	20	21	22	23	24	25
	26	27	28	29	30	1[a]	2
VAIŚĀKHA 2084	3	4	5	6	7	8	9
	10	11	12	13	14	15	16
	17	18	19	20	21	22	23
	24	25	26	27	28	29	30
	31	1	2	3	4	5	6
JYAISHTHA 2084	7	8	9	10	11	12	13
	14	15	16	17	18	19	20
	21	22	23	24	25	26	27
	28	29	30	31	1	2	3
ĀSHĀḌHA 2084	4	5	6	7	8	9	10
	11	12	13	14	15	16	17
	18	19	20	21	22	23	24
	25	26	27	28	29	30	31
	32	1	2	3	4	5	6
ŚRĀVAṆA 2084	7	8	9	10	11	12	13
	14	15	16	17	18	19	20
	21	22	23	24	25	26	27
	28	29	30	31	1	2	3
BHĀDRAPADA 2084	4	5	6	7	8	9	10
	11	12	13	14	15	16	17
	18	19	20	21	22	23	24
	25	26	27	28	29	30	31
ĀŚVINA 2084	1	2	3	4	5	6	7
	8	9	10	11	12	13	14
	15	16	17	18	19	20	21
	22	23	24	25	26	27	28
	29	30	31	1	2	3	4
KĀRTTIKA 2084	5	6	7	8	9	10	11
	12	13	14	15	16	17	18
	19	20	21	22	23	24	25
	26	27	28	29	30	1	2
MĀRGAŚĪRA 2084	3	4	5	6	7	8	9
	10	11	12	13	14	15	16
	17	18	19	20	21	22	23
	24	25	26	27	28	29	1
PAUSHA 2084	2	3	4	5	6	7	8
	9	10	11	12	13	14	15

ISLAMIC (ASTRONOMICAL) 1587/1588

Month	Sun	Mon	Tue	Wed	Thu	Fri	Sat
RAMAḌĀN 1587	10	11	12	13	14	15	16
	17	18	19	20	21	22	23
	24	25	26	27	28	29	30
SHAWWĀL 1587	1[f]	2	3	4	5	6	7
	8	9	10	11	12	13	14
	15	16	17	18	19	20	21
	22	23	24	25	26	27	28
DHU AL-QA'DA 1587	29	1	2	3	4	5	6
	7	8	9	10	11	12	13
	14	15	16	17	18	19	20
	21	22	23	24	25	26	27
DHU AL-ḤIJJA 1587	28	29	30	1	2	3	4
	5	6	7	8	9	10[g]	11
	12	13	14	15	16	17	18
	19	20	21	22	23	24	25
MUHARRAM 1588	26	27	28	29	30	1[a]	2
	3	4	5	6	7	8	9
	10[b]	11	12	13	14	15	16
	17	18	19	20	21	22	23
	24	25	26	27	28	29	30
SAFAR 1588	1	2	3	4	5	6	7
	8	9	10	11	12	13	14
	15	16	17	18	19	20	21
	22	23	24	25	26	27	28
RABĪ' I 1588	29	30	1	2	3	4	5
	6	7	8	9	10	11	12[c]
	13	14	15	16	17	18	19
	20	21	22	23	24	25	26
RABĪ' II 1588	27	28	29	1	2	3	4
	5	6	7	8	9	10	11
	12	13	14	15	16	17	18
	19	20	21	22	23	24	25
JUMĀDĀ I 1588	26	27	28	29	30	1	2
	3	4	5	6	7	8	9
	10	11	12	13	14	15	16
	17	18	19	20	21	22	23
JUMĀDĀ II 1588	24	25	26	27	28	29	1
	2	3	4	5	6	7	8
	9	10	11	12	13	14	15
	16	17	18	19	20	21	22
	23	24	25	26	27	28	29
RAJAB 1588	1	2	3	4	5	6	7
	8	9	10	11	12	13	14
	15	16	17	18	19	20	21
	22	23	24	25	26	27[d]	28
SHA'BĀN 1588	29	1	2	3	4	5	6
	7	8	9	10	11	12	13
	14	15	16	17	18	19	20
	21	22	23	24	25	26	27
RAMAḌĀN 1588	28	29	30	1[e]	2	3	4
	5	6	7	8	9	10	11
	12	13	14	15	16	17	18
	19	20	21	22	23	24	25

GREGORIAN 2162

Julian (Sun)	Sun	Mon	Tue	Wed	Thu	Fri	Sat	Month
Dec 13	27	28	29	30	31	1	2	JANUARY 2162
	3	4	5	6	7	8[a]	9	
Dec 27	10	11	12	13	14	15[b]	16	
	17	18	19	20	21	22	23	
Jan 10	24	25	26	27	28	29	30	
	31	1	2	3	4	5	6	FEBRUARY 2162
Jan 24	7	8	9	10	11	12	13	
	14	15	16	17[c]	18	19	20	
Feb 7	21	22	23	24	25	26	27	
	28[d]	1	2	3	4	5	6	MARCH 2162
Feb 21	7	8	9	10	11	12	13	
	14	15	16	17	18	19	20	
Mar 7	21	22	23	24	25	26	27	
	28	29	30	31	1	2	3	APRIL 2162
Mar 21	4[e]	5	6	7	8	9	10	
	11[f]	12	13	14	15	16	17	
Apr 4	18	19	20	21	22	23	24	
	25	26	27	28	29	30	1	MAY 2162
Apr 18	2	3	4	5	6	7	8	
	9	10	11	12	13	14	15	
May 2	16	17	18	19	20	21	22	
	23	24	25	26	27	28	29	
May 16	30	31	1	2	3	4	5	JUNE 2162
	6	7	8	9	10	11	12	
May 30	13	14	15	16	17	18	19	
	20	21	22	23	24	25	26	
Jun 13	27	28	29	30	1	2	3	JULY 2162
	4	5	6	7	8	9	10	
Jun 27	11	12	13	14	15	16	17	
	18	19	20	21	22	23	24	
Jul 11	25	26	27	28	29	30	31	
	1	2	3	4	5	6	7	AUGUST 2162
Jul 25	8	9	10	11	12	13	14	
	15	16	17	18	19	20	21	
Aug 8	22	23	24	25	26	27	28	
	29	30	31	1	2	3	4	SEPTEMBER 2162
Aug 22	5	6	7	8	9	10	11	
	12	13	14	15	16	17	18	
Sep 5	19	20	21	22	23	24	25	
	26	27	28	29	30	1	2	OCTOBER 2162
Sep 19	3	4	5	6	7	8	9	
	10	11	12	13	14	15	16	
Oct 3	17	18	19	20	21	22	23	
	24	25	26	27	28	29	30	
Oct 17	31	1	2	3	4	5	6	NOVEMBER 2162
	7	8	9	10	11	12	13	
Oct 31	14	15	16	17	18	19	20	
	21	22	23	24	25	26	27	
Nov 14	28[g]	29	30	1	2	3	4	DECEMBER 2162
	5	6	7	8	9	10	11	
Nov 28	12	13	14	15	16	17	18	
	19	20	21	22	23	24	25[h]	
Dec 12	26	27	28	29	30	31	1	

Persian: ‡Leap year; [a]New Year; [b]Sizdeh Bedar

Hindu Lunar: ‡Leap year; [a]New Year (Dundubhi); [b]Birthday of Rāma; [c]Birthday of Krishna; [d]Ganēśa Chaturthī; [e]Dashara; [f]Diwali; [g]Birthday of Vishnu; [h]Night of Śiva; [i]Holi

Hindu Solar: [a]New Year (Īśvara); [b]Pongal

Islamic: [a]New Year; [b]'Ashūrā'; [c]Prophet's Birthday; [d]Ascent of the Prophet; [e]Start of Ramaḍān; [f]'Id al-Fiṭr; [g]'Id al-'Aḍḥā

Gregorian: [a]Orthodox Christmas; [b]Julian New Year; [c]Ash Wednesday; [d]Feast of Orthodoxy; [e]Easter; [f]Orthodox Easter; [g]Advent; [h]Christmas

2163

GREGORIAN 2163 · Lunar Phases · ISO WEEK · JULIAN DAY

Month	Sun	Mon	Tue	Wed	Thu	Fri	Sat	Lunar Phases	ISO WEEK (Mon)	JULIAN DAY (Sun noon)
	26	27	28	◑	30	31	1[a]	7:25	52	2511074
JANUARY 2163	2	3	●	5	6	7	8	23:27	1	2511081
	9	10	11	◐	13	14	15	6:57	2	2511088
	16	17	18	19	○	21	22	10:28	3	2511095
	23	24	25	26	◑	28	29	16:46	4	2511102
	30	31	1	2	●	4	5	11:41	5	2511109
FEBRUARY 2163	6	7	8	9	10	◐	12	4:31	6	2511116
	13	14	15	16	17	18	○	1:42	7	2511123
	20	21	22	23	24	25	◑	0:37	8	2511130
	27	28	1	2	3	4	●	1:18	9	2511137
MARCH 2163	6	7	8	9	10	11	12		10	2511144
	◐	14	15	16	17	18	19	1:41	11	2511151
	○[b]	21	22	23	24	25	26	14:24	12	2511158
	◑	28	29	30	31	1	2	7:49	13	2511165
APRIL 2163	●	4	5	6	7	8	9	16:21	14	2511172
	10	◐	12	13	14	15	16	20:28	15	2511179
	17	18	○	20	21	22	23	0:45	16	2511186
	24	◑	26	27	28	29	30	15:25	17	2511193
MAY 2163	1	2	●	4	5	6	7	8:18	18	2511200
	8	9	10	◐	12	13	14	11:52	19	2511207
	15	16	17	○	19	20	21	9:07	20	2511214
	22	23	24	◑	26	27	28	0:29	21	2511221
	29	30	31	1	●	3	4	0:16	22	2511228
JUNE 2163	5	6	7	8	◐	10	11	23:46	23	2511235
	12	13	14	15	○	17	18	16:13	24	2511242
	19	20	21[c]	22	◑	24	25	11:51	25	2511249
	26	27	28	29	30	●	2	15:26	26	2511256
JULY 2163	3	4	5	6	7	8	◐	8:38	27	2511263
	10	11	12	13	14	○	16	23:03	28	2511270
	17	18	19	20	21	22	◑	1:52	29	2511277
	24	25	26	27	28	29	30		30	2511284
AUGUST 2163	●	1	2	3	4	5	6	5:26	31	2511291
	◐	8	9	10	11	12	13	15:13	32	2511298
	○	15	16	17	18	19	20	6:51	33	2511305
	◑	22	23	24	25	26	27	18:21	34	2511312
	28	●	30	31	1	2	3	18:18	35	2511319
SEPTEMBER 2163	4	◐	6	7	8	9	10	20:35	36	2511326
	11	○	13	14	15	16	17	16:49	37	2511333
	18	19	◑	21	22	23[d]	24	12:37	38	2511340
	25	26	27	●	29	30	1	6:15	39	2511347
OCTOBER 2163	2	3	4	◐	6	7	8	2:04	40	2511354
	9	10	11	○	13	14	15	5:46	41	2511361
	16	17	18	19	◑	21	22	7:42	42	2511368
	23	24	25	26	●	28	29	17:29	43	2511375
	30	31	1	2	◐	4	5	9:07	44	2511382
NOVEMBER 2163	6	7	8	9	○	11	12	21:50	45	2511389
	13	14	15	16	17	18	◑	2:25	46	2511396
	20	21	22	23	24	25	●	4:11	47	2511403
	27	28	29	30	1	◐	3	19:04	48	2511410
DECEMBER 2163	4	5	6	7	8	9	○	16:14	49	2511417
	11	12	13	14	15	16	17		50	2511424
	◑	19	20	21	22[e]	23	24	19:30	51	2511431
	●	26	27	28	29	30	31	14:36	52	2511438

HEBREW 5923‡/5924 · Molad

ISO WEEK	Month	Sun	Mon	Tue	Wed	Thu	Fri	Sat	Molad
52	TEVETH 5923	19	20	21	22	23	24	25	
1		26	27	28	29	1	2	3	Wed 10h56m13p
2	SHEVAT 5923	4	5	6	7	8	9	10	
3		11	12	13	14	15	16	17	
4		18	19	20	21	22	23	24	
5		25	26	27	28	29	30	1	Thu 23h40m14p
6	ADAR I 5923	2	3	4	5	6	7	8	
7		9	10	11	12	13	14	15	
8		16	17	18	19	20	21	22	
9		23	24	25	26	27	28	29	
10	ADAR II 5923	30	1	2	3	4	5	6	Sat 12h24m15p
11		7	8	9	10	11	12	13	
12		14[f]	15	16	17	18	19	20	
13		21	22	23	24	25	26	27	
14	NISAN 5923	28	29	1	2	3	4	5	Mon 1h8m16p
15		6	7	8	9	10	11	12	
16		13	14	15[g]	16	17	18	19	
17		20	21	22	23	24	25	26	
18	IYAR 5923	27	28	29	30	1	2	3	Tue 13h52m17p
19		4	5	6	7	8	9	10	
20		11	12	13	14	15	16	17	
21		18	19	20	21	22	23	24	
22	SIVAN 5923	25	26	27	28	29	1	2	Thu 2h37m0p
23		3	4	5	6[h]	7	8	9	
24		10	11	12	13	14	15	16	
25		17	18	19	20	21	22	23	
26		24	25	26	27	28	29	30	
27	TAMMUZ 5923	1	2	3	4	5	6	7	Fri 15h21m1p
28		8	9	10	11	12	13	14	
29		15	16	17	18	19	20	21	
30		22	23	24	25	26	27	28	
31	AV 5923	29	1	2	3	4	5	6	Sun 4h5m2p
32		7	8	9[i]	10	11	12	13	
33		14	15	16	17	18	19	20	
34		21	22	23	24	25	26	27	
35	ELUL 5923	28	29	30	1	2	3	4	Mon 16h49m3p
36		5	6	7	8	9	10	11	
37		12	13	14	15	16	17	18	
38		19	20	21	22	23	24	25	
39	TISHRI 5924	26	27	28	29	1[a]	2[a]	3	Wed 5h33m4p
40		4	5	6	7	8	9	10[b]	
41		11	12	13	14	15[c]	16	17	
42		18	19	20	21	22	23	24	
43	HESHVAN 5924	25	26	27	28	29	30	1	Thu 18h17m5p
44		2	3	4	5	6	7	8	
45		9	10	11	12	13	14	15	
46		16	17	18	19	20	21	22	
47		23	24	25	26	27	28	29	
48	KISLEV 5924	1	2	3	4	5	6	7	Sat 7h1m6p
49		8	9	10	11[d]	12	13	14	
50		15	16	17	18	19	20	21	
51		22	23	24	25[e]	26[e]	27[e]	28[e]	Sun 19h45m7p
52		29[e]	30[e]	1[e]	2[e]	3	4	5	

CHINESE Rén-Xū/Guǐ-Hài · Solar Term

ISO WEEK	Month	Sun	Mon	Tue	Wed	Thu	Fri	Sat	Solar Term
52	MONTH 11 Rén-Xū	21	22	23	24	25	26	27	
1	MONTH 12 Rén-Xū	28	29	30	*1*	2	3	4	Xiǎo hán
2		5	6	7	8	9	10	11	
3		12	13	14	15	***16***	17	18	Dà hán
4		19	20	21	22	23	24	25	
5		26	27	28	29	1[a]	*2*	3	Lì chūn
6	MONTH 1 Guǐ-Hài	4	5	6	7	8	9	10	
7		11	12	13	14	15[b]	16	***17***	Yǔ shuǐ
8		18	19*	20	21	22	23	24	
9		25	26	27	28	29	30	1	
10	MONTH 2 Guǐ-Hài	*2*	3	4	5	6	7	8	Jīng zhé
11		9	10	11	12	13	14	15	
12		16	***17***	18	19	20	21	22	Chūn fēn
13		23	24	25	26	27	28	29	
14		30	1	***2***[c]	3	4	5	6	Qīng míng
15	MONTH 3 Guǐ-Hài	7	8	9	10	11	12	13	
16		14	15	16	***17***	18	19*	20	Gǔ yǔ
17		21	22	23	24	25	26	27	
18		28	29	1	2	*3*	4	5	Lì xià
19	MONTH 4 Guǐ-Hài	6	7	8	9	10	11	12	
20		13	14	15	16	17	18	***19***	Xiǎo mǎn
21		20	21	22	23	24	25	26	
22		27	28	29	30	1	2	3	
23	MONTH 5 Guǐ-Hài	4	*5*[d]	6	7	8	9	10	Máng zhòng
24		11	12	13	14	15	16	17	
25		18	19	***20****	21	22	23	24	Xià zhì
26		25	26	27	28	29	1	2	
27	MONTH 6 Guǐ-Hài	3	4	5	6	*7*	8	9	Xiǎo shǔ
28		10	11	12	13	14	15	16	
29		17	18	19	20	21	22	***23***	Dà shǔ
30		24	25	26	27	28	29	30	
31	MONTH 7 Guǐ-Hài	1	2	3	4	5	6	7[e]	
32		*8*	9	10	11	12	13	14	Lì qiū
33		15[f]	16	17	18	19	20	21*	
34		22	23	***24***	25	26	27	28	Chǔ shǔ
35		29	30	1	2	3	4	5	
36	MONTH 8 Guǐ-Hài	6	7	8	9	*10*	11	12	Bái lù
37		13	14	15[g]	16	17	18	19	
38		20	21	22	23	24	***25***	26	Qiū fēn
39		27	28	29	1	2	3	4	
40	MONTH 9 Guǐ-Hài	5	6	7	8	9[h]	10	*11*	Hán lù
41		12	13	14	15	16	17	18	
42		19	20	21	22*	23	24	25	
43		***26***	27	28	29	30	1	2	Shuāng jiàng
44	MONTH 10 Guǐ-Hài	3	4	5	6	7	8	9	
45		10	*11*	12	13	14	15	16	Lì dōng
46		17	18	19	20	21	22	23	
47		24	25	***26***	27	28	29	1	Xiǎo xuě
48	MONTH 11* Guǐ-Hài	2	3	4	5	6	7	8	
49		9	10	11	*12*	13	14	15	Dà xuě
50		16	17	18	19	20	21	22	
51		23*	24	25	26	***27***[i]	28	29	Dōng zhì
52		1	2	3	4	5	6	7	

COPTIC 1879‡/1880 · ETHIOPIC 2155‡/2156

ISO WEEK	Coptic month	Sun	Mon	Tue	Wed	Thu	Fri	Sat	Ethiopic month
52	KOIAK 1879	16	17	18	19	20	21	22	TĀKHŚĀŚ 2155
1		23	24	25	26	27	28	29[c]	
2	TÔBE 1879	30	1	2	3	4	5	6[d]	ṬER 2155
3		7	8	9	10	11[e]	12	13	
4		14	15	16	17	18	19	20	
5		21	22	23	24	25	26	27	
6	MESHIR 1879	28	29	30	1	2	3	4	YAKĀTIT 2155
7		5	6	7	8	9	10	11	
8		12	13	14	15	16	17	18	
9		19	20	21	22	23	24	25	
10	PAREMOTEP 1879	26	27	28	29	30	1	2	MAGĀBIT 2155
11		3	4	5	6	7	8	9	
12		10	11	12	13	14	15	16	
13		17	18	19	20	21	22	23	
14		24	25	26	27	28	29	30	
15	PARMOUTE 1879	1	2	3	4	5	6	7	MIYĀZYĀ 2155
16		8	9	10	11	12	13	14	
17		15[f]	16	17	18	19	20	21	
18		22	23	24	25	26	27	28	
19	PASHONS 1879	29[g]	30	1	2	3	4	5	GENBOT 2155
20		6	7	8	9	10	11	12	
21		13	14	15	16	17	18	19	
22		20	21	22	23	24	25	26	
23	PAÔNE 1879	27	28	29	30	1	2	3	SANÉ 2155
24		4	5	6	7	8	9	10	
25		11	12	13	14	15	16	17	
26		18	19	20	21	22	23	24	
27	EPÊP 1879	25	26	27	28	29	30	1	ḤAMLĒ 2155
28		2	3	4	5	6	7	8	
29		9	10	11	12	13	14	15	
30		16	17	18	19	20	21	22	
31		23	24	25	26	27	28	29	
32	MESORÊ 1879	30	1	2	3	4	5	6	NAHASĒ 2155
33		7	8	9	10	11	12	13[h]	
34		14	15	16	17	18	19	20	
35		21	22	23	24	25	26	27	
36	EPAG. 1879	28	29	30	1	2	3	4	PĀG. 2155
37	THOOUT 1880	5	6	1[a]	2	3	4	5	MASKARAM 2156
38		6	7	8	9	10	11	12	
39		13	14	15	16	17[b]	18	19	
40		20	21	22	23	24	25	26	
41	PAOPE 1880	27	28	29	30	1	2	3	ṬEQEMT 2156
42		4	5	6	7	8	9	10	
43		11	12	13	14	15	16	17	
44		18	19	20	21	22	23	24	
45	ATHÔR 1880	25	26	27	28	29	30	1	HEDĀR 2156
46		2	3	4	5	6	7	8	
47		9	10	11	12	13	14	15	
48		16	17	18	19	20	21	22	
49		23	24	25	26	27	28	29	
50	KOIAK 1880	30	1	2	3	4	5	6	TĀKHŚĀŚ 2156
51		7	8	9	10	11	12	13	
52		14	15	16	17	18	19	20	

[a]New Year
[b]Spring (19:21)
[c]Summer (10:42)
[d]Autumn (3:52)
[e]Winter (2:59)
● New moon
◐ First quarter moon
○ Full moon
◑ Last quarter moon

‡Leap year
[a]New Year
[b]Yom Kippur
[c]Sukkot
[d]Winter starts
[e]Hanukkah
[f]Purim
[g]Passover
[h]Shavuot
[i]Fast of Av

[a]New Year (4861, Pig)
[b]Lantern Festival
[c]Qīngmíng
[d]Dragon Festival
[e]Qīqiǎo
[f]Hungry Ghosts
[g]Mid-Autumn Festival
[h]Double-Ninth Festival
[i]Dōngzhì
*Start of 60-name cycle

‡Leap year
[a]New Year
[b]Building of the Cross
[c]Christmas
[d]Jesus's Circumcision
[e]Epiphany
[f]Easter
[g]Mary's Announcement
[h]Jesus's Transfiguration

PERSIAN (ASTRONOMICAL) 1541/1542

Month	Sun	Mon	Tue	Wed	Thu	Fri	Sat
DEY 1541	5	6	7	8	9	10	11
	12	13	14	15	16	17	18
	19	20	21	22	23	24	25
	26	27	28	29	30	1	2
BAHMAN 1541	3	4	5	6	7	8	9
	10	11	12	13	14	15	16
	17	18	19	20	21	22	23
	24	25	26	27	28	29	30
ESFAND 1541	1	2	3	4	5	6	7
	8	9	10	11	12	13	14
	15	16	17	18	19	20	21
	22	23	24	25	26	27	28
	29	1[a]	2	3	4	5	6
FARVARDĪN 1542	7	8	9	10	11	12	13[b]
	14	15	16	17	18	19	20
	21	22	23	24	25	26	27
	28	29	30	31	1	2	3
ORDĪBEHEŠT 1542	4	5	6	7	8	9	10
	11	12	13	14	15	16	17
	18	19	20	21	22	23	24
	25	26	27	28	29	30	31
XORDĀD 1542	1	2	3	4	5	6	7
	8	9	10	11	12	13	14
	15	16	17	18	19	20	21
	22	23	24	25	26	27	28
	29	30	31	1	2	3	4
TĪR 1542	5	6	7	8	9	10	11
	12	13	14	15	16	17	18
	19	20	21	22	23	24	25
	26	27	28	29	30	31	1
MORDĀD 1542	2	3	4	5	6	7	8
	9	10	11	12	13	14	15
	16	17	18	19	20	21	22
	23	24	25	26	27	28	29
	30	31	1	2	3	4	5
SHAHRĪVAR 1542	6	7	8	9	10	11	12
	13	14	15	16	17	18	19
	20	21	22	23	24	25	26
	27	28	29	30	31	1	2
MEHR 1542	3	4	5	6	7	8	9
	10	11	12	13	14	15	16
	17	18	19	20	21	22	23
	24	25	26	27	28	29	30
ĀBĀN 1542	1	2	3	4	5	6	7
	8	9	10	11	12	13	14
	15	16	17	18	19	20	21
	22	23	24	25	26	27	28
	29	30	1	2	3	4	5
ĀZAR 1542	6	7	8	9	10	11	12
	13	14	15	16	17	18	19
	20	21	22	23	24	25	26
	27	28	29	30	1	2	3
DEY 1542	4	5	6	7	8	9	10

HINDU LUNAR 2219/2220

Month	Sun	Mon	Tue	Wed	Thu	Fri	Sat
MĀRGAŚĪRA 2219	20	21	22	23	24	25	26
	27	28	29	1	2	3	4
PAUSHA 2219	5	6	7	8	9	10	11
	11	12	13	14	15	16	17
	18	19	20	21	22	23	25
	26	27	28	29	30	1	2
MĀGHA 2219	3	4	5	6	7	8	9
	10	11	12	13	13	14	15
	16	18	19	20	21	22	23
	24	25	26	27	28[h]	29	1
PHĀLGUNA 2219	2	2	3	4	5	6	7
	8	9	10	11	12	13	14
	15[i]	16	17	18	19	20	21
	23	24	25	26	27	28	29
	30	1[a]	2	3	4	5	6
CHAITRA 2220	6	7	8[b]	9	10	11	12
	13	14	15	17	18	19	20
	21	22	23	24	25	26	27
	28	29	30	1	2	3	4
VAIŚĀKHA 2220	5	6	7	8	9	10	11
	12	13	14	15	16	17	18
	20	21	22	23	24	25	26
	27	28	29	30	1	1	2
JYAISHTHA 2220	3	4	5	6	7	8	9
	10	11	13	14	15	16	17
	18	19	20	21	22	23	24
	25	26	27	28	29	30	1
ĀSHĀḌHA 2220	2	3	4	5	6	7	8
	9	10	11	12	13	14	16
	17	18	19	20	21	22	23
	24	25	26	27	28	28	29
	30	1	2	3	4	5	6
ŚRĀVAṆA 2220	7	9	10	11	12	13	14
	15	16	17	18	19	20	21
	22	23[c]	24	25	26	27	28
	29	30	1	2	3	4[d]	5
BHĀDRAPADA 2220	6	7	8	9	10	12	13
	14	15	16	17	18	19	20
	21	22	23	24	24	25	26
	27	28	29	30	1	2	3
ĀŚVINA 2220	5	6	7	8[e]	9[e]	10[e]	11
	12	13	14	15	16	17	18
	19	20	21	22	23	24	25
	26	27	28	29	30	1[f]	2
KĀRTTIKA 2220	3	4	5	6	7	9	10
	11	12	13	14	15	16	17
	18	18	19	20	21	22	23
	24	25	26	27	28	29	30
MĀRGAŚĪRA 2220	1	3	4	5	6	7	8
	9	10	11[g]	12	13	14	15
	16	17	18	19	20	21	22
	22	23	24	26	27	28	29
	30	1	2	3	4	5	6

HINDU SOLAR 2084/2085

Month	Sun	Mon	Tue	Wed	Thu	Fri	Sat
	9	10	11	12	13	14	15
PAUSHA 2084	16	17	18	19	20	21	22
	23	24	25	26	27	28	29
	30	1[b]	2	3	4	5	6
MĀGHA 2084	7	8	9	10	11	12	13
	14	15	16	17	18	19	20
	21	22	23	24	25	26	27
	28	29	1	2	3	4	5
PHĀLGUNA 2084	6	7	8	9	10	11	12
	13	14	15	16	17	18	19
	20	21	22	23	24	25	26
	27	28	29	30	1	2	3
CHAITRA 2084	4	5	6	7	8	9	10
	11	12	13	14	15	16	17
	18	19	20	21	22	23	24
	25	26	27	28	29	30	1[a]
VAIŚĀKHA 2085	2	3	4	5	6	7	8
	9	10	11	12	13	14	15
	16	17	18	19	20	21	22
	23	24	25	26	27	28	29
	30	31	1	2	3	4	5
JYAISHTHA 2085	6	7	8	9	10	11	12
	13	14	15	16	17	18	19
	20	21	22	23	24	25	26
	27	28	29	30	31	32	1
ĀSHĀḌHA 2085	2	3	4	5	6	7	8
	9	10	11	12	13	14	15
	16	17	18	19	20	21	22
	23	24	25	26	27	28	29
	30	31	1	2	3	4	5
ŚRĀVAṆA 2085	6	7	8	9	10	11	12
	13	14	15	16	17	18	19
	20	21	22	23	24	25	26
	27	28	29	30	31	32	1
BHĀDRAPADA 2085	2	3	4	5	6	7	8
	9	10	11	12	13	14	15
	16	17	18	19	20	21	22
	23	24	25	26	27	28	29
	30	31	1	2	3	4	5
ĀŚVINA 2085	6	7	8	9	10	11	12
	13	14	15	16	17	18	19
	20	21	22	23	24	25	26
	27	28	29	30	1	2	3
KĀRTTIKA 2085	4	5	6	7	8	9	10
	11	12	13	14	15	16	17
	18	19	20	21	22	23	24
	25	26	27	28	29	30	1
MĀRGAŚĪRA 2085	2	3	4	5	6	7	8
	9	10	11	12	13	14	15
	16	17	18	19	20	21	22
	23	24	25	26	27	28	29
PAUSHA 2085	1	2	3	4	5	6	7
	8	9	10	11	12	13	14

ISLAMIC (ASTRONOMICAL) 1588/1589

Month	Sun	Mon	Tue	Wed	Thu	Fri	Sat
RAMAḌĀN 1588	19	20	21	22	23	24	25
	26	27	28	29	1[f]	2	3
SHAWWĀL 1588	4	5	6	7	8	9	10
	11	12	13	14	15	16	17
	18	19	20	21	22	23	24
	25	26	27	28	29	30	1
DHU AL-QA'DA 1588	2	3	4	5	6	7	8
	9	10	11	12	13	14	15
	16	17	18	19	20	21	22
	23	24	25	26	27	28	29
DHU AL-ḤIJJA 1588	1	2	3	4	5	6	7
	8	9	10[g]	11	12	13	14
	15	16	17	18	19	20	21
	22	23	24	25	26	27	28
	29	30	1[a]	2	3	4	5
MUḤARRAM 1589	6	7	8	9	10[b]	11	12
	13	14	15	16	17	18	19
	20	21	22	23	24	25	26
	27	28	29	30	1	2	3
ṢAFAR 1589	4	5	6	7	8	9	10
	11	12	13	14	15	16	17
	18	19	20	21	22	23	24
	25	26	27	28	29	30	1
RABĪ' I 1589	2	3	4	5	6	7	8
	9	10	11	12[c]	13	14	15
	16	17	18	19	20	21	22
	23	24	25	26	27	28	29
	30	1	2	3	4	5	6
RABĪ' II 1589	7	8	9	10	11	12	13
	14	15	16	17	18	19	20
	21	22	23	24	25	26	27
	28	29	1	2	3	4	5
JUMĀDĀ I 1589	6	7	8	9	10	11	12
	13	14	15	16	17	18	19
	20	21	22	23	24	25	26
	27	28	29	30	1	2	3
JUMĀDĀ II 1589	4	5	6	7	8	9	10
	11	12	13	14	15	16	17
	18	19	20	21	22	23	24
	25	26	27	28	29	1	2
RAJAB 1589	3	4	5	6	7	8	9
	10	11	12	13	14	15	16
	17	18	19	20	21	22	23
	24	25	26	27[d]	28	29	1
SHA'BĀN 1589	2	3	4	5	6	7	8
	9	10	11	12	13	14	15
	16	17	18	19	20	21	22
	23	24	25	26	27	28	29
RAMAḌĀN 1589	1[e]	2	3	4	5	6	7
	8	9	10	11	12	13	14
	15	16	17	18	19	20	21
	22	23	24	25	26	27	28
	29	30	1[f]	2	3	4	5

GREGORIAN 2163

Julian (Sun)	Sun	Mon	Tue	Wed	Thu	Fri	Sat	Month
Dec 12	26	27	28	29	30	31	1	JANUARY 2163
	2	3	4	5	6	7	8[a]	
Dec 26	9	10	11	12	13	14	15[b]	
	16	17	18	19	20	21	22	
Jan 9	23	24	25	26	27	28	29	
	30	31	1	2	3	4	5	FEBRUARY 2163
Jan 23	6	7	8	9	10	11	12	
	13	14	15	16	17	18	19	
Feb 6	20	21	22	23	24	25	26	
	27	28	1	2	3	4	5	MARCH 2163
Feb 20	6	7	8	9[c]	10	11	12	
	13[d]	14	15	16	17	18	19	
Mar 6	20	21	22	23	24	25	26	
	27	28	29	30	31	1	2	APRIL 2163
Mar 20	3	4	5	6	7	8	9	
	10	11	12	13	14	15	16	
Apr 3	17	18	19	20	21	22	23	
	24[e]	25	26	27	28	29	30	
Apr 17	1	2	3	4	5	6	7	MAY 2163
	8	9	10	11	12	13	14	
May 1	15	16	17	18	19	20	21	
	22	23	24	25	26	27	28	
May 15	29	30	31	1	2	3	4	JUNE 2163
	5	6	7	8	9	10	11	
May 29	12	13	14	15	16	17	18	
	19	20	21	22	23	24	25	
Jun 12	26	27	28	29	30	1	2	JULY 2163
	3	4	5	6	7	8	9	
Jun 26	10	11	12	13	14	15	16	
	17	18	19	20	21	22	23	
Jul 10	24	25	26	27	28	29	30	
	31	1	2	3	4	5	6	AUGUST 2163
Jul 24	7	8	9	10	11	12	13	
	14	15	16	17	18	19	20	
Aug 7	21	22	23	24	25	26	27	
	28	29	30	31	1	2	3	SEPTEMBER 2163
Aug 21	4	5	6	7	8	9	10	
	11	12	13	14	15	16	17	
Sep 4	18	19	20	21	22	23	24	
	25	26	27	28	29	30	1	OCTOBER 2163
Sep 18	2	3	4	5	6	7	8	
	9	10	11	12	13	14	15	
Oct 2	16	17	18	19	20	21	22	
	23	24	25	26	27	28	29	
Oct 16	30	31	1	2	3	4	5	NOVEMBER 2163
	6	7	8	9	10	11	12	
Oct 30	13	14	15	16	17	18	19	
	20	21	22	23	24	25	26	
Nov 13	27[g]	28	29	30	1	2	3	DECEMBER 2163
	4	5	6	7	8	9	10	
Nov 27	11	12	13	14	15	16	17	
	18	19	20	21	22	23	24	
Dec 11	25[h]	26	27	28	29	30	31	

Persian: [a]New Year; [b]Sizdeh Bedar

Hindu Lunar: [a]New Year (Rudhirodgārin); [b]Birthday of Rāma; [c]Birthday of Krishna; [d]Ganēśa Chaturthī; [e]Dashara; [f]Diwali; [g]Birthday of Vishnu; [h]Night of Śiva; [i]Holi

Hindu Solar: [a]New Year (Bahudhānya); [b]Pongal

Islamic: [a]New Year; [b]'Ashūrā'; [c]Prophet's Birthday; [d]Ascent of the Prophet; [e]Start of Ramaḍān; [f]'Īd al-Fiṭr; [g]'Īd al-'Aḍḥā

Gregorian: [a]Orthodox Christmas; [b]Julian New Year; [c]Ash Wednesday; [d]Feast of Orthodoxy; [e]Easter (also Orthodox); [g]Advent; [h]Christmas

2164

Gregorian 2164[‡]	Sun	Mon	Tue	Wed	Thu	Fri	Sat	Lunar Phases	ISO Week (Mon)	Julian Day (Sun noon)	Hebrew 5924/5925	Sun	Mon	Tue	Wed	Thu	Fri	Sat	Molad	Chinese Guǐ-Hài/Jiǎ-Zǐ[‡]	Sun	Mon	Tue	Wed	Thu	Fri	Sat	Solar Term	Coptic 1880/1881	Sun	Mon	Tue	Wed	Thu	Fri	Sat	Ethiopic 2156/2157
January 2164	◐[a]	2	3	4	5	6	7	8:41	1	2511445	Teveth 5924	6	7	8	9	10	11	12		Month 12 Guǐ-Hài	8	9	10	11	12	13	14	Xiǎo hán	Koiak 1880	21	22	23	24	25	26	27	Tākhśāś 2156
	8	○	10	11	12	13	14	11:38	2	2511452		13	14	15	16	17	18	19			15	16	17	18	19	20	21			28	29[c]	30	1	2	3	4	
	15	16	◑	18	19	20	21	9:48	3	2511459		20	21	22	23	24	25	26			22	23	24	25	26	27	28	Dà hán	Tōbe 1880	5	6[d]	7	8	9	10	11[e]	Ṭer 2156
	22	23	●	25	26	27	28	1:07	4	2511466		27	28	29	1	2	3	4	Tue 8h29m8p		29	30	1[a]	2	3	4	5			12	13	14	15	16	17	18	
	29	30	◐	1	2	3	4	1:42	5	2511473	Shevat 5924	5	6	7	8	9	10	11		Month 1 Jiǎ-Zǐ	6	7	8	9	10	11	12	Lì chūn		19	20	21	22	23	24	25	
February 2164	5	6	7	○	9	10	11	6:31	6	2511480		12	13	14	15	16	17	18			13	14	15[b]	16	17	18	19			26	27	28	29	30	1	2	
	12	13	14	◑	16	17	18	20:47	7	2511487		19	20	21	22	23	24	25			20	21	22	23	24*	25	26		Meshir 1880	3	4	5	6	7	8	9	Yakātit 2156
	19	20	21	●	23	24	25	12:06	8	2511494		26	27	28	29	30	1	2	Wed 21h13m9p		27	28	29	1	2	3	4	Yǔ shuǐ		10	11	12	13	14	15	16	
	26	27	28	◐	1	2	3	20:59	9	2511501	Adar 5924	3	4	5	6	7	8	9		Month 2 Jiǎ-Zǐ	5	6	7	8	9	10	11			17	18	19	20	21	22	23	
March 2164	4	5	6	7	○	9	10	23:30	10	2511508		10	11	12	13	14[f]	15	16			12	13	14	15	16	17	18	Jīng zhé		24	25	26	27	28	29	30	
	11	12	13	14	15	◑	17	4:49	11	2511515		17	18	19	20	21	22	23			19	20	21	22	23	24	25		Paremotep 1880	1	2	3	4	5	6	7	Magābit 2156
	18	19	20[b]	21	●	23	24	23:51	12	2511522		24	25	26	27	28	29	1	Fri 9h57m10p		26	27	28	29	30	1	2	Chūn fēn		8	9	10	11	12	13	14	
	25	26	27	28	29	◐	31	16:54	13	2511529		2	3	4	5	6	7	8		Month 3 Jiǎ-Zǐ	3	4	5	6	7	8	9			15	16	17	18	19	20	21	
April 2164	1	2	3	4	5	6	○	13:38	14	2511536	Nisan 5924	9	10	11	12	13	14	15[g]			10	11	12	13[c]	14	15	16	Qīng míng		22	23	24	25	26	27	28	
	8	9	10	11	12	13	◑	10:59	15	2511543		16	17	18	19	20	21	22			17	18	19	20	21	22	23		Parmoute 1880	29	30	1	2	3	4	5	Miyāzyā 2156
	15	16	17	18	19	20	●	12:27	16	2511550		23	24	25	26	27	28	29			24	25*	26	27	28	29	1	Gǔ yǔ		6[f]	7	8	9	10	11	12	
	22	23	24	25	26	27	28		17	2511557		30	1	2	3	4	5	6	Sat 22h41m11p	Month 4 Jiǎ-Zǐ	2	3	4	5	6	7	8			13	14	15	16	17	18	19	
	◐	30	1	2	3	4	5	12:00	18	2511564	Iyyar 5924	7	8	9	10	11	12	13			9	10	11	12	13	14	15	Lì xià		20	21	22	23	24	25	26	
May 2164	6	○	8	9	10	11	12	0:41	19	2511571		14	15	16	17	18	19	20			16	17	18	19	20	21	22		Pashons 1880	27	28	29[g]	30	1	2	3	Genbot 2156
	◑	14	15	16	17	18	19	16:43	20	2511578		21	22	23	24	25	26	27			23	24	25	26	27	28	29			4	5	6	7	8	9	10	
	20	●	22	23	24	25	26	1:52	21	2511585		28	29	1	2	3	4	5	Mon 11h25m12p	Leap Month 4 Jiǎ-Zǐ	30	1	2	3	4	5	6	Xiǎo mǎn		11	12	13	14	15	16	17	
	27	28	◐	30	31	1	2	5:10	22	2511592	Sivan 5924	6[h]	7	8	9	10	11	12			7	8	9	10	11	12	13			18	19	20	21	22	23	24	
June 2164	3	4	○	6	7	8	9	9:09	23	2511599		13	14	15	16	17	18	19			14	15	16	17	18	19	20	Máng zhòng	Paōne 1880	25	26	27	28	29	30	1	Sanē 2156
	10	◑	12	13	14	15	16	23:21	24	2511606		20	21	22	23	24	25	26			21	22	23	24	25	26*	27			2	3	4	5	6	7	8	
	17	18	●	20[c]	21	22	23	16:04	25	2511613		27	28	29	30	1	2	3	Wed 0h9m13p		28	29	30	1	2	3	4	Xià zhì		9	10	11	12	13	14	15	
	24	25	26	◐	28	29	30	19:38	26	2511620	Tammuz 5924	4	5	6	7	8	9	10		Month 5 Jiǎ-Zǐ	5[d]	6	7	8	9	10	11			16	17	18	19	20	21	22	
July 2164	1	2	3	○	5	6	7	16:05	27	2511627		11	12	13	14	15	16	17			12	13	14	15	16	17	18	Xiǎo shǔ	Epēp 1880	23	24	25	26	27	28	29	Hamlē 2156
	8	9	10	◑	12	13	14	7:58	28	2511634		18	19	20	21	22	23	24			19	20	21	22	23	24	25			30	1	2	3	4	5	6	
	15	16	17	18	●	20	21	6:57	29	2511641		25	26	27	28	29	1	2	Thu 12h53m14p		26	27	28	29	1	2	3			7	8	9	10	11	12	13	
	22	23	24	25	26	◐	28	7:10	30	2511648	Av 5924	3	4	5	6	7	8	9		Month 6 Jiǎ-Zǐ	4	5	6	7	8	9	10	Dà shǔ		14	15	16	17	18	19	20	
	29	30	31	1	○	3	4	22:45	31	2511655		10[i]	11	12	13	14	15	16			11	12	13	14	15	16	17		Mesorē 1880	21	22	23	24	25	26	27	Naḥasē 2156
August 2164	5	6	7	8	◑	10	11	19:17	32	2511662		17	18	19	20	21	22	23			18	19	20	21	22	23	24	Lì qiū		28	29	30	1	2	3	4	
	12	13	14	15	16	●	18	22:18	33	2511669		24	25	26	27	28	29	30			25	26	27*	28	29	30	1			5	6	7	8	9	10	11	
	19	20	21	22	23	24	◐	16:05	34	2511676	Elul 5924	1	2	3	4	5	6	7	Sat 1h37m15p	Month 7 Jiǎ-Zǐ	2	3	4	5	6	7[e]	8	Chǔ shǔ		12	13[h]	14	15	16	17	18	
	26	27	28	29	30	31	○	6:19	35	2511683		8	9	10	11	12	13	14			9	10	11	12	13	14	15[f]			19	20	21	22	23	24	25	
September 2164	2	3	4	5	6	7	◑	9:44	36	2511690		15	16	17	18	19	20	21			16	17	18	19	20	21	22	Bái lù	Epag. 1880	26	27	28	29	30	1	2	Pāg. 2156
	9	10	11	12	13	14	15		37	2511697		22	23	24	25	26	27	28			23	24	25	26	27	28	29		Thoout 1881	3	4	5	1[a]	2	3	4	Maskaram 2157
	●	17	18	19	20	21	22[d]	13:36	38	2511704	Tishri 5925	29	1[a]	2[a]	3	4	5	6	Sun 14h21m16p	Month 8 Jiǎ-Zǐ	1	2	3	4	5	6	7	Qiū fēn		5	6	7	8	9	10	11	
	◐	24	25	26	27	28	29	23:12	39	2511711		7	8	9	10[b]	11	12	13			8	9	10	11	12	13	14			12	13	14	15	16	17[b]	18	
	○	1	2	3	4	5	6	15:42	40	2511718		14	15[c]	16	17	18	19	20			15[g]	16	17	18	19	20	21	Hán lù		19	20	21	22	23	24	25	
October 2164	7	◑	9	10	11	12	13	3:19	41	2511725		21	22	23	24	25	26	27			22	23	24	25	26	27	28*		Paope 1881	26	27	28	29	30	1	2	Ṭeqemt 2157
	14	15	●	17	18	19	20	4:09	42	2511732		28	29	30	1	2	3	4	Tue 3h5m17p		29	30	1	2	3	4	5			3	4	5	6	7	8	9	
	21	22	◐	24	25	26	27	5:40	43	2511739	Heshvan 5925	5	6	7	8	9	10	11		Month 9 Jiǎ-Zǐ	6	7	8	9[h]	10	11	12	Shuāng jiàng		10	11	12	13	14	15	16	
	28	29	○	31	1	2	3	3:31	44	2511746		12	13	14	15	16	17	18			13	14	15	16	17	18	19			17	18	19	20	21	22	23	
November 2164	4	5	◑	7	8	9	10	23:25	45	2511753		19	20	21	22	23	24	25			20	21	22	23	24	25	26	Lì dōng	Athōr 1881	24	25	26	27	28	29	30	Ḫedār 2157
	11	12	13	●	15	16	17	17:29	46	2511760		26	27	28	29	30	1	2			27	28	29	30	1	2	3			1	2	3	4	5	6	7	
	18	19	20	◐	22	23	24	12:47	47	2511767	Kislev 5925	3	4	5	6	7	8	9	Wed 15h50m0p	Month 10 Jiǎ-Zǐ	4	5	6	7	8	9	10	Xiǎo xuě		8	9	10	11	12	13	14	
	25	26	27	○	29	30	1	18:00	48	2511774		10	11	12	13	14	15	16			11	12	13	14	15	16	17			15	16	17	18	19	20	21	
December 2164	2	3	4	5	◑	7	8	20:32	49	2511781		17	18	19	20	21[d]	22	23			18	19	20	21	22	23	24	Dà xuě		22	23	24	25	26	27	28	
	9	10	11	12	13	●	15	5:36	50	2511788		24	25[e]	26[e]	27[e]	28[e]	29[e]	30[e]		Month 11 Jiǎ-Zǐ	25	26	27	28*	29	1	2		Koiak 1881	29	30	1	2	3	4	5	Tākhśāś 2157
	16	17	18	19	◐	21[e]	22	21:36	51	2511795	Teveth 5925	1[e]	2[e]	3	4	5	6	7	Fri 4h34m1p		3	4	5	6	7	8[i]	9	Dōng zhì		6	7	8	9	10	11	12	
	23	24	25	26	27	○	29	11:03	52	2511802		8	9	10	11	12	13	14			10	11	12	13	14	15	16			13	14	15	16	17	18	19	
	30	31	1	2	3	4	◑	16:3[illegible]	1	2511809		15	16	17	18	19	20	21			17	18	19	20	21	22	23	Xiǎo hán		20	21	22	23	24	25	26	

‡Leap year
[a]New Year
[b]Spring (1:20)
[c]Summer (16:32)
[d]Autumn (9:32)
[e]Winter (8:42)
● New moon
◐ First quarter moon
○ Full moon
◑ Last quarter moon

[a]New Year
[b]Yom Kippur
[c]Sukkot
[d]Winter starts
[e]Hanukkah
[f]Purim
[g]Passover
[h]Shavuot
[i]Fast of Av

‡Leap year
[a]New Year (4862, Rat)
[b]Lantern Festival
[c]Qīngmíng
[d]Dragon Festival
[e]Qīqiǎo
[f]Hungry Ghosts
[g]Mid-Autumn Festival
[h]Double-Ninth Festival
[i]Dōngzhì
*Start of 60-name cycle

[a]New Year
[b]Building of the Cross
[c]Christmas
[d]Jesus's Circumcision
[e]Epiphany
[f]Easter
[g]Mary's Announcement
[h]Jesus's Transfiguration

PERSIAN (ASTRONOMICAL) 1542/1543

Month	Sun	Mon	Tue	Wed	Thu	Fri	Sat
DEY 1542	11	12	13	14	15	16	17
	18	19	20	21	22	23	24
BAHMAN 1542	25	26	27	28	29	30	1
	2	3	4	5	6	7	8
	9	10	11	12	13	14	15
	16	17	18	19	20	21	22
	23	24	25	26	27	28	29
ESFAND 1542	30	1	2	3	4	5	6
	7	8	9	10	11	12	13
	14	15	16	17	18	19	20
	21	22	23	24	25	26	27
FARVARDĪN 1543	28	29	1[a]	2	3	4	5
	6	7	8	9	10	11	12
	13[b]	14	15	16	17	18	19
	20	21	22	23	24	25	26
ORDĪBEHEŠT 1543	27	28	29	30	31	1	2
	3	4	5	6	7	8	9
	10	11	12	13	14	15	16
	17	18	19	20	21	22	23
	24	25	26	27	28	29	30
XORDĀD 1543	31	1	2	3	4	5	6
	7	8	9	10	11	12	13
	14	15	16	17	18	19	20
	21	22	23	24	25	26	27
TĪR 1543	28	29	30	31	1	2	3
	4	5	6	7	8	9	10
	11	12	13	14	15	16	17
	18	19	20	21	22	23	24
	25	26	27	28	29	30	31
MORDĀD 1543	1	2	3	4	5	6	7
	8	9	10	11	12	13	14
	15	16	17	18	19	20	21
	22	23	24	25	26	27	28
SHAHRĪVAR 1543	29	30	31	1	2	3	4
	5	6	7	8	9	10	11
	12	13	14	15	16	17	18
	19	20	21	22	23	24	25
MEHR 1543	26	27	28	29	30	31	1
	2	3	4	5	6	7	8
	9	10	11	12	13	14	15
	16	17	18	19	20	21	22
	23	24	25	26	27	28	29
ĀBĀN 1543	30	1	2	3	4	5	6
	7	8	9	10	11	12	13
	14	15	16	17	18	19	20
	21	22	23	24	25	26	27
ĀZAR 1543	28	29	30	1	2	3	4
	5	6	7	8	9	10	11
	12	13	14	15	16	17	18
	19	20	21	22	23	24	25
DEY 1543	26	27	28	29	30	1	2
	3	4	5	6	7	8	9
	10	11	12	13	14	15	16

[a]New Year
[b]Sizdeh Bedar

HINDU LUNAR 2220/2221‡

Month	Sun	Mon	Tue	Wed	Thu	Fri	Sat
PAUSHA 2220	**7**	9	10	*10*	11	12	13
	14	15	16	17	18	19	20
	21	22	23	24	25	26	27
MĀGHA 2220	28	29	**30**	2	3	4	5
	6	7	8	9	10	11	12
	13	*13*	14	15	16	17	18
	19	20	21	22	23	**24**	26
PHĀLGUNA 2220	27	28[h]	29	30	1	2	3
	4	5	6	7	8	9	10
	11	12	13	14	15[i]	16	17
	18	19	20	21	22	23	24
CHAITRA 2221	25	26	27	28	**29**	1[a]	2
	3	4	5	6	*6*	7	8[b]
	9	10	11	12	13	14	15
	16	17	18	19	20	21	**22**
	24	25	26	27	28	29	30
VAIŚĀKHA 2221	1	2	3	4	5	6	7
	8	9	10	*10*	11	12	13
	14	**15**	17	18	19	20	21
	22	23	24	25	26	27	28
JYAISHTHA 2221	29	30	1	2	3	4	5
	6	7	8	9	10	11	12
	13	14	15	16	17	**18**	20
	21	22	23	24	25	26	27
ĀSHĀDHA 2221	28	29	30	1	2	3	4
	5	6	*6*	7	8	9	10
	11	13	14	15	16	17	18
	19	20	21	22	**23**	25	26
LEAP ŚRĀVANA 2221	27	*27*	28	29	30	1	2
	3	4	5	6	7	8	9
	10	11	12	13	**14**	16	17
	18	19	20	21	22	23	24
ŚRĀVANA 2221	25	26	27	28	29	30	1
	2	3	*3*	4	5	**6**	8
	9	10	11	12	13	14	15
	16	17	**18**	20	21	22	23[c]
	24	*24*	25	26	27	28	29
BHĀDRAPADA 2221	30	1	2	3	4[d]	5	6
	7	8	9	**10**	12	13	14
	15	16	17	18	19	20	21
	22	23	24	25	26	27	28
ĀŚVINA 2221	*28*	29	30	1	2	**3**	5
	6	7	8[e]	9[e]	10[e]	11	12
	13	14	15	16	17	18	19
	20	21	22	23	24	25	26
KĀRTTIKA 2221	27	28	29	30	1[f]	2	3
	4	5	6	7	**8**	10	11
	12	13	14	15	16	17	18
	19	20	21	*21*	22	23	24
MĀRGAŚĪRA 2221	25	26	27	28	29	30	1
	2	4	5	6	7	8	9
	10	11[g]	12	13	14	15	16
	17	18	19	20	21	22	23

‡Leap year
[a]New Year (Raktāksha)
[b]Birthday of Rāma
[c]Birthday of Krishna
[d]Ganēśa Chaturthī
[e]Dashara
[f]Diwali
[g]Birthday of Vishnu
[h]Night of Śiva
[i]Holi

HINDU SOLAR 2085/2086‡

Month	Sun	Mon	Tue	Wed	Thu	Fri	Sat
PAUSHA 2085	15	16	17	18	19	20	21
	22	23	24	25	26	27	28
MĀGHA 2085	29	30	1[b]	2	3	4	5
	6	7	8	9	10	11	12
	13	14	15	16	17	18	19
	20	21	22	23	24	25	26
PHĀLGUNA 2085	27	28	29	1	2	3	4
	5	6	7	8	9	10	11
	12	13	14	15	16	17	18
	19	20	21	22	23	24	25
CHAITRA 2085	26	27	28	29	30	1	2
	3	4	5	6	7	8	9
	10	11	12	13	14	15	16
	17	18	19	20	21	22	23
	24	25	26	27	28	29	30
VAIŚĀKHA 2086	1[a]	2	3	4	5	6	7
	8	9	10	11	12	13	14
	15	16	17	18	19	20	21
	22	23	24	25	26	27	28
JYAISHTHA 2086	29	30	31	1	2	3	4
	5	6	7	8	9	10	11
	12	13	14	15	16	17	18
	19	20	21	22	23	24	25
	26	27	28	29	30	31	32
ĀSHĀDHA 2086	1	2	3	4	5	6	7
	8	9	10	11	12	13	14
	15	16	17	18	19	20	21
	22	23	24	25	26	27	28
ŚRĀVANA 2086	29	30	31	1	2	3	4
	5	6	7	8	9	10	11
	12	13	14	15	16	17	18
	19	20	21	22	23	24	25
	26	27	28	29	30	31	32
BHĀDRAPADA 2086	1	2	3	4	5	6	7
	8	9	10	11	12	13	14
	15	16	17	18	19	20	21
	22	23	24	25	26	27	28
ĀŚVINA 2086	29	30	31	1	2	3	4
	5	6	7	8	9	10	11
	12	13	14	15	16	17	18
	19	20	21	22	23	24	25
KĀRTTIKA 2086	26	27	28	29	30	1	2
	3	4	5	6	7	8	9
	10	11	12	13	14	15	16
	17	18	19	20	21	22	23
	24	25	26	27	28	29	30
MĀRGAŚĪRA 2086	1	2	3	4	5	6	7
	8	9	10	11	12	13	14
	15	16	17	18	19	20	21
	22	23	24	25	26	27	28
PAUSHA 2086	29	30	1	2	3	4	5
	6	7	8	9	10	11	12
	13	14	15	16	17	18	19

‡Leap year
[a]New Year (Pramāthin)
[b]Pongal

ISLAMIC (ASTRONOMICAL) 1589/1590‡

Month	Sun	Mon	Tue	Wed	Thu	Fri	Sat
SHAWWĀL 1589	6	7	8	9	10	11	12
	13	14	15	16	17	18	19
	20	21	22	23	24	25	26
DHU AL-QA'DA 1589	27	28	29	1	2	3	4
	5	6	7	8	9	10	11
	12	13	14	15	16	17	18
	19	20	21	22	23	24	25
DHU AL-ḤIJJA 1589	26	27	28	29	30	1	2
	3	4	5	6	7	8	9
	10[g]	11	12	13	14	15	16
	17	18	19	20	21	22	23
MUHARRAM 1590	24	25	26	27	28	29	1[a]
	2[d]	3	4	5	6	7	8
	9	10[b]	11	12	13	14	15
	16	17	18	19	20	21	22
	23	24	25	26	27	28	29
ṢAFAR 1590	30	1	2	3	4	5	6
	7	8	9	10	11	12	13
	14	15	16	17	18	19	20
	21	22	23	24	25	26	27
RABĪ' I 1590	28	29	30	1	2	3	4
	5	6	7	8	9	10	11
	12[c]	13	14	15	16	17	18
	19	20	21	22	23	24	25
RABĪ' II 1590	26	27	28	29	1	2	3
	4	5	6	7	8	9	10
	11	12	13	14	15	16	17
	18	19	20	21	22	23	24
JUMĀDĀ I 1590	25	26	27	28	29	30	1
	2	3	4	5	6	7	8
	9	10	11	12	13	14	15
	16	17	18	19	20	21	22
	23	24	25	26	27	28	29
JUMĀDĀ II 1590	30	1	2	3	4	5	6
	7	8	9	10	11	12	13
	14	15	16	17	18	19	20
	21	22	23	24	25	26	27
RAJAB 1590	28	29	1	2	3	4	5
	6	7	8	9	10	11	12
	13	14	15	16	17	18	19
	20	21	22	23	24	25	26
SHA'BĀN 1590	27[d]	28	29	1	2	3	4
	5	6	7	8	9	10	11
	12	13	14	15	16	17	18
	19	20	21	22	23	24	25
RAMAḌĀN 1590	26	27	28	29	30	1[e]	2
	3	4	5	6	7	8	9
	10	11	12	13	14	15	16
	17	18	19	20	21	22	23
SHAWWĀL 1590	24	25	26	27	28	29	1[f]
	2	3	4	5	6	7	8
	9	10	11	12	13	14	15
	16	17	18	19	20	21	22

‡Leap year
[a]New Year
[d]New Year (Arithmetic)
[b]'Āshūrā'
[c]Prophet's Birthday
[d]Ascent of the Prophet
[e]Start of Ramaḍān
[f]'Īd al-Fiṭr
[g]'Īd al-'Aḍḥā

GREGORIAN 2164‡

Julian† (Sun)	Month	Sun	Mon	Tue	Wed	Thu	Fri	Sat
Dec 18	JANUARY 2164	1	2	3	4	5	6	7
		8[a]	9	10	11	12	13	14
Jan 1		15[b]	16	17	18	19	20	21
		22	23	24	25	26	27	28
Jan 15	FEBRUARY 2164	29	30	31	1	2	3	4
		5	6	7	8	9	10	11
Jan 29		12	13	14	15	16	17	18
		19	20	21	22[c]	23	24	25
Feb 12	MARCH 2164	26	27	28	29	1	2	3
		4[d]	5	6	7	8	9	10
Feb 26		11	12	13	14	15	16	17
		18	19	20	21	22	23	24
Mar 11		25	26	27	28	29	30	31
	APRIL 2164	1	2	3	4	5	6	7
Mar 25		8[e]	9	10	11	12	13	14
		15[f]	16	17	18	19	20	21
Apr 8		22	23	24	25	26	27	28
	MAY 2164	29	30	1	2	3	4	5
Apr 22		6	7	8	9	10	11	12
		13	14	15	16	17	18	19
May 6		20	21	22	23	24	25	26
	JUNE 2164	27	28	29	30	31	1	2
May 20		3	4	5	6	7	8	9
		10	11	12	13	14	15	16
Jun 3		17	18	19	20	21	22	23
		24	25	26	27	28	29	30
Jun 17	JULY 2164	1	2	3	4	5	6	7
		8	9	10	11	12	13	14
Jul 1		15	16	17	18	19	20	21
		22	23	24	25	26	27	28
Jul 15	AUGUST 2164	29	30	31	1	2	3	4
		5	6	7	8	9	10	11
Jul 29		12	13	14	15	16	17	18
		19	20	21	22	23	24	25
Aug 12	SEPTEMBER 2164	26	27	28	29	30	31	1
		2	3	4	5	6	7	8
Aug 26		9	10	11	12	13	14	15
		16	17	18	19	20	21	22
Sep 9		23	24	25	26	27	28	29
	OCTOBER 2164	30	1	2	3	4	5	6
Sep 23		7	8	9	10	11	12	13
		14	15	16	17	18	19	20
Oct 7		21	22	23	24	25	26	27
	NOVEMBER 2164	28	29	30	31	1	2	3
Oct 21		4	5	6	7	8	9	10
		11	12	13	14	15	16	17
Nov 4		18	19	20	21	22	23	24
	DECEMBER 2164	25	26	27	28	29	30	1
Nov 18		2[g]	3	4	5	6	7	8
		9	10	11	12	13	14	15
Dec 2		16	17	18	19	20	21	22
		23	24	25[h]	26	27	28	29
Dec 16		30	31	1	2	3	4	5

‡Leap year
[a]Orthodox Christmas
[b]Julian New Year
[c]Ash Wednesday
[d]Feast of Orthodoxy
[e]Easter
[f]Orthodox Easter
[g]Advent
[h]Christmas

2165

GREGORIAN 2165	Sun Mon Tue Wed Thu Fri Sat	Lunar Phases	ISO WEEK (Mon)	JULIAN DAY (Sun noon)	HEBREW 5925/5926‡	Sun Mon Tue Wed Thu Fri Sat	Molad	CHINESE Jiǎ-Zǐ‡/Yǐ-Chǒu	Sun Mon Tue Wed Thu Fri Sat	Solar Term	COPTIC 1881/1882	Sun Mon Tue Wed Thu Fri Sat	ETHIOPIC 2157/2158
JANUARY 2165	30 31 1[a] 2 3 4 ◑	16:31	1	2511809	TEVETH 5925	15 16 17 18 19 20 21		MONTH 11 Jiǎ-Zǐ	17 18 19 20 21 22 23	Xiǎo hán	KOIAK 1881	20 21 22 23 24 25 26	TĀKHŚĀŚ 2157
	6 7 8 9 10 11 ●	16:48	2	2511816		22 23 24 25 26 27 28			24 25 26 27 28 29 30			27 28 29[c] 30 1 2 3	
	13 14 15 16 17 18 ◐	8:46	3	2511823	SHEVAT 5925	29 1 2 3 4 5 6	Sat 17h18m2p	MONTH 12 Jiǎ-Zǐ	1 2 3 4 5 6 7		TŌBE 1881	4 5 6[d] 7 8 9 10	ṬER 2157
	20 21 22 23 24 25 26		4	2511830		7 8 9 10 11 12 13			8 9 10 11 12 13 14	Dà hán		11[e] 12 13 14 15 16 17	
	○ 28 29 30 31 1 2	5:59	5	2511837		14 15 16 17 18 19 20			15 16 17 18 19 20 21			18 19 20 21 22 23 24	
FEBRUARY 2165	3 ◑ 5 6 7 8 9	9:26	6	2511844		21 22 23 24 25 26 27			22 23 24 25 26 27 28	Lì chūn		25 26 27 28 29 30 1	
	10 ● 12 13 14 15 16	3:26	7	2511851	ADAR 5925	28 29 30 1 2 3 4	Mon 6h2m3p	MONTH 1 Yǐ-Chǒu	29* 1[a] 2 3 4 5 6		MESHIR 1881	2 3 4 5 6 7 8	YAKĀTĪT 2157
	◐ 18 19 20 21 22 23	22:28	8	2511858		5 6 7 8 9 10 11			7 8 9 10 11 12 13	Yǔ shuǐ		9 10 11 12 13 14 15	
	24 25 ○ 27 28 1 2	1:23	9	2511865		12 13 14[f] 15 16 17 18			14 15[b] 16 17 18 19 20			16 17 18 19 20 21 22	
MARCH 2165	3 4 ◑ 6 7 8 9	22:23	10	2511872		19 20 21 22 23 24 25			21 22 23 24 25 26 27	Jīng zhé		23 24 25 26 27 28 29	
	10 11 ● 13 14 15 16	13:41	11	2511879	NISAN 5925	26 27 28 29 1 2 3	Tue 18h46m4p	MONTH 2 Yǐ-Chǒu	28 29 1 2 3 4 5		PAREMOTEP 1881	30 1 2 3 4 5 6	MAGĀBĪT 2157
	17 18 ◐ 20[b] 21 22 23	14:26	12	2511886		4 5 6 7 8 9 10			6 7 8 9 10 11 12	Chūn fēn		7 8 9 10 11 12 13	
	24 25 26 ○ 28 29 30	19:22	13	2511893		11 12 13 14 15[g] 16 17			13 14 15 16 17 18 19			14 15 16 17 18 19 20	
APRIL 2165	31 1 2 3 ◑ 5 6	7:39	14	2511900		18 19 20 21 22 23 24			20 21 22 23 24[c] 25 26	Qīng míng		21 22 23 24 25 26 27	
	7 8 9 ● 11 12 13	23:41	15	2511907	IYYAR 5925	25 26 27 28 29 30 1	Thu 7h30m5p	MONTH 3 Yǐ-Chǒu	27 28 29 30 1* 2 3		PARMOUTE 1881	28 29 30 1 2 3 4	MIYĀZYĀ 2157
	14 15 16 17 ◐ 19 20	8:02	16	2511914		2 3 4 5 6 7 8			4 5 6 7 8 9 10	Gǔ yǔ		5 6 7 8 9 10 11	
	21 22 23 24 25 ○ 27	10:31	17	2511921		9 10 11 12 13 14 15			11 12 13 14 15 16 17			12 13 14 15 16 17 18	
	28 29 30 1 2 ◑ 4	14:14	18	2511928		16 17 18 19 20 21 22			18 19 20 21 22 23 24			19 20 21 22 23 24 25	
MAY 2165	5 6 7 8 9 ● 11	9:43	19	2511935		23 24 25 26 27 28 29		MONTH 4 Yǐ-Chǒu	25 26 27 28 29 1 2	Lì xià	PASHONS 1881	26[f] 27 28 29[g] 30 1 2	GENBOT 2157
	12 13 14 15 16 17 ◐	2:23	20	2511942	SIVAN 5925	1 2 3 4 5 6[h] 7	Fri 20h14m6p		3 4 5 6 7 8 9			3 4 5 6 7 8 9	
	19 20 21 22 23 24 ○	22:28	21	2511949		8 9 10 11 12 13 14			10 11 12 13 14 15 16	Xiǎo mǎn		10 11 12 13 14 15 16	
	26 27 28 29 30 31 ◑	19:25	22	2511956		15 16 17 18 19 20 21			17 18 19 20 21 22 23			17 18 19 20 21 22 23	
JUNE 2165	2 3 4 5 6 7 ●	20:28	23	2511963		22 23 24 25 26 27 28			24 25 26 27 28 29 30	Máng zhòng		24 25 26 27 28 29 30	
	9 10 11 12 13 14 15		24	2511970	TAMMUZ 5925	29 30 1 2 3 4 5	Sun 8h58m7p	MONTH 5 Yǐ-Chǒu	1 2* 3 4 5[d] 6 7		PAŌNE 1881	1 2 3 4 5 6 7	SANĒ 2157
	◐ 17 18 19 20[c] 21 22	20:17	25	2511977		6 7 8 9 10 11 12			8 9 10 11 12 13 14	Xià zhì		8 9 10 11 12 13 14	
	23 ○ 25 26 27 28 29	7:53	26	2511984		13 14 15 16 17 18 19			15 16 17 18 19 20 21			15 16 17 18 19 20 21	
	30 ◑ 2 3 4 5 6	0:28	27	2511991		20 21 22 23 24 25 26			22 23 24 25 26 27 28	Xiǎo shǔ		22 23 24 25 26 27 28	
JULY 2165	7 ● 9 10 11 12 13	8:41	28	2511998	AV 5925	27 28 29 1 2 3 4	Mon 21h42m8p	MONTH 6 Yǐ-Chǒu	29 1 2 3 4 5 6		EPĒP 1881	29 30 1 2 3 4 5	ḤAMLĒ 2157
	14 15 ◐ 17 18 19 20	12:38	29	2512005		5 6 7 8 9[i] 10 11			7 8 9 10 11 12 13			6 7 8 9 10 11 12	
	21 22 ○ 24 25 26 27	15:48	30	2512012		12 13 14 15 16 17 18			14 15 16 17 18 19 20	Dà shǔ		13 14 15 16 17 18 19	
	28 29 ◑ 31 1 2 3	6:42	31	2512019		19 20 21 22 23 24 25			21 22 23 24 25 26 27			20 21 22 23 24 25 26	
AUGUST 2165	4 5 ● 7 8 9 10	22:52	32	2512026	ELUL 5925	26 27 28 29 30 1 2	Wed 10h26m9p	MONTH 7 Yǐ-Chǒu	28 29 30 1 2 3* 4	Lì qiū	MESORĒ 1881	27 28 29 30 1 2 3	NAḤASĒ 2157
	11 12 13 14 ◐ 16 17	2:49	33	2512033		3 4 5 6 7 8 9			5 6 7[e] 8 9 10 11			4 5 6 7 8 9 10	
	18 19 20 ○ 22 23 24	23:17	34	2512040		10 11 12 13 14 15 16			12 13 14 15[f] 16 17 18	Chǔ shǔ		11 12 13[h] 14 15 16 17	
	25 26 27 ◑ 29 30 31	15:20	35	2512047		17 18 19 20 21 22 23			19 20 21 22 23 24 25			18 19 20 21 22 23 24	
SEPTEMBER 2165	1 2 3 4 ● 6 7	14:49	36	2512054	TISHRI 5926	24 25 26 27 28 29 1[a]	Thu 23h10m10p	MONTH 8 Yǐ-Chǒu	26 27 28 29 1 2 3	Bái lù	EPAG. 1881	25 26 27 28 29 30 1	PĀG. 2157
	8 9 10 11 12 ◐ 14	14:46	37	2512061		2[a] 3 4 5 6 7 8			4 5 6 7 8 9 10		THOOUT 1882	2 3 4 5 1[a] 2 3	MASKARAM 2158
	15 16 17 18 19 ○ 21	7:13	38	2512068		9 10[b] 11 12 13 14 15[c]			11 12 13 14 15[g] 16 17	Qiū fēn		4 5 6 7 8 9 10	
	22[d] 23 24 25 26 ◑ 28	3:25	39	2512075		16 17 18 19 20 21 22			18 19 20 21 22 23 24			11 12 13 14 15 16 17[b]	
	29 30 1 2 3 4 ●	7:42	40	2512082		23 24 25 26 27 28 29			25 26 27 28 29 30 1			18 19 20 21 22 23 24	
OCTOBER 2165	6 7 8 9 10 11 12		41	2512089	ḤESHVAN 5926	30 1 2 3 4 5 6	Sat 11h54m11p	MONTH 9 Yǐ-Chǒu	2 3 4* 5 6 7 8	Hán lù	PAOPE 1882	25 26 27 28 29 30 1	TEQEMT 2158
	◐ 14 15 16 17 18 ○	0:53 16:14	42	2512096		7 8 9 10 11 12 13			9[h] 10 11 12 13 14 15			2 3 4 5 6 7 8	
	20 21 22 23 24 25 ◑	19:36	43	2512103		14 15 16 17 18 19 20			16 17 18 19 20 21 22	Shuāng jiàng		9 10 11 12 13 14 15	
	27 28 29 30 31 1 2		44	2512110		21 22 23 24 25 26 27			23 24 25 26 27 28 29			16 17 18 19 20 21 22	
NOVEMBER 2165	3 ● 5 6 7 8 9	0:21	45	2512117	KISLEV 5926	28 29 1 2 3 4 5	Mon 0h38m12p	MONTH 10 Yǐ-Chǒu	30 1 2 3 4 5 6	Lì dōng		23 24 25 26 27 28 29	
	10 ◐ 12 13 14 15 16	9:42	46	2512124		6 7 8 9 10 11 12			7 8 9 10 11 12 13		ATHŌR 1882	30 1 2 3 4 5 6	ḪEDĀR 2158
	17 ○ 19 20 21 22 23	2:56	47	2512131		13 14 15 16 17 18 19			14 15 16 17 18 19 20	Xiǎo xuě		7 8 9 10 11 12 13	
	24 ◑ 26 27 28 29 30	15:28	48	2512138		20 21 22 23 24 25[e] 26[e]			21 22 23 24 25 26 27			14 15 16 17 18 19 20	
DECEMBER 2165	1 2 ● 4 5 6 7	15:56	49	2512145	TEVETH 5926	27[e] 28[e] 29[e] 1[e] 2[e] 3[d][e] 4	Tue 13h22m13p	MONTH 11 Yǐ-Chǒu	28 29 1 2 3 4 5*	Dà xuě		21 22 23 24 25 26 27	
	8 9 ◐ 11 12 13 14	17:49	50	2512152		5 6 7 8 9 10 11			6 7 8 9 10 11 12		KOIAK 1882	28 29 30 1 2 3 4	TĀKHŚĀŚ 2158
	15 16 ○ 18 19 20 21[e]	15:52	51	2512159		12 13 14 15 16 17 18			13 14 15 16 17 18 19[i]	Dōng zhì		5 6 7 8 9 10 11	
	22 23 24 ◑ 26 27 28	13:24	52	2512166		19 20 21 22 23 24 25			20 21 22 23 24 25 26			12 13 14 15 16 17 18	
	29 30 31 1 ● 3 4	6:07	1	2512173		26 27 28 29 1 2 3	Thu 2h6m14p		27 28 29 30 1 2 3			19 20 21 22 23 24 25	

[a]New Year
[b]Spring (7:14)
[c]Summer (22:22)
[d]Autumn (15:27)
[e]Winter (14:38)
● New moon
◐ First quarter moon
○ Full moon
◑ Last quarter moon

‡Leap year
[a]New Year
[b]Yom Kippur
[c]Sukkot
[d]Winter starts
[e]Ḥanukkah
[f]Purim
[g]Passover
[h]Shavuot
[i]Fast of Av

‡Leap year
[a]New Year (4863, Ox)
[b]Lantern Festival
[c]Qīngmíng
[d]Dragon Festival
[e]Qīqiǎo
[f]Hungry Ghosts
[g]Mid-Autumn Festival
[h]Double-Ninth Festival
[i]Dōngzhì
*Start of 60-name cycle

[a]New Year
[b]Building of the Cross
[c]Christmas
[d]Jesus's Circumcision
[e]Epiphany
[f]Easter
[g]Mary's Announcement
[h]Jesus's Transfiguration

2165

PERSIAN (ASTRONOMICAL) 1543/1544‡

Month	Sun	Mon	Tue	Wed	Thu	Fri	Sat
DEY 1543	10	11	12	13	14	15	16
	17	18	19	20	21	22	23
	24	25	26	27	28	29	30
BAHMAN 1543	*1*	2	3	4	5	6	7
	8	9	10	11	12	13	14
	15	16	17	18	19	20	21
	22	23	24	25	26	27	28
ESFAND 1543	29	30	*1*	2	3	4	5
	6	7	8	9	10	11	12
	13	14	15	16	17	18	19
	20	21	22	23	24	25	26
FARVARDĪN 1544	27	28	29	*1*[a]	2	3	4
	5	6	7	8	9	10	11
	12	13[b]	14	15	16	17	18
	19	20	21	22	23	24	25
ORDĪBEHEŠT 1544	26	27	28	29	30	31	*1*
	2	3	4	5	6	7	8
	9	10	11	12	13	14	15
	16	17	18	19	20	21	22
	23	24	25	26	27	28	29
XORDĀD 1544	30	31	*1*	2	3	4	5
	6	7	8	9	10	11	12
	13	14	15	16	17	18	19
	20	21	22	23	24	25	26
TĪR 1544	27	28	29	30	31	*1*	2
	3	4	5	6	7	8	9
	10	11	12	13	14	15	16
	17	18	19	20	21	22	23
	24	25	26	27	28	29	30
MORDĀD 1544	31	*1*	2	3	4	5	6
	7	8	9	10	11	12	13
	14	15	16	17	18	19	20
	21	22	23	24	25	26	27
SHAHRĪVAR 1544	28	29	30	31	*1*	2	3
	4	5	6	7	8	9	10
	11	12	13	14	15	16	17
	18	19	20	21	22	23	24
	25	26	27	28	29	30	31
MEHR 1544	*1*	2	3	4	5	6	7
	8	9	10	11	12	13	14
	15	16	17	18	19	20	21
	22	23	24	25	26	27	28
ĀBĀN 1544	29	30	*1*	2	3	4	5
	6	7	8	9	10	11	12
	13	14	15	16	17	18	19
	20	21	22	23	24	25	26
ĀZAR 1544	27	28	29	30	*1*	2	3
	4	5	6	7	8	9	10
	11	12	13	14	15	16	17
	18	19	20	21	22	23	24
DEY 1544	25	26	27	28	29	30	*1*
	2	3	4	5	6	7	8
	9	10	11	12	13	14	15

‡Leap year
[a]New Year
[b]Sizdeh Bedar

HINDU LUNAR 2221‡/2222

Month	Sun	Mon	Tue	Wed	Thu	Fri	Sat
MĀRGAŚĪRA 2221	17	18	19	20	21	22	23
	24	25	26	27	28	29	30
PAUSHA 2221	1	2	3	4	5	6	**7**
	9	10	11	12	13	14	*14*
	15	16	17	18	19	20	21
	22	23	24	25	26	27	28
MĀGHA 2221	29	30	**1**	3	4	5	6
	7	8	9	10	11	12	13
	14	15	16	*16*	17	18	19
	20	21	22	23	24	**25**	27
PHĀLGUNA 2221	28	29[h]	30	1	2	3	4
	5	6	7	8	9	10	11
	12	13	14	15[i]	16	17	18
	19	20	21	22	23	24	25
CHAITRA 2222	26	27	28	**29**	1[a]	2	3
	4	5	6	7	8	9[b]	10
	10	11	12	13	14	15	16
	17	18	19	20	21	**22**	24
VAIŚĀKHA 2222	25	26	27	28	29	30	1
	2	3	4	5	6	7	8
	9	10	11	12	13	14	15
	16	17	18	19	20	21	22
	23	24	25	**26**	28	29	30
JYAISHṬHA 2222	1	2	3	4	5	*5*	6
	7	8	9	10	11	12	13
	14	15	16	17	18	**19**	21
	22	23	24	25	26	27	28
ĀSHĀḌHA 2222	29	30	1	2	3	4	5
	6	7	8	9	10	11	12
	13	14	15	16	17	18	19
	20	**21**	23	24	25	26	27
ŚRĀVAṆA 2222	28	29	30	1	2	*2*	3
	4	5	6	7	8	9	10
	11	12	13	**14**	16	17	18
	19	20	21	22	23[c]	24	25
BHĀDRAPADA 2222	26	27	28	29	30	1	2
	3	4[d]	5	6	7	8	9
	10	11	12	13	14	15	16
	17	**18**	20	21	22	23	24
	25	26	27	28	*28*	29	30
ĀŚVINA 2222	1	2	3	4	5	6	7
	8[e]	9[e]	10[e]	**11**	13	14	15
	16	17	18	19	20	21	22
	23	24	25	26	27	28	29
KĀRTTIKA 2222	30	1[f]	2	3	4	5	6
	7	8	9	10	11	12	13
	14	15	**16**	18	19	20	21
	21	22	23	24	25	26	27
MĀRGAŚĪRA 2222	28	29	30	1	2	3	4
	5	6	7	8	**9**	11[g]	12
	13	14	15	16	17	18	19
	20	21	22	23	24	*24*	25
	26	27	28	29	30	1	2

‡Leap year
[a]New Year (Krodhana)
[b]Birthday of Rāma
[c]Birthday of Krishna
[d]Ganēśa Chaturthī
[e]Dashara
[f]Diwali
[g]Birthday of Vishnu
[h]Night of Śiva
[i]Holi

HINDU SOLAR 2086‡/2087

Month	Sun	Mon	Tue	Wed	Thu	Fri	Sat
PAUSHA 2086	13	14	15	16	17	18	19
	20	21	22	23	24	25	26
MĀGHA 2086	27	28	29	1[b]	2	3	4
	5	6	7	8	9	10	11
	12	13	14	15	16	17	18
	19	20	21	22	23	24	25
PHĀLGUNA 2086	26	27	28	29	1	2	3
	4	5	6	7	8	9	10
	11	12	13	14	15	16	17
	18	19	20	21	22	23	24
CHAITRA 2086	25	26	27	28	29	30	1
	2	3	4	5	6	7	8
	9	10	11	12	13	14	15
	16	17	18	19	20	21	22
	23	24	25	26	27	28	29
VAIŚĀKHA 2087	30	31	1[a]	2	3	4	5
	6	7	8	9	10	11	12
	13	14	15	16	17	18	19
	20	21	22	23	24	25	26
JYAISHṬHA 2087	27	28	29	30	31	1	2
	3	4	5	6	7	8	9
	10	11	12	13	14	15	16
	17	18	19	20	21	22	23
	24	25	26	27	28	29	30
ĀSHĀḌHA 2087	31	1	2	3	4	5	6
	7	8	9	10	11	12	13
	14	15	16	17	18	19	20
	21	22	23	24	25	26	27
ŚRĀVAṆA 2087	28	29	30	31	32	1	2
	3	4	5	6	7	8	9
	10	11	12	13	14	15	16
	17	18	19	20	21	22	23
	24	25	26	27	28	29	30
BHĀDRAPADA 2087	31	1	2	3	4	5	6
	7	8	9	10	11	12	13
	14	15	16	17	18	19	20
	21	22	23	24	25	26	27
ĀŚVINA 2087	28	29	30	31	1	2	3
	4	5	6	7	8	9	10
	11	12	13	14	15	16	17
	18	19	20	21	22	23	24
	25	26	27	28	29	30	31
KĀRTTIKA 2087	1	2	3	4	5	6	7
	8	9	10	11	12	13	14
	15	16	17	18	19	20	21
	22	23	24	25	26	27	28
MĀRGAŚĪRA 2087	29	1	2	3	4	5	6
	7	8	9	10	11	12	13
	14	15	16	17	18	19	20
	21	22	23	24	25	26	27
PAUSHA 2087	28	29	30	1	2	3	4
	5	6	7	8	9	10	11
	12	13	14	15	16	17	18

‡Leap year
[a]New Year (Vikrama)
[b]Pongal

ISLAMIC (ASTRONOMICAL) 1590‡/1591

Month	Sun	Mon	Tue	Wed	Thu	Fri	Sat
SHAWWĀL 1590	16	17	18	19	20	21	22
	23	24	25	26	27	28	29
DHU AL-QA'DA 1590	30	*1*	2	3	4	5	6
	7	8	9	10	11	12	13
	14	15	16	17	18	19	20
	21	22	23	24	25	26	27
DHU AL-ḤIJJA 1590	28	29	1	*2*	3	4	5
	6	7	8	9	10[g]	11	12
	13	14	15	16	17	18	19
	20	21	22	23	24	25	26
MUḤARRAM 1591	27	28	29	30	*1*[a]	2	3
	4	5	6	7	8	9	10[b]
	11	12	13	14	15	16	17
	18	19	20	21	22	23	24
ṢAFAR 1591	25	26	27	28	29	1	*2*
	3	4	5	6	7	8	9
	10	11	12	13	14	15	16
	17	18	19	20	21	22	23
	24	25	26	27	28	29	30
RABĪ' I 1591	*1*	2	3	4	5	6	7
	8	9	10	11	12[c]	13	14
	15	16	17	18	19	20	21
	22	23	24	25	26	27	28
RABĪ' II 1591	29	1	*2*	3	4	5	6
	7	8	9	10	11	12	13
	14	15	16	17	18	19	20
	21	22	23	24	25	26	27
JUMĀDĀ I 1591	28	29	30	*1*	2	3	4
	5	6	7	8	9	10	11
	12	13	14	15	16	17	18
	19	20	21	22	23	24	25
JUMĀDĀ II 1591	26	27	28	29	30	*1*	2
	3	4	5	6	7	8	9
	10	11	12	13	14	15	16
	17	18	19	20	21	22	23
RAJAB 1591	24	25	26	27	28	29	*1*
	2	3	4	5	6	7	8
	9	10	11	12	13	14	15
	16	17	18	19	20	21	22
	23	24	25	26	27[d]	28	29
SHA'BĀN 1591	30	*1*	2	3	4	5	6
	7	8	9	10	11	12	13
	14	15	16	17	18	19	20
	21	22	23	24	25	26	27
RAMAḌĀN 1591	28	29	*1*[e]	2	3	4	5
	6	7	8	9	10	11	12
	13	14	15	16	17	18	19
	20	21	22	23	24	25	26
SHAWWĀL 1591	27	28	29	30	*1*[f]	2	3
	4	5	6	7	8	9	10
	11	12	13	14	15	16	17
	18	19	20	21	22	23	24
	25	26	27	28	29	*1*	2

‡Leap year
[a]New Year
[b]'Ashūrā'
[c]Prophet's Birthday
[d]Ascent of the Prophet
[e]Start of Ramaḍān
[f]'Id al-Fiṭr
[g]'Id al-'Aḍḥā

GREGORIAN 2165

Julian (Sun)	Sun	Mon	Tue	Wed	Thu	Fri	Sat	Month
Dec 16	*30*	31	1	2	3	4	5	JANUARY 2165
	6	7	8[a]	9	10	11	12	
Dec 30	*13*	14	15[b]	16	17	18	19	
	20	21	22	23	24	25	26	
Jan 13	*27*	28	29	30	31	1	2	FEBRUARY 2165
	3	4	5	6	7	8	9	
Jan 27	*10*	11	12	13[c]	14	15	16	
	17	18	19	20	21	22	23	
Feb 10	*24*	25	26	27	28	1	2	MARCH 2165
	3	4	5	6	7	8	9	
Feb 24	*10*	11	12	13	14	15	16	
	17	18	19	20	21	22	23	
Mar 10	*24*[d]	25	26	27	28	29	30	
	31[e]	1	2	3	4	5	6	APRIL 2165
Mar 24	*7*	8	9	10	11	12	13	
	14	15	16	17	18	19	20	
Apr 7	*21*	22	23	24	25	26	27	
	28	29	30	1	2	3	4	MAY 2165
Apr 21	*5*[f]	6	7	8	9	10	11	
	12	13	14	15	16	17	18	
May 5	*19*	20	21	22	23	24	25	
	26	27	28	29	30	31	1	JUNE 2165
May 19	*2*	3	4	5	6	7	8	
	9	10	11	12	13	14	15	
Jun 2	*16*	17	18	19	20	21	22	
	23	24	25	26	27	28	29	
Jun 16	*30*	1	2	3	4	5	6	JULY 2165
	7	8	9	10	11	12	13	
Jun 30	*14*	15	16	17	18	19	20	
	21	22	23	24	25	26	27	
Jul 14	*28*	29	30	31	1	2	3	AUGUST 2165
	4	5	6	7	8	9	10	
Jul 28	*11*	12	13	14	15	16	17	
	18	19	20	21	22	23	24	
Aug 11	*25*	26	27	28	29	30	31	
	1	2	3	4	5	6	7	SEPTEMBER 2165
Aug 25	*8*	9	10	11	12	13	14	
	15	16	17	18	19	20	21	
Sep 8	*22*	23	24	25	26	27	28	
	29	30	1	2	3	4	5	OCTOBER 2165
Sep 22	*6*	7	8	9	10	11	12	
	13	14	15	16	17	18	19	
Oct 6	*20*	21	22	23	24	25	26	
	27	28	29	30	31	1	2	NOVEMBER 2165
Oct 20	*3*	4	5	6	7	8	9	
	10	11	12	13	14	15	16	
Nov 3	*17*	18	19	20	21	22	23	
	24	25	26	27	28	29	30	
Nov 17	*1*[g]	2	3	4	5	6	7	DECEMBER 2165
	8	9	10	11	12	13	14	
Dec 1	*15*	16	17	18	19	20	21	
	22	23	24	25[h]	26	27	28	
Dec 15	*29*	30	31	1	2	3	4	

[a]Orthodox Christmas
[b]Julian New Year
[c]Ash Wednesday
[d]Feast of Orthodoxy
[e]Easter
[f]Orthodox Easter
[g]Advent
[h]Christmas

Gregorian 2166	Sun	Mon	Tue	Wed	Thu	Fri	Sat	Lunar Phases	ISO Week (Mon)	Julian Day (Sun noon)	Hebrew 5926‡/5927	Sun	Mon	Tue	Wed	Thu	Fri	Sat	Molad	Chinese Yǐ-Chǒu/Bǐng-Yín‡	Sun	Mon	Tue	Wed	Thu	Fri	Sat	Solar Term	Coptic 1882/1883‡	Sun	Mon	Tue	Wed	Thu	Fri	Sat	Ethiopic 2158/2159‡
January 2166	29	30	31	1[a]	●	3	4	6:07	1	2512173	Shevat 5926	26	27	28	29	1	2	3	Thu 2h 6m 14p	Month 12 Yǐ-Chǒu	27	28	29	30	1	2	3		Koiak 1882	19	20	21	22	23	24	25	Tāhśāś 2158
	5	6	7	8	◐	10	11	1:57	2	2512180		4	5	6	7	8	9	10			4	5	6	7	8	9	10	Xiǎo hán	Ṭōbe 1882	26	27	28	29[c]	30	1	2	Ṭer 2158
	12	13	14	15	○	17	18	7:20	3	2512187		11	12	13	14	15	16	17			11	12	13	14	15	16	17			3	4	5	6[d]	7	8	9	
	19	20	21	22	23	◑	25	10:56	4	2512194		18	19	20	21	22	23	24			18	**19**	20	21	22	23	24	Dà hán		10	11[e]	12	13	14	15	16	
	26	27	28	29	30	●	1	18:48	5	2512201	Adar I 5926	25	26	27	28	29	30	1	Fri 14h 50m 15p	Month 1 Bǐng-Yín	25	26	27	28	29	30	1[a]			17	18	19	20	21	22	23	
February 2166	2	3	4	5	6	◐	8	10:51	6	2512208		2	3	4	5	6	7	8			2	3	*4*	5*	6	7	8	Lì chūn		24	25	26	27	28	29	30	
	9	10	11	12	13	14	○	0:58	7	2512215		9	10	11	12	13	14	15			9	10	11	12	13	14	15[b]		Meshir 1882	1	2	3	4	5	6	7	Yakātit 2158
	16	17	18	19	20	21	22		8	2512222		16	17	18	19	20	21	22			16	17	**18**	19	20	21	22	Yǔ shuǐ		8	9	10	11	12	13	14	
	◑	24	25	26	27	28	1	5:56	9	2512229		23	24	25	26	27	28	29	Sun 3h 34m 16p		23	24	25	26	27	28	29			15	16	17	18	19	20	21	
March 2166	●	3	4	5	6	7	◐	5:56 21:19	10	2512236	Adar II 5926	30	1	2	3	4	5	6		Month 2 Bǐng-Yín	1	2	3	*4*	5	6	7	Jīng zhé		22	23	24	25	26	27	28	
	9	10	11	12	13	14	15		11	2512243		7	8	9	10	11	12	13			8	9	10	11	12	13	14		Paremotep 1882	29	30	1	2	3	4	5	Magābit 2158
	○	17	18	19	20[b]	21	22	19:28	12	2512250		14[f]	15	16	17	18	19	20			15	16	17	18	**19**	20	21	Chūn fēn		6	7	8	9	10	11	12	
	23	◑	25	26	27	28	29	21:15	13	2512257		21	22	23	24	25	26	27			22	23	24	25	26	27	28			13	14	15	16	17	18	19	
April 2166	30	●	1	2	3	4	5	15:30	14	2512264	Nisan 5926	28	29	1	2	3	4	5	Mon 16h 18m 17p	Month 3 Bǐng-Yín	29	1	2	3	4	5	6[c]	Qīng míng		20	21	22	23	24	25	26	
	6	◐	8	9	10	11	12	9:51	15	2512271		6	7	8	9	10	11	12			7*	8	9	10	11	12	13		Parmoute 1882	27	28	29	30	1	2	3	Miyāzyā 2158
	13	14	○	16	17	18	19	13:09	16	2512278		13	14	15[g]	16	17	18	19			14	15	16	17	18	19	20			4	5	6	7	8	9	10	
	20	21	22	◑	24	25	26	8:41	17	2512285		20	21	22	23	24	25	26			***21***	22	23	24	25	26	27	Gǔ yǔ		11[f]	12	13	14	15	16	17	
May 2166	27	28	●	30	1	2	3	23:55	18	2512292	Iyar 5926	27	28	29	30	1	2	3	Wed 5h 3m 0p	Month 4 Bǐng-Yín	28	29	30	1	2	3	4			18	19	20	21	22	23	24	
	4	5	6	◐	8	9	10	0:31	19	2512299		4	5	6	7	8	9	10			5	6	7	8	9	10	11	Lì xià	Pashons 1882	25	26	27	28	29[g]	30	1	Genbot 2158
	11	12	13	14	○	16	17	4:50	20	2512306		11	12	13	14	15	16	17			12	13	14	15	16	17	18			2	3	4	5	6	7	8	
	18	19	20	21	◑	23	24	16:42	21	2512313		18	19	20	21	22	23	24			19	20	21	**22**	23	24	25	Xiǎo mǎn		9	10	11	12	13	14	15	
	25	26	27	28	●	30	31	7:58	22	2512320	Sivan 5926	25	26	27	28	29	1	2	Thu 17h 47m 1p	Month 5 Bǐng-Yín	26	27	28	29	1	2	3			16	17	18	19	20	21	22	
June 2166	1	2	3	4	◐	6	7	16:53	23	2512327		3	4	5	6[h]	7	8	9			4	5[d]	6	7	8*	9	10	Máng zhòng		23	24	25	26	27	28	29	
	8	9	10	11	12	○	14	18:09	24	2512334		10	11	12	13	14	15	16			11	12	13	14	15	16	17		Paōne 1882	30	1	2	3	4	5	6	Sanē 2158
	15	16	17	18	19	◑	21[c]	22:16	25	2512341		17	18	19	20	21	22	23			18	19	20	21	22	23	**24**	Xià zhì		7	8	9	10	11	12	13	
	22	23	24	25	26	●	28	16:45	26	2512348		24	25	26	27	28	29	30		Month 6 Bǐng-Yín	25	26	27	28	29	30	1			14	15	16	17	18	19	20	
July 2166	29	30	1	2	3	4	◐	10:07	27	2512355	Tammuz 5926	1	2	3	4	5	6	7	Sat 6h 31m 2p		2	3	4	5	6	7	8			21	22	23	24	25	26	27	
	6	7	8	9	10	11	12		28	2512362		8	9	10	11	12	13	14			9	*10*	11	12	13	14	15	Xiǎo shǔ	Epēp 1882	28	29	30	1	2	3	4	Hamlē 2158
	○	14	15	16	17	18	19	5:24	29	2512369		15	16	17	18	19	20	21			16	17	18	19	20	21	22			5	6	7	8	9	10	11	
	◑	21	22	23	24	25	26	2:40	30	2512376		22	23	24	25	26	27	28			23	24	**25**	26	27	28	29	Dà shǔ		12	13	14	15	16	17	18	
August 2166	●	28	29	30	31	1	2	3:19	31	2512383	Av 5926	29	1	2	3	4	5	6	Sun 19h 15m 3p	Month 7 Bǐng-Yín	1	2	3	4	5	6	7[e]			19	20	21	22	23	24	25	
	3	◐	5	6	7	8	9	3:22	32	2512390		7	8	9[i]	10	11	12	13			8	9*	10	11	*12*	13	14	Lì qiū	Mesorē 1882	26	27	28	29	30	1	2	Nahasē 2158
	10	○	12	13	14	15	16	15:07	33	2512397		14	15	16	17	18	19	20			15[f]	16	17	18	19	20	21			3	4	5	6	7	8	9	
	17	◑	19	20	21	22	23	7:26	34	2512404		21	22	23	24	25	26	27			22	23	24	25	26	27	**28**	Chǔ shǔ		10	11	12	13[h]	14	15	16	
	24	●	26	27	28	29	30	16:18	35	2512411	Elul 5926	28	29	30	1	2	3	4	Tue 7h 59m 4p	Month 8 Bǐng-Yín	29	30	1	2	3	4	5			17	18	19	20	21	22	23	
September 2166	31	1	◐	3	4	5	6	19:57	36	2512418		5	6	7	8	9	10	11			6	7	8	9	10	11	12			24	25	26	27	28	29	30	
	7	8	○	10	11	12	13	23:56	37	2512425		12	13	14	15	16	17	18			*13*	14	15[g]	16	17	18	19	Bái lù	Epag. 1882 / Thoout 1883	1	2	3	4	5	1[a]	2	Pāg. 2158 / Maskaram 2159
	14	15	◑	17	18	19	20	14:10	38	2512432		19	20	21	22	23	24	25			20	21	22	23	24	25	26			3	4	5	6	7	8	9	
	21	22[d]	23	●	25	26	27	7:43	39	2512439	Tishri 5927	26	27	28	29	1[a]	2[a]	3	Wed 20h 43m 5p	Month 9 Bǐng-Yín	27	28	**29**	1	2	3	4	Qiū fēn		10	11	12	13	14	15	16	
October 2166	28	29	30	1	◐	3	4	11:23	40	2512446		4	5	6	7	8	9	10[b]			5	6	7	8	9[h]	10*	11			17[b]	18	19	20	21	22	23	
	5	6	7	8	○	10	11	8:29	41	2512453		11	12	13	14	15[c]	16	17			12	13	14	*15*	16	17	18	Hán lù		24	25	26	27	28	29	30	
	12	13	14	15	◑	17	18	0:17	42	2512460		18	19	20	21	22	23	24			19	20	21	22	23	24	25		Paope 1883	1	2	3	4	5	6	7	Ṭeqemt 2159
	19	20	21	22	23	●	25	0:58	43	2512467	Heshvan 5927	25	26	27	28	29	30	1	Fri 9h 27m 6p	Month 10 Bǐng-Yín	26	27	28	29	**30**	1	2	Shuāng jiàng		8	9	10	11	12	13	14	
	26	27	28	29	30	31	◐	1:11	44	2512474		2	3	4	5	6	7	8			3	4	5	6	7	8	9			15	16	17	18	19	20	21	
November 2166	2	3	4	5	6	○	8	17:31	45	2512481		9	10	11	12	13	14	15			10	11	12	13	14	*15*	16	Lì dōng		22	23	24	25	26	27	28	
	9	10	11	12	13	◑	15	14:35	46	2512488		16	17	18	19	20	21	22			17	18	19	20	21	22	23		Athōr 1883	29	30	1	2	3	4	5	Hedār 2159
	16	17	18	19	20	21	●	19:07	47	2512495		23	24	25	26	27	28	29			24	25	26	27	28	29	**30**	Xiǎo xuě		6	7	8	9	10	11	12	
	23	24	25	26	27	28	29		48	2512502	Kislev 5927	1	2	3	4	5	6	7	Sat 22h 11m 7p	*Leap Month 10* Bǐng-Yín	1	2	3	4	5	6	7			13	14	15	16	17	18	19	
December 2166	◐	1	2	3	4	5	6	12:57	49	2512509		8	9	10	11	12	13	14[d]			8	9	10*	11	12	13	14			20	21	22	23	24	25	26	
	○	8	9	10	11	12	13	3:45	50	2512516		15	16	17	18	19	20	21			*15*	16	17	18	19	20	21	Dà xuě	Koiak 1883	27	28	29	30	1	2	3	Tāhśāś 2159
	◑	15	16	17	18	19	20	8:51	51	2512523		22	23	24	25[e]	26[e]	27[e]	28[e]			22	23	24	25	26	27	28			4	5	6	7	8	9	10	
	21[e]	●	23	24	25	26	27	13:03	52	2512530	Teveth 5927	29[e]	30[e]	1[e]	2[e]	3	4	5	Mon 10h 55m 8p	Month 11 Bǐng-Yín	29	1[i]	2	3	4	5	6	Dōng zhì		11	12	13	14	15	16	17	
	28	◐	30	31	1	2	3	22:37	1	2512537		6	7	8	9	10	11	12			7	8	9	10	11	12	13			18	19	20	21	22	23	24	

Gregorian:
[a]New Year
[b]Spring (13:08)
[c]Summer (4:11)
[d]Autumn (21:19)
[e]Winter (20:31)
● New moon
◐ First quarter moon
○ Full moon
◑ Last quarter moon

Hebrew:
‡Leap year
[a]New Year
[b]Yom Kippur
[c]Sukkot
[d]Winter starts
[e]Ḥanukkah
[f]Purim
[g]Passover
[h]Shavuot
[i]Fast of Av

Chinese:
‡Leap year
[a]New Year (4864, Tiger)
[b]Lantern Festival
[c]Qīngmíng
[d]Dragon Festival
[e]Qīqiǎo
[f]Hungry Ghosts
[g]Mid-Autumn Festival
[h]Double-Ninth Festival
[i]Dōngzhì
*Start of 60-name cycle

Coptic/Ethiopic:
‡Leap year
[a]New Year
[b]Building of the Cross
[c]Christmas
[d]Jesus's Circumcision
[e]Epiphany
[f]Easter
[g]Mary's Announcement
[h]Jesus's Transfiguration

PERSIAN (ASTRONOMICAL) 1544‡/1545

Month	Sun	Mon	Tue	Wed	Thu	Fri	Sat
DEY 1544	9	10	11	12	13	14	15
	16	17	18	19	20	21	22
	23	24	25	26	27	28	29
BAHMAN 1544	30	1	2	3	4	5	6
	7	8	9	10	11	12	13
	14	15	16	17	18	19	20
	21	22	23	24	25	26	27
ESFAND 1544	28	29	30	1	2	3	4
	5	6	7	8	9	10	11
	12	13	14	15	16	17	18
	19	20	21	22	23	24	25
FARVARDĪN 1545	26	27	28	29	30	1[a]	2
	3	4	5	6	7	8	9
	10	11	12	13[b]	14	15	16
	17	18	19	20	21	22	23
	24	25	26	27	28	29	30
ORDĪBEHEŠT 1545	31	1	2	3	4	5	6
	7	8	9	10	11	12	13
	14	15	16	17	18	19	20
	21	22	23	24	25	26	27
XORDĀD 1545	28	29	30	31	1	2	3
	4	5	6	7	8	9	10
	11	12	13	14	15	16	17
	18	19	20	21	22	23	24
	25	26	27	28	29	30	31
TĪR 1545	1	2	3	4	5	6	7
	8	9	10	11	12	13	14
	15	16	17	18	19	20	21
	22	23	24	25	26	27	28
MORDĀD 1545	29	30	31	1	2	3	4
	5	6	7	8	9	10	11
	12	13	14	15	16	17	18
	19	20	21	22	23	24	25
SHAHRĪVAR 1545	26	27	28	29	30	31	1
	2	3	4	5	6	7	8
	9	10	11	12	13	14	15
	16	17	18	19	20	21	22
	23	24	25	26	27	28	29
MEHR 1545	30	31	1	2	3	4	5
	6	7	8	9	10	11	12
	13	14	15	16	17	18	19
	20	21	22	23	24	25	26
ABĀN 1545	27	28	29	30	1	2	3
	4	5	6	7	8	9	10
	11	12	13	14	15	16	17
	18	19	20	21	22	23	24
ĀZAR 1545	25	26	27	28	29	30	1
	2	3	4	5	6	7	8
	9	10	11	12	13	14	15
	16	17	18	19	20	21	22
	23	24	25	26	27	28	29
DEY 1545	30	1	2	3	4	5	6
	7	8	9	10	11	12	13

HINDU LUNAR 2222/2223

Month	Sun	Mon	Tue	Wed	Thu	Fri	Sat
	26	27	28	29	30	1	2
PAUSHA 2222	**3**	5	6	7	8	9	10
	11	12	13	14	15	16	17
	18	19	20	21	22	23	24
MĀGHA 2222	25	26	27	28	29	30	1
	2	3	4	5	6	7	**8**
	10	11	12	13	14	15	16
	16	17	18	19	20	21	22
	23	24	25	26	27	28[h]	29
PHĀLGUNA 2222	30	1	**2**	4	5	6	7
	8	9	10	11	12	13	14
	15[i]	16	17	18	19	19	20
	21	22	23	24	**25**	27	28
CHAITRA 2223	29	30	1[a]	2	3	4	5
	6	7	8[b]	9	10	11	12
	13	14	15	16	17	18	19
	20	21	22	23	24	25	26
VAIŚĀKHA 2223	27	28	**29**	1	2	3	4
	5	6	7	8	9	10	11
	12	13	13	14	15	16	17
	18	19	20	21	22	**23**	25
JYAISHṬHA 2223	26	27	28	29	30	1	2
	3	4	5	6	7	8	9
	10	11	12	13	14	15	16
	17	18	19	20	21	22	23
ĀSHĀḌHA 2223	24	25	**26**	28	29	30	1
	2	3	4	5	6	7	8
	9	10	10	11	12	13	14
	15	16	17	**18**	20	21	22
	23	24	25	26	27	28	29
ŚRĀVAṆA 2223	30	1	2	3	4	5	6
	7	8	9	10	11	12	13
	14	15	16	17	18	19	20
	21	23[c]	24	25	26	27	28
BHĀDRAPADA 2223	29	30	1	2	3	4[d]	5
	6	6	7	8	9	10	11
	12	13	**14**	16	17	18	19
	20	21	22	23	24	25	26
ĀŚVINA 2223	27	28	29	30	1	2	3
	4	5	6	7	8[e]	9[e]	10[e]
	11	12	13	14	15	16	17
	18	20	21	22	23	24	25
KĀRTTIKA 2223	26	27	28	29	30	1	1[f]
	2	3	4	5	6	7	8
	9	10	11	**12**	14	15	16
	17	18	19	20	21	22	23
	24	25	26	27	28	29	30
MĀRGAŚĪRA 2223	1	2	3	4	5	6	7
	8	9	10	**11**[g]	12	13	14
	15	**16**	18	19	20	21	22
	23	24	25	25	26	27	28
PAUSHA 2223	29	30	1	2	3	4	5
	6	7	8	9	**10**	12	13

HINDU SOLAR 2087/2088

Month	Sun	Mon	Tue	Wed	Thu	Fri	Sat
PAUSHA 2087	12	13	14	15	16	17	18
	19	20	21	22	23	24	25
MĀGHA 2087	26	27	28	29	1[b]	2	3
	4	5	6	7	8	9	10
	11	12	13	14	15	16	17
	18	19	20	21	22	23	24
PHĀLGUNA 2087	25	26	27	28	29	30	1
	2	3	4	5	6	7	8
	9	10	11	12	13	14	15
	16	17	18	19	20	21	22
	23	24	25	26	27	28	29
CHAITRA 2087	30	1	2	3	4	5	6
	7	8	9	10	11	12	13
	14	15	16	17	18	19	20
	21	22	23	24	25	26	27
VAIŚĀKHA 2088	28	29	30	1[a]	2	3	4
	5	6	7	8	9	10	11
	12	13	14	15	16	17	18
	19	20	21	22	23	24	25
JYAISHṬHA 2088	26	27	28	29	30	31	1
	2	3	4	5	6	7	8
	9	10	11	12	13	14	15
	16	17	18	19	20	21	22
	23	24	25	26	27	28	29
ĀSHĀḌHA 2088	30	31	1	2	3	4	5
	6	7	8	9	10	11	12
	13	14	15	16	17	18	19
	20	21	22	23	24	25	26
ŚRĀVAṆA 2088	27	28	29	30	31	32	1
	2	3	4	5	6	7	8
	9	10	11	12	13	14	15
	16	17	18	19	20	21	22
	23	24	25	26	27	28	29
BHĀDRAPADA 2088	30	31	1	2	3	4	5
	6	7	8	9	10	11	12
	13	14	15	16	17	18	19
	20	21	22	23	24	25	26
ĀŚVINA 2088	27	28	29	30	31	1	2
	3	4	5	6	7	8	9
	10	11	12	13	14	15	16
	17	18	19	20	21	22	23
	24	25	26	27	28	29	30
KĀRTTIKA 2088	31	1	2	3	4	5	6
	7	8	9	10	11	12	13
	14	15	16	17	18	19	20
	21	22	23	24	25	26	27
MĀRGAŚĪRA 2088	28	29	30	1	2	3	4
	5	6	7	8	9	10	11
	12	13	14	15	16	17	18
	19	20	21	22	23	24	25
PAUSHA 2088	26	27	28	29	1	2	3
	4	5	6	7	8	9	10
	11	12	13	14	15	16	17

ISLAMIC (ASTRONOMICAL) 1591/1592‡

Month	Sun	Mon	Tue	Wed	Thu	Fri	Sat
	25	26	27	28	29	1	2
DHU AL-QA'DA 1591	3	4	5	6	7	8	9
	10	11	12	13	14	15	16
	17	18	19	20	21	22	23
	24	25	26	27	28	29	30
DHU AL-HIJJA 1591	1	2	3	4	5	6	7
	8	9	10[g]	11	12	13	14
	15	16	17	18	19	20	21
	22	23	24	25	26	27	28
MUḤARRAM 1592	29	1[a]	2	3	4	5	6
	7	8	9	10[b]	11	12	13
	14	15	16	17	18	19	20
	21	22	23	24	25	26	27
ṢAFAR 1592	28	29	30	1	2	3	4
	5	6	7	8	9	10	11
	12	13	14	15	16	17	18
	19	20	21	22	23	24	25
RABĪʿ I 1592	26	27	28	29	1	2	3
	4	5	6	7	8	9	10
	11	12[c]	13	14	15	16	17
	18	19	20	21	22	23	24
RABĪʿ II 1592	25	26	27	28	29	30	1
	2	3	4	5	6	7	8
	9	10	11	12	13	14	15
	16	17	18	19	20	21	22
	23	24	25	26	27	28	29
JUMĀDĀ I 1592	1	2	3	4	5	6	7
	8	9	10	11	12	13	14
	15	16	17	18	19	20	21
	22	23	24	25	26	27	28
JUMĀDĀ II 1592	29	30	1	2	3	4	5
	6	7	8	9	10	11	12
	13	14	15	16	17	18	19
	20	21	22	23	24	25	26
RAJAB 1592	27	28	29	1	2	3	4
	5	6	7	8	9	10	11
	12	13	14	15	16	17	18
	19	20	21	22	23	24	25
SHA'BĀN 1592	26	27[d]	28	29	30	1	2
	3	4	5	6	7	8	9
	10	11	12	13	14	15	16
	17	18	19	20	21	22	23
RAMAḌĀN 1592	24	25	26	27	28	29	1[e]
	2	3	4	5	6	7	8
	9	10	11	12	13	14	15
	16	17	18	19	20	21	22
	23	24	25	26	27	28	29
SHAWWĀL 1592	30	1[f]	2	3	4	5	6
	7	8	9	10	11	12	13
	14	15	16	17	18	19	20
	21	22	23	24	25	26	27
DHU AL-QA'DA 1592	28	29	30	1	2	3	4
	5	6	7	8	9	10	11

GREGORIAN 2166

Julian (Sun)	Sun	Mon	Tue	Wed	Thu	Fri	Sat	Month
Dec 15	29	30	31	1	2	3	4	JANUARY 2166
	5	6	7	8[a]	9	10	11	
Dec 29	12	13	14	15[b]	16	17	18	
	19	20	21	22	23	24	25	
Jan 12	26	27	28	29	30	31	1	FEBRUARY 2166
	2	3	4	5	6	7	8	
Jan 26	9	10	11	12	13	14	15	
	16	17	18	19	20	21	22	
Feb 9	23	24	25	26	27	28	1	MARCH 2166
	2	3	4	5[c]	6	7	8	
Feb 23	9[d]	10	11	12	13	14	15	
	16	17	18	19	20	21	22	
Mar 9	23	24	25	26	27	28	29	
	30	31	1	2	3	4	5	APRIL 2166
Mar 23	6	7	8	9	10	11	12	
	13	14	15	16	17	18	19	
Apr 6	20[e]	21	22	23	24	25	26	
	27	28	29	30	1	2	3	MAY 2166
Apr 20	4	5	6	7	8	9	10	
	11	12	13	14	15	16	17	
May 4	18	19	20	21	22	23	24	
	25	26	27	28	29	30	31	
May 18	1	2	3	4	5	6	7	JUNE 2166
	8	9	10	11	12	13	14	
Jun 1	15	16	17	18	19	20	21	
	22	23	24	25	26	27	28	
Jun 15	29	30	1	2	3	4	5	JULY 2166
	6	7	8	9	10	11	12	
Jun 29	13	14	15	16	17	18	19	
	20	21	22	23	24	25	26	
Jul 13	27	28	29	30	31	1	2	AUGUST 2166
	3	4	5	6	7	8	9	
Jul 27	10	11	12	13	14	15	16	
	17	18	19	20	21	22	23	
Aug 10	24	25	26	27	28	29	30	
	31	1	2	3	4	5	6	SEPTEMBER 2166
Aug 24	7	8	9	10	11	12	13	
	14	15	16	17	18	19	20	
Sep 7	21	22	23	24	25	26	27	
	28	29	30	1	2	3	4	OCTOBER 2166
Sep 21	5	6	7	8	9	10	11	
	12	13	14	15	16	17	18	
Oct 5	19	20	21	22	23	24	25	
	26	27	28	29	30	31	1	NOVEMBER 2166
Oct 19	2	3	4	5	6	7	8	
	9	10	11	12	13	14	15	
Nov 2	16	17	18	19	20	21	22	
	23	24	25	26	27	28	29	
Nov 16	30[g]	1	2	3	4	5	6	DECEMBER 2166
	7	8	9	10	11	12	13	
Nov 30	14	15	16	17	18	19	20	
	21	22	23	24	25[h]	26	27	
Dec 14	28	29	30	31	1	2	3	

Persian:
‡Leap year
[a]New Year
[b]Sizdeh Bedar

Hindu Lunar:
[a]New Year (Kshaya)
[b]Birthday of Rāma
[c]Birthday of Krishna
[d]Ganēśa Chaturthī
[e]Dashara
[f]Diwali
[g]Birthday of Vishnu
[h]Night of Śiva
[i]Holi

Hindu Solar:
[a]New Year (Vṛisha)
[b]Pongal

Islamic:
‡Leap year
[a]New Year
[b]'Ashūrā'
[c]Prophet's Birthday
[d]Ascent of the Prophet
[e]Start of Ramaḍān
[f]'Īd al-Fiṭr
[g]'Īd al-'Aḍḥā

Gregorian:
[a]Orthodox Christmas
[b]Julian New Year
[c]Ash Wednesday
[d]Feast of Orthodoxy
[e]Easter (also Orthodox)
[g]Advent
[h]Christmas

2167

GREGORIAN 2167 / ISO WEEK / JULIAN DAY

Month	Sun	Mon	Tue	Wed	Thu	Fri	Sat	Lunar Phases	ISO WEEK (Mon)	JULIAN DAY (Sun noon)
	28	◐	30	31	1[a]	2	3	22:37	1	2512537
	4	○	6	7	8	9	10	15:44	2	2512544
JANUARY 2167	11	12	◑	14	15	16	17	5:48	3	2512551
	18	19	20	●	22	23	24	5:37	4	2512558
	25	26	27	◐	29	30	31	6:43	5	2512565
	1	2	3	○	5	6	7	5:37	6	2512572
FEBRUARY 2167	8	9	10	11	◑	13	14	3:28	7	2512579
	15	16	17	18	●	20	21	19:52	8	2512586
	22	23	24	25	◐	27	28	14:15	9	2512593
	1	2	3	4	○	6	7	21:02	10	2512600
	8	9	10	11	12	◑	14	23:51	11	2512607
MARCH 2167	15	16	17	18	19	20[b]	●	7:25	12	2512614
	22	23	24	25	26	◐	28	22:20	13	2512621
	29	30	31	1	2	3	○	13:15	14	2512628
	5	6	7	8	9	10	11		15	2512635
APRIL 2167	◑	13	14	15	16	17	18	17:22	16	2512642
	●	20	21	22	23	24	25	16:34	17	2512649
	◐	27	28	29	30	1	2	7:50	18	2512656
	3	○	5	6	7	8	9	5:34	19	2512663
MAY 2167	10	11	◑	13	14	15	16	7:07	20	2512670
	17	18	●	20	21	22	23	0:10	21	2512677
	24	◐	26	27	28	29	30	19:12	22	2512684
	31	1	○	3	4	5	6	21:21	23	2512691
	7	8	9	◑	11	12	13	17:02	24	2512698
JUNE 2167	14	15	16	●	18	19	20	7:18	25	2512705
	21[c]	22	23	◐	25	26	27	8:36	26	2512712
	28	29	30	1	○	3	4	12:07	27	2512719
	5	6	7	8	◑	10	11	23:53	28	2512726
JULY 2167	12	13	14	15	●	17	18	15:02	29	2512733
	19	20	21	22	◐	24	25	23:59	30	2512740
	26	27	28	29	30	31	○	1:27	31	2512747
	2	3	4	5	6	7	◑	4:57	32	2512754
AUGUST 2167	9	10	11	12	13	14	●	0:15	33	2512761
	16	17	18	19	20	21	◐	17:09	34	2512768
	23	24	25	26	27	28	29		35	2512775
	○	31	1	2	3	4	5	13:13	36	2512782
	◑	7	8	9	10	11	12	9:45	37	2512789
SEPTEMBER 2167	●	14	15	16	17	18	19	11:39	38	2512796
	20	◐	22	23[d]	24	25	26	11:32	39	2512803
	27	○	29	30	1	2	3	23:40	40	2512810
	4	◑	6	7	8	9	10	15:51	41	2512817
OCTOBER 2167	11	12	●	14	15	16	17	1:42	42	2512824
	18	19	20	◐	22	23	24	6:03	43	2512831
	25	26	27	○	29	30	31	9:27	44	2512838
	1	2	3	◑	5	6	7	0:31	45	2512845
	8	9	10	●	12	13	14	18:30	46	2512852
NOVEMBER 2167	15	16	17	18	◐	20	21	23:18	47	2512859
	22	23	24	25	○	27	28	19:22	48	2512866
	29	30	1	2	◑	4	5	12:33	49	2512873
	6	7	8	9	10	●	12	13:28	50	2512880
DECEMBER 2167	13	14	15	16	17	18	◐	14:04	51	2512887
	20	21	22[e]	23	24	25	○	5:56	52	2512894
	27	28	29	30	31	1	◑	4:10	53	2512901

HEBREW 5927/5928‡

ISO WEEK	Month	Sun	Mon	Tue	Wed	Thu	Fri	Sat	Molad
1		6	7	8	9	10	11	12	
2	TEVETH 5927	13	14	15	16	17	18	19	
3		20	21	22	23	24	25	26	
4		27	28	29	1	2	3	4	Tue 23h39m9p
5		5	6	7	8	9	10	11	
6	SHEVAT 5927	12	13	14	15	16	17	18	
7		19	20	21	22	23	24	25	
8		26	27	28	29	30	1	2	Thu 12h23m10p
9	ADAR 5927	3	4	5	6	7	8	9	
10		10	11	12	13	14[f]	15	16	
11		17	18	19	20	21	22	23	
12		24	25	26	27	28	29	1	Sat 1h7m11p
13		2	3	4	5	6	7	8	
14	NISAN 5927	9	10	11	12	13	14	15[g]	
15		16	17	18	19	20	21	22	
16		23	24	25	26	27	28	29	
17		30	1	2	3	4	5	6	Sun 13h51m12p
18		7	8	9	10	11	12	13	
19	IYYAR 5927	14	15	16	17	18	19	20	
20		21	22	23	24	25	26	27	
21		28	29	1	2	3	4	5	Tue 2h35m13p
22		6[h]	7	8	9	10	11	12	
23	SIVAN 5927	13	14	15	16	17	18	19	
24		20	21	22	23	24	25	26	
25		27	28	29	30	1	2	3	Wed 15h19m14p
26		4	5	6	7	8	9	10	
27	TAMMUZ 5927	11	12	13	14	15	16	17	
28		18	19	20	21	22	23	24	
29		25	26	27	28	29	1	2	Fri 4h3m15p
30		3	4	5	6	7	8	9	
31	AV 5927	10[i]	11	12	13	14	15	16	
32		17	18	19	20	21	22	23	
33		24	25	26	27	28	29	30	
34		1	2	3	4	5	6	7	Sat 16h47m16p
35		8	9	10	11	12	13	14	
36	ELUL 5927	15	16	17	18	19	20	21	
37		22	23	24	25	26	27	28	
38		29	1[a]	2[a]	3	4	5	6	Mon 5h31m17p
39		7	8	9	10[b]	11	12	13	
40	TISHRI 5928	14	15[c]	16	17	18	19	20	
41		21	22	23	24	25	26	27	
42		28	29	30	1	2	3	4	Tue 18h16m0p
43		5	6	7	8	9	10	11	
44	HESHVAN 5928	12	13	14	15	16	17	18	
45		19	20	21	22	23	24	25	
46		26	27	28	29	30	1	2	Thu 7h0m1p
47		3	4	5	6	7	8	9	
48	KISLEV 5928	10	11	12	13	14	15	16	
49		17	18	19	20	21	22	23	
50		24	25[e]	26[e]	27[e]	28[e]	29[e]	30[e]	
51		1[e]	2[e]	3	4	5	6	7	Fri 19h44m2p
52	TEVETH 5928	8	9	10	11	12	13	14	
53		15	16	17	18	19	20	21	

CHINESE Bǐng-Yín‡/Dīng-Mǎo

ISO WEEK	Month	Sun	Mon	Tue	Wed	Thu	Fri	Sat	Solar Term
1	MONTH 11 Bǐng-Yín	7	8	9	10	11	12	13	
2		14	15	16	17	18	19	20	Xiǎo hán
3		21	22	23	24	25	26	27	
4		28	29	30	1	2	3	4	Dà hán
5	MONTH 12 Bǐng-Yín	5	6	7	8	9	10	11*	
6		12	13	14	15	16	17	18	
7		19	20	21	22	23	24	25	Lì chūn
8		26	27	28	29	30	1[a]	2	Yǔ shuǐ
9	MONTH 1 Dīng-Mǎo	3	4	5	6	7	8	9	
10		10	11	12	13	14	15[b]	16	Jīng zhé
11		17	18	19	20	21	22	23	
12		24	25	26	27	28	29	1	Chūn fēn
13	MONTH 2 Dīng-Mǎo	2	3	4	5	6	7	8	
14		9	10	11	12*	13	14	15	
15		16[c]	17	18	19	20	21	22	Qīng míng
16		23	24	25	26	27	28	29	
17		30	1	2	3	4	5	6	Gǔ yǔ
18	MONTH 3 Dīng-Mǎo	7	8	9	10	11	12	13	
19		14	15	16	17	18	19	20	Lì xià
20		21	22	23	24	25	26	27	
21		28	29	1	2	3	4	5	Xiǎo mǎn
22	MONTH 4 Dīng-Mǎo	6	7	8	9	10	11	12	
23		13*	14	15	16	17	18	19	Máng zhòng
24		20	21	22	23	24	25	26	
25		27	28	29	1	2	3	4	Xià zhì
26	MONTH 5 Dīng-Mǎo	5[d]	6	7	8	9	10	11	
27		12	13	14	15	16	17	18	Xiǎo shǔ
28		19	20	21	22	23	24	25	
29		26	27	28	29	1	2	3	Dà shǔ
30	MONTH 6 Dīng-Mǎo	4	5	6	7	8	9	10	
31		11	12	13	14	15*	16	17	
32		18	19	20	21	22	23	24	Lì qiū
33		25	26	27	28	29	30	1	
34	MONTH 7 Dīng-Mǎo	2	3	4	5	6	7[e]	8	
35		9	10	11	12	13	14	15[f]	Chǔ shǔ
36		16	17	18	19	20	21	22	
37		23	24	25	26	27	28	29	Bái lù
38	MONTH 8 Dīng-Mǎo	1	2	3	4	5	6	7	
39		8	9	10	11	12	13	14	Qiū fēn
40		15[g]	16*	17	18	19	20	21	
41		22	23	24	25	26	27	28	Hán lù
42		29	30	1	2	3	4	5	
43	MONTH 9 Dīng-Mǎo	6	7	8	9[h]	10	11	12	Shuāng jiàng
44		13	14	15	16	17	18	19	
45		20	21	22	23	24	25	26	Lì dōng
46		27	28	29	30	1	2	3	
47	MONTH 10 Dīng-Mǎo	4	5	6	7	8	9	10	Xiǎo xuě
48		11	12	13	14	15	16*	17	
49		18	19	20	21	22	23	24	Dà xuě
50		25	26	27	28	29	1	2	
51	MONTH 11 Dīng-Mǎo	3	4	5	6	7	8	9	Dōng zhì
52		10	11	12[i]	13	14	15	16	
53		17	18	19	20	21	22	23	

COPTIC 1883‡/1884 — ETHIOPIC 2159‡/2160

ISO WEEK	Coptic Month	Sun	Mon	Tue	Wed	Thu	Fri	Sat	Ethiopic Month
1		18	19	20	21	22	23	24	
2	KOIAK 1883	25	26	27	28	29[c]	30	1	TĀKHŚĀŚ 2159
3		2	3	4	5	6[d]	7	8	
4		9	10	11[e]	12	13	14	15	
5	TŌBE 1883	16	17	18	19	20	21	22	ṬER 2159
6		23	24	25	26	27	28	29	
7		30	1	2	3	4	5	6	
8		7	8	9	10	11	12	13	
9	MESHIR 1883	14	15	16	17	18	19	20	YAKĀTIT 2159
10		21	22	23	24	25	26	27	
11		28	29	30	1	2	3	4	
12		5	6	7	8	9	10	11	
13	PAREMOTEP 1883	12	13	14	15	16	17	18	MAGĀBIT 2159
14		19	20	21	22	23	24	25	
15		26	27	28	29	30	1	2	
16		3[f]	4	5	6	7	8	9	
17	PARMOUTE 1883	10	11	12	13	14	15	16	MIYĀZYĀ 2159
18		17	18	19	20	21	22	23	
19		24	25	26	27	28	29[g]	30	
20		1	2	3	4	5	6	7	
21		8	9	10	11	12	13	14	
22	PASHONS 1883	15	16	17	18	19	20	21	GENBOT 2159
23		22	23	24	25	26	27	28	
24		29	30	1	2	3	4	5	
25		6	7	8	9	10	11	12	
26	PAŌNE 1883	13	14	15	16	17	18	19	SANĒ 2159
27		20	21	22	23	24	25	26	
28		27	28	29	30	1	2	3	
29		4	5	6	7	8	9	10	
30	EPĒP 1883	11	12	13	14	15	16	17	ḤAMLĒ 2159
31		18	19	20	21	22	23	24	
32		25	26	27	28	29	30	1	
33		2	3	4	5	6	7	8	
34		9	10	11	12	13[h]	14	15	
35	MESORĒ 1883	16	17	18	19	20	21	22	NAḤASĒ 2159
36		23	24	25	26	27	28	29	
37	EPAG. 1883	30	1	2	3	4	5	6	PĀG. 2159
38		1[a]	2	3	4	5	6	7	
39		8	9	10	11	12	13	14	
40	THOOUT 1884	15	16	17[b]	18	19	20	21	MASKARAM 2160
41		22	23	24	25	26	27	28	
42		29	30	1	2	3	4	5	
43		6	7	8	9	10	11	12	
44	PAOPE 1884	13	14	15	16	17	18	19	ṬEQEMT 2160
45		20	21	22	23	24	25	26	
46		27	28	29	30	1	2	3	
47		4	5	6	7	8	9	10	
48	ATHŌR 1884	11	12	13	14	15	16	17	HEDĀR 2160
49		18	19	20	21	22	23	24	
50		25	26	27	28	29	30	1	
51		2	3	4	5	6	7	8	
52	KOIAK 1884	9	10	11	12	13	14	15	TĀKHŚĀŚ 2160
53		16	17	18	19	20	21	22	

Gregorian notes:
[a]New Year
[b]Spring (18:58)
[c]Summer (10:03)
[d]Autumn (3:07)
[e]Winter (2:15)
● New moon
◐ First quarter moon
○ Full moon
◑ Last quarter moon

Hebrew notes:
‡Leap year
[a]New Year
[b]Yom Kippur
[c]Sukkot
[d]Winter starts
[e]Ḥanukkah
[f]Purim
[g]Passover
[h]Shavuot
[i]Fast of Av

Chinese notes:
‡Leap year
[a]New Year (4865, Hare)
[b]Lantern Festival
[c]Qīngmíng
[d]Dragon Festival
[e]Qǐqiǎo
[f]Hungry Ghosts
[g]Mid-Autumn Festival
[h]Double-Ninth Festival
[i]Dōngzhì
*Start of 60-name cycle

Coptic/Ethiopic notes:
‡Leap year
[a]New Year
[b]Building of the Cross
[c]Christmas
[d]Jesus's Circumcision
[e]Epiphany
[f]Easter
[g]Mary's Announcement
[h]Jesus's Transfiguration

PERSIAN (ASTRONOMICAL) 1545/1546

Month	Sun	Mon	Tue	Wed	Thu	Fri	Sat
DEY 1545	7	8	9	10	11	12	13
	14	15	16	17	18	19	20
	21	22	23	24	25	26	27
	28	29	30	*1*	2	3	4
BAHMAN 1545	5	6	7	8	9	10	11
	12	13	14	15	16	17	18
	19	20	21	22	23	24	25
	26	27	28	29	30	*1*	2
ESFAND 1545	3	4	5	6	7	8	9
	10	11	12	13	14	15	16
	17	18	19	20	21	22	23
	24	25	26	27	28	29	*1*[a]
FARVARDĪN 1546	2	3	4	5	6	7	8
	9	10	11	12	13[b]	14	15
	16	17	18	19	20	21	22
	23	24	25	26	27	28	29
	30	31	*1*	2	3	4	5
ORDĪBEHEŠT 1546	6	7	8	9	10	11	12
	13	14	15	16	17	18	19
	20	21	22	23	24	25	26
	27	28	29	30	31	*1*	2
XORDĀD 1546	3	4	5	6	7	8	9
	10	11	12	13	14	15	16
	17	18	19	20	21	22	23
	24	25	26	27	28	29	30
	31	*1*	2	3	4	5	6
TĪR 1546	7	8	9	10	11	12	13
	14	15	16	17	18	19	20
	21	22	23	24	25	26	27
	28	29	30	31	*1*	2	3
MORDĀD 1546	4	5	6	7	8	9	10
	11	12	13	14	15	16	17
	18	19	20	21	22	23	24
	25	26	27	28	29	30	31
SHAHRĪVAR 1546	*1*	2	3	4	5	6	7
	8	9	10	11	12	13	14
	15	16	17	18	19	20	21
	22	23	24	25	26	27	28
	29	30	31	*1*	2	3	4
MEHR 1546	5	6	7	8	9	10	11
	12	13	14	15	16	17	18
	19	20	21	22	23	24	25
	26	27	28	29	30	*1*	2
ĀBĀN 1546	3	4	5	6	7	8	9
	10	11	12	13	14	15	16
	17	18	19	20	21	22	23
	24	25	26	27	28	29	30
ĀZAR 1546	*1*	2	3	4	5	6	7
	8	9	10	11	12	13	14
	15	16	17	18	19	20	21
	22	23	24	25	26	27	28
DEY 1546	29	30	*1*	2	3	4	5
	6	7	8	9	10	11	12

[a]New Year
[b]Sizdeh Bedar

HINDU LUNAR 2223/2224‡

Month	Sun	Mon	Tue	Wed	Thu	Fri	Sat
PAUSHA 2223	6	7	8	9	**10**	12	13
	14	15	16	17	18	19	20
	21	22	23	24	25	26	27
MĀGHA 2223	*27*	28	29	30	1	2	3
	4	6	7	8	9	10	11
	12	13	14	15	16	17	18
	19	20	21	22	23	24	25
PHĀLGUNA 2223	26	27	28	29[h]	30	1	2
	3	4	5	6	7	8	**9**
	11	12	13	14	15[i]	16	17
	18	19	*19*	20	21	22	23
	24	25	26	27	28	29	30
CHAITRA 2224	1[a]	2	**3**	5	6	7	8
	9[b]	10	11	12	13	14	15
	16	17	18	19	20	21	22
	23	*23*	24	**25**	27	28	29
VAIŚĀKHA 2224	30	1	2	3	4	5	6
	7	**8**	10	11	12	13	*13*
	14	15	16	17	18	19	20
	21	22	23	24	25	26	27
LEAP JYAISHTHA 2224	28	29	**30**	2	3	4	5
	6	7	8	9	10	11	12
	13	14	15	16	17	18	*18*
	19	20	21	**22**	24	25	26
JYAISHTHA 2224	27	28	29	30	1	2	3
	4	6	7	8	9	*9*	10
	11	12	13	14	15	16	17
	18	19	20	21	22	23	24
ĀSHĀDHA 2224	25	**26**	28	29	30	1	2
	3	4	5	6	7	8	9
	10	11	12	13	14	15	*15*
	16	**17**	19	20	21	22	23
ŚRĀVANA 2224	24	25	26	27	28	**29**	1
	2	3	4	5	6	*6*	7
	8	9	10	11	12	13	14
	15	16	17	18	19	20	**21**
	23[c]	24	25	26	27	28	29
BHĀDRAPADA 2224	30	1	2	3	4[d]	5	6
	7	8	9	10	11	*11*	12
	13	15	16	17	18	19	20
	21	22	23	24	25	**26**	28
ĀŚVINA 2224	29	30	1	*1*	2	3	4
	5	6	7	8[e]	9[e]	10[e]	11
	12	13	14	15	16	17	**18**
	20	21	22	23	24	25	26
KĀRTTIKA 2224	27	28	29	30	1[f]	2	3
	4	*4*	5	6	7	8	9
	10	11	**12**	14	15	16	17
	18	19	20	21	22	23	24
MĀRGAŚĪRA 2224	25	26	27	28	29	30	1
	2	3	4	5	6	7	8
	9	10	11[g]	12	13	14	15
	16	**17**	19	20	21	22	23

‡Leap year
[a]New Year (Prabhava)
[b]Birthday of Rāma
[c]Birthday of Krishna
[d]Ganēśa Chaturthī
[e]Dashara
[f]Diwali
[g]Birthday of Vishnu
[h]Night of Śiva
[i]Holi

HINDU SOLAR 2088/2089

Month	Sun	Mon	Tue	Wed	Thu	Fri	Sat
PAUSHA 2088	11	12	13	14	15	16	17
	18	19	20	21	22	23	24
	25	26	27	28	29	30	1[b]
MĀGHA 2088	2	3	4	5	6	7	8
	9	10	11	12	13	14	15
	16	17	18	19	20	21	22
	23	24	25	26	27	28	29
PHĀLGUNA 2088	1	2	3	4	5	6	7
	8	9	10	11	12	13	14
	15	16	17	18	19	20	21
	22	23	24	25	26	27	28
	29	30	1	2	3	4	5
CHAITRA 2088	6	7	8	9	10	11	12
	13	14	15	16	17	18	19
	20	21	22	23	24	25	26
	27	28	29	30	1[a]	2	3
VAIŚĀKHA 2089	4	5	6	7	8	9	10
	11	12	13	14	15	16	17
	18	19	20	21	22	23	24
	25	26	27	28	29	30	31
JYAISHTHA 2089	1	2	3	4	5	6	7
	8	9	10	11	12	13	14
	15	16	17	18	19	20	21
	22	23	24	25	26	27	28
	29	30	31	32	1	2	3
ĀSHĀDHA 2089	4	5	6	7	8	9	10
	11	12	13	14	15	16	17
	18	19	20	21	22	23	24
	25	26	27	28	29	30	31
ŚRĀVANA 2089	1	2	3	4	5	6	7
	8	9	10	11	12	13	14
	15	16	17	18	19	20	21
	22	23	24	25	26	27	28
	29	30	31	32	1	2	3
BHĀDRAPADA 2089	4	5	6	7	8	9	10
	11	12	13	14	15	16	17
	18	19	20	21	22	23	24
	25	26	27	28	29	30	31
ĀŚVINA 2089	1	2	3	4	5	6	7
	8	9	10	11	12	13	14
	15	16	17	18	19	20	21
	22	23	24	25	26	27	28
	29	30	1	2	3	4	5
KĀRTTIKA 2089	6	7	8	9	10	11	12
	13	14	15	16	17	18	19
	20	21	22	23	24	25	26
	27	28	29	30	1	2	3
MĀRGAŚĪRA 2089	4	5	6	7	8	9	10
	11	12	13	14	15	16	17
	18	19	20	21	22	23	24
	25	26	27	28	29	1	2
PAUSHA 2089	3	4	5	6	7	8	9
	10	11	12	13	14	15	16

[a]New Year (Chitrabhānu)
[b]Pongal

ISLAMIC (ASTRONOMICAL) 1592‡/1593

Month	Sun	Mon	Tue	Wed	Thu	Fri	Sat
DHU AL-QA'DA 1592	5	6	7	8	9	10	11
	12	13	14	15	16	17	18
	19	20	21	22	23	24	25
	26	27	28	29	*30*	1	2
DHU AL-HIJJA 1592	3	4	5	6	7	8	9
	10[g]	11	12	13	14	15	16
	17	18	19	20	21	22	23
	24	25	26	27	28	29	*1*[a]
MUHARRAM 1593	2	3	4	5	6	7	8
	9	10[b]	11	12	13	14	15
	16	17	18	19	20	21	22
	23	24	25	26	27	28	29
ṢAFAR 1593	1	2	3	4	5	6	7
	8	9	10	11	12	13	14
	15	16	17	18	19	20	21
	22	23	24	25	26	27	28
	29	30	*1*	2	3	4	5
RABĪ' I 1593	6	7	8	9	10	11	12[c]
	13	14	15	16	17	18	19
	20	21	22	23	24	25	26
	27	28	29	1	2	3	4
RABĪ' II 1593	5	6	7	8	9	10	11
	12	13	14	15	16	17	18
	19	20	21	22	23	24	25
	26	27	28	29	30	*1*	2
JUMĀDĀ I 1593	3	4	5	6	7	8	9
	10	11	12	13	14	15	16
	17	18	19	20	21	22	23
	24	25	26	27	28	29	1
JUMĀDĀ II 1593	2	3	4	5	6	7	8
	9	10	11	12	13	14	15
	16	17	18	19	20	21	22
	23	24	25	26	27	28	29
RAJAB 1593	1	2	3	4	5	6	7
	8	9	10	11	12	13	14
	15	16	17	18	19	20	21
	22	23	24	25	26	27[d]	28
	29	30	1	2	3	4	5
SHA'BĀN 1593	6	7	8	9	10	11	12
	13	14	15	16	17	18	19
	20	21	22	23	24	25	26
	27	28	29	1[e]	2	3	4
RAMAḌĀN 1593	5	6	7	8	9	10	11
	12	13	14	15	16	17	18
	19	20	21	22	23	24	25
	26	27	28	29	30	1[f]	2
SHAWWĀL 1593	3	4	5	6	7	8	9
	10	11	12	13	14	15	16
	17	18	19	20	21	22	23
	24	25	26	27	28	29	30
DHU AL-QA'DA 1593	*1*	2	3	4	5	6	7
	8	9	10	11	12	13	14
	15	16	17	18	19	20	21

‡Leap year
[a]New Year
[b]'Ashūrā'
[c]Prophet's Birthday
[d]Ascent of the Prophet
[e]Start of Ramaḍān
[f]'Īd al-Fiṭr
[g]'Īd al-'Aḍḥā

GREGORIAN 2167

Julian (Sun)	Sun	Mon	Tue	Wed	Thu	Fri	Sat	Month
Dec 14	28	29	30	31	1	2	3	JANUARY 2167
	4	5	6	7	8[a]	9	10	
Dec 28	*11*	12	13	14	15[b]	16	17	
	18	19	20	21	22	23	24	
Jan 11	25	26	27	28	29	30	31	
	1	2	3	4	5	6	7	FEBRUARY 2167
Jan 25	8	9	10	11	12	13	14	
	15	16	17	18[c]	19	20	21	
Feb 8	22	23	24	25	26	27	28	
	1[d]	2	3	4	5	6	7	MARCH 2167
Feb 22	8	9	10	11	12	13	14	
	15	16	17	18	19	20	21	
Mar 8	22	23	24	25	26	27	28	
	29	30	31	1	2	3	4	APRIL 2167
Mar 22	5[e]	6	7	8	9	10	11	
	12[f]	13	14	15	16	17	18	
Apr 5	19	20	21	22	23	24	25	
	26	27	28	29	30	1	2	MAY 2167
Apr 19	3	4	5	6	7	8	9	
	10	11	12	13	14	15	16	
May 3	17	18	19	20	21	22	23	
	24	25	26	27	28	29	30	
May 17	31	1	2	3	4	5	6	JUNE 2167
	7	8	9	10	11	12	13	
May 31	14	15	16	17	18	19	20	
	21	22	23	24	25	26	27	
Jun 14	28	29	30	1	2	3	4	JULY 2167
	5	6	7	8	9	10	11	
Jun 28	*12*	13	14	15	16	17	18	
	19	20	21	22	23	24	25	
Jul 12	26	27	28	29	30	31	1	AUGUST 2167
	2	3	4	5	6	7	8	
Jul 26	9	10	11	12	13	14	15	
	16	17	18	19	20	21	22	
Aug 9	23	24	25	26	27	28	29	
	30	31	1	2	3	4	5	SEPTEMBER 2167
Aug 23	6	7	8	9	10	11	12	
	13	14	15	16	17	18	19	
Sep 6	20	21	22	23	24	25	26	
	27	28	29	30	1	2	3	OCTOBER 2167
Sep 20	*4*	5	6	7	8	9	10	
	11	12	13	14	15	16	17	
Oct 4	18	19	20	21	22	23	24	
	25	26	27	28	29	30	31	
Oct 18	*1*	2	3	4	5	6	7	NOVEMBER 2167
	8	9	10	11	12	13	14	
Nov 1	15	16	17	18	19	20	21	
	22	23	24	25	26	27	28	
Nov 15	29[g]	30	1	2	3	4	5	DECEMBER 2167
	6	7	8	9	10	11	12	
Nov 29	13	14	15	16	17	18	19	
	20	21	22	23	24	25[h]	26	
Dec 13	27	28	29	30	31	1	2	

[a]Orthodox Christmas
[b]Julian New Year
[c]Ash Wednesday
[d]Feast of Orthodoxy
[e]Easter
[f]Orthodox Easter
[g]Advent
[h]Christmas

2168

GREGORIAN 2168‡ — Lunar Phases — ISO WEEK — JULIAN DAY

Month	Sun	Mon	Tue	Wed	Thu	Fri	Sat	Lunar Phases	ISO Week (Mon)	Julian Day (Sun noon)
	27	28	29	30	31	1[a]	◑	4:10	53	2512901
JANUARY 2168	3	4	5	6	7	8	9		1	2512908
	●	11	12	13	14	15	16	9:06	2	2512915
	17	◐	19	20	21	22	23	1:54	3	2512922
	○	25	26	27	28	29	30	17:19	4	2512929
FEBRUARY 2168	◑	1	2	3	4	5	6	22:49	5	2512936
	7	8	●	10	11	12	13	3:24	6	2512943
	14	15	◐	17	18	19	20	11:06	7	2512950
	21	22	○	24	25	26	27	5:23	8	2512957
MARCH 2168	28	29	◑	2	3	4	5	19:20	9	2512964
	6	7	8	●	10	11	12	18:52	10	2512971
	13	14	15	◐	17	18	19	18:32	11	2512978
	20[b]	21	22	○	24	25	26	18:03	12	2512985
APRIL 2168	27	28	29	30	◑	1	2	15:54	13	2512992
	3	4	5	6	7	●	9	7:06	14	2512999
	10	11	12	13	14	◐	16	1:11	15	2513006
	17	18	19	20	21	○	23	7:31	16	2513013
	24	25	26	27	28	29	◑	10:39	17	2513020
MAY 2168	1	2	3	4	5	6	●	16:40	18	2513027
	8	9	10	11	12	13	◐	8:05	19	2513034
	15	16	17	18	19	20	○	21:58	20	2513041
	22	23	24	25	26	27	28		21	2513048
JUNE 2168	29	◑	31	1	2	3	4	2:16	22	2513055
	5	●	7	8	9	10	11	0:32	23	2513062
	◐	13	14	15	16	17	18	16:10	24	2513069
	19	○[c]	21	22	23	24	25	13:16	25	2513076
JULY 2168	26	27	◑	29	30	1	2	14:26	26	2513083
	3	4	●	6	7	8	9	7:37	27	2513090
	10	11	◐	13	14	15	16	2:21	28	2513097
	17	18	19	○	21	22	23	4:47	29	2513104
	24	25	26	◑	28	29	30	23:40	30	2513111
AUGUST 2168	31	1	2	●	4	5	6	14:48	31	2513118
	7	8	9	◐	11	12	13	15:23	32	2513125
	14	15	16	17	○	19	20	19:42	33	2513132
	21	22	23	24	25	◑	27	6:53	34	2513139
SEPTEMBER 2168	28	29	30	31	●	2	3	22:54	35	2513146
	4	5	6	7	8	◐	10	7:37	36	2513153
	11	12	13	14	15	16	○	9:30	37	2513160
	18	19	20	21	22[d]	23	◑	13:11	38	2513167
OCTOBER 2168	25	26	27	28	29	30	●	8:51	39	2513174
	2	3	4	5	6	7	8		40	2513181
	◐	10	11	12	13	14	15	2:36	41	2513188
	○	17	18	19	20	21	22	22:11	42	2513195
	◑	24	25	26	27	28	29	19:37	43	2513202
NOVEMBER 2168	●	31	1	2	3	4	5	21:33	44	2513209
	6	◐	8	9	10	11	12	22:57	45	2513216
	13	14	○	16	17	18	19	10:08	46	2513223
	20	21	◑	23	24	25	26	3:15	47	2513230
DECEMBER 2168	27	28	●	30	1	2	3	13:30	48	2513237
	4	5	6	◐	8	9	10	18:49	49	2513244
	11	12	13	○	15	16	17	21:41	50	2513251
	18	19	20	◑[e]	22	23	24	13:03	51	2513258
	25	26	27	28	●	30	31	8:15	52	2513265

HEBREW 5928‡/5929 — Molad

ISO Week	Month	Sun	Mon	Tue	Wed	Thu	Fri	Sat	Molad
53	TEVETH 5928	15	16	17	18	19	20	21	
1		22	23	24	25	26	27	28	
2	SHEVAT 5928	29	1	2	3	4	5	6	Sun 8h 28m 3p
3		7	8	9	10	11	12	13	
4		14	15	16	17	18	19	20	
5		21	22	23	24	25	26	27	
6	ADAR I 5928	28	29	30	1	2	3	4	Mon 21h 12m 4p
7		5	6	7	8	9	10	11	
8		12	13	14	15	16	17	18	
9		19	20	21	22	23	24	25	
10	ADAR II 5928	26	27	28	29	30	1	2	Wed 9h 56m 5p
11		3	4	5	6	7	8	9	
12		10	11	12	13	14[f]	15	16	
13		17	18	19	20	21	22	23	
14	NISAN 5928	24	25	26	27	28	29	1	Thu 22h 40m 6p
15		2	3	4	5	6	7	8	
16		9	10	11	12	13	14	15[g]	
17		16	17	18	19	20	21	22	
18		23	24	25	26	27	28	29	
19	IYAR 5928	30	1	2	3	4	5	6	Sat 11h 24m 7p
20		7	8	9	10	11	12	13	
21		14	15	16	17	18	19	20	
22		21	22	23	24	25	26	27	
23	SIVAN 5928	28	29	1	2	3	4	5	Mon 0h 8m 8p
24		6[h]	7	8	9	10	11	12	
25		13	14	15	16	17	18	19	
26		20	21	22	23	24	25	26	
27	TAMMUZ 5928	27	28	29	30	1	2	3	Tue 12h 52m 9p
28		4	5	6	7	8	9	10	
29		11	12	13	14	15	16	17	
30		18	19	20	21	22	23	24	
31	AV 5928	25	26	27	28	29	1	2	Thu 1h 36m 10p
32		3	4	5	6	7	8	9	
33		10[i]	11	12	13	14	15	16	
34		17	18	19	20	21	22	23	
35		24	25	26	27	28	29	30	
36	ELUL 5928	1	2	3	4	5	6	7	Fri 14h 20m 11p
37		8	9	10	11	12	13	14	
38		15	16	17	18	19	20	21	
39		22	23	24	25	26	27	28	
40	TISHRI 5929	29	1[a]	2[a]	3	4	5	6	Sun 3h 4m 12p
41		7	8	9	10[b]	11	12	13	
42		14	15[c]	16	17	18	19	20	
43		21	22	23	24	25	26	27	
44	HESHVAN 5929	28	29	30	1	2	3	4	Mon 15h 48m 13p
45		5	6	7	8	9	10	11	
46		12	13	14	15	16	17	18	
47		19	20	21	22	23	24	25	
48	KISLEV 5929	26	27	28	29	1	2	3	Wed 4h 32m 14p
49		4	5	6[d]	7	8	9	10	
50		11	12	13	14	15	16	17	
51		18	19	20	21	22	23	24	
52		25[e]	26[e]	27[e]	28[e]	29[e]	1[e]	2[e]	Thu 17h 16m 15p

CHINESE Dīng-Mǎo/Wù-Chén — Solar Term

ISO Week	Month	Sun	Mon	Tue	Wed	Thu	Fri	Sat	Solar Term
53	MONTH 11 Dīng-Mǎo	17	18	19	20	21	22	23	
1		24	25	26	27	28	29	30	Xiǎo hán
2	MONTH 12 Dīng-Mǎo	1	2	3	4	5	6	7	
3		8	9	10	***11***	12	13	14	
4		15	16	17*	18	19	20	21	Dà hán
5		22	23	24	25	*26*	27	28	
6	MONTH 1 Wù-Chén	29	30	1[a]	2	3	4	5	Lì chūn
7		6	7	8	9	10	***11***	12	
8		13	14	15[b]	16	17	18	19	Yǔ shuǐ
9		20	21	22	23	24	25	*26*	Jīng zhé
10	MONTH 2 Wù-Chén	27	28	29	30	1	2	3	
11		4	5	6	7	8	9	10	
12		***11***	12	13	14	15	16	17*	Chūn fēn
13		18	19	20	21	22	23	24	
14	MONTH 3 Wù-Chén	25	26[c]	27	28	29	1	2	Qīng míng
15		3	4	5	6	7	8	9	
16		10	11	***12***	13	14	15	16	Gǔ yǔ
17		17	18	19	20	21	22	23	
18	MONTH 4 Wù-Chén	24	25	26	27	*28*	29	30	Lì xià
19		1	2	3	4	5	6	7	
20		8	9	10	11	12	***13***	14	Xiǎo mǎn
21		15	16	17	18*	19	20	21	
22		22	23	24	25	26	27	28	
23	MONTH 5 Wù-Chén	29	1	2	3	4	5[d]	6	Máng zhòng
24		7	8	9	10	11	12	13	
25		14	15	***16***	17	18	19	20	Xià zhì
26		21	22	23	24	25	26	27	
27	MONTH 6 Wù-Chén	28	29	1	2	3	4	5	Xiǎo shǔ
28		6	7	8	9	10	11	12	
29		13	14	15	16	17	***18***	19	Dà shǔ
30		20*	21	22	23	24	25	26	
31	MONTH 7 Wù-Chén	27	28	29	1	2	3	4	
32		5	6	7[e]	8	9	10	11	Lì qiū
33		12	13	14	15[f]	16	17	18	
34		19	***20***	21	22	23	24	25	Chǔ shǔ
35	MONTH 8 Wù-Chén	26	27	28	29	30	1	2	
36		3	4	5	6	7	8	9	Bái lù
37		10	11	12	13	14	15[g]	16	
38		17	18	19	20	***21****	22	23	Qiū fēn
39	MONTH 9 Wù-Chén	24	25	26	27	28	29	1	
40		2	3	4	5	6	7	8	Hán lù
41		9[h]	10	11	12	13	14	15	
42		16	17	18	19	20	21	22	
43		***23***	24	25	26	27	28	29	Shuāng jiàng
44	MONTH 10 Wù-Chén	30	1	2	3	4	5	6	
45		7	*8*	9	10	11	12	13	Lì dōng
46		14	15	16	17	18	19	20	
47		21	22*	***23***	24	25	26	27	Xiǎo xuě
48	MONTH 11* Wù-Chén	28	29	1	2	3	4	5	
49		6	7	8	9	10	11	12	Dà xuě
50		13	14	15	16	17	18	19	
51		20	21	22	***23***[i]	24	25	26	Dōng zhì
52		27	28	29	30	1	2	3	

COPTIC 1884/1885 — ETHIOPIC 2160/2161

ISO Week	Coptic Month	Sun	Mon	Tue	Wed	Thu	Fri	Sat	Ethiopic Month
53	KOIAK 1884	16	17	18	19	20	21	22	TĀKHŠĀŠ 2160
1		23	24	25	26	27	28	29[c]	
2	TŌBE 1884	30	1	2	3	4	5	6[d]	TER 2160
3		7	8	9	10	11[e]	12	13	
4		14	15	16	17	18	19	20	
5		21	22	23	24	25	26	27	
6	MESHIR 1884	28	29	30	1	2	3	4	YAKĀTIT 2160
7		5	6	7	8	9	10	11	
8		12	13	14	15	16	17	18	
9		19	20	21	22	23	24	25	
10	PAREMOTEP 1884	26	27	28	29	30	1	2	MAGĀBIT 2160
11		3	4	5	6	7	8	9	
12		10	11	12	13	14	15	16	
13		17	18	19	20	21	22	23	
14		24	25	26	27	28	29	30	
15	PARMOUTE 1884	1	2	3	4	5	6	7	MIYĀZYĀ 2160
16		8	9	10	11	12	13	14	
17		15	16	17	18	19	20	21	
18		22[f]	23	24	25	26	27	28	
19	PASHONS 1884	29[g]	30	1	2	3	4	5	GENBOT 2160
20		6	7	8	9	10	11	12	
21		13	14	15	16	17	18	19	
22		20	21	22	23	24	25	26	
23	PAŌNE 1884	27	28	29	30	1	2	3	SANĒ 2160
24		4	5	6	7	8	9	10	
25		11	12	13	14	15	16	17	
26		18	19	20	21	22	23	24	
27	EPĒP 1884	25	26	27	28	29	30	1	HAMLĒ 2160
28		2	3	4	5	6	7	8	
29		9	10	11	12	13	14	15	
30		16	17	18	19	20	21	22	
31		23	24	25	26	27	28	29	
32	MESORĒ 1884	30	1	2	3	4	5	6	NAHASĒ 2160
33		7	8	9	10	11	12	13[h]	
34		14	15	16	17	18	19	20	
35		21	22	23	24	25	26	27	
36	EPAG. 1884	28	29	30	1	2	3	4	PĀG. 2160
37	THOOUT 1885	5	1[a]	2	3	4	5	6	MASKARAM 2161
38		7	8	9	10	11	12	13	
39		14	15	16	17[b]	18	19	20	
40		21	22	23	24	25	26	27	
41	PAOPE 1885	28	29	30	1	2	3	4	TEQEMT 2161
42		5	6	7	8	9	10	11	
43		12	13	14	15	16	17	18	
44		19	20	21	22	23	24	25	
45	ATHŌR 1885	26	27	28	29	30	1	2	HEDĀR 2161
46		3	4	5	6	7	8	9	
47		10	11	12	13	14	15	16	
48		17	18	19	20	21	22	23	
49		24	25	26	27	28	29	30	
50	KOIAK 1885	1	2	3	4	5	6	7	TĀKHŠĀŠ 2161
51		8	9	10	11	12	13	14	
52		15	16	17	18	19	20	21	

‡Leap year
[a]New Year
[b]Spring (0:45)
[c]Summer (16:01)
[d]Autumn (9:02)
[e]Winter (8:12)
● New moon
◐ First quarter moon
○ Full moon
◑ Last quarter moon

‡Leap year
[a]New Year
[b]Yom Kippur
[c]Sukkot
[d]Winter starts
[e]Hanukkah
[f]Purim
[g]Passover
[h]Shavuot
[i]Fast of Av

[a]New Year (4866, Dragon)
[b]Lantern Festival
[c]Qīngmíng
[d]Dragon Festival
[e]Qīqiǎo
[f]Hungry Ghosts
[g]Mid-Autumn Festival
[h]Double-Ninth Festival
[i]Dōngzhì
*Start of 60-name cycle

[a]New Year
[b]Building of the Cross
[c]Christmas
[d]Jesus's Circumcision
[e]Epiphany
[f]Easter
[g]Mary's Announcement
[h]Jesus's Transfiguration

PERSIAN (ASTRONOMICAL) 1546/1547

Month	Sun	Mon	Tue	Wed	Thu	Fri	Sat
DEY 1546	6	7	8	9	10	11	12
	13	14	15	16	17	18	19
	20	21	22	23	24	25	26
	27	28	29	30	1	2	3
BAHMAN 1546	4	5	6	7	8	9	10
	11	12	13	14	15	16	17
	18	19	20	21	22	23	24
	25	26	27	28	29	30	1
ESFAND 1546	2	3	4	5	6	7	8
	9	10	11	12	13	14	15
	16	17	18	19	20	21	22
	23	24	25	26	27	28	29
FARVARDĪN 1547	1[a]	2	3	4	5	6	7
	8	9	10	11	12	13[b]	14
	15	16	17	18	19	20	21
	22	23	24	25	26	27	28
	29	30	31	1	2	3	4
ORDĪBEHEŠT 1547	5	6	7	8	9	10	11
	12	13	14	15	16	17	18
	19	20	21	22	23	24	25
	26	27	28	29	30	31	1
XORDĀD 1547	2	3	4	5	6	7	8
	9	10	11	12	13	14	15
	16	17	18	19	20	21	22
	23	24	25	26	27	28	29
	30	31	1	2	3	4	5
TĪR 1547	6	7	8	9	10	11	12
	13	14	15	16	17	18	19
	20	21	22	23	24	25	26
	27	28	29	30	31	1	2
MORDĀD 1547	3	4	5	6	7	8	9
	10	11	12	13	14	15	16
	17	18	19	20	21	22	23
	24	25	26	27	28	29	30
	31	1	2	3	4	5	6
SHAHRĪVAR 1547	7	8	9	10	11	12	13
	14	15	16	17	18	19	20
	21	22	23	24	25	26	27
	28	29	30	31	1	2	3
MEHR 1547	4	5	6	7	8	9	10
	11	12	13	14	15	16	17
	18	19	20	21	22	23	24
	25	26	27	28	29	30	1
ĀBĀN 1547	2	3	4	5	6	7	8
	9	10	11	12	13	14	15
	16	17	18	19	20	21	22
	23	24	25	26	27	28	29
	30	1	2	3	4	5	6
ĀZAR 1547	7	8	9	10	11	12	13
	14	15	16	17	18	19	20
	21	22	23	24	25	26	27
	28	29	30	1	2	3	4
DEY 1547	5	6	7	8	9	10	11

HINDU LUNAR 2224‡/2225

Month	Sun	Mon	Tue	Wed	Thu	Fri	Sat
MĀRGAŚIRA 2224	16	**17**	19	20	21	22	23
	24	25	26	27	27	28	29
	30	1	2	3	4	5	6
PAUSHA 2224	7	8	9	10	**11**	13	14
	15	16	17	18	19	20	21
	22	23	24	25	26	27	28
	29	30	30	1	2	3	4
MĀGHA 2224	5	7	8	9	10	11	12
	13	14	15	16	17	18	19
	20	21	22	23	24	25	26
	27	28[h]	29	30	1	2	3
PHĀLGUNA 2224	4	5	6	7	8	9	**10**
	12	13	14	15[i]	16	17	18
	19	20	21	22	22	23	24
	25	26	27	28	29	30	1[a]
CHAITRA 2225	2	**3**	5	6	7	8	9[b]
	10	11	12	13	14	15	16
	17	18	19	20	21	22	23
	24	25	26	27	28	29	30
VAIŚĀKHA 2225	1	2	3	4	5	6	**7**
	9	10	11	12	13	14	15
	16	17	17	18	19	20	21
	22	23	24	25	26	27	28
	29	**30**	2	3	4	5	6
JYAISHTHA 2225	7	8	9	10	11	12	13
	14	15	16	17	18	19	20
	21	22	23	24	25	26	27
	28	29	30	1	2	**3**	5
ĀSHĀḌHA 2225	6	7	8	9	10	11	12
	13	14	14	15	16	17	18
	19	20	21	22	23	24	25
	26	28	29	30	1	2	3
ŚRĀVAṆA 2225	4	5	6	7	8	9	10
	11	12	13	14	15	16	17
	18	19	20	21	22	23[c]	24
	25	26	27	28	**29**	1	2
BHĀDRAPADA 2225	3	4[d]	5	6	7	8	9
	10	10	11	12	13	14	15
	16	17	18	19	20	21	**22**
	24	25	26	27	28	29	30
ĀŚVINA 2225	1	2	3	4	5	6	7
	8[e]	9[e]	10[e]	11	12	13	14
	15	16	17	18	19	20	21
	22	23	24	25	**26**	28	29
	30	1[f]	2	3	4	5	5
KĀRTTIKA 2225	6	7	8	9	10	11	12
	13	14	15	16	17	18	**19**
	21	22	23	24	25	26	27
	28	29	30	1	2	3	4
MĀRGAŚIRA 2225	5	6	7	8	8	9	10
	11[g]	12	**13**	15	16	17	18
	19	20	21	22	23	24	25
	26	27	28	29	30	1	2

HINDU SOLAR 2089/2090‡

Month	Sun	Mon	Tue	Wed	Thu	Fri	Sat
PAUSHA 2089	10	11	12	13	14	15	16
	17	18	19	20	21	22	23
	24	25	26	27	28	29	30
MĀGHA 2089	1[b]	2	3	4	5	6	7
	8	9	10	11	12	13	14
	15	16	17	18	19	20	21
	22	23	24	25	26	27	28
PHĀLGUNA 2089	29	1	2	3	4	5	6
	7	8	9	10	11	12	13
	14	15	16	17	18	19	20
	21	22	23	24	25	26	27
	28	29	30	1	2	3	4
CHAITRA 2089	5	6	7	8	9	10	11
	12	13	14	15	16	17	18
	19	20	21	22	23	24	25
	26	27	28	29	30	1[a]	2
VAIŚĀKHA 2090	3	4	5	6	7	8	9
	10	11	12	13	14	15	16
	17	18	19	20	21	22	23
	24	25	26	27	28	29	30
	31	1	2	3	4	5	6
JYAISHTHA 2090	7	8	9	10	11	12	13
	14	15	16	17	18	19	20
	21	22	23	24	25	26	27
	28	29	30	31	32	1	2
ĀSHĀḌHA 2090	3	4	5	6	7	8	9
	10	11	12	13	14	15	16
	17	18	19	20	21	22	23
	24	25	26	27	28	29	30
	31	1	2	3	4	5	6
ŚRĀVAṆA 2090	7	8	9	10	11	12	13
	14	15	16	17	18	19	20
	21	22	23	24	25	26	27
	28	29	30	31	32	1	2
BHĀDRAPADA 2090	3	4	5	6	7	8	9
	10	11	12	13	14	15	16
	17	18	19	20	21	22	23
	24	25	26	27	28	29	30
	31	1	2	3	4	5	6
ĀŚVINA 2090	7	8	9	10	11	12	13
	14	15	16	17	18	19	20
	21	22	23	24	25	26	27
	28	29	30	1	2	3	4
KĀRTTIKA 2090	5	6	7	8	9	10	11
	12	13	14	15	16	17	18
	19	20	21	22	23	24	25
	26	27	28	29	30	1	2
MĀRGAŚIRA 2090	3	4	5	6	7	8	9
	10	11	12	13	14	15	16
	17	18	19	20	21	22	23
	24	25	26	27	28	29	30
PAUSHA 2090	1	2	3	4	5	6	7
	8	9	10	11	12	13	14

ISLAMIC (ASTRONOMICAL) 1593/1594‡

Month	Sun	Mon	Tue	Wed	Thu	Fri	Sat
DHU AL-QA'DA 1593	15	16	17	18	19	20	21
	22	23	24	25	26	27	28
	29	30	1	2	3	4	5
DHU AL-ḤIJJA 1593	6	7	8	9	10[g]	11	12
	13	14	15	16	17	18	19
	20	21	22	23	24	25	26
	27	28	29	1[a]	2	3	4
MUḤARRAM 1594	5	6	7	8	9	10[b]	11
	12	13	14	15	16	17	18
	19	20	21	22	23	24	25
	26	27	28	29	30	1	2
ṢAFAR 1594	3	4	5	6	7	8	9
	10	11	12	13	14	15	16
	17	18	19	20	21	22	23
	24	25	26	27	28	29	1
RABĪ' I 1594	2	3	4	5	6	7	8
	9	10	11	12[c]	13	14	15
	16	17	18	19	20	21	22
	23	24	25	26	27	28	29
	30	1	2	3	4	5	6
RABĪ' II 1594	7	8	9	10	11	12	13
	14	15	16	17	18	19	20
	21	22	23	24	25	26	27
	28	29	1	2	3	4	5
JUMĀDĀ I 1594	6	7	8	9	10	11	12
	13	14	15	16	17	18	19
	20	21	22	23	24	25	26
	27	28	29	1	2	3	4
JUMĀDĀ II 1594	5	6	7	8	9	10	11
	12	13	14	15	16	17	18
	19	20	21	22	23	24	25
	26	27	28	29	30	1	2
RAJAB 1594	3	4	5	6	7	8	9
	10	11	12	13	14	15	16
	17	18	19	20	21	22	23
	24	25	26	27[d]	28	29	1
SHA'BĀN 1594	2	3	4	5	6	7	8
	9	10	11	12	13	14	15
	16	17	18	19	20	21	22
	23	24	25	26	27	28	29
	30	1[e]	2	3	4	5	6
RAMAḌĀN 1594	7	8	9	10	11	12	13
	14	15	16	17	18	19	20
	21	22	23	24	25	26	27
	28	29	1[f]	2	3	4	5
SHAWWĀL 1594	6	7	8	9	10	11	12
	13	14	15	16	17	18	19
	20	21	22	23	24	25	26
	27	28	29	30	1	2	3
DHU AL-QA'DA 1594	4	5	6	7	8	9	10
	11	12	13	14	15	16	17
	18	19	20	21	22	23	24
	25	26	27	28	29	30	1

GREGORIAN 2168‡

Julian† (Sun)	Sun	Mon	Tue	Wed	Thu	Fri	Sat	Month
Dec 13	27	28	29	30	31	1	2	
	3	4	5	6	7	8[a]	9	JANUARY 2168
Dec 27	10	11	12	13	14	15[b]	16	
	17	18	19	20	21	22	23	
Jan 10	24	25	26	27	28	29	30	
	31	1	2	3	4	5	6	
Jan 24	7	8	9	10[c]	11	12	13	FEBRUARY 2168
	14	15	16	17	18	19	20	
Feb 7	21	22	23	24	25	26	27	
	28	29	1	2	3	4	5	
Feb 21	6	7	8	9	10	11	12	MARCH 2168
	13	14	15	16	17	18	19	
Mar 6	20[d]	21	22	23	24	25	26	
	27[e]	28	29	30	31	1	2	
Mar 20	3	4	5	6	7	8	9	APRIL 2168
	10	11	12	13	14	15	16	
Apr 3	17	18	19	20	21	22	23	
	24	25	26	27	28	29	30	
Apr 17	1[f]	2	3	4	5	6	7	MAY 2168
	8	9	10	11	12	13	14	
May 1	15	16	17	18	19	20	21	
	22	23	24	25	26	27	28	
May 15	29	30	31	1	2	3	4	
	5	6	7	8	9	10	11	JUNE 2168
May 29	12	13	14	15	16	17	18	
	19	20	21	22	23	24	25	
Jun 12	26	27	28	29	30	1	2	
	3	4	5	6	7	8	9	JULY 2168
Jun 26	10	11	12	13	14	15	16	
	17	18	19	20	21	22	23	
Jul 10	24	25	26	27	28	29	30	
	31	1	2	3	4	5	6	
Jul 24	7	8	9	10	11	12	13	AUGUST 2168
	14	15	16	17	18	19	20	
Aug 7	21	22	23	24	25	26	27	
	28	29	30	31	1	2	3	
Aug 21	4	5	6	7	8	9	10	SEPTEMBER 2168
	11	12	13	14	15	16	17	
Sep 4	18	19	20	21	22	23	24	
	25	26	27	28	29	30	1	
Sep 18	2	3	4	5	6	7	8	OCTOBER 2168
	9	10	11	12	13	14	15	
Oct 2	16	17	18	19	20	21	22	
	23	24	25	26	27	28	29	
Oct 16	30	31	1	2	3	4	5	
	6	7	8	9	10	11	12	NOVEMBER 2168
Oct 30	13	14	15	16	17	18	19	
	20	21	22	23	24	25	26	
Nov 13	27[g]	28	29	30	1	2	3	
	4	5	6	7	8	9	10	DECEMBER 2168
Nov 27	11	12	13	14	15	16	17	
	18	19	20	21	22	23	24	
Dec 11	25[h]	26	27	28	29	30	31	

Persian: [a]New Year; [b]Sizdeh Bedar

Hindu lunar: ‡Leap year; [a]New Year (Vibhava); [b]Birthday of Rāma; [c]Birthday of Krishna; [d]Ganēśa Chaturthī; [e]Dashara; [f]Diwali; [g]Birthday of Vishnu; [h]Night of Śiva; [i]Holi

Hindu solar: ‡Leap year; [a]New Year (Subhānu); [b]Pongal

Islamic: ‡Leap year; [a]New Year; [b]'Ashūrā'; [c]Prophet's Birthday; [d]Ascent of the Prophet; [e]Start of Ramaḍān; [f]'Id al-Fiṭr; [g]'Id al-'Aḍḥā

Gregorian: ‡Leap year; [a]Orthodox Christmas; [b]Julian New Year; [c]Ash Wednesday; [d]Feast of Orthodoxy; [e]Easter; [f]Orthodox Easter; [g]Advent; [h]Christmas

2169

GREGORIAN 2169	Sun	Mon	Tue	Wed	Thu	Fri	Sat	Lunar Phases	ISO WEEK (Mon)	JULIAN DAY (Sun noon)	HEBREW 5929/5930	Sun	Mon	Tue	Wed	Thu	Fri	Sat	Molad	CHINESE Wù-Chén/Jǐ-Sì‡	Sun	Mon	Tue	Wed	Thu	Fri	Sat	Solar Term	COPTIC 1885/1886	Sun	Mon	Tue	Wed	Thu	Fri	Sat	ETHIOPIC 2161/2162
JANUARY 2169	1[a]	2	3	4	5	◐	7	12:33	1	2513272	TEVETH 5929	3[e]	4	5	6	7	8	9		MONTH 12 Wù-Chén	4	5	6	7	8	9	10	Xiǎo hán	KOIAK 1885	22	23	24	25	26	27	28	TĀKHŚĀŚ 2161
	8	9	10	11	12	○	14	8:52	2	2513279		10	11	12	13	14	15	16			11	12	13	14	15	16	17			29[c]	30	1	2	3	4	5	
	15	16	17	18	19	◑	21	1:47	3	2513286		17	18	19	20	21	22	23			18	19	20	21	22	23*	24	Dà hán	TŌBE 1885	6[d]	7	8	9	10	11[e]	12	ṬER 2161
	22	23	24	25	26	27	●	4:06	4	2513293		24	25	26	27	28	29	1	Sat 6h 0m 16p		25	26	27	28	29	30	1[a]			13	14	15	16	17	18	19	
FEBRUARY 2169	29	30	31	1	2	3	4		5	2513300	SHEVAT 5929	2	3	4	5	6	7	8		MONTH 1 Jǐ-Sì	2	3	4	5	6	7	8	Lì chūn		20	21	22	23	24	25	26	
	◐	6	7	8	9	10	○	3:11 19:32	6	2513307		9	10	11	12	13	14	15			9	10	11	12	13	14	15[b]			27	28	29	30	1	2	3	
	12	13	14	15	16	17	◑	17:35	7	2513314		16	17	18	19	20	21	22			16	17	18	19	20	21	22	Yǔ shuǐ	MESHIR 1885	4	5	6	7	8	9	10	YAKĀTIT 2161
	19	20	21	22	23	24	25		8	2513321		23	24	25	26	27	28	29			23	24	25	26	27	28	29			11	12	13	14	15	16	17	
	●	27	28	1	2	3	4	22:58	9	2513328		30	1	2	3	4	5	6	Sun 18h 44m 17p		30	1	2	3	4	5	6			18	19	20	21	22	23	24	
MARCH 2169	5	◐	7	8	9	10	11	14:26	10	2513335	ADAR 5929	7	8	9	10	11	12	13		MONTH 2 Jǐ-Sì	7	8	9	10	11	12	13	Jīng zhé		25	26	27	28	29	30	1	
	12	○	14	15	16	17	18	5:48	11	2513342		14[f]	15	16	17	18	19	20			14	15	16	17	18	19	20		PAREMOTEP 1885	2	3	4	5	6	7	8	MAGĀBIT 2161
	19	◑[b]	21	22	23	24	25	11:47	12	2513349		21	22	23	24	25	26	27			21	22	23*	24	25	26	27	Chūn fēn		9	10	11	12	13	14	15	
	26	27	●	29	30	31	1	15:24	13	2513356		28	29	1	2	3	4	5	Tue 7h 29m 0p		28	29	1	2	3	4	5			16	17	18	19	20	21	22	
APRIL 2169	2	3	◐	5	6	7	8	22:38	14	2513363	NISAN 5929	6	7	8	9	10	11	12		MONTH 3 Jǐ-Sì	6	7	8[c]	9	10	11	12	Qīng míng		23	24	25	26	27	28	29	
	9	10	○	12	13	14	15	16:07	15	2513370		13	14	15[g]	16	17	18	19			13	14	15	16	17	18	19			30	1	2	3	4	5	6	
	16	17	18	◑	20	21	22	6:58	16	2513377		20	21	22	23	24	25	26			20	21	22	23	24	25	26	Gǔ yǔ	PARMOUTE 1885	7	8	9	10	11	12	13	MIYĀZYĀ 2161
	23	24	25	26	●	28	29	4:56	17	2513384		27	28	29	30	1	2	3	Wed 20h 13m 1p		27	28	29	30	1	2	3			14[f]	15	16	17	18	19	20	
MAY 2169	30	1	2	3	◐	5	6	4:37	18	2513391	IYYAR 5929	4	5	6	7	8	9	10		MONTH 4 Jǐ-Sì	4	5	6	7	8	9	10	Lì xià		21	22	23	24	25	26	27	
	7	8	9	10	○	12	13	3:14	19	2513398		11	12	13	14	15	16	17			11	12	13	14	15	16	17			28	29[g]	30	1	2	3	4	
	14	15	16	17	18	◑	20	1:34	20	2513405		18	19	20	21	22	23	24			18	19	20	21	22	23	24*	Xiǎo mǎn	PASHONS 1885	5	6	7	8	9	10	11	GENBOT 2161
	21	22	23	24	25	●	27	15:48	21	2513412		25	26	27	28	29	1	2	Fri 8h 57m 2p		25	26	27	28	29	1	2			12	13	14	15	16	17	18	
	28	29	30	31	1	◐	3	9:41	22	2513419	SIVAN 5929	3	4	5	6[h]	7	8	9		MONTH 5 Jǐ-Sì	3	4	5[d]	6	7	8	9			19	20	21	22	23	24	25	
JUNE 2169	4	5	6	7	8	○	10	15:41	23	2513426		10	11	12	13	14	15	16			10	11	12	13	14	15	16	Máng zhòng		26	27	28	29	30	1	2	
	11	12	13	14	15	16	◑	18:26	24	2513433		17	18	19	20	21	22	23			17	18	19	20	21	22	23		PAŌNE 1885	3	4	5	6	7	8	9	SANĒ 2161
	18	19	20[c]	21	22	23	24		25	2513440		24	25	26	27	28	29	30			24	25	26	27	28	29	30	Xià zhì		10	11	12	13	14	15	16	
	●	26	27	28	29	30	◐	0:36 15:16	26	2513447	TAMMUZ 5929	1	2	3	4	5	6	7	Sat 21h 41m 3p	MONTH 6 Jǐ-Sì	1	2	3	4	5	6	7			17	18	19	20	21	22	23	
JULY 2169	2	3	4	5	6	7	8		27	2513454		8	9	10	11	12	13	14			8	9	10	11	12	13	14	Xiǎo shǔ		24	25	26	27	28	29	30	
	○	10	11	12	13	14	15	5:37	28	2513461		15	16	17	18	19	20	21			15	16	17	18	19	20	21		EPĒP 1885	1	2	3	4	5	6	7	ḤAMLĒ 2161
	16	◑	18	19	20	21	22	9:05	29	2513468		22	23	24	25	26	27	28			22	23	24	25*	26	27	28	Dà shǔ		8	9	10	11	12	13	14	
	23	●	25	26	27	28	29	8:04	30	2513475		29	1	2	3	4	5	6	Mon 10h 25m 4p	LEAP MONTH 6 Jǐ-Sì	29	1	2	3	4	5	6			15	16	17	18	19	20	21	
	◐	31	1	2	3	4	5	22:50	31	2513482	AV 5929	7	8	9[i]	10	11	12	13			7	8	9	10	11	12	13			22	23	24	25	26	27	28	
AUGUST 2169	6	○	8	9	10	11	12	20:42	32	2513489		14	15	16	17	18	19	20			14	15	16	17	18	19	20	Lì qiū		29	30	1	2	3	4	5	
	13	14	◑	16	17	18	19	21:29	33	2513496		21	22	23	24	25	26	27			21	22	23	24	25	26	27		MESORĒ 1885	6	7	8	9	10	11	12	NAHASĒ 2161
	20	21	●	23	24	25	26	15:05	34	2513503		28	29	30	1	2	3	4	Tue 23h 9m 5p		28	29	1	2	3	4	5	Chǔ shǔ		13[h]	14	15	16	17	18	19	
	27	28	◐	30	31	1	2	9:34	35	2513510	ELUL 5929	5	6	7	8	9	10	11		MONTH 7 Jǐ-Sì	6	7[e]	8	9	10	11	12			20	21	22	23	24	25	26	
SEPTEMBER 2169	3	4	5	○	7	8	9	12:24	36	2513517		12	13	14	15	16	17	18			13	14	15[f]	16	17	18	19	Bái lù	EPAG. 1885	27	28	29	30	1	2	3	PĀG. 2161
	10	11	12	13	◑	15	16	7:49	37	2513524		19	20	21	22	23	24	25			20	21	22	23	24	25	26			4	5	1[a]	2	3	4	5	
	17	18	19	●	21	22[d]	23	22:41	38	2513531		26	27	28	29	1[a]	2[a]	3	Thu 11h 53m 6p		27*	28	29	30	1	2	3	Qiū fēn	THOOUT 1886	6	7	8	9	10	11	12	MASKARAM 2162
	24	25	26	27	◐	29	30	0:07	39	2513538	TISHRI 5930	4	5	6	7	8	9	10[b]		MONTH 8 Jǐ-Sì	4	5	6	7	8	9	10			13	14	15	16	17[b]	18	19	
OCTOBER 2169	1	2	3	4	5	○	7	4:13	40	2513545		11	12	13	14	15[c]	16	17			11	12	13	14	15[g]	16	17			20	21	22	23	24	25	26	
	8	9	10	11	12	◑	14	16:26	41	2513552		18	19	20	21	22	23	24			18	19	20	21	22	23	24	Hán lù		27	28	29	30	1	2	3	
	15	16	17	18	19	●	21	7:59	42	2513559		25	26	27	28	29	30	1	Sat 0h 37m 7p		25	26	27	28	29	1	2		PAOPE 1886	4	5	6	7	8	9	10	ṬEQEMT 2162
	22	23	24	25	26	◐	28	18:14	43	2513566	HESHVAN 5930	2	3	4	5	6	7	8		MONTH 9 Jǐ-Sì	3	4	5	6	7	8	9[h]	Shuāng jiàng		11	12	13	14	15	16	17	
	29	30	31	1	2	3	○	19:41	44	2513573		9	10	11	12	13	14	15			10	11	12	13	14	15	16			18	19	20	21	22	23	24	
NOVEMBER 2169	5	6	7	8	9	10	◑	23:57	45	2513580		16	17	18	19	20	21	22			17	18	19	20	21	22	23	Lì dōng		25	26	27	28	29	30	1	
	12	13	14	15	16	17	●	19:52	46	2513587		23	24	25	26	27	28	29			24	25	26	27	28*	29	30		ATHŌR 1886	2	3	4	5	6	7	8	HEDĀR 2162
	19	20	21	22	23	24	25		47	2513594		30	1	2	3	4	5	6	Sun 13h 21m 8p	MONTH 10 Jǐ-Sì	1	2	3	4	5	6	7	Xiǎo xuě		9	10	11	12	13	14	15	
	◐	27	28	29	30	1	2	14:53	48	2513601	KISLEV 5930	7	8	9	10	11	12	13			8	9	10	11	12	13	14			16	17	18	19	20	21	22	
DECEMBER 2169	3	○	5	6	7	8	9	10:19	49	2513608		14	15	16	17[d]	18	19	20			15	16	17	18	19	20	21	Dà xuě		23	24	25	26	27	28	29	
	10	◑	12	13	14	15	16	7:20	50	2513615		21	22	23	24	25[e]	26[e]	27[e]			22	23	24	25	26	27	28			30	1	2	3	4	5	6	
	17	●	19	20	21[e]	22	23	10:40	51	2513622		28[e]	29[e]	30[e]	1[e]	2[e]	3	4	Tue 2h 5m 9p		29	1	2	3	4[i]	5	6	Dōng zhì	KOIAK 1886	7	8	9	10	11	12	13	TĀKHŚĀŚ 2162
	24	25	◐	27	28	29	30	12:20	52	2513629	TEVETH 5930	5	6	7	8	9	10	11		MONTH 11 Jǐ-Sì	7	8	9	10	11	12	13			14	15	16	17	18	19	20	
	31	1	○	3	4	5	6	23:37	1	2513636		12	13	14	15	16	17	18			14	15	16	17	18	19	20	Xiǎo hán		21	22	23	24	25	26	27	

[a]New Year
[b]Spring (6:41)
[c]Summer (21:46)
[d]Autumn (14:41)
[e]Winter (13:57)
● New moon
◐ First quarter moon
○ Full moon
◑ Last quarter moon

[a]New Year
[b]Yom Kippur
[c]Sukkot
[d]Winter starts
[e]Ḥanukkah
[f]Purim
[g]Passover
[h]Shavuot
[i]Fast of Av

‡Leap year
[a]New Year (4867, Snake)
[b]Lantern Festival
[c]Qīngmíng
[d]Dragon Festival
[e]Qīqiǎo
[f]Hungry Ghosts
[g]Mid-Autumn Festival
[h]Double-Ninth Festival
[i]Dōngzhì
*Start of 60-name cycle

[a]New Year
[b]Building of the Cross
[c]Christmas
[d]Jesus's Circumcision
[e]Epiphany
[f]Easter
[g]Mary's Announcement
[h]Jesus's Transfiguration

2169

PERSIAN (ASTRONOMICAL) 1547/1548‡

Month	Sun	Mon	Tue	Wed	Thu	Fri	Sat
DEY 1547	12	13	14	15	16	17	18
	19	20	21	22	23	24	25
	26	27	28	29	30	1	2
BAHMAN 1547	3	4	5	6	7	8	9
	10	11	12	13	14	15	16
	17	18	19	20	21	22	23
	24	25	26	27	28	29	30
ESFAND 1547	1	2	3	4	5	6	7
	8	9	10	11	12	13	14
	15	16	17	18	19	20	21
	22	23	24	25	26	27	28
FARVARDĪN 1548	29	1[a]	2	3	4	5	6
	7	8	9	10	11	12	13[b]
	14	15	16	17	18	19	20
	21	22	23	24	25	26	27
ORDĪBEHEŠT 1548	28	29	30	31	1	2	3
	4	5	6	7	8	9	10
	11	12	13	14	15	16	17
	18	19	20	21	22	23	24
	25	26	27	28	29	30	31
XORDĀD 1548	1	2	3	4	5	6	7
	8	9	10	11	12	13	14
	15	16	17	18	19	20	21
	22	23	24	25	26	27	28
TĪR 1548	29	30	31	1	2	3	4
	5	6	7	8	9	10	11
	12	13	14	15	16	17	18
	19	20	21	22	23	24	25
MORDĀD 1548	26	27	28	29	30	31	1
	2	3	4	5	6	7	8
	9	10	11	12	13	14	15
	16	17	18	19	20	21	22
	23	24	25	26	27	28	29
SHAHRĪVAR 1548	30	31	1	2	3	4	5
	6	7	8	9	10	11	12
	13	14	15	16	17	18	19
	20	21	22	23	24	25	26
MEHR 1548	27	28	29	30	31	1	2
	3	4	5	6	7	8	9
	10	11	12	13	14	15	16
	17	18	19	20	21	22	23
	24	25	26	27	28	29	30
ĀBĀN 1548	1	2	3	4	5	6	7
	8	9	10	11	12	13	14
	15	16	17	18	19	20	21
	22	23	24	25	26	27	28
ĀZAR 1548	29	30	1	2	3	4	5
	6	7	8	9	10	11	12
	13	14	15	16	17	18	19
	20	21	22	23	24	25	26
DEY 1548	27	28	29	30	1	2	3
	4	5	6	7	8	9	10
	11	12	13	14	15	16	17

‡Leap year
[a]New Year
[b]Sizdeh Bedar

HINDU LUNAR 2225/2226

Month	Sun	Mon	Tue	Wed	Thu	Fri	Sat
PAUSHA 2225	3	4	5	6	7	8	9
	10	11	12	13	14	15	16
	17	**18**	20	21	22	23	24
	25	26	27	28	29	30	*30*
MĀGHA 2225	1	2	3	4	5	6	7
	8	9	10	11	**12**	14	15
	16	17	18	19	20	21	22
	23	24	25	26	27	28[h]	29
PHĀLGUNA 2225	30	1	2	3	3	4	**5**
	7	8	9	10	11	12	13
	14	15[i]	16	17	**18**	20	21
	22	*22*	23	24	25	26	27
CHAITRA 2226	28	29	30	1[a]	2	3	4
	5	6	7	8	9[b]	**10**	12
	13	14	15	16	17	18	19
	20	21	22	23	24	25	26
VAIŚĀKHA 2226	*26*	27	28	29	30	1	2
	3	**4**	6	7	8	9	10
	11	12	13	14	15	16	17
	18	19	20	21	22	23	24
JYAISHTHA 2226	25	26	27	28	29	30	1
	2	3	4	5	6	**7**	9
	10	11	12	13	14	15	16
	17	18	19	20	21	22	*22*
	23	24	25	26	27	28	29
ĀSHĀDHA 2226	**30**	2	3	4	5	6	7
	8	9	10	11	12	13	14
	15	16	17	18	19	20	21
	22	23	24	25	26	27	28
ŚRĀVAṆA 2226	29	30	1	2	**3**	5	6
	7	8	9	10	11	12	13
	14	15	16	17	18	*18*	19
	20	21	22	23[c]	24	**25**	27
BHĀDRAPADA 2226	28	29	30	1	2	3	4[d]
	5	6	7	8	9	10	11
	12	13	14	15	16	17	18
	19	20	21	22	23	24	25
ĀŚVINA 2226	26	27	28	**29**	1	2	3
	4	5	6	7	8[e]	9[e]	10[e]
	11	12	13	14	*14*	15	16
	17	18	19	20	21	**22**	24
LEAP KĀRTTIKA 2226	25	26	27	28	29	30	1
	2	3	4	5	6	7	8
	9	10	11	12	13	14	15
	16	17	18	19	20	21	22
	23	24	25	**26**	28	29	30
KĀRTTIKA 2226	1[f]	2	3	4	5	6	7
	8	*8*	9	10	11	12	13
	14	15	16	17	18	19	**20**
	22	23	24	25	26	27	28
MĀRGAŚIRA 2226	29	30	1	2	3	4	5
	6	7	8	9	10	11	*11*[g]
	12	**13**	15	16	17	18	19

[a]New Year (Śukla)
[b]Birthday of Rāma
[c]Birthday of Krishna
[d]Ganēśa Chaturthī
[e]Dashara
[f]Diwali
[g]Birthday of Vishnu
[h]Night of Śiva
[i]Holi

HINDU SOLAR 2090‡/2091

Month	Sun	Mon	Tue	Wed	Thu	Fri	Sat
PAUSHA 2090	15	16	17	18	19	20	21
	22	23	24	25	26	27	28
MĀGHA 2090	29	1[b]	2	3	4	5	6
	7	8	9	10	11	12	13
	14	15	16	17	18	19	20
	21	22	23	24	25	26	27
PHĀLGUNA 2090	28	29	30	1	2	3	4
	5	6	7	8	9	10	11
	12	13	14	15	16	17	18
	19	20	21	22	23	24	25
CHAITRA 2090	26	27	28	29	1	2	3
	4	5	6	7	8	9	10
	11	12	13	14	15	16	17
	18	19	20	21	22	23	24
	25	26	27	28	29	30	31
VAIŚĀKHA 2091	1[a]	2	3	4	5	6	7
	8	9	10	11	12	13	14
	15	16	17	18	19	20	21
	22	23	24	25	26	27	28
JYAISHTHA 2091	29	30	31	1	2	3	4
	5	6	7	8	9	10	11
	12	13	14	15	16	17	18
	19	20	21	22	23	24	25
ĀSHĀDHA 2091	26	27	28	29	30	31	1
	2	3	4	5	6	7	8
	9	10	11	12	13	14	15
	16	17	18	19	20	21	22
	23	24	25	26	27	28	29
ŚRĀVAṆA 2091	30	31	32	1	2	3	4
	5	6	7	8	9	10	11
	12	13	14	15	16	17	18
	19	20	21	22	23	24	25
BHĀDRAPADA 2091	26	27	28	29	30	31	1
	2	3	4	5	6	7	8
	9	10	11	12	13	14	15
	16	17	18	19	20	21	22
	23	24	25	26	27	28	29
ĀŚVINA 2091	30	31	1	2	3	4	5
	6	7	8	9	10	11	12
	13	14	15	16	17	18	19
	20	21	22	23	24	25	26
KĀRTTIKA 2091	27	28	29	30	31	1	2
	3	4	5	6	7	8	9
	10	11	12	13	14	15	16
	17	18	19	20	21	22	23
	24	25	26	27	28	29	30
MĀRGAŚIRA 2091	1	2	3	4	5	6	7
	8	9	10	11	12	13	14
	15	16	17	18	19	20	21
	22	23	24	25	26	27	28
PAUSHA 2091	29	1	2	3	4	5	6
	7	8	9	10	11	12	13
	14	15	16	17	18	19	20

‡Leap year
[a]New Year (Tāraṇa)
[b]Pongal

ISLAMIC (ASTRONOMICAL) 1594‡/1595

Month	Sun	Mon	Tue	Wed	Thu	Fri	Sat
DHU AL-HIJJA 1594	2	3	4	5	6	7	8
	9	10[g]	11	12	13	14	15
	16	17	18	19	20	21	22
	23	24	25	26	27	28	29
MUHARRAM 1595	30[d]	1[a]	2	3	4	5	6
	7	8	9	10[b]	11	12	13
	14	15	16	17	18	19	20
	21	22	23	24	25	26	27
SAFAR 1595	28	29	1	2	3	4	5
	6	7	8	9	10	11	12
	13	14	15	16	17	18	19
	20	21	22	23	24	25	26
RABĪ' I 1595	27	28	29	30	1	2	3
	4	5	6	7	8	9	10
	11	12[c]	13	14	15	16	17
	18	19	20	21	22	23	24
RABĪ' II 1595	25	26	27	28	29	1	2
	3	4	5	6	7	8	9
	10	11	12	13	14	15	16
	17	18	19	20	21	22	23
	24	25	26	27	28	29	30
JUMĀDĀ I 1595	1	2	3	4	5	6	7
	8	9	10	11	12	13	14
	15	16	17	18	19	20	21
	22	23	24	25	26	27	28
JUMĀDĀ II 1595	29	1	2	3	4	5	6
	7	8	9	10	11	12	13
	14	15	16	17	18	19	20
	21	22	23	24	25	26	27
RAJAB 1595	28	29	1	2	3	4	5
	6	7	8	9	10	11	12
	13	14	15	16	17	18	19
	20	21	22	23	24	25	26
SHA'BĀN 1595	27[d]	28	29	30	1	2	3
	4	5	6	7	8	9	10
	11	12	13	14	15	16	17
	18	19	20	21	22	23	24
RAMAḌĀN 1595	25	26	27	28	29	1[e]	2
	3	4	5	6	7	8	9
	10	11	12	13	14	15	16
	17	18	19	20	21	22	23
	24	25	26	27	28	29	30
SHAWWĀL 1595	1[f]	2	3	4	5	6	7
	8	9	10	11	12	13	14
	15	16	17	18	19	20	21
	22	23	24	25	26	27	28
DHU AL-QA'DA 1595	29	1	2	3	4	5	6
	7	8	9	10	11	12	13
	14	15	16	17	18	19	20
	21	22	23	24	25	26	27
DHU AL-HIJJA 1595	28	29	30	1	2	3	4
	5	6	7	8	9	10[g]	11
	12	13	14	15	16	17	18

‡Leap year
[a]New Year
[d]New Year (Arithmetic)
[b]'Āshūrā'
[c]Prophet's Birthday
[d]Ascent of the Prophet
[e]Start of Ramaḍān
[f]'Īd al-Fiṭr
[g]'Īd al-'Aḍḥā

GREGORIAN 2169

Julian (Sun)	Sun	Mon	Tue	Wed	Thu	Fri	Sat	Month
Dec 18	1	2	3	4	5	6	7	JANUARY 2169
	8[a]	9	10	11	12	13	14	
Jan 1	15[b]	16	17	18	19	20	21	
	22	23	24	25	26	27	28	
Jan 15	29	30	31	1	2	3	4	FEBRUARY 2169
	5	6	7	8	9	10	11	
Jan 29	12	13	14	15	16	17	18	
	19	20	21	22	23	24	25	
Feb 12	26	27	28	1[c]	2	3	4	MARCH 2169
	5	6	7	8	9	10	11	
Feb 26	12[d]	13	14	15	16	17	18	
	19	20	21	22	23	24	25	
Mar 12	26	27	28	29	30	31	1	APRIL 2169
	2	3	4	5	6	7	8	
Mar 26	9	10	11	12	13	14	15	
	16[e]	17	18	19	20	21	22	
Apr 9	23[f]	24	25	26	27	28	29	
	30	1	2	3	4	5	6	MAY 2169
Apr 23	7	8	9	10	11	12	13	
	14	15	16	17	18	19	20	
May 7	21	22	23	24	25	26	27	
	28	29	30	31	1	2	3	JUNE 2169
May 21	4	5	6	7	8	9	10	
	11	12	13	14	15	16	17	
Jun 4	18	19	20	21	22	23	24	
	25	26	27	28	29	30	1	JULY 2169
Jun 18	2	3	4	5	6	7	8	
	9	10	11	12	13	14	15	
Jul 2	16	17	18	19	20	21	22	
	23	24	25	26	27	28	29	
Jul 16	30	31	1	2	3	4	5	AUGUST 2169
	6	7	8	9	10	11	12	
Jul 30	13	14	15	16	17	18	19	
	20	21	22	23	24	25	26	
Aug 13	27	28	29	30	31	1	2	SEPTEMBER 2169
	3	4	5	6	7	8	9	
Aug 27	10	11	12	13	14	15	16	
	17	18	19	20	21	22	23	
Sep 10	24	25	26	27	28	29	30	
	1	2	3	4	5	6	7	OCTOBER 2169
Sep 24	8	9	10	11	12	13	14	
	15	16	17	18	19	20	21	
Oct 8	22	23	24	25	26	27	28	
	29	30	31	1	2	3	4	NOVEMBER 2169
Oct 22	5	6	7	8	9	10	11	
	12	13	14	15	16	17	18	
Nov 5	19	20	21	22	23	24	25	
	26	27	28	29	30	1	2	DECEMBER 2169
Nov 19	3[g]	4	5	6	7	8	9	
	10	11	12	13	14	15	16	
Dec 3	17	18	19	20	21	22	23	
	24	25[h]	26	27	28	29	30	
Dec 17	31	1	2	3	4	5	6	

[a]Orthodox Christmas
[b]Julian New Year
[c]Ash Wednesday
[d]Feast of Orthodoxy
[e]Easter
[f]Orthodox Easter
[g]Advent
[h]Christmas

2170

Month	Sun	Mon	Tue	Wed	Thu	Fri	Sat	Lunar Phases	ISO WEEK (Mon)	JULIAN DAY (Sun noon)	Hebrew month	Sun	Mon	Tue	Wed	Thu	Fri	Sat	Molad	Chinese month	Sun	Mon	Tue	Wed	Thu	Fri	Sat	Solar Term	Coptic month	Sun	Mon	Tue	Wed	Thu	Fri	Sat	Ethiopic month
	GREGORIAN 2170										**HEBREW 5930/5931‡**									**CHINESE Jǐ-Sì‡/Gēng-Wǔ**									**COPTIC 1886/1887‡**	**ETHIOPIC 2162/2163‡**							
JANUARY 2170	31	1[a]	○	3	4	5	6	23:37	1	2513636	TEVETH 5930	12	13	14	15	16	17	18		MONTH 11 Jǐ-Sì	14	15	16	17	18	19	20	Xiǎo hán	KOIAK 1886	21	22	23	24	25	26	27	TÂKHŚÂŚ 2162
	7	8	◑	10	11	12	13	15:43	2	2513643		19	20	21	22	23	24	25	Wed 14h49m10p		21	22	23	24	25	26	27			28	29[c]	30	1	2	3	4	
	14	15	16	●	18	19	20	3:53	3	2513650	SHEVAT 5930	26	27	28	29	1	2	3		MONTH 12 Jǐ-Sì	28	29*	30	1	2	3	4	Dà hán	TÔBE 1886	5	6[d]	7	8	9	10	11[e]	TER 2162
	21	22	23	24	◐	26	27	8:39	4	2513657		4	5	6	7	8	9	10			5	6	7	8	9	10	11			12	13	14	15	16	17	18	
	28	29	30	31	○	2	3	11:18	5	2513664		11	12	13	14	15	16	17			12	13	14	15	16	17	18			19	20	21	22	23	24	25	
FEBRUARY 2170	4	5	6	7	◑	9	10	2:04	6	2513671		18	19	20	21	22	23	24	Fri 3h33m1p		19	20	21	22	23	24	25	Lì chūn		26	27	28	29	30	1	2	
	11	12	13	14	●	16	17	22:23	7	2513678	ADAR 5930	25	26	27	28	29	30	1			26	27	28	29	30	1[a]	2		MESHIR 1886	3	4	5	6	7	8	9	YAKÂTIT 2162
	18	19	20	21	22	23	◐	2:06	8	2513685		2	3	4	5	6	7	8		MONTH 1 Gēng-Wǔ	3	4	5	6	7	8	9	Yǔ shuǐ		10	11	12	13	14	15	16	
	25	26	27	28	1	○	3	21:27	9	2513692		9	10	11	12	13	14[f]	15			10	11	12	13	14	15[b]	16			17	18	19	20	21	22	23	
MARCH 2170	4	5	6	7	8	◑	10	14:49	10	2513699		16	17	18	19	20	21	22			17	18	19	20	21	22	23	Jīng zhé		24	25	26	27	28	29	30	
	11	12	13	14	15	16	●	16:48	11	2513706		23	24	25	26	27	28	29			24	25	26	27	28	29*	30		PAREMOTEP 1886	1	2	3	4	5	6	7	
	18	19	20[b]	21	22	23	24		12	2513713	NISAN 5930	1	2	3	4	5	6	7	Sat 16h17m12p	MONTH 2 Gēng-Wǔ	1	2	3	4	5	6	7	Chūn fēn		8	9	10	11	12	13	14	MAGÂBIT 2162
	◐	26	27	28	29	30	31	15:35	13	2513720		8	9	10	11	12	13	14			8	9	10	11	12	13	14			15	16	17	18	19	20	21	
APRIL 2170	○	2	3	4	5	6	7	6:37	14	2513727		15[g]	16	17	18	19	20	21			15	16	17	18[c]	19	20	21	Qīng míng		22	23	24	25	26	27	28	
	◑	9	10	11	12	13	14	5:44	15	2513734		22	23	24	25	26	27	28			22	23	24	25	26	27	28		PARMOUTE 1886	29[f]	30	1	2	3	4	5	
	15	●	17	18	19	20	21	9:56	16	2513741	IYYAR 5930	29	30	1	2	3	4	5	Mon 5h1m13p	MONTH 3 Gēng-Wǔ	29	1	2	3	4	5	6	Gǔ yǔ		6	7	8	9	10	11	12	MIYÂZYÂ 2162
	22	23	◐	25	26	27	28	1:01	17	2513748		6	7	8	9	10	11	12			7	8	9	10	11	12	13			13	14	15	16	17	18	19	
	29	○	1	2	3	4	5	15:30	18	2513755		13	14	15	16	17	18	19			14	15	16	17	18	19	20	Lì xià		20	21	22	23	24	25	26	
MAY 2170	6	◑	8	9	10	11	12	22:09	19	2513762		20	21	22	23	24	25	26			21	22	23	24	25	26	27		PASHONS 1886	27	28	29[g]	30	1	2	3	
	13	14	15	●	17	18	19	0:57	20	2513769	SIVAN 5930	27	28	29	1	2	3	4	Tue 17h45m14p	MONTH 4 Gēng-Wǔ	28	29	30*	1	2	3	4			4	5	6	7	8	9	10	GENBOT 2162
	20	21	22	◐	24	25	26	7:18	21	2513776		5	6[h]	7	8	9	10	11			5	6	7	8	9	10	11	Xiǎo mǎn		11	12	13	14	15	16	17	
	27	28	29	○	31	1	2	0:48	22	2513783		12	13	14	15	16	17	18			12	13	14	15	16	17	18			18	19	20	21	22	23	24	
JUNE 2170	3	4	5	◑	7	8	9	15:21	23	2513790		19	20	21	22	23	24	25			19	20	21	22	23	24	25	Máng zhòng		25	26	27	28	29	30	1	
	10	11	12	13	●	15	16	13:23	24	2513797	TAMMUZ 5930	26	27	28	29	30	1	2	Thu 6h29m15p	MONTH 5 Gēng-Wǔ	26	27	28	29	1	2	3		PAÔNE 1886	2	3	4	5	6	7	8	SANÊ 2162
	17	18	19	20	◐[c]	22	23	11:53	25	2513804		3	4	5	6	7	8	9			4	5[d]	6	7	8	9	10	Xià zhì		9	10	11	12	13	14	15	
	24	25	26	27	○	29	30	11:09	26	2513811		10	11	12	13	14	15	16			11	12	13	14	15	16	17			16	17	18	19	20	21	22	
JULY 2170	1	2	3	4	5	◑	7	8:41	27	2513818		17	18	19	20	21	22	23			18	19	20	21	22	23	24	Xiǎo shǔ		23	24	25	26	27	28	29	
	8	9	10	11	12	●	14	23:24	28	2513825	AV 5930	24	25	26	27	28	29	1	Fri 19h13m16p	MONTH 6 Gēng-Wǔ	25	26	27	28	29	30	1*		EPÊP 1886	30	1	2	3	4	5	6	
	15	16	17	18	19	◐	21	16:22	29	2513832		2	3	4	5	6	7	8			2	3	4	5	6	7	8			7	8	9	10	11	12	13	ḤAMLÊ 2162
	22	23	24	25	26	○	28	23:03	30	2513839		9[i]	10	11	12	13	14	15			9	10	11	12	13	14	15	Dà shǔ		14	15	16	17	18	19	20	
	29	30	31	1	2	3	4		31	2513846		16	17	18	19	20	21	22			16	17	18	19	20	21	22			21	22	23	24	25	26	27	
AUGUST 2170	◑	6	7	8	9	10	11	1:28	32	2513853		23	24	25	26	27	28	29			23	24	25	26	27	28	29	Lì qiū	MESORÊ 1886	28	29	30	1	2	3	4	
	●	13	14	15	16	17	◐	7:43 22:20	33	2513860	ELUL 5930	30	1	2	3	4	5	6	Sun 7h57m17p	MONTH 7 Gēng-Wǔ	1	2	3	4	5	6	7[e]			5	6	7	8	9	10	11	NAHASÊ 2162
	19	20	21	22	23	24	25		34	2513867		7	8	9	10	11	12	13			8	9	10	11	12	13	14	Chǔ shǔ		12	13[h]	14	15	16	17	18	
	○	27	28	29	30	31	1	12:52	35	2513874		14	15	16	17	18	19	20			15[f]	16	17	18	19	20	21			19	20	21	22	23	24	25	
SEPTEMBER 2170	2	◑	4	5	6	7	8	17:00	36	2513881		21	22	23	24	25	26	27			22	23	24	25	26	27	28	Bái lù	EPAG. 1886	26	27	28	29	30	1	2	PÂG. 2162
	9	●	11	12	13	14	15	15:23	37	2513888	TISHRI 5931	28	29	1[a]	2[a]	3	4	5	Mon 20h42m0p	MONTH 8 Gēng-Wǔ	29	1	2	3*	4	5	6		THOOUT 1887	3	4	5	1[a]	2	3	4	MASKARAM 2163
	16	◐	18	19	20	21	22[d]	7:01	38	2513895		6	7	8	9	10[b]	11	12			7	8	9	10	11	12	13			5	6	7	8	9	10	11	
	23	24	○	26	27	28	29	4:43	39	2513902		13	14	15[c]	16	17	18	19			14	15[g]	16	17	18	19	20	Qiū fēn		12	13	14	15	16	17[b]	18	
	30	1	2	◑	4	5	6	6:39	40	2513909		20	21	22	23	24	25	26			21	22	23	24	25	26	27			19	20	21	22	23	24	25	
OCTOBER 2170	7	8	●	10	11	12	13	23:32	41	2513916	HESHVAN 5931	27	28	29	30	1	2	3	Wed 9h26m1p	MONTH 9 Gēng-Wǔ	28	29	30	1	2	3	4	Hán lù	PAOPE 1887	26	27	28	29	30	1	2	ṬEQEMT 2163
	14	15	◐	17	18	19	20	19:17	42	2513923		4	5	6	7	8	9	10			5	6	7	8	9[h]	10	11			3	4	5	6	7	8	9	
	21	22	23	○	25	26	27	22:12	43	2513930		11	12	13	14	15	16	17			12	13	14	15	16	17	18	Shuāng jiàng		10	11	12	13	14	15	16	
	28	29	30	31	◑	2	3	18:07	44	2513937		18	19	20	21	22	23	24			19	20	21	22	23	24	25			17	18	19	20	21	22	23	
NOVEMBER 2170	4	5	6	7	●	9	10	9:04	45	2513944	KISLEV 5931	25	26	27	28	29	1	2	Thu 22h10m2p	MONTH 10 Gēng-Wǔ	26	27	28	29	1	2	3	Lì dōng		24	25	26	27	28	29	30	
	11	12	13	14	◐	16	17	11:25	46	2513951		3	4	5	6	7	8	9			4*	5	6	7	8	9	10		ATHÔR 1887	1	2	3	4	5	6	7	ḪEDÂR 2163
	18	19	20	21	22	○	24	16:11	47	2513958		10	11	12	13	14	15	16			11	12	13	14	15	16	17	Xiǎo xuě		8	9	10	11	12	13	14	
	25	26	27	28	29	30	◑	3:43	48	2513965		17	18	19	20	21	22	23			18	19	20	21	22	23	24			15	16	17	18	19	20	21	
DECEMBER 2170	2	3	4	5	6	●	8	20:25	49	2513972		24	25[e]	26[e]	27[e]	28[d,e]	29[e]	30[e]	Sat 10h54m3p	MONTH 11 Gēng-Wǔ	25	26	27	28	29	30	1	Dà xuě		22	23	24	25	26	27	28	
	9	10	11	12	13	14	◐	7:04	50	2513979	TEVETH 5931	1[e]	2[e]	3	4	5	6	7			2	3	4	5	6	7	8		KOIAK 1887	29	30	1	2	3	4	5	
	16	17	18	19	20	21[e]	22		51	2513986		8	9	10	11	12	13	14			9	10	11	12	13	14	15[i]	Dōng zhì		6	7	8	9	10	11	12	TÂKHŚÂŚ 2163
	○	24	25	26	27	28	29	9:11	52	2513993		15	16	17	18	19	20	21			16	17	18	19	20	21	22			13	14	15	16	17	18	19	
	◑	31	1	2	3	4	5	12:06	1	2514000		22	23	24	25	26	27	28			23	24	25	26	27	28	29	Xiǎo hán		20	21	22	23	24	25	26	

[a]New Year
[b]Spring (12:26)
[c]Summer (3:29)
[d]Autumn (20:32)
[e]Winter (19:42)
● New moon
◐ First quarter moon
○ Full moon
◑ Last quarter moon

‡Leap year
[a]New Year
[b]Yom Kippur
[c]Sukkot
[d]Winter starts
[e]Hanukkah
[f]Purim
[g]Passover
[h]Shavuot
[i]Fast of Av

‡Leap year
[a]New Year (4868, Horse)
[b]Lantern Festival
[c]Qīngmíng
[d]Dragon Festival
[e]Qīqiǎo
[f]Hungry Ghosts
[g]Mid-Autumn Festival
[h]Double-Ninth Festival
[i]Dōngzhì
*Start of 60-name cycle

‡Leap year
[a]New Year
[b]Building of the Cross
[c]Christmas
[d]Jesus's Circumcision
[e]Epiphany
[f]Easter
[g]Mary's Announcement
[h]Jesus's Transfiguration

PERSIAN (ASTRONOMICAL) 1548‡/1549

Month	Sun	Mon	Tue	Wed	Thu	Fri	Sat
DEY 1548	11	12	13	14	15	16	17
	18	19	20	21	22	23	24
	25	26	27	28	29	30	1
BAHMAN 1548	2	3	4	5	6	7	8
	9	10	11	12	13	14	15
	16	17	18	19	20	21	22
	23	24	25	26	27	28	29
ESFAND 1548	30	1	2	3	4	5	6
	7	8	9	10	11	12	13
	14	15	16	17	18	19	20
	21	22	23	24	25	26	27
FARVARDĪN 1549	28	29	30	1[a]	2	3	4
	5	6	7	8	9	10	11
	12	13[b]	14	15	16	17	18
	19	20	21	22	23	24	25
ORDĪBEHEŠT 1549	26	27	28	29	30	31	1
	2	3	4	5	6	7	8
	9	10	11	12	13	14	15
	16	17	18	19	20	21	22
	23	24	25	26	27	28	29
XORDĀD 1549	30	31	1	2	3	4	5
	6	7	8	9	10	11	12
	13	14	15	16	17	18	19
	20	21	22	23	24	25	26
TĪR 1549	27	28	29	30	31	1	2
	3	4	5	6	7	8	9
	10	11	12	13	14	15	16
	17	18	19	20	21	22	23
	24	25	26	27	28	29	30
MORDĀD 1549	31	1	2	3	4	5	6
	7	8	9	10	11	12	13
	14	15	16	17	18	19	20
	21	22	23	24	25	26	27
SHAHRĪVAR 1549	28	29	30	31	1	2	3
	4	5	6	7	8	9	10
	11	12	13	14	15	16	17
	18	19	20	21	22	23	24
	25	26	27	28	29	30	31
MEHR 1549	1	2	3	4	5	6	7
	8	9	10	11	12	13	14
	15	16	17	18	19	20	21
	22	23	24	25	26	27	28
ĀBĀN 1549	29	30	1	2	3	4	5
	6	7	8	9	10	11	12
	13	14	15	16	17	18	19
	20	21	22	23	24	25	26
ĀZAR 1549	27	28	29	30	1	2	3
	4	5	6	7	8	9	10
	11	12	13	14	15	16	17
	18	19	20	21	22	23	24
DEY 1549	25	26	27	28	29	30	1
	2	3	4	5	6	7	8
	9	10	11	12	13	14	15

‡Leap year
[a]New Year
[b]Sizdeh Bedar

HINDU LUNAR 2226/2227‡

Month	Sun	Mon	Tue	Wed	Thu	Fri	Sat
MĀRGAŚĪRA 2226	12	**13**	15	16	17	18	19
	20	21	22	23	24	25	26
MĀGHA 2226	**27**	29	*29*	30	1	2	3
	4	5	6	7	8	9	10
	11	12	13	14	15	16	17
	18	**19**	21	22	23	24	25
PHĀLGUNA 2226	26	27	28[h]	29	30	1	2
	3	*3*	4	5	6	7	8
	9	10	11	12	**13**	15[i]	16
	17	18	19	20	21	22	23
	24	25	26	27	28	29	30
LEAP CHAITRA 2227	1[a]	2	3	4	5	6	7
	8	9	10	11	12	13	14
	15	16	17	**18**	20	21	22
	23	24	25	26	*26*	27	28
CHAITRA 2227	29	30	1	2	3	4	5
	6	7	8	9[b]	10	**11**	13
	14	15	16	17	18	19	20
	21	22	23	24	25	26	27
VAIŚĀKHA 2227	28	29	30	*30*	1	2	**3**
	5	6	7	8	9	10	11
	12	13	14	**15**	17	18	19
	20	21	*21*	22	23	24	25
JYAISHṬHA 2227	26	27	28	29	30	1	2
	3	4	5	6	**7**	9	10
	11	12	13	14	15	16	17
	18	19	20	21	22	23	24
ĀSHĀḌHA 2227	25	26	27	*27*	**28**	30	1
	2	3	4	5	6	7	8
	9	**10**	12	13	14	15	16
	17	18	*18*	19	20	21	22
	23	24	25	26	27	28	29
ŚRĀVAṆA 2227	30	1	2	**3**	5	6	7
	8	9	10	11	12	13	14
	15	16	17	18	19	20	21
	22	23[c]	24	25	26	27	28
BHĀDRAPADA 2227	29	30	1	2	3	4[d]	5
	6	8	9	10	11	12	13
	14	*14*	15	16	17	18	19
	20	21	22	23	24	25	26
ĀŚVINA 2227	27	28	**29**	1	2	3	4
	5	6	7	8[e]	9[e]	10[e]	11
	12	13	14	15	16	17	18
	18	19	20	21	**22**	24	25
KĀRTTIKA 2227	26	27	28	29	30	1[f]	2
	3	4	5	6	7	8	9
	10	11	12	13	14	15	16
	17	18	19	20	21	22	23
MĀRGAŚĪRA 2227	24	25	26	**27**	29	30	1
	2	3	4	5	6	7	8
	9	10	11	*11*[g]	12	13	14
	15	16	17	18	19	20	**21**
	23	24	25	26	27	28	29

‡Leap year
[a]New Year (Pramoda)
[b]Birthday of Rāma
[c]Birthday of Krishna
[d]Ganēśa Chaturthī
[e]Dashara
[f]Diwali
[g]Birthday of Vishnu
[h]Night of Śiva
[i]Holi

HINDU SOLAR 2091/2092

Month	Sun	Mon	Tue	Wed	Thu	Fri	Sat
PAUSHA 2091	14	15	16	17	18	19	20
	21	22	23	24	25	26	27
MĀGHA 2091	28	29	1[b]	2	3	4	5
	6	7	8	9	10	11	12
	13	14	15	16	17	18	19
	20	21	22	23	24	25	26
PHĀLGUNA 2091	27	28	29	30	1	2	3
	4	5	6	7	8	9	10
	11	12	13	14	15	16	17
	18	19	20	21	22	23	24
CHAITRA 2091	25	26	27	28	29	30	1
	2	3	4	5	6	7	8
	9	10	11	12	13	14	15
	16	17	18	19	20	21	22
	23	24	25	26	27	28	29
VAIŚĀKHA 2092	30	1[a]	2	3	4	5	6
	7	8	9	10	11	12	13
	14	15	16	17	18	19	20
	21	22	23	24	25	26	27
JYAISHṬHA 2092	28	29	30	31	1	2	3
	4	5	6	7	8	9	10
	11	12	13	14	15	16	17
	18	19	20	21	22	23	24
	25	26	27	28	29	30	31
ĀSHĀḌHA 2092	1	2	3	4	5	6	7
	8	9	10	11	12	13	14
	15	16	17	18	19	20	21
	22	23	24	25	26	27	28
ŚRĀVAṆA 2092	29	30	31	32	1	2	3
	4	5	6	7	8	9	10
	11	12	13	14	15	16	17
	18	19	20	21	22	23	24
	25	26	27	28	29	30	31
BHĀDRAPADA 2092	1	2	3	4	5	6	7
	8	9	10	11	12	13	14
	15	16	17	18	19	20	21
	22	23	24	25	26	27	28
ĀŚVINA 2092	29	30	31	1	2	3	4
	5	6	7	8	9	10	11
	12	13	14	15	16	17	18
	19	20	21	22	23	24	25
KĀRTTIKA 2092	26	27	28	29	30	31	1
	2	3	4	5	6	7	8
	9	10	11	12	13	14	15
	16	17	18	19	20	21	22
	23	24	25	26	27	28	29
MĀRGAŚĪRA 2092	30	1	2	3	4	5	6
	7	8	9	10	11	12	13
	14	15	16	17	18	19	20
	21	22	23	24	25	26	27
PAUSHA 2092	28	29	1	2	3	4	5
	6	7	8	9	10	11	12
	13	14	15	16	17	18	19

[a]New Year (Pārthiva)
[b]Pongal

ISLAMIC (ASTRONOMICAL) 1595/1596

Month	Sun	Mon	Tue	Wed	Thu	Fri	Sat
DHU AL-ḤIJJA 1595	12	13	14	15	16	17	18
	19	20	21	22	23	24	25
MUḤARRAM 1596	26	27	28	29	30	1[a]	2
	3	4	5	6	7	8	9
	10[b]	11	12	13	14	15	16
	17	18	19	20	21	22	23
ṢAFAR 1596	24	25	26	27	28	29	1
	2	3	4	5	6	7	8
	9	10	11	12	13	14	15
	16	17	18	19	20	21	22
	23	24	25	26	27	28	29
RABĪ' I 1596	30	1	2	3	4	5	6
	7	8	9	10	11	12[c]	13
	14	15	16	17	18	19	20
	21	22	23	24	25	26	27
RABĪ' II 1596	28	29	30	1	2	3	4
	5	6	7	8	9	10	11
	12	13	14	15	16	17	18
	19	20	21	22	23	24	25
JUMĀDĀ I 1596	26	27	28	29	1	2	3
	4	5	6	7	8	9	10
	11	12	13	14	15	16	17
	18	19	20	21	22	23	24
JUMĀDĀ II 1596	25	26	27	28	29	30	1
	2	3	4	5	6	7	8
	9	10	11	12	13	14	15
	16	17	18	19	20	21	22
	23	24	25	26	27	28	29
RAJAB 1596	1	2	3	4	5	6	7
	8	9	10	11	12	13	14
	15	16	17	18	19	20	21
	22	23	24	25	26	27[d]	28
SHA'BĀN 1596	29	1	2	3	4	5	6
	7	8	9	10	11	12	13
	14	15	16	17	18	19	20
	21	22	23	24	25	26	27
RAMAḌĀN 1596	28	29	30	1[e]	2	3	4
	5	6	7	8	9	10	11
	12	13	14	15	16	17	18
	19	20	21	22	23	24	25
SHAWWĀL 1596	26	27	28	29	1[f]	2	3
	4	5	6	7	8	9	10
	11	12	13	14	15	16	17
	18	19	20	21	22	23	24
DHU AL-QA'DA 1596	25	26	27	28	29	30	1
	2	3	4	5	6	7	8
	9	10	11	12	13	14	15
	16	17	18	19	20	21	22
	23	24	25	26	27	28	29
DHU AL-ḤIJJA 1596	1	2	3	4	5	6	7
	8	9	10[g]	11	12	13	14
	15	16	17	18	19	20	21
	22	23	24	25	26	27	28

[a]New Year
[b]'Ashūrā'
[c]Prophet's Birthday
[d]Ascent of the Prophet
[e]Start of Ramaḍān
[f]'Id al-Fiṭr
[g]'Id al-'Aḍḥā

GREGORIAN 2170

Julian (Sun)	Sun	Mon	Tue	Wed	Thu	Fri	Sat	Month
Dec 17	31	1	2	3	4	5	6	JANUARY 2170
	7	8[a]	9	10	11	12	13	
Dec 31	14	15[b]	16	17	18	19	20	
	21	22	23	24	25	26	27	
Jan 14	28	29	30	31	1	2	3	FEBRUARY 2170
	4	5	6	7	8	9	10	
Jan 28	11	12	13	14[c]	15	16	17	
	18	19	20	21	22	23	24	
Feb 11	25[d]	26	27	28	1	2	3	MARCH 2170
	4	5	6	7	8	9	10	
Feb 25	11	12	13	14	15	16	17	
	18	19	20	21	22	23	24	
Mar 11	25	26	27	28	29	30	31	
	1[e]	2	3	4	5	6	7	APRIL 2170
Mar 25	8[f]	9	10	11	12	13	14	
	15	16	17	18	19	20	21	
Apr 8	22	23	24	25	26	27	28	
	29	30	1	2	3	4	5	MAY 2170
Apr 22	6	7	8	9	10	11	12	
	13	14	15	16	17	18	19	
May 6	20	21	22	23	24	25	26	
	27	28	29	30	31	1	2	JUNE 2170
May 20	3	4	5	6	7	8	9	
	10	11	12	13	14	15	16	
Jun 3	17	18	19	20	21	22	23	
	24	25	26	27	28	29	30	
Jun 17	1	2	3	4	5	6	7	JULY 2170
	8	9	10	11	12	13	14	
Jul 1	15	16	17	18	19	20	21	
	22	23	24	25	26	27	28	
Jul 15	29	30	31	1	2	3	4	AUGUST 2170
	5	6	7	8	9	10	11	
Jul 29	12	13	14	15	16	17	18	
	19	20	21	22	23	24	25	
Aug 12	26	27	28	29	30	31	1	SEPTEMBER 2170
	2	3	4	5	6	7	8	
Aug 26	9	10	11	12	13	14	15	
	16	17	18	19	20	21	22	
Sep 9	23	24	25	26	27	28	29	
	30	1	2	3	4	5	6	OCTOBER 2170
Sep 23	7	8	9	10	11	12	13	
	14	15	16	17	18	19	20	
Oct 7	21	22	23	24	25	26	27	
	28	29	30	31	1	2	3	NOVEMBER 2170
Oct 21	4	5	6	7	8	9	10	
	11	12	13	14	15	16	17	
Nov 4	18	19	20	21	22	23	24	
	25	26	27	28	29	30	1	DECEMBER 2170
Nov 18	2[g]	3	4	5	6	7	8	
	9	10	11	12	13	14	15	
Dec 2	16	17	18	19	20	21	22	
	23	24	25[h]	26	27	28	29	
Dec 16	30	31	1	2	3	4	5	

[a]Orthodox Christmas
[b]Julian New Year
[c]Ash Wednesday
[d]Feast of Orthodoxy
[e]Easter
[f]Orthodox Easter
[g]Advent
[h]Christmas

2171

Gregorian 2171								Lunar Phases	ISO Week	Julian Day	Hebrew 5931‡/5932								Molad	Chinese Gēng-Wǔ/Xīn-Wèi								Solar Term	Coptic 1887‡/1888								Ethiopic 2163‡/2164
	Sun	Mon	Tue	Wed	Thu	Fri	Sat		(Mon)	(Sun noon)		Sun	Mon	Tue	Wed	Thu	Fri	Sat			Sun	Mon	Tue	Wed	Thu	Fri	Sat			Sun	Mon	Tue	Wed	Thu	Fri	Sat	
January 2171	◑	31	1[a]	2	3	4	5	12:06	1	2514000	Teveth 5931	22	23	24	25	26	27	28		Month 12 Gēng-Wǔ	23	24	25	26	27	28	29	Xiǎo hán	Koiak 1887	20	21	22	23	24	25	26	Tākhśāś 2163
	●	7	8	9	10	11	12	9:38	2	2514007	Shevat 5931	29	1	2	3	4	5	6	Sun 23h38m4p		1	2	3	4	5*	6	7		Tôbe 1887	27	28	29[c]	30	1	2	3	Ṭer 2163
	13	◐	15	16	17	18	19	4:52	3	2514014		7	8	9	10	11	12	13			8	9	10	11	12	13	14			4	5	6[d]	7	8	9	10	
	20	21	○	23	24	25	26	0:03	4	2514021		14	15	16	17	18	19	20			15	16	17	18	19	20	21	Dà hán		11[e]	12	13	14	15	16	17	
February 2171	27	◑	29	30	31	1	2	20:11	5	2514028		21	22	23	24	25	26	27			22	23	24	25	26	27	28			18	19	20	21	22	23	24	
	3	4	●	6	7	8	9	0:31	6	2514035	Adar I 5931	28	29	30	1	2	3	4	Tue 12h22m5p	Month 1 Xīn-Wèi	29	30	1[a]	2	3	4	5	Lì chūn	Meshir 1887	25	26	27	28	29	30	1	Yakātit 2163
	10	11	12	◐	14	15	16	2:40	7	2514042		5	6	7	8	9	10	11			6	7	8	9	10	11	12			2	3	4	5	6	7	8	
	17	18	19	○	21	22	23	12:31	8	2514049		12	13	14	15	16	17	18			13	14	15[b]	16	17	18	19	Yǔ shuǐ		9	10	11	12	13	14	15	
March 2171	24	25	26	◑	28	1	2	4:45	9	2514056		19	20	21	22	23	24	25			20	21	22	23	24	25	26			16	17	18	19	20	21	22	
	3	4	5	●	7	8	9	16:50	10	2514063	Adar II 5931	26	27	28	29	30	1	2	Thu 1h6m6p	Month 2 Xīn-Wèi	27	28	29	30	1	2	3	Jīng zhé		23	24	25	26	27	28	29	
	10	11	12	13	◐	15	16	22:02	11	2514070		3	4	5	6	7	8	9			4	5*	6	7	8	9	10		Paremotep 1887	30	1	2	3	4	5	6	Magābit 2163
	17	18	19	20[b]	○	22	23	22:56	12	2514077		10	11	12	13	14[f]	15	16			11	12	13	14	15	16	17	Chūn fēn		7	8	9	10	11	12	13	
	24	25	26	27	◑	29	30	14:24	13	2514084		17	18	19	20	21	22	23			18	19	20	21	22	23	24			14	15	16	17	18	19	20	
April 2171	31	1	2	3	4	●	6	10:03	14	2514091	Nisan 5931	24	25	26	27	28	29	1	Fri 13h50m7p	Month 3 Xīn-Wèi	25	26	27	28	29	1[c]	2	Qīng míng		21	22	23	24	25	26	27	
	7	8	9	10	11	12	◐	13:29	15	2514098		2	3	4	5	6	7	8			3	4	5	6	7	8	9		Parmoute 1887	28	29	30	1	2	3	4	Miyāzyā 2163
	14	15	16	17	18	19	○	7:53	16	2514105		9	10	11	12	13	14	15[g]			10	11	12	13	14	15	16	Gǔ yǔ		5	6	7	8	9	10	11	
	21	22	23	24	25	26	◑	1:34	17	2514112		16	17	18	19	20	21	22			17	18	19	20	21	22	23			12	13	14	15	16	17	18	
May 2171	28	29	30	1	2	3	4		18	2514119		23	24	25	26	27	28	29			24	25	26	27	28	29	30			19[f]	20	21	22	23	24	25	
	●	6	7	8	9	10	11	3:09	19	2514126	Iyar 5931	30	1	2	3	4	5	6	Sun 2h34m8p	Month 4 Xīn-Wèi	1	2	3	4	5	6*	7	Lì xià	Pashons 1887	26	27	28	29[g]	30	1	2	Genbot 2163
	12	◐	14	15	16	17	18	0:45	20	2514133		7	8	9	10	11	12	13			8	9	10	11	12	13	14			3	4	5	6	7	8	9	
	○	20	21	22	23	24	25	15:57	21	2514140		14	15	16	17	18	19	20			15	16	17	18	19	20	21	Xiǎo mǎn		10	11	12	13	14	15	16	
June 2171	◑	27	28	29	30	31	1	14:35	22	2514147		21	22	23	24	25	26	27			22	23	24	25	26	27	28			17	18	19	20	21	22	23	
	2	●	4	5	6	7	8	18:58	23	2514154	Sivan 5931	28	29	1	2	3	4	5	Mon 15h18m9p	Month 5 Xīn-Wèi	29	30	1	2	3	4	5[d]	Máng zhòng		24	25	26	27	28	29	30	
	9	10	◐	12	13	14	15	8:36	24	2514161		6[h]	7	8	9	10	11	12			6	7	8	9	10	11	12		Paône 1887	1	2	3	4	5	6	7	Sanē 2163
	16	○	18	19	20	21[c]	22	23:46	25	2514168		13	14	15	16	17	18	19			13	14	15	16	17	18	19	Xià zhì		8	9	10	11	12	13	14	
	23	24	◑	26	27	28	29	5:36	26	2514175		20	21	22	23	24	25	26			20	21	22	23	24	25	26			15	16	17	18	19	20	21	
July 2171	30	1	2	●	4	5	6	8:42	27	2514182	Tammuz 5931	27	28	29	30	1	2	3	Wed 4h2m10p	Month 6 Xīn-Wèi	27	28	29	1	2	3	4			22	23	24	25	26	27	28	
	7	8	9	◐	11	12	13	14:15	28	2514189		4	5	6	7	8	9	10			5	6	7*	8	9	10	11	Xiǎo shǔ	Epêp 1887	29	30	1	2	3	4	5	Ḥamlē 2163
	14	15	16	○	18	19	20	8:08	29	2514196		11	12	13	14	15	16	17			12	13	14	15	16	17	18			6	7	8	9	10	11	12	
	21	22	23	◑	25	26	27	22:25	30	2514203		18	19	20	21	22	23	24			19	20	21	22	23	24	25	Dà shǔ		13	14	15	16	17	18	19	
August 2171	28	29	30	31	●	2	3	20:16	31	2514210	Av 5931	25	26	27	28	29	1	2	Thu 16h46m11p	Month 7 Xīn-Wèi	26	27	28	29	30	1	2			20	21	22	23	24	25	26	
	4	5	6	7	◐	9	10	19:01	32	2514217		3	4	5	6	7	8	9			3	4	5	6	7[e]	8	9	Lì qiū	Mesorê 1887	27	28	29	30	1	2	3	Nahasē 2163
	11	12	13	14	○	16	17	18:04	33	2514224		10[i]	11	12	13	14	15	16			10	11	12	13	14	15[f]	16			4	5	6	7	8	9	10	
	18	19	20	21	22	◑	24	16:18	34	2514231		17	18	19	20	21	22	23			17	18	19	20	21	22	23	Chǔ shǔ		11	12	13[h]	14	15	16	17	
	25	26	27	28	29	30	●	6:20	35	2514238		24	25	26	27	28	29	30		Month 8 Xīn-Wèi	24	25	26	27	28	29	1			18	19	20	21	22	23	24	
September 2171	1	2	3	4	5	6	◐	0:16	36	2514245	Elul 5931	1	2	3	4	5	6	7	Sat 5h30m12p		2	3	4	5	6	7	8*		Epag. 1887	25	26	27	28	29	30	1	Pāg. 2163
	8	9	10	11	12	13	○	6:32	37	2514252		8	9	10	11	12	13	14			9	10	11	12	13	14	15[g]	Bái lù	Thoout 1888	2	3	4	5	6	1[a]	2	Maskaram 2164
	15	16	17	18	19	20	21		38	2514259		15	16	17	18	19	20	21			16	17	18	19	20	21	22			3	4	5	6	7	8	9	
	◑	23[d]	24	25	26	27	28	10:09	39	2514266		22	23	24	25	26	27	28			23	24	25	26	27	28	29	Qiū fēn		10	11	12	13	14	15	16	
October 2171	●	30	1	2	3	4	5	15:45	40	2514273	Tishri 5932	29	1[a]	2[a]	3	4	5	6	Sun 18h14m13p	Month 9 Xīn-Wèi	1	2	3	4	5	6	7			17[b]	18	19	20	21	22	23	
	◐	7	8	9	10	11	12	7:16	41	2514280		7	8	9	10[b]	11	12	13			8	9[h]	10	11	12	13	14	Hán lù		24	25	26	27	28	29	30	
	○	14	15	16	17	18	19	22:04	42	2514287		14	15[c]	16	17	18	19	20			15	16	17	18	19	20	21		Paope 1888	1	2	3	4	5	6	7	Ṭeqemt 2164
	20	21	◑	23	24	25	26	2:52	43	2514294		21	22	23	24	25	26	27			22	23	24	25	26	27	28	Shuāng jiàng		8	9	10	11	12	13	14	
November 2171	27	28	●	30	31	1	2	1:19	44	2514301	Heshvan 5932	28	29	30	1	2	3	4	Tue 6h58m14p	Month 10 Xīn-Wèi	29	30	1	2	3	4	5			15	16	17	18	19	20	21	
	3	◐	5	6	7	8	9	17:13	45	2514308		5	6	7	8	9	10	11			6	7	8	9*	10	11	12	Lì dōng		22	23	24	25	26	27	28	
	10	11	○	13	14	15	16	16:13	46	2514315		12	13	14	15	16	17	18			13	14	15	16	17	18	19		Athôr 1888	29	30	1	2	3	4	5	Hedār 2164
	17	18	19	◑	21	22	23	17:44	47	2514322		19	20	21	22	23	24	25			20	21	22	23	24	25	26	Xiǎo xuě		6	7	8	9	10	11	12	
	24	25	26	●	28	29	30	11:24	48	2514329	Kislev 5932	26	27	28	29	30	1	2	Wed 19h42m15p	Month 11 Xīn-Wèi	27	28	29	1	2	3	4			13	14	15	16	17	18	19	
December 2171	1	2	3	◐	5	6	7	7:01	49	2514336		3	4	5	6	7	8	9[d]			5	6	7	8	9	10	11	Dà xuě		20	21	22	23	24	25	26	
	8	9	10	11	○	13	14	11:30	50	2514343		10	11	12	13	14	15	16			12	13	14	15	16	17	18		Koiak 1888	27	28	29	30	1	2	3	Tākhśāś 2164
	15	16	17	18	19	◑	21	6:24	51	2514350		17	18	19	20	21	22	23			19	20	21	22	23	24	25			4	5	6	7	8	9	10	
	22[e]	23	24	25	●	27	28	22:10	52	2514357		24	25[e]	26[e]	27[e]	28[e]	29[e]	30[e]		Month 12 Xīn-Wèi	26[i]	27	28	29	30	1	2	Dōng zhì		11	12	13	14	15	16	17	
	29	30	31	1	2	◐	4	0:48	1	2514364	Teveth 5932	1[e]	2[e]	3	4	5	6	7	Fri 8h26m16p		3	4	5	6	7	8	9			18	19	20	21	22	23	24	

[a]New Year
[b]Spring (18:07)
[c]Summer (9:20)
[d]Autumn (2:29)
[e]Winter (1:33)
● New moon
◐ First quarter moon
○ Full moon
◑ Last quarter moon

‡Leap year
[a]New Year
[b]Yom Kippur
[c]Sukkot
[d]Winter starts
[e]Ḥanukkah
[f]Purim
[g]Passover
[h]Shavuot
[i]Fast of Av

[a]New Year (4869, Sheep)
[b]Lantern Festival
[c]Qīngmíng
[d]Dragon Festival
[e]Qīqiǎo
[f]Hungry Ghosts
[g]Mid-Autumn Festival
[h]Double-Ninth Festival
[i]Dōngzhì
*Start of 60-name cycle

‡Leap year
[a]New Year
[b]Building of the Cross
[c]Christmas
[d]Jesus's Circumcision
[e]Epiphany
[f]Easter
[g]Mary's Announcement
[h]Jesus's Transfiguration

PERSIAN (ASTRONOMICAL) 1549/1550

Month	Sun	Mon	Tue	Wed	Thu	Fri	Sat
DEY 1549	9	10	11	12	13	14	15
	16	17	18	19	20	21	22
	23	24	25	26	27	28	29
BAHMAN 1549	30	1	2	3	4	5	6
	7	8	9	10	11	12	13
	14	15	16	17	18	19	20
	21	22	23	24	25	26	27
ESFAND 1549	28	29	30	1	2	3	4
	5	6	7	8	9	10	11
	12	13	14	15	16	17	18
	19	20	21	22	23	24	25
FARVARDĪN 1550	26	27	28	29	1[a]	2	3
	4	5	6	7	8	9	10
	11	12	13[b]	14	15	16	17
	18	19	20	21	22	23	24
	25	26	27	28	29	30	31
ORDĪBEHEŠT 1550	1	2	3	4	5	6	7
	8	9	10	11	12	13	14
	15	16	17	18	19	20	21
	22	23	24	25	26	27	28
XORDĀD 1550	29	30	31	1	2	3	4
	5	6	7	8	9	10	11
	12	13	14	15	16	17	18
	19	20	21	22	23	24	25
TĪR 1550	26	27	28	29	30	31	1
	2	3	4	5	6	7	8
	9	10	11	12	13	14	15
	16	17	18	19	20	21	22
	23	24	25	26	27	28	29
MORDĀD 1550	30	31	1	2	3	4	5
	6	7	8	9	10	11	12
	13	14	15	16	17	18	19
	20	21	22	23	24	25	26
SHAHRĪVAR 1550	27	28	29	30	31	1	2
	3	4	5	6	7	8	9
	10	11	12	13	14	15	16
	17	18	19	20	21	22	23
	24	25	26	27	28	29	30
MEHR 1550	31	1	2	3	4	5	6
	7	8	9	10	11	12	13
	14	15	16	17	18	19	20
	21	22	23	24	25	26	27
ĀBĀN 1550	28	29	30	1	2	3	4
	5	6	7	8	9	10	11
	12	13	14	15	16	17	18
	19	20	21	22	23	24	25
ĀZAR 1550	26	27	28	29	30	1	2
	3	4	5	6	7	8	9
	10	11	12	13	14	15	16
	17	18	19	20	21	22	23
	24	25	26	27	28	29	30
DEY 1550	1	2	3	4	5	6	7
	8	9	10	11	12	13	14

HINDU LUNAR 2227‡/2228

Month	Sun	Mon	Tue	Wed	Thu	Fri	Sat
MĀRGAŚĪRA 2227	23	24	25	26	27	28	29
PAUSHA 2227	30	1	2	3	4	5	6
	7	8	9	10	11	12	13
	14	15	16	17	18	19	20
	21	22	23	24	25	26	**27**
MĀGHA 2227	29	30	1	2	3	3	4
	5	6	7	8	9	10	11
	12	13	14	15	16	17	18
	19	**20**	22	23	24	25	26
PHĀLGUNA 2227	27	28[h]	29	30	1	2	3
	4	5	5	6	7	8	9
	10	11	12	13	**14**[i]	16	17
	18	19	20	21	22	23	24
CHAITRA 2228	25	26	27	28	29	30	1[a]
	2	3	4	5	6	7	8
	9[b]	10	11	12	13	14	15
	16	17	**18**	20	21	22	23
	24	25	26	27	28	29	30
VAIŚĀKHA 2228	30	1	2	3	4	5	6
	7	8	9	10	**11**	13	14
	15	16	17	18	19	20	21
	22	23	24	25	26	27	28
JYAISHTHA 2228	29	30	1	2	3	4	5
	6	7	8	9	10	11	12
	13	**14**	16	17	18	19	20
	21	22	23	24	25	26	*26*
ĀSHĀḌHA 2228	27	28	29	30	1	2	3
	4	5	6	**7**	9	10	11
	12	13	14	15	16	17	18
	19	20	21	22	23	24	25
ŚRĀVAṆA 2228	26	27	28	29	30	1	2
	3	4	5	6	7	8	9
	10	12	13	14	15	16	17
	18	19	20	21	22	23	*23*[c]
	24	25	26	27	28	29	30
BHĀDRAPADA 2228	1	2	**3**[d]	5	6	7	8
	9	10	11	12	13	14	15
	16	17	18	19	20	21	22
	23	24	25	26	27	28	29
ĀŚVINA 2228	30	1	2	3	4	5	**6**
	8[e]	9[e]	10[e]	11	12	13	14
	15	16	17	18	*18*	19	20
	21	22	23	24	25	26	27
KĀRTTIKA 2228	28	29	**30**[f]	2	3	4	5
	6	7	8	9	10	11	12
	13	14	15	16	17	18	19
	20	21	22	23	24	25	26
MĀRGAŚĪRA 2228	27	28	29	30	1	2	3
	4	**5**	7	8	9	10	11
	11[g]	12	13	14	15	16	17
	18	19	20	21	22	23	24
PAUSHA 2228	25	26	27	**28**	30	1	2
	3	4	5	6	7	8	9

HINDU SOLAR 2092/2093

Month	Sun	Mon	Tue	Wed	Thu	Fri	Sat
PAUSHA 2092	13	14	15	16	17	18	19
	20	21	22	23	24	25	26
MĀGHA 2092	27	28	29	30	1[b]	2	3
	4	5	6	7	8	9	10
	11	12	13	14	15	16	17
	18	19	20	21	22	23	24
PHĀLGUNA 2092	25	26	27	28	29	1	2
	3	4	5	6	7	8	9
	10	11	12	13	14	15	16
	17	18	19	20	21	22	23
	24	25	26	27	28	29	30
CHAITRA 2092	1	2	3	4	5	6	7
	8	9	10	11	12	13	14
	15	16	17	18	19	20	21
	22	23	24	25	26	27	28
VAIŚĀKHA 2093	29	30	1[a]	2	3	4	5
	6	7	8	9	10	11	12
	13	14	15	16	17	18	19
	20	21	22	23	24	25	26
JYAISHTHA 2093	27	28	29	30	31	1	2
	3	4	5	6	7	8	9
	10	11	12	13	14	15	16
	17	18	19	20	21	22	23
	24	25	26	27	28	29	30
ĀSHĀḌHA 2093	31	32	1	2	3	4	5
	6	7	8	9	10	11	12
	13	14	15	16	17	18	19
	20	21	22	23	24	25	26
ŚRĀVAṆA 2093	27	28	29	30	31	1	2
	3	4	5	6	7	8	9
	10	11	12	13	14	15	16
	17	18	19	20	21	22	23
	24	25	26	27	28	29	30
BHĀDRAPADA 2093	31	32	1	2	3	4	5
	6	7	8	9	10	11	12
	13	14	15	16	17	18	19
	20	21	22	23	24	25	26
ĀŚVINA 2093	27	28	29	30	31	1	2
	3	4	5	6	7	8	9
	10	11	12	13	14	15	16
	17	18	19	20	21	22	23
	24	25	26	27	28	29	30
KĀRTTIKA 2093	1	2	3	4	5	6	7
	8	9	10	11	12	13	14
	15	16	17	18	19	20	21
	22	23	24	25	26	27	28
MĀRGAŚĪRA 2093	29	30	1	2	3	4	5
	6	7	8	9	10	11	12
	13	14	15	16	17	18	19
	20	21	22	23	24	25	26
PAUSHA 2093	27	28	29	30	1	2	3
	4	5	6	7	8	9	10
	11	12	13	14	15	16	17

ISLAMIC (ASTRONOMICAL) 1596/1597/1598‡

Month	Sun	Mon	Tue	Wed	Thu	Fri	Sat
DHU AL-ḤIJJA 1596	22	23	24	25	26	27	28
MUḤARRAM 1597	29	30	1[a]	2	3	4	5
	6	7	8	9	10[b]	11	12
	13	14	15	16	17	18	19
	20	21	22	23	24	25	26
ṢAFAR 1597	27	28	29	1	2	3	4
	5	6	7	8	9	10	11
	12	13	14	15	16	17	18
	19	20	21	22	23	24	25
RABĪʿ I 1597	26	27	28	29	30	1	2
	3	4	5	6	7	8	9
	10	11	12[c]	13	14	15	16
	17	18	19	20	21	22	23
	24	25	26	27	28	29	30
RABĪʿ II 1597	1	2	3	4	5	6	7
	8	9	10	11	12	13	14
	15	16	17	18	19	20	21
	22	23	24	25	26	27	28
JUMĀDĀ I 1597	29	1	2	3	4	5	6
	7	8	9	10	11	12	13
	14	15	16	17	18	19	20
	21	22	23	24	25	26	27
JUMĀDĀ II 1597	28	29	30	1	2	3	4
	5	6	7	8	9	10	11
	12	13	14	15	16	17	18
	19	20	21	22	23	24	25
RAJAB 1597	26	27	28	29	30	1	2
	3	4	5	6	7	8	9
	10	11	12	13	14	15	16
	17	18	19	20	21	22	23
SHAʿBĀN 1597	24	25	26	27[d]	28	29	1
	2	3	4	5	6	7	8
	9	10	11	12	13	14	15
	16	17	18	19	20	21	22
	23	24	25	26	27	28	29
RAMAḌĀN 1597	1[e]	2	3	4	5	6	7
	8	9	10	11	12	13	14
	15	16	17	18	19	20	21
	22	23	24	25	26	27	28
SHAWWĀL 1567	29	30	1[f]	2	3	4	5
	6	7	8	9	10	11	12
	13	14	15	16	17	18	19
	20	21	22	23	24	25	26
DHU AL-QAʿDA 1597	27	28	29	30	1	2	3
	4	5	6	7	8	9	10
	11	12	13	14	15	16	17
	18	19	20	21	22	23	24
DHU AL-ḤIJJA 1597	25	26	27	28	29	1	2
	3	4	5	6	7	8	9
	10[g]	11	12	13	14	15	16
	17	18	19	20	21	22	23
MUḤARRAM 1598	24	25	26	27	28	29	1[a]
	2[a]	3	4	5	6	7	8

GREGORIAN 2171

Julian (Sun)	Sun	Mon	Tue	Wed	Thu	Fri	Sat	Month
Dec 16	*30*	31	1	2	3	4	5	JANUARY 2171
	6	7	8[a]	9	10	11	12	
Dec 30	*13*	14	15[b]	16	17	18	19	
	20	21	22	23	24	25	26	
Jan 13	*27*	28	29	30	31	1	2	FEBRUARY 2171
	3	4	5	6	7	8	9	
Jan 27	*10*	11	12	13	14	15	16	
	17	18	19	20	21	22	23	
Feb 10	*24*	25	26	27	28	1	2	MARCH 2171
	3	4	5	6[c]	7	8	9	
Feb 24	*10*	11	12	13	14	15	16	
	17[d]	18	19	20	21	22	23	
Mar 10	*24*	25	26	27	28	29	30	
	31	1	2	3	4	5	6	APRIL 2171
Mar 24	*7*	8	9	10	11	12	13	
	14	15	16	17	18	19	20	
Apr 7	*21*[e]	22	23	24	25	26	27	
	28[f]	29	30	1	2	3	4	MAY 2171
Apr 21	*5*	6	7	8	9	10	11	
	12	13	14	15	16	17	18	
May 5	*19*	20	21	22	23	24	25	
	26	27	28	29	30	31	1	JUNE 2171
May 19	*2*	3	4	5	6	7	8	
	9	10	11	12	13	14	15	
Jun 2	*16*	17	18	19	20	21	22	
	23	24	25	26	27	28	29	
Jun 16	*30*	1	2	3	4	5	6	JULY 2171
	7	8	9	10	11	12	13	
Jun 30	*14*	15	16	17	18	19	20	
	21	22	23	24	25	26	27	
Jul 14	*28*	29	30	31	1	2	3	AUGUST 2171
	4	5	6	7	8	9	10	
Jul 28	*11*	12	13	14	15	16	17	
	18	19	20	21	22	23	24	
Aug 11	*25*	26	27	28	29	30	31	
	1	2	3	4	5	6	7	SEPTEMBER 2171
Aug 25	*8*	9	10	11	12	13	14	
	15	16	17	18	19	20	21	
Sep 8	*22*	23	24	25	26	27	28	
	29	30	1	2	3	4	5	OCTOBER 2171
Sep 22	*6*	7	8	9	10	11	12	
	13	14	15	16	17	18	19	
Oct 6	*20*	21	22	23	24	25	26	
	27	28	29	30	31	1	2	NOVEMBER 2171
Oct 20	*3*	4	5	6	7	8	9	
	10	11	12	13	14	15	16	
Nov 3	*17*	18	19	20	21	22	23	
	24	25	26	27	28	29	30	
Nov 17	*1*[g]	2	3	4	5	6	7	DECEMBER 2171
	8	9	10	11	12	13	14	
Dec 1	*15*	16	17	18	19	20	21	
	22	23	24	25[h]	26	27	28	
Dec 15	*29*	30	31	1	2	3	4	

Persian notes:
[a]New Year
[b]Sizdeh Bedar

Hindu Lunar notes:
‡Leap year
[a]New Year (Prajāpati)
[b]Birthday of Rāma
[c]Birthday of Krishna
[d]Ganēśa Chaturthī
[e]Dashara
[f]Diwali
[g]Birthday of Vishnu
[h]Night of Śiva
[i]Holi

Hindu Solar notes:
[a]New Year (Vyaya)
[b]Pongal

Islamic notes:
‡Leap year
[a]New Year
[a]New Year (Arithmetic)
[b]ʿAshūrāʾ
[c]Prophet's Birthday
[d]Ascent of the Prophet
[e]Start of Ramaḍān
[f]ʿĪd al-Fiṭr
[g]ʿĪd al-ʾAḍḥā

Gregorian notes:
[a]Orthodox Christmas
[b]Julian New Year
[c]Ash Wednesday
[d]Feast of Orthodoxy
[e]Easter
[f]Orthodox Easter
[g]Advent
[h]Christmas

2172

Gregorian 2172‡, Lunar Phases, ISO Week, Julian Day

Gregorian 2172‡	Sun	Mon	Tue	Wed	Thu	Fri	Sat	Lunar Phases	ISO Week (Mon)	Julian Day (Sun noon)
January 2172	29	30	31	1[a]	2	◐	4	0:48	1	2514364
	5	6	7	8	9	10	○	6:03	2	2514371
	12	13	14	15	16	17	◑	16:49	3	2514378
	19	20	21	22	23	24	●	9:45	4	2514385
	26	27	28	29	30	31	◐	21:30	5	2514392
February 2172	2	3	4	5	6	7	8		6	2514399
	○	10	11	12	13	14	15	22:32	7	2514406
	16	◑	18	19	20	21	22	1:19	8	2514413
	●	24	25	26	27	28	29	22:27	9	2514420
March 2172	1	◐	3	4	5	6	7	19:00	10	2514427
	8	9	○	11	12	13	14	12:27	11	2514434
	15	16	◑	18	19[b]	20	21	8:33	12	2514441
	22	23	●	25	26	27	28	12:30	13	2514448
	29	30	31	◐	2	3	4	15:01	14	2514455
April 2172	5	6	7	○	9	10	11	23:50	15	2514462
	12	13	14	◑	16	17	18	15:34	16	2514469
	19	20	21	22	●	24	25	3:48	17	2514476
	26	27	28	29	30	◐	2	8:05	18	2514483
May 2172	3	4	5	6	7	○	9	9:00	19	2514490
	10	11	12	13	◑	15	16	23:29	20	2514497
	17	18	19	20	21	●	23	19:38	21	2514504
	24	25	26	27	28	29	◐	21:43	22	2514511
	31	1	2	3	4	5	○	16:32	23	2514518
June 2172	7	8	9	10	11	12	◑	9:20	24	2514525
	14	15	16	17	18	19	20[c]		25	2514532
	●	22	23	24	25	26	27	11:11	26	2514539
	28	◐	30	1	2	3	4	8:08	27	2514546
July 2172	○	6	7	8	9	10	11	23:18	28	2514553
	◑	13	14	15	16	17	18	21:48	29	2514560
	19	20	●	22	23	24	25	1:50	30	2514567
	26	27	◐	29	30	31	1	15:54	31	2514574
August 2172	2	3	○	5	6	7	8	6:26	32	2514581
	9	10	◑	12	13	14	15	13:01	33	2514588
	16	17	18	●	20	21	22	15:26	34	2514595
	23	24	25	◐	27	28	29	21:55	35	2514602
	30	31	1	○	3	4	5	15:13	36	2514609
September 2172	6	7	8	9	◑	11	12	6:35	37	2514616
	13	14	15	16	17	●	19	4:05	38	2514623
	20	21	22[d]	23	24	◐	26	3:21	39	2514630
	27	28	29	30	1	○	3	2:41	40	2514637
October 2172	4	5	6	7	8	9	◑	1:37	41	2514644
	11	12	13	14	15	16	●	15:56	42	2514651
	18	19	20	21	22	23	◐	9:34	43	2514658
	25	26	27	28	29	30	○	17:19	44	2514665
November 2172	1	2	3	4	5	6	7		45	2514672
	◑	9	10	11	12	13	14	20:58	46	2514679
	15	●	17	18	19	20	21	3:08	47	2514686
	◐	23	24	25	26	27	28	17:59	48	2514693
	29	○	1	2	3	4	5	10:47	49	2514700
December 2172	6	7	◑	9	10	11	12	15:19	50	2514707
	13	14	●	16	17	18	19	13:49	51	2514714
	20	21[e]	◐	23	24	25	26	5:42	52	2514721
	27	28	29	○	31	1	2	5:55	53	2514728

Hebrew 5932/5933

ISO Week	Month	Sun	Mon	Tue	Wed	Thu	Fri	Sat	Molad
1	Teveth 5932	1[e]	2[e]	3	4	5	6	7	Fri 8h26m16p
2		8	9	10	11	12	13	14	
3		15	16	17	18	19	20	21	
4		22	23	24	25	26	27	28	Sat 21h10m17p
5	Shevat 5932	29	1	2	3	4	5	6	
6		7	8	9	10	11	12	13	
7		14	15	16	17	18	19	20	
8		21	22	23	24	25	26	27	
9	Adar 5932	28	29	30	1	2	3	4	Mon 9h55m0p
10		5	6	7	8	9	10	11	
11		12	13	14[f]	15	16	17	18	
12		19	20	21	22	23	24	25	
13	Nisan 5932	26	27	28	29	1	2	3	Tue 22h39m1p
14		4	5	6	7	8	9	10	
15		11	12	13	14	15[g]	16	17	
16		18	19	20	21	22	23	24	
17	Iyyar 5932	25	26	27	28	29	30	1	Thu 11h23m2p
18		2	3	4	5	6	7	8	
19		9	10	11	12	13	14	15	
20		16	17	18	19	20	21	22	
21		23	24	25	26	27	28	29	
22	Sivan 5932	1	2	3	4	5	6[h]	7	Sat 0h7m3p
23		8	9	10	11	12	13	14	
24		15	16	17	18	19	20	21	
25		22	23	24	25	26	27	28	
26	Tammuz 5932	29	30	1	2	3	4	5	Sun 12h51m4p
27		6	7	8	9	10	11	12	
28		13	14	15	16	17	18	19	
29		20	21	22	23	24	25	26	
30	Av 5932	27	28	29	1	2	3	4	Tue 1h35m5p
31		5	6	7	8	9[i]	10	11	
32		12	13	14	15	16	17	18	
33		19	20	21	22	23	24	25	
34	Elul 5932	26	27	28	29	30	1	2	Wed 14h19m6p
35		3	4	5	6	7	8	9	
36		10	11	12	13	14	15	16	
37		17	18	19	20	21	22	23	
38	Tishri 5933	24	25	26	27	28	29	1[a]	Fri 3h3m7p
39		2[a]	3	4	5	6	7	8	
40		9	10[b]	11	12	13	14	15[c]	
41		16	17	18	19	20	21	22	
42		23	24	25	26	27	28	29	
43	Heshvan 5933	30	1	2	3	4	5	6	Sat 15h47m8p
44		7	8	9	10	11	12	13	
45		14	15	16	17	18	19	20	
46		21	22	23	24	25	26	27	
47	Kislev 5933	28	29	1	2	3	4	5	Mon 4h31m9p
48		6	7	8	9	10	11	12	
49		13	14	15	16	17	18	19	
50		20[d]	21	22	23	24	25[e]	26[e]	
51	Teveth 5933	27[e]	28[e]	29[e]	1[e]	2[e]	3[e]	4	Tue 17h15m10p
52		5	6	7	8	9	10	11	
53		12	13	14	15	16	17	18	

Chinese Xīn-Wèi/Rén-Shēn‡

ISO Week	Month	Sun	Mon	Tue	Wed	Thu	Fri	Sat	Solar Term
1	Month 12 Xīn-Wèi	3	4	5	6	7	8	9	
2		10*	11	12	13	14	15	16	Xiǎo hán
3		17	18	19	20	21	22	23	
4	Month 1 Rén-Shēn	24	25	26	27	28	29	1[a]	Dà hán
5		2	3	4	5	6	7	8	
6		9	10	11	12	13	14	15[b]	Lì chūn
7		16	17	18	19	20	21	22	
8		23	24	25	26	27	28	29	Yǔ shuǐ
9	Month 2 Rén-Shēn	30	1	2	3	4	5	6	
10		7	8	9	10	11*	12	13	Jīng zhé
11		14	15	16	17	18	19	20	
12		21	22	23	24	25	26	27	Chūn fēn
13	Month 3 Rén-Shēn	28	29	1	2	3	4	5	
14		6	7	8	9	10	11	12[c]	Qīng míng
15		13	14	15	16	17	18	19	
16		20	21	22	23	24	25	26	
17	Month 4 Rén-Shēn	27	28	29	30	1	2	3	Gǔ yǔ
18		4	5	6	7	8	9	10	
19		11	12*	13	14	15	16	17	Lì xià
20		18	19	20	21	22	23	24	
21	Month 5 Rén-Shēn	25	26	27	28	29	30	1	Xiǎo mǎn
22		2	3	4	5[d]	6	7	8	
23		9	10	11	12	13	14	15	Máng zhòng
24		16	17	18	19	20	21	22	
25		23	24	25	26	27	28	29	Xià zhì
26	Leap Month 5 Rén-Shēn	1	2	3	4	5	6	7	
27		8	9	10	11	12	13*	14	
28		15	16	17	18	19	20	21	Xiǎo shǔ
29		22	23	24	25	26	27	28	
30	Month 6 Rén-Shēn	29	30	1	2	3	4	5	Dà shǔ
31		6	7	8	9	10	11	12	
32		13	14	15	16	17	18	19	Lì qiū
33		20	21	22	23	24	25	26	
34	Month 7 Rén-Shēn	27	28	29	1	2	3	4	Chǔ shǔ
35		5	6	7[e]	8	9	10	11	
36		12	13	14*	15[f]	16	17	18	
37		19	20	21	22	23	24	25	Bái lù
38	Month 8 Rén-Shēn	26	27	28	29	30	1	2	
39		3	4	5	6	7	8	9	
40		10	11	12	13	14	15[g]	16	Qiū fēn
41		17	18	19	20	21	22	23	
42	Month 9 Rén-Shēn	24	25	26	27	28	29	1	Hán lù
43		2	3	4	5	6	7	8	Shuāng jiàng
44		9[h]	10	11	12	13	14	15*	
45		16	17	18	19	20	21	22	Lì dōng
46		23	24	25	26	27	28	29	
47	Month 10 Rén-Shēn	30	1	2	3	4	5	6	
48		7	8	9	10	11	12	13	Xiǎo xuě
49		14	15	16	17	18	19	20	
50		21	22	23	24	25	26	27	Dà xuě
51	Month 11 Rén-Shēn	28	29	1	2	3	4	5	
52		6	7[i]	8	9	10	11	12	Dōng zhì
53		13	14	15	16*	17	18	19	

Coptic 1888/1889, Ethiopic 2164/2165

ISO Week	Coptic Month	Sun	Mon	Tue	Wed	Thu	Fri	Sat	Ethiopic Month
1	Koiak 1888	18	19	20	21	22	23	24	Tākhśāś 2164
2	Ṭōbe 1888	25	26	27	28	29[c]	30	1	Ṭer 2164
3		2	3	4	5	6[d]	7	8	
4		9	10	11[e]	12	13	14	15	
5		16	17	18	19	20	21	22	
6		23	24	25	26	27	28	29	
7	Meshir 1888	30	1	2	3	4	5	6	Yakātīt 2164
8		7	8	9	10	11	12	13	
9		14	15	16	17	18	19	20	
10		21	22	23	24	25	26	27	
11	Paremotep 1888	28	29	30	1	2	3	4	Magābit 2164
12		5	6	7	8	9	10	11	
13		12	13	14	15	16	17	18	
14		19	20	21	22	23	24	25	
15	Parmoute 1888	26	27	28	29	30	1	2	Miyāzyā 2164
16		3	4	5	6	7	8	9	
17		10[f]	11	12	13	14	15	16	
18		17	18	19	20	21	22	23	
19		24	25	26	27	28	29[g]	30	
20	Pashons 1888	1	2	3	4	5	6	7	Genbot 2164
21		8	9	10	11	12	13	14	
22		15	16	17	18	19	20	21	
23		22	23	24	25	26	27	28	
24	Paōne 1888	29	30	1	2	3	4	5	Sanē 2164
25		6	7	8	9	10	11	12	
26		13	14	15	16	17	18	19	
27		20	21	22	23	24	25	26	
28	Epēp 1888	27	28	29	30	1	2	3	Ḥamlē 2164
29		4	5	6	7	8	9	10	
30		11	12	13	14	15	16	17	
31		18	19	20	21	22	23	24	
32	Mesorē 1888	25	26	27	28	29	30	1	Naḥasē 2164
33		2	3	4	5	6	7	8	
34		9	10	11	12	13[h]	14	15	
35		16	17	18	19	20	21	22	
36		23	24	25	26	27	28	29	
37	Epag. 1888 / Thout 1889	30	1	2	3	4	5	1[a]	Pāg. 2164 / Maskaram 2165
38		2	3	4	5	6	7	8	
39		9	10	11	12	13	14	15	
40		16	17[b]	18	19	20	21	22	
41		23	24	25	26	27	28	29	
42	Paope 1889	30	1	2	3	4	5	6	Ṭeqemt 2165
43		7	8	9	10	11	12	13	
44		14	15	16	17	18	19	20	
45		21	22	23	24	25	26	27	
46	Athōr 1889	28	29	30	1	2	3	4	Hedār 2165
47		5	6	7	8	9	10	11	
48		12	13	14	15	16	17	18	
49		19	20	21	22	23	24	25	
50	Koiak 1889	26	27	28	29	30	1	2	Tākhśāś 2165
51		3	4	5	6	7	8	9	
52		10	11	12	13	14	15	16	
53		17	18	19	20	21	22	23	

‡Leap year
[a]New Year
[b]Spring (23:59)
[c]Summer (15:07)
[d]Autumn (8:08)
[e]Winter (7:13)
● New moon
◐ First quarter moon
○ Full moon
◑ Last quarter moon

[a]New Year
[b]Yom Kippur
[c]Sukkot
[d]Winter starts
[e]Hanukkah
[f]Purim
[g]Passover
[h]Shavuot
[i]Fast of Av

‡Leap year
[a]New Year (4870, Monkey)
[b]Lantern Festival
[c]Qīngmíng
[d]Dragon Festival
[e]Qīqiǎo
[f]Hungry Ghosts
[g]Mid-Autumn Festival
[h]Double-Ninth Festival
[i]Dōngzhì
*Start of 60-name cycle

[a]New Year
[b]Building of the Cross
[c]Christmas
[d]Jesus's Circumcision
[e]Epiphany
[f]Easter
[g]Mary's Announcement
[h]Jesus's Transfiguration

2172

PERSIAN (ASTRONOMICAL) 1550/1551

Month	Sun	Mon	Tue	Wed	Thu	Fri	Sat
	8	9	10	11	12	13	14
DEY 1550	15	16	17	18	19	20	21
	22	23	24	25	26	27	28
	29	30	1	2	3	4	5
	6	7	8	9	10	11	12
BAHMAN 1550	13	14	15	16	17	18	19
	20	21	22	23	24	25	26
	27	28	29	30	1	2	3
	4	5	6	7	8	9	10
ESFAND 1550	11	12	13	14	15	16	17
	18	19	20	21	22	23	24
	25	26	27	28	29	1[a]	2
	3	4	5	6	7	8	9
FARVARDIN 1551	10	11	12	13[b]	14	15	16
	17	18	19	20	21	22	23
	24	25	26	27	28	29	30
	31	1	2	3	4	5	6
	7	8	9	10	11	12	13
ORDIBEHEŠT 1551	14	15	16	17	18	19	20
	21	22	23	24	25	26	27
	28	29	30	31	1	2	3
	4	5	6	7	8	9	10
XORDĀD 1551	11	12	13	14	15	16	17
	18	19	20	21	22	23	24
	25	26	27	28	29	30	31
	1	2	3	4	5	6	7
TĪR 1551	8	9	10	11	12	13	14
	15	16	17	18	19	20	21
	22	23	24	25	26	27	28
	29	30	31	1	2	3	4
	5	6	7	8	9	10	11
MORDĀD 1551	12	13	14	15	16	17	18
	19	20	21	22	23	24	25
	26	27	28	29	30	31	1
	2	3	4	5	6	7	8
SHAHRĪVAR 1551	9	10	11	12	13	14	15
	16	17	18	19	20	21	22
	23	24	25	26	27	28	29
	30	31	1	2	3	4	5
	6	7	8	9	10	11	12
MEHR 1551	13	14	15	16	17	18	19
	20	21	22	23	24	25	26
	27	28	29	30	1	2	3
	4	5	6	7	8	9	10
ĀBĀN 1551	11	12	13	14	15	16	17
	18	19	20	21	22	23	24
	25	26	27	28	29	30	1
	2	3	4	5	6	7	8
ĀZAR 1551	9	10	11	12	13	14	15
	16	17	18	19	20	21	22
	23	24	25	26	27	28	29
DEY 1551	30	1	2	3	4	5	6
	7	8	9	10	11	12	13

[a]New Year
[b]Sizdeh Bedar

HINDU LUNAR 2228/2229‡

Month	Sun	Mon	Tue	Wed	Thu	Fri	Sat
	3	4	5	6	7	8	9
PAUSHA 2228	10	11	12	13	13	14	15
	16	17	18	19	20	21	**22**
	24	25	26	27	28	29	30
	1	2	3	4	5	6	7
MĀGHA 2228	8	9	10	11	12	13	14
	15	16	17	18	19	20	21
	22	23	24	25	26	**27**	29[h]
	30	1	2	3	4	5	6
	6	7	8	9	10	11	12
PHĀLGUNA 2228	13	14	15[i]	16	17	18	19
	20	**21**	23	24	25	26	27
	28	29	30	1[a]	2	3	4
CHAITRA 2229	5	6	7	8	9[b]	9	10
	11	12	13	**14**	16	17	18
	19	20	21	22	23	24	25
	26	27	28	29	30	1	2
VAIŚĀKHA 2229	3	4	5	6	7	8	9
	10	11	12	13	14	15	16
	17	**18**	20	21	22	23	24
	25	26	27	28	29	30	1
	2	3	4	4	5	6	7
JYAISHṬHA 2229	8	9	10	**11**	13	14	15
	16	17	18	19	20	21	22
	23	24	25	26	27	28	29
	30	1	2	3	4	5	6
ĀSHĀḌHA 2229	7	8	9	10	11	12	13
	14	16	17	18	19	20	21
	22	23	24	25	26	27	28
	29	30	30	1	2	3	4
	5	6	**7**	9	10	11	12
ŚRĀVAṆA 2229	13	14	15	16	17	18	19
	20	21	22	23[c]	24	25	26
	27	28	29	30	1	2	3
	4	5	6	7	8	9	**10**
LEAP BHĀDRAPADA 2229	12	13	14	15	16	17	18
	19	20	21	22	23	24	25
	26	27	27	28	29	30	1
	2	**3**[d]	5	6	7	8	9
BHĀDRAPADA 2229	10	11	12	13	14	15	16
	17	18	19	20	21	22	23
	24	25	26	27	28	29	30
	1	2	3	4	5	6	**7**[e]
ĀŚVINA 2229	9[e]	10[e]	11	12	13	14	15
	16	17	18	19	20	21	21
	22	23	24	25	26	27	28
	29	30	1[f]	3	4	5	6
KĀRTTIKA 2229	7	8	9	10	11	12	13
	14	15	16	17	18	19	20
	21	22	23	24	25	26	27
	28	29	30	1	2	3	4
MĀRGAŚĪRA 2229	**5**	7	8	9	10	11[g]	12
	13	14	14	15	16	17	18

‡Leap year
[a]New Year (Aṅgiras)
[b]Birthday of Rāma
[c]Birthday of Krishna
[d]Ganēśa Chaturthī
[e]Dashara
[f]Diwali
[g]Birthday of Vishnu
[h]Night of Śiva
[i]Holi

HINDU SOLAR 2093/2094‡

Month	Sun	Mon	Tue	Wed	Thu	Fri	Sat
	11	12	13	14	15	16	17
PAUSHA 2093	18	19	20	21	22	23	24
	25	26	27	28	29	1[b]	2
MĀGHA 2093	3	4	5	6	7	8	9
	10	11	12	13	14	15	16
	17	18	19	20	21	22	23
	24	25	26	27	28	29	1
	2	3	4	5	6	7	8
PHĀLGUNA 2093	9	10	11	12	13	14	15
	16	17	18	19	20	21	22
	23	24	25	26	27	28	29
	30	1	2	3	4	5	6
	7	8	9	10	11	12	13
CHAITRA 2093	14	15	16	17	18	19	20
	21	22	23	24	25	26	27
	28	29	30	1[a]	2	3	4
	5	6	7	8	9	10	11
VAIŚĀKHA 2094	12	13	14	15	16	17	18
	19	20	21	22	23	24	25
	26	27	28	29	30	31	1
	2	3	4	5	6	7	8
JYAISHṬHA 2094	9	10	11	12	13	14	15
	16	17	18	19	20	21	22
	23	24	25	26	27	28	29
	30	31	32	1	2	3	4
	5	6	7	8	9	10	11
ĀSHĀḌHA 2094	12	13	14	15	16	17	18
	19	20	21	22	23	24	25
	26	27	28	29	30	31	32
	1	2	3	4	5	6	7
	8	9	10	11	12	13	14
ŚRĀVAṆA 2094	15	16	17	18	19	20	21
	22	23	24	25	26	27	28
	29	30	31	1	2	3	4
	5	6	7	8	9	10	11
BHĀDRAPADA 2094	12	13	14	15	16	17	18
	19	20	21	22	23	24	25
	26	27	28	29	30	31	1
	2	3	4	5	6	7	8
ĀŚVINA 2094	9	10	11	12	13	14	15
	16	17	18	19	20	21	22
	23	24	25	26	27	28	29
	30	1	2	3	4	5	6
	7	8	9	10	11	12	13
KĀRTTIKA 2094	14	15	16	17	18	19	20
	21	22	23	24	25	26	27
	28	29	30	1	2	3	4
	5	6	7	8	9	10	11
MĀRGAŚĪRA 2094	12	13	14	15	16	17	18
	19	20	21	22	23	24	25
	26	27	28	29	30	1	2
PAUSHA 2094	3	4	5	6	7	8	9
	10	11	12	13	14	15	16

‡Leap year
[a]New Year (Sarvajit)
[b]Pongal

ISLAMIC (ASTRONOMICAL) 1598‡/1599‡

Month	Sun	Mon	Tue	Wed	Thu	Fri	Sat
	2	3	4	5	6	7	8
MUHARRAM 1598	9	10[b]	11	12	13	14	15
	16	17	18	19	20	21	22
	23	24	25	26	27	28	29
	30	1	2	3	4	5	6
SAFAR 1598	7	8	9	10	11	12	13
	14	15	16	17	18	19	20
	21	22	23	24	25	26	27
	28	29	1	2	3	4	5
RABĪ' I 1598	6	7	8	9	10	11	12[c]
	13	14	15	16	17	18	19
	20	21	22	23	24	25	26
	27	28	29	30	1	2	3
RABĪ' II 1598	4	5	6	7	8	9	10
	11	12	13	14	15	16	17
	18	19	20	21	22	23	24
	25	26	27	28	29	1	2
JUMĀDĀ I 1598	3	4	5	6	7	8	9
	10	11	12	13	14	15	16
	17	18	19	20	21	22	23
	24	25	26	27	28	29	30
	1	2	3	4	5	6	7
	8	9	10	11	12	13	14
JUMĀDĀ II 1598	15	16	17	18	19	20	21
	22	23	24	25	26	27	28
	29	30	1	2	3	4	5
	6	7	8	9	10	11	12
RAJAB 1598	13	14	15	16	17	18	19
	20	21	22	23	24	25	26
	27[d]	28	29	1	2	3	4
SHA'BĀN 1598	5	6	7	8	9	10	11
	12	13	14	15	16	17	18
	19	20	21	22	23	24	25
	26	27	28	29	30	1[e]	2
	3	4	5	6	7	8	9
RAMAḌĀN 1598	10	11	12	13	14	15	16
	17	18	19	20	21	22	23
	24	25	26	27	28	29	30
	1[f]	2	3	4	5	6	7
SHAWWĀL 1598	8	9	10	11	12	13	14
	15	16	17	18	19	20	21
	22	23	24	25	26	27	28
	29	1	2	3	4	5	6
	7	8	9	10	11	12	13
DHU AL-QA'DA 1598	14	15	16	17	18	19	20
	21	22	23	24	25	26	27
	28	29	30	1	2	3	4
	5	6	7	8	9	10[g]	11
DHU AL-HIJJA 1598	12	13	14	15	16	17	18
	19	20	21	22	23	24	25
	26	27	28	29	1[a]	2	3
MUHARRAM 1599	4	5	6	7	8	9	10[b]
	11	12	13	14	15	16	17

‡Leap year
[a]New Year
[b]'Ashūrā'
[c]Prophet's Birthday
[d]Ascent of the Prophet
[e]Start of Ramaḍān
[f]'Id al-Fiṭr
[g]'Id al-'Aḍḥā

GREGORIAN 2172‡

Julian† (Sun)	Sun	Mon	Tue	Wed	Thu	Fri	Sat	Month
Dec 15	29	30	31	1	2	3	4	
	5	6	7	8[a]	9	10	11	JANUARY 2172
Dec 29	12	13	14	15[b]	16	17	18	
	19	20	21	22	23	24	25	
Jan 12	26	27	28	29	30	31	1	
	2	3	4	5	6	7	8	FEBRUARY 2172
Jan 26	9	10	11	12	13	14	15	
	16	17	18	19	20	21	22	
Feb 9	23	24	25	26[c]	27	28	29	
	1	2	3	4	5	6	7	
Feb 23	8[d]	9	10	11	12	13	14	MARCH 2172
	15	16	17	18	19	20	21	
Mar 8	22	23	24	25	26	27	28	
	29	30	31	1	2	3	4	
Mar 22	5	6	7	8	9	10	11	APRIL 2172
	12[e]	13	14	15	16	17	18	
Apr 5	19[f]	20	21	22	23	24	25	
	26	27	28	29	30	1	2	
Apr 19	3	4	5	6	7	8	9	
	10	11	12	13	14	15	16	MAY 2172
May 3	17	18	19	20	21	22	23	
	24	25	26	27	28	29	30	
May 17	31	1	2	3	4	5	6	
	7	8	9	10	11	12	13	JUNE 2172
May 31	14	15	16	17	18	19	20	
	21	22	23	24	25	26	27	
Jun 14	28	29	30	1	2	3	4	
	5	6	7	8	9	10	11	JULY 2172
Jun 28	12	13	14	15	16	17	18	
	19	20	21	22	23	24	25	
Jul 12	26	27	28	29	30	31	1	
	2	3	4	5	6	7	8	AUGUST 2172
Jul 26	9	10	11	12	13	14	15	
	16	17	18	19	20	21	22	
Aug 9	23	24	25	26	27	28	29	
	30	31	1	2	3	4	5	
Aug 23	6	7	8	9	10	11	12	SEPTEMBER 2172
	13	14	15	16	17	18	19	
Sep 6	20	21	22	23	24	25	26	
	27	28	29	30	1	2	3	
Sep 20	4	5	6	7	8	9	10	OCTOBER 2172
	11	12	13	14	15	16	17	
Oct 4	18	19	20	21	22	23	24	
	25	26	27	28	29	30	31	
Oct 18	1	2	3	4	5	6	7	
	8	9	10	11	12	13	14	NOVEMBER 2172
Nov 1	15	16	17	18	19	20	21	
	22	23	24	25	26	27	28	
Nov 15	29[g]	30	1	2	3	4	5	
	6	7	8	9	10	11	12	DECEMBER 2172
Nov 29	13	14	15	16	17	18	19	
	20	21	22	23	24	25[h]	26	
Dec 13	27	28	29	30	31	1	2	

‡Leap year
[a]Orthodox Christmas
[b]Julian New Year
[c]Ash Wednesday
[d]Feast of Orthodoxy
[e]Easter
[f]Orthodox Easter
[g]Advent
[h]Christmas

2173

Gregorian 2173	Sun	Mon	Tue	Wed	Thu	Fri	Sat	Lunar Phases	ISO WEEK (Mon)	JULIAN DAY (Sun noon)	Hebrew 5933/5934[‡]	Sun	Mon	Tue	Wed	Thu	Fri	Sat	Molad
	27	28	29	○	31	1[a]	2	5:55	53	2514728	TEVETH 5933	12	13	14	15	16	17	18	
JANUARY 2173	3	4	5	6	◑	8	9	7:20	1	2514735		19	20	21	22	23	24	25	
	10	11	12	13	●	15	16	0:15	2	2514742		26	27	28	29	1	2	3	Thu $5^h59^m11^p$
	17	18	19	◐	21	22	23	20:58	3	2514749	SHEVAT 5933	4	5	6	7	8	9	10	
	24	25	26	27	28	○	30	1:15	4	2514756		11	12	13	14	15	16	17	
FEBRUARY 2173	31	1	2	3	4	◑	6	20:04	5	2514763		18	19	20	21	22	23	24	
	7	8	9	10	11	●	13	10:51	6	2514770		25	26	27	28	29	30	1	Fri $18^h43^m12^p$
	14	15	16	17	18	◐	20	15:04	7	2514777	ADAR 5933	2	3	4	5	6	7	8	
	21	22	23	24	25	26	○	19:17	8	2514784		9	10	11	12	13	14[f]	15	
MARCH 2173	28	1	2	3	4	5	6		9	2514791		16	17	18	19	20	21	22	
	◑	8	9	10	11	12	●	5:27 21:59	10	2514798		23	24	25	26	27	28	29	
	14	15	16	17	18	19	20[b]		11	2514805	NISAN 5933	1	2	3	4	5	6	7	Sun $7^h27^m13^p$
	◐	22	23	24	25	26	27	10:35	12	2514812		8	9	10	11	12	13	14	
APRIL 2173	28	○	30	31	1	2	3	10:50	13	2514819		15[g]	16	17	18	19	20	21	
	4	◑	6	7	8	9	10	12:16	14	2514826		22	23	24	25	26	27	28	
	11	●	13	14	15	16	17	9:52	15	2514833	IYYAR 5933	29	30	1	2	3	4	5	Mon $20^h11^m14^p$
	18	19	◐	21	22	23	24	6:01	16	2514840		6	7	8	9	10	11	12	
MAY 2173	25	26	○	28	29	30	1	23:19	17	2514847		13	14	15	16	17	18	19	
	2	3	◑	5	6	7	8	17:52	18	2514854		20	21	22	23	24	25	26	
	9	10	●	12	13	14	15	22:36	19	2514861	SIVAN 5933	27	28	29	1	2	3	4	Wed $8^h55^m15^p$
	16	17	18	19	◐	21	22	0:08	20	2514868		5	6[h]	7	8	9	10	11	
	23	24	25	26	○	28	29	8:55	21	2514875		12	13	14	15	16	17	18	
JUNE 2173	30	31	1	◑	3	4	5	23:41	22	2514882		19	20	21	22	23	24	25	
	6	7	8	9	●	11	12	12:11	23	2514889	TAMMUZ 5933	26	27	28	29	30	1	2	Thu $21^h39^m16^p$
	13	14	15	16	17	◐	19	16:02	24	2514896		3	4	5	6	7	8	9	
	20[c]	21	22	23	24	○	26	16:27	25	2514903		10	11	12	13	14	15	16	
JULY 2173	27	28	29	30	1	◑	3	6:59	26	2514910		17	18	19	20	21	22	23	
	4	5	6	7	8	9	●	2:38	27	2514917	AV 5933	24	25	26	27	28	29	1	Sat $10^h23^m17^p$
	11	12	13	14	15	16	17		28	2514924		2	3	4	5	6	7	8	
	◐	19	20	21	22	23	○	5:11 23:07	29	2514931		9[i]	10	11	12	13	14	15	
	25	26	27	28	29	30	◑	16:44	30	2514938		16	17	18	19	20	21	22	
AUGUST 2173	1	2	3	4	5	6	7		31	2514945		23	24	25	26	27	28	29	
	●	9	10	11	12	13	14	17:50	32	2514952	ELUL 5933	30	1	2	3	4	5	6	Sun $23^h8^m0^p$
	15	◐	17	18	19	20	21	15:35	33	2514959		7	8	9	10	11	12	13	
	22	○	24	25	26	27	28	6:09	34	2514966		14	15	16	17	18	19	20	
SEPTEMBER 2173	29	◑	31	1	2	3	4	5:31	35	2514973		21	22	23	24	25	26	27	
	5	6	●	8	9	10	11	9:25	36	2514980	TISHRI 5934	28	29	1[a]	2[a]	3	4	5	Tue $11^h52^m1^p$
	12	13	◐	15	16	17	18	23:45	37	2514987		6	7	8	9	10[b]	11	12	
	19	20	○	22[d]	23	24	25	14:38	38	2514994		13	14	15[c]	16	17	18	19	
OCTOBER 2173	26	27	◑	29	30	1	2	21:36	39	2515001		20	21	22	23	24	25	26	
	3	4	5	6	●	8	9	0:43	40	2515008	HESHVAN 5934	27	28	29	30	1	2	3	Thu $0^h36^m2^p$
	10	11	12	13	◐	15	16	6:38	41	2515015		4	5	6	7	8	9	10	
	17	18	19	20	○	22	23	1:17	42	2515022		11	12	13	14	15	16	17	
	24	25	26	27	◑	29	30	16:43	43	2515029		18	19	20	21	22	23	24	
NOVEMBER 2173	31	1	2	3	4	●	6	15:00	44	2515036	KISLEV 5934	25	26	27	28	29	1	2	Fri $13^h20^m3^p$
	7	8	9	10	11	◐	13	13:28	45	2515043		3	4	5	6	7	8	9	
	14	15	16	17	18	○	20	14:29	46	2515050		10	11	12	13	14	15	16	
	21	22	23	24	25	26	◑	13:46	47	2515057		17	18	19	20	21	22	23	
DECEMBER 2173	28	29	30	1	2	3	4		48	2515064		24	25[e]	26[e]	27[e]	28[e]	29[e]	30[e]	
	●	6	7	8	9	10	◐	3:56 21:24	49	2515071	TEVETH 5934	1[e]	2[d,e]	3	4	5	6	7	Sun $2^h4^m4^p$
	12	13	14	15	16	17	18		50	2515078		8	9	10	11	12	13	14	
	○	20	21[e]	22	23	24	25	6:19	51	2515085		15	16	17	18	19	20	21	
	26	◑	28	29	30	31	1	10:48	52	2515092		22	23	24	25	26	27	28	

ISO WEEK	Chinese Rén-Shēn[‡]/Guǐ-Yǒu	Sun	Mon	Tue	Wed	Thu	Fri	Sat	Solar Term	Coptic 1889/1890	Sun	Mon	Tue	Wed	Thu	Fri	Sat	Ethiopic 2165/2166
53	MONTH 11 Rén-Shēn	13	14	15	16	17	18	19		KOIAK 1889	17	18	19	20	21	22	23	TĀKHŚĀŚ 2165
1		20	21	22	23	24	25	26	Xiǎo hán		24	25	26	27	28	29[c]	30	
2	MONTH 12 Rén-Shēn	27	28	29	30	1	2	3		ṬOBE 1889	1	2	3	4	5	6[d]	7	ṬER 2165
3		4	5	6	7	8	9	10	Dà hán		8	9	10	11[e]	12	13	14	
4		11	12	13	14	15	16	17			15	16	17	18	19	20	21	
5		18	19	20	21	22	23	24	Lì chūn		22	23	24	25	26	27	28	
6	MONTH 1 Guǐ-Yǒu	25	26	27	28	29	1[a]	2		MESHIR 1889	29	30	1	2	3	4	5	YAKĀTIT 2165
7		3	4	5	6	7	8	9	Yǔ shuǐ		6	7	8	9	10	11	12	
8		10	11	12	13	14	15[b]	16			13	14	15	16	17	18	19	
9		17*	18	19	20	21	22	23	Jīng zhé		20	21	22	23	24	25	26	
10		24	25	26	27	28	29	30		PAREMOTEP 1889	27	28	29	30	1	2	3	MAGĀBIT 2165
11	MONTH 2 Guǐ-Yǒu	1	2	3	4	5	6	7	Chūn fēn		4	5	6	7	8	9	10	
12		8	9	10	11	12	13	14			11	12	13	14	15	16	17	
13		15	16	17	18	19	20	21			18	19	20	21	22	23	24	
14		22[c]	23	24	25	26	27	28	Qīng míng	PARMOUTE 1889	25	26	27	28	29	30	1	MIYĀZYĀ 2165
15	MONTH 3 Guǐ-Yǒu	29	1	2	3	4	5	6			2	3	4	5	6	7	8	
16		7	8	9	10	11	12	13	Gǔ yǔ		9	10	11	12	13	14	15	
17		14	15	16	17	18*	19	20			16	17	18	19	20	21	22	
18		21	22	23	24	25	26	27	Lì xià		23	24	25	26	27	28	29[g]	
19	MONTH 4 Guǐ-Yǒu	28	29	30	1	2	3	4		PASHONS 1889	30[f]	1	2	3	4	5	6	GENBOT 2165
20		5	6	7	8	9	10	11	Xiǎo mǎn		7	8	9	10	11	12	13	
21		12	13	14	15	16	17	18			14	15	16	17	18	19	20	
22		19	20	21	22	23	24	25	Máng zhòng		21	22	23	24	25	26	27	
23	MONTH 5 Guǐ-Yǒu	26	27	28	29	1	2	3		PAŌNE 1889	28	29	30	1	2	3	4	SANĒ 2165
24		4	5[d]	6	7	8	9	10			5	6	7	8	9	10	11	
25		11	12	13	14	15	16	17	Xià zhì		12	13	14	15	16	17	18	
26		18	19*	20	21	22	23	24			19	20	21	22	23	24	25	
27	MONTH 6 Guǐ-Yǒu	25	26	27	28	29	30	1	Xiǎo shǔ	EPĒP 1889	26	27	28	29	30	1	2	ḤAMLĒ 2165
28		2	3	4	5	6	7	8			3	4	5	6	7	8	9	
29		9	10	11	12	13	14	15	Dà shǔ		10	11	12	13	14	15	16	
30		16	17	18	19	20	21	22			17	18	19	20	21	22	23	
31		23	24	25	26	27	28	29	Lì qiū		24	25	26	27	28	29	30	
32	MONTH 7 Guǐ-Yǒu	30	1	2	3	4	5	6		MESORĒ 1889	1	2	3	4	5	6	7	NAḤASĒ 2165
33		7[e]	8	9	10	11	12	13	Chù shǔ		8	9	10	11	12	13[h]	14	
34		14	15[f]	16	17	18	19*	20			15	16	17	18	19	20	21	
35		21	22	23	24	25	26	27			22	23	24	25	26	27	28	
36	MONTH 8 Guǐ-Yǒu	28	29	1	2	3	4	5	Bái lù	EPAG. 1889	29	30	1	2	3	4	5	PĀG. 2165
37		6	7	8	9	10	11	12		THOUT 1890	1[a]	2	3	4	5	6	7	MASKARAM 2166
38		13	14	15[g]	16	17	18	19	Qiū fēn		8	9	10	11	12	13	14	
39		20	21	22	23	24	25	26			15	16	17[b]	18	19	20	21	
40	MONTH 9 Guǐ-Yǒu	27	28	29	30	1	2	3	Hán lù		22	23	24	25	26	27	28	
41		4	5	6	7	8	9[h]	10		PAOPE 1890	29	30	1	2	3	4	5	ṬEQEMT 2166
42		11	12	13	14	15	16	17	Shuāng jiàng		6	7	8	9	10	11	12	
43		18	19	20*	21	22	23	24			13	14	15	16	17	18	19	
44	MONTH 10 Guǐ-Yǒu	25	26	27	28	29	1	2			20	21	22	23	24	25	26	
45		3	4	5	6	7	8	9	Lì dōng	ATHŌR 1890	27	28	29	30	1	2	3	ḪEDĀR 2166
46		10	11	12	13	14	15	16			4	5	6	7	8	9	10	
47		17	18	19	20	21	22	23	Xiǎo xuě		11	12	13	14	15	16	17	
48		24	25	26	27	28	29	30			18	19	20	21	22	23	24	
49	MONTH 11* Guǐ-Yǒu	1	2	3	4	5	6	7	Dà xuě	KOIAK 1890	25	26	27	28	29	30	1	TĀKHŚĀŚ 2166
50		8	9	10	11	12	13	14			2	3	4	5	6	7	8	
51		15	16	17[i]	18	19	20	21*	Dōng zhì		9	10	11	12	13	14	15	
52		22	23	24	25	26	27	28			16	17	18	19	20	21	22	

[a]New Year
[b]Spring (5:42)
[c]Summer (20:49)
[d]Autumn (13:57)
[e]Winter (13:09)
● New moon
◐ First quarter moon
○ Full moon
◑ Last quarter moon

[‡]Leap year
[a]New Year
[b]Yom Kippur
[c]Sukkot
[d]Winter starts
[e]Hanukkah
[f]Purim
[g]Passover
[h]Shavuot
[i]Fast of Av

[‡]Leap year
[a]New Year (4871, Fowl)
[b]Lantern Festival
[c]Qīngmíng
[d]Dragon Festival
[e]Qìqiǎo
[f]Hungry Ghosts
[g]Mid-Autumn Festival
[h]Double-Ninth Festival
[i]Dōngzhì
*Start of 60-name cycle

[a]New Year
[b]Building of the Cross
[c]Christmas
[d]Jesus's Circumcision
[e]Epiphany
[f]Easter
[g]Mary's Announcement
[h]Jesus's Transfiguration

PERSIAN (ASTRONOMICAL) 1551/1552‡

Month	Sun	Mon	Tue	Wed	Thu	Fri	Sat
DEY 1551	7	8	9	10	11	12	13
	14	15	16	17	18	19	20
	21	22	23	24	25	26	27
	28	29	30	1	2	3	4
BAHMAN 1551	5	6	7	8	9	10	11
	12	13	14	15	16	17	18
	19	20	21	22	23	24	25
	26	27	28	29	30	1	2
ESFAND 1551	3	4	5	6	7	8	9
	10	11	12	13	14	15	16
	17	18	19	20	21	22	23
	24	25	26	27	28	29	1[a]
FARVARDĪN 1552	2	3	4	5	6	7	8
	9	10	11	12	13[b]	14	15
	16	17	18	19	20	21	22
	23	24	25	26	27	28	29
	30	31	1	2	3	4	5
ORDĪBEHEŠT 1552	6	7	8	9	10	11	12
	13	14	15	16	17	18	19
	20	21	22	23	24	25	26
	27	28	29	30	31	1	2
XORDĀD 1552	3	4	5	6	7	8	9
	10	11	12	13	14	15	16
	17	18	19	20	21	22	23
	24	25	26	27	28	29	30
	31	1	2	3	4	5	6
TĪR 1552	7	8	9	10	11	12	13
	14	15	16	17	18	19	20
	21	22	23	24	25	26	27
	28	29	30	31	1	2	3
MORDĀD 1552	4	5	6	7	8	9	10
	11	12	13	14	15	16	17
	18	19	20	21	22	23	24
	25	26	27	28	29	30	31
	1	2	3	4	5	6	7
SHAHRĪVAR 1552	8	9	10	11	12	13	14
	15	16	17	18	19	20	21
	22	23	24	25	26	27	28
	29	30	31	1	2	3	4
MEHR 1552	5	6	7	8	9	10	11
	12	13	14	15	16	17	18
	19	20	21	22	23	24	25
	26	27	28	29	30	1	2
ĀBĀN 1552	3	4	5	6	7	8	9
	10	11	12	13	14	15	16
	17	18	19	20	21	22	23
	24	25	26	27	28	29	30
	1	2	3	4	5	6	7
ĀZAR 1552	8	9	10	11	12	13	14
	15	16	17	18	19	20	21
	22	23	24	25	26	27	28
	29	30	1	2	3	4	5
DEY 1552	6	7	8	9	10	11	12

‡Leap year
[a]New Year
[b]Sizdeh Bedar

HINDU LUNAR 2229‡/2230

Month	Sun	Mon	Tue	Wed	Thu	Fri	Sat
MĀRGAŚĪRA 2229	13	14	14	15	16	17	18
	19	20	21	22	23	24	25
	26	27	28	**29**	1	2	3
PAUSHA 2229	4	5	6	7	8	9	10
	11	12	13	14	15	16	16
	17	18	19	20	21	22	**23**
	25	26	27	28	29	30	1
MĀGHA 2229	2	3	4	5	6	7	8
	9	10	11	12	13	14	15
	16	17	18	19	20	21	22
	23	24	25	26	27	**28**[h]	30
PHĀLGUNA 2229	1	2	3	4	5	6	7
	8	9	9	10	11	12	13
	14	15[i]	16	17	18	19	20
	21	**22**	24	25	26	27	28
	29	30	1[a]	2	3	4	5
CHAITRA 2230	6	7	8	9[b]	10	11	12
	13	14	15	16	17	18	19
	20	21	22	23	24	25	**26**
	28	29	30	1	2	3	3
VAIŚĀKHA 2230	4	5	6	7	8	9	10
	11	12	13	14	15	16	17
	18	**19**	21	22	23	24	25
	26	27	28	29	30	1	2
JYAISHTHA 2230	3	4	5	6	7	8	9
	10	11	12	13	14	15	16
	17	18	19	20	21	**22**	24
	25	26	27	28	29	30	30
	1	2	3	4	5	6	7
ĀSHĀḌHA 2230	8	9	10	11	12	13	**14**
	16	17	18	19	20	21	22
	23	24	25	26	27	28	29
	30	1	2	3	4	5	6
ŚRĀVAṆA 2230	7	8	9	10	11	12	13
	14	15	16	**17**	19	20	21
	22	23[c]	24	25	26	27	27
	28	29	30	1	2	3	4[d]
BHĀDRAPADA 2230	5	6	7	8	9	**10**	12
	13	14	15	16	17	18	19
	20	21	22	23	24	25	26
	27	28	29	30	1	2	3
ĀŚVINA 2230	4	5	6	7	8[e]	9[e]	10[e]
	11	12	13	14	**15**	17	18
	19	20	21	21	22	23	24
	25	26	27	28	29	30	1[f]
KĀRTTIKA 2230	2	3	4	5	6	7	**8**
	10	11	12	13	14	15	16
	17	18	19	20	21	22	23
	24	24	25	26	27	28	29
MĀRGAŚĪRA 2230	30	**1**	3	4	5	6	7
	8	9	10	11[g]	12	13	14
	15	16	17	18	19	20	21
	22	23	24	25	26	27	28

‡Leap year
[a]New Year (Śrīmukha)
[b]Birthday of Rāma
[c]Birthday of Krishna
[d]Ganēśa Chaturthī
[e]Dashara
[f]Diwali
[g]Birthday of Vishnu
[h]Night of Śiva
[i]Holi

HINDU SOLAR 2094‡/2095

Month	Sun	Mon	Tue	Wed	Thu	Fri	Sat
PAUSHA 2094	10	11	12	13	14	15	16
	17	18	19	20	21	22	23
	24	25	26	27	28	29	1[b]
MĀGHA 2094	2	3	4	5	6	7	8
	9	10	11	12	13	14	15
	16	17	18	19	20	21	22
	23	24	25	26	27	28	29
	30	1	2	3	4	5	6
PHĀLGUNA 2094	7	8	9	10	11	12	13
	14	15	16	17	18	19	20
	21	22	23	24	25	26	27
	28	29	1	2	3	4	5
CHAITRA 2094	6	7	8	9	10	11	12
	13	14	15	16	17	18	19
	20	21	22	23	24	25	26
	27	28	29	30	31	1[a]	2
VAIŚĀKHA 2095	3	4	5	6	7	8	9
	10	11	12	13	14	15	16
	17	18	19	20	21	22	23
	24	25	26	27	28	29	30
	31	1	2	3	4	5	6
JYAISHTHA 2095	7	8	9	10	11	12	13
	14	15	16	17	18	19	20
	21	22	23	24	25	26	27
	28	29	30	31	1	2	3
ĀSHĀḌHA 2095	4	5	6	7	8	9	10
	11	12	13	14	15	16	17
	18	19	20	21	22	23	24
	25	26	27	28	29	30	31
	32	1	2	3	4	5	6
ŚRĀVAṆA 2095	7	8	9	10	11	12	13
	14	15	16	17	18	19	20
	21	22	23	24	25	26	27
	28	29	30	31	1	2	3
BHĀDRAPADA 2095	4	5	6	7	8	9	10
	11	12	13	14	15	16	17
	18	19	20	21	22	23	24
	25	26	27	28	29	30	31
	1	2	3	4	5	6	7
ĀŚVINA 2095	8	9	10	11	12	13	14
	15	16	17	18	19	20	21
	22	23	24	25	26	27	28
	29	30	31	1	2	3	4
KĀRTTIKA 2095	5	6	7	8	9	10	11
	12	13	14	15	16	17	18
	19	20	21	22	23	24	25
	26	27	28	29	30	1	2
MĀRGAŚĪRA 2095	3	4	5	6	7	8	9
	10	11	12	13	14	15	16
	17	18	19	20	21	22	23
	24	25	26	27	28	29	1
PAUSHA 2095	2	3	4	5	6	7	8
	9	10	11	12	13	14	15

‡Leap year
[a]New Year (Sarvadhārin)
[b]Pongal

ISLAMIC (ASTRONOMICAL) 1599‡/1600

Month	Sun	Mon	Tue	Wed	Thu	Fri	Sat
MUḤARRAM 1599	11	12	13	14	15	16	17
	18	19	20	21	22	23	24
	25	26	27	28	29	1	2
ṢAFAR 1599	3	4	5	6	7	8	9
	10	11	12	13	14	15	16
	17	18	19	20	21	22	23
	24	25	26	27	28	29	30
RABĪʿ I 1599	1	2	3	4	5	6	7
	8	9	10	11	12[c]	13	14
	15	16	17	18	19	20	21
	22	23	24	25	26	27	28
	29	1	2	3	4	5	6
RABĪʿ II 1599	7	8	9	10	11	12	13
	14	15	16	17	18	19	20
	21	22	23	24	25	26	27
	28	29	30	1	2	3	4
JUMĀDĀ I 1599	5	6	7	8	9	10	11
	12	13	14	15	16	17	18
	19	20	21	22	23	24	25
	26	27	28	29	1	2	3
JUMĀDĀ II 1599	4	5	6	7	8	9	10
	11	12	13	14	15	16	17
	18	19	20	21	22	23	24
	25	26	27	28	29	30	1
RAJAB 1599	2	3	4	5	6	7	8
	9	10	11	12	13	14	15
	16	17	18	19	20	21	22
	23	24	25	26	27[d]	28	29
SHAʿBĀN 1599	1	2	3	4	5	6	7
	8	9	10	11	12	13	14
	15	16	17	18	19	20	21
	22	23	24	25	26	27	28
	29	30	1[e]	2	3	4	5
RAMAḌĀN 1599	6	7	8	9	10	11	12
	13	14	15	16	17	18	19
	20	21	22	23	24	25	26
	27	28	29	30	1[f]	2	3
SHAWWĀL 1599	4	5	6	7	8	9	10
	11	12	13	14	15	16	17
	18	19	20	21	22	23	24
	25	26	27	28	29	30	1
DHU AL-QAʿDA 1599	2	3	4	5	6	7	8
	9	10	11	12	13	14	15
	16	17	18	19	20	21	22
	23	24	25	26	27	28	29
	30	1	2	3	4	5	6
DHU AL-ḤIJJA 1599	7	8	9	10[g]	11	12	13
	14	15	16	17	18	19	20
	21	22	23	24	25	26	27
	28	29[d]	1[a]	2	3	4	5
MUḤARRAM 1600	6	7	8	9	10[b]	11	12
	13	14	15	16	17	18	19
	20	21	22	23	24	25	26

‡Leap year
[a]New Year
[d]New Year (Arithmetic)
[b]ʿAshūrā'
[c]Prophet's Birthday
[d]Ascent of the Prophet
[e]Start of Ramaḍān
[f]ʿĪd al-Fiṭr
[g]ʿĪd al-'Aḍḥā

GREGORIAN 2173

Julian (Sun)	Sun	Mon	Tue	Wed	Thu	Fri	Sat	Month
Dec 13	27	28	29	30	31	1	2	
	3	4	5	6	7	8[a]	9	JANUARY 2173
Dec 27	10	11	12	13	14	15[b]	16	
	17	18	19	20	21	22	23	
Jan 10	24	25	26	27	28	29	30	
	31	1	2	3	4	5	6	
Jan 24	7	8	9	10	11	12	13	FEBRUARY 2173
	14	15	16	17[c]	18	19	20	
Feb 7	21	22	23	24	25	26	27	
	28	1	2	3	4	5	6	
Feb 21	7	8	9	10	11	12	13	MARCH 2173
	14	15	16	17	18	19	20	
Mar 7	21	22	23	24	25	26	27	
	28[d]	29	30	31	1	2	3	
Mar 21	4[e]	5	6	7	8	9	10	APRIL 2173
	11	12	13	14	15	16	17	
Apr 4	18	19	20	21	22	23	24	
	25	26	27	28	29	30	1	
Apr 18	2	3	4	5	6	7	8	
	9[f]	10	11	12	13	14	15	MAY 2173
May 2	16	17	18	19	20	21	22	
	23	24	25	26	27	28	29	
May 16	30	31	1	2	3	4	5	
	6	7	8	9	10	11	12	JUNE 2173
May 30	13	14	15	16	17	18	19	
	20	21	22	23	24	25	26	
Jun 13	27	28	29	30	1	2	3	
	4	5	6	7	8	9	10	JULY 2173
Jun 27	11	12	13	14	15	16	17	
	18	19	20	21	22	23	24	
Jul 11	25	26	27	28	29	30	31	
	1	2	3	4	5	6	7	
Jul 25	8	9	10	11	12	13	14	AUGUST 2173
	15	16	17	18	19	20	21	
Aug 8	22	23	24	25	26	27	28	
	29	30	31	1	2	3	4	
Aug 22	5	6	7	8	9	10	11	SEPTEMBER 2173
	12	13	14	15	16	17	18	
Sep 5	19	20	21	22	23	24	25	
	26	27	28	29	30	1	2	
Sep 19	3	4	5	6	7	8	9	OCTOBER 2173
	10	11	12	13	14	15	16	
Oct 3	17	18	19	20	21	22	23	
	24	25	26	27	28	29	30	
Oct 17	31	1	2	3	4	5	6	
	7	8	9	10	11	12	13	NOVEMBER 2173
Oct 31	14	15	16	17	18	19	20	
	21	22	23	24	25	26	27	
Nov 14	28[g]	29	30	1	2	3	4	
	5	6	7	8	9	10	11	DECEMBER 2173
Nov 28	12	13	14	15	16	17	18	
	19	20	21	22	23	24	25[h]	
Dec 12	26	27	28	29	30	31	1	

[a]Orthodox Christmas
[b]Julian New Year
[c]Ash Wednesday
[d]Feast of Orthodoxy
[e]Easter
[f]Orthodox Easter
[g]Advent
[h]Christmas

2174

Gregorian month	Gregorian 2174 (Sun Mon Tue Wed Thu Fri Sat)	Lunar Phases	ISO Week (Mon)	Julian Day (Sun noon)	Hebrew month	Hebrew 5934‡/5935 (Sun Mon Tue Wed Thu Fri Sat)	Molad	Chinese month	Chinese Guǐ-Yǒu/Jiǎ-Xū (Sun Mon Tue Wed Thu Fri Sat)	Solar Term	Coptic month	Coptic 1890/1891‡ / Ethiopic 2166/2167‡ (Sun Mon Tue Wed Thu Fri Sat)	Ethiopic month
	26 ◑ 28 29 30 31 1[a]	10:48	52	2515092	TEVETH 5934	22 23 24 25 26 27 28		MONTH 11* Guǐ-Yǒu	22 23 24 25 26 27 28		KOIAK 1890	16 17 18 19 20 21 22	TĀKHŚĀŚ 2166
JANUARY 2174	2 ● 4 5 6 7 8	15:41	1	2515099	SHEVAT 5934	29 1 2 3 4 5 6	Mon $14^{h}48^{m}5^{p}$	MONTH 12 Guǐ-Yǒu	29 1 2 3 4 5 6	Xiǎo hán		23 24 25 26 27 28 29[c]	
	9 ◐ 11 12 13 14 15	7:18	2	2515106		7 8 9 10 11 12 13			7 8 9 10 11 12 13		TŌBE 1890	30 1 2 3 4 5 6[d]	ṬER 2166
	16 17 ○ 19 20 21 22	0:23	3	2515113		14 15 16 17 18 19 20			14 15 16 17 **18** 19 20	Dà hán		7 8 9 10 11[e] 12 13	
	23 24 25 ◑ 27 28 29	5:33	4	2515120		21 22 23 24 25 26 27			21 22 23 24 25 26 27			14 15 16 17 18 19 20	
FEBRUARY 2174	30 31 1 ● 3 4 5	2:34	5	2515127	ADAR I 5934	28 29 30 1 2 3 4	Wed $3^{h}32^{m}6^{p}$	MONTH 1 Jiǎ-Xū	28 29 30 1[a] 2 3 4	Lì chūn		21 22 23 24 25 26 27	
	6 7 ◐ 9 10 11 12	19:34	6	2515134		5 6 7 8 9 10 11			5 6 7 8 9 10 11		MESHIR 1890	28 29 30 1 2 3 4	YAKĀTIT 2166
	13 14 15 ○ 17 18 19	19:40	7	2515141		12 13 14 15 16 17 18			12 13 14 15[b] 16 ***17*** 18	Yǔ shuǐ		5 6 7 8 9 10 11	
	20 21 22 23 ◑ 25 26	20:34	8	2515148		19 20 21 22 23 24 25			19 20 21 22* 23 24 25			12 13 14 15 16 17 18	
MARCH 2174	27 28 1 2 ● 4 5	12:54	9	2515155	ADAR II 5934	26 27 28 29 30 1 2	Thu $16^{h}16^{m}7^{p}$	MONTH 2 Jiǎ-Xū	26 27 28 29 1 2 3	Jīng zhé		19 20 21 22 23 24 25	
	6 7 8 9 ◐ 11 12	10:09	10	2515162		3 4 5 6 7 8 9			4 5 6 7 8 9 10		PAREMOTEP 1890	26 27 28 29 30 1 2	MAGĀBIT 2166
	13 14 15 16 17 ○ 19	14:27	11	2515169		10 11 12 13 14[f] 15 16			11 12 13 14 15 16 17			3 4 5 6 7 8 9	
	20[b] 21 22 23 24 25 ◑	7:34	12	2515176		17 18 19 20 21 22 23			***18*** 19 20 21 22 23 24	Chūn fēn		10 11 12 13 14 15 16	
APRIL 2174	27 28 29 30 31 ● 2	22:47	13	2515183	NISAN 5934	24 25 26 27 28 29 1	Sat $5^{h}0^{m}8^{p}$	MONTH 3 Jiǎ-Xū	25 26 27 28 29 30 1			17 18 19 20 21 22 23	
	3 4 5 6 7 8 ◐	2:41	14	2515190		2 3 4 5 6 7 8			2 3[c] 4 5 6 7 8	Qīng míng		24 25 26 27 28 29 30	
	10 11 12 13 14 15 16		15	2515197		9 10 11 12 13 14 15[g]			9 10 11 12 13 14 15		PARMOUTE 1890	1 2 3 4 5 6 7	MIYĀZYĀ 2166
	○ 18 19 20 21 22 23	7:01	16	2515204		16 17 18 19 20 21 22			16 17 18 ***19*** 20 21 22	Gǔ yǔ		8 9 10 11 12 13 14	
	◑ 25 26 27 28 29 30	15:16	17	2515211		23 24 25 26 27 28 29			23* 24 25 26 27 28 29			15[f] 16 17 18 19 20 21	
MAY 2174	● 2 3 4 5 6 7	8:29	18	2515218	IYAR 5934	30 1 2 3 4 5 6	Sun $17^{h}44^{m}9^{p}$	MONTH 4 Jiǎ-Xū	1 2 3 4 5 6 7	Lì xià		22 23 24 25 26 27 28	
	◐ 9 10 11 12 13 14	20:30	19	2515225		7 8 9 10 11 12 13			8 9 10 11 12 13 14		PASHONS 1890	29[g] 30 1 2 3 4 5	GENBOT 2166
	15 ○ 17 18 19 20 21	20:28	20	2515232		14 15 16 17 18 19 20			15 16 17 18 19 20 ***21***	Xiǎo mǎn		6 7 8 9 10 11 12	
	22 ◑ 24 25 26 27 28	20:54	21	2515239		21 22 23 24 25 26 27			22 23 24 25 26 27 28			13 14 15 16 17 18 19	
JUNE 2174	29 ● 31 1 2 3 4	18:33	22	2515246	SIVAN 5934	28 29 1 2 3 4 5	Tue $6^{h}28^{m}10^{p}$	MONTH 5 Jiǎ-Xū	29 30 1 2 3 4 5[d]			20 21 22 23 24 25 26	
	5 6 ◐ 8 9 10 11	14:36	23	2515253		6[h] 7 8 9 10 11 12			6 7 8 9 10 11 12	Máng zhǒng	PAŌNE 1890	27 28 29 30 1 2 3	SANĒ 2166
	12 13 14 ○ 16 17 18	7:02	24	2515260		13 14 15 16 17 18 19			13 14 15 16 17 18 19			4 5 6 7 8 9 10	
	19 20 21[c] ◑ 23 24 25	1:45	25	2515267		20 21 22 23 24 25 26			20 21 ***22*** 23 24* 25 26	Xià zhì		11 12 13 14 15 16 17	
JULY 2174	26 27 28 ● 30 1 2	5:45	26	2515274	TAMMUZ 5934	27 28 29 30 1 2 3	Wed $19^{h}12^{m}11^{p}$	MONTH 6 Jiǎ-Xū	27 28 29 1 2 3 4			18 19 20 21 22 23 24	
	3 4 5 6 ◐ 8 9	7:51	27	2515281		4 5 6 7 8 9 10			5 6 7 8 *9* 10 11	Xiǎo shǔ	EPĒP 1890	25 26 27 28 29 30 1	ḤAMLĒ 2166
	10 11 12 13 ○ 15 16	15:36	28	2515288		11 12 13 14 15 16 17			12 13 14 15 16 17 18			2 3 4 5 6 7 8	
	17 18 19 20 ◑ 22 23	7:08	29	2515295		18 19 20 21 22 23 24			19 20 21 22 23 ***24*** 25	Dà shǔ		9 10 11 12 13 14 15	
AUGUST 2174	24 25 26 27 ● 29 30	18:49	30	2515302	AV 5934	25 26 27 28 29 1 2	Fri $7^{h}56^{m}12^{p}$	MONTH 7 Jiǎ-Xū	26 27 28 29 30 1 2			16 17 18 19 20 21 22	
	31 1 2 3 4 ◐ 6	23:19	31	2515309		3 4 5 6 7 8 9			3 4 5 6 7[e] 8 9			23 24 25 26 27 28 29	
	7 8 9 10 11 ○ 13	23:17	32	2515316		10[i] 11 12 13 14 15 16			*10* 11 12 13 14 15[f] 16	Lì qiū	MESORĒ 1890	30 1 2 3 4 5 6	NAHASĒ 2166
	14 15 16 17 18 ◑ 20	14:21	33	2515323		17 18 19 20 21 22 23			17 18 19 20 21 22 23			7 8 9 10 11 12 13[h]	
	21 22 23 24 25 26 ●	9:58	34	2515330		24 25 26 27 28 29 30		MONTH 8 Jiǎ-Xū	24 25* ***26*** 27 28 29 1	Chǔ shǔ		14 15 16 17 18 19 20	
SEPTEMBER 2174	28 29 30 31 1 2 3		35	2515337	ELUL 5934	1 2 3 4 5 6 7	Sat $20^{h}40^{m}13^{p}$		2 3 4 5 6 7 8			21 22 23 24 25 26 27	
	◐ 5 6 7 8 9 10	12:39	36	2515344		8 9 10 11 12 13 14			9 10 11 *12* 13 14 15[g]	Bái lù	EPAG. 1890	28 29 30 1 2 3 4	PĀG. 2166
	○ 12 13 14 15 16 17	7:03	37	2515351		15 16 17 18 19 20 21			16 17 18 19 20 21 22		THOOUT 1891	5 1[a] 2 3 4 5 6	MASKARAM 2167
	◑ 19 20 21 22[d] 23 24	0:33	38	2515358		22 23 24 25 26 27 28			23 24 25 26 27 ***28*** 29	Qiū fēn		7 8 9 10 11 12 13	
OCTOBER 2174	25 ● 27 28 29 30 1	2:42	39	2515365	TISHRI 5935	29 1[a] 2[a] 3 4 5 6	Mon $9^{h}24^{m}14^{p}$	MONTH 9 Jiǎ-Xū	30 1 2 3 4 5 6			14 15 16 17[b] 18 19 20	
	2 ◐ 4 5 6 7 8	23:58	40	2515372		7 8 9 10[b] 11 12 13			7 8 9[h] 10 11 12 *13*	Hán lù		21 22 23 24 25 26 27	
	9 ○ 11 12 13 14 15	15:36	41	2515379		14 15[c] 16 17 18 19 20			14 15 16 17 18 19 20		PAOPE 1891	28 29 30 1 2 3 4	TEQEMT 2167
	16 ◑ 18 19 20 21 22	14:41	42	2515386		21 22 23 24 25 26 27			21 22 23 24 25 26* 27			5 6 7 8 9 10 11	
	23 24 ● 26 27 28 29	19:51	43	2515393	ḤESHVAN 5935	28 29 30 1 2 3 4	Tue $22^{h}8^{m}15^{p}$	MONTH 10 Jiǎ-Xū	***28*** 29 30 1 2 3 4	Shuāng jiàng		12 13 14 15 16 17 18	
NOVEMBER 2174	30 31 1 ◐ 3 4 5	9:39	44	2515400		5 6 7 8 9 10 11			5 6 7 8 9 10 11			19 20 21 22 23 24 25	
	6 7 8 ○ 10 11 12	1:31	45	2515407		12 13 14 15 16 17 18			12 *13* 14 15 16 17 18	Lì dōng	ATHŌR 1891	26 27 28 29 30 1 2	HEDĀR 2167
	13 14 15 ◑ 17 18 19	8:54	46	2515414		19 20 21 22 23 24 25			19 20 21 22 23 24 25			3 4 5 6 7 8 9	
	20 21 22 23 ● 25 26	12:19	47	2515421	KISLEV 5935	26 27 28 29 30 1 2	Thu $10^{h}52^{m}16^{p}$	MONTH 11 Jiǎ-Xū	26 27 ***28*** 29 1 2 3	Xiǎo xuě		10 11 12 13 14 15 16	
DECEMBER 2174	27 28 29 30 ◐ 2 3	18:16	48	2515428		3 4 5 6 7 8 9			4 5 6 7 8 9 10			17 18 19 20 21 22 23	
	4 5 6 7 ○ 9 10	13:20	49	2515435		10 11 12[d] 13 14 15 16			11 12 13 *14* 15 16 17	Dà xuě		24 25 26 27 28 29 30	
	11 12 13 14 15 ◑ 17	6:10	50	2515442		17 18 19 20 21 22 23			18 19 20 21 22 23 24		KOIAK 1891	1 2 3 4 5 6 7	TĀKHŚĀŚ 2167
	18 19 20 21[e] 22 23 ●	3:26	51	2515449		24 25[e] 26[e] 27[e] 28[e] 29[e] 30[e]		MONTH 12 Jiǎ-Xū	25 26 27* 28 ***29***[i] 30 1	Dōng zhì		8 9 10 11 12 13 14	
	25 26 27 28 29 30 ◐	2:24	52	2515456		1[e] 2[e] 3 4 5 6 7	Fri $23^{h}36^{m}17^{p}$		2 3 4 5 6 7 8			15 16 17 18 19 20 21	

[a]New Year
[b]Spring (11:26)
[c]Summer (2:31)
[d]Autumn (19:46)
[e]Winter (19:03)
● New moon
◐ First quarter moon
○ Full moon
◑ Last quarter moon

‡Leap year
[a]New Year
[b]Yom Kippur
[c]Sukkot
[d]Winter starts
[e]Ḥanukkah
[f]Purim
[g]Passover
[h]Shavuot
[i]Fast of Av

[a]New Year (4872, Dog)
[b]Lantern Festival
[c]Qīngmíng
[d]Dragon Festival
[e]Qīqiǎo
[f]Hungry Ghosts
[g]Mid-Autumn Festival
[h]Double-Ninth Festival
[i]Dōngzhì
*Start of 60-name cycle

‡Leap year
[a]New Year
[b]Building of the Cross
[c]Christmas
[d]Jesus's Circumcision
[e]Epiphany
[f]Easter
[g]Mary's Announcement
[h]Jesus's Transfiguration

PERSIAN (ASTRONOMICAL) 1552‡/1553

Month	Sun	Mon	Tue	Wed	Thu	Fri	Sat
DEY 1552	6	7	8	9	10	11	12
	13	14	15	16	17	18	19
	20	21	22	23	24	25	26
	27	28	29	30	1	2	3
BAHMAN 1552	4	5	6	7	8	9	10
	11	12	13	14	15	16	17
	18	19	20	21	22	23	24
	25	26	27	28	29	30	1
ESFAND 1552	2	3	4	5	6	7	8
	9	10	11	12	13	14	15
	16	17	18	19	20	21	22
	23	24	25	26	27	28	29
	30	1[a]	2	3	4	5	6
FARVARDĪN 1553	7	8	9	10	11	12	13[b]
	14	15	16	17	18	19	20
	21	22	23	24	25	26	27
	28	29	30	31	1	2	3
ORDĪBEHEŠT 1553	4	5	6	7	8	9	10
	11	12	13	14	15	16	17
	18	19	20	21	22	23	24
	25	26	27	28	29	30	31
XORDĀD 1553	1	2	3	4	5	6	7
	8	9	10	11	12	13	14
	15	16	17	18	19	20	21
	22	23	24	25	26	27	28
	29	30	31	1	2	3	4
TĪR 1553	5	6	7	8	9	10	11
	12	13	14	15	16	17	18
	19	20	21	22	23	24	25
	26	27	28	29	30	31	1
MORDĀD 1553	2	3	4	5	6	7	8
	9	10	11	12	13	14	15
	16	17	18	19	20	21	22
	23	24	25	26	27	28	29
	30	31	1	2	3	4	5
SHAHRĪVAR 1553	6	7	8	9	10	11	12
	13	14	15	16	17	18	19
	20	21	22	23	24	25	26
	27	28	29	30	31	1	2
MEHR 1553	3	4	5	6	7	8	9
	10	11	12	13	14	15	16
	17	18	19	20	21	22	23
	24	25	26	27	28	29	30
ABĀN 1553	1	2	3	4	5	6	7
	8	9	10	11	12	13	14
	15	16	17	18	19	20	21
	22	23	24	25	26	27	28
	29	30	1	2	3	4	5
ĀZAR 1553	6	7	8	9	10	11	12
	13	14	15	16	17	18	19
	20	21	22	23	24	25	26
	27	28	29	30	1	2	3
DEY 1553	4	5	6	7	8	9	10

HINDU LUNAR 2230/2231

Month	Sun	Mon	Tue	Wed	Thu	Fri	Sat
MĀRGAŚĪRA 2230	22	23	24	25	26	27	28
PAUSHA 2230	29	30	1	2	3	4	5
	6	8	9	10	11	12	13
	14	15	16	17	17	18	19
	20	21	22	23	24	25	26
MĀGHA 2230	27	28	29	30	2	3	4
	5	6	7	8	9	10	11
	12	13	14	15	16	17	18
	19	19	20	21	22	23	24
PHĀLGUNA 2230	26	27	28[h]	29	30	1	2
	3	4	5	6	7	8	9
	10	11	12	13	14	15[i]	16
	17	18	19	20	21	22	23
CHAITRA 2231	24	25	26	27	28	29	1[a]
	2	3	4	5	6	7	8
	9[b]	10	11	12	12	13	14
	15	16	17	18	19	20	21
	22	24	25	26	27	28	29
VAIŚĀKHA 2231	30	1	2	3	4	5	6
	7	8	9	10	11	12	13
	14	15	16	17	18	19	20
	21	22	23	24	25	26	28
JYAISHTHA 2231	29	30	1	2	3	4	5
	6	7	8	8	9	10	11
	12	13	14	15	16	17	18
	19	21	22	23	24	25	26
ĀSHĀDHA 2231	27	28	29	30	1	2	3
	4	5	6	7	8	9	10
	11	12	13	14	15	16	17
	18	19	20	21	23	24	25
ŚRĀVAṆA 2231	26	27	28	29	30	1	2
	3	4	5	5	6	7	8
	9	10	11	12	13	14	16
	17	18	19	20	21	22	23[c]
	24	25	26	27	28	29	30
BHĀDRAPADA 2231	1	2	3	4[d]	5	6	7
	8	9	10	11	12	13	14
	15	16	17	19	20	21	22
	23	24	25	26	27	28	29
ĀŚVINA 2231	30	30	1	2	3	4	5
	6	7	8[e]	9[e]	10[e]	11	13
	14	15	16	17	18	19	20
	21	22	23	24	25	26	27
KĀRTTIKA 2231	28	29	30	1[f]	2	3	4
	5	6	7	8	9	10	11
	12	13	14	15	17	18	19
	20	21	22	23	24	25	25
MĀRGAŚĪRA 2231	26	27	28	29	30	1	2
	3	4	5	6	7	8	9
	11[g]	12	13	14	15	16	17
	18	19	20	21	22	23	24
	25	26	27	27	28	29	30
PAUSHA 2231	1	2	4	5	6	7	8

HINDU SOLAR 2095/2096

Month	Sun	Mon	Tue	Wed	Thu	Fri	Sat
PAUSHA 2095	9	10	11	12	13	14	15
	16	17	18	19	20	21	22
	23	24	25	26	27	28	29
MĀGHA 2095	1[b]	2	3	4	5	6	7
	8	9	10	11	12	13	14
	15	16	17	18	19	20	21
	22	23	24	25	26	27	28
PHĀLGUNA 2095	29	30	1	2	3	4	5
	6	7	8	9	10	11	12
	13	14	15	16	17	18	19
	20	21	22	23	24	25	26
CHAITRA 2095	27	28	29	30	1	2	3
	4	5	6	7	8	9	10
	11	12	13	14	15	16	17
	18	19	20	21	22	23	24
VAIŚĀKHA 2096	25	26	27	28	29	30	1[a]
	2	3	4	5	6	7	8
	9	10	11	12	13	14	15
	16	17	18	19	20	21	22
	23	24	25	26	27	28	29
JYAISHTHA 2096	30	31	1	2	3	4	5
	6	7	8	9	10	11	12
	13	14	15	16	17	18	19
	20	21	22	23	24	25	26
ĀSHĀDHA 2096	27	28	29	30	31	1	2
	3	4	5	6	7	8	9
	10	11	12	13	14	15	16
	17	18	19	20	21	22	23
	24	25	26	27	28	29	30
ŚRĀVAṆA 2096	31	32	1	2	3	4	5
	6	7	8	9	10	11	12
	13	14	15	16	17	18	19
	20	21	22	23	24	25	26
BHĀDRAPADA 2096	27	28	29	30	31	1	2
	3	4	5	6	7	8	9
	10	11	12	13	14	15	16
	17	18	19	20	21	22	23
	24	25	26	27	28	29	30
ĀŚVINA 2096	31	1	2	3	4	5	6
	7	8	9	10	11	12	13
	14	15	16	17	18	19	20
	21	22	23	24	25	26	27
KĀRTTIKA 2096	28	29	30	31	1	2	3
	4	5	6	7	8	9	10
	11	12	13	14	15	16	17
	18	19	20	21	22	23	24
MĀRGAŚĪRA 2096	25	26	27	28	29	30	1
	2	3	4	5	6	7	8
	9	10	11	12	13	14	15
	16	17	18	19	20	21	22
	23	24	25	26	27	28	29
PAUSHA 2096	1	2	3	4	5	6	7
	8	9	10	11	12	13	14

ISLAMIC (ASTRONOMICAL) 1600/1601‡

Month	Sun	Mon	Tue	Wed	Thu	Fri	Sat
MUHARRAM 1600	20	21	22	23	24	25	26
SAFAR 1600	27	28	29	1	2	3	4
	5	6	7	8	9	10	11
	12	13	14	15	16	17	18
	19	20	21	22	23	24	25
RABĪ' I 1600	26	27	28	29	1	2	3
	4	5	6	7	8	9	10
	11	12[c]	13	14	15	16	17
	18	19	20	21	22	23	24
RABĪ' II 1600	25	26	27	28	29	30	1
	2	3	4	5	6	7	8
	9	10	11	12	13	14	15
	16	17	18	19	20	21	22
	23	24	25	26	27	28	29
JUMĀDĀ I 1600	1	2	3	4	5	6	7
	8	9	10	11	12	13	14
	15	16	17	18	19	20	21
	22	23	24	25	26	27	28
JUMĀDĀ II 1600	29	1	2	3	4	5	6
	7	8	9	10	11	12	13
	14	15	16	17	18	19	20
	21	22	23	24	25	26	27
RAJAB 1600	28	29	30	1	2	3	4
	5	6	7	8	9	10	11
	12	13	14	15	16	17	18
	19	20	21	22	23	24	25
SHA'BĀN 1600	26	27[d]	28	29	1	2	3
	4	5	6	7	8	9	10
	11	12	13	14	15	16	17
	18	19	20	21	22	23	24
RAMAḌĀN 1600	25	26	27	28	29	30	1[e]
	2	3	4	5	6	7	8
	9	10	11	12	13	14	15
	16	17	18	19	20	21	22
	23	24	25	26	27	28	29
SHAWWĀL 1600	30	1[f]	2	3	4	5	6
	7	8	9	10	11	12	13
	14	15	16	17	18	19	20
	21	22	23	24	25	26	27
DHU AL-QA'DA 1600	28	29	30	1	2	3	4
	5	6	7	8	9	10	11
	12	13	14	15	16	17	18
	19	20	21	22	23	24	25
DHU AL-HIJJA 1600	26	27	28	29	30	1	2
	3	4	5	6	7	8	9
	10[g]	11	12	13	14	15	16
	17	18	19	20	21	22	23
MUHARRAM 1601	24	25	26	27	28	29	1[a]
	2	3	4	5	6	7	8
	9	10[b]	11	12	13	14	15
	16	17	18	19	20	21	22
	23	24	25	26	27	28	29
	30	1	2	3	4	5	6

GREGORIAN 2174

Julian (Sun)	Sun	Mon	Tue	Wed	Thu	Fri	Sat	Month
Dec 12	26	27	28	29	30	31	1	
	2	3	4	5	6	7	8[a]	JANUARY 2174
Dec 26	9	10	11	12	13	14	15[b]	
	16	17	18	19	20	21	22	
Jan 9	23	24	25	26	27	28	29	
	30	31	1	2	3	4	5	
Jan 23	6	7	8	9	10	11	12	FEBRUARY 2174
	13	14	15	16	17	18	19	
Feb 6	20	21	22	23	24	25	26	
	27	28	1	2[c]	3	4	5	
Feb 20	6	7	8	9	10	11	12	MARCH 2174
	13[d]	14	15	16	17	18	19	
Mar 6	20	21	22	23	24	25	26	
	27	28	29	30	31	1	2	
Mar 20	3	4	5	6	7	8	9	APRIL 2174
	10	11	12	13	14	15	16	
Apr 3	17[e]	18	19	20	21	22	23	
	24[f]	25	26	27	28	29	30	
Apr 17	1	2	3	4	5	6	7	MAY 2174
	8	9	10	11	12	13	14	
May 1	15	16	17	18	19	20	21	
	22	23	24	25	26	27	28	
May 15	29	30	31	1	2	3	4	
	5	6	7	8	9	10	11	JUNE 2174
May 29	12	13	14	15	16	17	18	
	19	20	21	22	23	24	25	
Jun 12	26	27	28	29	30	1	2	
	3	4	5	6	7	8	9	JULY 2174
Jun 26	10	11	12	13	14	15	16	
	17	18	19	20	21	22	23	
Jul 10	24	25	26	27	28	29	30	
	31	1	2	3	4	5	6	
Jul 24	7	8	9	10	11	12	13	AUGUST 2174
	14	15	16	17	18	19	20	
Aug 7	21	22	23	24	25	26	27	
	28	29	30	31	1	2	3	
Aug 21	4	5	6	7	8	9	10	SEPTEMBER 2174
	11	12	13	14	15	16	17	
Sep 4	18	19	20	21	22	23	24	
	25	26	27	28	29	30	1	
Sep 18	2	3	4	5	6	7	8	OCTOBER 2174
	9	10	11	12	13	14	15	
Oct 2	16	17	18	19	20	21	22	
	23	24	25	26	27	28	29	
Oct 16	30	31	1	2	3	4	5	
	6	7	8	9	10	11	12	NOVEMBER 2174
Oct 30	13	14	15	16	17	18	19	
	20	21	22	23	24	25	26	
Nov 13	27[g]	28	29	30	1	2	3	
	4	5	6	7	8	9	10	DECEMBER 2174
Nov 27	11	12	13	14	15	16	17	
	18	19	20	21	22	23	24	
Dec 11	25[h]	26	27	28	29	30	31	

Persian: ‡Leap year; [a]New Year; [b]Sizdeh Bedar

Hindu Lunar: [a]New Year (Bhāva); [b]Birthday of Rāma; [c]Birthday of Krishna; [d]Ganēśa Chaturthī; [e]Dashara; [f]Diwali; [g]Birthday of Vishnu; [h]Night of Śiva; [i]Holi

Hindu Solar: [a]New Year (Virodhin); [b]Pongal

Islamic: ‡Leap year; [a]New Year; [b]'Ashūrā'; [c]Prophet's Birthday; [d]Ascent of the Prophet; [e]Start of Ramaḍān; [f]'Id al-Fiṭr; [g]'Id al-'Aḍḥā

Gregorian: [a]Orthodox Christmas; [b]Julian New Year; [c]Ash Wednesday; [d]Feast of Orthodoxy; [e]Easter; [f]Orthodox Easter; [g]Advent; [h]Christmas

2175

Gregorian 2175	Sun Mon Tue Wed Thu Fri Sat	Lunar Phases	ISO Week (Mon)	Julian Day (Sun noon)	Hebrew 5935/5936‡	Sun Mon Tue Wed Thu Fri Sat	Molad	Chinese Jiă-Xū/Yĭ-Hài‡	Sun Mon Tue Wed Thu Fri Sat	Solar Term	Coptic 1891‡/1892	Sun Mon Tue Wed Thu Fri Sat	Ethiopic 2167‡/2168
January 2175	1[a] 2 3 4 5 6 ○	3:29	1	2515463	Tevet 5935	8 9 10 11 12 13 14		Month 12 Jiă-Xū	9 10 11 12 13 14 15	Xiăo hán	Koiak 1891	22 23 24 25 26 27 28	Tāhśāś 2167
	8 9 10 11 12 13 14		2	2515470		15 16 17 18 19 20 21			16 17 18 19 20 21 22			29[c] 30 1 2 3 4 5	
	◑ 16 17 18 19 20 21	4:17	3	2515477		22 23 24 25 26 27 28			23 24 25 26 27 28 29	Dà hán	Tōbe 1891	6[d] 7 8 9 10 11[e] 12	Ṭer 2167
	● 23 24 25 26 27 28	16:59	4	2515484		29 1 2 3 4 5 6	Sun 12h21m0p		30 1[a] 2 3 4 5 6			13 14 15 16 17 18 19	
	◐ 30 31 1 2 3 4	10:45	5	2515491	Shevat 5935	7 8 9 10 11 12 13		Month 1 Yĭ-Hài	7 8 9 10 11 12 13	Lì chūn		20 21 22 23 24 25 26	
February 2175	○ 6 7 8 9 10 11	20:01	6	2515498		14 15 16 17 18 19 20			14 15[b] 16 17 18 19 20			27 28 29 30 1 2 3	
	12 13 ◑ 15 16 17 18	0:47	7	2515505		21 22 23 24 25 26 27			21 22 23 24 25 26 27*		Meshir 1891	4 5 6 7 8 9 10	Yakātit 2167
	19 20 ● 22 23 24 25	4:53	8	2515512		28 29 30 1 2 3 4	Tue 1h5m1p		28 29 1 2 3 4 5	Yŭ shuĭ		11 12 13 14 15 16 17	
	26 ◐ 28 1 2 3 4	20:09	9	2515519	Adar 5935	5 6 7 8 9 10 11		Month 2 Yĭ-Hài	6 7 8 9 10 11 12			18 19 20 21 22 23 24	
March 2175	5 6 ○ 8 9 10 11	14:04	10	2515526		12 13 14[f] 15 16 17 18			13 14 15 16 17 18 19	Jīng zhé		25 26 27 28 29 30 1	
	12 13 14 ◑ 16 17 18	18:00	11	2515533		19 20 21 22 23 24 25			20 21 22 23 24 25 26		Paremotep 1891	2 3 4 5 6 7 8	Magābit 2167
	19 20[b] 21 ● 23 24 25	15:05	12	2515540		26 27 28 29 1 2 3	Wed 13h49m2p		27 28 29 1 2 3 4	Chūn fēn		9 10 11 12 13 14 15	
	26 27 28 ◐ 30 31 1	7:17	13	2515547	Nisan 5935	4 5 6 7 8 9 10		Month 3 Yĭ-Hài	5 6 7 8 9 10 11			16 17 18 19 20 21 22	
April 2175	2 3 4 5 ○ 7 8	8:08	14	2515554		11 12 13 14 15[g] 16 17			12 13 14 15[c] 16 17 18	Qīng míng		23 24 25 26 27 28 29	
	9 10 11 12 13 ◑ 15	7:19	15	2515561		18 19 20 21 22 23 24			19 20 21 22 23 24 25		Parmoute 1891	30 1 2 3 4 5 6	Miyāzyā 2167
	16 17 18 19 ● 21 22	23:49	16	2515568		25 26 27 28 29 30 1			26 27 28 29* 30 1 2	Gŭ yŭ		7[f] 8 9 10 11 12 13	
	23 24 25 26 ◐ 28 29	20:33	17	2515575	Iyyar 5935	2 3 4 5 6 7 8	Fri 2h33m3p	Leap Month 3 Yĭ-Hài	3 4 5 6 7 8 9			14 15 16 17 18 19 20	
May 2175	30 1 2 3 4 5 ○	0:45	18	2515582		9 10 11 12 13 14 15			10 11 12 13 14 15 16	Lì xià		21 22 23 24 25 26 27	
	7 8 9 10 11 12 ◑	16:56	19	2515589		16 17 18 19 20 21 22			17 18 19 20 21 22 23			28 29[g] 30 1 2 3 4	
	14 15 16 17 18 19 ●	7:43	20	2515596		23 24 25 26 27 28 29			24 25 26 27 28 29 1		Pashons 1891	5 6 7 8 9 10 11	Genbot 2167
	21 22 23 24 25 26 ◐	11:50	21	2515603	Sivan 5935	1 2 3 4 5 6[h] 7	Sat 15h17m4p	Month 4 Yĭ-Hài	2 3 4 5 6 7 8	Xiăo măn		12 13 14 15 16 17 18	
	28 29 30 31 1 2 3		22	2515610		8 9 10 11 12 13 14			9 10 11 12 13 14 15			19 20 21 22 23 24 25	
June 2175	○ 5 6 7 8 9 10	15:11	23	2515617		15 16 17 18 19 20 21			16 17 18 19 20 21 22	Máng zhòng		26 27 28 29 30 1 2	
	◑ 12 13 14 15 16 17	23:35	24	2515624		22 23 24 25 26 27 28			23 24 25 26 27 28 29		Paōne 1891	3 4 5 6 7 8 9	Sanē 2167
	● 19 20 21[c] 22 23 24	15:49	25	2515631		29 30 1 2 3 4 5	Mon 4h1m5p		1* 2 3 4 5[d] 6 7	Xià zhì		10 11 12 13 14 15 16	
	25 ◐ 27 28 29 30 1	4:33	26	2515638	Tammuz 5935	6 7 8 9 10 11 12		Month 5 Yĭ-Hài	8 9 10 11 12 13 14			17 18 19 20 21 22 23	
July 2175	2 3 ○ 5 6 7 8	3:27	27	2515645		13 14 15 16 17 18 19			15 16 17 18 19 20 21	Xiăo shŭ		24 25 26 27 28 29 30	
	9 10 ◑ 12 13 14 15	4:23	28	2515652		20 21 22 23 24 25 26			22 23 24 25 26 27 28		Epēp 1891	1 2 3 4 5 6 7	Ḥamlē 2167
	16 17 ● 19 20 21 22	1:15	29	2515659		27 28 29 1 2 3 4			29 30 1 2 3 4 5			8 9 10 11 12 13 14	
	23 24 ◐ 26 27 28 29	21:52	30	2515666	Av 5935	5 6 7 8 9[i] 10 11	Tue 16h45m6p	Month 6 Yĭ-Hài	6 7 8 9 10 11 12	Dà shŭ		15 16 17 18 19 20 21	
	30 31 1 ○ 3 4 5	13:59	31	2515673		12 13 14 15 16 17 18			13 14 15 16 17 18 19			22 23 24 25 26 27 28	
August 2175	6 7 8 ◑ 10 11 12	8:47	32	2515680		19 20 21 22 23 24 25			20 21 22 23 24 25 26	Lì qiū	Mesorē 1891	29 30 1 2 3 4 5	Naḥasē 2167
	13 14 15 ● 17 18 19	12:56	33	2515687		26 27 28 29 30 1 2			27 28 29 1 2* 3 4			6 7 8 9 10 11 12	
	20 21 22 23 ◐ 25 26	15:01	34	2515694	Elul 5935	3 4 5 6 7 8 9	Thu 5h29m7p	Month 7 Yĭ-Hài	5 6 7[e] 8 9 10 11	Chŭ shŭ		13[h] 14 15 16 17 18 19	
	27 28 29 30 ○ 1 2	23:22	35	2515701		10 11 12 13 14 15 16			12 13 14 15[f] 16 17 18			20 21 22 23 24 25 26	
September 2175	3 4 5 6 ◑ 8 9	14:22	36	2515708		17 18 19 20 21 22 23			19 20 21 22 23 24 25	Bái lù	Epag. 1891	27 28 29 30 1 2 3	Pāg. 2167
	10 11 12 13 14 ● 16	3:13	37	2515715		24 25 26 27 28 29 1[a]	Fri 18h13m8p		26 27 28 29 30 1 2			4 5 6 1[a] 2 3 4	
	17 18 19 20 21 22 ◐[d]	7:24	38	2515722	Tishri 5936	2[a] 3 4 5 6 7 8		Month 8 Yĭ-Hài	3 4 5 6 7 8 9	Qiū fēn	Thoout 1892	5 6 7 8 9 10 11	Maskaram 2168
	24 25 26 27 28 29 ○	8:11	39	2515729		9 10[b] 11 12 13 14 15[c]			10 11 12 13 14 15[g] 16			12 13 14 15 16 17[b] 18	
October 2175	1 2 3 4 5 ◑ 7	22:40	40	2515736		16 17 18 19 20 21 22			17 18 19 20 21 22 23			19 20 21 22 23 24 25	
	8 9 10 11 12 13 ●	19:48	41	2515743		23 24 25 26 27 28 29			24 25 26 27 28 29 30	Hán lù		26 27 28 29 30 1 2	
	15 16 17 18 19 20 21		42	2515750		30 1 2 3 4 5 6	Sun 6h57m9p		1 2* 3 4 5 6 7		Paope 1892	3 4 5 6 7 8 9	Ṭeqemt 2168
	◐ 23 24 25 26 27 28	22:26	43	2515757	Heshvan 5936	7 8 9 10 11 12 13		Month 9 Yĭ-Hài	8 9[h] 10 11 12 13 14	Shuāng jiàng		10 11 12 13 14 15 16	
	○ 30 31 1 2 3 4	17:05	44	2515764		14 15 16 17 18 19 20			15 16 17 18 19 20 21			17 18 19 20 21 22 23	
November 2175	◑ 6 7 8 9 10 11	10:52	45	2515771		21 22 23 24 25 26 27			22 23 24 25 26 27 28	Lì dōng		24 25 26 27 28 29 30	
	12 ● 14 15 16 17 18	13:50	46	2515778		28 29 30 1 2 3 4	Mon 19h41m10p		29 1 2 3 4 5 6		Athōr 1892	1 2 3 4 5 6 7	Ḫedār 2168
	19 20 ◐ 22 23 24 25	11:34	47	2515785	Kislev 5936	5 6 7 8 9 10 11		Month 10 Yĭ-Hài	7 8 9 10 11 12 13	Xiăo xuě		8 9 10 11 12 13 14	
	26 27 ○ 29 30 1 2	2:46	48	2515792		12 13 14 15 16 17 18			14 15 16 17 18 19 20			15 16 17 18 19 20 21	
December 2175	3 4 ◑ 6 7 8 9	3:16	49	2515799		19 20 21 22 23[d] 24 25[e]			21 22 23 24 25 26 27	Dà xuě		22 23 24 25 26 27 28	
	10 11 12 ● 14 15 16	8:13	50	2515806		26[e] 27[e] 28[e] 29[e] 30[e] 1[e] 2[e]	Wed 8h25m11p		28 29 30 1 2 3* 4			29 30 1 2 3 4 5	Tāhśāś 2168
	17 18 19 ◐ 21 22[e] 23	22:29	51	2515813	Tevet 5936	3 4 5 6 7 8 9		Month 11 Yĭ-Hài	5 6 7 8 9 10[i] 11	Dōng zhì	Koiak 1892	6 7 8 9 10 11 12	
	24 25 26 ○ 28 29 30	13:52	52	2515820		10 11 12 13 14 15 16			12 13 14 15 16 17 18			13 14 15 16 17 18 19	
	31 1 2 ◑ 4 5 6	23:03	1	2515827		17 18 19 20 21 22 23			19 20 21 22 23 24 25	Xiăo hán		20 21 22 23 24 25 26	

[a]New Year
[b]Spring (17:14)
[c]Summer (8:14)
[d]Autumn (1:27)
[e]Winter (0:44)
● New moon
◐ First quarter moon
○ Full moon
◑ Last quarter moon

‡Leap year
[a]New Year
[b]Yom Kippur
[c]Sukkot
[d]Winter starts
[e]Ḥanukkah
[f]Purim
[g]Passover
[h]Shavuot
[i]Fast of Av

‡Leap year
[a]New Year (4873, Pig)
[b]Lantern Festival
[c]Qīngmíng
[d]Dragon Festival
[e]Qīqiǎo
[f]Hungry Ghosts
[g]Mid-Autumn Festival
[h]Double-Ninth Festival
[i]Dōngzhì
*Start of 60-name cycle

‡Leap year
[a]New Year
[b]Building of the Cross
[c]Christmas
[d]Jesus's Circumcision
[e]Epiphany
[f]Easter
[g]Mary's Announcement
[h]Jesus's Transfiguration

2175

PERSIAN (ASTRONOMICAL) 1553/1554

Month	Sun	Mon	Tue	Wed	Thu	Fri	Sat
DEY 1553	11	12	13	14	15	16	17
	18	19	20	21	22	23	24
	25	26	27	28	29	30	1
BAHMAN 1553	2	3	4	5	6	7	8
	9	10	11	12	13	14	15
	16	17	18	19	20	21	22
	23	24	25	26	27	28	29
ESFAND 1553	30	1	2	3	4	5	6
	7	8	9	10	11	12	13
	14	15	16	17	18	19	20
	21	22	23	24	25	26	27
FARVARDĪN 1554	28	29	1[a]	2	3	4	5
	6	7	8	9	10	11	12
	13[b]	14	15	16	17	18	19
	20	21	22	23	24	25	26
ORDĪBEHEŠT 1554	27	28	29	30	31	1	2
	3	4	5	6	7	8	9
	10	11	12	13	14	15	16
	17	18	19	20	21	22	23
	24	25	26	27	28	29	30
XORDĀD 1554	31	1	2	3	4	5	6
	7	8	9	10	11	12	13
	14	15	16	17	18	19	20
	21	22	23	24	25	26	27
TĪR 1554	28	29	30	31	1	2	3
	4	5	6	7	8	9	10
	11	12	13	14	15	16	17
	18	19	20	21	22	23	24
	25	26	27	28	29	30	31
MORDĀD 1554	1	2	3	4	5	6	7
	8	9	10	11	12	13	14
	15	16	17	18	19	20	21
	22	23	24	25	26	27	28
SHAHRĪVAR 1554	29	30	31	1	2	3	4
	5	6	7	8	9	10	11
	12	13	14	15	16	17	18
	19	20	21	22	23	24	25
MEHR 1554	26	27	28	29	30	31	1
	2	3	4	5	6	7	8
	9	10	11	12	13	14	15
	16	17	18	19	20	21	22
	23	24	25	26	27	28	29
ĀBĀN 1554	30	1	2	3	4	5	6
	7	8	9	10	11	12	13
	14	15	16	17	18	19	20
	21	22	23	24	25	26	27
ĀZAR 1554	28	29	30	1	2	3	4
	5	6	7	8	9	10	11
	12	13	14	15	16	17	18
	19	20	21	22	23	24	25
DEY 1554	26	27	28	29	30	1	2
	3	4	5	6	7	8	9
	10	11	12	13	14	15	16

[a]New Year
[b]Sizdeh Bedar

HINDU LUNAR 2231/2232‡

Month	Sun	Mon	Tue	Wed	Thu	Fri	Sat
PAUSHA 2231	9	10	11	12	13	14	15
	16	17	18	19	20	21	22
	23	24	25	26	27	28	29
MĀGHA 2231	30	1	2	3	4	5	6
	7	9	10	11	12	13	14
	15	16	17	18	19	19	20
	21	22	23	24	25	26	27
PHĀLGUNA 2231	28[h]	29	30	1	3	4	5
	6	7	8	9	10	11	12
	13	14	15[i]	16	17	18	19
	20	21	22	23	23	25	26
CHAITRA 2232	27	28	29	30	1[a]	2	3
	4	5	6	7	9[b]	10	11
	12	12	13	14	15	16	17
	18	19	20	21	22	23	24
VAIŚĀKHA 2232	25	26	27	28	29	1	2
	3	4	5	6	7	8	9
	10	11	12	13	14	15	16
	16	17	18	19	20	21	22
	24	25	26	27	28	29	30
JYAISHTHA 2232	1	2	3	4	5	6	7
	8	9	10	11	12	13	14
	15	16	17	18	19	20	21
	22	23	24	25	26	28	29
LEAP ĀSHĀḌHA 2232	30	1	2	3	4	5	6
	7	8	9	10	11	12	12
	13	14	15	16	17	18	20
	21	22	23	24	25	26	27
ĀSHĀḌHA 2232	28	29	30	1	3	3	4
	5	6	7	8	9	10	11
	12	13	14	15	16	17	18
	19	20	21	23	24	25	26
ŚRĀVAṆA 2232	27	28	29	30	1	2	3
	4	5	6	7	8	9	9
	10	11	12	13	14	16	17
	18	19	20	21	22	23[c]	24
BHĀDRAPADA 2232	25	26	28	29	30	30	1
	2	3	4[d]	5	6	7	8
	9	10	11	12	13	14	15
	16	17	18	20	21	22	23
	24	25	26	27	28	29	30
ĀŚVINA 2232	1	2	3	4	4	5	6
	7	8[e]	9[e]	10[e]	11	13	14
	15	16	17	18	19	20	21
	22	23	24	25	26	27	28
KĀRTTIKA 2232	29	30	1[f]	2	3	4	5
	6	7	8	9	10	11	12
	13	14	15	17	18	19	20
	21	22	23	24	25	26	27
MĀRGAŚĪRA 2232	27	28	29	30	1	2	3
	4	5	6	7	8	9	10[g]
	12	13	14	15	16	17	18
	19	20	21	22	23	24	25

‡Leap year
[a]New Year (Yuvan)
[b]Birthday of Rāma
[c]Birthday of Krishna
[d]Ganēśa Chaturthī
[e]Dashara
[f]Diwali
[g]Birthday of Vishnu
[h]Night of Śiva
[i]Holi

HINDU SOLAR 2096/2097‡

Month	Sun	Mon	Tue	Wed	Thu	Fri	Sat
PAUSHA 2096	15	16	17	18	19	20	21
	22	23	24	25	26	27	28
MĀGHA 2096	29	30	1[b]	2	3	4	5
	6	7	8	9	10	11	12
	13	14	15	16	17	18	19
	20	21	22	23	24	25	26
PHĀLGUNA 2096	27	28	29	1	2	3	4
	5	6	7	8	9	10	11
	12	13	14	15	16	17	18
	19	20	21	22	23	24	25
CHAITRA 2096	26	27	28	29	30	1	2
	3	4	5	6	7	8	9
	10	11	12	13	14	15	16
	17	18	19	20	21	22	23
	24	25	26	27	28	29	30
VAIŚĀKHA 2097	1[a]	2	3	4	5	6	7
	8	9	10	11	12	13	14
	15	16	17	18	19	20	21
	22	23	24	25	26	27	28
JYAISHTHA 2097	29	30	31	1	2	3	4
	5	6	7	8	9	10	11
	12	13	14	15	16	17	18
	19	20	21	22	23	24	25
	26	27	28	29	30	31	32
ĀSHĀḌHA 2097	1	2	3	4	5	6	7
	8	9	10	11	12	13	14
	15	16	17	18	19	20	21
	22	23	24	25	26	27	28
ŚRĀVAṆA 2097	29	30	31	1	2	3	4
	5	6	7	8	9	10	11
	12	13	14	15	16	17	18
	19	20	21	22	23	24	25
	26	27	28	29	30	31	32
BHĀDRAPADA 2097	1	2	3	4	5	6	7
	8	9	10	11	12	13	14
	15	16	17	18	19	20	21
	22	23	24	25	26	27	28
ĀŚVINA 2097	29	30	31	1	2	3	4
	5	6	7	8	9	10	11
	12	13	14	15	16	17	18
	19	20	21	22	23	24	25
KĀRTTIKA 2097	26	27	28	29	30	1	2
	3	4	5	6	7	8	9
	10	11	12	13	14	15	16
	17	18	19	20	21	22	23
	24	25	26	27	28	29	30
MĀRGAŚĪRA 2097	1	2	3	4	5	6	7
	8	9	10	11	12	13	14
	15	16	17	18	19	20	21
	22	23	24	25	26	27	28
PAUSHA 2097	29	30	1	2	3	4	5
	6	7	8	9	10	11	12
	13	14	15	16	17	18	19

‡Leap year
[a]New Year (Vikṛita)
[b]Pongal

ISLAMIC (ASTRONOMICAL) 1601‡/1602

Month	Sun	Mon	Tue	Wed	Thu	Fri	Sat
ṢAFAR 1601	7	8	9	10	11	12	13
	14	15	16	17	18	19	20
	21	22	23	24	25	26	27
RABĪʿ I 1601	28	29	1	2	3	4	5
	6	7	8	9	10	11	12[c]
	13	14	15	16	17	18	19
	20	21	22	23	24	25	26
RABĪʿ II 1601	27	28	29	1	2	3	4
	5	6	7	8	9	10	11
	12	13	14	15	16	17	18
	19	20	21	22	23	24	25
JUMĀDĀ I 1601	26	27	28	29	30	1	2
	3	4	5	6	7	8	9
	10	11	12	13	14	15	16
	17	18	19	20	21	22	23
JUMĀDĀ II 1601	24	25	26	27	28	29	1
	2	3	4	5	6	7	8
	9	10	11	12	13	14	15
	16	17	18	19	20	21	22
	23	24	25	26	27	28	29
RAJAB 1601	1	2	3	4	5	6	7
	8	9	10	11	12	13	14
	15	16	17	18	19	20	21
	22	23	24	25	26	27[d]	28
SHAʿBĀN 1601	29	30	1	2	3	4	5
	6	7	8	9	10	11	12
	13	14	15	16	17	18	19
	20	21	22	23	24	25	26
RAMAḌĀN 1601	27	28	29	1[e]	2	3	4
	5	6	7	8	9	10	11
	12	13	14	15	16	17	18
	19	20	21	22	23	24	25
SHAWWĀL 1601	26	27	28	29	30	1[f]	2
	3	4	5	6	7	8	9
	10	11	12	13	14	15	16
	17	18	19	20	21	22	23
	24	25	26	27	28	29	30
DHU AL-QAʿDA 1601	31	1	2	3	4	5	6
	7	8	9	10	11	12	13
	14	15	16	17	18	19	20
	21	22	23	24	25	26	27
DHU AL-ḤIJJA 1601	28	29	1	2	3	4	5
	6	7	8	9	10[g]	11	12
	13	14	15	16	17	18	19
	20	21	22	23	24	25	26
MUḤARRAM 1602	27	28	29	30[A]	1[a]	2	3
	4	5	6	7	8	9	10[b]
	11	12	13	14	15	16	17
	18	19	20	21	22	23	24
ṢAFAR 1602	25	26	27	28	29	1	2
	3	4	5	6	7	8	9
	10	11	12	13	14	15	16
	17	18	19	20	21	22	23

‡Leap year
[a]New Year
[A]New Year (Arithmetic)
[b]ʿĀshūrāʾ
[c]Prophet's Birthday
[d]Ascent of the Prophet
[e]Start of Ramaḍān
[f]ʿĪd al-Fiṭr
[g]ʿĪd al-ʾAḍḥā

GREGORIAN 2175

Julian (Sun)	Month	Sun	Mon	Tue	Wed	Thu	Fri	Sat
Dec 18	JANUARY 2175	1	2	3	4	5	6	7
		8[a]	9	10	11	12	13	14
Jan 1		15[b]	16	17	18	19	20	21
		22	23	24	25	26	27	28
Jan 15	FEBRUARY 2175	29	30	31	1	2	3	4
		5	6	7	8	9	10	11
Jan 29		12	13	14	15	16	17	18
		19	20	21	22[c]	23	24	25
Feb 12	MARCH 2175	26	27	28	1	2	3	4
		5[d]	6	7	8	9	10	11
Feb 26		12	13	14	15	16	17	18
		19	20	21	22	23	24	25
Mar 12	APRIL 2175	26	27	28	29	30	31	1
		2	3	4	5	6	7	8
Mar 26		9[e]	10	11	12	13	14	15
		16[f]	17	18	19	20	21	22
Apr 9		23	24	25	26	27	28	29
	MAY 2175	30	1	2	3	4	5	6
Apr 23		7	8	9	10	11	12	13
		14	15	16	17	18	19	20
May 7		21	22	23	24	25	26	27
	JUNE 2175	28	29	30	31	1	2	3
May 21		4	5	6	7	8	9	10
		11	12	13	14	15	16	17
Jun 4		18	19	20	21	22	23	24
	JULY 2175	25	26	27	28	29	30	1
Jun 18		2	3	4	5	6	7	8
		9	10	11	12	13	14	15
Jul 2		16	17	18	19	20	21	22
		23	24	25	26	27	28	29
Jul 16	AUGUST 2175	30	31	1	2	3	4	5
		6	7	8	9	10	11	12
Jul 30		13	14	15	16	17	18	19
		20	21	22	23	24	25	26
Aug 13	SEPTEMBER 2175	27	28	29	30	31	1	2
		3	4	5	6	7	8	9
Aug 27		10	11	12	13	14	15	16
		17	18	19	20	21	22	23
Sep 10		24	25	26	27	28	29	30
	OCTOBER 2175	1	2	3	4	5	6	7
Sep 24		8	9	10	11	12	13	14
		15	16	17	18	19	20	21
Oct 8		22	23	24	25	26	27	28
	NOVEMBER 2175	29	30	31	1	2	3	4
Oct 22		5	6	7	8	9	10	11
		12	13	14	15	16	17	18
Nov 5		19	20	21	22	23	24	25
	DECEMBER 2175	26	27	28	29	30	1	2
Nov 19		3[g]	4	5	6	7	8	9
		10	11	12	13	14	15	16
Dec 3		17	18	19	20	21	22	23
		24	25[h]	26	27	28	29	30
Dec 17		31	1	2	3	4	5	6

[a]Orthodox Christmas
[b]Julian New Year
[c]Ash Wednesday
[d]Feast of Orthodoxy
[e]Easter
[f]Orthodox Easter
[g]Advent
[h]Christmas

2176

GREGORIAN 2176‡	Sun	Mon	Tue	Wed	Thu	Fri	Sat	Lunar Phases	ISO WEEK (Mon)	JULIAN DAY (Sun noon)	HEBREW 5936‡/5937	Sun	Mon	Tue	Wed	Thu	Fri	Sat	Molad	CHINESE Yǐ-Hài‡/Bǐng-Zǐ	Sun	Mon	Tue	Wed	Thu	Fri	Sat	Solar Term	COPTIC 1892/1893	Sun	Mon	Tue	Wed	Thu	Fri	Sat	ETHIOPIC 2168/2169
JANUARY 2176	31	1[a]	2	◑	4	5	6	23:03	1	2515827	TEVETH 5936	17	18	19	20	21	22	23		MONTH 11 Yǐ-Hài	19	20	21	22	23	24	*25*	Xiǎo hán	KOIAK 1892	20	21	22	23	24	25	26	TĀKHŚĀŚ 2168
	7	8	9	10	11	●	13	1:44	2	2515834		24	25	26	27	28	29	1	Thu 21h9m12p	MONTH 12 Yǐ-Hài	26	27	28	29	30	1	2		TŌBE 1892	27	28	29[c]	30	1	2	3	
	14	15	16	17	18	◐	20	7:21	3	2515841	SHEVAT 5936	2	3	4	5	6	7	8			3	4	5	6	7	8	**9**	Dà hán		4	5	6[d]	7	8	9	10	ṬER 2168
	21	22	23	24	25	○	27	2:44	4	2515848		9	10	11	12	13	14	15			10	11	12	13	14	15	16			11[e]	12	13	14	15	16	17	
	28	29	30	31	1	◑	3	20:32	5	2515855		16	17	18	19	20	21	22			17	18	19	20	21	22	23			18	19	20	21	22	23	24	
FEBRUARY 2176	4	5	6	7	8	9	●	17:17	6	2515862		23	24	25	26	27	28	29			*24*	25	26	27	28	29	30	Lì chūn		25	26	27	28	29	30	1	
	11	12	13	14	15	16	◐	14:58	7	2515869	ADAR I 5936	30	1	2	3	4	5	6	Sat 9h53m13p	MONTH 1 Bǐng-Zǐ	1[a]	2	3*	4	5	6	7		MESHIR 1892	2	3	4	5	6	7	8	YAKĀTIT 2168
	18	19	20	21	22	23	○	17:15	8	2515876		7	8	9	10	11	12	13			8	**9**	10	11	12	13	14	Yǔ shuǐ		9	10	11	12	13	14	15	
	25	26	27	28	29	1	2		9	2515883		14	15	16	17	18	19	20			15[b]	16	17	18	19	20	21			16	17	18	19	20	21	22	
MARCH 2176	◑	4	5	6	7	8	9	17:41	10	2515890		21	22	23	24	25	26	27			22	23	*24*	25	26	27	28	Jīng zhé		23	24	25	26	27	28	29	
	10	●	12	13	14	15	16	6:09	11	2515897	ADAR II 5936	28	29	30	1	2	3	4	Sun 22h37m14p	MONTH 2 Bǐng-Zǐ	29	1	2	3	4	5	6		PAREMOTEP 1892	30	1	2	3	4	5	6	MAGĀBIT 2168
	◐	18	19[b]	20	21	22	23	22:28	12	2515904		5	6	7	8	9	10	11			7	8	9	**10**	11	12	13	Chūn fēn		7	8	9	10	11	12	13	
	24	○	26	27	28	29	30	8:53	13	2515911		12	13	14[f]	15	16	17	18			14	15	16	17	18	19	20			14	15	16	17	18	19	20	
	31	1	◑	3	4	5	6	12:42	14	2515918		19	20	21	22	23	24	25			21	22	23	24	*25*[c]	26	27	Qīng míng		21	22	23	24	25	26	27	
APRIL 2176	7	8	●	10	11	12	13	16:18	15	2515925	NISAN 5936	26	27	28	29	1	2	3	Tue 11h21m15p	MONTH 3 Bǐng-Zǐ	28	29	30	1	2	3	4*		PARMOUTE 1892	28	29	30	1	2	3	4	MIYĀZYĀ 2168
	14	15	◐	17	18	19	20	6:52	16	2515932		4	5	6	7	8	9	10			5	6	7	8	9	**10**	11	Gǔ yǔ		5	6	7	8	9	10	11	
	21	22	23	○	25	26	27	0:58	17	2515939		11	12	13	14	15[g]	16	17			12	13	14	15	16	17	18			12	13	14	15	16	17	18	
	28	29	30	1	◑	3	4	4:21	18	2515946		18	19	20	21	22	23	24			19	20	21	22	23	24	25			19	20	21	22	23	24	25	
MAY 2176	5	6	7	8	●	10	11	0:25	19	2515953	IYAR 5936	25	26	27	28	29	30	1	Thu 0h5m16p	MONTH 4 Bǐng-Zǐ	*26*	27	28	29	1	2	3	Lì xià	PASHONS 1892	26[f]	27	28	29[g]	30	1	2	GENBOT 2168
	12	13	14	◐	16	17	18	16:57	20	2515960		2	3	4	5	6	7	8			4	5	6	7	8	9	10			3	4	5	6	7	8	9	
	19	20	21	22	○	24	25	16:53	21	2515967		9	10	11	12	13	14	15			11	**12**	13	14	15	16	17	Xiǎo mǎn		10	11	12	13	14	15	16	
	26	27	28	29	30	◑	1	16:10	22	2515974		16	17	18	19	20	21	22			18	19	20	21	22	23	24			17	18	19	20	21	22	23	
JUNE 2176	2	3	4	5	6	●	8	7:30	23	2515981		23	24	25	26	27	28	29		MONTH 5 Bǐng-Zǐ	25	26	27	*28*	29	1	2	Máng zhòng		24	25	26	27	28	29	30	
	9	10	11	12	13	◐	15	5:02	24	2515988	SIVAN 5936	1	2	3	4	5	6[h]	7	Fri 12h49m17p		3	4	5[d]	6*	7	8	9		PAŌNE 1892	1	2	3	4	5	6	7	SANĒ 2168
	16	17	18	19	20[c]	21	○	8:09	25	2515995		8	9	10	11	12	13	14			10	11	12	13	**14**	15	16	Xià zhì		8	9	10	11	12	13	14	
	23	24	25	26	27	28	29		26	2516002		15	16	17	18	19	20	21			17	18	19	20	21	22	23			15	16	17	18	19	20	21	
JULY 2176	◑	1	2	3	4	5	●	0:30 19:15	27	2516009		22	23	24	25	26	27	28		MONTH 6 Bǐng-Zǐ	24	25	26	27	28	29	*1*	Xiǎo shǔ		22	23	24	25	26	27	28	
	7	8	9	10	11	12	◐	14:43	28	2516016	TAMMUZ 5936	29	30	1	2	3	4	5	Sun 1h34m0p		2	3	4	5	6	7	8		EPĒP 1892	29	30	1	2	3	4	5	ḤAMLĒ 2168
	14	15	16	17	18	19	20		29	2516023		6	7	8	9	10	11	12			9	10	11	12	13	14	15			6	7	8	9	10	11	12	
	○	22	23	24	25	26	27	22:19	30	2516030		13	14	15	16	17	18	19			16	**17**	18	19	20	21	22	Dà shǔ		13	14	15	16	17	18	19	
	28	◑	30	31	1	2	3	6:24	31	2516037		20	21	22	23	24	25	26			23	24	25	26	27	28	29			20	21	22	23	24	25	26	
AUGUST 2176	●	5	6	7	8	9	10	23:02	32	2516044	AV 5936	27	28	29	1	2	3	4	Mon 14h18m1p	MONTH 7 Bǐng-Zǐ	30	1	2	3	4	5	6	Lì qiū	MESORĒ 1892	27	28	29	30	1	2	3	NAḤASĒ 2168
	11	◐	13	14	15	16	17	11:31	33	2516051		5	6	7	8	9[i]	10	11			7[e]*	8	9	10	11	12	13			4	5	6	7	8	9	10	
	18	19	○	21	22	23	24	11:03	34	2516058		12	13	14	15	16	17	18			14	15[f]	16	17	**18**	19	20	Chǔ shǔ		11	12	13[h]	14	15	16	17	
	25	26	◑	28	29	30	31	11:16	35	2516065		19	20	21	22	23	24	25			21	22	23	24	25	26	27			18	19	20	21	22	23	24	
SEPTEMBER 2176	1	2	●	4	5	6	7	9:17	36	2516072	ELUL 5936	26	27	28	29	30	1	2	Wed 3h2m2p	MONTH 8 Bǐng-Zǐ	28	29	1	2	3	4	5	Bái lù	EPAG. 1892	25	26	27	28	29	30	1	PĀG. 2168
	8	9	10	◐	12	13	14	5:31	37	2516079		3	4	5	6	7	8	9			6	7	8	9	10	11	12		THOOUT 1893	2	3	4	5	1[a]	2	3	MASKARAM 2169
	15	16	17	○	19	20	21	22:22	38	2516086		10	11	12	13	14	15	16			13	14	15[g]	16	17	18	19			4	5	6	7	8	9	10	
	22[d]	23	24	◑	26	27	28	16:39	39	2516093		17	18	19	20	21	22	23			**20**	21	22	23	24	25	26	Qiū fēn		11	12	13	14	15	16	17[b]	
	29	30	1	●	3	4	5	22:02	40	2516100	TISHRI 5937	24	25	26	27	28	29	1[a]		MONTH 9 Bǐng-Zǐ	27	28	29	30	1	2	3	Hán lù		18	19	20	21	22	23	24	
OCTOBER 2176	6	7	8	9	10	◐	12	0:24	41	2516107		2[a]	3	4	5	6	7	8	Thu 15h46m3p		4	5	6	7	8*	9[h]	10		PAOPE 1893	25	26	27	28	29	30	1	ṬEQEMT 2169
	13	14	15	16	17	○	19	8:39	42	2516114		9	10[b]	11	12	13	14	15[c]			11	12	13	14	15	16	17			2	3	4	5	6	7	8	
	20	21	22	23	◑	25	26	23:59	43	2516121		16	17	18	19	20	21	22			18	19	20	**21**	22	23	24	Shuāng jiàng		9	10	11	12	13	14	15	
	27	28	29	30	31	●	2	13:35	44	2516128		23	24	25	26	27	28	29		MONTH 10 Bǐng-Zǐ	25	26	27	28	29	1	2			16	17	18	19	20	21	22	
NOVEMBER 2176	3	4	5	6	7	8	◐	18:47	45	2516135	ḤESHVAN 5937	30	1	2	3	4	5	6	Sat 4h30m4p		3	4	5	6	*7*	8	9	Lì dōng		23	24	25	26	27	28	29	
	10	11	12	13	14	15	○	18:37	46	2516142		7	8	9	10	11	12	13			10	11	12	13	14	15	16		ATHŌR 1893	30	1	2	3	4	5	6	ḪEDĀR 2169
	17	18	19	20	21	22	◑	10:18	47	2516149		14	15	16	17	18	19	20			17	18	19	20	21	**22**	23	Xiǎo xuě		7	8	9	10	11	12	13	
	24	25	26	27	28	29	30		48	2516156		21	22	23	24	25	26	27			24	25	26	27	28	29	30			14	15	16	17	18	19	20	
DECEMBER 2176	●	2	3	4	5	6	7	7:42	49	2516163	KISLEV 5937	28	29	1	2	3	4[d]	5	Sun 17h14m5p	MONTH 11 Bǐng-Zǐ	1	2	3	4	5	*6*	7	Dà xuě		21	22	23	24	25	26	27	
	8	◐	10	11	12	13	14	11:12	50	2516170		6	7	8	9	10	11	12			8	9*	10	11	12	13	14		KOIAK 1893	28	29	30	1	2	3	4	TĀKHŚĀŚ 2169
	15	○	17	18	19	20	21[e]	4:57	51	2516177		13	14	15	16	17	18	19			15	16	17	18	19	20	**21**[i]	Dōng zhì		5	6	7	8	9	10	11	
	22	◑	24	25	26	27	28	0:06	52	2516184		20	21	22	23	24	25[e]	26[e]			22	23	24	25	26	27	28			12	13	14.	15	16	17	18	
	29	30	●	1	2	3	4	3:20	1	2516191		27[e]	28[e]	29[e]	1[e]	2[e]	3[e]	4	Tue 5h58m6p		29	30	1	2	3	4	5			19	20	21	22	23	24	25	

‡Leap year
[a]New Year
[b]Spring (23:00)
[c]Summer (14:04)
[d]Autumn (7:19)
[e]Winter (6:38)
● New moon
◐ First quarter moon
○ Full moon
◑ Last quarter moon

‡Leap year
[a]New Year
[b]Yom Kippur
[c]Sukkot
[d]Winter starts
[e]Ḥanukkah
[f]Purim
[g]Passover
[h]Shavuot
[i]Fast of Av

‡Leap year
[a]New Year (4874, Rat)
[b]Lantern Festival
[c]Qīngmíng
[d]Dragon Festival
[e]Qīqiǎo
[f]Hungry Ghosts
[g]Mid-Autumn Festival
[h]Double-Ninth Festival
[i]Dōngzhì
*Start of 60-name cycle

[a]New Year
[b]Building of the Cross
[c]Christmas
[d]Jesus's Circumcision
[e]Epiphany
[f]Easter
[g]Mary's Announcement
[h]Jesus's Transfiguration

PERSIAN (ASTRONOMICAL) 1554/1555	Sun	Mon	Tue	Wed	Thu	Fri	Sat
DEY 1554	10	11	12	13	14	15	16
	17	18	19	20	21	22	23
	24	25	26	27	28	29	30
BAHMAN 1554	1	2	3	4	5	6	7
	8	9	10	11	12	13	14
	15	16	17	18	19	20	21
	22	23	24	25	26	27	28
ESFAND 1554	29	30	1	2	3	4	5
	6	7	8	9	10	11	12
	13	14	15	16	17	18	19
	20	21	22	23	24	25	26
FARVARDĪN 1555	27	28	29	1[a]	2	3	4
	5	6	7	8	9	10	11
	12	13[b]	14	15	16	17	18
	19	20	21	22	23	24	25
ORDĪBEHEŠT 1555	26	27	28	29	30	31	1
	2	3	4	5	6	7	8
	9	10	11	12	13	14	15
	16	17	18	19	20	21	22
	23	24	25	26	27	28	29
XORDĀD 1555	30	31	1	2	3	4	5
	6	7	8	9	10	11	12
	13	14	15	16	17	18	19
	20	21	22	23	24	25	26
TĪR 1555	27	28	29	30	31	1	2
	3	4	5	6	7	8	9
	10	11	12	13	14	15	16
	17	18	19	20	21	22	23
	24	25	26	27	28	29	30
MORDĀD 1555	31	1	2	3	4	5	6
	7	8	9	10	11	12	13
	14	15	16	17	18	19	20
	21	22	23	24	25	26	27
SHAHRĪVAR 1555	28	29	30	31	1	2	3
	4	5	6	7	8	9	10
	11	12	13	14	15	16	17
	18	19	20	21	22	23	24
	25	26	27	28	29	30	31
MEHR 1555	1	2	3	4	5	6	7
	8	9	10	11	12	13	14
	15	16	17	18	19	20	21
	22	23	24	25	26	27	28
ĀBĀN 1555	29	30	1	2	3	4	5
	6	7	8	9	10	11	12
	13	14	15	16	17	18	19
	20	21	22	23	24	25	26
ĀZAR 1555	27	28	29	30	1	2	3
	4	5	6	7	8	9	10
	11	12	13	14	15	16	17
	18	19	20	21	22	23	24
DEY 1555	25	26	27	28	29	30	1
	2	3	4	5	6	7	8
	9	10	11	12	13	14	15

HINDU LUNAR 2232‡/2233	Sun	Mon	Tue	Wed	Thu	Fri	Sat
MĀRGAŚĪRA 2232	19	20	21	22	23	24	25
PAUSHA 2232	26	27	28	29	30	1	1
	2	4	5	6	7	8	9
	10	11	12	13	14	15	16
	18	19	19	20	21	22	23
	24	25	26	27	28	29	30
MĀGHA 2232	1	2	3	4	5	6	7
	8	10	11	12	13	14	15
	16	17	18	19	20	21	22
	22	23	24	25	26	27	28[h]
PHĀLGUNA 2232	29	30	1	2	4	5	6
	7	8	9	10	11	12	13
	14	15[i]	16	17	18	19	20
	21	22	23	24	25	26	27
CHAITRA 2233	28	29	30	1[a]	2	3	4
	5	6	7	9[b]	10	11	12
	13	14	15	16	16	17	18
	19	20	21	22	23	24	25
VAIŚĀKHA 2233	26	27	28	29	30	2	3
	4	5	6	7	8	9	10
	11	12	13	14	15	16	17
	18	19	20	21	22	23	24
JYAISHTHA 2233	25	26	27	28	29	30	1
	2	3	5	6	7	8	9
	10	11	12	12	13	14	15
	16	17	18	19	20	21	22
	23	24	25	26	28	29	30
ĀSHĀDHA 2233	1	2	3	4	5	6	7
	8	9	10	11	12	13	14
	15	16	17	18	19	20	21
	22	23	24	25	26	27	28
ŚRĀVANA 2233	29	1	2	3	4	5	6
	7	8	9	9	10	11	12
	13	14	15	16	17	18	19
	20	21	22[c]	24	25	26	27
BHĀDRAPADA 2233	28	29	30	1	2	3	4[d]
	5	6	7	8	9	10	11
	12	13	14	15	16	17	18
	19	20	21	22	23	24	25
ĀŚVINA 2233	27	28	29	30	1	2	3
	4	4	5	6	7	8[e]	9[e]
	10[e]	11	12	13	14	15	16
	17	18	20	21	22	23	24
KĀRTTIKA 2233	25	26	27	28	29	30	1[f]
	2	3	4	5	6	7	8
	8	9	10	11	13	14	15
	16	17	18	19	20	21	22
	23	24	25	26	27	28	29
MĀRGAŚĪRA 2233	30	1	2	3	4	5	6
	7	8	9	10	11[g]	12	13
	14	15	16	18	19	20	21
	22	23	24	25	26	27	28
	29	30	30	1	2	3	4

HINDU SOLAR 2097‡/2098	Sun	Mon	Tue	Wed	Thu	Fri	Sat
PAUSHA 2097	13	14	15	16	17	18	19
	20	21	22	23	24	25	26
MĀGHA 2097	27	28	29	1[b]	2	3	4
	5	6	7	8	9	10	11
	12	13	14	15	16	17	18
	19	20	21	22	23	24	25
PHĀLGUNA 2097	26	27	28	29	1	2	3
	4	5	6	7	8	9	10
	11	12	13	14	15	16	17
	18	19	20	21	22	23	24
CHAITRA 2097	25	26	27	28	29	30	1
	2	3	4	5	6	7	8
	9	10	11	12	13	14	15
	16	17	18	19	20	21	22
	23	24	25	26	27	28	29
VAIŚĀKHA 2098	30	31	1[a]	2	3	4	5
	6	7	8	9	10	11	12
	13	14	15	16	17	18	19
	20	21	22	23	24	25	26
JYAISHTHA 2098	27	28	29	30	1	2	3
	4	5	6	7	8	9	10
	11	12	13	14	15	16	17
	18	19	20	21	22	23	24
	25	26	27	28	29	30	31
ĀSHĀDHA 2098	32	1	2	3	4	5	6
	7	8	9	10	11	12	13
	14	15	16	17	18	19	20
	21	22	23	24	25	26	27
ŚRĀVANA 2098	28	29	30	31	32	1	2
	3	4	5	6	7	8	9
	10	11	12	13	14	15	16
	17	18	19	20	21	22	23
	24	25	26	27	28	29	30
BHĀDRAPADA 2098	31	1	2	3	4	5	6
	7	8	9	10	11	12	13
	14	15	16	17	18	19	20
	21	22	23	24	25	26	27
ĀŚVINA 2098	28	29	30	31	1	2	3
	4	5	6	7	8	9	10
	11	12	13	14	15	16	17
	18	19	20	21	22	23	24
KĀRTTIKA 2098	25	26	27	28	29	30	1
	2	3	4	5	6	7	8
	9	10	11	12	13	14	15
	16	17	18	19	20	21	22
	23	24	25	26	27	28	29
MĀRGAŚĪRA 2098	30	1	2	3	4	5	6
	7	8	9	10	11	12	13
	14	15	16	17	18	19	20
	21	22	23	24	25	26	27
PAUSHA 2098	28	29	30	1	2	3	4
	5	6	7	8	9	10	11
	12	13	14	15	16	17	18

ISLAMIC (ASTRONOMICAL) 1602/1603	Sun	Mon	Tue	Wed	Thu	Fri	Sat
ṢAFAR 1602	17	18	19	20	21	22	23
RABĪ' I 1602	24	25	26	27	28	29	1
	2	3	4	5	6	7	8
	9	10	11	12[c]	13	14	15
	16	17	18	19	20	21	22
	23	24	25	26	27	28	29
RABĪ' II 1602	30	1	2	3	4	5	6
	7	8	9	10	11	12	13
	14	15	16	17	18	19	20
	21	22	23	24	25	26	27
JUMĀDĀ I 1602	28	29	1	2	3	4	5
	6	7	8	9	10	11	12
	13	14	15	16	17	18	19
	20	21	22	23	24	25	26
JUMĀDĀ II 1602	27	28	29	30	1	2	3
	4	5	6	7	8	9	10
	11	12	13	14	15	16	17
	18	19	20	21	22	23	24
RAJAB 1602	25	26	27	28	29	1	2
	3	4	5	6	7	8	9
	10	11	12	13	14	15	16
	17	18	19	20	21	22	23
SHA'BĀN 1602	24	25	26	27[d]	28	29	1
	2	3	4	5	6	7	8
	9	10	11	12	13	14	15
	16	17	18	19	20	21	22
	23	24	25	26	27	28	29
RAMAḌĀN 1602	30	1[e]	2	3	4	5	6
	7	8	9	10	11	12	13
	14	15	16	17	18	19	20
	21	22	23	24	25	26	27
SHAWWĀL 1602	28	29	30	1[f]	2	3	4
	5	6	7	8	9	10	11
	12	13	14	15	16	17	18
	19	20	21	22	23	24	25
DHU AL-QA'DA 1602	26	27	28	29	30	1	2
	3	4	5	6	7	8	9
	10	11	12	13	14	15	16
	17	18	19	20	21	22	23
DHU AL-ḤIJJA 1602	24	25	26	27	28	29	1
	2	3	4	5	6	7	8
	9	10[g]	11	12	13	14	15
	16	17	18	19	20	21	22
	23	24	25	26	27	28	29
MUḤARRAM 1603	30[d]	1[a]	2	3	4	5	6
	7	8	9	10[b]	11	12	13
	14	15	16	17	18	19	20
	21	22	23	24	25	26	27
ṢAFAR 1603	28	29	1	2	3	4	5
	6	7	8	9	10	11	12
	13	14	15	16	17	18	19
	20	21	22	23	24	25	26
	27	28	29	30	1	2	3

Julian† (Sun)	Sun	Mon	Tue	Wed	Thu	Fri	Sat	GREGORIAN 2176‡
Dec 17	31	1	2	3	4	5	6	JANUARY 2176
	7	8[a]	9	10	11	12	13	
Dec 31	14	15[b]	16	17	18	19	20	
	21	22	23	24	25	26	27	
Jan 14	28	29	30	31	1	2	3	FEBRUARY 2176
	4	5	6	7	8	9	10	
Jan 28	11	12	13	14[c]	15	16	17	
	18	19	20	21	22	23	24	
Feb 11	25	26	27	28	29	1	2	MARCH 2176
	3	4	5	6	7	8	9	
Feb 25	10	11	12	13	14	15	16	
	17	18	19	20	21	22	23	
Mar 10	24[d]	25	26	27	28	29	30	
	31[e]	1	2	3	4	5	6	APRIL 2176
Mar 24	7	8	9	10	11	12	13	
	14	15	16	17	18	19	20	
Apr 7	21	22	23	24	25	26	27	
	28	29	30	1	2	3	4	MAY 2176
Apr 21	5[f]	6	7	8	9	10	11	
	12	13	14	15	16	17	18	
May 5	19	20	21	22	23	24	25	
	26	27	28	29	30	31	1	JUNE 2176
May 19	2	3	4	5	6	7	8	
	9	10	11	12	13	14	15	
Jun 2	16	17	18	19	20	21	22	
	23	24	25	26	27	28	29	
Jun 16	30	1	2	3	4	5	6	JULY 2176
	7	8	9	10	11	12	13	
Jun 30	14	15	16	17	18	19	20	
	21	22	23	24	25	26	27	
Jul 14	28	29	30	31	1	2	3	AUGUST 2176
	4	5	6	7	8	9	10	
Jul 28	11	12	13	14	15	16	17	
	18	19	20	21	22	23	24	
Aug 11	25	26	27	28	29	30	31	
	1	2	3	4	5	6	7	SEPTEMBER 2176
Aug 25	8	9	10	11	12	13	14	
	15	16	17	18	19	20	21	
Sep 8	22	23	24	25	26	27	28	
	29	30	1	2	3	4	5	OCTOBER 2176
Sep 22	6	7	8	9	10	11	12	
	13	14	15	16	17	18	19	
Oct 6	20	21	22	23	24	25	26	
	27	28	29	30	31	1	2	NOVEMBER 2176
Oct 20	3	4	5	6	7	8	9	
	10	11	12	13	14	15	16	
Nov 3	17	18	19	20	21	22	23	
	24	25	26	27	28	29	30	
Nov 17	1[g]	2	3	4	5	6	7	DECEMBER 2176
	8	9	10	11	12	13	14	
Dec 1	15	16	17	18	19	20	21	
	22	23	24	25[h]	26	27	28	
Dec 15	29	30	31	1	2	3	4	

[a]New Year
[b]Sizdeh Bedar

‡Leap year
[a]New Year (Dhātṛi)
[b]Birthday of Rāma
[c]Birthday of Krishna
[d]Ganēśa Chaturthī
[e]Dashara
[f]Diwali
[g]Birthday of Vishnu
[h]Night of Śiva
[i]Holi

‡Leap year
[a]New Year (Khara)
[b]Pongal

[a]New Year
[d]New Year (Arithmetic)
[b]'Ashūrā'
[c]Prophet's Birthday
[d]Ascent of the Prophet
[e]Start of Ramaḍān
[f]'Id al-Fiṭr
[g]'Id al-'Aḍḥā

‡Leap year
[a]Orthodox Christmas
[b]Julian New Year
[c]Ash Wednesday
[d]Feast of Orthodoxy
[e]Easter
[f]Orthodox Easter
[g]Advent
[h]Christmas

2177

Gregorian 2177 (with Lunar Phases, ISO Week, Julian Day)

Month	Sun	Mon	Tue	Wed	Thu	Fri	Sat	Lunar Phases	ISO WEEK (Mon)	JULIAN DAY (Sun noon)
	29	30	●	1[a]	2	3	4	3:20	1	2516191
	5	6	7	◐	9	10	11	0:43	2	2516198
JANUARY 2177	12	13	○	15	16	17	18	15:57	3	2516205
	19	20	◑	22	23	24	25	17:12	4	2516212
	26	27	28	●	30	31	1	22:35	5	2516219
	2	3	4	5	◐	7	8	11:13	6	2516226
FEBRUARY 2177	9	10	11	12	○	14	15	3:34	7	2516233
	16	17	18	19	◑	21	22	12:45	8	2516240
	23	24	25	26	27	●	1	15:34	9	2516247
	2	3	4	5	6	◐	8	19:21	10	2516254
MARCH 2177	9	10	11	12	13	○	15	15:41	11	2516261
	16	17	18	19	20[b]	21	◑	9:19	12	2516268
	23	24	25	26	27	28	29		13	2516275
	●	31	1	2	3	4	5	5:20	14	2516282
	◐	7	8	9	10	11	12	2:07	15	2516289
APRIL 2177	○	14	15	16	17	18	19	4:26	16	2516296
	20	◑	22	23	24	25	26	5:02	17	2516303
	27	●	29	30	1	2	3	16:03	18	2516310
	4	◐	6	7	8	9	10	8:34	19	2516317
MAY 2177	11	○	13	14	15	16	17	18:07	20	2516324
	18	19	◑	21	22	23	24	22:16	21	2516331
	25	26	27	●	29	30	31	0:34	22	2516338
	1	2	◐	4	5	6	7	15:42	23	2516345
	8	9	10	○	12	13	14	8:50	24	2516352
JUNE 2177	15	16	17	18	◑	20[c]	21	12:12	25	2516359
	22	23	24	25	●	27	28	7:52	26	2516366
	29	30	1	2	◐	4	5	0:29	27	2516373
	6	7	8	9	10	○	12	0:16	28	2516380
JULY 2177	13	14	15	16	17	◑	19	22:58	29	2516387
	20	21	22	23	24	●	26	14:54	30	2516394
	27	28	29	30	31	◐	2	11:51	31	2516401
	3	4	5	6	7	8	○	15:40	32	2516408
AUGUST 2177	10	11	12	13	14	15	16		33	2516415
	◑	18	19	20	21	22	●	7:17 22:28	34	2516422
	24	25	26	27	28	29	30		35	2516429
	◐	1	2	3	4	5	6	2:26	36	2516436
	7	○	9	10	11	12	13	6:16	37	2516443
SEPTEMBER 2177	14	◑	16	17	18	19	20	14:08	38	2516450
	21	●[d]	23	24	25	26	27	7:27	39	2516457
	28	◐	30	1	2	3	4	20:15	40	2516464
	5	6	○	8	9	10	11	19:46	41	2516471
OCTOBER 2177	12	13	◑	15	16	17	18	20:33	42	2516478
	19	20	●	22	23	24	25	18:45	43	2516485
	26	27	28	◐	30	31	1	16:20	44	2516492
	2	3	4	5	○	7	8	8:19	45	2516499
NOVEMBER 2177	9	10	11	12	◑	14	15	3:36	46	2516506
	16	17	18	19	●	21	22	9:08	47	2516513
	23	24	25	26	27	◐	29	12:55	48	2516520
	30	1	2	3	4	○	6	20:16	49	2516527
	7	8	9	10	11	◑	13	12:14	50	2516534
DECEMBER 2177	14	15	16	17	18	19	●	2:39	51	2516541
	21[e]	22	23	24	25	26	27		52	2516548
	◐	29	30	31	1	2	3	8:07	1	2516555

Hebrew 5937/5938

ISO WEEK	Month	Sun	Mon	Tue	Wed	Thu	Fri	Sat	Molad
1		27[e]	28[e]	29[e]	1[e]	2[e]	3[e]	4	Tue 5h58m6p
2	TEVETH 5937	5	6	7	8	9	10	11	
3		12	13	14	15	16	17	18	
4		19	20	21	22	23	24	25	
5		26	27	28	29	1	2	3	Wed 18h42m7p
6		4	5	6	7	8	9	10	
7	SHEVAT 5937	11	12	13	14	15	16	17	
8		18	19	20	21	22	23	24	
9		25	26	27	28	29	30	1	Fri 7h26m8p
10		2	3	4	5	6	7	8	
11	ADAR 5937	9	10	11	12	13	14[f]	15	
12		16	17	18	19	20	21	22	
13		23	24	25	26	27	28	29	
14		1	2	3	4	5	6	7	Sat 20h10m9p
15		8	9	10	11*	12	13	14	
16	NISAN 5937	15[g]	16	17	18	19	20	21	
17		22	23	24	25	26	27	28	
18		29	30	1	2	3	4	5	Mon 8h54m10p
19		6	7	8	9	10	11	12	
20	IYYAR 5937	13	14	15	16	17	18	19	
21		20	21	22	23	24	25	26	
22		27	28	29	1	2	3	4	Tue 21h38m11p
23		5	6[h]	7	8	9	10	11	
24	SIVAN 5937	12	13	14	15	16	17	18	
25		19	20	21	22	23	24	25	
26		26	27	28	29	30	1	2	Thu 10h22m12p
27		3	4	5	6	7	8	9	
28	TAMMUZ 5937	10	11	12	13	14	15	16	
29		17	18	19	20	21	22	23	
30		24	25	26	27	28	29	1	Fri 23h6m13p
31		2	3	4	5	6	7	8	
32	AV 5937	9[i]	10	11	12	13	14	15	
33		16	17	18	19	20	21	22	
34		23	24	25	26	27	28	29	
35		30	1	2	3	4	5	6	Sun 11h50m14p
36		7	8	9	10	11	12	13	
37	ELUL 5937	14	15	16	17	18	19	20	
38		21	22	23	24	25	26	27	
39		28	29	1[a]	2[a]	3	4	5	Tue 0h34m15p
40		6	7	8	9	10[b]	11	12	
41	TISHRI 5938	13	14	15[c]	16	17	18	19	
42		20	21	22	23	24	25	26	
43		27	28	29	30	1	2	3	Wed 13h18m16p
44		4	5	6	7	8	9	10	
45	HESHVAN 5938	11	12	13	14	15	16	17	
46		18	19	20	21	22	23	24	
47		25	26	27	28	29	1	2	Fri 2h2m17p
48		3	4	5	6	7	8	9	
49	KISLEV 5938	10	11	12	13	14	15	16[d]	
50		17	18	19	20	21	22	23	
51		24	25[e]	26[e]	27[e]	28[e]	29[e]	30[e]	
52	TEVETH 5938	1[e]	2[e]	3	4	5	6	7	Sat 14h47m18p
1		8	9	10	11	12	13	14	

Chinese Bǐng-Zǐ/Dīng-Chǒu‡

ISO WEEK	Month	Sun	Mon	Tue	Wed	Thu	Fri	Sat	Solar Term
1		29	30	1	2	3	4	5	
2	MONTH 12 Bǐng-Zǐ	6	7	8	9	10	11	12	Xiǎo hán
3		13	14	15	16	17	18	19	
4		20	**21**	22	23	24	25	26	Dà hán
5		27	28	29	30	1[a]	2	3	
6		4	5	6	7	8	9*	10	Lì chūn
7	MONTH 1 Dīng-Chǒu	11	12	13	14	15[b]	16	17	
8		18	19	**20**	21	22	23	24	Yǔ shuǐ
9		25	26	27	28	29	1	2	
10		3	4	5	6	7	8	9	Jīng zhé
11	MONTH 2 Dīng-Chǒu	10	11	12	13	14	15	16	
12		17	18	19	20	**21**	22	23	Chūn fēn
13		24	25	26	27	28	29	30	
14		1	2	3	4	5	6[c]	7	Qīng míng
15		8	9	10*	11	12	13	14	
16	MONTH 3 Dīng-Chǒu	15	16	17	18	19	20	**21**	Gǔ yǔ
17		22	23	24	25	26	27	28	
18		29	30	1	2	3	4	5	
19		6	*7*	8	9	10	11	12	Lì xià
20	MONTH 4 Dīng-Chǒu	13	14	15	16	17	18	19	
21		20	21	**22**	23	24	25	26	Xiǎo mǎn
22		27	28	29	1	2	3	4	
23		5[d]	6	7	8	9	10	11*	Máng zhòng
24	MONTH 5 Dīng-Chǒu	12	13	14	15	16	17	18	
25		19	20	21	22	23	24	**25**	Xià zhì
26		26	27	28	29	1	2	3	
27		4	5	6	7	8	9	10	
28	MONTH 6 Dīng-Chǒu	*11*	12	13	14	15	16	17	Xiǎo shǔ
29		18	19	20	21	22	23	24	
30		25	26	**27**	28	29	1	2	Dà shǔ
31		3	4	5	6	7[e]	8	9	
32	MONTH 7 Dīng-Chǒu	10	11	12	13*	*14*	15[f]	16	Lì qiū
33		17	18	19	20	21	22	23	
34		24	25	26	27	28	**29**	30	Chǔ shǔ
35		1	2	3	4	5	6	7	
36	LEAP MONTH 7 Dīng-Chǒu	8	9	10	11	12	13	14	
37		*15*	16	17	18	19	20	21	Bái lù
38		22	23	24	25	26	27	28	
39		29	**1**	2	3	4	5	6	Qiū fēn
40		7	8	9	10	11	12	13	
41	MONTH 8 Dīng-Chǒu	14*	15[g]	16	*17*	18	19	20	Hán lù
42		21	22	23	24	25	26	27	
43		28	29	30	1	**2**	3	4	Shuāng jiàng
44		5	6	7	8	9[h]	10	11	
45	MONTH 9 Dīng-Chǒu	12	13	14	15	16	*17*	18	Lì dōng
46		19	20	21	22	23	24	25	
47		26	27	28	29	1	2	**3**	Xiǎo xuě
48		4	5	6	7	8	9	10	
49	MONTH 10 Dīng-Chǒu	11	12	13	14	15*	16	17	
50		*18*	19	20	21	22	23	24	Dà xuě
51		25	26	27	28	29	30	1	
52	MONTH 11 Dīng-Chǒu	2[i]	3	4	5	6	7	8	Dōng zhì
1		9	10	11	12	13	14	15	

Coptic 1893/1894 — Ethiopic 2169/2170

ISO WEEK	Coptic Month	Sun	Mon	Tue	Wed	Thu	Fri	Sat	Ethiopic Month
1	KOIAK 1893	19	20	21	22	23	24	25	TĀKHŚĀŚ 2169
2		26	27	28	29[c]	30	1	2	
3		3	4	5	6[d]	7	8	9	
4	TŌBE 1893	10	11[e]	12	13	14	15	16	ṬER 2169
5		17	18	19	20	21	22	23	
6		24	25	26	27	28	29	30	
7		1	2	3	4	5	6	7	
8		8	9	10	11	12	13	14	
9	MESHIR 1893	15	16	17	18	19	20	21	YAKĀTIT 2169
10		22	23	24	25	26	27	28	
11		29	30	1	2	3	4	5	
12		6	7	8	9	10	11	12	
13	PAREMOTEP 1893	13	14	15	16	17	18	19	MAGĀBIT 2169
14		20	21	22	23	24	25	26	
15		27	28	29	30	1	2	3	
16		4	5	6	7	8	9	10	
17	PARMOUTE 1893	11[f]	12	13	14	15	16	17	MIYĀZYĀ 2169
18		18	19	20	21	22	23	24	
19		25	26	27	28	29[g]	30	1	
20		2	3	4	5	6	7	8	
21	PASHONS 1893	9	10	11	12	13	14	15	GENBOT 2169
22		16	17	18	19	20	21	22	
23		23	24	25	26	27	28	29	
24		30	1	2	3	4	5	6	
25		7	8	9	10	11	12	13	
26	PAŌNE 1893	14	15	16	17	18	19	20	SANĒ 2169
27		21	22	23	24	25	26	27	
28		28	29	30	1	2	3	4	
29		5	6	7	8	9	10	11	
30	EPĒP 1893	12	13	14	15	16	17	18	ḤAMLĒ 2169
31		19	20	21	22	23	24	25	
32		26	27	28	29	30	1	2	
33		3	4	5	6	7	8	9	
34	MESORĒ 1893	10	11	12	13[h]	14	15	16	NAḤASĒ 2169
35		17	18	19	20	21	22	23	
36		24	25	26	27	28	29	30	
37	EPAG. 1893	1	2	3	4	5	1[a]	2	PĀG. 2169
38		3	4	5	6	7	8	9	
39	THOOUT 1894	10	11	12	13	14	15	16	MASKARAM 2170
40		17[b]	18	19	20	21	22	23	
41		24	25	26	27	28	29	30	
42		1	2	3	4	5	6	7	
43	PAOPE 1894	8	9	10	11	12	13	14	ṬEQEMT 2170
44		15	16	17	18	19	20	21	
45		22	23	24	25	26	27	28	
46		29	30	1	2	3	4	5	
47	ATHŌR 1894	6	7	8	9	10	11	12	ḪEDĀR 2170
48		13	14	15	16	17	18	19	
49		20	21	22	23	24	25	26	
50		27	28	29	30	1	2	3	
51	KOIAK 1894	4	5	6	7	8	9	10	TĀKHŚĀŚ 2170
52		11	12	13	14	15	16	17	
1		18	19	20	21	22	23	24	

[a]New Year
[b]Spring (5:00)
[c]Summer (19:47)
[d]Autumn (12:57)
[e]Winter (12:23)
● New moon
◐ First quarter moon
○ Full moon
◑ Last quarter moon

[a]New Year
[b]Yom Kippur
[c]Sukkot
[d]Winter starts
[e]Ḥanukkah
[f]Purim
[g]Passover
[h]Shavuot
[i]Fast of Av
*New solar cycle

‡Leap year
[a]New Year (4875, Ox)
[b]Lantern Festival
[c]Qīngmíng
[d]Dragon Festival
[e]Qīqiǎo
[f]Hungry Ghosts
[g]Mid-Autumn Festival
[h]Double-Ninth Festival
[i]Dōngzhì
*Start of 60-name cycle

[a]New Year
[b]Building of the Cross
[c]Christmas
[d]Jesus's Circumcision
[e]Epiphany
[f]Easter
[g]Mary's Announcement
[h]Jesus's Transfiguration

2177

PERSIAN (ASTRONOMICAL) 1555/1556‡

Month	Sun	Mon	Tue	Wed	Thu	Fri	Sat
DEY 1555	9	10	11	12	13	14	15
	16	17	18	19	20	21	22
	23	24	25	26	27	28	29
BAHMAN 1555	30	*1*	2	3	4	5	6
	7	8	9	10	11	12	13
	14	15	16	17	18	19	20
	21	22	23	24	25	26	27
ESFAND 1555	28	29	30	*1*	2	3	4
	5	6	7	8	9	10	11
	12	13	14	15	16	17	18
	19	20	21	22	23	24	25
FARVARDĪN 1556	26	27	28	29	*1*[a]	2	3
	4	5	6	7	8	9	10
	11	12	13[b]	14	15	16	17
	18	19	20	21	22	23	24
	25	26	27	28	29	30	31
ORDĪBEHEŠT 1556	*1*	2	3	4	5	6	7
	8	9	10	11	12	13	14
	15	16	17	18	19	20	21
	22	23	24	25	26	27	28
XORDĀD 1556	29	30	31	*1*	2	3	4
	5	6	7	8	9	10	11
	12	13	14	15	16	17	18
	19	20	21	22	23	24	25
TĪR 1556	26	27	28	29	30	31	*1*
	2	3	4	5	6	7	8
	9	10	11	12	13	14	15
	16	17	18	19	20	21	22
	23	24	25	26	27	28	29
MORDĀD 1556	30	31	*1*	2	3	4	5
	6	7	8	9	10	11	12
	13	14	15	16	17	18	19
	20	21	22	23	24	25	26
SHAHRĪVAR 1556	27	28	29	30	31	*1*	2
	3	4	5	6	7	8	9
	10	11	12	13	14	15	16
	17	18	19	20	21	22	23
	24	25	26	27	28	29	30
MEHR 1556	31	*1*	2	3	4	5	6
	7	8	9	10	11	12	13
	14	15	16	17	18	19	20
	21	22	23	24	25	26	27
ĀBĀN 1556	28	29	30	*1*	2	3	4
	5	6	7	8	9	10	11
	12	13	14	15	16	17	18
	19	20	21	22	23	24	25
ĀZAR 1556	26	27	28	29	30	*1*	2
	3	4	5	6	7	8	9
	10	11	12	13	14	15	16
	17	18	19	20	21	22	23
	24	25	26	27	28	29	30
DEY 1556	*1*	2	3	4	5	6	7
	8	9	10	11	12	13	14

‡Leap year
[a]New Year
[b]Sizdeh Bedar

HINDU LUNAR 2233/2234

Month	Sun	Mon	Tue	Wed	Thu	Fri	Sat
PAUSHA 2233	29	30	*30*	1	2	3	4
	5	6	7	8	9	10	**11**
	13	14	15	16	17	18	19
	20	21	22	23	24	25	26
MĀGHA 2233	27	28	29	30	1	2	3
	4	5	6	7	8	9	10
	11	12	13	14	15	**16**	18
	19	20	21	22	*22*	23	24
PHĀLGUNA 2233	25	26	27	28[h]	29	30	1
	2	3	4	5	6	7	8
	9	11	12	13	14	15[i]	16
	17	18	19	20	21	22	23
	24	25	*25*	26	27	28	29
CHAITRA 2234	30	1[a]	2	**3**	5	6	7
	8	9[b]	10	11	12	13	14
	15	16	17	18	19	20	21
	22	23	24	25	26	27	28
VAIŚĀKHA 2234	29	30	1	2	3	4	5
	6	**7**	9	10	11	12	13
	14	15	16	17	18	19	20
	20	21	22	23	24	25	26
JYAISHṬHA 2234	27	28	29	**30**	2	3	4
	5	6	7	8	9	10	11
	12	13	14	15	16	17	18
	19	20	21	22	23	24	25
ĀSHĀḌHA 2234	26	27	28	29	30	1	2
	3	5	6	7	8	9	10
	11	12	13	14	15	16	*16*
	17	18	19	20	21	22	23
ŚRĀVAṆA 2234	24	25	**26**	28	29	30	1
	2	3	4	5	6	7	8
	9	10	11	12	13	14	15
	16	17	18	19	20	21	22
	23[c]	24	25	26	27	28	**29**
BHĀDRAPADA 2234	1	2	3	4[d]	5	6	7
	8	9	10	11	12	13	*13*
	14	15	16	17	18	19	20
	21	**22**	24	25	26	27	28
ĀŚVINA 2234	29	30	1	2	3	4	5
	6	7	8[e]	9[e]	10[e]	11	12
	13	14	15	16	17	18	19
	20	21	22	23	24	**25**	27
KĀRTTIKA 2234	28	29	30	1[f]	2	3	4
	5	6	7	8	*8*	9	10
	11	12	13	14	15	16	17
	18	**19**	21	22	23	24	25
MĀRGAŚĪRA 2234	26	27	28	29	30	1	2
	3	4	5	6	7	8	9
	10	11[g]	12	13	14	15	16
	17	18	19	20	21	22	23
PAUSHA 2234	**24**	26	27	28	29	30	1
	1	2	3	4	5	6	7
	8	9	10	11	12	13	14

[a]New Year (Īśvara)
[b]Birthday of Rāma
[c]Birthday of Krishna
[d]Ganēśa Chaturthī
[e]Dashara
[f]Diwali
[g]Birthday of Vishnu
[h]Night of Śiva
[i]Holi

HINDU SOLAR 2098/2099

Month	Sun	Mon	Tue	Wed	Thu	Fri	Sat
PAUSHA 2098	12	13	14	15	16	17	18
	19	20	21	22	23	24	25
MĀGHA 2098	26	27	28	29	1[b]	2	3
	4	5	6	7	8	9	10
	11	12	13	14	15	16	17
	18	19	20	21	22	23	24
PHĀLGUNA 2098	25	26	27	28	29	30	1
	2	3	4	5	6	7	8
	9	10	11	12	13	14	15
	16	17	18	19	20	21	22
	23	24	25	26	27	28	29
CHAITRA 2098	1	2	3	4	5	6	7
	8	9	10	11	12	13	14
	15	16	17	18	19	20	21
	22	23	24	25	26	27	28
VAIŚĀKHA 2099	29	30	31	1[a]	2	3	4
	5	6	7	8	9	10	11
	12	13	14	15	16	17	18
	19	20	21	22	23	24	25
JYAISHṬHA 2099	26	27	28	29	30	31	1
	2	3	4	5	6	7	8
	9	10	11	12	13	14	15
	16	17	18	19	20	21	22
	23	24	25	26	27	28	29
ĀSHĀḌHA 2099	30	31	1	2	3	4	5
	6	7	8	9	10	11	12
	13	14	15	16	17	18	19
	20	21	22	23	24	25	26
ŚRĀVAṆA 2099	27	28	29	30	31	32	1
	2	3	4	5	6	7	8
	9	10	11	12	13	14	15
	16	17	18	19	20	21	22
	23	24	25	26	27	28	29
BHĀDRAPADA 2099	30	31	1	2	3	4	5
	6	7	8	9	10	11	12
	13	14	15	16	17	18	19
	20	21	22	23	24	25	26
ĀŚVINA 2099	27	28	29	30	31	1	2
	3	4	5	6	7	8	9
	10	11	12	13	14	15	16
	17	18	19	20	21	22	23
	24	25	26	27	28	29	30
KĀRTTIKA 2099	31	1	2	3	4	5	6
	7	8	9	10	11	12	13
	14	15	16	17	18	19	20
	21	22	23	24	25	26	27
MĀRGAŚĪRA 2099	28	29	30	1	2	3	4
	5	6	7	8	9	10	11
	12	13	14	15	16	17	18
	19	20	21	22	23	24	25
PAUSHA 2099	26	27	28	29	1	2	3
	4	5	6	7	8	9	10
	11	12	13	14	15	16	17

[a]New Year (Nandana)
[b]Pongal

ISLAMIC (ASTRONOMICAL) 1603/1604

Month	Sun	Mon	Tue	Wed	Thu	Fri	Sat
RABĪʿ I 1603	27	28	29	*30*	1	2	3
	4	5	6	7	8	9	10
	11	12[c]	13	14	15	16	17
	18	19	20	21	22	23	24
RABĪʿ II 1603	25	26	27	28	29	*1*	2
	3	4	5	6	7	8	9
	10	11	12	13	14	15	16
	17	18	19	20	21	22	23
	24	25	26	27	28	29	*30*
JUMĀDĀ I 1603	1	2	3	4	5	6	7
	8	9	10	11	12	13	14
	15	16	17	18	19	20	21
	22	23	24	25	26	27	28
JUMĀDĀ II 1603	29	*1*	2	3	4	5	6
	7	8	9	10	11	12	13
	14	15	16	17	18	19	20
	21	22	23	24	25	26	27
RAJAB 1603	28	29	*30*	1	2	3	4
	5	6	7	8	9	10	11
	12	13	14	15	16	17	18
	19	20	21	22	23	24	25
SHAʿBĀN 1603	26	27[d]	28	29	*1*	2	3
	4	5	6	7	8	9	10
	11	12	13	14	15	16	17
	18	19	20	21	22	23	24
RAMAḌĀN 1603	25	26	27	28	29	*1*[e]	2
	3	4	5	6	7	8	9
	10	11	12	13	14	15	16
	17	18	19	20	21	22	23
	24	25	26	27	28	29	30
SHAWWĀL 1603	*1*[f]	2	3	4	5	6	7
	8	9	10	11	12	13	14
	15	16	17	18	19	20	21
	22	23	24	25	26	27	28
DHU AL-QAʿDA 1603	29	*30*	1	2	3	4	5
	6	7	8	9	10	11	12
	13	14	15	16	17	18	19
	20	21	22	23	24	25	26
DHU AL-ḤIJJA 1603	27	28	29	*30*	1	2	3
	4	5	6	7	8	9	10[g]
	11	12	13	14	15	16	17
	18	19	20	21	22	23	24
MUḤARRAM 1604	25	26	27	28	29	*1*[a]	2
	3	4	5	6	7	8	9
	10[b]	11	12	13	14	15	16
	17	18	19	20	21	22	23
ṢAFAR 1604	24	25	26	27	28	29	1
	2	3	4	5	6	7	8
	9	10	11	12	13	14	15
	16	17	18	19	20	21	22
	23	24	25	26	27	28	29
RABĪʿ I 1604	30	*1*	2	3	4	5	6
	7	8	9	10	11	12	13

[a]New Year
[b]ʿAshūrāʾ
[c]Prophet's Birthday
[d]Ascent of the Prophet
[e]Start of Ramaḍān
[f]ʿĪd al-Fiṭr
[g]ʿĪd al-ʾAḍḥā

GREGORIAN 2177

Julian (Sun)	Month	Sun	Mon	Tue	Wed	Thu	Fri	Sat
Dec 15	JANUARY 2177	*29*	30	31	1	2	3	4
		5	6	7	8[a]	9	10	11
Dec 29		*12*	13	14	15[b]	16	17	18
		19	20	21	22	23	24	25
Jan 12	FEBRUARY 2177	*26*	27	28	29	30	31	1
		2	3	4	5	6	7	8
Jan 26		*9*	10	11	12	13	14	15
		16	17	18	19	20	21	22
Feb 9	MARCH 2177	*23*	24	25	26	27	28	1
		2	3	4	5[c]	6	7	8
Feb 23		*9*[d]	10	11	12	13	14	15
		16	17	18	19	20	21	22
Mar 9		*23*	24	25	26	27	28	29
	APRIL 2177	30	31	1	2	3	4	5
Mar 23		*6*	7	8	9	10	11	12
		13	14	15	16	17	18	19
Apr 6		*20*[e]	21	22	23	24	25	26
	MAY 2177	27	28	29	30	1	2	3
Apr 20		*4*	5	6	7	8	9	10
		11	12	13	14	15	16	17
May 4		*18*	19	20	21	22	23	24
		25	26	27	28	29	30	31
May 18	JUNE 2177	*1*	2	3	4	5	6	7
		8	9	10	11	12	13	14
Jun 1		*15*	16	17	18	19	20	21
		22	23	24	25	26	27	28
Jun 15	JULY 2177	*29*	30	1	2	3	4	5
		6	7	8	9	10	11	12
Jun 29		*13*	14	15	16	17	18	19
		20	21	22	23	24	25	26
Jul 13	AUGUST 2177	*27*	28	29	30	31	1	2
		3	4	5	6	7	8	9
Jul 27		*10*	11	12	13	14	15	16
		17	18	19	20	21	22	23
Aug 10		*24*	25	26	27	28	29	30
	SEPTEMBER 2177	31	1	2	3	4	5	6
Aug 24		*7*	8	9	10	11	12	13
		14	15	16	17	18	19	20
Sep 7		*21*	22	23	24	25	26	27
	OCTOBER 2177	28	29	30	1	2	3	4
Sep 21		*5*	6	7	8	9	10	11
		12	13	14	15	16	17	18
Oct 5		*19*	20	21	22	23	24	25
	NOVEMBER 2177	26	27	28	29	30	31	1
Oct 19		*2*	3	4	5	6	7	8
		9	10	11	12	13	14	15
Nov 2		*16*	17	18	19	20	21	22
		23	24	25	26	27	28	29
Nov 16	DECEMBER 2177	*30*[g]	1	2	3	4	5	6
		7	8	9	10	11	12	13
Nov 30		*14*	15	16	17	18	19	20
		21	22	23	24	25[h]	26	27
Dec 14		*28*	29	30	31	1	2	3

[a]Orthodox Christmas
[b]Julian New Year
[c]Ash Wednesday
[d]Feast of Orthodoxy
[e]Easter (also Orthodox)
[g]Advent
[h]Christmas

2178

Gregorian 2178	Sun	Mon	Tue	Wed	Thu	Fri	Sat	Lunar Phases	ISO Week (Mon)	Julian Day (Sun noon)	Hebrew 5938/5939‡	Sun	Mon	Tue	Wed	Thu	Fri	Sat	Molad	Chinese Dīng-Chǒu‡/Wù-Yín	Sun	Mon	Tue	Wed	Thu	Fri	Sat	Solar Term	Coptic 1894/1895‡	Sun	Mon	Tue	Wed	Thu	Fri	Sat	Ethiopic 2170/2171‡
January 2178	◐	29	30	31	1[a]	2	3	8:07	1	2516555	Teveth 5938	8	9	10	11	12	13	14		Month 11 Dīng-Chǒu	9	10	11	12	13	14	15		Koiak 1894	18	19	20	21	22	23	24	Tākhśāś 2170
	○	5	6	7	8	9	◑	7:45 23:21	2	2516562		15	16	17	18	19	20	21			16	17	18	19	20	21	22	Xiǎo hán		25	26	27	28	29[c]	30	1	
	11	12	13	14	15	16	17		3	2516569		22	23	24	25	26	27	28			23	24	25	26	27	28	29			2	3	4	5	6[d]	7	8	
	●	19	20	21	22	23	24	22:10	4	2516576	Shevat 5938	29	1	2	3	4	5	6	Mon 3h31m1p	Month 12 Dīng-Chǒu	30	1	2	3	4	5	6	Dà hán	Tōbe 1894	9	10	11[e]	12	13	14	15	Ṭer 2170
	25	26	◐	28	29	30	31	0:30	5	2516583		7	8	9	10	11	12	13			7	8	9	10	11	12	13			16	17	18	19	20	21	22	
February 2178	1	○	3	4	5	6	7	18:40	6	2516590		14	15	16	17	18	19	20			14	15*	16	17	18	19	20	Lì chūn		23	24	25	26	27	28	29	
	8	◑	10	11	12	13	14	13:26	7	2516597		21	22	23	24	25	26	27			21	22	23	24	25	26	27		Meshir 1894	30	1	2	3	4	5	6	Yakātit 2170
	15	16	●	18	19	20	21	17:42	8	2516604	Adar 5938	28	29	30	1	2	3	4	Tue 16h15m2p	Month 1 Wù-Yín	28	29	30	1[a]	2	3	4	Yǔ shuǐ		7	8	9	10	11	12	13	
	22	23	24	◐	26	27	28	13:29	9	2516611		5	6	7	8	9	10	11			5	6	7	8	9	10	11			14	15	16	17	18	19	20	
March 2178	1	2	3	○	5	6	7	4:57	10	2516618		12	13	14[f]	15	16	17	18			12	13	14	15[b]	16	17	18	Jīng zhé		21	22	23	24	25	26	27	
	8	9	10	◑	12	13	14	6:17	11	2516625		19	20	21	22	23	24	25			19	20	21	22	23	24	25		Paremotep 1894	28	29	30	1	2	3	4	Magābit 2170
	15	16	17	18	●	20[b]	21	11:22	12	2516632	Nisan 5938	26	27	28	29	1	2	3	Thu 4h59m3p	Month 2 Wù-Yín	26	27	28	29	1	2	3	Chūn fēn		5	6	7	8	9	10	11	
	22	23	24	25	◐	27	28	23:05	13	2516639		4	5	6	7	8	9	10			4	5	6	7	8	9	10			12	13	14	15	16	17	18	
	29	30	31	1	○	3	4	14:56	14	2516646		11	12	13	14	15[g]	16	17			11	12	13	14	15	16*	17[c]	Qīng míng		19	20	21	22	23	24	25	
April 2178	5	6	7	8	9	◑	11	0:52	15	2516653		18	19	20	21	22	23	24			18	19	20	21	22	23	24		Parmoute 1894	26	27	28	29	30	1	2	Miyāzyā 2170
	12	13	14	15	16	17	●	2:16	16	2516660	Iyyar 5938	25	26	27	28	29	30	1	Fri 17h43m4p	Month 3 Wù-Yín	25	26	27	28	29	30	1			3[f]	4	5	6	7	8	9	
	19	20	21	22	23	24	◐	5:56	17	2516667		2	3	4	5	6	7	8			2	3	4	5	6	7	8	Gǔ yǔ		10	11	12	13	14	15	16	
	26	27	28	29	30	1	○	1:17	18	2516674		9	10	11	12	13	14	15			9	10	11	12	13	14	15			17	18	19	20	21	22	23	
May 2178	3	4	5	6	7	8	◑	19:42	19	2516681		16	17	18	19	20	21	22			16	17	18	19	20	21	22	Lì xià		24	25	26	27	28	29[g]	30	
	10	11	12	13	14	15	16		20	2516688		23	24	25	26	27	28	29			23	24	25	26	27	28	29		Pashons 1894	1	2	3	4	5	6	7	Genbot 2170
	●	18	19	20	21	22	23	14:21	21	2516695	Sivan 5938	1	2	3	4	5	6[h]	7	Sun 6h27m5p	Month 4 Wù-Yín	1	2	3	4	5	6	7	Xiǎo mǎn		8	9	10	11	12	13	14	
	◐	25	26	27	28	29	30	11:10	22	2516702		8	9	10	11	12	13	14			8	9	10	11	12	13	14			15	16	17	18	19	20	21	
	○	1	2	3	4	5	6	12:46	23	2516709		15	16	17	18	19	20	21			15	16	17*	18	19	20	21	Máng zhòng		22	23	24	25	26	27	28	
June 2178	7	◑	9	10	11	12	13	13:26	24	2516716		22	23	24	25	26	27	28			22	23	24	25	26	27	28		Paōne 1894	29	30	1	2	3	4	5	Sanē 2170
	14	15	●	17	18	19	20	0:06	25	2516723	Tammuz 5938	29	30	1	2	3	4	5	Mon 19h11m6p	Month 5 Wù-Yín	29	30	1	2	3	4	5[d]			6	7	8	9	10	11	12	
	21[c]	◐	23	24	25	26	27	16:09	26	2516730		6	7	8	9	10	11	12			6	7	8	9	10	11	12	Xià zhì		13	14	15	16	17	18	19	
	28	29	○	1	2	3	4	1:48	27	2516737		13	14	15	16	17	18	19			13	14	15	16	17	18	19			20	21	22	23	24	25	26	
July 2178	5	6	7	◑	9	10	11	5:17	28	2516744		20	21	22	23	24	25	26			20	21	22	23	24	25	26	Xiǎo shǔ	Epēp 1894	27	28	29	30	1	2	3	Ḥamlē 2170
	12	13	14	●	16	17	18	8:10	29	2516751	Av 5938	27	28	29	1	2	3	4	Wed 7h55m7p	Month 6 Wù-Yín	27	28	29	1	2	3	4			4	5	6	7	8	9	10	
	19	20	◐	22	23	24	25	22:25	30	2516758		5	6	7	8	9[i]	10	11			5	6	7	8	9	10	11	Dà shǔ		11	12	13	14	15	16	17	
	26	27	28	○	30	31	1	16:18	31	2516765		12	13	14	15	16	17	18			12	13	14	15	16	17	18*			18	19	20	21	22	23	24	
August 2178	2	3	4	5	◑	7	8	19:00	32	2516772		19	20	21	22	23	24	25			19	20	21	22	23	24	25	Lì qiū	Mesorē 1894	25	26	27	28	29	30	1	Naḥasē 2170
	9	10	11	12	●	14	15	15:22	33	2516779	Elul 5938	26	27	28	29	30	1	2	Thu 20h39m8p	Month 7 Wù-Yín	26	27	28	29	1	2	3			2	3	4	5	6	7	8	
	16	17	18	19	◐	21	22	7:20	34	2516786		3	4	5	6	7	8	9			4	5	6	7[e]	8	9	10			9	10	11	12	13[h]	14	15	
	23	24	25	26	27	○	29	7:51	35	2516793		10	11	12	13	14	15	16			11	12	13	14	15[f]	16	17	Chǔ shǔ		16	17	18	19	20	21	22	
	30	31	1	2	3	4	◑	6:37	36	2516800		17	18	19	20	21	22	23			18	19	20	21	22	23	24			23	24	25	26	27	28	29	
September 2178	6	7	8	9	10	●	12	22:39	37	2516807	Tishri 5939	24	25	26	27	28	29	1[a]	Sat 9h23m9p	Month 8 Wù-Yín	25	26	27	28	29	30	1	Bái lù	Epag. 1894 / Thoout 1895	30	1	2	3	4	5	1[a]	Pāg. 2170 / Maskaram 2171
	13	14	15	16	17	◐	19	19:55	38	2516814		2[a]	3	4	5	6	7	8			2	3	4	5	6	7	8			2	3	4	5	6	7	8	
	20	21	22[d]	23	24	25	○	23:52	39	2516821		9	10[b]	11	12	13	14	15[c]			9	10	11	12	13	14	15[g]	Qiū fēn		9	10	11	12	13	14	15	
	27	28	29	30	1	2	3		40	2516828		16	17	18	19	20	21	22			16	17	18	19*	20	21	22			16	17[b]	18	19	20	21	22	
October 2178	◑	5	6	7	8	9	10	16:21	41	2516835		23	24	25	26	27	28	29			23	24	25	26	27	28	29	Hán lù		23	24	25	26	27	28	29	
	●	12	13	14	15	16	17	7:05	42	2516842	Heshvan 5939	30	1	2	3	4	5	6	Sun 22h7m10p	Month 9 Wù-Yín	1	2	3	4	5	6	7		Paope 1895	30	1	2	3	4	5	6	Ṭeqemt 2171
	◐	19	20	21	22	23	24	12:24	43	2516849		7	8	9	10	11	12	13			8	9[h]	10	11	12	13	14	Shuāng jiàng		7	8	9	10	11	12	13	
	25	○	27	28	29	30	31	15:51	44	2516856		14	15	16	17	18	19	20			15	16	17	18	19	20	21			14	15	16	17	18	19	20	
November 2178	1	2	◑	4	5	6	7	0:36	45	2516863		21	22	23	24	25	26	27			22	23	24	25	26	27	28	Lì dōng		21	22	23	24	25	26	27	
	8	●	10	11	12	13	14	17:42	46	2516870	Kislev 5939	28	29	30	1	2	3	4	Tue 10h51m11p	Month 10 Wù-Yín	29	30	1	2	3	4	5		Athōr 1895	28	29	30	1	2	3	4	Ḫedār 2171
	15	16	◐	18	19	20	21	8:04	47	2516877		5	6	7	8	9	10	11			6	7	8	9	10	11	12	Xiǎo xuě		5	6	7	8	9	10	11	
	22	23	24	○	26	27	28	7:15	48	2516884		12	13	14	15	16	17	18			13	14	15	16	17	18	19			12	13	14	15	16	17	18	
	29	30	1	◑	3	4	5	8:05	49	2516891		19	20	21	22	23	24	25[e]			20*	21	22	23	24	25	26			19	20	21	22	23	24	25	
December 2178	6	7	8	●	10	11	12	7:06	50	2516898	Teveth 5939	26[d,e]	27[e]	28[e]	29[e]	30[e]	1[e]	2[e]	Wed 23h35m12p	Month 11* Wù-Yín	27	28	29	1	2	3	4	Dà xuě	Koiak 1895	26	27	28	29	30	1	2	Tākhśāś 2171
	13	14	15	16	◐	18	19	5:29	51	2516905		3	4	5	6	7	8	9			5	6	7	8	9	10	11			3	4	5	6	7	8	9	
	20	21[e]	22	23	○	25	26	21:28	52	2516912		10	11	12	13	14	15	16			12	13	14[i]	15	16	17	18	Dōng zhì		10	11	12	13	14	15	16	
	27	28	29	30	◑	1	2	15:52	53	2516919		17	18	19	20	21	22	23			19	20	21	22	23	24	25			17	18	19	20	21	22	23	

[a]New Year
[b]Spring (10:48)
[c]Summer (1:31)
[d]Autumn (18:44)
[e]Winter (18:08)
● New moon
◐ First quarter moon
○ Full moon
◑ Last quarter moon

‡Leap year
[a]New Year
[b]Yom Kippur
[c]Sukkot
[d]Winter starts
[e]Ḥanukkah
[f]Purim
[g]Passover
[h]Shavuot
[i]Fast of Av

‡Leap year
[a]New Year (4876, Tiger)
[b]Lantern Festival
[c]Qīngmíng
[d]Dragon Festival
[e]Qīqiăo
[f]Hungry Ghosts
[g]Mid-Autumn Festival
[h]Double-Ninth Festival
[i]Dōngzhì
*Start of 60-name cycle

‡Leap year
[a]New Year
[b]Building of the Cross
[c]Christmas
[d]Jesus's Circumcision
[e]Epiphany
[f]Easter
[g]Mary's Announcement
[h]Jesus's Transfiguration

PERSIAN (ASTRONOMICAL) 1556‡/1557

Month	Sun	Mon	Tue	Wed	Thu	Fri	Sat
	8	9	10	11	12	13	14
DEY 1556	15	16	17	18	19	20	21
	22	23	24	25	26	27	28
	29	30	*1*	2	3	4	5
BAHMAN 1556	6	7	8	9	10	11	12
	13	14	15	16	17	18	19
	20	21	22	23	24	25	26
	27	28	29	30	*1*	2	3
	4	5	6	7	8	9	10
ESFAND 1556	11	12	13	14	15	16	17
	18	19	20	21	22	23	24
	25	26	27	28	29	30	*1*[a]
	2	3	4	5	6	7	8
FARVARDĪN 1557	9	10	11	12	13[b]	14	15
	16	17	18	19	20	21	22
	23	24	25	26	27	28	29
	30	31	*1*	2	3	4	5
	6	7	8	9	10	11	12
ORDĪBEHEŠT 1557	13	14	15	16	17	18	19
	20	21	22	23	24	25	26
	27	28	29	30	31	*1*	2
	3	4	5	6	7	8	9
XORDĀD 1557	10	11	12	13	14	15	16
	17	18	19	20	21	22	23
	24	25	26	27	28	29	30
	31	*1*	2	3	4	5	6
	7	8	9	10	11	12	13
TĪR 1557	14	15	16	17	18	19	20
	21	22	23	24	25	26	27
	28	29	30	31	*1*	2	3
	4	5	6	7	8	9	10
MORDĀD 1557	11	12	13	14	15	16	17
	18	19	20	21	22	23	24
	25	26	27	28	29	30	31
	1	2	3	4	5	6	7
	8	9	10	11	12	13	14
SHAHRĪVAR 1557	15	16	17	18	19	20	21
	22	23	24	25	26	27	28
	29	30	31	*1*	2	3	4
	5	6	7	8	9	10	11
MEHR 1557	12	13	14	15	16	17	18
	19	20	21	22	23	24	25
	26	27	28	29	30	*1*	2
	3	4	5	6	7	8	9
ABĀN 1557	10	11	12	13	14	15	16
	17	18	19	20	21	22	23
	24	25	26	27	28	29	30
	1	2	3	4	5	6	7
	8	9	10	11	12	13	14
ĀZAR 1557	15	16	17	18	19	20	21
	22	23	24	25	26	27	28
	29	30	*1*	2	3	4	5
DEY 1557	6	7	8	9	10	11	12

‡Leap year
[a]New Year
[b]Sizdeh Bedar

HINDU LUNAR 2234/2235‡

Month	Sun	Mon	Tue	Wed	Thu	Fri	Sat
	8	9	10	11	12	13	14
PAUSHA 2234	15	16	**17**	19	20	21	22
	23	24	25	26	27	28	29
	30	1	2	3	3	4	5
	6	7	8	9	10	11	**12**
MĀGHA 2234	14	15	16	17	18	19	20
	21	22	23	24	25	26	27
	28[h]	29	30	1	2	3	4
	5	6	7	8	9	10	11
PHĀLGUNA 2234	12	13	14	15[i]	16	**17**	19
	20	21	22	23	24	25	26
	26	27	28	29	30	1[a]	2
	3	4	5	6	7	8	9[b]
CHAITRA 2235	**10**	12	13	14	15	16	17
	18	19	20	21	22	23	24
	25	26	27	28	29	*29*	30
	1	2	**3**	5	6	7	8
VAIŚĀKHA 2235	9	10	11	12	13	14	15
	16	18	*18*	19	20	21	22
	23	24	25	26	27	28	29
	30	1	2	3	4	5	6
LEAP JYAISHTHA 2235	**7**	9	10	11	12	13	14
	15	16	17	18	19	20	21
	22	23	24	*24*	25	26	27
	28	29	**30**	2	3	4	5
	6	7	8	9	10	11	**12**
JYAISHTHA 2235	14	15	*15*	16	17	18	19
	20	21	22	23	24	25	26
	27	28	29	30	1	2	**3**
	5	6	7	8	9	10	11
ĀSHĀDHA 2235	12	13	14	15	16	17	18
	19	20	21	*21*	22	23	24
	25	27	28	29	30	1	2
	3	4	5	6	**7**	9	10
ŚRĀVAṆA 2235	11	12	*12*	13	14	15	16
	17	18	19	20	21	22	23[c]
	24	25	26	27	28	**29**	1
	2	3	4[d]	5	6	7	8
BHĀDRAPADA 2235	9	10	11	12	13	14	15
	16	17	*17*	18	19	20	**21**
	23	24	25	26	27	28	29
	30	1	2	3	4	5	6
ĀŚVINA 2235	7	8[e]	9[e]	10[e]	11	12	13
	14	15	16	17	18	19	20
	21	22	23	24	25	**26**	28
	29	30	1[f]	2	3	4	5
	6	7	8	9	10	11	*11*
KĀRTTIKA 2235	12	13	14	15	16	17	18
	19	**20**	22	23	24	25	26
	27	28	29	30	1	2	3
	4	5	6	7	8	9	10
MĀRGAŚĪRA 2235	11[g]	12	13	14	15	16	17
	18	19	20	21	22	23	24

‡Leap year
[a]New Year (Bahudhānya)
[b]Birthday of Rāma
[c]Birthday of Krishna
[d]Ganēśa Chaturthī
[e]Dashara
[f]Diwali
[g]Birthday of Vishnu
[h]Night of Śiva
[i]Holi

HINDU SOLAR 2099/2100

Month	Sun	Mon	Tue	Wed	Thu	Fri	Sat
	11	12	13	14	15	16	17
PAUSHA 2099	18	19	20	21	22	23	24
	25	26	27	28	29	1[b]	2
	3	4	5	6	7	8	9
MĀGHA 2099	10	11	12	13	14	15	16
	17	18	19	20	21	22	23
	24	25	26	27	28	29	30
	1	2	3	4	5	6	7
	8	9	10	11	12	13	14
PHĀLGUNA 2099	15	16	17	18	19	20	21
	22	23	24	25	26	27	28
	29	30	1	2	3	4	5
	6	7	8	9	10	11	12
CHAITRA 2099	13	14	15	16	17	18	19
	20	21	22	23	24	25	26
	27	28	29	30	1[a]	2	3
	4	5	6	7	8	9	10
VAIŚĀKHA 2100	11	12	13	14	15	16	17
	18	19	20	21	22	23	24
	25	26	27	28	29	30	31
	1	2	3	4	5	6	7
JYAISHṬHA 2100	8	9	10	11	12	13	14
	15	16	17	18	19	20	21
	22	23	24	25	26	27	28
	29	30	31	1	2	3	4
	5	6	7	8	9	10	11
ĀSHĀḌHA 2100	12	13	14	15	16	17	18
	19	20	21	22	23	24	25
	26	27	28	29	30	31	32
	1	2	3	4	5	6	7
ŚRĀVAṆA 2100	8	9	10	11	12	13	14
	15	16	17	18	19	20	21
	22	23	24	25	26	27	28
	29	30	31	32	1	2	3
	4	5	6	7	8	9	10
BHĀDRAPADA 2100	11	12	13	14	15	16	17
	18	19	20	21	22	23	24
	25	26	27	28	29	30	31
	1	2	3	4	5	6	7
	8	9	10	11	12	13	14
ĀŚVINA 2100	15	16	17	18	19	20	21
	22	23	24	25	26	27	28
	29	30	1	2	3	4	5
	6	7	8	9	10	11	12
KĀRTTIKA 2100	13	14	15	16	17	18	19
	20	21	22	23	24	25	26
	27	28	29	30	1	2	3
	4	5	6	7	8	9	10
MĀRGAŚĪRA 2100	11	12	13	14	15	16	17
	18	19	20	21	22	23	24
	25	26	27	28	29	1	2
PAUSHA 2100	3	4	5	6	7	8	9
	10	11	12	13	14	15	16

[a]New Year (Vijaya)
[b]Pongal

ISLAMIC (ASTRONOMICAL) 1604/1605‡

Month	Sun	Mon	Tue	Wed	Thu	Fri	Sat
	7	8	9	10	11	12[c]	13
RABĪ' I 1604	14	15	16	17	18	19	20
	21	22	23	24	25	26	27
	28	29	*1*	2	3	4	5
RABĪ' II 1604	6	7	8	9	10	11	12
	13	14	15	16	17	18	19
	20	21	22	23	24	25	26
	27	28	29	30	*1*	2	3
JUMĀDĀ I 1604	4	5	6	7	8	9	10
	11	12	13	14	15	16	17
	18	19	20	21	22	23	24
	25	26	27	28	29	30	*1*
JUMĀDĀ II 1604	2	3	4	5	6	7	8
	9	10	11	12	13	14	15
	16	17	18	19	20	21	22
	23	24	25	26	27	28	29
	1	2	3	4	5	6	7
	8	9	10	11	12	13	14
RAJAB 1604	15	16	17	18	19	20	21
	22	23	24	25	26	27[d]	28
	29	30	*1*	2	3	4	5
SHA'BĀN 1604	6	7	8	9	10	11	12
	13	14	15	16	17	18	19
	20	21	22	23	24	25	26
	27	28	29	*1*[e]	2	3	4
	5	6	7	8	9	10	11
RAMAḌĀN 1604	12	13	14	15	16	17	18
	19	20	21	22	23	24	25
	26	27	28	29	30	*1*[f]	2
SHAWWĀL 1604	3	4	5	6	7	8	9
	10	11	12	13	14	15	16
	17	18	19	20	21	22	23
	24	25	26	27	28	29	*30*
	1	2	3	4	5	6	7
	8	9	10	11	12	13	14
DHU AL-QA'DA 1604	15	16	17	18	19	20	21
	22	23	24	25	26	27	28
	29	*1*	2	3	4	5	6
	7	8	9	10[g]	11	12	13
DHU AL-ḤIJJA 1604	14	15	16	17	18	19	20
	21	22	23	24	25	26	27
	28	29	*1*[a]	2	3	4	5
	6	7	8	9	10[b]	11	12
MUḤARRAM 1605	13	14	15	16	17	18	19
	20	21	22	23	24	25	26
	27	28	29	1	2	3	4
	5	6	7	8	9	10	11
ṢAFAR 1605	12	13	14	15	16	17	18
	19	20	21	22	23	24	25
	26	27	28	29	30	*1*	2
	3	4	5	6	7	8	9
RABĪ' I 1605	10	11	12[c]	13	14	15	16
	17	18	19	20	21	22	23

‡Leap year
[a]New Year
[b]'Ashūrā'
[c]Prophet's Birthday
[d]Ascent of the Prophet
[e]Start of Ramaḍān
[f]'Id al-Fiṭr
[g]'Id al-'Aḍḥā

GREGORIAN 2178

Julian (Sun)	Sun	Mon	Tue	Wed	Thu	Fri	Sat	Month
Dec 14	*28*	29	30	31	1	2	3	
	4	5	6	7	8[a]	9	10	JANUARY 2178
Dec 28	*11*	12	13	14	15[b]	16	17	
	18	19	20	21	22	23	24	
Jan 11	*25*	26	27	28	29	30	31	
	1	2	3	4	5	6	7	
Jan 25	*8*	9	10	11	12	13	14	FEBRUARY 2178
	15	16	17	18[c]	19	20	21	
Feb 8	*22*	23	24	25	26	27	28	
	1[d]	2	3	4	5	6	7	
Feb 22	*8*	9	10	11	12	13	14	MARCH 2178
	15	16	17	18	19	20	21	
Mar 8	*22*	23	24	25	26	27	28	
	29	30	31	1	2	3	4	
Mar 22	*5*[e]	6	7	8	9	10	11	APRIL 2178
	12[f]	13	14	15	16	17	18	
Apr 5	*19*	20	21	22	23	24	25	
	26	27	28	29	30	1	2	
Apr 19	*3*	4	5	6	7	8	9	
	10	11	12	13	14	15	16	MAY 2178
May 3	*17*	18	19	20	21	22	23	
	24	25	26	27	28	29	30	
May 17	*31*	1	2	3	4	5	6	
	7	8	9	10	11	12	13	JUNE 2178
May 31	*14*	15	16	17	18	19	20	
	21	22	23	24	25	26	27	
Jun 14	*28*	29	30	1	2	3	4	
	5	6	7	8	9	10	11	
Jun 28	*12*	13	14	15	16	17	18	JULY 2178
	19	20	21	22	23	24	25	
Jul 12	*26*	27	28	29	30	31	1	
	2	3	4	5	6	7	8	
Jul 26	*9*	10	11	12	13	14	15	AUGUST 2178
	16	17	18	19	20	21	22	
Aug 9	*23*	24	25	26	27	28	29	
	30	31	1	2	3	4	5	
Aug 23	*6*	7	8	9	10	11	12	
	13	14	15	16	17	18	19	SEPTEMBER 2178
Sep 6	*20*	21	22	23	24	25	26	
	27	28	29	30	1	2	3	
Sep 20	*4*	5	6	7	8	9	10	
	11	12	13	14	15	16	17	OCTOBER 2178
Oct 4	*18*	19	20	21	22	23	24	
	25	26	27	28	29	30	31	
Oct 18	*1*	2	3	4	5	6	7	
	8	9	10	11	12	13	14	
Nov 1	*15*	16	17	18	19	20	21	NOVEMBER 2178
	22	23	24	25	26	27	28	
Nov 15	*29*[g]	30	1	2	3	4	5	
	6	7	8	9	10	11	12	
Nov 29	*13*	14	15	16	17	18	19	DECEMBER 2178
	20	21	22	23	24	25[h]	26	
Dec 13	*27*	28	29	30	31	1	2	

[a]Orthodox Christmas
[b]Julian New Year
[c]Ash Wednesday
[d]Feast of Orthodoxy
[e]Easter
[f]Orthodox Easter
[g]Advent
[h]Christmas

2179

GREGORIAN 2179 · ISO WEEK (Mon) · JULIAN DAY (Sun noon)

Month	Sun	Mon	Tue	Wed	Thu	Fri	Sat	Lunar Phases	ISO Week	Julian Day
JANUARY 2179	27	28	29	30	◑	1[a]	2	15:52	53	2516919
	3	4	5	6	●	8	9	23:10	1	2516926
	10	11	12	13	14	15	◐	2:43	2	2516933
	17	18	19	20	21	22	○	10:03	3	2516940
	24	25	26	27	28	29	◑	1:02	4	2516947
FEBRUARY 2179	31	1	2	3	4	5	●	17:04	5	2516954
	7	8	9	10	11	12	13		6	2516961
	◐	15	16	17	18	19	20	21:51	7	2516968
	○	22	23	24	25	26	27	20:52	8	2516975
MARCH 2179	◑	1	2	3	4	5	6	12:20	9	2516982
	7	●	9	10	11	12	13	11:30	10	2516989
	14	15	◐	17	18	19	20[b]	13:23	11	2516996
	21	22	○	24	25	26	27	6:18	12	2517003
APRIL 2179	28	29	◑	31	1	2	3	1:54	13	2517010
	4	5	6	●	8	9	10	5:14	14	2517017
	11	12	13	14	◐	16	17	0:45	15	2517024
	18	19	20	○	22	23	24	15:01	16	2517031
MAY 2179	25	26	27	◑	29	30	1	17:19	17	2517038
	2	3	4	5	●	7	8	21:16	18	2517045
	9	10	11	12	13	◐	15	8:25	19	2517052
	16	17	18	19	○	21	22	23:48	20	2517059
	23	24	25	26	27	◑	29	9:55	21	2517066
JUNE 2179	30	31	1	2	3	4	●	10:59	22	2517073
	6	7	8	9	10	11	◐	13:37	23	2517080
	13	14	15	16	17	18	○	9:22	24	2517087
	20	21[c]	22	23	24	25	26		25	2517094
JULY 2179	◑	28	29	30	1	2	3	3:08	26	2517101
	●	5	6	7	8	9	10	22:12	27	2517108
	◐	12	13	14	15	16	17	17:55	28	2517115
	○	19	20	21	22	23	24	20:18	29	2517122
	25	◑	27	28	29	30	31	20:20	30	2517129
AUGUST 2179	1	2	●	4	5	6	7	7:22	31	2517136
	8	◐	10	11	12	13	14	22:56	32	2517143
	15	16	○	18	19	20	21	9:05	33	2517150
	22	23	24	◑	26	27	28	12:48	34	2517157
SEPTEMBER 2179	29	30	31	●	2	3	4	15:23	35	2517164
	5	6	7	◐	9	10	11	6:06	36	2517171
	12	13	14	15	○	17	18	0:00	37	2517178
	19	20	21	22	23[d]	◑	25	3:46	38	2517185
OCTOBER 2179	26	27	28	29	●	1	2	23:20	39	2517192
	3	4	5	6	◐	8	9	16:30	40	2517199
	10	11	12	13	14	○	16	16:57	41	2517206
	17	18	19	20	21	22	◑	16:40	42	2517213
	24	25	26	27	28	29	●	8:16	43	2517220
NOVEMBER 2179	31	1	2	3	4	5	◐	6:44	44	2517227
	7	8	9	10	11	12	13		45	2517234
	○	15	16	17	18	19	20	11:05	46	2517241
	21	◑	23	24	25	26	27	3:27	47	2517248
DECEMBER 2179	●	29	30	1	2	3	4	18:48	48	2517255
	5	◐	7	8	9	10	11	0:45	49	2517262
	12	13	○	15	16	17	18	4:59	50	2517269
	19	20	◑	22[e]	23	24	25	12:31	51	2517276
	26	27	●	29	30	31	1	7:07	52	2517283

HEBREW 5939‡/5940

ISO Week	Month	Sun	Mon	Tue	Wed	Thu	Fri	Sat	Molad
53	TEVETH 5939	17	18	19	20	21	22	23	
1		24	25	26	27	28	29	1	Fri 12h19m13p
2	SHEVAT 5939	2	3	4	5	6	7	8	
3		9	10	11	12	13	14	15	
4		16	17	18	19	20	21	22	
5		23	24	25	26	27	28	29	
6	ADAR I 5939	30	1	2	3	4	5	6	Sun 1h3m14p
7		7	8	9	10	11	12	13	
8		14	15	16	17	18	19	20	
9		21	22	23	24	25	26	27	
10	ADAR II 5939	28	29	30	1	2	3	4	Mon 13h47m15p
11		5	6	7	8	9	10	11	
12		12	13	14[f]	15	16	17	18	
13		19	20	21	22	23	24	25	
14	NISAN 5939	26	27	28	29	1	2	3	Wed 2h31m16p
15		4	5	6	7	8	9	10	
16		11	12	13	14	15[g]	16	17	
17		18	19	20	21	22	23	24	
18	IYAR 5939	25	26	27	28	29	30	1	Thu 15h15m17p
19		2	3	4	5	6	7	8	
20		9	10	11	12	13	14	15	
21		16	17	18	19	20	21	22	
22		23	24	25	26	27	28	29	
23	SIVAN 5939	1	2	3	4	5	6[h]	7	Sat 4h0m0p
24		8	9	10	11	12	13	14	
25		15	16	17	18	19	20	21	
26		22	23	24	25	26	27	28	
27	TAMMUZ 5939	29	30	1	2	3	4	5	Sun 16h44m1p
28		6	7	8	9	10	11	12	
29		13	14	15	16	17	18	19	
30		20	21	22	23	24	25	26	
31	AV 5939	27	28	29	1	2	3	4	Tue 5h28m2p
32		5	6	7	8	9[i]	10	11	
33		12	13	14	15	16	17	18	
34		19	20	21	22	23	24	25	
35	ELUL 5939	26	27	28	29	30	1	2	Wed 18h12m3p
36		3	4	5	6	7	8	9	
37		10	11	12	13	14	15	16	
38		17	18	19	20	21	22	23	
39	TISHRI 5940	24	25	26	27	28	29	1[a]	Fri 6h56m4p
40		2[a]	3	4	5	6	7	8	
41		9	10[b]	11	12	13	14	15[c]	
42		16	17	18	19	20	21	22	
43		23	24	25	26	27	28	29	
44	HESHVAN 5940	30	1	2	3	4	5	6	Sat 19h40m5p
45		7	8	9	10	11	12	13	
46		14	15	16	17	18	19	20	
47		21	22	23	24	25	26	27	
48	KISLEV 5940	28	29	30	1	2	3	4	Mon 8h24m6p
49		5	6	7[d]	8	9	10	11	
50		12	13	14	15	16	17	18	
51		19	20	21	22	23	24	25[e]	
52		26[e]	27[e]	28[e]	29[e]	30[e]	1[e]	2[e]	Tue 21h8m7p

CHINESE Wù-Yín/Jǐ-Mǎo

ISO Week	Month	Sun	Mon	Tue	Wed	Thu	Fri	Sat	Solar Term
53	MONTH 11* Wù-Yín	19	20	21	22	23	24	25	
1	MONTH 12 Wù-Yín	26	27	28	29	30	1	2	Xiǎo hán
2		3	4	5	6	7	8	9	
3		10	11	12	13	14	15	16	Dà hán
4		17	18	19	20	21*	22	23	
5		24	25	26	27	28	29	30	Lì chūn
6	MONTH 1 Jǐ-Mǎo	1[a]	2	3	4	5	6	7	
7		8	9	10	11	12	13	14	Yǔ shuǐ
8		15[b]	16	17	18	19	20	21	
9		22	23	24	25	26	27	28	Jīng zhé
10	MONTH 2 Jǐ-Mǎo	29	1	2	3	4	5	6	
11		7	8	9	10	11	12	13	
12		14	15	16	17	18	19	20	Chūn fēn
13		21	22*	23	24	25	26	27	
14		28	29[c]	30	1	2	3	4	Qīng míng
15	MONTH 3 Jǐ-Mǎo	5	6	7	8	9	10	11	
16		12	13	14	15	16	17	18	Gǔ yǔ
17		19	20	21	22	23	24	25	
18		26	27	28	29	30	1	2	Lì xià
19	MONTH 4 Jǐ-Mǎo	3	4	5	6	7	8	9	
20		10	11	12	13	14	15	16	Xiǎo mǎn
21		17	18	19	20	21	22*	23	
22		24	25	26	27	28	29	1	Máng zhòng
23	MONTH 5 Jǐ-Mǎo	2	3	4	5[d]	6	7	8	
24		9	10	11	12	13	14	15	
25		16	17	18	19	20	21	22	Xià zhì
26		23	24	25	26	27	28	29	
27	MONTH 6 Jǐ-Mǎo	30	1	2	3	4	5	6	Xiǎo shǔ
28		7	8	9	10	11	12	13	
29		14	15	16	17	18	19	20	Dà shǔ
30		21	22	23*	24	25	26	27	
31	MONTH 7 Jǐ-Mǎo	28	29	1	2	3	4	5	Lì qiū
32		6	7[e]	8	9	10	11	12	
33		13	14	15[f]	16	17	18	19	
34		20	21	22	23	24	25	26	Chǔ shǔ
35	MONTH 8 Jǐ-Mǎo	27	28	29	1	2	3	4	
36		5	6	7	8	9	10	11	Bái lù
37		12	13	14	15[g]	16	17	18	
38		19	20	21	22	23	24	25*	Qiū fēn
39	MONTH 9 Jǐ-Mǎo	26	27	28	29	30	1	2	
40		3	4	5	6	7	8	9[h]	Hán lù
41		10	11	12	13	14	15	16	
42		17	18	19	20	21	22	23	Shuāng jiàng
43	MONTH 10 Jǐ-Mǎo	24	25	26	27	28	29	1	
44		2	3	4	5	6	7	8	Lì dōng
45		9	10	11	12	13	14	15	
46		16	17	18	19	20	21	22	Xiǎo xuě
47		23	24	25	26*	27	28	29	
48	MONTH 11 Jǐ-Mǎo	30	1	2	3	4	5	6	
49		7	8	9	10	11	12	13	Dà xuě
50		14	15	16	17	18	19	20	
51		21	22	23	24[i]	25	26	27	Dōng zhì
52		28	29	1	2	3	4	5	

COPTIC 1895‡/1896 · ETHIOPIC 2171‡/2172

ISO Week	Coptic Month	Sun	Mon	Tue	Wed	Thu	Fri	Sat	Ethiopic Month
53	KOIAK 1895	17	18	19	20	21	22	23	TĀKHŚĀŚ 2171
1		24	25	26	27	28	29[c]	30	
2	TŌBE 1895	1	2	3	4	5	6[d]	7	ṬER 2171
3		8	9	10	11[e]	12	13	14	
4		15	16	17	18	19	20	21	
5		22	23	24	25	26	27	28	
6	MESHIR 1895	29	30	1	2	3	4	5	YAKĀTIT 2171
7		6	7	8	9	10	11	12	
8		13	14	15	16	17	18	19	
9		20	21	22	23	24	25	26	
10	PAREMOTEP 1895	27	28	29	30	1	2	3	MAGĀBIT 2171
11		4	5	6	7	8	9	10	
12		11	12	13	14	15	16	17	
13		18	19	20	21	22	23	24	
14	PARMOUTE 1895	25	26	27	28	29	30	1	MIYĀZYĀ 2171
15		2	3	4	5	6	7	8	
16		9	10	11	12	13	14	15	
17		16	17	18	19	20	21	22	
18		23[f]	24	25	26	27	28	29[g]	
19	PASHONS 1895	30	1	2	3	4	5	6	GENBOT 2171
20		7	8	9	10	11	12	13	
21		14	15	16	17	18	19	20	
22		21	22	23	24	25	26	27	
23	PAŌNE 1895	28	29	30	1	2	3	4	SANĒ 2171
24		5	6	7	8	9	10	11	
25		12	13	14	15	16	17	18	
26		19	20	21	22	23	24	25	
27	EPĒP 1895	26	27	28	29	30	1	2	HAMLĒ 2171
28		3	4	5	6	7	8	9	
29		10	11	12	13	14	15	16	
30		17	18	19	20	21	22	23	
31		24	25	26	27	28	29	30	
32	MESORĒ 1895	1	2	3	4	5	6	7	NAḤASĒ 2171
33		8	9	10	11	12	13[h]	14	
34		15	16	17	18	19	20	21	
35		22	23	24	25	26	27	28	
36	EPAG. 1895	29	30	1	2	3	4	5	PĀG. 2171
37	THOOUT 1896	6	1[a]	2	3	4	5	6	MASKARAM 2172
38		7	8	9	10	11	12	13	
39		14	15	16	17[b]	18	19	20	
40		21	22	23	24	25	26	27	
41	PAOPE 1896	28	29	30	1	2	3	4	ṬEQEMT 2172
42		5	6	7	8	9	10	11	
43		12	13	14	15	16	17	18	
44		19	20	21	22	23	24	25	
45	ATHŌR 1896	26	27	28	29	30	1	2	HEDĀR 2172
46		3	4	5	6	7	8	9	
47		10	11	12	13	14	15	16	
48		17	18	19	20	21	22	23	
49		24	25	26	27	28	29	30	
50	KOIAK 1896	1	2	3	4	5	6	7	TĀKHŚĀŚ 2172
51		8	9	10	11	12	13	14	
52		15	16	17	18	19	20	21	

Gregorian notes:
[a]New Year
[b]Spring (16:30)
[c]Summer (7:27)
[d]Autumn (0:41)
[e]Winter (0:04)
● New moon
◐ First quarter moon
○ Full moon
◑ Last quarter moon

Hebrew notes:
‡Leap year
[a]New Year
[b]Yom Kippur
[c]Sukkot
[d]Winter starts
[e]Ḥanukkah
[f]Purim
[g]Passover
[h]Shavuot
[i]Fast of Av

Chinese notes:
[a]New Year (4877, Hare)
[b]Lantern Festival
[c]Qīngmíng
[d]Dragon Festival
[e]Qīqiǎo
[f]Hungry Ghosts
[g]Mid-Autumn Festival
[h]Double-Ninth Festival
[i]Dōngzhì
*Start of 60-name cycle

Coptic/Ethiopic notes:
‡Leap year
[a]New Year
[b]Building of the Cross
[c]Christmas
[d]Jesus's Circumcision
[e]Epiphany
[f]Easter
[g]Mary's Announcement
[h]Jesus's Transfiguration

PERSIAN (ASTRONOMICAL) 1557/1558								HINDU LUNAR 2235‡/2236								HINDU SOLAR 2100/2101‡								ISLAMIC (ASTRONOMICAL) 1605‡/1606‡								Julian (Sun)	GREGORIAN 2179							
	Sun	Mon	Tue	Wed	Thu	Fri	Sat		Sun	Mon	Tue	Wed	Thu	Fri	Sat		Sun	Mon	Tue	Wed	Thu	Fri	Sat		Sun	Mon	Tue	Wed	Thu	Fri	Sat		Sun	Mon	Tue	Wed	Thu	Fri	Sat	
	6	7	8	9	10	11	12	MĀRGAŚIRA 2235	18	19	20	21	22	23	24		10	11	12	13	14	15	16	RABĪ' I 1605	17	18	19	20	21	22	23	Dec 13	27	28	29	30	31	1	2	
DEY 1557	13	14	15	16	17	18	19		25	27	28	29	30	1	2	PAUSHA 2100	17	18	19	20	21	22	23		24	25	26	27	28	29	1		3	4	5	6	7	8[a]	9	
	20	21	22	23	24	25	26	PAUSHA 2235	3	3	4	5	6	7	8		24	25	26	27	28	29	30		2	3	4	5	6	7	8	Dec 27	10	11	12	13	14	15[b]	16	JANUARY 2179
	27	28	29	30	1	2	3		9	10	11	12	13	14	15		1[b]	2	3	4	5	6	7	RABĪ' II 1605	9	10	11	12	13	14	15		17	18	19	20	21	22	23	
	4	5	6	7	8	9	10		16	17	18	19	21	22	23		8	9	10	11	12	13	14		16	17	18	19	20	21	22	Jan 10	24	25	26	27	28	29	30	
BAHMAN 1557	11	12	13	14	15	16	17		24	25	26	27	28	29	30	MĀGHA 2100	15	16	17	18	19	20	21		23	24	25	26	27	28	29		31	1	2	3	4	5	6	
	18	19	20	21	22	23	24		1	2	3	4	5	5	6		22	23	24	25	26	27	28		30	1	2	3	4	5	6	Jan 24	7	8	9	10[c]	11	12	13	
	25	26	27	28	29	30	1		7	8	9	10	11	12	13		29	1	2	3	4	5	6		7	8	9	10	11	12	13		14	15	16	17	18	19	20	FEBRUARY 2179
	2	3	4	5	6	7	8	MĀGHA 2235	15	16	17	18	19	20	21		7	8	9	10	11	12	13	JUMĀDĀ I 1605	14	15	16	17	18	19	20	Feb 7	21	22	23	24	25	26	27	
ESFAND 1557	9	10	11	12	13	14	15		22	23	24	25	26	27	28[h]	PHĀLGUNA 2100	14	15	16	17	18	19	20		21	22	23	24	25	26	27		28	1	2	3	4	5	6	
	16	17	18	19	20	21	22		29	30	1	2	3	4	5		21	22	23	24	25	26	27		28	29	30	1	2	3	4	Feb 21	7	8	9	10	11	12	13	
	23	24	25	26	27	28	29		6	7	8	9	10	11	12		28	29	30	1	2	3	4		5	6	7	8	9	10	11		14	15	16	17	18	19	20	MARCH 2179
	1[a]	2	3	4	5	6	7	PHĀLGUNA 2235	13	14	15[i]	16	17	19	20		5	6	7	8	9	10	11	JUMĀDĀ II 1605	12	13	14	15	16	17	18	Mar 7	21[d]	22	23	24	25	26	27	
FARVARDĪN 1558	8	9	10	11	12	13[b]	14		21	22	23	24	25	26	27	CHAITRA 2100	12	13	14	15	16	17	18		19	20	21	22	23	24	25		28[e]	29	30	31	1	2	3	
	15	16	17	18	19	20	21		28	29	29	30	1[a]	2	3		19	20	21	22	23	24	25		26	27	28	29	30	1	2	Mar 21	4	5	6	7	8	9	10	
	22	23	24	25	26	27	28		4	5	6	7	8	9[b]	10		26	27	28	29	30	1[a]	2		3	4	5	6	7	8	9		11	12	13	14	15	16	17	APRIL 2179
	29	30	31	1	2	3	4	CHAITRA 2236	11	13	14	15	16	17	18		3	4	5	6	7	8	9	RAJAB 1605	10	11	12	13	14	15	16	Apr 4	18	19	20	21	22	23	24	
	5	6	7	8	9	10	11		19	20	21	22	23	24	25	VAIŚĀKHA 2101	10	11	12	13	14	15	16		17	18	19	20	21	22	23		25	26	27	28	29	30	1	
ORDĪBEHEŠT 1558	12	13	14	15	16	17	18		26	27	28	29	30	1	2		17	18	19	20	21	22	23		24	25	26	27[d]	28	29	1	Apr 18	2[f]	3	4	5	6	7	8	
	19	20	21	22	23	24	25		3	4	5	6	7	8	9		24	25	26	27	28	29	30		2	3	4	5	6	7	8		9	10	11	12	13	14	15	
	26	27	28	29	30	31	1	VAIŚĀKHA 2236	10	11	12	13	14	15	17		31	1	2	3	4	5	6	SHA'BĀN 1605	9	10	11	12	13	14	15	May 2	16	17	18	19	20	21	22	MAY 2179
	2	3	4	5	6	7	8		18	19	20	21	22	23	24	JYAISHṬHA 2101	7	8	9	10	11	12	13		16	17	18	19	20	21	22		23	24	25	26	27	28	29	
XORDĀD 1558	9	10	11	12	13	14	15		24	25	26	27	28	29	30		14	15	16	17	18	19	20		23	24	25	26	27	28	29	May 16	30	31	1	2	3	4	5	
	16	17	18	19	20	21	22		1	2	3	4	5	6	7		21	22	23	24	25	26	27		30	1[e]	2	3	4	5	6		6	7	8	9	10	11	12	
	23	24	25	26	27	28	29		9	10	11	12	13	14	15		28	29	30	31	32	1	2	RAMAḌĀN 1605	7	8	9	10	11	12	13	May 30	13	14	15	16	17	18	19	JUNE 2179
	30	31	1	2	3	4	5	JYAISHṬHA 2236	16	17	18	19	20	21	22		3	4	5	6	7	8	9		14	15	16	17	18	19	20		20	21	22	23	24	25	26	
	6	7	8	9	10	11	12		23	24	25	26	27	28	29	ĀSHĀḌHA 2101	10	11	12	13	14	15	16		21	22	23	24	25	26	27	Jun 13	27	28	29	30	1	2	3	
TĪR 1558	13	14	15	16	17	18	19		30	1	2	3	4	5	6		17	18	19	20	21	22	23		28	29	30	1[f]	2	3	4		4	5	6	7	8	9	10	
	20	21	22	23	24	25	26	ĀSHĀḌHA 2236	7	8	9	10	12	13	14		24	25	26	27	28	29	30	SHAWWĀL 1605	5	6	7	8	9	10	11	Jun 27	11	12	13	14	15	16	17	JULY 2179
	27	28	29	30	31	1	2		15	16	17	18	19	20	21		31	1	2	3	4	5	6		12	13	14	15	16	17	18		18	19	20	21	22	23	24	
	3	4	5	6	7	8	9		21	22	23	24	25	26	27	ŚRĀVAṆA 2101	7	8	9	10	11	12	13		19	20	21	22	23	24	25	Jul 11	25	26	27	28	29	30	31	
MORDĀD 1558	10	11	12	13	14	15	16		28	29	30	1	2	3	5		14	15	16	17	18	19	20		26	27	28	29	1	2	3		1	2	3	4	5	6	7	
	17	18	19	20	21	22	23	ŚRĀVAṆA 2236	6	7	8	9	10	11	12		21	22	23	24	25	26	27	DHU AL-QA'DA 1605	4	5	6	7	8	9	10	Jul 25	8	9	10	11	12	13	14	AUGUST 2179
	24	25	26	27	28	29	30		13	14	15	16	17	18	19		28	29	30	31	32	1	2		11	12	13	14	15	16	17		15	16	17	18	19	20	21	
	31	1	2	3	4	5	6		20	21	22	23[c]	24	25	26	BHĀDRAPADA 2101	3	4	5	6	7	8	9		18	19	20	21	22	23	24	Aug 8	22	23	24	25	26	27	28	
SHAHRĪVAR 1558	7	8	9	10	11	12	13	BHĀDRAPADA 2236	27	28	29	30	1	2	3		10	11	12	13	14	15	16		25	26	27	28	29	30	1		29	30	31	1	2	3	4	
	14	15	16	17	18	19	20		4[d]	5	6	8	9	10	11		17	18	19	20	21	22	23	DHU AL-ḤIJJA 1605	2	3	4	5	6	7	8	Aug 22	5	6	7	8	9	10	11	SEPTEMBER 2179
	21	22	23	24	25	26	27		12	13	14	15	16	17	17		24	25	26	27	28	29	30		9	10[g]	11	12	13	14	15		12	13	14	15	16	17	18	
	28	29	30	31	1	2	3		18	19	20	21	22	23	24		31	1	2	3	4	5	6		16	17	18	19	20	21	22	Sep 5	19	20	21	22	23	24	25	
	4	5	6	7	8	9	10		25	26	27	28	29	1	2	ĀŚVINA 2101	7	8	9	10	11	12	13		23	24	25	26	27	28	29[d]		26	27	28	29	30	1	2	
MEHR 1558	11	12	13	14	15	16	17	ĀŚVINA 2236	3	4	5	6	7	8[e]	9[e]		14	15	16	17	18	19	20		1[a]	2	3	4	5	6	7	Sep 19	3	4	5	6	7	8	9	OCTOBER 2179
	18	19	20	21	22	23	24		10[e]	11	12	13	14	15	16		21	22	23	24	25	26	27	MUḤARRAM 1606	8	9	10[b]	11	12	13	14		10	11	12	13	14	15	16	
	25	26	27	28	29	30	1		17	18	19	20	21	22	23		28	29	30	1	2	3	4		15	16	17	18	19	20	21	Oct 3	17	18	19	20	21	22	23	
	2	3	4	5	6	7	8		24	25	26	27	28	29	30	KĀRTTIKA 2101	5	6	7	8	9	10	11		22	23	24	25	26	27	28		24	25	26	27	28	29	30	
ĀBĀN 1558	9	10	11	12	13	14	15		1[f]	2	3	5	6	7	8		12	13	14	15	16	17	18		29	1	2	3	4	5	6	Oct 17	31	1	2	3	4	5	6	
	16	17	18	19	20	21	22	KĀRTTIKA 2236	9	10	11	11	12	13	14		19	20	21	22	23	24	25	ṢAFAR 1606	7	8	9	10	11	12	13		7	8	9	10	11	12	13	NOVEMBER 2179
	23	24	25	26	27	28	29		15	16	17	18	19	20	21		26	27	28	29	30	1	2		14	15	16	17	18	19	20	Oct 31	14	15	16	17	18	19	20	
	30	1	2	3	4	5	6		22	23	24	25	26	27	29	MĀRGAŚIRA 2101	3	4	5	6	7	8	9		21	22	23	24	25	26	27		21	22	23	24	25	26	27	
	7	8	9	10	11	12	13		30	1	2	3	4	5	6		10	11	12	13	14	15	16		28	29	1	2	3	4	5	Nov 14	28[g]	29	30	1	2	3	4	
ĀZAR 1558	14	15	16	17	18	19	20	MĀRGAŚIRA 2236	7	8	9	10	11[g]	12	13		17	18	19	20	21	22	23	RABĪ' I 1606	6	7	8	9	10	11	12[c]		5	6	7	8	9	10	11	DECEMBER 2179
	21	22	23	24	25	26	27		14	14	15	16	17	18	19		24	25	26	27	28	29	30		13	14	15	16	17	18	19	Nov 28	12	13	14	15	16	17	18	
	28	29	30	1	2	3	4		20	21	23	24	25	26	27	PAUSHA 2101	1	2	3	4	5	6	7		20	21	22	23	24	25	26		19	20	21	22	23	24	25[h]	
DEY 1558	5	6	7	8	9	10	11		28	29	30	1	2	3	4		8	9	10	11	12	13	14		27	28	29	30	1	2	3	Dec 12	26	27	28	29	30	31	1	

[a]New Year
[b]Sizdeh Bedar

‡Leap year
[a]New Year (Pramāthin)
[b]Birthday of Rāma
[c]Birthday of Krishna
[d]Ganēśa Chaturthī
[e]Dashara
[f]Diwali
[g]Birthday of Vishnu
[h]Night of Śiva
[i]Holi

‡Leap year
[a]New Year (Jaya)
[b]Pongal

‡Leap year
[a]New Year
[d]New Year (Arithmetic)
[b]'Āshūrā'
[c]Prophet's Birthday
[d]Ascent of the Prophet
[e]Start of Ramaḍān
[f]'Id al-Fiṭr
[g]'Id al-'Aḍḥā

[a]Orthodox Christmas
[b]Julian New Year
[c]Ash Wednesday
[d]Feast of Orthodoxy
[e]Easter
[f]Orthodox Easter
[g]Advent
[h]Christmas

2180

Gregorian 2180‡	Sun	Mon	Tue	Wed	Thu	Fri	Sat	Lunar Phases	ISO Week (Mon)	Julian Day (Sun noon)	Hebrew 5940/5941	Sun	Mon	Tue	Wed	Thu	Fri	Sat	Molad
January 2180	26	27	●	29	30	31	1[a]	7:07	52	2517283	Teveth 5940	26[e]	27[e]	28[e]	29[e]	30[e]	1[e]	2[e]	Tue 21h8m7p
	2	3	◐	5	6	7	8	21:43	1	2517290		3	4	5	6	7	8	9	
	9	10	11	○	13	14	15	21:09	2	2517297		10	11	12	13	14	15	16	
	16	17	18	◑	20	21	22	20:41	3	2517304		17	18	19	20	21	22	23	
	23	24	25	●	27	28	29	21:05	4	2517311	Shevat 5940	24	25	26	27	28	29	1	Thu 9h52m8p
February 2180	30	31	1	2	◐	4	5	19:47	5	2517318		2	3	4	5	6	7	8	
	6	7	8	9	10	○	12	10:50	6	2517325		9	10	11	12	13	14	15	
	13	14	15	16	17	◑	19	4:48	7	2517332		16	17	18	19	20	21	22	
	20	21	22	23	24	●	26	12:31	8	2517339		23	24	25	26	27	28	29	
March 2180	27	28	29	1	2	3	◐	16:34	9	2517346	Adar 5940	30	1	2	3	4	5	6	Fri 22h36m9p
	5	6	7	8	9	10	○	22:09	10	2517353		7	8	9	10	11	12	13	
	12	13	14	15	16	17	◑	13:37	11	2517360		14[f]	15	16	17	18	19	20	
	19[b]	20	21	22	23	24	25		12	2517367		21	22	23	24	25	26	27	
April 2180	●	27	28	29	30	31	1	5:06	13	2517374	Nisan 5940	28	29	1	2	3	4	5	Sun 11h20m10p
	2	◐	4	5	6	7	8	10:01	14	2517381		6	7	8	9	10	11	12	
	9	○	11	12	13	14	15	7:37	15	2517388		13	14	15[g]	16	17	18	19	
	◑	17	18	19	20	21	22	23:40	16	2517395		20	21	22	23	24	25	26	
	23	●	25	26	27	28	29	22:09	17	2517402	Iyyar 5940	27	28	29	30	1	2	3	Tue 0h4m11p
May 2180	30	1	◐	3	4	5	6	23:19	18	2517409		4	5	6	7	8	9	10	
	7	8	○	10	11	12	13	15:53	19	2517416		11	12	13	14	15	16	17	
	14	15	◑	17	18	19	20	11:23	20	2517423		18	19	20	21	22	23	24	
	21	22	23	●	25	26	27	14:37	21	2517430	Sivan 5940	25	26	27	28	29	1	2	Wed 12h48m12p
June 2180	28	29	30	31	◐	2	3	8:46	22	2517437		3	4	5	6[h]	7	8	9	
	4	5	6	○	8	9	10	23:35	23	2517444		10	11	12	13	14	15	16	
	11	12	13	14	◑	16	17	1:07	24	2517451		17	18	19	20	21	22	23	
	18	19	20[c]	21	22	●	24	5:26	25	2517458		24	25	26	27	28	29	30	
July 2180	25	26	27	28	29	◐	1	15:25	26	2517465	Tammuz 5940	1	2	3	4	5	6	7	Fri 1h32m13p
	2	3	4	5	6	○	8	7:28	27	2517472		8	9	10	11	12	13	14	
	9	10	11	12	13	◑	15	16:56	28	2517479		15	16	17	18	19	20	21	
	16	17	18	19	20	21	●	18:10	29	2517486		22	23	24	25	26	27	28	
	23	24	25	26	27	28	◐	20:33	30	2517493	Av 5940	29	1	2	3	4	5	6	Sat 14h16m14p
August 2180	30	31	1	2	3	4	○	16:25	31	2517500		7	8	9[i]	10	11	12	13	
	6	7	8	9	10	11	12		32	2517507		14	15	16	17	18	19	20	
	◑	14	15	16	17	18	19	10:26	33	2517514		21	22	23	24	25	26	27	
	20	●	22	23	24	25	26	5:04	34	2517521	Elul 5940	28	29	30	1	2	3	4	Mon 3h0m15p
September 2180	27	◐	29	30	31	1	2	1:29	35	2517528		5	6	7	8	9	10	11	
	3	○	5	6	7	8	9	3:31	36	2517535		12	13	14	15	16	17	18	
	10	11	◑	13	14	15	16	4:39	37	2517542		19	20	21	22	23	24	25	
	17	18	●	20	21	22[d]	23	14:56	38	2517549	Tishri 5941	26	27	28	29	1[a]	2[a]	3	Tue 15h44m16p
	24	25	◐	27	28	29	30	7:32	39	2517556		4	5	6	7	8	9	10[b]	
October 2180	1	2	○	4	5	6	7	17:35	40	2517563		11	12	13	14	15[c]	16	17	
	8	9	10	◑	12	13	14	22:22	41	2517570		18	19	20	21	22	23	24	
	15	16	17	18	●	20	21	0:35	42	2517577	Heshvan 5941	25	26	27	28	29	30	1	Thu 4h28m17p
	22	23	24	◐	26	27	28	15:55	43	2517584		2	3	4	5	6	7	8	
November 2180	29	30	31	1	○	3	4	10:41	44	2517591		9	10	11	12	13	14	15	
	5	6	7	8	9	◑	11	14:34	45	2517598		16	17	18	19	20	21	22	
	12	13	14	15	16	●	18	10:34	46	2517605		23	24	25	26	27	28	29	
	19	20	21	22	23	◐	25	3:44	47	2517612	Kislev 5941	1	2	3	4	5	6	7	Fri 17h13m0p
December 2180	26	27	28	29	30	1	○	5:47	48	2517619		8	9	10	11	12	13	14	
	3	4	5	6	7	8	9		49	2517626		15	16	17	18[d]	19	20	21	
	◑	11	12	13	14	15	●	4:38 21:05	50	2517633		22	23	24	25[e]	26[e]	27[e]	28[e]	
	17	18	19	20	21[e]	22	◐	19:31	51	2517640	Teveth 5941	29[e]	30[e]	1[e]	2[e]	3	4	5	Sun 5h57m1p
	24	25	26	27	28	29	30		52	2517647		6	7	8	9	10	11	12	
	31	○	2	3	4	5	6	1:02	1	2517654		13	14	15	16	17	18	19	

ISO Week	Chinese Jǐ-Mǎo/Gēng-Chén‡	Sun	Mon	Tue	Wed	Thu	Fri	Sat	Solar Term	Coptic 1896/1897	Sun	Mon	Tue	Wed	Thu	Fri	Sat	Ethiopic 2172/2173
52	Month 12 Jǐ-Mǎo	28	29	1	2	3	4	5		Koiak 1896	15	16	17	18	19	20	21	Tākhśāś 2172
1		6	7	8	9	*10*	11	12	Xiǎo hán		22	23	24	25	26	27	28	
2		13	14	15	16	17	18	19		Tōbe 1896	29[c]	30	1	2	3	4	5	Ṭer 2172
3		20	21	22	23	**24**	25	26	Dà hán		6[d]	7	8	9	10	11[e]	12	
4	Month 1 Gēng-Chén	27*	28	29	30	1[a]	2	3			13	14	15	16	17	18	19	
5		4	5	6	7	8	*9*	10	Lì chūn		20	21	22	23	24	25	26	
6		11	12	13	14	15[b]	16	17		Meshir 1896	27	28	29	30	1	2	3	Yakātit 2172
7		18	19	20	21	22	23	**24**	Yǔ shuǐ		4	5	6	7	8	9	10	
8	Month 2 Gēng-Chén	25	26	27	28	29	1	2			11	12	13	14	15	16	17	
9		3	4	5	6	7	8	9			18	19	20	21	22	23	24	
10		*10*	11	12	13	14	15	16	Jīng zhé	Paremotep 1896	25	26	27	28	29	30	1	Magābit 2172
11		17	18	19	20	21	22	23			2	3	4	5	6	7	8	
12		24	**25**	26	27	28*	29	30	Chūn fēn		9	10	11	12	13	14	15	
13	Month 3 Gēng-Chén	1	2	3	4	5	6	7			16	17	18	19	20	21	22	
14		8	9	10[c]	11	12	13	14	Qīng míng		23	24	25	26	27	28	29	
15		15	16	17	18	19	20	21		Parmoute 1896	30	1	2	3	4	5	6	Miyāzyā 2172
16		22	23	24	**25**	26	27	28	Gǔ yǔ		7[f]	8	9	10	11	12	13	
17	Month 4 Gēng-Chén	29	30	1	2	3	4	5			14	15	16	17	18	19	20	
18		6	7	8	9	10	*11*	12	Lì xià		21	22	23	24	25	26	27	
19		13	14	15	16	17	18	19		Pashons 1896	28	29[g]	30	1	2	3	4	Genbot 2172
20		20	21	22	23	24	25	**26**	Xiǎo mǎn		5	6	7	8	9	10	11	
21	Month 5 Gēng-Chén	27	28*	29	1	2	3	4			12	13	14	15	16	17	18	
22		5[d]	6	7	8	9	10	11			19	20	21	22	23	24	25	
23		12	*13*	14	15	16	17	18	Máng zhòng	Paōne 1896	26	27	28	29	30	1	2	Sanē 2172
24		19	20	21	22	23	24	25			3	4	5	6	7	8	9	
25	Month 6 Gēng-Chén	26	27	**28**	29	30	1	2	Xià zhì		10	11	12	13	14	15	16	
26		3	4	5	6	7	8	9			17	18	19	20	21	22	23	
27		10	11	12	13	*14*	15	16	Xiǎo shǔ		24	25	26	27	28	29	30	
28		17	18	19	20	21	22	23		Epēp 1896	1	2	3	4	5	6	7	Hamlē 2172
29		24	25	26	27	28	29*	**30**	Dà shǔ		8	9	10	11	12	13	14	
30	Leap Month 6 Gēng-Chén	1	2	3	4	5	6	7			15	16	17	18	19	20	21	
31		8	9	10	11	12	13	14			22	23	24	25	26	27	28	
32		15	*16*	17	18	19	20	21	Lì qiū	Mesorē 1896	29	30	1	2	3	4	5	Naḥasē 2172
33		22	23	24	25	26	27	28			6	7	8	9	10	11	12	
34	Month 7 Gēng-Chén	29	1	**2**	3	4	5	6	Chǔ shǔ		13[h]	14	15	16	17	18	19	
35		7[e]	8	9	10	11	12	13			20	21	22	23	24	25	26	
36		14	15[f]	16	17	*18*	19	20	Bái lù	Epag. 1896	27	28	29	30	1	2	3	Pāg. 2172
37		21	22	23	24	25	26	27		Thoout 1897	4	5	1[a]	2	3	4	5	Maskaram 2173
38	Month 8 Gēng-Chén	28	29	1*	2	3	**4**	5	Qiū fēn		6	7	8	9	10	11	12	
39		6	7	8	9	10	11	12			13	14	15	16	17[b]	18	19	
40		13	14	15[g]	16	17	18	*19*	Hán lù		20	21	22	23	24	25	26	
41		20	21	22	23	24	25	26		Paope 1897	27	28	29	30	1	2	3	Ṭeqemt 2173
42	Month 9 Gēng-Chén	27	28	29	30	1	2	3			4	5	6	7	8	9	10	
43		4	**5**	6	7	8	9[h]	10	Shuāng jiàng		11	12	13	14	15	16	17	
44		11	12	13	14	15	16	17			18	19	20	21	22	23	24	
45		18	19	*20*	21	22	23	24	Lì dōng	Athōr 1897	25	26	27	28	29	30	1	Hedār 2173
46	Month 10 Gēng-Chén	25	26	27	28	29	1	2*			2	3	4	5	6	7	8	
47		3	4	**5**	6	7	8	9	Xiǎo xuě		9	10	11	12	13	14	15	
48		10	11	12	13	14	15	16			16	17	18	19	20	21	22	
49		17	18	19	*20*	21	22	23	Dà xuě		23	24	25	26	27	28	29	
50		24	25	26	27	28	29	30		Koiak 1897	30	1	2	3	4	5	6	Tākhśāś 2173
51	Month 11 Gēng-Chén	1	2	3	4	5[i]	6	7	Dōng zhì		7	8	9	10	11	12	13	
52		8	9	10	11	12	13	14			14	15	16	17	18	19	20	
1		15	16	17	18	19	*20*	21	Xiǎo hán		21	22	23	24	25	26	27	

‡Leap year
[a]New Year
[b]Spring (22:25)
[c]Summer (13:22)
[d]Autumn (6:20)
[e]Winter (5:46)
● New moon
◐ First quarter moon
○ Full moon
◑ Last quarter moon

[a]New Year
[b]Yom Kippur
[c]Sukkot
[d]Winter starts
[e]Hanukkah
[f]Purim
[g]Passover
[h]Shavuot
[i]Fast of Av

‡Leap year
[a]New Year (4878, Dragon)
[b]Lantern Festival
[c]Qīngmíng
[d]Dragon Festival
[e]Qǐqiǎo
[f]Hungry Ghosts
[g]Mid-Autumn Festival
[h]Double-Ninth Festival
[i]Dōngzhì
*Start of 60-name cycle

[a]New Year
[b]Building of the Cross
[c]Christmas
[d]Jesus's Circumcision
[e]Epiphany
[f]Easter
[g]Mary's Announcement
[h]Jesus's Transfiguration

PERSIAN (ASTRONOMICAL) 1558/1559

Month	Sun	Mon	Tue	Wed	Thu	Fri	Sat
DEY 1558	5	6	7	8	9	10	11
	12	13	14	15	16	17	18
	19	20	21	22	23	24	25
BAHMAN 1558	26	27	28	29	30	1	2
	3	4	5	6	7	8	9
	10	11	12	13	14	15	16
	17	18	19	20	21	22	23
	24	25	26	27	28	29	30
ESFAND 1558	1	2	3	4	5	6	7
	8	9	10	11	12	13	14
	15	16	17	18	19	20	21
	22	23	24	25	26	27	28
FARVARDĪN 1559	29	1[a]	2	3	4	5	6
	7	8	9	10	11	12	13[b]
	14	15	16	17	18	19	20
	21	22	23	24	25	26	27
ORDĪBEHEŠT 1559	28	29	30	31	1	2	3
	4	5	6	7	8	9	10
	11	12	13	14	15	16	17
	18	19	20	21	22	23	24
	25	26	27	28	29	30	31
XORDĀD 1559	1	2	3	4	5	6	7
	8	9	10	11	12	13	14
	15	16	17	18	19	20	21
	22	23	24	25	26	27	28
TĪR 1559	29	30	31	1	2	3	4
	5	6	7	8	9	10	11
	12	13	14	15	16	17	18
	19	20	21	22	23	24	25
MORDĀD 1559	26	27	28	29	30	31	1
	2	3	4	5	6	7	8
	9	10	11	12	13	14	15
	16	17	18	19	20	21	22
	23	24	25	26	27	28	29
SHAHRĪVAR 1559	30	31	1	2	3	4	5
	6	7	8	9	10	11	12
	13	14	15	16	17	18	19
	20	21	22	23	24	25	26
MEHR 1559	27	28	29	30	31	1	2
	3	4	5	6	7	8	9
	10	11	12	13	14	15	16
	17	18	19	20	21	22	23
	24	25	26	27	28	29	30
ĀBĀN 1559	1	2	3	4	5	6	7
	8	9	10	11	12	13	14
	15	16	17	18	19	20	21
	22	23	24	25	26	27	28
ĀZAR 1559	29	30	1	2	3	4	5
	6	7	8	9	10	11	12
	13	14	15	16	17	18	19
	20	21	22	23	24	25	26
DEY 1559	27	28	29	30	1	2	3
	4	5	6	7	8	9	10
	11	12	13	14	15	16	17

[a]New Year
[b]Sizdeh Bedar

HINDU LUNAR 2236/2237‡

Month	Sun	Mon	Tue	Wed	Thu	Fri	Sat
PAUSHA 2236	28	29	30	1	2	3	4
	5	6	7	8	9	10	11
	12	13	14	15	16	17	18
	19	20	21	22	23	24	25
MĀGHA 2236	26	28	29	30	1	2	3
	4	5	6	6	7	8	9
	10	11	12	13	14	15	16
	17	18	19	20	22	23	24
PHĀLGUNA 2236	25	26	27	28[h]	29	30	1
	2	3	4	5	6	7	8
	8	9	10	11	12	13	15[i]
	16	17	18	19	20	21	22
	23	24	25	26	27	28	29
CHAITRA 2237	30	1[a]	2	3	4	5	6
	7	8	9[b]	10	11	12	13
	14	15	16	17	18	20	21
	22	23	24	25	26	27	28
VAIŚĀKHA 2237	29	30	1	2	2	3	4
	5	6	7	8	9	10	11
	13	14	15	16	17	18	19
	20	21	22	23	24	25	26
JYAIṢṬHA 2237	27	28	29	30	1	2	3
	4	5	6	7	8	9	10
	11	12	13	14	16	17	18
	19	20	21	22	23	24	25
ĀSHĀḌHA 2237	26	27	28	28	29	30	1
	2	3	4	5	6	7	9
	10	11	12	13	14	15	16
	17	18	19	20	21	22	23
	24	25	26	27	28	29	30
ŚRĀVAṆA 2237	1	2	3	4	5	6	7
	8	9	10	12	13	14	15
	16	17	18	19	20	21	22
	23[c]	24	25	25	26	27	28
BHĀDRAPADA 2237	29	30	1	2	3[d]	5	6
	7	8	9	10	11	12	13
	14	15	16	17	18	19	20
	21	22	23	24	25	26	27
LEAP ĀŚVINA 2237	28	29	30	1	2	3	4
	5	6	8	9	10	11	12
	13	14	15	16	17	18	19
	20	20	21	22	23	24	25
ĀŚVINA 2237	26	27	28	29	30	2	3
	4	5	6	7	8[e]	9[e]	10[e]
	11	12	13	14	15	16	17
	18	19	20	21	22	23	24
KĀRTTIKA 2237	25	26	27	28	29	30	1[f]
	2	3	4	6	7	8	9
	10	11	12	13	14	14	15
	16	17	18	19	20	21	22
	23	24	25	26	27	28	30
MĀRGAŚĪRA 2237	1	2	3	4	5	6	7
	8	9	10	11[g]	12	13	14
	15	16	17	17	18	19	20

‡Leap year
[a]New Year (Vikrama)
[b]Birthday of Rāma
[c]Birthday of Krishna
[d]Ganēśa Chaturthī
[e]Dashara
[f]Diwali
[g]Birthday of Vishnu
[h]Night of Śiva
[i]Holi

HINDU SOLAR 2101‡/2102

Month	Sun	Mon	Tue	Wed	Thu	Fri	Sat
PAUSHA 2101	8	9	10	11	12	13	14
	15	16	17	18	19	20	21
	22	23	24	25	26	27	28
MĀGHA 2101	29	1[b]	2	3	4	5	6
	7	8	9	10	11	12	13
	14	15	16	17	18	19	20
	21	22	23	24	25	26	27
PHĀLGUNA 2101	28	29	1	2	3	4	5
	6	7	8	9	10	11	12
	13	14	15	16	17	18	19
	20	21	22	23	24	25	26
CHAITRA 2101	27	28	29	30	1	2	3
	4	5	6	7	8	9	10
	11	12	13	14	15	16	17
	18	19	20	21	22	23	24
	25	26	27	28	29	30	31
VAIŚĀKHA 2102	1[a]	2	3	4	5	6	7
	8	9	10	11	12	13	14
	15	16	17	18	19	20	21
	22	23	24	25	26	27	28
JYAIṢṬHA 2102	29	30	31	1	2	3	4
	5	6	7	8	9	10	11
	12	13	14	15	16	17	18
	19	20	21	22	23	24	25
ĀSHĀḌHA 2102	26	27	28	29	30	31	1
	2	3	4	5	6	7	8
	9	10	11	12	13	14	15
	16	17	18	19	20	21	22
	23	24	25	26	27	28	29
ŚRĀVAṆA 2102	30	31	32	1	2	3	4
	5	6	7	8	9	10	11
	12	13	14	15	16	17	18
	19	20	21	22	23	24	25
BHĀDRAPADA 2102	26	27	28	29	30	31	1
	2	3	4	5	6	7	8
	9	10	11	12	13	14	15
	16	17	18	19	20	21	22
	23	24	25	26	27	28	29
ĀŚVINA 2102	30	31	1	2	3	4	5
	6	7	8	9	10	11	12
	13	14	15	16	17	18	19
	20	21	22	23	24	25	26
KĀRTTIKA 2102	27	28	29	30	1	2	3
	4	5	6	7	8	9	10
	11	12	13	14	15	16	17
	18	19	20	21	22	23	24
MĀRGAŚĪRA 2102	25	26	27	28	29	30	1
	2	3	4	5	6	7	8
	9	10	11	12	13	14	15
	16	17	18	19	20	21	22
	23	24	25	26	27	28	29
PAUSHA 2102	30	1	2	3	4	5	6
	7	8	9	10	11	12	13
	14	15	16	17	18	19	20

‡Leap year
[a]New Year (Manmatha)
[b]Pongal

ISLAMIC (ASTRONOMICAL) 1606‡/1607

Month	Sun	Mon	Tue	Wed	Thu	Fri	Sat
RABĪ' II 1606	27	28	29	30	1	2	3
	4	5	6	7	8	9	10
	11	12	13	14	15	16	17
	18	19	20	21	22	23	24
JUMĀDĀ I 1606	25	26	27	28	29	1	2
	3	4	5	6	7	8	9
	10	11	12	13	14	15	16
	17	18	19	20	21	22	23
	24	25	26	27	28	29	30
JUMĀDĀ II 1606	1	2	3	4	5	6	7
	8	9	10	11	12	13	14
	15	16	17	18	19	20	21
	22	23	24	25	26	27	28
RAJAB 1606	29	30	1	2	3	4	5
	6	7	8	9	10	11	12
	13	14	15	16	17	18	19
	20	21	22	23	24	25	26
SHA'BĀN 1606	27[d]	28	29	1	2	3	4
	5	6	7	8	9	10	11
	12	13	14	15	16	17	18
	19	20	21	22	23	24	25
RAMAḌĀN 1606	26	27	28	29	30	1[e]	2
	3	4	5	6	7	8	9
	10	11	12	13	14	15	16
	17	18	19	20	21	22	23
	24	25	26	27	28	29	30
SHAWWĀL 1606	1[f]	2	3	4	5	6	7
	8	9	10	11	12	13	14
	15	16	17	18	19	20	21
	22	23	24	25	26	27	28
DHU AL-QA'DA 1606	29	30	1	2	3	4	5
	6	7	8	9	10	11	12
	13	14	15	16	17	18	19
	20	21	22	23	24	25	26
DHU AL-ḤIJJA 1606	27	28	29	1	2	3	4
	5	6	7	8	9	10[g]	11
	12	13	14	15	16	17	18
	19	20	21	22	23	24	25
MUḤARRAM 1607	26	27	28	29	30[a]	1[a]	2
	3	4	5	6	7	8	9
	10[b]	11	12	13	14	15	16
	17	18	19	20	21	22	23
ṢAFAR 1607	24	25	26	27	28	29	1
	2	3	4	5	6	7	8
	9	10	11	12	13	14	15
	16	17	18	19	20	21	22
	23	24	25	26	27	28	29
RABĪ' I 1607	1	2	3	4	5	6	7
	8	9	10	11	12[c]	13	14
	15	16	17	18	19	20	21
	22	23	24	25	26	27	28
RABĪ' II 1607	29	1	2	3	4	5	6
	7	8	9	10	11	12	13
	14	15	16	17	18	19	20

‡Leap year
[a]New Year
[a]New Year (Arithmetic)
[b]'Ashūrā'
[c]Prophet's Birthday
[d]Ascent of the Prophet
[e]Start of Ramaḍān
[f]'Id al-Fiṭr
[g]'Id al-'Aḍḥā

GREGORIAN 2180‡

Julian† (Sun)	Sun	Mon	Tue	Wed	Thu	Fri	Sat	Month
Dec 12	26	27	28	29	30	31	1	JANUARY 2180
	2	3	4	5	6	7	8[a]	
Dec 26	9	10	11	12	13	14	15[b]	
	16	17	18	19	20	21	22	
Jan 9	23	24	25	26	27	28	29	
	30	31	1	2	3	4	5	FEBRUARY 2180
Jan 23	6	7	8	9	10	11	12	
	13	14	15	16	17	18	19	
Feb 6	20	21	22	23	24	25	26	
	27	28	29	1[c]	2	3	4	MARCH 2180
Feb 20	5[d]	6	7	8	9	10	11	
	12	13	14	15	16	17	18	
Mar 5	19	20	21	22	23	24	25	
	26	27	28	29	30	31	1	APRIL 2180
Mar 19	2	3	4	5	6	7	8	
	9	10	11	12	13	14	15	
Apr 2	16[e]	17	18	19	20	21	22	
	23	24	25	26	27	28	29	
Apr 16	30	1	2	3	4	5	6	MAY 2180
	7	8	9	10	11	12	13	
Apr 30	14	15	16	17	18	19	20	
	21	22	23	24	25	26	27	
May 14	28	29	30	31	1	2	3	JUNE 2180
	4	5	6	7	8	9	10	
May 28	11	12	13	14	15	16	17	
	18	19	20	21	22	23	24	
Jun 11	25	26	27	28	29	30	1	JULY 2180
	2	3	4	5	6	7	8	
Jun 25	9	10	11	12	13	14	15	
	16	17	18	19	20	21	22	
Jul 9	23	24	25	26	27	28	29	
	30	31	1	2	3	4	5	AUGUST 2180
Jul 23	6	7	8	9	10	11	12	
	13	14	15	16	17	18	19	
Aug 6	20	21	22	23	24	25	26	
	27	28	29	30	31	1	2	SEPTEMBER 2180
Aug 20	3	4	5	6	7	8	9	
	10	11	12	13	14	15	16	
Sep 3	17	18	19	20	21	22	23	
	24	25	26	27	28	29	30	
Sep 17	1	2	3	4	5	6	7	OCTOBER 2180
	8	9	10	11	12	13	14	
Oct 1	15	16	17	18	19	20	21	
	22	23	24	25	26	27	28	
Oct 15	29	30	31	1	2	3	4	NOVEMBER 2180
	5	6	7	8	9	10	11	
Oct 29	12	13	14	15	16	17	18	
	19	20	21	22	23	24	25	
Nov 12	26	27	28	29	30	1	2	DECEMBER 2180
	3[g]	4	5	6	7	8	9	
Nov 26	10	11	12	13	14	15	16	
	17	18	19	20	21	22	23	
Dec 10	24	25[h]	26	27	28	29	30	
	31	1	2	3	4	5	6	

‡Leap year
[a]Orthodox Christmas
[b]Julian New Year
[c]Ash Wednesday
[d]Feast of Orthodoxy
[e]Easter (also Orthodox)
[g]Advent
[h]Christmas

Month	Gregorian 2181 (Sun Mon Tue Wed Thu Fri Sat)	Lunar Phases	ISO Week (Mon)	Julian Day (Sun noon)	Hebrew month	Hebrew 5941/5942‡ (Sun Mon Tue Wed Thu Fri Sat)	Molad	Chinese month	Chinese Gēng-Chén‡/Xīn-Sì (Sun Mon Tue Wed Thu Fri Sat)	Solar Term	Coptic month	Coptic 1897/1898 – Ethiopic 2173/2174 (Sun Mon Tue Wed Thu Fri Sat)	Ethiopic month
January 2181	31 | ○[a] 2 3 4 5 6	1:02	1	2517654	Teveth 5941	13 14 15 16 17 18 19		Month 11 Gēng-Chén	15 16 17 18 19 20 21	Xiǎo hán	Koiak 1897	21 22 23 24 25 26 27	Tākhśāś 2173
	7 ◑ 9 10 11 12 13	16:20	2	2517661		20 21 22 23 24 25 26			22 23 24 25 26 27 28			28 29[c] 30 | 1 2 3 4	
	14 ● 16 17 18 19 20	8:13	3	2517668		27 28 29 | 1 2 3 4	Mon 18h41m2p	Month 12 Gēng-Chén	29 | 1 2 3* 4 5 6	Dà hán	Tōbe 1897	5 6[d] 7 8 9 10 11[e]	Ṭer 2173
	21 ◐ 23 24 25 26 27	14:51	4	2517675	Shevat 5941	5 6 7 8 9 10 11			7 8 9 10 11 12 13			12 13 14 15 16 17 18	
	28 29 ○ 31 | 1 2 3	18:43	5	2517682		12 13 14 15 16 17 18			14 15 16 17 18 19 20	Lì chūn		19 20 21 22 23 24 25	
February 2181	4 5 6 ◑ 8 9 10	1:45	6	2517689		19 20 21 22 23 24 25			21 22 23 24 25 26 27			26 27 28 29 30 | 1 2	
	11 12 ● 14 15 16 17	20:10	7	2517696		26 27 28 29 30 | 1 2	Wed 7h25m3p	Month 1 Xīn-Sì	28 29 30 | 1[a] 2 3 4		Meshir 1897	3 4 5 6 7 8 9	Yakātit 2173
	18 19 20 ◐ 22 23 24	12:04	8	2517703	Adar 5941	3 4 5 6 7 8 9			5 6 7 8 9 10 11	Yǔ shuǐ		10 11 12 13 14 15 16	
	25 26 27 28 | ○ 2 3	9:55	9	2517710		10 11 12 13 14[f] 15 16			12 13 14 15[b] 16 17 18			17 18 19 20 21 22 23	
March 2181	4 5 6 7 ◑ 9 10	9:25	10	2517717		17 18 19 20 21 22 23			19 20 21 22 23 24 25	Jīng zhé		24 25 26 27 28 29 30	
	11 12 13 14 ● 16 17	9:16	11	2517724		24 25 26 27 28 29 | 1	Thu 20h9m4p	Month 2 Xīn-Sì	26 27 28 29 | 1 2 3		Paremotep 1897	1 2 3 4 5 6 7	Magābit 2173
	18 19 20[b] 21 22 ◐ 24	8:54	12	2517731	Nisan 5941	2 3 4 5 6 7 8			4* 5 6 7 8 9 10	Chūn fēn		8 9 10 11 12 13 14	
	25 26 27 28 29 ○ 31	22:28	13	2517738		9 10 11 12 13 14 15[g]			11 12 13 14 15 16 17			15 16 17 18 19 20 21	
April 2181	1 2 3 4 5 ◑ 7	16:12	14	2517745		16 17 18 19 20 21 22			18 19 20 21[c] 22 23 24	Qīng míng		22 23 24 25 26 27 28	
	8 9 10 11 12 ● 14	23:42	15	2517752		23 24 25 26 27 28 29			25 26 27 28 29 30 | 1			29[f] 30 | 1 2 3 4 5	
	15 16 17 18 19 20 21		16	2517759		30 | 1 2 3 4 5 6	Sat 8h53m5p	Month 3 Xīn-Sì	2 3 4 5 6 7 8	Gǔ yǔ	Parmoute 1897	6 7 8 9 10 11 12	Miyāzyā 2173
	◐ 23 24 25 26 27 28	3:27	17	2517766	Iyyar 5941	7 8 9 10 11 12 13			9 10 11 12 13 14 15			13 14 15 16 17 18 19	
	○ 30 | 1 2 3 4 ◑	8:34 23:15	18	2517773		14 15 16 17 18 19 20			16 17 18 19 20 21 22	Lì xià		20 21 22 23 24 25 26	
May 2181	6 7 8 9 10 11 12		19	2517780		21 22 23 24 25 26 27			23 24 25 26 27 28 29			27 28 29[g] 30 | 1 2 3	
	● 14 15 16 17 18 19	15:06	20	2517787		28 29 | 1 2 3 4 5	Sun 21h37m6p	Month 4 Xīn-Sì	1 2 3 4 5* 6 7		Pashons 1897	4 5 6 7 8 9 10	Genbot 2173
	20 ◐ 22 23 24 25 26	18:47	21	2517794	Sivan 5941	6[h] 7 8 9 10 11 12			8 9 10 11 12 13 14	Xiǎo mǎn		11 12 13 14 15 16 17	
	27 ○ 29 30 31 | 1 2	16:44	22	2517801		13 14 15 16 17 18 19			15 16 17 18 19 20 21			18 19 20 21 22 23 24	
June 2181	3 ◑ 5 6 7 8 9	7:45	23	2517808		20 21 22 23 24 25 26			22 23 24 25 26 27 28	Máng zhòng		25 26 27 28 29 30 | 1	
	10 11 ● 13 14 15 16	6:44	24	2517815		27 28 29 30 | 1 2 3	Tue 10h21m7p	Month 5 Xīn-Sì	29 30 | 1 2 3 4 5[d]		Paōne 1897	2 3 4 5 6 7 8	Sanē 2173
	17 18 19 ◐[c] 21 22 23	6:49	25	2517822	Tammuz 5941	4 5 6 7 8 9 10			6 7 8 9 10 11 12	Xià zhì		9 10 11 12 13 14 15	
	24 25 ○ 27 28 29 30	23:41	26	2517829		11 12 13 14 15 16 17			13 14 15 16 17 18 19			16 17 18 19 20 21 22	
July 2181	1 2 ◑ 4 5 6 7	18:36	27	2517836		18 19 20 21 22 23 24			20 21 22 23 24 25 26	Xiǎo shǔ		23 24 25 26 27 28 29	
	8 9 10 ● 12 13 14	21:52	28	2517843		25 26 27 28 29 | 1 2	Wed 23h5m8p	Month 6 Xīn-Sì	27 28 29 30 | 1 2 3		Epēp 1897	30 | 1 2 3 4 5 6	Ḥamlē 2173
	15 16 17 18 ◐ 20 21	15:59	29	2517850	Av 5941	3 4 5 6 7 8 9			4 5* 6 7 8 9 10			7 8 9 10 11 12 13	
	22 23 24 25 ○ 27 28	6:27	30	2517857		10[i] 11 12 13 14 15 16			11 12 13 14 15 16 17	Dà shǔ		14 15 16 17 18 19 20	
	29 30 31 | 1 ◑ 3 4	8:20	31	2517864		17 18 19 20 21 22 23			18 19 20 21 22 23 24			21 22 23 24 25 26 27	
August 2181	5 6 7 8 9 ● 11	12:07	32	2517871		24 25 26 27 28 29 30			25 26 27 28 29 | 1 2	Lì qiū		28 29 30 | 1 2 3 4	
	12 13 14 15 16 ◐ 18	22:57	33	2517878	Elul 5941	1 2 3 4 5 6 7	Fri 11h49m9p	Month 7 Xīn-Sì	3 4 5 6 7[e] 8 9		Mesorē 1897	5 6 7 8 9 10 11	Naḥasē 2173
	19 20 21 22 23 ○ 25	14:17	34	2517885		8 9 10 11 12 13 14			10 11 12 13 14 15[f] 16	Chǔ shǔ		12 13[h] 14 15 16 17 18	
	26 27 28 29 30 31 | ◑	0:49	35	2517892		15 16 17 18 19 20 21			17 18 19 20 21 22 23			19 20 21 22 23 24 25	
September 2181	2 3 4 5 6 7 8		36	2517899		22 23 24 25 26 27 28			24 25 26 27 28 29 30	Bái lù	Epag. 1897	26 27 28 29 30 | 1 2	Pāg. 2173
	● 10 11 12 13 14 15	1:28	37	2517906	Tishri 5942	29 | 1[a] 2[a] 3 4 5 6	Sun 0h33m10p	Month 8 Xīn-Sì	1 2 3 4 5 6* 7		Thoout 1898	3 4 5 | 1[a] 2 3 4	Maskaram 2174
	◐ 17 18 19 20 21 22[d]	4:42	38	2517913		7 8 9 10[b] 11 12 13			8 9 10 11 12 13 14	Qiū fēn		5 6 7 8 9 10 11	
	○ 24 25 26 27 28 29	0:21	39	2517920		14 15[c] 16 17 18 19 20			15[g] 16 17 18 19 20 21			12 13 14 15 16 17[b] 18	
	◑ | 1 2 3 4 5 6	19:24	40	2517927		21 22 23 24 25 26 27			22 23 24 25 26 27 28			19 20 21 22 23 24 25	
October 2181	7 ● 9 10 11 12 13	13:59	41	2517934		28 29 30 | 1 2 3 4	Mon 13h17m11p	Month 9 Xīn-Sì	29 | 1 2 3 4 5 6	Hán lù		26 27 28 29 30 | 1 2	
	14 ◐ 16 17 18 19 20	10:30	42	2517941	Heshvan 5942	5 6 7 8 9 10 11			7 8 9[h] 10 11 12 13		Paope 1898	3 4 5 6 7 8 9	Ṭeqemt 2174
	21 ○ 23 24 25 26 27	13:29	43	2517948		12 13 14 15 16 17 18			14 15 16 17 18 19 20	Shuāng jiàng		10 11 12 13 14 15 16	
	28 29 ◑ 31 | 1 2 3	15:00	44	2517955		19 20 21 22 23 24 25			21 22 23 24 25 26 27			17 18 19 20 21 22 23	
November 2181	4 5 6 ● 8 9 10	1:46	45	2517962		26 27 28 29 | 1 2 3	Wed 2h1m12p	Month 10 Xīn-Sì	28 29 30 | 1 2 3 4	Lì dōng		24 25 26 27 28 29 30	
	11 12 ◐ 14 15 16 17	17:44	46	2517969	Kislev 5942	4 5 6 7 8 9 10			5 6 7* 8 9 10 11		Athōr 1898	1 2 3 4 5 6 7	Ḫedār 2174
	18 19 20 ○ 22 23 24	5:42	47	2517976		11 12 13 14 15 16 17			12 13 14 15 16 17 18	Xiǎo xuě		8 9 10 11 12 13 14	
	25 26 27 28 ◑ 30 | 1	10:18	48	2517983		18 19 20 21 22 23 24			19 20 21 22 23 24 25			15 16 17 18 19 20 21	
December 2181	2 3 4 5 ● 7 8	12:52	49	2517990		25[e] 26[e] 27[e] 28[e] 29[e][d] | 1[e] 2[e]	Thu 14h45m13p	Month 11 Xīn-Sì	26 27 28 29 | 1 2 3	Dà xuě		22 23 24 25 26 27 28	
	9 10 11 12 ◐ 14 15	3:43	50	2517997	Teveth 5942	3[e] 4 5 6 7 8 9			4 5 6 7 8 9 10		Koiak 1898	29 30 | 1 2 3 4 5	Tākhśāś 2174
	16 17 18 19 20 ○[e] 22	0:14	51	2518004		10 11 12 13 14 15 16			11 12 13 14 15 16[i] 17	Dōng zhì		6 7 8 9 10 11 12	
	23 24 25 26 27 28 ◑	3:52	52	2518011		17 18 19 20 21 22 23			18 19 20 21 22 23 24			13 14 15 16 17 18 19	
	30 31 | 1 2 3 ● 5	23:28	1	2518018		24 25 26 27 28 29 | 1	Sat 3h29m14p		25 26 27 28 29 30 | 1	Xiǎo hán		20 21 22 23 24 25 26	

Gregorian notes:
[a]New Year
[b]Spring (4:13)
[c]Summer (19:09)
[d]Autumn (12:13)
[e]Winter (11:40)
● New moon
◐ First quarter moon
○ Full moon
◑ Last quarter moon

Hebrew notes:
‡Leap year
[a]New Year
[b]Yom Kippur
[c]Sukkot
[d]Winter starts
[e]Ḥanukkah
[f]Purim
[g]Passover
[h]Shavuot
[i]Fast of Av

Chinese notes:
‡Leap year
[a]New Year (4879, Snake)
[b]Lantern Festival
[c]Qīngmíng
[d]Dragon Festival
[e]Qīqiǎo
[f]Hungry Ghosts
[g]Mid-Autumn Festival
[h]Double-Ninth Festival
[i]Dōngzhì
*Start of 60-name cycle

Coptic/Ethiopic notes:
[a]New Year
[b]Building of the Cross
[c]Christmas
[d]Jesus's Circumcision
[e]Epiphany
[f]Easter
[g]Mary's Announcement
[h]Jesus's Transfiguration

PERSIAN (ASTRONOMICAL) 1559/1560‡

Month	Sun	Mon	Tue	Wed	Thu	Fri	Sat
	11	12	13	14	15	16	17
DEY 1559	18	19	20	21	22	23	24
	25	26	27	28	29	30	*1*
	2	3	4	5	6	7	8
BAHMAN 1559	9	10	11	12	13	14	15
	16	17	18	19	20	21	22
	23	24	25	26	27	28	29
	30	*1*	2	3	4	5	6
ESFAND 1559	7	8	9	10	11	12	13
	14	15	16	17	18	19	20
	21	22	23	24	25	26	27
	28	29	*1*[a]	2	3	4	5
FARVARDĪN 1560	6	7	8	9	10	11	12
	13[b]	14	15	16	17	18	19
	20	21	22	23	24	25	26
	27	28	29	30	31	*1*	2
ORDĪBEHEŠT 1560	3	4	5	6	7	8	9
	10	11	12	13	14	15	16
	17	18	19	20	21	22	23
	24	25	26	27	28	29	30
	31	*1*	2	3	4	5	6
XORDĀD 1560	7	8	9	10	11	12	13
	14	15	16	17	18	19	20
	21	22	23	24	25	26	27
	28	29	30	31	*1*	2	3
TĪR 1560	4	5	6	7	8	9	10
	11	12	13	14	15	16	17
	18	19	20	21	22	23	24
	25	26	27	28	29	30	31
	1	2	3	4	5	6	7
MORDĀD 1560	8	9	10	11	12	13	14
	15	16	17	18	19	20	21
	22	23	24	25	26	27	28
	29	30	31	*1*	2	3	4
SHAHRĪVAR 1560	5	6	7	8	9	10	11
	12	13	14	15	16	17	18
	19	20	21	22	23	24	25
	26	27	28	29	30	31	*1*
MEHR 1560	2	3	4	5	6	7	8
	9	10	11	12	13	14	15
	16	17	18	19	20	21	22
	23	24	25	26	27	28	29
	30	*1*	2	3	4	5	6
ĀBĀN 1560	7	8	9	10	11	12	13
	14	15	16	17	18	19	20
	21	22	23	24	25	26	27
	28	29	30	*1*	2	3	4
ĀZAR 1560	5	6	7	8	9	10	11
	12	13	14	15	16	17	18
	19	20	21	22	23	24	25
	26	27	28	29	30	*1*	2
DEY 1560	3	4	5	6	7	8	9
	10	11	12	13	14	15	16

‡Leap year
[a]New Year
[b]Sizdeh Bedar

HINDU LUNAR 2237‡/2238

Month	Sun	Mon	Tue	Wed	Thu	Fri	Sat
MĀRGAŚĪRA 2237	15	16	17	*17*	18	19	20
	21	23	24	25	26	27	28
	29	30	1	2	3	4	5
PAUSHA 2237	6	7	8	9	10	11	12
	13	14	15	16	17	18	19
	20	21	22	23	24	25	26
	27	29	30	1	2	3	4
MĀGHA 2237	5	6	7	8	9	9	10
	11	12	13	14	15	16	17
	18	19	20	**21**	23	24	25
	26	27	28[h]	29	30	1	2
PHĀLGUNA 2237	3	4	5	6	7	8	9
	10	11	12	13	14	15[i]	16
	17	18	19	20	21	22	23
	24	25	**26**	28	29	30	1[a]
CHAITRA 2238	2	2	3	4	5	6	7
	8	9[b]	10	11	12	13	14
	15	16	17	**18**	20	21	22
	23	24	25	26	27	28	29
	30	1	2	3	4	5	6
VAIŚĀKHA 2238	*6*	7	8	9	10	**11**	13
	14	15	16	17	18	19	20
	21	22	**23**	25	26	27	*27*
	28	29	30	1	2	3	4
JYAISHṬHA 2238	5	6	7	8	9	10	11
	12	13	**14**	16	17	18	19
	20	21	22	23	24	25	26
	27	28	29	30	1	2	3
ĀSHĀḌHA 2238	3	4	5	**6**	8	9	10
	11	12	13	14	15	16	17
	18	20	21	22	23	24	25
	25	26	27	28	29	30	1
ŚRĀVAṆA 2238	2	3	4	5	6	7	8
	9	**10**	12	13	14	15	16
	17	18	19	20	21	22	23[c]
	24	25	26	27	28	29	30
BHĀDRAPADA 2238	*30*	1	**2**	4[d]	5	6	7
	8	9	10	11	12	13	**14**
	16	17	18	19	20	*20*	21
	22	23	24	25	26	27	28
	29	30	1	2	3	4	5
ĀŚVINA 2238	6	7[e]	9[e]	10[e]	11	12	13
	14	15	16	17	18	19	20
	21	22	23	24	*24*	25	26
	27	28	29	**30**[f]	2	3	4
KĀRTTIKA 2238	5	6	7	8	9	10	11
	12	13	14	15	16	17	18
	19	20	21	22	23	24	25
	26	27	28	29	30	1	2
MĀRGAŚĪRA 2238	3	4	**5**	7	8	9	10
	11[g]	12	13	14	15	16	17
	17	18	19	20	21	22	23
	24	25	26	27	28	**29**	1

‡Leap year
[a]New Year (Vṛisha)
[b]Birthday of Rāma
[c]Birthday of Krishna
[d]Ganēśa Chaturthī
[e]Dashara
[f]Diwali
[g]Birthday of Vishnu
[h]Night of Śiva
[i]Holi

HINDU SOLAR 2102/2103

Month	Sun	Mon	Tue	Wed	Thu	Fri	Sat
PAUSHA 2102	14	15	16	17	18	19	20
	21	22	23	24	25	26	27
	28	29	1[b]	2	3	4	5
MĀGHA 2102	6	7	8	9	10	11	12
	13	14	15	16	17	18	19
	20	21	22	23	24	25	26
	27	28	29	30	1	2	3
PHĀLGUNA 2102	4	5	6	7	8	9	10
	11	12	13	14	15	16	17
	18	19	20	21	22	23	24
	25	26	27	28	29	1	2
CHAITRA 2102	3	4	5	6	7	8	9
	10	11	12	13	14	15	16
	17	18	19	20	21	22	23
	24	25	26	27	28	29	30
	31	1[a]	2	3	4	5	6
VAIŚĀKHA 2103	7	8	9	10	11	12	13
	14	15	16	17	18	19	20
	21	22	23	24	25	26	27
	28	29	30	31	1	2	3
JYAISHṬHA 2103	4	5	6	7	8	9	10
	11	12	13	14	15	16	17
	18	19	20	21	22	23	24
	25	26	27	28	29	30	31
	1	2	3	4	5	6	7
ĀSHĀḌHA 2103	8	9	10	11	12	13	14
	15	16	17	18	19	20	21
	22	23	24	25	26	27	28
	29	30	31	32	1	2	3
ŚRĀVAṆA 2103	4	5	6	7	8	9	10
	11	12	13	14	15	16	17
	18	19	20	21	22	23	24
	25	26	27	28	29	30	31
	1	2	3	4	5	6	7
BHĀDRAPADA 2103	8	9	10	11	12	13	14
	15	16	17	18	19	20	21
	22	23	24	25	26	27	28
	29	30	31	1	2	3	4
ĀŚVINA 2103	5	6	7	8	9	10	11
	12	13	14	15	16	17	18
	19	20	21	22	23	24	25
	26	27	28	29	30	31	1
KĀRTTIKA 2103	2	3	4	5	6	7	8
	9	10	11	12	13	14	15
	16	17	18	19	20	21	22
	23	24	25	26	27	28	29
	30	1	2	3	4	5	6
MĀRGAŚĪRA 2103	7	8	9	10	11	12	13
	14	15	16	17	18	19	20
	21	22	23	24	25	26	27
	28	29	1	2	3	4	5
PAUSHA 2103	6	7	8	9	10	11	12
	13	14	15	16	17	18	19

[a]New Year (Durmukha)
[b]Pongal

ISLAMIC (ASTRONOMICAL) 1607/1608

Month	Sun	Mon	Tue	Wed	Thu	Fri	Sat
	14	15	16	17	18	19	20
RABĪʿ II 1607	21	22	23	24	25	26	27
	28	29	1	2	3	4	5
JUMĀDĀ I 1607	6	7	8	9	10	11	12
	13	14	15	16	17	18	19
	20	21	22	23	24	25	26
	27	28	29	30	1	2	3
JUMĀDĀ II 1607	4	5	6	7	8	9	10
	11	12	13	14	15	16	17
	18	19	20	21	22	23	24
	25	26	27	28	29	30	*1*
RAJAB 1607	2	3	4	5	6	7	8
	9	10	11	12	13	14	15
	16	17	18	19	20	21	22
	23	24	25	26	27[d]	28	29
SHAʿBĀN 1607	1	2	3	4	5	6	7
	8	9	10	11	12	13	14
	15	16	17	18	19	20	21
	22	23	24	25	26	27	28
	29	30	1[e]	2	3	4	5
RAMAḌĀN 1607	6	7	8	9	10	11	12
	13	14	15	16	17	18	19
	20	21	22	23	24	25	26
	27	28	29	30	1[f]	2	3
SHAWWĀL 1607	4	5	6	7	8	9	10
	11	12	13	14	15	16	17
	18	19	20	21	22	23	24
	25	26	27	28	29	*30*	1
DHU AL-QAʿDA 1607	2	3	4	5	6	7	8
	9	10	11	12	13	14	15
	16	17	18	19	20	21	22
	23	24	25	26	27	28	29
	30	1	2	3	4	5	6
DHU AL-ḤIJJA 1607	7	8	9	10[g]	11	12	13
	14	15	16	17	18	19	20
	21	22	23	24	25	26	27
	28	29[A]	1[a]	2	3	4	5
MUḤARRAM 1608	6	7	8	9	10[b]	11	12
	13	14	15	16	17	18	19
	20	21	22	23	24	25	26
	27	28	29	*1*	2	3	4
ṢAFAR 1608	5	6	7	8	9	10	11
	12	13	14	15	16	17	18
	19	20	21	22	23	24	25
	26	27	28	29	*1*	2	3
RABĪʿ I 1608	4	5	6	7	8	9	10
	11	12[c]	13	14	15	16	17
	18	19	20	21	22	23	24
	25	26	27	28	29	30	*1*
RABĪʿ II 1608	2	3	4	5	6	7	8
	9	10	11	12	13	14	15
	16	17	18	19	20	21	22
	23	24	25	26	27	28	29

[a]New Year
[A]New Year (Arithmetic)
[b]ʿAshūrāʾ
[c]Prophet's Birthday
[d]Ascent of the Prophet
[e]Start of Ramaḍān
[f]ʿĪd al-Fiṭr
[g]ʿĪd al-ʾAḍḥā

GREGORIAN 2181

Julian (Sun)	Sun	Mon	Tue	Wed	Thu	Fri	Sat	Month
Dec 17	31	1	2	3	4	5	6	
	7	8[a]	9	10	11	12	13	JANUARY 2181
Dec 31	14	15[b]	16	17	18	19	20	
	21	22	23	24	25	26	27	
Jan 14	28	29	30	31	1	2	3	
	4	5	6	7	8	9	10	FEBRUARY 2181
Jan 28	11	12	13	14[c]	15	16	17	
	18	19	20	21	22	23	24	
Feb 11	25[d]	26	27	28	1	2	3	
	4	5	6	7	8	9	10	MARCH 2181
Feb 25	11	12	13	14	15	16	17	
	18	19	20	21	22	23	24	
Mar 11	25	26	27	28	29	30	31	
	1[e]	2	3	4	5	6	7	
Mar 25	8[f]	9	10	11	12	13	14	APRIL 2181
	15	16	17	18	19	20	21	
Apr 8	22	23	24	25	26	27	28	
	29	30	1	2	3	4	5	
Apr 22	6	7	8	9	10	11	12	MAY 2181
	13	14	15	16	17	18	19	
May 6	20	21	22	23	24	25	26	
	27	28	29	30	31	1	2	
May 20	3	4	5	6	7	8	9	JUNE 2181
	10	11	12	13	14	15	16	
Jun 3	17	18	19	20	21	22	23	
	24	25	26	27	28	29	30	
Jun 17	1	2	3	4	5	6	7	
	8	9	10	11	12	13	14	JULY 2181
Jul 1	15	16	17	18	19	20	21	
	22	23	24	25	26	27	28	
Jul 15	29	30	31	1	2	3	4	
	5	6	7	8	9	10	11	AUGUST 2181
Jul 29	12	13	14	15	16	17	18	
	19	20	21	22	23	24	25	
Aug 12	26	27	28	29	30	31	1	
	2	3	4	5	6	7	8	
Aug 26	9	10	11	12	13	14	15	SEPTEMBER 2181
	16	17	18	19	20	21	22	
Sep 9	23	24	25	26	27	28	29	
	30	1	2	3	4	5	6	
Sep 23	7	8	9	10	11	12	13	OCTOBER 2181
	14	15	16	17	18	19	20	
Oct 7	21	22	23	24	25	26	27	
	28	29	30	31	1	2	3	
Oct 21	4	5	6	7	8	9	10	NOVEMBER 2181
	11	12	13	14	15	16	17	
Nov 4	18	19	20	21	22	23	24	
	25	26	27	28	29	30	1	
Nov 18	2[g]	3	4	5	6	7	8	DECEMBER 2181
	9	10	11	12	13	14	15	
Dec 2	16	17	18	19	20	21	22	
	23	24	25[h]	26	27	28	29	
Dec 16	30	31	1	2	3	4	5	

[a]Orthodox Christmas
[b]Julian New Year
[c]Ash Wednesday
[d]Feast of Orthodoxy
[e]Easter
[f]Orthodox Easter
[g]Advent
[h]Christmas

ISO Week (Mon)	Gregorian 2182	Sun	Mon	Tue	Wed	Thu	Fri	Sat	Lunar Phases	Julian Day (Sun noon)
1	January 2182	30	31	1[a]	2	3	●	5	23:28	2518018
2		6	7	8	9	10	◐	12	17:08	2518025
3		13	14	15	16	17	18	○	19:40	2518032
4		20	21	22	23	24	25	26		2518039
5	February 2182	◑	28	29	30	31	1	2	18:27	2518046
6		●	4	5	6	7	8	9	9:53	2518053
7		◐	11	12	13	14	15	16	9:45	2518060
8		17	○	19	20	21	22	23	14:28	2518067
9	March 2182	24	25	◑	27	28	1	2	5:28	2518074
10		3	●	5	6	7	8	9	20:32	2518081
11		10	11	◐	13	14	15	16	4:29	2518088
12		17	18	19	○[b]	21	22	23	7:19	2518095
13		24	25	26	◑	28	29	30	13:21	2518102
14	April 2182	31	1	2	●	4	5	6	7:47	2518109
15		7	8	9	◐	11	12	13	23:52	2518116
16		14	15	16	17	○	19	20	21:17	2518123
17		21	22	23	24	◑	26	27	19:15	2518130
18	May 2182	28	29	30	1	●	3	4	19:48	2518137
19		5	6	7	8	9	◐	11	18:36	2518144
20		12	13	14	15	16	17	○	8:11	2518151
21		19	20	21	22	23	24	◑	0:35	2518158
22	June 2182	26	27	28	29	30	31	●	8:42	2518165
23		2	3	4	5	6	7	8		2518172
24		◐	10	11	12	13	14	15	11:39	2518179
25		○	17	18	19	20	21[c]	22	16:35	2518186
26		◑	24	25	26	27	28	29	6:49	2518193
27	July 2182	●	1	2	3	4	5	6	22:33	2518200
28		7	8	◐	10	11	12	13	2:19	2518207
29		14	○	16	17	18	19	20	23:32	2518214
30		21	◑	23	24	25	26	27	15:04	2518221
31	August 2182	28	29	●	31	1	2	3	13:23	2518228
32		4	5	6	◐	8	9	10	14:16	2518235
33		11	12	13	○	15	16	17	6:18	2518242
34		18	19	20	◑	22	23	24	2:11	2518249
35	September 2182	25	26	27	28	●	30	31	4:58	2518256
36		1	2	3	4	◐	6	7	23:44	2518263
37		8	9	10	11	○	13	14	14:02	2518270
38		15	16	17	18	◑	20	21	16:37	2518277
39		22[d]	23	24	25	26	●	28	20:45	2518284
40	October 2182	29	30	1	2	3	4	◐	7:24	2518291
41		6	7	8	9	10	○	12	23:39	2518298
42		13	14	15	16	17	18	◑	10:24	2518305
43		20	21	22	23	24	25	26		2518312
44	November 2182	●	28	29	30	31	1	2	11:55	2518319
45		◐	4	5	6	7	8	9	14:20	2518326
46		○	11	12	13	14	15	16	11:39	2518333
47		17	◑	19	20	21	22	23	6:50	2518340
48	December 2182	24	25	●	27	28	29	30	1:48	2518347
49		1	◐	3	4	5	6	7	21:42	2518354
50		8	9	○	11	12	13	14	2:13	2518361
51		15	16	17	◑	19	20	21[e]	4:20	2518368
52		22	23	24	●	26	27	28	14:17	2518375
1		29	30	31	◐	2	3	4	6:32	2518382

ISO Week (Mon)	Hebrew 5942‡/5943	Sun	Mon	Tue	Wed	Thu	Fri	Sat	Molad
1	Shevat 5942	24	25	26	27	28	29	1	Sat 3h29m14p
2		2	3	4	5	6	7	8	
3		9	10	11	12	13	14	15	
4		16	17	18	19	20	21	22	
5		23	24	25	26	27	28	29	Sun 16h13m15p
6	Adar I 5942	30	1	2	3	4	5	6	
7		7	8	9	10	11	12	13	
8		14	15	16	17	18	19	20	
9		21	22	23	24	25	26	27	
10	Adar II 5942	28	29	30	1	2	3	4	Tue 4h57m16p
11		5	6	7	8	9	10	11	
12		12	13	14[f]	15	16	17	18	
13		19	20	21	22	23	24	25	
14	Nisan 5942	26	27	28	29	1	2	3	Wed 17h41m17p
15		4	5	6	7	8	9	10	
16		11	12	13	14	15[g]	16	17	
17		18	19	20	21	22	23	24	
18	Iyar 5942	25	26	27	28	29	30	1	Fri 6h26m0p
19		2	3	4	5	6	7	8	
20		9	10	11	12	13	14	15	
21		16	17	18	19	20	21	22	
22		23	24	25	26	27	28	29	
23	Sivan 5942	1	2	3	4	5	6[h]	7	Sat 19h10m1p
24		8	9	10	11	12	13	14	
25		15	16	17	18	19	20	21	
26		22	23	24	25	26	27	28	
27	Tammuz 5942	29	30	1	2	3	4	5	Mon 7h54m2p
28		6	7	8	9	10	11	12	
29		13	14	15	16	17	18	19	
30		20	21	22	23	24	25	26	
31	Av 5942	27	28	29	1	2	3	4	Tue 20h38m3p
32		5	6	7	8	9[i]	10	11	
33		12	13	14	15	16	17	18	
34		19	20	21	22	23	24	25	
35	Elul 5942	26	27	28	29	30	1	2	Thu 9h22m4p
36		3	4	5	6	7	8	9	
37		10	11	12	13	14	15	16	
38		17	18	19	20	21	22	23	
39	Tishri 5943	24	25	26	27	28	29	1[a]	Fri 22h6m5p
40		2[a]	3	4	5	6	7	8	
41		9	10[b]	11	12	13	14	15[c]	
42		16	17	18	19	20	21	22	
43		23	24	25	26	27	28	29	
44	Ḥeshvan 5943	30	1	2	3	4	5	6	Sun 10h50m6p
45		7	8	9	10	11	12	13	
46		14	15	16	17	18	19	20	
47		21	22	23	24	25	26	27	
48	Kislev 5943	28	29	30	1	2	3	4	Mon 23h34m7p
49		5	6	7	8	9	10[d]	11	
50		12	13	14	15	16	17	18	
51		19	20	21	22	23	24	25[e]	
52	Teveth 5943	26[e]	27[e]	28[e]	29[e]	30[e]	1[e]	2[e]	Wed 12h18m8p
1		3	4	5	6	7	8	9	

ISO Week (Mon)	Chinese Xīn-Sì/Rén-Wǔ	Sun	Mon	Tue	Wed	Thu	Fri	Sat	Solar Term
1	Month 12 Xīn-Sì	25	26	27	28	29	30	*1*	Xiǎo hán
2		2	3	4	5	6	7	8*	
3		9	10	11	12	13	14	15	
4		**16**	17	18	19	20	21	22	Dà hán
5		23	24	25	26	27	28	29	
6	Month 1 Rén-Wǔ	1[a]	2	3	4	5	6	7	Lì chūn
7		8	9	10	11	12	13	14	
8		15[b]	**16**	17	18	19	20	21	Yǔ shuǐ
9		22	23	24	25	26	27	28	
10	Month 2 Rén-Wǔ	29	30	*1*	2	3	4	5	Jīng zhé
11		6	7	8	9*	10	11	12	
12		13	14	15	**16**	17	18	19	Chūn fēn
13		20	21	22	23	24	25	26	
14	Month 3 Rén-Wǔ	27	28	29	1	2[c]	3	4	Qīng míng
15		5	6	7	8	9	10	11	
16		12	13	14	15	16	17	**18**	Gǔ yǔ
17		19	20	21	22	23	24	25	
18	Month 4 Rén-Wǔ	26	27	28	29	30	1	2	
19		3	4	5	6	7	8	9	Lì xià
20		10*	11	12	13	14	15	16	
21		17	18	**19**	20	21	22	23	Xiǎo mǎn
22	Month 5 Rén-Wǔ	24	25	26	27	28	29	1	
23		2	3	4	5[d]	6	7	8	Máng zhòng
24		9	10	11	12	13	14	15	
25		16	17	18	19	20	**21**	22	Xià zhì
26		23	24	25	26	27	28	29	
27	Month 6 Rén-Wǔ	30	1	2	3	4	5	6	
28		7	8	9	10	11*	12	13	Xiǎo shǔ
29		14	15	16	17	18	19	20	
30		21	**22**	23	24	25	26	27	Dà shǔ
31	Month 7 Rén-Wǔ	28	29	1	2	3	4	5	
32		6	7[e]	8	9	10	11	12	Lì qiū
33		13	14	15[f]	16	17	18	19	
34		20	21	22	23	24	**25**	26	Chǔ shǔ
35	Month 8 Rén-Wǔ	27	28	29	30	1	2	3	
36		4	5	6	7	8	9	*10*	Bái lù
37		11	12*	13	14	15[g]	16	17	
38		18	19	20	21	22	23	24	
39	Month 9 Rén-Wǔ	25	**26**	27	28	29	30	1	Qiū fēn
40		2	3	4	5	6	7	8	
41		9[h]	10	*11*	12	13	14	15	Hán lù
42		16	17	18	19	20	21	22	
43		23	24	25	**26**	27	28	29	Shuāng jiàng
44	Month 10 Rén-Wǔ	1	2	3	4	5	6	7	
45		8	9	10	11	*12*	13*	14	Lì dōng
46		15	16	17	18	19	20	21	
47		22	23	24	25	26	**27**	28	Xiǎo xuě
48	Month 11 Rén-Wǔ	29	30	1	2	3	4	5	
49		6	7	8	9	10	11	*12*	Dà xuě
50		13	14	15	16	17	18	19	
51		20	21	22	23	24	25	26	
52	Month 12 Rén-Wǔ	27[i]	28	29	1	2	3	4	Dōng zhì
1		5	6	7	8	9	10	11	

ISO Week (Mon)	Coptic 1898/1899‡	Sun	Mon	Tue	Wed	Thu	Fri	Sat	Ethiopic 2174/2175‡
1	Koiak 1898	20	21	22	23	24	25	26	Tākhśāś 2174
2	Tōbe 1898	27	28	29[c]	30	1	2	3	Ṭer 2174
3		4	5	6[d]	7	8	9	10	
4		11[e]	12	13	14	15	16	17	
5		18	19	20	21	22	23	24	
6	Meshir 1898	25	26	27	28	29	30	1	Yakātit 2174
7		2	3	4	5	6	7	8	
8		9	10	11	12	13	14	15	
9		16	17	18	19	20	21	22	
10		23	24	25	26	27	28	29	
11	Paremotep 1898	30	1	2	3	4	5	6	Magābit 2174
12		7	8	9	10	11	12	13	
13		14	15	16	17	18	19	20	
14		21	22	23	24	25	26	27	
15	Parmoute 1898	28	29	30	1	2	3	4	Miyāzyā 2174
16		5	6	7	8	9	10	11	
17		12	13	14	15	16	17	18	
18		19[f]	20	21	22	23	24	25	
19	Pashons 1898	26	27	28	29[g]	30	1	2	Genbot 2174
20		3	4	5	6	7	8	9	
21		10	11	12	13	14	15	16	
22		17	18	19	20	21	22	23	
23		24	25	26	27	28	29	30	
24	Paōne 1898	1	2	3	4	5	6	7	Sanē 2174
25		8	9	10	11	12	13	14	
26		15	16	17	18	19	20	21	
27		22	23	24	25	26	27	28	
28	Epēp 1898	29	30	1	2	3	4	5	Hamlē 2174
29		6	7	8	9	10	11	12	
30		13	14	15	16	17	18	19	
31		20	21	22	23	24	25	26	
32	Mesorē 1898	27	28	29	30	1	2	3	Naḥasē 2174
33		4	5	6	7	8	9	10	
34		11	12	13[h]	14	15	16	17	
35		18	19	20	21	22	23	24	
36	Epag. 1898	25	26	27	28	29	30	1	Pāg. 2174
37	Thoout 1899	2	3	4	5	1[a]	2	3	Maskaram 2175
38		4	5	6	7	8	9	10	
39		11	12	13	14	15	16	17[b]	
40		18	19	20	21	22	23	24	
41	Paope 1899	25	26	27	28	29	30	1	Ṭeqemt 2175
42		2	3	4	5	6	7	8	
43		9	10	11	12	13	14	15	
44		16	17	18	19	20	21	22	
45		23	24	25	26	27	28	29	
46	Athōr 1899	30	1	2	3	4	5	6	Hedār 2175
47		7	8	9	10	11	12	13	
48		14	15	16	17	18	19	20	
49		21	22	23	24	25	26	27	
50	Koiak 1899	28	29	30	1	2	3	4	Tākhśāś 2175
51		5	6	7	8	9	10	11	
52		12	13	14	15	16	17	18	
1		19	20	21	22	23	24	25	

[a]New Year
[b]Spring (10:01)
[c]Summer (0:56)
[d]Autumn (18:10)
[e]Winter (17:35)
● New moon
◐ First quarter moon
○ Full moon
◑ Last quarter moon

‡Leap year
[a]New Year
[b]Yom Kippur
[c]Sukkot
[d]Winter starts
[e]Ḥanukkah
[f]Purim
[g]Passover
[h]Shavuot
[i]Fast of Av

[a]New Year (4880, Horse)
[b]Lantern Festival
[c]Qīngmíng
[d]Dragon Festival
[e]Qīqiǎo
[f]Hungry Ghosts
[g]Mid-Autumn Festival
[h]Double-Ninth Festival
[i]Dōngzhì
*Start of 60-name cycle

‡Leap year
[a]New Year
[b]Building of the Cross
[c]Christmas
[d]Jesus's Circumcision
[e]Epiphany
[f]Easter
[g]Mary's Announcement
[h]Jesus's Transfiguration

PERSIAN (ASTRONOMICAL) 1560‡/1561

Month	Sun	Mon	Tue	Wed	Thu	Fri	Sat
DEY 1560	10	11	12	13	14	15	16
	17	18	19	20	21	22	23
	24	25	26	27	28	29	30
BAHMAN 1560	1	2	3	4	5	6	7
	8	9	10	11	12	13	14
	15	16	17	18	19	20	21
	22	23	24	25	26	27	28
ESFAND 1560	29	30	1	2	3	4	5
	6	7	8	9	10	11	12
	13	14	15	16	17	18	19
	20	21	22	23	24	25	26
FARVARDĪN 1561	27	28	29	30	1[a]	2	3
	4	5	6	7	8	9	10
	11	12	13[b]	14	15	16	17
	18	19	20	21	22	23	24
	25	26	27	28	29	30	31
ORDĪBEHEŠT 1561	1	2	3	4	5	6	7
	8	9	10	11	12	13	14
	15	16	17	18	19	20	21
	22	23	24	25	26	27	28
XORDĀD 1561	29	30	31	1	2	3	4
	5	6	7	8	9	10	11
	12	13	14	15	16	17	18
	19	20	21	22	23	24	25
TĪR 1561	26	27	28	29	30	31	1
	2	3	4	5	6	7	8
	9	10	11	12	13	14	15
	16	17	18	19	20	21	22
	23	24	25	26	27	28	29
MORDĀD 1561	30	31	1	2	3	4	5
	6	7	8	9	10	11	12
	13	14	15	16	17	18	19
	20	21	22	23	24	25	26
SHAHRĪVAR 1561	27	28	29	30	31	1	2
	3	4	5	6	7	8	9
	10	11	12	13	14	15	16
	17	18	19	20	21	22	23
	24	25	26	27	28	29	30
MEHR 1561	31	1	2	3	4	5	6
	7	8	9	10	11	12	13
	14	15	16	17	18	19	20
	21	22	23	24	25	26	27
ĀBĀN 1561	28	29	30	1	2	3	4
	5	6	7	8	9	10	11
	12	13	14	15	16	17	18
	19	20	21	22	23	24	25
ĀZAR 1561	26	27	28	29	30	1	2
	3	4	5	6	7	8	9
	10	11	12	13	14	15	16
	17	18	19	20	21	22	23
	24	25	26	27	28	29	30
DEY 1561	1	2	3	4	5	6	7
	8	9	10	11	12	13	14

‡Leap year
[a]New Year
[b]Sizdeh Bedar

HINDU LUNAR 2238/2239

Month	Sun	Mon	Tue	Wed	Thu	Fri	Sat
PAUSHA 2238	24	25	26	27	28	29	1
	2	3	4	5	6	7	8
	9	10	11	12	13	14	15
	16	17	18	19	20	20	21
	22	24	25	26	27	28	29
MĀGHA 2238	30	1	2	3	4	5	7
	8	8	9	10	11	12	13
	14	15	16	17	18	19	20
	21	22	23	24	25	26	27
PHĀLGUNA 2238	28[h]	30	1	2	3	4	5
	6	7	8	9	10	11	12
	12	13	14	15[i]	16	17	18
	19	20	21	22	24	25	26
CHAITRA 2239	27	28	29	30	1[a]	2	3
	4	5	6	7	8	9[b]	10
	11	12	13	14	15	16	17
	18	19	20	21	22	23	24
VAIŚĀKHA 2239	25	26	28	29	30	1	2
	3	4	5	6	6	7	8
	9	10	11	12	13	14	15
	16	17	18	19	21	22	23
	24	25	26	27	28	29	30
JYAISHṬHA 2239	1	2	3	4	5	6	7
	8	9	10	11	12	13	14
	15	16	17	18	19	20	21
	22	24	25	26	27	28	29
ĀSHĀḌHA 2239	30	1	2	2	3	4	5
	6	7	8	9	10	11	12
	13	14	16	17	18	19	20
	21	22	23	24	25	26	27
ŚRĀVAṆA 2239	28	29	30	1	2	3	4
	5	6	7	8	9	10	11
	12	13	14	15	16	17	19
	20	21	22	23[c]	24	25	26
BHĀDRAPADA 2239	27	28	29	29	30	1	2
	3	4[d]	5	6	7	8	9
	10	12	13	14	15	16	17
	18	19	20	21	22	23	24
ĀŚVINA 2239	25	26	27	28	29	30	1
	2	3	4	5	6	7	8[e]
	9[e]	10[e]	11	12	13	14	16
	17	18	19	20	21	22	23
	24	24	25	26	27	28	29
KĀRTTIKA 2239	30	1[f]	2	3	4	5	6
	7	9	10	11	12	13	14
	15	16	17	18	19	20	21
	22	23	24	25	26	27	28
MĀRGAŚIRA 2239	28	29	30	2	3	4	5
	6	7	8	9	10	11[g]	12
	13	14	16	16	17	18	19
	20	21	22	23	24	25	26
PAUSHA 2239	27	28	29	30	1	2	3
	4	5	6	8	9	10	11

[a]New Year (Chitrabhānu)
[b]Birthday of Rāma
[c]Birthday of Krishna
[d]Ganēśa Chaturthī
[e]Dashara
[f]Diwali
[g]Birthday of Vishnu
[h]Night of Śiva
[i]Holi

HINDU SOLAR 2103/2104

Month	Sun	Mon	Tue	Wed	Thu	Fri	Sat
PAUSHA 2103	13	14	15	16	17	18	19
	20	21	22	23	24	25	26
MĀGHA 2103	27	28	29	1[b]	2	3	4
	5	6	7	8	9	10	11
	12	13	14	15	16	17	18
	19	20	21	22	23	24	25
PHĀLGUNA 2103	26	27	28	29	30	1	2
	3	4	5	6	7	8	9
	10	11	12	13	14	15	16
	17	18	19	20	21	22	23
	24	25	26	27	28	29	30
CHAITRA 2103	1	2	3	4	5	6	7
	8	9	10	11	12	13	14
	15	16	17	18	19	20	21
	22	23	24	25	26	27	28
VAIŚĀKHA 2104	29	30	1[a]	2	3	4	5
	6	7	8	9	10	11	12
	13	14	15	16	17	18	19
	20	21	22	23	24	25	26
JYAISHṬHA 2104	27	28	29	30	31	1	2
	3	4	5	6	7	8	9
	10	11	12	13	14	15	16
	17	18	19	20	21	22	23
	24	25	26	27	28	29	30
ĀSHĀḌHA 2104	31	1	2	3	4	5	6
	7	8	9	10	11	12	13
	14	15	16	17	18	19	20
	21	22	23	24	25	26	27
ŚRĀVAṆA 2104	28	29	30	31	32	1	2
	3	4	5	6	7	8	9
	10	11	12	13	14	15	16
	17	18	19	20	21	22	23
	24	25	26	27	28	29	30
BHĀDRAPADA 2104	31	32	1	2	3	4	5
	6	7	8	9	10	11	12
	13	14	15	16	17	18	19
	20	21	22	23	24	25	26
ĀŚVINA 2104	27	28	29	30	31	1	2
	3	4	5	6	7	8	9
	10	11	12	13	14	15	16
	17	18	19	20	21	22	23
	24	25	26	27	28	29	30
KĀRTTIKA 2104	1	2	3	4	5	6	7
	8	9	10	11	12	13	14
	15	16	17	18	19	20	21
	22	23	24	25	26	27	28
MĀRGAŚIRA 2104	29	30	1	2	3	4	5
	6	7	8	9	10	11	12
	13	14	15	16	17	18	19
	20	21	22	23	24	25	26
PAUSHA 2104	27	28	29	1	2	3	4
	5	6	7	8	9	10	11
	12	13	14	15	16	17	18

[a]New Year (Hemalamba)
[b]Pongal

ISLAMIC (ASTRONOMICAL) 1608/1609

Month	Sun	Mon	Tue	Wed	Thu	Fri	Sat
	23	24	25	26	27	28	29
JUMĀDĀ I 1608	1	2	3	4	5	6	7
	8	9	10	11	12	13	14
	15	16	17	18	19	20	21
	22	23	24	25	26	27	28
JUMĀDĀ II 1608	29	30	1	2	3	4	5
	6	7	8	9	10	11	12
	13	14	15	16	17	18	19
	20	21	22	23	24	25	26
RAJAB 1608	27	28	29	1	2	3	4
	5	6	7	8	9	10	11
	12	13	14	15	16	17	18
	19	20	21	22	23	24	25
SHA'BĀN 1608	26	27[d]	28	29	30	1	2
	3	4	5	6	7	8	9
	10	11	12	13	14	15	16
	17	18	19	20	21	22	23
RAMAḌĀN 1608	24	25	26	27	28	29	1[e]
	2	3	4	5	6	7	8
	9	10	11	12	13	14	15
	16	17	18	19	20	21	22
	23	24	25	26	27	28	29
SHAWWĀL 1608	30	1[f]	2	3	4	5	6
	7	8	9	10	11	12	13
	14	15	16	17	18	19	20
	21	22	23	24	25	26	27
DHU AL-QA'DA 1608	28	29	30	1	2	3	4
	5	6	7	8	9	10	11
	12	13	14	15	16	17	18
	19	20	21	22	23	24	25
DHU AL-ḤIJJA 1608	26	27	28	29	30	1	2
	3	4	5	6	7	8	9
	10[g]	11	12	13	14	15	16
	17	18	19	20	21	22	23
MUḤARRAM 1609	24	25	26	27	28	29	1[a]
	2	3	4	5	6	7	8
	9	10[b]	11	12	13	14	15
	16	17	18	19	20	21	22
	23	24	25	26	27	28	29
ṢAFAR 1609	30	1	2	3	4	5	6
	7	8	9	10	11	12	13
	14	15	16	17	18	19	20
	21	22	23	24	25	26	27
RABĪ' I 1609	28	29	1	2	3	4	5
	6	7	8	9	10	11	12[c]
	13	14	15	16	17	18	19
	20	21	22	23	24	25	26
RABĪ' II 1609	27	28	29	1	2	3	4
	5	6	7	8	9	10	11
	12	13	14	15	16	17	18
	19	20	21	22	23	24	25
JUMĀDĀ I 1609	26	27	28	29	30	1	2
	3	4	5	6	7	8	9

[a]New Year
[b]'Ashūrā'
[c]Prophet's Birthday
[d]Ascent of the Prophet
[e]Start of Ramaḍān
[f]'Īd al-Fiṭr
[g]'Īd al-'Aḍḥā

GREGORIAN 2182

Julian (Sun)	Sun	Mon	Tue	Wed	Thu	Fri	Sat	Month
Dec 16	30	31	1	2	3	4	5	JANUARY 2182
	6	7	8[a]	9	10	11	12	
Dec 30	13	14	15[b]	16	17	18	19	
	20	21	22	23	24	25	26	
Jan 13	27	28	29	30	31	1	2	FEBRUARY 2182
	3	4	5	6	7	8	9	
Jan 27	10	11	12	13	14	15	16	
	17	18	19	20	21	22	23	
Feb 10	24	25	26	27	28	1	2	MARCH 2182
	3	4	5	6[c]	7	8	9	
Feb 24	10	11	12	13	14	15	16	
	17[d]	18	19	20	21	22	23	
Mar 10	24	25	26	27	28	29	30	
	31	1	2	3	4	5	6	APRIL 2182
Mar 24	7	8	9	10	11	12	13	
	14	15	16	17	18	19	20	
Apr 7	21[e]	22	23	24	25	26	27	
	28[f]	29	30	1	2	3	4	MAY 2182
Apr 21	5	6	7	8	9	10	11	
	12	13	14	15	16	17	18	
May 5	19	20	21	22	23	24	25	
	26	27	28	29	30	31	1	JUNE 2182
May 19	2	3	4	5	6	7	8	
	9	10	11	12	13	14	15	
Jun 2	16	17	18	19	20	21	22	
	23	24	25	26	27	28	29	
Jun 16	30	1	2	3	4	5	6	JULY 2182
	7	8	9	10	11	12	13	
Jun 30	14	15	16	17	18	19	20	
	21	22	23	24	25	26	27	
Jul 14	28	29	30	31	1	2	3	AUGUST 2182
	4	5	6	7	8	9	10	
Jul 28	11	12	13	14	15	16	17	
	18	19	20	21	22	23	24	
Aug 11	25	26	27	28	29	30	31	
	1	2	3	4	5	6	7	SEPTEMBER 2182
Aug 25	8	9	10	11	12	13	14	
	15	16	17	18	19	20	21	
Sep 8	22	23	24	25	26	27	28	
	29	30	1	2	3	4	5	OCTOBER 2182
Sep 22	6	7	8	9	10	11	12	
	13	14	15	16	17	18	19	
Oct 6	20	21	22	23	24	25	26	
	27	28	29	30	31	1	2	NOVEMBER 2182
Oct 20	3	4	5	6	7	8	9	
	10	11	12	13	14	15	16	
Nov 3	17	18	19	20	21	22	23	
	24	25	26	27	28	29	30	
Nov 17	1[g]	2	3	4	5	6	7	DECEMBER 2182
	8	9	10	11	12	13	14	
Dec 1	15	16	17	18	19	20	21	
	22	23	24	25[h]	26	27	28	
Dec 15	29	30	31	1	2	3	4	

[a]Orthodox Christmas
[b]Julian New Year
[c]Ash Wednesday
[d]Feast of Orthodoxy
[e]Easter
[f]Orthodox Easter
[g]Advent
[h]Christmas

2183

Month	GREGORIAN 2183 (Sun Mon Tue Wed Thu Fri Sat)	Lunar Phases	ISO WEEK (Mon)	JULIAN DAY (Sun noon)	Hebrew month	HEBREW 5943/5944 (Sun Mon Tue Wed Thu Fri Sat)	Molad	Chinese month	CHINESE Rén-Wǔ/Guǐ-Wèi‡ (Sun Mon Tue Wed Thu Fri Sat)	Solar Term	Coptic month	COPTIC 1899‡/1900 / ETHIOPIC 2175‡/2176 (Sun Mon Tue Wed Thu Fri Sat)	Ethiopic month
JANUARY 2183	29 30 31 ◐[a] 2 3 4	6:32	1	2518382	TEVETH 5943	3 4 5 6 7 8 9		MONTH 12 Rén-Wǔ	5 6 7 8 9 10 11		KOIAK 1899	19 20 21 22 23 24 25	TĀKHŚĀŚ 2175
	5 6 7 ○ 9 10 11	19:12	2	2518389		10 11 12 13 14 15 16			12 13 14* 15 16 17 18	Xiǎo hán	TŌBE 1899	26 27 28 29[c] 30 1 2	ṬER 2175
	12 13 14 15 16 ◑ 18	0:37	3	2518396		17 18 19 20 21 22 23			19 20 21 22 23 24 25			3 4 5 6[d] 7 8 9	
	19 20 21 22 23 ● 25	1:37	4	2518403		24 25 26 27 28 29 1	Fri 1h2m9p	MONTH 1 Guǐ-Wèi	26 27 28 29 30 1[a] 2	Dà hán		10 11[e] 12 13 14 15 16	
	26 27 28 29 ◐ 31 1	17:28	5	2518410	SHEVAT 5943	2 3 4 5 6 7 8			3 4 5 6 7 8 9			17 18 19 20 21 22 23	
FEBRUARY 2183	2 3 4 5 6 ○ 8	13:56	6	2518417		9 10 11 12 13 14 15			10 11 12 13 14 15[b] 16	Lì chūn		24 25 26 27 28 29 30	
	9 10 11 12 13 14 ◑	17:40	7	2518424		16 17 18 19 20 21 22			17 18 19 20 21 22 23		MESHIR 1899	1 2 3 4 5 6 7	YAKĀTIT 2175
	16 17 18 19 20 21 ●	12:07	8	2518431		23 24 25 26 27 28 29	Sat 13h46m10p	MONTH 2 Guǐ-Wèi	24 25 26 27 28 29 1	Yǔ shuǐ		8 9 10 11 12 13 14	
	23 24 25 26 27 28 ◐	6:39	9	2518438	ADAR 5943	30 1 2 3 4 5 6			2 3 4 5 6 7 8			15 16 17 18 19 20 21	
MARCH 2183	2 3 4 5 6 7 8		10	2518445		7 8 9 10 11 12 13			9 10 11 12 13 14 15*	Jīng zhé		22 23 24 25 26 27 28	
	○ 10 11 12 13 14 15	9:02	11	2518452		14[f] 15 16 17 18 19 20			16 17 18 19 20 21 22		PAREMOTEP 1899	29 30 1 2 3 4 5	MAGĀBIT 2175
	16 ◑ 18 19 20[b] 21 22	6:38	12	2518459		21 22 23 24 25 26 27			23 24 25 26 27 28 29	Chūn fēn		6 7 8 9 10 11 12	
	● 24 25 26 27 28 29	22:01	13	2518466	NISAN 5943	28 29 1 2 3 4 5	Mon 2h30m11p	MONTH 3 Guǐ-Wèi	30 1 2 3 4 5 6			13 14 15 16 17 18 19	
	◐ 31 1 2 3 4 5	21:56	14	2518473		6 7 8 9 10 11 12			7 8 9 10 11 12 13[c]	Qīng míng		20 21 22 23 24 25 26	
APRIL 2183	6 7 ○ 9 10 11 12	2:45	15	2518480		13 14 15[g] 16 17 18 19			14 15 16 17 18 19 20		PARMOUTE 1899	27 28 29 30 1 2 3	MIYĀZYĀ 2175
	13 14 ◑ 16 17 18 19	15:48	16	2518487		20 21 22 23 24 25 26			21 22 23 24 25 26 27			4[f] 5 6 7 8 9 10	
	20 21 ● 23 24 25 26	7:33	17	2518494	IYYAR 5943	27 28 29 30 1 2 3	Tue 15h14m12p	MONTH 4 Guǐ-Wèi	28 29 1 2 3 4 5	Gǔ yǔ		11 12 13 14 15 16 17	
	27 28 ◐ 30 1 2 3	14:53	18	2518501		4 5 6 7 8 9 10			6 7 8 9 10 11 12			18 19 20 21 22 23 24	
MAY 2183	4 5 6 ○ 8 9 10	17:43	19	2518508		11 12 13 14 15 16 17			13 14 15 16* 17 18 19	Lì xià	PASHONS 1899	25 26 27 28 29[g] 30 1	GENBOT 2175
	11 12 13 ◑ 15 16 17	22:15	20	2518515		18 19 20 21 22 23 24			20 21 22 23 24 25 26			2 3 4 5 6 7 8	
	18 19 20 ● 22 23 24	17:06	21	2518522	SIVAN 5943	25 26 27 28 29 1 2	Thu 3h58m13p	LEAP MONTH 4 Guǐ-Wèi	27 28 29 30 1 2 3	Xiǎo mǎn		9 10 11 12 13 14 15	
	25 26 27 28 ◐ 30 31	8:44	22	2518529		3 4 5 6[h] 7 8 9			4 5 6 7 8 9 10			16 17 18 19 20 21 22	
JUNE 2183	1 2 3 4 5 ○ 7	5:37	23	2518536		10 11 12 13 14 15 16			11 12 13 14 15 16 17	Máng zhòng		23 24 25 26 27 28 29	
	8 9 10 11 12 ◑ 14	3:14	24	2518543		17 18 19 20 21 22 23			18 19 20 21 22 23 24		PAŌNE 1899	30 1 2 3 4 5 6	SANĒ 2175
	15 16 17 18 19 ● 21[c]	3:25	25	2518550		24 25 26 27 28 29 30		MONTH 5 Guǐ-Wèi	25 26 27 28 29 1 2	Xià zhì		7 8 9 10 11 12 13	
	22 23 24 25 26 27 ◐	2:29	26	2518557	TAMMUZ 5943	1 2 3 4 5 6 7	Fri 16h42m14p		3 4 5[d] 6 7 8 9			14 15 16 17 18 19 20	
	29 30 1 2 3 4 ○	15:06	27	2518564		8 9 10 11 12 13 14			10 11 12 13 14 15 16			21 22 23 24 25 26 27	
JULY 2183	6 7 8 9 10 11 ◑	8:06	28	2518571		15 16 17 18 19 20 21			17* 18 19 20 21 22 23	Xiǎo shǔ	EPĒP 1899	28 29 30 1 2 3 4	HAMLĒ 2175
	13 14 15 16 17 18 ●	15:21	29	2518578		22 23 24 25 26 27 28		MONTH 6 Guǐ-Wèi	24 25 26 27 28 29 1			5 6 7 8 9 10 11	
	20 21 22 23 24 25 26		30	2518585	AV 5943	29 1 2 3 4 5 6	Sun 5h26m15p		2 3 4 5 6 7 8	Dà shǔ		12 13 14 15 16 17 18	
	◐ 28 29 30 31 1 2	19:02	31	2518592		7 8 9[i] 10 11 12 13			9 10 11 12 13 14 15			19 20 21 22 23 24 25	
AUGUST 2183	○ 4 5 6 7 8 9	23:11	32	2518599		14 15 16 17 18 19 20			16 17 18 19 20 21 22	Lì qiū	MESORĒ 1899	26 27 28 29 30 1 2	NAHASĒ 2175
	◑ 11 12 13 14 15 16	14:11	33	2518606		21 22 23 24 25 26 27			23 24 25 26 27 28 29			3 4 5 6 7 8 9	
	17 ● 19 20 21 22 23	5:27	34	2518613	ELUL 5943	28 29 30 1 2 3 4	Mon 18h10m16p	MONTH 7 Guǐ-Wèi	30 1 2 3 4 5 6	Chǔ shǔ		10 11 12 13[h] 14 15 16	
	24 25 ◐ 27 28 29 30	9:43	35	2518620		5 6 7 8 9 10 11			7[e] 8 9 10 11 12 13			17 18 19 20 21 22 23	
	31 1 ○ 3 4 5 6	6:57	36	2518627		12 13 14 15 16 17 18			14 15[f] 16 17 18* 19 20			24 25 26 27 28 29 30	
SEPTEMBER 2183	7 ◑ 9 10 11 12 13	22:43	37	2518634		19 20 21 22 23 24 25			21 22 23 24 25 26 27		EPAG. 1899 / THOOUT 1900	1 2 3 4 5 6 1[a]	PĀG. 2175 / MASKARAM 2176
	14 15 ● 17 18 19 20	21:37	38	2518641	TISHRI 5944	26 27 28 29 1[a] 2[a] 3	Wed 6h54m17p	MONTH 8 Guǐ-Wèi	28 29 30 1 2 3 4	Bái lù		2 3 4 5 6 7 8	
	21 22[d] 23 ◐ 25 26 27	22:20	39	2518648		4 5 6 7 8 9 10[b]			5 6 7 8 9 10 11	Qiū fēn		9 10 11 12 13 14 15	
	28 29 30 ○ 2 3 4	15:12	40	2518655		11 12 13 14 15[c] 16 17			12 13 14 15[g] 16 17 18			16 17[b] 18 19 20 21 22	
OCTOBER 2183	5 6 7 ◑ 9 10 11	10:50	41	2518662		18 19 20 21 22 23 24			19 20 21 22 23 24 25	Hán lù		23 24 25 26 27 28 29	
	12 13 14 15 ● 17 18	14:57	42	2518669	HESHVAN 5944	25 26 27 28 29 30 1	Thu 19h39m0p	MONTH 9 Guǐ-Wèi	26 27 28 29 1 2 3		PAOPE 1900	30 1 2 3 4 5 6	ṬEQEMT 2176
	19 20 21 22 23 ◐ 25	9:07	43	2518676		2 3 4 5 6 7 8			4 5 6 7 8 9[h] 10	Shuāng jiàng		7 8 9 10 11 12 13	
	26 27 28 29 30 ○ 1	0:32	44	2518683		9 10 11 12 13 14 15			11 12 13 14 15 16 17			14 15 16 17 18 19 20	
NOVEMBER 2183	2 3 4 5 6 ◑ 8	3:06	45	2518690		16 17 18 19 20 21 22			18 19* 20 21 22 23 24	Lì dōng		21 22 23 24 25 26 27	
	9 10 11 12 13 14 ●	8:10	46	2518697		23 24 25 26 27 28 29		MONTH 10 Guǐ-Wèi	25 26 27 28 29 30 1		ATHŌR 1900	28 29 30 1 2 3 4	ḪEDĀR 2176
	16 17 18 19 20 21 ◐	18:28	47	2518704	KISLEV 5944	1 2 3 4 5 6 7	Sat 8h23m1p		2 3 4 5 6 7 8	Xiǎo xuě		5 6 7 8 9 10 11	
	23 24 25 26 27 28 ○	11:25	48	2518711		8 9 10 11 12 13 14			9 10 11 12 13 14 15			12 13 14 15 16 17 18	
	30 1 2 3 4 5 ◑	23:08	49	2518718		15 16 17 18 19 20 21			16 17 18 19 20 21 22			19 20 21 22 23 24 25	
DECEMBER 2183	7 8 9 10 11 12 13		50	2518725		22[d] 23 24 25[e] 26[e] 27[e] 28[e]			23 24 25 26 27 28 29	Dà xuě	KOIAK 1900	26 27 28 29 30 1 2	TĀKHŚĀŚ 2176
	14 ● 16 17 18 19 20	0:14	51	2518732	TEVETH 5944	29[e] 30[e] 1[e] 2[e] 3 4 5	Sun 21h7m2p	MONTH 11* Guǐ-Wèi	30 1 2 3 4 5 6			3 4 5 6 7 8 9	
	21[e] ◐ 23 24 25 26 27	2:54	52	2518739		6 7 8 9 10 11 12			7 8[i] 9 10 11 12 13	Dōng zhì		10 11 12 13 14 15 16	
	28 ○ 30 31 1 2 3	0:22	1	2518746		13 14 15 16 17 18 19			14 15 16 17 18 19 20			17 18 19 20 21 22 23	

[a]New Year
[b]Spring (15:54)
[c]Summer (6:48)
[d]Autumn (23:59)
[e]Winter (23:17)
● New moon
◐ First quarter moon
○ Full moon
◑ Last quarter moon

[a]New Year
[b]Yom Kippur
[c]Sukkot
[d]Winter starts
[e]Ḥanukkah
[f]Purim
[g]Passover
[h]Shavuot
[i]Fast of Av

‡Leap year
[a]New Year (4881, Sheep)
[b]Lantern Festival
[c]Qīngmíng
[d]Dragon Festival
[e]Qīqiǎo
[f]Hungry Ghosts
[g]Mid-Autumn Festival
[h]Double-Ninth Festival
[i]Dōngzhì
*Start of 60-name cycle

‡Leap year
[a]New Year
[b]Building of the Cross
[c]Christmas
[d]Jesus's Circumcision
[e]Epiphany
[f]Easter
[g]Mary's Announcement
[h]Jesus's Transfiguration

PERSIAN (ASTRONOMICAL) 1561/1562

Month	Sun	Mon	Tue	Wed	Thu	Fri	Sat
DEY 1561	8	9	10	11	12	13	14
	15	16	17	18	19	20	21
	22	23	24	25	26	27	28
	29	30	1	2	3	4	5
BAHMAN 1561	6	7	8	9	10	11	12
	13	14	15	16	17	18	19
	20	21	22	23	24	25	26
	27	28	29	30	1	2	3
ESFAND 1561	4	5	6	7	8	9	10
	11	12	13	14	15	16	17
	18	19	20	21	22	23	24
	25	26	27	28	29	1[a]	2
FARVARDĪN 1562	3	4	5	6	7	8	9
	10	11	12	13[b]	14	15	16
	17	18	19	20	21	22	23
	24	25	26	27	28	29	30
	31	1	2	3	4	5	6
ORDĪBEHEŠT 1562	7	8	9	10	11	12	13
	14	15	16	17	18	19	20
	21	22	23	24	25	26	27
	28	29	30	31	1	2	3
XORDĀD 1562	4	5	6	7	8	9	10
	11	12	13	14	15	16	17
	18	19	20	21	22	23	24
	25	26	27	28	29	30	31
TĪR 1562	1	2	3	4	5	6	7
	8	9	10	11	12	13	14
	15	16	17	18	19	20	21
	22	23	24	25	26	27	28
	29	30	31	1	2	3	4
MORDĀD 1562	5	6	7	8	9	10	11
	12	13	14	15	16	17	18
	19	20	21	22	23	24	25
	26	27	28	29	30	31	1
SHAHRĪVAR 1562	2	3	4	5	6	7	8
	9	10	11	12	13	14	15
	16	17	18	19	20	21	22
	23	24	25	26	27	28	29
	30	31	1	2	3	4	5
MEHR 1562	6	7	8	9	10	11	12
	13	14	15	16	17	18	19
	20	21	22	23	24	25	26
	27	28	29	30	1	2	3
ĀBĀN 1562	4	5	6	7	8	9	10
	11	12	13	14	15	16	17
	18	19	20	21	22	23	24
	25	26	27	28	29	30	1
ĀZAR 1562	2	3	4	5	6	7	8
	9	10	11	12	13	14	15
	16	17	18	19	20	21	22
	23	24	25	26	27	28	29
DEY 1562	30	1	2	3	4	5	6
	7	8	9	10	11	12	13

[a]New Year
[b]Sizdeh Bedar

HINDU LUNAR 2239/2240‡

Month	Sun	Mon	Tue	Wed	Thu	Fri	Sat
PAUSHA 2239	4	5	**6**	8	9	10	11
	12	13	14	15	16	17	18
	19	20	*20*	21	22	23	24
	25	26	27	28	29	**30**	2
MĀGHA 2239	3	4	5	6	7	8	9
	10	11	12	13	14	15	16
	17	18	19	20	21	22	23
	24	25	26	27	28[h]	29	30
PHĀLGUNA 2239	1	2	3	4	**5**	7	8
	9	10	11	12	*12*	13	14
	15[i]	16	17	18	19	20	21
	22	23	24	25	26	27	28
CHAITRA 2240	**29**	1[a]	2	3	4	5	6
	7	8	9[b]	10	11	12	13
	14	15	*15*	16	17	18	19
	20	21	**22**	24	25	26	27
	28	29	30	1	2	3	4
VAIŚĀKHA 2240	5	6	7	8	9	10	11
	12	13	14	15	16	17	18
	19	20	21	22	23	24	25
	26	28	29	30	1	2	3
JYAISHṬHA 2240	4	5	6	7	8	9	10
	10	11	12	13	14	15	16
	17	18	**19**	21	22	23	24
	25	26	27	28	29	30	1
LEAP ĀSHĀḌHA 2240	2	3	4	5	6	7	8
	9	10	11	12	13	14	15
	16	17	18	19	20	21	**22**
	24	25	26	27	28	29	30
ĀSHĀḌHA 2240	1	2	3	4	5	6	7
	7	8	9	10	11	12	13
	14	16	17	18	19	20	21
	22	23	24	25	26	27	28
	29	30	1	2	3	4	5
ŚRĀVAṆA 2240	6	7	8	9	10	11	12
	13	14	15	16	**17**	19	20
	21	22	23[c]	24	25	26	27
	28	29	30	1	2	3	*3*[d]
BHĀDRAPADA 2240	4	5	6	7	8	9	**10**
	12	13	14	15	16	17	18
	19	20	21	22	23	24	25
	26	27	28	29	30	1	2
ĀŚVINA 2240	3	4	5	6	7	8[e]	9[e]
	10[e]	11	12	13	**14**	16	17
	18	19	20	21	22	23	24
	25	26	27	*27*	28	29	30
KĀRTTIKA 2240	1[f]	2	3	4	5	6	7
	8	10	11	12	13	14	15
	16	17	18	19	20	21	22
	23	24	25	26	27	28	29
MĀRGAŚĪRA 2240	30	1	2	3	4	5	6
	7	8	9	10	11[g]	12	**13**
	15	16	17	18	19	20	*20*

‡Leap year
[a]New Year (Subhānu)
[b]Birthday of Rāma
[c]Birthday of Krishna
[d]Ganēśa Chaturthī
[e]Dashara
[f]Diwali
[g]Birthday of Vishnu
[h]Night of Śiva
[i]Holi

HINDU SOLAR 2104/2105‡

Month	Sun	Mon	Tue	Wed	Thu	Fri	Sat
PAUSHA 2104	12	13	14	15	16	17	18
	19	20	21	22	23	24	25
	26	27	28	29	30	1[b]	2
MĀGHA 2104	3	4	5	6	7	8	9
	10	11	12	13	14	15	16
	17	18	19	20	21	22	23
	24	25	26	27	28	29	1
PHĀLGUNA 2104	2	3	4	5	6	7	8
	9	10	11	12	13	14	15
	16	17	18	19	20	21	22
	23	24	25	26	27	28	29
	30	1	2	3	4	5	6
CHAITRA 2104	7	8	9	10	11	12	13
	14	15	16	17	18	19	20
	21	22	23	24	25	26	27
	28	29	30	1[a]	2	3	4
VAIŚĀKHA 2105	5	6	7	8	9	10	11
	12	13	14	15	16	17	18
	19	20	21	22	23	24	25
	26	27	28	29	30	31	1
JYAISHṬHA 2105	2	3	4	5	6	7	8
	9	10	11	12	13	14	15
	16	17	18	19	20	21	22
	23	24	25	26	27	28	29
	30	31	32	1	2	3	4
ĀSHĀḌHA 2105	5	6	7	8	9	10	11
	12	13	14	15	16	17	18
	19	20	21	22	23	24	25
	26	27	28	29	30	31	1
ŚRĀVAṆA 2105	2	3	4	5	6	7	8
	9	10	11	12	13	14	15
	16	17	18	19	20	21	22
	23	24	25	26	27	28	29
	30	31	32	1	2	3	4
BHĀDRAPADA 2105	5	6	7	8	9	10	11
	12	13	14	15	16	17	18
	19	20	21	22	23	24	25
	26	27	28	29	30	31	1
ĀŚVINA 2105	2	3	4	5	6	7	8
	9	10	11	12	13	14	15
	16	17	18	19	20	21	22
	23	24	25	26	27	28	29
KĀRTTIKA 2105	30	1	2	3	4	5	6
	7	8	9	10	11	12	13
	14	15	16	17	18	19	20
	21	22	23	24	25	26	27
	28	29	30	1	2	3	4
MĀRGAŚĪRA 2105	5	6	7	8	9	10	11
	12	13	14	15	16	17	18
	19	20	21	22	23	24	25
	26	27	28	29	30	1	2
PAUSHA 2105	3	4	5	6	7	8	9
	10	11	12	13	14	15	16

‡Leap year
[a]New Year (Vilamba)
[b]Pongal

ISLAMIC (ASTRONOMICAL) 1609/1610

Month	Sun	Mon	Tue	Wed	Thu	Fri	Sat
JUMĀDĀ I 1609	3	4	5	6	7	8	9
	10	11	12	13	14	15	16
	17	18	19	20	21	22	23
	24	25	26	27	28	29	1
JUMĀDĀ II 1609	2	3	4	5	6	7	8
	9	10	11	12	13	14	15
	16	17	18	19	20	21	22
	23	24	25	26	27	28	29
	30	1	2	3	4	5	6
RAJAB 1609	7	8	9	10	11	12	13
	14	15	16	17	18	19	20
	21	22	23	24	25	26	27[d]
	28	29	1	2	3	4	5
SHA'BĀN 1609	6	7	8	9	10	11	12
	13	14	15	16	17	18	19
	20	21	22	23	24	25	26
	27	28	29	1[e]	2	3	4
RAMAḌĀN 1609	5	6	7	8	9	10	11
	12	13	14	15	16	17	18
	19	20	21	22	23	24	25
	26	27	28	29	30	1[f]	2
SHAWWĀL 1609	3	4	5	6	7	8	9
	10	11	12	13	14	15	16
	17	18	19	20	21	22	23
	24	25	26	27	28	29	30
DHU AL-QA'DA 1609	1	2	3	4	5	6	7
	8	9	10	11	12	13	14
	15	16	17	18	19	20	21
	22	23	24	25	26	27	28
	29	30	1	2	3	4	5
DHU AL-ḤIJJA 1609	6	7	8	9	10[g]	11	12
	13	14	15	16	17	18	19
	20	21	22	23	24	25	26
	27	28	29	1[a]	2	3	4
MUḤARRAM 1610	5	6	7	8	9	10[b]	11
	12	13	14	15	16	17	18
	19	20	21	22	23	24	25
	26	27	28	29	30	1	2
ṢAFAR 1610	3	4	5	6	7	8	9
	10	11	12	13	14	15	16
	17	18	19	20	21	22	23
	24	25	26	27	28	29	1
RABĪ' I 1610	2	3	4	5	6	7	8
	9	10	11	12[c]	13	14	15
	16	17	18	19	20	21	22
	23	24	25	26	27	28	29
	30	1	2	3	4	5	6
RABĪ' II 1610	7	8	9	10	11	12	13
	14	15	16	17	18	19	20
	21	22	23	24	25	26	27
	28	29	1	2	3	4	5
JUMĀDĀ I 1610	6	7	8	9	10	11	12
	13	14	15	16	17	18	19

[a]New Year
[b]'Ashūrā'
[c]Prophet's Birthday
[d]Ascent of the Prophet
[e]Start of Ramaḍān
[f]'Id al-Fiṭr
[g]'Id al-'Aḍḥā

GREGORIAN 2183

Julian (Sun)	Sun	Mon	Tue	Wed	Thu	Fri	Sat	Month
Dec 15	29	30	31	1	2	3	4	
	5	6	7	8[a]	9	10	11	JANUARY 2183
Dec 29	12	13	14	15[b]	16	17	18	
	19	20	21	22	23	24	25	
Jan 12	26	27	28	29	30	31	1	
	2	3	4	5	6	7	8	FEBRUARY 2183
Jan 26	9	10	11	12	13	14	15	
	16	17	18	19	20	21	22	
Feb 9	23	24	25	26[c]	27	28	1	
	2[d]	3	4	5	6	7	8	MARCH 2183
Feb 23	9	10	11	12	13	14	15	
	16	17	18	19	20	21	22	
Mar 9	23	24	25	26	27	28	29	
	30	31	1	2	3	4	5	
Mar 23	6	7	8	9	10	11	12	APRIL 2183
	13[e]	14	15	16	17	18	19	
Apr 6	20	21	22	23	24	25	26	
	27	28	29	30	1	2	3	
Apr 20	4	5	6	7	8	9	10	MAY 2183
	11	12	13	14	15	16	17	
May 4	18	19	20	21	22	23	24	
	25	26	27	28	29	30	31	
May 18	1	2	3	4	5	6	7	JUNE 2183
	8	9	10	11	12	13	14	
Jun 1	15	16	17	18	19	20	21	
	22	23	24	25	26	27	28	
Jun 15	29	30	1	2	3	4	5	
	6	7	8	9	10	11	12	JULY 2183
Jun 29	13	14	15	16	17	18	19	
	20	21	22	23	24	25	26	
Jul 13	27	28	29	30	31	1	2	
	3	4	5	6	7	8	9	AUGUST 2183
Jul 27	10	11	12	13	14	15	16	
	17	18	19	20	21	22	23	
Aug 10	24	25	26	27	28	29	30	
	31	1	2	3	4	5	6	
Aug 24	7	8	9	10	11	12	13	SEPTEMBER 2183
	14	15	16	17	18	19	20	
Sep 7	21	22	23	24	25	26	27	
	28	29	30	1	2	3	4	
Sep 21	5	6	7	8	9	10	11	OCTOBER 2183
	12	13	14	15	16	17	18	
Oct 5	19	20	21	22	23	24	25	
	26	27	28	29	30	31	1	
Oct 19	2	3	4	5	6	7	8	NOVEMBER 2183
	9	10	11	12	13	14	15	
Nov 2	16	17	18	19	20	21	22	
	23	24	25	26	27	28	29	
Nov 16	30[g]	1	2	3	4	5	6	DECEMBER 2183
	7	8	9	10	11	12	13	
Nov 30	14	15	16	17	18	19	20	
	21	22	23	24	25[h]	26	27	
Dec 14	28	29	30	31	1	2	3	

[a]Orthodox Christmas
[b]Julian New Year
[c]Ash Wednesday
[d]Feast of Orthodoxy
[e]Easter (also Orthodox)
[g]Advent
[h]Christmas

2184

Gregorian 2184‡

Month	Sun	Mon	Tue	Wed	Thu	Fri	Sat	Lunar Phases	ISO Week (Mon)	Julian Day (Sun noon)
January 2184	28	○	30	31	1[a]	2	3	0:22	1	2518746
	4	◑	6	7	8	9	10	21:11	2	2518753
	11	12	●	14	15	16	17	14:43	3	2518760
	18	19	◐	21	22	23	24	11:03	4	2518767
	25	26	○	28	29	30	31	15:38	5	2518774
February 2184	1	2	3	◑	5	6	7	18:46	6	2518781
	8	9	10	11	●	13	14	3:27	7	2518788
	15	16	17	◐	19	20	21	19:40	8	2518795
	22	23	24	25	○	27	28	8:51	9	2518802
March 2184	29	1	2	3	4	◑	6	13:44	10	2518809
	7	8	9	10	11	●	13	14:24	11	2518816
	14	15	16	17	18	◐[b]	20	5:34	12	2518823
	21	22	23	24	25	26	○	2:52	13	2518830
April 2184	28	29	30	31	1	2	3		14	2518837
	◑	5	6	7	8	9	●	4:59 17:24	15	2518844
	11	12	13	14	15	16	◐	23:39	16	2518851
	18	19	20	21	22	23	24		17	2518858
May 2184	○	26	27	28	29	30	1	20:09	18	2518865
	2	◑	4	5	6	7	8	16:21	19	2518872
	9	●	11	12	13	14	15	7:40	20	2518879
	16	◐	18	19	20	21	22	7:23	21	2518886
	23	24	○	26	27	28	29	11:37	22	2518893
June 2184	30	31	1	◑	3	4	5	0:22	23	2518900
	6	7	●	9	10	11	12	15:22	24	2518907
	13	14	◐	16	17	18	19	23:13	25	2518914
	20[c]	21	22	23	○	25	26	0:56	26	2518921
July 2184	27	28	29	30	◑	2	3	5:58	27	2518928
	4	5	6	●	8	9	10	23:51	28	2518935
	11	12	13	14	◐	16	17	16:15	29	2518942
	18	19	20	21	22	○	24	12:23	30	2518949
	25	26	27	28	29	◑	31	10:25	31	2518956
August 2184	1	2	3	4	5	●	7	10:15	32	2518963
	8	9	10	11	12	13	◐	9:40	33	2518970
	15	16	17	18	19	20	○	22:27	34	2518977
	22	23	24	25	26	27	◑	15:15	35	2518984
September 2184	29	30	31	1	2	3	●	23:14	36	2518991
	5	6	7	8	9	10	11		37	2518998
	12	◐	14	15	16	17	18	2:44	38	2519005
	19	○	21	22[d]	23	24	25	7:42	39	2519012
October 2184	◑	27	28	29	30	1	2	22:03	40	2519019
	3	●	5	6	7	8	9	14:51	41	2519026
	10	11	◐	13	14	15	16	18:51	42	2519033
	17	18	○	20	21	22	23	16:41	43	2519040
	24	25	◑	27	28	29	30	8:14	44	2519047
November 2184	31	1	2	●	4	5	6	8:27	45	2519054
	7	8	9	10	◐	12	13	9:22	46	2519061
	14	15	16	17	○	19	20	2:04	47	2519068
	21	22	23	◑	25	26	27	22:34	48	2519075
December 2184	28	29	30	1	2	●	4	3:00	49	2519082
	5	6	7	8	9	◐	11	21:41	50	2519089
	12	13	14	15	16	○	18	12:29	51	2519096
	19	20	21[e]	22	23	◑	25	16:48	52	2519103
	26	27	28	29	30	31	●	21:1	53	2519110

Hebrew 5944/5945‡

ISO Week	Month	Sun	Mon	Tue	Wed	Thu	Fri	Sat	Molad
1	Teveth 5944	13	14	15	16	17	18	19	
2		20	21	22	23	24	25	26	
3		27	28	29	1	2	3	4	Tue 9h51m3p
4	Shevat 5944	5	6	7	8	9	10	11	
5		12	13	14	15	16	17	18	
6		19	20	21	22	23	24	25	
7		26	27	28	29	30	1	2	Wed 22h35m4p
8	Adar 5944	3	4	5	6	7	8	9	
9		10	11	12	13	14[f]	15	16	
10		17	18	19	20	21	22	23	
11		24	25	26	27	28	29	1	Fri 11h19m5p
12	Nisan 5944	2	3	4	5	6	7	8	
13		9	10	11	12	13	14	15[g]	
14		16	17	18	19	20	21	22	
15		23	24	25	26	27	28	29	
16		30	1	2	3	4	5	6	Sun 0h3m6p
17	Iyyar 5944	7	8	9	10	11	12	13	
18		14	15	16	17	18	19	20	
19		21	22	23	24	25	26	27	
20		28	29	1	2	3	4	5	Mon 12h47m7p
21	Sivan 5944	6[h]	7	8	9	10	11	12	
22		13	14	15	16	17	18	19	
23		20	21	22	23	24	25	26	
24		27	28	29	30	1	2	3	Wed 1h31m8p
25	Tammuz 5944	4	5	6	7	8	9	10	
26		11	12	13	14	15	16	17	
27		18	19	20	21	22	23	24	
28		25	26	27	28	29	1	2	Thu 14h15m9p
29	Av 5944	3	4	5	6	7	8	9	
30		10[i]	11	12	13	14	15	16	
31		17	18	19	20	21	22	23	
32		24	25	26	27	28	29	30	
33	Elul 5944	1	2	3	4	5	6	7	Sat 2h59m10p
34		8	9	10	11	12	13	14	
35		15	16	17	18	19	20	21	
36		22	23	24	25	26	27	28	
37		29	1[a]	2[a]	3	4	5	6	Sun 15h43m11p
38	Tishri 5945	7	8	9	10[b]	11	12	13	
39		14	15[c]	16	17	18	19	20	
40		21	22	23	24	25	26	27	
41		28	29	30	1	2	3	4	Tue 4h27m12p
42	Heshvan 5945	5	6	7	8	9	10	11	
43		12	13	14	15	16	17	18	
44		19	20	21	22	23	24	25	
45		26	27	28	29	30	1	2	Wed 17h11m13p
46	Kislev 5945	3	4	5	6	7	8	9	
47		10	11	12	13	14	15	16	
48		17	18	19	20	21	22	23	
49		24	25[e]	26[e]	27[e]	28[e]	29[e]	30[e]	
50		1[e]	2[d][e]	3	4	5	6	7	Fri 5h55m14p
51	Teveth 5945	8	9	10	11	12	13	14	
52		15	16	17	18	19	20	21	
53		22	23	24	25	26	27	28	

Chinese Guǐ-Wèi‡/Jiǎ-Shēn

ISO Week	Month	Sun	Mon	Tue	Wed	Thu	Fri	Sat	Solar Term
1	Month 11* Guǐ-Wèi	14	15	16	17	18	19*	20	
2		21	22	23	24	25	26	27	Xiǎo hán
3		28	29	1	2	3	4	5	
4	Month 12 Guǐ-Wèi	6	7	**8**	9	10	11	12	Dà hán
5		13	14	15	16	17	18	19	
6		20	21	22	23	24	25	26	Lì chūn
7		27	28	29	30	1[a]	2	3	
8	Month 1 Jiǎ-Shēn	4	5	6	7	**8**	9	10	Yǔ shuǐ
9		11	12	13	14	15[b]	16	17	
10		18	19	20*	21	22	23	24	Jīng zhé
11		25	26	27	28	29	1	2	
12	Month 2 Jiǎ-Shēn	3	4	5	6	7	8	**9**	Chūn fēn
13		10	11	12	13	14	15	16	
14		17	18	19	20	21	22	23	
15		24[c]	25	26	27	28	29	30	Qīng míng
16		1	2	3	4	5	6	7	
17	Month 3 Jiǎ-Shēn	8	**9**	10	11	12	13	14	Gǔ yǔ
18		15	16	17	18	19	20	21*	
19		22	23	24	25	26	27	28	Lì xià
20		29	1	2	3	4	5	6	
21	Month 4 Jiǎ-Shēn	7	8	9	10	**11**	12	13	Xiǎo mǎn
22		14	15	16	17	18	19	20	
23		21	22	23	24	25	26	27	Máng zhòng
24		28	29	1	2	3	4	5[d]	
25	Month 5 Jiǎ-Shēn	6	7	8	9	10	11	12	
26		**13**	14	15	16	17	18	19	Xià zhì
27		20	21	22	23*	24	25	26	
28		27	28	29	30	1	2	3	Xiǎo shǔ
29	Month 6 Jiǎ-Shēn	4	5	6	7	8	9	10	
30		11	12	13	14	**15**	16	17	Dà shǔ
31		18	19	20	21	22	23	24	
32		25	26	27	28	29	1	2	Lì qiū
33	Month 7 Jiǎ-Shēn	3	4	5	6	7[e]	8	9	
34		10	11	12	13	14	15[f]	16	
35		**17**	18	19	20	21	22	23	Chǔ shǔ
36		24*	25	26	27	28	29	30	
37		1	2	3	4	5	6	7	Bái lù
38	Month 8 Jiǎ-Shēn	8	9	10	11	12	13	14	
39		15[g]	16	17	**18**	19	20	21	Qiū fēn
40		22	23	24	25	26	27	28	
41		29	1	2	3	4	5	6	Hán lù
42	Month 9 Jiǎ-Shēn	7	8	9[h]	10	11	12	13	
43		14	15	16	17	18	19	**20**	Shuāng jiàng
44		21	22	23	24	25*	26	27	
45		28	29	30	1	2	3	4	
46	Month 10 Jiǎ-Shēn	5	6	7	8	9	10	11	Lì dōng
47		12	13	14	15	16	17	18	
48		**19**	20	21	22	23	24	25	Xiǎo xuě
49		26	27	28	29	30	1	2	
50	Month 11 Jiǎ-Shēn	3	4	5	6	7	8	9	Dà xuě
51		10	11	12	13	14	15	16	
52		17	18	19[i]	20	21	22	23	Dōng zhì
53		24	25*	26	27	28	29	30	

Coptic 1900/1901 — Ethiopic 2176/2177

ISO Week	Coptic Month	Sun	Mon	Tue	Wed	Thu	Fri	Sat	Ethiopic Month
1	Koiak 1900	17	18	19	20	21	22	23	Tākhśāś 2176
2		24	25	26	27	28	29[c]	30	
3		1	2	3	4	5	6[d]	7	
4	Tōbe 1900	8	9	10	11[e]	12	13	14	Ṭer 2176
5		15	16	17	18	19	20	21	
6		22	23	24	25	26	27	28	
7		29	30	1	2	3	4	5	
8	Meshir 1900	6	7	8	9	10	11	12	Yakātīt 2176
9		13	14	15	16	17	18	19	
10		20	21	22	23	24	25	26	
11		27	28	29	30	1	2	3	
12	Paremotep 1900	4	5	6	7	8	9	10	Magābit 2176
13		11	12	13	14	15	16	17	
14		18	19	20	21	22	23	24	
15		25	26	27	28	29	30	1	
16	Parmoute 1900	2	3	4	5	6	7	8	Miyāzyā 2176
17		9	10	11	12	13	14	15	
18		16	17	18	19	20	21	22	
19		23[f]	24	25	26	27	28	29[g]	
20		30	1	2	3	4	5	6	
21	Pashons 1900	7	8	9	10	11	12	13	Genbot 2176
22		14	15	16	17	18	19	20	
23		21	22	23	24	25	26	27	
24		28	29	30	1	2	3	4	
25	Paōne 1900	5	6	7	8	9	10	11	Sanē 2176
26		12	13	14	15	16	17	18	
27		19	20	21	22	23	24	25	
28		26	27	28	29	30	1	2	
29	Epēp 1900	3	4	5	6	7	8	9	Hamlē 2176
30		10	11	12	13	14	15	16	
31		17	18	19	20	21	22	23	
32		24	25	26	27	28	29	30	
33	Mesorē 1900	1	2	3	4	5	6	7	Naḥasē 2176
34		8	9	10	11	12	13[h]	14	
35		15	16	17	18	19	20	21	
36		22	23	24	25	26	27	28	
37	Epag. 1900	29	30	1	2	3	4	5	Pāg. 2176
38	Thoout 1901	1[a]	2	3	4	5	6	7	Maskaram 2177
39		8	9	10	11	12	13	14	
40		15	16	17[b]	18	19	20	21	
41		22	23	24	25	26	27	28	
42		29	30	1	2	3	4	5	
43	Paope 1901	6	7	8	9	10	11	12	Ṭeqemt 2177
44		13	14	15	16	17	18	19	
45		20	21	22	23	24	25	26	
46		27	28	29	30	1	2	3	
47	Athōr 1901	4	5	6	7	8	9	10	Hedār 2177
48		11	12	13	14	15	16	17	
49		18	19	20	21	22	23	24	
50		25	26	27	28	29	30	1	
51	Koiak 1901	2	3	4	5	6	7	8	Tākhśāś 2177
52		9	10	11	12	13	14	15	
53		16	17	18	19	20	21	22	

‡Leap year
[a]New Year
[b]Spring (21:40)
[c]Summer (12:40)
[d]Autumn (5:56)
[e]Winter (5:16)
● New moon
◐ First quarter moon
○ Full moon
◑ Last quarter moon

‡Leap year
[a]New Year
[b]Yom Kippur
[c]Sukkot
[d]Winter starts
[e]Hanukkah
[f]Purim
[g]Passover
[h]Shavuot
[i]Fast of Av

‡Leap year
[a]New Year (4882, Monkey)
[b]Lantern Festival
[c]Qīngmíng
[d]Dragon Festival
[e]Qīqiǎo
[f]Hungry Ghosts
[g]Mid-Autumn Festival
[h]Double-Ninth Festival
[i]Dōngzhì
*Start of 60-name cycle

[a]New Year
[b]Building of the Cross
[c]Christmas
[d]Jesus's Circumcision
[e]Epiphany
[f]Easter
[g]Mary's Announcement
[h]Jesus's Transfiguration

PERSIAN (ASTRONOMICAL) 1562/1563

Month	Sun	Mon	Tue	Wed	Thu	Fri	Sat
DEY 1562	7	8	9	10	11	12	13
	14	15	16	17	18	19	20
	21	22	23	24	25	26	27
BAHMAN 1562	28	29	30	*1*	2	3	4
	5	6	7	8	9	10	11
	12	13	14	15	16	17	18
	19	20	21	22	23	24	25
ESFAND 1562	26	27	28	29	30	*1*	2
	3	4	5	6	7	8	9
	10	11	12	13	14	15	16
	17	18	19	20	21	22	23
FARVARDĪN 1563	24	25	26	27	28	29	*1*[a]
	2	3	4	5	6	7	8
	9	10	11	12	13[b]	14	15
	16	17	18	19	20	21	22
	23	24	25	26	27	28	29
ORDĪBEHEŠT 1563	30	31	*1*	2	3	4	5
	6	7	8	9	10	11	12
	13	14	15	16	17	18	19
	20	21	22	23	24	25	26
XORDĀD 1563	27	28	29	30	31	*1*	2
	3	4	5	6	7	8	9
	10	11	12	13	14	15	16
	17	18	19	20	21	22	23
	24	25	26	27	28	29	30
TĪR 1563	31	*1*	2	3	4	5	6
	7	8	9	10	11	12	13
	14	15	16	17	18	19	20
	21	22	23	24	25	26	27
MORDĀD 1563	28	29	30	31	*1*	2	3
	4	5	6	7	8	9	10
	11	12	13	14	15	16	17
	18	19	20	21	22	23	24
	25	26	27	28	29	30	31
SHAHRĪVAR 1563	*1*	2	3	4	5	6	7
	8	9	10	11	12	13	14
	15	16	17	18	19	20	21
	22	23	24	25	26	27	28
MEHR 1563	29	30	31	*1*	2	3	4
	5	6	7	8	9	10	11
	12	13	14	15	16	17	18
	19	20	21	22	23	24	25
ĀBĀN 1563	26	27	28	29	30	*1*	2
	3	4	5	6	7	8	9
	10	11	12	13	14	15	16
	17	18	19	20	21	22	23
	24	25	26	27	28	29	30
ĀZAR 1563	*1*	2	3	4	5	6	7
	8	9	10	11	12	13	14
	15	16	17	18	19	20	21
	22	23	24	25	26	27	28
DEY 1563	29	30	*1*	2	3	4	5
	6	7	8	9	10	11	12

[a]New Year
[b]Sizdeh Bedar

HINDU LUNAR 2240‡/2241

Month	Sun	Mon	Tue	Wed	Thu	Fri	Sat
MĀRGAŚIRA 2240	15	16	17	18	19	20	*20*
	21	22	23	24	25	26	27
PAUSHA 2240	28	29	30	1	2	3	4
	5	6	**7**	9	10	11	12
	13	14	15	16	17	18	19
	20	21	22	*22*	23	24	25
MĀGHA 2240	26	27	28	29	30	**1**	3
	4	5	6	7	8	9	10
	11	12	13	14	15	16	17
	18	19	20	21	22	23	24
PHĀLGUNA 2240	25	26	27	28	29[h]	30	1
	2	3	4	5	**6**	8	9
	10	11	12	13	14	15	*15*[i]
	16	17	18	19	20	21	22
	23	24	25	26	27	28	**29**
CHAITRA 2241	1[a]	2	3	4	5	6	7
	8	9[b]	10	11	12	13	14
	15	16	17	18	19	*19*	20
	21	23	24	25	26	27	28
VAIŚĀKHA 2241	29	30	1	2	3	**4**	6
	7	8	9	10	*10*	11	12
	13	14	15	16	17	18	19
	20	21	22	23	24	25	**26**
JYAISHTHA 2241	28	29	30	1	2	3	4
	5	6	7	8	9	10	11
	12	13	14	15	*15*	16	**17**
	19	20	21	22	23	24	25
ĀSHĀDHA 2241	26	27	28	**29**	1	2	3
	4	5	6	*6*	7	8	9
	10	11	12	13	14	15	16
	17	18	19	20	21	**22**	24
ŚRĀVAṆA 2241	25	26	27	28	29	30	1
	2	3	4	5	6	7	8
	9	10	11	12	13	14	15
	16	17	18	19	20	21	22
	23[c]	24	**25**	27	28	29	30
BHĀDRAPADA 2241	1	2	3	*3*[d]	4	5	6
	7	8	9	10	11	12	13
	14	15	16	17	**18**	20	21
	22	23	24	25	26	27	28
ĀŚVINA 2241	29	30	1	2	3	4	5
	6	7	*7*	8[e]	9[e]	**10**[e]	12
	13	14	15	16	17	18	19
	20	21	22	**23**	25	26	27
KĀRTTIKA 2241	*27*	28	29	30	1[f]	2	3
	4	5	6	7	8	9	10
	11	12	13	14	**15**	17	18
	19	20	21	22	23	24	25
MĀRGAŚIRA 2241	26	27	28	29	30	*30*	1
	2	3	4	5	6	7	8
	9	11[g]	12	13	14	15	16
	17	18	19	20	21	22	23
	24	25	26	27	28	29	30

‡Leap year
[a]New Year (Tāraṇa)
[b]Birthday of Rāma
[c]Birthday of Krishna
[d]Ganēśa Chaturthī
[e]Dashara
[f]Diwali
[g]Birthday of Vishnu
[h]Night of Śiva
[i]Holi

HINDU SOLAR 2105‡/2106

Month	Sun	Mon	Tue	Wed	Thu	Fri	Sat
PAUSHA 2105	10	11	12	13	14	15	16
	17	18	19	20	21	22	23
MĀGHA 2105	24	25	26	27	28	29	1[b]
	2	3	4	5	6	7	8
	9	10	11	12	13	14	15
	16	17	18	19	20	21	22
	23	24	25	26	27	28	29
PHĀLGUNA 2105	1	2	3	4	5	6	7
	8	9	10	11	12	13	14
	15	16	17	18	19	20	21
	22	23	24	25	26	27	28
CHAITRA 2105	29	30	1	2	3	4	5
	6	7	8	9	10	11	12
	13	14	15	16	17	18	19
	20	21	22	23	24	25	26
VAIŚĀKHA 2106	27	28	29	30	31	1[a]	2
	3	4	5	6	7	8	9
	10	11	12	13	14	15	16
	17	18	19	20	21	22	23
	24	25	26	27	28	29	30
JYAISHTHA 2106	31	1	2	3	4	5	6
	7	8	9	10	11	12	13
	14	15	16	17	18	19	20
	21	22	23	24	25	26	27
ĀSHĀDHA 2106	28	29	30	31	1	2	3
	4	5	6	7	8	9	10
	11	12	13	14	15	16	17
	18	19	20	21	22	23	24
	25	26	27	28	29	30	31
ŚRĀVAṆA 2106	32	1	2	3	4	5	6
	7	8	9	10	11	12	13
	14	15	16	17	18	19	20
	21	22	23	24	25	26	27
BHĀDRAPADA 2106	28	29	30	31	1	2	3
	4	5	6	7	8	9	10
	11	12	13	14	15	16	17
	18	19	20	21	22	23	24
	25	26	27	28	29	30	31
ĀŚVINA 2106	1	2	3	4	5	6	7
	8	9	10	11	12	13	14
	15	16	17	18	19	20	21
	22	23	24	25	26	27	28
KĀRTTIKA 2106	29	30	31	1	2	3	4
	5	6	7	8	9	10	11
	12	13	14	15	16	17	18
	19	20	21	22	23	24	25
MĀRGAŚIRA 2106	26	27	28	29	1	2	3
	4	5	6	7	8	9	10
	11	12	13	14	15	16	17
	18	19	20	21	22	23	24
PAUSHA 2106	25	26	27	28	29	30	1
	2	3	4	5	6	7	8
	9	10	11	12	13	14	15

‡Leap year
[a]New Year (Vikārin)
[b]Pongal

ISLAMIC (ASTRONOMICAL) 1610/1611

Month	Sun	Mon	Tue	Wed	Thu	Fri	Sat
JUMĀDĀ I 1610	13	14	15	16	17	18	19
	20	21	22	23	24	25	26
JUMĀDĀ II 1610	27	28	29	30	*1*	2	3
	4	5	6	7	8	9	10
	11	12	13	14	15	16	17
	18	19	20	21	22	23	24
RAJAB 1610	25	26	27	28	29	*1*	2
	3	4	5	6	7	8	9
	10	11	12	13	14	15	16
	17	18	19	20	21	22	23
	24	25	26	27[d]	28	29	30
SHA'BĀN 1610	*1*	2	3	4	5	6	7
	8	9	10	11	12	13	14
	15	16	17	18	19	20	21
	22	23	24	25	26	27	28
RAMAḌĀN 1610	29	*1*[e]	2	3	4	5	6
	7	8	9	10	11	12	13
	14	15	16	17	18	19	20
	21	22	23	24	25	26	27
SHAWWĀL 1610	28	29	30	*1*[f]	2	3	4
	5	6	7	8	9	10	11
	12	13	14	15	16	17	18
	19	20	21	22	23	24	25
DHU AL-QA'DA 1610	26	27	28	29	*1*	2	3
	4	5	6	7	8	9	10
	11	12	13	14	15	16	17
	18	19	20	21	22	23	24
DHU AL-ḤIJJA 1610	25	26	27	28	29	30	*1*
	2	3	4	5	6	7	8
	9	10[g]	11	12	13	14	15
	16	17	18	19	20	21	22
	23	24	25	26	27	28	29
MUḤARRAM 1611	*1*[a]	2	3	4	5	6	7
	8	9	10[b]	11	12	13	14
	15	16	17	18	19	20	21
	22	23	24	25	26	27	28
ṢAFAR 1611	29	*1*	2	3	4	5	6
	7	8	9	10	11	12	13
	14	15	16	17	18	19	20
	21	22	23	24	25	26	27
RABĪ' I 1611	28	29	30	*1*	2	3	4
	5	6	7	8	9	10	11
	12[c]	13	14	15	16	17	18
	19	20	21	22	23	24	25
RABĪ' II 1611	26	27	28	29	30	*1*	2
	3	4	5	6	7	8	9
	10	11	12	13	14	15	16
	17	18	19	20	21	22	23
JUMĀDĀ I 1611	24	25	26	27	28	29	*1*
	2	3	4	5	6	7	8
	9	10	11	12	13	14	15
	16	17	18	19	20	21	22
	23	24	25	26	27	28	29

[a]New Year
[b]'Ashūrā'
[c]Prophet's Birthday
[d]Ascent of the Prophet
[e]Start of Ramaḍān
[f]'Id al-Fiṭr
[g]'Id al-'Aḍḥā

GREGORIAN 2184‡

Julian† (Sun)	Sun	Mon	Tue	Wed	Thu	Fri	Sat	Month
Dec 14	*28*	29	30	31	1	2	3	JANUARY 2184
	4	5	6	7	8[a]	9	10	
Dec 28	*11*	12	13	14	15[b]	16	17	
	18	19	20	21	22	23	24	
Jan 11	*25*	26	27	28	29	30	31	
	1	2	3	4	5	6	7	FEBRUARY 2184
Jan 25	*8*	9	10	11[c]	12	13	14	
	15	16	17	18	19	20	21	
Feb 8	*22*	23	24	25	26	27	28	
	29	1	2	3	4	5	6	MARCH 2184
Feb 22	*7*	8	9	10	11	12	13	
	14	15	16	17	18	19	20	
Mar 7	*21*[d]	22	23	24	25	26	27	
	28[e]	29	30	31	1	2	3	APRIL 2184
Mar 21	*4*	5	6	7	8	9	10	
	11	12	13	14	15	16	17	
Apr 4	*18*	19	20	21	22	23	24	
	25	26	27	28	29	30	1	MAY 2184
Apr 18	*2*[f]	3	4	5	6	7	8	
	9	10	11	12	13	14	15	
May 2	*16*	17	18	19	20	21	22	
	23	24	25	26	27	28	29	
May 16	*30*	31	1	2	3	4	5	JUNE 2184
	6	7	8	9	10	11	12	
May 30	*13*	14	15	16	17	18	19	
	20	21	22	23	24	25	26	
Jun 13	*27*	28	29	30	1	2	3	JULY 2184
	4	5	6	7	8	9	10	
Jun 27	*11*	12	13	14	15	16	17	
	18	19	20	21	22	23	24	
Jul 11	*25*	26	27	28	29	30	31	
	1	2	3	4	5	6	7	AUGUST 2184
Jul 25	*8*	9	10	11	12	13	14	
	15	16	17	18	19	20	21	
Aug 8	*22*	23	24	25	26	27	28	
	29	30	31	1	2	3	4	SEPTEMBER 2184
Aug 22	*5*	6	7	8	9	10	11	
	12	13	14	15	16	17	18	
Sep 5	*19*	20	21	22	23	24	25	
	26	27	28	29	30	1	2	OCTOBER 2184
Sep 19	*3*	4	5	6	7	8	9	
	10	11	12	13	14	15	16	
Oct 3	*17*	18	19	20	21	22	23	
	24	25	26	27	28	29	30	
Oct 17	*31*	1	2	3	4	5	6	NOVEMBER 2184
	7	8	9	10	11	12	13	
Oct 31	*14*	15	16	17	18	19	20	
	21	22	23	24	25	26	27	
Nov 14	*28*[g]	29	30	1	2	3	4	DECEMBER 2184
	5	6	7	8	9	10	11	
Nov 28	*12*	13	14	15	16	17	18	
	19	20	21	22	23	24	25[h]	
Dec 12	*26*	27	28	29	30	31	1	

‡Leap year
[a]Orthodox Christmas
[b]Julian New Year
[c]Ash Wednesday
[d]Feast of Orthodoxy
[e]Easter
[f]Orthodox Easter
[g]Advent
[h]Christmas

2185

Gregorian 2185	Sun	Mon	Tue	Wed	Thu	Fri	Sat	Lunar Phases	ISO Week (Mon)	Julian Day (Sun noon)
	26	27	28	29	30	31	●[a]	21:16	53	2519110
	2	3	4	5	6	7	8		1	2519117
January 2185	◐	10	11	12	13	14	15	7:39	2	2519124
	○	17	18	19	20	21	22	0:24	3	2519131
	◑	24	25	26	27	28	29	13:36	4	2519138
	30	●	1	2	3	4	5	14:00	5	2519145
	6	◐	8	9	10	11	12	15:46	6	2519152
February 2185	13	○	15	16	17	18	19	13:58	7	2519159
	20	21	◑	23	24	25	26	11:02	8	2519166
	27	28	1	●	3	4	5	4:13	9	2519173
	6	7	◐	9	10	11	12	23:02	10	2519180
March 2185	13	14	15	○	17	18	19	4:52	11	2519187
	20[b]	21	22	23	◑	25	26	7:10	12	2519194
	27	28	29	30	●	1	2	15:35	13	2519201
	3	4	5	6	◐	8	9	6:37	14	2519208
April 2185	10	11	12	13	○	15	16	20:30	15	2519215
	17	18	19	20	21	22	◑	0:32	16	2519222
	24	25	26	27	28	29	●	0:29	17	2519229
	1	2	3	4	5	◐	7	15:28	18	2519236
	8	9	10	11	12	13	○	12:20	19	2519243
May 2185	15	16	17	18	19	20	21		20	2519250
	◑	23	24	25	26	27	28	14:17	21	2519257
	●	30	31	1	2	3	4	7:49	22	2519264
	◐	6	7	8	9	10	11	2:13	23	2519271
June 2185	12	○	14	15	16	17	18	3:51	24	2519278
	19	20[c]	◑	22	23	24	25	0:21	25	2519285
	26	●	28	29	30	1	2	14:44	26	2519292
	3	◐	5	6	7	8	9	15:09	27	2519299
July 2185	10	11	○	13	14	15	16	18:39	28	2519306
	17	18	19	◑	21	22	23	7:27	29	2519313
	24	25	●	27	28	29	30	22:21	30	2519320
	31	1	2	◐	4	5	6	6:19	31	2519327
	7	8	9	10	○	12	13	8:18	32	2519334
August 2185	14	15	16	17	◑	19	20	12:47	33	2519341
	21	22	23	24	●	26	27	7:33	34	2519348
	28	29	30	31	◐	2	3	23:34	35	2519355
	4	5	6	7	8	○	10	20:32	36	2519362
September 2185	11	12	13	14	15	◑	17	17:52	37	2519369
	18	19	20	21	22[d]	●	24	19:02	38	2519376
	25	26	27	28	29	30	◐	18:21	39	2519383
	2	3	4	5	6	7	8		40	2519390
October 2185	○	10	11	12	13	14	15	7:32	41	2519397
	◑	17	18	19	20	21	22	0:11	42	2519404
	●	24	25	26	27	28	29	9:16	43	2519411
	30	◐	1	2	3	4	5	13:29	44	2519418
	6	○	8	9	10	11	12	17:49	45	2519425
November 2185	13	◑	15	16	17	18	19	8:58	46	2519432
	20	21	●	23	24	25	26	2:16	47	2519439
	27	28	29	◐	1	2	3	7:22	48	2519446
	4	5	6	○	8	9	10	4:05	49	2519453
December 2185	11	12	◑	14	15	16	17	21:00	50	2519460
	18	19	20	●[e]	22	23	24	21:25	51	2519467
	25	26	27	28	◐	30	31	22:38	52	2519474

ISO Week	Hebrew 5945‡/5946	Sun	Mon	Tue	Wed	Thu	Fri	Sat	Molad
53	Teveth 5945	22	23	24	25	26	27	28	
1		29	1	2	3	4	5	6	Sat 18h 39m 15p
2		7	8	9	10	11	12	13	
3	Shevat 5945	14	15	16	17	18	19	20	
4		21	22	23	24	25	26	27	
5		28	29	30	1	2	3	4	Mon 7h 23m 16p
6		5	6	7	8	9	10	11	
7	Adar I 5945	12	13	14	15	16	17	18	
8		19	20	21	22	23	24	25	Tue 20h 7m 17p
9		26	27	28	29	30	1	2	
10		3	4	5	6	7	8	9	
11	Adar II 5945	10	11	12	13	14[f]	15	16	
12		17	18	19	20	21	22	23	Thu 8h 52m 0p
13		24	25	26	27	28	29	1	
14		2	3	4	5	6	7	8	
15	Nisan 5945	9	10	11	12	13	14	15[g]	
16		16	17	18	19	20	21	22	
17		23	24	25	26	27	28	29	Fri 21h 36m 1p
18		30	1	2	3	4	5	6	
19		7	8	9	10	11	12	13	
20	Iyar 5945	14	15	16	17	18	19	20	
21		21	22	23	24	25	26	27	
22		28	29	1	2	3	4	5	Sun 10h 20m 2p
23		6[h]	7	8	9	10	11	12	
24	Sivan 5945	13	14	15	16	17	18	19	
25		20	21	22	23	24	25	26	
26		27	28	29	30	1	2	3	Mon 23h 4m 3p
27		4	5	6	7	8	9	10	
28	Tammuz 5945	11	12	13	14	15	16	17	
29		18	19	20	21	22	23	24	
30		25	26	27	28	29	1	2	Wed 11h 48m 4p
31		3	4	5	6	7	8	9	
32	Av 5945	10[i]	11	12	13	14	15	16	
33		17	18	19	20	21	22	23	
34		24	25	26	27	28	29	30	Fri 0h 32m 5p
35		1	2	3	4	5	6	7	
36		8	9	10	11	12	13	14	
37	Elul 5945	15	16	17	18	19	20	21	
38		22	23	24	25	26	27	28	
39		29	1[a]	2[a]	3	4	5	6	Sat 13h 16m 6p
40		7	8	9	10[b]	11	12	13	
41	Tishri 5946	14	15[c]	16	17	18	19	20	
42		21	22	23	24	25	26	27	
43		28	29	30	1	2	3	4	Mon 2h 0m 7p
44		5	6	7	8	9	10	11	
45	Ḥeshvan 5946	12	13	14	15	16	17	18	
46		19	20	21	22	23	24	25	
47		26	27	28	29	1	2	3	Tue 14h 44m 8p
48		4	5	6	7	8	9	10	
49	Kislev 5946	11	12	13[d]	14	15	16	17	
50		18	19	20	21	22	23	24	
51	Teveth 5946	25[e]	26[e]	27[e]	28[e]	29[e]	1[e]	2[e]	Thu 3h 28m 9p
52		3[e]	4	5	6	7	8	9	

ISO Week	Chinese Jiă-Shēn/Yĭ-Yŏu	Sun	Mon	Tue	Wed	Thu	Fri	Sat	Solar Term
53		24	25	26	27	28	29	30	
1		1	2	3	4	5	6	7	Xiăo hán
2	Month 12 Jiă-Shēn	8	9	10	11	12	13	14	
3		15	16	17	18	19	20	21	
4		22	23	24	25	26	27	28	Dà hán
5		29	1[a]	2	3	4	5	6	Lì chūn
6	Month 1 Yĭ-Yŏu	7	8	9	10	11	12	13	
7		14	15[b]	16	17	18	19	20	Yŭ shuĭ
8		21	22	23	24	25	26*	27	
9		28	29	30	1	2	3	4	Jīng zhé
10	Month 2 Yĭ-Yŏu	5	6	7	8	9	10	11	
11		12	13	14	15	16	17	18	
12		19	20	21	22	23	24	25	Chūn fēn
13		26	27	28	29	1	2	3	
14	Month 3 Yĭ-Yŏu	4	5[c]	6	7	8	9	10	Qīng míng
15		11	12	13	14	15	16	17	
16		18	19	20	21	22	23	24	Gŭ yŭ
17		25	26	27*	28	29	30	1	
18		2	3	4	5	6	7	8	Lì xià
19	Month 4 Yĭ-Yŏu	9	10	11	12	13	14	15	
20		16	17	18	19	20	21	22	Xiăo măn
21		23	24	25	26	27	28	29	
22		1	2	3	4	5[d]	6	7	
23	Month 5 Yĭ-Yŏu	8	9	10	11	12	13	14	Máng zhòng
24		15	16	17	18	19	20	21	
25		22	23	24	25	26	27	28*	Xià zhì
26		29	1	2	3	4	5	6	
27	Month 6 Yĭ-Yŏu	7	8	9	10	11	12	13	Xiăo shŭ
28		14	15	16	17	18	19	20	
29		21	22	23	24	25	26	27	Dà shŭ
30		28	29	30	1	2	3	4	
31	Month 7 Yĭ-Yŏu	5	6	7[e]	8	9	10	11	
32		12	13	14	15[f]	16	17	18	Lì qiū
33		19	20	21	22	23	24	25	
34		26	27	28	29*	1	2	3	Chŭ shŭ
35	Month 8 Yĭ-Yŏu	4	5	6	7	8	9	10	
36		11	12	13	14	15[g]	16	17	Bái lù
37		18	19	20	21	22	23	24	
38		25	26	27	28	29	30	1	Qiū fēn
39	Month 9 Yĭ-Yŏu	2	3	4	5	6	7	8	
40		9[h]	10	11	12	13	14	15	Hán lù
41		16	17	18	19	20	21	22	
42		23	24	25	26	27	28	29	
43		1*	2	3	4	5	6	7	Shuāng jiàng
44	Month 10 Yĭ-Yŏu	8	9	10	11	12	13	14	
45		15	16	17	18	19	20	21	Lì dōng
46		22	23	24	25	26	27	28	
47		29	30	1	2	3	4	5	Xiăo xuě
48	Month 11 Yĭ-Yŏu	6	7	8	9	10	11	12	
49		13	14	15	16	17	18	19	Dà xuě
50		20	21	22	23	24	25	26	
51	Month 12 Yĭ-Yŏu	27	28	29	30[i]	1*	2	3	Dōng zhì
52		4	5	6	7	8	9	10	

ISO Week	Coptic 1901/1902	Sun	Mon	Tue	Wed	Thu	Fri	Sat	Ethiopic 2177/2178
53		16	17	18	19	20	21	22	
1	Koiak 1901	23	24	25	26	27	28	29[c]	Tākhśāś 2177
2		30	1	2	3	4	5	6[d]	
3		7	8	9	10	11[e]	12	13	
4	Tôbe 1901	14	15	16	17	18	19	20	Ṭer 2177
5		21	22	23	24	25	26	27	
6		28	29	30	1	2	3	4	
7		5	6	7	8	9	10	11	
8	Meshir 1901	12	13	14	15	16	17	18	Yakātit 2177
9		19	20	21	22	23	24	25	
10		26	27	28	29	30	1	2	
11		3	4	5	6	7	8	9	
12	Paremotep 1901	10	11	12	13	14	15	16	Magābit 2177
13		17	18	19	20	21	22	23	
14		24	25	26	27	28	29	30	
15		1	2	3	4	5	6	7	
16	Parmoute 1901	8	9	10	11	12	13	14	Miyāzyā 2177
17		15[f]	16	17	18	19	20	21	
18		22	23	24	25	26	27	28	
19		29[g]	30	1	2	3	4	5	
20		6	7	8	9	10	11	12	
21	Pashons 1901	13	14	15	16	17	18	19	Genbot 2177
22		20	21	22	23	24	25	26	
23		27	28	29	30	1	2	3	
24		4	5	6	7	8	9	10	
25	Paône 1901	11	12	13	14	15	16	17	Sanē 2177
26		18	19	20	21	22	23	24	
27		25	26	27	28	29	30	1	
28		2	3	4	5	6	7	8	
29	Epêp 1901	9	10	11	12	13	14	15	Ḥamlē 2177
30		16	17	18	19	20	21	22	
31		23	24	25	26	27	28	29	
32		30	1	2	3	4	5	6	
33	Mesorê 1901	7	8	9	10	11	12	13[h]	Naḥasē 2177
34		14	15	16	17	18	19	20	
35		21	22	23	24	25	26	27	
36		28	29	30	1	2	3	4	
37	Epag. 1901	5	1[a]	2	3	4	5	6	Pāg. 2177
38		7	8	9	10	11	12	13	
39	Thoout 1902	14	15	16	17[b]	18	19	20	Maskaram 2178
40		21	22	23	24	25	26	27	
41		28	29	30	1	2	3	4	
42		5	6	7	8	9	10	11	
43	Paope 1902	12	13	14	15	16	17	18	Ṭeqemt 2178
44		19	20	21	22	23	24	25	
45		26	27	28	29	30	1	2	
46		3	4	5	6	7	8	9	
47	Athôr 1902	10	11	12	13	14	15	16	Ḫedār 2178
48		17	18	19	20	21	22	23	
49		24	25	26	27	28	29	30	
50		1	2	3	4	5	6	7	
51	Koiak 1902	8	9	10	11	12	13	14	Tākhśāś 2178
52		15	16	17	18	19	20	21	

Gregorian:
[a]New Year
[b]Spring (3:37)
[c]Summer (18:27)
[d]Autumn (11:40)
[e]Winter (11:09)
● New moon
◐ First quarter moon
○ Full moon
◑ Last quarter moon

Hebrew:
‡Leap year
[a]New Year
[b]Yom Kippur
[c]Sukkot
[d]Winter starts
[e]Ḥanukkah
[f]Purim
[g]Passover
[h]Shavuot
[i]Fast of Av

Chinese:
[a]New Year (4883, Fowl)
[b]Lantern Festival
[c]Qīngmíng
[d]Dragon Festival
[e]Qīqiǎo
[f]Hungry Ghosts
[g]Mid-Autumn Festival
[h]Double-Ninth Festival
[i]Dōngzhì
*Start of 60-name cycle

Coptic/Ethiopic:
[a]New Year
[b]Building of the Cross
[c]Christmas
[d]Jesus's Circumcision
[e]Epiphany
[f]Easter
[g]Mary's Announcement
[h]Jesus's Transfiguration

PERSIAN (ASTRONOMICAL) 1563/1564‡

Month	Sun	Mon	Tue	Wed	Thu	Fri	Sat
DEY 1563	6	7	8	9	10	11	12
	13	14	15	16	17	18	19
	20	21	22	23	24	25	26
BAHMAN 1563	27	28	29	30	1	2	3
	4	5	6	7	8	9	10
	11	12	13	14	15	16	17
	18	19	20	21	22	23	24
ESFAND 1563	25	26	27	28	29	30	1
	2	3	4	5	6	7	8
	9	10	11	12	13	14	15
	16	17	18	19	20	21	22
	23	24	25	26	27	28	29
FARVARDĪN 1564	1[a]	2	3	4	5	6	7
	8	9	10	11	12	13[b]	14
	15	16	17	18	19	20	21
	22	23	24	25	26	27	28
ORDĪBEHEŠT 1564	29	30	31	1	2	3	4
	5	6	7	8	9	10	11
	12	13	14	15	16	17	18
	19	20	21	22	23	24	25
XORDĀD 1564	26	27	28	29	30	31	1
	2	3	4	5	6	7	8
	9	10	11	12	13	14	15
	16	17	18	19	20	21	22
	23	24	25	26	27	28	29
TĪR 1564	30	31	1	2	3	4	5
	6	7	8	9	10	11	12
	13	14	15	16	17	18	19
	20	21	22	23	24	25	26
MORDĀD 1564	27	28	29	30	31	1	2
	3	4	5	6	7	8	9
	10	11	12	13	14	15	16
	17	18	19	20	21	22	23
	24	25	26	27	28	29	30
SHAHRĪVAR 1564	31	1	2	3	4	5	6
	7	8	9	10	11	12	13
	14	15	16	17	18	19	20
	21	22	23	24	25	26	27
MEHR 1564	28	29	30	31	1	2	3
	4	5	6	7	8	9	10
	11	12	13	14	15	16	17
	18	19	20	21	22	23	24
ĀBĀN 1564	25	26	27	28	29	30	1
	2	3	4	5	6	7	8
	9	10	11	12	13	14	15
	16	17	18	19	20	21	22
	23	24	25	26	27	28	29
ĀZAR 1564	30	1	2	3	4	5	6
	7	8	9	10	11	12	13
	14	15	16	17	18	19	20
	21	22	23	24	25	26	27
DEY 1564	28	29	30	1	2	3	4
	5	6	7	8	9	10	11

‡Leap year
[a]New Year
[b]Sizdeh Bedar

HINDU LUNAR 2241/2242

Month	Sun	Mon	Tue	Wed	Thu	Fri	Sat
	24	25	26	27	28	29	30
PAUSHA 2241	1	2	3	4	5	6	7
	8	9	10	11	12	13	14
	16	17	18	19	20	21	22
	23	23	24	25	26	27	28
MĀGHA 2241	29	30	1	2	3	4	5
	6	7	8	10	11	12	13
	14	15	16	17	18	19	20
	21	22	23	24	25	25	26
PHĀLGUNA 2241	27	28[h]	29	30	1	2	4
	5	6	7	8	9	10	11
	12	13	14	15[i]	16	17	18
	19	20	21	22	23	24	25
CHAITRA 2242	26	27	28	29	30	1[a]	2
	3	4	5	6	8	9[b]	10
	11	12	13	14	15	16	17
	18	19	19	20	21	22	23
	24	25	26	27	28	29	30
VAIŚĀKHA 2242	2	3	4	5	6	7	8
	9	10	11	12	13	14	15
	16	17	18	19	20	21	22
	23	24	25	26	27	28	29
JYAISHTHA 2242	30	1	2	3	5	6	7
	8	9	10	11	12	13	14
	14	15	16	17	18	19	20
	21	22	23	24	25	26	28
ĀSHĀḌHA 2242	29	30	1	2	3	4	5
	6	7	8	9	10	11	12
	13	14	15	16	17	18	19
	20	21	22	23	24	25	26
ŚRĀVAṆA 2242	27	28	29	1	2	3	4
	5	6	7	8	9	10	11
	11	12	13	14	15	16	17
	18	19	20	21	22[c]	24	25
BHĀDRAPADA 2242	26	27	28	29	30	1	2
	3[d]	4	5	6	7	8	9
	10	11	12	13	14	15	16
	17	18	19	20	21	22	23
ĀŚVINA 2242	24	25	27	28	29	30	1
	2	3	4	5	6	7	7
	8[e]	9[e]	10[e]	11	12	13	14
	15	16	17	18	20	21	22
	23	24	25	26	27	28	29
KĀRTTIKA 2242	30	1[f]	2	3	4	5	6
	7	8	9	10	11	12	13
	14	15	16	17	18	19	20
	21	22	24	25	26	27	28
MĀRGAŚĪRA 2242	29	30	1	1	2	3	4
	5	6	7	8	9	10	11[g]
	12	13	14	15	16	18	19
	20	21	22	23	24	25	26
PAUSHA 2242	27	28	29	30	1	2	3
	3	4	5	6	7	8	9

[a]New Year (Pārthiva)
[b]Birthday of Rāma
[c]Birthday of Krishna
[d]Ganēśa Chaturthī
[e]Dashara
[f]Diwali
[g]Birthday of Vishnu
[h]Night of Śiva
[i]Holi

HINDU SOLAR 2106/2107

Month	Sun	Mon	Tue	Wed	Thu	Fri	Sat
	9	10	11	12	13	14	15
PAUSHA 2106	16	17	18	19	20	21	22
	23	24	25	26	27	28	29
MĀGHA 2106	1[b]	2	3	4	5	6	7
	8	9	10	11	12	13	14
	15	16	17	18	19	20	21
	22	23	24	25	26	27	28
PHĀLGUNA 2106	29	30	1	2	3	4	5
	6	7	8	9	10	11	12
	13	14	15	16	17	18	19
	20	21	22	23	24	25	26
CHAITRA 2106	27	28	29	1	2	3	4
	5	6	7	8	9	10	11
	12	13	14	15	16	17	18
	19	20	21	22	23	24	25
VAIŚĀKHA 2107	26	27	28	29	30	31	1[a]
	2	3	4	5	6	7	8
	9	10	11	12	13	14	15
	16	17	18	19	20	21	22
	23	24	25	26	27	28	29
JYAISHTHA 2107	30	31	1	2	3	4	5
	6	7	8	9	10	11	12
	13	14	15	16	17	18	19
	20	21	22	23	24	25	26
ĀSHĀḌHA 2107	27	28	29	30	31	1	2
	3	4	5	6	7	8	9
	10	11	12	13	14	15	16
	17	18	19	20	21	22	23
	24	25	26	27	28	29	30
ŚRĀVAṆA 2107	31	32	1	2	3	4	5
	6	7	8	9	10	11	12
	13	14	15	16	17	18	19
	20	21	22	23	24	25	26
BHĀDRAPADA 2107	27	28	29	30	31	1	2
	3	4	5	6	7	8	9
	10	11	12	13	14	15	16
	17	18	19	20	21	22	23
	24	25	26	27	28	29	30
ĀŚVINA 2107	31	1	2	3	4	5	6
	7	8	9	10	11	12	13
	14	15	16	17	18	19	20
	21	22	23	24	25	26	27
KĀRTTIKA 2107	28	29	30	31	1	2	3
	4	5	6	7	8	9	10
	11	12	13	14	15	16	17
	18	19	20	21	22	23	24
MĀRGAŚĪRA 2107	25	26	27	28	29	30	1
	2	3	4	5	6	7	8
	9	10	11	12	13	14	15
	16	17	18	19	20	21	22
	23	24	25	26	27	28	29
PAUSHA 2107	1	2	3	4	5	6	7
	8	9	10	11	12	13	14

[a]New Year (Śārvari)
[b]Pongal

ISLAMIC (ASTRONOMICAL) 1611/1612‡

Month	Sun	Mon	Tue	Wed	Thu	Fri	Sat
JUMĀDĀ I 1611	23	24	25	26	27	28	29
JUMĀDĀ II 1611	30	1	2	3	4	5	6
	7	8	9	10	11	12	13
	14	15	16	17	18	19	20
	21	22	23	24	25	26	27
RAJAB 1611	28	29	30	1	2	3	4
	5	6	7	8	9	10	11
	12	13	14	15	16	17	18
	19	20	21	22	23	24	25
SHA'BĀN 1611	26	27[d]	28	29	1	2	3
	4	5	6	7	8	9	10
	11	12	13	14	15	16	17
	18	19	20	21	22	23	24
RAMAḌĀN 1611	25	26	27	28	29	30	1[e]
	2	3	4	5	6	7	8
	9	10	11	12	13	14	15
	16	17	18	19	20	21	22
	23	24	25	26	27	28	29
SHAWWĀL 1611	1[f]	2	3	4	5	6	7
	8	9	10	11	12	13	14
	15	16	17	18	19	20	21
	22	23	24	25	26	27	28
DHU AL-QA'DA 1611	29	30	1	2	3	4	5
	6	7	8	9	10	11	12
	13	14	15	16	17	18	19
	20	21	22	23	24	25	26
DHU AL-ḤIJJA 1611	27	28	29	1	2	3	4
	5	6	7	8	9	10[g]	11
	12	13	14	15	16	17	18
	19	20	21	22	23	24	25
MUḤARRAM 1612	26	27	28	29	1[a]	2[d]	3
	4	5	6	7	8	9	10[b]
	11	12	13	14	15	16	17
	18	19	20	21	22	23	24
ṢAFAR 1612	25	26	27	28	29	30	1
	2	3	4	5	6	7	8
	9	10	11	12	13	14	15
	16	17	18	19	20	21	22
	23	24	25	26	27	28	29
RABĪ' I 1612	1	2	3	4	5	6	7
	8	9	10	11	12[c]	13	14
	15	16	17	18	19	20	21
	22	23	24	25	26	27	28
RABĪ' II 1612	29	30	1	2	3	4	5
	6	7	8	9	10	11	12
	13	14	15	16	17	18	19
	20	21	22	23	24	25	26
JUMĀDĀ I 1612	27	28	29	1	2	3	4
	5	6	7	8	9	10	11
	12	13	14	15	16	17	18
	19	20	21	22	23	24	25
JUMĀDĀ II 1612	26	27	28	29	30	1	2
	3	4	5	6	7	8	9

‡Leap year
[a]New Year
[a]New Year (Arithmetic)
[b]'Ashūrā'
[c]Prophet's Birthday
[d]Ascent of the Prophet
[e]Start of Ramaḍān
[f]'Id al-Fiṭr
[g]'Id al-'Aḍḥā

GREGORIAN 2185

Julian (Sun)	Sun	Mon	Tue	Wed	Thu	Fri	Sat	Month
Dec 12	26	27	28	29	30	31	1	JANUARY 2185
	2	3	4	5	6	7	8[a]	
Dec 26	9	10	11	12	13	14	15[b]	
	16	17	18	19	20	21	22	
Jan 9	23	24	25	26	27	28	29	
	30	31	1	2	3	4	5	FEBRUARY 2185
Jan 23	6	7	8	9	10	11	12	
	13	14	15	16	17	18	19	
Feb 6	20	21	22	23	24	25	26	
	27	28	1	2[c]	3	4	5	MARCH 2185
Feb 20	6	7	8	9	10	11	12	
	13[d]	14	15	16	17	18	19	
Mar 6	20	21	22	23	24	25	26	
	27	28	29	30	31	1	2	APRIL 2185
Mar 20	3	4	5	6	7	8	9	
	10	11	12	13	14	15	16	
Apr 3	17[e]	18	19	20	21	22	23	
	24[f]	25	26	27	28	29	30	
Apr 17	1	2	3	4	5	6	7	MAY 2185
	8	9	10	11	12	13	14	
May 1	15	16	17	18	19	20	21	
	22	23	24	25	26	27	28	
May 15	29	30	31	1	2	3	4	JUNE 2185
	5	6	7	8	9	10	11	
May 29	12	13	14	15	16	17	18	
	19	20	21	22	23	24	25	
Jun 12	26	27	28	29	30	1	2	JULY 2185
	3	4	5	6	7	8	9	
Jun 26	10	11	12	13	14	15	16	
	17	18	19	20	21	22	23	
Jul 10	24	25	26	27	28	29	30	
	31	1	2	3	4	5	6	AUGUST 2185
Jul 24	7	8	9	10	11	12	13	
	14	15	16	17	18	19	20	
Aug 7	21	22	23	24	25	26	27	
	28	29	30	31	1	2	3	SEPTEMBER 2185
Aug 21	4	5	6	7	8	9	10	
	11	12	13	14	15	16	17	
Sep 4	18	19	20	21	22	23	24	
	25	26	27	28	29	30	1	OCTOBER 2185
Sep 18	2	3	4	5	6	7	8	
	9	10	11	12	13	14	15	
Oct 2	16	17	18	19	20	21	22	
	23	24	25	26	27	28	29	
Oct 16	30	31	1	2	3	4	5	NOVEMBER 2185
	6	7	8	9	10	11	12	
Oct 30	13	14	15	16	17	18	19	
	20	21	22	23	24	25	26	
Nov 13	27[g]	28	29	30	1	2	3	DECEMBER 2185
	4	5	6	7	8	9	10	
Nov 27	11	12	13	14	15	16	17	
	18	19	20	21	22	23	24	
Dec 11	25[h]	26	27	28	29	30	31	

[a]Orthodox Christmas
[b]Julian New Year
[c]Ash Wednesday
[d]Feast of Orthodoxy
[e]Easter
[f]Orthodox Easter
[g]Advent
[h]Christmas

2186

Gregorian 2186

Month	Sun	Mon	Tue	Wed	Thu	Fri	Sat	Lunar Phases	ISO Week (Mon)	Julian Day (Sun noon)
January 2186	1[a]	2	3	4	○	6	7	14:47	1	2519481
	8	9	10	11	◑	13	14	12:24	2	2519488
	15	16	17	18	19	●	21	17:10	3	2519495
	22	23	24	25	26	27	◐	10:43	4	2519502
February 2186	29	30	31	1	2	3	○	2:02	5	2519509
	5	6	7	8	9	10	◑	6:40	6	2519516
	12	13	14	15	16	17	18		7	2519523
	●	20	21	22	23	24	25	11:28	8	2519530
March 2186	◐	27	28	1	2	3	4	19:55	9	2519537
	○	6	7	8	9	10	11	13:43	10	2519544
	12	◑	14	15	16	17	18	2:42	11	2519551
	19	20[b]	●	22	23	24	25	2:50	12	2519558
April 2186	26	27	◐	29	30	31	1	3:07	13	2519565
	2	3	○	5	6	7	8	1:51	14	2519572
	9	10	◑	12	13	14	15	22:50	15	2519579
	16	17	18	●	20	21	22	14:54	16	2519586
	23	24	25	◐	27	28	29	9:24	17	2519593
May 2186	30	1	2	○	4	5	6	14:43	18	2519600
	7	8	9	10	◑	12	13	17:21	19	2519607
	14	15	16	17	18	●	20	0:18	20	2519614
	21	22	23	24	◐	26	27	15:50	21	2519621
June 2186	28	29	30	31	1	○	3	4:40	22	2519628
	4	5	6	7	8	9	◑	8:59	23	2519635
	11	12	13	14	15	16	●	8:02	24	2519642
	18	19	20	21[c]	22	◐	24	23:26	25	2519649
	25	26	27	28	29	30	○	19:41	26	2519656
July 2186	2	3	4	5	6	7	8		27	2519663
	◑	10	11	12	13	14	15	21:24	28	2519670
	●	17	18	19	20	21	22	15:05	29	2519677
	◐	24	25	26	27	28	29	9:14	30	2519684
August 2186	30	○	1	2	3	4	5	11:13	31	2519691
	6	7	◑	9	10	11	12	7:02	32	2519698
	13	●	15	16	17	18	19	22:19	33	2519705
	20	◐	22	23	24	25	26	22:04	34	2519712
September 2186	27	28	29	○	31	1	2	2:29	35	2519719
	3	4	5	◑	7	8	9	14:44	36	2519726
	10	11	12	●	14	15	16	6:33	37	2519733
	17	18	19	◐	21	22[d]	23	14:21	38	2519740
	24	25	26	27	○	29	30	16:49	39	2519747
October 2186	1	2	3	4	◑	6	7	21:29	40	2519754
	8	9	10	11	●	13	14	16:41	41	2519761
	15	16	17	18	19	◐	21	9:37	42	2519768
	22	23	24	25	26	27	○	6:06	43	2519775
November 2186	29	30	31	1	2	3	◑	4:16	44	2519782
	5	6	7	8	9	10	●	5:32	45	2519789
	12	13	14	15	16	17	18		46	2519796
	◐	20	21	22	23	24	25	6:26	47	2519803
December 2186	○	27	28	29	30	1	2	18:34	48	2519810
	◑	4	5	6	7	8	9	12:05	49	2519817
	●	11	12	13	14	15	16	21:35	50	2519824
	17	18	◐	20	21[e]	22	23	2:46	51	2519831
	24	25	○	27	28	29	30	6:27	52	2519838
	31	◑	2	3	4	5	6	21:5	1	2519845

Hebrew 5946/5947‡

ISO Week	Month	Sun	Mon	Tue	Wed	Thu	Fri	Sat	Molad
1	Teveth 5946	10	11	12	13	14	15	16	
2		17	18	19	20	21	22	23	
3		24	25	26	27	28	29	1	Fri 16h12m10p
4	Shevat 5946	2	3	4	5	6	7	8	
5		9	10	11	12	13	14	15	
6		16	17	18	19	20	21	22	
7		23	24	25	26	27	28	29	
8		30	1	2	3	4	5	6	Sun 4h56m11p
9	Adar 5946	7	8	9	10	11	12	13	
10		14[f]	15	16	17	18	19	20	
11		21	22	23	24	25	26	27	
12		28	29	1	2	3	4	5	Mon 17h40m12p
13	Nisan 5946	6	7	8	9	10	11	12	
14		13	14	15[g]	16	17	18	19	
15		20	21	22	23	24	25	26	
16		27	28	29	30	1	2	3	Wed 6h24m13p
17	Iyyar 5946	4	5	6	7	8	9	10	
18		11	12	13	14	15	16	17	
19		18	19	20	21	22	23	24	
20		25	26	27	28	29	1	2	Thu 19h8m14p
21	Sivan 5946	3	4	5	6[h]	7	8	9	
22		10	11	12	13	14	15	16	
23		17	18	19	20	21	22	23	
24		24	25	26	27	28	29	30	
25		1	2	3	4	5	6	7	Sat 7h52m15p
26	Tammuz 5946	8	9	10	11	12	13	14	
27		15	16	17	18	19	20	21	
28		22	23	24	25	26	27	28	
29		29	1	2	3	4	5	6	Sun 20h36m16p
30	Av 5946	7	8	9[i]	10	11	12	13	
31		14	15	16	17	18	19	20	
32		21	22	23	24	25	26	27	
33		28	29	30	1	2	3	4	Tue 9h20m17p
34	Elul 5946	5	6	7	8	9	10	11	
35		12	13	14	15	16	17	18	
36		19	20	21	22	23	24	25	
37		26	27	28	29	1[a]	2[a]	3	Wed 22h5m0p
38	Tishri 5947	4	5	6	7	8	9	10[b]	
39		11	12	13	14	15[c]	16	17	
40		18	19	20	21	22	23	24	
41		25	26	27	28	29	30	1	Fri 10h49m1p
42	Heshvan 5947	2	3	4	5	6	7	8	
43		9	10	11	12	13	14	15	
44		16	17	18	19	20	21	22	
45		23	24	25	26	27	28	29	
46		30	1	2	3	4	5	6	Sat 23h33m2p
47	Kislev 5947	7	8	9	10	11	12	13	
48		14	15	16	17	18	19	20	
49		21	22	23	24[d]	25[e]	26[e]	27[e]	
50		28[e]	29[e]	30[e]	1[e]	2[e]	3	4	Mon 12h17m3p
51	Teveth 5947	5	6	7	8	9	10	11	
52		12	13	14	15	16	17	18	
1		19	20	21	22	23	24	25	

Chinese Yǐ-Yǒu/Bǐng-Xū‡

ISO Week	Month	Sun	Mon	Tue	Wed	Thu	Fri	Sat	Solar Term
1	Month 12 Yǐ-Yǒu	11	12	13	14	15	16	17	Xiǎo hán
2		18	19	20	21	22	23	24	
3		25	26	27	28	29	30	1[a]	Dà hán
4	Month 1 Bǐng-Xū	2	3	4	5	6	7	8	
5		9	10	11	12	13	14	15[b]	Lì chūn
6		16	17	18	19	20	21	22	
7		23	24	25	26	27	28	29	Yǔ shuǐ
8		1	2*	3	4	5	6	7	
9	Month 2 Bǐng-Xū	8	9	10	11	12	13	14	
10		15	16	17	18	19	20	21	Jīng zhé
11		22	23	24	25	26	27	28	
12		29	30	1	2	3	4	5	Chūn fēn
13	Leap Month 2 Bǐng-Xū	6	7	8	9	10	11	12	
14		13	14	15[c]	16	17	18	19	Qīng míng
15		20	21	22	23	24	25	26	
16		27	28	29	1	2	3*	4	Gǔ yǔ
17	Month 3 Bǐng-Xū	5	6	7	8	9	10	11	
18		12	13	14	15	16	17	18	Lì xià
19		19	20	21	22	23	24	25	
20		26	27	28	29	30	1	2	
21	Month 4 Bǐng-Xū	3	4	5	6	7	8	9	Xiǎo mǎn
22		10	11	12	13	14	15	16	
23		17	18	19	20	21	22	23	Máng zhòng
24		24	25	26	27	28	29	1	
25	Month 5 Bǐng-Xū	2	3	4*	5[d]	6	7	8	Xià zhì
26		9	10	11	12	13	14	15	
27		16	17	18	19	20	21	22	Xiǎo shǔ
28		23	24	25	26	27	28	29	
29	Month 6 Bǐng-Xū	1	2	3	4	5	6	7	Dà shǔ
30		8	9	10	11	12	13	14	
31		15	16	17	18	19	20	21	
32		22	23	24	25	26	27	28	Lì qiū
33		29	30	1	2	3	4	5*	
34	Month 7 Bǐng-Xū	6	7[e]	8	9	10	11	12	Chǔ shǔ
35		13	14	15[f]	16	17	18	19	
36		20	21	22	23	24	25	26	Bái lù
37		27	28	29	1	2	3	4	
38	Month 8 Bǐng-Xū	5	6	7	8	9	10	11	Qiū fēn
39		12	13	14	15[g]	16	17	18	
40		19	20	21	22	23	24	25	
41		26	27	28	29	30	1	2	Hán lù
42	Month 9 Bǐng-Xū	3	4	5	6*	7	8	9[h]	
43		10	11	12	13	14	15	16	Shuāng jiàng
44		17	18	19	20	21	22	23	
45		24	25	26	27	28	29	1	Lì dōng
46		2	3	4	5	6	7	8	
47	Month 10 Bǐng-Xū	9	10	11	12	13	14	15	Xiǎo xuě
48		16	17	18	19	20	21	22	
49		23	24	25	26	27	28	29	Dà xuě
50		30	1	2	3	4	5	6	
51	Month 11 Bǐng-Xū	7*	8	9	10	11	12[i]	13	Dōng zhì
52		14	15	16	17	18	19	20	
1		21	22	23	24	25	26	27	Xiǎo hán

Coptic 1902/1903‡ — Ethiopic 2178/2179‡

ISO Week	Coptic Month	Sun	Mon	Tue	Wed	Thu	Fri	Sat	Ethiopic Month
1	Koiak 1902	22	23	24	25	26	27	28	Tāḫśāś 2178
2		29[c]	30	1	2	3	4	5	
3	Tōbe 1902	6[d]	7	8	9	10	11[e]	12	Ṭer 2178
4		13	14	15	16	17	18	19	
5		20	21	22	23	24	25	26	
6		27	28	29	30	1	2	3	
7	Meshir 1902	4	5	6	7	8	9	10	Yakātīt 2178
8		11	12	13	14	15	16	17	
9		18	19	20	21	22	23	24	
10		25	26	27	28	29	30	1	
11	Paremotep 1902	2	3	4	5	6	7	8	Magābīt 2178
12		9	10	11	12	13	14	15	
13		16	17	18	19	20	21	22	
14		23	24	25	26	27	28	29	
15		30[f]	1	2	3	4	5	6	
16	Parmoute 1902	7	8	9	10	11	12	13	Miyāzyā 2178
17		14	15	16	17	18	19	20	
18		21	22	23	24	25	26	27	
19		28	29[g]	30	1	2	3	4	
20	Pashons 1902	5	6	7	8	9	10	11	Genbot 2178
21		12	13	14	15	16	17	18	
22		19	20	21	22	23	24	25	
23		26	27	28	29	30	1	2	
24	Paōne 1902	3	4	5	6	7	8	9	Sanē 2178
25		10	11	12	13	14	15	16	
26		17	18	19	20	21	22	23	
27		24	25	26	27	28	29	30	
28	Epēp 1902	1	2	3	4	5	6	7	Ḥamlē 2178
29		8	9	10	11	12	13	14	
30		15	16	17	18	19	20	21	
31		22	23	24	25	26	27	28	
32		29	30	1	2	3	4	5	
33	Mesorē 1902	6	7	8	9	10	11	12	Naḥasē 2178
34		13[h]	14	15	16	17	18	19	
35		20	21	22	23	24	25	26	
36		27	28	29	30	1	2	3	
37	Epag. 1902	4	5	1[a]	2	3	4	5	Pāg. 2178
38	Thoout 1903	6	7	8	9	10	11	12	Maskaram 2179
39		13	14	15	16	17[b]	18	19	
40		20	21	22	23	24	25	26	
41		27	28	29	30	1	2	3	
42	Paope 1903	4	5	6	7	8	9	10	Ṭeqemt 2179
43		11	12	13	14	15	16	17	
44		18	19	20	21	22	23	24	
45		25	26	27	28	29	30	1	
46	Athōr 1903	2	3	4	5	6	7	8	Ḫedār 2179
47		9	10	11	12	13	14	15	
48		16	17	18	19	20	21	22	
49		23	24	25	26	27	28	29	
50		30	1	2	3	4	5	6	
51	Koiak 1903	7	8	9	10	11	12	13	Tāḫśāś 2179
52		14	15	16	17	18	19	20	
1		21	22	23	24	25	26	27	

[a]New Year
[b]Spring (9:25)
[c]Summer (0:11)
[d]Autumn (17:28)
[e]Winter (16:58)
● New moon
◐ First quarter moon
○ Full moon
◑ Last quarter moon

‡Leap year
[a]New Year
[b]Yom Kippur
[c]Sukkot
[d]Winter starts
[e]Ḥanukkah
[f]Purim
[g]Passover
[h]Shavuot
[i]Fast of Av

‡Leap year
[a]New Year (4884, Dog)
[b]Lantern Festival
[c]Qīngmíng
[d]Dragon Festival
[e]Qīqiǎo
[f]Hungry Ghosts
[g]Mid-Autumn Festival
[h]Double-Ninth Festival
[i]Dōngzhì
*Start of 60-name cycle

‡Leap year
[a]New Year
[b]Building of the Cross
[c]Christmas
[d]Jesus's Circumcision
[e]Epiphany
[f]Easter
[g]Mary's Announcement
[h]Jesus's Transfiguration

PERSIAN (ASTRONOMICAL) 1564‡/1565

Month	Sun	Mon	Tue	Wed	Thu	Fri	Sat
DEY 1564	12	13	14	15	16	17	18
	19	20	21	22	23	24	25
	26	27	28	29	30	1	2
BAHMAN 1564	3	4	5	6	7	8	9
	10	11	12	13	14	15	16
	17	18	19	20	21	22	23
	24	25	26	27	28	29	30
ESFAND 1564	1	2	3	4	5	6	7
	8	9	10	11	12	13	14
	15	16	17	18	19	20	21
	22	23	24	25	26	27	28
	29	30*[â]	1[a]	2	3	4	5
FARVARDĪN 1565	6	7	8	9	10	11	12
	13[b]	14	15	16	17	18	19
	20	21	22	23	24	25	26
	27	28	29	30	31	1	2
ORDĪBEHEŠT 1565	3	4	5	6	7	8	9
	10	11	12	13	14	15	16
	17	18	19	20	21	22	23
	24	25	26	27	28	29	30
	31	1	2	3	4	5	6
XORDĀD 1565	7	8	9	10	11	12	13
	14	15	16	17	18	19	20
	21	22	23	24	25	26	27
	28	29	30	31	1	2	3
TĪR 1565	4	5	6	7	8	9	10
	11	12	13	14	15	16	17
	18	19	20	21	22	23	24
	25	26	27	28	29	30	31
MORDĀD 1565	1	2	3	4	5	6	7
	8	9	10	11	12	13	14
	15	16	17	18	19	20	21
	22	23	24	25	26	27	28
	29	30	31	1	2	3	4
SHAHRĪVAR 1565	5	6	7	8	9	10	11
	12	13	14	15	16	17	18
	19	20	21	22	23	24	25
	26	27	28	29	30	31	1
MEHR 1565	2	3	4	5	6	7	8
	9	10	11	12	13	14	15
	16	17	18	19	20	21	22
	23	24	25	26	27	28	29
	30	1	2	3	4	5	6
ABĀN 1565	7	8	9	10	11	12	13
	14	15	16	17	18	19	20
	21	22	23	24	25	26	27
	28	29	30	1	2	3	4
ĀZAR 1565	5	6	7	8	9	10	11
	12	13	14	15	16	17	18
	19	20	21	22	23	24	25
	26	27	28	29	30	1	2
DEY 1565	3	4	5	6	7	8	9
	10	11	12	13	14	15	16

‡Leap year
[a]New Year (or prior day)
*Near New Year: −1′48″
[â]New Year (Arithmetic)
[b]Sizdeh Bedar

HINDU LUNAR 2242/2243‡

Month	Sun	Mon	Tue	Wed	Thu	Fri	Sat
PAUSHA 2242	10	12	13	14	15	16	17
	18	19	20	21	22	23	24
	25	26	27	28	29	30	1
MĀGHA 2242	2	3	4	5	6	7	8
	9	10	11	12	13	14	15
	17	18	19	20	21	22	23
	24	25	26	26	27	28[h]	29
	30	1	2	3	4	5	6
PHĀLGUNA 2242	7	8	9	11	12	13	14
	15[i]	16	17	18	19	20	21
	22	23	24	25	26	27	28
	28	29	30	1[a]	2	4	5
CHAITRA 2243	6	7	8	9[b]	10	11	12
	13	14	15	16	17	18	19
	20	21	22	23	24	25	26
	27	28	29	30	1	2	3
VAIŚĀKHA 2243	4	5	6	7	9	10	11
	12	13	14	15	16	17	18
	19	20	21	22	22	23	24
	25	26	27	28	29	30	2
LEAP JYAISHTHA 2243	3	4	5	6	7	8	9
	10	11	12	13	14	15	16
	17	18	19	20	21	22	23
	24	25	26	27	28	29	30
JYAISHTHA 2243	1	2	3	5	6	7	8
	9	10	11	12	13	14	15
	16	17	18	19	19	20	21
	22	23	24	25	26	28	29
	30	1	2	3	4	5	6
ĀSHĀDHA 2243	7	8	9	10	11	12	13
	14	15	16	17	18	19	20
	21	22	23	24	25	26	27
	28	29	1	2	3	4	5
ŚRĀVANA 2243	6	7	8	9	10	11	12
	13	14	15	15	16	17	18
	19	20	21	23[c]	24	25	26
	27	28	29	30	1	2	3[d]
BHĀDRAPADA 2243	4	5	6	7	8	9	10
	11	12	13	14	15	16	17
	18	19	20	21	22	23	24
	25	27	28	29	30	1	2
ĀŚVINA 2243	3	4	5	6	7	8[e]	9[e]
	10[e]	10[e]	11	12	13	14	15
	16	17	18	19	21	22	23
	24	25	26	27	28	29	30
KĀRTTIKA 2243	1[f]	2	3	4	5	6	7
	8	9	10	11	12	13	14
	15	16	17	18	19	20	21
	22	23	25	26	27	28	29
	30	1	2	3	4	4	5
MĀRGAŚĪRA 2243	6	7	8	9	10	11[g]	12
	13	14	15	16	17	19	20
	21	22	23	24	25	26	27

‡Leap year
[a]New Year (Vyaya)
[b]Birthday of Rāma
[c]Birthday of Krishna
[d]Ganēśa Chaturthī
[e]Dashara
[f]Diwali
[g]Birthday of Vishnu
[h]Night of Śiva
[i]Holi

HINDU SOLAR 2107/2108

Month	Sun	Mon	Tue	Wed	Thu	Fri	Sat
PAUSHA 2107	15	16	17	18	19	20	21
	22	23	24	25	26	27	28
	29	1[b]	2	3	4	5	6
MĀGHA 2107	7	8	9	10	11	12	13
	14	15	16	17	18	19	20
	21	22	23	24	25	26	27
	28	29	30	1	2	3	4
PHĀLGUNA 2107	5	6	7	8	9	10	11
	12	13	14	15	16	17	18
	19	20	21	22	23	24	25
	26	27	28	29	30	1	2
CHAITRA 2107	3	4	5	6	7	8	9
	10	11	12	13	14	15	16
	17	18	19	20	21	22	23
	24	25	26	27	28	29	30
VAIŚĀKHA 2108	1[a]	2	3	4	5	6	7
	8	9	10	11	12	13	14
	15	16	17	18	19	20	21
	22	23	24	25	26	27	28
	29	30	31	1	2	3	4
JYAISHTHA 2108	5	6	7	8	9	10	11
	12	13	14	15	16	17	18
	19	20	21	22	23	24	25
	26	27	28	29	30	31	1
ĀSHĀDHA 2108	2	3	4	5	6	7	8
	9	10	11	12	13	14	15
	16	17	18	19	20	21	22
	23	24	25	26	27	28	29
	30	31	32	1	2	3	4
ŚRĀVANA 2108	5	6	7	8	9	10	11
	12	13	14	15	16	17	18
	19	20	21	22	23	24	25
	26	27	28	29	30	31	32
BHĀDRAPADA 2108	1	2	3	4	5	6	7
	8	9	10	11	12	13	14
	15	16	17	18	19	20	21
	22	23	24	25	26	27	28
	29	30	31	1	2	3	4
ĀŚVINA 2108	5	6	7	8	9	10	11
	12	13	14	15	16	17	18
	19	20	21	22	23	24	25
	26	27	28	29	30	1	2
KĀRTTIKA 2108	3	4	5	6	7	8	9
	10	11	12	13	14	15	16
	17	18	19	20	21	22	23
	24	25	26	27	28	29	30
MĀRGAŚĪRA 2108	1	2	3	4	5	6	7
	8	9	10	11	12	13	14
	15	16	17	18	19	20	21
	22	23	24	25	26	27	28
	29	1	2	3	4	5	6
PAUSHA 2108	7	8	9	10	11	12	13
	14	15	16	17	18	19	20

[a]New Year (Plava)
[b]Pongal

ISLAMIC (ASTRONOMICAL) 1612‡/1613

Month	Sun	Mon	Tue	Wed	Thu	Fri	Sat
JUMĀDĀ II 1612	10	11	12	13	14	15	16
	17	18	19	20	21	22	23
	24	25	26	27	28	29	30
RAJAB 1612	1	2	3	4	5	6	7
	8	9	10	11	12	13	14
	15	16	17	18	19	20	21
	22	23	24	25	26	27[d]	28
	29	30	1	2	3	4	5
SHA'BĀN 1612	6	7	8	9	10	11	12
	13	14	15	16	17	18	19
	20	21	22	23	24	25	26
	27	28	29	1[e]	2	3	4
RAMAḌĀN 1612	5	6	7	8	9	10	11
	12	13	14	15	16	17	18
	19	20	21	22	23	24	25
	26	27	28	29	30	1[f]	2
SHAWWĀL 1612	3	4	5	6	7	8	9
	10	11	12	13	14	15	16
	17	18	19	20	21	22	23
	24	25	26	27	28	29	1
DHU AL-QA'DA 1612	2	3	4	5	6	7	8
	9	10	11	12	13	14	15
	16	17	18	19	20	21	22
	23	24	25	26	27	28	29
	30	1	2	3	4	5	6
DHU AL-ḤIJJA 1612	7	8	9	10[g]	11	12	13
	14	15	16	17	18	19	20
	21	22	23	24	25	26	27
	28	29	1[a]	2	3	4	5
MUḤARRAM 1613	6	7	8	9	10[b]	11	12
	13	14	15	16	17	18	19
	20	21	22	23	24	25	26
	27	28	29	1	2	3	4
ṢAFAR 1613	5	6	7	8	9	10	11
	12	13	14	15	16	17	18
	19	20	21	22	23	24	25
	26	27	28	29	1	2	3
RABĪ' I 1613	4	5	6	7	8	9	10
	11	12[c]	13	14	15	16	17
	18	19	20	21	22	23	24
	25	26	27	28	29	30	1
RABĪ' II 1613	2	3	4	5	6	7	8
	9	10	11	12	13	14	15
	16	17	18	19	20	21	22
	23	24	25	26	27	28	29
	30	1	2	3	4	5	6
JUMĀDĀ I 1613	7	8	9	10	11	12	13
	14	15	16	17	18	19	20
	21	22	23	24	25	26	27
	28	29	1	2	3	4	5
JUMĀDĀ II 1613	6	7	8	9	10	11	12
	13	14	15	16	17	18	19
	20	21	22	23	24	25	26

‡Leap year
[a]New Year
[b]'Ashūrā'
[c]Prophet's Birthday
[d]Ascent of the Prophet
[e]Start of Ramaḍān
[f]'Id al-Fiṭr
[g]'Id al-'Aḍḥā

GREGORIAN 2186

Julian (Sun)	Sun	Mon	Tue	Wed	Thu	Fri	Sat	Month
Dec 18	1	2	3	4	5	6	7	JANUARY 2186
	8[a]	9	10	11	12	13	14	
Jan 1	15[b]	16	17	18	19	20	21	
	22	23	24	25	26	27	28	
Jan 15	29	30	31	1	2	3	4	FEBRUARY 2186
	5	6	7	8	9	10	11	
Jan 29	12	13	14	15	16	17	18	
	19	20	21	22[c]	23	24	25	
Feb 12	26[d]	27	28	1	2	3	4	MARCH 2186
	5	6	7	8	9	10	11	
Feb 26	12	13	14	15	16	17	18	
	19	20	21	22	23	24	25	
Mar 12	26	27	28	29	30	31	1	APRIL 2186
	2	3	4	5	6	7	8	
Mar 26	9[e]	10	11	12	13	14	15	
	16	17	18	19	20	21	22	
Apr 9	23	24	25	26	27	28	29	
	30	1	2	3	4	5	6	MAY 2186
Apr 23	7	8	9	10	11	12	13	
	14	15	16	17	18	19	20	
May 7	21	22	23	24	25	26	27	
	28	29	30	31	1	2	3	JUNE 2186
May 21	4	5	6	7	8	9	10	
	11	12	13	14	15	16	17	
Jun 4	18	19	20	21	22	23	24	
	25	26	27	28	29	30	1	JULY 2186
Jun 18	2	3	4	5	6	7	8	
	9	10	11	12	13	14	15	
Jul 2	16	17	18	19	20	21	22	
	23	24	25	26	27	28	29	
Jul 16	30	31	1	2	3	4	5	AUGUST 2186
	6	7	8	9	10	11	12	
Jul 30	13	14	15	16	17	18	19	
	20	21	22	23	24	25	26	
Aug 13	27	28	29	30	31	1	2	SEPTEMBER 2186
	3	4	5	6	7	8	9	
Aug 27	10	11	12	13	14	15	16	
	17	18	19	20	21	22	23	
Sep 10	24	25	26	27	28	29	30	
	1	2	3	4	5	6	7	OCTOBER 2186
Sep 24	8	9	10	11	12	13	14	
	15	16	17	18	19	20	21	
Oct 8	22	23	24	25	26	27	28	
	29	30	31	1	2	3	4	NOVEMBER 2186
Oct 22	5	6	7	8	9	10	11	
	12	13	14	15	16	17	18	
Nov 5	19	20	21	22	23	24	25	
	26	27	28	29	30	1	2	DECEMBER 2186
Nov 19	3[g]	4	5	6	7	8	9	
	10	11	12	13	14	15	16	
Dec 3	17	18	19	20	21	22	23	
	24	25[h]	26	27	28	29	30	
Dec 17	31	1	2	3	4	5	6	

[a]Orthodox Christmas
[b]Julian New Year
[c]Ash Wednesday
[d]Feast of Orthodoxy
[e]Easter (also Orthodox)
[g]Advent
[h]Christmas

2187

Gregorian 2187	Sun	Mon	Tue	Wed	Thu	Fri	Sat	Lunar Phases	ISO Week (Mon)	Julian Day (Sun noon)	Hebrew 5947‡/5948	Sun	Mon	Tue	Wed	Thu	Fri	Sat	Molad	Chinese Bĭng-Xū‡/Dīng-Hài	Sun	Mon	Tue	Wed	Thu	Fri	Sat	Solar Term	Coptic 1903‡/1904	Sun	Mon	Tue	Wed	Thu	Fri	Sat	Ethiopic 2179‡/2180
	31	◑[a]	2	3	4	5	6	21:51	1	2519845	TEVETH 5947	19	20	21	22	23	24	25		MONTH 11 Bĭng-Xū	21	22	23	24	25	26	27	Xiăo hán	KOIAK 1903	21	22	23	24	25	26	27	TĀKHŚĀŚ 2179
JANUARY 2187	7	8	●	10	11	12	13	16:18	2	2519852		26	27	28	29	1	2	3	Wed 1h1m4p	MONTH 12 Bĭng-Xū	28	29	30	1	2	3	4			28	29[c]	30	1	2	3	4	
	14	15	16	◐	18	19	20	20:51	3	2519859	SHEVAT 5947	4	5	6	7	8	9	10			5	6	7	8	9	10	11	Dà hán	TŌBE 1903	5	6[d]	7	8	9	10	11[e]	ṬER 2179
	21	22	23	○	25	26	27	17:42	4	2519866		11	12	13	14	15	16	17			12	13	14	15	16	17	18			12	13	14	15	16	17	18	
	28	29	30	◑	1	2	3	10:16	5	2519873		18	19	20	21	22	23	24			19	20	21	22	23	24	25			19	20	21	22	23	24	25	
	4	5	6	7	●	9	10	12:01	6	2519880		25	26	27	28	29	30	1	Thu 13h45m5p		26	27	28	29	1[a]	2	3	Lì chūn		26	27	28	29	30	1	2	
FEBRUARY 2187	11	12	13	14	15	◐	17	11:39	7	2519887	ADAR I 5947	2	3	4	5	6	7	8		MONTH 1 Dīng-Hài	4	5	6	7	8*	9	10		MESHIR 1903	3	4	5	6	7	8	9	YAKĀTIT 2179
	18	19	20	21	22	○	24	4:12	8	2519894		9	10	11	12	13	14	15			11	12	13	14	15[b]	16	17	Yŭ shuĭ		10	11	12	13	14	15	16	
	25	26	27	28	1	◑	3	1:32	9	2519901		16	17	18	19	20	21	22			18	19	20	21	22	23	24			17	18	19	20	21	22	23	
	4	5	6	7	8	9	●	6:42	10	2519908		23	24	25	26	27	28	29	Sat 2h29m6p		25	26	27	28	29	30	1	Jīng zhé		24	25	26	27	28	29	30	
MARCH 2187	11	12	13	14	15	16	◐	22:53	11	2519915		30	1	2	3	4	5	6		MONTH 2 Dīng-Hài	2	3	4	5	6	7	8			1	2	3	4	5	6	7	
	18	19	20[b]	21	22	23	○	14:04	12	2519922	ADAR II 5947	7	8	9	10	11	12	13			9	10	11	12	13	14	15	Chūn fēn	PAREMOTEP 1903	8	9	10	11	12	13	14	MAGABIT 2179
	25	26	27	28	29	30	◑	19:05	13	2519929		14[f]	15	16	17	18	19	20			16	17	18	19	20	21	22			15	16	17	18	19	20	21	
	1	2	3	4	5	6	7		14	2519936		21	22	23	24	25	26	27	Sun 15h13m7p		23	24	25	26	27[c]	28	29	Qīng míng		22	23	24	25	26	27	28	
	●	9	10	11	12	13	14	22:56	15	2519943		28	29	1	2	3	4	5			30	1	2	3	4	5	6			29	30	1	2	3	4	5	
APRIL 2187	15	◐	17	18	19	20	21	6:56	16	2519950	NISAN 5947	6	7	8	9	10	11	12		MONTH 3 Dīng-Hài	7	8*	9	10	11	12	13	Gŭ yŭ	PARMOUTE 1903	6	7	8	9	10	11	12	MIYĀZYĀ 2179
	○	23	24	25	26	27	28	23:53	17	2519957		13	14	15[g]	16	17	18	19			14	15	16	17	18	19	20			13	14	15	16	17	18	19	
	29	◑	1	2	3	4	5	13:42	18	2519964		20	21	22	23	24	25	26	Tue 3h57m8p		21	22	23	24	25	26	27	Lì xià		20[f]	21	22	23	24	25	26	
	6	7	●	9	10	11	12	12:18	19	2519971		27	28	29	30	1	2	3			28	29	1	2	3	4	5			27	28	29[g]	30	1	2	3	
MAY 2187	13	14	◐	16	17	18	19	12:41	20	2519978	IYAR 5947	4	5	6	7	8	9	10		MONTH 4 Dīng-Hài	6	7	8	9	10	11	12		PASHONS 1903	4	5	6	7	8	9	10	GENBOT 2179
	20	21	○	23	24	25	26	10:27	21	2519985		11	12	13	14	15	16	17			13	14	15	16	17	18	19	Xiăo măn		11	12	13	14	15	16	17	
	27	28	29	◑	31	1	2	7:56	22	2519992		18	19	20	21	22	23	24	Wed 16h41m9p		20	21	22	23	24	25	26			18	19	20	21	22	23	24	
	3	4	5	●	7	8	9	23:06	23	2519999		25	26	27	28	29	1	2			27	28	29	30	1	2	3	Máng zhòng		25	26	27	28	29	30	1	
JUNE 2187	10	11	12	◐	14	15	16	17:28	24	2520006	SIVAN 5947	3	4	5	6[h]	7	8	9		MONTH 5 Dīng-Hài	4	5[d]	6	7	8	9*	10		PAŌNE 1903	2	3	4	5	6	7	8	SANÉ 2179
	17	18	19	○	21[c]	22	23	22:26	25	2520013		10	11	12	13	14	15	16			11	12	13	14	15	16	17	Xià zhì		9	10	11	12	13	14	15	
	24	25	26	27	28	◑	30	0:46	26	2520020		17	18	19	20	21	22	23			18	19	20	21	22	23	24			16	17	18	19	20	21	22	
	1	2	3	4	5	●	7	7:56	27	2520027		24	25	26	27	28	29	30	Fri 5h25m10p		25	26	27	28	29	1	2	Xiăo shŭ		23	24	25	26	27	28	29	
JULY 2187	8	9	10	11	◐	13	14	22:46	28	2520034	TAMMUZ 5947	1	2	3	4	5	6	7		MONTH 6 Dīng-Hài	3	4	5	6	7	8	9			30	1	2	3	4	5	6	
	15	16	17	18	19	○	21	12:07	29	2520041		8	9	10	11	12	13	14			10	11	12	13	14	15	16		EPĒP 1903	7	8	9	10	11	12	13	ḤAMLĒ 2179
	22	23	24	25	26	27	◑	15:42	30	2520048		15	16	17	18	19	20	21			17	18	19	20	21	22	23	Dà shŭ		14	15	16	17	18	19	20	
	29	30	31	1	2	3	●	15:32	31	2520055		22	23	24	25	26	27	28	Sat 18h9m11p		24	25	26	27	28	29	1			21	22	23	24	25	26	27	
	5	6	7	8	9	10	◐	6:06	32	2520062		29	1	2	3	4	5	6		MONTH 7 Dīng-Hài	2	3	4	5	6	7[e]	8	Lì qiū		28	29	30	1	2	3	4	
AUGUST 2187	12	13	14	15	16	17	18		33	2520069	AV 5947	7	8	9[i]	10	11	12	13			9	10	11*	12	13	14	15[f]		MESORĒ 1903	5	6	7	8	9	10	11	NAHASÉ 2179
	○	20	21	22	23	24	25	3:14	34	2520076		14	15	16	17	18	19	20			16	17	18	19	20	21	22	Chŭ shŭ		12	13[h]	14	15	16	17	18	
	26	◑	28	29	30	31	1	4:38	35	2520083		21	22	23	24	25	26	27	Mon 6h53m12p		23	24	25	26	27	28	29			19	20	21	22	23	24	25	
	●	3	4	5	6	7	8	22:46	36	2520090		28	29	30	1	2	3	4			30	1	2	3	4	5	6	Bái lù	EPAG. 1903	26	27	28	29	30	1	2	PAG. 2179
SEPTEMBER 2187	◐	10	11	12	13	14	15	16:43	37	2520097	ELUL 5947	5	6	7	8	9	10	11		MONTH 8 Dīng-Hài	7	8	9	10	11	12	13			3	4	5	6	1[a]	2	3	
	16	○	18	19	20	21	22[d]	19:15	38	2520104		12	13	14	15	16	17	18			14	15[g]	16	17	18	19	20		THOOUT 1904	4	5	6	7	8	9	10	MASKARAM 2180
	23	24	◑	26	27	28	29	15:36	39	2520111		19	20	21	22	23	24	25			21	22	23	24	25	26	27	Qiū fēn		11	12	13	14	15	16	17[b]	
	30	1	●	3	4	5	6	6:39	40	2520118		26	27	28	29	1[a]	2[a]	3	Tue 19h37m13p		28	29	1	2	3	4	5			18	19	20	21	22	23	24	
OCTOBER 2187	7	8	◐	10	11	12	13	7:18	41	2520125	TISHRI 5948	4	5	6	7	8	9	10[b]		MONTH 9 Dīng-Hài	6	7	8	9[h]	10	11	12*	Hán lù		25	26	27	28	29	30	1	
	14	15	16	○	18	19	20	11:35	42	2520132		11	12	13	14	15[c]	16	17			13	14	15	16	17	18	19		PAOPE 1904	2	3	4	5	6	7	8	TEQEMT 2180
	21	22	23	24	◑	26	27	0:49	43	2520139		18	19	20	21	22	23	24			20	21	22	23	24	25	26	Shuāng jiàng		9	10	11	12	13	14	15	
	28	29	30	●	1	2	3	16:11	44	2520146		25	26	27	28	29	30	1	Thu 8h21m14p		27	28	29	30	1	2	3			16	17	18	19	20	21	22	
NOVEMBER 2187	4	5	6	7	◐	9	10	1:36	45	2520153	HESHVAN 5948	2	3	4	5	6	7	8		MONTH 10 Dīng-Hài	4	5	6	7	8	9	10	Lì dōng		23	24	25	26	27	28	29	
	11	12	13	14	15	○	17	3:38	46	2520160		9	10	11	12	13	14	15			11	12	13	14	15	16	17			30	1	2	3	4	5	6	
	18	19	20	21	22	◑	24	8:48	47	2520167		16	17	18	19	20	21	22			18	19	20	21	22	23	24	Xiăo xuĕ	ATHŌR 1904	7	8	9	10	11	12	13	HEDĀR 2180
	25	26	27	28	29	●	1	4:14	48	2520174		23	24	25	26	27	28	29	Fri 21h5m15p		25	26	27	28	29	1	2			14	15	16	17	18	19	20	
	2	3	4	5	6	◐	8	22:29	49	2520181	KISLEV 5948	1	2	3	4	5	6[d]	7		MONTH 11 Dīng-Hài	3	4	5	6	7	8	9	Dà xuĕ		21	22	23	24	25	26	27	
DECEMBER 2187	9	10	11	12	13	14	○	18:45	50	2520188		8	9	10	11	12	13	14			10	11	12	13*	14	15	16			28	29	30	1	2	3	4	
	16	17	18	19	20	21[e]	◑	16:24	51	2520195		15	16	17	18	19	20	21			17	18	19	20	21	22	23[i]	Dōng zhì	KOIAK 1904	5	6	7	8	9	10	11	TĀKHŚĀŚ 2180
	23	24	25	26	27	28	●	19:01	52	2520202		22	23	24	25[e]	26[e]	27[e]	28[e]	Sun 9h49m16p		24	25	26	27	28	29	30			12	13	14	15	16	17	18	
	30	31	1	2	3	4	5		1	2520209		29[e]	30[e]	1[e]	2[e]	3	4	5			1	2	3	4	5	6	7			19	20	21	22	23	24	25	

[a]New Year
[b]Spring (15:07)
[c]Summer (6:03)
[d]Autumn (23:25)
[e]Winter (22:55)
● New moon
◐ First quarter moon
○ Full moon
◑ Last quarter moon

‡Leap year
[a]New Year
[b]Yom Kippur
[c]Sukkot
[d]Winter starts
[e]Ḥanukkah
[f]Purim
[g]Passover
[h]Shavuot
[i]Fast of Av

‡Leap year
[a]New Year (4885, Pig)
[b]Lantern Festival
[c]Qīngmíng
[d]Dragon Festival
[e]Qīqiăo
[f]Hungry Ghosts
[g]Mid-Autumn Festival
[h]Double-Ninth Festival
[i]Dōngzhì
*Start of 60-name cycle

‡Leap year
[a]New Year
[b]Building of the Cross
[c]Christmas
[d]Jesus's Circumcision
[e]Epiphany
[f]Easter
[g]Mary's Announcement
[h]Jesus's Transfiguration

PERSIAN (ASTRONOMICAL) 1565/1566

Month	Sun	Mon	Tue	Wed	Thu	Fri	Sat
DEY 1565	10	11	12	13	14	15	16
	17	18	19	20	21	22	23
	24	25	26	27	28	29	30
BAHMAN 1565	1	2	3	4	5	6	7
	8	9	10	11	12	13	14
	15	16	17	18	19	20	21
	22	23	24	25	26	27	28
ESFAND 1565	29	30	1	2	3	4	5
	6	7	8	9	10	11	12
	13	14	15	16	17	18	19
	20	21	22	23	24	25	26
FARVARDĪN 1566	27	28	29	1[a]	2	3	4
	5	6	7	8	9	10	11
	12	13[b]	14	15	16	17	18
	19	20	21	22	23	24	25
ORDĪBEHEŠT 1566	26	27	28	29	30	31	1
	2	3	4	5	6	7	8
	9	10	11	12	13	14	15
	16	17	18	19	20	21	22
	23	24	25	26	27	28	29
XORDĀD 1566	30	31	1	2	3	4	5
	6	7	8	9	10	11	12
	13	14	15	16	17	18	19
	20	21	22	23	24	25	26
TĪR 1566	27	28	29	30	31	1	2
	3	4	5	6	7	8	9
	10	11	12	13	14	15	16
	17	18	19	20	21	22	23
	24	25	26	27	28	29	30
MORDĀD 1566	31	1	2	3	4	5	6
	7	8	9	10	11	12	13
	14	15	16	17	18	19	20
	21	22	23	24	25	26	27
SHAHRĪVAR 1566	28	29	30	31	1	2	3
	4	5	6	7	8	9	10
	11	12	13	14	15	16	17
	18	19	20	21	22	23	24
	25	26	27	28	29	30	31
MEHR 1566	1	2	3	4	5	6	7
	8	9	10	11	12	13	14
	15	16	17	18	19	20	21
	22	23	24	25	26	27	28
ĀBĀN 1566	29	30	1	2	3	4	5
	6	7	8	9	10	11	12
	13	14	15	16	17	18	19
	20	21	22	23	24	25	26
ĀZAR 1566	27	28	29	30	1	2	3
	4	5	6	7	8	9	10
	11	12	13	14	15	16	17
	18	19	20	21	22	23	24
DEY 1566	25	26	27	28	29	30	1
	2	3	4	5	6	7	8
	9	10	11	12	13	14	15

[a] New Year
[b] Sizdeh Bedar

HINDU LUNAR 2243‡/2244

Month	Sun	Mon	Tue	Wed	Thu	Fri	Sat
MĀRGAŚĪRA 2243	21	22	23	24	25	26	27
PAUSHA 2243	28	29	30	1	2	3	4
	5	6	6	7	8	9	10
	11	13	14	15	16	17	18
	19	20	21	22	23	24	25
MĀGHA 2243	26	27	28	29	30	1	2
	3	4	5	6	7	8	9
	10	11	12	13	14	15	**16**
	18	19	20	21	22	23	24
	25	26	27	28	28[h]	29	30
PHĀLGUNA 2243	1	2	3	4	5	6	7
	8	9	**10**	12	13	14	15[i]
	16	17	18	19	20	21	22
	23	24	25	26	27	28	29
CHAITRA 2244	30	1[a]	2	3	4	5	6
	7	8	9[b]	10	11	12	13
	14	16	17	18	19	20	21
	22	22	23	24	25	26	27
VAIŚĀKHA 2244	28	29	30	1	2	3	4
	5	6	**7**	9	10	11	12
	13	14	15	16	17	18	19
	20	21	22	23	24	25	26
JYAISHTHA 2244	27	27	**28**	30	1	2	3
	4	5	6	7	8	9	10
	11	13	14	15	16	17	18
	18	19	20	21	22	23	24
ĀSHĀḌHA 2244	25	26	27	28	29	30	1
	2	**3**	5	6	7	8	9
	10	11	12	13	14	15	16
	17	18	19	20	21	22	23
	24	25	26	27	28	29	30
ŚRĀVAṆA 2244	1	2	3	4	5	**6**	8
	9	10	11	12	13	14	15
	15	16	17	18	19	20	21
	22	23[c]	24	25	26	27	28
BHĀDRAPADA 2244	**29**	1	2	3	4[d]	5	6
	7	8	9	10	11	12	13
	14	15	16	17	18	19	20
	21	22	23	24	25	26	27
ĀŚVINA 2244	28	29	30	1	2	**3**	5
	6	7	8[e]	9[e]	10[e]	10[e]	11
	12	13	14	15	16	17	18
	19	20	21	22	23	24	25
KĀRTTIKA 2244	**26**	28	29	30	1[f]	2	3
	4	5	6	7	8	9	10
	11	12	13	14	14	15	16
	17	18	**19**	21	22	23	24
MĀRGAŚĪRA 2244	25	26	27	28	29	30	1
	2	3	4	5	6	7	8
	9	10	11[g]	12	13	14	15
	16	17	18	19	20	21	22
	23	**24**	26	27	28	29	30
	1	2	3	4	5	6	6

‡ Leap year
[a] New Year (Sarvajit)
[b] Birthday of Rāma
[c] Birthday of Krishna
[d] Ganēśa Chaturthī
[e] Dashara
[f] Diwali
[g] Birthday of Vishnu
[h] Night of Śiva
[i] Holi

HINDU SOLAR 2108/2109‡

Month	Sun	Mon	Tue	Wed	Thu	Fri	Sat
PAUSHA 2108	14	15	16	17	18	19	20
	21	22	23	24	25	26	27
MĀGHA 2108	28	29	30	1[b]	2	3	4
	5	6	7	8	9	10	11
	12	13	14	15	16	17	18
	19	20	21	22	23	24	25
PHĀLGUNA 2108	26	27	28	29	1	2	3
	4	5	6	7	8	9	10
	11	12	13	14	15	16	17
	18	19	20	21	22	23	24
CHAITRA 2108	25	26	27	28	29	30	1
	2	3	4	5	6	7	8
	9	10	11	12	13	14	15
	16	17	18	19	20	21	22
	23	24	25	26	27	28	29
VAIŚĀKHA 2109	30	1[a]	2	3	4	5	6
	7	8	9	10	11	12	13
	14	15	16	17	18	19	20
	21	22	23	24	25	26	27
JYAISHṬHA 2109	28	29	30	31	1	2	3
	4	5	6	7	8	9	10
	11	12	13	14	15	16	17
	18	19	20	21	22	23	24
	25	26	27	28	29	30	31
ĀSHĀḌHA 2109	32	1	2	3	4	5	6
	7	8	9	10	11	12	13
	14	15	16	17	18	19	20
	21	22	23	24	25	26	27
ŚRĀVAṆA 2109	28	29	30	31	1	2	3
	4	5	6	7	8	9	10
	11	12	13	14	15	16	17
	18	19	20	21	22	23	24
	25	26	27	28	29	30	31
BHĀDRAPADA 2109	32	1	2	3	4	5	6
	7	8	9	10	11	12	13
	14	15	16	17	18	19	20
	21	22	23	24	25	26	27
ĀŚVINA 2109	28	29	30	31	1	2	3
	4	5	6	7	8	9	10
	11	12	13	14	15	16	17
	18	19	20	21	22	23	24
KĀRTTIKA 2109	25	26	27	28	29	30	1
	2	3	4	5	6	7	8
	9	10	11	12	13	14	15
	16	17	18	19	20	21	22
	23	24	25	26	27	28	29
MĀRGAŚĪRA 2109	30	1	2	3	4	5	6
	7	8	9	10	11	12	13
	14	15	16	17	18	19	20
	21	22	23	24	25	26	27
PAUSHA 2109	28	29	30	1	2	3	4
	5	6	7	8	9	10	11
	12	13	14	15	16	17	18

‡ Leap year
[a] New Year (Śubhakṛit)
[b] Pongal

ISLAMIC (ASTRONOMICAL) 1613/1614‡

Month	Sun	Mon	Tue	Wed	Thu	Fri	Sat
JUMĀDĀ II 1613	20	21	22	23	24	25	26
RAJAB 1613	27	28	29	30	1	2	3
	4	5	6	7	8	9	10
	11	12	13	14	15	16	17
	18	19	20	21	22	23	24
SHA'BĀN 1613	25	26	27[d]	28	29	30	1
	2	3	4	5	6	7	8
	9	10	11	12	13	14	15
	16	17	18	19	20	21	22
	23	24	25	26	27	28	29
RAMAḌĀN 1613	30	1[e]	2	3	4	5	6
	7	8	9	10	11	12	13
	14	15	16	17	18	19	20
	21	22	23	24	25	26	27
SHAWWĀL 1613	28	29	1[f]	2	3	4	5
	6	7	8	9	10	11	12
	13	14	15	16	17	18	19
	20	21	22	23	24	25	26
DHU AL-QA'DA 1613	27	28	29	30	1	2	3
	4	5	6	7	8	9	10
	11	12	13	14	15	16	17
	18	19	20	21	22	23	24
DHU AL-ḤIJJA 1613	25	26	27	28	29	1	2
	3	4	5	6	7	8	9
	10[g]	11	12	13	14	15	16
	17	18	19	20	21	22	23
MUḤARRAM 1614	24	25	26	27	28	29	1[a]
	2	3	4	5	6	7	8
	9	10[b]	11	12	13	14	15
	16	17	18	19	20	21	22
	23	24	25	26	27	28	29
ṢAFAR 1614	30	1	2	3	4	5	6
	7	8	9	10	11	12	13
	14	15	16	17	18	19	20
	21	22	23	24	25	26	27
RABĪ' I 1614	28	29	1	2	3	4	5
	6	7	8	9	10	11	12[c]
	13	14	15	16	17	18	19
	20	21	22	23	24	25	26
RABĪ' II 1614	27	28	29	1	2	3	4
	5	6	7	8	9	10	11
	12	13	14	15	16	17	18
	19	20	21	22	23	24	25
JUMĀDĀ I 1614	26	27	28	29	30	1	2
	3	4	5	6	7	8	9
	10	11	12	13	14	15	16
	17	18	19	20	21	22	23
	24	25	26	27	28	29	30
JUMĀDĀ II 1614	1	2	3	4	5	6	7
	8	9	10	11	12	13	14
	15	16	17	18	19	20	21
	22	23	24	25	26	27	28
	29	1	2	3	4	5	6

‡ Leap year
[a] New Year
[b] 'Ashūrā'
[c] Prophet's Birthday
[d] Ascent of the Prophet
[e] Start of Ramaḍān
[f] 'Id al-Fiṭr
[g] 'Id al-'Aḍḥā

GREGORIAN 2187

Julian (Sun)	Month	Sun	Mon	Tue	Wed	Thu	Fri	Sat
Dec 17	JANUARY 2187	31	1	2	3	4	5	6
		7	8[a]	9	10	11	12	13
Dec 31		14	15[b]	16	17	18	19	20
		21	22	23	24	25	26	27
Jan 14	FEBRUARY 2187	28	29	30	31	1	2	3
		4	5	6	7[c]	8	9	10
Jan 28		11	12	13	14	15	16	17
		18	19	20	21	22	23	24
Feb 11	MARCH 2187	25	26	27	28	1	2	3
		4	5	6	7	8	9	10
Feb 25		11	12	13	14	15	16	17
		18[d]	19	20	21	22	23	24
Mar 11		25[e]	26	27	28	29	30	31
	APRIL 2187	1	2	3	4	5	6	7
Mar 25		8	9	10	11	12	13	14
		15	16	17	18	19	20	21
Apr 8		22	23	24	25	26	27	28
	MAY 2187	29[f]	30	1	2	3	4	5
Apr 22		6	7	8	9	10	11	12
		13	14	15	16	17	18	19
May 6		20	21	22	23	24	25	26
	JUNE 2187	27	28	29	30	31	1	2
May 20		3	4	5	6	7	8	9
		10	11	12	13	14	15	16
Jun 3		17	18	19	20	21	22	23
		24	25	26	27	28	29	30
Jun 17	JULY 2187	1	2	3	4	5	6	7
		8	9	10	11	12	13	14
Jul 1		15	16	17	18	19	20	21
		22	23	24	25	26	27	28
Jul 15	AUGUST 2187	29	30	31	1	2	3	4
		5	6	7	8	9	10	11
Jul 29		12	13	14	15	16	17	18
		19	20	21	22	23	24	25
Aug 12	SEPTEMBER 2187	26	27	28	29	30	31	1
		2	3	4	5	6	7	8
Aug 26		9	10	11	12	13	14	15
		16	17	18	19	20	21	22
Sep 9		23	24	25	26	27	28	29
	OCTOBER 2187	30	1	2	3	4	5	6
Sep 23		7	8	9	10	11	12	13
		14	15	16	17	18	19	20
Oct 7		21	22	23	24	25	26	27
	NOVEMBER 2187	28	29	30	31	1	2	3
Oct 21		4	5	6	7	8	9	10
		11	12	13	14	15	16	17
Nov 4		18	19	20	21	22	23	24
	DECEMBER 2187	25	26	27	28	29	30	1
Nov 18		2[g]	3	4	5	6	7	8
		9	10	11	12	13	14	15
Dec 2		16	17	18	19	20	21	22
		23	24	25[h]	26	27	28	29
Dec 16		30	31	1	2	3	4	5

[a] Orthodox Christmas
[b] Julian New Year
[c] Ash Wednesday
[d] Feast of Orthodoxy
[e] Easter
[f] Orthodox Easter
[g] Advent
[h] Christmas

2188

Gregorian 2188‡	Sun	Mon	Tue	Wed	Thu	Fri	Sat	Lunar Phases	ISO Week (Mon)	Julian Day (Sun noon)	Hebrew 5948/5949	Sun	Mon	Tue	Wed	Thu	Fri	Sat	Molad	Chinese Dīng-Hài/Wù-Zǐ‡	Sun	Mon	Tue	Wed	Thu	Fri	Sat	Solar Term	Coptic 1904/1905	Sun	Mon	Tue	Wed	Thu	Fri	Sat	Ethiopic 2180/2181
January 2188	30	31	1[a]	2	3	4	5		1	2520209	Teveth 5948	29[e]	30[e]	1[e]	2[e]	3	4	5	Sun 9h49m16p	Month 12 Dīng-Hài	1	2	3	4	5	6	7		Koiak 1904	19	20	21	22	23	24	25	Tākhśāś 2180
	◐	7	8	9	10	11	12	20:09	2	2520216		6	7	8	9	10	11	12			8	9	10	11	12	13	14	Xiǎohán	Tōbe 1904	26	27	28	29[c]	30	1	2	Ṭer 2180
	13	○	15	16	17	18	19	8:19	3	2520223		13	14	15	16	17	18	19			15	16	17	18	19	20	21			3	4	5	6[d]	7	8	9	
	20	◑	22	23	24	25	26	0:42	4	2520230		20	21	22	23	24	25	26			22	23	24	25	26	27	28	Dàhán		10	11[e]	12	13	14	15	16	
February 2188	27	●	29	30	31	1	2	12:02	5	2520237	Shevat 5948	27	28	29	1	2	3	4	Mon 22h33m17p	Month 1 Wù-Zǐ	29	1[a]	2	3	4	5	6			17	18	19	20	21	22	23	
	3	4	◐	6	7	8	9	16:37	6	2520244		5	6	7	8	9	10	11			7	8	9	10	11	12	13	Lìchūn		24	25	26	27	28	29	30	
	10	11	○	13	14	15	16	20:00	7	2520251		12	13	14	15	16	17	18			14*	15[b]	16	17	18	19	20		Meshir 1904	1	2	3	4	5	6	7	Yakātīt 2180
	17	18	◑	20	21	22	23	10:42	8	2520258		19	20	21	22	23	24	25			21	22	23	24	25	26	27	Yǔshuǐ		8	9	10	11	12	13	14	
March 2188	24	25	26	●	28	29	1	6:10	9	2520265	Adar 5948	26	27	28	29	30	1	2	Wed 11h18m0p	Month 2 Wù-Zǐ	28	29	30	1	2	3	4			15	16	17	18	19	20	21	
	2	3	4	5	◐	7	8	10:05	10	2520272		3	4	5	6	7	8	9			5	6	7	8	9	10	11	Jīngzhé		22	23	24	25	26	27	28	
	9	10	11	12	○	14	15	5:57	11	2520279		10	11	12	13	14[f]	15	16			12	13	14	15	16	17	18		Paremotep 1904	29	30	1	2	3	4	5	Magābīt 2180
	16	17	18	◑[b]	20	21	22	22:51	12	2520286		17	18	19	20	21	22	23			19	20	21	22	23	24	25	Chūnfēn		6	7	8	9	10	11	12	
	23	24	25	26	27	●	29	0:11	13	2520293	Nisan 5948	24	25	26	27	28	29	1	Fri 0h2m1p	Month 3 Wù-Zǐ	26	27	28	29	30	1	2			13	14	15	16	17	18	19	
April 2188	30	31	1	2	3	◐	5	23:31	14	2520300		2	3	4	5	6	7	8			3	4	5	6	7	8[c]	9	Qīngmíng		20	21	22	23	24	25	26	
	6	7	8	9	10	○	12	14:44	15	2520307		9	10	11	12	13	14	15[g]			10	11	12	13	14*	15	16		Parmoute 1904	27	28	29	30	1	2	3	Miyāzyā 2180
	13	14	15	16	17	◑	19	13:03	16	2520314		16	17	18	19	20	21	22			17	18	19	20	21	22	23	Gǔyǔ		4	5	6	7	8	9	10	
	20	21	22	23	24	25	●	17:01	17	2520321		23	24	25	26	27	28	29			24	25	26	27	28	29	30			11[f]	12	13	14	15	16	17	
May 2188	27	28	29	30	1	2	3		18	2520328	Iyyar 5948	30	1	2	3	4	5	6	Sat 12h46m2p	Month 4 Wù-Zǐ	1	2	3	4	5	6	7			18	19	20	21	22	23	24	
	◐	5	6	7	8	9	○	8:54 23:11	19	2520335		7	8	9	10	11	12	13			8	9	10	11	12	13	14	Lìxià	Pashons 1904	25	26	27	28	29[g]	30	1	Genbot 2180
	11	12	13	14	15	16	17		20	2520342		14	15	16	17	18	19	20			15	16	17	18	19	20	21			2	3	4	5	6	7	8	
	◑	19	20	21	22	23	24	4:49	21	2520349		21	22	23	24	25	26	27			22	23	24	25	26	27	28	Xiǎomǎn		9	10	11	12	13	14	15	
	25	●	27	28	29	30	31	7:52	22	2520356	Sivan 5948	28	29	1	2	3	4	5	Mon 1h30m3p	Month 5 Wù-Zǐ	29	1	2	3	4	5[d]	6			16	17	18	19	20	21	22	
June 2188	1	◐	3	4	5	6	7	15:07	23	2520363		6[h]	7	8	9	10	11	12			7	8	9	10	11	12	13	Mángzhòng		23	24	25	26	27	28	29	
	8	○	10	11	12	13	14	8:04	24	2520370		13	14	15	16	17	18	19			14	15*	16	17	18	19	20		Paōne 1904	30	1	2	3	4	5	6	Sanē 2180
	15	◑	17	18	19	20[c]	21	21:36	25	2520377		20	21	22	23	24	25	26			21	22	23	24	25	26	27	Xiàzhì		7	8	9	10	11	12	13	
	22	23	●	25	26	27	28	20:21	26	2520384	Tammuz 5948	27	28	29	30	1	2	3	Tue 14h14m4p	Month 6 Wù-Zǐ	28	29	30	1	2	3	4			14	15	16	17	18	19	20	
July 2188	29	30	◐	2	3	4	5	19:38	27	2520391		4	5	6	7	8	9	10			5	6	7	8	9	10	11			21	22	23	24	25	26	27	
	6	7	○	9	10	11	12	18:06	28	2520398		11	12	13	14	15	16	17			12	13	14	15	16	17	18	Xiǎoshǔ	Epēp 1904	28	29	30	1	2	3	4	Ḥamlē 2180
	13	14	15	◑	17	18	19	14:50	29	2520405		18	19	20	21	22	23	24			19	20	21	22	23	24	25			5	6	7	8	9	10	11	
	20	21	22	23	●	25	26	6:34	30	2520412	Av 5948	25	26	27	28	29	1	2	Thu 2h58m5p	Leap Month 6 Wù-Zǐ	26	27	28	29	1	2	3	Dàshǔ		12	13	14	15	16	17	18	
August 2188	27	28	29	30	◐	1	2	0:05	31	2520419		3	4	5	6	7	8	9			4	5	6	7	8	9	10			19	20	21	22	23	24	25	
	3	4	5	6	○	8	9	5:50	32	2520426		10[i]	11	12	13	14	15	16			11	12	13	14	15	16*	17	Lìqiū	Mesorē 1904	26	27	28	29	30	1	2	Naḥasē 2180
	10	11	12	13	14	◑	16	7:55	33	2520433		17	18	19	20	21	22	23			18	19	20	21	22	23	24			3	4	5	6	7	8	9	
	17	18	19	20	21	●	23	15:12	34	2520440		24	25	26	27	28	29	30	Fri 15h42m6p	Month 7 Wù-Zǐ	25	26	27	28	29	1	2	Chǔshǔ		10	11	12	13[h]	14	15	16	
	24	25	26	27	28	◐	30	6:01	35	2520447	Elul 5948	1	2	3	4	5	6	7			3	4	5	6	7[e]	8	9			17	18	19	20	21	22	23	
September 2188	31	1	2	3	4	○	6	19:42	36	2520454		8	9	10	11	12	13	14			10	11	12	13	14	15[f]	16			24	25	26	27	28	29	30	
	7	8	9	10	11	12	13		37	2520461		15	16	17	18	19	20	21			17	18	19	20	21	22	23	Báilù	Epag. 1904 / Thoout 1905	1	2	3	4	5	1[a]	2	Pāg. 2180 / Maskaram 2181
	◑	15	16	17	18	19	●	0:01 14:43	38	2520468		22	23	24	25	26	27	28			24	25	26	27	28	29	30			3	4	5	6	7	8	9	
	21	22[d]	23	24	25	26	◐	23:14	39	2520475	Tishri 5949	29	1[a]	2[a]	3	4	5	6	Sun 4h26m7p	Month 8 Wù-Zǐ	1	2	3	4	5	6	7	Qiūfēn		10	11	12	13	14	15	16	
October 2188	28	29	30	1	2	3	4		40	2520482		7	8	9	10[b]	11	12	13			8	9	10	11	12	13	14			17[b]	18	19	20	21	22	23	
	○	6	7	8	9	10	11	11:49	41	2520489		14	15[c]	16	17	18	19	20			15[g]	16	17*	18	19	20	21	Hánlù		24	25	26	27	28	29	30	
	12	◑	14	15	16	17	18	14:22	42	2520496		21	22	23	24	25	26	27			22	23	24	25	26	27	28		Paope 1905	1	2	3	4	5	6	7	Ṭeqemt 2181
	19	●	21	22	23	24	25	7:46	43	2520503	Heshvan 5949	28	29	30	1	2	3	4	Mon 17h10m8p	Month 9 Wù-Zǐ	29	1	2	3	4	5	6	Shuāngjiàng		8	9	10	11	12	13	14	
November 2188	26	◐	28	29	30	31	1	3:01	44	2520510		5	6	7	8	9	10	11			7	8	9[h]	10	11	12	13			15	16	17	18	19	20	21	
	2	3	○	5	6	7	8	5:43	45	2520517		12	13	14	15	16	17	18			14	15	16	17	18	19	20	Lìdōng		22	23	24	25	26	27	28	
	9	10	11	◑	13	14	15	2:31	46	2520524		19	20	21	22	23	24	25			21	22	23	24	25	26	27		Athōr 1905	29	30	1	2	3	4	5	Ḫedār 2181
	16	17	●	19	20	21	22	17:35	47	2520531	Kislev 5949	26	27	28	29	30	1	2	Wed 5h54m9p	Month 10 Wù-Zǐ	28	29	30	1	2	3	4	Xiǎoxuě		6	7	8	9	10	11	12	
	23	24	◐	26	27	28	29	19:13	48	2520538		3	4	5	6	7	8	9			5	6	7	8	9	10	11			13	14	15	16	17	18	19	
December 2188	30	1	2	3	○	5	6	0:10	49	2520545		10	11	12	13	14	15	16[d]			12	13	14	15	16	17	18*	Dàxuě		20	21	22	23	24	25	26	
	7	8	9	10	◑	12	13	12:36	50	2520552		17	18	19	20	21	22	23			19	20	21	22	23	24	25		Koiak 1905	27	28	29	30	1	2	3	Tākhśāś 2181
	14	15	16	17	●	19	20	5:04	51	2520559		24	25[e]	26[e]	27[e]	28[e]	29[e]	30[e]		Month 11* Wù-Zǐ	26	27	28	29	1	2	3			4	5	6	7	8	9	10	
	21[e]	22	23	24	◐	26	27	14:52	52	2520566	Teveth 5949	1[e]	2[e]	3	4	5	6	7	Thu 18h38m10p		4[i]	5	6	7	8	9	10	Dōngzhì		11	12	13	14	15	16	17	
	28	29	30	31	1	○	3	17:31	1	2520573		8	9	10	11	12	13	14			11	12	13	14	15	16	17			18	19	20	21	22	23	24	

‡Leap year
[a]New Year
[b]Spring (21:07)
[c]Summer (11:55)
[d]Autumn (5:04)
[e]Winter (4:36)
● New moon
◐ First quarter moon
○ Full moon
◑ Last quarter moon

[a]New Year
[b]Yom Kippur
[c]Sukkot
[d]Winter starts
[e]Ḥanukkah
[f]Purim
[g]Passover
[h]Shavuot
[i]Fast of Av

‡Leap year
[a]New Year (4886, Rat)
[b]Lantern Festival
[c]Qīngmíng
[d]Dragon Festival
[e]Qīqiǎo
[f]Hungry Ghosts
[g]Mid-Autumn Festival
[h]Double-Ninth Festival
[i]Dōngzhì
*Start of 60-name cycle

[a]New Year
[b]Building of the Cross
[c]Christmas
[d]Jesus's Circumcision
[e]Epiphany
[f]Easter
[g]Mary's Announcement
[h]Jesus's Transfiguration

PERSIAN (ASTRONOMICAL) 1566/1567

Month	Sun	Mon	Tue	Wed	Thu	Fri	Sat
	9	10	11	12	13	14	15
DEY 1566	16	17	18	19	20	21	22
	23	24	25	26	27	28	29
	30	1	2	3	4	5	6
BAHMAN 1566	7	8	9	10	11	12	13
	14	15	16	17	18	19	20
	21	22	23	24	25	26	27
	28	29	30	1	2	3	4
ESFAND 1566	5	6	7	8	9	10	11
	12	13	14	15	16	17	18
	19	20	21	22	23	24	25
	26	27	28	29	1[a]	2	3
FARVARDĪN 1567	4	5	6	7	8	9	10
	11	12	13[b]	14	15	16	17
	18	19	20	21	22	23	24
	25	26	27	28	29	30	31
ORDĪBEHEŠT 1567	1	2	3	4	5	6	7
	8	9	10	11	12	13	14
	15	16	17	18	19	20	21
	22	23	24	25	26	27	28
	29	30	31	1	2	3	4
XORDĀD 1567	5	6	7	8	9	10	11
	12	13	14	15	16	17	18
	19	20	21	22	23	24	25
	26	27	28	29	30	31	1
TĪR 1567	2	3	4	5	6	7	8
	9	10	11	12	13	14	15
	16	17	18	19	20	21	22
	23	24	25	26	27	28	29
	30	31	1	2	3	4	5
MORDĀD 1567	6	7	8	9	10	11	12
	13	14	15	16	17	18	19
	20	21	22	23	24	25	26
	27	28	29	30	31	1	2
SHAHRĪVAR 1567	3	4	5	6	7	8	9
	10	11	12	13	14	15	16
	17	18	19	20	21	22	23
	24	25	26	27	28	29	30
	31	1	2	3	4	5	6
MEHR 1567	7	8	9	10	11	12	13
	14	15	16	17	18	19	20
	21	22	23	24	25	26	27
	28	29	30	1	2	3	4
ĀBĀN 1567	5	6	7	8	9	10	11
	12	13	14	15	16	17	18
	19	20	21	22	23	24	25
	26	27	28	29	30	1	2
ĀZAR 1567	3	4	5	6	7	8	9
	10	11	12	13	14	15	16
	17	18	19	20	21	22	23
	24	25	26	27	28	29	30
DEY 1567	1	2	3	4	5	6	7
	8	9	10	11	12	13	14

[a]New Year
[b]Sizdeh Bedar

HINDU LUNAR 2244/2245‡

Month	Sun	Mon	Tue	Wed	Thu	Fri	Sat
	1	2	3	4	5	6	6
PAUSHA 2244	7	8	9	10	11	12	13
	14	15	16	17	**18**	20	21
	22	23	24	25	26	27	28
	29	30	1	2	3	4	5
MĀGHA 2244	6	7	8	9	9	10	**11**
	13	14	15	16	17	18	19
	20	21	22	23	24	**25**	27
	28	28[h]	29	30	1	2	3
PHĀLGUNA 2244	4	5	6	7	8	9	10
	11	12	13	14	15[i]	16	**17**
	19	20	21	22	23	24	25
	26	27	28	29	30	1[a]	1
CHAITRA 2245	2	3	4	5	6	7	8[b]
	9	10	**11**	13	14	15	16
	17	18	19	20	21	22	23
	24	25	26	27	28	29	30
VAIŚĀKHA 2245	1	2	3	4	5	6	7
	8	9	10	11	12	13	**14**
	16	17	18	19	20	21	22
	23	24	25	26	26	27	28
	29	30	1	2	3	4	5
JYAISHTHA 2245	6	**7**	9	10	11	12	13
	14	15	16	17	18	19	20
	21	22	23	24	25	26	27
	28	29	30	1	2	3	4
ĀSHĀḌHA 2245	5	6	7	8	9	**10**	12
	13	14	15	16	17	18	19
	20	21	22	23	23	24	25
	26	27	28	29	30	1	2
ŚRĀVAṆA 2245	**3**	5	6	7	8	9	10
	11	12	13	14	15	16	17
	18	19	20	21	22	23[c]	24
	25	26	27	28	29	30	1
BHĀDRAPADA 2245	2	3	4[d]	5	**6**	8	9
	10	11	12	13	14	15	16
	17	18	19	19	20	21	22
	23	24	25	26	27	28	**29**
ĀŚVINA 2245	1	2	3	4	5	6	7
	8[e]	9[e]	10[e]	11	12	13	14
	15	16	17	18	19	20	21
	22	23	24	25	26	27	28
	29	30	1	2	**3**	5	6
LEAP KĀRTTIKA 2245	7	8	9	10	11	12	13
	14	14	15	16	17	18	19
	20	21	22	23	24	25	26
	27	29	30	1[f]	2	3	4
KĀRTTIKA 2245	5	6	7	8	9	10	11
	12	13	14	15	16	17	17
	18	**19**	21	22	23	24	25
	26	27	28	29	30	1	2
MĀRGAŚĪRA 2245	**3**	5	6	6	7	8	9
	10	11[g]	12	13	14	15	16

‡Leap year
[a]New Year (Sarvadhārin)
[b]Birthday of Rāma
[c]Birthday of Krishna
[d]Ganēśa Chaturthī
[e]Dashara
[f]Diwali
[g]Birthday of Vishnu
[h]Night of Śiva
[i]Holi

HINDU SOLAR 2109‡/2110

Month	Sun	Mon	Tue	Wed	Thu	Fri	Sat
PAUSHA 2109	12	13	14	15	16	17	18
	19	20	21	22	23	24	25
	26	27	28	29	1[b]	2	3
MĀGHA 2109	4	5	6	7	8	9	10
	11	12	13	14	15	16	17
	18	19	20	21	22	23	24
	25	26	27	28	29	1	2
PHĀLGUNA 2109	3	4	5	6	7	8	9
	10	11	12	13	14	15	16
	17	18	19	20	21	22	23
	24	25	26	27	28	29	30
	1	2	3	4	5	6	7
CHAITRA 2109	8	9	10	11	12	13	14
	15	16	17	18	19	20	21
	22	23	24	25	26	27	28
	29	30	31	1[a]	2	3	4
VAIŚĀKHA 2110	5	6	7	8	9	10	11
	12	13	14	15	16	17	18
	19	20	21	22	23	24	25
	26	27	28	29	30	31	1
JYAISHTHA 2110	2	3	4	5	6	7	8
	9	10	11	12	13	14	15
	16	17	18	19	20	21	22
	23	24	25	26	27	28	29
	30	31	1	2	3	4	5
ĀSHĀḌHA 2110	6	7	8	9	10	11	12
	13	14	15	16	17	18	19
	20	21	22	23	24	25	26
	27	28	29	30	31	32	1
ŚRĀVAṆA 2110	2	3	4	5	6	7	8
	9	10	11	12	13	14	15
	16	17	18	19	20	21	22
	23	24	25	26	27	28	29
	30	31	1	2	3	4	5
BHĀDRAPADA 2110	6	7	8	9	10	11	12
	13	14	15	16	17	18	19
	20	21	22	23	24	25	26
	27	28	29	30	31	1	2
ĀŚVINA 2110	3	4	5	6	7	8	9
	10	11	12	13	14	15	16
	17	18	19	20	21	22	23
	24	25	26	27	28	29	30
	31	1	2	3	4	5	6
KĀRTTIKA 2110	7	8	9	10	11	12	13
	14	15	16	17	18	19	20
	21	22	23	24	25	26	27
	28	29	1	2	3	4	5
MĀRGAŚĪRA 2110	6	7	8	9	10	11	12
	13	14	15	16	17	18	19
	20	21	22	23	24	25	26
	27	28	29	30	1	2	3
PAUSHA 2110	4	5	6	7	8	9	10
	11	12	13	14	15	16	17

‡Leap year
[a]New Year (Śobhana)
[b]Pongal

ISLAMIC (ASTRONOMICAL) 1614‡/1615

Month	Sun	Mon	Tue	Wed	Thu	Fri	Sat
	29	1	2	3	4	5	6
RAJAB 1614	7	8	9	10	11	12	13
	14	15	16	17	18	19	20
	21	22	23	24	25	26	27[d]
	28	29	30	1	2	3	4
SHA'BĀN 1614	5	6	7	8	9	10	11
	12	13	14	15	16	17	18
	19	20	21	22	23	24	25
	26	27	28	29	30	1[e]	2
RAMAḌĀN 1614	3	4	5	6	7	8	9
	10	11	12	13	14	15	16
	17	18	19	20	21	22	23
	24	25	26	27	28	29	1[f]
SHAWWĀL 1614	2	3	4	5	6	7	8
	9	10	11	12	13	14	15
	16	17	18	19	20	21	22
	23	24	25	26	27	28	29
	30	1	2	3	4	5	6
DHU AL-QA'DA 1614	7	8	9	10	11	12	13
	14	15	16	17	18	19	20
	21	22	23	24	25	26	27
	28	29	30	1	2	3	4
DHU AL-ḤIJJA 1614	5	6	7	8	9	10[g]	11
	12	13	14	15	16	17	18
	19	20	21	22	23	24	25
	26	27	28	29	1[a]	2	3
MUḤARRAM 1615	4	5	6	7	8	9	10[b]
	11	12	13	14	15	16	17
	18	19	20	21	22	23	24
	25	26	27	28	29	1	2
ṢAFAR 1615	3	4	5	6	7	8	9
	10	11	12	13	14	15	16
	17	18	19	20	21	22	23
	24	25	26	27	28	29	30
RABĪ' I 1615	1	2	3	4	5	6	7
	8	9	10	11	12[c]	13	14
	15	16	17	18	19	20	21
	22	23	24	25	26	27	28
	29	1	2	3	4	5	6
RABĪ' II 1615	7	8	9	10	11	12	13
	14	15	16	17	18	19	20
	21	22	23	24	25	26	27
	28	29	30	1	2	3	4
JUMĀDĀ I 1615	5	6	7	8	9	10	11
	12	13	14	15	16	17	18
	19	20	21	22	23	24	25
	26	27	28	29	1	2	3
JUMĀDĀ II 1615	4	5	6	7	8	9	10
	11	12	13	14	15	16	17
	18	19	20	21	22	23	24
	25	26	27	28	29	30	1
RAJAB 1615	2	3	4	5	6	7	8
	9	10	11	12	13	14	15

‡Leap year
[a]New Year
[b]'Ashūrā'
[c]Prophet's Birthday
[d]Ascent of the Prophet
[e]Start of Ramaḍān
[f]'Īd al-Fiṭr
[g]'Īd al-'Aḍḥā

GREGORIAN 2188‡

Julian‡ (Sun)	Sun	Mon	Tue	Wed	Thu	Fri	Sat	Month
Dec 16	30	31	1	2	3	4	5	
	6	7	8[a]	9	10	11	12	JANUARY 2188
Dec 30	13	14	15[b]	16	17	18	19	
	20	21	22	23	24	25	26	
Jan 13	27	28	29	30	31	1	2	
	3	4	5	6	7	8	9	FEBRUARY 2188
Jan 27	10	11	12	13	14	15	16	
	17	18	19	20	21	22	23	
Feb 10	24	25	26	27[c]	28	29	1	
	2	3	4	5	6	7	8	MARCH 2188
Feb 24	9[d]	10	11	12	13	14	15	
	16	17	18	19	20	21	22	
Mar 9	23	24	25	26	27	28	29	
	30	31	1	2	3	4	5	
Mar 23	6	7	8	9	10	11	12	APRIL 2188
	13[e]	14	15	16	17	18	19	
Apr 6	20[f]	21	22	23	24	25	26	
	27	28	29	30	1	2	3	
Apr 20	4	5	6	7	8	9	10	MAY 2188
	11	12	13	14	15	16	17	
May 4	18	19	20	21	22	23	24	
	25	26	27	28	29	30	31	
May 18	1	2	3	4	5	6	7	JUNE 2188
	8	9	10	11	12	13	14	
Jun 1	15	16	17	18	19	20	21	
	22	23	24	25	26	27	28	
Jun 15	29	30	1	2	3	4	5	
	6	7	8	9	10	11	12	JULY 2188
Jun 29	13	14	15	16	17	18	19	
	20	21	22	23	24	25	26	
Jul 13	27	28	29	30	31	1	2	
	3	4	5	6	7	8	9	AUGUST 2188
Jul 27	10	11	12	13	14	15	16	
	17	18	19	20	21	22	23	
Aug 10	24	25	26	27	28	29	30	
	31	1	2	3	4	5	6	
Aug 24	7	8	9	10	11	12	13	SEPTEMBER 2188
	14	15	16	17	18	19	20	
Sep 7	21	22	23	24	25	26	27	
	28	29	30	1	2	3	4	
Sep 21	5	6	7	8	9	10	11	OCTOBER 2188
	12	13	14	15	16	17	18	
Oct 5	19	20	21	22	23	24	25	
	26	27	28	29	30	31	1	
Oct 19	2	3	4	5	6	7	8	NOVEMBER 2188
	9	10	11	12	13	14	15	
Nov 2	16	17	18	19	20	21	22	
	23	24	25	26	27	28	29	
Nov 16	30[g]	1	2	3	4	5	6	
	7	8	9	10	11	12	13	DECEMBER 2188
Nov 30	14	15	16	17	18	19	20	
	21	22	23	24	25[h]	26	27	
Dec 14	28	29	30	31	1	2	3	

‡Leap year
[a]Orthodox Christmas
[b]Julian New Year
[c]Ash Wednesday
[d]Feast of Orthodoxy
[e]Easter
[f]Orthodox Easter
[g]Advent
[h]Christmas

2189

GREGORIAN 2189	Sun	Mon	Tue	Wed	Thu	Fri	Sat	Lunar Phases	ISO WEEK (Mon)	JULIAN DAY (Sun noon)	HEBREW 5949/5950‡	Sun	Mon	Tue	Wed	Thu	Fri	Sat	Molad	CHINESE Wù-Zǐ‡/Jǐ-Chǒu	Sun	Mon	Tue	Wed	Thu	Fri	Sat	Solar Term	COPTIC 1905/1906	Sun	Mon	Tue	Wed	Thu	Fri	Sat	ETHIOPIC 2181/2182
JANUARY 2189	28	29	30	31	1[a]	○	3	17:31	1	2520573	TEVETH 5949	8	9	10	11	12	13	14		MONTH 11* Wù-Zǐ	11	12	13	14	15	16	17		KOIAK 1905	18	19	20	21	22	23	24	TĀḪŚĀŚ 2181
	4	5	6	7	8	◑	10	21:12	2	2520580		15	16	17	18	19	20	21			18	19	20	21	22	23	24	Xiǎo hán	TŌBE 1905	25	26	27	28	29[c]	30	1	ṬER 2181
	11	12	13	14	15	●	17	18:10	3	2520587		22	23	24	25	26	27	28		MONTH 12 Wù-Zǐ	25	26	27	28	29	30	1			2	3	4	5	6[d]	7	8	
	18	19	20	21	22	23	◐	12:37	4	2520594	SHEVAT 5949	29	1	2	3	4	5	6	Sat 7h22m11p		2	3	4	5	6	7	8	Dà hán		9	10	11[e]	12	13	14	15	
	25	26	27	28	29	30	31		5	2520601		7	8	9	10	11	12	13			9	10	11	12	13	14	15			16	17	18	19	20	21	22	
FEBRUARY 2189	○	2	3	4	5	6	7	8:33	6	2520608		14	15	16	17	18	19	20			16	17	18	19*	20	21	22	Lì chūn		23	24	25	26	27	28	29	
	◑	9	10	11	12	13	14	5:12	7	2520615		21	22	23	24	25	26	27			23	24	25	26	27	28	29		MESHIR 1905	30	1	2	3	4	5	6	YAKĀTIT 2181
	●	16	17	18	19	20	21	8:43	8	2520622	ADAR 5949	28	29	30	1	2	3	4	Sun 20h6m12p	MONTH 1 Jǐ-Chǒu	1[a]	2	3	4	5	6	7	Yǔ shuǐ		7	8	9	10	11	12	13	
	22	◐	24	25	26	27	28	10:15	9	2520629		5	6	7	8	9	10	11			8	9	10	11	12	13	14			14	15	16	17	18	19	20	
MARCH 2189	1	○	3	4	5	6	7	20:58	10	2520636		12	13	14[f]	15	16	17	18			15[b]	16	17	18	19	20	21	Jīng zhé		21	22	23	24	25	26	27	
	8	◑	10	11	12	13	14	13:24	11	2520643		19	20	21	22	23	24	25			22	23	24	25	26	27	28		PAREMOTEP 1905	28	29	30	1	2	3	4	MAGĀBIT 2181
	15	16	●	18	19	20[b]	21	0:31	12	2520650	NISAN 5949	26	27	28	29	1	2	3	Tue 8h50m13p	MONTH 2 Jǐ-Chǒu	29	30	1	2	3	4	5	Chūn fēn		5	6	7	8	9	10	11	
	22	23	24	◐	26	27	28	5:30	13	2520657		4	5	6	7	8	9	10			6	7	8	9	10	11	12			12	13	14	15	16	17	18	
APRIL 2189	29	30	31	○	2	3	4	7:09	14	2520664		11	12	13	14	15[g]	16	17			13	14	15	16	17	18	19[c]	Qīng míng		19	20	21	22	23	24	25	
	5	6	◑	8	9	10	11	22:28	15	2520671		18	19	20	21	22	23	24			20*	21	22	23	24	25	26		PARMOUTE 1905	26	27	28	29	30	1	2	MIYĀZYĀ 2181
	12	13	14	●	16	17	18	17:10	16	2520678	IYYAR 5949	25	26	27	28	29	30	1	Wed 21h34m14p		27	28	29	30	1	2	3	Gǔ yǔ		3[f]	4	5	6	7	8	9	
	19	20	21	22	◐	24	25	20:51	17	2520685		2	3	4	5	6	7	8		MONTH 3 Jǐ-Chǒu	4	5	6	7	8	9	10			10	11	12	13	14	15	16	
MAY 2189	26	27	28	29	○	1	2	15:48	18	2520692		9	10	11	12	13	14	15			11	12	13	14	15	16	17			17	18	19	20	21	22	23	
	3	4	5	6	◑	8	9	8:58	19	2520699		16	17	18	19	20	21	22			18	19	20	21	22	23	24	Lì xià		24	25	26	27	28	29[g]	30	
	10	11	12	13	14	●	16	9:53	20	2520706		23	24	25	26	27	28	29		MONTH 4 Jǐ-Chǒu	25	26	27	28	29	1	2		PASHONS 1905	1	2	3	4	5	6	7	GENBOT 2181
	17	18	19	20	21	22	◐	8:09	21	2520713	SIVAN 5949	1	2	3	4	5	6[h]	7	Fri 10h18m15p		3	4	5	6	7	8	9	Xiǎo mǎn		8	9	10	11	12	13	14	
	24	25	26	27	28	○	30	23:33	22	2520720		8	9	10	11	12	13	14			10	11	12	13	14	15	16			15	16	17	18	19	20	21	
JUNE 2189	31	1	2	3	4	◑	6	21:22	23	2520727		15	16	17	18	19	20	21			17	18	19	20	21*	22	23	Máng zhòng		22	23	24	25	26	27	28	
	7	8	9	10	11	12	13		24	2520734		22	23	24	25	26	27	28			24	25	26	27	28	29	30		PAŌNE 1905	29	30	1	2	3	4	5	SANĒ 2181
	●	15	16	17	18	19	20[c]	1:33	25	2520741	TAMMUZ 5949	29	30	1	2	3	4	5	Sat 23h2m16p	MONTH 5 Jǐ-Chǒu	1	2	3	4	5[d]	6	7	Xià zhì		6	7	8	9	10	11	12	
	◐	22	23	24	25	26	27	16:07	26	2520748		6	7	8	9	10	11	12			8	9	10	11	12	13	14			13	14	15	16	17	18	19	
JULY 2189	○	29	30	1	2	3	4	7:07	27	2520755		13	14	15	16	17	18	19			15	16	17	18	19	20	21	Xiǎo shǔ		20	21	22	23	24	25	26	
	◑	6	7	8	9	10	11	11:56	28	2520762		20	21	22	23	24	25	26			22	23	24	25	26	27	28		EPĒP 1905	27	28	29	30	1	2	3	ḤAMLĒ 2181
	12	●	14	15	16	17	18	15:24	29	2520769	AV 5949	27	28	29	1	2	3	4	Mon 11h46m17p	MONTH 6 Jǐ-Chǒu	29	1	2	3	4	5	6	Dà shǔ		4	5	6	7	8	9	10	
	19	◐	21	22	23	24	25	21:56	30	2520776		5	6	7	8	9[i]	10	11			7	8	9	10	11	12	13			11	12	13	14	15	16	17	
AUGUST 2189	26	○	28	29	30	31	1	15:21	31	2520783		12	13	14	15	16	17	18			14	15	16	17	18	19	20			18	19	20	21	22	23	24	
	2	3	◑	5	6	7	8	4:38	32	2520790		19	20	21	22	23	24	25			21	22*	23	24	25	26	27	Lì qiū	MESORĒ 1905	25	26	27	28	29	30	1	NAḤASĒ 2181
	9	10	11	●	13	14	15	3:19	33	2520797	ELUL 5949	26	27	28	29	30	1	2	Wed 0h31m0p	MONTH 7 Jǐ-Chǒu	28	29	30	1	2	3	4			2	3	4	5	6	7	8	
	16	17	18	◐	20	21	22	2:54	34	2520804		3	4	5	6	7	8	9			5	6	7[e]	8	9	10	11	Chǔ shǔ		9	10	11	12	13[h]	14	15	
	23	24	25	○	27	28	29	1:14	35	2520811		10	11	12	13	14	15	16			12	13	14	15[f]	16	17	18			16	17	18	19	20	21	22	
SEPTEMBER 2189	30	31	1	◑	3	4	5	22:45	36	2520818		17	18	19	20	21	22	23			19	20	21	22	23	24	25	Bái lù		23	24	25	26	27	28	29	
	6	7	8	9	●	11	12	13:49	37	2520825	TISHRI 5950	24	25	26	27	28	29	1[a]	Thu 13h15m1p	MONTH 8 Jǐ-Chǒu	26	27	28	29	1	2	3		EPAG. 1905 / THOOUT 1906	30	1	2	3	4	5	1[a]	PĀG. 2181 / MASKARAM 2182
	13	14	15	16	◐	18	19	8:19	38	2520832		2[a]	3	4	5	6	7	8			4	5	6	7	8	9	10	Qiū fēn		2	3	4	5	6	7	8	
	20	21	22[d]	23	○	25	26	13:47	39	2520839		9	10[b]	11	12	13	14	15[c]			11	12	13	14	15[g]	16	17			9	10	11	12	13	14	15	
OCTOBER 2189	27	28	29	30	1	◑	3	17:08	40	2520846		16	17	18	19	20	21	22			18	19	20	21	22	23*	24			16	17[b]	18	19	20	21	22	
	4	5	6	7	8	●	10	23:44	41	2520853		23	24	25	26	27	28	29			25	26	27	28	29	30	1	Hán lù		23	24	25	26	27	28	29	
	11	12	13	14	15	◐	17	15:28	42	2520860	HESHVAN 5950	30	1	2	3	4	5	6	Sat 1h59m2p	MONTH 9 Jǐ-Chǒu	2	3	4	5	6	7	8		PAOPE 1906	30	1	2	3	4	5	6	ṬEQEMT 2182
	18	19	20	21	22	23	○	5:30	43	2520867		7	8	9	10	11	12	13			9[h]	10	11	12	13	14	15	Shuāng jiàng		7	8	9	10	11	12	13	
	25	26	27	28	29	30	31		44	2520874		14	15	16	17	18	19	20			16	17	18	19	20	21	22			14	15	16	17	18	19	20	
NOVEMBER 2189	◑	2	3	4	5	6	7	10:32	45	2520881		21	22	23	24	25	26	27			23	24	25	26	27	28	29	Lì dōng		21	22	23	24	25	26	27	
	●	9	10	11	12	13	14	9:44	46	2520888	KISLEV 5950	28	29	1	2	3	4	5	Sun 14h43m3p	MONTH 10 Jǐ-Chǒu	1	2	3	4	5	6	7		ATHŌR 1906	28	29	30	1	2	3	4	ḪEDĀR 2182
	◐	16	17	18	19	20	21	1:29	47	2520895		6	7	8	9	10	11	12			8	9	10	11	12	13	14	Xiǎo xuě		5	6	7	8	9	10	11	
	○	23	24	25	26	27	28	23:56	48	2520902		13	14	15	16	17	18	19			15	16	17	18	19	20	21			12	13	14	15	16	17	18	
DECEMBER 2189	29	30	◑	2	3	4	5	2:02	49	2520909		20	21	22	23	24	25[e]	26[e]			22	23	24*	25	26	27	28	Dà xuě		19	20	21	22	23	24	25	
	6	●	8	9	10	11	12	20:08	50	2520916	TEVETH 5950	27[d,e]	28[e]	29[e]	1[e]	2[e]	3[e]	4	Tue 3h27m4p	MONTH 11 Jǐ-Chǒu	29	30	1	2	3	4	5		KOIAK 1906	26	27	28	29	30	1	2	TĀḪŚĀŚ 2182
	13	◐	15	16	17	18	19	15:15	51	2520923		5	6	7	8	9	10	11			6	7	8	9	10	11	12	Dōng zhì		3	4	5	6	7	8	9	
	20	21[e]	○	23	24	25	26	19:30	52	2520930		12	13	14	15	16	17	18			13	14[i]	15	16	17	18	19			10	11	12	13	14	15	16	
	27	28	29	◑	31	1	2	15:09	53	2520937		19	20	21	22	23	24	25			20	21	22	23	24	25	26			17	18	19	20	21	22	23	

[a]New Year
[b]Spring (2:58)
[c]Summer (17:38)
[d]Autumn (10:53)
[e]Winter (10:26)
● New moon
◐ First quarter moon
○ Full moon
◑ Last quarter moon

‡Leap year
[a]New Year
[b]Yom Kippur
[c]Sukkot
[d]Winter starts
[e]Ḥanukkah
[f]Purim
[g]Passover
[h]Shavuot
[i]Fast of Av

‡Leap year
[a]New Year (4887, Ox)
[b]Lantern Festival
[c]Qīngmíng
[d]Dragon Festival
[e]Qīqiǎo
[f]Hungry Ghosts
[g]Mid-Autumn Festival
[h]Double-Ninth Festival
[i]Dōngzhì
*Start of 60-name cycle

[a]New Year
[b]Building of the Cross
[c]Christmas
[d]Jesus's Circumcision
[e]Epiphany
[f]Easter
[g]Mary's Announcement
[h]Jesus's Transfiguration

PERSIAN (ASTRONOMICAL) 1567/1568‡	Sun	Mon	Tue	Wed	Thu	Fri	Sat
	8	9	10	11	12	13	14
DEY 1567	15	16	17	18	19	20	21
	22	23	24	25	26	27	28
	29	30	1	2	3	4	5
BAHMAN 1567	6	7	8	9	10	11	12
	13	14	15	16	17	18	19
	20	21	22	23	24	25	26
	27	28	29	30	1	2	3
ESFAND 1567	4	5	6	7	8	9	10
	11	12	13	14	15	16	17
	18	19	20	21	22	23	24
	25	26	27	28	29	1[a]	2
FARVARDĪN 1568	3	4	5	6	7	8	9
	10	11	12	13[b]	14	15	16
	17	18	19	20	21	22	23
	24	25	26	27	28	29	30
	31	1	2	3	4	5	6
ORDĪBEHEŠT 1568	7	8	9	10	11	12	13
	14	15	16	17	18	19	20
	21	22	23	24	25	26	27
	28	29	30	31	1	2	3
XORDĀD 1568	4	5	6	7	8	9	10
	11	12	13	14	15	16	17
	18	19	20	21	22	23	24
	25	26	27	28	29	30	31
TĪR 1568	1	2	3	4	5	6	7
	8	9	10	11	12	13	14
	15	16	17	18	19	20	21
	22	23	24	25	26	27	28
	29	30	31	1	2	3	4
MORDĀD 1568	5	6	7	8	9	10	11
	12	13	14	15	16	17	18
	19	20	21	22	23	24	25
	26	27	28	29	30	31	1
SHAHRĪVAR 1568	2	3	4	5	6	7	8
	9	10	11	12	13	14	15
	16	17	18	19	20	21	22
	23	24	25	26	27	28	29
	30	31	1	2	3	4	5
MEHR 1568	6	7	8	9	10	11	12
	13	14	15	16	17	18	19
	20	21	22	23	24	25	26
	27	28	29	30	1	2	3
ĀBĀN 1568	4	5	6	7	8	9	10
	11	12	13	14	15	16	17
	18	19	20	21	22	23	24
	25	26	27	28	29	30	1
ĀZAR 1568	2	3	4	5	6	7	8
	9	10	11	12	13	14	15
	16	17	18	19	20	21	22
	23	24	25	26	27	28	29
DEY 1568	30	1	2	3	4	5	6
	7	8	9	10	11	12	13

‡Leap year
[a]New Year
[b]Sizdeh Bedar

HINDU LUNAR 2245‡/2246	Sun	Mon	Tue	Wed	Thu	Fri	Sat
MĀRGAŚIRA 2245	10	11	12	13	14	15	16
	17	18	19	20	21	22	23
	24	**25**	27	28	29	30	1
PAUSHA 2245	2	3	4	5	6	7	8
	9	9	10	11	12	13	14
	15	16	17	18	**19**	21	22
	23	24	25	26	27	28	29
	30	1	2	3	4	5	6
LEAP PHĀLGUNA 2245	7	8	9	10	11	12	13
	14	15	16	17	18	19	20
	21	22	23	**24**	26	27	28
	29[h]	30	1	2	2	3	4
PHĀLGUNA 2245	5	6	7	8	9	10	11
	12	13	14	15[i]	16	17	**18**
	20	21	22	23	24	25	26
	27	28	29	30	1[a]	2	3
CHAITRA 2246	4	5	5	6	7	8[b]	9
	10	**11**	13	14	15	16	17
	18	19	20	21	22	23	24
	25	26	27	28	29	30	1
VAIŚĀKHA 2246	2	3	4	5	6	7	8
	9	10	11	12	13	**14**	16
	17	18	19	20	21	22	23
	24	25	26	27	28	29	30
	30	1	2	3	4	5	6
JYAISHTHA 2246	**7**	9	10	11	12	13	14
	15	16	17	18	19	20	21
	22	23	24	25	26	27	28
	29	30	1	2	3	4	5
ĀSHĀDHA 2246	6	7	8	9	**10**	12	13
	14	15	16	17	18	19	20
	21	22	23	24	25	26	27
	27	28	29	30	1	**2**	4
ŚRĀVAṆA 2246	5	6	7	8	9	10	11
	12	13	14	**15**	17	18	18
	19	20	21	22	23[c]	24	25
	26	27	28	29	30	1	2
BHĀDRAPADA 2246	3	4[d]	5	**6**	8	9	10
	11	12	13	14	15	16	17
	18	19	20	21	22	23	23
	24	25	26	27	28	**29**	1
ĀŚVINA 2246	2	3	4	5	6	7	8[e]
	9[e]	10[e]	11	12	13	14	15
	16	17	18	19	20	21	22
	23	24	25	26	27	28	29
	30	1[f]	2	**3**	5	6	7
KĀRTTIKA 2246	8	9	10	11	12	13	14
	15	16	17	17	18	19	20
	21	22	23	24	25	26	**27**
	29	30	1	2	3	4	5
MĀRGAŚIRA 2246	6	7	8	9	10	11[g]	12
	13	14	15	16	17	18	19
	20	21	22	23	24	25	26

‡Leap year
[a]New Year (Virodhin)
[b]Birthday of Rāma
[c]Birthday of Krishna
[d]Ganēśa Chaturthī
[e]Dashara
[f]Diwali
[g]Birthday of Vishnu
[h]Night of Śiva
[i]Holi

HINDU SOLAR 2110/2111	Sun	Mon	Tue	Wed	Thu	Fri	Sat
PAUSHA 2110	11	12	13	14	15	16	17
	18	19	20	21	22	23	24
	25	26	27	28	29	1[b]	2
MĀGHA 2110	3	4	5	6	7	8	9
	10	11	12	13	14	15	16
	17	18	19	20	21	22	23
	24	25	26	27	28	29	30
PHĀLGUNA 2110	1	2	3	4	5	6	7
	8	9	10	11	12	13	14
	15	16	17	18	19	20	21
	22	23	24	25	26	27	28
	29	30	1	2	3	4	5
CHAITRA 2110	6	7	8	9	10	11	12
	13	14	15	16	17	18	19
	20	21	22	23	24	25	26
	27	28	29	30	1[a]	2	3
VAIŚĀKHA 2111	4	5	6	7	8	9	10
	11	12	13	14	15	16	17
	18	19	20	21	22	23	24
	25	26	27	28	29	30	31
JYAISHTHA 2111	1	2	3	4	5	6	7
	8	9	10	11	12	13	14
	15	16	17	18	19	20	21
	22	23	24	25	26	27	28
	29	30	31	1	2	3	4
ĀSHĀDHA 2111	5	6	7	8	9	10	11
	12	13	14	15	16	17	18
	19	20	21	22	23	24	25
	26	27	28	29	30	31	32
ŚRĀVAṆA 2111	1	2	3	4	5	6	7
	8	9	10	11	12	13	14
	15	16	17	18	19	20	21
	22	23	24	25	26	27	28
	29	30	31	1	2	3	4
BHĀDRAPADA 2111	5	6	7	8	9	10	11
	12	13	14	15	16	17	18
	19	20	21	22	23	24	25
	26	27	28	29	30	31	1
ĀŚVINA 2111	2	3	4	5	6	7	8
	9	10	11	12	13	14	15
	16	17	18	19	20	21	22
	23	24	25	26	27	28	29
	30	31	1	2	3	4	5
KĀRTTIKA 2111	6	7	8	9	10	11	12
	13	14	15	16	17	18	19
	20	21	22	23	24	25	26
	27	28	29	30	1	2	3
MĀRGAŚIRA 2111	4	5	6	7	8	9	10
	11	12	13	14	15	16	17
	18	19	20	21	22	23	24
	25	26	27	28	29	1	2
PAUSHA 2111	3	4	5	6	7	8	9
	10	11	12	13	14	15	16

[a]New Year (Krodhin)
[b]Pongal

ISLAMIC (ASTRONOMICAL) 1615/1616	Sun	Mon	Tue	Wed	Thu	Fri	Sat
RAJAB 1615	9	10	11	12	13	14	15
	16	17	18	19	20	21	22
	23	24	25	26	27[d]	28	29
SHA'BĀN 1615	1	2	3	4	5	6	7
	8	9	10	11	12	13	14
	15	16	17	18	19	20	21
	22	23	24	25	26	27	28
	29	30	1[e]	2	3	4	5
RAMAḌĀN 1615	6	7	8	9	10	11	12
	13	14	15	16	17	18	19
	20	21	22	23	24	25	26
	27	28	29	1[f]	2	3	4
SHAWWĀL 1615	5	6	7	8	9	10	11
	12	13	14	15	16	17	18
	19	20	21	22	23	24	25
	26	27	28	29	30	1	2
DHU AL-QA'DA 1615	3	4	5	6	7	8	9
	10	11	12	13	14	15	16
	17	18	19	20	21	22	23
	24	25	26	27	28	29	30
DHU AL-ḤIJJA 1615	1	2	3	4	5	6	7
	8	9	10[g]	11	12	13	14
	15	16	17	18	19	20	21
	22	23	24	25	26	27	28
	29	1[a]	2	3	4	5	6
MUḤARRAM 1616	7	8	9	10[b]	11	12	13
	14	15	16	17	18	19	20
	21	22	23	24	25	26	27
	28	29	30	1	2	3	4
ṢAFAR 1616	5	6	7	8	9	10	11
	12	13	14	15	16	17	18
	19	20	21	22	23	24	25
	26	27	28	29	1	2	3
RABĪ' I 1616	4	5	6	7	8	9	10
	11	12[c]	13	14	15	16	17
	18	19	20	21	22	23	24
	25	26	27	28	29	30	1
RABĪ' II 1616	2	3	4	5	6	7	8
	9	10	11	12	13	14	15
	16	17	18	19	20	21	22
	23	24	25	26	27	28	29
JUMĀDĀ I 1616	1	2	3	4	5	6	7
	8	9	10	11	12	13	14
	15	16	17	18	19	20	21
	22	23	24	25	26	27	28
	29	30	1	2	3	4	5
JUMĀDĀ II 1616	6	7	8	9	10	11	12
	13	14	15	16	17	18	19
	20	21	22	23	24	25	26
	27	28	29	1	2	3	4
RAJAB 1616	5	6	7	8	9	10	11
	12	13	14	15	16	17	18
	19	20	21	22	23	24	25

[a]New Year
[b]'Ashūrā'
[c]Prophet's Birthday
[d]Ascent of the Prophet
[e]Start of Ramaḍān
[f]'Id al-Fiṭr
[g]'Id al-'Aḍḥā

Julian (Sun)	Sun	Mon	Tue	Wed	Thu	Fri	Sat	GREGORIAN 2189
Dec 14	28	29	30	31	1	2	3	
	4	5	6	7	8[a]	9	10	JANUARY 2189
Dec 28	11	12	13	14	15[b]	16	17	
	18	19	20	21	22	23	24	
Jan 11	25	26	27	28	29	30	31	
	1	2	3	4	5	6	7	FEBRUARY 2189
Jan 25	8	9	10	11	12	13	14	
	15	16	17	18[c]	19	20	21	
Feb 8	22	23	24	25	26	27	28	
	1[d]	2	3	4	5	6	7	MARCH 2189
Feb 22	8	9	10	11	12	13	14	
	15	16	17	18	19	20	21	
Mar 8	22	23	24	25	26	27	28	
	29	30	31	1	2	3	4	APRIL 2189
Mar 22	5[e]	6	7	8	9	10	11	
	12[f]	13	14	15	16	17	18	
Apr 5	19	20	21	22	23	24	25	
	26	27	28	29	30	1	2	MAY 2189
Apr 19	3	4	5	6	7	8	9	
	10	11	12	13	14	15	16	
May 3	17	18	19	20	21	22	23	
	24	25	26	27	28	29	30	
May 17	31	1	2	3	4	5	6	JUNE 2189
	7	8	9	10	11	12	13	
May 31	14	15	16	17	18	19	20	
	21	22	23	24	25	26	27	
Jun 14	28	29	30	1	2	3	4	JULY 2189
	5	6	7	8	9	10	11	
Jun 28	12	13	14	15	16	17	18	
	19	20	21	22	23	24	25	
Jul 12	26	27	28	29	30	31	1	AUGUST 2189
	2	3	4	5	6	7	8	
Jul 26	9	10	11	12	13	14	15	
	16	17	18	19	20	21	22	
Aug 9	23	24	25	26	27	28	29	
	30	31	1	2	3	4	5	SEPTEMBER 2189
Aug 23	6	7	8	9	10	11	12	
	13	14	15	16	17	18	19	
Sep 6	20	21	22	23	24	25	26	
	27	28	29	30	1	2	3	OCTOBER 2189
Sep 20	4	5	6	7	8	9	10	
	11	12	13	14	15	16	17	
Oct 4	18	19	20	21	22	23	24	
	25	26	27	28	29	30	31	
Oct 18	1	2	3	4	5	6	7	NOVEMBER 2189
	8	9	10	11	12	13	14	
Nov 1	15	16	17	18	19	20	21	
	22	23	24	25	26	27	28	
Nov 15	29[g]	30	1	2	3	4	5	DECEMBER 2189
	6	7	8	9	10	11	12	
Nov 29	13	14	15	16	17	18	19	
	20	21	22	23	24	25[h]	26	
Dec 13	27	28	29	30	31	1	2	

[a]Orthodox Christmas
[b]Julian New Year
[c]Ash Wednesday
[d]Feast of Orthodoxy
[e]Easter
[f]Orthodox Easter
[g]Advent
[h]Christmas

2190

Gregorian 2190

Month	Sun	Mon	Tue	Wed	Thu	Fri	Sat	Lunar Phases	ISO Week (Mon)	Julian Day (Sun noon)
	27	28	29	◑	31	1[a]	2	15:09	53	2520937
JANUARY 2190	3	4	5	●	7	8	9	6:58	1	2520944
	10	11	12	◐	14	15	16	8:50	2	2520951
	17	18	19	20	○	22	23	14:13	3	2520958
	24	25	26	27	28	◑	30	1:46	4	2520965
	31	1	2	3	●	5	6	18:22	5	2520972
FEBRUARY 2190	7	8	9	10	11	◐	13	5:12	6	2520979
	14	15	16	17	18	19	○	6:44	7	2520986
	21	22	23	24	25	26	◑	10:11	8	2520993
	28	1	2	3	4	5	●	6:38	9	2521000
MARCH 2190	7	8	9	10	11	12	13		10	2521007
	◐	15	16	17	18	19	20[b]	2:19	11	2521014
	○	22	23	24	25	26	27	20:32	12	2521021
	◑	29	30	31	1	2	3	17:07	13	2521028
APRIL 2190	●	5	6	7	8	9	10	20:08	14	2521035
	11	◐	13	14	15	16	17	22:02	15	2521042
	18	19	○	21	22	23	24	7:43	16	2521049
	25	◑	27	28	29	30	1	23:39	17	2521056
MAY 2190	2	3	●	5	6	7	8	10:49	18	2521063
	9	10	11	◐	13	14	15	14:57	19	2521070
	16	17	18	○	20	21	22	16:41	20	2521077
	23	24	25	◑	27	28	29	7:01	21	2521084
	30	31	1	2	●	4	5	2:14	22	2521091
JUNE 2190	6	7	8	9	10	◐	12	4:39	23	2521098
	13	14	15	16	17	○	19	0:03	24	2521105
	20[c]	21	22	23	◑	25	26	16:21	25	2521112
	27	28	29	30	1	●	3	17:36	26	2521119
JULY 2190	4	5	6	7	8	9	◐	15:19	27	2521126
	11	12	13	14	15	16	○	6:45	28	2521133
	18	19	20	21	22	23	◑	4:26	29	2521140
	25	26	27	28	29	30	31		30	2521147
AUGUST 2190	●	2	3	4	5	6	7	8:23	31	2521154
	◐	9	10	11	12	13	14	23:28	32	2521161
	○	16	17	18	19	20	21	13:54	33	2521168
	◑	23	24	25	26	27	28	19:31	34	2521175
	29	●	31	1	2	3	4	22:22	35	2521182
SEPTEMBER 2190	5	6	◐	8	9	10	11	5:53	36	2521189
	12	○	14	15	16	17	18	22:46	37	2521196
	19	20	◑	22[d]	23	24	25	13:15	38	2521203
	26	27	28	●	30	1	2	11:34	39	2521210
OCTOBER 2190	3	4	5	◐	7	8	9	11:41	40	2521217
	10	11	12	○	14	15	16	10:22	41	2521224
	17	18	19	20	◑	22	23	8:41	42	2521231
	24	25	26	27	●	29	30	23:59	43	2521238
	31	1	2	3	◐	5	6	18:09	44	2521245
NOVEMBER 2190	7	8	9	10	11	○	13	1:10	45	2521252
	14	15	16	17	18	19	◑	4:35	46	2521259
	21	22	23	24	25	26	●	11:40	47	2521266
	28	29	30	1	2	3	◐	2:41	48	2521273
DECEMBER 2190	5	6	7	8	9	10	○	18:45	49	2521280
	12	13	14	15	16	17	18		50	2521287
	◑	20	21[e]	22	23	24	25	23:27	51	2521294
	●	27	28	29	30	31	1	22:37	52	2521301

Hebrew 5950‡/5951

ISO Week	Month	Sun	Mon	Tue	Wed	Thu	Fri	Sat	Molad
53	TEVETH 5950	19	20	21	22	23	24	25	
1		26	27	28	29	1	2	3	Wed 16h11m5p
2	SHEVAT 5950	4	5	6	7	8	9	10	
3		11	12	13	14	15	16	17	
4		18	19	20	21	22	23	24	
5		25	26	27	28	29	30	1	Fri 4h55m6p
6	ADAR I 5950	2	3	4	5	6	7	8	
7		9	10	11	12	13	14	15	
8		16	17	18	19	20	21	22	
9		23	24	25	26	27	28	29	
10		30	1	2	3	4	5	6	Sat 17h39m7p
11	ADAR II 5950	7	8	9	10	11	12	13	
12		14[f]	15	16	17	18	19	20	
13		21	22	23	24	25	26	27	
14		28	29	1	2	3	4	5	Mon 6h23m8p
15	NISAN 5950	6	7	8	9	10	11	12	
16		13	14	15[g]	16	17	18	19	
17		20	21	22	23	24	25	26	
18		27	28	29	30	1	2	3	Tue 19h7m9p
19	IYAR 5950	4	5	6	7	8	9	10	
20		11	12	13	14	15	16	17	
21		18	19	20	21	22	23	24	
22		25	26	27	28	29	1	2	Thu 7h51m10p
23	SIVAN 5950	3	4	5	6[h]	7	8	9	
24		10	11	12	13	14	15	16	
25		17	18	19	20	21	22	23	
26		24	25	26	27	28	29	30	Fri 20h35m11p
27	TAMMUZ 5950	1	2	3	4	5	6	7	
28		8	9	10	11	12	13	14	
29		15	16	17	18	19	20	21	
30		22	23	24	25	26	27	28	
31		29	1	2	3	4	5	6	Sun 9h19m12p
32	AV 5950	7	8	9[i]	10	11	12	13	
33		14	15	16	17	18	19	20	
34		21	22	23	24	25	26	27	
35		28	29	30	1	2	3	4	Mon 22h3m13p
36	ELUL 5950	5	6	7	8	9	10	11	
37		12	13	14	15	16	17	18	
38		19	20	21	22	23	24	25	
39		26	27	28	29	1[a]	2[a]	3	Wed 10h47m14p
40	TISHRI 5951	4	5	6	7	8	9	10[b]	
41		11	12	13	14	15[c]	16	17	
42		18	19	20	21	22	23	24	
43		25	26	27	28	29	30	1	Thu 23h31m15p
44	HESHVAN 5951	2	3	4	5	6	7	8	
45		9	10	11	12	13	14	15	
46		16	17	18	19	20	21	22	
47		23	24	25	26	27	28	29	
48		1	2	3	4	5	6	7	Sat 12h15m16p
49	KISLEV 5951	8	9[d]	10	11	12	13	14	
50		15	16	17	18	19	20	21	
51		22	23	24	25[e]	26[e]	27[e]	28[e]	
52		29[e]	30[e]	1[e]	2[e]	3	4	5	Mon 0h59m17p

Chinese Jǐ-Chǒu/Gēng-Yín

ISO Week	Month	Sun	Mon	Tue	Wed	Thu	Fri	Sat	Solar Term
53	MONTH 11 Jǐ-Chǒu	20	21	22	23	24	25	26	
1		27	28	*29*	1	2	3	4	Xiǎo hán
2	MONTH 12 Jǐ-Chǒu	5	6	7	8	9	10	11	
3		12	13	14	**15**	16	17	18	Dà hán
4		19	20	21	22	23	24	25*	
5		26	27	28	*29*	30	1[a]	2	Lì chūn
6	MONTH 1 Gēng-Yín	3	4	5	6	7	8	9	
7		10	11	12	13	**14**	15[b]	16	Yǔ shuǐ
8		17	18	19	20	21	22	23	
9		24	25	26	27	28	*29*	1	Jīng zhé
10	MONTH 2 Gēng-Yín	2	3	4	5	6	7	8	
11		9	10	11	12	13	14	**15**	Chūn fēn
12		16	17	18	19	20	21	22	
13		23	24	25	26*	27	28	29	
14		*30*[c]	1	2	3	4	5	6	Qīng míng
15	MONTH 3 Gēng-Yín	7	8	9	10	11	12	13	
16		14	15	**16**	17	18	19	20	Gǔ yǔ
17		21	22	23	24	25	26	27	
18		28	29	1	*2*	3	4	5	Lì xià
19	MONTH 4 Gēng-Yín	6	7	8	9	10	11	12	
20		13	14	15	16	17	**18**	19	Xiǎo mǎn
21		20	21	22	23	24	25	26	
22		27*	28	29	30	1	2	3	Máng zhòng
23	MONTH 5 Gēng-Yín	4	5[d]	6	7	8	9	10	
24		11	12	13	14	15	16	17	
25		18	**19**	20	21	22	23	24	Xià zhì
26		25	26	27	28	29	30	1	
27	MONTH 6 Gēng-Yín	2	3	4	*5*	6	7	8	Xiǎo shǔ
28		9	10	11	12	13	14	15	
29		16	17	18	19	**20**	21	22	Dà shǔ
30		23	24	25	26	27*	28	29	
31		1	2	3	4	5	6	*7*[e]	Lì qiū
32	MONTH 7 Gēng-Yín	8	9	10	11	12	13	14	
33		15[f]	16	17	18	19	20	21	
34		22	**23**	24	25	26	27	28	Chǔ shǔ
35		29	30	1	2	3	4	5	
36	MONTH 8 Gēng-Yín	6	7	*8*	9	10	11	12	Bái lù
37		13	14	15[g]	16	17	18	19	
38		20	21	22	23	**24**	25	26	Qiū fēn
39		27	28*	29	1	2	3	4	
40	MONTH 9 Gēng-Yín	5	6	7	8	9[h]	*10*	11	Hán lù
41		12	13	14	15	16	17	18	
42		19	20	21	22	23	24	**25**	Shuāng jiàng
43		26	27	28	29	30	1	2	
44	MONTH 10 Gēng-Yín	3	4	5	6	7	8	9	
45		*10*	11	12	13	14	15	16	Lì dōng
46		17	18	19	20	21	22	23	
47		24	**25**	26	27	28	29*	1	Xiǎo xuě
48	MONTH 11 Gēng-Yín	2	3	4	5	6	7	8	
49		9	10	*11*	12	13	14	15	Dà xuě
50		16	17	18	19	20	21	22	
51		23	24	25	**26**[i]	27	28	29	Dōng zhì
52		30	1	2	3	4	5	6	

Coptic 1906/1907‡ — Ethiopic 2182/2183‡

ISO Week	Coptic Month	Sun	Mon	Tue	Wed	Thu	Fri	Sat	Ethiopic Month
53	KOIAK 1906	17	18	19	20	21	22	23	TĀKHŚĀŚ 2182
1		24	25	26	27	28	29[c]	30	
2	TÔBE 1906	1	2	3	4	5	6[d]	7	ṬER 2182
3		8	9	10	11[e]	12	13	14	
4		15	16	17	18	19	20	21	
5		22	23	24	25	26	27	28	
6	MESHIR 1906	29	30	1	2	3	4	5	YAKĀTIT 2182
7		6	7	8	9	10	11	12	
8		13	14	15	16	17	18	19	
9		20	21	22	23	24	25	26	
10	PAREMOTEP 1906	27	28	29	30	1	2	3	MAGĀBIT 2182
11		4	5	6	7	8	9	10	
12		11	12	13	14	15	16	17	
13		18	19	20	21	22	23	24	
14	PARMOUTE 1906	25	26	27	28	29	30	1	MIYĀZYĀ 2182
15		2	3	4	5	6	7	8	
16		9	10	11	12	13	14	15	
17		16[f]	17	18	19	20	21	22	
18		23	24	25	26	27	28	29[g]	
19	PASHONS 1906	30	1	2	3	4	5	6	GENBOT 2182
20		7	8	9	10	11	12	13	
21		14	15	16	17	18	19	20	
22		21	22	23	24	25	26	27	
23	PAÔNE 1906	28	29	30	1	2	3	4	SANÉ 2182
24		5	6	7	8	9	10	11	
25		12	13	14	15	16	17	18	
26		19	20	21	22	23	24	25	
27	EPÊP 1906	26	27	28	29	30	1	2	ḤAMLÉ 2182
28		3	4	5	6	7	8	9	
29		10	11	12	13	14	15	16	
30		17	18	19	20	21	22	23	
31		24	25	26	27	28	29	30	
32	MESORÊ 1906	1	2	3	4	5	6	7	NAHASÉ 2182
33		8	9	10	11	12	13[h]	14	
34		15	16	17	18	19	20	21	
35		22	23	24	25	26	27	28	
36	EPAG. 1906	29	30	1	2	3	4	5	PāG. 2182
37	THOOUT 1907	1[a]	2	3	4	5	6	7	MASKARAM 2183
38		8	9	10	11	12	13	14	
39		15	16	17[b]	18	19	20	21	
40		22	23	24	25	26	27	28	
41	PAOPE 1907	29	30	1	2	3	4	5	TEQEMT 2183
42		6	7	8	9	10	11	12	
43		13	14	15	16	17	18	19	
44		20	21	22	23	24	25	26	
45	ATHÔR 1907	27	28	29	30	1	2	3	HEDĀR 2183
46		4	5	6	7	8	9	10	
47		11	12	13	14	15	16	17	
48		18	19	20	21	22	23	24	
49	KOIAK 1907	25	26	27	28	29	30	1	TĀKHŚĀŚ 2183
50		2	3	4	5	6	7	8	
51		9	10	11	12	13	14	15	
52		16	17	18	19	20	21	22	

Gregorian notes:
[a]New Year
[b]Spring (8:42)
[c]Summer (23:22)
[d]Autumn (16:45)
[e]Winter (16:20)
● New moon
◐ First quarter moon
○ Full moon
◑ Last quarter moon

Hebrew notes:
‡Leap year
[a]New Year
[b]Yom Kippur
[c]Sukkot
[d]Winter starts
[e]Ḥanukkah
[f]Purim
[g]Passover
[h]Shavuot
[i]Fast of Av

Chinese notes:
[a]New Year (4888, Tiger)
[b]Lantern Festival
[c]Qīngmíng
[d]Dragon Festival
[e]Qīqiǎo
[f]Hungry Ghosts
[g]Mid-Autumn Festival
[h]Double-Ninth Festival
[i]Dōngzhì
*Start of 60-name cycle

Coptic/Ethiopic notes:
‡Leap year
[a]New Year
[b]Building of the Cross
[c]Christmas
[d]Jesus's Circumcision
[e]Epiphany
[f]Easter
[g]Mary's Announcement
[h]Jesus's Transfiguration

2190

PERSIAN (ASTRONOMICAL) 1568‡/1569	Sun	Mon	Tue	Wed	Thu	Fri	Sat
DEY 1568	7	8	9	10	11	12	13
	14	15	16	17	18	19	20
	21	22	23	24	25	26	27
	28	29	30	*1*	2	3	4
BAHMAN 1568	5	6	7	8	9	10	11
	12	13	14	15	16	17	18
	19	20	21	22	23	24	25
	26	27	28	29	30	*1*	2
ESFAND 1568	3	4	5	6	7	8	9
	10	11	12	13	14	15	16
	17	18	19	20	21	22	23
	24	25	26	27	28	29	30*
FARVARDĪN 1569	1[a]	2	3	4	5	6	7
	8	9	10	11	12	13[b]	14
	15	16	17	18	19	20	21
	22	23	24	25	26	27	28
	29	30	*31*	1	2	3	4
ORDĪBEHEŠT 1569	5	6	7	8	9	10	11
	12	13	14	15	16	17	18
	19	20	21	22	23	24	25
	26	27	28	29	30	*31*	1
XORDĀD 1569	2	3	4	5	6	7	8
	9	10	11	12	13	14	15
	16	17	18	19	20	21	22
	23	24	25	26	27	28	29
	30	*31*	1	2	3	4	5
TĪR 1569	6	7	8	9	10	11	12
	13	14	15	16	17	18	19
	20	21	22	23	24	25	26
	27	28	29	30	*31*	1	2
MORDĀD 1569	3	4	5	6	7	8	9
	10	11	12	13	14	15	16
	17	18	19	20	21	22	23
	24	25	26	27	28	29	30
	31	1	2	3	4	5	6
SHAHRĪVAR 1569	7	8	9	10	11	12	13
	14	15	16	17	18	19	20
	21	22	23	24	25	26	27
	28	29	30	*31*	1	2	3
MEHR 1569	4	5	6	7	8	9	10
	11	12	13	14	15	16	17
	18	19	20	21	22	23	24
	25	26	27	28	29	*30*	1
ĀBĀN 1569	2	3	4	5	6	7	8
	9	10	11	12	13	14	15
	16	17	18	19	20	21	22
	23	24	25	26	27	28	29
	30	1	2	3	4	5	6
ĀZAR 1569	7	8	9	10	11	12	13
	14	15	16	17	18	19	20
	21	22	23	24	25	26	27
	28	29	*30*	1	2	3	4
DEY 1569	5	6	7	8	9	10	11

HINDU LUNAR 2246/2247	Sun	Mon	Tue	Wed	Thu	Fri	Sat
MĀRGAŚĪRA 2246	20	21	22	23	24	25	26
	27	28	29	30	1	2	**3**
PAUSHA 2246	5	6	7	8	9	9	10
	11	12	13	14	15	16	17
	18	19	20	21	22	23	24
	25	**26**	28	29	30	1	2
MĀGHA 2246	3	4	5	6	7	8	9
	10	11	12	*12*	13	14	15
	16	17	18	19	**20**	22	23
	24	25	26	27	28[h]	29	30
PHĀLGUNA 2246	1	2	3	4	5	6	7
	8	9	10	11	12	13	14
	15[i]	16	17	18	19	20	21
	22	23	24	**25**	27	28	29
	30	1[a]	2	3	4	5	5
CHAITRA 2247	6	7	8	9[b]	10	11	12
	13	14	15	16	17	**18**	20
	21	22	23	24	25	26	27
	28	29	30	1	2	3	4
VAIŚĀKHA 2247	5	6	7	8	9	10	11
	12	13	14	15	16	17	18
	19	20	21	**22**	24	25	26
	27	28	29	30	*30*	1	2
JYAISHTHA 2247	3	4	5	6	7	8	9
	10	11	12	13	14	**15**	17
	18	19	20	21	22	23	24
	25	26	27	28	29	30	1
ĀSHĀḌHA 2247	2	3	4	5	6	7	8
	9	10	11	12	13	14	15
	16	17	**18**	20	21	22	23
	24	25	26	27	*27*	28	29
	30	1	2	3	4	5	6
ŚRĀVAṆA 2247	7	8	9	**10**	12	13	14
	15	16	17	18	19	20	21
	22	23[c]	24	25	26	27	28
	29	30	1	2	3	4[d]	5
BHĀDRAPADA 2247	6	7	8	9	10	11	12
	13	15	16	17	18	19	20
	21	22	23	*23*	24	25	26
	27	28	29	30	1	2	3
ĀŚVINA 2247	4	5	6	7[e]	9[e]	10[e]	11
	12	13	14	15	16	17	18
	19	20	21	22	23	24	25
	26	27	28	*28*	30	1[f]	2
KĀRTTIKA 2247	3	4	5	6	7	8	9
	10	**11**	13	14	15	16	17
	17	18	19	20	21	22	23
	24	25	26	27	28	29	30
MĀRGAŚĪRA 2247	1	2	3	**4**	6	7	8
	9	10	11[g]	12	13	14	15
	16	17	18	19	20	*20*	21
	22	23	24	25	26	27	**28**
	30	1	2	3	4	5	6

HINDU SOLAR 2111/2112	Sun	Mon	Tue	Wed	Thu	Fri	Sat
PAUSHA 2111	10	11	12	13	14	15	16
	17	18	19	20	21	22	23
	24	25	26	27	28	29	1[b]
MĀGHA 2111	2	3	4	5	6	7	8
	9	10	11	12	13	14	15
	16	17	18	19	20	21	22
	23	24	25	26	27	28	29
	30	1	2	3	4	5	6
PHĀLGUNA 2111	7	8	9	10	11	12	13
	14	15	16	17	18	19	20
	21	22	23	24	25	26	27
	28	29	30	1	2	3	4
CHAITRA 2111	5	6	7	8	9	10	11
	12	13	14	15	16	17	18
	19	20	21	22	23	24	25
	26	27	28	29	30	1[a]	2
VAIŚĀKHA 2112	3	4	5	6	7	8	9
	10	11	12	13	14	15	16
	17	18	19	20	21	22	23
	24	25	26	27	28	29	30
	31	1	2	3	4	5	6
JYAISHTHA 2112	7	8	9	10	11	12	13
	14	15	16	17	18	19	20
	21	22	23	24	25	26	27
	28	29	30	31	32	1	2
ĀSHĀḌHA 2112	3	4	5	6	7	8	9
	10	11	12	13	14	15	16
	17	18	19	20	21	22	23
	24	25	26	27	28	29	30
	31	1	2	3	4	5	6
ŚRĀVAṆA 2112	7	8	9	10	11	12	13
	14	15	16	17	18	19	20
	21	22	23	24	25	26	27
	28	29	30	31	32	1	2
BHĀDRAPADA 2112	3	4	5	6	7	8	9
	10	11	12	13	14	15	16
	17	18	19	20	21	22	23
	24	25	26	27	28	29	30
	31	1	2	3	4	5	6
ĀŚVINA 2112	7	8	9	10	11	12	13
	14	15	16	17	18	19	20
	21	22	23	24	25	26	27
	28	29	30	1	2	3	4
KĀRTTIKA 2112	5	6	7	8	9	10	11
	12	13	14	15	16	17	18
	19	20	21	22	23	24	25
	26	27	28	29	30	1	2
MĀRGAŚĪRA 2112	3	4	5	6	7	8	9
	10	11	12	13	14	15	16
	17	18	19	20	21	22	23
	24	25	26	27	28	29	1
PAUSHA 2112	2	3	4	5	6	7	8
	9	10	11	12	13	14	15

ISLAMIC (ASTRONOMICAL) 1616/1617	Sun	Mon	Tue	Wed	Thu	Fri	Sat
RAJAB 1616	19	20	21	22	23	24	25
	26	27[d]	28	29	30	*1*	2
SHA'BĀN 1616	3	4	5	6	7	8	9
	10	11	12	13	14	15	16
	17	18	19	20	21	22	23
	24	25	26	27	28	29	1[e]
RAMAḌĀN 1616	2	3	4	5	6	7	8
	9	10	11	12	13	14	15
	16	17	18	19	20	21	22
	23	24	25	26	27	28	29
SHAWWĀL 1616	1[f]	2	3	4	5	6	7
	8	9	10	11	12	13	14
	15	16	17	18	19	20	21
	22	23	24	25	26	27	28
	29	30	*1*	2	3	4	5
DHU AL-QA'DA 1616	6	7	8	9	10	11	12
	13	14	15	16	17	18	19
	20	21	22	23	24	25	26
	27	28	29	30	*1*	2	3
DHU AL-ḤIJJA 1616	4	5	6	7	8	9	10[g]
	11	12	13	14	15	16	17
	18	19	20	21	22	23	24
	25	26	27	28	29	1[a]	2[d]
MUHARRAM 1617	3	4	5	6	7	8	9
	10[b]	11	12	13	14	15	16
	17	18	19	20	21	22	23
	24	25	26	27	28	29	30
ṢAFAR 1617	1	2	3	4	5	6	7
	8	9	10	11	12	13	14
	15	16	17	18	19	20	21
	22	23	24	25	26	27	28
	29	30	*1*	2	3	4	5
RABĪ' I 1617	6	7	8	9	10	11	12[c]
	13	14	15	16	17	18	19
	20	21	22	23	24	25	26
	27	28	29	1	2	3	4
RABĪ' II 1617	5	6	7	8	9	10	11
	12	13	14	15	16	17	18
	19	20	21	22	23	24	25
	26	27	28	29	30	*1*	2
JUMĀDĀ I 1617	3	4	5	6	7	8	9
	10	11	12	13	14	15	16
	17	18	19	20	21	22	23
	24	25	26	27	28	29	30
JUMĀDĀ II 1617	*1*	2	3	4	5	6	7
	8	9	10	11	12	13	14
	15	16	17	18	19	20	21
	22	23	24	25	26	27	28
	29	*1*	2	3	4	5	6
RAJAB 1617	7	8	9	10	11	12	13
	14	15	16	17	18	19	20
	21	22	23	24	25	26	27[d]
	28	29	1	2	3	4	5

Julian (Sun)	GREGORIAN 2190	Sun	Mon	Tue	Wed	Thu	Fri	Sat
Dec 13	JANUARY 2190	*27*	28	29	30	31	1	2
		3	4	5	6	7	8[a]	9
Dec 27		*10*	11	12	13	14	15[b]	16
		17	18	19	20	21	22	23
Jan 10		*24*	25	26	27	28	29	30
	FEBRUARY 2190	31	1	2	3	4	5	6
Jan 24		*7*	8	9	10	11	12	13
		14	15	16	17	18	19	20
Feb 7		*21*	22	23	24	25	26	27
	MARCH 2190	28	1	2	3	4	5	6
Feb 21		*7*	8	9	10[c]	11	12	13
		14[d]	15	16	17	18	19	20
Mar 7		*21*	22	23	24	25	26	27
	APRIL 2190	28	29	30	31	1	2	3
Mar 21		*4*	5	6	7	8	9	10
		11	12	13	14	15	16	17
Apr 4		*18*	19	20	21	22	23	24
	MAY 2190	25[e]	26	27	28	29	30	1
Apr 18		*2*	3	4	5	6	7	8
		9	10	11	12	13	14	15
May 2		*16*	17	18	19	20	21	22
		23	24	25	26	27	28	29
May 16	JUNE 2190	*30*	31	1	2	3	4	5
		6	7	8	9	10	11	12
May 30		*13*	14	15	16	17	18	19
		20	21	22	23	24	25	26
Jun 13	JULY 2190	*27*	28	29	30	1	2	3
		4	5	6	7	8	9	10
Jun 27		*11*	12	13	14	15	16	17
		18	19	20	21	22	23	24
Jul 11		*25*	26	27	28	29	30	31
	AUGUST 2190	1	2	3	4	5	6	7
Jul 25		*8*	9	10	11	12	13	14
		15	16	17	18	19	20	21
Aug 8		*22*	23	24	25	26	27	28
	SEPTEMBER 2190	29	30	31	1	2	3	4
Aug 22		*5*	6	7	8	9	10	11
		12	13	14	15	16	17	18
Sep 5		*19*	20	21	22	23	24	25
	OCTOBER 2190	26	27	28	29	30	1	2
Sep 19		*3*	4	5	6	7	8	9
		10	11	12	13	14	15	16
Oct 3		*17*	18	19	20	21	22	23
		24	25	26	27	28	29	30
Oct 17	NOVEMBER 2190	*31*	1	2	3	4	5	6
		7	8	9	10	11	12	13
Oct 31		*14*	15	16	17	18	19	20
		21	22	23	24	25	26	27
Nov 14	DECEMBER 2190	28[g]	29	30	1	2	3	4
		5	6	7	8	9	10	11
Nov 28		*12*	13	14	15	16	17	18
		19	20	21	22	23	24	25[h]
Dec 12		*26*	27	28	29	30	31	1

Persian:
‡Leap year
[a]New Year (or prior day)
*Near New Year: −0′2″
[d]New Year (Arithmetic)
[b]Sizdeh Bedar

Hindu Lunar:
[a]New Year (Vikṛita)
[b]Birthday of Rāma
[c]Birthday of Krishna
[d]Ganēśa Chaturthī
[e]Dashara
[f]Diwali
[g]Birthday of Vishnu
[h]Night of Śiva
[i]Holi

Hindu Solar:
[a]New Year (Viśvāvasu)
[b]Pongal

Islamic:
[a]New Year
[d]New Year (Arithmetic)
[b]'Ashūrā'
[c]Prophet's Birthday
[d]Ascent of the Prophet
[e]Start of Ramaḍān
[f]'Id al-Fiṭr
[g]'Id al-'Aḍḥā

Gregorian:
[a]Orthodox Christmas
[b]Julian New Year
[c]Ash Wednesday
[d]Feast of Orthodoxy
[e]Easter (also Orthodox)
[g]Advent
[h]Christmas

2191

GREGORIAN 2191	Sun Mon Tue Wed Thu Fri Sat	Lunar Phases	ISO WEEK (Mon)	JULIAN DAY (Sun noon)	HEBREW 5951/5952	Sun Mon Tue Wed Thu Fri Sat	Molad	CHINESE Gēng-Yín/Xīn-Mǎo‡	Sun Mon Tue Wed Thu Fri Sat	Solar Term	COPTIC 1907‡/1908	Sun Mon Tue Wed Thu Fri Sat	ETHIOPIC 2183‡/2184
JANUARY 2191	● 27 28 29 30 31 1[a]	22:37	52	2521301	TEVETH 5951	29[e] 30[e] 1[e] 2[e] 3 4 5	Mon 0h59m1p	MONTH 12 Gēng-Yín	30 1 2 3 4 5 6		KOIAK 1907	16 17 18 19 20 21 22	TĀKHŚĀŚ 2183
	◐ 3 4 5 6 7 8	14:17	1	2521308		6 7 8 9 10 11 12			7 8 9 10 11 12 13	Xiǎo hán		23 24 25 26 27 28 29[c]	
	9 ○ 11 12 13 14 15	13:56	2	2521315		13 14 15 16 17 18 19			14 15 16 17 18 19 20		TŌBE 1907	30 1 2 3 4 5 6[d]	ṬER 2183
	16 17 ◑ 19 20 21 22	15:49	3	2521322		20 21 22 23 24 25 26			21 22 23 24 25 26 27	Dà hán		7 8 9 10 11[e] 12 13	
	23 24 ● 26 27 28 29	9:05	4	2521329	SHEVAT 5951	27 28 29 1 2 3 4	Tue 13h44m0p	MONTH 1 Xīn-Mǎo	28 29 1[a]* 2 3 4 5			14 15 16 17 18 19 20	
FEBRUARY 2191	30 31 ◐ 2 3 4 5	5:13	5	2521336		5 6 7 8 9 10 11			6 7 8 9 10 11 12	Lì chūn		21 22 23 24 25 26 27	
	6 7 8 ○ 10 11 12	9:12	6	2521343		12 13 14 15 16 17 18			13 14 15[b] 16 17 18 19		MESHIR 1907	28 29 30 1 2 3 4	YAKĀTIT 2183
	13 14 15 16 ◑ 18 19	4:42	7	2521350		19 20 21 22 23 24 25			20 21 22 23 24 25 26	Yǔ shuǐ		5 6 7 8 9 10 11	
	20 21 22 ● 24 25 26	19:26	8	2521357	ADAR 5951	26 27 28 29 30 1 2	Thu 2h28m1p	MONTH 2 Xīn-Mǎo	27 28 29 30 1 2 3			12 13 14 15 16 17 18	
MARCH 2191	27 28 1 ◐ 3 4 5	22:47	9	2521364		3 4 5 6 7 8 9			4 5 6 7 8 9 10	Jīng zhé		19 20 21 22 23 24 25	
	6 7 8 9 10 ○ 12	3:05	10	2521371		10 11 12 13 14[f] 15 16			11 12 13 14 15 16 17		PAREMOTEP 1907	26 27 28 29 30 1 2	MAGĀBIT 2183
	13 14 15 16 17 ◑ 19	14:01	11	2521378		17 18 19 20 21 22 23			18 19 20 21 22 23 24			3 4 5 6 7 8 9	
	20[b] 21 22 23 24 ● 26	6:07	12	2521385	NISAN 5951	24 25 26 27 28 29 1	Fri 15h12m2p	MONTH 3 Xīn-Mǎo	25 26 27 28 29 1 2*	Chūn fēn		10 11 12 13 14 15 16	
APRIL 2191	27 28 29 30 31 ◐ 2	17:44	13	2521392		2 3 4 5 6 7 8			3 4 5 6 7 8 9			17 18 19 20 21 22 23	
	3 4 5 6 7 8 ○	18:29	14	2521399		9 10 11 12 13 14 15[g]			10 11 12[c] 13 14 15 16	Qīng míng		24 25 26 27 28 29 30	
	10 11 12 13 14 15 ◑	20:37	15	2521406		16 17 18 19 20 21 22			17 18 19 20 21 22 23		PARMOUTE 1907	1 2 3 4 5 6 7	MIYĀZYĀ 2183
	17 18 19 20 21 22 ●	17:27	16	2521413		23 24 25 26 27 28 29			24 25 26 27 28 29 30	Gǔ yǔ		8[f] 9 10 11 12 13 14	
	24 25 26 27 28 29 30		17	2521420	IYYAR 5951	30 1 2 3 4 5 6	Sun 3h56m3p	MONTH 4 Xīn-Mǎo	1 2 3 4 5 6 7			15 16 17 18 19 20 21	
MAY 2191	◐ 2 3 4 5 6 7	12:42	18	2521427		7 8 9 10 11 12 13			8 9 10 11 12 13 14	Lì xià		22 23 24 25 26 27 28	
	8 ○ 10 11 12 13 14	6:49	19	2521434		14 15 16 17 18 19 20			15 16 17 18 19 20 21		PASHONS 1907	29[g] 30 1 2 3 4 5	GENBOT 2183
	15 ◑ 17 18 19 20 21	1:53	20	2521441		21 22 23 24 25 26 27			22 23 24 25 26 27 28	Xiǎo mǎn		6 7 8 9 10 11 12	
	22 ● 24 25 26 27 28	5:38	21	2521448	SIVAN 5951	28 29 1 2 3 4 5	Mon 16h40m4p	MONTH 5 Xīn-Mǎo	29 1 2 3* 4 5[d] 6			13 14 15 16 17 18 19	
JUNE 2191	29 30 ◐ 1 2 3 4	6:35	22	2521455		6[h] 7 8 9 10 11 12			7 8 9 10 11 12 13			20 21 22 23 24 25 26	
	5 6 ○ 8 9 10 11	16:20	23	2521462		13 14 15 16 17 18 19			14 15 16 17 18 19 20	Máng zhòng	PAŌNE 1907	27 28 29 30 1 2 3	SANĒ 2183
	12 13 ◑ 15 16 17 18	7:20	24	2521469		20 21 22 23 24 25 26			21 22 23 24 25 26 27			4 5 6 7 8 9 10	
	19 20 ●[c] 22 23 24 25	18:48	25	2521476	TAMMUZ 5951	27 28 29 30 1 2 3	Wed 5h24m5p	LEAP MONTH 5 Xīn-Mǎo	28 29 30 1 2 3 4	Xià zhì		11 12 13 14 15 16 17	
JULY 2191	26 27 28 ◐ 30 1 2	22:33	26	2521483		4 5 6 7 8 9 10			5 6 7 8 9 10 11			18 19 20 21 22 23 24	
	3 4 5 ○ 7 8 9	23:52	27	2521490		11 12 13 14 15 16 17			12 13 14 15 16 17 18	Xiǎo shǔ	EPĒP 1907	25 26 27 28 29 30 1	ḤAMLĒ 2183
	10 11 12 ◑ 14 15 16	14:16	28	2521497		18 19 20 21 22 23 24			19 20 21 22 23 24 25			2 3 4 5 6 7 8	
	17 18 19 20 ● 22 23	9:04	29	2521504	AV 5951	25 26 27 28 29 1 2	Thu 18h8m6p	MONTH 6 Xīn-Mǎo	26 27 28 29 1 2 3	Dà shǔ		9 10 11 12 13 14 15	
AUGUST 2191	24 25 26 27 28 ◐ 30	12:03	30	2521511		3 4 5 6 7 8 9			4* 5 6 7 8 9 10			16 17 18 19 20 21 22	
	31 1 2 3 4 ○ 6	6:37	31	2521518		10[i] 11 12 13 14 15 16			11 12 13 14 15 16 17			23 24 25 26 27 28 29	
	7 8 9 10 ◑ 12 13	23:46	32	2521525		17 18 19 20 21 22 23			18 19 20 21 22 23 24	Lì qiū	MESORĒ 1907	30 1 2 3 4 5 6	NAḤASĒ 2183
	14 15 16 17 18 19 ●	0:23	33	2521532		24 25 26 27 28 29 30		MONTH 7 Xīn-Mǎo	25 26 27 28 29 30 1			7 8 9 10 11 12 13[h]	
	21 22 23 24 25 26 ◐	22:59	34	2521539	ELUL 5951	1 2 3 4 5 6 7	Sat 6h52m7p		2 3 4 5 6 7[e] 8	Chǔ shǔ		14 15 16 17 18 19 20	
SEPTEMBER 2191	28 29 30 31 1 2 ○	13:50	35	2521546		8 9 10 11 12 13 14			9 10 11 12 13 14 15[f]			21 22 23 24 25 26 27	
	4 5 6 7 8 9 ◑	12:28	36	2521553		15 16 17 18 19 20 21			16 17 18 19 20 21 22	Bái lù	EPAG. 1907	28 29 30 1 2 3 4	ṖĀG. 2183
	11 12 13 14 15 16 17		37	2521560		22 23 24 25 26 27 28			23 24 25 26 27 28 29		THOOUT 1908	5 6 1[a] 2 3 4 5	MASKARAM 2184
	● 19 20 21 22[d] 23 24	16:22	38	2521567	TISHRI 5952	29 1[a] 2[a] 3 4 5 6	Sun 19h36m8p	MONTH 8 Xīn-Mǎo	30 1 2 3 4* 5 6	Qiū fēn		6 7 8 9 10 11 12	
OCTOBER 2191	25 ◐ 27 28 29 30 1	7:44	39	2521574		7 8 9 10[b] 11 12 13			7 8 9 10 11 12 13			13 14 15 16 17[b] 18 19	
	○ 3 4 5 6 7 8	22:32	40	2521581		14 15[c] 16 17 18 19 20			14 15[g] 16 17 18 19 20	Hán lù		20 21 22 23 24 25 26	
	9 ◑ 11 12 13 14 15	4:39	41	2521588		21 22 23 24 25 26 27			21 22 23 24 25 26 27		PAOPE 1908	27 28 29 30 1 2 3	ṬEQEMT 2184
	16 17 ● 19 20 21 22	8:14	42	2521595	HESHVAN 5952	28 29 30 1 2 3 4	Tue 8h20m9p	MONTH 9 Xīn-Mǎo	28 29 1 2 3 4 5			4 5 6 7 8 9 10	
	23 24 ◐ 26 27 28 29	15:09	43	2521602		5 6 7 8 9 10 11			6 7 8 9[h] 10 11 12	Shuāng jiàng		11 12 13 14 15 16 17	
NOVEMBER 2191	30 31 ○ 2 3 4 5	9:24	44	2521609		12 13 14 15 16 17 18			13 14 15 16 17 18 19			18 19 20 21 22 23 24	
	6 7 8 ◑ 10 11 12	0:01	45	2521616		19 20 21 22 23 24 25			20 21 22 23 24 25 26	Lì dōng	ATHŌR 1908	25 26 27 28 29 30 1	ḪEDĀR 2184
	13 14 15 ● 17 18 19	23:06	46	2521623	KISLEV 5952	26 27 28 29 30 1 2	Wed 21h4m10p	MONTH 10 Xīn-Mǎo	27 28 29 30 1 2 3			2 3 4 5 6 7 8	
	20 21 22 ◐ 24 25 26	22:20	47	2521630		3 4 5 6 7 8 9			4 5* 6 7 8 9 10	Xiǎo xuě		9 10 11 12 13 14 15	
DECEMBER 2191	27 28 29 ○ 1 2 3	22:44	48	2521637		10 11 12 13 14 15 16			11 12 13 14 15 16 17			16 17 18 19 20 21 22	
	4 5 6 7 ◑ 9 10	21:25	49	2521644		17 18 19 20[d] 21 22 23			18 19 20 21 22 23 24	Dà xuě		23 24 25 26 27 28 29	
	11 12 13 14 15 ● 17	12:30	50	2521651		24 25[e] 26[e] 27[e] 28[e] 29[e] 30[e]		MONTH 11 Xīn-Mǎo	25 26 27 28 29 1 2		KOIAK 1908	30 1 2 3 4 5 6	TĀKHŚĀŚ 2184
	18 19 20 21[e] 22 ◐ 24	6:24	51	2521658	TEVETH 5952	1[e] 2[e] 3 4 5 6 7	Fri 9h48m11p		3 4 5 6 7[i] 8 9	Dōng zhì		7 8 9 10 11 12 13	
	25 26 27 28 29 ○ 31	14:33	52	2521665		8 9 10 11 12 13 14			10 11 12 13 14 15 16			14 15 16 17 18 19 20	

[a]New Year
[b]Spring (14:33)
[c]Summer (5:14)
[d]Autumn (22:27)
[e]Winter (21:59)
● New moon
◐ First quarter moon
○ Full moon
◑ Last quarter moon

[a]New Year
[b]Yom Kippur
[c]Sukkot
[d]Winter starts
[e]Ḥanukkah
[f]Purim
[g]Passover
[h]Shavuot
[i]Fast of Av

‡Leap year
[a]New Year (4889, Hare)
[b]Lantern Festival
[c]Qīngmíng
[d]Dragon Festival
[e]Qīqiǎo
[f]Hungry Ghosts
[g]Mid-Autumn Festival
[h]Double-Ninth Festival
[i]Dōngzhì
*Start of 60-name cycle

‡Leap year
[a]New Year
[b]Building of the Cross
[c]Christmas
[d]Jesus's Circumcision
[e]Epiphany
[f]Easter
[g]Mary's Announcement
[h]Jesus's Transfiguration

PERSIAN (ASTRONOMICAL) 1569/1570

Month	Sun	Mon	Tue	Wed	Thu	Fri	Sat
	5	6	7	8	9	10	11
DEY 1569	12	13	14	15	16	17	18
	19	20	21	22	23	24	25
	26	27	28	29	30	1	2
BAHMAN 1569	3	4	5	6	7	8	9
	10	11	12	13	14	15	16
	17	18	19	20	21	22	23
	24	25	26	27	28	29	30
ESFAND 1569	1	2	3	4	5	6	7
	8	9	10	11	12	13	14
	15	16	17	18	19	20	21
	22	23	24	25	26	27	28
	29	1[a]	2	3	4	5	6
FARVARDĪN 1570	7	8	9	10	11	12	13[b]
	14	15	16	17	18	19	20
	21	22	23	24	25	26	27
	28	29	30	31	1	2	3
ORDĪBEHEŠT 1570	4	5	6	7	8	9	10
	11	12	13	14	15	16	17
	18	19	20	21	22	23	24
	25	26	27	28	29	30	31
XORDĀD 1570	1	2	3	4	5	6	7
	8	9	10	11	12	13	14
	15	16	17	18	19	20	21
	22	23	24	25	26	27	28
	29	30	31	1	2	3	4
TĪR 1570	5	6	7	8	9	10	11
	12	13	14	15	16	17	18
	19	20	21	22	23	24	25
	26	27	28	29	30	31	1
MORDĀD 1570	2	3	4	5	6	7	8
	9	10	11	12	13	14	15
	16	17	18	19	20	21	22
	23	24	25	26	27	28	29
	30	31	1	2	3	4	5
SHAHRĪVAR 1570	6	7	8	9	10	11	12
	13	14	15	16	17	18	19
	20	21	22	23	24	25	26
	27	28	29	30	31	1	2
MEHR 1570	3	4	5	6	7	8	9
	10	11	12	13	14	15	16
	17	18	19	20	21	22	23
	24	25	26	27	28	29	30
ĀBĀN 1570	1	2	3	4	5	6	7
	8	9	10	11	12	13	14
	15	16	17	18	19	20	21
	22	23	24	25	26	27	28
	29	30	1	2	3	4	5
ĀZAR 1570	6	7	8	9	10	11	12
	13	14	15	16	17	18	19
	20	21	22	23	24	25	26
DEY 1570	27	28	29	30	1	2	3
	4	5	6	7	8	9	10

[a]New Year
[b]Sizdeh Bedar

HINDU LUNAR 2247/2248‡

Month	Sun	Mon	Tue	Wed	Thu	Fri	Sat
	30	1	2	3	4	5	6
PAUSHA 2247	7	8	9	10	11	12	13
	14	15	16	17	18	19	20
	21	22	23	24	25	26	27
	28	29	30	1	2	3	5
MĀGHA 2247	6	7	8	9	10	11	12
	12	13	14	15	16	17	18
	19	20	21	22	23	24	25
	26	27	29[h]	30	1	2	3
PHĀLGUNA 2247	4	5	6	7	8	9	10
	11	12	13	14	14	15[i]	16
	17	18	19	20	21	23	24
	25	26	27	28	29	30	1[a]
CHAITRA 2248	2	3	4	5	6	7	8
	9[b]	10	11	12	13	14	15
	16	17	18	19	20	21	22
	23	24	25	27	28	29	30
	1	2	3	4	5	6	7
VAIŚĀKHA 2248	8	8	9	10	11	12	13
	14	15	16	17	18	19	21
	22	23	24	25	26	27	28
	29	30	1	2	3	4	5
JYAISHTHA 2248	6	7	8	9	10	11	12
	13	14	15	16	17	18	19
	20	21	22	24	25	26	27
	28	29	30	1	2	3	4
ĀSHĀDHA 2248	5	5	6	7	8	9	10
	11	12	13	14	16	17	18
	19	20	21	22	23	24	25
	26	27	28	29	30	1	2
LEAP ŚRĀVAṆA 2248	3	4	5	6	7	8	9
	10	11	12	13	14	15	16
	17	19	20	21	22	23	24
	25	26	27	28	29	30	1
ŚRĀVAṆA 2248	1	2	3	4	5	6	7
	8	9	10	12	13	14	15
	16	17	18	19	20	21	22
	23[c]	24	25	26	27	28	29
	30	1	2	3	4[d]	5	6
BHĀDRAPADA 2248	7	8	9	10	11	12	13
	14	16	17	18	19	20	21
	22	23	24	25	26	27	27
	28	29	30	1	2	3	4
ĀŚVINA 2248	5	6	7[e]	9[e]	10[e]	11	12
	13	14	15	16	17	18	19
	20	21	22	23	24	25	26
	27	28	29	30	1[f]	2	3
KĀRTTIKA 2248	4	5	6	7	8	9	10
	11	12	14	15	16	17	18
	19	20	20	21	22	23	24
	25	26	27	28	29	30	1
MĀRGAŚĪRA 2248	2	3	4	5	7	8	9
	10	11[g]	12	13	14	15	16

‡Leap year
[a]New Year (Khara)
[b]Birthday of Rāma
[c]Birthday of Krishna
[d]Ganēśa Chaturthī
[e]Dashara
[f]Diwali
[g]Birthday of Vishnu
[h]Night of Śiva
[i]Holi

HINDU SOLAR 2112/2113‡

Month	Sun	Mon	Tue	Wed	Thu	Fri	Sat
	9	10	11	12	13	14	15
PAUSHA 2112	16	17	18	19	20	21	22
	23	24	25	26	27	28	29
	30	1[b]	2	3	4	5	6
MĀGHA 2112	7	8	9	10	11	12	13
	14	15	16	17	18	19	20
	21	22	23	24	25	26	27
	28	29	1	2	3	4	5
PHĀLGUNA 2112	6	7	8	9	10	11	12
	13	14	15	16	17	18	19
	20	21	22	23	24	25	26
	27	28	29	30	1	2	3
CHAITRA 2112	4	5	6	7	8	9	10
	11	12	13	14	15	16	17
	18	19	20	21	22	23	24
	25	26	27	28	29	30	1[a]
VAIŚĀKHA 2113	2	3	4	5	6	7	8
	9	10	11	12	13	14	15
	16	17	18	19	20	21	22
	23	24	25	26	27	28	29
	30	31	1	2	3	4	5
JYAISHTHA 2113	6	7	8	9	10	11	12
	13	14	15	16	17	18	19
	20	21	22	23	24	25	26
	27	28	29	30	31	32	1
ĀSHĀDHA 2113	2	3	4	5	6	7	8
	9	10	11	12	13	14	15
	16	17	18	19	20	21	22
	23	24	25	26	27	28	29
	30	31	1	2	3	4	5
ŚRĀVAṆA 2113	6	7	8	9	10	11	12
	13	14	15	16	17	18	19
	20	21	22	23	24	25	26
	27	28	29	30	31	32	1
BHĀDRAPADA 2113	2	3	4	5	6	7	8
	9	10	11	12	13	14	15
	16	17	18	19	20	21	22
	23	24	25	26	27	28	29
	30	31	1	2	3	4	5
ĀŚVINA 2113	6	7	8	9	10	11	12
	13	14	15	16	17	18	19
	20	21	22	23	24	25	26
	27	28	29	30	1	2	3
KĀRTTIKA 2113	4	5	6	7	8	9	10
	11	12	13	14	15	16	17
	18	19	20	21	22	23	24
	25	26	27	28	29	30	1
MĀRGAŚĪRA 2113	2	3	4	5	6	7	8
	9	10	11	12	13	14	15
	16	17	18	19	20	21	22
	23	24	25	26	27	28	29
PAUSHA 2113	30	1	2	3	4	5	6
	7	8	9	10	11	12	13

‡Leap year
[a]New Year (Parābhava)
[b]Pongal

ISLAMIC (ASTRONOMICAL) 1617/1618‡

Month	Sun	Mon	Tue	Wed	Thu	Fri	Sat
	28	29	1	2	3	4	5
SHA'BĀN 1617	6	7	8	9	10	11	12
	13	14	15	16	17	18	19
	20	21	22	23	24	25	26
	27	28	29	30	1[e]	2	3
RAMAḌĀN 1617	4	5	6	7	8	9	10
	11	12	13	14	15	16	17
	18	19	20	21	22	23	24
	25	26	27	28	29	1[f]	2
SHAWWĀL 1617	3	4	5	6	7	8	9
	10	11	12	13	14	15	16
	17	18	19	20	21	22	23
	24	25	26	27	28	29	1
DHU AL-QA'DA 1617	2	3	4	5	6	7	8
	9	10	11	12	13	14	15
	16	17	18	19	20	21	22
	23	24	25	26	27	28	29
	30	1	2	3	4	5	6
DHU AL-ḤIJJA 1617	7	8	9	10[g]	11	12	13
	14	15	16	17	18	19	20
	21	22	23	24	25	26	27
	28	29	1[a]	2[A]	3	4	5
MUḤARRAM 1618	6	7	8	9	10[b]	11	12
	13	14	15	16	17	18	19
	20	21	22	23	24	25	26
	27	28	29	30	1	2	3
ṢAFAR 1618	4	5	6	7	8	9	10
	11	12	13	14	15	16	17
	18	19	20	21	22	23	24
	25	26	27	28	29	30	1
RABĪ' I 1618	2	3	4	5	6	7	8
	9	10	11	12[c]	13	14	15
	16	17	18	19	20	21	22
	23	24	25	26	27	28	29
	1	2	3	4	5	6	7
RABĪ' II 1618	8	9	10	11	12	13	14
	15	16	17	18	19	20	21
	22	23	24	25	26	27	28
	29	30	1	2	3	4	5
JUMĀDĀ I 1618	6	7	8	9	10	11	12
	13	14	15	16	17	18	19
	20	21	22	23	24	25	26
	27	28	29	30	1	2	3
JUMĀDĀ II 1618	4	5	6	7	8	9	10
	11	12	13	14	15	16	17
	18	19	20	21	22	23	24
	25	26	27	28	29	30	1
RAJAB 1618	2	3	4	5	6	7	8
	9	10	11	12	13	14	15
	16	17	18	19	20	21	22
	23	24	25	26	27[d]	28	29
SHA'BĀN 1618	1	2	3	4	5	6	7
	8	9	10	11	12	13	14

‡Leap year
[a]New Year
[A]New Year (Arithmetic)
[b]'Ashūrā'
[c]Prophet's Birthday
[d]Ascent of the Prophet
[e]Start of Ramaḍān
[f]'Īd al-Fiṭr
[g]'Īd al-'Aḍḥā

GREGORIAN 2191

Julian (Sun)	Month	Sun	Mon	Tue	Wed	Thu	Fri	Sat
Dec 12		26	27	28	29	30	31	1
	JANUARY 2191	2	3	4	5	6	7	8[a]
Dec 26		9	10	11	12	13	14	15[b]
		16	17	18	19	20	21	22
Jan 9		23	24	25	26	27	28	29
		30	31	1	2	3	4	5
Jan 23	FEBRUARY 2191	6	7	8	9	10	11	12
		13	14	15	16	17	18	19
Feb 6		20	21	22	23[c]	24	25	26
		27	28	1	2	3	4	5
Feb 20	MARCH 2191	6[d]	7	8	9	10	11	12
		13	14	15	16	17	18	19
Mar 6		20	21	22	23	24	25	26
		27	28	29	30	31	1	2
Mar 20	APRIL 2191	3	4	5	6	7	8	9
		10[e]	11	12	13	14	15	16
Apr 3		17[f]	18	19	20	21	22	23
		24	25	26	27	28	29	30
Apr 17	MAY 2191	1	2	3	4	5	6	7
		8	9	10	11	12	13	14
May 1		15	16	17	18	19	20	21
		22	23	24	25	26	27	28
May 15		29	30	31	1	2	3	4
	JUNE 2191	5	6	7	8	9	10	11
May 29		12	13	14	15	16	17	18
		19	20	21	22	23	24	25
Jun 12		26	27	28	29	30	1	2
	JULY 2191	3	4	5	6	7	8	9
Jun 26		10	11	12	13	14	15	16
		17	18	19	20	21	22	23
Jul 10		24	25	26	27	28	29	30
		31	1	2	3	4	5	6
Jul 24	AUGUST 2191	7	8	9	10	11	12	13
		14	15	16	17	18	19	20
Aug 7		21	22	23	24	25	26	27
		28	29	30	31	1	2	3
Aug 21	SEPTEMBER 2191	4	5	6	7	8	9	10
		11	12	13	14	15	16	17
Sep 4		18	19	20	21	22	23	24
		25	26	27	28	29	30	1
Sep 18	OCTOBER 2191	2	3	4	5	6	7	8
		9	10	11	12	13	14	15
Oct 2		16	17	18	19	20	21	22
		23	24	25	26	27	28	29
Oct 16		30	31	1	2	3	4	5
	NOVEMBER 2191	6	7	8	9	10	11	12
Oct 30		13	14	15	16	17	18	19
		20	21	22	23	24	25	26
Nov 13		27[g]	28	29	30	1	2	3
	DECEMBER 2191	4	5	6	7	8	9	10
Nov 27		11	12	13	14	15	16	17
		18	19	20	21	22	23	24
Dec 11		25[h]	26	27	28	29	30	31

[a]Orthodox Christmas
[b]Julian New Year
[c]Ash Wednesday
[d]Feast of Orthodoxy
[e]Easter
[f]Orthodox Easter
[g]Advent
[h]Christmas

2192

Gregorian 2192‡	Sun	Mon	Tue	Wed	Thu	Fri	Sat	Lunar Phases	ISO Week (Mon)	Julian Day (Sun noon)	Hebrew 5952/5953‡	Sun	Mon	Tue	Wed	Thu	Fri	Sat	Molad	Chinese Xīn-Mǎo‡/Rén-Chén	Sun	Mon	Tue	Wed	Thu	Fri	Sat	Solar Term	Coptic 1908/1909	Sun	Mon	Tue	Wed	Thu	Fri	Sat	Ethiopic 2184/2185
January 2192	1[a]	2	3	4	5	6	◑	18:45	1	2521672	Teveth 5952	15	16	17	18	19	20	21		Month 11 Xīn-Mǎo	17	18	19	20	21	22	23	Xiǎo hán	Koiak 1908	21	22	23	24	25	26	27	Tākhśāś 2184
	8	9	10	11	12	13	14		2	2521679		22	23	24	25	26	27	28			24	25	26	27	28	29	30			28	29[c]	30	1	2	3	4	
	●	16	17	18	19	20	◐	0:27 16:09	3	2521686		29	1	2	3	4	5	6	Sat 22h32m12p		1	2	3	4	5	6*	7	Dà hán	Tōbe 1908	5	6[d]	7	8	9	10	11[e]	Ṭer 2184
	22	23	24	25	26	27	28		4	2521693	Shevat 5952	7	8	9	10	11	12	13		Month 12 Xīn-Mǎo	8	9	10	11	12	13	14			12	13	14	15	16	17	18	
	○	30	31	1	2	3	4	8:26	5	2521700		14	15	16	17	18	19	20			15	16	17	18	19	20	21	Lì chūn		19	20	21	22	23	24	25	
February 2192	5	◑	7	8	9	10	11	13:41	6	2521707		21	22	23	24	25	26	27			22	23	24	25	26	27	28			26	27	28	29	30	1	2	
	12	●	14	15	16	17	18	11:18	7	2521714		28	29	30	1	2	3	4	Mon 11h16m13p		29	1[a]	2	3	4	5	6		Meshir 1908	3	4	5	6	7	8	9	Yakātīt 2184
	19	◐	21	22	23	24	25	3:59	8	2521721	Adar 5952	5	6	7	8	9	10	11		Month 1 Rén-Chén	7	8	9	10	11	12	13	Yǔ shuǐ		10	11	12	13	14	15	16	
	26	27	○	29	1	2	3	3:24	9	2521728		12	13	14[f]	15	16	17	18			14	15[b]	16	17	18	19	20			17	18	19	20	21	22	23	
March 2192	4	5	6	◑	8	9	10	4:44	10	2521735		19	20	21	22	23	24	25			21	22	23	24	25	26	27	Jīng zhé		24	25	26	27	28	29	30	
	11	12	●	14	15	16	17	21:21	11	2521742		26	27	28	29	1	2	3	Wed 0h0m14p		28	29	30	1	2	3	4			1	2	3	4	5	6	7	
	18	19[b]	◐	21	22	23	24	17:56	12	2521749	Nisan 5952	4	5	6	7	8	9	10		Month 2 Rén-Chén	5	6	7*	8	9	10	11	Chūn fēn	Paremotep 1908	8	9	10	11	12	13	14	Magābīt 2184
	25	26	27	○	29	30	31	21:51	13	2521756		11	12	13	14	15[g]	16	17			12	13	14	15	16	17	18			15	16	17	18	19	20	21	
April 2192	1	2	3	4	◑	6	7	15:41	14	2521763		18	19	20	21	22	23	24			19	20	21	22[c]	23	24	25	Qīng míng		22	23	24	25	26	27	28	
	8	9	10	11	●	13	14	6:49	15	2521770		25	26	27	28	29	30	1	Thu 12h44m15p		26	27	28	29	1	2	3			29	30	1	2	3	4	5	
	15	16	17	18	◐	20	21	9:46	16	2521777	Iyyar 5952	2	3	4	5	6	7	8		Month 3 Rén-Chén	4	5	6	7	8	9	10	Gǔ yǔ	Parmoute 1908	6	7	8	9	10	11	12	Miyāzyā 2184
	22	23	24	25	26	○	28	14:11	17	2521784		9	10	11	12	13	14	15			11	12	13	14	15	16	17			13	14	15	16	17	18	19	
	29	30	1	2	3	◑	5	23:17	18	2521791		16	17	18	19	20	21	22			18	19	20	21	22	23	24	Lì xià		20	21	22	23	24	25	26	
May 2192	6	7	8	9	10	●	12	16:02	19	2521798		23	24	25	26	27	28	29			25	26	27	28	29	30	1			27[f]	28	29[g]	30	1	2	3	
	13	14	15	16	17	18	◐	2:59	20	2521805		1	2	3	4	5	6[h]	7	Sat 1h28m16p	Month 4 Rén-Chén	2	3	4	5	6	7	8*		Pashons 1908	4	5	6	7	8	9	10	Genbot 2184
	20	21	22	23	24	25	26		21	2521812	Sivan 5952	8	9	10	11	12	13	14			9	10	11	12	13	14	15	Xiǎo mǎn		11	12	13	14	15	16	17	
	○	28	29	30	31	1	2	3:33	22	2521819		15	16	17	18	19	20	21			16	17	18	19	20	21	22			18	19	20	21	22	23	24	
June 2192	◑	4	5	6	7	8	9	4:45	23	2521826		22	23	24	25	26	27	28			23	24	25	26	27	28	29	Máng zhòng		25	26	27	28	29	30	1	
	●	11	12	13	14	15	16	1:39	24	2521833		29	30	1	2	3	4	5	Sun 14h12m17p		1	2	3	4	5[d]	6	7			2	3	4	5	6	7	8	
	◐	18	19	20[c]	21	22	23	20:47	25	2521840	Tammuz 5952	6	7	8	9	10	11	12		Month 5 Rén-Chén	8	9	10	11	12	13	14	Xià zhì	Paōne 1908	9	10	11	12	13	14	15	Sanē 2184
	24	○	26	27	28	29	30	14:09	26	2521847		13	14	15	16	17	18	19			15	16	17	18	19	20	21			16	17	18	19	20	21	22	
July 2192	1	◑	3	4	5	6	7	9:27	27	2521854		20	21	22	23	24	25	26			22	23	24	25	26	27	28	Xiǎo shǔ		23	24	25	26	27	28	29	
	8	●	10	11	12	13	14	12:31	28	2521861		27	28	29	1	2	3	4	Tue 2h57m0p		29	1	2	3	4	5	6			30	1	2	3	4	5	6	
	15	16	◐	18	19	20	21	14:05	29	2521868	Av 5952	5	6	7	8	9[i]	10	11		Month 6 Rén-Chén	7	8	9	10*	11	12	13		Epēp 1908	7	8	9	10	11	12	13	Ḥamlē 2184
	22	23	○	25	26	27	28	22:54	30	2521875		12	13	14	15	16	17	18			14	15	16	17	18	19	20	Dà shǔ		14	15	16	17	18	19	20	
	29	30	◑	1	2	3	4	14:43	31	2521882		19	20	21	22	23	24	25			21	22	23	24	25	26	27			21	22	23	24	25	26	27	
August 2192	5	6	7	●	9	10	11	1:26	32	2521889		26	27	28	29	30	1	2	Wed 15h41m1p		28	29	30	1	2	3	4	Lì qiū		28	29	30	1	2	3	4	
	12	13	14	15	◐	17	18	5:58	33	2521896	Elul 5952	3	4	5	6	7	8	9		Month 7 Rén-Chén	5	6	7[e]	8	9	10	11		Mesorē 1908	5	6	7	8	9	10	11	Naḥasē 2184
	19	20	21	22	○	24	25	6:51	34	2521903		10	11	12	13	14	15	16			12	13	14	15[f]	16	17	18	Chǔ shǔ		12	13[h]	14	15	16	17	18	
	26	27	28	◑	30	31	1	21:50	35	2521910		17	18	19	20	21	22	23			19	20	21	22	23	24	25			19	20	21	22	23	24	25	
September 2192	2	3	4	5	●	7	8	16:42	36	2521917		24	25	26	27	28	29	1[a]	Fri 4h25m2p		26	27	28	29	30	1	2	Bái lù		26	27	28	29	30	1	2	
	9	10	11	12	13	◐	15	19:55	37	2521924		2[a]	3	4	5	6	7	8		Month 8 Rén-Chén	3	4	5	6	7	8	9		Epag. 1908	3	4	5	1[a]	2	3	4	Pāg. 2184
	16	17	18	19	20	○	22[d]	14:56	38	2521931	Tishri 5953	9	10[b]	11	12	13	14	15[c]			10*	11	12	13	14	15[g]	16	Qiū fēn	Thoout 1909	5	6	7	8	9	10	11	Maskaram 2185
	23	24	25	26	27	◑	29	8:02	39	2521938		16	17	18	19	20	21	22			17	18	19	20	21	22	23			12	13	14	15	16	17[b]	18	
	30	1	2	3	4	5	●	9:47	40	2521945		23	24	25	26	27	28	29			24	25	26	27	28	29	1			19	20	21	22	23	24	25	
October 2192	7	8	9	10	11	12	13		41	2521952		30	1	2	3	4	5	6	Sat 17h9m3p		2	3	4	5	6	7	8	Hán lù		26	27	28	29	30	1	2	
	◐	15	16	17	18	19	○	7:55 22:14	42	2521959	Heshvan 5953	7	8	9	10	11	12	13		Month 9 Rén-Chén	9[h]	10	11	12	13	14	15		Paope 1909	3	4	5	6	7	8	9	Ṭeqemt 2185
	21	22	23	24	25	26	◑	23:50	43	2521966		14	15	16	17	18	19	20			16	17	18	19	20	21	22	Shuāng jiàng		10	11	12	13	14	15	16	
	28	29	30	31	1	2	3		44	2521973		21	22	23	24	25	26	27			23	24	25	26	27	28	29			17	18	19	20	21	22	23	
November 2192	4	●	6	7	8	9	10	3:28	45	2521980		28	29	1	2	3	4	5	Mon 5h53m4p		30	1	2	3	4	5	6	Lì dōng		24	25	26	27	28	29	30	
	11	◐	13	14	15	16	17	18:14	46	2521987	Kislev 5953	6	7	8	9	10	11	12		Month 10 Rén-Chén	7	8	9	10	11*	12	13		Athōr 1909	1	2	3	4	5	6	7	Ḫedār 2185
	18	○	20	21	22	23	24	10:00	47	2521994		13	14	15	16	17	18	19			14	15	16	17	18	19	20	Xiǎo xuě		8	9	10	11	12	13	14	
	25	◑	27	28	29	30	1	16:33	48	2522001		20	21	22	23	24	25[e]	26[e]			21	22	23	24	25	26	27			15	16	17	18	19	20	21	
December 2192	2	3	●	5	6	7	8	20:26	49	2522008		27[e]	28[e]	29[e]	1[e]	2[d][e]	3[e]	4	Tue 18h37m5p		28	29	30	1	2	3	4	Dà xuě		22	23	24	25	26	27	28	
	9	10	11	◐	13	14	15	3:16	50	2522015	Teveth 5953	5	6	7	8	9	10	11		Month 11 Rén-Chén	5	6	7	8	9	10	11			29	30	1	2	3	4	5	
	16	17	○	19	20	21[e]	22	21:53	51	2522022		12	13	14	15	16	17	18			12	13	14	15	16	17[i]	18	Dōng zhì	Koiak 1909	6	7	8	9	10	11	12	Tākhśāś 2185
	23	24	25	◑	27	28	29	13:55	52	2522029		19	20	21	22	23	24	25			19	20	21	22	23	24	25			13	14	15	16	17	18	19	
	30	31	1	2	●	4	5	11:55	1	2522036		26	27	28	29	1	2	3	Thu 7h21m6p		26	27	28	29	1	2	3	Xiǎo hán		20	21	22	23	24	25	26	

‡Leap year
[a]New Year
[b]Spring (20:14)
[c]Summer (11:02)
[d]Autumn (4:16)
[e]Winter (3:51)
● New moon
◐ First quarter moon
○ Full moon
◑ Last quarter moon

‡Leap year
[a]New Year
[b]Yom Kippur
[c]Sukkot
[d]Winter starts
[e]Ḥanukkah
[f]Purim
[g]Passover
[h]Shavuot
[i]Fast of Av

‡Leap year
[a]New Year (4890, Dragon)
[b]Lantern Festival
[c]Qīngmíng
[d]Dragon Festival
[e]Qīqiǎo
[f]Hungry Ghosts
[g]Mid-Autumn Festival
[h]Double-Ninth Festival
[i]Dōngzhì
*Start of 60-name cycle

[a]New Year
[b]Building of the Cross
[c]Christmas
[d]Jesus's Circumcision
[e]Epiphany
[f]Easter
[g]Mary's Announcement
[h]Jesus's Transfiguration

PERSIAN (ASTRONOMICAL) 1570/1571

Month	Sun	Mon	Tue	Wed	Thu	Fri	Sat
DEY 1570	11	12	13	14	15	16	17
	18	19	20	21	22	23	24
	25	26	27	28	29	30	1
BAHMAN 1570	2	3	4	5	6	7	8
	9	10	11	12	13	14	15
	16	17	18	19	20	21	22
	23	24	25	26	27	28	29
	30	1	2	3	4	5	6
ESFAND 1570	7	8	9	10	11	12	13
	14	15	16	17	18	19	20
	21	22	23	24	25	26	27
	28	29	1[a]	2	3	4	5
FARVARDĪN 1571	6	7	8	9	10	11	12
	13[b]	14	15	16	17	18	19
	20	21	22	23	24	25	26
	27	28	29	30	31	1	2
ORDĪBEHEŠT 1571	3	4	5	6	7	8	9
	10	11	12	13	14	15	16
	17	18	19	20	21	22	23
	24	25	26	27	28	29	30
	31	1	2	3	4	5	6
XORDĀD 1571	7	8	9	10	11	12	13
	14	15	16	17	18	19	20
	21	22	23	24	25	26	27
	28	29	30	31	1	2	3
TĪR 1571	4	5	6	7	8	9	10
	11	12	13	14	15	16	17
	18	19	20	21	22	23	24
	25	26	27	28	29	30	31
MORDĀD 1571	1	2	3	4	5	6	7
	8	9	10	11	12	13	14
	15	16	17	18	19	20	21
	22	23	24	25	26	27	28
	29	30	31	1	2	3	4
SHAHRĪVAR 1571	5	6	7	8	9	10	11
	12	13	14	15	16	17	18
	19	20	21	22	23	24	25
	26	27	28	29	30	31	1
MEHR 1571	2	3	4	5	6	7	8
	9	10	11	12	13	14	15
	16	17	18	19	20	21	22
	23	24	25	26	27	28	29
	30	1	2	3	4	5	6
ĀBĀN 1571	7	8	9	10	11	12	13
	14	15	16	17	18	19	20
	21	22	23	24	25	26	27
	28	29	30	1	2	3	4
ĀZAR 1571	5	6	7	8	9	10	11
	12	13	14	15	16	17	18
	19	20	21	22	23	24	25
	26	27	28	29	30	1	2
DEY 1571	3	4	5	6	7	8	9
	10	11	12	13	14	15	16

[a]New Year
[b]Sizdeh Bedar

HINDU LUNAR 2248‡/2249

Month	Sun	Mon	Tue	Wed	Thu	Fri	Sat
MĀRGAŚĪRA 2248	17	18	19	20	21	22	22
	23	24	25	26	27	28	29
PAUSHA 2248	1	2	3	4	5	6	7
	8	9	10	11	12	13	14
	15	16	17	18	19	20	21
	22	23	24	25	26	27	28
	29	30	1	2	3	4	6
MĀGHA 2248	7	8	9	10	11	12	13
	14	15	15	16	17	18	19
	20	21	22	23	24	25	26
	27	28[h]	30	1	2	3	4
PHĀLGUNA 2248	5	6	7	8	9	10	11
	12	13	14	15[i]	16	17	18
	18	19	20	21	23	24	25
	26	27	28	29	30	1[a]	2
CHAITRA 2249	3	4	6	7	8	8[b]	9
	10	11	12	13	14	15	16
	17	18	19	20	21	22	23
	24	25	26	28	29	30	1
VAIŚĀKHA 2249	2	3	4	5	6	7	8
	9	10	11	12	12	13	14
	15	16	17	18	20	21	22
	23	24	25	26	27	28	29
	30	1	2	3	4	5	6
JYAISHTHA 2249	7	8	9	10	11	12	13
	14	15	16	17	18	19	20
	21	22	24	25	26	27	28
	29	30	1	2	3	4	5
ĀSHĀḌHA 2249	6	7	8	9	9	10	11
	12	13	14	16	17	18	19
	20	21	22	23	24	25	26
	28	29	30	1	1	2	3
ŚRĀVAṆA 2249	4	5	6	7	8	9	10
	11	12	13	14	15	16	17
	19	20	21	22	23[c]	24	25
	26	27	28	29	30	1	2
BHĀDRAPADA 2249	3	4[d]	5	6	6	7	8
	9	10	12	13	14	15	16
	17	18	19	20	21	22	24
	25	26	26	27	28	29	30
ĀŚVINA 2249	1	2	3	4	5	6	7
	8[e]	9[e]	10[e]	11	12	13	14
	16	17	18	19	20	21	22
	23	24	25	26	27	28	29
	30	30	1[f]	2	3	4	5
KĀRTTIKA 2249	6	7	8	10	11	12	13
	14	15	16	17	18	19	20
	21	22	23	24	25	26	27
	28	29	30	1	2	3	4
MĀRGAŚĪRA 2249	5	6	7	8	9	10	11[g]
	12	14	15	16	17	18	19
	20	21	22	23	23	24	25
	26	27	28	29	30	1	2

‡Leap year
[a]New Year (Nandana)
[b]Birthday of Rāma
[c]Birthday of Krishna
[d]Ganēśa Chaturthī
[e]Dashara
[f]Diwali
[g]Birthday of Vishnu
[h]Night of Śiva
[i]Holi

HINDU SOLAR 2113‡/2114

Month	Sun	Mon	Tue	Wed	Thu	Fri	Sat
PAUSHA 2113	14	15	16	17	18	19	20
	21	22	23	24	25	26	27
	28	29	1[b]	2	3	4	5
MĀGHA 2113	6	7	8	9	10	11	12
	13	14	15	16	17	18	19
	20	21	22	23	24	25	26
	27	28	29	1	2	3	4
PHĀLGUNA 2113	5	6	7	8	9	10	11
	12	13	14	15	16	17	18
	19	20	21	22	23	24	25
	26	27	28	29	30	1	2
CHAITRA 2113	3	4	5	6	7	8	9
	10	11	12	13	14	15	16
	17	18	19	20	21	22	23
	24	25	26	27	28	29	30
	31	1[a]	2	3	4	5	6
VAIŚĀKHA 2114	7	8	9	10	11	12	13
	14	15	16	17	18	19	20
	21	22	23	24	25	26	27
	28	29	30	31	1	2	3
JYAISHTHA 2114	4	5	6	7	8	9	10
	11	12	13	14	15	16	17
	18	19	20	21	22	23	24
	25	26	27	28	29	30	31
ĀSHĀḌHA 2114	1	2	3	4	5	6	7
	8	9	10	11	12	13	14
	15	16	17	18	19	20	21
	22	23	24	25	26	27	28
	29	30	31	32	1	2	3
ŚRĀVAṆA 2114	4	5	6	7	8	9	10
	11	12	13	14	15	16	17
	18	19	20	21	22	23	24
	25	26	27	28	29	30	31
BHĀDRAPADA 2114	1	2	3	4	5	6	7
	8	9	10	11	12	13	14
	15	16	17	18	19	20	21
	22	23	24	25	26	27	28
	29	30	31	1	2	3	4
ĀŚVINA 2114	5	6	7	8	9	10	11
	12	13	14	15	16	17	18
	19	20	21	22	23	24	25
	26	27	28	29	30	31	1
KĀRTTIKA 2114	2	3	4	5	6	7	8
	9	10	11	12	13	14	15
	16	17	18	19	20	21	22
	23	24	25	26	27	28	29
MĀRGAŚĪRA 2114	1	2	3	4	5	6	7
	8	9	10	11	12	13	14
	15	16	17	18	19	20	21
	22	23	24	25	26	27	28
	29	30	1	2	3	4	5
PAUSHA 2114	6	7	8	9	10	11	12
	13	14	15	16	17	18	19

‡Leap year
[a]New Year (Plavaṅga)
[b]Pongal

ISLAMIC (ASTRONOMICAL) 1618‡/1619

Month	Sun	Mon	Tue	Wed	Thu	Fri	Sat
SHA'BĀN 1618	15	16	17	18	19	20	21
	22	23	24	25	26	27	28
	29	1[e]	2	3	4	5	6
RAMAḌĀN 1618	7	8	9	10	11	12	13
	14	15	16	17	18	19	20
	21	22	23	24	25	26	27
	28	29	30	1[f]	2	3	4
SHAWWĀL 1618	5	6	7	8	9	10	11
	12	13	14	15	16	17	18
	19	20	21	22	23	24	25
	26	27	28	29	1	2	3
DHU AL-QA'DA 1618	4	5	6	7	8	9	10
	11	12	13	14	15	16	17
	18	19	20	21	22	23	24
	25	26	27	28	29	1	2
DHU AL-ḤIJJA 1618	3	4	5	6	7	8	9
	10[g]	11	12	13	14	15	16
	17	18	19	20	21	22	23
	24	25	26	27	28	29	30
MUḤARRAM 1619	1[a]	2	3	4	5	6	7
	8	9	10[b]	11	12	13	14
	15	16	17	18	19	20	21
	22	23	24	25	26	27	28
	29	1	2	3	4	5	6
ṢAFAR 1619	7	8	9	10	11	12	13
	14	15	16	17	18	19	20
	21	22	23	24	25	26	27
	28	29	30	1	2	3	4
RABĪ' I 1619	5	6	7	8	9	10	11
	12[c]	13	14	15	16	17	18
	19	20	21	22	23	24	25
	26	27	28	29	1	2	3
RABĪ' II 1619	4	5	6	7	8	9	10
	11	12	13	14	15	16	17
	18	19	20	21	22	23	24
	25	26	27	28	29	30	31
JUMĀDĀ I 1619	1	2	3	4	5	6	7
	8	9	10	11	12	13	14
	15	16	17	18	19	20	21
	22	23	24	25	26	27	28
	29	30	1	2	3	4	5
JUMĀDĀ II 1619	6	7	8	9	10	11	12
	13	14	15	16	17	18	19
	20	21	22	23	24	25	26
	27	28	29	1	2	3	4
RAJAB 1619	5	6	7	8	9	10	11
	12	13	14	15	16	17	18
	19	20	21	22	23	24	25
	26	27[d]	28	29	30	1	2
SHA'BĀN 1619	3	4	5	6	7	8	9
	10	11	12	13	14	15	16
	17	18	19	20	21	22	23
	24	25	26	27	28	29	1

‡Leap year
[a]New Year
[b]'Ashūrā'
[c]Prophet's Birthday
[d]Ascent of the Prophet
[e]Start of Ramaḍān
[f]'Id al-Fiṭr
[g]'Id al-'Aḍḥā

GREGORIAN 2192‡

Julian† (Sun)	Sun	Mon	Tue	Wed	Thu	Fri	Sat	Month
Dec 18	1	2	3	4	5	6	7	JANUARY 2192
	8[a]	9	10	11	12	13	14	
Jan 1	15[b]	16	17	18	19	20	21	
	22	23	24	25	26	27	28	
Jan 15	29	30	31	1	2	3	4	FEBRUARY 2192
	5	6	7	8	9	10	11	
Jan 29	12	13	14	15[c]	16	17	18	
	19	20	21	22	23	24	25	
Feb 12	26	27	28	29	1	2	3	MARCH 2192
	4	5	6	7	8	9	10	
Feb 26	11	12	13	14	15	16	17	
	18	19	20	21	22	23	24	
Mar 11	25[d]	26	27	28	29	30	31	
	1[e]	2	3	4	5	6	7	APRIL 2192
Mar 25	8	9	10	11	12	13	14	
	15	16	17	18	19	20	21	
Apr 8	22	23	24	25	26	27	28	
	29	30	1	2	3	4	5	MAY 2192
Apr 22	6[f]	7	8	9	10	11	12	
	13	14	15	16	17	18	19	
May 6	20	21	22	23	24	25	26	
	27	28	29	30	31	1	2	JUNE 2192
May 20	3	4	5	6	7	8	9	
	10	11	12	13	14	15	16	
Jun 3	17	18	19	20	21	22	23	
	24	25	26	27	28	29	30	
Jun 17	1	2	3	4	5	6	7	JULY 2192
	8	9	10	11	12	13	14	
Jul 1	15	16	17	18	19	20	21	
	22	23	24	25	26	27	28	
Jul 15	29	30	31	1	2	3	4	AUGUST 2192
	5	6	7	8	9	10	11	
Jul 29	12	13	14	15	16	17	18	
	19	20	21	22	23	24	25	
Aug 12	26	27	28	29	30	31	1	SEPTEMBER 2192
	2	3	4	5	6	7	8	
Aug 26	9	10	11	12	13	14	15	
	16	17	18	19	20	21	22	
Sep 9	23	24	25	26	27	28	29	
	30	1	2	3	4	5	6	OCTOBER 2192
Sep 23	7	8	9	10	11	12	13	
	14	15	16	17	18	19	20	
Oct 7	21	22	23	24	25	26	27	
	28	29	30	31	1	2	3	NOVEMBER 2192
Oct 21	4	5	6	7	8	9	10	
	11	12	13	14	15	16	17	
Nov 4	18	19	20	21	22	23	24	
	25	26	27	28	29	30	1	DECEMBER 2192
Nov 18	2[g]	3	4	5	6	7	8	
	9	10	11	12	13	14	15	
Dec 2	16	17	18	19	20	21	22	
	23	24	25[h]	26	27	28	29	
Dec 16	30	31	1	2	3	4	5	

‡Leap year
[a]Orthodox Christmas
[b]Julian New Year
[c]Ash Wednesday
[d]Feast of Orthodoxy
[e]Easter
[f]Orthodox Easter
[g]Advent
[h]Christmas

2193

Month	Sun	Mon	Tue	Wed	Thu	Fri	Sat	Lunar Phases	ISO Week (Mon)	Julian Day (Sun noon)
January 2193	30	31	1[a]	2	●	4	5	11:55	1	2522036
	6	7	8	9	◐	11	12	11:31	2	2522043
	13	14	15	16	○	18	19	11:54	3	2522050
	20	21	22	23	24	◑	26	12:03	4	2522057
February 2193	27	28	29	30	31	1	●	1:36	5	2522064
	3	4	5	6	7	◐	9	19:42	6	2522071
	10	11	12	13	14	15	○	4:04	7	2522078
	17	18	19	20	21	22	23		8	2522085
March 2193	◑	25	26	27	28	1	2	8:31	9	2522092
	●	4	5	6	7	8	9	13:24	10	2522099
	◐	11	12	13	14	15	16	4:39	11	2522106
	○	18	19	20[b]	21	22	23	21:38	12	2522113
	24	25	◑	27	28	29	30	1:39	13	2522120
April 2193	31	●	2	3	4	5	6	23:20	14	2522127
	7	◐	9	10	11	12	13	15:08	15	2522134
	14	15	○	17	18	19	20	15:13	16	2522141
	21	22	23	◑	25	26	27	14:55	17	2522148
May 2193	28	29	30	●	2	3	4	7:42	18	2522155
	5	6	7	◐	9	10	11	3:42	19	2522162
	12	13	14	15	○	17	18	7:32	20	2522169
	19	20	21	22	23	◑	25	0:32	21	2522176
June 2193	26	27	28	29	●	31	1	15:16	22	2522183
	2	3	4	5	◐	7	8	18:23	23	2522190
	9	10	11	12	13	○	15	21:54	24	2522197
	16	17	18	19	20[c]	21	◑	7:14	25	2522204
	23	24	25	26	27	●	29	23:04	26	2522211
July 2193	30	1	2	3	4	5	◐	10:45	27	2522218
	7	8	9	10	11	12	13		28	2522225
	○	15	16	17	18	19	20	10:19	29	2522232
	◑	22	23	24	25	26	27	12:08	30	2522239
August 2193	●	29	30	31	1	2	3	8:18	31	2522246
	4	◐	6	7	8	9	10	4:05	32	2522253
	11	○	13	14	15	16	17	21:10	33	2522260
	18	◑	20	21	22	23	24	16:38	34	2522267
	25	●	27	28	29	30	31	19:56	35	2522274
September 2193	1	2	◐	4	5	6	7	21:36	36	2522281
	8	9	10	○	12	13	14	6:58	37	2522288
	15	16	◑	18	19	20	21	22:19	38	2522295
	22[d]	23	24	●	26	27	28	10:19	39	2522302
October 2193	29	30	1	2	◐	4	5	14:35	40	2522309
	6	7	8	9	○	11	12	16:15	41	2522316
	13	14	15	16	◑	18	19	6:42	42	2522323
	20	21	22	23	24	●	26	3:10	43	2522330
November 2193	27	28	29	30	31	1	◐	6:19	44	2522337
	3	4	5	6	7	8	○	1:33	45	2522344
	10	11	12	13	14	◑	16	18:56	46	2522351
	17	18	19	20	21	22	●	21:34	47	2522358
	24	25	26	27	28	29	30		48	2522365
December 2193	◐	2	3	4	5	6	7	20:05	49	2522372
	○	9	10	11	12	13	14	11:29	50	2522379
	◑	16	17	18	19	20	21[e]	11:18	51	2522386
	22	●	24	25	26	27	28	16:17	52	2522393
	29	30	◐	1	2	3	4	7:24	1	2522400

HEBREW 5953‡/5954

Week	Month	Sun	Mon	Tue	Wed	Thu	Fri	Sat	Molad
1		26	27	28	29	1	2	3	Thu 7h21m6p
2	Shevat 5953	4	5	6	7	8	9	10	
3		11	12	13	14	15	16	17	
4		18	19	20	21	22	23	24	
5		25	26	27	28	29	30	1	Fri 20h5m7p
6	Adar I 5953	2	3	4	5	6	7	8	
7		9	10	11	12	13	14	15	
8		16	17	18	19	20	21	22	
9		23	24	25	26	27	28	29	Sun 8h49m8p
10		30	1	2	3	4	5	6	
11	Adar II 5953	7	8	9	10	11	12	13	
12		14[f]	15	16	17	18	19	20	
13		21	22	23	24	25	26	27	
14		28	29	1	2	3	4	5	Mon 21h33m9p
15	Nisan 5953	6	7	8	9	10	11	12	
16		13	14	15[g]	16	17	18	19	
17		20	21	22	23	24	25	26	
18		27	28	29	30	1	2	3	Wed 10h17m10p
19	Iyar 5953	4	5	6	7	8	9	10	
20		11	12	13	14	15	16	17	
21		18	19	20	21	22	23	24	
22		25	26	27	28	29	1	2	Thu 23h1m11p
23	Sivan 5953	3	4	5	6[h]	7	8	9	
24		10	11	12	13	14	15	16	
25		17	18	19	20	21	22	23	
26		24	25	26	27	28	29	30	Sat 11h45m12p
27	Tammuz 5953	1	2	3	4	5	6	7	
28		8	9	10	11	12	13	14	
29		15	16	17	18	19	20	21	
30		22	23	24	25	26	27	28	
31		29	1	2	3	4	5	6	Mon 0h29m13p
32	Av 5953	7	8	9[i]	10	11	12	13	
33		14	15	16	17	18	19	20	
34		21	22	23	24	25	26	27	
35		28	29	30	1	2	3	4	Tue 13h13m14p
36	Elul 5953	5	6	7	8	9	10	11	
37		12	13	14	15	16	17	18	
38		19	20	21	22	23	24	25	
39		26	27	28	29	1[a]	2[a]	3	Thu 1h57m15p
40	Tishri 5954	4	5	6	7	8	9	10[b]	
41		11	12	13	14	15[c]	16	17	
42		18	19	20	21	22	23	24	
43		25	26	27	28	29	30	1	Fri 14h41m16p
44	Heshvan 5954	2	3	4	5	6	7	8	
45		9	10	11	12	13	14	15	
46		16	17	18	19	20	21	22	
47		23	24	25	26	27	28	29	
48		1	2	3	4	5	6	7	Sun 3h25m17p
49	Kislev 5954	8	9	10	11	12	13[d]	14	
50		15	16	17	18	19	20	21	
51		22	23	24	25[e]	26[e]	27[e]	28[e]	
52		29[e]	30[e]	1[e]	2[e]	3	4	5	Mon 16h10m0p
53	Teveth 5954	6	7	8	9	10	11	12	

CHINESE Rén-Chén/Guǐ-Sì

Week	Month	Sun	Mon	Tue	Wed	Thu	Fri	Sat	Solar Term
1		26	27	28	29	1	2	3	Xiǎo hán
2	Month 12 Rén-Chén	4	5	6	7	8	9	10	
3		11	12*	13	14	15	16	**17**	Dà hán
4		18	19	20	21	22	23	24	
5		25	26	27	28	29	30	1[a]	
6	Month 1 Guǐ-Sì	2	3	4	5	6	7	8	Lì chūn
7		9	10	11	12	13	14	15[b]	
8		16	**17**	18	19	20	21	22	Yǔ shuǐ
9		23	24	25	26	27	28	29	
10		1	2	3	4	5	6	7	Jīng zhé
11	Month 2 Guǐ-Sì	8	9	10	11	12	13*	14	
12		15	16	17	**18**	19	20	21	Chūn fēn
13		22	23	24	25	26	27	28	
14		29	30	1	2	3[c]	4	5	Qīng míng
15	Month 3 Guǐ-Sì	6	7	8	9	10	11	12	
16		13	14	15	16	17	**18**	19	Gǔ yǔ
17		20	21	22	23	24	25	26	
18		27	28	29	1	2	3	4	
19	Month 4 Guǐ-Sì	5	6	7	8	9	10	11	Lì xià
20		12	13	14*	15	16	17	18	
21		19	**20**	21	22	23	24	25	Xiǎo mǎn
22		26	27	28	29	1	2	3	
23	Month 5 Guǐ-Sì	4	5[d]	6	7	8	9	10	Máng zhòng
24		11	12	13	14	15	16	17	
25		18	19	20	21	22	**23**	24	Xià zhì
26		25	26	27	28	29	30	1	
27	Month 6 Guǐ-Sì	2	3	4	5	6	7	*8*	Xiǎo shǔ
28		9	10	11	12	13	14	15*	
29		16	17	18	19	20	21	22	
30		23	**24**	25	26	27	28	29	Dà shǔ
31		1	2	3	4	5	6	7[e]	
32	Month 7 Guǐ-Sì	8	9	10	*11*	12	13	14	Lì qiū
33		15[f]	16	17	18	19	20	21	
34		22	23	24	25	**26**	27	28	Chǔ shǔ
35		29	30	1	2	3	4	5	
36	Month 8 Guǐ-Sì	6	7	8	9	10	11	*12*	Bái lù
37		13	14	15[g]	16*	17	18	19	
38		20	21	22	23	24	25	26	
39		**27**	28	29	1	2	3	4	Qiū fēn
40	Month 9 Guǐ-Sì	5	6	7	8	9[h]	10	11	
41		12	13	*14*	15	16	17	18	Hán lù
42		19	20	21	22	23	24	25	
43		26	27	28	**29**	30	1	2	Shuāng jiàng
44	Month 10 Guǐ-Sì	3	4	5	6	7	8	9	
45		10	11	12	13	*14*	15	16	Lì dōng
46		17*	18	19	20	21	22	23	
47		24	25	26	27	28	**29**	30	Xiǎo xuě
48		1	2	3	4	5	6	7	
49	Month 11* Guǐ-Sì	8	9	10	11	12	*13*	14	Dà xuě
50		15	16	17	18	19	20	21	
51		22	23	24	25	26	27	**28**[i]	Dōng zhì
52		29	30	1	2	3	4	5	
53	Month 12 Guǐ-Sì	6	7	8	9	10	11	12	

COPTIC 1909/1910 — ETHIOPIC 2185/2186

Week	Coptic Month	Sun	Mon	Tue	Wed	Thu	Fri	Sat	Ethiopic Month
1	Koiak 1909	20	21	22	23	24	25	26	Tākhśāś 2185
2		27	28	29[c]	30	1	2	3	
3	Ṭōbe 1909	4	5	6[d]	7	8	9	10	Ṭer 2185
4		11[e]	12	13	14	15	16	17	
5		18	19	20	21	22	23	24	
6		25	26	27	28	29	30	1	
7	Meshir 1909	2	3	4	5	6	7	8	Yakātit 2185
8		9	10	11	12	13	14	15	
9		16	17	18	19	20	21	22	
10		23	24	25	26	27	28	29	
11		30	1	2	3	4	5	6	
12	Paremotep 1909	7	8	9	10	11	12	13	Magābit 2185
13		14	15	16	17	18	19	20	
14		21	22	23	24	25	26	27	
15		28	29	30	1	2	3	4	
16	Parmoute 1909	5	6	7	8	9	10	11	Miyāzyā 2185
17		12	13	14	15	16	17	18	
18		19[f]	20	21	22	23	24	25	
19		26	27	28	29[g]	30	1	2	
20	Pashons 1909	3	4	5	6	7	8	9	Genbot 2185
21		10	11	12	13	14	15	16	
22		17	18	19	20	21	22	23	
23		24	25	26	27	28	29	30	
24	Paōne 1909	1	2	3	4	5	6	7	Sanē 2185
25		8	9	10	11	12	13	14	
26		15	16	17	18	19	20	21	
27		22	23	24	25	26	27	28	
28		29	30	1	2	3	4	5	
29	Epēp 1909	6	7	8	9	10	11	12	Hamlē 2185
30		13	14	15	16	17	18	19	
31		20	21	22	23	24	25	26	
32		27	28	29	30	1	2	3	
33	Mesorē 1909	4	5	6	7	8	9	10	Nahasē 2185
34		11	12	13[h]	14	15	16	17	
35		18	19	20	21	22	23	24	
36		25	26	27	28	29	30	1	
37	Epag. 1909	2	3	4	5	1[a]	2	3	Ṗāg. 2185
38	Thoout 1910	4	5	6	7	8	9	10	Maskaram 2186
39		11	12	13	14	15	16	17[b]	
40		18	19	20	21	22	23	24	
41		25	26	27	28	29	30	1	
42	Paope 1910	2	3	4	5	6	7	8	Ṭeqemt 2186
43		9	10	11	12	13	14	15	
44		16	17	18	19	20	21	22	
45		23	24	25	26	27	28	29	
46		30	1	2	3	4	5	6	
47	Athōr 1910	7	8	9	10	11	12	13	Hedār 2186
48		14	15	16	17	18	19	20	
49		21	22	23	24	25	26	27	
50		28	29	30	1	2	3	4	
51	Koiak 1910	5	6	7	8	9	10	11	Tākhśāś 2186
52		12	13	14	15	16	17	18	
53		19	20	21	22	23	24	25	

Gregorian notes:
[a] New Year
[b] Spring (2:06)
[c] Summer (16:45)
[d] Autumn (9:56)
[e] Winter (9:38)
● New moon
◐ First quarter moon
○ Full moon
◑ Last quarter moon

Hebrew notes:
‡ Leap year
[a] New Year
[b] Yom Kippur
[c] Sukkot
[d] Winter starts
[e] Ḥanukkah
[f] Purim
[g] Passover
[h] Shavuot
[i] Fast of Av

Chinese notes:
[a] New Year (4891, Snake)
[b] Lantern Festival
[c] Qīngmíng
[d] Dragon Festival
[e] Qǐqiǎo
[f] Hungry Ghosts
[g] Mid-Autumn Festival
[h] Double-Ninth Festival
[i] Dōngzhì
* Start of 60-name cycle

Coptic/Ethiopic notes:
[a] New Year
[b] Building of the Cross
[c] Christmas
[d] Jesus's Circumcision
[e] Epiphany
[f] Easter
[g] Mary's Announcement
[h] Jesus's Transfiguration

	PERSIAN (ASTRONOMICAL) 1571/1572		HINDU LUNAR 2249/2250		HINDU SOLAR 2114/2115		ISLAMIC (ASTRONOMICAL) 1619/1620‡	Julian (Sun)	GREGORIAN 2193	
	Sun Mon Tue Wed Thu Fri Sat		Sun Mon Tue Wed Thu Fri Sat		Sun Mon Tue Wed Thu Fri Sat		Sun Mon Tue Wed Thu Fri Sat		Sun Mon Tue Wed Thu Fri Sat	
DEY 1571	10 11 12 13 14 15 16	PAUSHA 2249	26 27 28 29 30 1 2	PAUSHA 2114	13 14 15 16 17 18 19	RAMAḌĀN 1619	24 25 26 27 28 29 1[e]	Dec 16	30 31 1 2 3 4 5	JANUARY 2193
	17 18 19 20 21 22 23		3 4 5 6 8 9 10		20 21 22 23 24 25 26		2 3 4 5 6 7 8		6 7 8[a] 9 10 11 12	
	24 25 26 27 28 29 30		11 12 13 14 15 16 17		27 28 29 1[b] 2 3 4		9 10 11 12 13 14 15	Dec 30	13 14 15[b] 16 17 18 19	
BAHMAN 1571	1 2 3 4 5 6 7		18 19 20 21 22 23 24	MĀGHA 2114	5 6 7 8 9 10 11		16 17 18 19 20 21 22		20 21 22 23 24 25 26	
	8 9 10 11 12 13 14		25 25 26 27 28 29 30		12 13 14 15 16 17 18		23 24 25 26 27 28 29	Jan 13	27 28 29 30 31 1 2	
	15 16 17 18 19 20 21	MĀGHA 2249	2 3 4 5 6 7 8		19 20 21 22 23 24 25	SHAWWĀL 1619	1[f] 2 3 4 5 6 7		3 4 5 6 7 8 9	FEBRUARY 2193
	22 23 24 25 26 27 28		9 10 11 12 13 14 15		26 27 28 29 30 1 2		8 9 10 11 12 13 14	Jan 27	10 11 12 13 14 15 16	
	29 30 1 2 3 4 5		16 17 18 19 20 21 22	PHĀLGUNA 2114	3 4 5 6 7 8 9		15 16 17 18 19 20 21		17 18 19 20 21 22 23	
ESFAND 1571	6 7 8 9 10 11 12		23 24 25 26 27 28[h] 29		10 11 12 13 14 15 16		22 23 24 25 26 27 28	Feb 10	24 25 26 27 28 1 2	
	13 14 15 16 17 18 19	PHĀLGUNA 2249	30 1 2 3 4 5 7		17 18 19 20 21 22 23	DHU AL-QA'DA 1619	29 30 1 2 3 4 5		3 4 5 6[c] 7 8 9	MARCH 2193
	20 21 22 23 24 25 26		8 9 10 11 12 13 14		24 25 26 27 28 29 30		6 7 8 9 10 11 12	Feb 24	10 11 12 13 14 15 16	
FARVARDĪN 1572	27 28 29 1[a] 2 3 4		15[i] 16 17 18 18 19 20	CHAITRA 2114	1 2 3 4 5 6 7		13 14 15 16 17 18 19		17[d] 18 19 20 21 22 23	
	5 6 7 8 9 10 11		21 22 23 24 25 26 27		8 9 10 11 12 13 14		20 21 22 23 24 25 26	Mar 10	24 25 26 27 28 29 30	
	12 13[b] 14 15 16 17 18	CHAITRA 2250	28 29 1[a] 2 3 4 5		15 16 17 18 19 20 21	DHU AL-ḤIJJA 1619	27 28 29 1 2 3 4		31 1 2 3 4 5 6	APRIL 2193
	19 20 21 22 23 24 25		6 7 8 9[b] 10 11 12		22 23 24 25 26 27 28		5 6 7 8 9 10[g] 11	Mar 24	7 8 9 10 11 12 13	
	26 27 28 29 30 31 1		13 14 15 16 17 18 19	VAIŚĀKHA 2115	29 30 1[a] 2 3 4 5		12 13 14 15 16 17 18		14 15 16 17 18 19 20	
ORDIBEHEŠT 1572	2 3 4 5 6 7 8		20 21 22 23 24 25 26		6 7 8 9 10 11 12		19 20 21 22 23 24 25	Apr 7	21[e] 22 23 24 25 26 27	
	9 10 11 12 13 14 15	VAIŚĀKHA 2250	27 28 29 30 1 2 3		13 14 15 16 17 18 19	MUḤARRAM 1620	26 27 28 29 1[a] 2[â] 3		28[f] 29 30 1 2 3 4	MAY 2193
	16 17 18 19 20 21 22		5 6 7 8 9 10 11		20 21 22 23 24 25 26		4 5 6 7 8 9 10[b]	Apr 21	5 6 7 8 9 10 11	
	23 24 25 26 27 28 29		12 12 13 14 15 16 17	JYAISHṬHA 2115	27 28 29 30 31 1 2		11 12 13 14 15 16 17		12 13 14 15 16 17 18	
	30 31 1 2 3 4 5		18 19 20 21 22 23 24		3 4 5 6 7 8 9		18 19 20 21 22 23 24	May 5	19 20 21 22 23 24 25	
XORDĀD 1572	6 7 8 9 10 11 12	JYAISHṬHA 2250	25 26 28 29 30 1 2		10 11 12 13 14 15 16	ṢAFAR 1620	25 26 27 28 29 30 1		26 27 28 29 30 31 1	JUNE 2193
	13 14 15 16 17 18 19		3 4 5 6 7 8 9		17 18 19 20 21 22 23		2 3 4 5 6 7 8	May 19	2 3 4 5 6 7 8	
	20 21 22 23 24 25 26		10 11 12 13 14 15 16		24 25 26 27 28 29 30		9 10 11 12 13 14 15		9 10 11 12 13 14 15	
TĪR 1572	27 28 29 30 31 1 2		17 18 19 20 21 22 23	ĀSHĀḌHA 2115	31 1 2 3 4 5 6		16 17 18 19 20 21 22	Jun 2	16 17 18 19 20 21 22	
	3 4 5 6 7 8 9	ĀSHĀḌHA 2250	24 25 26 27 28 29 1		7 8 9 10 11 12 13	RABĪ' I 1620	23 24 25 26 27 28 29		23 24 25 26 27 28 29	
	10 11 12 13 14 15 16		2 3 4 5 6 7 8		14 15 16 17 18 19 20		1 2 3 4 5 6 7	Jun 16	30 1 2 3 4 5 6	JULY 2193
	17 18 19 20 21 22 23		9 9 10 11 12 13 14		21 22 23 24 25 26 27		8 9 10 11 12[c] 13 14		7 8 9 10 11 12 13	
	24 25 26 27 28 29 30		15 16 17 18 19 20 21	ŚRĀVAṆA 2115	28 29 30 31 32 1 2		15 16 17 18 19 20 21	Jun 30	14 15 16 17 18 19 20	
MORDĀD 1572	31 1 2 3 4 5 6	ŚRĀVAṆA 2250	22 24 25 26 27 28 29		3 4 5 6 7 8 9	RABĪ' II 1620	22 23 24 25 26 27 28		21 22 23 24 25 26 27	
	7 8 9 10 11 12 13		30 1 2 3 4 5 6		10 11 12 13 14 15 16		29 30 1 2 3 4 5	Jul 14	28 29 30 31 1 2 3	AUGUST 2193
	14 15 16 17 18 19 20		7 8 9 10 11 12 13		17 18 19 20 21 22 23		6 7 8 9 10 11 12		4 5 6 7 8 9 10	
	21 22 23 24 25 26 27		14 15 16 17 18 19 20		24 25 26 27 28 29 30		13 14 15 16 17 18 19	Jul 28	11 12 13 14 15 16 17	
SHAHRĪVAR 1572	28 29 30 31 1 2 3	BHĀDRAPADA 2250	21 22 23[c] 24 25 27 28	BHĀDRAPADA 2115	31 1 2 3 4 5 6	JUMĀDĀ I 1620	20 21 22 23 24 25 26		18 19 20 21 22 23 24	
	4 5 6 7 8 9 10		29 30 1 2 3 4[d] 5		7 8 9 10 11 12 13		27 28 29 30 1 2 3	Aug 11	25 26 27 28 29 30 31	
	11 12 13 14 15 16 17		5 6 7 8 9 10 11		14 15 16 17 18 19 20		4 5 6 7 8 9 10		1 2 3 4 5 6 7	SEPTEMBER 2193
	18 19 20 21 22 23 24		12 13 14 15 16 17 18		21 22 23 24 25 26 27		11 12 13 14 15 16 17	Aug 25	8 9 10 11 12 13 14	
	25 26 27 28 29 30 31		20 21 22 23 24 25 26	ĀŚVINA 2115	28 29 30 31 1 2 3		18 19 20 21 22 23 24		15 16 17 18 19 20 21	
MEHR 1572	1 2 3 4 5 6 7	ĀŚVINA 2250	27 28 29 30 1 2 3		4 5 6 7 8 9 10	JUMĀDĀ II 1620	25 26 27 28 29 30 1	Sep 8	22 23 24 25 26 27 28	
	8 9 10 11 12 13 14		4 5 6 7 8[e] 9[e] 10[e]		11 12 13 14 15 16 17		2 3 4 5 6 7 8		29 30 1 2 3 4 5	OCTOBER 2193
	15 16 17 18 19 20 21		11 12 13 14 15 16 17		18 19 20 21 22 23 24		9 10 11 12 13 14 15	Sep 22	6 7 8 9 10 11 12	
	22 23 24 25 26 27 28		18 19 20 21 23 24 25		25 26 27 28 29 30 31		16 17 18 19 20 21 22		13 14 15 16 17 18 19	
	29 30 1 2 3 4 5	KĀRTTIKA 2250	26 27 28 29 30 30 1[f]	KĀRTTIKA 2115	1 2 3 4 5 6 7	RAJAB 1620	23 24 25 26 27 28 29	Oct 6	20 21 22 23 24 25 26	
ĀBĀN 1572	6 7 8 9 10 11 12		2 3 4 5 6 7 8		8 9 10 11 12 13 14		30 1 2 3 4 5 6		27 28 29 30 31 1 2	NOVEMBER 2193
	13 14 15 16 17 18 19		9 10 11 12 13 14 15		15 16 17 18 19 20 21		7 8 9 10 11 12 13	Oct 20	3 4 5 6 7 8 9	
	20 21 22 23 24 25 26		17 18 19 20 21 22 23		22 23 24 25 26 27 28		14 15 16 17 18 19 20		10 11 12 13 14 15 16	
ĀZAR 1572	27 28 29 30 1 2 3		24 25 26 27 28 29 30	MĀRGAŚĪRA 2115	29 30 1 2 3 4 5	SHA'BĀN 1620	21 22 23 24 25 26 27[d]	Nov 3	17 18 19 20 21 22 23	
	4 5 6 7 8 9 10	MĀRGAŚĪRA 2250	1 2 3 3 4 5 6		6 7 8 9 10 11 12		28 29 1 2 3 4 5		24 25 26 27 28 29 30	
	11 12 13 14 15 16 17		7 8 10 11[g] 12 13 14		13 14 15 16 17 18 19		6 7 8 9 10 11 12	Nov 17	1[g] 2 3 4 5 6 7	DECEMBER 2193
	18 19 20 21 22 23 24		15 16 17 18 19 20 21		20 21 22 23 24 25 26		13 14 15 16 17 18 19		8 9 10 11 12 13 14	
DEY 1572	25 26 27 28 29 30 1		22 23 24 25 26 27 28	PAUSHA 2115	27 28 29 1 2 3 4	RAMAḌĀN 1620	20 21 22 23 24 25 26	Dec 1	15 16 17 18 19 20 21	
	2 3 4 5 6 7 8	PAUSHA 2250	29 30 1 2 3 4 5		5 6 7 8 9 10 11		27 28 29 1[e] 2 3 4		22 23 24 25[h] 26 27 28	
	9 10 11 12 13 14 15		6 7 8 9 10 11 12		12 13 14 15 16 17 18		5 6 7 8 9 10 11	Dec 15	29 30 31 1 2 3 4	

Persian: [a]New Year; [b]Sizdeh Bedar

Hindu lunar: [a]New Year (Vijaya); [b]Birthday of Rāma; [c]Birthday of Krishna; [d]Gaṇēśa Chaturthī; [e]Dashara; [f]Diwali; [g]Birthday of Vishnu; [h]Night of Śiva; [i]Holi

Hindu solar: [a]New Year (Kīlaka); [b]Pongal

Islamic: ‡Leap year; [a]New Year; [â]New Year (Arithmetic); [b]'Ashūrā'; [c]Prophet's Birthday; [d]Ascent of the Prophet; [e]Start of Ramaḍān; [f]'Id al-Fiṭr; [g]'Id al-'Aḍḥā

Gregorian: [a]Orthodox Christmas; [b]Julian New Year; [c]Ash Wednesday; [d]Feast of Orthodoxy; [e]Easter; [f]Orthodox Easter; [g]Advent; [h]Christmas

2194

Gregorian 2194 / ISO week / Julian Day

Month	Sun	Mon	Tue	Wed	Thu	Fri	Sat	Lunar Phases	ISO Week (Mon)	Julian Day (Sun noon)
January 2194	29	30	◐	1[a]	2	3	4	7:24	1	2522400
	5	○	7	8	9	10	11	22:36	2	2522407
	12	13	◑	15	16	17	18	6:56	3	2522414
	19	20	21	●	23	24	25	10:02	4	2522421
February 2194	26	27	28	◐	30	31	1	16:24	5	2522428
	2	3	4	○	6	7	8	11:14	6	2522435
	9	10	11	12	◑	14	15	4:10	7	2522442
	16	17	18	19	20	●	22	1:36	8	2522449
March 2194	23	24	25	26	◐	28	1	23:51	9	2522456
	2	3	4	5	6	○	8	1:17	10	2522463
	9	10	11	12	13	14	◑	1:01	11	2522470
	16	17	18	19	20[b]	21	●	14:20	12	2522477
	23	24	25	26	27	28	◐	6:56	13	2522484
April 2194	30	31	1	2	3	4	○	16:21	14	2522491
	6	7	8	9	10	11	12		15	2522498
	◑	14	15	16	17	18	19	19:49	16	2522505
	20	●	22	23	24	25	26	0:16	17	2522512
May 2194	◐	28	29	30	1	2	3	14:47	18	2522519
	4	○	6	7	8	9	10	7:52	19	2522526
	11	12	◑	14	15	16	17	11:24	20	2522533
	18	19	●	21	22	23	24	8:07	21	2522540
	25	26	◐	28	29	30	31	0:14	22	2522547
June 2194	1	2	○	4	5	6	7	23:26	23	2522554
	8	9	10	◑	12	13	14	23:19	24	2522561
	15	16	17	●	19	20[c]	21	15:01	25	2522568
	22	23	24	◐	26	27	28	11:47	26	2522575
July 2194	29	30	1	2	○	4	5	14:36	27	2522582
	6	7	8	9	10	◑	12	7:54	28	2522589
	13	14	15	16	●	18	19	22:05	29	2522596
	20	21	22	23	24	◐	26	1:40	30	2522603
August 2194	27	28	29	30	31	1	○	4:59	31	2522610
	3	4	5	6	7	8	◑	14:06	32	2522617
	10	11	12	13	14	15	●	6:23	33	2522624
	17	18	19	20	21	22	◐	17:55	34	2522631
	24	25	26	27	28	29	30		35	2522638
September 2194	○	1	2	3	4	5	6	18:10	36	2522645
	◑	8	9	10	11	12	13	19:18	37	2522652
	●	15	16	17	18	19	20	16:42	38	2522659
	21	◐[d]	23	24	25	26	27	12:11	39	2522666
October 2194	28	29	○	1	2	3	4	6:01	40	2522673
	5	6	◑	8	9	10	11	0:58	41	2522680
	12	13	●	15	16	17	18	5:36	42	2522687
	19	20	21	◐	23	24	25	7:35	43	2522694
November 2194	26	27	28	○	30	31	1	16:50	44	2522701
	2	3	4	◑	6	7	8	8:28	45	2522708
	9	10	11	●	13	14	15	21:20	46	2522715
	16	17	18	19	20	◐	22	2:36	47	2522722
	23	24	25	26	27	○	29	3:14	48	2522729
December 2194	30	1	2	3	◑	5	6	18:51	49	2522736
	7	8	9	10	11	●	13	15:38	50	2522743
	14	15	16	17	18	19	◐	19:35	51	2522750
	21[e]	22	23	24	25	26	○	13:48	52	2522757
	28	29	30	31	1	2	◑	8:30	1	2522764

Hebrew 5954/5955‡

ISO Week	Month	Sun	Mon	Tue	Wed	Thu	Fri	Sat	Molad
1		6	7	8	9	10	11	12	
2	Teveth 5954	13	14	15	16	17	18	19	
3		20	21	22	23	24	25	26	
4		27	28	29	1	2	3	4	Wed 4h54m1p
5	Shevat 5954	5	6	7	8	9	10	11	
6		12	13	14	15	16	17	18	
7		19	20	21	22	23	24	25	
8		26	27	28	29	30	1	2	Thu 17h38m2p
9	Adar 5954	3	4	5	6	7	8	9	
10		10	11	12	13	14[f]	15	16	
11		17	18	19	20	21	22	23	
12		24	25	26	27	28	29	1	Sat 6h22m3p
13		2	3	4	5	6	7	8	
14	Nisan 5954	9	10	11	12	13	14	15[g]	
15		16	17	18	19	20	21	22	
16		23	24	25	26	27	28	29	
17		30	1	2	3	4	5	6	Sun 19h6m4p
18	Iyyar 5954	7	8	9	10	11	12	13	
19		14	15	16	17	18	19	20	
20		21	22	23	24	25	26	27	
21		28	29	1	2	3	4	5	Tue 7h50m5p
22	Sivan 5954	6[h]	7	8	9	10	11	12	
23		13	14	15	16	17	18	19	
24		20	21	22	23	24	25	26	
25		27	28	29	30	1	2	3	Wed 20h34m6p
26	Tammuz 5954	4	5	6	7	8	9	10	
27		11	12	13	14	15	16	17	
28		18	19	20	21	22	23	24	
29		25	26	27	28	29	1	2	Fri 9h18m7p
30	Av 5954	3	4	5	6	7	8	9	
31		10[i]	11	12	13	14	15	16	
32		17	18	19	20	21	22	23	
33		24	25	26	27	28	29	30	
34		1	2	3	4	5	6	7	Sat 22h2m8p
35	Elul 5954	8	9	10	11	12	13	14	
36		15	16	17	18	19	20	21	
37		22	23	24	25	26	27	28	
38		29	1[a]	2[a]	3	4	5	6	Mon 10h46m9p
39	Tishri 5955	7	8	9	10[b]	11	12	13	
40		14	15[c]	16	17	18	19	20	
41		21	22	23	24	25	26	27	
42		28	29	30	1	2	3	4	Tue 23h30m10p
43	Heshvan 5955	5	6	7	8	9	10	11	
44		12	13	14	15	16	17	18	
45		19	20	21	22	23	24	25	
46		26	27	28	29	30	1	2	Thu 12h14m11p
47	Kislev 5955	3	4	5	6	7	8	9	
48		10	11	12	13	14	15	16	
49		17	18	19	20	21	22	23[d]	
50		24	25[e]	26[e]	27[e]	28[e]	29[e]	30[e]	
51	Teveth 5955	1[e]	2[e]	3	4	5	6	7	Sat 0h58m12p
52		8	9	10	11	12	13	14	
1		15	16	17	18	19	20	21	

Chinese Guǐ-Sì/Jiǎ-Wǔ‡

ISO Week	Month	Sun	Mon	Tue	Wed	Thu	Fri	Sat	Solar Term
1		6	7	8	9	10	11	12	
2	Month 12 Guǐ-Sì	13	14	15	16	17*	18	19	Xiǎo hán
3		20	21	22	23	24	25	26	
4		27	28	29	1[a]	2	3	4	Dà hán
5	Month 1 Jiǎ-Wǔ	5	6	7	8	9	10	11	
6		12	13	14	15[b]	16	17	18	Lì chūn
7		19	20	21	22	23	24	25	
8		26	27	28	29	30	1	2	Yǔ shuǐ
9	Month 2 Jiǎ-Wǔ	3	4	5	6	7	8	9	
10		10	11	12	13	14	15	16	Jīng zhé
11		17	18*	19	20	21	22	23	
12		24	25	26	27	28	29	1	Chūn fēn
13		2	3	4	5	6	7	8	
14	Month 3 Jiǎ-Wǔ	9	10	11	12	13	14[c]	15	Qīng míng
15		16	17	18	19	20	21	22	
16		23	24	25	26	27	28	29	
17		30	1	2	3	4	5	6	Gǔ yǔ
18	Leap Month 3 Jiǎ-Wǔ	7	8	9	10	11	12	13	
19		14	15	16	17	18	19*	20	Lì xià
20		21	22	23	24	25	26	27	
21		28	29	1	2	3	4	5	Xiǎo mǎn
22	Month 4 Jiǎ-Wǔ	6	7	8	9	10	11	12	
23		13	14	15	16	17	18	19	Máng zhòng
24		20	21	22	23	24	25	26	
25		27	28	29	1	2	3	4	Xià zhì
26	Month 5 Jiǎ-Wǔ	5[d]	6	7	8	9	10	11	
27		12	13	14	15	16	17	18	
28		19	20	21*	22	23	24	25	Xiǎo shǔ
29		26	27	28	29	30	1	2	
30	Month 6 Jiǎ-Wǔ	3	4	5	6	7	8	9	Dà shǔ
31		10	11	12	13	14	15	16	
32		17	18	19	20	21	22	23	Lì qiū
33		24	25	26	27	28	29	1	
34		2	3	4	5	6	7[e]	8	Chǔ shǔ
35	Month 7 Jiǎ-Wǔ	9	10	11	12	13	14	15[f]	
36		16	17	18	19	20	21	22*	
37		23	24	25	26	27	28	29	Bái lù
38		30	1	2	3	4	5	6	
39	Month 8 Jiǎ-Wǔ	7	8	9	10	11	12	13	Qiū fēn
40		14	15[g]	16	17	18	19	20	
41		21	22	23	24	25	26	27	Hán lù
42		28	29	1	2	3	4	5	
43	Month 9 Jiǎ-Wǔ	6	7	8	9[h]	10	11	12	Shuāng jiàng
44		13	14	15	16	17	18	19	
45		20	21	22	23*	24	25	26	Lì dōng
46		27	28	29	30	1	2	3	
47	Month 10 Jiǎ-Wǔ	4	5	6	7	8	9	10	Xiǎo xuě
48		11	12	13	14	15	16	17	
49		18	19	20	21	22	23	24	
50		25	26	27	28	29	1	2	Dà xuě
51	Month 11 Jiǎ-Wǔ	3	4	5	6	7	8	9	
52		10[i]	11	12	13	14	15	16	Dōng zhì
1		17	18	19	20	21	22	23	

Coptic 1910/1911‡ — Ethiopic 2186/2187‡

ISO Week	Coptic Month	Sun	Mon	Tue	Wed	Thu	Fri	Sat	Ethiopic Month
1	Koiak 1910	19	20	21	22	23	24	25	Tākhśāś 2186
2		26	27	28	29[c]	30	1	2	
3	Tōbe 1910	3	4	5	6[d]	7	8	9	Ṭer 2186
4		10	11[e]	12	13	14	15	16	
5		17	18	19	20	21	22	23	
6		24	25	26	27	28	29	30	
7	Meshir 1910	1	2	3	4	5	6	7	Yakātit 2186
8		8	9	10	11	12	13	14	
9		15	16	17	18	19	20	21	
10		22	23	24	25	26	27	28	
11		29	30	1	2	3	4	5	
12	Paremotep 1910	6	7	8	9	10	11	12	Magābit 2186
13		13	14	15	16	17	18	19	
14		20	21	22	23	24	25	26	
15		27	28	29	30	1	2	3	
16	Parmoute 1910	4[f]	5	6	7	8	9	10	Miyāzyā 2186
17		11	12	13	14	15	16	17	
18		18	19	20	21	22	23	24	
19		25	26	27	28	29[g]	30	1	
20	Pashons 1910	2	3	4	5	6	7	8	Genbot 2186
21		9	10	11	12	13	14	15	
22		16	17	18	19	20	21	22	
23		23	24	25	26	27	28	29	
24		30	1	2	3	4	5	6	
25	Paōne 1910	7	8	9	10	11	12	13	Sané 2186
26		14	15	16	17	18	19	20	
27		21	22	23	24	25	26	27	
28		28	29	30	1	2	3	4	
29	Epēp 1910	5	6	7	8	9	10	11	Hamlé 2186
30		12	13	14	15	16	17	18	
31		19	20	21	22	23	24	25	
32		26	27	28	29	30	1	2	
33	Mesorē 1910	3	4	5	6	7	8	9	Nahasé 2186
34		10	11	12	13[h]	14	15	16	
35		17	18	19	20	21	22	23	
36		24	25	26	27	28	29	30	
37	Epag. 1910 / Thoout 1911	1	2	3	4	5	1[a]	2	Pāg. 2186 / Maskaram 2187
38		3	4	5	6	7	8	9	
39		10	11	12	13	14	15	16	
40		17[b]	18	19	20	21	22	23	
41		24	25	26	27	28	29	30	
42	Paope 1911	1	2	3	4	5	6	7	Teqemt 2187
43		8	9	10	11	12	13	14	
44		15	16	17	18	19	20	21	
45		22	23	24	25	26	27	28	
46		29	30	1	2	3	4	5	
47	Athōr 1911	6	7	8	9	10	11	12	Hedār 2187
48		13	14	15	16	17	18	19	
49		20	21	22	23	24	25	26	
50		27	28	29	30	1	2	3	
51	Koiak 1911	4	5	6	7	8	9	10	Tākhśāś 2187
52		11	12	13	14	15	16	17	
1		18	19	20	21	22	23	24	

[a]New Year
[b]Spring (7:54)
[c]Summer (22:26)
[d]Autumn (15:42)
[e]Winter (15:17)
● New moon
◐ First quarter moon
○ Full moon
◑ Last quarter moon

‡Leap year
[a]New Year
[b]Yom Kippur
[c]Sukkot
[d]Winter starts
[e]Ḥanukkah
[f]Purim
[g]Passover
[h]Shavuot
[i]Fast of Av

‡Leap year
[a]New Year (4892, Horse)
[b]Lantern Festival
[c]Qīngmíng
[d]Dragon Festival
[e]Qīqiǎo
[f]Hungry Ghosts
[g]Mid-Autumn Festival
[h]Double-Ninth Festival
[i]Dōngzhì
*Start of 60-name cycle

‡Leap year
[a]New Year
[b]Building of the Cross
[c]Christmas
[d]Jesus's Circumcision
[e]Epiphany
[f]Easter
[g]Mary's Announcement
[h]Jesus's Transfiguration

PERSIAN (ASTRONOMICAL) 1572/1573‡

Month	Sun	Mon	Tue	Wed	Thu	Fri	Sat
DEY 1572	9	10	11	12	13	14	15
	16	17	18	19	20	21	22
	23	24	25	26	27	28	29
	30	1	2	3	4	5	6
BAHMAN 1572	7	8	9	10	11	12	13
	14	15	16	17	18	19	20
	21	22	23	24	25	26	27
	28	29	30	1	2	3	4
ESFAND 1572	5	6	7	8	9	10	11
	12	13	14	15	16	17	18
	19	20	21	22	23	24	25
	26	27	28	29	1[a]	2*	3
FARVARDĪN 1573	4	5	6	7	8	9	10
	11	12	13[b]	14	15	16	17
	18	19	20	21	22	23	24
	25	26	27	28	29	30	31
ORDĪBEHEŠT 1573	1	2	3	4	5	6	7
	8	9	10	11	12	13	14
	15	16	17	18	19	20	21
	22	23	24	25	26	27	28
	29	30	31	1	2	3	4
XORDĀD 1573	5	6	7	8	9	10	11
	12	13	14	15	16	17	18
	19	20	21	22	23	24	25
	26	27	28	29	30	31	1
TĪR 1573	2	3	4	5	6	7	8
	9	10	11	12	13	14	15
	16	17	18	19	20	21	22
	23	24	25	26	27	28	29
	30	31	1	2	3	4	5
MORDĀD 1573	6	7	8	9	10	11	12
	13	14	15	16	17	18	19
	20	21	22	23	24	25	26
	27	28	29	30	31	1	2
SHAHRĪVAR 1573	3	4	5	6	7	8	9
	10	11	12	13	14	15	16
	17	18	19	20	21	22	23
	24	25	26	27	28	29	30
	31	1	2	3	4	5	6
MEHR 1573	7	8	9	10	11	12	13
	14	15	16	17	18	19	20
	21	22	23	24	25	26	27
	28	29	30	1	2	3	4
ĀBĀN 1573	5	6	7	8	9	10	11
	12	13	14	15	16	17	18
	19	20	21	22	23	24	25
	26	27	28	29	30	1	2
ĀZAR 1573	3	4	5	6	7	8	9
	10	11	12	13	14	15	16
	17	18	19	20	21	22	23
	24	25	26	27	28	29	30
DEY 1573	1	2	3	4	5	6	7
	8	9	10	11	12	13	14

‡Leap year
[a]New Year (or next day)
*Near New Year: 1′59″
[b]Sizdeh Bedar

HINDU LUNAR 2250/2251‡

Month	Sun	Mon	Tue	Wed	Thu	Fri	Sat
PAUSHA 2250	6	7	8	9	10	11	12
	13	15	16	17	18	19	20
	21	22	23	24	25	26	26
	27	28	29	30	1	2	3
MĀGHA 2250	4	5	6	7	8	10	11
	12	13	14	15	16	17	18
	19	20	21	22	23	24	25
	26	27	28	29[h]	29	30	2
PHĀLGUNA 2250	3	4	5	6	7	8	9
	10	11	12	13	14[i]	16	17
	17	18	19	20	21	22	23
	24	25	26	27	28	29	30
CHAITRA 2251	1[a]	2	3	4	5	6	8
	9[b]	10	11	12	13	14	15
	16	17	18	19	20	21	21
	22	23	24	25	26	27	28
VAIŚĀKHA 2251	29	30	2	3	4	5	6
	7	8	9	10	11	12	13
	14	15	16	17	18	19	20
	21	22	23	24	25	26	27
	28	29	30	1	2	3	5
JYAISHTHA 2251	6	7	8	9	10	11	12
	13	14	15	16	16	17	18
	19	20	21	22	23	24	25
	26	28	29	30	1	2	3
LEAP ĀSHĀDHA 2251	4	5	6	7	8	9	10
	11	12	13	14	15	16	17
	18	19	20	21	22	23	24
	25	26	27	28	29	1	2
ĀSHĀDHA 2251	3	4	5	6	7	8	9
	10	11	12	13	13	14	15
	16	17	18	19	20	21	23
	24	25	26	27	28	29	30
ŚRĀVANA 2251	1	2	3	4	5	6	7
	8	9	10	11	12	13	14
	15	16	17	18	19	20	21
	22	23[c]	24	25	27	28	29
	30	1	2	3	4[d]	5	6
BHĀDRAPADA 2251	7	8	9	9	10	11	12
	13	14	15	16	17	18	20
	21	22	23	24	25	26	27
	28	29	30	1	2	3	4
ĀŚVINA 2251	5	6	7	8[e]	9[e]	10[e]	11
	12	13	14	15	16	17	18
	19	20	21	22	24	25	26
	27	28	29	30	1[f]	2	3
KĀRTTIKA 2251	4	4	5	6	7	8	9
	10	11	12	13	14	15	16
	18	19	20	21	22	23	24
	25	26	27	28	29	30	1
MĀRGAŚĪRA 2251	2	3	4	5	6	7	7
	8	10	11[g]	12	13	14	15
	16	17	18	19	20	21	22

‡Leap year
[a]New Year (Jaya)
[b]Birthday of Rāma
[c]Birthday of Krishna
[d]Ganēśa Chaturthī
[e]Dashara
[f]Diwali
[g]Birthday of Vishnu
[h]Night of Śiva
[i]Holi

HINDU SOLAR 2115/2116

Month	Sun	Mon	Tue	Wed	Thu	Fri	Sat
PAUSHA 2115	12	13	14	15	16	17	18
	19	20	21	22	23	24	25
	26	27	28	29	30	1[b]	2
MĀGHA 2115	3	4	5	6	7	8	9
	10	11	12	13	14	15	16
	17	18	19	20	21	22	23
	24	25	26	27	28	29	1
PHĀLGUNA 2115	2	3	4	5	6	7	8
	9	10	11	12	13	14	15
	16	17	18	19	20	21	22
	23	24	25	26	27	28	29
	30	1	2	3	4	5	6
CHAITRA 2115	7	8	9	10	11	12	13
	14	15	16	17	18	19	20
	21	22	23	24	25	26	27
	28	29	30	1[a]	2	3	4
VAIŚĀKHA 2116	5	6	7	8	9	10	11
	12	13	14	15	16	17	18
	19	20	21	22	23	24	25
	26	27	28	29	30	31	1
JYAISHTHA 2116	2	3	4	5	6	7	8
	9	10	11	12	13	14	15
	16	17	18	19	20	21	22
	23	24	25	26	27	28	29
	30	31	32	1	2	3	4
ĀSHĀDHA 2116	5	6	7	8	9	10	11
	12	13	14	15	16	17	18
	19	20	21	22	23	24	25
	26	27	28	29	30	31	1
ŚRĀVANA 2116	2	3	4	5	6	7	8
	9	10	11	12	13	14	15
	16	17	18	19	20	21	22
	23	24	25	26	27	28	29
	30	31	32	1	2	3	4
BHĀDRAPADA 2116	5	6	7	8	9	10	11
	12	13	14	15	16	17	18
	19	20	21	22	23	24	25
	26	27	28	29	30	31	1
ĀŚVINA 2116	2	3	4	5	6	7	8
	9	10	11	12	13	14	15
	16	17	18	19	20	21	22
	23	24	25	26	27	28	29
	30	1	2	3	4	5	6
KĀRTTIKA 2116	7	8	9	10	11	12	13
	14	15	16	17	18	19	20
	21	22	23	24	25	26	27
	28	29	30	1	2	3	4
MĀRGAŚĪRA 2116	5	6	7	8	9	10	11
	12	13	14	15	16	17	18
	19	20	21	22	23	24	25
	26	27	28	29	1	2	3
PAUSHA 2116	4	5	6	7	8	9	10
	11	12	13	14	15	16	17

[a]New Year (Saumya)
[b]Pongal

ISLAMIC (ASTRONOMICAL) 1620‡/1621‡

Month	Sun	Mon	Tue	Wed	Thu	Fri	Sat
RAMAḌĀN 1620	5	6	7	8	9	10	11
	12	13	14	15	16	17	18
	19	20	21	22	23	24	25
	26	27	28	29	30	1[f]	2
SHAWWĀL 1620	3	4	5	6	7	8	9
	10	11	12	13	14	15	16
	17	18	19	20	21	22	23
	24	25	26	27	28	29	1
DHU AL-QA'DA 1620	2	3	4	5	6	7	8
	9	10	11	12	13	14	15
	16	17	18	19	20	21	22
	23	24	25	26	27	28	29
	30	1	2	3	4	5	6
DHU AL-ḤIJJA 1620	7	8	9	10[g]	11	12	13
	14	15	16	17	18	19	20
	21	22	23	24	25	26	27
	28	29	1[a]	2	3	4	5
MUḤARRAM 1621	6	7	8	9	10[b]	11	12
	13	14	15	16	17	18	19
	20	21	22	23	24	25	26
	27	28	29	1	2	3	4
ṢAFAR 1621	5	6	7	8	9	10	11
	12	13	14	15	16	17	18
	19	20	21	22	23	24	25
	26	27	28	29	30	1	2
RABĪ' I 1621	3	4	5	6	7	8	9
	10	11	12[c]	13	14	15	16
	17	18	19	20	21	22	23
	24	25	26	27	28	29	1
RABĪ' II 1621	2	3	4	5	6	7	8
	9	10	11	12	13	14	15
	16	17	18	19	20	21	22
	23	24	25	26	27	28	29
	30	1	2	3	4	5	6
JUMĀDĀ I 1621	7	8	9	10	11	12	13
	14	15	16	17	18	19	20
	21	22	23	24	25	26	27
	28	29	30	1	2	3	4
JUMĀDĀ II 1621	5	6	7	8	9	10	11
	12	13	14	15	16	17	18
	19	20	21	22	23	24	25
	26	27	28	29	30	1	2
RAJAB 1621	3	4	5	6	7	8	9
	10	11	12	13	14	15	16
	17	18	19	20	21	22	23
	24	25	26	27[d]	28	29	1
SHA'BĀN 1621	2	3	4	5	6	7	8
	9	10	11	12	13	14	15
	16	17	18	19	20	21	22
	23	24	25	26	27	28	29
RAMAḌĀN 1621	1[e]	2	3	4	5	6	7
	8	9	10	11	12	13	14
	15	16	17	18	19	20	21

‡Leap year
[a]New Year
[b]'Ashūrā'
[c]Prophet's Birthday
[d]Ascent of the Prophet
[e]Start of Ramaḍān
[f]'Id al-Fiṭr
[g]'Id al-'Aḍḥā

GREGORIAN 2194

Julian (Sun)	Sun	Mon	Tue	Wed	Thu	Fri	Sat	Month
Dec 15	29	30	31	1	2	3	4	JANUARY 2194
	5	6	7	8[a]	9	10	11	
Dec 29	12	13	14	15[b]	16	17	18	
	19	20	21	22	23	24	25	
Jan 12	26	27	28	29	30	31	1	
	2	3	4	5	6	7	8	FEBRUARY 2194
Jan 26	9	10	11	12	13	14	15	
	16	17	18	19[c]	20	21	22	
Feb 9	23	24	25	26	27	28	1	
	2[d]	3	4	5	6	7	8	MARCH 2194
Feb 23	9	10	11	12	13	14	15	
	16	17	18	19	20	21	22	
Mar 9	23	24	25	26	27	28	29	
	30	31	1	2	3	4	5	APRIL 2194
Mar 23	6[e]	7	8	9	10	11	12	
	13[f]	14	15	16	17	18	19	
Apr 6	20	21	22	23	24	25	26	
	27	28	29	30	1	2	3	MAY 2194
Apr 20	4	5	6	7	8	9	10	
	11	12	13	14	15	16	17	
May 4	18	19	20	21	22	23	24	
	25	26	27	28	29	30	31	
May 18	1	2	3	4	5	6	7	JUNE 2194
	8	9	10	11	12	13	14	
Jun 1	15	16	17	18	19	20	21	
	22	23	24	25	26	27	28	
Jun 15	29	30	1	2	3	4	5	JULY 2194
	6	7	8	9	10	11	12	
Jun 29	13	14	15	16	17	18	19	
	20	21	22	23	24	25	26	
Jul 13	27	28	29	30	31	1	2	AUGUST 2194
	3	4	5	6	7	8	9	
Jul 27	10	11	12	13	14	15	16	
	17	18	19	20	21	22	23	
Aug 10	24	25	26	27	28	29	30	
	31	1	2	3	4	5	6	SEPTEMBER 2194
Aug 24	7	8	9	10	11	12	13	
	14	15	16	17	18	19	20	
Sep 7	21	22	23	24	25	26	27	
	28	29	30	1	2	3	4	OCTOBER 2194
Sep 21	5	6	7	8	9	10	11	
	12	13	14	15	16	17	18	
Oct 5	19	20	21	22	23	24	25	
	26	27	28	29	30	31	1	NOVEMBER 2194
Oct 19	2	3	4	5	6	7	8	
	9	10	11	12	13	14	15	
Nov 2	16	17	18	19	20	21	22	
	23	24	25	26	27	28	29	
Nov 16	30[g]	1	2	3	4	5	6	DECEMBER 2194
	7	8	9	10	11	12	13	
Nov 30	14	15	16	17	18	19	20	
	21	22	23	24	25[h]	26	27	
Dec 14	28	29	30	31	1	2	3	

[a]Orthodox Christmas
[b]Julian New Year
[c]Ash Wednesday
[d]Feast of Orthodoxy
[e]Easter
[f]Orthodox Easter
[g]Advent
[h]Christmas

2195

Month	Sun	Mon	Tue	Wed	Thu	Fri	Sat	Lunar Phases	ISO WEEK (Mon)	JULIAN DAY (Sun noon)
GREGORIAN 2195										
	28	29	30	31	1[a]	2	◑	8:30	1	2522764
	4	5	6	7	8	9	10		2	2522771
JANUARY 2195	●	12	13	14	15	16	17	11:22	3	2522778
	18	◐	20	21	22	23	24	9:25	4	2522785
	25	○	27	28	29	30	31	0:45	5	2522792
	1	◑	3	4	5	6	7	1:16	6	2522799
FEBRUARY 2195	8	9	●	11	12	13	14	6:38	7	2522806
	15	16	◐	18	19	20	21	20:01	8	2522813
	22	23	○	25	26	27	28	12:05	9	2522820
	1	2	◑	4	5	6	7	20:20	10	2522827
MARCH 2195	8	9	10	●	12	13	14	23:32	11	2522834
	15	16	17	18	◐	20[b]	21	4:02	12	2522841
	22	23	24	○	26	27	28	23:43	13	2522848
	29	30	31	1	◑	3	4	16:24	14	2522855
APRIL 2195	5	6	7	8	9	●	11	13:08	15	2522862
	12	13	14	15	16	◐	18	10:29	16	2522869
	19	20	21	22	23	○	25	11:53	17	2522876
	26	27	28	29	30	1	◑	11:44	18	2522883
	3	4	5	6	7	8	●	23:41	19	2522890
MAY 2195	10	11	12	13	14	15	◐	16:29	20	2522897
	17	18	19	20	21	22	23		21	2522904
	○	25	26	27	28	29	30	0:59	22	2522911
	31	◑	2	3	4	5	6	4:51	23	2522918
JUNE 2195	7	●	9	10	11	12	13	8:03	24	2522925
	◐	15	16	17	18	19	20	23:09	25	2522932
	21[c]	○	23	24	25	26	27	15:18	26	2522939
	28	29	◑	1	2	3	4	18:57	27	2522946
JULY 2195	5	6	●	8	9	10	11	15:19	28	2522953
	12	13	◐	15	16	17	18	7:33	29	2522960
	19	20	21	○	23	24	25	6:38	30	2522967
	26	27	28	29	◑	31	1	6:05	31	2522974
	2	3	4	●	6	7	8	22:23	32	2522981
AUGUST 2195	9	10	11	◐	13	14	15	18:39	33	2522988
	16	17	18	19	○	21	22	22:15	34	2522995
	23	24	25	26	27	◑	29	14:53	35	2523002
	30	31	1	2	3	●	5	6:05	36	2523009
SEPTEMBER 2195	6	7	8	9	10	◐	12	9:10	37	2523016
	13	14	15	16	17	18	○	13:21	38	2523023
	20	21	22[d]	23	24	25	◑	22:15	39	2523030
	27	28	29	30	1	2	●	15:15	40	2523037
OCTOBER 2195	4	5	6	7	8	9	10		41	2523044
	◐	12	13	14	15	16	17	3:10	42	2523051
	18	○	20	21	22	23	24	3:27	43	2523058
	25	◑	27	28	29	30	31	5:07	44	2523065
	1	●	3	4	5	6	7	2:45	45	2523072
NOVEMBER 2195	8	◐	10	11	12	13	14	23:38	46	2523079
	15	16	○	18	19	20	21	16:34	47	2523086
	22	23	◑	25	26	27	28	12:26	48	2523093
	29	30	●	2	3	4	5	17:15	49	2523100
DECEMBER 2195	6	7	8	◐	10	11	12	20:41	50	2523107
	13	14	15	16	○	18	19	4:56	51	2523114
	20	21[e]	22	◑	24	25	26	21:08	52	2523121
	27	28	29	30	●	1	2	10:46	53	2523128

ISO WEEK	Month	Sun	Mon	Tue	Wed	Thu	Fri	Sat	Molad
	HEBREW 5955‡/5956								
1	TEVETH 5955	15	16	17	18	19	20	21	
2		22	23	24	25	26	27	28	
3		29	1	2	3	4	5	6	Sun 13h42m13p
4	SHEVAT 5955	7	8	9	10	11	12	13	
5		14	15	16	17	18	19	20	
6		21	22	23	24	25	26	27	
7		28	29	30	1	2	3	4	Tue 2h26m14p
8	ADAR I 5955	5	6	7	8	9	10	11	
9		12	13	14	15	16	17	18	
10		19	20	21	22	23	24	25	
11		26	27	28	29	30	1	2	Wed 15h10m15p
12	ADAR II 5955	3	4	5	6	7	8	9	
13		10	11	12	13	14[f]	15	16	
14		17	18	19	20	21	22	23	
15		24	25	26	27	28	29	1	Fri 3h54m16p
16		2	3	4	5	6	7	8	
17	NISAN 5955	9	10	11	12	13	14	15[g]	
18		16	17	18	19	20	21	22	
19		23	24	25	26	27	28	29	
20		30	1	2	3	4	5	6	Sat 16h38m17p
21	IYAR 5955	7	8	9	10	11	12	13	
22		14	15	16	17	18	19	20	
23		21	22	23	24	25	26	27	
24		28	29	1	2	3	4	5	Mon 5h23m0p
25	SIVAN 5955	6[h]	7	8	9	10	11	12	
26		13	14	15	16	17	18	19	
27		20	21	22	23	24	25	26	
28		27	28	29	30	1	2	3	Tue 18h7m1p
29	TAMMUZ 5955	4	5	6	7	8	9	10	
30		11	12	13	14	15	16	17	
31		18	19	20	21	22	23	24	
32		25	26	27	28	29	1	2	Thu 6h51m2p
33	AV 5955	3	4	5	6	7	8	9	
34		10[i]	11	12	13	14	15	16	
35		17	18	19	20	21	22	23	
36		24	25	26	27	28	29	30	
37		1	2	3	4	5	6	7	Fri 19h35m3p
38	ELUL 5955	8	9	10	11	12	13	14	
39		15	16	17	18	19	20	21	
40		22	23	24	25	26	27	28	
41		29	1[a]	2[a]	3	4	5	6	Sun 8h19m4p
42	TISHRI 5956	7	8	9	10[b]	11	12	13	
43		14	15[c]	16	17	18	19	20	
44		21	22	23	24	25	26	27	
45		28	29	30	1	2	3	4	Mon 21h3m5p
46	ḤESHVAN 5956	5	6	7	8	9	10	11	
47		12	13	14	15	16	17	18	
48		19	20	21	22	23	24	25	
49		26	27	28	29	30	1	2	
50	KISLEV 5956	3	4[d]	5	6	7	8	9	Wed 9h47m6p
51		10	11	12	13	14	15	16	
52		17	18	19	20	21	22	23	
53		24	25[e]	26[e]	27[e]	28[e]	29[e]	30[e]	

ISO WEEK	Month	Sun	Mon	Tue	Wed	Thu	Fri	Sat	Solar Term
	CHINESE Jiǎ-Wǔ‡/Yǐ-Wèi								
1	MONTH 11 Jiǎ-Wǔ	17	18	19	20	21	22	23	
2		24*	25	26	27	28	29	30	Xiǎo hán
3	MONTH 12 Jiǎ-Wǔ	1	2	3	4	5	6	7	
4		8	9	10	11	12	13	14	Dà hán
5		15	16	17	18	19	20	21	
6		22	23	24	25	26	27	28	Lì chūn
7		29	30	1[a]	2	3	4	5	
8	MONTH 1 Yǐ-Wèi	6	7	8	9	10	11	12	Yǔ shuǐ
9		13	14	15[b]	16	17	18	19	
10		20	21	22	23	24*	25	26	Jīng zhé
11		27	28	29	30	1	2	3	
12	MONTH 2 Yǐ-Wèi	4	5	6	7	8	9	10	Chūn fēn
13		11	12	13	14	15	16	17	
14		18	19	20	21	22	23	24	
15		25[c]	26	27	28	29	1	2	Qīng míng
16	MONTH 3 Yǐ-Wèi	3	4	5	6	7	8	9	
17		10	11	12	13	14	15	16	Gǔ yǔ
18		17	18	19	20	21	22	23	
19		24	25*	26	27	28	29	30	Lì xià
20		1	2	3	4	5	6	7	
21	MONTH 4 Yǐ-Wèi	8	9	10	11	12	13	14	Xiǎo mǎn
22		15	16	17	18	19	20	21	
23		22	23	24	25	26	27	28	Máng zhòng
24		29	1	2	3	4	5[d]	6	
25	MONTH 5 Yǐ-Wèi	7	8	9	10	11	12	13	
26		14	15	16	17	18	19	20	Xià zhì
27		21	22	23	24	25	26*	27	
28		28	29	1	2	3	4	5	Xiǎo shǔ
29	MONTH 6 Yǐ-Wèi	6	7	8	9	10	11	12	
30		13	14	15	16	17	18	19	Dà shǔ
31		20	21	22	23	24	25	26	
32		27	28	29	30	1	2	3	Lì qiū
33	MONTH 7 Yǐ-Wèi	4	5	6	7[e]	8	9	10	
34		11	12	13	14	15[f]	16	17	
35		18	19	20	21	22	23	24	Chǔ shǔ
36		25	26	27*	28	29	1	2	
37	MONTH 8 Yǐ-Wèi	3	4	5	6	7	8	9	Bái lù
38		10	11	12	13	14	15[g]	16	
39		17	18	19	20	21	22	23	Qiū fēn
40		24	25	26	27	28	29	1	
41	MONTH 9 Yǐ-Wèi	2	3	4	5	6	7	8	Hán lù
42		9[h]	10	11	12	13	14	15	
43		16	17	18	19	20	21	22	Shuāng jiàng
44		23	24	25	26	27	28	29*	
45		30	1	2	3	4	5	6	Lì dōng
46	MONTH 10 Yǐ-Wèi	7	8	9	10	11	12	13	
47		14	15	16	17	18	19	20	
48		21	22	23	24	25	26	27	Xiǎo xuě
49		28	29	30	1	2	3	4	
50	MONTH 11 Yǐ-Wèi	5	6	7	8	9	10	11	Dà xuě
51		12	13	14	15	16	17	18	
52		19	20	21[i]	22	23	24	25	Dōng zhì
53		26	27	28	29*	1	2	3	

ISO WEEK	Coptic Month	Sun	Mon	Tue	Wed	Thu	Fri	Sat	Ethiopic Month
	COPTIC 1911‡/1912								ETHIOPIC 2187‡/2188
1	KOIAK 1911	18	19	20	21	22	23	24	TĀKHŚĀŚ 2187
2		25	26	27	28	29[c]	30	1	
3	ṬŌBE 1911	2	3	4	5	6[d]	7	8	ṬER 2187
4		9	10	11[e]	12	13	14	15	
5		16	17	18	19	20	21	22	
6		23	24	25	26	27	28	29	
7		30	1	2	3	4	5	6	
8	MESHIR 1911	7	8	9	10	11	12	13	YAKĀTIT 2187
9		14	15	16	17	18	19	20	
10		21	22	23	24	25	26	27	
11		28	29	30	1	2	3	4	
12	PAREMOTEP 1911	5	6	7	8	9	10	11	MAGĀBIT 2187
13		12	13	14	15	16	17	18	
14		19	20	21	22	23	24	25	
15		26	27	28	29	30	1	2	
16	PARMOUTE 1911	3	4	5	6	7	8	9	MIYĀZYĀ 2187
17		10	11	12	13	14	15	16	
18		17	18	19	20	21	22	23	
19		24[f]	25	26	27	28	29[g]	30	
20		1	2	3	4	5	6	7	
21	PASHONS 1911	8	9	10	11	12	13	14	GENBOT 2187
22		15	16	17	18	19	20	21	
23		22	23	24	25	26	27	28	
24		29	30	1	2	3	4	5	
25	PAŌNE 1911	6	7	8	9	10	11	12	SANĒ 2187
26		13	14	15	16	17	18	19	
27		20	21	22	23	24	25	26	
28		27	28	29	30	1	2	3	
29	EPĒP 1911	4	5	6	7	8	9	10	HAMLĒ 2187
30		11	12	13	14	15	16	17	
31		18	19	20	21	22	23	24	
32		25	26	27	28	29	30	1	
33	MESORĒ 1911	2	3	4	5	6	7	8	NAḤASĒ 2187
34		9	10	11	12	13[h]	14	15	
35		16	17	18	19	20	21	22	
36		23	24	25	26	27	28	29	
37	EPAG. 1911	30	1	2	3	4	5	6	PĀG. 2187
38		1[a]	2	3	4	5	6	7	
39	THOOUT 1912	8	9	10	11	12	13	14	MASKARAM 2188
40		15	16	17[b]	18	19	20	21	
41		22	23	24	25	26	27	28	
42		29	30	1	2	3	4	5	
43	PAOPE 1912	6	7	8	9	10	11	12	ṬEQEMT 2188
44		13	14	15	16	17	18	19	
45		20	21	22	23	24	25	26	
46		27	28	29	30	1	2	3	
47	ATHŌR 1912	4	5	6	7	8	9	10	HEDĀR 2188
48		11	12	13	14	15	16	17	
49		18	19	20	21	22	23	24	
50		25	26	27	28	29	30	1	
51	KOIAK 1912	2	3	4	5	6	7	8	TĀKHŚĀŚ 2188
52		9	10	11	12	13	14	15	
53		16	17	18	19	20	21	22	

[a]New Year
[b]Spring (13:30)
[c]Summer (4:13)
[d]Autumn (21:38)
[e]Winter (21:10)
● New moon
◐ First quarter moon
○ Full moon
◑ Last quarter moon

‡Leap year
[a]New Year
[b]Yom Kippur
[c]Sukkot
[d]Winter starts
[e]Ḥanukkah
[f]Purim
[g]Passover
[h]Shavuot
[i]Fast of Av

‡Leap year
[a]New Year (4893, Sheep)
[b]Lantern Festival
[c]Qīngmíng
[d]Dragon Festival
[e]Qīqiǎo
[f]Hungry Ghosts
[g]Mid-Autumn Festival
[h]Double-Ninth Festival
[i]Dōngzhì
*Start of 60-name cycle

‡Leap year
[a]New Year
[b]Building of the Cross
[c]Christmas
[d]Jesus's Circumcision
[e]Epiphany
[f]Easter
[g]Mary's Announcement
[h]Jesus's Transfiguration

PERSIAN (ASTRONOMICAL) 1573‡/1574

Month	Sun	Mon	Tue	Wed	Thu	Fri	Sat
DEY 1573	8	9	10	11	12	13	14
	15	16	17	18	19	20	21
	22	23	24	25	26	27	28
BAHMAN 1573	29	30	1	2	3	4	5
	6	7	8	9	10	11	12
	13	14	15	16	17	18	19
	20	21	22	23	24	25	26
ESFAND 1573	27	28	29	30	1	2	3
	4	5	6	7	8	9	10
	11	12	13	14	15	16	17
	18	19	20	21	22	23	24
FARVARDĪN 1574	25	26	27	28	29	30	1[a]
	2	3	4	5	6	7	8
	9	10	11	12	13[b]	14	15
	16	17	18	19	20	21	22
	23	24	25	26	27	28	29
ORDĪBEHEŠT 1574	30	31	1	2	3	4	5
	6	7	8	9	10	11	12
	13	14	15	16	17	18	19
	20	21	22	23	24	25	26
XORDĀD 1574	27	28	29	30	31	1	2
	3	4	5	6	7	8	9
	10	11	12	13	14	15	16
	17	18	19	20	21	22	23
	24	25	26	27	28	29	30
TĪR 1574	31	1	2	3	4	5	6
	7	8	9	10	11	12	13
	14	15	16	17	18	19	20
	21	22	23	24	25	26	27
MORDĀD 1574	28	29	30	31	1	2	3
	4	5	6	7	8	9	10
	11	12	13	14	15	16	17
	18	19	20	21	22	23	24
	25	26	27	28	29	30	31
SHAHRĪVAR 1574	1	2	3	4	5	6	7
	8	9	10	11	12	13	14
	15	16	17	18	19	20	21
	22	23	24	25	26	27	28
MEHR 1574	29	30	31	1	2	3	4
	5	6	7	8	9	10	11
	12	13	14	15	16	17	18
	19	20	21	22	23	24	25
ĀBĀN 1574	26	27	28	29	30	1	2
	3	4	5	6	7	8	9
	10	11	12	13	14	15	16
	17	18	19	20	21	22	23
	24	25	26	27	28	29	30
ĀZAR 1574	1	2	3	4	5	6	7
	8	9	10	11	12	13	14
	15	16	17	18	19	20	21
	22	23	24	25	26	27	28
DEY 1574	29	30	1	2	3	4	5
	6	7	8	9	10	11	12

‡Leap year
[a]New Year
[b]Sizdeh Bedar

HINDU LUNAR 2251‡/2252

Month	Sun	Mon	Tue	Wed	Thu	Fri	Sat
MĀRGAŚIRA 2251	16	17	18	19	20	21	22
	24	25	25	26	27	28	29
PAUSHA 2251	30	1	2	3	4	5	6
	7	8	9	10	11	12	13
	14	16	17	18	19	20	21
	22	23	24	25	26	27	28
MĀGHA 2251	28	29	30	1	2	3	4
	5	6	7	8	9	11	12
	13	14	15	16	17	18	19
	20	21	22	23	24	25	26
PHĀLGUNA 2251	27	28	29[h]	30	1	2	3
	4	5	6	7	8	9	10
	11	12	13	15[i]	16	17	18
	19	20	21	21	22	23	24
CHAITRA 2252	25	26	27	28	29	30	1[a]
	2	3	4	5	6	7	9[b]
	10	11	12	13	14	15	16
	17	18	19	20	21	22	23
	24	25	25	26	27	28	29
VAIŚĀKHA 2252	1	2	3	4	5	6	7
	8	9	10	11	12	14	15
	15	16	17	18	19	20	21
	22	23	24	25	26	27	28
JYAISHTHA 2252	29	30	1	2	3	5	6
	7	8	9	10	11	12	13
	14	15	16	17	18	19	20
	21	21	22	23	24	25	27
ĀSHĀḌHA 2252	28	29	30	1	2	3	4
	5	6	7	9	10	11	12
	13	13	14	15	16	17	18
	19	20	21	22	23	24	25
ŚRĀVAṆA 2252	26	27	28	29	1	2	3
	4	5	6	7	8	9	10
	11	12	13	14	15	16	17
	18	19	19	20	22	23[c]	24
BHĀDRAPADA 2252	25	26	27	28	29	30	1
	2	3[d]	5	6	7	8	9
	9	10	11	12	13	14	15
	16	17	18	19	20	21	22
	23	24	25	27	28	29	30
ĀŚVINA 2252	1	2	3	4	5	6	7
	8[e]	9[e]	10[e]	11	12	13	13
	14	15	16	17	18	20	21
	22	23	24	25	26	27	28
KĀRTTIKA 2252	29	30	1[f]	2	3	4	5
	6	7	8	9	10	11	12
	13	14	15	16	17	18	19
	20	21	22	23	25	26	27
MĀRGAŚIRA 2252	28	29	30	1	2	3	4
	5	6	6	7	8	9	10
	11[g]	12	13	14	15	16	17
	19	20	21	22	23	24	25
	26	27	28	29	30	1	2

‡Leap year
[a]New Year (Manmatha)
[b]Birthday of Rāma
[c]Birthday of Krishna
[d]Ganēśa Chaturthī
[e]Dashara
[f]Diwali
[g]Birthday of Vishnu
[h]Night of Śiva
[i]Holi

HINDU SOLAR 2116/2117‡

Month	Sun	Mon	Tue	Wed	Thu	Fri	Sat
PAUSHA 2116	11	12	13	14	15	16	17
	18	19	20	21	22	23	24
MĀGHA 2116	25	26	27	28	29	30	1[b]
	2	3	4	5	6	7	8
	9	10	11	12	13	14	15
	16	17	18	19	20	21	22
	23	24	25	26	27	28	29
PHĀLGUNA 2116	1	2	3	4	5	6	7
	8	9	10	11	12	13	14
	15	16	17	18	19	20	21
	22	23	24	25	26	27	28
CHAITRA 2116	29	30	1	2	3	4	5
	6	7	8	9	10	11	12
	13	14	15	16	17	18	19
	20	21	22	23	24	25	26
VAIŚĀKHA 2117	27	28	29	30	1[a]	2	3
	4	5	6	7	8	9	10
	11	12	13	14	15	16	17
	18	19	20	21	22	23	24
	25	26	27	28	29	30	31
JYAISHTHA 2117	1	2	3	4	5	6	7
	8	9	10	11	12	13	14
	15	16	17	18	19	20	21
	22	23	24	25	26	27	28
ĀSHĀḌHA 2117	29	30	31	32	1	2	3
	4	5	6	7	8	9	10
	11	12	13	14	15	16	17
	18	19	20	21	22	23	24
	25	26	27	28	29	30	31
ŚRĀVAṆA 2117	1	2	3	4	5	6	7
	8	9	10	11	12	13	14
	15	16	17	18	19	20	21
	22	23	24	25	26	27	28
BHĀDRAPADA 2117	29	30	31	32	1	2	3
	4	5	6	7	8	9	10
	11	12	13	14	15	16	17
	18	19	20	21	22	23	24
	25	26	27	28	29	30	31
ĀŚVINA 2117	1	2	3	4	5	6	7
	8	9	10	11	12	13	14
	15	16	17	18	19	20	21
	22	23	24	25	26	27	28
KĀRTTIKA 2117	29	30	1	2	3	4	5
	6	7	8	9	10	11	12
	13	14	15	16	17	18	19
	20	21	22	23	24	25	26
MĀRGAŚIRA 2117	27	28	29	30	1	2	3
	4	5	6	7	8	9	10
	11	12	13	14	15	16	17
	18	19	20	21	22	23	24
PAUSHA 2117	25	26	27	28	29	30	1
	2	3	4	5	6	7	8
	9	10	11	12	13	14	15

‡Leap year
[a]New Year (Sādhāraṇa)
[b]Pongal

ISLAMIC (ASTRONOMICAL) 1621‡/1622

Month	Sun	Mon	Tue	Wed	Thu	Fri	Sat
RAMAḌĀN 1621	15	16	17	18	19	20	21
	22	23	24	25	26	27	28
SHAWWĀL 1621	29	30	1[f]	2	3	4	5
	6	7	8	9	10	11	12
	13	14	15	16	17	18	19
	20	21	22	23	24	25	26
DHU AL-QA'DA 1621	27	28	29	30	1	2	3
	4	5	6	7	8	9	10
	11	12	13	14	15	16	17
	18	19	20	21	22	23	24
DHU AL-ḤIJJA 1621	25	26	27	28	29	1	2
	3	4	5	6	7	8	9
	10[g]	11	12	13	14	15	16
	17	18	19	20	21	22	23
	24	25	26	27	28	29	30[a]
MUḤARRAM 1622	1[a]	2	3	4	5	6	7
	8	9	10[b]	11	12	13	14
	15	16	17	18	19	20	21
	22	23	24	25	26	27	28
ṢAFAR 1622	29	1	2	3	4	5	6
	7	8	9	10	11	12	13
	14	15	16	17	18	19	20
	21	22	23	24	25	26	27
RABĪ' I 1622	28	29	1	2	3	4	5
	6	7	8	9	10	11	12[c]
	13	14	15	16	17	18	19
	20	21	22	23	24	25	26
RABĪ' II 1622	27	28	29	30	1	2	3
	4	5	6	7	8	9	10
	11	12	13	14	15	16	17
	18	19	20	21	22	23	24
JUMĀDĀ I 1622	25	26	27	28	29	30	1
	2	3	4	5	6	7	8
	9	10	11	12	13	14	15
	16	17	18	19	20	21	22
	23	24	25	26	27	28	29
JUMĀDĀ II 1622	1	2	3	4	5	6	7
	8	9	10	11	12	13	14
	15	16	17	18	19	20	21
	22	23	24	25	26	27	28
RAJAB 1622	29	30	1	2	3	4	5
	6	7	8	9	10	11	12
	13	14	15	16	17	18	19
	20	21	22	23	24	25	26
SHA'BĀN 1622	27[d]	28	29	1	2	3	4
	5	6	7	8	9	10	11
	12	13	14	15	16	17	18
	19	20	21	22	23	24	25
RAMAḌĀN 1622	26	27	28	29	1[e]	2	3
	4	5	6	7	8	9	10
	11	12	13	14	15	16	17
	18	19	20	21	22	23	24
	25	26	27	28	29	30	1

‡Leap year
[a]New Year
[a]New Year (Arithmetic)
[b]'Ashūrā'
[c]Prophet's Birthday
[d]Ascent of the Prophet
[e]Start of Ramaḍān
[f]'Id al-Fiṭr
[g]'Id al-'Aḍḥā

GREGORIAN 2195

Julian (Sun)	Sun	Mon	Tue	Wed	Thu	Fri	Sat	Month
Dec 14	28	29	30	31	1	2	3	JANUARY 2195
	4	5	6	7	8[a]	9	10	
Dec 28	11	12	13	14	15[b]	16	17	
	18	19	20	21	22	23	24	
Jan 11	25	26	27	28	29	30	31	
	1	2	3	4	5	6	7	FEBRUARY 2195
Jan 25	8	9	10	11[c]	12	13	14	
	15	16	17	18	19	20	21	
Feb 8	22	23	24	25	26	27	28	
	1	2	3	4	5	6	7	MARCH 2195
Feb 22	8	9	10	11	12	13	14	
	15	16	17	18	19	20	21	
Mar 8	22[d]	23	24	25	26	27	28	
	29[e]	30	31	1	2	3	4	APRIL 2195
Mar 22	5	6	7	8	9	10	11	
	12	13	14	15	16	17	18	
Apr 5	19	20	21	22	23	24	25	
	26	27	28	29	30	1	2	MAY 2195
Apr 19	3[f]	4	5	6	7	8	9	
	10	11	12	13	14	15	16	
May 3	17	18	19	20	21	22	23	
	24	25	26	27	28	29	30	
May 17	31	1	2	3	4	5	6	JUNE 2195
	7	8	9	10	11	12	13	
May 31	14	15	16	17	18	19	20	
	21	22	23	24	25	26	27	
Jun 14	28	29	30	1	2	3	4	JULY 2195
	5	6	7	8	9	10	11	
Jun 28	12	13	14	15	16	17	18	
	19	20	21	22	23	24	25	
Jul 12	26	27	28	29	30	31	1	AUGUST 2195
	2	3	4	5	6	7	8	
Jul 26	9	10	11	12	13	14	15	
	16	17	18	19	20	21	22	
Aug 9	23	24	25	26	27	28	29	
	30	31	1	2	3	4	5	SEPTEMBER 2195
Aug 23	6	7	8	9	10	11	12	
	13	14	15	16	17	18	19	
Sep 6	20	21	22	23	24	25	26	
	27	28	29	30	1	2	3	OCTOBER 2195
Sep 20	4	5	6	7	8	9	10	
	11	12	13	14	15	16	17	
Oct 4	18	19	20	21	22	23	24	
	25	26	27	28	29	30	31	
Oct 18	1	2	3	4	5	6	7	NOVEMBER 2195
	8	9	10	11	12	13	14	
Nov 1	15	16	17	18	19	20	21	
	22	23	24	25	26	27	28	
Nov 15	29[g]	30	1	2	3	4	5	DECEMBER 2195
	6	7	8	9	10	11	12	
Nov 29	13	14	15	16	17	18	19	
	20	21	22	23	24	25[h]	26	
Dec 13	27	28	29	30	31	1	2	

[a]Orthodox Christmas
[b]Julian New Year
[c]Ash Wednesday
[d]Feast of Orthodoxy
[e]Easter
[f]Orthodox Easter
[g]Advent
[h]Christmas

2196

GREGORIAN 2196‡	Sun	Mon	Tue	Wed	Thu	Fri	Sat	Lunar Phases	ISO WEEK (Mon)	JULIAN DAY (Sun noon)	HEBREW 5956/5957	Sun	Mon	Tue	Wed	Thu	Fri	Sat	Molad	CHINESE Yǐ-Wèi/Bǐng-Shēn‡	Sun	Mon	Tue	Wed	Thu	Fri	Sat	Solar Term	COPTIC 1912/1913	Sun	Mon	Tue	Wed	Thu	Fri	Sat	ETHIOPIC 2188/2189
	27	28	29	30	●	1[a]	2	10:46	53	2523128		24	25[e]	26[e]	27[e]	28[e]	29[e]	30[e]			26	27	28	29	1	2	3			16	17	18	19	20	21	22	
JANUARY 2196	3	4	5	6	7	◐	9	16:15	1	2523135		1[e]	2[e]	3	4	5	6	7	Thu 22h31m7p	MONTH 12 Yǐ-Wèi	4	5	6	7	8	9	10	Xiǎo hán	KOIAK 1912	23	24	25	26	27	28	29[c]	TĀKHŚĀŚ 2188
	10	11	12	13	14	○	16	16:36	2	2523142	TEVETH 5956	8	9	10	11	12	13	14			11	12	13	14	15	16	17			30	1	2	3	4	5	6[d]	
	17	18	19	20	21	◑	23	8:02	3	2523149		15	16	17	18	19	20	21			18	19	20	**21**	22	23	24	Dà hán	TŌBE 1912	7	8	9	10	11[e]	12	13	ṬER 2188
	24	25	26	27	28	29	●	6:09	4	2523156		22	23	24	25	26	27	28	Sat 11h15m8p		25	26	27	28	29	30	1[a]			14	15	16	17	18	19	20	
	31	1	2	3	4	5	6		5	2523163		29	1	2	3	4	5	6		MONTH 1 Bǐng-Shēn	2	3	4	5	6	7	8	Lì chūn		21	22	23	24	25	26	27	
FEBRUARY 2196	◐	8	9	10	11	12	13	8:52	6	2523170	SHEVAT 5956	7	8	9	10	11	12	13			9	10	11	12	13	14	15[b]			28	29	30	1	2	3	4	
	○	15	16	17	18	19	◑	3:25 21:39	7	2523177		14	15	16	17	18	19	20			16	17	18	19	20	**21**	22	Yǔ shuǐ	MESHIR 1912	5	6	7	8	9	10	11	YAKĀTIT 2188
	21	22	23	24	25	26	27		8	2523184		21	22	23	24	25	26	27			23	24	25	26	27	28	29			12	13	14	15	16	17	18	
	28	●	1	2	3	4	5	1:28	9	2523191		28	29	30	1	2	3	4	Sun 23h59m9p		30*	1	2	3	4	5	6	Jīng zhé		19	20	21	22	23	24	25	
MARCH 2196	6	◐	8	9	10	11	12	21:53	10	2523198	ADAR 5956	5	6	7	8	9	10	11		MONTH 2 Bǐng-Shēn	7	8	9	10	11	12	13			26	27	28	29	30	1	2	
	13	○	15	16	17	18	19[b]	13:23	11	2523205		12	13	14[f]	15	16	17	18			14	15	16	17	18	19	20		PAREMOTEP 1912	3	4	5	6	7	8	9	
	20	◑	22	23	24	25	26	13:51	12	2523212		19	20	21	22	23	24	25	Tue 12h43m10p		**21**	22	23	24	25	26	27	Chūn fēn		10	11	12	13	14	15	16	MAGĀBIT 2188
	27	28	●	30	31	1	2	18:54	13	2523219		26	27	28	29	1	2	3			28	29	30	1	2	3	4			17	18	19	20	21	22	23	
APRIL 2196	3	4	5	◐	7	8	9	7:23	14	2523226	NISAN 5956	4	5	6	7	8	9	10		MONTH 3 Bǐng-Shēn	5	6[c]	7	8	9	10	11	Qīng míng		24	25	26	27	28	29	30	
	10	11	○	13	14	15	16	22:53	15	2523233		11	12	13	14	15[g]	16	17			12	13	14	15	16	17	18			1	2	3	4	5	6	7	
	17	18	19	◑	21	22	23	7:47	16	2523240		18	19	20	21	22	23	24			19	20	**21**	22	23	24	25	Gǔ yǔ	PARMOUTE 1912	8	9	10	11	12	13	14	MIYĀZYĀ 2188
	24	25	26	27	●	29	30	9:37	17	2523247		25	26	27	28	29	30	1	Thu 1h27m11p		26	27	28	29	1*	2	3			15[f]	16	17	18	19	20	21	
MAY 2196	1	2	3	4	◐	6	7	14:03	18	2523254	IYYAR 5956	2	3	4	5	6	7	8		MONTH 4 Bǐng-Shēn	4	5	6	7	8	9	10	Lì xià		22	23	24	25	26	27	28	
	8	9	10	11	○	13	14	8:43	19	2523261		9	10	11	12	13	14	15			11	12	13	14	15	16	17			29[g]	30	1	2	3	4	5	
	15	16	17	18	19	◑	21	2:09	20	2523268		16	17	18	19	20	21	22			18	19	20	21	22	**23**	24	Xiǎo mǎn	PASHONS 1912	6	7	8	9	10	11	12	GENBOT 2188
	22	23	24	25	26	●	28	21:36	21	2523275		23	24	25	26	27	28	29			25	26	27	28	29	30	1			13	14	15	16	17	18	19	
	29	30	31	1	2	◐	4	19:02	22	2523282		1	2	3	4	5	6[h]	7	Fri 14h11m12p	MONTH 5 Bǐng-Shēn	2	3	4	5[d]	6	7	8			20	21	22	23	24	25	26	
JUNE 2196	5	6	7	8	9	○	11	19:42	23	2523289	SIVAN 5956	8	9	10	11	12	13	14			9	10	11	12	13	14	15	Máng zhòng		27	28	29	30	1	2	3	
	12	13	14	15	16	17	◑	19:42	24	2523296		15	16	17	18	19	20	21			16	17	18	19	20	21	22		PAŌNE 1912	4	5	6	7	8	9	10	SANĒ 2188
	19	20[c]	21	22	23	24	25		25	2523303		22	23	24	25	26	27	28			23	**24**	25	26	27	28	29	Xià zhì		11	12	13	14	15	16	17	
	●	27	28	29	30	1	◐	7:21 23:46	26	2523310		29	30	1	2	3	4	5	Sun 2h55m13p		1	2*	3	4	5	6	7			18	19	20	21	22	23	24	
JULY 2196	3	4	5	6	7	8	9		27	2523317	TAMMUZ 5956	6	7	8	9	10	11	12		MONTH 6 Bǐng-Shēn	8	9	10	*11*	12	13	14	Xiǎo shǔ		25	26	27	28	29	30	1	
	○	11	12	13	14	15	16	8:23	28	2523324		13	14	15	16	17	18	19			15	16	17	18	19	20	21		EPĒP 1912	2	3	4	5	6	7	8	ḤAMLĒ 2188
	17	◑	19	20	21	22	23	11:43	29	2523331		20	21	22	23	24	25	26			22	23	24	25	26	**27**	28	Dà shǔ		9	10	11	12	13	14	15	
	24	●	26	27	28	29	30	15:33	30	2523338		27	28	29	1	2	3	4	Mon 15h39m14p		29	1	2	3	4	5	6			16	17	18	19	20	21	22	
	31	◐	2	3	4	5	6	5:49	31	2523345	AV 5956	5	6	7	8	9[i]	10	11		MONTH 7 Bǐng-Shēn	7[e]	8	9	10	11	12	*13*	Lì qiū		23	24	25	26	27	28	29	
AUGUST 2196	7	○	9	10	11	12	13	22:49	32	2523352		12	13	14	15	16	17	18			14	15[f]	16	17	18	19	20			30	1	2	3	4	5	6	
	14	15	16	◑	18	19	20	1:53	33	2523359		19	20	21	22	23	24	25	Wed 4h23m15p		21	22	23	24	25	26	27		MESORĒ 1912	7	8	9	10	11	12	13[h]	NAHASĒ 2188
	21	22	●	24	25	26	27	22:58	34	2523366		26	27	28	29	30	1	2			28	**29**	30	1	2	3*	4	Chǔ shǔ		14	15	16	17	18	19	20	
	28	29	◐	31	1	2	3	14:36	35	2523373	ELUL 5956	3	4	5	6	7	8	9		LEAP MONTH 7 Bǐng-Shēn	5	6	7	8	9	10	11			21	22	23	24	25	26	27	
SEPTEMBER 2196	4	5	6	○	8	9	10	14:34	36	2523380		10	11	12	13	14	15	16			12	13	14	*15*	16	17	18	Bái lù	EPAG. 1912	28	29	30	1	2	3	4	PĀG. 2188
	11	12	13	14	◑	16	17	14:07	37	2523387		17	18	19	20	21	22	23			19	20	21	22	23	24	25			5	1[a]	2	3	4	5	6	
	18	19	20	21	●[d]	23	24	6:32	38	2523394		24	25	26	27	28	29	1[a]	Thu 17h7m16p		26	27	28	29	**1**	2	3	Qiū fēn	THOOUT 1913	7	8	9	10	11	12	13	MASKARAM 2189
	25	26	27	28	◐	30	1	3:10	39	2523401		2[a]	3	4	5	6	7	8		MONTH 8 Bǐng-Shēn	4	5	6	7	8	9	10			14	15	16	17[b]	18	19	20	
OCTOBER 2196	2	3	4	5	6	○	8	7:02	40	2523408	TISHRI 5957	9	10[b]	11	12	13	14	15[c]			11	12	13	14	15[g]	*16*	17	Hán lù		21	22	23	24	25	26	27	
	9	10	11	12	13	14	◑	0:31	41	2523415		16	17	18	19	20	21	22			18	19	20	21	22	23	24			28	29	30	1	2	3	4	
	16	17	18	19	20	●	22	15:16	42	2523422		23	24	25	26	27	28	29			25	26	27	28	29	1	**2**	Shuāng jiàng	PAOPE 1913	5	6	7	8	9	10	11	ṬEQEMT 2189
	23	24	25	26	27	◐	29	19:45	43	2523429		30	1	2	3	4	5	6	Sat 5h51m17p	MONTH 9 Bǐng-Shēn	3	4	5*	6	7	8	9[h]			12	13	14	15	16	17	18	
	30	31	1	2	3	4	○	23:35	44	2523436	ḤESHVAN 5957	7	8	9	10	11	12	13			10	11	12	13	14	15	16			19	20	21	22	23	24	25	
NOVEMBER 2196	6	7	8	9	10	11	12		45	2523443		14	15	16	17	18	19	20			*17*	18	19	20	21	22	23	Lì dōng		26	27	28	29	30	1	2	
	◑	14	15	16	17	18	19	9:18	46	2523450		21	22	23	24	25	26	27			24	25	26	27	28	29	30		ATHŌR 1913	3	4	5	6	7	8	9	ḪEDĀR 2189
	●	21	22	23	24	25	26	2:05	47	2523457		28	29	1	2	3	4	5	Sun 18h36m18p		1	**2**	3	4	5	6	7	Xiǎo xuě		10	11	12	13	14	15	16	
	◐	28	29	30	1	2	3	15:38	48	2523464	KISLEV 5957	6	7	8	9	10	11	12		MONTH 10 Bǐng-Shēn	8	9	10	11	12	13	14			17	18	19	20	21	22	23	
DECEMBER 2196	4	○	6	7	8	9	10	15:30	49	2523471		13	14	15[d]	16	17	18	19			15	16	*17*	18	19	20	21	Dà xuě		24	25	26	27	28	29	30	
	11	◑	13	14	15	16	17	17:07	50	2523478		20	21	22	23	24	25[e]	26[e]	Tue 7h20m19p		22	23	24	25	26	27	28			1	2	3	4	5	6	7	
	18	●	20	21[e]	22	23	24	15:32	51	2523485	TEVETH 5957	27[e]	28[e]	29[e]	1[e]	2[e]	3[e]	4		MONTH 11 Bǐng-Shēn	29	1	2	3[i]	4	5	6*	Dōng zhì	KOIAK 1913	8	9	10	11	12	13	14	TĀKHŚĀŚ 2189
	25	26	◐	28	29	30	31	13:15	52	2523492		5	6	7	8	9	10	11			7	8	9	10	11	12	13			15	16	17	18	19	20	21	

‡Leap year
[a]New Year
[b]Spring (19:25)
[c]Summer (10:06)
[d]Autumn (3:19)
[e]Winter (2:54)
● New moon
◐ First quarter moon
○ Full moon
◑ Last quarter moon

[a]New Year
[b]Yom Kippur
[c]Sukkot
[d]Winter starts
[e]Ḥanukkah
[f]Purim
[g]Passover
[h]Shavuot
[i]Fast of Av

‡Leap year
[a]New Year (4894, Monkey)
[b]Lantern Festival
[c]Qīngmíng
[d]Dragon Festival
[e]Qīqiǎo
[f]Hungry Ghosts
[g]Mid-Autumn Festival
[h]Double-Ninth Festival
[i]Dōngzhì
*Start of 60-name cycle

[a]New Year
[b]Building of the Cross
[c]Christmas
[d]Jesus's Circumcision
[e]Epiphany
[f]Easter
[g]Mary's Announcement
[h]Jesus's Transfiguration

PERSIAN (ASTRONOMICAL) 1574/1575

Month	Sun	Mon	Tue	Wed	Thu	Fri	Sat
	6	7	8	9	10	11	12
DEY 1574	13	14	15	16	17	18	19
	20	21	22	23	24	25	26
	27	28	29	30	*1*	2	3
	4	5	6	7	8	9	10
BAHMAN 1574	11	12	13	14	15	16	17
	18	19	20	21	22	23	24
	25	26	27	28	29	30	*1*
	2	3	4	5	6	7	8
ESFAND 1574	9	10	11	12	13	14	15
	16	17	18	19	20	21	22
	23	24	25	26	27	28	29
	1[a]	2	3	4	5	6	7
FARVARDIN 1575	8	9	10	11	12	13[b]	14
	15	16	17	18	19	20	21
	22	23	24	25	26	27	28
	29	30	31	*1*	2	3	4
	5	6	7	8	9	10	11
ORDIBEHEST 1575	12	13	14	15	16	17	18
	19	20	21	22	23	24	25
	26	27	28	29	30	31	*1*
	2	3	4	5	6	7	8
XORDĀD 1575	9	10	11	12	13	14	15
	16	17	18	19	20	21	22
	23	24	25	26	27	28	29
	30	31	*1*	2	3	4	5
	6	7	8	9	10	11	12
TĪR 1575	13	14	15	16	17	18	19
	20	21	22	23	24	25	26
	27	28	29	30	31	*1*	2
	3	4	5	6	7	8	9
MORDĀD 1575	10	11	12	13	14	15	16
	17	18	19	20	21	22	23
	24	25	26	27	28	29	30
	31	*1*	2	3	4	5	6
	7	8	9	10	11	12	13
SHAHRĪVAR 1575	14	15	16	17	18	19	20
	21	22	23	24	25	26	27
	28	29	30	31	*1*	2	3
MEHR 1575	4	5	6	7	8	9	10
	11	12	13	14	15	16	17
	18	19	20	21	22	23	24
	25	26	27	28	29	30	*1*
	2	3	4	5	6	7	8
ĀBĀN 1575	9	10	11	12	13	14	15
	16	17	18	19	20	21	22
	23	24	25	26	27	28	29
	30	*1*	2	3	4	5	6
ĀZAR 1575	7	8	9	10	11	12	13
	14	15	16	17	18	19	20
	21	22	23	24	25	26	27
DEY 1575	28	29	30	*1*	2	3	4
	5	6	7	8	9	10	11

[a]New Year
[b]Sizdeh Bedar

HINDU LUNAR 2252/2253

Month	Sun	Mon	Tue	Wed	Thu	Fri	Sat
	26	27	28	29	30	1	2
PAUSHA 2252	3	4	5	6	7	8	9
	10	11	12	13	14	15	16
	17	18	19	20	21	**22**	24
	25	26	27	28	29	*29*	30
	1	2	3	4	5	6	7
MĀGHA 2252	8	9	10	11	12	13	14
	15	**16**	18	19	20	21	22
	23	24	25	26	27	28	29[h]
	30	1	*1*	2	3	4	5
PHĀLGUNA 2252	6	7	8	9	**10**	12	13
	14	15[i]	16	17	18	19	20
	21	22	23	24	25	26	27
	28	29	30	1[a]	2	3	4
CHAITRA 2253	5	6	7	8	9[b]	10	11
	12	13	**14**	16	17	18	19
	20	21	22	23	24	25	*25*
	26	27	28	29	30	1	2
VAIŚĀKHA 2253	3	4	5	6	**7**	9	10
	11	12	13	14	15	16	17
	18	19	20	21	22	23	24
	25	26	27	28	29	30	1
	2	3	4	5	6	7	8
JYAISHTHA 2253	9	10	**11**	13	14	15	16
	17	18	19	20	21	*21*	22
	23	24	25	26	27	28	29
	30	1	2	**3**	5	6	7
ĀSHĀDHA 2253	8	9	10	11	12	13	14
	15	16	17	18	19	20	21
	22	23	24	25	26	27	28
	29	30	1	2	3	4	5
ŚRĀVANA 2253	**6**	8	9	10	11	12	13
	14	15	16	17	18	*18*	19
	20	21	22	23[c]	24	25	26
	27	28	**29**	1	2	3	4[d]
BHĀDRAPADA 2253	5	6	7	8	9	10	11
	12	13	14	15	16	17	18
	19	20	21	22	23	24	25
	26	27	28	29	30	1	**2**
ĀŚVINA 2253	4	5	6	7	8[e]	9[e]	10[e]
	11	12	13	*13*	14	15	16
	17	18	19	20	21	22	23
	24	25	**26**	28	29	30	1[f]
	2	3	4	5	6	7	8
KĀRTTIKA 2253	9	10	11	12	13	14	15
	16	17	18	19	20	21	22
	23	24	25	26	27	28	29
	30	2	3	4	5	6	7
MĀRGAŚĪRA 2253	*7*	8	9	10	11[g]	12	13
	14	15	16	17	18	19	20
	21	22	23	**24**	26	27	28
PAUSHA 2253	29	30	1	2	3	4	5
	6	7	8	9	*9*	10	11

[a]New Year (Durmukha)
[b]Birthday of Rāma
[c]Birthday of Krishna
[d]Ganēśa Chaturthī
[e]Dashara
[f]Diwali
[g]Birthday of Vishnu
[h]Night of Śiva
[i]Holi

HINDU SOLAR 2117‡/2118

Month	Sun	Mon	Tue	Wed	Thu	Fri	Sat
	9	10	11	12	13	14	15
PAUSHA 2117	16	17	18	19	20	21	22
	23	24	25	26	27	28	29
	1[b]	2	3	4	5	6	7
MĀGHA 2117	8	9	10	11	12	13	14
	15	16	17	18	19	20	21
	22	23	24	25	26	27	28
	29	1	2	3	4	5	6
PHĀLGUNA 2117	7	8	9	10	11	12	13
	14	15	16	17	18	19	20
	21	22	23	24	25	26	27
	28	29	30	1	2	3	4
CHAITRA 2117	5	6	7	8	9	10	11
	12	13	14	15	16	17	18
	19	20	21	22	23	24	25
	26	27	28	29	30	31	1[a]
VAIŚĀKHA 2118	2	3	4	5	6	7	8
	9	10	11	12	13	14	15
	16	17	18	19	20	21	22
	23	24	25	26	27	28	29
	30	31	1	2	3	4	5
JYAISHTHA 2118	6	7	8	9	10	11	12
	13	14	15	16	17	18	19
	20	21	22	23	24	25	26
	27	28	29	30	31	1	2
ĀSHĀDHA 2118	3	4	5	6	7	8	9
	10	11	12	13	14	15	16
	17	18	19	20	21	22	23
	24	25	26	27	28	29	30
	31	32	1	2	3	4	5
ŚRĀVANA 2118	6	7	8	9	10	11	12
	13	14	15	16	17	18	19
	20	21	22	23	24	25	26
	27	28	29	30	31	1	2
BHĀDRAPADA 2118	3	4	5	6	7	8	9
	10	11	12	13	14	15	16
	17	18	19	20	21	22	23
	24	25	26	27	28	29	30
	31	1	2	3	4	5	6
ĀŚVINA 2118	7	8	9	10	11	12	13
	14	15	16	17	18	19	20
	21	22	23	24	25	26	27
	28	29	30	31	1	2	3
KĀRTTIKA 2118	4	5	6	7	8	9	10
	11	12	13	14	15	16	17
	18	19	20	21	22	23	24
	25	26	27	28	29	30	1
MĀRGAŚĪRA 2118	2	3	4	5	6	7	8
	9	10	11	12	13	14	15
	16	17	18	19	20	21	22
	23	24	25	26	27	28	29
PAUSHA 2118	1	2	3	4	5	6	7
	8	9	10	11	12	13	14

‡Leap year
[a]New Year (Virodhakṛit)
[b]Pongal

ISLAMIC (ASTRONOMICAL) 1622/1623

Month	Sun	Mon	Tue	Wed	Thu	Fri	Sat
	25	26	27	28	29	30	*1*[f]
SHAWWĀL 1622	2	3	4	5	6	7	8
	9	10	11	12	13	14	15
	16	17	18	19	20	21	22
	23	24	25	26	27	28	29
	30	1	2	3	4	5	6
DHU AL-QA'DA 1622	7	8	9	10	11	12	13
	14	15	16	17	18	19	20
	21	22	23	24	25	26	27
	28	29	*1*	2	3	4	5
DHU AL-ḤIJJA 1622	6	7	8	9	10[g]	11	12
	13	14	15	16	17	18	19
	20	21	22	23	24	25	26
	27	28	29	30	*1*[a]	2	3
MUḤARRAM 1623	4	5	6	7	8	9	10[b]
	11	12	13	14	15	16	17
	18	19	20	21	22	23	24
	25	26	27	28	29	30	*1*
ṢAFAR 1623	2	3	4	5	6	7	8
	9	10	11	12	13	14	15
	16	17	18	19	20	21	22
	23	24	25	26	27	28	29
	1	2	3	4	5	6	7
RABĪ' I 1623	8	9	10	11	12[c]	13	14
	15	16	17	18	19	20	21
	22	23	24	25	26	27	28
	29	30	*1*	2	3	4	5
RABĪ' II 1623	6	7	8	9	10	11	12
	13	14	15	16	17	18	19
	20	21	22	23	24	25	26
	27	28	29	*1*	2	3	4
JUMĀDĀ I 1623	5	6	7	8	9	10	11
	12	13	14	15	16	17	18
	19	20	21	22	23	24	25
	26	27	28	29	30	*1*	2
JUMĀDĀ II 1623	3	4	5	6	7	8	9
	10	11	12	13	14	15	16
	17	18	19	20	21	22	23
	24	25	26	27	28	29	*1*
RAJAB 1623	2	3	4	5	6	7	8
	9	10	11	12	13	14	15
	16	17	18	19	20	21	22
	23	24	25	26	27[d]	28	29
	30	*1*	2	3	4	5	6
SHA'BĀN 1623	7	8	9	10	11	12	13
	14	15	16	17	18	19	20
	21	22	23	24	25	26	27
	28	29	*1*[e]	2	3	4	5
RAMAḌĀN 1623	6	7	8	9	10	11	12
	13	14	15	16	17	18	19
	20	21	22	23	24	25	26
SHAWWĀL 1623	27	28	29	*1*[f]	2	3	4
	5	6	7	8	9	10	11

[a]New Year
[b]'Ashūrā'
[c]Prophet's Birthday
[d]Ascent of the Prophet
[e]Start of Ramaḍān
[f]'Id al-Fiṭr
[g]'Id al-'Aḍḥā

GREGORIAN 2196‡

Julian‡ (Sun)	Sun	Mon	Tue	Wed	Thu	Fri	Sat	Month
Dec 13	27	28	29	30	31	1	2	
	3	4	5	6	7	8[a]	9	JANUARY 2196
Dec 27	*10*	11	12	13	14	15[b]	16	
	17	18	19	20	21	22	23	
Jan 10	*24*	25	26	27	28	29	30	
	31	1	2	3	4	5	6	
Jan 24	7	8	9	10	11	12	13	FEBRUARY 2196
	14	15	16	17	18	19	20	
Feb 7	*21*	22	23	24	25	26	27	
	28	29	1	2[c]	3	4	5	
Feb 21	6	7	8	9	10	11	12	MARCH 2196
	13[d]	14	15	16	17	18	19	
Mar 6	*20*	21	22	23	24	25	26	
	27	28	29	30	31	1	2	
Mar 20	3	4	5	6	7	8	9	APRIL 2196
	10	11	12	13	14	15	16	
Apr 3	*17*[e]	18	19	20	21	22	23	
	24[f]	25	26	27	28	29	30	
Apr 17	*1*	2	3	4	5	6	7	
	8	9	10	11	12	13	14	MAY 2196
May 1	*15*	16	17	18	19	20	21	
	22	23	24	25	26	27	28	
May 15	*29*	30	31	1	2	3	4	
	5	6	7	8	9	10	11	JUNE 2196
May 29	*12*	13	14	15	16	17	18	
	19	20	21	22	23	24	25	
Jun 12	*26*	27	28	29	30	1	2	
	3	4	5	6	7	8	9	JULY 2196
Jun 26	*10*	11	12	13	14	15	16	
	17	18	19	20	21	22	23	
Jul 10	*24*	25	26	27	28	29	30	
	31	1	2	3	4	5	6	
Jul 24	*7*	8	9	10	11	12	13	AUGUST 2196
	14	15	16	17	18	19	20	
Aug 7	*21*	22	23	24	25	26	27	
	28	29	30	31	1	2	3	
Aug 21	*4*	5	6	7	8	9	10	SEPTEMBER 2196
	11	12	13	14	15	16	17	
Sep 4	*18*	19	20	21	22	23	24	
	25	26	27	28	29	30	1	
Sep 18	*2*	3	4	5	6	7	8	OCTOBER 2196
	9	10	11	12	13	14	15	
Oct 2	*16*	17	18	19	20	21	22	
	23	24	25	26	27	28	29	
Oct 16	*30*	31	1	2	3	4	5	
	6	7	8	9	10	11	12	NOVEMBER 2196
Oct 30	*13*	14	15	16	17	18	19	
	20	21	22	23	24	25	26	
Nov 13	*27*[g]	28	29	30	1	2	3	
	4	5	6	7	8	9	10	DECEMBER 2196
Nov 27	*11*	12	13	14	15	16	17	
	18	19	20	21	22	23	24	
Dec 11	25[h]	26	27	28	29	30	31	

‡Leap year
[a]Orthodox Christmas
[b]Julian New Year
[c]Ash Wednesday
[d]Feast of Orthodoxy
[e]Easter
[f]Orthodox Easter
[g]Advent
[h]Christmas

2197

Gregorian 2197	Sun	Mon	Tue	Wed	Thu	Fri	Sat	Lunar Phases	ISO Week (Mon)	Julian Day (Sun noon)	Hebrew 5957/5958‡	Sun	Mon	Tue	Wed	Thu	Fri	Sat	Molad	Chinese Bǐng-Shēn‡/Dīng-Yǒu	Sun	Mon	Tue	Wed	Thu	Fri	Sat	Solar Term	Coptic 1913/1914	Sun	Mon	Tue	Wed	Thu	Fri	Sat	Ethiopic 2189/2190
JANUARY 2197	1[a]	2	3	○	5	6	7	6:05	1	2523499	TEVETH 5957	12	13	14	15	16	17	18		MONTH 11 Bǐng-Shēn	14	15	16	17	18	19	20	Xiǎo hán	KOIAK 1913	22	23	24	25	26	27	28	TĀKHŚĀŚ 2189
	8	9	10	◑	12	13	14	0:57	2	2523506		19	20	21	22	23	24	25			21	22	23	24	25	26	27			29[c]	30	1	2	3	4	5	
	15	16	17	●	19	20	21	7:27	3	2523513	SHEVAT 5957	26	27	28	29	1	2	3		MONTH 12 Bǐng-Shēn	28	29	30	1	2	3	4	Dà hán	TŌBE 1913	6[d]	7	8	9	10	11[e]	12	ṬER 2189
	22	23	24	25	◐	27	28	10:37	4	2523520		4	5	6	7	8	9	10	Wed 20h4m2p		5	6	7	8	9	10	11			13	14	15	16	17	18	19	
FEBRUARY 2197	29	30	31	1	○	3	4	18:46	5	2523527		11	12	13	14	15	16	17			12	13	14	15	16	17	18	Lì chūn		20	21	22	23	24	25	26	
	5	6	7	8	◑	10	11	9:52	6	2523534		18	19	20	21	22	23	24			19	20	21	22	23	24	25			27	28	29	30	1	2	3	
	12	13	14	15	16	●	18	1:01	7	2523541	ADAR 5957	25	26	27	28	29	30	1	Fri 8h48m3p	MONTH 1 Dīng-Yǒu	26	27	28	29	30	1[a]	2	Yǔ shuǐ	MESHIR 1913	4	5	6	7	8	9	10	YAKĀTIT 2189
	19	20	21	22	23	24	◐	5:45	8	2523548		2	3	4	5	6	7	8			3	4	5	6*	7	8	9			11	12	13	14	15	16	17	
MARCH 2197	26	27	28	1	2	3	○	5:26	9	2523555		9	10	11	12	13	14[f]	15			10	11	12	13	14	15[b]	16			18	19	20	21	22	23	24	
	5	6	7	8	9	◑	11	20:39	10	2523562		16	17	18	19	20	21	22			17	18	19	20	21	22	23	Jīng zhé	PAREMOTEP 1913	25	26	27	28	29	30	1	MAGĀBIT 2189
	12	13	14	15	16	17	●	19:01	11	2523569		23	24	25	26	27	28	29			24	25	26	27	28	29	30			2	3	4	5	6	7	8	
	19	20[b]	21	22	23	24	25		12	2523576	NISAN 5957	1	2	3	4	5	6	7	Sat 21h32m4p	MONTH 2 Dīng-Yǒu	1	2	3	4	5	6	7	Chūn fēn		9	10	11	12	13	14	15	
APRIL 2197	◐	27	28	29	30	31	1	21:15	13	2523583		8	9	10	11	12	13	14			8	9	10	11	12	13	14			16	17	18	19	20	21	22	
	○	3	4	5	6	7	8	14:33	14	2523590		15[g]	16	17	18	19	20	21			15	16	17[c]	18	19	20	21	Qīng míng		23	24	25	26	27	28	29	
	◑	10	11	12	13	14	15	9:31	15	2523597		22	23	24	25	26	27	28			22	23	24	25	26	27	28		PARMOUTE 1913	30[f]	1	2	3	4	5	6	MIYĀZYĀ 2189
	16	●	18	19	20	21	22	12:22	16	2523604	IYYAR 5957	29	30	1	2	3	4	5	Mon 10h16m5p	MONTH 3 Dīng-Yǒu	29	1	2	3	4	5	6	Gǔ yǔ		7	8	9	10	11	12	13	
	23	24	◐	26	27	28	29	8:34	17	2523611		6	7	8	9	10	11	12			7*	8	9	10	11	12	13			14	15	16	17	18	19	20	
MAY 2197	30	○	2	3	4	5	6	22:52	18	2523618		13	14	15	16	17	18	19			14	15	16	17	18	19	20	Lì xià		21	22	23	24	25	26	27	
	7	8	◑	10	11	12	13	0:14	19	2523625		20	21	22	23	24	25	26			21	22	23	24	25	26	27		PASHONS 1913	28	29[g]	30	1	2	3	4	GENBOT 2189
	14	15	16	●	18	19	20	4:10	20	2523632	SIVAN 5957	27	28	29	1	2	3	4	Tue 23h0m6p	MONTH 4 Dīng-Yǒu	28	29	30	1	2	3	4	Xiǎo mǎn		5	6	7	8	9	10	11	
	21	22	23	◐	25	26	27	16:12	21	2523639		5	6[h]	7	8	9	10	11			5	6	7	8	9	10	11			12	13	14	15	16	17	18	
JUNE 2197	28	29	30	○	1	2	3	7:14	22	2523646		12	13	14	15	16	17	18			12	13	14	15	16	17	18			19	20	21	22	23	24	25	
	4	5	6	◑	8	9	10	16:18	23	2523653		19	20	21	22	23	24	25			19	20	21	22	23	24	25	Máng zhòng	PAŌNE 1913	26	27	28	29	30	1	2	SANĒ 2189
	11	12	13	14	●	16	17	17:51	24	2523660	TAMMUZ 5957	26	27	28	29	30	1	2	Thu 11h44m7p	MONTH 5 Dīng-Yǒu	26	27	28	29	30	1	2			3	4	5	6	7	8	9	
	18	19	20[c]	21	◐	23	24	21:22	25	2523667		3	4	5	6	7	8	9			3	4	5[d]	6	7*	8	9	Xià zhì		10	11	12	13	14	15	16	
JULY 2197	25	26	27	28	○	30	1	16:27	26	2523674		10	11	12	13	14	15	16			10	11	12	13	14	15	16			17	18	19	20	21	22	23	
	2	3	4	5	6	◑	8	9:17	27	2523681		17	18	19	20	21	22	23			17	18	19	20	21	22	23	Xiǎo shǔ		24	25	26	27	28	29	30	
	9	10	11	12	13	14	●	5:14	28	2523688	AV 5957	24	25	26	27	28	29	1	Sat 0h28m8p	MONTH 6 Dīng-Yǒu	24	25	26	27	28	29	1		EPĒP 1913	1	2	3	4	5	6	7	ḤAMLĒ 2189
	16	17	18	19	20	21	◐	1:39	29	2523695		2	3	4	5	6	7	8			2	3	4	5	6	7	8	Dà shǔ		8	9	10	11	12	13	14	
	23	24	25	26	27	28	○	3:11	30	2523702		9[i]	10	11	12	13	14	15			9	10	11	12	13	14	15			15	16	17	18	19	20	21	
AUGUST 2197	30	31	1	2	3	4	5		31	2523709		16	17	18	19	20	21	22			16	17	18	19	20	21	22			22	23	24	25	26	27	28	
	◑	7	8	9	10	11	12	2:36	32	2523716		23	24	25	26	27	28	29			23	24	25	26	27	28	29	Lì qiū	MESORĒ 1913	29	30	1	2	3	4	5	NAHASĒ 2189
	●	14	15	16	17	18	19	14:42	33	2523723	ELUL 5957	30	1	2	3	4	5	6	Sun 13h12m9p	MONTH 7 Dīng-Yǒu	1	2	3	4	5	6	7[e]			6	7	8	9	10	11	12	
	◐	21	22	23	24	25	26	6:40	34	2523730		7	8	9	10	11	12	13			8	9*	10	11	12	13	14	Chǔ shǔ		13[h]	14	15	16	17	18	19	
SEPTEMBER 2197	○	28	29	30	31	1	2	15:56	35	2523737		14	15	16	17	18	19	20			15[f]	16	17	18	19	20	21			20	21	22	23	24	25	26	
	3	◑	5	6	7	8	9	19:32	36	2523744		21	22	23	24	25	26	27			22	23	24	25	26	27	28	Bái lù	EPAG. 1913	27	28	29	30	1	2	3	PĀG. 2189
	10	●	12	13	14	15	16	23:05	37	2523751	TISHRI 5958	28	29	1[a]	2[a]	3	4	5	Tue 1h56m10p	MONTH 8 Dīng-Yǒu	29	30	1	2	3	4	5		THOOUT 1914	4	5	1[a]	2	3	4	5	MASKARAM 2190
	17	◐	19	20	21	22[d]	23	13:51	38	2523758		6	7	8	9	10[b]	11	12			6	7	8	9	10	11	12	Qiū fēn		6	7	8	9	10	11	12	
OCTOBER 2197	24	25	○	27	28	29	30	7:01	39	2523765		13	14	15[c]	16	17	18	19			13	14	15[g]	16	17	18	19			13	14	15	16	17[b]	18	19	
	1	2	3	◑	5	6	7	11:10	40	2523772		20	21	22	23	24	25	26			20	21	22	23	24	25	26			20	21	22	23	24	25	26	
	8	9	10	●	12	13	14	7:27	41	2523779	ḤESHVAN 5958	27	28	29	30	1	2	3	Wed 14h40m11p	MONTH 9 Dīng-Yǒu	27	28	29	1	2	3	4	Hán lù	PAOPE 1914	27	28	29	30	1	2	3	ṬEQEMT 2190
	15	16	17	◐	19	20	21	0:18	42	2523786		4	5	6	7	8	9	10			5	6	7	8	9[h]	10*	11			4	5	6	7	8	9	10	
	22	23	24	25	○	27	28	0:18	43	2523793		11	12	13	14	15	16	17			12	13	14	15	16	17	18	Shuāng jiàng		11	12	13	14	15	16	17	
NOVEMBER 2197	29	30	31	1	2	◑	4	0:48	44	2523800		18	19	20	21	22	23	24			19	20	21	22	23	24	25			18	19	20	21	22	23	24	
	5	6	7	8	●	10	11	16:43	45	2523807	KISLEV 5958	25	26	27	28	29	1	2	Fri 3h24m12p	MONTH 10 Dīng-Yǒu	26	27	28	29	30	1	2	Lì dōng	ATHŌR 1914	25	26	27	28	29	30	1	HEDĀR 2190
	12	13	14	15	◐	17	18	14:36	46	2523814		3	4	5	6	7	8	9			3	4	5	6	7	8	9			2	3	4	5	6	7	8	
	19	20	21	22	23	○	25	18:53	47	2523821		10	11	12	13	14	15	16			10	11	12	13	14	15	16	Xiǎo xuě		9	10	11	12	13	14	15	
DECEMBER 2197	26	27	28	29	30	1	◑	12:09	48	2523828		17	18	19	20	21	22	23			17	18	19	20	21	22	23			16	17	18	19	20	21	22	
	3	4	5	6	7	8	●	3:28	49	2523835		24	25[e]	26[e]	27[d,e]	28[e]	29[e]	30[e]		MONTH 11 Dīng-Yǒu	24	25	26	27	28	29	1	Dà xuě	KOIAK 1914	23	24	25	26	27	28	29	TĀKHŚĀŚ 2190
	10	11	12	13	14	15	◐	8:38	50	2523842	TEVETH 5958	1[e]	2[e]	3	4	5	6	7	Sat 16h8m13p		2	3	4	5	6	7	8			30	1	2	3	4	5	6	
	17	18	19	20	21[e]	22	23		51	2523849		8	9	10	11	12	13	14			9	10	11*	12	13[i]	14	15	Dōng zhì		7	8	9	10	11	12	13	
	○	25	26	27	28	29	30	13:11	52	2523856		15	16	17	18	19	20	21			16	17	18	19	20	21	22			14	15	16	17	18	19	20	
	◑	1	2	3	4	5	6	21:3	1	2523863		22	23	24	25	26	27	28			23	24	25	26	27	28	29	Xiǎo hán		21	22	23	24	25	26	27	

[a]New Year
[b]Spring (1:11)
[c]Summer (15:48)
[d]Autumn (9:06)
[e]Winter (8:47)
● New moon
◐ First quarter moon
○ Full moon
◑ Last quarter moon

‡Leap year
[a]New Year
[b]Yom Kippur
[c]Sukkot
[d]Winter starts
[e]Ḥanukkah
[f]Purim
[g]Passover
[h]Shavuot
[i]Fast of Av

‡Leap year
[a]New Year (4895, Fowl)
[b]Lantern Festival
[c]Qīngmíng
[d]Dragon Festival
[e]Qīqiǎo
[f]Hungry Ghosts
[g]Mid-Autumn Festival
[h]Double-Ninth Festival
[i]Dōngzhì
*Start of 60-name cycle

[a]New Year
[b]Building of the Cross
[c]Christmas
[d]Jesus's Circumcision
[e]Epiphany
[f]Easter
[g]Mary's Announcement
[h]Jesus's Transfiguration

PERSIAN (ASTRONOMICAL) 1575/1576

Month	Sun	Mon	Tue	Wed	Thu	Fri	Sat
DEY 1575	12	13	14	15	16	17	18
	19	20	21	22	23	24	25
	26	27	28	29	30	1	2
BAHMAN 1575	3	4	5	6	7	8	9
	10	11	12	13	14	15	16
	17	18	19	20	21	22	23
	24	25	26	27	28	29	30
ESFAND 1575	1	2	3	4	5	6	7
	8	9	10	11	12	13	14
	15	16	17	18	19	20	21
	22	23	24	25	26	27	28
FARVARDIN 1576	29	1[a]	2	3	4	5	6
	7	8	9	10	11	12	13[b]
	14	15	16	17	18	19	20
	21	22	23	24	25	26	27
ORDIBEHEŠT 1576	28	29	30	31	1	2	3
	4	5	6	7	8	9	10
	11	12	13	14	15	16	17
	18	19	20	21	22	23	24
	25	26	27	28	29	30	31
XORDĀD 1576	1	2	3	4	5	6	7
	8	9	10	11	12	13	14
	15	16	17	18	19	20	21
	22	23	24	25	26	27	28
TĪR 1576	29	30	31	1	2	3	4
	5	6	7	8	9	10	11
	12	13	14	15	16	17	18
	19	20	21	22	23	24	25
MORDĀD 1576	26	27	28	29	30	31	1
	2	3	4	5	6	7	8
	9	10	11	12	13	14	15
	16	17	18	19	20	21	22
	23	24	25	26	27	28	29
SHAHRĪVAR 1576	30	31	1	2	3	4	5
	6	7	8	9	10	11	12
	13	14	15	16	17	18	19
	20	21	22	23	24	25	26
MEHR 1576	27	28	29	30	31	1	2
	3	4	5	6	7	8	9
	10	11	12	13	14	15	16
	17	18	19	20	21	22	23
	24	25	26	27	28	29	30
ĀBĀN 1576	1	2	3	4	5	6	7
	8	9	10	11	12	13	14
	15	16	17	18	19	20	21
	22	23	24	25	26	27	28
ĀZAR 1576	29	30	1	2	3	4	5
	6	7	8	9	10	11	12
	13	14	15	16	17	18	19
	20	21	22	23	24	25	26
DEY 1576	27	28	29	30	1	2	3
	4	5	6	7	8	9	10
	11	12	13	14	15	16	17

[a]New Year
[b]Sizdeh Bedar

HINDU LUNAR 2253/2254‡

Month	Sun	Mon	Tue	Wed	Thu	Fri	Sat
PAUSHA 2253	12	13	14	15	16	17	18
	20	21	22	23	24	25	26
MĀGHA 2253	27	28	29	30	1	2	3
	4	5	6	7	8	9	10
	11	12	13	14	15	16	17
	18	19	20	21	22	23	25
PHĀLGUNA 2253	26	27	28	29[h]	30	1	2
	2	3	4	5	6	7	8
	9	10	11	12	13	14	15[i]
	16	17	19	20	21	22	23
	24	25	26	27	28	29	30
CHAITRA 2254	1[a]	2	3	4	4	5	6
	7	8[b]	9	10	12	13	14
	15	16	17	18	19	20	21
	22	23	24	25	26	27	28
LEAP VAIŚĀKHA 2254	29	30	1	2	3	4	5
	6	7	8	9	10	11	12
	13	14	16	17	18	19	20
	21	22	23	24	25	26	27
VAIŚĀKHA 2254	28	29	29	30	1	2	3
	4	5	6	7	9	10	11
	12	13	14	15	16	17	18
	19	20	21	22	23	24	25
JYAISHTHA 2254	26	27	28	29	30	1	2
	3	4	5	6	7	8	9
	10	12	13	14	15	16	17
	18	19	20	21	22	23	24
	25	25	26	27	28	29	30
ĀSHĀḌHA 2254	1	2	3	5	6	7	8
	9	10	11	12	13	14	15
	16	17	18	19	20	21	22
	23	24	25	26	27	28	29
ŚRĀVAṆA 2254	30	1	2	3	4	5	6
	8	9	10	11	12	13	14
	15	16	17	18	19	20	21
	22	22	23[c]	24	25	26	27
BHĀDRAPADA 2254	28	29	1	2	3	4[d]	5
	6	7	8	9	10	11	12
	13	14	15	16	17	18	19
	20	21	22	23	24	25	26
ĀŚVINA 2254	27	28	29	30	1	2	3
	5	6	7	8[e]	9[e]	10[e]	11
	12	13	14	15	16	16	17
	18	19	20	21	22	23	24
KĀRTTIKA 2254	25	26	28	29	30	1[f]	2
	3	4	5	6	7	8	9
	10	11	12	13	14	15	16
	17	18	19	20	21	22	23
	24	25	26	27	28	29	30
MĀRGAŚIRA 2254	1	3	4	5	6	7	8
	9	10	10	11[g]	12	13	14
	15	16	17	18	19	20	21
	22	23	24	25	27	28	29

‡Leap year
[a]New Year (Hemalamba)
[b]Birthday of Rāma
[c]Birthday of Krishna
[d]Ganēśa Chaturthī
[e]Dashara
[f]Diwali
[g]Birthday of Vishnu
[h]Night of Śiva
[i]Holi

HINDU SOLAR 2118/2119

Month	Sun	Mon	Tue	Wed	Thu	Fri	Sat
PAUSHA 2118	15	16	17	18	19	20	21
	22	23	24	25	26	27	28
MĀGHA 2118	29	1[b]	2	3	4	5	6
	7	8	9	10	11	12	13
	14	15	16	17	18	19	20
	21	22	23	24	25	26	27
PHĀLGUNA 2118	28	29	30	1	2	3	4
	5	6	7	8	9	10	11
	12	13	14	15	16	17	18
	19	20	21	22	23	24	25
CHAITRA 2118	26	27	28	29	30	1	2
	3	4	5	6	7	8	9
	10	11	12	13	14	15	16
	17	18	19	20	21	22	23
	24	25	26	27	28	29	30
VAIŚĀKHA 2119	1[a]	2	3	4	5	6	7
	8	9	10	11	12	13	14
	15	16	17	18	19	20	21
	22	23	24	25	26	27	28
JYAISHTHA 2119	29	30	31	1	2	3	4
	5	6	7	8	9	10	11
	12	13	14	15	16	17	18
	19	20	21	22	23	24	25
ĀSHĀḌHA 2119	26	27	28	29	30	31	1
	2	3	4	5	6	7	8
	9	10	11	12	13	14	15
	16	17	18	19	20	21	22
	23	24	25	26	27	28	29
ŚRĀVAṆA 2119	30	31	32	1	2	3	4
	5	6	7	8	9	10	11
	12	13	14	15	16	17	18
	19	20	21	22	23	24	25
BHĀDRAPADA 2119	26	27	28	29	30	31	1
	2	3	4	5	6	7	8
	9	10	11	12	13	14	15
	16	17	18	19	20	21	22
	23	24	25	26	27	28	29
ĀŚVINA 2119	30	31	1	2	3	4	5
	6	7	8	9	10	11	12
	13	14	15	16	17	18	19
	20	21	22	23	24	25	26
KĀRTTIKA 2119	27	28	29	30	31	1	2
	3	4	5	6	7	8	9
	10	11	12	13	14	15	16
	17	18	19	20	21	22	23
	24	25	26	27	28	29	30
MĀRGAŚIRA 2119	1	2	3	4	5	6	7
	8	9	10	11	12	13	14
	15	16	17	18	19	20	21
	22	23	24	25	26	27	28
PAUSHA 2119	29	1	2	3	4	5	6
	7	8	9	10	11	12	13
	14	15	16	17	18	19	20

[a]New Year (Paridhāvin)
[b]Pongal

ISLAMIC (ASTRONOMICAL) 1623/1624

Month	Sun	Mon	Tue	Wed	Thu	Fri	Sat
SHAWWĀL 1623	12	13	14	15	16	17	18
	19	20	21	22	23	24	25
DHU AL-QA'DA 1623	26	27	28	29	30	1	2
	3	4	5	6	7	8	9
	10	11	12	13	14	15	16
	17	18	19	20	21	22	23
DHU AL-ḤIJJA 1623	24	25	26	27	28	29	1
	2	3	4	5	6	7	8
	9	10[g]	11	12	13	14	15
	16	17	18	19	20	21	22
	23	24	25	26	27	28	29
MUḤARRAM 1624	30	1[a]	2	3	4	5	6
	7	8	9	10[b]	11	12	13
	14	15	16	17	18	19	20
	21	22	23	24	25	26	27
ṢAFAR 1624	28	29	30	1	2	3	4
	5	6	7	8	9	10	11
	12	13	14	15	16	17	18
	19	20	21	22	23	24	25
RABĪ' I 1624	26	27	28	29	1	2	3
	4	5	6	7	8	9	10
	11	12[c]	13	14	15	16	17
	18	19	20	21	22	23	24
RABĪ' II 1624	25	26	27	28	29	30	1
	2	3	4	5	6	7	8
	9	10	11	12	13	14	15
	16	17	18	19	20	21	22
	23	24	25	26	27	28	29
JUMĀDĀ I 1624	30	1	2	3	4	5	6
	7	8	9	10	11	12	13
	14	15	16	17	18	19	20
	21	22	23	24	25	26	27
JUMĀDĀ II 1624	28	29	30	1	2	3	4
	5	6	7	8	9	10	11
	12	13	14	15	16	17	18
	19	20	21	22	23	24	25
RAJAB 1624	26	27	28	29	1	2	3
	4	5	6	7	8	9	10
	11	12	13	14	15	16	17
	18	19	20	21	22	23	24
SHA'BĀN 1624	25	26	27[d]	28	29	1	2
	3	4	5	6	7	8	9
	10	11	12	13	14	15	16
	17	18	19	20	21	22	23
RAMAḌĀN 1624	24	25	26	27	28	29	1[e]
	2	3	4	5	6	7	8
	9	10	11	12	13	14	15
	16	17	18	19	20	21	22
	23	24	25	26	27	28	29
SHAWWĀL 1624	1[f]	2	3	4	5	6	7
	8	9	10	11	12	13	14
	15	16	17	18	19	20	21
	22	23	24	25	26	27	28

[a]New Year
[b]'Ashūrā'
[c]Prophet's Birthday
[d]Ascent of the Prophet
[e]Start of Ramaḍān
[f]'Id al-Fiṭr
[g]'Id al-'Aḍḥā

GREGORIAN 2197

Julian (Sun)	Sun	Mon	Tue	Wed	Thu	Fri	Sat	Month
Dec 18	1	2	3	4	5	6	7	JANUARY 2197
	8[a]	9	10	11	12	13	14	
Jan 1	15[b]	16	17	18	19	20	21	
	22	23	24	25	26	27	28	
Jan 15	29	30	31	1	2	3	4	FEBRUARY 2197
	5	6	7	8	9	10	11	
Jan 29	12	13	14	15	16	17	18	
	19	20	21	22[c]	23	24	25	
Feb 12	26[d]	27	28	1	2	3	4	MARCH 2197
	5	6	7	8	9	10	11	
Feb 26	12	13	14	15	16	17	18	
	19	20	21	22	23	24	25	
Mar 12	26	27	28	29	30	31	1	APRIL 2197
	2	3	4	5	6	7	8	
Mar 26	9[e]	10	11	12	13	14	15	
	16	17	18	19	20	21	22	
Apr 9	23	24	25	26	27	28	29	
	30	1	2	3	4	5	6	MAY 2197
Apr 23	7	8	9	10	11	12	13	
	14	15	16	17	18	19	20	
May 7	21	22	23	24	25	26	27	
	28	29	30	31	1	2	3	JUNE 2197
May 21	4	5	6	7	8	9	10	
	11	12	13	14	15	16	17	
Jun 4	18	19	20	21	22	23	24	
	25	26	27	28	29	30	1	JULY 2197
Jun 18	2	3	4	5	6	7	8	
	9	10	11	12	13	14	15	
Jul 2	16	17	18	19	20	21	22	
	23	24	25	26	27	28	29	
Jul 16	30	31	1	2	3	4	5	AUGUST 2197
	6	7	8	9	10	11	12	
Jul 30	13	14	15	16	17	18	19	
	20	21	22	23	24	25	26	
Aug 13	27	28	29	30	31	1	2	SEPTEMBER 2197
	3	4	5	6	7	8	9	
Aug 27	10	11	12	13	14	15	16	
	17	18	19	20	21	22	23	
Sep 10	24	25	26	27	28	29	30	
	1	2	3	4	5	6	7	OCTOBER 2197
Sep 24	8	9	10	11	12	13	14	
	15	16	17	18	19	20	21	
Oct 8	22	23	24	25	26	27	28	
	29	30	31	1	2	3	4	NOVEMBER 2197
Oct 22	5	6	7	8	9	10	11	
	12	13	14	15	16	17	18	
Nov 5	19	20	21	22	23	24	25	
	26	27	28	29	30	1	2	DECEMBER 2197
Nov 19	3[g]	4	5	6	7	8	9	
	10	11	12	13	14	15	16	
Dec 3	17	18	19	20	21	22	23	
	24	25[h]	26	27	28	29	30	
Dec 17	31	1	2	3	4	5	6	

[a]Orthodox Christmas
[b]Julian New Year
[c]Ash Wednesday
[d]Feast of Orthodoxy
[e]Easter (also Orthodox)
[g]Advent
[h]Christmas

2198

Gregorian 2198	Sun	Mon	Tue	Wed	Thu	Fri	Sat	Lunar Phases	ISO Week (Mon)	Julian Day (Sun noon)
January 2198	◑	1[a]	2	3	4	5	6	21:34	1	2523863
	●	8	9	10	11	12	13	15:46	2	2523870
	14	◐	16	17	18	19	20	5:31	3	2523877
	21	22	○	24	25	26	27	5:35	4	2523884
	28	29	◑	31	1	2	3	5:47	5	2523891
February 2198	4	5	●	7	8	9	10	5:28	6	2523898
	11	12	13	◐	15	16	17	3:26	7	2523905
	18	19	20	○	22	23	24	19:18	8	2523912
	25	26	27	◑	1	2	3	13:39	9	2523919
March 2198	4	5	6	●	8	9	10	20:26	10	2523926
	11	12	13	14	15	◐	17	0:02	11	2523933
	18	19	20[b]	21	22	○	24	6:27	12	2523940
	25	26	27	28	◑	30	31	21:58	13	2523947
April 2198	1	2	3	4	5	●	7	12:27	14	2523954
	8	9	10	11	12	13	◐	17:22	15	2523961
	15	16	17	18	19	20	○	15:38	16	2523968
	22	23	24	25	26	27	◑	7:23	17	2523975
	29	30	1	2	3	4	5		18	2523982
May 2198	●	7	8	9	10	11	12	5:01	19	2523989
	13	◐	15	16	17	18	19	6:38	20	2523996
	○	21	22	23	24	25	26	23:36	21	2524003
	◑	28	29	30	31	1	2	18:26	22	2524010
June 2198	3	●	5	6	7	8	9	21:12	23	2524017
	10	11	◐	13	14	15	16	16:11	24	2524024
	17	18	○	20[c]	21	22	23	7:03	25	2524031
	24	25	◑	27	28	29	30	7:39	26	2524038
July 2198	1	2	3	●	5	6	7	12:02	27	2524045
	8	9	10	◐	12	13	14	23:00	28	2524052
	15	16	17	○	19	20	21	14:45	29	2524059
	22	23	24	◑	26	27	28	23:12	30	2524066
	29	30	31	1	2	●	4	1:01	31	2524073
August 2198	5	6	7	8	9	◐	11	4:21	32	2524080
	12	13	14	15	○	17	18	23:38	33	2524087
	19	20	21	22	23	◑	25	16:46	34	2524094
	26	27	28	29	30	31	●	12:21	35	2524101
September 2198	2	3	4	5	6	7	◐	9:30	36	2524108
	9	10	11	12	13	14	○	10:46	37	2524115
	16	17	18	19	20	21	22[d]		38	2524122
	◑	24	25	26	27	28	29	11:23	39	2524129
October 2198	●	1	2	3	4	5	6	22:42	40	2524136
	◐	8	9	10	11	12	13	15:43	41	2524143
	14	○	16	17	18	19	20	0:58	42	2524150
	21	22	◑	24	25	26	27	5:43	43	2524157
	28	29	●	31	1	2	3	8:51	44	2524164
November 2198	4	5	◐	7	8	9	10	0:13	45	2524171
	11	12	○	14	15	16	17	18:18	46	2524178
	18	19	20	◑	22	23	24	22:35	47	2524185
	25	26	27	●	29	30	1	19:12	48	2524192
December 2198	2	3	4	◐	6	7	8	12:03	49	2524199
	9	10	11	12	○	14	15	13:40	50	2524206
	16	17	18	19	20	◑[e]	22	13:12	51	2524213
	23	24	25	26	27	●	29	5:54	52	2524220
	30	31	1	2	3	◐	5	3:42	1	2524227

Julian Day	Hebrew 5958‡/5959	Sun	Mon	Tue	Wed	Thu	Fri	Sat	Molad
2523863	Teveth 5958	22	23	24	25	26	27	28	
2523870	Shevat 5958	29	1	2	3	4	5	6	Mon 4h52m14p
2523877		7	8	9	10	11	12	13	
2523884		14	15	16	17	18	19	20	
2523891		21	22	23	24	25	26	27	
2523898	Adar I 5958	28	29	30	1	2	3	4	Tue 17h36m15p
2523905		5	6	7	8	9	10	11	
2523912		12	13	14	15	16	17	18	
2523919		19	20	21	22	23	24	25	
2523926	Adar II 5958	26	27	28	29	30	1	2	Thu 6h20m16p
2523933		3	4	5	6	7	8	9	
2523940		10	11	12	13	14[f]	15	16	
2523947		17	18	19	20	21	22	23	
2523954	Nisan 5958	24	25	26	27	28	29	1	Fri 19h4m17p
2523961		2	3	4	5	6	7	8	
2523968		9	10	11	12	13	14	15[g]	
2523975		16	17	18	19	20	21	22	
2523982		23	24	25	26	27	28	29	
2523989	Iyar 5958	30	1	2	3	4	5	6	Sun 7h49m0p
2523996		7	8	9	10	11	12	13	
2524003		14	15	16	17	18	19	20	
2524010		21	22	23	24	25	26	27	
2524017	Sivan 5958	28	29	1	2	3	4	5	Mon 20h33m1p
2524024		6[h]	7	8	9	10	11	12	
2524031		13	14	15	16	17	18	19	
2524038		20	21	22	23	24	25	26	
2524045	Tammuz 5958	27	28	29	30	1	2	3	Wed 9h17m2p
2524052		4	5	6	7	8	9	10	
2524059		11	12	13	14	15	16	17	
2524066		18	19	20	21	22	23	24	
2524073	Av 5958	25	26	27	28	29	1	2	Thu 22h1m3p
2524080		3	4	5	6	7	8	9	
2524087		10[i]	11	12	13	14	15	16	
2524094		17	18	19	20	21	22	23	
2524101		24	25	26	27	28	29	30	
2524108	Elul 5958	1	2	3	4	5	6	7	Sat 10h45m4p
2524115		8	9	10	11	12	13	14	
2524122		15	16	17	18	19	20	21	
2524129		22	23	24	25	26	27	28	
2524136	Tishri 5959	29	1[a]	2[a]	3	4	5	6	Sun 23h29m5p
2524143		7	8	9	10[b]	11	12	13	
2524150		14	15[c]	16	17	18	19	20	
2524157		21	22	23	24	25	26	27	
2524164	Heshvan 5959	28	29	30	1	2	3	4	Tue 12h13m6p
2524171		5	6	7	8	9	10	11	
2524178		12	13	14	15	16	17	18	
2524185		19	20	21	22	23	24	25	
2524192	Kislev 5959	26	27	28	29	30	1	2	Thu 0h57m7p
2524199		3	4	5	6	7[d]	8	9	
2524206		10	11	12	13	14	15	16	
2524213		17	18	19	20	21	22	23	
2524220		24	25[e]	26[e]	27[e]	28[e]	29[e]	30[e]	Fri 13h41m8p
2524227		1[e]	2[e]	3	4	5	6	7	

Julian Day	Chinese Dīng-Yǒu/Wù-Xū	Sun	Mon	Tue	Wed	Thu	Fri	Sat	Solar Term
2523863	Month 12 Dīng-Yǒu	23	24	25	26	27	28	29	Xiǎo hán
2523870		1	2	3	4	5	6	7	
2523877		8	9	10	11	12	13	14	Dà hán
2523884		15	16	17	18	19	20	21	
2523891		22	23	24	25	26	27	28	Lì chūn
2523898	Month 1 Wù-Xū	29	30	1[a]	2	3	4	5	
2523905		6	7	8	9	10	11	12*	
2523912		13	14	15[b]	16	17	18	19	Yǔ shuǐ
2523919		20	21	22	23	24	25	26	
2523926	Month 2 Wù-Xū	27	28	29	30	1	2	3	Jīng zhé
2523933		4	5	6	7	8	9	10	
2523940		11	12	13	14	15	16	17	Chūn fēn
2523947		18	19	20	21	22	23	24	
2523954	Month 3 Wù-Xū	25	26	27	28[c]	29	1	2	Qīng míng
2523961		3	4	5	6	7	8	9	
2523968		10	11	12	13*	14	15	16	Gǔ yǔ
2523975		17	18	19	20	21	22	23	
2523982		24	25	26	27	28	29	30	Lì xià
2523989	Month 4 Wù-Xū	1	2	3	4	5	6	7	
2523996		8	9	10	11	12	13	14	
2524003		15	16	17	18	19	20	21	Xiǎo mǎn
2524010		22	23	24	25	26	27	28	
2524017	Month 5 Wù-Xū	29	30	1	2	3	4	5[d]	Máng zhòng
2524024		6	7	8	9	10	11	12	
2524031		13*	14	15	16	17	18	19	Xià zhì
2524038		20	21	22	23	24	25	26	
2524045	Month 6 Wù-Xū	27	28	29	1	2	3	4	Xiǎo shǔ
2524052		5	6	7	8	9	10	11	
2524059		12	13	14	15	16	17	18	
2524066		19	20	21	22	23	24	25	Dà shǔ
2524073	Month 7 Wù-Xū	26	27	28	29	30	1	2	
2524080		3	4	5	6	7[e]	8	9	Lì qiū
2524087		10	11	12	13	14*	15[f]	16	
2524094		17	18	19	20	21	22	23	Chǔ shǔ
2524101	Month 8 Wù-Xū	24	25	26	27	28	29	1	
2524108		2	3	4	5	6	7	8	Bái lù
2524115		9	10	11	12	13	14	15[g]	
2524122		16	17	18	19	20	21	22	Qiū fēn
2524129		23	24	25	26	27	28	29	
2524136	Month 9 Wù-Xū	30	1	2	3	4	5	6	
2524143		7	8	9[h]	10	11	12	13	Hán lù
2524150		14	15*	16	17	18	19	20	
2524157		21	22	23	24	25	26	27	Shuāng jiàng
2524164	Month 10 Wù-Xū	28	29	1	2	3	4	5	
2524171		6	7	8	9	10	11	12	Lì dōng
2524178		13	14	15	16	17	18	19	
2524185		20	21	22	23	24	25	26	Xiǎo xuě
2524192	Month 11* Wù-Xū	27	28	29	30	1	2	3	
2524199		4	5	6	7	8	9	10	Dà xuě
2524206		11	12	13	14	15	16*	17	
2524213		18	19	20	21	22	23[i]	24	Dōng zhì
2524220	Month 12 Wù-Xū	25	26	27	28	29	1	2	
2524227		3	4	5	6	7	8	9	Xiǎo hán

Julian Day	Coptic 1914/1915‡	Sun	Mon	Tue	Wed	Thu	Fri	Sat	Ethiopic 2190/2191‡
2523863	Koiak 1914	21	22	23	24	25	26	27	Tākhśāś 2190
2523870	Tōbe 1914	28	29[c]	30	1	2	3	4	Ṭer 2190
2523877		5	6[d]	7	8	9	10	11[e]	
2523884		12	13	14	15	16	17	18	
2523891		19	20	21	22	23	24	25	
2523898	Meshir 1914	26	27	28	29	30	1	2	Yakātīt 2190
2523905		3	4	5	6	7	8	9	
2523912		10	11	12	13	14	15	16	
2523919		17	18	19	20	21	22	23	
2523926		24	25	26	27	28	29	30	
2523933	Paremotep 1914	1	2	3	4	5	6	7	Magābīt 2190
2523940		8	9	10	11	12	13	14	
2523947		15	16	17	18	19	20	21	
2523954		22	23	24	25	26	27	28	
2523961	Parmoute 1914	29	30	1	2	3	4	5	Miyāzyā 2190
2523968		6	7	8	9	10	11	12	
2523975		13	14	15	16	17	18	19	
2523982		20[f]	21	22	23	24	25	26	
2523989	Pashons 1914	27	28	29[g]	30	1	2	3	Genbot 2190
2523996		4	5	6	7	8	9	10	
2524003		11	12	13	14	15	16	17	
2524010		18	19	20	21	22	23	24	
2524017	Paōne 1914	25	26	27	28	29	30	1	Sanē 2190
2524024		2	3	4	5	6	7	8	
2524031		9	10	11	12	13	14	15	
2524038		16	17	18	19	20	21	22	
2524045		23	24	25	26	27	28	29	
2524052	Epēp 1914	30	1	2	3	4	5	6	Ḥamlē 2190
2524059		7	8	9	10	11	12	13	
2524066		14	15	16	17	18	19	20	
2524073		21	22	23	24	25	26	27	
2524080	Mesorē 1914	28	29	30	1	2	3	4	Naḥasē 2190
2524087		5	6	7	8	9	10	11	
2524094		12	13[h]	14	15	16	17	18	
2524101		19	20	21	22	23	24	25	
2524108	Epag. 1914	26	27	28	29	30	1	2	Pāg. 2190
2524115	Thoout 1915	3	4	5	1[a]	2	3	4	Maskaram 2191
2524122		5	6	7	8	9	10	11	
2524129		12	13	14	15	16	17[b]	18	
2524136		19	20	21	22	23	24	25	
2524143	Paope 1915	26	27	28	29	30	1	2	Ṭeqemt 2191
2524150		3	4	5	6	7	8	9	
2524157		10	11	12	13	14	15	16	
2524164		17	18	19	20	21	22	23	
2524171		24	25	26	27	28	29	30	
2524178	Athōr 1915	1	2	3	4	5	6	7	Ḫedār 2191
2524185		8	9	10	11	12	13	14	
2524192		15	16	17	18	19	20	21	
2524199		22	23	24	25	26	27	28	
2524206	Koiak 1915	29	30	1	2	3	4	5	Tākhśāś 2191
2524213		6	7	8	9	10	11	12	
2524220		13	14	15	16	17	18	19	
2524227		20	21	22	23	24	25	26	

[a]New Year
[b]Spring (6:53)
[c]Summer (21:32)
[d]Autumn (15:02)
[e]Winter (14:48)
● New moon
◐ First quarter moon
○ Full moon
◑ Last quarter moon

‡Leap year
[a]New Year
[b]Yom Kippur
[c]Sukkot
[d]Winter starts
[e]Ḥanukkah
[f]Purim
[g]Passover
[h]Shavuot
[i]Fast of Av

[a]New Year (4896, Dog)
[b]Lantern Festival
[c]Qīngmíng
[d]Dragon Festival
[e]Qīqiǎo
[f]Hungry Ghosts
[g]Mid-Autumn Festival
[h]Double-Ninth Festival
[i]Dōngzhì
*Start of 60-name cycle

‡Leap year
[a]New Year
[b]Building of the Cross
[c]Christmas
[d]Jesus's Circumcision
[e]Epiphany
[f]Easter
[g]Mary's Announcement
[h]Jesus's Transfiguration

PERSIAN (ASTRONOMICAL) 1576/1577‡

Month	Sun	Mon	Tue	Wed	Thu	Fri	Sat
DEY 1576	11	12	13	14	15	16	17
	18	19	20	21	22	23	24
	25	26	27	28	29	30	1
BAHMAN 1576	2	3	4	5	6	7	8
	9	10	11	12	13	14	15
	16	17	18	19	20	21	22
	23	24	25	26	27	28	29
	30	1	2	3	4	5	6
ESFAND 1576	7	8	9	10	11	12	13
	14	15	16	17	18	19	20
	21	22	23	24	25	26	27
	28	29	1[a]	2	3	4	5
FARVARDĪN 1577	6	7	8	9	10	11	12
	13[b]	14	15	16	17	18	19
	20	21	22	23	24	25	26
	27	28	29	30	31	1	2
ORDĪBEHEŠT 1577	3	4	5	6	7	8	9
	10	11	12	13	14	15	16
	17	18	19	20	21	22	23
	24	25	26	27	28	29	30
	31	1	2	3	4	5	6
XORDĀD 1577	7	8	9	10	11	12	13
	14	15	16	17	18	19	20
	21	22	23	24	25	26	27
	28	29	30	31	1	2	3
TĪR 1577	4	5	6	7	8	9	10
	11	12	13	14	15	16	17
	18	19	20	21	22	23	24
	25	26	27	28	29	30	31
MORDĀD 1577	1	2	3	4	5	6	7
	8	9	10	11	12	13	14
	15	16	17	18	19	20	21
	22	23	24	25	26	27	28
	29	30	31	1	2	3	4
SHAHRĪVAR 1577	5	6	7	8	9	10	11
	12	13	14	15	16	17	18
	19	20	21	22	23	24	25
	26	27	28	29	30	31	1
MEHR 1577	2	3	4	5	6	7	8
	9	10	11	12	13	14	15
	16	17	18	19	20	21	22
	23	24	25	26	27	28	29
	30	1	2	3	4	5	6
ĀBĀN 1577	7	8	9	10	11	12	13
	14	15	16	17	18	19	20
	21	22	23	24	25	26	27
	28	29	30	1	2	3	4
ĀZAR 1577	5	6	7	8	9	10	11
	12	13	14	15	16	17	18
	19	20	21	22	23	24	25
	26	27	28	29	30	1	2
DEY 1577	3	4	5	6	7	8	9
	10	11	12	13	14	15	16

‡Leap year
[a]New Year
[b]Sizdeh Bedar

HINDU LUNAR 2254‡/2255

Month	Sun	Mon	Tue	Wed	Thu	Fri	Sat
MĀRGAŚĪRA 2254	22	23	24	25	27	28	29
PAUSHA 2254	30	1	2	3	4	5	6
	7	8	9	10	11	12	12
	13	14	15	16	17	18	19
	21	22	23	24	25	26	27
	28	29	30	1	2	3	4
MĀGHA 2254	5	6	7	8	9	10	11
	12	13	14	15	16	17	18
	19	20	21	22	23	24	26
	27	28	29[h]	30	1	2	3
PHĀLGUNA 2254	4	5	5	6	7	8	9
	10	11	12	13	14	15[i]	16
	17	19	20	21	22	23	24
	25	26	27	28	29	30	1[a]
CHAITRA 2255	2	3	4	5	6	7	8
	9[b]	9	11	12	13	14	15
	16	17	18	19	20	21	22
	24	25	26	27	28	28	29
	30	1	2	3	4	5	6
VAIŚĀKHA 2255	7	8	9	10	11	12	13
	14	15	17	18	19	20	21
	22	23	24	25	26	27	28
	29	30	1	2	3	3	4
JYAISHṬHA 2255	5	6	8	9	10	11	12
	13	14	15	16	17	18	20
	21	22	23	24	25	25	26
	27	28	29	30	1	2	3
ĀSHĀḌHA 2255	4	5	6	7	8	9	10
	12	13	14	15	16	17	18
	19	20	21	22	23	24	25
	26	27	28	29	30	1	2
ŚRĀVAṆA 2255	3	4	5	6	7	8	9
	10	11	12	13	14	16	17
	18	19	20	21	22	22	23[c]
	24	25	26	27	28	29	30
	1	2	3	4[d]	5	6	8
BHĀDRAPADA 2255	9	10	11	12	13	14	15
	16	17	18	19	20	21	22
	23	24	25	26	27	27	28
	30	1	2	3	4	5	6
ĀŚVINA 2255	7	8[e]	9[e]	10[e]	12	13	14
	15	16	16	17	18	19	20
	21	22	23	24	25	26	27
	28	29	30	1[f]	2	3	5
KĀRTTIKA 2255	6	7	8	9	10	11	12
	13	14	15	16	17	18	19
	20	20	21	22	23	24	25
	26	27	29	30	1	2	3
MĀRGAŚĪRA 2255	4	5	6	7	8	9	10
	11[g]	12	13	14	15	16	17
	18	19	20	21	22	23	24
	25	26	27	28	29	30	1
PAUSHA 2255	2	4	5	6	7	8	9

‡Leap year
[a]New Year (Vilamba)
[b]Birthday of Rāma
[c]Birthday of Krishna
[d]Ganēśa Chaturthī
[e]Dashara
[f]Diwali
[g]Birthday of Vishnu
[h]Night of Śiva
[i]Holi

HINDU SOLAR 2119/2120

Month	Sun	Mon	Tue	Wed	Thu	Fri	Sat
PAUSHA 2119	14	15	16	17	18	19	20
	21	22	23	24	25	26	27
	28	29	30	1[b]	2	3	4
MĀGHA 2119	5	6	7	8	9	10	11
	12	13	14	15	16	17	18
	19	20	21	22	23	24	25
	26	27	28	29	1	2	3
PHĀLGUNA 2119	4	5	6	7	8	9	10
	11	12	13	14	15	16	17
	18	19	20	21	22	23	24
	25	26	27	28	29	30	1
CHAITRA 2119	2	3	4	5	6	7	8
	9	10	11	12	13	14	15
	16	17	18	19	20	21	22
	23	24	25	26	27	28	29
	30	1[a]	2	3	4	5	6
VAIŚĀKHA 2120	7	8	9	10	11	12	13
	14	15	16	17	18	19	20
	21	22	23	24	25	26	27
	28	29	30	31	1	2	3
JYAISHṬHA 2120	4	5	6	7	8	9	10
	11	12	13	14	15	16	17
	18	19	20	21	22	23	24
	25	26	27	28	29	30	31
	32	1	2	3	4	5	6
ĀSHĀḌHA 2120	7	8	9	10	11	12	13
	14	15	16	17	18	19	20
	21	22	23	24	25	26	27
	28	29	30	31	1	2	3
ŚRĀVAṆA 2120	4	5	6	7	8	9	10
	11	12	13	14	15	16	17
	18	19	20	21	22	23	24
	25	26	27	28	29	30	31
	32	1	2	3	4	5	6
BHĀDRAPADA 2120	7	8	9	10	11	12	13
	14	15	16	17	18	19	20
	21	22	23	24	25	26	27
	28	29	30	31	1	2	3
ĀŚVINA 2120	4	5	6	7	8	9	10
	11	12	13	14	15	16	17
	18	19	20	21	22	23	24
	25	26	27	28	29	30	1
KĀRTTIKA 2120	2	3	4	5	6	7	8
	9	10	11	12	13	14	15
	16	17	18	19	20	21	22
	23	24	25	26	27	28	29
	30	1	2	3	4	5	6
MĀRGAŚĪRA 2120	7	8	9	10	11	12	13
	14	15	16	17	18	19	20
	21	22	23	24	25	26	27
	28	29	30	1	2	3	4
PAUSHA 2120	5	6	7	8	9	10	11
	12	13	14	15	16	17	18

[a]New Year (Pramādin)
[b]Pongal

ISLAMIC (ASTRONOMICAL) 1624/1625

Month	Sun	Mon	Tue	Wed	Thu	Fri	Sat
SHAWWĀL 1624	22	23	24	25	26	27	28
DHU AL-QA'DA 1624	29	30	1	2	3	4	5
	6	7	8	9	10	11	12
	13	14	15	16	17	18	19
	20	21	22	23	24	25	26
	27	28	29	1	2	3	4
DHU AL-ḤIJJA 1624	5	6	7	8	9	10[g]	11
	12	13	14	15	16	17	18
	19	20	21	22	23	24	25
	26	27	28	29	30	1[a]	2
MUḤARRAM 1625	3	4	5	6	7	8	9
	10[b]	11	12	13	14	15	16
	17	18	19	20	21	22	23
	24	25	26	27	28	29	30
	1	2	3	4	5	6	7
ṢAFAR 1625	8	9	10	11	12	13	14
	15	16	17	18	19	20	21
	22	23	24	25	26	27	28
	29	30	1	2	3	4	5
RABĪ' I 1625	6	7	8	9	10	11	12[c]
	13	14	15	16	17	18	19
	20	21	22	23	24	25	26
	27	28	29	1	2	3	4
RABĪ' II 1625	5	6	7	8	9	10	11
	12	13	14	15	16	17	18
	19	20	21	22	23	24	25
	26	27	28	29	30	1	2
JUMĀDĀ I 1625	3	4	5	6	7	8	9
	10	11	12	13	14	15	16
	17	18	19	20	21	22	23
	24	25	26	27	28	29	30
	1	2	3	4	5	6	7
JUMĀDĀ II 1625	8	9	10	11	12	13	14
	15	16	17	18	19	20	21
	22	23	24	25	26	27	28
	29	30	1	2	3	4	5
RAJAB 1625	6	7	8	9	10	11	12
	13	14	15	16	17	18	19
	20	21	22	23	24	25	26
	27[d]	28	29	1	2	3	4
SHA'BĀN 1625	5	6	7	8	9	10	11
	12	13	14	15	16	17	18
	19	20	21	22	23	24	25
	26	27	28	29	1[e]	2	3
RAMAḌĀN 1625	4	5	6	7	8	9	10
	11	12	13	14	15	16	17
	18	19	20	21	22	23	24
	25	26	27	28	29	1[f]	2
SHAWWĀL 1625	3	4	5	6	7	8	9
	10	11	12	13	14	15	16
	17	18	19	20	21	22	23
	24	25	26	27	28	29	1
DHU AL-QA'DA 1625	2	3	4	5	6	7	8

[a]New Year
[b]'Ashūrā'
[c]Prophet's Birthday
[d]Ascent of the Prophet
[e]Start of Ramaḍān
[f]'Id al-Fiṭr
[g]'Id al-'Aḍḥā

GREGORIAN 2198

Julian (Sun)	Sun	Mon	Tue	Wed	Thu	Fri	Sat	Month
Dec 17	31	1	2	3	4	5	6	
	7	8[a]	9	10	11	12	13	JANUARY 2198
Dec 31	14	15[b]	16	17	18	19	20	
	21	22	23	24	25	26	27	
Jan 14	28	29	30	31	1	2	3	
	4	5	6	7[c]	8	9	10	FEBRUARY 2198
Jan 28	11	12	13	14	15	16	17	
	18	19	20	21	22	23	24	
Feb 11	25	26	27	28	1	2	3	
	4	5	6	7	8	9	10	MARCH 2198
Feb 25	11	12	13	14	15	16	17	
	18[d]	19	20	21	22	23	24	
Mar 11	25[e]	26	27	28	29	30	31	
	1	2	3	4	5	6	7	
Mar 25	8	9	10	11	12	13	14	APRIL 2198
	15	16	17	18	19	20	21	
Apr 8	22	23	24	25	26	27	28	
	29[f]	30	1	2	3	4	5	
Apr 22	6	7	8	9	10	11	12	
	13	14	15	16	17	18	19	MAY 2198
May 6	20	21	22	23	24	25	26	
	27	28	29	30	31	1	2	
May 20	3	4	5	6	7	8	9	
	10	11	12	13	14	15	16	JUNE 2198
Jun 3	17	18	19	20	21	22	23	
	24	25	26	27	28	29	30	
Jun 17	1	2	3	4	5	6	7	
	8	9	10	11	12	13	14	JULY 2198
Jul 1	15	16	17	18	19	20	21	
	22	23	24	25	26	27	28	
Jul 15	29	30	31	1	2	3	4	
	5	6	7	8	9	10	11	AUGUST 2198
Jul 29	12	13	14	15	16	17	18	
	19	20	21	22	23	24	25	
Aug 12	26	27	28	29	30	31	1	
	2	3	4	5	6	7	8	
Aug 26	9	10	11	12	13	14	15	SEPTEMBER 2198
	16	17	18	19	20	21	22	
Sep 9	23	24	25	26	27	28	29	
	30	1	2	3	4	5	6	
Sep 23	7	8	9	10	11	12	13	OCTOBER 2198
	14	15	16	17	18	19	20	
Oct 7	21	22	23	24	25	26	27	
	28	29	30	31	1	2	3	
Oct 21	4	5	6	7	8	9	10	NOVEMBER 2198
	11	12	13	14	15	16	17	
Nov 4	18	19	20	21	22	23	24	
	25	26	27	28	29	30	1	
Nov 18	2[g]	3	4	5	6	7	8	DECEMBER 2198
	9	10	11	12	13	14	15	
Dec 2	16	17	18	19	20	21	22	
	23	24	25[h]	26	27	28	29	
Dec 16	30	31	1	2	3	4	5	

[a]Orthodox Christmas
[b]Julian New Year
[c]Ash Wednesday
[d]Feast of Orthodoxy
[e]Easter
[f]Orthodox Easter
[g]Advent
[h]Christmas

2199

Gregorian 2199	Sun	Mon	Tue	Wed	Thu	Fri	Sat	Lunar Phases	ISO Week (Mon)	Julian Day (Sun noon)	Hebrew 5959/5960	Sun	Mon	Tue	Wed	Thu	Fri	Sat	Molad
JANUARY 2199	30	31	1[a]	2	3	◐	5	3:42	1	2524227	TEVETH 5959	1[e]	2[e]	3	4	5	6	7	Fri $13^h41^m8^p$
	6	7	8	9	10	11	○	9:07	2	2524234		8	9	10	11	12	13	14	
	13	14	15	16	17	18	19		3	2524241		15	16	17	18	19	20	21	
	◑	21	22	23	24	25	●	1:12 16:57	4	2524248		22	23	24	25	26	27	28	
FEBRUARY 2199	27	28	29	30	31	1	◐	22:44	5	2524255	SHEVAT 5959	29	1	2	3	4	5	6	Sun $2^h25^m9^p$
	3	4	5	6	7	8	9		6	2524262		7	8	9	10	11	12	13	
	10	○	12	13	14	15	16	2:53	7	2524269		14	15	16	17	18	19	20	
	17	◑	19	20	21	22	23	10:40	8	2524276		21	22	23	24	25	26	27	
MARCH 2199	24	●	26	27	28	1	2	4:34	9	2524283	ADAR 5959	28	29	30	1	2	3	4	Mon $15^h9^m10^p$
	3	◐	5	6	7	8	9	19:33	10	2524290		5	6	7	8	9	10	11	
	10	11	○	13	14	15	16	18:01	11	2524297		12	13	14[f]	15	16	17	18	
	17	18	◑	20[b]	21	22	23	18:07	12	2524304		19	20	21	22	23	24	25	
	24	25	●	27	28	29	30	17:09	13	2524311	NISAN 5959	26	27	28	29	1	2	3	Wed $3^h53^m11^p$
APRIL 2199	31	1	2	◐	4	5	6	15:59	14	2524318		4	5	6	7	8	9	10	
	7	8	9	10	○	12	13	6:23	15	2524325		11	12	13	14	15[g]	16	17	
	14	15	16	17	◑	19	20	0:30	16	2524332		18	19	20	21	22	23	24	
	21	22	23	24	●	26	27	6:58	17	2524339	IYYAR 5959	25	26	27	28	29	30	1	Thu $16^h37^m12^p$
MAY 2199	28	29	30	1	2	◐	4	10:18	18	2524346		2	3	4	5	6	7	8	
	5	6	7	8	9	○	11	16:18	19	2524353		9	10	11	12	13	14	15	
	12	13	14	15	16	◑	18	7:03	20	2524360		16	17	18	19	20	21	22	
	19	20	21	22	23	●	25	21:51	21	2524367		23	24	25	26	27	28	29	
JUNE 2199	26	27	28	29	30	31	1		22	2524374	SIVAN 5959	1	2	3	4	5	6[h]	7	Sat $5^h21^m13^p$
	◐	3	4	5	6	7	8	1:36	23	2524381		8	9	10	11	12	13	14	
	○	10	11	12	13	14	◑	0:17 15:00	24	2524388		15	16	17	18	19	20	21	
	16	17	18	19	20	21[c]	22		25	2524395		22	23	24	25	26	27	28	
	●	24	25	26	27	28	29	13:11	26	2524402	TAMMUZ 5959	29	30	1	2	3	4	5	Sun $18^h5^m14^p$
JULY 2199	30	◐	2	3	4	5	6	13:50	27	2524409		6	7	8	9	10	11	12	
	7	○	9	10	11	12	13	7:09	28	2524416		13	14	15	16	17	18	19	
	14	◑	16	17	18	19	20	1:25	29	2524423		20	21	22	23	24	25	26	
	21	22	●	24	25	26	27	4:19	30	2524430	AV 5959	27	28	29	1	2	3	4	Tue $6^h49^m15^p$
AUGUST 2199	28	29	◐	31	1	2	3	23:20	31	2524437		5	6	7	8	9[i]	10	11	
	4	5	○	7	8	9	10	13:55	32	2524444		12	13	14	15	16	17	18	
	11	12	◑	14	15	16	17	14:54	33	2524451		19	20	21	22	23	24	25	
	18	19	20	●	22	23	24	18:52	34	2524458	ELUL 5959	26	27	28	29	30	1	2	Wed $19^h33^m16^p$
	25	26	27	28	◐	30	31	6:44	35	2524465		3	4	5	6	7	8	9	
SEPTEMBER 2199	1	2	3	○	5	6	7	21:50	36	2524472		10	11	12	13	14	15	16	
	8	9	10	11	◑	13	14	7:25	37	2524479		17	18	19	20	21	22	23	
	15	16	17	18	19	●	21	8:42	38	2524486	TISHRI 5960	24	25	26	27	28	29	1[a]	Fri $8^h17^m17^p$
	22[d]	23	24	25	26	◐	28	12:54	39	2524493		2[a]	3	4	5	6	7	8	
OCTOBER 2199	29	30	1	2	3	○	5	8:02	40	2524500		9	10[b]	11	12	13	14	15[c]	
	6	7	8	9	10	11	◑	2:18	41	2524507		16	17	18	19	20	21	22	
	13	14	15	16	17	18	●	21:49	42	2524514		23	24	25	26	27	28	29	
	20	21	22	23	24	25	◐	19:03	43	2524521	HESHVAN 5960	30	1	2	3	4	5	6	Sat $21^h2^m0^p$
NOVEMBER 2199	27	28	29	30	31	1	○	21:19	44	2524528		7	8	9	10	11	12	13	
	3	4	5	6	7	8	9		45	2524535		14	15	16	17	18	19	20	
	◑	11	12	13	14	15	16	22:24	46	2524542		21	22	23	24	25	26	27	
	17	●	19	20	21	22	23	10:08	47	2524549	KISLEV 5960	28	29	30	1	2	3	4	Mon $9^h46^m1^p$
	24	◐	26	27	28	29	30	2:28	48	2524556		5	6	7	8	9	10	11	
DECEMBER 2199	1	○	3	4	5	6	7	13:41	49	2524563		12	13	14	15	16	17	18[d]	
	8	9	◑	11	12	13	14	18:13	50	2524570		19	20	21	22	23	24	25[e]	
	15	16	●	18	19	20	21[e]	21:36	51	2524577	TEVETH 5960	26[e]	27[e]	28[e]	29[e]	30[e]	1[e]	2[e]	Tue $22^h30^m2^p$
	22	23	◐	25	26	27	28	12:26	52	2524584		3	4	5	6	7	8	9	
	29	30	31	○	2	3	4	8:15	1	2524591		10	11	12	13	14	15	16	

ISO Week (Mon)	Chinese Wù-Xū/Jǐ-Hài‡	Sun	Mon	Tue	Wed	Thu	Fri	Sat	Solar Term	Coptic 1915‡/1916	Sun	Mon	Tue	Wed	Thu	Fri	Sat	Ethiopic 2191‡/2192
1	MONTH 12 Wù-Xū	3	4	5	6	7	8	9	Xiǎo hán	KOIAK 1915	20	21	22	23	24	25	26	TĀKHŚĀŚ 2191
2		10	11	12	13	14	15	16			27	28	29[c]	30	1	2	3	
3		17	18	19	20	21	22	23		TÔBE 1915	4	5	6[d]	7	8	9	10	ṬER 2191
4		**24**	25	26	27	28	29	30	Dà hán		11[e]	12	13	14	15	16	17	
5	MONTH 1 Jǐ-Hài	1[a]	2	3	4	5	6	7			18	19	20	21	22	23	24	
6		8	*9*	10	11	12	13	14	Lì chūn		25	26	27	28	29	30	1	
7		15[b]	16	17*	18	19	20	21		MESHIR 1915	2	3	4	5	6	7	8	YAKĀTIT 2191
8		22	**23**	24	25	26	27	28	Yǔ shuǐ		9	10	11	12	13	14	15	
9	MONTH 2 Jǐ-Hài	29	1	2	3	4	5	6			16	17	18	19	20	21	22	
10		7	8	*9*	10	11	12	13	Jīng zhé		23	24	25	26	27	28	29	
11		14	15	16	17	18	19	20		PAREMOTEP 1915	30	1	2	3	4	5	6	MAGĀBIT 2191
12		21	22	23	**24**	25	26	27	Chūn fēn		7	8	9	10	11	12	13	
13	MONTH 3 Jǐ-Hài	28	29	30	1	2	3	4			14	15	16	17	18	19	20	
14		5	6	7	8	*9*[c]	10	11	Qīng míng		21	22	23	24	25	26	27	
15		12	13	14	15	16	17	18*		PARMOUTE 1915	28	29	30	1	2	3	4	MIYĀZYĀ 2191
16		19	20	21	22	23	24	**25**	Gǔ yǔ		5	6	7	8	9	10	11	
17	MONTH 4 Jǐ-Hài	26	27	28	29	1	2	3			12[f]	13	14	15	16	17	18	
18		4	5	6	7	8	9	10			19	20	21	22	23	24	25	
19		*11*	12	13	14	15	16	17	Lì xià	PASHONS 1915	26	27	28	29[g]	30	1	2	GENBOT 2191
20		18	19	20	21	22	23	24			3	4	5	6	7	8	9	
21	MONTH 5 Jǐ-Hài	25	26	**27**	28	29	30	1	Xiǎo mǎn		10	11	12	13	14	15	16	
22		2	3	4	5[d]	6	7	8			17	18	19	20	21	22	23	
23		9	10	11	*12*	13	14	15	Máng zhòng		24	25	26	27	28	29	30	
24		16	17	18	19*	20	21	22		PAÔNE 1915	1	2	3	4	5	6	7	SANÉ 2191
25		23	24	25	26	27	**28**	29	Xià zhì		8	9	10	11	12	13	14	
26	MONTH 6 Jǐ-Hài	1	2	3	4	5	6	7			15	16	17	18	19	20	21	
27		8	9	10	11	12	13	14			22	23	24	25	26	27	28	
28		*15*	16	17	18	19	20	21	Xiǎo shǔ	EPÊP 1915	29	30	1	2	3	4	5	ḤAMLĒ 2191
29		22	23	24	25	26	27	28			6	7	8	9	10	11	12	
30	LEAP MONTH 6 Jǐ-Hài	29	**30**	1	2	3	4	5	Dà shǔ		13	14	15	16	17	18	19	
31		6	7	8	9	10	11	12			20	21	22	23	24	25	26	
32		13	14	15	*16*	17	18	19	Lì qiū	MESORĒ 1915	27	28	29	30	1	2	3	NAHASĒ 2191
33		20*	21	22	23	24	25	26			4	5	6	7	8	9	10	
34	MONTH 7 Jǐ-Hài	27	28	29	30	1	**2**	3	Chǔ shǔ		11	12	13[h]	14	15	16	17	
35		4	5	6	7[e]	8	9	10			18	19	20	21	22	23	24	
36		11	12	13	14	15[f]	16	*17*	Bái lù	EPAG. 1915	25	26	27	28	29	30	1	PĀG. 2191
37		18	19	20	21	22	23	24		THOOUT 1916	2	3	4	5	6	1[a]	2	MASKARAM 2192
38	MONTH 8 Jǐ-Hài	25	26	27	28	29	1	2			3	4	5	6	7	8	9	
39		3	**4**	5	6	7	8	9	Qiū fēn		10	11	12	13	14	15	16	
40		10	11	12	13	14	15[g]	16			17[b]	18	19	20	21	22	23	
41		17	18	*19*	20	21*	22	23	Hán lù		24	25	26	27	28	29	30	
42		24	25	26	27	28	29	30		PAOPE 1916	1	2	3	4	5	6	7	ṬEQEMT 2192
43	MONTH 9 Jǐ-Hài	1	2	3	**4**	5	6	7	Shuāng jiàng		8	9	10	11	12	13	14	
44		8	9[h]	10	11	12	13	14			15	16	17	18	19	20	21	
45		15	16	17	18	*19*	20	21	Lì dōng		22	23	24	25	26	27	28	
46		22	23	24	25	26	27	28		ATHÔR 1916	29	30	1	2	3	4	5	ḪEDĀR 2192
47	MONTH 10 Jǐ-Hài	29	1	2	3	4	**5**	6	Xiǎo xuě		6	7	8	9	10	11	12	
48		7	8	9	10	11	12	13			13	14	15	16	17	18	19	
49		14	15	16	17	18	19	*20*	Dà xuě		20	21	22	23	24	25	26	
50		21	22*	23	24	25	26	27		KOIAK 1916	27	28	29	30	1	2	3	TĀKHŚĀŚ 2192
51	MONTH 11 Jǐ-Hài	28	29	30	1	2	3	4			4	5	6	7	8	9	10	
52		**5**[i]	6	7	8	9	10	11	Dōng zhì		11	12	13	14	15	16	17	
1		12	13	14	15	16	17	18			18	19	20	21	22	23	24	

[a]New Year
[b]Spring (12:50)
[c]Summer (3:26)
[d]Autumn (20:48)
[e]Winter (20:31)
● New moon
◐ First quarter moon
○ Full moon
◑ Last quarter moon

[a]New Year
[b]Yom Kippur
[c]Sukkot
[d]Winter starts
[e]Ḥanukkah
[f]Purim
[g]Passover
[h]Shavuot
[i]Fast of Av

‡Leap year
[a]New Year (4897, Pig)
[b]Lantern Festival
[c]Qīngmíng
[d]Dragon Festival
[e]Qīqiǎo
[f]Hungry Ghosts
[g]Mid-Autumn Festival
[h]Double-Ninth Festival
[i]Dōngzhì
*Start of 60-name cycle

‡Leap year
[a]New Year
[b]Building of the Cross
[c]Christmas
[d]Jesus's Circumcision
[e]Epiphany
[f]Easter
[g]Mary's Announcement
[h]Jesus's Transfiguration

2199

PERSIAN (ASTRONOMICAL) 1577‡/1578

Month	Sun	Mon	Tue	Wed	Thu	Fri	Sat
DEY 1577	10	11	12	13	14	15	16
	17	18	19	20	21	22	23
	24	25	26	27	28	29	30
BAHMAN 1577	1	2	3	4	5	6	7
	8	9	10	11	12	13	14
	15	16	17	18	19	20	21
	22	23	24	25	26	27	28
ESFAND 1577	29	30	1	2	3	4	5
	6	7	8	9	10	11	12
	13	14	15	16	17	18	19
	20	21	22	23	24	25	26
FARVARDIN 1578	27	28	29	30	1[a]	2	3
	4	5	6	7	8	9	10
	11	12	13[b]	14	15	16	17
	18	19	20	21	22	23	24
	25	26	27	28	29	30	31
ORDIBEHEŠT 1578	1	2	3	4	5	6	7
	8	9	10	11	12	13	14
	15	16	17	18	19	20	21
	22	23	24	25	26	27	28
XORDĀD 1578	29	30	31	1	2	3	4
	5	6	7	8	9	10	11
	12	13	14	15	16	17	18
	19	20	21	22	23	24	25
TĪR 1578	26	27	28	29	30	31	1
	2	3	4	5	6	7	8
	9	10	11	12	13	14	15
	16	17	18	19	20	21	22
	23	24	25	26	27	28	29
MORDĀD 1578	30	31	1	2	3	4	5
	6	7	8	9	10	11	12
	13	14	15	16	17	18	19
	20	21	22	23	24	25	26
SHAHRĪVAR 1578	27	28	29	30	31	1	2
	3	4	5	6	7	8	9
	10	11	12	13	14	15	16
	17	18	19	20	21	22	23
	24	25	26	27	28	29	30
MEHR 1578	31	1	2	3	4	5	6
	7	8	9	10	11	12	13
	14	15	16	17	18	19	20
	21	22	23	24	25	26	27
ABĀN 1578	28	29	30	1	2	3	4
	5	6	7	8	9	10	11
	12	13	14	15	16	17	18
	19	20	21	22	23	24	25
ĀZAR 1578	26	27	28	29	30	1	2
	3	4	5	6	7	8	9
	10	11	12	13	14	15	16
	17	18	19	20	21	22	23
	24	25	26	27	28	29	30
DEY 1578	1	2	3	4	5	6	7
	8	9	10	11	12	13	14

‡Leap year
[a]New Year
[b]Sizdeh Bedar

HINDU LUNAR 2255/2256‡

Month	Sun	Mon	Tue	Wed	Thu	Fri	Sat
PAUSHA 2255	**2**	4	5	6	7	8	9
	10	11	12	12	13	14	15
	16	17	18	19	20	21	22
	23	24	25	**26**	28	29	30
MĀGHA 2255	1	2	3	4	5	6	7
	8	9	10	11	12	13	14
	15	15	16	17	18	**19**	21
	22	23	24	25	26	27	28[h]
PHĀLGUNA 2255	29	30	1	2	3	4	5
	6	7	8	9	10	11	12
	13	14	15[i]	16	17	18	19
	20	21	22	23	**24**	26	27
CHAITRA 2256	28	29	30	1[a]	2	3	4
	5	6	7	8	8[b]	9	10
	11	12	13	14	15	16	17
	18	20	21	22	23	24	25
VAIŚĀKHA 2256	26	27	28	29	30	1	2
	3	4	5	6	7	8	9
	10	11	12	13	14	15	16
	17	18	19	20	21	**22**	24
JYAISHTHA 2256	25	26	27	28	29	30	1
	2	3	3	4	5	6	7
	8	9	10	11	12	13	14
	15	17	18	19	20	21	22
	23	24	25	26	27	28	29
ĀSHĀDHA 2256	30	1	2	3	4	5	6
	7	8	9	10	11	12	13
	14	15	16	17	**18**	20	21
	22	23	24	25	26	27	28
ŚRĀVAṆA 2256	29	29	30	1	2	3	4
	5	6	7	8	9	**10**	12
	13	14	15	16	17	18	19
	20	21	22	23[c]	24	25	26
LEAP BHĀDRAPADA 2256	27	28	29	30	1	2	3
	4	5	6	7	8	9	10
	11	12	**13**	15	16	17	18
	19	20	21	22	23	24	25
BHĀDRAPADA 2256	26	26	27	28	29	30	1
	2	3	4[d]	5	6	**7**	9
	10	11	12	13	14	15	16
	17	18	19	20	21	22	23
	24	25	26	27	28	29	30
ĀŚVINA 2256	1	2	3	4	5	6	7
	8[e]	9[e]	**10**[e]	12	13	14	15
	16	17	18	19	20	20	21
	22	23	24	25	26	27	28
KĀRTTIKA 2256	29	30	1[f]	2	3	**4**	6
	7	8	9	10	11	12	13
	14	15	16	17	18	19	20
	21	22	23	23	24	25	26
MĀRGAŚĪRA 2256	**27**	29	30	1	2	3	4
	5	6	7	8	9	10	11[g]
	12	13	14	15	16	17	18

‡Leap year
[a]New Year (Vikārin)
[b]Birthday of Rāma
[c]Birthday of Krishna
[d]Gaṇēśa Chaturthī
[e]Dashara
[f]Diwali
[g]Birthday of Vishnu
[h]Night of Śiva
[i]Holi

HINDU SOLAR 2120/2121‡

Month	Sun	Mon	Tue	Wed	Thu	Fri	Sat
PAUSHA 2120	12	13	14	15	16	17	18
	19	20	21	22	23	24	25
MĀGHA 2120	26	27	28	29	1[b]	2	3
	4	5	6	7	8	9	10
	11	12	13	14	15	16	17
	18	19	20	21	22	23	24
PHĀLGUNA 2120	25	26	27	28	29	1	2
	3	4	5	6	7	8	9
	10	11	12	13	14	15	16
	17	18	19	20	21	22	23
	24	25	26	27	28	29	30
CHAITRA 2120	1	2	3	4	5	6	7
	8	9	10	11	12	13	14
	15	16	17	18	19	20	21
	22	23	24	25	26	27	28
VAIŚĀKHA 2121	29	30	1[a]	2	3	4	5
	6	7	8	9	10	11	12
	13	14	15	16	17	18	19
	20	21	22	23	24	25	26
JYAISHTHA 2121	27	28	29	30	31	1	2
	3	4	5	6	7	8	9
	10	11	12	13	14	15	16
	17	18	19	20	21	22	23
	24	25	26	27	28	29	30
ĀSHĀDHA 2121	31	32	1	2	3	4	5
	6	7	8	9	10	11	12
	13	14	15	16	17	18	19
	20	21	22	23	24	25	26
ŚRĀVAṆA 2121	27	28	29	30	31	1	2
	3	4	5	6	7	8	9
	10	11	12	13	14	15	16
	17	18	19	20	21	22	23
	24	25	26	27	28	29	30
BHĀDRAPADA 2121	31	32	1	2	3	4	5
	6	7	8	9	10	11	12
	13	14	15	16	17	18	19
	20	21	22	23	24	25	26
ĀŚVINA 2121	27	28	29	30	31	1	2
	3	4	5	6	7	8	9
	10	11	12	13	14	15	16
	17	18	19	20	21	22	23
	24	25	26	27	28	29	30
KĀRTTIKA 2121	1	2	3	4	5	6	7
	8	9	10	11	12	13	14
	15	16	17	18	19	20	21
	22	23	24	25	26	27	28
MĀRGAŚĪRA 2121	29	30	1	2	3	4	5
	6	7	8	9	10	11	12
	13	14	15	16	17	18	19
	20	21	22	23	24	25	26
PAUSHA 2121	27	28	29	30	1	2	3
	4	5	6	7	8	9	10
	11	12	13	14	15	16	17

‡Leap year
[a]New Year (Rākshasa)
[b]Pongal

ISLAMIC (ASTRONOMICAL) 1625/1626‡

Month	Sun	Mon	Tue	Wed	Thu	Fri	Sat
DHU AL-QA'DA 1625	2	3	4	5	6	7	8
	9	10	11	12	13	14	15
	16	17	18	19	20	21	22
	23	24	25	26	27	28	29
DHU AL-HIJJA 1625	30	1	2	3	4	5	6
	7	8	9	10[g]	11	12	13
	14	15	16	17	18	19	20
	21	22	23	24	25	26	27
MUHARRAM 1626	28	29	1[a]	2[d]	3	4	5
	6	7	8	9	10[b]	11	12
	13	14	15	16	17	18	19
	20	21	22	23	24	25	26
SAFAR 1626	27	28	29	30	1	2	3
	4	5	6	7	8	9	10
	11	12	13	14	15	16	17
	18	19	20	21	22	23	24
RABĪ' I 1626	25	26	27	28	29	30	1
	2	3	4	5	6	7	8
	9	10	11	12[c]	13	14	15
	16	17	18	19	20	21	22
	23	24	25	26	27	28	29
RABĪ' II 1626	1	2	3	4	5	6	7
	8	9	10	11	12	13	14
	15	16	17	18	19	20	21
	22	23	24	25	26	27	28
JUMĀDĀ I 1626	29	30	1	2	3	4	5
	6	7	8	9	10	11	12
	13	14	15	16	17	18	19
	20	21	22	23	24	25	26
JUMĀDĀ II 1626	27	28	29	30	1	2	3
	4	5	6	7	8	9	10
	11	12	13	14	15	16	17
	18	19	20	21	22	23	24
RAJAB 1626	25	26	27	28	29	30	1
	2	3	4	5	6	7	8
	9	10	11	12	13	14	15
	16	17	18	19	20	21	22
	23	24	25	26	27[d]	28	29
SHA'BĀN 1626	1	2	3	4	5	6	7
	8	9	10	11	12	13	14
	15	16	17	18	19	20	21
	22	23	24	25	26	27	28
RAMAḌĀN 1626	29	1[e]	2	3	4	5	6
	7	8	9	10	11	12	13
	14	15	16	17	18	19	20
	21	22	23	24	25	26	27
SHAWWĀL 1626	28	29	30	1[f]	2	3	4
	5	6	7	8	9	10	11
	12	13	14	15	16	17	18
	19	20	21	22	23	24	25
DHU AL-QA'DA 1626	26	27	28	29	1	2	3
	4	5	6	7	8	9	10
	11	12	13	14	15	16	17

‡Leap year
[a]New Year
[d]New Year (Arithmetic)
[b]'Ashūrā'
[c]Prophet's Birthday
[d]Ascent of the Prophet
[e]Start of Ramaḍān
[f]'Id al-Fiṭr
[g]'Id al-'Aḍḥā

GREGORIAN 2199

Julian (Sun)	Month	Sun	Mon	Tue	Wed	Thu	Fri	Sat
Dec 16	JANUARY 2199	30	31	1	2	3	4	5
		6	7	8[a]	9	10	11	12
Dec 30		13	14	15[b]	16	17	18	19
		20	21	22	23	24	25	26
Jan 13	FEBRUARY 2199	27	28	29	30	31	1	2
		3	4	5	6	7	8	9
Jan 27		10	11	12	13	14	15	16
		17	18	19	20	21	22	23
Feb 10	MARCH 2199	24	25	26	27[c]	28	1	2
		3	4	5	6	7	8	9
Feb 24		10[d]	11	12	13	14	15	16
		17	18	19	20	21	22	23
Mar 10		24	25	26	27	28	29	30
	APRIL 2199	31	1	2	3	4	5	6
Mar 24		7	8	9	10	11	12	13
		14[e]	15	16	17	18	19	20
Apr 7		21[f]	22	23	24	25	26	27
	MAY 2199	28	29	30	1	2	3	4
Apr 21		5	6	7	8	9	10	11
		12	13	14	15	16	17	18
May 5		19	20	21	22	23	24	25
	JUNE 2199	26	27	28	29	30	31	1
May 19		2	3	4	5	6	7	8
		9	10	11	12	13	14	15
Jun 2		16	17	18	19	20	21	22
		23	24	25	26	27	28	29
Jun 16	JULY 2199	30	1	2	3	4	5	6
		7	8	9	10	11	12	13
Jun 30		14	15	16	17	18	19	20
		21	22	23	24	25	26	27
Jul 14	AUGUST 2199	28	29	30	31	1	2	3
		4	5	6	7	8	9	10
Jul 28		11	12	13	14	15	16	17
		18	19	20	21	22	23	24
Aug 11		25	26	27	28	29	30	31
	SEPTEMBER 2199	1	2	3	4	5	6	7
Aug 25		8	9	10	11	12	13	14
		15	16	17	18	19	20	21
Sep 8		22	23	24	25	26	27	28
	OCTOBER 2199	29	30	1	2	3	4	5
Sep 22		6	7	8	9	10	11	12
		13	14	15	16	17	18	19
Oct 6		20	21	22	23	24	25	26
	NOVEMBER 2199	27	28	29	30	31	1	2
Oct 20		3	4	5	6	7	8	9
		10	11	12	13	14	15	16
Nov 3		17	18	19	20	21	22	23
		24	25	26	27	28	29	30
Nov 17	DECEMBER 2199	1[g]	2	3	4	5	6	7
		8	9	10	11	12	13	14
Dec 1		15	16	17	18	19	20	21
		22	23	24	25[h]	26	27	28
Dec 15		29	30	31	1	2	3	4

[a]Orthodox Christmas
[b]Julian New Year
[c]Ash Wednesday
[d]Feast of Orthodoxy
[e]Easter
[f]Orthodox Easter
[g]Advent
[h]Christmas

2200

GREGORIAN 2200 · Lunar Phases · ISO WEEK (Mon) · JULIAN DAY (Sun noon)

Month	Sun	Mon	Tue	Wed	Thu	Fri	Sat	Lunar Phases	ISO Week	Julian Day
	29	30	31	○[a]	2	3	4	8:15	1	2524591
January 2200	5	6	7	8	◑	10	11	12:12	2	2524598
	12	13	14	15	●	17	18	8:19	3	2524605
	19	20	21	22	◐	24	25	1:36	4	2524612
	26	27	28	29	30	○	1	3:38	5	2524619
February 2200	2	3	4	5	6	7	◑	3:00	6	2524626
	9	10	11	12	13	●	15	18:36	7	2524633
	16	17	18	19	20	◐	22	17:44	8	2524640
	23	24	25	26	27	28	○	22:18	9	2524647
March 2200	2	3	4	5	6	7	8		10	2524654
	◑	10	11	12	13	14	15	14:02	11	2524661
	●	17	18	19	20[b]	21	22	4:53	12	2524668
	◐	24	25	26	27	28	29	11:52	13	2524675
	30	○	1	2	3	4	5	14:58	14	2524682
April 2200	6	◑	8	9	10	11	12	21:46	15	2524689
	13	●	15	16	17	18	19	15:36	16	2524696
	20	21	◐	23	24	25	26	6:41	17	2524703
	27	28	29	○	1	2	3	4:46	18	2524710
May 2200	4	5	6	◑	8	9	10	3:23	19	2524717
	11	12	13	●	15	16	17	3:03	20	2524724
	18	19	20	21	◐	23	24	1:03	21	2524731
	25	26	27	28	○	30	31	15:34	22	2524738
June 2200	1	2	3	4	◑	6	7	8:24	23	2524745
	8	9	10	11	●	13	14	15:28	24	2524752
	15	16	17	18	19	◐	21[c]	18:03	25	2524759
	22	23	24	25	26	○	28	23:58	26	2524766
	29	30	1	2	3	◑	5	14:16	27	2524773
July 2200	6	7	8	9	10	11	●	5:02	28	2524780
	13	14	15	16	17	18	19		29	2524787
	◐	21	22	23	24	25	26	8:57	30	2524794
	○	28	29	30	31	1	◑	7:00 22:15	31	2524801
August 2200	3	4	5	6	7	8	9		32	2524808
	●	11	12	13	14	15	16	19:51	33	2524815
	17	◐	19	20	21	22	23	21:24	34	2524822
	24	○	26	27	28	29	30	13:55	35	2524829
	31	◑	2	3	4	5	6	9:13	36	2524836
September 2200	7	8	●	10	11	12	13	11:43	37	2524843
	14	15	16	◐	18	19	20	7:28	38	2524850
	21	22	○[d]	24	25	26	27	21:54	39	2524857
	28	29	◑	1	2	3	4	23:40	40	2524864
October 2200	5	6	7	8	●	10	11	4:01	41	2524871
	12	13	14	15	◐	17	18	15:43	42	2524878
	19	20	21	22	○	24	25	7:44	43	2524885
	26	27	28	29	◑	31	1	17:38	44	2524892
November 2200	2	3	4	5	6	●	8	19:47	45	2524899
	9	10	11	12	13	◐	15	23:06	46	2524906
	16	17	18	19	20	○	22	19:55	47	2524913
	23	24	25	26	27	28	◑	14:22	48	2524920
	30	1	2	3	4	5	6		49	2524927
December 2200	●	8	9	10	11	12	13	10:12	50	2524934
	◐	15	16	17	18	19	20	6:43	51	2524941
	○	22[e]	23	24	25	26	27	10:30	52	2524948
	28	◑	30	31	1	2	3	12:10	1	2524955

HEBREW 5960/5961‡ · Molad

ISO Week	Month	Sun	Mon	Tue	Wed	Thu	Fri	Sat	Molad
1	Teveth 5960	10	11	12	13	14	15	16	
2		17	18	19	20	21	22	23	
3		24	25	26	27	28	29	1	Thu 11h14m9p
4	Shevat 5960	2	3	4	5	6	7	8	
5		9	10	11	12	13	14	15	
6		16	17	18	19	20	21	22	
7		23	24	25	26	27	28	29	
8		30	1	2	3	4	5	6	Fri 23h58m4p
9	Adar 5960	7	8	9	10	11	12	13	
10		14[f]	15	16	17	18	19	20	
11		21	22	23	24	25	26	27	
12		28	29	1	2	3	4	5	Sun 12h42m5p
13	Nisan 5960	6	7	8	9	10	11	12	
14		13	14	15[g]	16	17	18	19	
15		20	21	22	23	24	25	26	
16		27	28	29	30	1	2	3	Tue 1h26m6p
17	Iyyar 5960	4	5	6	7	8	9	10	
18		11	12	13	14	15	16	17	
19		18	19	20	21	22	23	24	
20		25	26	27	28	29	1	2	Wed 14h10m7p
21	Sivan 5960	3	4	5	6[h]	7	8	9	
22		10	11	12	13	14	15	16	
23		17	18	19	20	21	22	23	
24		24	25	26	27	28	29	30	
25	Tammuz 5960	1	2	3	4	5	6	7	Fri 2h54m8p
26		8	9	10	11	12	13	14	
27		15	16	17	18	19	20	21	
28		22	23	24	25	26	27	28	
29		29	1	2	3	4	5	6	Sat 15h38m9p
30	Av 5960	7	8	9[i]	10	11	12	13	
31		14	15	16	17	18	19	20	
32		21	22	23	24	25	26	27	
33		28	29	30	1	2	3	4	Mon 4h22m10p
34	Elul 5960	5	6	7	8	9	10	11	
35		12	13	14	15	16	17	18	
36		19	20	21	22	23	24	25	
37		26	27	28	29	1[a]	2[a]	3	Tue 17h6m11p
38	Tishri 5961	4	5	6	7	8	9	10[b]	
39		11	12	13	14	15[c]	16	17	
40		18	19	20	21	22	23	24	
41		25	26	27	28	29	30	1	Thu 5h50m12p
42	Heshvan 5961	2	3	4	5	6	7	8	
43		9	10	11	12	13	14	15	
44		16	17	18	19	20	21	22	
45		23	24	25	26	27	28	29	
46	Kislev 5961	1	2	3	4	5	6	7	Fri 18h34m13p
47		8	9	10	11	12	13	14	
48		15	16	17	18	19	20	21	
49		22	23	24	25[e]	26[e]	27[e]	28[e]	
50		29[d][e]	1[e]	2[e]	3[e]	4	5	6	Sun 7h18m14p
51	Teveth 5961	7	8	9	10	11	12	13	
52		14	15	16	17	18	19	20	
1		21	22	23	24	25	26	27	

CHINESE Jǐ-Hài‡/Gēng-Zǐ · Solar Term

ISO Week	Month	Sun	Mon	Tue	Wed	Thu	Fri	Sat	Solar Term
1	Month 11 Jǐ-Hài	12	13	14	15	16	17	18	
2		19	20	21	22	23	24	25	Xiǎo hán
3		26	27	28	29	1	2	3	
4	Month 12 Jǐ-Hài	4	5	6	7	8	9	10	Dà hán
5		11	12	13	14	15	16	17	
6		18	19	20	21	22	23*	24	Lì chūn
7		25	26	27	28	29	30	1[a]	
8	Month 1 Gēng-Zǐ	2	3	4	5	6	7	8	Yǔ shuǐ
9		9	10	11	12	13	14	15[b]	
10		16	17	18	19	20	21	22	Jīng zhé
11		23	24	25	26	27	28	29	
12	Month 2 Gēng-Zǐ	1	2	3	4	5	6	7	Chūn fēn
13		8	9	10	11	12	13	14	
14		15	16	17	18	19	20	21[c]	Qīng míng
15		22	23	24*	25	26	27	28	
16		29	1	2	3	4	5	6	
17	Month 3 Gēng-Zǐ	7	8	9	10	11	12	13	Gǔ yǔ
18		14	15	16	17	18	19	20	
19		21	22	23	24	25	26	27	Lì xià
20		28	29	30	1	2	3	4	
21	Month 4 Gēng-Zǐ	5	6	7	8	9	10	11	Xiǎo mǎn
22		12	13	14	15	16	17	18	
23		19	20	21	22	23	24	25*	Máng zhòng
24		26	27	28	29	1	2	3	
25	Month 5 Gēng-Zǐ	4	5[d]	6	7	8	9	10	Xià zhì
26		11	12	13	14	15	16	17	
27		18	19	20	21	22	23	24	
28		25	26	27	28	29	30	1	Xiǎo shǔ
29	Month 6 Gēng-Zǐ	2	3	4	5	6	7	8	
30		9	10	11	12	13	14	15	Dà shǔ
31		16	17	18	19	20	21	22	
32		23	24	25	26*	27	28	29	Lì qiū
33		30	1	2	3	4	5	6	
34	Month 7 Gēng-Zǐ	7[e]	8	9	10	11	12	13	Chǔ shǔ
35		14	15[f]	16	17	18	19	20	
36		21	22	23	24	25	26	27	
37		28	29	1	2	3	4	5	Bái lù
38	Month 8 Gēng-Zǐ	6	7	8	9	10	11	12	
39		13	14	15[g]	16	17	18	19	Qiū fēn
40		20	21	22	23	24	25	26	
41		27*	28	29	30	1	2	3	Hán lù
42	Month 9 Gēng-Zǐ	4	5	6	7	8	9[h]	10	
43		11	12	13	14	15	16	17	Shuāng jiàng
44		18	19	20	21	22	23	24	
45		25	26	27	28	29	30	1	Lì dōng
46	Month 10 Gēng-Zǐ	2	3	4	5	6	7	8	
47		9	10	11	12	13	14	15	Xiǎo xuě
48		16	17	18	19	20	21	22	
49		23	24	25	26	27*	28	29	
50	Month 11 Gēng-Zǐ	1	2	3	4	5	6	7	Dà xuě
51		8	9	10	11	12	13	14	
52		15	16[i]	17	18	19	20	21	Dōng zhì
1		22	23	24	25	26	27	28	

COPTIC 1916/1917 · ETHIOPIC 2192/2193

ISO Week	Coptic Month	Sun	Mon	Tue	Wed	Thu	Fri	Sat	Ethiopic Month
1	Koiak 1916	18	19	20	21	22	23	24	Tākhśāś 2192
2		25	26	27	28	29[c]	30	1	
3	Ṭōbe 1916	2	3	4	5	6[d]	7	8	Ṭer 2192
4		9	10	11[e]	12	13	14	15	
5		16	17	18	19	20	21	22	
6		23	24	25	26	27	28	29	
7	Meshir 1916	30	1	2	3	4	5	6	Yakātit 2192
8		7	8	9	10	11	12	13	
9		14	15	16	17	18	19	20	
10		21	22	23	24	25	26	27	
11	Paremotep 1916	28	29	30	1	2	3	4	Magābit 2192
12		5	6	7	8	9	10	11	
13		12	13	14	15	16	17	18	
14		19	20	21	22	23	24	25	
15	Parmoute 1916	26[f]	27	28	29	30	1	2	Miyāzyā 2192
16		3	4	5	6	7	8	9	
17		10	11	12	13	14	15	16	
18		17	18	19	20	21	22	23	
19		24	25	26	27	28	29[g]	30	
20	Pashons 1916	1	2	3	4	5	6	7	Genbot 2192
21		8	9	10	11	12	13	14	
22		15	16	17	18	19	20	21	
23		22	23	24	25	26	27	28	
24	Paōne 1916	29	30	1	2	3	4	5	Sanē 2192
25		6	7	8	9	10	11	12	
26		13	14	15	16	17	18	19	
27		20	21	22	23	24	25	26	
28	Epēp 1916	27	28	29	30	1	2	3	Ḥamlē 2192
29		4	5	6	7	8	9	10	
30		11	12	13	14	15	16	17	
31		18	19	20	21	22	23	24	
32	Mesorē 1916	25	26	27	28	29	30	1	Naḥasē 2192
33		2	3	4	5	6	7	8	
34		9	10	11	12	13[h]	14	15	
35		16	17	18	19	20	21	22	
36		23	24	25	26	27	28	29	
37	Epag. 1916	30	1	2	3	4	5	1[a]	Pāg. 2192
38	Thoout 1917	2	3	4	5	6	7	8	Maskaram 2193
39		9	10	11	12	13	14	15	
40		16	17[b]	18	19	20	21	22	
41		23	24	25	26	27	28	29	
42	Paope 1917	30	1	2	3	4	5	6	Teqemt 2193
43		7	8	9	10	11	12	13	
44		14	15	16	17	18	19	20	
45		21	22	23	24	25	26	27	
46	Athōr 1917	28	29	30	1	2	3	4	Ḫedār 2193
47		5	6	7	8	9	10	11	
48		12	13	14	15	16	17	18	
49		19	20	21	22	23	24	25	
50	Koiak 1917	26	27	28	29	30	1	2	Tākhśāś 2193
51		3	4	5	6	7	8	9	
52		10	11	12	13	14	15	16	
1		17	18	19	20	21	22	23	

Gregorian:
[a]New Year
[b]Spring (18:40)
[c]Summer (9:15)
[d]Autumn (2:40)
[e]Winter (2:26)
● New moon
◐ First quarter moon
○ Full moon
◑ Last quarter moon

Hebrew:
‡Leap year
[a]New Year
[b]Yom Kippur
[c]Sukkot
[d]Winter starts
[e]Ḥanukkah
[f]Purim
[g]Passover
[h]Shavuot
[i]Fast of Av

Chinese:
‡Leap year
[a]New Year (4898, Rat)
[b]Lantern Festival
[c]Qīngmíng
[d]Dragon Festival
[e]Qīqiǎo
[f]Hungry Ghosts
[g]Mid-Autumn Festival
[h]Double-Ninth Festival
[i]Dōngzhì
*Start of 60-name cycle

Coptic/Ethiopic:
[a]New Year
[b]Building of the Cross
[c]Christmas
[d]Jesus's Circumcision
[e]Epiphany
[f]Easter
[g]Mary's Announcement
[h]Jesus's Transfiguration

PERSIAN (ASTRONOMICAL) 1578/1579

Month	Sun	Mon	Tue	Wed	Thu	Fri	Sat
DEY 1578	8	9	10	11	12	13	14
	15	16	17	18	19	20	21
	22	23	24	25	26	27	28
BAHMAN 1578	29	30	1	2	3	4	5
	6	7	8	9	10	11	12
	13	14	15	16	17	18	19
	20	21	22	23	24	25	26
ESFAND 1578	27	28	29	30	1	2	3
	4	5	6	7	8	9	10
	11	12	13	14	15	16	17
	18	19	20	21	22	23	24
FARVARDIN 1579	25	26	27	28	29	1[a]	2
	3	4	5	6	7	8	9
	10	11	12	13[b]	14	15	16
	17	18	19	20	21	22	23
	24	25	26	27	28	29	30
ORDIBEHEST 1579	31	1	2	3	4	5	6
	7	8	9	10	11	12	13
	14	15	16	17	18	19	20
	21	22	23	24	25	26	27
XORDAD 1579	28	29	30	31	1	2	3
	4	5	6	7	8	9	10
	11	12	13	14	15	16	17
	18	19	20	21	22	23	24
	25	26	27	28	29	30	31
TIR 1579	1	2	3	4	5	6	7
	8	9	10	11	12	13	14
	15	16	17	18	19	20	21
	22	23	24	25	26	27	28
MORDAD 1579	29	30	31	1	2	3	4
	5	6	7	8	9	10	11
	12	13	14	15	16	17	18
	19	20	21	22	23	24	25
SHAHRIVAR 1579	26	27	28	29	30	31	1
	2	3	4	5	6	7	8
	9	10	11	12	13	14	15
	16	17	18	19	20	21	22
	23	24	25	26	27	28	29
MEHR 1579	30	31	1	2	3	4	5
	6	7	8	9	10	11	12
	13	14	15	16	17	18	19
	20	21	22	23	24	25	26
ABAN 1579	27	28	29	30	1	2	3
	4	5	6	7	8	9	10
	11	12	13	14	15	16	17
	18	19	20	21	22	23	24
AZAR 1579	25	26	27	28	29	30	1
	2	3	4	5	6	7	8
	9	10	11	12	13	14	15
	16	17	18	19	20	21	22
	23	24	25	26	27	28	29
DEY 1579	30	1	2	3	4	5	6
	7	8	9	10	11	12	13

HINDU LUNAR 2256‡/2257

Month	Sun	Mon	Tue	Wed	Thu	Fri	Sat
MĀRGAŚIRA 2256	12	13	14	15	16	17	18
	19	20	21	22	23	24	25
PAUSHA 2256	26	27	28	29	30	1	2
	3	5	6	7	8	9	10
	11	12	13	14	15	*15*	16
	17	18	19	20	21	22	23
MĀGHA 2256	24	25	26	**27**	29	30	1
	2	3	4	5	6	7	8
	9	10	11	12	13	14	15
	16	17	18	19	*19*	21	22
	23	24	25	26	27	28[h]	29
PHĀLGUNA 2256	30	1	2	**3**	5	6	7
	7	8	9	10	11	12	13
	14	15[i]	16	17	18	19	20
	21	22	23	24	**25**	27	28
CHAITRA 2257	29	30	1[a]	2	3	4	5
	6	7	8	9[b]	10	11	*11*
	12	13	14	15	16	17	**18**
	20	21	22	23	24	25	26
VAIŚĀKHA 2257	27	28	29	30	1	2	3
	4	5	6	7	8	9	10
	11	12	13	14	15	16	17
	18	19	20	21	**22**	24	25
JYAISHTHA 2257	26	27	28	29	30	1	2
	3	4	5	6	7	*7*	8
	9	10	11	12	13	**14**	16
	17	18	19	20	21	22	23
	24	25	26	27	28	29	30
ĀSHĀḌHA 2257	1	2	3	4	5	6	7
	8	9	10	11	12	13	14
	15	16	**17**	19	20	21	22
	23	24	25	26	27	28	29
ŚRĀVAṆA 2257	30	1	2	3	4	*4*	5
	6	7	8	9	**10**	12	13
	14	15	16	17	18	19	20
	21	22	23[c]	24	25	26	27
BHĀDRAPADA 2257	28	29	30	1	2	3	4[d]
	5	6	7	8	9	10	11
	12	13	**14**	16	17	18	19
	20	21	22	23	24	25	26
ĀŚVINA 2257	27	28	29	*29*	30	1	2
	3	4	5	6	7[e]	9[e]	10[e]
	11	12	13	14	15	16	17
	18	19	20	21	22	23	24
KĀRTTIKA 2257	25	26	27	28	29	30	1[f]
	2	3	4	5	6	7	8
	9	10	**11**	13	14	15	16
	17	18	19	20	21	22	23
	23	24	25	26	27	28	29
MĀRGAŚIRA 2257	30	1	2	3	4	**5**	7
	8	9	10	11[g]	12	13	14
	15	16	17	18	19	20	21
	22	23	24	25	26	27	*27*

HINDU SOLAR 2121‡/2122

Month	Sun	Mon	Tue	Wed	Thu	Fri	Sat
PAUSHA 2121	11	12	13	14	15	16	17
	18	19	20	21	22	23	24
MĀGHA 2121	25	26	27	28	29	1[b]	2
	3	4	5	6	7	8	9
	10	11	12	13	14	15	16
	17	18	19	20	21	22	23
	24	25	26	27	28	29	30
PHĀLGUNA 2121	1	2	3	4	5	6	7
	8	9	10	11	12	13	14
	15	16	17	18	19	20	21
	22	23	24	25	26	27	28
CHAITRA 2121	29	1	2	3	4	5	6
	7	8	9	10	11	12	13
	14	15	16	17	18	19	20
	21	22	23	24	25	26	27
VAIŚĀKHA 2122	28	29	30	31	1[a]	2	3
	4	5	6	7	8	9	10
	11	12	13	14	15	16	17
	18	19	20	21	22	23	24
	25	26	27	28	29	30	31
JYAISHTHA 2122	1	2	3	4	5	6	7
	8	9	10	11	12	13	14
	15	16	17	18	19	20	21
	22	23	24	25	26	27	28
ĀSHĀḌHA 2122	29	30	31	1	2	3	4
	5	6	7	8	9	10	11
	12	13	14	15	16	17	18
	19	20	21	22	23	24	25
	26	27	28	29	30	31	32
ŚRĀVAṆA 2122	1	2	3	4	5	6	7
	8	9	10	11	12	13	14
	15	16	17	18	19	20	21
	22	23	24	25	26	27	28
BHĀDRAPADA 2122	29	30	31	1	2	3	4
	5	6	7	8	9	10	11
	12	13	14	15	16	17	18
	19	20	21	22	23	24	25
ĀŚVINA 2122	26	27	28	29	30	31	1
	2	3	4	5	6	7	8
	9	10	11	12	13	14	15
	16	17	18	19	20	21	22
	23	24	25	26	27	28	29
KĀRTTIKA 2122	30	31	1	2	3	4	5
	6	7	8	9	10	11	12
	13	14	15	16	17	18	19
	20	21	22	23	24	25	26
MĀRGAŚIRA 2122	27	28	29	30	1	2	3
	4	5	6	7	8	9	10
	11	12	13	14	15	16	17
	18	19	20	21	22	23	24
PAUSHA 2122	25	26	27	28	29	1	2
	3	4	5	6	7	8	9
	10	11	12	13	14	15	16

ISLAMIC (ASTRONOMICAL) 1626‡/1627‡

Month	Sun	Mon	Tue	Wed	Thu	Fri	Sat
DHU AL-QA'DA 1626	11	12	13	14	15	16	17
	18	19	20	21	22	23	24
DHU AL-ḤIJJA 1626	25	26	27	28	29	1	*2*
	3	4	5	6	7	8	9
	10[g]	11	12	13	14	15	16
	17	18	19	20	21	22	23
	24	25	26	27	28	29	30
MUḤARRAM 1627	*1*[a]	2	3	4	5	6	7
	8	9	10[b]	11	12	13	14
	15	16	17	18	19	20	21
	22	23	24	25	26	27	28
ṢAFAR 1627	29	1	2	3	4	5	6
	7	8	9	10	11	12	13
	14	15	16	17	18	19	20
	21	22	23	24	25	26	27
RABĪ' I 1627	28	29	30	*1*	2	3	4
	5	6	7	8	9	10	11
	12[c]	13	14	15	16	17	18
	19	20	21	22	23	24	25
RABĪ' II 1627	26	27	28	29	1	2	3
	4	5	6	7	8	9	10
	11	12	13	14	15	16	17
	18	19	20	21	22	23	24
JUMĀDĀ I 1627	25	26	27	28	29	30	*1*
	2	3	4	5	6	7	8
	9	10	11	12	13	14	15
	16	17	18	19	20	21	22
	23	24	25	26	27	28	29
JUMĀDĀ II 1627	30	*1*	2	3	4	5	6
	7	8	9	10	11	12	13
	14	15	16	17	18	19	20
	21	22	23	24	25	26	27
RAJAB 1627	28	29	*30*	1	2	3	4
	5	6	7	8	9	10	11
	12	13	14	15	16	17	18
	19	20	21	22	23	24	25
SHA'BĀN 1627	26	27[d]	28	29	*30*	1	2
	3	4	5	6	7	8	9
	10	11	12	13	14	15	16
	17	18	19	20	21	22	23
RAMAḌĀN 1627	24	25	26	27	28	29	1[e]
	2	3	4	5	6	7	8
	9	10	11	12	13	14	15
	16	17	18	19	20	21	22
	23	24	25	26	27	28	29
SHAWWĀL 1627	1[f]	2	3	4	5	6	7
	8	9	10	11	12	13	14
	15	16	17	18	19	20	21
	22	23	24	25	26	27	28
DHU AL-QA'DA 1627	29	*30*	1	2	3	4	5
	6	7	8	9	10	11	12
	13	14	15	16	17	18	19
	20	21	22	23	24	25	26

GREGORIAN 2200

Julian† (Sun)	Sun	Mon	Tue	Wed	Thu	Fri	Sat	Month
Dec 15	29	30	31	1	2	3	4	JANUARY 2200
	5	6	7	8[a]	9	10	11	
Dec 29	*12*	13	14	15[b]	16	17	18	
	19	20	21	22	23	24	25	
Jan 12	26	27	28	29	30	31	1	FEBRUARY 2200
	2	3	4	5	6	7	8	
Jan 26	9	10	11	12	13	14	15	
	16	17	18	19[c]	20	21	22	
Feb 9	23[d]	24	25	26	27	28	1	MARCH 2200
	2	3	4	5	6	7	8	
Feb 23	9	10	11	12	13	14	15	
	16	17	18	19	20	21	22	
Mar 8	23	24	25	26	27	28	29	
	30	31	1	2	3	4	5	APRIL 2200
Mar 22	6[e]	7	8	9	10	11	12	
	13	14	15	16	17	18	19	
Apr 5	20	21	22	23	24	25	26	
	27	28	29	30	1	2	3	MAY 2200
Apr 19	4	5	6	7	8	9	10	
	11	12	13	14	15	16	17	
May 3	18	19	20	21	22	23	24	
	25	26	27	28	29	30	31	
May 17	1	2	3	4	5	6	7	JUNE 2200
	8	9	10	11	12	13	14	
May 31	15	16	17	18	19	20	21	
	22	23	24	25	26	27	28	
Jun 14	29	30	1	2	3	4	5	JULY 2200
	6	7	8	9	10	11	12	
Jun 28	13	14	15	16	17	18	19	
	20	21	22	23	24	25	26	
Jul 12	27	28	29	30	31	1	2	AUGUST 2200
	3	4	5	6	7	8	9	
Jul 26	10	11	12	13	14	15	16	
	17	18	19	20	21	22	23	
Aug 9	24	25	26	27	28	29	30	
	31	1	2	3	4	5	6	SEPTEMBER 2200
Aug 23	7	8	9	10	11	12	13	
	14	15	16	17	18	19	20	
Sep 6	21	22	23	24	25	26	27	
	28	29	30	1	2	3	4	OCTOBER 2200
Sep 20	5	6	7	8	9	10	11	
	12	13	14	15	16	17	18	
Oct 4	19	20	21	22	23	24	25	
	26	27	28	29	30	31	1	NOVEMBER 2200
Oct 18	2	3	4	5	6	7	8	
	9	10	11	12	13	14	15	
Nov 1	16	17	18	19	20	21	22	
	23	24	25	26	27	28	29	
Nov 15	30[g]	1	2	3	4	5	6	DECEMBER 2200
	7	8	9	10	11	12	13	
Nov 29	14	15	16	17	18	19	20	
	21	22	23	24	25[h]	26	27	
Dec 13	28	29	30	31	1	2	3	

Persian:
[a]New Year
[b]Sizdeh Bedar

Hindu Lunar:
‡Leap year
[a]New Year (Śārvari)
[b]Birthday of Rāma
[c]Birthday of Krishna
[d]Ganēśa Chaturthī
[e]Dashara
[f]Diwali
[g]Birthday of Vishnu
[h]Night of Śiva
[i]Holi

Hindu Solar:
‡Leap year
[a]New Year (Anala)
[b]Pongal

Islamic:
‡Leap year
[a]New Year
[b]'Ashūrā'
[c]Prophet's Birthday
[d]Ascent of the Prophet
[e]Start of Ramaḍān
[f]'Īd al-Fiṭr
[g]'Īd al-'Aḍḥā

Gregorian:
†Julian leap year
[a]Orthodox Christmas
[b]Julian New Year
[c]Ash Wednesday
[d]Feast of Orthodoxy
[e]Easter (also Orthodox)
[g]Advent
[h]Christmas

Warnings

Changes in font (roman or italic, lightface or bold) are important in the tables. The section "Reading the Tables" explains the significance for each calendar. xiv

Times for lunar phases, equinoxes, and solstices are given in Universal Time. The times are close approximations, but may be in error by a few minutes. xv

Julian day numbers count days from noon to noon, but modified Julian day numbers and fixed day numbers count days from midnight to midnight. xviii

On the Hebrew calendar each day begins the prior evening at local sunset. xix

Historically, on the Chinese calendar for the Gregorian year 1906, Month 4 began on April 24, not April 23 as shown; it thus had 29 days instead of the 30 days shown. The disagreement occurs because our calculations of times of solar and lunar events are more accurate than the seventeenth-century methods used by the Chinese until 1913. xxii

The year number we give for Chinese New Year is the popular version of the Huángdi era. xxii

Our Persian calendar is astronomical and the decision to use it or one of the proposed arithmetic forms is uncertain. xxiv

When the equinox occurs very close to noon, our Persian calendar may be off by a day. xxiv

There are numerous variants of the Hindu calendar, human calendar calculators use approximations, and dates are determined regionally. Some calendar makers prefer modern astronomical methods. xxvi

For the Hindu lunar calendar, we follow the rules of the Sūrya-Siddhānta, as amended by Gaṇesa Daivajna, except that the actual time of sunrise in Ujjain is used. xxvi

Hindu lunar months are shown from new moon to new moon; in many regional variants full moon to full moon would be used. The day numbers of the second ("dark") half of each lunar month typically start over from 1; we use 16–30, instead. xxvi

Our Hindu solar calendar follows the Orissa rule and actual sunrise in Calcutta, which can differ by a day or two from the rules used elsewhere. xxvi

The sequence of Hindu months, and their names, differ regionally. Ours begins the solar year with Vaiśākha, the name of the second month of the lunar year. xxvi

On the Hindu calendars each day begins at local sunrise. xxvi

There is very wide variance in the precise date of celebration of the various Hindu holidays, and in the length of the celebration. xxvi

Our Islamic calendar is an approximation based on astronomical determination of when the new crescent moon is likely to be visible in Los Angeles, California; however, the actual date depends on human observation of the crescent moon. Thus, month beginnings and endings can be in error by a day or so, and vary from country to country. Holiday dates are therefore also only approximate and vary from country to country. xxvii

On the Islamic calendar each day begins the prior evening at local sunset. xxviii

The italicized dates of the arithmetic Islamic calendar indicated in the tables are based on a fixed thirty-year cycle in which years 2, 5, 7, 10, 13, 16, 18, 21, 24, 26, and 29 are leap years. xxviii

Printed in the United States
By Bookmasters